THE
NEW MATTHEW HENRY
COMMENTARY

The Classic Work with Updated Language

THE
NEW MATTHEW HENRY
COMMENTARY

The Classic Work with Updated Language

MATTHEW HENRY

Edited by Martin H. Manser

ZONDERVAN®

ZONDERVAN.com/
AUTHORTRACKER
follow your favorite authors

ZONDERVAN

The New Matthew Henry Commentary
Copyright © 2010 by Zondervan

This title is also available as a Zondervan ebook.
Visit www.zondervan.com/ebooks.

Requests for information should be addressed to:
Zondervan, *Grand Rapids, Michigan* 49530

Library of Congress Cataloging-in-Publication Data

Henry, Matthew (1662 – 1714).
    [Commentary on the whole Bible]
    The new Matthew Henry Commentary / Matthew Henry ; edited and updated by Martin H.
Manser. — Abridged ed. with updated language.
      p. cm.
    ISBN 978 – 0 – 310 – 25399 – 0 (hardcover, printed)
    1. Bible — Commentaries. I. Manser, Martin H. II. Title.
  BS491.3.H46 2008b
  220.7 — dc22
                                                     2008029109

For the most part, Scripture quotations are taken from the King James Version of the Bible (also called The
Authorized Version). On many occasions, to help explain the KJV text, the reviser consulted and used the text
of the Holy Bible, *New International Version®. NIV®.* Copyright © 1973, 1978, 1984 by Biblica, Inc.®. Used by
permission of Zondervan. All rights reserved worldwide.

Any Internet addresses (websites, blogs, etc.) and telephone numbers printed in this book are offered as a
resource. They are not intended in any way to be or imply an endorsement by Zondervan, nor does Zondervan
vouch for the content of these sites and numbers for the life of this book.

Edited by Martin H. Manser, www.martinmanser.com.

Interior design: Ruth Bandstra & Nancy Wilson
Interior design management: Ben Fetterley

Printed in China

CONTENTS

REVISER'S PREFACE

Matthew Henry wrote his commentary about three hundred years ago; he began writing in November 1704, and the first volume was first published in 1708. Before he died at the age of 52 in 1714, he had completed up to and including Acts. After his death, the New Testament letters and Revelation were prepared by thirteen Nonconformist ministers.

This work has had a significant influence on many ministers and individual Christians in the last three hundred years. Thus, when the publishers of Zondervan approached me in 2002 about editing a version in contemporary English, I immediately felt humbled at the sheer privilege of the task. The work itself was immense; the original text contained over eight million words, and on average, Matthew Henry's comments take up more than 200 words on every verse of the Bible.

My remit was to update the wording of the original to clear, contemporary, natural-sounding English, so that it reads as a modern, practical, and devotional commentary on the KJV. I had to make the original more readable and understandable to present-day generations and future generations. This meant, for example, shortening his lengthy sentences and updating the author's language.

I have sought to ensure that this commentary will have the same impact on contemporary readers that Matthew Henry had on his original readers in terms of clarity of expression. Where his text was clear but awkward by today's standards, I have edited his text. On other occasions, when his original text was unclear, I have provided a thought-for-thought recasting of his original sense. I have had to ask myself many times day after day for six years, "If Matthew Henry were here today, how would he have expressed this?"

I have not, generally speaking, sought to update the scholarship on which the text was originally based: in many cases, he draws out points that are timeless. In a few places, I have added an editor's note on Matthew Henry's text such as the following at Genesis 7:11 – 12: "[Ed. note: Many Christians today use significantly longer dates.]" Matthew Henry was, as is understandable, a person of his time; therefore, on occasion, I have softened his stance toward, for example, the Roman Catholic church.

I wish to thank many people for their collaboration: Rosalind Desmond, Inna Frampton, and Nicky Bull have assisted my work, refining and correcting my text. At the publishers, Stan Gundry offered vital support and encouragement throughout the project from its inception; Verlyn Verbrugge and Jack Kuhatschek provided me with invaluable help to make sense of the original Hebrew and Greek. I would also like to thank Robert Banning for his editorial changes. Andrew White assisted by proofreading the entire typeset book. We gladly acknowledge the great usefulness of the Oxford English Dictionary in helping us understand archaic words and senses. I have also gathered around me a group of friends who have supported me in prayer over the last six years, and I am very grateful for their encouragement.

The task has been humbling. As I have attempted to present Matthew Henry's text in contemporary English, I have realized I have been standing on the shoulders of a giant, and inwardly at least, I have also knelt alongside this giant in adoration of the Lamb.

Martin H. Manser
Aylesbury, England
May 2008
www. martinmanser.com

A HISTORICAL NOTE ON
MATTHEW HENRY

Matthew Henry was born on October 18, 1662, at Broad Oak, a farmhouse on the border between Wales and England. His father, Philip Henry, was a clergyman who had been ejected from the church along with two thousand others by the Act of Uniformity 1662, since he refused to go along with the rites and ceremonies of the Book of Common Prayer. Unlike many of his fellow sufferers, however, Philip was able to give his son a good education.

For much of his early education, Matthew was tutored by his father. In 1685 he began formal studies in the area of law, but he also did some preaching on the side in his father's neighborhood. In January 1687 he went to Chester, where he continued preaching. His reception was so positive that the people there asked him to become their minister, and two years later he was privately ordained as an ordained clergyman to serve the Presbyterian congregation at Chester. The number of communicant members continued to grow under his preaching.

An exposition of the New Testament by a certain Mr. Burkitt—first on the Gospels, and then on Acts and the Epistles—had been very well received by preachers in Matthew Henry's day. But Mr. Burkitt died shortly after finishing the New Testament, and some of Matthew Henry's friends encouraged him to do something similar for the Old Testament. He was minded to do the same thing himself, and in 1704 he began writing his exposition of the Old Testament. His first volume on the Pentateuch was completed 1706 and was published in 1708. Every two years he completed another volume, so that the writing of the Old Testament was completed in 1710. In 1712 he moved to a larger church in Hackney, London, and finding the necessary time to continue writing became much more difficult. Two years later, on June 22, 1714, he suddenly collapsed and died on a journey from Chester to London.

By the time he died, Matthew Henry had completed the writing of his commentary through Acts, but he did not live to see the publication of volume 5, on the Gospels. Moreover, it was left to other non-Conformist ministers to do the actual writing of New Testament books from Romans to Revelation. They worked from extensive shorthand notes had been made on expositions he gave of these books. Here is a list, then, of those who completed the Matthew Henry Commentary:

Romans – Mr. [later Dr.] John Evans
1 Corinthians – Mr. Simon Browne
2 Corinthians – Mr. Daniel Mayo
Galatians – Mr. Joshua Bayes
Ephesians – Mr. Samuel Rosewell
Philippians and Colossians – Mr. [later Dr.] William Harris
1 and 2 Thessalonians – Mr. Daniel Mayo
1 and 2 Timothy – Mr. Benjamin Andrews Atkinson
Titus and Philemon – Mr. Jeremiah Smith
Hebrews – Mr. William Tong
James – Dr. S. Wright
1 Peter – Mr. Zech. Merrill
2 Peter – Mr. Joseph Hill
1, 2, and 3 John – Mr. John Reynolds of Shrewsbury
Jude – Mr. John Billingsley
Revelation – Mr. William Tong

A Practical and Devotional Exposition
of the First Book of Moses,

Genesis

Here before us is the Holy Bible, or *book*, for this is what the word *bible* means. We call it *the Book*, for it is incomparably the best book that has ever been written: it is the book of books. We call it the Holy Book, because it was written by holy prophets, moved by the Holy Spirit. The great things of God's Law and Gospel are here *written* for us, that they might be transmitted to distant lands and ages in a purer and more complete way than they could possibly be by word of mouth or tradition. This is the *light that shines in a dark place* (2Pe 1:19), and a dark place indeed the world would be without the Bible.

We have before us that part of the Bible which we call the *Old Testament*. This is called a *testament* or *covenant* because it was a settled declaration of the *will* of God concerning the entire human race, and had its force *from* the designed death of the great One who died, leaving his will, *the Lamb slain from the foundation of the world* (Rev 13:8). It is called the *Old Testament*. This stands with reference to the *New Testament*, which does not cancel and supersede the Old, but crowns and perfects it, by bringing in the better hope which was prefigured and foretold in it.

We have before us that part of the Old Testament that we call the *Pentateuch*, or the five books of Moses. In our Savior's division of the books of the Old Testament into the *Law*, the *Prophets*, and the *Psalms*, or *Hagiographa*, these are the *Law*.

We have before us the first and longest of those five books, which we call *Genesis*, written, some think, when Moses was in Midian, for the instruction and encouragement of his suffering brothers and sisters in Egypt. We prefer to think that he wrote it in the desert, after he had been on the mountain with God, where, probably, he received full and detailed instructions as to what to write.

Genesis is a name taken from the Greek. It means the "original" or "generation": it is a history of originals—the creation of the world, the entrance of sin and death into it, the invention of arts, the rise of nations, and especially the formation of the church, and its state in its early days. It is also a history of the generations of Adam, Noah, Abraham, etc. The beginning of the New Testament is called *Genesis* too (Mt 1:1); *biblos geneseos*, the book of the *genesis*, or *generation*, of Jesus Christ. Blessed be God for that book which shows us our healing, as this book opens up our wounds. Lord, open our eyes, that we may see the wonderful things of both your Law and your Gospel!

CHAPTER 1

Here is a plain and full account of the creation of the world—in answer to that first inquiry, "Where is God my Maker?" Unbelieving philosophers have made a grave mistake in this matter, some asserting the world's eternity and self-existence, others ascribing it to a chance convergence of atoms: thus "the world by wisdom knew not God," but took great pains to lose him. The aim of revealed Holy Scripture is to revive the principles of the laws of nature, the first being that this world was, in the beginning of time, created by a Being of infinite wisdom and power, who was himself before all time and all worlds. The first verse of the Bible gives us a surer and better, a more satisfying and more useful, knowledge of the origin of the universe, than all the volumes of the philosophers.

We have three things in this chapter: 1. A general idea given to us of the work of creation (vv. 1–2). 2.

A detailed account of the work of several days, put down in the form of a journal, distinctly and in order (vv. 3–30). 3. The review and approval of the whole work (v. 31).

Verses 1–2

Here is the work of creation in its essence and in its embryo.

1. The work of creation in its essence in v. 1, where we find the first line of our creed, that *God the Father Almighty is the Maker of heaven and earth.*

1.1. Notice in this verse four things:

1.1.1. What is produced: The world is like a great house, consisting of upper and lower stories, the structure grand and magnificent, uniform and fitting, and every room well and wisely furnished. The heavens are not only beautiful to our eyes with glorious lights which decorate its outside, the creation of which we read about here, but

1

they are also filled inside with glorious beings, out of our sight. In the visible world it is easy to observe:

- Great variety, several sorts of creatures differing vastly in their nature and being from one another.
- Great beauty. The blue sky and green earth are delightful to the eye of the careful spectator. How much more superlative must be the beauty of the Creator!
- Great precision. To those who with the help of microscopes closely examine the works of nature, they appear far more impressive than any works of art.
- Great power. The earth is not a lump of dead and inactive matter; the earth itself has an energy.
- Great order, a mutual dependence of beings, an exact harmony of movement, and a wonderful linking of the various causes.
- Great mystery. There are phenomena in nature which cannot be solved. But from what we see of heaven and earth we may deduce the eternal power and godhead of the great Creator. Our duty as Christians is always to keep heaven in our sight and the earth under our feet.

1.1.2. Who caused this great work: God. The Hebrew word is *Elohiym*, which speaks of:

1.1.2.1. The power of God the Creator. *El* signifies *the strong God*; and what less than almighty strength could bring all things out of nothing?

1.1.2.2. The plurality of persons in the Godhead: Father, Son, and Holy Spirit. This plural name of God in Hebrew, which speaks of him as many, though he is one, confirms our faith in the doctrine of the Trinity, which, though only barely intimated in the Old Testament, is clearly revealed in the New. We are often told that the world was made by the Son, and nothing was made without him (Jn 1:3, 10; Eph 3:9; Col 1:16; Heb 1:2).

1.1.3. How this work was carried out: *God created it*, that is, made it out of nothing. There was not any preexistent matter out of which the world was produced. Craftspeople cannot work unless they have something to work on. But with God it is different. The God of nature is not subject to the laws of nature. By the almighty power of God it is not only possible that something be made out of nothing, but in the creation it is impossible that it be otherwise, for nothing so dishonors the eternal mind more than to suppose in the existence of eternal matter.

1.1.4. When this work was produced: *In the beginning*, that is, in the beginning of time, when that clock was first set going: time began with the production of those beings which are measured by time. Before the beginning of time there was nothing but that infinite Being that lives in eternity. But for us it is enough to say, *In the beginning was the Word* (Jn 1:1).

1.2. Let us learn from this:

- That those who deny God's existence are foolish, for they see there is a world that could not make itself, and yet they will not acknowledge that there is a God who made it.
- That God is the sovereign Lord over all by his indisputable right.
- That with God everything is possible, and so the people that have him for their God can be happy: they are the ones who receive his help and who stand in his name (Ps 121:2; 124:8).
- That the God we serve is worthy of all blessing and praise (Ne 9:5–6). If everything comes from him, everything must be given to him.

2. The work of creation in its embryo in v. 2, where we have an account of primordial matter and the Prime Mover.

2.1. Chaos was the primordial matter. It is here called the earth; it is also called *the deep*, both for its vastness and because the waters which were afterward separated from the earth were now mixed with it. The Creator could have made his work perfect to begin with, but by using a gradual process he showed what is the normal method of his providence and grace. Notice the description of this formless earth, this chaos:

2.1.1. There was nothing in it desirable to be seen, for it was *without form and void*. *Tohu* and *bohu*, *confusion* and *emptiness* are the translation of these words in Isa 34:11. To those whose hearts are in heaven, this lower world, when compared with that upper, still appears to be nothing but chaos and desolation.

2.1.2. If there had been anything desirable to be seen, there was no light to see it by; for *darkness*, thick darkness, *was upon the face of the deep*. This chaos represents the state of an unregenerate, graceless soul: there is disorder, confusion, and every evil work; it is empty of all good, for it is without God; it is dark till almighty grace brings about a blessed change.

2.2. The Spirit of God was the Prime Mover: He *moved upon the face of the waters*. The Spirit of God begins to work, and, if he is at work, who or what can hinder him? God is said to make the world by his Spirit (Job 26:13; Ps 33:6); and by the same mighty worker the new creation is brought into being. He moved upon the face of the deep. God is not only the author of everything living, but the fountain of life and spring of every change. Dead matter would remain dead if he did not bring it alive. And this makes us believe that it is possible for God to raise the dead.

Verses 3–5

We have here a further account of the first day's work, in which notice:

1. That the first of all visible beings which God created was light. We needed light so that we might see his works and his glory in them, and might carry out our work while it is day (Jn 9:4). Light is the great beauty and blessing of the universe. In the new creation, the first thing created in the soul is *light*: the blessed Spirit captivates the will, mind, and heart by giving light to the understanding. Those that by sin were darkness become by grace light in the world.

2. That the light was made by the word of God's power. He said, *Let there be light*; he willed and appointed it, and it was done immediately. The word of God is quick and powerful. Christ is the Word, the essential eternal Word, and by him the light was produced, for *in him was light, and he is the true light, the light of the world* (Jn 1:9; 9:5). The divine light which shines in sanctified souls is created by the power of God, giving the knowledge of the glory of God in the face of Christ, as, at first, *God commanded the light to shine out of darkness* (2Co 4:6).

3. That the light which God willed, when it was produced, God approved of: *God saw the light, that it was good*. If the light is good, how good is the One that is the fountain of light, from whom we receive it.

4. That God *divided the light from the darkness*. Yet he divided the time between them, the day for light and the night for darkness, constantly and regularly following each other. Though the darkness was now scattered by the light, yet it takes its turn with the light, and has its place, because it has its use; for, as the light of the morning is

the friend of the business of the day, so the shadows of the evening are the friend of the rest of the night, and draw the curtains around us, so that we may sleep the better.

5. That God divided them from each other by distinguishing names: *He called the light day, and the darkness he called night.* He gave them names, as the Lord of both. Let us acknowledge God in the constant sequence of day and night, and set apart both to his honor, by working for him every day and resting in him every night.

6. That this was the first day's work, and a good day's work it was. *The evening and the morning were the first day.* This was not only the first day of the world, but the first day of the week. Let us observe the honor of that day, because the new world began on the first day of the week in the same way in the resurrection of Christ, as the light of the world, early in the morning. In him the rising sun has come to us from heaven (Lk 1:78).

Verses 6–8

We have here an account of the second day's work, the creation of the firmament. Notice:

1. God's command concerning it: *Let there be a firmament,* "an expansion" or "great space," for this is what the Hebrew word means, like a sheet spread, or a curtain drawn out. This firmament is not a wall of partition, but a way of passage. See Job 26:7; 37:18; Ps 104:3; Am 9:6.

2. Its creation. So that it should not seem as if God had only commanded it to be done, and someone else had carried out the work, he adds, *And God made the firmament.* What God requires of us he himself works in us, or it is not done. He that commands faith, holiness, and love creates them in us by the power of his grace alongside his word.

3. Its use and design: to *divide the waters from the waters,* that is, to distinguish between the waters enveloped in the clouds and those that cover the sea. God has, in the firmament of his power, heavenly palaces, from which he *watereth the earth.* O how great God is! He has provided for the comfort of all that serve him.

4. Its naming: *He called the firmament heaven.* It is the visible heaven, the sky, the pavement of the holy city; above the firmament God is said to have his throne (Eze 1:26). We should be led by the contemplation of the heavens that are in our sight to consider *our Father who is in heaven.* The height of the skies above us should remind us of God's supremacy and the infinite distance there is between us and him; the brightness of the heavens and their purity should remind us of his glory, majesty, and perfect holiness. The vastness of the heavens, their surrounding of the earth, and the influence they have upon it, should remind us of God's immensity and providence for all.

Verses 9–13

Until this time the power of the Creator had been applied in the upper part of the visible world; the light of heaven was lit, and the firmament of heaven fixed: but now our God comes down to this lower world, the earth, which was designed for the human race, designed both for us to live in and also to support us. Here we have an account of how the world is suitable for both purposes: its building and its provision:

1. How the earth was prepared to be lived in by human beings, by the gathering of the waters together, and the making of the dry land to appear (vv. 9–10).

1.1. The waters which had covered the earth were ordered to withdraw, and to gather into one place. The waters collected in this way he called *seas.* Waters and seas often, in Scripture, stand for troubles and affliction (Ps 42:7; 69:2, 14–15). God's own people are not exempt from these in this world; but it is their comfort that they are only waters under the heaven (there are none in heaven), and that they are all in the place that God has appointed them and within the limits that he has set for them.

1.2. The dry land was made to appear, and emerge from the waters, and was called *earth,* and given to us. The earth, it seems, existed beforehand; but it was of no use, because it was underwater. Similarly, many of God's gifts are received in vain, because they are buried; if we make them appear, they become of use to others.

2. How the earth was made suitable to keep and support the human race (vv. 11–12). God made provision by the immediate products of the newly made earth. It became fruitful, and brought forth vegetation: plants and trees, for livestock and people. Provision was similarly made for the future, every one *having its seed in itself after its kind,* that, as long as we live on the earth, there might be food for our use and benefit. Notice here:

2.1. That not only the earth is the Lord's, but *the fullness thereof,* and he is the rightful owner and sovereign disposer, not only of it, but of all that is within it. The earth was *emptiness* (v. 2), but now, by a word that was spoken, it has become full of God's riches.

2.2. That common providence is a continued creation, and in it *our Father worketh hitherto.* The earth still remains under the effectiveness of this command, to produce vegetation and its annual products. They are continuing instances of the unwearied power and inexhaustible goodness of the world's great Maker and Master.

2.3. That though God commonly makes use of the means of secondary causes, according to their nature, yet he neither needs them nor is bound by them.

2.4. That it is good to provide what is necessary—before we have occasion to use them: before the animals and human beings were made, plants and trees were prepared for them.

2.5. That God must have the glory from all the benefits we receive from the products of the earth.

Verses 14–19

This is the account of the fourth day's work, the creating of the sun, moon, and stars, that embellishment which is not only the great beauty of the upper world, but also so much the blessing of this lower. We now have an account of the creation of the lights of the heavens:

1. In general in vv. 14–15, where we have:

1.1. The command given concerning them: *Let there be lights in the firmament of heaven.* God had said, *Let there be light* (v. 3), and there was light; but that was, as it were, light in disarray, scattered and confused: now it was collected and formed, so making light both more glorious and more useful. God is the God of order, not of confusion; and, as he is light, so he is the Father and former of lights.

1.2. The uses they were intended to be to the earth:

- They distinguish the times of day and night, summer and winter, and so, *under the sun,* there is *a season to every purpose* (Ecc 3:1).
- They direct our actions. They are the signs of changes in weather, that farmers may know whether the weather will be fair or stormy (Mt 16:2–3) and so can plan their work accordingly. They also *give light upon the earth,* that we may *walk* (Jn 11:9), and *work* (Jn 9:4) as the duties of each day require. The lights of heaven shine for us, for our pleasure and benefit. The

lights of heaven are made to serve us, and they do it faithfully, and shine in their seasons without fail: but we are set as lights in this world to serve God. Do we in the same way fulfill the purpose of our creation? We burn our Master's candles, but all too often do not care for our Master's work.

2. In detail in vv. 16–18, where we have:

2.1. The lights of heaven are the sun, moon, and stars; and all these are the work of God's hands.

2.1.1. The sun is the greatest light of all. Let us learn from Ps 19:1–6 how to give God the glory that he deserves, as the Maker of the sun.

2.1.2. The moon is a lesser light, but is here considered as one of the greater lights. The most useful are the most valuable; and the greatest lights are not those who have the best gifts, but those who humbly and faithfully do the most good with what God has given them.

2.1.3. *He made the stars also*, for the Scriptures were written, not to satisfy our curiosity and make us astronomers, but to lead us to God, and make us saints. Now these lights are deputy-governors, rulers under him. Here the lesser light, the moon, is said to *rule the night*; but in Ps 136:9 the stars are mentioned as sharers in that rule: *The moon and stars to rule by night.* The best and most honorable way of ruling is by giving light and doing good: those who live a useful life and so shine as lights are those who command respect.

2.2. We can learn from all this:

2.2.1. The sin and folly of that ancient form of idolatry, the worshiping of the sun, moon, and stars. The account given of them here plainly shows that they are both created by God and for the service of human beings, and therefore it is both a great affront to God and a great reproach to ourselves to make gods of them and give them divine honor.

2.2.2. The duty and wisdom of daily worshiping that God who made all these things what they are and to offer a solemn sacrifice of prayer and praise every morning and evening.

Verses 20–23

We do not read of the creation of any living creature till the fifth day, of which these verses give us an account. It was on the fifth day that the fish and birds were created, both from the waters. Notice:

1. The making of the sea creatures and birds, originally (vv. 20–21). God commanded them to be produced. God said, *Let the waters bring forth abundantly*, and he himself carried out this command: *God created great whales, and every living creature that moveth.* Insects, which perhaps are as various and as numerous as any species of animals, and their structure as ingenious, were part of this day's work. We can, with Mr. Boyle, wonder at the Creator's wisdom and power as much in an ant as in an elephant. The masterly formation of the bodies of animals, with their different sizes and shapes and with their great sensory powers, serves not only to silence and shame the objections of those who do not believe, but also to raise high thoughts and praises of God in godly souls (Ps 104:25, etc.).

2. The blessing of these creatures and their continuing existence. All living creatures grow weak. Life's strength is not the strength of stones. It is a candle that will burn out, if it is not first itself blown out; and therefore the wise Creator not only made individuals, but also provided for their reproduction in several different ways: *God blessed them, saying, Be fruitful, and multiply* (v. 22).

Verses 24–25

We have here the first part of the sixth day's work and on this day the animals of the earth, livestock and wild animals, were made. Here, as before, *the Lord gave the word*; he said, *Let the earth bring forth.* God also did the work; he made them all in their own kind, in various shapes, sizes, natures, and food—some living upon grass and plants, others upon meat—some bold, and others timorous—some (like the horse) to be used for the service of human beings, and not our sustenance; others (like the sheep) for our sustenance, and not our service, while others (like the ox), for both; while still others (like the wild animals) for neither.

Verses 26–28

We have here the second part of the sixth day's work, the creation of human beings. Notice:

1. That of all the creatures human beings were made last, that it might not be suspected that we had, in any way, helped God in the creation of the world. Yet it was both an honor and a favor to us that we as human beings were made last. It was an honor, for the method of the creation was to move from the less perfect to the more perfect. It was a favor, for it was not right that we should stay in the palace designed for us until it was completely fitted and furnished for our reception. As soon as the first human beings were made, they had the whole visible creation before them, both to contemplate and to take comfort in.

2. That the creation of human beings was a more significant and immediate act of divine wisdom and power than that of the other creatures. Up to now, it has been said, "Let there be light," "Let there be a firmament," and "Let the earth, or waters, bring forth"; but now the word of command is turned into a word of council, "*Let us make man*, for whose sake the rest of the creatures were made: this is a work we must take into our own hands." In the former he speaks as one having authority, in this as one having affection. It is as if he had said, "Having at last settled the preliminaries, let us now apply ourselves to the real work, *Let us make man.*" Human beings were to be creatures that were different from all that had been made up to that time. Flesh and spirit, heaven and earth, must be put together in human beings, and they must be allied to both worlds. And therefore God himself not only undertakes to make human beings, but also is pleased to express himself as if he called together a council to consider their making: *Let us make man.* The three persons of the Trinity—Father, Son, and Holy Spirit—meet in council and agree. Let the One who said, *Let us make man*, rule over us.

3. That human beings were made in God's image and his likeness, two words that express the same thing and make each other the more expressive. *Image* and *likeness* denote the most alike image. Still between God and human beings there is an infinite distance. Only Christ is the *express* image of God's person, as the Son of his Father, having the same nature. It is only some of God's honor that is put upon human beings, who are God's image only as the shadow in a mirror, or the monarch's imprint on coins. God's image on human beings consists in these things:

3.1. In God's nature and constitution, not those of his body (for God does not have a body), but those of his soul. This honor God has indeed put on our bodies, that the Word was made flesh, the Son of God was clothed with a body like ours and will soon clothe ours with a glory like his. But it is the great soul of human beings that especially bears God's image. The soul of human beings, considered in its three noble faculties — understanding, will, and active power — is perhaps the brightest, clearest mirror in nature, in which we can see God.

3.2. In God's place and authority: *Let us make man in our image, and let him have dominion.* As human beings have power over the lesser creatures, we are, as it were, God's representatives, or viceroys, on earth. But the government of ourselves by the freedom of our will has in it more of God's image than our government of creatures.

3.3. In God's purity and justice. God's image on human beings consists in knowledge, righteousness, and true holiness (Eph 4:24; Col 3:10). It was in this holy and happy state that our first parents were, bearing the image of God on them.

4. That human beings were made male and female, and blessed with the blessing of fruitfulness and increase. God said, *Let us make man,* and immediately it follows, *So God created man;* he carried out what he decided. With us saying and doing are two things, but they are not so with God. It would seem that of the rest of the creatures God made many couples, but of human beings *did not he make one?* From this Christ infers an argument against divorce (Mt 19:4–5). Our first father, Adam, was limited to one wife; and, if he had put her away, there would be no other woman for him to marry, which clearly showed that the marriage bond was not to be dissolved at pleasure. God originally made only one male and one female, that the whole human race might know that they themselves are made of one blood and are descendants from one common ancestry, and so might be led to love one another. He gave them:

4.1. A large inheritance: *Replenish the earth;* it is this that is given to the whole human race. We were made *to dwell on the face of all the earth* (Ac 17:26). This is the place in which God has set us to be apprentices to learn how to serve him more fully.

4.2. A numerous, lasting family to enjoy this inheritance.

5. That God gave to human beings, when he had made them, a dominion over the lower creatures, over the fish of the sea and over the fowl of the air. Although as human beings we provide for neither fish nor birds, we have power over both. In this God wanted to honor us. God's providence continues to human beings as is necessary for our safety and support.

Verses 29–30

We have here the third part of the sixth day's work, a gracious provision of food for all flesh (Ps 136:25).

1. Food provided for human beings (v. 29). They were to eat all kinds of plants, grain, and fruit. Notice here:

1.1. That this should make us humble. As we were made from the earth, so we are kept by it. There is food that endures to everlasting life; Lord, evermore give us this.

1.2. That this should make us thankful. Our bodies belong to the Lord; from him we receive all the supports and comforts of this life. He gives us all things richly to enjoy, not only necessities, but also great variety and luxuries for our enjoyment and delight.

1.3. That this should make us moderate and content with what we are given. If God gives us food for our lives, let us not, with murmuring Israel, ask food for our cravings (Ps 78:18); see Da 1:15.

2. Food provided for the animals (v. 30). *Doth God take care for oxen?* Yes, certainly, he provides the right food for them, and not for oxen only, but even the young lions and the young ravens come under his providential care. God is like a very rich and abundant housekeeper, who

satisfies the desires of every living thing. The God who feeds the birds will not starve his little ones.

Verse 31

Here is God's approval and conclusion of his whole work of creation. We see here:

1. The review God undertook of his work: He *saw every thing that he had made.* God does this still; he watches over all the works of his hands. God's complete knowledge of everything cannot be separated from his complete power over everything. But this was the eternal Mind's solemn reflection upon the results of its own wisdom and power. In this way God has set us an example of reviewing our works. When we have finished a day's work and are coming to rest at night, we should meditate within our own hearts (Ps 4:4) about what we have been doing that day.

2. The satisfaction that God took in his work. He did not pronounce it good till he had seen it to be good: this teaches us not to respond to a matter before we have heard it.

2.1. It was good. Good, for everything is pleasant to the mind of the Creator, just as he would have it to be. Good, for it fulfills the purpose for which it was designed. Good, for it is useful to human beings, whom God appointed lords of the visible creation. Good, for it is all for God's glory.

2.2. It was very good. Of each day's work (except the second) it was said that it was good, but now, it is *very good.* This is because:

2.2.1. Human beings, the high point of creation, were made; human beings, who were designed to be the visible image of the Creator's glory and the mouth of the creation in their praises.

2.2.2. Everything was made; every part was good, but all together it was very good. The glory and goodness, the beauty and harmony, of God's works, both of providence and grace, will best appear when they are perfected. So the lesson is: judge nothing before the right time.

3. The time when this work was concluded: *The evening and the morning were the sixth day;* so that in six days God made the world. God could have made the world in an instant. He that said, *Let there be light, and there was light,* could have said, "Let there be a world," and there would have been a world, *in a moment, in the twinkling of an eye,* as at the Resurrection (1Co 15:52). But he did it in his own way and in his own time. The Sabbath would be so significant in keeping religion in the world that God considered it important in the timing of his creation.

CHAPTER 2

This chapter is an appendix to the history of the Creation, more particularly enlarging on and explaining that part of the history which relates immediately to human beings. We have in it: 1. The institution of the Sabbath (vv. 1–3). 2. A more detailed account of the creation of the first man (vv. 4–7). 3. A description of the Garden of Eden, and the placing of the man in it under the obligations of a law and covenant (vv. 8–17). 4. The creation of the woman, her marriage to the man, and the institution of the ordinance of marriage (vv. 18–25).

Verses 1–3

Here is:

1. The completion of God's work of Creation and God's rest from that work (vv. 1–2). Notice:

1.1. The creatures made both in heaven and on earth are disciplined, and under God's command. Every one knows and keeps their place.

1.2. The heavens and the earth are finished works, and so are all the creatures in them.

1.3. After the end of the first six days God finished all his works of creation. He has ended his work. In miracles, he has controlled nature, but never changed its settled course.

1.4. The eternal God did not rest, as one who is weary, but as one who is well pleased.

2. The beginning of the kingdom of grace, in making the Sabbath day holy (v. 3). Notice:

2.1. The solemn observance of one day in seven, as a day of holy rest and holy work to God's honor, is the indispensable duty of all those to whom God has revealed his holy Sabbath.

2.2. Sabbaths are as ancient as the world; and we see no reason to doubt that the Sabbath, being now begun before the Fall, was observed by the people of God throughout the patriarchal age.

2.3. The Sabbath of the Lord is to be fully honored for the sake of its great Author, since our God himself and our first parents also obeyed God in this way.

2.4. The Sabbath day is a blessed day, for God blessed it, and what he blesses is blessed indeed. God has promised to meet us and bless us on that day.

2.5. The Sabbath day is a holy day, for God has made it holy.

Verses 4–7

Notice in these verses:

1. Here is a name given to the Creator which we have not yet met with, and that is *Jehovah*—the LORD, in capital letters, which is used in our English Bible translations to show that in the original it is *Jehovah*. In the first chapter of Genesis, he was called *Elohiym*, a God of power; but now *Jehovah Elohiym*, a God of power and perfection, a God who completes his work. *Jehovah* is that great and incommunicable name of God which shows that he has being of himself, and that he has given existence to all things. It is the personal and covenant name of God, the Redeemer of his people.

2. A further note of the production of plants and shrubs, because they were made and appointed to be food for human beings (vv. 5–6). Here notice:

2.1. The earth did not produce its fruits by itself, but purely by God's almighty power. Similarly, the work of grace in the soul does not grow naturally within us, but is the work of God's own hand.

2.2. Rain also is the gift of God; it did not come until *the Lord God caused it to rain*.

2.3. Though God normally works by ordinary means, he is not limited to them.

2.4. In some way or other God will take care of watering the plants that he has planted. Though as yet there was no rain, God made a mist equivalent to a shower or streams, and so *watered the whole face of the ground*. Divine grace descends like a mist or silent dew and waters the church noiselessly (Dt 32:2).

3. A more detailed account of the creation of the first man (v. 7). Human beings are a little world, consisting of heaven and earth, soul and body. Now here we have an account of the origin of both.

3.1. The lowly origin, and the skillfully woven form, of the body of the man.

3.1.1. The substance that the man was made from was contemptible. He was made *of the dust of the ground*, a very unlikely thing to make a human being of; but the same infinite power that made the world out of nothing made human beings, its masterpiece, out of next to nothing. The man was not made of fine particles of gold, pearls, or diamonds, but common dust, the dust of the ground. Our form is earthly, and the fashioning of it like that of an earthen vessel (Job 10:9). What have we then to be proud of?

3.1.2. The Maker was great, and what he made was fine. Of the other creatures it is said that they were *created* and *made*; but of the man that he was *formed*, which shows a gradual process in the work with great precision. The workmanship exceeded the materials. Let us present our bodies to God as living sacrifices (Ro 12:1).

3.2. The high origin, and the great usefulness, of the human soul.

3.2.1. The soul has its origin in the breath of heaven. It was not made from the earth, as the body was; and so it came directly from God. Let the soul which God has breathed into us breathe after him. Into his hands let us commit our spirits, for from his hands we received them.

3.2.2. The soul is the person. The body would be a worthless, useless, loathsome carcass, if the soul did not give it life. Since the origin of the soul is so noble, and its nature and faculties are so excellent, let us not be foolish and despise our own souls, by favoring our bodies instead (Pr 15:32). The One who made the soul is alone able to make it new.

Verses 8–15

We have just read that human beings are made up of body and soul, a body made from the earth and a rational, immortal soul from the breath of heaven. In these verses we now see the provision that God made for the happiness of both body and soul. The One that made the man took care to make him happy. It would have been good if the man could have kept himself in such a state.

1. A description of the Garden of Eden, which was intended to be the stately home and grounds of this great lord, the palace of this ruler. The inspired writer, in this account, was writing first of all for Jews, and developing this account for the early church, and describes things by their outward perceptible appearances, and leaves us, by further discoveries of God's light, to be led into the understanding of the mysteries surrounding them. Therefore he does not so much emphasize the happiness of Adam's mind as his outward state.

1.1. The place where Adam was to stay was a garden; not an ivory tower or a palace overlaid with gold, but a garden, decorated simply by nature, not by art. The heavens were the roof of Adam's house, and never was any roof so skillfully lined and painted. The earth was his floor, and never was any floor so richly inlaid. The shadow of the trees was where he rested; under them were his dining-rooms, his living-rooms, and never were any rooms so finely decorated as these: Solomon's, in all their splendor, were not dressed like them (Mt 6:29). Nature is content with a little and with what is most natural, grace is content with less, but covetousness is content with nothing.

1.2. The planning and furnishing of this garden were the immediate work of God's wisdom and power. The Lord God planted this garden. No delights can be pleasant or satisfying to a soul except those that God himself has provided and given; no true paradise, except when God has planted it.

1.3. The location of this garden was extremely pleasant. It was in *Eden*, which signifies "delight" and "pleasure." The location is here described by lines and boundaries that were sufficient, we suppose, when Moses wrote. Let us be sure of a place in the heavenly paradise, and then we do not need to become bewildered in our search for the location of the earthly paradise.

1.4. The trees with which this garden was planted.

1.4.1. It had all the best and most select trees. God as a tender Father provided not only for Adam's good, but also for his gratification. There is a gratification, a pleasure, consistent with innocence; there is even a true and transcendent pleasure in innocence. But:

1.4.2. It contained two trees that were found exclusively in this garden; they were not to be found anywhere else on earth.

1.4.2.1. There was *the tree of life in the midst of the garden*, which was chiefly meant to be a sign and seal to Adam. It assured him of the continuance of life and happiness, even to immortality and everlasting happiness, through the grace and favor of his Maker, on condition that he persevered in his state of innocence and obedience. He could eat from and live off this tree. Christ has now become the tree of life (Rev 2:7; 22:2) to us.

1.4.2.2. There was *the tree of the knowledge of good and evil*, so called, not because it had any power in it to create or increase useful knowledge, but:

- Because there was an express and explicit revelation of the will of God concerning this tree, so that by it the man might know good and evil. What is good? It is good not to eat from this tree. What is evil? It is evil to eat from this tree. The distinction between all other good and evil was naturally written on the heart of the man; but this, which resulted from the instituted law of God, was written on this tree.
- Because in the event it proved to give Adam the experience and knowledge of good and evil when he and the woman took its fruit and ate it (3:6): they lost the good as they perceived the evil. As the covenant of grace contained, not only *Believe and be saved*, but also *Believe not and be damned* (Mk 16:16), so the covenant of innocence contained not only "Do this and live," which was sealed and confirmed by the tree of life, but also "Fail and die," which Adam was assured of by this other tree: "Touch it at your peril." So we see that in these two trees, God set before the man *good and evil, the blessing and the curse* (Dt 30:19). These two trees were like two ordinances.

1.5. The rivers with which this garden was watered (vv. 10–14). These four rivers (or one river branched into four streams) contributed a lot to the pleasantness and also to the fruitfulness of this garden. In the heavenly paradise there is a river infinitely surpassing these; for it is a river of the water of life, not coming out of Eden, like this, but proceeding from the throne of God and of the Lamb (Rev 22:1), a river that *makes glad the city of our God* (Ps 46:4). Havilah had gold, spices, and precious stones; but Eden had what was infinitely better, the tree of life and fellowship with God. Some people may have gold, but not have the Gospel. Their gold is good, but the riches of the Gospel are infinitely better.

2. The placing of the man in this Paradise of delight (v. 15). Notice:

2.1. How God put him in the garden:

2.1.1. The man was made *outside* Paradise; for, after God had formed him, he put him into the garden: he was made out of common clay, not of paradise dust. He could not plead the right of a tenant to the garden, for he was not born there. He had nothing he could call his own; all that he had he had received, so that all boasting may be excluded (Ro 3:27).

2.1.2. The same God that was the author of his existence was the author of his enjoyment. He that made us is alone able to make us happy.

2.1.3. It adds much to the comfort of any situation if we have clearly seen God going before us and putting us into it. If we have not forced Providence, but taken the hints of direction that Providence has given us, we may hope to find a paradise. See Ps 47:4.

2.2. How God appointed him to tend the garden and to take care of it. Paradise itself was not a place of exemption from work. Note here:

2.2.1. None of us was sent into the world to be lazy. The One who made these souls and bodies has given us something to work with; the One who made us living wants us to labor, to serve him and our society, and to work out our salvation.

2.2.2. Secular employment can run alongside a state of innocence and a life of fellowship with God.

2.2.3. The farmer's calling is an ancient and honorable calling; it was needed even in Paradise. It was a calling giving the man an opportunity to wonder at the Creator. While his hands were concerned with the trees, his heart might be with his God.

2.2.4. There is a true pleasure in the work which God calls us to and uses us in.

3. The command which God gave to the man in his innocence, and the covenant he then took him into. Up to this time we have seen God as the man's powerful Creator and his generous benefactor; now he appears as his Ruler and Lawgiver.

Verses 16–17

Notice here:

1. God's authority over the man, as a creature that had reason and freedom of will. The Lord God commanded the man, who stood now as the father and representative of the whole human race, to receive law, as he had a short time before received a nature. Even the lower animals have their own instincts; but human beings were given minds to perform their service to their Lord, and so received, not only the command of a Creator, but the command of a Ruler and Master.

2. The particular act of this authority, in stipulating to him what he should do.

2.1. A confirmation to him of his present happiness, in the conferring of the privileges, *Of every tree in the garden thou mayest freely eat*. This was not only a gift of liberty to him, but it was in addition an assurance of life to him, immortal life, if he obeyed it. So, on condition of perfect personal and perpetual obedience, Adam was sure of Paradise to himself and his heirs forever.

2.2. A testing of his obedience. If he disobeyed God's command, he would forfeit his happiness: "Adam, know that you are on your best behavior; in Paradise you are, as it were, in a court of law. Observe my law and you will live forever. If you disobey my law you will be as miserable as much as you are happy now." Here:

2.2.1. Adam is warned of death if he disobeys. Notice that even Adam, in his state of innocence, was in awe of God's warning. The punishment threatened is death, which was threatened as the immediate consequence of sin.

2.2.2. Adam is tried by an instituted law, not to eat of the fruit *of the tree of knowledge* for two reasons:

- Command is purely the will of the Lawmaker. Adam had in his nature a hatred to what was evil in itself, and so he is tested in something which was evil only because it was forbidden.

• The restraint of it is laid on the desires of the flesh and of the mind, which, in corrupt human nature, are the two great sources of sin. This prohibition restrained both his appetite toward sensuous delights and his ambitions toward clever knowledge, that his body might be ruled by his soul and his soul by his God.

Verses 18–20

Here is:

1. An instance of the Creator's care of the man and his fatherly concern for his comfort (v. 18). He lets him know, for encouragement in his obedience, that he is a friend. Notice:

1.1. How God graciously took pity on his solitude. The One that made him knew both him and what was good for him, and indeed knew him better than he did himself, so he said, "It is not good that he should continue alone in this way."

1.1.1. Such a state of solitude did not bring him comfort, for we are social beings. Perfect solitude would turn a paradise into a desert, and a palace into a dungeon.

1.1.2. Such a state of solitude would not increase or reproduce his kind. God could originally have made a world of people to fill the earth. God saw fit to make up that number by a succession of generations, which, as God had formed the man, must be from two, and those male and female. One on your own is always one.

1.2. How God graciously decided to provide company for him. The result of this line of thought concerning him was this kind decision, *I will make an help meet for him*. Note from this:

1.2.1. In our best state in this world we still need one another's help.

1.2.2. It is God only who perfectly knows all our needs, and he is perfectly able to supply them all (Php 4:19). In him alone is our help, and from him come all our helpers.

1.2.3. A suitable wife is a companion and is from the Lord.

1.2.4. Family life, if it is pleasant, deals with the deep sense of loneliness. The man who has a good God, a good heart, and a good wife to talk to, but still complains he lacks conversation, would not have been easy or happy in Paradise.

2. An instance of the creatures' subjection to the man, and the man's dominion over them (vv. 19–20). So it was that God delivered to the man full possession of all that he had given him and put him in possession of his dominion over the creatures. God brought them to him, that he might name them, and so might show:

2.1. His knowledge, as a creature endowed with the faculties of both reason and speech.

2.2. His power. It is an act of authority to impose names (Da 1:7). God gave names to the day and night, the heavens, the earth, the sea; and he *calleth the stars by their names*, to show that he is the supreme Lord of these. But he allowed Adam to name the animals and birds, as their secondary lord; for, having made him in his own image, he put some of his own honor on him.

3. An instance of the creatures' inadequacy in bringing happiness to the man: *But* (among them all) *for Adam there was not found an help meet for him*. Notice here the dignity and excellence of human nature and the futility of this world and everything in it. Everything in the world will not make a suitable companion for the man. They will not suit the nature of his soul, nor supply its needs, nor satisfy its right desires, nor run parallel with its never-failing span of life.

Verses 21–25

Here we have:

1. The making of the woman to be a suitable companion for Adam. Notice:

1.1. That Adam was first formed, then Eve (1Ti 2:13). If man is the head, she is the crown, a crown to her husband, the crown of the visible creation. The man was dust refined, but the woman was dust double-refined, one stage further from the earth.

1.2. That Adam slept while his wife was being made as one who had given all his anxieties to God, with a cheerful submission of himself and all his life to his Maker's will and wisdom. *Jehovah-jireh*, let the Lord provide when and whom he pleases.

1.3. That *God caused a sleep to fall on Adam*, and made it a deep sleep. While Adam does not know sin, God will see that he will not feel any pain.

1.4. That the woman was *made of a rib out of the side of Adam*; not made out of his head to rule over him, or out of his feet to be trampled upon by him, but out of his side to be equal with him, under his arm to be protected by him, and near his heart to be loved by him.

2. The marriage of the woman to Adam. Marriage is honorable, but this surely was the most honorable marriage ever, one in which God himself had all along an immediate hand. Marriages, it is said, are made in heaven: we are sure that this was, for the man and the woman were matched by God's own work; he, by his power, made them *both*, and now, by his ordinance, made them *one*.

2.1. God, as *her* Father, brought the woman to the man, as the man's second self, and as a suitable companion for him. The wife that is of God's making by his special grace, and of God's bringing by his special providence, is likely to prove a suitable companion for a man.

2.2. From God, as *his* Father, Adam received her (v. 23). God's gifts to us are to be received with a humble, thankful acknowledgment of his wisdom in making them suitable for us, and of his favor in giving them to us. Further, as a sign of his acceptance of her, he gave her a name, not special to her, but common to her sex: *She shall be called woman, Ishshah*, differing from man in sex only, not in nature.

3. The institution of the ordinance of marriage and the establishment of its law (v. 24). The Sabbath and marriage were two ordinances instituted before the Fall, the former for the preservation of the church, the latter for the preservation of the human race. It appears (from Mt 19:4–5) that it was God himself who said here, "A man must leave all his relations, to be united to his wife."

3.1. See here how great is the power of a divine ordinance; its ties are stronger even than those of nature.

3.2. See how necessary it is that children should take their parents' agreement with them in their marriage.

3.3. See what need there is of both carefulness and prayer in the choice of this relationship, which is so close and so lasting.

3.4. See how firm the bond of marriage is, not to be divided and weakened by having many wives (Mal 2:15) or to be broken or ended by divorce, for any cause except marital unfaithfulness or voluntary desertion.

3.5. See how dear the affection ought to be between husband and wife, such as there is for our own bodies (Eph 5:28).

4. Evidence of the purity and innocence of the state in which our first parents were created (v. 25). They were both naked. They needed no clothes for protection against cold or heat. No, they needed none to become decent; they were naked but had no reason to be ashamed. "They did

not know what shame was" is the reading in Aramaic. Those that had no sin in their conscience might well have no shame on their faces, even though they had no clothes on their backs.

CHAPTER 3

We have here an account of the sin and misery of our first parents, the wrath and curse of God against them, the peace of creation disturbed, and its beauty stained and sullied, all bad, very bad. 1. The innocent tempted (vv. 1–5). 2. The tempted rebelling (vv. 6–8). 3. The rebels brought to trial (vv. 9–10). 4. The rebels found guilty at their trial (vv. 11–13). 5. The rebels' sentence (vv. 14–19). 6. The rebels' reprieve (vv. 20–21). 7. Despite their reprieve, the sentence partly carried out (vv. 22–24). And were it not for the gracious intimations given in this chapter of redemption by the promised descendants, they and all the rest of their degenerate guilty race would have been left to endless despair.

Verses 1–5

1. Here is the tempter, and that was the Devil, in the shape and likeness of a serpent.

1.1. It is certain that it was the Devil that deceived Eve. The Devil (Satan) is the old Serpent (Rev 12:9), an evil spirit, by creation an angel of light and a direct attendant on God's throne, but by sin he became apostate from his first state and a rebel against God's crown and dignity. He knew that the only way he could ruin the first human beings was to lead them astray. So the ploy which Satan had to use was to draw our first parents to sin, and so to separate them and their God. The whole human race could be struck at one point, as it were, and Satan struck at that.

1.2. It was the Devil in the likeness of a serpent. Many a dangerous temptation comes to us in apparently fine colors that are only skin-deep, and seems to come from above; for Satan can appear as an angel of light. The serpent is a subtle creature. Many instances are given of the subtlety of the Serpent. There is not anything by which the Devil serves himself and his own interest more than by unholy subtlety.

2. The person tempted was the woman, now by herself and at a distance from her husband, but near the forbidden tree. It was the Devil's subtlety:

- To attack the weaker partner with his temptations.
- To engage her in conversation when she was alone. There are many temptations to which solitude gives great advantage; but the fellowship of believers contributes much to their strength and safety.
- To find her near the forbidden tree, probably gazing on its fruit, simply to satisfy her curiosity. Those that would not eat the forbidden fruit must not go near the forbidden tree.
- To tempt Eve, that by her he might tempt Adam.

3. Here we have the temptation itself, and the contrived management of it. What the Devil aimed at was to persuade Eve to eat of forbidden fruit; and, to do this, he used the same method that he does still. He questioned whether it was a sin or not (v. 1). He denied that there was any danger in it (v. 4). He suggested benefits from it (v. 5). And these are the ways he still uses.

3.1. The Devil questioned whether it was a sin or not to eat of this tree, and whether the fruit of it really was forbidden. Notice:

3.1.1. *He said to the woman, Yea, hath God said, Ye shall not eat?* The first word hinted at something said earlier, perhaps some conversation Eve had with herself, which Satan took hold of, and joined this question to. Notice here:

- Satan does not reveal his aim at first, but puts a question which seems innocent: "I hear some information—is it true? Has God forbidden you to eat of this tree?"
- Satan misquotes the command as if it were a prohibition, not only of that tree, but of all.
- Satan seems to speak as a taunt, rebuking the woman for her shyness in meddling with that tree.
- It is the subtlety of Satan to damage the reputation of the divine law as uncertain or unreasonable, and so to draw people to sin.

3.1.2. In answer to this question the woman gives him a plain and full account of the law they were under (vv. 2–3). Here notice:

3.1.2.1. It was a sign of her weakness that she entered into conversation with the Serpent. It is a dangerous thing to discuss terms with a temptation. Instead the temptation should at the outset be rejected with disdain and hatred. The garrison that calls for a conference to discuss terms is not far from being surrendered.

3.1.2.2. It was a sign of her wisdom to take notice of the liberty that God had given them. "Yes," she says, "we may eat of the fruit of the trees, thanks to our Maker. There is plenty and great variety for us."

3.1.2.3. It was a sign of her decisiveness that she adhered to the command, and faithfully repeated it, as of unquestionable certainty: "We must not eat, and so we will not touch. It is forbidden to the highest degree, and the authority of the prohibition is sacred to us."

3.1.2.4. She seems to waver a little about the warning; all she makes of that is, *Lest you die.*

3.2. The Devil denied that there was any danger in their disobedience, insisting that, although it might be the breaking of a command, it would not incur a penalty: *You shall not surely die* (v. 4). Either:

3.2.1. "It is not certain that you will die," according to some. Satan teaches people first to doubt and then to deny; he makes them skeptics first, and so gradually makes them atheists. Or:

3.2.2. "It is certain you will not die," according to others. He declares his contradiction, with the same phrase of assurance that God had used in confirming his warning. He concealed his own misery, that he might draw them into the same: so it is that he still deceives sinners to their own ruin. Hope is a great support to all iniquity.

3.3. The Devil promises them benefits from their disobedience (v. 5). He could not have persuaded them to run the risk of ruining themselves if he had not suggested to them a great probability of improving themselves.

3.3.1. The Devil suggests to them how their lives would be better if they ate this fruit. He tailors the temptation to the pure state they were now in, proposing to them intellectual delight and satisfaction. These were the baits that he put on his hook:

- "*Your eyes shall be opened*; you will have much more of the power and pleasure of contemplation than now you have; you will see further into things than you do now."
- "*You shall be as gods*, as *Elohiym*, mighty gods; not only all-knowing, but also all-powerful."
- "You will *know good and evil*, that is, everything that is desirable to be known." To support this part of the

temptation, he abuses the name given to this tree. He corrupts the sense of it, as if this tree would give them a speculative, notional knowledge of the nature, kind, and origins of good and evil. And:

• All this immediately: *"In the day you eat thereof* you will find a sudden and immediate change for the better."* Now in all these suggestions he aims to create in them discontent with their present state and ambition to advance themselves, as if they were fit to be gods.

3.3.2. The Devil suggests to them that God had no good plans for them, in forbidding them this fruit, as if he dare not let them eat of that tree because then they would know their own strength, and would be able to contend with him. This was a great affront to God, and the highest indignity that could be done him. It was a reproach to his power, as if he feared his creatures, and also even more a reproach to his goodness, as if he hated the work of his own hands and would not want those whom he has made to be happy. It was also a most dangerous trap to our first parents, as it tended to distance their sensibilities from God.

Verses 6–8

Satan eventually wins his point, and the stronghold is taken by his scheming. Here we have:

1. The inducements that moved them to disobey God's command.

1.1. Eve saw no more harm in this tree than in any of the rest of the trees. It seemed as good for food as any of them: "Why should this tree be forbidden to them rather than any of the rest?" We are often betrayed into snares by an excessive desire to have our senses gratified. It was coveted all the more because it was prohibited. In us (that is, in our flesh, in our sinful nature) there dwells a strange spirit of contradiction. *Nitimur in vetitum,* "We desire what is prohibited."

1.2. She imagined more power in this tree than in any of the rest, that it was a tree not only not to be in awe of, but *to be desired to make one wise.* Notice here how the desire for unnecessary knowledge, under the mistaken notion of wisdom, proves hurtful and destructive to many. Our first parents, who knew so much, did not know this—that they knew enough.

2. The steps of the disobedience, not steps upward, but downward:

2.1. She *saw.* She should have turned away her eyes from looking at something futile and worthless; but she enters into temptation, by looking with pleasure at the forbidden fruit. Notice, a great deal of sin comes in through our eyes.

2.2. She *took.* It was her own act and deed. The Devil did not take it, and put it into her mouth, to see whether she would eat it or not, but she herself took it. Satan may tempt, but he cannot force; he may persuade us to throw ourselves down, but he cannot throw us down (Mt 4:6).

2.3. She *did eat.* Perhaps she did not intend, when she looked, to take; nor when she took, to eat; but this was the result. The way of sin is downhill; we cannot stop ourselves when we want to. Suppress the first emotions of sin, and stop it before we join company with it. *Obsta principiis,* "Nip evil in the bud."

2.4. She *gave also to her husband with her.* She gave it to him, persuading him with the same arguments that the Serpent had used with her, adding this to all the rest, that she herself had eaten of it, and had found that it did not bring death; no, it was extremely pleasant and gratifying. As was the Devil, so was Eve, no sooner a sinner than a tempter.

2.5. *He did eat,* overcome by his wife's boldness. In neglecting the tree of life from which he was allowed to eat, and eating from the tree of knowledge which was forbidden, he plainly showed a contempt for the favors God had given to him, and a preference for what God did not consider fit for him. He would be both his own carver and his own master, he would have and do what he pleased: his sin was, in one word, *disobedience* (Ro 5:19). Since this human nature was lodged entirely in our first parents, from that point onward it could not but be transmitted from them with the penalty of guilt, a stain of dishonor, and a hereditary disease of sin and corruption. Can we say, then, that Adam's sin had but little harm in it?

3. The immediate consequences of the disobedience:

3.1. Shame came on them (v. 7). Notice:

3.1.1. The strong conviction they fell under, in their own selves: *The eyes of them both were opened.* By this is not meant the eyes in their heads, but the eyes of their consciences were opened, and they were conscience-stricken for what they had done. Now, when it was too late, they saw the folly of eating the forbidden fruit. They saw the happiness they had fallen from, and the misery they had fallen into. They saw a law in their bodies at war against the law of their minds. The text tells us that they saw *that they were naked,* that is:

3.1.1.1. That they were stripped, deprived of all the honors and joys of their state of paradise. They were disarmed; they were vulnerable; their defense had departed from them.

3.1.1.2. That they were shamed. They saw themselves laid open to the contempt and reproach of heaven, and earth, and their own consciences. Now see here:

• What a dishonor and restlessness sin brings; it causes trouble wherever it is admitted.

• What a deceiver Satan is. He told our first parents, when he tempted them, that their eyes would be opened; and so they were, but not as they understood it; they were opened to their shame and grief.

3.1.2. The pitiful attempt they made to try to dull these convictions, and to arm themselves against them: *They sewed,* or plaited, *fig leaves together;* and to cover, at least, part of their shame from each other, they *made themselves aprons,* coverings. See here what is commonly the folly of those that have sinned:

3.1.2.1. That they are more concerned with saving face before their fellows than obtaining pardon from their God.

3.1.2.2. That the excuses people make, to cover and explain away their sins, are foolish and futile. Like the coverings of fig leaves, they never make the matter better, but worse: the shame, hidden in this way, becomes even more shameful.

3.2. Fear came upon them as soon as they ate the forbidden fruit (v. 8). Notice here:

3.2.1. What was the cause and occasion of their fear: They *heard the voice of the Lord God walking in the garden in the cool of the day.* It was the approach of the Judge that frightened them; and yet he came in such a way as it was formidable only to guilty consciences. In the cool of the day, not in the night, when all fears are doubly fearful, nor in the heat of day, for he came not in the heat of his anger. They heard his voice, and probably it was a still small voice, a gentle whisper, as he came when he was seeking Elijah.

3.2.2. What was the effect and evidence of their fear: *They hid themselves from the presence of the Lord God*—a sad change! God had become a terror to them, and so it is no surprise that they had become a terror to themselves. Their own consciences accused them, and set their sin before them in its true colors. Their fig leaves failed them, and were of no use to them. Knowing themselves guilty, they did not dare stand trial, but ran off, fleeing from justice. See here:

- The falsehood of the tempter. He promised them they would be safe, but now it seems inconceivable that they could think they were; he promised them they would be knowing, but they see themselves at a loss, and do not know even where to hide themselves; he promised them they should be like gods—great, bold, and daring—but they are as criminals discovered.
- The folly of sinners, to think it either possible or desirable to hide themselves from God.
- The fear that accompanies sin. All that terrifying fear of God's appearances, the accusations of conscience, the approaches of trouble, the attacks of lower creatures, and the captivity of death, which are common among the whole human race, are all the effects of sin.

Verses 9–10

Here we have the accusation of these fugitives before the righteous Judge.

1. The startling question with which God went after Adam and laid hold of him: *Where art thou?* Not in what *place?* but, in what *condition?* "Is this all the effect of eating the forbidden fruit?" We can learn from this:

1.1. This inquiry concerning Adam may be thought of as God graciously and kindly seeking him, in order to bring about his restoration.

1.2. If sinners will only consider where they are, they will not rest till they return to God.

2. The trembling answer which Adam gave to this question: *I heard thy voice in the garden, and I was afraid* (v. 10). He does not acknowledge his guilt, and yet in effect confesses it by owning up to his shame and fear.

Verses 11–13

Here the offenders are found guilty by their own confession and yet endeavor to excuse and make allowances for their fault. See:

1. How their confession was drawn from them. God put it to the man: *Who told thee that thou wast naked?* (v. 11). "How did you become aware of your nakedness and your shame?" *Hast thou eaten of the forbidden tree?* Although God knows all our sins, yet he wants to know them from us, and requires from us a simple confession of them; not so that he may be informed, but that we may be humbled. The question put to the woman was, *What is this that thou hast done?* (v. 13). Those who have eaten forbidden fruit themselves, and especially those who have enticed others to eat it, should seriously consider what they have done. In eating forbidden fruit, we have offended a great and gracious God. In enticing others to eat of it, we do the Devil's work, make ourselves guilty of others' sins, and contribute to their ruin.

2. How their crime was excused by them in their confession. It was to no effect to plead *not guilty.* Instead of increasing the offensiveness of the sin and taking the shame to themselves, they try to explain away the sin and lay the shame and blame on others.

2.1. Adam lays all the blame on his wife. Learn from this never to be delivered to sin by what will not deliver us from judgment; let us therefore never act against our consciences, nor ever displease God, to please the best

friend we have in the world. But this is not the worst of it. He not only lays the blame on his wife, but he also puts it in such a way as tacitly to reflect on God himself. He suggests that God contributed to his sin: he gave him the woman, and she gave him the fruit. There is a strange tendency in those that are tempted to say that they are tempted by God, as if our abusing of God's gifts would excuse our violation of God's laws.

2.2. Eve lays all the blame on the Serpent: *The serpent beguiled me.* Sin is a wretch that nobody is willing to own, a sign that it is a scandalous thing. Satan's temptations are all deceiving, his arguments are all false, his enticements are all fraudulent. Sin deceives us, and, by deceiving, cheats us. It is by the *deceitfulness of sin* that the heart is hardened. See Ro 7:11; Heb 3:13. Satan's subtlety will not put us right in sin: though he is the tempter, we are the sinners; and indeed it is our own evil desires that draw us aside and entice us (Jas 1:14).

Verses 14–15

God immediately proceeds to pass sentence; and, in these verses, he begins with the Serpent, which is where the sin began, because he was already convicted of rebelling against God.

1. The sentence passed on the tempter may be considered as coming upon the Serpent. The Devil's instruments must share in the Devil's punishments. Now:

1.1. The Serpent is here laid under the curse of God: *Thou art cursed above all cattle.* Unsanctified subtlety often proves a great curse to human beings; and the more cunning people are to do evil the more trouble they make.

1.2. The Serpent is here laid under human reproach and enmity.

1.2.1. He is to be forever looked upon as a vile and despicable creature. His crime was that he tempted Eve to eat what she should not; his punishment was that he had to eat what he did not want: *Dust shalt thou eat.*

1.2.2. He is to be forever looked on as a venomous destructive creature, and a true object of hatred and detestation. The Serpent is hurtful to the human race, and often strikes their heel, because it can reach no higher; no, notice is taken of his biting the horse's heels (49:17). But human beings are victorious over the Serpent, and crush his head, that is, give him a mortal wound, aiming to destroy the whole generation of snakes. This sentence pronounced upon the Serpent is strengthened greatly by that promise of God to his people, *Thou shalt tread upon the lion and adder* (Ps 91:13), and that of Christ to his disciples, *They shall take up serpents* (Mk 16:18). Notice here, the Serpent and the woman had just been very friendly and intimate in conversation about the forbidden fruit, and they had wonderfully agreed, but how soon they are irreconcilably set at variance! Sinful friendships justly end in mortal feuds: those that unite in wickedness will not stay united for long.

2. This sentence may be considered as leveled at the Devil, who only made use of the Serpent as his instrument in this appearance, but was himself the principal agent.

2.1. A perpetual reproach is here fixed on that great enemy of both God and the human race. Under the cover of the Serpent, he is here sentenced to be:

2.1.1. Degraded and cursed by God. *How art thou fallen, O Lucifer!* The one who would be higher than God, and would lead a rebellion against him, is here justly exposed to contempt, and God will humble those that will not humble themselves.

2.1.2. Detested and hated by the whole human race. He is here condemned to a state of war and irreconcilable enmity.

2.1.3. Destroyed and ruined eventually by *the great Redeemer*, signified by the crushing of his head. His subtle scheming will be totally thwarted, his usurped power will be entirely crushed.

2.2. A perpetual quarrel is here begun between the kingdom of God and the kingdom of the Devil among human beings. It is the fruit of this enmity that there is a continual conflict between grace and sin in the hearts of God's people and that there is similarly a continual struggle between the wicked and the godly in this world.

2.3. A gracious promise is here made of Christ, as the deliverer of fallen humanity from the power of Satan. It was said in the earshot of our first parents, who, doubtless, saw a door of hope opened to them. Here was the dawning of the Gospel day. No sooner was the wound given than the remedy was provided and revealed. They are told three things concerning Christ:

2.3.1. His incarnation, that he would be *the seed of the woman*, the offspring of *that* woman; therefore his genealogy (Lk 3:23–38) goes so far as to show him to be the son of Adam, but God does the woman the honor to call him rather her offspring, because it was she whom the Devil had deceived, and Adam had laid the blame on her. In this we can see that God magnifies his grace, in that, though the woman was first in the rebellion, it is she who will be saved by childbearing, that is, by the promised offspring who will descend from her (1Ti 2:15). He was similarly to be the offspring of a woman only, of a virgin.

2.3.2. His sufferings and death, pointed at in Satan's *bruising his heel*, that is, his human nature. Satan tempted Christ in the wilderness, to draw him into sin; and some think it was Satan that terrified Christ in his agony, to drive him to despair. It was the Devil that put it into the heart of Judas to betray Christ, of Peter to deny him, of the chief priests to try him, of the false witnesses to accuse him, and of Pilate to condemn him. In all this, they aimed at destroying the Savior, and so destroying salvation. But on the contrary, it was by death that Christ *destroyed him that had the power of death* (Heb 2:14). Christ's heel was bruised when his feet were pierced and nailed to the cross, and Christ's sufferings are continued in the sufferings of the saints for his name. The Devil tempts them, throws them into prison, persecutes and kills them, and so strikes the heel of Christ, who is afflicted in their afflictions. But while the heel is bruised on earth, it is well that the head is safe in heaven.

2.3.3. His victory over Satan in this. Satan had now trampled on the woman, and insulted her; but the offspring of the woman would be raised up in the fullness of time to *triumph over him* (Col 2:15). *He shall bruise his head*, that is, he shall destroy all his schemings and all his powers, and overthrow completely his kingdom and concerns. Christ thwarted Satan's temptations; by his death, he gave a fatal blow to the Devil's kingdom, a wound to the head of this Beast that can never be healed.

Verse 16

We have here the sentence passed on the woman for her sin:

1. She is here put into a state of sorrow, of which only one detail is specified, that of childbearing; but it includes grief and fear. Sin brought sorrow into the world; if we had known no guilt, we would have known no grief. The sorrows are here said to be increased: *greatly multiplied*. No wonder that our sorrows are multiplied when our sins are: both are innumerable evils. The sorrows of childbearing are multiplied; and if the children turn out evil and foolish, they are more than ever a heaviness to her that bore them.

2. She is put into a state of submission. *Wives, be in subjection to your own husbands* (1Pe 3:1); but the entrance of sin has made that duty a punishment, which otherwise it would not have been. If Eve had not eaten the forbidden fruit herself, and tempted her husband to eat it, she would never have complained of her subjection; and so it should never be complained of, even though it is harsh. It is sin that must be complained of, it is sin that made it so. Those wives who not only despise and disobey their husbands, but also domineer over them, do not consider that they are violating a divine law, and thwarting a divine sentence.

3. Notice here how mercy is mixed with wrath in this punishment. The woman will have sorrow, but it shall be childbearing, and the sorrow will be forgotten for joy *when a child is born* (Jn 16:21). The punishment was not a curse to bring about her ruin, but a discipline to bring about her repentance.

Verses 17–19

Here is the sentence passed on Adam, which is introduced with a description of his offense.

1. God put marks of his displeasure on Adam in three ways:

1.1. Where he lives is, by this sentence, cursed: *Cursed is the ground for thy sake*; and the effect of that curse is, *Thorns and thistles shall it bring forth to thee*. What good fruits it does produce must be forced from it by human ingenuity and industry. But notice a mixture of mercy in this sentence. Adam himself is not cursed, as the Serpent was (v. 14). God had blessings in store for him. He is still above the ground. The earth does not open and swallow him up in spite of its degeneration from its original beauty and fruitfulness.

1.2. His work and enjoyments are all made bitter to him:

1.2.1. His work will from this time on become a toil to him, and he will go on with it *in the sweat of his face* (v. 19). His work, before he sinned, was a constant pleasure to him; the garden was then tended and kept without any difficulty or drudgery. If Adam had not sinned, he would not have sweated. Labor is our duty, which we must faithfully perform.

1.2.2. His food will from this time on become unpleasant to him, in comparison with what it had been. *In sorrow* (v. 17) and *in the sweat of his face* (v. 19) he must eat of it. All, even the happiest in this world, have illnesses, disasters, and death that entered the world with sin and still lay waste to it and detract from our joy. Yet, in this part of the punishment, there is also a mixture of mercy. He will sweat, but his toil will make his rest all the more welcome when he returns to his earth, as to his bed; he will grieve, but he will not starve; he will have sorrow, but in that sorrow he will eat food, which will strengthen his heart in his sorrows.

1.3. His life also is but short. Considering how full of trouble his days are, it is out of kindness to him that they are few. Although death is dreadful to nature (even though life itself is at times unpleasant) death concludes the sentence. "Thou shalt *return to the ground out of which thou wast taken*; your body, that part of you which was taken out of the ground, will return to it again; for *dust thou art*." "Your body will be abandoned by your soul, and will become itself a lump of dust; and then it will be lodged in the grave, its proper place, and be mixed with the dust of the earth," *our dust* (Ps 104:29). "Earth to earth, dust to dust." Notice here:

1.3.1. That human beings are lowly and frail creatures, *little* as dust, the small dust of the balance—*light* as dust, altogether lighter than futility—*weak* as dust, and of no consistency.

1.3.2. That human beings are mortal, dying creatures, great masses of dust, and must return to the earth.

1.3.3. That sin brought death into the world. If Adam had not sinned, he would not have died (Ro 5:12).

2. We must not leave this sentence on our first parents till we have considered two things:

2.1. How fittingly the sad consequences of sin on the soul of Adam and his sinful race were represented. Although the only misery that is mentioned is the one which affected the body, yet that was a pattern of spiritual miseries, the curse that entered the soul.

2.1.1. The pains of a woman in childbearing represent the terrors and pangs of a guilty conscience awakened to a sense of sin.

2.1.2. The state of submission to which the woman was reduced represents that loss of spiritual liberty and freedom of will which is the effect of sin.

2.1.3. The curse of barrenness which was brought upon the earth, and its product of briers and thorns, are a suitable representation of the barrenness of a corrupt and sinful soul in that which is good and its fruitfulness in evil.

2.1.4. The toil and sweat speak of the difficulty which, through the weakness of the flesh, we labor under in the service of God and the work of religion.

2.2. How wonderfully the satisfaction our Lord Jesus made by his death and sufferings fulfills the sentence here passed on our first parents. Did travailing pains come in with sin? We read of the *travail of his soul*, the soul of Christ, the suffering servant (Isa 53:11). Did subjection come in with sin? Christ was born under law (Gal 4:4). Did the curse come in with sin? Christ became a curse for us, died a cursed death (Gal 3:13). Did thorns come in with sin? He was crowned with thorns for us. Did sweat come in with sin? For us his sweat was like drops of blood. Did sorrow come in with sin? He was a man of sorrows, in his agony his soul was extremely sorrowful. Did death come in with sin? He became obedient to death. And so the plaster covers the whole wound completely. Blessed be God for Jesus Christ!

Verse 20

God having named the man and called him *Adam,* meaning "ground," Adam named the woman, *Eve*, that is, "living." Adam bears the name of dying matter, Eve that of the living soul. The reason for the name is given here: *Because she was* (that is, was to be) *the mother of all living.* He had before called her *Ishshah*—*woman*, as a wife; here he calls her *Hawwah*, "living," as a mother. Now:

1. If this was done by divine direction, it was an instance of God's favor, and was a seal of the covenant, and an assurance to them that he had not reversed that blessing with which he had blessed them: *Be fruitful and multiply.* It was similarly a confirmation of the promise now made, that the offspring of the woman, of this woman, should crush the Serpent's head.

2. If Adam did it by himself, it was an instance of his faith in the word of God. It was done depending on the blessing of a reprieve, that he should spare such sinners to be the parents of all living, and the blessing of a Redeemer, the promised offspring, to whom Adam was looking in calling his wife Eve—"life."

Verse 21

We have here a further instance of God's care for our first parents, in spite of their sin. Although he corrects his disobedient children, he does not disinherit them, but like a tender father provides the plants of the field for their food and *coats of skins* for their clothing. God is to be acknowledged with thankfulness, for giving us not only food, but clothes also (28:20). The wool and the linen are his, as well as *the corn and the wine* (Hos 2:9). Adam and Eve made for themselves coverings of fig leaves, coverings too narrow for them to *wrap themselves in* (Isa 28:20). Such are all the rags of our own righteousness. But God made them garments of skin: large, strong, and durable, and fitting for them; such is the righteousness of Christ. Therefore *put on the Lord Jesus Christ* (Ro 13:14).

Verses 22–24

After the sentence had been passed upon the offenders, we see the punishment carried out, in part, on them immediately. See:

1. How they were justly disgraced and shamed before God and the holy angels, by the ironic rebuke of them with the outcome of their undertaking: "*Behold, the man has become as one of us, to know good and evil.* What a fair god he is, is he not?" This was said to waken and humble them, and to bring them to a sense of their sin and folly. It was also to lead them to repentance for that sin. So God *fills their faces with shame, that they may seek his name* (Ps 83:16). He disgraces them that he might deliver them.

2. How they were justly driven out of and excluded from Paradise.

2.1. The reason God gave why he shut the man out of Paradise; not only because he had disobeyed God by putting out his hand and taking from the tree of knowledge, which was his sin, but also so that he should not again put out his hand and take also from the tree of life and flatter himself with the thought that in so doing he should live forever.

2.2. The method God used in expelling and excluding him from this garden of pleasure. He turned him out, and kept him out.

2.2.1. God turned him out, from the garden to the common land. This meant that he and all his guilty race were excluded from that fellowship with God which was the bliss and glory of Paradise. His knowledge of God was lessened and lost, and that relationship which had been settled between the man and his Maker was interrupted and broken off. But where did God send him to when he turned him out of Eden? He might justly have banished him out of the world (Job 18:18), but he only drove him out of the garden. But man was only sent to work the ground out of which he was taken. He was sent to a place of toil, not to a place of torment. He was sent to the ground, not to the grave—to a place of work not to a place of confinement or prison—to hold the plow, not to drag the chain. His working the ground would be rewarded by his eating of its fruits; and his dealings with the earth from which he was taken could be used for good purposes to keep him humble and to remind him of the end of his life. Notice then, that although our first parents were excluded from the privileges of their state of innocence, they were not abandoned to despair. God's thoughts of love appointed them a second test of their character on new terms.

2.2.2. God kept him out, and forbade him all hopes of reentry; for he *placed at the east of the garden of Eden* a detachment of *cherubim*. These were God's hosts, armed with a dreadful and irresistible power. They guarded the way that led to the tree of life, so that he could neither force an entry or gain entry secretly. Now this suggested to Adam:

- That God was displeased with him.
- That the angels were at war with him; there was no peace with the heavenly hosts, while he was in rebellion against their Lord and ours.
- That the way to the tree of life was closed, namely, that way which, at first, he was put into, the way of spotless innocence. In vain could Adam and Eve expect righteousness, life, and happiness, because of the first covenant, for it was irreparably broken. We are all undone if we are judged by that covenant. God revealed this to Adam, not to drive him to despair, but to constrain and stir him to look for life and happiness in the promised offspring, by whom the flaming sword is removed. God and his angels are reconciled to us, and a new and living way into the holiest is consecrated and laid open for us.

CHAPTER 4

In this chapter we have both the world and the church in a family. As the whole human race was represented in Adam, so that great distinction of the human race into saints and sinners was here represented in Cain and Abel, and an early example is given of the enmity which was later put between the descendants of the woman and the descendants of the Serpent.

We have here: 1. The birth, names, and callings of Cain and Abel (vv. 1–2). 2. Their religion, and different successes in it (vv. 3–5a). 3. Cain's anger at God, and his rebuke for that anger (vv. 5b–7). 4. Cain's murder of his brother, and the proceedings against him for that murder. The murder committed (v. 8). The proceedings against him. 4.1. His accusation (v. 9a). 4.2. His plea (v. 9b). 4.3. His conviction (v. 10). 4.4. The sentence passed on him (vv. 11–12). 4.5. His complaint against the sentence (vv. 13–14). 4.6. The confirmation of the sentence (v. 15). 4.7. The sentence carried out (vv. 15–16). 5. The family and descendants of Cain (vv. 17–24). 6. The birth of another son and grandson of Adam (vv. 25–26).

Verses 1–2

Adam and Eve had many sons and daughters (5:4). But Cain and Abel seem to have been the two eldest.

1. Here are the names of their two sons:

1.1. The name *Cain* sounds like the Hebrew for "brought forth"; for Eve, when she bore him, said with joy, thankfulness, and great expectation, *I have gotten a man from the Lord* (v. 1). Children are God's gifts, and God must be acknowledged when our families are built up. It doubles and blesses our comfort in them when we see them coming to us from the hand of God, who will not abandon the works and gifts of his own hand.

1.2. The name *Abel* means "meaningless." When Eve thought she had obtained the promised descendant in Cain, she was so taken up with that possession that another son was meaningless or futile to her.

2. Here is the work that Cain and Abel had:

2.1. They both had a calling. God gave their father Adam a calling, even in innocence, and Adam gave them one. It is the will of God that each one of us should have something to do in this world. Parents ought to bring up their children to work. As the commentator Mr. Dod noted, "Give them a Bible and a calling, and God be with them."

2.2. They had different jobs, that they might trade with each other, as there was occasion. The members of society need one another, and mutual love is helped by mutual business.

2.3. Their work was connected to their father's profession as a farmer.

2.4. Abel, although he was the younger brother, entered first into his calling, and probably his example drew in Cain.

2.5. Abel chose the work that most suited contemplation and devotion, for a pastoral life has been looked on as being especially favorable to these.

Verses 3–5

Here we have:

1. The devotions of Cain and Abel. *In the process of time* Cain and Abel brought to Adam, as the priest of the family, each of them *an offering to the Lord*. In this way, God tested Adam's faith in the promise and his obedience to the law, which was intended to provide a remedy for sin. He would also establish harmony again between heaven and earth, and give *a shadow of good things to come* (Heb 10:1). Notice here:

1.1. That the religious worship of God is no innovation but an ancient institution. It is that which was *from the beginning* (1Jn 1:1); it is the *good old way* (Jer 6:16).

1.2. That it is a good thing for children to be well taught when they are young, and trained up early in their lives in religious services, that when they come to be capable to act for themselves they may, of their own accord, *bring an offering to God*.

1.3. That every one of us should honor God with what we have, as he has prospered us.

1.4. That hypocrites and evildoers may be found to go as far as the best of God's people in external religious services. Cain brought an offering with Abel; no, Cain's offering is mentioned first, as if he were the more forward of the two. The Pharisee and the tax collector went to the temple to pray (Lk 18:10).

2. The different successes of their devotions. Our aim in all acts of religion is God's acceptance: we do well if we reach this, and we worship in vain if we miss it (2Co 5:9). God had *respect to Abel and to his offering*, and showed his acceptance of it, probably by fire from heaven; but to *Cain and his offering he had not respect*, he did not look on it with favor.

2.1. There was a difference in the character of those making the offerings. Cain was a wicked man and therefore his sacrifice was *a vain oblation* (Isa 1:13). God did not look with favor on Cain himself, nor on his offering. But Abel was a righteous man; he is called *righteous Abel* (Mt 23:35); his heart was upright and his life was devout. God looked with favor on Abel as a holy man, and so considered his offering a holy offering.

2.2. There was a difference in the offerings they brought. It is expressly said (Heb 11:4), Abel's was *a more excellent sacrifice* than Cain's: either in its nature or in the qualities of the offering. Cain brought *of the fruit of the ground* (v. 3), anything that was close at hand, what he did not need for himself. But Abel was careful in the choice of his offering: not the lame, nor the lean, nor the worthless leftovers, but the *firstlings of his flock* (v. 4)—the best he had, *and the fat thereof*—the best of the best.

2.3. The great difference was this: that Abel made his offering in faith, and Cain did not. There was a difference in the principle or motive in which they brought their offering. Abel offered his sacrifice with an eye on God's will as his rule, and God's glory as his aim, Cain did what he did to keep company or to save his reputation. He did not come in faith, and so it turned into sin to him. Abel was penitent. Cain was unhumbled, his confidence was in himself.

3. Cain's displeasure at the difference God made between his sacrifice and Abel's. Cain was very angry, which immediately appeared in his very looks. This anger speaks of:

3.1. Cain's enmity toward God. He should really have been angry at himself for his own unfaithfulness and hypocrisy, by which he had forfeited God's acceptance. It is a certain sign of an unhumbled heart to quarrel with those rebukes which we have by our own sin brought on ourselves.

3.2. Cain's envy of his brother. He conceived a hatred of him as an enemy. We can learn from this:

3.2.1. It is common for those who have rendered themselves unworthy of God's favor to be indignant toward those who are honored by it. The Pharisees walked in this way of Cain, when they *neither entered into the kingdom of God themselves* but rather *hindered those that were entering in* (Lk 11:52).

3.2.2. Envy is a sin that commonly carries with it its own punishment, in the wasting away of its bones.

Verses 6–7

God here reasons with Cain, to convince him of the sin and folly of his anger and discontent, and to bring him back into a composed state of mind, that further harm might be prevented. In the same way, the father of the prodigal argued the case with the elder son (Lk 15:28–32).

1. God seeks for Cain himself to inquire into the cause of his discontent: *Why is thy countenance fallen?* (v. 6). God takes note of all our sinful passions and discontented moods. *"Why am I wroth?* Is there a real cause, a just cause, a reasonable cause for it? Why am I angry so quickly?"

2. It is here made clear to Cain to put Cain back into his right mind:

2.1. That he had no reason to be angry with God.

2.1.1. God sets before Cain life and a blessing: either: "If you had done well, as your brother did, you would have been accepted, as he was." Or: "If now you do well, if you repent of your sin, reform your heart and life, and bring your sacrifice in a better manner, you will be accepted, your sin will be pardoned, your comfort and honor restored, and all will be well." See how early the Gospel was preached, and the benefit of it here offered even to one of the chief of sinners.

2.1.2. God sets before Cain death and a curse: "If now you will not do well, if you persist in this anger, and, instead of humbling yourself before God, harden yourself against him, *sin lies at the door,*" that is further sin. "Now that anger is in your heart, murder is at the door" and also the punishment of sin. So close are sin and punishment that the same word in Hebrew signifies both. If sin is harbored in the house, the curse waits at the door, like a bailiff ready to arrest sinners whenever they look out. "If you do not do well, *sin* (that is, *the sin offering*), lies at the door, and you may take the benefit of it." The same word signifies "sin" and "a sacrifice for sin." Christ, the great sin offering, is said to *stand at the door* (Rev 3:20). All this considered, Cain had no reason to be angry with God, but only with himself.

2.2. That he had no reason to be angry with his brother: *Unto thee shall be his desire* (v. 7), "He shall continue his respect to you as an elder brother, and you, as the firstborn, will rule over him as much as ever." God's acceptance of Abel's offering did not transfer the birthright to him. God did not intend it in this way and neither did Abel interpret it. Why then should he be so exasperated?

Verse 8

Here is Abel's murder, which may be considered in two ways:

1. As Cain's sin; and a scarlet, crimson, sin it was, a sin of the first magnitude. Notice in it:

1.1. Adam's eating the forbidden fruit seemed just a little sin, but it opened the door to the greatest.

1.2. A fruit of the enmity which is in the descendant of the Serpent against the descendant of the woman. So early did he who was after the flesh *persecute him that was after the Spirit.*

1.3. See also what comes of envy, hatred, and malice. If these sins are indulged and cherished in the soul, they are in danger of involving people in the horrid guilt of murder itself. Cain's sin was serious in many ways:

1.3.1. It was his own brother that he murdered, his younger brother, whom he ought to have protected.

1.3.2. He was a good brother, one who had never done him any wrong.

1.3.3. God himself had told him what would come of it, yet he persisted in his brutal plans.

1.3.4. He covered it with a show of friendship and kindness. According to the Septuagint Cain said to Abel, "Let us go into the field." The Aramaic paraphrase adds that Cain maintained that there was no judgment to come, no future state, and that when Abel spoke in defense of the truth Cain took that occasion to attack him. However:

1.3.5. What the Scripture tells us was the reason that he killed him was a sufficient cause of the murder; it was *because his own works were evil and his brother's righteous.*

1.3.6. In killing his brother, he struck directly at God himself; he hated Abel because God loved him.

2. As Abel's suffering. Death reigned ever since Adam sinned, but we do not read of any taken captive by death till now; and now:

2.1. The first that dies is a saint, one that was accepted and beloved of God. The first that went to the grave went to heaven.

2.2. The first that dies is in fact a martyr, and dies for his religion. Abel's death has not only no curse in it, but also it has a crown in it.

Verses 9–12

Here is the trial and condemnation of the first murderer:

1. The accusation of Cain: *The Lord said unto Cain, Where is Abel thy brother?* (v. 9). He asks him, that he may draw from him a confession of his crime, for those who would be justified before God must accuse themselves, and those who are penitent will do so.

2. Cain's plea: he pleads *not guilty,* and adds rebellion to his sin. For:

2.1. He endeavors to cover a deliberate murder with a deliberate lie: *I know not.* So in Cain, the Devil was both a murderer and a liar from the beginning. Those are strangely blind that think it possible to conceal their sins from a God that sees everything, and those are strangely hardhearted that think it desirable to conceal their sins from a God who pardons only those that confess.

2.2. He impertinently charges his Judge with folly and injustice, in putting this question to him: *Am I my brother's keeper?* (v. 9). He should have humbled himself, and have said, "Am I not my brother's murderer?" Some think he reflects on God and his providence, as if he had said, "Are you not his keeper? If he is missing, the blame must be on you, and not on me, who never undertook to keep him." Those who are not concerned for the welfare of their brothers and sisters, and are not careful when they have opportunity to prevent their hurt in their bodies, goods, or good name, especially in their souls, do in effect speak Cain's language. See Lev 19:17; Php 2:4.

3. The conviction of Cain (v. 10). The evidence against him is clear and incontestable: *The voice of thy brother's blood cries.* He speaks as if the blood itself were both witness and prosecutor, because God's own knowledge testified against him. Notice here:

3.1. Murder is a crying sin, none more so. The patient sufferers cried for pardon (*Father, forgive them,* Lk 23:34), but their blood cries out for vengeance.

3.2. The blood is said to cry from the ground, the earth, which is said *to open her mouth to receive his brother's blood from his hand* (v. 11).

3.3. In the original the word is plural, *thy brother's* "bloods," not only his blood, but the blood of all those that might have descended from him. How well it is for us that the blood of Christ speaks a better word than that of Abel! (Heb 12:24). Abel's blood cried for vengeance, Christ's blood cries for pardon.

4. The sentence passed on Cain: *And now art thou cursed from the earth* (v. 11).

4.1. He is cursed. The curse for Adam's disobedience terminated on the ground: *Cursed is the ground for thy sake;* but that for Cain's rebellion fell immediately on himself: *Thou art cursed.* We have all deserved this curse, and it is only in Christ that believers are saved from it and inherit the blessing (Gal 3:10, 13).

4.2. He is cursed from the ground. Cain found his punishment where he chose his lot, his destiny, and where he set his heart. Two things we expect from the ground, and by this curse both are denied to Cain and taken from him: *sustenance* and *settlement.*

4.2.1. Sustenance from the ground is here withheld from him. It is a curse on him in his pleasures, and particularly in his calling: *When thou tillest the ground, it shall not henceforth yield unto thee her strength.*

4.2.2. Settlement on the earth is here denied him: *A fugitive and a vagabond shalt thou be in the earth.* By this he was condemned to perpetual disgrace and reproach among his fellows and perpetual disquiet and horror in his own mind. His own guilty conscience would haunt him wherever he went, and make him "a terror round about." What rest can those find, what settlement, that carry their own disturbance with them in their breasts wherever they go? Those must be fugitives who are tossed about in this way.

4.3. This was the sentence passed on Cain; and even in this there was mercy mixed, inasmuch as he was not immediately cut off, but was given room to repent; for God is patient toward us, not willing that any should perish (2Pe 3:9).

Verses 13 – 15

A further account of the proceedings against Cain:

1. Here is Cain's complaint at the sentence passed on him as hard and severe. Some make him speak the language of despair. There is forgiveness with the pardoning God for the greatest of sins and sinners; but those who despair of it forfeit it. Just before, Cain made nothing of his sin, but now he goes to the other extreme: Satan drives his servants from presumption to despair. He thinks that he has been strictly dealt with when in reality he has been favorably treated; and he cries from his wrong when he has more reason to wonder that he is not in hell. Now, to justify this complaint, Cain comments on the sentence:

- He sees himself excluded by it from the favor of his God.
- He sees himself expelled from all the comforts of this life, and concludes that being a fugitive, he is in effect *driven out this day from the face of the earth* (v. 13).
- He sees himself exposed by it to the hatred and ill will of the whole human race: *It shall come to pass that every one that finds me shall slay me.* Wherever he wanders, he goes in danger of his life, or at least he thinks so; and, like someone in debt, thinks everyone he meets a bailiff. There were none alive but his near relatives; yet he, who had himself been so barbarous to his brother, is justly afraid even of them. He sees the whole creation bearing arms against him.

2. Here is God's confirmation of the sentence; for when he judges he will rule (v. 15). Notice:

2.1. How Cain is protected in wrath by this declaration, notified, we may suppose, to all the world which was then in being: *Whosoever slayeth Cain, vengeance shall be taken on him sevenfold,* because in such a slaying the sentence he was under (that he should be a restless wanderer) would be defeated. God having said in Cain's case, *Vengeance is mine, I will repay* (Ro 12:19), it would be a daring usurper who would take the sword out of God's hand.

2.2. *The Lord set a mark upon Cain* (v. 15), to distinguish him from the rest of the human race and to point out that he was the man that murdered his brother.

Verses 16 – 18

Here is a further account of Cain, and what became of him after he was rejected by God.

1. He obediently submitted to that part of his sentence by which he was hidden from God's face; for *he went out from the presence of the Lord* (v. 16), that is, he willingly renounced God and religion, and was content to forgo its privileges, so that he might not be under its precepts. Cain went out now from the presence of the Lord, and we never find that he came into it again, to his comfort.

2. He endeavored to face up to that part of the sentence by which he was made a restless wanderer:

2.1. He chose his land. He went and *dwelt on the east of Eden* (v. 16), somewhere distant from the place where Adam and his family lived. But his attempt to settle was in vain; for the land he dwelled in was to him *the land of Nod* (that is, of "wandering"), because of the continual restlessness and unease of his own spirit. Those that reject God cannot find rest anywhere else. After Cain went out from the presence of the Lord, he never rested. *Return therefore to thy rest, O my soul* (Ps 116:7), to your rest in God, or forever you will be restless.

2.2. He built a city to live in (v. 17). "He was building a city," as some read it, constantly building it, but, because a curse was on him and the work of his hands, he could not finish it. Notice:

2.2.1. Cain's defiance at the divine sentence. God said he should be a *fugitive and a vagabond.* If he had humbled himself and repented, this curse might have been turned into a blessing.

2.2.2. What was Cain's choice after he had forsaken God; he pitched a settlement in this world as his rest forever.

2.2.3. What method Cain took to defend himself against the terrors with which he was perpetually haunted. He undertook this building to divert his thoughts from the consideration of his own misery, and to drown out the clamors of a guilty conscience with the noise of axes and hammers. Many confuse their convictions in this way, throwing themselves into a hurry of worldly business.

2.2.4. How wicked people often get the start on God's people, and outdo them in outward prosperity. Cain and his cursed race live in a city, while Adam and his blessed family live in tents.

2.3. His family also was built up. Here is an account of his descendants, at least the heirs of his family, for several generations.

Verses 19–22

Here are some particulars concerning Lamech, the descendant of Adam in the line of Cain. Though Lamech sinned in marrying two wives, he was still blessed with children by both marriages. His children became famous in their generation, not for their godliness but for their ingenuity. They were not only people who worked, but also people who were useful to the world, and famous for the invention, or at least the improvement, of some useful skills. Jabal was a famous shepherd. Jubal was a famous musician, and particularly a flautist, and the first who gave the rules for the noble art of music. While Jabal made them rich, Jubal made them radiant. Jabal was their Pan and Jubal their Apollo. Tubal-Cain was a famous smith, who greatly improved the art of working in bronze and iron, for the service of both war and farming. He was their Vulcan. Even those who are destitute of the knowledge and grace of God may be given many excellent and useful talents, which may make them famous and useful in their generation. Common gifts are given to bad people, while God chooses to himself the foolish things of the world.

Verses 23–24

From this speech of Lamech, which is here recorded and was probably much talked about in those times, he further appears to have been a wicked man, as Cain's cursed race generally were. He confesses himself a man of a fierce and cruel disposition who would attack others without mercy, and kill all that stood in his way. His wives, knowing what manner of spirit he had, how inclined he was both to give and to resent provocation, were afraid lest somebody or other would be the death of him. "Never fear," he says, "I defy any man to attack me; whoever does, I will show him who is the better fighter, I will slay him, whether he is young or old."

Verses 25–26

This is the first mention of Adam in this chapter. Undoubtedly the murder of Abel, and the impenitence and apostasy of Cain, were a cause of very great grief to him and Eve, and all the more so because the disobedience and backsliding of Adam and Eve now reprimanded and corrected them. But here we have what was a relief to our first parents in their suffering.

1. God let them see the rebuilding of their family, which was sorely shaken and weakened by the sad episode of Cain and Abel. For:

1.1. They saw their child, *another seed instead of Abel* (v. 25). Notice God's kindness and tenderness toward his people in his providential dealings with them; when he takes away one comfort from them, he gives them another instead, which may prove a greater blessing to them than

the one in which their lives were bound up. Those who kill God's servants hope to wear out the saints of the Most High in this way; but they will be deceived. Christ will still see his seed; God can raise up children for him even from stones. The blood of the martyrs is the seed of the church. This son, by a prophetic spirit, they called *Seth* (that is, "granted" or "settled"), because, in his descendants, the human race would continue to the end of time, and from him the Messiah would descend. While Cain, the head of the apostasy, is made a wanderer, Seth, from whom the true church was to come, is the secure one. In Christ and his church is the only true security.

1.2. They saw their child's child (v. 26). *To Seth was born a son called Enosh.*

2. God let them see the revival of religion in their family: *Then began men to call upon the name of the Lord* (v. 26). It is small comfort to godly people to see their children's children, if they do not also see peace upon Israel, and those that come of them walking in the truth. The worshipers of God began to stir up themselves to do more in religion than they had done before. Now people began to worship God, not only in their own homes and families, but in public and solemn assemblies. The worshipers of God began to distinguish themselves. The margin reads, "Then began men to be called by the name of the Lord," or to call themselves by it.

CHAPTER 5

We have here an account concerning: 1. Adam (vv. 1–5). 2. Seth (vv. 6–8). 3. Enos (Enosh) (vv. 9–11). 4. Cainan (Kenan) (vv. 12–14). 5. Mahalaleel (Mahalalel) (vv. 15–17). 6. Jared (vv. 18–20). 7. Enoch (vv. 21–24). 8. Methuselah (vv. 25–27). 9. Lamech and his son Noah (vv. 28–32). All Scripture, being given by inspiration of God, is profitable, though not all profitable to the same extent.

Verses 1–5

The first words of the chapter are the title or argument of the whole chapter: it is *the book of the generations of Adam,* his line. The line begins with Adam himself.

1. Here is Adam's creation in vv. 1–2, where we have a brief reiteration of what was related before concerning the creation of human beings. Notice here:

1.1. That *God created man.* The human race is not its own maker, therefore we must not be our own master; but the Author of our being must be the director of our activities and the center of them.

1.2. That there was a day on which God created the first man. He was not from eternity, but of yesterday.

1.3. That God made people in his own likeness, righteous and holy, and therefore, undoubtedly, happy.

1.4. That God created them male and female (v. 2), for their mutual comfort as well as for the preservation and increase of their kind.

2. Here is the birth of Adam's son *Seth* (v. 3). What is most noteworthy here concerning Seth is that Adam had him *in his own likeness, after his image.* Adam was made in the image of God; but, when he was fallen and corrupt, he had a son in his own image.

Verses 6–20

We have here all that the Holy Spirit thought fit to leave on record concerning five of the patriarchs before the Flood, Seth, Enos (Enosh), Cainan (Kenan), Mahalaleel (Mahalalel), and Jared. There is nothing particularly noteworthy concerning any of these, though we have reason to think they were renowned in their day both for their discretion and devotion. Concerning each of them, except Enoch, it is said, *and he died*. It is implied in the numbering of the years of their lives that their lives, when those years were numbered and finished, came to an end. However, *and he died* is still repeated to show that death came to all without exception. This one was a strong, healthy man, but he died; that one was a great and rich man, but he died; this one was a wise and astute man, but he died; that one was a very good man, perhaps a very useful man, but he died.

What is especially noticeable is that they all lived very long. Long life to the devout patriarchs was a blessing and made them a blessing.

Verses 21–24

The accounts here run on for several generations without anything remarkable, or any variation except in the names and numbers; but eventually comes one that must not be passed over in this way, one of whom special notice must be taken, and that is *Enoch*, the seventh from Adam. The others, we may suppose, lived good lives, but he surpassed them all, and was the brightest star of the patriarchal age. Little is recorded concerning him; but this little is enough to make his name great, greater than the name of the other Enoch, who had a city called by his name. Here are two things concerning him:

1. His gracious behavior in this world, which is twice spoken of: *Enoch walked with God after he begat Methuselah* (v. 22), and again, *Enoch walked with God* (v. 24).

1.1. The nature of his religion and the scope and tenor of his behavior: he *walked with God*, which stands for:

1.1.1. True religion; what is godliness, but walking with God? The ungodly and worldly are without God in the world, they walk contrary to him: but the godly walk with God, which presupposes reconciliation with God, for two cannot *walk together except they be agreed* (Am 3:3). To walk with God is to set God always before us, and to act as those that are always under his eye. It is to live a life of fellowship with God both in worship of him and wisdom in our dealings with others. It is to make God's word our rule and his glory our aim in all our actions. It is to obey his will, to agree with his intentions, and to be workers together with him.

1.1.2. Distinguished religion. He was entirely dead to this world; he not only walked with God, as all good people do, but he walked with God, as if he were in heaven already.

1.1.3. Activity in promoting religion among others. Executing the priest's office is called *walking before God* (1Sa 2:30, 35), and see Zec 3:7. Enoch, it would seem, was a priest of the Most High God. Now the Holy Spirit, instead of saying, Enoch *lived*, says, Enoch *walked with God*; for it is the life of a good person to walk with God. This was the business, the joy, and support of his life.

2. His glorious taking away to a better world. As he did not live as others do, so he did not die as others do (v. 24): *He was not, for God took him*; that is, as it is explained (Heb 11:5), *He was translated that he should not see death; and was not found, because God had translated him*. Whenever good people die, God takes, leads, and receives them to himself. The writer to the Hebrews adds concerning Enoch that, *before his translation, he had this testimony, that he pleased God*. Those whose behavior in the world is truly holy will find their being taken from it truly happy.

Verses 25–27

Methuselah may mean "man of the dart," "man of [the deity] Lach," or "a sending forth." However, it is signifi-

cant that even the person who lived the longest carried death in his name, that he might be reminded of its certain coming, although it came slowly.

Verses 28–32

Here is the first mention of Noah, of whom we will read much in the following chapters. Notice:

1. His name, with the reason of it: *Noah* signifies "rest" or "comfort"; his parents gave him that name, with a prospect of his being a more than ordinary blessing to his generation.

2. His children: Shem, Ham, and Japheth. It would seem that Japheth was the eldest (10:21), but Shem is put first because on him the covenant was bestowed, as appears by 9:26, where God is called the *Lord God of Shem*. To him, it is probable, the birthright was given, and from him, it is certain, both Christ the head, and the church the body, were to descend. Therefore he is called *Shem*, which means "name," because in his descendants the name of God would always remain, until the One whose name is above every name would come from his body, so that in putting Shem first Christ was in effect put first, who in all things must have the preeminence.

CHAPTER 6

The most remarkable thing we have on record concerning the old world is the destruction of it by the universal Deluge, the account of which begins in this chapter, in which we have: 1. The abundant iniquity of that wicked world (vv. 1–5 and vv. 11–12). 2. The righteous God's indignation at that great iniquity, and his holy resolution to punish it (vv. 6–7). 3. The special favor of God to his servant Noah. 3.1. In the character recorded of him (vv. 8–10). 3.2. In the communication of God's purpose to him (vv. 13, 17). 3.3. In the directions he gave him to build an ark for his own safety (vv. 14–16). 3.4. In the using of him to preserve the rest of the animals (vv. 18–21). Lastly, Noah's obedience to the instructions given him (v. 22).

Verses 1–2

Here we have an account of two things which brought about the wickedness of the old world:

1. The increase of the human race: *Men began to multiply on the face of the earth*. This was the effect of the blessing (1:28), and yet human corruption so abused and perverted this blessing that it was turned into a curse. The more sinners, the more sin. Infectious diseases are most destructive in populous cities; and sin is like a spreading skin disease.

2. Mixed marriages (v. 2): *The sons of God* (that is, those who professed religion) *married the daughters of men*, that is, those that were irreligious and strangers to God and godliness. The descendants of Seth did not keep themselves to themselves, as they ought to have done. They intermarried with the excommunicated race of Cain: *They took them wives of all that they chose*. But what was wrong in these marriages?

2.1. They chose only by the eye: *They saw that they were fair*, which was all they looked at.

2.2. They followed the choice which their own corrupt hearts made. But:

2.3. What proved to have such bad results for them was that they *married strange wives* (Ne 13:27), *were unequally yoked with unbelievers* (2Co 6:14). The bad will sooner lead astray the good than the good reform the bad.

Verse 3

Here is a sign of God's displeasure:

1. God's resolution not always to contend with human beings by his Spirit. We can learn from this:

1.1. The blessed Spirit strives with sinners, by the convictions and warnings of conscience, to turn them from sin to God.

1.2. If the Spirit is resisted, quenched, and fought against, although he will contend for a long time, he will not contend always (Hos 4:17).

2. The reason for this resolution: *For that he also is flesh*, that is, incurably corrupt, worldly, and sensual. It is the corrupt nature and the inclination of the soul toward the flesh that oppose the Spirit's exertions and make them ineffective. None lose the Spirit's exertions except those who have first forfeited them.

3. A postponement of the punishment is granted, despite this: *Yet his days shall be one hundred and twenty years.* The time of God's patience and forbearance toward offending sinners is sometimes long, but always limited: reprieves are not pardons.

Verses 4–5

Here is a further account of the corruption of the former world:

1. The temptation they were under to oppress others violently. They were *giants* (Nephilim), and they were *men of renown*.

1.1. With their great bulk, as the sons of Anak, see Nu 13:33.

1.2. With their great name, as the king of Assyria, see Isa 37:11. Those that have so much power over others as to be able to oppress them seldom have as much power over themselves not to engage in oppression.

2. The charge demonstrated and proved against them (v. 5). Now what did God take notice of?

2.1. He observed all the streams of sin that flowed in the people's lives, and the breadth and depth of those streams. The oppressors were *mighty men* and *men of renown*; and, *then, God saw that the wickedness of man was great*. The wickedness of a people is great indeed when the most notorious sinners are those of renown among them. Wickedness is then great when great people are wicked. All the sins of sinners are known to God the Judge.

2.2. He observed the fountain of sin that was in the people's hearts. Anyone might see that *the wickedness of man was great*, for they declared their sin as Sodom; but God's eye went farther: *He saw that every imagination of the thoughts of his heart was only evil continually.* The thoughts of the heart were so. The imagination of the thoughts of the heart was so, that is, their purposes and plots were wicked. They did not do evil through mere carelessness, but they did evil with deliberation and determination contriving how to make trouble.

Verses 6–7

Here is:

1. God's indignation at human wickedness. He did not watch as an unconcerned spectator, but as one injured and offended by it. He saw it as a tender father sees the folly and stubbornness of a rebellious and disobedient child, which not only angers him, but also grieves him.

1.1. This language does not imply any passion or uneasiness in God (nothing can disturb the eternal Mind), but it expresses his just and holy displeasure against sin and sinners. Does God hate sin in this way? And should we not hate it? Has our sin grieved him to the heart? And should we not be grieved and distressed to the heart for it?

1.2. It does not imply any change of God's mind, but it expresses a change of his way. But, now that human beings had turned away from God, he could not have acted in any other way than show himself displeased; so that the change was in human beings, not in God. God was grieved that he had made human beings; but we never find him grieving that he redeemed human beings.

2. God's intention to destroy human beings for their wickedness (v. 7). We mock God in saying that we are sorry for our sin, and that it grieves us to the heart, if we then continue to indulge in it. The original word is very significant: "I will wipe man off the earth," as some read it, as dirt or filth is wiped off a place which should be clean. Those forfeit their lives who do not fulfill the purpose of their living. God made this decision concerning human beings after his Spirit had long been contending with them in vain. None are destroyed by the justice of God except those who hate to be reformed by the grace of God.

Verses 8–10

We have here Noah distinguished from the rest of the world, and a special mark of honor put on him.

1. When God was displeased with the rest of the world, he favored Noah: there being one good man, he found him out and smiled on him. He was made an object of God's mercy. God made him greater and more truly honorable than all the *giants that were in those days*, who became *mighty men* and *men of renown*. Those are highly favored whom God favors.

2. Noah kept his integrity: *Noah was a just man* (v. 9). This aspect of Noah's character is either:

2.1. The reason for God's favor to him. God loves those that love him: or:

2.2. The effect of God's favor on him. It was God's goodwill to him that produced this good work in him. He was a very good man, but he was no better than the grace of God made him (1Co 15:10). Now notice his character:

2.2.1. He *was a just man*, that is, justified in the sight of God by faith in the promised offspring; for he was an *heir of the righteousness which is by faith* (Heb 11:7). God has sometimes chosen the foolish things of the world, but he never chose the unprincipled things of it.

2.2.2. He was *perfect*, not with a sinless perfection, but with uprightness and a blamelessness among the people of his time. It is good for us that because of the covenant of grace on the record of Christ's righteousness, sincerity is accepted under the Gospel.

2.2.3. He *walked with God*. He lived a life of fellowship with God. God looks down with an eye of favor on those who sincerely look up to him with an eye of faith. It is easy to be religious when religion is in fashion; but it is an evidence of strong faith and resolve to swim against the tide to heaven, and to stand up for God when no one else stands up for him.

Verses 11–12

The wickedness of that generation is here again spoken of:

1. All kinds of sin were found among them, for it is said (v. 11) that the earth was *corrupt before God. The earth was also filled with violence* and injustice toward human beings. Wickedness, as it is the shame of human nature, is also the ruin of human society. If you take away conscience and the fear of God, human beings become animals and devils to one another. Sin fills the earth with violence, and so turns the world into a wilderness, into a battlefield.

2. The proof and evidence of it were undeniable; for *God looked upon the earth*, and was himself an eyewitness of its corruption, as we have read.

3. What worsened the matter most was that the contagion had spread universally: *All flesh had corrupted his way*. When wickedness has become general then universal ruin is not far off. While there is a remnant of praying people in a nation, to prevent sin from being complete, judgments may be restrained for a great while.

Verses 13–21

It appears indeed that Noah *found grace in the eyes of the Lord*.

1. God here makes Noah the *man of his counsel*, communicating to him his purpose to destroy this wicked world by water as, afterward, he told Abraham his decision concerning Sodom (18:17). *The secret of the Lord* was with *his servants the prophets* (Am 3:7), by a spirit of revelation, informing them particularly of his purposes; it is with all believers by a spirit of wisdom and faith, enabling them to understand.

1.1. God told Noah, in general, that he would destroy the world (v. 13). Noah, it is likely, in preaching to his neighbors, had warned them. Now God backs up his endeavors.

1.2. God told Noah, particularly, that he would destroy the world by a flood of waters: *And behold, I, even I, do bring a flood of waters upon the earth* (v. 17). The reasons, we may be sure, were wise and just, though unknown to us. God has many arrows in his quiver, and he may use the ones that he wants. These words show the certainty of the judgment: *I, even I*, will do it.

2. God here makes Noah the *man of his covenant*, a Hebrew expression for a friend (v. 18): *But with thee will I establish my covenant*:

2.1. The covenant of providence, that the course of nature will be continued to the end of time, despite the interruption which the Flood would give to it. This promise was immediately made to Noah and his sons (9:8–11). They were as trustees for all this part of the creation.

2.2. The covenant of grace, that God would be to him a God and that from his offspring would call to himself a people.

3. God here makes Noah a memorial of salvation. Special devoutness will be rewarded with special instances of salvation.

3.1. God directs Noah to *make an ark* (vv. 14–16). This ark was like the hulk of a ship, fitted not to sail on the waters (there was no need for that, as there would be no shore to sail to), but to float on the waters, waiting for them to subside. God chose, however, to use him to make what would be the means of his preservation, both to test his faith and obedience and to teach us that none will be saved by Christ except those who *work out their salvation* (Php 2:12). We cannot do this without God, and he will not do this without us. God gave him very particular instructions concerning the building:

- It must be made of *gopher-wood*.
- He must make it three stories high inside.
- He must divide it into cabins, with partitions, rooms suitable for the different sorts of creature, so as to lose no space.
- Exact dimensions were given him. Those that work for God must take their standards from him and carefully observe them.
- He must *pitch it within and without*—outside, to keep off the rain, and to prevent the water from soaking in—inside, to take away the bad smell of the animals when kept near to one another.

- He must make a little window toward the top, to let in light.
- He must make a door in the side of it, as a means of entrance and exit.

3.2. God promises Noah that he and his family will be preserved alive in the ark (v. 18): *Thou shalt come into the ark*. Notice:

3.2.1. The care of good parents; they are concerned not only for their own salvation, but also for the salvation of their families, especially their children.

3.2.2. The happiness of those children that have godly parents. Their parents' devoutness often secures them an earthly salvation, as here; and it furthers them on the way to eternal salvation, if they make the most of its benefits.

4. God here makes Noah a means of great blessing to the world, and in so doing makes him a notable type of the Messiah.

4.1. God made him a preacher to the people of that generation.

4.2. God made him a savior to the lower creatures, to keep the different kinds of them from perishing and being lost in the Deluge (vv. 19–21).

4.2.1. He was to provide shelter for them, so that they would not be drowned.

4.2.2. He was to provide sustenance for them, that they might not starve (v. 21). In this he was also a type of Christ, to whom we owe the fact that the world stands, in whom all things hold together, and who preserves the human race from being totally cut off and destroyed by sin. Noah saved those whom he was to rule over, as does Christ (Heb 5:9).

Verse 22

Noah's care and diligence in building the ark may be considered:

1. As an effect of his faith in the word of God.

2. As an act of obedience to the command of God. His neighbors would ridicule him for his credulity, and he would be the song of the drunkards; his building would be called "Noah's folly." But Noah overcame by faith these and a thousand such objections. He did all exactly according to the instructions given him, and having begun to build, did not leave off till he had finished it. As he did, so must we. We must prepare to meet the Lord in his judgments on earth, especially prepare to meet him at death and in the judgment of the great day, build on Christ the Rock (Mt 7:24), and go into Christ the ark. Every blow of his axes and hammers was a call to repentance, a call to them to prepare arks too.

CHAPTER 7

In this chapter we have the fulfillment of what was foretold in the previous chapter, concerning both the destruction of the old world and the salvation of Noah. Here we see the conclusion of the building, his labors and the laxity of others. We have in this chapter: 1. God's gracious call to Noah and his family to come into the ark (vv. 1–4). 2. Noah's obedience to this heavenly vision (vv. 5–10), an account of which is repeated (vv. 13–16), to which is added God's tender care to shut him in. Also, the coming of the threatened Deluge (v. 10). 3. The causes of it (vv. 11–12). 4. The extensiveness of it (vv. 17–20). 5. The dreadful desolation that was made by it (vv. 21–23) and the continuance of it as a high tide, before it began to ebb, 150 days (v. 24).

Verses 1–4

1. Here is a gracious invitation of Noah and his family to come into a place of safety.

1.1. The call itself is very kind, like that of a tender father to his children, to come indoors, when he sees nightfall or a storm coming. God does not command him *go* into the ark, but *come* into it, implying that God would go with him, would lead him into it, accompany him in it, and in due time bring him safely out of it. It was this that made Noah's ark, which was a prison, to be not only a refuge, but also a palace. This call to Noah was a type of the call which the Gospel gives to humble sinners. Christ is an ark already prepared, in whom alone we can be safe when death and judgment come.

1.2. The reason for this invitation is a very honorable testimony to Noah's integrity. Notice:

- Those are righteous indeed that are righteous before God, who searches the heart and cannot be deceived by human character.
- God takes notice of and is pleased with those that are righteous before him: *The Lord knows those that are his.*
- God, who is a witness to, will shortly be a witness for his people's integrity.
- God is, in a special way, pleased with those who are good in bad times and bad places.
- Those who keep themselves pure in times of general wickedness God will keep safe in times of general calamity.

2. Here are necessary orders given concerning the animals that were to be kept alive with Noah in the ark (vv. 2–3). They were not capable of receiving the warning, and so Noah is charged with the care of them. Being under his power, they must be under his protection.

3. Here notice is given of the now imminent approach of the Flood.

3.1. "It will be seven days from now, before I do it." God grants them a reprieve of seven days longer. But all these are in vain; these seven days were trifled away, just like all the others; they continued worldly and unworried until the day that the Flood came.

3.2. "It shall be only seven days." While Noah told them of the judgment far off, they were tempted to put off their repentance, because the vision was for a great while to come. But now he is ordered to tell them that it is close at hand.

Verses 5–10

Here is Noah's ready obedience to the commands that God gave him. Notice:

1. He went into the ark, having been given notice that the Flood would come after seven days, though probably as yet there was no visible sign of its approach. He went into it by faith in this warning that it would come quickly, though he did not see that the secondary causes had yet begun to work. In every step he took, he walked by faith, and not by sense.

2. He took all his family along with him, his wife, his sons, and his sons' wives, that by them, not only his family, but also the whole human race might be built up.

3. The animals readily went in with him.

Verses 11–12

Here is the date of this great event; this is carefully recorded, for the greater certainty of the story.

1. The years of the old world are reckoned, not by the reigns of the giants, but by the lives of the patriarchs; saints are of more account with God than rulers. Noah was now a very old man, even as human ages went then. We can learn from this:

1.1. The longer we live in this world, the more we see of its miseries and calamities.

1.2. Sometimes God exercises his older servants with extraordinary trials of obedient patience. The oldest of Christ's soldiers must not promise themselves a discharge from their warfare until death discharges them. They must continue to put on their harness, and not boast as though they had put it off.

2. Here are the secondary causes that coincided with this Deluge. In the very same day that Noah was established in the ark, the inundation began. See what was done on that day, that fatal day to the world of the ungodly. *The fountains of the great deep were broken up.* The waters of the sea returned to cover the earth, as they had done at first (1:9). *The windows of heaven were opened,* and *the waters which were above the firmament* were poured out on the world. The rain, which ordinarily descends in drops, then came down in streams, as the floodgates of the heavens were opened in cloudbursts and torrents much more violent than we have ever seen in the heaviest shower.

3. Now learn from this:

3.1. That all the creatures are at God's disposal, and that he makes what use he pleases of them, whether *for correction, or for mercy.*

3.2. That God often makes what *should be for our welfare to become a trap* (Ps 69:22). Nothing is more needed or useful than water, both the springs of the earth and the showers from heaven; and yet now nothing was more hurtful, nothing more destructive: all of God's created acts are to us what God makes them.

3.3. That it is impossible to escape the righteous judgments of God when they come authoritatively against sinners.

Verses 13–16

Here is repeated what was related before of Noah's entrance into the ark, with his family and the creatures that were marked for preservation.

1. It is repeated in this way for the honor of Noah, whose faith and obedience shone so brightly in them.

2. We notice that the wild animals go in *each after his kind,* according to the phrase used in the history of the creation (1:21–25), and that this preservation was a kind of new creation. A life remarkably protected is, as it were, a new life.

3. It is added, *The Lord shut him in* (v. 16). As Noah continued his obedience to God, so God continued his care of Noah. God shut the door to secure him, and keep him safe in the ark and also to exclude all others. Up to this time the door of the ark stood open, and if anyone, even during the previous seven days, had repented and believed, for all we know they might have been welcomed into the ark; but now the door was shut.

4. There is much of our duty and privilege in relation to the Gospel to be seen in Noah's preservation in the ark. Notice then:

4.1. It is our great duty in obedience to the Gospel call to come by a living faith in Christ into that way of salvation which God has provided for poor sinners. When Noah came into the ark, he left his own house and land. In the same way, we must leave our own righteousness and our worldly possessions, whenever they compete with Christ. Noah must for a while submit to the confinements and inconveniences of the ark, in order to secure his preservation for a new world. In the same way, those who come into Christ to be saved by him must deny themselves, both in sufferings and services.

4.2. Those who come into the ark themselves should bring as many as they can in with them, by good teaching, by persuasion, and by a good example. There is room enough in Christ for all who come.

4.3. Those who by faith come into Christ, the ark, will be shut in by the power of God and will be kept as in a stronghold *by the power of God* (1Pe 1:5).

Verses 17–20

Here we see:

1. How long the flood was increasing—*forty days* (v. 17). The secular world, which did not believe that it would come, probably when it came flattered themselves with the hope that it would soon abate, but it lasted. The gradual approaches of God's judgments, which are designed to bring sinners to repentance, are often abused in their presumption to their hardening.

2. To what degree the waters increased: they rose so high that not only the low flat countries were deluged, but to ensure that none might definitely escape, the tops of the highest mountains were also overflowed—*fifteen cubits*, that is, twenty feet (about seven meters). So the refuge of lies was swept away. There is no place on earth so high that people can there escape God's judgments (Jer 49:16; Ob 3–4).

3. What became of Noah's ark when the waters rose in this way: *It was lifted up above the earth* (v. 17), *and went upon the face of the waters* (v. 18). Notice:

3.1. The waters which broke down everything else supported the ark.

3.2. The more the waters rose, so the higher the ark was lifted up toward heaven. We can learn from this that sanctified afflictions lift us spiritually.

Verses 21–24

1. Here is the general destruction of every living thing by the waters of the Flood:

1.1. All the wild animals, birds, all the creatures died, except the few that were in the ark. Notice the destruction of the creatures was their deliverance from the bondage of corruption, the deliverance from which the whole creation now groans after (Ro 8:21–22).

1.2. All the men, women, and children who were in the world (except those who were in the ark) died.

1.2.1. We may easily imagine what terror and consternation seized them when they saw themselves surrounded.

1.2.2. We may suppose that they tried every possible means to preserve their lives, but it was all in vain. Those who are not found in Christ, the ark, are certainly ruined.

1.2.3. Let us now pause awhile and consider this awful judgment! Eliphaz appeals to this story as a standing warning to a careless world (Job 22:15–16), *Hast thou marked the old way, which wicked men have trodden, who were cut down out of time*, and sent into eternity, *whose foundation was overflown with the flood?*

2. Here is the special preservation of Noah and his family. Notice:

2.1. Noah lives. When all around him bore witness to God's justice, thousands falling at his right hand and ten thousands at his left, he bore witness to God's mercy. We have reason to think that, while God in his patience waited, Noah not only preached to, but also prayed for that wicked world, and would have turned away the wrath; but his prayers return to his very self, and are answered only in his own escape, which is plainly referred to (Eze 14:14), *Noah, Daniel, and Job, shall but deliver their own souls.*

2.2. Only Noah lives. Noah remains alive, and this is all; he is in effect buried alive—cooped up in an enclosed place. But he comforts himself with this, that he is in the place of duty and in the place of deliverance.

CHAPTER 8

At the close of the previous chapter we left the world in ruins. Now the scene alters, the brighter side of that cloud appears which formerly looked so black and dark—for, although God contends for a long time, he will not contend forever, nor will there always be wrath. We have here: 1. The earth made new, by the receding of the waters, and the appearing of the dry land. 1.1. The rising of the waters is stopped (vv. 1–2). 1.2. They begin to abate noticeably (v. 3). 1.3. After sixteen days' receding, the ark rests (v. 4). 1.4. After sixty days' receding, the tops of the mountains appeared (v. 5). 1.5. After forty days' receding, and twenty days before the mountains appeared, Noah began to send out his spies, a raven and a dove, to see the lay of the land (vv. 6–12). 1.6. Two months after the appearing of the tops of the mountains, the waters had gone, and the face of the earth was dry (v. 13), though not dried sufficiently for human habitation until almost two months afterward (v. 14). 2. Human beings again put on the earth. 2.1. Noah's dismissal and departure from the ark (vv. 15–19). 2.2. His sacrifice of praise, which he offered to God on his liberation (v. 20). 2.3. God's acceptance of his sacrifice, and the promise he made here not to drown the world again (vv. 21–22). And so eventually, mercy triumphs over judgment.

Verses 1–3

Here is:

1. An act of God's grace: *God remembered Noah and every living thing*. This is an expression about God that uses human language; for not any of his creatures (Lk 12:6), much less any of his people, are forgotten by God (Isa 49:15–16). God's remembering of Noah was the return of his mercy to the human race, whom he would not destroy completely. Noah himself, even though he was the one that had found grace in the eyes of the Lord, still seemed to be forgotten in the ark, and perhaps began to think of himself in this way, for we do not find that God had told him how long he should be confined for and when he would be released. Very good people have sometimes been ready to conclude that they have been forgotten by God, especially when their suffering has been unusually distressing and long. Perhaps Noah, though a great believer, when he found the Flood still continuing so long after it might reasonably be presumed to have completed its work, was tempted to fear that the One who shut him in would keep him in, and began to take issue with God. *How long wilt thou forget me?* (Ps 13:1). But eventually God returned in mercy to him, and this is expressed by God remembering him.

2. An act of God's power over wind and water, both of which are at his command, though neither of them is under human control.

2.1. He commanded the wind, and said to it, *Go*, and it went, to carry away the Flood: *God made a wind to pass over the earth*. See here:

2.1.1. What was God's remembrance of Noah: it was to bring relief to Noah.

2.1.2. What sovereign authority God has over the winds. Even stormy winds do his bidding (Ps 148:8). Now God sent a wind, a drying wind, such as the one God sent to divide the Red Sea before Israel (Ex 14:21).

2.2. He commanded the waters, and said to them, *Come*, and they came.

2.2.1. He took away the cause. As God has a key to open, so he has a key to shut up again, and to slowing down the progress of judgments by stopping the causes of them. The same hand that brings the desolation must bring the deliverance. He that wounds is alone able to heal. See Job 12:14.

2.2.2. Then the effects stopped, not all at once, but gradually. God usually works deliverance for his people gradually, that the day of small things may not be despised, nor the day of great things despaired of (Zec 4:10). See Pr 4:18.

Verses 4 – 5

Here we have the effects and evidence of the receding of the waters:

1. The ark rested. This no doubt pleased Noah, to feel the house he was in resting on firm ground, and no longer movable. It came to rest on a mountain, to where it was directed, not by Noah's prudence (he did not steer it), but by the wise and gracious providence of God, that it might rest all the sooner. God has times and places of rest for his people after their disturbances, and many a time he provides timely strength and support without their own contriving and quite beyond their own foresight.

2. The tops of the mountains were seen, like little islands, appearing above the water. We must suppose that they were seen by Noah and his sons; for there were no other people who could see them. It is probable that they had looked through the window of the ark every day, like yearning mariners after a long and tiring voyage, to see if they could discover land. They felt ground more than forty days before they saw it, according to the reckoning of the commentator Dr. Lightfoot, from which he infers that, if the waters decreased proportionately, the ark displaced eleven cubits of water, that is, sixteen and a half feet (five and a half meters).

Verses 6 – 12

Here is an account of the spies, a raven and a dove, which Noah sent out to bring him news from the outside world. Note:

1. That though God had told Noah particularly when the Flood would come, he did not reveal to him particular details of the time at which and the steps by which it would *go away*, because:

1.1. The knowledge of the former was necessary to his preparing of the ark, but the knowledge of the latter would serve only to gratify his curiosity. Concealing the latter from him would exercise his faith and patience. And:

1.2. He could not have predicted the Flood, but known about it only by revelation. He might, by ordinary means, find out about the receding of the waters.

2. That though Noah by faith expected his liberation, and by patience waited for it, yet he was curious about it, as anyone would be who had been confined in this way for such a long time. *He that believes does not make haste* to run before God, but he does make haste to go out to meet him (Isa 28:16). Note that:

2.1. Noah sent out a raven through the window of the ark. The raven went out, as the Hebrew phrase is "returning and going forth," that is, flying about and returning

to the ark for rest; probably not in it, but on it. This gave Noah little satisfaction, and so:

2.2. Noah sent out a dove, which returned the first time with no good news, but probably came back wet and dirty. The second time, however, it brought an olive leaf in its bill, which appeared to be first plucked off, a clear indication that now the trees, the fruit trees, had begun to appear above the water. Note here:

2.2.1. That Noah sent out the dove the second time seven days after the first time, and the third time was after seven days too. Probably the first sending out of the dove was seven days after the sending out of the raven. This suggests that it was done on the Sabbath day, which, it would seem, Noah religiously observed in the ark.

2.2.2. The dove is an emblem of a gracious soul, which finding no home in which to rest, no solid peace or satisfaction in this world, returns to Christ as to its ark. The worldly heart, like the raven, is taken up with the world, and feeds on the dead flesh it finds there. And as Noah put out his hand, took the dove, and pulled it in to him, into the ark, so Christ will graciously preserve, help, and welcome those that fly to him for rest.

2.2.3. The olive branch, which was an emblem of peace, was brought, not by the raven, a bird of prey, nor by a bright and proud peacock, but by a mild, patient, humble dove. It is a dovelike disposition that brings into the soul a sense of assurance, rest, and joy.

2.2.4. Some commentators make these things an allegory. The Law was first sent forth like the raven, but brought no news; therefore, in the fullness of time, God sent forth his Gospel, as the dove, in the likeness of which the Holy Spirit descended, and this presents us with an olive branch symbolizing peace and hope.

Verses 13 – 14

Here is:

1. The ground dry (v. 13), that is, all the water carried away from it, of which, on the first day of the first month (a joyful New Year's Day it was), Noah was himself an eyewitness. He *removed the covering of the ark*, to give him a view of the earth around it—and what a comforting view he had! He saw the wonderful sight, *the face of the ground was dry*. We can learn from this:

- It is a great mercy to see ground around us. Noah was more aware of it than we are; for restored mercies are much more touching than continued mercies.
- The divine power which now renewed the face of the earth can renew the face of an afflicted, troubled soul and of a distressed, persecuted church.

2. The ground dried up (v. 14), so as to be a suitable place for Noah to live in. God considers our welfare rather than our desires. We would tend to leave the ark before the ground is completely dried: and perhaps, if the door is shut, we are even ready to remove the covering. God's time of showing his mercy is certainly the best time. This will be when the mercy is ripe for us and we are ready for it.

Verses 15 – 19

Here is:

1. Noah's dismissal from the ark (vv. 15 – 17). Notice:

1.1. Noah did not stir till God commanded him. It is only those who follow God's direction and submit to his rule that come under his protection.

1.2. Though God confined him for a long time, he eventually commanded him to leave.

1.3. God had said, *Come into the ark*, which suggested that God went in with him; now he does not say, "Come forth," but, *Go forth*, which suggests that God, who went in with him, stayed with him all the time, until he sent him out safely.

2. Noah's departure when he had his dismissal. When he found himself kept there, not only for a new life, but also for a new world, he saw no reason to complain of his long confinement. Notice that Noah and his family came out alive and he brought out all the creatures that went in with him, except the raven and the dove, which, probably, were ready to meet their mates when they left the ark. Noah was able to give a very good account of his responsibility, for of all that were given to him he had lost none.

Verses 20–22

Here is:

1. Noah's thankful acknowledgment of God's favor to him, in completing the mercy of his deliverance (v. 20).

1.1. He *built an altar*. God is pleased with freewill offerings and praises that await him. Noah was now turned out into a cold and desolate world, where, you would have thought, his first task would have been to build a house for himself; but we see that he begins with an altar for God. God, who is the first, must be first served; and he that begins with God begins well.

1.2. He offered a sacrifice upon his altar, *of every clean beast, and of every clean fowl*. Here notice:

1.2.1. He offered only those that were clean.

1.2.2. Though his livestock were so small in number, and those that there were had been rescued from ruin with a great deal of care, yet he did not grudge to give God his due from it. Serving God with the little we have is the way to make it more; and we must never think that what God is honored with is wasted.

1.2.3. The antiquity of religion: the first thing we find done in the new world was an act of worship (Jer 6:16). We are now to express our thankfulness, not by burnt offerings, but by the sacrifices of praise and the sacrifices of righteousness, by godly devotion and godly behavior.

2. God's gracious acceptance of Noah's thankfulness.

2.1. God was well pleased with the performance (v. 21). He *smelled a sweet savour*, or, as it is in the Hebrew, "a savor of rest," from it. He was well pleased with Noah's godly zeal and these hopeful beginnings of the new world. Having caused his anger to rest on the world of sinners, God here caused his love to rest on this little remnant of believers.

2.2. Immediately following this, God resolved never to drown the world again. Solid assurance is here given, which may be relied on:

2.2.1. That this judgment would never be repeated. Noah might think, "Why should the world be restored, if in all probability, because of its wickedness, it will quickly be similarly destroyed again?" "No," says God, "it never will be." *Neither will I again smite any more every living thing*. I will no longer follow this severe method"; for:

2.2.1.1. "Human beings are instead to be pitied, for it is all the effect of sin living in them, and it is only what might be expected from such a degenerate race: they are called *transgressors from the womb*, and therefore it is not strange that they behave so very treacherously" (Isa 48:8). So God *remembers that they are flesh*.

2.2.1.2. "He will be utterly ruined, for, if he is dealt with according to his just deserts, one flood must succeed another until everything is destroyed." Notice:

• That outward judgments, though they may terrify and restrain people, cannot of themselves sanctify and renew them; the grace of God must work with those judgments.

• That God's reasons for mercy are all drawn from himself, not from anything in us.

2.2.2. That the course of nature would never be discontinued (v. 22): "*While the earth remaineth*, and human beings on it, there shall be *summer and winter* (not all winter as had been the previous year), *day and night*," not all night, as probably it was while the rain was falling. It is clearly shown that this earth is not to remain always. As long as the world does remain, God's providence will carefully preserve the regular succession of times and seasons, and cause each to know its place. To this we owe the fact that the world stands, and the wheel of nature keeps on its course. See here how changeable the times are and yet how also unchangeable.

2.2.2.1. The course of nature is always changing: *day and night, summer and winter*, changing one for the other.

2.2.2.2. The course of nature never changes. It is constant in its inconstancy. These seasons have never ceased, nor will cease, while the sun continues to be such a steady measurer of time and the moon such a *faithful witness in heaven* (Ps 89:37). This is *God's covenant of the day and of the night*, the stability of which is mentioned to confirm our faith in the covenant of grace, which is sacrosanct and cannot be broken (Jer 33:20).

CHAPTER 9

Both the world and the church were now again reduced to a family, the family of Noah, the details of which this chapter describes. Here is: 1. The covenant of providence established with Noah and his sons (vv. 1–11). In this covenant: 1.1. God promises them that he will take care of their lives, so that: 1.1.1. They would replenish the earth (vv. 1, 7). 1.1.2. They would be safe from the insults of the wild animals (v. 2). 1.1.3. They would be allowed to eat flesh; only they must not eat blood (vv. 3–4). 1.1.4. The world would never be drowned again (vv. 8–11). 1.2. God requires of them to take care of one another's lives and of their own (vv. 5–6). 2. The seal of that covenant, namely, the rainbow (vv. 12–17). 3. A story concerning Noah and his sons: 3.1 Noah's family and work (vv. 18–19). 3.2. Noah's sin and shame (vv. 20–21). 3.3. Ham's impudence and impiety (v. 22). 3.4. The godly modesty of Shem and Japheth (v. 23). 3.5. The curse of Canaan, and the blessing of Shem and Japheth (vv. 21–27). 4. The age and death of Noah (vv. 28–29).

Verses 1–7

In general, *God blessed Noah and his sons* (v. 1), that is, he assured them of his goodwill to them and his gracious intentions concerning them. We read (8:20) how Noah blessed God, by his altar and sacrifice.

Now here we have the *Magna Carta*, the great charter of this new kingdom of nature which was now to be established and incorporated, the former charter having been established and then forfeited.

1. The privileges of this charter are kind and gracious to the human race.

1.1. The privilege of lands of vast extent, and a promise of a great increase of people to occupy and enjoy them. The first blessing is here renewed: *Be fruitful, and multiply, and replenish the earth* (v. 1).

1.1.1. God sets the whole earth before all human beings, tells them it is all their own, *while it remains*, to them and their heirs. Though it is not a paradise, but instead a wilderness, it is still better than we deserve. Blessed be God that it is not hell.

1.1.2. God gives them a blessing, so that in a little time all the habitable parts of the earth would indeed be more or less inhabited. Though death would still reign, the earth would never again be depopulated as now it was but would be filled (Ac 17:24–26).

1.2. The privilege of power over the lower creatures (v. 2). Human beings in innocence rule by love, fallen humans rule by fear. Now this promise remains in force, and so far we still have the benefit of it. Now here see:

1.2.1. That God is a good Master, and provides, not only that we may live, but that we may live comfortably, in his service; not only for our necessity, but also for our delight.

1.2.2. That every *creature of God is good*, and nothing is to be rejected (1Ti 4:4).

2. The precepts and provisos of this charter are no less kind and gracious, and are instances of God's goodwill to people. The Jewish teachers spoke so often of the seven precepts of Noah, or of the sons of Noah, which they say were to be observed by all nations, that it may not be wrong to set them down. The first is against the worship of idols. The second is against blasphemy, and requires blessing the name of God. The third is against murder. The fourth is against incest and all uncleanness. The fifth is against theft, pillage, and robbery. The sixth requires the administration of justice. The seventh is against eating of meat that still has its lifeblood in it.

2.1. People must not harm their own lives by eating food that is unwholesome and detrimental to their health (v. 4); they must not be greedy and hasty in taking their food; they must not be brutal and cruel to the lower creatures. While the law of sacrifices continued, in which the blood made *atonement for the soul* (Lev 17:11), meaning that the life of the sacrifice was accepted for the life of the sinner, blood must not be looked on as a common thing, but must be *poured out unto the Lord* (2Sa 23:16). But now that the great and true sacrifice has been offered, the obligation of the law ends along with the reason for it.

2.2. Human beings must not take their own lives: *Your blood of your lives will I require* (v. 5). Our lives are not so much our own that we may leave them at our own pleasure, but they are God's.

2.3. The animals must not be allowed to hurt human life. This was confirmed by the Law of Moses (Ex 21:28), and we think it would not be unsafe to observe it still. In this way God showed his hatred of the sin of murder, that we might hate it all the more, and not only punish it, but also prevent it.

2.4. Willful murderers must be put to death. This is the sin which is here designed to be restrained by the terror of punishment.

2.4.1. God will punish murderers. At one time or other, in this world or in the next, he will both discover concealed murders, which are hidden from human eyes, and punish declared and justified murders, which are too great for human hands.

2.4.2. The judge must punish murderers (v. 6). There are those who are servants of God for this purpose, to protect the innocent, by being a terror to the malicious and evildoers, and they must not *bear the sword in vain* (Ro 13:4). It is a sin *which the Lord would not pardon* in a ruler (2Ki 24:3–4), and which therefore a ruler should not pardon in a subject. To this law there is a reason attached: *For in the image of God made he man* originally. As human beings we are so dear to our Creator, and so we should be to one another. God put honor upon us, and so

let us not have contempt for one another. Such remains of God's image are still on us even in our fallen state that the one who unjustly kills another human being defaces the image of God and dishonors him.

Verses 8–11

Here is:

1. The general establishment of God's covenant with this new world, and the extent of that covenant (vv. 9–10). Here notice:

1.1. That God is graciously pleased to deal with human beings by way of covenant, in which God greatly encourages our duty and obedience.

1.2. That all God's covenants with human beings are of his own making: *I, behold, I.*

1.3. That God's covenants are established more firmly than the pillars of heaven or the foundations of the earth, and cannot be revoked.

1.4. That God's covenants are made with the covenanters and with their descendants: the promise is to them and their children.

2. The particular purposes of this covenant. It was designed to keep the world safe from another Deluge: *There shall not any more be a flood.* It is because of God's goodness and faithfulness, not because of any reformation of the world, that it has not often been flooded, and that it is not flooded now. As the old world was destroyed to be a memorial to justice, so this world remains to this day as a memorial to mercy, according to the oath of God, that the waters of Noah would never again cover the earth (Isa 54:9). If the sea would flow only for a few days as it does twice every day for a few hours, what desolation would it make! Let us give him the glory of his mercy in promising and the glory of his truth in performing this.

Verses 12–17

Human contracts are usually sealed, and so God, being *willing more abundantly to show to the heirs of promise the immutability of his counsel*, has confirmed his covenant by a seal or oath (Heb 6:17). The seal of this covenant of nature was natural enough; it was the *rainbow*. Concerning this seal of the covenant, notice:

1. Alongside this seal come repeated assurances of the truth of the promise which it was designed to ratify: *I do set my bow in the cloud* (v. 13); it *shall be seen in the cloud* (v. 14), that the eye might affect the heart and so confirm the faith; and it shall be *the token of the covenant* (vv. 12–13), *and I will remember my covenant, that the waters shall no more become a flood* (v. 15).

2. The rainbow appears when the clouds are most inclined to rain, and returns after the rain, when we have most reason to fear the prevalent rain. In this way God removes our fears.

3. The thicker the cloud, the brighter the rainbow in the clouds. In the same way, just as sufferings come to us in abundance, God showers his encouragement and comfort upon us all the more (2Co 1:5).

4. The rainbow appears when one part of the sky is clear, which is a sign of mercy remembered at a time of wrath; and the clouds are enclosed, as it were, by the rainbow, that they may not spread over the heavens, for a rainbow is colored rain or the edges of a gilded cloud.

5. A bow speaks of terror, but this bow has neither string nor arrow, and a bow alone will not achieve much. It is a bow, but it is directed upward, not toward the earth; for the seals of the covenant were intended to comfort, not to terrify.

Verses 18–23

Here is:

1. Noah's family and work. The work that Noah applied himself to was that of *a husbandman*, a farmer (Hebrew, "a man of the earth"), that is, one dealing in the earth, who kept soil in his hand, and lived on the land. Noah was by his calling led to trade in the fruits of the earth. He *began to be a husbandman*, that is he returned to his old work, from which he had first been diverted by the building of the ark, and probably afterward by the building of a house on dry land for himself and his family. For all this time he had been a carpenter, but now he began again to be a farmer.

2. Noah's sin and shame: *He planted a vineyard*; and when he had gathered his grape harvest, probably he appointed a day of joy and feasting in his family, and had his sons and their children with him, to rejoice with him in the growth of his house as well as in the growth of his vineyard; and perhaps he appointed this feast with the aim, at the end, of blessing his sons. At this feast he *drank of the wine*. But he drank too liberally, for he was *drunk*. Notice how he now came to be overtaken in this fault. It was his sin, and a great sin, so much the worse for its coming so soon after a great deliverance; but God left him to himself, and has left this failure of his on record, to teach us:

2.1. That the most beautiful compositions that ever mere mortals wrote since the Fall have had their blots and false strokes.

2.2. That sometimes those who with watchfulness and resolution have by the grace of God kept their integrity in the midst of temptation have, through confidence, carelessness, and neglect of the grace of God, surprisingly fallen into sin when the hour of temptation is over.

2.3. That we need to be very careful, when we use what God has created plentifully, so that we do not use it to excess. Now the consequence of Noah's sin was shame. He was made naked to his shame, as Adam was when he had eaten the forbidden fruit. Notice here the great evil of the sin of drunkenness:

- It uncovers people. Whatever weaknesses they have, they betray when they are drunk, and what secrets they are entrusted with are then easily got out of them. Drunken porters keep open gates.
- It disgraces people, and exposes them to contempt. People say and do things when they are drunk which when they are sober they would blush at the thought of (Hab 2:15–16).

3. Ham's impudence and impiety: He *saw the nakedness of his father, and told his two brethren* (v. 22).

3.1. He pleased himself with the sight. Perhaps Ham had sometimes been himself drunk. It is common for those who walk in false ways themselves to delight in the false steps which they sometimes see others make. But love does not delight in evil.

3.2. *He told his two brethren* in a scornful deriding manner, that his father might seem offensive to them. It is very wrong to make fun of sin (Pr 14:9) and to make known the faults of any, especially of our parents, whom it is our duty to honor.

4. The faithful care of Shem and Japheth to cover their poor father's shame (vv. 2–3). There is a covering of love to be thrown over the faults of all (1Pe 4:8). Besides this, there is a robe of reverence to be thrown over the faults of parents.

Verses 24–27

1. Noah comes to himself. He *awoke from his wine*.

2. The spirit of prophecy comes on him, and, like dying Jacob (49:1), he tells his sons what will happen to them.

2.1. He pronounces a curse on Canaan, the son of Ham (v. 25). The particular curse is, *A servant of servants* (that is, the lowest and most despised slave) *shall he be*, even *to his brethren*. We can learn from this that:

2.1.1. God sometimes punishes the children for the sins of their fathers (Ex 20:5), when the children inherit their fathers' wicked dispositions, and imitate their fathers' wicked practices, and do nothing to cut off the transmission of the curse.

2.1.2. Disgrace is justly put on those who put disgrace on others, especially those who dishonor and grieve their own parents.

2.2. He passes on a blessing to Shem and Japheth.

2.2.1. He blesses Shem, or rather blesses God for him. Notice:

2.2.1.1. He calls the Lord *the God of Shem*. All blessings are included in this. Shem is sufficiently rewarded for his respect to his father in this, that the Lord himself puts this honor upon him, *to be his God*.

2.2.1.2. He gives to God the glory of that good work which Shem had done. When we see the good works of others we should glorify, not them, but *our Father* (Mt 5:16). It is an honor and a favor to be used by God in doing good.

2.2.1.3. He foresees that God's gracious dealings with Shem and his family would be evidence to all the world that he was the God of Shem.

2.2.1.4. It is intimated that the church should be built up and continued in the descendants of Shem; for from him came the Jews, who were for a great while the only professing people God had in the world.

2.2.2. He blesses Japheth and in him, *the isles of the Gentiles* (10:5) which were populated by his descendants: *God shall enlarge Japheth, and he shall dwell in the tents of Shem* (v. 27). Some make this to belong wholly to Japheth, and to denote either:

2.2.2.1. His outward prosperity, that his descendants would be so numerous and so victorious that they would be masters of the tents of Shem, which was fulfilled when the people of the Jews, the most eminent of Shem's race, paid tribute to the Greeks first and afterward to the Romans, both from Japheth's descendants. Or:

2.2.2.2. It denotes the conversion of the Gentiles and the bringing of them into the church; and then we should read it, "God shall persuade Japheth" (for this is what the word means), and then, being so persuaded, *he shall dwell in the tents of Shem*, that is, Jews and Gentiles shall be united together in the Gospel fold. It is only God who can bring those again into the church who have separated themselves from it. Souls are brought into the church, not by force, but by persuasion (Ps 110:3). They are persuaded by reason to turn to God.

Verses 28–29

Here we see:

1. How God prolonged the life of Noah; this long life was a further reward of his great godliness, and a great blessing to the world.

2. How God put an end to his life at last. Noah lived to see two worlds, but being an heir of the righteousness which is by faith (Heb 11:7), when he died he went to see one that is better than either.

CHAPTER 10

This chapter shows the origin of nations; and yet perhaps there is no nation except that of the Jews that can be confident from which of these seventy fountains (for there are as many here) it derives its streams. Through the lack of early records, the mixture of people, the revolutions of nations, and the distance of time, the knowledge of the lineal descent of the present inhabitants of the earth is lost. Here is a brief account: 1. Of the descendants of Japheth (vv. 2–5). 2. Of the descendants of Ham (vv. 6–20), and in this particular notice is taken of Nimrod (vv. 8–10). 3. Of the descendants of Shem (vv. 21–32).

Verses 1–5

The descendants of Japheth were allotted to *the isles of the Gentiles* (v. 5), which were divided among them, and possibly this island of ours among the rest. They became maritime peoples. All places beyond the sea from Judea are called *isles* (Jer 25:22), and this directs us to understand that promise (Isa 42:4), *the isles shall wait for his law*, of the conversion of the Gentiles to the faith of Christ.

Verses 6–14

What is noteworthy and useful in these verses is the account here given of Nimrod (vv. 8–10). He is here represented as a great man in his day: he was resolved to tower above his neighbors. The same spirit that moved the giants before the Flood now revived in him. There are some in whom ambition and aspirations of dominion seem to be bred in the bone. Nothing on this side of hell will humble and break the proud spirits of some people. Now:

1. Nimrod was a great hunter; with this he began, and for this he became proverbially famous.

1.1. Some think he did well with his hunting, served his country by ridding it of the wild animals which pervaded it.

1.2. Others think that under pretense of hunting he gathered warriors under his command, in pursuit of another game he had to play, which was to make himself ruler of the country. Great conquerors are only great hunters. Alexander and Caesar would not figure so much in scriptural history as they do in general history. Nimrod was a mighty hunter "against" the Lord, as in the Septuagint (a Greek version of the Old Testament); that is:

1.2.1. He set up idolatry; so that he might set up a new government, he set up a new religion. *Babel* (Babylon) *was the mother of harlots* (Rev 17:5). Or:

1.2.2. He carried on his oppression and violence in defiance of God himself.

2. Nimrod was a great ruler: *The beginning of his kingdom was Babel* (Babylon) (v. 10). Some way or other, by art or arms, he got into power, and so laid the foundations of a monarchy. If Nimrod and his neighbors began, other nations soon learned to incorporate their affairs under one leader for their common safety and welfare, which, however it began, proved so great a blessing to the world that things were reckoned to go badly indeed when there *was no king in Israel* (Jdg 17:6).

3. Nimrod was a great builder. Probably he was architect in the building of Babylon, and there he began his kingdom; but, when his project to rule all the sons of Noah was thwarted by the confusion of tongues, "out of that land he went forth into Assyria" (so the margin reads it, v. 11) *and built Nineveh.*

Verses 15–20

Here is the account of the descendants of Canaan, of the families and nations that derived from him, and of the land they possessed, which was very pleasantly situated. Canaan here has a better land than either Shem or Japheth, and yet they have a better lot, for they inherit the blessing.

Verses 21–32

Two things especially are noteworthy in this account of Shem's descendants:

1. The description of Shem (v. 21). We have not only his name, *Shem*, which signifies "a name," but two titles to distinguish him by:

1.1. He was *the father of all the children of Eber.* Eber was his great-grandson; but why should he be called the father of all *his* children, rather than of all Arphaxad's, or Salah's (Shelah's), etc.? Probably because Abraham and his descendants, God's covenant people, not only descended from Heber, but from him were called *Hebrews*; (14:13), *Abram the Hebrew*. Since the holy language was commonly called from him *Hebrew*, it is probable that he retained it in his family, in the confusion of Babel, as a special sign of God's favor to him. Now, when the inspired author wants to give Shem an honorable title, he calls him *the father of the Hebrews*. As Ham, though he had many sons, is disowned by being called *the father of Canaan*, so Shem, though he had many sons, is dignified with the title of *the father of Eber*, to whose descendants the blessing was passed on. Godliness is true greatness.

1.2. He was *the brother of Japheth the elder.* The sacred writer had mentioned it as Shem's honor that he was the father of the Hebrews; but, so that Japheth's seed should not therefore be looked on as forever excluded from the church, he here reminds us that he *was the brother of Japheth*, not only in birth, but also in blessing; for *Japheth was to dwell in the tents of Shem* (9:27).

CHAPTER 11

We have in this chapter: 1. The dispersion of the people at Babel (vv. 1–9), where we have: 1.1. Their presumptuous and defiant plan to build a city and a tower (vv. 1–4). 1.2. The righteous judgment of God on them by confusing their languages and scattering them (vv. 5–9). 2. The genealogy from Shem to Abraham (vv. 10–26), with a general account of his family, and move from his native country (vv. 27–32).

Verses 1–4

The end of the previous chapter tells us that *by* the sons of Noah, or *among* the sons of Noah, *the nations were divided in the earth after the flood* (10:32), that is, were divided into several tribes, and it was either decided by Noah or agreed on among his sons, which way each tribe or community should steer its course. But it would seem that the people were loath to disperse to distant places; they thought, to put it in terms of proverbs: "the more the merrier" and "there is safety in numbers"; and so they planned to stay together, thinking themselves wiser than either God or Noah. Here we have:

1. The advantages which accompanied their plan to stay together:

1.1. They were all of *one language* (v. 1). Now while they all understood one another, they would be all the more likely to love one another, and the more capable of helping one another, and less inclined to separate one from another.

1.2. They found a very suitable and spacious place to settle in (v. 2), *a plain in the land of Shinar*, an extensive plain, able to contain them all, and a fruitful plain, able according to their present numbers, to support them all.

2. The method they took to stay close to one another, and to settle together in one body. Instead of wanting to enlarge their borders by peacefully leaving under the divine protection, they planned to strengthen their borders. Their unanimous resolution is, *Let us build ourselves a city and a tower*. Notice here:

2.1. How they excited and encouraged one another to set about this work. They said, *Go to, let us make brick* (v. 3), and again (v. 4), *Go to, let us build us a city*; their spurring one another on made them all the more daring and resolute.

2.2. What materials they used in their building. Since the country was a plain, it produced neither stone nor mortar, but this did not discourage them from their undertaking. They made brick serve instead of stone, and slime or tar instead of mortar. What efforts those make who are resolute in their purposes: if we were as zealous to pursue good, we would not stop our work as often as we do, pretending that we lack the personal resources to carry it on.

2.3. For what purpose they built. Three things, it seems, they aimed at in building this tower:

2.3.1. It seems designed as an insult to God himself; for they wanted to build a tower — *whose top might reach to heaven*, which speaks of a defiance of God, or at least a desire to rival him.

2.3.2. They hoped to make for themselves a reputation, and to give future generations the knowledge that there had been such people as they in the world. They would leave this memorial to their pride, ambition, and folly. We do not find in any history the name of so much as one of these Babel-builders.

2.3.3. They did it to prevent their dispersion. It is probable that the hand of ambitious Nimrod was in all this. He aimed at universal monarchy, so that, in the pretense of uniting for their common safety, he planned to keep them in one body, watch over them all, and keep them under his power. It is God's prerogative to be universal monarch, Lord of all and King of kings; the person who aims at it offers to step into the throne of God, but he will not give his glory to another.

Verses 5–9

We have here the quashing of the project of the Babel-builders.

1. The discernment God gave toward the plans that were afoot. God is incontestably just and fair in all his dealings with sin and sinners, and condemns none without a hearing. They were "the sons of Adam," so it is in the Hebrew, of that sinful disobedient Adam, whose children are by nature children of disobedience. Devout Eber is not found among these ungodly people; for he and his are called the children of God.

2. The decisions and counsels of the eternal God concerning this matter.

2.1. God allowed them to proceed some way in their enterprise before he put a stop to it, that they might have opportunity to repent.

2.2. God had tried, by his commands and warnings, to turn them away from this project, but in vain, and so he must take another course to keep the world in some order and to tie the hands of those who do not want to be restrained by law. Now notice here the mercy of God, in limiting the punishment, and not making it proportionate to the offense; for *he deals not with us according to our sins* (Ps 103:10). He does not say, "*Let us go down* now in thunder and lightning, and consume those rebels in a moment." No; only, "*Let us go down*, and scatter them." They deserved death, but are only banished and dispersed; for the patience of God is very great toward a world that provokes his anger.

3. Three things were done:

3.1. Their language was confused. Those unfortunate questions concerning disagreements over words that arise from our misunderstanding of one another's language are, for all we know, owing to this confusion of tongues.

3.2. Their building was stopped: *They left off to build the city* (v. 8). This was the effect of the confusion of their languages, for it not only made them unable to help one another, but also probably dampened their spirits so much that they could not proceed, since they saw in this the hand of the Lord against them. It is wisdom to leave off what we see God fighting against.

3.3. The builders were scattered over the whole earth (vv. 8–9). They departed in companies, after their clans, and after their languages (10:5, 20, 31), to the different countries and places allotted to them. They left behind them forever a memorial of their reproach, in the name given to the place. It was called *Babel*, which sounds like the Hebrew for "confused." Those that aim at a great name commonly end up with a *bad* name. The people were now finally scattered, and never did, nor ever will, come all together again, till the great day, when the Son of Man sits on the throne of his glory, and all the nations will be gathered before him (Mt 25:31–32).

Verses 10–26

We have here a genealogy, not an endless genealogy, for here it ends in Abram, the friend of God, and leads further to Christ, the promised seed, who was the son of Abram. From Abraham the genealogy of Christ is reckoned (Mt 1:1–17).

1. Nothing is left on record concerning those of this line of descent except their names and ages, the Holy Spirit seeming to move on through them to the story of Abram. How little do we know of those that have gone before us in this world, even those that lived in the same places where we live, as we likewise know little of those that are our contemporaries in distant places! We have enough to do to mind the work of our own day, and to let God alone call the past to account (Ecc 3:15).

2. There was a noticeable gradual decrease in the years of their lives. Shem reached 600 years, which still fell short of the age of the patriarchs before the Flood; the next three came short of 500; the next three did not reach to 300; after them we read of none that reached to 200, except Terah; and, not many ages after this, Moses reckoned seventy or eighty to be the most people ordinarily live to.

3. Eber, from whom the Hebrews were named, was the longest-living person born after the Flood, which perhaps was the reward of his special godliness and loyal devotion to the ways of God.

Verses 27–32

Here begins the story of Abram, whose name is famous from this time on in both Testaments. Here we see:

1. Abram's country: *Ur of the Chaldees* (v. 28). This was the land of his birth, an idolatrous country, where even the ways of the children of Eber themselves had

become worse. Those who are heirs of the Land of Promise through grace ought to remember what the land of their birth was, what their corrupt and sinful state was by nature, the rock from which they were cut (Isa 51:1).

2. Abram's relatives, mentioned for his sake, and because of their part in the following story.

2.1. His father was *Terah*, of whom it is said (Jos 24:2) that he served other gods, on the other side of the River (i.e., Euphrates). So early it was that idolatry gained a footing in the world, and so hard it is even for those that have some good principles to swim against the stream. We have:

2.2. Some account of his brothers:

2.2.1. *Nahor*, out of whose family both Isaac and Jacob had their wives.

2.2.2. *Haran*, the father of Lot, of whom it is here said (v. 28) *that he died before his father Terah*. Children cannot be sure that they will survive their parents; for death does not go by seniority, taking the eldest first. *The shadow of death is without any order* (Job 10:22). It is likewise said that he died *in Ur of the Chaldees*, before the fortunate move of the family out of that idolatrous country.

2.3. His wife was *Sarai*; Abram himself says of her that she was the daughter of his father, but not the daughter of his mother (20:12). She was ten years younger than Abram.

3. Abram's departure from Ur of the Chaldees, with his father Terah, his nephew Lot, and the rest of his family, in obedience to the call of God, of which we will read more in the next chapter. This chapter leaves them in Haran, or Charran (Ac 7:4), a place about midway between Ur and Canaan, where they lived until Terah died, probably because the old man was unable, through the infirmities of age, to proceed any farther in his journey. Many reach Haran, and yet fall short of Canaan; they are not far from the kingdom of God, but never quite reach it.

CHAPTER 12

From now onward Abram and his descendants are almost the only subject of the sacred history. In this chapter we have: 1. God's call of Abram to the land of Canaan (vv. 1–3). 2. Abram's obedience to this call (vv. 4–5). 3. His welcome to the land of Canaan (vv. 6–9). 4. His journey to Egypt, with an account of what happened to him there: 4.1. Abram's fleeing and fault (vv. 10–13). 4.2. Sarai's danger and deliverance (vv. 14–20).

Verses 1–3

1. We have here the call by which Abram was moved from the land of his birth to the Land of Promise, which was designed both to test his faith and obedience and also to set him apart for God and for special services. We may be somewhat helped in the knowledge of the circumstances of the call by Stephen's speech (Ac 7:2), where we are told:

1.1. That the God of glory appeared in such a display of his glory that it left Abram no room to doubt the divine authority of this call. God spoke to him afterward in various ways; but this first time, when the agreement was to be set up, he appeared to him as *the God of glory* and spoke to him.

1.2. That this call was given him in Mesopotamia, before he dwelt in Charran (Haran). Some think that Haran was in Chaldea, and so was still a part of Abram's country, or that Abram, having stayed there five years, began to

call it his country, and to put down roots there, till God let him know this was not the place he was intended to stay in. If God loves us and has mercy in store for us, he will not allow us to take up our rest anywhere short of Canaan, but will graciously repeat his calls, till the good work that he has begun is truly carried out and our souls rest only in God. In the call itself we have a precept and a promise:

2. A trying precept: *Get thee out of thy country* (v. 1).

2.1. By this precept Abram was tested to see whether he loved his native land and dearest friends, and whether he could willingly leave all to go along with God. His country had become idolatrous, his family and his father's house were a constant temptation to him, and he could not continue with them without danger of being contaminated by them. This command which God gave to Abram is much the same with the Gospel call by which all the spiritual descendants of faithful Abram are brought into covenant with God. For:

2.1.1. Natural affection must give way to divine grace.

2.1.2. Sin, and all occasions of it, must be forsaken, particularly bad company; we must abandon all the idols of wickedness which have been set up in our hearts, willingly parting with what is dearest to us, when we cannot keep it without risking our integrity.

2.1.3. The world and all our enjoyments in it must be looked on with a holy indifference; we must no longer look on it as our country or home, but where we are staying for a while, and must accordingly sit loose to it, be independent of it, live above it, and make sure that it does not hold our deepest affection.

2.2. By this precept Abram was tested to see whether he could trust God further than he saw him, for he has to leave his own country, to go to a *land that God would show him*. He does not say, "It is a land that I will give you," but merely, "a land that I will show you." He must follow God with an implicit faith, though he had no particular security given him that he would gain something by leaving his country to follow God.

3. An encouraging promise, or rather a combination of promises, exceedingly many great and precious promises. All God's precepts are accompanied by promises to the obedient. If we obey the command, God will not fail to fulfill the promise. Here are six promises:

3.1. *I will make of thee a great nation* (v. 2). When God took him from his own people, he promised to make him the head of another; he cut him off from being the branch of a wild olive tree to make him the root of a good olive tree. This promise was:

- A great relief to Abram's burden; for he had now no child. God knows how to make his favors fit the needs and necessities of his children. He who has a bandage for every sore will first provide one for what is most painful.

- A great test of Abram's faith; for his wife had been long barren.

3.2. *I will bless thee* (v. 2). Leave your father's house, and I will give you a father's blessing.

3.3. *I will make thy name great* (v. 2). By leaving his country, he lost his name there. Having no child, he feared he would have no name; but God will make him a great nation, and so make him a great name.

3.4. *Thou shalt be a blessing* (v. 2); that is:

- "Your happiness will be an example of happiness, so that those who want to bless their friends will only pray that God would make them like Abram," as Ru 4:11.

- "Your life will be a blessing to the places where you will stay."

3.5. *I will bless those that bless thee and curse him that curseth thee* (v. 3). This made it a kind of alliance, offensive and defensive, between God and Abram.

3.6. *In thee shall all the families of the earth be blessed* (v. 3). This was the promise that crowned all the rest; for it points to the Messiah, in whom *all the promises are yea and amen* (2Co 1:20). Jesus Christ is the great blessing of the world, the greatest blessing that the world has ever known. He is a family blessing, by him salvation is brought to the house (Lk 19:9).

Verses 4–5

Here is:

1. Abram's departure from his country, out of Ur first and afterward out of Haran, in obedience to the call of God. He *went out, not knowing whither he went* (Heb 11:8), but knowing whom he followed.

2. His age when he departed: he was *seventy-five years old*, an age when he would rather have settled and have had rest, but, if God wanted to have him begin the world again now in his old age, he would submit to him. Here is an example of someone converted at, by our reckoning, an old age.

3. What he took: he took his wife, and his nephew Lot, with him. It is very comforting when husband and wife agree to go together along the way to heaven. Lot also, his nephew, was influenced by Abram's good example, who was perhaps his guardian after the death of his father, and he was willing to go along with him too. They took all their possessions with them—*all their substance* and movable goods, *that they had gathered*. To have thrown away their possessions, because God had promised to bless them, would have been to tempt God, not to trust him.

4. Their happy arrival at their journey's end: *They went forth to go into the land of Canaan* (v. 5); so they did before (11:31), and then stopped far short, but now they continued on their way, and with the good hand of their God on them, they came to the land of Canaan, where by a fresh revelation they were told that this was the land God promised to show them.

Verses 6–9

You would have expected, after Abram had had such an extraordinary call to Canaan, that some great event would have happened upon his arrival there. Little notice is taken of him, for God wanted him to live by faith. Notice:

1. How little comfort he had in the land he came to; for:

1.1. He did not have it to himself: he found the country populated and possessed by Canaanites, who were likely to be bad neighbors and worse landlords.

1.2. He did not settle in it. All good people must look on themselves as foreigners and tenants in this world, and by faith sit loose to it as a strange country. We must continue our journey, going on from strength to strength, as having not yet reached our goal.

2. How much comfort he had in the God he followed.

2.1. God spoke to him good and encouraging words: *Unto thy seed will I give this land*. Enemies may part us and our homes, us and our altars, but not us and our God. Mercies to the children are mercies to the parents. "I will give it, not to you, but to your offspring"; it is a privilege to his descendants, which Abram understood also as a privilege to himself, for he looked for a heavenly country (Heb 11:16).

2.2. Abram *built an altar unto the Lord who appeared to him, and called on the name of the Lord* (vv. 7–8). So he decided, on his part, to maintain fellowship with God. Wherever he had a tent, God had an altar, an altar that was sanctified by prayer. The *souls he had gotten in Haran*, being discipled, must be further taught. The way of family worship is a good and old way; it is not a novel invention but is the time-honored practice of all the saints. Wherever we go, let us not fail to take our faith along with us.

Verses 10–13

Here is:

1. A famine in the land of Canaan, *a grievous famine*. It was a severe time of testing; it tested what Abram would think. Nothing short of a strong faith could maintain good thoughts of God under such circumstances. He was tested to see whether he would maintain his unshaken confidence that the God who brought him to Canaan would keep him there, and whether he could rejoice in him as the God of his salvation when the fig tree did not blossom (Hab 3:17–18). We can see from this that it is possible for us to be in the line of duty, and on the way to happiness, and still meet with great troubles and disappointments.

2. Abram's move to Egypt, on the occasion of this famine. See how wisely God provides that there should be plenty in one place when there was scarcity in another. We must not expect unneeded miracles. When he must leave Canaan for a time, he chose to go to Egypt, which lay southwest, the opposite way, that he might not so much as seem to look back (Heb 11:15–16).

3. A great fault that Abram was guilty of, in denying his wife and pretending that she was his sister. Scripture is impartial in relating the misdeeds of the most celebrated saints, which are recorded, not for us to imitate but to warn us that he *who thinks he stands may take heed lest he fall* (1Co 10:12). What lay at its root was a jealous and apprehensive notion he had that some of the Egyptians would be so charmed with the beauty of Sarai that, if they were to know he was her husband, they would find some way or other to lead him away and kill him, that they might marry her. The grace Abram was most famous for was faith, but he still sinned through unbelief and distrust of the divine Providence, even *after God had appeared to him twice*. What will become of the slender willows, when the sturdy cedars are thus shaken in this way?

Verses 14–20

Here is:

1. The danger Sarai was in of having her chastity violated by the king of Egypt. They recommended her to the king, and she was immediately taken into Pharaoh's house, as Esther into the harem of King Xerxes (Est 2:8), in order for her to be taken into his bed.

2. The deliverance of Sarai from this danger. For if God did not deliver us we would soon be ruined. He does not deal with us according to what we deserve.

2.1. God punished Pharaoh, and so prevented the progress of his sin. They are fortunate punishments that prevent us from acting sinfully and effectively bring us back to our duty.

2.2. Pharaoh reproved Abram, and then dismissed him with respect.

2.2.1. The reproof was calm, but very just: *What is this that thou hast done?* Pharaoh reasons with him: *Why didst thou not tell me that she was thy wife?* intimating that, if he had known this, he would not have taken her into his house. We have often found more virtue, honor, and conscience in some people than we thought they possessed. It ought to be a pleasure to us to be disappointed in this way, as Abram was here, when he found Pharaoh to be a better man than he expected. Goodwill teaches us to hope for the best.

2.2.2. The dismissal was kind and very generous. Pharaoh restored Abram's wife to Abram without offering any injury to her honor. *Pharaoh commanded his men concerning him.* He appointed them, when Abram was about to return home, after the famine, to escort him safely out of the country. Note a resemblance between this deliverance of Abram from Egypt and the deliverance of his offspring from there: after Abram went into Egypt on occasion of a famine they went there on occasion of a famine also; he was drawn out with great plagues on Pharaoh, so were they. For God's care of his people is the same *yesterday, today, and for ever.*

CHAPTER 13

In this chapter we have a further account concerning Abram. 1. In general, of his life and ways in the Land of Promise. His moves (vv. 1, 3–4, 18), his riches (v. 2), his devotion (vv. 4, 18). 2. A particular account of a quarrel that happened between him and Lot. The unhappy occasion of their disagreement (vv. 5–6); the different parties in the disagreement and its development (v. 7); the making up of the quarrel, by the prudence of Abram (vv. 8–9). 3. Lot's departure from Abram to the plain of Sodom (vv. 10–13). 4. God's appearance to Abram to confirm the promise of the land of Canaan to him (vv. 14–18).

Verses 1–4

Here is:

1. Abram's return from Egypt (v. 1). He came himself and brought all his own with him.

2. His wealth: *He was very rich* (v. 2). He was very "heavy," so the Hebrew word means; for riches are a burden. There is a burden of care in gaining them, a fear in keeping them, a temptation in using them, guilt in abusing them, sorrow in losing them, and finally a burden of the responsibility in giving an account of how they have been used. God, in his providence, sometimes makes good people rich people, and teaches them how to live in plenty, as well as how to live in want. Though it is hard for the rich to get to heaven, yet it is not impossible (Mk 10:23–24). Outward prosperity, if well managed, provides an opportunity of doing even more good.

3. His move to Bethel (vv. 3–4). He went there not only because that was where he formerly had his tent, but also because he formerly had his altar there. Long afterward God sent Jacob to this same place on that errand (31:13; 35:1). We need to be reminded of our solemn vows. Perhaps the place where they were made may help to bring them afresh to mind, and so it may do us good to go there.

4. His devotion there. His altar was gone, so that he could not offer sacrifice; but *he called on the name of the Lord* (v. 3), as he had done (12:8). Abram did not leave his religion behind him in Egypt, as many do in their travels.

Verses 5–9

We have here a sad disagreement between Abram and Lot, who had up to this time been inseparable companions.

1. The reason for their quarrel was their riches. Riches are often a reason for strife and contention. Poverty and trials, being in want while wandering, could not separate Abram and Lot; but riches did. Friends are soon lost; but God is a friend from whose love neither the height of prosperity nor the depth of adversity will separate us.

2. The quarrel began *between the herdsmen of Abram's cattle and the herdsmen of Lot's cattle* (v. 7). They argued who should have the better pastureland or the better water.

3. The worsening of the quarrel was that *the Canaanite and the Perizzite dwelt then in the land* (v. 7). This made the quarrel very dangerous and very scandalous. The arguments of those who profess a godly faith are the reproach of our godly faith, and give reason, as much as anything, to the enemies of the Lord to blaspheme.

4. The making up of this quarrel was fortunate. It is best to preserve the peace, so that it is not broken; but the next best thing is, if differences do come about, that they are resolved as quickly as possible. The movement to settle the quarrel was made by Abram.

4.1. His petition for peace was very affectionate: *Let there be no strife, I pray thee.* Abram knew how to turn away wrath with a gentle answer; he made the first overture of reconciliation. The people of God should always demonstrate themselves to be a peaceable people; whatever others are in favor of, they must be in favor of peace.

4.2. His plea for peace was very compelling:

4.2.1. "Let there be no strife *between me and thee.* Let the Canaanites and Perizzites argue about trivialities; but let not you and me fall out, who know better things, and look for a better country." The remembrance of old friendships should quickly put an end to new quarrels which can happen at any time.

4.2.2. Let it be remembered that *we are brethren.* We are rational creatures, and should be ruled by reason. We are people, not wild animals; adults, not children. We are brothers and sisters, those of the same nature, of the same family, of the same religion, companions in obedience, companions in patience.

4.3. His proposal for peace was very fair. "Why should we quarrel for room, while there is room enough for us both?" Abram offers Lot a sufficient share of the land they were in. Abram gives Lot his choice, and offers to take what is left: *If thou wilt take the left hand, I will go to the right.* There was all the reason in the world for Abram to choose first; yet he renounces his right. It is a noble conquest to be willing to yield for the sake of peace; it is the conquest of ourselves, and our own pride and passion (Mt 5:39–40).

Verses 10–13

We have here the choice that Lot made when he parted company with Abram. After Abram had offered Lot the choice, Lot accepted it without a word of thanks, and made his election. Passion and selfishness make people rude.

1. Lot had an eye on the goodness of the land. He *beheld all the plain of Jordan,* the flat country in which Sodom stood, that it was extraordinarily *well-watered everywhere.* It would be somewhere where he could comfortably settle, and in such a fruitful soil he would certainly prosper, and grow very rich. This was all he looked at. But what came of it? Why, the next news we hear of him is that he is caught up among them; he and his possessions are taken away captive (14:12). Eventually God burned the city over his head and forced him to the mountains for safety, the one who had chosen the plain for wealth and pleasure.

Sensual choices are sinful choices, and seldom work out well. In all our choices this principle should overrule us: what is best for us is what is best for our souls.

2. *But the men of Sodom were wicked* (v. 13). Some sinners are the worse for living in a good land. So the Sodomites were. Depraved Sodomites live in a city, in a fruitful plain, while devout Abram and his godly family live in tents on the barren mountains. Now Lot's coming to live among the Sodomites may be considered a great mercy to them, and a likely means of bringing them to repentance; for now they had a prophet among them and a preacher of righteousness, and, if they had listened to him, they might have been mended in their ways, and the ruin prevented.

Verses 14 – 18

Here we see:

1. An account of a gracious appearance by God to Abram, to confirm the promise to him and his offspring. Note when it was that God renewed and ratified the promise:

- After the quarrel was over.
- After Abram humbly and with self-denial condescended to Lot to keep the peace.
- After he had lost the encouraging company of his relative, and his heart was saddened, then God came to him with these good and encouraging words. Lot perhaps had the better land, but Abram still had the better *title*. Lot had the paradise, such as it was, but Abram had the promise.

2. The promises themselves with which God now comforted and enriched Abram. Two things he assures him of — a good land, and numerous offspring to enjoy it:

2.1. Here is the promise of a good land, a land famous above all lands, for it was to be the holy land, and Emmanuel's land. What God has to show is infinitely better and more desirable than anything that the world has to offer to our view. He secures this land to him and his offspring forever (v. 15).

2.2. Here is the promise of numerous offspring to fill this good land, so that it should never be lost for lack of heirs (v. 16). The same God that provides the inheritance provides the heirs.

3. What Abram did when God had confirmed his promise to him (v. 18). He *removed his tent*. In compliance with God's will in this, *he removes his tent*, conforming himself to the life of a pilgrim. He *built there an altar*, as a sign of his thankfulness to God.

CHAPTER 14

We have four things in this chapter: 1. A war with the king of Sodom and his allies (vv. 1–11) and the captivity of Lot in that war (v. 12). 2. Abram's rescue of Lot from being captured (vv. 13–16). 3. Abram's return from the expedition (v. 17), with an account of what passed between him and the king of Salem (vv. 18–20). 4. What passed between him and the king of Sodom (vv. 21–24). Here we have the promise to Abram fulfilled in part, that God would make his name great.

Verses 1 – 12

Here is an account of the first war that ever we read of in Scripture.

1. The parties engaged in it. The invaders were four kings, two of them no less than kings of Shinar and Elam (that is, Babylonia and the plain of Khuzistan). The

invaded were the kings of five cities that lay near one another in the plain of Jordan, namely, Sodom, Gomorrah, Admah, Zeboiim, and Zoar.

2. The occasion of this war was the revolt of the five kings from under the rule of Chedorlaomer (Kedorlaomer). They served him for twelve years. They had small joy from their fruitful land, while they paid tribute to a foreign power, and could not call what they had their own. In the thirteenth year, beginning to be weary of their subjection, they rebelled, refused to pay their tribute, and attempted to shake off the tyranny and retrieve their old liberties. In the fourteenth year, after some pause and preparation, Chedorlaomer, in conjunction with his allies, set himself to chastise and bring back the rebels.

3. The progress and success of the war. The four kings laid waste to the neighboring countries and enriched themselves with their spoils (vv. 5 – 7). The forces of the king of Sodom and his allies were routed. The cities were plundered (v. 11). Lot was taken captive (v. 12). They took Lot among the rest, and his goods. Many upright people fare the worse because of their wicked neighbors. It is therefore our wisdom to separate ourselves and so not receive their punishments (Rev 18:4). When we leave the line of duty, we take ourselves away from under God's protection, and cannot expect that the choices which are made by our sinful desires should result in our comfort.

Verses 13 – 16

We have here an account of the only military action we ever find Abram engaged in, and this he was prompted to, not by his greed or ambition, but purely by the principle of charity; it was not to enrich himself, but to help his friend. We read here of:

1. The news brought to Abram of his relative's distress. He is here called *Abram the Hebrew*, that is, the son and follower of Eber, in whose family the profession of the true religion was kept up in those corrupt times. The news was brought by one who had escaped with his life.

2. The preparations Abram made for this expedition. This shows that Abram was:

- A great man, who had so many servants depending on him.
- A good man, who not only served God himself, but instructed all those around him in the service of God.
- A wise man, for, though he was a man of peace, he still disciplined his servants for war. Though our holy religion teaches us to be in favor of peace, it does not forbid us from preparing for war.

3. Abram's allies and confederates in this expedition. He prevailed with his neighbors, *Aner, Eshcol, and Mamre*, to go along with him. Those who depend on God's help, in times of distress still ought to make use of the help of other people, as Providence offers it; else they tempt God.

4. Abram's courage and conduct, which were very remarkable:

4.1. There was a great deal of bravery in the enterprise itself, considering the disadvantages he was under. What could one family of farmers and shepherds do against the armies of four rulers, who now came fresh from bloodshed and victory? Religion tends to make us, not cowardly, but truly courageous. The true Christian is the true hero.

4.2. Careful and suitable planning is a good friend both to our safety and to our usefulness. The serpent's head (provided it is nothing like the old Serpent) may well turn into the body of a true Christian, especially if it has the eye of a peace-loving dove in it (Mt 10:16).

5. Abram's success, which was very great (vv. 15–16). He defeated his enemies and rescued his friends; and we do not find that he sustained any loss.

5.1. Abram rescued his relative; twice here he is called his *brother Lot*. Remembering the relationship that was between them, both by nature and grace, made him forget the little quarrel that had been between them. We ought to be ready, whenever it is in the power of our hands, to help and relieve those that are in distress. Though others may be lacking in their duty to us, we must still not therefore deny our duty to them. Some have said that they can more easily forgive their enemies than their friends, but we see ourselves obliged to forgive both.

5.2. Abram rescued the rest of the captives, for Lot's sake, though they were strangers to him and as such he was under no obligation to them at all. As we have opportunity we must do good to all people.

Verses 17–20

This paragraph begins with the mention of the respect which the king of Sodom paid to Abram, but, before a detailed account is given of this, the story of Melchizedek is briefly related:

1. Who he was. He was *king of Salem* and *priest of the Most High God* (v. 18); and other glorious things are said of him (Heb 7:1–10).

1.1. Some commentators conclude that Melchizedek was Shem the son of Noah. But why should his name be changed? And how did he come to settle in Canaan?

1.2. Many Christian commentators have thought that this was an appearance of the Son of God himself. He appeared to him as a righteous king, with a righteous cause, and giving peace. It is difficult to imagine that any mere man should be said to *be without father, without mother, and without descent, having neither beginning of days nor end of life* (Heb 7:3).

1.3. It is possible that Melchizedek was a Canaanite ruler who reigned in Salem, and maintained the true religion there. If so, why should his name occur here only in all the story of Abram? The *Arabic Catena* gives this account of Melchizedek, that he was the son of Heraclim, the son of Peleg, the son of Eber, and that his mother's name was Salathiel, the daughter of Gomer, the son of Japheth, the son of Noah.

2. What he did:

2.1. He *brought forth bread and wine*, to refresh Abram and his soldiers, and to congratulate them on their victory. This he did as a king.

2.2. As priest of the Most High God, he blessed Abram, which we may suppose was a greater refreshment to Abram than his bread and wine were. In this way, God, having raised up his Son Jesus, has sent him as having authority to bless us. Those whom he blesses are blessed indeed.

3. What he said (vv. 19–20). Two things were said by him:

3.1. He blessed Abram from God. Notice the titles he here gives to God, which are very glorious: *The Most High God* and *possessor of heaven and earth*, that is, rightful owner and sovereign Lord of all creatures, because he made them.

3.2. He blessed God for Abram (v. 20): and *blessed be the Most High God*.

4. What was done to him: *Abram gave him tithes of all*, that is, of the plunder (Heb 7:4). This may be looked on:

4.1. As a gift presented to Melchizedek, to repay his expressions of respect.

4.2. As an offering vowed and dedicated to the Most High God, and so put into the hands of Melchizedek his priest. We can learn from this that:

- When we have received some significant mercy from God, it is fitting that we should express our thankfulness in some special act of godly kindness.
- The tenth of our income is a fitting proportion to be set apart for the honor of God and the service of his sanctuary.
- Jesus Christ, our great Melchizedek, is to have homage paid to him and is to be humbly acknowledged by every one of us as our king and priest. Not only the tithe of all, but all we have, must be surrendered and given up to him.

Verses 21–24

We have here an account of what passed between Abram and the king of Sodom:

1. The king of Sodom's grateful offer to Abram: *Give me the persons, and take the goods to thyself* (v. 21). "Give me the soul, and you take the substance," is the Hebrew reading. Here he begs for the people, but freely says that Abram may keep all the goods for himself.

2. Abram's generous refusal of this offer. He not only relinquished the people to him, but he restored all the goods too. He would not take *from a thread to a shoe-latchet*. What are all the mere fripperies of life and sensory delights to those who have God and heaven always in their sight?

2.1. Abram confirms this resolution with a solemn oath. Notice the practice used in this oath: *I have lifted up my hand* (v. 22). In religious swearing, we appeal to God's knowledge of our truth and sincerity. We invoke his wrath if we swear falsely, and the *lifting up of the hand* is very significant and expressive of both aspects.

2.2. Abram supports his refusal with a good reason: *Lest thou shouldest say, I have made Abram rich*, which would reflect discredit on the promise and covenant of God and on the piety and compassion of Abram. The people of God must, for their credit's sake, take heed of doing anything that looks mean or mercenary or that smacks of covetousness or self-seeking.

CHAPTER 15

In this chapter we have a solemn treaty between God and Abram concerning a covenant that was to be established between them. In the former chapter we saw Abram dealing with kings; here we find him dealing with God; and, though there he looked great, here we think he looks much greater. The covenant to be set up between God and Abram was a covenant of promises; and so here is: 1. A general assurance of God's kindness and goodwill to Abram (v. 1). 2. A special declaration of the purposes of his love concerning him, in two things: that he would give him innumerable descendants (vv. 2–6); and that he would give him Canaan as an inheritance (vv. 7–21). What made the promised offspring and the promised land true encouragements to this great believer was that they were both types of those two invaluable blessings, Christ and heaven.

Verse 1

Here we see:

1. The time when God made this treaty with Abram:

1.1. After that famous act of generous kindness which Abram had carried out in rescuing his friends and neighbors from distress, and that, *not for price nor reward* (Isa 45:13).

1.2. After that victory which he had won over four kings.

2. The way in which God spoke to Abram: which supposes Abram was awake, and some visible appearance of the *Shechinah* or some perceptible expression of the presence of the divine glory.

3. The gracious assurance God gave of his favor to him:

3.1. He called him by name: *Abram*. God's good word does us good when it is spoken by his Spirit to us specifically. The word says, *Ho, every one* (Isa 55:1), the Spirit says, *Ho, such a one* (Ru 4:1).

3.2. He cautioned him against being uneasy and unnerved: *Fear not, Abram*. Let the sinners in Zion be afraid, but Abram, do not be afraid.

3.3. He assured him of safety and happiness, that he would forever be:

3.3.1. As safe as God himself could keep him. God would be not only the God of Israel, but also a God to Israel.

3.3.2. As happy as God himself could make him: I will be *thy exceeding great reward*; not only your rewarder, but also your reward. Abram had generously refused the rewards which the king of Sodom offered him.

Verses 2–6

Here is the assurance given to Abram of numerous offspring which would descend from him:

1. Abram's repeated complaint (vv. 2–3). This was what gave rise to this promise. The great affliction that lay heavily on Abram was the lack of a child. Though we must never complain about God, we may still complain to him, and it is some ease to a burdened spirit to open up to a faithful and compassionate friend: God is such a friend. Now his complaint is fourfold:

1.1. That he had no child (v. 3).

1.2. That he was never likely to have any, which he intimated by saying, *I go*, or "I am going," *childless*, going into years, fast getting on in years.

1.3. That his servants were all he had for the present and were likely to take the place of sons.

1.4. That the lack of a son was so great a trouble to him that it took away the comfort of all his enjoyments: "All is nothing to me, if I do not have a son." But, if we suppose that Abram in this had his sights set on the promised seed, the importunity of his desire was very commendable. Everything was nothing to him, if he did not have an assurance of his relationship with the Messiah, of which God had already encouraged him to maintain an expectation. "I have this thing and another, but what use are these to me if I go Christless?"

2. God's gracious answer to this complaint:

2.1. God gave him the explicit promise of a son (v. 4). The one who is born in your house *shall not be thy heir*, as you fear, but one who will *come forth out of thy own bowels shall be thy heir*.

2.2. To influence him all the more with this promise, God took him out, and showed him the stars, and then told him, *So shall thy seed be* (v. 5):

2.2.1. So innumerable; the stars seem countless to the ordinary eye: Abram feared he would have no child at all.

2.2.2. So illustrious, resembling the stars in splendor. Abram's descendants, according to his flesh, were like the dust of the earth (13:16), but his spiritual descendants are like the stars of heaven, not only numerous, but also glorious and very precious.

3. Abram's firm belief in the promise God now made to him, and God's favorable acceptance of his faith (v. 6). See how the apostle magnifies this faith of Abram, and makes it an outstanding example (Ro 4:19–21). *God counted it to him for righteousness*; that is, on the record of this he was accepted by God, and, as the rest of the patriarchs, by faith he *obtained witness that he was righteous* (Heb 11:4). This is urged in the New Testament to show that we are justified by faith apart from the works of the law (Ro 4:4; Gal 3:6). All believers are justified as Abram was, and it was his faith that was *counted to him for righteousness*.

Verses 7–11

Here is the assurance given to Abram of the land of Canaan as an inheritance:

1. God declares his purpose concerning it (v. 7). Those who are sure they share in the promised seed will see no reason to doubt ownership of a share in the promised land. If Christ is ours, heaven is also ours. When he believed the former promise (v. 6), then God explained and confirmed this to him. God reminds Abram of three things here, for his encouragement concerning the promise of this good land:

1.1. What God is in himself: *I am the Lord Jehovah.* "I can give it to you, whatever opposition there may be, whatever its source." God never promises more than he is able to perform, as we humans often do.

1.2. What God had done for Abram. He had brought him out of Ur of the Chaldees. The Jewish writers have a tradition that Abram was cast into a fiery furnace for refusing to worship idols and was miraculously delivered. This was the start of mercy, special mercy to Abram, and so a pledge and deposit guaranteeing further mercy to come (Isa 66:9).

1.3. What God intended to do still further for Abram: "*I brought thee* here, on purpose *to give thee this land to inherit it*, not only to possess it, but to possess it as an inheritance, which is the most satisfying and most sure ownership." The great thing God designs in all his dealings with his people is to bring them safely to heaven.

2. Abram desires a sign: *Whereby shall I know that I shall inherit it?* (v.8):

2.1. To strengthen and confirm his own faith; he believed (v. 6), but here he prays, *Lord, help me* against *my unbelief* (Mk 9:24). *Now* he believed, but he desired a sign to be held dear for the hour of temptation.

2.2. To confirm the promise to his descendants, that they also might be brought to believe it.

3. God directs Abram to make preparations for a sacrifice, intending by so doing to give him a sign, and Abram makes preparation accordingly (vv. 9–11). Those who want to receive the assurances of God's favor and want to have their faith confirmed, must attend to the ordinances that God has given and expect to meet with him in them. Abram did as God appointed him, though as yet he did not know how these things would become a sign to him. This was not the first instance of Abram's implicit obedience. He divided the animals in two, according to the ceremony used in confirming covenants (Jer 34:18–19),

where it is said, They cut *the calf in twain, and passed between the parts*. While God's acknowledgment of his sacrifice was deferred, Abram continued waiting, and his expectations were raised by the delay; when *the fowls came down upon the carcases*, birds of prey to seize them, *Abram drove them away* (v. 11). When vain thoughts, like these birds of prey, come down on our sacrifices, we must drive them away, and *attend on God without distraction* (1Co 7:35).

Verses 12–16

Here is a full and detailed revelation made to Abram of God's purposes concerning his descendants.

1. The time when God came to him with this revelation: *When the sun was going down*, or declining, about the time of the *evening sacrifice* (1Ki 18:36; Da 9:21). God often keeps his people waiting in expectation of the comforts he plans for them, to confirm their faith; but though the answers to prayer, and the fulfillment of the promises, come slowly, yet they come surely.

2. The preparations for this revelation:

2.1. *A deep sleep fell upon Abram*, not a common sleep through weariness or carelessness, but a divine ecstasy. The doors of the body were locked up, that the soul might be secluded and retired, and might act the more freely.

2.2. With this sleep, *a horror of great darkness fell upon him*. This great darkness, which brought horror with it, was designed:

2.2.1. To strike awe on the spirit of Abram and to give him such a holy reverence. Holy fear prepares the soul for holy joy; the spirit of slavery makes way for the spirit of adoption.

2.2.2. To be an example of the methods of God's dealings with his offspring. They must first be in the horror and darkness of Egyptian slavery and then enter with joy into the good land.

3. The prediction itself. Several things are here foretold:

3.1. The suffering state of Abram's descendants for a long time (v. 13). He must know that the promised seed would be a persecuted seed. Now we have here:

3.1.1. The details of their sufferings:

- They will be strangers. In the same way, the heirs of heaven are first of all strangers on earth.
- They will be servants. The Canaanites serve under a curse, the Hebrews under a blessing.
- They will be sufferers. Those whom they serve will oppress them (Ex 1:11).

3.1.2. The continuance of their sufferings—*four hundred years*. This was a long time, but a limited time.

3.2. The judgment of the enemies of Abram's seed: *That nation whom they shall serve*, even the Egyptians, *will I judge* (v. 14). Though God may allow persecutors and oppressors to abuse his people a great while, he will certainly eventually bring them to account, for his *day is coming* (Ps 37:12–13).

3.3. The deliverance of Abram's descendants from Egypt. That great event is here foretold: *afterward shall they come out with great substance*. It is here promised:

3.3.1. That they would be set free. The destruction of oppressors is the redemption of the oppressed.

3.3.2. That they would be made rich. God took care they would have, not only a good land to go to, but also good merchandise to carry with them.

3.4. Their happy settlement in Canaan (v. 16). They will not only come out of Egypt, but also *they shall come hither again*, to the land of Canaan, in which they now are.

3.5. Abram's peaceful and quiet death and burial, before these things would come to pass (v. 15). Good people are sometimes greatly favored by being *taken away from the evil to come* (Isa 57:1). Let this satisfy Abram, that for his part:

3.5.1. He shall *go to his fathers in peace*. Notice that:

- Even the friends and favorites of heaven are not exempt from the blow of death.
- Good people die willingly; they are not snatched, they are not forced, but they go.
- At death we go to our ancestors, to our godly ancestors who have gone before us to the state of the blessed (Heb 12:23). Outward peace is promised to Abram to the end: peace, truth, and security in his days, whatever would come afterward (2Ki 20:19). Peace with God and everlasting peace are certain to be received by all his descendants.

3.5.2. He will be *buried in a good old age*. He will not only die in peace, but also die in honor. Old age is a blessing, a great opportunity to be useful.

Verses 17–21

Here is:

1. The covenant ratified (v. 17); the sign which Abram desired was eventually given.

1.1. The *smoking furnace* stood for the suffering of his descendants in Egypt.

1.2. The *burning lamp* stands for comfort in this suffering; and God showed this to Abram at the same time that he showed him the *smoking furnace*.

1.2.1. Light stands for deliverance from the furnace:

1.2.2. The lamp refers to direction in the smoke. God's word was their lamp (Ps 119:105): this word to Abram was like this—it was a light shining in a dark place.

1.2.3. The burning lamp refers to the destruction of their enemies who kept them so long in the furnace.

1.3. The passing of these between the pieces was confirmation of the covenant God now made with Abram. It is probable that the furnace (firepot) and lamp (torch), which passed between the pieces, burned and consumed them, and so completed the sacrifice, bearing witness to God's acceptance of it, as of Gideon's (Jdg 6:21). So it shows:

1.3.1. That God's covenants with human beings are made by sacrifice (Ps 50:5), by Christ, the great sacrifice: there is no reconciliation without atonement.

1.3.2. God's acceptance of our spiritual sacrifices is a deposit, guaranteeing further favors.

2. The covenant repeated and explained: *Unto thy seed have I given this land* (v. 18). Here is:

2.1. A repetition of the privilege. God's promises are God's gifts, and are to be reckoned as such. The possession of the privilege is as certain, in due time, as if it were now actually delivered to them. What God has promised is as certain as if it were already done; and so it is said, whoever *believes hath everlasting life* (Jn 3:36), for all that believe will as surely go to heaven as if they were there already.

2.2. A rendering of the particulars given, as is usual in the granting of lands. The land granted is here described in its utmost extent because it was to be a type of the heavenly inheritance, where there is enough room: in our Father's house are many mansions (Jn 14:2).

CHAPTER 16

Hagar is the person this chapter is mostly concerned with, an obscure Egyptian woman. Probably she was one of those maidservants whom the king of Egypt gave to Abram (14:16). Concerning her, we have four things in this chapter: 1. Her marriage to Abram her master (vv. 1–3). 2. Her misbehavior toward Sarai her mistress (vv. 4–6). 3. Her conversation with an angel that met her in her fleeing (vv. 7–14). 4. Her giving birth to a son (vv. 15–16).

Verses 1–3

We have here the marriage of Abram to Hagar, who was his wife in a secondary sense. It seems to have proceeded from an improper desire to build up families to populate the world and the church all the more quickly. Certainly it must not be so now. Christ has brought this matter to the institution of marriage: the union that is to be between one man and one woman only.

1. Who would have thought that the maker of this match was Sarai herself? It is the policy of Satan to tempt us by our nearest and dearest relatives. It would have been much more in Sarai's interest if Abram had kept to the rule of God's law instead of being guided by her foolish ideas.

2. The inducement to this match was Sarai's barrenness. She used this as an argument that Abram should marry his maidservant, and he was persuaded by this argument to do so. Abram's agreement to Sarai's proposal, we have reason to think, was from an earnest desire for the promised offspring, on whom the privileges of the covenant depended. God had told him that his heir would be a son of his body but had not yet told him that it would be a son by Sarai, and so he thought, "Why not by Hagar, since Sarai herself proposed it?" Let us notice that:

- Worldly wisdom, as it moves ahead of God's time of mercy, puts us out of God's way.
- This would be happily avoided if we were to seek God's guidance by the word and by prayer, before we attempt what is important and suspicious.

Verses 4–6

Here are the immediate bad consequences of Abram's unhappy marriage to Hagar. It caused a great deal of trouble quickly. When we do not do good, both sin and trouble lie close at the door. See it in this story:

1. Sarai is despised and so is provoked and set into a rage (v. 4). Hagar thinks herself a better woman than Sarai, more favored by heaven, and likely to be more greatly loved by Abram, and so she will not submit as she had done. We justly suffer at the hands of those whom we have sinfully indulged, and it is a righteous thing if God makes those instruments of our trouble the ones whom we have made instruments of our sin.

2. Sarai raises an outcry against Abram. He was not allowed to rest as long as Sarai is angry. She unjustly charges him with causing the harm (v. 5). She rashly appeals to God in the case: *The Lord judge between me and thee,* as if Abram had refused to set her right. When passion is on the throne, reason has been thrown outdoors and is neither heard nor spoken. Those who are most loud and forward in appealing to God are not always in the right. Rash and bold language is commonly evidence of guilt and bad motives.

3. Hagar is afflicted and driven from the house (v. 6). She herself had first provoked matters by despising her mistress.

Verses 7–9

Here is the first mention we have in Scripture of an angel's appearance. Note:

1. How the angel stopped her fleeing (v. 7). She was going toward her own country, toward Egypt. It would be good if our sufferings made us think of our home. But Hagar was now out of the line of duty and going farther astray. God allows those who have gone astray to wander for a while, so that when they see their folly, they may be all the more inclined to return. Hagar was not stopped till she was in the desert. God brings us into a desert and meets with us there (Hos 2:14).

2. How the angel questioned her (v. 8). Notice:

2.1. He called her *Hagar, Sarai's maid.* Though she was Abram's wife, yet he calls her *Sarai's maid,* to humble her. Although courtesy teaches us to call others by their highest titles, humility and wisdom teach us to call ourselves by the lowest. Sarai's maidservant ought to be in Sarai's tent, not wandering in the desert and strolling by a spring of water.

2.2. The questions the angel put to her were proper and very relevant.

2.2.1. *"Whence camest thou?* (v. 8). Consider that you are running away from duty."

2.2.2. *"Whither wilt thou go?* You are running yourself into sin in Egypt and into danger in the desert." Those who abandon God and their duty would do well to remember not only *whence they have fallen,* but *whither they are falling.*

2.3. Her answer was honest and a reasonable confession: *I flee from the face of my mistress.*

3. How he sent her back with suitable and compassionate counsel: *Return to thy mistress, and submit thyself under her hands* (v. 9).

Verses 10–14

We may suppose that, the angel having given Hagar good guidance (v. 9) to *return to her mistress,* she immediately promised to do so, and was setting out homeward; and then the angel went on to encourage her with an assurance of the mercy God had in store for her and her descendants: for God will meet those with mercy who are returning to their duty. *I said, I will confess, and thou forgavest* (Ps 32:5). Here is:

1. A prediction concerning her descendants given to comfort her in her present distress. It is a great comfort to pregnant women to think that they are under the particular watchful care of divine Providence. Now:

1.1. The angel assures her of a safe delivery, and that she will give birth to a *son,* which Abram desired. She was saved in childbearing, not only by Providence, but also by promise.

1.2. He names her child, which was an honor both to her and the child: Call him *Ishmael,* meaning "God hears"; and the reason is that the Lord has heard. Even where there is little cry of devotion, the God of pity sometimes graciously hears the cry of our misery. Tears speak as well as prayers.

1.3. He promises her numerous descendants (v. 10). It has traditionally been thought that this promise has been fulfilled through the Arab peoples.

1.4. He gives the character of the child she would bear. He *will be a wild man;* "a wild donkey of a man" (so the word is), rude and bold, and fearing no one—untamed, unmanageable, living on the loose, impatient of anyone's service and restraint. *His hand will be against every man*—this is his *sin; and every man's hand against him*—this is his *punishment.* Those who have turbulent spirits commonly have troublesome lives. Many who are greatly exposed by their own lack of caution are strangely preserved by divine Providence, so much better is God to them than they deserve.

2. Hagar's devout reflection on this gracious appearance of God to her (vv. 13–14). Notice in what she said:

2.1. Her awed adoration of God's perfect knowledge and providence, with the application of it to herself: *Thou God seest me*; this would be with her his name forever. *God is* (as the ancients expressed it) "all eye." He that sees all sees me, as David writes (Ps 139:1), *O Lord, thou hast searched me, and known me*. It is a proper word for one who repents: "You see the sincerity and seriousness of my returning and repenting."

2.2. Her humble wonder at God's favor to her: "*Have I also here looked after him that seeth me?* (v. 13)." Probably she did not know who it was that talked with her till he was departing, and then she looked after him, with a thought like that of the two disciples (Lk 24:31–32). Not only in Abram's tent and at his altar, but "*Here* also, in this desert? Here, where I never expected it, where I had left my line of duty? *Lord, how is it?*" (Jn 14:22).

3. The name which this story gave to the place: *Beerlahairoi* (Beer Lahai Roi) meaning "the well of the Living One who sees me" (v. 14). This was the place where the God of glory manifested the special care he gave to a poor woman in distress.

Verses 15–16

It is here taken for granted that Hagar did as the angel commanded her, returning to her mistress and then, in the fullness of time, she gave birth to her son.

CHAPTER 17

This chapter contains the articles of the covenant decided and agreed on between the Father of mercies, on the one part, and Abram, the father of the faithful, on the other part. Abram is therefore called "the friend of God," not only because he was the man of God's counsel, but because he was the man of God's covenant; both these secrets were with him. Mention has already been made of this covenant (15:18), but here it is put into the form of a covenant. Here are: 1. The circumstances of the making of this covenant, the time and manner (v. 1), and the position Abram took up (v. 3). 2. The covenant itself, that he would be the father of many nations (vv. 4, 6), and, as a sign of this, his name was changed (v. 5). 3. That God would be a God to him and his descendants and would give them the land of Canaan (vv. 7–8). The seal of this part of the covenant was circumcision (vv. 9–14). 4. That he should have a son by Sarai, and as a sign of that, her name was changed (vv. 15–16). This promise Abram received (v. 17), and his request for Ishmael (v. 18) was answered (vv. 19–22). 5. The circumcision of Abram and his family, as God had appointed (vv. 23–27).

Verses 1–3

Here is:

1. The time when God graciously appeared to Abram: a full thirteen years after the birth of Ishmael. There are some special encouragements from God which are not our daily bread, no, not even of the best saints. God favors us with them only now and then. On this side of heaven we have the food we need, but not a continual feast. The promise of Isaac was postponed for such a long time, perhaps to correct Abram's overhasty marrying of Hagar.

2. The way in which God made this covenant with him: *The Lord appeared to Abram*, in the *Shechinah*, some visible display of God's immediate glorious presence with him.

3. The position Abram put himself into on this occasion: *He fell on his face while God talked with him* (v. 3) as one overcome by the brightness of the divine glory and as one ashamed of himself and blushing to think of the honors done to one so unworthy.

4. The general scope and summary of the covenant laid down, which is the foundation on which all the rest was built; it is no other than the covenant of grace still made with all believers in Jesus Christ (v. 1). Notice:

4.1. What we may expect God to be to us: *I am the Almighty God*. By this name he chose to make himself known to Abram rather than by his name *Jehovah* (Ex 6:3). He used it to Jacob (28:3; 43:14; 48:3). After Moses, *Jehovah* is more frequently used, and this, *El-Shaddai*, very rarely; it speaks of the almighty power of God, either as an avenger or as a benefactor. He is a God that is enough; or, as an older English translation reads here: "I am God all-sufficient."

4.2. What God requires that we should be for him. The covenant is mutual: *Walk before me, and be thou perfect*. Notice:

4.2.1. That to be religious is to walk before God in integrity. It is to live *inwardly with him*, in all the duties of religious worship, for in them particularly we walk before God (1Sa 2:30). We know of no religion except blamelessness.

4.2.2. That upright walking with God is the condition of the privilege of sharing in his all-sufficiency.

Verses 4–6

The covenant of grace is a covenant of God's own making; this he glories in (*as for me*, v. 4), and so may we.

1. It is promised to Abram that he should be a *father of many nations*; that is:

- That his descendants would be very numerous.
- That all believers in every age would be looked on as his spiritual descendants, and that he would be called, not only *the friend of God*, but *the father of the faithful*.

2. As a sign of this his name was changed from *Abram*, "the father is exalted," to *Abraham*, "the father of a multitude." This was to put an honor on him and to encourage and confirm his faith.

Verses 7–14

Here is:

1. The continuation of the covenant, suggested by three things:

1.1. It is established; it is not to be altered or revoked.

1.2. It is, to use the legal term, entailed: his inheritance is settled on a designated line of heirs. It is a covenant, not with Abraham only but also with his descendants after him, not only the descendants from his body, but also his spiritual descendants.

1.3. It is eternal in a Gospel sense. The covenant of grace is everlasting.

2. The content of the covenant: it is a covenant of promises. There are two which indeed are all-sufficient:

2.1. That God would be their God (vv. 7–8). What God is himself, that he will be to his people: his wisdom is theirs, to guide and counsel them; his power is theirs, to protect and support them; his goodness is theirs, to provide for and comfort them.

2.2. That Canaan would be their everlasting possession (v. 8). It must be looked on as a type of heaven's happiness, that everlasting rest which remains for the people of

God (Heb 4:9). Canaan is here said to be the land in which Abraham was a foreigner; and the heavenly Canaan is a land in which we are all foreigners, for what we will be has not yet been made known (1Jn 3:2).

3. The sign of the covenant, circumcision, and that is why the covenant is itself called the *covenant of circumcision* (Ac 7:8). It is called a sign and seal (Ro 4:11), for it was:

3.1. A confirmation to Abraham and his descendants of those promises which were God's part of the covenant.

3.2. An ordinance that involved the shedding of blood, for all things by the Law were purified by blood (Heb 9:22). See Ex 24:8. But since the blood of Christ has been shed, all ordinances that involve the shedding of blood are now abolished, and so circumcision gives way to baptism.

3.3. Exclusively for males, though the women were also included in the covenant, for the man is the head of the woman (1Co 11:3).

3.4. The flesh of the foreskin that was to be cut off, because it is by normal reproduction that sin is spread. Since Christ had not yet offered himself for us, God wanted man to enter into the covenant by the offering of some part of his own body. It is a hidden part of the body; for the true circumcision is that of the heart (1Co 12:23–24).

3.5. To be administered to children when they were eight days old.

3.6. To be administered to the children of the foreigners, of whom the master of the family was the true domestic owner (vv. 12–13). This looked favorably on the Gentiles, who would in due time be brought into the family of Abraham by faith. See Gal 3:14.

3.7. To be obeyed with respect. To hold circumcision in contempt meant holding the covenant in contempt. If the parents did not circumcise their children, they were in danger, as in the case of Moses (Ex 4:24–25).

Verses 15–22

Here is:

1. The promise made to Abraham of a son by *Sarai*, for *she also shall be a mother of nations, and kings of people shall be of her* (v. 16). Notice that:

1.1. God gradually reveals the purposes of his goodwill to his people. God had told Abraham long before that he would have a son, but never till now that he would have a son by *Sarai*.

1.2. The blessing of the Lord brings fruit and adds no trouble to it (Pr 10:22), no such trouble as was in Hagar's case.

1.3. Civil government and order are a great blessing to the church. It is promised, not only that *people*, but *kings of people*, would come from her; not a leaderless mob, but a well-modeled, well-governed society.

2. The ratification of this promise in the change of *Sarai's* name to *Sarah* (v. 15). *Sarai* means "my princess," as if her honor were confined to one family only. *Sarah* means "*a princess*," namely, of multitudes.

3. Abraham's joyful, thankful reception of this gracious promise (v. 17). On this occasion he expressed:

3.1. Great humility: He *fell on his face*.

3.2. Great joy: He *laughed*. It was a laughter of delight, not of distrust. There is the joy of faith as well as the joy of fruitfulness.

3.3. Great wonder: *Shall a child be born to him that is a hundred years old?*

4. Abraham's prayer for Ishmael: *O that Ishmael might live before thee!* (v. 18). Abraham says this, not wishing that Ishmael might be preferred to the son he would have by Sarah, but dreading that Ishmael might be abandoned by God. Though we must not dictate to God, yet he allows us, in prayer, humbly to be free with him and in particular to make known our requests (Php 4:6). It is the duty of parents to pray for their children, for all their children, as Job did. He offered a burnt offering for each of them (Job 1:5). The great thing we should desire of God for our children is that they may live in his presence, that is, that they may be held in covenant with him, and may have grace to walk before him in uprightness.

5. God's answer to his prayer, and it is an answer of peace.

5.1. Common blessings are secured to Ishmael (v. 20): *As for Ishmael*, whom you are so anxious about, *I have heard thee*; he will find favor for your sake; *I have blessed him*. His descendants will be numerous: *I will multiply him exceedingly*, more than his neighbors. They will be notable: *Twelve princes shall he beget*.

5.2. Covenant-blessings are reserved for Isaac and are assigned to him (vv. 19, 21).

5.2.1. God repeats to him the promise of a son by Sarah.

5.2.2. He names that child—calls him *Isaac*, meaning "he laughs," because Abraham was glad in his spirit when this son was promised him. God's promised mercies will in due time be our *exceeding* joy. Christ will be laughter to those who look for him.

5.2.3. He passes on the covenant to that child.

Verses 23–27

We have here Abraham's obedience to the law of circumcision. He himself and all his family were circumcised, so receiving the sign of the covenant and distinguishing themselves from other families that had no part nor share in the matter.

1. It was an implicit obedience.

2. It was a speedy obedience: *In the selfsame day* (vv. 23, 26). Sincere obedience does not delay (Ps 119:60).

3. It was a universal obedience: he did not circumcise his family but excuse himself, but he set them an example. Ishmael is blessed and therefore circumcised.

CHAPTER 18

We have an account in this chapter of another meeting between God and Abraham. Here is: 1. The kind visit which God made him (vv. 1–8). 2. The matters discussed between them and the purposes of God's love concerning Sarah (vv. 9–15). 3. The purposes of God's wrath concerning Sodom and the revelation God made to Abraham of his plan to destroy Sodom (vv. 16–22). 4. The intercession Abraham made for Sodom (vv. 23–33).

Verses 1–8

This appearance of God to Abraham seems to have had in it freedom and familiarity, and so is like that great appearance when the Word would be made flesh and appear as one of us. Here we see:

1. How Abraham expected strangers, and how richly his expectations were answered. God graciously comes to those in whom he has first raised an expectation of him. Those who have been open to showing hospitality to strangers have entertained angels to their unspeakable

honor and enjoyment. Where we see no reason to suspect ill, love teaches us to hope for the best and to show kindness accordingly. It is better to feed five drones or wasps than to starve one bee.

2. How Abraham showed hospitality to those strangers, and how kindly his reception was accepted. Forgetting his age and seriousness, he *ran to meet them* in the most obliging manner, and with all due courtesy. Religion does not destroy, but improve, good manners, and teaches us to honor all people. It is right that those whom God has blessed with plenty should be generous and openhearted. His hospitality, though it was very generous, was also plain and ordinary. His dining-room was an arbor under a tree. The meal was a joint or two of veal, and some cakes baked on the hearth. Here there was no wide range of delicacies, but good, plain, wholesome food, though Abraham was very rich and his guests were very honorable. He and his wife were busy, in accommodating their guests with the best they had. Sarah herself is cook and baker; Abraham runs to fetch the calf, brings out the milk and butter, and thinks it not beneath him to wait at table. Genuine friendship will stoop to anything but sin. Christ himself has taught us to wash one another's feet in humble love (Jn 13:14–17).

Verses 9–15

Here we see that these heavenly guests return his kindness. He receives angels and has angels' rewards—a gracious message from heaven (Mt 10:41).

1. Care is taken that Sarah should be within hearing. Modesty forbade women from sitting to eat with men, at least with strangers, but confined them to their own rooms. Sarah is therefore here out of sight: but she must not be out of hearing. *Where is Sarah thy wife?* the angels say. "*Behold, in the tent*," Abraham says. "Where else should she be? There she is in her usual place. Those are most likely to receive comfort from God and his promises who are in their place of duty (Lk 2:8).

2. The promise is then renewed and confirmed, that she would have a son. The same blessings which others have from common providence believers receive from the promise, which makes them very precious and sure. The spiritual offspring of Abraham owe their life, joy, and hope, indeed everything, to the promise. They are born by the word of God (1Pe 1:23).

3. Sarah thinks this too good news to be true, and so cannot find it in her heart to believe it: *Sarah laughed within herself*—a laughter of doubting and mistrust. The great objection which Sarah could not get over was her age: "*I am waxed old*, and past childbearing in the natural course of things." Human improbability often sets itself up in contradiction to the divine promise. It is hard to remain united to the first Cause, when secondary causes perplex us.

4. The angel rebukes her for the improper expressions of her distrust (vv. 13–14). God gave this rebuke to Sarah by Abraham her husband. God said to him, *Why did Sarah laugh?* Our unbelief and distrust are a great offense to the God of heaven. He justly considers it wrong to have the objections of our senses set up in contradiction to his promise (Lk 1:18). *Is anything too hard for the Lord?*

5. Sarah foolishly tries to conceal her fault (v. 15): *She denied, saying, I did not laugh*; she told this lie, because *she was afraid*. There seems to be in Sarah a withdrawal of her distrust. Now that she realized by putting the circumstances together that it was a divine promise which had been made concerning her, she gave up all her doubting, distrusting

thoughts about it. There was also a sinful attempt to cover up a sin with a lie. It is shameful to do wrong, but it is even more shameful to deny it.

Verses 16–22

The messengers from heaven had now carried out one part of their business, which was an assignment of grace to Abraham and Sarah, but now they have before them work of another nature. Sodom is to be destroyed. Here we see:

1. The honor Abraham did to his guests: *He went with them to bring them on the way* (v. 16), as one that was loath to part with such good company, and who wanted to pay his utmost respects to them.

2. The honor they did to him; for those who honor God he will honor. God communicated to Abraham his purpose to destroy Sodom. But why must Abraham be a member of the cabinet council? Some Jewish writers suggest that because God had granted the land of Canaan to Abraham and his descendants he therefore would not destroy those cities which were a part of that land without his knowledge and consent. But God here gives two other reasons:

2.1. Abraham has to know, for he is God's friend and a favorite. Those who by faith live a life of friendship with God must know more of his mind than other people do. They have a better insight than others into what is present (Ps 107:43; Hos 14:9), and a better foresight of what is to come.

2.2. Abraham has to know, for he is to teach his household. Those who expect family blessings must conscientiously undertake family duties. If our children are the Lord's they must be nurtured for him; if they wear his uniform, they must be trained up in his work. Abraham made it his concern and business to promote practical religion in his family. He did not fill their heads with matters of subtle speculation or disputable matters; but he taught them to keep *the way of the Lord, and to do judgment and justice*, that is, to be serious and devout in the worship of God and to be honest in their dealings with all people. Abraham was careful that his future household would keep the way of the Lord, that religion might flourish in his family when he was in his grave.

2.3. Here we have also God's friendly talk with Abraham. He tells him of the evidence there was against Sodom. Some sins, and the sins of some sinners, are crying out to heaven for vengeance. As human beings we are prone to suggest that his ways are not just, but we need to know that his judgments are the result of his eternal counsels and are never rash or sudden decisions. Perhaps the decree is here spoken of as not yet conclusive, that room and encouragement might be given to Abraham to make intercession for them. In so doing, God looked to see if there was anyone to intercede (Isa 59:16).

Verses 23–33

Fellowship with God is maintained by the word and by prayer. In the word, God speaks to us; in prayer we speak to him. God had revealed to Abraham his purposes concerning Sodom; now from this Abraham takes the opportunity to speak to God on Sodom's behalf. God's word does us good when it provides us with matter for prayer and stirs us to it. Notice:

1. The solemnity of Abraham's address to God on this occasion: *Abraham drew near* (v. 23). The expression shows a holy concern: *He engaged his heart* to approach God (Jer 30:21) and a holy confidence: He drew near *with an assurance of faith*.

2. The general scope of this prayer. It is the first solemn prayer we have on record in the Bible; and it is a prayer for the sparing of Sodom. Though sin is to be hated, sinners are to be pitied and prayed for. God does not delight in their death, and we should not desire, but pray for deliverance from, the day of destruction.

2.1. He begins with a prayer that the righteous among them might be spared, thinking particularly of the righteous Lot.

2.2. He turns this into a petition that all might be spared for the sake of the righteous that were among them, God himself considering this request.

3. The gracious qualities that are obvious in this prayer:

3.1. Here is great faith; and it is the prayer of faith that is the effective prayer. The righteous are mixed in with the wicked in this world. Among the best there are, commonly, some bad, and among the worst some good: even in Sodom, there was one Lot. Though the righteous live among the wicked, the righteous God will certainly not destroy the righteous with the wicked. Note, too, that the righteous shall not *be as the wicked* (v. 25). Though they may suffer with them, they do not suffer like them.

3.2. Here is great humility:

3.2.1. A deep sense of his own unworthiness (v. 27): *Behold now, I have taken upon me to speak unto the Lord, who am but dust and ashes*; and again in v. 31. He speaks as one amazed at his own boldness. The access we have to the throne of grace, and the freedom of speech allowed us, are rightfully a matter of humble wonder (2Sa 7:18).

3.2.2. An awed dread of God's displeasure. But he with whom we have to do is *God and not man*; and, however he may seem, is not really *angry with the prayers of the upright* (Ps 80:4), for they are *his delight* (Pr 15:8), and he is pleased when he is wrestled with.

3.3. Here is great love:

3.3.1. A loving opinion of Sodom's character: as bad as it was, he thought there were several good people in it. It is right for us to hope the best of the worst places. Of the two it is better to err to that extreme.

3.3.2. A loving desire for Sodom's welfare: he used all his privileges at the throne of grace to pray for mercy for them.

3.4. Here is great boldness, believing confidence. Suppose there are fifty (v. 24). As God conceded more, so Abraham explored the way forward more and more.

4. The success of the prayer. God's general goodwill appears in this, that he agreed to spare the wicked for the sake of the righteous. See what great blessings good people are to any place. His particular favor to Abraham appeared in this, that he did not stop giving way until Abraham stopped asking. Such is the power of prayer.

CHAPTER 19

This chapter records the history of Sodom's destruction and Lot's rescue from that destruction. In the last chapter we read of God's viewing of the present state of Sodom. Now here we have the result of that inquiry. 1. It emerged that Lot was very good (vv. 1–3), and it did not appear that there were any more of the same character. 2. It was found that the Sodomites were very wicked and vile (vv. 4–11). 3. Special care was therefore taken to move Lot and his family to a secure place of safety (vv. 12–23). 4. Mercy having been displayed in this, justice shows itself in the destruction of Sodom and the
death of Lot's wife (vv. 24–26), with a general repetition of the story (vv. 27–29). 5. Lot becomes guilty of an evil sin, in committing incest with his two daughters (vv. 30–38).

Verses 1–3

Notice here:

1. There was but one good man in Sodom, and these heavenly messengers soon found him out.

2. Lot distinguished himself sufficiently from the rest of his neighbors, at this time, which plainly set a mark on him. He who did not behave like the rest would not be destroyed like the rest. Lot sat in the gate of Sodom in the evening. He was hospitable and very free and generous in his invitations and hospitality. He sought to invite these strangers to his house and to the best accommodation he had and gave them all the assurances that he could of his sincerity. When the angels accepted his invitation, he treated them splendidly. Good people should be wise and generous people.

Verses 4–11

Now it appeared, beyond contradiction, that the outcry of Sodom was as great as there was reason for. We find here:

1. That they were all wicked (v. 4). Wickedness had become universal, and they were unanimous in any evil design.

2. That they had arrived at the highest point of wickedness; they were *sinners before the Lord exceedingly* (v. 13); for:

2.1. It was the most unnatural and detestable wickedness that they were now set on, a sin that still bears their name and is called *sodomy*.

2.2. We can learn from this that those who have become insolent in sin generally turn out to be impenitent in sin; and it will be their destruction. Those who arrogantly sin have hard hearts indeed (Jer 6:15).

2.3. When Lot tried to interrupt them, with all the mildness imaginable, to restrain the rage and fury of their sinful desire, they were most defiantly rude and abusive to him. Being greatly disturbed at their evil endeavors, he unadvisedly and unjustifiably offered to give his two daughters to be sexually abused by them (v. 8). It is true, of two evils we must choose the lesser; but of two sins we must choose neither and never do evil that good may come of it. They threaten him and violently lay hands on him.

3. That nothing less than the power of an angel could save a good man from their wicked hands.

3.1. They rescue Lot (v. 10). The saints, at death, are pulled like Lot into a house of perfect safety, and the door shut forever against those who pursue them.

3.2. They punish the arrogance of the Sodomites: *They smote them with blindness* (v. 11). Yet these Sodomites, after they were struck blind, continued looking for the door, to break it down, till they were tired. No judgments will, of themselves, change the corrupt natures and purposes of wicked people. If their minds had not been blinded as well as their bodies, they would have said, as the magicians, *This is the finger of God* (Ex 8:19) and would have submitted themselves to God.

Verses 12–14

We have here the preparation for Lot's deliverance:

1. Notice is given to Lot of Sodom's impending destruction: *We will destroy this place* (v. 13).

2. Lot is directed to warn his friends and relatives, that they, if they wanted to, might be saved with him (v. 12). Those who through grace are themselves delivered from a sinful state should do what they can to deliver others, especially their relatives. This directive is also the offer of great favor. The angels ask what relatives he had there, that, whether they are righteous or unrighteous, they might be saved with him. We see from this that bad people often fare better in this world because of their good relatives. It is good to be related to a godly person.

3. Accordingly, Lot turns himself to his sons-in-law (v. 14). Notice:

3.1. The fair warning that Lot gave them: *Up, get you out of this place.*

3.2. The snub they gave to this warning: *He seemed to them as one that mocked* (v. 14). They thought, perhaps, that the attack which the Sodomites had previously made on his house had disturbed his mind. Those who led a godless life and joked at everything made fun of this warning, and so they perished in the destruction.

Verses 15–23

Here is:

1. The rescue of Lot from Sodom (vv. 15–17). Early in the morning his own guests, out of kindness to him, urge him and his family to leave. His married daughters perished with their unbelieving husbands, but those who went with him were preserved with him. Notice:

1.1. With what a gracious forcefulness Lot was brought out of Sodom (v. 16). It seems he did not make as much haste as was needed. It might have led to his death if the angels had not *laid hold of his hand, and brought him forth,* and saved him with fear (Jude 23). The salvation of the most righteous people must be attributed to God's mercy, not to their own merit. We are all saved by grace (Eph 2:8).

1.2. With what a gracious forthrightness he was urged to make the best of his way, when he was *brought forth* (v. 17). He must not long for Sodom: *Look not behind thee.* He must not linger by the way: *Stay not in all the plain.* He must not stop short of the place of refuge appointed him: *Escape to the mountain.* Such commands as these are given to those who through grace are delivered from a sinful state:

• Do not return to sin and Satan, for that is looking back to Sodom.

• Do not rely on yourself and the world, for that is staying in the plain.

• Reach toward Christ and heaven, for that is escaping to the mountain, short of which we must not stop.

2. The establishing of a place of refuge for him. The mountain was first appointed for him to flee to, but:

2.1. He begged to go to a city of refuge, one of the five that lay together, called *Bela* (14:2; vv. 18–20). It was Lot's weakness to think a city of his own choice would be safer than the mountain of God's appointing. Could not the One that saved him from greater evils save him from the lesser? In his begging he stresses the smallness of the place: *It is a little one, is it not?* This gave a new name to the place; it was called *Zoar,* meaning "small."

2.2. God granted him his request, even though there was much weak about it (vv. 21–22). See what favor God showed to a true saint, even though he was weak. Zoar was spared, to please Lot.

3. The rising of the sun when Lot reached Zoar, for when good people come into a place they bring light with them, or at least they should.

Verses 24–25

Then, when Lot had safely reached Zoar, then this destruction came; for good people are taken away from the evil to come. *Then,* when the sun had risen bright and clear, promising a fine day, then this storm arose, to show that it did not come from natural causes. It was a *strange punishment* (Job 31:3). The likes of it were not seen before and have not been seen since. It was a judgment that destroyed everything: *He overthrew the cities,* and destroyed all the inhabitants of them, the plain, and all that grew on the ground (v. 25). It was complete destruction and irrevocable. That fruitful valley remains to this day a great lake, or dead sea; it is called *the Salt Sea* (Nu 34:12). It is about forty-eight miles (about seventy-seven kilometers) long and six to nine miles (about ten to fourteen kilometers) broad; it has no living creature in it; it is not moved by the wind; the smell of it is offensive; things do not easily sink in it. The Greeks call it *Asphaltites,* from the kind of pitch which it throws up. Jordan falls into it and is lost there. It was a punishment that was the consequence of their sin. Those who *went after strange flesh* were destroyed by strange fire (Jude 7). It is often referred to in Scripture and made an example of the destruction of Israel (Dt 29:23), of Babylon (Isa 13:19), of Edom (Jer 49:17–18), of Moab and Ammon (Zep 2:9).

Verse 26

This also is written to warn us. Our Savior refers to it (Lk 17:32), *Remember Lot's wife.* As from the example of Sodom the wicked are warned to turn away from their wickedness, so from the example of Lot's wife the righteous are warned not to turn from their righteousness. See Eze 3:18, 20.

1. The sin of Lot's wife: *She looked back from behind him.* She disobeyed an express command. Probably she hankered after her home and possessions in Sodom and was loath to leave them. Christ intimates this was her sin (Lk 17:31–32); she too much regarded her *stuff.* Her looking back revealed an inclination to go back, and so our Savior uses it as a warning against apostasy, turning back from our Christian profession. We have all renounced the world and the flesh, and have set our faces heavenward; we are in the plain, serving, as it were, a probationary period in this life. We risk losing everything if we return to the interests we profess to have abandoned.

2. The punishment of Lot's wife for this sin. Though she was a memorial to special mercy in her deliverance from Sodom, God still did not ignore her disobedience. Since it is such a dangerous thing to look back, let us always press forward (Php 3:13–14).

Verses 27–29

1. Here is Abraham's devout looking to God in this event. *He got up early* to look toward Sodom; and, to show that he wanted to see what became of his prayers. We must direct our prayer as we send a letter and then look up to wait for a reply. We must direct our prayer as an arrow and then look up to see whether it reaches its mark (Ps 5:3).

2. Here is God's favorable regard to Abraham (v. 29). As before, when Abraham prayed for Ishmael, God heard him for Isaac, so now, when he prayed for Sodom, he heard him for Lot. *He remembered Abraham, and,* for his

sake, brought Lot out of the catastrophe. We can learn from this that God will certainly give an answer of peace to the prayer of faith, in his own way and time. Though, for a while, it seems to be forgotten, yet sooner or later, it will appear to be remembered.

Verses 30–38

Here is:

1. The great trouble and distress that Lot was brought into after his deliverance (v. 30).

1.1. He was frightened out of Zoar; he did not dare live there, probably because he found it as wicked as Sodom, and so he decided Zoar could not long survive God's judgment either. Settlements and shelters that are of our own choosing, and in which we do not follow God, commonly seem uneasy to us.

1.2. He was forced to go to the mountain and to live in a cave as his home. Notice:

1.2.1. He was now glad to go to the mountain, the place which God had appointed as his shelter.

1.2.2. He who a while before could not find space enough for himself and his livestock in the whole land, but had to compete with Abraham, and get as far from him as he could, is now confined to a mere hole in a hill, where he has scarcely space to turn himself, and there he is solitary and trembling.

2. The great sin that Lot and his daughters were guilty of, when they were in this desolate place. It is a tragic story:

2.1. His daughters hatched a very wicked plot to make him sin; and theirs was, doubtless, the greater guilt.

2.1.1. Some think that their pretense was plausible. Their father had no sons, they had no husbands; they did not know that they belonged to Abraham's line of inheritance of the holy seed, and that, therefore, if they had children by others, their father's name would not be preserved in them. But:

2.1.2. Whatever their pretense was, it is certain that their plan was very wicked and evil, and an impudent insult to the very light and law of nature.

2.2. Lot himself, by his own folly and carelessness, was shamefully defeated, and allowed himself so to be deceived and imposed on by his own children as, on two successive nights, to be drunk and to commit incest (v. 33, etc.). *Lord, what is man!* (Ps 144:3). What are the best people, when God leaves them to themselves! Notice:

2.2.1. The danger of security. Lot, who kept himself sober and chaste in Sodom, was on the mountain, where he was alone and thought he was completely out of the line of temptation, shamefully overpowered. Let those who think they are standing firm be careful that they do not fall! (1Co 10:12). No mountain, on this side of the holy hill above, can put us out of reach of Satan's fiery darts.

2.2.2. The danger of drunkenness. It is not only a great sin itself, but it allows in many sins; it may turn out to allow in the worst and most unnatural of sins.

2.3. At the close of this chapter we have an account of the birth of the two sons, or grandsons (call them which you will), of Lot, Moab and Ammon, the fathers of two nations, neighbors of Israel, and which we often read of in the Old Testament; both together are called *the children of Lot* (Ps 83:8).

2.4. Note that, after this, we never read any more of Lot, but from the silence of Scripture concerning him from this time on we may learn that drunkenness makes people not only forgetful, it also makes them forgotten.

CHAPTER 20

We return here to the story of Abraham, but that part of it which is here recorded is not to his honor. The most beautiful marble has its flaws, and, while there are spots in the sun, we must not expect anything spotless under it. Scripture, it should be noted, is impartial in relating the blemishes even of its most celebrated characters. We have here: 1. Abraham's sin in denying his wife, and Abimelech's sin in then taking her (vv. 1–2). 2. God's conversation with Abimelech in a dream on this occasion, in which God shows him his error (v. 3), accepts his plea (vv. 4–6), and directs him to make restitution (v. 7). 3. Abimelech's conversation with Abraham, in which he rebukes him for cheating him (vv. 8–10), and Abraham excuses it as well as he can (vv. 11–13). 4. The good outcome of the story, in which Abimelech restores to Abraham his wife (vv. 14–16), and Abraham, by prayer, prevails with God for the judgment Abimelech was under to be removed (vv. 17–18).

Verses 1–2

Here is:

1. Abraham's move from Mamre. We are not told on what occasion he moved.

2. His sin in denying his wife was worsened in two ways:

2.1. He had been guilty of this same sin before, and had been rebuked for it. It is possible that a good person may not only fall into sin but lapse into the same sin through the unexpectedly powerful attacks of temptation and the weakness of the flesh.

2.2. Sarah, it would seem, was now with child of the promised descendants; he ought therefore to have taken special care of her at that time (Jdg 13:4).

Verses 3–7

It appears from this that God revealed himself by dreams even to those who were beyond the reaches of the church and covenant.

1. God warns Abimelech of his danger (v. 3): his danger of *sin*, telling him that the woman is already married, so if he takes her, he will wrong her husband; and his danger of death for this sin: *Thou art a dead man.* If you are a bad person, certainly you are a dead person.

2. Abimelech pleads ignorance that Abraham and Sarah had agreed to deceive him, and not told him that they were any more than brother and sister (v. 6). Our hearts do not condemn us (1Jn 3:21). If our consciences bear witness to our integrity, and, however we may have been cheated and have fallen into a trap, we have not intentionally sinned against God, so it will be to our joy in the day of disaster.

3. God gives a very full answer to what Abimelech had said:

3.1. God allows Abimelech's plea, and acknowledges that what he did he did out of the integrity of his heart: *Yea, I know it* (v. 6). It is a matter of strength and support to those who are honest that God knows their honesty and integrity, and will acknowledge it, though perhaps people who are prejudiced against them either cannot be convinced of it or will not acknowledge it.

3.2. God instructs Abimelech to make restitution: *Now therefore*, now that you are better informed, *restore the man his wife* (v. 7). Ignorance will excuse no longer than it continues. If we have entered on a wrong course of action through ignorance, this does not excuse our knowingly persisting in it (Lev 5:3–5).

Verses 8–13

Abimelech, being warned by God in this way in a dream, heeds the warning, and, as one truly afraid of sin and its consequences, he rises early to obey the directions given him:

1. He cautions his servants (v. 8).
2. He chides Abraham. Notice:

2.1. The serious rebuke which Abimelech gave to Abraham (vv. 9–10). His reasoning with Abraham on this occasion was very strong, and yet also very mild. Nothing could be said better; he does not reproach him or insult him. He does not say, "Is this the life that you profess? I see, even though you do not swear, you will lie. If these are prophets, I beg not ever to see them." Instead he represents justly the injury Abraham had done him and calmly indicates his anger at it.

2.1.1. He calls that sin which he now found he had been in danger of committing a great sin.

2.1.2. He realizes that both he and his kingdom would have been exposed to the wrath of God if he had been guilty of this sin, even out of ignorance. The sins of rulers often cause the plagues of kingdoms; rulers should therefore, for their people's sake, dread sin.

2.1.3. He charges Abraham with doing what was not justifiable in disowning his marriage.

2.1.4. He takes it as a very great injury to himself and his family that Abraham had exposed them to sin in this way: "*What have I offended thee?*" (v. 9). If I had been your worst enemy, you could not have done me a worse turn, nor taken a more effective course to be revenged on me."

2.1.5. He challenges him to assign a cause for his suspecting them as dangerous people. "What reason did you have to think that if we had known her to be your wife you would have been exposed to any danger by it?" A suspicion of our goodness is justly reckoned as a greater insult than a slight on our greatness.

2.2. The poor excuse that Abraham made for himself:

2.2.1. He pleaded the bad opinion he had of the place (v. 11). *Surely the fear of God is not in this place; and they will slay me.* There are many places and people that have more fear of God in them than we think they have. Perhaps they are not called by our distinctive name, they do not wear our badges, they do not associate themselves with what we have an opinion about; and so we conclude they have not the fear of God in their hearts, which is very damaging both to Christ and Christians and is offensive to God's judgment (Mt 7:1). An unloving and critical spirit is a sin that is the cause of many other sins. People would not do wrong if they did not first think wrong.

2.2.2. He excused himself from the guilt of a downright lie by making it appear that, in a sense, she was his sister (v. 12). But those to whom he said, *She is my sister,* understood that she was his sister insofar as she was not his wife. He was fudging the issue, trying to deceive.

2.2.3. He clears himself from the imputation of an insult against Abimelech by alleging that it had been his practice before, according to an agreement between him and his wife, when they first became wanderers (v. 13).

Verses 14–18

Here is:

1. The kindness which Abimelech showed to Abraham. See how unjust Abraham's jealousies were. Abimelech gives Abraham his royal permission to live where he pleased in his country. He gives him his royal gifts. He gave these when he restored Sarah, by way of settling the wrong he had offered to do, in taking her to his house.

According to the Law, when restitution was made, something should be added to it (Lev 6:5).

2. The kindness of a prophet which Abraham showed to Abimelech: he *prayed for him* (vv. 17–18). In the same way, God healed Miriam, when Moses, whom she had insulted, prayed for her (Nu 12:13), and Job's friends were reconciled to God when Job, whom they had grieved, showed care and prayed for them (Job 42:8–10). The prayers of good people may be a kindness to great people and ought to be valued.

CHAPTER 21

In this chapter we have: 1. Isaac, the child of promise, born into Abraham's family (vv. 1–8). 2. Ishmael, the son of the slave woman, driven out of it (vv. 9–21). 3. Abraham's treaty with his neighbor Abimelech (vv. 22–32). 4. Abraham's devotion to his God (vv. 33–34).

Verses 1–8

Few people in Old Testament times were brought into the world with such expectation as Isaac was, not for the sake of any great personal fame which he was to achieve, but because he was to be in this a type of Christ, that offspring which the holy God had long promised and holy people had long expected. Here is:

1. The fulfilling of God's promise in the conception and birth of Isaac (vv. 1–2):

1.1. Isaac was born according to the promise. He was born *at the set time of which God had spoken* (v. 2). God is always punctual according to his timing. Though his promised mercies do not come at the time we set, they will certainly come at the time he sets, and that is the best time.

1.2. It was not by the power of common providence, but by the power of a special promise that Isaac was born. True believers, by means of God's promises, are enabled to do what is above the power of human nature, for *by his great and precious promises they partake of a divine nature* (2Pe 1:4).

2. Abraham's obedience to God's command concerning Isaac. He named him as God commanded him (v. 3). There was good reason for the name, for:

- When Abraham received the promise of him, he laughed for joy (17:17).
- When Sarah received the promise, she laughed with distrust and insecurity.
- Isaac was himself afterward laughed at by Ishmael (v. 9), and perhaps his name led him to expect it.
- The promise which he was the heir of was to be the joy of all the saints in all ages.

3. The effect which this mercy had on Sarah:

3.1. It filled her with joy (v. 6): "*God has made me to laugh;* he has given me both a reason to rejoice and a heart to rejoice." So it was also with the mother of our Lord (Lk 1:46–47). Whatever is the source of our joy, God must be acknowledged as its author, unless it is the *laughter of the fool* (Ecc 7:6). It adds to the comfort of any mercy for our friends to share our joy in it: *All that hear will laugh with me,* for laughter is infectious. See Lk 1:58.

3.2. It filled her with wonder (v. 7). "What was so highly improbable, so nearly impossible, that if anyone but God had said it, we would not have believed it." God's favors to his covenant-people are those that exceed both their own and others' thoughts and expectations. Who would have thought that God would send his Son to die for us, his Spirit to make us holy, his angels to minister to us? Who would have thought that our great sins would be pardoned?

4. A short account of Isaac's infancy: *The child grew* (v. 8). He grew so that he did not always need milk but was able to take in solid food, and then he was weaned. See Heb 5:13–14. Abraham held a feast on the day that he was weaned, because God's blessing on the nursing of children, and the preservation of them through the dangers of infancy, are special occasions of the care and tenderness of divine Providence. See Ps 22:9–10; Hos 11:1.

Verses 9–13

The sending away of Ishmael is here considered:

1. Ishmael himself gave rise to the occasion by making fun of Isaac his little brother. Sarah herself was an eyewitness of the events. Ishmael is here called the *son of the Egyptian*, because, as some think, the 400 years' suffering of the offspring of Abraham under the Egyptians began now (15:13). Ishmael was fourteen years older than Isaac, and it showed that Ishmael had a nasty and contemptible streak in him that he was abusive to a child who was in no way a match for him.

2. Sarah set matters in motion: *Cast out this bondwoman* (v. 10). This seems to be spoken in a moment of anger, yet it is quoted (Gal 3:30) as if it had been prompted by a spirit of prophecy. It is the sentence passed on all hypocrites and worldly people, even though they have a place and a name in the visible church.

3. Abraham was distressed by this: *The thing was very grievous in Abraham's sight* (v. 11). It distressed him that Ishmael had treated Isaac so contemptuously. It also distressed him that Sarah insisted on such a punishment. "Might it not be sufficient to discipline him? Couldn't we do something less than expel him?"

4. God decided it (vv. 12–13). The covenant seed of Abraham must be a special people, a people by themselves, from the very beginning, distinguished, not mixed in with those who were outside the covenant; for this reason Ishmael must be separated. The driving out of Ishmael would not destroy him (v. 13). He will be a *nation, because he is thy seed*. It is presumptuous to say that all those who are left out of the external administration of God's covenant are therefore excluded from all his mercies. Though he was chased out of the church, he was not *chased out of the world* (Job 18:18). *I will make him a nation* (v. 13). We can learn from this:

- Nations are of God's making: he founds them, he forms them, he fixes them.
- Many are full of the blessings of God's providence who are foreigners to the blessings of his covenant.

Verses 14–21

Here is:

1. The driving out of the slave woman and her son from the family of Abraham (v. 14). Abraham's obedience to the divine command in this matter was speedy—*early in the morning*. It was also submissive; it was contrary to his own personal inclinations to do it. But as soon as he realizes that it is the mind of God, he makes no objections but silently does as he is asked.

2. Their wandering in the desert, missing their way to the place Abraham arranged for them to settle.

2.1. They were humbled to a great distress there. Their provisions were used up, and Ishmael became ill. Hagar is in tears, subdued and humbled. She despairs of relief and reckons on nothing except *the death of the child* (vv. 15–16).

2.2. God heard *the voice of the lad* (v. 17). An angel was sent to comfort Hagar, and it was not the first time that she had met with God's comforts in a desert.

2.2.1. The angel assures her: *God has heard the voice of the lad where he is*, though he is in a desert (for, wherever we are, there is a way open to heaven), so *lift up the lad, and hold him in thy hand* (v. 18).

2.2.2. The angel repeats the promise concerning her son, that he would be *a great nation*, as a reason why she should stir herself to help him.

2.2.3. God shows her a present supply (v. 19), and then *she saw a well of water*. Many who have reason enough to be strong go about mourning from day to day. There is a well of water by them in the covenant of grace, but they are not aware of it till the same God that opened their eyes to see their sorrow opens them to see their salvation (Jn 16:6–7). Now the apostle tells us that those things concerning Hagar and Ishmael are *allegoroumena* (Gal 4:24), they are an allegory: they are to be taken figuratively. This illustrates the folly:

2.2.3.1. Of those who, like the unbelieving Jews, look for righteousness by the Law and its worldly ordinances, and not by the promise made in Christ.

2.2.3.2. Of those who look for satisfaction and happiness in the world and worldly things. Those who abandon the comforts of the covenant and fellowship with God wander endlessly in pursuit of satisfaction and eventually come to rest still lacking it.

3. The settlement of Ishmael, eventually, in the desert of Paran (vv. 20–21), a wild place, fit for a wild man such as him (16:12). Notice:

3.1. He had some signs of God's presence: *God was with the lad* (v. 20).

3.2. By trade he became an archer.

3.3. His mother arranged a marriage for him from Egypt: as great an archer as he was, he did not think he could take his aim well in the matter of marriage, if he proceeded without his mother's advice and agreement.

Verses 22–32

We have here an account of the treaty between Abimelech and Abraham. Abraham's friendship is valued, is sought, even though he is a stranger and a tenant in a land that was not his own.

1. The treaty is proposed by Abimelech and Phichol (Phicol), the commander of his army.

1.1. The inducement to it was God's favor to Abraham (v. 22): "*God is with thee in all that thou doest*, and we have to take notice of it." It is good to be in favor with those who are in favor with God. *We will go with you, for we have heard that God is with you* (Zec 8:23). We do well for ourselves if we have fellowship with those who have fellowship with God (1Jn 1:3).

1.2. The tenor of it was, in general, that there should be a firm and constant friendship between the two families. He wanted his children, his descendants, and his land, to benefit from it.

2. It is agreed to by Abraham, with a particular clause inserted about a well. In Abraham's part of this transaction, notice:

2.1. Abraham was ready to enter into this treaty with Abimelech, finding him to be a man of honor and conscience, and one with the fear of God before his eyes.

2.2. Abraham prudently settled the matter concerning a well, about which Abimelech's servants had quarreled with him. Wells of water, it seems, were very special in that country. Abraham mildly told Abimelech about it (v. 25), and no more can be expected from honorable people than that they are ready to do right as soon as they know that they have done wrong.

2.3. Abraham made a very handsome present to Abimelech (v. 27). The exchanging of kind services between people makes the most of love: what is mine is my friend's.

2.4. Abraham confirmed the covenant by an oath, and registered it by giving a new name to the place (v. 31), *Beer-sheba,* meaning "well of the oath."

Verses 33–34

Abraham stayed many days, as many as would be consistent with his character as Abraham the traveler. He made there, not only a constant practice, but also an open profession, of his religion: *There he called on the name of the Lord, the everlasting God,* maybe by the grove or tree he planted, which was his oratory or house of prayer. Christ prayed in a garden, on a mountain. In calling on the Lord, we must consider him as *the everlasting God. The everlasting God,* who was before all worlds and will be, when time and days will be no more. See Isa 40:28.

CHAPTER 22

We have here the famous story of Abraham's offering of his son Isaac, that is, his offering to sacrifice him. Here is: 1. The strange command which God gave to Abraham (vv. 1–2). 2. Abraham's strange obedience to this command (vv. 3–10). 3. The strange outcome of this testing. The sacrificing of Isaac was revoked (vv. 11–12), and another sacrifice was provided (vv. 13–14). 4. The covenant renewed with Abraham (vv. 15–19). 5. An account of some of Abraham's relatives (vv. 20–24).

Verses 1–2

Here is:

1. The testing of Abraham's faith. It was made to appear that he loved God better than his father; now he loved him better than his son. Now, perhaps, he was beginning to think the storms of life had all blown over; but after everything, this encounter comes, which is more intense than any before.

2. The author of the testing: *God* tested him, not to draw him to sin, but to discover his graces, how strong they were, that they might be *found to praise, and glory, and honor* (1Pe 1:7). So it was that God tested Job, that he might appear not only as a good man, but also as a great man. *God did tempt Abraham;* he "lifted up Abraham," as some read it; as a scholar who is doing well is advanced to a higher level. Probably he expected some renewed promise as those in 15:1 and 17:1. But, to his great terror, what God has to say to him is, in short, "Abraham, go and kill your son." Every word here is a sword in his bones: the testing is braced with traumatic phrases.

3. The person to be offered. *"Take thy son,* not your bullocks or your lambs. No, *I will take no bullock out of thy house* (Ps 50:9). I must have your son: take *Isaac,* him, by name, 'he laughs,' that son indeed, that son *whom thou lovest."* In Hebrew it is expressed more emphatically and might very well be read, "Take now that son of yours, that only one of yours, whom you love, that Isaac."

4. The place: *In the land of Moriah,* three days' journey away, so that he might have time to consider it, that it might be a service all the more proper and honorable.

5. The manner: *Offer him for a burnt offering.* He must not only kill his son but also kill him as a sacrifice.

Verses 3–10

Here is Abraham's obedience to this extreme command. *Being tried, he offered up Isaac* (Heb 11:17):

1. The difficulties which he overcame in this act of obedience.

1.1. It seemed directly against the previous law of God, which forbids murder under a severe penalty (9:5–6).

1.2. How could it be consistent with his natural affection for his own son?

1.3. God gave him no reason for it. When Ishmael was to be driven out, a just cause was given, but here Isaac must die, and Abraham must kill him, and neither the one nor the other knows why. If Isaac were to die as a martyr for the truth, or if his life were to be the ransom of some other life more precious, it would have been another matter. But the case is not so: he is a dutiful, obedient, and hopeful son. "Lord, *what profit is there in his blood?"* (Ps 30:9).

1.4. How would this be consistent with the promise? Was it not said that *in Isaac shall thy seed be called?* (21:12).

1.5. How could he ever look Sarah in the face again?

1.6. What would the Egyptians say, and the Canaanites and the Perizzites who dwelled then in the land? It would be a disgrace to Abraham and his sacrifices forever. "If this is grace, then I'm turning away from this back to the ways of the world."

2. Several steps of obedience:

2.1. He rises early (v. 3), for the command was categorical; it was nonnegotiable. Those who do the will of God sincerely will do it speedily.

2.2. He gets things ready for a sacrifice.

2.3. It is very probable that he said nothing about it to Sarah.

2.4. He carefully looked around him, to discover the place appointed for this sacrifice, when he said (v. 5), *"We will go yonder,* where you see the light, *and worship."*

2.5. He left his servants some distance off (v. 5), so that they would not intervene in his strange sacrifice. Similarly, when Christ was entering on his agony in the Garden of Gethsemane, he took only three of his disciples with him (Mk 14:32) and left the rest at the entrance to the garden.

2.6. He had Isaac carry the wood while he himself carried the deadly knife and fire (v. 6).

2.7. Without any fuss or bother, he talks it over with Isaac, as if it were an ordinary sacrifice that he was going to offer (vv. 7–8).

2.7.1. It was a very poignant question that Isaac asked him, as they were going together: *My father,* said Isaac; it was such a heartfelt word, which, you would think, would strike deeper into Abraham's breast than his knife would into Isaac's breast. But somehow he keeps his composure and keeps his face from showing his true feelings. He calmly waits for his son's question, and this is it: *Behold the fire and the wood, but where is the lamb?* This is:

2.7.1.1. A trying question for Abraham. How could he still think that Isaac was himself the lamb? It is like this but Abraham dares not tell him so yet.

2.7.1.2. A searching question for us all, that when we are going to worship God, we should seriously consider: Where is the heart? Is that ready to be offered up to God, to rise to him as a burnt offering?

2.7.2. It was a very prudent answer which Abraham gave him: *My son, God will provide himself a lamb.* This was the language, either of his obedience or of his faith. A sacrifice was provided instead of Isaac. In the same way, firstly, Christ, the great sacrifice of atonement, was provided by God. Secondly, all our sacrifices of acknowledgment are provided by God too. It is he that *prepares the heart* (Ps 10:17). *The broken and contrite spirit* is a sacrifice of God (Ps 51:17), one that he provides.

2.8. He goes on with a holy deliberation, after many a weary step, and with a heavy heart he eventually arrives at the fatal place, builds the altar, the saddest that he ever built, lays the wood in order for Isaac's funeral pile, and now tells him the fearful news: "Isaac, you are the lamb which God has provided." Isaac, for all that appears, is as willing as Abraham; we do not find that he attempted to make his escape or resisted in any way. Yet it is necessary that a sacrifice be bound. But with what heart could tender Abraham tie those guiltless hands, which perhaps had often been raised to ask his blessing, and outstretched to embrace him, and were now the more narrowly bound with the bonds of love and duty? However, it must be done. Having bound him, he lays him on the altar and his hand on the head of his sacrifice. Then, we may suppose, with floods of tears, he gives and takes the final farewell with a parting kiss. With an unswerving heart and an eye lifted up to heaven, he takes the knife, and stretches out his hand. Be stunned, heavens, at this! Wonder, O earth! Here is an act of faith and obedience, which deserves to be a spectacle to God, angels, and the whole of humanity. This obedience of Abraham in *offering* up Isaac is a personification of:

2.8.1. The love of God to us, in delivering up his only-begotten Son to suffer and die for us, as a sacrifice. It *pleased the Lord* himself to *bruise him* (Isa 53:10; Zec 13:7).

2.8.2. Our duty to God, in return for that love. We must follow in the footsteps of Abraham's faith. God, by his word, calls us to leave all for Christ.

Verses 11–14

Up to this point this story has been very sad, and seems to have moved quickly toward a most tragic end; but here the sky suddenly clears up, the sun breaks through, and a bright and pleasant scene opens up. The same hand that had wounded and thrown down here heals and lifts up:

1. Isaac is rescued (vv. 11–12). The command to offer him up was intended only as a test, and so the order is revoked: *Lay not thy hand upon the lad* (v. 12). The closer the danger, the more wonderful and the more welcome is the rescue, when God finally brings it.

2. Abraham is not only approved of; he is also acclaimed: *Now I know that thou fearest God*. The best evidence of our fearing God is our being willing to serve and honor him with what is dearest to us.

3. Another sacrifice is provided instead of Isaac (v. 13). God must be acknowledged with thankfulness for Isaac's rescue. Abraham's words must be implemented: *God will provide himself a lamb*. Reference must be made to the promised Messiah, the blessed offspring. Christ was sacrificed in our place, as this ram instead of Isaac, and his death released us. Though that blessed offspring had so recently been promised, and was now typified by Isaac, his being offered up would be delayed: and in the meantime the sacrifice of animals would be accepted, as this ram was, as a pledge of that great sacrifice of atonement which would one day be made. And it is noteworthy that the temple, the place of sacrifice, was afterward built on this Mount Moriah (2Ch 3:1), and Calvary (Golgotha), where Christ was crucified, was not far off.

4. A new name is given to the place, and for the encouragement of all believers, cheerfully to trust in God: *Jehovah-jireh*, "The Lord will provide" or "The Lord will see (to it)" (v. 14), alluding to what he had said (v. 8), *God will provide himself a lamb*.

Verses 15–19

Abraham's obedience was graciously accepted; but this was not all: here we have it greatly rewarded. Notice:

1. God is pleased to make mention of Abraham's obedience as a factor in the covenant and he speaks of it with praise: *Because thou hast done this thing, and hast not withheld thy son, thine only son* (v. 16).

2. God now confirmed the promise with an oath. It was stated and sealed before, but now it is sworn: *By myself have I sworn*; for he could swear by no greater one (Heb 6:13). He did (to speak with reverence) even condescend to our human frailty and pledge his own life and being on it (*As I live*), that by all those unchangeable things, in which it was impossible for God to lie, he and his people might be greatly encouraged.

3. The particular promise renewed here is that of a numerous offspring: *Multiplying, I will multiply thee* (v. 17). What a prominent part the offspring of Abraham play in history! How numerous, how famous, were his known descendants who, to this day, triumph in this, that they have Abraham as their father!

4. The promise, doubtless, points to the Messiah and the grace of the Gospel. This is the oath sworn to our father Abraham, which Zechariah refers to (Lk 1:73–75). And so here is a promise:

- Of the great blessing of the Spirit: *In blessing, I will bless thee*, namely, with the best of blessings, the gift of the Holy Spirit.
- Of the growth of the church, that believers, his spiritual offspring, would be as numerous as the stars of heaven.
- Of spiritual victories. Probably Zechariah refers to this part of the oath, *That we being delivered out of the hand of our enemies, might serve him without fear* (Lk 1:74).
- Of the incarnation of Christ. This is the crown of all the promises. *In thy seed*, one particular person who will descend from you (for he speaks not of many, but of one, as the apostle notes, Gal 3:16), *shall all the nations of the earth be blessed*.

Verses 20–24

This is recorded here to show that although Abraham saw his own family greatly honored with special privileges, yet he was glad to hear of the growth and prosperity of his relatives' families.

CHAPTER 23

Here is: 1. Abraham a mourner for the death of Sarah (vv. 1–2). 2. Abraham a purchaser of a burial place for Sarah. The purchase humbly proposed by Abraham (vv. 3–4), and the purchase discussed and agreed to, with a great deal of mutual politeness and respect (vv. 5–15). 3. The purchase price paid (v. 16), the land securely transferred to Abraham (vv. 17–18), and Sarah's funeral (vv. 19–20).

Verses 1–2

We have here:

1. Sarah's age (v. 1). She died in the land of Canaan, where she had lived for over sixty years as a pilgrim.

2. Abraham's mourning for Sarah. Two words are used: he came both to *mourn* and to *weep* (v. 1). Tears are a tribute due to our deceased friends. When the body is sown, it must be watered. But we must not grieve as those that have no hope (1Th 4:13); for we have a good hope through grace both concerning them and also concerning ourselves.

Verses 3–15

Here is:

1. The humble request which Abraham made to his neighbors, the Hittites, for a burial place among them (vv. 3–4), and the fitting diversion which this matter provided, for the present, from Abraham's grief: *He stood up from before his dead.* For those who grieve for their dead relatives, there must be a time of rising up from beside their dead and bringing their mourning to an end. Weeping must not hinder sowing. The death of a relative should serve as an effective reminder to us that we are not at home in this world. When they are gone, we should say, "We are going too."

2. The generous offer which the Hittites made to him (vv. 5–6). They compliment him:

2.1. With a title of respect: *Thou art a mighty prince among us* (v. 6).

2.2. With an offer of the best of their burial places. Even ordinary and natural manners teach us to be civil and respectful toward all, even though they are strangers and foreigners.

3. The particular proposal which Abraham made to them (vv. 7–9). He returns to them his thanks. Though a great man, an old man, and now a mourner, he still stands up and bows himself humbly before them (v. 7). Religion teaches good manners; and those who connect it with ignorance and rudeness do it a great injustice.

4. The present which Ephron made to Abraham of his field: *The field give I thee* (vv. 10–11). Abraham thought he would have to be pleaded with to sell it, but when it is first mentioned, without pleading, Ephron freely gives it. Some people have more generosity than they are thought to have.

5. Abraham's modest and sincere refusal of Ephron's kind offer (vv. 12–13). Abraham gives him great thanks for it (v. 12), but decides to give him money for the field, even its full value. Abraham was rich in silver and gold (13:2) and was able to pay for the field and so did not want to take advantage of Ephron's generosity. Honesty as well as honor forbids us from sponging on our neighbors.

6. The price of the land fixed by Ephron but not insisted on: *The land is worth four hundred shekels of silver, but what is that between me and thee?* (vv. 14–15). He would rather oblige his friend than have so much money in his pocket. When we are tempted to be high-handed in demanding our rights, or hardheaded in denying a kindness, we should answer the temptation with this question: "What is that between me and my friend?"

Verses 16–20

We have here the conclusion of the contract between Abraham and Ephron about the burial place. The agreement was publicly made before all the neighbors, *in the presence and audience of the sons of Heth* (vv. 16–17). Abraham then takes possession and buries Sarah in the cave which was in the field that had been bought. It is worth noting:

1. That a burial place was the first piece of ground Abraham possessed in Canaan. When we come into the world it is good to think of our departing from it; for, as soon as we are born, we begin to die.

2. That it was the only piece of land he ever possessed, though all the country was all his own according to God's promise still to be fulfilled. Abraham was longing for a better country, that is, a heavenly one. Abraham is content still to move from one place to another, as long as he lives, but assures himself of a place where, when he dies, his flesh may rest in hope.

CHAPTER 24

Marriages and funerals bring changes in families and are the general news among the inhabitants of villages. In the previous chapter we read of Abraham burying his wife; here we have him marrying his son. These stories concerning his family, with their tiny details, are related in depth, while the histories of the kingdoms of the then world with all their major changes are buried in silence. Here is: 1. Abraham's concern for the woman whom his son is to marry (vv. 1–9). 2. His servant's journey to Abraham's country, to try to find a wife for his young master from among his own relatives (vv. 10–14), and the kind providence which brought him to come to know Rebekah, whose father was Isaac's first cousin (vv. 15–28). 3. The agreement of marriage with her relatives (vv. 29–49), and their consent given (vv. 50–60). 4. The happy meeting and marriage between Isaac and Rebekah (vv. 61–67).

Verses 1–9

Three things we may notice here concerning Abraham:

1. The concern he had to see his son well married. Now Abraham's godly concern for his son was:

1.1. That he should not marry a daughter of Canaan, but one of his own relatives. He saw that the Canaanites were falling into great wickedness.

1.2. That he should not leave the land of Canaan, to go himself among his family, not even for the purpose of choosing a wife, so that he would not be tempted to settle there.

2. The responsibility he gave to his oldest and cleverest servant, probably Eliezer of Damascus, one whose conduct, trustworthiness, and affection to him and his family, he had had long experience of. He trusted him with this great matter, and not Isaac himself, because he did not want Isaac to go at all into that country, but marry there by proxy; and there was no representative so suitable as this *steward of his house.*

2.1. The servant must be bound by an oath to do all he could to find a wife for Isaac from among his relatives (vv. 2–4).

2.2. He must not be bound by this oath if, when he had done all he could, he could not succeed.

3. The confidence he put in a good God, who, he does not doubt, will give his servant success in this undertaking (v. 7). He remembers also the promise God had made and confirmed to him that he would give Canaan to his offspring and so deduces that God would acknowledge him in his endeavors to find a wife for his son, not from among the Canaanites, but from ones who were suited to be the mother of such an offspring. God's promises, and our own experiences, are sufficient to encourage our dependence on God, and our expectations from him, in all the matters of this life.

Verses 10-28

Abraham's servant is not named, but much is here recorded to his honor:

1. How faithful Abraham's servant demonstrates himself to be to his master. Having received his responsibility, he quickly set out on his journey, with all that was necessary and suitable to the task before him (v. 10).

2. How devoutly Abraham's servant acknowledged God in this matter, as one of that happy household which Abraham had *commanded to keep the way of the Lord* (18:19). He arrived early in the evening after many days' traveling at the place of his destination, and rested by a well of water, to consider how he might best proceed from then onward. And:

2.1. He acknowledges God in a detailed prayer (vv. 12-14), in which:

2.1.1. He asks for prosperity and good success in this matter: *Send me good speed, this day*. Those who want to have success must pray for it.

2.1.2. He pleads God's covenant with his master Abraham: *O God of my master Abraham, show kindness to him*.

2.1.3. He desires that his master's wife should be a humble and industrious woman, brought up to care and work, willing to put her hand to any work that had to be done; and that she might be pleasant and hospitable. When he came to try to find a wife for his master, he did not go to the theater or amusement park and pray that he might meet one there, but to *the well of water*, expecting to find one there already well employed.

2.2. God acknowledges him in details of Providence. The answer to this prayer was:

2.2.1. Speedy: *before he had done speaking* (v. 15).

2.2.2. Satisfactory: the first person who came to draw water was, and did in everything, according to his own heart.

2.2.2.1. She was so well qualified that in all respects she fulfilled the characteristics he wished for in the woman who was to be his master's wife, beautiful and healthy, humble and industrious, very polite and helpful to a stranger, having all the marks of a good disposition. When she came to the well (v. 16), she went down and *filled her pitcher, and came up* to go home with it. She did not stand to gaze on the strange man and his camels, but minded her own business and would not have been diverted from it except for an opportunity to do good.

2.2.2.2. Providence so ordered it that she did what exactly fulfilled his sign, and wonderfully paralleled his proposal: she not only gave him a drink, but, what was more than could have been expected, she offered her services to give his camels a drink too, which was the very sign he had looked for. Rebekah, quite beyond her expectation at this time, was brought in this way into the line of Christ and the covenant. There may be a great deal of helpful kindness in what costs us only a little: our Savior has promised a reward even for a cup of cold water (Mt 10:42).

2.2.2.3. Upon inquiry he found, to his great satisfaction, that she was a near relative of his master, and that the family she came from was significant and able to show him hospitality (vv. 23-25).

2.3. He acknowledges God in a special thanksgiving. He first paid his respects to Rebekah, in gratitude for her politeness (v. 22). Having done this, he turns his wonder (v. 21) into worship. He had prayed for success (v. 12), and now that he had received success, he gives thanks. What we gain by prayer we must be grateful for with

praise. He thinks himself very happy, that he was led to the *house of his master's brethren* (v. 27), those of them who had come from Ur of the Chaldees. They were not idolaters, but worshipers of the true God and inclined to the religion of Abraham's family.

Verses 29-53

We have here the making of the marriage between Isaac and Rebekah:

1. The very kind reception given to Abraham's servant by Rebekah's relatives.

1.1. The invitation was kind: *Come in, thou blessed of the Lord* (v. 31). Perhaps because they heard from Rebekah (v. 28) of the gracious words which came from his mouth. We should welcome those who are blessed by God. It is good to acknowledge those whom God acknowledges.

1.2. The hospitality was generous (vv. 32-33). Particular care was taken of the camels; for *a good man regardeth the life of his beast* (Pr 12:10).

2. The full account which he gave them of his task, and the attention he gave to them for their agreement respecting Rebekah. Notice:

2.1. How intent he was on his business; though he had finished his journey and come to a good house, he would *not eat, till he had told his errand* (v. 33).

2.2. How intelligent he was in managing this task:

2.2.1. He gives a short account of the state of his master's family (vv. 34-36). He suggests two things, to commend his proposal:

- That his master Abraham, through the blessing of God, had become wealthy; and:
- That he had given everything to Isaac, on whose behalf the servant was now petitioning.

2.2.2. He tells them the responsibility his master had given him, to find a wife for his son from among his father's family and clan, with the reason behind it (vv. 37-38). The highest degrees of divine affection must not relieve us of natural affection.

2.2.3. He relates to them the wonderful convergence of the details of God's providence, to support and further the proposal, showing clearly the hand of God in it.

2.2.4. They freely and happily accept the proposal on the very good principle (v. 50): "*The thing proceedeth from the Lord*. Providence smiles on it, and we have nothing to say against it."

2.2.5. Abraham's servant thankfully acknowledges the good success he had met with: *He worshipped the Lord* (v. 52). God sent his angel before him, and so gave him success (vv. 7, 40). But when he has the desired success, he worships God, not the angel.

Verses 54-61

Rebekah here takes leave of her father's house. Rebekah's relatives, out of their natural affection and according to the usual expression of kindness in such instances, ask her to stay some time among them (v. 55). They had agreed to the marriage but were loath to part with her. Rebekah herself decided the matter. She agreed, not only to go, but also to go immediately. At this, she is sent away with Abraham's servant, with suitable attendants, and with sincere good wishes. Now that she was going to be a wife, they prayed that she might be a mother both of a numerous and of a victorious offspring.

Verses 62-67

Isaac and Rebekah are finally and happily brought together.

1. Isaac was well employed when he met Rebekah: *He went out to meditate*, or pray, *in the field, at the eventide* (vv. 62–63). He went to take advantage of a quiet evening and a solitary field for meditation and prayer, those divine exercises by which we speak with God and our own hearts. We can learn from this:

1.1. Holy souls love retirement. It will do us good to be left alone often, walking alone and sitting alone; and, if we are able to make the most of solitude, we will find we are never less alone than when we are alone, for God is with us.

1.2. Meditation and prayer ought to be both our business and our delight when we are alone.

1.3. The exercises of devotion should be the refreshment and means of relaxation in the evening, to relieve us from the tiredness occasioned by the care and business of the day, and to prepare us for the rest and sleep of the night. Some think Isaac was now praying for success in this imminent matter, and now, when he sets himself, as it were, on his watchtower to see what God would answer him, as the prophet (Hab 2:1), *he sees the camels coming* (v. 63).

2. Rebekah behaved herself very gracefully when she met Isaac: understanding who he was, she *alighted off her camel* (v. 64), and *took a veil, and covered herself* (v. 65), as a sign of her humility, modesty, and submission.

3. They were brought together to their mutual comfort (v. 67). Notice here:

3.1. What an affectionate son he was to his mother: it had been about three years since her death, and yet he was not, till now, comforted concerning it.

3.2. What an affectionate husband he was to his wife.

CHAPTER 25

The holy writer, in this chapter: 1. Takes his leave of Abraham, with an account: of his children by another wife (vv. 1–4); of his last will and testament (vv. 5–6); of his age, death, and burial (vv. 7–10). 2. Takes his leave of Ishmael, with a short account of Ishmael's children (vv. 12–16) and of Ishmael's age and death (vv. 17–18). 3. Begins the history of Isaac: his prosperity (v. 11), the conception and birth of his two sons, with the word of God concerning them (vv. 19–26) and their different characters (vv. 27–28). 4. Describes Esau's selling his birthright to Jacob (vv. 29–34).

Verses 1–10

Abraham lived, after the marriage of Isaac, thirty-five years, and all that is recorded concerning him during that time is here in a very few verses. We hear no more of God's extraordinary appearances to him or testings of him; for not all the days, even of the best and greatest saints, are noteworthy days; some slide by silently, and neither come nor go with special note; such were these last days of Abraham. We read here of:

1. An account of his children by Keturah, another wife whom he married after the death of Sarah.

2. The disposal which Abraham made of his estate (vv. 5–6). After the birth of these sons, he put his house in order, with prudence and justice.

2.1. He made Isaac his heir, as he was bound to do, in justice to Sarah his first and principal wife and to Rebekah who married Isaac on the assurance of this (24:36). God having already made Isaac the heir of the promise, Abraham therefore made him heir of his property.

2.2. He gave gifts to the rest of his children, both to Ishmael, though at first he was sent empty away, and to his sons by Keturah. It was just to provide for them; parents who are not like him in this are worse than unbelievers. It was prudent that they should settle in places far away from Isaac, that they might not pretend to divide the inheritance with him, nor be in any way a care or expense to him. Notice, he did this *while he yet lived*, fearing that it would not be done, or not so well done, afterward.

3. The age and death of Abraham (vv. 7–8). He lived 175 years, and died just 100 years after he came to Canaan; so long was he a foreigner in a strange country.

3.1. He *gave up the ghost*. His life was not extracted from him, but he cheerfully submitted it to God. Into the hands of the Father of spirits he committed his spirit.

3.2. He *died in a good old age, an old man*; God had promised him this. His death released him from the burdens of his age. It was also the crown of the glory of his old age.

3.3. He was *full of years*, or "full of life." He did not live till the world was weary of him, but till he was weary of the world; he had had enough of it and desired no more. Good people, though they should not die old, die full of days, satisfied with living here and longing to live in a better place.

3.4. He *was gathered to his people*. His body was gathered to the congregation of the dead, and his soul to the congregation of the blessed. Death gathers us to our people. Those who are our people while we live, whether the people of God or the children of this world, are the people to whom death will gather us.

4. Abraham's burial (vv. 9–10). Notice:

4.1. Who buried him: *His sons Isaac and Ishmael*. It was the last duty of respect they had to pay to their good father. There had formerly been some distance between Isaac and Ishmael; but it seems either that Abraham had himself brought them together while he lived or at least that his death reconciled them.

4.2. Where they buried him: in his own burial place, which he had bought, and in which he had buried Sarah.

Verses 11–18

Immediately after the account of Abraham's death, Moses begins the story of Isaac (v. 11), and tells us where he dwelled and how remarkably God blessed him. But he immediately digresses from the story of Isaac to give a short account of Ishmael, inasmuch as he also was a son of Abraham, and God had made some promises concerning him:

1. Concerning his children. He had twelve sons, *twelve princes* (twelve tribal rulers) they are called (v. 16), heads of families, which in the process of time became nations, distinct tribes, numerous and very significant. They populated Arabia. The names of his twelve sons are recorded. We often read about Kedar and Midian in Scripture. And some expositors have taken notice of the meaning of those three names which are put together (v. 14), as containing good advice to us all, *Mishma, Dumah*, and *Massa*, that may be, "hear" (or "fame"), "keep silence," and "bear"; we have them together in the same order in Jas 1:19: *Be swift to hear, slow to speak, slow to wrath*. The descendants of Ishmael not only had tents in the fields, in which they grew rich in times of peace; they also had settlements and camps (v. 16), in which they fortified themselves in time of war.

2. Concerning himself. Here is an account of his age: he *lived 137 years* (v. 17), which is recorded to show the

effectiveness of Abraham's prayer for him (17:18), *O that Ishmael might live before thee!* Here is also an account of his death; he too *was gathered to his people*; but it is not said that he was *full of days*, though he lived to so great an age. He died with his friends about him, which is encouraging.

Verses 19–28

We have here an account of the birth of Jacob and Esau, the twin sons of Isaac and Rebekah: their entrance into the world was (which is not usual) one of the most significant parts of their story. Isaac seems not to have been a man of great action, not tested much, but to have spent his days in quietness and silence. Now concerning Jacob and Esau we are here told:

1. That they were prayed for. Their parents, after they had been childless for a long time, obtained them by prayer (vv. 20–21). *Isaac was forty years old when he was married.* He was sixty years old when his sons were born (v. 26), so that, after he got married, he had no child for twenty years. But:

1.1. He prayed *for* his wife; some read it "with his wife." Husbands and wives should pray together. The Jews have a tradition that Isaac eventually took his wife with him to Mount Moriah, where God had promised that he would multiply Abraham's seed (22:17), and there, in his prayer with her and for her, pleaded the promise made in that very place.

1.2. God heard and answered his prayer and entreaty.

2. That they were prophesied of before they were born, and great mysteries were wrapped up in the prophecies which went before them (vv. 22–23). Now Rebekah being pregnant with these two sons, notice here:

2.1. How she was perplexed in her mind concerning her present case: *The children struggled together within her* (v. 22). This struggle between Jacob and Esau in the womb represents the struggle that is maintained between the kingdom of God and the kingdom of Satan. A holy war is better than the peace of the Devil's palace.

2.2. What course she took for her relief: *She went to enquire of the Lord* (v. 22). It is a great relief to the mind to spread out our case before the Lord and ask his advice. *Go into the sanctuary* (Ps 73:17).

2.3. The information given her, on her inquiry, which explained the mystery: *Two nations are in thy womb* (v. 23). She was now pregnant, not with two children, but with two nations, which would not only greatly differ from each other in their manners and temperaments, but clash and contend with each other in their interests. The outcome of the contest would be that the elder would serve the younger, which was fulfilled in the subjection of the Edomites, for many ages, to the house of David, till they rebelled (2Ch 21:8). In the struggle between grace and corruption in the soul, grace, the younger, will certainly gain the upper hand in the end.

3. That when they were born there was a great difference between them:

3.1. There was a great difference in their bodies (v. 25). Esau, when he was born, was rough and hairy, as if he were already a grown man; his name may mean "hairy" or "made, reared already." This was an indication of a very strong constitution and gave cause to expect that he would be a very robust, daring, and active man. But Jacob was smooth and tender as other children. It is God's usual way to choose the weak things of the world and to overlook the strong (1Co 1:26–27).

3.2. There was a clear competition in their births.

3.3. They were very different in their temperaments and the way of living they chose (v. 27):

3.3.1. Esau was a man of this world. He was a man devoted to recreation, for he was a skillful hunter. He was a man of the field, like Nimrod and Ishmael.

3.3.2. Jacob was a man of the other world. He was not cut out to be a leader, nor did he pretend to look great, but he was *a plain man, dwelling in tents*, an honest man who always meant well and dealt fairly, who preferred the true delights of quiet solitude and retirement to all the pretended pleasure of busy and noisy sports. He dwelled in tents:

• As a shepherd. He was attached to that safe and quiet employment of keeping sheep, to which also he brought up his children (46:34). Or:
• As a student. He frequented the tents of Melchizedek, or Heber, as some understand it, to be taught divine things by them. And this was that son of Isaac on whom the covenant was settled as one in the designated line of heirs.

3.4. Their claims on the affections of their parents were likewise different. They had only these two children, and, it seems, one was the father's darling and the other the mother's (v. 28):

3.4.1. Isaac loved to see his son active. Esau knew how to please his father, and showed a great respect for him, by treating him often with wild game.

3.4.2. Rebekah was mindful of the prophecy of God, which had given the preference to Jacob, and therefore she preferred him in her affection.

Verses 29–34

We have here the deal struck between Jacob and Esau about the birthright, which was Esau's by providence but Jacob's by promise. It was a spiritual privilege, such a birthright as then had the blessing attached to it and the inheritance of the promise.

1. Jacob's godly desire for the birthright, which he still sought to obtain by indirect means. He is to be commended for this: that he coveted earnestly the best gifts. But he cannot be vindicated in this: that he took advantage of his brother's necessity to make him a very hard bargain (v. 31): *Sell me this day thy birthright.* It is quiet people who live their lives in simple and godly sincerity and without worldly wisdom, who are often found the wisest of all for their souls and eternity. Jacob's wisdom appeared in two things:

1.1. He chose the most suitable time.

1.2. Having made the bargain, he made it certain, and got it confirmed by Esau's oath: *Swear to me* this day (v. 33).

2. Esau's godless contempt of the birthright, and his foolish sale of it. He is called *profane Esau* for it, godless (Heb 12:16), because *for one morsel of meat he sold his birthright*, as dear a meal as ever was eaten since the forbidden fruit; and he lived to regret it when it was too late. There are those who are penny-wise and pound-foolish, thrifty in small matters, while careless in larger matters, cunning people who can outwit others and draw them into their snares, but are themselves put on by Satan's schemes and taken captive by him at his will. Notice the instances of Esau's folly:

2.1. His appetite was very strong (vv. 29–30). Poor Jacob had gotten some bread and stew (vv. 29, 34) for his dinner, when Esau came in from hunting, hungry and weary. Give me, he says, some of "that red, that red," as it is in the original. The gratifying of the sensual appetite is what ruins thousands of precious souls: surely, if Esau was hungry and faint, he might have gotten the food for a meal more cheaply than at the expense of his birthright.

2.2. His reasoning was very weak (v. 32): *Behold, I am at the point to die*; and, if he were, would nothing keep him alive except this stew? Even if the famine were now in the land (26:1), as Dr. Lightfoot supposes, we cannot suppose that Isaac was so poor, or Rebekah so bad a housekeeper, that he might not have been supplied with suitable food in other ways. It is a terrible folly to part with our privileges with God, Christ, and heaven, for the riches, honors, and pleasures of this world, as bad a bargain as his that sold a birthright for a bowl of stew.

2.3. Repentance was hidden from his eyes (v. 34): *He did eat and drink*; the food pleased his taste buds. He then carelessly stood up and went on his way, without any signs whatsoever of regret. So it was that Esau despised his birthright.

CHAPTER 26

In this chapter we have: 1. Isaac in adversity, because of a famine, which means that he has to move (v. 1). But God comes to him with direction and encouragement (vv. 2–5). 2. Isaac foolishly denying his wife (vv. 6–11). 3. Isaac in prosperity (vv. 12–14a) and the Philistines being envious (vv. 14b–17); he continued diligently (vv. 18–23); God encouraged him (vv. 24–25). 4. The Philistines eventually agreeing to a covenant with him (vv. 26–33). 5. The difficult marriage of his son Esau (vv. 34–35).

Verses 1–5

Here:

1. In his providence, God tested Isaac. Now there *is a famine in the land* (v. 1). What is he to think of the promise when the Promised Land will not find him bread? Yes, Isaac will still cling to the covenant. The intrinsic value of God's promises cannot be lessened in a believer's eye by any difficult providences.

2. God directed Isaac in this testing according to his word. Isaac must go somewhere for supplies. He set out for Egypt, where his father went in a similar predicament, but he takes in Gerar on his way. God told him to stay where he was and *not go down into Egypt: Sojourn in this land* (vv. 2–3). There was a famine in Jacob's days, and God told him to *go down into Egypt* (46:3–4), a famine in Isaac's days, and God told him *not to go down*, a famine in Abraham's days, and God left him to choose for himself. Some see this variety in the divine procedure as being based on the different characters of these three patriarchs. Abraham was a man of very high achievements and intimate fellowship with God, and to him all places and conditions were alike. Isaac was a very good man, but not cut out for hardship, and so he is forbidden to go to Egypt. Jacob was already hardened by difficulties; he was strong and patient; and so he must go down to Egypt. In this way God matches his tests of his people to their strength. "*Abraham obeyed my voice*; you are to do so too, and the promise will be certain to you." Abraham's obedience is here celebrated to his honor, for this is what he was commended for both by God and his fellows.

Verses 6–11

Isaac had now stayed in Gerar, the country in which he was born (v. 6). But there he enters into temptation to deny his wife, and to suggest that she was his sister. Notice:

1. How he sinned (v. 7). Because his wife was beautiful, he thought that the Philistines would find some way or other to take him away, so that one of them might marry her, and so he pretended that she was his sister.

2. How he was detected, and the deceit discovered, by the king himself. Abimelech (not the same that was in Abraham's days, 20:1–18, for this was at least sixty years later, but this was a common name of the Philistine kings) saw that Isaac was more intimate with Rebekah than he knew he would be with his sister (v. 8): he saw him *sporting with her*, caressing her or "*laughing*"; it is the same word from which Isaac had his name. Nowhere may a man allow himself to be more innocently happy than with his own wife and children. Abimelech charged him with the deceit (v. 9) and showed him what might have been its bad consequences (v. 10). Then, to convince Isaac how groundless and unjust his jealousy of them was, Abimelech took him and his family under his particular protection, forbidding any injury to be done to him or his wife on pain of death (v. 11).

Verses 12–25

Here are:

1. The signs of God's goodwill to Isaac.

1.1. His crops multiplied greatly (v. 12). He had no land of his own but took some land of the Philistines, and planted crops in it; and (may those who are poor tenants and honestly and industriously occupy other people's lands be encouraged by this) God blessed him with a great increase. He reaped *a hundredfold* that *same year* when there was a famine in the land.

1.2. His cattle also increased (v. 14). And then:

1.3. He had *great store of servants*, whom he employed and kept.

2. The signs of the Philistines' ill will to him. They *envied him* (v. 14). That is a bad principle which makes us *grieve at the good of others*, as if something must be wrong with me because things are going well with my neighbor. Because they did not have their own flocks to water at these wells, they did not want to leave them for others to use; see how absurd malice is. The king of Gerar began to look on him with jealousy. Isaac's house was like a monarch's court and he must go farther away. A wise and a good person will rather retire into obscurity, as Isaac does here into a valley, than sit high and be the target of envy and ill will.

3. Isaac's constancy and continuation in his work:

3.1. He kept up his farming and continued diligently to find wells of water. He set himself to make the best of the country he had come into, which every person should seek to do.

3.1.1. He reopened the wells that his father had dug (v. 18). In our search after truth, that fountain of living water, it is good to make use of the revelations of former ages, which may have been clouded by the corruptions of later times. Inquire for the old way, the wells which our ancestors dug, which the adversaries of truth have stopped up.

3.1.2. His servants dug new wells (v. 19). Though we must use the light of former ages, it does not therefore follow that we must rest in it, stopping there and not moving on. We must still build on their foundation.

3.1.3. In digging his wells he met with much opposition (vv. 20–21). Those who open the fountains of truth must expect resistance. The first two wells which they dug were called *Esek* and *Sitnah*, "dispute" and "opposition."

3.1.4. Eventually he moved to a quiet settlement (Ps 120:6). He preferred quietness to victory. Those who follow peace will, sooner or later, find peace. This well they called *Rehoboth*, "room," space enough: in the two former wells we saw what the earth is, "dispute" and "opposition." This well shows us what heaven is like; it is roomy and peaceful, for there are many mansions in it.

3.2. He kept up his faith and his fellowship with God. He came weary and uneasy to Beersheba. *Fear not*, God says to him, *I am with thee, and will bless thee*. If we are sure of God's presence with us wherever we go, then we may move on with God's encouragement. *There he built an altar, and called upon the name of the Lord* (v. 25).

Verses 26–33

We have here the strife that there had been between Isaac and the Philistines resulting in a harmonious peace and reconciliation:

1. Abimelech pays a friendly visit to Isaac, as a sign of the respect he had for him (v. 26).

2. Isaac prudently and cautiously questions Abimelech's sincerity in this visit (v. 27).

3. Abimelech professes his sincerity in his reply to Isaac and earnestly seeks his friendship (vv. 28–29). Isaac complained they had *hated him, and sent him away* (v. 27). No, said Abimelech, *we sent thee away in peace* (v. 29). He acknowledges the signs of God's favor to him and makes this the reason for their desire to be in alliance with him: *The Lord is with thee, and thou art the blessed of the Lord.*

4. Isaac receives him and his company and enters into an alliance of friendship with him (vv. 30–31). Religion teaches us to be neighborly, and as much as in us lies, to *live peaceably with all men* (Ro 12:18).

5. Providence smiled on what Isaac did; for the very day that he made this covenant with Abimelech his servants brought him the news of a well of water they had found (vv. 32–33).

Verses 34–35

Here is:

1. Esau's foolish marriage—foolish, in marrying Canaanites, who were strangers to the blessing of Abraham, for which he is called *profane*; for in this he showed that he neither desired the blessing of God nor feared the curse of God.

2. The grief and trouble it created for his caring parents. It grieved them that he married the daughters of Hittites, who had no religion among them.

CHAPTER 27

In this chapter we return to the story of the struggle between Esau and Jacob. Esau had godlessly sold the birthright to Jacob. This story is explained in Heb 12:16–17: "Because he sold the birthright, when he would have inherited the blessing, he was rejected." We have here: 1. Isaac's purpose to pass on the blessing to Esau (vv. 1–5). 2. Rebekah's scheme to obtain it for Jacob (vv. 6–17). 3. Jacob's successful arranging of the scheme, and his obtaining the blessing (vv. 18–29). 4. Esau's indignation at this; his great audacity with his father to try to obtain a blessing (vv. 30–40). 5. His great

enmity toward his brother for defrauding him of the first blessing (vv. 41–46).

Verses 1–5

Here is:

1. Isaac's purpose in making his will, to declare Esau his heir.

2. The directions Isaac gave to Esau, in accordance with his plan. Isaac calls Esau to him (v. 1). For Esau, though he had greatly grieved his parents by his marriage, yet they had not expelled him but made the best of it. Parents who are justly offended at their children must not be implacable toward them.

2.1. Isaac tells Esau what he has decided to do (v. 2).

2.2. Isaac asks Esau to get things ready for the solemn task of executing his last will and testament, by which he intended to make him his heir (vv. 3–4). Esau must go hunting, and bring some wild game, which his father will eat and then bless him. Prayer is the work of the soul, not only of the lips; as the soul must be occupied in blessing God (Ps 103:1), so it must also be engaged in blessing ourselves and others. The blessing will not come to the heart if it does not come from the heart.

Verses 6–17

Rebekah here contrives to obtain for Jacob the blessing which was intended for Esau.

1. Her purpose was good. God had said it would be so, that the elder would *serve the younger* (25:23); and so Rebekah decides it will be so. But:

2. The means she tried to use were bad and in no way justifiable. If it was not wronging Esau to deprive him of the blessing (he himself having forfeited it by selling the birthright), yet it was wronging Isaac, taking advantage of his infirmity to deceive him. It was wronging Jacob too, whom she taught to deceive. It would likewise expose him to endless scruples about the blessing, if he were to obtain it fraudulently in this way. If Rebekah had gone to Isaac, and made him remember what God had said concerning their sons—if further she had shown him how Esau had forfeited the blessing both by selling his birthright and by marrying foreign women—it is probable that Isaac would have been prevailed on to confer the blessing on Jacob.

Verses 18–29

Notice here:

1. The skill and self-assurance with which Jacob carried out this scheme. Who would have thought that this quiet man could have played his part so well in a plan of this nature? Lying is soon learned. We wonder how honest Jacob could so readily speak the words (v. 19), *I am Esau thy firstborn*. How could he say, *I have done as thou badest me*, when he had received no command from his father, but was doing what his mother had asked him to do? How could he say, *Eat of my venison*, when he knew it had not come from the field, but from the fold? But especially we wonder how he could have the audacity to trace the deceit back to God (v. 20): *The Lord thy God brought it to me*. Is this Jacob? Is this Israel, indeed, without deceit? These things are certainly written, not that we may imitate them, but to warn us.

2. The success of this plan. Jacob won the point with some difficulty and obtained the blessing.

2.1. Isaac was at first not satisfied, and would have discovered the deceit if he had trusted his own ears, for *the voice was Jacob's voice* (v. 22). His voice is Jacob's voice, but his hands are Esau's. He speaks the language of a saint, but does the works of a sinner; and the judgment will be, as here, at his hands.

2.2. Eventually he gave in to the power of the deceit, *because the hands were hairy* (v. 23), not considering how easy it was to falsify that; and now Jacob carries it out skillfully. What in some small degree mitigates the crime of Rebekah and Jacob is that the deceit was intended, not so much to speed up the fulfillment, as to prevent the frustration, of God's prophecy: the blessing was going to be put on the wrong head, and they thought it was time to stir themselves into action. Now let us see how Isaac gave Jacob his blessing (vv. 26–29):

2.2.1. He embraced him as a sign of a particular affection to him.

2.2.2. He praised him. *He smelt the smell of his raiment, and said, See, the smell of my son is as the smell of a field which the Lord hath blessed.*

2.2.3. He prayed for him, and in so doing prophesied concerning him. Jacob is here blessed with three things:

• Plenty (v. 28).
• Power (v. 29).
• Privileges of sharing with God and in heaven: Cursed be every one that curseth thee and blessed be he that blesseth thee.

Verses 30–40

Here is:

1. The covenant-blessing denied to Esau. He who had made so light of the birthright *would now have inherited the blessing.* Notice:

1.1. How carefully he sought it. When he understood that Jacob had obtained it surreptitiously, he *cried with a great and exceedingly bitter cry* (v. 34). Those who will not so much as ask and seek now, will soon knock, and cry, *Lord, Lord* (Mt 7:22). Those who insult Christ now will then seek him humbly.

1.2. How he was rejected. Isaac, when first made aware of the deceit that had been practiced on him, *trembled exceedingly* (v. 33). But he soon recovers himself and confirms the blessing he had given to Jacob: *I have blessed him, and he shall be blessed.* Having found himself more than ordinarily filled with the Holy Spirit when he gave the blessing to Jacob, he perceived that God did, as it were, say Amen to it now. In this we see:

1.2.1. Jacob was confirmed in his possession of the blessing.

1.2.2. Isaac rested in the will of God, though it contradicted his own expectations and affections.

1.2.3. Esau was cut off from the expectation of that special blessing which he thought he had preserved for himself when he sold his birthright. The Jews, like Esau, pursued *the law of righteousness* (Ro 9:31), but missed out on the blessing of righteousness, *because they sought it by the works of the law* (Ro 9:32); while the Gentiles, who, like Esau, sought it by faith in God's prophecy, obtained it *by force*, with that violence of the kingdom of heaven. See Mt 11:12. Those who undervalue their spiritual birthright and can afford to sell it for a single meal forfeit spiritual blessings. Those who part with their wisdom and grace, with their faith and a good conscience, for the honors, wealth, or pleasures of this world, however much they may pretend to be zealous for God's blessing, have already judged themselves unworthy of it.

2. A common blessing given to Esau:

2.1. He wanted this: *Bless me also* (v. 34). *Hast thou not reserved a blessing for me?* (v. 36). It is the folly of most people that they are willing to be satisfied with

the smallest good thing (Ps 4:6), as Esau was here, who desired only a second-rate blessing, a blessing separated from the birthright. It is as if he had said, "I will be satisfied with anything: even though I have not the blessing of the church, let me still have some blessing."

2.2. He received this (vv. 39–40); let him then make his best of it.

2.2.1. He was promised:

2.2.1.1. An adequate livelihood—the *fatness of the earth, and the dew of heaven.* Those who come short of the blessings of the covenant may still have a very good share in outward blessings.

2.2.1.2. A gradual recovery of his liberty. He will serve, but he will not starve; and, eventually after many skirmishes, he will break the yoke of slavery and wear the badges of freedom. This was fulfilled (2Ki 8:20–22) when the Edomites revolted.

2.2.2. But it was still far short of Jacob's blessing. God had reserved some better thing for Jacob:

2.2.2.1. In Jacob's blessing *the dew of heaven* is put first, as what he most valued. In Esau's *the fatness of the earth* is put first, for this is what he had looked for most.

2.2.2.2. Jacob will have authority over his brothers and sisters: so the Israelites often ruled over the Edomites. But the great difference is that there is nothing in Esau's blessing that points to Christ, nothing that brings him or his family into the church and covenant of God, without which the richness of the earth will be of no lasting value.

Verses 41–46

Here is:

1. The grudge Esau bore against Jacob because of the blessing which he had obtained (v. 41). Esau's hatred of Jacob was:

1.1. A hatred without cause. He hated him for no other reason than that his father blessed him and God loved him.

1.2. A cruel hatred. Nothing less would satisfy him than to kill his brother.

1.3. A hatred based on power. He expected his father to die soon, and then claims and entitlements would be fought over by the brothers, which would give him a fair opportunity for revenge.

2. The method Rebekah followed to stop the trouble from happening:

2.1. She warned Jacob of the danger he was in and advised him to withdraw for a while and move for his own safety. Notice here:

2.1.1. What Rebekah feared, that she *should be deprived of them both in one day* (v. 45).

2.1.2. What Rebekah hoped, that if Jacob kept out of sight for a while, the resentment which his brother held so fiercely would gradually leave him.

2.2. She impressed on Isaac the necessity of Jacob's going among her relatives for another reason, which was to take a wife (v. 46).

CHAPTER 28

We have here: 1. Jacob leaving his parents, to go to Paddan Aram; the commands his father gave him (vv. 1–2), the blessing he sent him away with (vv. 3–4), his obedience to the orders given him (vv. 5, 10), and the influence this had on Esau (vv. 6–9). 2. Jacob meeting with God and his fellowship with him. And then his vision of the ladder or stairway (vv. 11–12), and the gracious promises God made him (vv. 13–15). 3. The impression this made on him (vv. 16–19) and the vow he made to God on this occasion (vv. 20–22).

Verses 1–5

Jacob had no sooner obtained the blessing than he was immediately forced to flee from his country. Now *Jacob fled into Syria* (Hos 12:12). He was blessed with plenty of grain and wine, but he went away poor; was blessed as a ruler, but went out to hard labor. This was:

- Perhaps to correct him for his deceitful dealings with his father. The blessing will be confirmed to him, but he would suffer for the deceitful way in which he went about obtaining it.
- To teach us that those who inherit the blessing must also expect persecution; those who have peace in Christ will have trouble in the world (Jn 16:33). Now Jacob is here dismissed by his father:

1. With a solemn commandment: *He blessed him, and charged him* (vv. 1–2). Those who have the blessing must keep the commands attached to it and not think of separating what God has joined together. If Jacob is to be an heir of promise, he must *not take a wife of the daughters of Canaan*; those who profess religion should not marry those who are irreligious.

2. With a solemn blessing (vv. 3–4). He had before blessed him unintentionally; now he does so deliberately, to give greater encouragement to Jacob in the sad situation to which he was now moving. This blessing is more specific and fuller than the former; it is the inheritance of the blessing of Abraham. The blessing of Abraham is a Gospel blessing; it is a blessing from God Almighty, by which name God appeared to the patriarchs (Ex 6:3). Isaac gives Jacob:

2.1. The promise of heirs: *God make thee fruitful, and multiply thee* (v. 3).

2.1.1. Never was such a multitude of people so often gathered into one assembly as the tribes of Israel were in the desert and afterward.

2.1.2. From his body would descend from Abraham that person in whom all the families of the earth would be blessed, for all things in heaven and earth are united in Christ (Eph 1:10).

2.2. The promise of an inheritance for those heirs: *That thou mayest inherit the land wherein thou art a stranger* (v. 4). In this way Canaan was passed on to the descendants of Jacob, excluding the descendants of Esau. He is told here that he would inherit the land in which he now lived as a stranger. Those have the best enjoyment of present things who sit most loose to them. This was the better country, which Jacob, with the other patriarchs, had in his sights, when he confessed himself *a stranger and pilgrim upon the earth* (Heb 11:13). Away he went to Paddan Aram (v. 5).

Verses 6–9

This passage concerning Esau comes in the middle of Jacob's story, either:

1. To show the influence of a good example. Esau, though the greater man, now begins to think Jacob the better man, and is not ashamed to use him as his example in this particular instance of marrying a daughter of Abraham. Or:

2. To show the folly of an afterthought. Esau did well, but he did it when it was too late. He *saw that the daughters of Canaan pleased not his father*, and he might have

seen that long before if he had considered his father's judgment as much as he did his own taste. And how did he now resolve the matter? Why, so as to make bad matters even worse. He married a daughter of Ishmael, the son of the slave woman, who was got rid of. He did it only to please his father, not to please God. He rested in a partially reformed life.

Verses 10–15

We see here Jacob on his journey toward Syria, in a very desolate condition. The first night, he had made a long day's journey from Beersheba to Bethel, about fifty miles (about eighty kilometers). There he had:

1. A hard resting-place (v. 11), the *stones for his pillows*, and the sky for his canopy and curtains.

2. In his hard resting-place, a pleasant dream. Indeed any Israelite would be willing to rest on Jacob's pillow, if they might have Jacob's dream. There and then, he *heard the words of God, and saw the visions of the Almighty* (Nu 24:4). It was the best night's sleep he had ever had in his life. Notice:

2.1. The encouraging vision Jacob saw (v. 12). He saw a ladder or stairway, which reached from earth to heaven, with angels ascending and descending on it and God himself at its head. Now this represents:

2.1.1. The providence of God, by which there is a constant fellowship kept up between heaven and earth. Providence does its work gradually. The wisdom of God is at the upper end of the stairway, directing all the movement of secondary causes to the glory of the Prime Mover, the First Cause. This vision gave comfort to Jacob just at the right time, letting him know that he had both a good guide and a good guard, in his going out and coming in.

2.1.2. The mediation of Christ. Christ is this stairway, the foot on earth in his human nature, the top in heaven in his divine nature: or the former in his humiliation, the latter in his exaltation. If God lives with us, and we live with him, it is because of Christ. We have no way of getting to heaven, except by this stairway; if we climb up any other way, we are thieves and robbers (Jn 10:8). Our Savior alludes to this vision when he speaks of the angels of God *ascending and descending upon the Son of man* (Jn 1:51).

2.2. The encouraging words Jacob heard:

2.2.1. The former promises made to his father were repeated and confirmed to him (vv. 13–14). In general, God showed to him that he would be the same to him that he had been to Abraham and Isaac. The land of Canaan is settled on him. He is promised that his descendants would multiply exceedingly as the dust of the earth. It is added that the Messiah would come from his body, in whom all the families of the earth would be blessed.

2.2.2. Fresh promises were made to him:

2.2.2.1. Jacob was apprehensive of the danger from his brother Esau; but God promises to keep him.

2.2.2.2. Jacob had now a long journey before him and had to travel alone, along unknown ways, to an unknown country; but, *behold, I am with thee*, says God.

2.2.2.3. Jacob did not know, but God knew, what hardships he would encounter in his uncle's service, and so God promises to preserve him in all places. He was now going as an exile to a faraway place, but God promises to bring him back again to this land. He seemed to be abandoned by all his friends, but God here gives him this assurance, *I will not leave thee.* Those whom God loves, he never leaves.

Verses 16–22

Jacob's sleep had been very pleasant to him. Here we are told about his devotion on this occasion:

1. He expressed a great surprise at the signs he had received of God's special presence with him in that place: *Surely the Lord is in this place and I knew it not* (v. 16). God can give undeniable demonstrations of his presence and assurances that cannot be communicated to others, but that are convincing to themselves. No place excludes divine appearances (16:13); wherever we are, in the city or in the desert, in the house or in the field, in the shop or in the street.

2. He was awestruck (v. 17): *He was afraid*. He said, *How dreadful is this place!* What he saw there at this time was, as it were, *the house of God*, and *the gate of heaven*.

3. He took care to mark its remembrance in two ways:

3.1. He set up the stone as a pillar (v. 18), because he did not then have time to build an altar there, as Abraham did in the places where God appeared to him (12:7). He therefore *poured oil on the top of this stone*, an altar when he was able to, as he later did, in gratitude to God for this vision (35:7). The privilege of receiving God's mercy calls for a response of duty, and the sweet fellowship we have with God ought always to be remembered.

3.2. He gave a new name to the place (v. 19). It had been called *Luz*, meaning "an almond tree"; but he wanted it from now on to be called *Beth-el*, meaning "the house of God."

4. He made a solemn vow on this occasion (vv. 20–22). When God confirms his promises to us, it is proper for us to repeat our promises back to him. Now in this vow notice:

4.1. Jacob's faith. God had said (v. 15), *I am with thee, and will keep thee*. Jacob takes hold of this and infers, "I will depend on this." God's promises are to guide and rule our desires and expectations.

4.2. Jacob's great modesty and great moderation in his desires. He is cheerfully content to have bread to eat and clothes to put on. By nature we are content with a little and by grace it can be even less.

4.3. Jacob's godliness and his concern for God, which appear here:

4.3.1. In what he desired, that God would be with him and keep him.

4.3.2. In what he decided. His decision is:

4.3.2.1. In general, to remain faithful to the Lord, as his God in the covenant: *Then shall the Lord be my God.*

4.3.2.2. In particular, to perform some special acts of devotion, as a sign of his gratitude. Firstly, "This pillar will stay here till I come back in peace, and then an altar will be erected here to the honor of God." Secondly, "The house of God will not be unfurnished, nor his altar without a sacrifice: *Of all that thou shalt give me I will surely give the tenth unto thee*, to be spent either on God's altars or on his poor," both of which receive from him in the world.

CHAPTER 29

This chapter gives us an account of God's providences concerning Jacob. 1. How he was brought safely to his journey's end (vv. 1–14). 2. How he was married (vv. 15–30). 3. How his family was built up in the birth of four sons (vv. 31–35).

Verses 1–8

1. We are here told how cheerfully he proceeded in his journey after the sweet fellowship he had with God at Bethel: "Then Jacob lifted up his feet"; so the margin reads (v. 1).

2. Notice how happily he arrived at his journey's end. Providence brought him to the very field where his uncle's flocks were to be watered, and there he met Rachel, who was to be his wife. Divine Providence is to be acknowledged in all the detailed circumstances which go to make a journey or any other undertaking encouraging and successful. If we meet with those who can direct us, we must not say that it was by chance, but that it was at such times God in his providence who was favoring us. What is here said of the constant care of the shepherds concerning their sheep (vv. 2–3, 7–8) may serve to illustrate the tender concern which our Lord Jesus, the great Shepherd of the sheep, has for his flock, the church; for he is the Good Shepherd, who knows his sheep, and is known by them (Jn 10:14). When all the shepherds came together with their flocks, then, like loving neighbors, at watering-time, they watered their flocks together.

It is right that we should speak politely and respectfully to strangers. *The law of kindness in the tongue* has a commanding power (Pr 31:26).

Verses 9–14

Here we see:

1. Rachel's humility and industry: *She kept her father's sheep* (v. 9).

2. Jacob's tenderness and affection. When he understood that this was a relative, he was greatly attentive and keen to serve her.

3. It is without reason that some of the Jewish writers think that Jacob, when he kissed Rachel, wept because he had been robbed on his journey by Eliphaz the eldest son of Esau, at the command of his father, of all his money and jewels, which his mother had given him when she sent him away. It is clear that it was his passion for Rachel and the surprise of this happy meeting that drew these tears from his eyes.

4. Laban, though not the best-humored of men, made him welcome and was satisfied with the account he gave of himself and the reason for coming in such poor circumstances.

Verses 15–30

Here is:

1. The reasonable agreement made between Laban and Jacob, during the month that Jacob spent there as a guest (v. 14). Now Jacob had a good opportunity to make known to Laban the affection he had for his daughter Rachel; and, owning no worldly goods which he could endow her with, he promises him seven years' service, on condition that, at the end of the seven years, Laban would give Rachel to Jacob as his wife.

2. Jacob's honest performance of his part of the bargain (v. 20). Jacob honestly served out his seven years. *They seemed to him but a few days, for the love he had to her* (v. 20), as if it were more his desire to earn her than to have her.

3. Laban's deceitful fraud in his part of the bargain, when at the end of seven years, he put Leah into Jacob's arms instead of Rachel (v. 23). This was Laban's sin; he wronged both Jacob and Rachel. It is easy to observe here how Jacob was treated as he had treated others. He had cheated his own father when he pretended to be Esau, and now his father-in-law cheated him.

4. The excuse and amends Laban made for the deception:

4.1. The excuse was a lame one: *It must not be so done in our country* (v. 26). There was no such custom in his country as he pretended. He mocks Jacob with it and scorns his mistake.

4.2. His adding to the matter only made things even worse: *We will give thee this also* (v. 27). In so doing he drew Jacob into the sin, trap, and distress of having several wives, which remains a stain on his reputation. Honest Jacob did not plan this. He could not refuse Rachel, for he was pledged to be married to her; still less could he refuse Leah, for he had married her. The polygamy of the patriarchs was to some degree excusable in them, because, though there was a reason against it as old as Adam's marriage (Mal 2:15), there still was no explicit command against it; they acted sinfully out of ignorance. It by no means justifies this practice now, when God's will is plainly made known, that one man and one woman only must be joined together in marriage (1Co 7:2). Dr. Lightfoot considers that Leah and Rachel prefigure the two churches, the Jews under the Law and the Gentiles under the Gospel: the younger the more beautiful, and more in the thoughts of Christ when he came in the form of a servant; but the other, like Leah, first taken into marriage.

Verses 31–35

We have here the birth of four of Jacob's sons, all by Leah. Notice:

1. That Leah, who was less loved, was blessed with children, while Rachel was denied that blessing (v. 31).

2. The names she gave her children showed her great respect both to God and to her husband. She called her firstborn *Reuben*, meaning "see a son"; the name sounds like the Hebrew for "he has seen my misery": with that this pleasant thought, *Now will my husband love me*. She called her second son *Simeon*, which probably means "one who hears": *because the Lord had heard*; her third son *Levi* (derived from the Hebrew for "joined"), with this expectation, *Now will my husband be joined unto me* (v. 34). She thankfully acknowledges the kind providence of God in it: *The Lord hath looked upon my affliction* (v. 32). "*The Lord hath heard that I was hated, he has therefore given me this son.*" Her fourth she called *Judah* (meaning "praise"), saying, *Now will I praise the Lord* (v. 35). And this was the one from whom, in his human ancestry, Christ came. He descended from the one whose name meant "praise," for he is our praise. Is Christ formed in my heart? *Now will I praise the Lord.*

CHAPTER 30

In this chapter we have an account of the growth: 1. Of Jacob's family. Eight children more we find recorded in this chapter (vv. 1–24). 2. Of Jacob's wealth. He makes a new agreement with Laban (vv. 25–34). And in the seven years' further service he did for Laban, God wonderfully blessed him, so that his stock of cattle became very large (vv. 35–43).

Verses 1–13

We have here the bad consequences of that strange marriage which Jacob made with the two sisters. Here is:

1. An unhappy disagreement between him and Rachel (vv. 1–2), which was brought about, not so much by her own barrenness as by her sister's fruitfulness.

1.1. Rachel becomes jealous. She *envied her sister* (v. 1). Envy is desiring to have the advantage that another person has; this is a sin in God's sight and hurts our neighbor and ourselves.

1.2. Jacob rebukes her and justly so. He loved Rachel and so rebuked her for what she wrongly said (v. 2). Faithful rebukes are products and instances of true affection (Ps 141:5; Pr 27:5–6). He was angry, not at the person, but at the sin; he expressed himself so as to show his displeasure. It was a very serious and devout reply which Jacob gave to Rachel's fractious demand: *Am I in God's stead?* The Aramaic has, "Do you ask sons of me? Ought you not to ask them from before the Lord?" The Arabic reads, "Am I above God? Can I give you what God denies you?"

2. An unhappy agreement between him and the two maidservants.

2.1. At the persuasion of Rachel, he took her maidservant Bilhah as his wife, that, according to the custom of those times, his children by her might be adopted and acknowledged as her mistress's children (vv. 3–8). Rachel would rather have children to preserve her good name than none at all, children that she might consider to be her own, and call her own, though they were not so. She takes pleasure in giving them names that carry in them nothing but marks of imitation of her sister, as if she had overcome her:

2.1.1. In law. She calls the first son of her maidservant Dan ("he has vindicated"), saying, *God hath judged me* (v. 6), that is, "God has vindicated me."

2.1.2. In battle. She calls the next Naphtali ("my struggle"), saying, *I have wrestled with my sister, and have prevailed* (v. 8); as if all Jacob's sons must be born men of war.

2.2. At the persuasion of Leah, he took Zilpah her maidservant to be his wife as well (v. 9). Zilpah bore two sons to Jacob, and one she called *Gad* (v. 11), meaning "good fortune" or "a troop": she promised herself a little "troop" of children. The other she called *Asher*, "happy," thinking herself happy in him. There was much that was wrong in the contest and competition between these two sisters, but God brought good out of this evil. In this way, Jacob's family was stocked with twelve sons, heads of the thousands of Israel, from whom the celebrated twelve tribes descended and were named.

Verses 14–24

Here we see:

1. That Reuben, a little boy, perhaps about seven years old, playing in the field, found *mandrakes, dudaiym*. It is uncertain exactly what these plants were, but they were very pleasant to the smell and were superstitiously thought to induce pregnancy when eaten. There are products of the earth in open fields, as well as in protected gardens, that are very valuable and useful. It is a praiseworthy custom of the devout Jews, when they find pleasure, for example, in eating an apple, to lift up their hearts, and say, "Blessed be he that made this fruit pleasant!" Or, in smelling a flower, "Blessed be he that made this flower sweet." Whatever the mandrakes were, Rachel could not bear to see them in Leah's hands, where the child had placed them; she longed for them. Bishop Patrick very well suggests here that the true reason of this contest between Jacob's wives for his company, and their giving him their maidservants to be his wives, was the earnest desire they had to fulfill the promise made to Abraham that his descendants should be as many as the stars of heaven. And he thinks it would have been below the dignity of this sacred history to take such particular notice of these things if there had not been some such great significance in them. Leah was now blessed with two sons; the first she called *Issachar*

(which sounds like the Hebrew for "reward"), considering herself well repaid for her mandrakes. The other she called *Zebulun* ("honor"), acknowledging God's goodness to her: *God has endowed me with a good dowry* (v. 20). She reckons a family of children not in purely monetary terms but as a precious gift (Ps 113:9). Mention is made (v. 21) of the birth of a daughter, *Dinah*, because of the following story concerning her (34:1–31).

2. Rachel fruitful at last (v. 22). She gives birth to a son and said, *He has taken away my reproach*. Then Rachel called her son *Joseph*, which in Hebrew means "may he add": *The Lord shall add to me another son*.

Verses 25–36

We have here:

1. Jacob's thoughts of home. He faithfully completed his time with Laban, even his second time of testing. He retained his affection for the land of Canaan, not only because it was the land of his birth, and his father and mother were there, whom he longed to see, but also because it was the Land of Promise.

2. Laban's desire that he should stay (v. 27). Out of love to himself, not to Jacob or to his wives or children, Laban tries to persuade him to continue as his chief shepherd. Rude and selfish people know how to give good words when it serves their own ends. Laban found that his livestock and wealth had wonderfully increased with Jacob's good management, and he acknowledges it, with expressions of respect both toward God and Jacob: *I have learned by experience that the Lord has blessed me for thy sake*.

3. The new agreement they came to. Laban's cunning and covetousness took advantage of Jacob's plainness, honesty, and good nature. Jacob accordingly makes a proposal.

3.1. He shows what reason he had to insist on so much, considering:

3.1.1. That Laban was bound in gratitude to see him well looked after. But here note how he speaks, like himself, very modestly. Humble saints take more pleasure in doing good than in hearing about their actions.

3.1.2. That he himself was bound in duty to take care of his own family.

3.2. He is willing to turn to the providence of God, which, he knew, extends to the smallest things, even the appearance of the cattle; and he will be content to have for his wages the sheep and goats of such and such a color, speckled, spotted, and dark-colored, which would later be brought out (vv. 32–33). Laban was willing to agree to this because he thought if the few he had that were now speckled and spotted were separated from the rest, which they agreed was to be done immediately, the body of the flock which Jacob was to tend, all being of one color, either all black or all white, would produce few or none of mixed colors, and so he would have Jacob's service for nothing or next to nothing.

Verses 37–43

Now Jacob's plan was to set peeled branches before the cattle where they were watered, that, looking a great deal at those unusual parti-colored sticks, by the power of imagination they might produce young ones that were parti-colored in the same way (vv. 37–39). Probably this custom was commonly used by the shepherds of Canaan, who wanted their cattle to have this motley color. When he began to have a stock of *ringstraked* and dark, he planned to put them first and to set the faces of the rest toward them, with the same intention as in the former plan. Thus *Jacob increased exceedingly* (v. 43), and grew very rich in a short time. Those who, while their beginning is small, are humble and upright, contented and industrious, are likely to see great increase later in life. Those who are faithful in a little will be entrusted with more. Those who are faithful in what belongs to others will be entrusted with something of their own. Jacob, who had been a just servant, became a rich master.

CHAPTER 31

Jacob was a man of great devotion and integrity, but he had more trouble and anxiety than any of the patriarchs. Here is: 1. His decision to return (vv. 1–16). 2. His secret departure (vv. 17–21). 3. Laban's angry pursuit of him (vv. 22–25). 4. The angry words that passed between them (vv. 26–42). 5. Their amicable agreement eventually (vv. 43–55).

Verses 1–16

Jacob here decides immediately to leave his uncle's service, to take what he had and go back to Canaan. He was provoked into this decision:

1. For Laban and his sons had become very ill natured toward him. Laban's sons showed their ill will in what they said (v. 1). Laban himself said little, but his attitude toward Jacob was not what it used to be, and Jacob noticed it (vv. 2, 5). He was always churlish, but now he was even more churlish than before.

2. By divine direction and in accordance with a promise: *The Lord said unto Jacob, Return, and I will be with thee* (v. 3). He had gone there by orders from heaven, and he would stay there till he was ordered back. It is our duty to put ourselves under God's guidance, in all the comings and goings of our lives. Jacob was also encouraged by what is said in v. 13, *I am the God of Beth-el*. This was the place where the covenant was renewed with him. *Now arise* (v. 13) *and return*:

2.1. To your devotions in Canaan, the seriousness of which had perhaps been greatly interrupted while he was with Laban.

2.2. To your comforts in Canaan: *Return to the land of thy kindred* (v. 13).

3. With the knowledge and agreement of his wives. He sent for Rachel and Leah to come to him in the field (v. 4), so that he might speak with them more privately. Husbands who love their wives will communicate their thoughts and intentions to them. Where there is a mutual affection, there will be a mutual confidence. He told them of the command God had given him, in a dream, to return to his own country (v. 13), so that they might not suspect his decision to be as a result of a lack of devotion or any dislike of their country or family, but might see that it came from the desire to obey his God. His wives happily agreed to his decision. They were willing to go along with their husband and put themselves with him under divine direction: *Whatsoever God hath said unto thee do* (v. 16).

Verses 17–24

Here is:

1. Jacob's fleeing from Laban. It was honorably undertaken: he took no more than his own with him, the *cattle of his getting* (v. 18). He took what Providence gave him and was content with that. But Rachel was not as honest as her husband; she *stole her father's images* (v. 19)

and carried them away with her. The Hebrew calls them *teraphim*. Some think they were only little representations of the ancestors of the family, in statues or pictures, which Rachel had a particular fondness for, and wanted to have with her, now that she was going to another country. Or they may have been idols for religious use, household gods, either worshiped or consulted as oracles. We are willing to hope that she took them away with the aim of convincing her father of the folly of his regard for those gods which could not keep themselves safe (Isa 46:1–2).

2. Laban's pursuit of Jacob. News was brought to him on the third day that Jacob had fled. He pursued him seven days (v. 23). But the truth is, bad people are more passionate in their anger than in their love. God intervened in the quarrel, rebuking Laban and sheltering Jacob, and charging Laban not to *speak unto him either good or bad* (v. 24). A similar Hebrew expression occurs in 24:50. God comes to him, and with one word ties his hands, though he does not turn his heart. The safety of good people owes a lot to the grip God has on the consciences of bad people and the access he has to them.

Verses 25–35

We have here the reasoning, not to say the rallying, that took place between Laban and Jacob at their meeting in that mountain which was afterward called *Gilead* (v. 25). Here is:

1. The grave charge which Laban brought against him. He accuses him:

1.1. As a renegade who had unjustly deserted his service. To represent Jacob as a criminal, he will have it thought that he intended to be kind to his daughters (vv. 27–28). It is common for bad people, when they are disappointed in their wicked plans, to pretend that their intentions were purely kind and fair.

1.2. As a thief (v. 30): *Wherefore hast thou stolen my gods?* How foolish! To call his own those gods that could be stolen! Could he expect protection from those that could neither resist nor reveal who had taken them? Enemies may steal our goods, but not our God.

2. Jacob's defense of himself.

2.1. As to the charge of carrying off his own wives, he clears himself by giving the true reason (v. 31). He feared that Laban would take away his daughters by force, and so make him, because of his affection for his wives, to continue in his service.

2.2. As to the charge of stealing Laban's gods, he pleads not guilty (v. 32). He not only did not take them himself (he did not want them), but also he did not know that they were taken.

3. The diligent search Laban made for his gods (vv. 33–35). We do not find that he searched Jacob's flocks for stolen cattle; but he searched the tent for stolen gods. Laban, after all his searches, did not find his gods, but was frustrated in all his rummaging: Rachel had put them inside her camel's saddle (v. 34). Our God will not only be found by those who seek him, but they will find him to be their rich rewarder.

Verses 36–42

See in these verses:

1. The power of provocation. Jacob's natural temper was mild and calm, but Laban's unreasonable behavior toward him made him very angry (vv. 36–37).

2. The comfort of a good conscience. Those who in any employment have dealt faithfully, if they cannot gain the honor from it with others, will still be able to draw strength from it within their own selves.

3. The character of a good servant and particularly of a faithful shepherd:

3.1. He was very careful, so that the sheep did not miscarry through his oversight or neglect.

3.2. He was very honest and took nothing to eat which was not allowed him.

3.3. He was very hard-working (v. 40). He stuck to his business in all weathers.

4. The character of a hard taskmaster. Laban had been such to Jacob. Those are bad masters:

4.1. Who exact from their servants what is unjust, by obliging them to make good what is not damaged through any fault of theirs. Laban did this (v. 39).

4.2. Who deny to their servants what is just and equitable. Laban did this (v. 41). It was unreasonable for him to make Jacob serve time for his daughters, when he had the prospect of inheriting a great estate secured to him by the promise of God himself.

5. The care of Providence for the protection of injured innocence (v. 42). God took notice of the wrong done to Jacob and rewarded him whom Laban would otherwise have sent away empty. Jacob speaks of God as the God of Abraham, and the fear of Isaac, for Abraham was dead, and had gone to that world where perfect love drives out fear; but Isaac was still alive, sanctifying the Lord in his heart, as the One whom he had fear and awe for.

Verses 43–55

We have here the compromise agreed on between Laban and Jacob. Laban had nothing to say in reply to Jacob's protest: he could neither justify himself nor condemn Jacob, but was convicted by his own conscience of the wrong he had done him.

1. Laban begins with a profession of kindness for Jacob's wives and children (v. 43): *These daughters are my daughters.* When he cannot excuse what he has done, he does, in effect, acknowledge what he should have done; he should have treated them as his own, but he had regarded them as strangers (v. 15).

2. Laban proposes a covenant of friendship between them, to which Jacob readily agrees, without insisting on Laban's submission, much less his restitution. Peace and love are such valuable jewels that we can scarcely pay too much for them. It is better to sit down as losers than to go to war.

2.1. The substance of this covenant. Jacob left it wholly to Laban to settle:

2.1.1. That Jacob should be a good husband to his wives. Jacob had never given him any cause to suspect that he would be anything other than a kind husband, but as if he had, he was willing to commit himself to this.

2.1.2. That Jacob should never be a bad neighbor to Laban (v. 52). It was agreed that Jacob would forgive and forget all the wrongs he had received.

2.2. The ceremony of this covenant. It was made and confirmed with great solemnity, according to the practice in those times:

2.2.1. A pillar was erected (v. 45), and a heap of stones raised (v. 46), to mark its remembrance forever.

2.2.2. A sacrifice was offered (v. 54), a sacrifice of peace offerings. Our peace with God is what puts true strength into our peace with our friends. If different groups strive against each other, the reconciliation of both to him will facilitate their reconciliation to one another.

2.2.3. They ate bread together (v. 46), jointly sharing in the food of the sacrifice (v. 54). Covenants of friendship were in ancient times confirmed by the parties eating and drinking together. It was like a love feast.

2.2.4. They solemnly appealed to God concerning their sincerity in it:

2.2.4.1. As a witness (v. 49): *The Lord watch between me and thee.* When we are out of one another's sight, let this restrain us, that wherever we are we are under God's eye.

2.2.4.2. As a Judge (v. 53). *The God of Abraham* (from whom Jacob was descended), *and the God of Nahor* (from whom Laban was descended), *the God of their father* (the common ancestor, from whom they both were descended), *judge between us.* God's relationship with them is expressed to show that they worshiped one and the same God, as a result of which there ought to be no enmity between them.

2.2.5. They gave a new name to the place (vv. 47–48). Laban called it in Aramaic, and Jacob in Hebrew, "the heap of witness"; and (v. 49) it was called *Mizpah,* "a watchtower." These names are applicable to the seals of the Gospel covenant, which are witnesses to us if we are faithful, but witnesses against us if we are false. The name Jacob gave this heap (*Galeed*) remained with it, not the name Laban gave it. In all this encounter, Laban was noisy and wordy, saying much; Jacob was silent and said little.

Lastly, after all this angry talk, they part company as friends (v. 55).

CHAPTER 32

We have here Jacob still on his journey toward Canaan. Never did so many memorable things occur on any journey as on this journey of Jacob's little family. On his way he: 1. Meets with good news from his God (vv. 1–2). 2. Meets with bad news from his brother, to whom he sent a message to inform him of his return (vv. 3–6). In his distress he divides his company (vv. 7–8). 3. Makes his prayer to God (vv. 9–12). 4. Sends a present to his brother (vv. 13–23). 5. Wrestles with the angel (vv. 24–32).

Verses 1–2

Here is:

1. Jacob's escort on his journey (v. 1): *The angels of God met him,* in a visible appearance. Whether he saw them in a vision by day or in a dream by night, as when he saw them on the ladder (28:12), is uncertain. They had accompanied him invisibly all along, but now they appeared to him, because he had greater dangers before him than those he had encountered up to that time. God, however, wants us, when we are at peace, to prepare for trouble, and, when trouble comes, to live on our former observations and experiences, for *we walk by faith, not by sight* (2Co 5:7). God's people, at death, return to Canaan, to their Father's house, and then the angels of God will meet them.

2. The encouraging notice he took of this escort (v. 2). *This is God's host.* To remember this favor, Jacob gave a name to the place, *Mahanaim,* "two encampments," one on either side, or one in the front and the other in the rear, to protect him from Laban at the back and Esau in front, that they might guard him completely. In this way, he is surrounded by God's favor. Perhaps in allusion to this the church is called *two armies* (SS 6:13). Here were Jacob's family, which made one army, represent-

ing the church militant at war on earth; and the angels, another army, representing the church triumphant at rest in heaven.

Verses 3–8

Jacob takes the occasion to remind himself of the enemies he had, particularly Esau. It is probable that Rebekah had sent him word of Esau's settlement in Seir, and that his hostility to him continued. What will poor Jacob do? He longs to see his father, and yet he dreads to see his brother.

1. He sends a very kind and humble message to Esau. Kind and polite acts may help to end hostilities.

1.1. He calls Esau his *lord,* himself his servant, to show that he did not insist on the prerogatives of the birthright and blessing he had obtained for himself.

1.2. He gives him a brief account of himself, that he was not a restless wanderer, and that he was not a beggar, nor did he come home like the prodigal son empty-handed and likely to be a burden to his relatives. And:

1.3. He seeks his favor: *I have sent, that I might find grace in thy sight.*

2. He receives a very formidable account of Esau's warlike preparations against him (v. 6), *He comes to meet thee, and four hundred men with him.*

2.1. He remembers the old quarrel and wants now to be avenged on him for the birthright and blessing, and if possible to defeat Jacob's expectations of both. Angry people have long memories.

2.2. He envies Jacob what little possessions he had, and although he himself now has much more, he only wants to gloat over Jacob's ruin and fill his fields with Jacob's possessions.

2.3. He concludes that it is easy to destroy him, now that he was on the road, a poor, weary traveler with no settled abode, and, as he thinks, unguarded.

2.4. He decides to act suddenly, and before Jacob had come to his father, in case he should intervene and mediate between them. He marches out, spurred on with rage; he had with him 400 men, and now breathing out murderous threats. A tenth of this number would be enough to completely destroy poor Jacob and his innocent, helpless family. Jacob, even though he had great faith, was now very afraid. A real awareness and fear of danger may very well exist alongside a humble confidence in God's power and promises. Christ himself, in his agony, was greatly troubled.

3. He puts himself into the best defensive position that his present circumstances will permit. It was absurd to think of resisting; his only plan is to escape (vv. 7–8). He divided his company, not as Abraham (14:15) to fight, but to flee.

Verses 9–12

We should call on God in times of trouble; and here we have an example of this. Its success encourages us to follow this example. In his distress he sought the Lord, and he heard him. Times of fear should become times of prayer; whatever frightens us should drive us to our knees and to our God. Now it is worthwhile inquiring what was so extraordinary in this prayer that it should gain all this honor for Jacob.

1. The request itself is one and very explicit: *Deliver me from the hand of my brother* (v. 11).

2. The pleas are many and very powerful; no case has ever been put as carefully (Job 23:4). He makes his request with great faith, fervency, and humility.

2.1. He speaks to God as the God of his fathers (v. 9). Such was his humble self-denial and the sense he had of his own unworthiness that he did not call God his own God, but a God in covenant with his ancestors. God's covenant with our fathers may encourage us when we are in distress.

2.2. He brings out his authorization: *Thou saidst unto me, Return unto thy country.* We may be going where God calls us and still think our way is obstructed by thorns and thistles. If God is our guide, he will also be our guard.

2.3. He humbly acknowledges his own unworthiness to receive any favor from God (v. 10): *I am not worthy*; it is an unusual plea. Christ never commended any of his petitioners so much as him who said, *Lord, I am not worthy* (Mt 8:8), and her who said, *Truth, Lord, yet the dogs eat of the crumbs which fall from their master's table* (Mt 15:27). Now notice:

2.3.1. How honorably and awesomely he speaks of the mercies of God to him.

2.3.2. How simply and humbly he speaks of himself, renouncing all thought of his own merit: "*I am not worthy of the least of all thy mercies*, much less am I worthy of so great a favor as this I am now seeking." "I am less than all thy mercies," is the meaning. It is those who are best prepared for the greatest mercies who see themselves unworthy of the least.

2.4. He acknowledges with gratitude God's goodness to him in his travels and how much it had exceeded his expectations: "*With my staff I passed over this Jordan,* poor and desolate, like a forlorn and despised pilgrim"; "*and now I have become two bands,* now I am surrounded by a numerous and strong retinue of children and servants."

2.5. He pleads the extremity of the danger he was in: *Lord, deliver me from Esau, for I fear him* (v. 11). The people of God have not been reluctant to tell God their fears. The fear that stirs us to pray can itself be prayed about.

2.6. He especially asserts the promise God had made him (v. 9): *Thou saidst, I will deal well with thee,* and again, at the end (v. 12): *Thou saidst, I will surely do thee good.* The best we can say to God in prayer is what he has already said to us.

Verses 13–23

Jacob, having devoutly made God his friend in prayer, here prudently tries to make Esau his friend by a present. He had prayed to God to deliver him from Esau's hand, and his prayer did not make him presume on God's mercy without doing anything. When we have prayed to God for any mercy, we must back up our prayers with our endeavors. To pacify Esau:

1. Jacob sent him a very noble present of cattle, 580 in all (vv. 13–15). It was a present that he thought would be acceptable to Esau, who had dealt so much in hunting wild animals that perhaps he had few tame cattle in his livestock. Peace and love, even though they cost us a great deal, will prove the expense well spent. Jacob forgives and forgets.

2. Jacob sent him a very humble message, which he ordered his servants to deliver most courteously (vv. 17–18). They must call Esau their *lord,* and Jacob his *servant;* they must tell him the cattle they had were a small present which Jacob had sent him. They must especially take care to tell him that Jacob was coming behind (vv. 18–20), that he might not suspect he had fled through fear. If Jacob seems not to be afraid of Esau, Esau, it may be hoped, will not be a terror to Jacob.

Verses 24–32

We have here the remarkable story of Jacob's wrestling with the angel and prevailing, which is referred to in Hos 12:4. Very early in the morning, a great while before day, Jacob had helped his wives and his children over the stream, and he wanted to be by himself and was alone, so that he could again fully spread out his cares and fears before God in prayer. While Jacob was earnest in prayer, *stirring up himself to take hold on God,* an angel takes hold of him. Some think this was the *angel of his presence* (Isa 63:9), one of those that wait on the *Shechinah,* the divine majesty. Others think it was the eternal Word, the Angel of the covenant. Notice:

1. How Jacob and this angel struggled (v. 24). Jacob was now full of anxiety and fear about the meeting he expected the next day with his brother, and God himself seemed to oppose his entrance into the Land of Promise. We are told by the prophet (Hos 12:4) how *Jacob wrestled:* he *wept, and made supplication;* prayers and tears were his weapons.

2. What the outcome was of the struggle:

2.1. Jacob kept his ground; though the struggle continued for a long time, the angel *prevailed not against him* (v. 25), that is, this discouragement did not overpower him by shaking his faith or silencing his prayer. It was not in his own strength that he wrestled, nor by his own strength that he prevailed, but in and by strength derived from heaven. We cannot prevail with God except in God's own strength. It is his Spirit that intercedes in us and *helps our infirmities* (Ro 8:26).

2.2. The angel put the socket of Jacob's thigh out of joint. Some think that Jacob felt little or no pain from this hurt; he probably did not, for he did not stop until the struggle was over (v. 31), and, if so, this was evidence of a truly divine touch, which wounded and healed at the same time.

2.3. The angel, with extraordinary condescension, mildly requests Jacob to let him go (v. 26), as God said to Moses (Ex 32:10), *Let me alone.* In this way, he wanted to honor Jacob's faith and prayer and also test his faithfulness.

2.4. Jacob persists in his holy boldness: *I will not let thee go, except thou bless me.* The gaining of a conquest will do him no good without the benefit of a blessing. In begging this blessing he acknowledges his inferiority, though he seemed to have the upper hand in the struggle.

2.5. The angel puts a lasting mark of honor upon Jacob, by changing his name (vv. 27–28): "You are a brave fighter," the angel says, "a man of heroic resolution; what is your name?" "Jacob," he says, meaning "he grasps the heel" (Hos 12:3), figuratively, "he deceives." "Well," the angel says, "you will be called *Israel, a prince with God,* a name greater than those of the great people of the earth." Jacob is here knighted in the field, as it were, and has a title of honor which will remain to his praise to the end of time. Yet this was not all; having power with God, he will have power with human beings too.

2.6. He dismisses him with a blessing (v. 29). Instead of telling him his name, he gave him his blessing, which was the thing he wrestled for. Sharing in the angel's blessing is better than knowing his name. The tree of life is better than the tree of knowledge.

2.7. Jacob gives a new name to the place; he calls it *Peniel,* meaning "face of God" (v. 30). The name he gives to the place preserves forever not the honor of his valor or victory, but only the honor of God's free grace. "In this place I saw God face to face, and my life was preserved";

not, "It was to my praise that I came out as a conqueror," but, "It was because of God's mercy that I escaped with my life."

3. The record Jacob carried of this in his bones: *He halted on his thigh* (v. 31). The honor and encouragement he obtained by this struggle more than compensated for the hurt he received, even though he went limping to his grave. Notice is here made of the sun's rising on him when he passed over *Penuel* (Peniel); for it is sunrise with the soul that has fellowship with God. The inspired writer mentions a traditional custom which the descendants of Jacob had, never to eat of the tendon attached to the socket of the hip in an animal. In this way, they preserve the memory of this story.

CHAPTER 33

We read in the previous chapter how Jacob had power with God and prevailed; here we find what power he had with people too, and how his brother Esau was placated and suddenly reconciled to him. Here is: 1. A very friendly meeting between Jacob and Esau (vv. 1–4). 2. Their conversation at their meeting, in which they compete with each other to be polite. Their conversation is: about Jacob's family (vv. 5–7), about the present he had sent (vv. 8–11), and about the progress of their journey (vv. 12–15). 3. Jacob's settlement in Canaan, his home, field, and altar (vv. 16–20).

Verses 1–4

Here:

1. Jacob sees Esau's approach (v. 1). Some think that his lifting up his eyes shows his cheerfulness and confidence, in contrast to a sad face. Having committed his case to God in prayer, he went on his way, *and his countenance was no more sad* (1Sa 1:18).

2. Jacob arranged his family into the best order he could to receive Esau. Notice what a different figure these two brothers made. Esau is attended by a guard of 400 men, and looks big; Jacob is followed by an awkward retinue of women and children who are in his care, and he looks tenderhearted and anxious for their safety. But it is Jacob who had the birthright and was to rule, and he was in every way the better man. Jacob, at the head of his household, set a better example than Esau at the head of his regiment.

3. At their meeting, the expressions of kindness were exchanged in the best manner between them:

3.1. Jacob bowed to Esau (v. 3). Though he feared Esau as an enemy, he still respected him as an elder brother. Many preserve themselves by humbling themselves: the bullet flies over the person who stoops.

3.2. Esau embraced Jacob (v. 4): *He ran to meet him,* not in anger, but in love; and, as one heartily reconciled to him. If there was not some wonderful change worked in the spirit of Esau at this time, we do not see how wrestling Jacob could be said to have such power with people as to call him a *prince* (32:28). God has the hearts of all people in his hands and can turn them when and how he pleases by a secret, silent, and irresistible power. He can suddenly convert enemies into friends, as he did two Sauls, one by restraining grace (1Sa 26:21, 25), the other by renewing grace (Ac 9:21–22).

3.3. They both wept. Jacob wept for joy, to be so kindly received by his brother, and Esau wept perhaps out of grief and shame.

Verses 5–15

We have here the conversation between the two brothers at their meeting. They talk:

1. About Jacob's retinue (vv. 5–7). Eleven or twelve little ones, the eldest of them not fourteen years old, followed Jacob closely: *Who are these?* says Esau. Jacob gives a serious answer: *They are the children which God hath graciously given thy servant.* Jacob speaks of his children as God's gifts; they are a *heritage of the Lord* (Ps 127:3; cf. 107:41; 112:9; 128:2).

2. About the present Jacob had sent him:

2.1. Esau modestly refused it because he had enough and did not need it (v. 9). It is a good thing for those who have a lot to know that they have enough, even though they do not have so much as some others have. Even Esau can say, *I have enough.*

2.2. Jacob affectionately urges him to accept it and prevails (vv. 10–11). Jacob sent it, in fear (v. 20), but, the fear having now passed, he is now so bold as to seek his acceptance of it out of love, to show that he desires his brother's friendship and did not merely dread his anger. It is a very high compliment that he passes on him: *I have seen thy face, as though I had seen the face of God.* The meaning is that Jacob saw God's favor to him in Esau's face: it was a sign of good to him that God had accepted his prayers. Jacob also acknowledges the sufficiency he had of this world's goods: *God has dealt graciously with me.* "And *I have enough*; I have all I need." Esau's enough was a lot, but Jacob's enough was all he needed. He has all in prospect; he will have all soon, when he reaches heaven: on this principle Jacob urged Esau, and he took his present.

3. About the progress of their journey:

3.1. Esau offers himself to be his guide and companion, as a sign of sincere reconciliation (v. 12). Esau has become fond of Jacob's company and wants to accompany him to Mount Seir. Let us never despair of any, nor distrust God in whose hand are all hearts. But Jacob saw reason to modestly refuse this offer (vv. 13–14), in which he shows a tender concern for his own family and flocks, like a good shepherd and a good father. He must consider the children, and the flocks with their young, and not lead the one, nor drive the other, too fast. This prudence and tenderness of Jacob ought to be imitated by those who have the care and charge of young people in the things of God. They must not be driven hard at first by heavy tasks in religious services, but led on, as they can bear, having their work made as easy to them as possible. Christ, the Good Shepherd, does so (Isa 40:11).

3.2. Esau offers some of his people to be his guard and escort (v. 15). Jacob is humble and does not need it to look great, and he is under the divine protection and does not need it for safety.

Verses 16–20

Here:

1. Having in a friendly manner parted company with Esau, who had gone to his own country (v. 16), Jacob comes to a place where, it would seem, he rested for some time. The place was afterward known by the name of Succoth, a city in the tribe of Gad, on the other side of Jordan (it means "booths" or "shelters"), that when his descendants afterward dwelled in houses of stone, they might remember that *the Syrian ready to perish* was their father (Dt 26:5).

2. Jacob comes to Shechem; the text reads *to Shalem, a city of Shechem.* After a dangerous journey, in which he

had met with many difficulties, he eventually came safely to Canaan. Here:

2.1. He buys a field (v. 19). Even though the land of Canaan was his by promise, and the time for taking possession had not yet come, he is content to pay for his own land.

2.2. He builds an altar (v. 20) in thankfulness to God and so that he might maintain the worship of God in his family. Where we have a tent, God must have an altar; where we have a house, he must have a church in it. He dedicated this altar to the honor of *El-elohe-Israel*, "God, the God of Israel." God had recently called him by the name of *Israel*, and now he calls God *the God of Israel*; though he is styled *a prince with God*, God will still be a prince, a ruler, with him, his Lord and his God.

CHAPTER 34

This chapter records the beginning of the story of Jacob's suffering in his children, which is recorded to show: 1. The futility of this world. What is dearest to us may cause us the greatest trouble. 2. The general suffering of good people. Jacob's sons, although they caused him grief in some things, were still all taken into the covenant with God. In this chapter we have: 1. Dinah raped (vv. 1–5). 2. An agreement of marriage between her and Shechem, who had defiled her (vv. 6–17). 3. The circumcision of the Shechemites following on from that agreement (vv. 18–24). 4. The treacherous and bloody revenge which Simeon and Levi took on them (vv. 25–31).

Verses 1–5

Dinah, Jacob's only daughter, is reckoned to be fifteen or sixteen years of age when she here caused so much trouble. Notice:

1. Her vain curiosity. She went to *see*, but that was not all, she went to be *seen* too; she went to see the daughters of the land, but it may be, with some thoughts of the sons of the land too. We fear she went in order to get acquainted with the Canaanites and to learn their ways.

2. The loss of her honor by this means (v. 2). Dinah went away to look around her; but, if she had looked around her as she ought, she would not have fallen into this trap.

3. The affection Shechem had for her, after he had raped her.

4. The news came to poor Jacob (v. 5). Jacob *held his peace*, as one who was dismayed, not knowing what to say. He had left the management of his affairs very much, too much we fear, to his sons, and he would do nothing without them. Things never go well when the authority of a parent runs low in a family.

Verses 6–17

Jacob's sons, when they heard of the injury done to Dinah, showed very great indignation at it, influenced possibly by jealousy for the honor of their family rather than by a sense of virtue. Many are concerned at the shamefulness of sin who never take to heart its sinfulness. It is here called *folly in Israel* (v. 7):

- Uncleanness is folly; for it sacrifices the favor of God, peace of conscience, and all the soul can claim that is sacred and honorable, to evil and brutal desires.
- This folly is most disgraceful in *Israel*, in the clan of Israel, where God is known and worshiped.

Hamor came to talk to Jacob himself, but he turns him over to his sons; and here we have a particular account of the agreement, in which the Canaanites were more honest than the Israelites:

1. Hamor and Shechem propose this agreement in all fairness, to bring about trade. Shechem is deeply in love with Dinah, and he wants her on any terms (vv. 11–12). His father not only agrees but asks for him and solemnly declares the benefits that would follow from the union of the families (vv. 9–10).

2. Jacob's sons deceitfully pretend to insist on an agreement based on religion, when really they planned the opposite. They are thinking only of revenge. The Shechemites must be circumcised; not to make them holy (the vengeful brothers never intended that), but to make them hurt, that while they were still sore they might become easier victims to the sword. The pretense of Jacob's sons was false. Their intention was malicious, as is seen by the outcome of the story; their only intention was to get them ready to be killed. Religion is never more harmed, nor are God's ordinances more profaned, than when they are used in this way as a cloak of maliciousness.

Verses 18–24

Here:

1. Hamor and Shechem allowed themselves to be circumcised (vv. 18–19). They were moved to undertake this by what they might have heard of the sacred and honorable intentions of this sign in the family of Abraham. Probably, they had some confused ideas about circumcision. Many who know little of religion know a certain amount that makes them willing to join themselves with those who are religious.

2. Jacob's sons were hard-working, thriving people, and promised themselves and their neighbors benefits from an alliance with them; it would improve the land and trade of the Shechemites and bring money into their country. Now:

2.1. It was bad enough to marry for this reason.

2.2. It was worse to be circumcised for this reason. There are many whose religion is to desire more and more, and who are more controlled and influenced by their worldly thoughts of having more, than by any principle of religion.

Verses 25–31

Here we have Simeon and Levi, two of Jacob's sons, young men not much more than twenty years old, cutting the throats of the Shechemites, and in so doing breaking the heart of their good father:

1. The cruel murder of the Shechemites.

1.1. Slaughtering the inhabitants of Shechem—*all the males*, Hamor and Shechem particularly, with whom they had been dealing in a friendly manner so recently, but in reality intending to take their lives. As nothing makes us safer than true religion, so nothing exposes us to danger more than pretended religion. But Simeon and Levi were most unrighteous.

1.1.1. It was true that Shechem had *wrought folly against Israel* (v. 7) in raping Dinah; but it ought also to have been considered how far Dinah herself had been accessory to it.

1.1.2. It was true that Shechem had done wrong; but he was trying to atone for it, and was as honest and honorable, *ex post facto*, "after the deed," as the case would allow.

1.1.3. It was true that Shechem had done wrong; but what was that to all the Shechemites? Must the innocent fall with the guilty?

1.1.4. But what above all aggravated the cruelty was the great treachery that was in it.

1.2. Seizing the prey of Shechem and looting the town. The Shechemites were willing to please the sons of Jacob by submitting to the penance of circumcision, on this principle, *Shall not their cattle and their substance be ours?* (v. 23), and notice what the outcome is. Instead of making themselves masters of the wealth of Jacob's family, Jacob's family become masters of their wealth.

2. Jacob's indignation at this bloody deed of Simeon and Levi (v. 30). Two things he complains of bitterly:

2.1. The disgrace they had brought on him by their actions: "What will they say of us and our religion?"

2.2. The ruin they had exposed him to. What could be expected, except that the Canaanites, who were numerous and formidable, would join forces against him, and he and his little family would become an easy target to them? When sin is in the house, there is reason to fear destruction just outside. You would have thought this would have made them repent, but instead of this, they justify themselves and give him this arrogant reply, *Should he deal with our sister as with a harlot?*

CHAPTER 35

In this chapter we have three times of fellowship and three funerals. 1. Three times of fellowship between God and Jacob. God ordered Jacob to go to Bethel (vv. 1 – 5). Jacob built an altar at Bethel to the honor of God, who had appeared to him (vv. 6 – 7). God appeared to him again and confirmed the change of his name and the covenant with him (vv. 9 – 13), for which Jacob made a grateful acknowledgment (vv. 14 – 15). 2. Three funerals: Deborah's (v. 8), Rachel's (vv. 16 – 20), and Isaac's (vv. 27 – 29). 3. Here is also Jacob's journey (v. 21), Reuben's incest (v. 22), and an account of Jacob's sons (vv. 23 – 26).

Verses 1 – 5

Here:

1. God reminds Jacob of his vow at Bethel, and sends him there to fulfill it (v. 1). Jacob had said on the day of his distress, *If I come again in peace, this stone shall be God's house* (28:22). It was now seven or eight years since he came to Canaan; he had bought ground there and had built an altar in remembrance of God's last appearance to him when he called him *Israel*; but Bethel is still forgotten (33:19 – 20). Those whom God loves, he reminds of neglected duties, using one way or another, for example by conscience or by his providence. When we have made a vow to God, it is best not to delay in fulfilling it (Ecc 5:4), but better late than never. We should desire to live in Bethel, the house of God (Ps 27:4). That should be our home, not our hotel. God does not remind him explicitly of his vow, but of its occasion: *When thou fleddest from the face of Esau.*

2. Jacob commands his household to prepare for this solemn act; not only for the journey and move, but also for the religious services that were to be performed (vv. 2 – 3). Notice the commands he gives his household, like Abraham (18:19):

2.1. They must *put away the strange gods.* Strange gods in Jacob's family! Strange things indeed! Could such a family, that was taught the good knowledge of the Lord, allow them in their home? In those families where there is an appearance of religion and an altar to God, there is often much amiss and more strange gods than you would suspect.

2.2. They must be clean, and *change their garments.* Simeon and Levi had their hands full of blood, and they particularly needed to wash themselves clean and take off their clothes that were so stained. These were only ceremonies, standing for purification and a change of heart. What are clean clothes and new clothes, without a clean heart and a new heart?

2.3. They must go with him to Bethel (v. 3).

3. Jacob's family gave up all they had that was idolatrous or superstitious (v. 4). Jacob took care to bury their idols, that they might not afterward find them and return to them.

4. Jacob moves without being harassed from Shechem to Bethel (v. 5). *The terror of God was upon the cities.* The way of duty is the way of safety. While there was sin in Jacob's house, he was afraid of his neighbors; but now that the strange gods have been put away, and they were all going together to Bethel, his neighbors were afraid of him.

Verses 6 – 15

Jacob and his retinue having safely arrived at Bethel, we are here told what happened there:

1. There he built an altar (v. 7) and offered sacrifice on it. With these sacrifices he no doubt praised God for former mercies. And he called the place (that is, *the altar*) *El-beth-el*, "the God of Bethel." The strength which saints draw from holy ordinances is not so much from *Beth-el*, "the house of God," as from *El-beth-el*, "the God of the house." The ordinances are purely empty, if we do not meet with God in them.

2. There he buried Deborah, Rebekah's nurse (v. 8). Rebekah was probably dead, but her old nurse (of whom mention is made, 24:59) survived her. Honor was done to this nurse at her death by Jacob's family, though she was not related to them, and though she was elderly. Trouble may come to a family even when that family is devout and religious.

3. There God appeared to him (v. 9), to acknowledge his altar, to answer to the name by which he had called him, *the God of Beth-el* (v. 7), and to comfort him in his trouble (v. 8). He renewed and confirmed the covenant with him, by the name *El-Shaddai. I am God Almighty*, "God all-sufficient" (v. 11), able to fulfill the promise in due time. Two things are promised:

3.1. That he would be the father of a great nation.

3.2. That he would be given a good land (v. 12). He will not have children without possessions, which is often the case of the poor, nor possessions without children, which is often to the grief of the rich; but both. These two promises had a spiritual meaning, for, without doubt, Christ is the promised seed, and heaven is the Promised Land. God then *went up from him*, or "from over him," in some visible display of glory, which had hovered over Jacob while God talked with him (v. 13).

4. There Jacob erected a memorial of this (v. 14). He set up a pillar. As a sign of his wanting it to be a sacred memorial of his fellowship with God, he poured oil and the other ingredients of a drink offering on it. His vow was, "This stone shall be God's house," that is, it will be set up for his honor, as houses are dedicated to the praise of their builders.

Verses 16 – 20

We have here the story of the death of Rachel, Jacob's dear wife. She went into labor on the way, and was not able to reach Bethlehem, the next town, though they were near it. Her labor brought about the life of the child but her own death. Her dying is here called the *departing of her soul*. The death of the body is the departure of the soul to the world of spirits. Her dying lips called her newborn son *Ben-oni*, "the son of my sorrow." But Jacob, because he did not want to go through the sorrowful remembrance of the mother's death every time he called his son by his name, changed his name, and called him *Benjamin*, "the son of my right hand"; that is, "very dear to me, set at my right hand for a blessing, the support of my age, as the staff in my right hand." Jacob buried her near the place where she died. If the soul is at rest after death, it does not matter much where the body lies. Jacob set up a pillar on her grave, so that it was known, long after, as Rachel's tomb (1Sa 10:2), and Providence so ordered it that this place afterward fell to Benjamin's lot.

Verses 21–29

Here is:

1. Jacob's journey (v. 21). Immediately after the story of Rachel's death he is here called Israel (vv. 21–22), and not often afterward: the Jews say, "The writer honors him here because he bore that affliction with such admirable patience and submission to Providence."

2. Reuben's sin. He was guilty of a heinous wickedness (v. 22). Though perhaps Bilhah was the greater criminal, and probably was abandoned by Jacob because of it, Reuben's crime was so offensive that, because of it, he lost his birthright and blessing (49:4). This was Reuben's sin, but it was Jacob's suffering.

3. A complete list of the sons of Jacob, now that the youngest, Benjamin, was born. This is the first time we have the names of these heads of the twelve tribes together.

4. The visit which Jacob made to his father Isaac at Hebron. Probably he did this now on the death of Rebekah, which had left Isaac by himself.

5. A record of the age and death of Isaac. Isaac, a mild, quiet man, lived the longest of all the patriarchs. Special note is taken of the friendly agreement of Esau and Jacob in solemnizing their father's funeral (v. 29), to show how wonderfully God had changed Esau's heart since he vowed his brother's murder immediately after his father's death (27:41).

CHAPTER 36

In this chapter we have an account of the descendants of Esau, who were called Edomites. Firstly, because he was the son of Isaac, for whose sake this honor is put on him; secondly, because the Edomites were neighbors to Israel; and thirdly, to show the fulfillment of the promise to Abraham, that he would be the father of many nations (17:4–5) and of that answer which Rebekah had from the prophecy she considered, Two nations are in thy womb *(25:23) and of the blessing of Isaac,* Thy dwelling shall be the fatness of the earth *(27:39). We have here: 1. Esau's wives (vv. 1–5) and his move to Mount Seir (vv. 6–8). 2. The names of his sons (vv. 9–14) and the chiefs among Esau's descendants (vv. 15–19). 3. The chiefs of the Horites (vv. 20–30). 4. The rulers of Edom (vv. 31–43). This chapter is abridged in 1Ch 1:35–54.*

Verses 1–8

Notice here:

1. Concerning Esau himself (v. 1). He is called *Edom* (and again, v. 8), that name by which he was remembered

for the foolish bargain he made, when he sold his birthright for *that red pottage* (25:30).

2. Concerning his wives, and the children they bore him in the land of Canaan.

3. Concerning his move to Mount Seir, which was the country God had given him as a possession, when he reserved Canaan for the seed of Jacob. God acknowledges it long afterward: *I gave to Esau Mount Seir* (Dt 2:5; Jos 24:4), which was the reason why the Edomites must not be troubled in their possession. He withdrew wholly to Mount Seir, took with him what was his share of his father's personal estate, and left Canaan to Jacob, not only because it was promised to him, but also because Esau noticed that if they should continue to prosper as they had begun,there would not be room for them both.

Verses 9–19

Notice here:

1. That only the names of Esau's sons and grandsons are recorded, only their names, not their histories. Nor does the genealogy go any further than the third and fourth generations. It is only the ancestry of the Israelites—who were to be the heirs of Canaan, and from whom were to come the promised seed, and the holy seed—that is extrapolated, as far as there was occasion for it, even out of all the tribes, until Canaan was divided among them; and this Israelite ancestry is the royal line from which Christ came.

2. That these sons and grandsons of Esau are called *dukes* (vv. 15–19) or captains, who had soldiers under them; for Esau and his family lived *by the sword* (27:40). Esau's sons were chiefs when Jacob's sons were ordinary shepherds (47:3). This is not a reason why such titles should not be used among Christians; but it is a reason why people should not think of themselves too highly or of others for their sake.

3. Esau increases and is enriched first. God's promise to Jacob began its work late, but the effect of it remained longer, and it was completely fulfilled in the spiritual Israel.

Verses 20–30

In the midst of this genealogy of the Edomites is inserted the genealogy of the Horites, those Canaanites or Hittites (compare 26:34), that were the original inhabitants of Mount Seir. This comes in here, not only to give light to the story, but also to bring discredit to the Edomites for intermarrying with them. Since Esau, having sold his birthright, lost his blessing, and entered into an alliance with the Hittites, his descendants and the sons of Seir are here considered together.

Verses 31–43

Gradually it seems, the Edomites drove out the Horites, gaining full possession of the country, and had a government of their own.

1. They were ruled by kings, and, as Bishop Patrick notes, seem to have come to the throne by election and not because of their family line. These kings reigned in *Edom before there reigned any king over the children of Israel.* Esau's blood becomes royal long before any of Jacob's did. We may suppose it was a great testing to the faith of God's Israel to hear of the pomp and power of the kings of Edom, while they were slaves in Egypt, but those who look for great things from God must be content to wait for them; God's time is the best time.

2. They were afterward governed by chiefs, again named here, who, we suppose, ruled all at the same time in several places in the country. We read of the chiefs of Edom (Ex 15:15), but long afterward of their kings again.

3. Mount Seir is called *the land of their possession* (v. 43). While the Israelites dwelled in the land of slavery, and their Canaan was only the Land of Promise, the Edomites dwelled in their own places and Seir was in their possession. The children of this world have everything in their hand, but have nothing to hope for in the future (Lk 16:25); while the children of God have everything to hope for, and next to nothing in their hands. But, all things considered, it is better to have Canaan as a promise than Mount Seir as a possession.

CHAPTER 37

The story of Joseph begins at this chapter. In every subsequent chapter except one to the end of this book he is the major figure. His story is so markedly distinguished by his humiliation and his exaltation that we cannot avoid seeing something of Christ in it, who was first humbled and then exalted. It also shows what happens to Christians, who must enter the kingdom through many hardships. In this chapter we have: 1. The malice his brothers bore against him, because he informed his father of their wickedness (vv. 1–2) and because his father loved him (vv. 3–4). 2. They also hated him because he dreamed of his authority over them (vv. 5–11). 3. The harm his brothers intended and did to him. The visit Joseph made gave them an opportunity (vv. 12–17). They plotted to kill him, determined to starve him (vv. 18–22). 4. They changed their minds and sold him as a slave (vv. 23–30). 5. They made their father believe that he was torn to pieces (vv. 31–35) and sold him into Egypt to Potiphar (v. 36). And all this was working together for good.

Verses 1–4

The story of Jacob's family: *These are the generations of Jacob.* His is not a bare genealogy like that of Esau (36:1), but a more memorable history. Here is:

1. Jacob staying with his father Isaac, who was still alive (v. 1).

2. Joseph, a shepherd, *feeding the flock with his brethren* (v. 2). Though he was his father's darling, he was not brought up in idleness or luxury. Those who are brought up to do nothing are likely to be good for nothing.

3. Joseph, beloved by his father (v. 3), being the greatest comfort of his father's old age. Jacob declared his affection for him by dressing him in finer clothes than the rest of his children: He *made him a coat of many colours.*

4. Joseph hated by his brothers:

• Because his father loved him. When parents make a difference between their children, the children soon notice it, and it often gives rise to feuds and quarrels in families.

• Because he *brought to his father their evil report.* Jacob's sons did things, when they were out from under his gaze, which they would not have dared do if they had been at home with him, but Joseph gave his father an account of their bad behavior.

Verses 5–11

Here:

1. Joseph relates the prophetic dreams he had (vv. 6–7, 9–10). His dreams were:

1.1. That his brothers' sheaves all bowed down to his, suggesting the occasion on which they would be brought to pay homage to him, namely, in seeking grain from him. Their empty sheaves would bow down to his full one.

1.2. That the sun, moon, and eleven stars bowed down to him (v. 9). Joseph was more of a prophet than a politician or he would have kept this to himself, when he must have known that his brothers already hated him and that this would exasperate them even further.

2. His brothers take it very badly and become more and more angry toward him (v. 8): *Shalt thou indeed reign over us?* How scornfully they resented it: "*Shalt thou, who are but one, reign over us,* who are many? Will you, the youngest, rule over us who are older?"

3. His father gently rebukes him for it but still takes note of the saying (vv. 10–11). He probably restrained him for it. He suggested that it was just an idle dream. Jacob, like Mary (Lk 2:51), kept these things in his heart, and no doubt remembered them long afterward, when things turned out in accordance with the prediction.

Verses 12–22

Here is:

1. The visit which Joseph, in obedience to his father's command, made to his brothers, who were feeding the flock at Shechem, many miles off. In Joseph we can see an example of:

1.1. Dutifulness to his father. Even though he was his father's darling, he was still willing to be his father's servant. He awaits his father's orders readily.

1.2. Kindness to his brothers. Though he knew they hated him and envied him, he still made no objections to his father's commands. Joseph was sent by his father to Shechem, to see whether his brothers were well there, and whether the inhabitants had risen up against them and destroyed them as revenge for their brutal murder of the Shechemites some years before.

2. The bloody and malicious plot by his brothers against him, the one who gave good for evil. It was not in a sudden passion or provocation that they thought to kill him, but it was a cold-blooded, premeditated act. The more advance planning there is in a sin the worse it is; it is bad to do evil, but even worse to intend it. They scornfully rebuked him for his dreams (v. 19): *This dreamer cometh* and (v. 20), *We shall see what will become of his dreams.* This shows what it was that got them worked up and enraged them. They could not bear the thought of bowing down to him. They agreed to cover up the murder with a lie: *We will say, Some evil beast hath devoured him.*

3. Reuben's plan to deliver him (vv. 21–22). Reuben, of all the brothers, had most reason to be jealous of Joseph, for he was the firstborn, but in fact he turns out to be Joseph's best friend. Reuben made a proposal which they thought would satisfy their desires to destroy Joseph, but which he had in mind would satisfy his desire to rescue Joseph from their hands and see him restored to his father. But God overruled matters to serve his own purposes of making Joseph an instrument to save the lives of many people.

Verses 23–30

We see here their plot carried out against Joseph:

1. They stripped him of his coat of many colors (v. 23). In so doing, they stripped him of the birthright, of which perhaps this was the emblem. In the same way, our Lord Jesus was stripped of his seamless garment, and suffering saints have first been stripped of their privileges and honors and then made the refuse of this world.

2. They were going to starve him, by throwing him into a dry cistern and leaving him there to die with hunger. Where envy reigns, compassion is banished, and humanity itself is forgotten (Pr 27:4). Is this the one to whom his brothers will bow down? God's providence often seems to contradict his purposes, even when God's providence serves his purposes.

3. They insulted him when he was in distress and were not sorry to see him suffer; they neglected him and *sat down to eat bread* (v. 25). They felt no remorse whatsoever for their sin. If they had, it would have spoiled their appetite for food and its taste. They were now pleased to think how they had been released from the fear of their brother's authority over them.

4. They sold him. A caravan of merchants happened to be passing by, and Judah suggested that they should sell Joseph to them, to be carried far enough away to Egypt, where he would probably be lost and never heard of again.

4.1. Judah made this proposal out of compassion for Joseph (v. 26): *What profit is it if we slay our brother?*

4.2. They accepted this, because they thought that if he was sold as a slave he would never be a lord. Reuben thought himself doomed, because the child was sold: *I, whither shall I go?* (v. 30). Since he was the eldest, his father would expect from him an account of what had happened to Joseph; but, as it turned out, they would all have been doomed if he had not been sold.

Verses 31–36

1. Joseph would soon be missed, he would be widely asked after, and so his brothers have a further plan, to make the world believe that Joseph was torn to pieces by a wild animal. They did this:

1.1. To clear themselves, that they might not be suspected of having caused him any harm. When the Devil has taught people to commit one sin, he then teaches them to cover it up by committing another, theft and murder with lying and perjury; but those who try to hide their sin will not succeed in this forever.

1.2. To make their father sorry. It seems to be their deliberate plan to take revenge on him for the special love their good father had for Joseph. They sent him Joseph's coat of many colors with one color more than it originally had, the color of blood (v. 32). They pretended they had found it in the fields, and Jacob himself would be scornfully asked, *Is this thy son's coat?* Let those who know a parent's heart imagine the agonies that poor Jacob has to go through. Sleeping or waking, he imagines a wild animal attacking Joseph. He imagines how the beast tore him limb from limb, leaving no remains except the coat of many colors. Now:

1.2.1. They tried to comfort him. His sons hypocritically pretended to do this (v. 35), but they were all miserable comforters. If they really wanted to comfort him, they might easily have done so by telling him the truth, "Joseph is alive, he is indeed sold into Egypt, but it will be easy to go there and redeem him."

1.2.2. It was all in vain: *Jacob refused to be comforted* (v. 35).

2. The Ishmaelites and Midianites only bought Joseph to trade with him and now sell him on to Potiphar (v. 36). How soon was the land of Egypt made a house of slavery to the descendants of Jacob! Jacob never thought that his dear Joseph would be bought and sold in this way as a servant.

CHAPTER 38

This chapter gives us an account of Judah and his family. If we were to form a description of him from this story, we would not say, Judah, thou art he whom thy brethren shall praise *(49:8). We have in this chapter: 1. Judah's marriage and children and the untimely death of his two eldest sons (vv. 1–11). 2. Judah's incest with his daughter-in-law Tamar, without his knowledge (vv. 12–23). 3. His shame, when it was discovered (vv. 24–26), and the birth of his twin sons, in whom his family was built up (vv. 27–30).*

Verses 1–11

Here is:

1. Judah's foolish friendship with a Canaanite man.

2. His foolish marriage with a Canaanite woman, a match made, not by his father, who, it would seem, was not consulted, but by his new friend Hirah (v. 2).

3. His three sons by her, Er, Onan, and Shelah. Judah married too young and very rashly; he also married his sons too young, when they had neither the knowledge nor grace to control themselves, and the consequences were very bad.

3.1. His firstborn, *Er*, was notoriously wicked; he was so *in the sight of the Lord* (v. 7), that is, he defied God and his Law.

3.2. The next son, *Onan*, was, according to the ancient custom, married to the widow, to preserve the name of his deceased brother who died childless. The custom of marrying the brother's widow was afterward made one of the laws of Moses (Dt 25:5). Onan, though he agreed to marry the widow, as an outrage against his own body, against the wife whom he had married, and against the memory of his brother who was gone, refused to have children for his brother.

3.3. *Shelah*, the third son, was reserved for the widow (v. 11), but with a plan that he should not marry as young. However, Tamar accepted the matter at that time and awaited the outcome.

Verses 12–23

It is a very unfortunate and foolish story told here concerning Judah. He was unjust to his daughter-in-law, either through negligence or intention, in not giving her his surviving son, and this exposed her to temptation.

1. Tamar wickedly gave herself as a prostitute to Judah, that, if the son might not, the father might, raise up offspring to the deceased. Bishop Patrick thinks it probable that she hoped Shelah, who was her husband by right, might have come along with his father, and that he might have been tempted by her embraces.

1.1. She took her opportunity when Judah was enjoying a feast and a time of happiness with his sheep-shearers.

1.2. She exposed herself as a prostitute *in an open place* (v. 14). It would seem it was the custom of prostitutes in those times to cover their faces, that, though they were not ashamed, they might seem to be so. The sin of immorality was not as shameless as it is now.

2. Judah was caught in the trap, and though he did not know he was guilty of incest with his daughter-in-law (since he did not know who she was), he was willfully guilty of sexual immorality: whoever she was, he knew she was not his wife and so was not to be touched. Notice:

2.1. Judah's sin began with the eye (v. 15): *He saw her.* We need to make a covenant with our eyes (Job 31:1), and to turn them away from vain things, in case our eyes contaminate our heart.

2.2. It added to the scandal that the notorious hire of a prostitute (a most infamous thing) was demanded, offered, and accepted — *a kid from the flock* (v. 17), a good price at which her chastity and honor were valued! If the price had been thousands of rams and ten thousand rivers of oil, it would not have been a high enough price. The favor of God, the purity of the soul, the peace of conscience, and the hope of heaven are too precious to be put up for sale at such rates.

2.3. It was Judah's disgrace that he pledged his *signet* (seal), *bracelets* (cord), *and staff* for a young goat.

3. He lost what he gave her in the bargain; he sent the young goat, according to his promise, to redeem his pledge, but the supposed prostitute could not be found. Judah sits down content to lose his seal and its cord and forbids his friend to ask further about them, giving this reason, *lest we be shamed* (v. 23). He expresses no concern about the sin, to see that forgiven; he is only concerned to prevent the shame.

Verses 24–30

Here is:

1. Judah's strictness to Tamar, when he heard she had committed adultery. She was, in the eye of the law, Shelah's wife, and so her being with child by another man was looked on as bringing harm and disgrace on Judah's family: *Bring her forth therefore*, says Judah, the master of the family, and *let her be burnt*; not burned to death, but burned in the cheek or forehead, stigmatized as a prostitute. It is a common thing for people to be severe toward those very sins in others which they still allow in themselves, and so, in judging others, they condemn themselves (Ro 2:1; 14:22).

2. Judah's shame, when it came out that he was the adulterer. She produced *the ring and the bracelets* in court, which showed that Judah was the father of the child (vv. 25–26). He acknowledges that he, who had been so much an accessory to the matter, would be perpetually marked with notoriety.

3. The building up of Judah's family in this, nevertheless, in the birth of Pharez (Perez) and Zarah (Zerah), from whom descended the most important families of the illustrious tribe of Judah. The four eldest sons of Jacob were guilty of grave sins. Reuben and Judah were guilty of the sin of incest, Simeon and Levi of that of murder, but they were patriarchs, and from Levi descended the priests, and from Judah the kings and Messiah. In this way they became examples of repentance and memorials to forgiveness and mercy.

CHAPTER 39

In this chapter we return to the story of Joseph. We see him here: 1. A servant, a slave in Potiphar's house (v. 1), and yet there greatly honored and favored, and, by the providence of God, in effect, a master (vv. 2–6). 2. By the grace of God, more than a conqueror over a strong temptation to sexual immorality (vv. 7–12). 3. Suffering, falsely accused (vv. 13–18). 4. Imprisoned (vv. 19–20), but his imprisonment made both honorable and encouraging by the signs of God's special presence with him (vv. 21–23).

Verses 1–6

Here is:

1. Joseph sold to one of Pharaoh's officials, through whom he might get to know public people and business and so be made more suitable for the promotion which

God had in store for him. What God intends for people he will certainly qualify them for in one way or another.

2. Joseph blessed, wonderfully blessed, even in the house where he served.

2.1. God prospered him (vv. 2–3). Though, at first, we may suppose that he was doing the lowliest tasks, even in those his intelligence and industriousness became apparent; a particular blessing of heaven accompanied him, which, as he rose in his employment, became more and more discernible. Joseph's brothers had stripped him of his coat of many colors, but they could not strip him of his goodness and wisdom. Joseph was separated from his brothers, but not from his God; banished from his father's house, but *the Lord was with him*, and this gave him great strength.

2.2. His master promoted him and gradually put him in charge of his household (v. 4). It is wise of those who are in any sort of authority to take notice of and employ those who appear to have the presence of God with them (Ps 101:6). Potiphar knew what he was doing when he put everything into Joseph's hands.

2.3. God favored his master for his sake (v. 5): *He blessed the Egyptian's house*, even though he was an Egyptian, a stranger to the true God, *for Joseph's sake*. Good people are the blessings of the places where they live.

Verses 7–12

Here is:

1. A most shameful instance of immodesty and scandal from Potiphar's wife, having lost all virtue and honor.

1.1. Her sin began in her eyes: *She cast her eyes upon Joseph* (v. 7), who *was a goodly person, and well-favoured* (v. 6). We really need to make a covenant with our eyes (Job 31:1), so that our eyes do not contaminate our heart.

1.2. She was daring and shameless in her sin.

1.3. She was importunate and forceful in her temptation. *She spoke to him day by day* (v. 10). This showed her great wickedness and was also a great temptation to Joseph.

2. A most illustrious example of virtue and decisive purity in Joseph, who, by the grace of God, was enabled to resist and overcome this temptation; and, all things considered, his escape was as great an example of divine power as the deliverance of the three children from the fiery furnace.

2.1. The temptation that attacked him was very strong. The tempter was his master's wife, a strong-minded woman, whom it was his place to obey and his work to please, whose favor would contribute more than anything to his promotion. On the other hand, it was his greatest danger if he insulted her and made her his enemy. Opportunity favored the temptation. The tempter was in the house with him; his business led him to be, without any suspicion, where she was.

2.2. His resistance to the temptation was very brave and the victory truly honorable. God's almighty grace enabled him to overcome this attack of the enemy:

2.2.1. Because he did not want to wrong his master. He did not want to offend his God. This is the chief argument which he uses to support his hatred of this sin. *How can I do this?* Not only, How will I? or, How dare I? but, *How can I? Id possumus, quod jure possumus*, "We can do that which we can do lawfully." Joseph urges on himself three arguments. Firstly, he considers who he was that was tempted. "*I*; others may perhaps be free, but *I* cannot." Secondly, what the sin was to which he was tempted: *This* great wickedness. Others might look on it as a small matter, a peccadillo, a mere youthful prank; but Joseph saw it in a completely different light. Let sin be recognized as sin (Ro 7:13); we should call it by its name and never lessen it. Thirdly, against whom he was tempted to sin— *against God*, against his nature and his authority, against his love and his purposes. Those who love God hate sin for this reason.

2.2.2. By steadfast determination. The grace of God enabled him to overcome the temptation by avoiding the tempter. He would not stay so much as to discuss the temptation but flew away from it with the utmost horror; he left his garment, as one escaping for his life. It is better to lose a good coat than a good conscience.

Verses 13–18

Potiphar's wife, having tried in vain to make Joseph a criminal, now endeavors to represent him as one and takes revenge on him for his virtue. Pure and holy love will continue, though insulted; but sinful love, like Amnon's to Tamar (2Sa 13), is easily changed to sinful hatred. She accused him to his fellow-servants (vv. 13–15) and gave him a bad reputation among them. She accused him to her husband, who had the power to punish him. She tells an improbable story, but it was told to take revenge on his virtue and was a most malicious lie. But she manages to make her husband angry with him, blaming her husband for bringing this Hebrew servant among them.

Verses 19–23

Here we read:

1. Joseph was wronged by his master. Potiphar believed the accusation. There is no way out; he is condemned to imprisonment (vv. 19–20). He would be shut up with the king's prisoners, the prisoners of state. Potiphar, it is likely, chose that prison because it was the worst. He was confined in the king's prison, so that he might be promoted from there to the king himself.

2. Joseph was far away from all his friends, but *the Lord was with Joseph, and showed him mercy* (v. 21). No gates or bars can shut out his gracious presence from his people, for he has promised that he will never leave them. Those who have a good conscience in prison have a good God with them there. Joseph is not a prisoner for long before he becomes a leader. God *gave him favour in the sight of the keeper of the prison.* God can raise up friends for his people even where they do not expect to find them. The warden saw that God was with him and that everything was successful in his hand, and so he entrusted Joseph with the management of the affairs of the prison (vv. 22–23).

CHAPTER 40

In this chapter things are working, though slowly, toward Joseph's promotion. 1. Two of Pharaoh's servants are sent to prison, and to Joseph's care there, and so witness his extraordinary behavior (vv. 1–4). 2. They each dreamed a dream, which Joseph interpreted (vv. 5–19), and the events showed the interpretation to be true (vv. 20–22), and so they became witnesses of his extraordinary ability. 3. Joseph commends his case to one of them (whose promotion he foresaw, vv. 14–15), but unsuccessfully (v. 23).

Verses 1–4

We would not have had this story of Pharaoh's butler (cupbearer) and baker recorded in Scripture if it had not been part of the story of Joseph's promotion. Notice:

1. Two of the great officials of Pharaoh's court, having offended the king, are sent to prison. There are many thoughts concerning the possible offenses of these servants of Pharaoh; some consider that they were making an attempt on his life, others no more than the casual putting of a fly in his cup and a little sand in his bread.

2. The *captain of the guard* himself, who was Potiphar, assigned Joseph to look after them (v. 4), which suggests that he now began to be reconciled to him and perhaps to be convinced of his innocence, though he did not dare release him for fear of offending his wife.

Verses 5–19

Notice:

1. The special providence of God, which filled the heads of these two prisoners with unusual dreams, which had an extraordinary impression on them and brought with them evidence of divine origin, both in one night.

2. The impression which was made on these prisoners by their dreams (v. 6): *They were sad.*

3. Joseph's great tenderness and compassion toward them. He asked with concern, *Wherefore look you so sadly today?* (v. 7). Joseph was their keeper, was now a prisoner with them, and had been a dreamer too. Sharing in suffering helps bring compassion toward those who suffer. It is some relief to those who are in trouble to be taken notice of.

4. The dreams themselves and their interpretation. *There is no interpreter* here in prison (v. 8). Here, Joseph directed them which way to look: *Do not interpretations belong to God?* Joseph suggests, "If interpretations belong to God, he can do freely as he wishes and may pass this ability to anyone he wants. So tell me your dreams."

4.1. The dream of the chief butler (cupbearer) was a happy prediction of his release, and restoration to his former position within three days; and so Joseph explained it to him (vv. 12–13).

4.2. The chief baker's dream foresaw his ignominious death (vv. 18–19). The fortunate interpretation of the other's dream encouraged him to relate his. It was not Joseph's fault that he brought him no better news. Ministers are only interpreters; they cannot make things different from what they are.

5. How Joseph made the most of this opportunity to have a friend at court (vv. 14–15). He modestly asked for the favor of the chief butler (cupbearer), whose promotion he foretold: *But think of me when it shall be well with thee.* Notice how modestly he presents his own case (v. 15). He does not discredit his brothers who sold him. Neither does he mention the wrong done to him in his imprisonment by his master's wife in her false accusation, and by his master who was his judge. Instead, he mildly asserts his own innocence. When we are called to vindicate ourselves we should carefully avoid, as far as possible, speaking badly of others. Let us be content to prove ourselves innocent and not be fond of rebuking others for their guilt.

Verses 20–23

Here is the verifying of Joseph's interpretation of the dreams on the very day that had been appointed. The chief butler (cupbearer) and baker were both promoted, one to his office, the other to the gallows, and both at the end of three days. Some observe the resemblance between Joseph and Christ in this story. Joseph's fellow-sufferers were like the two thieves who were crucified with Christ—the one saved, the other condemned. One of these, when Joseph said to him, *Think on me when it shall be well with thee*

(v. 14), forgot him; but one of those, when he said to Christ, *Remember me when thou comest into thy kingdom* (Lk 23:42), was not forgotten.

CHAPTER 41

Providence here brings about two things: Joseph is promoted and Jacob and his family are kept in a time of famine. 1. Pharaoh's dreams (vv. 1–8). 2. The recommendation of Joseph to Pharaoh as an interpreter (vv. 9–16). 3. The interpretation of the dreams, and the prediction of seven years' plenty and seven years' famine in Egypt, with the prudent advice given to Pharaoh about this (vv. 17–32). 4. The promotion of Joseph to the position of highest power and trust in Egypt (vv. 33–45). 5. The fulfillment of Joseph's prediction and his faithfulness to his trust (vv. 46–57).

Verses 1–8

Notice:

1. The delay in Joseph's release. It was not till *the end of two full years* (v. 1). There is a time set when God's people are to be rescued, and that time will come, even though it seems to delay. When it comes, it will appear to have been the best time.

2. The means of Joseph's release, which were Pharaoh's dreams, and are related here. If we were to think of them as ordinary dreams, we might see how foolish and absurd their creativity seems to be, how tame cows are represented as wild animals (in fact, even more ravenous than ordinary wild animals; these ones eat up those of their own kind) and ears of corn as swallowing up one another. Foolish dreams told only make for foolish talk. But these dreams which Pharaoh dreamed brought their own evidence that they were sent by God; and so when he woke up, his mind was troubled (v. 8). His magicians were puzzled, the rules and their abilities failed them. This made Joseph's achievement with the help of the Spirit of God all the more extraordinary. Compare with this story Da 2:27; 4:7; 5:8. Joseph's own dreams were the reason for his troubles, and now Pharaoh's dreams were the reason for his release.

Verses 9–16

Here is:

1. The recommending of Joseph to Pharaoh as an interpreter. The chief butler (cupbearer) acted more out of a compliment to Pharaoh, to please him, than in gratitude to Joseph or out of compassion for his situation. The story he had to tell was, in short, that there was some unknown young man in the king's prison, who had rightly interpreted the dreams he and the chief baker had had. Events had, in both cases, turned out just as Joseph had interpreted. He was now recommending this man to his master the king as an interpreter. God's time for the release of his people will eventually be seen to be the best time. If the chief butler had initially used his privileged position for Joseph's release, and had obtained it, it is probable that on his release Joseph would have gone back to the *land of the Hebrews* again, which he spoke of so intensely (40:15), and then he would neither have been so blessed himself, nor been such a blessing to his family, as afterward he proved to be. But by staying two years longer, and coming now eventually to interpret the king's dreams, he found the way was made for his very great promotion.

2. The introducing of Joseph to Pharaoh. It is done as quickly as possible, and Joseph is brought in, perhaps

almost as surprised as Peter was (Ac 12:9). Immediately Pharaoh, without even asking who he is or where he comes from, tells him that he expected him to interpret his dream (v. 15). Joseph very modestly replies to this (v. 16), in which:

- He gives honor to God. "It is not in my power to do this; God must do it."
- He shows respect to Pharaoh and deep goodwill to him and his government, in supposing that the interpretation would be a peaceful one.

Verses 17–32

Here:

1. Pharaoh tells Joseph his dream. He dreamed that he stood on the bank of the River Nile, and saw the cows, both the fat ones and the lean ones, coming up out of the river.

2. Joseph interprets his dream and tells him that it meant seven years' plenty about to happen, which would be followed by as many years' famine. Notice:

2.1. The two dreams signified the same thing, but the repetition showed the indisputability, the imminence, and the importance of the event (v. 32).

2.2. The two dreams distinctly referred to the two things in which we most experience plenty and scarcity, namely, grass and grain. The plenty and scarcity of grass for the cattle were signified by the fat cows and the lean ones; the plenty and scarcity of grain for the service of human beings, by the full heads of grain and the thin ones.

2.3. What changes the comforts of this life are subject to. After great plenty great scarcity may come.

2.4. The goodness of God in sending seven years' plenty before those of famine, that provision might be made accordingly. How wisely and wonderfully has the great housekeeper of Providence arranged the affairs of the vast family of the human race from the beginning until now! There has been a wide variety of seasons, and the products of the earth are sometimes more and sometimes fewer. If one time is compared with another, however, what was miraculous concerning the provision of manna is also shown to be true in the common course of Providence, *He that gathers much has nothing over, and he that gathers little has no lack* (Ex 16:18).

2.5. The deteriorating nature of our worldly enjoyments. The great increase of the years of plenty was completely lost and swallowed up in the years of famine; and the surplus of it, which seemed very large, only just kept the people alive (vv. 29–31).

2.6. God revealed this beforehand to Pharaoh, who, as king of Egypt, was to be the leader of his country, so that he could make prudent provision for them.

Verses 33–45

Here is:

1. The good advice that Joseph gave to Pharaoh, which was:

1.1. That in the years of plenty he should store up grain for the years of famine, to buy up grain when it was cheap, so that he might both enrich himself and also supply the country when grain would become dear and scarce.

1.2. Because what is everybody's work commonly proves to be nobody's work, he advises Pharaoh to appoint commissioners who should make it their business, and to select one person to be in charge of the whole matter (v. 33).

2. The great honor that Pharaoh did to Joseph.

2.1. He gave honorable testimony to his character: He is *a man in whom the Spirit of God is*, and this puts a great excellence on any person. Such people ought to be valued (v. 38). He is the epitome of wisdom: *There is none so discreet and wise as thou art* (v. 39). Now he is greatly rewarded for the disgrace done to him.

2.2. He gave him an honorable position. He not only employed him to buy up grain, but also made him prime minister of state, in charge of his palace.

2.3. He gave him all imaginable marks of honor, to commend him to the respect of the people as the king's favorite, and one whom he delighted to honor. He gave him a new name, to show his authority over him, but also a name that spoke of the value he had for him, *Zaphnath-paaneah*—which may mean "revealer of secrets." He married him honorably to a priest's daughter. Where God had been generous in giving wisdom and other benefits, Pharaoh was not sparing in conferring honors.

Verses 46–57

Notice here:

1. The building of Joseph's family in the birth of two sons, Manasseh and Ephraim (vv. 50–52). In the names he gave them, he acknowledged divine Providence in fortunately turning his affairs around. He was made *fruitful in the land of his affliction*. It had been the land of his affliction, and in some sense it was still so, for it was not Canaan, the Land of Promise. His distance from his father was still his affliction. The afflictions of the saints further their fruitfulness. *Ephraim* sounds like the Hebrew for "twice fruitful," and Manasseh means "making to forget," for these two often go together. When Jeshurun grew fat, he forgot God, his Maker (Dt 32:15).

2. The confirmation of Joseph's predictions. Pharaoh had great confidence in his truth. The seven years of plenty came (v. 47), and, eventually, they came to an end (v. 54). Years of plenty will end, and so, *Whatsoever thy hand finds to do, do it* (Ecc 9:10). We are to harvest at harvest time. *The seven years of dearth began to come* (v. 54). This famine, it seems, was not only in Egypt, but in other lands also, in *all lands*, that is, all the neighboring countries. It is said here that *in the land of Egypt there was bread*.

3. The fulfillment of Joseph's trust. He was found faithful in what was entrusted to him, as a steward ought to be. He was diligent in storing up grain, while there was plenty (vv. 48–49). He was wise and careful in distributing grain, when the famine came, and kept the markets low by supplying them at reasonable rates from his stores. The people in distress cried to Pharaoh. He sent them to his treasurer, *Go to Joseph*. Joseph, no doubt, wisely and justly fixed the price of the grain he sold, so that the country might not be oppressed, nor unfair advantage taken of the general deprivation. And the price was determined by that golden rule of justice, to do as we would be done by.

CHAPTER 42

In this and the following chapters we have the fulfilling of the dreams which Joseph himself had dreamed, that his father's family should pay homage to him. The story mostly concerns what happened between Joseph and his brothers, because it is very instructive and it gave reason for Jacob's family to move to Egypt, on which so many great events afterward depended. We have, in this chapter: 1. The humble request of Jacob's sons to
Joseph to buy grain (vv. 1–6). 2. The shock Joseph put them into, to test them (vv. 7–20). 3. The conviction they were now under because of their sin to Joseph long before (vv. 21–24). 4. Their return to Canaan with grain and the great distress of their good father on hearing the account of their expedition (vv. 25–38).

Verses 1–6

Though Jacob's sons were all married, they were still joined as one community, under the leadership of their father Jacob. We have here:

1. The orders he gave them to go and buy grain in Egypt (vv. 1–2). Notice:

1.1. The famine was severe in the land of Canaan. It is noteworthy that all three patriarchs, to whom Canaan was the Land of Promise, met with famine in that land, which was not only to test their faith, to see whether they would trust God even though he should starve them, but also to teach them to look for a better country, that is, the heavenly one (Heb 11:14–16).

1.2. While there was famine in Canaan, there was grain in Egypt. Providence has ordered things, so that one place should help and supply another; for we are all brothers and sisters.

1.3. *Jacob saw that there was corn in Egypt.*

1.4. Jacob rebuked his sons for delaying to provide grain for their families. *Why do you look one upon another?*

1.5. Jacob spurred them on to go to Egypt: *Get you down thither.*

2. Their obedience to these orders (v. 3). They *went down to buy corn*; they did not send their servants but very wisely went themselves to spend their own money. Let none think themselves too great or too good to put themselves out. Benjamin did not go with them, for he was his father's darling. They came to Egypt, and, having a considerable quantity of grain to buy, they were taken before Joseph himself, *they bowed down themselves before him* (v. 6). Now their empty sheaves were bowing down to his full one.

Verses 7–20

We may well wonder that Joseph, during the twenty years that he had now been in Egypt, never made a journey to Canaan to visit his aged father, when he was on the border of Egypt, which lay next to Canaan. It is probable that his whole dealings with himself in this matter were at the special direction from heaven, that the purpose of God concerning Jacob and his family might be fulfilled. When Joseph's brothers came, he knew them by many convincing signs, but they did not know him, little thinking to find him there (v. 8). In his behavior toward his brothers, Joseph had in mind his dreams, and he aimed at bringing his brothers to repentance for their former sins.

1. Joseph showed himself very rigorous and harsh with his brothers. He charged them with evil purposes against the government (v. 9) and treated them as dangerous people, saying, *You are spies*. Why was Joseph so hard toward his brothers? We may be sure it was not from a spirit of revenge. It was to bring them to repentance. It was to draw from them an account of their family's state, which he longed to know. Not seeing his brother Benjamin with them, perhaps he began to suspect that they had done away with him too, and so he gives them occasion to speak of their father and brother.

2. They were very submissive at this. They spoke to him with all the greatest of respect: *Nay, my lord* (v. 10)—a

great change since they said, *Behold, this dreamer comes* (37:19). They very modestly deny the charge: *We are no spies*. They tell him their business, that they have come to buy food.

3. He had them all put in prison for three days (v. 17).

4. He finished with them eventually by telling them that one of them would be left as a hostage, and the rest should go home and fetch Benjamin. It was a very encouraging word he said to them (v. 18): *I fear God*; it is as if he had said, "You may assure yourselves I will do you no wrong; I dare not, for I know that, even though I am in a high position, there is one higher than I." With those who fear God we have reason to expect fair treatment. The fear of God will restrain those who are in power from abusing that power to oppress and tyrannize others. Those who have no one else to stand in awe of ought to stand in awe of their own consciences. See Ne 5:15, *So did not I, because of the fear of God.*

Verses 21–28

Here is:

1. The penitent reflection Joseph's brothers showed for the wrong they had formerly done to him (v. 21). They talked the matter over in Hebrew, not suspecting that Joseph, whom they took to be a native of Egypt, understood them, much less that he was the person they spoke of. They remembered with regret how they had cruelly and brutally treated him. Now see here:

1.1. The role of conscience. As time will not wear away the guilt of sin, so it will also not blot out the records of our conscience.

1.2. The benefit of suffering. Suffering sometimes turns out to be a fortunate and effective means of awakening our conscience.

2. Joseph's tenderness toward them on this occasion. This represents the tender mercies of our God toward repenting sinners. See Jer 31:20, *Since I spoke against him I do earnestly remember him still.* See also Jdg 10:16.

3. The binding of Simeon (v. 24). Joseph chose Simeon as the hostage probably because he remembered him to have been his most bitter enemy, or because he noticed him now to be the one who was least humbled and concerned.

4. The dismissal of the rest of them. They came for grain, and grain they had; and not only so, but each one of them had his money restored in the mouth of his sack.

4.1. It was in fact a mercy, for we hope they had no wrong done to them when their money was given them back. It was a kindness, but they were still terrified by it. Guilty consciences are inclined to take good providences badly. If they had been robbed of their money, they could not have been more frightened than they were now when they found their money back in their sacks.

4.2. They knew that the Egyptians hated Hebrews (43:32), and so, since they could not expect to receive any kindness from them, they concluded that this was done with the aim of picking a quarrel with them, because the lord of the land had accused them of being spies. Their own consciences had also been aroused, and their sins set out before them, and this put them into a state of turmoil. When the human spirit is sinking, it seems that everything is working toward its destruction.

Verses 29–38

Here is:

1. The report which Jacob's sons made to their father of the great trouble they had been in in Egypt, and how

they had been suspected and threatened and made to leave Simeon a prisoner there, till they should take Benjamin back with them.

2. The deep impression this made on the good man. The very pouches of silver which Joseph returned in kindness to his father frightened him (v. 35), for he concluded it was done with some evil purpose.

2.1. He has very sad thoughts about the present state of his family. Jacob gives Joseph up as dead, and Simeon and Benjamin as being in danger; and he concludes, *All these things are against me*. It turned out otherwise, that all these were for him, were working together for his good and the good of his family. Through our ignorance and mistakes and the weakness of our faith, we often think that what is really for us is against us.

2.2. He is at present determined that Benjamin should not go. Jacob's present thoughts are, *My son shall not go down with you*. He clearly distrusts them, remembering that he had never seen Joseph since he had been with them.

CHAPTER 43

Here the story of Joseph's brothers is continued: 1. Their sad parting with their father Jacob in Canaan (vv. 1–14). 2. Their pleasant meeting with Joseph in Egypt (vv. 15–34).

Verses 1–10

Here:

1. Jacob urges his sons to go and buy more grain in Egypt (vv. 1–2). The famine continued, and the grain they had bought was all used up.

2. Judah urges Jacob to agree to Benjamin going with them. Judah's conscience had just struck him for what he had done a long time before against Joseph (42:21); and, as evidence of the truth of his repentance, he tried to make some amends for the irreparable injury he had done him by redoubling his care for Benjamin.

Verses 11–14

Notice here:

1. Jacob's persuasibleness. He was to be ruled by reason: "*If it must be so now, take your brother.* If grain can only be obtained on those terms, so be it. We may as well expose him to such a dangerous journey as allow ourselves and our families, Benjamin included, to die for lack of bread." Faithfulness is a virtue, but obstinacy is not.

2. Jacob's wisdom and justice, which is seen in three things:

2.1. He sent back the money which they had found in the mouths of the sacks, with the wise interpretation, *Peradventure it was an oversight*. Even though we receive something because of someone's mistake, if we keep it when the mistake is discovered, we are keeping it deceitfully.

2.2. He sent double the money, as much again as they took the time before, supposing that the price of grain might have risen, or to show a generous spirit, that they might be all the more likely to receive generous treatment from *the man, the lord of the land.*

2.3. He sent gifts of such things as the land offered, which were scarce in Egypt—*balm and honey, spices, myrrh, nuts, and almonds* (v. 11), the commodities that Canaan exported (37:25). Honey and spice will never make up for the lack of grain for bread. The famine was severe in Canaan, and yet they had balm, myrrh, and so on. We may live well enough on plain food without any delicacies, but we cannot live on delicacies without plain food. Let us thank God that what is most necessary and useful is generally the cheapest and most widely available.

3. Jacob's piety, as is seen appearing in his prayer: *God Almighty give you mercy before the man!* (v. 14). Jacob had formerly turned an angry brother into a kind one with a present and a prayer, and here he tries to use the same method, and it is successful.

Verses 15–25

Jacob's sons, having received permission to take Benjamin with them, went down the second time to Egypt to buy grain. If we should ever know what is meant by a famine of the word (Am 8:11), let us not think much of traveling as far for spiritual food as they did for physical food. Here we have an account of what passed between them and Joseph's steward. *They were afraid, because they were brought into Joseph's house* (v. 18). Now they thought they would be held responsible for the money in the mouths of the sacks, and would be accused of being cheats. They therefore put the case before the steward. To actually prove their honesty, they produced the money before they were even accused of taking it. The steward encouraged them (v. 23): *Peace be to you, fear not.* He directs them to look to divine Providence in the return of their money: *Your God, and the God of your father, has given you treasure in your sacks.* In this he rules out further discussion of it. "Don't ask how it came to be there; Providence brought it to you, and let that satisfy you." It appears from what he said, by his good master's instructions, that he was brought to the knowledge of the true God, the God of the Hebrews.

Verses 26–34

Here is:

1. The great respect that Joseph's brothers paid to him. When they brought him the gifts, *they bowed themselves before him* (v. 26), and again, when they gave him an account of their father's health, *they made obeisance,* and called him, *Thy servant our father* (v. 28). In this way Joseph's dreams were gradually fulfilled.

2. The great kindness that Joseph showed to them, while they little realized it was brotherly kindness. Here is:

2.1. His kind inquiry concerning Jacob: *Is he yet alive?*

2.2. The kind note he took of Benjamin, his own brother. He spoke a prayer for him: *God be gracious unto thee, my son* (v. 29). He shed some tears for him (v. 30). Tears of tenderness and affection are nothing to scorn, even in great and wise people.

2.3. When his weeping had subsided so that he could control himself, he sat down to dinner with them, treated them nobly, showing them generous hospitality.

2.3.1. He ordered three tables to be spread, one for his brothers, another for the Egyptians who dined with him (for so different were their customs that they did not want to eat together), another for himself, who did not dare acknowledge himself as a Hebrew, but would not sit with the Egyptians.

2.3.2. He placed his brothers according to their seniority (v. 33).

2.3.3. He gave them lavish hospitality, sending servings of food to them from his own table (v. 34). This was all the more generous of him, and the more pleasant for them, because of the present scarcity of food. Their cares

and fears were now over, and they ate their bread with joy, concluding they were now on good terms with the man, the lord of the land. Joseph gave them to understand that Benjamin was his favorite, for his serving of food was *five times as much as any of theirs.*

CHAPTER 44

Joseph, having shown hospitality to his brothers, now dismissed them; but here we have them brought back in an even greater shock than any they had been in before. Notice: 1. What method Joseph took both to humble them further and also to test their affection for his brother Benjamin, by which he would be able to judge how sincere their repentance was for what they had done against himself. He wanted to be satisfied about this before he showed his reconciliation to them. He did this by causing distress to Benjamin (vv. 1–17). 2. The success of the test; he found them all deeply concerned, particularly Judah, both for the safety of Benjamin and for the comfort of their aged father (vv. 18–34).

Verses 1–17

Joseph pours further kindnesses on his brothers, fills their sacks, returns their money, and sends them away happy; but he also tests them further. Joseph ordered his steward to put his fine silver cup (which was probably used at his table when they dined with him) into the mouth of Benjamin's sack, that it might seem as if he had stolen it from the table, and put it there himself, after his grain was delivered to him. Notice:

1. How the pretend criminals were pursued and arrested, on suspicion of having stolen the silver cup. The steward accused them of ingratitude.

2. How they pleaded for themselves. They solemnly protested their innocence and offered to submit to the severest punishment if they were found guilty (vv. 9–10).

3. How the theft was attributed to Benjamin. The cup was found in his sack. They dare not denounce Joseph's sense of justice, nor so much as suggest that perhaps whoever had put their money in the mouths of their sacks had also put the cup there, but they throw themselves on Joseph's mercy.

4. Their humble submission (v. 16):

4.1. They acknowledge the righteousness of God: *God hath found out the iniquity of thy servants,* perhaps referring to the harm they had formerly done to Joseph, for which they thought God was now holding them responsible.

4.2. They surrender themselves as prisoners to Joseph: *We are my lord's servants.* Now Joseph's dreams were completely fulfilled.

5. How Joseph, with an expression of justice, passes sentence that only Benjamin should be kept as a slave, and the rest should be dismissed; for why should any suffer except the guilty? It is clear he intended this to test the affection of his brothers toward Benjamin and their father. If they had gone away contentedly and left Benjamin as a slave, no doubt Joseph would soon have released and promoted him and informed Jacob and would have left the rest of his brothers justly to suffer for their hardheartedness. They turned out, however, to be more caring toward Benjamin than he feared. The ones who had sold Joseph would not now abandon Benjamin. Even the worst people may improve in time.

Verses 18–34

We have here a noble and poignant speech which Judah made to Joseph on Benjamin's behalf, to release him. Perhaps Judah was a closer friend to Benjamin than the rest were, or the rest chose him to speak for them, because he had a greater command of language, than any of them.

1. There is a great deal of unaffected, unforced rhetoric in this speech.

1.1. He addressed himself to Joseph with a great deal of respect and deference.

1.2. He represented Benjamin as one worthy of his compassionate consideration (v. 20); he was a *little one*, compared with the rest of them; the youngest, brought up tenderly with his father. It made the case all the more pitiable that he is the only one of his mother's sons left, his brother, namely *Joseph*, being dead.

1.3. He reminded Joseph that he himself had constrained them to bring Benjamin with them. Was he not brought to Egypt, purely in obedience to the command of Joseph? Would he then not show him some mercy?

1.4. The great argument he insisted on delivering was the inconsolable grief it would be to his aged father if Benjamin were left behind in slavery: "*If he should leave his father, his father would die*; much more so if he is now left behind, never more to return to him." So Judah urges this with a great deal of earnestness: "*His life is bound up in the lad's life*" (v. 30).

1.5. Judah, out of honor to the justice of Joseph's sentence, and to show his sincerity in this plea, offers himself to become a slave instead of Benjamin (v. 33). Neither Jacob nor Benjamin needed an intercessor with Joseph, for he himself loved them.

2. Let us note about the whole matter:

2.1. How wisely Judah suppressed all mention of the crime that Benjamin was accused of.

2.2. What good reason dying Jacob had to say, *Judah, thou art he whom thy brethren shall praise* (49:8), for he surpassed them all in boldness, wisdom, eloquence, and especially tenderness for their father and family.

2.3. Judah's faithful devotion to Benjamin in his distress was rewarded long afterward by the faithfulness of the tribe of Benjamin to the tribe of Judah, when all the other ten tribes deserted it.

2.4. How well does the writer to the Hebrews, in describing the mediation of Christ, notice, that *our Lord sprang out of Judah* (Heb 7:14), for, like his father Judah, he not only *made intercession for the transgressors*, but he also became a guarantee for them.

CHAPTER 45

It is a pity that this chapter and the previous one are divided and can be read separately. There we had Judah's intercession for Benjamin. Joseph let him continue without interruption, heard all he had to say, and then answered it all with the words, "I am Joseph." Now he found his brothers humbled for their sins, mindful of himself (for Judah had mentioned him twice in his speech), respectful toward their father, and very tender toward their brother Benjamin. To Joseph's brothers it was like a clear sky after a storm, or rather, it was like life from the dead. Here is: 1. Joseph's revelation of himself to his brothers (vv. 1–15). 2. The orders Pharaoh then gave to bring Jacob and his family to Egypt and Joseph's dispatch of his brothers back to his father with those orders (vv. 16–24). 3. The joyful news of this brought to Jacob (vv. 25–28).

Verses 1–15

Judah and his brothers were waiting for an answer.

1. Joseph ordered all his attendants to leave (v. 1). The private conversations among friends are the most free. So it is that Christ graciously shows himself and his loving-kindness to his people out of the sight and hearing of the world.

2. Tears introduced his speech (v. 2). These were tears of tenderness and strong affection.

3. He very abruptly tells them who he was: *I am Joseph*. They knew him only by his Egyptian name, *Zaphnath-paaneah* (41:45), his Hebrew name being lost and forgotten in Egypt; but now he teaches them to call him by that. So when Christ wanted to convince Paul he said, *I am Jesus* (Ac 9:5), and when he wanted to comfort his disciples he said, *It is I, be not afraid* (Mt 14:27). So when Christ shows himself to his people, he encourages them to draw near to him with a true heart.

4. He tries to soften their sorrow for the harm they had caused him, by showing them that God had brought much good out of it (v. 5): *Be not grieved, nor angry with yourselves*. Sinners must be sorry for their sins. Those who truly repent should be greatly moved when they see God bringing good out of evil. Now he tells them how long the famine was likely to last—*five years*, but (v. 6) what a position he was in to be kind to his relatives and friends. *God sent me before you* (vv. 5, 7).

4.1. God in his providence especially looks after God's Israel.

4.2. Providence looks a great way forward and reaches far into the future. The psalmist praises God for this (Ps 105:17): *He sent a man before them, even Joseph*. God sees his work from the beginning to the end, but we do not (Ecc 3:11).

4.3. God often works by opposites. Many of those who put Christ to death were saved by his death.

4.4. God must have all the glory. *It was not you that sent me hither, but God* (v. 8). They must not be proud of it, because it was God's doing, not theirs.

5. He promises to take care of his father and all the family during the remaining years of famine:

5.1. His brothers must go quickly to Canaan and tell Jacob that his son Joseph was *lord of all Egypt* (v. 9). If anything would make him young again, this would.

5.2. He is very serious about his father and all his family coming to him to Egypt: *Come down unto me, tarry not* (v. 9). He says that they will live in Goshen. He promises to provide for him: *I will nourish thee* (v. 11). Our Lord Jesus, being like Joseph, exalted to the highest honor and power in heaven, says he wants all those who are his to be with him where he is (Jn 17:24).

6. Deep affection is expressed by Joseph and his brothers. Joseph began with the youngest, his own brother Benjamin, who was very young when Joseph was separated from his brothers. After he had embraced Benjamin, he similarly kissed them all (v. 15), and then *his brethren talked with him*.

Verses 16–24

Here is:

1. The kindness of Pharaoh to Joseph and to his relatives for Joseph's sake: Pharaoh made his brothers welcome (v. 16), though it was a time of scarcity, and they were likely to be a burden to him. He told Joseph to send for his father to come back to Egypt and promised to provide them with all the facilities they needed both for his move and settlement there. If the best of all the land of

Egypt would be sufficient for him, he was welcome to it all, so that they need not worry about their belongings (v. 20). What they had in Canaan he considered merely *stuff* in comparison with what he had in store for them in Egypt.

2. The kindness of Joseph to his father and brothers. Pharaoh was respectful to Joseph, in gratitude, because Joseph had been instrumental in bringing much good to him. Joseph likewise was respectful to his father and brothers. He gave them carts and provisions for the way, both going and coming. To each of his brothers he gave a set of clothes, to Benjamin sets of clothes and also money in his pocket (v. 22). To his father he sent a very generous present of the best things of Egypt (v. 23). He dismissed them with a well-timed warning: *See that you fall not out by the way* (v. 24). Now Joseph, having forgiven them all, puts this obligation on them, not to rebuke one another. Our Lord Jesus has given us this responsibility, *that we love one another* (Jn 13:34). For:

- We are brothers and sisters; we all have one Father.
- We are his brothers and sisters, and we put to shame our relationship with him *who is our peace*, if we quarrel.
- We are guilty, *verily guilty* (42:21), and, instead of quarreling with one another, have a great deal of reason to quarrel with ourselves.

Verses 25–28

We have here the good news brought to Jacob. When he first heard it, he was stunned, for he could not believe it. To hear that *Joseph is alive* is too good news to be true; his heart fainted, for he cannot believe it. Our hearts faint, because we do not believe. Jacob had easily believed his sons formerly when they told him, *Joseph is dead*; but he can hardly believe them now that they tell him, *Joseph is alive*. Weak and tender spirits are influenced more by fear than hope. But eventually Jacob is convinced of the truth of the story, especially when he sees the carts which were sent to carry him, for seeing is believing. He says nothing of Joseph's glory, which they told him about; it was enough to him that Joseph was alive.

CHAPTER 46

Jacob here moves to Egypt in his old age, forced to go there by a famine and invited there by a son. Here: 1. How he acknowledged God in this way (vv. 1–4). 2. All his family go with him (vv. 5–27). 3. Joseph makes him welcome (vv. 28–34).

Verses 1–4

Jacob has here a very serious concern in front of him. We are told:

1. How he acknowledged God in this way. He *came to Beer-sheba*, from Hebron, where he now dwelled, and there *he offered sacrifices to the God of his father Isaac* (v. 1). Abraham called on God there (21:33) and so did Isaac (26:25). In his devotion:

1.1. He saw God as the God of his father Isaac, that is, a God in covenant with him.

1.2. He *offered sacrifices*:

1.2.1. To thank God for the recent fortunate changes in his family, for the good news he had received concerning Joseph, and for the hopes he had of seeing him.

1.2.2. To ask for the presence of God with him on his intended journey.

1.2.3. To seek God. The nations consulted their oracles by sacrifice. Jacob would not go till he had asked God's will.

2. How God directed his paths: *In the visions of the night God spoke unto him*. If we speak to him as we ought, he will not fail to speak to us. What has God to say to him?

2.1. He renews the covenant with him: *I am God, the God of thy father* (v. 3).

2.2. He encourages him to move with his family: *Fear not to go down into Egypt*. We must always rejoice with trembling. Jacob had many anxious thoughts about this journey, which God cared about.

2.2.1. He was old. It was a long journey.

2.2.2. He feared that his sons might be tainted with the idolatry of Egypt, forget the God of their fathers, or fall for the pleasures of Egypt, and forget the Land of Promise.

2.3. He promises him comfort in his move:

2.3.1. That he would multiply in Egypt.

2.3.2. That he would have God's presence with him: *I will go down with thee into Egypt*.

2.3.3. That neither he nor his descendants would be lost in Egypt. Though Jacob died in Egypt, this promise was still fulfilled:

2.3.3.1. In the bringing of his body to be buried in Canaan.

2.3.3.2. In the bringing of his descendants to be settled in Canaan. Whatever low or dark valley we are called into at any time, we may be confident, if God is with us in it, that he will surely bring us up again. If he goes with us down to death, he will surely bring us up again to glory.

2.3.4. That living and dying, his beloved Joseph would be a comfort to him: *Joseph shall put his hand upon thine eyes*.

Verses 5–27

Old Jacob here leaves Beersheba. Little did he think of ever leaving Canaan. He expected, no doubt, *to die in his nest*, and to leave his descendants in actual possession of the Promised Land, but Providence arranges it otherwise. It is good to be ready, not only for the grave, but for whatever may happen between us and the grave. We have here a detailed account of the names of Jacob's family, *his sons' sons*, most of whom are afterward mentioned as heads of houses in the several tribes. When Jacob himself moved to a land of plenty, he did not leave any of his children behind to starve in a barren land. It was now 215 years since God had promised Abraham to make of him a great nation (12:2), but yet that branch of his descendants on which the promise was settled had increased only to seventy. When God pleases, *a little one shall become a thousand* (Isa 60:22).

Verses 28–34

We have here:

1. The joyful meeting between Jacob and his son Joseph, in which notice:

1.1. Jacob's wisdom in sending Judah before him to Joseph, to give him advance notice of his arrival in Goshen.

1.2. Joseph's filial respect to him. He went in his chariot to meet him, and in the interview, showed how much he honored him and how much he loved him. Time did not wear out the sense of his obligation, but the tears which he plentifully shed as he threw his arms around his father, out of joy to see him, were real indications of the sincere and strong affection he had for him.

1.3. Jacob's great satisfaction at this meeting.

2. Joseph's wise care concerning his brothers' settlement. There was a time when they were plotting to get rid of him; now he is making plans to see them settled to their satisfaction and advantage: this is repaying good for evil. Now:

2.1. He wanted them to live *in the land of Goshen*, which lay nearest to Canaan, and which perhaps was more thinly populated by the Egyptians and well supplied with pasture for cattle. He wanted them to live separately, so that they might be in less danger both of being contaminated by the vices of the Egyptians and of being insulted by the ill will of the Egyptians.

2.2. He wanted them to continue as shepherds, and not to be ashamed to have that as their occupation before Pharaoh. It is better to be a source of honor in a lowly position than a source of shame in a high one.

CHAPTER 47

In this chapter we see: 1. Joseph presenting first his brothers and then his father to Pharaoh (vv. 1–10), settling them in Goshen (vv. 11–12), and paying his respects to his father when he sent for him (vv. 27–31). 2. Joseph's justice between ruler and people in the difficult matter of selling Pharaoh's grain to his subjects at a reasonable profit to Pharaoh (vv. 13–26). In this he showed himself wise and good, both in his private and in his public capacity.

Verses 1–12

Here is:

1. The respect which Joseph, as a subject, showed to his ruler. Though he had had particular orders from Pharaoh to send for his father back to Egypt, he would not allow him to settle until he had given notice of it to Pharaoh (v. 1).

2. The respect which Joseph, as a brother, showed to his brothers.

2.1. Though he was a great man, and they were comparatively lowly and disrespected, especially in Egypt, he still acknowledged them. Every branch of the tree cannot be a top branch, but, because it is a lower branch, does it not still belong to the tree? Our Lord Jesus, like Joseph here, is not *ashamed to call us brethren* (Heb 2:11).

2.2. Since they were strangers and not courtiers, he introduced some of them to Pharaoh. Being presented to Pharaoh, according to the instructions which Joseph had given them, they tell him:

2.2.1. What was their business — that they were shepherds (v. 3). Everyone who has a place in the world should have an employment in it according to their ability. Rulers, as those who have the care of the public welfare, should ask about their subjects' jobs. Idle people are good-for-nothings, like drones in a hive, unprofitable burdens to the state.

2.2.2. What was their business in Egypt — to stay there for a time, while there was famine in Canaan. He obtained for them the right to settle in the land of Goshen (vv. 5–6). This was an example of Pharaoh's gratitude to Joseph. For those with special ability, he offered to put them in charge of his own livestock.

3. The respect Joseph, as a son, showed to his father: he presented him to Pharaoh (v. 7). And here:

3.1. Pharaoh asks Jacob a common question: *How old art thou?* (v. 8). A question usually put to old men, for it is natural to us to marvel at old age and to revere it (Lev 19:32).

3.2. Jacob gives Pharaoh an uncommon answer (v. 9). He speaks as a patriarch, with a serious air to instruct Pharaoh. Notice here:

3.2.1. He calls his life *a pilgrimage*, looking on himself as a stranger in this world and a traveler toward another world: this earth is like a hotel, not a home.

3.2.2. He reckons his life by *days*; for, even so, the days soon add up, and we are not sure how many days it will go on for. We may be turned out of the tent of this body at less than an hour's warning. Let us therefore number our days (Ps 90:12) and measure them (Ps 39:4).

3.2.3. How he describes them. First, they were few. Secondly, they were evil. Jacob's life, particularly, had been made up of evil days, and the most pleasant days of his life lay still before him. Thirdly, they were fewer than the days of his fathers, not as many, not as pleasant, as their days.

3.3. Jacob both addresses himself to Pharaoh and takes leave of him with a blessing: *Jacob blessed Pharaoh* (vv. 7, 10); he prayed for him, as one with the authority of a prophet and a patriarch.

Verses 13–26

Joseph now returns to managing the great trust which Pharaoh had placed in his hands. It would have been pleasant enough for him to have gone and lived with his father and brothers in Goshen, but his work would not allow it. In Joseph's dealings with the Egyptians notice:

1. The dire need that Egypt and adjacent lands were reduced to by the famine.

1.1. Notice from this how much we depend on God's providence. If its usual favors are suspended just for a while, we die, we all perish. All our wealth would not keep us from starving if the rain of heaven were withheld for just two or three years. Seeing how much we are indebted to God's mercy, let us always keep ourselves in his love.

1.2. Notice how much we suffer by our own improvidence. If all the Egyptians had done for themselves in the seven years' plenty what Joseph did for Pharaoh, they would not now have been in this predicament.

2. The price that had been paid for the supply of grain in this emergency:

2.1. They parted with all their money which they had hoarded (v. 14). Silver and gold would not feed them; they must have grain.

2.2. When the money failed, they parted with all their cattle; those used in their work, such as the horses and donkeys, and those for food, such as the flocks and the herds (v. 17). Pharaoh saw in reality what he had seen before in a vision, nothing but lean cows.

2.3. When they had sold off their livestock, it was easy to persuade themselves to sell their land too; for what good would that be for them, when they had neither grain to sow it nor cattle to eat on it? So next they sold that for a further supply of grain.

2.4. When their land was sold, so that they had nothing to live on, they of course had to sell themselves, that they might live purely on their labor. *Skin for skin, and all that a man hath, will he give for his life* (Job 2:4); for life is sweet.

3. The method which Joseph took to work out the matter between ruler and people.

3.1. For their lands, he did not need to come to any bargain with them while the years of famine lasted; but when these were over, he came to an agreement, which it seems pleased both sides, that the people should occupy and enjoy the lands, as he thought fit to assign them, and they should also have seed to plant in them from the king's stores, for their own proper use and benefit. They would then pay a fifth part of the yearly profits as rent to the crown. This became an established law (v. 26). It is observable how faithful Joseph was to him who appointed him. He did not put the money into his own pocket, nor settle the lands on his own family, but put both entirely at Pharaoh's disposal.

3.2. For their persons, he moved them to cities (v. 21). However hard this seems to have been for them, they were at this time aware of it as a very great kindness and were thankful that life was not even worse for them: *Thou hast saved our lives* (v. 25).

4. The exception Joseph made of the priests. They were freely maintained, so that they did not need to sell their lands (v. 22).

Verses 27–31

Notice:

1. The comfort Jacob lived in (vv. 27–28); while the Egyptians were impoverished in their own land, Jacob was restored in a strange land.

2. The care Jacob died in. At last *the time drew nigh that Israel must die* (v. 29). Now Jacob's anxiety was about his burial:

2.1. He wanted to be buried in Canaan, because it was the Land of Promise, and because it was a type of heaven, that better country which he who said these things showed that they are looking for (Heb 11:14). He aimed at a good land, where he would find rest and happiness on the other side of death.

2.2. He wanted Joseph to swear that he would take him there to be buried (vv. 29–31). When this was done, *Israel bowed himself upon the bed's head*, submitting himself, as it were, to the stroke of death.

CHAPTER 48

The time has drawn near that Israel must die. He takes leave of his grandchildren by Joseph. God's gifts and graces shine out much more in some saints than in others on their deathbeds. In this chapter: 1. Joseph, hearing of his father's illness, goes to visit him and takes his two sons with him (vv. 1–2); Jacob solemnly adopts Joseph's two sons and takes them as his own (vv. 3–7). 2. He blesses them (vv. 8–16); he explains and justifies the crossing of his hands in blessing them (vv. 17–20); and he leaves a particular legacy to Joseph (vv. 21–22).

Verses 1–7

Here:

1. Joseph goes to see his elderly father (v. 1). It is our duty to visit the sick, and those to whom we have the opportunity of doing good, either in body or soul. Joseph took his sons with him, that they might receive their dying grandfather's blessing. We think it unlikely that Manasseh and Ephraim would ever forget what happened at this time.

2. Jacob, having been told that his son was coming, prepared himself as well as he could to receive him (v. 2). It is very good for sick and elderly people to be as active and happy as they can, that they may not give up in the day of trouble. *Strengthen thyself*, as Jacob here, and God will strengthen you.

3. As a reward to Joseph for all his care for him, he adopted his two sons. In this adoption certificate there is:

3.1. A particular recalling of God's promise to him, which is referred to: "*God blessed me* (v. 3), and let that blessing be passed on to them."

3.2. An explicit receiving of Joseph's sons into his family: "Your sons are mine (v. 5), not only my grandchildren, but they are to be reckoned as my own children." He explains this at v. 16, *Let my name be named upon them, and the name of my fathers*. In this way, the elderly dying patriarch teaches these young people not to look on Egypt as their home, nor to join themselves to the Egyptians, but to accept their lot with the people of God, as Moses afterward did in a similar temptation (Heb 11:24–26). Those are worthy of double honor who, through God's grace, break through the temptations of worldly wealth and advancement, to take up religion with any shame or poverty that it may bring. Mention is made of the death and burial of Rachel, Joseph's mother, and Jacob's most loved wife (v. 7), referring to the story (35:19). Those who were as close to us as our own souls are dead and buried. Do we think it too much to follow them in the same path?

Verses 8–22

Here is:

1. The blessing with which Jacob blessed the two sons of Joseph, which is all the more remarkable because the writer to the Hebrews mentions it (Heb 11:21).

1.1. Jacob's eyes were failing because of old age (v. 10). Jacob, like his father before him, when he was old, had failing eyesight. Those who have the honor of age must also be content to accept the burdens it brings. The eye of faith may be very clear even when the eye of the body is very much obscured.

1.2. Jacob was very fond of Joseph's sons. With what satisfaction does Jacob say here (v. 11), *I had not thought to see thy face* (having for many years assumed Joseph to be lost), *and, lo, God has shown me also thy seed!*

1.3. Before he passes on his blessing, he recalls his experiences of God's goodness to him:

1.3.1. He had *fed him all his life long unto this day* (v. 15). As long as we have lived in this world we have continually experienced God's goodness to us, in providing for our normal everyday support. He who has fed us all our life long surely will not fail us at the end.

1.3.2. He had *redeemed him from all evil* by the Angel (v. 16).

1.4. When he confers the blessing and name of Abraham and Isaac on them, he commends the pattern and example of Abraham and Isaac to them (v. 15). He calls God the *God before whom his fathers Abraham and Isaac walked*, that is, in whom they believed, whom they followed and obeyed.

1.5. In blessing them, he *crossed hands*. Joseph put them so that Jacob's right hand should be put on the head of Manasseh the elder (vv. 12–13). Jacob, however, wanted to put it on the head of Ephraim the younger (v. 14). But Jacob gave him to understand that he knew what he was doing, and that he did not do it by mistake, as a whim, or from a greater affection for one more than the other, but from a spirit of prophecy, and in fulfillment of the divine plan. Manasseh would be great, but Ephraim would be truly greater. Joshua was of that tribe, so was Jeroboam. The tribe of Manasseh was divided, one half on one side of the Jordan, the other half on the other side, which made it less powerful and important. Foreseeing this, *Jacob crossed hands*. Grace does not follow the order of nature, nor does God use those whom we think most suitable to be used, but he does as he pleases. It is remarkable how often God, according to the special favors of his covenant, advanced the younger above the elder, Abel above Cain, Shem above Japheth, Abraham above Nahor and Haran, Isaac above Ishmael, Jacob above Esau, Judah and Joseph before Reuben, Moses before Aaron, and David and Solomon before their elder brothers (1Sa 16:7).

2. The special signs of Jacob's favor to Joseph. He left with him the promise of their return out of Egypt as a sacred trust: *I die, but God shall be with you, and bring you again* (v. 21). These words of Jacob provide us with comfort regarding the death of our friends. He will bring us to the land of our fathers, the heavenly Canaan, where our godly ancestors have gone before us. If God is with us while we stay behind in this world and will soon receive us to be with those who have gone on ahead to a better world, we ought not to grieve as those who have no hope.

CHAPTER 49

This chapter is a prophecy. Jacob is here on his deathbed, making his will. The twelve sons of Jacob were, in their day, famous men, but the twelve tribes of Israel, which came from and were named after them, were even more famous. In prospect of this, their dying father says something remarkable to each son or to the tribe that bore his name. Here is: 1. The introduction (vv. 1–2). 2. The prediction concerning each tribe (vv. 3–28). 3. The instruction repeated concerning his burial (vv. 29–32). 4. His death (v. 33).

Verses 1–4

Here is:

1. The introduction to the prophecy, in which:

1.1. The group is called together (v. 2). It was a comfort to Jacob, now that he was dying, to see all his children around him. His calling on them twice (vv. 1–2) to gather together was an instruction to them to unite in love and all make one people.

1.2. A general idea is given of what he intends to say (v. 1): *That I may tell you that which shall befall you* (not only you, but also your descendants) *in the last days.*

1.3. Their attention is called for (v. 2): "*Hearken to Israel your father*; let Israel, who has prevailed with God, prevail with you."

2. The prophecy concerning Reuben. He begins with him (vv. 3–4), for he was the firstborn. By committing sexual immorality with his father's wife, he forfeited the privileges of the birthright. He will have all the privileges of a son, but not of a firstborn. No judge, prophet, or ruler, is found to come from that tribe, nor any famous person except Dathan and Abiram, who were noted for their ungodly rebellion against Moses (Nu 16). Reuben himself seems to have lost all that influence on his brothers to which his birthright entitled him, for *when he spoke unto them they would not hear* (42:22). Reuben's infamous characteristic is that he was *unstable as water.* His nature was unstable; he could not control himself and his own appetites. Consequently, his honor was unstable; it left him, and became as water spilled on the ground. Those who throw away their goodness must not expect to save their reputation.

Verses 5–7

Notice:

1. The character of Simeon and Levi: they were brothers by disposition; but, unlike their father, they were passionate and vengeful, fierce and uncontrollable; their swords, which should have been used only as weapons of defense, were (as the margin reads it, v. 5) "weapons of violence." It is not in the power of parents, nor in their upbringing, to form the temperaments of their children. Jacob brought up his sons to everything that was mild and quiet, but they turned out to be a fierce, angry people.

2. Proof of this is the murder of the Shechemites, which troubled Jacob deeply at the time (34:30) and still continued to trouble him. Simeon and Levi would not listen to the advice of their elderly and experienced father; no, they wanted to be ruled by their own passions rather than by his wisdom.

3. Jacob's protest against their brutal act: *O my soul, come not thou into their secret.* He is showing in this that not only does he hate such practices in general, but also he is innocent particularly in this matter.

4. His hatred of those brutal desires that led them to this wickedness: *Cursed be their anger.* He does not curse their persons, but their passions. We ought carefully to distinguish between the sinner and the sin, so as not to love the sin for the sake of the person, nor to hate the person for the sake of the sin.

5. A sign of displeasure which he foretells their descendants would come under for this: *I will divide them.* The Levites were scattered throughout all the tribes, and Simeon's allotment lay in different places. This curse was afterward turned into a blessing to the Levites, but for the Simeonites, because of Zimri's sin (Nu 25:14), there was no release.

Verses 8–12

Glorious things are here said about Judah. Judah's name means "praise," in allusion to which he says, *Thou art he whom thy brethren shall praise* (v. 8). It is prophesied that:

1. The tribe of Judah would be victorious and successful in war.

2. It would be superior to the rest of the tribes; not only in itself more numerous and famous, but having authority over them. Judah was the *lawgiver* (Ps 60:7). That tribe led the vanguard through the desert and in the conquest of Canaan (Jdg 1:2).

3. It would be a strong and courageous tribe, one qualified for command and conquest: *Judah is a lion's whelp* (v. 9). The lion may be considered the ruler of animals; when it seizes its prey none can resist. By this it is foretold that the tribe of Judah would become very formidable. It would not only obtain great victories, but it would also peaceably and quietly enjoy what was obtained from those victories. They would wage war, not for its own sake, but for the sake of peace. Judah is compared, not to a lion standing, always tearing, raging, and ranging; but to a lion lying down, enjoying the satisfaction of his power and success, without being a nuisance to others. This is true greatness.

4. It would be the royal tribe, and the tribe from which Messiah the Prince would come: *The sceptre shall not depart from Judah, till Shiloh come* (v. 10). Jacob here foresees and foretells:

4.1. That the scepter would come to the tribe of Judah, which was fulfilled in David, onto whose family the crown was settled by inheritance.

4.2. That Shiloh would be of this tribe—his offspring, that promised offspring, in whom the earth would be blessed: *that peaceable and prosperous one*, or "the Savior," as others translate it, will come out of Judah.

4.3. That after the coming of the scepter to the tribe of Judah it would continue in that tribe. Till the Captivity, all along from David's time, the scepter was in Judah, and subsequently the governors of Judea came from that tribe, or of the Levites that joined it (which was the same thing), till Judea became a province of the Roman Empire, just at the time of our Savior's birth, and was numbered as one of the provinces in the census (Lk 2:1). And at the time of his death the Jews explicitly acknowledged, *We have no king but Caesar* (Jn 19:15). So it is undeniably reasoned against the thinking of the Jews, that our Lord Jesus is the One who would come.

5. It would be a very fruitful tribe, especially that it should bring much milk for babes and wine to gladden the human heart (vv. 11–12). Much of what is here said concerning Judah can be applied to our Lord Jesus. In him there is plenty of everything that is nourishing and refreshing to the soul, and which maintains and comforts the divine life in it. In him we may have wine and milk, the riches of Judah's tribe, without money and without cost (Isa 55:1).

Verses 13–21

Here we have Jacob's prophecy about six of his sons:

1. Concerning Zebulun (v. 13), that his descendants would live by the seashore, that they would be merchants, mariners, and sea traders. This was fulfilled when, about four hundred years later, the land of Canaan was divided by lot, and the *border of Zebulun went up towards the sea* (Jos 19:11).

2. Concerning Issachar (vv. 14–15), that the descendants of that tribe would be strong and industrious, fit for and inclined to labor, particularly the work of farming, like the donkey that patiently carries its burden, and, by getting used to it, makes it easier. Issachar submitted to two burdens, tilling the soil and forced labor. It was a tribe that took pains, and, being successful, was called on to pay rents and taxes.

3. Concerning Dan (vv. 16–17). What is said concerning Dan refers to that tribe in general, that though Dan was one of the sons of the concubines, he still would by skill, cunning, and surprise gain advantages over his enemies, like a serpent suddenly biting the heel of a traveler. Dan will be legally integrated as well as any of the other tribes. Some, like Dan, may excel in the subtlety of the serpent, while others, like Judah, may excel in the courage of the lion. Both may give good service to the cause of God against the Canaanites. Jacob was carrying on with his prophecy; but now, having almost finished speaking, and ready to fade away, he refreshes himself with the words which come as an aside (v. 18), *I have waited for thy salvation, O Lord.*

4. Concerning Gad (v. 19). He alludes to his name, which means "a troop," and foresees the character of that tribe, that it would be a warlike tribe, and so we find (1Ch 12:8), the *Gadites were men of war fit for the battle.* He foresees that the situation of that tribe on the other side of Jordan would expose it to the attacks of its neighbors, the Moabites and Ammonites. He also foretells that the troops of their enemies would overcome them in many skirmishes. But he assures them that they should *overcome at the last*, which was fulfilled when in Saul's time and David's the Moabites and Ammonites were wholly subdued: see 1Ch 5:18–22. *Vincimur in praelio, sed non in bello*, "We are foiled in a battle, but not in a campaign." Grace in the soul is often frustrated in its conflicts, but the cause is God's and grace will eventually be seen as the conqueror, even *more than conqueror* (Ro 8:37).

5. Concerning Asher (v. 20), that it should be a very rich tribe, filled not only with bread for necessity, but with delicacies. These were exported from Asher to other tribes, perhaps to other lands.

6. Concerning Naphtali (v. 21), a tribe that carries struggles in its name; it means "my struggle," and the blessing given to it refers to prevailing; it is a *hind let loose*. This tribe was:

- Like a loving deer, friendly and obliging.
- Like a liberated deer, zealous for its liberty.
- Like a swift deer (Ps 18:33), quick in dispatching its business.

Among God's Israel there is to be found a great variety of temperaments, all different from one another, but all contributing to the beauty and strength of the body, Judah like a lion, Issachar like a donkey, Dan like a serpent, Naphtali like a deer.

Verses 22–27

He closes with the blessings of his best-beloved sons, Joseph and Benjamin. He breathes his last with these.

1. The blessing of Joseph, which is very large and full. He is compared (v. 22) to *a fruitful bough* or vine, for God had made him fruitful in the land of his suffering, which he acknowledged (41:52). His two sons were like branches of a vine, or other spreading plants, *running over the wall*. Here are:

1.1. The providences of God concerning Joseph (vv. 23–24):

1.1.1. Joseph's predicaments and troubles (v. 23). Though he now lived comfortably and in honor, Jacob reminds him of the difficulties he had formerly struggled with. He had had many enemies, here called *archers*, being good at making trouble. His brothers, in his father's house, thought they were getting rid of him. Potiphar's wife dared to attack his purity, shooting arrows against which there is little defense except the hold God has on the consciences of bad people. Doubtless he had enemies in the court of Pharaoh, who were jealous of his promotion and sought to undermine him.

1.1.2. Joseph's strength and support in all these troubles (v. 24): *His bow abode in strength*, that is, his faith did not fail. The *arms of his hands were made strong*, that is, his other gracious qualities played their part: his wisdom, courage, and patience, which are better than weapons of war.

1.1.3. The origin and fountain of this strength: it was *by the hands of the mighty God. All* our strength to resist temptation and to endure suffering comes from God. His grace is sufficient and his strength is made perfect in our weakness.

1.1.4. The state of honor and usefulness to which he was later advanced. In this, Joseph was a type of Christ and of the church in general.

1.2. The promises of God to Joseph. Our experiences of God's power and goodness in strengthening us up to the present time encourage us still to hope for help from him. We may build a lot on our *Eben-ezers* (1Sa 7:12). Notice the blessings given to Joseph:

1.2.1. *Blessings of heaven above* (rain in its season, good weather in its season, and the temperate influences of the heavenly bodies); *blessings of the deep that lieth under* this earth, which compared with the upper world, is great in depth with underground caverns and springs.

1.2.2. Surpassing and superior blessings, which *prevail above the blessings of my progenitors* (v. 26).

1.2.3. Long-lasting and extensive blessings: *Unto the utmost bounds of the everlasting hills*, including all the products of the most fruitful hills, and lasting as long as they last (Isa 54:10).

2. The blessing of Benjamin (v. 27): He *shall ravin as a wolf*, he is a ravenous wolf; it is clear from this that Jacob was guided in what he said by a spirit of prophecy, not by natural affection, or he would have spoken with more tenderness of his beloved son Benjamin. Concerning Benjamin he foresees and foretells only that his descendants would be a warlike tribe, strong and daring, and that they would enrich themselves with the plunder of their enemies—that they would be active and busy in the world and be a tribe as much feared by their neighbors as any other. Blessed Paul was of this tribe (Ro 11:1; Php 3:5). In his early years, he devoured the prey as a persecutor, but, in his later years, he distributed the plunder as a preacher.

Verses 28–33

Here is:

1. The summing up of the blessings of Jacob's sons (v. 28). Though Reuben, Simeon, and Levi were under the marks of their father's displeasure, he is still said to *bless them every one according to his blessing*; for none of them were rejected as Esau was.

2. The solemn instructions Jacob gave them concerning his burial, which are a repetition of what he had given to Joseph before. See how he speaks of death: *I am to be gathered unto my people* (v. 29). Though death separates us from our children and our people in this world, it gathers us to our ancestors and to our people in the other world.

3. The death of Jacob (v. 33), as one happily resting, now that he was weary. *I will lay me down, and sleep* (Ps 4:8). He freely submitted his spirit into the hand of God, the Father of spirits: *He yielded up the ghost*. His separated soul went to the assembly of the souls of the faithful, which, after they are delivered from physical burdens, are in a state of joy and bliss: he was *gathered to his people*.

CHAPTER 50

Here is: 1. The preparation for Jacob's funeral (vv. 1–6). 2. The funeral itself (vv. 7–14). 3. The establishing of a good understanding between Joseph and his brothers after the death of Jacob (vv. 15–21). 4. The age and death of Joseph (vv. 22–26). In this way, the book of Genesis, which began with the origins of light and life, ends with nothing but death and darkness. Sin has made such a sad change.

Verses 1–6

Joseph here pays his last respects to his dead father:

1. With tears and kisses and all the tender expressions of a son's affection, he takes leave of his body (v. 1). The departed soul is beyond the reach of our tears and kisses, but it is right to show our respect to the poor body, of which we look forward to a glorious and joyful resurrection.

2. Joseph ordered the body to be embalmed (v. 2), not only because he died in Egypt, and that was the custom of the Egyptians, but also because he was to be carried to Canaan.

3. He observed the ceremony of solemn mourning for him (v. 3). Even many Egyptians, out of the great respect they had for Joseph, put themselves into mourning for his father.

4. He asked and obtained leave from Pharaoh to go to Canaan, to attend the funeral of his father there (vv. 4–6). He promised to return: *I will come again*. When we return to our own houses from burying the bodies of our relatives, we say, "We have left them behind"; but, if their souls have gone to our heavenly Father's house, we may with more reason say, "They have left us behind."

Verses 7–14

We have here an account of Jacob's funeral. He dies in honor, and is followed to the grave by all his children.

1. It was a dignified funeral. He was accompanied to the grave, not only by his own family, but also by the courtiers and all the great people of the kingdom, who as a sign of their gratitude to Joseph, showed this respect to his father for his sake and honored him at his death. Good old Jacob had conducted himself so well among them as to gain universal esteem. Those who profess religion should try, by wisdom and love, to remove the prejudices which many may have against them because they do not know them.

2. It was a sad funeral (vv. 10–11). The solemn mourning for Jacob gave a name to the place, *Abel-mizraim*, "the mourning of the Egyptians," which served as a testimony against the next generation of Egyptians, who oppressed the descendants of Jacob to whom their ancestors showed such respect.

Verses 15–21

We have here the establishing of an agreement between Joseph and his brothers, now that their father was dead. When Providence has removed parents by death, every effort ought to be made to preserve acquaintance and love, that unity may continue even when that center of unity has been taken away.

1. Joseph's brothers humbly seek his favor:

1.1. While their father lived, they thought themselves safe in his shadow; but now that he was dead they feared the worst from Joseph. A guilty conscience exposes people to continual shocks. Those who want to be without fear should keep themselves without guilt.

1.2. They humbled themselves before him, confessed their fault, and begged his pardon: *Forgive the trespass. We are thy servants*.

1.3. They pleaded their relationship with Jacob and with Jacob's God:

1.3.1. With Jacob, urging that he directed them to make this submission: *Thy father did command*.

1.3.2. With Jacob's God. They plead (v. 17), *We are the servants of the God of thy father*; not only children of the same Jacob, but worshipers of the same Jehovah.

2. Joseph with a great deal of compassion confirms his reconciliation and affection to them; his compassion appears (v. 17): *He wept when they spoke to him*. These were tears of sorrow for their suspicion of him, and tears of tenderness on their submission. In his reply:

2.1. He directs them to look to God in their repentance (v. 19): *Am I in the place of God?* "Make your peace with God, and then you will find it relatively easy to make your peace with me."

2.2. He lessens their fault, out of consideration of the great good which God wonderfully brought out of it, which, though it should not make them less sorry for their sin, might make him more willing to forgive it (v. 20). God often brings good out of evil, and furthers the purposes of his providence even by human sins. Not that he is the author of sin; far be it from us to think so; but his infinite wisdom so overrules events that the outcome ends in his praise which in its own nature had a direct tendency to dishonor him, as, for example, the putting of Christ to death (Ac 2:23).

2.3. He assures them that his kindness will continue to them: *Fear not; I will nourish you* (v. 21).

Verses 22–26

Here is:

1. The prolonging of Joseph's life in Egypt: he lived to be *a hundred and ten years old* (v. 22).

2. The building up of Joseph's family: he lived to see his great-grandchildren by both his sons (v. 23), and probably he saw his two sons solemnly acknowledged as heads of distinct tribes, equal to any of his brothers.

3. The last will and testament of Joseph declared in the presence of his brothers, when he saw his death approaching. To those of them who still survived, and to the sons of those who were gone, who stood up in their fathers' places, he said this:

3.1. To comfort them with the assurance of their return to Canaan in due time: *I die, but God will surely visit you* (v. 24). He tells them to be confident: *God will bring you out of this land*, and so:

3.1.1. They must not look on it as their rest forever; they must set their hearts on the Land of Promise and call that their home.

3.1.2. They must not be afraid of failing and being ruined there: "*God will bring you* in triumph *out of this land* eventually."

3.2. To confess his own faith and confirm theirs. He charges them to keep him unburied till they would settle in the Land of Promise (v. 25). He makes them promise him with an oath that they would bury him in Canaan.

4. The death of Joseph, and the keeping of his body for a burial in Canaan (v. 26). He was *put in a coffin in Egypt*, but not buried till his children had received their inheritance in Canaan (Jos 24:32).

A Practical and Devotional Exposition of the Second Book of Moses,

Exodus

In the first book of Moses' history, he preserved and transmitted the records of the church, while it existed in private families. In this second book, he comes to give us an account of its growth into a great nation. The beginning of the former book shows us how God formed the world for himself; the beginning of this shows us how he formed Israel for himself, and both to proclaim his praise (Isa 43:21). There we have the history of the creation of the world; here we have the type of the redemption of the world.

The Greek translators called this book *Exodus* (which means "a departure" or "going out") because it begins with the story of the going out of the children of Israel from Egypt. The forming of Israel into a people was a new creation. This book gives us: 1. The fulfillment of the promises made before to Abraham (1:1 – 19:25). 2. The establishment of the ordinances which were afterward observed by Israel (20:1 – 40:38). Moses, in this book, begins, like Caesar, to write his own commentaries. But from now on, the writer is himself the hero and gives us the history of those things of which he was himself an eyewitness and earwitness, *et quorum pars magna fuit*, "and in which he bore a conspicuous part." There are more types of Christ in this book than perhaps in any other book of the Old Testament, for Moses wrote about him (Jn 5:46). The way of human reconciliation to God and coming into covenant and fellowship with him by a Mediator is here represented in various ways, and it is of great use to us to illustrate the New Testament, now that we have that to help us to explain the Old.

CHAPTER 1

We have here: 1. God's kindness to Israel, in multiplying them exceedingly (vv. 1 – 7). 2. The Egyptians' wickedness to them, oppressing and enslaving them (vv. 8 – 14). 3. The murder of their children (vv. 15 – 22). In this way, those whom the court of heaven blessed, the country of Egypt cursed because they were God's people.

Verses 1 – 7

We have:

1. A register of the names of the *twelve patriarchs*, as they are called (Ac 7:8).

2. The account which was kept of the number of Jacob's family, when they went down to Egypt. Notice is here taken of this that their increase in Egypt might appear even more surprising.

3. The death of Joseph (v. 6). *All that generation* gradually died off. Perhaps all Jacob's sons died much about the same time, for there was not many years' difference in age between the eldest and the youngest of them, except Benjamin.

4. The strange increase of Israel in Egypt (v. 7). Here are four words used to express it: They were fruitful and increased abundantly. They multiplied and waxed exceedingly mighty. This wonderful increase was the fulfillment of the promise made long before to the fathers.

Verses 8 – 14

The land of Egypt here eventually becomes a house of slavery to Israel, though up to that time it had been a happy shelter and settlement for them. Notice here:

1. The obligations the Egyptians were under to Israel on Joseph's account were forgotten: *There arose a new king*, after several successors in Joseph's time, *who knew not Joseph* (v. 8). If we work only for our fellow human beings, our works at best will die with us; if we work for God, they will follow us (Rev 14:13).

2. Purely political reasons were suggested for the Egyptians' harsh dealing with Israel (vv. 9 – 10).

2.1. They are represented as greater and mightier than the Egyptians; certainly they were not so, but the king of Egypt, when he decided to oppress them, wanted his people to think so, and looked on them as a formidable group.

2.2. So it is implied that if care is not taken to subdue them, they would become dangerous to the government. The thing the Egyptians feared was that Israel would *get them up out of the land*, probably having heard them speak of the promise made to their fathers that they would settle in Canaan.

2.3. It is therefore proposed that a course of action be followed to prevent them from increasing: *Come on, let us deal wisely with them, lest they multiply.*

3. The method the Egyptians took to suppress them and restrain their growth (vv. 11, 13 – 14).

3.1. They took care to keep them poor, by charging them heavy taxes.

3.2. They effectively made them slaves by this means. The Israelites, it would seem, were much more hardworking than the Egyptians, and so Pharaoh was careful to find them work, both in building and in farming. All this

81

was exacted from them with the utmost rigor and severity. They had *taskmasters* set over them, who were directed *to afflict them with their burdens*. They made them *serve with rigour*, so that their lives became bitter to them. In this they intended:

• To break their spirits.
• To ruin their health and shorten their days, and so reduce their numbers.
• To discourage them from marrying, since their children would be born into slavery. It is to be feared that the oppression they were under led many of them to join with the Egyptians in their idolatrous worship. However, they were kept as a separate group that did not associate with the Egyptians, and that by their other customs was separate from them, which was *the Lord's doing, and marvellous* (Mt 21:42).

4. The wonderful increase of the Israelites: *The more they afflicted them the more they multiplied*, greatly to the annoyance of the Egyptians. The blood of the martyrs was the seed of the church.

Verses 15–22

The Egyptians' indignation at Israel's increase, despite the many hardships they put on them, eventually drove them to the most inhuman and brutal methods of suppressing them: by murdering their children. Pharaoh and Herod proved themselves sufficient agents for that *great red dragon, who stood to devour the man-child as soon as it was born* (Rev 12:3–4). Pilate handed Christ over to be crucified, after he had confessed that he found no fault in him. It is well for us that, though human beings can kill the body, this is all they can do.

1. The midwives were commanded to murder them. Notice:

1.1. The orders given them (vv. 15–16). It added much to the brutality of the intended executions that the *midwives* were appointed to be the executioners. Pharaoh's project was that the midwives would secretly kill any male children as soon as they were born, and then put it down to a difficult or unfortunate birth (Job 3:11).

1.2. Their godly disobedience to this ungodly command (v. 17). *They feared God*, regarded his Law, and dreaded God's wrath more than Pharaoh's, and so kept the male children alive and safe.

1.3. Their justifying themselves in this disobedience, when they were charged with it as a crime (v. 18). They gave their reason for it, that they came too late to carry it out, for generally the children were born before they arrived (v. 19). Some of the old Jewish teachers explain it in this way, "Before the midwife comes to them, they pray to their Father in heaven, and he answers them and they give birth."

1.4. The reward God gave them for their tenderness toward his people: *He dealt well with them* (v. 20). In particular, *he made them houses* (v. 21), built them up into families, blessed their children, and prospered them in all they did.

2. When this plan did not succeed, Pharaoh gave public orders to all his people to drown all the male children of the Hebrews (v. 22).

CHAPTER 2

This chapter begins the story of Moses, that man who is famous for his intimate acquaintance with heaven and his great usefulness on earth, and the most remarkable type of Christ, as a prophet, savior, lawgiver, and mediator,

in the whole Old Testament. In this chapter we have: 1. The dangers of his birth and infancy (vv. 1–4). 2. His preservation through those dangers and the advances of his childhood and youth (vv. 5–10). 3. The devout choice of his more mature years, which was to acknowledge the people of God. He offered them his service at that time, if they wanted to accept it (vv. 11–14). 4. His withdrawal that he might keep himself for further service later (vv. 15–22). 5. The dawning of the day of Israel's rescue (vv. 23–25).

Verses 1–4

Moses was a Levite, both by his father and mother. Jacob left Levi under marks of disgrace (Ge 49:5), but soon after, Moses appears as a descendant from him, that he might be a type of Christ, who came in the likeness of sinful flesh and was made a curse for us. This tribe began to be distinguished from the rest by the birth of Moses, as afterward it became significant in many other matters. Notice:

1. How he was hidden. The parents of Moses had Miriam and Aaron, both older than he, born to them before the cruel law was declared. Probably the mother of Moses was full of anxiety in expecting his birth, now that this law was in force. But this child turns out to be the glory of his father's house. Just at the time when Pharaoh's cruelty rose to its height, the deliverer was born. When people are plotting the church's ruin, God is preparing for its salvation.

1.1. His parents observed him to be *a goodly child*, more than commonly beautiful; he was *fair to God* (Ac 7:20).

1.2. They were all the more concerned to preserve his life, because they looked on this as an indication of some good purpose of God concerning him and a happy sign of something great to come. *Three months* they hid him in some private room of their own house. In this Moses was a type of Christ, who, in his infancy, was forced to escape, and to Egypt too (Mt 2:13), and was wonderfully preserved, when many innocent children were massacred. It is our responsibility to live for God; it is his responsibility to work out the events. Faith in God will set us above the traps and fears that human beings set for us.

2. How he was exposed. At the end of three months they put him in an ark of bulrushes (a papyrus basket) by the *river's brink* (v. 3), and set his little sister at some distance to watch what would happen to him and into whose hands he would come (v. 4). God put it into their hearts to do this, to bring about his own purposes, that Moses might by this means be brought into the hands of Pharaoh's daughter. Moses seemed quite abandoned by his friends; his own mother did not dare acknowledge him, but now the Lord took him up and protected him (Ps 27:10).

Verses 5–10

Here is:

1. Moses saved from perishing. He lay in a bulrush-basket by the riverside. If he had been left to lie there, he would have quickly died from hunger, if he had not been sooner washed away by the river or devoured by a crocodile. If he had fallen into any other hands than those he did fall into, they certainly would have thrown him into the river straightaway. Providence, however, brings no less a person there than Pharaoh's daughter, just at that point, and guides her to the place where this poor sad infant lay. Providence inclines her heart to pity the child,

which she dares do when no one else dared. Never did a poor child cry at such the right time, as this one did. God often raises up friends for his people even among their enemies. Pharaoh cruelly seeks Israel's destruction, but his own daughter has care and compassion on a Hebrew child, and not only so, but, beyond her intention, actually preserves Israel's deliverer.

2. Moses well provided for with a good nurse, no less than his own dear mother (vv. 7–9). Pharaoh's daughter thinks it right that he should have a Hebrew nurse, rather than be looked after by an Egyptian woman, and the sister of Moses, with skill and good management, introduces the mother as a nurse to the great advantage of the child. Mothers are the best nurses.

3. Moses advanced to be the son of Pharaoh's daughter (v. 10). The tradition of the Jews is that Pharaoh's daughter had no child of her own, and that she was the only child of her father, so that when Moses was adopted as her son he was likely to receive the crown. Those whom God has in mind for great services he finds ways to qualify and prepare beforehand. Moses, by having his education at court, is more suited to be a prince and *king in Jeshurun* (Dt 33:25); by having his education at the learned court of the Egyptians, he is more suited to be a writer; and by having his education at the court of Egypt he is more suited to work in God's name as an ambassador to that court.

4. Moses named. Pharaoh's daughter called him *Moses,* meaning "drawn out of the water," ultimately from Egyptian. The calling of the Jewish lawgiver by an Egyptian name is a happy sign to the gentile world and gives hopes of that day when it will be said, *Blessed be Egypt my people* (Isa 19:25). His tuition at court was a pledge of the fulfillment of that promise (Isa 49:23), *Kings shall be thy nursing fathers, and queens thy nursing mothers.*

Verses 11–15

Moses had now passed the first forty years of his life in Pharaoh's court, preparing himself for his work, and now it was time for him to undertake that.

1. He boldly acknowledges and embraces the cause of God's people: *When Moses was grown he went out unto his brethren, and looked on their burdens* (v. 11). The best exposition of these words comes from the inspired writer (Heb 11:24–26), where we are told that by this he expressed:

1.1. His holy contempt of the honors and pleasures of the Egyptian court; he *refused to be called the son of Pharaoh's daughter.*

1.2. His tender concern for his poor brothers in slavery, with whom, though he might easily have avoided it, he *chose to suffer affliction.*

2. He gives an example of the great things he was afterward to do for God and his Israel in two cases, related particularly by Stephen (Ac 7:23–53):

2.1. Moses killed the Egyptian who was beating the Hebrew (vv. 11–12); probably it was one of the Egyptian slave drivers, whom he found mistreating his Hebrew slave. The Jews' tradition is that he did not kill him with any weapon, but, as Peter struck Ananias and Sapphira, with the word of his mouth.

2.2. Moses was afterward to be used to govern Israel, and as an example of this we have him here trying to end a quarrel between two Hebrews. Notice:

2.2.1. The unfortunate quarrel which Moses observed between two Hebrews (v. 13). When God raises up instruments of salvation for the church, they will find enough to do, not only to restrain oppressing Egyptians, but also to reconcile quarrelsome Israelites.

2.2.2. The way he took of dealing with them; he noticed the one who caused the quarrel, who did the wrong, and gently reasoned with him: *Wherefore smitest thou thy fellow?* Moses kindly tried to reconcile them. The rebuke Moses gave on this occasion may still be of use, *Wherefore smitest thou thy fellow?*

2.2.3. The failure of his attempt (v. 14): *He said, Who made thee a prince?* A person needs no great authority to give a mild rebuke; it is an act of kindness. This man, however, interprets it as an authoritarian act and sees the one who rebuked him as acting in a high-handed way. Sometimes people reject a good talk or a timely warning with the thought that they are being preached at, or as if it were too much for someone to speak out a word for God and against sin. He rebukes Moses for what he had done in killing the Egyptian: *Intendest thou to kill me?* If the Hebrews had taken the hint and accepted Moses as their head and leader, they probably would have been rescued by then. But they despised their deliverer, and their rescue was justly delayed, and their slavery prolonged forty years, as afterward their despising of Canaan kept them out of it forty years more. We must take heed of being prejudiced against the ways and people of God by the pettiness and follies of some who profess religion. Christ himself was rejected by the builders and is still rejected by those he wants to save.

2.2.4. The fleeing of Moses to Midian as a result. God arranged it for wise and holy purposes. Things were not yet ready for Israel's rescue. Moses has to be further prepared for service and so is directed to withdraw for the present. God guided Moses to Midian because the Midianites were of the seed of Abraham. And through this country he was afterward to lead Israel. He came here and sat down by a well, tired and thoughtful, not really knowing what to do, and waiting to see which way Providence would direct him. It was a great change with him, since he had only recently been at ease in Pharaoh's court. God tested his faith in this way.

Verses 16–22

Moses here settles in Midian, just as his father Jacob had in Syria (Ge 29:2). Events that seem insignificant, and purely accidental, afterward appear to have been intended by the wisdom of God for very good purposes. A brief and casual incident has sometimes brought about the greatest and happiest turn of events in a person's life. Notice:

1. Concerning the seven daughters of Reuel the priest (or margin, "prince") of Midian:

1.1. They were humble and very hard-working; they *drew water for their father's flock* (v. 16). Idleness is an honor to no one.

1.2. They were modest and did not ask this strange Egyptian to come home with them till their father sent for him. Modesty is an attractive quality in a woman.

2. Concerning Moses. He was thought to be an Egyptian (v. 19). Note:

2.1. How ready he was to help Reuel's daughters to water their flocks. Those who have had a liberal education should not be strangers to humble work, because they do not know what necessity Providence may give them to work for themselves, or what opportunity Providence may give them to be useful to others. He loved to do good. Wherever the providence of God places us we should desire and try to be useful; and, when we cannot do the good we want to, we must be ready to do the good that we can do.

2.2. How well he was repaid for his usefulness. When the young women told their father, he asked them to invite him to his house and treated him with great courtesy (v. 20). Moses soon commended himself to the respect and good of this priest of Midian, who took him into his house, and in the course of time married one of his daughters to him (v. 21), by whom he had a son, whom he called *Gershom*, "a stranger there" (v. 22). Now this settlement of Moses in Midian was designed by Providence to protect him for the present and to prepare him for the great service he was further intended for. His way of life in Midian would be of use to him:

2.2.1. To acclimatize him to hardship and poverty.

2.2.2. To acclimatize him to contemplation and devotion. Egypt made him a scholar, a gentleman, a statesman, a soldier, but he still lacked one thing, which the court of Egypt could not help him with. He must learn what it was to live a life of fellowship with God. To achieve this, he would be greatly helped by the solitude and retirement of a shepherd's life in Midian. By his life in Egypt he was prepared to rule in Jeshurun, but by his life in Midian he was prepared to speak with God on Mount Horeb, near which mountain he had spent much of his time.

Verses 23–25

Here is:

1. The continuation of the Israelites' slavery in Egypt (v. 23). Probably the murder of their infants did not continue. The Egyptians were now content with the number of the children of Israel, finding that Egypt was enriched by their labor. Since they took them as slaves, they did not care how many they were. When one Pharaoh died, another rose up in his place. He was ruled by the same principles and was as cruel to Israel as his predecessors.

2. The introduction to their eventual rescue.

2.1. *They cried* (v. 23). Now, at last, they began to think of God in their troubles and to return to him from the idols they had served (Eze 20:8). But before God unties them he put it into their hearts to cry to him, as it is explained in Nu 20:16.

2.2. God heard (vv. 24–25):

• *God heard their groaning.* He knows the burdens they groan under and the blessings they long for.

• *God remembered his covenant.*

• *God looked upon the children of Israel.* Moses looked on them and pitied them (v. 11), but now God looked on them and helped them.

• *God had a respect unto them,* he was concerned about them as his own people.

CHAPTER 3

Here is: 1. The revelation God was pleased to make of his glory to Moses at the bush, which Moses was forbidden to come too close to (vv. 1–5), and a general declaration of God's grace and goodwill to his people, who were loved for their fathers' sakes (v. 6). 2. A special declaration of God's purposes for the rescue of Israel from Egypt. He assures Moses it would be done now (vv. 7–9), and he gives him a commission to act as his ambassador both to Pharaoh (v. 10) and to Israel (v. 16). 3. He answers the objection Moses made of his own unworthiness (vv. 11–12). He gives him full instructions about what to say both to Pharaoh and to Israel

(vv. 13–18). He tells him beforehand what the outcome would be (vv. 19–22).

Verses 1–6

The years of the life of Moses are remarkably divided into three forties: the first forty he spent as a ruler in Pharaoh's court, the second as a shepherd in Midian, and the third as a king in Jeshurun. He had now finished his second forty years, when he received his commission to bring Israel out of Egypt. Sometimes it is a long while before God calls his servants to do that work which he has intended them for and has been graciously preparing them for. Notice:

1. How this appearance of God to him found him working. He was keeping the flock, tending sheep, near Mount Horeb (v. 1). This was a poor work for a man of his talents and education. It was the lot of Moses, who foresaw nothing except that he should die, as he had lived a long life, and as a poor lowly shepherd. When we are alone, the Father is with us. Moses saw more of God in a desert than he had ever seen in Pharaoh's court.

2. What the appearance was. To his great surprise he saw a bush burning, when he could see no fire either from earth or heaven to set it alight, and, what was even stranger, the bush did not burn up (v. 2). It was an extraordinary revelation of God's presence and glory.

2.1. He saw a flame of fire. When Israel's rescue from Egypt was promised to Abraham, he saw a burning lamp, a blazing torch, which represented the light of joy which that rescue would bring about (Ge 15:17). But now it shines more brightly, as a flame of fire.

2.2. This fire was not in a tall and imposing cedar, but in a bush, "a thorny bush," for this is what the word means.

2.3. The bush burned, but was not consumed.

3. The interest Moses showed in this extraordinary sight: *I will turn aside and see* (v. 3).

4. The invitation he had to draw near, but with a warning not to come too near, nor too quickly:

4.1. God gave him a gracious call, to which he readily responded (v. 4). When he went over to look, God called to him. *Draw nigh to God, and he will draw nigh to you* (Jas 4:8). God called him by name, *Moses, Moses.* The word of the Lord always accompanied the glory of the Lord, for every divine vision was intended for divine revelation (Job 4:16–21; 32:14–15). Divine calls are effective when we respond with an obedient answer to them, as Moses here, *Here am I, what saith my Lord unto his servant?* (Jos 5:14).

4.2. God gave him a necessary warning. Moses must draw near, but not too near. His conscience must be satisfied, but not his curiosity. Moses must express his reverence and his readiness to obey: "Take your sandals off your feet, as a servant." Removing your sandal was then what lifting off your hat is now, a sign of respect and submission.

5. The solemn declaration God made of his name, by which he wanted to be known to Moses: *I am the God of thy father* (v. 6). Abraham was dead, but God is still the God of Abraham. This means that Abraham's soul lives, which God stands in relationship with. To make Abraham's soul completely happy, his body must live again in due time. By these words it appears that God remembered his covenant (2:24).

6. The awe-inspiring impression this made on Moses. He hid his face, as one both ashamed and afraid to look on God. He was not afraid of a burning bush till he was aware that God was in it.

Verses 7–10

Now, after forty years of Israel's slavery and Moses' exile, when we may suppose both he and they began to despair, eventually the time has come: the year of redemption. Here is:

1. The notice God takes of the misery and suffering of Israel (vv. 7, 9): *Seeing I have seen*; not only, *I have surely seen*, but I have noticed this closely and considered the matter. God took notice of three things:

- Their sorrows (v. 7). It is likely they were not permitted to complain about their grievances to Pharaoh. But God saw their tears.
- Their cry: *I have heard their cry* (v. 7); it *has come unto me* (v. 9).
- The tyranny of their persecutors: *I have seen the oppression* (v. 9).

2. The promise God makes of their quick rescue and liberation: *I have come down to deliver them* (v. 8). When God does something very extraordinary he is said to *come down* to do it, as in Isa 64:1. This rescue was a type of our redemption by Christ, in which the eternal Word came down from heaven to rescue us. He promises also that they will settle happily in the land of Canaan, that they would exchange slavery for liberty, poverty for plenty, labor for rest.

3. The commission God gives to Moses to achieve this (v. 10). Moses is sent not only as a prophet to Israel, but also as an ambassador to Pharaoh, to entreat him. He is also sent as a ruler to Israel, to lead and command them. The same hand that now took a shepherd out of a desert, to be the planter of a Jewish church, afterward took fishermen from their boats, to be the planters of the Christian church.

Verses 11–15

God, having spoken to Moses, gives him the opportunity to speak.

1. He says that he is not capable of the service he was called to (v. 11): *Who am I?* He thinks himself unworthy of the honor. He thinks he lacks courage. He thinks he lacks skill, and so cannot rescue the children of Israel from Egypt; they are unarmed, undisciplined, and demoralized.

1.1. Moses was incomparably the most suitable person living to undertake this work, noted for his learning, wisdom, experience, bravery, faith, and holiness, but he says, *Who am I?* The more suitable people are for service usually the lower the opinion they have of themselves: see Jdg 9:8, etc.

1.2. The difficulties of the work were indeed very great. But Moses is the man who eventually does it, for God gives grace to the humble.

2. God answers this objection (v. 12). He promises him his presence: *Certainly I will be with thee*, and that is enough. He assures him of success and that the Israelites should serve God on this mountain.

3. Moses asks instructions about fulfilling his commission and wants to know by what name God wants to make himself known at this time (v. 13).

3.1. He supposes the children of Israel would ask him, *What is his name?* This they would ask either to confuse Moses, or for their own information.

3.2. He wants to know what answer to give them: "*What shall I say to them?* What name will guarantee to them proof of my authority?"

4. God would now be known by two names:

4.1. A name that shows what he is in himself (v. 14): *I AM THAT I AM.* This explains his name *Jehovah*, and means:

4.1.1. That he is self-existent; he has his being from himself, and has no dependence on any other. Being self-existent, he must also be self-sufficient and the inexhaustible fountain of being and bliss.

4.1.2. That he is eternal and unchangeable.

4.1.3. That we cannot fathom him out by searching. Let Israel know this, *I AM hath sent me unto you. Jehovah* is the personal and covenant name of God, the Redeemer of his people.

4.2. A name that shows what he is to his people. *The Lord God of your fathers hath sent me unto you* (v. 15). God had made himself known to him with this name (v. 6), and so he must pass on this name to them:

4.2.1. That he might revive among them the religion of their fathers.

4.2.2. That he might raise their expectations of the quick fulfillment of the promises made to their fathers. God wants this to be his name forever, and it has been, is, and will be his name, by which his worshipers know him and distinguish him from all false gods; see 1Ki 18:36.

Verses 16–22

Moses is here instructed in detail concerning his work and informed beforehand of his success:

1. He must go and meet with the elders of Israel, and raise their expectations that they will move promptly to Canaan (vv. 16–17). He is told that he will be successful with the elders of Israel (v. 18): *They shall hearken to thy voice* and not drive you away as they did forty years before.

2. He must go and meet with the king of Egypt (v. 18), he and the elders of Israel. They must not begin with a demand, but with a humble petition. *We beseech thee, let us go.* Moreover, they must only ask Pharaoh to allow them to go as far as Mount Sinai to worship God. If he would not give them permission to go and sacrifice at Sinai, they would justly go without permission and settle in Canaan. As to his success with Pharaoh, Moses is here told:

2.1. That petitions would not win him over: *I am sure he will not let you go* (v. 19).

2.2. That plagues would compel him to it: I will smite Egypt, and then he will let you go (v. 20).

2.3. That his people would supply Israel at their departure with articles and jewels, to enrich them: *I will give this people favour in the sight of the Egyptians* (vv. 21–22).

CHAPTER 4

This chapter: 1. Continues and concludes God's conversation with Moses at the bush concerning the great matter of bringing Israel out of Egypt. Moses raises the objection of the people's unbelief (v. 1), and God answers that objection by giving him the power to work miracles: to turn his rod into a serpent (his staff into a snake) and then back into a rod again (vv. 2–5); to make his hand leprous and then restored and whole again (vv. 6–8); and to turn water into blood (v. 9). 2. Is where Moses raises the objection of his own slowness of speech (v. 10) and asks to be excused (v. 13), but God answers this objection: by promising him his presence (vv. 11–12), by commissioning Aaron with him (vv. 14–16), and by putting an honor on the staff in his hand (v. 17). 3. Begins Moses' fulfillment of his commission. He obtains permission from his father-in-law to return to Egypt (v. 18). He receives further instructions and encouragements from God (vv. 19, 21–23). He departs and takes his family with him (v. 20). 4. Has Moses meeting with some difficulty on the way over the circumcising of his son (vv. 24–26). He has the joy of meeting his brother Aaron (vv. 27–28). He tells the elders of Israel about his commission to their great joy (vv. 29–31). So the plan was set in motion for the great rescue of Israel from Egypt.

Verses 1–9

1. Moses objects that the people would probably not *hearken to his voice* (v. 1), that is, they would not accept his word, unless he showed them some sign. If there were some people among them who were to contradict or question his commission, how would he deal with them?

2. God empowers him to work miracles, and directs him to three in particular, two of which were now immediately performed for his own assurance:

2.1. The rod, the staff, in his hand is made the subject of a miracle, a double miracle: it is thrown out of his hand and it becomes a snake; he takes hold of it and it becomes a rod again (vv. 2–4). Here was an honor put on Moses, that this change was brought about by his throwing the rod down and taking the snake up, without any spell, charm, or incantation. His being empowered to act in this way under God, beyond the normal course of nature and Providence, was a demonstration of his authority under God to set up a new dispensation of the kingdom of grace. There was significance in the miracle itself. Pharaoh had turned the rod of government into the snake of oppression, from which Moses had himself fled into Midian, but by means of Moses the scene was altered again.

2.2. His hand itself is next made the subject of a miracle. He puts it once into his cloak, and it comes out leprous; he puts it back again into the same place, and it comes out restored (vv. 6–7). This showed:

2.2.1. That Moses, by the power of God, would bring painful diseases on Egypt, and that they would be removed at his prayer.

2.2.2. That whereas the Israelites in Egypt had become leprous, contaminated with sin, by being taken into Moses' cloak they would be made clean and cured.

2.2.3. That Moses was not to work miracles using his own power.

2.3. He is directed, when he comes to Egypt, to turn some of the water of the river into blood (v. 9).

Verses 10–17

Moses is still reluctant to undertake the service for which God had intended him. We can no longer put his reluctance down to his humility and modesty, but must accept that here there was too much cowardice, laziness, and unbelief. Notice:

1. How Moses tries to excuse himself:

1.1. He pleads that he was not a powerful speaker: *O my Lord, I am not eloquent* (v. 10). God is pleased sometimes to choose those people as his messengers who have fewest natural advantages of skill. Christ's disciples were no great speakers, till the Spirit made them such.

1.2. When this plea was overruled, and all his excuses were answered, he begged that God would send somebody else on this errand and leave him to keep sheep in Midian (v. 13).

2. How God condescends to answer all his excuses. Though *the anger of the Lord was kindled against him* (v. 14), God still continued to reason with him, till he had won him over.

2.1. To make up for Moses' weakness, he here reminds him of his own power (v. 11): *Who has made man's mouth? Have not I the Lord?* Moses knew that God made human beings, but he must now be reminded that God made the human mouth too and of his power in general over the other faculties. The perfections of our faculties come from him; he makes *the seeing*; he formed the eye (Ps 94:9) and he opens the understanding, the eyes of the mind (Lk 24:45).

2.2. To encourage him in this great undertaking, he repeats the promise of his presence, not only generally, *I will be with thee* (3:12), but specifically, "*I will be with thy mouth,* so that your lack of eloquence will not spoil your message." If others spoke more gracefully, none spoke more powerfully, than he did.

2.3. He commissions Aaron with him. He promises that Aaron will meet him soon, and that he will be glad to see him, they probably not having seen each other for many years (v. 14). He directs him to use Aaron as his spokesman (v. 16), that their natural affection for each other might help them together more strongly fulfill their commission. Christ sent his disciples out two by two, and some of the twos were brothers. Aaron's tongue, with the head and heart of Moses, would make one complete unit for this delegation. God promises, *I will be with thy mouth, and with his mouth.* Even Aaron, who could speak well, could not speak God's word unless God was with his mouth.

2.4. He asks him to take the rod (staff) with him in his hand (v. 17). The rod he carried as a shepherd must be his staff of authority and must, for him, take the place of a sword and scepter.

Verses 18–23

Here:

1. Moses obtains permission from his father-in-law to return to Egypt (v. 18).

2. He receives from God further encouragements and directions in his work. And:

2.1. He assures Moses that the way ahead was clear. Whatever new enemies he might make in his undertaking, his old enemies were *all dead, all that sought his life* (v. 19).

2.2. He orders him to do the miracles, not only before the elders of Israel, but before Pharaoh (v. 21).

2.3. So that Pharaoh's obstinacy might be no surprise or discouragement to him, God tells him before that he would *harden his heart*.

2.4. Words are put into his mouth with which to address Pharaoh (vv. 22–23).

2.4.1. He must deliver his message in the name of the great Jehovah: *Thus saith the Lord*. This is the first time that introduction is used by anyone which afterward is used so frequently by all the prophets.

2.4.2. He must let Pharaoh know Israel's relationship with God and God's concern for Israel.

2.4.3. He must demand they be released: "*Let my son go*; not only my servant whom you have no right to detain, but my son whose liberty and honor I am very jealous for."

2.4.4. He must threaten Pharaoh with the death of the firstborn of Egypt, if he refuses: *I will slay thy son, even thy firstborn*.

3. Moses embarks on this journey.

Verses 24–31

Moses is here going to Egypt, and we are told:

1. How God met him in anger (vv. 24–26). This is a very difficult passage. These are our thoughts on:

1.1. The sin of Moses in neglecting to circumcise his son. This was probably the effect of his being *unequally yoked* (2Co 6:14) with a Midianite, who was too indulgent toward her child.

1.2. God's displeasure against him. Omissions are sins. God takes notice of, and is angry with, the sins of his own people. If they neglect their duty, they should expect to hear of it in their consciences and perhaps feel it in adverse circumstances.

1.3. The prompt fulfillment of the duty, for the neglect of which God had been angry with him. His son must be circumcised; Moses is unable to circumcise him, and so, out of necessity, his wife Zipporah does it.

1.4. The release of Moses after this: *So he let him go*; and all was well: only Zipporah could not forget the shock she was in, and on this occasion he probably sent his family back to his father-in-law.

2. How Aaron met him in love (vv. 27–28). God sent Aaron to meet him and directed him where to find him, in the desert that lay toward Midian. He met him *in the mount of God*, the place where God had met with him. They embraced each other as a pledge of their sincere agreement in the work to which they were called together. Moses informed his brother of the commission he had received (v. 28).

3. How the elders of Israel met him in faith and obedience. When Moses and Aaron first started their commission in Egypt, they met with a better reception than they promised themselves (vv. 29–31). *The people believed* (v. 31), as God had foretold (3:18). *They bowed their heads and worshipped.*

CHAPTER 5

Moses and Aaron here have dealings with Pharaoh, to ask permission from him to go and worship in the desert. 1. They ask permission in the name of God (v. 1), and he answers their demand by defying God (v. 2). 2. They ask permission in the name of Israel (v. 3), and he answers their request with further orders to oppress Israel (vv. 4–9). 3. These cruel orders were executed by the slave drivers (vv. 10–14). 4. They were complained about to Pharaoh, but in vain (vv. 15–19), complained about by the people to Moses (vv. 20–21), and by him to God (vv. 22–23).

Verses 1–2

Moses and Aaron now have to deal with Pharaoh.

1. Their demand is reverently bold: *Thus saith the Lord God of Israel, Let my people go* (v. 1). Moses, in dealing with the elders of Israel, is directed to call God *the God of their fathers*, but in dealing with Pharaoh, they call him *the God of Israel*. This is the first time we find him so called in Scripture: he was called the *God of Israel*, the *person* (Ge 33:20), but here it is Israel, the *people*. They are just beginning to be formed into a people when God is called their God. In this great name they deliver their message: *Let my people go.*

2. Pharaoh's answer is irreverently bold: *Who is the Lord, that I should obey his voice?* (v. 2). He does not stop to discuss the matter or even consider it for a moment. How scornfully he speaks of the God of Israel: "Who is Jehovah? I do not know him nor care for him. I neither value him nor fear him." Ignorance and contempt of God are at the root of all the wickedness that is in the world. How proudly he speaks of himself: "*That I should obey his voice.* Will I, who rule over the Israel of God, obey the

God of Israel?" This is the heart of the matter: God must rule, but people do not want to be ruled.

Verses 3–9

Finding that Pharaoh had no trace of worship of God in him at all, Moses and Aaron next see whether he has any compassion on Israel.

1. Their request is very humble and modest (v. 3). They make no complaint of the rigor they met with. What they ask is very reasonable, only for a short time away, while they went three days' journey into the desert, "*We will sacrifice unto the Lord our God*, as other people do to theirs."

2. Pharaoh's denial of their request is very brutal and unreasonable (vv. 4–9).

2.1. He suggested that the people were lazy, and that is why they talked of going to offer sacrifices. But the cities they built for Pharaoh were sure signs they were not lazy. The malice of Satan has often represented the service and worship of God as work fit only for those who have nothing else to do.

2.2. His decisions were very brutal:

2.2.1. Moses and Aaron themselves must get to *their burdens* (v. 4). They must share in the work and common slavery of their nation.

2.2.2. The usual quota of bricks must be demanded, but without the usual allowance of straw to mix with the clay or to burn the bricks with.

Verses 10–14

Pharaoh's orders are here implemented; straw is denied, but the work not reduced.

1. The Egyptian slave drivers were very harsh. These slave drivers insisted on the same daily quotas as when there was straw (v. 13).

2. The people were scattered throughout all the land of Egypt to gather stubble (v. 12).

3. The Israelite supervisors were treated with particular harshness (v. 14). We can learn from this:

3.1. What a miserable thing slavery is, and what reason we have to be thankful to God that we are free, not oppressed. Liberty and property are valuable jewels in the eyes of those whose services and possessions lie at the mercy of a despotic power.

3.2. What strange steps God sometimes takes in rescuing his people. The lowest ebbs come before the highest tides, and very cloudy mornings commonly introduce the finest days (Dt 32:36).

Verses 15–23

It was a grave predicament that the supervisors were in. Notice:

1. How justly they complained to Pharaoh: They came and cried unto Pharaoh (v. 15). Thy servants are beaten but the fault is in thy own people, the slave drivers, who deny us what is necessary to carry on our work. But what was the result of this complaint? It only made matters even worse. Pharaoh taunted them (v. 17). When they had almost killed themselves by working so hard, he told them they were idle. It is good for us that people are not to be our judges, but God who knows what the motives are from which we act.

2. How unjustly they complained about Moses and Aaron: *The Lord look upon you, and judge* (v. 21). This was not fair. Moses and Aaron had shown that they were genuinely concerned for Israel's freedom, but because things were not immediately successful they were criticized for

worsening their slavery. Now what did Moses do in this predicament?

2.1. He turned back to the Lord (v. 22) to tell him about it. When we find ourselves, at any time, perplexed and confused in our duty, we should turn to God in faithful and fervent prayer. If we withdraw, let us withdraw to him, but no farther.

2.2. Moses asks, *Wherefore hast thou so evil entreated this people? Why is it thou hast sent me?* So:

2.2.1. He complains of his lack of success: "Pharaoh has done evil to this people, and not one step seems to have been taken toward their rescue."

2.2.2. He asks what could be done further: *Why hast thou sent me?* that is, "What other method can I take to fulfill my commission?"

CHAPTER 6

In this chapter: 1. God satisfies Moses in answering his complaints at the end of the previous chapter (v. 1). He gives him fuller instructions than before on what to say to the children of Israel, to satisfy them (vv. 2–8), but with little effect (v. 9). 2. He sends him again to Pharaoh (vv. 10–11). But Moses objects to that (v. 12), and so the command is given to him and his brother to vigorously fulfill their commission (v. 13). 3. Is a summary of the genealogy of the tribes of Reuben and Simeon and an introduction to that of Levi, so that the ancestry of Moses and Aaron might be made clear (vv. 14–25). The chapter concludes with a repetition of as much of the preceding story as is necessary to make way for the following chapter (vv. 26–30).

Verses 1–9

Here:

1. God silences Moses' complaints with the assurance of success in his negotiations, repeating the promise made him in 3:20, *After that, he will let you go. Then the Lord said unto Moses,* to quiet his mind, *"Now shalt thou see what I will do to Pharaoh"* (v. 1). See Ps 12:5, *Now will I arise.* Human extremity is God's opportunity to help and save. God takes the work into his own hands. *With a strong hand,* that is, being forced to it by a strong hand, *he shall let them go.*

2. God gives Moses further instructions, that both he and the people of Israel might be encouraged to hope for a glorious outcome of this matter. Take comfort:

2.1. From God's name, Jehovah (vv. 2–3). God would now be known by his name Jehovah, that is:

2.1.1. A God who fulfilled what he had promised.

2.1.2. A God who perfected what he had begun. In the history of the creation, God is never called Jehovah till the heavens and the earth were finished (Ge 2:4). When the salvation of the saints is completed in eternal life, then he will be known by his name Jehovah (Rev 22:13); in the meantime they will find him, for their strength and support, *El-Shaddai,* God Almighty and all-sufficient, a God that is enough.

2.2. From God's covenant: *I have established my covenant* (v. 4). We can pin all our hopes on that.

2.3. From God's compassions (v. 5): I have heard the groaning of the children of Israel.

2.4. From God's present decisions (vv. 6–8): I will bring you out. I will rid you. I will redeem you. I will bring you into the land of Canaan, and I will give it to you.

2.5. From God's gracious intentions in all these (v. 7):

2.5.1. He wanted their happiness: "I will take you to be a people for me."

2.5.2. He wanted to bring glory to himself: "You will know that I am the Lord." Their despondency was such that it made them not take any notice of God's promises (v. 9): *They hearkened not unto Moses for anguish of spirit.* By being worried and unhappy, we deprive ourselves of the comfort we might receive from God's word and from his providence and only have ourselves to thank if we continue not being encouraged.

Verses 10–13

Here:

1. God sends Moses the second time to Pharaoh (v. 11) on the same mission as before, to command him at risk to his life that he *let the children of Israel go.*

2. Moses makes objections. He pleads:

2.1. The unlikelihood of Pharaoh's hearing: "The children of Israel have not listened to me. They do not believe what I have said. How then can I expect that Pharaoh should hear me?" If God's professing people do not listen to his messengers, how can it be thought that his professed enemy should?

2.2. His own infirmity and lack of skill in speaking: *I am of uncircumcised lips.* God had given a sufficient answer to this objection, for the sufficiency of grace can make up for what is naturally missing at any time.

3. God again joins Aaron with Moses in the commission and puts an end to the argument by introducing his own authority and giving them both a solemn command. Moses himself needed to be commanded, as Timothy did (1Ti 6:13; 2Ti 4:1).

Verses 14–30

1. We have here a genealogy, not an endless one, such as the apostle condemns (1Ti 1:4), for it ends with those two great patriots Moses and Aaron, and is introduced here to show that they were Israelites, bone of their bone and flesh of their flesh, whom they were sent to rescue. The heads of the houses of three of the tribes are here named, agreeing with the accounts we had earlier (Ge 46:1–34). Dr. Lightfoot thinks that Reuben, Simeon, and Levi are honored here by themselves because they were left in notoriety by their dying father, and so Moses honors them particularly, to magnify God's mercy in their repentance and forgiveness. The two former seem rather to be mentioned only for the sake of a third, which was Levi, from whom Moses and Aaron descended, and all the priests of the Jewish church. Notice here:

1.1. That Kohath, from whom Moses and Aaron and all the priests derived their ancestry, was a younger son of Levi (v. 16).

1.2. That Aaron married Elisheba, daughter of Amminadab, one of the fathers of the tribe of Judah; for the tribes of Levi and Judah often intermarried (v. 23).

2. At the close of the chapter Moses returns to his narrative, from which he had broken off somewhat abruptly (v. 13), and repeats:

2.1. The command God had given him to deliver his message to Pharaoh (v. 29): *Speak all that I say unto thee,* as a faithful ambassador.

2.2. His objection to it (v. 30). Those who have at any time spoken unadvisedly with their lips ought often to reflect on it with regret, as Moses seems to do here.

CHAPTER 7

In this chapter: 1. The differences between God and Moses are dealt with, and Moses applies himself to his commission in obedience to God's command (vv. 1–7).

2. *The dispute between Moses and Pharaoh begins, and what a famous test of skill it was. Moses, in God's name, demands Israel's release; Pharaoh dismisses it. The contest is between the power of the great God and the power of a proud ruler. Moses confirms the demand he had made to Pharaoh, by a miracle, turning his rod (staff) into a snake, but Pharaoh hardens his heart against this conviction (vv. 8–13). 3. God punishes Pharaoh's disobedience by a plague, the first of the ten, turning the water to blood, but Pharaoh hardens his heart against this correction (vv. 14–25).*

Verses 1–7

Here:

1. God encourages Moses to go to Pharaoh.

1.1. He endows him with great power and authority (v. 1): *I have made thee a god to Pharaoh*; that is, my representative in this matter, just as judges are called *gods*, because they are God's vice-gerents. He was authorized to speak and act in God's name and place. Moses was a god, but he was only *made* a god, not essentially one by nature; he was a god only by commission. He was a god, but he was a god only to Pharaoh; the living and true God is a God to all the world.

1.2. He again nominates an assistant for him, his brother Aaron, a notable speaker: "He will be *thy prophet.* You will, as a god, inflict and take away the plagues, and Aaron, as a prophet, will announce them and threaten Pharaoh with them."

1.3. He tells him that Pharaoh would not listen to him, but the work would eventually be done. The Egyptians, who did not want to know the Lord, would be made to know him.

2. Moses and Aaron apply themselves to their work without further objection: *They did as the Lord commanded them* (v. 6). Their obedience was worthy of celebration by the psalmist (Ps 105:28), *They rebelled not against his word*, namely, Moses and Aaron, whom he mentions (Ps 105:26). In the same way, Jonah, though at first he was very averse to it, eventually went to Nineveh.

Verses 8–13

The first time that Moses asked Pharaoh, Moses gave only his instructions; now he is directed to produce his credentials, and he does so.

1. Pharaoh says, *Show a miracle*; not with any desire to be convinced, but in the hope that none will be performed.

2. Orders are therefore given to turn the rod (staff) into a snake, according to the instructions (4:3). Aaron threw his rod to the ground, and immediately it became a snake (v. 10). This was right, not only to move Pharaoh to wonder, but also to strike terror into him.

3. This miracle, even though it is too clear to be dismissed, is weakened, and the conviction of it lessened, by the magicians' imitation of it (vv. 11–12). Moses had been originally instructed in the learning of the Egyptians, and was suspected of having learned magic in his long retirement. So the magicians are sent for, to compete with him. Their rods became snakes, some think, by the power of God, to harden Pharaoh's heart; others think, by the power of evil angels. God allows the lying spirit to do strange things, so that the faith of some may be tried and made evident (Dt 13:3; 1Co 11:19). In this contest, however, Moses clearly gains the victory. The snake which Aaron's rod was turned into swallowed up the others,

which was sufficient to have convinced Pharaoh on which side the right lay. But Pharaoh was not persuaded by this. After the magicians had produced snakes, he had this to say: that there was a case between them and Moses.

Verses 14–25

Here is the first of the ten plagues, the turning of the water to blood, which was:

• An awful plague. Fish was their food (Nu 11:5), but the changing of the water led to the death of the fish; it was a plague in their natural habitat (v. 21): *The fish died. He slew their fish*; and when another destruction of Egypt, long afterward, is threatened, the disappointment of those *that make sluices and ponds for fish* is particularly noticed (Isa 19:10).

• A righteous plague, and justly inflicted on the Egyptians, for the Nile was personified and worshiped as a god (Hapi) in Egypt. The Egyptians and their land derived so much benefit from it that they served and worshiped it more than the Creator. God punished them, and turned what they had turned into a god into blood. The creature which we idolize God justly removes from us or makes us bitter toward. He makes what we make a competitor to him to be a torment to us.

• A significant plague. Egypt depended greatly on their river (Zec 14:18), so that in striking the river, they were warned of the destruction of all the products of their country, till it came at last to their firstborn; and this red river proved a dreadful omen of the destruction of Pharaoh and all his forces in the Red Sea. One of the first miracles Moses performed was turning water into blood, but one of the first miracles our Lord Jesus performed was turning water into wine (Jn 2:1–11), for the Law was given by Moses, and it was a dispensation of death and terror, but grace and truth, which like wine give joy to the heart, came through Jesus Christ.

1. Moses is directed to warn Pharaoh of this plague. "*Pharaoh's heart is hardened* (v. 14), therefore go and see what this will do to soften it" (v. 15). Moses is directed to meet him at the riverbank, where God knew he would come in the morning to pay his morning devotions to the river. Moses must be ready to give him a new summons to surrender there, and in case he refuses, to tell him of the judgment that was coming on that very river on the banks of which they then stood. So notice is given him of it beforehand, that they might have no opportunity to say it was by chance or to attribute it to any other cause, but that it might appear to be carried out by the power of the God of the Hebrews. We can learn from this that God warns before he wounds, for he is *longsuffering, not willing that any should perish, but that all should come to repentance* (2Pe 3:9).

2. Aaron, who carried the rod (staff), is directed to command the plague to come by striking the river with his rod (vv. 19–20). This shows:

2.1. The almighty power of God. Every creature is what God makes it to be to us, water or blood.

2.2. The changeability of everything under the sun, and what changes we may encounter in them. A river, at best, is transient; but divine justice can quickly make it harmful.

2.3. How troublesome sin is. If the things that have been our comforts turn to troubling us, we only have ourselves to thank. It is sin that turns our water to blood.

3. Pharaoh tries to confront the miracle, because he decides not to humble himself under the plague. He sends

for the magicians, and, by God's permission, they imitate the miracle by their secret arts (v. 22). Pharaoh uses this as an excuse not to accept the miracle (v. 23), and what a pitiful excuse it was. If they had been able to turn the river of blood back to water again, it would have been to the point. Then they would have proved their power, and Pharaoh would have been obliged to them as those who had done him good.

4. The Egyptians, in the meantime, seek relief from the plague, digging along the river for water to drink (v. 24). Probably they found some, with great difficulty, since God remembered mercy in his wrath; for he is full of compassion, and would not let the subjects suffer too severely because of the obstinacy of their ruler.

5. The plague lasted for seven days (v. 25), and in all that time Pharaoh's proud heart would not let him so much as ask Moses to intercede for it to be removed.

CHAPTER 8

Three more of the plagues against Egypt are related in this chapter: 1. The plague of frogs, which is threat-ened (vv. 1–4), inflicted (vv. 5–6), imitated by the magicians (v. 7), and removed at the humble request of Pharaoh (vv. 8–14), who hardens his heart again, despite his promise while the plague was on him (v. 8), and refuses to let Israel go (v. 15). 2. The plague of lice (gnats) (vv. 16–17), by which the magicians were frus-trated (vv. 18–19), and Pharaoh was hardened (v. 19). 3. The plague of flies. Pharaoh is warned of it before (vv. 20–21) and told that the land of Goshen would be exempt from this plague (vv. 22–23). The plague is brought (v. 24). Pharaoh negotiates with Moses about the release of Israel and humbles himself (vv. 25–29). Moses then prays, the plague is then removed (v. 31), and Pharaoh's heart is hardened (v. 32).

Verses 1–15

Pharaoh is here first threatened and then plagued with frogs—as afterward in this chapter he is plagued with lice (gnats) and flies—lowly and loathsome creatures, and by their vast numbers the source of severe plagues on the Egyptians. Some have thought that the power of God is shown as much in making an ant as in making an elephant. His providence serves his own purposes with the lowliest creatures as effectively as with the strongest, to show that he might humble Pharaoh's pride and correct his defiance. It would be a great humiliation for this proud monarch to see himself brought to his knees and forced to submit by such lowly means! As to the plague of frogs we may notice:

1. How it was threatened. Moses is here directed to warn Pharaoh of another judgment to come on him, if he continues to be obstinate. God does not punish people for sin unless they persist in it. The plague threatened, if he refused, was formidable and extensive.

2. How it was inflicted. Since Pharaoh did not consider the warning and was not at all inclined to yield to the summons, Aaron is ordered to give the signal of battle. Armies of frogs invade the land, and the Egyptians cannot halt their progress. Compare this with that prophecy of an army of locusts and caterpillars (Joel 2:2; Jer 51:27).

3. How the magicians were allowed to imitate it (v. 7). They also brought up frogs, but could not move those that God sent. The magicians intended to deceive, but God intended to use the frogs to destroy those who would be deceived.

4. How Pharaoh relented under this plague: it was the first time he did so (v. 8). He begs Moses to intercede for the frogs to be removed and promises that he will let the people go.

5. How Moses sets the time with Pharaoh, and then prevails with God in prayer for the frogs to be removed. Pharaoh sets the time for the next day (v. 10). In answer to the prayer of Moses, the frogs that came up one day died the next day, or the day after that.

6. What the outcome of this plague was (v. 15): *When Pharaoh saw there was a respite*, without considering either what he had just felt or what he had reason to fear, he hardened his heart. We can learn from this:

6.1. Until the heart is renewed by the grace of God, the effects made by suffering do not remain; the convic-tions wear off, and the promises that were made are soon forgotten.

6.2. God's patience is shamefully mistreated by sinners who do not repent. He graciously calls a truce, in order for them to make their peace. They take that opportunity to rally again the frustrated forces of their stubbornness and unfaithfulness. See Ecc 8:11; Ps 78:34; etc.

Verses 16–19

Here is a short account of the plague of lice (gnats). Notice:

1. How this plague of lice was inflicted on the Egyp-tians (vv. 16–17). The frogs were produced from the waters, but these lice out *of the dust of the earth*. The second woe was past, but the third woe followed very quickly.

2. How the magicians were frustrated by it (v. 18). They attempted to imitate it, but they could not. This forced them to confess that they were defeated: *This is the finger of God* (v. 19). Sooner or later God will draw out, even from his enemies, an acknowledgment of his own sovereignty and overruling power. It is certain they must all knuckle under eventually, just as Julian, "the apostate," did, when his dying lips confessed, "Thou hast overcome me, O thou Galilean!" God will not only be hard on all opposers but will also force them to acknowledge him.

3. How Pharaoh, despite this, was made more and more obstinate (v. 19). Those who are not reformed by God's word and providence are often made worse by them.

Verses 20–32

Here is the story of the plague of flies, in which we are told:

1. How it was threatened, like that of frogs, before it was inflicted. Moses is directed (v. 20) to rise early in the morning, to confront Pharaoh when he came out to the water. Moses must *stand before Pharaoh*, proud as Pha-raoh was, tell him what was most humbling, and must challenge him, if he refused to release his captives, to engage with an army of flies, which would obey God's orders if Pharaoh did not.

2. How the Egyptians and the Hebrews were to be espe-cially distinguished in this plague (vv. 22–23). Pharaoh must be made to know that *God is the Lord in the midst of the earth*, and in this it will be indisputable. Notice how it is repeated: *I will put a division between my people and thy people* (v. 23). The Lord knows those who are his, and will make it appear, perhaps in this world and certainly in the next, that he has set them apart for himself. A day will come when he shall *return and discern between the righteous and the wicked* (Mal 3:18), *the sheep and the goats* (Mt 25:32; Eze 34:17), though now the two mix freely with each other.

3. How it was inflicted, the day after it was threatened: *There came a grievous swarm of flies* (v. 24).

4. How Pharaoh, on this attack, entered into a treaty with Moses and Aaron about surrendering his captives; but notice the reluctance with which he gives in.

4.1. He is content they should sacrifice to their God, provided they do it in the land of Egypt (v. 25). But Moses will not accept his concession; he cannot (v. 26). So Moses insists: *We will go three days' journey into the wilderness* (v. 27). Those who want to offer an acceptable sacrifice to God must withdraw from the distractions of the world. Israel cannot keep the feast of the Lord either among the brick kilns or among the fleshpots of Egypt. Though they were indeed slaves to Pharaoh, in the worship of God they must observe his commands and not Pharaoh's.

4.2. When this proposal is rejected, he agrees that they can go into the desert, provided they do not go *very far away*. We see here a struggle between Pharaoh's convictions and his sinful nature; his convictions said, "Let them go"; his sinful nature said, "But not very far away." He sided with his sinful nature in preference to his convictions, and this was his ruin. Moses accepted this proposal, insofar as he promised to pray for this plague to be removed if Pharaoh did not change his mind (v. 29).

4.3. The outcome of it all was that God graciously removed the plague (vv. 30–31), but Pharaoh unfaithfully returned to his hardness of heart, and *would not let the people go* (v. 32). His pride would not let him part with such a jewel in his crown as his authority over Israel, nor would his covetousness let him part with such a major part of his income as their labors brought in.

CHAPTER 9

In this chapter we have an account of three more of the plagues against Egypt: 1. The plague on the livestock, which was fatal to them (vv. 1–7). 2. The plague of boils (vv. 8–12). 3. The plague of hail with thunder and lightning. Warning is given of this plague (vv. 13–21). 4. It is inflicted to their great dismay (vv. 22–26). Pharaoh, in shock, renews his agreement with Moses, but immediately breaks his word (vv. 27–35).

Verses 1–7

Here is:

1. Warning given of another plague, namely, a plague on livestock.

1.1. *Let my people go* (v. 1). They are my people, so let them go.

1.2. God describes the plague that would come, if Pharaoh refused (vv. 2–3). *The hand of the Lord is upon the cattle,* many of which would die in the plague. *Tomorrow* it will be done. We do not know what any day will produce, and so we cannot say what we will do tomorrow, but it is not so with God.

2. The plague itself inflicted. The cattle died (v. 6). The Egyptians afterward, and (some think) now, worshiped their cattle; it was among them that the Israelites learned to make a god out of a calf. So the plague here spoken of deals with them justly.

3. The distinction put between the cattle of the Egyptians and the cattle of the Israelites, according to the word of God: *not one of the cattle of the Israelites died* (vv. 6–7).

Verses 8–12

Concerning the plague of boils, notice:

1. When they were not persuaded by the death of their cattle, God sent a plague that took hold of their own bod-

ies and struck them painfully. If minor judgments do not do their work, God will send major ones.

2. The signal by which this plague was summoned. Sometimes God shows people their sin in their punishment; they had oppressed Israel in the furnaces, and now the ashes of the furnace are made as much a terror to them as their slave drivers had been to the Israelites.

3. The plague itself was very severe: these eruptions were inflammations, like Job's. This is afterward called the *botch of Egypt* (Dt 28:27).

4. The magicians themselves were struck with these boils (v. 11). They were punished in this way for helping to harden Pharaoh's heart. God will deal severely with those who strengthen the hands of the wicked in their wickedness.

5. Pharaoh continued to be obstinate, for now *the Lord hardened* his heart (v. 12). Before, he had hardened his own heart and resisted the grace of God, and now God justly gave him up to his own heart's sinful desires.

Verses 13–21

Here is:

1. A general declaration of the wrath of God against Pharaoh for his obstinacy. Though God has hardened his heart (v. 12), Moses must still repeat his application to him. In the same way, God wants to show an example of patience, and how he waits to be gracious to a *disobedient and gainsaying people* (Ro 10:21). Six times the demand had been made in vain, but Moses must make it still for a seventh time: *Let my people go* (v. 13). Moses is here ordered to deliver a most dreadful message to him, whether he will hear it or not. "I will send my plagues *upon thy heart*, not only physical plagues on your body, but spiritual plagues on your soul." He must tell him that he is to remain in history as a constant memorial to the justice and power of God's wrath (v. 16), "*For this cause have I raised thee up* to the throne at this time, and made you stand the shock of the plagues up to this time, *to show in thee my power*." Everything worked together to show this, that God's name (that is, his incontestable sovereignty, his irresistible power, and his unwavering justice) might be declared throughout all the earth, not only to all places, but through all ages while the earth remains. Pharaoh was a great king; God's people were poor shepherds at best and now poor slaves, but Pharaoh will be ruined if he sets himself up against them, for it is considered as setting himself up against God.

2. A particular prediction of the plague of hail (v. 18) and gracious advice to Pharaoh and his people to send their servants and cattle out of the field, that they might be sheltered from the hail (v. 19). Notice here what care God took to distinguish, not only between Egyptians and Israelites, but between some Egyptians and others. *Some believed the things that were spoken,* and they feared and took their servants and cattle inside (v. 20), like Noah (Heb 11:7), and it was to their wisdom. Even among the servants of Pharaoh there were some who trembled at God's word.

Verses 22–35

The threatened plague of hail is here summoned. We are told:

1. What destruction it caused on the earth. It killed both people and cattle, and struck down, not only the plants and crops, but also the trees (v. 25). The grain that was growing above the ground was destroyed, and only what had not yet sprouted from the ground was preserved

(vv. 31–32). Notice is taken here (v. 26) of the land of Goshen being preserved from receiving any damage from this plague.

2. What distress it caused Pharaoh. He humbled himself to Moses with the language of repentance (vv. 27–28). He condemns himself and his land: "*I and my people are wicked* and deserve what is brought on us." He asks Moses to pray for him: "*Entreat the Lord* for me, that this awful plague may be removed." And, lastly, he promises to release his prisoners: *I will let you go.* Moses now becomes an intercessor for him with God. Though Moses had every reason in the world to think that he would immediately turn away from his repentance, and told him so (v. 30), he still promises to be his friend in the court of heaven. We should continue to pray for and to teach even those whom we have little hope for (1Sa 12:23). Peace with God makes people safe from thunder, for thunder is the voice of their Father. The success of it: Moses prevailed with God (v. 33), but he could not prevail with Pharaoh: *He sinned yet more, and hardened his heart* (vv. 34–35). Little credit is to be given to confessions made on the spur of the moment.

CHAPTER 10

The eighth and ninth plagues of Egypt, of locusts and of darkness, are recorded in this chapter. 1. Concerning the plague of locusts: God instructs Moses in the meaning of these terrifying displays of his providence (vv. 1–2). He threatens the locusts (vv. 3–6). Pharaoh, on the persuasion of his servants, is willing to negotiate again with Moses (vv. 7–9), but they cannot agree (vv. 10–11). 2. The locusts come (vv. 12–15). Pharaoh cries, Peccavi, "I have offended" (vv. 16–17), and Moses prays for the plague to be taken away, and it is; but Pharaoh's heart is still hardened (vv. 18–20). 3. Concerning the plague of darkness: it is inflicted (vv. 21–23). Pharaoh again negotiates with Moses about a surrender (vv. 24–25), but the agreement breaks off in a fit of anger (vv. 26–29).

Verses 1–11

Here:

1. Moses is instructed. These plagues are constant memorials to the greatness of God, the happiness of the church, and the sinfulness of sin, and constant reminders to the whole human race not to *provoke the Lord to jealousy* (1Co 10:22) nor to *strive with their Maker*.

2. Pharaoh is rebuked (v. 3): this is what the Lord God of the poor, despised, and persecuted Hebrews says: "How long will you refuse to humble yourself before me?" Those who do not want to humble themselves will be humbled by God.

3. The plague of locusts is threatened (vv. 4–6). The hail had broken down the crops of the earth, but these locusts would come and devour what was left of them. Moses, after he had delivered his message, did not expect any better answer than he had before, so turned and left Pharaoh's presence (v. 6). In the same way, Christ appointed his disciples to depart from those who would not receive them, and to shake off the dust of their feet as a testimony against them (Mk 6:11).

4. Pharaoh's officials, his ministers of state or privy councilors, intervene to persuade him to negotiate terms with Moses (v. 7). The Israelites had become a weighty stone to the Egyptians, and now, eventually, the rulers of Egypt wanted to get rid of them (Zec 12:3).

5. A new agreement is now made between Pharaoh and Moses, in which Pharaoh agrees that the Israelites may go into the desert to make their sacrifices, but the matter now in dispute was who should go (v. 8).

5.1. Moses insists that they should take their whole families and all their belongings along with them (v. 9).

5.2. Pharaoh will in no way allow this: he will allow only the men to go, pretending that this was all they wanted, though this matter had never been mentioned in any of the former agreements, but, as for the *little ones*, he decides to keep them as hostages, to force them to return (vv. 10–11).

5.3. The agreement is then abruptly broken off.

Verses 12–20

Here is:

1. The invasion of the land by the locusts—*God's great army* (Joel 2:11). The locusts obey the call and fly on the wings of the wind, the east wind, and *caterpillars without number*, as we are told (Ps 105:34–35). A formidable army of cavalry and soldiers might have been more easily resisted than this army of insects.

2. The bleakness they caused in the land (v. 15): They covered the face of the earth, and ate up the fruit of it. Plants grow for the service of man, but when God pleases, those contemptible insects will not only be fellow-consumers with us, but also will plunder us and eat the bread from our mouths.

3. Pharaoh's admission (vv. 16–17):

3.1. Pharaoh confesses his fault: *I have sinned against the Lord your God, and against you.* He now sees his own folly in insulting and snubbing God and his ambassadors, and *seems*, at least, to repent of it.

3.2. He asks for pardon, not from God, as those who repent ought to, but from Moses.

3.3. He entreats Moses and Aaron to pray for him. Pharaoh asks for their prayers *that this death* only might be taken away, not *this sin*: he deplores the plague of locusts, but not the plague of a hard heart, which was much more dangerous.

4. The removal of the judgment after Moses prayed (vv. 18–19). This was:

4.1. As great an example of the power of God as the judgment itself. An east wind brought the locusts, and now a west wind took them away. Whichever point of the compass the wind is in, it fulfills God's word and turns around according to his will.

4.2. A great proof of the authority of Moses and confirmation of his commission.

4.3. As strong an argument for their repentance as the judgment itself, for by this it appeared that God is ready to forgive and quick to show mercy.

5. Pharaoh's return to his ungodly determination not to let the people go (v. 20).

Verses 21–29

Here is:

1. The plague of darkness. Notice particularly concerning this plague:

1.1. That it was a total darkness. They saw not one another. Hell is utter darkness. The light of a candle shall shine no more at all in thee (Rev 18:23).

1.2. That it was darkness which *might be felt* (v. 21).

1.3. No doubt it stunned and terrified them. The tradition of the Jews is that in this darkness they were terrified by the apparitions of evil spirits, or rather by the awful sounds and murmurs which they made, or, which is as frightening, by the horrors of their own consciences.

1.4. It continued *three days*, "six nights in one," says Bishop Hall. Spiritual darkness is spiritual slavery; while Satan blinds people's eyes so that they do not see, he binds their hands and feet so that they do not work for God or move toward heaven. They *sit in darkness* (Ps 107:10). Never was someone's mind so blinded as Pharaoh's; never was air so darkened as Egypt's. In their cruelty, the Egyptians wanted to extinguish the lamp of Israel and quench their flame, and so God justly puts out their lights.

2. The effects on Pharaoh of this plague:

2.1. It woke him up to the extent that he renewed his agreement with Moses and Aaron and now eventually agreed that they could take their little ones with them, but he wanted them to leave their cattle behind (v. 24). Moses decides not to lower his terms: *Our cattle shall go with us* (v. 26). Moses gives a very good reason why they must take their cattle with them; they must go to offer sacrifices, and so they must take everything necessary for that.

2.2. But it exasperated him to the extent that, when he could not set his own terms, he suddenly broke off the meeting. Moses is angrily dismissed and forbidden on penalty of death to enter the court. Moses takes him at his word (v. 29): *I will see thy face no more*. The result was that after this interview Moses did not come till he was sent for.

CHAPTER 11

We have in this chapter: 1. The instructions God had given to Moses, which he was now to follow (vv. 1–2), together with the respect Israel and Moses had with the Egyptians (v. 3). 2. The last message Moses delivered to Pharaoh, concerning the death of the firstborn (vv. 4–8), a repetition of the prediction of Pharaoh's hardening his heart (v. 9), and the response that it meets (v. 10).

Verses 1–3

Here is:

1. The high regard Moses and Israel had with God. Moses longed to see an end to this terrible work, to see the end of the plagues on Egypt and the end of the oppression on Israel. The Israelites were favorites of heaven. This was the last day of their slavery; they were about to go away, and their slave drivers, who had mistreated them in their work, wanted now to defraud them of their wages and send them away empty-handed. Though the patient Israelites were content to lose their wages, God would not let them go without them.

2. The high regard Moses and Israel had with the Egyptians (v. 3).

2.1. Even the people who had been hated and despised now came to be respected.

2.2. *The man Moses was very great.* How could it be otherwise when they saw what power he was endowed with, and what wonders were performed by his hand? In the same way, the apostles, though otherwise lowly people, came to be held in high esteem (Ac 5:13). Those who honor God he will honor. Though Pharaoh hated Moses, there were some of Pharaoh's servants who respected him. Similarly, in Caesar's household, even Nero's, there were some who had a high opinion of Paul (Php 1:13).

Verses 4–10

Pharaoh is warned here of the last plague which was now to be inflicted. This was the *death of all the first-*

born *in* Egypt at one time, which had been threatened originally in 4:23 (*I will slay thy son, thy firstborn*), but is now to be carried out. If the death of their cattle had humbled and reformed them, their children would have been spared. The extent of this plague is described (v. 5). It would include everyone: from the ruler who was to succeed to the throne down to the slaves at the mill. When Moses had delivered his message, it is said, *He went out from Pharaoh in a great anger*, though he was the meekest person in all the earth. Probably he expected that the very threat of the death of the firstborn would have led Pharaoh to give way. But it did not have that effect; his proud heart would not yield, not even to save all the firstborn of his kingdom. Moses was provoked to a holy indignation at this, being grieved, as our Savior was later, at the *hardness of his heart* (Mk 3:5). It is a great trouble to the spirits of good ministers to see people deaf to all the just warnings given them, and running headlong to destruction, despite all the kind methods taken to prevent it. In the same way, Ezekiel went in the *bitterness of his spirit* (Eze 3:14), because God had told him that the house of Israel would not listen to him (v. 7). To be angry at nothing except sin is the way not to sin in anger.

CHAPTER 12

1. Not one of all the ordinances of the Jewish church was more well known than that of the Passover, nor is any one more frequently mentioned in the New Testament. The ordinance consisted of three parts: 1.1. The killing and eating of the paschal lamb (vv. 1–6, 8–11). 1.2. The sprinkling of the blood on the doorposts, spoken of as a special thing (Heb 11:28) and exclusive to this first Passover (v. 7) with its reason (v. 13). 1.3. The Feast of Unleavened Bread for seven days following (vv. 14–20). This institution is communicated to the people, and they are instructed to observe: 1.3.1. This first Passover (vv. 21–23). 1.3.2. Later Passovers (vv. 24–27). The Israelites' obedience to these orders (v. 28). 2. Not one of all the providences of God concerning the Jewish church was more famous or is more frequently mentioned than the rescue of the children of Israel from Egypt. 2.1. The firstborn of the Egyptians are killed (vv. 12, 29–30). 2.2. Orders are given immediately for their release (vv. 31–33). 2.3. They begin their march: 2.3.1. Carrying their own belongings (v. 34). 2.3.2. Enriched with the plunder of Egypt (vv. 35–36). 2.3.3. Accompanied by a mixed multitude (vv. 37–38). 2.3.4. Brought into a predicament as regards their present supplies (v. 39). The event is dated (vv. 40–42). 3. A summary at the end of this memorable ordinance, with some additions (vv. 43–49), and of this memorable providence (vv. 50–51).

Verses 1–20

Moses and Aaron here *receive of the Lord* what they were afterward to *deliver to the people* concerning the ordinance of the Passover, which is introduced by an order for a new calendar to be inaugurated (vv. 1–2): *This shall be to you the beginning of months*. Up to that time, they had begun their year in the middle of September, but from now on they were to begin it from the middle of March, at least in all their religious reckonings. It is good to begin the day, to begin the year, and especially to begin our lives, with God. This new calendar began the year with spring, which *reneweth the face of the earth*, and used as a type of the coming of Christ (SS 2:11–12). While Moses was bringing the ten plagues on the Egyptians, he was directing the Israelites to prepare for their departure at an hour's warning. Their terror and hurry, it is easy to suppose, were great, but now they must apply themselves to observe a sacred ceremony, to honor God.

1. God appointed that on the night on which they were to go out of Egypt they should in each of their families *kill a lamb*, or that two or three families, if they were small, should share one with their nearest neighbor. The lamb was to be gotten ready four days before, and that afternoon they were to *kill it* (v. 6) as a religious ceremony, acknowledging God's goodness to them, not only in preserving them, but also in rescuing them, from the plagues inflicted on the Egyptians.

2. The lamb that was killed they were then to eat, roasted, with unleavened bread and bitter herbs, because they were to *eat it in haste* (v. 11), and to leave none of it until the morning, for God wanted them to depend on him for their daily bread. The One who led them would feed them.

3. Before they ate the flesh of the lamb, they were to sprinkle the blood on the doorposts (v. 7). This was the means that would distinguish their houses from those of the Egyptians.

4. This was to be annually observed as a festival to the Lord for generations to come, to which the *Feast of Unleavened Bread* was attached, during which, for seven days, they were to eat no bread except what was unleavened, to remember that they had to be confined to such bread for many days after they left Egypt (vv. 14–20).

4.1. The paschal lamb was a type. Christ is *our Passover* (1Co 5:7).

4.1.1. It was to be a lamb, and Christ is the Lamb of God (Jn 1:29), often in Revelation called the Lamb, meek and innocent as a lamb, silent before the shearers.

4.1.2. It was to be a *male of the first year* (v. 5), in its prime; Christ offered up himself in the middle of his life, not in infancy with the babies of Bethlehem.

4.1.3. It was to be *without blemish* (v. 5), showing the purity of the Lord Jesus, a Lamb *without spot* (1Pe 1:19).

4.1.4. It was to be set aside four days before (vv. 3, 6), to show that the Lord Jesus was set apart to be a Savior. It is significant that as Christ was crucified at the Passover, so he solemnly entered into Jerusalem four days before, the very day that the paschal lamb was set apart.

4.1.5. It was to be killed, and *roasted with fire* (vv. 6–9), showing the intensely painful sufferings of the Lord Jesus, even to death, death on the cross.

4.1.6. It was to be killed by the whole congregation. Christ suffered at the *end of the world* (Heb 9:26), by the hand of the Jews, the whole multitude of them (Lk 23:18), and for the good of all his spiritual Israel.

4.1.7. Not *a bone of it must be broken* (v. 46), which is explicitly said to be fulfilled in Christ (Jn 19:33, 36), showing the unbroken strength of the Lord Jesus.

4.2. The sprinkling of the blood was a type.

4.2.1. It was not enough that the blood of the lamb was shed; it also had to be sprinkled, showing the application of the benefits of Christ's death to our souls; we must *receive the atonement* (Ro 5:11).

4.2.2. It was to be sprinkled with *a bunch of hyssop* (v. 22) *dipped in the basin*. Faith is the bunch of hyssop by which we apply the promises to ourselves.

4.2.3. It was to be sprinkled on the doorposts, showing the open profession we are to make of faith in Christ and obedience to him.

4.2.4. It was to be sprinkled on the *lintel* and the side posts but not on the *threshold* (v. 7), which warns us against trampling on and spurning the blood of the covenant (Heb 10:29).

4.2.5. The blood sprinkled in this way preserved the Israelites from the destroying angel, who could do nothing where the blood was.

4.3. The solemn eating of the lamb was a type of our Gospel duty to Christ.

4.3.1. The paschal lamb was killed, not only to be looked on, but also to be fed on. So we must make Christ ours by faith. As we gain energy from our food, so we must receive spiritual strength and nourishment from him.

4.3.2. All of it was to be eaten; those who by faith feed on Christ must feed on a whole Christ; they must take Christ and his yoke, Christ and his cross, as well as Christ and his crown.

4.3.3. It was to be eaten immediately, not delayed till morning (v. 10). Christ is offered *today* and is to be accepted while it is still today.

4.3.4. It was to be eaten *with bitter herbs* (v. 8), in remembrance of the bitterness of their slavery in Egypt. Christ will be sweet to us if sin is bitter.

4.3.5. It was to be eaten in readiness to leave (v. 11); when we feed on Christ by faith we must leave totally the authority and reign of sin. We must leave all for Christ and consider it something very good (Heb 13:13–14).

4.4. The Feast of Unleavened Bread was a type of the Christian life (1Co 5:7–8). Having received Christ Jesus the Lord:

4.4.1. We must celebrate the festival with holy joy, continually delighting ourselves in Christ Jesus. If true believers do not enjoy a festival continually, it is their own fault.

4.4.2. It must be a Feast of Unleavened Bread, marked by love, without the yeast of malice, insincerity, or hypocrisy.

Verses 21–28

1. Here is Moses, as a faithful steward in God's house. It is added:

1.1. That this night, when the firstborn were to be destroyed, no Israelite must *go out of doors till morning*. They must not go outdoors, so that they do not drift and fail to be there when they would be called to leave.

1.2. That in the future they would carefully teach their children the meaning of this ceremony (vv. 26–27).

1.2.1. The question which the children would ask: "*What mean you by this service?* Why are we making all this fuss about eating this lamb and this unleavened bread more than our usual food?" We should all be concerned to understand the meaning of the holy ordinances with which we worship God, what is their nature, purpose, and meaning; what privileges they give and what responsibilities they lead to.

1.2.2. The answer which the parents were to give to this question (v. 27): *You shall say, It is the sacrifice of the Lord's passover*, that is, "By killing and sacrificing this lamb, we remember the work of wonder and grace which God did for our ancestors, when to prepare for our rescue from slavery, he killed the firstborn of the Egyptians. Though there were *with us, even with us, sins against the Lord our God* (2Ch 28:10), God graciously appointed and accepted the sacrifice by a family of a lamb—as before the ram was accepted instead of Isaac—and in every house where the lamb was killed the firstborn were saved." The word *pesach* means "pass over" or "spring over." It is a passing over, for the destroying angel passed over the houses of the Israelites and did not destroy their firstborn. It was intended to look forward as a sure sign of the great sacrifice of the Lamb of God in the fullness of time, instead of us and our firstborn. *Christ our passover was sacrificed for us* (1Co 5:7), his death was our life, and so he was the *Lamb slain from the foundation of the world* (Rev 13:8), from the foundation of the Jewish church: Moses kept the Passover by faith in Christ, for Christ was *the end of the law for righteousness* (Ro 10:4).

2. The people received these instructions with reverence and ready obedience. They *bowed the head and worshipped* (v. 27). They *went away and did* as they were commanded (v. 28). Here was none of that grumbling and murmuring among them which we read of earlier (5:20–21). The plagues of Egypt had done them good and raised their expectations of a glorious rescue, which before they had despaired of but now they went out ready for.

Verses 29–36

Here we have:

1. The Egyptians' sons, even their firstborn, killed (vv. 29–30). If Pharaoh had heeded the warning given him of this plague and released Israel, how many precious lives might have been preserved! But notice what trouble obstinate faithlessness brings on people. It reached from the throne to the dungeon. Ruler and rustic stand on the same level before God's judgments, for all are equal before him; see Job 34:19–20. Let us learn from this:

• To tremble before God, and to be *afraid of his judgments* (Ps 119:120).
• To be thankful to God for his keeping ourselves and our families daily.

2. Pharaoh's pride humbled, and Pharaoh submits to everything that Moses had insisted on: *Serve the Lord as you have said* (v. 31), and *take your flocks as you have said* (v. 32).

2.1. They are commanded to depart: *Rise up and get you forth* (v. 31). Pharaoh had told Moses he should *see his face no more* (10:28), but now he sent for him. He sent them out, not as hated people but as feared people, as can be clearly seen in his humble request to them (v. 32): "*Bless me also*, let me have your prayers, that I may not be plagued for what is past when you are gone."

2.2. They are induced to depart by the Egyptians. The Egyptians cried out (v. 33), *We be all dead men*. When the Egyptians urged them to go, it was easy for them to say that the Egyptians had kept them poor, that they could not undertake such a journey with empty purses, but that, if they were to give them the resources to pay for their expenses, they would go. The Israelites might receive and keep what they asked for and needed from the Egyptians as justly as servants receive wages from their masters for work done and pursue matters if it is delayed.

Verses 37–42

Here is the departure of the children of Israel out of Egypt. Pharaoh was now in a good frame of mind, but they had reason to think he would not long remain like this, and so now was no time to linger. We have here an account:

1. Of their number, about 600,000 men (v. 37), besides women and children, which we cannot suppose to make less than 1,200,000 more. What a vast increase was this, to grow from seventy souls in little more than 400 years!

2. Of their retinue (v. 38): *A mixed multitude went up with them*, many others beside that great family, some perhaps willing to leave their country because it had been devastated by the plagues, others going out of curiosity, to see how seriously the Israelites would offer sacrifices to their God, which had been talked about so much. Maybe they expected to see some glorious appearance of their God in the desert. Probably the greatest part of this great number was an ignorant, unthinking rabble, who just followed the crowd. We afterward find that they proved to be a trap to them (Nu 11:4), and probably when soon afterward they understood that the children of Israel were to continue forty years in the desert, they left them and returned to Egypt.

3. Of their belongings. They had with them *flocks and herds, even very much cattle*.

4. Of the provision made for the camp, which was very poor and slight. They took some dough with them out of Egypt in their knapsacks (v. 34). They had prepared to bake the next day in advance of their supposed departure, thinking it was very near; but, being hurried away some hours sooner than they had thought, they took the dough as it was, unleavened. When they came to Succoth, their first resting-place, they baked unleavened cakes, and though these were of course tasteless, the freedom that they had gained made this the most tasty and joyful meal they had ever eaten. It was just 430 years from the promise made to Abraham (as the apostle explains it, Gal 3:17) at his first coming into Canaan. [Ed. note: The 430 years of vv. 40–41 are now generally reckoned to refer to the length of time the Israelites were in Egypt rather than the time from Abraham to the exodus.] The promise of a settlement lay dormant and unfulfilled for a long time, but now, eventually, it was renewed. The first Passover night was a night of the Lord *much to be observed*; but the last Passover night, in which Christ was betrayed (and in which the Passover, with the rest of the ceremonial institutions, was superseded and abolished), was a night of the Lord *much more to be observed*, when a yoke heavier than that of Egypt was removed from our necks, and a land better than that of Canaan set before us. That was a physical rescue to be celebrated *in their generation*; this is an eternal redemption to be celebrated in the praises of his glorious saints, *world without end*.

Verses 43–51

Some further commands are here given concerning the Passover, as it should be observed in times to come:

1. *All the congregation of Israel shall keep it* (v. 47). All who share in God's mercies should join in thankful praises for them. The New Testament Passover, the Lord's Supper, ought not to be neglected by any who are capable of celebrating it.

1.1. No foreigner who was uncircumcised was allowed to eat it (vv. 43, 45, 48). We must be born again by the word before we can ever be nourished by it. None can share in and enjoy the benefits of Christ's sacrifice except those who are first circumcised in heart (Col 2:11).

1.2. Any stranger who had been circumcised was welcome to eat the Passover, even *servants* (v. 44). If we give ourselves sincerely and zealously to God, we will also want to give up all we have to him and do all we can to see that all who belong to us may be his too. Here is an early indication of favor to lowly Gentiles, that the stranger, if circumcised, stands on the same level as the native-born Israelite. It was their dedication to God, not their descent from Abraham, that entitled them to their privileges.

2. *In one house shall it be eaten* (v. 46), that they might rejoice together, and build up one another in eating it.

3. The chapter concludes with a repetition of the whole matter, that the children of Israel did as they were asked, and God did for them as he promised (vv. 50–51).

CHAPTER 13

In this chapter we have: 1. The commands God gave to Israel: to consecrate all their firstborn to him (vv. 1–2), to be sure to remember their rescue from Egypt (vv. 3–4) and in remembering it to keep the Feast of Unleavened Bread (vv. 5–7), and to pass on carefully the knowledge of it to their children (vv. 8–10). 2. The command to set apart to God the first offspring of their cattle (vv. 11–13) and to explain that also to their children (vv. 14–16). 3. The care God took of Israel, when he brought them out of Egypt: choosing the way for them (vv. 17–18) and guiding them in the way (vv. 20–22). Their care of Joseph's bones (v. 19).

Verses 1–10

Care is here taken to keep alive the remembrance:

1. Of the preservation of Israel's firstborn. God here lays claim in particular to the firstborn of the Israelites for their protection: *Sanctify to me all the firstborn.* God, who is the first and best, should have the first and best, and we should give to him what is most dear to us and most valuable. The firstborn were the joy and hope of their families. Therefore *they shall be mine,* says God. It is the *church of the firstborn* that is sanctified to God (Heb 12:23). Christ is *the firstborn among many brethren* (Ro 8:29), and because of their union with him, all who are born again and born from above are reckoned as firstborn. There is an *excellency of dignity and power* (Ge 49:3) belonging to them, and *if children, then heirs* (Ro 8:17).

2. Of their coming out of Egypt: "*Remember this day* (v. 3). Remember it by a good sign, as the most significant day of your lives, the birthday of your nation, or the day of its coming of age, no longer to be slaves under the Egyptians." In the same way, the day of Christ's resurrection is to be remembered, for we were raised up on it with Christ out of death's *house of bondage.*

2.1. They must be sure to *keep the feast of unleavened bread* (vv. 5–7). It was not enough that they remembered it; they must also celebrate it in that way which God had appointed. Notice how strict the prohibition of yeast is (v. 7); not only must no yeast be eaten, but none must be anywhere within their borders. The Jews' custom before the Feast of the Passover was therefore to throw anything that had yeast in it out of their houses: they burned it, buried it, or broke it in small pieces and scattered them in the wind. They searched diligently with lighted candles in all the corners of their houses, so that there would be no yeast there.

2.2. They must instruct their children in its meaning and tell them the story of their rescue from Egypt (v. 8). When they were celebrating the ordinance, they must explain it.

Verses 11–16

Here we have:

1. Further directions concerning the dedication of their firstborn to God. The first offspring of their cattle were to be dedicated to God as part of their possessions.

2. A warning that the firstborn of their children were to be redeemed and in no way sacrificed, as the Gentiles sacrificed their children to Moloch. The price of the redemption of the firstborn was fixed by the Law (Nu 18:16) at *five shekels.*

3. Further directions concerning the teaching of their children and all those of the rising generation from time to time in this matter. We can learn from this:

3.1. Children should be directed and encouraged to ask their parents questions concerning the things of God.

3.2. We should all be able to show the reasons for what we do in religion. As ordinances are sanctified by the word, so they must also be explained and understood by it. God's service is reasonable, and so it is acceptable when we perform it intelligently in our minds, knowing what we do and why we do it.

3.3. Mercies to our fathers are ancestors to us; we reap their benefits. This is all the more reason we have to say that in the death and resurrection of Jesus Christ we were redeemed.

Verses 17–22

Here is:

1. The choice God made in their way (vv. 17–18). He was their guide. Moses gave them direction, as he received it from the Lord. There were two ways from Egypt to Canaan. One was a short way from the north of Egypt to the south of Canaan, several days' journey; the other was much farther, through the desert, and that was the way by which God chose to lead his people Israel (v. 18).

1.1. There were many reasons why God led them *through the way of the wilderness of the Red Sea.* The Egyptians were to be drowned in the Red Sea. The Israelites were to be humbled and tested in the wilderness (Dt 8:2). Matters must first be settled between them and their God, laws must be given, ordinances instituted, covenants sealed, and the original contract confirmed. God's way is the right way, though it seems *about.* If we think he is not leading his people the quickest way, we can be sure he is leading them the best way, and so it will appear when we come to our journey's end.

1.2. There was one reason why God did not lead them the quickest way, because they were not then ready for war, much less for war with the Philistines (v. 17). Their spirits were broken with slavery; it was not easy for them to turn their hands suddenly from a spade to a sword. The Philistines were formidable enemies, too fierce to be fought against by raw recruits. God is said to bring Israel out of Egypt as the eagle *brings up her young ones* (Dt 32:11), gradually teaching them to fly. After orders had been given as to which way they should go, we are told:

1.2.1. That they went up themselves, not as a confused throng, but in good order, rank and file: they *went up harnessed* (v. 18).

1.2.2. That they took the *bones of Joseph* along with them (v. 19). Joseph had seen particularly to it that his bones should be taken there when God should appear to them (Ge 50:25–26). They might have thought, "Joseph's bones must rest in the end, and then we too will rest."

2. The guidance they were blessed with on the way: *The Lord went before them,* the *Shechinah* (the appearance of divine Majesty, which was a type of Christ) or an early revelation of the eternal Word, which, in the fullness of time, was to be *made flesh* and *dwell among us* (Jn 1:14). Christ was with the church in the wilderness (1Co 10:9). Those whom God leads into a desert he will not leave or lose there, but will take care to lead them through it. Those who make the glory of God their aim, the word of God their rule, the Spirit of God the guide of their senses,

and the providence of God the guide of their lives, may be confident that *the Lord goes before them,* as truly as he went before Israel in the desert, even though we may not sense him as much as they did; we must live by faith.

2.1. They all saw an appearance from heaven of a pillar, which in the bright day appeared as a cloud, and in the dark night appeared as a fire. God gave them this visible demonstration of his presence, out of compassion for the weakness of their faith.

2.2. They received perceptible effects of God's going before them in this pillar. For:

2.2.1. It led the way through that wasteland, in which there was no road, no track, for which they had no maps, and through which they had no guides. When they marched, this pillar went before them, at a speed at which they could follow.

2.2.2. It sheltered them by day from the heat.

2.2.3. It gave them light by night and at all times made the wilderness they were in less frightening.

3. The use of constant miracles (v. 22): He *took not away the pillar of cloud.* It never left them, till it brought them to the borders of Canaan. It was a cloud which the wind could not scatter. There was something spiritual in this pillar of cloud and fire. Some consider this cloud to be a type of Christ. The cloud of his human nature was a veil to the light and fire of his divine nature. Christ is our way, the light of our way, and its guide.

CHAPTER 14

The departure of the children of Israel out of Egypt, which was in fact the birth of the Jewish church, is made even more unforgettable. See the records of this chapter, its contents together with its key (Heb 11:29). Here is: 1. The extreme danger that Israel was in at the Red Sea. Moses was warned of this earlier (vv. 1–4). The cause of it was Pharaoh's pursuit of them (vv. 5–9). 2. Israel's great fear about it (vv. 10–12). Moses tries to encourage them (vv. 13–14). 3. The wonderful rescue that God brought about. Moses is instructed about it (vv. 15–18). A way could not be forced between the camp of Israel and Pharaoh's camp (vv. 19–20). 4. The Red Sea divided by divine power (v. 21) and made a way for the Israelites, who marched safely through it (vv. 22, 29). But to the Egyptians it was made an ambush which they were drawn into (vv. 23–25) and a grave which they were all buried in (vv. 26–28). The effects all this had on the Israelites (vv. 30–31).

Verses 1–9

We have here:

1. Instructions given to Moses concerning Israel's movements and encampments.

1.1. So that there might be no hesitation nor dissatisfaction about it, Moses is told before where they must go to (vv. 1–2). They had gotten to the edge of the wilderness (13:20), and a stage or two more would have brought them to Horeb, the place appointed for them to serve God, but instead of going forward they are ordered to turn off short, on the right hand from Canaan, and to march toward the Red Sea.

1.2. Moses will know that Pharaoh intends to ruin Israel (v. 3), and therefore God intends to ruin Pharaoh, and he uses this way to bring it about (v. 4).

2. Pharaoh's pursuit of Israel, in which, while he indulges his own ill will and revenge, he is furthering the fulfillment of God's plans for him. *It was told him that the people fled* (v. 5). Now:

2.1. He reflects with regret that he had allowed their departure. He and his servants were now angry with themselves for it: *Why have we done thus?*

2.1.1. They were angry that Israel were now free, that they had lost the profit from their labors and the pleasure of punishing them. The liberty of God's people grieves their enemies greatly (Est 5:12–13; Ac 5:17, 33).

2.1.2. It made their anger greater that they themselves had agreed to it. In this way, God makes the envy and rage of the wicked against his people turn into a torment to themselves (Ps 112:10).

2.2. He decides, if possible, either to lower their numbers or to get his revenge on them. In order to do this, he calls up an army, musters all his forces of chariots and charioteers (vv. 17–18), not doubting that he will make them slaves again (vv. 6–7). It is said (v. 8) that the children of Israel went out with a great deal of courage. *But the Egyptians pursued after them* (v. 9). Those who keenly set their faces heavenward, and want to live godly lives in Christ Jesus, must expect to be attacked by Satan's temptations and terrors. He will not feebly part with any from his service or go out without raging (Mk 9:26).

Verses 10–14

We have here:

1. The shock that the children of Israel were in when they perceived that Pharaoh pursued them (v. 10). They knew very well the strength and rage of the enemy and their own weakness. On the one hand was Pi Hahiroth, possibly a range of impassable craggy rocks; on the other hand were Migdol and Baal Zephon. In front of them was the sea; behind them were the Egyptians: so that there was no way open for them but upward, and that is where their rescue came from.

1.1. Some of them cried out to the Lord; their fear set them praying, and that was its good effect. God brings us into difficulties that he may bring us to our knees.

1.2. Others of them cried out against Moses; their fear set them murmuring (vv. 11–12). This was its bad effect. How inexcusable was their distrust! Here they express:

1.2.1. Withering contempt of their freedom, preferring slavery because it was accompanied by only some difficulties. A generous spirit would have said, "It is better to live as free people in the open air of a desert than as the Egyptians' slaves in the smoke of the brick kilns."

1.2.2. Complete ingratitude to Moses, who had been the faithful means of their rescue. They had as soon forgotten the miracles of mercy as the Egyptians had forgotten the miracles of wrath, and they as well as the Egyptians hardened their hearts, eventually to their own destruction. As Egypt did after ten plagues, so Israel did after ten provocations, of which this was the first (Nu 14:22); they were sentenced to die in the desert.

2. The well-timed encouragement that Moses gave them in this distress (vv. 13–14). He did not answer these fools according to their folly. Instead of correcting them, he comforts them, and with an extraordinary presence and composure of mind. He quiets their murmuring with the assurance of a fast and complete rescue: *Fear you not.* It is our duty and our privilege, that when we cannot leave our troubles, we can still rise above our fears, so that they may stimulate our prayers and endeavors and may not succeed in silencing our faith and hope. He directs them to leave matters to God, in silent expectation of the event: "*Stand still;* do not think you can save yourselves either by fighting or fleeing. Wait for God's orders. God is now about to work for you."

Verses 15–20

We have here:

1. Directions given to Israel's leader.

1.1. What he must himself do. He must, for the present, stop praying and turn to action (v. 15): *Wherefore cryest thou unto me?* Is God displeased with Moses for praying? No, he asks this question, *Wherefore cryest thou unto me?*

1.1.1. To assure Moses' faith. "Why should you press your petition any further, when it is already granted? I have answered your prayer."

1.1.2. To stir Moses to action. Moses had something else to do besides praying; he was to command the Israelites, and it was now necessary that he should be at his post.

1.2. What he must order Israel to do. *Speak to them, that they go forward.* Moses had told them to stand still and expect orders from God, and now orders are given. They thought they would be directed either to the right hand or to the left. "No," God says, "tell them to go forward, directly to the edge of the sea"; as if there were a fleet of transport ships ready for them to embark on.

2. A guard set on Israel's camp where it now lay most exposed, which was *in the rear* (vv. 19–20). *The angel of God,* whose ministry was made use of in the pillar of cloud and fire, went from *before the camp of Israel,* where they did not now need a guide, since there was no danger of missing their way through the sea, and they did not need any other word of command than to go forward. The angel of God withdrew and went behind them, where they now needed a guard and so there was a wall of partition between them.

Verses 21–31

We have here the account of that marvelous work which is so often mentioned both in the Old and New Testaments, the dividing of the Red Sea before the children of Israel. It was the dread of the Canaanites (Jos 2:9–10) and the praise and triumph of the Israelites (Ps 106:9; 114:3; 136:13–14). It was a type of baptism (1Co 10:1–2). Israel's passage through it was a type of the conversion of souls (Isa 11:15). We have here:

1. An example of God's almighty power in the kingdom of nature, in dividing the sea. It was a bay, gulf, or arm of the sea, maybe over six to nine miles (ten to fifteen kilometers), which was divided (v. 21). The natural sign was a strong east wind, showing that it was done by the power of God, whom the winds and the seas obey.

2. An example of his wonderful favor to his Israel.

2.1. They went through the sea to the opposite shore. They walked upon dry land in the midst of the sea (v. 29). The waters were a wall on their right hand and on their left. Probably Moses and Aaron ventured first onto the untrodden path, and then all Israel after them. This march through the paths of the great waters would make their later march, through the desert, less formidable. Those who had followed God through the sea did not fear following him wherever he led them.

2.2. This was done and recorded in order to encourage God's people in all ages to trust in him in the greatest difficulties. We find the saints long afterward sharing in the triumph of this march (Ps 66:6).

3. An example of his just and righteous wrath on his and his people's enemies, the Egyptians. Notice:

3.1. How they were confounded. The Egyptians had more chariots and horses, while the Israelites were on foot.

3.2. How they were confused (vv. 24–25). But, in the morning watch, the Lord looked upon the host of the Egyptians, and troubled them.

3.2.1. They had bullied and boasted as if everything belonged to them; but now they were panic-stricken.

3.2.2. They had driven furiously; but now they had difficulty driving, and found the wheels of their chariots jammed. As soon as the children of Israel had safely reached the shore, the waters returned to their place and overwhelmed all the Egyptians' army (vv. 27–28). Pharaoh and his servants, who had hardened one another in sin, now died together: not one escaped. An ancient tradition says that Pharaoh's court magicians, Jannes and Jambres, died with the rest. God dealt with Pharaoh for all his proud and defiant behavior toward Moses his ambassador. Come and see the desolations he made, and write it down, not in water, but *with an iron pen in the rock for ever* (Job 19:23). This is Pharaoh and all his horde (Eze 31:18).

4. The attention which the Israelites paid to this wonderful work which God did for them. They were ashamed of their former distrust and murmuring; they would never again quarrel with Moses or talk of returning to Egypt. They were now baptized into Moses in the sea (1Co 10:2). Being brought triumphantly out of Egypt in this way, they did not doubt that they would soon be in Canaan, having such a God to trust in, and such a mediator between them and him. Oh that there had in fact been such a heart in them as now there seemed to be! How good it would be for us if we were always in such good spirits as we are sometimes in!

CHAPTER 15

In this chapter: 1. Israel looks back on Egypt with a song of praise for their rescue. Here is the song itself (vv. 1–19) and the solemn singing of it (vv. 20–21). 2. Israel marches forward into the desert (v. 22). Their discontent at the waters of Marah (vv. 23–24), the relief given to them (vv. 25–26), and their satisfaction in the waters of Elim (v. 27).

Verses 1–21

Having read how that complete victory of Israel over the Egyptians was gained, we are told here how it was celebrated. Moses was divinely inspired to sing this song, and he delivered it to the children of Israel, that it should be sung before they moved from the place where they saw the Egyptians dead on the shore. They expressed their joy in God and thankfulness to him by singing. It was a song of faith. Here is:

1. The song itself.

1.1. We may notice concerning this, that it is:

• An ancient song, one of the earliest pieces of Hebrew poetry.

• An awe-inspiring composition, with a high and spectacular style, with vivid and true images and very moving.

• A holy song, consecrated to the honor of God, and intended to exalt his name and celebrate his praise, and only his.

1.2. What Moses chiefly points to in this song:

1.2.1. He gives glory to God and triumphs in him; this is his first intention (v. 1): *I will sing unto the Lord.* Israel rejoiced in God:

• As their own God and so their strength, song, and salvation (v. 2).

• *As their fathers' God.* They take notice of this, because, being conscious in themselves of their own unworthiness and defiant spirits, they had reason to think that what God had now done for them was for their *fathers' sake* (Dt 4:37).

• As a God of infinite power (v. 3).

• As a God of matchless and incomparable perfection (v. 11). This is expressed generally: *Who is like unto thee, O Lord, among the gods!* Egypt was notorious for having many gods, but the *God of the Hebrews* was too hard for them and confused them all (Dt 32:23–39). This is also expressed particularly: *He is glorious in holiness;* his holiness is his glory. God is *rich in mercy:* this is his treasure; *glorious in holiness:* this is his honor. *He is fearful in praises.* What is the subject of our praise is joyful to God's servants, but is fearful to his enemies (Ps 66:1–3). God is *doing wonders,* wonderful to all, since they are beyond the power and normal course of nature. They were wonders of power and wonders of grace, and God was to be humbly adored in both.

1.2.2. He describes the rescue they were now triumphing in, because the song was intended, not only to express and excite their thankfulness at the present time, but also to preserve and perpetuate the remembrance of this wonder for the future. Two things were to be taken notice of:

1.2.2.1. The destruction of the enemy and the waters being divided (v. 8). *The floods stood upright as a heap.* Pharaoh and all his army were buried in the waters. The proud waters went over the proud sinners. Their sin had made them as hard as a stone, and so they justly sank like a stone.

1.2.2.2. The protection and guidance of Israel (v. 13): *Thou in thy mercy hast led forth the people,* led them out of slavery in Egypt and out of the dangers of the Red Sea (v. 19).

1.2.3. He sets himself to make the most of this wonderful appearance of God for them. God had preserved them, so they decide to spare no cost or trouble in setting up a tabernacle to his honor, and they will exalt him there. The psalmist was so confident of the happy outcome of the salvation which was so gloriously begun that he looks on it as in effect already finished: *Thou hast guided them to thy holy habitation* (v. 13). This great rescue was encouraging in three ways:

1.2.3.1. It was such an example of God's power as would terrify their enemies and completely discourage them (vv. 14–16). It had this effect: the Edomites were afraid of them (Dt 2:4) and so were the Moabites (Nu 22:3) and the Canaanites (Jos 2:9–10; 5:1).

1.2.3.2. It was the beginning of God's favor to them as a pledge of the perfection of his kindness. *Thou shalt bring them in* (v. 17). If he *brought them out of Egypt,* despite their unworthiness and the difficulties that prevented their escape, no doubt he will bring them into Canaan.

1.2.3.3. It was a sign of unspeakable encouragement to all God's faithful subjects, that he will reign eternally, and his authority will never end. *The Lord shall reign for ever and ever* (v. 18).

2. The solemn singing of this song (vv. 20–21). Moses led the psalm and sang it for the men, and then Miriam for the women. Famous victories were usually applauded by the daughters of Israel (1Sa 18:6–7).

Verses 22–27

It would seem, it was with some difficulty that Moses persuaded Israel to leave that triumphant shore on which they had sung the previous song. Now here we are told:

1. That they had no water in the Desert of Shur (v. 22).

2. That they had water at Marah, but it was bitter, so that although they had gone three days without water they could not drink it. Now in this distress:

2.1. The people became angry and quarreled with Moses, as if he had done wrong to them. *What shall we drink?* they grumble (v. 24).

2.2. Moses prayed: *He cried unto the Lord* (v. 25). God is the guide of the church's guides; and to him, as the Chief Shepherd, the undershepherds must turn on all occasions.

2.3. God directed Moses to a piece of wood, which he threw into the water, as a result of which, the water was suddenly made sweet. Some think this wood had special powers in it for this purpose, because it is said, *God showed him the tree.* God is to be acknowledged, not only in the creation of things useful for us, but also in our discovering their usefulness. Some make this tree a type of the cross of Christ, which sweetens the bitter waters of suffering of the faithful and enables them to have joy in the midst of troubles.

2.4. *There he* [God] *made a statute and an ordinance* and decided matters with them. *There he proved them,* that is, he tested them there, put them on trial, allowing them to be probationers. In short, he tells them (v. 26):

2.4.1. What he expected from them, and that was, in a word, obedience. They must not think, now that they had been rescued from slavery in Egypt, that they were their own masters; they must look on themselves as God's servants, because he had *loosed their bonds* (Ps 116:16; Lk 1:74–75).

2.4.2. What they might then expect from him: *I will put none of these diseases upon thee,* that is, "I will not bring on you any of the plagues of Egypt." Let not the Israelites think God would then ignore their sins and let them do as they wanted. No, God shows no favoritism; a rebellious Israelite will fare no better than a rebellious Egyptian, which they found to their cost before they reached Canaan.

3. That they had good water and enough at Elim (v. 27). Here were twelve wells for their supply, one for every tribe, that they might not fight over water, as their ancestors had sometimes done; and, for their pleasure, there were seventy palm trees.

CHAPTER 16

This chapter gives us an account of the feeding of the camp of Israel. 1. They complain for lack of food (vv. 1–3). The notice God gave them beforehand of the provision he was going to make for them (vv. 4–12). 2. The sending of the manna (vv. 13–15) and the laws and commands concerning the manna. They should gather it daily as their daily bread (vv. 16–21). 3. They should gather a double portion on the sixth day (vv. 22–26) and should expect none on the seventh day (vv. 27–31). 4. They should preserve a certain amount of the manna as a memorial (vv. 32–36).

Verses 1–12

It seems that the army of Israel took along with them out of Egypt a month's provisions, which, by the fifteenth day of the second month, were all used up, and so here we have:

1. Their grumbling and murmuring on that occasion (vv. 2–3).

1.1. They thought they were going to die in the desert—nothing less, at the first sight of disaster. It shows great distrust in God if we talk of nothing but being killed quickly.

1.2. They picked on Moses and accused him of intending to starve them when he brought them out of Egypt.

1.3. They underrated their rescue so much that they wished they had died in Egypt. They would rather die near the fleshpots (pots of meat) of Egypt, where they had provisions, than live under the guidance of the heavenly pillar in the desert and be provided for by the hand of God! We do not think that they had plenty in Egypt, however much they are now talking of the fleshpots; nor could they be afraid of dying of hunger in the desert, while they had their flocks and herds with them. But discontent makes what is past seem bigger and condemns what is present, without consideration of truth or reason.

2. The care God graciously took to provide for them. Notice:

2.1. How God makes known his kind intentions to Moses, that he might not get worked up about their grumblings or be tempted to wish he had left them alone in Egypt.

2.1.1. He takes notice of the people's complaints.

2.1.2. He promises them a speedy, sufficient, and sustained supply (v. 4). Notice what God intended in making this provision for them: *That I may prove them, whether they will walk in my law or no.*

2.1.2.1. He tested them to see whether they would trust him and walk in the law of faith or not, whether they could be satisfied with the bread of the day for that day and depend on God for fresh supplies the next day.

2.1.2.2. He tested them to see whether they would serve him and always be faithful.

2.2. How Moses made known these intentions to Israel, as God directed him. Here Aaron was his prophet, as he had been to Pharaoh. Moses directed Aaron as to what to *speak to the congregation of Israel* (v. 9). God condescends to give a fair hearing even to those who grumble.

2.2.1. He convinces them that their grumbling was wrong. They thought they were complaining only to Moses and Aaron, but here they are told that God also was struck by their grumbling (vv. 7–8). When we grumble, justly or unjustly, against those who seem to be the cause of a difficulty, we would do well to consider that we are actually grumbling against God; human beings are simply the agents of his hand.

2.2.2. He assures them of the supply of their needs, and since they had harped on about fleshpots (pots of meat) so much, they would for once have plenty of meat that evening, bread the next morning, and so on, every day from then on (vv. 8, 12). There are many of whom it could be said that they are better fed than taught, but the Israelites were fed in this way, that they might be taught:

2.2.2.1. *By this you shall know that the Lord hath brought you out from the land of Egypt* (v. 6). The fact that they were brought out of Egypt was clear enough, but they were so strangely foolish and shortsighted that they said it was Moses who had brought them out (v. 3).

2.2.2.2. *By this you shall know that I am the Lord your God* (v. 12). When God brought the plagues on the Egyptians, it was to make them know that he was the Lord. When he provided for the Israelites, it was to make them know that he was their God.

3. How God himself revealed his glory, to quiet the grumbling of the people, and to make sure that Moses and Aaron were highly regarded (v. 10). While Aaron was speaking, *the glory of the Lord appeared in the cloud.*

Verses 13–21

Now they begin to be provided for by the direct hand of God.

1. He makes them a feast, at night, of tasty fowl. Quail (the game bird) came and covered the camp, so tame that they might take as many of them as they pleased.

2. Next morning he rained down manna on them, which was to become a constant supply for their daily bread.

2.1. What was provided for them was manna, itself of such consistency that it served as nourishing and strengthening food on its own. They called it *manna*, meaning, "What is it?"

2.2. They were to gather it every morning (v. 21), each day's portion every day (v. 4). Our Savior seems to allude to this daily raining down and gathering of manna when he teaches us to pray, *Give us this day our daily bread* (Mt 6:11). We are taught in this:

2.2.1. To carefully provide proper food for ourselves and our families. What God gives us graciously we must industriously gather.

2.2.2. To be content and satisfied with what is sufficient. They must gather, *every man according to his eating.* As the proverb puts it, "Enough is as good as a feast," and more than enough is as bad as a surfeit.

2.2.3. To depend on Providence: *Let no man leave till morning* (v. 19). "Let them learn to go to bed and sleep quietly, even though they do not have any bread in their tent or in all their camp. Let them trust that God will bring them their daily bread the following day." See here the folly of hoarding. The manna that was stored by some went bad, became full of maggots, and became good for nothing.

2.3. Let us learn from this to think:

2.3.1. Of the great power of God which fed Israel in the desert and made miracles their daily bread. Never was there such a superstore of provisions as this, where 600,000 men and their families were daily provided for, without money and without cost. Never was there such an open house kept as God kept in the desert for forty years, nor was such free and plentiful hospitality ever given.

2.3.2. Of the constant providence of God. The same wisdom, power, and goodness that then brought food daily from the clouds, are used in the present constant cycle of nature, bringing food every year from the earth and giving us all things richly to enjoy.

Verses 22–31

We have here the setting apart of one day in seven for holy work, and, in order to do that, for holy rest. This was a divine appointment ever since God created human beings on earth, and the oldest good law. Notice also the double provision which God made for the Israelites, and which they were to make for themselves, on the sixth day. God gave them *on the sixth day the bread of two days* (v. 29). Appointing them to rest on the seventh day, he took care that they would not be losers by it, and none will ever be losers by serving God. On that day, they were to gather in enough for two days and prepare it (v. 23). The law was very strict, that they must do their baking and boiling the day before, not on the Sabbath. This does not now mean it is unlawful for us to prepare food on the Lord's Day, but it does direct us to arrange our family affairs so that they may hinder us as little as possible from the work of the Sabbath. What they kept for their food on the Sabbath did not rot (v. 24). Some of them, it seems, went out on the seventh day, expecting to find manna (v. 27); but *they found none*, for those who want to find must seek at the appointed time. God on this occasion said to Moses, *How long refuse you to keep my commandments?* (v. 28). Why did he say this to Moses? He was not disobedient. No, but he was the ruler of a disobedient people; *you* is plural in Hebrew in this verse. God makes this charge against Moses that he might pass this charge on to the people; their disobedience was not through any neglect or default of his.

Verses 32–36

After God had provided manna for his people's food in the desert, we are told here:

1. How the memory of it was preserved. An omer of this manna was to be kept in *a golden pot*, as we are told in Heb 9:4, and kept *before the Testimony*, or the ark, when it was afterward made (vv. 32–34). Once we have eaten our food, we should not forget it. God's miracles and mercies are to be remembered forever, as an encouragement to trust him at all times.

2. How the mercy of it was continued as long as they needed it. The manna did not stop till they came to the border of Canaan, where there was bread enough and to spare (v. 35). The manna is called *spiritual meat* (1Co 10:3), because it was a type of spiritual blessings of heavenly things. Christ himself is the true manna, the bread of life, which was prefigured in the physical manna (Jn 6:49–51). The word of God is the manna by which our souls are nourished (Mt 4:4). The encouragements of the Spirit are hidden manna (Rev 2:17). These come from heaven, as the manna did, and support, encourage, and strengthen the divine life in the soul, while we are in the wilderness of this world. It is to be *gathered*; Christ in the word is to be applied to the soul, and the means of grace are to be used. Every one of us must gather for ourselves, and gather in the morning of our days, the morning of our opportunities, which if we allow to pass, it may be too late to gather. The manna they gathered must not be stored up, but eaten; those who have received Christ must by faith live on him and not receive his grace in vain. But those who ate the manna became hungry again, died eventually, and God was not pleased with many of them; while those who feed on Christ by faith will never hunger, will never die, and God will be well pleased with them forever. *Lord, evermore give us this bread* (Jn 6:34)!

CHAPTER 17

Two matters are recorded in this chapter: 1. The provision of water for the Israelites. They lacked water in the desert (v. 1). They complained to Moses about this (vv. 2–3). Moses cried out to God (v. 4). God ordered him to strike the rock, and water came out of that; Moses did so (vv. 5–6). The place named after it (v. 7). 2. The defeating of the army of Amalek. The victory obtained by the prayer of Moses (vv. 8–12), by the sword of Joshua (v. 13), and a record kept of it (vv. 14–16). These things which happened to them are written to instruct us on our life journey and in our spiritual warfare.

Verses 1–7

Here is:

1. The difficulty that the children of Israel were in because of lack of water.

2. Their discontent and distrust in this difficulty. It is said (v. 3), They *thirsted there for water*. This intimates that their passion sharpened their appetites and they were forceful and impatient in their desires. Notice the language of their excessive desires.

2.1. They challenged Moses to supply them (v. 2): *Give us water, that we may drink*, demanding it as a right.

2.2. They quarreled with Moses for bringing them out of Egypt, as if, instead of rescuing them, he intended to kill them. Their ill feeling against Moses rose so high that they were *almost ready to stone him* (v. 4).

2.3. They began to question whether God was with them or not: They *tempted the Lord, saying, Is the Lord among us or not?* (v. 7). They question his real presence, whether there was a God or not; his common providence, whether God ruled the world; and his special promise, whether he would be true to his word to them. This is called their *tempting God*. They think, in effect, that Moses was an impostor, that the long series of miracles which had rescued them, served them, and fed them was a series of frauds, and the promise of Canaan a mere joke to them. If *the Lord was not among them*, it was all so.

3. The action that Moses took:

3.1. He rebuked those who grumbled (v. 2): *Why chide you with me?* Notice how mildly he answered them. He showed them whom their grumblings dishonored, and that the slurs they directed to him actually fell on God himself: *You tempt the Lord*; that is, "By distrusting his power, you test his patience, and so arouse his wrath."

3.2. He made his complaint to God (v. 4): *Moses cried unto the Lord*. When people unjustly criticize us and quarrel with us, it is a great relief to us to go to God, and in prayer lay our case before him and leave it with him. If people will not listen to us, God will. Moses begs God to direct him what he should do, for he was completely at a loss to know what to do next.

4. God's gracious appearance to relieve them (vv. 5–6). He orders Moses to walk on ahead before the people. He must take his rod (staff) with him, not to call up some plague to punish them, but to get water for them. How wonderfully patient God is! If God had only shown Moses a fountain of water in the desert, as he did for Hagar, that would have been a great favor. But so that he might show his power as well as his pity, and make it a miracle of mercy, he gave them water from a rock. He directed Moses where to go to and appointed him to take some of the elders to be witnesses to what was done, that they might themselves be assured of the certainty of God's presence with them. He promised to meet him there in the cloud of glory, and ordered him to strike the rock. Moses obeyed, and immediately water came out of the rock in great gushes. It is called *a fountain of waters* (Ps 114:8). This fine water that came out of the rock is called *honey and oil* (Dt 32:13), because the people's thirst made it doubly pleasant. Coming when they were in extreme need, it was like honey and oil to them. God can open up fountains for our supply where we least expect them, *waters in the wilderness* (Isa 43:20), because he makes *a way in the wilderness* (Isa 43:19). Those who keep to God's way in the wilderness of this world may trust him to provide for them. The graces and encouragements of the Spirit are compared to *rivers of living water* (Jn 7:38–39; 4:14). These flow from Christ, who is the rock struck by the Law of Moses, for he was made under the Law. Nothing will supply the needs, and satisfy the desires, of a soul except water from this rock, this living fountain. Sensual pleasures are mere puddles in comparison; spiritual delights are water from the rock, so pure, so clear, so refreshing: rivers of deep, lasting joy.

5. A new name given to the place on this occasion, to preserve the remembrance of the sin of their murmuring— *Massah*, "testing" or "temptation," because they tempted

God; *Meribah*, "quarreling," because they quarreled with Moses (v. 7).

Verses 8–16

We have here the story of the war with Amalek. Amalek was the first of the nations that Israel fought with (Nu 24:20). Notice:

1. Amalek's attack: They *came out, and fought with Israel* (v. 8). The Amalekites were the descendants of Esau, who hated Jacob because of the birthright and blessing, and this was an example of their hereditary enmity. Consider this as Israel's affliction and as Amalek's sin (Dt 25:17–18). They wickedly attacked their rear and struck those who were faint and weak and who could not resist or escape. In vain they attacked a camp guarded by and fed on miracles. They did not know what they were doing.

2. Israel's defense against the aggressors:

2.1. The position assigned to Joshua, who is mentioned here for the first time: he is nominated commander in chief in this expedition, that he might be trained up in the services he was intended for after Moses died.

2.2. The position taken up by Moses: I will stand on the top of the hill with the rod of God in my hand (v. 9). Joshua fights, and Moses prays and holds up the rod of God in his hand. This rod Moses held up to Israel, to stir them; it was held up as a banner to encourage the soldiers. Moses also held up this rod to God, to appeal to him. Moses was not only a standard bearer, but also an intercessor, pleading for success and victory with God. It is here the praying power that proves to be the victorious power. Notice:

2.2.1. How Moses was tired (v. 12): *His hands were heavy.* We do not find that Joshua's hands were heavy from fighting, but Moses' hands were heavy from praying. The more spiritual any service is, the more likely we are to fail and flag in it.

2.2.2. What influence the rod of Moses had on the battle (v. 11): "When Moses held up his hand in prayer," as the Aramaic explains it, "Israel prevailed," but, "when he let down his hand from prayer, Amalek prevailed."

2.2.3. The care that was taken to support Moses. When he could not stand any longer, he sat down on a stone (v. 12). When he could not hold up his hands, he was helped to hold them up. Moses, the man of God, is happy to have the assistance of Aaron his brother, and Hur, who possibly was, according to some, e.g., Josephus, his brother-in-law, the husband of Miriam. Moses' hands, held up in this way, were *steady till the going down of the sun.* No doubt it was a great encouragement to the people to see Joshua in front of them in the field of battle and Moses above them on the top of the hill. Christ is both to us: our Joshua, the captain of our salvation who fights our battles, and our Moses, who in heaven always lives to make intercession, that our faith will not fail (Lk 22:32; Heb 7:25).

3. The defeat of Amalek. Victory had swung for a while between the camps, but Israel won the day (v. 13). Though Joshua fought with great disadvantages—his soldiers undisciplined, poorly armed, long used to slavery, and liable to grumble—God used them to achieve a great salvation.

4. The memorial of this victory established.

4.1. Moses took care that God would have the glory for it (v. 15). Instead of setting up a triumphal arch to the honor of Joshua, he builds an altar to the honor of God. What is most carefully recorded is the inscription on the altar, *Jehovah-nisi*, "The Lord is my banner," which

probably refers to the lifting up of the rod (staff) of God as a banner in the battle. The presence and power of Jehovah were the banner under which they enlisted, by which they were kept alert together, and so which they erected on the day of their triumph.

4.2. God took care that descendants would derive encouragement and benefit from it: "Write this for a memorial, and then rehearse it in the ears of Joshua, let him be entrusted with this permanent record, to pass it on to generations to come." Moses must now begin to keep a diary or journal of events. It is the first mention of writing that we find in Scripture, and perhaps the command was not given till after the writing of the Law on the tablets of stone: "Write it *in perpetuam rei memoriam* — 'that the event may be held in perpetual remembrance'; that which is written remains."

4.2.1. "Write what has been done. Let future ages know that God fights for his people, and *he that touches them touches the apple of his eye*" (Zec 2:8).

4.2.2. Write what will be done:

4.2.2.1. That in the course of time Amalek will be totally ruined and blotted out (v. 14). Israel will in the end undoubtedly triumph in the destruction of Amalek. This sentence was carried out partly by Saul (1Sa 15:1–35), and completely by David (1Sa 30:1–31; 2Sa 1:1; 8:12). After his time we never read further mention of the name of Amalek.

4.2.2.2. That in the meantime God would be in continual dispute with him (v. 16). This was written to direct Israel never to make any alliance with the Amalekites.

CHAPTER 18

This chapter concerns Moses himself and the affairs of his own family. 1. His father-in-law Jethro brings his wife and children to him (vv. 1–6). 2. Moses receives his father-in-law with great respect (v. 7), with good conversation (vv. 8–11), and with a sacrifice and a feast (v. 12). 3. Jethro advises him (vv. 13–23), and Moses, after some time, takes his advice (vv. 24–26), and so they part (v. 27).

Verses 1–6

Jethro comes:

1. To congratulate the good fortune of Israel and particularly the honor of Moses his son-in-law. Jethro must have heard what was the talk of all the country, the glorious appearances of God for his people Israel (v. 1), and he comes to find out for himself and to rejoice with them, as one who had a true respect both for them and for their God. Though he, as a Midianite, was not to share with them in the Promised Land, he still shared with them in the joy of their rescue.

2. To bring Moses' wife and children to him. It seems he had sent them back home to his father-in-law. Jethro, we may suppose, was glad of his daughter's company and fond of her children, but he did not want to keep her from her husband or them from their father (vv. 5–6). Moses must have his family with him, so that while he ruled the church of God he might set a good example of wisdom in family government (1Ti 3:5). Moses now had a great deal of honor and care put on him, and it was right that his wife should be with him to share with him in both. Notice is taken of the significant names of his two sons:

2.1. The eldest was called *Gershom* (v. 3), "a stranger there."

2.2. The other he called *Eliezer* (v. 4), "My God is helper," as we translate it; it looks back to his deliverance from Pharaoh. It could also be translated so as to look forward, "The Lord is my help and will deliver me" from the sword of Pharaoh.

Verses 7–12

Notice here:

1. The kind greeting that took place between Moses and his father-in-law (v. 7). Those who stand high in God's favor are not therefore discharged from the duty they owe to their fellow human beings. Moses went out to meet Jethro, bowed down, and *kissed him*. Religion does not destroy good manners. *They asked each other of their welfare.*

2. The account that Moses gave his father-in-law of the great things God had done for Israel (v. 8).

3. The impressions this story made on Jethro:

3.1. He congratulated God's Israel: Jethro was delighted (v. 9). He was not only delighted at the honor done to his son-in-law, but also at all the goodness done for Israel (v. 9). If we declare God's blessings publicly, the spirits of all who are present are encouraged. While the Israelites were themselves grumbling despite all God's goodness to them, here was a Midianite who was joyful.

3.2. He gave the glory to Israel's God (v. 10).

3.3. His faith was confirmed by this, and he took this occasion to solemnly profess it: *Now know I that the Lord is greater than all gods* (v. 11). Notice:

3.3.1. The subject of his faith: that the God of Israel is greater than all who claim sovereignty and all false and counterfeit gods.

3.3.2. The confirmation and building up of his faith. Now he knows; he knew it before, but now he knows it better; his faith grew to a full assurance on this fresh evidence.

3.3.3. The ground on which he built his faith. God was far above all the arrogance of the magicians. The magicians were confounded, the idols were shaken, Pharaoh was humbled and his powers broken, and, in spite of all their plotting and scheming, God's Israel was rescued from their hands.

4. The expressions of their joy and thankfulness. They had fellowship with one another both in a feast and in a sacrifice (v. 12). Jethro was gladly admitted, though a Midianite, into fellowship with Moses and the elders of Israel, *forasmuch as he also was a son of Abraham*, though of a less important family.

4.1. They joined in a sacrifice of thanksgiving: *Jethro took a burnt offering for God*, and probably offered it himself, for he was a priest in Midian and a worshiper of the true God.

4.2. They joined in a joyful feast of sacrifice.

Verses 13–27

Here is:

1. The great zeal and industriousness of Moses as a judge.

1.1. Having been used to redeem Israel from slavery, he is here a further type of Christ, in that he is a lawgiver and a judge among them.

1.1.1. He was to tell them God's will when they were not sure about it and to explain God's laws and decrees that were already given them, concerning the Sabbath, the manna, etc., besides the laws of nature, relating both to godliness and justice (v. 15). He made them *know the statutes of God and his laws* (v. 16). His business was, not

to make laws, but to make God's laws known; his role was only that of a servant.

1.1.2. He was to settle disputes, judging between one person and another (v. 16). And, if the people were as quarrelsome with one another as they were with God, no doubt he had a great many causes brought before him.

1.2. Such was the business Moses was called to, and it appears that he did it:

- With great consideration.
- With great condescension to the people, who stood *by him* (v. 14).
- With great constancy.

2. The great wisdom and consideration of Jethro as a friend:

2.1. He disliked the method that Moses was using, and felt free enough to tell him so (vv. 14, 17–18). He thought it was too much work for Moses to undertake alone. It is possible to overdo our doing good.

2.2. He advised him to adopt such a model of government as would better respond to the people's needs, which was:

2.2.1. That he should continue to bring all their disputes to God (v. 19): *Be thou for the people to God-ward*; that was an honor which it was not fitting that any other should share with him (Nu 12:6–8). Also whatever concerned the whole congregation in general must pass through him (v. 20). But:

2.2.2. That he should appoint judges in the different tribes and families, who would try cases between one person and another and decide them. This would be done with less fuss and more speed than in the general assembly over which Moses himself presided. But:

2.2.3. An appeal might come, if there were just cause, from these lower courts to Moses himself. *Every great matter they shall bring unto thee* (v. 22).

2.3. He adds two qualifications to his counsel:

2.3.1. That great care should be taken in the choice of the people who would receive this trust (v. 21); they must *be able men*, etc. They needed to be of the very best character:

- In judgment and determination — *able men*. Clear heads and resolute hearts make good judges.
- In godliness and religion — those who *fear God*, who were conscientious, who dare not commit wrong, even though they could do it secretly.
- In integrity and honesty — *men of truth*.
- In hating dishonest gain, having a deep contempt of worldly wealth — *hating covetousness*.

2.3.2. That he should seek God's direction in this matter (v. 23): If thou shalt do this thing, and God command thee so. Now Moses did not despise this advice, but he hearkened to the voice of his father-in-law (v. 24).

3. Jethro's return to his own land (v. 27). It is supposed that the Kenites (mentioned in 1Sa 15:6) were the descendants of Jethro (compare Jdg 1:16), and they are there taken under special protection because of the kindness their ancestor showed here to Israel.

CHAPTER 19

This chapter introduces the solemnity of the giving of the Law on Mount Sinai. We have here: 1. The circumstances of time and place (vv. 1–2). The covenant between God and Israel established in general. The gracious proposal God made to them (vv. 3–6) and their agreement to this (vv. 7–8). 2. Two days' notice given of God's intention to declare the Law from a dense cloud on the third day (vv. 9–10). Orders are given to prepare the people to receive the Law (vv. 10–13) and care taken to carry out those orders (vv. 14–15). 3. The awesome appearance of God's glory on Mount Sinai (vv. 16–20). Silence declared (vv. 21–25).

Verses 1–8

Here is:

1. The date of that great covenant into which Israel was about to enter.

1.1. Its time (v. 1) *in the third month* after they came out of Egypt.

1.2. Its place: *Sinai,* the highest in all that range of mountains. In this way, God scorned cities, palaces, and magnificent structures, setting up his canopy on the top of a high mountain in a waste and barren desert to initiate this covenant. It is called *Sinai,* "a bush," from the many thorny bushes that spread over it.

2. The covenant itself. Moses was called up the mountain and was the messenger of the covenant: *Thus shalt thou say to the house of Jacob, and tell the children of Israel* (v. 3). Notice:

2.1. That the Maker and Prime Mover of the covenant is God himself. In all our dealings with God, free grace comes before the blessings of goodness to us, and all our comfort is owing, not to our knowing God, but rather to our being *known of him* (Gal 4:9).

2.2. That the subject of the covenant is kind and gracious, giving them the greatest privileges and advantages imaginable.

2.2.1. He reminds them of what he had done for them (v. 4). *I bore you on eagles' wings,* a noble expression of the wonderful tenderness God had shown to them. It is explained in Dt 32:11–12. It shows great speed. God not only came on wings to rescue them, but he also made them move out quickly, as it were on their wings. He did it with the strength as well as with the swiftness of an eagle. Egypt, that iron furnace, was the nest in which these young ones were hatched, where they were first formed as the embryo of a nation. Then, when their numbers increased, they grew to maturity and were taken out of that nest. Other birds carry their young in their talons, but the eagle, it is said, carries its young on its wings, so that even those archers who shoot flying birds cannot hurt the young ones, unless they first shoot through the eagle itself. *I brought you unto myself.* They were brought not only into a state of liberty and honor, but also into the covenant and fellowship with God. This was the glory of their rescue, as it is of ours by Christ, that he died, *the just for the unjust, that he might bring us to God* (1Pe 3:18). God aims at this in all his providence and grace, to bring us back to himself, from whom we have rebelled, and to bring us home to himself, in whom alone we can be happy. Some have well noticed that the Old Testament church is said to be carried on eagles' wings, but the New Testament church is said to be gathered by the Lord Jesus, *as a hen gathers her chickens under her wings* (Mt 23:37), showing the grace and compassion of that dispensation, and the extraordinary condescension and humiliation of the Redeemer.

2.2.2. He tells them clearly (v. 5) that they should *obey his voice indeed and keep his covenant.* Having saved them in this way, God insisted that they should be ruled by him.

2.2.3. He assures them of the honor he would put on them and the kindness he would show them, if they kept his covenant in this way (vv. 5–6), *Then you shall be a peculiar treasure to me.*

2.2.3.1. God here asserts his sovereignty over, and ownership of, the whole visible creation: *All the earth is mine.*

2.2.3.2. He calls Israel to himself, to be a people dear to him. *You shall be a peculiar treasure.* By giving them divine revelation, special ordinances, and promises of eternal life, by sending his prophets among them and pouring out his Spirit on them, he distinguished them from, and honored them above, all people.

3. Israel's acceptance of this covenant and agreement to its conditions:

3.1. Moses faithfully delivered God's message to them (v. 7): he *laid before their faces all those words.* His *laying* it *before their faces* shows his laying it on their consciences.

3.2. They readily agreed to the covenant. *All that the Lord hath spoken we will do.* 3.3. Moses, as a mediator, brought the words of the people back to God (v. 8). In the same way, Christ, the Mediator between us and God, as a prophet reveals God's will to us, and then as a priest offers up to God our spiritual sacrifices. So he is the great *daysman who lays his hand upon us both* (Job 9:33), the arbitrator who brings us together.

Verses 9–15

Here:

1. God shows to Moses his purpose in coming down on Mount Sinai in a visible appearance of his glory, in *a thick cloud* (v. 9). God would *come down in the sight of all the people* (v. 11). Though they would not see his form, they would see so much as would convince them that God was really among them. The agreement was to begin with a perceptible appearance of divine glory, which was afterward continued more silently by the ministry of Moses. In the same way, the Holy Spirit descended visibly on Christ at his baptism, and all who were present heard God speak to him (Mt 3:17), that afterward, without the repetition of such visible signs they might believe him. Similarly, the Spirit descended in divided tongues on the apostles (Ac 2:3), that they might be believed.

2. God orders Moses to prepare for this great ceremony, giving him two days' notice of it.

2.1. He must *sanctify the people* (v. 10). *Sanctify them,* that is, "Call them away from their worldly business, and call them to religious exercises, meditation and prayer, that they may receive the Law from God's mouth with reverence and devotion. *Let them be ready*" (v. 11). Wandering thoughts must be reined in, impure feelings abandoned, unruly passions suppressed, even all cares about secular business must, for the present, be dismissed and put to one side, so that our hearts may be preoccupied with approaching God. As a sign of their cleansing they must *wash their clothes* (v. 10), and they did so (v. 14). Not that God considers our clothes, but while they were washing their clothes he wanted them to think of washing their souls in repenting. It is right that we should wear clean clothes when we come before great people, and so clean hearts are necessary when we come before the great God, who sees them as clearly as people see our clothes.

2.2. He must *set bounds about the mountain* (vv. 12–13). Probably he drew a line, or ditch, around the foot of the hill, which none were to pass over except on penalty of death. This was to show the humble reverence which ought to occupy the minds of all those who worship God.

2.3. He must order the people to wait for the call that would be given (v. 13), *"When the trumpet soundeth long, then let them take their places at the foot of the mountain and sit down at God's feet."* No one's voice could have reached so many, but the voice of God did.

Verses 16–25

Now eventually that memorable day comes. Never was such a sermon preached, before or since, as the one that was preached here to the church in the desert. For:

1. The preacher was God himself (v. 18): *The Lord descended in fire*, and (v. 20), *The Lord came down upon Mount Sinai*. The *Shechinah*, or glory of the Lord, appeared in the sight of all the people.

2. The pulpit (or rather, throne) was Mount Sinai, with *a thick cloud* over it (v. 16), covered with *smoke* (v. 18), and made to *quake* greatly.

3. The congregation was called together by the *sound of a trumpet, exceedingly loud* (v. 16), and *waxing louder and louder* (v. 19).

4. Moses brought the hearers to the place of meeting (v. 17). He who had led them out of slavery in Egypt now led them to receive the Law from God's mouth. Moses, leading an assembly worshiping God, was as great as Moses leading an army in the field.

5. The introduction to the service brought *thunders and lightnings* (v. 16). Thunder and lightning have natural causes, but Scripture directs us to take particular notice of the power of God and his terribleness in them.

6. Moses is God's minister, who is spoken to, to command silence and keep the congregation in order: *Moses spoke* (v. 19). God stilled his fear by his special favor to him, in calling him up to the top of the mountain (v. 20), in which also he tested his faith and courage. Neither the priests nor the people should try to force their way through the limits that had been set, to *come up unto the Lord*, but only Moses and Aaron, those whom God delighted to honor. Notice what it was that God forbade them from doing—breaking through *to gaze*. Enough was provided to waken their consciences, but they were not allowed to indulge their vain curiosity. They might see, but not gaze. We are in danger if we break through the limits that God has set us, and encroach on what he does not allow for us.

CHAPTER 20

All things are now ready for the solemn declaration of the divine Law. We have in this chapter: 1. The Ten Commandments, as God himself spoke them on Mount Sinai (vv. 1–17). 2. The effects made on the people by them (vv. 18–21). 3. Some detailed instructions which God gave privately to Moses for him to communicate to the people, relating to his worship (vv. 22–26).

Verses 1–11

Here is:

1. The introduction of the lawwriter, Moses: *God spoke all these words* (v. 1). The Law of the Ten Commandments is:

1.1. A law of God's making.

1.2. A law of his own speaking. God has many ways of speaking to the human race (Job 33:14); he has not spoken, at any time or on any occasion, as he spoke the Ten Commandments. God had given this Law to human beings before—it was inherently written on their hearts—but sin had so defaced this writing, that it was necessary to revive knowledge of it in this way.

2. The introduction by the Lawmaker: *I am the Lord thy God* (v. 2). In this:

2.1. God asserts his own authority to make this law in general.

2.2. God proposes that he is to be the sole object of the religious worship which is instructed in the first four of the commandments. The people are here bound to obedience by *a threefold cord*:

2.2.1. Because God *is the Lord*. The One who gives being may give Law, and so he is able to support and reward us in our obedience and to punish our disobedience.

2.2.2. He was their God, a God in covenant with them, their God with their own agreement. Though that exclusive covenant has ended, it has been surpassed by one, in which all who are baptized are taken into relationship to him as their God, and so are unjust, unfaithful, and very ungrateful, if they do not obey him.

2.2.3. He had *brought them out of the land of Egypt*. Even by redeeming them, he obtained a further right to rule them; they owed their service to the One to whom they owed their freedom. In the same way, Christ, having rescued us from the slavery of sin, is entitled to the best service we can give him (Lk 1:74).

3. The Law itself. We have in these verses the first four of the Ten Commandments, sometimes called "the first table," which concern our duty to God. It is right that these should be put first, because we have a Maker to love before we had a neighbor to love, and justice and love are acceptable acts of obedience to God only when they flow from the motives of goodness. It cannot be expected that we can be true to our brothers and sisters if we are false to our God.

3.1. The first commandment concerns whom we are to worship, Jehovah, and him only (v. 3), *Thou shalt have no other gods before me*. The Egyptians and other neighboring nations had many gods, creations of their own imagination, strange gods, *new gods* (Dt 32:17). The sin against this commandment which we are most in danger of is giving the glory and honor to any creature which are due only to God himself. Pride makes a god of self, covetousness makes a god of money, sensuality makes a god of the stomach; whatever is honored or loved, feared or served, delighted in or depended on, more than God, whatever it is, we are in effect making a god of. In the last words, *before me*, it is intimated that we cannot have any other God without him certainly knowing it. It is a sin that defies him to his face, which he cannot, in fact he will not, overlook or ignore. See Ps 44:20–21.

3.2. The second commandment concerns the ordinances of worship, or how God is to be worshiped.

3.2.1. The prohibition: we are here forbidden to worship even the true God by means of idols (vv. 4–5). The Jews, at least after the Captivity, thought themselves forbidden by this commandment to make any idol or picture whatever. And so even the images which the Roman armies had on their flags are called *an abomination* to them (Mt 24:15), especially when they were set up *in the holy place*. It is called exchanging the truth of God for a lie (Ro 1:25), for an idol is a teacher of lies; it implies to us that God has a body, whereas he is an infinite spirit (Hab 2:18). It also forbids us to make images of God in our imagination, as if he were human like us. Our religious worship must be governed by the power of faith, not by the power of imagination.

3.2.2. The reasons for this prohibition (vv. 5–6), which are:

3.2.2.1. God's jealousy in the matter of his worship: "*I the Lord* Jehovah, and *thy God, am a jealous God,* especially in things of this nature."

3.2.2.2. The punishment of idolaters. God looks on them as those who hate him. He will *visit it upon the children*. It is not an unrighteous thing for God—if the parents died in their sins and the children follow in their steps, continuing their false worship, because they received them by tradition from their parents—when their sins reach their limit, to come in his judgment and judge them for these. Though he is patient for a long time with an idolatrous people, he will not always be patient, but by the fourth generation, at the latest, he will begin his punishment.

3.2.2.3. The favor God wants to show to his faithful worshipers: *Keeping mercy for thousands* (v. 6; 34:7) of persons, thousands of generations *of those that love me, and keep my commandments*. As the first commandment requires the inward worship of love, desire, joy, hope, and wonder, so the second requires the outward worship of prayer and praise, and reverent attention to God's word. Those who truly love God will consistently try to keep his commandments, particularly those that relate to his worship. Those who love God and keep those commandments will receive grace to keep his other commandments. Gospel worship will have a good effect on obedience to the Gospel in a range of spheres of life. This mercy will extend to thousands, much farther than the wrath threatened to those who hate him.

3.3. The third commandment concerns how we are to worship God. We have here:

3.3.1. A strict prohibition: *Thou shalt not take the name of the Lord thy God in vain*. We take God's name in vain, we misuse it:

3.3.1.1. By hypocrisy, professing God's name, but not living up to that profession. Those who acknowledge the name of Christ, but have not left their sinful ways, misuse that name.

3.3.1.2. By covenant-breaking; if we make promises to God, committing our souls to what is good, but not carrying out our vows to the Lord, we are misusing his name (Mt 5:33).

3.3.1.3. By rash swearing, mentioning the name of God as a casual form of contempt.

3.3.1.4. By false swearing. One part of the religious respect the Jews were taught to pay to their God was to *swear by his name* (Dt 10:20). But they insulted him, instead of honoring him, if they called him to witness to a lie.

3.3.2. A severe penalty: *The Lord will not hold him guiltless*. Those members of the judiciary who punish other offenses may not think that they should be concerned to take notice of this, because it does not immediately affect either private property or the public peace. Sinners may perhaps consider themselves innocent. God will *not hold him guiltless*, and they will find it a fearful thing to fall into the hands of the living God (Heb 10:31).

3.4. The fourth commandment concerns when God is to be worshiped. He is to be served and honored daily, but one day in seven is to be specially dedicated to his honor and spent in his service. Here is:

3.4.1. The command itself (v. 8): *Remember the sabbath day to keep it holy* and (v. 10), *In it thou shalt do no manner of work*. We read of God's blessing and making a seventh day holy from the beginning (Ge 2:3), so this was not making a new law, but reviving an old one.

3.4.1.1. They are told what is the day they must religiously observe—a *seventh, after six days' labour*. Whether this was the seventh counting from the first seventh, or from the day of their coming out of Egypt, or both, is not certain.

3.4.1.2. They are told how it must be observed. First, as a day of rest; they were to do no kind of work on this day with regard to their callings or worldly business. Secondly, as a holy day, set apart for the honor of the holy God, and to be spent in holy exercises. God, by blessing it, had made it holy; they, by solemnly blessing him, must keep it holy.

3.4.1.3. They are told who must observe it: *Thou, and thy son, and thy daughter*; the wife is not mentioned, because she is supposed to be one with her husband and present with him. God takes notice of what we do, particularly what we do on Sabbath days, even though we are in a strange place.

3.4.1.4. They are given a particular reminder of this duty: *Remember it*. It is indicated that the Sabbath was instituted and observed before, but in their slavery in Egypt they had let observance of it fall into neglect. Some think it refers to the preparation we should make for the Sabbath; we must think of it before it comes, so that, when it does come, we may keep it holy.

3.4.2. The reasons for this command.

3.4.2.1. We have time enough for ourselves on the other six days: *Six days must thou labour*. We have time enough to serve ourselves. On the seventh day let us serve God. On the seventh it is a kindness to us to be obliged to rest.

3.4.2.2. This is God's day: it is the *sabbath of the Lord thy God*, not only instituted by him, but also made holy for him.

3.4.2.3. It is intended to remind us of the creation of the world and so is to be observed to the glory of the Creator. By keeping the Sabbath holy, the Jews declared that they worshiped the God who made the world, and so distinguished themselves from all other nations, who worshiped gods which they themselves made.

3.4.2.4. God has given us an example of rest, after six days' work: he *rested the seventh day*.

3.4.2.5. He has himself *blessed the sabbath day and hallowed it*. He has put blessings on it, which he has encouraged us to expect from him in the religious observance of that day. It is the *day which the Lord hath made* (Ps 118:24), so let us not do anything to destroy it.

Verses 12–17

We have here the laws of the "second table," as they are sometimes called, the last six of the Ten Commandments, encompassing our duty to ourselves and to one another, and commenting on the second great commandment, *Thou shalt love thy neighbour as thyself* (Mk 12:31).

1. The fifth commandment concerns the duties we owe to our relatives; those of children to their parents are specified by themselves: *Honour thy father and thy mother*, which includes:

1.1. A decent respect for them, an inward respect for them outwardly expressed on all occasions in our behavior.

1.2. Obedience to their lawful commands, as it is explained in Eph 6:1–3: *Children, obey your parents*, from a motive of love. Though you have said, "We will not," later change your mind and obey (Mt 21:29).

1.3. Submission to their rebukes, instructions, and corrections. Children, whether they are well behaved or naughty, should obey their parents, because they fear God.

1.4. Trying in everything to encourage their parents and to make them content in their old age, maintaining them if they are in need of support, which our Savior makes particular reference to in Mt 15:4–6. The reason attached to this commandment is a promise: *That thy days may be long upon the land which the Lord thy God giveth thee.* Here, at the beginning of the second table, he mentions his bringing them into Canaan. A long life in that good land is promised particularly to obedient children.

2. The sixth commandment concerns our own and our neighbor's life (v. 13): *"Thou shalt not kill;* you will not do anything hurtful or injurious to the health, peace, and life of your own body, or any other person's, unjustly." It does not forbid killing in lawful war, or in our own necessary defense. But it forbids all maliciousness and hatred—for everyone who hates a brother or sister is a murderer—to any person, and all personal revenge arising from that. It also forbids all rash anger caused by sudden provocation and hurt said or done, or aimed to be done, in rage: our Savior expounds this commandment in this way (Mt 5:22).

3. The seventh commandment concerns our own and our neighbor's purity: *Thou shalt not commit adultery* (v. 14). This is put before the sixth by our Savior (Mk 10:19): *Do not commit adultery, do not kill;* for our purity should be as precious to us as our lives, and we should be as afraid of what defiles the body as of what destroys it. This commandment forbids all acts of sexual immorality, with all those sinful desires which produce those acts and wage war against the soul, and all those practices which arouse or feed those sexual desires, such as looking at others lustfully, which, Christ tells us, is forbidden in this commandment (Mt 5:28).

4. The eighth commandment concerns our own and our neighbor's wealth, possessions, and goods: *Thou shalt not steal* (v. 15). This command forbids us from robbing ourselves of what we have by spending money sinfully, sinful saving, robbing others by invading our neighbors' rights, taking their money, possessions, house, or field, by force or secretly, cheating them in trading deals, not restoring what is borrowed or found, moving ancient boundary stones, withholding just debts, rents, or wages, and robbing the state of income or what is dedicated to the service of religion.

5. The ninth commandment concerns our own and our neighbor's good name: *Thou shalt not bear false witness* (v. 16). This forbids:

5.1. Speaking falsely in any matter, lying, equivocating, and in any way plotting or scheming to deceive our neighbor.

5.2. Speaking unjustly against our neighbor, to prejudice their reputation.

5.3. Bearing false testimony against them, accusing them of things they know nothing about, slandering, backbiting, taletelling, aggravating what is done wrong and making it worse than it is, and in any way trying to raise our own reputation to the ruin of our neighbor's.

6. The tenth commandment strikes at the root of sin: *Thou shalt not covet* (v. 17). The previous commands implicitly forbid all desire of doing what will hurt or harm our neighbor; this forbids all inordinate desire of having what will gratify ourselves. The apostle Paul, when the grace of God caused the scales to fall from his eyes, realized that this law, *Thou shalt not covet,* forbade all those abnormal appetites and desires which are the beginnings of all sin committed by us.

Verses 18–21

Here we read of:

1. The formidable terror with which the Law was given. It was intended to give a perceptible awareness of the glorious majesty of God, to prepare the soul for the comfort of the Gospel. In this way, the Law was given by Moses in such a way that it might humble us, that the *grace and truth which came by Jesus Christ* (Jn 1:17) might be all the more welcome.

2. The effects which this then made on the people: They removed, and stood afar off (v. 18). They entreated that the word should not be so spoken to them any more (Heb 12:19), but begged that God would speak to them by Moses (v. 19). They also teach us in this to accept that method which infinite Wisdom takes, of speaking to us through people like ourselves.

3. The encouragement Moses gave them, by explaining the intention of God in his terror (v. 20): *Fear not,* that is, "Do not think that the thunder and fire are intended to consume you." They were intended:

3.1. To test them, to see how they would cope with God directly, without a mediator.

3.2. To keep them acting responsibly and prevent them from sinning against God. He encourages them, saying, *Fear not,* but also tells them that God had spoken to them in this way, *that his fear might be before their face.* We must not have a terrifying fear, but we must always have in our minds a reverence of God's majesty, a fearsome respect for his displeasure, and an obedient consideration of his sovereign authority over us. Such fear will quicken us in our duty and make us careful in our behavior.

4. The progress of their fellowship with God by the mediation of Moses (v. 21). While the people continued to stand at a distance, *Moses drew near unto the thick darkness;* he "was made to draw near." Some of the rabbis suppose God sent an angel to take him by the hand and led him up.

Verses 22–26

After Moses had gone into *the thick darkness, where God was,* God spoke there in his hearing only, privately and without terror, all that follows from here to the end of chapter 23, which is mostly an expansion on and exposition of the Ten Commandments. He was to transmit it by word of mouth first, and afterward in writing, to the people. The laws in these verses related to God's worship:

1. They are here forbidden to make idols for worship (vv. 22–23).

1.1. The repetition of the second commandment comes in here to point to what might properly be inferred from God's speaking to them as he had done. He had demonstrated his presence sufficiently to them; they did not need to make idols of him, as if he were absent.

1.2. Though they pretended to worship them only as representations of God, in reality they made them rivals with God, which he would not tolerate.

2. They are here directed to make altars for use in their worship.

2.1. To make their altars very plain, either *of earth* or of *unhewn stone* (vv. 24–25). So that they might not be tempted to think of an idol, they must not dress or shape the stones that they made their altars of, but pile them up roughly as they were. Plainness should be accepted as the best decoration of the external services of religion, and Gospel-worship should not be performed with any outward showy decoration. The beauty of holiness does not need to be painted.

2.2. To make their altars very low (v. 26), so that they might not go up steps to them. Thinking that the higher the altar was, and the closer to heaven, the more acceptable the sacrifice was, was a foolish idea of the nations, who therefore chose high places. In contrast to this, and to show that it is the elevation of the heart, not of the sacrifice, that God looks at, they were here ordered to make their altars low.

3. They are here assured of God's gracious acceptance of their devotions, wherever they were made according to his will (v. 24). Under the Gospel, when we are encouraged to pray everywhere, this promise is fulfilled in its full extent, that, wherever God's people meet in his name to worship him, he will be *in the midst of them* (Mt 18:20). There he will come to them and will bless them, and we need not desire more than this to enhance our meetings for worship.

CHAPTER 21

The laws recorded in this chapter relate to the fifth and sixth commandments; and though they do not fit our natural temperaments, nor are the penalties attached to them binding on us, they are still very useful in explaining the moral law and the rules of natural justice. Here are elaborations: 1. Of the fifth commandment, which concerns particular relationships. The duty of masters toward their servants (vv. 2–11). The punishment of disobedient children (vv. 15, 17). 2. Of the sixth commandment, which forbids all violence by the one person to another, concerning: murder (vv. 12–14), kidnapping (v. 16), assault and battery (vv. 18–19), correcting a slave (vv. 20–21), hurting a pregnant woman (vv. 22–23), the law of retaliation (vv. 24–25), maiming a servant (v. 26–27), an ox (bull) goring (vv. 28–32), damage by leaving a pit uncovered (vv. 33–34), cattle fighting (vv. 35–36).

Verses 1–11

The first verse is the general title of the laws contained in this and the following two chapters, most of them relating to human relationships. These laws are called *judgments*, because they are framed in infinite wisdom and justice, and because their judges were to give judgment according to them. God delivered them privately to Moses, and he was to communicate them to the people. He begins with the laws concerning servants, commanding mercy and moderation toward them. Here is:

1. A law concerning male servants, sold, either by themselves or their parents, through poverty, or by the judges, for their crimes; even those of the latter sort, if Hebrews, were to continue in slavery for seven years at the most. At the end of seven years either the servant should go out free (vv. 2–3) or his servitude should from that time onward be his choice (vv. 5–6).

1.1. By this law God taught:

1.1.1. The Hebrew servants generosity and a noble love of liberty, for they were the Lord's freemen. In this way, Christians, being *bought with a price* (Gal 5:13) *and called unto liberty*, must not be the slaves of human beings or of their sinful desires (1Co 7:23). He likewise taught:

1.1.2. The Hebrew masters not to trample on their poor servants.

1.2. This law will be further useful to us to illustrate the right God has to the children of believing parents, as such, and the place they have in his church.

2. A law concerning female servants, whom their parents through extreme poverty had sold when they were very young to masters who they hoped would marry them when they grew up. If the masters did not marry them, they must not sell them to foreigners, but rather try to make sure that they are properly compensated for the disappointment; if they did marry them, they must maintain them well (vv. 7–11).

Verses 12–21

Here is:

1. A law concerning murder. He had just said, *Thou shalt not kill*. Here he provides:

1.1. For the punishing of intentional murder (v. 12): *Whoso sheddeth man's blood, by man shall his blood be shed.*

1.2. For the relief of those killed accidentally, when a person, without intending to hurt anyone, unintentionally kills another. In such cases, God provided cities of refuge to protect those whose misfortune it was, but not their fault, to cause the death of another person (v. 13). We have our judicial system to carry out justice; we do not need avengers of blood. The law itself is a sufficient sanctuary.

2. A law concerning rebellious children. It is here made a capital crime, to be punished by death, for children either to strike their parents (v. 15) or to curse their parents (v. 17). The disrespectful behavior of children toward their parents is very offensive to God our Father; and, if people will not punish it, he will.

3. A law against kidnapping (v. 16): *He that steals a man*, that is, any person, man, woman, or child, with the intention of selling them to the Gentiles (for no Israelite would buy him), was condemned to death by this statute.

4. Care taken that reparation is made for hurt done to a person, even though death does not result (vv. 18–19). The one that did the hurt must be accountable for damages, and pay, not only for the healing, but also for the loss of time.

5. Direction is given as to what should be done if a slave died because of his master's punishment. But if the slave died under their master's hand, the master should be punished for cruelty, at the discretion of the judges and on consideration of the circumstances (v. 20).

Verses 22–36

Notice here:

1. The particular care which the Law took of pregnant women, that no hurt should be done to them which might cause them to miscarry. The general law of retaliation comes now, which our Savior refers to (Mt 5:38), *An eye for an eye*. Now:

1.1. The carrying out of this law is not put into the hands of private people. The tradition of the elders seems to have explained this corruptly, in contrast to which our Savior commands us to forgive injuries and not think of revenge (Mt 5:39).

1.2. God often carries out this law in the course of his Providence, making the punishment in many cases correspond to the sin, as Jdg 1:7; Isa 33:1; Hab 2:13; Mt 26:52.

1.3. Judges ought to consider this rule when punishing offenders and doing right to those who are injured. Consideration must be made of the nature, quality, and degree of the wrong done, that reparation may be made to the party injured, and others deterred from acting similarly.

2. The care God took of servants. If their masters maimed them, even though it was only the knocking out of a tooth, they should let them go free (vv. 26–27).

3. Does God take care for oxen (bulls)? Yes, it appears from the following laws in this chapter that he does, *for our sakes* (1Co 9:9–10). The Israelites are here directed what to do:

3.1. In case of harm done by bulls or any other wild animal.

3.1.1. As an instance of God's care for human life. If a bull killed any man, woman, or child, the bull was to be *stoned* (v. 28). In this way, God wanted to keep in the minds of his people a deep abhorrence of the sin of murder and everything brutal.

3.1.2. To make people see to it that none of their cattle might do any harm, but that, by all possible means, trouble might be prevented.

3.2. In case of hurt done to oxen or other cattle.

3.2.1. If they fall into a pit and die there, the person who left the pit uncovered must pay for the loss (vv. 33–34). Trouble committed maliciously is a serious breaking of the law, but trouble committed through negligence is not without fault.

3.2.2. If cattle fight and one kills another, the owners are to share in the loss equally (v. 35). In the wilderness where they lay closely camped together, and had their flocks and herds with them, such trouble as is described at the end of this chapter was likely to occur.

CHAPTER 22

The laws of this chapter relate: 1. To the eighth commandment, concerning theft (vv. 1–4), trespass by cattle (v. 5), damage by fire (v. 6), what is entrusted to others (vv. 7–13), and borrowing cattle (vv. 14–15) or money (vv. 25–27). 2. To the seventh commandment, against sexual immorality (vv. 16–17) and bestiality (v. 19). 3. To the first four commandments, forbidding sorcery (v. 18) and idolatry (v. 20), and commanding the offering of the firstfruits (vv. 29–30). 4. To the poor (vv. 21–24). 5. To the civil government (v. 28) and to the special distinction of the Jewish nation (v. 31).

Verses 1–6

Here are laws:

1. Concerning theft:

1.1. If someone steals any cattle, which made up most of the wealth of those times, and they are found in that person's custody, that person must pay back double (v. 4).

1.2. If someone had killed or sold the sheep or ox they had stolen and persisted in this crime, they must restore *five oxen for an ox, and four sheep for a sheep* (22:1).

1.3. If the thief was not able to make restitution, the thief must be sold as a slave (v. 3).

1.4. If a thief broke into a house at night and was killed in so doing, the thief's blood was on their own head.

2. Concerning trespass (v. 5). The person who willfully put their cattle into a neighbor's field must make restitution of the best of their own.

3. Concerning damage done by fire (v. 6). A person who intended to burn only thorn bushes might become accessory to the burning of grain, and should not be held guiltless. People must suffer for their carelessness, as well as for their malice.

Verses 7–15

These laws:

1. Concern what is entrusted to others (vv. 7–13). If a person delivers goods, and if special confidence is put in the person they are lodged with, if these goods are then stolen or lost, perish or are damaged, if it appears that it was not because of any fault of the trustee, the owner must stand the loss, or else the one who has been false to the trust must be compelled to make restitution. This teaches us:

1.1. It is unjust and wrong, and what is widely considered shameful, to betray a trust.

1.2. That there is such a general failing of truth and justice on earth as gives too much reason to suspect people's honesty whenever it is in their interest to be dishonest. The religion of an oath is very ancient, and a clear indication of the universal belief in a God, Providence, and a judgment to come.

2. Concern loans (vv. 14–15). If someone lent an animal to a neighbor, if the owner was with it or was to receive profit for its loan, whatever harm came to the cattle, the owner must stand the loss of. However, if the owner was so kind to the borrower as to lend it to the borrower for nothing, then, if any harm happened, the borrower must make it good.

Verses 16–24

Here is:

1. A law that the man who seduced a young woman should be obliged to marry her (vv. 16–17). This law puts an honor on marriage and shows how improper it is that children should marry without their parents' agreement.

2. A law which makes sorcery a capital crime (v. 18).

3. A law which says that having sexual relations with an animal is a "capital offense"; such a person is unfit to live (v. 19): *Whosoever lies with a beast shall die.*

4. Idolatry also made a "capital offense" (v. 20).

5. A caution against oppression. Because those who were empowered to punish other crimes were themselves most in danger of this, God takes the punishing of it into his own hands.

5.1. Foreigners must not be mistreated (v. 21), not wronged in judgment by the judges, nor deceived in contracts, nor must any advantage be taken of their ignorance or need. They must not be taunted, trampled on, treated with contempt, or rebuked for being foreign. We can learn form this:

5.1.1. Humanity is one of the laws of religion. Those who are foreigners to us are known to God, and he preserves them (Ps 146:9).

5.1.2. Those who profess religion should try to please foreigners, that in so doing they may commend their religion.

5.2. Widows and the fatherless must not be taken advantage of unfairly (v. 22): *You shall not afflict them,* that is, "You shall comfort and assist them." Their condition must be considered: they have lost those who should look after them and protect them. It is a great comfort to those who are oppressed or hurt by others that they have a God to go to who will do more than *give them the hearing.*

Verses 25–31

Here is:

1. A law against extortion in lending. The strictness of this law seems to have been exclusive to the Jews, but its justice leads us to show mercy to those of whom we might take unfair advantage, and to be content to share in loss as well as in profit. It seems as lawful to receive interest for my money, which another person may take pains with and may use with the risk of losing it in trade, as it is to receive rent for my land, which another takes pains with

and may use with the risk of losing it in farming. They must not take a poor person's cloak in pawn; but, if they did, it must be restored by sunset (vv. 26–27).

2. A law against the contempt of authority (v. 28): *Thou shalt not revile the gods*, that is, the rulers and judges, who carry out these laws. They must do their duty, whoever suffers by it.

3. A law concerning the offering of their firstfruits to God (vv. 29–30). It was appointed before (13:1–22), and it is here repeated: *The firstborn of thy sons shalt thou give unto me*, and we have much more reason to give ourselves and all we have to God, who *spared not his own Son, but delivered him up for us all* (Ro 8:32). They must not delay in offering the first crop of their corn. Let not young people delay in offering God the firstfruits of their time and strength.

4. A distinction put between the Jews and all other people: *You shall be holy men unto me*, and one mark of that special distinction is to be in their diet, which was, that they should not *eat any flesh that was torn of beasts* (v. 31), not only because it was unhealthy, but also because eating the leftovers of animals killed by wild animals was worthless.

CHAPTER 23

This chapter continues and concludes the acts passed in the first session, if we may call it that, on Mount Sinai. Here are: 1. Some laws relating especially to the ninth commandment, against bearing false testimony (v. 1) and giving false judgment (vv. 2–3, 6–8). A law of doing good to our enemies (vv. 4–5) and not oppressing foreigners (v. 9). 2. Some laws special to the Jews. The sabbatical year (vv. 10–11), a repetition of the fourth commandment and a prohibition against invoking other gods (vv. 12–13), the three annual feasts (vv. 14–17), and some laws relating to them. 3. Gracious promises of the fulfilling of the mercy God had begun for them, on condition of their obedience. That God would lead them through the wilderness (vv. 20–24), that he would prosper all they had (vv. 25–26), and that he would lead them to possess Canaan (vv. 27–31). But they must not associate with the other nations (vv. 32–33).

Verses 1–9

Here are:

1. Cautions concerning judicial proceedings.

1.1. Witnesses are here warned against causing an innocent person to be accused by spreading false reports or helping prosecute an innocent person *by putting their hand* in swearing as witnesses against that person (v. 1). Bearing false testimony has in it all the guilt of lying, perjury, malice, theft, and murder. There is scarcely any one act of wickedness that a person can possibly be guilty of which has a greater unscrupulousness than this. But the first part of this warning is to be extended to ordinary conversation, so that slandering and backbiting are kinds of bearing false testimony. A person's reputation lies as much at the mercy of all those they have dealings with as their wealth or life does at the mercy of a judge or jury. So, people who spread false reports against others sin as much against the laws of truth, justice, and love as a false witness does.

1.2. The judges are here warned against perverting the course of justice:

1.2.1. They must not be persuaded to follow the crowd and to go against their consciences in giving judgment

(v. 2). The junior judge voted first, so that this judge might not be swayed or overruled by the authority of the senior. We must ask what we ought to do, not what the majority do, because we must be judged by our Master and not by our fellow-servants. It is too great a compliment to be willing to go to hell to be with our friends.

1.2.2. They must not pervert the course of justice, either in favor of the poor (v. 3) or against them (v. 6). Let them not fare the better or the worse for being poor. Judges must have nothing to do with false charges (v. 7). They themselves are accountable to the great Judge. They must not oppress a foreigner (v. 9). Though foreigners might not inherit the Israelites' lands, they must still have justice done them, must peaceably enjoy their own, and be given redress if they have been wronged, even though they were strangers to the citizenship of Israel.

2. Commands concerning neighborly kindnesses. We must be ready to act kindly, as needs arise, toward anybody, even toward those who have done us harm (vv. 4–5). The command of loving our enemies is not only *a new*, but an *old* commandment (Pr 25:21–22). We can learn from this:

2.1. If we must do this kindness for an enemy, we should do much more for a friend.

2.2. If it is wrong not to prevent our enemy's loss and damage, how much worse is it to cause harm and loss to our enemy or their possessions.

2.3. If we must bring back our neighbors' cattle when they go astray, how much more should we try, using careful instructions and warnings, to bring back our neighbors themselves, when they wander in any sinful path, see Jas 5:19–20. And, if we must endeavor to help up a fallen donkey, how much more should we try to comfort and encourage those with a sinking spirit, *saying to those that are of a fearful heart, Be strong* (Isa 35:4).

Verses 10–19

Here is:

1. The institution of the sabbatical year (vv. 10–11). The land was to rest every seventh year. They must not plow or sow it at the beginning of the year, and then they could not expect any great harvest at the end of the year. This was intended:

1.1. To show what a plentiful land God was bringing them into.

1.2. To remind them of their dependence on God their great landlord and their obligation to use the fruit of their land as he should direct. Afterward, we find that their disobedience to this command meant that the promises were forfeited (2Ch 36:21).

1.3. To teach them confidence in divine Providence.

2. The repetition of the law of the fourth commandment concerning the weekly Sabbath (v. 12). Some have tried to take away the observance of the Sabbath by pretending that every day must be a Sabbath day.

3. A prohibition against invoking the names of gods of the nations (v. 13). A general warning is attached to this, which refers to all these commands: *In all things that I have said unto you, be circumspect.*

4. The strict requirement of solemn religious attendance on God in the place of his choosing (vv. 14–17). All the men must come together three times a year in a holy congregation. They must come together *before the Lord* (v. 17), to bow before him. They must not *appear before God empty* (v. 15). They must bring some freewill offering or other, and, as they were not allowed to come empty-handed, so we must not come to worship God

emptyhearted; our souls must be filled with grace, with holy, godly, and devout desires toward him and dedication of ourselves to him. The Passover, Pentecost, and Feast of Tabernacles, in spring, summer, and autumn, were the three times appointed for them to celebrate to God.

5. Some particular directions given about the three festivals, though not as detailed as later.

5.1. As to the Passover, it was not to be offered with leavened bread, nor was the fat of the offering to remain until the morning, or it would become offensive (v. 18).

5.2. At the Feast of Pentecost, when they were to begin their harvest, they must bring *the first of their firstfruits* to God: the whole harvest was sanctified by the devout presentation of these (v. 19).

5.3. At the Feast of Ingathering, as it is called (v. 16), they must give God thanks for the mercies of the harvest they had received and must depend on him for the next harvest. They must not think of following the superstitious custom of some Gentiles, who, it is said, at the end of their harvest, *seethed a kid in its dam's milk* (v. 19), and sprinkled that milk stew magically on their gardens and fields, to make them more fruitful next year.

Verses 20–33

Here are three gracious promises made to Israel, to call them to their duty and to encourage them in it:

1. It is promised that they would be guided and kept in their way through the wilderness to the Land of Promise: *Behold, I send an Angel before thee* (v. 20), *my Angel* (v. 23), a created angel, some say, a minister of God's providence, to lead and protect the camp of Israel. Others suppose it to be the Son of God, the Angel of the covenant; and we may take it that he is God's messenger and the church's Redeemer before his incarnation, as *the Lamb slain from the foundation of the world* (Rev 13:8). It is promised that this blessed angel would *keep them in the way*. It is also promised that he would bring them into the place which God had not only intended but also prepared for them, and so Christ has prepared a place for his followers.

2. It is promised that they would settle comfortably in the land of Canaan. Notice:

2.1. How reasonable the conditions of this promise are—only that they should serve their God, the only true God.

2.2. How rich the details of this promise are:

2.2.1. The comfort of their food. He shall bless thy bread and thy water.

2.2.2. The continuation of their health: "*I will take sickness away*, either prevent it or remove it."

2.2.3. The increase of their wealth. Their cattle would not be barren.

2.2.4. The prolonging of their lives to old age: "*The number of thy days I will fulfil*, and they will not be cut off by untimely deaths." In this way, godliness has the *promise of the life that now is* (1Ti 4:8).

3. It is promised that they would conquer and subdue their enemies, the present inhabitants of the land of Canaan, who would be driven out to make room for them. Hosts of hornets made way for the hosts of Israel; God can make use of such lowly creatures to punish his people's enemies, as he did in the plagues of Egypt. When God pleases, hornets can drive out Canaanites, as well as lions could (Jos 24:12). The command linked to this promise is that they should not make any friendship, or have any acquaintance, with idolaters (vv. 32–33). Idolaters must not even stay in their land, unless they renounced their idolatry. Those who want to avoid bad ways must avoid bad company.

CHAPTER 24

In this chapter: 1. Moses comes down to the people, tells them the laws he had received and receives their agreement to those laws (v. 3), writes the laws, reads them to the people, who repeat their agreement (vv. 4–7), and then by sacrifice and the sprinkling of blood, confirms the covenant between them and God (vv. 5–6, 8). 2. He returns to God again to receive further directions. When he was dismissed from his previous session with God, he was ordered to come again (vv. 1–2). He did so with seventy elders, to whom God revealed his glory (vv. 9–11). 3. Moses is ordered up onto the mountain (vv. 12–13); the rest are ordered to go down to the people (v. 14). The cloud of glory is seen by all the people on the top of Mount Sinai (vv. 15–17), and Moses stays there with God forty days and forty nights (v. 18).

Verses 1–8

Moses is directed to bring Aaron, his sons, and the seventy elders of Israel, that they might be witnesses of the glory of God, and that their testimony might confirm the people's faith. They must all be very reverent: *Worship you afar off* (v. 1). In the following verses, we have the solemn covenant made between God and Israel and the exchange of confirmations.

1. Moses told the people the words of the Lord (v. 3). He laid before them all the instructions and stipulations, general and particular, of the previous chapters. He then put it to them whether they were willing to submit to these laws or not.

2. The people unanimously agreed to the proposed terms, without reservation or exception: *All the words which the Lord hath said will we do*. This is the tenor of the covenant. If they observed the previous precepts, God would fulfill the previous promises. "Obey and be happy." Notice:

2.1. How it was engrossed in the Book of the Covenant: *Moses wrote the words of the Lord* (v. 4).

2.2. How it was sealed by the blood of the covenant, that Israel might receive great encouragement from God's confirmation of his promises to them and might come under great obligation from the confirmation of their promises to God. The covenant must be made by sacrifice (Ps 50:5), because since Adam and Eve sinned and forfeited the Creator's favor, there can be no fellowship by covenant until there is first atonement and reconciliation by sacrifice.

2.2.1. In preparation for this:

2.2.1.1. Moses builds an altar, to the honor of God, which was the main intention in all the altars that were built, and which was the first thing to be looked at in the covenant they were now to seal.

2.2.1.2. He erects twelve pillars, according to the number of the tribes. These were to represent the people, the other party to the covenant; and we may suppose that they were set up against the altar, and that Moses, as mediator, passed backward and forward between them. Probably each tribe set up and knew its own pillar, and their elders stood by it.

2.2.1.3. He appointed sacrifices to be offered on the altar (v. 5), burnt offerings and peace offerings (fellowship offerings), which were always intended to be atoning sacrifices.

2.2.2. After preparations had been made, the confirmations were very solemnly exchanged:

2.2.2.1. The blood of the sacrifice which the people offered was partly sprinkled on the altar (v. 6), which represented the people's dedication of themselves and their lives to God and to his honor.

2.2.2.2. The blood of the sacrifice which God had acknowledged and accepted was—the remainder of it—sprinkled either on the people themselves (v. 8) or on the pillars that represented them. This represented God's graciously giving his favor to them. In the same way, our Lord Jesus, the Mediator of the new covenant (of whom Moses was a type), having offered up himself a sacrifice on the cross, that his blood might indeed be the blood of the covenant, sprinkled it on the altar in his intercession (Heb 9:12) and sprinkles it on his church by his word and ordinances and the activity of his promised Spirit, by whom we are sealed. Christ himself seemed to allude to this ceremony when in the institution of the Lord's Supper he said, *This cup is the new testament* (or covenant) *in my blood* (Lk 22:20). Compare with this Heb 9:19–20.

Verses 9–11

God gives to their representatives some special signs of his favor to them and allows them to come closer to him than they could have expected. Notice:

1. *They saw the God of Israel* (v. 10), that is, they caught a glimpse of his glory, in light and fire, though they saw *no manner of similitude* (Dt 4:15), and his being *no man hath seen nor can see* (1Ti 6:16). They saw the place where the God of Israel stood (as the Septuagint, a Greek version of the Old Testament, reads), something that came near the form of God, but was not. Whatever they saw, it was certainly something of which no idol or picture could be made, but was enough to satisfy them that God was truly with them. Nothing is described except what was under his feet, for our conceptions of God are all below him and fall infinitely short of being adequate. At the bottom of the brightness, and as its footstool or pedestal, they saw a most rich and splendid pavement, as it had been made of sapphire, azure or sky-colored.

2. *Upon the nobles* (or elders) *of Israel, he laid not his hand* (v. 11). Though they were human, the dazzling splendor of his glory was so restrained (Job 26:9), that they were able to bear it.

3. *They saw God, and did eat and drink.* Not only were their lives spared, but also their vigor, courage, and strength increased; the experience did not dampen their joy, but rather increased it.

Verses 12–18

After the public ceremony of sealing the covenant is over, Moses is now called up to receive further instructions.

1. He is called to go up to God on the mountain, and there he remains six days at some distance. "Come up, and *I will give thee a law, that thou mayest teach them*." Having received these orders:

1.1. He appointed Aaron and Hur to be as vice-regents in his absence to keep the peace and good order in the congregation (v. 14).

1.2. He took Joshua up with him on the mountain (v. 13). Joshua was his minister, and it would be good for him to have him as a companion during the six days that he waited on the mountain, before God called to him. Joshua was to be his successor, and so he was honored before the people above the rest of the elders, that they might afterward more readily accept him as their new leader. Joshua was prepared for service in this way, by being trained in fellowship with God.

1.3. A cloud covered the mountain six days, a visible sign of God's special presence there. During these six days, Moses stayed waiting on the mountain for a call into God's presence (vv. 15–16).

2. He is called into the cloud on the seventh day, probably on the Sabbath day (v. 16). Now:

2.1. The thick cloud opened up in the sight of all Israel, and the glory of the Lord burst forth *like devouring fire* (v. 17).

2.2. The entrance of Moses into the cloud was very awesome: *Moses went into the midst of the cloud* (v. 18), sure that he who called him would protect him.

2.3. His continuing in the cloud was no less awesome; he was there *forty days and forty nights*. When Moses was called *into the midst of the cloud*, he left Joshua outside it, and Joshua continued to eat and drink daily while he waited for Moses' return, but from then on Moses fasted.

CHAPTER 25

This chapter begins the account of the instructions God gave to Moses on the mountain to set up and furnish a tabernacle to the honor of God. We have here: 1. Orders given for a collection to be made among the people for this purpose (vv. 1–9). 2. Detailed instructions concerning the ark of the covenant (vv. 10–22). 3. The table of shewbread (bread of the Presence) (vv. 23–30). 4. The golden candlestick (lampstand) (vv. 31–40).

Verses 1–9

We suppose that when Moses went into the cloud and stayed there so long, he saw and heard glorious things relating to the heavenly world, but they were inexpressible. In these verses God tells Moses his intention in general, that the children of Israel should build a sanctuary for him, because he intended to *dwell among them* (v. 8). God had chosen the people of Israel (v. 8). As their King, he had already given them laws to govern themselves and for their dealings with one another, with some general rules for religious worship.

1. He orders a royal palace to be set up among them for himself, here called *a sanctuary* or holy place, of which it is said (Jer 17:12), *A glorious high throne from the beginning is the place of our sanctuary*. This sanctuary is to be considered:

1.1. As ceremonial, in accordance with other institutions of that dispensation, which consisted of external regulations (Heb 9:10), and so it is called a *worldly* (earthly) *sanctuary* (Heb 9:1).

1.1.1. He revealed his presence among them there, a sign of his presence, that, while they had that in the midst of them, they might never again ask, *Is the Lord among us or not?* (17:7). And, because they lived in tents in the desert, even this royal palace was ordered to be a tabernacle that it might be portable and move with them.

1.1.2. He ordered his subjects to come before him with their praise and worship. They must bring their sacrifices. All Israel must meet there, to come together to declare their reverence to the God of Israel.

1.2. As a type. The holy places made with hands were the *figures of the true* (Heb 9:24). The body of Christ, in and by which he made atonement, was the *greater and more perfect tabernacle* (Heb 9:11). The *Word was made flesh, and dwelt among us* (Jn 1:14), as in a tabernacle.

2. When Moses was to erect this palace, it was necessary that he should first be instructed where he must get the materials from, and on what he must model it:

2.1. The people must provide him with the materials, not by a tax imposed on them, but by a voluntary contribution.

2.1.1. *Speak unto the children of Israel that they bring me an offering.* Since we live on what he provides, we must also live for him.

2.1.2. This offering must be given willingly, and with the heart. We should ask, not only, "What must we do?" but, "What may we do for God?"

2.1.3. The details here mention what they must offer (vv. 3–7), all of them things that would be needed in the tabernacle. Some note that here was gold, silver, and bronze, but no iron; that is the military metal, and this was to be a house of peace.

2.2. God himself would provide him with the model: *According to all that I show thee* (v. 9).

Verses 10–22

The first thing which is here ordered to be made is the ark with its accessories, the furniture of the Most Holy Place, and the special sign of God's presence, which the tabernacle was set up to contain.

1. The ark itself was a chest, or coffer, in which the two tablets of the Law were to be honorably and carefully kept. This chest or cabinet was about three and three-quarter feet (about 1.1 meters) long and about two and a quarter feet (about 0.7 meter) broad and deep. It was overlaid inside and outside with thin plates of gold. It had a molding, or cornice, of gold around it, with rings and poles to carry it with, and in it he must put the Testimony (vv. 10–16). The tablets of the Law are called the *testimony* because God testified his will in them. The Gospel of Christ is also called a testimony or witness (Mt 24:14). It is noteworthy:

1.1. That the tablets of the Law were carefully preserved in the ark for the purpose of teaching us to make much of the word of God, and to hide it in our hearts, in our innermost thoughts, as the ark was placed in the Holy of Holies.

1.2. That this ark was the chief sign of God's presence, and it teaches us that the first and great evidence and assurance of God's favor is the putting of his Law in our hearts. God lives where that rules (Heb 8:10).

1.3. That provision was made for the carrying of this ark around with them in all their moves, which shows us that, wherever we go, we should take our religion along with us, always behaving according to the love of the Lord Jesus and his Law.

2. The mercy seat (atonement cover) was the covering of the ark or chest, made of solid gold, exactly to fit the dimensions of the ark (vv. 17, 21).

3. The cherubim of gold were fixed to the mercy seat (atonement cover), and of a piece with it, and spread their wings over it (v. 18). It is supposed that these cherubim were intended to represent the holy angels, who always accompanied the *Shechinah* or divine Majesty, not by a statue of an angel, but some sign of the angelic nature, possibly like one of those four faces described in Eze 1:10. Whatever the faces were, they looked toward one another, and both downward toward the ark, while their wings were stretched out to overshadow the cover. The writer to the Hebrews calls them *cherubim of glory shadowing the mercy seat* (Heb 9:5). God is said to live or sit enthroned, *between the cherubim*, on the mercy seat (Ps 80:1), and there he promises in the future to meet with Moses, and to *commune with him* (v. 22). In allusion to the mercy seat, we are said to come boldly to *the throne of grace* (Heb 4:16), for we *are not under the law*, which is covered, *but under grace* (Ro 6:14), which is revealed. Its wings are stretched out, and we are invited to come and take refuge under the shadow of them (Ru 2:12).

Verses 23–30

Here is:

1. A table ordered to be made of wood overlaid with gold, which was to stand, not in the Holy of Holies (nothing was in that except the ark with its accessories), but in the outer part of the tabernacle, called the *sanctuary* or *holy place* (Heb 9:2, 23, etc.). There must also be plates and dishes, etc., and all *of gold* (v. 29).

2. A provision for it to be always spread and furnished with the shewbread (bread of the Presence) (v. 30) or "bread of the face (of God)," twelve loaves, one for each tribe, set in two rows, six in a row; see the law concerning them (Lev 25:5–10). In the royal palace it was right that there should be a royal table. Some make the twelve loaves represent the twelve tribes. As the ark represented God's presence with them, so the twelve loaves represented their being presented to God. This bread was intended to be:

2.1. A thankful acknowledgment of God's goodness to them, in giving them their daily bread, manna in the wilderness, where he prepared a table for them, and, in Canaan, the grain of the land. Christ has taught us to pray every day for daily bread.

2.2. A sign of their fellowship with God. As this bread on God's table was made of the same grain as the bread on their own tables, God and Israel, as it were, ate together as a sign of their friendship and fellowship; he ate with them, and they with him.

2.3. A type of the spiritual provision which is made in the church by the Gospel of Christ, for all who are made priests to our God. *In our Father's house there is bread enough and to spare* (Lk 15:17), a loaf for every tribe.

Verses 31–40

1. The next thing to be made for the tabernacle furnishing was a rich, stately candlestick (lampstand) of pure gold. The particular directions here given concerning it show:

1.1. That it was ornamental. It had many branches drawn from the main shaft, which not only had their bowls or cups necessary for the oil and the kindled wick, but also knops and flowers (buds and blossoms) for ornament.

1.2. That it was suitable and well designed both to disperse light and to keep the tabernacle clean from smoke and snuffs.

1.3. That it was significant. The tabernacle had no windows to let in daylight; all its light was candlelight. But God did not leave himself without witness, nor them without instruction; the commandment was a lamp, the Law a light, and the prophets were the branches of that lamp, which gave light through the ages to the Old Testament church. The church is still dark, as the tabernacle was, in comparison with what it will be in heaven; but the word of God is *a light shining in a dark place* (2Pe 1:19), and the world would be a really dark place without it. The Spirit of God, in his various gifts and graces, is compared to the *seven lamps* which *burn before the throne* (Rev 4:5). The churches are golden candlesticks, the lights of the world, *holding forth the word of life* as the candlestick does the light (Php 2:15–16). Ministers are to light the lamps (v. 37), by opening up the Scriptures.

2. In the middle of these instructions an express caution is given to Moses, to beware varying from his model: *Make them after the pattern shown thee* (v. 40).

CHAPTER 26

Moses here receives instructions: 1. Concerning the inner curtains of the tent or tabernacle and the joining of those curtains (vv. 1–6). 2. Concerning the outer curtains, which were of goat hair, to strengthen the former (vv. 7–13), and concerning the case or cover which was to keep it safe from the elements (v. 14). 3. Concerning the boards (frames) which were used to support the curtains, with their crossbars and sockets (bases) (vv. 15–30). 4. Concerning the partition between the Holy Place and the Most Holy Place (vv. 31–35) and the curtain for the door (vv. 36–37).

Verses 1–6

1. The house must be a *tabernacle* or tent. God revealed his presence among them in a tabernacle:

1.1. To fit in with their present conditions in the desert, that they might have him with them wherever they went.

1.2. To represent the state of God's church in this world: it is *a tabernacle, a sanctuary* (Ps 15:1). *We have here no continuing city* (Heb 13:14); we are strangers in this world and travelers toward a better one. We will never be completely settled till we come to heaven.

2. The curtains of the tabernacle must correspond to a divine pattern:

2.1. They were to be very rich, the best of the kind, fine twined linen, and very pleasant, blue, and purple, and scarlet.

2.2. They were to be embroidered with cherubim (v. 1), to show that the angels of God pitch their tents around the church (Ps 34:7).

2.3. There were to be two hangings, five widths in each, sewn together, and the two hangings coupled together with golden clasps so that it might be all one tabernacle (v. 6). In this way, the churches of Christ and the saints, though they are many, are still one, being *fitly framed together* in holy love, and by the *unity of the Spirit*, so growing into one *holy temple* in *the Lord* (Eph 2:21–22; 4:3, 16).

Verses 7–14

Moses is here ordered to make a double covering for the tabernacle, that the elements might not cause damage.

1. There was to be a covering of goat-hair curtains, which were somewhat larger than the inner curtains, because they were to enclose them, and probably were stretched out at a little distance from them (v. 7, etc.). These were coupled together with bronze clasps.

2. Over this there was to be another covering, and that a double one (v. 14), one of *rams' skins dyed red*, probably dressed with the wool on; another of *badgers' skins*, or the hide of sea cows, some strong sort of fine leather, for we read of the best sort of shoes being made of it (Eze 16:10). Notice that the outside of the tabernacle was rough, but its beauty was in the inner curtains. Those in whom God lives must try to be better than they seem to be. Let our finest parts be those of our inner selves, which God values (1Pe 3:4).

Verses 15–30

Very particular directions are here given about the boards (frames) of the tabernacle, which were to bear the curtains, as the stakes of a tent which needed to be strong (Isa 54:2). These boards had tenons (projections) which fell into the mortises that were made for them in silver bases. God took care to have everything strong, as well as fine, in his tabernacle. The boards were coupled together with gold rings at the top and bottom (v. 24) and kept firm with crossbars that ran through golden staples in every board (v. 26), and the boards and crossbars were all overlaid with gold (v. 29).

Verses 31–37

Here, two curtains are ordered to be made:

1. One as a partition between the Holy Place and the Most Holy Place, which not only forbade anyone to enter, but also forbade them so much as to look into the holiest of all (vv. 31, 33). Under that dispensation, divine grace was veiled, but now we contemplate it with unveiled faces (2Co 3:18). The writer to the Hebrews tells us (Heb 9:8–9) what the meaning of this curtain was: it showed that the ceremonial law *could not make the comers thereunto perfect* (Heb 10:1), nor would the observance of it bring people to heaven. The *way into the holiest of all was not made manifest while the first tabernacle was standing. Life and immortality* were hidden till they were *brought to light by the gospel* (2Ti 1:10), which was represented by the tearing of this curtain at the death of Christ (Mt 27:51). We have now *boldness to enter into the holiest*, in all acts of devotion, *by the blood of Jesus* (Heb 10:19), but also with a holy reverence and humility before God.

2. Another curtain for the outer door of the tabernacle (vv. 36–37). Through this first curtain the priests, but not the people, went in every day to minister in the Holy Place (Heb 9:6). This curtain, which was the only defense the tabernacle had against thieves and robbers, might easily be broken through, for it could be neither locked nor barred, and the abundance of wealth in the tabernacle might be a temptation to such people. By leaving it exposed, however:

2.1. The priests and Levites would be even more obliged to keep a strict watch on it, and:

2.2. God would show his care of his church on earth, though it is weak and defenseless and continually exposed. A curtain will be, if God is pleased to make it so, as strong a defense to his house as gates of bronze and bars of iron.

CHAPTER 27

In this chapter directions are given concerning: 1. The bronze altar of burnt offering (vv. 1–8). 2. The courtyard of the tabernacle, with its curtains (vv. 9–19). 3. Oil for the lamp (vv. 20–21).

Verses 1–8

1. In the tabernacle God wanted to reveal his presence among his people. The people were to pay their devotions to him there, not in the tabernacle itself—only the priests entered that, as God's domestic servants—but in the courtyard of the tabernacle. There an altar was ordered to be set up, to which they must bring their sacrifices. Moses is here given directions about the altar:

1.1. Its dimensions: it was square (vv. 1–2).

1.2. Its horns (v. 2), which were both decorative and functional. The sacrifices were bound with cords to the horns of the altar; they were symbols of help and refuge (1Ki 1:50; 2:28).

1.3. Its material; it was made of wood overlaid with bronze (vv. 1–2).

1.4. Its utensils (v. 3), which were all made of bronze.

1.5. The grating, which was let into the hollow of the altar, about the middle of it, in which the fire was kept and the sacrifice burned.

1.6. The staves (poles) with which it must be carried (vv. 6–7). Moses is referred to the pattern that was shown him (v. 8).

2. This bronze altar was a type of Christ dying to make atonement for our sins. Helpless sinners fly for refuge to

the horns of this altar when justice pursues them, and they are kept safe because of the sacrifice offered there.

Verses 9–19

The courtyard of the tabernacle was enclosed with curtains of the finest linen that was used for tents. This courtyard was 150 feet (about 46 meters) long and seventy-five feet (about 23 meters) wide. Pillars (posts) were set up at convenient distances with brass sockets (bronze bases) with silver hooks and bands, on which the linen curtains were fastened: the curtain which served for the entrance was finer than the rest (v. 16). Thanks be to God, now, under the Gospel, the enclosure is taken down. God's will is that people should *pray everywhere* (1Ti 2:8), and there is space for all who in every place call on the name of Jesus Christ.

Verses 20–21

Here an instruction is given for the lamps to be kept constantly burning in it. In every candlestick (lampstand) there should be a burning and shining light: candlesticks without candles are as *wells without water* (2Pe 2:17) or as *clouds without water* (Jude 12). Now:

1. The people were to provide the oil.
2. The priests were to light the lamps and to keep them burning. In the same way, it is the work of ministers, by the preaching and expounding of the Scriptures, which are like a lamp, to give light to the church, God's tabernacle on earth.

CHAPTER 28

This and the following chapter deal with the priests who were to minister in this holy place. In this chapter: 1. God names those who were to be his servants (v. 1) and appoints their garments in keeping with the glory of the house which was now to be established (vv. 2–5). 2. He appoints the garments of his chief servant, the high priest. An ephod and girdle (sash or waistband) (vv. 6–14). 3. A breastplate (breastpiece) of judgment (vv. 15–29), in which the Urim and Thummim must be put (v. 30). 4. The robe of the ephod (vv. 31–35), and the miter (turban) (vv. 36–39). 5. The garments of the lesser priests (vv. 40–43). And these also were shadows of good things to come.

Verses 1–5

We have here:

1. The priests named: Aaron and his sons (v. 1). Moses, who had officiated up to that time as one of the priests of the Lord (Ps 99:6), had enough to do as their prophet to speak God's words, and as their ruler to judge among them. And so he was very pleased to see his brother Aaron invested in this office. Aaron, who had humbly served as a prophet to his younger brother Moses, and did not decline the office (7:1), is now put forward to be a priest, a high priest, to God. Because it was necessary that those who ministered at the altar should give themselves wholly to the service, and because what is everybody's work soon becomes nobody's work, God chose from among them one to be a family of priests, the father and his four sons. From Aaron's body descended all the priests of the Jewish church, of whom we read so often, both in the Old Testament and in the New.

2. The priests' garments appointed, to give dignity and honor (v. 2). The garments that were appointed:

2.1. For both the high priest and the lesser priests were four in number, namely, the linen breeches (undergarments), the linen coat (tunic), the linen girdle (sash) which fastened it to them, and the bonnet (headband) or turban; what the high priest wore is called a miter.

2.2. Only for the high priest were four more, namely, the ephod, with its skillfully woven waistband, the breastplate (breastpiece) of judgment, the long robe with the bells and pomegranates at the bottom of it, and the golden plate on his forehead. The decorative features that we now bear under the Gospel are not to be of gold, pearl, and expensive clothes, but the garments of salvation and the robe of righteousness (Ps 132:9, 16; Isa 61:10).

Verses 6–14

Directions are here given concerning the ephod, the sleeveless vestment which was the outermost garment of the high priest. Linen ephods were worn by the lesser priests (1Sa 22:18). Samuel wore one when he was a child (1Sa 2:18), and David when he danced before the ark (2Sa 6:14). The one, however, which only the high priest wore was called a golden ephod, because there was a great deal of gold woven into it. It was a short coat without sleeves, buttoned closely to him, with a skillfully woven waistband of the same material (vv. 6–8); the shoulder pieces were buttoned together with two precious stones set in gold, one on each shoulder, on which were engraved the names of the children of Israel (vv. 9–12).

Verses 15–30

The most important of the ornaments of the high priest was the breastplate (breastpiece), a rich piece of cloth, skillfully worked with gold, purple, etc., two spans long and a span broad, so that, being doubled, it was a span square (v. 16). This was fastened to the ephod with braided chains of gold (vv. 13–14, 22, etc.) both at the top and the bottom, so that the breastplate might not go loose from the ephod (v. 28). The ephod was the garment of service; *the breastplate of judgment* was an emblem of honor: these two must not be separated.

1. In this breastplate the tribes of Israel were commended to God's favor in twelve precious stones (vv. 17–21, 29). Aaron was to bear their names as a memorial before the Lord continually, being ordained to represent all Israel in things concerning God, in so doing being a type of Christ, our great High Priest, who always appears in the presence of God for us.

1.1. The people were forbidden to come near, but by the high priest, who had their names on his breastplate, they entered the holiest. In the same way, believers, even while they are here on earth, not only enter into the holiest, but by faith are made to sit with Christ in the heavenly realms (Eph 2:6).

1.2. The name of each tribe was engraved on a precious stone, to show how precious and honored believers are in God's sight (Isa 43:4). They will be his in the day he makes up his treasured possession (Mal 3:17).

1.3. The high priest had the names of the tribes both on his shoulders and on his chest, showing both the power and love with which our Lord Jesus intercedes for his people. He not only carries them in his arms with an almighty strength, but he also bears them *upon his heart*, as the expression here is (v. 29), carries them close to himself (Isa 40:11), with the most tender affection.

2. The Urim and Thummim, by which the will of God was made known in doubtful cases, were put in this breastplate, which is therefore called the breastplate of judgment

(v. 30). Urim and Thummim represent light and integrity. We think the words may be read thus, "And you will give, add, or deliver, to the breastplate of judgment, the lights and perfections, and they will be on the heart of Aaron"; that is, "He will be endowed with a power of knowing and making known the mind of God in all difficult or doubtful cases, relating either to the civil or ecclesiastical state of the nation." Their government was a theocracy: God was their King, the high priest was, under God, their ruler, the Urim and Thummim were his cabinet. Probably Moses wrote on the breastplate, or wove into it, these words, *Urim* and *Thummim*, to show that the high priest, having this breastplate on him, and asking to know the will of God in any emergency relating to the people, would be directed to take those measures and give that advice which God would acknowledge. The answer was given either by a voice from heaven or rather by an impulse on the mind of the high priest, which is perhaps indicated in the expression, *He shall bear the judgment of the children of Israel upon his heart.* The Urim and Thummim were of great use to Israel; Joshua inquired of the Urim (Nu 27:21), and, it is likely, the judges after him. It was lost in the Captivity and never recovered afterward. But it was a shadow of good things to come, and the substance, the full reality, is Christ. He makes known God's will; by him God has in these last days made known himself and his mind to us (Jn 1:18; Heb 1:2). Divine revelation centers on him and comes to us through him.

Verses 31–39

Here are directions given:

1. Concerning the robe of the ephod (vv. 31–35). This was worn under the ephod, and reached down to the knees, and was without sleeves. The hole on the top, through which the head was put, was reinforced with a woven edge so that it might not tear when put on. Around the hem of the robe were hung golden bells, and the representations of pomegranates made of yarn of different colors. The pomegranates added to the beauty of the robe, and the sound of the bells gave notice to the people in the outer court when the high priest went into the Holy Place to burn incense, that they might then turn to their devotions at the same time (Lk 1:10). Some consider the bells of the holy robe to be a type of the sound of the Gospel of Christ in the world, making known his entrance within the curtain for us. The adding of the pomegranates, which are a fragrant fruit, shows the sweet savor of the Gospel.

2. Concerning the golden plate fixed on Aaron's forehead, on which must be engraved, *HOLINESS TO THE LORD* (vv. 36–37), Aaron is reminded by this that God is holy and that his priests must be holy. Aaron must have this on his forehead, that he may *bear the iniquity of the holy things* (v. 38), and that *they may be accepted before the Lord*. In this he was a type of Christ, the great Mediator between God and humanity, through whom we may come to God.

2.1. Through him what is defective in our services is forgiven. In many things we fall short of our duty, so that we are very conscious in ourselves of much iniquity that there is in our holy things. But Christ, our High Priest, bears this iniquity himself, bears it for us in such a way that he takes it from us, and through him it is forgiven to us and not counted against us.

2.2. Through him what is good is accepted; our lives and how we lead them are pleasing to God on account of Christ's intercession, and not otherwise (1Pe 2:5). Having *such a high priest*, we come *boldly to the throne of grace* (Heb 4:14–16).

3. The rest of the garments are only named (v. 39). The embroidered coat (tunic) of fine linen was worn under the robe. It reached to the feet, had sleeves that reached to the wrists, and was tied around the body with an embroidered girdle or sash. The miter (turban) was of linen, such as kings wore in the east in ancient times; this is a type of the kingly office of Christ.

Verses 40–43

We have here:

1. Detailed instructions about the garments of the lesser priests. They were to have coats (tunics) and girdles (sashes) and bonnets (headbands) of the same materials as those of the high priest; but there was a difference in shape between their bonnets and his miter. Theirs, as his, were to be *for glory and beauty* (v. 40), but all this glory was nothing compared with the glory of grace. This beauty was as nothing compared to the beauty of holiness, of which these holy garments were types.

2. A general rule concerning the garments both of the high priest and of the lesser priests, that they were to be put on them at first when they were ordained as a sign, and then they were to wear them in all their services, but not at other times (v. 43). These garments are types to us of the righteousness of Christ—if we do not appear before God in this, we will *bear iniquity and die*—and of *the armour of God*, described in Eph 6:13–17.

CHAPTER 29

Particular instructions are given in this chapter concerning: 1. The consecration of the priests and the sanctification of the altar (vv. 1–37). 2. The daily sacrifice (vv. 38–41), to which gracious promises are attached that God would acknowledge and bless them in all their services (vv. 42–46).

Verses 1–37

Here is:

1. The law concerning the consecration of Aaron and his sons to the priest's office.

1.1. The ceremonies with which it was to be done were very fully explained, because nothing of this kind had been done before. Now:

1.1.1. The work to be done was the ordination of those whom God had chosen to be priests, by which they devoted themselves to the service of God and God declared his acceptance of them. The people were made to know that they *glorified not themselves* to be made priests, but were *called of God* (Heb 5:4–5). All who are to be used by God are to be sanctified to him. The person must first be accepted, and then their work may be carried out.

1.1.2. The person whom God appointed to do it was Moses. By God's special appointment, he now did the priest's work, and so what was the priest's part of the sacrifice was here ordered to be his (v. 26).

1.1.3. The place was at the *door of the tabernacle of the congregation* (Tent of Meeting) (v. 4). They were ordained at the door, for they were to be doorkeepers.

1.1.4. It was done with many ceremonial acts:

1.1.4.1. They were to be washed (v. 4), showing that those who *bear the vessels of the Lord* (Isa 52:11) must be clean. Those who want perfect holiness must *cleanse themselves from all filthiness of flesh and spirit* (Isa 1:16–18; 2Co 7:1).

1.1.4.2. They were to be clothed with the holy garments (vv. 5–6, 8–9), to show that it was not enough for them to put away the contamination of sin, but they must also put on the graces of the Spirit and be clothed with righteousness (Ps 132:9).

1.1.4.3. The high priest was to be anointed with the holy anointing oil (v. 7), that the church might be filled and delighted with the sweet savor of his ministry and as a sign of the pouring out of the Spirit on him, to qualify him for his work.

1.1.4.4. Sacrifices were to be offered for them. The covenant of priesthood, as all other covenants, must be made by sacrifice: firstly, there must be a sin offering, to make atonement for them (vv. 10–14). It was used as other sin offerings were; only, whereas the flesh of other sin offerings was eaten by the priest (Lev 10:18) as a sign of the priest's taking away the sin of the people, this was appointed to be all burned outside the camp (v. 14), to show the imperfection of the legal dispensation. Secondly, there must be a burnt offering, a ram wholly burned to the honor of God, as a sign of the total dedication of themselves to God and to his service as living sacrifices, kindled with the fire and ascending in the flame of holy love (vv. 15–18). Thirdly, there must be a peace offering (fellowship offering). It is called the *ram of consecration*, because there was more in this offering that was special to the occasion than in the other two offerings. In the burnt offering, God had the glory of their priesthood; in this offering they had the encouragement of the priesthood; and, as a sign of a mutual covenant between God and them:

1.1.4.4.1. The blood of the sacrifice was divided between God and them (vv. 20–21); part of the blood was sprinkled on all sides of the altar, and part on their bodies (v. 20) and on their garments (v. 21). The blood of Christ and the graces of the Spirit form the beauty of holiness and commend us to God; robes are *made white with the blood of the Lamb* (Rev 7:14).

1.1.4.4.2. The flesh of the sacrifice, with the meat offering (grain offering) attached to it, was likewise divided between God and them, that, if we may put it reverently, God and they might enjoy a feast together as a sign of their friendship and fellowship. Their eating of the things with which the atonement was made represented their receiving the atonement, as it is expressed in Ro 5:11, their thankful acceptance of its benefit and their joyful fellowship with God on that basis, which was the true meaning of a feast on a sacrifice.

1.2. The time that was to be spent in this ordination: *Seven days shalt thou consecrate them* (v. 35). Though all the ceremonies were performed on the first day:

1.2.1. They were not to look on their ordination as complete till the end of the seven days, which made admission into the priesthood all the more solemn, put a distance between this and their former state, and obliged them to enter on their work with a pause, so giving them time to weigh up how serious it was.

1.2.2. Every day of the seven, a bull was to be sacrificed as a sin offering (v. 36), which was to show to them:

1.2.2.1. That though atonement was made and they had received its benefits, they must still maintain a penitent sense of sin and often repeat their confession of sin.

1.2.2.2. That those sacrifices which were offered in this way day by day to make atonement could not make perfect those who draw near to worship, for then they would have stopped being offered, as the writer to the Hebrews argues (Heb 10:1–2). They must therefore expect the *bringing in of a better hope* (Heb 7:19).

1.3. This ordination of the priests was a shadow of good things to come:

1.3.1. Our Lord Jesus is the great High Priest of our profession, clothed with the holy garments of glory and beauty, having obtained eternal redemption for us by his own blood, not that of bulls and rams (Heb 9:12), made perfect, or consecrated, through sufferings (Heb 2:10).

1.3.2. All believers are spiritual priests, to offer spiritual sacrifices (1Pe 2:5), washed in the blood of Christ. It is through Christ, the great sacrifice, that they are dedicated to this service.

2. The consecration of the altar, which seems to have coincided with that of the priests. The sin offerings which were offered every day for seven days together referred to the altar as well as the priests (vv. 36–37). The altar was also sanctified and purified, not only set apart for sacred use, but also made so holy that it could sanctify the gifts offered on it (Mt 23:19). Christ is our altar; for our sakes he sanctified himself, that we and our lives might be sanctified and commended to God (Jn 17:19).

Verses 38–46

In this paragraph:

1. The daily service is appointed. A lamb was to be offered on the altar every morning and a lamb every evening, each with a meat offering (grain offering), both made by fire, as *a continual burnt offering throughout their generations* (vv. 38–41). Now:

1.1. This is a type of the continual intercession which Christ always lives to make because of his atonement, for the continual sanctification of his church: though he offered himself *once for all* (Heb 10:10), that one offering becomes in this way a continual offering.

1.2. This teaches us to offer to God the spiritual sacrifices of prayer and praise every day, morning and evening, in humble acknowledgment of our dependence on him and our obligations to him.

2. Great and precious promises are made of God's favor to Israel and the signs of his special presence with them. Faithfulness in religion brings in its comfort. If we do our part, God will do his and will mark out and establish for himself what is sincerely given to him.

CHAPTER 30

In this chapter, Moses is further instructed concerning: 1. The altar of incense (vv. 1–10). 2. The ransom money (atonement money) which the Israelites were to pay, when they were numbered (vv. 11–16). 3. The brass laver (bronze basin), which was set for the priests to wash in (vv. 17–21). 4. The making up of the anointing oil and its use (vv. 22–33) and the incense and perfume which were to be burned on the golden altar (vv. 34–38).

Verses 1–10

1. The orders given concerning the altar of incense are:

1.1. That it was to be made of wood and covered with gold, with horns at the corners, a golden molding around it, with rings and staves (poles) of gold, for carrying it (vv. 1–5). The measurements of the altar of incense in Ezekiel's temple are about double what they are here (Eze 41:22), and it is there called *an altar of wood*, and there is no mention of gold, to show that the incense in Gospel times should be spiritual, the worship clear and direct, and the service of God made wider.

1.2. That it was to be placed in front of the mercy seat (atonement cover), which was within the curtain (v. 6).

For although the one who ministered at the altar could not see the mercy seat, since the curtain came in between, he must still look toward it and direct his incense that way, to teach us that though we cannot physically see the throne of grace, we must in prayer by faith set ourselves before it, direct our prayer, and look up.

1.3. That Aaron was to burn fragrant incense on this altar, every morning and every evening, intended, not only to take away the foul smell of the meat that was burned daily on the bronze altar, but to show that his people's services were acceptable (vv. 7–8). As the offerings on the bronze altar brought atonement for what had been done that was displeasing to God, so by this offering what they did well was, as it were, commended to divine acceptance; for our two great concerns with God are to be acquitted from guilt and accepted as righteous in his sight.

2. This incense altar was a type of:

2.1. The mediation of Christ. The bronze altar in the courtyard was a type of Christ dying on earth; the golden altar in the sanctuary was a type of Christ interceding in heaven. This altar was before the mercy seat (atonement cover), for Christ always appears in the presence of God for us: he is our *advocate with the Father* (1Jn 2:1), and his intercession is a sweet-smelling savor to God. This altar had a crown fixed to it; for Christ intercedes as a king.

2.2. The devotions of the saints. When the priest was burning incense, the people were praying (Lk 1:10), to show that prayer is the true incense. The lamps were dressed or trimmed at the same time that the incense was burned, to teach us that the reading of the Scriptures, which are our light and lamp, is part of our daily work and should normally accompany our prayers and praises. When we speak to God we must hear what God says to us, and so the fellowship is complete. And, if the heart and life are not holy, even *incense is an abomination* (Isa 1:13), and he that offers it is *as if he blessed an idol* (Isa 66:3).

Verses 11–16

Moses is here ordered to levy money on the people by way of tax, so much per head, for the service of the tabernacle. He must do this when he numbered the people. Some think that it refers only to the first numbering of them. Others think that it was afterward repeated in any emergency and always when the people were numbered. But many of the Jewish writers are of the opinion that it was to be an annual tribute. This was that tribute money which Christ paid, so as not to offend his adversaries (Mt 17:27). Now:

1. The tribute to be paid was *half a shekel*. The rich were not to give more, nor the poor less (v. 15), to show that the souls of the rich and poor are alike precious, and that God is *no respecter of persons* (Ac 10:34; Job 34:19). In other offerings people were to give according to their ability, but this, which was the *ransom of the soul*, must be the same for all.

2. This tribute was to be paid as a ransom of the soul, that there might be no plague among them.

3. The money that was raised was to be used in the service of the tabernacle (v. 16); with it they bought sacrifices, flour, incense, wine, oil, fuel, salt, and priests' garments. Those who receive the benefit of God's tabernacle must be willing to cover its expenses.

Verses 17–21

Instructions are given here:

1. For the making of a laver (basin) of bronze, a large vessel, that would contain a good quantity of water, which was to be set near the door of the tabernacle (v. 18).

2. For the use of this laver. Aaron and his sons must wash their hands and feet at this laver every time they went in to minister, every morning, at least (vv. 19–21). This was intended:

2.1. To teach them purity in all their ministry. The person who may *stand in God's holy place* has *clean hands and a pure heart* (Ps 24:3–4). And:

2.2. To teach us, who daily wait on God, to daily renew our repentance of sin. Cleanse your hands and purify your hearts, and then draw nigh to God (Jas 4:8).

Verses 22–38

Directions are here given for making the holy anointing oil and the incense that were to be used in the service of the tabernacle.

1. Instructions are given concerning how the holy anointing oil is to be made up; the ingredients and their quantities are prescribed (vv. 23–25). It was to be compounded *after the art of the apothecary* (v. 25); the fine spices were to be infused in about four quarts (about four liters) of oil, and then strained out, leaving a wonderful sweet smell in the oil. God's tent and all its furniture were to be anointed with this oil. It was to be used also in the consecration of the priests (vv. 26–30). Solomon was anointed with it (1Ki 1:39), as were some of the other kings, and all the high priests. Christ's name is said to be *as ointment poured forth* (SS 1:3), and the good name of Christians better than *precious ointment* (Ecc 7:1).

2. The incense which was burned on the golden altar was prepared similarly with sweet spices, though not so rich as those of which the anointing oil was made (vv. 34–35).

3. Concerning both these preparations the same law is here given (vv. 32–33, 37–38), that they should not be made for any common use.

CHAPTER 31

God is here drawing toward a conclusion of what he had to say to Moses on the mountain, where he had now been with him forty days and forty nights. This concludes God's instructions (from chapter 25 onward) to Moses concerning the tabernacle. In this chapter: 1. He appoints workers to be employed in building and furnishing the tabernacle (vv. 1–11). 2. He repeats the law of the Sabbath and its observance (vv. 12–17), and he delivers to Moses the two tablets of the Testimony at their parting (v. 18).

Verses 1–11

God had ordered a great deal of fine work to be done around the tabernacle. The people were to provide the materials, but who must put them together? Moses himself was well versed in all the learning of the Egyptians, but he did not know how to engrave or embroider. We may suppose that there were some very clever people among the Israelites, but having lived all their days in slavery in Egypt, we cannot think any of them were instructed in the creative arts. They knew how to make brick and to work with clay, but they had never been brought up to work in gold and in cutting diamonds. They had no goldsmiths or jewelers; their experts were masons and bricklayers. *Who was sufficient for these things?* (2Co 2:16). But God takes care of this matter also.

1. He names the people to be employed in this way.

1.1. Bezaleel (Bezalel) was to be the architect or leading skilled worker (v. 2). He was of the tribe of Judah, a tribe that God delighted to honor; the grandson of Hur, probably that Hur who had helped to hold up Moses' hands (17:8–16).

1.2. Aholiab (Oholiab), of the tribe of Dan, is appointed next to Bezaleel, to be his partner (v. 6). Aholiab was of the tribe of Dan, which was one of the less honorable tribes, so that the tribes of Judah and Levi might not be advanced, and so that it would not seem that they secured all the eminent positions. Huram-Abi, who was the skilled craft worker in the building of Solomon's temple, was also of the tribe of Dan (2Ch 2:14).

1.3. There were others employed by and under these in the several activities around the tabernacle (v. 6).

2. He qualifies these people for service (v. 3): I have filled him with the Spirit of God; and (v. 6) in the hearts of all that are wise-hearted I have put wisdom.

2.1. All skill, in creative arts and generally, is the gift of God; from him come both the ability and the means of making the most of the ability. He teaches the farmer (Isa 28:26) and traders too, and he must receive the praise for it.

2.2. God distributes his gifts widely, one gift to one person, another to another person, and all for the good of the whole body, both of the human race and of the church. Moses was the most suitable person to govern Israel, but Bezaleel was more suitable than Moses to build the tabernacle.

2.3. Those whom God calls to any service he will equip for it. The work that was to be done here was to make the tabernacle and its furnishings, which are here listed (v. 7). The people employed in these tasks were enabled to *work in gold, and silver, and brass.* When Christ sent his apostles to raise the Gospel tabernacle, he poured out his Spirit on them, to enable them to speak with tongues of the wonderful works of God. They were not called to work with metal, but to work with people. The gifts were even greater, as the tabernacle to be pitched was *a greater and more perfect tabernacle,* as the writer to the Hebrews calls it (Heb 9:11).

Verses 12–18

Here is:

1. A strict command for the sanctification of the Sabbath day (vv. 13–17). The law of the Sabbath had been given before any other law, by way of preparation (16:23). It had been put into the body of the moral law in the fourth commandment. It had been attached to the judicial law (23:12), and here it is added to the first part of the ceremonial law, because the observance of the Sabbath can be thought of as the beginning and end of the whole law. Where in conscience it is not observed, godliness and integrity are left behind, for it stands between the two tables in the moral law. *Verily* (or nevertheless), *my sabbaths you shall keep.* Though they must do the work quickly, they must not put speed above doing the job well. They must not break the law of the Sabbath in their desire to finish the work quickly. Even tabernacle work must give way to the Sabbath rest. Note what is said here concerning the Sabbath:

1.1. The nature and significance of the Sabbath, by declaring of which God honors it and teaches us to value it. Several different things are here said about the Sabbath:

1.1.1. *It is a sign between me and you* (v. 13 and again v. 17). The institution of the Sabbath was a sign that he had set them apart from all other people. God, by sanctifying this day among them, let them know that he sanctified them and set them apart for himself and his service.

1.1.2. *It is holy unto you* (v. 14), that is, "It is intended for your benefit as well as for God's honor"; *the sabbath was made for man* (Mk 2:27).

1.1.3. It is the *sabbath of rest, holy to the Lord* (v. 15). It is to be separated from ordinary use and intended for the honor and service of God.

1.1.4. It was to be observed throughout their generations, in every age, for a perpetual covenant (v. 16).

1.2. The law of the Sabbath. They must keep it (vv. 13–14, 16), keep it as a trust, as something precious.

1.3. The reason for the Sabbath, for God's laws are not only backed by the highest authority, but are also supported by the best reason. God's own example is the best reason given (v. 17).

1.4. The penalty to be imposed if this law was broken: "Every one that defileth the sabbath, by doing any work therein except works of devotion and mercy, shall be cut off from among his people (v. 14); he shall surely be put to death" (v. 15).

2. The delivering of the two tablets of the Testimony to Moses.

2.1. The Ten Commandments which God had spoken on Mount Sinai in the hearing of all the people were now written, *in perpetuam rei memoriam,* "for a perpetual memorial," because what is written down remains.

2.2. They were written in *tables of stone.* The Law was written on *tables of stone,* to show that it would last forever.

2.3. They were written *with the finger of God,* that is, directly by his will and power. Only God can write his Law on the heart; by his Spirit, which is the *finger of God,* he writes his will in the *fleshy tables of the heart* (2Co 3:3).

2.4. They were written on two tablets, intended to instruct us in our duty both toward God and toward our fellow human beings.

2.5. They are called *tables of testimony* (tablets of the Testimony) because this written Law testified both to the will of God concerning them and his goodwill toward them and would be a testimony against them if they were disobedient.

CHAPTER 32

This chapter records a very sad interruption to the account of the establishment of the church and of religion among the Jews. Things were moving well toward a happy settlement: God had shown himself very favorable, and the people also had seemed fairly amenable. Moses had now almost completed his forty days on the mountain, and, we may suppose, had pleasant thoughts of the very joyful welcome he would receive from the camp of Israel at his return, and of the quick setting up of the tabernacle among them. But God's plans are frustrated: the sin of Israel turns away from good and puts a stop to the flow of God's favors. The sin that caused the trouble was worshiping a golden calf. The marriage was ready to be solemnized between God and Israel, but Israel commits adultery, and so the match is broken, and putting the pieces together again will not be easy. Here is: 1. The sin of Israel, and of Aaron particularly, in making the golden calf as a god (vv. 1–4) and worshiping it (vv. 5–6). 2. The warning which God gave of this to Moses, who was then on the mountain with him (vv. 7–8), and the condemnation of his wrath against them (vv. 9–10). The intercession which Moses immediately made for them on the mountain (vv. 11–13)

*and the success of that intercession (v. 14). 3. Moses'
coming down from the mountain, when he became an
eyewitness of their idolatry (vv. 15–19), out of hatred
of which, he broke the tablets in just indignation (v. 19)
and burned the golden calf (v. 20). 4. The questioning
of Aaron about it (vv. 21–24) and the execution of the
ringleaders for the idolatry (vv. 25–29). 5. The further
intercession Moses made for them, to turn away the
wrath of God from them (vv. 30–32), and a reprieve
then granted, reserving them for further punishment
(vv. 33–35).*

Verses 1–6

While Moses was on the mountain, receiving the Law
from God, the people had time to meditate on what had
been delivered. However, there were those among them
that were trying to work out how to break the laws they
had already received. On the thirty-ninth day of the forty,
the plot broke out in rebellion against the Lord. Here is:

1. The unrestrained request which the people made to
Aaron, who was entrusted with the government in Moses'
absence: *Up, make us gods, which shall go before us*
(v. 1).

1.1. Notice the adverse effects of Moses' absence from
them.

1.2. Notice the anger and violence of a crowd when
they are influenced and corrupted by those who wait to
deceive.

1.2.1. They were weary of waiting for the Promised
Land. They want to move on to the land *flowing with milk
and honey* (3:8, etc.) and cannot wait to take their religion
along with them. We must first wait for God's Law before
we can lay hold of his promises.

1.2.2. They were weary of waiting for Moses to return.
*As for this Moses, the man that brought us up out of Egypt,
we wot not what has become of him.* Notice how scornfully they speak of his person—*this Moses.* This shows
how ungrateful they are to Moses, who had shown such
tender care for them, and in so doing they oppose God. If
he was in the cloud a long time, it was because God had
a great deal to say to him, for their good; he stayed on the
mountain as their ambassador. He would certainly return
as soon as he had finished the business he went up there
for. But they still make this the cover for their wicked statement. Misinterpretations of our Redeemer's delays cause a
great deal of wickedness. Our Lord Jesus has gone up onto
the mountain of glory, where he appears in the presence
of God for us, but out of our sight. The heavens must keep
him in and hide him, so that we may live by faith. Weariness in waiting can lead us into a great many temptations.
Israel here, if they could just have stayed one day longer,
would have seen what had become of Moses.

1.2.3. They were weary of waiting for a divine institution of religious worship among them. They were told that
they must *serve God in this mountain,* but, because that
was not decided on as soon as they wished, they would
put their own senses to work out signs of God's presence
with them; they would glory in them and worship something of their own invention, probably such as they had
seen among the Egyptians. To say, "Moses is lost, make us
a god," was completely ridiculous. *Make us gods, which
shall go before us*! Gods! How many did they want? Is
not one enough? *Make us gods!* What good would gods
of their own making do them?

2. The demand which Aaron then makes for their
jewels: *Bring me your golden earrings* (v. 2). We do not
find that he said one word to object to their proposal, but

seemed to approve of the idea and showed himself not
unwilling to indulge in it. You would have hoped that he
intended to begin by making fun of the whole idea, putting it over as something ridiculous in order to expose
it and to show them its folly. Some charitably suppose
that when Aaron told them to break off their earrings and
bring them to him, he did it with the aim of putting an end
to their proposal, believing that though their covetousness
would have let them *lavish gold out of the bag* to make an
idol of (Isa 46:6), their pride would not have allowed them
to part with their golden earrings.

3. The making of the golden calf (vv. 3–4).

3.1. The people brought their earrings to Aaron, whose
request, instead of discouraging them, gratified their
superstition and produced in them the idea that the gold
taken from their ears would be most acceptable and would
make a most valuable god.

3.2. Aaron melted down their rings, and having a mold
prepared for the purpose, poured the molten gold into it
and then produced it in the shape of a calf or ox. Some
think that Aaron chose this figure as a sign of the divine
presence, because he thought the head and horns of an
ox a proper emblem of divine power, and because it was
so plain and common a thing, he hoped the people would
not be so foolish as to worship it. But they had probably
learned the form of their idols from the Egyptians, for
it is said (Eze 20:8), *They did not forsake the idols of
Egypt,* and (Eze 23:8), *Neither left she her whoredoms
brought from Egypt. Thus they changed their glory into
the similitude of an ox* (Ps 106:20) and declared their own
folly, beyond that of other idolaters who worshiped the
stars of heaven.

4. The worship of the golden calf. Having made the calf
in Horeb, they *worshipped the molten image* (Ps 106:19).
Aaron, seeing the people fond of their calf, was willing to
humor them still further, and he built an altar before it and
announced a festival in its honor (v. 5), a feast of dedication. Note that he calls it a *feast to Jehovah*; for, animal-
like as they were, they did not imagine that this idol was
itself a god, but they made it as a representation of the true
God, whom they intended to worship in and through this
idol. The people are bold enough to celebrate this festival
(v. 6): *They rose up early on the morrow,* to show how
pleased they were with the ceremony, and according to
the ancient rites of worship, they offered sacrifices to this
new-made god of theirs and then feasted on the sacrifice.
At the expense of their earrings, they had made their god,
and they now try, at the expense of their animals, to atone
for their sins. Now:

4.1. It was strange that any of the people, especially so
many of them, should do such a thing. Had they not, only
the other day and at that very place, heard the voice of the
Lord God speaking to them out of the midst of the fire,
Thou shalt not make to thyself any graven image (20:4)?
Had they not even solemnly entered into a covenant with
God and promised that everything that he had said to them
they *would do, and would be obedient* (24:7)? *They made
a calf in Horeb,* the very place where the Law was given.
It was different with those who received the Gospel; they
immediately *turned from idols* (1Th 1:9).

4.2. It was especially strange that Aaron should be so
deeply implicated in this sin, that he should make the
calf and announce the festival. Is this Aaron, who had
been with Moses on the mountain (19:24), and knew that
there was no form of God seen there, of which they might
make an idol? Is he aiding and abetting in this rebellion
against the Lord? How was it possible that he should ever

do such a sinful thing? Either he was strangely taken by surprise and did it when he was half asleep, or he was frightened into it by the outrages of the crowd. The Jews have a tradition that when his colleague Hur opposed it, the people fell on him and stoned him and so we never read of him after, and that this frightened Aaron into going along with them.

Verses 7–14

Here:

1. God tells Moses what was going on in the camp while he was absent (vv. 7–8). He says to Moses concerning this sin:

1.1. That they had *corrupted themselves*. Sin is the depraved corruption of the sinner, and it is a self-corruption.

1.2. That they had *turned aside out of the way*. Sin is a deviation from the way of our duty into a byway.

1.3. That they had turned aside quickly, after the Law had been given them and they had promised to obey it.

1.4. He tells him in detail what they had done: *They have made a calf, and worshipped it*. Those sins which are concealed from our rulers are open and exposed before God. We could not bear to see a thousandth part of that offensiveness which God sees every day but keeps silence about.

1.5. He seems to disown them, in saying to Moses, They are *thy people whom thou broughtest up out of the land of Egypt*. Those who corrupt themselves not only shame themselves, but even make God himself ashamed of them and of his kindness to them.

1.6. He sends Moses down to them quickly: *Go, get thee down*.

2. God expresses his displeasure against Israel for this sin (vv. 9–10):

2.1. He describes the people's true character: *It is a stiffnecked people*. The righteous God sees, not only what we do, but what we are.

2.2. He declares their just deserts — that his wrath would *wax hot against them*. Sin exposes us to the wrath of God; and that wrath, if it is not lessened by divine mercy, will burn us up like stubble.

2.3. He holds out inducements to Moses not to intercede for them: *Therefore, let me alone*. So he wanted to honor the means of grace of prayer, indicating that nothing except the intercession of Moses could save them from destruction.

3. Moses passionately intercedes with God on their behalf (vv. 11–13): he sought the Lord his God. If God would not be called *the God of Israel*, he still hoped he might address him as *his own God*. He wisely took the hint which God gave him when he said, *Let me alone*, which, though it seemed to forbid his interceding, in fact really encouraged him, by showing what power the prayer of faith has with God. Notice:

3.1. His prayer (v. 12): *Turn from thy fierce wrath*; not as if he thought God was not justly angry, but he begs God that he would not be so greatly angry as to consume them.

3.2. His pleas. He fills his mouth with arguments, not to move God, but to express his own faith and to arouse his own fervency in prayer.

3.2.1. He urges God's claims on them and the great things he had already done for them. God had said to Moses (v. 7), They are *thy people, whom thou broughtest up out of Egypt*; but Moses humbly turns them back on God again: "They are *thy people*, you are their Lord

and owner; I am only their servant. *Thou broughtest them forth out of Egypt*. I was only the instrument in your hand. Thou *broughtest them out of Egypt*, though they were unworthy and had served the gods of the Egyptians there (Jos 24:15). If you did that for them, despite their sins in Egypt, will you undo all that for their sins of the same nature in the desert?"

3.2.2. He pleads the concern of God's glory (v. 12): *Wherefore should the Egyptians say, For mischief did he bring them out?* He cannot bear to hear God discredited, and so he insists, *Lord, what will the Egyptians say?* If a people saved so strangely should be suddenly ruined, what would the world say of it, especially the Egyptians, who implacably hate both Israel and the God of Israel? They would say, "God was either so weak and could not, or so fickle, and would not complete the salvation he began." What will the Egyptians say? We ought always to be careful that the name of God and his teaching are not blasphemed through us.

3.2.3. He pleads God's promise to the patriarchs that he would multiply their offspring and give them the land of Canaan. We are to use God's promises as our pleas in prayer.

4. God graciously reduced the rigor of the sentence and *repented of the evil he thought to do* (v. 14). See here:

4.1. The power of prayer; God allows himself to be prevailed upon by the humble, believing boldness of intercessors.

4.2. The compassion of God toward poor sinners, and how ready he is to forgive.

Verses 15–20

Here is:

1. The favor of God to Moses, in trusting him with the two tablets of the Testimony, which, though made of ordinary stone, were far more valuable than all the precious stones that decorated the breastpiece of Aaron.

2. The familiarity between Moses and Joshua. While Moses was in the cloud, in the presence of God, Joshua stayed as close as possible. When Moses came down, he came with him, and not till then. Joshua, who was a soldier, feared there was *a noise of war in the camp*, and that he would be missed. Moses, however, having received warning of it from God, was more able to distinguish the sound and was aware that it was *the voice of those that sing*.

3. The great and just displeasure of Moses against Israel for their idolatry. He resented it as an offense against God and the dishonor of his people. Moses was the meekest person on earth, but when he saw *the calf, and the dancing*, his *anger waxed hot*. We are not breaking the law of meekness when we show our displeasure at wickedness. It is right that we should be cold when it comes to our own reputation, but warm with God's.

3.1. To convince them that they had lost the favor of God, *he broke the tables* (v. 19), that the sight of it might move them deeply and unsettle them greatly, when they saw what blessings they had lost.

3.2. To convince them that they had turned to a god that could not help them, he *burnt the calf* (v. 20), melted it down, and then ground it to powder. Then, so that this powder might be noticed throughout the camp, he scattered it on the water that they drank. So that it might be seen that *an idol is nothing in the world* (1Co 8:4), he reduced it to dust, that it might be as close to nothing as possible.

Verses 21–29

Here we see how Moses, having shown his righteous anger against the sin of Israel by breaking the tablets and burning the calf, now moves on to deal with the sinners and to call them to account. In this he acts as the representative of God. Now:

1. He begins with Aaron, as God began with Adam, because he was the main, though not the first, person in the sin; he was the one drawn into it. Notice here:

1.1. The just rebuke Moses gives him (v. 21). Since Moses prevailed with God for him to save him from destruction, he now remonstrates with him, to bring him to repentance. He calls on Aaron to consider:

1.1.1. What he had done to this people: *Thou hast brought so great a sin upon them.* The people, who initiated it, could have been said to have brought the sin on Aaron; but he, being a judge who should have suppressed it, aided and abetted the sin and might truly be said to have brought it on them, because he hardened their hearts and strengthened their hands in it.

1.1.2. What moved him to it: *What did this people unto thee?* People can only tempt us to sin; they cannot force us. People can only frighten us; if we do not give in to their demands, they cannot hurt us.

1.2. The feeble excuse Aaron makes for himself.

1.2.1. He asks that Moses should not be angry with him, whereas Aaron should not have moved God to anger in the first place: *Let not the anger of my lord wax hot* (v. 22).

1.2.2. He shifts all the blame on the people: *They are set on mischief, and they said, Make us gods.* It is natural to us to try to transfer our guilt. Sin is a brat that nobody is willing to own up to.

1.2.3. We hope he did not intend to discredit Moses and make him an accessory to the sin by unnecessarily repeating the suspicion of the people (when Moses had stayed so long on the mountain), *As for this Moses, we wot not what is become of him* (v. 23).

1.2.4. He tries to lessen and hide his own share of the sin. He childishly insinuates that when he threw the gold into the fire it somehow came out in the shape of a calf. He does not say a word about his fashioning it (v. 24).

2. The people are next to be judged for this sin. The approach of Moses turned their dancing into trembling. Those who badgered Aaron into going along with them in their sin did not dare look Moses in the face. Notice:

2.1. How they were exposed to shame by their sin: *The people were naked* (v. 25), not so much because some of them had lost their earrings, but because they had lost their integrity. It was a shame to them forever, that they *changed their glory into the similitude of an ox* (Ps 106:20). They were *made naked*, stripped of their ornaments and exposed to contempt.

2.2. The course that Moses took to remove this disgrace, not by concealing the sin or making it appear in any false light, but by punishing it, and so bearing public testimony against it. Notice:

2.2.1. By whom vengeance was taken—by the children of Levi (vv. 26, 28); not by the direct hand of God himself, as on Nadab and Abihu, but by the sword, to teach them that idolatry was an *iniquity to be punished by the judge*, being a *denial of the God that is above* (Dt 13:9; Job 31:28). The innocent must be chosen to execute the guilty. We are told here:

2.2.1.1. How the Levites were called to this service. Moses *clad himself with zeal* (Isa 59:17), as with a robe, and summoned all those to appear immediately who were on God's side, against the golden calf. *Who is on the Lord's side?* The cause of sin and wickedness is the Devil's cause, and all wicked people side with that cause. The cause of truth and holiness is God's cause, with which all godly people side. There cannot be neutrality.

2.2.1.2. How the Levites were commissioned for this service (v. 27): *Slay every man his brother*, that is, "Slay all those whom you know to have been active in making and worshiping the golden calf, even though they were your own closest relatives or dearest friends." But it would seem, they were to kill only those whom they found *abroad in the streets* of the camp; for it might be hoped that those who had withdrawn to their tents were ashamed of what they had done, and were on their knees, repenting.

2.2.2. On whom vengeance is taken: *There fell of the people that day about 3,000 men* (v. 28). Probably these were only few, in comparison with the many who were guilty; but these were those who had led the rebellion and so were picked out, to be made examples of, to instill fear in all the others.

Verses 30–35

Moses, having executed justice on the principal offenders, here deals both with the people and with God.

1. With the people, to bring them to repentance (v. 30).

1.1. When some were killed—so that the rest should not imagine that because they were exempt from the capital punishment, they were therefore looked on as free from guilt—Moses here tells the survivors, *You have sinned a great sin.* To move them with the greatness of their sin, he shows them how difficult it would be to be reconciled with God. The depth of the awfulness of sin is seen in the price of forgiveness.

1.2. It was, however, some encouragement to the people, when they were told that they had *sinned a great sin*, to hear that Moses would *go up unto the Lord to make atonement* for them. Christ, the great Mediator, had a greater certainty than this, for he had been in the closest possible relationship with the Father and perfectly knew all his will.

2. With God, interceding for mercy. Notice:

2.1. How stirring his address was. *Moses returned unto the Lord*, not to receive further instructions about the tabernacle. Moses in this address expresses:

2.1.1. His great loathing of the people's sin (v. 31). *Oh, this people have sinned a great sin.* God had first told him about it (v. 7), and now he tells God about it, by way of lamentation. He does not try to excuse or extenuate the sin; but what he had said to them in conviction he says to God in confession: *They have sinned a great sin.* He did not come to make apologies, but to make atonement.

2.1.2. His great desire for the people's welfare (v. 32): *Yet now* it is not too great a sin for infinite mercy to pardon, and therefore *if thou wilt forgive their sin.* It is an abrupt expression, *If thou wilt forgive*, is as much as, "O that you would forgive!" as Lk 19:42, *If thou hadst known* is, *O that thou hadst known.* "But *if not, blot me, I pray thee, out of the book which thou hast written*"; that is, "If they must be cut off, let me be cut off with them, and cut short of Canaan; if all Israel must die, I am content to die with them; let me not be the only one to survive and receive the Land of Promise." In the same way, he expresses his tender affection for the people and is a type of the good Shepherd, who *lays down his life for the sheep* (Jn 10:11), who was to be *cut off from the land of the living for the transgression of my people* (Isa 53:8; Da 9:26). He is also an example of public-spiritedness to all, especially to those in public positions.

2.2. How successful his address was. God would not take him at his word. He will not blot anyone out of his book except those who by their willful disobedience have forfeited the honor of being enrolled in it (v. 33). This was also a sign of mercy to the people. In answer to the address of Moses:

2.2.1. God promises to continue with his intention of giving them the land of Canaan. So he sends Moses back to them to lead them, even though they were unworthy of him, and he promises that his angel would go before them.

2.2.2. God threatens to remember this sin against them when later he should have reason to punish them for other sins. The Jews have a saying that takes this as a basis, that from then on no judgment fell on Israel unless there was in it an ounce of the powder of the golden calf. Stephen says that when they *made a calf, and offered sacrifice to the idol, God turned, and gave them up to worship the host of heaven* (Ac 7:41–42); so that the strange devotion of the people to the sin of idolatry was a just judgment on them for making and worshiping the golden calf and a judgment they were never quite freed from till the Captivity of Babylon. See Ro 1:23–25. Aaron was not struck with a plague, but the people were, for his was a sin of weakness, but theirs was a sin of arrogance.

CHAPTER 33

In this chapter we continue the account of the mediation of Moses between God and Israel, to repair the separation that sin had made between them. 1. Moses brings a very humbling message from God to them (vv. 1–3, 5), which helps to prepare them for mercy (vv. 4, 6). 2. He establishes good relations between God and them (vv. 7–11). 3. Moses fervently pleads with God in prayer and prevails for a promise of his presence with the people (vv. 12–17) and for a sight of his glory for himself (vv. 18–23).

Verses 1–6

Here is:

1. The message which God sent by Moses to the children of Israel.

1.1. He disciplines them by telling them their true character—*a stiffnecked people* (vv. 3, 5). God wanted to bring them under the restraint of his Law and into the bond of his covenant, but their necks were too stiff to bow to them. God judges people by the character of their minds. We know what people do; God knows what people are like. We know what comes out of people; God knows what is in people, and nothing is more displeasing to him than stubbornness.

1.2. He tells them what they deserved. If he had dealt with them according to their sins, he would have destroyed them swiftly.

1.3. He tells them to *depart and go up hence* to the land of Canaan (v. 1).

1.4. Though he promises to fulfill his covenant with Abraham in giving them Canaan, he denies them the extraordinary signs of his presence. "*I will send an angel before thee*, to protect you, otherwise the evil angels would soon destroy you; but *I will not go up in the midst of thee, lest I consume thee*" (vv. 2–3). Justice said, "Destroy them; consume them." Mercy said, *How shall I give thee up, Ephraim?* (Hos 11:8). Well, God says, *put off thy ornaments, that I may know what to do with thee;* that is, "Be ashamed of your sins, that mercy may rejoice over judgment" (v. 5). Calls to repentance are clear signs of intended mercy.

2. The people's sad acceptance of this message:

2.1. *They mourned* (v. 4) for their sin which had caused God to withdraw from them and mourned for this as the most severe punishment of their sin. Of all the bitter fruits and effects of sin, what true penitents dread most is God's departure from them.

2.2. As a sign of great shame and humiliation, those who were not fully dressed did *not put on their ornaments* (v. 4), and those who were fully dressed *stripped themselves of their ornaments, by the mount*; as some read it, "at a distance from the mount" (v. 6), standing *afar off* like the tax collector (Lk 18:13).

Verses 7–11

Here is:

1. One mark of displeasure put on them to humiliate them further: *Moses took the tabernacle*, the tent in which he gave audience, heard cases, and inquired of God, the town hall, as it were, of their camp, and *pitched it without, afar off from the camp* (v. 7), to show them that they had made themselves unworthy of it, and that unless peace was made and they were reconciled, it would never return to them.

2. Much encouragement given them, nevertheless, to hope that God would still be reconciled with them.

2.1. Though the Tent of Meeting was moved, everyone who was inclined to seek the Lord was welcome to follow it (v. 7). A place was appointed for them to go to outside the camp, to ask for God to return to them. When God intends to grant mercy, he stirs up prayer.

2.2. Moses undertook to mediate between God and Israel. He *went out to the tabernacle*, the place of agreement, probably pitched between them and the mountain (v. 8), and he *entered into the tabernacle* (v. 9).

2.3. The people seemed to be in very good spirits and well disposed toward reconciliation.

2.3.1. When Moses went out to go to the tent, the people *looked after him* (v. 8) as a sign of their respect to him whom before they had insulted and of their complete dependence on his mediation.

2.3.2. When they saw the pillar of cloud, that symbol of God's presence, they all *worshipped, every man at his tent door* (v. 10). The fact that they worshiped at the entrance of their tents showed clearly that they were not ashamed publicly to acknowledge their respect for God and Moses, just as they had publicly worshiped the calf.

2.4. God was, in Moses, reconciling Israel to himself and revealed himself very willing to be at peace.

2.4.1. God met Moses at the place of agreement (v. 9). If our hearts go out toward God to meet him, he will graciously come to meet us.

2.4.2. God *talked with Moses* (v. 9), *spoke to him face to face, as a man speaks to his friend* (v. 11), which shows that God revealed himself to Moses, not only with greater clearness and authentication of divine light than to any other of the prophets, but also with greater expressions of particular kindness and grace. *Moses turned again into the camp* but because he intended to return quickly to the Tent of Meeting, he left Joshua there, for it was not right that the place should be left empty, as long as the cloud of glory *stood at the door* (v. 9).

Verses 12–23

Moses, having returned to the entrance of the tent, humbly but boldly asks two great favors, and as a ruler he has power with God.

1. Moses fervently asks God for the privilege of knowing his presence with Israel in the rest of their march to Canaan, despite their sins. Notice how Moses states his case before God:

1.1. Notice how he pleads:

1.1.1. He insists on the commission God had given him to *bring up this people* (v. 12). He begins with this: "Lord, it is you for whom I am working. Will you not acknowledge me?"

1.1.2. He makes the most of the rightful claims he himself has with God and pleads God's gracious kindness to him: *Thou hast said, I know thee by name. Now, therefore*, Moses says, if it really is so, that *I have found grace in thy sight, show me thy way* (v. 13). He lays hold of God: "Lord, if you will do anything for me, do this for the people." In the same way, our Lord Jesus in his intercession presents himself to the Father as One in whom he is always well pleased and so obtains mercy for us with whom he is, in his justice, displeased; and we are *accepted in the beloved* (Eph 1:6).

1.1.3. He implies that the people, even though they are unworthy, were still in some relationship with God: "*Consider that this nation is thy people*, a people whom you have done great things for, redeemed to yourself, and taken into covenant with yourself; Lord, they are your own, do not leave them." The offended father considers this: "My children are foolish and self-willed, but they are still my children and I cannot abandon them."

1.1.4. He expresses the great value he put on the presence of God. When God said, *My presence shall go with thee*, he laid hold of that word eagerly, as something he could not live without: *If thy presence go not with me, carry us not up hence* (v. 15).

1.1.5. He concludes with an argument taken from God's glory (v. 16): "Wherein shall it be known to the nations that I and thy people have found grace in thy sight, so as to be separated from all people on earth? How will it appear that we are honored in this way? Is it not in that thou goest with us?"

1.2. Notice how successful he is. He obtained an assurance of God's favor:

1.2.1. To himself (v. 14): *I will give thee rest*. Moses never entered Canaan, but God fulfilled his word that he would give him rest (Da 12:13).

1.2.2. To the people for his sake. Gracious souls think it not enough to get to heaven themselves; they want all their friends to go there too. God grants as long as he asks, *gives liberally*, and *does not upbraid* him. Notice the power of prayer, and be stirred to ask, seek, and knock, and to *continue instant in prayer* (Ro 12:12), to *pray always and not to faint* (Lk 18:1). See this as a type of the effective power of Christ's intercession, who always lives to make intercession for all those who come to God by him. The grounds of that effective power are purely Christ's own merit, not anything in those for whom he intercedes; it is because *thou hast found grace in my sight*. And now that the matter is settled, God is perfectly reconciled to them; his presence in the pillar of cloud returns to them and will continue with them. All is well again, and from now on we hear no more of the golden calf.

2. Having gained this point, Moses next begs *a sight of God's glory* and is heard in this matter also. Notice:

2.1. The humble request Moses makes: *I beseech thee, show me thy glory* (v. 18). Moses had wonderfully prevailed with God for one favor after another, and the success of his prayers made him bold to go on seeking God. The more he had, the more he asked for: *Show me thy glory*; "Let me see it," is the sense, "Make it visible in some way or other, and enable me to bear its sight." He was not so ignorant as to think God's essence could be seen with the physical eyes; but, having up to that time only heard a voice out of a pillar of cloud or fire, he wanted to see some representation of divine glory that God saw fit to give him. Some think that Moses desired a sight of God's glory as a sign of his reconciliation and as a pledge of that presence which he had promised them, but he did not know what he asked.

2.2. The gracious reply God made to this request:

2.2.1. God denied what could not be granted and what Moses could not bear: *Thou canst not see my face* (v. 20). A full revelation of the glory of God would completely overwhelm any mortal in this present state, even Moses himself. There is a knowledge and enjoyment of God which must be waited for in another world, when we shall *see him as he is* (1Jn 3:2). In the meantime, let us adore him for the extent of what we do know of God and the depths of what we do not.

2.2.2. God gave what would be greatly satisfying:

2.2.2.1. Moses would hear what would please him (v. 19): *I will make all my goodness pass before thee*. He had shown him wonderful examples of his goodness in being reconciled to Israel, but that was only a mere trickle of goodness; he would now show him the full measure of his goodness: *all his goodness*. This was a sufficient answer to his request. "Show me your glory," Moses says. "I will show you my goodness," God says in reply. God's goodness is his glory, and he wants us to know him by the glory of his mercy more than by the glory of his majesty. It is never said, "I will be angry with whom I will be angry," for his wrath is always just and holy; but *I will show mercy on whom I will show mercy*, for his grace is always free. His divine right is never to condemn people; his divine right is to save.

2.2.2.2. Moses would see what he could bear, and what would be enough for him. First, safe in a *cleft of the rock* (vv. 21–22). *That rock was Christ* (1Co 10:4). And it is only through Christ that we have *the knowledge of the glory of God* (2Co 4:6). None can see his glory except those who stand on this rock and take shelter in it. Secondly, he would see more of God than anyone ever saw on earth, but not as much as those see who are in heaven. Moses was not given that sight of God, but such a sight as we have of someone who has gone past us, so that we only see their back and catch a glimpse of them. When we see what God has done in his works, the actions of our God, our King, we see, as it were, his back. If we faithfully make the most of the revelation God gives us of himself while we are here, a brighter and more glorious scene will soon be opened up to us, for *to him that hath shall be given* (Mt 25:29).

CHAPTER 34

In the previous chapter God indicated to Moses his reconciliation to Israel, and here he gives proofs of it and proceeds to establish his covenant and fellowship with them. In this chapter we read of: 1. The orders he gives to Moses to come up to the mountain the next morning and bring two tablets of stone with him (vv. 1–4). 2. His meeting him there and the proclamation of his name (vv. 5–9). 3. The instructions he gave him there and his conversation with him for forty days without interruption (vv. 10–27). 4. The honor he put on him when he sent him down with his face shining (vv. 28–35). In all this God dealt with Moses as one who affected Israel as a whole, as mediator between him and Israel, and as a type of the great Mediator, Jesus Christ.

Verses 1–4

Such agreement as was in existence between God and Israel was broken off abruptly by their worshiping the golden calf, so when peace was made everything must begin again.

1. Moses must prepare for the tablets to be renewed (v. 1). So, in the first writing of the Law on the human heart in innocence, both the tablets and the writing were the work of God, but when these were broken and defaced by sin and the divine Law was to be preserved in the Scriptures, God made use of human ministry and Moses to begin with. But the prophets and apostles only chiseled out the tablets, as it were; the writing was God's still, for all scripture is given by inspiration of God (2Ti 3:16). Notice, when God was reconciled to them, he ordered the tablets to be renewed and wrote his Law on them, which clearly shows us:

1.1. That even under the Gospel of peace and reconciliation by Christ, of which the intercession of Moses was a type, the moral law should continue to be binding on believers. When our Savior in his Sermon on the Mount expounded the moral law and justified it against the corrupt interpretations with which the scribes and Pharisees had broken it (Mt 5:19), he in effect renewed the tablets and made them like the first, that is, he brought the Law back to its original sense and intention.

1.2. That the best proof of forgiveness of sin and peace with God is the writing of the Law on the heart.

1.3. That, if we want God to write the Law on our hearts, we must prepare our hearts to receive it.

2. Moses must go again on the top of Mount Sinai and present himself to God there (v. 2). Moses, then, rose up early (v. 4), to go to the appointed place. It is good to spend the early part of the morning at our devotions. The morning is perhaps as good a friend to the graces as it was to the Muses.

Verses 5–9

No sooner had Moses reached the top of the mountain than God met with him there (v. 5): The Lord descended, by some perceptible sign of his presence and revelation of his glory. He descended in the cloud. His making a cloud his canopy showed that, though he revealed much of himself, there was still much more that remained hidden. Notice:

1. How God declared his name (vv. 6–7): he did it in transitu, "as he passed by him." Lasting views of God are reserved for the future state; the best we have in this world are transient. God now performed what he had promised Moses the day before, that his glory should pass by (33:22). He proclaimed the name of the Lord, by which he made himself known. He had made himself known to Moses in the glory of his self-existence and self-sufficiency when he declared that name, I AM THAT I AM (3:14); now he makes himself known in the glory of his grace, goodness, and all-sufficiency to us. This comes before the revelation of his mercy, to teach us to think and to speak even of God's grace and goodness

with great seriousness and holy awe. His greatness and goodness illustrate and enhance each other. Many words are here put together, to teach, show, and convince us of God's goodness:

1.1. He is merciful. This speaks of his tender compassion, like that of a father to his children.

1.2. He is gracious. His mercy is gracious, freely gracious; this teaches us to be not only compassionate, but also humble (1Pe 3:8).

1.3. He is long-suffering, that is, he is slow to anger and delays carrying out his justice; he waits to be gracious and extends his offers of mercy.

1.4. He is abundant in goodness and truth. This speaks of his promised goodness, goodness and truth put together, goodness committed by promise, and his faithfulness committed for its security.

1.5. He keeps mercy for thousands.

1.6. He forgiveth iniquity, transgression, and sin. Pardoning mercy is spoken of because it is this which opens the door to all other gifts of his divine grace.

2. How Moses received this declaration which God made of himself, his grace, and his mercy. It would seem as if Moses accepted this as an adequate reply to his request that God would show him his glory. Now we are told here:

2.1. What impression it made on him: Moses made haste, and bowed his head (v. 8).

2.2. How he made the most of it. He immediately based a fervent and loving prayer on it (v. 9):

2.2.1. For the presence of God with his people Israel in the wilderness: "I pray thee, go among us, for your presence means everything to our safety and success."

2.2.2. For forgiveness of sin: "O pardon our iniquity and our sin, or we cannot expect you to go among us." And:

2.2.3. For the privileges of a special people: "Take us as thy inheritance." God had already promised these things and given Moses assurances of them, but he prays for them, not because he doubted the sincerity of God's gifts, but as one concerned to see them confirmed. Those who have some good hope through grace that their sins are forgiven, must still continue to pray for forgiveness, for the renewing of their forgiveness, and the cleansing of it more and more from their souls. Moses is truly public-spirited and intercedes even for the children still to be born. But it is a strange plea he urges: For it is a stiff-necked people. God had given this as a reason why he would not go along with them (33:3). "Yes," Moses says, "all the more reason that we need you to go along with us; for the worse they are, the more they need your presence and grace to make them better."

Verses 10–17

After reconciliation has been made, a covenant of friendship is established here between God and Israel. The traitors are not only forgiven, but also elevated and made favorites again. It is right that the assurances of this are introduced by behold, a word that commands attention and wonder: Behold, I make a covenant. Here is:

1. God's part of this covenant, what he would do for them (vv. 10–11).

1.1. In general: Before all thy people, I will do marvels. Marvels indeed, for they were without precedent, such as have not been done in all the earth. They were the joy of Israel, and they confirmed their faith: Thy people shall see and acknowledge the work of the Lord. And their enemies were in awe of them: It is a terrible thing that I will do. Even God's own people would look on them with fear.

1.2. In particular: *I drive out before thee the Amorite.*

2. Their part of the covenant: *Observe that which I command thee.* We cannot expect the benefit of God's promises unless we conscientiously follow God's commands.

2.1. *Thou shalt worship no other gods* (v. 14), not give divine honor to any creature, any name, or any creation of the imagination. If we do not worship only God, we do not worship God rightly.

2.2. So that they might not be tempted to worship other gods, they must not join in marriage or friendship with those who did (v. 12): *Make no covenant with the inhabitants of the land.* If God out of kindness to them drove out the Canaanites, they ought in their duty to God not to shelter them. They must particularly beware of intermarrying with them (vv. 15–16). If they chose their children as partners in marriage, they would be in danger of choosing their gods as partners in sin. So that they might not be tempted to make molten gods, they must destroy completely those they found and everything associated with them, *the altars and groves* (v. 13).

Verses 18–27

Here are several instructions relating to their festivals. When they had made the calf, they declared a feast in its honor; now, so that they might never do so again, they are here instructed to observe the festivals which God had instituted. We do not need to be drawn away from our religion by the temptations of mere human geniality, for we serve a Master who has provided abundantly for the joy of his servants.

1. Once a week they must rest (v. 21), *in earing* (plowing) *time, and in harvest,* the busiest times of the year. Harvesting will be more successful if the Sabbath is kept at harvest.

2. They must hold special festivals three times a year (v. 23); they must then appear *before the Lord God, the God of Israel.* The country will be left exposed to the insults of their neighbors; and what would become of the poor women, children, sick, and aged who were left at home? Trust God with them (v. 24): *Neither shall any man desire thy land;* not only will they not invade it, but also they will not even so much as think of invading it. The line of duty is the line of safety.

3. The three festivals are mentioned here:

3.1. The Passover, and the Feast of Unleavened Bread, in remembrance of their rescue from Egypt. The law of the redemption of the firstborn is attached to this (vv. 18–20). This feast was instituted (12:13) and urged again (23:15).

3.2. The Feast of Weeks, that is, Pentecost, seven weeks after Passover, and to this is attached the law of the first-fruits.

3.3. The Feast of Ingathering at the year end, which was the Feast of Tabernacles (v. 22): he had also spoken before of these (23:16).

4. These laws are repeated here to show that not one jot or tittle of the law should pass away. And at the end:

4.1. Moses is ordered to write these words (v. 27), that the people might know them better by reading them frequently, and that they might be passed on to the generations to come. We can never be thankful enough to God for the written word.

4.2. He is told that according to the tenor of these words God had made a covenant with Moses and Israel; not with Israel directly, but with them through Moses as mediator.

Verses 28–35

Here is:

1. Moses staying on the mountain, where he was miraculously sustained (v. 28). When we are weary of an hour or two spent waiting on God and worshiping him, we should remember how many days and nights Moses spent with him. He continued so long without food and drink, probably without sleep too, for:

1.1. The power of God supported him, so that he did not need it.

1.2. He ate food which the world did not know, for it was his food and drink to hear the word of God and pray. When God dealt with his favorite Moses, it was not with food and drink, but with his light, Law, and love, with the knowledge of himself and his will. As Moses fasted forty days and forty nights, so did Elijah and Christ too.

2. Moses coming down from the mountain, enriched and miraculously radiant. He came down:

2.1. Rich with the best treasure; for he brought in his hands the two tablets of the Law.

2.2. Radiating the best beauty, for the *skin of his face shone* (v. 29).

2.2.1. This may be looked on:

2.2.1.1. As a great honor to Moses, that the people might never again question his mission. He carried his authority on his very face. The Israelites could not look him in the face, but they must have read his commission there. But after this, they murmured against him.

2.2.1.2. As also a great favor to the people and an encouragement to them, that God put this glory on him, who was their intercessor, so giving them assurance that he was accepted, and they through him.

2.2.1.3. As the effect of his sight of God. When we have been on the mountain with God, we should let our *light shine before men* (Mt 5:16), that everyone we meet with may *take knowledge of us that we have been with Jesus* (Ac 4:13).

2.2.2. Concerning the shining of Moses' face notice here:

2.2.2.1. Moses was not aware of it himself: *He wist not that the skin of his face shone* (v. 29). Whatever beauty God puts on us, we should still be filled with such a humble sense of our own unworthiness and many weaknesses as will make us ignore and forget what makes our faces shine.

2.2.2.2. Aaron and the children of Israel saw it and *were afraid* (v. 30). Probably they were not sure whether it was a sign of God's favor or of his displeasure; being conscious of guilt, they feared the worst.

2.2.2.3. Moses put a *veil upon his face,* when he perceived that it shone (vv. 33, 35). This teaches us all a lesson of modesty and humility.

2.2.2.4. When Moses *went in before the Lord,* to speak with him in the Tent of Meeting, he *put off the veil* (v. 34). There was no need for it then, and, before God, every person does and must appear unveiled. This represented also, as it is explained (2Co 3:16), that when a soul turns to the Lord the veil is taken away, that with open face it may *behold his glory.*

CHAPTER 35

What would have been said and done when Moses first came down the mountain now begins to be said and done again, after reconciliation had been made with great difficulty. 1. Moses gives Israel those instructions, received from God, which needed to be obeyed immediately:

Concerning the Sabbath (vv. 1–3). Concerning the contribution that was to be made for setting up the tabernacle (vv. 4–9). Concerning what must be made in the tabernacle and its materials (vv. 10–19). 2. The people bring their contributions (vv. 20–29). 3. The leading workers are named (vv. 30–35).

Verses 1–19

The setting up and furnishing of the tabernacle is the work to which they now immediately applied themselves, and here particular mention is made of instructions concerning it:

1. All the congregation is summoned to attend (v. 1).

2. Moses instructed them in everything which God had commanded him. Both sides put their trust in him, and he was true to the trust. He was faithful only as a servant, but *Christ as a Son* (Heb 3:5–6).

3. Moses begins with the law of the Sabbath: *Six days shall work be done*, work on the tabernacle, *But on the seventh day* you must not work at all. It is a Sabbath rest. It is a "Sabbath of Sabbaths," as some read it, greater and more honorable than any of the other festivals, and would outlast them all. A "Sabbath of sabbatism," as others read it, being a type of that rest, both spiritual and eternal, which *remains for the people of God* (Heb 4:9). It is "a Sabbath and a little Sabbath," as some Jews read it; not only observing the whole day as a Sabbath, but an hour before it begins and an hour after it ends, "a little Sabbath," to show how glad they are of the approach of the Sabbath and how loath they are to part with it.

4. Moses orders preparation to be made for the tabernacle to be set up. Two things were to be done:

4.1. All who were able must contribute: *Take you from among you an offering* (v. 5). The rule is, *Whosoever is of a willing heart let him bring.* It was not to be a tax that was imposed on them, but a voluntary contribution. This shows us:

• That God has not made our yoke heavy.
• That God loves a cheerful giver and is most pleased with freewill offerings. Those services are acceptable to him that come from the willing heart of a willing people (Ps 110:3).

4.2. All who were skilled must work: *Every wise hearted among you shall come, and make ...* (v. 10). Notice how diversely God distributes his gifts, and, *as every man hath received the gift, so he must minister* (1Pe 4:10). Those who were rich must bring materials to work on; those who were able must serve the tabernacle with their abilities. As they needed one another, so the tabernacle needed them both (1Co 12:12–21).

Verses 20–29

Notice here:

1. The offerings that were brought for the service of the tabernacle (v. 21, etc.):

1.1. It seems that they brought their offerings immediately. "There is no time like the present."

1.2. It is said that *their spirits made them willing* (v. 21) and *their hearts* (v. 29).

1.3. When it is said that *as many as were willing hearted* brought their offerings (v. 22), it would seem as if there were some who were not as willing, who loved their gold better than their God and would not part with it, not even for the service of the tabernacle. They want true religion, as long as it is cheap and costs them nothing.

1.4. The offerings were of different kinds, according to what they had. Those who could not bring precious stones brought goats' hair and rams' skins. The gift of the widow's mites was more pleasing than the large amounts put in by the rich (Mk 12:41–44). God looks on the heart of the giver more than the value of the gift.

1.5. Many of the things they offered were their ornaments, bracelets (brooches) and rings, and tablets or lockets (v. 22), and even the women parted with these. If we think the New Testament guidelines about clothing are too strict (1Ti 2:9–10; 1Pe 3:3–4), maybe we would scarcely have done what these Israelites did. The rich things they offered were probably mostly the plunder of the Egyptians. Who would have thought that even the wealth of Egypt would have been used so well? Let every man give *according as God hath prospered him* (1Co 16:2). Exceptional successes should be acknowledged by exceptional offerings. But great care must be taken to make sure that Egypt's gods do not associate with Egypt's gold.

2. The work that was done for the service of the tabernacle (v. 25): *The women did spin with their hands.* Some spun fine embroidery of blue and purple, others spun coarse goats' hair, which was said to be done *in wisdom* (v. 26). As it is not only rich gifts, so it is not only fine work that God accepts. Notice is here taken of the women's good work for God, as well as of Bezaleel's (Bezalel's) and Aholiab's (Oholiab's). The woman's anointing of Christ will be told in memory of her (Mt 26:13), and a record is kept of the women who labored in the Gospel tabernacle (Php 4:3) and were helpers to Paul in Christ Jesus (Ro 16:3). The poor may relieve the poor, and those that have nothing except their physical bodies and their senses may still carry out works of love.

Verses 30–35

Here is the divine appointment of the leading skilled workers, that there might be no argument over who was to undertake this task. God is the God of order and not of confusion.

1. Those whom God called by name to this service he *filled with the Spirit of God*, to qualify them for it (vv. 30–31). Skill in secular employments is God's gift and comes from above (Jas 1:17). When the apostles were appointed to be skilled leaders in building the Gospel tabernacle, they were filled with the Spirit of God in wisdom and understanding.

2. They were appointed, not only to make artistic designs (v. 32), but also to carry out work.

3. They were not only to make designs and work themselves, but they were also to teach others (v. 34). Not only had Bezaleel authority to command, but he was also to be careful to instruct. Those who lead should teach, and those to whom God has given knowledge should be willing to communicate it for the benefit of others and not keep it to themselves.

CHAPTER 36

In this chapter: 1. The work of the tabernacle is begun (vv. 1–4), and an end is put to the people's contributions (vv. 5–7). 2. A particular account is given of the making of the tabernacle itself; its fine curtains (vv. 8–13); the coarse ones (vv. 14–19); the boards (frames) (vv. 20–30); the bars (crossbars) (vv. 31–34). 3. An account is given of the making of the partition curtain (vv. 35–36) and the curtain for the door (vv. 37–38).

Verses 1–7

1. The workers started without delay. Then *they wrought* (v. 1). When God had qualified them for the work, they then applied themselves to it. They began when Moses called them (v. 2). Those people are called to build the Gospel tabernacle whom God has by his grace equipped in some measure for the work and also made free to undertake it. Ability and willingness, with determination, are the things to be regarded in the call of ministers. The materials which the people had contributed were delivered by Moses to the workers (v. 3). Precious souls are the materials of the Gospel tabernacle; they are *built up a spiritual house* (1Pe 2:5). The people are to offer themselves as a freewill offering to the Lord, for the purpose of serving him (Ro 15:16). They are then committed to be looked after by his ministers, who will form them and build them up so that they increase in holiness, till they all come, like the curtains of the tabernacle, *in the unity of the faith to be a holy temple* (Eph 2:21–22; 4:12–13).

2. The contributions were restrained. The people continued to bring *free offerings every morning* (v. 3). Now notice:

2.1. The honesty of the workers. When they had finished their work and found how far all the material went, they went as a group to Moses to tell him that they did not need any more contributions (vv. 4–5). They were people of integrity who would not even consider doing something so shabby as to use the people's offering to line their own pockets. Those who cheat the public are the greatest cheats.

2.2. The generosity of the people. This is very rare! Most people need to be spurred on to give an offering; it is very few who need to be restrained from doing so, but these did.

Verses 8–13

The first work they undertook was to put together the house, not made of bricks or wood but of curtains elaborately embroidered and joined together. This served as a type of the state of the church in this world, the palace of God's kingdom among the human race. The church is lowly; it is not static; it is the church militant; its shepherds dwelled in tents. God is the shepherd of Israel; the Lord is a warrior; his soldiers dwelled in tents. His church marches on and must fight its way through enemy country. The kings of the earth enclose themselves in cedar (Jer 22:15), but the ark of God was enfolded only in curtains. But there is a beauty in holiness; the curtains were embroidered, so the church is made attractive with the gifts and graces of the Spirit, that *raiment of needlework* (Ps 45:14).

Verses 14–34

1. The shelter and special protection that the church is under is represented by the curtains of hair cloth, which were spread over the tabernacle, and the covering of rams' skins and badgers' skins (hides of sea cows) over them (vv. 14–19). God has provided for his people a *shadow from the heat, and a covert from storm and rain* (Isa 4:6). Those who live in God's house will find, even if the storm is extremely violent, or the rain falls continually, that the rain does not actually come in.

2. The strength and stability of the church, even though it is only a tabernacle, are represented by the boards (frames) and bars (crossbars) which held the curtains up (vv. 20–34).

Verses 35–38

1. There was a curtain made as a partition between the Holy Place and the Most Holy Place (vv. 35–36). This represented the darkness and distance of that order, compared with the New Testament, which shows us the glory of God more clearly and invites us to draw near to it (1Th 4:17; 1Jn 3:2).

2. There was a curtain made for the entrance to the tent (vv. 37–38). The people gathered at this entrance, although they were forbidden to enter, for while we are in this present state, we must come as near to God as we can.

CHAPTER 37

Bezaleel (Bezalel) and his workers are still busy, making: 1. The ark with the mercy seat (atonement cover) and the cherubim (vv. 1–9). 2. The table with its vessels (vv. 10–16) and the candlestick (lampstand) with its accessories (vv. 17–24). 3. The golden altar of incense (vv. 25–28) and the holy oil and incense (v. 29).

Verses 1–9

1. Moses had recorded in such detail the instructions given him on the mountain for making all these things. Why then are so many chapters taken up with this narrative? We must consider:

1.1. Moses wrote primarily for the people of Israel, to whom it would be very useful often to read and hear about these divine and holy treasures with which they were entrusted. We need to have instilled in us again and again the great things of God's Law and Gospel.

1.2. Moses wants to show us the great care which he and his workers took to make everything exactly according to the pattern shown him on the mountain. Having before given us the original, here he gives us the copy, that we may compare them and notice how exactly they correspond with each other.

2. In these verses we have an account of the making of the ark, with its glorious and most significant accessories, the mercy seat (atonement cover) and the cherubim. If we consider these three together, they represent the glory of a holy God, the sincerity of a holy heart, and the fellowship between them, in and through a Mediator.

Verses 10–24

Here is:

1. The making of the table on which the shewbread was to be constantly placed. God is a good housekeeper, One who always keeps a table full of food. Is the world his tabernacle? His providence in it spreads a table for all his creatures: he *provides food for all flesh* (Ps 136:25). Is the church his tabernacle? His grace in it spreads a table for all believers, with the delightful spread of the bread of life. But notice how far the new order of the Gospel surpasses that of the Law. Though this was a furnished table, it was only furnished with *shewbread*, bread to be looked on, not to be eaten, while it was on this table, and afterward to be eaten only by the priests. But Christ invites all true Christians to the table which he has spread for us in the new covenant. It is said to them, *Eat, O friends, come eat of my bread* (Pr 9:5). What the Law made visible at a distance, the Gospel gives real enjoyment of and a sincere welcome to.

2. The making of the candlestick (lampstand), which was hammered only out of pure gold (vv. 17, 22). The Bible is a golden candlestick; it is of pure gold (Ps 19:10). From it, light spreads to every part of God's tabernacle.

Verses 25-29

Here is:

1. The making of the golden altar, on which incense was to be daily burned, which represented both the prayers of saints and the intercession of Christ. The rings and staves (poles) and all the accessories of this altar were overlaid with gold, as all the vessels of the table and candlestick were of gold, for these were used in the Holy Place.

2. The preparing of the incense which was to be burned on this altar, and with it the holy anointing oil (v. 29).

CHAPTER 38

Here is an account: 1. Of the making of the altar of burnt offering (vv. 1-7) and the laver (basin) (v. 8). 2. Of the preparing of the curtains for enclosing the court in which the tabernacle was to stand (vv. 9-20). 3. Of the gold, silver, and bronze contributed to and used in the preparation of the tabernacle (vv. 21-31).

Verses 1-8

After Bezaleel (Bezalel) had finished the gold work, which though the richest, was still ordered to be most out of sight in the tabernacle itself, he here goes on to prepare the court, which lay open to everyone's view. The court was furnished with two things, both made of bronze:

1. An altar of burnt offering (vv. 1-7). On this all their sacrifices were offered.

2. A laver (basin), to hold water for the priests to wash in when they went in to minister (v. 8). This is here said to be made of the *looking-glasses* (or mirrors) of the women who gathered at the entrance to the Tent of Meeting.

2.1. It would seem these women were particularly noted for their devotion. Anna was one such woman a long time afterward, who *departed not from the temple, but served God with fastings and prayers night and day* (Lk 2:37).

2.2. These women gave up their mirrors for use in the tabernacle. Rather than the workers lacking bronze, or not having the best, they wanted to give up their mirrors, even though they could hardly manage without them.

2.3. These mirrors were used to make the basin with. Either they were skillfully put together or they were melted down and cast again.

Verses 9-20

The walls of the courtyard were, like the rest, curtains or hangings, made according to the instructions (27:9-19). This represented the state of the Old Testament church: it was an enclosed garden; the worshipers were then confined to a small area. But since the enclosure was only made of curtains, this was an indication that the confinement of the church to one particular nation would not last forever. The dispensation itself was a tabernacle-dispensation, movable and changeable, and so was in due time taken down and folded up, when the place of the tent was to be enlarged and its cords lengthened to make room for the Gentile world, as is foretold (Isa 54:2-3).

Verses 21-31

Here we have an account which, at Moses' command, the Levites took and kept of the gold, silver, and bronze that were brought in for the tabernacle's use, and how these were used. Ithamar, the son of Aaron, was appointed to draw up this account and so was trained up in lesser services and fitted for greater (v. 21). Bezaleel (Bezalel) and Aholiab (Oholiab) must bring in the account (vv. 22-23), and Ithamar must audit it and give it to Moses. And this is what happened. All the gold was a freewill offering and the silver was levied by way of tax; every person was assessed at half a shekel, a kind of poll tax.

CHAPTER 39

This chapter describes the completion of the work of the tabernacle: 1. The last things prepared were the holy garments: the ephod and its skillfully woven sash or waistband (vv. 1-5); the onyx stones for the shoulder pieces (vv. 6-7); the breastplate (breastpiece) with the precious stones in it (vv. 8-21); the robe of the ephod (vv. 22-26); the coats (tunics), bonnets (headbands), and breeches (undergarments) for the lesser priests (vv. 27-29); and the plate of the holy crown or diadem (vv. 30-31). 2. A summary of the whole work, as it was presented to Moses when everything had been finished (vv. 32-43).

Verses 1-31

In this account of the making of the priests' garments, according to the instructions given (ch. 28), we may notice:

1. That the priests' garments are called here *clothes of service* (v. 1). It is said of those who are dressed in white robes that they *are before the throne of God, and serve him day and night in his temple* (Rev 7:13-15).

2. That all the six paragraphs here, which particularly describe the making of these holy garments, conclude with the words *as the Lord commanded Moses* (vv. 5, 7, 21, 26, 29, 31). This shows that all the Lord's ministers should make the word of God their rule in all their service and in observing and obeying God's commands.

3. That these garments, like the other furnishings of the tabernacle, were rich and magnificent. The infant church was taught to be pleased with such basic principles.

4. That they were all shadows of good things to come, but the reality is Christ and the grace of the Gospel. So when the reality has come, it is absurd to be fond of mere shadows.

4.1. Christ is our great High Priest. When he undertook the work of our redemption, he put on the clothes of service.

4.2. True believers are spiritual priests. The clean linen with which all their clothes of service must be made is *the righteousness of saints* (Rev 19:8).

Verses 32-43

1. The builders of the tabernacle worked efficiently and quickly. It may not have been much more than five months from when they began to when they finished.

2. They carried out their orders promptly and did not depart from them in the slightest. They did everything *according to all that the Lord commanded Moses* (vv. 32, 42).

3. They brought all their work to Moses, and submitted it to his inspection and examination (v. 33). Though they knew how to do the work better than Moses, Moses had a better and more exact idea of the model than they had, and so they could not be pleased with their own work unless they also had his approval.

4. After Moses had inspected their work, he found that everything had been done according to the rule (v. 43). Moses saw they had done it according to the pattern shown him, for the same Being that showed him the pattern also guided their hands to complete the work.

5. Moses blessed them:

5.1. He commended them, and showed his approval of all they had done. He did not find fault where there was none, as some do, who think they discredit their own judgment if they do not find something wrong even in the best achievements. In all this work there was probably the odd stitch that was amiss or stroke that had gone wrong, but Moses was too wise to notice small faults where there were no great ones.

5.2. He not only praised them, but he also prayed for them.

CHAPTER 40

In this chapter: 1. Orders are given to set up the tabernacle and to place all its furnishings in their proper places (vv. 1–8), and to consecrate it (vv. 9–11) and the priests (vv. 12–15). 2. Care is taken to do all this as God commanded it to be done (vv. 16–33). 3. God fills the tabernacle by the cloud of his glory (vv. 34–38).

Verses 1–15

The materials and furnishings of the tabernacle had been viewed individually and now they are put together.

1. The time for doing this is fixed as *the first day of the first month* (v. 2). It is good to begin the year with some good work. Let God who is the first have the first, and let the things of his kingdom be sought first. In Hezekiah's time we find they began to sanctify the temple *on the first day of the first month* (2Ch 29:17). Moses is specially ordered to set up the tabernacle itself first, in which God would dwell and be served (v. 2), then to put the ark in its place, shielded by the curtain (v. 3), then to fix the table, the candlestick (lampstand), and the altar of incense outside the curtain (vv. 4–5), and to put the curtain at the entrance to the tabernacle. Then in the courtyard he must place the bronze altar of burnt offering and the laver (basin) (vv. 6–7), and lastly he must set up the curtains of the courtyard and a hanging at the entrance to the courtyard.

2. God directs Moses, when he had set up the tabernacle and all its furnishings, to consecrate it and them by anointing them with the oil which was prepared for the purpose according to instructions given by God earlier (30:25–29, etc.). Everything was sanctified when it was put in its proper place. As everything is beautiful in its season, so everything is beautiful in its place (Ecc 3:11).

3. God directs him to consecrate Aaron and his sons.

Verses 16–33

When the tabernacle and its furnishings were prepared, they set it up in the midst of their camp, while they were still in the wilderness. Here we have an account of that New Year's Day's work. What was to be veiled he hung the shielding curtain in front of (v. 21), and what was to be used he used immediately. What he did he did by special authority and direction from God, more as a prophet or lawgiver than as a priest. He set the wheels in motion and then left the work in the hands of the appointed ministers.

1. When he had put the table in place, he set the shewbread in order on it (v. 23).

2. As soon as he had put the candlestick (lampstand) in place, *he lighted the lamps before the Lord* (v. 25).

3. When he had put the golden altar in its place, immediately he *burnt sweet incense thereon* (v. 27).

4. The altar of burnt offering was no sooner set up in the court of the tabernacle than he had a *burnt offering and a meat offering* ready to offer on it (v. 29).

5. When he had put the laver (basin) in place, Moses himself washed his hands and feet.

Verses 34–38

As in creation when God had finished this earth—which he intended for human habitation—he then made human beings so that they could occupy it, so when Moses had finished the tabernacle—which was intended as God's dwelling place among the human race—God came and occupied it. Where God has a throne and an altar in the soul, there is a living temple. Accordingly, when God came down to occupy his house, the *cloud covered it* on the outside, and *the glory of the Lord filled it* within:

1. The cloud covered the tent. This cloud was intended to be:

1.1. A sign of God's presence that was constantly visible day and night (v. 38) to all Israel, even to those who lay in the farthest corners of the camp, that they might never again question it, *Is the Lord among us, or is he not?* (17:7).

1.2. A hiding of the tabernacle and the glory of God in it. God really did dwell among them, but he dwelled in a cloud.

1.3. A protection for the tabernacle. The people had protected it with one covering on another, but after all that, the cloud that covered it was its best protection. Those who dwell in the house of the Lord are safe under divine protection (Ps 27:4–5).

1.4. A guide to the camp of Israel in their march through the wilderness (vv. 36–37). While the cloud stayed on the tabernacle, they rested; when it moved, they moved and followed it, as being only under divine direction.

2. *The glory of the Lord filled the tabernacle* (vv. 34–35). It was in light and fire, and, for all we know, not in any other way, that the *Shechinah* made itself visible, for *God is light* (1Jn 1:5).

A Practical and Devotional Exposition of the Third Book of Moses,

Leviticus

There is nothing historical in the whole book of Leviticus except the accounts of the consecration of the priesthood (8:1–9:24), of the punishment of Nadab and Abihu by the hand of God for offering strange (unauthorized) fire (10:1–20), and of the punishment of Shelomith's son by the hand of the judge for blasphemy (24:1–23). All the rest of the book is taken up with the laws, chiefly ecclesiastical laws, which God gave to Israel through Moses, concerning their sacrifices and offerings, their food and drinks, and cleansings; and other special laws and regulations by which God set that people apart for himself and distinguished them from other nations. All of these were shadows of good things to come and are fulfilled and superseded by the Gospel of Christ. We call the book *Leviticus*, from the Septuagint (a Greek version of the Old Testament), because it contains the laws and ordinances of the *Levitical priesthood* (as it is called, Heb 7:11) and its services. The Levites were principally responsible for carrying out these laws and ordinances, both to do them and also to teach the people their responsibilities. We read at the close of the previous book of the setting up of the tabernacle, which was to be the place of worship. As that was modeled on the pattern God gave, so must also the ordinances of worship be.

CHAPTER 1

This book begins with the laws concerning sacrifices, of which the most ancient were the burnt offerings, about which God gives Moses instructions in this chapter (vv. 1–2). Directions are given here about how that sacrifice must be carried out: 1. Burnt offerings of cattle from herds (vv. 3–9). 2. Burnt offerings of sheep and goats from flocks (vv. 10–13) or of birds (vv. 14–17). The offering was more or less valuable in itself, if it was offered with an upright heart, and according to these laws it was accepted by God.

Verses 1–2

Notice here that it is taken for granted that people would be inclined to bring offerings to the Lord. Revealed religion supposes natural religion to be an ancient institution, because the Fall had necessitated people to glorify God by sacrifice. They implicitly acknowledged in sacrifices that as creatures they had received everything from God and as sinners they had forfeited everything to him. Provision is made that people should not follow their own whims and indulgences, nor become futile in their own thoughts about their sacrifices, so that they would not in reality dishonor God while they pretended to honor him. Everything therefore is directed to be done so that their sacrifices might be most expressive of both the great sacrifice of atonement which Christ was to offer in the fullness of time and also the spiritual sacrifices of praise which believers should offer daily. God gave those laws to Israel by Moses. Through other prophets God sent messages to his people, but through Moses he gave them laws.

As soon as the *Shechinah* had occupied its new home, God talked with Moses from the mercy seat (atonement cover), while he was outside the curtain or, rather, was at the entrance, hearing only a voice. The tabernacle was set up to be a place of fellowship between God and Israel. There, where they carried out their services to God, God revealed his will to them. The moral law was given with terror from a burning mountain in thunder and lightning; but the remedial law of sacrifice was given more gently from a mercy seat (atonement cover), because that was a type of the grace of the Gospel, which is the ministry of life and peace.

Verses 3–9

If the person bringing the sacrifice was rich and could afford it, it is said that a burnt sacrifice, intended to honor God, would be brought from their herd of cattle.

1. The animal to be offered must be male, without defect, and the best in that person's pasture.

2. The owner must offer it voluntarily. What is done in religion to please God must be done by no other constraint except that of love.

3. It must be offered at the entrance to the tabernacle, where the bronze altar of burnt offerings stood, which sanctified the gift. It must be offered at the entrance, since the one bringing the offering was unworthy to enter. In this way, it was acknowledged that there can be no admission for a sinner into covenant and fellowship with God, except by sacrifice.

4. The offerer must put their hand on the head of the offering (v. 4), showing in this way:

4.1. The transfer of all rights to, and claims on, the animal to God.

4.2. An acknowledgment that the offerer deserved to die and would have been willing to die if God had required it.

4.3. A dependence on the sacrifice as an ordained type of the great sacrifice on which the iniquities of us all were to be laid. Though the burnt offering was not for any one particular sin, as the sin offering was, yet the burnt offerings were to make atonement for sin in general.

5. The sacrifice was to be killed by the priests or Levites, *before the Lord* (v. 5), that is, in a devout, religious manner.

6. The priests were to *sprinkle the blood upon the altar* (v. 5), for the blood being the life, it was this that made atonement for the soul.

7. The animal was to be skinned and properly cut up, divided into several pieces, and then all the pieces, with the head and the fat, were to be burned together on the altar (vv. 6–9).

8. This is said to be *an offering of a sweet savour*, or "savor of rest," *unto the Lord* (v. 13). The burning of flesh is unsavory in itself, but this as an act of obedience to a divine command and as a type of Christ was pleasing to God. He was reconciled to the offerer. Christ's offering of himself to God is said to be of *a sweet-smelling savour* (Eph 5:2), and the spiritual sacrifices of Christians are said to be *acceptable to God, by Christ* (1Pe 2:5).

Verses 10–17

Here we have the laws concerning the burnt offerings that were from flocks or birds. Those people of the middle classes who could not afford to offer cattle would bring a sheep or a goat, and those who were not able to do that would be accepted by God if they brought a turtledove (dove) or a pigeon. It is noticeable that those creatures that were chosen for sacrifice were most mild and gentle, harmless and inoffensive. In this, they are a type of the innocence and meekness in Christ; they show us the innocence and meekness that should be in Christians. Directions are here given:

1. Concerning the burnt offerings of the flock (v. 10). The method of making the sacrifice is much the same as that of sacrificing the cattle.

2. Concerning the burnt offerings of the birds. They must be either turtledoves or pigeons, and if pigeons, they must be young. The turtledoves or young pigeons of the poor are here said to be *an offering of a sweet savour*, as much as that of an ox or young bull with horns or hoofs. For after all, to *love God with all our heart, and to love our neighbour as ourselves, is better than all burnt offerings and sacrifices* (Mk 12:33).

CHAPTER 2

In this chapter we have the law concerning the meat offering (grain offering). 1. Its elements were flour with oil and incense (vv. 1, 6); it was to be baked in the oven (v. 4), on a plate (v. 5), or in a frying pan (v. 7). How the elements were to be used: the flour (vv. 2–3) and the cakes (vv. 8–10). 2. Some particular rules concerning it: that leaven (yeast) and honey must never be allowed (vv. 11–12), and salt never omitted in the meat offering (v. 13). The law concerning the offering of firstfruits of new grain (vv. 14–16).

Verses 1–10

The law of this chapter concerns those meat offerings that were offered by themselves, whenever worshipers wanted to express their devotion in this way. The first offering we read of in Scripture was of this kind (Ge 4:3): *Cain brought of the fruit of the ground an offering.*

1. This sort of offering was given:

1.1. To include the poor, according to their ability, that those who themselves lived only on bread and cakes might offer an acceptable offering to God out of what was their own rough and ordinary food.

1.2. To be a proper acknowledgment of the mercy of God to them in their food. This was like a rent, by which they declared their dependence on God, their thankfulness to him, and their expectations from him. Those who with kind and generous hearts now share their bread with the hungry give an acceptable offering to God.

2. The laws of the meat offerings were:

2.1. The ingredients must always be fine flour and oil, two staple commodities of the land of Canaan (Dt 8:8). In those days, oil was to them for their food what butter is to us now.

2.2. If it was unbaked flour, besides the oil it must have frankincense (incense) put on it, which was to be burned with it (vv. 1–2), to give a sweet scent to the altar.

2.3. If it was prepared, this could be done in various ways. The offerer could bake it, fry it, or mix the flour and oil on a plate. The Law was very precise even about those offerings that were least costly.

2.4. It was to be presented by the offerer to the priest, which is called *bringing it to the Lord* (v. 8).

2.5. Part of it was to be burned on the altar as a memorial portion, that is, as a sign of their need to remember God's generosity to them in giving them all things richly to enjoy.

2.6. The rest of the meat offering was to be given to the priests (vv. 3, 10). In this way, God provided that those who served at the altar would live on the altar, and live comfortably.

Verses 11–16

1. Leaven (yeast) and honey are forbidden to be put in any of their meat offerings.

1.1. The yeast was forbidden in order to remind them of the unleavened bread they ate when they came out of Egypt.

1.2. Honey was forbidden, although Canaan flowed with it. Some think the chief reason why these two things, yeast and honey, were forbidden, was that the Gentiles used them a lot in their sacrifices, and God's people must not follow the ways of the nations. Some also consider yeast to represent grief and sadness of spirit (Ps 73:21, "My heart was leavened") and honey to represent sensual pleasure and indulgence.

2. Salt was required in all their offerings (v. 13). The altar was the table of the Lord, and since salt is always set on our tables, God wants it always used at his. It is called *the salt of the covenant*, because as people confirmed their covenants with each other by eating and drinking together—on all of which occasions salt was used—so God, by accepting his people's gifts and receiving the feast of his people's sacrifices—eating with them and they with him (Rev 3:20)—confirmed his covenant with them. Among ancient people, salt was a symbol of friendship. The salt for the sacrifice was not brought by the offerers, but was provided in unlimited supplies (Ezr 7:22). There was a room in the court of the temple called "the chamber of salt," in which they stored it all. Christianity is the salt of the earth.

3. Directions are given about the firstfruits:

3.1. The sacrifice of their firstfruits at harvest, of which we read also in Dt 26:2. These were offered to the Lord, not to be burned on the altar, but to be given to the priests as a benefit of their office (v. 12).

3.2. A meat offering (grain offering) of their firstfruits. The meat offering was required by the law, but this was a freewill offering (vv. 14–16).

3.2.1. The offerer must be sure to bring the first ripe and full ears, not those that were small and withered.

3.2.2. These fresh green heads of grain must be dried and roasted on the fire, so that the edible part of the grain might be beaten out of the full heads.

3.2.3. Oil and frankincense (incense) must be put on it. In this way, wisdom and humility must soften, sweeten, and mellow the spirits and services of young people. God takes a particular delight in the first ripe fruits of the Spirit and the expressions of young godliness and devotion.

3.2.4. It must be used as other meat offerings were (v. 16); compare v. 9. He shall *offer all the frankincense; it is an offering made by fire.* Holy love to God is the fire by which all our offerings must be made, or otherwise they are not a sweet aroma to God. Frankincense represents the mediation and intercession of Christ, by which all our services are made sweet and commended to God's gracious acceptance.

CHAPTER 3

In this chapter we have the law concerning the peace offerings (fellowship offerings), whether they were: 1. Cattle from the herd (vv. 1–5). Or: 2. Of the flock, either a lamb (vv. 6–11) or a goat (vv. 12–17).

Verses 1–5

The burnt offerings expressed pure adoration and so were wholly burnt. But the peace offerings (fellowship offerings) considered God as the generous giver of all things to his creatures, and so these were divided between the altar, the priest, and the owner. Peace signifies:

• Reconciliation, harmony, and fellowship. And so these were called *peace offerings*, because in them God and his people, as it were, held a feast together, as a sign of their friendship.

• Prosperity and happiness: *Peace be to you* was equivalent to "All good be to you," and so the peace offerings were offered either as a request for some good that was wanted, or as a thanksgiving for some particular mercy received. It is called "a peace offering of thanksgiving" (7:12–13), for so it was sometimes, as in other cases *a vow* (7:15–16). The sacrifice of praise will please the Lord better than any cattle.

Verses 6–17

Directions are here given concerning the peace offering (fellowship offering), if it was a sheep or a goat. Turtledoves (doves) or young pigeons, which could be brought as whole burnt offerings, were not allowed as peace offerings, because they do not have enough fat to be burned on the altar, and so they would not amount to much if they were divided according to the law of the peace offerings. The laws concerning a lamb or goat offered as a peace offering are much the same as those concerning cattle.

CHAPTER 4

This chapter concerns the sin offering, which was intended to make atonement for sin committed unintentionally: 1. By the priest himself (vv. 1–12). 2. By the whole community (vv. 13–21). 3. By a leader (vv. 22–26). 4. By an ordinary person (vv. 27–35).

Verses 1–12

Here begin the statutes of another session, another day. From the throne of glory between the cherubim, God gave these orders. It would seem that burnt offerings, meat offerings (grain offerings), and peace offerings (fellowship offerings) had been offered before the giving of the Law on Mount Sinai. But since the Law was now added *because of transgressions* (Gal 3:19), the people were given a way of making atonement for sin particularly by sacrifice.

1. Here is the general case (v. 2). Notice:

1.1. Concerning sin in general, that it is described to be against *any of the commandments of the Lord* (v. 2), for *sin is the transgression of the law* (1Jn 3:4), the divine law. It is said, *if a soul sin*—for it is not sin if it is not in some way or other an act of the soul—it is called the *sin of the soul* (Mic 6:7), and it is the soul that is harmed by it (Pr 8:36).

1.2. Concerning the sins for which those offerings were appointed:

1.2.1. They are considered to be explicit acts, for if they had been required to bring a sacrifice for every sinful thought or word, the task would have been endless. Atonement was made for those generally once a year on the Day of Atonement, but these sins are considered to be done against the commandments.

1.2.2. They are considered to be sins of commission, things which ought not to be done.

1.2.3. They are considered to be sins committed through ignorance. But if the offender was either ignorant of the Law—as we may suppose many were in some instances, since the prohibitions were so numerous and varied—or if the offender was caught unawares in sin, relief was provided by the remedial law of the sin offering.

2. The Law begins with the case of the anointed priest, that is, the high priest, if he should sin unintentionally, for *the law made men priests who had infirmity* (Heb 7:28). Though he of all people was least excusable for ignorance, he was still allowed to bring his offering. The law concerning the sin offering for the high priest is:

2.1. That he must bring a young bull without defect as a sin offering (v. 3), as valuable an offering as that for the whole community (v. 14).

2.2. The hand of the offerer must be laid on the head of the offering (v. 4), with a solemn, penitent confession of the sin that had been committed, putting it on the head of the sin offering (16:21).

2.3. The young bull must be killed, and there was a great deal of ceremony concerning the disposing of the blood, for it was *the blood that made atonement* (17:11), and *without shedding of blood* there *was no remission* (Heb 9:22). Some of the blood of the high priest's sin offering was to be *sprinkled seven times before the veil* (v. 6) with an eye toward the mercy seat (atonement cover), even though it was hidden behind the curtain. Some of it was to be put on the horns of the golden altar, because the priest himself served at that altar. In this way, it represented the putting away of the pollution from his sins which clung to his services. When this was done, the remainder of the blood was poured at the foot of the bronze altar. In this ceremony, sinners acknowledged that they deserved to have their blood poured out like water in this way. It also represented the pouring out of the soul before God in true repentance and was a type of our Savior's *pouring out his soul unto death* (Isa 53:12).

2.4. The fat of the innards was to be burned on the altar of burnt offering (vv. 8–10). By this, the intention of the offering and the atonement made by it were directed to the glory of God, who, having been dishonored by the sin, was honored by the sacrifice.

Verses 13–21

This is the law for making atonement for the guilt of a sin by the whole community by means of a sin offering. If the leaders of the people caused them to err through mistakes concerning the Law, when the mistake was discovered, an offering must be brought, so that God's wrath might not come on the whole community.

1. It is possible that the church may err, and that its leaders may mislead the church. It is said here that the whole congregation may sin unintentionally. God will always have a church on earth, but he has never said that it would be infallible or perfectly pure from corruption on this side of heaven.

2. When a sacrifice was to be offered for the whole community, at least three of the elders, as representatives of the people and agents for them, were to lay their hands on the animal's head.

3. The blood of this sin offering, as it was in the former instructions, was to be *sprinkled seven times before the Lord* (v. 17). It was not to be poured out there, but only to be sprinkled, for the cleansing power of the blood of Christ was and still is sufficiently represented by sprinkling (Isa 52:15). It was to be sprinkled seven times. Seven is a perfect number, because when God had made the world in six days he rested on the seventh. This therefore represented the perfect atonement Christ made and the complete cleansing of the souls of the faithful that it achieved; see Heb 10:14. When the offering is completed, it is said, *atonement is made, and the sin shall be forgiven* (v. 20). The promise of forgiveness rests on the atonement.

Verses 22–26

Notice here:

1. God takes notice of and is displeased with the sins of rulers and leaders.

2. The sins of the leaders which they committed unintentionally may afterward come to their knowledge (v. 23). This must be either by the restraints of their own conscience or by the rebuke of friends.

3. The sin offering for a leader was to be *a kid of the goats*, not a young bull as it was for the priest and the whole community; nor was the blood of the leader's sin offering to be brought into the tabernacle, as for the other two, but it was all put on the bronze altar (v. 25). Neither was its flesh to be burned, as it was for the other two, outside the camp. This showed that the sin of a ruler, though worse than that of an ordinary person, was still not as offensive, or of such awful significance, as the sin of the high priest or of the whole community.

4. It is promised that the atonement would be accepted and the sin forgiven (v. 26), that is, if the leader repented and mended his ways.

Verses 27–35

1. Here is the law of the sin offering for an ordinary person, which differs from that for a leader only in this: that a private person could bring either a goat or a lamb, whereas a leader could only bring a goat, and also that for a leader the goat must be male, for the ordinary person, female. Notice:

1.1. The case described: *If any one of the common people sin through ignorance* (v. 27). If they sinned unintentionally, they must bring a sin offering. We all need to pray with David that we would be cleansed from *secret faults*, the hidden errors which we ourselves do not understand or are not aware of (Ps 19:12).

1.2. That the sins inadvertently committed by a single insignificant person required a sacrifice.

1.3. That a sin offering was not only admitted, but also accepted, even from one of the ordinary people, and atonement was made by it (vv. 31, 35). Here both rich and poor, ruler and rustic, meet together; they are both welcome to come to Christ on the same terms. See Job 34:19.

2. From all these laws concerning the sin offerings we may learn:

2.1. To hate sin and to guard against it.

2.2. To value Christ, the great and true sin offering, whose blood cleanses us from all sin, which it was not possible that the *blood of bulls and of goats should take away* (Heb 10:4). Perhaps there was some allusion to this law concerning sacrifices for unintentional sins in that prayer of Christ's, when he was offering up himself as a sacrifice, *Father, forgive them, for they know not what they do* (Lk 23:34).

CHAPTER 5

This chapter, and part of the next, concerns the trespass offering (guilt offering). The difference between this and the sin offering lay not so much in the sacrifices themselves as in the occasions on which they were offered. They were both intended to make atonement for sin, but the sin offering was more general and the trespass offering applied in some particular instances. Notice what is said here: 1. Concerning the trespass. If a person sins: 1.1. In not speaking up when they hear a public charge to testify about something they have witnessed (v. 1); in touching something ceremonially unclean (vv. 2–3); in swearing (v. 4). 1.2. In sinning against holy things (vv. 14–16); in any sin of weakness (vv. 17–19). There are some other cases in which these offerings were to be offered (6:2–4; 14:12; 19:21; Nu 6:12). 2. Concerning the trespass offerings: 2.1. From the flock (vv. 5–6). 2.2. Of birds (vv. 7–10); of flour (vv. 11–13). 2.3. Especially, of a ram without defect (vv. 14–19).

Verses 1–6

1. The offenses here described are:

1.1. Someone concealing the truth by not speaking up when they are sworn as a witness to testify about something they have witnessed. Such a person should speak the truth, the whole truth, and nothing but the truth. Judges among the Jews had power to put on oath not only witnesses as with us, but also the person suspected, as appears by the demand of the high priest to our Savior, who answered, even though before he had been silent (Mt 26:63–64). Now (v. 1), *If a soul sin*—that is, a person, for the soul is the person—if that person *hears the voice of swearing*—that is, if they are put on oath to testify what they know—if in such a case the person refuses to give evidence or only gives it partly, *he shall bear his iniquity*. Let all who are called on at any time to bear witness remember this law and be free and open in their evidence and make sure they are not evasive. An oath of the Lord is something light and not to be toyed with frivolously.

1.2. A person's touching anything ceremonially unclean (vv. 2–3). If a person defiled by such touch came carelessly into the sanctuary, or if they neglected to wash themselves according to the Law, then they were to look on themselves as guilty and must bring an offering.

1.3. Rash swearing. If a person binds themselves by an oath that they will do or not do a certain thing and the carrying out of the oath afterward proves either unlawful or impracticable, by which the person is discharged from the obligation, they must still bring an offering to atone for their foolishness in swearing so rashly.

2. Now in these cases:

2.1. The offender must confess their sin and bring an offering (vv. 5–6), and the offering was not accepted unless it was accompanied by confession of sin and a humble prayer for forgiveness.

2.2. The priest must *make an atonement for him* (v. 6).

Verses 7–13

Provision is here made for the poor among God's people and the soothing of their conscience under a sense of guilt. Those who were not able to bring a lamb could bring a pair of *turtledoves* (doves) or *two young pigeons* as a sin offering (v. 7). In fact, if any were so poor that they were not able to obtain these, they could bring an ephah, that is about two quarts (about two liters), of fine flour, and this would be accepted. In this way, the expense of the sin offering was brought lower than that of any other offering, to teach us that poverty will never prevent someone from receiving forgiveness. No person will ever be able to say that they did not have the resources to pay the cost of a journey to heaven.

1. If the sinner brought two turtledoves, one was to be offered as a sin offering and the other as a burnt offering (v. 7). Notice:

1.1. Before the person offered the burnt offering, which was for the honor and praise of God, they must offer the sin offering to make atonement.

1.2. After the sin offering, which made atonement, came the burnt offering, as an acknowledgment of the great mercy of God in ordaining and accepting the atonement.

2. If the offerer brought fine flour, a handful of it was to be offered, but without either oil or frankincense (incense) (v. 11), not only because this would make it too expensive for the poor, but also because it was a sin offering. To show the offensiveness of the sin for which it was offered, it must not be made pleasant to the taste by oil or to the smell by frankincense.

Verses 14–19

Here we have the law concerning those that were properly *trespass offerings* (guilt offerings), which were offered to atone for trespasses done against a neighbor. Now injuries done to another may be either in holy things or in ordinary things: of the former we have the law in these verses; of the latter at the beginning of the next chapter. Now if someone unintentionally transferred the ownership of or took for their own use anything that was dedicated to God, they were to bring this sacrifice. Possible examples of trespasses are inadvertent use of tithes, firstfruits, or the firstborn of cattle, or if they had eaten any parts of the sacrifices which were appropriate only for the priests. If they were done in deliberate contempt of the Law, the offender died without mercy (Heb 10:28). But this sacrifice was established in cases of unintentional negligence. The trespasser must bring an offering to the Lord, which in all those that were purely trespass offerings, must be *a ram without blemish*. The trespasser must likewise make restitution to the priest, according to the proper value of the thing, adding a fifth to its value.

CHAPTER 6

1. Vv. 1–7 might more properly have been added to the previous chapter, since they are a continuation of the law of the trespass offering (guilt offering). 2. From v. 8 comes the description of the several ceremonies concerning: the burnt offering (vv. 8–13). 3. The meat offering (grain offering) (vv. 14–18), particularly that at the consecration of the priest (vv. 19–23). 4. The sin offering (vv. 24–30).

Verses 1–7

This is the latter part of the law of the trespass offering. Notice here:

1. The trespass described (vv. 2–3). Though all the instances relate to our neighbor, it is still called a *trespass against the Lord*. The person who speaks evil of his brother or sister is said to speak evil of the Law, and so of the Lawmaker (Jas 4:11). The trespasses specified are:

1.1. Denying a trust: *If a man lie unto his neighbour in that which was delivered him to keep*, or what is worse, what was lent him for his use.

1.2. Defrauding a partner: *If a man lie in fellowship*, claiming a sole interest in something in which he has only a joint interest.

1.3. Disowning a clear wrong: *If a man* has the audacity to *lie in a thing taken away by violence*, which normally cannot be hidden.

1.4. Deceiving in commerce, or as some think, by false accusation.

1.5. Detaining what is found and denying it (v. 3).

2. The trespass offering ordained:

2.1. *In the day of his trespass offering* the offender must make restitution to the wronged person. Let the offerer faithfully restore all that was gained by fraud, extortion, or oppression, with a fifth part added.

2.2. The offerer must *then come and offer his gift*, must *bring his trespass offering to the Lord* whom he had offended, and the priest must make an atonement for the offerer (vv. 6–7).

Verses 8–13

Moses was directed to give instructions to the priests; he must *command Aaron and his sons* (v. 9). In these verses we have the law of the burnt offering, as far as it was the special responsibility of the priests. The daily sacrifice of a lamb, which was offered morning and evening for the whole congregation, is here mainly referred to:

1. The priest must take care of the ashes of the burnt offering, that they may be properly disposed of (vv. 10–11). He must clear the altar of them every morning and put them on the east side of the altar, which was farthest from the sanctuary. He must do this in his linen clothes, which he always wore when he did any service at the altar, and then he must put on other clothes and must *carry the ashes into a clean place without* (outside) *the camp*. The priest himself must not only kindle the fire, but also clean the hearth and take out the ashes. God's servants must think nothing beneath them except sin.

2. The priest must take care of the fire on the altar. *The fire shall ever be burning upon the altar, it shall never go out* (v. 13). Though we are not always offering sacrifices, we must still keep the fire of holy devotion always burning, and so we should *pray without ceasing* (1Th 5:17).

Verses 14–23

The meat offering (grain offering) was either what was offered by the people or what was offered by the priests at their consecration. Now:

1. Concerning the ordinary meat offering (grain offering):

1.1. Only a handful of fine flour and oil was to be burned on the altar; all the rest was allowed for the priests as their food.

1.2. The laws concerning the eating of the offering were:

- It must be *eaten unleavened* (v. 16).
- It must be eaten in *the court of the tabernacle* (here called the *Holy Place*, v. 16).
- Only the males may eat of it (v. 18).
- Only the priests who were clean may eat it.

2. Concerning the consecration meat offering (grain offering), which was offered for the priests themselves, it was to be *wholly burnt, and none of it eaten* (v. 23). The Jewish writers say that the high priest was bound to offer it every day of his life, from the day on which he was anointed. Josephus says, "The high priest sacrificed twice every day at his own expense, and this was his sacrifice." The meat offering of the priest was to be baked as if it were to be eaten, but it must be completely burned.

Verses 24–30

We have here so much of the law of the sin offering as specially concerned the priests who offered it:

1. It must be killed *in the place where the burnt offering was killed* (v. 25).

2. The priest who offered it for the sinner was, with his sons or other priests (v. 29), to eat its flesh, after the blood and fat had been offered to God, in the *court of the tabernacle* (v. 26).

3. The blood of the sin offering was very reverently to be washed out of the clothes on which it happened to be spattered (v. 27).

4. The pot in which the flesh of the sin offering was boiled must be broken if it was earthen (clay), and if bronze it was to be washed well (v. 28).

CHAPTER 7

Here is: 1. The law of the trespass offering (guilt offering) (vv. 1–7), with some further directions concerning the burnt offering and the meat offering (grain offering) (vv. 8–10). 2. The law of the peace offering (fellowship offering). Instructions concerning the eating of it (vv. 11–21), at which time the prohibition of eating fat or blood is repeated (vv. 22–27), and concerning the priests' share of it (vv. 28–34). 3. A summary of those offerings (vv. 35–38).

Verses 1–10

Notice here:

1. Concerning the trespass offering (guilt offering), that as it was of much the same nature as the sin offering, it was to be governed by the same rules (v. 6). When the blood and fat were offered to God to make atonement, the priests were to eat the flesh, like that of the sin offering, in the Holy Place. The Jews have a tradition, as noted by Bishop Patrick, concerning the sprinkling of the blood of the trespass offering *round about upon the altar* (v. 2), "that there was a scarlet line which went around the altar exactly in the middle, and the blood of the burnt offerings was sprinkled around above the line, but that of the trespass offerings and peace offerings around below the line." It seems the offerers themselves were not to have any share of the trespass offering, as they were to have of the peace offering; but it was all divided between the altar and the priest. They offered peace offerings in thankfulness

for mercy, and then it was right to celebrate a feast; but they offered trespass offerings in sorrow for sin, and then fasting was more proper, as a sign of holy mourning and a determination to renounce sin.

2. Concerning the burnt offering, the instruction here is that the priest who offered it should have the skin or hide (v. 8), which no doubt he could make money from.

3. Concerning the meat offering (grain offering), if it was cooked, it was fit to be eaten immediately; and so the priest who offered it was to have it (v. 9).

Verses 11–34

1. The nature and purpose of the peace offering (fellowship offering) are here described. It was offered:

1.1. In thankfulness for some special mercy received, such as recovery from sickness, preservation on a journey, deliverance at sea, or redemption from captivity. Or:

1.2. In carrying out a vow which someone made when they were in distress (v. 16). Or:

1.3. In asking God for some special mercy, and then it was called a *voluntary offering* (a freewill offering) (v. 16). This accompanied a person's prayers, as the peace offering brought in thanksgiving did their praises.

2. The ceremonies of the peace offerings are described more fully:

2.1. If the peace offering was offered in thanksgiving, a meat offering (grain offering) must be offered with it, cakes of several sorts and wafers (v. 12), and—what was special about the peace offerings—leavened bread must be offered. Unleavened bread was less pleasant to the taste, and so although it was commanded in the Passover for a particular reason, in other festivals, leavened bread—which was lighter and more pleasant—was appointed, so that people might feast at God's table as well as at their own.

2.2. The flesh of the peace offerings, both what was the priest's share and what was the offerer's, must be eaten promptly, and not kept long, either raw, or cooked, cold. Though they did not have to eat it in the Holy Place, as those offerings that are called most holy, but could take it to their own tents and eat it there, yet God wanted them by this law to know the difference between that and other meat:

2.2.1. Because God did not want that holy flesh to be in danger of going bad.

2.2.2. Because God did not want his people to be stingy and sparing, distrusting Providence.

2.2.3. The flesh of the peace offerings was God's special treat, and so God ordered it to be used generously to be hospitable to the friends of the offerers and to be used charitably for the relief of the poor.

2.3. The flesh, and those who eat it, must be pure:

2.3.1. The flesh must *touch no unclean thing*; if it did, it must not be eaten, but burned (v. 19).

2.3.2. The flesh must not be eaten by any unclean person. If people who for any reason were ceremonially unclean were presumptuous enough to eat the flesh of the peace offerings, they were in danger (vv. 20–21). If anyone who is defiled by unrepented sin dare eat at the table of the Lord, they are desecrating holy things and eat and drink judgment on themselves in their uncleanness (1Co 11:29), as those did who ate the peace offerings (v. 20).

2.4. The eating of blood and the fat of the innards is here again prohibited, and the prohibition is attached as before to the law of the peace offerings (3:17). To eat the flesh of an animal that died by itself or was torn by wild animals was unlawful, but to eat the fat of such animals was doubly unlawful (v. 24). The prohibition of blood is more general (vv. 26–27), because the fat was offered to God only as an acknowledgment, but the blood *made atonement for the soul* (17:11) and so was a type of Christ's sacrifice even more than the burning of the fat was. Greater reverence must therefore be paid to this, till these types were fulfilled in the offering up of the body of Christ once for all.

2.5. The priest's share of the peace offerings is here stated. Jesus Christ is our great peace offering, for he made himself a sacrifice, not only to atone for sin and so save us from the curse, but also to buy a great blessing for us. By joyfully sharing in the benefits of redemption we *feast upon the sacrifice*, as a sign of which the Lord's Supper was instituted.

Verses 35–38

Here is the conclusion of these laws concerning the sacrifices. They are to be considered:

1. As a share given to the priests (vv. 35–36).

2. As a statute forever to the people, that they should bring these offerings according to the rules that were established and cheerfully give the priests their share of them. *God commanded the children of Israel to offer their oblations* (v. 38). The solemn acts of religious worship are commanded. Observing the laws of Christ cannot be less important than observing the laws of Moses.

CHAPTER 8

This chapter gives us an account of the solemn ordination of Aaron and his sons to the office of priest. 1. It was done in public, and the whole assembly, the entire congregation, was called together to witness it (vv. 1–4); it was done exactly according to God's commandments (v. 5). Aaron's sons were washed and clothed (vv. 6–9, 13); the tabernacle and its utensils were anointed and then the priests (vv. 10–12). 2. A sin offering was offered for them (vv. 14–17); a burnt offering (vv. 18–21); and the ram of consecration (ram for the ordination) (vv. 22–30). 3. This ceremony continued for seven days (vv. 31–36).

Verses 1–13

God had given Moses orders to ordain Aaron and his sons to the office of priest when he was with him the first time on Mount Sinai (Ex 28:1–29:46). We have here:

1. The orders repeated. The tabernacle had just been set up, but was without the priests, which would be like a candlestick without a candle. The law concerning sacrifices had just been given but could not be observed without priests. Aaron and his sons were close relatives of Moses, and so he would not ordain them till he had received further orders, so as not to seem too forward in bringing honor on his own family.

2. The congregation, the assembly, called together, *at the door* of the tabernacle of the congregation, that is, at the entrance of the Tent of Meeting (v. 4). The ceremony was performed in public:

2.1. Because it was a solemn transaction between God and Israel, and so it was right that both sides should come and acknowledge the appointment at the entrance of the Tent of Meeting.

2.2. To instill a great respect for the priests and their office by those who saw the ceremony. It was strange that any of those who witnessed what was done here should say afterward, as some of them did, *You take too much upon you, you sons of Levi* (Nu 16:7).

3. The commission read (v. 5). Moses, who was God's representative in this ceremony, produced his orders before the congregation: *This is the thing which the Lord commanded to be done.*

4. The ceremony performed according to the divine ritual:

4.1. Aaron and his sons were *washed with water* (v. 6), as a sign that they ought now to purify themselves from all sinful inclinations and keep themselves pure at all times in the future.

4.2. They were clothed with the holy garments, Aaron with his (vv. 7–9), which were a type of the supreme dignity and honor of Christ our great High Priest, and his sons with theirs (v. 13), which were a type of the holiness of Christians, who are spiritual priests. Christ wears the breastplate (breastpiece) of judgment and the holy crown, for the church's High Priest is her Prophet and King. All believers are clothed with the robe of righteousness, and have the girdle of truth, commitment, and devotion buckled around their waist, and their heads are *bound*, as the word is here, with the bonnet (headband) or diadem of beauty, the beauty of holiness.

4.3. The high priest was anointed. The tabernacle and all its utensils received some of the anointing oil put on them by Moses' finger (v. 10), and so did the altar (v. 11), but he poured it out more plentifully on the head of Aaron (v. 12), so that it ran down to the *skirts of his garments* (Ps 133:2), because his anointing was a type of the anointing of Christ with the Spirit, who was given without limit to him.

Verses 14–30

Sacrifices of each kind must be offered for the priests, that they might tenderly and carefully offer the gifts and sacrifices of the people, with *compassion on the ignorant*, and on *those that were out of the way* (Heb 5:2), remembering that they themselves had had sacrifices offered for them, being *compassed with infirmity* (Heb 5:2).

1. A bull, the largest sacrifice, was offered as a sin offering (v. 14). Ministers, who are to declare the forgiveness of sins to others, should make sure that they themselves have received forgiveness for their own sins. Those to whom is *committed the ministry of reconciliation* (2Co 5:18) must themselves first be reconciled to God.

2. A ram was offered as a burnt offering (vv. 18–21). By this, they gave God the glory of this great honor which was now put on them and praised him for it, as Paul thanked Christ Jesus for *putting him into the ministry* (1Ti 1:12).

3. Another ram, called the *ram of consecration* (ram for the ordination), was offered as a peace offering (fellowship offering) (vv. 22–29). All the ceremonies of this offering, like those before, were appointed by the explicit command of God.

Verses 31–36

Moses, having done his part of the ceremony, now leaves Aaron and his sons to do theirs:

1. They must cook the flesh of their peace offering (fellowship offering) and eat it in the court of the tabernacle, at the entrance of the Tent of Meeting, and they must burn up the remains with fire (vv. 31–32).

2. They must not leave the court of the tabernacle, the entrance of the Tent of Meeting, for seven days (v. 33).

2.1. Since the priesthood unavoidably demanded warfare, they must learn to endure hardness, and not to get involved in *the affairs of this life* (2Ti 2:3–4). The work lasted seven days, for it was a kind of creation. This time was set in honor of the Sabbath, which was probably the last day of the seven, for which they were to prepare during the six days.

2.2. They were faithful to *keep the charge of the Lord* (v. 35): each one of us must do what God requires. We have a responsibility before God to fulfill, an eternal God to glorify, an immortal soul to provide for, necessary duties to be done, our generation to serve. We must make sure that we carry out our responsibilities every day, for they come from the Lord our Master.

2.3. Lastly, we are told (v. 36) that *Aaron and his sons did all that was commanded*. But after all the ceremonies of their ordination there was one point of confirmation which was reserved to be the honor and establishment of Christ's priesthood, which was this, that they were *made priests without an oath*, but *Christ with an oath* (Heb 7:21), for neither such priests nor their priesthood would last forever, but Christ's priesthood is eternal and unchangeable.

CHAPTER 9

After Aaron and his sons had been ceremonially ordained into the priesthood, this chapter records the beginning of their ministry the very next day after their ordination had been completed. 1. Moses calls a meeting between God and his priests, as the representatives of his people, instructing them to serve him and assuring them that he would appear to them (vv. 1–7). 2. The meeting is held according to the appointment. Aaron serves God with sacrifices, offering a sin offering and a burnt offering for himself (vv. 8–14), and then the offerings for the people, whom he blessed in the name of the Lord (vv. 15–22). 3. God shows his acceptance: of their lives by showing them his glory (v. 23) and of their sacrifices by consuming them with fire from heaven (v. 24).

Verses 1–7

Orders are here given for another ceremony on the eighth day. The priests were not even given one day's rest from service, but were busily employed the very next day, for their consecration was the *filling of their hands*. Now:

1. Moses raises their expectations of a glorious appearance of God to them on that very day (v. 4): *"Today the Lord will appear to you* who are priests." We are not now to expect such appearances; we Christians walk more by faith, and less by sight, than they did. But we may be sure that God draws near to those who draw near to him, and that the offerings of faith are in reality acceptable to him, even though, since the sacrifices are spiritual, the signs of the acceptance are likewise spiritual, as it is right that they should be.

2. Moses prepares both priests and people to receive this favor which God intended to give them. *Aaron and his sons* and the *elders of Israel* are all summoned to attend (v. 1):

2.1. Aaron is instructed to prepare his offerings: *A young calf for a sin offering* (v. 2). The Jewish writers suggest that a calf was appointed as a sin offering to remind him of his sin in making the golden calf.

2.2. Aaron must direct the people to get their sacrifices ready.

2.3. Aaron must offer his own sacrifice first, and then the people's (v. 7).

2.3.1. The high priest made atonement for himself, as one who was a sinner, but we have a High Priest who was separate from sinners and needed no atonement. When our Messiah was cut off as a sacrifice, it was not for himself, for he knew no sin.

2.3.2. He must *make an atonement for the people* (v. 7) by offering their sacrifices. He must *make atonement as the Lord commanded* (v. 7). Here is the mercy of God, that he not only allows atonement to be made, but also commands it. There can therefore be no possible doubt that the atonement which is commanded will be accepted.

Verses 8–22

Since these were the first offerings ever offered by the Levitical priesthood, according to the newly enacted law of sacrifices, the way in which they were offered is recorded in detail:

1. Aaron *slew the offering* with his own hands (v. 8), and did the work of the lesser priests. So like Moses before, Aaron now offered some of each of the several sorts of sacrifice that had been instituted.

2. He offered these *besides the burnt sacrifice of the morning*, which was offered first every day (v. 17). When Aaron had done everything that was to be done by him for the sacrifices, he *lifted up his hand towards the people, and blessed them* (v. 22). Aaron *lifted up his hands* to bless them, to show where he wanted and expected the blessing to come from, from heaven, which is God's throne. Aaron could only long for a blessing; it is God's right to give it. Aaron, when he blessed, came down; Christ, when he blessed, went up.

Verses 23–24

We are not told what Moses and Aaron went into the tabernacle, the Tent of Meeting, to do (v. 23). Some of the Jewish writers say that they went in to pray for the appearance of the divine glory. But when they came out, they both joined in blessing the people, who stood expecting the promised appearance of divine glory, and it was now — when Moses and Aaron agreed in their praying — that they received what they waited for. God's revelations of himself, of his glory and grace, are normally given in answer to prayer. The glory of God appeared, not while the sacrificers were making the offerings, but when the priests prayed, which shows that the prayers and praises of God's spiritual priests are more pleasing to God than all burnt offerings and sacrifices.

1. *The glory of the Lord appeared unto all the people* (v. 23). What it looked like precisely we are not told; no doubt it was such that it showed its own evidence. Those who are in God's house with an eye of faith may *behold the beauty of the Lord* (Ps 27:4).

2. *There came a fire out from before the Lord, and consumed the sacrifice* (v. 24). Whether this fire came from heaven, from the Most Holy Place, or from that visible appearance of the glory of God which all the people saw, it was a clear sign of God's acceptance of their service.

2.1. This fire consumed (or, as the word is, "ate up") the present sacrifice. It showed:

- That God turned away his wrath from them. Its being directed on the sacrifice and consuming that showed God's acceptance of that as an atonement for the sinner.
- God's entering into covenant and communion with them.

2.2. This fire took possession, as it were, of the altar. This was also a type of good things to come. The Spirit descended on the apostles in *fire* (Ac 2:3). The descent of this holy fire into our souls is to kindle godly and devout affections toward God and a holy zeal that burns up our sinful nature with its sinful desires. These are a sure sign of God's gracious acceptance of our lives.

3. We are here told how the people were moved by this revelation of God's glory and grace. They received it:

3.1. With the greatest joy: *They shouted* (v. 24), stirring themselves up to a state of holy jubilation.

3.2. With the humblest reverence: *They fell on their faces* (v. 24), submissively adoring the majesty of the God who condescended to reveal himself to them in this way.

CHAPTER 10

The story of this chapter is as sad an interruption to the institutions of the Levitical law as that of the golden calf was to the account of the setting up of the tabernacle. Here is: 1. The sin and death of Nadab and Abihu, the sons of Aaron (vv. 1–2). 2. The pacifying of Aaron under this severe trial (v. 3); orders given and observed about the funeral and mourning (vv. 4–7). 3. A command to the priests not to drink wine when they went in to minister (vv. 8–11). 4. The care Moses took that they should go on with their work, despite the disturbance produced by this event (vv. 12–20).

Verses 1–2

Here is:

1. The great sin that Nadab and Abihu were guilty of. But what was their sin? All the account here given of it is that they *offered strange fire before the Lord, which he commanded them not* (v. 1), and the same is in Nu 3:4.

1.1. Nadab and Abihu were so proud of the honor that they had just been promoted to and so ambitious to get on immediately with the highest and most honorable part of their work, that though the service of this day was exceptional and done under special direction of Moses, they took their censers, and without receiving an order, they wanted to enter the tabernacle (the Tent of Meeting) and burn incense. Their *offering strange fire* is the same as *offering strange incense*, which is expressly forbidden (Ex 30:9).

1.2. They presumed to burn incense of their own that had not been authorized, and it is no wonder that they made a further mistake, and instead of taking the fire from the altar, which had just been kindled by the Lord and which from that time on must be used in offering both sacrifice and incense (Rev 8:5), they took ordinary fire, probably from the fire with which the flesh of the peace offerings (fellowship offerings) was cooked, and they made use of this in burning incense. Since it was not holy fire, it is called *strange fire* (v. 1).

1.3. Incense was always to be burned by only one priest at a time, but here they both wanted to go together to burn it.

1.4. They did it rashly and impetuously. They "snatched" their censers, without due reverence.

1.5. It is possible that they were drunk when they did it, because of the law which was given on this occasion (v. 8). They had been feasting on the peace offerings and the drink offerings, and so their heads may have been light.

1.6. No doubt it was done presumptuously.

2. The dreadful punishment of this sin: *There went out fire from the Lord, and devoured them* (v. 2). But why did the Lord deal so severely with them? Were they not the sons of Aaron, the saint of the Lord, nephews of Moses, the great favorite of heaven?

2.1. The sin was a grave sin. It was carried out in clear contempt of Moses and the divine law given by Moses. Up to that time it had been explicitly noticed concerning everything that had been done that they did it *as the Lord commanded Moses*. This is in contrast to what is said here, that they did that *which the Lord commanded them not*, and acted of their own volition. God was now teaching his people obedience, and in everything to observe his rules, as is right for servants. And so for priests to disobey and break the rules was so offensive that it could not go unpunished.

2.2. Their punishment was a necessary act of justice, now that the ceremonial institutions had been established. And no doubt the example that was made of them in this justice prevented many later acts of disobedience. In the same way, Ananias and Sapphira were also punished, when they presumed to lie to the Holy Spirit, who had then so recently fallen as tongues of fire.

Verses 3–7

We may well think that when Nadab and Abihu were struck down and killed, all around them were struck with horror. Moses remained composed, though it touched him at a very tender spot. He remained self-possessed.

1. He tried to pacify Aaron in this sad matter (v. 3). Notice:

1.1. What it was that Moses suggested to his poor brother on this occasion: *This is it that the Lord spoke.* What was it that God spoke? It was this—and may the Lord by his grace speak it to all our hearts! *I will be sanctified in those that come nigh me*, whoever they are, and *before all the people I will be glorified* (v. 3). What was there in this to pacify Aaron? Two things:

1.1.1. It must silence him to know that his sons deserved death, for they were cut off from their people because they did not sanctify and glorify God.

1.1.2. It must satisfy him to know that the death of his sons resulted in God being honored, and his impartial justice, for it would be praised and adored forever.

1.2. What good effects this had on him: *Aaron held his peace* (v. 3), that is, he patiently submitted to the holy will of God in this sad providence. When God corrects us or our families for sin, it is our duty to be silent in the correction, and not to quarrel with God, not to call on him to explain his justice or accuse him of acting foolishly, but to rest in all that God does—we should not only bear, but also accept, the punishment for our sin. The most effective ways of soothing a suffering spirit are those that are taken from God's glory. Far be it from him that he should honor his sons more than God, or wish that God's name, house, or Law would be exposed to contempt or disgrace just to preserve his family's reputation.

2. He gives orders about the dead bodies. It was not right that they should be left to lie where they fell. But Moses takes care of this matter, so that even though they died by the hand of justice in the act of sin, they would still be decently buried—and this was seen to (vv. 4–5). Two cousins of Nadab and Abihu carried them out of the camp to be buried. It was a terrible sight that moved the people. The names of Nadab and Abihu had become very great and honorable among them. Nadab and Abihu, who had been on the mountain with God (Ex 24:1), were looked on as the great favorites of heaven and the hopes of their people. Now suddenly, when the news of the event had scarcely

reached their ears, to see them both carried out dead, with the visible marks of divine vengeance on them, as sacrifices to the justice of God, they could only cry out, *Who is able to stand before this holy Lord God?* (1Sa 6:20).

3. He gives directions about the mourning:

3.1. The priests must not mourn. This was forbidden both to Aaron and his sons, because:

3.1.1. They were now actually waiting to do a great work, which must by no means stop (Ne 6:3), and it was very much to the honor of God that their waiting on him should be given priority over the respects that they should pay to their relatives, and that all services should give way to those of their ministry.

3.1.2. Their brothers were cut off because of their sin directly by the hand of God. They must not mourn for them so that they would not seem to encourage the sin, or challenge the justice of God in the punishment. It was very hard, no doubt, for Aaron and his sons to restrain themselves from excessive grief on such an exceptional occasion, but reason and grace controlled their passions and they bore the affliction with obedient patience. Happy are those who place themselves under God's government and have their passions ruled by their own self-control.

3.2. The people must mourn: *Let the whole house of Israel bewail the burning which the Lord has kindled* (v. 6). The congregation must lament, not only the loss of their priests, but also and especially the displeasure of God which came about.

Verses 8–11

Because Aaron had observed very closely what God had said to him through Moses, God now does him the honor of speaking to him directly (v. 8): *The Lord spoke unto Aaron. Do not drink wine, nor strong drink, when you go into the tabernacle*; they would do this at their peril, *lest you die* (v. 9). Probably they had seen the ill effects of it in Nadab and Abihu, and so must note the warning of what happened to them. Notice here:

1. The prohibition itself, *Do not drink wine nor strong drink*. At other times they were allowed it—it was not expected that every priest should be a Nazarite—but during the time of their ministry it was forbidden them. This was one of the laws in Ezekiel's temple (Eze 44:21), and so it is also required of Gospel ministers that they be not given to wine (1Ti 3:3).

2. The penalty attached to the prohibition, *Lest you die. Lest you die* when you drink, and so that day come upon you unawares (Lk 21:34). Or, "So that you will not be liable to be cut off by the hand of God."

3. The reasons given for this prohibition. They must be sober and clearminded, or they could not carry out their responsibilities properly; they would be in danger of *erring through wine* (Isa 28:7). They must be sure to keep sober:

3.1. That in their ministry they might be able to distinguish between what was holy and what was common and might never confuse them (v. 10).

3.2. That they might be able to teach the people (v. 11), for that was part of the priests' work (Dt 33:10). Those who are addicted to drink are most unsuitable to teach God's laws to people, both because those who live according to the sinful nature cannot know the things of the Spirit, and also because such teachers pull down with one hand what they build up with the other.

Verses 12–20

Moses here directs Aaron to continue his service after this interruption. Suffering should stir us to do our duty rather than take us away from it. Notice (v. 12), God spoke to Aaron and to his *sons that were left*. The notice taken of those who survived shows:

• That Aaron should be encouraged by the loss of two of his sons to the extent that God had graciously spared the other two.

• That God's sparing them should encourage them to proceed in his service, and not to depart from it quickly. Here were four priests ordained together: two were taken away and two were left. The two who were left should therefore try to fill the places of those who were gone, by being doubly careful and diligent in the services of the priesthood.

1. Moses repeats the directions he had formerly given them about eating their share of the sacrifices (vv. 12–15).

2. He asks about one deviation from the appointed rules, which seems to have happened on this occasion, which was this—that a goat was to be sacrificed as *a sin offering for the people* (9:15).

2.1. The law of sin offerings stated that if the blood was brought into the Holy Place, as that of the sin offerings for the priest was, then the flesh was to be burned outside the camp. Now the blood of this goat was not brought into the Holy Place but, it would seem, was burned outside the camp.

2.2. Moses blamed the fault on Eleazar and Ithamar (v. 16), but it is probable that what they did was at Aaron's direction, and so he apologized for it. He makes the event of the death of his two oldest sons and the suffering that he was going through his excuse (v. 19). *Such things have befallen me*, such sad things which were very dear and close to his heart and made it very heavy. He was a high priest *taken from among men* (Heb 5:1) and could not put off his natural feelings when he put on his holy clothes. He held his peace (v. 3), but his sorrow was stirred. He makes this an excuse for his varying from the appointed rule about the sin offering. He could not have eaten it except in his mourning and with a sorrowful spirit, and would this have been accepted? Moses accepted this excuse: *He was content* (v. 20). Perhaps he thought it justified what they had done. God had provided that what could not be eaten might be burned.

CHAPTER 11

The ceremonial law is described by the writer to the Hebrews (Heb 9:9–10) as consisting, not only of "gifts and sacrifices," but also "meats, and drinks, and divers washings," that is, food, drink, and various ceremonial washings from uncleanness, the laws concerning which begin with this chapter. These put a difference between some sorts of flesh or meat and others, allowing some to be eaten as clean and forbidding others as unclean. But there is: 1. Another kind of flesh of animals, concerning which the Law directs here (vv. 1–8). 2. Another law for fish (vv. 9–12); another for birds (vv. 13–19). 3. Another for flying insects (vv. 20–28) and animals that move about on the ground (vv. 29–43). The Law concludes with the general rule of holiness and reasons for it (vv. 44–47).

Verses 1–8

Now that Aaron was ordained as high priest over the house of God, God spoke to him with Moses, and appointed them both as joint commissioners to deliver his will to the people.

1. The priests were specially required to make a difference between what was ceremonially clean and unclean and also teach the people to do so. They might eat flesh, but not all kinds of flesh. They must consider some as unclean and forbidden to them, others as clean and allowed them.

2. But what reason can be given for this law? Most of the meats forbidden as unclean are such as were really unwholesome and not fit to be eaten; and those that we think wholesome enough and use accordingly, such as rabbits, hares, and pigs, might perhaps have been harmful in those countries and to their bodies. The Lord is all for the body, and it is not only foolish, but also a sin against God to harm our health for the sake of pleasing our appetites. It would seem that before this there had been some differences between the Hebrews and other nations in their food, which had been kept up by tradition, for the Egyptians and the Hebrews would not eat together (Ge 43:32).

3. Scholars also notice that most of the creatures which according to this law were to be detested as unclean were those that were highly revered by followers of other religions, not so much for food as for divination and sacrifice to their gods. Those that are mentioned here as unclean and detestable are therefore those which they would not be tempted in any way to eat, so that they might continue to detest for religious reasons what the Gentiles valued for superstitious reasons. The pig was with the later Gentiles holy to Venus, the owl to Minerva, the eagle to Jupiter, the dog to Hecate, etc., and all these are here considered unclean.

4. As to the animals, there is a general rule laid down, that those which both had a split hoof and chewed the cud were clean, and only those: these are particularly mentioned when this law is repeated in Dt 14:4–5, where it appears that the Israelites had enough variety allowed them and did not need to complain of the restrictions they were under. Those animals that did not both *chew the cud and divide the hoof* (have a split hoof) (v. 4) were unclean, by which rule the flesh of pigs, hares, and rabbits was prohibited to them, though more commonly used among us. Of all the creatures here forbidden as unclean, none has been more feared and detested by devout Jews than the flesh of pigs. Many were put to death by Antiochus because they would not eat it.

5. Some suggest that the prohibition of these animals as unclean was intended as a warning to the people against the bad qualities of these creatures. We must not be filthy or wallow in the mud like pigs, or be as timid and faint-hearted as hares, or live in the earth as rabbits do. Let us not as honored human beings make ourselves like these animals that perish.

Verses 9–19

Here is:

1. A general rule concerning which fish were clean and which not. They were allowed to eat every fish that had fins and scales, and only those odd kinds of marine creatures that do not were forbidden (vv. 9–10). Concerning the prohibited fish it is said, *They shall be an abomination to you* (vv. 10–12), that is, "You shall count them as unclean, and not only not eat them, but also keep your distance from them." In the same way, God's spiritual Israel, as they are honored above others by the Gospel covenant of adoption and friendship, must be disciplined more than others by the Gospel commands of self-denial and taking up the cross.

2. No general rule concerning birds. However, a list is given of those birds that they must not eat because they are unclean, which implies that all others are allowed. Of the birds here forbidden:

2.1. Some are birds of prey, such as the eagle and vulture. God wants his people to detest everything that is cruel and not live by blood or pillaging. Doves that are preyed on were proper food for people to eat and to be offered to God, but kites and hawks that prey on them must be looked on as detestable to God and human beings.

2.2. Others of them are solitary birds, such as the owl (Ps 102:6), the cormorant, and ravens (Isa 34:11), that live in dark and desolate places, for God's Israel should not be a sad people or be constantly alone.

2.3. Others of them, such as the stork, feed on what is impure, e.g., on worms, and we must not only keep away from all impurity ourselves but also from fellowship with those who continue in it.

2.4. Further birds were used by the Egyptians and other Gentiles in their divinations. Some birds were reckoned to bring good luck, others bad luck, and their soothsayers closely watched the flights of these birds, all of which therefore must be detestable to God's people, who must not follow the ways of other religions.

Verses 20–43

Here is the law:

1. Concerning flying or swarming insects, such as flies, wasps, and bees. They were not to eat these (v. 20); in fact, they are not fit to be eaten. They are here allowed to eat locusts (vv. 21–22), and there were several sorts of locust which in those countries were eaten as good food: John the Baptist lived on them in the desert.

2. Concerning creatures that move about on the ground: these were all forbidden (vv. 29–30 and again vv. 41–42). Dust is the food of creatures that move about on the ground, and so they are not fit for human consumption.

3. Concerning the dead carcasses of all these unclean animals:

3.1. Everyone who touched them was to be unclean until the evening (vv. 24–28). They contracted a ceremonial uncleanness, which forbade them for a time from coming into the tabernacle, eating any of the holy things, or even dealing with their neighbors. But the uncleanness continued only till the evening. And we must learn, by daily renewing our repentance every night for the sins of the day, to cleanse ourselves from the defilement of our sins, that we may not go to sleep in our uncleanness.

3.2. Even the article, object, or other things they fell on were made unclean until the evening (v. 32), and if they were earthen vessels (clay pots), they must be broken (v. 33). We ought to be as conscientious in keeping our precious souls from the defilement of sin, and as quick to cleanse them when they are defiled, as the Israelites were to keep and cleanse their bodies and household goods from ceremonial uncleanness.

Verses 44–47

Here is:

1. The explanation of this law or a key to allow us to understand its meaning. It was not intended merely as a menu, or as a list of directions to follow when we go on a diet, but God wanted to teach them to sanctify themselves and to be holy (v. 44). These *rudiments* (basic principles) *of the world* (Col 2:8) were their *tutors and governors* (Gal 4:2–3), to bring them to a revival of our first state in

Adam and to the pledge of our best state in Christ, that is, holiness, without which no one shall see the Lord. It is the true and great intention of all the ordinances that by them we may sanctify ourselves and learn to be holy. Even this law concerning their food, which seemed to stoop so very low, aimed so high. *Without holiness no man shall see the Lord* (Heb 12:14). If it was so offensive for a person to eat the meat of pigs, much more so must it be to offer the blood of pigs at God's altar; see Pr 15:8.

2. The reasons for this law:

2.1. *I am the Lord your God* (v. 44). "Therefore you are bound to do this in perfect obedience."

2.2. *I am holy* (v. 44 and again v. 45). If God is holy, we must be also, or otherwise we cannot expect him to accept us. All these ceremonial restraints were intended to teach us that we must not *fashion ourselves according to our former lusts in our ignorance* (1Pe 1:14).

2.3. *I am the Lord that bringeth you out of the land of Egypt* (v. 45). He who had done more for them than for any other people might justly expect more from them.

3. A summary of this law: *This is the law of the beasts, and of the fowl*, etc. (vv. 46–47). This law was to be a statute to them forever, that is, as long as that era lasted; but under the Gospel we find it explicitly repealed by a voice from heaven to Peter (Ac 10:15), as it had before been virtually set aside by the death of Christ, with the other ordinances that *perished in the using*. And now we are sure that *meat commends us not to God* (1Co 8:8), and that *nothing is unclean of itself* (Ro 14:14), nor is it what goes into our mouth that makes us unclean, but what comes out from our heart (Mt 15:11). Let us therefore:

• Give thanks to God that we are not bound by these chains of slavery, but everything created by God is allowed to us as good.

• Stand fast in the liberty wherewith Christ has made us free (Gal 5:1).

• Be strictly and conscientiously self-restrained in the use of the good things created by God and allowed to us. Nature is content with little, grace with less, but sinful desires with nothing.

CHAPTER 12

After the laws concerning clean and unclean food come the laws concerning clean and unclean people: 1. The law concerning the ceremonial uncleanness of women in childbirth (vv. 1–5). 2. The law concerning their purification from that uncleanness (vv. 6–8).

Verses 1–5

The Law here pronounces women in childbirth as ceremonially unclean. The Jews say, "The law extended even to a premature delivery, if the child was so formed that the sex could be identified."

1. There was some time of strict separation immediately after the birth. During these days, the mother was separated from her husband and friends, and those who had to be with her were ceremonially unclean, which was one reason why the males were not circumcised till the eighth day, because they participated in the mother's uncleanness during the days of her separation.

2. There was also a longer time appointed for her purification. During this time she was only separated from the sanctuary and forbidden to eat the Passover or peace offerings (fellowship offerings), or if she was a priest's wife, to eat anything that was holy to the Lord. If sin had

not entered, nothing but purity and honor would have accompanied all that came from that great blessing, *Be fruitful and multiply* (Ge 1:28). The exclusion of the woman for so many days from the sanctuary and from joining in holy things showed that our original corruption would have excluded us forever from the enjoyment of God and his favors if he had not graciously provided a way for us to be purified.

Verses 6–8

When the time came for the woman who had given birth to return to the sanctuary, she must bring her offerings (v. 6):

1. A *burnt offering*: a lamb if she was able; if poor, a pigeon. She was to offer this in thankfulness to God for his mercy to her, in bringing her safely through the pain and dangers of childbirth, and hoping and wanting to see God's further favor both to her and to the child. When a child is born, there is joy and hope, and so it was right to bring this offering. But besides this, she must offer:

2. A *sin offering*, which must be the same for poor and rich, a turtledove (dove) or a young pigeon, for whatever difference there may be between rich and poor in the sacrifices of acknowledgment, that of atonement is the same for both. This sin offering was intended either:

2.1. To complete her purification from that ceremonial uncleanness, which though it was not sinful in itself, was a type of moral corruption, or:

2.2. To make atonement for what was really sin, either an excessive desire for the blessing of children or dissatisfaction or impatience in the pain of childbirth. According to this law, we find that the mother of our blessed Lord, though he was not conceived in sin like others, still *accomplished the days of purification* (Lk 2:22) and then presented her son to the Lord, being a firstborn, and brought her own offering, *a pair of turtledoves* (Lk 2:22–24). Christ's parents were so poor that they were not able to bring a lamb as a burnt offering, and so *when the fulness of the time was come*, Christ was *made under the law, to redeem those that were under it* (Gal 4:4–5).

CHAPTER 13

The next ceremonial uncleanness is that of infectious skin diseases, concerning which the Law went into great detail. [Ed. note: The KJV translates the Hebrew word tsara'at *as "leprosy," although this word referred to various skin conditions, not necessarily leprosy.] In this chapter we have the regulations by which the priest must judge whether a person had an infectious skin disease, according to the symptoms that appeared; in the next, the regulations for the cleansing of a person who had contracted such a disease. Scarcely any one thing in all the Levitical law has so much space devoted to it as this. Regulations given here instruct the priest how to judge a symptom: 1. If it was a swelling, a scab (rash), or a bright white spot (vv. 1–17). 2. If it was a boil (vv. 18–23); if it was a burn (vv. 24–28); and if it was on the head or in the beard (vv. 29–37). 3. If it was a bright white spot (vv. 38–39); if it was on a bald head (vv. 40–44). Direction is given how a person with such a disease must be dealt with (vv. 45–46). 4. Regulations are given concerning leprosy (mildew) in garments (vv. 47–59).*

Verses 1–17

1. Concerning infectious skin diseases, we may notice in general that they were uncleanness rather than diseases;

or at least this is how the Law considered them, and so it employed priests rather than doctors to deal with them.

1.1. Christ is said to cleanse those who suffered from such diseases, not to cure them. We do not read of any who died of such diseases, but the diseases buried them alive, rendering them unfit to associate with others except those who were defiled like themselves.

1.2. It is said to have begun first in Egypt, from where it spread to Syria. The Jews continued with the idolatrous customs they had learned in Egypt, and so God justly caused this infectious skin disease with some other diseases of Egypt to go with them. We also read of Naaman the Syrian, who suffered from an infectious skin disease (2Ki 5:1).

1.3. There were other physical eruptions on the body which were like infectious skin diseases, but were not infectious; they could cause a great deal of soreness and were repulsive but did not make the person ceremonially unclean. The judgment of them was referred to the priests. Those who suffered from infectious skin diseases were looked on as stigmatized by the justice of God, and so it was left to his servants the priests, who were thought to know best in such matters, to declare which of those who were suffering in this way were unclean and which were not.

1.4. The diseases symbolized the moral defilement of the human mind by sin, which is the disease of the soul and sullies the conscience, and from which only Christ can cleanse us. The power of his grace infinitely transcends that of the legal priesthood, in that the priest could only declare a person ceremonially unclean—for through the law comes the knowledge of sin—but Christ can cure those who are unclean: he can take away sin. *Lord, if thou wilt, thou canst make me clean*: this was more than the priests could do (Mt 8:2). It is very important, but also very difficult, to judge our own spiritual state. We all have reason to think that we are guilty: we are conscious of sores and spots in ourselves, but the most important question is whether we are clean or unclean.

2. Several principles are here laid down as tests for the priests:

2.1. If the sore was only *skin deep*, it was to be hoped it was not an infectious skin disease (v. 4). But if it was *deeper than the skin*, the person must be declared unclean (v. 3). The weaknesses that exist alongside grace do not sink deep into the soul, but *the mind* still *serves the law of God*, and the *inward man delights in it* (Ro 7:22, 25). But if the matter is really worse than it shows, and the infection is deep, then the case is dangerous.

2.2. If the sore *be at a stay* and does not *spread*, the priest may declare that person clean (vv. 5–6). But if it *spread much abroad* and continues to do so after several examinations, the case is bad (vv. 7–8). If people do not grow worse, but an end is put to the course of their sins and the error of their ways is restrained, it is to be hoped they will become better. But if sin gains ground and they get worse each day, they are going downhill.

2.3. If there was prominent raw flesh in the swelling, the priest need not wait any longer; it was certainly a chronic skin disease (vv. 10–11). This shows that there are no more certain indicators of the bad spiritual state of the human heart than its rising up in self-conceit, confidence in the flesh, and resistance to the rebukes of the word and the striving of the Spirit.

2.4. If the eruption of the skin, whatever it was, *covered all the skin* from head to foot, that person could be declared clean (vv. 12–13), for it was proof that the vital organs were sound and strong, and nature puts itself right in this, rejecting what was oppressive, and harms the surface of the body. The breaking out of blisters in chicken pox is like coming out with our sins when we freely confess them, not hiding them. On the other hand, those who cover up their sins are in the greatest possible danger. Some take this to mean that there is more hope for the worldly than for hypocrites. The tax collectors and prostitutes went into the kingdom of heaven before the teachers of the Law and the Pharisees. In one respect, the sudden outbreaks of passion, though bad enough, are not as dangerous as hatred that is hidden. Others take this to show that if we judge ourselves, we will not be judged. If we see and acknowledge that there is *no soundness in our flesh* (Ps 38:3), because of our sin, we will *find grace in the eyes of the Lord* (Ge 6:8).

2.5. The priest must take time in coming to a decision and not give it rashly.

Verses 18–37

The priest is here instructed what decision to come to if there was any appearance of an infectious skin disease:

1. In an old boil that had healed (vv. 18–23). When old sores, which seemed to be healed, break out again, it is to be feared that the disease is infectious and the person is unclean. Such is the danger of those who, having escaped the world's defilements, are again *entangled therein and overcome* (2Pe 2:20).

2. In a burn by accident, for this may be meant (vv. 24–28). Times when we are beside ourselves in red-hot anger are occasions for the outbreak of sins that show us to be unclean.

Verses 38–46

We have here:

1. Provisos that neither a *freckled skin* (rash) nor a *bald head* should be mistaken for an infectious skin disease (vv. 38–41). Every deformity must not immediately be considered to be a ceremonial defilement.

2. A declaration made on the person if the infectious skin disease appeared at any time on *a bald head*. *The plague is in his head, he is utterly unclean* (v. 44). If the disease of sin has overtaken our minds, if our judgment is defiled, and wrong principles which support wrong practices are embraced, it is an *utter uncleanness*. Soundness in the faith keeps diseases from our minds.

3. Directions as to what must be done with the person who has an infectious skin disease. When the priest, on mature deliberation, had formally declared the person unclean:

3.1. The person must put themselves into the posture of a mourner and cry out, *Unclean, unclean* (v. 45). Such people must therefore:

3.1.1. Humble themselves under the mighty hand of God, not insisting on their cleanness when the priest had declared them unclean. Such a person must show this by *rending his clothes, uncovering* his head, and *covering his upper lip* (v. 45): all signs of shamefulness, disgrace, and humiliation which should fill the hearts of those who repent, who judge themselves truly.

3.1.2. Warn others to beware of coming near them. Wherever those who suffered from infectious diseases went, they must cry out to those they saw at a distance, "I am *unclean, unclean*, do not touch me." By touching someone who suffered from an infectious skin disease, a person contracted ceremonial uncleanness. And this was all that the Law could do. The Law only shows us our disease; the Gospel shows us our help in Christ.

3.2. The person must be shut out of the camp, and afterward when they came to Canaan, out of the city, town, or village where they lived, and *dwell alone* (v. 46), associating with none but others who were unclean because they suffered infectious skin diseases like themselves.

Verses 47–59

This is the law concerning *the plague of leprosy in a garment* (mildew), whether linen or woolen. Mildew in clothing, with signs that could be discerned, is something that seems inexplicable to us. The process was much the same as for a person who was suspected of having an infectious skin disease. The garment that was thought to be tainted was not to be burned immediately but must be *shown to the priest* (v. 19). If on closer examination there was found to be an area that had been affected by mildew, it must be *burnt*. If the cause of the suspected mildew was gone, the garment must be washed, and then could be used again (v. 58).

CHAPTER 14

Chapter 13 described how the priests determine whether a person has an infectious skin disease, whether the person is ceremonially unclean or clean. The remedy here relates only to the ceremonial part of the person's disease, but the authority Christ gave to his ministers was to heal those suffering from infectious skin diseases and so cleanse them. We have here: 1. The formal declaration of the person as being clean (vv. 1–9). 2. The sacrifices which that person was to offer to God eight days later (vv. 10–20). 3. The sacrifices which that person was to offer to God eight days later, if they were poor (vv. 21–32). 4. How to deal with a house in which signs of leprosy (mildew) appeared (vv. 33–53). 5. The conclusion and summary (vv. 54–57).

Verses 1–9

1. It is supposed that the infectious skin disease was not incurable. Uzziah's continued to the day of his death, but Miriam's lasted only seven days: we may suppose that it often wore off in the process of time. [Ed. note: The KJV translates the Hebrew word *tsara'at* as "leprosy," although this word refers to various skin conditions, not necessarily leprosy.]

2. The determination of the cure, as well as that of the disease, was referred to the priest.

2.1. The priest must go outside the camp to examine the person suffering from the infectious skin disease, to see whether they have been healed (v. 3). It was out of mercy to those who were unclean from infectious skin diseases that the priests had special orders to look after them. When the person who was unclean because of an infectious skin disease was excluded from the community and could not go to the priests, it was good that the priests might come to them. *Is any sick? Let him send for the elders,* the ministers (Jas 5:14).

2.2. If we apply this to the spiritual uncleanness of sin, it shows that when we no longer associate with those who lead disobedient lives, so that they become ashamed, we must not consider them to be enemies, but warn them as brothers and sisters (2Th 3:15). And when God by his grace has brought to repentance those who were excluded from fellowship because of some immoral behavior, they ought to be received again with tenderness, joy, and warm affection. In this way, Paul writes concerning the excommunicated Corinthian, that when he had given evidence of

his repentance they should forgive him, comfort him, and *confirm their love towards him* (2Co 2:7–8).

3. If it was found that the person has been healed of the infectious skin disease, the priest must declare it with a special ceremony. The person or their friends were to get ready two birds caught for this purpose—any sort of wild birds that were clean—and cedar wood, scarlet yarn, and hyssop.

3.1. Some blood and water were to be mixed, with which the person must be sprinkled. One of the birds was to be killed over an earthen (clay) pot of fresh water, so that the blood of the bird might discolor the water.

3.2. The living bird, with a little scarlet wool and a bunch of hyssop, must be attached to a cedar stick, dipped in the water and blood, and then used to sprinkled the blood and water on the person who was to be cleansed (vv. 6–7). The cedar wood represented the restoring of the person to strength and sound health, for that kind of wood does not rot. The scarlet wool represented the person's recovery of a ruddy complexion, for the infectious skin disease made the person as white as snow. The hyssop represented the removing of the unpleasant smell which commonly accompanied the disease. The cedar is a grand tree and hyssop a lowly plant, and here both are used together in this service (see 1Ki 4:33). The person must be sprinkled *seven times,* to represent a complete purification, in allusion to which David prays, *Wash me thoroughly* (Ps 51:2). Naaman was directed to wash *seven times* (2Ki 5:10).

3.3. The living bird was then to be released into the open fields, to show that because the person had been cleansed, they were now no longer restrained or confined but were at liberty to go where they pleased. The flying of the bird toward heaven was a sign that the person should from that time on set their heart on heavenly things and not spend the new life which God had restored to them pursuing merely earthly things. Those whose souls before *bowed down to the dust* (Ps 44:25) in grief and fear now fly high to the open skies of heaven and soar upward on the wings of faith and hope, holy love and joy.

3.4. The priest must on this occasion declare the person to be clean. Those are clean indeed whom Christ declares so, and they do not need to pay any attention to what others may say about them. But though Christ was the *end of the law for righteousness* (Ro 10:4), he was still physically *made under the law* (Gal 4:4)—which had not yet been repealed—and so he ordered the man with the skin disease whom he had miraculously healed to go and *show himself to the priest* and *offer for their cleansing according to the law* (Mt 8:4; Lk 17:14).

3.5. When the person had been declared clean, he must wash his body and clothes, and *shave off all his hair* (v. 8), must wait seven days outside the camp, and on the seventh day must do it all again (v. 9). After the priest had declared them clean from the disease, they must take time to make themselves as clean as they possibly could from all remnants of it and from all other defilements.

Verses 10–20

Notice:

1. To complete the person's purification, on the eighth day after the formal ceremony outside the camp, they were to come to *the door of the tabernacle,* to the entrance to the Tent of Meeting, to be *presented to the Lord* there, with an offering (v. 11). Notice here:

1.1. That the only reasonable response to the mercies of God is for us to present ourselves to him (Ro 12:1).

1.2. When God has restored to us the liberty of taking part in religious services, after being restrained by illness, work commitments away from home, etc., we should take the first opportunity of showing our respect to God and our desire to worship him with his people.

2. The cleansed person was to bring three lambs, with a meat offering (a grain offering) and a log of oil, which was about two-thirds of a pint (about 0.3 liter). Now:

2.1. Most of the ceremony that was special to this case was like the ceremony in the trespass offering (guilt offering), the lamb for which was offered first (v. 12). The Jews say that the person with an infectious skin disease stood outside the entrance of the tabernacle and the priest inside, and so the ceremony was performed through the entrance, showing that now the person was allowed to come into the courts of the Lord's house again with other Israelites and was as welcome as ever, though perhaps the name might stick with them throughout their life—as we read of one who probably was cleansed by our Lord Jesus, but who afterward is called *Simon the leper* (Mt 26:6). Cleansed people, who formerly were unclean because of their infectious skin disease, are as welcome to receive the blood and the oil as ordained priests are.

2.2. Besides this there must be a sacrifice of a sin offering and a burnt offering, a lamb for each (vv. 19–20). By each of these offerings, it is said, the priests will *make atonement for him*:

2.2.1. The person's moral guilt will be removed.

2.2.2. The person's ceremonial uncleanness will be removed, which had kept them from sharing in the holy things. And this is called *making atonement for him*, because our restoration to the privileges of God's children, which the ceremonies are types of, is only because of Christ's atoning sacrifice. The burnt offering, besides the atonement that was made by it, was a thankful acknowledgment of God's mercy, and the more direct the hand of God was in the illness and in its cure, the more reason the person had to give glory to God, and so, as our Savior says (Mk 1:44), to *offer for his cleansing* all *those things which Moses commanded for a testimony unto them*.

Verses 21–32

We have here the gracious provision which the Law made for the cleansing of *poor lepers*. If they were not able to bring three lambs, and three-tenths of an ephah of flour, they must bring one lamb, and one-tenth of an ephah of flour, and instead of the other two lambs, two turtledoves (doves) or two young pigeons (vv. 21–22). Here we notice:

1. That the poverty of the person concerned would not excuse them if they brought no offering at all. Let no one think that because they are poor God requires no service from them, since he has considered them and still demands what it is in the power of the poorest to give. "*My son, give me thine heart*" (Pr 23:26), and with that the *calves of our lips* (Hos 14:2) will be accepted instead of the *calves of the stall*" (Mal 4:2).

2. That God expected an offering from the poor only according to their ability. If there is first a willing mind and an honest heart, two pigeons—when they are the most a person is able to bring—are as acceptable to God as two lambs.

Verses 33–53

This is the law concerning *leprosy* (mildew) in a house. Mildew in a house may seem as inexplicable as mildew in clothing, but if we do not understand its natural causes, we may consider it to come from the power of the God of nature. Now:

1. It is supposed that even in Canaan itself, the Land of Promise, their houses might be infected with mildew.

2. It is taken for granted that the owner of the house will let the priest know about it, as soon as the owner sees there is reason to suspect there is mildew there. Where sin reigns in a house, it is like a cancer there, as it is in a heart. Leaders of families should be aware and afraid of the first appearance of blatant sin in their families and remove the sin, whatever it is, far away from their tent (Job 22:23).

3. If the priest, on examination, found that the mildew had gotten into the house, the priest must try to heal it, by taking out the part of the building that was contaminated (vv. 40–41). This was like cutting off a gangrened leg, in order to preserve the rest of the body.

4. If the mildew remained in the house, the whole house must be pulled down, and all the materials carried to the unclean place (vv. 44–45).

5. If removing the infected stones healed the house, and the mildew did not spread any further, then the house must be cleansed. It must not only be aired, that it might be hygienic; it must also be purified from the ceremonial uncleanness, so that it might be fit for an Israelite to live in. The ceremony of its cleansing was much the same as that of cleansing an unclean person with an infectious skin disease (vv. 49–53). And we should take the same care to reform whatever is wrong in our families, that we and our houses may serve the Lord: see Ge 35:2.

Verses 54–57

This is the conclusion of this law concerning leprosy (infectious skin diseases and mildew). We may see in this law:

1. The gracious care God took of his people Israel. When Naaman the Syrian was healed of his skin disease, he was not instructed to show himself to the priest, even though he was cured in Jordan, as the Jews that were healed by our Savior were.

2. The religious care we ought to take of ourselves, to keep our minds from being controlled by sinful attitudes and ways, which cause disease and defilement, so that we may be fit for the service of God.

CHAPTER 15

In this chapter we have laws concerning other ceremonial uncleannesses either contracted by physical disease, such as an infectious skin disease, or occurring naturally in: 1. Men (vv. 1–18). 2. Women (vv. 19–33). We need not explain these laws in intricate detail; it is enough for us to notice their general intention. We need, however, to be very careful so that sin does not have reason through the commandment to become completely sinful in us.

Verses 1–18

We have here the law concerning the ceremonial uncleanness that was contracted by male discharges, usually the effect of dissolute living. It is an evil disease that is evil deserts for sin. Now whoever had this disease on him:

1. He was himself unclean (v. 2). He must not dare come near the sanctuary.

2. He made every person and thing unclean that he touched or that touched him (vv. 4–12). This represented the defilement of sin, the danger we are in of being defiled by associating with those who are defiled.

3. When he was cured of the disease, he still could not be cleansed from the defilement without a sacrifice, for which he was to prepare by bathing in fresh water (vv. 13–15). This represented the great Gospel responsibilities of faith and repentance, and the great Gospel privileges of applying Christ's blood to our souls for our justification and applying his grace for our sanctification.

Verses 19–33

These verses deal with the ceremonial uncleanness of women because of their discharges.

1. This made the woman unclean (v. 25) and everything she touched unclean (vv. 26–27). If the woman's discharge of blood cleared up, and she found that she was perfectly free from it for seven days, she was to be cleansed by the offering of two turtledoves (doves) or two young pigeons, to make atonement for her (vv. 28–29). By these laws they were taught that they were *purified unto God a peculiar people* (Tit 2:14), the holy God's own people whom he intended to be a kingdom of priests, a holy nation They were also taught to preserve the honor of their purity, and to keep themselves from all sinful defilements. In all these laws there seems to be special consideration given to the honor of the tabernacle, which no one must approach in their uncleanness, that they *defile not my tabernacle* (v. 31). In this way, they were taught never to draw near to God except with a fearful and humble sense of their remoteness and vulnerability.

1.2. Let us bless God that we are not tied to the chains of these physical ordinances, that as nothing can destroy us, so nothing can defile us, except sin. There are those who did not dare eat the peace offerings who may now share in the Lord's Supper. Let us all see how absolutely necessary real holiness is to our future happiness, and make sure that our hearts are cleansed by faith so that we may see God.

CHAPTER 16

In this chapter we have the institution of the annual ceremony of the Day of Atonement, which contains as much of the Gospel as perhaps any of the appointed ordinances of the ceremonial law, as appears by the reference the writer to the Hebrews makes to it (Heb 9:7, etc.). The chapter concerns the sacrifice in which the whole community was involved. The whole service of the day is committed to the high priest: 1. He must never come into the Most Holy Place except on this day (vv. 1–2); he must come wearing linen garments (v. 4); he must bring a sin offering and a burnt offering for himself (v. 3). 2. He must bring his sin offering (vv. 6–11), then go into the innermost sanctuary behind the curtain with some of the blood of his sin offering, burn incense, and sprinkle the blood in front of the mercy seat (atonement cover) (vv. 12–14). 3. Two goats and a ram must be provided for the people (v. 5) and lots cast for the goats; one of them must be a sin offering for the people (vv. 7–9), and the blood of it must be sprinkled on the mercy seat (vv. 15–17), and then some of the blood of both of the sin offerings must be sprinkled on the altar (vv. 18–19). 4. The other goat is to be a scapegoat (v. 10): the sins of Israel must be confessed over it, and then it must be sent away into the desert (vv. 20–22); the person who releases the goat has become ceremonially unclean (v. 26). The burnt offerings were then to be offered, the fat of the sin offerings burned on the altar, and their flesh burned outside the camp (vv. 23–25, 27–28). 5. The people were to observe the day religiously by holy rest and holy mourning for sin; and this was to be a permanent ordinance (vv. 29–34).

Verses 1–4

Here is:

1. The date of this law concerning the Day of Atonement: it was *after the death of the two sons of Aaron* (v. 1), which we read about in chapter 10:

1.1. So that Aaron need not fear that any remaining guilt of that sin would cling to his family, he is directed as to how to make atonement for his household.

1.2. Because the priests were warned by the death of Nadab and Abihu to approach God with reverence and godly fear, directions are given here as to how they should approach God.

2. The purpose of this law. One intention was to preserve a respect for the Most Holy Place, behind the curtain, where the *Shechinah*, or divine glory, was pleased to dwell between the cherubim. Behind the curtain none must ever come except only the high priest, and he only one day in the year. But notice what a blessed change is made by the Gospel of Christ: all true Christians now have *boldness to enter into the holiest, through the veil*, every day (Heb 10:19–20); and we *come boldly* (not as Aaron must have done, with fear and trembling) to the *throne of grace*, the mercy seat (Heb 4:16). The more dealings we have with objects of faith, the more they reveal their greatness and goodness. We are now welcome to come at all times into the *holy place not made with hands* (Heb 9:24). Aaron must not come near at all times, *lest he die*; we, however, may now come near at all times so that we may live. It is only separation from God that leads to death.

3. The person to whom the work of this day was committed, and that was only the high priest: *Thus shall Aaron come into the holy place* (v. 3).

4. The clothes of the high priest for this service. He was not to be dressed up in his rich garments, he was not to put on the ephod, with its precious stones, but only the linen clothes (tunic) which he wore in common with the lesser priests (v. 4). It was right that he should wear such lowlier clothes on this day of humiliation.

Verses 5–14

The Jewish writers say that for seven days before the Day of Atonement, the high priest was to live in a chamber of the temple, that he might prepare himself. During those seven days he himself did the work of the lesser priests.

1. He was to begin the service of the day very early with the usual morning sacrifice, after he had first washed his whole body before he dressed himself, and his hands and feet again afterward. He then burned the daily incense, lit the lamps, and offered the exceptional sacrifice appointed (Nu 29:8).

2. He must then take off his rich robes, bathe himself, put on the linen clothes, and present to the Lord his own young bull, which was to be a sin offering for himself and his household (v. 6).

3. He must cast lots for the two goats, which were both together to make one sin offering for the community. One of these goats must be killed, as a sign of atonement for sin, to satisfy God's justice; the other must be sent away, as a sign of the forgiveness or removal of sin by the mercy of God. Both must be presented together to God (v. 7) before the lot was cast for them, and afterward the scapegoat by itself (v. 10). Some think that goats were chosen for the sin offering because the offensiveness of sin is represented by their unpleasant smell.

4. The next thing to be done was to kill the young bull as the sin offering for the high priest and his household (v. 11).

5. He took a censer of burning coals and a dish full of fragrant incense and then went into the Most Holy Place, set the coals down on the floor, and scattered the incense on them, so that the room was immediately filled with smoke. The Jews say that he was to "go in sideways," that he might not look directly at the ark where the divine glory was, then he must "come out backwards," out of reverence to the divine Majesty; and after a short prayer, he was to show himself to the people.

6. He then took the blood of the young bull and took that in with him the second time into the Most Holy Place, which was now filled with the smoke of the incense. With his finger he sprinkled some of the blood toward the mercy seat (atonement cover), once toward its top and then seven times toward its lower part (v. 14).

Verses 15–19

When the priest had come out from sprinkling the blood of the young bull before the mercy seat (atonement cover):

1. He must next kill the goat which was the sin offering for the people (v. 15) and go a third time into the Most Holy Place to sprinkle the blood of the goat, as he had done that of the young bull, and so he was to *make atonement for the holy place* (v. 16), so that God, being reconciled to them, might continue with them.

2. He must then do the same for the outer part of the tabernacle as he had done for the inner room. The reason is that *the tabernacle remained among them in the midst of their uncleanness* (v. 16). God wanted to show them how much their hearts needed to be purified.

3. He must then put some of the blood, both of the young bull and of the goat mixed together, on the horns of the altar that is before the Lord (vv. 18–19).

Verses 20–28

After the high priest had presented the atoning sacrifices to the Lord, by the sprinkling of their blood:

1. He is next to confess the sins of Israel, with both his hands placed on the head of the scapegoat (vv. 20–21). Whenever hands were laid on the head of any sacrifice, it was always done with confession. In the latter and, according to some, more corrupt ages of the Jewish church, a set form of confession was prepared for the high priest. By this confession, Aaron must *put the sins of Israel upon the head of the goat* (v. 21).

2. The goat was then to be sent away immediately by the hand of a person into a wilderness, an uninhabited desert. God allowed the people to understand that the sending away of the goat was the sending away of their sins, freely and fully forgiving them: *He shall bear upon him all their iniquities* (v. 22). In later times, the Jews had a custom of tying one piece of scarlet cloth to the horns of the goat and another to the gate of the temple, or to the top of the rock where the goat was released, and they concluded that if it turned white—as they say it usually did—the sins of Israel were forgiven, as it is written, *Though your sins have been as scarlet, they shall be as wool* (Isa 1:18). They add that for forty years before the destruction of Jerusalem by the Romans the scarlet cloth never changed color at all, which is a fair admission of their rejection of the reality, as well as its shadow.

3. The high priest must then take off his linen clothes in the Tent of Meeting and leave them there, according to the Jews never to be worn again by himself or any other person, for they made new clothes every year. He must then bathe himself in water, put on his normal high-priestly clothes, and then offer both his own and the people's burnt offerings (vv. 23–24). When we receive the encouragement of forgiveness, God must have all the glory for it.

4. The flesh of both of those sin offerings whose blood was taken behind the curtain was to be all burned at a distance outside the camp, as a sign both of putting away sin by true repentance and God's putting it away by full forgiveness, so that it will never again rise up in judgment against us.

5. The person who released the scapegoat into the wilderness and the people who burned the sin offering were to be looked on as ceremonially unclean and defiled by sin. They must not come into the camp till they had washed their clothes and bathed their bodies in water.

6. When all this was done, the high priest went again into the Most Holy Place to fetch his censer. He then returned to his own house with joy, because he had done his duty and had not died.

Verses 29–34

1. We have here some additional directions referring to this great ceremony:

1.1. The day appointed for it. It must be observed yearly on the *tenth day of the seventh month* (v. 29).

1.2. The duty of the people on this day:

1.2.1. They must rest from all their labors: *It shall be a sabbath of rest* (v. 31).

1.2.2. They must humble their souls. They must exercise self-denial; they must not enjoy any physical refreshments or delights, to show that they are inwardly humbled and contrite in their souls for their sins. All of them, except children and those who were ill, fasted on this day from food and took off their jewelry.

1.3. The duration of this ordinance: *It shall be a statute for ever* (vv. 29, 34). It must not be discontinued any year or even ever be allowed to lapse until the type was to be superseded by its fulfillment. The annual repetition of the sacrifices showed that they could only faintly and weakly make atonement. It could be done effectively only by the *offering up of the body of Christ once for all* (Heb 10:10), and that once was sufficient: that sacrifice did not need to be repeated.

2. Let us notice what can be seen of the Gospel in all this:

2.1. Here are types of the two great Gospel privileges of the forgiveness of sins and access to God, both of which we owe to the mediation of our Lord Jesus. Here then let us see:

2.1.1. The atoning sacrifice which Christ made for us. He is himself both the Sacrificer and the Sacrifice of the atonement, for he is:

2.1.1.1. The Priest, in fact the High Priest, who *makes reconciliation for the sins of the people* (Heb 2:17). No one was to be with the high priest when he made atonement (v. 17), for our Lord Jesus was to *tread the winepress alone*, and of the people there must be *none with him* (Isa 63:3). And so when he began his sufferings, *all his disciples forsook him and fled* (Mt 26:56), for if any of them had been taken and put to death with him, it might have looked as if they had assisted in making the atonement. But whereas the atonement which the high priest made was only for the people of Israel, Christ is the atoning sacrifice, not only for the sins of the Jews, but also for the sins of the whole Gentile world. In this also, Christ infinitely surpassed Aaron, because Aaron needed to offer a sacrifice for his own sin first, for which he had to make confession on the head of his sin offering, but our Lord Jesus had no sin of his own to be punished for.

2.1.1.2. Also the sacrifice with which atonement is made, for he is everything in our reconciliation with God. In this way he was prefigured by the two goats, which both made one offering: the goat that was killed was a type of Christ dying for our sins, and the scapegoat was a type of Christ rising again for our justification.

2.1.1.2.1. The atonement is said to be made by transferring the sins of Israel onto the goat. The people deserved to have been abandoned and sent into a land where the dead are forgotten, but that punishment was here transferred onto the goat that took away their sins. This refers to the fact that God is said to have laid on our Lord Jesus—the reality of all these shadows—*the iniquity of us all* (Isa 53:6), and he is said to have *borne our sins*, even the punishment of them, *in his own body upon the tree* (1Pe 2:24).

2.1.1.2.2. The consequence of this was that all the sins of Israel were carried into a *land of forgetfulness* (Ps 88:12), a place of oblivion where the dead are forgotten. In the same way, Christ, the Lamb of God, *takes away the sin of the world*, by taking it on himself (Jn 1:29). And when God forgives sin, he is said to remember it no more (Heb 8:12), *to cast it behind his back* (Isa 38:17), *into the depths of the sea* (Mic 7:19), and to separate it *as far as the east is from the west* (Ps 103:12).

2.1.2. The high priest's entrance into the Most Holy Place is a type of the entrance into heaven which Christ made for us. The writer to the Hebrews explains it in this way (Heb 9:7, etc.), showing:

2.1.2.1. That heaven is the holiest place of all, not the tabernacle, and that the way into it by faith, hope, and prayer through a Mediator was not then so clearly revealed as it is to us now in the Gospel.

2.1.2.2. That Christ our High Priest entered into heaven at his ascension once for all.

2.1.2.3. That Christ entered *by his own blood* (Heb 9:12), sprinkling his blood, as it were, before the mercy seat (atonement cover), where it promised better things than the blood of bulls and goats could. And so he is said to appear in the midst of the throne as *a lamb that had been slain* (Rev 5:6). The intercession of Christ is there set out before God as incense. And just as the high priest interceded for himself first, then for his household, and then for all Israel, so our Lord Jesus, in Jn 17, first commended himself to his Father, then commended his disciples, and then all Israel and all who would believe in him through their word.

2.2. Here are types of the two great Gospel duties of faith and repentance, by which we are eligible to receive the atonement and come to receive its benefits:

2.2.1. By faith we must put our hands on the head of the offering, relying on Christ as the Lord our Righteousness, pleading only his atonement to receive forgiveness for our sins. "I only have you, Lord."

2.2.2. By repentance we must humble our souls, not only fasting for a time from the delights of the body, but inwardly being deeply sorry for our sins, and living a life of self-denial.

CHAPTER 17

In this chapter we have two prohibitions necessary to keep the honor of that atonement: 1. That no sacrifice should be offered by anyone other than the priests, or anywhere except at the door of the tabernacle (the entrance to the Tent of Meeting). If this was not observed, then the offerer would be killed (vv. 1–9). 2. That no

blood should be eaten, for which there was the same penalty (vv. 10–16).

Verses 1–9

This ordinance required that all the people of Israel should bring all the sacrifices to be offered to God's altar. Notice:

1. What the previous arrangements were:

1.1. The people were allowed to build altars and offer sacrifices to God where they pleased.

1.2. This liberty had sometimes led to idolatry. The Israelites themselves had learned in Egypt to sacrifice to demons. And it seemed that some of them had indulged in such a practice ever since the God of Israel had so gloriously appeared to them.

2. How this law arranged matters: It is hard to consider this as a temporary law, when it is expressly said to be *a statute for ever* (v. 7), and so it would seem instead to forbid only the killing of animals for sacrifice anywhere except at God's altar. They must not offer sacrifice, as they had done, *in the open field* (v. 5). If the sacrifices were to the true God, they must be brought to the priest, to be offered on the altar of the Lord. If anyone should disobey this law and offer sacrifice anywhere except at the tabernacle:

2.1. The guilt was great: *Blood shall be imputed to that man; he hath shed blood* (v. 4). Idolatrous sacrifices were looked on, not only as adultery, but also as murder: he that *offereth them is as if he slew a man* (Isa 66:3).

2.2. The punishment would be severe: *That man shall be cut off from among his people* (vv. 4, 9).

3. How this law was observed:

3.1. While the Israelites kept their integrity, they were committed to this law, as can be seen from their zeal against the altar which was set up by the two tribes and the half-tribe, which they would not in any way have allowed to stand if they had not been satisfied that it was never intended, and would never be used, for sacrifice or offering (Jos 22:12, etc.).

3.2. Disobedience to this law was for many ages the corruption of the Jewish church, as can be seen from the complaint which so often occurs in the history even of the good kings—*Howbeit the high places were not taken away* (2Ki 14:4; 2Ch 20:33)—and it allowed gross idolatry to come in.

4. How the matter stands now and what use we are to make of this law:

4.1. It is certain that the spiritual sacrifices we are now to offer are not limited to any one place. We now have no temple or altar that consecrates the gift. Similarly, Gospel unity does not lie in one place, but in one heart and the *unity of the Spirit* (Eph 4:1).

4.2. Christ is our altar and the *true tabernacle* (Heb 8:2; 13:10). In him, God dwells among us, and it is in him that our sacrifices are acceptable to God, and only in him (1Pe 2:5).

Verses 10–16

We have here a repetition and confirmation of the law against eating blood. We have read of this prohibition twice before in the Levitical law (3:17; 7:26), as well as in the place it had in the instructions to Noah (Ge 9:4). But here:

1. The prohibition is repeated again and again, and the former laws are referred to with this intention (v. 12). Great emphasis is laid on it, as a law which has more to it than you would think at first.

2. The law is made binding, not only on the *house of Israel*, but also on the *strangers that sojourned among them* (v. 10).

3. The penalty attached to this law is very severe (v. 10).

4. A reason is given for this law (v. 11): because *it is the blood that makes atonement for the soul* (v. 11). The life of the body is in the blood. The sinner deserved to die, and so the sacrifice must die. Now the blood being the life—and animals were usually killed for human use by the drawing out of all their blood—God appointed the sprinkling or pouring out of the blood of the sacrifice on the altar to represent the fact that the life of the sacrifice was given to God instead of the sinner's life, and as a ransom or price paid for it. In the New Testament, we read that *without shedding of blood there was no remission* (Heb 9:22). For this reason they must eat no blood, and:

4.1. It was then a very good reason, for God by this means preserved the honor of that way of atonement which he had ordained. But:

4.2. This reason is now superseded, which indicates that the law itself was ceremonial, and is now no longer in force: the blood of Christ, who has come, is alone what makes atonement for the soul. The blood of the sacrifices was an imperfect type of his atoning sacrifice. The blood, provided it is prepared in such a way that it is not unhealthy, is now allowed to give nourishment to our bodies, because it is no longer appointed as a means of making atonement for the soul.

CHAPTER 18

Here is: 1. A general law against conformity to the evil customs of the followers of other religions (vv. 1–5). 2. Particular laws: against incest (vv. 6–18). 3. Against immoral sexual acts and barbaric idolatry (vv. 19–23); the enforcement of these laws, to be seen in the destruction of the Canaanites (vv. 24–30).

Verses 1–5

After several ceremonial ordinances, God returns here to the enforcement of moral instructions. The former are still of use to us as types, and the latter are still binding as laws. We have here:

1. The holy authority by which these laws are given: *I am the Lord your God* (vv. 2, 4, 30).

2. A strict warning against holding on to the surviving traces of the idolatrous ways of Egypt, where they had lived before, and against being defiled by the idolatries of Canaan, to where they were now going (v. 3). If we genuinely keep God's commandments, even though we come short of leading sinless and perfect lives, we will find that our line of duty is the way of strength, encouragement, and happiness from God. It is the description of the *righteousness which is of the law, that the man which doeth those things shall live by them* (Ro 10:5). *The law is not of faith* (Gal 3:12). The change which the Gospel has made is in the word *live: the man that does them shall live* (Gal 3:12), not live by them, for the Law could not give life, because we could not perfectly keep it. Such a person will owe their life to the grace of Christ, and not to any goodness of their own; see Gal 3:21–22.

Verses 6–18

These laws relate to the seventh commandment:

1. What is forbidden for the close relatives mentioned here is *approaching to them to uncover their nakedness* (v. 6), to have sexual relations with them.

1.1. It is chiefly meant to forbid marriage to any of these close relatives. Marriage is a divine institution intended for the comfort of human life and the decent and honorable reproduction of the human race, which is right for the dignity of human nature above that of the animals. These prohibitions, besides being given by a sovereign authority, are also in themselves very just and reasonable.

1.1.1. In marriage, two were to become one flesh, and so it would be a contradiction if those who were already natural family members and, in a way one flesh, were to become one flesh through marriage.

1.1.2. Marriage puts an equality between husband and wife. The inequality between master and servant, employer and employee, high and lowly, rests on human custom and consent, and there is no harm done if that inequality is taken away by marriage. However, the inequality between parents and children, uncles and nieces, aunts and nephews, either by blood or marriage, rests on the natural order of things, and cannot—except by bringing extreme confusion and disturbance—be taken away by marriage.

1.1.3. No relatives of the same generation are forbidden, except brothers and sisters, whether full, half, or step brothers and sisters. Making use of the ordinance of marriage to support incestuous marriage in no way justifies such relationships or lessens their guilt. In fact, it adds to the guilt of disobeying an ordinance of God, and abusing for evil purposes what was instituted for the best reasons. But:

1.2. Sexual immorality committed with any of these relatives outside of marriage is likewise prohibited.

2. The sexual relationships forbidden are mostly clearly described, and it is generally laid down as a rule that those relatives of a man's own whom he is restricted from marrying are the same as those relatives of his wife whom he is forbidden to marry, for the two are one. That law which forbids marrying a brother's wife (v. 16) had a special exception for the Jews, that if a man died without children, his brother or next of kin should marry the widow and bring up children for the deceased (Dt 25:5). This was for reasons that held good only in that community.

Verses 19–30

Here is:

1. A law to preserve the honor of the marriage-bed, that it should not be used at the wrong time (v. 19) or violated by an adulterer (v. 20).

2. A law against what was the most unnatural idolatry, causing their children to *pass through the fire to Molech* (v. 21). Some think Molech was the idol that they used for worshiping the sun, that great fire of the world, and so in their worship they made their own children either sacrifices to this idol, burning them to death in front of it, or devotees of it, causing them to pass between two fires or to be thrown through one, to the honor of this pretended deity. They were thought to have done all this to Molech, imagining that the consecrating of only one of their children would obtain good fortune for all the other children.

3. A law against the unnatural sexual acts of homosexuality and bestiality, sins that should not be discussed or even thought about except with complete abhorrence (vv. 22–23). Other sins put people on the same level as animals, but these put them much lower.

4. Arguments against these and similarly detestable immoral acts:

4.1. Sinners defile themselves with these evil acts. All sin defiles the conscience, but these sins have a particularly great depravity.

4.2. *The souls that commit them shall be cut off* (v. 29). Sinful desires war against the soul and will certainly destroy it unless God's mercy and grace bring about a change. For these and similar sins the Canaanites were to be destroyed.

5. The chapter concluding with a sovereign answer to such defilement. "Keep my laws so that you do not commit any of these detestable customs" (v. 30). A close and constant devotion to God's laws is the most effective way of keeping free from the defilements of gross sin. It is only the grace of God that will keep us safe, and we can really only expect to receive that grace if we make use of the means of grace.

CHAPTER 19

1. The laws of this chapter, which were special to the Jews, are: 1.1. Concerning their peace offerings (fellowship offerings) (vv. 5–8). 1.2. Concerning the gleanings of their fields (vv. 9–10). 1.3. Against mixing their cattle, seed, and cloth (v. 19). 1.4. Concerning their trees (vv. 23–25). 1.5. Against some superstitious customs (vv. 26–28). But: 2. Many of these instructions are binding on us, for they explain most of the Ten Commandments. 2.1. Here the introduction to the Ten Commandments, "I am the Lord," is repeated fifteen times. 2.2. A summary of the Ten Commandments. All the first table is summed up in this, "Be you holy" (v. 2); all the second table in this, Thou shalt love thy neighbour (v. 18), and an answer to the question, "Who is my neighbor?" (vv. 33–34). 2.3. Something of each commandment: 2.3.1. The first commandment implied in what is often repeated here, "I am your God." And here is a prohibition of enchantment (divination) (v. 26) and witchcraft (v. 31), which make a god of the Devil. 2.3.2. Idolatry, against the second commandment, is forbidden (v. 4). 2.3.3. Profanation of God's name, against the third commandment (v. 12). 2.3.4. Keeping the Sabbath holy (the fourth commandment) is urged (vv. 3, 30). 2.3.5. Children are required to honor their parents (the fifth commandment) (v. 3) and the aged (v. 32). 2.3.6. Hatred and revenge are forbidden here, against the sixth commandment (vv. 17–18). 2.3.7. Against adultery (the seventh commandment) (vv. 20–22), and whoredom (prostitution) (v. 29). 2.3.8. The eighth commandment: justice is required here in judgment (v. 15); theft forbidden (v. 11); fraud and withholding dues (v. 13); and false weights (vv. 35–36). 2.3.9. Against the ninth commandment: lying (v. 11); slandering (v. 14); taletelling, and false-witness bearing (v. 16). 2.3.10. The tenth commandment lays a restraint on the heart (v. 17): Thou shalt not hate thy brother in thy heart. And here is a solemn command to observe all these decrees and laws (v. 37). Now these are things which do not need a lot of understanding, but rather constant care and watchfulness to observe them. A good understanding have all those that do these commandments (Ps 111:10).

Verses 1–10

Moses is ordered to speak the summary of the laws to all the assembly of the people of Israel (v. 2). They had already received many of the instructions given here, but they needed to be repeated, so that they might be remembered. We need to constantly receive God's detailed commands and instructions in our lives. In these verses it is required:

1. That Israel should be a holy people, because the God of Israel is a holy God (v. 2). And this is now the law of

Christ. "You shall be holy, for I am holy" (1Pe 1:15–16). Israel was made holy by types and shadows (20:8), but we are made holy by the truth, the reality of all those shadows (Jn 17:17; Tit 2:14).

2. That children should be obedient to their parents: "You shall fear every man his mother and his father" (v. 3).

2.1. The fear required here includes inward reverence and esteem, outward expressions of respect, obedience to the lawful commands of parents, trying to please them and make them content, and avoiding everything that may offend them, grieve them, or incur their displeasure. The Jewish teachers ask, "What is this fear that is due to a father?" And they answer, "It is not to stand in his way nor to sit in his place, not to contradict what he says nor to complain about it, not to call him by his name, either living or dead, but 'My Father'; it is to provide for him if he is poor, and the like."

2.2. Children, when they grow up to be adults, must not think they are discharged from this duty: everyone, even though they are wise or famous, must still respect their parents, simply because they are their parents.

2.3. The mother is put first, which is unusual, to show that the duty is equally owing to both.

2.4. It is added, *keep my Sabbaths*. If God provides by his Law for parents to be continually honored, parents must also exercise authority over their children to preserve God's honor, particularly the honor of his Sabbaths. The destruction of young people has sometimes been noticed to begin with the contempt of their parents and the godlessness of the Sabbath day.

2.5. The reason given for both these instructions is, "I am the Lord your God; the Lord of the Sabbath and the God of your parents."

3. That only God is to be worshiped, and not by means of idols (v. 4): "Do not turn to idols, to vain things of no power, no value, gods that are not really gods at all. You are the work of God's hands, so do not be so foolish as to worship gods that are the work of your own hands."

4. That the sacrifices of their peace offerings (fellowship offerings) should always be offered and eaten according to the Law (vv. 5–8).

5. That they should leave the gleanings of their harvest and vineyard for the poor (vv. 9–10). When they gathered in their grain, they must leave some standing at the corners of the field; the Jewish teachers say, "It should be a sixtieth part of the field"; and they must also leave the gleanings and the small clusters of grapes, which they missed the first time they gathered in the grapes.

Verses 11–18

We are taught here:

1. To be honest and true in all our dealings (v. 11). Whatever we have in the world, we must see to it that it is honestly come by, for we cannot be truly rich, or rich for a long time, with what is not.

2. To maintain a reverent respect for the holy name of God (v. 12).

3. Not to take or keep something that rightly belongs to another person (v. 13). We must not take what does not belong to us, by either fraud or robbery, or keep what belongs to someone else. Let the workers receive the wages for their day's work as soon as they have finished their work, if they want it.

4. To honor the deaf and see that the way of the blind is safe. We should be particularly respectful toward those who cannot help themselves (v. 14):

4.1. The deaf: *Thou shalt not curse the deaf*, that is, not only those who are naturally deaf, who cannot hear at all, but also those who are absent and are at present out of earshot.

4.2. The blind. We must also care for the safety and security of the blind and not put any stumbling block in their way. If we were to put a stumbling block in their way, it would be adding a further burden to those who were already suffering. This prohibition implies an instruction to help the blind and to remove stumbling blocks from their way. The Jewish writers, thinking it impossible that any should be so cruel as to put a stumbling block in the way of the blind, understood it figuratively. They said that it forbids giving bad advice to those who are simple and easily deceived, by which they may be led to do something that would hurt or harm them.

5. That judges and all in authority are to give a verdict and judgment without partiality (v. 15) by showing favoritism to the poor (Ex 23:3). Be charitable to the poor, but only give to them what is their right and what they are legally entitled to, and do not let their poverty excuse them from receiving any just punishment for a wrong. The Jews say, "Judges were obliged by this law to be so impartial as not to let one of the contending parties sit while the other stood, or permit one to say what they pleased and ask the other to be brief"; see also Jas 2:1–4.

6. Not to do anything that would harm or hurt our neighbor's good name (v. 16), either:

6.1. In ordinary conversation: we are not to go about *as a talebearer*, slandering others. The word used for a *talebearer* refers to a peddler or a petty or unauthorized trader, for talebearers, slanderers, and gossips pick up malicious stories at one house and then pass them on at another and commonly exchange or barter slanderous words. Notice how this sin is condemned (Pr 11:13; 20:19; Jer 9:4–5; Eze 22:9). Or:

6.2. In bearing witness. We are not to stand as witnesses *against the blood of our neighbour* (v. 16) if they are innocent or harmless. The Jewish teachers go further: "If by your testimony you can clear someone who is accused, then you are obliged by this law to do it"; see also Pr 24:11–12.

7. To rebuke our neighbor in love (v. 17):

7.1. It is better to rebuke our neighbors than hate them for an injury done to ourselves. If we discover that our neighbors have in any way wronged us, we must not harbor a grudge against them and alienate ourselves from them. We must rather try to show the one who has wronged us that they have wronged us. We must reason our case fairly with them. This is the rule our Savior gives in such instances (Lk 17:3).

7.2. We are to rebuke our neighbors for their sin against God, because we love our neighbors. Friendly rebuke is a duty we owe to one another, and we ought both to give it and receive it in love. *Let the righteous smite me; it shall be a kindness* (Ps 141:5).

8. To put off all malice or hatred and to put on love (v. 18). We must not be hostile to anyone. We must be loving to all: *Thou shalt love thy neighbor as thyself*. We must do to our neighbor what we would have them do to us (Mt 7:12), putting our souls in their place (Job 16:4–5). In many cases, we may even need to deny ourselves for our neighbor's good, as Paul did (1Co 9:19, etc.). In this matter, the Gospel goes beyond even the excellent instruction of the Law, for Christ, by laying down his life for us, has taught us even to lay down our lives for our brothers and sisters in some cases (1Jn 3:16), and so to love our neighbor more than ourselves.

Verses 19–29

Here is:

1. A law against mixed breeding (v. 19). In the beginning God made the cattle according to their kinds (Ge 1:25), and we must rest in the order of nature that God has established, believing that it is best and sufficient, and not want to create malformed freaks of nature. The sowing of two different kinds of seed and the wearing of garments made of two different kinds of material are forbidden here, either because these were ungodly customs, or to show how careful the people should be not to associate themselves closely with the ungodly or to try to weave any of the gentile customs into God's ways. Mr. Ainsworth suggests that it was to lead Israel to have a simple and sincere religion.

2. A law for punishing adultery committed with a woman who was a slave girl already promised to be married (vv. 20–22). It was for the honor of marriage, though at that time only the promise of marriage, that the crime should be punished; but it was for the honor of freedom that it should not be punished as the violating of a free woman was. So great was the difference then made between slave and free (Gal 4:30), but the Gospel of Christ knows no such distinction (Col 3:11).

3. A law concerning fruit trees, that for the first three years after they had been planted, if they should happen to be so forward as to bear fruit in that time, no use should be made of the fruit (vv. 23–25). It was therefore the practice of the Jews to pluck off the fruit, as soon as they saw that it was forming on the young trees, as gardeners do sometimes, because early fruitbearing may hinder future growth. If any fruit did reach maturity, it was not to be used in the service either of God or human beings, but the fruit that was borne the fourth year was to be holy to the Lord, either given to the priests or eaten before the Lord with joy, as their second tithe. From that time onward, it was all their own. This law in the case of fruit trees seems to be parallel with that of animals, that no creature should be accepted as an offering till it was more than eight days old; children were not to be circumcised until that day; see 22:27. God wanted the firstfruits of their trees, but because for the first three years they were as insignificant as a lamb or a calf less than eight days old, God did not want them, for it is right that he should have everything at its best. However, he would not allow them to be used, because his firstfruits were not offered by then. They must therefore be counted as uncircumcised, that is, as an animal less than eight days old, and not fit for any use.

4. A law against the superstitious practices of the nations (vv. 26–28):

4.1. Eating meat with the blood still in it, as the Gentiles did, who gathered the blood of their sacrifices into a container for their demons, so they thought, to drink. The blood of God's sacrifices was to be sprinkled on the altar, and then poured at the foot of it, and then taken away.

4.2. Enchantment (divination) and sorcery, a superstitious consideration of some times as lucky and others as unlucky. These kinds of magic may have been invented by the Egyptian priests. It would be unforgivable for those to whom were committed the words of God to seek advice from the Devil, and still worse in Christians to whom the Son of God is revealed, who has destroyed the works of the Devil. For Christians to follow astrology and look up their horoscopes, to have their fortunes told, to use spells and charms to try to heal illnesses and drive away evil spirits, to be affected by such superstitions as having to throw salt over your shoulder or not walking under a ladder, all these are grave insults to the Lord Jesus and support paganism and idolatry. Those who hold such views dishonor both themselves and the worthy name by which they are called.

4.3. Trimming hair at the sides of their head or off the edges of their beard as the nations did. There was a superstition even in this, and it must not be imitated by the people of God: *You shall not round the corners of your heads* (v. 27). Those who worshiped the stars in the sky cut their hair in honor of them so that their heads might resemble the earth, but as the custom was foolish in itself, so if it were done with respect to their false gods, it was idolatrous.

4.4. The rituals by which other nations expressed their sorrow at their funerals (v. 28). The Israelites must not make cuts on their bodies or put tattoos on their bodies for the dead, for these were the practices of the nations to pacify the diabolical deities. Christ by his sufferings has altered the power of death and made it a true friend to every true Israelite, and now, as nothing is needed to make death favorable toward us, we do not need to grieve as those who have no hope.

4.5. The degrading of their daughters to become prostitutes (v. 29). It seems to have been practiced by the nations in their idolatrous worship.

Verses 30–37

Here is:

1. A law to preserve the honor of the time and place set aside for the service of God (v. 30).

1.1. Sabbaths must be religiously observed.

1.2. The sanctuary must be held in reverence. Though there is now no place that is holy by divine institution, as the tabernacle and temple then were, this law should still make us respect and have reverence for meetings of Christian worship, because they have the promise of Christ's special presence in them.

2. A warning against all fellowship with mediums or spiritists: *"Regard them not, seek not after them* (v. 31). Do not fear any evil from them or hope to receive any good from them."

3. A command to young people to show respect to the aged: *Thou shalt rise up before the hoary head* (v. 32). Those whom God has honored with the blessing of long life we ought to honor. Those who are wise and good in their old age are worthy of double honor. Their authority and encouragement should be carefully consulted, and their advice asked and listened to (Job 32:6–7). Religion teaches us good manners and requires us to give honor to those to whom honor is due.

4. A command to the Israelites to be kind toward foreigners (vv. 33–34). *"Thou shalt not vex a stranger*, but *love him as thyself* (vv. 33–34), and as one of your own people." God takes special care of foreigners, as he does of widows and children without fathers, because it is his honor to help the helpless (Ps 146:9). We need to be generous and have a godly attitude to God as Father of all if we are to be kind to foreigners. But here is a reason added that is special to the Jews: *"For you were strangers in the land of Egypt* (v. 34). God then favored you, and so you should now favor foreigners."

5. A command for justice in weights and measures: that they should not cheat in using them (v. 35), that they should be honest and accurate (v. 36).

6. A general command as a conclusion to this chapter (v. 37): *You shall observe all my statutes, and do them.*

CHAPTER 20

In this chapter we have: 1. Many particular crimes that are made capital offenses: giving their children to Molech (vv. 1–5); consulting mediums and spiritists (vv. 6, 27); cursing parents (v. 9). 2. More capital crimes of: adultery (v. 10); incest (vv. 11–12, 14, 17, 19–21); and immoral sexual acts (vv. 13, 15–16, 18). 3. General commands given to be holy (vv. 7–8, 22–26).

Verses 1–9

1. In these verses, three sins are threatened with death:

1.1. Parents abusing their children, by sacrificing them to Molech (vv. 2–3). It was not enough to tell them they might spare their children but they must be told:

1.1.1. That the person who committed such a crime would themselves be put to death as a murderer: *The people of the land shall stone him with stones* (v. 2), which was looked on as the worst capital punishment among the Jews.

1.1.2. That all those who assisted in committing this sin would also be cut off by the righteousness of God. If neighbors concealed such a person and would not appear as witnesses against them—if the judges turned a blind eye to the offense and would not pass sentence on them, pitying their foolishness rather than hating their ungodliness—God himself would reckon with these people for their complicity (vv. 4–5).

1.2. Children abusing their parents, by cursing them (v. 9). If children are spiteful or scornful toward their parents, or wish them harm, then this was a sin that was to be punished by the judges, who were employed to preserve both God's honor and also the public peace, which were both attacked by such unnatural, defiant behavior.

1.3. People abusing themselves by consulting mediums or spiritists, those who are *familiar spirits* (v. 6). By this, as much as anything, people devalue, disparage, and deceive themselves, and so abuse themselves. What could be more insane than for someone to go to a liar for information and to an enemy for advice? Those who do so turn to those who deal in devilish matters and know the depths of Satan.

2. In the midst of these particular laws comes that general command in vv. 7–8, where we have:

2.1. Two duties required:

2.1.1. That in our motives, aims, and our heart, we should be holy: *Sanctify yourselves and be you holy* (v. 7).

2.1.2. That in all our actions and our behavior we should be obedient to the laws of God: *You shall keep my statutes* (v. 8). Make the tree good, and the fruit will then be good.

2.2. The reasons for these duties:

2.2.1. *I am the Lord your God* (vv. 7, 24), and so be holy, that you may please him and become like the One whose people you are. Holiness is the characteristic of God's people.

2.2.2. *I am the Lord who sanctifieth you* (v. 8). God sanctified them by special privileges, laws, and favors, which set them apart from all other nations and honored them as God's people. He gave them his word and ceremonies so that they would increase in holiness, and he gave his Holy Spirit to instruct them.

Verses 10–21

Sins against the seventh commandment are ordered here to be severely punished:

1. Committing adultery with another man's wife was made a capital crime. The adulterer and the adulteress

who had joined in the sin must both come under the sentence: they will both be *put to death* (v. 10).

2. Incestuous relationships, whether by marriage or not,were to be punished with either death or barrenness.

3. The shocking sins of homosexual acts and bestiality were to be punished by death.

Verses 22–27

The last verse is a specific law, which comes after the general conclusion, as if it were omitted from its proper place: it describes putting to death those who were mediums or spiritists (v. 27). Those who are in league with the Devil have in effect made a covenant with death.

The rest of these verses repeat and instill what had been said before concerning the people:

1. Their dignity. They had the *Lord for their God* (v. 24). They were his, his concern, his choice, his treasure.

2. Their duty; this may be seen from their dignity. God had done more for them than he had for others, and so more was expected from them than from others.

3. Their danger. They were going into a defiled place (v. 24): *You shall inherit their land*, a land *flowing with milk and honey*, which they would fully enjoy if they kept their integrity; but it was also a land full of idols, idolatries, and superstitious customs, which they would all too likely fall in love with, having brought with them from Egypt the tendency to be struck down with that defilement.

CHAPTER 21

This chapter is a law obliging priests to take the greatest care to preserve the honor of their priesthood. 1. The lesser priests are here given commands concerning mourning and also their marriages and their children (vv. 1–9). 2. More restrictions are put on the high priest than on any of them (vv. 10–15). 3. Neither one nor the other must have any deformity (vv. 16–24).

Verses 1–9

It had been appointed before that the priests should teach the people the laws God had given concerning the *difference between clean and unclean* (10:10–11). Now here the priests are instructed that they should themselves observe what they were to teach the people. The priests were to draw nearer to God than any of the people, and to deal more intimately with holy things, and so they needed to keep farther away than others from anything that might defile them.

1. They must take care not to dishonor themselves in mourning for the dead. It made a person ceremonially unclean to come within six feet (two meters) of a dead corpse. It is even declared (Nu 19:14) that all who come into the tent where a dead body lies will be unclean for seven days.

1.1. The priests should never disqualify themselves from coming into the sanctuary, unless it was for one of their closest relatives (vv. 1–3).

1.2. They must not be exaggerated in the expressions of their mourning. Their mourning must be neither:

1.2.1. Superstitious, according to the nations, whose followers cut off their hair and lacerated their bodies, in honor of the imaginary deities which ruled, so they thought, over the congregation of the dead, so that the deities might be favorable toward their friends who had just died. Nor:

1.2.2. Excessive. God's ministers must set an example to others of patience in suffering, particularly when it is

a matter of something as sensitive as the death of their close relatives.

2. They must take care not to disgrace themselves in their marriage (v. 7). A priest must not marry a woman defiled by prostitution, who either had been guilty, or was suspected, of such sexual immorality.

3. Their children must be afraid of doing anything to discredit them (v. 9): *If the daughter of any priest play the whore*, her crime is great; she not only defiles but also *profaneth herself*: other women do not have that honor to lose which she has, who as one of a priest's family, has eaten holy things and is supposed to have been better educated than others.

Verses 10–15

More was expected from a priest than from other people, but more from the high priest than from other priests, because on his head the *anointing oil was poured*. It is called the *crown of the anointing oil of his God* (v. 12), for the anointing of the Spirit is, for all who have it, *a crown of glory* and *a diadem of beauty* (Isa 28:5). Because the high priest was honored in this way:

1. He must not defile himself at all for the dead, not even for his closest relatives, *his father or his mother*, much less his child or brother (v. 11). Our Lord Jesus, the great High Priest of our profession, touched the dead body of Jairus' daughter, the coffin of the widow's son, and the grave of Lazarus, to show that he came to change the power of death, to take away its terrors, by breaking its power. Now that death cannot destroy, it does not defile.

2. He must not marry a widow (as other priests could), much less a divorced woman, or a prostitute (vv. 13–14). The reason for this was to put a difference between him and other priests in this matter.

3. He must not dishonor his offspring among his people (v. 15). It may be a warning to him in seeing whom his children married; he must not dishonor his offspring by seeing them marry unsuitable partners. Ministers' children are dishonored if they are joined to unbelievers.

Verses 16–24

Because the priesthood was confined to one particular family and was passed on to all the male children of that family throughout their generations, it was very likely that some people born into the priesthood at later times would have natural defects and deformities.

1. The law concerning priests who had deformities was:

1.1. That they could live on the altar: *he shall eat the bread of his God, both of the most holy, and of the holy* (v. 22). He will eat the sacrifices with the other priests, even the *most holy things*, such as the consecrated bread and the sin offerings, as well as the *holy things*, such as the tithes and firstfruits, and the priests' share of the peace offerings (fellowship offerings). The deformities were such as they could not help, and so, although they could not work, they must not starve.

1.2. But he must not approach and serve at the altar, at either of the altars, or be admitted to be present at or assist the other priests in offering sacrifices or burning incense (vv. 17, 21, 23). It was to inspire trustworthiness in the sanctuary that no one should appear there who was in any way disfigured, either naturally or accidentally.

2. Under the Gospel:

2.1. Those who have any such defects as the ones mentioned should thank God that these abnormalities do not exclude them from offering spiritual sacrifices to God, or if they are otherwise qualified for it, from the office of the ministry. There is many a healthy and beautiful soul that is stuck inside an infirm and deformed body. But:

2.2. We ought to learn from this how incapable people are to serve God acceptably whose minds are defective and whose lives are deformed by any compulsive sin. People who are spiritually blind, lame, and deformed are unworthy to be called Christians, and unsuitable to be employed as ministers. Their sins render them offensive to God, and the offerings of the Lord are detested for their sakes.

CHAPTER 22

In this chapter we have various laws concerning the priests and sacrifices, all intended to preserve the honor of the sanctuary: 1. When the priests are ceremonially unclean, they should not eat holy things (vv. 1–9). 2. No outsider who did not belong to a family of the priests should eat the holy things (vv. 10–13), but if they did so unintentionally, they must make restitution (vv. 14–16). 3. The sacrifices which were offered must be without any defect or blemish (vv. 17–25); the offerings must be more than eight days old (vv. 26–28); and the sacrifices of thanksgiving must be eaten the same day they were offered (vv. 29–33).

Verses 1–9

Those who had natural deformities, even though they were forbidden to do the priests' work, were still allowed to eat holy things. The Jewish writers say that to keep them from being idle they were employed in the wood-room, to pick out what was worm-eaten, so that it would not be used in the fire on the altar. They could also be employed in determining whether someone was suffering from an infectious skin disease, but:

1. Those who were ceremonially unclean, which might have come about through their own fault, were not allowed even to eat the holy things while they continued in their defiled state.

2. As to the intention of this law, we may notice:

2.1. It obliged the priests to carefully preserve their purity and to fear everything that would defile them.

2.2. It impressed the people with reverence for the holy things.

Verses 10–16

The holy things were to be eaten by the priests and their families.

1. Here is a law that no one outside a priest's family may eat them, that is, no person whatsoever except the priests and those who belonged to them (v. 10). The priests are given this responsibility: they must not *profane the holy things* by permitting outsiders to eat them (v. 15) and must not allow them *to bear the iniquity of trespass* (v. 16). We must not only be careful that we do not bring guilt onto ourselves, but we must also do what we can to prevent others from bringing it onto themselves.

2. Here is an explanation of the law, showing who were to be looked on as belonging to the priest's family, and who not.

2.1. The guests of a priest or his hired workers who had not lived in the house forever were in the family, but did not belong to it, and so were not allowed to eat holy things (v. 10). However, the slave who was born in the house or bought with money, being the personal property of the family, was allowed to eat holy things (v. 11).

2.2. As to the children of the family, there could be no dispute concerning the sons, since they themselves were priests, but concerning the daughters a distinction was made. While the daughters continued living in their father's house, they were allowed to eat holy things, but if they married men who were not priests, they lost that right (v. 12).

3. Here is a demand for restitution to be made by the person who had no right to holy things, but ate them unintentionally (v. 14).

4. This law could be disregarded in cases of necessity, as it was when David and his men ate the consecrated bread (1Sa 21:6). And our Savior justifies them, and gives a reason for it, which provides us with a lasting rule in all such cases, that *God will have mercy and not sacrifice* (Mt 12:3–4, 7; Hos 6:6). Ritual must give way to right actions.

Verses 17–33

Here are four laws concerning sacrifices:

1. Whatever was offered in sacrifice to God should be without defect, or otherwise it would not be accepted. Moreover, a distinction is made between what was brought as a freewill offering and what was brought in fulfillment of a vow (v. 23). According to this law, great care was taken to examine all the animals that were brought to be sacrificed, that the people might be sure that there was no defect or blemish in them. Many of the priests of other religions were not so strict in this matter; they would receive sacrifices for their gods which were blemished, but foreigners and outsiders must know that the God of Israel does not want to be served in such ways. It is an instruction to us to offer to God the best we have in our spiritual sacrifices. If our devotions are unthinking, cold, insignificant, and easily distracted, we are offering *the blind, and the lame, and the sick* as sacrifices.

2. No animal should be offered in sacrifice before it was eight days old (vv. 26–27). The Law had previously stated that the first offspring of their cattle, which were to be dedicated to God, should not be brought to him till after the eighth day (Ex 22:30). Here it is declared that no creature should be offered in sacrifice till it was a full eight days old. If it was sooner than that, it was not fit to be used at human tables, and so also not at God's altar.

3. The female animal and its young should not both be killed on the same day, whether in sacrifice or for ordinary use (v. 28). It would have seemed cruel toward the species to kill two generations at once, as if you were intending to destroy the whole species.

4. The flesh of their thank offerings should be eaten on the same day that they were sacrificed (vv. 29–30). This is a repetition of what had been instructed before (7:15; 19:6–7). The chapter concludes with such a general command as we have often met with, to *keep God's commandments*, and not to *profane his holy name* (vv. 31–32).

CHAPTER 23

Up to this point, the Levitical law has been chiefly concerned with holy people, holy things, and holy places; in this chapter we have the institution of holy times (vv. 1–2). 1. The weekly feast of the Sabbath (v. 3). 2. The yearly feasts: the Passover and the Feast of Unleavened Bread (vv. 4–8), to which was attached the offering of the sheaf of firstfruits (vv. 9–14). 3. Pentecost (vv. 15–22). 4. The ceremonies of the seventh month: the

Feast of Trumpets on the first day (vv. 23–25), the Day of Atonement on the tenth day (vv. 26–32). 5. The Feast of Tabernacles on the fifteenth (vv. 33–44).

Verses 1–3

Here is:

1. A general description of the holy times which God appointed (v. 2). He is the only one who can declare that a time is holy; for he is the Lord of time, and as soon as he had set the wheels in motion, it was he who sanctified and blessed one day above the others (Ge 2:3). We may decide to make *a good day* (Est 9:19), but it is God's divine right to make a holy day. Now, concerning the holy times ordained here, notice:

1.1. They are called *feasts*. The Day of Atonement, which was one of them, was a fast; but because most of them were to be times of joy, they are generally called feasts. Some read it, "These are my assemblies," but we prefer to read it, "These are my solemnities"; and reading it in this way here, we learn that the Day of Atonement was as solemn a ceremony as any of them.

1.2. They are the feasts of the Lord (*my feasts*).

1.3. They were declared; for they were to be observed not only by the priests who came to the sanctuary, but by all the people.

1.4. They were to be sanctified and celebrated as holy assemblies, so that the services of these feasts might appear more honorable and respected, and the people more united in celebrating them.

2. A repetition of the law of the Sabbath in the first place. Though the annual feasts were made more significant by the people's general attendance at the sanctuary, these must not obscure the brightness of the Sabbath (v. 3). Christ appointed the New Testament Sabbath to be a holy assembly by meeting his disciples more than once on the first day of the week. "Whether you have opportunity of sanctifying it in a holy assembly or not, may it still be *the sabbath of the Lord in all your dwellings* (v. 3). In your family life, make a difference between that day and other days."

Verses 4–14

Here again the feasts are called the *feasts of the Lord* (v. 4), because he appointed them. Mostly they were times of joy and rejoicing. The weekly Sabbath is like this, and all their yearly ceremonies, except the Day of Atonement. God wanted to teach them by this that the ways of wisdom are pleasant. He wanted to draw them into his service by encouraging them to be cheerful in it and to sing at their work. Seven days were days of strict rest and holy assemblies; the first and the seventh days of the Feast of Unleavened Bread, the Day of Pentecost, the day of the Feast of Trumpets, the first and the eighth days of the Feast of Tabernacles, and the Day of Atonement: here were six for holy joy and only one for holy mourning. Here is:

1. A repetition of the law of the Passover, which was to be observed on the fourteenth day of the first month, in remembrance of their rescue from Egypt and the special preservation of their firstborn, acts of mercy that were never to be forgotten.

2. An order for the offering of a sheaf of the firstfruits, on the second day of the Feast of Unleavened Bread; the first is called the *sabbath*, because it was observed as a Sabbath (v. 11), and on the day after, they held this ceremony.

2.1. A sheaf or handful of new grain was brought to the priest, who was to wave it, as a sign of his presenting it to

the God of heaven, backward and forward before the Lord, as the Lord of the whole earth, and this would be accepted by God as a thankful acknowledgment of God's mercy to them in giving grain to their fields, of their dependence on God, and of their desire for him to keep the land for their use. The offering of this sheaf of firstfruits in the name of the whole congregation consecrated, as it were, their whole harvest to them.

2.2. We find that when they came into Canaan, the manna stopped on the very day that the sheaf of firstfruits was offered. They had eaten the old grain the day before (Jos 5:11), and then on that day they offered the firstfruits, by which they became entitled to the new grain too (Jos 5:12), so that there was no further need for manna.

2.3. This sheaf of firstfruits was a type of our Lord Jesus, who has risen from the dead as the *firstfruits of those that slept* (1Co 15:20). The people were not to eat their new grain till God's part of it had first been offered to him (v. 14), for we must always begin with God, begin our lives with him, begin every day with him, begin every meal with him and begin every business with him. *Seek first the kingdom of God* (Mt 6:33).

Verses 15–22

Here is the institution of the Feast of Pentecost, or *weeks*, as it is called (Dt 16:9), because it was observed fifty days, or seven weeks, after the Passover. It is also called the *feast of harvest* (Ex 23:16). For just as the presenting of the sheaf of firstfruits was an introduction to the harvest and gave them the freedom to begin reaping, so they celebrated the end of the grain harvest at this feast.

1. For their firstfruits, they offered a handful of ears of barley; now, they offered *two loaves of fine flour* (v. 17). These were baked with yeast. At the Passover they ate unleavened bread, but now at Pentecost it was made with yeast, because it was an acknowledgment of God's goodness to them in their ordinary food, which was made with yeast.

2. With that sheaf of firstfruits they offered only one lamb as a burnt offering, but with these loaves of firstfruits they offered seven lambs, two rams, and one young bull, all as a burnt offering to give glory to God, as the Lord of their harvest. Similarly, they offered a male goat as a sin offering, and lastly, two lambs were brought as a sacrifice of a peace offering (fellowship offering), to ask for a blessing on the grain they had gathered in.

3. One day was to be kept as a holy assembly (v. 21). It was one of the days on which all Israel was to meet God and one another, at the place which the Lord would choose. Some suggest that whereas seven days were designated for the Feast of Unleavened Bread, only one day was appointed for the Feast of Pentecost, because this was a busy time of the year for them, and God allowed them quickly to return to their work in the country. This annual feast was established to mark the giving of the Law on Mount Sinai, the fiftieth day after they came out of Egypt. But the consummation and perfection of this feast was the outpouring of the Spirit on the apostles on the day of this feast (Ac 2:1), in which the law of faith was given, fifty days after Christ our Passover was sacrificed for us.

4. To the institution of the Feast of Pentecost is attached a repetition of that law by which they were instructed to leave the gleanings of their fields and the grain that grew on the ends of the stalks, for the poor (v. 22). It also taught them that the joy of harvest should express itself in acts of kindness to the poor.

Verses 23–32

Here is:

1. The institution of the Feast of Trumpets, on the first day of the seventh month (vv. 24–25). What is made special about this festival here is that it was *a memorial of blowing of trumpets* (v. 24). They blew the trumpet every New Moon (Ps 81:3), but at the New Moon of the seventh month it was to be done with more than a usual sense of occasion; for they began to blow at sunrise and continued till sunset. Now:

1.1. This is here said to be a *memorial*, perhaps of the sound of the trumpet on Mount Sinai when the Law was given, which must never be forgotten.

1.2. The Jewish writers believe it to have a spiritual significance. At the beginning of the year, they were called by this sound of the trumpets to shake off their spiritual drowsiness and lethargy, to examine their ways, and to put them right. The Day of Atonement was the ninth day after this, and so they were woken up to prepare for that day by genuine and deep repentance.

1.3. It was a type of the preaching of the Gospel, by which joyful sound souls were to be called to serve God and keep a spiritual feast with him.

2. A repetition of the law of the Day of Atonement, that is, as much of it as concerned the people:

2.1. On this day they must rest from all kinds of work. The reason is: *For it is a day of atonement* (v. 28). The person who wanted to do the work of the Day of Atonement as it should be done had to put aside thoughts about everything else.

2.2. They must humble their souls. If they did not, they would be cut off by the hand of God (vv. 27, 29, 32). They must mortify their bodies and deny its appetites.

2.3. The whole day must be kept: *From even to even you shall afflict your souls* (v. 32).

Verses 33–44

We have here:

1. The institution of the Feast of Tabernacles, which was one of the three great festivals at which all the males were committed to attend, and which was celebrated with more joy than any of them.

1.1. Notice the instructions for this festival:

1.1.1. It was to be observed five days after the Day of Atonement. We may suppose that though they were not all committed to be present at the Day of Atonement—as they were at the three great festivals—many devout Jews came up these few days before the Feast of Tabernacles so that they could enjoy the opportunity of being present at the Day of Atonement. The humbling of their souls on the Day of Atonement prepared them for the joy of the Feast of Tabernacles. The more sorry and humbled for sin we are, the more qualified we are to receive the encouragements of the Holy Spirit.

1.1.2. It was to continue eight days, the first and last of which were to be observed as Sabbaths.

1.1.3. During the first seven days of this feast, all the people were to leave their houses, including the women and children, and to live in booths made of the boughs of thick trees, particularly palm trees (vv. 40, 42).

1.1.4. They were to *rejoice before the Lord God* during all the time of this feast (v. 40). The tradition of the Jews is that they were to express their joy by dancing and singing hymns of praise to God with musical instruments.

1.2. Notice the purpose of this festival:

• It was to be kept in remembrance of their living in tents in the desert.

• It was a Feast of Ingathering, as it is called (Ex 23:16).

2. The summary and conclusion of these institutions. God appointed these festivals (vv. 37–38), *besides the sabbaths and your freewill offerings*. God's institutions leave room for freewill offerings. The feasts of the Lord that have been declared to us are not so numerous, and observing them is not so burdensome or sacrificial, as theirs were then, but more spiritual and significant. They are more definite and joyful pledges of the eternal feast, at the last ingathering.

CHAPTER 24

In this chapter we have: 1. A repetition of the laws concerning the lamps and the consecrated bread (vv. 1–9). 2. A breach of the law against blasphemy, with the imprisonment, trial, condemnation, and execution of the blasphemer (vv. 10–14, 23); the law against blasphemy reinforced (vv. 15–16), and various other laws (vv. 17–23).

Verses 1–9

Instructions are given here that the candlestick (lampstand) and table in God's house should be properly taken care of:

1. The lamps must always be kept burning.

1.1. The people were to provide oil (v. 2), the best, *pure olive oil, beaten* (pressed); probably it was double-filtered. Ministers are like burning and shining lights in Christ's church, but it is the duty of people to provide resources for their ministers, as Israel provided for the lamps. If ministers are inadequately resourced, then the people have no right to complain about an inadequate ministry.

1.2. The priests were to look after the lamps; they must clear and snuff them, clean the candlestick, and supply them with oil morning and evening (vv. 3–4). In the same way, it is the work of ministers of the Gospel to *hold forth that word of life* (Php 2:16), not to set up new lights, but by opening up and preaching the word, to make its light clearer and to apply it more widely.

2. The table must always be kept spread. Instructions were given about this before (Ex 25:30).

2.1. There was a loaf for every tribe, for *in our Father's house there is bread enough* (Lk 15:17). Even after the rebellion of the ten tribes this number of loaves was continued (2Ch 13:11), for the sake of those few of each tribe who kept up their affection for the temple and continued to be present there.

2.2. A handful of frankincense (incense) was put along each row. When the bread was removed and given to the priests, this frankincense was burned on the golden altar, as a memorial portion instead of the bread, as a humble acknowledgment, and all the loaves were presented to the priests.

2.3. Every Sabbath the bread was renewed. Christ's ministers should provide new bread for his house every Sabbath day, the product of their fresh studies of the Scriptures, that *their profiting may appear to all* (1Ti 4:15).

Verses 10–23

Bad manners, it has sometimes been said, produce good laws. We have here an account of the bad manners of a certain nameless Israelite, and the good laws brought about by it:

1. The offender was the son of an Egyptian father and an Israelite mother (v. 10); his mother was of the tribe of Dan (v. 11). The fact that his parents are noted is intended to show:

1.1. What caused the quarrel he was involved in. The Jews say, "He offered to set up his tent among the Danites according to the rights of his mother, but was justly opposed by someone or other of that tribe, and was informed that since his father was an Egyptian he had no part or share in the matter, but must consider himself an outsider." Or:

1.2. The common adverse effects of such mixed marriages.

2. The cause of the offense was a fight: He *strove with a man of Israel*.

3. The offense itself was blasphemy and cursing (v. 11). He *blasphemed the name of the Lord*. Probably finding himself resentful at God's decree, which separated Israelites and outsiders, he arrogantly and defiantly rebuked both the Law and the Lawmaker. He cursed either God himself or the person with whom he fought.

4. The offender received a warning for this sin. Moses himself would not give a quick judgment, but put the offender into custody, until God's will became clear in this case. They waited to know what was *the mind of the Lord*, whether the man was to be put to death by the hand of the judge or to be left to the judgment of God.

5. The sentence was passed on this offender by the righteous Judge of heaven and earth himself: *Let all the congregation stone him* (v. 14).

6. A law was established on this occasion for blasphemers to be stoned (vv. 15–16). Judges are the guardians of both tables of the Ten Commandments and ought to be as jealous to safeguard the honor of God against those who speak contemptuously about him as they should be to safeguard the public peace and safety from those who want to disturb them.

7. A repetition of some other laws was attached to this new law:

7.1. That murder would be punished by death (v. 17 and again v. 21).

7.2. That those who injure others should in the same way be punished by the law of retaliation (vv. 19–20). We have had this law before (Ex 21:22–25; 22:4–5). And it corresponded more to that era, in which the rigor of the law and the punishment of sin were revealed, than to the present era, in which the grace of the Gospel and the forgiveness of sins are revealed. Our Savior has therefore set aside extremist use of this law (Mt 5:38–39), not to restrain judges from enforcing public justice, but to restrain us from making excessive retribution in returning personal injuries and to make us forgive others as we are forgiven.

7.3. That harm done willfully to the cattle of a neighbor should be punished by making restitution for the damage (vv. 18, 21).

7.4. That foreigners, as well as native Israelites, should both be entitled to the benefit of this law, so as not to suffer wrong, and also be liable to the punishment of this law if they did wrong.

CHAPTER 25

The law of this chapter concerns the lands of the Israelites in Canaan, the occupying and transferring ownership of which were to be under divine direction, as well as their religious worship, for just as the tabernacle was a holy house, so also Canaan was a holy land. God appointed: 1. That every seventh year should be a year of rest from farming the land, a sabbatical year (vv. 1–7). 2. That every fiftieth year should be a Year of Jubilee, that is, a year of release from debts and mortgages, and a return to the possession of their transferred lands (vv. 8–17). 3. That they should follow special instructions for the sale and redemption of land (vv. 23–28); of houses in cities and villages, with a proviso for Levite cities (vv. 29–34); and a law for the kind treatment of poor debtors (vv. 35–38). 4. That they should observe the Year of Jubilee by obeying the law for the release of all Israelites who were sold as servants, if they had not been redeemed before, if they had been sold to Israelites (vv. 39–46), and if sold to converts (vv. 47–55).

Verses 1–7

The Law of Moses emphasized the Sabbath. That law not only revived the observance of the weekly Sabbath, but also, to further advance its honor, added the institution of a sabbatical year: *In the seventh year shall be a sabbath of rest unto the land* (v. 4). This sabbatical year began in September, at the end of harvest, the seventh month of their ecclesiastical year: and the law was:

1. That at the seedtime which immediately followed the end of their ingathering, they should sow no grain in their land, and that in the spring they should not prepare their vineyards, and so they would not expect a grain or a grape harvest the next year.

2. That what their ground produced by itself they should not claim possession of or use, except from hand to mouth, but leave it for the poor, servants, foreigners who lived with them, and cattle (vv. 5–7).

2.1. It must be a Sabbath rest for the land. They must neither do any work on it, nor expect any fruit from it. All annual labors must be interrupted in the seventh year, as much as daily labors on the seventh day. It was an act of kindness to the land to give it a rest for a time—so that it would be in prime condition for the long-term future, which God wanted them to consider—and not only to use the land as if it were intended simply for the short term.

2.2. This year of rest was a type of the spiritual rest which all believers enter into through Christ, our true Noah, who gives us comfort and rest *concerning our work, and the toil of our hands, because of the ground which the Lord hath cursed* (Ge 5:29).

Verses 8–22

Here is:

1. The general institution of the Year of Jubilee:

1.1. When it was to be observed: after *seven sabbaths of years* (v. 8).

1.2. How it was to be declared, with the sound of trumpet in all parts of the country (v. 9), both to give notice to everyone about it and also to express their joy and triumph in it. The word *yobel*, or "jubilee," refers to a particular sound of the trumpet. The trumpet was sounded at the close of the Day of Atonement. When their peace was made with God, then freedom was declared.

1.3. What was to be done in that exceptional year, besides the general rest of the land, which was observed every sabbatical year (vv. 11–12): the release of personal debts (Dt 15:2–3) and the legal restoration to every Israelite of all the property and all the freedom that had been sold by them since the last Jubilee.

1.3.1. The property which everyone had in their share of the land of Canaan could not be transferred any longer than up to the Year of Jubilee (vv. 13, 28). This did not wrong the purchaser, because the Year of Jubilee was fixed, and everyone knew when it would come and so could arrange the financial details accordingly. They will not have power to sell, but only to make leases for a certain term of years, not going beyond the next Jubilee. This made sure that the distinction between the various tribes would be kept; that none would grow exorbitantly rich, by accumulating *house to house, and field to field* (Isa 5:8), but that they would instead give themselves to cultivating what they had rather than obtaining further property and possessions.

1.3.2. The liberty which everyone was born into, if it was sold or forfeited, would similarly return to them at the Year of Jubilee: *You shall return every man to his family* (v. 10). In this way, those who were sold into other families became strangers to their own, but they were to return in this year of redemption.

2. A law on this occasion against oppression in buying and selling of land; neither the buyer nor the seller must overreach themselves (vv. 14–17). The yearly value of the land must be clearly agreed on, and then how many years' purchase it was worth till the Year of Jubilee. It is easy to notice that the nearer the Jubilee was, the less the value of the land had to be: *According to the fewness of the years thou shalt diminish the price* (v. 16).

3. Assurance given them that they would not be losers, but gainers, by observing these years of rest. It is promised:

3.1. That they would be kept safe: *You shall dwell in the land in safety* (v. 18 and again v. 19). The word refers to both outward safety and inward security and confidence of spirit.

3.2. That they would be rich: *You shall eat your fill* (v. 19).

3.3. That they would not lack food in the year in which they did not sow or reap: *I will command my blessing in the sixth year, and it shall bring forth fruit for three years* (v. 21). This was intended to be an encouragement to all God's people in all ages to trust him in their duty and to give all their cares to him.

Verses 23–38

Here is:

1. A law concerning the property of the Israelites in the land of Canaan and the transferring of it.

1.1. No land should be permanently sold from the family to whom it was allotted in the division of the land. And the reason given is, *The land is mine, and you are strangers and sojourners with me* (v. 23). If a person was forced through poverty to sell their land to keep their family alive, and if afterward they were able to redeem it before the Year of Jubilee, they were permitted to do so (vv. 24, 26–27). The price must be agreed on according to the number of years since the sale and before the Jubilee.

1.2. If the person himself was not able to redeem it, their closest relative could (v. 25). The closest relative is called *go'el*, the redeemer (Nu 5:8; Ru 3:9), to whom belonged the right of redeeming the land.

1.2.1. This was a type of Christ, who took on himself our nature, that he might be our closest relative, our Kinsman-Redeemer. If the land was not redeemed before the Year of Jubilee, then it would of course revert to the one who had sold or mortgaged it: *In the jubilee it shall go out* (v. 28). This prefigured the free grace of God toward us in Christ, by which we are restored to the favor of God, and become entitled to paradise, from which our first parents were expelled for disobedience.

1.2.2. A difference was made between houses in walled cities and houses in country villages. Houses in walled cities were more the product of their own industry, and houses

in villages with no fortified walls were more the direct gift of God's goodness. So if a person sold a house in a city, it might be redeemed at any time within a year after the sale, but otherwise it was confirmed to the purchaser permanently and would not revert, not even at the Year of the Jubilee (vv. 29–30).

1.2.3. This provision was made to encourage foreigners and converts to come and settle among them. Though they could not buy land in Canaan for themselves and their heirs, they still could buy houses in walled cities. A clause is added in favor of the Levites, as an exception to these rules.

2. A law to help the poor, and to carefully look after poor debtors. These are more general and permanent obligations than the previous ones.

2.1. The poor must be helped (v. 35). Here is:

2.1.1. The case if one of their own people becomes poor. Every human being is to be looked on and treated as a brother or sister, for *we have all one Father* (Mal 2:10).

2.1.2. The commitment that is to be shown: *Thou shalt relieve him* (v. 35). How? By showing sympathy, having compassion on the poor; by service, doing acts of kindness for them; and by giving to them what they need according to our ability.

2.2. Poor debtors must not be oppressed: *If thy brother be waxen poor*, and needs to borrow money from you to support his family, *take thou no usury of him.* Do not charge interest when lending money or make a profit when selling food (vv. 36–37).

Verses 39–55

We have here the laws concerning slavery, intended to preserve the honor of the Jewish nation as a free people, who were rescued by divine power from slavery into the glorious liberty of the children of God, his firstborn. Now the law is:

1. That native Israelites should never be made slaves forever. If they were sold for debt or for a crime by the law court, they were to serve only six years and go free on the seventh; this was the law (Ex 21:2). But if the person sold themselves through extreme poverty, having nothing at all to live on, and if they sold themselves to one of their own nation, then in such cases:

1.1. That person should not *serve as a bondservant* (slave) (v. 39), nor be *sold as bondmen* (slaves) (v. 42). The person will serve you as *a hired servant*, a worker whom the master may use. God had redeemed them from Egypt, and so they must never be exposed to sale as slaves.

1.2. While the person worked, they should not be treated harshly, as the Israelites were in Egypt (v. 43). Both the work and the treatment of the worker must be those appropriate for children of Abraham.

1.3. At the Year of Jubilee the person should *go out free*, with *his children*, and should *return to his own family* (v. 41). For ten days before the Jubilee trumpet sounded, the servants who were then to be discharged expressed their great joy by feasting and wearing garlands on their heads.

2. That they could buy slaves from the nations that were around them, for the Year of Jubilee did not discharge them (vv. 44, 46).

3. That if an Israelite sold themselves as a servant to a wealthy convert who stayed among them, care should be taken that they should have the same advantages as if they had sold themselves to an Israelite, and in some respects greater:

3.1. That they should not serve as slaves, but as hired workers. Further, they were to go free at the Year of Jubilee (v. 54).

3.2. That they should have the further advantage that they might be redeemed again before the Year of Jubilee (vv. 48–49).

CHAPTER 26

This chapter brings the main body of the Levitical law to a formal conclusion. The instructions that follow in this and the next book are repetitions and explanations. This chapter gives a general enforcement of all those laws by promising a reward in case of obedience, and threats of punishment for disobedience, the former to produce hope, the latter fear, those two ways of taking hold of the soul. Here is: 1. A repetition of two or three of the main commandments (vv. 1–2), leading to a promise of good things, if they kept God's commandments (vv. 3–13). 2. A terrible threat of destructive judgments which would be brought on them if they were perverse and disobedient (vv. 14–39). 3. A gracious promise of mercy to those who repented and reformed their ways (vv. 40–46). Dt 28:1–20 is a parallel passage to this.

Verses 1–13

Here:

1. Those instructions of the Law which were most important are instilled, by which the obedience of the Israelites would be especially tested (vv. 1–2). They are a summary of the second and fourth commandments:

1.1. "Be sure you never worship idols or ever make any sorts of image for religious use" (v. 1). Next to God's Being, unity, and universal influence, it is necessary that we know and believe that he is an infinite Spirit, and so to represent him by an idol or to worship and bow down to an idol *changes his truth into a lie* (Ro 1:25) and *his glory into shame* (Ps 4:2), as much as anything.

1.2. "Be sure you greatly respect Sabbaths and religious assemblies" (v. 2). As nothing leads more to corrupt religion than using idols in worship, so nothing contributes more to true religion than *keeping the sabbaths* and *reverencing the sanctuary* (v. 2). These form the means of religion, by which its essentials are maintained.

2. Great encouragements are given them to live in constant obedience to all God's commandments. Human governments enforce their laws with penalties that are inflicted if the laws are disobeyed, but God wants to be known as *the rewarder of those that seek him* (Heb 11:6). God promises:

2.1. Plentiful fruits of the earth. Before they had reaped their corn and threshed it, the grape harvest would be ready, and before they had finished their grape harvest, it would be time to begin sowing again. The plenty would be so great that they would need to *bring forth the old* (v. 10), to give it away to the poor *because of the new*, to make room for it in their barns.

2.2. Peace under the divine protection: "*You shall dwell in your land safely* (v. 5); safe in your own perception. You will lie down to rest in the power and promise of God, and not only will no one hurt you, but also no one will so much as *make you afraid*" (v. 6). See Ps 4:8.

2.3. Victory and success in their wars abroad, while they had peace and tranquility at home (vv. 7–8).

2.4. Increase in the numbers of their people: *I will make you fruitful and multiply you* (v. 9).

2.5. His favor, which is the fountain of all good: *I will have respect unto you* (v. 9). If we are looking by faith to God, he will look with his favor on us.

2.6. Signs of his presence in and by his ordinances: *I will set my tabernacle among you* (v. 11).

2.7. The grace of the covenant, as the fountain and foundation, the sweetness and security, of all these blessings: *I will establish my covenant with you* (v. 9). If they fulfill their part of the covenant, God will not fail to fulfill his. All covenant blessings are summed up in the covenant-relationship (v. 12): *I will be your God, and you shall be my people*, and they are all based on their redemption: *I am your God*, because I *brought you forth out of the land of Egypt* (v. 13).

Verses 14–39

After God had set these blessings of a good and happy life before them, he here sets curses before them. If they were disobedient, then death and evil would make them miserable. Notice:

1. How their sin is described, which would bring all this misery on them. Not sins of ignorance and infirmity, since God had provided sacrifices for those. Not the sins they repented of and abandoned, but the sins arrogantly committed and stubbornly persisted in. Two things would certainly bring this ruin on them:

1.1. Contempt of God's commandments (v. 14). Their sin is said to begin in mere carelessness, neglect, and omission.

- *Despising God's statutes*, both the duties that were instructed and the authority instructing them, having a low opinion of the Law and the Lawmaker.
- *Abhorring his judgments* (v. 15), their very souls hating them. Those who turn away from it will turn against it, and their hearts will rise up against it.
- *Breaking his covenant* (v. 15). When people have come to such a level of ungodliness as to despise and hate God's commandment, the next step will be to turn their backs on God and everything to do with him. Those who reject God's principles will eventually come to renounce the covenant.

1.2. Contempt of God's corrections. Even their disobedience would not have led to their destruction if they had not been stubborn and refused to repent, despite the efforts God made to win them back. This is expressed in three ways:

- *If you will not for all this hearken to me* (vv. 18, 21, 27).
- *If you walk contrary to me* (vv. 21, 23, 27). All sinners are hostile to God, to his truths, laws, and counsels, but especially those who refuse to be influenced by his judgments.
- *If you will not be reformed by these things* (v. 23). God's intention in disciplining his people is to reform them, by giving them a clear sense of the evil of sin and making them seek him for relief. But those who will not be reformed by the judgments of God must expect to be destroyed by them.

2. How the misery is described which their sin would bring on them, in two ways:

2.1. God himself would be against them, and this is the root of all their misery. Those who drive God away deserve that he should drive them away. When those who are stubborn and refuse to be corrected have weathered one storm, they must expect another, more violent one.

2.2. The whole creation would be at war against them. Here:

2.2.1. Material judgments are threatened:

2.2.1.1. Diseases of body would be widespread among them.

2.2.1.2. Famine and scarcity of bread would come on them.

2.2.1.3. "Your best soldiers will die in battle, and *those that hate you shall reign over you*, and justly so, since you are not willing that the God who loved you should reign over you" (2Ch 12:8).

2.2.1.4. Wild animals — lions, bears, and wolves — would come in increasing numbers.

2.2.1.5. They would be scattered in captivity or dispersion: *I will scatter you among the heathen* (v. 33), *in your enemies' land* (v. 34). Never was any people so united among themselves as the Israelites were, but God would scatter them because of their sin, so that they would be lost among the nations, from whom God had graciously set them apart, but with whom they had wrongly associated.

2.2.1.6. Their land would be completely destroyed and become desolate; the destruction would be so massive that even their enemies, who had been instrumental in bringing it about, would be appalled by it (v. 32):

• Their cities would be laid waste.
• Their sanctuaries would be destroyed.
• The country itself would become desolate, not cultivated or farmed (vv. 34–35).

2.2.1.7. Their idols would be destroyed: *I will destroy your high places* (v. 30). Those who do not want to leave their sins by the commands of God will be parted from them by his judgments. Since they would not destroy their high places, God would do so himself.

2.2.2. Spiritual judgments are threatened. These would seize the mind, for the One who made the mind can, when he pleases, make his sword come near it. It is threatened here:

• That they would find no acceptance with God: *I will not smell the savour of your sweet odours* (v. 31).
• That they would have no courage in their wars, but would be completely demoralized.
• That they would have no hope of the forgiveness of their sins (v. 39).

Verses 40–46

Here the chapter concludes with gracious promises of the return of God's favor to them if they repent, that they might not, unless it were their own fault, *pine* (waste) *away in their iniquity* (v. 39). As terrible as things are, *there is* still *hope in Israel*. Notice:

1. How the repentance which would qualify them for this mercy is described (vv. 40–41). There are three conditions:

1.1. Confession, by which they must give glory to God, and be ashamed of themselves. They must call sin sin when they confess it: it is *walking contrary to God* (vv. 40–41).

1.2. A broken, contrite heart and godly sorrow for sin: *If their uncircumcised heart be humbled* (v. 41). An impenitent, unbelieving, unhumbled heart is called an *uncircumcised* heart, the heart of a Gentile that is a stranger to God, rather than the heart of an Israelite in covenant with him. True circumcision is *of the heart* (Ro 2:29), without which the circumcision of the flesh is of no value (Jer 9:26). A humble heart under humbling providences is a good preparation for receiving God's rescue and true comfort.

1.3. Submission to the justice of God in all his dealings. If they *accept of the punishment of their iniquity*

(v. 41 and again v. 43), that is, if they justify God and condemn themselves, then they will show they have truly repented.

2. How the mercy which they would receive if they repented is described:

2.1. They would not be abandoned: *Though they have despised my judgments, yet for all that, I will not cast them away* (vv. 43–44). God speaks as a tender Father who cannot find it in his heart to disinherit his disobedient children.

2.2. They would be remembered: *I will remember the land* with favor, which is based on the promise before, *I will remember my covenant* (v. 42 and again v. 45). God is said *to remember the covenant* when he fulfills its promises, purely because of his faithfulness. The word *covenant* is repeated three times in v. 42, to show that God always remembers it and wants us to also. When those who have walked against God's ways return to him in sincere repentance, even though God has walked contrary to them in judgment, he will return to them in special mercy, according to the covenant of redemption and grace. No one is more ready to repent than God is to forgive, when a sinner repents, through Christ under the new covenant.

CHAPTER 27

Having given laws concerning his institutions, God through Moses here gives directions concerning vows and voluntary services, the freewill offerings of their mouths. Perhaps some godly people among them might have been so moved by what Moses had delivered to them in the previous chapter that in the heat of the moment they zealously dedicated themselves, their children, or property to him. Here is the law: 1. Concerning what was dedicated to God: people (vv. 2–8), cattle, clean or unclean (vv. 9–13), houses and lands (vv. 14–25); with an exception of the firstborn (vv. 26–27). 2. Concerning what was devoted (vv. 28–29). 3. Concerning tithes (vv. 30–34).

Verses 1–13

This is part of the law concerning exceptional vows, which though God did not explicitly insist on, he would gladly accept, if they were consistent with his general commands.

1. People dedicated to God by a special vow (v. 2). If a person dedicated themselves or a child to the service of the tabernacle to be employed there in some lowly work such as sweeping the floor, carrying out ashes, or running errands, *the person* dedicated in this way *shall be for the Lord*, that is, "God will graciously accept the goodwill." *Thou didst well that it was in thy heart* (2Ch 6:8). But because there was no need for their service in the tabernacle, as a whole tribe was employed in those duties, those who were promised in this way were to be redeemed, and the money paid for their redemption was to be used in the repair of the sanctuary, or for other uses, as appears in 2Ki 12:4, where the margin reads "the money of the souls of his estimation." A record of prices is therefore provided, by which the priests were to make their valuations. The poor will be valued according to their ability (v. 8). Something must be paid, so that they might learn not to make rash vows to God. But the price to be paid should be no more than what the person could afford, that they might not ruin themselves and their families by their overzealousness.

2. Animals vowed to God.

Verses 14–25

Here is the law concerning property dedicated to God's service by a special vow:

1. Suppose a person in their zeal for God's honor should *sanctify his house to God* (v. 14). The house must be valued by the priest, and the money gained from the sale must be converted for use in the sanctuary, which gradually came to be greatly enriched with *dedicated things* (1Ki 15:15). If the owner was inclined to redeem it themselves, they must not have it as cheaply as another, but must add a fifth to the price, for they should have thought about that before they vowed it (v. 15).

2. Suppose a person wants to dedicate part of their land to the Lord, giving it over to godly uses. Then a difference must be made between land that came to the donor through the family line and what came through being bought, and the cases were dealt with differently.

Verses 26–34

1. A warning is given that no one should make light of dedicating things to the Lord by dedicating any firstborn to him, for that was already his according to the law (v. 26).

2. A distinction is made between things or people that were devoted, and things or people that were only dedicated.

2.1. Devoted things were most holy to the Lord, and could be neither sold nor redeemed: they could not revert nor have their ownership transferred (v. 28).

2.2. Devoted (or banned) people were to be put to death (v. 29). Not that it was in the power of any parent or master to devote a child or a servant to death in this way, but it must be meant to refer to the public enemies of Israel.

3. A law concerning tithes, which were paid for the service of God before the law was instituted, as appears by Abraham's payment of them (Ge 14:20) and Jacob's promise of them (Ge 28:22). They are instructed here to pay a tithe of all their grain, trees, and cattle (vv. 30, 32). We are taught in general to *honour the Lord with our substance* (Pr 3:9), and in particular to support and maintain his ministers, to *communicate* to them (Gal 6:6; 1Co 9:11). We cannot see how this may be done in a more appropriate and more equal proportion than a tenth, which God himself ordained.

4. The last verse seems to refer to this whole book, of which it is the conclusion: *These are the commandments which the Lord commanded Moses, for the children of Israel.* Many of these commandments are moral and are binding forever; others, which were ceremonial and special to the Jewish dispensation, have nevertheless spiritual significance, and are instructive to us who have been given the key to allow us into their mysteries. Generally, we have cause to bless God that *we have not come to Mount Sinai* (Heb 12:18):

4.1. That we are not under the *dark shadows* of the Law, but enjoy the clear light of the Gospel, which shows us *Christ the end of the law for righteousness* (Ro 10:4). The doctrine of our reconciliation to God through a Mediator is not obscured with the smoke of burning sacrifices, but cleared by the knowledge of *Christ and him crucified* (1Co 2:2).

4.2. That we are not under the *heavy yoke* (1Ki 12:4) of the Law and its *carnal ordinances* — as the writer to the Hebrews calls them (Heb 9:10) — external regulations, till the time of the new order, a yoke which *neither they nor their fathers were able to bear* (Ac 15:10), but under the pleasant and light ways of the Gospel, which declares those the *true worshippers that worship the Father in spirit and truth* (Jn 4:23), only by Christ, and in his name, who is our Priest, temple, altar, sacrifice, purification, and everything. *Having boldness to enter into the holiest by the blood of Jesus, let us draw near with a true heart, and in full assurance of faith* (Heb 10:19), worshiping God with a deep joy and humble confidence and saying, *Blessed be God for Jesus Christ!*

A Practical and Devotional Exposition of the Fourth Book of Moses,

Numbers

The titles of the five books of Moses which we use in our Bibles are all taken from the Septuagint, a Greek translation of the Old Testament. But it is only the title of this book that we turn into English; in all the rest we retain the Greek word itself. This book was given this title because of the numbers of the children of Israel, so often mentioned in it and so worthy to give it its title, because it was the remarkable achievement of God's promise to Abraham that his descendants would be as many as the stars in the sky. It also relates to two censuses, one at Mount Sinai (ch. 1), the other in the plains of Moab, thirty-nine years later (ch. 26). The book is almost equally divided between histories and laws, mixed together.

We have here: 1. The histories of the numbering and marshaling of the tribes (chs. 1–4), the dedication of the altar and Levites (chs. 7–8), their march (chs. 9–10), their grumbling and unbelief, for which they were sentenced to wander forty years in the desert (chs. 11–14), supplementary offerings (ch. 15), the rebellion of Korah (chs. 16–17), the history of the last year of the forty (chs. 20–26), the conquest of Midian, and the settlement of the two tribes (chs. 31–32), with an account of their journeys (ch. 33). 2. Various laws about the camp purity (ch. 5), the Nazarites (ch. 6), supplementary offerings (ch. 15), the priests' duties (chs. 18–19), festivals (chs. 28–29), and vows (ch. 30), relating to their settlement in Canaan (chs. 27; 34–36). A summary of much of this book is given in a few words in Ps 95:10: *Forty years long was I grieved with this generation*, and an application of it to ourselves in Heb 4:1: *Let us fear lest we seem to come short*. Many significant nations that lived in cities and fortified towns now existed, but no notice is taken of them, no record kept, by sacred history. But very exact records are kept of the affairs of a handful of people who lived in tents and wandered strangely in a desert, because they were the children of the covenant. *For the Lord's portion is his people, Jacob is the lot of his inheritance* (Dt 32:9).

CHAPTER 1

Israel was now to be formed into a community, or rather a kingdom, for "the Lord was their King" (1Sa 12:12), their government a theocracy, and Moses was king under him in Jeshurun (Dt 33:5). So that this holy state might be rightly established, after good laws had been instituted it was necessary to have good order instituted. And so a census must be taken of the subjects of this kingdom, which is done in this chapter, where we have: 1. Orders given to Moses to number the people (vv. 1–4). The people named who are to help him in this (vv. 5–16). 2. The particular number of each tribe, as it was given in to Moses (vv. 17–43). 3. The total of all the tribes together (vv. 44–46). 4. The exception of the Levites (vv. 47–54).

Verses 1–16

1. We have here a commission issued for the numbering of the people of Israel, and much later David paid dearly for doing it without a commission. Here is:

1.1. The date of this commission (v. 1).

1.1.1. The place: it is given at God's court in the wilderness of Sinai, from his royal palace, the tabernacle of the congregation, the Tent of Meeting.

1.1.2. The time: in the second year after they came up out of Egypt; we may call it the second year of that reign.

The laws in Leviticus were given in the first month of that year; these orders were given in the beginning of the second month.

1.2. The directions given for carrying it out (vv. 2–3):

1.2.1. Only the males were to be numbered, and only those who were able to go to war.

1.2.2. None who were unfit for war because of age, bodily weakness, blindness, lameness, or chronic diseases were numbered.

1.2.3. The account was to be taken *according to their families*, that not only would it be known how many they were and what their names were, but also from which tribe and family or clan, and even from which particular house every person came, or considering the total number of troops of an army, to which regiment every soldier belonged, that all the soldiers might each know their place and the leaders might know where to find each one. They were numbered a little before this, when a poll tax was paid for the service of the tabernacle (Ex 38:25–26). But it would seem they were not then registered *by the house of their fathers*, as they now are.

1.3. Commissioners are named to undertake this work. Moses and Aaron were to preside (v. 3), and one man of every tribe, who was prominent in his tribe, and was presumed to know it well, was to assist in it.

2. Why was this account ordered to be taken and kept? For several reasons:

2.1. To prove the fulfillment of the promise made to Abraham, that God would *multiply his seed exceedingly* (Ge 16:10), which promise was renewed to Jacob (Ge 28:14), that *his seed should be as the dust of the earth.*

2.2. To show the special care which God himself would take of his Israel. God is called the *Shepherd of Israel* (Ps 80:1). Now shepherds always kept count of their flocks and delivered them by number to their undershepherds, that they might know if any were missing. In the same way, God numbers his flock.

2.3. To put a difference between the truly born Israelites and the many other people who were among them; it was only the Israelites who were numbered.

2.4. To marshal them into several districts, so that justice could be administered more easily, and so that they could make a more orderly march through the desert.

Verses 17–43

We see here that the orders given for the numbering of the people were quickly acted on. The census was begun on the same day that the orders were given, *the first day of the second month* (vv. 1, 18). In the details here recorded, we may observe:

1. That the numbers are registered in full words, not figures; for every one of the twelve tribes it is repeated, to give greater formality to the record, that they were numbered *by their generations, after their families, by the house of their fathers, according to the number of the names* (vv. 20, 22, 24, 26, 28, 30, 32, 34, 36, 38, 40, 42). In this way, every man might know who were his relatives or next of kin, on which some laws already considered depended.

2. That they all end with hundreds, only Gad with *fifty* (v. 25), but none of the numbers go into units or tens.

3. That Judah is the most numerous of them all, more than double those of Benjamin and Manasseh, and almost 12,000 more than any other tribe (v. 27). It was Judah whom his *brethren shall praise* (Ge 49:8), because the Messiah, the Ruler, was to descend from him. Judah was to lead the way through the desert and so was given greater strength than any other tribe.

Verses 44–46

We have here the total at the close of the record; they were in all 603,550 fighting men (v. 46). Some think that when this was their number some months before (Ex 38:26), the Levites were counted with them, but now that this tribe was set apart for the service of God, so many more had by this time reached the age of twenty years that they were still the same number. This shows that whatever we part with for the honor and service of God will certainly be made up to us one way or another.

Verses 47–54

Care is taken here to distinguish the tribe of Levi from the rest of the tribes. The tribe of Levi had distinguished itself in the episode with the golden calf (Ex 32:26). Exceptional service for God will be rewarded by exceptional honors.

1. The Levites were honored by being made guardians of spiritual matters. The care of the tabernacle and its treasures was committed to the Levites both in the camps of the Israelites and on their journeys.

1.1. When they moved, the Levites were to take down the tabernacle, to carry it and everything that belonged

to it, and then to set it up again at the appointed place (vv. 50–51). The holy things were held in such a position of honor that no one was allowed to see them or touch them, except those who had been called by God to the service.

1.2. When the people rested, the Levites were to *encamp round about the tabernacle* (vv. 50, 53), that they might be near their work and stay near what was their responsibility, always being readily available and guarding the tabernacle to keep it from being plundered or desecrated.

2. Just as Israel, being a holy people, were not *reckoned among the nations* (23:9), so the Levites were also honored as a holy tribe by not being counted among other Israelites, but numbered by themselves afterward (v. 49).

CHAPTER 2

The thousands of Israel, after they had been mustered—which we read about in the previous chapter—are in this chapter marshaled, and the camp is arranged in a regular way by divine appointment. Here is: 1. A general order (vv. 1–2). 2. Particular directions for the positioning of each of the tribes in four distinct divisions, three tribes in each division. In the vanguard on the east Judah, Issachar, and Zebulun were positioned (vv. 3–9); on the right wing on the south, Reuben, Simeon, and Gad (vv. 10–16); at the rear on the west, Ephraim, Manasseh, and Benjamin (vv. 18–24); on the left wing on the north, Dan, Asher, and Napthali (vv. 25–31). The tabernacle is in the center (v. 17). 3. The conclusion of this arrangement (vv. 32–34).

Verses 1–2

Here is the general arrangement given for both the people's orderly formation when they rested and their orderly march when they moved:

1. They all lived in tents, and when they marched, they carried all their tents along with them.

2. The people of each tribe were to set up their tents together, *every man by his own standard* (1:52). Those who are related to each other should, as far as they can, get to know one another deeply. We should make the most of natural relationships to strengthen the ties of Christian fellowship.

3. Every one must know their place and keep to it.

4. Every tribe had its standard, flag, or ensign, and it would seem that every family had a special ensign for their own house. It is uncertain how these standards were distinguished: some think that the standard of each tribe had the same color as the precious stone in which the name of that tribe was written on the high priest's ephod. Some of them say the four principal standards were: Judah a lion, Reuben a man, Joseph an ox, and Dan an eagle, making the appearances in Ezekiel's vision (Eze 1:10) allude to it.

5. They were to set up camp around the tabernacle, which was to be in the middle of them, as the tent or pavilion of a general is in the center of an army, so that they might guard and defend the tabernacle and the Levites on every side.

6. But they were to set up their tents far away, out of due reverence to the sanctuary. It is thought (Jos 3:4), that the distance between the nearest part of the camp and the tabernacle was 2,000 cubits, that is, about 1,000 yards (about 900 meters).

Verses 3–34

We have here the particular arrangement of the twelve tribes into four divisions, three tribes in a division, one of which was to lead the other two.

1. God himself appointed their places, to prevent strife and envy among them. If God in his providence promotes others above us and humbles us, we ought to be as satisfied with what he has done as if he had done it in the way that he did here, by a voice out of the tabernacle. And as far as our place is concerned, our Savior has given us a rule in Lk 14:8: *Sit not down in the highest room* (place of honor); and another in Mt 20:27: *He that will be chief, let him be your servant*. Those who are most humble and most useful are those who are really most honorable.

2. Every tribe had a leader, whom God himself nominated, the same as the one who had been appointed to number them (1:5). Some believe the significance of the names of these leaders, at least in general, shows how much God was in the thoughts of those who gave them their names, for most of them have *El*, "God," at one end or the other of their names. *Nethaneel* (Nethanel), "God gives"; *Eliab*, "God is Father"; *Elizur*, "God is rock"; *Shelumiel*, "God is peace"; *Eliasaph*, "God has added"; *Elishama*, "God is hearer"; *Gamaliel*, "God is my reward"; *Pagiel*, "God has met me."

3. Those tribes were placed together under the same standard that were most closely related to one another; Judah, Issachar, and Zebulun were the three younger sons of Leah, and so they were put together; and Issachar and Zebulun would not object to being under Judah, since they were his younger brothers. Reuben and Simeon would not have been happy in their place. And so Reuben, Jacob's eldest son, is made leader of the next division; Simeon, no doubt, is willing to be under him, and Gad, the son of Zilpah, Leah's maidservant, is suitably added to them in Levi's place. Ephraim, Manasseh, and Benjamin are all the descendants of Rachel. Dan, the eldest son of Bilhah, is made a leading tribe so that greater honor might be given to what lacked, him being only the son of a concubine; and it was said, *Dan should judge his people* (Ge 49:16), and to him were added the two younger sons of the maidservants. In this way, exception could not be taken to the order in which they were placed.

4. The tribe of Judah was given the first position of honor, toward the rising sun, and in their marches led the vanguard, not only because it was the most numerous tribe, but also mainly because Christ was to come from that tribe. Judah was the first of the twelve sons of Jacob who was blessed. The one who was first in blessing, though not in birth, is put first, to teach children how to value the smiles of their godly parents and fear their frowns.

5. The tribe of Levi set up camp close to the tabernacle, in the middle of the rest of the tribes (v. 17). They must defend the sanctuary, and then the rest of the tribes must defend them. Civil powers should protect the religious interests of a nation and defend that glory.

6. The camp of Dan, though positioned on the left wing when they camped, was ordered to bring up the rear in their marching (v. 31). They were the most numerous next to Judah, and so were ordered to take up a position which next to the front required the most strength.

CHAPTER 3

This chapter and the next deal with the tribe of Levi, which was to be gathered and marshaled by itself. In this chapter the Levites are considered: 1. As attendants on, and assistants to, the priests in the temple service. We have an account of the priests themselves (vv. 1–4), their work (v. 10), and the gift of the Levites to them (vv. 5–9). 2. As people to be numbered (vv. 14–16), and the total is worked out (v. 39). Each particular family is gathered and is assigned its position and its responsibility: the Gershonites (vv. 17–26), the Kohathites (vv. 27–32), the Merarites (vv. 33–39). 3. As equivalents for the firstborn (vv. 11–13): the firstborn are numbered, and the Levites taken instead of them, as far as the number of the Levites went (vv. 40–45). The number of firstborn Israelites to be redeemed was greater than the number of Levites (vv. 46–51).

Verses 1–13

1. The family of Aaron is confirmed in the priests' office (v. 10). They had been called to it before and ordained. Here they are appointed to *wait on their priests' office*: the apostle Paul uses this phrase (Ro 12:7), *Let us wait on our ministry*. The office of the ministry requires constant alertness and great dedication. Its work is so constant and its favorable opportunities so brief, that we must always be ready to serve. *The stranger that cometh nigh shall be put to death*, which forbids any other person whatever from taking over the priests' office. No one else must come near to minister except Aaron and his sons; all others are not authorized to do so. The office also places a responsibility on the priests as doorkeepers in God's house, to take care that no one forbidden by the Law would come near.

2. A detailed record is given of the family of Aaron. What we have read about them before is repeated here. The two younger sons, Eleazar and Ithamar, ministered *in the sight of Aaron* (v. 4). They stayed under their father's eye, and took instruction from him in all they did, because probably Nadab and Abihu were out of their father's sight when they offered unauthorized fire.

3. The privilege is given to the Levites to be assistants to the priests in their work: *Give the Levites to Aaron* (v. 9). Aaron was to have a greater ownership of, and authority over, the tribe of Levi than any of the other leaders had over their respective tribes. Here is:

3.1. The service which the Levites were intended to fulfill: they were to *minister to the priests* in their service to the Lord (v. 6) and to *keep Aaron's charge* (v. 7). The Levites killed the sacrifices, and then the priests only needed to sprinkle the blood and burn the fat. The Levites prepared the incense, the priests burned it. They were to fulfill, not only Aaron's responsibilities, but also those of *the whole congregation* (v. 7).

3.2. The significance of the Levites; they were taken instead of the firstborn.

Verses 14–39

Since the Levites were given to Aaron to minister to him, they are here given to him in certain numbers, that he might know how many he had and employ them accordingly. Notice:

1. According to what rule they were numbered: *Every male from a month old and upward* (v. 15). The rest of the tribes were numbered only from twenty years old and upward, and of them only those who were *able to go forth to war* (1:3, etc.), but they must include both infants and infirm in the number of the Levites. Since they were exempted from going to war, it was not insisted that they be of the age and strength for war. Though it appears

afterward that little more than a third of the Levites were fit to be employed in the service of the tabernacle (about 8,000 out of 22,000; see 4:47–48), God wanted them all numbered as dependents in his family.

2. How they were distributed into three clans, according to the number of the sons of Levi—Gershon, Kohath, and Merari—and these subdivided into several families (vv. 17–20).

2.1. We have a record concerning each of these three clans:

• Of their number.
• Of their position around the tabernacle at which they were to serve. The Gershonites set up their tents behind the tabernacle, to the west (v. 23). The Kohathites on the right hand, to the south (v. 29). The Merarites on the left hand, to the north (v. 35). And to complete the square, Moses and Aaron with the priests set up camp in the front, to the east (v. 38).
• Of their leader. As each clan had its own place, so each also had its own leader.
• Of their responsibilities, when the camp moved. The Gershonites were responsible for the care and transport of all the curtains and coverings of the tabernacle and court (vv. 25–26); the Kohathites of all the furnishings of the tabernacle—the ark, altar, table, etc. (vv. 31–32); the Merarites of the heavy equipment: boards (frames), bars, pillars (posts), etc. (vv. 36–37).

2.2. Here we may notice:

2.2.1. That the Kohathites, although they were the second house, were preferred to the elder family of the Gershonites. Moreover, Aaron and the priests came from that family; they were more numerous, and their position and responsibility more honorable, which probably was arranged to give honor to Moses, who came from that family. But:

2.2.2. That the descendants of Moses were not honored or privileged in any way, but stood on the same level as other Levites.

3. The total numbers of this tribe. They are worked out as being 22,000 in all (v. 39). What is especially significant here is that the tribe of Levi was by far the smallest in number of all the tribes.

Verses 40–51

Here the exchange is made of the Levites for the first-born:

1. The firstborn were numbered from a month old (vv. 42–43). Bishop Patrick is of the firm opinion that none were numbered except those who were born since they had left Egypt, when the firstborn were consecrated (Ex 13:2). If there were 22,000 firstborn males and we may suppose as many females, and if all these were born in the first year after they came out of Egypt, we must deduce from this that in the last year of their slavery—when they were in greatest difficulty—many marriages took place among the Israelites. They were not discouraged by their then current distress, but married in faith, expecting that God would soon come to them in mercy, and that their children, though born in slavery, would live in freedom and honor. They were not only kept alive, but also greatly increased, in a barren desert.

2. The number of the firstborn, and that of the Levites, by special providence, came quite near to each other.

3. The small number of firstborn which exceeded the number of the Levites (273 in all) were to be redeemed, at five shekels each, and the redemption money given to Aaron, for it would not be good to have them added to the Levites.

CHAPTER 4

In the last chapter, a record was given of the whole tribe of Levi. In this chapter, we have a record of those who were in the prime of their life of service, between thirty and fifty years old. Here we read of the useful men of: 1. The Kohathites, who are ordered to be numbered, and of the responsibilities given them (vv. 1–20). 2. The Gershonites (vv. 21–28) and the Merarites (vv. 29–33). 3. The numbers of each, with the totals recorded (vv. 34–49).

Verses 1–20

We have here a second gathering of the tribe of Levi. As that tribe was taken out of all Israel to be God's own, so the middle-aged men of that tribe were taken from among the rest to be actually employed in the service of the tabernacle:

1. Who were to be taken into this number. All the males from thirty years old to fifty. The service of God requires the best of our strength and the prime of our lives, which cannot be better spent than in honoring him who is the first and best. A person may make a good soldier much sooner than a good minister.

1.1. They were not to be employed till they were thirty years old. They started as probationers at twenty-five years old (8:24), and in David's time, when there was more work to be done, at twenty (1Ch 23:24; Ezr 3:8), but they must spend five years in learning and waiting, to equip themselves for service. In David's time they were ten years in preparation, from twenty to thirty. John the Baptist began his public ministry, and Christ his, at thirty years old. This gives us two sound principles:

1.1.1. That ministers must not be recently converted (1Ti 3:6). It is a work that requires maturity of judgment and great steadiness.

1.1.2. That they must learn before they may teach, serve before they may lead, and must first be tested (1Ti 3:10).

1.2. They were discharged at fifty years old from the burdensome part of the service, particularly that of carrying the tabernacle.

2. How their work is described. They are said to enter into the *host* (service), or "warfare" (v. 3, margin), *to do the work in the tabernacle.* Those who enter into the ministry must look on themselves as entering into the service and show themselves to be *good soldiers* (2Ti 2:3). As regards the sons of Kohath in particular, here:

2.1. Their service is appointed, in the moving of the tabernacle. Afterward, when the tabernacle was fixed, they had other work assigned them, but this was the work of the day, which was to be done in its day. The Kohathites were to carry all the holy things of the tabernacle.

2.1.1. Aaron and his sons the priests must pack up the things which the Kohathites were to carry, as is directed here (v. 5).

2.1.2. All the holy things must be covered, the ark and table with three coverings, all the rest with two. Even the ashes of the altar, in which the holy fire was carefully preserved and raked, must have a purple cloth spread over them (v. 13). The bronze altar, though it stood open to the view of all in the court of the sanctuary, was covered when it was transported. This represented the darkness of that era. What is now brought to light by the Gospel and revealed to little children was then hidden from the wise. They saw only the coverings, not the holy things themselves (Heb 10:1), but now Christ has *destroyed the face of the covering* (Isa 25:7).

2.1.3. When all the holy things were covered, then the Kohathites were to carry them on their shoulders.

2.2. Eleazar, now the eldest son of Aaron, was appointed overseer of the Kohathites in this service (v. 16).

2.3. Great care must be taken to preserve the lives of these Levites, by preventing their irreverent approach to the most holy things: *Cut you not off the Kohathites* (v. 18).

2.3.1. The Kohathites must not see the holy things till the priests had covered them (v. 20). And:

2.3.2. When the holy things were covered, they were not permitted to touch them, at least not the ark, called here *the holy thing*, without incurring the punishment of death (v. 15). In this way, the Lord's ministers themselves were then kept in fear, and that was a dispensation of terror as well as darkness, but now through Christ the situation has changed: we have *seen with our eyes*, and our *hands have handled the word of life* (1Jn 1:1), and we are encouraged to *come boldly to the throne of grace* (Heb 4:16).

Verses 21–33

We have here the responsibilities of the other two families of the Levites, which, though not as honorable as the first, were still necessary and were to be done regularly:

1. The Gershonites were given the responsibility of transporting all the drapery of the tabernacle, the curtains and coverings, including those of badgers' skins (hides of sea cows) (vv. 22–26).

2. The Merarites were given the responsibility of transporting the boards (frames) and bars, the pillars (posts) and sockets (bases), the pins (pegs) and cords (ropes), and these were given to them by name (vv. 31–32).

Verses 34–49

We have here a detailed record of the numbers of the three families of the Levites respectively, that is, of the men fit for work, between thirty years old and fifty. The whole number of the able men of the tribe of Levi who entered into God's service was only 8,580, whereas the able men of the other tribes who entered the service of Israel to wage war were many more. The least of the tribes had almost four times as many able men as the Levites, and some of them more than eight times as many, for those who are engaged in the service of this world and *war after the flesh* (2Co 10:3) are many more than those who are devoted to the service of God and *fight the good fight of faith* (1Ti 6:12).

CHAPTER 5

In this chapter we have: 1. An order, in accordance with laws already made, for removing the unclean from the camp (vv. 1–4); a repetition of the laws concerning restitution, in case of a wrong done to a neighbor (vv. 5–8), and concerning the appropriating of holy things by the priests (vv. 9–10). 2. A new law made concerning the trial of a wife suspected of adultery, by the waters of jealousy (vv. 11–31).

Verses 1–10

Here is:

1. A command to purify the camp, by expelling from within it all those who were ceremonially unclean from a bodily discharge, an infectious skin disease, or touching a dead body, until they were cleansed according to the Law (vv. 2–3). [Ed. note: The KJV translates the Hebrew word used here as "leper" although the word used refers to a person suffering from various skin conditions, not necessarily leprosy.]

1.1. These orders were carried out immediately (v. 4). The camp had been recently newly modeled, and so to complete its reformation, it should next be cleansed. God's tabernacle was now established in the middle of their camp, and so they must be careful to keep it clean. The person, the place, *in the midst of which God dwells*, must not be defiled, for if it is, he will be greatly insulted and offended and led to withdraw from it (1Co 3:16–17).

1.2. The expulsion of the unclean from the camp was to represent:

1.2.1. What the leaders of the church ought to do: they must *separate between the precious and the vile* (Jer 15:19) and remove immoral people. It is to glorify Christ and to build up his church that those who are openly ungodly and immoral and refuse to be corrected should be expelled and kept from Christian fellowship until they repent.

1.2.2. What God himself will do at the last day: he will *thoroughly purge his floor* (Mt 3:12) and *gather out of his kingdom all things that offend* (Mt 13:41). As here the unclean were excluded from the camp, so *no unclean thing shall enter* into the new Jerusalem (Rev 21:27).

2. A law concerning restitution, in case of wrong done to a neighbor.

2.1. The person must *confess his sin* (v. 7), confess it to God, confess it to the person wronged, and so be ashamed of themselves.

2.2. The person must bring a sacrifice, *a ram of atonement* (v. 8). Atonement must be made for the offense done against God, whose law is broken, as well as for the loss sustained by the neighbor. In this case, restitution is not sufficient without faith and repentance.

2.3. The sacrifices would not be accepted until full restitution has also been made to the party wronged, not only the original cost, but also with a fifth of its value added (v. 7). If the party wronged was dead, and there was no close relative who was entitled to the debt, it must be given to the priest (v. 8). Some work of godliness or kindness is a necessary justice to be done by those who are themselves conscious that they have done wrong, but do not know how to make restitution otherwise.

3. A general rule concerning holy things given on this occasion, that whatever was given to the priest, *his it shall be* (vv. 9–10).

Verses 11–31

We have here the law concerning the holy trial of a wife whose husband was jealous of her. Notice:

1. What was the case: that a man had some reason to suspect his wife to have committed adultery (vv. 12–14). The sin of adultery is justly represented as a great sin. It is committing a sin against the husband, robbing him of his honor, violating his right, introducing illegitimate children into his family to share with his own children in his estate, and destroying her marriage covenant with him.

1.1. Let all wives be warned by this not to give anyone the least occasion to suspect them of impurity.

1.2. Let all husbands be warned not to entertain any unfounded or unjust suspicions of their wives. Love in general, and much more so the love between husband and wife, teaches to *think no evil* (1Co 13:5).

2. What was the course prescribed in this case, so that if the suspected wife was innocent, she might not continue under the disgrace and uneasiness of her husband's jealousy, and if guilty, her sin might be found out, and others might hear, fear, and accept the warning: her husband must *bring her to the priest* (v. 15), with the witnesses who

could prove the reasons for his suspicion, and the desire that she might be put on trial. If she confessed, saying, "I am defiled," she was not put to death, but was divorced and lost her dowry; if she said, "I am pure," then they proceeded. God will find some way or other to make plain the innocence of the innocent, and to *bring forth their righteousness as the light* (Ps 37:6). To *the pure all things are pure*, but *to the defiled nothing* is so (Tit 1:15).

CHAPTER 6

In this chapter we have: 1. The law concerning Nazarites. The obligations of a Nazarite (vv. 1–8); a remedial law in case a Nazarite happened to be defiled by touching a dead body (vv. 9–12). The formal ceremony of discharge when their time had been completed (vv. 13–21). 2. Instructions given to the priests on how they should bless the people (vv. 22–27).

Verses 1–21

After the law for recognizing and shaming those who had sinned by corrupting themselves, it is appropriate that it should be followed by words of encouragement and direction for those who by their outstanding godliness and devotion had made themselves honorable. There were those who were called *Nazarites*, and were consecrated by that title as people whom professed a greater devotion and zeal in religion than others. Joseph is called a Nazarite among his brothers (Ge 49:26). Notice:

1. The general character of a Nazarite: it is a person *separated unto the Lord* (v. 2). Some were Nazarites for life, either by divine appointment, like Samson (Jdg 13:5) and John the Baptist (Lk 1:15), or by their parents' vow concerning them, like Samuel (1Sa 1:11). This law does not speak about this. Others were Nazarites for a limited time and by their own voluntary commitment, and rules are given about them in this law. A woman could bind herself with the vow of a Nazarite, with the restrictions we find in 30:3. The Nazarites were:

1.1. Devoted to the Lord during the time of their Nazariteship, and they probably spent much of their time studying the Law, in acts of devotion, and instructing others.

1.2. Separated from ordinary people and ordinary things.

1.3. Separated by making a vow. All the Israelites were committed by the divine Law to love God with all their heart, but the Nazarites committed themselves by their own act and deed to some religious observances, as expressions of that love, which other Israelites were not committed to. Christ was called a Nazarene as a term of reproach — *He shall be called a Nazarene* (Mt 2:23) — and so were his followers, but he was not a Nazarite according to this law. He drank wine and touched dead bodies, but in him this type was fulfilled, for in him all purity and perfection met, and every true Christian is a spiritual Nazarite, separated by a vow to the Lord.

2. The particular obligations that the Nazarites were under:

2.1. They must have nothing to do with *the fruit of the vine* (vv. 3–4). They must drink no wine or strong drink, nor eat grapes, not the kernel or the husk, or even a raisin. Those who gave the Nazarites wine to drink did the tempter's work (Am 2:12), persuading them to take the forbidden fruit. The fact that it was considered something perfect and praiseworthy not to drink wine appears from the example of the Rechabites (Jer 35:6). They were to *drink no* wine:

2.1.1. That they might be examples of moderation and mortification. Drinking *a little wine for the stomach's sake* is allowed, to help that (1Ti 5:23). But drinking much wine for the palate's sake, to please that, is inconsistent with those who profess to walk not *after the flesh, but after the Spirit* (Ro 8:1, 4).

2.1.2. That they might be qualified to employ themselves in the service of God. They must not drink, so that they would not *forget the law* (Pr 31:5), so that they would not *err through wine* (Isa 28:7). Let all Christians be moderate in their use of wine and strong drink, for if the love of these once gets control of a person, then that person becomes a very easy target for Satan.

2.2. They must not *cut their hair* (v. 5). They must neither cut short the hair on their heads nor shave their beards. This was that mark of Samson's Nazariteship which we often read of in his story. Now:

2.2.1. This represented a virtuous lack of concern for the body and physical comfort and beauty, which was right for those who because they were set apart for God ought to be wholly taken up with their souls, to secure their spiritual peace and beauty.

2.2.2. Some notice that long hair is spoken of as a sign of submission (1Co 11:5, etc.), so that the long hair of the Nazarites was a sign of their submission to God and their putting themselves under his authority.

2.3. They must not go near any dead body (vv. 6–7).

2.4. All *the days of their separation* they must be *holy to the Lord* (v. 8).

3. The provision made for the cleansing of Nazarites, if they unavoidably happened to contract ceremonial defilement by touching a dead body. The person must be purified from the ceremonial defilement they had contracted, as others must, on the seventh day (v. 9). In fact, more was required to purify the Nazarite than any other person who had touched a dead body. The Nazarite must bring a sin offering and a burnt offering, and an atonement must be *made for him* (v. 11). This teaches us that sins that we commit because of our weaknesses and those that catch us unawares must be firmly repented of. We must apply the benefits of Christ's sacrifice to our souls to forgive such sins every day (1Jn 2:1–2).

4. The law for the formal discharge of Nazarites from the vow, when they had completed the set time. The Jews say that the length of a Nazarite's vow could not be less than thirty days, and if a man said, "I will be a Nazarite, but only for two days," he was still committed for thirty. However, it would seem that Paul's vow was for only seven days (Ac 21:27). When the time of the vowed separation was over, the person was to be set free:

4.1. *Publicly, at the door of the tabernacle* (v. 13).

4.2. With sacrifices (v. 14). The person must bring one of each sort of the instituted offerings:

- A burnt offering.
- A sin offering.
- A peace offering (fellowship offering), in thankfulness to God, who had enabled the Nazarite to fulfill their vow.
- The meat offerings (grain offerings) and drink offerings.
- Part of the peace offering, with a cake and wafer, to be waved as a wave offering (vv. 19–20). This was a gift to the priest, who received it for his efforts, after it had been first presented to God.
- Besides all this, the person could bring freewill offerings, *such as his hand shall get* (v. 21). And to enable more to be given at the ceremony, it was common on this occasion to have their friends to be at *charges with them* (Ac 21:24), to pay their expenses.

4.3. With one further ceremony, which was like the canceling of the bond when the conditions were fulfilled, and that was the *cutting off of his hair*, which had been allowed to grow all the time that the person was a Nazarite. The hair was to be burned in the fire over which the peace offerings were boiling (v. 18). This showed that the complete fulfillment of the vow was acceptable to God in Christ, the great sacrifice.

Verses 22–27

Here:

1. The priests, among other good duties which they were to do, are formally appointed to bless the people in the *name of the Lord* (v. 23). Though the priest by himself could do no more than ask a blessing, yet because he was an intercessor by office and interceded in the name of the One who commands the blessing, the prayer carried with it a promise, and he pronounced it as one who had authority, with his hands lifted up and his face toward the people. Now:

1.1. This was a type of Christ's mission into the world, which was to *bless us* (Ac 3:26), as *the High Priest of our profession* (Heb 3:1).

1.2. It was an example to ministers of the Gospel and leaders of meetings to end their formal gatherings with a blessing in the same way. Those who teach God's words to his people are likewise to bless them.

2. A form of blessing is set down here for them. Notice here:

2.1. That the blessing is commanded to each individual person: *The Lord bless thee* (v. 24). If we take the Law to ourselves, we may take the blessing to ourselves and include our own names personally in its benefits.

2.2. That the name *Jehovah* is repeated three times in the blessing, on each occasion with a different accent in the original.

2.3. That the favor of God is everything in this blessing, for that is the fountain of all good:

- *The Lord bless thee!* (v. 24).
- *The Lord make his face shine upon thee* (v. 25), alluding to the shining of the sun on the earth, to give it light and comfort and to renew its face.
- *The Lord lift up his countenance upon thee* (v. 26). This has the same purpose as the previous one and seems to allude to the smiles of a parent on their child or of a person on a friend whom they take pleasure in.

2.4. That the fruits of this favor given in this blessing are protection, pardon, and peace:

- Protection from evil (v. 24). The Lord *keep thee*.
- Pardon from sin (v. 25). The Lord be *gracious* or *merciful* to you.
- Peace (v. 26), including all good which goes to make up complete happiness.

3. God here promises to confirm the blessing: *They will put my name on the children of Israel* (v. 27).

CHAPTER 7

After God had set up his house, as it were, in the midst of the camp of Israel, the leaders of Israel here come to visit. They brought offerings: 1. At the dedication of the tabernacle, for its service (vv. 1–9). 2. At the dedication of the altar, for its use (vv. 10–88). God graciously showed his acceptance of them (v. 89). The two previous chapters were the records of additional laws which God gave to Israel, and this chapter records the history of the additional services which Israel performed to God.

Verses 1–9

Here is the offering of the leaders to the service of the tabernacle. Notice:

1. When the gifts were made: it was not till *the tabernacle was fully set up* (v. 1), when all things were done both around the tabernacle itself and around the camp of Israel which surrounded it.

2. Who it was who offered the gifts: *The princes* (leaders) *of Israel, heads of the house of their fathers* (v. 2).

3. What was offered: six wagons (carts), each of which had two oxen to draw it (v. 3).

4. How the offering was dealt with, and what use was made of it: the wagons and oxen were given to the Levites to be used in carrying the tabernacle.

4.1. The Gershonites, who had the lighter things to carry, the curtains and hangings, had only two wagons and two pairs of oxen (v. 7).

4.2. The Merarites, who had the heavier things to carry, and what was most unwieldy—the boards (frames), pillars (posts), sockets (bases), etc.—had four wagons and four pairs of oxen allotted them (v. 8). Notice here how God wisely and graciously gave the most resources to those who had the most work. Each had wagons *according to their service* (v. 7), as their work required.

4.3. The Kohathites, who carried the most holy things, had no wagons at all, because they were to carry what they were responsible for on their shoulders (v. 9), with particular care and respect.

Verses 10–89

We have here an account of the great ceremony of dedicating the altars, both that of burnt offerings and that of incense. They had been sanctified before, when they were anointed (Lev 8:10–11), but now they were inaugurated, as it were, by the leaders with their freewill offerings. They began with rich presents, considerable expressions of joy and gladness, and great respect for those signs of God's presence with them. Notice here:

1. That the leaders were first and most forward in the service of God. It is right to expect that those who have more than others should do more good than others with what they have. If they do not do so, they are unfaithful stewards and will not give an *account* for their lives *with joy* (Heb 13:17).

2. That the offerings they brought were very rich and valuable.

2.1. They brought some things to remain for lasting service, twelve large silver plates, each about 3.25 pounds (about 1.5 kilograms) in weight, and as many large silver cups, or bowls, of about 1.75 pounds (about 0.8 kilogram) in weight—the former to be used for the meat offerings (grain offerings), the latter for the drink offerings—the former for the flesh of the sacrifices, the latter for the blood. The probable purpose of the gold spoons (dishes) being filled with incense was the service of the golden altar, for both altars were anointed at the same time.

2.2. They brought some things to be used immediately, offerings of each sort. By these means, they showed their thankful acceptance of, and happy submission to, all those laws concerning the sacrifices which God had just delivered to them through Moses. And though it was a time of joy and rejoicing, it is significant that in the midst of their sacrifices we still find a *sin offering*.

2.3. They each brought their offerings on a separate day, in the order that they had just been arranged into, so the ceremony lasted twelve days.

2.4. All their offerings were exactly the same, though probably neither the leaders nor the tribes were all rich to the same degree, and this uniformity showed that all the tribes of Israel had an equal share in the altar and an equal claim to the sacrifices that were offered on it.

2.5. Nahshon, the leader of the tribe of Judah, brought the first offering, because God had given that tribe the first position of honor in the camp, and the rest of the tribes accepted this.

2.6. Though the offerings were all the same, the record of them is repeated in detail for each tribe in the same words. We find Christ taking particular notice of what was thrown into the treasury (Mk 12:41). Though what is offered is only a little, if it is given according to our ability, it will be noted.

2.7. The grand total is added at the end of the account (vv. 84–88), to show how greatly God was pleased with the mention of his freewill offerings, and what a great deal they amounted to in total, when every leader brought their quota.

2.8. God showed his gracious acceptance of these presents that were brought to him, by speaking intimately to Moses, as a man speaks to his friend, from the mercy seat (atonement cover) (v. 89; 12:8). In speaking to him, God in effect spoke to all Israel, showing them this sign for good (Ps 103:7).

CHAPTER 8

This chapter deals with the lamps or lights of the sanctuary. 1. The burning lamps in the candlestick (lampstand), which the priests were given the responsibility of looking after (vv. 1–4). 2. The living lamps, if they may be so called, the Levites, who as ministers were burning and shining lights. We had an account of the ordination of the priests (Lev 8:1–36). Here we have an account of the ordination of the Levites, the lesser clergy: how they were purified (vv. 5–8); how they were set apart from the people (vv. 9–10); how they were presented to God instead of the firstborn (vv. 11–18); how they were assigned to Aaron and his sons, to be ministers to them (v. 19); how all these orders were duly carried out (vv. 20–22). And lastly, the age appointed for their ministry (vv. 23–26).

Verses 1–4

Directions had been given long before this for the golden candlestick (lampstand) to be made (Ex 25:31), and it was made according to the pattern shown to Moses on the mountain (Ex 37:17). But it was now that the lamps were first ordered to be lit, when other things began to be used. Notice:

1. Who must light the lamps: Aaron himself *lighted the lamps* (v. 3). As the representative of the people before God, he performed the duty of a servant in God's house, lighting his Master's candle. Scripture is *a light shining in a dark place* (2Pe 1:19). The work of ministers is to light these lamps, by opening up and applying the word of God. The priest lit the middle lamp from the fire of the altar, and the rest of the lamps he lit from one another, which, according to Mr. Ainsworth, shows that the fountain of all light and knowledge is in Christ, who has the *seven Spirits of God* represented by the *seven lamps of fire* (Rev 4:5), and in the explaining of Scripture one passage borrows light from another. He also says that since seven is a perfect number, the seven branches of the candlestick show the full perfection of the Scriptures, which are able to *make us wise to salvation* (2Ti 3:15).

2. For what purpose the lamps were lit. They were not lit like tapers in a hollow pot or urn, to burn for themselves, but to give light to other areas of the tabernacle, and it is for this reason that lamps are lit (Mt 5:15). We have been given light, so that we may give out light.

Verses 5–26

We read before of the setting apart of the Levites from among the children of Israel when they were counted (3:6, 15), that they might be employed in the service of the tabernacle. Here we have directions given for their consecration (v. 6), and this is carried out (v. 20). All Israel must know that they did not take this honor on themselves, but were called by God to it. It was not enough that they were set apart from their neighbors; they must also be formally devoted to God. All who serve God must be dedicated to him, according to the kind of service they carry out. Christians must be baptized, ministers must be ordained; we must first give ourselves, and then our services, to the Lord. Notice how this was to be done:

1. The Levites must be cleansed, and this happened. The ritual and ceremonies of their cleansing were to be performed:

- By themselves. Those who perform ministry for the Lord must themselves be clean.
- By Moses. He must *sprinkle the water of purifying upon them* (v. 7) which was prepared by divine direction. It is our duty to cleanse ourselves, and it is God's promise that he will cleanse us.

2. After the Levites had been prepared in this way, they must be brought before the Lord in a formal assembly of all Israel, and the *children of Israel* must *put their hands upon them* (v. 10), so transferring their claims on them and their service—to which the whole body of the people was entitled—to God and to his sanctuary. This laying on of hands by the children of Israel on the Levites did not make them ministers of the sanctuary, but only represented the releasing of that tribe from all secular service in order that they might be made ministers by Aaron, who was to present them to the Lord.

3. Sacrifices were to be offered for them, a sin offering first (v. 12) and then a burnt offering, to make *atonement for the Levites*. Notice here:

3.1. That we are all completely unworthy and unfit to be admitted into and used in the service of God, until atonement has been made for sin and our peace has so been made with God.

3.2. That we are reconciled to God, and made fit to be offered to him by sacrifice, by Christ the great sacrifice. It is by him that Christians are sanctified to the work of their Christian faith, and ministers to the work of their ministry.

4. The Levites themselves were *offered before the Lord for an offering of the children of Israel* (v. 11). Aaron presented them to God, after they had first presented themselves to the children of Israel.

5. God declares his acceptance of them: *The Levites shall be mine* (v. 14). All who belong to God he uses in some way; even angels themselves have their services to carry out.

6. The Levites are then given as a gift to Aaron and his sons (v. 19), and the benefits flowed to the children of Israel:

6.1. The Levites must serve under the priests as attendants on them. Aaron presented them to God (v. 11), and then God gave them back to Aaron (v. 19). Our hearts, our children, and our possessions are never more truly and assuredly ours than when we have first offered them up to God.

6.2. The Levites must act for the people. God's ministers, when they keep within the sphere of their office and conscientiously discharge its duties, must be looked on as some of the most useful servants of their country.

7. The time of their ministry is fixed:

7.1. They were to enter the service at the age of twenty-five years (v. 24), a very good age for ministers to begin their public work.

7.2. They were to serve until they were fifty years old; then they were to "return from the warfare," as the expression is (v. 25, margin), not dismissed with disgrace, but moved on to the rest which their age brought, to be given the honor of their office, as up to that time they had been loaded down by its burdens. If God's grace provides people with abilities according to their work, we should take care that people have work only according to their ability. Older people are the most suitable to be trusted with supervision; the younger ones are the most suitable for the actual works of service.

CHAPTER 9

This chapter concerns: 1. The great ordinance of the Passover. Orders are given for its observance at the turn of the year (vv. 1–5). Provisos are added in regard to those who were ceremonially unclean, or otherwise disabled, at the time that the Passover was to be kept (vv. 6–14). 2. The great mercy of the pillar of cloud, which guided Israel through the wilderness (vv. 15–23).

Verses 1–14

Here we have:

1. An order given for the celebration of the Passover, twelve months after they came out of Egypt, on the fourteenth day of the first month of the second year, some days before they were counted, for that was done at the beginning of the second month. Notice:

1.1. God gave particular orders for this Passover to be kept. It appears that after this they kept no Passover until they came to Canaan (Jos 5:10). This was an early indication of the final abolition of the ceremonial institutions. The ordinance of the Lord's Supper—which took the place of the Passover—was not discontinued in the first days of the Christian church, although those were more difficult and distressing days than Israel knew in the desert. In fact in times of persecution, the Lord's Supper was celebrated more frequently than afterward. The Israelites in the desert could not forget their rescue from Egypt. Danger lay when they came to Canaan. However, because the first Passover was celebrated in a hurry, it was the will of God that at the turn of the year, when they were more rested and more familiar with the divine Law, they should observe it again, so that their children might more clearly understand the ceremony and remember it better in the future.

1.2. Moses faithfully passed on to the people the orders given him (v. 4).

1.3. The people observed the orders given them (v. 5). They kept the Passover even in the wilderness. In this way, God provided for his Israel in the desert.

2. Instructions concerning those who were ceremonially unclean when they were to eat the Passover. The law of the Passover required every Israelite to eat it. They must therefore wash themselves and then come near to God's altar (Ps 26:6).

2.1. *Certain men were defiled by the dead body of a man* (v. 6) for seven days (19:11) and during that time were not allowed to eat the holy things (Lev 7:20). This was unfortunate and to be regretted, but it was not because of their sin.

2.2. God gave directions in this case, and in other similar cases, that explained the law of the Passover. The unfortunate incident produced good laws. Those who happened to be ceremonially unclean at the time when the Passover should be eaten were allowed to eat it that day a month later, when they were clean; so were those that happened to be *in a journey afar off* (vv. 10–11).

Verses 15–23

We have here a record of the cloud. It is not something natural, for *who knows the balancings of the clouds?* (how they are poised) (Job 37:16), but something divine. The cloud was appointed to be the visible sign and symbol of God's presence with Israel.

1. When the tabernacle was finished, this cloud—which before had hung high over their camp—settled on the tabernacle and covered it, to show that God reveals his presence with his people in and through his ordinances.

2. What appeared as a cloud by day appeared as a fire all night. Similarly, we are taught to *set the Lord always before* us (Ps 16:8), and to see him near us both night and day. Something of the divine revelation which the Old Testament church was governed by might also be represented by these visible signs of God's presence, the cloud standing for the darkness and the fire for the terror of the Old Testament era, in comparison with the more clear and encouraging revelation God has made of his glory in the face of Jesus Christ.

3. This pillar of cloud and fire directed and decided all the movements, marches, and encampments of Israel in the desert. The guidance of this cloud is spoken of as representing the guidance of the Holy Spirit. We are not now to expect such visible signs of God's presence and guidance as this, but the firm promise still stands for all God's spiritual Israel that he will *guide them by his counsel* (Ps 73:24), *even unto death* (Ps 48:14), that all the children of God will be *led by the Spirit of God* (Ro 8:14). In our actions and senses we must follow the direction of his word and Spirit. All the activities of our souls must be guided by God's will. Our hearts should always move and rest at the commandment of the Lord.

CHAPTER 10

In this chapter we have: 1. Orders given concerning the making and use of silver trumpets. These orders are actually one commandment, and it seems to have been the last of all those God gave on Mount Sinai, and one of the least; but it is not without significance (vv. 1–10). 2. The account of the move of Israel's camp from Mount Sinai and their orderly march to the Desert of Paran (vv. 11–28). 3. Moses' entreaty with Hobab, his brother-in-law (vv. 29–32); Moses' prayer at the moving and resting of the ark (vv. 33–36).

Verses 1–10

Here we have directions concerning the public notifications that were to be given to the people on several occasions by the sound of the trumpet. The trumpets were to be sounded:

1. At the *calling of assemblies* (v. 2). In the same way, they were told to blow the trumpet in Zion to call a sacred assembly, to declare a holy fast (Joel 2:15). But so that the trumpet might not *give an uncertain sound* (1Co 14:8),

they were directed, if only the leaders and elders were to meet, to blow only one of the trumpets. If the body of the people was to be called together, however, both the trumpets must be sounded.

2. At the *journeying of the camps* (v. 2), to give notice when each division must move. When the trumpets were blown for this purpose, they must *sound an alarm* (v. 5), perhaps a broken, quavering blast, which was meant to arouse and encourage the minds of the people in marching against their enemies. On the other hand, a constant, even sound was perhaps used to call the assembly together (v. 7). When the people were called together to pray to be saved from God's judgments, we find an alarm sounded (Joel 2:1). At the first blast, Judah's division marched, at the second Reuben's, at the third Ephraim's, at the fourth Dan's (vv. 5–6).

3. To stir and encourage their armies, when they went out in battle (v. 9).

4. To celebrate their sacred feasts (v. 10). One of their feasts was called *a memorial of the blowing of trumpets* (Lev 23:23–25). Holy work should be done with holy joy.

Verses 11–28

Here is:

1. A general account of the move of the camp of Israel from Mount Sinai, before which they had stayed for about a year, during which time much significant work had been completed. Notice:

1.1. The signal given (v. 11): *The cloud was taken up.*

1.2. The march begun: *They took their journey according to the commandment of the Lord*, just as the cloud led them (v. 13). *The commandment of the Lord* (v. 13) leading and guiding them in all their travels is mentioned frequently in this and the previous chapter, in order, some think, to avoid the disgrace and misrepresentation which Israel was afterward accused of, that they stayed so long in the desert because they had gotten lost there and could not find the way out. Those who have given themselves up to the direction of God's word and Spirit steer a steady course, even when they seem at times perplexed.

1.3. The place they rested in after three days' march: they went *out of the wilderness of Sinai* and rested *in the wilderness of Paran* (v. 12).

2. A detailed schedule of the order of their march, according to the model given:

2.1. Judah's division marched first (vv. 14–16). The leading standard, now lodged with that tribe, was a pledge of the scepter which in David's time would be committed to it. It looked beyond that to the captain of our salvation, of whom it was similarly foretold that *unto him should the gathering of the people be* (Ge 49:10).

2.2. Then came those two families of the Levites which were entrusted to carry the tabernacle.

2.3. Reuben's division marched forward next, taking their place after Judah, *according to the commandment of the Lord* (v. 13).

2.4. The Kohathites then followed with their responsibility, the sacred furniture of the tabernacle, *in the midst of the camp*, the safest and most honorable place (v. 21).

2.5. Ephraim's division followed next after the ark (vv. 22–24).

2.6. Dan's division came last (vv. 25–27). It is called the *rearward* (rear guard) of all the camps, because it gathered up all who were left behind; not the women and children—these we presume were looked after by the heads of their families in their respective tribes—but all the unclean, the mixed multitude, and all who were weak and dawdled at the back of the main group.

Verses 29–36

Here is:

1. An account of what happened between Moses and Hobab on the journey which the camp of Israel made toward Canaan. Some think that Hobab was the same as Jethro, Moses' father-in-law, and that the story in Ex 18:1–27 should be included here. It seems more probable, however, that Hobab was the son of Jethro, and that when the elderly father went to his own land (Ex 18:27), he left his son Hobab with Moses. This Hobab was content to stay with Israel while they camped at Mount Sinai, near his own country, but now that they were moving, he wanted to go back to his own country, family, and his father's house. Here is:

1.1. The kind invitation Moses gives him to go with them to Canaan (v. 29). Those who have the heavenly Canaan in their sights should invite and encourage all their friends to go along with them.

1.2. Hobab's desire and decision to go back to his own country (v. 30). He was indeed a son of Abraham's body, for the Midianites descended from Abraham by Keturah, but not an heir of Abraham's faith (Heb 11:8), or he would not have given Moses this answer.

1.3. The great boldness Moses used with him to try to get him to change his mind (vv. 31–32). He urges that Hobab might be useful to them: *We are to encamp in the wilderness*—a country well known to Hobab—*and thou mayest be to us instead of eyes.* We do not find any reply given by Hobab to Moses, and so we hope that this silence showed his agreement, and he did not leave them. And we find that his family was no loser by it (Jdg 1:16; 1Sa 15:6).

2. An account of the fellowship between God and Israel in this move. They left the mountain of the Lord (v. 33), Mount Sinai, where they had seen his glory and heard his voice. But when they left the mountain of the Lord, they took with them the ark of the covenant of the Lord, by which their regular fellowship with God was to be maintained. For by it:

2.1. God directed their paths. The ark of the covenant went before them, some think actually physically in front, at least in this move; others think it was only in influence and that it had a greater priority. The ark—that is, the God of the ark—is said to *search out*, to find them a resting-place.

2.2. They acknowledged God in all their ways. Moses, as the mouthpiece of the congregation, lifted up a prayer both when the ark moved on and when it rested. This is an example to us to begin and end every day's journey and every day's work with prayer:

2.2.1. Moses' prayer whenever the ark set out: *Rise up, Lord, and let thy enemies be scattered* (v. 35). We can learn from this:

- There are those in the world who are enemies and haters of God: secret and open enemies; enemies of his truths, his laws, his ordinances, and his people.
- The scattering and defeating of God's enemies is something to be passionately desired and faithfully expected by all the Lord's people.

2.2.2. Moses' prayer whenever the ark came to rest (v. 36):

- That God would cause his people to rest. Some read it, "*Return, O Lord, the many thousands of Israel*, return them to their rest again after this tiring work."
- That God himself would take up his rest among them. So we read it: *Return to the thousands of Israel*, "the ten

thousand thousands" (v. 36, margin), so the word is. The welfare and happiness of the Israel of God are expressed by the constant presence of God among them.

CHAPTER 11

Up to this time, things had gone pretty well for Israel. There had been little interruption in God's favor to them since the incident with the golden calf; the people seemed teachable in marshaling and purifying the camp, the leaders godly and generous in dedicating the altar, and they hoped to be in Canaan soon. But at this chapter a sad scene begins: 1. Their complaints sparked off a fire among them, which was soon quenched by Moses' prayer (vv. 1–3). 2. No sooner had the fire of judgment been quenched than the fire of sin breaks out again. The people are troubled because of a lack of meat (vv. 4–9). Moses is troubled because of a lack of help (vv. 10–15). 3. God promises to satisfy them both, to give help to Moses (vv. 16–17) and to give meat to the people (vv. 18–23). 4. He soon acts on both these promises. The Spirit of God qualifies the seventy elders for leadership (vv. 24–30). 5. The power of God brings quail for the people to feast on (vv. 31–32). However, the justice of God struck them with a plague because of their grumblings (vv. 33–35).

Verses 1–3

Here is:

1. The people's sin. They *complained* (v. 1). The Law revealed sin but could not remove it; it controlled it, but could not conquer it. They *complained*. When they had been given so much reason for thanksgiving, you may justly wonder where they could find any cause for complaint.

2. God's righteous anger at the insult given him by this sin: *The Lord heard it* (v. 1) and his *anger was kindled* (v. 1).

3. The judgment with which God punished them for this sin. We have read about their murmurings several times before, when they first left Egypt (Ex 15:22–17:16). But we do not read about any plagues inflicted on them then for their murmurings, as happened now, for by now they had enjoyed great experiences of God's care for them, and so to distrust him had become even more inexcusable.

4. The people's cry to Moses, who was their proven intercessor (v. 2). *When he slew them, then they sought him* (Ps 78:34). They turned to Moses to stand as their friend.

5. The success of Moses' intercession for them: *When Moses prayed unto the Lord*, God respected him and his offering, and *the fire was quenched* (v. 2).

6. A new name then given to the place, to record forever the shame of a murmuring people. The place was called *Taberah*, meaning "burning" (v. 3), so that others might hear, fear, and accept the warning not to sin as the people of Israel did.

Verses 4–15

These verses record sadly unsettling events in Israel, with both the people and their leader made anxious.

1. Here the people murmured and spoke against God himself. Notice:

1.1. Who the criminals were:

1.1.1. The *mixed multitude* began the sin when they *fell a lusting* (v. 4); they had cravings for other food. The rabble that came with them out of Egypt expected only the

Land of Promise, not to be put on probation on the way to it. These were the diseased sheep that infected the whole flock, the yeast that affected the whole batch of dough.

1.1.2. Even *the children of Israel* were caught up in this condition, as we are told (v. 4).

1.2. What their offense was:

1.2.1. They emphasized how much they had and the delicacies they had in Egypt (v. 5), as if God had dealt with them wrongly in leading them out of there. They remember the cucumbers, melons, leeks, onions, and garlic—precious food indeed to be fond of!—but they conveniently forget the brick kilns and the slave drivers, the voice of their oppressors, and the cracking of the whip.

1.2.2. They were fed up with the good provision God had made for them (v. 6). It was bread from heaven, angels' food. While they lived on manna, they seemed to be exempt from the curse which sin has brought on the human race, that in the sweat of our brow we should eat our food. But they speak of the manna so scornfully, as if it were not good enough to be given to pigs: *Our soul is dried away* (v. 6); they had lost their appetites.

1.2.3. They could not be satisfied unless they had meat to eat.

1.2.4. They distrusted the power and goodness of God as insufficient for their supply—*Who will give us flesh to eat?* (v. 4)—assuming that God was not able to do so.

1.2.5. They were eager and demanding in their desires; they *fell a lusting*: "they desired a desire" is the literal meaning; they craved greatly and greedily, till they *wept again* in their dissatisfaction.

1.2.6. Meat is good to eat and may lawfully be eaten, but they are said to have set their hearts on evil things. What is lawful in itself becomes evil to us when it is what God does not allow for us and we still set our hearts on it.

2. Moses himself, though so humble and good a man, is troubled and displeased on this occasion. Now:

2.1. It must be confessed that the offense was very great. The murmurings of the people reflected great dishonor on God, and Moses took this dishonor to heart.

2.2. But Moses fell short of his duty both to God and Israel in his rebukes:

2.2.1. He undervalues the honor God had put on him.

2.2.2. He complains too much of the heavy burdens he feels God has placed on him, and takes too personally their problems, all the noise, and his tiredness.

2.2.3. He emphasizes his own achievements, that the whole burden of the people lay on him.

2.2.4. He is not as aware as he ought to be of the obligation he was under—because of the divine commission and command—to do all he could for his people.

2.2.5. He takes too much on himself when he asks, *Whence should I have flesh to give them?* (v. 13), as if he were the housekeeper, not God.

2.2.6. He speaks distrustfully of God's grace when he despairs of being able to carry all the people (v. 14).

2.2.7. Worst of all, he passionately wished to die, to be killed. Is this Moses? Is this the humblest person on the whole earth? The best people have their weaknesses and sometimes fail in exercising that grace for which they are most eminent. Lord, *lead us not into temptation* (Mt 6:13).

Verses 16–23

We have here God's gracious answer to both of the previous complaints:

1. Provision is made to put right the grievances Moses complains of. If he finds the burdens of leadership are too heavy for him, though he was too angry and passionate

in his rebuke, he will be relieved, not by being discarded from leadership, but by having assistants appointed to help him. Moses is directed to nominate the persons (v. 16). The number of elders he is to choose is seventy, according to the number of the souls that went down into Egypt (Ge 46:27). God promises to qualify these assistants.

2. Even the mood of the discontented people will be satisfied too, that every mouth may be silenced. They are ordered to *sanctify themselves* (v. 18), that is, to put themselves into such a position as to be able to receive proof of God's power that would be a sign of both mercy and judgment.

2.1. God promises, or rather threatens, that they will have their fill of meat, and if they do not control their appetites better than now it appears they have, they will be given an excess of it (vv. 19–20).

2.2. Moses breaks in to raise the objection that it is improbable that this can be achieved (vv. 21–22). It is like the objection that the disciples made (Mk 8:4), *Whence can a man satisfy these men?* He raises the objection of the number of the people, as if the One who provided bread for them all could not by his same limitless power provide meat too. He thinks it must be the flesh either of animals or fish, little thinking that the flesh of little birds could serve the purpose.

2.3. God gives a short but sufficient answer to the objection in that question: *Has the Lord's hand waxed short?* (v. 23). God here brings Moses back to learn again the first principles of the old name of God, *The Lord God Almighty* (Rev 21:22).

Verses 24–30

We have here God's word to Moses fulfilled that Moses should have help in leading Israel:

1. Here is the situation with the seventy privy councilors in general. Moses, though a little disturbed by the tumults of the people, was soon completely composed by the fellowship he had with God and came to himself again.

- Moses fulfilled his part; he presented the seventy elders before the Lord around the tabernacle (v. 24), that they might stand there ready to receive the grace of God in the place where he revealed himself.
- God was not lacking in fulfilling his part. *He gave of his Spirit to the seventy elders* (v. 25).

2. Here is the situation with two of them, *Eldad* and *Medad*, possibly two brothers, in particular:

2.1. They were named by Moses to be assistants in leadership, but they *went not out unto the tabernacle* as the rest did (v. 26).

2.2. The Spirit of God found them out in the camp, where they were hidden, and there they prophesied, that is, they exercised their gift of praying, preaching, and praising God, in some private tent. It was by a special providence that these two were absent, for it showed that it was truly a divine Spirit which the elders were moved by, and that God gave them that Spirit, not Moses.

2.3. Moses was told about this (v. 27): *Eldad and Medad do prophesy in the camp.* Whoever it was who brought the news seems to have looked on it as something improper.

2.4. Joshua wanted to have them silenced: *My lord Moses, forbid them* (v. 28). It is probable that Joshua himself was one of the seventy. He does not want them to be punished for what they had done, but only restrained in the future.

2.5. Moses rejected the suggestion and rebuked the one who made it (v. 29): *Enviest thou for my sake?* Though Joshua was Moses' special friend and confidant, though he said this out of respect to Moses — whose honor he did not want to see diminished by the call of those elders — Moses still rebukes him. We must not be forward in condemning and silencing those who differ from us, as if they do not follow Christ because they do not follow *him with us* (Mk 9:38). Will we reject those whom Christ has acknowledged, or restrain anyone from doing good because they are not of our mind in everything? Moses had another spirit: so far from silencing these two and quenching the Spirit in them, he wished *all the Lord's people were prophets*, that is, that he would *put his Spirit upon them* (v. 29).

3. The elders, now newly ordained, immediately began their administrative work (v. 30). When their call was sufficiently confirmed by their prophesying, they went with Moses to the camp and got down to work.

Verses 31–35

After God had fulfilled his promise to Moses by giving him assistants in the leadership, he here fulfills his promise to the people by giving them meat. Notice:

1. How the people were satisfied by meat given in plenty: *A wind* (a southeast wind, as appears in Ps 78:26) *brought quails* (v. 31). It is uncertain what sort of animals they were; the psalmist calls them *feathered fowl* or "fowl of wing" (Ps 78:27). Bishop Patrick inclines to agree with those writers who think they were locusts, a delicious sort of food well known in those parts, rather because they were brought in by a wind, lay in heaps, and were dried in the sun for use. Whatever they were, they fulfilled the intention and served as a month's feast for Israel: such an indulgent Father was God to his perverse children.

2. How greedily the people ate this meat that God sent them. They pounced on the plunder with an insatiable appetite, not regarding what Moses had told them from God, that they would have too much of it (v. 32).

3. How dearly they paid for their feasts, when it came to the reckoning: *The Lord smote them with a very great plague* (v. 33), some physical disease, which probably was the effect of their eating too much and led to the death of many of them. The remembrance of this is preserved in the name given to the place (v. 34). Moses called it *Kibroth-hattaavah*, the "graves of craving."

CHAPTER 12

In the previous chapter we had the trouble which the people gave to Moses; in this we see his patience tried by his own relatives: 1. Miriam and Aaron, his own brother and sister, verbally attack him (vv. 1–3). 2. God called them to give an account for it (vv. 4–9). 3. Miriam was struck by leprosy (a skin disease) because of it (v. 10). Aaron submits and Moses humbly intercedes for Miriam (vv. 11–13). Miriam is healed, but is shamed for seven days (vv. 14–16). This is recorded to show that even the best people and families are foolish and have to suffer trouble.

Verses 1–3

Here is:

1. The uncharacteristic anger of Aaron and Miriam: they *spoke against* Moses (v. 1). It would seem that Miriam began the quarrel, and Aaron, not having been involved or consulted in the choice of the seventy elders,

was offended and was quickly drawn in to take his sister's side. They quarreled with Moses about two things:

1.1. About his marriage: some think it was a late marriage with a Cushite or Arabian; others think it was his marriage to Zipporah, whom on this occasion Miriam and Aaron contemptuously called *an Ethiopian woman*, and who, they implied, had too great an influence on Moses in choosing the seventy elders.

1.2. About his leadership; not that he was mismanaging it, but that he was monopolizing it (v. 2): *Hath the Lord spoken only by Moses?*

2. The wonderful patience of Moses under this provocation. He, as one who was deaf to their inflammatory words, did not listen to them. When God's honor was at stake, as in the incident with the golden calf, no one was more zealous than Moses, but when his own honor was at stake, no one was more humble. He was as bold as a lion in the cause of God, but as mild as a lamb in his own cause. Sometimes the unkindness of our friends is a greater test of our humility than the hatred of our enemies.

Verses 4–9

Moses did not resent the wrong done to him; he did not complain about it to God or make any appeal to him; but God was angry about it. The more silent we are concerning our own cause, the more committed God is to protect it. Those who are innocent but are accused need only say a little if they know that the judge will speak up for them as their advocate.

1. The case is called, and the parties are summoned immediately to come to the door of the tabernacle, the Tent of Meeting (vv. 4–5).

2. Aaron and Miriam were made to know that although they were great, they must not pretend to be equal to Moses or set themselves up as rivals to him (vv. 6–8).

2.1. It was true that God honored the prophets very much. God *made himself known to them* (v. 6), either by dreams when they were asleep or by visions when they were awake, and he made himself known through them to others. He now makes himself known not by dreams and visions, as he did in former times, but by the *Spirit of wisdom and revelation* (Eph 1:17).

2.2. But God honored Moses far more (v. 7): *My servant Moses is not so*, he surpasses them all. To reward Moses for humbly and patiently bearing the insults of Miriam and Aaron, God not only cleared him, but also praised him.

2.2.1. Moses was a man of great integrity and tried and tested faithfulness. He is *faithful in all my house* (v. 7). This is put first in his character, because grace surpasses gifts, love surpasses knowledge, and sincerity in the service of God honors a person more greatly and commends them to God's favor more highly than learning, arguing over obscure details, and an ability to *speak with tongues* (1Co 14:18–39).

2.2.2. Moses was therefore honored with clearer revelations of God's mind and more intimate fellowship with God than any other prophet.

2.2.3. Now let Miriam and Aaron consider whom they insulted: *Were you not afraid to speak against my servant Moses?*

3. After God had shown them their fault and foolishness, he next shows them his displeasure (v. 9): *The anger of the Lord was kindled against them*. But it was a sure sign of his displeasure that he left and would not even listen to their excuse. The removal of God's presence from us is the surest and saddest sign of God's displeasure against us. We are ruined if he leaves us, but he never

leaves us until we have first driven him away by our sin and foolishness.

Verses 10–16

Here is:

1. God's judgment on Miriam (v. 10): *The cloud departed from off* that part of the tabernacle, as a sign of God's displeasure, and immediately Miriam was struck by *leprosy*, a skin disease. [Ed. note: The KJV translates the Hebrew word *tsara'at* as "leprosy," although this refers to various conditions affecting the skin, not necessarily leprosy.] According to Bishop Hall, the foulness of her words is justly punished by the foulness of her looks. Moses needs a veil to hide his glory, but Miriam needs one to hide her shame. Miriam was struck with a skin disease, but not Aaron, because she was the leader in the sin and God wanted to make a difference between those who wrongly lead and those who are wrongly led. Aaron, as priest, was to be the judge of the skin disease. He was convicted by what he saw and could not declare her to have a skin disease without blushing and trembling, knowing himself to be equally to blame.

2. Aaron's submission to this (vv. 11–12); he humbles himself before Moses, confesses his fault, and asks for pardon. He who had just joined with his sister in speaking against Moses is here forced to come with his sister and penitently speak to him. In his submission, he confesses his own and his sister's sin (v. 11) and asks Moses' pardon: *Lay not this sin upon us* (v. 11). He also commends the awful condition of his sister to Moses' compassion (v. 12): *Let her not be as one dead.*

3. The intercession Moses made for Miriam (v. 13): He *cried unto the Lord* with a loud voice, because the cloud, the symbol of his presence, had moved on and stood some distance away, and to express his intense passion in this request, *Heal her now, O Lord, I beseech thee*. So Miriam was healed here by the prayer of Moses, whom she had abused.

4. The resolution of the matter so that mercy and justice might come together:

- Mercy is given insofar as Miriam will be healed; Moses forgives her and God will. See 2Co 2:10. But:
- Justice is fulfilled insofar as Miriam will be humbled (v. 14): *Let her be shut out from the camp seven days*.

5. The obstacle this was to the people's progress: *The people journeyed not till Miriam was brought in again* (v. 15). God did not move the cloud, and so they did not move their camp. This was intended:

5.1. As a rebuke to the people, who were themselves conscious of having sinned in the same way as Miriam in speaking against Moses.

5.2. As a mark of respect to Miriam. If the camp had moved on during the days of her confinement, her trouble and shame would have been greater. Those who have been punished and rebuked for sin ought to be treated very tenderly and not be overloaded with the shame they have deserved or *counted as enemies* (2Th 3:15), but *forgiven and comforted* (2Co 2:7). Sinners must be driven out with grief, but those who repent taken back with joy.

CHAPTER 13

A memorable and very sad story is related in this and the following chapter, of the turning back of Israel from the borders of Canaan, just when they were ready to set foot in it, and the sentencing of them to wander and perish in the desert because of their unbelief and murmuring. It is referred to in Ps 95:7–11 and is given as a warning to Christians (Heb 3:7–19). In this chapter we have: 1. The sending of twelve spies before the people into Canaan (vv. 1–16); the instructions given to these spies (vv. 17–20). 2. The commission carried out according to the instructions given and their return from the search (vv. 21–25). 3. The report they brought back to the camp of Israel (vv. 26–33).

Verses 1–20

Here we have:

1. Orders given to send spies to explore the land of Canaan. It is said here that God directed Moses to send them (vv. 1–2), but it appears (Dt 1:22) that the suggestion came originally from the people. They came to Moses and said, *We will send men before us.* They would not take God's word for it that it was a good land. How absurd it was for them to send people to spy out a land which God himself had spied out for them. But in the same way, we often bring ruin on ourselves by giving more credit to what we see, hear, or feel than we do to divine revelation; we tend to walk by sight, not by faith. When the people made this suggestion to Moses, he consulted God about it, who told him to please the people in this matter and send spies before them: "Let them follow their own ways."

2. The people named who were to be used in this service (vv. 4–15), one from each tribe, that it might be seen to be an act of the people generally. This was intended to be the best way, but it turned out to have an adverse effect: these so-called quality people brought the faithless report that influenced the people's beliefs. Some think that they are all named for the sake of the two faithful ones among them, Caleb and Joshua. Notice is taken here of the change of Joshua's name on this occasion (v. 16). The name by which he was generally called and known in his own tribe was *Oshea* (Hoshea), but Moses called him *Joshua,* and now he ordered others to call him so. *Oshea* means a prayer for salvation, "Save!"; *Joshua* means a promise of salvation, "The Lord is salvation," in answer to that prayer. The relationship between prayer and promise is so close. Prayers are successful in applying the promises, and promises direct and encourage prayers. *Jesus* is the same name as *Joshua,* and it is the name of our Lord Christ, of whom Joshua was a type as successor to Moses, Israel's leader, and conqueror of Canaan. Joshua was the savior of God's people from the powers of Canaan, but Christ is their Savior from the powers of hell.

3. The instructions given to those spies. They were sent into the land of Canaan to take note of what it was like (v. 17). They were given two lines of inquiry to follow up:

3.1. To see the land itself: to see whether it was *good or bad,* and (v. 20) *whether it be fat or lean,* fertile or poor. Moses himself was satisfied that Canaan was a very good land, but he sent these spies to bring a report to satisfy the people.

3.2. To see the inhabitants themselves—their number, whether they were few or many—their size and stature, and whether they were strong or weak.

4. The dismissal of the spies by Moses with this command, *Be of good courage* (v. 20), showing that they should bring an encouraging report back to the people and make the best of everything.

Verses 21–25

We have here a short account of the survey which the spies made of the Promised Land:

1. They went completely through it, from Zin in the south, to Rehob, near Hamath in the north (v. 21). They divided themselves into several groups and so passed unsuspected as groups of travelers.

2. They took particular note of Hebron (v. 22), probably because near there was the field of Machpelah, where the patriarchs were buried (Ge 23:2). They made a special visit to this grave and found the adjacent city in the possession of the children of Anak. Where the bodies of their ancestors kept possession for them, the giants kept possession against them.

3. They took a bunch of grapes with them, and some other fruits of the land, as evidence of the exceptional goodness of the country. The place from where they took it was called the Valley of Eshcol, *Eshcol* meaning "cluster," that famous cluster which was both a pledge and example to Israel of all the fruits of Canaan.

Verses 26–33

At last, the messengers return, but they do not agree in their report.

1. Most of them recommend that the people should not go forward to Canaan.

1.1. Notice their report:

1.1.1. They could not deny that the land of Canaan was very fruitful: the bunch of grapes they brought with them clearly demonstrated that (v. 27). But afterward they contradict themselves, when they say (v. 32), *It is a land that eateth up the inhabitants thereof.* Some think there was a great plague in the country at the time they explored it. They wrongly put it down it to the fact that the air was unhealthy and so took occasion to find fault with the country. But:

1.1.2. They presented the conquest of the land as being totally impracticable, and as if there were no point even in attempting it. Nothing served their faithless purposes more than a description of the giants, whom they emphasized. They therefore concluded, *We are not able to go up against them* (v. 31), and so they must think of taking some other course.

1.2. Now even if they were to judge only by human probabilities, they could not have been excused from the accusation that they were cowards. Were not the hosts of Israel numerous? They were effective men, well marshaled and modeled, closely grouped, and completely united in purpose and heart. Moses, their commander in chief, was wise and brave, and if the people had been determined and behaved courageously, what could have gotten in their way?

1.3. But though they deserved to be considered cowards, this was not the worst of it, for Scripture brands them as unbelievers.

1.3.1. They had signs of God's presence with them. The Canaanites were stronger than Israel; but even if they were, were the Canaanites stronger than the God of Israel? Their cities may be fortified against us, but can they be fortified against heaven? Besides this:

1.3.2. They had had very great experiences of the power of God revealed on their behalf. Had not the Egyptians also been stronger than the Israelites just as the Canaanites were now? But without so much as a sword being drawn by Israel or a stroke struck, the chariots and charioteers of Egypt were completely routed and ruined. The Amalekites were defeated.

1.3.3. They had special promises given to them of victory and success in their wars against the Canaanites. God had given Abraham every possible assurance that he would give his descendants possession of that land (Ge 15:18; 17:8). He had explicitly promised them through Moses that he would *drive out the Canaanites* from before them (Ex 33:2), and that he would do it *by little and little* (Ex 23:30). And after all this for them then to say, *We are not able to go up against them* (v. 31), was in effect saying, "God himself is not able to fulfill his word."

2. Caleb, however, encouraged the people to go forward, though he was supported only by Joshua (v. 30): *Caleb stilled the people.* Caleb may mean "all heart," and he was true to his name, was himself wholehearted and would have made the people so if they had listened to him.

2.1. He speaks very confidently of success: *We are well able to overcome them* (v. 30), strong though they are.

2.2. He stirs the people to go on, and since he was in the leading division, he speaks as one determined to lead them on bravely: *Let us go up at once. Let us go up and possess it* (v. 30).

CHAPTER 14

This chapter records that fatal quarrel between God and Israel which, because of their grumbling and unbelief, he concluded by declaring on oath in his anger that they would not enter into his rest. Here is: 1. The rebellion of Israel against God, on the report of the faithless spies (vv. 1–4). 2. The futile attempts of Moses and Aaron, Caleb, and Joshua to quiet the uproar (vv. 5–10). 3. Their complete destruction justly threatened by an offended God (vv. 11–12) and the humble intercession of Moses for them (vv. 13–19). 4. A reduction in the punishment in answer to the prayer of Moses; they will not all be destroyed, but the decree goes out confirmed with an oath, is declared to the people, and again and again is repeated, that this whole congregation would die in the desert, and none of them would enter Canaan except only Caleb and Joshua (vv. 20–35). 5. The immediate death of the faithless spies (vv. 36–39), and the rebuke given to those who nevertheless attempted to go forward (vv. 40–45). And this is written to warn us, that we fall not after the same example of unbelief (Heb 4:11).

Verses 1–4

Here we see what trouble the faithless spies made by their pessimistic report. Notice:

1. How uproar broke out among the people: *They lifted up their voices and cried* (v. 1). They believed the report of the spies rather than the word of God. Those who cried when nothing hurt them deserved to be given something to cry about.

2. How they turned on their leaders—they *murmured against Moses and Aaron*, and through them rebuked the Lord (v. 2). The congregation of elders began the discontent (v. 1).

2.1. They look back with an anger that is without foundation. They wish they had died in Egypt. Never were so many months spent so pleasantly as those which they had spent since they had left Egypt. How evil and faithless were the spirits of these corrupt Israelites, who wanted instead to die in the desert.

2.2. They look forward with a despair that is without foundation, assuming (v. 3) that if they continued, they would fall by the sword. This is an evil blasphemy against God himself, as if he had deliberately brought them there that their poor, innocent wives and children would become plunder for the enemy.

3. How they eventually came to the dreadful decision that instead of going forward to Canaan, they would go back again to Egypt. *Were it not better for us to return into Egypt? Let us make a captain and return to Egypt.*

3.1. It was foolish to wish they were back in Egypt, or to think that if they were there, things would be better than they were at the present.

3.2. It was nonsensical and ridiculous to talk of returning through the desert. We are restless with our present situations, we complain about where we live and what is happening to us, and we want to move, but is there any place or condition in this world that does not contain something that would unsettle us if we are as we are now? The way to improve our condition is to get our spirits into a better state, and instead of asking, "Would it not be better to go to Egypt?" we should ask, "Would it not be better to be content, and make the best of what my life is at the moment?"

Verses 5–10

The friends of Israel here intervene to save them if possible from destroying themselves, but in vain.

1. Best endeavors were used to still the uproar.

1.1. The clamor and noise of the people were so great that Moses and Aaron could not be heard. To gain a hearing in the sight of all the assembly, they fell on their faces. This expressed:

- Their humble prayers to God to still the tumult of the people.
- The great concern of their own spirits. They fell down as those who were stunned and flabbergasted, dismayed at seeing a people throw away God's mercy. What they said to the people, Moses relates in the repetition of this story. *Be not afraid; the Lord your God shall fight for you* (Dt 1:29–30).

1.2. Caleb and Joshua did their part: they tore their clothes in holy anger at the sin of the people and a holy fear of the wrath of God, which they saw as ready to break out against them. No reasoning could have been fuller of pathos and pleading than theirs was (vv. 7–9), and they spoke with authority:

1.2.1. They assured them of the goodness of the land they had surveyed, and that it was really worth going into.

1.2.2. They made nothing of the difficulties that seemed to lie in the way of gaining possession of the land: "Do not be afraid of the people of the land" (v. 9). However formidable they might have appeared to you, the lions are not so fierce as they are painted. *They are bread for us,* that is, "they are set before us to be fed on rather than to be fought with." Though the Canaanites lived in walled cities, they are exposed: their defenses have left them. The other spies took notice of the Canaanites' strength, but these took notice of the Canaanites' evil and inferred that God had abandoned them, and so their defense had departed.

1.2.3. They showed them clearly that all the danger they were in was of their own discontented making, and that they would succeed against all their enemies if they did not make God their enemy.

2. It was all futile; the people were deaf to this good reasoning. In fact, they were exasperated by it and became even angrier: *All the congregation bade stone them with stones* (v. 10). Caleb and Joshua knew they were standing for God and his glory, and so did not doubt that God would come to rescue them and keep them safe. And they were not disappointed, for immediately *the glory of the Lord appeared* (v. 10), to the dismay and terror of those who wanted to stone the servants of God.

Verses 11–19

1. When *the glory of the Lord appeared in the tabernacle* (v. 10), we may suppose Moses took that as a call for him to come immediately and wait on God there. We are now told what God said to him there:

1.1. He showed him the great evil of the people's sin (v. 11). God justly complains about two things to Moses:

• Their sin. They *provoke me* (v. 11); the word means they "reject; despise; rebuke" me, for *they will not believe me.* It was their unbelief that made this a day of rebellion in the desert (Heb 3:8).
• Their continuing in sin: *How long will they do so?* The more God has done for us, the greater he is offended by our rebellion and distrust of him.

1.2. He showed him the punishment which his justice demanded of them for it (v. 12). What remains to be done except that I should destroy them completely? They wanted to die; and so let them die, and not one of them will be left.

2. Moses made humble intercession for them.

2.1. The prayer of his petition can be summed up in brief, *Pardon, I beseech thee, the iniquity of this people* (v. 19), that is, "Do not bring on them the destruction they deserve." This was Christ's prayer for those who crucified him, *Father, forgive them.*

2.2. He has many urgent pleas:

2.2.1. He pleads the glory of God (vv. 13–16). "If this people who have caused such an uproar are all destroyed, if all their mighty huffing and puffing comes to nothing and their light is snuffed out, the news will be given with much pleasure in Gath and the streets of Askelon (Ashkelon) (2Sa 1:20). How will the followers of other religions view it? It will be impossible to make them understand it as an act of God's justice. They will put it down to a failure of God's power."

2.2.2. He pleads God's declaration of his name at Horeb (vv. 17–18): *Let the power of the Lord be great.* To reinforce this petition, Moses refers to the word which God had spoken: *The Lord is long-suffering and of great mercy* (v. 18). God's goodness had there been spoken of as his glory; God gloried in it (Ex 34:6–7). Now he prays here on this occasion that God would glorify it. He does not ask that they may not be disciplined, but that they may not be disinherited.

2.2.3. He pleads past experience: *As thou hast forgiven this people from Egypt* (v. 19). Moses looks on it as something good to plead, *Lord, forgive, as thou hast forgiven* (v. 19). To forgive now will bring no more dishonor to your justice and make your mercy no less praiseworthy than formerly.

Verses 20–35

Here is God's answer to the prayer of Moses, which speaks both of mercy and judgment.

1. The most severe penalty of the punishment is withdrawn (v. 20). Notice what support and encouragement God gives to our intercessions for others, that we may pray widely and boldly. Here is a whole nation rescued from destruction by *the effectual fervent prayer of one righteous man* (Jas 5:16).

2. The glorifying of God's name is in general decided on (v. 21). Moses in his prayer had shown great concern for the glory of God. All the world will see how God hates sin even in his own people and will judge it, but how gracious and merciful he is, and how slow to anger. And so, when our Savior prayed, *Father, glorify thy name*, he was immediately answered, *I have glorified it, and will glorify it yet again* (Jn 12:28).

3. The sin of this people which had offended had God and given him reason to act against them is emphasized (vv. 22, 27). They tested God—tested his power. They

tested his justice, whether he would be angry at their rebellions and punish them or not. They grumbled against him (v. 27). They did this after they had seen God's miracles in Egypt and in the desert (v. 2). They had rebelled ten times, that is, very often.

4. Judgment is passed on them for this sin:

4.1. That they would not see the Promised Land (v. 23) or *come into it* (v. 30). The promise of God would be fulfilled by their descendants, but not by them.

4.2. That they would immediately *turn back into the wilderness* (v. 25). Their next move would be a retreat.

4.3. That all those who had now reached adulthood would die in the desert, not immediately, but gradually. They wanted to die in the desert, and God agreed to their fervent wish.

4.4. That as a consequence of this sentence they would wander backward and forward in the desert like lost travelers for forty years:

4.4.1. So that this might lead them to repentance, and they might find mercy with God in the next world, whatever happened to them in this.

4.4.2. So that they might become aware of how dangerous it is for God's covenant-people to reject him, for God never leaves any till they first leave him.

4.4.3. That a new generation might be raised up during this time, which could not happen suddenly. The children, being brought up under the signs of God's displeasure against their ancestors, might beware following in the footsteps of their ancestors' disobedience.

5. Mercy was given with this harsh punishment:

5.1. Mercy to Caleb and Joshua, that though they would wander with the rest of the people in the desert, they and only they — out of all who were older than twenty — would survive the years of banishment and live to enter Canaan. Caleb only is spoken of (v. 24), and a special mark of honor is put on him:

5.1.1. In the character described of him: he had *another spirit*, unlike the rest of the spies; he had a different spirit, which gave him second thoughts, and he *followed the Lord fully*. He kept close to his duty and went through with it, even though he was abandoned and threatened, and:

5.1.2. In the reward promised to him: *Him will I bring in due time into the land whereinto he went* (v. 24). When Caleb is mentioned again (v. 30), Joshua is standing with him, surrounded by the same favors and crowned with the same honors, having stood with him in the same services.

5.2. Mercy to the children even of the rebels. Their descendants would be preserved, and Canaan would be kept safe for those descendants: *Your little ones*, now under twenty years old, *which you*, in your unbelief, *said should be a prey* (plunder), *them will I bring in* (v. 31).

Verses 36–45

Here is:

1. The sudden death of the ten unfaithful spies. While the sentence was passed on the people, before it was declared, they *died of the plague before the Lord* (vv. 36–37).

1.1. They sinned themselves, in giving an untrue report of the Land of Promise. It is those who misrepresent religious faith, bring disgrace on it, and raise prejudices in people's minds against it, who offend God greatly.

1.2. They *made Israel to sin*. They intentionally *made all the congregation murmur* (v. 36) against God.

2. The special preservation of Caleb and Joshua: *They lived still* (v. 38).

3. The declaration of judgment on all the people. The Lord told them the whole decree, which could not be reversed. They must all die in the desert. Canaan must be reserved for the next generation.

4. The foolish, fruitless attempts of some of the Israelites to enter Canaan, despite the judgment:

4.1. They were now eager to go forward toward Canaan (v. 40). They were up early, energetically gathered together as one body, and begged Moses to lead them on against the enemy. But, though God was glorified by confession of sin, they gained no benefit from it, because it came too late.

4.2. Moses completely forbids them from moving on: *Go not up* (vv. 41–43). "*The Canaanites are before you* (v. 43) to attack you, and *the Lord is not among you* (v. 43) to protect you and fight for you. You need to look to yourselves *that you be not smitten before your enemies* (v. 42)." Those who have left the way of their duty are no longer under God's protection, and go at their peril.

4.3. Nevertheless, the people moved on. Never was a people so perverse and so desperately determined to go against God. God told them to go, and they did not; he forbade them, and they went.

4.4. The expedition moves on (v. 45). The enemy had positioned themselves on the top of the hill, to secure that pass against the invaders, and being informed by their scouts of their approach, went out to them and defeated them, and probably many of the Israelites were killed.

CHAPTER 15

This chapter, which deals mostly with sacrifices and offerings, comes between the stories of two rebellions (one in chapter 14 and the other in chapter 16), to show that these legal institutions were types of the gifts which Christ was to receive even from rebels (Ps 68:18). In the previous chapter, Israel had provoked God and he had decided to destroy them. As a sign of his wrath, he had sentenced them to die in the desert. But on Moses' intercession, God said, "I have pardoned them," and as a sign of that mercy, he repeats and explains in this chapter some of the laws concerning offerings, to show that he was reconciled to them. Here is: 1. The law concerning the meat offerings (grain offerings) and drink offerings (vv. 1–12) both for Israelites and for foreigners (vv. 13–16), and a law concerning the heave offerings of the first of their dough (ground meal) (vv. 17–21). 2. The law concerning sacrifices for unintentional sins (vv. 22–29). 3. The punishment of defiant sins (vv. 30–31), and an example made of the Sabbath-breaker (vv. 32–36). 4. A law concerning fringes (tassels) as reminders on the borders of their garments (vv. 37–41).

Verses 1–21

Here we have:

1. Full instructions given concerning the meat offerings (grain offerings) and drink offerings, which were additions to all the sacrifices of animals. The beginning of this law is very encouraging: *When you come into the land of your habitation which I give unto you*, then you will do such and such (v. 2). This was a clear sign, not only that God was reconciled to them, but also that he would keep the Promised Land safe for their descendants. The purpose of this law is to show what proportion the meat offering and drink offering should have to the different sacrifices to which they were attached.

2. Natives and foreigners set on the same level in this as in other matters (vv. 13–16): "*One law shall be for you and for the stranger* who is converted to the Jewish religion." Now:

2.1. This was an invitation to the Gentiles to convert and to embrace the faith and worship of the true God. In civil things, a difference was made between foreigners and native-born Israelites, but not in the things of God.

2.2. This was an obligation on the Jews to be kind to foreigners and not oppress them, because they saw they were acknowledged and accepted by God. Fellowship in religion should remove all hostilities. It was a favorable prophecy of the calling of the Gentiles and of their admission into the church. If the Law made so little difference between Jew and Gentile, much less would the Gospel make. The Gospel broke down the wall of partition and reconciled both to God in one sacrifice, without the observance of legal ceremonies.

3. A law for the offering of the first of their dough (ground meal) to the Lord. This, like the former law, assumes their having *come into the promised land* (v. 18). Not only must they offer him the firstfruits and tithes of the grain in their fields, but when they had it in their houses, in their kneading troughs, when it was almost ready to be set on their tables, God must have a further tribute. Part of their dough must be heaved or offered up to God (vv. 20–21), and the priest must have it for the use of his family. They must acknowledge their dependence on God for their daily bread in this way. Christ has not taught us to pray, "Give us this year our yearly harvest," but he has taught us to pray, *Give us this day our daily bread* (Mt 6:11).

Verses 22–29

We have here the laws concerning sacrifices for unintentional sins; the Jews understand it as false worship through the error of their teachers. If they had failed in the offerings, they must bring an offering of atonement, even though the omission had been because of their forgetfulness or a mistake.

1. The case is supposed of a national sin committed through ignorance, which has become common practice through general error (v. 24). If there should appear to have been a general neglect of that service, then a sacrifice must be offered for the whole congregation.

2. The case is considered of the sin of a particular person. In this way, atonement will be made *for the soul that sins, when he sins through ignorance* (v. 28). Sins committed unintentionally will be forgiven through Christ, the great sacrifice, who, when he offered up himself once for all on the cross, may have explained the intention of his offering in that prayer, *Father, forgive them, for they know not what they do* (Lk 23:34). The apostle Paul also seems to allude to this law concerning sins committed unintentionally (1Ti 1:13): *I obtained mercy, because I did it ignorantly and in unbelief*. And it was favorable for the Gentiles that this law of atonement for unintentional sins is explicitly made to extend to those who were foreigners to the community of Israel (v. 29), but who were converts to righteousness. In this way, the blessing of Abraham comes on the Gentiles.

Verses 30–36

Here is:

1. The general condemnation of defiant sinners. Those are to be reckoned *presumptuous* sinners who sin "with a high hand," as the margin reads (v. 30), who fight against

God and shake their fists at him, daring him to do his worst; see Job 15:25. Such people call infinite Wisdom foolish; they dare to call the righteous Judge of heaven and earth sinful. Such is the evil hatred of willful sin. The judgment passed on such sin is terrible. There remains no sacrifice for those sins; the Law provided none.

2. A particular example of arrogance in the sin of Sabbath-breaking.

2.1. The offense was the gathering of wooden sticks on the Sabbath day (v. 32), which were probably to be used to make a fire with, whereas they were commanded to bake and boil what they needed on the day before (Ex 16:23). It appears from the context to have been done arrogantly as an insult both to the Law and to the Lawmaker.

2.2. It seems that even ordinary Israelites, though there was much that was wrong among them, were not content to see the Sabbath dishonored. The Law had already made desecrating the Sabbath a capital crime (Ex 31:14; 35:2), but they were in doubt, either concerning the offense — whether what had been done should be considered a desecration or not — or concerning the punishment, what kind of death he should die.

2.3. Sentence was passed; the prisoner was judged a Sabbath-breaker, according to the law, and as such he must be put to death. To show how great the crime was, and how displeasing it was to God, and so that others might hear and fear and not act arrogantly in the same way, the death that was appointed for him was looked on as most terrible. He must be *stoned with stones* (v. 35). God jealously protects the honor of his Sabbaths, and will not hold those guiltless, whatever people do, who desecrate them.

2.4. The sentence was carried out (v. 36). He was *stoned* to death *by the congregation*. The whole assembly carried out the execution, so that many who threw a stone at the Sabbath-breaker might themselves be afraid of breaking the Sabbath. This shows that open desecration of the Sabbath is a sin which ought to be punished and restrained by the civil magistrate, who as far as overt acts go, is keeper of both tables of the Law. See Ne 13:17. You would have thought there could be little harm in gathering a few sticks, whichever day it was, but God intended to make the punishment of the Sabbath-breaker an example to us all to conscientiously keep the Sabbath holy.

Verses 37–41

Provision had just now been made by the law to forgive sins committed unintentionally and in weakness. Here a course of action is provided to prevent such sins. The people are ordered to make fringes (tassels) on the corners of their garments, which were to remind them of their duty. The appointed sign is a fringe of silk, and a blue cord bound on the top to keep it tight (v. 38). Our Savior, being made under the Law, wore these tassels; and so we read of the hem or edge of his garment (Mt 9:20). The Pharisees enlarged these borders, so that they might be thought more holy and devout than other people. Many look on their decorative features to feed their pride, but the Israelites must look on the fringes to awaken their consciences to a sense of duty. The chapter closes with that great and fundamental law of religion, *Be holy unto your God* (v. 40).

CHAPTER 16

The date of the events in this chapter is uncertain. Probably these rebellions happened after their move back again from Kadesh Barnea. Immediately after the new laws were given comes the record of a further rebellion. Here is: 1. A defiant and dangerous rebellion against Moses and Aaron, by Korah, Dathan, and Abiram (vv. 1–15). Korah and his accomplices compete for the priesthood with Aaron (v. 3). Moses reasons with them and appeals to God for a decision in the dispute (vv. 4–11). 2. Dathan and Abiram quarrel with Moses and refuse to obey his summons, which makes him very sad and angry (vv. 12–15). Those who claim the priesthood solemnly appear before God, and the glory of the Lord appears to all the people, which would have consumed them if Moses and Aaron had not interceded (vv. 16–22). 3. The deciding of the dispute, and the crushing of the rebellion, by cutting off the rebels. Those in their tents were buried alive (vv. 23–34). 4. Those at the door of the tabernacle (entrance to the Tent of Meeting) were consumed by fire (v. 35), and their censers were preserved as a memorial (vv. 36–40). 5. A further rebellion by the people (vv. 41–43). God threatened to consume them (vv. 44–45) and stopped the rebellion with a plague (v. 48); Aaron stopped the plague by offering incense (vv. 46–50). The way in which this story is recorded clearly shows the uproar was very great.*

Verses 1–11

Here is:

1. A record of the rebels, who and what they were, prominent and distinguished men. Korah was the ringleader: he formed and headed the faction. Dathan and Abiram joined him, chief men of the tribe of Reuben, the eldest son of Jacob. Probably Korah took offense at the promotion of Aaron to the priesthood and the designating of Elizaphan to lead the Kohathites (3:30). Perhaps the Reubenites were angry that the tribe of Judah had the most honorable position in the camp. And since these were themselves well known, they persuaded *two hundred and fifty princes* (leaders) *of the assembly* (v. 2) to join them in the conspiracy.

2. The rebels' complaints (v. 3). What they are quarreling about is the settlement of the priesthood on Aaron and his family.

2.1. They proudly boast of the holiness of the community and the presence of God in it. In fact, they had little reason to boast of the people's purity or of God's favor, as the people had just been so deeply defiled by sin.

2.2. They unjustly accuse Moses and Aaron of taking the honor upon themselves, whereas it was clear that they were called by God to do it (Heb 5:4). Notice here:

2.2.1. The spirit of those who want to have no differences in rank between people. They despise authority and resist the government that God has set over them. They are proud, jealous, ambitious, unstable, evil, and unreasonable.

2.2.2. The treatment even the best and most useful people may expect to receive.

3. Moses' behavior when they declared their opposition to him:

3.1. He *fell on his face* (v. 4), as he had done before (14:5). He turned to God in prayer, asking for direction as to what to say and do on this sad occasion.

3.2. He takes the case to God and leaves it to him to decide, as one who was assured that he was entitled to his leadership position, but also content to resign, if God thought fit, in order to satisfy this discontented people and bring another name to them.

3.3. He argues the case justly with them, to silence the rebellion with sound reasons if possible, before the appeal came to God's tribunal, for if it came to that, he knew it would lead to those complaining being confounded.

3.3.1. He calls them *the sons of Levi* (v. 7 and again v. 8). Can they be Levites and also rebels at one and the same time?

3.3.2. He turns the charge back on them. They had unjustly accused Moses and Aaron of taking too much on themselves, although they had done no more than what God had given them, but Moses says to them, *You take too much upon you, you sons of Levi.*

3.3.3. He shows them the privileges they had as Levites. These were surely enough for them, and they did not need to aspire to the honor of the priesthood (vv. 9–10).

3.3.4. He convicts them of the sin of underrating those privileges: *Seemeth it a small thing unto you?* (Eze 34:18).

3.3.5. He interprets their rebellion to be against God (v. 11). While they pretended to assert the holiness and liberty of the Israel of God, they really took up arms against the God of Israel: *You are gathered together against the Lord* (v. 11).

Verses 12–22

Here is:

1. The defiance of Dathan and Abiram and their treacherous complaints. Moses had heard what Korah had to say and had answered it. Now he calls Dathan and Abiram to bring their complaints (v. 12). They, however, did not obey his summons. Dathan and Abiram send their challenge to Moses, and their accusations are very great:

1.1. They accuse him of having done them a great deal of wrong in leading them out of Egypt, unfairly calling that *a land flowing with milk and honey* (v. 13).

1.2. They accuse him of intending to *kill them in the wilderness.*

1.3. They accuse him of intending to infringe their liberties, that he was going to lord it over them and enslave them, by *making himself a prince* (ruler) *over them* (v. 13). A ruler over them indeed! Was he not a tender father to them? Was he not their devoted servant for the Lord's sake?

1.4. They accuse him of deceiving them, of raising their expectations of a good land, and then disappointing them (v. 14): *Thou hast not brought us,* as you promised us, *into a land that floweth with milk and honey.* Whose fault was that? He had brought them to its borders and was ready, under God, to give them possession of it. It was they who had pushed it away from themselves and shut the door on it. It was purely their own fault that they were not now in Canaan, but Moses has to bear the blame.

2. Moses' just anger at their defiance (v. 15). In this anxiety:

2.1. He appeals to God concerning his own integrity. God knew very well:

2.1.1. That he had never gained anything from them: *I have not taken one ass from them* (v. 15) not only not by way of bribery and extortion, but also not by way of reward or as a perk for all the good works he had done them. He profited more when he kept Jethro's flock than when he came to be king in Jeshurun.

2.1.2. That they had never lost anything by him: *Neither have I hurt any one of them* (v. 15).

2.2. He pleads his case, imploring God. He asks God to clear him by showing his displeasure at the incense which Korah and his associates were to offer, with whom Dathan and Abiram were in league. "Lord," he says, "Do not accept their offering."

3. The argument between Moses and his accusers:

3.1. Moses challenges them to appear with Aaron the next morning at the time of the offering of the morning incense and refer the matter to God's judgment (vv. 16–17).

3.2. Korah accepts the challenge and appears with Moses and Aaron at the door of the tabernacle, to fulfill his claims (vv. 18–19). Then each one of the 250 took his censer. Perhaps some of the censers were those which these heads of the families had used at their family altars.

4. The judgment pronounced, and the Judge takes the tribunal and threatens to pass sentence on the whole community.

4.1. The glory of the Lord appeared (v. 19). The same glory that appeared when Aaron was originally installed into his office (Lev 9:23) now appeared to confirm him in it and to confound those who opposed him.

4.2. God threatened to consume them all in a moment, and in order to do that, he asked Moses and Aaron to stand apart from them (v. 21).

5. The humble intercession of Moses and Aaron for the community (v. 22):

5.1. Their posture was petitioning: they fell on their faces, prostrating themselves before God, asking God fervently that in his mercy he would spare them. Though the people had treacherously deserted Moses and Aaron and fallen in with those who were up in arms against them, they still showed themselves to be faithful to the trust committed to them, as shepherds of Israel who were to stand in the gap when they saw the flock in danger. If others fail in their duty to us, it does not discharge us from our duty to them or remove the obligation we are under to seek their welfare.

5.2. Their prayer was pleading, and it turned out to be effective. Notice in the prayer:

5.2.1. The title they give to God: *The God of the spirits of all flesh* (v. 22). Notice what human beings are: spirits in flesh, souls embodied, creatures wonderfully made by heaven and earth. See what God is: he is the God of the spirits of the whole human race.

5.2.2. The argument they insist on; it is much the same as Abraham's in his urgent intercession for Sodom (Ge 18:23): *Wilt thou destroy the righteous with the wicked?* This is the plea here: will one man sin and will you be angry with the whole assembly?

Verses 23–34

We have here the deciding of the dispute with Dathan and Abiram, who rebelled against Moses, as in the next section we have the deciding of the dispute with Korah and his company, who set themselves up as rivals to Aaron. It would seem that Dathan and Abiram had established a spacious tabernacle in the middle of the tents of their families, where they held court, met in council, and hung out their flag of defiance against Moses; it is called *the tabernacle of Korah, Dathan, and Abiram* (vv. 24, 27).

1. Public warning is given to the assembly to withdraw immediately from the tents of the rebels:

1.1. God tells Moses to speak to this effect (v. 24). This was in answer to Moses' prayer. He had begged that God would not *destroy the whole congregation.* God never promised to save by special miracles those who do not want to save themselves by ordinary means. The Moses who had prayed for them must also preach this to them and warn them to *flee from this wrath to come* (Mt 3:7).

1.2. So Moses returns to the headquarters of the rebels, leaving Aaron at the door of the tabernacle (v. 25). Dathan and Abiram had stubbornly refused to go up to him (v. 12), but he humbly condescends to go down to them, to see if he could still try to convince and win them back.

1.3. It is declared that all the people, if they were concerned for their own safety, should immediately *depart from the tents of these wicked men* (v. 26).

2. The assembly heed the warning, but the rebels themselves continue to be obstinate (v. 27).

2.1. God in his mercy inclined the people to leave the rebels.

2.2. God in his justice left the rebels to the obstinacy and hardness of their own hearts. They defiantly *stood in the doors of their tents* (v. 27), as if to challenge God himself and dare him to do his worst.

3. Sentence is solemnly pronounced on them by Moses in the name of the Lord, and the outcome of the dispute is seen in the execution of the judgment by the almighty power of God.

4. Execution is immediately carried out. It appeared that God and his servant Moses had a very close relationship and understood each other very well, for as soon as Moses had spoken the word, God did the work, and the earth *clave asunder* (v. 31), *opened her mouth, and swallowed them all up*, them and all their possessions (v. 32), and then *closed upon them* (v. 33). This judgment was:

- Unparalleled.
- Very terrible for the sinners themselves: they went down alive into their own graves.
- Harsh on their poor children, though we cannot tell in detail how bad they might have been to deserve God's anger or how good God might otherwise have been to them to make up for it. We are sure that infinite Justice did them no wrong.

5. All Israel is alarmed at the judgment: *They fled at the cry of them* (v. 34). The ruin of others should act as a warning to us.

Verses 35–40

We must now look back to the door of the tabernacle, the entrance to the Tent of Meeting, where we left those claiming the priesthood with their censers in their hands, ready to offer incense. Here we find:

1. Vengeance taken on them (v. 35). This punishment was no less strange or dreadful, and in it we can see:

1.1. That *our God is a consuming fire* (Heb 12:29).

1.2. That we are in danger if we meddle with what does not belong to us. God jealously protects the honor of his own institutions and will not see them violated. If they had been content with their positions as Levites, which were holy and honorable—and more than they deserved—they might have lived and died with joy and reputation.

2. Care taken to remember this vengeance forever. Orders are given about their censers:

2.1. That they should be kept safe, because they are holy. Eleazar is given this responsibility (v. 37). Now Eleazar is ordered to scatter the fire with the incense that was kindled with it in some unclean place outside the camp, to show that God detested their offering as something defiled: *The sacrifice of the wicked is an abomination to the Lord* (Pr 15:8). But he is to gather up the censers from the mixed fires, God's fire and theirs, because *they are hallowed* (vv. 37–38).

2.2. That they may be used in the service of the sanctuary. They must be beaten into *broad plates for a covering of the brazen altar* (vv. 38–40). These people thought of destroying the altar by opening up the priesthood to all, but to show that Aaron's office was not shaken by their malice and was instead confirmed by it, their censers—which they had tried to make rivals to his—were used both to decorate and preserve the altar at which he ministered.

These censers were preserved so that others might hear and fear and not behave defiantly toward God.

Verses 41–50

Here is:

1. A further rebellion breaking out the very next day against Moses and Aaron. *On the morrow* (v. 41) the community rebelled:

1.1. Though they had just been so terrified at the sight of the punishment of the rebels. The same sins came out again and all these warnings were completely ignored.

1.2. Though they had only just been saved from sharing in the same punishment. Their accusation is strong: *You have killed the people of the Lord.* Could anything have been more unjust or malicious? It was perfectly clear that Moses and Aaron were not involved in their death in any way—in fact, they had done what they could to save them—so that in accusing them of murder the people were in effect accusing God himself of that. The terrors of his judgments as they were carried out on the disobedient show how necessary the grace of God is to bring about powerful and definite changes in human hearts and lives. Love will do what fear cannot do.

2. God's prompt appearance against the rebels. When they had *gathered against Moses and Aaron*, perhaps with the intention of deposing or murdering them, they *looked towards the tabernacle*, as if the apprehension of their consciences expected to receive some disapproval from there, and *behold, the glory of the Lord appeared* (v. 42), to protect his servants and to confound the accusers and enemies.

3. The intercession which Moses and Aaron made for them:

3.1. They both *fell on their faces* (v. 45), humbly to intercede with God for mercy. They had done this several times before on similar occasions, and though the people had repaid them badly for it, God had graciously accepted their intercession, and they use the same method again. This is what is meant by praying always.

3.2. Moses, noticing that the *plague had begun in the congregation* of the rebels, sent Aaron to undertake his priestly office and make atonement for them (v. 46). Aaron went quickly and burned incense between the living and the dead. By this it appeared:

3.2.1. That Aaron was a very good man, and a man with a true love for his people, even though they were jealous of him and hated him.

3.2.2. That Aaron was a very bold man, bold to risk his life as he ran among the angry rabble. He was bold enough to venture into the midst of the defilement. In order to save their lives he put his own life at risk, not counting it dear to him, so that he might fulfill his ministry.

3.2.3. That Aaron was a man of God and *ordained for men, in things pertaining to God* (Heb 5:1). His call to the priesthood was greatly confirmed by this and put beyond all contradiction.

3.2.4. That Aaron was a type of Christ, who came into the world to make atonement for sin.

4. The result of all these events. God showed them what he could do by his power and his justice, but then he showed them what he could do in his love and pity. He would, despite all this, keep them as a people for himself in and through a mediator.

CHAPTER 17

Enough had been done in the previous chapter to quash all claims of the families of the tribe of Levi to set themselves up in competition with Aaron, but the leaders of the other tribes began to grumble. If the head of a tribe must be a priest, why not the head of a tribe other than Levi? The One who searches the heart knew this thought to be in some of them, and before it broke out into any overt act he graciously anticipated it, to prevent bloodshed; and it is answered by a miracle in this chapter, not a miracle of wrath, as before, but a miracle of grace. 1. The matter is put on trial by the bringing of twelve rods (staffs), one for each leader, before the Lord (vv. 1–7). 2. The matter is determined by the miraculous blossoming of Aaron's rod (vv. 8–9). The decision of the dispute is seen in the preservation of the rod (vv. 10–11). The people accept this with some reluctance (vv. 12–13).

Verses 1–7

Here we have:

1. Orders given for bringing in a rod (staff) for every tribe, so that God might perform a miracle to declare whom he had given the honor of the priesthood to.

1.1. It seems the priesthood was then a position that the leaders of the tribes tried to reach.

1.2. It seems there were those who did not accept the divine appointment, but who tried to oppose it. God wants to rule, but Israel does not want to be ruled; and this is what they are arguing about.

1.3. It is an example of the grace of God that, having performed many different miracles to punish sin, he is going to do one more to prevent it. The directions are:

1.3.1. That twelve rods or staffs should be brought in. They were probably all from the almond tree. It would seem they were only twelve in all, with Aaron's, for when Levi comes into the story, Ephraim and Manasseh are only one, in the name of Joseph.

1.3.2. That the name of each leader should be written on their rod.

1.3.3. That they should be placed in the tabernacle for a night, before the Testimony, that is, before the ark, which with its mercy seat (atonement cover) was a symbol or sign of God's presence with them.

1.3.4. That they were to expect that the rod of the tribe or leader whom God chose to the priesthood would bud and blossom (v. 5).

2. The preparing of the rods accordingly. The leaders brought them in, and *Moses laid them up before the Lord.*

Verses 8–13

Here is:

1. The final decision of the dispute concerning the priesthood by the performing of a miracle (vv. 8–9). The rods or staffs were brought from the Most Holy Place, where they had been placed, and publicly brought out to the people, and while all the other rods remained as they were, only Aaron's rod, a dry stick, had become a living branch that budded, blossomed, and produced almonds. This was a miracle and took away all suspicion of any deception, as if Moses had taken away Aaron's rod at night and put a living branch from an almond tree in its place, for no ordinary branch would bear buds, blossoms, and fruits all at once. Now:

1.1. This was a clear indication to the people that Aaron was chosen to the priesthood. Bishop Hall comments from this that fruitfulness is the best evidence of a divine call, and that the plants that God puts into the ground and the branches cut from them will flourish. See Ps 92:12–14. The trees of the Lord, although they may seem dry, are full of sap.

1.2. It was an appropriate sign to represent the priesthood, which was confirmed to Aaron in this. It showed that:

1.2.1. The priesthood would be fruitful and useful to the church of God.

1.2.2. There would be a succession of priests. Here were not only almonds for the present, but also buds and blossoms that brought the promise of more later.

1.2.3. This priesthood would not last forever, but in the course of time, like the branches and blossoms of a tree, it would fail and wither.

1.3. It was a type of Christ and his priesthood. He was to *grow up before God*, as this did before the ark, *like a tender plant, and a root out of a dry ground* (Isa 53:2).

2. The record of this decision, by the preserving of the rod before the Testimony, that it might be remembered forever (vv. 10–11).

2.1. The intention of God in all his providences is to take away sin and to prevent it.

2.2. What God does to take away sin is done out of his real kindness to us, *that we die not.* All the bitter medicines he gives, all the unpleasant methods he uses with us, are to heal a disease which otherwise would certainly be fatal.

3. The outcry of the people at this (vv. 12–13): *Behold, we die, we perish, we all perish. Shall we be consumed with dying?* This may be considered as the language either:

3.1. Of a resentful people quarreling with the judgments of God, which their own pride and obstinacy had brought on them. They seem to speak with despair, as if God were a hard Master who sought to take advantage of them. Or:

3.2. Of a repenting people. We submit to God's will in this decision. We will not oppose him anymore, so that none of us will die.

CHAPTER 18

Now that Aaron was fully established in the priesthood, God gives him full instructions in this chapter concerning his office, or rather he repeats those which he had given him before. He tells him: 1. What his work must be and the responsibilities committed to him, and what assistance he would have from the Levites in that work (vv. 1–7). 2. What would be his and the Levites' wages for this work, the perks or fees that were for the priests (vv. 8–19). 3. What would be the settled maintenance of the Levites (vv. 20–24); and the portion which must be paid to the priests out of the Levites' maintenance (vv. 25–32). In this way, everyone knew what they had to do and what they had to live on.

Verses 1–7

The connection of this chapter with the previous one is significant:

1. The people, at the end of that chapter, had complained of the difficulty and danger they had in drawing near to God. In answer to this complaint, God here gives them to understand through Aaron that the priests would come near for them as their representatives.

2. God had recently greatly honored Aaron. God comes to him to remind him of the burdens put on him and the duties required of him as a priest. He would then see reason to receive the honors of his office with reverence and holy fear, when he considered how great the duties were that were committed to him.

2.1. God tells him of the danger that accompanied his dignified position (v. 1):

2.1.1. That both the priests and the Levites (*thou, and thy sons, and thy father's house*) would *bear the iniquity of the sanctuary*, that is, if the sanctuary was desecrated by the intrusion of unauthorized people, such as those who were unclean, the blame would fall on the Levites and priests, who ought to have kept them away.

2.1.2. That the priests would themselves *bear the iniquity of the priesthood* (v. 1); that is, if they either neglected any part of their work or allowed other people to usurp their office and take their work out of their hands, they would bear the blame for it.

2.2. God tells him of the duty that accompanied his dignity:

2.2.1. That he and his sons must *minister before the tabernacle of witness* (v. 2), that is, according to Bishop Patrick, "before the Most Holy Place," in which the ark was, outside the curtain of that tent, but within the entrance of the Tent of Meeting. They were to serve at the golden altar, the table, and the candlestick (lampstand), which no Levite might approach. *You shall serve* (v. 7). Not, "You will rule." Ministers must remember that they are ministers, that is, servants, and they should be humble, diligent, and faithful.

2.2.2. That the Levites must assist him and his sons and minister to them in all the *service of the tabernacle* (vv. 2–4), though they must not come near the furnishings of the sanctuary.

2.2.3. That both priests and Levites must carefully make sure that holy things are not desecrated. The Levites must *keep the charge of the tabernacle*. And the priests must *keep the charge of the sanctuary* (v. 5); they must teach the people and warn them of the due distance they were to keep.

Verses 8–19

The priest's service is called "warfare"; and who goes to war at their own expense? As they were well employed, so they were well provided for. Those who *served at the altar lived upon the altar*. So those who *preach the gospel should live upon the gospel*, and live lives free of hardship (1Co 9:13–14). If ministers are paid an inadequate salary, then an inadequate ministry follows. Notice:

1. That much of the provision made for them resulted from the sacrifices which they themselves were employed to offer.

2. That their maintenance was such that it left them completely *disentangled from the affairs of this life* (2Ti 2:4). In this way, provision is made that a Gospel ministry would continue until Christ comes, by an ordinance forever. *Lo, I am with you*, to maintain and support you, *always, even to the end of the world* (Mt 28:20).

Verses 20–32

Here is a further account of the provision made both for the Levites and for the priests, from the country:

1. They must have *no inheritance in the land*. Later they were allowed to live in towns, but they could not possess any land. God variously distributes his favors. The Levites have the honor of serving at the tabernacle, which is denied the Israelites, but then the Israelites have the honor of inheritances in Canaan, which is denied the Levites.

2. But they must both have tithes of the land. Besides the firstfruits which were taken by the priests, the tithe was also taken possession of.

2.1. The Levites received the tithes of the people's produce (v. 21). The Levites were the smallest tribe of the twelve, and besides all the other advantages, they had a tenth part of the yearly profits, without the trouble and expense of plowing and sowing.

2.2. The priests had the tenths of the Levites' tithes passed on to them. Moses is directed to give the order for this to the Levites, whom God wanted to see pay it cheerfully, rather than the priests have to demand it with authority.

2.2.1. The Levites were to give God his dues from their tithes, just as the Israelites gave from their produce. Those who are employed to help in the devotions of others must be sure to make their own, as a heave offering (wave offering) to the Lord. Prayers and praises lifted up to God — with the heart lifted up in them — are our present heave offerings.

2.2.2. This was to be given to *Aaron the priest* (v. 28) and to his successors the high priests, to be divided and disposed of in such proportions as they thought fit among the lesser priests.

CHAPTER 19

This chapter deals with the preparation and use of the ashes to infuse the water of purification (water of cleansing). The people had complained of the strictness of the Law, which forbade them from coming near the tabernacle (17:13). In answer to this complaint, they are here instructed to cleanse themselves, so that they might come as far as they could without fear. Here is a description of: 1. How the ashes were to be prepared, by burning a red heifer, with a great deal of ceremony (vv. 1–10). 2. The way the ashes were to be used. They were intended to cleanse people from the defilement contracted by a dead body (vv. 11–16); they were to be put into running water, with which the person to be cleansed must be purified (vv. 17–22). The fact that this ceremonial purification was a type of the cleansing of the consciences of believers from the defilement of sin is seen in Heb 9:13–14, where the effectiveness of the blood of Christ is compared with the sanctifying power that was in the ashes of a heifer sprinkling the unclean.

Verses 1–10

We have here the divine requirement concerning the ceremonial burning of a red heifer to ashes. The ashes were to be kept, so that they might be used not to make something attractive, but to cleanse water. That was the farthest the Law reached; it could not make something attractive, as the Gospel does, but could only cleanse.

1. There was a great deal of care taken in the choice of the heifer that was to be burned, much more than in the choice of any other offering (v. 2). The heifer must not only be without blemish, being a type of the spotless purity and sinless perfection of the Lord Jesus, but it must also be a red heifer, because of the rarity of the color, that it might be more significant. The heifer also had to be one on which a yoke had never come, which was not insisted on in other sacrifices, but this was a type of the willing sacrifice of the Lord Jesus, when he said, *Lo, I come* (Heb 10:7, 9). He was bound and held with no other cords except those of his own love.

2. There was to be a great deal of ceremony when it was burned. The responsibility of doing it was committed to Eleazar, the one who was next to Aaron in rank. Now:

2.1. The heifer was to be killed outside the camp as an impure thing, which speaks of the inadequacy of the ways of the ceremonial law to take away sin.

2.2. Eleazar was to *sprinkle the blood directly before the door of the tabernacle*, looking steadfastly toward it (v. 4). This made it a kind of atoning sacrifice, for the sprinkling of the blood before the Lord was the main ceremony in all the sacrifices of atonement.

2.3. The heifer was to be wholly *burnt* (v. 5). The priest was to throw into the fire, while it was burning, cedar wood, hyssop, and scarlet wool, which were used in the cleansing of those with infectious skin diseases (Lev 14:6–7), that the ashes of these might be mixed in with the ashes of the heifer, because they were intended for cleansing.

2.4. The ashes of the heifer—separated as much as they could be from the ashes of the wood with which it was burned—were to be carefully gathered up by the hand of a clean person and, according to the Jews, pounded, sifted, and stored for use by the community as need be (v. 9).

2.5. All those who were employed in this service were made ceremonially unclean by it; even Eleazar himself, though he only sprinkled the blood (v. 7). All the sacrifices which were offered for sin were looked on as impure, because human sins were laid on them, as all our sins were laid on Christ, who therefore is said to be *made sin for us* (2Co 5:21).

Verses 11–22

Directions are given here concerning the use and application of the ashes which were prepared for cleansing:

1. When the ashes were to be used to cleanse. Nothing is mentioned here except the ceremonial uncleanness contracted by contact with a dead body, a dead human bone or a grave, or being in the tent or house where a dead body lay (vv. 11, 14–16). The Law could not conquer death, abolish it, nor change its power, as the Gospel does by bringing life and immortality to light, and so introducing a better hope. Since our Redeemer was dead and buried, death is no longer destructive to the Israel of God, and so dead bodies are no longer defiling. While the church was under the Law, however, the defilement contracted by dead bodies must have brought sad and distressing thoughts to their minds concerning death. But believers now through Christ can triumph over it. *O grave, where is thy victory?* (1Co 15:55). Where is its defilement now?

2. How the ashes were to be used and applied in these cases:

2.1. A small quantity of the ashes must be put into a cup of spring water, and mixed with the water, which then became what was called *a water of separation* (vv. 9, 13, 20–21), because it was to be sprinkled on those who were separated or removed from the sanctuary because of their uncleanness. As the ashes of the heifer represented the merits of Christ, so the running water represented the power and grace of the blessed Holy Spirit, who is compared to rivers of living water, and it is by his activity that the righteousness of Christ is applied to cleanse us.

2.2. This water must be applied by a bunch of hyssop dipped in it, with which the person or thing to be cleansed must be sprinkled (v. 18), in allusion to which David prays, *Purge me with hyssop* (Ps 51:7). Faith is the bunch of hyssop with which the conscience is sprinkled and the heart cleansed. The blood of Christ is said to be the *blood of sprinkling* (Heb 12:24), and with it we are said to be *sprinkled from an evil conscience* (Heb 10:22), that is, we are freed from a sense of uneasiness that arises from guilt. And it is foretold that Christ, by his baptism, would *sprinkle many nations* (Isa 52:15).

CHAPTER 20

This chapter begins the record of the fortieth year, which was the last of the Israelites' wandering in the desert. Since the beginning of their second year, when they were sentenced to be isolated in the desert, to while away the tedious stretch of forty years, little is recorded about them until this last year, which brought them to the borders of Canaan. The record of this year is almost as detailed as the record of the first year. This chapter gives an account of: 1. The death of Miriam (v. 1). The bringing of water from the rock, in which we notice the distress Israel was in because of a lack of water (v. 2); their discontent and grumbling in that distress (vv. 3–5); God's pity and power seen in supplying them with water from the rock (vv. 6–9); the weakness of Moses and Aaron on this occasion (vv. 10–11); God's displeasure against them (vv. 12–13). 2. Negotiations with the Edomites: Israel's request (vv. 14–17) and the rebuff of the Edomites (vv. 18–21). 3. The death of Aaron the high priest on Mount Hor, the investiture of Eleazar in his place, and the people's mourning for him (vv. 22–29).

Verses 1–13

After thirty-eight years' tedious marching, or rather tedious rests, in the desert back toward the Red Sea, the armies of Israel now eventually were facing toward Canaan again. They had not come far from the place where they had been when God had righteously sentenced them to begin their wanderings. Up to this time, they had been led around as if they were in a maze. They were now brought back to the right way again: they stayed at Kadesh (v. 1).

1. Here Miriam, the sister of Moses and Aaron, dies, who it would seem was older than either of them. She must have been so if she was the sister who was set to watch Moses when he was put into the ark of bulrushes, the papyrus basket (Ex 2:4). *Miriam died there* (v. 1). She was a prophet and had been instrumental in bringing a great deal of good to Israel (Mic 6:4). When Moses and Aaron with their rod (staff) went before them to work wonders for them, Miriam went before them with her tambourine to praise God for his wonderful works (Ex 15:20). But she had once grumbled (12:1–16) and was not allowed to enter Canaan.

2. Here there is another Meribah:

2.1. *There was no water for the congregation* (v. 2). They had probably been for some time in a country where they were supplied in an ordinary way, and when common providence supplied them it was right that the miracle should stop. But in this place it so happened that there was no water—or not enough—for the community.

2.2. Here they grumbled, they rebelled (v. 2): *they gathered themselves together against Moses and Aaron.* They wished they had died as evildoers at the hands of God's justice, rather than be neglected—or so they thought—by his mercy. They were angry that they had been brought out of Egypt and led through the desert (vv. 4–5). Although what they lacked at that time was water, now that they are in the mood for finding fault, they will no doubt soon be considering it intolerable that they do not have vines and figs.

2.3. Moses and Aaron did not reply to them but withdrew to the door of the tabernacle (the entrance to the Tent of Meeting) to know God's will (v. 6).

2.4. God came and decided the matter; he did not appear on the throne as a judge, to punish the rebels according to what they deserved. But he came:

2.4.1. On his throne of glory, to silence their unjust grumbling (v. 6). A believing sight of the glory of the Lord would powerfully restrain our sinful desires and would control our tongues.

2.4.2. On his throne of grace, to satisfy their just desires. They needed to have water. For a second time, Moses must command in God's name that water should flow from a rock for them, to show that God is as able as ever to supply his people with good things.

2.4.3. God tells him to speak to the rock, which would do as it was asked, to shame the people who had been so often spoken to and who refused to listen and obey.

2.4.4. God promises that the rock would produce water (v. 8), and it did so (v. 11).

2.5. Moses and Aaron acted improperly in carrying out God's orders, so much so that God was displeased with them and told them immediately that they would not have the honor of leading Israel into Canaan (vv. 10–12).

2.5.1. It is not completely certain what they had done that offended God so much. Their errors were complex:

2.5.1.1. God told them to *speak to the rock*, and they spoke *to the people*. They *smote* (struck) *the rock*, which on this occasion they had not been ordered to do, but they thought that simply speaking to the rock would not be enough.

2.5.1.2. They took too much of the glory of this miracle to themselves: *Must we fetch water?* (v. 10). It is as if it had to be done by some power or worthiness of their own.

2.5.1.3. Their great sin was unbelief (v. 12): *You believed me not.* Dr. Lightfoot thinks that their unbelief is seen in the fact that they doubted whether now eventually, after forty years had expired, they would enter Canaan, and whether they must not because of the people's grumblings be condemned to a further period of toil, because a new rock had opened up to supply them, which they took as a sign that they were to stay longer.

2.5.1.4. They said and did everything in a vehement passion.

2.5.1.5. What made everything else worse and more offensive was that their actions were made in public, before the eyes of *the children of Israel*, to whom they should have been examples of faith, hope, and humility.

2.5.2. From all this we may learn that even the best people have their failings and that God judges not as we judge concerning sin.

3. The place is then called *Meribah* (v. 13). It is called *Meribah-Kadesh* (Dt 32:51), to distinguish it from the other Meribah. It is the "water of strife" (27:14), to be a perpetual reminder of the people's sin, and Moses', but also of God's mercy, who nevertheless supplied them with water and acknowledged and honored Moses.

Verses 14–21

Here we have Israel seeking permission from the Edomites to pass through their land. The most direct way to Canaan from the place where Israel was now camped was through the country of Edom. Now:

1. Moses sends messengers to negotiate with the king of Edom for permission to pass through his country.

1.1. They are to claim family ties with the Edomites. Both nations descended from Abraham and Isaac, their common ancestors.

1.2. They are to give a short account of the history and present state of Israel. In this, there was a double plea:

• Israel had been mistreated by the Egyptians and so ought to be pitied and helped by their relatives.
• Israel had been wonderfully saved by the Lord and so ought to be supported and favored (v. 16).

1.3. They are humbly to ask for authorization to pass through their country.

1.4. They are to guarantee the good behavior of the Israelites in their journey.

2. The messengers returned with a refusal (v. 18). Edom, that is, the king of Edom, threatened, if they attempted to enter his country, that their lives would be in danger. This was because of their jealousy of the Israelites and the old hostilities between Esau and Israel. If they had no reason to fear being wronged by them, they were still not willing even to show kindness to them. Esau hated Jacob because of the blessing.

Verses 22–29

The chapter began with the funeral of Miriam, and it ends with the funeral of her brother Aaron.

1. God tells Aaron that he is going to die (v. 24).

1.1. There is a note of displeasure in these orders. Aaron would not be allowed to enter Canaan, because he had failed in his duty at Meribah. The reference to this doubtless went straight to Moses' heart, who knew himself perhaps at that time to have been the guiltier of the two.

1.2. There is much that is merciful in them. Although Aaron died because of his sin, he is not put to death as an evildoer by a plague or fire from heaven but dies contentedly and in honor. He is not *cut off from his people*, as the death of those who die at the hand of divine justice is usually expressed, but he is *gathered to his people* (v. 24), as one who died in the arms of divine grace.

1.3. There is much about them that expresses a type. Aaron must not enter Canaan, to show that the Levitical priesthood could make nothing perfect. That must be done by bringing in a better hope.

2. Aaron accepts God's will and dies in the way God appointed, with it seems as much cheerfulness as if he had been simply going to bed.

2.1. Aaron puts on his holy garments to take his leave of them and goes up with his brother and son to the top of Mount Hor, and probably some of the elders of Israel with him (v. 27). His going up the hill to die showed that the death of saints is their ascension. They go up rather than down to death. Aaron is called *the saint of the Lord* (Ps 106:16).

2.2. Moses, whose hands had first dressed Aaron in his priestly garments, now removes them from him, for it was not right that he should die in them, out of reverence for the priesthood.

2.3. Moses immediately puts the priestly garments on Eleazar his son, clothes him with his father's robe, and *strengthens him with his girdle* (Isa 22:21). Now:

2.3.1. This was a great comfort to Moses, a welcome promise to the church of the care God would take that as one generation of ministers and Christians (spiritual priests) passes away, another generation would come up to take its place.

2.3.2. It was a great satisfaction to Aaron to see his son, who was dear to him, honored in this way, and his office, which was even dearer, preserved in this way.

2.3.3. It was a great kindness to the people.

CHAPTER 21

The armies of Israel now begin to emerge from the desert, and to come into an inhabited land, to begin to take possession of the frontiers of the Land of Promise. Here is: 1. The defeat of Arad the Canaanite (vv. 1–3).

2. *The disciplining of the people with venomous snakes because they grumbled, and the relief given them on their submission to the bronze snake (vv. 4 – 9). 3. The journey forward, and some events on the way (vv. 10 – 20). 4. The famous conquest of Sihon king of the Amorites (vv. 21 – 32) and of Og king of Bashan (vv. 33 – 35), and possession taken of their land.*

Verses 1 – 3

Here is:

1. The attack by Arad the Canaanite on the camp of Israel, hearing that they came *by the way of the spies* (v. 1), for though the spies which Moses had sent thirty-eight years before then had passed unnoticed, their arrival and their mission probably later became known to the Canaanites. It must have been a warning to them and induced them to watch Israel.

2. Arad's initial success. His advance guards picked up some straggling Israelites and took them prisoner (v. 1).

3. Israel's humbly turning to God on this occasion (v. 2). They were tempted to grumble like their fathers and to despair of ever gaining possession of Canaan, but God, who tested them by his providence, gave them grace to act rightly and to trust him for relief.

4. The victory which the Israelites won over the Canaanites (v. 3). A strong division was sent out, probably under the command of Joshua, which not only drove back these Canaanites, but followed them to their towns and completely destroyed them, and returned to the camp. *Vincimur in praelio, sed non in bello,* "We lose a battle, but we finally triumph." What is said of the tribe of Gad is true of all God's Israel, a band of raiders may overcome them, but they will overcome eventually (Ge 49:19).

Verses 4 – 9

Here is:

1. The tiredness of Israel from their long march around the land of Edom, because they were not allowed to pass through it by the most direct way: *The soul of the people was much discouraged because of the way* (v. 4).

2. Their unbelief and grumbling on this occasion (v. 5). They have *bread enough and to spare* (Lk 15:17), but they complain *there is no bread* (v. 5). Although it is angels' food that they are eating, they have become bored with it. They are sick and tired of manna every day, which they call *light bread* (v. 5): they see it as fit only for children, not for adults and soldiers. If they are not pleased with manna, then what will they be pleased with? Let not the contempt that some have for the word of God cause us to value it less: it is the bread of life; it is substantial, not light, and will nourish those who by faith feed on it to eternal life, whatever anyone else calls it.

3. The righteous judgment which God brought on them for their grumbling (v. 6). He sent *fiery serpents* (venomous snakes) *among them,* which bit or stung many of them to death. The desert through which they had passed was overrun by poisonous snakes (Dt 8:15). God had miraculously kept his people from being hurt by them until this point, when they murmured. The snakes are called *fiery,* from their color, their rage, or the effects of their bite. The people had arrogantly lifted themselves up against God and Moses, but God now humbled and disciplined them by sending these contemptible creatures on them.

4. Their repentance and prayer to God at this judgment (v. 7). *We have sinned.* It might have been that they would not have acknowledged their sin if they had not suffered as they did. They ask Moses to pray for them. Suffering

often changes people's feelings toward God's people; they learn to value their prayers, which they had previously scorned. Moses, to show that he had genuinely forgiven them, blesses those who had cursed him, and *prays for those who had despitefully used him* (Lk 6:28). In this he was a type of Christ, who interceded for his persecutors. He is an example for us to go and do likewise, and so show that we *love our enemies* (Lk 6:27).

5. The wonderful provision which God made to bring relief to them. God ordered Moses to make an image of a venomous snake, which he did, using bronze, and he set it up on a very high pole, so that it might be seen from all parts of the camp, and looking up to this bronze snake healed all those who had been stung by a venomous snake. The people prayed that God would *take away the serpents from them* (v. 7), but God saw fit not to do this, for he brings complete relief to us in the way he thinks best, which may not be the way that we think. The Jews themselves say that it was not the sight of the bronze snake that healed them, but when they looked to it, they looked to God as the Lord who healed them. The Gospel can be seen in this; our Savior has told us so (Jn 3:14 – 15), that *as Moses lifted up the serpent in the wilderness so the Son of man must be lifted up,* that *whosoever believeth in him should not perish.* Notice then a likeness:

5.1. Between their disease and ours. The Devil is the old Serpent, a fiery Serpent, and so he appears (Rev 12:3) as *a great red dragon. Sin* is the bite of this fiery Serpent; it is painful to the startled conscience and poisonous to the seared conscience. Satan's temptations are called his *fiery darts* (Eph 6:16).

5.2. Between their treatment and ours:

5.2.1. It was God himself who prescribed this antidote against the venomous snakes, and so our salvation in Christ was planned by infinite Wisdom. God himself has found the means of redemption.

5.2.2. It was a very unlikely way of healing. Similarly, our salvation by the death of Christ is *to the Jews a stumbling block and to the Greeks foolishness* (1Co 1:23).

5.2.3. What brought healing was shaped in the likeness of what wounded. So Christ, though perfectly free from sin himself, was *made in the likeness of sinful flesh* (Ro 8:3), so that it was taken for granted that this *man* was a *sinner* (Jn 9:24).

5.2.4. The bronze snake was lifted up, and so was Christ. He was lifted up on the cross (Jn 12:33 – 34), for he was displayed to the world. He was lifted up by the preaching of the Gospel. The word used here for a *pole* means "a banner; ensign," for Christ crucified *stands for an ensign of the people* (Isa 11:10). Some see the lifting up of the snake to be a type of Christ's triumph over Satan, the old Serpent, whose head he struck, when on the cross he made a public spectacle of the principalities and powers which he had disarmed and destroyed (Col 2:15).

5.3. Between the application of their healing and ours. They looked and lived, and we, if we believe, will not die. It is by faith that we look to Jesus (Heb 12:2). *Look unto me, and be you saved* (Isa 45:22). Whoever looked up to this healing sign, even from the farthest point in the camp, and even though they looked only weakly and with tears, was certainly healed. Similarly, whoever believes in Christ, even though they have only a weak faith, will not die.

Verses 10 – 20

We have here a record of the several stages and moves of the children of Israel, till they came to the plains of Moab, from which they eventually passed over Jordan into

Canaan, as we read at the beginning of book of Joshua. Natural movements become quicker the nearer they get to their center. The Israelites were now drawing near to the promised rest, and now they *set forward* (v. 10). It would be good if we were to follow their example as we journey to heaven, and if, the nearer we came to heaven, the more active and zealous we became in the work of the Lord. Two things especially are noticeable:

1. The wonderful success which God blessed his people with, near the brooks of Arnon (vv. 13–15). They had now gone around the land of Edom. It is good that there are more ways than one into Canaan. The enemies of God's people may slow down their passage but cannot prevent their ultimate entrance into the promised rest. Care is taken to let us know that the Israelites on their journey strictly observed the instructions which God gave them not to provoke the Moabites to war in any way (Dt 2:9), because they were the descendants of righteous Lot.

2. The wonderful supply which God blessed his people with at *Beer* (v. 16), which means "a well." Up to this time, we have found that when they were supplied with water, they asked for it with unjust discontent, and God gave it to them in his just displeasure, but here we find:

2.1. That God gave it in love (v. 16): *Gather the people together*, to witness the wonder and to share in the favor, *and I will give them water*. Before they prayed, God answered.

2.2. That they received it with joy and thankfulness, which made the mercy doubly sweet to them (v. 17). Then they sang this song, to the glory of God and the encouragement of one another, *Spring up, O well!* They prayed this so that it may spring up, for promised mercies must be sought in prayer. Just as the bronze snake was a type of Christ, who is lifted up to heal us, so this well is a type of the Spirit, who is poured out to give us assurance, and from whom flow to *us rivers of living waters* (Jn 7:38).

2.3. That whereas before, the miracle was perpetually remembered by the names given to places which represented the people's grumbling, now it was perpetually remembered by a song of praise. *The princes digged the well.* The seventy elders dug holes with their staffs into the soft, sandy ground, and God caused the water to miraculously spring up in the holes which they made. God promised to give them water, but they had to open the ground to receive it, and allow it to come. We must expect to receive God's favors by using those means which lie within our power, but nevertheless the all-surpassing power comes from God.

Verses 21–35

We have here a record of the victories gained by Israel over Sihon and Og:

1. Israel sent a peaceful message to Sihon king of the Amorites (v. 21), but received a hostile reply. Not only was Sihon's army routed, but also all his country came to be possessed by Israel (vv. 24–25). This occupation is justified:

1.1. Against the Amorites themselves, for they were the aggressors, and provoked the Israelites to battle.

1.2. Against the Moabites, who had formerly ruled this country.

1.2.1. The justification itself is that though it was true that this country had belonged to the Moabites, the Amorites had taken it from them some time before, and were now in full and settled possession of it (v. 26). Because this country was intended in due time to be possessed by Israel, it is beforehand put into the hands of the Amorites,

who little think that they have it only as trustees until Israel takes it at the right time, and then they must surrender it. We do not understand the vast reaches of Providence, but all God's works are known to him, as can be seen in this instance.

1.2.2. For proof of the allegation, he refers to the authentic records of the country, their proverbs or songs, one of which he quotes from (vv. 27–30), which sufficiently proves what is affirmed, namely:

1.2.2.1. That the places named here, although they had been in the possession of the Moabites, had been won in war by Sihon king of the Amorites.

1.2.2.2. That the Moabites were prevented completely from ever regaining possession, and even Chemosh their god had given them up and was unable to rescue them from the hands of Sihon (v. 29).

2. Og king of Bashan, instead of being warned by what happened to his neighbors to make peace with Israel, is prompted by it to make war with them, which turns out to lead to his destruction in the same way. Og was also an Amorite, and more likely to win because of his own massive strength and stature. Notice:

2.1. That the Amorite begins the war (v. 33). His country was very rich and pleasant. Bashan was famous for the best timber, as is seen from the oaks of Bashan, and the best breeds, as is seen in the famous cattle, lambs, and rams of that country (Dt 32:14).

2.2. That God involves himself and tells Israel not to fear this threatening force. Giants are mere worms when God's power is at work.

2.3. That Israel not only routs the enemies' army, but gains the enemies' country, which later was part of the inheritance of the two and a half tribes that were first established on the other side of Jordan.

CHAPTER 22

The famous story of Balak and Balaam begins at this chapter, with their attempt to curse Israel, and the frustration of that attempt; God's people are long afterward told to remember what Balak the king of Moab advised, and what Balaam the son of Beor answered, that they might know the righteousness of the Lord (Mic 6:5). In this chapter we have: 1. Balak's fear of Israel, and the plan he conceived to see them cursed (vv. 1–4); the messengers he sent to Balaam, a seer, to bring him back for that purpose, and the disappointment he met with in the first mission (vv. 5–14). 2. Balaam's coming to him with his second message (vv. 15–21). 3. The opposition Balaam met with on the way (vv. 22–35). 4. The eventual meeting between Balak and Balaam (vv. 36–41).

Verses 1–14

The children of Israel have now at last finished their wanderings in the desert, from which they went up (21:18), and are now camped in the plains of Moab near Jordan, where they continued till they passed through Jordan under Joshua after the death of Moses. Here we have:

1. The shock which the Moabites were in when Israel approached (vv. 2–4). Despite the old friendship between Abraham and Lot, the Moabites were determined to ruin Israel if they could. They therefore assume, without any proper grounds for their suspicion, that Israel is determined to destroy them. They communicated these fears to their neighbors, the elders of Midian, so that some joint action might be worked out between them for their common security. They had reason to seek Israel's

friendship and to come to their aid, but having abandoned the religion of their father Lot and fallen into idolatry, they hated the people of the God of Abraham.

2. The plan which the king of Moab devised to see the people of Israel cursed, that is, to set God against them. He trusted more in his magic power than in his military power and thought that if he could just get some prophet or other to cast a spell and call down evil on them, and at the same time pronounce a blessing on himself and his forces, then although he was weak by himself, he would be able to deal with them. This thought arose from:

2.1. The remnants of some religion, for it acknowledges a dependence on some hidden powers that rule over human affairs.

2.2. The ruins of true religion, for if the Midianites and Moabites had not turned away so perversely from the faith and worship of their godly ancestors, Abraham and Lot, they could not have imagined it possible to stir up trouble with their curses toward a people who followed only the true God, and from whom they themselves had rebelled.

3. The attention which Balak the Moabite king paid to Balaam the son of Beor, a famous seer, to hire him to curse Israel. This Balaam lived a long way away, in the country from where Abraham came and where Laban lived. In order to gain him, he makes him his friend and in effect also makes him his god, according to the great power he attributes to his word.

4. The restraint God places on Balaam, forbidding him to curse Israel. He stays overnight with the messengers, taking his time to consider what he will do, sleeping on the matter, and waiting to receive instructions from God (v. 8). God comes to him at night, probably in a dream, and asks what business those strangers had with him. God knows what it is, but he wants Balaam to tell him. Balaam tells him why they have come (vv. 9–11), and God then instructs him not to go with them or attempt to curse that blessed people (v. 12). Balaam is commanded not only not to go to Balak, but also not to offer to curse this people, which he might have tried to do from a distance. The reason is given: *They are blessed.*

5. The return of the messengers without Balaam. Balaam is not faithful in giving God's complete answer to the messengers (v. 13). He only tells them, *the Lord refuseth to give me leave to go with you.* He did not tell them, as he should have done, that Israel was a blessed people and must not be cursed at all.

Verses 15–21

We have here a second mission sent to Balaam to win him over to curse Israel. Notice:

1. The temptation Balak laid before Balaam. He now tempted him with honors, offering enticement not only for his greed, but also for his pride and ambition. Notice how scheming Balak is in offering the temptation:

• The messengers he sent were *more,* and *more honourable* (v. 15).

• The request was very urgent. The powerful ruler Balak becomes a suitor to Balaam: *"Let nothing, I pray thee, hinder thee* (v. 16), nothing, not God, conscience, or any fear of sin or shame."

• The offers were high: *"I will promote thee to very great honour* among the rulers of Moab."

2. Balaam's seeming resistance of, but in reality giving in to, this temptation. We may here discern in Balaam a struggle between his conviction and his corruption:

2.1. His conviction assured him he must observe the command of God, and he expressed that conviction

(v. 18). In fact, no one could have expressed it better: *"If Balak would give me his house full of silver and gold,* and that is more than he can give or I can ask, *I cannot go beyond the word of the Lord my God."*

2.2. At the same time, his corruption strongly inclined him to disobey the command. He seemed to refuse the temptation (v. 18). But even then he expressed no aversion to it, as Christ did when the kingdoms of the world were offered him: *Get thee hence, Satan* (Mt 4:10); and as Peter did when Simon Magus offered him money: *Thy money perish with thee* (Ac 8:20). But it appears (v. 19) that he had a strong inclination to accept their offer, for he wants to consider the matter further, to know what God wants to say to him, hoping that God might change his mind and give him permission to go. This reflected badly on God Almighty, as if he could change his mind. It is a grave insult to God, and shows how corruption controls the heart, if we ask permission to sin.

3. The permission God gave him to go (v. 20). God came to him, probably by an angel, and told him he could, if he pleased, go with Balak's messengers. *So he gave him up to his own heart's lust* (Ps 81:12). As God sometimes denies the prayers of his people in love, so also sometimes he gives the desires of the wicked in wrath.

Verses 22–35

We read here of an account of the opposition God brought to Balaam on his journey toward Moab. Notice:

1. God's displeasure against Balaam for undertaking this journey: God's *anger was kindled because he went* (v. 22). Note:

1.1. The sin of sinners is not to be thought less offensive to God simply because he allows it.

1.2. Nothing is more displeasing to God than evil intentions against his people. Those who want to strike them are striking the apple of his eye, his most valued possession.

2. The way God let Balaam know of his displeasure against him: *An angel stood in the way for an adversary* (v. 22).

2.1. Balaam was warned of God's displeasure by the donkey, but this did not startle him. The *ass saw the angel* (v. 23). How arrogantly Balaam boasted that he was a man whose *eyes were open,* and that he *saw the visions of the Almighty* (24:3–4), but when the donkey he rode on saw more than he did, his eyes were blinded by greed and ambition. Let no one become conceited because of visions and revelations, when we remember that a donkey saw an angel. To save both itself and its foolish rider:

2.1.1. It *turned aside out of the way* (v. 23). Balaam should have taken the hint and considered whether he had not left his line of duty, but instead of this, he beat the donkey to get it back on the road. Similarly, those who willfully sin and are running headlong toward a lost eternity are angry with those who try to stop their destruction.

2.1.2. It had not gone much farther before it saw the angel again, and then to avoid him, *ran up to a wall,* and *crushed her rider's foot* (vv. 24–25). The crushing of Balaam's foot, though its purpose was to save his life, offended him so much that he struck his donkey a second time.

2.1.3. On the next encounter with the angel, the donkey lay down under Balaam (vv. 26–27). Balaam struck the donkey a third time, though it had now done him the best service it had ever done him, saving him from the sword of the angel, and by its falling down trying to teach him to do likewise.

2.1.4. When all this did not have any effect, God went so far as to open the donkey's mouth, and it spoke to him twice, but even this did not affect him in the slightest. Here Mr. Ainsworth notices that the Devil, when he tempted our first parents to sin, used a wily serpent, but that God, when he wanted to convince Balaam, employed a silly donkey, an animal that is proverbially foolish:

2.1.4.1. The donkey complained of Balaam's cruelty (v. 28): *What have I done unto thee, that thou hast smitten me?* God in his righteousness will not stand by and watch while the lowliest and weakest are mistreated; either they will be enabled to speak up in their own defense or he will use some means or other to speak up for them. His wild, headstrong passions blinded him so much that he did not even notice that something strange had happened. Nothing makes a person so foolish as unbridled anger.

2.1.4.2. The donkey reasoned with him (v. 30). God enabled not only a mute creature to speak, but a slow-witted creature to speak to the point.

2.2. Balaam eventually became aware of God's displeasure from the angel, and this startled him. When God opened his eyes, *he saw the angel* (v. 31), and then he himself *fell flat upon his face.* God has many ways of breaking and humbling the hard and proud heart.

2.2.1. The angel rebuked him for his outrageous behavior (vv. 32–33): *Wherefore hast thou smitten thy ass?*

2.2.2. Balaam then seemed to back down (v. 34): *"I have sinned.* I have sinned in undertaking this journey. I have sinned in pushing ahead so forcefully." However, he made the excuse that he had not seen the angel, but now that he did see him, he was willing to go back again. There is no sign that his heart has turned, but if his hands are tied, he cannot help it. In this way, many leave their sins simply because their sins have left them. There seems to be a reformation of the life, but what use is this if there is no renewal of the heart?

2.2.3. The angel, however, continued with his permission: *"Go with the men* (v. 35). Go ahead if you want to make a fool of yourself and be shamed before Balak and all the princes of Moab. *Go, only the word that I shall speak unto thee, that thou shalt speak* (v. 35), whether you want to or not." The angel's words seem not to be an instruction, but a prediction of what would happen, that he would not only not be able to curse Israel, but also be forced to bless them.

Verses 36–41

Here is the meeting between Balak and Balaam, allied enemies against God's Israel, but here they seem to have different expectations of the success:

1. Balak speaks of it with confidence, not doubting that he will be successful now that Balaam had come.

2. Balaam speaks with doubt about the outcome and asks Balak not to depend too much on him (v. 38): *"Have I now any power at all to say anything?* I would gladly curse Israel, but I must not, I cannot, God will not allow me."

3. They get down to business quickly. Balaam is well entertained overnight, with a sacrifice of thanksgiving offered to the gods of Moab for the safe arrival of this welcome guest, and he is treated with a feast of the sacrifice (v. 40). And the next morning, so that no time would be lost, Balak takes Balaam in his chariot to the high places of his kingdom. And now Balaam is really as concerned to please Balak as ever he had pretended to be to please God.

CHAPTER 23

In this chapter we see Balak and Balaam busy at work to cause trouble for Israel, and it appears that neither Moses nor the elders of Israel know anything about what is going on, but God frustrates the attempt, without any intercession or interference by Israel. Here is: 1. The first attempt to curse Israel: the preparation made for it by sacrifice (vv. 1–3); the opposite instruction God gave Balaam (vv. 4–5); the blessing Balaam was compelled to pronounce on Israel, instead of a curse (vv. 6–10); and Balak's great disappointment (vv. 11–12). 2. The second attempt, made in the same way and frustrated in the same way (vv. 13–26), and preparations made for a third attempt (vv. 27–30), the outcome of which we have in the next chapter.

Verses 1–12

Here:

1. Great preparations are made to curse Israel. What they were aiming at was to get the God of Israel to abandon his people, and either to be on Moab's side or to be neutral. It is absurd for him to *eat the flesh of bulls or drink the blood of goats* (Ps 50:13). It is nonsense to think that these would please God and gain his favor, when there was no faith or obedience involved in them. But it would seem that they offered these sacrifices to the God of heaven, the supreme Deity, and not to any of their local gods.

2. The curse is turned into a blessing by the overruling power of God, because of his love for Israel, which is how Moses expresses it (Dt 23:5).

2.1. God puts the blessing into the mouth of Balaam. While the sacrifices were burning, Balaam withdrew; he went by himself ("went solitary," v. 3, margin) to some dark grove on the top of the high place (v. 3). He knew this much, that solitude gives a good opportunity for fellowship with God. But Balaam withdrew only with the thought that God might perhaps meet him. He was aware of his guilt and knew that God had just met him in anger and so had reason to speak doubtfully: *Peradventure the Lord will come to meet me* (v. 3). But whatever he intended, God intended to serve his own glory by him and so *met Balaam* (v. 4). God would compel Balaam to make such a declaration as would not only honor God and Israel but would also be a warning to any who opposed Israel in the future. When Balaam was aware that God met with him, he boasted of what he had done: *I have prepared seven altars, and offered upon every altar a bullock and a ram* (v. 4). However, even though the sacrifice was detestable to God, God used the occasion of Balaam's expectancy to *put a word into his mouth* (v. 5):

2.2. Balaam pronounces the blessing to Balak's ears. He pronounces Israel safe and fortunate. He blesses them:

2.2.1. He declares them safe and out of the reach of his poisonous darts:

2.2.1.1. He acknowledges that his original intention was to curse them, that Balak sent for him from his own country, and that he came with that intention in mind (v. 7).

2.2.1.2. He acknowledges that the intention has been defeated and that he is unable to accomplish it. He could not so much as speak out one bad word or wish: *How shall I curse those whom God has not cursed?* (v. 8). It was not that he would not do it; it was that he simply could not do it. This is a reasonable confession:

• Of the weakness and ineffectiveness of his own magic powers.

• Of the sovereignty of God's power. He acknowledges that he could do no more than God allowed him to do.
• Of the absolute security of the people of God.

2.2.2. He declares them fortunate in three things:
2.2.2.1. Fortunate that they are special; they are distinct from the other nations: *From the top of the rock I see him* (v. 9). And it seems to have been a great surprise to Balaam that while they probably appeared to him as a rowdy, disorderly, and rambling rabble that invaded the neighboring countries, he portrayed them in his oracle as a regular, united camp that appeared well disciplined and ordered. It is the duty and honor of those who are dedicated to God to be separate from the world. Those who conscientiously undertake special duties may be assured of special privileges.
2.2.2.2. Fortunate in their numbers, not so few and lowly as they appeared to Balaam, but an innumerable group, which made them both honorable and formidable (v. 10): *Who can count the dust of Jacob?* Balak was worried about the number of the people (22:3). Balaam takes notice of the number:

• Of the *dust of Jacob* (v. 10), that is, the people of Jacob, concerning whom it was foretold that they would be like the dust in number (Ge 28:14).
• Of the *fourth part of Israel* (v. 10), alluding to the form of their camp, which was formed into four divisions, under four standards.

2.2.2.3. Fortunate in their final destiny: *Let me die the death of the righteous* (v. 10) Israelites, who are in covenant with God, and let my *last end*, my future state, be *like theirs*, my reward, namely, in the other world. Here:

• It is taken for granted that death is the destiny of all people. The righteous themselves must die. It is good for us to think of this and apply it to ourselves, as Balaam himself does here, speaking of his own death.
• He believes in the soul's immortality and a different state beyond death; this is clear evidence of its being known and believed long ago.
• He pronounces the righteous truly blessed, not only while they live, but also when they die.
• He shows his thoughts about religion to be better than his resolve. There are many who want to die the death of the righteous, but who do not try to live the life of the righteous. They want their destiny to be like that of the righteous, but are not prepared to live that way. They want to be saints in heaven, but not saints on earth. Now:

3. We are told:
3.1. How Balak was distressed at it (v. 11). He pretended to honor the Lord with his sacrifices and wait for the answer God was going to give him, but when the answer was not the one he was looking for, he forgot God.
3.2. How Balaam was forced to accept it. He submits because he can do nothing else.

Verses 13–30

Here is:
1. Preparation made for a second attempt to curse Israel. The place is changed (v. 13). The sacrifices are repeated: new altars are built, a young bull and a ram offered on every altar, and Balak waits at his sacrifice as closely as ever (vv. 14–15). Balaam renews his waiting on God, and God meets him a second time and puts another word into his mouth, not to reverse the first message, but to confirm it (vv. 16–17).

2. A second transformation of the curse into a blessing by the overruling power of God. This blessing is both fuller and stronger than the first one and completely destroys any hope of it being changed. Because Balak had been so forward in asking what the Lord had spoken (v. 17), Balaam now turns particularly to him (v. 18): *Rise up, Balak, and hear.*

2.1. In his message, Balaam tells Balak two things:
2.1.1. That he had no reason to hope that he would destroy Israel:
2.1.1.1. It would be futile to attempt to destroy them:

• Because God is unchangeable. He never changes his mind and so never needs to recall his promise.
• Because Israel are at present unblamable. There was no idolatry among them, which is particularly iniquitous. Balaam knew that nothing would separate them and God except sin.
• Because the power of God's unchangeableness and Israel's present blamelessness was irresistible. Firstly, they had the presence of God with them. Secondly, they had the joy of that presence and were always made to triumph in it.

2.1.1.2. From all this he reasons that it would be futile if he thought he could cause trouble by all his magic arts (v. 23). The curses of hell can never take the place of the blessings of heaven.
2.1.2. That he had more reason to fear being destroyed by them, for they were likely to wage war among his neighbors, and if Balak and his country escaped, it was not because he was too great for Israel to fight against, but because he did not fall among the nations that God had commissioned them to subdue (v. 24).
2.2. What was the outcome of this disappointment?
2.2.1. Balak and Balaam were both fed up with the matter. Balak is now willing to have his diviner silenced. "If you cannot curse them, then at least don't bless them." Balaam is still willing to acknowledge himself overruled and appeals to what he had said at the beginning (22:38): *All that the Lord speaketh, that I must do* (v. 26).
2.2.2. But they decide to make another attempt. The place which Balak now took Balaam to was the top of Peor, a famous high place in his country, probably where Baal was worshiped, and for this reason it was called *Baal-peor.*

CHAPTER 24

This chapter continues and concludes the history of the defeat of the counsels of Balak and Balaam against Israel, not by might, nor by power, but by the Spirit of the Lord of hosts (Zec 4:6). In this chapter we are told: 1. What the blessing was into which the intended curse was turned (vv. 1–9). 2. How Balak then dismissed Balaam from his service (vv. 10–13). 3. The predictions Balaam left behind him concerning Israel and some of the neighboring nations (vv. 14–25).

Verses 1–9

The blessing itself which Balaam here pronounces on Israel is much the same as the two we read about in the previous chapter, but its introduction is different:
1. The way he proceeds is different here. Balaam laid aside the sorcery which he had depended on up to that time. He used no spells, charms, or magic arts, having found them to be useless. It was futile to deal with the Devil to obtain a curse, when it was clear that God was

resolutely determined to bless (v. 1). He did not now withdraw to a solitary place as before, but set his face directly toward the desert where Israel lay camped. Now *the Spirit of God came upon him*, that is, the Spirit of prophecy. He now used a different introduction from the one he had used before (vv. 3–4), but one suggestive very much, some think, of pride and boasting. He takes all the praise of this prophecy for himself and exalts himself as a member of the leading council of heaven. When he attempted to curse Israel, he acknowledges he made a mistake, but now he begins to see his error. Unfortunately, he is still blinded by his foolish and harmful covetousness and ambition. Many have their eyes open who do not have their hearts open. They are enlightened but not sanctified.

2. But the blessing is substantially the same as those before. He marvels at several things about Israel:

2.1. Their beauty (v. 5): *How goodly are thy tents, O Jacob!* Though they did not live in stately palaces, but in rough, simple, and no doubt weather-beaten tents, Balaam still sees a beauty in those tents, because of their extraordinary order, according to their tribes (v. 2). Nothing commends religious faith more to the good opinion of outsiders than the unity and harmony of those who profess to follow it (Ps 133:1).

2.2. Their fruitfulness and increase. This may be intended by the comparisons (v. 6) of the valleys, gardens, and trees, as well as by the expressions (v. 7), *He shall pour the water out of his buckets*, that is, God will water them with his blessing like rain from heaven, and then his *seed shall be in many waters*.

2.3. Their honor and advancement. As the multitude of a people is the honor of a ruler, so the magnificence of the ruler is the honor of the people. Balaam therefore prophesies that their *king shall be higher than Agag* (v. 7). Agag was probably the most powerful monarch in those parts.

2.4. Their power and victory (v. 8). He looks back on what they had done, or rather what had been done for them: *God brought them forth out of Egypt*; he had spoken about this before (23:22). He looks out at their present strength and also looks forward to their future conquests.

2.5. Their courage and security: *He lay down as a lion, as a great lion* (v. 9). Lions do not withdraw into places of shelter to sleep, but lie down anywhere, knowing that no other creature dare interfere with them.

2.6. Their interests in, and influence on, their neighbors. Their friends, and those in alliance with them, were happy.

Verses 10–14

We have here the conclusion of this futile attempt to curse Israel, and the complete abandonment of the plan.

1. Balak made the worst of it. He broke out in a rage against Balaam (v. 10). He told him to leave his presence, expelled him from his country, and rebuked him with the advancements he had intended to give him, but which he now refused to give (v. 11).

2. Balaam made the best of it:

2.1. He tries to excuse his disappointment. Balak could not say that Balaam had deceived him, since he had given him reasonable warnings of the restraint he found himself under.

2.2. He endeavors to make up for it (v. 14). He will satisfy Balak's curiosity with some predictions concerning the nations around him. He will satisfy him with an assurance that, whatever this formidable people would do to his people, it would not be till later. He will give him a way of causing trouble for Israel without needing to resort

to sorcery or cursing. Since he could not gain permission from God to curse them, he sets him thinking about getting help from the Devil to tempt them.

Verses 15–25

The role of prophets was both to bless and to prophesy in the name of the Lord.

1. He plays the part of a true prophet very well, God allowing and directing him to do so, because *whatever his character, the prophecy itself was true*. He *saw the vision of the Almighty* (v. 16), but it was not a vision by which he was *changed into the same image* (2Co 3:18). He calls God the *Most High*, and the *Almighty*, but he had no true fear of him, no love for him or faith in him. A person may go so far toward heaven, but still come short of it and not reach it.

2. Here is his prophecy concerning the person who would be the crown and glory of his people Israel. This person is:

2.1. David, the type under whom the forces of Israel would *do valiantly* (v. 18). This was fulfilled when David struck Moab. At the same time the Edomites were similarly brought into obedience to Israel (v. 14).

2.2. Our Lord Jesus, the promised Messiah, who is especially pointed to in the fulfillment. It is a significant prophecy of him. It was the will of God that not only the Jews, but also the peoples of other nations, should be told about his coming a great while before, because his Gospel and kingdom were to extend far beyond the borders of the land of Israel. It is here foretold:

2.2.1. That his coming would not be for a great while yet: "*I shall see him, but not now* (v. 17); I do see him in a vision, but far away at a great distance, through the intervening time of 1,500 years at least."

2.2.2. That he would come out of Jacob, and Israel, as a star and a scepter, the former representing his glory and luster, the *bright and morning star* (Rev 22:16), the latter representing his power and authority. It is *he that shall have dominion* (v. 19).

2.2.3. That his kingdom would be universal and victorious over all opposition. David's victories over Moab and Edom were types of such triumphs. Christ will be king, not only of Jacob and Israel, but also of all the world.

3. Here is his prophecy concerning the Amalekites and Kenites, part of whose country he probably then had in view:

3.1. The Amalekites were now *the first of the nations* (v. 20). Here Balaam confirms the condemnation of Amalek, which Moses had described (Ex 15:14, 16).

3.2. The Kenites were now the most secure of the nations; nature had given them a strongly fortified position: "*Thou puttest thy nest* (like the eagle) *in a rock* (v. 21). You think you are safe, but the *Kenites shall be wasted* (v. 22) and gradually destroyed, till they are carried away captive by the Assyrians," which was done at the Captivity of the ten tribes. Even a nest in a rock is not eternally secure.

4. Here is a prophecy that looks as far forward as the Greeks and Romans, for they may be intended by the *coast of Chittim* (v. 24).

4.1. The introduction to this prophecy is significant (v. 23): *Alas! who shall live when God doeth this?* Either:

4.1.1. These events are so far off in the future that it is hard to say *who shall live till they come*. Or:

4.1.2. They will be so awful and cause such desolation, that scarcely anyone will escape or be left alive.

4.2. The prophecy itself is significant. Much of Greece and Italy lies on the sea, and so their armies were sent out mostly in ships. Now he seems here to prophesy:

4.2.1. That the forces of the Greeks would humble and defeat the Assyrians, who were united with the Persians, which was fulfilled when the eastern country was overrun by Alexander the Great.

4.2.2. That theirs and the Roman forces would torment the Hebrews, or Jews, who were called *the children of Eber* (Ge 10:21). This was partly fulfilled when the Greek Empire oppressed the Jewish nation, but chiefly when the Roman Empire destroyed it. But:

4.2.3. That *Chittim*, that is, the Roman Empire, in which the Greeks were eventually swallowed up, would itself perish when *the stone cut out of the mountain without hands* (Da 2:45) will consume all these kingdoms, especially the *feet of iron and clay* (Da 2:34). According to Dr. Lightfoot, all this shows that Balaam, instead of cursing the church, curses Amalek the first, and then Rome the last enemy of the church.

CHAPTER 25

After Israel had escaped Balaam's curse, they experienced great suffering and disgrace, which may have been because of the advice Balaam gave Balak before he left him. It was more effective than trying to come between the Israelites and their God. Those who succumb to sinful desires are in deadly danger. Here is: 1. The sin of Israel; they were enticed by the women of Moab to commit both sexual immorality and idolatry (vv. 1–3); the punishment of this sin by the hand of the judges (vv. 4–5) and directly by God (v. 9). 2. The godly zeal of Phinehas in killing Zimri and Cozbi, two outrageous sinners (vv. 6–8, 14, 15), and God's commendation of the zeal of Phinehas (vv. 10–13). 3. Enmity put between the Israelites and the Midianites, their tempters, as originally between the woman and the Serpent (vv. 16–18).

Verses 1–5

Here is:

1. The sin of Israel, to which they were enticed by the women of Moab and Midian. They were guilty of both physical and spiritual adultery, for *Israel joined himself unto Baal-peor* (v. 3). Not all, or most, but very many, were trapped by this snare. Notice that sexual immorality and idolatry went together. They first defiled and depraved their consciences by committing sexual immorality with the women, and then were easily drawn on, out of a desire to please them further and in contempt of the God of Israel, to bow down to their idols. And they were more likely to do this if, as it is commonly supposed and seems probable by the fact that sexual immorality and idolatry are put together, the immorality they committed was part of the worship and service performed to the Baal of Peor. It was a very serious sin, for *Israel abode in Shittim* (v. 1), where the land of Canaan was in view, and they were just about ready to enter and take possession of it.

2. God's just displeasure against them for this sin. Israel's immorality did what all Balaam's sorcery could not do.

2.1. A plague immediately broke out. Epidemic diseases are the just punishments of epidemic sins; one infection follows the other.

2.2. The ringleaders are ordered to be put to death at the hand of public justice, which is the only way to stop the plague (v. 4). The judges must first order them to be

slain with the sword (v. 5), and their dead bodies must be hanged up, so that the ignorant Israelites might have a sense of the evil of the sin.

Verses 6–15

Here is a remarkable contest between evil and right. Righteousness wins, as it undoubtedly eventually will.

1. Never was vice more daring than that of Zimri, *a prince* (leader) *of a chief house* (v. 14) in the tribe of Simeon. He publicly appeared with a Midianite prostitute in full view of Moses and all the people of Israel. It insulted the justice of the nation and it insulted the religion of the nation.

2. Never was virtue more daring than that of Phinehas. Being aware of the shamelessness of Zimri, Phinehas rises up from his prayers in holy indignation at the offenders and takes his sword. He follows those defiant sinners into their tent, and stabs them both (vv. 7–8). It is not at all difficult to justify Phinehas in what he did, for because he was now heir to the high priesthood, he no doubt was one of the judges of Israel whom Moses had ordered by divine appointment to kill those whom they knew to have joined themselves to the Baal of Peor. God showed his acceptance of the godly zeal of Phinehas. He honored Phinehas. Phinehas did no more than it was his duty to do as a judge, but because he undertook it with extraordinary zeal against sin and he did it when the other judges—out of respect to Zimri's character as a leader—were afraid, God showed himself particularly pleased with him, and it *was counted to him for righteousness* (Ps 106:31). Although Phinehas is only a young man, he is now declared to be his country's patriot and best friend (v. 11). The priesthood is passed on by covenant to his family. It had been intended before that it would be his, but now it was confirmed as his.

Verses 16–18

God had punished the Israelites for their sin with a plague, as a father disciplined his own children with a rod. The trouble which the Midianites caused Israel by enticing them to commit immorality must be remembered and punished with as much severity as what the Amalekites did in fighting with them when they came out of Egypt (Ex 17:14).

CHAPTER 26

This book is called Numbers, from the numberings of the children of Israel which it describes. In the first year after they left Egypt they were numbered at Mount Sinai, which was recorded in 1:1–2:34. And now they were numbered a second time on the plains of Moab, just before they entered Canaan, and we have a record of this in this chapter. We have: 1. Orders given for the census to be taken (vv. 1–4). 2. A register of the families and numbers of each tribe (vv. 5–50), with the sum total (v. 51). 3. Directions given to divide the land among them (vv. 52–56). 4. The families and numbers of the Levites by themselves (vv. 57–62). 5. Notice taken of the fulfilling of the threat in the death of all those who were originally numbered (vv. 63–65). Special regard may have been taken to this in making and keeping this record.

Verses 1–4

Notice here that Moses numbered the people only when God commanded him. David in his time did it without a command, and paid dearly for it. God now appointed him to take a census of them. Eleazar was commissioned with him, as Aaron had been before. This showed the honor God gave to Eleazar in front of the elders of his people and confirmed his succession. They were now to count according to the same rules that they had used in the earlier census, counting only those who were able to go out to war, for this was the duty that was now ahead of them.

Verses 5–51

This is the register of the tribes as they were now enrolled, in the same order in which they were numbered in 1:1–54. Notice:

1. The record noted here of the families of each tribe, which must not be understood in the same way as we understand families, those that live in the same house together. Rather, families or clans were the descendants of the different sons of the patriarchs. The families of the twelve tribes are numbered in this way: of Dan only one clan, for Dan had only one son, but that tribe was the most numerous of all except Judah (vv. 42–43). Zebulun was divided into three clans, Ephraim into four, Issachar into four, Naphtali into four, and Reuben into four; Judah, Simeon, and Asher had five clans each, Gad and Benjamin seven each, and Manasseh eight. Benjamin brought ten sons into Egypt (Ge 46:21), but three of them, it seems, either died childless or had families that died out, for here we find only seven of their names preserved.

2. The numbers of each tribe. In this record we may notice:

2.1. That all the three tribes camped under the standard of Judah, who was the ancestor of Christ, had increased.

2.2. That none of the tribes had increased so much as that of Manasseh, which in the former account was the smallest of all the tribes, only 32,200, while here it is among the largest.

2.3. That none of the tribes decreased as much as Simeon did, from 59,300 down to 22,000, little more than a third of what it was. Some think that most of those 24,000 who were destroyed by the plague for the sin of Baal of Peor came from that tribe, for Zimri—who was a ringleader in that sin—was a leader of that tribe.

3. In the record of the tribe of Reuben, there is mentioned the rebellion of the Reubenites Dathan and Abiram, in alliance with Korah, a Levite (vv. 9–11).

Verses 52–56

If anyone should ask why such a detailed record needed to be kept of the tribes, clans, and numbers of the people of Israel, an answer is given here. As their numbers grew, so they were allotted land, not according to common Providence, but according to promise. To support the honor of divine revelation, God wants the fulfillment of the promise noted both in their increase in numbers and in their inheritance of land.

Verses 57–62

Because Levi was God's tribe, it was a tribe that was to have no inheritance with the others in the land of Canaan, and so was not numbered with the rest, but by itself. It had been numbered in this way at the beginning of this book at Mount Sinai, and so it did not come under the sentence passed on all those who were numbered then, that none of them would enter Canaan except Caleb and Joshua. Of the Levites, who were not numbered with the rest of Israel and who were not to go out to war, Eleazar and Ithamar, and perhaps others who were then more than twenty years old, as appears in 4:16, 28, entered Canaan, but this tribe

now at its second census had increased by only 1,000, and was still one of the smallest tribes.

Verses 63–65

What is significant in the conclusion of this record is the execution of the sentence passed on those who grumbled (14:29), that not one of those who *were numbered from twenty years old and upwards* would enter Canaan, except Caleb and Joshua. In the census now held it appeared that no one was counted now who had been counted then, except Caleb and Joshua (vv. 64–65). In this we see:

1. The righteousness of God and his faithfulness to his threats, when once the *decree has gone forth* (Zep 2:2).

2. The goodness of God to this people, despite their offenses. And though the number was a little below what it was at Mount Sinai, those numbered now had the advantage that they were all middle-aged men, between twenty and sixty, in the prime of their lives, and during the thirty-eight years of Israel's wandering and dying in the desert they had the opportunity of coming to know the laws and ordinances of God.

CHAPTER 27

Here: 1. The case of Zelophehad's daughters is decided (vv. 1–11). 2. Notice is given to Moses of his approaching death (vv. 12–14). 3. Provision is made for a successor in the leadership: by the prayer of Moses (vv. 15–17) and by the appointment of God (vv. 18–23).

Verses 1–11

Mention had been made of the case of the daughters of Zelophehad in the previous chapter (26:33). It was a special case and did not generally occur in Israel at that time, that the head of a family had no sons, but only daughters. Another aspect of their case is discussed again (36:1–13), and according to the judgments given in their case, we find them given an inheritance as their possession (Jos 17:3–4). It could be thought that their personal character added weight to their case.

Here is:

1. Their case stated by themselves, and their request presented to the highest judicial court. We do not find that they had an advocate to speak up for them, but they managed their own cause cleverly enough, which they could do well because it was clear and honest and spoke for itself.

1.1. What they ask for: that they might have property in the land of Canaan, *among the brethren of their father* (v. 4). God had said to Moses (26:53) that the land of Canaan was to be divided among those who were then counted. But these daughters knew they were not counted, and so according to this rule could not expect any inheritance. If they had had a brother, they would not have turned to Moses to obtain the inheritance, but because they had no brother, they had to ask for property. There is a debt which children owe to the memory of their parents, which is required by the fifth commandment: *Honour thy father and mother* (Ex 20:12).

1.2. On what basis they ask. Their father had not died because he had committed a crime, which would have meant that his estate could not be passed on as an inheritance, but he had died in his own sin (v. 3): he was subject only to the sins shared in common by the whole human race. He was responsible to his own God to be declared innocent or guilty, but was not responsible to any legal process with Moses or the leaders.

2. Their case decided by God. What they ask for is granted (v. 7). The matter is settled for all future occasions. These daughters of Zelophehad considered not only their own family's means and name, but also more widely the honor and happiness of all their sex. On this particular occasion a general law was made that in cases where a man had no son, his estate would go to his daughters (v. 8), not to the eldest, as the eldest son, but to them all in copartnership in equal shares. "If a man has no children at all, his estate will go to his brothers; if there are no brothers, then it shall pass to his father's brothers, and if there are none of those, then to his nearest relative."

Verses 12–14

Here:

1. God tells Moses of his error, when he spoke out of order at the waters of quarreling, where he did not have proper regard for the honor of God and of Israel (v. 14).

2. God tells Moses of his death. He is told about it in such a way that it would lighten and take the edge off the sentence and help him to come to terms with it.

2.1. Moses has to die, but he will first have the satisfaction of seeing the Land of Promise (v. 12).

2.2. Moses must die, but death does not *cut him off*. Death only gathers him to his people and brings him to join the holy patriarchs who had gone before him and to the rest they were enjoying.

2.3. Moses must die, as Aaron had died before him (v. 13). Moses had seen how readily and happily Aaron had first put off the priesthood and then his body. And so Moses is not to be afraid of dying; he was simply to be *gathered to his people* (v. 13), just as Aaron had been gathered.

Verses 15–23

Here:

1. Moses prays for a successor. Those who are always jealously looking over their shoulders at others do not love their successors, but Moses was not like that. We should be concerned, both in our prayers and in our actions, for the rising generation, that religious faith may prosper. Moses expresses in his prayer:

1.1. A tender concern for the people of Israel: *That the congregation of the Lord be not as sheep which have no shepherd* (v. 17).

1.2. A believing dependence on God, as the *God of the spirits of all flesh* (v. 16). Moses prays to God, not to send an angel but to *set a man over the congregation*, that is, to name and appoint one whom he would qualify and acknowledge as ruler of his people Israel.

2. God, in answer to his prayer, appoints a successor for him, Joshua, who had long since shown his remarkable courage in fighting Amalek, his great humility in serving Moses, and his outstanding faith and integrity in witnessing against the report of the faithless spies.

2.1. God directs Moses how Joshua was to succeed him:

2.1.1. Moses must ordain him: *Lay thy hand upon him* (v. 18). This was done as a sign of Moses' transference of the leadership to him, as the laying on of hands on the sacrifice put the offering in the place of the offerer. It also is a sign of the gift of God's blessing of the Spirit on him, which Moses gained through prayer. It is said, *Joshua was full of the spirit of wisdom, for Moses had laid his hands on him* (Dt 34:9). This ceremony of the laying on of hands is used in the New Testament to set apart Gospel ministers, showing they are formally appointed to that office with the desire that God would qualify them for it and

acknowledge them in it. It is the offering of them to Christ and his church as living sacrifices.

2.1.2. Moses must present him to Eleazar and the people, set him before them, that they might know that he has been appointed by God to be entrusted with that great work.

2.1.3. Moses must *give him a charge*, he must commission him (v. 19).

2.1.4. Moses must *put some of his honour upon him* (v. 20).

2.1.5. Moses must appoint Eleazar the high priest, with his breastpiece, to be his privy council (v. 21). This was a direction to Joshua. Though he was full of the Spirit and had all this honor put on him, he must still do nothing without asking for God's direction, *not leaning to his own understanding* (Pr 3:5). In this way, the leadership of Israel was now purely divine, in both the appointing and the directing of leaders.

2.2. Moses acts according to these directions (vv. 22–23). He happily ordained Joshua:

2.2.1. Though it diminished his own position and was tantamount to stepping down from the leadership.

2.2.2. Though it might have appeared as an insult to his family, first to ordain Eleazar as high priest, and then Joshua who came from a different tribe as leader, while his own children were not advanced in any way but were left at the rank of ordinary Levites. This was a great example of self-denial and submission to the will of God. It was more to God's glory than the highest advancement of his family could have been.

CHAPTER 28

Now that the people had been counted, orders had been given for the allotting of the land, and a general of the forces had been named and commissioned, you would have expected that the next chapter would begin the history of the military campaign. This chapter records the services of worship, and shows that now that they were on the point of entering Canaan, they should make sure they take their religious faith with them and not forget it while they pursue their wars (vv. 1–2). The laws are repeated here and summed up concerning the sacrifices that were to be offered: 1. Daily (vv. 3–8). 2. Weekly (vv. 9–10) and monthly (vv. 11–15). 3. Yearly at the Passover (vv. 16–25) and at Pentecost (vv. 26–31). And the next chapter concerns the annual ceremonies of the seventh month.

Verses 1–8

Here is:

1. A general order given concerning the offerings of the Lord, which were to be brought at the right time (v. 2). God thought it right to repeat the law of sacrifices now:

1.1. Because this was a new generation of people, most of whom had not been born when the former laws were given.

1.2. Because they were now about to start waging war and might be tempted to think that while they were involved with that, they could be excused from offering sacrifices. The law tends to be neglected in times of war. They were particularly concerned to keep their peace with God when they were at war with their enemies.

1.3. Because they were now to be given possession of the Land of Promise, that land flowing with milk and honey, where they would have plenty of good things. God says, "Now, when you are feasting yourselves, do not forget to offer sacrifices as the food of your God."

2. The particular law of the daily sacrifice, a lamb in the morning and a lamb in the evening, which because of its constant regularity every day is called *a continual burnt offering* (v. 3). This teaches us that when we are instructed to *pray always, and to pray without ceasing* (1Th 5:17), we are to offer our reverent prayers and praises to God at least every morning and every evening.

Verses 9–15

The New Moon festivals and the Sabbaths are often spoken of together as great ceremonies in the Jewish church. Here we have the sacrifices appointed:

1. On the Sabbaths. Every Sabbath day the offering must be doubled.

2. At the New Moon festivals. Some suggest that as the Sabbath was observed in consideration of the creation of the world, so the New Moon festivals were made holy in consideration of divine providence that *appoints the moon for seasons* (Ps 104:19) and guides the months by its changes.

Verses 16–31

Here is the appointment of the Passover sacrifices; not the main one, the paschal lamb—sufficient instructions had already been given about that—but those that were to be offered on the seven days of unleavened bread which followed it (vv. 17–25). The first and last of those seven days were to be kept holy as Sabbaths by holy rest and a holy assembly. On each of the seven days they were to be generous in their sacrifices as a sign of their great and constant thankfulness for their rescue from Egypt. The sacrifices are also appointed which were to be offered at the Feast of Pentecost, here called the *day of the firstfruits* (v. 26). At the Feast of Unleavened Bread they offered *a sheaf of their firstfruits* of barley—which was their first ripe cereal—to the priest (Lev 23:10). This was an introduction to the harvest, but now, about seven weeks later, they were to bring *a new meat offering* (grain offering) *to the Lord* (v. 26) at the end of the harvest. It was at this feast that the Spirit was poured out (Ac 2:1–13), and thousands were converted by the preaching of the apostles and were presented to Christ, to be *a kind of firstfruits of his creatures* (Jas 1:18).

CHAPTER 29

In this chapter the offerings to be made by fire to the Lord at the three great ceremonies of the seventh month are appointed: 1. At the Feast of Trumpets on the first day of that month (vv. 1–6) and on the Day of Atonement on the tenth day (vv. 7–11). 2. At the Feast of Tabernacles on the fifteenth day and the seven days following (vv. 12–38), and then the conclusion of these ordinances (vv. 39–40).

Verses 1–11

There were more holy ceremonies in the seventh month than in any other month of the year, not only because until Israel had been rescued from Egypt it had been the first month, but also because it still continued to be the first month for their civil calculations of the Jubilees and years of release. It was also because it was the time of holiday between harvest and seedtime, when they had most spare time to attend the sanctuary. We have here the appointment of the sacrifices to be offered:

1. On the first day of the month, the day of *blowing the trumpets* (v. 1), which was a preparation for the two great ceremonies: that of holy mourning on the Day of Atonement and that of holy joy at the Feast of Tabernacles.

2. On the *day of atonement*. Besides all the services of that day, which we had the institution of in Lev 16:1–34, burnt offerings are also ordered to be brought (vv. 8–10).

Verses 12–40

Soon after the Day of Atonement, that day on which the people were to humble their souls, came the Feast of Tabernacles, at which they were to express their joy before the Lord, for those who *sow in tears* will soon *reap in joy* (Ps 126:5). Directions are added to the former laws about this feast, which we had in Lev 23:34–44, about the *offerings made by fire* which they were to bring to the Lord during the *seven days of that feast* (Lev 23:36). Notice here:

1. Their days of joy were to be days of sacrifice.

2. They must offer sacrifices every day that they stayed in booths.

3. The sacrifices for each of the seven days, though only differing by the number of the young bulls, are described in detail for the different days.

4. The number of the young bulls—which were the most expensive part of the sacrifice—decreased every day. The multitude of their sacrifices would end in one great sacrifice, infinitely more worthy than all of them. It was on the last day of the feast, after all the sacrifices had been offered, that our Lord Jesus stood and cried out to those who still thirsted for righteousness *to come unto him and drink* (Jn 7:37). Such people were aware that these sacrifices could not put them right with God.

5. The meat offerings (grain offerings) and drink offerings accompanied all the sacrifices.

6. Every day a sin offering must be presented, as we noticed in the other feasts.

7. Even when all these sacrifices were offered, the regular burnt offering must not be left out either morning or evening. Every day, this had to be offered first thing in the morning and last thing in the evening. This shows us that special services should not squeeze out our regular devotions.

8. All these sacrifices were required to be presented by the body of the assembly, at the public expense. As well as these, however, individual people might glorify God also with their vows and their freewill offerings (v. 39).

CHAPTER 30

In this chapter we have a law concerning vows, which had been mentioned at the end of the previous chapter. 1. Here is a general rule laid down that all vows must be carefully fulfilled (vv. 1–2). 2. Some special exceptions to this rule are given: the vows of daughters should not be binding unless allowed by the father (vv. 3–5), and the vows of wives should not be binding unless allowed by the husband (vv. 6–16).

Verses 1–2

This law was delivered to the heads of the tribes so that they might instruct those who were their responsibility.

1. The case discussed is that a person makes a vow to the Lord, making God one party to the promise. The subject of the vow is something lawful: no one can be committed to a promise to do something that they are already forbidden by God to do. The person who vows is here said to *bind his soul with a bond* (v. 2). It is a vow to God, who is Spirit, and the soul with all its powers must be committed to him. A promise to a person is a

commitment of physical things, but a promise to God is a commitment of the soul.

2. The command given is that these vows should be conscientiously fulfilled.

Verses 3 – 16

It is assumed here that the people making the vows are fully responsible, have sound understanding and memory, and are normally committed to fulfill whatever they vow which is lawful and possible. But if the person making the vow is under the authority and direction of another, the case is different. Two similar cases are discussed and decided here:

1. In the case of a daughter in her father's house, the general rule is: if a man makes a vow, he must fulfill it. But for a daughter it is explicitly said: her vow is not valid until her father knows it, and — we may suppose — knows about it from her, for when it comes to his knowledge, it is in his power either to confirm it or nullify it. In favor of the vow:

1.1. Even his silence is enough to confirm it: if he *hold his peace* and says nothing, her *vows shall stand* (v. 4). As the phrase is, "Silence gives consent." But:

1.2. If he protests against the vow, it will be made completely void, because it is possible that such a vow might prejudice the affairs of his family. She showed her goodwill in making the vow, and if her intentions in making it were sincere, she will be accepted, and to obey her father will be counted better than sacrifice.

2. The case of a wife is similar. As for a woman who is widowed or divorced, she is not under the authority of her father or husband, so whatever vow she commits her soul to will be binding and *stand against her* (v. 9). If she turns her back on it, she is in danger.

CHAPTER 31

This chapter belongs to the Book of the Wars of the Lord, in which it may possibly have been included. It is the history of a holy war, a war with Midian. Here is: 1. A divine command for the war (vv. 1 – 2) and the undertaking of the war (vv. 3 – 6). 2. Its glorious success (vv. 7 – 12). 3. The soldiers' triumphant return from the war: the respect Moses paid to them (v. 13); the rebuke he gave them for sparing the women (vv. 14 – 18); and the directions he gave them to purify themselves and their goods (vv. 19 – 24). 4. The division of the spoils they had taken: one half to the soldiers, the other to the community, and a tribute to the Lord from each (vv. 25 – 47). 5. The freewill offering of the officers (vv. 48 – 54).

Verses 1 – 6

Here:

1. The Lord gives orders to Moses to make war on the Midianites. The Midianites were descended from Abraham by Keturah (Ge 25:2). Some of them settled south of Canaan, among whom Jethro lived, and they maintained the worship of their true God; but these settled east of Canaan and fell into idolatry, since they were neighbors to and in league with the Moabites. They made themselves offensive to the Israelites by sending their immoral women among them to draw them into idolatry and adultery. This was the cause of the offense, their quarrel. For this reason, God says, *avenge Israel of the Midianites* (v. 2).

1.1. God wanted to discipline the Midianites. Israel's quarrel with Amalek, who fought against them, was not avenged till long afterward, but their quarrel with Midian,

who seduced them, was quickly avenged, for they were looked on as the more dangerous enemy.

1.2. God wanted it done through Moses in his lifetime, so that he who had become so deeply angered by that wrong would have the satisfaction of seeing it avenged.

2. Moses gives orders to the people to prepare for this expedition (v. 3).

3. A body of troops is sent out to undertake this service, 1,000 *out of every tribe*, 12,000 in all, a small number in comparison with what they could have sent. But God wanted to teach them that it does not matter to him *to save by many or by few* (1Sa 14:6).

4. Phinehas, the son of Eleazar, is sent along with them. This was a holy war, and Phinehas was their common leader. He therefore took with him the holy articles or vessels, probably the breastplate of judgment (breastpiece), by means of which God might be consulted in any emergency.

Verses 7 – 12

Here is:

1. The descent which this little army of Israelites made on the country of Midian. They probably made a public declaration against them first, showing the reasons for the war, and requiring them to give up the ringleaders of the trouble to justice. Afterward this was the *law* (Dt 20:10) and the *practice* (Jdg 20:12 – 13).

2. The military execution of their attack:

2.1. They *slew all the males* (v. 7), that is, all they met with; they killed them all and showed no mercy.

2.2. They *slew the kings of Midian* (v. 8), the same who are called *elders of Midian* (22:4) and the *dukes of Sihon* (Jos 13:21). Five of these princes are named here, one of whom is *Zur*, probably the same Zur whose daughter was Cozbi (25:15).

2.3. They killed Balaam. Whatever the reason for his being there, God's sovereign providence brought him there, and God's righteous vengeance found him there.

2.4. They took all the *women and children captives* (v. 9).

2.5. They *burnt their cities and goodly castles* (v. 10).

2.6. They plundered the country and took away all the cattle and valuable goods, and so returned to the camp of Israel loaded with a very rich booty (vv. 9, 11 – 12).

Verses 13 – 24

Here we have the triumphant return of the army of Israel from the war with Midian:

1. They were met with great respect (v. 13).

2. They were severely rebuked for keeping the women alive. Because the order of execution referred to their crime of drawing them in to the worship of Peor, it was easy to conclude that the women, who were the principal criminals, must not be spared. "It is dangerous to let them live; they will still continue to tempt the Israelites to be sexually immoral, and so those whom you have taken captive will be your conquerors and will destroy you a second time."

3. They were obliged to purify themselves according to the ceremony of the Law, and to remain outside the camp for seven days until their purification was completed, for God wanted to keep in their minds the fact that murder is something dreadful and detestable.

4. They must likewise purify the spoil they had taken, the captives (v. 19) and all the goods (vv. 21 – 23). What would withstand fire must pass through the fire, and what would not must be washed with water.

Verses 25–47

We have here the division of the spoils which were taken in this expedition against Midian:

1. The spoils are to be divided into two parts, one for the 12,000 men who waged the war and the other for the rest of the community. The spoils which were divided seem to have been only the captives and the cattle; as for the gold, jewels, and other goods, every man kept what he took, as is suggested by vv. 50–53. Only what would be useful to stock the good land into which they were going was divided.

2. God was to have a tribute from it, as an acknowledgment of his sovereignty over them in general, that he was their king to whom *tribute was due*.

Verses 48–54

Here is a great example of godly devotion by the officers of the army. They came to Moses as their general and commander in chief, and humbly and respectfully turned to him, calling themselves his *servants*. They devoutly take note of God's wonderful goodness to them in this recent expedition, in preserving not only their own lives, but also the lives of all the soldiers under them; so that when they counted how many there were, not one was missing (v. 49). They looked on it as a mercy to themselves that not one of those under their command had died. Instead of coming to Moses to demand a reward for the good service they had done in *avenging the Lord of Midian*, or to set up a war memorial to commemorate their victory and to preserve the memory of their own names forever, they bring an offering to *make atonement for their souls*.

CHAPTER 32

In this chapter we have: 1. The humble request of the tribes of Reuben and Gad for an inheritance on that side of the Jordan where the people of Israel were now camped (vv. 1–5). 2. Moses' misinterpretation of their request (vv. 6–15). 3. Their explanation of it, stating it rightly (vv. 16–19). 3. The granting of their request with the conditions and limitations that they themselves proposed (vv. 20–42).

Verses 1–15

Israel's tents were now pitched on the plains of Moab. While they paused, the disposal of the conquests they had already made was settled here, not by any special order or appointment by God, but at the special request of two of the tribes, to which Moses agreed. Here is:

1. A proposal made by the Reubenites and Gadites, that the land which they had just gained possession of and which by right of conquest belonged to Israel generally, might be particularly assigned to them as their inheritance. Two things which are common in this life made these tribes suggest this proposal, the *lust of the eye* and the *pride of life* (1Jn 2:16):

1.1. The *lust of the eye*. The land which they wanted was not only beautiful in its situation and attractive to look at, but it was also suitable for food for their cattle. They had a great many cattle, more than the rest of the tribes. Now because they had these large stocks of cattle, they wanted a proportionate amount of land for them.

1.2. Perhaps there was also something of the *pride of life* in it. Reuben was the firstborn of Israel, but he had lost his birthright. He tries here to take hold of the first allotment, even though it was not in Canaan and was far

away from the tabernacle. The tribe of Gad descended from the firstborn of Zilpah, and their claim was similar to that of the Reubenites. Manasseh, too, was a firstborn, but knew he was to be eclipsed by Ephraim his younger brother, and so he also wanted to have priority.

2. Moses' dislike of this proposal, and the severe rebuke he gives them for it, as a faithful ruler and prophet.

2.1. It must be confessed that at first sight, the matter seemed wrong, especially from the closing words of their request: *Bring us not over Jordan* (v. 5). It seemed to arise from a wrong motive, a contempt of the Land of Promise. There also seemed to be more than an element of greed in it, for what they kept going on about was that it was suitable for their cattle. It seemed to show a neglect of their brothers and sisters, as if they did not care what happened to Israel, as long as they themselves were all right and were well looked after.

2.2. Moses is therefore very impatient with them:

2.2.1. He shows them what he understood to be wrong in their suggestion, that it would discourage the hearts of their compatriots (vv. 6–7).

2.2.2. He reminds them of the fatal results of the unbelief and faintheartedness of their fathers, when they were about to enter Canaan, just as they themselves now were. He goes over the story in detail (vv. 8–13).

2.2.3. He gives them a reasonable warning of the trouble that would likely result from this separation which they were about to make from the camp of Israel. They would be in danger of bringing wrath on all the people, and would lead them all back again into the desert (vv. 14–15).

Verses 16–27

We have here the compromise between Moses and the two tribes about their settlement on this side of the Jordan. After some deliberation, they return with this suggestion, that their men of war would go and help their brothers in conquering Canaan, and they would leave their families and flocks behind them in this land. If this request was granted, no harm would be done.

1. Their proposal is very reasonable and generous and, far from discouraging their brothers, would actually encourage them. They propose:

1.1. That their *men of war*, who were fit for service, would go *ready armed before the children of Israel* (v. 17) into the land of Canaan.

1.2. That they would leave behind them their families and cattle—which would otherwise be something of an impediment—so they would be more useful to their brothers (v. 16).

1.3. That they would not return to their homes till the conquest of Canaan was completed (v. 18).

1.4. That they would not expect any share of the land still to be conquered (v. 19).

2. Moses then grants their request, as long as they followed their proposals:

2.1. He insists very much that they should never lay down their arms till their brothers laid down theirs. They promised to go armed *before the children of Israel* (v. 17). "No," Moses says, "you will go armed *before the Lord* (vv. 20–21). It is God's cause more than your brothers'."

2.2. He grants them this land as their possession on this condition. But:

2.3. He warns them of the danger of breaking their word: "If you fail, you *sin against the Lord* (v. 23), and not only against your brothers, and *be sure your sin will find you out*." Note that sin will without doubt find out the sinner sooner or later. We should therefore make sure that we find out our own sins, that we may repent of them and abandon them, so that they do not find us out and we do not end up shamed and destroyed.

3. They unanimously agree to the conditions of what Moses granted, and enter, as it were, into a formal contract to carry out what has been ordered: *Thy servants will do as my lord commandeth* (v. 25).

Verses 28–42

1. Moses settles this matter with Eleazar and with Joshua, who was to be his successor, knowing that he himself would not live to see it fulfilled (vv. 28–30). He gives land to Reuben and Gad conditionally, leaving it to Joshua, if they fulfilled the condition, to declare the land absolutely theirs. They again repeat their promise to stand by their brothers (vv. 31–32).

2. Moses settles them in the land they desired. Here is the first mention of the half tribe of Manasseh joining them in a share. Notice, concerning the settlement of these tribes, that they built the cities, or rather, rebuilt them, and that they changed the names of cities (v. 38). Nebo and Baal were names of the cities' gods which the Israelites were forbidden to call upon (Ex 23:13). By changing the names of these cities, they tried to forget them forever.

CHAPTER 33

In this chapter we have: 1. A detailed record of the moves and camp sites of the children of Israel, from their escape from Egypt to their entry into Canaan, forty-two in all, with some significant events that happened at some of those places (vv. 1–49). 2. A strict command given to them to drive out all the inhabitants of the land of Canaan, which they were now going to conquer and take possession of (vv. 50–56). The former part of the chapter looks back on their journey through the desert; the latter looks forward to their settlement in Canaan.

Verses 1–49

This is a review and brief repetition of the travels of the children of Israel through the desert. Notice:

1. How the account was kept: *Moses wrote their goings out* (v. 2). It may be useful to individual Christians, especially those in more public positions, to preserve in writing an account of the providences of God concerning them and the constant mercies they experience. Details of those twists and turns in life that make some days remarkable would be especially useful. Our memories are deceitful and need this help, that we may *remember all the way which the Lord our God has led us in this wilderness* (Dt 8:2).

2. What the account itself was. It began with their departure out of Egypt, continued with their journey through the desert, and ended up on the plains of Moab, where they were now camped.

2.1. Some things are noted here concerning their escape from Egypt, which they are always to remember as miraculous. They went out with their armies (v. 1), people in rank and file, like an army with banners. They did not slip away secretly (Isa 52:12) but boldly and in defiance of their enemies, to whom God had made them such a burden they could not or dare not oppose them.

2.2. Concerning their travels toward Canaan, notice:

2.2.1. They were continually on the move. Such is our state in this world: we have no continuing city here.

2.2.2. Most of their way lay through a desert, uninhabited and desolate, without tracks, and without the necessities of human life. Their journey exalts the wisdom and power of God, whose miraculous guidance and goodness kept thousands of them alive for forty years. In fact, they came out at least as numerous and as strong as they went in. At first they pitched *in the edge of the wilderness* (v. 6), but afterward in the middle of it. God gives his people little difficulties to prepare them for greater ones.

2.2.3. They were led backward and forward as if they were in a maze, but all the time they were under the direction of the pillar of cloud and fire. The way which God takes to bring his people to himself is always the best way, although it does not always seem to us to be the most direct.

Verses 50–56

While the children of Israel were in the desert, their complete separation from all other people kept them from being tempted to idolatry. But now that they were to cross over the Jordan, they were again entering into that temptation and so:

- They are here strictly commanded to completely destroy all the remnants of idolatry.
- They were assured that if they did so, God would gradually give them full possession of the Land of Promise (vv. 53–54).
- They were threatened that if they spared either the idols or the idolaters, their own sin would certainly bring punishment on them. If we do not drive sin out of our lives, sin will drive us out. If we do not put to death our sinful desires, those sinful desires will lead to the death of our souls.

CHAPTER 34

In this chapter God directs Moses, and he is to direct Israel: 1. Concerning the boundaries of the land of Canaan (vv. 1–15). 2. Concerning its division and distribution to the tribes of Israel (vv. 16–29).

Verses 1–15

Here is a detailed draft of the lines by which the land of Canaan was to be measured and bordered on all sides. A much larger possession was promised them, which in due time they would have possessed if they had been obedient, reaching as far as the River Euphrates (Dt 11:24). And the dominion of Israel did extend that far in David's and Solomon's times (2Ch 9:26). But what is described here is only Canaan, which was the allotment of the nine and a half tribes, for the other two and a half were already settled (vv. 14–15). Notice concerning the limits of Canaan:

1. That it was limited within certain boundaries:

1.1. That they might know whom they were to drive out and the extent of their commission (33:53) to *drive out the inhabitants* (33:55).

1.2. That they might know what land they could expect to possess themselves.

2. That it lay within a comparatively small area: as the boundaries are given here, it is reckoned to be only about 160 miles (about 250 kilometers) in length and about fifty miles (about eighty kilometers) wide, but this is the country which was promised to the father of the faithful and was the possession of the descendants of Israel. This was that little plot of ground in which for many years only *God was known, and his name was great* (Ps 76:1). Notice

how small a part of the world God has for himself and how small a share of the world God often gives to his own people.

3. It is significant what its boundaries were:

3.1. Canaan was itself *a pleasant land* (Da 8:9), but it bordered on deserts and seas, and was surrounded by many depressing views.

3.2. Many of its borders were its defenses and natural fortifications.

3.3. The border reached to the *river of Egypt* (v. 5), that the sight of that country which they could look into from their own country might remind them of their times of slavery there and their miraculous rescue from it.

3.4. Their border is here made to begin at the *Salt Sea* (v. 3) and end there (v. 12). That pleasant, fruitful valley in which Sodom and Gomorrah stood before their destruction became a dreary, sterile, and desolate region with a lake which then carried no boats, and still has no fish or living creature of any sort found in it and so is called the *Dead Sea.*

3.5. Their western border was the *Great Sea* (v. 6), which is now called the Mediterranean.

Verses 16–29

God here appoints commissioners to divide the land for them. The conquest of it is taken for granted, though as yet they have not even begun it. The principal commissioners of the leaders were Eleazar and Joshua (v. 17). Besides these, so that there could be no accusations of bias, a leader from each tribe was appointed to supervise the matter, and to see that the tribe they represented was not wronged in any way.

CHAPTER 35

Orders having been given before for the dividing of the land of Canaan among the "lay tribes," as we may call them, care is taken here that the clergy, the tribe of Levi, which ministered in holy things, would be suitably provided for. 1. Forty-eight towns were to be assigned to them, with their pasturelands, some in every tribe (vv. 1–8). 2. Six cities out of these were to be cities of refuge, for anyone who killed another person unintentionally (vv. 9–15). Notice in the law when asylum was not allowed: in cases of willful murder (vv. 16–21); and in what cases it was allowed (vv. 22–24); and what the law was for those who took shelter in the cities of refuge (vv. 25–34).

Verses 1–8

The laws about the tithes and offerings had provided abundantly for the maintenance of the Levites, but it was not to be thought—nor indeed was it for the public good—that when they came to Canaan they should all live around the tabernacle as they had done in the desert. Care must therefore be taken to provide places where they could live comfortably and usefully. This is noted here:

1. Towns were allotted them, with their *suburbs* (pasturelands) (v. 2). They were not to have any land for cultivating.

1.1. Towns were allotted to them, that they might live close together and discuss the Law with one another, including matters about which they were unsure.

1.2. These towns had pasturelands attached to them for their cattle (v. 3); 1,000 cubits, about 1,500 feet (about 450 meters) from the wall, was allowed for them to keep their cattle in, and then 2,000 cubits, about 3,000 feet (about 900 meters), for fields to graze their cattle in (vv. 4–5).

2. These towns were to be assigned them from the possessions of each tribe (v. 8):

• That each tribe might gratefully acknowledge God.
• That each tribe might receive the benefit of the Levites living among them, to *teach them the good knowledge of the Lord* (2Ch 30:22).

3. The number allotted them was forty-eight in all from the twelve tribes.

Verses 9–34

We have here the orders given concerning the cities of refuge. Here we can discern a great deal both of good Law and of pure Gospel:

1. Here is a great deal of good Law, in the case of murder and manslaughter.

1.1. That willful murder should be punished by death, and in that case no asylum should be allowed, no ransom accepted, nor any reduction of the punishment permitted. Where wrong has been done, restitution must be made, and since the murderer cannot restore the life wrongfully taken away, the murderer's own life must be taken instead, not as some have thought, to satisfy the spirit of the person who has been killed, but to satisfy the law and the justice of a nation and to be a warning to all others not to do the same. Not only the prosecution, but also the execution, of the murderer is committed to the murdered person's next of kin, who, as they were to be the redeemer of the estate of their relative if it was mortgaged, should also be the *avenger of his blood if he were murdered* (v. 19). *The revenger* (avenger) *of blood himself shall slay the murderer* (vv. 19, 21).

1.2. But if the homicide was done accidentally, unintentionally, or without hostility (v. 22), not seeing the person or not seeking their harm (v. 23)—which our law calls manslaughter or homicide—in this case cities of refuge were appointed for the offender to flee to. By our law they lose their possessions, but in exceptional circumstances a pardon may be granted. Concerning the cities of refuge the law was:

1.2.1. That if the offender killed a person, that offender was safe in these cities and under the protection of the law, until their trial before the assembly, that is, before the judges in open court.

1.2.2. If on trial the murder was found to be willful, the city of refuge would no longer be an option; the case was already decided: *Thou shalt take him from my altar, that he may die* (Ex 21:14).

1.2.3. But if the manslaughter was found to be unintentional or accidental and the striking was made without any intentions on the life of the person killed or any other person, then the offender could continue to be safe in the city of refuge, and the avenger of blood could not interfere with them (v. 25). There the offender was to remain in exile from their own house, property, and inheritance till the death of the high priest. Now:

1.2.3.1. By the preserving of the life of the offender God wants to teach us that people ought not to suffer for an unfortunate accident.

1.2.3.2. By the banishment of the offender from their own town and their confinement to the city of refuge, God wants to teach us to have a dread and horror of the guilt of bloodshed, and to take great care of the sanctity of life.

1.2.3.3. By limiting the time of the offender's banishment to the death of the high priest, God put an honor on that sacred office. The cities of refuge were all Levite cities, and because the high priest was the head of that tribe, those who were confined to them could be considered to be his prisoners, and so his death meant that they could be released.

2. Here is a great deal of the Gospel expressed in the type of the cities of refuge. The writer to the Hebrews seems to allude to them in speaking of our fleeing for *refuge to lay hold upon the hope set before us* (Heb 6:18), and the apostle Paul seems to allude to them in speaking of being found in Christ (Php 3:9).

2.1. There were several cities of refuge, and they were arranged in different parts of the country so that wherever the offender lived in Israel, they might reach one or another of them within half a day. This teaches us that although there is only one Christ appointed for our refuge, wherever we are, he is always a constantly available and close refuge, an ever-present help, for the word is close to us and Christ is in the word.

2.2. The offender was safe in any of these cities. Similarly, in Christ believers who flee to him and rest in him are protected from the wrath of God and the curse of the Law. *There is no condemnation to those that are in Christ Jesus* (Ro 8:1).

2.3. They were all Levite cities. It was a kindness to the poor offender that the Levites would make them welcome and strengthen and encourage them. It is the work of Gospel ministers to welcome sinners to Christ, and to give help and guidance to those who through grace belong to him.

2.4. Even foreigners and strangers, though they were not native-born Israelites, could take advantage of these cities of refuge (v. 15). Similarly, in Christ Jesus no difference is made between Greek and Jew.

2.5. Even the limits or pasturelands of the city were sufficient security to the offender (vv. 26–27). This teaches us that there is power even in the hem of Christ's clothing (Mt 14:36) to heal and save sinners.

CHAPTER 36

We have in this chapter the resolution of another question which arose from the case of the daughters of Zelophehad. God had appointed that they should have property as an inheritance (27:7). Now here: 1. A difficulty is suggested: what would happen if they married into any other tribe (vv. 1–4)? 2. The answer is given: God says that they should marry only within their own tribe and tribal clan (vv. 5–7), and this is settled as a rule in similar cases (vv. 8–9). This is what happened: they married some of their own relatives (vv. 10–12), and the book concludes with this (v. 13).

Verses 1–4

We have here the humble words that the heads of the tribe of Manasseh spoke to Moses and the leaders after the order had been given concerning the daughters of Zelophehad.

1. They justly repeat what had formerly been decided in this case. They do not want to set that aside, but are very willing to accept it (v. 2).

2. They present the difficulty which might possibly result if the daughters of Zelophehad wanted to marry men from any other tribe (v. 3). They aimed at two things in their statement:

- It would disrupt the divine appointment if such a considerable part of the lot of Manasseh were to be transferred by their marriage to any other tribe.
- To prevent arguments and strife among their descendants. If those of other tribes were to come among them, perhaps it might lead to conflict.

Verses 5–13

Here:

1. The matter between the daughters of Zelophehad and the rest of the tribe of Manasseh is settled by an explicit command from God. The appeal is considered and care is taken to prevent the difficulty that had been feared from actually happening: *The tribe of the sons of Joseph hath said well* (v. 5).

1.1. They do not have to marry any particular named men; there was enough choice among the family of their father: *Let them marry to whom they think best* (v. 6). As children must preserve the authority of their parents, and not marry against their parents' wishes, so parents must consider the affections of their children in thinking about whom they should marry, and not compel them to marry those they cannot love. Forced marriages are not likely to prove a blessing.

1.2. But they are confined to their own relatives, so that their inheritance may not go to another tribe.

2. The law, in this particular case, was made binding forever.

3. The daughters of Zelophehad submit to this arrangement.

4. This whole book concludes, referring to its final part: *These are the judgments which the Lord commanded in the plains of Moab* (v. 13), these previous commands and regulations from 26:1, related mostly to their settlement in Canaan, which they were now entering. Whatever new condition God by his providence brings us into, we must ask him to teach us its duties and ask him also to enable us to fulfill them. In this way, we may do the work of the day at its right time and place.

A PRACTICAL AND DEVOTIONAL EXPOSITION OF THE FIFTH BOOK OF MOSES,

Deuteronomy

This book is very much a repetition of both the history and the laws contained in the three previous books. There is no new history here, except the death of Moses in the final chapter. The former laws are repeated and commented on, explained and enlarged on, and some individual commands are added, with detailed reasons to back them up. The Greek interpreters call it *Deuteronomy*, which means the "second law," or a "second edition of the law"; not that it had amendments, for none were needed, but it had additions, to give further directions to the people in different cases not mentioned before. 1. It was much for the honor of the divine law that it should be repeated in this way. 2. There might be a particular reason for their repetition now. The people of the generation to which the Law was first given were all dead, and a new generation had arisen, to whom God wanted it repeated by Moses himself, so that if possible it might make a lasting impression on them. Now that they were about to take possession of the land of Canaan, Moses must read the stipulations of the agreement to them, that they might know on what terms and conditions they were to possess and enjoy that land. 3. It would be very useful to the people to have those parts of the Law collated and put together which were of more immediate concern to them and their practice, for the laws concerning the priests and Levites and their responsibilities are not repeated. The great and vital truths of the Gospel should be often impressed on people by ministers of Christ. *To write the same things*, writes Paul (Php 3:1), *to me indeed is not grievous, but for you it is safe*. What God has spoken once we need to hear twice, in fact, to hear many times, and it is good if we eventually realize it and obey it. The Gospel is a kind of Deuteronomy, a second law, a spiritual law, a law of salvation, and a law of faith.

This book of Deuteronomy begins with a brief repetition of the most significant events that had happened to the Israelites since they came from Mount Sinai. In chapter 4 we have a fervent encouragement to obedience. In chapters 12 to 26 many details are repeated, which are supported (chs. 27–28) by promises and threats, blessings and curses, and formed into a covenant (chs. 29–30). They should be careful to remember these things forever (ch. 31), particularly in a song (ch. 32), and so Moses concludes with a blessing (ch. 33). All this was delivered by Moses to Israel in the last month of his life. When our Savior answered the Devil's temptations with, *It is written*, he took all his quotations from this book (Mt 4:4, 7, 10).

CHAPTER 1

The first part of Moses' farewell sermon to Israel begins with this chapter and continues almost to the end of the fourth chapter. 1. In the first five verses of this chapter we have the date of the sermon, the place where it was preached (vv. 1–2, 5), and the time when it was preached (vv. 3–4). The narrative in this chapter reminds them: of the promise God made them of the land of Canaan (vv. 6–8). 2. Of the provision made for leaders for them (vv. 9–18). 3. Of their unbelief and grumbling at the report of the spies (vv. 19–33), the sentence passed on them for it, and the confirmation of that sentence (vv. 34–46).

Verses 1–8

We have here:
1. The date that this sermon was preached by Moses to the people of Israel.
1.1. The place where they were now camped was *in the plain, in the land of Moab* (vv. 1, 5), where they were

about to enter Canaan and wage war against the Canaanites. But he does not talk to them about military matters, but about their duty to God.

1.2. The time was near the end of the fortieth year since they came out of Egypt. Now that they were to enter new and more pleasant territory, Moses repeats the Law to them as a sign of good things to come.

2. The speech itself. In general, Moses spoke to them *all that the Lord had given him in commandment* (v. 3). He begins his narrative with their move from Mount Sinai (v. 6) and describes here:

2.1. The orders that God gave them to break camp and proceed on their journey (vv. 6–7): *You have dwelt long enough in this mount*. God took them there to humble them, and to prepare them by the terrors of the law for the Land of Promise. Though God brings his people into trouble and affliction of different kinds, he knows when they have lived through enough of it. He will certainly find a

201

time to move them on from the terrors of the spirit of slavery to the assurance of the spirit of adoption (Ro 8:15).

2.2. The prospect which he gave them of a joyful and early settlement in Canaan. When God commands us to go forward in our Christian lives, he sets the heavenly Canaan before us to encourage us.

Verses 9–18

Moses here reminds them of the fortunate arrangement of their leadership, which was intended to make them all safe and secure as long as they were responsible. He suggests to them in this part of his narrative:

1. That he is joyful at the increase of their numbers. He acknowledges that God's promise to Abraham has been fulfilled: *You are as the stars of heaven for multitude* (v. 10); *God make you a thousand times more* (v. 11). We are not constrained by the power and goodness of God, so why should we be confined in our own faith and hope, which ought to be as wide as the promise? They could not be wider. The people might become a thousand times more than they were now, since they were now ten thousand times more than they were when they went into Egypt.

2. That he was not ambitious of monopolizing all the honor of leadership, and ruling over the people alone as an absolute monarch (v. 9).

3. That he did not want to advance individuals of his own choice, or those who would be dependent on him. He leaves it to the people to choose their own judges, to whom he would grant commissions. He directs them to *take wise men and understanding* (v. 13), whose personal merits commended them.

4. That he was very willing in this matter to please the people. They agreed to the proposal. The leadership they later quarreled with was what they themselves had agreed to.

5. That he aimed to build them up as well as to please them, for:

5.1. He appointed people of good character (v. 15), *wise men and men known,* leaders who would be faithful to their trust and to the public interest.

5.2. He gave them serious responsibilities (vv. 16–17). He commands them:

5.2.1. To be diligent and patient. Hear both sides of a case, hear them fully, hear them carefully, for nature has provided us with two ears. A listening ear is necessary for the person with an instructed tongue (Isa 50:4).

5.2.2. To be just and impartial. There must be no prejudice in the judgment. Bribes must not be accepted; the verdicts must always be given with unbiased justice.

5.2.3. To be resolute and courageous. You are God's vice-regents, you are acting for him, and so you must act like him. You are his representatives, but if you judge unjustly, you are misrepresenting him.

5.3. He allowed them to bring all the difficult cases to him, and he would always be ready to hear and decide cases, to put both the judges and the people at their ease.

Verses 19–46

Moses here describes again that fatal error of the people's sin. It was a memorable story; we read it in Nu 13–14, but different circumstances are found here which are not related there:

1. He reminds them of their journey from Horeb to Kadesh Barnea (v. 19), through *that great and terrible wilderness.* He takes notice of this to make them aware of God's great goodness to them, in guiding them through so vast a desert. Remembering the dangers we have passed through should make us thankful for the ways God has rescued us.

2. He shows them how they were about to enter Canaan at that time (vv. 20–21). He lets them see how close they were to a happy settlement when they themselves shut the open door.

3. He puts the blame on them for sending the spies, though he had not done so in Numbers. There it is said (Nu 13:1–2) that the Lord directed the sending of them, but here we find that the people first wanted it, and God, in allowing it, allowed them to follow their own ways: *You said, We will send men before us* (v. 22). Moses had given them God's word (vv. 20–21), but in their hearts they did not want to rely on that. They think they know better than God's wisdom; it is as if they want to light a candle to add to sunlight!

4. He repeats the report that the spies brought of the goodness of the land they were sent to survey (vv. 24–25) and reminds the people that they had believed that the difficulties of conquering were too much for them (v. 28).

5. He tells them how hard he had tried to encourage them, when their brothers had said so much to discourage them (v. 29). He assured them that God was present with them. If they wanted proof of his power over their enemies, he told them to think back to what they had seen in Egypt. And if they wanted proof of God's goodwill to them, he told them to think back to what *they had seen in the wilderness* (vv. 31, 33). They had been guided through the desert with as much care and tenderness as had ever been shown to any child in the arms of a tender father. Was there therefore any room left to distrust this God?

6. He accuses them of the sin they were guilty of on this occasion:

- Disobedience and rebellion against God's Law.
- Unjust reflections on God's goodness.
- An unbelieving heart, which lay at the root of all this: *You did not believe the Lord your God* (v. 32).

7. He repeats the sentence passed on them:

7.1. They were all condemned to die in the desert, and none of them would be allowed to enter Canaan except Caleb and Joshua (vv. 34–38). It was not for breaking any of the commands of the Law that they were excluded from Canaan, nor for the incident with the golden calf, but for their disbelief of the promise which was a type of Gospel grace. No sin will destroy us except unbelief, which is a sin against the way of salvation.

7.2. Moses himself afterward incurred God's displeasure for the rash word which they provoked him to speak: *The Lord was angry with me for your sakes* (v. 37).

7.3. But here mercy is mixed with wrath:

7.3.1. Though Moses was not allowed to lead them into Canaan, Joshua would (v. 38).

7.3.2. Though this generation would not enter into Canaan, the next generation would (v. 39).

8. He reminds them of their foolish and futile attempts to reverse this sentence when it was too late:

8.1. They tried to reverse it by reforming their lives; whereas they had refused to go up against the Canaanites, now they said they would go up. But this act, which looked like a reformation of their lives, turned out to be only a further rebellion. They were chased and destroyed.

8.2. They tried by their prayers and tears to get the sentence reversed: *They returned and wept before the Lord* (v. 45). These were tears of repentance and humiliation *before* God. But their weeping was all futile. *The Lord would not hearken to your voice* (v. 45), because you would not listen to his.

CHAPTER 2

*In this chapter Moses proceeds to recount God's provi-
dences concerning Israel on their way to Canaan, but he
does not give any record of what happened during their
long and tedious journeys back to the Red Sea, which took
almost thirty-eight years. He starts his narrative when
they turned toward Canaan (vv. 1–3) and drew near to
the countries that were inhabited. God here gives them
directions as to which nations they must not disturb: 1.
The Edomites (vv. 4–8). 2. The Moabites (v. 9); of their
land and that of the Edomites he gives some background
history (vv. 10–12). He also includes here an account
of their passing the River Zered (vv. 13–16). They must
also not disturb the Ammonites, whose country is again
discussed here (vv. 17–23). 3. What nations they should
attack and conquer. They must begin with Sihon king of
the Amorites (vv. 24–25), and so they had occasion to
quarrel with him (vv. 26–32). God gave them a complete
victory over him (vv. 33–37).*

Verses 1–7

Here we have:

1. A short account of the long stay of Israel in the
desert: *We compassed Mount Seir many days* (v. 1).
They wandered in the deserts of Seir for nearly thirty-
eight years. They probably stayed several years in some
places.

2. Orders given to them to turn toward Canaan.

3. A command given them not to attack the Edomites.
They must not provoke them to war: *Meddle not with them*
(vv. 4–5). They must do business with them as neighbors,
buy food and water from them, and pay for what they
bought (v. 6). Religion must never be made a cloak for
behaving unjustly.

Verses 8–23

It is significant here that when Moses speaks of the
Edomites (v. 8), he calls them *our brethren, the children
of Esau.* Although they had been unkind to Israel in refusing to allow them to pass peaceably through their country,
he still calls them *brethren*. Now in these verses we have
the account which Moses gives:

1. Of the origin of the Moabites, Edomites, and Ammonites. He tells us here how they came to those countries
in which Israel found them. They were not the indigenous
inhabitants, but:

1.1. The Moabites lived in a country which had
belonged to a populous race of giants, called *Emim*
(Emites), meaning "terrifying ones," as tall as the Anakim
(Anakites), and perhaps fiercer (vv. 10–11).

1.2. In the same way, the Edomites drove out the Horim
(Horites) from Mount Seir, and took their country (v. 12
and again v. 22), of which we read in Ge 36:20.

1.3. The Ammonites similarly gained possession of a
country that had formerly been inhabited by giants, called
Zamzummim (Zamzummites), "whisperers" or "wicked
people" (vv. 20–21), perhaps the same as the *Zuzim* (Zuzites) (Ge 14:5). He illustrates these comments by recalling
an even older incident: the Caphtorim (Caphtorites), who
were related to the Philistines (Ge 10:14), drove the Avim
(Avvites) out of their country and took possession of it
(v. 23). Bishop Patrick presumes that these Avvites, after
they had been expelled from there, then settled in Assyria,
and are the same people that we read about with that name
in 2Ki 17:31.

2. Of the advances which Israel made toward Canaan.
They *passed by the way of the wilderness of Moab* (v. 8),

and then went over the brook or vale of Zered (v. 13).
There Moses notes the fulfillment of the word God had
spoken concerning them, that none of those who were
counted at Mount Sinai would see the land that God had
promised (Nu 14:23).

3. Of the warning given to them not to provoke the
Moabites or Ammonites to war. They must not dispossess
them or even disturb their possessions: *Distress them not,
nor contend with them* (v. 9). But why must the Moabites
and Ammonites not be provoked?

- Because they were the *children of Lot* (vv. 9, 19), righteous Lot, who kept his integrity in Sodom.
- Because the land they possessed was given them by
God, and it was not his will that Israel should possess it.

Verses 24–37

After God had tested his people to see if they could
exercise self-denial when he forbade them from provoking the Moabites and Ammonites to go to war—and they
had quietly passed by those rich countries—and although
they were superior in numbers, they did not make any
attack on them—he here rewards them for their obedience by giving them possession of the country of Sihon
king of the Amorites:

1. God commissions them to go to war against the
country of Sihon king of Heshbon (vv. 24–25). This was
in those days God's way of disposing of kingdoms, but
in our day such particular authority should be neither
expected nor claimed.

2. Moses sends to Sihon a message of peace and asks
permission to pass through his land. He promises that he
will not disturb his country in any way but wants to take
advantage of trading for money with so great a kingdom
(vv. 26–29).

3. Sihon began the war (v. 32).

4. Israel was victorious. Israel struck down all the Amorites, men, women, and children (vv. 33–34). They died not
as Israel's enemies, but as sacrifices to divine justice. In
the offering of these sacrifices, Israel was used as a kingdom of priests. Israel took possession of all they had: their
towns (v. 34), their goods (v. 35), and their land (v. 36).

CHAPTER 3

*In this chapter, Moses relates: 1. The conquest of Og,
king of Bashan, and the seizing of his country (vv. 1–11).
2. The division of these new conquests among the two
and a half tribes (vv. 12–17), with certain conditions
and restrictions (vv. 18–20). 3. The encouragement
given to Joshua to carry on the war which had been so
gloriously begun (vv. 21–22); Moses' request to go over
into Canaan (vv. 23–25), with the denial of that request,
but the giving of something equivalent (vv. 26–29).*

Verses 1–11

We have here another country, Bashan, boldly given
into the hands of Israel. Notice:

1. How they conquered Og, who was a very formidable
ruler:

1.1. He was very strong, for he was the last remaining giant (v. 11). When God pleads his people's cause,
he can deal with giants as he does with grasshoppers. No
person's power can keep them safe against the Almighty.
The army of Og was very powerful, for he commanded
sixty fortified cities, besides unwalled villages (v. 5).

1.2. He was very bold and daring. He trusted in his own strength and so was hardened to his destruction. God told Moses not to be afraid of him (v. 2). If Moses himself was so strong in his faith that he did not need this advice, the people probably needed it. These fresh assurances are intended for them: *I will deliver him into thy hand* (v. 2).

2. How they gained possession of Bashan, a very desirable country. They took all the cities (v. 4) and all their plunder (v. 7). They made them all their own (v. 10). This means they then had in their hands all the fruitful country which lay east of the Jordan, from *the river Arnon unto Hermon* (v. 8).

Verses 12–20

Having shown how this country which they were now in was conquered, Moses goes on to show in these verses how it was settled on the Reubenites, Gadites, and the half tribe of Manasseh. We read this story before (Nu 32:1–42):

1. He specifies the particular parts of the country that were allotted to each tribe, especially the division of the allotment to the half tribe of Manasseh, the subdividing of which tribe is significant.

2. He repeats the condition on which the two and a half tribes' title to the land would depend, according to an agreement they already made (vv. 18–20). They were to send a strong detachment over the Jordan to lead the soldiers in the conquest of Canaan, and the detachment would not return to their families until they had seen their brothers have as full possession of their allotted land as they themselves now had of theirs. Good people cannot be joyful about the comforts of their own families unless they also see *peace upon Israel* (Ps 128:6).

Verses 21–29

Here is:

1. The encouragement that Moses gave to Joshua, who was to succeed him in the leadership (vv. 21–22). He commanded him not to be afraid. Moses wanted Joshua to consider two things for his encouragement:

1.1. What God has done. Joshua had seen how God had given victory to the forces of Israel over those two kings. He must not only reason from that that the Lord *can* deal with all the others in the same way, for he is as strong, but also that the Lord *will* actually do this, for his purposes have not changed. What he has begun, he will finish.

1.2. What God had promised. The *Lord your God he shall fight for you* (v. 22), and the cause which almighty God fights for must be victorious.

2. The prayer which Moses made for himself, and the answer which God gave to that prayer:

2.1. His prayer was that if it was God's will, he might go before Israel over the Jordan into Canaan. *Let me go over and see the good land* (v. 25). Not, "Let me go over and be a ruler there." He does not seek his own honor; he is happy to leave the leadership to Joshua, but, "Let me go and see your kindness to Israel and see what I believe concerning the goodness of the Land of Promise."

2.2. God's answer to this prayer contained both mercy and judgment so that he might sing to God of both:

2.2.1. There was judgment in the denial of his request, and also a note of anger in that: *The Lord was wroth with me for your sakes* (v. 26). But why was he angry with Moses *for the sake of Israel*? There are three possible reasons:

2.2.1.1. For that sin which they aroused him to; see Ps 106:32–33. Or:

2.2.1.2. Because the removal of Moses at that time, when he could hardly be spared, was a rebuke to all Israel and a punishment of their sin. Or:

2.2.1.3. It was for their sakes, that it might be a warning to them to make sure they did not offend God at any time by rash and unbelieving words such as those by which Moses had sinned. Even though Moses—one of the descendants of Jacob who wrestled—did not seek God in vain, he still did not receive what he sought for. God may accept our prayers, but he may still not give us the very things we are praying for.

2.2.2. Here is mercy mixed with this wrath in several ways:

2.2.2.1. God quieted the spirit of Moses: *Let it suffice thee* (v. 26). With this word, no doubt, divine power came to reconcile Moses to the will of God and to help him come to terms with it. If God does not by his providence give us what we want, but by his grace makes us content without it, it comes to much the same thing.

2.2.2.2. God honored his prayer in directing him not to insist any further on his request: *Speak no more to me of this matter* (v. 26).

2.2.2.3. God promised him a sight of Canaan *from the top of Pisgah* (v. 27). Though he would not possess it, he would still have a sight of it, not to tease him, but to give him such a sight as would give him true satisfaction and would enable him to form a clear and pleasant idea of the Promised Land.

2.2.2.4. God provided him with a successor, one who would support the honor of Moses and carry on and complete that glorious work which the heart of Moses was so set on, the bringing of Israel to Canaan and settling them there (v. 28).

CHAPTER 4

In this chapter we have: 1. A most fervent and heartfelt encouragement to obedience, backed up by arguments, repeated again and again, and set before the people in a most moving and tender way (vv. 1–40). 2. The appointing of the cities of refuge on that side of the Jordan (vv. 41–43); the particular description of the place where Moses delivered the following repetition of the Law (vv. 44–49).

Verses 1–40

This striking and fine address may be well known.

1. In general, it takes and applies the people's previous history. We should review God's providences concerning our own lives, to stir us and commit ourselves more deeply to duty and obedience.

2. The scope and tenor of his address is to persuade them to keep close to God and to his service, and not to abandon him for any other god.

2.1. Notice how he commands them and shows them *what the Lord requires of them* (Mic 6:8):

2.1.1. He demands that they give diligent attention to the word of God: *Hearken, O Israel* (v. 1). He means not only that they must now listen to him, but also that whenever the Book of the Law was read to them, or read by them, they should be attentive to it.

2.1.2. He commands them to keep the divine Law pure and whole among them (v. 2). Keep it pure, and do not add to it; keep it whole, and do not take away from it.

2.1.3. He commands them to keep God's *commandments* (v. 2), to *do them* (vv. 5, 14), to *keep and do them* (v. 6), to *perform the covenant* (v. 13). Hearing must lead to doing, and knowing must lead to practice.

2.1.4. He commands them to be very strict and careful in their observance of the Law (v. 9): *Only take heed to thyself, and keep thy soul diligently,* and (v. 15), *Take you therefore good heed unto yourselves,* and again (v. 23), *Take heed to yourselves.*

2.1.5. He commands them to be especially aware of the sin of idolatry. He warns them against two kinds of idolatry:

2.1.5.1. The worship of idols, however they might intend to use them to worship the true God, as they had done in the golden calf, so changing the *truth of God into a lie* (Ro 1:25) and his *glory into shame* (Ps 4:2). The second commandment is explicitly directed against this and is here enlarged on (vv. 15–18). To represent an infinite Spirit by an idol, and the great Creator by the idol of something created is a great insult to God and a deception to ourselves. As an argument against their making idols of God, he makes it plain that when God made himself known to them at Horeb he did it by a voice of words which sounded in their ears, to teach them that *faith comes by hearing* (Ro 10:17), and God in the word is close to us. No idol was presented to their eye, however, for to see God as he is is kept for our enjoyment in the next world, and to see him as he is not will harm us and do us no good in this world. You saw *no similitude* (v. 12), *no manner of similitude* (v. 15), no form of God.

2.1.5.2. The worship of the sun, moon, and stars (v. 19). This was the most ancient kind of idolatry and the most plausible. The plausibleness of it made it all the more dangerous. *When thou seest the sun, moon, and stars* (v. 19), you will wonder at their brightness and distance, their regular movements and powerful influences, and you will be strongly tempted to give the glory to them which is due only to the One who made them. It seems they needed to be given a great deal of strong determination to arm them against this temptation, because their faith in an invisible God and an invisible world was so weak. These pretended deities, the *sun, moon, and stars,* were only blessings which the Lord their God had given to all nations. It is absurd to worship them, for they are the servants of the human race; they were made and ordained to give light on earth.

2.1.6. He instructs them to teach their children to observe the laws of God: *Teach them to thy sons, and thy sons' sons* (v. 9), *that they may teach their children* (v. 10).

2.1.7. He instructs them never to forget their duty: *Take heed lest you forget the covenant of the Lord your God* (v. 23).

2.2. Let us now see what the motivations and arguments are that he uses to back up these encouragements:

2.2.1. He urges them to remember the greatness, glory, and goodness of God. If we stopped to consider what a God he is with whom we have to do, we would surely be more conscientious in our duty to him and not dare sin against him. He reminds them here: that the Lord Jehovah is the one only *living and true God* (1Th 1:9). All the gods of the nations were counterfeit and usurped what rightfully belonged to him. None of them pretended to be a universal ruler of heaven and earth, but claimed to be only local deities. The Israelites, who worshiped none other than the supreme God, were forever without excuse if they either changed their God or neglected him. Make sure that you do not offend him, for he must have our complete devotion and adoration. He will by no means tolerate any rival. Even in the New Testament we find the same argument urged on us as a reason why we should serve *God with reverence* (Heb 12:28–29), because though he is our God and a joyful light to those who serve him faithfully,

he is also a consuming fire to those who trifle with him. He is also *a merciful God* (v. 31). This is included here as an encouragement to repentance, but it might also be a motivation to obedience, and something for them to think about to stop them from turning away from God.

2.2.2. He urges them to remember their relationship with this God, his authority over them, and their obligations to him. He is the *Lord God of your fathers* (v. 1), so that you are his by inheritance. Your fathers were his, and you were born in his house. "He is the *Lord your God* (v. 2), so you are his by your own agreement. He is the *Lord my God* (v. 5), so I am discussing these terms with you as his agent and ambassador."

2.2.3. He urges them to remember the wisdom of observing his decrees: *For this is your wisdom in the sight of the nations* (v. 6). Great things may justly be looked for from those who are guided by divine revelation and to whom are entrusted the very words of God.

2.2.4. He urges them to remember the special advantages which they enjoyed because of the fortunate leadership they were under (vv. 7–8). Our fellowship with God—which is the highest honor and happiness we are capable of in this world—is maintained by the word and prayer. In both of these, Israel was more fortunate than any other people under heaven. The Law of God is far more excellent than the laws of nations. No law is so consistent with the principles of natural justice and the unbiased principles of right reason, so in harmony within itself in every part, and so conducive to the welfare and interests of the human race as the Law of Scripture (Ps 119:128). Those who exalt the Law will be exalted by it.

2.2.5. He urges them to remember God's glorious appearances to them at Mount Sinai, when he gave them this Law. He insists on this. Take heed *lest thou forget the day that thou stoodest before the Lord thy God in Horeb* (v. 10). What we see of God is sufficient basis for our faith in him as a Being of infinite power and perfection, but it gives us absolutely no reason for us to think that he has a physical body like ours. What they heard at Mount Sinai (v. 12): "*The Lord spoke unto you* with a voice you could understand, in your own language, and you heard it." God reveals himself to all the world in the works of creation without speech or language, and their voice is heard (Ps 19:1–3), but he made himself known to Israel by speech and language, bringing himself down to the lowly level of the church's infant state.

2.2.6. He urges them to consider God's gracious appearances for them, in bringing them out of Egypt, from the iron furnace where they labored in the fire, forming them into a people, and then taking them to be his own people, a *people of inheritance* (v. 20). He mentions this again (vv. 34, 37–38). They were intended to settle happily in Canaan (v. 38).

2.2.7. He urges them to remember God's righteous appearances against them for their sins. He specifies particularly the matter of Peor (vv. 3–4). This had happened recently: their eyes had only just seen the sudden destruction of those who joined themselves to the Baal of Peor and the preservation of those who were faithful to the Lord. They might easily reason from this the danger of turning away from God and the benefit of remaining faithful to him.

2.2.8. He urges them to remember the clear advantage of obedience.

2.2.9. He urges them to remember the fatal consequences if they turned away from God, that it would undoubtedly lead to the destruction of their nation. This he develops (vv. 25–31). Notice here:

2.2.9.1. That whatever place we are in we may *thence seek the Lord our God*, even though it is far away from our own country or his holy temple. There is no part of this earth that has a chasm fixed between it and heaven.

2.2.9 2. Only those who seek God with all their heart will find God to be their assurance, encouragement, and strength.

2.2.9.3. Suffering is sent to draw us back to God, to stir our spiritual lives to see God afresh. By the grace of God working with them, many are turned back to their right mind.

3. If all these arguments are put together, who dare challenge that religion has reason on its side? It is only those who have first abandoned true human understanding who reject the authority of their God.

Verses 41–49

Here is:

1. The naming of the cities of refuge on that side of Jordan where Israel was now camped. Three cities were appointed for that purpose, one in the allotment of Reuben, another in that of Gad, and another in that of the half tribe of Manasseh (vv. 41–43).

2. The introduction to another sermon that Moses preached to Israel, which we have in the following chapters. It was probably preached the following Sabbath, when the assembly gathered to receive instruction. He had in general encouraged them to obedience; here he comes to repeat the Law that they were to observe, for he demands a universal but not unquestioning obedience. How can we do our duty if we do not know it? He therefore here sets the Law before them as the rule they were to live by.

CHAPTER 5

In this chapter we have the "second edition" of the Ten Commandments: 1. Their general intention: they were in the nature of a covenant between God and Israel (vv. 1–5). 2. The individual commands are repeated (vv. 6–21), with their twofold delivery in word and in writing (v. 22). 3. The settling of the agreement from then onward between God and Israel by the mediation and ministry of Moses. This is what Israel humbly requested (vv. 23–27), and it was God's gracious provision and privilege that it should be so (vv. 28–31). And so Moses reasons from that the obligation they were under to obey God (vv. 32–33).

Verses 1–5

Here:

1. Moses summons the assembly. He *called all Israel*.

2. Moses demands their attention.

3. Moses refers them to the covenant made with them at Horeb, as the covenant that they must govern their whole lives by. Notice here the wonderful condescension of God's grace, that he turns the command into a covenant. Notice:

3.1. The parties to this covenant. The covenant was made either with them or with their immediate parents, who represented them and made it on their behalf before Mount Sinai,.

3.2. The declaration of this covenant. God himself, as it were, read out the articles of the covenant to them (v. 4): he *talked with you face to face*; the Aramaic reads, "word to word."

3.3. The mediator of the covenant: *Moses stood between God and them*, at the foot of the mountain (v. 5). Here

Moses was a type of Christ, who *stands between God and man, to show us the word of the Lord* (v. 5). He is a blessed mediator, One who has laid his hand on us that we may both hear from God and speak to him without trembling.

Verses 6–22

Here is the repetition of the Ten Commandments, in which notice:

1. Though they had been spoken and written before, they are repeated.

2. There are a few differences between the record here and that given in Ex 20:1–26.

3. The most significant difference is in the fourth commandment. In Ex 20:8–11 the reason attached is taken from the creation of the world; here it is taken from their rescue from Egypt, because that was a type of our redemption by Jesus Christ, in remembrance of which the Christian Sabbath was to be observed: *Remember that thou wast a servant, and God brought thee out* (v. 15). Therefore:

3.1. "It is right that your servants should be favored by the Sabbath rest, for you know the heart of a servant, and how welcome one day's rest will be after six days' labor."

3.2. "It is right that your God should be honored by what you do on the Sabbath, in the religious services of that day, considering the great things he has done for you." In the resurrection of Christ, we were brought into the glorious liberty of the children of God, *with a mighty hand and an outstretched arm* (26:8), and so the Gospel rendition of the Law directs us to observe the first day of the week in remembrance of that glorious work of power and grace.

4. To the fifth commandment is added, *That it may go well with thee* (v. 16), which the apostle Paul quotes and puts first (Eph 6:3), *that it may be well with thee, and that thou mayest live long*.

5. The last five commandments are connected or coupled together, which they are not in Exodus: *Neither shalt thou commit adultery, neither shalt thou steal* (vv. 18–19), which shows that God's commands are all consistent.

6. These commandments were given with a great deal of frightening solemnity (v. 22).

Verses 23–33

1. Moses reminds them of the agreement of both of the parties of the negotiations through his mediation. Here is:

1.1. The fear that the people were in because of the extreme terror with which the Law was given. They acknowledged that they could not bear it any more: "*This great fire will consume us*; this terrible voice will kill us; we will certainly die if we hear it any more" (v. 25).

1.2. Their fervent request that God would from that time onward speak to them through Moses, with the promise that they would listen to what he said as coming from God himself and do it (v. 27).

1.3. God's approval of their request. He appoints Moses to be his messenger to them, to receive the Law from his mouth and to communicate it to them (v. 31). God would from that time onward speak to us by human beings like ourselves, by Moses and the prophets, by the apostles and evangelists. If we do not believe them, neither would we be persuaded even if God spoke to us as he did to Israel at Mount Sinai.

2. Moses reasons from this a command for them to observe all that God had commanded them, to *walk in all the ways that God had commanded them* (v. 33).

CHAPTER 6

In this chapter, Moses continues with his commands to Israel, that Israel must maintain their religion in Canaan. It is much the same as 4:1–40. 1. His introduction is a persuasive call to obedience (vv. 1–3). 2. He lays down the great principles of obedience. The first truth to be believed is that God is one (v. 4). The first duty to be fulfilled is to love him with all our heart (v. 5). He instructs them on how to maintain their religious faith (vv. 6–9). He warns them against those things which would destroy their religious faith—not handling prosperity in the right way (vv. 10–12) and their inclination to idolatry (vv. 14–15)—and gives them some general commands (vv. 13, 16–19). 3. He tells them what instructions they are to give their children (vv. 20–25).

Verses 1–3

Notice here:

1. That Moses taught the people everything that God commanded him to teach them (v. 1), no more and no less. In the same way, Christ's ministers are to teach his churches *all that he has commanded* (Mt 28:20).

2. That the purpose of their being taught was that they might do as they were taught (v. 1), that they might *keep God's statutes* (v. 2) and *observe to do them* (v. 3).

3. That Moses carefully tried to establish them in the ways of God and godly living now that they were entering the land of Canaan.

Verses 4–16

Here is:

1. A brief summary of religion, containing the basic principles of faith and obedience (vv. 4–5). The Jews consider these two verses to be one of the finest passages of Scripture: they write it in their phylacteries and think that they are not only obliged to say it at least twice every day, but that they are also very happy to have to do so. They have this saying among them, "Blessed are we, who every morning and evening say, 'Hear, O Israel, the Lord our God is one Lord.'" Notice:

1.1. What we are taught here to believe concerning God: Jehovah our God is one Jehovah:

1.1.1. That the God whom we serve is Jehovah, a Being who is infinitely and eternally perfect, self-existent, and self-sufficient.

1.1.2. That God is the one and only living and true God; only he is God, and he is one. The firm belief of this self-evident truth would powerfully defend them from idolatry, which came in with the basic error that there are many gods. Happy are those who have this one Lord as their God, for they have only one master to please and one benefactor to seek. It is better to have one fountain than a thousand broken or dried-up wells, one all-sufficient God than a thousand inadequate ones.

1.2. What we are taught here concerning the duty that God requires of human beings. It is summed up in this one principle, *Thou shalt love the Lord thy God with all thy heart* (Mt 22:37). Has a king or queen ever made a law that their subjects should love them? But God in his grace condescends that this is the first and great commandment of God's Law, that we are to love him, and that we are to carry out all other aspects of our duty to him from that motive of love. This love is to be intelligent love; it is explained in this way in Mk 12:33. To love him with all our heart, and with all our understanding, we must know him and love him as those who have good reason to love him.

2. The means as to how to maintain religious faith in our hearts and homes so that it might not die out or decay. These are:

2.1. Meditation: *These words which I command thee will be in thy heart* (v. 6).

2.2. The religious education of children (v. 7): "*Thou shalt teach them diligently to thy children*; and by communicating your knowledge you will increase it." Take every opportunity to talk with those around you about the things of God; do not try to impress others by talking about unrevealed mysteries or get sidetracked into discussing matters where there are differences of opinion, but simply talk about the plain truths and laws of God and the things that belong to our peace. The more familiar we are with them, the more we will wonder at them and be moved by them, and so we may be instrumental in communicating God's light and heart to others. God appointed them, at least for the present, to write some selected sentences of the Law—those which were most significant and comprehensive—on their walls, or on scrolls of parchment to be worn around their wrists. Some think that the phylacteries, much used among the Jews, arose from this. Christ blames the Pharisees not for wearing them, but for wearing them wider than other people's (Mt 23:5). It was wise and godly of the first reformers of the English church to see to it that when Bibles were scarce, some select portions of Scripture were written on the walls and pillars of the churches, so that the people might become familiar with them.

3. A warning not to forget God when things are going well and there is plenty (vv. 10–12). He raises their expectations of the goodness of God, assuming that he would lead them into the good land that he had promised (v. 10), that they would no longer live in tents as shepherds and poor travelers, but would settle in large and flourishing cities, that they would no longer wander in a barren wilderness, but would enjoy houses that were well furnished and gardens that were well planted (v. 11). *Cities which thou buildedst not, houses which thou filledst not.*

4. Some special commands and prohibitions requiring that they give honor to God on every occasion (v. 13). Take your oaths in his name in all treaties and covenants with the neighboring nations, and do not even think of paying them the compliment of taking oaths by their gods. Israel must make sure they do not dishonor God by *tempting him* (v. 16). "You shall not in any situation, especially a critical one, test God by distrusting his power, presence, and providence."

Verses 17–25

1. Moses commands them to keep God's commandments: *You shall diligently keep God's commandments* (vv. 17–19).

2. Moses commands them to teach the commandments of God to their children, not only so that they might at a younger age intelligently and warmly join in religious services, but so that also in later years they might keep up their religious faith and pass it on to those who came after them. Now:

2.1. Here is a good question which it is thought the children might ask (v. 20): "What do all these terms and rules mean? What is the meaning of the feasts we observe, the sacrifices we offer, and the many special customs we respect?" Notice:

2.1.1. All divine institutions have a certain meaning, and there is something significant in them.

2.1.2. We should be concerned to know and understand their meaning, so that we may use our minds when we serve God and may not offer improper things as a sacrifice.

2.2. Here a full answer is put into the parents' mouths to be given to this good question. Have the children asked about the meaning of God's laws? If so, then let them be told so that the laws could be observed:

2.2.1. In grateful remembrance of God's former favors to them, especially their rescue from Egypt (vv. 21–23).

2.2.2. As the specified condition of his further favors (v. 24): *The Lord commanded us all these statutes for our good.* If we could perfectly fulfill only that one command of loving God with all our heart, soul, and might, and if we could say that we have never done otherwise, this would be our righteousness such that we would be entitled to the benefits of the covenant of innocence before the Fall. If we had obeyed everything that is written in the Book of the Law to do, the Law would have justified us. But we cannot pretend to do this, and so our sincere obedience will be accepted through a Mediator.

CHAPTER 7

Moses in this chapter encourages Israel: 1. In general, to keep God's commandments (vv. 11–12). 2. In particular, to keep themselves pure from all association with idolaters: they must completely destroy the seven devoted nations (vv. 1–2, 16, 24); they must not intermarry with them (vv. 3–4); they must break down and destroy their altars and idols, and not even take their silver and gold from them to use for themselves (vv. 5, 25–26). By way of support for this command, he shows that they were committed to do so because of their duty: considering their election by God (v. 6), the reason for that election (vv. 7–8), and the terms they stood on with God (vv. 9–10); and because of their privileges of being God's people: they are promised that if they served God, he would bless and prosper them (vv. 12–15), and if they drove out the nations, so that the nations might not be a source of temptation to them, God himself would drive them out, so that they would not cause Israel any trouble (vv. 17–26).

Verses 1–11

Here:

1. A very strict warning is given against all friendship and fellowship with idols and idolaters.

1.1. These devoted nations are named and numbered (v. 1). They are specified so that Israel might know the boundaries and limits of their commission. The confining of this commission to the nations mentioned here clearly shows that people were not to see this later as a precedent. It cannot be used to justify those barbaric laws which show no mercy. Yet if God drives them out, Israel must not take them in as tenants, vassals, or servants. The sin of the Amorites had now reached its limit, and the longer it had been in reaching that limit, the more extreme the vengeance was when it finally came. The people of these detestable nations must not be mixed in with the holy descendants, so that they do not defile them. This shows us how we must deal with the sinful desires that war against our souls; God has delivered them into our hands by that promise, *Sin shall not have dominion over you* (Ro 6:14) unless it is our own fault; let us then not make a covenant with them or show them any mercy, but put them to death, crucify them, and destroy them completely .

1.2. They must not enter into any marriages with those of them who were not killed (vv. 3–4). There is more reason to fear in mixed marriages that the good will be cor-

rupted than there is reason to hope that the bad will be improved and converted. One of the Aramaic paraphrases adds as a reason of this command (v. 3), "For the one who marries idolaters does in effect marry their idols."

1.3. They must destroy all the remnants of their idolatry (v. 5). Their altars and pillars, their groves (Asherah poles) and graven images (idols), must all be destroyed, both in righteous anger against idolatry and to prevent defilement.

2. Very good reasons are given to back up this warning:

- The choice which God had made of this people as his own (v. 6).
- The freeness of that grace which made this choice: God chose them purely because of his own character (v. 8). All those whom God loves, he loves freely (Hos 14:4).
- The tenor of the covenant into which they were taken; in short, as they were to God, so God would be to them.

Verses 12–26

1. The warning against idolatry is repeated, as is also the warning against fellowship with those who practice idolatry. Here is also a repetition of the command to destroy the idols (vv. 25–26). The idols which were worshiped in other religions were detestable to God, and so must be detestable to them too. All who truly love God hate what he hates.

2. The promise of God's favor to them if they were obedient is developed. Every possible assurance is given them. Let us continue to do our duty, and then we cannot question God's mercy. If they kept themselves pure from the idolatries of Egypt, God would keep them clear of the *diseases of Egypt* (v. 15). This seems to refer not only to those plagues of Egypt which Israel was rescued from, but also to some other epidemic disease which they remembered had afflicted the Egyptians, and which God had used as a punishment for the sins of that nation. Let them not be discouraged by the slow progress of the warfare, or think that the Canaanites would never be subdued if it did not all happen in the first year. No, they would be driven out *little and little*, not *all at once* (v. 22). We must not think that, because the church is not rescued and its enemies are not destroyed immediately, God's plan will therefore never be carried out. God will complete his own work in his own time and in his own way, and we are to rest assured that they are always the best. In the same way, corruption is driven out of believers' hearts *little and little.* The work of sanctification is carried on gradually, but judgment will in the end be brought to complete victory.

CHAPTER 8

Moses had commanded parents to teach their children to instill the word of God in them (6:7) by frequently repeating the same things over and over again. He here uses the same method himself to instruct the Israelites as his children, frequently impressing on them the same commands and warnings. In this chapter, Moses gives them: 1. General encouragements to obedience (vv. 1, 6); a review of the great things God had done for them in the desert, as good grounds for their obedience (vv. 2–5, 15–16); a view of the good land into which God was now going to bring them (vv. 7–9). 2. An important warning against the temptations of prosperity (vv. 10–14, 17–18), and a necessary warning of the tragic consequences of turning away from God (vv. 19–20).

Verses 1–9

The command given them here is the same as before, to keep and do all God's commandments. He directs them:

1. To look back on the desert through which God had now brought them. Now that they had come of age and were entering into their inheritance, they must be reminded of the discipline they had been under in their earlier years and of the ways God had trained them to be his own people. The desert was the school in which they had lived and been taught for forty years, and now the time came for it to be remembered. Let us set up our Ebenezers here (1Sa 7:12).

1.1. They must remember the difficulties they had sometimes been led into for two purposes: to put to death their pride and to reveal their perverseness. God tested them in this to see whether they would trust his promises, the word which he commanded to a thousand generations, and whether, depending on his promises, they would obey his commands.

1.2. They must remember that they had always been provided for. Although God has appointed bread as a means of strengthening our human bodies, and it is part of our staple diet, God can when he pleases still call on support and nourishment from other sources and make something else, even something unlikely, fulfill that intention as well. We might live on air if God had honored it to be used in that way, *sanctified by the word of God* (1Ti 4:5). Our Savior quotes this Scripture in answer to that temptation of Satan, *Command that these stones be made bread.* "There is no need for that," Christ says; "my heavenly Father can keep me alive without bread" (Mt 4:3–4). It may be applied spiritually: the *word of God*—the revelation of God's will and grace duly received by faith—is food for the soul. The life which is supported by that is the human life, not only that life which is supported by bread. The manna was a type of Christ, *the bread of life* (Jn 6:35). He is *the Word of God*; we live by him.

1.3. They must also remember the rebukes they had been under (v. 5). During those years of training, they had been kept under a strict discipline, and with good reason too. They were chastened so they would not be condemned, chastened by human agency, not as soldiers wound and kill their enemies whose destruction they are intent on, but as parents discipline their children, because they want to see their children happy and good. God disciplined and taught them in this way (Ps 94:12).

2. To look forward to Canaan, into which God was now bringing them. Whichever way we look, both looking back and also looking forward will provide us with reasons for obedience.

Verses 10–20

After Moses had described the abundant life they would find in the land of Canaan, he finds it necessary to warn them against abusing that plenty, which was a sin they would be more inclined to commit immediately after they had left behind a barren desert and came into that vineyard of the Lord.

1. He directs them to the responsibilities given them in their prosperous condition (v. 10). God must have the glory for whatever they gained comfort from. As our Savior has taught us to give thanks before we eat (Mt 14:19–20), so we are taught here to give thanks after food. That is our *Hosanna*, "God bless"; it is our *Hallelujah*, "Blessed be God." *In every thing we must give thanks* (1Th 5:18). From this law, the religious Jews took up the commendable custom of giving thanks to God, not only at their formal meals, but also on other occasions. If they drank a cup of wine, they lifted up their hands and said, "Blessed be the One who created the fruit of the vine to make the heart glad." If they only smelled a flower, they said, "Blessed be the One who made this flower sweet."

2. He warns them against the temptations of their prosperous condition:

2.1. "Then be on your guard against pride." When your possessions mount up, the mind is inclined to rise along with it in self-conceit, self-complacency, and self-confidence.

2.2. "Then be on your guard against forgetting God." When people grow rich, they are tempted to think that having a religious faith is something completely unnecessary. They are happy without it and think of it as something beneath them and too narrow for their indulgent lifestyle. Their pride forbids them from humbling themselves, and their liberty forbids them from serving God or others.

CHAPTER 9

In this chapter, Moses' purpose is to convince the people of Israel of their complete unworthiness to receive those great favors from God which were now to be given to them. 1. He assures them of victory over their enemies (vv. 1–3). He warns them not to attribute their successes to their own merit, but to God executing his justice on their enemies, and to him showing his faithfulness to their fathers (vv. 4–6). 2. To make it clear that they had no reason to boast of their own righteousness, he mentions their faults. In general, they had been a people who had constantly offended God (vv. 7–24). In particular, in the incident with the golden calf, which he relates in detail (vv. 8–21); he also mentions some other examples of their rebellion (vv. 22–23) and returns (v. 25) to speak of the intercession he had made for them at Horeb (vv. 26–29), to prevent their being destroyed because of the golden calf.

Verses 1–6

The call to attention (v. 1), *Hear, O Israel*, indicates that this was a new address.

1. Moses tells the people about the formidable strength of the enemies which they were now about to encounter (v. 1). This statement is similar to the one that the faithless spies had made (Nu 13:28, 33), but it was made with a very different intention. The purpose of that earlier one was to drive them away from God and to discourage their hope in him; the purpose of this one is to drive them to God and to stimulate their hope in him.

2. He assures them of victory by the presence of God with them, despite the strength of the enemy (v. 3).

3. He warns them not to entertain the slightest thought about their own righteousness, as if that had gained them this favor from God in any way. Just as our gaining possession of the heavenly Canaan must be attributed to God's power and not our own abilities, so it must be ascribed solely to God's grace and not to anything good in ourselves.

4. He shows them the true reasons why God would take this good land from the hands of the Canaanites to give it to Israel.

Verses 7–29

1. So that they might not pretend that God brought them to Canaan *for their righteousness,* Moses here shows them what a miracle of mercy it was that they had not

been destroyed in the desert long before this: *"Remember, and forget not, how thou provokedst the Lord thy God* (v. 7). Far from obtaining his favor, you have often exposed yourselves to his displeasure." They had angered God ever since they left Egypt (v. 7). Though the Mosaic history records little more than the events of the first and last years out of the forty, it still seems from this general account that the remaining years were not much better, but that they offended God continually.

2. If all the offenses that Moses enumerates are put together, it would appear that whatever favor God would later show them in subduing their enemies and bringing them into the land of Canaan, it was not because of their righteousness. It is good for us often to remind ourselves of our former sins, to our sorrow and shame, and to review the record that our conscience keeps of them, that we may see how much we are indebted to God's free grace and may humbly acknowledge that all that we have ever deserved from God's hand is his wrath and punishment.

CHAPTER 10

In this chapter, Moses sets before them God's great mercy to them, despite their offenses against God. 1. He mentions various signs of God's favor and reconciliation toward them which they must never forget: the renewing of the tablets of the covenant (vv. 1–5); the giving of orders for their progress toward Canaan (vv. 6–7); the choice of the tribe of Levi as his own (vv. 8–9) to continue the priesthood after the death of Aaron (v. 6); and the acknowledgment and acceptance of the intercession of Moses for them (vv. 10–11). 2. From all these, he reasons what obligations they were under to fear, love, and serve God (vv. 12–22).

Verses 1–11

God showed that he was reconciled to Israel by means of four things, which made them truly great and blessed:

1. He gave them his Law; he gave it to them in writing, as a constant pledge of his favor. God's putting his Law into our hearts and writing it on our inner beings provides the best evidence of our reconciliation to him and the most certain sign of our blessedness in him. God will send his Law and Gospel to those whose hearts are prepared like arks to receive them. Christ is the ark in which our salvation is now kept safely, so that it may not be lost as it was in the First Adam, when he was responsible for it. These two tablets, engraved in this way, were faithfully placed in the ark. *And there they be,* they are there now, said Moses, probably pointing toward the sanctuary (v. 5). He passed on to the people the good thing which was committed to him and left it whole and pure in their hands. Let them look to it now or suffer the consequences. And so we can say to the rising generation, "God has entrusted us with Bibles, Sabbaths, his holy services, etc., as signs of his presence and favor. They are there; we leave them with you" (2Ti 1:13–14).

2. He led them forward toward Canaan, though in their hearts they turned back toward Egypt, so that he might justly have let them follow their delusions (vv. 6–7).

3. He appointed a constant ministry among them to serve them in holy things. This shows us that a settled ministry is a great blessing to a people and a special sign of God's favor. Under the Law, a succession in the ministry was maintained by the office being passed on as an inheritance to a certain tribe and family. But now under the Gospel, when the Spirit has been poured out more plentifully

and powerfully, the succession is maintained by the Spirit's activity in human hearts, qualifying people for, and inclining them to, that work, certain ones in every age.

4. He accepted Moses as an advocate or intercessor for them, and so made him their ruler and leader (vv. 10–11): *The Lord hearkened to me and said, Arise, go before the people.* It was a mercy to them that they had such a friend, faithful both to the One who appointed him and also to those whom he was appointed to serve.

Verses 12–22

Here is a very powerful encouragement to obedience:

1. We are taught our duty to God, our neighbor, and ourselves:

1.1. We are taught our duty to God. We must *fear the Lord our God* (v. 12 and again v. 20). We must fear him as a great God and Lord, and love him as a good God and Father and most generous giver. We must *serve him* (v. 20), *serve him with all our heart and soul* (v. 12). What we do for him we must do cheerfully and with a good will. We must *keep his commandments and his statutes* (v. 13).

1.2. We are taught our duty to our neighbor (v. 19): *Love the stranger* (foreigner), and if we are to love foreigners, then how much more should we love our brothers and sisters as ourselves? Two arguments are here urged to back up this responsibility:

1.2.1. God's common providence, which reaches out to every country, since everyone is made of the same flesh and blood. God *loveth the stranger* (v. 18), that is, to all people he gives life, and breath, and everything, even to those who are Gentiles and foreigners to citizenship in Israel and to Israel's God.

1.2.2. The suffering which the Israelites themselves had experienced, when they had been foreigners in Egypt. Those who themselves have been in distress and have found mercy with God should sympathize most dearly with those who are in a similar distress and should be ready to show kindness to them. However, the Jews developed a deep-rooted hatred toward the Gentiles, and this finally brought destruction on the Jews themselves.

1.3. We are taught our duty to ourselves (v. 16): *Circumcise the foreskin of your hearts,* that is, "Drive out all sinful desires and inclinations which hinder you from fearing and loving God." The circumcision of the heart makes it ready to submit to God and his discipline.

2. We are very powerfully persuaded to do our duty. If reason rules us, then our religious faith will. Therefore:

2.1. Consider the greatness and glory of God, and so fear him. Let that be a great motivation for you to serve and obey him.

2.2. Consider the goodness and grace of God, and so love him. Let that too be a great motivation for you to serve and obey him. His goodness is his glory as much as his greatness.

CHAPTER 11

With this chapter, Moses concludes his introduction to the repetition of the laws and decrees which they must observe. He repeats the general command (v. 1), and having at the end of the previous chapter begun to mention the great things God had done among them, in this chapter: 1. He specifies several great works which God had done before their eyes (vv. 2–7). 2. He sets before them for the future, life and death, the blessing and the curse, according to whether they would keep, or not keep, God's commandments (vv. 8–17, 22–25). 3. He directs them how they might keep God's law in their minds (vv. 18–21). 4. He concludes with solemnly commanding them to choose which they wanted: the blessing or curse (vv. 26–32).

Verses 1–7

They are to *keep his charge* (v. 1), that is, the commands of his word and the ordinances of his worship, with which they were entrusted and for which they were responsible. It is a phrase often used concerning the office of the priests and Levites, for all Israel was a kingdom of priests, a holy nation. Notice the link between these two: *Thou shalt love the Lord* and *keep his charge* (v. 1), since love will work out in obedience, and the only acceptable obedience is what is motivated by love (1Jn 5:3).

Verses 8–17

1. Moses continues on the same subject, being reluctant to finish until he has made his point firmly. *"If thou wilt enter into life* (Mt 19:17), if you want to enter into Canaan, which is a type of that life, and you find it to be a good land, keep the commandments: Keep all the commandments which I command you this day* (v. 8). Love God and serve him with all your heart."

2. Moses does not set about teaching them the art of warfare, how to draw the bow, use the sword, and keep ranks, so that they might be strong and go in and possess the land. No; the way to be strong and successful is to stay true to God's commandments and to their religious faith. Sin tends to reduce the days of individual people and to reduce the days of a people's prosperity. Obedience, however, will extend their tranquillity. This teaches us that the better God has provided for our outward condition and our comforts, the more zealous we should be to serve him. The less we have to do for our bodies, the more we should do for God and our souls.

3. To wake them up to the fact that they must be careful, Moses tells them clearly that if they were to *turn aside to other gods* (v. 16):

• They would cause God to be angry with them.
• Good things would be turned away from them. Heaven would withhold its rain, and then the earth would not yield its fruit.

Verses 18–25

1. Moses repeats the directions he had given to guide and help the people in their obedience. Let us all be guided by the three rules given here:

1.1. Let our hearts be filled with the word of God: *Lay up these words in your heart and in your soul* (v. 18).

1.2. Let our eyes be fixed on the word of God. Bind these words as a sign *upon your hand*, which is always in view (Isa 49:16), *and as frontlets* (symbols) *between your eyes* (v. 18).

1.3. Let us talk about the word of God. Let it be the subject of our ordinary speech, wherever we are, especially with our children.

2. Moses repeats the assurances he had given them before, in God's name, of prosperity and success if they were obedient. Nothing leads more to the international significance of a country, to its being valuable to its friends and formidable to its enemies, than to have religious faith reigning in it, for who can be against people who have God for them? And he is definitely on the side of those who sincerely follow him (Pr 14:34).

Verses 26–32

Moses concludes his general encouragements to obedience:

1. He sums up all his arguments for obedience in two words, *the blessing and the curse* (v. 26). The promise of blessing and the threat of curse lay hold of hope and fear, the two handles of the soul, by which our lives are restrained, kept, and managed.

2. He appoints a public and formal declaration to be made of the blessing and curse which he had set before them, on the two mountains of Gerizim and Ebal (vv. 29–30). We have more detailed directions for this ceremony in 27:11–28:68 and an account of its performance in Jos 8:33. It was to be done, and was done, immediately on their coming into Canaan, so that when they first took possession of that land they might know on what terms they stood.

CHAPTER 12

In this chapter, Moses comes to the particular statutes which he had to command Israel about. He begins with those that relate to the worship of God, and particularly those which explain the second commandment, about which God is especially jealous: 1. They must utterly destroy all relics and remnants of idolatry (vv. 1–3). 2. They must keep close to the tabernacle (vv. 4–5). The former command was intended to prevent all false worship; the latter to preserve the worship God had instituted. By this latter law they are commanded to bring all their offerings to the altar of God, and all their holy things to the place which he would choose (vv. 6–32).

Verses 1–4

From those great original truths, that there is a God, and that there is only one God, come those great fundamental laws, that God is to be worshiped, and only he. We are therefore to have no other God before him: this is the first commandment. The second commandment is a means of protecting and guarding the first. To prevent us from turning to false gods, the true God forbids us to worship him in such a way as the false gods were worshiped. We are commanded to observe the instituted ways of worship so that we may continue to observe the proper object of worship. For this reason, Moses is very detailed in his explanation of the second commandment. What is contained in this and the four following chapters refers mostly to that.

1. They are commanded to abolish and destroy all those things that the Canaanites had served their idols with (vv. 2–3). The places that had been used, and were now to be destroyed, were enclosures for their worship on *mountains and hills*—as if the height of the ground might help their devotions rise—and under green trees, either because such places were pleasant or because they helped the worshipers to be reverent. He begins the decrees about divine worship with these, because they must first learn to detest what is evil before they can go on with what is good (Ro 12:9). The kingdom of God must be set up, both in people and in places, on the ruins of Satan's kingdom, for they cannot stand together, just as there can be no fellowship between Christ and Belial.

2. They are commanded not to transfer the rites and customs of idolaters to the worship of God. They might be tempted to do this in an attempt to make it more attractive (v. 4).

Verses 5–32

There is not any one particular command, as far as we can recall, in all the Law of Moses, which is so insisted on and instilled as this one, by which the people are all committed to bring their sacrifices to that one altar which was set up in the court of the tabernacle, and there to perform all the ceremonies of their religion. As regards other spiritual duties, people could no doubt, then as now, pray everywhere, as the Jews later did in their synagogues. But this command concerns the sacrifices and ceremonies of worship, and it is repeated, along with the prohibition of the contrary:

- Because of the strange inclination in the hearts of the people to idolatry and superstition.
- Because of the great use which the observance of this appointment would be to preserve unity and mutual love among them, that by meeting all together in one place, they might continue to be united in their ways and their hearts.
- Because of the significance of this appointment. They must keep to one place as a sign of their belief of those two great truths, which we find together (1Ti 2:5), that *there is one God*, and *one mediator between God and man*.

Let us now consider this command under different headings:

1. It is promised here that when they had settled in Canaan, when they had *rest from their enemies, and dwelt in safety*, God would choose a certain place, which he would appoint to be the center of their unity, to which they should bring all their offerings (vv. 10–11). He does not choose the place now, as he had appointed Mounts Gerizim and Ebal for declaring the blessings and curses (11:29), but keeps back from doing that till later, so that they might expect further directions from heaven and divine guidance after Moses died. The ark was the sign of God's presence, and where that was put, there God put his name, and that was his dwelling place. The place which God first chose for the ark was in Shiloh, and after that place had had this honor removed because of its sin, we find the ark at Kiriath Jearim and other places, but eventually in David's time, it was established in Jerusalem, and God expressed himself more explicitly about Solomon's temple than he had ever done about any other place, *This I have chosen for a house of sacrifice* (2Ch 7:12). Compare 2Ch 6:5. Now under the Gospel we have no temple that sanctifies the gold, no altar that sanctifies the gift, but only Christ, and as to the places of worship, the prophets foretold that *in every place* the spiritual *incense should be offered* (Mal 1:11). Our Savior has in fact declared that those who worship God in spirit and truth are accepted as true worshipers, without regard either to this mountain or Jerusalem (Jn 4:23).

2. They are commanded to bring all their burnt offerings and sacrifices to the place that God would choose (v. 6 and again v. 11).

3. They are commanded to feast on their holy things with holy joy before the Lord. If we glorify God, we edify ourselves and, through his grace, cultivate our own minds by increasing our knowledge and faith, inspiring our devout affections, and confirming our godly habits and decisions. The soul is nourished in this way.

3.1. While they were before the Lord they must rejoice (v. 12). It is the will of God that we should serve him gladly. No one displeased him more than those that *covered his altar with tears* (Mal 2:13). See what a good Master we serve, who has made it our duty to sing at our work.

3.2. It would seem that while they were in the desert, they did not eat the meat of any of those kinds of animals that were used as sacrifices, except what was killed at the door of the tabernacle (the entrance to the Tent of Meeting), part of which was presented to God as a peace offering (fellowship offering) (Lev 17:3–4). But when they came to Canaan, where they had to live far away from the tabernacle, they could kill whatever they pleased for their own use from their flocks and herds, without bringing a part to the altar. They must not eat blood (v. 16 and again v. 23). When they could not bring the blood to the altar, they must pour it out on the earth, as not belonging to them, because it was the life. In so doing they acknowledged: that it was the life; that it belonged to God, who gives life; and that also as an atonement it belonged to God, to whom life is surrendered. Bishop Patrick thinks one reason why they were so strictly forbidden from eating the blood was to prevent the superstitions held by former idolaters, who thought that their demons delighted in the eating of blood and who imagined that in the eating of it they had fellowship with those demons.

3.3. Never was there a better ruler than Moses, and you would never have thought never a better opportunity of keeping good order and discipline among the people of Israel than now, when they were camped so closely under the eye of their ruler. It seems, however, that there was much that was wrong and that many irregularities had crept in among them. But, Moses says, when you come to Canaan, you *shall not do as we do here* (v. 8). When the people of God are in an unsettled condition, certain things may be tolerated and dispensed with which would not be tolerated at all at another time. Moses was now about to lay down his life and leadership, and it was an encouragement to him to foresee that Israel would be better under a future leadership than they had been under his.

CHAPTER 13

In this chapter, Moses warns the people against the possibility of idolatry arising among themselves. They must make sure that they are not drawn into idolatry: 1. Under the pretense of prophecy (vv. 1–5). 2. Under the pretense of friendship and relationships (vv. 6–11). 3. Under the pretense of numbers (vv. 12–18).

Verses 1–5

Here is:

1. A very unusual case considered (vv. 1–2):

1.1. It is unusual that someone pretending to have a vision or prophecy would appear among them and entice them to *go and serve other gods* (vv. 6, 13). Could an Israelite ever be guilty of such ungodliness? We see it in our own day and so may think it less unusual: many who profess both learning and religious faith encouraging themselves and others not only to worship God by means of idols, but also to give divine honor to saints and angels.

1.2. It is considered here in order to strengthen them against the danger of impostors and counterfeit miracles (2Th 2:9).

2. A very necessary command given:

2.1. Not to give in to the temptation: "*Thou shalt not hearken to the words of that prophet* (v. 3). Not only are you not to do what the prophet tempts you to, but you are also not even to listen to the temptation. It is so detestable that you are to reject it scornfully. Keep close to following your God-given duty, and keep out of harm's way. God never leaves us until we leave him."

2.2. Not to spare the tempter (v. 5). They must keep the infection from spreading by cutting off the gangrened limb and by putting away the evildoers. Such dangerous diseases as these must be nipped in the bud and dealt with strictly.

Verses 6–11

In this part of the decree further provision is made against being defiled by idolatry from those who are near and dear to us. Satan tempted Adam through Eve and he tempted Christ through Peter.

Verses 12–18

Here the case is considered of a city rebelling against its allegiance to the God of Israel *and serving other gods* (v. 13).

1. The crime is supposed as having been committed:
1.1. By one of the cities of Israel, which lay within the jurisdiction of their courts. The city here considered to have become idolatrous is one that formerly worshiped the true God, but had now withdrawn to follow other gods. The treatment here give to this case shows how great the crime is.
1.2. By most of the inhabitants of the city; by *certain men, the children of Belial* (v. 13). Belial stands for the Devil (2Co 6:15), and the children of Belial are his children.
2. The case is to be considered very carefully (v. 14): *Thou shalt inquire and make search.*
3. If the crime was proved and the criminals were unrepentant, the city was to be wholly destroyed. If there were a few righteous in it, no doubt they would move themselves and their families out of such a dangerous place. The faithful worshipers of the true God must take every occasion to show their righteous indignation against idolatry, and not only idolatry but also atheism, godlessness, and ungodliness. They might think it unwise and against the interests of their nation to destroy a whole city because of a crime which was "only religious," and that they should be more sparing of the blood of Israelites, but Moses says, "Do not be afraid of that. God will multiply you all the more; the main part of your nation will lose nothing by shedding this sinful blood." Though idolaters may escape human punishment—and this letter of the law is not binding now under the Gospel—the Lord our God will not allow them to escape his righteous judgments.

CHAPTER 14

In this chapter, Moses teaches the people: 1. That they must set themselves apart from their neighbors by being different from all the nations around them in their mourning (vv. 1–2) and in what they eat (vv. 3–21). 2. That they are to devote themselves to God, and, as a sign of that, to give him what is due to him from their produce, both the yearly tithe and the tithe due every third year for the maintenance of their religious feasts, the Levites, and the poor (vv. 22–29).

Verses 1–21

Moses tells the people of Israel:
1. How God had honored them as his own people with three special privileges:
1.1. The privilege of election: *The Lord hath chosen thee* (v. 2). He did not choose them because they were a more dedicated and submissive people than other nations, but he chose them that they might be so by his grace.

1.2. The privilege of adoption (v. 1): "*You are the children of the Lord your God,* formed by him into a people, recognized by him as his people. In fact, you are his family, *a people near unto him* (Ps 148:14), closer than any other."
1.3. The privilege of sanctification (v. 2): "*Thou art a holy people,* set apart for God, devoted to his service, designed for his praise, governed by a holy law, and graced by a holy tabernacle and its holy ordinances."
2. How they ought to set themselves apart by being different from all the nations around them. The Septuagint (a Greek version of the Old Testament) reads it as a command, "Be the children of the Lord your God" (v. 1), that is, "Behave in a way that is characteristic of the children of God. Do nothing to disgrace the honor and cause the privileges of the relationship to be withdrawn." They must set themselves apart particularly in two things:
2.1. In their mourning: *You shall not cut yourselves* (v. 1). Some think this prohibits them not only from cutting themselves at their funerals, either to express their grief or to try to satisfy the deities of hell with their own blood, but also from mutilating and slashing themselves in the worship of their gods, as Baal's prophets did (1Ki 18:28). But it means at least that they are forbidden from disturbing and afflicting their own minds with excessive grief at the loss of their close and dear relatives. We who have a God to hope in and a heaven to hope for must encourage ourselves with that hope when we face burdens of this kind.
2.2. In what they eat. Notice:
2.2.1. They must religiously abstain from many kinds of flesh which were wholesome enough and which other people commonly ate but which were ceremonially unclean:
2.2.1.1. Here is a more detailed listing of those animals which they were allowed to eat than was in Leviticus.
2.2.1.2. There is only one general rule given concerning fish, that whatever did not have fins and scales, such as shellfish and eels—as well as leeches and other animals that live in the water but are not proper food—was *unclean* and forbidden (vv. 9–10).
2.2.1.3. No general rule is given concerning birds, but those are particularly mentioned which were to be ceremonially unclean to them. There are few or none which are forbidden here that are commonly eaten now.
2.2.1.4. They are further prohibited from:

- Eating the flesh of any creature which they found already dead, because the blood was not separated from it; and, besides being under a ceremonial uncleanness (Lev 11:39), it is not wholesome food.
- *Seething a kid* (cooking a young goat) *in its mother's milk* (v. 21), either to please their own fancies, or to go along with some superstitious custom of another religion.

2.2.2. Now as to all these commands concerning their food:
2.2.2.1. It is clear in the Law itself that they belonged only to the Jews, were not moral, and were not intended to last forever, because not everyone was universally obliged to keep them. The Israelites could give to a stranger what they were not permitted to eat themselves. Or they could sell it to a foreigner, a Gentile, who came to their country on business.
2.2.2.2. It is clear in the Gospel that these laws are now outdated and have been repealed. For *every creature of God is good, and nothing now to be refused,* or called common and unclean (1Ti 4:4).

Verses 22–29

We have here part of the statute concerning tithes. The products of the ground were tithed twice, so that by putting both together, the people devoted to God a fifth out of their produce, and only four-fifths was for their own ordinary use. The first tithe was given to maintain their Levites. But it is the second tithe that is spoken of here, which was to be taken out of the remainder when the Levites had had theirs:

1. They are commanded to set it apart for God: *Thou shalt truly tithe all the increase of thy seed* (v. 22).

2. They are instructed as to how they should use it when they had set it apart. This second tithe was to be:

• Used in godly works for the first two years after the year of release.

• Distributed at home in works of charity every third year (vv. 28–29): *Lay it up within thy own gates*. Let it be given to the poor. "Let them come there, eat, and be satisfied."

CHAPTER 15

In this chapter, Moses gives orders about: 1. The cancellation of debts every seventh year (vv. 1–6), with a warning that this should not hinder their charitable lending (vv. 7–11). 2. The release of servants after seven years' service (vv. 12–18). 3. The sanctification of the firstborn of their cattle to God (vv. 19–23).

Verses 1–11

Here is:

1. A law to relieve poor debtors. Every seventh year was a year of cancellation or release, in which the ground had a rest from cultivation and servants were released from their service. Among other acts of grace, this was one which said that those who had borrowed money and had not been able to pay it back before should be released from it in that year. If they were able, they were afterward bound by their consciences to repay it, but from that time on, a creditor could never recover it by law. Some commentators think this law only forbids exacting repayment of debt in the year of cancellation, because no harvest was gathered that year and it could not be expected that people would repay their debts then, but afterward it might be pursued and recovered. This meant that the cancellation did not wipe out the debt, but only delayed its repayment for a time. Other commentators think it was a cancellation of the debt forever, and this seems more probable. The law is not that the creditor will not receive the debt, if the debtor or the debtor's friends can pay it, but that the creditor will not exact it by a legal process. The reasons for this law are:

1.1. To honor the sabbatical year: *Because it is called the Lord's release* (v. 2).

1.2. To prevent any Israelite from falling into extreme poverty; and so the margin reads (v. 4), "To the end that there be no poor among you."

1.3. To give a security from God, by way of his promise that whatever they lost by their poor debtors would be made up to them in God's blessing on all they had and did (vv. 4–6).

2. A law in favor of poor borrowers, so that they might not suffer harm from the law of the year of release:

2.1. It is assumed that there would be poor among them, who would have occasion to borrow (v. 7), and that there would never cease to be some who needed such charity (v. 11).

2.2. In such cases, the command here is to lend or give according to our ability and the need: *Thou shalt not harden thy heart, nor shut thy hand* (v. 7). You are to *open thy hand wide unto him,* to *lend him sufficient* (v. 8). Furthermore, sometimes there is as much love in wise lending as in giving, as it makes the borrower work hard and honestly, so that they learn to help themselves. When we have occasion to lend charitably, if we cannot trust the borrower, we must trust God and lend without expecting to get anything back in this world, but expecting it to be repaid at the resurrection of the righteous (Lk 6:35; 14:14).

3. A command to give cheerfully whenever we give in charity: *Thy heart shall not be grieved when thou givest* (v. 10).

Verses 12–18

Here is:

1. A repetition of the law that had been given concerning Hebrew servants who had sold themselves as servants, or who were sold by their parents through extreme poverty, or were sold by a law court for some crime committed. The law was:

1.1. That they should serve only six years, and should go free in the seventh (v. 12). Compare Ex 21:2. And if the Year of Jubilee came round before they served out their time, they would then be released.

1.2. That if when their six years' service had expired, they did not want to go free, but preferred to continue in service, they must put themselves under an obligation to serve forever, that is, for life, by having *their ears bored to the door posts* (vv. 16–17).

2. An addition to this law, requiring the masters to give some supplies to their servants to help them set themselves up when they left their masters' service (vv. 13–14).

Verses 19–23

Here is:

1. A repetition of the law concerning the firstborn of their cattle.

2. An addition to that law, to explain it further, directing them what to do with the firstborn that were:

2.1. Females: "You are to *do no work with the* female *firstlings of the cow,* nor shear those of the sheep" (v. 19).

2.2. Blemished, for example, blind or lame, or something more serious (v. 21). Whether it was male or female, it must not be brought near the sanctuary or used as a sacrifice or in a holy festival, for it would not be right to honor God with something defective. What a mercy it is that we are not weighed down with this burden! Our food is not prescribed as theirs was; we make no difference between a first calf or lamb and others which follow. Let us therefore realize the Gospel meaning of this law, giving ourselves and the first part of our time and strength to God, as a kind of firstfruits of his creation.

CHAPTER 16

In this chapter, we have: 1. A repetition of the laws concerning the three yearly feasts, in particular, Passover (vv. 1–8), Pentecost (vv. 9–12), and the Feast of Tabernacles (vv. 13–15); and the general law concerning the people's presence at them (vv. 16–17). 2. The institution of a lesser judiciary system, and the general rules of justice given to those called to that office (vv. 18–20); and a warning against groves and idols (vv. 21–22).

Verses 1–17

The three yearly feasts maintained fellowship between God and his people Israel and preserved an outward appearance of religion in the nation. Several times we have met with the institution and the laws of these feasts. They are repeated here:

1. They must observe the law of the Passover, which was such a great ceremony that it gave significance to the whole month that it came in the middle of: *Observe the month of Abib* (v. 1). Though only one week of this month was to be kept as a festival, their preparations for it, their reflections on it, and their resolutions after it were so serious that they amounted to an observance of the whole month. The laws concerning it are:

1.1. That they must be sure to sacrifice the Passover in the place where God would choose (v. 2) and in no other place (vv. 5–7).

1.2. That they must eat unleavened bread for seven days, and no leavened bread must be seen in their territory (vv. 3–4, 8). The apostle Paul gives us the Gospel meaning of this Feast of Unleavened Bread in the expression (1Co 5:7) *Christ our passover being sacrificed for us.* Because we receive strength and encouragement as we take part in the blessed fruits of that sacrifice, *let us keep the feast* (v. 10) in holy living, free from *the leaven of malice* toward our brothers and sisters and free from hypocrisy toward God, and *with the unleavened bread of sincerity* (1Co 5:8) and love.

2. Seven weeks after the Passover, the Feast of Pentecost (the Feast of Weeks) was to be observed. They must *bring an offering unto God* (v. 10). It is here called a *tribute of a freewill offering.* The Law did not specify the amount, but it was left to everyone's generosity to bring what they chose. But whatever they did bring must be given cheerfully, and so it is called *a freewill offering.*

3. They must keep the Feast of Tabernacles (vv. 13–15). When we express our joy in God ourselves, we should do what we can to help others also to express their joy in him, by comforting the mourners and providing for the needy, so that even *the stranger, the fatherless, and the widow may rejoice with us* (v. 11). See also Job 29:13. Those who make God their joy may *rejoice in hope* (Ro 5:2), for he who has promised is faithful.

4. The laws concerning the three great festivals are summed up (vv. 16–17). The general commands concerning them are that all the males must come personally to God and that none must appear before God empty-handed, but every man must bring some offering or other.

Verses 18–22

Here:

1. They must make sure that justice is properly administered among them, so that disputes might be settled, matters of conflict dealt with, the wronged compensated, and those who commit the wrongs punished. While they were camped in the desert, they had *judges and officers* (v. 18) according to their numbers, officials over thousands and hundreds (Ex 18:25). When they came to Canaan, they must have them in their *gates*, their towns and cities, for the law courts met in the gates.

2. They must make sure that they do not conform in any way to the idolatrous customs of the nations (vv. 21–22). They must not plant a grove or even a tree near God's altar, so that they would not make it look like the altars of the false gods. Nothing tends more to corrupt and deprave the human mind, than to use idols to represent and worship the God who is an infinite and eternal Spirit.

CHAPTER 17

The commands of this chapter concern: 1. The purity and perfection of all the animals offered in sacrifice (v. 1). 2. The punishment of the people who worshiped idols (vv. 2–7). 3. Appeals from the lower courts to the higher court (vv. 8–13). 4. The choice and duties of a king (vv. 14–20).

Verses 1–7

Here is:

1. A law to preserve the honor of God's worship, by providing that no creature with any defect or flaw should be offered as a sacrifice to him (v. 1). Here we see that the Old Testament sacrifices had to be perfect because they were types of Christ, who is *a Lamb without blemish or spot* (1Pe 1:19). In the later times of the Jewish church, when they were curbed in their idolatry by the Captivity in Babylon, they were still charged with breaking this law, with *offering the blind, and the lame, and the sick for sacrifice* (Mal 1:8).

2. A law to punish those who worshiped false gods.

2.1. What is specified—the worship of the sun, moon, and stars—was the oldest and most plausible form of idolatry, but if that was so detestable, then how much more would it be to worship mere blocks of wood, slabs of stone, or representations of the lowly animals? Where such a crime was suspected, the people must investigate the matter and bring evidence, including the testimony of at least two witnesses. In so doing they would acknowledge both that the crime was very detestable and that, however detestable and awful it was, no one must be punished for it unless there was solid proof against them.

2.2. With proof, such an extreme punishment as death and such an extreme form of death as stoning must be inflicted on the idolater, whether man or woman, for the excuse of being a woman was not accepted (v. 5). The hands of the witnesses, in this as in other cases, must be the first to be laid on the offender, that is, they must be the first to throw a stone at the offender. This meant that they confirmed their testimony and solemnly invoked the guilt of the offender's blood on themselves if their evidence were false. This custom was meant to deter people from giving false testimony.

Verses 8–13

Law courts were ordered to be set up in every town (16:18), and they were given authority to hear and decide cases according to the Law, both criminal law and civil law. It is probable that they settled the matters brought before them and their sentence was definitive, but it is assumed here that sometimes a case might come to their court that was too difficult for these lower judges to decide. These difficult cases, which according to Jethro's advice up to that time had been brought to Moses, were after Moses' death to be brought to the supreme authority, wherever it was vested, whether in a judge (when an extraordinary person was raised up and qualified for that great service, such as Othniel, Deborah, or Gideon) or in the high priest (when he, because of the greatness of his gifts, was called by God to lead in public affairs, such as Eli). Alternatively, if no single person was chosen by God for this honor, then this authority was given to the priests and Levites.

Verses 14–20

After the laws which concerned subjects, it is appropriate that they are given laws which concern kings, for those who rule others must themselves remember that they are under a command. Here are laws given:

1. To the electors, about what rules they must go by in making their choice (vv. 14–15):

1.1. It is thought that the people would in due time want a king, whose royal pomp and power would be thought of as making their nation look great among their neighbors.

1.2. They are directed in their choice. If they wanted to have a king over them, as God foresaw they would—though it does not appear that the suggestion was made till almost 400 years later—then they must:

1.2.1. Ask for God's guidance and make the man whom God chooses their king. Accordingly, when the people wanted a king, they turned to Samuel, a prophet of the Lord; and afterward David, Solomon, Jeroboam, Jehu, and others were chosen by the prophets.

1.2.2. Not choose a foreigner under pretense of strengthening their alliances. The reason for this is that God did not want a foreign king to introduce foreign customs.

2. To the king who would be elected, about how to administer the government properly:

2.1. He must carefully avoid everything that would distract him from God and religion. Riches, honors, and pleasures are the three great hindrances of godliness (*the lusts of the flesh, the lusts of the eye, and the pride of life*, 1Jn 2:16), especially to those in high positions: the king is therefore warned against these.

2.2. He must know the Law of God thoroughly and make that his rule for life. This must be more important to him than all riches, honors, and pleasures, than many horses or many wives, better than vast sums of gold and silver.

2.2.1. He must himself write out a copy of the Law from the original, which was kept by the priests who served in the sanctuary (v. 18). We can learn from this that we will find it very useful if we write down what builds us up spiritually, from the Scriptures, good books, and sermons we hear. Writing words of wisdom may go far toward making up for any deficiencies in our memory, and it will also fill our storerooms so that we can bring out new treasures and old (Mt 13:52).

2.2.2. His writing and reading were all meaningless if he did not put into practice what he wrote and read (vv. 19–20). May the king know what authority his religious faith must have over him, and what influence it must have on him:

• It must give him a reverent and fearful regard for God's majesty and authority.
• It must draw him to constantly and conscientiously observe God's Law because of that fear.
• It must keep him humble. However advanced he is, may he keep his spirit low, and let him not think he is better than his people.

CHAPTER 18

In this chapter: 1. The rights and income of the church are established, and rules are given concerning the Levites' ministry and maintenance (vv. 1–8). 2. The warning against the detestable, idolatrous customs of the nations is repeated (vv. 9–14). 3. A promise is given to them that the spirit of prophecy would continue among them, which would finally center on Christ, the great Prophet (vv. 15–18); wrath is threatened against those who despise prophecy (v. 19) or falsify it (v. 20), and a rule is given to test the false prophet (vv. 21–22).

Verses 1–8

The judiciary and ministry are two divine institutions that support and advance the kingdom of God among the human race. We had laws concerning the former at the end of the previous chapter, and directions concerning the latter are given in this chapter. Boundaries are put here between the possessions of the priests and those of the people:

1. Care is taken that the priests do not get involved in worldly matters, or become rich with the wealth of this world; they are to be concerned with better things.

2. Care is similarly taken that they should not lack any of the comforts and conveniences of this life. Though God, who is a Spirit, is their inheritance, it does not therefore follow that they must live on nothing material. The people must provide for them. They must receive their *due from the people* (v. 3). Their maintenance must not depend on the generosity of the people, but by the Law they are entitled to it.

Verses 9–14

You would not have thought it would have been so necessary to strengthen the people of Israel against the defilements of the idolatrous customs of the Canaanites. Yet after many warnings, they are commanded here once again not to imitate the detestable practices of those nations (v. 9):

1. Some details are mentioned, such as:

1.1. The sacrificing of their children to Molech, an idol that represented the sun, by making them *pass through the fire*, and sometimes consuming them as sacrifices in the fire (v. 10). We had the law against this before (Lev 18:21).

1.2. Using divination to try to obtain unnecessary knowledge of things to come, for example, *enchantments* (sorcery), *witchcraft*, and *charms* (casting spells).

2. Some reasons are given against following the practices of the Gentiles:

2.1. Because it would make them detestable to God.

2.2. Because these detestable practices had led to the destruction of the Canaanites. They were not only witnesses to but also instruments of this destruction.

2.3. Because they were better taught (vv. 13–14). It is a similar argument to the one the apostle Paul uses against Christians living as the Gentiles do (Eph 4:17–18, 20): *You have not so learned Christ.*

Verses 15–22

Here is:

1. The promise of the great Prophet, with a command to receive him and listen to him.

1.1. Some think it is the promise of a succession of prophets, who would be maintained in Israel for many years. As well as the priests and Levites—their ordinary ministers, whose office it was to teach Israel God's Law—they would have prophets, extraordinary ministers, to rebuke them for their faults, remind them of their duty, and foretell things to come, judgments to warn them and rescues to strengthen them.

1.2. Whether a succession of prophets is included in this promise or not, we are sure that it is primarily intended as a promise of Christ, and it is the clearest promise of him in the whole Law of Moses. It is explicitly applied to our Lord Jesus as the promised Messiah (Ac 3:22; 7:37), and the people considered this promise when they said concerning him, *This is of a truth that prophet that should come into the world* (Jn 6:14). It was his Spirit who spoke in all the other prophets (1Pe 1:11). It is also a command given to all people to hear, believe, and obey this great promised Prophet: *Unto him you shall hearken* (v. 15). Whoever will not listen to him will be severely dealt with for showing such disrespect (v. 19): *I will require it of him.*

2. A warning against false prophets. Whatever directly opposes common sense, the light and law of nature, and the plain meaning of the written word, is not, we may be sure, what the Lord has spoken. Similarly, we are to reject what supports or encourages sin or shows a clear tendency to undermine godliness or love.

CHAPTER 19

The laws which Moses had repeated and urged up to this time had mostly dealt with acts of religion and devotion toward God, but here he comes to urge more fully the duties of righteousness between human beings. This chapter concerns: 1. The sixth commandment, Thou shalt not kill *(vv. 1–13). 2. The eighth commandment,* Thou shalt not steal *(v. 14), and the ninth commandment,* Thou shalt not bear false witness *(vv. 15–21).*

Verses 1–13

One of the commands given to the sons of Noah was that *whoso sheddeth man's blood by man shall his blood be shed,* that is, by the avenger of blood (Ge 9:6). Here we have the law established between blood and blood, between the blood of the murdered and the blood of the murderer, and effective provision was made:

1. That the cities of refuge would function to protect someone who killed another person unintentionally, so that the person who killed the other would not die for a crime which was not deliberate but which was a most unfortunate event. Instructions are given for:

1.1. The appointing of three cities in Canaan for this purpose. The country was to be divided into three districts, and a city of refuge put at the center of each, so that every corner of the land might have one within reach.

1.2. The use to be made of these cities (vv. 4–6):

1.2.1. It is thought that it might happen that a person might unintentionally cause the death of their neighbor, not from a fit of rage or malice aforethought, but purely by accident, as for instance, if the head of an ax should fly off. Other cases were to be considered in the light of this example.

1.2.2. It is presumed that the relatives of the person killed would want to avenge the blood. Though the law did not allow the avenging of any other wrong or injury with death, a concession was made that the avenger of blood, the next of kin of the person who was killed, could kill the offender, even though the killing was accidental, and it would not be counted as murder if the avenger of blood did this before the offender reached the city of refuge.

1.2.3. It is provided that if an avenger of blood were to be so unreasonable as to demand satisfaction for blood shed only accidentally, then the city of refuge would protect the offender.

1.3. The appointing of three more cities to be used in this way if God later extended their territories and the authority of their religion, so that all those places which came under the jurisdiction of the Law of Moses might also enjoy the benefit of this law (vv. 8–10).

2. That the cities of refuge would not be a sanctuary or shelter to a deliberate murderer, but the murderer would be taken from there and handed over to the avenger of blood (vv. 11–13). Before the Reformation, there were some churches and religious houses which served as sanctuaries to protect all kinds of criminals who fled to them, not excluding intentional murderers, so that as Stamford says, in his *Pleas of the Crown,* the government followed not Moses but Rome, and it was not till about the end of Henry VIII's time that this privilege of sanctuary for intentional murder was taken away.

Verses 14–21

Here is a decree to prevent fraud and perjury, for God's Law takes care of and protects human rights and property:

1. A law against fraud (v. 14):

1.1. An implicit instruction is given to the first settlers in Canaan to set up boundary stones, according to the allotting of the land to the different tribes and families.

1.2. An explicit law is given to later generations not to remove the boundary stones. It prohibits us from:

1.2.1. Invading anyone's rights, and taking for ourselves what is not our own by any fraudulent practice, such as forgery; concealing, destroying, or altering deeds and other legal documents (which are kinds of boundary stones, and to which appeals are made); and moving boundary stones.

1.2.2. Sowing discord among neighbors, and doing anything which causes strife or legal action.

2. A law against perjury, which describes two situations:

2.1. That only one witness should never be allowed to give evidence in a criminal case, so that sentence should not be passed on that person's testimony alone (v. 15).

2.2. That a false witness would incur the same punishment which was to have been inflicted on the accused (vv. 16–21).

CHAPTER 20

This chapter establishes the militia and the laws and ordinances of war. It concerns: 1. The soldiers: those who were ready for battle must be encouraged (vv. 1–4); those whose personal affairs meant that they had to be at home must be discharged and sent home again (vv. 5–7), and so must those whose weakness and fearfulness made them unfit for service in the battlefield (vv. 8–9). 2. The enemies they made war with: the negotiations they must make with the cities that were far off (vv. 10–15); the destruction they must make of the people into whose land they were going (vv. 16–18); and the care they must take, in besieging cities, not to destroy the fruit trees (vv. 19–20).

Verses 1–9

Israel was at this time considered to be more like a camp than a kingdom, since they were entering on an enemy's country and not yet settled in a country of their own. Even after they had settled in their land, they could neither protect nor enlarge their territory without hearing the call to arms. It was therefore necessary that they be instructed about their military affairs.

1. Those who were willing to fight must be given encouragement and support even in their fears, and motivate themselves with two things in their minds:

1.1. The presence of God with them: *"The Lord thy God is with thee* (v. 1), and so you are not in danger, and you do not need to be afraid." See Isa 41:10.

1.2. The experience they and their fathers had had of God's power and goodness in *bringing them out of the land of Egypt* (v. 1), defying Pharaoh and all his powers: "Let not your hearts be tender" (v. 3, margin), sensitive to every fearful impression. Instead, be strengthened by a confident trust in the power and promises of God. "Fear not, and do not make haste" (v. 3, margin), for the proverb holds true, "The more haste, the less speed." "Do not make haste either rashly to anticipate your advantages or wrongly to flee at every disadvantage." This encouragement must be particularly addressed to the common soldiers by a priest who was appointed for that purpose. This shows:

1.2.1. That it is very important that armies should have chaplains, not only to pray for them, but also to preach to them, both to deal with anything which might prevent their success and also to raise their hopes of success.

1.2.2. That it is the work of Christ's ministers to encourage his good soldiers in their spiritual conflict with the world and the sinful nature, and to assure them that they are conquerors—in fact, more than conquerors—through Christ who loved us.

2. Those who were unwilling to fight must be discharged:

2.1. The Jewish writers agree that this freedom to return was allowed only in those wars which they made voluntarily, not those which were made at God's command against Amalek and the Canaanites, in which everyone had to fight.

2.2. If the man's unwillingness to fight came from a weakness of spirit, he was allowed to return from war (v. 8). It was partly out of kindness to such soldiers that they were discharged—and they no doubt felt ashamed, as well as relieved—but in fact it was more out of kindness to the rest of the army, because the remaining warriors were freed from being saddled with those who were useless. The danger of their cowardice spreading to others was also prevented.

3. It is ordered that when all the cowards had been dismissed, then *captains* (commanders) should be named (v. 9), for it was especially important that the leaders and commanders should be courageous.

Verses 10–20

They are directed here as to how to deal with the cities on which they made war. Only the cities are mentioned (v. 10), but doubtless the armies in the field and the nations they had to deal with are also intended. They must not launch an attack on any of their neighbors until they had first warned them and publicly declared the reasons for their quarrel.

1. An offer of terms of peace must form part of the declaration of war, to see if the enemy would accept it on reasonable terms. Israel must first declare peace to them. This shows:

1.1. God's grace in dealing with sinners: though he might justly and quickly destroy them, yet because he takes no pleasure in destroying them, he declares peace and begs them to be reconciled.

1.2. The responsibility we have in dealing with our brothers and sisters. If a quarrel should break out, then let us not only be ready to listen to proposals of peace, but also be bold in actually being first to make such proposals. We should never resort to legal action until we have first tried to sort out a conflict in a friendly way at no cost or trouble. *We* must be for peace, whoever else is for war.

2. If the offer of peace is not accepted, then they must go ahead with war.

3. The nations of Canaan are excluded from the merciful provisions of this law. Remnants might be left of the cities which were far away (v. 15), because Israel was not in so much danger of being defiled by their idolatry, but no remnants must be left of the inhabitants of the cities which were given to Israel as an inheritance (v. 16), because since it could not be expected that the Canaanites would be healed of their disease of idolatry, if they were allowed to live while still infected with it, they would be in danger of defiling God's Israel, who were very inclined to fall into this sin.

4. Care is taken here that when they laid siege to the cities they should not destroy their fruit trees (vv. 19–20). The intention of many of God's commands is to restrain us from destroying what we need and what is good for us. Armies and their commanders are not allowed to make what devastation they please in the countries that they are at war with. No fruit tree is to be destroyed unless it is barren and is using up the ground. The Jews maintain that this applies to any deliberate waste whatsoever, and that those who deliberately break a pot, tear clothes, stop up a well, pull down a building, or destroy food, break this law: *Thou shalt not destroy* (v. 19).

CHAPTER 21

In this chapter provision is made: 1. To put away the guilt of blood from the land, when the person who shed it had fled from justice (vv. 1–9). 2. To preserve the honor of a captive woman (vv. 10–14). 3. To secure the right of a firstborn son, even though he was not a favorite (vv. 15–17). 4. To restrain and punish a rebellious son (vv. 18–21) and to maintain the honor of human bodies, which must not be hanged in chains, but decently buried, even the bodies of the worst evildoers (vv. 22–23).

Verses 1–9

Care had been taken in the preceding laws to vigorously and effectively prosecute a deliberate murderer (19:11–13). When such a murderer was put to death, the guilt from the shedding of human blood was put away from the land. If this could not be done, however—if the murderer could not be discovered—they must not think that the land was not in danger of being defiled just because it was not through any neglect of theirs that the murderer was unpunished. A great ceremony is provided here to put away the guilt, to express their abhorrence of that sin.

1. The case described is that *one is found slain, and it is not known who slew him* (v. 1).

2. Directions are given concerning what is to be done in this case. The priests were to pray to God for the country and nation, that God would be merciful to them, and that he would not bring on them the judgments which involvement in the sin of murder would deserve.

Verses 10–14

This law permits a soldier to marry a captive woman if he so pleased. Moses gave them permission to do this because of the hardness of their hearts. Otherwise, if they had not been given this freedom, the men would have taken the liberty of defiling themselves with these women, and the camp would have been troubled by such evil. The man is thought to have a wife already, and to take this wife as "a secondary wife," as the Jews called them. This satisfying of a man's excessive desires, in which their hearts followed their eyes, does not in any way conform to the law of Christ, which in this respect among others is far more glorious than the Law of Moses.

Verses 15–17

This law restrains men from disinheriting their eldest sons out of a mere whim and without just provocation.

1. The case described here (v. 15) teaches us much:

1.1. It shows the great trouble caused by having more than one wife, a practice which the Law of Moses did not restrain.

1.2. It shows how Providence commonly sides with the weaker side, for the firstborn son is here presumed to be *hers that was hated* (v. 15). This was the situation in Jacob's family: *the Lord saw that Leah was hated* (Ge 29:31).

2. The law in this case is still binding on parents. They must be impartial in giving their children what is rightly due to them. In the case described here, although the eldest son is the son of the wife who is not loved, he must still have the privilege of his birthright. This privilege was a double portion of the father's estate, because he was born when his father was at the beginning of his strength. No son should be abandoned by his father until he clearly appears to be abandoned by God, which is hard to say of any as long as they live.

Verses 18–23

Here is:

1. A law to punish a rebellious son. The previous law provided that parents should not deprive their children of what was rightly due to them, and so it is appropriate that this law should make sure that children fulfill their duty to their parents by honoring them. Notice:

1.1. How the criminal is described. He is a *stubborn and rebellious son* (v. 18). A son was not to come off worse because he was weak or slow in understanding, but because he was willful and obstinate. He is particularly thought of (v. 20) as *a glutton or a drunkard*. This shows either:

- That these were sins which his parents warned him against particularly. Or:
- That these sins led to his defiance and obstinacy toward his parents. When people take to drink, they forget all the law (Pr 31:5), even the basic law of honoring their parents.

1.2. How this criminal is to be brought to justice. His own father and mother are to prosecute him (vv. 19–20).

1.3. What judgment is to be executed on the criminal: he must be publicly *stoned to death by the men of his city* (v. 21).

2. A law for the burial of the bodies of evildoers which had been hanged (v. 22). It was usually ordered by the judges, that the dead bodies of those who were stoned to death should hang on a post for some time on public display, to show how awful their crime was. The law provides here that whatever time of day the bodies were hanged up, at sunset they should be taken down and buried. Now:

2.1. God wanted in this way to preserve the honor of human bodies and to be humanitarian toward even the worst of criminals.

2.2. It is also clear that there was something ceremonial in it. According to the Law of Moses, contact with a dead body was defiling, and so dead bodies must not be left hanging up in the country, because by the same rule, this would defile the land.

2.3. *He that is hanged is accursed of God* (v. 23), that is, it is the most shameful disgrace that a human being can suffer, and it declares that they are under the curse of God as much as any outward punishment can. Those who see

him hang between heaven and earth will conclude that he has been abandoned by both and is not worthy of either, and so let him not hang all night, for that would take the matter too far.

CHAPTER 22

The laws of this chapter provide: 1. For the preservation of love and good neighborliness in looking after strayed or fallen cattle (vv. 1–4). 2. For the preservation of the distinction between men and women, that they should not wear one another's clothes (v. 5); and that other unnecessary mixtures should be avoided (vv. 9–11); for the preservation of birds (vv. 6–7); of life (v. 8); and of the commandments (v. 12). 3. For the preservation of the reputation of an abused wife, if she was innocent (vv. 13–19), but for her punishment if she was guilty (vv. 20–21). For the preservation of the purity of wives (v. 22) and of girls pledged to be married (vv. 23–27) or not (vv. 28–29); and lastly, a command against incest (v. 30).

Verses 1–4

The kindness that was commanded to be shown to an enemy (Ex 23:4–5) is required here to be shown even more to neighbors, although they are not Israelites.

1. Cattle which had strayed should be brought back, either to the owner or to the pasture from which they had strayed (vv. 1–2). If such care is to be taken of a neighbor's ox or donkey that has gone astray, then how much more care should be taken if we see our neighbor straying from God and the path of duty. We should do all we can to bring them back, to restore them (Jas 5:19), not forgetting ourselves (Gal 6:1).

2. Possessions that are lost should be brought back to the owner (v. 3). The Jews say, "The person who found the lost goods was to publicly announce it via the town crier three or four times."

Verses 5–12

These verses contain several laws which seem to deal with very lowly and minute details of life.

1. The sexes are to be kept distinct by their clothing, to keep pure our own lives and those of our neighbors (v. 5).

1.1. Some think this refers to the idolatrous custom of the Gentiles according to which, in the worship of Venus, women appeared in armor, and men in women's clothes.

1.2. This forbids the confusing of the roles and characters of the sexes. Probably this confusing of clothes had been used to allow opportunity for some to commit sexual immorality, and so it is forbidden.

2. In coming across a bird's nest, one must let the mother bird go (vv. 6–7). But *doth God take care* of birds (1Co 9:9)? Yes, of course he does. Perhaps our Savior alludes to this law: *Are not five sparrows sold for two farthings, and not one of them is forgotten before God?* (Lk 12:6). This law:

2.1. Forbids us to be cruel to animals or to take pleasure in destroying them.

2.2. Teaches us to be compassionate to those of our own kind and to hate the thought of everything that is cruel and wrong, especially in matters concerning women, who always ought to be treated with the greatest respect, because of the sorrow which they suffer in childbirth.

3. In building a house, one must take care to make it safe, so that no one might be injured by falling from it (v. 8). The roofs of Israelite houses were flat for people to walk on. The owners must surround them with parapets,

which the Jews say must be three and a half feet (about one meter) high. Notice here:

3.1. How precious human life is to God, who protects it not only by his providence, but also by his Law.

3.2. How precious, therefore, human life ought to be to us, and what care we should take to put a fence around, and remove obstacles from, everything which might endanger life, covering up deep wells, keeping bridges in a good state of repair, etc. We would do well to follow this example.

4. Odd mixtures are forbidden (vv. 9–10). We have read of this before (Lev 19:19). There does not appear to be anything at all immoral or evil in these things, and now we cheerfully sow wheat and rye together, plow with horses and oxen together, and wear clothes of wool and linen woven together, but in the Law of Moses these are forbidden either because they were an idolatrous custom of another religion, or because they were contrary to the pure and distinctive lives of Israelites. They must not satisfy their own vanity and curiosity by putting those things together which God in his infinite wisdom had separated.

5. The law concerning fringes (tassels) on their garments, to remind them of the commandments, which we had before (Nu 15:38–39), is repeated here (v. 12). These distinguished them from other people, so that it might be said when someone first saw them, "There goes an Israelite."

Verses 13–30

These laws relate to the seventh commandment, putting a restraint on those sinful desires which war against the soul, by imposing penalties:

1. If a man who sexually desires another woman wants to get rid of his wife and so slanders his wife and falsely accuses her, he must be punished if his slander is disproved (vv. 13–19). The closer anyone is in a personal relationship with us, the greater sin it is to tell lies about them and harm their reputation.

2. If the woman who was married as a virgin was in fact found not to have been one she was to be stoned to death at the door of her father's house (vv. 20–21). Now:

2.1. This gave a powerful warning to young women to avoid sexual immorality, since however much it was hidden before a marriage, it would probably be discovered afterward, to the couple's tragic loss and destruction.

2.2. Parents are shown that they must do all they can to preserve their children's purity, by giving them good advice, warning them, setting them good examples, keeping them from bad company, praying for them, and restraining them where necessary.

3. If any single or married man slept with a married woman, they were both to be put to death (v. 22). We had this law before (Lev 20:10).

4. If a girl was pledged to be married but was not yet married, she was not under the eye of her intended husband, and so she and her purity were taken under the special protection of the Law.

CHAPTER 23

The laws of this chapter provide: 1. For the preservation of the purity and honor of the families of Israel, by excluding those who would disgrace them (vv. 1–8). 2. For the preservation of the purity and honor of the camp of Israel when they went to battle (vv. 9–14). 3. For the encouragement and reception of slaves who fled to them

(vv. 15–16); for the prohibition of sexual immorality (vv. 17–18), of charging interest (vv. 19–20), and of breaking vows (vv. 21–23); and for determining what a person could take from a neighbor's field and vineyard, and what not (vv. 24–25).

Verses 1–8

Interpreters do not agree about what is meant here by *entering into the congregation of the Lord* (vv. 1–3), which is forbidden forever to eunuchs, people born illegitimately, Ammonites, and Moabites, but to Edomites and Egyptians only till the third generation.

1. Some think this means they are excluded from sharing with the people of God in their religious services.

2. Others think this means they are excluded from bearing office in the congregation.

3. Others think they are excluded only from marrying Israelites. It would seem that the men of Israel could marry the daughters of the nations of Canaan if the women were completely converted to the Jewish religion, but the men of these nations could not marry the daughters of Israel, and neither could those men be naturalized, except as provided for here.

Verses 9–14

Israel was now settled in their camp, and this vast army was about to enter into military action which was likely to keep them together for a long time, and so it was appropriate to give them detailed directions on how to keep their camp in good order. The command is, in a word, to be *clean.* They must take care to keep their camp pure from moral, ceremonial, and natural defilements:

1. From moral defilement (v. 9): *When the host* (army) *goes forth against thy enemy,* then make sure that you are especially committed to *keep thyself from every wicked thing.*

1.1. The soldiers themselves must beware of sin, for sin takes the edge off bravery; guilt turns soldiers into cowards. Soldiers must keep themselves from the idols or devoted things which they found in the camps they plundered.

1.2. Even every individual who stayed at home must also keep away from evil. Times of war should be times of reformation, for how else can we expect God to hear and answer our prayers for success (Ps 66:18)? See 1Sa 7:3.

2. From ceremonial defilement. This trouble and disgrace, which came upon the men even for nocturnal emissions, taught them to maintain a deep fear of all sinful desires.

3. From natural defilement caused by relieving oneself. The camp of the Lord must have nothing detestable in it (vv. 12–14). If such care must be taken to keep our bodies decent and clean, how much more should we be concerned to keep our minds like this too? This is the reason given here: *For the Lord thy God walketh* by his ark, the special sign of his presence, *in the midst of thy camp* (v. 14). Because of that external symbol, this external purity is required, which teaches us to preserve inward purity in our souls, because we know that God sees all we do.

Verses 15–25

Orders are given here about five different things which bear no relationship with one another:

1. The land of Israel is made a sanctuary, or a city of refuge, for slaves who had been wronged and abused by their masters and who had fled there for shelter from the neighboring countries (vv. 15–16).

1.1. It is honorable to shelter and protect the weak, provided they are not evil. The angel told Hagar to return to her mistress, and Paul sent Onesimus back to his master Philemon, because neither of them had any cause to go away, and neither was exposed to any danger by returning.

1.2. If it appeared that the slave had been unfairly taken advantage of, then the people must not only protect the slave, but if the slave wants to embrace their religion, the slave must be given every encouragement to settle among them.

2. The land of Israel must not become a shelter for the unclean. No prostitute or pimp must be allowed to live among them (vv. 17–18). No brothels must be kept by either men or women.

3. The matter of charging interest is settled here (vv. 19–20):

3.1. They must not charge an Israelite interest. It was seldom or never that they needed to borrow great sums. It was necessary to borrow at all only when they had to support their families, for example when they had a disastrous harvest one year. Where the borrower makes a profit, on the other hand, or hopes to make one, then in such situations it is fair that the lender should share in the gain. But where a person borrows to buy food and other necessities, compassion must be shown, and we must lend without expecting to get anything back, if we have the means to do so (Lk 6:35).

3.2. They could charge interest when lending to foreigners, those who engaged in business and who, as we put it, want to "earn a quick buck." They made a profit on what was borrowed and came among the Israelites hoping to do so. From this it seems that charging interest is not in itself oppressive, for they must not oppress foreigners, but could charge them interest.

4. The fulfillment of the vows which we have committed ourselves to is required:

4.1. We are free to choose whether to make a vow or not. God had already shown he would accept a freewill offering vowed in this way, even though it was only a little fine flour (Lev 2:4–7). But so that the priests, who had the largest share of those vows and voluntary offerings, would not sponge off the people, by pressing them to make such vows as their duty and beyond what they were able and willing to do, they are here explicitly told that it would not be counted as a sin if they did not make such vows.

4.2. We are here put under the highest obligation, that when we have made a vow, we are to fulfill it promptly.

5. A concession is given that when they passed through a grainfield or vineyard, they could pluck and eat the grain or grapes growing by the roadside. This law:

- Showed them they would have plenty of grain and wine in Canaan.
- Provided for the support of poor travelers, to relieve the tiredness of their journey.
- Teaches us not to insist on our ownership in small matters, of which it is easy to say, *What is that between me and thee?* (Ge 23:15).
- Got them used to hospitality.

CHAPTER 24

In this chapter, we have: 1. The toleration of divorce (vv. 1–4). 2. The releasing of newly married men from war (v. 5); laws: concerning pledges as security for debts (vv. 6, 10–13, 17), against kidnapping (v. 7),

and concerning leprosy (vv. 8–9). 3. Laws against the injustice of masters toward their servants (vv. 14–15); what judges should do in capital cases (v. 16) and civil matters (vv. 17–18); commands to be kind to the poor (vv. 19–22).

Verses 1–4

This is the permission which the Pharisees wrongly referred to as a command, when they said, *Moses commanded to give a writing of divorcement* (Mt 19:7). It was not so; our Savior told them that Moses only allowed it, because if they had not had the liberty to divorce their wives, men would have ruled them harshly, maybe causing their death. It is probable that divorces had been granted before—they are assumed in Lev 21:14—and Moses thought it necessary to give some rules concerning them:

1. That a man could not divorce his wife unless he *found some uncleanness* (indecency) *in her* (v. 1). It was not enough to say that he did not like her, or that he liked another woman more, but he must show cause for his dislike.

2. That divorce must be done, not by word of mouth, for that might be spoken in haste, but in writing, in the proper way, and formally declared before witnesses as a man's own act. This was something that could not be done rashly, but took time and allowed opportunity for consideration.

3. That the husband must hand to his wife a certificate of divorce and send her away. Some think this meant that he had to give her the resources to live.

4. That after she had been divorced, it was lawful for her to marry again (v. 2). The divorce had dissolved the bond of marriage as effectively as death could dissolve it. She was therefore free to marry again as if her first husband had died naturally.

5. That if her second husband died or divorced her, then still she might marry a third, but her first husband was not allowed to marry her again (vv. 3–4). The Jewish writers say that this was to prevent the Egyptians' evil practice of changing wives.

Verses 5–13

Here is:

1. Provision made to keep and confirm the love between newlyweds (v. 5). This appropriately follows the laws concerning divorce, which would be prevented if the couple's affection for each other was well established when they first got married. If the husband was away from his wife too much during the first year of their marriage, his love for her would be in danger of cooling off. He would be in danger of being drawn aside to other women whom he would meet with in his travels. So his service to his country in times of war, or the times when he was away on special missions or involved in other public business, should be dispensed with, *that he may cheer up the wife that he has taken* (v. 5).

1.1. It is very important that love should be maintained between a husband and wife.

1.2. One of the duties of that relationship is to bring happiness to each other in all the adversities of life, to encourage each other's joy, for happiness is a good medicine.

2. A law against kidnapping (v. 7). Stealing cattle or goods was not a capital offense under the Law of Moses, but kidnapping a child, a weak or vulnerable person, or one who was in someone else's custody and treating them

as a slave, was a capital crime. It was taking away someone's liberty, the liberty of a freeborn Israelite, which was worth almost as much as their life.

3. A reminder as to what to do concerning leprosy (vv. 8–9). [Ed. note: The KJV translates the Hebrew word *tsara'at* as "leprosy," although this word refers to various skin conditions, not necessarily leprosy.] The laws concerning it must be carefully observed. We had laws concerning leprosy before (Lev chapters 13 and 14).

4. Some necessary orders given about pledges for the security of money lent.

4.1. They must not take a millstone as a security for a debt (v. 6), for people used that to grind the grain which was to be bread for their families. This law therefore forbids a lender to take as a security for a debt anything whose loss would lead to the debtor's ruin. This is consistent with the old English law which provides that the tools of a person's trade, such as the ax of a carpenter or the books of a scholar, should not be used to pay debts. The creditor who does not care if the debtor and their family starve, as long as the creditor gets the money back, goes against not only the law of Christ, but also the Law of Moses.

4.2. They must not go into the borrower's house to fetch the pledge. It is provided that the lender should not go into the home and take whatever they please, but rather the lender should have what the borrower can best spare. A poor man's cloak should never be taken as a pledge (vv. 12–13). We had this before (Ex 22:26–27). If the cloak was taken in the morning, it must be brought back again at night, which is in effect saying that it must not be taken at all.

Verses 14–22

1. Masters are commanded to be just to their poor servants (vv. 14–15):

1.1. They must not oppress them. "For *thou wast a bondman* in the land where you were a stranger (v. 18), and you know how oppressive it is to be mistreated by a slave driver, so *Thou shalt not oppress a servant*" (v. 14).

1.2. They must be faithful and prompt in paying them their wages. Those who work for wages paid by the day are those who live from hand to mouth. They do not have tomorrow's bread for their families until they are paid for today's work.

2. Magistrates and judges are commanded to be fair in administering justice.

3. The rich are commanded to be kind and charitable to the poor. The Law of Moses orders them to be so in many ways. The particular kind act commanded here is that they should not be greedy when gathering in their grain, grapes, and olives. They should not worry about leaving any behind, but instead they should be willing to overlook some and let the poor have the gleanings (vv. 19–22).

CHAPTER 25

Here is: 1. A law to regulate the flogging of evildoers (vv. 1–3); a law in favor of the ox that is treading out the grain (v. 4). 2. A law to disgrace the person who refused to marry his brother's widow (vv. 5–10) and also a law to punish an immodest woman (vv. 11–12). 3. A law for just weights and measures (vv. 13–16) and a command to destroy Amalek (vv. 17–19).

Verses 1–4

Here is:

1. An instruction to the judges in flogging evildoers (vv. 1–3). We have read of many commands which do not

have any particular penalty attached to them. The punishment for breaking most of these commands was flogging, according to the practice of the Jews. The instructions given here for the flogging of criminals are:

1.1. That it should be done formally, not noisily and with great show through the streets, but in the open court before the judge, and carefully so that the lashes might be counted. The Jews say that while the punishment was being carried out, the chief justice of the court read out loud 28:58–59 and 29:9 and concluded with the words (Ps 78:38), *But he, being full of compassion, forgave their iniquity*. In this way, it became a sort of religious act, and was likely to reform the offender and to be a warning to others.

1.2. That it should be done in proportion to the crime.

1.3. That however great the crime was, the number of lashes should never exceed *forty* (v. 3). *Forty save one* was the general custom, as appears from 2Co 11:24. They reduced it by one for fear of having miscounted, because they would never go to the harshest extreme, or because the execution was usually done with a whip of three lashes, so that thirteen lashes—each one being counted as three—made up thirty-nine, and one more by that reckoning would have been forty-two.

2. An instruction to farmers not to prevent their cattle from eating while the cattle were working, if food was within their reach (v. 4).

Verses 5–12

Here is:

1. The law established concerning the marrying of a brother's widow. It appears from the story of Judah's family that this had been an old custom (Ge 38:8). The case put is one that often happens, of a man's dying without children, while his brothers were still young enough to be unmarried. Now in such a situation:

1.1. The widow was not to marry again into any other family unless all the relatives of her husband refused her, so that the estate she was endowed with might not be transferred to the ownership of another person.

1.2. The husband's brother, or next of kin, must marry her, partly out of respect for her, who having given up her own people and her father's house should be treated with the greatest kindness by the family which she married into, and partly out of respect for her deceased husband, so that though he was dead, he might not be forgotten or lost from his family tree. The firstborn child, which the brother or next of kin would have by the widow, should be named after the brother who had died, and recorded as his child in the family tree (vv. 5–6). But:

1.3. If the brother or next of kin refused to carry out this responsibility to the memory of the dead brother, what must be done then? He will not be compelled to marry her (v. 7), but he will be publicly disgraced for not marrying her.

2. A law for punishing an immodest woman (vv. 11–12).

Verses 13–19

Here is:

1. A law against deceitful weights and measures. They must not only not use them, but they must not have them, for if they had them, they would be strongly tempted to use them. They must not have a great weight or measure to use when buying and a small one to use when selling, for that was cheating both ways. But *thou shalt have a perfect and just weight* (v. 15).

2. A command to eliminate Amalek:

2.1. The trouble Amalek caused to Israel must be remembered (vv. 17–18). They had no reason at all to quarrel with Israel; neither did they give Israel any notice by declaring war, but took unfair advantage of them when they had just come out of slavery and were, as far as Amalek could tell, only going to *sacrifice to God in the wilderness*.

2.2. This trouble must in due time be avenged (v. 19). It was nearly 400 years after this that Saul was ordered to carry out this sentence (1Sa 15:1–35), but he was rejected by God because he did not do it properly.

CHAPTER 26

With this chapter, Moses concludes the decrees which he thought fit to pass on to Israel as commands when he left them. What follows comes as confirmation, rewards, and penalties. In this chapter: 1. Moses gives them a form of confession to be made by the offerer of the basket of firstfruits (vv. 1–11). 2. Moses tells them the declaration and prayer that are to be made after the third year's tithe has been distributed (vv. 12–15). 3. Moses commits them to obey all the commands he had given them; he commits them by divine authority—"Not I, but the Lord thy God has commanded thee to do these statutes" (v. 16)—and by the mutual covenant between God and them (vv. 17–19).

Verses 1–11

Here Moses commands:

1. A good work to be done, which is the presentation of a basket of their firstfruits to God every year (vv. 1–2). When people went into the field or vineyard at the time when the fruits were ripening, they were to notice what was most advanced and to put it by as firstfruits: wheat, barley, grapes, figs, pomegranates, olives, and dates. Some of each must be put into the same basket, with leaves between them, and presented to God in the place of his choice. We may learn from this law:

1.1. To acknowledge God as the giver of all those good things which support and strengthen our natural life.

1.2. To deny ourselves. We tend to be especially fond of what is the first to be ripe and what is particularly tasty and mouth-watering. We must discipline ourselves not to eat the fruit when it is first brought in from the harvest.

1.3. To give to God the first and best that we have. Those who dedicate the days of their youth and the prime of their lives to the service and honor of God are bringing him their firstfruits.

2. Good words to be put into their mouths which they are to speak when they do this good work. They must acknowledge two things in this:

2.1. The lowliness of their common ancestor: *A Syrian ready to perish was my father* (v. 5). Jacob is here called an Aramean or *Syrian*, because he lived twenty years in Paddan Aram.

2.2. The miserable conditions of their nation in its infancy. They lived in Egypt as strangers and served there as slaves (v. 6).

Verses 12–15

We had before (14:28–29) a record of how the tithe was to be distributed every third year. The second tithe, which in the other two years was to be spent on a special feast, was in the third year to be spent at home in entertaining the poor.

1. They must formally affirm (vv. 13–14):

1.1. That no sacred portions had been hoarded by them: *"I have brought them away out of my house* (v. 13). Nothing remains there except what is mine."

1.2. That the poor, and particularly poor ministers, poor foreigners, and poor widows, had received their portions according to the commandment.

1.3. That none of this tithe had been put to any ordinary use, much less to any wrong use. The Jews say that this declaration of their integrity was to be made with a low voice, because it looked like self-commendation, but that the previous confession of God's goodness was to be made with a loud voice to his glory. The person who did not dare make this declaration must bring a *trespass offering* (Lev 5:15).

2. They must add a solemn prayer to this solemn declaration (v. 15), not so much for themselves, but for *God's people Israel*, for when there is a general peace and prosperity, every individual prospers and has peace.

Verses 16–19

Moses urges two things to support all these commands:

1. They were the commands of God (v. 16). They were not thought up by Moses' own wisdom and neither did they come about because of his own authority. No; infinite Wisdom framed them, and the power of the King of Kings committed them to the people: *The Lord thy God commands thee.*

2. Their covenant with God obliged them to keep these commands.

CHAPTER 27

Up to this chapter, Moses has set out in detail the people's duties. At the end of the previous chapter, Moses put them under the obligation to keep both the commands and the covenant. In this chapter, he now comes to give them the outward means: 1. To help their memories. They must write all the words of this Law on stones (vv. 1–10). 2. To move their feelings, so that they might not be indifferent to the Law and treat it disrespectfully. When they came to Canaan, the blessings and curses which were the rewards and penalties of the Law were to be solemnly declared in the hearing of all Israel, who were to say Amen *to them (vv. 11–26).*

Verses 1–10

Here is:

1. A general command to the people to keep God's commandments. This is urged on them with authority. *Moses with the elders of Israel*, the rulers of each tribe (v. 1), and again, *Moses and the priests the Levites* (v. 9), commanded their people to *keep all the commandments* (v. 1).

2. A particular command to them to register with due ceremony and reverence the words of this Law as soon as they reach Canaan. There was a solemn confirmation of the covenant between God and Israel at Mount Sinai, when an altar was set up, with twelve pillars, and the Book of the Covenant was produced (Ex 24:4). What is appointed here has a similar solemnity. They must set up a monument on which they must *write the words of this law* (v. 3). They must also set up an altar. God spoke to them by means of the words of the Law which were written on the plastered stones. They spoke to God by means of the altar and the sacrifices offered on it, and so fellowship was maintained between them and God.

Verses 11–26

It seems that in Canaan, in the part which later was allotted to Ephraim (Joshua's tribe), there were two mountains near each other, with a valley between, one called *Gerizim* and the other *Ebal*. On the sides of these two mountains, which faced one another, all the tribes were to be drawn up, six on one side and six on the other. Then when silence was declared and attention called for, one of the priests declared loudly one of the curses that come here, and all the people who stood on the side and foot of Mount Ebal said *Amen*. Then the opposite blessing was declared, "Blessed is the one who does not do so or so," and then those that stood on the side, and at the foot, of Mount Gerizim, said *Amen*.

1. Something is to be generally observed concerning this ceremony, which was to be done only once, but which would be talked about forever:

1.1. God appointed which tribes should stand on Mount Gerizim and which on Mount Ebal (vv. 12–13). The six tribes that were appointed to bless the people were all the children of the free women (Leah and Rachel), for the promise belongs to such (Gal 4:31). Levi is here put among the rest, though earlier God had separated this tribe from the others for work of the tabernacle (Nu 3:7, 12, 41, 45). This teaches ministers to apply to themselves the blessing and curse which they preach to others, and by faith to express their own *Amen* to it.

1.2. It is said of the tribes that were to say *Amen* to the blessings, *They stood to bless the people* (v. 12), but of the others, *They stood to curse* (v. 13), not mentioning the people, as if any of the people whom God had taken as his own would be reluctant to put themselves under the curse.

1.3. Those Levites and priests who were appointed for that purpose were to declare the curses as well as the blessings.

1.4. The curses are expressed here, but not the blessings. In Christ's Sermon on the Mount, which was the true Mount Gerizim, we only have blessings (Mt 5:3–11).

1.5. The people were to say *Amen* to each curse. The Jews have a saying to encourage people to say *Amen* to the public prayers: "Whoever answers 'Amen' after the one who blesses, that person is like the one who blesses." But how could they say *Amen* to the curses? They could do it because when they said *Amen*, they declared their faith in God; they were in effect saying not only, "It is certain it will be so," but also, "It is right it should be so."

2. Let us now notice what the particular sins are against which the curses are announced. They are sins:

2.1. Against the second commandment. This flaming sword is set to keep that commandment first (v. 15). A curse is declared here not only on those who worship idols or images, but also on those who make or keep them. Such people are—or are like—idolaters who worship false gods.

2.2. Against the fifth commandment (v. 16). Having contempt for parents is such a detestable sin that it is put next to having contempt for God himself.

2.3. Against the eighth commandment. The curse of God is here attached:

• To an unjust neighbor who *removes the landmarks*, boundary stones (v. 17). See 19:14.
• To an unjust counselor.
• To an unjust judge who *perverteth the judgment of the stranger, fatherless, and widow*, whom the judge should protect and vindicate (v. 19).

2.4. Against the seventh commandment. Incest with a sister, a father's wife, or a mother-in-law is a cursed sin (vv. 20, 22–23).

2.5. Against the sixth commandment. Two of the worst kinds of murder are mentioned here:

2.5.1. Murder which is committed in secret: when someone does not attack their neighbor in a way that gives the neighbor an opportunity to defend themselves, but *smites him secretly* (v. 24), for example by using poison. The person who is murdered does not see who is causing the hurt. See Ps 10:8–9.

2.5.2. Murder under the pretense of the Law. The person who is hired or bribed to accuse, convict, or condemn and so *slay an innocent person* is cursed (v. 25). See Ps 15:5.

3. The ceremony concludes with a general curse on the person *that confirmeth not all the words of this law to do them* (v. 26). When we obey the Law, we set our seal on it, and so confirm it. When we disobey the Law, we are breaking it, making it void (Ps 119:126).

CHAPTER 28

This chapter is a detailed explanation of two words in the previous chapter, blessing *and* curse. *1. Moses describes the blessings that would come on them if they were obedient. The blessings would be in their personal, family, and especially national life, for it is particularly as a nation that they are dealt with here (vv. 1–14). 2. He describes more fully the curses which would come on them if they were disobedient. These would bring extreme trouble and distress on them (vv. 15–44). 3. He describes their final complete ruin and destruction (vv. 45–68). This chapter has much the same intention as Lev 26:1–46, setting before them life and death, good and evil. The promise at the close of that chapter, of their restoration when they repented, is similarly repeated in detail (30:1–20).*

Verses 1–14

The blessings are here put before the curses, to show:

• That God is slow to anger, but quick to show mercy. He has declared on oath that he prefers us to obey and live rather than sin and die.
• That the obedience that pleases God most springs from the motive of delighting in his goodness.

1. The details of this blessing are given. It is promised that God's providence would prosper them in all their outward concerns. These blessings are said to *overtake them* (v. 2). On the Day of Judgment the blessing will come on the righteous who *say, Lord, when saw we thee hungry and fed thee?* (Mt 25:37).

1.1. Several things are listed to show the various ways in which God in his providence would bless them:

1.1.1. They would be safe and comfortable; a blessing would rest on them wherever they were, *in the city or in the field* (v. 3). Their own persons would be protected, and they would know success in what they did in life.

1.1.2. Their families would be built up by having many children.

1.1.3. They would be rich and have plenty of all the good things of this life. A blessing is promised:

1.1.3.1. On everything outside their homes, grain and cattle in the field (vv. 4, 11), especially their cows and sheep.

1.1.3.2. On everything they had inside their homes, their basket and their kneading trough (*store*) (v. 5), their storehouses or barns (v. 8). We depend on God and his blessing, not only for the annual harvest, but also for our daily bread from our own baskets, and so are taught to pray for it every day.

1.1.4. They would be successful in all their work; God would acknowledge their diligence and *bless the work of their hand* (v. 12).

1.1.5. They would be honored among their neighbors (v. 1). Two things would help make them great among the nations:

1.1.5.1. Their wealth (v. 12): "*Thou shalt lend to many nations* on interest," which they were allowed to take from the neighboring nations, "but you will have no need to borrow."

1.1.5.2. Their power (v. 13): *The Lord shall make thee the head, and not the tail.* They would be leaders, not followers. They would give law to all around them, exact tribute from them, and settle all disputes among them. Religious faith among them, and the blessing of God on them, would make them formidable to all their neighbors, as frightening as a powerful army arrayed against them.

1.1.6. They would be victorious over their enemies and succeed in all their wars.

1.2. We learn from all this that religious faith and godliness are related to outward prosperity. It would be good if everyone believed it. Even though ordinary, temporal blessings are not dealt with so much in the promises of the New Testament as they are in the Old Testament, it is enough that our Lord Jesus has given us his word that if we *seek first the kingdom of God, and the righteousness thereof, all other things* will be added to us, as far as infinite Wisdom sees good to give us. Surely we are to take him at his word. Who can want more than this (Mt 6:33)?

2. It is also promised that the grace of God would *establish them* as *a holy people* (v. 9). This establishing of their religious faith would mean that their reputations were well established (v. 10).

Verses 15–44

Having viewed the bright side of the cloud, which is toward the obedient, we are now presented with the dark side, which is toward the disobedient. If we do not keep God's commandments, we not only fall short of the blessings promised, but we also put ourselves under the curse, which is as tragic as the blessing is joyful. Notice:

1. The justice of this curse. It is not a curse that is without reason, or only for some trivial reasons. God does not take unfair advantage of us, and neither does he want to pick a quarrel with us. What is mentioned here as bringing the curse is:

1.1. Despising God, refusing to *hearken to his voice* (v. 15), which speaks of the greatest possible contempt for him.

1.2. Disobeying God, *not doing his commandments* (v. 15).

1.3. Deserting God. He never rejects us until we have first rejected him.

2. The extent of this curse:

2.1. In general, it is declared, "*All these curses shall come upon thee* from above, *and shall overtake thee* (v. 15), even if you try to escape them." You cannot run away from God except by running to him. There is no fleeing from his justice except by fleeing to his mercy. See Ps 21:7–8. To those whose *mind and conscience are defiled* everything else is so (Tit 1:15). This curse is exactly the opposite of the blessing in the first part of the chapter.

2.2. Many specific judgments are listed here as the fruits of the curse. These judgments threatened are of various kinds, including disease, want, defeat by enemies, and captivity. But God's judgments can fill people's minds, as well as their bodies and possessions, with darkness and horror. These mental difficulties are the most painful of all judgments. They can make people a terror to themselves, and even destroy themselves.

Verses 45–68

You would have thought that enough had been said for them to fear the *wrath of God* which is *revealed from heaven against the ungodliness and unrighteousness of men* (Ro 1:18). But to show how deep the storehouse of that wrath is, and that still there is worse to come, Moses—when you would have thought that he had concluded this sad subject—begins again and adds to this scroll of curses many similar words, as Jeremiah did to his (Jer 36:32). Here, in this latter part, he prophesies their destruction by the Romans and then their dispersion. The present sad state of the Jewish nation, and of all who have joined them by embracing their religion, fulfills completely the prediction in these verses. In fact, it does this so much that it is incontrovertible proof of the truth of prophecy and so of the divine authority of Scripture. And since this final destruction is here represented as even more terrible than the former, it shows that their sin in rejecting Christ and his Gospel was more detestable. Under this final destruction now for more than 1,600 years they continue to be hostile toward the Lord Jesus.

1. It is terrifying to think that a people who had for so long been the favorites of heaven would be so completely abandoned and rejected, that a people so closely joined together would be so universally dispersed, and yet that a people so scattered among all nations would preserve themselves so distinctly and not mix with any, but still be marked out and be restless wanderers like Cain.

2. The destruction threatened is described. Moses speaks here about the same sad subject that our Savior spoke about to his disciples in his farewell sermon (Mt 24:4–28), namely, the destruction of Jerusalem and the Jewish nation.

2.1. Five things are prophesied as steps to their destruction:

2.1.1. That they would be invaded by a foreign enemy (vv. 49–50): *A nation from far*, namely, the Romans, as *swift as the eagle* flying to its prey. Our Savior makes use of this comparison in foretelling this destruction when he says, *where the carcase is, there will the eagles be gathered together* (Mt 24:28). Bishop Patrick observes that the ensign of the Roman armies was an eagle.

2.1.2. That the country would be devastated and all its crops devoured by this army of foreigners. This is the natural consequence of an invasion, especially when it is made, as that by the Romans was, to punish rebels.

2.1.3. That their cities would be besieged, and that those being besieged would be so stubborn and those besieging so strong, that their cities would be put in the situation of most extreme need and would eventually fall into the hands of the enemy (v. 52).

2.1.4. That many of them would perish, so that they would become *few in number* (v. 62).

2.1.5. That the remnant would be scattered throughout the nations. This completes their sorry state: *The Lord shall scatter thee among all people* (v. 64).

2.2. Generally:

2.2.1. The fulfillment of these predictions for the Jewish nation shows that Moses spoke by the Spirit of God.

2.2.2. Let us all learn from this to have awe and reverence for God and not to sin. One evil man read the threats of this chapter and was so angry that he tore the page out of the Bible, as Jehoiakim cut Jeremiah's scroll (Jer 36). But nothing is achieved if a copy is defaced, when the original remains on record in the divine plan. God has unchangeably determined that the wages of sin is death, whether people listen or refuse to listen to his word.

CHAPTER 29

The first words of this chapter describe its contents: These are the words of the covenant (v. 1). Here is: 1. A repetition of God's dealings with them, through which he brought them into this covenant (vv. 2–8); a solemn command to them to keep the covenant (v. 9). 2. A summary of the covenant itself (vv. 12–13); specification of the people taken into the covenant (vv. 10–11, 14–15); a warning of the great purpose of this covenant against idolatry (vv. 16–17); an awful and terrible declaration of the wrath of God against those who sinfully promise themselves peace (vv. 18–28). The conclusion of this covenant, with a distinction between the secret things and the revealed things (v. 29).

Verses 1–9

Now that Moses had repeated the commands which the people were to observe as their part of the covenant, and the promises and threats which God would fulfill as his part of the covenant, according to whether the people obeyed or not, the whole is summed up in a covenant transaction. The covenant that had formerly been made is renewed. Moses, who was its mediator before, is its mediator again (v. 1): *The Lord commanded Moses to make it.* It is probable that some were now living who, though they were too young to be recruited at Horeb, were old enough to agree to the covenant made there, but it is renewed here. But by far the majority of them were a new generation, and so the covenant had to be made afresh with them, for it is right that the covenant should be renewed to the children of the covenant.

1. It is usual for a contract to begin with a preamble of background statements. This one does, with a repetition of the great things God had done for them:

1.1. To encourage them to believe that God would indeed be their God, for he would not have done so much for them if he had not intended more. Everything he had done up to that time was only a beginning.

1.2. To commit them to be a people who would obey him because of what he had done for them.

2. Moses appeals to their own eyes (v. 2) to prove what he here says: *You have seen all that the Lord did.* Their own senses were incontrovertible evidence of the facts: *Keep therefore the words of this covenant* (v. 9).

3. Moses mentions the following things to show the power and goodness of God that were evident when God came to them:

3.1. God's rescuing them from Egypt (vv. 2–3).

3.2. Their behavior through the desert for forty years (vv. 5–6). They were miraculously led, clothed, and fed there. These miracles taught them that the Lord was God, and that he was their God by these blessings.

3.3. The victory they had recently gained over Sihon and Og, and the good land which they had taken possession of (vv. 7–8).

4. Moses reasons from these recollections and laments their stupidity: *Yet the Lord has not given you a heart to perceive* (v. 4):

4.1. The hearing ear, the seeing eye, and the understanding heart are all the gift of God.

4.2. God gives not only food and clothes, but also wealth and great possessions to many whom he does not give grace to. Many people enjoy the gifts but do not have the hearts to acknowledge the One who has given them, or to understand the true intention and use of the gifts.

4.3. God's readiness to do us good in other things is clear evidence that if we do not have grace, which is the best gift, then it is our own fault, not his.

Verses 10–29

It appears by the length of the sentences, and by the fullness and powerfulness of the expressions, that Moses became very zealous, now that he was drawing near to the close of his address. He very much wanted to impress his message on the minds of this unthinking people. To commit them more closely to God and their duty, he makes an everlasting covenant between them and God. He does not ask for their explicit agreement, but puts the matter clearly before them and then leaves it between God and their own consciences. We have here:

1. The parties to this covenant:

1.1. It is the Lord their God whom they are to covenant with (v. 12).

1.2. They are all to be taken into covenant with him. They were all summoned to attend (v. 2).

1.2.1. Even their great leaders, the commanders of their tribes, their elders and officials, must not think it any dishonor to submit to the terms of this covenant.

1.2.2. Not only the men, but also their wives and children, must come into this covenant.

1.2.3. Not only the people of Israel, but also the foreigners who were in their camp, provided they had converted to the Israelite religion and renounced all false gods, were taken into this covenant. This was an early sign of God's favor to the Gentiles and of the kindness God had in store for them.

1.2.4. Not only those who were free, but also *the hewers of wood and drawers of water* (v. 11), those who did the lowliest work among them.

1.2.5. Not only those who were now present before God in this solemn assembly, but also those who were not there with them, were taken into the covenant (v. 15). By this is meant:

1.2.5.1. Those who stayed at home were included, even though they were prevented from coming because of illness or necessary business.

1.2.5.2. The generations to come are included. And so when we take this covenant as a type of the dispensation of the covenant of grace, it is a noble testimony to the Mediator of that covenant, who is *the same yesterday, today, and for ever* (Heb 13:8).

2. The summary of this covenant. All the commands and promises of the covenant are included in the covenant-relationship between God and them (v. 13).

3. The main purpose in renewing this covenant at this time: to strengthen them against temptations to idolatry.

3.1. Idolaters were like drunkards, violently set on their idols themselves and keen to draw others into their evil ways. Orgies commonly accompanied their idolatries (1Pe 4:3), so this speaks ruin to drunkards. Drunkenness is a sin that hardens the heart and leads the conscience astray as much as any other sin. It is a sin to which people are strangely tempted even when they have recently experienced the trouble it causes. It is also a sin which they are strangely fond of drawing others into (Hab 2:15).

3.2. Idolatry would bring about the destruction of their nation. It would bring plagues on the land, a land which took no notice of this root of bitterness and allowed the infection to spread. And just as the sin spread, so the judgment would also similarly spread.

3.3. He concludes with a distinction between *the secret things* and *those things which are revealed* (v. 29):

3.3.1. We are forbidden to be overinquisitive about the secret counsels of God. A full answer is given to the question why the Lord has acted in this way to this land. The answer is sufficient to justify God and to warn us. But if we ask further why God would go to such miraculous lengths to mold such a people, whose apostasy and destruction he clearly foresaw, why he did not act in his almighty grace to prevent it, or what he still intends to do with them, then we should know that such questions cannot be answered. See Ac 1:7; Jn 21:22; Col 2:18.

3.3.2. We are directed and encouraged to diligently ask about what God has made known: things *revealed belong to us and to our children* (v. 29). We can learn from this that although God has kept much of his counsel secret, enough is revealed to satisfy and save us. He has *kept back nothing that is profitable for us* (Ac 20:20). We and our children ought to get to know the things of God that are revealed. We are not only allowed to search into them, but should actively do so. It is in the interest of each of us and our families to do so. These things are the rules, the privileges, and the promises that we are to live by. We are therefore to learn them diligently for ourselves and to teach them diligently to our children. All our knowledge must be put into practice, because this is the purpose of all divine revelation. It is not given to provide us with things that we and our friends can merely think about and discuss, *but that we may do all the words of this law* (v. 29), and be blessed in doing them.

CHAPTER 30

You would have thought that the threats at the end of the previous chapter would have completely destroyed the people of Israel and would have left their situation completely desperate, but in this chapter we have clear signs of the mercy God had in store for them in later days, so that mercy finally triumphs over judgment. Here we have: 1. Very great and precious promises made to them, conditioned on their repentance and turning back to God (vv. 1–10). 2. The righteousness of faith set before them in the clarity and ease of the commandment now given them (vv. 11–14). 3. A powerful conclusion stating the great choice before them (vv. 15–20).

Verses 1–10

These verses may be considered either as a promise or as a prediction:

1. They are chiefly to be considered as a promise for all people, not only Israel. Their purpose is to assure us that if the greatest sinners repent and are converted, their sins will be forgiven and they will be restored to God's favor. This is the intention of the covenant of grace. It leaves room for repentance when our behavior is wrong and promises forgiveness when we repent. Notice here:

1.1. How the repentance is described. This is the condition of these promises:

1.1.1. It begins with serious consideration (v. 1): *"Thou shalt call to mind* what you had forgotten or not

considered." Consideration is the first step toward conversion. *Bring to mind, O you transgressors* (Isa 46:8). The prodigal son came to himself first, and then to his father. What they should call to mind is the blessing and the curse. If sinners would only seriously consider the happiness they have lost because of their sin and the misery they have brought on themselves, and if they realized that if they repented they would escape that misery and recover that happiness, then they would not delay to *return to the Lord their God* (Hos 7:10). The prodigal son *called to mind the blessing and the curse* (v. 1) when he considered his poverty and the plentiful bread *in his father's house* (Lk 15:17).

1.1.2. It consists of sincere conversion. The effect of the consideration must be godly sorrow and shame (Eze 6:9; 7:16). But the essence of repentance, its life and soul, without which the most passionate expressions are mere words, is *returning to the Lord our God* (v. 2). *If thou turn with all thy heart and with all thy soul* (v. 10).

1.1.3. It is shown by a sustained conformity to the holy will of God. We are to constantly obey him. If you will *obey his voice* (v. 2), says Moses.

- This obedience must be toward God: *Thou shalt obey his voice* (v. 8), and *hearken* to it, listen to it and obey it (v. 10).
- It must be sincere, joyful, and complete: *With all thy heart, and with all thy soul* (v. 2).
- It must be from a motive of love, and that love must be *with all thy heart and with all thy soul* (v. 6).

1.2. What the favor is which is promised if these conditions of repentance are fulfilled. Even though they are brought to God by their trouble and distress from among the nations to which they were driven (v. 1), God will graciously accept them nevertheless. This is why afflictions are sent: to bring us to repentance. There is the same way to heaven from every place. It is promised here:

1.2.1. That God would have compassion on them as objects of his pity (v. 3).

1.2.2. That God would *turn their captivity, and gather them from the nations whither they were scattered* (v. 3), even though they were very distant (v. 4).

1.2.3. That God would *bring them into their land again* (v. 5). Sinners who repent are not only rescued from their misery but also restored to true happiness and the favor of God.

2. This may also be considered as a prediction of the repentance and restoration of the Jews: *When all these things shall come upon thee* (v. 1), the blessing first, and after that the curse, then the mercy kept in reserve will come on them. Although their hearts were terribly hardened, the grace of God would still soften and change them. Then even though their case was wretched, the providence of God would deal with all their grievances. Now:

2.1. It is certain that this was fulfilled in their return from their captivity in Babylon. It was a wonderful example of their repentance and reformation that Ephraim, who had been devoted to idols, abandoned them and said, *What have I to do any more with idols?* (Hos 14:8). That captivity effectively healed them of idolatry, and then God planted them again in their own land and did them good. But:

2.2. Some think that it is still further to be fulfilled in the conversion of the Jews who are now dispersed, in their repentance for the sin of their ancestors in crucifying Christ, in their return to God through him, and in their becoming part of the Christian church.

Verses 11–14

Moses here urges them to obey God when they consider how clear and practicable the command is:

1. This is true of the Law of Moses. They could never plead as an excuse for their disobedience that God had commanded them to do what was either unintelligible or impracticable, something impossible to be known or to be done (v. 11): *It is not hidden from thee.* That is:

1.1. "It is not too high for you; you do not need to send messengers to heaven (v. 12), to ask what you must do to please God. Neither do you need to go *beyond the sea* (v. 13), as the philosophers did, who traveled to many and distant lands in pursuit of learning."

1.2. "It is not too *hard* nor *heavy* for you," is the reading of the Septuagint (a Greek version of the Old Testament) (v. 11). "There is something in you which *consents to* (agrees with) *the law that it is good* (Ro 7:16). You therefore have no reason to complain of any insuperable difficulty in observing it."

2. This is true of the Gospel of Christ, to which the apostle Paul applies this statement of Moses. Paul considers 30:11–14 to be the language of the *righteousness which is of faith* (Ro 10:6–8). This appeal of Moses is now God's commandment under the Gospel that we *believe in the name of his Son Jesus Christ* (1Jn 3:23). The word is near us, and Christ is near us in that word, so that if we believe with the heart that the promises of the incarnation and resurrection of the Messiah are fulfilled in our Lord Jesus and we receive him as such and confess him with our mouth, then we have Christ with us and we will be saved. The One who justifies us is very near us. The Law was clear and easy, but the Gospel is even more so. See also Mt 11:28–30.

Verses 15–20

Moses here concludes very powerfully, so that the message he has preached might enter the understanding and affections of this unthinking people.

1. He states the case very attractively:

1.1. Everyone wants to gain life and good, to escape death and evil. Everyone desires happiness and dreads misery. So Moses says, "I have shown you the way to gain all the happiness you could ever want and to avoid every possible misery. Be obedient, and everything will be well, and nothing will go wrong."

1.2. Everyone is moved and controlled in their actions by hope and fear: hope of good and fear of evil, whether real or apparent. Moses comments on this situation by saying, "There are two ways of coming to obedience: either you will be drawn to obedience by the certain prospect of what you will gain by it, or you will be driven to obedience by the equally certain prospect of the destruction you will incur if you are disobedient. Whichever way you are dealt with, you will be kept close to God and your duty. But if you decide to disobey, you will be completely without excuse."

2. Having stated the case in this way, he reasonably sets before them the choice, with the direction that they should choose well.

3. In the last verse he shows them briefly what their duty is, *to love God,* and to love him as *the Lord,* a most precious Being, and as *their God,* a God in covenant with them. *He is thy life, and the length of thy days* (v. 20).

CHAPTER 31

In this chapter after Moses had finished his sermon: 1. He encourages the people who were now to enter Canaan (vv. 1–6), and also Joshua who was to lead them (vv. 7–8,

23). 2. He takes care that after his death they would always remember certain things by means of: 2.1. The Book of the Law, which was written, given to be looked after by the priests (vv. 9, 24–27), and ordered to be read publicly every seventh year (vv. 10–13). 2.2. A song which God orders Moses to write, to instruct and warn them. He calls Moses and Joshua to the door of the tabernacle, the Tent of Meeting (vv. 14–15); he foretells that Israel would turn away from God in due course, and thereby bring judgments on themselves (vv. 16–18); he gives the following song to be a witness against them (vv. 19–21). 4. Moses wrote it (v. 22) and gave it to Israel, indicating its purpose, which he had received from the Lord (vv. 28–30).

Verses 1–8

If we do not want to leave people, sometimes it seems that we say good-by to them often. So with Moses as he takes his leave of the children of Israel. It is not that he does not want to go to God, but that he does not want to leave them, for fear that when he has left them they will leave God. Here he calls them together to give them a word of encouragement. It was discouraging to them that Moses was to be taken away from them at a time when he could not be spared. Even though Joshua continued to fight for them in the valley, they wanted Moses to intercede for them on the hill, as he had before (Ex 17:10).

• He is 120 *years old,* and it is time for him to think of giving up his honor and returning to his rest.
• He is under a divine sentence: *Thou shalt not go over Jordan* (v. 2).

1. He encourages the people. Never did any general stir their soldiers for such good reasons as those for which Moses encourages Israel:

1.1. He assures them of the constant presence of God with them (v. 3): *The Lord thy God,* who has led you and kept you up to this point, will *go over before thee.* The writer to the Hebrews applies this to all God's spiritual Israel, to encourage their faith and hope. This Gospel is preached to us, as well as them: *He will never fail thee, nor forsake thee* (Heb 13:5).

1.2. He commends Joshua to them as a leader. He was one whose leadership, courage, and sincere regard for their interests they had long experience of. He was one whom God had ordained and appointed to be their leader, and so God would no doubt acknowledge and bless him and make him a blessing to them. See Nu 27:18.

1.3. He assures them of their success. Their hopes of this were encouraged by two things:

1.3.1. The victories they had already gained over Sihon and Og (v. 4). They could use these as an assurance of both the power of God—that he could do what he had done—and the purpose of God—that he would finish what he had begun.

1.3.2. The command God had given them to destroy the Canaanites (7:2; 12:2), from which they might reason that no doubt he would enable them to do so.

2. He encourages Joshua (vv. 7–8). Notice:

2.1. Although Joshua was an experienced general and a man of proven boldness, he did not take Moses' command as an implied criticism but was very pleased to be encouraged by Moses to be *strong and of good courage* (v. 6).

2.2. Moses commands him *in the sight of all Israel* (v. 7), so that they might observe more seriously the one whom they saw inducted in this way.

2.3. Moses gives him the same assurance of the divine presence, and so of glorious success, that he had given the people.

Verses 9 – 13

Jn 1:17 says, *The law was given by Moses.* Moses was not only entrusted with communicating it to that generation, but also with transmitting it to the generations to come. Here we read that he was faithful to that trust:

1. *Moses wrote this law* (v. 9):

1.1. So that those who had heard it might often review it for themselves and call it to mind.

1.2. So that it might be the more securely handed down to future generations. The church has received many advantages from the writings of divine things, as well as from preaching. Faith comes not only by hearing, but also by reading. We can be thankful that the same care which was taken of the Law is taken of the Gospel too. It was written soon after it was preached, so that it might reach those on whom the fulfillment of the ages will come.

2. Having written it, Moses committed it to the custody of the priests and elders. He passed one true copy to the priests to be placed beside the ark (v. 26), to remain there as a standard by which all other copies must be approved.

3. Moses appointed the public reading of this Law in a general assembly of all Israel every seventh year. The godly Jews probably read the Law daily in their families, and *Moses of old time was read in the synagogue every sabbath day* (Ac 15:21). But once every seven years it must be read at a general assembly, so that the Law would be exalted and honored. Here he gives instructions:

3.1. When the Law must be solemnly read, so that the time might add to the ceremony. It must be done:

3.1.1. In the year for canceling debts. The land rested that year, so they could better spare the time to attend this service. Servants who were discharged then, and poor debtors who were released then from their debts, must know that because they had the benefit of the Law, they were justly expected to obey it. They should therefore give themselves to be God's servants, because he had loosened their chains and restraints. The year for canceling debts was a type of Gospel grace, and it is therefore called the *acceptable year of the Lord* (Lk 4:19). The forgiveness and freedom we receive in Christ commit us to keep his commandments (Lk 1:74–75).

3.1.2. At the Feast of Tabernacles in that year. They were particularly required to *rejoice before God* at that feast (Lev 23:40).

3.2. To whom it must be read: to *all Israel* (v. 11), *men, women, and children, and the strangers* (v. 12). The women and children were not obliged to go up to the other feasts, but only this one, when the Law was read.

3.3. By whom it must be read: *Thou shalt read it* (v. 11), "You, Israel," by a person appointed for that purpose, or, "You, Joshua," their chief ruler. We therefore find that he read the Law himself (Jos 8:34–35). So did Josiah (2Ch 34:30) and Ezra (Ne 8:3).

3.4. For what purpose it must be solemnly read: so that the present generation might maintain their knowledge of the Law of God (v. 12). They must hear so that they may *learn, and fear God, and observe* to do their duty. This should be our aim when we listen to the word. We must listen, so that we may learn and grow in knowledge. Every time we read the Scriptures we will find there is still more to be learned from them.

Verses 14 – 21

Here:

1. Moses and Joshua are summoned to come to the divine Majesty at the door of the tabernacle, the Tent of Meeting (v. 14). Moses is again told that he must die soon.

He must also bring Joshua with him to be presented to God as a successor and to receive his commission and charge.

2. God graciously meets with them: *He appeared in the tabernacle*—as the *Shechinah* used to appear—*in a pillar of a cloud* (v. 15).

3. God tells Moses that after his death, the covenant between Israel and their God which he had given so much attention to would certainly be broken.

3.1. That Israel would *forsake God* (v. 16). Worshiping the gods of the Canaanites would undoubtedly be considered as breaking the covenant. In the same way, those who make a god of money by allowing greed to reign or who make a god of their stomachs by allowing sensuality to reign are those who rebel against Christ. Those who *turn to other gods* (v. 18) abandon their own mercies.

3.2. That God would then abandon Israel. He is righteous when he rejects those who have wrongly rejected him (v. 17). Those who have rejected their God by sinning will find that they cause trouble to come on their own heads.

4. God instructs Moses to speak a song to them. He would be divinely inspired in composing this, and it would be an enduring testimony that God was faithful to them and would thereby serve as a warning to them. Human wisdom has devised many ways of communicating the knowledge of good and evil, such as laws, history, prophecies, proverbs, and songs. Each style has its own advantages. The wisdom of God has made use of them all in Scripture, so that the ignorant and negligent might be left without excuse.

4.1. This song could be a way of preventing them from turning away from God, if its message was taken to heart and acted on.

4.2. If this song did not prevent them from turning away from God, it might still help to bring them to repentance. When troubles come on them, this *song shall not be forgotten* (v. 21). It could act as a mirror to show them their own faces, so that they might humble themselves and return to the One from whom they have rebelled. God may allow to fall those for whom he has mercy in store, but he will provide a way for them to come back to him. Medicines are prepared beforehand for their cure.

Verses 22 – 30

Here:

1. The command is given to Joshua, which God had said (v. 14) that he would give him. Joshua had now heard from God so much about the evil of the people he was to lead that it must have been a discouragement to him. But God says, "No; however bad they are, you will complete your undertaking, for *I will be with thee.* Therefore *be of good courage.*"

2. The solemn giving of the Book of the Law to the Levites to be placed beside the ark is related here again (vv. 24–26). Here they are directed where to store this precious original, not in the ark, where only the two tablets were preserved, but in another box by the side of the ark. It is probably this very book that was found in the house of the Lord in the days of Josiah (2Ch 34:14), after it had somehow been misplaced.

3. The song which follows in the next chapter is given to Moses, and by him to the people.

3.1. He declares what little joy he had had in them while he was with them (v. 27). He does not mention the rebellions against himself. He had long since forgiven and forgotten these, but the people must be reminded of their rebellions against God, so that they may be repented of and never repeated.

3.2. He declares what little hopes he had in them now that he was leaving them. *I know that after my death you will utterly corrupt yourselves* (v. 29). In the same way, our Lord Jesus foretold the rise of false Christs and false prophets a little before his death (Mt 24:24); but despite these and despite all the apostasy of later times, we may be confident that *the gates of hell shall not prevail against the church* (Mt 16:18), for the *foundation of God stands sure* (2Ti 2:19).

CHAPTER 32

In this chapter we have: 1. The song which Moses gave to the children of Israel at God's appointment: 1.1. Its introduction (vv. 1–2). 1.2. The noble character of God and, in contrast to that, the bad character of the people of Israel (vv. 3–6). 1.3. A repetition of the great things God had done for them and, in contrast to that, an account of their evil behavior toward him (vv. 7–18). 1.4. A prediction of the devastating and destructive judgment of God on them for their sins (vv. 19–35). 1.5. A promise of the final destruction of their enemies and oppressors and the glorious rescue of a remnant of Israel (vv. 36–43). The chapter concludes with: 2. The encouragement with which Moses gave this song to them (vv. 44–47). 3. The orders God gave to Moses to go up to Mount Nebo and die (vv. 48–52).

Verses 1–6

Here is:

1. A commanding introduction to the Song of Moses (vv. 1–2). He begins:

1.1. With a solemn appeal to heaven and earth concerning the truth and importance of what he was about to say, and the justice of God against a rebellious and backsliding people. Heaven and earth will be witnesses against sinners. They will be witnesses of the warning given them and of their refusal to accept the warning (see Job 20:27).

1.2. With a solemn application to the people of what he was about to say (v. 2): *My doctrine* (teaching) *shall drop as the rain.* "It will be sweeping rain that beats down on the rebellious" is one of the Aramaic paraphrases. Rain is sometimes sent as judgment, and the word of God, which to some people is refreshing as a *savour of life unto life*, is also terrifying to others (2Co 2:16). It will come as sweet and comforting dew to those who are rightly prepared to receive it. Notice:

1.2.1. The subject of this song is teaching; he had given them a song of praise and thanksgiving (Ex 15:1–21), but this is a song of instruction, for we are to use *psalms, and hymns, and spiritual songs* not only to give glory to God, but also to *teach and admonish one another* (Col 3:16). This is the reason that many of David's psalms are entitled *Maschil* (Maskil), "to give instruction."

1.2.2. It is appropriate that this teaching is compared to rain and showers that fall from above to make the earth fruitful.

1.2.3. He promises that his teaching will drop and distill as the dew and the fine rain which descend silently. The preached word is likely to be profitable when it comes gently and when it sweetly plants itself in the hearts and minds of the hearers.

1.2.4. He asks for their acceptance and reception of it.

2. A fearful declaration of the greatness and righteousness of God (vv. 3–4):

2.1. He begins with this and expresses it as his underlying motive. To justify God in his dealings with them, we must acknowledge that God is righteous, even when his *judgments are a great deep* (Jer 12:1; Ps 36:6).

2.2. He here sets himself to *publish* (proclaim) *the name of the Lord* (v. 3), so that Israel might never be so foolish as to exchange him for a false god. *Ascribe greatness to our God* (v. 3). If we always have high and honorable thoughts of God and take every occasion to express them, then we will find that that helps prevent sin and will keep us following our duty. Notice that when Moses wants to declare the greatness of God, he does not explain his eternity and infinity or describe his great glory in heaven, but he shows the faithfulness of his word, the perfection of his works, and the wisdom and justice of all his leading, for his glory shines most clearly to us in these. These are the things that are revealed concerning him, which *belong to us and our children* (29:29).

2.2.1. *He is the rock* (v. 4). God is the rock, for he is unchangeable and immovable in himself. He is an impregnable shelter to everyone who seeks him and runs to him. He is an everlasting foundation for all who trust in him.

2.2.2. *His work is perfect* (v. 4). His work of creation *was very good* (Ge 1:31). His works of providence are also, or will be so in due course. And when the mystery of God is finished, the perfection of his works will appear to all the world. Nothing that God does can be added to (Ecc 3:14). God was now perfecting what he had promised and had begun for his people Israel.

2.2.3. *All his ways are judgment* (justice) (v. 4). The purposes of all his ways are righteous. He is wise in how he chooses to fulfill those purposes. *Judgment* means both wisdom and justice.

2.2.4. He is *a God of truth* (v. 4). We may accept his word and rely on it, for the One who is faithful to all his promises cannot lie, and neither will his threats fall empty to the ground.

2.2.5. He *is without iniquity* (v. 4). He has never cheated anyone who trusted in him. He has never wronged anyone who appealed to his justice, and he has never been harsh toward anyone who has thrown themselves on his mercy.

2.2.6. *Just and right is he* (v. 4). As he will not wrong anyone by punishing them more than they deserve, so he will not fail to reward all those who serve him or suffer for him.

3. A great accusation declared against the Israel of God, whose character was in every respect the opposite of that of the *God of Israel*.

3.1. *They have corrupted themselves* (v. 5).

3.2. *Their spot is not the spot of his children*; they are not his children because of their blemish (v. 5). Even God's children have spots and blemishes while they are in this imperfect state, for if we say we have no sin or spot, we deceive ourselves. But the sin of Israel was none of those; it was not a weakness that they fought, watched, and prayed against, but an evil which their hearts were fully set on. For:

3.3. They were *a perverse and crooked generation* (v. 5). They were moved by a corrupt and perverse spirit, which would do something forbidden just because it was forbidden.

4. A poignant argument with the offensive people for their ingratitude (v. 6): *Do you thus requite* (repay) *the Lord?*

4.1. He reminds them of the obligations God had given them to serve him and to stay close to him. He had been a Father to them. And are not our responsibilities as baptized Christians equally great and strong to our Creator who made us, our Redeemer who bought us, and our Sanctifier who has established us?

4.2. He reasons from this the evil of abandoning God and rebelling against him. For it was evil ingratitude and wild madness.

Verses 7–14

After Moses had in general presented God to them as the One who was the generous giver, he now shows them particular examples of God's kindness to them and his concern for them:

- Some examples were ancient, and he appeals to the records to prove them (v. 7): *Remember the days of old*. This shows us how the true records of ancient times are of special use, particularly the history of the church in its early times, of both the Old Testament and the New Testament church.
- Other examples were more modern, and he appeals to their fathers and elders who were now alive and with them to confirm them.

Moses describes three things as examples of God's kindness to his people Israel:

1. The early gift of the land of Canaan as their inheritance. It was ordained and prepared beforehand in God's mind (v. 8) and was a type of our heavenly inheritance. Notice:

1.1. When the earth was divided among the human race, God had Israel in his thoughts.

1.2. The reason given for the special care God took of this people, so long before they were either born or thought of in our world—if we may put it that way—only serves to emphasize God's kindness and puts his people under a greater obligation (v. 9): *For the Lord's portion is his people*.

2. The forming of them into a people, so that they might be ready to enter into this inheritance, like an heir coming of age at the time that the Father set. In this also, Canaan was a type of the heavenly inheritance, for just as it was from eternity proposed and intended for all God's spiritual Israel, so also they were made ready and fit for it in the course of time (Col 1:12). A great deal was done to model this people, to mold them into shape, and to prepare them for the great things intended for them in the Land of Promise.

2.1. *He found him* [Jacob, as metaphor for the nation] *in a desert land* (v. 10). This no doubt refers to the wilderness through which God brought the people to Canaan, and in which he took so much care over them. It is called *the church in the wilderness*, the assembly in the desert (Ac 7:38). It was born, nursed, and educated there:

2.1.1. Their condition was sad. Egypt was a desert land for them, and a *waste howling wilderness*, as they were slaves in it.

2.1.2. Their character was very unpromising. Most of them did not know anything much about the things of God. They were foolish and did not want to accept those things; they were perverse and quarrelsome; they wanted their own way all the time. In that respect it is well said that they were found in a desert land.

2.2. *He led him about and instructed him* (v. 10). When God had his people in the desert, he did not bring them straight to Canaan, but made them go a long way round, and so he instructed them. Learners need time to learn. He tested their faith, patience, and dependence on God, and got them used to the hardships of the desert, and used these

experiences to teach them. Every stage contained something that was instructive. We may well imagine how unfit that people would have been for Canaan if they had not first gone through the disciplines of living in the desert.

2.3. *He kept him as the apple of his eye* (v. 10). He guarded the people with every possible care and tenderness from the harmful influences of the open air and all the dangers of an inhospitable desert. The pillar of cloud and fire guided and guarded them.

2.4. He did for them what the eagle does for its nest of young ones (vv. 11–12). The simile was touched on before, when God said (Ex 19:4), *I bore you on eagles' wings*. It is expanded on here. The eagle is known to have a strong affection for its young, by protecting them and making provision for them, by teaching them to fly. For this purpose the eagle stirs them out of the nest where they lie dozing; the eagle flutters over them to show them how they must use their wings, and then gets them used to flying on their wings until they have learned to fly on their own. This is also an example to parents of how to train their children to hard work and not to allow them to laze about idly. God acted in this way with Israel: when Israel was in love with slavery, and reluctant to leave it, God through Moses stirred them up to want their freedom. He carried them out of Egypt, led them into the desert, and now finally led them through it.

3. Their settlement in a good land. This was partly done already, in the satisfactory establishing of the two and a half tribes, which was a pledge of what would certainly and quickly be done for the rest of the tribes. They were blessed with plenty of all good things: *honey out of the rock, and oil out of the flinty rock*. Mr. Ainsworth compares the abundance of good things in Canaan with the fruitfulness of Christ's kingdom and the heavenly comforts of his word and Spirit. Our loving heavenly Father gives to his children butter and milk, the sincere milk of the word, strong meat for those who are strong, and wine that makes people glad.

Verses 15–18

We have here a description of how Israel turned away from God. This apostasy would come about soon, because it was already in their hearts. Here are two clear examples of their evil ways:

1. False security and sensuality, pride and defiance, and the other common ways that plenty and prosperity are misused (v. 15). They *kicked*; they grew proud and defiant, and *lifted up the heel* (Ps 41:9) even against God himself. They *kicked against the pricks* (Ac 9:5) or kicked as *a bullock* (an unruly calf) *unaccustomed to the yoke* (Jer 31:18). They angrily persecuted the prophets and defied Providence itself.

2. Idolatry, which was the greater way in which they turned away from God. Their materialism led them to it, as it made them sick of their religion, self-willed, and foolish in their ways. Notice:

2.1. What sort of gods they chose and offered sacrifice to when they abandoned the God who made them (vv. 16–17). The very services which they should have done for the true God they did: to *strange* (foreign) *gods* (v. 16)—these gods could not claim to have been kind to them—and to *new gods, that came newly up*, gods that recently appeared (v. 17). A new god! Can there be anything more absurd?

2.1.1. These so-called "gods" were not gods at all. Their names had been made up by the human imagination, and their idols were the work of human hands.

2.1.2. In fact, they were devils. Far from being *gods*, they really were "destroyers"—for this is what the word means—whose purpose was to cause trouble.

2.2. What a great insult this was to Jehovah their God. It was justly considered as neglecting and forgetting him (v. 18): *Of the Rock that begat thee thou art unmindful*, and it was justly considered an inexcusable offense.

Verses 19–25

The song continues to follow the outline of the predictions of the previous chapter.

1. He had delighted in them, but now he would reject them. The closer any are to God by professing to be his people, the more offensive they are to him if they defile themselves in sin (Ps 106:39–40).

2. He had given them the signs of his presence with them and his favor toward them, but now he would withdraw and *hide his face from them* (v. 20). His *hiding his face* shows his great displeasure. It also shows how slow God is in judging them. They were perverse and willful and were unfaithful and a people that could not be trusted.

3. He had done everything to make them secure, but now the punishment corresponds to the sin (v. 21).

3.1. They had offended God with detestable gods which were not gods at all.

3.2. God would therefore strike them with detestable enemies. The more evil the people that tyrannized them, the more cruel they would be—there is no one so arrogant as an undeserving person given power.

4. He had planted them in a good land and filled them with good things, but now he would remove every comfort from them and destroy them. The judgments threatened are: famine; plagues; the insults of the lower creatures, *the teeth* (fangs) *of beasts and the poison of serpents* (the venom of vipers) (v. 24); and war and its fatal consequences (v. 25).

Verses 26–38

After many terrible threats of deserved wrath and vengeance, here are some surprising signs of undeserved mercy, which triumphs over judgment, and by which it appears that God has *no pleasure in the death of sinners*, but would rather they should *turn and live* (Eze 33:11).

1. To protect his own honor, he will not destroy them completely (vv. 26–28). Mercy prevails to spare a remnant and to save that unworthy people from complete destruction: *I feared the wrath of the enemy* (v. 27). It is a very human expression; it is certain that God fears the wrath of no human being, but because the few good people remaining in Israel feared God's name being mocked, he acted here as if he had feared it. He did not need Moses to plead it with him, but he reminded himself of it: what will the Egyptians say? However much we deserve to be disgraced, God will never disgrace the throne of his glory.

2. He deeply desires their conversion out of concern for their welfare. God takes no delight in seeing sinners destroy themselves, but he wants them to help themselves, and if they want to be helped, he is ready to give them that help. If sinners seriously consider what will happen to them in the end, in the future state, that will help them return to God. Here is a particular description of what God had foretold through Moses concerning this people in the future, but it may also be applied more generally.

3. He calls to mind the great things he had formerly done for them, as a reason why he should not reject them

totally. This seems to be the meaning of vv. 30–31, "How could one Israelite have been too hard for a thousand Canaanites, as they have been many times, except that God, who is greater than all gods, fought for them?" This corresponds with Isa 63:10–11. When God was their enemy and when he fought against them because of their sins, he then remembered the former days, saying, *Where is he that brought them out of the sea?* God would soon have subdued their enemies (Ps 81:14), except that the evil of Israel gave them into their enemies' hands.

4. He decides finally to destroy those who had been the persecutors and oppressors of Israel. God will bring down the church's enemies in due time:

4.1. In displeasure at their evil, which he notices and keeps an account of (vv. 34–35). Some understand it as the sin of Israel, especially their persecution of the prophets, which was kept in store against them since *the blood of righteous Abel* was shed (Mt 23:35). Whether this is so or not, it teaches us that God's righteous anger, as his just response to the evil of evildoers, would come on them in due course.

4.2. In compassion for his own people, who, although they had greatly offended him, were still in relationship with him. Their misery appealed to his mercy (v. 36). This clearly points to the ways in which God used judges to rescue Israel from the hands of those to whom they had been sold for their sins (see Jdg 2:11–18), and to how *his soul was grieved for the misery of Israel* (Jdg 10:16), when they reached crisis point. God helped them when they could not help themselves.

4.3. To disgrace the idol-gods (vv. 37–38). Where are their gods? This may be understood in two ways:

4.3.1. That God would do for his people what the idols which they had served could not do for them. Or:

4.3.2. That God would do the things against their enemies which the idols they had served could not save them from. Sennacherib and Nebuchadnezzar boldly challenged the God of Israel to rescue his worshipers (Isa 37:10; Da 3:15), and God did rescue them to the shame of their enemies. But the God of Israel challenged Bel and Nebo to rescue their worshipers, to rise up and help and protect them (Isa 47:12–13), and far from them being able to help, the idols—which was all they were—were themselves taken into captivity (Isa 46:1–2).

Verses 39–43

This conclusion of the song speaks of three things:

1. Glory to God (v. 39). The great God here requires the glory:

1.1. Of self-existence: *I, even I, am he* (v. 39). In this way, Moses is concluding with the name of God by which God was first made to know him (Ex 3:14): "*I AM THAT I AM*. I am he that I have been, that I will be, that I have promised to be, that I have threatened to be; all will find me true to my word." One of the Targums paraphrases it in this way: "When the Word of the Lord reveals himself to redeem his people, he will say to all people, 'See that I now am what I am, and have been, and I am what I will be,'" which we know very well applies to the One who said to John, *I am he who is, and was, and is to come* (Rev 1:8). We read these words, *I, even I, am he* (v. 39) often in those chapters of Isaiah where God is encouraging his people to hope for their rescue from Babylon (Isa 41:4; 43:11, 13, 15, 25; 46:4).

1.2. Of sole supremacy. "There *is no god with* (besides) *me* (v. 39). There is none to help me and none to contend with me." See Isa 43:10–11.

1.3. Of absolute and universal sovereignty: *I kill, and I make alive* (v. 39).

1.4. Of irresistible power.

2. Terror to God's enemies (vv. 40–42). This is terror to those who hate him, that is, those who serve other gods, who willfully persist in disobeying his Law, and who persecute his faithful servants. In order to strike fear in such people to repent:

2.1. The divine sentence is confirmed with an oath (v. 40): he *lifts up his hand to heaven,* where he lives in his holiness. This was an ancient and significant sign used in swearing (Ge 14:22). The sin of sinners will lead to their destruction if they continue in their sin.

2.2. Preparation is made for the sentence to be carried out: the *glittering sword is whet,* the flashing sword is sharpened (v. 41). See Ps 7:12.

2.3. The execution itself will be terrible.

3. Comfort to his own people (v. 43): *Rejoice, O you nations, with his people.* He concludes the song with words of joy, for there is a remnant in God's Israel whose conclusion will be peace. God's people will finally be joyful; they will rejoice forever. Three things are mentioned here as causes for joy:

3.1. The enlarging of the church's boundaries. The apostle Paul applies the first words of this verse to the conversion of the Gentiles: *Rejoice you Gentiles with his people* (Ro 15:10)

3.2. The taking of vengeance on the church's adversaries.

3.3. The mercy God has in store for his church and for all who belong to it. He will be *merciful to his land, and to his people* (v. 43), that is, to people everywhere who fear and serve him.

Verses 44–52

Here is:

1. The solemn giving of this song to the children of Israel (vv. 44–45). Moses spoke it to as many people as could hear him, while Joshua, in another assembly at the same time, recited it to as many as his voice would reach. Though the people changed their commander, there was no change in the divine command. Joshua, as well as Moses, would be a witness against them if they ever abandoned God.

2. A serious command to them to observe these words and all the other good words Moses had spoken to them.

2.1. He gives them the responsibilities that:

2.1.1. They should think carefully about these things for themselves: "Set your hearts on the laws, and also on the promises and threats, the blessings and curses, and finally on this song."

2.1.2. They should faithfully pass on these things to those who would come after them. Those who themselves are good must want their children to be likewise.

2.2. The reasons he uses to persuade them to make their religious faith real in their lives and to persevere in it are:

2.2.1. The immense importance of what he had commanded them (v. 47): *It is not a vain thing, because it is your life.* He had not spoken idle words, but words of vital importance.

2.2.2. The immense benefits it would bring them: *Through this thing you shall prolong your days* (v. 47) in Canaan, which was a type of the promise of the eternal life Christ has assured for those who keep God's commandments (Mt 19:17).

3. An order given to Moses concerning his death. Now that this renowned witness for God had finished his testimony, he must go up to Mount Nebo and die. Orders

were given to Moses that same day (v. 48). Now that he had completed his work, why should he desire to live a day longer? He had indeed formerly prayed that he might go over the Jordan, but now he is fully satisfied, and as God had asked him, *saith no more of that matter* (3:26).

3.1. God reminds him of the sin he had been guilty of, which was why he was excluded from Canaan (v. 51).

3.2. God reminds him of the death of his brother Aaron (v. 50), to make his own death less difficult and less formidable.

3.3. God sends him up a high hill, to look onto the land of Canaan from there and then die (vv. 49–50). Remembering his sin might make death terrible, but the sight God gave him of Canaan took away its terror, because it was a sign that he had been reconciled to God. It also clearly showed him that though his sin excluded him from the earthly Canaan, it would not deprive him of that better country which can only be seen in this world with the eye of faith.

CHAPTER 33

Moses has not yet finished with the children of Israel, however, even though he had preached them a farewell sermon. But it had been a long sermon, and then he had given them a long psalm, and now nothing remains except to dismiss them with a blessing. He pronounces that blessing in this chapter in the name of the Lord, and then takes his final leave of them: 1. He declares them all to be blessed in what God had done for them already, especially in giving them his Law (vv. 1–5). 2. He declares a blessing on each tribe, which is both a prayer for and a prophecy of their happiness: Reuben (v. 6); Judah (v. 7). 3. Levi (vv. 8–11). 4. Benjamin (v. 12) and Joseph (vv. 13–17). 5. Zebulun and Issachar (vv. 18–19); Gad (vv. 20–21). 6. Dan (v. 22); Naphtali (v. 23); and Asher (vv. 24–25). 7. He declares them all blessed in general if they remain obedient (vv. 26–29).

Verses 1–5

The first verse of this chapter is its title: the chapter is a blessing. In the previous chapter the terrors of the Lord had thundered out against Israel for their sin. Now, so that he might not seem to be angrily taking his leave of them, he adds a blessing. In the same way, Christ's last work on earth was to bless his disciples (Lk 24:50), as Moses did here, as a sign of parting as friends. Moses blessed them:

- As a prophet—a *man of God* (v. 1).
- As a parent to Israel, for good rulers are like parents to their subjects. Jacob blessed his sons on his deathbed (Ge 49:1). Moses now follows his example and blesses the tribes that were descended from Jacob's sons. He wanted them to be happy, although he had to die and could not share their happiness. He begins his blessing with a grand description of the glorious appearances of God to them when he gave them the Law, and the great benefits they gained from it:

1. There was a visible and radiant revelation of the divine Majesty, enough to convince and silence forever all non-believers, to awaken and stir those who were foolish and negligent, and to put to shame all secret inclinations to follow other gods (v. 2). His retinue was glorious; he came with his holy myriads, as Enoch had long since foretold he would come on the last day to judge the world (Jude 14). This is why the Law is said to *be given by the disposition of angels* (Ac 7:53; Heb 2:2).

2. He gave them his Law, which:

2.1. Is called *a fiery law* (v. 2), because it was given them *out of the midst of the fire* (4:33), and its effects are like fire. If it is received, it melts, warms, purifies, and burns up the dross of corruption. If it is rejected, it hardens, sears, torments, and destroys. The Spirit descended in divided tongues as of fire, for the Gospel also is a fiery law.

2.2. Is said to *go from his right hand* (v. 2), to show the power and energy of the Law and the divine strength that goes along with it, so that it may not return empty. It came as a strong and precious gift to them.

2.3. Was an example of the special kindness he had for them: *Yea, he loved the people* (v. 3), and so although it was a fiery law, it is still said to *go for them* (v. 2), that is, in their favor. This shows us that when the Law of God is written on the heart, it is definite evidence that the love of God has been poured out there. We must consider God's Law to be one of the gifts of his grace. *All his saints are in his hand* (v. 3). They were in his hand to be covered, protected, and used as the seven stars were in the hand of Christ (Rev 1:16).

3. He made them willing to receive the Law which he gave them: *They sat down at thy feet* (v. 3); they bowed down reverently as scholars at the feet of their teacher, waiting for and humbly submitting to what is taught. Israel was like this at the foot of Mount Sinai and promised to hear and do whatever God would say. Everyone then stood ready to receive God's words and did so again when the Law was publicly read to them, as in Jos 8:34.

3.1. They are taught to speak with great respect of the Law, and to call it *the inheritance of the congregation of Jacob* (v. 4).

3.2. They are taught to speak with great respect of Moses. They were particularly obliged to keep his name because he had not provided for it to be kept in his family. His descendants were never called the *sons of Moses* as the priests were called the *sons of Aaron*.

Verses 6–7

Here is:

1. The blessing of Reuben. Though Reuben had lost the honor of his birthright, Moses still begins with him, for we should not gloat over those who are disgraced, nor should we want to remember people's mistakes forever (v. 6). Moses wants and foretells:

1.1. The preservation of this tribe. Although it was a frontier tribe on the other side of Jordan, still, "*Let it live*, and not be destroyed by its neighbors or lost among them." Perhaps he is referring to those chosen men of that tribe who, having had the allotment assigned to them already, left their families there, and were now ready to *go over armed before their brethren* (Nu 32:27, 32).

1.2. The increase of this tribe: *Let not his men be few*, or, "Let his men be a number." "Let Reuben live and not die, though his men be few" (v. 6) is Bishop Patrick's rendering. All the Aramaic paraphrases refer this to the other world: "Let Reuben live in eternal life, and not die the second death," is the reading of the Targum Onkelos. "Let Reuben live in this world, and not die that death which the wicked die in the world to come," read the Jonathan and the Jerusalem Targums.

2. The blessing of Judah, which is put before Levi because our *Lord sprang out of* (descended from) *Judah* (Heb 7:14). The blessing (v. 7) may refer either:

2.1. To the whole tribe in general. Moses prays for and prophesies the great prosperity of that tribe. It is taken for granted that the tribe of Judah would be both a praying tribe and an active tribe. Or:

2.2. In particular to David, as a type of Christ, in which case Moses would be praying that God *would hear his prayers* (Ps 20:1) that he would give David victory over his enemies and success in his great undertakings. The prayer that God would *bring him to his people* (v. 7) seems to refer to Jacob's prophecy concerning Shiloh, that *to him should the gathering of the people be* (Ge 49:10). The tribe of Simeon is omitted in the blessing, because Jacob had left it under a curse (Ge 49:5–7), and it had never done anything, as Levi had done, to regain its honor. It was reduced in numbers in the desert more than any of the other tribes, and Zimri, who had been so notoriously guilty in the matter of Peor, came from that tribe (Nu 25:14–18). Or perhaps because Simeon's allotment was part of that of Judah, that tribe is included in the blessing of Judah.

Verses 8–11

In blessing the tribe of Levi, Moses expresses himself more fully, not so much because it was his own tribe—for he does not mention his own relationship with it—but because it was God's special tribe. The blessing of Levi refers:

1. To the high priest, here called God's *holy one* (v. 8), because his office was holy, as a sign of which, *HOLINESS TO THE LORD* (Ex 28:36) was written on a seal attached to his turban.

1.1. Moses seems to acknowledge that God might justly have removed Aaron and his descendants because of his sin at Meribah (Nu 20:12–14). Many understand the verse in this way. However, it seems more probable to us that Moses is pleading with God the zeal and faithfulness of Aaron, and his boldness in stemming the tide of the people's grumblings at the other Meribah (Ex 17:7). All the Aramaic paraphrases agree that the time referred to in v. 8 was a time of testing in which Aaron was "found perfect and faithful."

1.2. Moses prays that the office of the high priest might always remain: *Let thy Thummim and thy Urim be with him* (v. 8). The office was given him for some distinguished service, as appears in Mal 2:5. "Lord, let this office never be taken away from him." Despite this blessing, the Urim and Thummim were lost in the Captivity, and never restored under the second temple. *Thummim* signifies integrity, and *Urim* illumination. "May these *be with thy holy one*, that is, Lord, let the high priest always be a man who is upright and who has understanding." This is a good prayer to lift up for the ministers of the Gospel, that they may have clear heads and honest hearts; light and integrity make a complete minister.

2. To the lesser priests and Levites (vv. 9–11):

2.1. He commends the zeal of this tribe for God when they sided with Moses, and so with God, against the worshipers of the golden calf (Ex 32:26–28). And those who not only keep themselves pure from the general sins of the times and places in which they live, but also bear witness against them as they are able and *stand up for God against the evildoers* (Ps 94:16), will be given special honors. Perhaps Moses was thinking of the sons of Korah, who refused to join in the rebellion led by their father (Nu 16:1–3, 32; 26:11). He may also have been thinking of Phinehas, who *executed judgment*, intervened, and *stayed the plague* (Ps 106:30).

2.2. He confirms the commission granted to this tribe to minister holy things, which was the reward for their zeal and faithfulness (v. 10).

2.2.1. They were to have dealings with God for the people: "They will teach *Jacob thy judgments and Israel thy law*, both as preachers in the religious assemblies, reading and explaining the Law (Ne 8:7–8), and as judges, deciding doubtful and difficult cases that were brought to them" (2Ch 17:8–9).

2.2.2. They were to have dealings with God for the people also in burning incense to the praise and glory of God, and in offering sacrifices to make atonement for sin and to gain God's favor. This was the work of the priests, but the Levites also helped.

2.3. He prays for them (v. 11):

2.3.1. That God would prosper them in their possessions. *Bless, Lord, his substance*, his skills. "Bless, Lord, his power," is how some understand it. "Lord, increase your graces in them and make them more and more fit to do your work."

2.3.2. That God would accept them in their services: "Be pleased to accept the work of his hands, both for himself and for the people to whom he ministers."

2.3.3. That God would act against all his enemies.

Verses 12–17

Here is:

1. The blessing of Benjamin (v. 12). Benjamin is put next to Levi because the temple, where the priests' work was, lay on the edge of this tribe's allotment, and it is put before Joseph because of the renown of Jerusalem—part of which was in this tribe—above Samaria, which was in the tribe of Ephraim. It was also put next to Levi because Benjamin remained faithful to the house of David and to the temple of the Lord, when the other tribes deserted the house of David and the temple with Jeroboam (1Ki 12:21).

1.1. Benjamin is here called the *beloved of the Lord* (v. 12); the father of this tribe was Jacob's beloved son, the "son of my right hand" (the meaning of the name *Benjamin*). Saul the first king and Paul the great apostle both came from this tribe.

1.2. Benjamin is here assured of God's protection: he will *dwell in safety*.

1.3. It is suggested that the temple in which God would dwell would be built at the borders of this tribe. Jerusalem the holy city was in this tribe's allotted land (Jos 18:28), and although Zion, the city of David, belonged to Judah, Mount Moriah, on which the temple was built, was in Benjamin's allotted land. God is *therefore* said to dwell *between his shoulders* (v. 12), because the temple stood on that mount, as the head is on a person's shoulders.

2. The blessing of Joseph, including both Manasseh and Ephraim. When Jacob blessed his sons (Ge 49:1–27), his blessing on Joseph was the largest, and so it is here. Moses uses the title Jacob had given to Joseph (v. 16), noting that he was *separated from his brethren* (Ge 49:26). His brothers set him apart from them by making him a slave, but God set him apart from them by making him a ruler among them. This tribe's blessings are of great plenty and great power.

2.1. Great plenty (vv. 13–16). In general: *Blessed of the Lord be his land* (v. 13). The lands which were allotted to Ephraim and Manasseh were fruitful, but Moses prays they might be watered by the blessing of God.

2.1.1. He lists many details which he prays may lead to the wealth and abundance of those two tribes. He prays:

2.1.1.1. For rain and dew in their seasons, *the precious things of heaven* (v. 13). They are so precious, though only pure water, that without them all the earth's crops would fail completely.

2.1.1.2. For plentiful springs, which help to make the earth fruitful, called here *the deep that coucheth beneath*, the deep waters that lie below (v. 13).

2.1.1.3. For the favorable influences of the heavenly bodies (v. 14), *for the precious fruits* produced by the reviving heat of the sun and the cooling moisture of the moon.

2.1.1.4. For the fruitfulness of their hills and mountains, which in other countries were barren (v. 15).

2.1.1.5. For the products of the lower lands (v. 16): *For the precious things of the earth*. Although the earth itself seems a worthless lump of matter, precious things are produced from it to support and strengthen human life. Some consider these precious things prayed for to be pictures of *spiritual blessings in heavenly things by Christ* (Eph 1:3): the gifts, graces, and comforts of the Spirit.

2.1.2. He crowns all with the goodwill, the favorable acceptance, of the One who *dwelled in the bush* (v. 16), that is, of God, who appeared to Moses in the burning bush which was not consumed (Ex 3:2), to give him the commission to lead Israel out of Egypt. Though God's glory appeared there only for a while, it is still said to dwell there. The verse might be read, "the goodwill of the *Shechinah* in the bush," for *Shechinah* means "that which dwells" or "the one who dwells." God had appeared to Moses many times, but now that Moses is dying he seems to have the most pleasant remembrance of the first time God appeared to him, when he first came to have visions of the Almighty. That time of intimacy was never forgotten. So when Moses prays for the goodwill of him that *dwelled in the bush* (v. 16), he is considering the covenant renewed then and there, on which all our hopes of God's favor must be based.

2.2. Great power (v. 17). Three examples of Joseph's power are foretold:

2.2.1. His authority among his brothers: *His glory is like the firstling* (firstborn) *of his bullock* (v. 17), or young bull, which is a dignified animal and so was formerly used as a sign of royal majesty.

2.2.2. His force against his enemies and victory over them: *His horns are like the horn of a unicorn* (wild ox) (v. 17), that is, "The forces he will bring into the field will be very strong and formidable, and *with them he shall push the people*" (v. 17).

2.2.3. The numbers of his people, in which Ephraim, although the younger family, outnumbered Manasseh as Jacob foretold when he crossed hands and blessed Ephraim above Manasseh (Ge 48:19); *they are the ten thousands of Ephraim, and the thousands of Manasseh* (v. 17).

Verses 18–21

Here we have:

1. The blessings of Zebulun and Issachar put together, for they were both the sons of Jacob by Leah, and were neighbors in their allotted lands in Canaan. It is foretold:

1.1. That they would both be comfortably settled and employed (v. 18). Zebulun must rejoice, for he will have cause to rejoice; and Moses prays that he may have cause to rejoice in his *going out*, either to war or to sea, for Zebulun was *a haven of ships* (Ge 49:13). And Issachar must rejoice in his tents, that is, in his business at home, his farming, to which that tribe generally confined themselves. Notice here:

1.1.1. That the providence of God, just as it marks out the different boundaries for people to live in—some in the city and some in the country, some in seaports and some in towns—so also it wisely inclines people to different employments. The genius of some people leads them to writing, of others to the sea, of others to the armed forces. Some take up a job in the country; others take up a trade, and still others are good at engineering. It is good that it is so. *If the whole body were an eye, where were the hearing?* (1Co 12:17). It was for the common good of Israel that the tribe of Zebulun were merchants and the tribe of Issachar farmers.

1.1.2. That whatever our place and business are, we will do well if we adapt ourselves to our circumstances, and then we will be happy.

1.2. That they would both be useful in the work to which they were called, for the honor of God and for the good of the religious faith of the nation (v. 19). It has often been observed that though those who like Zebulun travel widely and meet many people often know more of the *light* of religion, those who stay like Issachar and live in the country know more of its *life* and *energy.*

1.2.1. It is here foretold that both these tribes would grow rich. Zebulun, who travels widely, will *suck of* (feast on) *the abundance of the seas* (v. 19), the good things that merchants enjoy, while Issachar, who stays at home, will be enriched with *treasures hid in the sands* (v. 19), either the fruits of the earth or the underground treasures of metals and minerals, or—because the word for *sand* here properly refers to the sand of the sea—the rich things thrown up by the sea, for Issachar's allotted land reached to the coast.

1.2.2. It is foretold that after these tribes had been enriched in this way, they would *consecrate their gain unto the Lord, and their substance unto the Lord of the whole earth* (Mic 4:13).

2. The blessing of the tribe of Gad (vv. 20–21). This was one of the tribes already positioned on that side of the Jordan where Moses now was.

2.1. He foretells what this tribe would be (v. 20):

2.1.1. That it would be expanded, even though they already had a spacious allotment. We find how this tribe gained more land because of their success in a war—which it seems they carried out very religiously against the Hagrites (1Ch 5:19–20, 22).

2.1.2. That it would be a brave and victorious tribe. If they were left alone, they would live as securely and fearlessly as a lion, but if provoked, they would, like a lion, *tear the arm with the crown of the head* (v. 20). He would pull to pieces all who stood in his way, both the arm—the strength—and the crown of the head—the skill and authority—of his enemies.

2.2. He commends this tribe for what they had done and were now doing (v. 21).

Verses 22–25

Here is:

1. The blessing of Dan (v. 22). When Jacob blessed him, he compared him to a serpent in his cunning. Moses compares him to a lion in his courage and resolution. What could stand before a people with the head of a serpent and the heart of a lion? He is compared to the lions that leaped from Bashan, a mountain noted for its fierce lions, from where they came down to seize on their prey on the plains. A group from this tribe—after they had found out about the security of Laish, which was in the most distant part of Canaan from them—launched a surprise attack on it and soon conquered it. See Jdg 18:27. And because the mountains of Bashan lay far not far from that city, they probably made their descent on it from there, and so are said to *leap from Bashan* (v. 22).

2. The blessing of Naphtali (v. 23). He looks on this tribe with wonder and applauds it: "O Naphtali, you are happy, you will be so, and may you always be so!" Jacob had described this tribe to be generally a polite and friendly people, giving kind words like a loving deer (Ge 49:21). Now what would they gain by being so? Moses here tells them they would gain a share in the affections of their neighbors and be satisfied with favor. The Jews say that the portion of the tribe of Naphtali was so fruitful, and the products so advanced, that although it lay north, those from this tribe were generally the first to bring their firstfruits to the temple. They therefore were the first to receive the blessing from the priest, which was the blessing of the Lord. Capernaum, where Christ mainly stayed, was on land belonging to this tribe. Naphtali would also *Possess the west and the south* (v. 23), or "the sea and the south," that is, the sea which will lie south of your allotted land, the Sea of Galilee, which we read about so much in the Gospels, directly north of which was the allotted territory of this tribe, and which was of great advantage to the tribe of Naphtali, as can be seen from the wealth of Capernaum and Bethsaida.

3. The blessing of Asher (vv. 24–25). He prays for and prophesies four things about this tribe, which carries blessedness in its name, for Leah called the father of it *Asher,* saying, *Happy am I* (Ge 30:13):

3.1. The increase of their numbers.

3.2. Favor with their neighbors: *Let him be acceptable to* (favored by) *his brethren* (v. 24).

3.3. The richness of their land:

3.3.1. Above the ground: *Let him dip* (bathe) *his foot in oil* (v. 24), that is, "Let him have plenty of oil in his allotted land so that he may not only anoint his head with it, but also if he wants, wash his feet in it."

3.3.2. Under the ground: *Thy shoes* (the bolts of your gates) *shall be iron and brass* (bronze) (v. 25), that is, "You will have plenty of these metals and mines in your own land." The Aramaic paraphrases understand this figuratively: "You will be strong and bright like iron and bronze."

3.4. The continuance of their strength and energy: *As thy days, so shall thy strength be*; your strength will equal your days (v. 25). Many paraphrase it, "The strength of your old age will be like that of your youth. You will not feel that your body is decaying, or that you are becoming the worse for wear, but you will renew your youth. It will be as if your shoes and your bones will be as strong as iron and bronze." Is work given them? They will have strength to do it. Have they been given burdens? They will have strength to bear them. They will never be *tempted above that they are able* (1Co 10:13).

Verses 26–29

Moses, the man of God, exalts with his last breath both the God of Israel and the Israel of God:

1. There is no God like the God of Israel. None of the gods of the nations could do for their worshipers what Jehovah did for his: *There is none like unto the God of Jeshurun* (v. 26).

1.1. His sovereign power and authority: *He rides upon the heavens* (v. 26). When he has anything to do for his people, he *rides upon the heavens* (v. 26) to do it, for he does this strongly and quickly. No enemy can either know in advance or obstruct the progress of the One who rides on the heavens.

1.2. His infinite eternity. He is the eternal God. His arms are *everlasting* (v. 27). The gods of the nations had only just been thought up and would soon be forgotten, but the God of Jeshurun is eternal. He was before all worlds and will be when all time and days finish. See Hab 1:12.

2. There are no people like the Israel of God. Having declared a blessing on each tribe, at the end he declares them all together to be blessed, so blessed in all respects that there was no nation under the sun comparable to them (v. 29). If Israel honors God as the incomparable One, he will favor them and make them an incomparable people. What is here said of the church of Israel can certainly be applied to *the church of the firstborn* (Heb 12:23), whose names are written in heaven. The Christian church is the Israel of God, as the apostle calls it (Gal 6:16).

2.1. Never was a people so well established or sheltered (v. 27): *The eternal God is thy refuge.* The word *refuge* means "dwelling place, where you are as safe, secure, and at rest as people feel in their own houses." Every Israelite indeed is at home in God; the soul returns to him and has him as its resting-place (Ps 116:7) and hiding-place (Ps 32:7).

2.2. Never was a people so well supported and carried: *Underneath are the everlasting arms* (v. 27). Here is the almighty power of God. The everlasting covenant and the everlasting comforts flowing from it are true everlasting arms. They sustain believers and keep them cheerful in dark times. God's grace is sufficient for them (2Co 12:9).

2.3. Never was a people so well commanded and led into battle: "*He shall thrust* (drive) *out the enemy from before thee* (v. 27) by his almighty power, which will open up the way before you." Believers are more than conquerors over their spiritual enemies through Christ who loved them. The author of our salvation *thrust out the enemy from before us* (v. 27) when he overcame the world and disarmed the powers and authorities on the cross.

2.4. Never was a people so well secured and protected (v. 28): *Israel shall then dwell in safety alone.* Those who dwell in God and make his name their strong tower, *dwell in safety*; the *place of their defense is the munitions of rocks* (the mountain fortress) (Isa 33:16). They will live in safety *alone*:

2.4.1. Even though they are alone; though they make no alliances with their neighbors.

2.4.2. Because they are alone. They will live in safety as long as they continue to lead pure lives. They were not to closely associate with the nations.

2.5. Never was a people so well provided for: *The fountain of Jacob* (v. 28)—that present generation of people, which is like a fountain to all the streams that will descend from it—will now immediately be established in a good land. "The eye of Jacob," as it might be read—for the word *fountain* also means "eye"—*is upon the land of corn and wine* (v. 28), directly in front of them on the other side of the river.

2.6. Never was a people so well helped. If they were in any difficulty, God himself rode on the heavens for *their help* (v. 26). And they were *a people saved by the Lord* (v. 29).

2.7. Never was a people so well armed. God himself was the shield with which they were armed defensively. He was also the *sword of their excellency*, with which they were armed offensively. This made them formidable.

2.8. Never was a people so well assured of victory over their enemies: *They shall be found liars unto thee* (v. 29); they will be forced to cower before you and submit to you against their will. It will be a false submission. "If you find your enemies to be liars," is how some read it, "*thou shalt tread upon their high places.*"

CHAPTER 34

Having read how Moses finished his testimony, we are told here that immediately after that his life came to an end. We have had an account of his dying words, and here we have an account of his dying work, which is a work we must all do soon. It had to be done well. Here is: 1. The view Moses had of the land of Canaan just before he died (vv. 1–4). 2. His death and burial (vv. 5–6); his age (v. 7). Israel's mourning for him (v. 8). 3. His successor (v. 9) and his character (vv. 10–12).

Verses 1–4

1. Moses climbs upward toward heaven, as high as the top of Pisgah, to die there, for that was the appointed place (32:49–50). Israel was camped on the flat land in the plains of Moab, and he went up from there as he was ordered to climb the highest point or ridge of Mount Nebo, which was called *Pisgah* (v. 1). Pisgah is a generic name for all such peaks. It would seem that Moses went up to the top of Pisgah alone and without help. When he had completed blessing Israel, we suppose that he solemnly took leave of Joshua, Eleazar, and the rest of his friends, who probably took him to the foot of the hill. But then he commanded them as Abraham commanded his servants at the foot of another hill: *Abide ye here ... and I ... will go yonder* (Ge 22:5). He went up:

1.1. To show that he was willing to die. When he knew the place of his death, far from avoiding it, he happily climbed a steep hill to reach it.

1.2. To show that he looked on death as his ascension. When the soul of a good person leaves the body, it *goes upwards* (Ecc 3:21). When God's servants are sent for from this world, the call comes, *Go up and die.*

2. Moses looks downward again toward this world, to see the earthly Canaan which he can never enter. But he also looks forward by faith to the heavenly Canaan which he would now enter immediately.

2.1. If he went up alone to the top of Pisgah, he was not really alone, for the Father was with him (Jn 16:32).

2.2. This shows us that we are indebted to the grace of God for all the pleasant prospects we have of the better country, for he gives the spirit of wisdom as well as the spirit of revelation, the ability to see as well as the object seen.

2.3. He saw it at a distance. Through grace, believers now have such a sight of the bliss and glory of their future state. The word and ordinances are to them what Mount Pisgah was to Moses.

2.4. He saw it, but could never enjoy it. Glorious things are spoken about the kingdom of Christ in the last days, its progress, growth, and expansion. We foresee it but are unlikely to live to see it. We hope that those who come after us will enter that Promised Land, which comforts us.

2.5. Canaan was Immanuel's land (Isa 8:8), so when he viewed it, he was viewing the blessings we enjoy in Christ.

Verses 5–8

Here is:

1. Moses' death (v. 5): *Moses the servant of the Lord died.* It was hard on Moses himself, when he had gone through all the tiring years in the desert, to be prevented from enjoying the pleasures of Canaan. But *the man Moses was very meek* (Nu 12:3); it is God's will, and Moses gladly submits to it.

1.1. He is called *the servant of the Lord* (v. 5). He was not only a good person—all the saints are God's servants—but he was also exceptionally useful. He had nobly served God's purposes in leading Israel out of Egypt and through the desert.

1.2. But he dies. Neither his godliness nor his usefulness could save him from the deathblow. God's servants must die so that they may rest from their labors, receive their reward, and make room for others. When God's servants are moved on, they are no longer serving him on earth but go to serve him in a better world, *day and night in his temple* (Rev 7:15). He dies *according to the word of the Lord* (v. 5), meaning "at the mouth of the Lord." The Jews say, "with a kiss from the mouth of God." When the servants of the Lord have completed all their work, they must eventually die in obedience to their Master. They must be freely willing to go home whenever he sends for them (Ac 21:13).

2. Moses' burial (v. 6). God takes care of the dead bodies of his servants: just as their death is precious, so is their dust, and the covenant with it will be remembered. He was buried in a valley *over against* (opposite) *Beth-peor* (v. 6). If the soul is at rest with God, where the body rests does not matter so much. The particular place was not known, so that the children of Israel, who were so inclined to idolatry, could not make a shrine of the place and worship the dead body of Moses, who founded their nation and did so much good for them.

3. Moses' age (v. 7). His life was prolonged:

3.1. To old age. He was 120 years old, which, although far short of the years of the patriarchs, was still far longer than the age of most of his contemporaries. Moses' age was three forties. The first forty he lived as a courtier at ease and in honor at Pharaoh's court; the second forty he lived as a poor, desolate shepherd in Midian; the third forty he lived as a king in Jeshurun with honor and power, but weighed down with a great deal of care and hard work.

3.2. To a good old age: *His eye was not dim*, as Isaac's (Ge 27:1) and Jacob's were (Ge 48:10), *nor was his natural force abated* (v. 7).

4. The solemn mourning for Moses (v. 8). Notice:

4.1. Who the mourners were: *The children of Israel* (v. 8).

4.2. How long they mourned: *Thirty days* (v. 8). Yet the *ending of the days of weeping and mourning* (v. 8) for Moses is a sign that however great our losses have been, we must not grieve forever. We must allow the wounds to heal with time. If we hope to go to heaven with joy, why should we go to the grave with sadness?

Verses 9–12

Here is an honorable eulogy for both Moses and Joshua. Each receives praise, as each should. Let God be glorified in both:

1. Joshua is praised as a man extraordinarily well qualified for the work which he was called to (v. 9). Moses brought Israel to the borders of Canaan and then died and

left them. This showed that *the law made nothing perfect* (Heb 7:19). The Law brings people into the desert, where they are convicted of their sin, but not into Canaan, where they find rest and the settled peace of forgiveness of their sins. It is an honor reserved for our Joshua—our Lord Jesus, of whom Joshua was a type—to do for us what *the law could not do, in that it was weak through the flesh* (Ro 8:3). Through him we enter into rest, the spiritual rest of conscience and eternal rest in heaven. Three things worked together to bring about Joshua's call to this great undertaking:

1.1. God equipped him for it: *He was full of the spirit of wisdom* (v. 9). Leadership qualities are as necessary in a general as courage.

1.2. Moses had ordained him to this role under God: *He had laid his hands upon him* (v. 9), so substituting Joshua as Moses' successor and praying that God would equip him for the service to which he had called him.

1.3. The people happily acknowledged him and submitted to him.

2. Moses is praised (vv. 10–12) and with good reason:

2.1. He was indeed a very great man, especially in two respects:

2.1.1. His intimacy with the God of nature: *God knew him face to face* (v. 10), and so he knew God. See Nu 12:8.

2.1.2. His privileges and power in the kingdom of nature. The miracles of judgment he performed in Egypt before Pharaoh and the miracles of mercy he performed in the desert before Israel showed that he was a special favorite of heaven and that he had an extraordinary commission to act as he did on earth. Never was there any man whom Israel had more reason to love, or whom the enemies of Israel had more reason to fear.

2.2. He was greater than any other of the Old Testament prophets. Though these prophets had great privileges in heaven and great influence on earth, none of them could compare with this great man. None of them either received or carried out such a commission from heaven as Moses did. This eulogy to Moses seems to have been written long after his death, but then no prophet had risen *like unto Moses* (v. 10). God gave the Law through Moses and molded and formed the Jewish church. God only sent particular rebukes, directions, and predictions through the other prophets. The last of the prophets concludes with a charge *to remember the law of Moses* (Mal 4:4). Christ himself often appealed to the writings of Moses, and appealed to him as a witness, as one who *saw his day* at a distance *and spoke of him* (Jn 8:56). Moses was faithful as a servant, but Christ as a Son. The record of Moses leaves him buried in the plains of Moab and concludes with the period of his government, but the record of our Savior leaves him sitting *at the right hand of the Majesty on high* (Heb 1:3), and we are assured that *of the increase of his government and peace there shall be no end* (Isa 9:7).

A Practical and Devotional Exposition of the Book of

Joshua

1. We have before us the history of the Jewish nation in this book and those that follow to the end of the book of Esther. They were a part of the words of God which were committed to the Jews and were received as such and referred to by our Savior and the apostles. In the five books of Moses we had a very full account of the rise, advance, and constitution of the Old Testament church; the family from which it was raised; the promise which was the great charter of its constitution; the miracles by which it was built up; and the laws and ordinances by which it was to be ruled. A nation that had such righteous decrees and laws would, you would think, have been holy and very happy. But the sad truth is that a great part of the history is a sorry record of its sins and unfortunate condition. If we compare the history of the Christian church with its constitution, we will find the same cause for wonder there, for its errors and corrupt ways, too, have been many; for the *Gospel* does not *make anything perfect* in this world any more than the Law, but leaves us still expecting a *better hope* in the future state.

2. We have now before us the *book of Joshua*. The reason for the book's title may not be that it was written by him, for that is uncertain. Dr. Lightfoot thinks that Phinehas wrote it. Bishop Patrick is sure that Joshua wrote it himself. Whoever is the author, we know that it is written concerning Joshua, and if any other person wrote it, it was collected from his journals or memoirs. It contains the history of Israel under the command and leadership of Joshua, how he presided as general of their armies: 2.1. In their entrance into Canaan (chs. 1–5). 2.2. In their conquest of Canaan (chs. 6–12). 2.3. In the distribution of the land of Canaan among the tribes of Israel (chs. 13–21). 2.4. In the settlement and establishment of religion among them (chs. 22–24). We may also see in it: 2.4.1. Much of God and his *providence*—his power, his justice, his faithfulness, and his kindness to his people Israel, despite their disobedience. 2.4.2. Much of Christ and his grace. Though Joshua is not expressly mentioned in the New Testament as a type of Christ, all agree that he was an outstanding one. He had our Savior's name, as did also another type of him, Joshua the high priest (Zec 6:11–12). The Septuagint (a Greek version of the Old Testament), giving the name *Joshua* a Greek ending, calls him all along *Iesous*, "Jesus," and he is called this also in the New Testament (Ac 7:45; Heb 4:8). His name means "He will save." Joshua saved God's people from the Canaanites; our Lord Jesus saves them from their sins. Christ, as Joshua, is the author of our salvation, a leader and commander of the people, to crush Satan under their feet, to give them possession of the heavenly Canaan, and to give them rest, which it is said (Heb 4:8) Joshua did not.

CHAPTER 1

In this chapter: 1. God appoints him to be the leader to replace Moses and gives him a full commission, detailed instructions, and great encouragements (vv. 1–9). 2. Joshua accepts the leadership and turns immediately to its work. He gives orders to the officers of the people in general (vv. 10–11) and in particular to the two and a half tribes (vv. 12–15). 3. The people agree to it and declare their loyalty to him (vv. 16–18).

Verses 1–9

Joshua is honored here, and great power is given into his hands by the One who is the fountain of all honor and power, and by whom monarchs reign. God speaks to him (v. 1) probably as he spoke to Moses (Lev 1:1), *out of the tabernacle of the congregation*, from the Tent of Meeting.

God speaks to him directly, to greatly encourage him, some think by a dream or vision (Job 33:15). Concerning Joshua's call, notice here:

1. The time when the call was given to him: *After the death of Moses* (v. 1). As soon as Moses was dead, Joshua took over the administration from him, because of his solemn ordination in Moses' lifetime. However, God probably did not tell him to go forward toward Canaan until after the thirty days of mourning for Moses had ended. God wanted to give the people time to grieve their loss of him and to repent of their failures toward him.

2. The place Joshua had been in before he was made leader. He was *Moses' minister*, that is, an aide or assistant in his work. The Septuagint (a Greek version of the Old Testament) translates it as *hypourgos*, a worker under his direction. Notice:

2.1. He had long been trained to work.

2.2. He was trained to be submissive and under the command of others. Those who have learned to obey are the most fit to rule.

2.3. He who was to succeed Moses knew him intimately, so that he might take the same action and walk in the same spirit as Moses had, and thus be able to carry on the same work.

2.4. In all these ways Joshua was a type of Christ. Christ himself, therefore, could be called Moses' minister, because he was born under the Law and fulfilled all its righteousness.

3. The call itself that God gave him:

3.1. The reason why he was called to rule and lead: *Moses my servant is dead* (v. 2). When Moses had completed his work as a servant, he died and went to rest from his labors *and entered into the joy of his Lord* (Mt 25:21).

3.2. The call itself: *Now therefore arise* (v. 2):

3.2.1. "Though Moses is dead, the work must go on. Get ready to go about it." When God has work to do, he will find or make instruments who are equipped to carry it on. Moses the *servant* is dead, but God the *Master* is not: he lives forever.

3.2.2. "Because Moses is dead, the work is to be given to you as his successor." Joshua must get up and finish what Moses had begun. In this way, later generations enter into the labors of earlier ones. And so Christ, our Joshua, does for us what could never be done by the Law of Moses—he *justifies* (Ac 13:39) and *sanctifies* (Ro 8:3). The life of Moses made way for Joshua and prepared the people for what was to be done by him. In the same way, the Law is a schoolteacher to bring us to Christ.

3.3. The particular service he was now called to: "*Arise, go over this Jordan* (v. 2), this river which you are looking at, and on the banks of which you are camped." This was to test Joshua's faith. He had no pontoons or boats with which he could make a bridge that they could use to cross, but he must believe that the God who had ordered them over would open up a way for them. Crossing over the Jordan was going into Canaan.

3.4. A repetition of the gift of the land of Canaan to the children of Israel (vv. 2–4): *I do give it them*. It was promised to the patriarchs—*I will give it*—but now that several generations had passed, the time had come for the promise to be fulfilled (v. 3): "*I have given it*. Even though it has not yet been conquered, it is as certain to you as if it were already in your hands." Notice:

3.4.1. The people to whom the land is transferred: *To them, even to the children of Israel* (v. 2), because they are the descendants of Jacob, who was called *Israel* at the time when this promise was made to him (Ge 35:10, 12).

3.4.2. The land itself that is transferred: from the River Euphrates east of them to the Mediterranean Sea west of them (v. 4). Had they been obedient, God would have given them this and much more. Out of all these countries, and many others, there were in the course of time converts to the Jewish religion, as can be seen from Ac 2:5–11.

3.4.3. The condition on which this gift is made is implied in the words, *as I said unto Moses* (v. 3), that is, "on the terms Moses told you about many times: *if you will keep my statutes*, you will go in and possess that good land. The only way to possess it is under these terms and conditions, and not otherwise."

3.4.4. "*Every place that the sole of your foot shall tread upon* (v. 3) will—within the boundaries mentioned—be your own. You have only to set your foot on it and it will be yours."

3.5. The promises God made to Joshua for his encouragement:

3.5.1. That he would be certain of God's presence (v. 5): "*As I was with Moses*, in leading Israel out of Egypt and through the desert, so I will be with you, to enable you to settle in Canaan." Moses was able to do what he did because of the presence of God with him, and although Joshua did not always have the same presence of mind as Moses, yet if he always had the same presence of God, he would do well enough. It is a great comfort to the rising generation of ministers and Christians that the same grace which was sufficient for those who went before them will also be sufficient for them if they make the most of it. The promise is repeated (v. 9). Those who go where God sends them will have him with them wherever they go.

3.5.2. That the presence of God would never be withdrawn from him: *I will not fail thee, nor forsake thee* (v. 5). Moses had assured him of this (Dt 31:8), saying that although he would have to leave Joshua, God never would. We can be sure that the Lord is with us while we follow him. The promise made here to Joshua may be applied to all believers.

3.5.3. That he would gain a victory over all the enemies of Israel (v. 5): *There shall not any man* that comes against you *be able to stand before thee*. No one will be able to stand up against those who have God on their side. *If he be for us, who can be against us?* (Ro 8:31).

3.5.4. That he would himself lead the people of Israel to possess the land and would distribute it among them (v. 6). He would have to be very courageous because of the bad character of the people whom he must lead to inherit that land. He well knew what a willful, discontented people they were and how perverse they had been under his predecessor.

3.6. The command God gave to Joshua:

3.6.1. That he should obey everything in the Law of God (vv. 7–8). God put the Book of the Law, as it were, into Joshua's hand. He was commanded:

3.6.1.1. *To meditate therein day and night* (v. 8). If ever anyone's work might have excused them from meditation and other devotions, you would think Joshua's might at this time. A great trust had been placed into his hands. It was enough for the work of ten people, but he must still find time and thoughts for meditation.

3.6.1.2. Not to let it *depart out of his mouth* (v. 8), that is, all his orders to the people must be consistent with the Law of God. He must on every occasion *speak according to this word* (Isa 8:20). This was no time for making new laws; instead he must carefully and faithfully keep *that good thing which was committed to him* (2Ti 1:14).

3.6.1.3. *To observe to do according to all this law* (v. 7). Joshua was a man of great power and authority, but he himself must be under command and do as he is told. The dignity or authority of no person, however great they are, sets them above the Law of God:

- He must do what was written, not only hear and know it.
- He must do *according to what was written*, observing all the Law precisely in its written form.
- He must be careful to observe the restraints of conscience, the hints of Providence, and all the advantages that opportunities gave him.
- He must *not turn from it* (v. 7) to the right or to the left, either in his own personal behavior or in his leadership and rule, for the right way is the middle way.
- He must be *strong and courageous* (v. 7).
- He was assured that if he observed the Law in all these ways, he would "do wisely" (v. 7, margin) and *make his way prosperous* (v. 8).

3.6.2. That he should encourage himself in these things with the promise and presence of God. These were to be his foundation (vv. 6–7 and again v. 9). Joshua had long since shown his bravery in the war with Amalek and when he disagreed with the report of the faithless spies. Yet although he was humble and did not distrust God, he was diffident about himself and his sufficiency for the work. This is why God repeated so often, "*Be strong and of a good courage* (v. 6). *Have not I commanded thee?* (v. 9) I have commanded the work to be done, and so it will be done." It will greatly help to stir us and make us bold if we keep our eyes on God's authority and hear him say, "*Have not I commanded thee?* (v. 9) I will therefore help you, accept you, and reward you by giving you success."

Verses 10–15

Now that Joshua is settled as Israel's leader, he gets down to business immediately to further the work of God among the people over whom God has set him:

1. He issues orders to the people to get ready for the journey. The officers of the people who, under Joshua, command their respective tribes and families wait on him for orders, which they pass on to the people. What could Joshua have done without officers? We are required to be subject, not only to *the king as supreme, but to governors as to those that are sent by him* (1Pe 2:13–14). By these officers:

1.1. Joshua gives public notice that they are *to pass over Jordan within three days* (v. 11). Notice the great assurance with which Joshua says to the people—because God said it to him—*You shall pass over Jordan, and shall possess the land* (v. 11). We greatly honor the truth of God when we do not waver through unbelief at the promise of God.

1.2. Joshua gives them directions to prepare their provisions, not their transport. The One who carried them out of Egypt would take them the same way into Canaan (Ex 19:4). But those who wanted other provisions besides manna, which had not yet stopped, must get it ready by the set time. Perhaps although the manna did not stop completely until they came to Canaan (5:12), it did not fall so plentifully anymore, since they had come *into a land inhabited* (Ex 16:35), where they could be partly supplied with other provisions. See Ex 19:10–11.

2. He reminds the two and a half tribes of the obligations they are under to go over the Jordan with their brothers, even though they will leave their possessions and families on this side. This was an act of self-denial and went against the grain, and so it was necessary to refer to the agreement which Moses made with them (v. 13): *Remember the word which Moses commanded you*. Although Moses had died, his commands and their promises were still in force. He reminds them:

2.1. Of the benefits they received in being settled first: "*The Lord your God hath given you rest* (v. 13). He has given your minds rest. You are not like the other tribes who first have to wait for the outcome of the war and then the allotting of the land. He has also given rest to your families in giving you this good land." When God by his providence has given us rest, we ought to consider what service we may do for our brothers and sisters who are not as settled. When God had given David rest (2Sa 7:1), notice how restless he was till he *found out a habitation* for the ark (Ps 132:4–5).

2.2. Of their agreement to help their brothers in the wars of Canaan until God had given them rest in the same way (vv. 14–15). This:

2.2.1. Was reasonable in itself.

2.2.2. Had been commanded by Moses, the servant of the Lord.

2.2.3. Was their only way to avoid having it count as a great sin for them to settle on that side of the Jordan, a sin which would find them out at one time or another (Nu 32:23).

2.2.4. Was the condition on which Moses had granted them *the land of their possession*, as it is called (v. 15).

2.2.5. Was an agreement that they had accepted and had covenanted to keep (Nu 32:25): *Thy servants will do as my Lord commandeth*.

Verses 16–18

This answer was given by the *officers of all the people* (v. 10) as their representatives:

1. They promise to obey Joshua (v. 16), as subjects to their ruler and as soldiers to their general; they commit themselves to Joshua: "*All that thou commandest us we will do* (v. 16), willingly and without complaining." This is how we must declare our loyalty to our Lord Jesus as the author of our salvation. We are to commit ourselves to do what he commands us by his word and to go where he sends us by his providence. The people have no reason to boast of their obedience to Moses; he found them a stubborn people (Dt 9:24). But they mean that they will follow Joshua as most of them at least sometimes followed Moses. This shows us that we must not so exalt those who are gone that we fail to honor and respect those who follow them. Obedience for the sake of conscience will continue even though Providence changes the hands by which it rules and acts.

2. They pray for the presence of God with him (v. 17): "*Only the Lord thy God be with thee* to bless and prosper you and to give you success, *as he was with Moses*." The best thing we can ask of God for those in authority is that they may have the presence of God with them. We should honor and respect those who we have reason to think have favor from God. Some understand the people's prayer as a limitation on their obedience: "We will obey you only as far as we think the Lord is with you, but no further. While you keep close to God, we will keep close to you. We will obey you up to that point, but no further." But there is no need for such a condition.

3. They make it a capital offense for any Israelite to disobey Joshua's orders or to *rebel against his commandment* (v. 18). There is a special reason for this law to be made now, when they are beginning the wars of Canaan, for in times of war the harshness of military discipline is more necessary than at other times.

4. They stir him to continue cheerfully with the work to which God has called him. Leaders are greatly encouraged if those who follow do so with goodwill. Even though Joshua's bravery was proven, yet when the people told him to be strong and courageous, he did not take it wrongly and feel insulted but accepted their words as an act of kindness.

CHAPTER 2

In this chapter we have an account of the scouts who were sent to report to Joshua about the city of Jericho. Notice: 1. How Joshua sent them (v. 1); how Rahab received them and protected them. 2. The account she gave them of what Jericho was like, and of the panic its citizens were struck with when Israel approached (vv. 8–11); the agreement she made with them for the safety of herself and her relatives (vv. 12–21). 3. Their safe return to Joshua and the account they gave him of their expedition (vv. 22–24). Rahab is twice celebrated in the New Testament: as a great believer (Heb 11:31) and as one whose faith was proved by good works (Jas 2:25).

Verses 1–7

In these verses we have:

1. The wisdom of Joshua in sending spies to see what this important route was like, which would probably be fought over when Israel entered Canaan (v. 1): *Go view the land, even Jericho.* Moses had sent spies (Nu 13:1–33); Joshua himself had been one of them. Joshua now sent spies, not to survey the whole land as the former spies had been sent to do, but to survey only Jericho. He was particularly careful to make sure the first step was taken well and that he did not stumble at the threshold. Notice:

1.1. Great people must see with other people's eyes. This makes it necessary that they be cautious in choosing who will work for them.

1.2. Faith in God's promises ought not to take the place of, but encourage, our diligence in using proper means. We are distrusting God and presumptuously testing him if our expectations and hopes make us fail to try hard.

1.3. How ready the spies were to go out on this dangerous undertaking. In obedience to Joshua their general, they were zealous for the service of the camp. They depended on the power of God.

2. The providence of God in directing the spies to the house of Rahab. We are not told how they got over the Jordan, but they came into Jericho, which was about five miles (about eight kilometers) from the river. There they looked for a convenient inn and were directed to the house of Rahab, here called *a harlot,* a woman who was or had formerly been a prostitute. That disgrace stayed with her name even though she may have repented and reformed before the spies came. And so she is called Rahab the prostitute in the New Testament, where both her faith and her good works are praised, to teach us:

2.1. That great sin is no restriction on receiving mercy and forgiveness if it is truly repented of. We read of tax collectors and prostitutes entering into the kingdom of the Messiah and being welcomed into all the privileges of the kingdom (Mt 21:31).

2.2. That there are many who were evil before their conversion but who later come to great faith and holiness.

2.3. That even those who through grace have repented of the sins of their youth must expect to bear their disgrace. It seems that God's Israel had only one well-wisher in all Jericho, and that was Rahab the prostitute. God has often served his own purposes and his church's interests by using people with uncertain morals. If these scouts had gone to any other house than this, they would certainly have been betrayed. But God knew where they could find a friend, although they did not know this, and he directed them there. God *will guide with his eye* (Ps 32:8) those who faithfully acknowledge him in their ways. See Jer 36:19, 26.

3. The godliness of Rahab in receiving and protecting these Israelites. Rahab showed her guests more than ordinary civility. It was *by faith* that she welcomed those against whom her king and country had declared war (Heb 11:31).

3.1. She made them welcome to her house, and they stayed there, even though she knew both where they came from and what their business was.

3.2. She hid them on the roof of the house, which was flat, by covering them with stalks of flax (v. 6). These stalks, which she herself had laid out on the roof to dry in the sun, in order to beat them and make them ready for the spinning wheel, show that she had one of the good qualities of the woman of noble character (Pr 31:13).

3.3. When she was asked about the spies, she denied they were in her house. It is no wonder that the king of Jericho sent a message to inquire after them (vv. 2–3). Rahab not only denied that she knew them, but so that no further search might be made for them in the city, she told the pursuers that the spies had gone away again and that in all probability they could be overtaken (vv. 4–5). Now:

3.3.1. We are sure that this was a good work: it is blessed in Jas 2:25, where she is said to be *justified by works,* and it is said that *she received the messengers, and sent them out another way.* She did this by faith, which set her above the fear of other people, even fear of the king's wrath. When she heard of the wonders done for Israel, she believed that their God was the only true God and that therefore their declared intentions for Canaan would undoubtedly take effect. This shows us that those who by faith take the Lord as their God take his people as their people, and throw in their lot with them. Those who have God as their refuge must shelter his people when a need arises. *Let my outcasts* (fugitives) *dwell with thee* (Isa 16:3–4). And we must be glad to have an opportunity to prove we are sincere and zealous in our love for God by putting ourselves at risk to serve his church and kingdom. But:

3.3.2. There is something in it which is not easy to justify.

3.3.2.1. It is clear that she betrayed her country by harboring its enemies. What justifies her in this is that *she knew the Lord had given Israel this land* (v. 9). She knew it by the incontrovertible miracles God had done for them, which confirmed that gift. She also knew that her obligations to God were higher than her obligations to any other. If she knew *God had given them* (v. 9) this land, it would have been a sin to join with those who prevented them from possessing it.

3.3.2.2. It is clear that she deceived the officers who examined her with a lie. What can we say about this? If she had either told the truth or been silent, she would have betrayed the spies, and it does not appear that she had any other way of hiding them than by her false direction to the officers to go after them another way. Yet this case was exceptional and so cannot in any way be used as a precedent. Commentators generally consider Rahab's deception a sin, though one that was extenuated by her ignorance: being a Canaanite, she may not have been taught that lying was a sin. Whatever was right in this case, we are sure that every one of us should speak the truth to their neighbor, should fear and hate lying, and should never *do evil, that good may come of it* (Ro 3:8). But God accepts what is sincerely and honestly intended, even though it contains elements of weakness and foolishness, and he is not so strict and harsh as to keep a record of our sins.

Verses 8–21

Here Rahab and the spies settle the matter concerning the service she is now going to do for them and the favor they are afterward to show to her.

1. Having gotten rid of the officers, she comes up to them on the *roof of the house* (v. 6), where they have hidden.

1.1. She tells them that the report of the great things God has done for them has come to Jericho (v. 10) to the terror of everyone.

1.2. She tells them what impressions the news of these things has made on the Canaanites: *your terror has fallen upon us* (v. 9); *our hearts did melt* (v. 11). If she kept a public house, her dealings with customers would give her the opportunity to understand how travelers from other parts of the country were thinking and feeling. It would have encouraged even the most cowardly Israelite to hear how their enemies were discouraged, and it was easy to conclude that those who now fainted before them would most certainly fall before them. This news would therefore be a pledge that all the other promises God had made to them would also be fulfilled. Let God's Israel not be afraid of their most powerful enemies.

1.3. She then makes a profession of her faith in God and his promise:

1.3.1. She believes God has power and authority over all the world (v. 11): "Jehovah your God, whom you worship and call on, is so far above all gods that he is the only true God, for *he is God in heaven above and in earth beneath* and is served by all the powers of both."

1.3.2. She believes his promise to his people Israel (v. 9): *I know that the Lord hath given you the land*. The most powerful, persuasive means will not in themselves fulfill their purpose without divine grace. It is by grace that Rahab the prostitute, who had only heard of the wonders God had done, speaks with greater assurance of the truth of the promise made to the fathers of Israel than had all the elders of Israel, all of whom were eyewitnesses of those wonders and many of whom died through unbelief in this promise.

2. She committed them to take her and her relatives under their protection (vv. 12–13). Now:

2.1. This was evidence of the sincerity and strength of her faith. Those who truly believe the divine revelation concerning the destruction of sinners and the gift of the heavenly land to God's Israel will diligently flee from the wrath to come. They will lay hold of eternal life by joining themselves to God and to his people.

2.2. The provision she made for the safety of her relatives as well as of her own family is a commendable example of natural affection. It shows us that we too should do all we can for the salvation of the souls of those who are dear to us.

2.3. Her request that they would swear to her by Jehovah (v. 12) is an example of her knowledge of the only true God and her faith in him.

2.4. Her request is fair and reasonable: that since she had protected them, they should also protect her. This teaches us that those who show mercy may expect to find mercy. Rahab was afterward advanced to become a princess in Israel, the wife of Salmon, and one of the ancestors of Christ (Mt 1:5).

3. They solemnly commit themselves to preserve the lives of Rahab and her clan in the general destruction (v. 14): *Our life for yours*. She had pledged her life for theirs, and now in return they pledge their lives for hers. They also pledge the good faith and reputation of their nation. The law of thankfulness is one of the laws of nature. Notice:

3.1. The promises they made to her. In general, *"We will deal kindly and truly with thee"* (v. 14). We will not only be kind in promising now, but also kind in exceeding your demands and expectations."

3.2. The conditions and limitations of their promises. Although they were in a hurry, we still find that they were very careful about the terms they included in the agreement. They did not want to commit themselves to more than they could fulfill. This shows us that covenants must be made with care. Those who are conscientious in keeping their promises will be careful about making them. The spies' promise was here accompanied by three conditions. They would always protect Rahab and all her relatives, provided:

3.2.1. That she tie in her window, as a sign, the scarlet cord with which she was now about to let them down (v. 18), so that the soldiers, informed about the sign, would not use force against that house. This was like the blood sprinkled on the doorframe, which kept the firstborn safe from the destroying angel (Ex 12). The same cord which she used to preserve these Israelites was to be used for her preservation. Similarly, we find that when we serve and honor God, he uses our service to bless, encourage, and strengthen us.

3.2.2. That she bring into her house, and keep there, all those whose safety she wanted to protect. When the city was to be occupied, none of them should dare move outdoors (vv. 18–19). It was reasonable that, because they were saved purely for Rahab's sake, her house should have the honor of being their refuge. It was also a significant condition, suggesting to us that those who are added to the church so that they may be saved must keep close to the society of the faithful.

3.2.3. That she keep the matter secret (vv. 14, 20): "*If thou utter this our business*, that is, if you betray us when we are gone, we will not be bound by your oath." Those who do not know how to keep a secret are unworthy of *the secret of the Lord*, unworthy to have him confide in them (Ps 25:14).

4. She then took great care to make sure her new friends were safe and *sent them out another way* (Jas 2:25), and in this way the location of her house proved very useful to them. Paul made a similar escape out of Damascus (2Co 11:33). She also directed them as to which way to go for their own safety. She instructed them to leave the high road and go off into the mountains until the pursuers returned. Those who follow God may expect Providence to protect them, but this will not excuse them from taking wise precautions to ensure their own safety. Providence must be trusted, but not tempted.

Verses 22–24

Here we have the safe return of the spies Joshua had sent and the great encouragement they brought with them to Israel to proceed in their attack on Canaan. The spies might have told Israel what they had noticed of the height and strength of the walls of Jericho. But they had a different spirit and, depending on God's promise, they inspired Joshua to depend on it too.

1. Their safe return was itself an encouragement to Joshua and a sign for good. The fact that they had come back in one piece was an example of God's great care for them for the sake of Israel. It gave the people a deep assurance of God's guidance and care. The One who had so wonderfully protected their scouts would surely also preserve their soldiers.

2. The report they brought was even more encouraging (v. 24): "*All the inhabitants of the country*, though determined to resist, still *do faint because of us*. They do not have the wisdom to surrender or the courage to fight." They conclude from this, *Truly the Lord has delivered into our hands all the land*. The fear of sinners is sometimes a definite sign of their imminent fall. If we resist our spiritual enemies, they will run away from us.

CHAPTER 3

This chapter and what follows give us the history of Israel's crossing the Jordan to go into Canaan. At Joshua's orders they marched up to the river's side (v. 1), and then God's almighty power led them through it. They passed through the Red Sea unexpectedly and at night, but here they are given notice some time before of their passing through the Jordan, and their expectations are raised. 1. The people are directed to follow the ark of the covenant (vv. 2–4). They are commanded to consecrate themselves (v. 5). The priests with the ark are ordered to go on ahead of the people (v. 6). 2. Joshua is exalted and made commander in chief (vv. 7–8). Notice is publicly given of what God is about to do for them (vv. 9–13). 3. The miracle takes place: the Jordan is divided and Israel is brought safely through it (vv. 14–17). This was the Lord's doing, and it is marvellous in our eyes (Mt 21:42).

Verses 1–6

When Rahab mentioned to the spies the *drying up of the Red Sea* (2:10), she showed that those on the other side of the river expected that the great defensive Jordan would give way to Israel in the same manner. Whether Israel expected this is not mentioned. God often *did things for them which they looked not for* (Isa 64:3). Now we are told:

1. They *came to Jordan and lodged there* (v. 1). Although they had not yet been told how they would cross the river, they still went forward in faith, having been told (1:11) that they would cross it. Let us proceed as far as we can, and let us depend on God's resources. Joshua led them in this journey, and special notice is taken of the fact that he got up early (v. 1; also 6:12; 7:16; 8:10). This shows how little he loved taking things easy. Those who want to see great things happen must get up early.

2. The people were directed to follow the ark of the covenant.

2.1. They could depend on the ark to lead them, that is, on God himself, of whose presence the ark was an appointed sign. It is called the *ark of the covenant of the Lord their God* (v. 3). What greater encouragement could they have than this, that the Lord was their God, a God in covenant with them? Here was the *ark of the covenant* (v. 3). Formerly the ark was carried in the middle of the camp, but now it went before them to *search out a resting place* for them (Nu 10:33) and, as it were, to give them formal possession of the Promised Land. In the ark were the tablets of the Law, and over it the mercy seat (atonement cover), for God's Law and grace in the heart are the most certain pledges of God's presence and favor.

2.2. They could depend on the priests and Levites, who were appointed for carrying the ark before them. The work of ministers is to declare the word of life and to carefully administer those ordinances which are the signs of God's presence and the instruments of his power and grace.

2.3. The people must follow the ark: *Remove* (move out) *from your place and go after it* (v. 3).

2.3.1. Wherever God's ordinances go, there we must go. If they move, then we must move on and go after them.

2.3.2. In the same way, we must follow the rule of the word and the direction of the Spirit in everything, and then peace will come on us as it then came on the Israel of God. They must follow the priests as far as they carried the ark, but no farther. We, too, must follow our ministers only as far as they follow Christ.

2.4. In following the ark, they must keep their distance (v. 4). None of them must come within 1,000 yards (about 900 meters) of the ark.

2.4.1. In this they showed their fearful, reverent regard to the sign of God's presence, so that its familiarity with them would not breed contempt. The command corresponded to that era of darkness, slavery, and terror; but now through Christ we have access with boldness to come right into the presence of God.

2.4.2. The ark was able to protect itself and did not need to be guarded by the soldiers, but was itself a guard to them.

2.4.3. It was made more visible to those who were to be led by it: *That you may know the way by which you must go* (v. 4). They would be encouraged to see it. *For you have not passed this way heretofore* (v. 4). They had followed an untrodden path all their way through the wilderness, but this one through the Jordan was especially so. Our way through the *valley of the shadow of death* (Ps 23:4) is a way we have not gone before. But if we have the assurance of God's presence, we do not need to be afraid.

3. They were commanded to *sanctify themselves, for tomorrow the Lord will do wonders among you* (v. 5). Joshua could tell beforehand what God would do and when. This shows us what preparation we must make to receive the revelations of God's glory and the assurances of his grace: we must consecrate ourselves; we must turn away from all other cares and devote ourselves to God's honor. We are to *cleanse ourselves from all filthiness* that contaminates *flesh and spirit* (2Co 7:1).

4. The priests were ordered to take up the ark and carry it *before the people* (v. 6). It was usually the Levites' work to carry the ark (Nu 4:15). We might expect that the Israelites now used the prayer Moses had spoken when the ark set out (Nu 10:35), *Rise up, Lord, and let thine enemies be scattered.* By this command of Joshua to the priests, judges are instructed to stir up ministers to their work. Ministers must likewise learn to go on ahead in God's ways. They must expect to be attacked most, but they *know whom they have trusted* (2Ti 1:12).

Verses 7–13

God honors Joshua, and Joshua honors God. God honors those who honor him.

1. God honored Joshua greatly by speaking to him (vv. 7–8), as God had spoken to Moses from the mercy seat (atonement cover).

1.1. God's purpose was to *magnify him in the sight of all Israel* (v. 7). He had told him before that he would be with him (1:5), but now all Israel would see it. The people whom God is with and those whom he uses and acknowledges in his service are truly great. Godly judges are to be highly honored and respected as blessings to the public. The more we see of God with them and in them, the more we should honor them. By dividing the Jordan, God would now convince them that he was with Joshua in leading them into Canaan. It was on the banks of the Jordan that God began to exalt Joshua, and it was at the same place that he began to exalt our Lord Jesus as Mediator. John was baptizing at *Bethabara* (Bethany) (Jn 1:28), "the house of passage," and there it was that when our Savior was baptized it was declared, *This is my beloved Son* (Mt 3:17).

1.2. God gave orders through Joshua to the priests themselves, that they should stand still at the edge of the waters of the Jordan while the waters parted *at the presence of the Lord* (Ps 114:5, 7). God could have divided the river without the priests, but they could not have done it without him.

2. Joshua speaks to the people and so honors God:

2.1. He earlier commanded them to consecrate themselves, and so he calls them to *hear the word of God*, for that is the usual way of sanctification (Jn 17:17).

2.2. He then tells them how they will be able to cross the Jordan, namely, by the stopping of its flow (v. 13): *The waters of Jordan shall be cut off*. The miracle of dividing waters, performed earlier at the Red Sea, is repeated here, to show that God has the same power to complete the salvation of his people that he had to begin it; that is, the miracle is repeated to show that he is as truly with Joshua as he was with Moses. The God whom they worship is the same God who made the world, and the power he used in creation is the same power that is committed to and working for them.

2.3. After the people have been directed to follow the ark, they are told that it must *pass before them into Jordan* (v. 11). Notice:

2.3.1. The ark of the covenant must be their guide. Divine grace in the Mosaic era was wrapped up as in a cloud and covered with a veil, but with Christ, our Joshua, it is revealed in the unveiled ark of the covenant.

2.3.2. It is called *the ark of the covenant of the Lord of all the earth* (v. 11). "It is your honor and happiness to have him in covenant with you. If he is yours, the whole creation is at your service, and when he pleases he will work for you."

2.3.3. They are told that the ark will *pass before them into Jordan* (v. 11). They can safely go even into the Jordan itself if the ark of the covenant leads them. So also will all their descendants (Isa 43:2): *When thou passest through the waters I will be with thee; and through the rivers, they shall not overflow thee.*

2.4. From what God has promised to do for them now, Joshua infers an assurance of what God would do still further. The dividing of the Jordan was intended to be to them:

2.4.1. A certain sign of God's presence with them.

2.4.2. A certain pledge of the conquest of Canaan. If the living God is among you, then (as it reads the Hebrew) "expelling he will expel" *from before you the Canaanites* (v. 10). God's forcing a way through the Jordan for Israel was a sure sign that all the powers of the Canaanites would be destroyed. The assurance which Joshua gave them had such a strong basis that it would enable one Israelite to chase 1,000 Canaanites. We ought to use God's glorious appearances for his church and his people to encourage our faith and hope for the future. *As for God, his work is perfect* (2Sa 22:31). If the Jordan's flood cannot keep them back, then Canaan's forces cannot drive them back.

2.5. Joshua instructs them to get twelve men ready, one from each tribe, who must be readily available to receive orders.

Verses 14–17

Here we have a short and clear account of the dividing of the River Jordan. We are told:

1. This river was now broader and deeper than it usually was at other times of the year (v. 15). The melting of the snow on the mountains of Lebanon, near which this river had its source, meant that at the time of the spring barley harvest, Jordan was at flood stage and overflowed all its banks. This great flood exalted the power of God and his kindness to Israel. Even if the banks of the Jordan are filled till they are under water, it is as easy for almighty God to divide them and dry them as if they were very narrow or shallow.

2. As soon as the feet of the priests dipped in the water's edge, the flow immediately stopped (vv. 15–16). The waters upstream swelled, piled up in a heap, and flowed back, but did not spread. The waters on the other side of this invisible dam ran down and left the bottom of the river dry. When they passed through the Red Sea, the waters were a wall on either side, but here only on the right side. Is there anything that God cannot do? What will he not do to perfect his people's salvation? When we have finished our pilgrimage through this desert, death will be like this Jordan between us and the heavenly Canaan, but the ark of the covenant has prepared a way through it for us; it is the last enemy that will be destroyed.

3. *The people passed over right against* (opposite) *Jericho* (v. 16), which was an example of their boldness and their open defiance of their enemies. To have this city in their sights was also an encouragement to them to go through Jordan, for Jericho was a notable city and the country around it very pleasant. It would also bring fear on and confound Israel's enemies to see them so close.

4. The priests *stood still in the midst of Jordan while all the people passed over* (v. 17). The ark was appointed to be in the middle of the Jordan to show that the same power which parted the waters kept them separate as long as they needed to be. The priests were appointed to stand still there:

4.1. To test their faith. Just as they made a bold step when they had first set foot in the Jordan, so now they also made a bold stand when they waited for a long time in the Jordan, but they knew they carried their own protection with them.

4.2. To encourage the faith of the people, so that they might go triumphantly into Canaan and *fear no evil* in this *valley of the shadow of death* (Ps 23:4), because they were assured of God's presence, which came between them and the proud waters that otherwise would have killed them.

CHAPTER 4

This chapter gives a further account of the miraculous passage of Israel through the Jordan. 1. The setting up of twelve stones in the Jordan (v. 9) and the taking from the Jordan of a further twelve stones (vv. 1–8). 2. The journey of the people through the river channel (vv. 10–14); the closing of the waters again (vv. 15–19). 3. The setting up of the monument in Gilgal (vv. 20–24).

Verses 1–9

How busy Joshua and all the fighting men were while they crossed the Jordan, marching into enemy country. They had their wives, children, cattle, tents, and baggage to take over this unknown and untrodden path. Nevertheless, he must make sure that this miracle of God would be remembered forever. This shows us that however busy we are, we must not neglect to do what we have to do for the glory of God. That, in fact, is the best work we could do. Now:

1. God gave orders for a memorial to be prepared. If Joshua had proceeded without divine direction, it might have looked as though he wanted his own name to be remembered. God's command here shows us that his miracles should be remembered forever. Some of the Israelites did not care whether this miracle was remembered. Others may have been so deeply impressed by it that they thought that no memorial needed be set up. But God knew what they were like and how quickly they would forget his works, and so he decided that something had to be

done to make sure this miracle would be remembered by all generations.

1.1. Joshua, as commander, must give directions about it (v. 1): *When all the people had clean* (completely) *passed over Jordan,* God spoke to Joshua about providing materials for this monument.

1.2. One man was to be chosen from each tribe to prepare materials so that each tribe would be able to hear the story from one of its own members and each tribe might contribute something to the glory of God (vv. 2, 4): *Out of every tribe a man.*

1.3. The stones of which this memorial was to be made must be taken out of the middle of the channel and as near as possible to the very place where the priests stood *with the ark* (vv. 3, 5). Future generations must know from this memorial that the Jordan was driven back, because these very stones were taken out of it.

1.4. The use of the stones was appointed as *a sign* (v. 6) and as *a memorial* (v. 7). They would cause children to ask their parents in times to come, *What mean ye by these stones?* (v. 6).

2. The Israelites acted according to these orders:

2.1. Twelve stones were taken up from the middle of the Jordan. As the people took up these stones according to God's orders, God was, as it were, giving them formal possession of the land. It all belonged to them; let them enter into it and take possession of it. What these twelve did was what the children of Israel are said to do (v. 8), because the twelve were the representatives of their respective tribes. When the Lord Jesus, our Joshua, had overcome the agony of death, dried up a path across the Jordan into heaven, and opened the kingdom of heaven to all believers, he appointed his twelve apostles to remember the Gospel and communicate it to distant places and future ages.

2.2. A further twelve stones were set up *in the midst of Jordan* (v. 9) to show the exact place where the ark stood.

Verses 10–19

Joshua observed the orders God gave him and did nothing without divine direction, completing all that *the Lord had commanded* him (v. 10).

1. *The people hasted* (hurried) *and passed over* (v. 10). Some hurried because they were not able to trust God; others hurried because they did not really think that God would keep the miracle going for any longer than necessary; others hurried because they were eager to be in Canaan. Those that thought about these things the least still hurried simply because the others did. *He that believeth doth not make haste* to go ahead of God's purposes, but hurries to put them into action (Isa 28:16).

2. The two and a half tribes led the way (vv. 12–13). They were all chosen men, fit for service and ready-armed. The two tribes had no reason to complain: the position of danger is the position of honor.

3. When all the people had finished crossing to the other side, the priests with the ark came up out of the Jordan. Joshua did not order them to leave the Jordan until God directed him to do so (vv. 15–17). However lowly a condition God may bring his priests or people into at any time, they must wait patiently until God in his providence calls them up out of it. As long as they have the signs of God's presence with them, let them not become tired of waiting, even in the depths of their trouble.

4. As soon as the priests and the ark had come up out of the Jordan, the waters of the river, which had stood up in a heap, gradually flowed down according to their usual, natural course. When the purpose had been fulfilled, and the sign of God's presence had been taken away, the waters immediately flowed again.

5. Joshua was exalted by all this (v. 14): *On that day the Lord magnified Joshua,* both by the fellowship into which God took him with himself and also by the authority in which God confirmed him over the priests and people. The best and most certain way of commanding respect from subordinates is not by blustering and threatening, but by showing holiness, love, and a constant concern for their welfare and for God's will and honor. Those who are sanctified are truly exalted and are worthy of double honor.

6. A record was kept of the time of this great event (v. 19): it was *on the tenth day of the first month,* just forty years since they came out of Egypt, minus five days. God had said in his anger that they would wander for forty years in the desert. He eventually brought them into Canaan five days before the forty years were over, to show how little pleasure God takes in administering punishment and how quick he is to show mercy. God ordered it so that they would enter Canaan four days before the annual ceremony of the Passover, and on the exact day when preparations for it were to begin (Ex 12:3), because he wanted them to remember their rescue from Egypt.

Verses 20–24

The twelve stones which were *laid down in Gilgal* (v. 8) are now arranged together. Perhaps they were set one on top of the other; on the other hand, they may have been set one next to another in rows, for after they are set up, they are not called *a heap of stones,* but simply *these stones.*

1. Future generations would ask about their meaning: *Your children shall ask their fathers, What mean these stones?* (v. 21). This shows us that those who want to be wise when they are old must be inquisitive when they are young. Similarly, our Lord Jesus—although he had in himself the fullness of knowledge—has taught children and young people by his example to hear and ask questions (Lk 2:46).

2. The parents are directed as to how to answer this question (v. 22): "*You shall let your children know* what you yourselves have learned from the written word and from your fathers." This teaches us that it is the duty of parents to help their children come to know the word and works of God in their early years.

2.1. The people must let their children know that the Jordan was driven back before Israel, who *went through it upon dry land,* and that this was the very place where they crossed. This shows us that God's mercies to our ancestors are mercies to us; and we should remember the great things God did for our ancestors in former times.

2.2. They must also use that occasion to tell their children about the Red Sea drying up forty years before: *As the Lord your God did to the Red Sea* (v. 23). We can learn from this:

2.2.1. That by comparing later mercies to former mercies, we can see that God is the same yesterday, today, and forever.

2.2.2. That later mercies should remind us of former mercies and renew our thankfulness for them.

2.3. They must direct their children to use these miracles to edify themselves spiritually, and the children could do this in two ways. First, they would see that the power of God was exalted in this miracle, for the rescues of God's people are instructive for all people. They serve as a reasonable warning not to fight against almighty God. Second, remembering this miracle would powerfully restrain them from worshiping other gods and would constrain them to stay close to and serve their own God fully.

CHAPTER 5

Israel has now crossed the Jordan. The people now have a foothold in Canaan and must turn to its conquest, so this chapter tells us: 1. How their enemies were discouraged (v. 1) and what was done when they first landed to help and encourage them: the covenant of circumcision was renewed (vv. 2–9). 2. The Feast of the Passover was celebrated (v. 10); their camp was provided with the grain of the land, after which the manna stopped (vv. 11–12). 3. The commander of the Lord's army himself appeared to Joshua to encourage and direct him (vv. 13–15).

Verses 1–9

The numerous camp of Israel must no doubt have been a great display of military strength in the plains of Jericho where they had pitched their tents. The *church in the wilderness has now come up from the wilderness, fair as the moon, clear as the sun, and terrible as an army with banners* (Ac 7:38; Hos 13:15; SS 6:10). We are told here how fearsome Israel was in the eyes of its enemies (v. 1). We are told in the following verses how fair and clear it had been made in the eyes of its friends by the removing of the disgrace of Egypt:

1. Here is the impression which the news made on the kings of this land: *Their heart melted* like wax before the fire, *neither was there spirit in them any more* (v. 1). The kings had until now kept up their spirits fairly well and had promised themselves that because they possessed their land and because it was a populous country with fortified cities, they would be able to stand up to the invaders. But when they heard not only that Israel had come over the Jordan but also that they had come over miraculously, that the God of nature was clearly fighting for them, then *their hearts melted* too (v. 1), and they did not know what to do. And:

1.1. They had every reason to be afraid. Israel itself was a formidable body, and much more so with almighty God at its head.

1.2. God impressed these fears on them and discouraged them, just as he had promised (Ex 23:27).

2. *At that time* (v. 2), when the country around them was in that state of great fear, God ordered Joshua to circumcise the children of Israel. Now notice:

2.1. The occasion for this general circumcision. All who left Egypt were circumcised (v. 5). While they lived peacefully in Egypt, they doubtless kept the ordinance. But when the decree went out for the destruction of their male infants, the administration of this ordinance was interrupted. Many of those born after this interruption were uncircumcised, and of those there was a general circumcision. It is with reference to that earlier general circumcision that this is called a *second* one (v. 2). To have all the children born for thirty-eight years left uncircumcised, even under the leadership of Moses himself, is inexplicable, except if brought about by divine direction:

2.1.1. Some think circumcision was omitted because it was unnecessary: it was appointed as a mark of distinction between the Israelites and other nations, and so in the desert there was no need for it.

2.1.2. Others think that they did not look on the command of circumcision as compulsory until they came to settle in Canaan.

2.1.3. Others think that God favorably waived the observance of this ordinance because they were unsettled.

2.1.4. It seems to us to have been a continued sign of God's displeasure against them for their unbelief and grumbling. And this was just as significant an indication of God's wrath as was the breaking of the tablets of the covenant when Israel had broken the covenant by making the golden calf. Whatever the reason was, it seems that this great ordinance was neglected in Israel for almost forty years, which is a clear indication that it was not absolutely necessary nor forever compulsory.

2.2. The orders given to Joshua for this general circumcision (v. 2). Why was this ordered to be done now?

2.2.1. Because now the promise was fulfilled of which circumcision was instituted as the seal. The descendants of Israel had been safely brought into the land of Canaan.

2.2.2. Because now the judgment was fully executed by the expiring of the forty years, and so the seal of the covenant was now renewed again.

2.2.2.1. God wanted to show them that the camp of Israel was not governed by ordinary rules and standards of war but by the immediate direction of God.

2.2.2.2. God wanted to prepare his people Israel for the difficulties they were now to encounter by confirming his covenant with them. This gave them an indisputable assurance of victory and success and full possession of the Land of Promise.

2.2.2.3. God wanted to teach them, and us with them, to *begin with God* in all great undertakings by offering ourselves to him as *a living sacrifice* (Ro 12:1)—for that is what was meant by the blood of circumcision—so that we may be sure of his favor.

2.2.2.4. The reviving of circumcision, after it had fallen into disuse for such a long time, was intended to revive the observance of other institutions.

2.2.2.5. This *second* circumcision, as it is called here, was a type of the spiritual circumcision with which the people of the Israel of God are circumcised when they enter into the Gospel rest. It points to *Jesus as the true circumciser*, the author of *another circumcision* than that *of the flesh*, commanded by the Law: the *circumcision of the heart* (Ro 2:29), called the *circumcision of Christ* (Col 2:11).

2.3. The people's obedience to these orders. Joshua *circumcised the children of Israel* (v. 3), and their submission to this painful ordinance was an example of their dutiful obedience.

3. Their circumcision rolled away the reproach of Egypt.

3.1. They were tainted with the disgrace of the idolatry of Egypt, but now that they were circumcised, one might have hoped that they would be so completely devoted to God that the disgrace would be rolled away.

3.2. Their coming safely to Canaan rolled away the reproach of Egypt, for it silenced the malicious suggestion by the Egyptians that Israel had been brought out with evil intent and *the wilderness had shut them in* (Ex 14:3).

Verses 10–12

We may well imagine that the people of Canaan were dismayed. Joshua began his military campaign with one act of devotion after another. What begins with God is likely to end well. Here is:

1. A solemn Passover kept, at the time appointed by the law, *the fourteenth day of the first month*, and at the same place where they were circumcised (v. 10). While they were wandering in the desert, they were denied the benefit and comfort of this ordinance, but now God comforted them again, and so that joyful ordinance is revived. The solemn Passover followed immediately after the solemn circumcision. In the same way, those who received the word were baptized, and we find them immediately *breaking bread* (Ac 2:41–42). They kept this Passover in the plains of Jericho, defying, as it were, the Canaanites. He now *prepared a table before them in the presence of their enemies* (Ps 23:5).

2. Provision made for their camp from the *corn* (grain) *of the land*, and the *ceasing of the manna* after that (vv. 11–12). Manna was a wonderful mercy to them when they needed it, but it was the mark of their life in the desert; it would be more acceptable to them to eat of the *corn of the land* (v. 11), and they are now provided with this.

2.1. The country people, having withdrawn for safety into Jericho, had left their barns, fields, and everything in them. And the supply came just at the right time, for:

2.1.1. After the Passover they were to keep the Feast of Unleavened Bread, which they could not observe in the appointed way when they had nothing except manna to live on, but now they found enough old grain in the barns of the Canaanites to be a plentiful supply for them on that occasion.

2.1.2. On the day after the Passover Sabbath they were to *wave the sheaf of firstfruits before the Lord* (Lev 23:10–11). They were particularly ordered to do this when they *came into the land which God would give them* (Lev 23:9). They were provided with the *fruit of the land that year* (v. 12), which was then growing and beginning to ripen.

2.2. The manna stopped as soon as they had eaten the *old corn of the land* (vv. 11–12):

2.2.1. It came just when they needed it, and it continued for as long as they needed it and no longer.

2.2.2. This teaches us not to expect extraordinary provision when provision may be received in an ordinary way. Now that they did not need it, God withdrew it. Our heavenly Father is a wise Father. He knows the needs of his children, and he adjusts his gifts to those needs, not to their whims. The word and ordinances of God are spiritual manna, with which God nourishes his people in the wilderness of this world. But when we come to the heavenly Canaan, this manna will stop, for we will no longer need it.

Verses 13–15

Up to this time we have found God often speaking to Joshua, but it is only now that we read of an appearance of God's glory to him. Now that his difficulties increased, his encouragements were also increased in proportion. Notice:

1. The time when he was favored with this vision. It was immediately after Joshua had carried out the great ceremonies of circumcision and the Passover. We can learn from this that we may expect revelations of God's grace when we follow our duty.

2. The place where he had this vision. It was *by Jericho*. It would seem that he was all alone there, unafraid of the dangers because he was sure of divine protection. Some think he was meditating and praying, or perhaps he was viewing the city to work out how to attack it. God

came and directed him. God will help those who help themselves. As the saying goes, "The law helps those who watch, not those who sleep." Joshua was in his position as a general when God came and made himself known as the supreme Commander.

3. The appearance itself. Joshua, as is usual with those who are full of thought and care, was looking downward, his eyes fixed on the ground, when suddenly he was surprised by the appearance of a man who stood in front of him. This made him lift up his eyes. Now:

3.1. We have reason to think that this man was the Son of God, the eternal Word, who, before he assumed human nature for eternity, frequently appeared in human form.

3.2. He appeared here as a soldier, with *his sword drawn in his hand* (v. 13). He appeared to Abraham in his tent as a traveler, but to Joshua in the field as a man of war. Christ will be to his people what their faith expects and wants him to be. He came to encourage Joshua to carry on boldly and strongly, for Christ's sword drawn in his hand shows how ready he is to defend and save his people, who will be courageous through him.

4. The bold question with which Joshua confronted him. Here we see:

4.1. His great courage and determination. He was not put off by the suddenness of the appearance.

4.2. His great concern for the people and their cause. It would seem that he suspected the man was an enemy. In the same way, we are all too often inclined to look on something that is overwhelmingly for us as being against us. The cause between the Israelites and the Canaanites, between Christ and Beelzebub, does not allow neutrality: *he that is not against us is for us* (Lk 9:50).

5. The account the man gave of himself (v. 14): "No, I am not for your enemies, you may be sure, but *as captain of the host of the Lord have I now come*. I am not only for you as a friend, but over you as commander in chief." He, as commander of both, leads the army of Israel and commands the host of angels to help them. It is perhaps in allusion to this that Christ is called the *captain of our salvation* (Heb 2:10) *and a leader and commander to the people* (Isa 55:4).

6. The realization that he was a divine person, and not a mere man:

6.1. Joshua worshiped him: *He fell on his face to the earth and did worship* (v. 14). Joshua was himself general of the forces of Israel, but he joyfully submitted to him as his commander.

6.2. Joshua asked to receive commands and directions from him: *What saith my lord unto his servant?* (v. 14). This question was just as devout and saintlike as his previous question had been bold and soldierlike. Nor did it in any way lessen the greatness of Joshua's spirit: even crowned heads cannot bow too low before the throne of the Lord Jesus, who is *King of Kings* (Ps 2:10–11; 72:10–11; Rev 19:16). Notice:

6.2.1. The relationship he acknowledged between himself and Christ, in which Christ was his Lord and he was Christ's servant and under his command. Christ was his Captain, and he himself was a soldier under him, to do as he was told to do (Mt 8:9).

6.2.2. The inquiry he made as part of this relationship: *What saith my Lord?* (v. 14). This implied a sincere desire to know the will of Christ, and a joyful readiness and determination to do it. This frame of mind shows that he was well qualified for the position he was in, for it is those who know how to obey who best know how to command.

7. The further expressions of reverence which this divine commander required from Joshua (v. 15): *Loose thy shoe from off thy foot*, as a sign of reverence and respect — attitudes which with us are represented by uncovering the head. We are used to saying of a person for whom we have a great affection that we love the very ground which that person treads on. Outer expressions of inner reverence are both befitting and required whenever we approach God in solemn ceremonies. Bishop Patrick is right when he notes here that the very same order which God gave to Moses at the bush (Ex 3:5), he gave here to Joshua; as God had been with Moses, so he would be with Joshua (1:5).

CHAPTER 6

Joshua began the campaign with the siege of Jericho, a city which trusted greatly in the strength of its walls as its defense. Here we have the story of the taking of Jericho: 1. The directions and assurances which the commander of the Lord's army gave for it (vv. 1–5). 2. His testing of the people's patient obedience by requiring them to walk around the city for six days (vv. 6–14). 3. The wonderful transfer of it into their hands on the seventh day, with a solemn command to them to treat it as a devoted thing (vv. 15–21, 24); the preservation of Rahab and her relatives (vv. 22–23, 25); a curse declared on anyone who would dare rebuild this city (vv. 26–27). We have a summary of this story among the trophies of faith (Heb 11:30).

Verses 1–5

Here we have the controversy between God and the people of Jericho:

1. Jericho determined that Israel would *not* be its master (v. 1). There were no deserters; none went out to negotiate peace, and none were allowed in to offer peace.

2. God determined that Israel *would* be its master, and that this would happen quickly:

2.1. The commander of the Lord's army gives directions on how the city must be besieged. No trenches are to be opened, nor any military preparations made, but the ark of God must be carried by the priests around the city once a day on six successive days, and seven times on the seventh day. The fighting men are to march around the city in silence, with the priests blowing trumpets of rams' horns all that time (vv. 3–4). This is all they have to do.

2.2. The commander of the Lord's army assures them that before nightfall on the seventh day they will without fail have conquered the city. When a signal is given, they must all shout, and immediately the wall will collapse. God appointed this way:

2.2.1. To exalt his own power, so that he might be *exalted in his own strength* (Ps 21:13), not in the strength of the instruments he had chosen to use.

2.2.2. To honor his ark, the appointed sign of his presence, and to give a reason for the laws that required the people to look on it with the deepest reverence and respect.

2.2.3. To honor the priests, who were appointed on this occasion to carry the ark and sound the trumpets.

2.2.4. To test the faith, obedience, and patience of the people, to see whether they would observe a command which to their merely human thinking seemed foolish to obey and whether they would believe a promise which according to human probability could not possibly be fulfilled. In this way, it was by faith, not by force, that the walls of Jericho fell down.

2.2.5. To encourage the hope of Israel concerning the difficulties still before them. The strongest and highest walls cannot hold out against almighty God.

Verses 6–16

Here is a record of the march that Israel made around Jericho, the orders Joshua gave concerning it, as he had received them from the Lord, and their prompt observance of these orders.

1. The people accompanied the ark wherever it went (v. 9). The armed guard went before it to clear its way. It is an honor to the greatest people to carry out any good work for the ark and to serve the interests of religious faith in their country. The *rereward* (rear guard) (v. 9) followed the ark; this was another body of armed soldiers, or perhaps the division of Dan, which was at the rear on their journey through the desert, or it may have been the multitude of the people who were not armed.

2. Seven priests went directly in front of the ark, with trumpets in their hands, which they continually sounded (vv. 4–5, 9, 13).

2.1. They declared war on the Canaanites, and so struck terror into them. In the same way, when God's ministers solemnly declare his wrath against all evil and ungodliness, they must blow the trumpet in Zion, so that sinners in Zion may fear.

2.2. They declared God's gracious presence with Israel, and so revitalized and encouraged them.

3. The trumpets they used were not silver trumpets, but trumpets of rams' horns, which some think were bored out hollow for this purpose. These trumpets were of the lowliest matter, produced the dullest sound, and were the least showy, to demonstrate that the all-surpassing power came from God. In the same way, by the *foolishness of preaching* (1Co 1:21) — rightly compared to the sounding of these rams' horns — the Devil's kingdom is thrown down. The *weapons of our warfare*, though not worldly, are still *mighty through God to the pulling down of strongholds* (2Co 10:4–5).

4. All the people were commanded to be silent, not to speak a word, nor make any noise (v. 10), so that they might listen very carefully to the sound of the holy trumpets, which they must now consider to be the voice of God among them — and it is not right for us to speak when God is speaking.

5. They were to do this once a day for six successive days and seven times on the seventh day. This is what they did (vv. 14–15). Just as God's promised rescues must be expected to come in his way, so also they must be expected to come in his time.

6. One of these days must have been a Sabbath, and the Jews say that it was the last, although this is not certain. However, if the One who appointed them to rest on the other Sabbath days appointed them to walk on this one, then that was sufficient justification for them to do it. He never intended to be bound by his own laws, and so he could overrule them when he wanted. And, besides, the law of the Sabbath forbids our own secular and worldly work, but what they did was a religious act. Doing Sabbath work is certainly not breaking the Sabbath rest.

7. They continued to do this for the appointed time, and seven times on the seventh day, although they did not see that it had any effect. We may suppose that their odd behavior at first amused those who were besieged. They probably made fun of those laying siege, as did the enemies mentioned in Ne 4:2: *What do these feeble Jews?*

8. Eventually the people were to give a shout, and they did so, and immediately the walls collapsed (v. 20). This was a triumphant shout, a shout of prayer, and an echo of the sound of the trumpets which declared the promise that God would remember them. And at the end of time, when our Lord descends from heaven with a shout and the sound of a trumpet, Satan's kingdom will be completely torn down. But the victory will not be complete until then, when all opposition and every principality and power will be completely and eternally destroyed.

Verses 17–27

The people had religiously observed the orders given them concerning the siege of Jericho, and now finally Joshua told them (v. 16), "*The Lord hath given you the city*; enter and take possession." We have:

1. The rules they were to observe in taking possession:

1.1. The city and everything in it would be a *herem*, a devoted thing, to the Lord. It was set apart in a special way to be destroyed. No life in it could be redeemed on any terms. The only exceptions to this judgment were Rahab and her family: *She shall live and all that are with her* (v. 17). She had set herself apart from her neighbors by the kindness she had shown to Israel.

1.2. All the treasury of Jericho, the money, silver, gold, and valuable goods, must be consecrated to the service of the tabernacle. God had promised them a land *flowing with milk and honey* (5:6), not a land with plenty of silver and gold. He also wanted to see them consider themselves rich as they enriched the tabernacle.

1.3. A particular warning is given to them to make sure they do not interfere with the forbidden plunder: "*In any wise keep yourselves from the accursed thing*; restrain yourselves, and be afraid of having anything to do with it." He speaks as if he foresees the sin of Achan, which we have a record of in the next chapter.

2. The entrance that was opened up for them into the city by the sudden collapse of the walls. What the inhabitants trusted in as their defense turned out to be their destruction. The sudden collapse of the wall doubtless put the inhabitants into such a state of fear that they had no strength or heart left to offer any resistance, and they became easy targets for Israel's attack. Satan's kingdom will fall in this way, and those who harden themselves against God will suffer the same destiny.

3. The orders carried out concerning this devoted city:

3.1. Every living thing was killed. If they had not received divine authority under the confirmation of miracles to carry out this judgment, it could not have been justified. Moreover, something like this cannot be justified now, when we are sure no such authority can be produced. The spirit of the Gospel is completely different, for Christ came not to destroy human life but to save it (Lk 9:56). Christ's victories were of a completely different character.

3.2. The city was *burnt with fire, and all that was in it* (v. 24).

3.3. All the silver and gold and all the articles which could be purified by fire were brought into the treasury of the house of the Lord.

4. The preservation of Rahab the prostitute or innkeeper, who *perished not with those that believed not* (Heb 11:31). The two spies had committed the Israelites to keeping her safe, and the Israelite honor was at stake, and so although they were in a great hurry to take the city, Joshua must first ensure her safety. The same people whom she had kept safe were used to keep her safe (vv. 22–23). All her family and all who belonged to her were saved with her. Now that Rahab was alive:

4.1. She was left for some time outside the camp to be purified from her gentile superstitions. She was to renounce these in preparation for her admission as a convert into the Israel of God.

4.2. She became in due time part of the church of Israel, and she and her descendants lived in Israel. Her family was significant long after. We read that she was the wife of Salmon, ruler of Judah; the mother of Boaz; and an ancestor of our Savior (Mt 1:5).

5. Jericho condemned to desolation forever, and a curse pronounced on anyone who at any time later would attempt to rebuild it (v. 26). The city was in a very pleasant situation, and its closeness to the Jordan was probably an advantage, so people would be tempted to build at the same place, but they were told here that their lives would be in danger if they did. People build for their descendants, but the one who built Jericho would have no descendants to enjoy what was built. This curse did come on the man who long after rebuilt Jericho (1Ki 16:34), but we are not to think that it made the place worse when it was built or brought any harm on those who inhabited it. We find Jericho afterward graced with the presence, not only of those two great prophets Elijah and Elisha, but also of our blessed Savior himself (Lk 18:35; 19:1; Mt 20:29).

CHAPTER 7

More than once we have found in the life of Israel, even when they were in the most fortunate situations, that they were confused and embarrassed by sin, and in this chapter we have another instance of interruption to their progress because of sin. But because it was only the sin of one person or family, and soon atoned for, the consequences were not as troublesome. We have here: 1. The sin of Achan in acting unfaithfully with the devoted things (v. 1); the defeat of Israel at Ai because of that (vv. 2–5). 2. How Joshua humbled himself and prayed after that tragedy (vv. 6–9). 3. The directions God gave him to put away the guilt (vv. 10–15). 4. The discovery, trial, conviction, condemnation, and execution of Achan (vv. 16–26). We can learn from this story that just as the laws made nothing perfect (Heb 7:19), neither did Canaan itself. The perfection both of holiness and of peace for God's Israel is to be expected only in the heavenly Canaan.

Verses 1–5

The story of this chapter begins with a *but* (v. 1). The previous chapter ends by saying, *The Lord was with Joshua, and his fame was noised through all* (spread throughout) *that country* (6:27). *But the children of Israel committed a trespass* (v. 1), and so set God against them. If we lose our God, we lose our friends, who cannot help us unless God is for us. Here is:

1. The sin of Achan (v. 1). The sin is here said to be *taking of the accursed thing*, the devoted things (v. 1), disobeying Joshua's command and defying his threat (6:18). When Jericho was devastated, Israel submitted to the law in the first prohibition and showed no compassion, but they disobeyed the second prohibition and indulged their covetousness. The love of the world is the root of bitterness which is the hardest to dig out. But the record of Achan's sin is a clear sign that out of all the thousands of Israel he was the only offender in this matter. And yet, although it was only one person who sinned, the Israelites are said *to commit the trespass* (v. 1), because one of their body did it, and he was not then separated from

them or disowned by them. They did it, that is, Achan's act brought guilt on the whole community of which he was a member. This should warn us against sin in ourselves, so that many may not be defiled or troubled by it (Heb 12:15). Many diligent business executives have been ruined because they have had careless partners. We should watch over one another to prevent sin.

2. The camp of Israel suffering because of Achan's sin: *The anger of the Lord was kindled against Israel* (v. 1). God saw the offense even though they did not, and he found a way of making them see it:

2.1. Joshua sent a detachment to attack the next city in their way, which was Ai. Only 3,000 men were sent, because he was advised by his spies that the place was insignificant and did not need a stronger force to conquer it (vv. 2–3). The spies said, *They are but few* (v. 3), but although they may have been only a few, that still proved too many for the detachment that was sent. Remembering that *we wrestle with principalities and powers* (Eph 6:12) will make us aware of the need to be diligent in our Christian warfare.

2.2. The party Joshua sent in their first attack on the city was repelled with some loss (vv. 4–5). It served:

• To humble God's Israel.
• To harden the Canaanites and make them feel the more secure.
• To show God's anger against Israel and call them to *purge out the old leaven*, to get rid of the old yeast (1Co 5:7). This was the main purpose of their defeat. The retreat of this party in disarray scared the whole camp of Israel: *The hearts of the people melted* (v. 5), not so much because of their loss as because of their disappointment. It appeared to any one of them who thought about it that it was a sign of God's displeasure.

Verses 6–9

We have here a record of Joshua's deep concern on this sad occasion. Notice:

1. How he grieved: he *rent* (tore) *his clothes* (v. 6) as a sign of great sorrow for this disaster and in awe of God's displeasure, which had certainly been its cause. One of the bravest soldiers there have ever been acknowledged that his *flesh trembled for fear of God* (Ps 119:120). As one *humbling himself under the mighty hand of God* (1Pe 5:6), *he fell to the earth upon his face* (v. 6). Because the elders of Israel were interested in the cause and influenced by his example, they prostrated themselves with him, and as a sign of deep humility and shame *put dust upon their heads* (v. 6). They were not only mourners but also penitents. Joshua's eye was on God, and he knew that God was displeased, which troubled him.

2. How he prayed. He humbly pleaded the case before God, and was not sullen, as David was when *the Lord had made a breach upon Uzzah* (2Sa 6:8), when the Lord's wrath had broken out against Uzzah, but was deeply moved. His spirit seemed to be unsettled, but not so much that he was put out of a spirit of prayer, and by expressing his trouble humbly to God he kept his temper, and all ended well.

2.1. He wished that they had all stayed with the allotment of the two tribes on the other side of the Jordan (v. 7). The words *wherefore hast thou brought us over Jordan to destroy us?* (v. 7) are too similar to those that the murmurers often spoke (Ex 14:11–12; 16:3; 17:3; Nu 14:2–3). However, the One who searches all hearts knew they came from a different spirit, and he was not so harsh as to keep a record of Joshua's wrong words.

2.2. He spoke as one who was at a loss concerning the meaning of this event (v. 8). Has the Lord become weak? This shows us that the methods of Providence are often intricate and perplexing, in such a way that the wisest and best people cannot always understand, but *they shall know hereafter* (Jn 13:7).

2.3. He pleaded the danger Israel was now in of being destroyed. In this way, even good people, when things go against them a little, tend too readily to fear the worst. But this is included here as a plea: "Lord, let not Israel's name, which has been so dear to you and so great in the world, be wiped off the face of the earth."

2.4. He pleaded the disgrace that would fall on God, and that if Israel were destroyed, his glory would suffer. He feared it would reflect badly on God, on his wisdom and power, his goodness and faithfulness. What would the Egyptians say? This shows us that nothing is more painful to a gracious soul than dishonor to God's name. We cannot urge a better plea than this: Lord, *What wilt thou do for thy great name?* (v. 9). Let God be glorified in everything, and then let us welcome his whole will.

Verses 10–15

Here we have God's answer to Joshua's address. And let those who find themselves under God's displeasure never complain *about* him, but complain *to* him, and they will receive an answer of peace. The answer came immediately:

1. God encouraged Joshua to move on from his present unhappy state: "*Get thee up*, do not allow your spirits to sink in this way; *wherefore liest thou thus upon thy face?*" Now God told him that it was enough. God did not want him to continue any longer in such a sad position, for God does not delight in the grief of those who repent when they humble their souls more than is necessary to receive forgiveness and peace. Joshua continued his mourning *till eventide* (v. 6). It was time for him to take off his mourning clothes and put on his judge's robes. He had to *clothe himself with zeal as a cloak* (Isa 59:17). Weeping must not prevent sowing, and one religious duty must not push out another.

2. God informs Joshua of the true and only reason for this disaster (v. 11): *Israel hath sinned.* The sinner is not named, but the sin is described, and it is spoken of as the act of Israel in general. Notice how the sin is here made to appear totally sinful:

2.1. *They have transgressed my covenant* (v. 11), an explicit command with a penalty attached to it. It was agreed that God would have all the plunder from Jericho, and they would have the plunder from the rest of the cities of Canaan. So when they robbed God of his part, they *transgressed this covenant* (v. 11).

2.2. *They have even taken of the accursed* (devoted) *thing* (v. 11).

2.3. They *have also stolen* (v. 11); they did it secretly, thinking they could hide it from God's knowledge of everything.

2.4. They have *dissembled* (lied) (v. 11) also. Achan joined with the rest in generally declaring his innocence, and did not own up to what he had done wrong, like the adulteress who *eats and wipes her mouth, and says, I have done no wickedness* (Pr 30:20). In fact:

2.5. They have put the devoted things *among their own stuff* (v. 11), as if they were entitled to it as their own possession. God could now have told him who the person was who had committed this sin, but he does not, so that he may:

2.5.1. Exercise the zeal of Joshua and Israel in searching out the criminal.

2.5.2. Give the sinner an opportunity to repent and confess the sin. But Achan did not make himself known until the casting of lots found him out. This showed his hardness of heart, and so he found no mercy.

3. God stirs Joshua to ask further, by telling him:

3.1. That this is the only reason why God is against them, so when these devoted things have been put away, he need not fear.

3.2. That if these devoted things are not destroyed, the people cannot expect the return of God's gracious presence. When we personally repent and our lives are reformed, we destroy the devoted things in our own hearts, and unless we do this, we can never expect to receive the grace and favor of God.

4. God directs Joshua as to how he should investigate the matter and bring the offender to justice:

4.1. Joshua must *sanctify the people*, immediately, overnight, that is, he is to command the people to *sanctify themselves* (v. 13). What more can judges or ministers do toward sanctification? The people must prepare themselves to have the right attitude to come before God and submit to God's scrutiny.

4.2. Joshua must bring them all under the scrutiny of the casting of lots (v. 14). The tribe which contained the guilty person would first be discovered by lot, then the family, then the household, and last of all the person. In this way, the conviction came on the person gradually so that that individual might have had the opportunity to come and give themselves up, for God is *not willing that any should perish, but that all should come to repentance* (2Pe 3:9).

4.3. When the criminal was found out, that person must be put to death *without mercy* (Heb 10:28). This crime had to be severely punished in this way as a warning to people in every age to make sure they do not rob God of what is rightfully his.

Verses 16–26

We have in these verses:

1. The discovery of Achan by the casting of lots. Notice in the investigation:

1.1. That the guilty tribe was the tribe of Judah, which was and was to become the most honorable and illustrious of all the tribes. According to the Jewish tradition, when the tribe of Judah was taken, the brave men of that tribe drew their swords and professed that they would not put them back in their sheaths until they saw the criminal punished and until they themselves were cleared, knowing they were innocent.

1.2. That the guilty person was eventually discovered. The language of the casting of lots was *Thou art the man* (2Sa 12:7) (v. 18). It was strange that when Achan was conscious of his guilt and when he saw the casting of lots pointing ever closer to him, he did not have either the good sense to escape or the grace to confess. Notice here:

1.2.1. The foolishness of those who think their sin will remain secret: God in his righteousness has many ways of bringing to light the hidden deeds of darkness.

1.2.2. How concerned we should be, when God is striving against us, to find out what the particular sin is, to pray earnestly with holy Job, *Lord, show me wherefore thou contendest with me*, tell me what charges you have against me (Job 10:2).

2. Achan's examination and trial (v. 19). Joshua himself is the judge and urges him to repent and confess, so that through his repentance his soul may be saved in the other world. Notice:

2.1. How Joshua comes to Achan with the greatest possible tenderness. He might justly have called him "thief" and "rebel," "Raca" and "you fool," but he calls him "son." He might have commanded him to confess, as the high priest did our blessed Savior, or threatened him with torture to draw out a confession, but for love's sake he begs him instead: *I pray thee make confession* (v. 19). This is an example to all not to gloat over those who are in trouble, even if they have brought their misery on themselves by their own evil. It is also an example to judges never to be carried away into indecent behavior or language even toward those who have caused the greatest offense. *The wrath of man worketh not the righteousness of God* (Jas 1:20).

2.2. What Joshua wants Achan to do: to confess his sin. Joshua stands before Achan in God's place, so that in confessing to Joshua, Achan confesses to God. This shows us that in confessing sin and becoming ashamed of ourselves, we give glory to God as a righteous God. We acknowledge that he is just in being displeased with us. We acknowledge that he is good and that he will not use our confessions as evidence against us, but *he is faithful and just to forgive us* (1Jn 1:9) when we are brought to acknowledge that he would be faithful and just if he did punish us. Our sin has wronged God's honor. By his death, Jesus Christ has made atonement for the wrong, but we have to show our goodwill for his honor by repenting, and, as far as we are able, give glory to him.

3. Achan's confession, which finally — when he saw that it was useless to hide his crime any further — was open and honest (vv. 20–21). Here is:

3.1. A penitent acknowledgment of his sin.

3.2. A full record of his sin: *Thus and thus have I done* (v. 20). This shows us that when we repent of our sins to God, it befits us to be detailed in our confessions. We should not say only, "I have sinned," but, "I have sinned in this and that." He confesses:

3.2.1. What he took. When he plundered a house in Jericho, he found a beautiful Babylonian robe. The word refers to the kind of robe worn by rulers when they appeared in state. He thought, "It would be an enormous pity if it were burned. I'll be able to use it as my best robe for several years." He starts off small in this way, but the beginnings of his claims are nevertheless bold. And once he has started, he goes on to take a bag of money, *two hundred shekels* (v. 21), that is, about five pounds (about 2.3 kilograms) of silver, and a *wedge of gold* which weighed *fifty shekels* (v. 21), about 1.25 pounds (about 0.6 kilogram). In taking these, he could not plead that he was saving them *from the fire* — for the *silver and gold* were to be stored in *the treasury* — but those who make up a slight excuse for daring to commit one sin will move on to the next without such an excuse, for the path of sin goes downhill. It was for such a meager prize that Achan was risking his life. See Mt 16:26.

3.2.2. How he took them:

3.2.2.1. The sin began with his eyes. First he saw these fine things, just as Eve saw the forbidden fruit, and he was strangely charmed with the sight. This is what happens when we allow our hearts to follow our eyes. We need to make a covenant with our eyes (Job 31:1), that if they wander they will be sure to weep. *Look not thou upon the wine that is red* (Pr 23:31); do not look at a beautiful woman lustfully.

3.2.2.2. The sin came from the heart. He acknowledges, *I coveted them* (v. 21). In this way, after desire has conceived, it gives birth to sin. Those who want to be kept from sinful actions must put to death and restrain their sinful desires. It was not simply looking, but looking lustfully, that destroyed him.

3.2.2.3. When he had committed the sin, he was careful to cover it up. Notice the *deceitfulness of sin* (Heb 3:13); what is pleasing in being carried out is bitter when it is reflected on. The sin has a sting in its tail.

4. Achan's conviction. God had convicted him by the casting of lots; he had convicted himself by his own confession. Joshua has Achan further convicted by having his tent searched. There the goods which he confessed to were found.

5. Achan's condemnation. Joshua passes sentence on him (v. 25): *Why hast thou troubled us?* Sin is very troublesome, not only to sinners themselves, but also to everyone around them. Now, Joshua says, *God shall trouble thee* (v. 25). Notice why Achan was dealt with so severely: not only because he had robbed God, but also because he had troubled Israel. The accusation was written over his head, as it were, "Achan, *the troubler of Israel*" (1Ch 2:7), as Ahab was (1Ki 18:18). Some of the Jewish teachers reason, on the basis of the word which determines that he will be troubled *this day*, that therefore he would not be troubled in the world to come. The flesh was destroyed so that the spirit might be saved. If this is so, the administration of justice was less severe than it seemed.

6. Achan's execution:

6.1. The place of execution. The execution was at a distance, so that the camp which had been disturbed by Achan's sin might not be defiled by his death.

6.2. The people used in his execution. It was done by *all Israel* (vv. 24–25).

6.3. What and who shared with him in the punishment, for *he perished not alone in his iniquity* (22:20):

• The stolen goods were destroyed with him.

• All his other goods were similarly destroyed, not only his tent and its furnishings, but also his *oxen, asses, and sheep* (v. 24). Those who want to grasp at more than they have lose what they already have.

• His sons and daughters were put to death with him. Some indeed think that they were *brought out* (v. 24) only to watch their father's punishment. Yet perhaps his sons and daughters had aided and abetted in the evil act and had helped carry off the devoted things. They probably helped to hide them. If they had joined in only a small way in the crime, the crime was so detestable that they justly shared in the punishment.

6.4. The punishment itself that was inflicted on him. He was stoned—some think he was stoned as a Sabbath-breaker because they believe that the sacrilege was committed on the Sabbath day—and then his dead body was burned.

6.5. The satisfying of God's wrath in this (v. 26): *The Lord turned from the fierceness of his anger.* If you take away the cause, then the effect will cease.

7. The record of Achan's conviction and execution. Care was taken that it would be remembered by future generations to serve as a warning and instruction:

7.1. A large pile of rocks was set up on the place where Achan was executed. Perhaps each member of the community threw a stone onto the heap as a sign of their abhorrence at the crime.

7.2. A new name was given to the place; it was called the *Valley of Achor* (v. 26), *Achor* meaning "trouble." The *Valley of Achor* is said to be given as *a door of hope*, because when we put away the devoted things, then there is *a door of hope* in Israel (Hos 2:15; Ezr 10:2).

CHAPTER 8

In this chapter we have: 1. The glorious progress of the war in Israel's capture of Ai, in contrast to the recent previous attack, which ended in disgrace. God encourages Joshua to attack Ai, giving him the assurance of success (vv. 1–2). 2. Joshua giving orders accordingly to his men of war (vv. 3–8). The strategy is successful (vv. 9–22). 3. Joshua conquering the city. He kills all the inhabitants, burns it, and hangs the king, but gives the plunder to the soldiers (vv. 23–29). 4. The great ceremony of writing and reading the Law before a general assembly of all Israel, drawn up for that purpose on the two mountains of Gerizim and Ebal (vv. 30–35).

Verses 1–2

It would seem that Joshua was now in a state of perplexity, and he could not think of pushing ahead without fear and trembling, in case there might be another Achan in the camp. But then God spoke to him, either in a vision as we had before (5:13–15), as a man of war with his sword drawn, or by the Urim and Thummim. It is when we have faithfully put away the cursed thing of sin that we may expect to hear from God words of assurance, encouragement, and strength. God's directing us how to go on in our Christian work and warfare is a good sign that we are reconciled with him. Notice:

1. The encouragement God gives to Joshua to proceed: *Fear not, neither be thou dismayed* (v. 1). Evil in the church weakens the hands and dampens the spirits of the church's leaders and helpers more than opposition from outside. Traitorous Israelites are to be feared more than evil Canaanites. But God tells Joshua not to be dismayed. The same power that keeps Israel from being destroyed by their enemies will keep them from destroying themselves. To encourage him:

1.1. He assures him of success against Ai. He tells him it will all belong to him; he only has to take it as God's gift.

1.2. He allows the people to carry off the plunder for themselves. Here the plunder is not consecrated to God as it was in Jericho.

2. The instructions God gives Joshua for attacking Ai. It must not take as long as it took to capture Jericho. Nor is it, as Jericho was, to be taken by miraculous means, but now they must courageously exert themselves. They had seen God at work for them, and now they must get going. God instructs him to take all his army and to set an ambush behind the city.

Verses 3–22

Here is an account of the taking of Ai by strategic warfare. Nothing was pretended; nothing falsified except a retreat. The enemy should have been on their guard and kept within the defense of their own walls. Common wisdom should have warned them not to risk pursuing an army which they saw was far superior to them in numbers. They should not have left their city unguarded, but as the Latin phrase puts it, *si populus vult decipi, decipiatur,* "If the people will be deceived, then let them be."

1. There is some difficulty in reckoning the numbers used to carry out the attack. Mention is made (v. 3) of 30,000 that were *chosen and sent away by night,* to whom the command was given to surprise the city as soon as they noticed it was evacuated (vv. 4, 7–8). But afterward (v. 12) it is said that Joshua *took* 5,000 *men and set them to lie in ambush* behind the city, and that *ambush entered the city* and *set it on fire* (v. 19). Now:

1.1. Some think there were two parties sent out to lie in ambush, and that Joshua made his open attack on the city with all the thousands of Israel. But:

1.2. Others think that all the people were taken only to set up camp in front of the city, and that out of them Joshua chose 30,000 men to be employed in the action, out of which he sent 5,000 to lie in ambush, which were as many as could be supposed to march incognito.

2. The main parts of the story are, however, clear enough: that a detachment was secretly marched behind the city, on the side opposite that on which the main body of the army lay, and that Joshua and his forces faced the city. The garrison from Ai made a strong raid out toward them, and immediately Joshua and his troops withdrew, gave ground, and retreated in apparent disorder toward the desert. Noticing this, the people of Ai sent out all their forces to pursue them. This was a good opportunity for those who had lain in ambush to conquer the city. They set it on fire, and the column of smoke was a signal for Joshua and all his forces to turn on the pursuers. The people of Ai became aware too late of the snare they were drawn into, and, their retreat being intercepted, they were all killed. Notice:

2.1. How brave a commander Joshua was. Though an army of Israelites had been repelled at Ai, he is courageous enough to decide to lead them in person the second time (v. 5). He *went that night into the midst of the valley* to make the necessary arrangements for an attack. Bishop Patrick thinks that he went into the valley alone, to pray to God. When he had stretched out his javelin toward the city (v. 18)—a javelin almost as fatal and formidable to the enemies of Israel as Moses' staff was—he never drew back his hand until the work was completed. Those who have stretched out their hands against their spiritual enemies must never draw them back. Joshua conquered by surrendering, as if he had himself been conquered. In the same way, when our Lord Jesus bowed his head and gave up his spirit, it seemed as if death had triumphed over him, and as if he and all he stood for had been completely destroyed, but in his resurrection he came back and totally defeated the powers of darkness. He broke the serpent's head by allowing him to strike his heel. What a glorious strategy!

2.2. What an obedient people Israel was. They did what *Joshua commanded them to do, according to the commandment of the Lord* (v. 8) without complaining or arguing.

2.3. How foolish an enemy the king of Ai was. He did not discover by means of his scouts those who lay in ambush behind the city (v. 14). Moreover, his reasoning was unsound: he expected to rout such a great army as he now had to deal with as easily as he had routed the earlier, smaller army (v. 6): *They flee before us as at the first*. He reasoned, perhaps, that Israelite soldiers were quick to retreat: the last time they had attacked, they had retreated so quickly that only thirty-six men out of 3,000 were killed. Notice how the prosperity of fools destroys them and hardens them to their destruction.

2.4. What a complete victory Israel won over them because of God's favor and blessing. Each did their part.

Verses 23–29

We have here an account of how the Israelites were victorious over Ai:

1. They killed everyone. Here it is said (v. 26) that *Joshua drew not his hand back wherewith he stretched out the spear* (see v. 18). Some think the javelin he held out was not to kill the enemies, but to encourage his own soldiers. He kept to the subordinate post of standard-bearer and did not leave it until the work was finished. He held out the javelin to direct the people to expect their help from God and to give God all the praise.

2. They plundered the city and took all the spoils for themselves (v. 27).

3. They burned the city to ashes, and left it to remain like that (v. 28). Israel still had to live in tents, and so this city, as well as Jericho, had to be burned down.

4. The king of Ai was taken prisoner and hanged, and his dead body was thrown at the gate of his own city, *under a heap of stones* (vv. 23, 29). It is likely that he had been a notoriously evil blasphemer of the God of Israel, perhaps when he repelled the first attack by the forces of Israel.

Verses 30–35

The religious ceremony recorded here is included somewhat surprisingly in the middle of the history of the wars of Canaan. Here a scene of quite a different kind comes; the camp of Israel is drawn out into the field, not to engage the enemy, but to offer sacrifice, to hear the Law read, and to say *Amen* to the blessings and the curses. It is a remarkable instance:

- Of the zeal of Israel for the service of God and for his honor. The warfare must come to a standstill while they make the long journey to the appointed place and there observe this ceremony. The way to succeed is to begin with God (Mt 6:33).
- Of the care of God for his faithful servants and worshipers. Although they were in enemy country that was still unconquered, they were safe in the service of God. It was a covenant transaction: the covenant was now renewed between God and Israel upon their taking possession of the Land of Promise, so that they might be encouraged in conquering it, know the terms on which they held it, and come under a fresh obligation to obey God. As a sign of the covenant:

1. They built an altar and offered sacrifice to God (vv. 30–31). This showed their dedication of themselves to God as living sacrifices to his honor in and by a Mediator, who is represented by the altar that sanctifies this gift. This altar was erected on Mount *Ebal*. The curses pronounced on Mount Ebal would have been carried out immediately if atonement had not been made by sacrifice. By the sacrifices offered on this altar they gave God the glory for the victories they had already obtained, as in Ex 17:15. The altar they built was of rough, unhewn, and undressed stone according to the Law (Ex 20:25), for God is most pleased with worship that is plain and natural and not showy or ostentatious.

2. They received the Law from God. Those who want to find favor with God and who expect to have their offerings accepted must do this. Now here:

2.1. The Law of the Ten Commandments was written on stones in the presence of all Israel, as an abridgment of the whole (v. 32). The stones were coated with plaster, and the Law was written on the plaster (Dt 27:4, 8). It was written so that everyone might see what they agreed to.

2.2. The blessings and the curses, the rewards and punishments of the Law, were publicly read (vv. 33–34), and we think the people said *Amen* to them as Moses had appointed them to do.

2.2.1. The audience was very large: the highest ruler was not excused and the lowliest foreigner was not excluded. This was an encouragement to converts, and a fortunate sign of the kindness to be shown to lowly Gentiles in later days.

2.2.2. The tribes were positioned, as Moses directed, six toward Gerizim and six toward Ebal. The ark in the middle of the valley was between them, for it was the *ark of the covenant* (v. 33). The ark contained the closely written rolls of that law which was copied out and declared openly on the stones. The covenant was commanded, and the command was covenanted. After the people had all taken their places and silence was declared, the priests who accompanied the ark or some of the Levites who accompanied them pronounced clearly the blessings and the curses, as Moses had drawn them up. The tribes said *Amen* to these, but it is only said here that they should *bless the people* (v. 33), for the blessing was what God intended first and foremost when he gave the Law. If they fell under the curse, then that was their own fault.

2.3. The Law itself, which also contained the commands and prohibitions, was read (v. 35), probably by Joshua himself.

CHAPTER 9

In this chapter we see: 1. The unwise confederacy of the kings of Canaan against Israel (vv. 1–2). 2. The wise confederacy of the inhabitants of Gibeon with Israel: how it was craftily proposed and asked for by the Gibeonites, who pretended to come from a distant country (vv. 3–13). 3. How it was unwisely agreed to by Joshua and the Israelites, to the disgust of the community when the deception was discovered (vv. 14–18). 4. How the matter was resolved to the satisfaction of all sides, by giving these Gibeonites their lives because Israel had covenanted with them but at the same time depriving them of their liberties because the covenant was not gained fairly (vv. 19–27).

Verses 1–2

Up to this time, the Canaanites had acted defensively; the Israelites were the aggressors against Jericho and Ai. But here, when the Canaanite kings *heard thereof* (v. 1), they met together to attack Israel, and they vigorously joined together as united forces to restrain the progress of Israel's victorious army. They *heard*, not only of the conquest of Jericho and Ai, but also of the Israelites' meeting at Mount Ebal: how Joshua—as if he already thought himself to be master of the country—had gathered all his people together, had read the laws to them by which they must be governed, and had heard their promises to submit to those laws; and so now they realized that the Israelites were serious in their intentions, and they thought it was time for them to take action. Although they were kings of many different nations, Hittites, Amorites, Perizzites, etc., who no doubt had their different interests and had often been in conflict with one another, they still unanimously determined to unite against Israel.

Verses 3–14

1. The Gibeonites wanted to make peace with Israel, because they were alarmed at the news they heard of the destruction of Jericho (v. 3). Other people heard that news and so were angry enough to make war on Israel, but the Gibeonites heard the news and decided to make peace with them. The same sun softens wax but hardens clay. These four united cities (mentioned in v. 17) seem to have been governed by elders, or senators (v. 11), who looked after the common safety more than their personal dignity. The inhabitants of Gibeon did well for themselves.

2. They contrived a method. They knew that all the inhabitants of the land of Canaan were to be destroyed.

There was therefore no way of saving their lives from the sword of Israel unless they could disguise themselves and make Joshua believe that they had come from some distant country, for the Israelites had not been commanded to make war on those countries and were not forbidden to *make peace with* them, but were especially appointed to *offer peace to* them (Dt 20:10, 15). This therefore is the only plan they could follow, and notice:

2.1. They followed it very cunningly and successfully. Never was any such thing more craftily managed:

2.1.1. They came as a delegation from a foreign state, which they thought would please the rulers of Israel and make them proud of the honor of being courted by distant countries.

2.1.2. They pretended to be very weary because of the long journey and produced what passed for tangible evidence. They pretended that when they brought their provisions from home, they were new and fresh, but now they appeared to be old and dry. Their shoes and clothes were in a worse state than those of the Israelites after forty years, and their bread was moldy (vv. 4–5) and again vv. 12–13).

2.1.3. When suspicions of deception were aroused and they were closely examined as to where they came from, they were careful to avoid disclosing the name of their country until the agreement had been settled.

2.1.3.1. The men of Israel suspected that this was a deception (v. 7): "*Peradventure* (perhaps) *you dwell among us*, and then we may not, we must not, make any treaty with you."

2.1.3.2. Joshua puts questions to them: *Who are you? and whence come you?* (v. 8).

2.1.3.3. They will not say where they have come from but still repeat the same thing: *We have come from a very far country* (v. 9).

2.1.4. They profess a respect for the God of Israel, to ingratiate themselves with Joshua, but we charitably believe they were sincere in this profession: *We have come because of the name of the Lord thy God* (v. 9).

2.1.5. They claim to be motivated by what had been done some time before in Moses' reign—the plagues of Egypt and the destruction of Sihon and Og (vv. 9–10). But they wisely do not mention the destruction of Jericho and Ai at all, because they want it thought that they came from home long before those conquests were made.

2.1.6. They offer general submission—We *are your servants*—and humbly seek a general agreement—*Make a league with us* (v. 11). But:

2.2. There is a mixture of good and evil in their behavior:

2.2.1. Their deception cannot be justified, and it should not be used as a precedent. It is significant that when they had once said, *We have come from a far country* (v. 6), they found themselves having to say it again (v. 9), and to say what was completely false about their bread, their wineskins, and their clothes (vv. 12–13), for one lie leads to a second, and then to a third, and so on. But:

2.2.2. Their faith and wisdom are to be greatly commended. Our Lord *commended* even *the unjust steward*, the shrewd manager, *because he had done wisely* and well for himself (Lk 16:8). In submitting to the God of Israel, the Gibeonites submitted to the God of Israel, which implied a renunciation of the god they had served. They did not wait till Israel had besieged their cities. It would then have been too late to surrender, but when they were still some distance away, they wanted to make peace. The way to avoid judgment is to repent. Let us imitate these Gibeonites and make our peace with God in the rags of our humiliation and godly sorrow, so that our sin will not destroy us. Let us be the servants of Jesus, our blessed Joshua, and make a peace treaty with him and the Israel of God, and then we will live.

Verses 15–21

Here is:

1. The treaty agreed to quickly with the Gibeonites (v. 15). The matter was not accomplished with long formalities, but, to put it briefly:

1.1. Israel agreed to let them live, and the Gibeonites did not ask for more.

1.2. This agreement was made not only by Joshua, but also by the leaders of the assembly together with him.

1.3. It was confirmed by an oath. The Israelites swore an oath to the Gibeonites, not by any of the gods of Canaan, but only by the God of Israel (v. 19).

1.4. Nothing appears to have been reprehensible in all this except that it was done rashly. The Israelites used only their senses, not their reason, and "they received the men by reason of their victuals" (v. 14, margin), from the view and taste of the bread. But *they asked not counsel at the mouth of the Lord* (v. 14). Joshua himself was not altogether without blame in this. This shows us that we are acting with more haste and less speed in any business when we do not wait to take God along with us, by consulting him in the word and prayer.

2. The deception soon discovered by which this treaty was obtained. *A lying tongue is but for a moment* (Pr 12:19), and sooner or later the truth will out. Within three days they found to their great surprise that the cities for which the delegation had negotiated were very near them, just one night's march from the camp at Gilgal (10:9).

3. The disgust of the assembly at this. They did indeed submit to the restraints which the terms of the treaty imposed on them. They did not strike the cities of the Gibeonites, nor did they kill the people or seize the plunder, but they were annoyed to have their hands tied in this way, and they *murmured against the princes* (leaders) (v. 18).

4. The wise attempts of the leaders to quiet the discontented assembly no doubt helped the people to calm down.

4.1. They decided to spare the lives of the Gibeonites, for they had expressly sworn to let them live (v. 15).

4.1.1. The oath was lawful.

4.1.2. Because the oath was lawful, both the leaders and the people for whom they made the commitment were bound by it. They were bound by their consciences and in honor of the God of Israel, by whom they had sworn and whose name would have been blasphemed by the Canaanites if Israel had violated this oath. The leaders would keep their word:

4.1.2.1. Although they lost out by it. A citizen of Zion *swears to his own hurt and changes not*, keeps his oath even when it hurts (Ps 15:4).

4.1.2.2. Although the people were uneasy at it, and their discontent might have ended in rebellion, the leaders still would not break their commitment to the Gibeonites. We must never be overawed, either by majesty or numbers, into doing something sinful and going against our consciences.

4.1.2.3. Although they were drawn into this treaty by deception and might have had a plausible reason to declare it null and void, they still adhered to it. Let this convince us all how religiously we ought to fulfill our promises and agreements. We ought to deal conscientiously with a promise when we make one. If a covenant obtained by so many lies and deceits is not to be broken, how can it be right to evade the obligations of those that have been made with the greatest honesty and fairness?

4.2. Although they spared the lives of the Gibeonites, they removed their liberty and sentenced them to be *hewers of wood and drawers of water to the congregation* (v. 21). The assembly was pacified by this proposal.

Verses 22–27

The matter is here settled between Joshua and the Gibeonites.

1. Joshua rebukes them for their deception (v. 22), and they excuse it as best they can (v. 24).

1.1. Joshua rebukes them mildly: *Wherefore have you beguiled us?* (v. 22).

1.2. They make the best excuse they can under the circumstances (v. 24). They considered that God's sovereignty is incontrovertible, his justice inflexible, and his power irresistible, and so they decided to throw themselves on his mercy, and they found that that was not in vain. They do not try to justify their lie, but in effect beg forgiveness for it. They plead that they acted in this way purely to save their lives.

2. Joshua condemns them to slavery as a punishment of their deception (v. 23), they submit to the sentence (v. 25), and it seems that both sides are pleased.

2.1. Joshua declares that they are to be slaves forever. Notice how the judgment is given against them:

2.1.1. Their slavery is made a curse to them.

2.1.2. But this curse is turned into a blessing; they must be servants, but it will be for *the house of my God* (v. 23). The leaders wanted them to be slaves *unto all the congregation* (v. 21). Joshua commutes the sentence, both in honor to God and in favor to the Gibeonites. Even menial work becomes honorable when it is done for the house of our God and its offices.

2.1.2.1. Their work excluded them from the liberties and privileges of trueborn Israelites. But:

2.1.2.2. They were employed in the service that required their personal attendance on *the altar of God in the place which he should choose* (v. 27). This would bring them to the knowledge of God's Law.

2.1.2.3. It would benefit the priests and Levites greatly to have so many men, and such *mighty men* (10:2), as constant attendants who were committed to the chores of the tabernacle. A great deal of wood must be cut for fuel for God's house. And a great deal of water must be carried for the various washings prescribed in the Law.

2.1.2.4. They served the whole community in this, for whatever furthers the worship of God is a real service to the community. Gibeonites afterward became temple servants (1Ch 9:2), given to the Levites in the same way as the Levites were given to the priests (Nu 3:9), to minister to them in the service of God.

2.1.2.5. This may be looked on as a type of the admission of the Gentiles into the Gospel church.

2.2. They submit to this condition (v. 25). *Do as it seemeth right unto thee* (v. 25). This is how the matter was determined. And so Israel's slaves became the Lord's free people, for to serve him in lowly ways is liberty, and his work is its own wages. Let us in the same way submit to our Lord Jesus and give our lives to him. If he asks us to carry his cross, help with his work, or serve at his altar, this will bring us no shame or sadness.

CHAPTER 10

In this chapter we have an account of the conquest of the kings and kingdoms of the southern part of the land of Canaan, as in the next chapter we have an account of the conquest of the northern parts. Here we have: 1. The routing of the Canaanite forces in the field, in which notice: their confederacy against the Gibeonites (vv. 1–5); the Gibeonites' request to Joshua to help them (v. 6). 2. Joshua's speedy march, with God's encouragement, for their relief (vv. 7–9); the defeat of the armies of these confederate kings (vv. 10–11); the miraculous prolonging of the day by the sun standing still in favor of the conquerors (vv. 12–14). 3. The execution of the kings who escaped the battle (vv. 15–27). 4. The conquest of particular cities and the total destruction of all that were found in them: Makkedah (v. 28), Libnah (vv. 29–30), Lachish (vv. 31–32) and the king of Gezer who attempted its rescue (v. 33), Eglon (vv. 34–35), Hebron (vv. 36–37), and Debir (vv. 38–39). Joshua subdues the whole region (vv. 40–42), and, lastly, the army returns to the headquarters (v. 43).

Verses 1–6

Joshua and the armies of Israel had conquered Jericho by a miracle, Ai by strategy, and Gibeon by surrender, and that was all. There were no doubt some among them who were impatient at the delays and complained about Joshua's slowness, asking why they did not immediately penetrate into the heart of the country, before the enemy could rally their forces. They may well have attacked Joshua's caution as laziness, cowardice, and faintheartedness. But:

- Canaan was not to be conquered in a day. God had said that *by little and little* he would drive out the Canaanites (Ex 23:30).
- Joshua was waiting for the Canaanites to attack first. Then their destruction would be—or at least appear to be—more just and more justifiable.

After Israel had waited awhile for an occasion to make war on the Canaanites, an opportunity presented itself:

1. Five kings joined forces against the Gibeonites. Adoni-Zedek king of Jerusalem initiated, and was the ringleader of, this confederacy. It seems he was a bad man and an implacable enemy of the descendants of Abraham, to whom his predecessor, Melchizedek, was such a faithful friend. So he said, *Come, and help me, that we may smite Gibeon* (v. 4). He decided to do this either:

- As a political act, so that he might recapture the city, because it was a strong city, and important to the country in whose hands it was; or:
- In an act of passion, so that he might attack the citizens for making peace with Joshua, pretending that they had treacherously betrayed their country.

2. The Gibeonites send word to Joshua of the distress and danger they are in (v. 6). They think Joshua is obliged to help them for conscience's sake, because they are his servants, and for the sake of honor, because the reason for their enemies' quarrel with them is the respect they have shown to Israel. When our spiritual enemies set themselves up against us and threaten to swallow us up, may we turn in faith and prayer to Christ, our Joshua, for strength and support, as Paul did, and we will receive the same answer of peace, *My grace is sufficient for thee* (2Co 12:8–9).

Verses 7–14

Here:

1. Joshua decides to help the Gibeonites, and God encourages him in this decision:

1.1. He marches up from Gilgal (v. 7), determined to relieve Gibeon. Joshua knew that when the Gibeonites embraced the faith and worship of the God of Israel, they

came to take refuge under the shadow of his wings (Ru 2:12), and so because they were God's servants, Joshua was committed to protecting them.

1.2. God encouraged him in his undertaking (v. 8): *Fear not*, that is: "Do not doubt the goodness of your cause and the clearness of your call. Do not fear the power of the enemy. *I have delivered them into thy hand.*"

2. Joshua applies himself to carry out this decision, and God helps him to do so. Here we have:

2.1. The great diligence of Joshua, and the power of God working with him, to defeat the enemy. In this action, Joshua showed his goodwill in going quickly to relieve Gibeon (v. 9). Now that things were ready to be carried out, no one was quicker off the mark than Joshua, who before had seemed so slow. He marched all night, deciding not to sleep a wink until he had completed this enterprise. Let the *good soldiers of Jesus Christ* (2Ti 2:3) learn from this to endure hardness in *following the Lamb whithersoever he goes* (Rev 14:4). Let them not think themselves ruined if their religious faith causes them now and then to lose a night's sleep; there will be enough rest when we come to heaven. But why did Joshua need to put himself and his army under so much pressure? Had not God promised him that he would without fail *deliver the enemies into his hand* (v. 8)? It is true he had; yet God's promises are intended not to slacken and replace our endeavors, but to encourage and enliven them. *The Lord discomfited them* (threw them into confusion) *before Israel* (v. 10). Israel did what they could, but God did everything.

2.2. The great faith of Joshua, and the power of God crowning it with the miraculous stopping of the sun, so that the day of Israel's victories might be prolonged and the enemy totally defeated. The hailstones came from no higher than the clouds, but to show that Israel's help came from above the clouds, the sun itself, which by its constant movement serves the whole earth, came to a standstill when it was needed to serve the Israelites and show them kindness. *The sun and moon stood still in their habitation, at the light of thy arrows* which gave the signal (Hab 3:11). Here is:

2.2.1. The prayer of Joshua that the sun might stand still. This prayer showed his great faith. It showed greatness for Joshua to say, *Sun, stand thou still* (v. 12). His ancestor Joseph had indeed dreamed that the sun and moon paid homage to him; but who would have thought, after it had been fulfilled figuratively, that it would again be fulfilled literally to one of his descendants? He told the sun to stand still over Gibeon, the place of action and the theater of war, showing that what he was asking for was for Israel to gain an advantage over its enemies. The sun was probably now setting, and he mentions here the Valley of Aijalon, which was near Gibeon, because he was there at that time. Moreover, it was bold for Joshua to speak out such a prayer in the presence of Israel, and it shows a great assurance of faith.

2.2.2. The wonderful answer to this prayer. It was no sooner said than done (v. 13): *The sun stood still, and the moon stayed*. The same God who rules in heaven above rules on earth at the same time, and when he pleases, even *the heavens shall hear the earth* (Hos 2:21), as here. Concerning this great miracle it is said:

2.2.2.1. That it continued *a whole day* (v. 13), that is, the sun continued to be seen above the horizon for as long as the daylight of another whole day.

2.2.2.2. That it gave the people ample time to avenge themselves on their enemies and to defeat them totally. Sometimes God completes a great salvation in a short time and makes only one day's work of it. An account of this miracle is said to be written *in the book of Jasher* (v. 13), an early chronicle of Israel's wars, perhaps in poems, in which case the poem written down on this occasion was preserved among the rest. The words *Sun, stand thou still upon Gibeon, and thou, Moon, in the valley of Ajalon* (v. 12) sound metrical, and it is supposed that they were taken from the narrative of this event as it was found in the Book of Jashar. The sun, the eye of the world, must be fixed for some hours upon Gibeon and the Valley of Aijalon, as if to contemplate the great works of God there for Israel, and so to attract people to look that way and *inquire of this wonder done in the land* (2Ch 32:31). God wanted to convince and confound those idolaters who worshiped the sun and moon and gave divine honors to them, by showing that those creatures were subject to the command of the God of Israel. This miracle signified that in the last days, when the light of the world was tending toward a night of darkness, the *Sun of righteousness*, even our Joshua, would arise (Mal 4:2), restraining the approaching night and being the true light.

Verses 15–27

The five kings were all routed. And now Joshua thought that his work was done and he could go with his army into a place of refreshment, but he soon found that he had more work to do. The victory must be followed up so that the plunder might be divided.

1. The forces that had dispersed must be followed. He directed his men to pursue the common soldiers, as many as there might be, to prevent their escaping to the garrisons. The result of this energetic pursuit was:

1.1. That most of the enemies of God and Israel were killed. And:

1.2. The battlefield was cleared of them, so that none were left except those who reached their fortified cities.

1.3. *None moved his tongue against any of the children of Israel* (v. 21). This expression shows:

1.3.1. Israel's perfect safety and tranquility. They were not threatened by any danger at all after their victory, no, not even so much as by the barking of a dog.

1.3.2. Their honor and reputation: no one insulted them; there was not a bad word said about them.

2. The kings who had hidden themselves must now be brought to account as rebels against the Israel of God. Notice:

2.1. How they were kept secure. The cave which they fled to and trusted in for refuge became their prison. They were confined there until Joshua judged them (v. 18).

2.2. How they were triumphed over. Joshua ordered them to be brought out of the cave and set before him as in a court of law, and their names to be called out (vv. 22–23). And whether they were tied up and thrown onto the ground helpless, or whether they threw themselves on the ground and humbly begged for their lives, Joshua called for the general officials and great men, and commanded them to trample on these kings, and put their feet on their necks. Glorying over these miserable kings, who had fallen so suddenly from the place of highest honor to such a lowly and disgraceful position, does indeed look cruel. It definitely ought not to be used as a precedent, for the case was extraordinary.

2.2.1. God wanted to punish the detestable evil of these kings. The public act of justice carried out on these ringleaders of the sins of the Canaanites would fill the people with a greater fear and abhorrence of the sins of *these nations that the Lord doth drive out from before them* (Dt 9:4), sins which the Israelites would be tempted to imitate.

2.2.2. God saw to the fulfillment of the promise made by Moses (Dt 33:29), *Thou shalt tread upon their high places*.

2.2.3. God wanted to encourage the faith and hope of his people Israel with reference to the wars that lay ahead of them. And so Joshua said (v. 25), *Fear not, nor be dismayed*. "Do not be afraid of these kings, nor any of their people. Do not be afraid of any other kings, who may at any time join forces against you. Be encouraged that you brought down these kings whom you thought formidable."

2.2.4. God wanted to show this as a type of Christ's victories over the powers of darkness, and believers' victories through him. All the enemies of the Redeemer will be *made his footstool* (Ps 110:1). Sooner or later we will see all things put under him (Heb 2:8), and *principalities and powers* made a show of (Col 2:15).

2.3. How they were put to death. Joshua struck them with the sword and then hanged their bodies until evening, when they were taken down and thrown *into the cave in which they had hidden themselves* (vv. 26–27). If these five kings had humbled themselves in time and if they had begged for peace instead of waging war, they might have saved their lives.

Verses 28–43

Here is:

1. A full account of the several cities which Joshua immediately conquered:

1.1. He went and took possession of the cities of three of the kings whom he had defeated, Lachish (vv. 31–32), Eglon (vv. 34–35), and Hebron (vv. 36–37). The other two, Jerusalem and Jarmuth, were not captured at this time.

1.2. He conquered three other cities, and royal cities they were, too: Makkedah (v. 28) and Libnah (vv. 29–30) and Debir (vv. 38–39).

1.3. One king who brought in his forces to relieve Lachish, Horam king of Gezer, was struck down with all his forces (v. 33).

2. A general account of the country which was conquered in this way and brought into Israel's hands (vv. 40–42), which lay south of Jerusalem and afterward mostly fell to the allotment of the tribe of Judah. Notice in this narrative:

2.1. How quickly Joshua took these cities.

2.2. How severely Joshua dealt with those he conquered. He was not merciful to any man, woman, or child. He put to the sword *all the souls* (vv. 28, 30, 32, 35), *utterly destroyed all that breathed* (v. 40), and *left none remaining*. In having Joshua do this, God wanted to:

2.2.1. Show his hatred of the idolatry and other detestable practices which the Canaanites had been guilty of.

2.2.2. Exalt his love to his people Israel.

2.3. The great success of this expedition. The Lord *fought for Israel* (v. 42). They could not have gained the victory if God had not undertaken the battle.

CHAPTER 11

This chapter continues and concludes the history of the conquest of Canaan. In the previous chapter we had an account of the conquest of the southern parts, after which we may presume Joshua allowed his forces some time to rest. Here we have the story of the war in the north and the success of that war. 1. The confederacy of the northern kings against Israel (vv. 1–5); the encouragement which God gave to Joshua to engage them in war (v. 6);

his victory over them (vv. 7–9). 2. The conquest of their cities (vv. 10–15). 3. The destruction of the Anakites (vv. 21–22) and the conclusion of the story of this war (vv. 16–20, 23).

Verses 1–9

Here we enter on the story of another campaign that Joshua made. It was lesser with respect to glorious miracles when compared with his former campaigns. The wonders God had carried out for them in that earlier campaign were intended to stir and encourage them to act vigorously themselves. In the same way, the war carried on by the preaching of the Gospel against Satan's kingdom at first advanced by miracles, but because the miracles showed sufficiently that the war was of God, those who declare it now are left to the more ordinary help of God's grace in using the sword of the Spirit. We must not expect hailstones or the standing still of the sun. In this story we have:

1. The Canaanites opening the military campaign against Israel. They were the aggressors. Sinners bring ruin on their own heads, so that *God will be justified when he speaks* (Ps 51:4), and they alone will bear the blame forever. Now:

1.1. Several nations joined in this alliance, some *in the mountains* and some *in the plains* (v. 2). They all united against Israel as the common enemy. In the same way, *the children of this world* are sometimes more united—speaking with one voice—and are *wiser than the children of light* (Lk 16:8). The unity of the church's enemies should shame the church's friends out of their disagreements and divisions and cause them to be united.

1.2. The head of this alliance was *Jabin king of Hazor* (v. 1). When they had all drawn their forces together, they were a huge army. They had very many horses and chariots, which we do not find that the southern kings had.

2. The encouragement God gave to Joshua to appoint a place for them to meet, even on the ground of their own choosing (v. 6): *Be not afraid because of them.* Joshua was remarkable for his courage—it was his strongest quality—but it seems he needed again and again to be encouraged not to be afraid. For Joshua's encouragement:

2.1. God assured him of success and established the time: *Tomorrow about this time* (v. 6).

2.2. God appointed him to *hough* (hamstring) *their horses,* lame them, and *burn their chariots* (v. 6), not only so that Israel could not use them afterward, but also so that they would not fear them now, because God intended them to be treated with contempt. Israel must look on their chariots merely as rotten wood to be thrown onto the fire, and their horses of war as disabled, scarcely good enough to pull a cart.

3. Joshua's march against these confederate forces (v. 7). He *came upon them suddenly* and surprised them where they were.

4. Joshua's success (v. 8). He obtained the honor and advantage of a complete victory; he struck them and chased them. They fled in different directions.

5. Joshua's obedience to the orders given him, in destroying the horses and chariots (v. 9), which showed his care to keep the people having the same confidence in God, by taking away from them what they would be tempted to trust too much in. This was *cutting off a right hand* (Mt 5:30).

Verses 10–14

We have here the same use made of this victory as was made of that in the previous chapter:

1. The destruction of Hazor is particularly recorded, because its king had been the head of all the kingdoms that had plotted against Israel (vv. 10–11).

2. Of the rest of the cities in that part of the country it is only said generally that Joshua conquered them all, but he did not burn them as he did Hazor, for Israel was to live in *great and goodly cities which they builded not* (Dt 6:10), in these among others.

Verses 15–23

We have here the conclusion of this whole matter:

1. A short account is given of what was done about four things:

1.1. The obstinacy of the Canaanites in their opposition to the Israelites. It is suggested that other cities might have made good terms for themselves, without ragged clothes and worn-out shoes, if they had humbled themselves, but they never so much as *desired conditions of peace.* God left them to this to punish them for all their other foolish acts and to cause those whom they might have made their friends to become their enemies.

1.2. The faithfulness of the Israelites in pursuing this war (v. 18): *Joshua made war a long time.* Some reckon it as five years, others seven, that were spent in subduing this land.

1.3. The eventual conquest of the Anakites (vv. 21–22). Either this was done as they fought them where they were scattered, as some think, or more probably it would seem that the Anakites withdrew to their strongholds and so were hunted down and were eventually destroyed after the rest of Israel's enemies had been destroyed. The mountains of Judah and Israel were where these huge men lived, but nothing could save them from the sword of Joshua—not their height, the strong defense of their caves, or the difficulty of the terrain. The destroying of the descendants of Anak is particularly mentioned because they had been such a terror to the spies roughly forty years earlier, and their bulk and strength had been thought an insuperable difficulty in conquering the land of Canaan (Nu 13:28, 33). Giants are as tiny as grasshoppers before almighty God, but this struggle with the Anakites was kept back to the later stages of the war, when the Israelites had become more expert in the art of warfare and had more experience of the power and goodness of God. This shows us that God sometimes holds back the most severe trials of affliction and temptation for the final part of the lives of his people. Death, that tremendous descendant of Anak, is the last enemy to be encountered, but it is *to be destroyed* (1Co 15:26).

1.4. The conclusion and outcome of this long war. The Canaanites were rooted out: *Joshua took all that land* (vv. 16–17). And we suppose that the people scattered themselves and their families into the countries they had conquered, at least those which were nearest to the headquarters at Gilgal.

2. What was now done is compared with what had been said to Moses. Notice in closing:

2.1. That all the commands God had given to Moses about the conquest of Canaan were obeyed by the people, at least while Joshua lived. Joshua himself was a great commander, but nothing commended him more than his obedience. Because Joshua was zealous for almighty God, he spared neither the idols nor the idolaters. Saul's disobedience, or rather his partial obedience, to the command of God to completely destroy the Amalekites cost him his kingdom.

2.2. That all the promises God had given to Moses relating to this conquest were accomplished *on his part* (v. 23). God had promised to drive out the nations before them (Ex 33:2; 34:11) and to *bring them down* (Dt 9:3). And now it was done.

CHAPTER 12

This chapter is a summary of Israel's conquests: 1. Their conquests under Moses on the other side of the Jordan. Here is a synopsis of that history (vv. 1–6). 2. Their conquests under Joshua on this side of the Jordan, to the west: the country they conquered (vv. 7–8); the kings they subdued, thirty-one in all (vv. 9–24). And this is included here not only as a conclusion of the history of the wars of Canaan, but also as an introduction to the history of the distribution of the land of Canaan, so that all they were now to distribute might be put together.

Verses 1–6

Before Joshua, or whoever is the writer, comes to sum up the conquests Israel had made, he recounts in these verses their former conquests in Moses' time, under whom they conquered the great and powerful kingdoms of Sihon and Og. Joshua's services and achievements are truly great, but let those of Moses not be overlooked and forgotten. Here is:

1. A description of this conquered country (v. 1): *From the River Arnon* in the south, to *Mount Hermon* in the north. In particular, here is a description of the kingdom of Sihon (vv. 2–3) and that of Og (vv. 4–5). Moses had described this country in detail (Dt 2:36; 3:4; etc.), and the description here corresponds to his. King Og is said to have reigned in Ashtaroth and Edrei (v. 4), as they were probably both his royal cities. He had palaces in both. But Israel took both from him and made one grave for him who could not be content with one palace.

2. The distribution of this country. Moses assigned it to the two and a half Transjordan tribes, who had requested it, and he divided it among them (v. 6). We had this story in detail in Nu 32:1–42. The dividing of it when it was conquered by Moses is mentioned here as an example to Joshua of what he must do now that he had conquered the country on the other side of the Jordan. In Moses' time, he gave a very rich and fruitful country to one part of Israel, but it was on the east of the Jordan. Joshua, however, gave to all Israel the holy land, the mountain of God's sanctuary, over the Jordan.

Verses 7–24

We have here a short account of Joshua's conquests:

1. The limits of the country he conquered. It lay between the Jordan on the east and the Mediterranean Sea on the west, and extended from Baal Gad near Lebanon in the north to Mount Halak, which lay in the country of Edom in the south (v. 7). The boundaries are more fully described in Nu 34:2–12. God had been true to his word and had given them possession of all he had promised them by Moses.

2. The various kinds of land that were found in this country, which contributed to both its pleasantness and its fruitfulness (v. 8). There were mountains, not craggy, rocky, and barren, but fruitful hills which produced *precious things* (Dt 33:15). The valleys were not mossy and boggy but *covered with corn* (Ps 65:13). There were plains, with springs to water them. In that rich land there were even areas of wilderness or forests.

3. The various nations who had possessed this country—the Hittites, Amorites, Canaanites, etc., all of them descended from Canaan, the cursed son of Ham (Ge 10:15–18). They are called seven nations (Dt 7:1), and this number is given there, but only six are mentioned here, with the Girgashites being either lost or left out, though we find them in Ge 10:16; 15:21. Either they were

incorporated into one of the other nations, or as the tradition of the Jews has it, when Israel approached under Joshua's leadership, they all withdrew and went to Africa.

4. A list of the kings that were conquered and subdued by the sword of Israel: the kings of Jericho and Ai; the king of Jerusalem and the rulers of the south who were in league with him; and then those of the north. This shows what a fruitful country Canaan was at that time and why it could support so many kingdoms.

CHAPTER 13

The account of dividing the land of Canaan among the tribes of Israel by lot begins at this chapter. The preserving of this account of the division would be very useful to the Jewish nation, whose people were obliged by the Law to maintain this first division and not to transfer inheritances from tribe to tribe (Nu 36:9). Similarly, the chapter is useful to explain other Scriptures, for the geographical description of a country illuminates its history. In this chapter: 1. God tells Joshua what parts of the country were intended in the gift to Israel but are not yet conquered (vv. 1–6). 2. He appoints Joshua nevertheless to allocate what was conquered (v. 7). To complete this account, there comes a repetition of the distribution Moses had made of the land on the other side of the Jordan: in general (vv. 8–14); in particular, the lots of Reuben (vv. 15–23), of Gad (vv. 24–28), and of the half tribe of Manasseh (vv. 29–33).

Verses 1–6

Here:

1. God reminds Joshua of his old age (v. 1):

1.1. It is said that Joshua was *old and stricken in years*, and he and Caleb were at this time the only old men among the thousands of Israel. They were the only old men still alive out of all those who had been counted at Mount Sinai. Joshua did not have the same strength and energy in his old age as Moses had. Those who reach old age do not all find it pleasant to the same extent.

1.2. God makes Joshua aware of his age: *God said to him, Thou art old* (v. 1), as a reason why:

1.2.1. He should now put aside the thoughts of pursuing the war. Just as he entered into the labors of Moses, so others will enter into his, and set up the capstone, which is to be reserved for David long after.

1.2.2. He should quickly turn to allocating the land that he has conquered. That work must be done now. Because he is *old and stricken in years* (v. 1), and not likely to continue to live for very much longer, this may be his final act of service to God and Israel.

2. God gives Joshua a detailed account of the land intended for Israel that is still not conquered, which in due time they will control if they do not sin and come under God's judgment. Different places are mentioned here, some in the south, such as the country of the Philistines governed by five rulers and the land that lay toward Egypt (vv. 2–3); some westward, such as the land toward the Sidonians (v. 4); some eastward, including all Lebanon (v. 5); and some toward the north, such as that toward Hamath (v. 5).

3. God promises that he himself will give the Israelites victory over all those countries that have still not been subdued, even though Joshua is old. God will complete his own work in his own time (v. 6): *I will drive them out.* This promise that he will drive them out from before the children of Israel clearly presupposes as a condition of the promise that the children of Israel must themselves

attempt to destroy those people, or else they cannot be said to be driven out before Israel. If the Israelites sit back and leave them alone through laziness or cowardice, then they only have themselves to blame, and not God, if the Canaanites are not driven out. We must work out our salvation, and then God will work in us and work with us.

Verses 7–33

Here we have:

1. Orders given to Joshua to allocate a part of the land to each tribe, including what was not yet subdued.

1.1. The land must be allocated to the different tribes, and they must not always live sharing a common land, as they did then.

1.2. The land must be divided as an inheritance, though they gained it by conquest.

1.2.1. The promise of it came to them as an inheritance from their fathers; the Land of Promise belonged to the children of promise.

1.2.2. The possession of it was to be passed on as an inheritance to their children.

1.3. Joshua must not allocate the land according to his own will. Although he was very wise, just, and good, it must not be left to him to give what he pleased to each tribe. No; he must do it by casting lots, which referred the matter wholly to God and to his will. Yet Joshua must have the honor of allocating the land because he had experienced the hard work of conquering it and so that he might become a type of Christ, who has not only conquered the gates of hell for us, but has also opened the gates of heaven to us. He has purchased the eternal inheritance for all believers and will in due time give them all possession of it.

2. An account given of the distribution of the land on the other side of the Jordan among the Reubenites, the Gadites, and the half tribe of Manasseh. Notice:

2.1. How this account is introduced. It is included:

2.1.1. As the reason why this land to the west of the Jordan must be divided only among the nine and a half tribes, because the other two and a half tribes were already provided for.

2.1.2. As a pattern for Joshua in the work he now had to do.

2.1.3. As a motivation to Joshua to allocate the land promptly, so that the nine and a half tribes might not be kept waiting any longer than necessary for their possession, since their brothers and sisters of the two and a half tribes were so well settled in theirs.

2.2. The details of this account. Here is:

2.2.1. A general description of the country given to the two and a half tribes, *which Moses gave them, even as Moses gave them* (v. 8). The repetition implies a confirmation of the gift by Joshua. Here we have:

2.2.1.1. The establishing of the boundaries of this country, by which Israel was separated from the neighboring nations (vv. 9–12). Israel must know its own boundaries and keep to them.

2.2.1.2. The exclusion of one part of this country from Israel's possession even though it was in their gift, namely, the lands of Geshur and Maacah (v. 13).

2.2.2. A very detailed account of the inheritances of these two and a half tribes. This is set down as a full and exact record in order that future generations might be moved by reading about the goodness of God to their ancestors. Moreover, the detailed setting down of the limits of each tribe in this authentic record would prevent any disputes from developing.

2.2.2.1. Here is the allotment of the tribe of Reuben, Jacob's firstborn, who, although he had lost the dignity and authority which belonged to the birthright, still seems to have had the advantage of being the first to be served. The separation of this tribe from the rest by the River Jordan was what Deborah mourned; and she attacked the preference they gave to their private interests (Jdg 5:15–16). In this tribe's territory Heshbon and Sibmah were also situated, famous for their fruitful fields and vineyards. This tribe and Gad were overpowered by Hazael king of Syria (2Ki 10:32–33) and later removed and taken into captivity by the king of Assyria (1Ch 5:26), maybe twenty years before the general captivity of the ten tribes.

2.2.2.2. Here is the allotment of the tribe of Gad (vv. 24–28). This was north of Reuben's allotment; the country of Gilead, famous for its balm, was situated in this tribe's territory, as were the cities of Jabesh Gilead and Ramoth Gilead, which we often read about in Scripture. So also were Succoth and Penuel, which we read about in the story of Gideon. Sharon, famous for roses, was also in this tribe's territory. And within the limits of this tribe lived those Gadarenes who loved their pigs more than their Savior; they were more suitably called *Girgashites* than *Israelites*.

2.2.2.3. Here is the allotment of the half tribe of Manasseh (vv. 29–31). Bashan, the kingdom of Og, was in this allotment, famous for the best timber, as can be seen in references to the oaks of Bashan, and for the best breed of cattle, as can be seen in references to the bulls and rams of Bashan. This tribe was situated north of Gad, extended as far as Mount Hermon, and contained part of Gilead. Mizpah was in this half tribe, and Jephthah was one of its distinguished inhabitants; so was Elijah, for in this tribe was Tishbe, from which he is called the *Tishbite* (1Ki 17:1); and Jair was another. At the edge of the tribe stood Korazin, honored with Christ's miracles but judged by his righteous anger for not making the most of them.

2.2.2.4. To the tribe of Levi *Moses gave no inheritance* (vv. 14, 33), for this is what God had appointed (Nu 18:20). They were to live scattered throughout all the tribes, and their maintenance must come from all the tribes (Dt 10:9; 18:2).

CHAPTER 14

Here is: 1. The general method that was taken in dividing the land (vv. 1–5). 2. The request Caleb made for Hebron, as his by promise, and so not to be included in the allotment with the rest (vv. 6–12). Joshua's agreement to that request (vv. 13–15). This was done at Gilgal, which was their base camp.

Verses 1–5

The writer now comes to tell us what they did with the territories in the land of Canaan. They were not conquered to be left as desert. Canaan would have been subdued in vain if it had not been inhabited. But everyone could not go and settle where they pleased. God had given Moses directions as to how this distribution should be made. See Nu 26:53–56.

1. The organizers of this great affair were Joshua the chief judge, Eleazar the chief priest, and ten leaders, one from each of the tribes who were now to receive their inheritance, whom God himself had named (Nu 34:17–29).

2. The tribes among whom the land was to be divided were nine and a half. This excluded the tribe of Levi,

which was to be provided for in different ways. Joseph made two tribes, Manasseh and Ephraim, in accordance with Jacob's adoption of Joseph's two sons, and so the number of tribes was kept to twelve, though Levi was excluded, which is indicated here (v. 4).

3. The rule which they followed was the casting of lots (v. 2), *the disposal* of which is *of the Lord* (Pr 16:33). It was here used in a significant matter, which could not otherwise be settled to everyone's satisfaction. It was used as an appeal to God in a solemn religious manner, with the approval of the parties.

Verses 6–15

Before the lot was cast to determine the allocations of the respective tribes, the particular portion of Caleb was assigned to him. He was now, besides Joshua, not only the oldest man in all Israel, but also twenty years older than any of them, for all who were older than twenty had died in the desert when he was forty. It was therefore right that this paragon of age should be honored in some special way in the dividing of the land.

1. Caleb here makes his request that Hebron be given him as a possession (*this mountain* he calls it, v. 12) and that it not be included with the other parts of the country. To justify his demand, he shows that God long ago, through Moses, promised him *the land that he hath trodden upon* (Dt 1:36). Notice:

1.1. To support his petition:

• He brings the children of Judah, that is, the heads and leaders of that tribe, along with him to present it.

• He appeals to Joshua himself concerning the truth of the allegations which he bases his petition on: *Thou knowest the thing* (v. 6).

1.2. In his request he sets out:

1.2.1. The testimony of his conscience concerning the spying out of the land:

1.2.1.1. That he made his report as it was on his heart (Nu 13:30; 14:7–9). He did not do it merely to please Moses or to keep the people quiet, and he certainly did not do it from a perverse spirit against his fellows, but he was fully convinced of the truth of what he said and firmly believed in God's promise.

1.2.1.2. That in this he *wholly followed the Lord his God*, and so he was not boasting when he spoke about it, just as it is not boasting when people have *God's Spirit witnessing with their spirits* (Ro 8:16) that they are the children of God, and then humbly and thankfully tell others, for their encouragement, what God has done for their souls.

1.2.1.3. That he did this when all his brothers and companions in that service, except Joshua, did otherwise.

1.2.2. The experience he had had of God's goodness to him ever since, up to that day:

1.2.2.1. That he had been kept alive in the desert, not only despite the general dangers and toils of that tedious journey, but also despite the destruction of that whole generation of Israelites—except himself and Joshua—in one way or another by death. Notice how grateful he was for God's goodness to him (v. 10). *Now behold*—behold and wonder—*the Lord hath kept me alive these forty and five years*, thirty-eight years in the desert, through the plagues of the desert, and seven years in Canaan through the perils of war. We can learn from this that the longer we live, the more aware we should be of God's goodness to us in keeping us alive: his care in prolonging our weak lives, and his patience in prolonging our sinful lives.

1.2.2.2. That he was ready to serve God now that he was in Canaan. Although he was eighty-five years old, he was still as strong and energetic as he was when he was forty (v. 11): *As my strength was then, so is it now*. This was the fruit of the promise, and it exceeded what was said, for God not only gives what he promises, but he gives more: the promise of life is life, health, and strength, and all that makes the promised life a blessing and comfort.

1.2.3. The promise Moses had made him in God's name that he would have *this mountain* (v. 12). This was the place, more than any other, on the basis of which the spies made their report, for it was here they met the descendants of Anak (Nu 13:22), the sight of whom made such an impression on them (Nu 13:33). We may presume that Caleb had noted how much emphasis they had put on the difficulty of conquering Hebron, a city garrisoned by the giants, and that he bravely wanted to have that city which they had regarded as invincible (Nu 13:31) assigned to himself as his own portion: "I will undertake to deal with it, and if I cannot gain it as my inheritance, I will go without." He chose this place only because it was the most difficult to be conquered. And to show that his soul did not wear out any more than his body, now forty-five years later he still abides by his choice and is still of the same mind.

1.2.4. The hopes he had of conquering it, although the descendants of Anak still possessed it (v. 12): *If the Lord will be with me, then I shall be able to drive them out*. Joshua had already conquered the city of Hebron (10:37), but the mountain which belonged to it and which was inhabited by the descendants of Anak was not yet conquered. Caleb seemed to speak doubtfully of God's being with him from a humble sense of his own unworthiness. But he expressed without the least doubt his assurance that if God was with him he would be able to remove the descendants of Anak. In all this Caleb fulfilled his name, which may mean "all heart."

2. Joshua grants Caleb's petition (v. 13): *Joshua blessed him*, commended his bravery, applauded his request, and gave him what he asked. Hebron became the inheritance of Caleb and his heirs (v. 14), *because he wholly followed the Lord God of Israel*. Hebron had been the city of Arba, the greatest man among the Anakites (v. 15); we find it called *Kirjath-arba* (Ge 23:2), as the place where Sarah died. This was where Abraham, Isaac, and Jacob lived during most of their time in Canaan, and near it was the cave of Machpelah, where they were buried, which perhaps had led Caleb here when he went to spy out the land and had made him want this rather than any other part as his inheritance. It later became one of the cities belonging to the priests (21:13) and was designated as a city of refuge (20:7). When Caleb had it, he was content with the country around it, and cheerfully gave the city to the priests, the Lord's ministers. Still later it became a royal city and, in the beginning of David's reign, the chief town of the kingdom of Judah; it was there that the people turned to him, and there he reigned seven years.

CHAPTER 15

In this chapter, we have the allotment of the tribe of Judah, which in this, as in other things, took precedence. Here we have: 1. The boundaries of the inheritance of Judah (vv. 1–12). 2. The particular assignment of Hebron and the surrounding country to Caleb and his family (vv. 13–19). 3. The names of the various towns that came within Judah's allotment (vv. 20–63).

Verses 1–12

Judah and Joseph were the two sons of Jacob who received the birthright that Reuben lost through sin. Judah had the birthright passed onto him, and Joseph received a double portion, and so these two tribes were the first ones to be established, Judah in the southern part of the land of Canaan and Joseph in the northern part. In these verses, we have the borders of the lot of Judah, which are said to be, like the borders of the rest of the tribes, *by their families* (v. 1), that is, clan by clan. This phrase also shows that when Joshua and Eleazar, and the rest of the commissioners, had by lot given each tribe its portion, they later subdivided those larger portions and assigned the inheritance to each clan and family and then each household.

1. The eastern border was the Salt Sea (v. 5).

2. The southern border was that of the land of Canaan in general, as will appear by comparing vv. 1–4 with Nu 34:3–5. The result was that the powerful and warlike tribe of Judah guarded the frontiers of the whole land on the side which faced their old sworn enemies—the Edomites.

3. The northern border divided it from the allotment of Benjamin. Here *the stone of Bohan*, a Reubenite, is mentioned (v. 6), who died in the camp at Gilgal, and was buried not far away under this stone. The Valley of Achor also lay on this boundary (v. 7), to remind the people of Judah of the trouble which Achan, one of their tribe, gave to the community of Israel. This northern line was close to Jerusalem (v. 8); it was so close that Mount Zion and Mount Moriah were included in this tribe's allotment, although most of the city was in Benjamin's allotment.

4. The western border went near the Great Sea (the Mediterranean) originally (v. 12), but later Dan's allotment took away a good part of Judah's allotment on that side. Judah's inheritance had its boundaries established.

Verses 13–19

The writer seems pleased every time he has occasion to mention Caleb, because he had honored God. Notice:

1. It is repeated here that Joshua gave him the mountain of Hebron as his inheritance (v. 13).

2. After Caleb had obtained this gift, we are told:

2.1. How he showed his bravery in conquering Hebron (v. 14): *He* and those who helped him in this service *drove thence the three sons of Anak.*

2.2. How he encouraged the bravery of those around him in the conquest of Debir (vv. 15–19). It seems that although Joshua had once conquered Debir (10:39), the Canaanites had still regained possession of it in the absence of the army. This city therefore had to be conquered a second time. When Caleb had finished conquering Hebron, which was for himself and his own family, he pressed on with conquering Debir. This shows how zealous he was to be active for the good of the whole community as well as for his own private interests.

2.2.1. Caleb offered his daughter, and a good dowry with her, to anyone who would capture that city. Caleb's family was not only honorable and wealthy, but also religious, so his daughter was no doubt a very desirable match. The position was bravely taken by Othniel, a nephew of Caleb, whom Caleb had probably thought about when he made the offer (v. 17). And so Othniel married his first cousin Acsah, Caleb's daughter. The writer gives us an account of Acsah's dowry: some land she obtained by Caleb's free gift. He *gave her a south land* (v. 19). Land indeed, but *a south land*, dry and likely to be parched.

2.2.1.1. She obtained more on her request. She urged her husband to ask her father for a field, but her husband

thought the request would be more likely to be successful if she asked. And so she asked, submitting to her husband's judgment. When her father brought her home to her husband's house, she got off her donkey (v. 18) as a sign of respect and reverence for her father. She was sure that, because she married not only with her father's approval but also in obedience to his command, he would not deny her his blessing.

2.2.1.2. She asked only for the *water* (v. 19), without which the ground she had would not be of much use for cultivation or pasture, but she was referring to the field in which the springs of water were. Acsah was successful. Her father gave her what she asked, and perhaps more, for *he gave her the upper springs and the nether* (lower) *springs* (v. 19), two fields so called from the springs that were in them, just as we commonly distinguish between a higher field and a lower field.

2.2.2. From this story we learn:

- It is not breaking the tenth commandment to moderately desire those comforts and conveniences of this life which we see we can gain in a fair and proper way.
- Husbands and wives should discuss together and jointly agree on what is for the good of their family.
- Parents must never regard as lost what is given to their children for their advantage.

Verses 20–63

Here is a list of the various towns which came within the allotment of the tribe of Judah:

1. The towns are named and counted in several groups:

1.1. Some are said to be the southernmost towns *towards the coast* (boundary) *of Edom* (vv. 21–32). Thirty-eight are named here, but there are said to be only *twenty-nine* (v. 32), because nine of these were afterward transferred to the allotment of Simeon.

1.2. Other towns that are said to be *in the valley*, in the western foothills (v. 33), are counted as fourteen, but fifteen are named. This is probably because Gederah and Gederothaim (v. 36) were either alternative names or two parts of the same town.

1.3. Sixteen are then named without any distinctive heading (vv. 37–41), and nine more (vv. 42–44).

1.4. Then come the three Philistine towns, Ekron, Ashdod, and Gaza (vv. 45–47).

1.5. There were also towns *in the mountains.*

2. Now here:

2.1. We do not find Bethlehem, which was afterward the city of David and was given the special honor of being the birthplace of our Lord Jesus. That city, however, was but *little among the thousands of Judah* (Mic 5:2), except that it was honored in this way. Christ came to give honor to the places he was related to, not to receive honor from them.

2.2. Jerusalem is said to continue in the hands of the Jebusites (v. 63), *for the children of Judah could not drive them out* because of their slowness, stupidity, and unbelief.

2.3. Among the towns of Judah (in all 114) we came across Libnah, which in Jehoram's days rebelled and probably set itself up as a free, independent state (2Ki 8:22), and Lachish, where King Amaziah was killed (2Ki 14:19). Lachish took the lead in idolatry (Mic 1:13); it was the *beginning of sin to the daughter of Zion.* Many of the towns of this tribe come in the history of David's troubles. Adullam, Ziph, Keilah, Maon, En Gedi, and Ziklag are all included in this tribe and were places near which David had most of his haunts.

CHAPTER 16

It is a pity that this and the following chapter have been separated, for both of them give us the allotment of the children of Joseph, Ephraim and Manasseh; these two, next to Judah, were to have the position of honor, and so had the first and best portion in the northern part of Canaan, as Judah had in the southern part. In this chapter, we have: 1. A general account of the allotment of these two tribes together (vv. 1–4). 2. The boundaries of the allotment of Ephraim in particular (vv. 5–10). The boundaries of Manasseh come in the next chapter.

Verses 1–4

Although Joseph was one of the younger sons of Jacob, he was still his eldest by Jacob's first desired and best-loved wife Rachel (Ge 29:30); he was himself *his best-beloved son* (Ge 37:3). His descendants were very much favored by what was allotted to them. Their part lay in the heart of the land of Canaan. It extended from the Jordan in the east (v. 1) to the Mediterranean Sea in the west, so that the fruitfulness of the soil fulfilled the blessings of both Jacob and Moses (Ge 49:25–26; Dt 33:13–17). The allotments to Ephraim and Manasseh are not described in such detail as those of the other tribes. We are told only about their limits and boundaries, not the particular towns in them.

Verses 5–10

Here:

1. The border of the allotment of Ephraim is established, by which it was divided to the south from Benjamin and Dan, which lay between it and Judah, and to the north from Manasseh. To the east and west it reached from the Jordan to the Mediterranean.

2. Some individual towns are described in v. 9 that did not come within these borders—at least not if the line was drawn in a direct way—but lay within Manasseh's allotment; this verse might better be read, "and there were separate towns for the children of Ephraim among the inheritance of the children of Manasseh."

3. A mark of disgrace is put on the Ephraimites because they did not drive out the Canaanites from Gezer (v. 10) but instead subjected them to forced labor. The Ephraimites disgraced themselves in this because it shows that they spared the Canaanites out of greed, in order to profit from their labors, and because through their continued interactions with the Canaanites they were in danger of being defiled with their idolatry. Some think, however, that when they subjected them to forced labor, they also made them abandon their idols. Samaria, built by Omri after the burning of the royal palace of Tirzah, was in this tribe's territory, and was for a long time the royal city of the kingdom of the ten tribes. Not far from it were Shechem, the mountains Ebal and Gerizim, and Sychar, near which was Jacob's well, where Christ talked with the Samaritan woman. We read much about the hill country of Ephraim in the story of the Judges, and about a town called *Ephraim*, probably in this tribe's territory, to which Christ withdrew (Jn 11:54). The whole kingdom of the ten tribes is often called *Ephraim* in the Prophets, especially in Hosea.

CHAPTER 17

The half tribe of Manasseh is the next to be provided for, and here we have: 1. The clans of that tribe who were to receive the allotment (vv. 1–6). 2. The country that was included in their allotment (vv. 7–13). 3. The joint
request of the two tribes who descended from Joseph for their allotment to be enlarged, and Joshua's answer to that request (vv. 14–18).

Verses 1–6

Manasseh was itself only one half of the tribe of Joseph, but it was divided and subdivided:

1. It was divided into two parts, one already settled on the other side of the Jordan, consisting of those who were the descendants of Makir (v. 1). This Makir was born to Manasseh in Egypt; he had distinguished himself there as a warrior, probably in the conflicts between the Ephraimites and the men of Gath (1Ch 7:21).

2. The part on this side of the Jordan was subdivided into ten clans or families (v. 5). Here is:

2.1. The claim which the daughters of Zelophehad made, based on the command God gave to Moses concerning them (v. 4). When they were young, they had themselves pleaded their own case before Moses and obtained the gift of an inheritance with their brothers, and now they did not wish to lose the benefit of that gift by not speaking to Joshua.

2.2. The assignment of their portions according to their claim. Joshua knew very well what God had ordered in their case, and he did not object that because they had not served in the wars of Canaan there was no reason why they should share in the possessions of Canaan, but readily *gave them an inheritance among the brethren of their father* (v. 4).

Verses 7–13

We have here a short account of the allotment of this half tribe. It extended from the Jordan in the east to the Mediterranean Sea in the west; to the south it lay adjacent to Ephraim, but to the north it joined Asher and Issachar. Some things are particularly noted about this allotment:

1. That there were many dealings between this tribe and the tribe of Ephraim. The town of Tappuah belonged to Ephraim, but the country adjoined Manasseh (v. 8); there were likewise many towns of Ephraim that lay within the border of Manasseh (v. 9), which we read about before (16:9).

2. That Manasseh likewise had towns with their surrounding settlements in the tribes of Issachar and Asher (v. 11), since God had arranged matters so that although every tribe had its own special inheritance—which could not be transferred from it—they would still mix with one another. Although they were of different tribes, they were all one Israel.

3. That they allowed the Canaanites to live among them, contrary to the command of God, serving their own ends by taking no notice of them, for they subjected the Canaanites to forced labor (vv. 12–13). The most significant person of this half tribe in later times was Gideon, whose great deeds were achieved within this allotment.

Verses 14–18

1. The children of Joseph quarrel with their allotment. Joshua, however, lets them know that in fulfilling his responsibility as one acting on behalf of the wider community he has no more regard to his own tribe than any other. They suggest two things:

1.1. That they are very numerous because of God's blessing on them (v. 14): *I am a great people, for the Lord has blessed me.* We have reason to hope that the One who has sent mouths will also send food.

1.2. That a good part of that country which has now come to their allotment is in the hands of the Canaanites, who are formidable enemies and bring *chariots of iron* onto the battlefield (v. 16), perhaps chariots with long scythes fastened to their sides or axles, which brought great destruction to all in their path, mowing them down like corn.

2. Joshua tries to reconcile them to their lot. He acknowledges that they are *a great people*, and because they are two tribes, they ought to have more than *one lot only* (v. 17). He tells them that what has come to their share will be sufficient for both of them if they will only work at it and fight for it. "If you have many mouths to fill, then you have twice as many hands that can work for it. Earn your wages, and then you can eat."

2.1. He tells them to work for more (v. 15): "*Get thee up to the wood country*, which is within your own borders, and set everyone to work to cut down the trees and clear the land. Work away diligently and make the ground ready for cultivation so that you can grow crops on it." We can learn from this that many want larger possessions but are not making the best of what they already have.

2.2. When they plead that they cannot get to the woodlands he spoke about because in the valley in between are Canaanites whom they dare not fight with, he tells them that, nonetheless, to fight for more is what they must do (vv. 17–18).

CHAPTER 18

In this chapter we have: 1. The setting up of the tabernacle (Tent of Meeting) at Shiloh (v. 1). 2. The motivating of the seven tribes who were still not settled to look after their lot, and the establishing of a plan of action by Joshua (vv. 2–7); the distributing of the land into seven lots by certain men employed for that purpose (vv. 8–9); and the determining of these seven portions for the seven tribes who were still not provided for by lot (v. 10). 3. The particular allotment of the tribe of Benjamin, with its borders (vv. 11–20) and towns (vv. 21–28). The other six tribes we will find well provided for in the next chapter.

Verse 1

In the middle of the story of the dividing of the land an account is included of the setting up of the tabernacle, the Tent of Meeting. Until that time, it had continued in its old place at the center of their camp, but now that three of the four divisions that used to surround it in the desert were incomplete and reduced in numbers, it was time to think of moving the tabernacle itself into a city. The priests and Levites had taken it down many times, carried it, and set it up again in the desert, according to the directions they had been given (Nu 4:5–33). But now they must do it one last time. Notice:

1. The place to which the Tent of Meeting was moved, and where it was set up. It was *Shiloh*, a city in the allotment of Ephraim, but close to the allotment of Benjamin.

1.1. This place was chosen because it was in the heart of the country. The tabernacle had been in the middle of their camp in the desert, and so it must now be in the middle of their nation.

1.2. The setting up of the tabernacle (Tent of Meeting) in Shiloh showed them that in the Shiloh spoken about by Jacob (Ge 49:10) all the ordinances of this worldly sanctuary would be fulfilled in a greater and more perfect tabernacle (Heb 9:1, 11).

2. The solemn manner in which it was done: *The whole congregation assembled together* (v. 1) to attend the ceremony, to honor the ark of God as the sign of his presence. When their first thought was to see the ark established as

soon as they had a safe place ready for it to be settled in, it was a good sign that they would settle down well in Canaan. The ark remained in Shiloh for about 300 years, until the sins of Eli's house forfeited the ark, lost it, and ruined Shiloh, and its ruins were long after used as warnings to Jerusalem: *Go, see what I did to Shiloh* (Jer 7:12; Ps 78:60).

Verses 2–10

1. Joshua rebukes those tribes which are still not settled because they have not yet stirred themselves to gain a settlement in the land God has given them. Joshua reasons with them (v. 3): *How long are you slack?*

1.1. They were too happy with their present condition. They were living very comfortably off the plunder they had taken from the cities, and they put out of their minds any thoughts of the future.

1.2. They were lazy and wanted to put off actually making a move. This shows us that many are distracted from their real duties and do not enjoy real comforts because of apparent difficulties. By his grace, God has entitled us to receive a good land, the heavenly Canaan, but we may be *slack to take possession* (v. 3). We are not entering into that rest, as we should, with faith, hope, and holy joy. We are not living in heaven, as we could if we were to truly set our hearts on things above and have our citizenship there.

2. Joshua sets out a plan of action:

2.1. The remaining land must be surveyed and a description made of the towns and their territories (v. 4). These must be divided into seven equal parts. The Levites were to own no land personally. Gad, Reuben, and the half tribe of Manasseh were already settled and did not need to be looked after in this way.

2.1.1. The surveyors consisted of three men from each of the seven tribes (v. 4).

2.1.2. The survey was made by these twenty-one and brought to Joshua (vv. 8–9). Notice in it:

- The faith and courage of those who surveyed the land. Many Canaanites remained in the land, and all were set against Israel, *as a bear robbed of her whelps* (Pr 17:12).
- The good providence of God in protecting them from the many dangers of death they were exposed to. They all came back safely to the camp at Shiloh.

2.2. After the land had been surveyed and divided into seven lots, Joshua then appealed to God to direct and determine which of these lots would belong to each tribe (v. 6): *That I may cast lots for you here* at the Tent of Meeting — because it was a sacred transaction — *before the Lord our God.*

Verses 11–28

Here we have the allotted territory of the tribe of Benjamin, which Providence put next to Joseph on the one side, because "little" Benjamin (Ps 68:27) was Joseph's only full brother, who needed the protection of powerful Joseph. Benjamin was put next to Judah on the other side, so that this tribe might later join with Judah in supporting the throne of David and the temple at Jerusalem. Here we have:

1. The exact borders and limits of this tribe. The western border is said to *compass* (go around) *the corner of the sea southward* (v. 14). Bishop Patrick thinks the meaning is that it ran parallel to — though at a distance from — the Mediterranean Sea.

2. The individual cities and towns in this tribe, not all of them, but the most important ones. Twenty-six are

named here. Jericho is put first because, although it had been destroyed, and forbidden to be rebuilt as a city with gates and walls, it could still be built and inhabited as a village. Gilgal, where Israel first camped when Saul was made king (1Sa 11:15), was in this tribe's territory. It was afterward a very worldly place. *All their wickedness is in Gilgal* (Hos 9:15). Bethel, a famous place, was also in this tribe's territory.

CHAPTER 19

In the description of the allotments of Judah and Benjamin we have an account of both their borders and their towns. In that of Ephraim and Manasseh we have the borders, but not the towns. In this chapter, Simeon and Dan are described only by their towns, not their borders, because they lay very much within Judah, especially Simeon. The others have both their borders described and their towns and cities named. Here is: 1. The allotment for Simeon (vv. 1–9). 2. The allotment for Zebulun (vv. 10–16). 3. The allotment for Issachar (vv. 17–23). 4. The allotment for Asher (vv. 24–31). 5. The allotment for Naphtali (vv. 32–39). 6. The allotment for Dan (vv. 40–48). 7. Lastly, the inheritance assigned to Joshua himself and his own family (vv. 49–51).

Verses 1–9

Simeon's lot was drawn after Judah's, Joseph's, and Benjamin's, because Jacob had put that tribe to shame. There is not one notable person, neither judge nor prophet, who came from this tribe, as far as we know.

1. The situation of their allotment was within the territory of Judah (v. 1) and was taken from it (v. 9).

1.1. The men of Judah did not oppose the taking away of some of those towns which according to the first distribution fell within their borders, because they were convinced they had more than their fair share.

1.2. What was taken away from Judah was to be put into a new allotment which Providence directed to the tribe of Simeon. The towns of Simeon were scattered throughout Judah. This brought them into a league with the tribe of Judah (Jdg 1:3) and afterward brought about the joining of many of this tribe with the house of David, at the time of the rebellion of the ten tribes with Jeroboam.

2. The towns within their allotment are named here. Beersheba, or Sheba, for these names seem to refer to the same place, is put first. Ziklag, which we read of in David's story, is one of them.

Verses 10–16

This is the allotment for Zebulun, who although born of Leah after Issachar, was still blessed by Jacob and Moses before him.

1. The allotment of this tribe had the Great Sea (Mediterranean Sea) to the west, and the Sea of Tiberias to the east, fulfilling Jacob's prophecy (Ge 49:13): *Zebulun shall be a haven of ships,* trading ships on the Great Sea and fishing ships on the Sea of Galilee.

2. Although there were some places in this tribe which were famous in the Old Testament, especially *Mount Carmel,* it was much more famous in the New Testament. Within the allotment of this tribe was Nazareth, where our blessed Savior spent so much of his time on earth, and that coast of the Sea of Galilee on which Christ preached so many sermons and performed so many miracles.

Verses 17–23

The allotment of Issachar extended from the Jordan in the east to the Great Sea (Mediterranean Sea) to the west,

Manasseh to the south, and Zebulun to the north. Among the places in this tribe were:

1. Jezreel, where Ahab's palace was, and near it Naboth's vineyard (1Ki 21:1).

2. Shunem, where the good Shunammite lived who received Elisha (2Ki 4:8).

3. The Kishon River, on the banks of which in this tribe's territory Sisera was beaten by Deborah and Barak (Jdg 4:7).

4. Mount Gilboa, on which Saul and Jonathan were killed (1Sa 31:8), which was not far from Endor, where Saul consulted the witch (1Sa 28:7).

5. The plain of Megiddo, where Josiah was killed near Hadad Rimmon (2Ki 23:29; Zec 12:11).

Verses 24–31

The lot of Asher lay on the coast of the Great Sea (Mediterranean Sea). The only famous person we read of who came from this tribe was the prophet Anna, who was a constant resident in the temple at the time of our Savior's birth (Lk 2:36). But close to this tribe were the famous seaports of Tyre and Sidon.

Verses 32–39

The allotment for Naphtali lay farthest north of all the tribes, bordering on Mount Libanus. The town of Leshem, or Laish, lay on its northernmost edge, and so when the Danites conquered it and called it *Dan,* the length of Canaan from north to south was reckoned as "from Dan to Beersheba." It was in the lot of this tribe, near the Waters of Merom, that Joshua fought and routed Jabin (11:1–14). In this tribe's territory lay Capernaum and Bethsaida, at the north end of the Sea of Tiberias, where Christ did so many miracles.

Verses 40–48

Dan was commander of one of the four divisions of the camp of Israel in the desert, bringing up the rear, and was the last tribe to be provided for in Canaan. The allotment for this tribe fell in the southern part of Canaan, between Judah on the east and the land of the Philistines on the west, Ephraim to the north and Simeon to the south. Providence arranged for this populous and powerful tribe to be put into a dangerous position, as the one best able to deal with the troublesome neighbors the Philistines, as was discovered in Samson's life. *Japho* (Joppa) was in this allotment.

Verses 49–51

Here is an account of the particular inheritance assigned to Joshua:

1. He was the last to be served, although the eldest and greatest person in all Israel. In everything he did he sought the good of his country, not any private interest of his own. He was content to remain unsettled until he saw everyone else settled first.

2. He had his lot *according to the word of the Lord* (v. 50). It is probable that when God told Caleb through Moses what inheritance he would have (14:9), he gave a similar promise to Joshua.

3. He chose it in the hill country of Ephraim, which belonged to his own tribe.

4. The *children of Israel* are said to *give an inheritance to him* (v. 49), which speaks of his humility: he would not take it for himself without the people's agreement and approval.

5. It was a town that had to be built before it was fit to be lived in.

CHAPTER 20

This short chapter concerns the cities of refuge. We read about these often in the writings of Moses, but this is the last time that they are mentioned, for now that matter was completely settled. Here is: 1. The law God gave concerning them (vv. 1–6). 2. The people's appointment of the particular cities for that use (vv. 7–9). This law of salvation prefigured good things to come.

Verses 1–6

The Law of Moses ordered many things to be done when they came into Canaan, including the appointment of cities of refuge. These were sanctuaries to protect those who were guilty of manslaughter. It was for the benefit of the land that the blood of an innocent person—the hand of whom was guilty but not the heart—should not be shed by the avenger of blood. God therefore reminded them of this law, which was for their good.

1. Orders were given for these cities to be appointed (v. 2); see also Dt 19:3. This was probably not done until after the Levites had had their portion assigned them, because the cities of refuge were all to be Levite towns. As soon as God had given them towns of rest, he told them to appoint cities of refuge, to which any one of them might need to escape. It shows what God's spiritual Israel has and will have in Christ and heaven: not only rest to enjoy, but also refuge to keep them safe.

2. Instructions were given on how these cities were to be used. We had the laws in this matter in detail before (Nu 35:10–34; Dt 4:41–43; 19:1–14): it is provided that if in the trial it came out that the murder took place purely accidentally, with no intention—either to satisfy a grudge or in a sudden fit of rage—then the offender would be sheltered from the avenger of blood in any of these cities (vv. 4–6). This law entitled the offenders to live in that city, but also confined them to it, as prisoners free to roam but only within it.

Verses 7–9

We have here the naming of the cities of refuge in the land of Canaan.

1. The Israelites "sanctified" these cities (v. 7, margin), the ones that were *appointed* (v. 7). There was no ceremony to consecrate them, except that the people publicly and legally declared them to be cities of refuge, and as such sacred to the honor of God, who protected those shown to be innocent.

2. These cities—like those on the other side of the Jordan—stood in the three different parts of the country, conveniently placed, it is thought, so that someone might reach one of them within half a day from any corner of the country.

3. They were all Levite towns, and in this way God's tribe was honored, being made judges in those cases in which God's providence was closely concerned and made protectors of those who although innocent were persecuted. If the offender had to be confined, then it was to be within a Levite town, where they could, if they wished, make the most of their time.

4. These cities were on hills which could be seen from far away, for although this meant that the final section was uphill, it would still be comforting that the place of safety was drawing nearer and would be reached quickly.

5. Some notice that the names of these cities are significant when they are applied to Christ, our refuge. *Kedesh* means "holy," and our refuge is the holy Jesus. *Shechem,*

"a shoulder," and the government is on his shoulders. *Hebron,* "fellowship," and believers are called into the fellowship of Christ Jesus our Lord. *Bezer,* "a fortification," for he is a stronghold to all who trust in him. *Ramoth,* "high" or "exalted," for God has exalted him with his own right hand. *Golan* may mean "joy" or "exultation," for all believers are justified and glory in him.

6. Besides all these, the horns of the altar, wherever it was, were a refuge to those who took hold of them if the crime was such as sanctuary allowed. This is implied in the law (Ex 21:14) that said an intentional murderer would be taken from God's altar to be put to death.

CHAPTER 21

It had been often said that the tribe of Levi would have no inheritance with their brethren, no particular part of the country assigned them, as the other tribes had. It appears, however, from the provision made for them in this chapter that they were no losers by their being dispersed. We have here: 1. The request the Levites made to have towns assigned them, according to God's appointment (vv. 1–2); the naming of the towns accordingly from the different tribes, and the distribution of them to the respective families of this tribe (vv. 3–8). 2. A catalog of the towns, forty-eight in all (vv. 9–42). 3. A fulfillment of everything God had promised to his people Israel (vv. 43–45).

Verses 1–8

Here is:

1. The Levites' request presented to this general assembly of leaders, now sitting at Shiloh (vv. 1–2). Notice:

1.1. They did not receive what was assigned to them until they made their claim. They based their claim on a very good foundation, not their service or what they deserved, but the divine command: *"The Lord commanded by the hand of Moses to give us cities* (v. 2). He commanded you to give us cities, which implies a command for us to ask for them." This shows us that the maintenance of ministers is not something arbitrary to be left purely to the goodwill of the people, who may let them starve if they want to. No; just as the God of Israel commanded that the Levites should be well provided for, so the Lord Jesus, the King of the Christian church, has ordained that *those who preach the gospel should live of the gospel* (1Co 9:14).

1.2. They did not make their claim till all the rest of the tribes had been provided for, and then they did it immediately. They were willing to be served last, and they did not come off the worse for it. God's ministers should not complain if at any time they find themselves ignored in human thoughts and cares, but they should make sure of God's favor and the honor that comes from him, and then they will be able to bear human insults and neglect.

2. The Levites' request granted immediately, without any argument.

2.1. The Israelites are said to give the towns to the Levites. God had appointed how many they should be: forty-eight in all. God had appointed, *Every one shall give of his cities to the Levites* (Nu 35:8). It appears from the list which follows that the towns they gave the Levites were generally some of the best and most important in each tribe.

2.2. They gave them *at the commandment of the Lord* (v. 3).

2.3. After the forty-eight towns had been chosen, they were divided into four lots, each lot having towns that were nearest each other, and then they were assigned by lot to the four different families of the tribe of Levi.

2.3.1. The family of Aaron, whose men were the only priests, received as their share the thirteen towns given by the tribes of Judah, Simeon, and Benjamin (v. 4).

2.3.2. The Kohathites, among whom were the descendants of Moses—although his descendants were never distinguished from the rest of the clan—had the towns that lay in the allotment of Dan, which lay next to Judah, and in the allotments of Ephraim and the half tribe of Manasseh, which lay next to Benjamin. So those who descended from Aaron's father were nearest to Aaron's sons.

2.3.3. Gershon was the eldest son of Levi, and so although the younger house of the Kohathites was given preferential treatment over his, his children still had precedence over the other family of Merari (v. 6).

2.3.4. The Merarites, the youngest house, had their lot last, and it lay farthest away from Jerusalem (v. 7).

Verses 9–42

Several things may be noticed in this account, besides what was already observed in the Law (Nu 35:1–34):

1. That the Levites were scattered throughout all the tribes and were not allowed to live all together in any one part of the country. Christ left his twelve disciples together as a group, but left orders that they should in due time be dispersed, so that they might *preach the gospel to every creature* (Mk 16:15).

2. That every tribe of Israel was enriched with its share of Levite towns in proportion to its extent, even those that were the most remote. They all had the Levites among them:

• So that they could show the Levites kindness, as God directed them (Dt 12:19; 14:29).
• So that they could all receive advice and instruction from the Levites. When they could not go up to the tabernacle to consult those who served there, they could go to a Levite town and there be taught the knowledge of the Lord. In this way, God set a candle in every room of his house, to give light to all his family.

3. That there were thirteen towns, and those some of the best, appointed for the priests, the sons of Aaron (v. 19). Aaron left only two sons, Eleazar and Ithamar, but his family had now grown so much, and it was foreseen that it would in due time become so numerous, as to fill all these towns. We read in both Testaments of such numbers of priests that we may suppose that none of all the families of Israel who came from Egypt increased as much as that of Aaron. The promise later to the house of Aaron is, *God shall increase you more and more, you and your children* (Ps 115:12, 14).

4. That some of the Levite towns were later famous for other reasons. Hebron was the city in which David began his reign, and in Mahanaim, another Levite town (v. 38), David stayed and had his headquarters when he fled from Absalom. The first Israelite who ever bore the title of king, namely, Abimelech, the son of Gideon, reigned in Shechem, another Levite town (v. 21).

Verses 43–45

We have here the previous account summed up:

1. God had promised to give the descendants of Abraham the land of Canaan as their possession, and now at last he fulfilled this promise (v. 43): *They possessed it, and dwelt therein.*

2. God had promised to give them peace in that land, and now they had peace around them, peace from their travels through the desert, and peace after wars in Canaan. They now lived, not only in dwelling places of their own, but also in ones that were quiet and peaceful. This peace continued until their own sin and foolishness gave them great trouble.

3. God had promised to give them victory and success in their wars, and this promise likewise was fulfilled: *There stood not a man before them* (v. 44). These verses, then, both narrate Israel's experience of God's faithfulness and document their acknowledgment of that faithfulness; and in this acknowledgment, God is honored, his promise—which has so often been distrusted—is vindicated, and all believers to the end of the world are encouraged: *There failed not any good thing*, no, *not aught of any good thing, which the Lord had spoken unto the house of Israel*, but in due time *all came to pass* (v. 45).

CHAPTER 22

We have read many particular things concerning the two and a half Transjordan tribes, though nothing separated them from the rest of the tribes except the River Jordan. This chapter is wholly about them. We have here: 1. Joshua's dismissal of the militia of those tribes from the camp of Israel, in which they had served as auxiliaries during all the wars of Canaan, and their return to their own country (vv. 1–9). 2. The altar they built on the borders of the Jordan as a sign of their fellowship with the land of Israel (v. 10); the offense which the rest of the tribes took at this altar, and the message they then sent (vv. 11–20). 3. The two and a half tribes' defense of what they had done (vv. 21–29). 4. The satisfaction which their defense gave to the rest of the tribes (vv. 30–34).

Verses 1–9

Now that the war has ended so gloriously, Joshua as a wise general disbands his army. The intention never was for war to become their trade, and so he sends them home to enjoy what they had conquered and to beat their swords into plowshares and their spears into pruning hooks. This is particularly true for the forces of those separate tribes that had received their inheritance on the other side of the Jordan. Joshua publicly and formally discharges them in Shiloh. We are not sure exactly when this was done, but it was certainly not done till after Shiloh was made the headquarters (21:2), which means that the land had begun to be divided (14:6). This army of Reubenites and Gadites, which had been in the vanguard in all the wars of Canaan, had probably sometimes crossed over the Jordan to visit their families, for it was not far, but still these two and a half tribes had their quota of troops ready, 40,000 in all, which, whenever they were needed, presented themselves at their respective posts. These now came as a group to be discharged. We, too, must stay on earth till our warfare has been completed. We must wait until we are discharged. We must not move until we are told we may go.

1. Joshua dismisses them to the *land of their possession* (v. 4). Those who were first to be assigned an allotment were the last to enjoy it.

2. Joshua dismisses them with their pay, for who serves as a soldier at their own expense? *Return with much riches unto your tents* (v. 8). Joshua says, "Go home to your tents," that is, "your houses," which he calls *tents*, because they had been used to tents in the desert. "Go home *with*

much riches (v. 8), not only cattle, the plunder of the country, but also silver and gold, the plunder of the cities. Let your families whom you go to, who guarded your belongings on the other side of the Jordan, also have some share of the plunder: *Divide the spoil with your brethren* (v. 8)."

3. Joshua dismisses them with a commendation:

• For their readiness to obey their commanders (v. 2).
• For their constant affection for and loyalty to the other Israelites: *You have not left them these many days* (v. 3).
• For their faithfulness and obedience to the divine Law. They had not only done their duty to Joshua and Israel, but—what was best of all—they had conscientiously fulfilled their duty to God: *You have kept the charge* (v. 3), or, as it could read, "You have kept the keeping," that is, "You have carefully kept the *commandment of the Lord your God* (v. 3), not only in this particular instance of continuing to serve Israel to the end of the war, but also more generally in maintaining your religious faith in your part of the camp. This is something rare and excellent among soldiers and is very commendable."

4. Joshua dismisses them with good advice: not to cultivate their ground, fortify their cities, and—because they were now used to war and victory—invade their neighbors in an attempt to expand their own territories; no, instead they should continue to be godly and depend on God's power.

5. Joshua dismisses them with a blessing (v. 6), particularly the half tribe of Manasseh. To them Joshua, as an Ephraimite, was somewhat more closely related than to the other two, and they were perhaps more reluctant to depart because they left one half of their own tribe behind them, and so in all the farewells and lingering behind they received a second dismissal and blessing (v. 7). Joshua not only prayed for them, taking the role of a friend, but also, taking the role of a father, blessed them in the name of the Lord, commending them, their families, and their lives to the grace of God.

Verses 10–20

Here is:

1. The godly care of the separated tribes to keep their hold on Canaan's religion—the worship of the Lord—even when they were leaving Canaan's land. In order to do this, they built an imposing altar by the Jordan to be a witness for them that they were Israelites and as such were *partakers of the altar of* the Lord (1Co 10:18). When they came to the Jordan (v. 10), they wanted only to preserve their relationship with the church of God and to continue to share in the fellowship of believers. Therefore they built this altar without delay, to serve as a bridge to maintain their fellowship with the other tribes in the things of God. This altar, then, was built with innocent and honorable intentions; however, it would still have been better if they had consulted God before they built it, since it might appear evil and so might cause offense to their brothers and sisters. Or at least it would have been better to tell their fellow Israelites what they were planning to do, explaining their reasons for building the altar before rather than afterward, to prevent any misunderstanding.

2. The holy protectiveness by the other tribes for the honor of God and his altar at Shiloh. The leaders of Israel were told immediately about the building of this altar (v. 11). They soon became apprehensive that the building of another altar was an insult to God and his decision to put his name in a certain place. They interpreted it as a direct rebellion and a desire to worship some other god. Now:

2.1. Their suspicion was excusable, for what the separated tribes were doing looked wrong at first sight. It seemed to imply an intention to set up a competitor to the altar at Shiloh.

2.2. Their zeal arising from their suspicion was very commendable (v. 12). They all gathered together at Shiloh, because they were defending the divine charter that had just been given there. They wanted to behave as a kingdom of priests, who were devoted to God and his service; they did not *acknowledge their brethren* or *know their own children* (Dt 33:9). They would immediately go *up to war against them* (v. 12) if it appeared they were rebelling against God.

2.3. Their wisdom in pursuing this zealous resolution is no less commendable. They decided not to send out their army and wage war until they had first sent a delegation to investigate what the two and a half tribes were trying to achieve. The delegation consisted of ten of the chief men, one from each tribe, with Phinehas at their head as their spokesperson (vv. 13–14).

2.4. The delegation's dealing with this matter clearly shows both their zeal and their wisdom:

2.4.1. The accusation they brought against their brothers is a very strong one. The delegation was very zealous for the honor of God. They wanted to justify the anger of the assembly at Shiloh and to arouse the supposed offenders to clear themselves.

2.4.2. In the way they expressed their accusation they went rather too far: *Is the iniquity of Peor too little for us?* (v. 17). The building of this altar seemed something minor, but it might have led to a sin as evil as that of Peor, and so it must be crushed in its early stages.

2.4.3. The reason they gave for being so concerned about this matter is significant. They were obliged to be concerned, for their own defense, by the law of self-preservation: "If you rebel against God today, who knows but tomorrow his judgment may break out on the *whole congregation* (v. 18), as in the case of Achan? (v. 20) (7:1–26). He sinned, and we all suffered for it."

2.4.4. The offer they made is kind and reasonable (v. 19), that if the two and a half tribes thought that the land they possessed was defiled because it had no altar and that they therefore could not be at ease without one, then rather than building another as a competitor to the one at Shiloh, they should consider themselves welcome to come back to the land *where the Lord's tabernacle was* and settle there, and the tribes in Canaan would very willingly make adjustments to make room for them.

Verses 21–29

The reply of the two and a half tribes to the rebuke of the ten tribes was reasonable and straightforward. They did not make an aggressive reply to the accusation. Neither did they rebuke them for their rash and ill-thought-out criticism. No; they gave them a gentle answer which turns away wrath. They did not take exception to their attempts to apply what is right under God to them. They did not say that they were not accountable to them for their actions. Neither did they tell them to mind their own business. What they did was this: they freely and openly declared their sincere intentions in their actions. In so doing, they freed themselves from the charges they were under and set themselves right in the opinion of their brothers.

1. They solemnly objected to the suggestion that the intention of the altar was that it would be used for sacrifice or offering. Far from setting it up as a competitor to the altar at Shiloh, they did not have the slightest thought

of abandoning that authorized place of worship. They had indeed built what had the form of an altar, but they had not dedicated it to religious use. To support this objection, they make:

1.1. A solemn appeal to God about it, with which they begin their defense, intending to give glory to God first and then to satisfy their brothers (v. 22).

1.1.1. They have a deep reverence for God, expressed in the form of their appeal: *The Lord God of gods, the Lord God of gods, he knows* (v. 22). This brief confession of faith would help to avoid and remove their brothers' suspicion that they intended to abandon the God of Israel to worship other gods.

1.1.2. They have a great confidence in their own integrity, expressed in the substance of their appeal. Nothing but a clear conscience would have invoked divine justice in this way to avenge the rebellion if there had been any hint of idolatry.

1.2. A solemn defense to their brothers: *Israel, he shall know* (v. 22).

1.3. A solemn renunciation of the intentions which they were suspected of being guilty of. They conclude their defense with this (v. 29): "*God forbid that we should rebel against the Lord*. We have as great a value and respect for the altar of the Lord at Shiloh as any of the tribes of Israel have. We are as firmly resolved to remain loyal to it and to constantly attend it. We have the same concern that you have for the purity of God's worship and for the unity of his church. Far be it from us to think of turning away from following God."

2. They fully explained their true intention and purpose in building this altar. To justify themselves, they said that when they built this altar they were far from seeing it as a step toward separating from their brothers and from the altar of the Lord at Shiloh. On the contrary, it was really intended as a promise of their continued fellowship with their brothers and with the altar of God and as a sign of their determination to *do the service of the Lord before him* (v. 27).

2.1. They described the fears they had that over time their descendants, who were established far away from the tabernacle, would be looked on and treated as strangers to the citizenship of Israel (v. 24). Those who are cut off from taking part in public services are likely to lose all their religious faith. They will gradually stop fearing the Lord. Although the form and profession of godliness are maintained by many without its life or power, its life and power cannot be kept up for long without its form and profession. If you take away the means of grace, you take away grace itself.

2.2. They explained the idea they had to prevent this (vv. 26–28). "Therefore, to keep our rights to the altar of God for those who will come after us and to prove their entitlement to it, *we said, Let us build an altar, to be a witness between us and you*," so that because they kept this copy of the altar, it might be produced as evidence of their right to the privileges of the original.

Verses 30–34

Here is the good outcome of this dispute, which, if both sides had not had a peaceful disposition as much as they had a zeal for God, might have had very unfortunate consequences, because quarrels about religion, for lack of wisdom and love, often prove the most heated and the most difficult to resolve.

1. The delegation was very pleased with the objections the separate tribes had raised in defense of their innocent intentions in building this altar. The delegation did not question their sincerity. They did not rebuke them for their rash and ill-advised action. Much less did they go about fishing for evidence to support their accusation, because they had already expressed it, but they were glad to see that their mistake was put right, and were not at all ashamed to acknowledge it. When people are touchy, quick-tempered, and angrily and unjustly attack their brothers and sisters, they will stand by their attack and cannot be persuaded to withdraw it, even though much convincing evidence is brought of the injustice of their accusation.

2. The assembly was fully satisfied when their delegation reported back to them their brothers' defense of what they had done.

3. The separate tribes were satisfied, and since they decided to keep among them this pattern of the altar of God—even though there was not likely to be the need for it which they imagined—Joshua and the leaders went along with them and did not give orders for the altar to be demolished. Care was taken that, now that they had explained the meaning of their altar—that it was intended as no more than a testimony to their fellowship with the altar at Shiloh—this explanation would be recorded, by giving it a name to show its meaning (v. 34). They called it *Ed*, meaning "a witness" to that, and no more, a witness of the relationship they stood in with God and Israel.

CHAPTER 23

In this and the following chapter we have two farewell sermons which Joshua preached to the people of Israel shortly before his death. If he had intended to satisfy the curiosity of succeeding ages, he would have recorded how Israel had settled into their new conquests, but instead what he intended to do by means of the official records in this book was to pass on a sense of religious faith and duty to God to future generations. He therefore communicated to his readers the methods he used to persuade Israel to be faithful to their covenant with their God. In this chapter, we have: 1. A calling together of all the leaders of Israel (vv. 1–2). Joshua's speech to them comes at the opening, or possibly the conclusion, of their meeting, to show the main purpose of their coming together. In it, Joshua reminds them of what God had done for them (vv. 3–4, 9, 14) and what he was ready to do further (vv. 5, 10). He encourages them to carefully and resolutely persevere in their duty to God (vv. 6, 8, 11). He warns them against all familiarity with their idolatrous neighbors (v. 7). 2. He gives them a reasonable warning of the fatal consequences of turning away from God in rebellion and turning to idols (vv. 12–13, 15, 16).

Verses 1–10

Notice:

1. As to the place and time of this address by Joshua:

1.1. No mention at all is made of the place where this general assembly was held. Some think it was at Timnath Serah, Joshua's own town where he lived, and from where, because he was old, he could not move easily. It is more probable that this meeting took place at Shiloh, where the Tent of Meeting was.

1.2. There is only a general mention of the time when this was done. It was *long after the Lord had given them rest*, but it is not said how long (v. 1). It was:

1.2.1. Long enough for Israel to experience the joy and comforts of their rest and possessions in Canaan and to enjoy the benefits of that good land.

1.2.2. Long enough for Joshua to observe which ways they were in danger of being corrupted, namely, by their intimate dealings with the Canaanites who remained, against which he is therefore careful to warn them.

2. The people to whom Joshua made this speech: "To all Israel, even their elders." V. 2 might be read in this way.

3. Joshua's circumstances when he gave them this command: he *was old and stricken* (well advanced) *in age* (v. 1). It was probably in the last year of his life, and he lived to be 110 years old (24:29). *I am old and stricken in age* (v. 2). He uses this:

3.1. As an argument to himself that he should give them this command, that because he is old he can expect to be with them for only a little while longer, to advise and instruct them.

3.2. As an argument for them to pay attention to what he said. He was old and experienced, and he had grown old in their service and had devoted himself for their good. He therefore should be the more respected by them.

4. The address itself:

4.1. He reminds them of the great things God has done for them in his days. He appeals to their own eyes for the proof of this (v. 3): "*You have seen all that the Lord your God has done*; not what I have done or what you have done, but what God himself has done through me and for you."

4.1.1. Many great and powerful nations—according to how nations were determined then—were driven out from a country as fine as any that could be found at that time, to make room for Israel.

4.1.2. Those nations were not only driven out, but they were still subdued by Israel, which made the possessing of their land even more glorious.

4.1.3. They had not only conquered the Canaanites but also fully possessed their land (v. 4).

4.2. He assures them of God's readiness to continue and complete this glorious work in due time. He tells them how little they need care about the numbers of their forces: *One man of you shall chase a thousand* (v. 10), as Jonathan believed (1Sa 14:6). "*The Lord your God, he it is that fighteth for you* (v. 10), and how many is he equivalent to?"

4.3. He commands them from his heart to remain faithful to their duty, to go on and persevere in the ways of the Lord in which they have started so well. He encourages them:

4.3.1. To be courageous (v. 6): "God is fighting for you against your enemies; therefore, *behave yourselves valiantly* (1Ch 19:13) for him."

4.3.2. To be cautious:

• They must not associate closely with idolaters, go among them to visit them, or be present at any of their feasts or entertainments, for if they had intimate dealings with them, they would be liable to become defiled.

• They must not show the slightest respect to any idol, nor *make mention of the name of their gods* (v. 7), but they were to try to bury every memory of them, so that their worship would never be revived.

• They must not support others in showing respect to any idol. They must not only not invoke the names of idols or swear by them themselves, but they must also not make others swear by them. This implies that they must not make any covenants with idolaters, because in confirming their covenants, they would swear by their idols. Israelites are not to take such oaths.

4.3.3. To be constant (v. 8): *Cleave unto the Lord your God*, that is, "hold fast to him, stay faithful to him, delight in him, depend on him, devote yourselves to his glory, and continue to do so to the end."

Here:

1. Joshua directs them what to do so that they may remain faithful to their religious faith (v. 11). If we want to remain true to the Lord and not abandon him:

1.1. We must always be on our guard, for many precious souls have lost their way and and have been ruined through carelessness: "Take heed, therefore, *take good heed to yourselves*, to your 'souls' (v. 11, margin)."

1.2. What we do in our religious life must be done from a motive of love, not because we are forced or out of a slavish fear of God but because we want to and because we delight in him. "*Love the Lord your God* (v. 11), and you will not leave him."

2. Joshua urges God's faithfulness to them as a reason why they should be faithful to him (v. 14): "*I am going the way of all the earth*; I am old and dying. Now that I am coming near the end of my life, it is right for me to look back over the past years. You know that *not one thing hath failed of all the good things which the Lord spoke concerning you*, and he spoke a great many" (v. 14); see also 21:45.

3. Joshua gives them a reasonable warning of what the fatal consequences of apostasy would be (vv. 12–13, 15–16): "If you turn back, then you must definitely know that that will lead to your destruction."

3.1. He describes the apostasy which he warns them against. Its first step would be becoming on intimate terms with idolaters (v. 12). The next step would be to intermarry with them. The result would be (v. 16) that they *served other gods*—the pretended ancient deities of the country—and bowed down to them.

3.2. He describes the destruction which he warns them of. He tells them:

3.2.1. That if they associated with, harbored, or went along with the remaining Canaanites, then they would discover that the Canaanites would be a snare and a trap to them. They would draw them back to sin and into foolish relationships, unprofitable projects, and every kind of bad way.

3.2.2. That the anger of the Lord would rise up against them. If they entered into close associations with the Canaanites, then this would not only give the idolaters the opportunity of causing them trouble, but it would also show how ungrateful they were to God, cause him to become their enemy, and arouse his displeasure against them.

3.2.3. That all the threats of the word would be fulfilled, just as the promise had been, for the God of eternal truth is faithful to both (v. 15): "*As all good things have come upon you* according to the promise so long as you have kept close to God, so also all evil things will come on you according to the threats if you abandon him."

CHAPTER 24

This chapter concludes the life and reign of Joshua. We have here: 1. The great care and effort he took to confirm the people of Israel in the true faith and worship of God, so that after his death they might persevere in that. In order to do this, he called another general assembly of the leaders of the tribes of Israel (v. 1) and talked with them. He recounted the narrative of the great things God had done for them and their ancestors (vv. 2–13). He commanded them to consider God's actions for them and so serve God (v. 14). 2. The agreement with them that he outlined, in which he aimed to bring them to deliberately choose their religious faith. They did so, giving the reasons for their choice (vv. 15–18); they made it their determined choice and decided to remain faithful to it (vv. 19–24). We then have the covenant of that agreement (vv. 25–28). 3. The conclusion of this history, with the death and burial of Joshua (vv. 29–30) and Eleazar (v. 33), and the mention of the burial of Joseph's bones on that occasion (v. 32); A general account of the state of Israel at that time (v. 31).

Verses 1–14

Joshua thought he had taken his final farewell of Israel in the solemn command he gave them in the previous chapter, when he said, *I go the way of all the earth* (23:14), but God graciously continued his life longer than expected. Joshua wanted to make the most of his remaining time for the good of Israel. He summoned them together again, so that he might see what more he could do to make them committed to God.

1. The place appointed for their meeting is *Shechem*, not only because that was nearer to Joshua than Shiloh, and so more convenient now that he was weak and not fit to travel, but also because it was the place where Abraham, the first trustee of God's covenant with this people, settled when he came to Canaan, and where God appeared to him (Ge 12:6–7). Near there stood Mounts Gerizim and Ebal, where the people had renewed their covenant with God when they had first come to Canaan (8:30).

2. They presented themselves in this assembly not only before Joshua but also before God. Joshua ordered the ark of God to be brought by the priests to Shechem, which, they say, was roughly twelve miles (about twenty kilometers) from Shiloh, and to be set down in the place where they met, which is therefore called (v. 26) *the sanctuary of the Lord*, since the presence of the ark made it sacred at that time. We do not now have any such visible signs of God's presence but are to believe that *where two or three are gathered together* (Mt 18:20) in Christ's name, he is really with them as much as God was where the ark was.

3. Joshua spoke to them in God's name, and as from him, in the language of a prophet (v. 2): *Thus saith the Lord.* This shows us that the word of God is to be received by us as his word, whoever the messenger is who brings it. The greatness of the messenger cannot add to it, nor can the lowliness of the messenger detract from it.

3.1. The doctrinal part is a history of the great things God had done for his people and for their ancestors before them:

3.1.1. He brought Abraham out of Ur of the Chaldeans (vv. 2–3). Abraham, who afterward was the friend of God and the great favorite of heaven, was brought up in idolatry and lived for a long time in it, until God by his grace snatched him as a burning stick out of the fire. In this way, Abraham's justification is given by the apostle Paul as an example of God's *justifying the ungodly* (Ro 4:5).

3.1.2. He brought Abraham to Canaan, built up his family, and led him through the land to Shechem, where they now were. He multiplied Abraham's descendants through Ishmael, whose offspring included twelve rulers, but at last gave him Isaac, the promised son, and multiplied his descendants through him. When Isaac had two sons, Jacob and Esau, God provided an inheritance for Esau elsewhere in Mount Seir so that the land of Canaan might be kept wholly for the descendants of Jacob, and the descendants of Esau might not lay claim to it.

3.1.3. He boldly rescued the descendants of Jacob from Egypt (vv. 5–6), out of the hands of Pharaoh and his army at the Red Sea (vv. 6–7). The same waters that were a

guard for the Israelites were also a grave for the Egyptians. This was an answer to prayer, for although we find in the story that they grumbled against God in their distress (Ex 14:11–12), notice is here taken that they *cried unto God* (v. 7). He graciously accepted those who prayed to him and overlooked the foolishness of those who quarreled with him—the same people.

3.1.4. He protected them in the desert, where they are here said not to have wandered but to have *dwelt for a long season* (v. 7).

3.1.5. He gave them the land of the Amorites, on the other side of the Jordan (v. 8), and there they defeated the plot of Balak and Balaam against them, so that Balaam could not curse them as he wanted to. And so Balak dared not fight them, but because he had intended to, he is said here to have done it.

3.1.6. He brought them safely and triumphantly into Canaan, gave the Canaanites into their hands (v. 11), and *sent hornets before them* (v. 12) when they were actually waging war with the enemy, which tormented them with their stings and terrified them with their noise, so that the Canaanites became an easy target for Israel.

3.1.7. He gave them peaceful possession of a good land, and they lived comfortably on the fruit of other people's labors (v. 13).

3.2. The application of this history of God's mercies to them is given as an exhortation that they should fear and serve God in gratitude for his favor so that it might continue for them (v. 14). It would seem from this command, which is repeated in v. 23, that some of them privately kept in their rooms the idols or pictures of these false gods, which came into their hands from their ancestors as family heirlooms, even though perhaps they did not worship them. Joshua earnestly urges them to throw them away: "Get rid of them. Destroy them, so that you won't be tempted to serve them."

Verses 15–28

Never was an agreement better managed, nor brought to a better outcome, than this one between Joshua and the people, to commit them to serve God.

1. Would their service to God be an obligation for them if they chose it? It would; yet Joshua here put it before them as a choice because it would have a great influence on their perseverance in their faith if they embraced it fully with all human reason and determination. He leads them to two things:

1.1. He wants them to embrace their religious faith rationally and intelligently, for it is a reasonable service. And so:

1.1.1. Joshua puts the matter to them as a reasonable choice (v. 15). Here:

1.1.1.1. He proposes the candidates who are standing for election. The Lord, Jehovah, is on the one side. On the other side are either the gods of their ancestors or the *gods of* their neighbors, *the Amorites*, in *whose land they dwell*, which will worm their way into the affections of those who want to please others and who enjoy good company.

1.1.1.2. He supposes there are those to whom, for some reason or other, it will *seem evil to serve the Lord* (v. 15). There are prejudices and objections which some people raise against religion. It seems undesirable, hard, and unreasonable to them to have to deny themselves, mortify the flesh, take up their cross, and so on.

1.1.1.3. He calls on them to make a decision themselves: "*Choose you whom you will serve* (v. 15). Choose today, now that the matter has been clearly put before you.

Bring matters swiftly to a conclusion. Don't stand around hesitating." Much later, in the dispute between Jehovah and Baal, Elijah committed the decision to the consciences of those with whom he was dealing (1Ki 18:21). Joshua's putting the matter here to the issue clearly shows two things:

- That it is the will of God that every one of us should make a serious and deliberate choice of our religious faith.
- That faith in God has so much plain reason and righteousness on its side that it may safely be committed to everyone who allows themselves freedom of thought to choose it or refuse it. The merits of the cause are so plain that no considerate person can do otherwise than choose it.

1.1.1.4. He directs their choice in this matter by openly declaring his own decision: "*But as for me and my house, whatever you do, we will serve the Lord* (v. 15). I hope you too will all be of the same mind."

1.1.2. After the choice has been put to them, they immediately decide by a free, rational, and intelligent declaration to serve the God of Israel, rejecting all other competitors (vv. 16–18): *We will also serve the Lord.* They give substantial reasons for their choice, to show that they have not made their decision purely to please Joshua but have made it because they are fully convinced that it is reasonable and right.

1.2. He wants them to embrace their religious faith with determination, and to express a wholeheartedness in staying faithful to the Lord. Now that he has them in a good frame of mind, he follows up his blow and "hits the nail on the head" so that the nail might, if possible, be hammered in securely. If you fasten things securely when you leave, they will still be there when you return.

1.2.1. In order to do this, he sets before them the difficulties of religious faith and those things that might be thought discouraging (vv. 19–20): *You cannot serve the Lord, for he is a holy God. He will not forgive. And, if you forsake him, he will do you hurt.* Joshua definitely does not want to put the people off from serving God as something impracticable or dangerous. But:

1.2.1.1. He perhaps intended to present the suggestions of the seducers, those who tempted Israel away from their God with insinuations that God was a hard taskmaster and that they would not be able to do his work or please him. This was probably a common objection against the Jewish religion.

1.2.1.2. He was expressing a godly jealousy for them and his fear concerning them, that despite the profession they were now making of zealously choosing God and his service, they would later turn away.

1.2.1.3. He decided to paint them the blackest picture, "*You cannot serve the Lord* (v. 19), except if you put away all other gods." In this way, although our Master has assured us that *his yoke is easy* (Mt 11:30), he does not want us to become overconfident, negligent, and careless. He has also told us that the gate is small, and the way is

narrow, that leads to life, that we may therefore do our best to enter it, not simply seek it.

1.2.1.4. He was showing them the apparent discouragements in their way so that he might sharpen up their resolution.

1.2.2. Despite this statement of the difficulties of a religious faith, they declare a firm determination to continue and persevere (v. 21): *Nay; but we will serve the Lord.*

2. After they have deliberately decided to serve God, Joshua commits them to this by a solemn covenant (v. 25). Moses twice publicly confirmed this covenant between God and Israel, at Mount Sinai (Ex 24) and in the plains of Moab (Dt 29:1). Joshua himself has already done it once (8:31–35), and now he does it a second time. Now, to give it the formalities of a covenant:

2.1. He calls witnesses, no other than themselves (v. 22): *You are witnesses that you have chosen the Lord.*

2.2. He put it in writing and recorded it as we find it here in the sacred canon: he *wrote it in the book of the law* (v. 26). He *set up a great stone under an oak* as a monument to this covenant. He may perhaps have written an inscription on it showing its intention, to give "a voice" to the stone, as it were.

Verses 29–33

We have here:

1. The burial of Joseph (v. 32). He died perhaps approximately 430 years before in Egypt but *gave commandment concerning his bones* (Heb 11:22) that they should not rest in their grave until Israel enjoyed rest in the Land of Promise. And so the children of Israel, who had brought this coffin full of bones with them from Egypt, carried it along with them in all their journeys through the desert and kept it in their camp till Canaan had been completely conquered. Now eventually they laid his bones in the plot of ground which his father gave him near Shechem (Ge 48:22). Probably the sermon in this chapter served both as Joseph's funeral sermon and Joshua's own farewell sermon.

2. The death and burial of Joshua (vv. 29–30). Here he is called the *servant of the Lord*, the same title that was given to Moses (1:1) when his death was mentioned. Joshua's burial place is here said to be *on the north side of the hill Gaash* (Jdg 2:9), or "the trembling hill." The Jews say it was so called because it trembled at the burial of Joshua, to rebuke the people of Israel because they were stupid not to mourn the death of that great and good man as they should have done.

3. The death and burial of Eleazar the chief priest, who probably died at about the same time as Joshua, just as Aaron died in the same year as Moses (v. 33). He was buried in a hill that belonged to Phinehas his son.

4. A general idea given us of the state of Israel at this time (v. 31). While Joshua lived, religious faith was maintained among them under his care and influence, but soon after he and his contemporaries died, it decayed. How good it is for the Gospel church that Christ, our Joshua, still supports the church by his Spirit and always will do so, even *unto the end of the world* (Mt 28:20)!

A Practical and Devotional Exposition of the Book of

Judges

This is called in the Hebrew *Shepher Shoptim*, "the *book of Judges*," which the Syriac and Arabic versions expand on and call "The book of the judges of the children of Israel." The Septuagint (a Greek version of the Old Testament) entitles it only *Kritai*, "Judges." It is the history of the community of Israel during the leadership of the judges from Othniel to Eli. It contains the history, according to Dr. Lightfoot's reckoning, of about 299 years. This can be calculated by assigning the following periods to the respective judges, according to the figures given in the book: to Othniel of Judah forty years, to Ehud of Benjamin eighty years, to Deborah of Ephraim and Barak of Naphtali forty years, to Gideon of Manasseh forty years, to Abimelech his son three years, to Tola of Issachar twenty-three years, to Jair of Manasseh twenty-two years, to Jephthah of Manasseh six years, to Ibzan of Judah seven years, to Elon of Zebulun ten years, to Abdon of Ephraim eight years, to Samson of Dan twenty years, in all about 299.

The judges here appear to have come from eight different tribes. We see therefore that this honor was spread out among them, until at last it centered on Judah. Eli and Samuel, the two judges who do not come within this book, came from Levi. It seems that no judge came from Reuben or Simeon, Gad or Asher. We have the chronological history of these judges in this book in chs. 1–16. And then in chs. 17–21 we have an account of some particularly memorable events that happened—as did those of the story of Ruth (Ru 1:1)—*in the days when the judges ruled*, though it is not certain in which judges' days. What was the state of the community of Israel during this period?

1. They do not appear to be either so great or so good as you might have expected the character of such a special people to be, who were governed by such laws and enriched by such promises. We find them miserable and corrupt, and oppressed by the neighbors around them. But:

2. We may hope that though the writer in this book deals fully with the people's offenses and grievances, there was still some evidence of religious practice in the land. Although there were among them those who were sidetracked to idolatry, the tabernacle service, according to the Law of Moses, was still maintained, and there were many who attended it.

3. It would seem that in those days each tribe very much had its ordinary government within itself and acted separately without one common head or council. This led to many differences among themselves and kept them from being or doing anything significant.

4. The leadership of the judges was not constant, but occasional: when it is said that after Ehud's victory *the land rested eighty years* (3:30) and after Deborah's *forty* (5:31), it is not certain that they lived, much less that they governed, for such a long time; but they and the others were raised up and inspired by the Spirit of God to do a particular service to the public when there was occasion, to *avenge Israel of their enemies* (Isa 1:24) and to cleanse Israel from their idolatries, which are the two things principally meant by their judging Israel. But the prophet Deborah was judging Israel before she was needed to deliver Israel from Jabin, king of Hazor (4:4).

5. During the leadership of the judges, God was in a more special way Israel's king; this is what Samuel tells them when they decide to reject this form of government (1Sa 12:12). Four of the judges of Israel are mentioned in the great chapter of heroes of faith (Heb 11:32): Gideon, Barak, Samson, and Jephthah. As to the authorship of this book, Bishop Patrick thinks the author was the prophet Samuel.

CHAPTER 1

This chapter gives us a detailed account of the progress that the different tribes of Israel made in conquering Canaan after Joshua died. He, as we put it, broke the back of that work, and put Israel into such a position *that they could easily have completed it in due time if they had not failed because of themselves. We read here of what progress they did make and also of their failures: 1. The united tribes of Judah and Simeon were brave in their achievements. God appointed Judah to begin with (vv. 1–2). Judah called on Simeon to work with them (v. 3). They succeeded in their enterprises against Bezek (vv. 4–7) and Jerusalem (v. 8). 2. We read of their success in Hebron and Debir (vv. 9–15), Hormah, Gaza, and other places (vv. 17–19). But where there were iron chariots, their hearts failed (v. 19). It is mentioned that the Kenites settled among them (v. 16). 3. The other tribes, in comparison with these, were cowardly. Benjamin failed (v. 21). The house of Joseph did well against Bethel (vv. 22–26) but in other places did not make the most of their advantages, and neither did Manasseh (vv. 27–28) nor Ephraim (v. 29). Zebulun spared the Canaanites (v. 30). Asher yielded more than any of the tribes to the Canaanites (vv. 31–32). Naphtali was kept from fully possessing several settlements (v. 33). Dan was restricted by the Amorites (vv. 34–36). No account is given of Issachar, nor of the two and a half tribes on the other side of the Jordan.*

Verses 1–8

Here:

1. The children of Israel asked the Lord for direction as to which out of all the tribes should be the first to attempt to clear their country of the Canaanites. The question they asked was, *Who shall go up first?* (v. 1). We may suppose that by this time there were so many of them that the places they possessed began to be too confined for them. Whether each tribe ambitiously wanted to be first and so fought for that honor, or whether each tribe was afraid of being first, and so was keen to refuse that honor, is not stated.

2. God appointed Judah to go first and promised them success (v. 2): "*I have delivered the land into his hand*, to be possessed. I will give the enemy into Judah's hand and destroy those who stop Judah from possessing the land." Why must Judah be first in this undertaking?

2.1. Judah was the most numerous and powerful tribe.

2.2. Judah was first in honor and so must be first in duty. Judah was the tribe from which our Lord was to come, which meant that in Judah, Christ, the lion of the tribe of Judah, went before them. Christ waged war with the powers of darkness first and defeated them. This inspires us in our conflicts; it is in him that we are *more than conquerors* (Ro 8:37).

3. Judah prepares to go, but the men of Judah want their brother and neighbor, the tribe of Simeon, to join forces with them (v. 3). Notice that the stronger should not despise the help of the weaker; on the contrary, they should want it. Judah is the most significant of all the tribes, and Simeon the most insignificant, but Judah asks for Simeon's friendship and help. The head cannot say to the foot, *I have no need of thee* (1Co 12:21), for we are *members one of another* (Ro 12:5).

4. The joint forces of Judah and Simeon took to the battlefield: *Judah went up* (v. 4), and Simeon with Judah (v. 3). Caleb was probably commander in chief of this expedition. It would seem also from what follows (vv. 10–11) that Caleb did not yet possess his own allotted territory. It was fortunate for them that they had a general who was so wholehearted.

5. God gave Israel great success. Whether they invaded the enemy or the enemy first sounded the call to battle, the Lord gave them into their hands (v. 4). We are told:

5.1. How the army of the Canaanites was routed in the field, in or near Bezek, the place where they set themselves up, which afterward Saul made the place of a general mustering (1Sa 11:8). The Israelites killed 10,000 men in Bezek (v. 4). If they had followed through after such a devastating blow, it would certainly have weakened those who were already brought so low.

5.2. How their king was taken and humiliated. His name was Adoni-Bezek, which means "lord of Bezek." He was taken prisoner after the battle, and we are told how they mutilated him; they cut off his thumbs, to make him unfit for fighting, and his big toes, so that he could not run away (v. 6). It was cruel to triumph over a miserable person who lay at their mercy, except he was a Canaanite, and one who had abused others in a similar way. Notice here:

5.2.1. How great Adoni-Bezek had been, but how he now found himself a prisoner and was reduced to the most shameful disgrace.

5.2.2. What devastations he had brought about among his neighbors. He had wholly subdued seventy kings. Dr. Lightfoot says, "When Judah conquered Adoni-Bezek, he was, in effect, conquering seventy kings."

5.2.3. How justly he was treated in the same way as he treated others.

5.2.4. How honorably he acknowledged the righteousness of God in this: *As I have done, so God has requited (repaid) me* (v. 7).

6. Particular notice is taken of the conquest of Jerusalem (v. 8).

Verses 9–20

We have here a further account of that glorious and successful campaign which Judah and Simeon made:

1. Judah's allotment had been pretty well cleared of the Canaanites, but not completely. Those who *dwelt in the mountain*, the hill country around Jerusalem, were driven out (vv. 9, 19), but those in the valley and plain kept their ground against them, having *chariots of iron*, such as we read of in Jos 17:16. They had iron chariots, and so it was not thought safe to attack them, but did not Israel have God on their side, *whose chariots are thousands of angels* (Ps 68:17)? But they allowed their fears to be stronger than their faith, and so they could not trust God when circumstances went against them. Instead, they passively withdrew their forces. What they should have done was make one bold strike against the Canaanites, and then they would have completed their victories.

2. Caleb was put in possession of Hebron, which, although it had been given him by Joshua ten or twelve years before, was still used for settling the affairs of all the tribes, which he put before his own private interests. It seems he did not make use of what had been given him until now, so content was he as a good man to serve others, leaving himself until last. But now the men of Judah all came to his assistance to subdue Hebron (v. 10), killed the sons of Anak, and gave him possession of it (v. 20). They gave Hebron to Caleb; and now Caleb wanted to repay the kindness of his compatriots and was impatient to see Debir conquered and put into the hands of the men of Judah. So to see that happen, he offered his daughter to the man who would undertake to be in command in the siege of that important place (vv. 11–12). Othniel bravely undertook it and so won the city and Caleb's daughter (v. 13).

3. Simeon gained ground from the Canaanites in their territory (vv. 17–18). In the eastern part of Simeon's allotment, they destroyed the Canaanites in Zephath, calling that city *Hormah*, meaning "destruction." In the western part they took Gaza, Ashkelon, and Ekron, cities of the Philistines; they gained possession of the cities at that time but did not destroy the inhabitants, and so the Philistines over time regained the cities and turned out to be long-standing enemies of the Israel of God, and the Israelites could expect no better, because they had only half-completed their work.

4. The Kenites gained a settlement in the tribe of Judah, choosing it there rather than in any other tribe, because Judah was the strongest, and they hoped that they would be safe and secure there (v. 16). These were the descendants of Jethro. They had at first established themselves in Jericho, *the city of palm trees* (v. 16), a city which never was to be rebuilt and so was more suitable for those who lived in tents and did not want to build. But afterward they moved to the Desert of Judah. Israel respected them enough to allow them to settle where they wanted to. They were a quiet people and were happy wherever they were, with only a little. Those who did not attack others were themselves not attacked by anyone. *Blessed are the meek, for they shall inherit the earth* (Mt 5:5).

Verses 21–36

1. We are told here how the other tribes got along in their wars with the remaining Canaanites:

1.1. Benjamin failed to drive the Jebusites out of that part of the city of Jerusalem which came in their allotment (v. 21). Judah had set them a good example and gained great advantages for them by what they did (v. 9), but Benjamin did not follow up the attack because they lacked determination.

1.2. The house of Joseph:

1.2.1. Stirred themselves a little to gain possession of Bethel (v. 22). That city is mentioned earlier as being allotted to the tribe of Benjamin (Jos 18:22). But it is spoken of there (Jos 18:13) as a city on the border of that tribe, and it would seem that the boundary went right through it, so that one half of it belonged to Benjamin, the other half to Ephraim. Notice in this account of the mission of the Ephraimites against Bethel:

1.2.1.1. The privilege they had that *the Lord was with them* (v. 22). He would also have been with the other tribes if they had exerted themselves.

1.2.1.2. The wise measures they took to capture the city. They sent spies to discover which part of the city was the weakest (v. 23). These spies gained very useful information from a man they met, who showed them a private way into the city. It seems he did not want to attach himself to the people of Israel, and so he moved later to a settlement of the Hittites, who had gone into Arabia and settled there when Joshua invaded the country. This man chose to live with these people and built a city. In naming the city, he preserved the ancient name of his native city, *Luz,* "an almond tree," preferring this to its new name, which included a religious meaning, *Bethel,* "the house of God."

1.2.1.3. Their success. The spies brought or sent to the army this information they had gained, which gave them the advantage, and they surprised the city and killed all its inhabitants (v. 25).

1.2.2. Did nothing remarkable, it seems, besides this achievement.

1.3. Zebulun, perhaps because they were involved with sea trade — for it was foretold that their land would be a haven for ships (Ge 49:13) — failed to conquer Kitron and Nahalol (v. 30) and only subjected the inhabitants of those places to forced labor.

1.4. Asher did the least out of all the tribes (vv. 31–32). They not only left more towns than any of the other tribes in the hands of the Canaanites, but actually submitted themselves to the Canaanites instead of subjecting them to forced labor.

1.5. Naphtali also allowed the Canaanites to live among them (v. 33) and only gradually managed to press them into forced labor.

1.6. Dan was far from extending their conquests where their allotment lay, because they lacked the spirit to make any headway against the Amorites. Instead, Dan was forced by them to withdraw into the mountainous hill country and live in the settlements there, and did not dare venture into the valley and plains, where the iron chariots probably were (v. 34). In Jacob's blessing, Judah is compared to a lion, Dan to a serpent, but notice how Judah's lionlike courage brought prosperity and success, while Dan's cunning subtlety gained no ground at all. Artful and sly machinations do not always bring about the wonders they claim.

2. Generally it appears that the people of Israel were negligent toward both their duty and their interest in making progress against the Canaanites. They did not take active steps to drive out the Canaanites and make room for themselves. They distrusted God. The unbelief that kept their fathers out of Canaan for forty years now kept them from fully possessing it. Distrusting God's power and promise lost them their advantage and led them into great trouble.

CHAPTER 2

In this chapter we have: 1. A special message which God sent to Israel by an angel, and the impression it made on them (vv. 1–5). 2. A general idea of the state of Israel during the leadership of the judges, in which notice: they remained faithful to God while Joshua and the elders lived (vv. 6–10); they later rebelled and served idols (vv. 11–13); God was displeased with them and judged them for it (vv. 14–15); he showed mercy toward them by raising up judges for them (vv. 16–18); they relapsed into idolatry after the judgment was over (vv. 17–19); God in his anger completely stopped their successes (vv. 20–23).

Verses 1–5

Israel enjoyed the privilege of particular messages sent from heaven, as needs arose, to rebuke, correct, and instruct. Besides the written word which was theirs to be read, they often *heard a word behind them, saying, This is the way* (Isa 30:21). This is how God now begins to deal with them. In these verses we have a sermon that is preached to them to wake them up when they are beginning to cool off in their religious faith.

1. The preacher was an *angel of the Lord* (v. 1). We sometimes find in this book that extraordinary messengers were used to raise up the judges who rescued Israel, such as Gideon and Samson. Here, to show how many and varied are the services these messengers perform for God's Israel, one is sent to preach to them, to prevent them from falling into sin and trouble.

2. The people to whom this sermon was preached were *all the children of Israel* (v. 4). Here is a great congregation for a great preacher! The place is called *Bochim* (v. 1) because it gained that name on this occasion. All Israel needed the rebuke and warning given here.

3. The sermon itself is short and condensed. God told them clearly:

3.1. What he had done for them (v. 1). He had brought them out of Egypt, a land of slavery and toil, into Canaan, a land of rest, liberty, and plenty.

3.2. What he had promised them: *I said, I will never break my covenant with you* (v. 1).

3.3. What were his reasonable expectations from them (v. 2). Because they were taken into covenant with God, it was right that they should have no association with the Canaanites. The Canaanites were both his enemies and theirs, and now that they had set up his altar, they should get rid of the Canaanite altars so that they would not be tempted to serve the Canaanite gods.

3.4. How they had disobeyed him in this very thing which he had most insisted on: "In such a small matter as this you have not obeyed my voice."

3.5. How they must expect to suffer because of their foolishness (v. 3). Those who expect to benefit from being friends with those who are God's enemies are only deceiving themselves.

4. The success of this sermon is significant: the people *lifted up their voice and wept* (v. 4). But this was not enough; they wept, but we do not find that they reformed their behavior, that they went home and destroyed all remnants of idolatry and idolaters among them. Many are softened by the word but become hard again before they are formed into a new mold. However, this general weeping:

4.1. Gave a new name to the place (v. 5): they called it *Bochim*, "Weepers."

4.2. Gave opportunity for a solemn sacrifice: they *sacrificed there unto the Lord* (v. 5), having probably met at Shiloh, where God's altar was.

Verses 6–23

The angel had foretold that the Canaanites and their idols would be a snare to Israel; now the writer shows that this is what happened. So that this may become clearer, the writer looks back a little and notices:

- Their happy settlement in the land of Canaan. After Joshua had distributed this land among them, he dismissed them to quietly and comfortably possess it (v. 6).
- Their continuance in the faith and fear of God's holy name as long as Joshua lived (v. 7).
- The death and burial of Joshua, which was a fatal blow to the faithful religious practices among the people (vv. 8–9).
- The rising of a new generation (v. 10). They were so completely wrapped up in this world, so intent on its business and so concerned to satisfy themselves and to take things easy in a life of self-indulgence, that they had no time for the true God and his holy religion. They were so readily drawn aside to false gods and their detestable superstitions.

And so the writer comes to give us a general idea of the series of things undertaken in Israel during the time of the judges.

1. The people of Israel abandoned the God of Israel. In general, *they did evil* (v. 11); nothing could be more evil, more offensive to God, or cause greater harm to them, and it was *in the sight of the Lord*. In particular:

1.1. They *forsook the Lord* (v. 12 and again v. 13). This was one of the two great evils they were guilty of (Jer 2:13). They had been joined to the Lord in covenant, but now they abandoned him, as an unfaithful wife *treacherously departs from her husband* (Jer 3:20).

1.2. When they abandoned the only true God, they did not become so foolish as to deny God's existence and say, *There is no God* (Ps 14:1), but they followed other gods. There still remained traces in them of a nature that acknowledged God, but there was so much of their corrupt nature in them as to multiply their gods and to follow others they came across. They wanted to "follow the crowd," follow the latest fashion, rather than God's ways of religious worship. *Baalim* means "lords," and

Ashtaroth, "blessed ones," and both are plural, for when they abandoned Jehovah, who is one, they served many gods and lords.

2. This provoked the God of Israel to anger, and he handed them over to their enemies (vv. 14–15).

2.1. The scale of victory was tipped against them. God would rather give success to those who had never known or acknowledged him than to those who had both known and acknowledged him but had now abandoned him.

2.2. The balance of power then turned against them.

3. The God of infinite mercy took pity on them in their distress even though they had brought such distress on themselves by their own foolish sin, and he rescued them. Notice here:

3.1. The motivation for their rescue. It came purely from within God himself, from his mercy and tender compassion, not because of their repentance. It was not so much the burden of sin as the burden of affliction that they groaned under. Indeed, they deserved to die eternally under his curse, but because this was the day of his patience and he wanted to give them another chance, he did not destroy them.

3.2. The method of their rescue. God raised up judges from among the Israelites themselves, when it was necessary, those whom God qualified in an extraordinary way to reform and rescue Israel, and he crowned their endeavors with great success: *The Lord was with the judges* (v. 18) when he raised them up, and so they became deliverers and saviors. We can learn from this:

3.2.1. In the days of the church's lowest points, when it is most corrupt and distressed, God will either find or equip some people to set things right.

3.2.2. God gives such people wisdom, courage, and boldness. All who in any way bless their country must be looked on as the gifts of God.

4. The degenerate Israelites were not fully or thoroughly reformed, not even by their judges (vv. 17–19). They had been promised in marriage to God, but they broke faith with the marriage covenant and joined themselves to other gods and worshiped them. Idolatry is spiritual adultery. *They corrupted themselves more than their fathers*; they tried to outdo them in multiplying their foreign gods and thinking up godless and ungodly ceremonies of worship that went completely against what the reformers were trying to do.

5. In his righteousness, God decided to continue to discipline them. After Joshua's death, little was done for a long time against the Canaanites: Israel indulged them and became familiar with them, and so God would not drive them out anymore (v. 21). God *chose their delusions* (harsh treatment) (Isa 66:4). In the same way, people pander to their own corrupt appetites and passions, and so God justly leaves them to themselves under the power of their sins, which will destroy them. This is their destiny; they themselves have decided it.

CHAPTER 3

We have in this chapter: 1. A general account of Israel's enemies and the trouble they caused (vv. 1–7). 2. A particular account of the brave exploits done by the first three of the judges: 2.1. Othniel, whom God raised up to fight Israel's battles against the king of Mesopotamia (vv. 8–11). 2.2. Ehud, who rescued Israel from the hands of the Moabites (vv. 12–30). 2.3. Shamgar, who distinguished himself in an encounter with the Philistines (v. 31).

Verses 1–7

We are told here what remained of the former inhabitants of Canaan. Some of them remained together in united groups (v. 3): *The five lords of the Philistines*, namely, Ashdod, Gaza, Ashkelon, Gath, and Ekron (1Sa 6:17). There was a particular nation called the *Canaanites*, whose land was alongside that of the Sidonians (Ge 10:19), on the coast of the Great Sea, the Mediterranean. And in the north, the Hivites held much of the Lebanon mountains. But besides these, throughout the country various nations (v. 5), Hittites, Amorites, etc., were scattered. Notice concerning these remaining Canaanites:

1. How wise it was of God to allow them to remain. At the end of the previous chapter it was mentioned that, as an act of God's justice, he let them remain to discipline Israel. But here another interpretation is put on it, and God's wisdom is said to consist in letting them remain for Israel's positive benefit, that is, so that those who *had not known the wars of Canaan* might *learn war* (vv. 1–2). Because their country lay very much in the midst of enemies, they therefore should be well disciplined, so that they might defend their territory when it was invaded and might later expand their territory as God had promised them.

2. How Israel entered into wrong associations with those who remained:

2.1. They married the Canaanites (v. 6) even though they could not advance their honor or their estates by doing so.

2.2. In marrying the Canaanites they were led to join in worship with them; they *served their gods* (v. 6), *Baalim and the groves* (v. 7), that is, the Asherah images that were worshiped in groves of thick trees, which were a sort of natural temple. In such unequal alliances there is more reason to fear that the bad will corrupt the good than to hope that the good will reform the bad, just as there is in placing two pears side by side, the one rotten and the other sound. When they began to worship other gods, they *forgot the Lord their God* (v. 7).

Verses 8–11

We come now to the records of the leadership of the individual judges, the first of whom was Othniel, whose ministry is closely linked with that of Joshua. In this short account of Othniel's period as judge we see:

1. The distress that Israel was brought into for their sin (v. 8). In his righteousness, God was displeased with them and he laid them open to the other nations. They were "put up for sale" as goods he could part with, and the first to lay hands on them was Cushan-Rishathaim, king of that part of Syria between the two great rivers Tigris and Euphrates, called *Mesopotamia*, which means "between the rivers." Aiming to expand his territories, he immediately invaded the two tribes on the side of the Jordan closer to him, and he later perhaps gradually penetrated into the heart of the country, and as far as he went, he harshly subjected them for eight years, perhaps imposing soldiers on them.

2. Israel's return to God in this distress: *When he slew them, then they sought him* (Ps 78:34), the One whom they had spurned before. The *children of Israel cried unto the Lord* (v. 9). When everything went well, they had cried out to the Baals and the Asherahs, but they were now in trouble, and so they cried out to the Lord.

3. God's mercy in coming to rescue Israel. Notice:

3.1. The deliverer was Othniel, who married Caleb's daughter, one of the old generation who had *seen the works of the Lord* (Ps 107:24). He was now probably very old when God raised him up to this honor.

3.2. Where Othniel received his commission from. It did not come from or by a fellow human being; rather, *the Spirit of the Lord came upon him* (v. 10), a spirit of wisdom and courage that equipped him for service and a spirit of power that inspired him to do it.

3.3. How Othniel set about his work. He first judged Israel, rebuked them, and reformed them, and then went to war. This was the right way. Sin at home must first be conquered, and then enemies away from home will more easily be dealt with. In the same way, let Christ be our Judge and Lawgiver, and then *he will save us*, and on no other terms (Isa 33:22).

3.4. How successful Othniel was. He broke the chains of the oppression, for it is said, *The Lord delivered Chushan-rishathaim into his hand* (v. 10).

3.5. The beneficial result of Othniel's good service. The land had peace for forty years. The benefit would have lasted forever if they had kept close to God and their duty.

Verses 12–30

Ehud is the next judge whose achievements are related in this history, and here is an account of his actions:

1. When Israel sinned again, God raised up a new oppressor (vv. 12–14). Perhaps they thought they might be even bolder with their former sins because they saw that they were in no danger from their old oppressor, since the powers of that kingdom had been weakened and brought low. But God *strengthened Eglon king of Moab against them* (v. 12). This oppressor was nearer to them than the former one and so could cause more trouble. The king of Moab received help from the Ammonites and Amalekites (v. 13), and this made him even more powerful. We are told how they were successful:

1.1. They defeated Israel on the battlefield: they *went and smote Israel* (v. 13), not only those tribes nearest to them on the other side of the Jordan, but also those also on the west side of the Jordan, for they defeated *the city of palm trees*, which was probably near the place where Jericho had stood, for Jericho had been called by that name (Dt 34:3).

1.2. They subjected the Israelites to their rule (v. 14), that is, they exacted tribute from them, either the crops of the earth or money instead.

2. When Israel prayed again, God raised up a new deliverer (v. 15), named Ehud. We are told:

2.1. That he was a Benjamite. The City of Palms lay within this tribe's allotment, and so they probably suffered most and were therefore the first to try to shake off the rule. That tribe was probably the weakest of all the tribes, but out of it God raised up this deliverer.

2.2. That he was left-handed, as it seems many of that tribe were (20:16). *Benjamin* means "the son of the right hand," but many of them were left-handed, for there is not always a complete correspondence between human nature and a name. God, however, chose this left-handed person to be his right-hand man, whom he would *make strong for himself* (Ps 80:17). It was *God's right hand* that gained Israel the victory (Ps 44:3), not the right hand of the instruments he used.

2.3. What Ehud did to rescue Israel from the hands of the Moabites:

2.3.1. He put to death Eglon the king of Moab; he did not murder or assassinate him, but as a judge, or minister of divine justice, he carried out God's judgment on him:

2.3.1.1. He had occasion to gain access to the king. Because Ehud was an ingenious and active man, and ready to stand before rulers, his people chose him to carry *a present* (v. 15) in the name of all Israel, over and above their tribute, to their great lord the king of Moab, so that they might find favor in his eyes (v. 15). Ehud went on his mission to Eglon and offered his tribute with the usual ceremony and expressions of respect, to support what he intended to do and to prevent any suspicion from being aroused.

2.3.1.2. It would seem that from the outset he intended to put him to death. The fact that he planned and thought through the death of this tyrant can be seen from the preparation he made of a weapon for this purpose, a dagger or sword, which might easily be hidden under his clothing (v. 16). He wore this on his right thigh so that it might be easily drawn by his left hand and might arouse little suspicion.

2.3.1.3. He found a way of being alone with the king, which he could easily do now that he had not only made himself known to him but also ingratiated himself by the gift of the tribute. He sought a private audience with the king and gained it in a drawing room, here called a *summer parlour*. He told the king he had a secret message for him, and so the king ordered all his attendants to withdraw (v. 19).

2.3.1.4. When he had him alone, he soon put him to death. Ehud called his attention to *a message from God* (v. 20), and that message was a sword. The message was delivered, not to his ear, but directly and literally to his heart, into which the fatal sword was driven and was left (vv. 21–22). *Eglon* means "a calf," and he fell like a fattened calf killed by the sword as an acceptable sacrifice to divine justice. No such commissions are now given, and to claim them is to blaspheme God, and make him support the most notorious acts.

2.3.1.5. Providence wonderfully favored Ehud's escape when he had carried out the execution. The tyrant fell silently, without any shriek or cry, which might have been overheard by his servants a little ways away. The one who had boldly carried out this act of vengeance shut the doors after him, took the key with him, and passed through the guards with an innocent air and lack of concern. The servants who waited in the vestibule came to the door of the inner parlor when Ehud had gone, to receive further orders from their master, but finding it locked and quiet, they concluded he had lain down to sleep. In this way their desire not to disturb his sleep meant that they lost the opportunity of avenging his death. The servants eventually opened the door and found that their master had fallen to the floor, dead (v. 25). Ehud by this means made his escape to Seirah, which according to some means "a thick wood."

2.3.2. After he had put to death the king of Moab, he totally routed the forces of the Moabites among them and thereby effectively ended their oppressive rule:

2.3.2.1. He immediately raised an army in the hill country of Ephraim, some distance away from the headquarters of the Moabites, with himself as the leader (v. 27). The trumpet he blew was a true Jubilee trumpet which declared liberty. It was a joyful sound to the oppressed Israelites, who for a long time had heard no trumpets except those of their enemies.

2.3.2.2. As a godly person and as one who had done all this in faith, he took encouragement himself, and gave encouragement to his soldiers, from the power of God committed for them (v. 28): *"Follow me, for the Lord hath delivered your enemies into your hands."*

2.3.2.3. As a wise general, he first secured the fords of Jordan and set strong guards on all those crossing points,

to cut off the communication lines. He then struck the Moabites and killed them all: *There escaped not a man* of them. The consequence of this victory was that the power of the Moabites was wholly broken in the land of Israel. The country was cleared of these oppressors, and *the land had rest eighty years* (v. 30).

Verse 31

The other side of the country which lay southwest was at that time plagued by the Philistines, against whom Shamgar held his own.

1. It seems Israel needed to be rescued, for *he delivered Israel*; the extent of their distress was later related by Deborah in her song (5:6–7), when she said that *in the days of Shamgar the highways were unoccupied, and the travellers walked through byways. The inhabitants of the villages ceased.*

2. God raised up Shamgar to rescue them, it would seem, while Ehud was still living. The number of the enemies was so insignificant that it seems the killing of 600 of them amounted to a rescue for Israel, and he struck down that many with an oxgoad, or as some read it, "a plowshare." God with his remnant of the Spirit could, when he pleased, make plowmen into judges and generals and turn fishermen into apostles. It does not matter how weak the weapon is if God gives direction and power. An oxgoad, when God pleases, will do more than Goliath's sword.

CHAPTER 4

Here is the story of Deborah and Barak: 1. Israel rebelling from God (v. 1); Israel oppressed by Jabin (vv. 2–3). 2. Israel judged by Deborah (vv. 4–5); Israel rescued from the hands of Jabin: their rescue is arranged through an agreement between Deborah and Barak (vv. 6–9). 3. Barak takes the field (v. 10). Sisera, Jabin's general, meets him (vv. 12–13). Deborah encourages him (v. 14), and God gives him a complete victory (vv. 15–16). 4. The general is forced to flee (v. 17). And where he expected shelter (vv. 11, 17), he has his life stolen from him by Jael while he is asleep (vv. 18–21), which completes Barak's triumph (v. 22) and Israel's rescue (vv. 23–24).

Verses 1–3

Here is:

1. Israel backsliding from God: they again *did evil in his sight*. Notice in this:

1.1. The strange power of corruption, which rushes people headlong into sin even though they frequently experience its fatal consequences.

1.2. The common adverse effects of a long peace. The land had peace for eighty years, and this time should have been long enough to see them well established in their religious faith. But the opposite happened; the long period of peace made them secure in themselves, rebellious, and immoral.

1.3. The great loss which a people sustains by the death of good leaders. "They did evil, because Ehud was dead" is a possible reading of v. 1.

2. Israel oppressed by their enemies. When the Israelites abandoned God, he abandoned them, and then they became an easy target to anyone who wanted to plunder them. Jabin reigned in Hazor, as another of the same name—who perhaps was his ancestor—had done before him; Joshua routed and killed that earlier Jabin and burned his city (Jos 11:1, 10). But it seems that in the course of

time, the city was rebuilt. Jabin and his general, Sisera, powerfully oppressed Israel. What made this oppression even worse was that these Canaanites had formerly been conquered and subdued by Israel, were condemned to be their slaves in early times (Ge 9:25), and might now have been in subjection to them, if Israel's own laziness, cowardice, and unbelief had not allowed the Canaanites to gain the upper hand.

3. Israel returning to their God. Their distress was so severe—and they saw no other way of relief—that it drove them to cry to the Lord.

Verses 4–9

The time of redemption eventually came, when Israel was to be rescued from the hands of Jabin. Now here we have:

1. The preparation of the people for their rescue, by the prophetic behavior and leadership of Deborah (vv. 4–5). Her name means "a bee," and her name corresponded to her diligence, wisdom, and usefulness to the people, her sweetness to her friends, and her sharpness to her enemies. She is said to be *the wife of Lapidoth* (v. 4), but since the ending of that word is not commonly found in a man's name, some consider this to be the name of a place: she was "a woman of Lapidoth." Others take it as a description, with *Lapidoth* meaning "lamps." The rabbis say she had employed herself in making wicks for the lamps of the tabernacle. Or perhaps she was an enlightened or magnificent woman, one who was extraordinarily wise. We are told about her:

1.1. That she knew God intimately: she was a *prophetess.*

1.2. That she was completely devoted to the service of Israel. She judged Israel at the time that Jabin oppressed them. She judged, not as a princess by any civil authority given to her, but as a prophet and as God's mouthpiece to them. It is said that she *dwelt*, or as some read it, she "sat" under a palm tree, which was afterward called *the palm tree of Deborah* (v. 5). Either she had her home under that tree, or this was where she held court in the open air, under the shadow of that tree, which was a sign of the justice she administered there. Such justice would grow and prosper even when it was opposed, just as palm trees grow under stress.

2. The plan for their rescue. Since she was a woman, she was not herself qualified to command an army, but she named one who was qualified, Barak from Naphtali. He could do nothing without her mind, and she could do nothing without his hands. But together they both made a complete rescuer, and the rescue they carried out was complete.

2.1. By God's direction, Deborah orders Barak to raise an army and fight Jabin's forces, who are under Sisera's command (vv. 6–7). Barak may have been thinking of launching an attack against the common enemy, but two things discouraged him:

2.1.1. He needed a commission to enlist forces. Deborah gave him this with the seal of heaven, which as a prophet she was authorized to give: *Hath not the Lord God of Israel commanded it?* (v. 6). *Go and draw towards Mount Tabor* (v. 6). She directs him:

• How many warriors he is to muster: 10,000.
• From where he should raise them—only from of his own tribe, Naphtali, and the adjacent tribe of Zebulun.
• Where to make his rendezvous—at Mount Tabor, in his own neighborhood.

2.1.2. When he has raised an army, he does not know how he will have an opportunity to fight the enemy. "Well," Deborah says, "*I will draw* (lure) *unto thee Sisera and his army.*" She expressly promises success: *I will*—that is, God will, in whose name I speak—*deliver them into thy hand* (v. 7).

2.2. At Barak's request, she promises to go along with him to the battlefield.

2.2.1. Barak insisted very much that she also be there. Her presence would mean more to him than a council of war (v. 8): "*If thou wilt go with me* to direct and advise me, and let me know God's mind in every difficult case, *then I will go* with all my heart, and I will not fear the iron chariots. But if you don't go with me, then I won't go." Nothing would give him greater assurance than to have Deborah the prophet with him so that she could encourage the soldiers and he could consult her to know God's mind on every occasion.

2.2.2. Deborah promised to go with him (v. 9). The arduousness of the task or its danger would not discourage her from doing all she could do to serve her country. Deborah was the *weaker vessel* (1Pe 3:7), but she had the stronger faith. Yet although she agreed to go with Barak if he insisted, she also gave him enough of a hint to make the soldier in him not want to insist on it: "*The journey thou takest shall not be for thy honour.* It will not gain you as much honor as if you had gone by yourself, for *the Lord shall sell Sisera into the hands of a woman*" (v. 9); that is, the world would attribute the victory to Deborah, and God would complete the victory by the hand of Jael, which would somewhat eclipse his glory and honor. But Barak values the success of his undertaking more than his honor, and so he does not withdraw his request.

Verses 10–16

Here:

1. Barak mustered a volunteer force and soon had his soldiers ready (v. 10). Although the tribes of Zebulun and Naphtali were chiefly depended on, it appears from the Song of Deborah that some had also come from other tribes (Manasseh and Issachar), and more were expected who did not come, from Reuben, Dan, and Asher (5:14–17). Then comes v. 11, concerning the move of Heber—one of the families of the Kenites—from the Desert of Judah in the south into the northern country, which is included for the sake of what follows concerning the exploits of Jael, a wife of that family.

2. Sisera took to the battlefield with a very strong army (vv. 12–13). Sisera's confidence was chiefly in his chariots, and so particular notice is taken of them, 900 *chariots of iron* (v. 13), which caused terrible bloodshed when they were driven, scythes protruding from their axles, into an army of foot soldiers.

3. Deborah gave orders to engage the enemy (v. 14). Josephus says that when Barak saw Sisera's army drawn up and attempting to surround the mountain on the top of which he and his forces were camped, his heart failed him, but Deborah encouraged him to descend on Sisera: *The Lord hath delivered Sisera into thy hand* (v. 14). It was good that Barak had Deborah with him, for she made up what was deficient in his leadership by telling him, *This is the day* (v. 14), and also what was deficient in his courage by assuring him of God's presence.

4. God himself routed the enemy's army (v. 15). It was not so much the bold and unexpected attack that Barak made on their camp which discouraged and dispersed them, but rather God's terror, which seized their spirits.

The stars, it seems, fought against them (5:20). Josephus says that a violent hailstorm beat in their faces, driving them back. They then became a very easy target to the army of Israel, and Deborah's words were fulfilled: *The Lord has delivered them into thy hand* (v. 14).

5. Barak chases the scattered forces as far as their general's headquarters at Harosheth (v. 16). He spares none of those whom God has given into his hands to be destroyed: *There was not a man left.*

Verses 17–24

We have seen the army of the Canaanites totally routed. Here we have:

1. The fall of their general, Sisera, commander of their forces. Let us trace the steps of this mighty man's fall:

1.1. He leaves his chariot and takes to his feet (vv. 15, 17). Sisera is so miserable now that he has gotten off his chariot. The one who has just trusted so fully in his arms now finds he has little confidence as he trusts his feet.

1.2. He flees for shelter to the tents of the Kenites, because he has no stronghold or any other secure place of his own that he can easily withdraw to. What encourages him to go there is that at this time there is peace between his master and the house of Heber. Sisera thinks he will therefore be safe among them.

1.3. Jael invited him in and made him very welcome. She probably stood at the entrance to the tent and asked what news there was from the army and how successful he had been in the battle that had been fought nearby.

1.3.1. She invited him in. Perhaps she was waiting for an opportunity to show kindness to any distressed Israelite, if there should be such an opportunity.

1.3.2. She looked after him very hospitably and seemed concerned that he should be put at his ease as her invited guest. We suppose too that she kept her tent as quiet as she could, and free from noise, so that he might go to sleep more quickly and soundly. Now, when Sisera felt he was most secure, he was in fact the least safe.

1.4. When he lay fast asleep, Jael hammered a long tent peg through his temple, so fastening his head to the ground and killing him (v. 21). She was divinely authorized to do this, and so, because no such extraordinary commissions can be claimed now, what she did must on no account be imitated. The rules of friendship and hospitality must be religiously observed, and we must detest even the thought of betraying any whom we have invited and encouraged to put confidence in us. And in this act of Jael—like that of Ehud in the previous chapter—we have reason to think she was sure she had been prompted by God and that that task had been well done. The one who had thought to destroy Israel with his many iron chariots is himself destroyed with one iron tent peg.

2. The glory and joy of Israel at this:

2.1. Their leader, Barak, found his enemy dead (v. 22), and no doubt he was very pleased to find the work so well done, to the glory of God and to the shame of his enemies.

2.2. Israel was completely rescued from the hands of Jabin king of Canaan (vv. 23–24). They not only shook off his rule by this day's victory, but they also later pursued the war against him until they had destroyed him.

CHAPTER 5

This chapter contains the triumphant song which was composed and sung on the occasion of the glorious victory which Israel won over the forces of Jabin king of Canaan, and it records the fortunate results of that victory.
1. It begins with praise to God (vv. 1–3). The substance

of this song communicates the remembrance of this great achievement. God's appearances for them on this occasion are compared with his appearances to them on Mount Sinai (vv. 4–5). 2. Their rescue from the awful conditions they had been in is emphasized (vv. 6–8). They are called to join in the praise because they shared in the success (vv. 9–13). 3. Honor is reflected on those tribes who were forward and active in that war, and disgrace on those who did not serve (vv. 14–19, 23). 4. Notice is taken of how God himself fought for them (vv. 20–22). The honor of Jael, who killed Sisera, is especially celebrated (vv. 24–30). The song concludes with a prayer to God (v. 31).*

Verses 1–5

1. God is praised by a song, which is:

1.1. A very natural expression of rejoicing. *Is any merry? Let him sing* (Jas 5:13). Holy joy is right at the root of praise and thanksgiving.

1.2. A very good way of remembering great events forever. Neighbors would learn this song from one another, and children would learn it from their parents. In this way, *one generation* would *praise God's works to another* and *declare his mighty acts* (Ps 145:4).

2. Deborah herself wrote this song, as appears in v. 7.

2.1. She used her gifts as a prophet in writing the song, and the tone throughout is fine and noble, the images are lively, the expressions elegant, and there is a wonderful mixture of sweetness and majesty.

2.2. We may suppose she used her authority as a princess to make the conquering army of Israel learn and sing this song. She set things in motion in battle, and this is also how it was in the thanksgiving.

3. Deborah looks back on the times when God has come to them in the past and compares this occasion with those. What God is doing now should bring to our mind what he has done, for he is the same yesterday, today, and forever (v. 4): *Lord, when thou wentest out of Seir.* This may be understood as referring to either:

3.1. The times when God's power and justice came against the enemies of Israel to subdue and conquer them. God had led his people Israel from the country of Edom, and he subjected Sihon and Og to them, striking them and their armies with such terror and fear that they thought the world was coming to an end. Or perhaps the verse notes the glorious display of God's majesty and the amazing effects of his power, which are enough to make the earth tremble, the heavens drop like snow before the sun, and the mountains melt. Or:

3.2. The appearances of God's glory and majesty to Israel when he gave them his Law at Mount Sinai. It was then literally true that *the earth trembled, and the heavens dropped* (v. 4). The Aramaic paraphrase considers the verse to refer to the giving of the Law but has a strange comment on those words, *the mountains melted.* "Tabor, Hermon, and Carmel fought among themselves. One said, 'Let the divine majesty dwell on me'; the other said, 'Let it dwell on me'; but God made it to dwell on Mount Sinai, the least and lowliest of all the mountains." We suppose "the least" means "the least valuable," because it is barren and rocky.

Verses 6–11

Here:

1. Deborah describes the distressed state of Israel under the tyranny of Jabin. *From the days of Shamgar*, who did something toward rescuing Israel from the Philistines, to the days of Jael, the present day, in which Jael had so distinguished herself, the country had been desolate. There had been:

1.1. No trade. All commerce ceased, the highways were empty: there were no caravans of merchants, as there had been before.

1.2. No traveling.

1.3. No cultivation. The fields had been devastated and vacated when the inhabitants of the villages were obliged to take shelter for themselves and their families in walled and fenced cities.

1.4. No administration of justice. There was conflict in the gates where their courts were kept (v. 8).

1.5. No peace for those who went out or for those who came in. The gates which they passed through had been invaded by the enemy; even the places where they drew water were attacked by archers. What a great feat, to terrify those who came to draw water.

1.6. Neither arms nor courage for the Israelites to help themselves with, not *a shield nor spear seen among forty thousand* (v. 8).

2. Deborah briefly shows what it was that brought all this misery on them: *They chose new gods* (v. 8). It was their idolatry that offended God so much that he gave them into the hands of their enemies.

3. Deborah notes God's goodness to Israel in raising up those who would put these things right. She includes herself first (v. 7): *Till that I Deborah arose*, to restrain and punish those who disturbed the public peace. In this way, she became a mother to Israel, one who looked after the people as a nursing mother does. Such was the affection she had for her people. Under her, there were other *governors of Israel* (v. 9). Of these leaders she says, *My heart is towards them* (v. 9).

4. Deborah calls on those who received a particular share in the advantages of this great salvation to offer special thanks to God (vv. 10–11):

4.1. *You that ride on white asses* (v. 10), that is, the nobility and gentry. Let such people speak out God's praises: they have had their salvation restored and have been given back not only their liberty, as other Israelites have been, but also their dignity.

4.2. Let those who *sit in judgment* (v. 10) be aware of it and be thankful that the sword of justice is not struck from their hand by the sword of war.

4.3. Let those who *walk by the way* (v. 10), who do not encounter anyone to make them afraid, speak about the goodness of God in removing bandits from the roads which they had taken over for a long time.

4.4. Let those who do not have their wells taken from them or find them stopped up, and who are not in danger of being caught by the enemy when they go there to draw water, *rehearse* (recite) *the acts of the Lord* (v. 11). They are not to recount Deborah's acts, or Barak's, but the Lord's. He is the One who made peace in their borders. Notice in his acts:

• Justice is carried out on his bold enemies.
• Kindness is shown to his trembling people, *the inhabitants of the villages* (v. 7), who were most exposed to the enemy. It is the glory of God to protect those who are most vulnerable, and to help the weakest.

Verses 12–23

Here:

1. Deborah stirs herself and Barak to celebrate this victory in a holy, grand, and awe-inspiring way:

1.1. Deborah, as a prophet, must praise God in song. She has composed and now sings this song which inspires her: *Awake, awake*, and again, *awake, awake* (v. 12).

1.2. Barak, as a general, must praise God in victory: *Lead thy captivity captive* (v. 12). Although the army of Sisera was cut off in the field, and no mercy was shown them, we may also suppose that as the victory was followed up, when the war was carried into enemy country, many who were not armed were seized and taken as prisoners of war.

2. Deborah gives good reason for this praise and triumph (v. 13):

2.1. The Israelites had become few and insignificant, but God gave them authority over nobles. As long as any of God's Israel remains—and God will keep a remnant in the worst times—there is hope, even if it is a very small remnant, for God can make the one who remains, even just one person, triumph over those who are the most proud and powerful.

2.2. Deborah was herself of the weaker sex, the sex that from the Fall had been made to submit, but the Lord authorized her to rule over the mighty men of Israel. They willingly submitted to her direction and enabled her to triumph over the mighty men of Canaan.

3. Deborah makes particular comments about the different parties involved in this great action, noting who fought against them, who fought for them, and who was neutral:

3.1. Who fought against them. Jabin and Sisera had been mentioned in the story, but here it appears that:

3.1.1. Amalek was in league with Jabin. Ephraim is here said to act against Amalek (v. 14), probably intercepting and cutting off some of the Amalekite forces who were traveling to join Sisera.

3.1.2. Other kings of Canaan, who had recovered somewhat since their defeat by Joshua, joined with Jabin and strengthened his army with their forces. These kings *came and fought* (v. 19). It is said of these kings that *they took no gain of money* (v. 19), that they were not mercenary troops hired to serve Jabin.

3.2. Who fought for them. The different tribes who helped in this great achievement are here spoken of with honor:

3.2.1. Ephraim and Benjamin, those tribes among whom Deborah herself lived, acted bravely. The people of Benjamin had set them a good example in this: "Ephraim moved, *after thee, Benjamin*" (v. 14); Benjamin was at this time the junior and subordinate tribe to Ephraim both in numbers and wealth, but when they led, Ephraim followed.

3.2.2. Because the ice had been broken by Ephraim and Benjamin, Makir (the half tribe of Manasseh beyond the Jordan) and Zebulun sent people who were very useful to their plan.

3.2.3. Issachar gave good service, too. Although their forefather *saw that rest was good, and so bowed his shoulder to bear*—which was also the character of their tribe (Ge 49:15)—they still hated the oppressiveness of Jabin's rule and preferred the hard toil of war to subjection.

3.2.4. Zebulun and Naphtali were the most bold and active of all the tribes, not only out of special affection for Barak their compatriot, but also because they lay nearest to Jabin, and so they felt the rule of oppression more heavily than any other tribe.

3.2.5. The stars from heaven appeared, or acted at least, on Israel's side (v. 20): *The stars in their courses*, according to the order and direction of the One who is the great Lord of their powers, *fought against Sisera*, either by their evil influences or by causing the storms of hail and thunder which led to the routing of Sisera's army.

3.2.6. The *river of Kishon* fought against their enemies. It swept away multitudes of those who hoped to escape through it (v. 21). It was usually a shallow river, but now, probably because of the great rain that fell, the river had swollen. This meant that the stream was so deep and strong that those who attempted to cross it were drowned.

3.2.7. Deborah's own soul fought against them. She speaks of this with holy exultation (v. 21): *O, my soul, thou hast trodden down strength.*

3.3. Who was neutral, who did not side with Israel as might have been expected. No mention is made of Judah or Simeon among the tribes concerned, because they were so remote from the scene of action and did not have an opportunity to appear.

3.3.1. Reuben failed to serve (vv. 15–16). Two things prevented them from being committed:

3.3.1.1. Their division. This refers not only to their division from Canaan by the River Jordan, which need not have been a problem if they had really wanted to help, but it also means either:

• That they were divided among themselves — they could not agree who should go or who should lead. Or:
• That they were divided from the rest of the tribes in their opinion of this war. They thought the attempt not justifiable or not practicable.

3.3.1.2. Their business in the world: *Reuben abode among the sheepfolds* (v. 16), a warmer and safer place than the camp, pretending they could not conveniently leave the sheep they were looking after.

3.3.2. Dan and Asher also failed to serve (v. 17). These two were situated on the seacoast, and:

3.3.2.1. Dan pretended he could not leave his ships because that would leave them exposed, and so *I pray thee have me excused* (Lk 14:18).

3.3.2.2. Asher pretended he had to stay at home to repair the breaches which the sea had made on his land in some places, and to fortify his works against the encroachment of the sea; he stayed in his coves, or small havens, where his trading ships were, so that he could attend to them.

3.3.3. But most of all, Meroz is condemned, and a curse is declared on its inhabitants, *because they came not to the help of the Lord* (v. 23). This was probably a town situated near the scene of action, and so the inhabitants had a reasonable opportunity of showing their obedience to God and their concern for Israel, and of doing good to the common cause. But they were evil and refused to help, for fear of Jabin's iron chariots; they did not want to be wounded or injured. God looks on those who are not with him as being against him. This town of Meroz seems to have been a significant place at this time, since something great was expected from it.

Verses 24–31

Deborah concludes this triumphant song:

1. With the praises of Jael, her joint hero, whose brave act had completed and crowned the victory. Her poetry is at its finest and most florid here in the final part of this song. Notice how honorably she speaks of Jael (v. 24), who preferred her peace with the God of Israel to her peace with the king of Canaan. *Blessed shall she be above women in the tent* (v. 24). Those whose lot is cast in the tent in a very low and narrow sphere of activity, if they serve God there according to their ability, will in no way lose their reward.

2. With a prayer to God:

2.1. For the destruction of all his enemies: "*So, so* shamefully and miserably, *let all thy enemies perish, O Lord* (v. 31).

2.2. For the exaltation and comfort of all his friends. "But may those who love him and who genuinely have good wishes for his kingdom on earth *be as the sun when he goeth forth in his might* (v. 31)."

3. The victory celebrated by this song had such a fortunate effect on Israel that for about a generation they enjoyed the peace which it opened the way to: *The land had rest forty years* (v. 31).

CHAPTER 6

Nothing that occurred in the quiet and peaceful times of Israel is recorded: the forty years' peace after the conquest of Jabin is passed over in silence. Here begins the story of another distress and another rescue, by Gideon, the fourth of the judges. Here is: 1. The disastrous condition of Israel because of the invasion of the Midianites (vv. 1–6). 2. The message God sent them by a prophet (vv. 7–10). 3. The raising up of Gideon to rescue them; a commission which God sent him, which was confirmed by a sign (vv. 11–24). 4. The firstfruits of his leadership in reforming his father's house (vv. 25–32). 5. The preparations he made for a war against the Midianites (vv. 33–40).

Verses 1–6

Here we have:

1. Israel's sin renewed: *They did evil in the sight of the Lord* (v. 1).

2. Israel's troubles repeated. This follows naturally. All who sin should expect to suffer. All who return to their foolish ways should expect to return to misery. This trouble:

2.1. Arose from a terrible enemy. God gave them into the hands of the Midianites (v. 1), whose land bordered Moab (Nu 22:4). They were a people whom everyone despised as uneducated and unintelligent, a people that Israel had formerly subdued and had in some way destroyed (see Nu 31:7). But by this time they had grown so much that they were capable of being made a severe scourge for Israel's punishment.

2.2. Arose to a formidable intensity (v. 2): *The hand of Midian prevailed*; their power, purely because of their numbers, became very oppressive. God had promised to increase Israel to be as many as the grains of sand on the seashore, but their sin stopped their growth and made them fewer, and then their enemies, although in every other respect inferior to them, overpowered them by sheer force of numbers. Here we see that:

2.2.1. The Israelites were imprisoned, or rather they imprisoned themselves, in shelters and caves (v. 2). This was purely because of their own cowardice. They preferred to flee rather than fight. This was the effect of a guilty conscience.

2.2.2. The Israelites were greatly impoverished (v. 6). The Midianites frequently invaded the land of Canaan. This fruitful land was a great temptation to them. They came up against Israel (v. 3), camped among them (v. 4), and penetrated to the heart of the country as far as Gaza in the west (v. 4). They left the Israelites alone to sow their ground, but toward harvest time they came and seized everything, ate it up, and destroyed it, both grass and grain. When they went away, they took with them the sheep and oxen. We may see in this the justice of God in punishing their sin and the consequence of God's departing from a people. When God leaves, all good goes and all trouble breaks out.

3. Israel's sense of God's hand revived at last. They were handed over to the Midianites for seven years, each probably worse than the previous (v. 1), until finally Israel found that there was no help elsewhere and so *Israel cried unto the Lord* (v. 6).

Verses 7–10

Note here:

1. The notice God took of the cries of Israel when those cries were eventually directed toward him. This shows how ready he is to forgive, how quick he is to show mercy, and how inclined he is to hear prayer.

2. The method God took to rescue them:

2.1. Before he sent an angel to raise up a savior for them, he sent a prophet to rebuke them for their sin and to bring them to repentance (v. 8). His mission was to convict them of sin so that in their crying to the Lord, they might confess their sin with sorrow and shame and not waste their breath only complaining about their troubles.

2.1.1. We have reason to hope that God intends to be merciful to us if we find he is preparing us for it by his grace.

2.1.2. The sending of prophets to a people, and the giving of faithful ministers to a land, is a good sign and certain evidence that God has mercy in store for them.

2.2. We have here the main contents of the message which this prophet delivered to Israel in the name of the Lord:

2.2.1. He sets before them the great things God has done for them (vv. 8–9):

2.2.1.1. He brought them out of Egypt, where otherwise they would have continued in poverty and slavery forever.

2.2.1.2. He *delivered them out of the hands of all that oppressed them* (v. 9). This is mentioned to show that the reason they were not now rescued from the hands of the oppressing Midianites was not any lack of power or goodwill by God.

2.2.1.3. He gave them quiet possession of this good land. This not only worsened their sin and meant they could be rightly considered very ungrateful, but it also justified God and cleared him from any blame for the trouble they were now in.

2.2.2. He shows how right and fair God's demands and expectations were of them (v. 10): *"I am the Lord your God*, to whom you are under the greatest obligation; *fear not the gods of the Amorites."*

2.2.3. He charges them with rebelling against God, who had therefore made this accusation against them: *But you have not obeyed my voice* (v. 10).

Verses 11–24

It is not said what effect the prophet's sermon had on the people, but we may hope it had a good effect and that at least some of them repented and changed their ways, for immediately afterward comes the dawning of the day when they are rescued by the calling of Gideon to take on the command of their forces against the Midianites.

1. The person to be commissioned for this service was Gideon, the son of Joash (v. 11). The father kept the worship of Baal in his own family (v. 25), which we may suppose this son objected to as far as was in his power. He came from the half tribe of Manasseh that was in Canaan, from the clan of Abiezer, the eldest house of that tribe (Jos 17:2).

2. The person who commissioned him was an *angel of the Lord* (v. 11). This angel is here called *Jehovah*, the incommunicable personal covenant name of God (vv. 14, 16), and he said, *I will be with thee.*

2.1. This divine person appeared here to Gideon, and it should be noted how he found him:

2.1.1. All alone. God often shows himself to his people when they have withdrawn from the noise and rush of this world.

2.1.2. Employed in threshing wheat with a staff or rod, probably because he had only a little to thresh and did not need oxen to tread it out. The work he undertook was a sign of that greater work to which he was now to be called, as the disciples' fishing was. From threshing wheat he is called to thrash the Midianites (Isa 41:15).

2.1.3. Distressed; he was threshing his wheat, not on a threshing floor, the proper place, but *by the winepress* (v. 11), in some private, forgotten corner, for fear of the Midianites.

2.2. Let us now see what took place between the angel and Gideon, who did not know with certainty that he was an angel until after he was gone, but thought he was a prophet:

2.2.1. The angel appeared to him with respect and assured him of the presence of God with him (v. 12). By this word:

- He gives him his commission.
- He inspires him with all necessary qualifications to carry out his commission.
- He assures him of success, for *if God be for us, who can* succeed *against us?* (Ro 8:31).

2.2.2. Gideon gave a sad response to this joyful greeting (v. 13): *O my Lord! If the Lord be with us why then has all this befallen us?* Gideon is not conscious within himself of anything great or encouraging in his own spirit. He simply holds on to the assurance the angel had given him of God's presence. Notice that the angel spoke particularly to him: *The Lord is with thee* (v. 11); but Gideon widens it out to all: *If the Lord be with us* (v. 13). He groups himself with the thousands of Israel. He wants no comfort except what they all might share in. He is far from thinking of monopolizing God's presence, though he received great encouragement from it. Gideon was a *mighty man of valour*, but he was still weak in faith. This was Gideon's weakness. We must not expect that the miracles which were performed when a church was being formed and great truths were being settled will be continued and repeated when the formation and settlement have been completed. Nor should we expect that the mercies God showed to our ancestors who served him and kept close to him will be renewed for us if we turn away from him and rebel against him.

2.2.3. The angel gave him a very powerful answer to his objections by commissioning him to rescue Israel from the hands of the Midianites. The angel assured him of success in that task (v. 14). Now the angel is called *Jehovah*, for he spoke as one with authority, not simply as a mere messenger.

2.2.3.1. There was something extraordinary in the look he now gave to Gideon. He looked on him and smiled at the objections he made. He strengthened him with such power as would soon enable him to answer those objections himself and make him ashamed that he had ever raised them. It was a look that "spoke volumes," as we say, as when Christ looked at Peter (Lk 22:61). It was a powerful look which unexpectedly breathed new life and light into Gideon's breast.

2.2.3.2. But there was much more in what he said to him:

2.2.3.2.1. He commissioned him to appear and act as the one who would rescue Israel. The few spiritually aware people in the nation, including Gideon, were now expecting such a person to be raised up. But now Gideon was told, "You are the one. *Go in this thy might* (v. 14), this strength with which you have been threshing wheat. Go and use it for a nobler purpose; *I will make thee a thresher of men.*" "*Go*, not in your own natural strength, but go in *this* power and strength which you have now received. *Go in the strength of the Lord God* (Ps 71:16). That is the power with which you must strengthen yourself."

2.2.3.2.2. He assured him of success. *Thou shalt save Israel from the hand of the Midianites* (v. 14). You will be not only an eyewitness to this event but also a glorious instrument in performing such wonders as your ancestors told you about. Gideon probably looked stunned at this strange and surprising power which was given to him.

2.2.4. Gideon modestly objected to this commission (v. 15): *O my Lord! Wherewith shall I save Israel?* This question shows that he is:

2.2.4.1. Distrusting of God and his power.

2.2.4.2. Inquisitive concerning the methods he has to use: "Lord, I labor under all imaginable disadvantages. If I have to do it, you must set things in motion." Or:

2.2.4.3. Humble, diffident, and self-denying. The angel has honored him, but notice in what lowly terms he speaks of himself: "My clan is comparatively poor and weak in Manasseh, and I am the least. I have the least honor and privilege *in my father's house* (v. 15). What can I possibly do? I am completely unqualified for such service and am unworthy of the honor." But God delights to advance the humble.

2.2.5. This objection was soon answered by a repetition of the promise that God would be with him (v. 16). "*Surely I will be with thee*, to direct and strengthen you. Be assured *thou shalt smite the Midianites as one man* (v. 16), as easily as if they were only one person and as effectively. All the thousands of Midian will be as if they had only one head, and you will be the one who will cut it off."

2.2.6. Gideon desires to have his faith confirmed concerning this commission. He therefore humbly asks this divine person, whoever he is:

2.2.6.1. To give him a sign (v. 17). In this dispensation of the Spirit, we are not now to expect physical signs, as Gideon wanted here, but we must fervently pray to God that, if *we have found grace in his sight*, he would show us a sign in our heart, by the powerful activity of his Spirit there, *fulfilling the work of faith* (2Th 1:11).

2.2.6.2. To give him a further and longer opportunity of conversation with him (v. 18). When the angel assures him he will stay for dinner with him, he intends:

- To show his grateful and generous respect for this stranger, and through him, for God, who sent him. Out of the little which the Midianites had left him, he would gladly spare enough to entertain a friend, especially a messenger from heaven.
- To see if he could find out who and what this extraordinary person was. What he brought out is called his *present* (v. 18). It is the same word that is used for a meat offering (grain offering). If the visitor ate it as ordinary meat, Gideon would think he was a human being, a prophet; if something else happened, as in fact it did, then Gideon would know him to be an angel.

2.2.7. The angel ordered him to take the meat and bread from the basket, place it on a hard and cold rock, and pour out the soup on it, which if he had brought it hot, would soon be cold. *Gideon did so* (v. 20), believing that the angel appointed it with an intention of giving him a sign.

2.2.7.1. He turned the *meat into an offering made by fire, of a sweet savour* (Lev 1:13).

2.2.7.2. He brought fire *out of the rock* to burn up this sacrifice. This was a sign that Gideon had *found grace in his sight* (v. 17; Ex 33:13). This acceptance of Gideon's sacrifice was evidence of the acceptance of his person and confirmed his commission.

2.2.7.3. The angel *departed out of his sight* (v. 21) immediately.

2.2.8. Although Gideon was no doubt confirmed in his faith by the signs, he was in a state of shock until God removed his fears.

2.2.8.1. Gideon realized he was in danger (v. 22): *When he perceived that he was an angel*, he cried out, *Alas, O Lord God!* Be merciful to me, I am ruined, for *I have seen an angel*. In this physical world, it is fearful to have any perceptible dealings with the spiritual world, to which we are very much strangers. Gideon's courage failed him now.

2.2.8.2. God speaks peace to him (v. 23). The Lord has *departed out of his sight* (v. 21). But although he must no longer walk by sight, he may still live by faith, for the Lord says to him, *Peace be unto thee, thou shalt not die* (v. 23).

2.3. Gideon set up a memorial to this vision in the form of an altar and called it *Jehovah-shalom* (v. 24), "The Lord is peace." This is:

- The title of the Lord who spoke to him. Or:
- The substance of what the Lord said to him: "The Lord spoke peace." Or:
- A prayer based on what he had said: "The Lord send peace" (v. 24, margin), that is, rest from the present troubles, for the good of the nation still lay closest to Gideon's heart.

Verses 25–32

Here:

1. Orders are given to Gideon to begin his leading role with the reformation of his father's house (vv. 25–26). The same night that he had seen God, when he was full of thoughts about what had happened, *The Lord said unto him* in a dream, "Do this." If we make God welcome, he will come again to us. Gideon was appointed:

1.1. To tear down Baal's altar, which it seems belonged to his father and was kept for use by either his own family or perhaps the whole town. He must likewise *cut down the grove that was by it* (v. 25).

1.2. To build an altar to God, *to Jehovah his God* (v. 26). God directs him to the place where he should build it, on the *top of the rock* (v. 26). The word here used for *the rock* on which the altar was to be built refers to a fortress or stronghold that was built, some think, to keep them safe from the Midianites. On this altar:

1.2.1. He was to offer sacrifices. He must offer two young bulls: his father's *young bullock, and the second bullock of seven years old* (v. 25). He was probably to offer the former for himself, the latter for the sins of the people (Lev 9:7), whom he was to rescue.

1.2.2. Baal's grove, image, or whatever it was that was the sanctity or beauty of the altar, must not only be burned but also be used as fuel for God's altar. God ordered Gideon to do this:

1.2.2.1. To see if he was zealous in his religious faith, which he must be proved to be before he went on the battlefield.

1.2.2.2. So that some steps might be taken toward Israel's reformation, steps which were to prepare the way for their rescue. Sin, the cause, must be removed, or else how could the trouble, which was the effect of sin, come to an end?

2. Gideon was *obedient to the heavenly vision* (Ac 26:19) (v. 27). The one who was to command the Israel of God must first *save his people from their sins* (Mt 1:21) and then save them from their enemies.

2.1. He had servants of his own, whom he could confide in.

2.2. He had no scruples about taking his father's young bull and offering it to God without his father's approval, because God, who expressly commanded him to do so, was more entitled to it than his father, and it was the greatest and best kindness he could do for his father, to prevent his sin.

2.3. He expected to incur the displeasure of his father's household by it; while he was sure of God's favor, he was not afraid of the anger of his fellows. But:

2.4. To prevent them from opposing it being done, he wisely chose to do it at night.

3. Gideon was brought into danger of his life for doing it (vv. 28–30):

3.1. What had been done was soon discovered, for the men of the town *rose early in the morning* (v. 28) to say their morning prayers at Baal's altar.

3.2. It was soon discovered who had done it.

3.3. After Gideon had been found guilty of the act, these immoral Israelites required his own father to hand him over: *Bring out thy son, that he may die* (v. 30).

4. Gideon was rescued from the hands of his persecutors by his own father (v. 31):

4.1. There were those who stood against Gideon, who wanted to have him put to death. Despite the severe judgment they were suffering at this time because of their idolatry, they still hated to change their behavior.

4.2. But then Gideon's father, Joash, stood up for him; he was one of the chief men of the town.

4.2.1. This Joash had patronized Baal's altar, but he now protected the one who had destroyed it:

4.2.1.1. Out of natural affection for his son. If Joash showed kindness to Baal, he showed even more kindness to his son. Or:

4.2.1.2. Out of a desire for the public peace. The mob was growing out of control, he feared, and so, some think, he acted to restrain the tumult. Or:

4.2.1.3. Out of a conviction that Gideon had done well. Let us do our duty, and then we may trust God with our safety.

4.2.2. Joash urged two things:

4.2.2.1. That it was absurd for them to champion the cause of Baal. It is bad to commit sin, but it is far worse to stand up for it, especially to defend Baal, that idol— whatever it is—that occupies the place in the heart which God should have.

4.2.2.2. That it was unnecessary for them to defend Baal. If he was not a god, as was claimed, there was no point in speaking for him. If he was a god, then he was well able to stand up for himself.

4.2.3. Gideon's father then gave him a new name (v. 32). He called him *Jerubbaal*: "Let Baal contend; let him stand against Gideon if he can. If he has anything to say for himself against his destroyer, then let him say it."

Verses 33–40

Here we have:

1. The descent which the enemies of Israel made on them (v. 33). A vast number of Midianites, Amalekites, and Arabians made their headquarters in the valley of Jezreel, in the heart of Manasseh's tribe, not far from Gideon's city. But it turned out that the limit of their sins had been reached; the time of judgment had come; they must now *cease to spoil* and *be spoiled* (Isa 33:1); they must stop destroying and be destroyed themselves. They are *gathered as sheaves to the floor* (Mic 4:12–13) for Gideon to thresh.

2. The preparation which Gideon makes to attack them in their camp (vv. 34–35):

2.1. God, by his Spirit, put life into Gideon: *The Spirit of the Lord came upon Gideon*; the word is "clothed"; the Spirit clothed him as a robe, put honor on him, clothed him as a coat of armor and defense. God will qualify and encourage those whom he calls to his work.

2.2. Gideon puts life into his neighbors by blowing his trumpet, and God works with him.

2.2.1. The men of Abiezer, though they had just been angry with him for tearing down the altar of Baal, and though they had condemned him to death as a criminal, were now convinced of their error and bravely came to help him.

2.2.2. Distant tribes, even Asher and Naphtali, which were far away and were strangers to him, obeyed his summons.

3. The signs which God satisfied Gideon with, to confirm both his own faith and that of his followers. Notice:

3.1. His request for a sign (vv. 36–37): "May I by this *know that thou wilt save Israel by my hand*: let *a fleece of wool*, spread in the open air, be *wet with the dew*, and may the ground around it be dry." The thrust of this is, *Lord, I believe, help thou my unbelief* (Mk 9:24). When he repeated his request for a second sign, the reverse of the former, he did it with a very humble apology, wanting to be saved from God's displeasure and anger, because it looked so much like self-willed and irrational distrust of God. God's favor must be sought with great reverence and a due sense of our distance.

3.2. God's gracious granting of his request. Here we see how sensitive God is to true believers even though they are weak. Gideon wanted to have *the fleece wet* and the *ground dry*; but then in case anyone should raise the objection, "It is natural for wool, if a little moisture falls, to take it in and retain it, and so there was nothing extraordinary in this"—though the quantity wrung out was sufficient to prevent such an objection—he wants the reverse to happen on the next night. He wants the ground to be wet and the fleece dry, and this is what happens. God is so willing to *give to the heirs of promise strong consolation* (Heb 6:17–18), even by two unchangeable things. He allows himself not only to be prevailed on by their bold requests, but also to deal with their doubts and dissatisfaction in the way they ask. Does Gideon want the dew of divine grace to come on himself especially? He can be assured that this will be so, because he sees the fleece is wet with dew. Does he want God to be as the dew to all Israel? Then he will see that all the ground is wet.

CHAPTER 7

This chapter shows us Gideon on the battlefield, commanding the army of Israel and routing the army of the Midianites. We are told here: 1. What directions God gave to Gideon to model his army, by which it was reduced to 300 soldiers (vv. 1–8). 2. What encouragement God gave Gideon to attack the enemy, by sending him secretly into their camp to hear a Midianite tell his dream (vv. 9–15). How Gideon formed his attack on the enemy's camp with his 300 soldiers, not to fight them but to frighten them (vv. 16–20). 3. The success of this attack: it put them to flight and totally routed them (vv. 21–25).

Verses 1–8

Here:

1. Gideon sets about fulfilling the role of a wise general. He pitched his camp near a famous well, so that his army might not become distressed for lack of water, and he gained the higher ground, which possibly might be some advantage to him, for the Midianites *were beneath him in the valley* (v. 1). This shows us that faith in God's promises must not slacken, but rather speed up, our endeavors.

2. The army consisted of 32,000 soldiers, a small army in comparison with what Israel might have raised, and very small in comparison with what the Midianites were now bringing onto the field. Gideon was ready to think they were too few, but God tells him they are *too many* (v. 2).

2.1. He wanted to silence them and exclude any boasting on their part. This is the reason given here by the One who knows the pride that is in the human heart: *Lest Israel vaunt themselves against me* (so that Israel may not boast against me) (v. 2).

2.2. God used two ways to reduce their numbers:

2.2.1. He ordered all those who were afraid or fearful to leave (v. 3). You would have thought there would be scarcely one Israelite against such an enemy as the Midianites and under such a leader as Gideon who would acknowledge that he was fearful, but more than two-thirds of them took advantage of this declaration, and went off. Some think that the oppression they had suffered for so long had broken their spirits. Others think—and we tend to agree with them—that an awareness of their own guilt deprived them of their courage. Their sin stared them in the face, and so they dared not look death in the face.

2.2.2. He directed the dismissal of all who remained except for 300 soldiers. He did this by a sign: *The people are yet too many* for me to make use of (v. 4). God said they are still *too many*, which may help us understand those circumstances which sometimes seem to weaken the church and its interests: its friends are too many, too powerful, and too wise for God to bring about his rescue, so that he may be *exalted in his own strength* (Ps 21:13). Gideon is ordered to bring his soldiers to the watering place, probably to the spring of Harod (v. 1) and the stream which flowed from it. Some—no doubt most of them—would get down on their knees to drink and put their mouths into the water as horses do. Others perhaps would not make such a formality of it, but be more like a dog lapping with its tongue, quickly taking up a little water in their hands, cooling their mouths with that, and then rushing away. Three hundred, and no more, were of this second kind and drank quickly, and it was those whom God told Gideon he would rout the Midianites with (v. 7). This second separation meant that the soldiers who were to be used had to be:

2.2.2.1. Strong, able to cope with being exhausted without complaining that they were thirsty or tired.

2.2.2.2. Quick, thinking it was taking a long time for them to fight the enemy, preferring the service of God

and their country to their own personal refreshment. It was a great test for the faith and courage of Gideon when God told him to let all the rest of the people except for these 300 *go every man to his place* (v. 7). So it was in this strange way that Gideon's army was cleansed, modeled, and reduced instead of being recruited. Let us see how this little, miserable regiment, on which the main thrust of the action must lie, was equipped and fitted out. Every soldier took responsibility for his own provisions. They *took victuals* (provisions) *in their hands* (v. 8). They left their bag and baggage behind, and each one had to carry his own provisions, which tested their faith, to see whether they could trust God when they had no more provisions with them than what they could carry. It was also a trial of their diligence, to see whether they could carry as much as they needed. This was truly living from hand to mouth. Every soldier became a trumpeter as if they had been going to play a sport rather than fight a battle.

Verses 9–15

After Gideon's army had been reduced in this way, he must decide either to fight by faith or not to fight at all. God knows this and so gives him recruits for his faith rather than recruits for his forces:

1. He provides him with a good foundation to build his faith on. Nothing but a word from God will be a solid basis for faith. Here is:

1.1. A word of command to authorize the action: *Arise, get thee down* with this handful of soldiers *unto the host* (camp) (v. 9).

1.2. A word of promise to assure him of success: *I have delivered it into thy hand* (v. 9); it is all your own. This word of the Lord probably came to him the same night as when he was anxious and worried about what would happen; *in the multitude of his thoughts within him these comforts did delight his soul* (Ps 94:19).

2. He provides him with a good support for his faith:

2.1. He ordered him to be his own spy, and now at the dead of night to go down privately into the camp of the Midianites to see what information he could gain: "*If thou fear to go down* to fight, go first of all only with your own servant (v. 10) and *hear what they say*" (v. 11). The suggestion is that he would hear what would greatly strengthen his faith. He must take with him *Phurah his servant* (v. 10), probably one of the ten who had helped him to tear down the altar of Baal.

2.2. This being so, God ordered him to see something that was discouraging. To be able to make out, perhaps in the moonlight, the vast numbers of the enemy (v. 12) was enough to frighten him. They were as numerous as grasshoppers or locusts, though they turned out no better than grasshoppers for strength and courage. The camels were innumerable, as many as grains of sand. But:

2.3. He caused them to hear what was a very good sign for him. He overheard two enemy soldiers, who were friends, talking:

2.3.1. One of them tells the other his dream: he saw a round loaf of barley bread rolling down the hill into the camp of the Midianites, he says, and "I thought this rolling cake struck one of our tents with such force that it overturned the tent, forced down the stakes, and broke the ropes all at once and buried its inhabitants" (v. 13).

2.3.2. The other friend tries to interpret this dream: *This is nothing else save the sword of Gideon* (v. 14). Gideon, who had threshed corn for his family and made cakes for his friend (6:11–19), was appropriately represented by a loaf: he and his army were as insignificant as a loaf made of a little flour, as inferior as a barley loaf—hurriedly gotten ready like a loaf quickly baked on coals—and as unlikely to conquer this great army as a loaf of bread was to overthrow a tent. It was also evidence that the enemy was quite discouraged and that the name of Gideon had become so formidable to them that it even disturbed their sleep.

2.4. Gideon was greatly encouraged. He was pleased to hear himself compared to a loaf of barley bread when he learned that it was to bring about such great things. He gave the glory for it to God, and in a short exclamation thanked God for the victory he was now certain of and for the encouragement God had given that he should expect it. He gave his friends a share in the encouragement he had received: *Arise, prepare to march immediately; the Lord has delivered Midian into your hand* (v. 14).

Verses 16–22

Here is:

1. The fright which Gideon gave the camp of Midian at the dead of night, for the intention was that those who had terrorized Israel for so long should themselves be routed and destroyed purely by terror. Gideon:

1.1. Divided his army, small as it was, into three companies (v. 16), one of which he himself commanded (v. 19).

1.2. Ordered them all to do as he did (v. 17). This is like the word of command which our Lord Jesus, the author of our salvation, gives his soldiers, for he has *left us an example* (1Pe 2:21), with a command to follow it: *As I do, so shall you do* (v. 17).

1.3. Made his descent at night, when the Midianites felt secure and least expected an attack, and when the small-ness of his army would not be discovered. At night, every shock is very frightening. He equipped each soldier in his army with a trumpet in his right hand, and a torch in it in his left. The small number of his soldiers was advantageous for his plan. Gideon managed to strike terror into this army in three ways:

1.3.1. With a loud noise. Every soldier must blow his trumpet in the most terrible way and smash his clay jar to pieces at the same time.

1.3.2. With a great blaze. The lit torches were hidden in the jars, and then because they were all suddenly brought out together, they would make a dazzling display. Perhaps they used these to set on fire some of the tents on the outside of the camp.

1.3.3. With a great shout. Every soldier must cry out, "For the Lord and for Gideon," which is how some think v. 18 should be read, for there *the sword* is not in the origi-nal, although it is in v. 20, *The sword of the Lord, and of Gideon.* The sword of the Lord is the key to the success of the sword of Gideon, but the sword of Gideon must still be used, always subordinate to God.

2. The method that was used to defeat the Midianites, which may be referred to as a type of the destruction of the Devil's kingdom in the world by the preaching of the eternal Gospel, the sounding of that trumpet, and the hold-ing out of the light from of jars of clay (2Co 4:6–7). In this way, God chose the *foolish things of the world to confound* (shame) *the wise* (1Co 1:27), a loaf of barley bread to over-throw the tents of Midian, that the *excellency of the power* (this all-surpassing power) *might be only of God* (2Co 4:7). The Gospel is a sword, not in the hand, but in the mouth.

3. The wonderful success of this attack. Gideon's sol-diers carried out their orders and *stood every man in his place round about the camp* (v. 21), sounding their trum-pets to encourage one another to fight and holding out their torches to light the Midianites to their destruction. Notice how the intentions were fulfilled:

3.1. They feared the Israelites. *All the host* were immedi-ately afraid. They had reason to suspect that all those trum-peters and torchbearers were leading a very great army. But there was more of a supernatural power that impressed this terror on them. God himself brought it on. We see here the power of the imagination, how much it may become a ter-ror at times, just as it is a pleasure at other times.

3.2. They turned on one another: *The Lord set every man's sword against his fellow* (v. 22). God often makes the enemies of his church instruments that destroy one another.

3.3. They ran for their lives.

Verses 23–25

Here we have the culmination of this glorious victory:

1. Gideon's soldiers who had been dismissed came together again and hotly pursued those whom they had not dared face. Those who were fearful and afraid to fight (v. 3) now took heart when the worst was over and were ready enough to distribute the spoils, even though they had been hesitant in making the attack.

2. The Ephraimites were called by Gideon and came unanimously. They secured the crossing places over the Jordan at several different fords to cut off the enemies' retreat into their own country.

3. Two of the chief commanders of the camp of Mid-ian were taken and killed by the Ephraimites on this side of the Jordan (v. 25). Their names perhaps showed their nature: *Oreb* means "a raven," and *Zeeb* means "a wolf."

CHAPTER 8

This chapter gives us a further account of Gideon's vic-tory over the Midianites, with the remainder of the story of his life and leadership. 1. Gideon wisely pacifies the Ephraimites (vv. 1–3). 2. He bravely pursues the Midian-ites (vv. 4, 10–12). He justly rebukes the rudeness of the people of Succoth and Peniel (vv. 5–9 and vv. 13–17). 3. He honorably kills the two kings of Midian (vv. 18–21). 4. After all this he modestly declines to rule Israel (vv. 22–23). But he foolishly indulges the superstitious whims of his people by setting up an ephod in his own town (vv. 24–27). He kept the country at peace for forty years (v. 28). 5. He died in honor and left a large family behind him (vv. 29–32). But both he and his God were soon forgotten by an ungrateful Israel (vv. 33–35).

Verses 1–3

No sooner had the Midianites, the common enemy, been subdued than the children of Israel began to quar-rel among themselves. When the Ephraimites brought the heads of Oreb and Zeeb to Gideon as general, they picked a quarrel with him and became very angry with him:

1. Their accusations were selfish and unreasonable: *Why didst thou not call us when thou wentest to fight with the Midianites?* (v. 1). Ephraim was very jealous of Manasseh, and wanted to make sure Manasseh did not at any time overshadow their honor. How unjust their quarrel was with Gideon! But:

1.1. Gideon was called by God, and neither took the honor for himself nor himself gave out honors, but left matters to God to do everything as he wanted. The result was that in this quarrel the Ephraimites dishonored God's leadership.

1.2. Why had the Ephraimites not offered themselves willingly in the service? The situation produced its own call, and they did not need to wait for a special call from Gideon. Cowards may appear brave when the danger has passed, but it is those who think only of their own reputation who do not test their courage when danger is near.

2. Gideon's answer was intended not so much to justify himself as to please and quiet them (vv. 2 – 3). He answered them:

2.1. With a great deal of humility. In so doing, he won as much true honor now by the command he had over his own passions as he had won earlier in his victory over the Midianites.

2.2. With a great deal of modesty, exalting what they have done above his own: *Is not the gleaning of the grapes of Ephraim*, who picked up the stragglers of the enemy and destroyed those who escaped, *better than the vintage* (full grape harvest) *of Abiezer* — is not Ephraim's action a greater honor to them, and better service to the country, than the honor Gideon won in the first attack he made on the Midianites? Making the most of a victory is often more honorable, and of greater significance, than winning it. Gideon shows us that humility is the best way of dealing with jealousy and that it is also the best way of dealing with conflict.

3. What was the outcome of this dispute? The Ephraimites had *chidden with* (criticized) *him sharply* (v. 1), but Gideon's *soft answer turned away their wrath* (Pr 15:1).

Verses 4 – 17

In these verses we have:

1. Gideon as a brave general pursuing the remaining Midianites. It seems that the two kings of Midian were better prepared for an escape than the others, and they, together with 15,000 men, crossed the Jordan before the crossing places could be secured by the Ephraimites, and they made their way toward their own country. But Gideon thought he was not fully carrying out his orders to save Israel if he allowed them to escape.

1.1. His determination was exemplary under very great disadvantages and discouragements:

1.1.1. He took with him only his 300 soldiers. He expected more from 300 soldiers supported by that particular promise than from many more thousands supported only by their own bravery.

1.1.2. They were *faint, yet pursuing* (v. 4).

1.1.3. He met with discouragement from his own people. If those who should help us to fulfill our duty turn out to hinder us, let this not turn us away from pursuing what we believe to have come from God.

1.1.4. He made a very long march by *the way of those that dwelt in tents* (v. 11). Now he found it an advantage to have his 300 soldiers who could bear hunger, thirst, and hard work.

1.2. His success encouraged his determination and diligence in pursuing a good cause. He routed the army (v. 11) and took the two kings prisoners (v. 12).

2. Gideon as a righteous judge rebuking the defiance of the disaffected Israelites, the people of Succoth and the people of Peniel.

2.1. Their crime was great. Gideon, with a handful of weak troops, was pursuing the enemy to complete Israel's rescue. His way led him through the town of Succoth first and afterward to Peniel. He begged some necessary food for his soldiers, who were ready to faint from hunger. He asked very humbly but boldly: *Give, I pray you, loaves of bread unto the people that follow me* (v. 5). The request

would have been reasonable if they had been poor travelers in distress. But considering that they were soldiers whom God had highly honored and to whom Israel was greatly indebted, nothing could be more just than that their brothers should give them the best provisions their town could afford. But the officials of Succoth neither *feared God nor regarded man* (Lk 18:2). For:

2.1.1. They had contempt for God. They refused to respond to the just request of the one whom God had raised up to save them. They were very willing to believe that the remaining forces of Midian, which they had now seen march through their country, would be too hard for Gideon.

2.1.2. They had no compassion on their brothers. They were as devoid of love as they were of faith and would not even give morsels of bread to those who were ready to die. The people of Peniel gave the same answer to the same request, defying *the sword of the Lord and of Gideon* (7:18).

2.2. The warning he gave them of the punishment for their crime was reasonable:

2.2.1. He did not punish them immediately. He did not want to do it in the heat of passion, but:

2.2.2. He told them how he would punish them (vv. 7, 9), to show the confidence he had of success in God's strength, and so that they might have second thoughts, repent of their foolishness, and send him help and supplies. God gives notice of danger and opportunity to repent so that sinners may *flee from the wrath to come* (Mt 3:7).

2.3. The warning was ignored, and so the punishment, even though it was severe, was also just:

2.3.1. The officials of Succoth were first made examples of. He punished them with thorns and briers, but not, it would seem, to death. With these he tormented their bodies and instructed their minds; with these *he taught the men of Succoth* (v. 16). The correction he gave them was not intended to destroy them, but to be a wholesome discipline for them, to make them wiser and better for the future. He "made them know," so the word is; he made them know both themselves and their foolishness, God and their duty. This shows us that many are taught with the briers and thorns of suffering who will not learn any other way.

2.3.2. The condemnation of the people of Peniel comes next:

2.3.2.1. He *beat down their tower*, in which they trusted. Perhaps they had scornfully advised Gideon and his soldiers to keep themselves safe in the tower rather than pursue the Midianites.

2.3.2.2. He *slew the men of the city* who had abusively taunted him the most, to frighten the rest, and *so he taught the men of Penuel*.

Verses 18 – 21

The kings of Midian must now be judged:

1. They are accused of the murder of Gideon's brothers some time before at Mount Tabor. When the children of Israel, for fear of the Midianites, had made themselves *dens in the mountains* (6:2), those young men probably took shelter in that mountain, where they were found by these two kings, and they were barbarically killed in cold blood.

2. Being found guilty of this murder by their own confession, by him must *their blood be shed* (Ge 9:6), even though they were kings.

3. The execution was done by Gideon himself with his own hand, because he was the avenger of blood. He told his son to kill them, but:

3.1. The young man wanted to be excused *because he was yet a youth* (v. 20).

3.2. The prisoners themselves wanted Gideon to excuse his son (v. 21): "You are at your full strength. Your son has not yet reached that point, and so you are to be the executioner."

Verses 22–28

Here is:

1. Gideon's commendable modesty after his great victory, in refusing to be Israel's ruler, which the people wanted him to be.

1.1. It was honorable of them to offer it: *Rule thou over us, for thou hast delivered us* (v. 22).

1.2. It was honorable of him to refuse it: *I will not rule over you* (v. 23). What he wanted to do was not to rule them but to serve them. He wanted to make them secure, happy, and at ease rather than make himself great or honorable. "*The Lord shall* still *rule over you* and designate your judges by the special appointment of his own Spirit, as he has done." This shows:

- His modesty and the lowly opinion he had of himself and his own character.
- His godliness and the high opinion he had of God's rule.

2. Gideon's mistaken zeal to remember this victory forever by making an ephod out of the best of the plunder. He asked the Israelites to give him the earrings from their share of the plunder. He himself added the plunder he took from the kings of Midian. He made an ephod out of this (v. 27):

2.1. The act seems commendable enough, and Gideon may well have intended by it that a memorial of such a divine victory would be preserved in the judge's own town. But it was ill advised to make a sacred ephod a memorial. We want to put the best interpretation on the actions of good people, and we are sure Gideon was such a person. But we have reason to suspect that this ephod had, as they usually had, *teraphim* (idols) attached to it (Hos 3:4), and that, having an altar already built by divine appointment (6:26)—which he mistakenly imagined he might still use for sacrifice—he intended this to be used when he wanted to inquire of the Lord in doubtful cases. This is the view of Dr. Spencer. Each tribe now had its leadership very much within itself, and they were too inclined to keep their worship local. We read very little of Shiloh, and the ark there, in all the story of the Judges. We can learn from this that many are led into false ways by one false step of a good person. The beginning of sin, particularly idolatry and worship according to merely human fancy, without divine authority, *is as the letting forth of water* (Pr 17:14), and such worship has been found in the corruptions of the Church of Rome. It is better therefore to *leave it off before it be meddled with* (Pr 17:14).

2.2. It became a snare to Gideon himself, diminishing his zeal for the house of God in his old age, and an even greater snare to his family, who were drawn into sin by it, and it turned out to be the ruin of the family.

3. Gideon's fortunate role in giving Israel peace (v. 28). Although Gideon would not assume the honor and power of a king, he led the people as a judge and did everything he could for them. The result was that *the country was in quietness forty years* (v. 28). Up to then, the times of Israel had been reckoned by forties. Othniel judged forty years, Ehud eighty—just two forties—Barak forty, and now Gideon forty; Providence so arranged matters to call to mind the forty years of their wandering in the wilderness. After these, Eli led Israel for forty years (1Sa 4:18), Samuel and Saul forty (Ac 13:21), David forty, and Solomon forty. Forty years is about one generation.

Verses 29–35

We have here the conclusion of the story of Gideon:

1. He withdrew to the house he had lived in before his advancement and quietly lived there (v. 29). When the action was over, that brave soldier who was suddenly called from the plow to command the army returned to his plow again.

2. His family was multiplied.

3. He died in honor at a good old age.

4. After his death the people became corrupt and unfaithful to God. As soon as Gideon had died, they *went a whoring after Baalim*, they prostituted themselves to the Baals (v. 33). False worship made way for false gods. They now chose a new god (5:8), a god of a new name, *Baal-berith* (v. 33), a goddess, according to some; Berith, some think, was Berytus, the place where the Phoenicians worshiped this idol. The name means "the Lord of a covenant." Perhaps he was so called because his worshipers joined themselves by covenant to him, in imitation of Israel's covenanting with God, for the Devil apes God. Israel's rebellion toward idolatry showed:

- Great ingratitude to God (v. 34). *They remembered not the Lord.*
- Great ingratitude to Gideon (v. 35). For the *goodness he had shown unto Israel*, they ought to have been kind to his family when he was gone, but Israel did not show this kindness to Gideon's family. It is no wonder if those who forget their God also forget their friends.

CHAPTER 9

The apostasy of Israel after the death of Gideon is punished by internal strife among themselves. This chapter is an account of the usurpation and tyranny of Abimelech, who was an evil son of Gideon; we would prefer to call him this rather than describe him as his natural son: he was so unlike him. We are told: 1. How he thrust himself forward into the government at Shechem (vv. 1–6). 2. How his condemnation was read in a parable by Jotham, Gideon's youngest son (vv. 7–21). 3. The conflict between Abimelech and his friends the Shechemites (vv. 22–41). How this ended in the destruction of the Shechemites (vv. 42–49). 4. Finally, the destruction of Abimelech himself (vv. 50–57).

Verses 1–6

Here we are told how Abimelech gained a position of authority and made himself great. His mother had perhaps instilled into him some very ambitious thoughts, and the name his father gave him, because it carried royalty with it, may have helped to puff up these sparks. He had no call from God to undertake this honor as his father did, nor was there any need at that time for a judge to save Israel as there had been when his father was advanced. Notice:

1. How cunningly he gained his mother's relatives to be on his side. Shechem was a significant city in the tribe of Ephraim. Joshua had held his last assembly there. If only that city would support him and establish him, then he thought matters would go far in his favor. But no one would have dreamed of making such a man a king unless he had dreamed of it himself. We see here:

1.1. How he wheedled his way into their choice (vv. 2–3). He was so evil as to suggest that because Gideon had left seventy sons, they intended to keep in their hands the power which their father had. "Now," he says, "it would be better if you had one king rather than so many. *Remember that I am your bone and your flesh* (your flesh and blood)" (v. 2). The plan took root immediately. The leaders of Shechem were pleased to think of their city as a royal city and as the capital of Israel, and so they "*inclined to follow him; for they said, He is our brother* (v. 3). If he is advanced, then that will be to our advantage."

1.2. How he gained money from them to cover the costs of his claim (v. 4): *They gave him seventy pieces of silver*, money from the house of Baal-Berith, that is, the public treasury, which, out of respect for their idol, they placed in his temple to be protected by him. How unfit Abimelech was to rule over Israel, and how unlikely he was to defend them. Instead of restraining and punishing idolatry, he received money from an idol!

1.3. The soldiers he enlisted. He hired into his service *vain and light persons* (v. 4), reckless adventurers who were the scum of the country, scoundrels with broken fortunes, foolish people who led dissolute lives.

2. How cruelly he removed his father's sons:

2.1. The first thing he did with the rabble he led was to kill all his brothers at once, publicly, and in cold blood, all seventy of them, except one who escaped. All were killed on one stone. How the power of ambition turns people into wild animals! How dangerous is the honor of high birth!

2.2. When the way had been made open for Abimelech's election, the citizens of Shechem proceeded to choose him as their king (v. 6). God was not consulted as to whether they should have any king at all, much less who it should be. But:

2.2.1. The Shechemites aided and abetted him in murdering his brothers (v. 24), and then they *made him king* (v. 6). His evil was rewarded with a crown.

2.2.2. The rest of the Israelites were so very foolish as to just sit by and remain unconcerned. It is for this that they are accused of ingratitude (8:35): *Neither showed they kindness to the house of Jerubbaal.*

Verses 7–21

Only Jotham, the youngest son of Gideon, who by God's special providence had escaped the general destruction of his family (v. 5), dealt plainly with the Shechemites. Jotham did not set about raising an army out of the other cities of Israel—he only gave a faithful rebuke to the Shechemites and a reasonable warning of the fatal consequences.

1. His introduction is serious: *Hearken unto me, you men of Shechem, that God may hearken unto you* (v. 7).

2. His parable is clever—that when the trees wanted to choose a king, the government was offered to those valuable trees, the olive, the fig tree, and the vine, but they refused it, choosing to serve rather than rule, to do good rather than exercise power. But when the same suggestion was made to the *bramble* (thornbush) (v. 14), that bush accepted it with boastful exultation.

2.1. In this, he was applauding the generous modesty of Gideon and the other judges who came before him, and perhaps also of the sons of Gideon, who had declined to accept the state and power of kings when they might have had them. It similarly shows that it is generally wise and good people who are inclined to refuse advancement and choose to be useful rather than to be great.

2.1.1. There was no need at all for the trees to choose a king. Nor was there any need for Israel to talk of setting a king over them, for *the Lord was their king.*

2.1.2. When they had it in their thoughts to choose a king, they did not offer the government to the stately cedar or the lofty pine, which are only for show and to provide shade. They are not useful in other ways until they are cut down. But the leadership position was offered to the fruit trees, the vine and the olive. Those who bear fruit for the public good are justly respected and honored.

2.1.3. The reason which all these fruit trees gave for their refusal was much the same. The olive pleads (v. 9), *Should I leave my fatness* (give up my oil)? And the vine, *Should I leave my wine* (v. 13), with which both God and people are served and honored? Oil and wine were both used at God's altars and at the meals people enjoyed. *And shall I leave my sweetness, saith the fig tree, and my good fruit* (v. 11), *and go to be promoted* (hold sway) *over the trees?* Or, as the margin reads it, "go up and down for other trees." It is suggested:

2.1.3.1. That leadership roles involve people in a great deal of both hard work and anxious care.

2.1.3.2. That those who are advanced to positions of public trust and power must decide to give up their private interests and advantages and sacrifice them to the good of the community.

2.1.3.3. That those who are advanced to positions of honor and dignity are in great danger of losing their oil and fruitfulness. Promotion is likely to make people become proud and lazy. Their usefulness is spoiled, and this is a good reason why those who want to do good should be afraid of becoming too great.

2.2. He exposes the ridiculous ambition of Abimelech, whom he compares to the bramble (thornbush) or thistle (v. 14). The thornbush is a worthless plant, not to be numbered among the trees. It is useless and fruitless; in fact it is harmful and troublesome. It scratches, tears, and causes trouble. It began with the curse, and its destiny is to be burned. Abimelech was such a one, but he was still chosen to the leadership *by the trees, by all the trees* (v. 14). Let us not think it strange if we *see folly set in great dignity* (Ecc 10:6), the *vilest men exalted* (Ps 12:8), and people blind to their own interests in their choice of guides for themselves.

3. His application is very clear and detailed:

3.1. He reminds them of the many good services his father had done for them (v. 17).

3.2. He highlights their unkindness to his father's family. They had not *done to him according to the deserving of his hands* (v. 16). Gideon had left many sons who were an honor to his name and family, but Abimelech and the Shechemites had barbarically murdered them. Only one son was left, *the son of his maidservant, whom all* (v. 18) who had any respect for Gideon's honor would try to cover up. But he was the one they made king.

3.3. He leaves it to the outcome of events to determine whether they had done well.

3.3.1. If they were successful for a long time in their sinful ways, he would allow them to say they had done well (v. 19). But:

3.3.2. If they had, as he was sure they had, dealt wrongly in this matter, then let them never expect to prosper (v. 20).

4. After Jotham had given them this rebuke, he fled and ran for his life (v. 21). And because he was afraid of Abimelech, he lived in exile in some obscure, remote place.

Verses 22–49

Abimelech reigned for three years, after a sort, without any disturbance. It is not said that he judged Israel or did any service at all for his country, but he enjoyed the title and dignity of a king for that time. But the triumphing of the wicked is short. The destruction of these confederates in their evil ways came from the righteous hand of God. *He sent an evil spirit between Abimelech and the Shechemites* (v. 23), that is, they grew bitter and jealous of each another and distrusting toward each other. This was from God. He allowed that great troublemaker the Devil to sow seeds of discord between them. He *is an evil spirit* (v. 23), whom God not only restrains but also sometimes uses to serve his own purposes. Their own desires were evil spirits. Such desires are demons in the human heart, and fights and quarrels come from them. God gave Abimelech and the Shechemites up to these, and so he may be said to have *sent the evil spirits between them* (v. 23). When human sin becomes a punishment, although God is not the author of the sin, the punishment still comes from him. The Shechemites who supported Abimelech's claims, who aided and abetted him in his bloody plan and acknowledged their part in the deed by making him king after he had done it, must also fall with him; in fact they will fall by him and fall first.

1. The Shechemites began to insult Abimelech.

1.1. They *dealt treacherously with him* (v. 23). It is not said that they repented of their sin in acknowledging him.

1.2. They aimed to seize him when he was at his home at Arumah (v. 41). Expecting him to come to the city, they *set liers* (an ambush) *in wait for him* (v. 25). When those who positioned themselves there discovered that he was not coming, they took the opportunity of robbing travelers.

1.3. They received a man named Gaal and set him as their leader in opposition to Abimelech (v. 26). This Gaal is said to be the son of *Ebed*, which means "a servant." As Abimelech was the son of a servant by his mother's side, so was Gaal by his father's. Here was one thornbush fighting against another. Gaal was a bold and ambitious man, so he went over to the Shechemites to stir up trouble and fan the flames of discord, and they *put their confidence in him* (v. 26).

1.4. They treated Abimelech's name with as much contempt as they could (v. 27). They *went into the house of their god* to celebrate their feast of ingathering, and there *they did eat, and drink, and cursed Abimelech*, praying to their idol to destroy him. That very temple from which they had taken money to set him up as their ruler was the one they now met in to curse him and plan his destruction.

1.5. They pleased themselves with Gaal's boastful defiance of Abimelech (vv. 28–29). They loved to hear that impudent upstart speak scornfully:

- Of Abimelech.
- Of his good father, Gideon, in similar terms: *Is not he the son of Jerubbaal?* (v. 28).
- Of his prime minister of state, *Zebul his officer, and ruler of the city* (vv. 28, 30). Gaal did not aim to recover Shechem's liberty, only to change their tyrant: *O that this people were under my hand* (command)*!* (v. 29). This pleased the Shechemites, who were now as sick of Abimelech as they had ever been fond of him. Those who have no conscience also have no commitment.

2. Abimelech turned all his force on them and quickly destroyed them. Notice the steps of their overthrow:

2.1. The plans were betrayed to Abimelech by Zebul, his confidant, the ruler of the city, who continued to be on his side. *His anger was kindled* (v. 30). Abimelech thinks it best that he should march his forces into the neighborhood at night. How could the Shechemites hope to be successful in their attempt when the ruler of their city was on the side of the enemy?

2.2. Gaal, who led their faction, having been betrayed by Zebul, Abimelech's confidant, was then scornfully ridiculed by him. When, in the morning, Gaal noticed Abimelech's army approaching and asked Zebul about it, Zebul said, "It *is* but *the shadow of the mountains* which you take to be *an* army." He intended by this:

2.2.1. To ridicule him.

2.2.2. To detain him while the forces of Abimelech were coming closer. Then Zebul used another way to ridicule him, rebuking Gaal with what Gaal himself had said just a day or two earlier, in contempt of Abimelech (v. 38). Now Zebul, in Abimelech's name, challenges him: *go out, and fight with them* (v. 38), if you dare.

2.3. Abimelech routed Gaal's forces that came out of the city (vv. 39–40).

2.4. That night Zebul drove Gaal out of the city along with the party he had brought with him into Shechem (v. 41), sending him to the place from which he had come.

2.5. The next day, Abimelech attacked the city and totally destroyed it because of its treacherous dealings with him. He decided to follow up his blow and punish them completely for their treachery:

2.5.1. He received information that the people of Shechem had come out *into the field* (v. 42) to do the work of plowing and sowing. Others think they went out onto the battlefield; although Gaal was driven out, they would not lay down their arms.

2.5.2. Abimelech himself, with a strong detachment of troops, cut off the communication lines between them and the city. He then sent two companies of troops, who were too strong for them, and those troops killed them all, and *ran on those that were in the fields and slew them*.

2.5.3. He then attacked the city itself, and scattered salt all over it so that it might remain a lasting monument of the punishment of treachery. Yet Abimelech did not succeed in making its desolation last forever, for it was rebuilt later and became such a significant place that all Israel came there to make Rehoboam king (1Ki 12:1).

2.6. Those who had withdrawn into the stronghold of their idol temple were all destroyed there. These are called *the men of the tower of Shechem* (vv. 46–47), some stronghold that belonged to the city but was situated some distance from it. But what they hoped would turn out for their good proved to be a snare and trap for them, as those who run to idols for shelter will certainly find. All that were in it were either burned in the fire set by Abimelech and his soldiers or suffocated by the smoke. What wild ways people dream up to destroy one another! These cruel fights and quarrels come from their evil desires. About 1,000 men and women died in this fire, many of whom were probably totally unconnected with the quarrel between Abimelech and the Shechemites but nevertheless came to such a wretched end in this civil war. People with factious, turbulent spirits do not suffer alone in their sin, but involve many more who simply follow them and suffer the same disaster as them.

Verses 50–57

Thebez was a small city, probably not far from Shechem, and was dependent on it and in confederacy with it. Now:

1. Abimelech attempted to destroy this city (v. 50). He drove all the inhabitants of the city into the castle or citadel (v. 51).

2. He himself was destroyed in the attempt, having his brains knocked out with a millstone (v. 53). Three circumstances are significant in the death of Abimelech:

2.1. That he was killed with a stone, as he had killed his brothers all *upon one stone* (v. 18).

2.2. That he had his skull broken. This was vengeance aimed at the guilty head which had worn the usurped crown.

2.3. That the stone was thrown on him by a woman (v. 53). Nothing troubled him so much as this, that it should be said, *A woman slew him* (v. 54). Notice:

2.3.1. His foolish pride, in taking this small disgrace so much to heart. He took no care of his precious soul; he was not concerned about what would become of that. He uttered no prayer to God for mercy. All he was concerned about was patching up his shattered reputation, whereas his shattered skull could not be patched up. "O let it never be said that such a powerful man as Abimelech was killed by a mere woman!"

2.3.2. His foolish plan to avoid this disgrace, although in fact nothing could be more ridiculous. He asked his own servant to strike his sword through him, not to get rid of his pain more quickly, but so *that men say not, A woman slew him* (v. 54).

3. The outcome of everything is that Abimelech is killed:

3.1. Israel's peace was restored, and an end was put to this civil war.

3.2. God's justice was glorified (vv. 56–57). Although evil may prosper for a while, it will not succeed forever.

CHAPTER 10

In this chapter, we have: 1. The peaceful times Israel enjoyed under two judges, Tola and Jair (vv. 1–5). 2. The troublesome times which followed: Israel's sin that brought them into trouble (v. 6) and the trouble itself (vv. 7–9). 3. Their repentance and humiliation, their prayers and reformation, and the mercy they found with God (vv. 10–16); preparation made for their rescue from their oppressors (vv. 17–18).

Verses 1–5

The reigns of the two judges Tola and Jair were quiet and peaceful. They did not play conspicuous parts, and they take up only a little space in this history. But no doubt they were both raised up by God to serve their country in the position of judges, not claiming, as Abimelech had, the grand status of kings, nor, like him, assuming an honor which was not theirs by right, but having received the honor of their position by being called by God to it.

1. Concerning Tola it is said that he rose after Abimelech to save Israel (v. 1). God appointed this good man to rise in order to reform the abuses, put down the idolatry, pacify the turmoil, and heal the wounds caused by Abimelech's usurping.

2. Jair was a Gileadite, as was his successor Jephthah, and both came from that half tribe of Manasseh which lay on the other side of the Jordan. What is significant about Jair is the growth and honor of his family: *He had thirty sons* (v. 4). And:

2.1. They had good positions, for they *rode on thirty ass colts* (v. 4); that is, they were itinerant judges who, as deputies to their father, rode from place to place to administer justice on their different circuits.

2.2. They had good possessions, each one a town, from those which were called, from their ancestor of the same name as their father, *Havoth-jair,* "the settlements or villages of Jair"; but they are called *cities* (v. 4). Villages become cities to a happy mind.

Verses 6–9

While those two judges, Tola and Jair, led the affairs of Israel, things went well, but afterward:

1. Israel returned to their idolatry.

1.1. They worshiped many gods: not only their old demons the Baals and Ashtoreths, which the Canaanites had worshiped, but also the gods of Aram, Sidon, Moab, Ammon, and the Philistines—as if they wanted to announce their foolishness to all their neighbors. It looks as if the chief trade of Israel had become to import gods from every country. It is hard to say whether it was more ungodly or unwise to do this. Those nations which by their evil ways they tried to make friends with became their enemies and oppressors by the righteous judgments of God.

1.2. They did not even allow the God of Israel to be one of those many gods they worshiped but totally rejected him. Those who think they can serve both God and mammon will soon come to completely abandon God and serve only mammon. If God does not have all the heart, he will soon have none of it.

2. God renewed his judgments on them, bringing them under the power of oppressing enemies. God had appointed that if any of the cities of Israel were to return to idolatry, then the rest should make war on them and destroy them (Dt 13:12–18; etc.). God brought the neighboring nations on them to discipline them for turning away from him. The oppression of Israel by the Ammonites, the descendants of Lot, was very long—it continued eighteen years—and very painful. They began by attacking those tribes that were closest to them on the other side of the Jordan, here called *the land of the Amorites* (v. 8) because the Israelites had fallen into such sin, and had made themselves so like the other nations, that they had in a way become perfect Amorites (Eze 16:3). But the Ammonites gradually pressed forward, came over the Jordan, and invaded Judah, Benjamin, and Ephraim (v. 9); these were three of the most famous tribes of Israel, but when they abandoned God, they were trampled on, and they could not make any headway against the invading forces.

Verses 10–18

Here is:

1. A humble confession which Israel makes to God in their distress (v. 10). They confess their sins of omission, for that is where their sin began: "We have abandoned our God"; and they confess their sins of commission: "We have served the Baals, which was very foolish, treacherous, and evil."

2. A humbling message which God then sends to Israel, though it is not certain whether it comes by an angel (2:1) or by a prophet (6:8). Now in this message:

2.1. He rebukes them for their great ingratitude. He reminded them of the great things he had done for them. In his justice, God had corrected them, and in his mercy he had rescued them, and so they might reasonably be expected either through fear or love to remain close to him and his service.

2.2. He shows them how it would be just of him now to abandon them to destruction, by abandoning them to *gods that they had served* (v. 13). To wake them up to repent thoroughly and reform their ways, he lets them see:

2.2.1. Their foolishness in serving the Baals. "*Go, and cry unto the gods which you have chosen* (v. 14); see what they can do for you now." This shows us that in true repentance it is necessary that we be fully convicted that all those things we have idolized are completely insufficient to help us. We must be convinced that neither the physical pleasures we love nor the wealth of the world that we covet can truly satisfy us. We cannot be happy or at ease anywhere except in God.

2.2.2. Their misery and danger in abandoning God.

3. A humble submission which Israel then made to God's justice, with a humble request for his mercy (v. 15). They not only repeat their confession, *We have sinned* (v. 15), but:

- They surrender themselves to God's justice: *Do thou unto us whatsoever seemeth good unto thee* (v. 15).
- They ask for God's mercy.

4. A blessed reformation put into action. They produced fruits in keeping with repentance (v. 16): *They put away the* "gods of strangers," as the word means literally, foreign or strange gods; they *served the Lord*. This is true repentance not only for sin, but also from sin.

5. God's gracious mercy in coming to them, which is expressed very tenderly (v. 16): *His soul was grieved for the misery of Israel.* As he wants to put himself into the relationship of a father to his people who are in covenant with him, so also he wants to show his goodness to them by the compassion of a father toward his children. He is the Father of lights and also the Father of mercies.

6. Everything now working toward their rescue from the Ammonites' oppression (vv. 17–18). God said, "I will rescue you no more," but now they are not what they were; they are different. They are new people, and he will rescue them now.

6.1. The Ammonites are hardened to their own destruction. They gather together in one body so that they may be destroyed at one fell swoop (Rev 16:16).

6.2. The Israelites act vigorously for their own rescue. They also gather together (v. 17). During their eighteen years' oppression, as in the former times of their subjection, they had been oppressed by their enemies because they would not join with one another. Each family, clan, city, town, or tribe stood by itself and acted independently, and so they all became an easy target to the oppressors, because they lacked a proper sense of a common interest to join together. Whenever they did act together, however, they did well, as they did here. When God's Israel becomes united to move toward a common good and to oppose a common enemy, what difficulty can stand in their way?

CHAPTER 11

This chapter gives the history of Jephthah, who did great things by faith (Heb 11:32). 1. The disadvantages of his origin (vv. 1–3). 2. The Gileadites' choice of him to be their commander against the Ammonites (vv. 4–11). 3. His earnest negotiation with the king of Ammon about the rights of the two nations, so that the matter might be settled, if possible, without bloodshed (vv. 12–28). 4. His war with the Ammonites, which he entered on with a solemn vow (vv. 29–31), pursued with bravery (v. 32), and ended with a glorious victory (v. 33); the difficulties he came into at his return to his own house because of the vow he had made (vv. 34–40).

Verses 1–3

At the end of the previous chapter we left the leaders and people of Gilead discussing the choice of a general. Now all agreed that Jephthah, the Gileadite, was *a mighty man of valor* (v. 1) and eminently suitable for that purpose. In fact, there was no one better qualified than he was, but there were three disadvantages about choosing him:

1. He was *the son of a harlot* (prostitute) (v. 1), of *a strange woman* (v. 2). The Jews say his mother was an Ishmaelite. If his mother was a prostitute, that was not his fault, however, although it was still his disgrace. People ought not to be made to feel ashamed of any unfortunate aspects of their parentage or ancestry. The child of a prostitute, if born again, born from above, will be accepted by God and be as welcome as any other child to enjoy the glorious liberties of being one of his children.

2. He had been forced out of his country by his brothers. His father's legitimate children had insisted on applying the Law rigorously and had driven him out of sharing any inheritance with them. They did not consider his extraordinary qualifications, which surely meant that special exemption should be made for him. If they had done this, he would have been a great asset to their family and would have made it more illustrious. God often humbles those whom he intends to exalt, then takes that *stone which the builders rejected* and makes it *the head of the corner* (Lk 20:17). Joseph, Moses, and David, the three most eminent shepherds of Israel, were all driven out by their fellows before they were called by God to their great positions.

3. In his exile, he had led a rabble (v. 3). After he had been driven out by his brothers, he would not allow himself either to dig or to beg, but knew he had to live by his sword. Others who were reduced to similar difficulties were stirred into action by such a spirit and followed him. They are called *vain men* (v. 3). They were a group of adventurers—outcasts and misfits—who had run out of money and had to seek a livelihood. Such people followed him, not to rob or plunder, but to hunt wild animals. This is the man who must save Israel.

Verses 4–11

Here is:

1. The distress which the Israelites were in when the Ammonites invaded their country (v. 4).

2. The request which the elders made to Jephthah to come and help them. They did not write a letter or send a messenger to him but went themselves to fetch him. They knew he was a bold man and was well able to fight with the sword, and so he must be the man. Notice how God prepares people for the service he intends for them, and even makes their troubles work to guide them on their way. If Jephthah had not been brought into such a difficult situation by his brothers' unkindness, he would not have had such occasion as this gave him to exercise and make the most of his military skills, and so to distinguish himself and become famous. An army without a general is like a body without a head. Leadership is so necessary in every society that any community would rather humbly beg the favor of being commanded than let everyone be their own commander. Let us thank God for good government.

3. The objections Jephthah made against accepting the elders' offer: *Did you not hate me, and expel me?* (v. 7). Jephthah was not unwilling to serve his country, but he thought it right that he should note their former unkindness to him, so that they might repent of their sin in mistreating him. In the same way, Joseph humbled his brothers before he made himself known to them. Many offend God and good people until they themselves come into a distressing situation, and then they want God's mercy and the prayers of good people.

4. The urgency of the elders toward him to accept the leadership they offer him (v. 8). Let this situation be:

4.1. A warning to us not to trample on or despise anyone because they are lowly. We are to make no one our enemy, because we do not know how soon our distresses may be such that we may very much want to make them our friends.

4.2. An encouragement to worthy people who are offended or mistreated. Let them endure such difficulties with humility and cheerfulness and leave it to God to make their light shine out of obscurity.

5. The agreement he comes to with them. God has forgiven Israel for their offenses against him (10:16), and so Jephthah will also forgive.

5.1. He puts a fair question to them (v. 9): "Now if God blesses us and I come home as conqueror, then tell me clearly, *shall I be your head?* (v. 9). If I, under God, rescue you, then will I, under God, also reform you?" The same question is put to those who want salvation by Christ. "If he saves you, will you be willing for him to rule over your life? There are no other terms under which he will save you. If he makes you happy, will he also make you holy? If he is your helper, then will he also be your head?"

5.2. They immediately give him a positive answer (v. 10): "We *will do according to thy words*; command us in war, and you will command us in peace." Then the elders confirm their agreement with an oath. In this way the original contract is confirmed between Jephthah and the Gileadites, and all Israel, it seems, agrees to it later, for it is said (12:7), *he judged Israel*. He then goes with the elders (v. 11), to the place where all the Israelites are assembled (10:17), and there they all agree and *make him head and captain*. To obtain this small honor, Jephthah is willing to risk his life for them (12:3). The question comes to us, will we be discouraged in our Christian warfare by any of the difficulties we may meet with in it, when Christ himself has promised *a crown of life to him that overcometh* (Rev 2:10)?

6. Jephthah's godly acknowledgment of God in this great matter (v. 11): *He uttered all his words before the Lord in Mizpeh*, that is, when he was advanced, he immediately withdrew to his own devotions and spread the whole matter out in prayer before God. He spoke out before God all his thoughts and cares in this matter, for God allows us to be free with him.

6.1. "Lord, the people have made me their leader; will you confirm the choice and acknowledge me as your people's leader under you and for you?" Jephthah says, "Lord, I will not accept this role unless it is your will."

6.2. In this way, Jephthah opened the campaign with prayer. Its outcome was likely to be glorious, since it had begun in such a godly way.

Verses 12–28

We have here the negotiation between Jephthah, now judge of Israel, and the king of the Ammonites.

1. Jephthah, as one having authority, sent messengers to the king of Ammon, who was the aggressor in this war, to demand his reasons for invading the land of Israel. Now this reasonable demand shows:

1.1. That Jephthah did not delight in war, even though he was a mighty warrior, but was willing to prevent it by peaceful reconciliation. War should be the last resort and should not be used until all other methods of ending a dispute have been tried. This rule should also be observed in going to court. The sword of justice, as well as the sword of war, must not be appealed to until the disputing parties have first tried by gentler means to reconcile their differences and settle conflicting matters (1Co 6:1).

1.2. That Jephthah delighted in justice, and that this was all he wanted.

2. The king of the Ammonites now gives his demand, which he should have declared before he had invaded Israel (v. 13). His claim is, "Israel took away my lands long ago; so now restore those lands."

3. Jephthah gives a very full and satisfactory answer to this demand, showing that the Ammonites are in no way entitled to claim as theirs the land which lies between the rivers Arnon and Jabbok and which is now in the possession of the tribes of Reuben and Gad.

3.1. Israel never took any land away from either the Moabites or the Ammonites. He puts them together because they were brothers, the children of Lot, near neighbors with united interests, having the same god, Chemosh, and perhaps sometimes the same king. Israel took away the lands in question from Sihon king of the Amorites. If the Amorites, before Israel came into that country, had taken these lands from the Moabites or Ammonites—as it would seem they had (Nu 21:26; Jos 13:25)—then that was not the concern or responsibility of Israel.

3.2. So far were the Israelites from invading the property of any other nations, except the descendants of Canaan who were set apart in a special way to be destroyed—one of the branches of whom the Amorites were (Ge 10:16)—that they would not even force a passage through the country either of the Edomites, the descendants of Esau, or of the Moabites, the descendants of Lot.

3.3. In that war in which they took this land from Sihon king of the Amorites, he was the aggressor, and not they (vv. 19–20). They sent a humble petition to him for permission to go through his land and were willing to give him any security for their good behavior in their march. Sihon not only denied them this courtesy but had also gathered all his forces and fought against Israel (v. 20). And so, in their war with him, Israel stood up in their own just and necessary defense, and having routed his army, could justly, as further revenge for the wrong that had been committed, seize his country as something Israel gained by right. This is how Israel came to possess this country. It is unreasonable for the Ammonites to question their rights.

3.4. Jephthah pleads that the land was a gift from the crown and makes his claims on that basis (vv. 23–24). God gave them the land by a special transfer, which vested the right to ownership in them, which they could validate against all the world (Dt 2:24): *I have given into thy hand Sihon and his land*. To support this plea, he uses an argument that involves the Ammonites' character. *Wilt not thou possess that which Chemosh thy god giveth thee?* (v. 24). It was not that Jephthah thought Chemosh a god, but only that he was *thy god*, and the worshipers of even those foreign gods which could do neither good nor evil still thought themselves indebted to them for all they had (Hos 2:12). "Now," Jephthah says, "we are as entitled to our country as you are to yours."

3.5. He pleads Israel's claim on the basis that they have been there a long time:

3.5.1. Their legal right to the land was not disputed when they first entered it (v. 25).

3.5.2. Their possession has not yet been disturbed (v. 26). He pleads that they have kept this country as their own now for about 300 years, and the Ammonites in all that time have never attempted to take it from them. So, even supposing Israel's legal claim had not been clear originally, the right of the children of Ammon was without doubt excluded forever because no claim in opposition to it had been made for so many generations. A legal claim that had been for so long unchallenged will be presumed unchallengeable.

3.6. By these arguments Jephthah justifies himself and his own cause and condemns the Ammonites: *"Thou doest me wrong to war against me* and must expect disaster" (v. 27). The Israelites, in the days of their prosperity and power — for there were some such days in the times of the judges — had conducted themselves very inoffensively to all their neighbors. The king of the Ammonites, when he was looking for a reason to quarrel with them, was forced to look back 300 years to support his claim.

3.7. To settle the dispute, he turns to God and his justice (v. 27): *The Lord the Judge be judge this day.* The king of Ammon proceeds against him (v. 28).

4. Neither Jephthah's defense nor his appeal had any effect on the king of the Ammonites. They had found the spoils of Israel to be sweet in the eighteen years in which they had oppressed them (10:8), and they now hoped to conquer the tree, the fruit of which they had so often enjoyed.

Verses 29–40

Here we have Jephthah's triumph, but he is troubled and distressed by an ill-advised vow:

1. Jephthah's victory was clear.

1.1. God gave him an excellent spirit, and he used it bravely (v. 29). The Spirit of the Lord came on him. The Spirit vastly enhanced his natural faculties, endowing him with power from heaven. God used this to confirm him in his office and assure him of success in his undertaking. Spurred into action in this way, he lost no time, but with undaunted determination took to the battlefield.

1.2. God gave him notable success, and he bravely used that (v. 32). Having routed their forces on the battlefield, he chased them to their towns. But it does not appear that he completely destroyed the people or that he offered to make himself ruler of the country. Though the attempts by others to wrong us will justify us in defending our own rights, those attempts will not authorize us to wrong them in return.

2. Jephthah's vow is tragic and casts a dark shadow over his success. When he was leaving his own house on this dangerous undertaking, as he prayed to God for his presence with him, he made a secret but solemn vow or religious promise to God, that if God would graciously bring him back as conqueror, whoever or whatever would be first to come out of his house to meet him would be devoted to God and offered as a burnt offering. At his return, news of his victory came home before him, and his one and only daughter met him with the prompt expression of joy. He was very dismayed, but there was no way out. After she had taken some time to mourn her own unfortunate situation, she cheerfully submitted to the fulfillment of his vow. Now:

2.1. There are several lessons to be learned from this story:

2.1.1. That there may be remnants of distrust and doubt even in the hearts of true and great believers. Jephthah may have had a vain thought that he could not promise himself a victory unless he offered something significant to God in exchange for the victory.

2.1.2. That it is still very good, when we are serving him, to make vows to God when we are seeking or expecting any help. We should do this not to "buy" the favor we want, but as an expression of our gratitude to him and the deep sense we have of our obligations to respond to him for the benefits we have received.

2.1.3. That we should be very careful and wise in making such vows, so that we do not, by satisfying a present emotion — even of godly zeal — entangle our own consciences.

2.1.4. That what we have solemnly vowed to God we must conscientiously perform, if it is possible and lawful, even though it is very difficult and painful to us.

2.1.5. That it is good for children to obediently and cheerfully submit to their parents in the Lord, and particularly to fulfill their parents' godly decisions to honor God and to maintain a religious faith in their families, even though the commands are harsh and rigorous, as with the Rechabites, who for many generations strictly observed the commands of Jonadab their father in refusing wine, and also as with Jephthah's daughter here, who, for the satisfying of her father's conscience, and for the honor of God and her country, submitted herself as one set apart in a special way to be destroyed (v. 36).

2.1.6. That our friends' sufferings should be our sorrows. Where Jephthah's daughter went to mourn her terrible fate, her companions, the virgins, joined with her in weeping (v. 38). Those who only rejoice with us and do not also weep with us are unworthy of being called our friends.

2.1.7. That heroic zeal for the honor of God and Israel, even though it is mixed with weakness and indiscretion, is worth being remembered forever. It was a good custom that young women of Israel annually preserved the honorable memory of Jephthah's daughter, who made light even of her own life.

2.2. But there are some difficult questions that arise from this story:

2.2.1. It is difficult to say what Jephthah actually did to his daughter in fulfilling his vow:

2.2.1.1. Some think he only shut her up, that she totally set herself apart from all the affairs of this life, including marriage, and gave herself wholly to acts of devotion for the rest of her life. What supports this view is that she is *said to bewail her virginity* (vv. 37–38) and that *she knew no man* (v. 39).

2.2.1.2. It seems more probable that he offered her up as a sacrifice, according to the literal words of his vow, misunderstanding that law which spoke of people set apart by the curse of God (Lev 27:29): *None devoted shall be redeemed, but shall surely be put to death*; he acted as if this law were to be applied to those who were set apart by human vows in the same way as to those set apart by God's curse. Since he had made such a vow, he thought it would be better to kill his daughter than break his vow; he would let Providence bear the blame for bringing her out to meet him.

2.2.2. But if Jephthah did sacrifice his daughter, the question then is whether he did the right thing:

2.2.2.1. Some justify him in it and think he did the right thing. They think he was acting as one who preferred the honor of God before what was dearest to him in this world. But:

2.2.2.2. Most condemn Jephthah. He was wrong to make such a rash vow and acted even more wrongly in fulfilling it. He could not be bound by his vow to what God had forbidden by the sixth commandment: *thou shalt not kill* (Ex 20:13). God had forbidden human sacrifices, so that it was (according to Dr. Lightfoot) in effect a sacrifice to Molech.

CHAPTER 12

In this chapter, we have: 1. Jephthah's conflict with the Ephraimites, the blood which was shed on that unfortunate occasion (vv. 1–6), and the conclusion of Jephthah's life and leadership (v. 7). 2. A short account of three other judges of Israel: Ibzan (vv. 8–10), Elon (vv. 11–12), and Abdon (vv. 13–15).

Verses 1–7

Here is:

1. The unreasonable resentment the Ephraimites felt toward Jephthah, because he had not called on them to help him against the Ammonites so that they might share in the triumphs and plunder (v. 1). Pride lay at the root of the quarrel. Proud people want to draw attention to themselves and think they are the only ones who should be honored, and then *who can stand before envy?* (Pr 27:4). The anger of the Ephraimites at Jephthah was:

1.1. Without reason and unjust. Why *didst thou not call us to go with thee?* (v. 1). Jephthah had not asked for their help for a good reason. It was the people of Gilead, not the Ephraimites, who had made him their commander, and so he had no authority to call them.

1.2. Cruel and outrageous. They were furious at being left out and so gathered their forces together, crossed over the Jordan as far as Mizpah in Gilead, where Jephthah lived, and wanted to take out their anger on him by burning down his house with him in it. Often, those resentments which are the most unreasonable contain the most anger. Jephthah was now in mourning for his daughter, and the Ephraimites should have comforted him. Cruel people take pleasure in adding further suffering to those who are already suffering.

2. Jephthah's warm justification of his actions:

2.1. Whether they would be pacified or not, Jephthah is careful to justify himself (vv. 2–3). He says that they have no reason at all to quarrel with him, for:

2.1.1. He had not waged war in order to gain glory, but because he had to defend his country.

2.1.2. He had invited the Ephraimites to come and join with him, but they had refused to help. He had more reason to quarrel with them for abandoning the common interests of Israel at a time of need, than they with him for his supposed slight against them. It is nothing new when those who are themselves most to blame shout the loudest in their accusations of those who are innocent.

2.1.3. The undertaking was very dangerous. The honor they were jealous of had been bought with a high price, and so they did not need to begrudge him that honor, for few of them would have risked their lives in such a way.

2.1.4. He does not take the glory of the success to himself but gives it all to God: "*The Lord delivered them into my hands* (v. 3). If God wanted to make use of me for his glory, then why should you be offended at that?"

2.2. When this just answer, although it was not as gentle an answer as Gideon's, did not succeed in turning away their wrath, he made sure he both defended himself from their anger and rebuked their defiance with the sword, because of his authority as Israel's judge.

2.2.1. The Ephraimites had not only quarreled with Jephthah but also mistreated his neighbors and friends when they appeared in order to support him. "Who cares about you? All your neighbors know what you are. You are no better than fugitives and vagabonds, separated from your brothers, and now you are driven into a corner." It is wrong to attach shameful names or qualities to people or countries, as commonly happens, especially to people who are outwardly disadvantaged. Such name-calling often leads to quarrels that have harmful consequences, as happened here.

2.2.2. This insult greatly angers the Gileadites, and the indignity done to themselves, as well as to their commander, must be revenged:

2.2.2.1. They struck down the Ephraimites on the battlefield (v. 4).

2.2.2.2. The Gileadites, who perhaps knew the fords of the Jordan better than the Ephraimites, secured them with strong guards and were ordered to kill every Ephraimite who tried to cross the river. Here was:

- Cruelty. There was no need to be so severe as to kill all who escaped. Will the sword forever consume?
- Cunning in the way they were discovered. It seems that the Ephraimites, although they spoke the same language as the other Israelites, still had kept up a customary dialect of their country and pronounced the Hebrew letter *Shin* like *Samek*. Those who first used "s" for "sh" did so either because it was shorter or because it was finer, and their children learned to speak like them, so that you could tell a person was an Ephraimite from the way they spoke; as in England we know someone from the West Country (e.g., Cornwall) or from the North (e.g., Cheshire) by their style of pronunciation. A New Testament example is *Thou art a Galilean, and thy speech betrays thee* (Mt 26:73). If the Gileadites took a man that they suspected to be an Ephraimite, but he denied it, they asked him to say *Shibboleth*, but either he *could not*, or he did not pronounce it correctly, but said *Sibboleth*, and so showed himself to be an Ephraimite and was killed immediately. *Shibboleth* means "a river in flood": "Ask permission to cross Shibboleth, the river."

2.3. The punishment of these proud and angry Ephraimites corresponded in several ways to their sin:

2.3.1. They were proud of the honor of their tribe, but how soon were they brought to be ashamed or afraid to own up to their country! *Art thou an Ephraimite? No* (v. 5); now they prefer to come from any other tribe except that one.

2.3.2. They had gone angrily over the Jordan to burn down Jephthah's house, but now they came back to the Jordan as furtively as before they had crossed it indignantly. They were prevented from ever returning to their own houses.

2.3.3. They had rebuked the Gileadites about the unfortunate state of their country, which lay at such a distance, and now it was their turn to suffer because of a speech impediment which was peculiar to *their* own country, in not being able to pronounce the word *Shibboleth* correctly.

2.3.4. They had unjustly called the Gileadites *fugitives*, and now it was they who really became fugitives. Those who unjustly disgrace someone should themselves expect to be justly disgraced.

3. The end of Jephthah's leadership. He judged Israel for only six years and then died (v. 7). Perhaps the death of his daughter depressed him so much that he never looked up again; perhaps it shortened his life and he went to his grave mourning.

Verses 8–15

1. Here is a brief account of the short reigns of three more judges of Israel, the first of whom governed only seven years, the second ten, and the third eight:

1.1. Ibzan of Bethlehem, most probably Bethlehem of Judah, David's city, not that in Zebulun, which is mentioned only once (Jos 19:15). He ruled for only seven years, but from the number of his children, and his looking after them all in marriage, it appears that he lived a long life. What is significant about him is:

1.1.1. That he had many children, sixty in all.

1.1.2. That he had an equal number of each sex, thirty sons and thirty daughters, something which does not often happen in the same family, but in the great family of the human race, the One who originally made two, male and female, by his wise providence preserves a succession of both in some measure of equality as far as is needed to keep up the generations of people on earth.

1.1.3. That he took care to see that they were all married. The Jews say that every father owes three things to his son: to teach him to read the Law, to give him a trade, and to get him a wife.

1.2. Elon of Zebulun, in the north of Canaan, was next raised up to lead in public affairs, to administer justice, and to reform abuses. He continued to bless Israel for ten years and then died (vv. 11–12). Dr. Lightfoot reckons that it was at the beginning of his time that the forty years' oppression by the Philistines began (which is described in 13:1), and it was about that time that Samson was born.

1.3. Abdon, of the tribe of Ephraim, came next, and in him that illustrious tribe began to recover its reputation. This Abdon was famous for his many children (v. 14): he had forty sons and thirty grandsons, all of whom he lived to see grown up. It was greatly satisfying for him to be able to see his children's children, but he did not see peace in Israel, for by this time the Philistines had begun to disturb them.

2. It is very strange that in the history of all these judges, some of whose actions are related very fully, there is not so much as one mention of the high priest, or any other priest or Levite, appearing either to give guidance or take action in any public matter, from Phinehas (20:28) to Eli, which may well be reckoned as approximately 250 years. It is only the names of the high priests at that time which are preserved (1Ch 6:4–7; Ezr 7:3–5). How can the strange obscurity of that priesthood for such a long time, now at the beginning of its days, be consistent with the mighty splendor with which it was introduced and the prominent part which the institution played in the Law of Moses? Surely it suggests that the institution was chiefly intended to be a type of what was to come, and that the great benefits that seemed to be promised by it were to be mainly looked for in its fulfillment, the eternal and much more glorious priesthood of our Lord Jesus, in comparison with which that priesthood had no glory (2Co 3:10).

CHAPTER 13

The story of Samson begins at this chapter. He was the last of the judges of Israel whose story is recorded in this book, and the one before Eli. He plays a very prominent part in this record, vastly different from that of his predecessors. We never find him leading either a court or an army, never on the throne of judgment or on the battlefield, but in his own person he was a great patriot of his country and a terrible scourge and restraint on its enemies and oppressors. The history of each of the rest of the judges begins with their promotion to that position, but Samson's begins with his birth. 1. The occasion of the raising up of this deliverer is the oppression of Israel by the Philistines (v. 1). His birth is foretold by an angel to his mother (vv. 2–5). She relates the prediction to his father (vv. 6–7). 2. They both together receive it again from the angel (vv. 8–14). 3. They treat the angel with respect (vv. 15–18), and he, to their great amazement, reveals his high standing when he leaves (vv. 19–23). 4. Samson is born (vv. 24–25).

Verses 1–7

The first verse gives us a short account of the great distress that Israel was in, which was the occasion for the raising up of a deliverer. They did evil, as they had done,

in the sight of the Lord (v. 1). The enemies whom God now sold them to were the Philistines, their closest neighbors, an insignificant people compared with Israel—they had only five cities of any note—but when God made use of them as the rod in his hand, they were very oppressive and troublesome. This trouble lasted longer than any trouble had up to that time: it continued forty years, though it was probably not always violent to the same extent. It was when Israel was in this time of distress that Samson was born, and here his birth is foretold by an angel. Notice:

1. His ancestry. He came from the tribe of Dan (v. 2). *Dan* means "a judge; judgment" (Ge 30:6). The land allotted to the tribe of Dan was next to the country of the Philistines, and so one from that tribe was most suitable to act as a restraint on them. His parents had been childless for a long time. Many famous people have been born of mothers who have been childless for a long time, so that the mercy might be even more welcome when it actually comes. Think of such children as Isaac, Joseph, Samuel, and John the Baptist.

2. The good news brought to his mother that she would give birth to a son. The messenger was an *angel of the Lord* (v. 3), but he appeared in human form, with the appearance and clothes of a prophet, a man of God. It was not so much for the sake of Manoah and his wife, who were simply obscure Danites, that this extraordinary message was sent, but for the sake of Israel, whom he was to save. And it was still more than this. It was also for the Messiah's sake, whose type he was to be, and whose birth must be prophesied by an angel, as his was. In the message which the angel brings:

2.1. He takes notice of her suffering: *Behold now, thou art barren and bearest not* (v. 3). "*Now* you are barren, but you will not always be so," as she fears, "and not for a long time to come."

2.2. He assures her that she will *conceive and bear a son* (v. 3), and then he repeats the assurance (v. 5). To show the power of a divine word, the strongest person ever was a child of promise.

2.3. He specifies that the child will be a Nazarite from his birth, which means that the mother will be subject to the law of the Nazarites, though not under the vow of a Nazarite, and must *drink no wine or strong drink* (v. 4) for as long as this child is to have his nourishment from her, either in the womb or from her breast (vv. 4–5). Other judges had corrected Israel's rebellions from God, but Samson must appear, more than any of them, as one consecrated to God, and despite what we read of his faults, we have reason to think that as a Nazarite of God's making he was an example not only of the ceremony but also of the substance of that *separation to the Lord* of Nazariteship (Nu 6:2). The mother of this judge must therefore deny herself and not eat any unclean thing. What was lawful at another time was now to be avoided. Women who are pregnant ought to conscientiously avoid whatever they have reason to think will in any way harm the health or good constitution of the child within them. And perhaps Samson's mother was to avoid wine and strong drink not only because he was intended to be a Nazarite, but also because he was intended to be a man of great strength, which his mother's temperance would contribute to.

2.4. He foretells the service which this child will perform for his country. Notice that *He shall begin to deliver Israel*. This suggested that the oppression of the Philistines would last for a long time, for Israel's rescue from it would not so much as begin till this child had grown up. But he would not complete the deliverance: he would only *begin* to deliver Israel, which suggests that the trouble would be prolonged. In this Samson was a type of Christ:

2.4.1. As a Nazarite to God, a Nazarite from the womb. For although our Lord Jesus was not a Nazarite himself, the Nazarites were still a type of him, since he was perfectly pure from all sin. He was not conceived in sin and was completely devoted to his Father's honor.

2.4.2. As a savior of Israel, for he is a type of Jesus, the Savior who saves his people from their sins. But there is this difference: Samson only began to save Israel — David was later raised up to complete the destruction of the Philistines — but our Lord Jesus is both Samson and David too, both the *author and finisher of our faith* (Heb 12:2).

3. The report which Manoah's wife brought joyfully and quickly to her husband of this surprising message (vv. 6 – 7):

3.1. Of the messenger. It was *a man of God* (v. 6). She could describe his appearance. It was awesome: he had such a majesty about him. In fact, from her ideas of what angels looked like, this man looked like one. But she could not say anything about his name or to which tribe or city of Israel he belonged. She was certain that he was a servant of God. She knew that his person and message brought their own evidence along with them, and she had asked no more.

3.2. Of the message. She gives Manoah a detailed account both of the promise and of the command (v. 7), so that he also might believe the promise. In the same way, husbands and wives in Christ should share with one another their experiences of fellowship with God, so that they may one another in the ways of holiness.

Verses 8 – 14

We have here an account of the second visit the angel of God made to Manoah and his wife:

1. Manoah prayed with all his heart for it (v. 8).

1.1. He takes it for granted that this child of promise will in due time be given them. He speaks without hesitation of *the child that shall be born* (v. 8). *Blessed are those that have not seen and yet*, as Manoah here, *have believed* (Jn 20:29).

1.2. All his concern is *what they should do to the child* (v. 8) who was to be born. This shows us that good people are more concerned to know what responsibilities they should fulfill than to know the events that will happen to them, for our responsibility is up to us, while events are up to God.

1.3. He therefore prays to God to send the same blessed messenger again, to give them further instructions concerning what rules they should follow for this Nazarite's life and work. He is afraid that his wife's joy at the promise may have made her forget some part of the command. He wants to share in receiving full information and not be under any mistake. Do we want God's messengers, the ministers of his Gospel, to bring a special word to us and to instruct us? *Entreat the Lord* to send them to us to teach us (Ro 15:30, 32).

2. God graciously answered his prayer: *God hearkened to the voice of Manoah* (v. 9).

2.1. The angel appears a second time, again to his wife, when she is sitting alone, probably looking after the flocks. Solitude is often a good opportunity for fellowship with God. Good people need never think of themselves as alone if God is with them.

2.2. She quickly goes to call her husband, no doubt humbly asking this blessed messenger to stay until she returns with her husband (vv. 10 – 11). The man of God is very willing that she should call her husband (Jn 4:16). See also Jn 4:28 – 30. Manoah is not offended that the angel did not appear to him on this second occasion, but

is very willing to follow his wife to the man of God. If the wife takes the lead, let the husband not think it beneath him to follow her in what is noble and commendable.

2.3. After Manoah has come to the angel and is satisfied with the angel's affirmation that he is the same messenger who appeared to his wife, Manoah humbly:

2.3.1. Welcomes the promise (v. 12): *Now let thy words come to pass*. This was the language, not only of his desire, but also of his faith, like that of the Virgin Mary (Lk 1:38): "*Be it according to thy word*. Lord, I take hold of what you have said and depend on it; *let it come to pass*. May your words be fulfilled."

2.3.2. Begs that the instructions which were given may be repeated: *How shall we order the child?* (v. 12), What is to be the rule for the boy's life and work? The directions were given to his wife, but he considers it his concern to help her in carefully looking after this promised descendant, according to the command. The greatest care of both parents, and their constant joint endeavor, are not too much to ask for in the good upbringing of children who are devoted to God and who are to be brought up for him. One parent should not try to pass the responsibility on to the other, but both should do their best. Those to whom God has given children must take great care how they discipline and guide them, and what they do to them, so that they may drive out the *foolishness* that *is bound up in their hearts* (Pr 22:15), form their minds and manners at an early age, and train them in *the way wherein they should go* (Pr 22:6). Godly parents will gladly recognize that they need divine help to do these things: "Lord, teach us how we may guide our children, so that they may be Nazarites in their rule of life, living sacrifices to you."

2.4. The angel repeats the directions he gave before (vv. 13 – 14). We need to exercise a good deal of caution and observance to rightly order both our own lives and also those of our children. Those who want to keep their lives pure must keep away from what borders on sin or leads to it. When she was pregnant with a Nazarite, she must not eat *any unclean thing* (v. 14). It is the same for those *in whom Christ is formed* (Gal 4:19). They must carefully *cleanse themselves from all filthiness of flesh and spirit* (2Co 7:1), purify themselves from everything that contaminates body and spirit, doing nothing that might harm the new creation that we are.

Verses 15 – 23

We have here an account:

1. Of what then passed between Manoah and the angel at this meeting. It was out of kindness to Manoah that while the angel was with him, he did not realize he was an angel. We could not bear the sight of God's unveiled glory. God decided to speak to us by human beings like ourselves, prophets and ministers, and even when he spoke by his angels, or by his Son, they appeared in human likeness, and were assumed to be people who had come from God. Now:

1.1. The angel declined to accept his gift and directed him to turn it into a sacrifice. Manoah begged that he would take some refreshment with him (v. 15), but the angel told him (v. 16) that he would *not eat of his bread*, any more than he would of Gideon's, but directed him to offer it to God (6:20 – 21). Though we cannot live without food and drink, we still eat and drink to the glory of God, and so turn even our ordinary meals into sacrifices.

1.2. The angel declined to tell him his name. Manoah wanted to know his name (v. 17) and from which tribe he came so *that when thy sayings come to pass, we may do thee honour* (v. 17). What Manoah asked for as regards instruction in his responsibility and duty he was readily told about (vv. 12–13), but what he asked to satisfy his curiosity was denied. God has in his word given us full directions concerning our responsibilities and duties, but he never intended to answer all the speculative questions we may have. We must never seek to satisfy our idle curiosity concerning these things (Col 2:18). To be willingly ignorant of the things that our great Master refuses to teach us is to be both ignorant and wise.

1.3. The angel was present at and acknowledged their sacrifice. First, Manoah brought his burnt offering as directed by the angel. "Lord, here it is, do what you please with it." This is how we must bring our hearts to God as living sacrifices and submit them to the activity of his Spirit. Then the angel *wondrously* made fire come to burn up the sacrifice and ascended *in the flame of the altar* (vv. 19, 20). Prayer is the ascent of the soul to God, but it is Christ in the heart by faith who makes it an offering that is fragrant: without him our services are offensive smoke, but in him, an acceptable flame. We may apply it to Christ's sacrifice of himself for us: he ascended in the flame of his own offering, for *by his own blood he entered in once into the holy place* (Heb 9:12).

2. Of the impressions which this vision made on Manoah and his wife:

2.1. In Manoah's contemplation there is great fear (v. 22). Manoah had spoken with great assurance of the son who would soon be born to them (vv. 8, 12), but he was now confounded: *We shall surely die* (v. 22). It was a general opinion among the ancient Jews that seeing God or an angel meant immediate death, and this idea completely overcame his faith at that time, as it did Gideon's (6:22).

2.2. In his wife's contemplation there is great faith (v. 23). Here the weaker partner was the stronger believer, which perhaps was the reason why the angel chose both times to appear to her. Husbands and wives should devoutly help each other's faith and joy as need be. None could argue better than Manoah's wife did. Her husband said, *We shall surely die* (v. 22), but she said, "No, the signs of his favor which we have received forbid us to think that he intends to destroy us. If he had wanted to kill us:

- "He would not have accepted our sacrifice.
- "He would not have shown us all these things, nor would he have given these very great and precious promises of a son who would be a Nazarite and a deliverer of Israel." God does not desire the death of sinners: he has accepted the great sacrifice which Christ offered for their salvation. And let those Christians who have had fellowship with God in the word and prayer, to whom he has graciously revealed himself, be encouraged by this in difficult times. "God would not have done what he has done for my soul if he had wanted to abandon me and leave me to die, for his work is perfect, nor will he mock his people with his favors." We should learn to reason as Manoah's wife did.

Verses 24–25

Here is:

1. Samson's birth. The woman who had been barren for so long gave birth to a son, according to the promise.

2. His name, *Samson*. Some have derived it from *shemesh*, "the sun," turned into a diminutive, so that it would mean "the sun in miniature," perhaps because, being born like Moses to be a deliverer, he was like him in being exceedingly fair, and his face shone like a little sun because of his great strength. The sun is compared to *a strong man* (Ps 19:5). A little sun, because he was the glory of, and a light to, his people Israel, as a type of Christ, the Sun of righteousness.

3. His childhood. He far outgrew other children of his age; it appeared that the Lord blessed him and qualified him in both body and mind for something great and extraordinary.

4. His youth. When he grew up a little, *the Spirit of the Lord began to move him* (v. 25). The Spirit of God moved Samson in the camp of Dan to oppose the raids of the Philistines. It was there that the child Samson appeared among them and distinguished himself by some brave actions, surpassing them all in bold exercises and trials of strength. He probably showed himself more than usually zealous against the enemies of his country.

CHAPTER 14

The idea which this chapter gives of Samson is not what you might have expected for one who had been specially marked out by heaven to be a Nazarite to God and a deliverer of Israel, but he was both. Here is: 1. Samson's courtship of a daughter of the Philistines and his marriage to her (vv. 1–5, 7–8). 2. His conquest of a lion, and the prize he found in its carcass (vv. 5–6, 8–9). Samson's riddle given to his companions (vv. 10–14) and solved by means of the treachery of his wife (vv. 15–18); the occasion this gave him to kill thirty Philistines (v. 19) and to break off his new alliance (v. 20).

Verses 1–9

Here:

1. Samson, under the extraordinary guidance of Providence, seeks an occasion to quarrel with the Philistines by joining in marriage with them. This was something strange, but the truth is that Samson was himself a riddle and a paradox. He did what was great and good by what seemed weak and evil.

1.1. Since the process of deciding whom Samson should marry followed a common pattern, we may notice:

1.1.1. That it was foolish to set his affections on a daughter of the Philistines. Shall one who is not only an Israelite but also a Nazarite, dedicated to the Lord, want to become one with a worshiper of Dagon? Shall one marked out as a patriot of his country find his life partner from among those who are its sworn enemies? His parents did well to dissuade him from joining in marriage with unbelievers. "*Is there never a woman among the daughters of thy brethren, or*, if none of our tribe, *among all thy people* (v. 3), not an Israelite whom you like or who you think could be worthy of your affection, that you should marry a Philistine?"

1.1.2. If there had not been a special reason for it, it certainly would have been improper of him to insist on his choice, and of them to finally agree to it. This Nazarite, in submitting to his parents and asking their approval, and not proceeding until he had it, was an example to all children.

1.2. But this contract of marriage is explicitly said to be *of the Lord* (v. 4). It was not only that God later overruled it to serve his purposes against the Philistines, but also that he put it into Samson's heart to make this choice, that he *might have occasion against the Philistines*. It seems that the way in which the Philistines oppressed Israel was not by great armies, but by secret raids of their giants and of small parties of their plunderers. In the same way, therefore, Samson must deal with them. If he could by this marriage get among them, then he would be a constant source of trouble to them.

2. Samson, by special Providence, is encouraged to attack the Philistines. God prepared him for it by two events:

2.1. By enabling him to *kill a lion* on a journey to Timnah (vv. 5–6).

2.1.1. Samson's encounter with the lion was dangerous. It was a young lion, one of the fiercest sort, which attacked him, roaring for his prey. He was all alone in the vineyards, into which he had wandered away from his father and mother, probably to eat grapes. If Samson had met with this lion on the road, he might have had more reason to expect help from both God and his parents than here alone and in a remote vineyard. But there was a special providence in it, and because the encounter was more dangerous:

2.1.2. The victory was even more remarkable. It was obtained without any difficulty. He strangled the lion and tore his throat as easily as he could have strangled a young goat. Christ fought the roaring lion and defeated him at the beginning of his public work (Mt 4:1–11) and later disarmed the powers and authorities, triumphing over them *in himself*. He was *exalted in his own strength* (Ps 21:13). But Samson did not boast about this victory. He did *not even tell his father nor mother* (v. 6) what many people would soon have told throughout the whole country. Modesty and humility are the brightest crown of great actions.

2.2. By providing him on the next journey with honey in the carcass of this lion (vv. 8–9). When he went down the next time, he found the carcass of the lion. The wild birds or animals had probably eaten the flesh, and in its skeleton a swarm of bees had settled. They had made their hive there and had not been idle but had laid up a good supply of honey, which was one of the staple commodities of Canaan. Samson had a more definite claim to the hive than anyone else, and so he seized the honey with his hands. This involved an encounter with the bees, but since he had not once dreaded the lion's paws, he had no reason to fear the sting of the bees. By dislodging the bees he was taught not to fear the large number of Philistines. Although they *compassed him about* (swarmed around him) *like bees, yet in the name of the Lord he should destroy them* (Ps 118:12). From the honey he found there:

2.2.1. He ate some himself. John the Baptist, that Nazarite of the New Testament, lived in part on wild honey.

2.2.2. He gave some to his parents, and they ate it. He did not eat it all himself. He let his parents share with him. Let those who by the grace of God have found the delights of religious faith share that experience with their friends and relatives and invite them to come and join with them. He did not tell his parents where he got it from, so that they would not hesitate to eat it. Honey is still honey, even though it is in a dead lion.

Verses 10–20

We have here an account of Samson's wedding feast and the occasion it gave him to attack the Philistines:

1. Samson conformed to the custom of the country in making his wedding a feast, which lasted seven days (v. 10). It is not part of religion to go against the harmless customs of the places where we live. Rather, it dishonors religion when those who profess it give just cause to others to call them greedy, sly, or morose. Good people should be concerned to make themselves good companions in the best sense.

2. Samson's wife's relatives paid him the usual respect of the place on that occasion and brought him thirty young men to keep him company during the ceremony, as his attendants (v. 11): *When they saw him*, they brought him these companions. Or perhaps they brought them to him seemingly as his companions, but in reality as guards for him, or as spies to observe him.

3. Samson decided to entertain the company and gave them a riddle to solve. He challenged them to give him the answer within seven days (vv. 12–14). It seems that this was an old custom on such occasions. Samson had thought up the riddle himself, for it was his own achievement that gave rise to it: *Out of the eater came forth meat, and out of the strong came forth sweetness* (v. 14). What does the riddle mean? This riddle can be applied to many of the ways of divine Providence and grace. When God, in his overruling providence, brings good out of evil to his church and people—when what threatens their destruction turns to their advantage—when their enemies are made useful to them, and human wrath turns to God's praise—then *meat* comes *out of the eater* and *sweetness out of the strong* (v. 14). See also Php 1:12.

4. When Samson's companions could not solve the riddle themselves, they made his wife extract the explanation from him (v. 15). If she did not entice the bridegroom into letting them in on its meaning, then they would *burn her and her father's house with fire* (v. 15). Could anything be more ridiculous?

5. By her unreasonable persistence, his wife gained the key to the riddle from him. It was *on the seventh day* (v. 15), that is, the seventh day of the week—as Dr. Lightfoot thinks—but on the fourth day of the feast, that they asked her to entice her husband (v. 15), and she did it skillfully (v. 16) and successfully. Eventually Samson became worn out by her pestering and told her the meaning of his riddle, and though we may suppose she promised to keep the answer a secret—and no doubt said that if he told her she would tell no one else—she immediately went and told it to the *children of her people* (v. 17). He could not have expected anything better from a Philistine. The riddle was finally solved (v. 18): *What is sweeter than honey*, or better food (Pr 24:13)? *What is stronger than a lion*, or a greater devourer? Samson generously acknowledged that they had won the wager. But he thought fit to tell them, *If you had not ploughed with my heifer*, taken advantage of my wife, *you would not have found out my riddle* (v. 18). Satan, in his temptations, could not cause us the trouble he does if he did not "plow with the heifer" of our own sinful nature.

6. Samson pays his wager to these Philistines with the plunder from their other compatriots (v. 19).

7. The result turned out to be a good occasion of weaning Samson away from his new relatives. He found how his companions had mistreated him and how his wife had betrayed him, and so *his anger was kindled* (v. 19). After he received this unpleasant treatment from them, he *went up to his father's house* (v. 19). It would be good for us if the unkind acts and disappointments we meet with from the world had the good effect on us of making us return to our heavenly Father's house with faith, prayer, and rest. The difficulties we meet with in life should make us love home and long to be there.

CHAPTER 15

When Samson was seeking an alliance with the Philistines, he was looking for a good reason to confront them (14:4). 1. He took the treachery of his wife and her father as reason to burn the Philistines' grain (vv. 1–5).

He took the Philistines' cruelty to his wife and her father as reason strike down many of them (vv. 6–8). 2. He took the treachery of his compatriots, who tied him up and handed him over to the Philistines, as reason to kill 1,000 of the Philistines with the jawbone of a donkey (vv. 9–17). 3. God took the distress he was then in, for lack of water, as an occasion to show him his favor by supplying him at just the right time (vv. 18–20).

Verses 1–8

Here is:

1. Samson's return to his wife, whom he had left in displeasure. Time had slightly cooled down his resentment, and he came back to her and *visited her with a kid* (young goat) (v. 1). This was meant as a sign of reconciliation, and perhaps such a gift was commonly used in this way in those times. When differences come between close relatives, the wisest are those who are most forward in forgiving and forgetting wrongs.

2. The rejection Samson met with. Her father forbade him to come near her, for the father had married her to another man (v. 2). The father tries:

2.1. To justify himself in this wrong: *I verily thought that thou hadst utterly hated her* (v. 2).

2.2. To pacify Samson by offering him his younger daughter. Samson scorned his proposal; he knew better than *to take a wife to her sister* (Lev 18:18).

3. The revenge Samson took on the Philistines for this mistreatment. He looked on himself as acting on behalf of all Israel. He considered the offense as having been committed against the whole nation of Israel. Now the way Samson took revenge on them was by setting their grainfields on fire, which would greatly weaken and impoverish the country (vv. 4–5).

3.1. The method he used was very strange. He caught 300 foxes, tied them in pairs tail to tail, and sent them into the grainfields. Each pair had a torch of fire fastened between their tails, which terrified them so that they ran into the grain for protection. There they set fire to the grain. The fire broke out in many different places all at the same time. We never find Samson, in any of his exploits, making use of any other person whatever, servant or soldier. The lowliness and weakness of the animals he used showed his contempt for the enemies he fought against. This plan is often alluded to in order to show how the church's enemies have often united in coming up with some unscrupulous, destructive plan to try to devastate the church of God, particularly to set alight fires of division.

3.2. The trouble this caused to the Philistines was very great. It was at the time of the wheat harvest (v. 1), and because the straw was dry, it soon burned the sheaves of grain that had been cut and stacked as well as *the standing corn, and the vineyards and olives* (v. 5).

4. The Philistines' outrage against Samson's treacherous wife and her father. Realizing that they had provoked Samson to get his revenge on the country, the rabble attacked his wife and her father and burned them to death, perhaps in their own house (v. 6). The Philistines had threatened Samson's wife, that if she would not get the riddle out of him, they would burn her and her father's household to death (14:15). To save herself and to please her compatriots, she had betrayed her husband. Now, the very thing that she feared and had sought by sin to avoid came on her: she and her father's household were burned to death. This shows us that the trouble we may try to escape from by following unlawful practices will often come back on our own heads.

5. How Samson took this violence of the Philistines as a reason to cause them even more trouble, which affected their own flesh and blood (vv. 7–8). "Representing the community of Israel as a whole, I am going to plead Israel's cause and take revenge for the wrongs done to them. *I will be avenged on you.*" So he *smote them hip and thigh with a great slaughter*, "with a great stroke," as the word literally means. And when he had completed his slaughter, he withdrew to a natural fortress in a cave in the rock of Etam, where he waited to see whether the Philistines would be subdued by the way he had disciplined them.

Verses 9–17

Here:

1. Samson is forcefully pursued by the Philistines. They set up camp in Judah and spread themselves throughout the country to look for Samson, who they heard had come that way (v. 9). An army was sent against one man, for indeed he was himself an army. In the same way, a whole band of men was sent to seize our Lord Jesus, that blessed Samson, although a tenth would have been enough when his hour had come, and ten times as many would have done nothing if he had not submitted.

2. Samson is wickedly betrayed and handed over by the men of Judah (v. 11). They were corrupt branches of that noble tribe. Perhaps they were discontented with Samson because he did not come from their tribe: because they were foolishly preoccupied with wanting to be first—a right they had forfeited—they preferred to be oppressed by Philistines rather than be rescued by a Danite. So also the church's rescue has often been obstructed by such petty jealousies and pretended points of honor. Sin discourages people; in fact, it confounds them and hides from their eyes the things that would give them peace. Probably Samson went to the border of Judah to offer his services, *supposing his brethren would have understood how that God by his hand would deliver them*, as Moses did (Ac 7:25). But instead of accepting his offer, they begged him to allow them to tie him up and hand him over to the Philistines. They were miserable cowards.

3. Samson submissively allowed himself to be tied up by his compatriots and handed over to the hands of his angry enemies (vv. 12–13). He patiently submitted:

3.1. So that he might be an example of great humility, coupled with great strength and courage. He was one who could control his own spirit and who knew how to submit as well as conquer.

3.2. So that by being handed over to the Philistines, he might have the opportunity to kill some of them. Justice is done when misery is prolonged for those who, in order to please their worst enemies, mistreat their best friend. Never did any people so foolishly deceive themselves as did these men of Judah, except those who mistreated our blessed Savior.

4. Samson successfully defended himself even when he was handed over firmly tied up with two new ropes. When the Philistines had him among them, they *shouted against him* (v. 14), glorying in their success and gloating over him. When they shouted at him as a man held captive, confident that everything was now theirs, then the *Spirit of the Lord came upon him* (v. 14). Because he was stirred in this way:

4.1. He immediately got clear of the ropes that were tying him. The two new ropes gave way with his first exertion. They broke and "were melted" (v. 14, margin) off from his hands, no doubt to the great dismay and terror of those who had shouted at him, whose shouts now became shrieks. Notice that *where the Spirit of the Lord is there is liberty* (2Co 3:17), and those who are freed in this way are really free. This was a type of the resurrection of Christ by the power of the Spirit of holiness (Ro 1:4). Christ, in his resurrection, loosed the bands of death, and its cords, the graveclothes, fell from his hands without being loosed, as Lazarus' were, because it was impossible that the mighty Savior should be held by them. He triumphed over the powers of darkness, though they shouted against him as if they held him securely in their grip.

4.2. He brought great destruction among the Philistines, who had all gathered around him to make fun of him (v. 15). Notice how poorly he was armed: he had no better weapon than the jawbone of a donkey; but what great destruction he caused with it! It never left his hand till he had used it to strike 1,000 Philistines dead on the spot. If it had been the jawbone of a lion, especially one he himself had killed, it might have made him boastful and made him think he was even more formidable, but to take the bone of that lowly animal was to do miracles with *the foolish things of the world* (1Co 1:27), so that the *excellency of the power might be of God and not of man* (2Co 4:7).

5. Samson celebrated his own victory, since the men of Judah would not do even that for him. He composed a short song, which he sang to himself. The thrust of this song was, *With the jawbone of an ass, heaps on heaps, have I slain a thousand men* (v. 16). The Hebrew word for "donkey" (*hamor*) sounds like the Hebrew for "heap," so this is a pun, representing the Philistines falling as weakly as a mass of donkeys. He also gave a name to the place, to remember the Philistines' disgrace forever (v. 17): *Ramath-lehi*, "the lifting up of the jawbone."

Verses 18–20

Here is:

1. The distress which Samson suffered after this great victory (v. 18). He found himself in a critical condition for lack of water and was about to faint. Josephus says that it was intended to rebuke him for not mentioning God in the song by which he memorialized the victory he had gained, and instead taking all the praise to himself: *I have slain a thousand men* (v. 16).

2. Samson's prayer to God in this distress. Those who forget to come to God with their praises may perhaps be forced to come to him with their prayers. Suffering is sometimes sent to bring unthankful people to God. He pleads two things with God in support of his petition:

2.1. His having experienced the power and goodness of God in his recent success as God's servant. He calls his victory *a great deliverance*, for if God had not helped him, he would not merely have failed to conquer the Philistines but would have been overwhelmed by them. This teaches us that it is good if we plead past experiences of God's power and goodness in prayer for further mercy.

2.2. His now being exposed to his enemies: "So that I do not fall into the hands of the uncircumcised and give them cause to tell it in Gath. Won't God be dishonored?" The best pleas are those that refer to God's glory.

3. The prompt relief God sent Samson. God heard his prayer and sent him water from *a hollow place that was in the jaw*. But I prefer the marginal reading of v. 19: God opened up a hollow place that was in "Lehi": the place of this action was, from the jawbone, called *Lehi*; even before the action it is so called (vv. 9, 14). And there God caused a plentiful supply of water to spring up. He drank this fine water, and his spirits revived. We would be more thankful for the mercy of water if we stopped to consider how badly off we would be without it.

4. The memorial of this provision, in the name Samson gave to this new fountain, *En-hakkore*, "the well of the one who called," so remembering both his own distress and God's favor to him. God opens up to his people many springs of comfort which may be rightly called by this name: it is the well of the one who called. Samson had given a name to the place which showed him great and triumphant, *Ramath-lehi*, "the lifting up of the jawbone," but here he gives it another name, which shows him to be needy and dependent.

5. The continuation of Samson's leadership after these achievements (v. 20). Israel finally submitted to the one whom they had betrayed. It was a mercy to Israel that although they were oppressed by a foreign enemy, they still had a judge who preserved order and kept them from destroying one another. His leadership continued for twenty years, but the details of that time are not included, except for the beginning of his leadership in this chapter and the end of it in the next.

CHAPTER 16

Samson's name means "a little sun." We have seen this sun rising very bright, and we assume that the middle of the day, while he led Israel for twenty years, was proportionally brilliant, but this chapter gives us an account of the evening of his life that does not commend to us its daytime. This little sun set under a cloud. But as it set, it darted out one last strong and glorious beam that made him a type of Christ, conquering by death. Here is Samson: 1. Greatly endangered by his intimacy with a prostitute, and only just escaping (vv. 1–3). 2. Completely destroyed by his intimacy with another harlot, Delilah. Notice how he was betrayed to her by his own sinful desires (v. 4); how he was betrayed by her to his sworn enemies, the Philistines, who eventually made him divulge the secret of his great strength (vv. 5–17). 3. Robbed of his strength (vv. 18–20). 4. Seized, blinded, imprisoned, mistreated, and, at a solemn festival, made to entertain the Philistines (vv. 21–25). But finally he took his revenge on them by pulling down the theater onto their heads, so dying with them (vv. 26–31).

Verses 1–3

Here is:

1. Samson's sin (v. 1). When he took a Philistine as his wife at the beginning of his life, that was excusable to some extent, but to have sexual relations with a prostitute whom he happened to see among them dishonors him greatly as an Israelite and as a Nazarite. *Tell it not in Gath* (2Sa 1:20).

2. Samson's danger. Notice was given to the magistrates of Gaza, perhaps by the treacherous prostitute herself, that Samson was in the city (v. 2). The gates of the city were then shut, guards were set, and all was kept quiet, so that Samson would suspect no danger. They thought they now had him in prison and did not doubt that it would lead to his death the next morning. If only all those who satisfy their sensual appetites in drunkenness, immorality, or any sinful desires would see themselves surrounded in this way by their spiritual enemies!

3. Samson's escape (v. 3). He got up at midnight, wakened perhaps by the restraints of his own conscience. He got up in repentance, horrified, we hope, at the sin he was now committing, and at himself because of that sin, and devoutly decided not to return to it. It was bad that he lay down without thinking about such matters, but it would

have been even worse if he had continued to lie in them. He immediately went toward the city gate, and once there, he did not stay to break open the gates but lifted them up along with their posts and their bars and carried them *up to the top of a hill* (v. 3), scorning the Philistines' attempt to restrain him with gates and bars, to prove the great strength God had given him. In this, he was a type of Christ's victory over death and the grave. He not only rolled away the stone from the door of the grave and so came out himself, but also carried away the gates of the grave, bar and all, and so left it forever to be an open prison to all who are his.

Verses 4–17

Children who have burned themselves dread the fire, but Samson, who has more than the strength of an ordinary man, does not even have the wisdom of a child in this matter, for although he has more than once fallen into great trouble, difficulty, and danger because of his love and desire for women, he still will not accept a warning but again falls into the same trap, and after this third fall he pays for it dearly. This evil woman, who was the ruin of Samson, is here called *Delilah*, a notorious name that suitably describes a person who by flattery or falsehood brings destruction on those to whom they pretend kindness. Notice:

1. The affection Samson had for Delilah: *he loved her* (v. 4). Whether she was an Israelite or a Philistine is not certain. If she was an Israelite, which is unlikely, she had the heart of a Philistine.

2. The desire of the rulers of the Philistines for her to betray Samson (v. 5):

2.1. What they told her they wanted to do was to *afflict* him, to humble and subdue him. They promised not to harm him at all; they just wanted to render him harmless so that he could not hurt them in any way.

2.2. What they wanted to find out was where his great strength lay and how they might tie him up. They involved Delilah in getting the secret out of him, telling her what a kindness it would be to them, and perhaps assuring her that it would not cause any real trouble, either to him or to her.

2.3. The price for doing this was high. Each of them promised to give her 1,100 pieces of silver, 5,500 in all. This was the price of betraying the one she pretended to love.

3. The ways in which Samson put her off on different occasions. She asked him *where his great strength lay*, and how he could be tied up and subdued (v. 6), pretending that she thought it was impossible for him to be tied up except by her charms.

3.1. When she urged him very much, he told her:

3.1.1. That he could be tied up with *seven green withs* (fresh thongs) (v. 7). This was tried (v. 8), but he *broke the withs* as easily *as a thread of tow is broken when it toucheth the fire* (v. 9), as easily as a piece of string snaps when it comes close to a flame.

3.1.2. When she continued to plead (v. 10), he told her that he could be held so tight by two new ropes that he would be as weak as any other man (v. 11). This was also tried, but it failed: the *new ropes* broke off from his arm *like a thread* (v. 12).

3.1.3. He then told her that the weaving of the seven locks or braids of his head would greatly affect him (v. 13). This came nearer the truth than anything he had said up to that time. His strength appeared to be very much in his hair, and when this was put to the test, he carried away the *pin of the beam* and *the web* purely by the strength of his hair (v. 14); he pulled up the pin and the loom with the fabric.

3.2. In making all these tests, it is hard to say which is seen more: Samson's weakness or Delilah's wickedness.

3.2.1. Could anything be more evil than her restless and unreasonable pleading with him to find out a secret which she knew would put his life in danger? What could be more evil, false, or treacherous than to lay his head in her lap, as one whom she loved, and at the same time to think of betraying him to those who hated him?

3.2.2. Could anything be weaker than for him to continue in a relationship with one who was so clearly intent on causing him trouble?

4. Samson's eventual disclosure of his great secret; and if the disclosure turned out to lead to his death, then he had only himself to blame, because he had not kept his secret from one who clearly wanted to destroy him. The name *Delilah* may mean "one who destroys"; and this is what she did to him. Notice:

4.1. How she teased him, telling him she did not believe he loved her unless he pleased her in this matter (v. 15): *How canst thou say, I love thee, when thine heart is not with me?* She continued to nag and annoy him for many days with her constant pestering, so that he became sick and tired of it (v. 16).

4.2. How she conquered him (v. 17): he *told her all his heart*; he told her everything. God left him to his own foolish devices to punish him for indulging his lust. *No razor should come upon his head* (13:5). His consecration to God was to be his strength, and so the sign of his consecration—his hair—was the promise of his strength. If he lost the former, he knew he would forfeit the latter. "If I am shaved, I will no longer be a Nazarite, and then all my strength will be lost." God's making his physical strength depend so much on his hair—which would not by nature influence his strength one way or the other—teaches us to exalt divine institutions and to expect God's grace to be given, and continue to be given, only as we use those means of grace which he has appointed for us so that we might wait on him: the word, sacraments, and prayer.

Verses 18–21

We have here the fatal consequences of Samson's foolish betrayal of his own strength. Notice:

1. How carefully Delilah made sure of taking the money for herself. It would have been heartbreaking to see one of the boldest people in the world sold and bought, just as a mere sheep to be slaughtered.

2. How she handed him over to them according to what had been arranged. Notice how treacherous she was (v. 19): she *made him sleep upon her knees*. Here we see the fatal consequences of thinking we are secure. Satan destroys people by rocking them to sleep, flattering them into thinking they are safe, and so making them care about nothing and fear nothing. He then deprives them of their strength and honor and makes them captive to his will. When Samson was asleep, Delilah had someone ready to cut off his hair, which they did so silently and so quickly that it did not wake him up.

3. How little concerned he himself was about it (v. 20). He must have missed his hair as soon as he woke up, but he said, "*I will shake myself as at other times*" after sleep. He soon found that he had changed, but did not know *that the Lord had departed from him*: he did not consider that this was the reason for the change. Many have lost the favorable presence of God and have not been aware of it; they have provoked God to withdraw from them but are not conscious of their loss.

4. What use the Philistines soon made of their advantage over him (v. 21). The Philistines took him when God had left him. If we sleep in the lap of our sinful desires, we will certainly wake up in the hands of the Philistines. They had probably promised Delilah not to kill him, but they made sure they rendered him harmless. The first thing they did, when they had him in their hands and found they could control him, was to *put* (gouge) *out his eyes* (v. 21), by "applying fire to them," says the Arabic. They considered that his eyes would never come back, as perhaps his hair might, and that the strongest arms could do little without eyes to guide them, and so they thought that if they now made him blind, then he would be blind forever. His eyes were what allowed his sin to enter—he saw the prostitute at Gaza, and *went in to her* (v. 1)—and so it was there that his punishment began. *They brought him down to Gaza* (v. 21) so that he might appear in weakness at the place where he had so recently given such proofs of his strength (v. 3). They *bound him*—who had before been tied up in the ropes of his own sin—*with fetters of brass* (bronze shackles) (v. 21), and he did *grind in the prison* (v. 21); they set him grinding in the prison. Poor Samson, how the mighty has fallen! Your honor is now laid in the dust!

Verses 22–31

Though the last stage of Samson's life was not glorious, there was honor in his death. No doubt he greatly repented of his sin, for the fact that God was reconciled to him can be seen:

- By the return of the sign of his Nazariteship (v. 22): *His hair began to grow again, as when he was shaven,* that is, to be as thick and as long as it had been before it had been cut off. The growth seems to have been extraordinary and intended as a special indication of the return of God's favor to him when he repented.
- By the use God made of him to destroy the enemies of his people, and at a time when it would do most to vindicate the honor of God, rather than directly defend and rescue Israel. Notice:

1. How the Philistines defiantly offended the God of Israel:

1.1. By the sacrifices they offered to Dagon, his rival. They called Dagon their *god*, but it was a god of their own making. He was represented by an idol, the upper part of which had a human form and the lower part the form of a fish. It was purely a creation of their own imagination, but they used it as a rival to the true and living God. It was only such a false god as Dagon that could be considered to support such an evil act.

1.2. By the entertainment they made of Samson, God's champion, which dishonored God himself. They made one another laugh to see how he stumbled and floundered in his blindness. They probably said, *Where is thy God?* (Ps 42:10). But because he had repented, his godly sorrow made him patient, and he accepted the shame as the punishment for his sin.

2. How justly the God of Israel brought sudden destruction on them by the hands of Samson. Thousands of the Philistines had gathered together to be present with their rulers for the sacrifices and joys of that day. They had come together to watch this comedy, but they were all killed. Notice:

2.1. Who were destroyed: all the *lords* (rulers) *of the Philistines* (v. 27), those who had corruptly bribed Delilah into betraying Samson to them. Samson had been drawn into sin by the Philistine women, and now many of them are killed.

2.2. When they were destroyed:

2.2.1. When they were in high spirits; when they felt safe and secure; when they were happy and did not think for a moment that they were in the slightest danger.

2.2.2. When they were praising Dagon, their god.

2.2.3. When they had as their entertainment an Israelite, a Nazarite, and when they gloated over him, persecuting the one whom God had struck down. When people make fun of a good person, they do not know what they are doing, nor whom they are offending.

2.3. How they were destroyed. Samson pulled the house down on them.

2.3.1. He gained strength to do it by prayer (v. 28). The strength which he had lost by sin he regained by prayer, as one who had truly repented. He prayed to God to remember him and strengthen him just once more. In so doing, he acknowledged that his strength for what he had already done had come from God. He begged that this power might be given to him just once more, to give them all a parting blow. Samson died praying, and so did our blessed Savior. Samson, however, prayed for revenge; Christ prayed for forgiveness.

2.3.2. He gained the opportunity to do it by leaning against the two pillars which were the chief, central supports of the building. The vast crowd of people on the roof contributed to its fall. Few escaped without being suffocated or crushed to death. Now in this:

2.3.2.1. The Philistines were greatly humbled. All their rulers and great people were killed. The temple of Dagon—as many think the house was—collapsed, and Dagon was buried in it.

2.3.2.2. Samson may very well be justified and declared not guilty of any sinful murder either of himself or the Philistines. Neither was this an act of suicide, for it was not his own life that he was trying to destroy.

2.3.2.3. God was glorified in forgiving Samson's great disobedience, and this act of God was evidence of that forgiveness.

2.3.2.4. Samson was a clear type of Christ. Samson pulled down Dagon's temple; Christ tore down Satan's kingdom. When Christ died, he gained the most glorious victory over the powers of darkness. When his arms were stretched out on the cross, as Samson's reached out to the two pillars, he fatally shook the gates of hell, and, *through death, destroyed him that had the power of death, that is, the devil* (Heb 2:14–15). In this Christ surpassed Samson, in that Christ not only died with the Philistines, but also rose again to triumph over them.

3. How the story of Samson concludes:

- With an account of his burial.
- With the repetition of the account we had before of the continuance of his leadership: *He judged Israel twenty years* (v. 31).

CHAPTER 17

What is related in this and the remaining chapters to the end of this book happened soon after the death of Joshua, in the days of Phinehas the son of Eleazar (20:28). But it is included here so that it might not interrupt the history of the judges. We read how unhappy the nation was when there were no judges, so that it might be seen how fortunate they were with judges. Idolatry began in these days in the family of Micah (ch. 17). It spread into the tribe of Dan (ch. 18). Notorious sin was committed in Gibeah of Benjamin (ch. 19). That whole tribe was destroyed for supporting it (ch. 20). Strange methods were used to keep up that tribe (ch. 21). In this chapter we are told how Micah, an Ephraimite, provided himself: 1. With an idol for his god (vv. 1–6). 2. With a Levite—such as he was—as his priest (vv. 7–13).

Verses 1–6

Here we have:

1. Micah and his mother quarreling:

1.1. A son robs his mother. The old woman had managed to hoard, through scrimping and saving for a long time, a great sum of money, 1,100 shekels of silver. She probably intended, when she died, to leave it to her son.

1.2. The mother curses the son or whoever has taken her money. Notice what trouble the love of money causes, how it destroys the responsibility and comfort of every relationship. Outward losses drive good people to pray, but they drive bad people to curse.

2. Micah and his mother reconciled:

2.1. The son was so terrified of his mother's curses that he gave back the money.

2.2. The mother was so pleased with her son's repentance that she recalled her curses and turned them into prayers for her son's welfare: *Blessed be thou of the Lord, my son* (v. 2).

3. Micah and his mother agreeing to turn their money into a god and set up an idol in their family. And although this was only the worship of the true God by an idol, against the second commandment, this still opened the door to the worship of other gods, Baals and the Asherahs, against the first and great commandment. Notice:

3.1. The mother's scheming in this matter. When the silver was recovered, she pretended she had consecrated it to the Lord (v. 3), either before it was stolen or afterward—it is uncertain which. "Come," she said to her son, "the money is mine, but you want it. Let it be neither mine nor yours, but let us both agree to make it into an idol for religious use." Probably this old woman was one of those who came out of Egypt, and would have had such idols made as she had seen there. Perhaps she told her son that this way of worshiping God by idols was, to her knowledge, the old religion.

3.2. The son agreed with her. It seems that when she first suggested the plan, he took offense at it, knowing the second commandment. But when the idols were made, Micah, through his mother's persuasion, was not only reconciled to them, but also greatly pleased. Strong as the old woman's superstition was, however, notice how her greed overcame, in part, even that. She had wholly consecrated the silver to make the carved and cast idols (v. 3), but when the time came to do it, she used less than a fifth, 200 shekels (v. 4). Now notice:

3.2.1. What was the corruption that was introduced (v. 5). Micah had a shrine, *a house of gods*; "a house of God" is the reading of the Septuagint (a Greek version of the Old Testament), for this was how he viewed it, considering it as good as that at Shiloh, and better, because it was his own, for people love to have their religion as something that they can control. "A house of error" is the Aramaic reading, for it really was so, a deviation from the truth, which allowed in all kinds of deceit. He made teraphim (household gods), which he could consult as necessary, and from which he could receive information, direction, and predictions. In this way, while the honor of Jehovah was claimed (v. 3), yet because the worship he instituted had been abandoned, these Israelites unavoidably lapsed into downright idolatry and demon worship.

For these teraphim, some room in the house of Micah was set up as the temple or house of God. An ephod, or holy garment, was provided for his priest to officiate in, to imitate those used at the tabernacle of God, and he consecrated one of his sons, probably the eldest, to be his priest. This is where idolatry began, and it spread like an all-consuming cancer. Dr. Lightfoot notes that just as 1,100 pieces of silver were here devoted to make an idol, which destroyed religious faith especially in the tribe of Dan, so 1,100 pieces of silver were given by each Philistine ruler to destroy Samson.

3.2.2. What was the cause of this corruption (v. 6): *There was no king in Israel*, no judge or sovereign ruler to take notice that these idols were being set up. Everyone did what was *right in his own eyes*, and then they soon did what was *evil in the sight of the Lord*. This shows us what a mercy good leadership is and why not only *prayers and intercessions, but giving of thanks should be made for kings and all in authority* (1Ti 2:1–2). Nothing contributes more under God to support religious faith in the world than the right administration of these two great ordinances: good judges and good Christian ministers.

Verses 7–13

We have here an account of Micah's provision for himself of a Levite as his chaplain. Notice:

1. On his mother's side the Levite came from the family of Judah, and he lived at Bethlehem. He left that place looking for somewhere else to stay, and in his travels he came to the house of Micah in the hill country of Ephraim (v. 8). Some think that it was because of some misfortune that he had moved on, that perhaps he was neglected and starved at Bethlehem. If that was the case, Israel's neglect of God began with their neglect of the Levites. It is a sign that religious faith is on the decline when good ministers are neglected and are suffering for their livelihood.

2. What agreement Micah came to with him. Micah takes him into his family (v. 10) and promises him:

2.1. Good prospects: *Be unto me a father and a priest.* He does not ask for references or credentials. Even if the Levite turns out to be a perfect scoundrel, thinks Micah, he will still be good enough to serve as a priest to a carved image. Such a priest would be like Jeroboam's priest of the *lowest of the people* (1Ki 12:31). It is not surprising if those who can make anything serve as a god can also make anyone serve as a priest.

2.2. A tolerable upkeep. He will allow him food, drink, and clothes (v. 10); "a double suit" is the reading in the margin, an ordinary suit and a best suit, one for everyday wear and one for holy days, and ten shekels (a few dollars) each year as spending money, a poor salary in comparison with what God provided for Levites who behaved well, but those who neglect God's service will never improve themselves or find a better master. The ministry is the best calling but remuneratively one of the lowest paid in the world.

3. The Levite's settlement with Micah (v. 11): he was *content to dwell with the man*, although his work was superstitious and his wages were scandalous. Micah thought himself holier than any of his neighbors and presumed to consecrate this Levite (v. 12).

4. Micah's satisfaction at this (v. 13): *Now know I that the Lord will do me good*:

4.1. He thought it was a sign of God's favor to him and his idols that God had at just the right time sent a Levite to him.

4.2. He now thought that the errors of his priesthood had all been put right and that everything would now go smoothly, even though he still kept his carved and cast idols. Many deceive themselves into good thoughts about their own condition by only partly mending their ways. They think they are as good as they should be, because they are not as bad as they were in one particular example.

4.3. He thought that making a Levite into a priest was a very commendable act, while in fact it was a presumptuous usurping.

4.4. He thought that having a Levite in the house with him would naturally make him entitled to receive God's favor. But having a Levite as your priest is by no means a security ensuring that God will do you good, unless you yourself are good and make good use of these advantages.

CHAPTER 18

We had an account in the previous chapter of how idolatry crept into the family of Micah, and in this chapter we read how it was transferred from there into the tribe of Dan. The tribe of Dan had been the last tribe to be assigned their allotment, and so a significant town in the most northerly corner of Canaan was added to it. Here we are told: 1. How, to get a report of the place, they sent spies, who in their traveling came to know Micah's priest (vv. 1–6). 2. What an encouraging report these spies brought back (vv. 7–10); what forces were sent to conquer Laish (vv. 11–13). 3. How they also plundered Micah of his gods (vv. 14–26). 4. How easily they conquered Laish (vv. 27–29) and, when they had captured it, set up the carved idol there (vv. 30–31).

Verses 1–6

We read here:

1. How these Danites had their eye on Laish, not the whole tribe of Dan, but one clan, in whose allotment that town came in the subdivision of Canaan. Up to that time this clan had stayed with their brothers, who had taken possession of their allotment, which lay between Judah and the Philistines, and had declined to go to their own town, because there was *no king in Israel* to rule over them (v. 1). But eventually necessity forced them to stir themselves, and they began to think of a place of their own where they could settle.

2. They sent *five men to search the land* (v. 2). The people they sent were brave warriors, who, if they fell into enemy hands, knew how to look danger in the face.

3. How the spies got to know Micah's priest. It seems they had known this Levite beforehand, that sometimes on his journeys he had been in their country. They recognized him by his voice (v. 3). Because they realized that he had in his possession a means of finding out God's will, they wanted him to tell them whether their journey would be successful (v. 5). They seem to have had a greater opinion of Micah's household gods of God's Urim, for they had passed by Shiloh and, it seems, had not asked for guidance from God's high priest, but they do not hesitate to consult Micah's contemptible Levite. He made them believe he had an answer from God that encouraged them to go on and assured them of good success (v. 6).

Verses 7–13

Here is:

1. The observation which the spies made of the town of Laish (v. 7). Never would a place so badly ruled and so badly guarded, which would make it a very easy target to an invading force:

1.1. It was badly governed, for everyone could be as evil as they wanted, and there was *no magistrate* (v. 7), no "heir of restraint" (margin): there was no one who would restrain them, so their shameless immorality offended God's wrath, and they weakened and devoured one another by all sorts of trouble. Notice here:

1.1.1. What the office of magistrate (judge or ruler) is. Magistrates are "heirs of restraint," to restrain what is evil. They are "possessors of restraint" (v. 7, margin), entrusted with authority to restrain everything that is evil and to be *a terror to evildoers* (Ro 13:3). It is only God's grace that can renew the corrupt human mind and turn people's hearts to him, but the judge's power may restrain their bad practices and tie their hands, so that their evil may not be so harmful or spread so much as otherwise it would.

1.1.2. What method must be used to restrain evil. Sinners must be put to shame, so that those who will not be restrained by the shamefulness of their sin before God and their own consciences may be restrained by the shamefulness of the punishment before other people. Every possible way must be tried to make sin appear unattractive and contemptible and make people ashamed of their laziness, drunkenness, cheating, lying, and other sins, by showing them that a good reputation always depends on leading a good life.

1.1.3. How miserable and how close to ruin are those places that have neither judges nor anyone who can bear the sword for any purpose.

1.2. It was badly guarded. The people of Laish were careless, peaceful, and falsely secure. They left their gates wide open. Their walls were in a bad state of repair. They lived like this because they did not think they were in any danger. It was a sign that the Israelites, through their laziness and cowardice, were not now such a terror to the Canaanites as they were when they first came among them, or otherwise the town of Laish, which probably knew it belonged to Israel, would not have felt so secure. And lastly, they had *no business with any man* (v. 7); they had no relationship with anyone else, which shows either their lives of laziness or the independence they pursued. They despised being either in subjection to or in alliance with any of their neighbors. The people of Laish kept themselves to themselves. They took no notice of anyone, and so no one took any notice of them.

2. The encouragement which they then gave to their compatriots who sent them to pursue their attack on this town (vv. 8–10).

- They describe the place as desirable (v. 9), better than the mountainous country into which they were crowded by the Philistines.
- They describe the place as within their reach. They do not doubt at all that, with God's blessing, they may soon gain possession of it, for *the people are secure* (v. 10).

3. The Danites' mission against Laish. This particular clan, to whose lot that town fell, now eventually set out for it (vv. 11–13). The military men were only a total of 600. It was strange that none of their brothers from their own tribe came to help them, but it was long after Israel came to Canaan before there appeared anything of a community spirit among them. It appears (from v. 21) that these 600 were the total that went to settle there, for they had their families and possessions with them, their *little ones and cattle*. The second day's march brought them to the hill country of Ephraim, near Micah's house (v. 13), and it is there that we pause a while.

Verses 14–26

The Danites had sent out their spies to locate a country for themselves. Now that the settlers came to the place, their spies let them know something else: they could tell them where there were gods: "Here, *in these houses*, there are an ephod, teraphim (household gods), and a great many fine devotional things, the like of which we do not have in our own country. *Now therefore consider what you have to do* (v. 14). We asked their guidance and received a good reply from them. They are worth having, and if we can only master these gods, we may hope to be successful and conquer Laish itself." They were right in thinking that it was desirable to have God's presence with them, but they were miserably mistaken in assuming that these idols—which were more suitable for use in a puppet play than in devotion to God—were signs of God's presence. The place they were going to settle in was so far from Shiloh that they thought they had greater need *of a house of gods* among themselves than Micah had, who lived so close to Shiloh. And so they were determined to take these gods along with them, and we are told how they stole the idols, flattered the priest, and frightened Micah from attempting to rescue them.

1. The five men who knew the house and its approaches, especially the chapel, went in and took the idols, with the ephod, household gods, and all the things that went with them, while the 600 kept the priest talking at the gate (vv. 16–18). This shows us what little care this poor priest took of his gods. This also shows us how powerless these poor gods were, which could not even prevent themselves from being stolen. How foolish these Danites were! They must have *gods to go before them*, not gods that they themselves had made, but what was as bad, gods that they themselves had stolen. Their idolatry began with theft, which was a fitting introduction for such a work. In order to break the second commandment, they began by breaking the eighth and took their neighbor's goods to make them their gods.

2. They spoke to the priest and flattered him into a good mood, not only persuading him to let the gods go, but also to go along with them, for without him they would not know how to use the gods. Notice:

2.1. How they tempted him (v. 19). They assured him of better prospects with them than those he had then.

2.2. How they won him over. A little persuasion was enough: *His heart was glad* (v. 20). He took the idols with him and spread the infection of idolatry to a whole town. If ten shekels won him over—as Bishop Hall expresses it—eleven would have lost him, for what can keep those who have shipwrecked their conscience? *The hireling flees because he is a hireling* (Jn 10:13).

3. They frightened Micah away when he chased them to recover his gods. His neighbors all went together and pursued the robbers, who, having their children and cattle in front of them (v. 21), could not move quickly. The pursuers called after them, wanting to speak with them. Those at the back turned around and asked Micah what he wanted (v. 23). He argued with them and pleaded his right, which he thought would prevail, but they answered and pleaded their power, which, it turned out, did prevail.

3.1. He insists on the wrong they have done to him (v. 24): "*You have taken away my gods*, my idols of God. I made them myself." How foolish it was for him to call things of his own making his *gods*, when only the One who made us is to be worshiped as God!

3.2. They insist on the trouble they will certainly make for him if he continues with his demand. They will not listen to reason or act justly. They do not even offer to pay him for the direct costs he has incurred in having the idols made. They will not even speak to him pleasantly, but decide to justify their robbery with murder unless he immediately drops his claims (v. 25). Micah does not have enough courage to risk his life to rescue his gods: that is how low his opinion is of their being able to protect and support him; and so he weakly gives the gods up (v. 26). If the loss of our idols heals us of the love of them and makes us say, *What have we to do any more with idols?* (Hos 14:8), then that loss will be our unspeakable gain. See also Isa 2:20; 30:22.

Verses 27–31

Here:

1. Laish is conquered by the Danites. They continued on their journey, and because they met with no disaster, they perhaps concluded that they had not done anything wrong in robbing Micah. Many people use their success to justify their ungodliness. Notice:

1.1. The people of Laish were peaceful and falsely secure, which made them a soft target for this little handful of men who attacked them (v. 27).

1.2. What a complete victory they gained over them: they *put all the people to the sword* (v. 27) and burned down as much of the town as they thought fit to rebuild (vv. 27–28).

1.3. How the conquerors settled themselves in the place of the people they had killed (vv. 28–29). They built the town, or much of it, afresh and *called the name of it Dan*, as a witness to them that although it was separated by a great distance from their brothers, they were nevertheless Danites by birth.

2. Idolatry is immediately set up. God had graciously fulfilled his promise in giving them possession of what was allotted to them. But the first thing they did after they are settled was to break his precepts and statutes. As soon as they began to settle down, they *set up the graven image* (v. 30), perversely attributing their success to that idol. Their Levite, who officiated as priest, is finally named here: *Jonathan, the son of Gershom, the son of Manasseh* (v. 30). The word *Manasseh*, in the original, has the Hebrew letter *Nun, n*, set as a superscript letter, which according to some of the Jewish rabbis is a sign that it should be left out, and that *Manasseh* here is *Moses*, and this Levite, they say, was grandson of the famous Moses, who indeed had a son named Gershom. The Vulgate reads *Moses*. And if in fact Moses had a grandson who was immoral, and was taken up as a tool to be used to set up idolatry, it is not the only example of the unfortunate corruption of the descendants of great and good people. Children's children are not always the crown of the old. But Bishop Patrick takes this as an idle thought of the rabbis, and thinks this Jonathan came from some other Levite family. We are told at the close of the chapter how long these corruptions went on. The descendants of this Jonathan continued to act as priests to this family of Dan that was established. These idols continued till Samuel's time, for that is how long *the ark of God was at Shiloh* (v. 31), and in his time effective care was probably taken to suppress and do away with this idolatry. This shows us how dangerous it is to allow an infection to break out, for spiritual illnesses are not as quickly healed as they are caught.

CHAPTER 19

The three remaining chapters of this book contain a most tragic story of the evil of the men of Gibeah, supported by the tribe of Benjamin. This seems to have been when there was no king or judge in Israel (v. 1; 21:25). These evils — the Danites' idolatry and the Benjamites' immorality — allowed a general apostasy to break out (3:7). The rape of the Levite's concubine is related here. 1. Her unfaithfulness to him (vv. 1–2); his reconciliation to her and the journey he took to bring her home (v. 3); her father's kind reception of him (vv. 4–9); the bad treatment he met with at Gibeah. He was neglected by the men of Gibeah (vv. 10–15). 2. He was received by an Ephraimite who stayed among them (vv. 16–21). 3. They attacked him in his quarters, as the Sodomites did Lot's guests (vv. 22–24). They shamelessly raped and abused his concubine to death (vv. 25–28). He sent notice of this to all the tribes of Israel (vv. 29–30).

Verses 1–15

This Levite came from the hill country of Ephraim (v. 1). He married a wife of Bethlehem in Judah. It does not seem that he had any other wife, and the margin of v. 1 says she is "a wife, a concubine."

1. This Levite's concubine was unfaithful to him and left him (v. 2). The Aramaic reads that she behaved defiantly toward him, or despised him; and because he showed his displeasure at it, she went away from him, and she was received at her father's house. When she treacherously departed from her husband to have a relationship with a stranger, her father ought not to have supported her sin. Children's ruin often owes a lot to their parents' indulgence.

2. The Levite himself went to seek her return. She is addressed in the kindest terms by her wronged husband, who deliberately takes a long journey to ask her to be reconciled (v. 3). This is part of the character of the wisdom from above: it is gentle, submissive, and open to reason. He spoke *friendly* to her, or comfortingly, for this is what the Hebrew phrase here, *speaking to the heart*, commonly refers to. This shows that she was sorry and penitent for the wrong she had done.

3. The woman's father made the Levite very welcome.

3.1. Her father received him kindly, was pleased to see him (v. 3), and gave him generous hospitality for three days (v. 4). The Levite wanted to show that he was perfectly reconciled, and so he accepted his father-in-law's kindness. We do not find that he rebuked him or his daughter for what had been done wrong. It befits everyone, but especially Levites, to forgive as God does. Everything gave the couple a hopeful prospect of living comfortably together for the future.

3.2. Her father was very keen for him to stay, to continue his generous welcome even further. The affection he had for him, and the pleasure he took in his company, came:

3.2.1. From a polite respect for the Levite as his son-in-law and as a grafted-in branch of his own house. This shows us that love and duty are due to those to whom we are related by marriage as well as to those who are our own flesh and blood.

3.2.2. From a godly respect for him as a Levite, a servant of God's house.

3.2.2.1. He wanted him to stay as long as he possibly could. Although the Levite was nobly treated, he was keen to go soon. A good person's heart is where their business is. When people want to enjoy being away from home for a long time where there is nothing to do, it is a sign that they either have little to do at home or do not want to do what has to be done.

3.2.2.2. He forced him to stay till the afternoon of the fifth day, and this, as it turned out, was unkind (vv. 8–9).

If the couple had set out earlier, they might have reached some better lodging place than the one they then had to stay at; in fact, they might even have reached Shiloh.

4. On his way home the Levite was forced to stay at Gibeah, a city in the tribe of Benjamin, afterward called *Gibeah of Saul* (1Sa 11:4), which lay on his way toward Shiloh and the hill country of Ephraim. When night came, they could not carry on their journey.

4.1. The servant proposed that they lodge in Jebus, which was later called Jerusalem but was then still in the possession of the Jebusites. If they had done so, they would probably have been treated much better than they were at Gibeah of Benjamin. Corrupt and dissolute Israelites are worse and much more dangerous than Canaanites.

4.2. Having passed by Jebus, they stopped at Gibeah (vv. 13–15). They sat down in the street or square because nobody offered them any lodging. Although this traveler was a Levite — and it was to those of that tribe that God had particularly commanded his people to be kind on all occasions — he met with a frosty reception in Gibeah: *No man took them into his house* (v. 15).

Verses 16–21

When the Levite, his wife, and his servant were beginning to fear that they must spend the night in the city square — which was as good as going into a lions' den — they were eventually invited into a house, and we are told:

1. Who the kind man was who invited them in:

1.1. He was a man from the hill country of Ephraim who was staying in Gibeah (v. 16). Out of all the tribes of Israel, the Benjamites had most reason to be kind to poor travelers, because their ancestor, Benjamin, was born on the road, as his mother was then on a journey which was very near this place (Ge 35:16–17). But they were hardhearted to a traveler in distress, while an honest Ephraimite had compassion on him; and no doubt the Ephraimite was even more kind to him when, by asking him about himself, he discovered that he was his compatriot, also from the hill country of Ephraim.

1.2. He was an old man, but one who kept some of the old virtues of the Israelites. The rising generation was entirely corrupt. If there was any goodness still among them, it was only among those who were old and getting on in years.

1.3. He was coming home from his work in the fields in the evening. The rest had given themselves up to lazy and indulgent ways, and so it was no wonder there was much sexual immorality among them, as there was in Sodom, since there were many people who were not in the least concerned about others (Eze 16:49), just as in Sodom.

2. How free and generous he was in his invitation. He did not wait till they turned to him to beg for a night's accommodation. In the same way, our God answers us before we call out to him. We can learn from this that a charitable disposition expects opportunities, rather than importunity, to do good, and will give help when it sees a need without having to be asked. Love is not inclined to distrust, but *hopeth all things* (1Co 13:7).

Verses 22–30

Here is:

1. The great evil of the men of Gibeah. The sinners are here called *sons of Belial* (v. 22), that is, obscene and perverted men, men without any self-control, children of the Devil (for he is Belial), who were like him and were joining him in rebelling against God and his rule.

1.1. They made a contemptuous and barbaric attack on the house of an honest man at night. He not only lived at peace among them but also kept a good house that was a blessing and an attractive feature of their city.

1.2. They had a particular hatred for strangers who were within their gates, who wanted a night's accommodation among them. They acted against the laws of hospitality, which all civilized nations consider sacred, and which the owner of the house pleaded with them (v. 23).

1.3. They intended to abuse the Levite in the most obscene and detestable way, which is not to be thought of without horror and revulsion: *Bring him forth that we may know him*, so we can have sex with him (v. 22). Now:

1.3.1. This was the sin of Sodom, and it is therefore called *sodomy*. What use was it if they had the ark of God in Shiloh when they had Sodom in their square—God's Law in their fringes, but the Devil in their hearts?

1.3.2. This was the punishment for their idolatry, that sin to which they were devoted above all others. God gave them up to these immoral ways, by which they dishonored themselves just as they had by their idolatry dishonored him and turned his glory into shame (Ro 1:24, 28).

1.4. They turned a deaf ear to the reasoning and rebukes of the owner of the house, who probably knew about the story of Lot and the Sodomites and set himself to imitate Lot (vv. 23–24). Compare Ge 19:6–8. But in one thing he went too far in following Lot's example: in offering them his daughter to do with her what they wanted. He did not have the right to prostitute his daughter, nor should he have done this evil so that good might come. But *they would not hearken to him* (v. 25). Willful, sinful desires are like the deaf adder that stops up its ear (Ps 58:4–5); they make the conscience insensitive.

1.5. They got the Levite's wife among them and raped and abused her to death (v. 25). They snubbed the old man's offer to let them satisfy their lusts with his daughter.

2. The notice that was sent of this evil to all the tribes of Israel. The poor, abused woman who had been so brutally raped made her way toward her husband's lodging place as soon as dawn came, for daybreak made these sons of Belial let her go (v. 25): such works of darkness hate and dread the light. She fell down at the door with her hands on the threshold, and in that position as one who was repenting, with her mouth in the dust, she breathed her last. He found her there (vv. 26–27), soon became aware that she was dead (v. 28), took up her dead body, gave up his original purpose of going to Shiloh, and went straight home. There was no king in Israel to appeal to and demand justice from. He therefore had no other way open to him but to appeal to the people: let the community be the judge. To each of the tribes, in their respective meetings, he sent by special messengers a complaint about the wrong that had been done to him, in all its aggravating circumstances, and with it a piece of the dead body of his wife (v. 29) to show how brutally she had been treated. All who saw the pieces of the dead body and were told about it expressed the same feelings about it:

2.1. That the men of Gibeah had been guilty of an obscene and detestable evil, the like of which had never been known before in Israel (v. 30).

2.2. That a general assembly of all Israel should be called to debate what would be a fitting punishment for this evil, so that an end might be put to this threatening inundation of corruption and the wrath of God might not be poured out on the whole nation as a result. We have here the three great rules which those who sit in council should go by in every difficult matter:

- Let everyone withdraw and consider the matter impartially, seriously, calmly, and fully in their own thoughts, without prejudice on either side, before they speak about it.
- Let them talk it over freely, and let everyone take the advice of their friends, to know their thoughts and reasons, and to weigh them up carefully.
- Then let everyone speak their mind and give their vote according to their conscience. *In the multitude of such counselors there is safety* (Pr 11:14).

CHAPTER 20

The story of this chapter must be brought into the Book of the Wars of the Lord, but it is the most sad and most unfortunate episode in that history, for there is nothing in it that is cheerful or pleasant in the least, except the godly zeal of Israel against the evil men of Gibeah. And yet this happened soon after the glorious settlement of Israel in the Land of Promise, after which you would have expected everything to be calm and prosperous. We have in this chapter: 1. The Levite's cause heard in a general assembly of the tribes (vv. 1–7); a unanimous decision to avenge his quarrel on the men of Gibeah (vv. 8–11). 2. The Benjamites appearing in defense of the criminals (vv. 12–17). 3. The defeat of Israel in the first and second days' battles (vv. 18–25). 4. Their humbling themselves before God on that occasion (vv. 26–28); the total rout of the Benjamites on the third encounter by a strategy which meant that they were all destroyed except for 600 men (vv. 29–48).

Verses 1–11

Here is:

1. A general meeting of all the assembly of Israel to examine the matter concerning the Levite's concubine and to consider what was to be done about it (vv. 1–2). They came together by general agreement, as it were, as one, fired with a holy zeal for the honor of God and Israel.

1.1. The place of their meeting was *Mizpeh*; they gathered together to the Lord there, for Mizpah was so close to Shiloh that their camp might well have been supposed to extend from Mizpah to Shiloh. Shiloh was a small town, and so when there was a general meeting of the people to present themselves before God, they chose Mizpah as their headquarters.

1.2. The people who met were all Israel, from Dan in the north to Beersheba in the south, with the land of Gilead—that is, the tribes on the other side of the Jordan—all as one: they were unanimous in their concern for the public well-being. In this assembly of all Israel, the chiefs of the people presented themselves as the representatives of the rest. The leaders were like cornerstones of the people and kept them all together. They took their places at their respective posts, as the heads of thousands and hundreds, fifties and tens, which they led, for we suppose there was a great deal of order and government among them, even though they had no general or commander in chief. Here was:

- A general congress of the states to give guidance.
- A general meeting of the soldiers, who were warriors armed with swords (v. 17), for action.

2. Notice of this meeting given to the tribe of Benjamin (v. 3): *They heard that the children of Israel had gone up to Mizpeh*. But the notice they received of this meeting hardened and angered them rather than stirred them to think of the things concerning their peace and honor.

3. A solemn examination of the crime of which the men of Gibeah were accused. The Levite gave a detailed report of the matter. He concluded his declaration with an appeal to the judgment of the court (v. 7): *You are all children of Israel*, and so you *know law and judgment* (Est 1:13). So give your advice and guidance on what is to be done.

4. The decision they then came to, which was that, being now together, they would not separate until they had seen vengeance taken on this evil city which had brought shame and disgrace on their nation. Notice:

4.1. Their zeal against the terrible immoral act that had been committed. They would not return to their houses, however much their families and their lives at home needed them, until they had vindicated the honor of God and Israel.

4.2. Their wisdom in sending out a considerable group of forces to get provisions for the rest (vv. 9 – 10).

4.3. Their unanimity in making these decisions and carrying them out. The decision was unanimous, with no dissent (v. 8). This was their glory and strength, that the different tribes had no separate interests as far as the common good was concerned.

Verses 12 – 17

Here is:

1. The fair and just demand which the tribes of Israel, now camped, sent to the tribe of Benjamin, to hand over the evildoers of Gibeah to justice (vv. 12 – 13). The Israelites were zealous against the evil that had been committed, but they were prudent in their zeal and did not think they were justified in falling on the whole tribe of Benjamin unless, by refusing to give up the criminals and protecting them from justice, the tribe would make themselves guilty as accessories after the fact.

2. The wretched stubbornness and perverseness of the men of Benjamin, who seem to have been as unanimous and zealous in their determination to stand by the criminals as the rest of the tribes were to punish them. So little was their sense of honor, duty, and rights.

2.1. They objected to the other tribes' interfering with their concerns. They would not do what they knew was their duty, because they were reminded of it by their brothers, whom they objected to being taught and controlled by.

2.2. They were so arrogant as to advance against the united force of all Israel. How could they expect to succeed when they fought against justice, and thus against God himself in his justice, against those who had the high priest and divine wisdom on their side — and so acted in outright rebellion against the sacred and supreme authority of the nation? It would seem they depended on the skill of their men to make up what was lacking in their numbers. They depended especially on a regiment of 700 warriors who could sling a stone. These soldiers were left-handed but were so skillful at slinging stones that they could sling a stone at a single hair and not miss (v. 16). But these expert slingers were far off course as far as fighting for the right cause was concerned.

Verses 18 – 25

We have here the defeat of the men of Israel in their first and second battles with the Benjamites:

1. Before their first encounter they asked God for guidance concerning the order of their battle and were given direction, but they were still severely beaten. The whole army laid siege to Gibeah (v. 19). The Benjamites went forward to lift the siege, and the Israelite army prepared to give them a fierce reception (v. 20) and turned on them to fight them. But between the Benjamites who attacked them in the front with incredible ferocity, and the men of Gibeah who came out to their rear, they were put into confusion and lost 22,000 soldiers (v. 21).

2. Before their second encounter they again *asked counsel of God*. This time they asked more seriously than before, for it is said that they *wept before the Lord until evening* (v. 23). Further, this time they did not ask who should go first, but whether they should go up at all. God told them to go up; he allowed the attempt, for although Benjamin was their brother, he was a cancerous part of their body and must be cut out. Hearing this response, they took courage, perhaps more in their own strength than in the divine commission, and made a second attempt on the forces of the rebels, at the same place where the former battle was fought (v. 22). But they were repelled again this second time, with the loss of 18,000 soldiers (v. 25). What may we say about these things, that such a just and honorable cause was defeated in this way once again? Were they not fighting God's battles against sin?

2.1. God's judgments are very deep, and his ways are as mysterious as the movements of the sea. We may be sure that God's ways of advancing his purposes are righteous, even when we cannot see the reasons for those ways.

2.2. God wanted to show them, and us also, that *the race is not to the swift nor the battle to the strong* (Ecc 9:11), that our confidence is not to be in numbers, which perhaps the Israelites depended too much on. We must never trust merely in human strength, but instead we should trust in the Rock of ages.

2.3. God wanted to discipline Israel for their sins. They did well to show such zeal against the evil of Gibeah, but *were there not with them, even with them, sins against the Lord their God?* (2Ch 28:10). Some think the defeat was a rebuke to them for not witnessing against the idolatry of Micah and the Danites.

2.4. God wants to teach us not to think it strange if a good cause suffers defeat for a while, nor to evaluate its merits by its success. The advantage of grace in the heart and the validity of the Christian religion in the world may be thwarted, suffer great loss, and seem to be weak, but judgment will eventually be brought out victoriously: "We may lose a battle, but we will win the war." Right may fall, but it will always rise again.

Verses 26 – 48

We have here a full account of the complete victory of the Israelites over the Benjamites in their third encounter: the righteous cause finally gained the victory. Notice:

1. How the victory was gained. In the earlier encounters they had trusted too much in two matters: the goodness of their cause and the superiority of their numbers. It was true that they had both right and strength on their side, which were great advantages, but they depended too much on them, to the neglect of those duties which they turned to on this third attempt — after they saw the error of their ways.

1.1. Previously, they were so confident of the goodness of their cause that they thought it unnecessary to turn to God for his presence and blessing. They took it for granted that God would bless them; in fact, they perhaps concluded that he owed them his favor. They only inquired of God, *Who shall go up first?* And, *Shall we go up?* (v. 18). But now they begged his favor; they fasted, prayed, and *offered burnt offerings and peace offerings* (v. 26), in order to make atonement for sin and to acknowledge their dependence on God. And when they were in this spiritual attitude and sought the Lord, he not only ordered them to go up against the Benjamites a third time but also gave them a promise of victory: *Tomorrow I will deliver them into thy hand* (v. 28).

1.2. Previously, they were so confident of the greatness of their strength that they thought it unnecessary to use any special means, set up an ambush, or even formulate a strategy. They did not doubt that they would win by sheer weight of numbers. Now, however, they saw that they needed to make a plan as if their enemy were superior in numbers. And so they set up an ambush (v. 29) and were victorious, as their fathers were at Ai (Jos 8:1–35).

1.2.1. Notice the method they used. The main forces of the army faced the city of Gibeah, as they had done before, advancing toward the gates (v. 30). The Benjamites, whose main forces were now quartered at Gibeah, boldly charged out to engage in battle with them. The besiegers withdrew quickly, as if their hearts failed them when they saw the Benjamites. But when the Benjamites were all drawn out of the city, the ambush seized the city (v. 37) and gave a signal to the main forces of the army (vv. 38, 40), which immediately turned on the Benjamites (v. 41), and it would seem another considerable body of troops positioned at Baal Tamar attacked them at the same time (v. 33). The result was that the Benjamites were completely surrounded, which put them into a great panic. A sense of guilt now discouraged them. Everyone was against them.

1.2.2. Notice in this story:

- At the beginning of the battle, the Benjamites were confident that the day would belong to them. Sometimes God allows evildoers to flourish so that their ruin may be more complete. Their joy is short-lived, and their triumph lasts only for a moment.
- Evil was near them, but they did not know it (v. 34).
- Although the men of Israel played their part well in this encounter, the victory is still ascribed to God (v. 35).
- They *trode down* (overran) *the men of Benjamin with ease* when God fought against them (v. 43).

2. How the Israelites followed up their victory and made the most of it by the military operation they carried out against these sinners and their souls:

- Gibeah itself, that den of iniquity, was destroyed.
- The army on the battlefield was completely routed and cut off.
- Those who escaped from the battlefield were chased and cut off in their flight.
- Even those who stayed at home were caught in the destruction. It seems that only 600 men remained out of all the tribe of Benjamin, who took shelter in the rock of Rimmon and stayed there for four months (v. 47).

3. How the whole matter affected Israel: what happened at Gibeah is spoken about twice by the prophet Hosea as the beginning of the corruption of Israel and a pattern of everything that followed (Hos 9:9): *They have deeply corrupted themselves as in the days of Gibeah*, and (Hos 10:9), *Thou hast sinned from the days of Gibeah*. It is also added that *the battle in Gibeah against the children of iniquity did not* — that is, did not at first — overtake them.

CHAPTER 21

At the end of the previous chapter we read about the destruction of the tribe of Benjamin. Here we have: 1. The mourning of Israel over this destruction (vv. 1–4, 6, 15).

2. The provision the Israelites made to rebuild the tribe out of the 600 men who escaped, for whom they found wives: 2.1. From the virgins of Jabesh Gilead (vv. 5, 7–14). 2.2. From the daughters of Shiloh (vv. 16–25).

Verses 1–15

We may notice here:

1. The ardent zeal which the Israelites had expressed against the evil of the men of Gibeah, as it was supported by the tribe of Benjamin.

1.1. While the general assembly of the people was gathering together, they bound themselves, by putting themselves under the great curse which they called the *cherem*, to completely destroy all those cities that would not send their representatives, for they looked on those who refused as not being angry at the crime that had been committed, as showing no concern for keeping the nation from God's judgments by administering justice, and as having no regard for the authority of a common agreement, by which they were summoned to meet.

1.2. When they had met and heard the cause, they made another solemn oath that none of all the thousands of Israel then present, nor any of those whom they represented — not intending to commit their descendants — would give his daughter in marriage to a Benjamite (v. 1), if they could help it. They made this decision not with any intention to destroy the tribe, but because they generally wanted to treat those who had joined or helped in this evil as they treated the nations of Canaan which had been set apart in a special way to be destroyed. They were not only obliged to destroy these nations; they were also forbidden to take husbands or wives from among them.

2. The deep concern which the Israelites expressed at the destruction of the tribe of Benjamin when it was carried out. Notice:

2.1. Though the tide of their anger at Benjamin's crime was high and strong before, yet the tide of their grief at Benjamin's destruction was just as high and as strong afterward: *They repented* (grieved) *for Benjamin their brother* (vv. 6, 15). They did not grieve at their zeal against the sin but at the sad consequences of what they had done, for they had taken matters further than was either just or necessary. It would have been enough to destroy all they found who bore arms, and it was unnecessary for them to kill the women and children, the farmers and shepherds. We can learn from this:

2.1.1. We can be too enthusiastic about doing good. We must take great care in controlling our zeal, so that what seemed supernatural in its causes does not turn out to be unnatural in its effects. That which swallows up our humanity cannot be good theology. Many wars which began well end badly.

2.1.2. Even necessary justice is to be done with compassion. God does not enjoy punishing people, and neither should we.

2.1.3. Strong passions can bring about the need for later repentance. What we say and do in an angry temper we often wish we could undo in calmer moments. Now:

2.2. How did they express their concern?

2.2.1. By their grief for the rift that had occurred. They came to the house of God, for that is where they brought all their doubts, opinions, cares, and sorrows. They poured out their complaint (v. 3): *There is one tribe lacking*. What if Benjamin became a *Benoni* — if the "son of the right hand" became a "son of sorrow"? In this trouble they built an altar, to atone for their own foolishness in pursuing victory and to ask for God's favor in their present difficulty. Everything that grieves us should bring us closer to God.

2.2.2. By their amicable treaty with the poor, distressed refugees who were hidden in the rock of Rimmon, to whom they sent an offer of peace, assuring them, in the name of the whole community, that Israel would now no longer treat them as enemies but receive them as brothers (v. 13).

2.2.3. By the care they took to find wives for them, so that their tribe might be built up again, and its destruction repaired. They all worked out ways to rebuild this tribe. While the poor, distressed Benjamites who were hidden in the rock feared that their brothers were plotting their destruction, those brothers were in fact planning to move them on. Four hundred virgins who were eligible for marriage were found at Jabesh Gilead, and these were married to that number of the surviving Benjamites (v. 14). Perhaps the alliance that was effected between Benjamin and Jabesh Gilead through these marriages made Saul, who was a Benjamite, even more concerned for that place than he would otherwise have been (1Sa 11:4), even though in his time it was inhabited by new families.

Verses 16 – 25

Here is how wives were found for the 200 remaining Benjamites.

1. At Shiloh, in the fields, all the young women of that city met to dance, in honor of *a feast of the Lord*, probably the Feast of Tabernacles (v. 19), for that festival was the only season at which the Jewish virgins were allowed to dance, and it was allowed not so much for their own recreation as to express their holy joy, as David did when he danced before the ark. The dancing was modest and chaste. However, their dancing in public in this way made them an easy target for those who wished to take advantage of them.

2. The elders of Israel gave authority to the Benjamites to *lie in wait in the vineyards*; take wives, each man one wife for himself; and carry them straight to their own country (vv. 20 – 21). It was preposterous for the elders to presume, in their matchmaking, that both the mutual affection of the young people and the approval of the parents must come later. The case was extraordinary and may not be used as a precedent in any way. As the proverb puts it, "Marry in haste, repent at leisure," and what comfort can be expected from a match made either by force or by fraud?

3. They undertook to pacify the fathers of these young women. Some of the fathers, whose consciences were tender, might fear that they were still subject to the oath they had taken not to give their daughters to Benjamites. The elders would argue that the necessity had been urgent (v. 22): *We reserved not to each man his wife.* They acknowledged now that they had done wrong in destroying all the women. In order to make up for their too rigorous interpretation of their vow to destroy the Benjamites, they gave the most lenient interpretation to their vow not to give their daughters to them.

4. Lastly, at the close of this book we have:

• The resettling of the tribe of Benjamin. The few who remained returned to the inheritance of that tribe (v. 23). And soon after, Ehud came from among them. He was famous in his generation as the second judge of Israel (3:15).

• The disbanding and dispersing of the army of Israel (v. 24). They did not set up a standing army or claim to make any changes in, or establish any laws for, the government, but quietly departed with God's peace when the episode which they were called together for was over, everyone to his family.

A PRACTICAL AND DEVOTIONAL EXPOSITION OF THE BOOK OF

Ruth

This short story of the domestic affairs of one particular family is a suitable book to follow the book of Judges—the events related here happened in the days of the judges—and is also a suitable book to go before the books of Samuel, because David is introduced at the end. It does not relate any miracles, laws, wars, or victories, or the overthrow of states, but first the suffering and then the comfort of Naomi; and first the conversion, and later the advance, of Ruth. The intention of this book is: 1. To lead us to Providence, to show us how it is informed by God's knowledge of our private concerns. See also 1Sa 2:7–8; Ps 113:7–9. 2. To lead us to Christ, who was a descendant of Ruth, and part of whose genealogy concludes the book, which is the source of the genealogy in Mt 1:3–5. In the conversion of Ruth the Moabite woman and the bringing of her into the family line of the Messiah, we have a type of the calling of the Gentiles in due time into the fellowship of our Lord Jesus Christ. We have an account of the suffering of Naomi and Ruth (ch. 1); examples of their diligence and humility (ch. 2); the bringing of them into a relationship with Boaz (ch. 3); and finally, their happy settlement (ch. 4). And let us remember that the scene is set in Bethlehem, where our Redeemer was born.

CHAPTER 1

In this chapter we have Naomi's suffering and troubles: 1. As a distressed mother running a home and forced by famine to move to the land of Moab (vv. 1–2); as a mournful widow and mother, mourning the death of her husband and her two sons (vv. 3–5). 2. As a caring mother-in-law, wanting to be kind to her two daughters (vv. 6–18). 3. As a poor woman sent back to the place where she had originally settled (vv. 19–22).

Verses 1–5

The first words give the date of this story. It was *in the days when the judges ruled* (v. 1). It must have been toward the beginning of the judges' time, for Boaz, who married Ruth, was born of Rahab, who received the spies in Joshua's time. Some think it was in the days of Ehud; others think it was in the days of Deborah. Bishop Patrick is inclined to think it was in the days of Gideon, because it was only in his days that we read of a famine, the one caused by the Midianites' invasion (Jdg 6:3–4). Here is:

1. A famine in the land of Canaan, the *land flowing with milk and honey* (Ex 3:8; etc.). This was one of the judgments which God had threatened to bring on them for their sins (Lev 26:19–20). When the land had rest, it still did not have plenty; even in Bethlehem, which means "house of bread," there was scarcity. *A fruitful land is turned into barrenness* (Ps 107:34), to rebuke and restrain the self-indulgent and dissolute ways of those who lived there.

2. An account of one particular family distressed in the famine, the family of Elimelech. His name means "my God a king." His wife was Naomi, which means "pleasant." But his son's names were Mahlon and Kilion, "sickness" and "failing," perhaps because they were weak, sickly children.

3. The move of this family from Bethlehem to the country of Moab, to live on the other side of the Jordan because of the famine (vv. 1–2). It seems there was plenty in the country of Moab while there was scarcity of bread in the land of Israel. Elimelech goes to stay there for a time during the famine, just as Abraham did on a similar occasion when he went to Egypt and as Isaac did in the land of the Philistines. Notice here:

3.1. Elimelech's care for his family and his taking his wife and children with him were no doubt commendable. But:

3.2. We do not see how his move to Moab could be justified on this occasion. The seed of Israel was now established and ought not to move to the territories of the nations. What reason did Elimelech have more than any of his neighbors? If he could not be content with the small allowances that his neighbors endured, if he could not live in hope that the years of plenty would come again, or could not wait patiently for those years to come, then that was his fault, and it was dishonoring to God and the good land he had given them. It would weaken, not *strengthen, the hands of his brethren* (Isa 35:3), with whom he should have been willing to share his lot. He set a poor example to others. It is a sign of a discontented, distrustful, and unstable spirit if we are weary of the place in which God has set us, and if we always want to leave the moment something disturbs or inconveniences us. Or if he wanted to move, why did he go to the country of Moab? If he had asked, he would probably have found plenty in some of the tribes of Israel, for example those on the other side of the Jordan, which bordered on the land of Moab. If he had had that zeal for God and that affection for his brothers and sisters which were consistent with being an Israelite, he would not have persuaded himself so readily to go and stay among the Moabites.

4. The marriage of his two sons to two of the daughters of Moab after his death (v. 4). All agree that this was wrong. The Aramaic says, "They violated the decree of the word of the Lord in taking foreign wives." It does not appear that the women they married had converted to the Jewish religion, for Orpah is said to return to her gods (v. 15). On the other hand, it is a tradition of the Jews without any foundation that Ruth was the daughter of Eglon king of Moab.

5. The death of Elimelech and his two sons and the unhappiness this brought on Naomi. Her husband died (v. 3), and her two sons (v. 5) also died soon after their marriage, and the Aramaic says that "their days were shortened" because they broke the law in marrying foreign wives. When Naomi lost her husband, the main source of her pleasure was her sons, whom she then trusted more than before for her sustenance. The spirit of poor Naomi was very unhappy when she was *left of* (without) *her two sons and her husband* (v. 5). When *these two things, loss of children and widowhood, come upon her in a moment, by whom shall she be comforted?* (Isa 47:9; 51:19). It is God alone who has the resources to comfort those who are so dejected in this way.

Verses 6–18

We read of:

1. The affection Naomi had for the land of Israel (v. 6). Although the country of Moab had given her shelter and supplies in her time of need, she did not want to stay there forever. The only land which we should want to stay in forever is the holy land, where the sanctuary of God is.

1.1. God finally acted in mercy toward his people. God finally and graciously came to help his people and *visited them in giving them bread* (v. 6). God loves to give plenty, and it is by his coming that he provides the staple food of bread and *holds our souls in life* (Ps 66:9). Although this mercy is more striking when it comes after famine, we are not to value it any less if we have constantly enjoyed it and have never known what famine is.

1.2. Naomi finally had good news brought to her of plenty in Bethlehem, and so she could then think of nothing except returning there. Although there may be a reason for our being in bad places, when the reason comes to an end, we do not have to stay there. Forced absence from God's ordinances and forced companionship with evildoers are great afflictions, but when we are no longer forced and yet continue in such a situation by choice, then it becomes a sin. The land of Moab had now become a sad place for her. She now wanted to go to Canaan again. Earth is made bitter to us so that heaven may become more precious to us.

2. The affection which her two daughters-in-law, and one of them especially, had for her, and her generous repayment of their affection.

2.1. They were both so kind as to accompany her, part of the way at least, when she returned toward the land of Judah. By this we see both that Naomi, as was right for an Israelite, had been very kind to them and had gained their love, and also that Orpah and Ruth had a due sense of her kindness. They had lived together in unity, though the men had died by whom the relationship between them had come about. Although they kept their affection for the gods of Moab (v. 15), and Naomi was still faithful to the God of Israel, that did not prevent either side from being loving and from carrying out the good and kind

acts that the relationship required. Mothers-in-law and daughters-in-law are too often in conflict (Mt 10:35), and so it is more commendable if they live together harmoniously in love.

2.2. When they had gone a little way with her, Naomi, with a great deal of affection, urged them to go back (vv. 8–9): *Return each to her mother's house.* Naomi suggests that life with their own mothers would be more pleasant for them than life with their mother-in-law, especially when their own mothers had houses and their mother-in-law was not sure what she could call her own. She dismisses them:

2.2.1. With commendation.

2.2.2. With prayer. It is good for friends, when they part, to part with prayer. She sends them home with her blessing, and the blessing of a mother-in-law is not to be treated lightly. In this blessing she twice mentions the name *Jehovah*, Israel's God, and the only true God, so that she may direct her daughters to look to him as the fountain of all good. She prays that they may be happily married again: *The Lord grant that you may find rest, each of you in the house of her husband* (v. 9).

2.2.3. With affection: *She kissed them* (v. 9). She wished she had more to give them, but she did not have any silver or gold. However, this parting kiss would be the seal of true friendship.

2.3. The two young widows could not think of taking their leave of their mother-in-law, since, in her godliness, she had made such a deep impression on them. "*Surely we will return with thee unto thy people* and share our lives with you." It is a rare example of affection for a mother-in-law and a sign that for her sake they had a high opinion of the people of Israel. Even Orpah, who later went back to her gods, now seemed to have made the decision to go forward with Naomi.

2.4. Naomi set herself to dissuade them from going along with her (vv. 11–13):

2.4.1. Naomi spoke deeply about her afflicted condition. If she had had any sons in Canaan, or any close male relatives, whom she could have expected to marry the widows, it might have been some encouragement to them to hope that they would settle down comfortably at Bethlehem. The most terrible aspect of her suffering was that she was not in a position to do things for them as she would have wanted. She mourned most the trouble that came on them because of it. A gracious, generous spirit can bear its own burden better than it can bear to see that burden bring suffering to others or to see others in any way drawn into trouble by it. Naomi is more willing to be in need herself than to see her daughters in need.

2.4.2. Did Naomi do well to discourage her daughters from going with her in this way, when by taking them with her she might have saved them from the idolatry of Moab and have brought them to the faith and worship of the God of Israel? Naomi, no doubt, wanted to do so. But:

2.4.2.1. If they were to come with her, she did not want them to come because of her. Those who profess a religious faith only to please their relatives or friends, or for the sake of company, will be converts of little value who do not last long.

2.4.2.2. If they were to come with her, she would want it to be their deliberate choice. She wanted them to sit down first and count the cost, as is right for those who want to follow a religious faith. It is good for us to be told the worst possible scenario. This was the line taken by our Savior with a man who in the heat of the moment spoke out zealously and boldly, *Master, I will follow thee whithersoever thou goest.* "Come," Christ says, "can you live my life as I do? *The Son of man has not where to lay his head.* Stop and consider this. Reflect on whether you can find it in your heart to join forces with him" (Mt 8:19–20). This is how Naomi deals with her daughters-in-law. Thoughts which mature into decisions after serious thought are likely to be kept always in the mind and heart, whereas what ripens quickly also quickly rots.

2.5. Orpah was easily persuaded to give in to her own corrupt inclinations and to go back to her country, her relatives, and her father's house, now that she was in a favorable position to receive a call from it. Both daughters-in-law *lifted up their voice and wept again* (v. 14), as they were very much affected by the tender things that Naomi had said. But her words had different effects on the two of them. Orpah was sent back to the country of Moab by Naomi's description of the inconveniences they would have to deal with if they went to Canaan, and to her Naomi's words were a smell of death. Ruth, on the other hand, was strengthened in her determination, and to her those words were the fragrance of life.

2.5.1. *Orpah kissed her mother-in-law* (v. 14), that is, she took affectionate leave of her and said her final farewell (Mt 8:21). Orpah's kiss showed she had warm affection for Naomi and was reluctant to part with her, but she did not love her enough to leave her country for her sake. In the same way, many value Christ and have an affection for him but come short of receiving salvation from him because they cannot find it in their hearts to leave other things for him. They love him but they still leave him, because they do not love him enough, but love other things more. This is the fate of the young man who went away from Christ sad (Mt 19:22). But:

2.5.2. *Ruth clave* (clung) *unto her* (v. 14). It is not clear whether she had already decided, when she started the journey with Naomi, that she would go forward with her.

2.6. Naomi tries to persuade Ruth to go back, urging her sister's example as a further inducement. Now, *return thou after thy sister* (v. 15), that is, "If you ever want to return, then now is the time to do so. Go back with her. This is the greatest test of your faithfulness. If you withstand this test, you will be mine forever."

2.7. Ruth puts an end to any argument by a most solemn profession of her steadfast determination never to abandon Naomi, nor to go back to her own country and her old relatives again (vv. 16–17).

2.7.1. Nothing could be said that is finer or braver than this. She seems to have had a different spirit and a different way of talking, now that her sister was gone, and it is an example of the grace of God inclining the soul to the firm choice of the better part (Lk 10:42).

2.7.1.1. She begs her mother-in-law to say nothing more about her going: *Entreat me not to leave thee, or to return from following after thee* (v. 16).

2.7.1.2. She expresses her firm determination to cling to Naomi and never leave her. She speaks the language of one who is determined to follow God and go to heaven.

- She will travel with Naomi: *Whither thou goest I will go* (v. 16), even though it is to a country I have never seen. Even though it is far away from my own country, every road will be pleasant with you.
- She will stay with her: *Where thou lodgest I will lodge* (v. 16), even though it is in a humble cottage, in fact, even if it is no better lodging than Jacob had when he had stones as his pillow.
- She will join with her interests: *Thy people shall be my people* (v. 16).

- She will join in her religious faith. In this way, she determines to be Naomi's to the very altar. *Thy God shall be my God* (v. 16).
- She will gladly die in the same place as Naomi: *Where thou diest will I die* (v. 17).
- She wants to be buried in the same grave and to place her bones next to Naomi's: *There will I be buried* (v. 17). She does not even want her dead body to be taken back to the country of Moab, as a sign of any remaining longing for it. No; Naomi and she have joined together; they are soul mates. She wants their ashes to mix, in the hope of their both rising together and being together forever in the next world.

2.7.1.3. She backs up her decision to cling to Naomi with a solemn oath: *The Lord do so to me, and more also*—which was an old form of curse—*if aught but death part thee and me* (v. 17).

2.7.2. This is a model for those who follow God and the Christian faith. We must be agreed on this:

2.7.2.1. We must take the Lord as our God. "This God is my God for ever and ever; I declare that he is mine."

2.7.2.2. When we take God as our God, we must take his people as our people in every condition. Even though they are poor and despised, if they are his then they must be ours too.

2.7.2.3. Having thrown in our lot with them, we must be willing to take our lot with them and live as they live.

2.8. Naomi is silenced by all this (v. 18): *When she saw that Ruth was stedfastly minded to go with her*—which was the very thing Naomi had aimed at in everything she had said, to bring Ruth to a firm resolution to go with her—when Naomi saw that she had succeeded, she was satisfied and *left off speaking to her* (v. 18); she stopped urging her.

Verses 19–22

After a long, tiring journey, Naomi and Ruth eventually came to Bethlehem. And they came at just the right time, *in the beginning of the barley harvest* (v. 22), which was the first of their harvests, with the wheat harvest coming later. Now they had opportunity to provide for winter. Notice is here taken:

1. That the neighbors were unsettled on this occasion (v. 19): *All the city was moved* (stirred) *about them.* Her old acquaintances gathered around her, to ask how she was and to welcome her back to Bethlehem. Or perhaps they were "moved about her," that is, disturbed about her, concerned that she might be a burden on the town, as she looked so needy. And they said, *Is this Naomi?* (v. 19). Her close friends were surprised to see how she was. She was so broken and changed by her suffering. *Is this Naomi?* Most of them asked out of compassion and commiseration: "Is this the woman who used to live such a full life, who kept such a good house, and was so charitable to the poor?" Suffering can make great and surprising changes in a little time. When we see how old age and illness change people, their faces and their attitudes, we may think of what the Bethlehemites said: *Is this Naomi?* May God, by his grace, prepare us for all such changes, especially the great change!

2. That Naomi's spirit was calm. If some people rebuked her for her poverty, she was not stirred up by them, as she would have been if she had been poor and proud: "*Call me not Naomi, call me Mara. Naomi* means 'pleasant,' but all my pleasant things have been destroyed. Instead, call me *Mara*, 'bitter,' for I am now a woman with a heavy and sad spirit." Notice:

2.1. The change of her state, and how it is described, with a godly consideration of divine Providence, and without any angry murmurings or complaints. She now *came home again empty* (v. 21), a widow and childless. She had probably sold her goods, and out of all the belongings which she took with her she came home with no more than the clothes on her back. She acknowledges the all-powerful hand of God in her suffering. "It is the Lord who has *brought me home again empty*; it is the Almighty who has brought trouble on me." We can learn from this that nothing is more likely to lead to the assurance of a gracious soul in suffering or trouble than to consider the hand of God in it. The One who empties us of the creation knows how to fill us with himself.

2.2. The submission of her spirit to this change: "*Call me not Naomi* (v. 20), for I am no longer pleasant, either to myself or to my friends, *but call me Mara* (v. 20), a name which corresponds to my present state." If God has dealt bitterly with her, she will make the necessary adjustments for her present state of affairs. She is willing to be called *Mara*, "bitter." *Tribulation works patience*, suffering produces perseverance (Ro 5:3).

CHAPTER 2

Here we have: 1. Ruth's humility and diligence in gleaning corn, when Providence directed her to Boaz' field (vv. 1–3). 2. The great favor which Boaz showed to her in many ways (vv. 4–16). 3. The completion of Ruth's work for the day and her return to her mother-in-law (vv. 17–23).

Verses 1–3

Naomi had now settled down in Bethlehem among her old friends; and here we have a description:

1. Of her rich relative, Boaz, *a mighty man of wealth* (v. 1). The Aramaic reads, "mighty in the law." He even has power in his name, for *Boaz* means "in him is strength." He came from the family of Elimelech, the family that had now been reduced to such lowly circumstances.

2. Of her poor daughter-in-law, Ruth:

2.1. Her condition is very lowly and poor, which is a great test for the faith and faithfulness of this young convert. The only way Naomi and her daughter-in-law had of getting the food they needed was to pick up the leftover grain.

2.2. Her character, in this condition, is very good (v. 2). She is *not mindful of the country from which she came out* (Heb 11:15), or else that would be a good reason for returning. The God of Israel will be her God, and *though he slay her, yet will she trust in him* (Job 13:15) and never leave him. *Let me go to the field, and glean ears of corn,* pick up the leftover grain (v. 2). Let us remember Ruth, for she is a great example:

2.2.1. Of humility. When Providence has made her poor, she does not say, "I am ashamed to pick up leftovers, which is like begging." She does not tell her mother-in-law she was never brought up to live on crumbs. Even though she was not brought up to do such a thing, she is brought down to it, and she is not uncomfortable with it.

2.2.2. Of diligence. "*Let me go and glean ears of corn* (v. 2), which will be to our advantage." A diligent heart is a sign of something good both in this world and in the next. We must not be reluctant to undertake any honest employment, even if it is lowly. No form of work is a disgrace.

2.2.3. Of consideration for one's mother-in-law. Although she was only Ruth's mother-in-law, Ruth dutifully looked after her.

2.2.4. Of dependence on Providence, which is suggested when she says, I will *glean after him in whose sight I shall find grace*, behind anyone in whose eyes I find favor (v. 2). She does not know which way to turn or whom she should ask for help, but she trusts that Providence will raise up some friend for her or someone who will be kind to her. And things went well for Ruth, for when she went out alone, without any guide or companion, to pick up the leftover grain, *her hap was to light on* (she happened to come to) *the field of Boaz* (v. 3). To her it seemed purely fortuitous, but Providence directed her steps to this field. Many great matters have happened because of a small turn of events which seemed fortuitous to us but was intentionally directed by Providence.

Verses 4–16

Now Boaz himself appears, and he is seen as a very honorable person in his behavior:

1. Toward his own servants and those who were employed by him in reaping and gathering in his corn. Harvest time is a busy time, and many people must be involved in that work. Boaz is an example of a good master:

1.1. He had a servant who was set over the reapers (v. 6).

1.2. But he himself came to his reapers to see how the work was progressing. He came to encourage his servants, who would continue their work more cheerfully when their master had supported them by coming to see them.

1.3. Kind and devout greetings were exchanged between Boaz and his reapers:

1.3.1. He said to them, *The Lord be with you,* and they replied, *The Lord bless thee* (v. 4). They expressed in this:

- Their mutual respect for one another. Things are likely to be successful in a house where there is such goodwill as this between master and servants.
- Their joint dependence on divine Providence. They express their kindness to each other by praying for each other.

1.3.2. Let us learn from this to use:

- Polite greetings to express sincere goodwill to our friends.
- Godly praises, lifting up our hearts to God in response to his favor in such short prayers as these. We must make sure they do not degenerate into merely formal words.

1.4. He received an account from his reapers about a foreigner he had met in the field, and gave the necessary orders concerning her, that they should not touch her (v. 9) or rebuke her (v. 15). He also ordered them to be kind to her and *let fall some of the handfuls on purpose for her,* pull out some stalks deliberately for her from the bundles (v. 16).

2. Toward Ruth. He was very kind to her, and showed her a great deal of favor. He was motivated to do so by the account he received of her and what he noticed about her.

2.1. The supervisor gave Boaz a favorable account of her, one that commended her to his favor (vv. 6–7).

2.1.1. That she was a foreigner and therefore one of those who by the Law of God were to *gather the gleanings of the harvest* (Lev 19:9–10).

2.1.2. That she was related to his family; she had come back with Naomi, the widow of Elimelech, a relative of Boaz.

2.1.3. That she was a convert, for she had left the country of Moab to settle in the land of Israel.

2.1.4. That she was very modest and had not gone to pick up the leftover grain until she had asked permission.

2.1.5. That she was very hard-working and had continued to work from morning until now. Now, in the heat of the day, she was having a short rest in the shelter that was set up in the field to give protection.

2.2. Boaz was then extremely obliging to her:

2.2.1. He told her to go with his reapers to every field they gathered in and not to glean in the field of another. He told her she would not find anywhere better (v. 8).

2.2.2. He told all his servants to be very kind and respectful toward her. She was a foreigner, and her language, clothes, and behavior were probably very different from theirs.

2.2.3. He made her welcome to the refreshment he had provided for his own servants. He told her to drink the water which was drawn for them. He also invited her at *mealtime to come and eat of their bread* (v. 14). He even offered her the wine vinegar for her to dip the bread in to make it savory (v. 14). And he himself was present when the reapers sat down to eat; and he *reached her parched corn* (v. 14)—offered her some roasted grain—to eat.

2.2.4. He commended her for her dutiful respect toward her mother-in-law, whom, although he did not know her by sight, he had heard about (v. 11). But what he especially commended Ruth for was that she had left her own country and converted to the Jewish religion.

2.2.5. He prayed for her (v. 12): *The Lord recompense thy work.* Those who come under the wings of divine grace by faith may be sure that they will receive a full reward for doing so. The Jews describe a convert as one who "is gathered under the wings of the divine Majesty."

2.2.6. He encouraged her to go on gleaning. Boaz ordered his servants to let her glean among the sheaves and not to rebuke her.

2.3. Ruth received his favors with a great deal of humility and gratitude. She paid every possible respect to him and gave him honor according to the custom of the country (v. 10): *She fell on her face, and bowed herself to the ground.* She humbly acknowledged herself unworthy of his favors: "*I am a stranger* (v. 10) and *not like one of thy handmaids* (v. 13). She begged that his goodwill would continue. When Boaz gave her her dinner with his reapers, she only ate as much as she needed and immediately got up to glean (vv. 14–15).

Verses 17–23

Here:

1. Ruth finishes her day's work (v. 17):

1.1. She took care not to waste any time, and she gleaned until evening.

1.2. She took care not to lose what she had gathered, but threshed it herself so that she might more easily carry it home and have it ready for use. Ruth had gathered it ear by ear, but when she had put it all together, it was an ephah of barley, about three-fifths of a bushel (about twenty-two liters).

2. Ruth paid respect to her mother-in-law and *showed her what she had gleaned* (v. 18), so that Naomi might see that she had not been doing nothing all day. She told her about her day's work, and how Providence had kindly favored her in it. Naomi asked her where she had been: *Where hast thou gleaned today?* (v. 19). Ruth gave her a detailed account of the kindness she had received from Boaz (v. 19), and of the hopes she had of receiving further kindnesses from him because he had told her to stay with his servants throughout the harvest (v. 21). Naomi,

even before she knew who he was, prayed sincerely for the man who had been so kind to her daughter-in-law (v. 19): *Blessed be he,* whoever he was, *that did take knowledge* (notice) *of thee*; thus she shot the arrow of prayer at random. But when she was told who he was, she remembered the former kindnesses Boaz had shown to her husband and sons and added those to this: he has not *left off* (stopped showing) *his kindness to the living and to the dead* (v. 20). She told Ruth about the relationship of their family to Boaz: *The man is near of kin to us*; he is our close relative (v. 20). Notice the chain of thoughts here—and also a chain of providential circumstances—which brings about what was intended for Ruth. Ruth names Boaz as one who had been kind to her. Naomi thinks to herself, "Who could that be?" and immediately remembers: "*The man is near of kin to us*, he is our close relative (v. 20)." This thought leads to another: "He is *our next kinsman*, our go'el, our kinsman-redeemer; he has the right to redeem our estate." She told Ruth to stay in the fields of Boaz (v. 22): "*Let them not meet thee in any other field*, for that could be interpreted as showing contempt for his politeness." Has the Lord dealt bountifully with us? If so, let us not be found in any other field or seek happiness and satisfaction in the creation. Ruth dutifully observed her mother's directions. She continued to glean not only to the end of the barley harvest, but also through the wheat harvest, which followed it, so that she might gather food at the harvest to be used in winter (Pr 6:6–8).

CHAPTER 3

We have here: 1. The directions Naomi gave to her daughter-in-law on how to claim Boaz as her husband (vv. 1–5). 2. Ruth's prompt observance of those directions (vv. 6–7). The kind and honorable way in which Boaz treated her (vv. 8–15). 3. Her return to her mother-in-law (vv. 16–18).

Verses 1–5

Here:

1. Naomi's care for her daughter-in-law's comfort is without doubt very commendable. She is full of ways of seeing how she can get Ruth married. Her wisdom planned things for her daughter-in-law which her daughter-in-law's modesty prevented her from planning for herself (v. 1). She did this:

1.1. Out of justice to the dead, to raise up descendants for those who had died, and so to prevent the family from dying out.

1.2. Out of kindness and gratitude to her daughter-in-law, who had behaved very dutifully and respectfully to her. "*My daughter,*" she said, looking on her in every way as her own, "*shall I not seek rest for thee,* should I not try to find a home for you (v. 1), so that you can settle down and get married?" A married state is, or should be, a state of rest for young people. Wandering affections are then fixed, and the heart must be at rest. A woman's heart is at rest in the house of a husband and in his heart (1:9). Those who are not brought to rest by marriage must be very fickle indeed.

2. The course she took in order to advance her daughter was very unusual and looks suspicious. If there was anything improper about it, the fault must lie with Naomi, who put her daughter up to it, and who knew, or should have known, the laws and customs of Israel better than Ruth did.

2.1. On the one hand, it was true that Boaz was obliged by divine Law to marry the widow of Mahlon, who was the eldest son of Elimelech and who had died without children (v. 2): Boaz was a close relative of the deceased and—for all that Naomi knew—the closest relative of any who were now alive. So Naomi asks, "Why should we not remind him of his duty?"

2.2. Also, it was a convenient time to remind him of it, now that he had gotten to know Ruth so well as she had worked tirelessly with his reapers during the whole harvest, which had now come to an end. And when he held a winnowing feast at his threshing floor (v. 2), there would be a good opportunity to turn to him.

2.3. Naomi thought Ruth the most proper person to do it herself, and perhaps it was the custom in that country that in this case the woman should make the demand. The Law suggests this (Dt 25:7–9). "*Wash thyself and anoint thee*; put on your best clothes, and go down to the floor." That was where the supper was which she was probably invited to. She must not make herself known, however—that is, she should not make known why she was going—until the company had gone their separate ways and Boaz had retired for the night. So far, all is well. But:

2.4. Her coming to lie down at his feet when he was asleep in his bed seems so immoral that we do not know how we can justify it. All agree that it is not to be used as a precedent, and neither our laws nor our times are the same as theirs were. However, I am willing to see what happened in the best light. If Boaz was, as the women presumed, the closest relative, she was his wife before God, as we say, and little ceremony was needed to complete the marriage. Naomi did not intend that Ruth should approach him in any other way than as his wife. She knew Boaz to be a serious and sober man, a noble and religious man, and one who feared God. She knew Ruth to be a modest woman, *chaste, and a keeper at home* (Tit 2:5). Naomi herself intended nothing except what was honest and honorable. If what she advised had been as indecent and immodest according to the custom of the country in those times as it seems to us now, still we cannot think that Naomi would have had so little wisdom as to put her daughter-in-law up to it and risk repelling such a serious and good man as Boaz. We must therefore think that the thing did not look so wrong then as it does now. We may be sure that if Ruth had thought there was anything wrong in what her mother advised her to do, she was a woman of too much virtue and sense to promise, as she did (v. 5), *All that thou sayest unto me I will do.*

Verses 6–13

Here is:

1. Boaz' good management of the day's business. Probably, according to the custom of those days:

1.1. When his servants winnowed, he was with them to prevent any carelessness in winnowing.

1.2. When he had more than ordinary work to be done, he treated his servants with extraordinary kindness and, to encourage them, had his meal with them.

1.3. When he had eaten with his workers and had spent a pleasant time with them, he went to bed early, so early, in fact, that he had already had his best sleep by midnight (v. 8).

1.4. He had his bed or couch laid *at the end of the heap of corn*, at the far end of the grain pile (v. 7). He was like his father Jacob, a simple man, who knew that if need be he could make his bed in a barn, and if he had to, could sleep contentedly in the straw.

2. Ruth's confidence in managing her business. When he woke up in the night, noticed there was somebody at his feet, and asked who it was, she told him her name and then why she had come (v. 9). She explained that she had come to put herself under his protection, as the person appointed by divine Law to be her protector: "You are the one who has a right to redeem a family and an estate from perishing, and so *let this ruin be under thy hand*, take charge of this 'heap of ruins' (Isa 3:6), and *spread thy skirt over me* (v. 9). Be pleased to take me and my cause."

3. The acceptance Ruth gained with Boaz. He knew her demand to be just and honorable and treated her accordingly. Boaz knew it was not any sinful desire that had brought her there, and so he boldly kept both his own honor and hers.

3.1. He commended her, spoke kindly to her, called her his *daughter*, and spoke honorably of her as a woman of great virtue. She had been very kind in leaving her own country and coming along with her mother-in-law to the land of Israel, to live with her and help maintain her, and he had blessed her for this (2:12). But now he says, "You have *shown more kindness in the latter end than at the beginning* (v. 10)," in that she did not think about her own wishes, but her husband's family, in remarrying.

3.2. He promised her marriage (v. 11): "*Fear not* that I will spurn you or treat you disrespectfully. No; *I will do all that thou requirest*, for this is what the Law requires from the next of kin, and I have no reason to decline it, *for all the city of my people doth know that thou art a virtuous woman*" (v. 11).

3.3. He made his promise conditional, and could not do otherwise, for it seems there was a kinsman-redeemer who was a closer relative than he was, to whom the right of redemption belonged (v. 12).

3.3.1. He himself would present the matter to the other relative to find out his thoughts.

3.3.2. If the other relative refused to act as the kinsman-redeemer, he would take on that role. He would marry the widow, redeem the land, and so restore the family. Bishop Hall sums up the matter by observing that Boaz, instead of touching her as someone who was immoral, as a father blesses her, as a friend encourages her, as a kinsman makes a promise to her, as a patron supports her, and sends her away showered with hopes and gifts, not less virtuous, but happier, than when she came.

Verses 14–18

We are told here:

1. How Ruth was sent away by Boaz. He sent her away:

1.1. Telling her to keep the matter a secret (v. 14): *Let it not be known that a woman came into the floor* and lay all night so near Boaz.

1.2. With a gift of barley, which would be very acceptable to her poor mother-in-law at home and would be a sign for Naomi that he had not sent Ruth away because he disliked her, which Naomi might have suspected if he had sent her away empty-handed. He measured it out and poured it into her *veil* or shawl.

2. How Ruth was welcomed by her mother-in-law. Naomi asked her, "*Who art thou, my daughter?* (v. 16). How did you get along? Are you a bride or not? Are congratulations in order?" So Ruth told her how matters stood (v. 17), and then her mother-in-law:

2.1. Advised her to rest assured in what was done: *Sit still, my daughter, till thou know how the matter will fall* (v. 18).

2.2. Assured her that Boaz, having made his promise in this matter, would turn out to be a faithful and careful friend: *He will not be at rest till he have finished the matter* (v. 18).

CHAPTER 4

In this chapter we are told about: 1. How Boaz got past his rival and justly replaced him (vv. 1–8). 2. How his marriage with Ruth was publicly solemnized and accompanied by the good wishes of his neighbors (vv. 9–12). 3. The happy child who descended from this marriage, Obed, the grandfather of David (vv. 13–17). And so the book concludes with the family line of David (vv. 18–22).

Verses 1–8

Here:

1. Boaz immediately convened a court. He was probably one of the elders (or aldermen) of the town. But why did Boaz act so quickly; why was he so keen to get married? Ruth was not rich, but a poor and lowly foreigner. But what made Boaz love her and made him concerned to see things happen quickly was that all her neighbors agreed that she was a woman of noble character. He therefore wanted to bring matters to a speedy conclusion. It was not a day on which the court normally sat, but he arranged for ten of the elders of the town to meet him at the town hall over the gate, where public business was customarily transacted (v. 2). It was probably the custom of the town that ten constituted a full court.

2. Boaz summoned his rival to come and hear the matter presented to him (v. 1).

3. Boaz proposed to the other relative that he redeem Naomi's land, which had probably been mortgaged for money to buy bread when the famine was in the land (v. 3): *Naomi has a parcel of land to sell.* He brought this to the attention of the relative (v. 4) so that the relative might have the first refusal of it.

4. The relative seemed willing to redeem the land till he was told that if he did that, he must marry the widow, and then he drew back. "*I cannot redeem it for myself. I will* not take it on these terms, because in so doing I might spoil my own inheritance." The land, he thought, would improve his inheritance, but the land with the woman would not; in fact he thought that would spoil it.

5. The right of redemption is justly given to Boaz. If this nameless relative lost a good bargain, good lands, and a good wife, he had only himself to blame for not paying more attention to it. Boaz would thank him for making the way clear for him to gain what he valued and wanted above anything else. In those ancient times it was not the custom to transfer estate in written documents, as happened later (Jer 32:10–12), but by some sign or ceremony; similarly, under our own law possession of property is formally delivered by giving the key to a house or by cutting and giving a piece of turf from the plot of land as a sign of transfer of possession. The ceremony used here was that the one who surrendered his right *plucked off his shoe*, took off his sandal (v. 7), and gave it to the one to whom he transferred the right, so showing that, whatever right he had to walk on the land, he conveyed and transferred it, in exchange for something of value, to the purchaser. This was a *testimony in Israel* (v. 7); it was the method of legalizing transactions in Israel which was used in this case (v. 8).

Verses 9–12

Boaz now sees his way clear in fulfilling his promise to Ruth that he would take up the role of kinsman-redeemer. And so at the gate of the town, before the elders and all the people, he declares a marriage contract between himself and Ruth, the Moabite woman, and, along with the marriage, the purchase of all the estate that belonged to the family of Elimelech. We read about this marriage:

1. That it was solemnized, or at least declared, before many witnesses (vv. 9–10).

1.1. "I have bought the estate. Whoever has it, or any part of it, mortgaged to them, let them come to me and they will have their money."

1.2. "I have bought the widow to be my wife." He had no dowry to expect from her; what joint estate she had left to her was mortgaged, and he could not have it without giving as much for it as it was worth, and so he might well say he bought her. His intention in marrying her was to preserve the memory of the dead, so that the name of Mahlon, even though he left no son to carry it on, might be preserved. Notice, too, that because Boaz did this honor to the dead as well as this kindness to the living, God also honored him by bringing him into the genealogy of the Messiah, by which his family was given a dignity above that of all the families of Israel. The other relative, however—the one who was so afraid of lowering himself and spoiling his inheritance by marrying the widow—has his name, family, and inheritance buried in oblivion and disgrace. Our Lord Jesus is our *Go'el*, our "Kinsman-Redeemer," our eternal Redeemer. Like Boaz, he looked with compassion on the desperate state of the fallen human race. At vast expense he redeemed the heavenly inheritance for us, which was mortgaged by sin and forfeited into the hands of divine justice, and which we would never have been able to redeem for ourselves.

2. That it was accompanied by many prayers. When the elders and all the people witnessed it, they wished them well and blessed them (vv. 11–12).

2.1. It was probably the senior elder who spoke this prayer, and the rest of the elders, with the people, joined in, and so it is spoken of as made by them all, for in public prayers, although only one person speaks, we must all pray. Marriages ought to be blessed and accompanied by prayer. We should pray for the welfare and prosperity of one another.

2.2. Here:

2.2.1. They prayed for Ruth, *The Lord make the woman that has come into thy house like Rachel and Leah* (v. 11), that is, "God, make her a good wife and a fruitful mother."

2.2.2. They prayed for Boaz. They wanted the wife to be a blessing in the private affairs of the home, and the husband to be a blessing in the public business of the town, so that each in their sphere of influence might be wise, noble, and successful.

2.2.3. They prayed for the family: "*Let thy house be like the house of Pharez* (Perez)" (v. 12), that is, "May your family be very numerous, may it increase and multiply greatly, as the house of Perez did." The Bethlehemites came from the house of Perez. Now they prayed that the family of Boaz, which was one branch of that clan, might in the process of time become as numerous and great as the whole clan was then.

Verses 13–22

Here is:

1. Ruth as a wife. Boaz took her into his house with the usual ceremonies, and *she became his wife* (v. 13).

Boaz had prayed that this devout convert would receive a full reward for her courage and faithfulness from the God of Israel, *under whose wings she had come to trust* (2:12). Now he had become an instrument of that kindness which was an answer to his prayer, and helped fulfill his own words.

2. Ruth as a mother: *The Lord gave her conception,* enabled her to conceive (v. 13), for *the fruit of the womb is his reward* (Ps 127:3).

3. Ruth as a daughter-in-law still, as she always was, to Naomi, who, far from being forgotten, comes to share significantly in these new joys. Prayer to God accompanied the marriage (v. 11), and praise to him accompanies the birth of the child. It is a great pity that such godly words have either fallen into disuse among Christians or degenerated into a mere formality. "*Blessed be the Lord,*

who has sent you this grandson" (vv. 14–15). They say of Ruth that she loves Naomi and so is better to her than seven sons. The ties of love prove stronger than those of blood, so here is a daughter-in-law who is better to her mother-in-law than her own child. Here:

3.1. The child is named by the neighbors (v. 17). The women wanted to call the child *Obed*, "a servant," either to remember the lowliness and poverty of the mother or to look forward to his later becoming a servant, and very useful, to his grandmother.

3.2. The child is nursed by his grandmother. Grandmothers are often the most loving people.

4. Ruth as an ancestor of David and Christ, which was the greatest honor. The genealogy is here drawn from Perez, through Boaz and Obed, to David, and so leads on toward the Messiah.

A Practical and Devotional Exposition of
The Book of

1 Samuel

～⁕～

This book and the next bear the name of Samuel in the title, not because he was the author of them but because the first book begins with a detailed account of him: his birth and childhood, his life and leadership. The rest of these two books that bear his name contains the history of the reigns of Saul and David, who were both anointed by him. And because the history of these two kings takes up the greatest part of these books, the Vulgate calls them the *First* and *Second Books of the Kings*, and the two that follow, the *Third* and *Fourth Books of the Kings*, which the titles in some English Bibles take notice of with the subtitles "otherwise called the First Book of the Kings," "otherwise called the Second Book of the Kings," etc. The Septuagint (a Greek version of the Old Testament) calls them the *First* and *Second Books of the Kingdoms*. These two books contain the history of the last two of the judges, Eli and Samuel—who were not, like the rest, warriors, but priests—and therefore much of these books is an appendix to the book of Judges; similarly, the books contain the history of the first two of the kings, Saul and David, and therefore much of them makes way for the history of the kings. This first book gives us a full account of Eli's fall and Samuel's rise and good leadership (chs. 1–8) and of Samuel's stepping down from government and Saul's rise and failure (chs. 9–15); the choice of David, his struggles with Saul, Saul's final downfall, and the opening of the way for David to become king (chs. 16–31).

CHAPTER 1

The story of Samuel begins here at an early age—even before he was born. Samuel is introduced as a child of prayer. Samson's birth was foretold by an angel to his mother; Samuel was asked for of God by his mother. Samuel's mother was Hannah, the main person in the story of this chapter. Here is: 1. Her suffering: she was childless, and her misery was made worse by her rival's arrogant taunts but to some extent balanced out by her husband's kindness (vv. 1–8). 2. The prayer and vow she made to God in her suffering. When Eli the high priest saw her doing this, he at first criticized her, but later encouraged her (vv. 9–18). 3. The birth and nursing of Samuel (vv. 19–23); the dedication of him to the Lord (vv. 24–28).

Verses 1–8

We have here an account of what the family was like into which Samuel the prophet was born. His father was Elkanah, a Levite of the family of the Kohathites (the most honorable house of that tribe), as appears in 1Ch 6:33–34. His ancestor Zuph was an *Ephrathite*, that is, of Bethlehem in Judah, which was called *Ephrathah* (Ru 1:2). This family of Levites had at first settled there, but one branch of it, in the course of time, moved to the hill country of Ephraim, from which Elkanah came. This Elkanah lived at Ramah, or Ramathaim, which means "the double Ramah," the higher and lower town.

1. It was a devout family. All the families of Israel should be so, but Levites' families should be so especially.

Ministers should set an example in family religious life. Elkanah went up at the solemn feasts to the tabernacle at Shiloh, to *worship and to sacrifice to the Lord of hosts* (v. 3). The prophet Samuel was probably the first to use this title of God in Scripture. He used it to strengthen and encourage Israel, at times during his judgeship when their armies were small and weak and the armies of their enemies great and powerful. It would then strengthen them to think that the God they served was Lord of hosts, the Lord Almighty, God of all the powers both in heaven and on earth. Elkanah was a country Levite, and it appears he did not have any position or office which required his attendance at the tabernacle, but he went up as an ordinary Israelite with his own sacrifices to encourage his neighbors and set them a good example. And what was even more commendable was:

1.1. That there was a general decay and neglect of religious faith around him in the nations.

1.2. That Hophni and Phinehas, the sons of Eli, were the men who were now mainly employed in the service of the house of God. They were men who behaved very badly in that place, but Elkanah still went up to sacrifice. If the priests did not do their duty, he would still do his.

2. But it was a divided family, and its divisions brought both guilt and grief.

2.1. The original cause of this division was Elkanah's marrying two wives, which was a violation of the original institution of marriage, which our Savior refers to (Mt 19:5, 8): *From the beginning it was not so.* It caused trouble in Abraham's family, Jacob's, and here in Elkanah's.

2.2. What followed from this error was that the two wives could not agree. They had different blessings: Peninnah, like Leah, was fruitful and had many children, which should have made her feel thankful and secure even though she was his second wife and was less loved. Hannah, like Rachel, was childless, but she was very precious to her husband, and this should have made her feel thankful and secure too. But instead they had different attitudes: Peninnah could not cope with the blessing of fruitfulness and became proud and arrogant; Hannah could not cope with the affliction of barrenness and became discontented and depressed. Elkanah had a difficult role standing between them.

2.2.1. Elkanah maintained his attendance at God's altar despite these unhappy differences in his family. He also took his wives and children with him, so that if they could not agree in other things, they might still agree to worship God together. If the devotions of our family do not succeed in ending its divisions, then let us make sure that the divisions do not stop the devotions.

2.2.2. Elkanah did everything he could to encourage Hannah and keep her spirits up amidst her suffering (vv. 4–5). At the festival, he offered peace offerings (fellowship offerings) to ask for peace in his family:

2.2.2.1. He worked hard to show his love for Hannah even more because she was suffering, insulted, and in low spirits.

2.2.2.2. He showed his great love for her in the share he gave her of his peace offerings. In the same way, we should show our affection for our friends and relatives by praying for them a great deal.

2.2.3. Peninnah was extremely self-willed and provocative:

2.2.3.1. She rebuked Hannah in her troubles, despised her because she was barren, and taunted her with the fact that God had not shown her his favor by giving her children.

2.2.3.2. She was jealous of the love Hannah received from Elkanah.

2.2.3.3. She abused Hannah especially when they *went up to the house of the Lord* (v. 7), perhaps because they were more together then than at other times, or because it was then that Elkanah was most affectionate toward Hannah. Her intention was to irritate Hannah so much that she would feel depressed. Perhaps she wanted to break her heart, so that she might possess her husband's heart totally.

2.2.4. Poor Hannah could not bear the provocation: *She wept, and did not eat* (v. 7). But she was weak in that she gave way so much to the sorrow of the world as to make herself unfit to express her holy joy in God. Those who tend toward depression, who are too ready to take to heart the provocative behavior of others, are their own worst enemies and rob themselves of many comforts of life and godliness.

2.2.5. Elkanah said what he could to her to try to comfort Hannah. *Hannah, why weepest thou?* Those who by marriage are made one flesh should also go so far in being of one spirit as to share in each other's troubles, so that one cannot be at ease while the other is not. He then suggests that nothing was lacking on his part to make up for her unhappiness: *"Am not I better to thee* (do I not mean more to you) *than ten sons?* (v. 8). You know you have all my affection. That should give you strength and encouragement." This shows us that we should take note of our blessings, to keep ourselves from being too troubled by the crosses we have to bear, for we deserve our crosses,

but we have lost the right to enjoy our blessings. To keep a balance, we need to look both at what is going right for us and at what is going against us. If we do otherwise, we are unjust to Providence and unkind to ourselves.

Verses 9–18

Elkanah had gently rebuked Hannah for her excessive sorrow, and we see here the good effects of that rebuke:

1. It brought her back to her food. She ate and drank (v. 9). She did not become stubborn in her misery and surly when she was rebuked for it. It is as great an act of self-denial to control our passions as it is to control our appetites.

2. It brought her to her prayers. "Instead of keeping the burden to myself, would it not be better if I unloaded it and gave it to the Lord in prayer?" If she was ever going to speak to God on this weighty matter, now was the time. They are at Shiloh, at the entrance of the tabernacle, the place where God had promised to meet his people, the *house of prayer* (Isa 56:7). They had recently offered their peace offerings. We may notice concerning Hannah's prayer:

2.1. The warm and vital devotion it contained, which appeared in several ways, and which should also direct our prayers:

2.1.1. She used her present grief and trouble in her spirit to stir and quicken her godly devotion in prayer: *Being in bitterness of soul, she prayed* (v. 10). *We should put our suffering to good use.* Our suffering should make us more intense in praying to God. Our blessed Savior himself, *being in an agony, prayed more earnestly* (Lk 22:44).

2.1.2. She mixed tears with her prayers. It was not a dry prayer: she wept bitterly.

2.1.3. She was very specific, but also very modest, in her request. She asked for a child; she asked for a son, so that he might be eligible to serve in the tabernacle.

2.1.4. She made a solemn vow, or promise, that if God would give her a son, she would *give him up to God* (v. 11). He would be a Levite by birth and so would be devoted to the service of God, but she vowed he would be a Nazarite, and his very childhood would be sacred. This also teaches us that when we are seeking any mercy, it is right that we commit our own souls with a promise. Not that in doing so we may pretend to deserve the gift, but that we may thus be prepared for it and for the strength and encouragement it brings. In hoping for mercy, let us promise to do our duty.

2.1.5. She spoke all this so softly that no one could hear her. Her lips moved, but *her voice was not heard* (v. 13). She trusted God's knowledge of her heart. Thoughts are words to him.

2.2. The strong rebuke Hannah came under because of it. Eli was then high priest and judge in Israel. He sat on a chair in the temple to oversee what was done there (v. 9). The tabernacle is here called the *temple* because it was now fixed and served all the purposes of a temple. Eli sat there to receive requests and to give direction, and he noticed Hannah praying somewhere, probably in a private corner. He looked, noticed her unusual behavior, and thought she was drunk, and so he spoke to her accordingly (v. 14): *How long wilt thou be drunken?* This was the very same accusation brought against Peter and the apostles when the Holy Spirit *gave them utterance* (Ac 2:4, 13). Perhaps it was nothing strange to see drunken women at the entrance to the tabernacle in that corrupt age. When a disease has reached epidemic proportions, everyone is suspected of being contaminated. She had been rebuked by Elkanah because she would not eat and drink, and now to be scolded by Eli for eating and drinking too much was very hard on her.

2.3. Hannah's humble justification of herself against the charge brought against her.

2.3.1. Out of justice to herself, she explicitly denied the accusation. "No, my lord, it is not as you suspect. I have not drunk wine or any strong drink. In fact, I've drunk nothing at all; *count not thy handmaid for a daughter of Belial*, do not think your servant is a wicked woman" (v. 16). The very way in which she spoke in her own defense was enough to show she was not drunk.

2.3.2. Out of justice to him, she explained why she was behaving as she did. She had been more than usually fervent in her prayer to God, and so she tells him this was the real reason why she had seemed to be carried away and distraught.

2.4. The way Eli made up for his rash and unfriendly criticism, by giving a kind and fatherly blessing (v. 17). He now encouraged Hannah's devotions as much as he had discouraged them before. He showed he was convinced of her innocence by the words, *Go in peace* (v. 17), and then added his blessing: *The God of Israel grant thee thy petition*, whatever it is, *that thou hast asked of him* (v. 17).

2.5. The great assurance with which Hannah now went away (v. 18). She went her way and ate what remained of the peace offerings, *and her countenance was no more sad*. Where did this sudden happy change come from? She had committed her cause to God in prayer, had left it with him, and now she was no longer perplexed about it. She had prayed for herself, and Eli had prayed for her. She believed that God would either give her the blessing she had prayed for or make up to her the lack of it in some other way. Prayer releases the heart of a gracious soul.

Verses 19–28

Here is:

1. The return of Elkanah and his family to their own home, when the days appointed for the festival were over (v. 19). They had a journey before them and a family of children to take along with them, but they would not stir till they had worshiped God together. Prayer and provisions speed a journey on.

2. The birth and name of this desired son. At last the Lord remembered Hannah, for she then conceived and gave birth to a son. The mother called her son *Samuel* (v. 20). Some consider the origin of this name to be much the same as that of *Ishmael*, "heard by God," because the mother's prayers were heard in a remarkable way, and he was an answer to them. Others, because of the reason she gives for the name, think it means *asked of God* (v. 20). Blessings that come in answer to prayer should be remembered with special expressions of thankfulness, as in Ps 116:1–2. How many timely rescues and supplies have we experienced that we may call *Samuels, asked of God* (v. 20)? He was asked for of God and was at the same time dedicated to him.

3. The close attention Hannah gave to nursing him, not only because he was dear to her but also because he was dedicated to God. Although Hannah felt a warm regard for the courts of God's house, she asked her husband if she could stay at home, for the women were not under any obligation to go up to the three annual festivals, as the men were. Hannah had been used to going, but she now wanted to be excused:

3.1. Because she did not want to be away for such a long time from caring for her child. God desires mercy, not sacrifice. Those who are detained from public services because they have to look after their young children may take encouragement from this example, and believe that if they are doing that work with God in mind, then he will graciously accept them in that.

3.2. Because she did not want to go up to Shiloh till her son was old enough to be not only taken there but also left there. Once she took him there, she thought she would never find it in her heart to take him back again.

4. The solemn entrance of this child into the service of the sanctuary. Some think this was as soon as he stopped being breast-fed, which according to the Jews was not until he was three years old. Others think it was not till he was weaned from childish things, at about eight to ten years old. It is said (v. 24), *The child was young*. Notice how she presented her child:

4.1. With a sacrifice; no less than three bullocks, with a meat offering (grain offering) for each (v. 24). Perhaps there was a bullock for each year of the child's life, or perhaps one for a burnt offering, another for a sin offering, and the third for a peace offering.

4.2. With a grateful acknowledgement of God's goodness in answer to her prayer. She spoke to Eli, because he had encouraged her to hope for an answer of peace (vv. 26–27): *For this child I prayed.*

4.3. With full surrender of all her rights to this child to the Lord (v. 28): *I have lent him to the Lord as long as he liveth.*

4.3.1. Whatever we give to God, it is what we have first asked for and received from him. *Of thy own, Lord, have we given thee* (1Ch 29:14, 16).

4.3.2. Whatever we give to God may on this account be said to be *lent* to him. When we dedicate our children to God by baptism, let us remember that they belonged to him before by his sovereign right, and that they are still ours for our strength and encouragement.

5. The child Samuel doing his part beyond what could have been expected from one of his age, for it seems to be spoken about him, *He worshipped the Lord there* (v. 28), that is, he said his prayers. Little children should learn at an early age to worship God. Their parents should instruct them in worshiping God and take them to it. They should encourage them to become involved in it as much as they can, and God will graciously accept them and teach them to do even better.

CHAPTER 2

We have in this chapter: 1. Hannah's song of thanksgiving to God for giving her Samuel (vv. 1–10). 2. Their return to their family, with Eli's blessing (vv. 11, 20); the growth of their family (v. 21); Samuel's growth in stature and favor with God (vv. 11, 18, 21, 26) and the care Hannah took to clothe him (v. 19); the great evil of Eli's sons (vv. 12–17, 22); the too gentle rebuke that Eli gave them (vv. 23–25). 3. The justly terrible message God sent him by a prophet (vv. 27–36).

Verses 1–10

Here is Hannah's thanksgiving, dictated not only by the spirit of prayer, but also by the spirit of prophecy. Notice in general:

• When she received a blessing from God, she acknowledged it, expressing her thankfulness to his praise.

Praise is what we owe God; it is our tribute to him. We are unjust if we do not give him what is rightfully his.

- The blessing she received was an answer to prayer, and so she thought she was especially obliged to give thanks for it.
- Her thanksgiving is here called a prayer: *Hannah prayed* (v. 1); for thanksgiving is an essential part of prayer. *Her voice was not heard* (1:13) when she had prayed for a son, but in her thanksgiving she spoke out loud so that everyone might hear her. She had made her request *with groanings that could not be uttered* (Ro 8:26), but now her lips were opened to *show forth God's praise* (Ps 51:15).

We have three things in this thanksgiving:

1. Hannah's triumph in God, in his glorious perfections and in the great things he had done for her (vv. 1–3). Notice:

1.1. What great things she says about God. She is not concerned about the particular mercy she is now expressing her joy for. She looks beyond the gift and praises the giver, whereas most forget the giver and are concerned only with the gift. Hannah celebrates four of God's glorious qualities:

- His perfect purity. *There is none holy as the Lord* (v. 2).
- His almighty power: *Neither is there any rock like our God* (v. 2).
- His unsearchable wisdom: *The Lord*, the Judge of all, *is a God of knowledge* (v. 3).
- His unerring justice: *By him actions are weighed* (v. 3).

1.2. How she comforts herself in these things. What we give God the glory for, we may take comfort from. Hannah does so:

1.2.1. With holy joy: *My heart rejoiceth in the Lord* (v. 1). She does not rejoice so much in her son as in her God.

1.2.2. With holy triumph: "*My horn is exalted* (v. 1). Not only is my reputation saved by my having a son, but it is also lifted high by having such a son as this one." *My horn is exalted* means "My praises are lifted up to an unusually high degree." *My mouth is enlarged* (v. 1), that is, "Now I have the resources to respond to those who wanted to shame me."

1.3. How she silences those who have set themselves up as rivals to God and as rebels against him (v. 3): Talk no more so exceedingly proudly.

2. The note Hannah takes of the wisdom and sovereignty of divine Providence in his direction of the affairs of human beings.

2.1. The strong are soon made weak, and the weak are soon made strong, when God pleases (v. 4). On the one hand, if he speaks the word, *the bows of the mighty men are broken*; they are disarmed and prevented from doing what they have done before and what they had intended to do. On the other hand, if the Lord speaks the word, those who stumble through weakness — who were so feeble that they could not walk straight or steadily — are *girded with strength* (v. 4) in body and mind, and are able to make great things happen.

2.2. The rich are soon made poor, and the poor strangely and suddenly made rich (v. 5). *Riches flee away* (Pr 23:5) and leave those miserable who, when they had them, placed their happiness in them. To those

who have been full and free, poverty and slavery must be especially painful. But on the other hand, Providence sometimes so orders it that *those who are hungry cease* (v. 5), that is, they stop working for bread as they had done. It may also be understood to describe the same person. God makes poor those who were rich and after a while makes them rich again, like Job. He gave, he takes away, and then he gives again. Let the rich not become proud and secure in themselves, for God can soon make them poor. Neither should the poor be despondent and fall into despair, for God can in due time make them rich again.

2.3. Empty families are increased, and populous families are reduced and made few. *The barren hath borne seven* children (v. 5), meaning herself, for although at that present time she had only one son, yet because that one was a Nazarite, devoted to God and employed directly in his service, he was as good as seven children to her. Or perhaps it is the language of her faith: now that she had one, she hoped for more and was not disappointed.

2.4. God is the sovereign Lord of life and death (v. 6): *The Lord killeth and maketh alive*. Nothing is too hard for God, not even the bringing back to life of the dead and putting life into dry bones.

2.5. Advancement and abasement both come from him. He brings some people low and lifts others up (v. 7). He humbles the proud and gives grace and honor to the lowly. He lays in the dust those who want to compete with God and crushes all about them (Job 40:12–13). But he lifts up with his salvation those who humble themselves before him (Jas 4:10). Joseph and Daniel, Moses and David were strangely advanced, from a prison to a palace, from a shepherd's crook to a scepter.

2.6. A reason is given for all these acts which makes us accept them, however surprising they are: *For the pillars of the earth are the Lord's* (v. 8).

2.6.1. If we understand this literally, it shows God's almighty power, which cannot be controlled. He upholds the whole creation; he founded the earth and still sustains it by the word of his power. What is there that he cannot do in the lives of families and kingdoms, he *who hangs the earth upon nothing* (Job 26:7)? He can do anything, however far beyond our conception and expectation it may be. But:

2.6.2. If we understand it figuratively, it shows his incontrovertible sovereignty, which cannot be disputed. The rulers and great ones of the earth, the leaders of states and governments, are the *pillars of the earth* (Ps 75:3). The affairs of the world seem to turn on these hinges, but in fact they are the Lord's (Ps 47:9). They have their power from him, and so he may advance those whom he pleases, and who may say, *What doest thou?* (Job 9:12).

3. A prediction of the preservation and advancement of all God's faithful friends, and the destruction of all his and their enemies. Having expressed her joyful triumph in what God has done and is doing, she now concludes with joyful hopes of what he will do (vv. 9–10). Godly devotions rose to the height of prophecy many times in those days.

3.1. This prophecy may refer more immediately to the leadership of Israel by Samuel, and by David, whom he was used to anoint. Israel — which at the time of the judges had become so insignificant and had spent all its time just surviving — would soon become great and significant and give the Law to all its neighbors. That was an extraordinary change, and the birth of Samuel was, as it were, the dawn of that day. But:

3.2. We have reason to think that this prophecy looks further ahead, to the kingdom of Christ and the rule of that kingdom of grace, of which she now comes to speak, having spoken in such detail about the kingdom of Providence. This is the first time we read the name "Messiah" or *his Anointed*. The old expositors, both Jewish and Christian, believe that this looks beyond David to the Son of David. Glorious things are spoken here about the kingdom of the Mediator. We are assured:

3.2.1. That all its loyal subjects will be carefully and powerfully protected (v. 9): *He will keep the feet of his saints.* If he will keep their feet, he will keep their heads and hearts even better. Or perhaps it means that he will secure the ground they stand on and give them a firm place to stand. He will set a guard of grace on their desires and actions, so that their feet may neither wander from the way nor stumble on the way.

3.2.2. That all the powers that attack it will not be able to destroy it.

3.2.3. That all its enemies will certainly be broken and defeated: *The wicked shall be silent in darkness* (v. 9).

3.2.4. That the conquests of this kingdom will extend to distant regions: *The Lord shall judge the ends of the earth* (v. 10). David's victories and authority reached far, but the *uttermost parts of the earth* are promised to the Messiah for his *possession* (Ps 2:8).

3.2.5. That the power and honor of Messiah the king will increase more and more: *He shall give strength unto his king* (v. 10) for the accomplishment of his great undertaking (Ps 89:21; Lk 22:43); the Lord will strengthen his King to go through the difficulties of his humiliation. In the exaltation of his King the Lord will *lift up the head* (Ps 110:7), lift up the horn, the power and honor, of his *anointed*, and *make him higher than the kings of the earth* (Ps 89:27).

Verses 11–26

In these verses we have the good character of Elkanah's family, and the bad character of Eli's family.

1. Let us see how well things went in Elkanah's family and how much better than before.

1.1. Eli sent them away from the house of the Lord with a blessing when they had presented their small son there (v. 20). If Hannah had had many children then, it would not have been such a generous act of godliness for her to part with one out of many for the service of the tabernacle, but when she had only one, dedicating him to the Lord was an act of heroic godliness that would by no means lose its reward. As when Abraham offered Isaac, he received the promise of numerous descendants (Ge 22:16–17), so did Hannah, when she dedicated Samuel to the Lord as a living sacrifice.

1.2. They returned to their own home. This is mentioned twice (v. 11 and again v. 20).

1.3. They went every year to the house of God with their *yearly sacrifice* (v. 19). They did not think that because their son ministered there, they had an excuse not to go. They probably went to see their child more often than once a year—for it was approximately fifteen miles (twenty-five kilometers) from Ramah—but their annual visit is especially noted because that was when they brought their yearly sacrifice, and then Hannah gave her son a new suit of clothes, *a little coat* or robe (v. 19) and everything that went with it. Some think she did this more often than once a year.

1.4. The child Samuel did very well. He is mentioned four separate times in these verses, and we are told about two things:

1.4.1. The service he did for the Lord. He did well indeed, for he *ministered to the Lord* (vv. 11, 18). Perhaps he waited directly on Eli. He could light a candle, hold a utensil, run an errand, or shut a door. Because he did all these activities with a godly attitude, it is called *ministering to the Lord*.

1.4.2. The blessing he received from the Lord. He *grew before the Lord* like a tender plant (v. 21), *grew on* (v. 26) in strength and stature, and especially in wisdom and understanding: *He was in favour with the Lord and with man* (v. 26). What is here said of Samuel is also said of our blessed Savior, our great example (Lk 2:52).

2. Let us now see how badly things went in Eli's family, even though they were seated at the very door of the tabernacle, the entrance to the Tent of Meeting. The nearer they were to the church, the farther away from God they were.

2.1. The detestable evil of Eli's sons (v. 12): *The sons of Eli were sons of Belial.* The expression is emphatic. *They knew not the Lord* (v. 12). They were living at the seat of both the judiciary and the ministry, but nevertheless they were *sons of Belial* (v. 12), and their honor, power, and learning made them even worse. It is hard to say which dishonors God more, idolatry or godlessness, especially the godlessness of the priests.

2.1.1. They dishonored the offerings of the Lord and made them into a means to profit themselves, or rather to indulge their appetites.

2.1.1.1. They robbed those who brought the offerings, taking for themselves some of the offerers' part of the sacrifice of the peace offerings (fellowship offerings). The priests had the *wave breast* and the *heave shoulder* as their share (Lev 7:34), but Eli's sons were not content with that share.

2.1.1.2. They stepped in before God himself, and encroached on his rights too. *As if it were a small thing to weary men, they wearied my God also* (Isa 7:13). The effects were:

- That God was displeased: *The sin of the young men was very great before the Lord* (v. 17).
- That religious observance suffered: *Men abhorred the offerings of the Lord* (v. 17). In the midst of this sad story, Samuel's devotion is mentioned repeatedly (vv. 11, 18, 21, 26; 3:1). *But Samuel ministered before the Lord* (v. 18) as an example of the power of God's grace, which kept him pure and godly in the midst of these evil men. This helped to stop the reputation of the sanctuary from sinking too low in the minds of the people.

2.1.2. They slept with the women who came to worship at the door of the tabernacle, the entrance to the Tent of Meeting (v. 22).

2.2. The rebuke which Eli gave his sons for this evil: *Eli was very old* (v. 22) and could not himself oversee the service of the tabernacle as he had done, but left everything to his sons. Because of the weaknesses of his old age, however, they ignored him and did whatever they wanted. It seems he did not even rebuke them till he heard about their sleeping with the women, and it was only then that he decided to restrain them. Notice concerning the rebuke he gave them:

2.2.1. That it was very just and reasonable. What he said was very proper:

2.2.1.1. He tells them that the facts of the matter are too plain to be denied and too public to be hidden: *I hear of your evil dealings by all this people* (v. 23).

2.2.1.2. He shows them the disastrous consequences of their sin. Not only have they sinned, but they have also caused Israel to sin. They will be held responsible for the people's sin as well as their own.

2.2.1.3. He warns them of the danger they have brought on themselves by their sin (v. 25). He shows them what God afterward will tell him, that the *iniquity* will not be *purged with sacrifice nor offering* (3:14).

2.2.2. That it was too gentle. He should have rebuked them severely. Their crimes deserved a stern rebuke; their attitude needed it; the softness of his dealing with them would only harden them even more. What he said was right, but it did not go far enough.

2.3. Their stubbornness toward this rebuke. They *hearkened not to their father* (v. 25); they did not listen to him, even though he was also a judge. Samuel's submissive attitude is again mentioned (v. 26) to put their obstinacy to shame: *The child Samuel grew.* God's grace is his own; he denied it to the sons of the high priest but gave it to the child of an obscure country Levite.

Verses 27–36

Eli rebuked his sons too gently and did not threaten them as he should have, and so God sent a prophet to him to rebuke him sharply. The message is sent to Eli himself, because God wanted to bring him to repentance and save him. The message did not come to his sons, whom God had determined to destroy.

1. The prophet reminds Eli of the great things God has done for his ancestors and family line. God appeared to Aaron in slavery in Egypt (Ex 4:27) as a sign of the further favor which he intended to show him (v. 27). He advanced him to the priesthood and passed that on to his family as an inheritance, so setting it above all the other families of Israel.

2. He brings a very serious accusation against Eli and his family. His children have done evil, and he has turned a blind eye to it and so has incriminated himself in the guilt. The indictment is therefore against them all (v. 29):

2.1. His sons had godlessly dishonored the holy things of God: "*You kick at* (scorn) *my sacrifice which I have commanded.*"

2.2. He had supported them in their actions by not punishing their ungodly disrespect: "Thou *honourest thy sons above me*" (v. 29).

2.3. They had all shared in the profits of the sacrilege. It is feared that Eli himself, even though he disliked and criticized the abuses they committed, did not refuse to eat the roast meat they had gained sacrilegiously (v. 15).

3. He declares that the inheritance of the high priesthood will be cut off from Eli's family (v. 30). *I said, indeed, that thy house, and the house of thy father,* Ithamar—for Eli descended from that younger son of Aaron—*should walk before me for ever.* We are not told here when the honor of the high priesthood was transferred from the family of Eleazar to that of Ithamar, but it seems this had been done, and Eli was likely to have that honor passed on to his descendants forever. But notice that the promise included its own condition: *They shall walk before me forever,* that is, "they will have the honor, provided they serve faithfully." *Walking before God* is the great condition of the covenant (Ge 17:1). "If they put themselves in my presence, then I will put them continually in my presence (Ps 41:12), but not otherwise." But now the Lord says, *Be it far from me* (v. 30). "Now that you have rejected me, you can expect nothing other than that I should reject you. You choose not to walk before me as you should, and so you shall not."

4. He gives a good reason for the revoking of this privilege, based on an established rule God uses in his government, a rule by which all must expect to be dealt with—the rule Cain was tried by (Ge 4:7): *Those that honour me I will honour, and those that despise me shall be lightly esteemed* (disdained) (v. 30). The way to be truly great is to be truly good. If we humble and deny ourselves in anything to honor God, and give him undivided supremacy in our lives, we may depend on this promise, and he will honor us. See also Jn 12:26.

5. He foretells the particular judgments which would come on Eli's family, to its eternal disgrace:

5.1. That their power would be broken (v. 31): *I will cut off thy arm* (cut short your strength), and *the arm* (strength) *of thy father's house.* They would be stripped of all their authority; they would be deposed and have none of the influence on the people that they had before.

5.2. That their lives would be shortened. It is mentioned twice: *There shall not be an old man in thy house for ever* (vv. 31–32), and again (v. 33), "*All the increase of thy house,* from generation to generation, *shall die in the flower of their age.*"

5.3. That all their comforts would become unpleasant to them:

5.3.1. The comfort they had in the sanctuary, in its wealth and prosperity: *Thou shalt see an enemy in my habitation,* you will see distress in my dwelling (v. 32). This was fulfilled in the Philistines' invasions and the trouble they caused to Israel.

5.3.2. The comfort of their children: "*The man of thine whom I shall not cut off* by an untimely death (v. 33) will be spared to live only to be a blot on the family and a burden to them." Grief for a dead child is great, but grief for a bad child is even greater.

5.4. That their resources would be depleted, and they would be reduced to extreme poverty (v. 36): "*He that is left* alive *in thy house* will have little joy in life, for lack of a livelihood. He will come and bow before those who come after him and beg for means to live on."

5.4.1. They will beg for the smallest gift, a *piece of silver* (and the word means "the least piece") and *a morsel of bread.* Being in want is the just punishment for rebellion and sexual immorality. Those, and the families of those, who could not be content without a wide variety of the luxuries of life are made to lack the necessities of life.

5.4.2. They will beg for the lowliest office: "Put me into somewhat about (some position related to) the priesthood" (v. 36), as it reads in the margin; *make me as one of the hired servants* (Lk 15:19), the most suitable position for a prodigal. The rights to plenty and power are given up when they are abused. This was probably fulfilled when Abiathar, who came from Eli's family line, was deposed by Solomon for treason, and he and his family were turned out of their office in the temple (1Ki 2:26–27).

5.5. That God would soon begin to carry out these judgments in the death of Hophni and Phinehas, the sad news of which Eli himself would live to hear: *This shall be a sign to thee* (v. 34).

6. In the midst of all these threats against the house of Eli, mercy is promised to Israel (v. 35): *I will raise me up a faithful priest.*

6.1. This was fulfilled in Zadok, of the family of Eleazar, who took Abiathar's place at the beginning of Solomon's reign and was faithful to his trust. If some people betray their trust, others will be raised up who will be true to it. God's work will never fall to the ground for lack of hands to carry it on.

6.2. It has its complete fulfillment in the priesthood of Christ.

CHAPTER 3

In the previous chapter we read about Samuel as a young priest, for, though only a Levite by birth, he ministered before the Lord in a linen ephod. In this chapter we have him as a young prophet, with God revealing himself to him and in him reviving, if not beginning, prophecy in Israel. Here is: 1. God's first revelation of himself in an extraordinary way to Samuel (vv. 1–10). 2. The message God sent by Samuel to Eli (vv. 11–14); the faithful communication of that message to Eli and Eli's submission to the righteousness of God in it (vv. 15–18). 3. The recognition of Samuel as a prophet in Israel (vv. 19–21).

Verses 1–10

We are told here:

• How diligent Samuel was in serving God. The fact that the child Samuel shamed Eli's sons made their evil even worse. They rebelled against the Lord, but Samuel ministered to him. They insulted their father by spurning his admonitions, but Samuel heeded them. He ministered before Eli, under his eye and direction. It is those who have learned to obey that are the most qualified to rule.

• How rare prophecy was then, which made the call of Samuel a greater surprise to himself and a greater favor to Israel: *The word of the Lord was precious* (rare) *in those days* (v. 1). It was rare, for it seems the prophecy that did occur was private: *There was no open vision* (v. 1). Perhaps the ungodliness and impurity that prevailed in the tabernacle, and which no doubt corrupted the whole nation, had provoked God to withdraw the Spirit of prophecy as a sign of his displeasure. The way in which God revealed himself to Samuel is related in detail because it was uncommon:

1. Eli had retired to bed. Samuel had helped him to his bed (v. 2): *Eli was laid down in his place.*

2. Samuel had lain down to sleep in a side room near Eli's room, ready and within call if the old man should need anything in the night. When his own sons caused him grief, his little attendant brought him joy. *Samuel was laid down ere* (before) *the lamp of God went out* (v. 3).

3. God called Samuel by name, and he thought it was Eli calling him and ran to him (vv. 4–5). This shows us:

3.1. Samuel's diligence and his readiness to wait on Eli. "Here I am," he said. He set a good example to servants in this, to come when they are called, and also an example to those who are younger, not only to submit to their elders but also to take tender care of them.

3.2. Samuel's ignorance of the visions of the Almighty, in that he took what was really the call of God to be Eli's call. We make such mistakes more often than we think. God calls us by his word, and we take it to be only the call of the minister and respond accordingly. God calls us by his providences, and we look only at the instruments he uses. Eli assured him that he did not call him, but gently told him to lie down again. *So Samuel went and lay down* (v. 9).

4. The same call was repeated, and the same mistake made, a second and third time (vv. 6–9).

4.1. God continued to call the child yet again (v. 6), and again the third time (v. 8).

4.2. Samuel still did not realize that it was the Lord who called him (v. 7): *Samuel did not yet know the Lord.* The witness of the Spirit in the hearts of the faithful is often misinterpreted in this way, and so they miss the

comforts of the Spirit; the strivings of the Spirit with the consciences of sinners are similarly often misinterpreted, and so they lose the benefit of being convicted of their sins. Samuel went to Eli a second and third time, and he told Eli with great conviction, *"Thou didst call me"* (vv. 6–8). It could not be anyone else." But there was a special providence in his going so many times to Eli, for it was then, eventually, that *Eli perceived that the Lord had called the child* (v. 8). This would humble Eli, and he would realize that it was a step toward his family's degradation: when God had something to say, he chose to say it to the child Samuel, Eli's servant who waited on him, and not to Eli.

5. Eventually, Samuel was put into the right spiritual attitude for receiving a message from God.

5.1. Eli realized it was the voice of God that Samuel had heard, and so he instructed him what to say (v. 9). The instruction was, when God called the next time, to say, *Speak, Lord, for thy servant heareth* (v. 9). We may expect God to speak to us when we set ourselves to listen to what he says (Ps 85:8; Hab 2:1). When we come to read the word of God, and to listen to it being preached, we should come with such an attitude, submitting ourselves to its commanding light and power: *Speak, Lord, for thy servant heareth* (v. 9).

5.2. It would seem that God spoke a fourth time in a way which was somewhat different from the other times. Now *he stood and called* (v. 10), which suggests that there was some visible appearance of divine glory to Samuel. This convinced him that it was not Eli who called. Again, the call came twice, *Samuel, Samuel,* as if God delighted in mentioning his name.

5.3. Samuel said, as he was told to, *Speak, for thy servant heareth* (v. 10). Samuel did not now get up and run as he had before when he thought Eli had called him, but he lay still and listened. The quieter and more composed our spirits are, the better prepared they are to receive divine revelation. All must be silent when he speaks. But notice that Samuel left out one word; he did not say, "Speak, Lord," but only, *Speak, for thy servant heareth* (v. 10), perhaps because, as Bishop Patrick suggests, he was uncertain whether it was God who was speaking to him or not.

Verses 11–18

Here is:

1. The message which, after all this introduction, God then gave to Samuel about Eli's family. The message is short, not nearly so long as the one that the man of God brought (2:27). But it is a sad message, to confirm the message of the former chapter and the sentence declared there:

1.1. About the sin: it is the *iniquity that he knoweth* (v. 13). The man of God had told him about it, and his own conscience had told him many times about it. *His sons made themselves vile* (contemptible), *and he restrained them not* (v. 13). The Hebrew reads, "he frowned not upon them."

1.2. About the punishment: it is *that which I have spoken concerning his house* (vv. 12–13). When that sentence began to be executed, it would be terrible and fearful to all Israel (v. 11): *Both the ears of every one that heareth it shall tingle.* Every Israelite would be struck with terror and horror to hear of the killing of Eli's sons, the breaking of Eli's neck, and the scattering of Eli's family. "The *iniquity of Eli's house shall not be purged with sacrifice nor offering for ever* (v. 14). No atonement will be made for the sin, and no reduction will be made in the punishment."

This showed the imperfect nature of the legal sacrifices, that there were sins which they did not reach, which they could not purify, *but the blood of Christ cleanseth from all sin* (1Jn 1:7), and keeps safe from eternal death—the wages of sin—all those who share in it by faith.

2. The delivery of this message to Eli. Notice:

2.1. Samuel's modest concealment of it (v. 15):

2.1.1. He *lay till the morning*, and we suppose he lay awake pondering what he had heard.

2.1.2. *He opened the doors of the house of the Lord* (v. 15) in the morning, as he was used to doing, being up first in the tabernacle. That he should do so at other times was an example of the great helpfulness of this child, but that he should do so this morning was an example of his great humility. God had highly honored him above all the children of his people; yet he did not become proud of the honor, but as happily as ever, he went and opened the doors of the tabernacle.

2.1.3. *He feared to show Eli the vision* (v. 15) because he was afraid to grieve and trouble the good old man.

2.2. Eli's careful questioning about it (vv. 16–17). As soon as he had heard that Samuel was up and about in the morning, he called for him, probably to come to his bedside. He had reason enough to fear that the message prophesied nothing good about him, but evil. However, because it was a message from God, he could not be content to be ignorant about it. Good people want to know all the will of God, whether it is for them or against them.

2.3. Samuel's eventual faithful communication of his message (v. 18): *He told him every whit* (everything).

2.4. Eli's devout acceptance of it. He did not question Samuel's integrity. He was not cross with him, and he did not raise any objection to the justice of the sentence. *It is the Lord, let him do what seemeth him good* (v. 18). *It is the Lord* (v. 18), in whom there is no unrighteousness, who never did and never will do anything wrong to any of his creatures. He will not exact more than their sin deserves. *"Let him do what seemeth him good* (v. 18). I have nothing to say against his dealings."

Verses 19–21

After Samuel had come to know the visions of God, we have here an account of the further honor given to him as a prophet:

1. God honored him. Having begun to favor him, God continued to do so and crowned his own work in him: *Samuel grew, for the Lord was with him* (v. 19). God honored Samuel:

1.1. By further revelations of himself to him: *The Lord revealed himself again to Samuel in Shiloh* (v. 21).

1.2. By fulfilling what he spoke by him: *God did let none of his words fall to the ground* (v. 19). Whatever Samuel said as a prophet, it turned out to be true and was fulfilled at the right time.

2. Israel honored him. They all knew and acknowledged *that Samuel was established to be a prophet* (v. 20). He became famous and useful to his generation. He who began at an early age to *be* good soon came to *do* good.

CHAPTER 4

The predictions concerning the destruction of Eli's house now begin to be fulfilled. Here is: 1. The disgrace and loss Israel sustained in an encounter with the Philistines (vv. 1–2); their foolish plan to fortify themselves by bringing the ark of God into their camp on the shoulders of Hophni and Phinehas (vv. 3–4), which made them feel secure *(v. 5) and struck fear into the Philistines. Such fear, however, roused them (vv. 6–9). 2. The fatal consequences of this plan: Israel was defeated, and the ark was captured (vv. 10–11). 3. The news of this brought to Shiloh, and the sad reception of that news: the town was put into confusion (vv. 12–13); Eli fainted, fell, and broke his neck (vv. 14–18); on hearing what had occurred, his daughter-in-law went into labor and gave birth to a son, but died immediately (vv. 19–22).*

Verses 1–9

Here is:

1. A war entered into with the Philistines (v. 1). It was an attempt to throw off their oppression and would have succeeded if they had first repented and reformed, thus doing their work in the right order.

2. The defeat of Israel in that war (v. 2). The Israelites, who were the aggressors, were struck down, and 4,000 of them were killed on the spot. Sin, which was under God's curse, was in the camp and gave their enemies every advantage against them they could wish for.

3. The measures they arranged for another encounter.

3.1. They quarreled with God for appearing against them (v. 3): *Wherefore* (Why) *has the Lord smitten* (brought defeat on) *us?* They boldly complained to God about it. They were displeased with what he had done and took the matter up with him.

3.2. They imagined that they could make God appear for them the next time by bringing the ark into their camp. They sent men to Shiloh to bring back the ark, and Eli did not have enough courage to detain it, but sent his ungodly sons, Hophni and Phinehas, along with it, or at least allowed them to go. Notice here:

3.2.1. The deep respect the people had for the ark. They said, "Let's send for that, and it will work wonders for us." The ark was, by institution, a visible sign of God's presence. They thought that by giving great respect to this sacred chest, they would prove they were true Israelites and engage God Almighty to appear for them. It is common for those who have given up their living religious faith to still be attracted to its ritual and outward ceremonies. And so also here, Israel made an idol of the ark and looked to it to be as much an image of the God of Israel as those idols of other nations were images of the gods that they worshiped.

3.2.2. Their outrageous foolishness in thinking that if they had the ark in their camp, it would certainly *save them out of the hand of their enemies* (v. 3) and bring victory to their side. What good would the ark do them? It would be like a shell without a kernel. Instead of honoring God by what they did, in reality they were defying him. In fact, if there had been nothing else to cancel out their expectations of the presence of the ark, how could they expect it would bring a blessing when it was carried by Hophni and Phinehas?

4. The great joy in the camp of Israel when the ark was brought into it (v. 5): *They shouted, so that the earth rang again.* Now they thought they were sure of victory.

5. The fear which the bringing of the ark into the camp of Israel put into the Philistines. The two armies were camped so close together that the Philistines heard the shout the Israelites raised on this great occasion. They soon understood that it was the Israelites triumphed in (v. 6) and were afraid of its consequences. For:

5.1. It had never happened like that in their days: *God has come into their camp*, and so *woe unto us* (v. 7), and again, *woe unto us* (v. 8). See how blatantly wrong their ideas of God's presence were: they thought that the God of Israel was not as much in the camp before the ark came there. Yet they may well be excused for this, since the ideas the Israelites themselves had of that presence were no better.

5.2. When it had been done in former times, it had worked wonders: *These are the gods that smote the Egyptians with all the plagues in the wilderness* (v. 8). Here they were as wrong in their history as they were in their religious knowledge: the plagues of Egypt were inflicted before the ark was made and before Israel went into the desert. It would seem, however, that they scarcely believed themselves when they spoke formidably of these mighty gods (v. 8), but were only mocking, for they stirred one another up to fight even more boldly.

Verses 10–11

Here is a short account of the outcome of this battle:

1. Israel was defeated, and the army was dispersed and totally routed:

1.1. Even though they had the better cause and were the people of God. They failed, for *their rock had sold* (deserted) *them* (Dt 32:30). A good cause often suffers because of the bad people who undertake it.

1.2. Even though they had the greater confidence and were the more courageous. Having the ark in the camp will add nothing to its strength when there is an Achan in it (Jos 7).

2. The ark itself was taken by the Philistines, and Hophni and Phinehas were *both slain* (v. 11).

2.1. The killing of the priests, considering their bad character, was no great loss to Israel, but it was a terrible judgment on Eli's family. The word which God had spoken was fulfilled (2:34). But:

2.2. The taking of the ark was a very great judgment on Israel, and a sure sign of God's anger against them. Now they are made to see how foolish they were to trust in their outward privileges when they had forfeited those privileges by their evil, and how foolish to think that the ark would save them when God had already left them.

Verses 12–18

News was brought to Shiloh of the fatal outcome of the battle with the Philistines. Bad news flies fast. And so a messenger was sent there immediately. The messenger was a man of Benjamin; the Jews think it was Saul. *He rent* (tore) *his clothes, and put earth* (dust) *upon his head* (v. 12), and these signs declared the sad news. He went straight to Shiloh with the news. We are told:

1. How the town received it. *Eli sat in the gate* (vv. 13, 18), but the messenger passed him by and told the people in the town what had happened, with all its gory details, and now *both the ears of every one that heard it tingled*, as had been foretold (3:11). Their hearts trembled, and every face turned ashen. *All the city cried out* (v. 13), and well they might, for it was also a special loss for Shiloh, and the ruin of that place: although the ark was soon rescued from the hands of the Philistines, it never returned to Shiloh again. Jerusalem is much later reminded of this abandonment of Shiloh and told to heed the warning (Jer 7:12): *Go see what I did to Shiloh.*

2. What a fatal blow it was to old Eli. Let us see:

2.1. With what fear he expected the news. Even though he was old, blind, and heavy, he could not keep to his room when he was aware that the glory of Israel was at risk, but set himself by the roadside to receive the first information, for *his heart trembled for the ark of God* (v. 13). He knew what a dishonor it would be to God, and what a loss to Israel, if the ark were to fall into the hands of the Philistines. He also knew how imminent the danger was that that would happen. Israel—his own sons especially—had lost the right to have the ark. Now there comes to his mind the threat that he would *see an enemy in God's habitation* (dwelling) (2:32), and perhaps his own heart rebuked him for not using his authority to prevent the ark from being brought into the camp. All good people put the interests of God's church closer to their hearts than any secular interests or concerns of their own. How can we be at ease if the ark is not safe?

2.2. With what sadness he received the news. Although he could not see, he could still hear the *tumult* and *crying of the city* (v. 14). He realized it was mourning. He was told that a messenger had come from the army, and the messenger related the story to him in detail, having himself been an eyewitness of it (vv. 16–17). The account of the defeat of the army and of the killing of a great many soldiers was very painful to him as a judge, and the news of the death of his two sons, who he had reason to fear died without having repented, touched his heart as a father. He did not interrupt the story with any passionate mourning for his sons, like David for Absalom, but waited until the end of the story, not doubting that the messenger, being an Israelite, would, without being asked, say something about the ark. If only the messenger could have said, "But the ark of God is safe, and we are bringing that home," Eli's joy would have overcome his grief at all the other disasters. When the messenger concluded his story with, *The ark of God is taken* (vv. 17, 22), Eli was struck to the heart, and, it would seem, he fainted. He died immediately. His heart was broken first, then his neck. The foolishness and evil of his sons, whom he had indulged, was his final ruin. But we must notice, to Eli's praise, that it was the loss of the ark that led to his death, not the killing of his sons.

Verses 19–22

Here is another sad story, which continues the losses to Eli's family and the sad feeling which the news of the ark's capture aroused. The story is about the wife of Phinehas, one of those ungracious sons of Eli who had brought all this trouble on Israel. From what is told us about her it appears:

1. She was a woman of a very weak spirit. When the news came, she was about to give birth. When she heard of the death of her father-in-law, whom she respected, and her husband, whom, bad as he was, she loved, but especially when she heard of the loss of the ark, *she travailed* (went into labor), *for her pains came upon her*. She was overcome by labor pains (v. 19), and although she had enough strength to give birth to the child, soon afterward she fainted and died, being very willing to let go of life when she had lost the greatest comforts of her life.

2. She was a woman of a very gracious spirit. Her concern for the death of her husband and father-in-law was evidence of her natural affections, but her much greater concern for the loss of the ark was evidence of her godly and devout affection for God and sacred things. *She said, The glory has departed from Israel.*

2.1. The women who looked after her *said unto her, Fear not, now the worst is past, for thou hast borne a son*—perhaps he was her firstborn—*but she answered not, neither did she regard it* (v. 20). What is the joy of having borne a son, to one who is mourning the loss of the ark? She would gain small comfort from a child born in Israel, in Shiloh, considering that the ark is lost, has been captured, and has been taken to the land of the Philistines.

2.2. This made her give her child a name which would recall the calamity and her response to it. She tells them to call him *Ichabod*, which means, "Where is the glory?" or, "Alas for the glory!" or, "There is no glory" (v. 21). She explains this with her dying lips (v. 22): *The glory has departed from Israel; for the ark of God is taken*. If God leaves, the glory leaves, and all good leaves.

CHAPTER 5

It is now time to ask what has happened to the ark of God, but we do not find any moves made, because there was so little zeal or courage left. "It is gone, and let it go" seems to be their thought. They were unworthy of the name of Israelites when they could so tamely part with the glory of Israel. God therefore took the work into his own hands. We are told in this chapter: 1. How the Philistines triumphed over the ark (vv. 1–2). 2. How the ark triumphed over the Philistines: 2.1. Over Dagon their god (vv. 3–5). 2.2. Over the Philistines themselves, who were severely afflicted with tumors: the men of Ashdod first (vv. 6–7), then the men of Gath (vv. 8–9), and lastly those of Ekron (v. 10). These afflictions made them finally decide to send the ark back to the land of Israel (vv. 11–12).

Verses 1–5

Here is:

1. The Philistines' triumph over the ark, which they were very pleased about. They were proud to control it, because before the battle they had been very afraid of it (4:7). When they had it in their hands, however, God restrained them, so that they did not use any force against it. They carried it carefully to a safe place: to Ashdod, one of their five cities, the city in which Dagon's temple was situated. They placed the ark of God there, *by Dagon* (v. 2), either:

1.1. As a sacred thing, which they intended to give some religious respect to, together with Dagon, for the gods of other religions were never looked on as being averse to partners. Although the nations would not change their gods, they would still multiply them and add to them. But they were mistaken about the God of Israel when they tried to honor him by putting his ark next to Dagon's idol, for he is not worshiped at all if he is not worshiped alone. Or, more likely:

1.2. As a trophy of victory, in honor of Dagon their god.

1.2.1. God wants to show how insignificant the ark of the covenant is if the covenant itself is broken and neglected. Even sacred signs are not things that he is bound to or that we can trust in.

1.2.2. God allows them to have the ark for a time, so that he may receive more glory in judging those who defy him and gain honor for himself from them. Having punished Israel, who betrayed the ark by giving it into the hands of the Philistines, he will now deal with those who abused it, and he will take it out of their hands again.

2. The ark's triumph over Dagon. Dagon was made to fall before it twice. The first time was the next morning. When the worshipers of Dagon came to make their devotions at his shrine, they found their happiness short-lived (Job 20:5).

2.1. Dagon had *fallen upon his face to the earth before the ark* (v. 3). Great care was taken when setting up the

idols of their gods to make sure they were firmly fixed. The prophet notes it (Isa 41:7): *He fastened it with nails that it should not be moved*; and again in Isa 46:7. But Dagon's secure fastenings were useless. The kingdom of Satan will certainly fall before the kingdom of Christ, error will fall before truth, godlessness will fall before godliness, and corruption will fall before grace in the hearts of the faithful. When the interests of religion seem to be downtrodden and dying, even then we may still be confident that the day of their triumph will come.

2.2. When the priests found their idol on the floor, they acted as quickly as they could to put him back in his place again before the matter became known. It was a very sad state of affairs when a god who had fallen needed help to be put up again. The people were miserable and foolish if they prayed to receive help from an idol who himself needed—and in effect begged—their help. How could they attribute their victory to the power of Dagon when Dagon himself could not stand up on his own before the ark? But they were firmly determined that Dagon would still be their god, and so they set him back in his place.

2.3. Dagon fell a second time the next night (v. 4). The head and hands were *cut off upon the threshold* (v. 4), so that nothing remained except the stump, or as the margin reads it, "the fishy part of Dagon," for some commentators believe the upper part of this idol had a human form and the lower part the form of a fish, as mermaids are painted. Falling in this way, the misshapen monster is made to appear:

2.3.1. Ridiculous and worthy to be despised. Dagon was a shameful object, now that the fall had broken it into different parts and shown how the human and fishy parts were artificially joined together.

2.3.2. Powerless and unworthy to be prayed to or trusted in. Losing his head and hands proved that he was totally devoid of any wisdom and power and completely unable to act for or guide his worshipers.

2.4. From then on, the threshold of Dagon's temple was always looked on as sacred, and not to be stepped on (v. 5). Some see a reference to this superstitious custom of Dagon's worshipers in Zep 1:9, where God threatens to punish those who, in imitation of the Philistines, *leaped on the threshold*. Instead of despising Dagon because of the threshold which had cut his head off, they were almost ready to worship the threshold because it was the block on which he had been beheaded.

Verses 6–12

If the people had used the downfall of Dagon to good effect and if it had brought them to repent of their idolatry, humble themselves before the God of Israel, and seek his face, then it might have prevented the vengeance which God proceeded to take on them for the dishonor done to his ark.

1. He destroyed them (v. 6). At Gath it is called *a great destruction* (v. 9), *a deadly destruction* (v. 11). It is expressly said (v. 12) that those who were *smitten with the emerods* (afflicted with tumors) *were the men that died not* by this other *destruction*, which probably was the plague.

2. Those who were not destroyed *he smote with emerods*, he afflicted them with tumors (v. 6), *in their secret parts* (in the groin) (v. 9). The tumors were so painful that (v. 12) the *cry went up to heaven*, that is, the outcry could be heard from far away. Perhaps in their extreme pain and misery, they cried, not to Dagon, but to the God of heaven. This was both a painful and a shameful disease. God wanted to use it to humble their pride, to

show them contempt, as they had shown to his ark. The disease, perhaps unknown among them before, became an epidemic. *Ashdod was smitten, and the coasts thereof* (v. 6), the vicinity around the city.

3. The men of Ashdod soon became aware that it was *the hand of God, the God of Israel* (v. 7). They were constrained to acknowledge his power and authority in this way. They had to confess that they came under his jurisdiction, but they still would not renounce Dagon and submit to Jehovah. No; now that he was affecting their bodies, they were ready instead to curse him to his face. Rather than making their peace with him and wanting the ark to stay with them on better terms, they wanted to get clear of it. When worldly hearts are suffering under the judgments of God, they would rather, if possible, put him far away from them than enter into covenant and fellowship with him and make him their friend. So the men of Ashdod decided, *The ark of the God of Israel shall not abide* (stay) *with us* (v. 7).

4. It was decided to change the place where it was held captive. It was agreed that it should be moved to Gath (v. 8). They superstitiously thought that there was something wrong with the place and that the ark would be happier if it stayed somewhere else, farther away from Dagon's temple. And so, instead of returning it to its rightful place, as they should have done, they planned to send it somewhere else. Gath was chosen, a place that was famous for its race of giants, but their strength and stature were no defense against the plague and the tumors: all the people of that city were afflicted, *both great and small* (v. 9), both the tall and the short; all alike came under God's judgment.

5. Eventually they all became weary of the ark and wanted to get rid of it. It was sent from Gath to Ekron, and because it came by order of the council, the people of Ekron could not refuse it, but they were very angry with their leaders for sending them such a fatal present (v. 10): *They have sent it to us to slay us and our people.* A general assembly is called urgently, to advise about *sending the ark again to its place* (v. 11). While they are considering the matter, the hand of God is carrying out its work, and their plans to evade the judgment only spread it. Many drop down dead among them. Many more are desperately ill because of the tumors (v. 12). What can they do?

CHAPTER 6

In this chapter we have the return of the ark to the land of Israel. Notice: 1. How the Philistines sent it away, under the advice of their priests (vv. 1–11), with rich presents to the God of Israel to make atonement for their sin (vv. 3–5), but also with a plan to bring it back unless Providence directed the cows, against their inclination, to go to the land of Israel (vv. 8–9). 2. How the Israelites received it with great joy and sacrifices of praise (vv. 12–18). 3. How they overconfidently and curiously looked into it, for which many of them were struck down dead (vv. 19–21).

Verses 1–9

The ark was in the country of the Philistines seven months (v. 1). So long as they held it captive, they would find that it brought a curse on them. Now:

• It was seven months that Israel was punished by the absence of the ark, that special sign of God's presence. It was no doubt a sad time, but they could comfort themselves with the thought that wherever the ark may be, *the Lord is in his holy temple*. By faith and prayer we may have access with boldness to come to God. God can be with us even when the ark is far away.

• It was seven months that the Philistines were punished by the presence of the ark. It was a plague to them for so long because they did not want to send it home any sooner. This shows us that sinners extend their own misery by stubbornly refusing to leave their sins. But it was finally decided that the ark must be sent back.

1. The priests and the diviners were consulted about what to do (v. 2). They were supposed to be the ones who were best informed about the rules of wisdom and the ceremonies of worship and atonement, and so it was right to ask them, *What shall we do to the ark of the Lord?* (v. 2).

2. They gave their detailed advice and seemed to be unanimous in it.

2.1. Referring to the example of Pharaoh and the Egyptians (v. 6), they urgently impressed upon the Philistines that it was absolutely necessary to send the ark back.

2.2. They advised that, when the Philistines sent the ark back, they should send a trespass offering (guilt offering) with it (v. 3). They knew that the God of Israel was a jealous God, and those with whom he had such a quarrel must by all means *return him a trespass offering* (v. 3), and they could not expect to be healed on any other terms. But when the advisers began to work out what that atonement should be, they became wrong in their thinking.

2.3. They directed the Philistines to prepare this trespass offering as an acknowledgment of the punishment of their people's sin. The Philistines must make models of the *emerods*, that is, of the tumors and sores with which they had been afflicted, thus making the shame of that awful disease everlasting by their own deed (Ps 78:66). They were also to make models of the *mice that had marred* (rats that had destroyed) *the land* (v. 5), thus acknowledging the almighty power of the God of Israel, who could rebuke and humble them, even in the day of their triumph, by such small and contemptible creatures. These models must be made of gold, the most precious metal, to show that they would gladly buy their peace with the God of Israel at any price. The *golden emerods* must number five according to the *number of the lords* (rulers) (v. 4), who were probably all afflicted with them and were content to acknowledge it in this way. It was advised that the *golden mice* (rats) should number five too.

2.4. They encourage the Philistines to hope that if they do this, then they will effectively get rid of the plague: *You shall be healed* (v. 3). "Let them therefore send back the ark, and then," they say, "*It shall be known to you why his hand is not removed from you* (v. 3), that is, you will know whether it is because you kept the ark that you have been afflicted by the plague. If that is so, then when you hand over the ark, the plague will stop."

2.5. But the Philistines' advisers directed them to test even further whether it was the hand of the God of Israel that had struck them with these plagues. They must put the ark on a new cart or carriage, to honor it, and this vehicle was to be drawn by two cows that had calved (v. 7) but had never pulled a cart before and were inclined to return home. No one must lead or drive them, but they must make their own way, which you would reason would be homeward again, that is, unless the God of Israel, after all the other miracles he had worked, would work one more, and by an invisible power lead these cows contrary to their natural instincts and inclination to the land of Israel, particularly to Beth Shemesh. Unless this happened, the advisers would withdraw their former opinion and would not believe that it was the hand of God that struck them but would conclude that it was by chance that they had suffered as they had (vv. 8–9).

Verses 10–18

We are told here:

1. How the Philistines sent the ark away (vv. 10–11). They were as glad to part with it as they had been to capture it.

- They received no money or price for its redemption, though they had hoped to get even more than "a king's ransom." In fact:
- They gave gold jewels, as the Egyptians did to the Israelites, to get rid of it.

2. How the cows brought it to the land of Israel (v. 12). They took the straight way to Beth-shemesh, the nearest town in the land of Israel, a priests' town, and turned not aside; they did not turn to the right or left. This was a wonderful example of the power of God over these animals, that cattle who were not used to pulling a cart would go along the road straight to Beth Shemesh, a town about ten miles (about sixteen kilometers) away. They did not lose their way; they did not turn aside into the fields to feed themselves, and they did not turn back home to feed their calves.

3. How it was welcomed in the land of Israel: *The men of Beth-shemesh were reaping their wheat harvest* (v. 13). They were going about their ordinary worldly business and were not concerned about the ark. God will rescue his church in his own time, even though it is not only fought against by its enemies but also neglected by its friends. The same invisible hand that directed the cows to the land of Israel brought them to the field of Joshua of Beth Shemesh, because of the large rock in that field, which was convenient to rest the ark on, and which is spoken about in vv. 14–15, 18. Notice:

3.1. When the reapers *saw the ark, they rejoiced* (v. 13). Although they did not have enough zeal and courage to try to rescue or redeem it, they still welcomed it genuinely when it did come.

3.2. They offered the cows as a burnt offering, to honor God, and made use of the wood of the cart for fuel (v. 14). In sending the cows, the Philistines probably intended them to be a part of their trespass offering (guilt offering), to make atonement (vv. 3, 7).

3.3. They placed the ark, with the chest of jewels that the Philistines presented, on the large rock in the open field. This was a cold and lowly place for the ark of the Lord to rest, but it was much better than in Dagon's temple or in the hands of the Philistines. As the burning of the cart and cows which brought home the ark might be interpreted to mean that they hoped it would never again be taken out of the land of Israel, so the placing of it on a large rock might mean they hoped it would again be established on a firm foundation. The church is built on a rock.

3.4. They offered sacrifices of thanksgiving to God. Some think they did this on the large rock, but more probably it was on an altar of earth made for the purpose (v. 15). The accidental bringing of the ark to this town was a sign of its intended settlement there in the course of time. It was one of those cities which were assigned out of the allotted territory of Judah to the *sons of Aaron* (Jos

21:16). Where should the ark go except to a priests' town? It was good that they had those of that sacred order ready to take down the ark and to offer the sacrifices.

3.5. The rulers of the Philistines returned to Ekron. They were probably very moved by what they had seen of the glory of God and the zeal of the Israelites, but they had not yet abandoned the worship of Dagon.

Verses 19–21

Here is:

1. The sin of the men of Beth Shemesh: *They looked into the ark of the Lord* (v. 19). We were all ruined by the thirst for forbidden knowledge. What made this looking into the ark a great sin was that it came from a very low and inferior opinion of the ark. Maybe they presumed on the present lowly circumstances of the ark, that it had just come out of captivity and was still unsettled. It is an offense against God if we have a low opinion of his ordinances because of the lowly way in which they are administered. If they had looked with understanding on the ark, and not judged purely by outward appearance, they would have realized that the ark never shone with greater majesty than it did now.

2. Their punishment for this sin: *He smote the men of Beth-shemesh, many of them, with a great slaughter*; also, *He smote 50,070 men* (v. 19). This is expressed in a very unusual way in the original, which has caused many commentators to question whether we are reading the text in the right way. Josephus says that only seventy were struck down.

3. The terror that came on the men of Beth Shemesh because of this severe blow. They said, as well they might, *Who is able to stand before this holy Lord God?* (v. 20). To stand in God's presence to worship him is, thankfully, not impossible; through Christ we are invited, encouraged, and enabled to do so. But we are not able to stand in God's presence to contend with him.

4. Their desire to get rid of the ark. They asked, *To whom shall he go up from us?* (v. 20). They sent messengers to the elders of Kiriath Jearim, a strong city further up in the country, and begged them to come and take the ark there (v. 21). This city lay on the way from Beth Shemesh to Shiloh, and so we may suppose that when the people of Beth Shemesh sent this message, they intended that the elders of Shiloh would take the ark from Kiriath Jearim once it had been brought there, but God intended otherwise. And so it was sent from town to town, and the community was unconcerned about it, a sign that there was no king in Israel.

CHAPTER 7

In this chapter we have the overshadowing of the glory of the ark by its seclusion in Kiriath Jearim for many years (vv. 1–2). We also read of the appearing of the glory of Samuel as he undertook service for the good of Israel, for whom he was raised up as a judge, and he was the last such person. We see him here active: 1. In the reforming of the Israelites from their idolatry (vv. 3–4). 2. In the reviving of true religion among them (vv. 5–6). 3. In praying for them against the invading Philistines (vv. 7–9), over whom God, in answer to his prayer, gave them a glorious victory (vv. 10–11); in setting up a memorial to express their gratitude for that victory (v. 12). 4. In their making the most of that victory (vv. 13–14); in the administration of justice (vv. 15–17).

Verses 1–2

Here we accompany the ark to Kiriath Jearim, not hearing any more about it except once (14:18) till David took it from there about forty years later (1Ch 13:6).

1. The men of Beth Shemesh have foolishly turned what might have been a blessing into a burden. Notice:

1.1. The men of Kiriath Jearim happily brought it among them (v. 1). They were no less glad to receive it than their neighbors, the people of Beth Shemesh, were to get rid of it, for they knew very well that the killing the ark had made at Beth Shemesh was not an act of despotic power but of necessary justice. Those who suffered had only themselves, not the ark, to blame.

1.2. They carefully provided for its proper reception among them with true affection, respect, and reverence.

1.2.1. They provided a proper place to receive it in the house of Abinadab, which stood on the hill and was probably the best house in their city. The men of Beth Shemesh left it exposed on a rock in an open field, but the men of Kiriath Jearim found room for it in one of their houses. God will find a resting place for his ark. If some people reject it, the hearts of others will still be inclined to receive it. Nor is it anything new for God's ark to be put into a private house.

1.2.2. They provided a proper person to guard it: *They sanctified Eleazar his son to keep it* (v. 1). They did not consecrate the father, because he was old and infirm. Eleazar's business was to guard the ark, to protect it not only from being seized by malicious Philistines, but also from being touched or looked into by overcurious Israelites. He was to regularly clean the room in which the ark was and to keep the room respectable, so that it might not look as though it was neglected. It does not seem that this Eleazar came from the tribe of Levi, much less from the house of Aaron. We may suppose that some devout Israelites came and prayed in the presence of the ark, and he was there ready to attend and assist those who did so. The men of Kiriath Jearim consecrated him for this purpose, set him apart for this work in the name of all their citizens. This was unusual and irregular but was excusable because of the present distressing circumstances.

2. But we are very reluctant to leave the ark there, wishing it were back at Shiloh again. That place, however, has been made desolate (Jer 7:14), and so the ark must lie by the wayside for lack of some people with a good community spirit to take it to its proper place.

2.1. The time that it stayed there was very long. For more than forty years it lay in a remote, obscure, private place, off the beaten track and almost completely neglected (v. 2). It was very strange that during all the time that Samuel governed, the ark was never brought to the Most Holy Place, and this was a sign that the Israelites were becoming less zealous for God. God allowed this to happen in order to punish them for their neglect when it was in its place.

2.2. Twenty years passed before the house of Israel became aware of the lack of the ark. The Septuagint (a Greek version of the Old Testament) expresses it somewhat more clearly than the KJV: "and it was twenty years, and [that is, it had been twenty years when] the whole house of Israel looked up again after the Lord" (v. 2). While the ark was away from the tabernacle, the sign of God's special presence was lacking, nor could they keep the Day of Atonement as it should be kept. They were content to have the altars but not the ark. Those whose profession of religious faith is merely formal are easily satisfied with external ceremonies that lack any signs of God's presence or acceptance. But eventually the Israelites came to themselves and began to mourn and seek after the Lord. They were probably stirred into doing this by the preaching of Samuel, which was accompanied by an extraordinary working of the Spirit of God. A general attitude of repentance and reformation now appeared throughout all Israel. True repentance and conversion begin in mourning and seeking after the Lord. Things went better with the Israelites when they lacked the ark and mourned it than when they had the ark and were prying into it or priding themselves in it.

Verses 3–6

We may well wonder where Samuel had been and what he had been doing all this time, but his labors among his people are not mentioned until their fruit appears. When he noticed that they began to *lament after the Lord* (v. 2), he struck while the iron was hot, and he tried to do two things for them:

1. He endeavored to separate them from their idols, for reformation must begin there. He *spoke to all the house of Israel* (v. 3), going, it seems, from place to place as an itinerant preacher—for we do not find that they were gathered together till v. 5—and wherever he went, this was his encouragement: "*If you do indeed return to the Lord* (v. 3), then know:

1.1. "That you must renounce and abandon your idols. Put away Baals, the foreign gods, and Ashtoreths, the foreign goddesses," for they also had these. *Ashtaroth* is particularly named because it was the best-loved idol. True repentance strikes at our favorite sin and wants with a special zeal and resolution to put away that sin, the sin which most *easily besets us* (Heb 12:1).

1.2. "That you must be serious about returning to God, and do that with careful consideration and firm resolution, for both are included in *preparing the heart* (v. 3), which means directing the heart to the Lord and establishing it for him.

1.3. "That you must be wholly committed to God, to him and no other. *Serve him only* (v. 3), or else you will not be serving him in any way that pleases him. Take this course, and *he will deliver you out of the hand of the Philistines* (v. 3)." This was the thrust of Samuel's preaching, and it had a wonderfully favorable effect (v. 4): *They put away Baalim and Ashtaroth.* They not only stopped worshiping them but also destroyed their idols, demolished their altars, and totally abandoned them.

2. He tried to get them to commit themselves to God and his service forever:

2.1. He summoned all Israel, at least their elders as their representatives, to meet him at Mizpah (v. 5), and he promised to pray for them there. When we come together in religious meetings, we must remember that we have as great a responsibility to join in public prayers as we have to listen to a sermon.

2.2. They obeyed his summons, and they not only came to the meeting but also went along with his intentions for it, and when they came they seemed to be in very good spirits (v. 6).

2.2.1. They drew water and poured it out before the Lord. This showed:

2.2.1.1. Their humiliation and contrition for sin. They acknowledged themselves to be like water that has been spilled on the ground and cannot be recovered (2Sa 14:14). The Aramaic reads, "They poured out their hearts in repentance before the Lord."

2.2.1.2. Their fervent prayers and supplications to God for mercy.

2.2.1.3. Their universal reformation. They expressed their willingness to part with all their sins, so that no more of the delight or savor of those sins would remain in their mouths than there remains of water in a container from which it has been poured out.

2.2.1.4. Their joy — according to some interpreters — at the hope of God's mercy, which Samuel had assured them of.

2.2.2. *They fasted* (v. 6); they abstained from food and humbled their souls, so expressing their repentance.

2.2.3. They made a public confession: *We have sinned against the Lord* (v. 6). They gave glory to God and expressed their shame.

2.3. *Samuel judged* them at that time *in Mizpah* (v. 6), that is, when they repented, he assured them in God's name that their sins were forgiven and that God was reconciled with them. It was a judgment of declaring God's forgiveness. Whereas before he acted only as a prophet, now he began to act as a judge, to prevent them from falling back into those sins which they then seemed to have renounced.

Verses 7–12

Here:

1. The Philistines attacked Israel (v. 7), being resentful of that general assembly for repentance and prayer as if it had been a council to declare war. Notice:

1.1. How evil sometimes seems to come out of good. The religious meeting of the Israelites at Mizpah brought trouble on them from the Philistines. When sinners begin to repent and reform, they must expect Satan to muster all his forces against them and set his instruments to do all they can to oppose and discourage them. But:

1.2. How good is finally brought out of that evil. There could not have been a more opportune time for Israel to be threatened than when they were repenting and praying, nor could they have been better prepared to receive the enemy.

2. Israel clung closely to Samuel, as their best friend under God in this distress. Even though he was no military man or famous warrior, they called on Samuel to pray for them: *Cease not to cry unto the Lord our God for us* (v. 8). They were here unarmed and unprepared for war. They had come together to fast and pray, not to fight. Prayers and tears were the only weapons many of them were now supplied with, and so they turned to these.

3. Samuel interceded with God for them and did so *by sacrifice* (v. 9). Samuel's sacrifice without his prayer would have been a meaningless shadow, and his prayer without the sacrifice would not have been so successful, but both together teach us what great things we may expect from God in answer to those prayers which are made with faith in Christ's sacrifice. Note that this was a burnt offering, that is, one that was offered purely for the glory of God. Yet it was only one suckling lamb that he offered, for it is the integrity and intention of the heart that God looks at, more than the amount or number of offerings. Samuel was no priest, but he was a Levite and a prophet. The case was extraordinary, and what he did was by special direction, and so it was accepted by God.

4. God graciously answered Samuel's prayer (v. 9): *The Lord heard him*. He was himself a *Samuel*, "asked of God," and God gave him many Samuels, many mercies in answer to prayer. The prayer of Samuel was honored, for at the very time he was offering his sacrifice and his prayer, the battle began and turned immediately against the Philistines. Just as, in a former encounter with the Philistines, God had justly rebuked their presumptuous confidence in the presence of the ark on the shoulders of two godless priests, so also now he graciously accepted their humble dependence on the prayer of faith from the mouth and heart of a godly prophet.

5. Samuel set up a memorial of thanksgiving for this victory, to give glory to God and encouragement to Israel (v. 12). He set up an *Eben-ezer*, "stone of help." The place where this memorial was set up was the same where, twenty years before, the Israelites had been defeated by the Philistines, for that was beside Ebenezer (4:1). The reason he gives for the name Ebenezer is, *Hitherto* (thus far) *the Lord hath helped us* (v. 12). Here he speaks thankfully of what was past, but he speaks somewhat doubtfully about the future: "Thus far things have gone well, but we do not know what God may still do with us. We are leaving the future to him, but let us praise him for what he has done so far." *Having obtained help from God, I continue hitherto*, says Paul (Ac 26:22).

Verses 13–17

It appears (2Ch 35:18) that in the days of Samuel the prophet, the people of Israel kept the ordinance of the Passover with more than ordinary devotion, despite the distance of the ark and the desolation at Shiloh. No doubt he did much good for Israel, but here we are told only how instrumental he was:

1. In securing the public peace (v. 13): *In his days the Philistines came no more into the coast* (territory) *of Israel*. Samuel was a protector and deliverer of Israel, not by means of the sword, like Gideon, or by virtue of bodily strength, like Samson, but by the power of prayer to God and by carrying on the work of reformation among the people. True religious faith and godliness are the best security for a nation.

2. In regaining the community's rights (v. 14). Under his influence, Israel had the courage to demand the cities which the Philistines had unjustly captured from them. It is added, *There was peace between Israel and the Amorites* (v. 14), that is, the Canaanites, the remainder of the indigenous people.

3. In administering public justice (vv. 15–16): *He judged Israel*. Even after Saul was made king, he promised them (12:23), *I will* not fail to *teach you the good and the right way*. He set up courts in Bethel, Gilgal, and Mizpah, all in the tribe of Benjamin, but his base was at Ramah, his father's town, and he judged Israel there.

4. In maintaining the public exercise of religious faith. Where he lived, he built an altar to the Lord. He did not do this in contempt of the altar at Nob or Gibeon. Rather, because no place had yet been chosen for the Israelites to bring their offerings to (Dt 12:11) instead of to Shiloh, he did as the patriarchs did and built an altar where he lived, both for the use of his own family and for the good of the people who turned to it.

CHAPTER 8

Israel's good days rarely continued long. We have here: 1. Samuel becoming old (v. 1); his sons becoming worse (vv. 2–3). 2. Israel discontented with the present government and anxious to see a change. They ask Samuel to set a king over them (vv. 4–5). Samuel brings the matter before God (v. 6). God shows him what answer to give them, by way of rebuke (vv. 7–8) and by way of objection, setting out the consequences of a change of government and showing them how insecure they would soon be under it (vv. 8–18). Nevertheless they insist on their petition (vv. 19–20). Samuel promises them from God that they will soon have their request granted (vv. 21–22).

Verses 1–3

Here are two sad, but not unusual, things:

1. A good and useful man growing old and unfit for service (v. 1): *Samuel was old* and could not judge Israel as he had done. It is thought that he was not more than sixty years old now, perhaps not even that much, but he had been a man at a very early age, had been full of thoughts and responsibilities even as a child. The fruits that are the first to ripen are the ones that keep the most poorly. He had spent his strength and spirits on the hard work and troubles of public life, and if he now thought he could stir himself as he had been able to in earlier life, he found he was mistaken. Old age had limited his abilities. Those who are in the prime of their lives ought to be busy doing the work of life.

2. The children of a good man turning aside and not following in his steps. We have good grounds for thinking that the reason Samuel commissioned them was not that they were his sons but that, for all it appeared, they were men qualified to be entrusted with such a task. But unfortunately *his sons walked not in his ways* (v. 3), and because their character was the opposite of his, their relationship with such a good person, which otherwise would have been their honor, was in reality their disgrace. When Samuel's sons were made judges and settled far away from him, then they showed their true colors. In the same way, many who have done well in a state of subjection have been spoiled by promotion and power. Honors change people's minds, and too often for the worse. It does not appear that Samuel's sons were as godless and evil as Eli's sons, but whatever they were in other respects, they were still corrupt judges. They *turned aside after lucre*, dishonest gain (v. 3), after "the mammon of unrighteousness," according to the Aramaic. In deciding disputes, they considered the bribe, not the law. They asked, "Who will pay the most?" rather than, "Which side is right?"

Verses 4–22

Here is the beginning of a completely new and unexpected matter: the setting up of kingly government in Israel. Here we have:

1. The speech by the elders to Samuel about this (vv. 4–5). They came to him at his house at Ramah. Their speech contained:

1.1. A declaration of their grievances. In short, *Thou art old, and thy sons walk not in thy ways* (v. 5).

1.1.1. It was true that Samuel was old, but it also meant that he was wiser, more experienced, and so more qualified to govern.

1.1.2. It was true that his sons did not walk in his ways. That made him sad, but the elders could not say it was his fault; he had not, like Eli, indulged them in their bad ways, but was ready to receive complaints against them.

1.2. A request to redress these grievances by setting a king over them: *Make us a king to judge us like all the nations* (v. 5). They had done well so far, in that they had not rebelled against Samuel and set up a king for themselves. But it appears from what followed that it was an outrageous proposal and displeased God. They had to have a king to lead them with a show of outward power, like *all the nations* (v. 5). A poor prophet in a cloak, even though he knew the visions of the Almighty, looked inferior in the eyes of those who judged by outward appearance, but a king in a purple robe, with guards and officers of state, would appear great. And that was the kind of leader they had to have.

2. Samuel's indignation at what they said (v. 6):

2.1. It cut him to the heart. It probably came as a surprise to him. Also, it *displeased him when they said, Give us a king to judge us* (v. 6), because that reflected badly on God and his honor.

2.2. It drove him to his knees; he gave them no immediate answer but took time to consider what they proposed and prayed to the Lord for direction on what to do.

3. The instruction God gives him about this. He tells Samuel:

3.1. What will pacify Samuel's displeasure. Samuel was very disturbed at the proposal, but God told him he must not think it either hard to bear or strange.

3.1.1. He must not think it hard to bear this disrespect they had shown toward him, for they were showing their disrespect for God himself. If God's reputation is involved in the indignities that are done to us, then we may well afford to bear them patiently. Samuel must not complain if they were tired of his leadership, for in reality they were tired of God's leadership. The government of Israel had up to that time been a theocracy, a divine government. Their judges received their call and commission directly from God, and the affairs of their nation were under his special direction. But they were tired of this way of doing things.

3.1.2. He must not think it strange, for they were now doing as they always had done. They had always been rude to their leaders, for example, Moses and Aaron.

3.2. How to answer the elders' demand. Samuel would not have known what to say unless God had instructed him, but now he would give them, with conviction, the answer God sent them:

3.2.1. He must tell them that *they shall have a king. Hearken to the voice of the people* (v. 7 and again v. 9). God told Samuel to yield to them in this matter:

- So that they might be beaten with their own rod of discipline and might feel, to their cost, the difference between his government and the government of a king.
- To prevent something worse. If they were not yielded to, they would rise up in rebellion against Samuel or universally rebel from their religion and begin to worship the gods of other nations so that they might have kings like them.

3.2.2. But he must also tell them that when they have a king, they will soon have enough of him, and will want to repent of their decision when it is too late.

4. Samuel's faithful communication of God's mind to them (v. 10). He *told them all the words of the Lord*: how their request displeased the Lord greatly, and that he interpreted it as a rejection of him and compared it with their serving other gods. Samuel laid before them in detail what would be, not the rights of a king in general, but *the manner of the king that should reign over them*, who would follow the pattern of the kings of the other nations (v. 11):

4.1. If they want such a king as the other nations have, then let them consider that:

4.1.1. A king will have to have a great retinue, many attendants. And where would such servants and attendants come from? "Why, he will take your sons, and he will *appoint them for himself*" (v. 11). They must wait on him, *ear* (plow) *his ground, and reap his harvest* (v. 12). They were to think they were being promoted when they did these things (v. 16).

4.1.2. A king will have to keep a great table, a lavish diet.

4.1.3. A king will have to have a standing army for guards and garrisons.

4.1.4. A king will probably have favorites, whom he will dignify and make noble. "He will then make them rich out of your inheritances (v. 14). How will you like that?"

4.1.5. A king will have to have a great income to maintain his grandeur and power. "He will take a tenth of your grain (v. 15) and your cattle (v. 17)."

4.2. These would be their grievances, and when they complained to God, he *would not hear them* (v. 18).

5. The people's stubbornness in their demand (vv. 19–20). *"We will have a king over us* (v. 19), whatever God or Samuel may say to the contrary. We want a king, whatever it costs us, and whatever misfortune we bring on ourselves or our descendants because of it." They were completely deaf to reason and blind to what was good for them. They could not wait for God's time. God had indicated to them in the Law that in due time Israel would have a king (Dt 17:14–15). If only they could have waited a few more years; they would have had David, a king of God's giving in mercy, and all the disasters Israel suffered under Saul might have been avoided.

6. The people sent away with an indication that they would very soon have what they asked for.

6.1. *Samuel rehearsed* (repeated) *all their words in the ears of the Lord* (v. 21). This shows a holy intimacy, to which God graciously admits his people. They speak into the Lord's ears, as one friend whispers a confidence to another.

6.2. God gave direction that they should have a king, since they were so desperately set on it (v. 22): *"Make them a king,* and let them make the best of him." *So he gave them up to their own hearts' lusts* (sinful desires) (Ro 1:24). Samuel sent them home for the present, *every man to his city* (v. 22), for the identity of the person who was to become king must be left with God, and there was nothing more for them to do.

CHAPTER 9

Most governments began with the ambition of a prince to rule, but Israel's began with the ambition of the people to be ruled. Because God, in the Law, claimed for himself the right to choose their king (Dt 17:15), they all sit still and wait to hear from heaven, and they do indeed hear in this chapter, where the story of Saul, their first king, begins. We read here about the strange steps of Providence, which brings Saul to be privately anointed by Samuel, and so to be prepared for an election by lot and for the public recommendation of him to the people by Samuel, which we read about in the next chapter. Here is: 1. A short account of Saul's parents and person (vv. 1–2). 2. A long and detailed account of his coming to Samuel, to whom he had before been a total stranger. 2.1. By revelation, God had told Samuel to expect him (vv. 15–16). 2.2. By providence, God led him to Samuel: Being sent to find his father's donkeys, Saul did not know which way to turn (vv. 3–5); by the advice of his servant, Saul decided to consult Samuel (vv. 6–10); by the direction of the young girls, Saul found him (vv. 11–14); Samuel was informed by God about Saul (v. 17); Samuel treated Saul with respect (vv. 18–27).

Verses 1–2

We are told here:

1. What a good family Saul came from (v. 1). He came from the tribe of Benjamin; so did the New Testament Saul, who also was called *Paul,* and the apostle mentions his membership in that tribe as his honor, for Benjamin was a favorite (Ro 11:1; Php 3:5). Although that tribe was fewest in number, it was foremost in honor. Saul's father was *Kish, a mighty man of power* (v. 1), or as the margin reads, "in substance." He was bold in spirit, strong in body, and wealthy in his possessions; in short, he was a man of standing.

2. What a good appearance Saul had (v. 2). No mention is made of his wisdom or virtue, his learning or godliness, or any of his mental achievements, but instead it is said that he was a tall, handsome man who carried himself gracefully and had a great presence. *Among all the children of Israel there was not a goodlier person than he.* He was head and shoulders taller than any of the people. When God chose a king after his own heart, he chose one who was not at all remarkable for his height and who had nothing special about his looks except his natural innocence and ruddiness (16:7, 12). But when he chose a king as the people wanted — who wanted nothing less than stateliness and grandeur — he chose this huge, tall man, who, even if he had no other good qualities, would still look great.

Verses 3–10

Here is:

1. A great man rising from small beginnings. It does not appear that Saul had any advancement at all or any position of honor or trust until he was chosen as king of Israel.

2. A great event arising from small occurrences. Notice how lowly the beginnings of history are. If we want to trace Saul's path to the crown, we must first see him employed as humbly as any others we meet who are later advanced.

2.1. Saul's father sends him with one of his servants to seek some donkeys that he had lost. Saul and his servant traveled far, probably on foot, looking for the donkeys, but in vain: they did not find them. He missed what he was looking for, but he met with the kingdom, which he never dreamed of.

2.2. When he could not find them, he decided to return to his father (v. 5). He cared about his father's tender concern for him.

2.3. His servant proposed that since they were now at Ramah, they should call on Samuel and take his advice in this important matter. They were close to the town where Samuel lived, and that put it into their minds to consult him (v. 6). *He is a man of God, and an honourable man* (v. 6). This was Samuel's honor as a man of God: that *all he saith comes surely to pass* (v. 6). They agreed to ask him concerning *the way that they should go; peradventure* (perhaps) *he can show us* (v. 6). Most people would rather be told their fortune than their duty, how to be rich than how to be saved. If it were the business of ministers to give directions on how to recover lost donkeys, they would be consulted much more than they are now consulted for directions on how to recover lost souls, which is their business. Saul gave thought to what present they should take to the man of God. They could not present him with loaves and cakes (1Ki 14:3), for their bread was used up, but the servant realized that he had a quarter of a shekel of silver in his pocket. "That will do," Saul says; *"let us go"* (v. 10). Some think he came to Samuel regarding him as a fortune-teller rather than as a prophet, and so he thought a quarter of a shekel of silver was enough to give him. But to me it seems rather to be an example of the principle that those who sowed spiritual things should reap, not only eternal things from God, who employed them, but also physical things from the people whom God employed them for. Even though Saul's gift was only a little, it was still the widow's mite. And yet it is true that Saul himself did not acknowledge that he had money in his pocket, and only agreed to go to the prophet when the servant generously offered to bear the cost himself. Most people love to have religion on the cheap, and they like it best when they can pass on its expense to others. The writer here takes note of the name then given to the prophets: they called them *Seers*, or "seeing men" (v. 9). It was not that the term *prophet* was not used then and applied to such people, but the term *seers* was more commonly used. Those who are prophets must first be seers; those who undertake to speak about the things of God to others must first have gained an insight for themselves.

Verses 11–17

Here:

1. Saul is directed to Samuel by ordinary inquiry (vv. 11–14). Gibeah of Saul was not ten miles (about sixteen kilometers) from Ramah, where Samuel lived, and was near Mizpah, where he often judged Israel:

1.1. The girls of Ramah, whom they met at the places of drawing water, could give him and his servant information about Samuel:

1.1.1. That there was a sacrifice that day at the high place. Samuel had built an altar at Ramah (7:17), and here we see him making use of that altar.

1.1.2. That Samuel was to come to the town that day.

1.1.3. That this was just the time of their meeting to eat the sacrifice before the Lord.

1.1.4. That the people would not eat till Samuel came, because *he* must bless the sacrifice, both as an ordinary meal and as a religious meeting. When the sacrifice was offered, it needed to be blessed in a special way, as is the Christian Eucharist.

1.2. Saul and his servant followed the directions given them. They met Samuel at just the right time, as he was going to the high place, the synagogue of the town (v. 14).

2. Samuel was informed concerning Saul by extraordinary revelation. He was a seer, and so he must see this in a way that was special to himself:

2.1. God had told him the day before that he would at this time send him the man who would serve the people of Israel as the kind of king they wished to have. He *told him in his ear*, that is, he had revealed it to him privately, by a secret whisper to his mind, or perhaps by a still small voice. The Hebrew means, literally, "uncovered the ear of Samuel." When God wants to reveal himself to a soul, he uncovers the ear; he says, *Ephphatha*, "Be opened" (Mk 7:34), and he takes *the veil from off the heart* (2Co 3:16). Although God has in his displeasure answered their request for a king, he still speaks tenderly to Israel.

2.1.1. He calls them again and again *my people*. Although they are an obstinate and self-willed people who have offended him, they are still his people.

2.1.2. He sends them a man to be their leader.

2.1.3. He does it with a gracious consideration of them and their cry: *I have looked upon my people*, and *their cry has come unto me* (v. 16).

2.2. When Saul came up toward him in the road, God again whispered into Samuel's ear (v. 17): *Behold the man whom I spoke to thee of*. That he might be fully convinced, God told him explicitly, *That is the man* who will restrain — for this is the work of magistrates — *my people Israel* (v. 16).

Verses 18–27

Having seen how Providence eventually brought Samuel and Saul together, we now have an account of what took place between them in the gateway, at the feast, and in private:

1. In the gateway of the town. Saul found Samuel passing through it (v. 18) and asked him the way to Samuel's house. Samuel answered him, "*I am the seer*, the person you are asking about" (v. 19). Samuel knew Saul before Saul knew Samuel. Now:

1.1. Samuel compels him to stay with him till the next day. Saul has nothing on his mind except finding his donkeys, but Samuel wants to take him away from that worry and direct him to exercise godliness, and so he tells him to *go to the high place*.

1.2. Samuel assures him about his donkeys (v. 20): "*Set not thy mind on them*, don't worry anymore about them; *they are found*." Saul would be able to tell from this that the man was a prophet.

1.3. Samuel surprises him with an indication of the advancement which lies before him: "*On whom is all the desire of Israel?* (v. 20). Is it not a king that they are set on? And there is never a man in Israel who will be more suitable than you."

1.4. Saul gives a modest answer to this strange suggestion (v. 21). He thinks that Samuel is mocking him because he is a tall man but very unlikely to be a king. *I am a Benjamite, my family the least* (v. 21), probably a younger clan, not in any place of honor or trust, not even in their own tribe.

2. At the public feast; Samuel took him and his servant there. Samuel did not treat him as a common person, but as a person of quality and distinction, to prepare both him and the people for what was to follow. He put two marks of honor on him:

2.1. He set him in the best place.

2.2. He presented him with the *best dish*. And what would this precious dish be for the king-elect? It was a plain *shoulder* (leg) of mutton (vv. 23–24). The right shoulder (thigh) of the peace offerings (fellowship offerings) was to be given to the priests, who were God's receivers (Lev 7:32); the next in honor to that was the left shoulder, which probably was always given to those who sat at the upper end of the table, and was usually Samuel's share at other times. So his giving it to Saul now was an implicit stepping down from his position in favor of Saul.

3. In private. Both that evening and early the next morning Samuel talked with Saul on the flat roof of the house (vv. 25–26). We may suppose Samuel now told him the whole story of the people's desire for a king, the reasons for their desire, and God's giving it. He sent him toward home early in the morning, brought him part of the way, and told him to send his servant on ahead, so that they might be in private (v. 27). There, as we find at the beginning of the next chapter, he anointed him and so showed him the *word of the Lord*.

CHAPTER 10

We have here: 1. The anointing of Saul (v. 1); the signs (vv. 2–6) and the instructions (vv. 7–8) that Samuel gave him. 2. The fulfillment of those signs to assure Saul (vv. 9–13); Saul's return to his father's house (vv. 14–16). 3. Saul's public election by lot and his solemn inauguration (vv. 17–25); Saul's return to his own home (vv. 26–27).

Verses 1–8

Here Samuel carried out the office of a prophet, fully assuring Saul from God that he would be king.

1. Samuel *anointed him* and *kissed him* (v. 1). This was not done in the solemn assembly, but it was done by divine appointment, which made up for the lack of external ceremony.

1.1. By anointing Saul, Samuel assured him that it was God's act to make him king: *Is it not because the Lord hath anointed thee?*

1.2. By kissing him, Samuel assured Saul of his own approval of the choice, even though it would reduce his power and eclipse his glory and the glory of his family. Similarly, it was a kiss of loyalty: it showed that he recognized him not only as king but also as his king, and in this sense we are commanded to *kiss the Son* (Ps 2:12). Samuel reminds him:

1.2.1. Of the nature of the government to which he is called. He was anointed to be a captain, a true leader and commander in war, which means worry, sweat, and danger.

1.2.2. Of the origin of the government: *The Lord hath anointed thee* (v. 1). He was given his rule by the Lord, and so he must rule for him, depending on him, and considering his glory.

1.2.3. Of the purpose of the government. It is a government over his inheritance, and it must take care of that inheritance, protect it, and arrange all of its affairs for the best. He is like a steward whom a great person sets over an estate.

2. To assure him further, Samuel gave Saul some signs, which would come to pass immediately that very day:

2.1. He would immediately meet with some people who would bring him news from home of about how his father was worried about him (v. 2). He would meet these people near Rachel's tomb. Two men would meet him there, and they would tell him the donkeys had been found.

2.2. He would next meet with others going to Bethel, where, it would seem, there was a high place for religious worship, and these men would be taking their sacrifices there (vv. 3–4). It is supposed that the young goats, the loaves of bread, and the skin of wine which the three men had with them were intended as a sacrifice, with the meat offerings (grain offerings) and drink offerings that were to accompany the sacrifice, but Samuel told Saul that they would give him two of their loaves of bread, and he must take them. It would be interpreted as a suitable gift for a ruler, and Saul must receive it as such, the first gift brought to him as king, by those who did not know what they were doing, or why they did it, but had it put into their hearts by God, which made it an even more suitable sign for him.

2.3. The most remarkable sign of all would be that, under the influence of a spirit of prophecy that would then come on him, he would join a procession of prophets he would meet. What God works in us by his Spirit serves much more to confirm our faith than anything worked for us by his providence. Samuel tells Saul (vv. 5–6):

2.3.1. Where this would happen: *At the hill of God*, where there was *a garrison* (outpost) of the Philistines (v. 5). It seems that, since the beginning of Samuel's judgeship, the Philistines had regained so much ground as to force this outpost to that place, and so God raised up the man who would overthrow them. There was a place that was called the *hill of God* (v. 5), or the Gibeah of God, because one of the schools of the prophets was built on it. Even the Philistines paid such respect to religion that an outpost of their soldiers allowed a school of God's prophets to live at peace near them. They did not disturb the public expressions of their devotion.

2.3.2. When and how it would happen: he would meet *a company of prophets with music before them, prophesying* (v. 5), and he himself would join them. These prophets occupied themselves in studying the Law, in instructing their neighbors, and in acts of godliness, especially in praising God. What a pity it was that Israel would be tired of the government of such a man as Samuel, who, as a man of God, had established schools of prophets. These prophets had been at the high place, probably to offer a sacrifice, and now they were on their way back singing psalms. Saul would find himself compelled to join them and so would be turned *into another man* (v. 6); he would be changed into a person who was different from what he had been in his private capacity.

3. Samuel directs Saul to proceed to administer his government as Providence would lead him and as Samuel would advise him.

3.1. He must follow Providence in ordinary cases (v. 7): "*Do as occasion shall serve thee.* Do whatever your hand finds to do; take such measures as your own wisdom directs you to." But:

3.2. In the extraordinary circumstances that he would later find himself in at Gilgal, which would be the most critical moment of all, when he would especially need divine help, he must wait for Samuel to come to him, must stay there *seven days* expecting him to come (v. 8). His failure in this matter proved his downfall later (13:11).

Verses 9–16

Saul has now taken his leave of Samuel, and Saul is probably stunned. We are told:

1. What occurred on the way (v. 9). The signs that Samuel had given him were promptly fulfilled, but what gave him the greatest assurance of all was that he immediately found that God had given him *another heart*. A new fire was kindled within him. He had now forgotten all about looking for the donkeys, and all he could think about was fighting the Philistines, setting right the grievances of Israel, making laws, administering justice, and providing for the security of the community: these were the things that now filled his mind. He no longer had the heart of a lowly agricultural worker who is concerned only about grain and cattle, but had the heart of a leader, a general, a ruler. God equips those whom he calls to any service.

2. What occurred when he came near home. They came to *the hill* (v. 10), that is, to *Gibeah*. He met with the prophets as Samuel had told him he would, and *the Spirit of God came on him*, strongly and suddenly—for this is what the word means—but not in such a way that the Spirit would rest and remain on him. For the present, however, the Spirit had a strange effect on him, for he immediately joined the prophets in their devotion: *He prophesied among them.* Now:

2.1. His prophesying was publicly noticed (vv. 11–12). He was among those who knew what he was like before. When they saw him among the prophets, they called out to one another to come and see this strange sight. This would prepare them to accept him as king. Now:

2.1.1. They were all amazed to see Saul among the prophets: *What is this that has come to the son of Kish?* (v. 11). Although this group of prophets was near his father's house, he had never associated with them. When the townspeople now saw him prophesying among them, it came as a great surprise to them, just as it was a surprise when, long after, his namesake in the New Testament preached the Gospel which he had previously persecuted (Ac 9:21). Where God gives another heart, it will soon reveal itself.

2.1.2. One of them, who was wiser than the others, asked, "*Who is their father* (v. 12), or instructor? Isn't it God? Aren't they all taught by him? Isn't he the source of all their gifts? Does God restrict himself as to how he acts? Can't he make Saul a prophet, as much as any of them, if he wants to?" Or perhaps the questioner meant, "Isn't Samuel their father?"

2.1.3. It became a common saying in Israel, which they used when they wanted to express their wonder at a bad person making good or at least being found in good company: *Is Saul among the prophets?* (v. 11).

2.2. His being anointed was kept private. When he had finished prophesying:

2.2.1. He went straight *to the high place* (v. 13) to give thanks to God for his mercies to him and to pray that those mercies would continue. But:

2.2.2. He was diligent in hiding from his relatives what had taken place. His uncle, who met him either at the high place or as soon as he came home, questioned him (v. 14). Saul acknowledged, for his servant knew, that they had been with Samuel and that Samuel had told them the donkeys had been found, but he did not say a word of *the kingdom* (vv. 14–15), his kingship. This was an example of his humility and his wisdom. If he had been forward in declaring his kingship, he would have been envied, and he did not want to begin to think about what difficulties that might have caused him.

Verses 17–27

Saul's nomination to the throne is here made public in a general assembly of the elders of Israel, the representatives of their respective tribes at Mizpah. When the people had met in a solemn assembly, in which God was present in a special way—and so it is said they were *called together unto the Lord* (v. 17)—Samuel acted on behalf of God among them:

1. He rebuked them for rejecting the government of a prophet and wanting that of a commander.

1.1. He showed them (v. 18) how successful they had been under divine government; when God ruled them, he delivered them out of the hand of those that oppressed them, and what more could they want?

1.2. He showed them similarly (v. 19) how they had defied God: "*You have this day rejected your God* (v. 19). This is what you have done, and because you have rejected God, he would be justified in rejecting you."

2. He advised them to choose their king by lot. Benjamin is chosen out of all the tribes (v. 20), and out of that tribe Saul the son of Kish (v. 21). This method would show the people, as it already appeared to Samuel, that Saul was appointed by God to be king, for *the disposal of the lot is of the Lord* (Pr 16:33).

3. It was with a lot of trouble, and not without further inquiries of the Lord, that Saul was eventually produced. When the lot fell on him, everyone expected he would answer when his name was first called out, but that did not happen, and none of his friends could find him (v. 21): he had *hidden himself among the stuff*, the baggage (v. 22).

3.1. He withdrew, in the hope that if he did not appear, they would proceed to choose someone else. We may suppose that at this time he did not want to take on the government:

3.1.1. Because he was aware within himself that he was not qualified for such a great trust.

3.1.2. Because it would expose him to the envy of his neighbors.

3.1.3. Because he understood, from what Samuel had said, that the people had sinned in asking for a king.

3.1.4. Because the affairs of Israel were at this time in a bad condition. The Philistines were strong and the Ammonites were threatening, and it would be a very bold captain who would set sail in a storm.

3.2. But the assembly believed that the choice had been well made, since God himself had made it, and they would leave no stone unturned to find the one who had been chosen by lot.

4. Samuel presented Saul to the people, and they accepted him. He did not need to go up to a raised platform or take a special seat to be seen, for he was taller than any of them by *head and shoulders* (v. 23). "Look," Samuel said, "this is the king that God has chosen for you. He is the one you wished for; *there is none like him among all the people* (v. 24), none who has so much majesty in his face and such a graceful stateliness in his demeanor. He rises up like a cedar among the shrubs of a crowd." The people then showed their approval of the choice and their acceptance of him. They *shouted and said* (v. 24), *God save the king*, that is, "Long live the king! May he reign over us for many years in health and prosperity."

5. Samuel made an original contract between them and put it on record (v. 25). He defined the positions of the king and the people, so that neither might encroach on the other. Let them rightly understand one another from the outset, and let the agreement be in writing, in black and white, which will help ensure that they remain on good terms with one another ever after.

6. The assembly came to an end when the ceremony was over: *Samuel sent every man to his house* (v. 25). *Saul also went home to Gibeah* (v. 26), to his father's house, not conceited about having a kingdom under him. At Gibeah there was no palace, throne, or court for him, but he still went there. If he must be a king, then let him remember the rock from which he was cut. He would make his own city the royal city, and he would not be ashamed of his lowly relatives—as many are when they are promoted to an advanced position.

6.1. What was the people's attitude toward their new king? It seems most of them were not particularly concerned: they *went every man to his own house*. But:

6.1.1. There were some who were so faithful as to accompany him: *A band of men whose hearts God had touched* (v. 26). A small group went with him to Gibeah as his bodyguard. Since *God had touched their hearts* (v. 26), they wanted in this situation to do their duty by showing proper respect to their king.

6.1.2. There were others so spiteful as to look down on him; *children of Belial* (v. 27), troublemakers who would not stand any discipline. In the same way, people have different responses to our exalted Redeemer. God has set him as king on the holy hill of Zion. There is a remnant *whose hearts God has touched* (v. 26), whom he has *made willing in the day of his power* (Ps 110:3). But there are others who despise him, who ask, *How shall this man save us?*

6.2. How did Saul respond to the bad behavior of those who were hostile to his government? *He held his peace* (v. 27). The margin reads, "He was as though he had been deaf."

CHAPTER 11

Here is: 1. The crisis which the town of Jabesh Gilead, on the other side of the Jordan, was reduced to by the Ammonites (vv. 1–3). 2. Saul's great readiness to come to

their relief, in which he distinguished himself (vv. 4–10);
the success of his attempt, by which God honored Saul
(v. 11). 3. Saul's tenderness, despite this, toward those
who had opposed him (vv. 12–13); the public confirma-
tion and recognition of his election to the government
(vv. 14–15).

Verses 1–4

The Ammonites were bad neighbors to those tribes of
Israel that were closest to them, even though they were
descendants of righteous Lot and even though Israel had
for that reason dealt civilly with them. See Dt 2:19. The
town of Jabesh Gilead had been destroyed by Israel's
sword of justice some time before, for not fighting against
the evil of Gibeah (Jdg 21:10), and now, because it had
become repopulated—probably by the descendants of
those who had then escaped the sword—it was in danger of being destroyed by the Ammonites, as if the place
were jinxed. Nahash, king of the Ammonites (1Ch 19:1),
besieged it. Now here:

1. The besieged people wanted to discuss terms (v. 1):
"*Make a covenant with us, and we will* surrender and *serve
thee.*" They had lost the virtue of Israelites, or else they
would not have lost the bravery of Israelites, weakly given
in to an Ammonite, and agreed to be subject to him.

2. The besiegers offered them barbaric terms: the
Ammonites would spare their lives and make them their
servants on condition that they would let the Ammonites
put (gouge) *out their right eyes* (v. 2). The Gileadites were
content to part with their freedom and lands. But their
pitiful submission made the Ammonites even bolder in
their demands.

2.1. They must torment the Gileadites and make them
suffer the intense pain of each having their right eye
gouged out.

2.2. They must render them unfit to fight in battle. In
those times soldiers fought with shields in their left hands,
which covered their left eyes, so that soldiers without their
right eyes were in effect blind.

3. The besieged people wanted, and gained, seven days
to consider this proposal (v. 3). Nahash, not imagining it
possible that they could be helped in such a short time
and being very sure of the advantages he thought he had
against them, dared to give them seven days, so that the
disgrace on Israel for not rescuing them might be even
greater and his triumphs even more glorious.

4. Notice was sent to Gibeah of the crisis. They said
they would send messengers *to all the coasts* (territory)
of Israel (v. 3), which made Nahash feel even more
secure, for he thought that would take time. But the
messengers, either of their own accord or by order of
their masters, went straight to Gibeah, and because they
did not find Saul there, told their news to the people,
who began to weep aloud when they heard what had happened (v. 4).

Verses 5–11

What is described here is very much to the honor of
Saul and shows the happy fruits of the other spirit that he
had been endowed with. Notice here:

1. His humility. Although he had been anointed king
and accepted by his people, he still did not think it beneath
him to know the condition of his own flocks, and so he
went himself to see them. He came back in the evening
with his servants, *after the herd out of the field* (v. 5); he
returned from the fields, behind his oxen. Like Paul, he
worked with his hands, for if he neglected his farming,
how could he maintain himself and his family?

2. His concern for his neighbors. When he noticed they
were crying, he asked, "*What ails the people that they
weep?* (v. 5). Why are they weeping? Let me know, so
that if it is caused by a grievance which can be put right,
I may do my best to help them, and if not, I may weep
with them."

3. His zeal for the security and honor of Israel. When
he heard of the arrogance of the Ammonites and the distress of a town in Israel, *the Spirit of God came upon him*
and put great thoughts into his mind, *and his anger was
kindled greatly* (v. 6). He was angry at the defiance of the
Ammonites, angry at the lowly and cowardly spirit of the
men of Jabesh Gilead, angry to see his neighbors in tears
when it would have been better for them to be preparing
for war.

4. The authority and power he exerted on this important occasion. He soon let Israel know that he still cared
very much for the community. He knew how to command
soldiers on the battlefield as well as how to drive out
cattle from an ordinary field (vv. 5, 7). He sent a summons throughout Israel and ordered all the military men
to immediately appear armed at a general assembly at
Bezek. Notice:

4.1. His modesty in making Samuel part of the joint
commission with himself. He did not want to carry out
the office of a king without due regard to the office of
a prophet.

4.2. His mildness in the penalty threatened against
those who would disobey his orders. He cut a pair of
oxen in pieces and sent the pieces to the different towns
of Israel to illustrate the punishment that would come to
those who refused to serve; his threat was not, however,
"This is what will happen to *you*," but "This is what will
happen to your *oxen*" (v. 7). The effect of this summons
was that the militia, or trained bands, of the nation *came
out as one man*, and the reason given is that *the fear of
the Lord fell upon them* (v. 7). Those who fear God will
conscientiously do their duty to all people, particularly
to their rulers.

5. His wise dealings in this matter (v. 8). He numbered
those who were mustered and who had come to him, so
that he might know his own strength and the best way to
distribute his forces. In this muster, it seems that although
Judah was numbered by itself, it did not make up a prominent figure, for it was only an eleventh part of the whole
number, 30,330, even though the assembly took place at
Bezek, in that tribe.

6. His faith and confidence and his courage and determination in this undertaking. He now sends the Gileadite
messengers back with the assurance, "*Tomorrow*, at such
and such an hour, before the enemy can try to say that the
seven days have elapsed, *you shall have deliverance* (v. 9).
Be ready to do your part, and we will not fail to do ours.
If you rush out and attack the besiegers, we will surround
them." Saul knew he had a just cause, a clear call, and
God on his side, and so he did not doubt that he would
be successful. This was good news to the besieged Gileadites. When they heard it, they were glad, relying on the
assurances that were given them. They sent a message into
the enemies' camp (v. 10) to tell them that the next day
they would be ready to meet them. The enemies understood as a sign that the Gileadites despaired of relief, and
so they were made more confident by it.

7. His industry and close diligence in this work. When
the Spirit of the Lord comes on people, he will make
them experts even without experience. Saul now had a
vast army—especially in comparison with those that

are raised nowadays—at his disposal, and a long march before him, nearly twenty miles (about thirty-two kilometers), and over the Jordan too. There were no cavalry in his army, only infantry, which he divided into three battalions (v. 11). Notice:

- With what incredible speed he rushed to the enemy. He was better than his word, for he promised help the next day, *by that time the sun was hot* (v. 9), but he brought it before daybreak, *in the morning watch* (v. 11).
- With what incredible bravery he rushed on the enemy. Early in the morning he was in the midst of their forces. His troops, having marched against them in three columns, surrounded them on every side, so that they had neither the heart nor the time to advance against them.

8. To complete his honor, God crowned all these virtues with success. Jabesh Gilead was rescued, and the Ammonites were totally defeated.

Verses 12–15

We see here how Saul made the most of the glorious victory he had gained:

1. The people used this occasion to show how much they would defend the honor of Saul and how angry they were at the dishonor that had been done to him. The sons of Belial who did not want him to reign over them should be brought out and killed, they said (v. 12). When Saul looked lowly, the people did not have the courage to suggest the prosecution of those who had opposed him (1Sa 10:27), but now that his victory made him appear great, they decided that the sons of Belial ought to be put to death.

2. Saul used this occasion to give further proofs of his mercy, for without even waiting for Samuel's answer, he himself quashed the suggestion (v. 13): *There shall not a man be put to death this day*:

2.1. Because it was a day of joy and triumph: *"Today the Lord has wrought salvation in Israel*, and since God has been so good to us all, let us not be harsh with one another."

2.2. Because he hoped that this day's work had brought those who had opposed him into a better frame of mind. Now, he hoped, they were convinced that this man, under God, could save them, and so they would now honor him even though they had earlier despised him. If they were reformed, he would be safe from any trouble from them, and so he would have won his point. If an enemy is turned into a friend, that is better than having them killed.

3. Samuel used this occasion to call the people together *before the Lord in Gilgal* (vv. 14–15). The purpose was:

- To publicly give God thanks for the victory they had just won.
- To confirm Saul in the government, more solemnly than had been done thus far, so that he might not withdraw again into an obscure capacity.

CHAPTER 12

In this chapter we have the speech Samuel made to the people when he resigned as leader of the government and transferred that part of his authority into the hands of Saul. In this speech: 1. He clears himself of every suspicion and imputation that he might have mismanaged the administration while it was in his hands (vv. 1–5). 2. He reminds them of the great things God has done for

them and their ancestors (vv. 6–13). He sets before them good and evil, the blessing and the curse (vv. 14–15). 3. He awakens them to consider what he has said to them by calling to God for thunder (vv. 16–19). He encourages them with the hope that all will go well (vv. 20–25). This is his farewell sermon to that distinguished assembly, and it is also Saul's coronation sermon.

Verses 1–5

1. Samuel gives them a short account of the recent change in their government and of the present state of it, to introduce what he is going to say to them (vv. 1–2):

1.1. For his own part, he had spent his days in serving them: *"I have walked before you*, as a guide to direct you and as a shepherd to lead a flock (Ps 80:1), *from my childhood unto this day*. And now my best days are finished: *I am old and grayheaded* (v. 2)." It was thus very unkind of them to reject him, but he was willing to resign. And yet he would warn them, "Perhaps I may never be given the opportunity to speak to you again, and so take notice of what I say."

1.2. As for his sons, he says, *"Behold, they are with you* (v. 2). If you want to, you may hold them responsible for anything they have done wrong."

1.3. As for their new king, Samuel had given in to them in setting him over them (v. 1). *"Behold, the king walketh before you* (v. 2). Now that you have made yourselves like the nations in your civil government and have rejected the divine administration in that, make sure you do not follow the ways of other nations in their religion and reject the worship of God."

2. Samuel solemnly appeals to them concerning his own integrity in the administration of the government (v. 3): *Witness against me, whose ox have I taken?*

2.1. Notice his intention in this appeal. By it, he wanted:

2.1.1. To convince them of the wrong they had done him in rejecting him.

2.1.2. To preserve his own reputation. Those who heard of Samuel's rejection would be ready to suspect that he must have done something evil, or he would never have been so badly treated.

2.1.3. To leave his successor a good example before him, just as he wanted to leave a good name behind him. Let the king take Samuel as his example, and he will not go far wrong.

2.2. Notice in the appeal itself:

2.2.1. What it is that Samuel here acquits himself of:

2.2.1.1. He had never taken what was not his own, be it an ox or a donkey. He had never seized their cattle to pay tributes, penalties, or fines. He had never used their service without paying for it.

2.2.1.2. He had never cheated those with whom he dealt or oppressed those who were in his power.

2.2.1.3. He had never taken bribes to pervert the course of justice.

2.2.2. How he calls on those who have looked down on him to bear witness about his leadership: *Here I am; witness* (testify) *against me* (v. 3).

3. Samuel is honorably acquitted as a result of this appeal. His only wish had been that they would do him justice, and they did that (v. 4).

4. This honorable testimony that was brought in support of Samuel's integrity is left on record to his honor (v. 5): *"The Lord is witness*, who searches the heart, *and his anointed is witness*, who tries observable acts." The people agreed to it: *He is witness.*

Verses 6–15

After Samuel had made his own reputation secure, he did not rebuke the people for their unkindness to him but set himself to instruct them in the path of duty.

1. He reminds them of the great goodness of God to them and to their ancestors, gives them a summary history of their nation, so that if they consider the great things God has done for them, they may be committed to love him and serve him forever. He reminds them not only of what God has done for them in their days but also of what he did in previous times, in the days of their ancestors, because the present generation has received the benefit of God's former favors.

1.1. He reminds them of their rescue from Egypt.

1.2. He reminds them of the miseries and calamities which their ancestors brought on themselves by forgetting God and serving other gods (v. 9).

1.3. He reminds them of their ancestors' repentance and humiliation before God for their idolatry: *They said, We have sinned* (v. 10).

1.4. He reminds them of God's glorious deliverances of them, of the victories he had blessed them with, and of the many times they had been happily settled after days of trouble and distress (v. 11). He mentions some of their judges by name, including Gideon and Jephthah, great conquerors in their time.

1.5. He finally reminds them of God's recent favor to the present generation in gratifying them by giving them a king, when they wanted to dictate to God that he ought to use such a king to save them from the hands of Nahash king of the Ammonites (vv. 12–13). It now comes out that this was the immediate reason for their wanting a king: Nahash had threatened them. They wanted Samuel to name a general; he told them that God was their commander in chief in all their wars and they needed no one else. What was lacking in them would be made up by his power: *The Lord is your king.* But they insisted on it: *Nay* (no); *but a king shall reign over us* (v. 12). "And now," he said, "you have a king, a king of your own asking — that is said to your shame; but he is a king of God's making — let that be spoken of to his honor and to the glory of his grace."

2. He shows them that they and their king are now expected to behave themselves. They must not think that they had now cut themselves off from depending completely on God.

2.1. Their obedience to God would certainly result in their happiness (v. 14). If they did not turn away from God to idols, if only they kept up their allegiance to him, then they and their king would certainly be happy.

2.1.1. "You will continue in the path of your duty to God, which will be to your honor and strength."

2.1.2. "You will continue under divine guidance and protection." The original reads: "You shall be after the Lord," that is, "he will go before you to lead and prosper you, and make your way clear. *The Lord is with you while you are with him*" (2Ch 15:2).

2.2. Their disobedience would just as certainly lead to their destruction (v. 15).

Verses 16–25

Samuel aims at two things:

1. To convince the people of their sin in wanting a king. They were now rejoicing before God in and with their king (11:15), and offering to God sacrifices of praise, which they hoped God would accept. Perhaps this made them think that there was no harm in asking for a king. Notice:

1.1. The expressions of God's displeasure against them for asking for a king. At Samuel's word, God sent tremendous thunder and rain on them at a season of the year when nothing like that had ever been seen or known in that country before (vv. 16–18). Thunder and rain have natural causes and sometimes have terrible effects. But Samuel made it clear that this was deliberately intended by the almighty power of God to convince them that they had done very *wickedly in asking a king* (v. 17). It not only came at a very unusual time but also was announced beforehand by Samuel, and thus could be no less than a miracle: *Stand and see this great thing* (vv. 16–17). If what he said in a *still small voice* (1Ki 19:12) did not reach their hearts, and his teaching that fell like the dew made no impact on them, then they would hear God speaking to them in terrible thunderclaps and in his heavy and powerful rain. Samuel, that son of prayer, was still famous for his successes in prayer. He showed them that however calm and prosperous their condition seemed to be now that they had a king — like the weather in wheat harvest — nevertheless, if God so pleased, he could still quickly change the sky.

1.2. The impressions which this made on the people. It shocked them very much, as well it might.

1.2.1. *They greatly feared the Lord and Samuel* (v. 18).

1.2.2. They acknowledged how sinful and foolish they were in wanting a king: *We have added to all our sins this evil* (v. 19).

1.2.3. They fervently begged Samuel's prayers (v. 19): *Pray for thy servants, that we die not.* They were apprehensive of the danger they were in from the wrath of God and could not expect that he would hear their prayers for themselves, and so they humbly asked Samuel to pray for them. They now saw their need of the one whom they had looked down on a short time before.

2. To confirm the people in their religious faith and get them to commit themselves forever to remain faithful to the Lord. The intention of his speech is much the same as that of Joshua's (23:1–24:22).

2.1. He does not want the terrors of the Lord to frighten them away from him, for the purpose of those terrors was to frighten them toward him (v. 20): "*Fear not; though you have done all this wickedness*, and though God is angry with you for it, this is no reason to leave his service or *turn from following him.*" *Fear not*, that is, "Don't despair or be terrified, the weather will clear up after the storm. Don't be afraid, for although God will frown on his people, yet *for his great name's sake* he still will not reject them (v. 22), and so you should not reject him."

2.2. He warns them against idolatry: "*Turn not aside* from God and the worship of him" (v. 20 and again v. 21), "for if you turn away from God, whatever you turn away to, you will find that it is useless. It will never fulfill your expectations but will certainly deceive you if you trust in it. It is a broken reed, a broken cistern."

2.3. He comforts them with an assurance that he will continue to be concerned for them and look after them (v. 23). They asked him only to pray for them, but he promised to do more for them, not only to pray for them, but also to teach them. Although they were not willing to be governed by him as a judge, he would not therefore deny them his instructions as a prophet.

2.4. He concludes with a fervent encouragement to practical religion and dedicated godliness (vv. 24–25).

CHAPTER 13

While Samuel was jointly commissioned with Saul, things went well (11:7). But now that Saul began to reign alone, everything went downhill, and Samuel's words began to be fulfilled: "You will be consumed, both you and your king" (12:25). In this chapter: 1. Saul appears as a stupid ruler: confounded in his thoughts (vv. 1–3), invaded by his neighbors (vv. 4–5), and deserted by his soldiers (vv. 6–7). 2. Saul is mixed up in his own spirit and sacrificing in confusion (vv. 8–10), rebuked by Samuel (vv. 11–13), and rejected by God from being king (v. 14). 3. The people are miserable: discouraged and dispersed (vv. 6–7), diminished (vv. 15–16), plundered (vv. 17–18), and disarmed (vv. 19–23).

Verses 1–7

We are not told how the people of Israel offended God, but no doubt they left God, or else he would not have left them, as it appears he did, for:

1. Saul was very weak and not shrewd, and he did not order his affairs wisely. Saul *reigned one year* (v. 1), and nothing happened that was significant; it was a year in which nothing much happened. But in his second year he did as follows:

1.1. He chose a band of 3,000 men, of whom he himself commanded 2,000, and his son Jonathan 1,000 (v. 2). He sent the rest of the people away to their tents. If he intended these only to be his personal guards and honorary attendants, it was unwise to have so many. If he intended them to be a standing army, for fear of danger from the Philistines, it was no less unwise to have so few. Perhaps the confidence he put in this select number, and his disbanding of the rest of the brave army with which he had just defeated the Ammonites (11:8–11), was looked on as an insult to the kingdom, aroused general disgust, and was the reason he had so few at his call when he needed them.

1.2. He ordered his son Jonathan to surprise and destroy the outpost of the Philistines that was situated near him at Geba (v. 3).

1.3. When he had angered the Philistines, it was then that he began to raise forces, which, if he had acted wisely, he would have done before. As many as thought fit came to Saul at Gilgal (v. 4). Most men, however, probably drew back from this call, either because they disliked Saul's politics or because they dreaded the Philistines' power.

2. Never did the Philistines appear such a formidable army as they did now, after Saul had provoked them. If Saul had asked for guidance from God before he had given the Philistines this provocation, he and his people might have dealt better with such a threat than they now could, having brought this trouble on themselves by their own foolishness.

3. Never were the people of Israel so fainthearted, cringing, and cowardly as they were now. They may have come in considerable numbers to Saul at Gilgal, but when they heard of the Philistines' numbers and preparations, their spirits sank within them because, some think, they did not find Samuel there with Saul. Now that they saw the Philistines making war on them but not Samuel coming to help them, they did not know what to do; *men's hearts failed them for fear* (Lk 21:26). And:

3.1. Some hid themselves. A single person can by faith say, *I will not be afraid of 10,000* (Ps 3:6), but here thousands of degenerate Israelites tremble at the approach of a great crowd of Philistines. Guilt turns people into cowards.

3.2. Others ran away (v. 7): they *went over Jordan to the land of Gilead*, to a place where they had just been victorious over the Ammonites. They hoped to be sheltered in the place where they had triumphed.

3.3. Those who stayed with Saul *followed him trembling* (v. 7), quaking with fear and fully expecting to be killed. Their hands and hearts had been made much weaker by the desertion of so many of their troops.

Verses 8–14

Here is:

1. Saul's offense in offering a sacrifice before Samuel came. When Samuel had anointed him, he had ordered Saul to wait seven days at Gilgal for him (10:8). Perhaps that order had just been repeated with reference to this particular occasion, but in any case it is clear that Saul understood the order as obliging him under God to wait, and he disobeyed it.

1.1. He presumed to offer a sacrifice without Samuel.

1.2. He determined to engage the Philistines without Samuel's direction. Saul was so self-sufficient that he thought it not worthwhile to wait around for a prophet of the Lord to pray for him or advise him.

1.2.1. He did not send any messenger to Samuel to find out his thoughts on the matter.

1.2.2. When Samuel came, Saul seemed to boast of what he had done rather than repent of it, for he *went forth to salute* (greet) *him* (v. 10) as his fellow-sacrificer. He went out to "bless him" (so the Hebrew reads), as if he now thought himself a complete priest.

1.2.3. He accused Samuel of breaking his promise: *Thou camest not within the days appointed* (v. 11).

1.2.4. When he was charged with disobedience, he justified himself in what he had done and showed no signs at all of repentance. See what excuses he made (vv. 11–12). He wanted this act of disobedience to be thought of as an example of his diligence and devoutness. He wanted to be thought of as godly and as very careful not to take on the Philistines until he had prayed and offered a sacrifice to get God on his side: "*The Philistines,*" he said, "*will come down upon me, before I have made my supplication to the Lord* (v. 12), and then I am ruined." But lastly he acknowledged that it went against his conscience to do it: *I forced myself* (felt compelled) *and offered a burnt offering* (v. 12).

2. The sentence passed on Saul for this offense:

2.1. Samuel shows him how great is the crime he is charged with. He accuses him of being an enemy of himself and his own interests: *Thou hast done foolishly*. And he charges him with rebelling against God and his government. "*Thou hast not kept the commandment of the Lord thy God* (v. 13), that commandment with which he wanted to test your obedience." Sin is foolish, and sinners are the greatest fools.

2.2. Samuel reads out his condemnation (v. 14). He shows that there is no sin which is "little," because the God who is sinned against is not a "little god." By every sin we commit we give up our right to the heavenly kingdom, which we were in a good position to enter but for that sin. Saul lost his kingdom for lack of two or three hours' patience.

Verses 15–23

1. Samuel departs in displeasure. Saul had set himself up, and he was now left to himself: *Samuel gat him* (went up) *from Gilgal* (v. 15). But in going up to Gibeah in Benjamin, which was Saul's city, Samuel showed that he had not completely abandoned him.

2. Saul goes after him to Gibeah and there musters his army and finds his total number to be only 600 men (vv. 15–16).

3. The Philistines ravage the country. The main troops of their army were situated in an advantageous pass at Michmash, but from there they sent out three separate parties or detachments that went their different ways to plunder the country. The land of Israel was both terrified and impoverished by these raiders, and the Philistines were excited and enriched.

4. The Israelites who take to the battlefield with Saul are unarmed and have only slings and clubs, not a sword or spear among them all, except what Saul and Jonathan themselves have (vv. 19, 22). Notice here:

4.1. How wise the Philistines were. They closed down all the smiths' workshops, transferred the smiths to their own country, and forbade any Israelite, under severe penalties, to exercise the trade or art of working in bronze (or copper) or iron. The Israelites had to go to one or another of the Philistine outposts to get all their ironwork done, and an Israelite could use only a file (vv. 20–21).

4.2. How unwise Saul was, that he did not, at the beginning of his reign, put right this grievance.

4.3. How lazy and smallminded the Israelites were, who allowed the Philistines to impose themselves on them and had no thought or spirit to help themselves. If they had not been discouraged, they could not have been disarmed, but it was sin that exposed them to their shame.

CHAPTER 14

1. Jonathan (vv. 1–3) attacked the Philistines bravely, with only his armor-bearer, encouraging himself in the Lord his God (vv. 4–7). He challenged them (vv. 8–12) and, on their acceptance of the challenge, charged them with such fury, or rather such faith, that he made them flee and set them against one another (vv. 13–15). 2. This attack gave Saul, his forces, and other Israelites the opportunity to follow through and gain a victory (vv. 16–23). 3. The army of Israel was troubled and perplexed by the rash and foolish action of Saul, who put the people under oath to eat no food until nightfall. This order put Jonathan into a predicament (vv. 24–30) and caused the people to be tempted, when the time of their fast had elapsed, to eat meat with blood (vv. 31–35). 4. The error Jonathan committed through ignorance should have caused his death, but the people rescued him (vv. 36–46). 5. At the close, we have a general account of Saul's exploits (vv. 47–48) and of his family (vv. 49–52).

Verses 1–15

Notice here:

1. The goodness of God in restraining the Philistines, who had a vast army of brave troops on the battlefield, from attacking that little handful of fearful, trembling people who were with Saul.

2. The weakness of Saul, who seems to have been quite at a loss as to what to do and unable to help himself:

2.1. He pitched his tent under a tree and had only 600 men with him (v. 2). He did not dare stay at Gibeah, but went to some obscure place on the outskirts of the city under a pomegranate tree, under *Rimmon*, which is the Hebrew word. See also Jdg 20:47.

2.2. He sent for a priest and the ark, a priest from Shiloh and the ark from Kiriath Jearim (vv. 3, 18). Samuel, the Lord's prophet, had left him, but he thought he could make

up for that loss by commanding Ahijah, the Lord's priest, to come to him. He also wanted the ark to be brought. Perhaps he hoped that having the ark would make up the deficiency of his forces. You would have thought that they would never have brought the ark into the camp again, because the last time they did that, the ark not only did not save them, but also itself fell into the Philistines' hands. But it is common for those who have lost the substance of their religious faith to be most fond of its shadows, as here a deserted ruler courts a deserted priest.

3. The bravery and godliness of Jonathan, the son of Saul, who was much more suitable than his father to wear the crown. Bishop Hall says he is "a sweet imp out of a crab-stock," a sweet-apple shoot grown from a crab-apple stock.

3.1. He decided to go as an unknown person to the camp of the Philistines. Access to the enemies' camp is described (vv. 4–5) as being particularly difficult, and their natural entrenchments were impregnable, but this does not discourage him. The power and sharpness of the rocks only hardened and sharpened his determination. Great and generous souls are stirred by opposition and take pleasure in breaking through it.

3.2. He encouraged his armor-bearer, a young man who served him, to go along with him in this bold undertaking (v. 6): "*Come, and let us* put our lives in our hands, *and go over to the* enemy *garrison*, and see what we can do to confound them, for:

3.2.1. "They are uncircumcised. Don't be afraid, we'll make out all right, because they are not under the protection of God's covenant as we are." If those who are our enemies are also strangers to God, we do not need to be afraid of them.

3.2.2. "God is able to make us two people victorious over their unnumbered regiments. *There is no restraint in the Lord to save by many or by few*" (v. 6). This is a truth easily stated in general, but it is not so easy to apply in particular instances, when we are only few in number—not easy to believe that God can not only save us, but also save by us. This is an example of faith, which will be commended wherever it is found.

3.2.3. "Who knows but the One who can use us for his glory will do it? *It may be the Lord will work for us* (v. 6)." An active faith will venture far in God's cause. It will take as its basis even an *it may be*. Jonathan's armor-bearer, or the one who carried his shield, behaved as one who had learned to carry, not only Jonathan's weapons, but also his heart: he promised to stand by him and follow him wherever he went (v. 7).

3.3. However bold his determination was, he decided to follow Providence in carrying out the plan. "Come," he says to his confidant, "we will show ourselves to the enemy. We are not afraid to look them in the face (v. 8), and then, if they are so cautious as to tell us to stay where we are, we will advance no further. We will take that as a sign from Providence that God wants us to act defensively (v. 9). But if they challenge us, and the first guard we meet tells us to march on, we will press forward and launch a firm attack. We will have come to the conclusion that it is God's will for us to go on the offensive. Then we will not doubt that he will *stand by us*" (v. 10). This is how he states the issue, firmly believing:

3.3.1. That God is sovereign over the hearts and tongues of all people. Jonathan knew that God could show his mind to him as surely by the mouth of a Philistine as by the mouth of a priest.

3.3.2. That God would somehow direct the steps of those who *acknowledge him in all their ways* (Pr 3:6).

3.4. Providence gave him the sign he expected, and he responded to the signal. He and his armor-bearer did not surprise the Philistines when they were asleep, but showed themselves to them by daylight (v. 11). The guards of the Philistines:

3.4.1. Disdained them. *Behold, the Hebrews come forth out of their holes* (v. 11).

3.4.2. Defied them (v. 12): *Come, and we will show you a thing*. They mocked them, which made Jonathan even bolder. He encouraged his servant with this. Beforehand (v. 6) he had spoken with uncertainty: *It may be the Lord will work for us*; but he now speaks with assurance (v. 12): *The Lord has delivered them into the hand of Israel*. After his faith had been strengthened in this way, no difficulty could stand before him. He climbed up the rock on all fours (v. 13), even though he had nothing to cover him, no one but his servant to support him, and, humanly speaking, only death before him.

3.5. This daring enterprise succeeded wonderfully. Instead of falling on Jonathan to kill him or take him prisoner, the Philistines fell before him (v. 13) inexplicably, at the first blow he gave. They fell, that is:

3.5.1. Many of them were killed by him and his armor-bearer (v. 14). It was God's right hand and his power that gained him this victory.

3.5.2. The rest were made to run for their lives and fell in panic on one another (v. 15): *There was trembling in the host*. It is called "a trembling of God." The One who made the heart knows how to make it tremble. To complete the confusion, even the earth quaked, making them ready to fear that it would sink beneath them.

Verses 16–23

We read here about how Jonathan and his armor-bearer followed up the great advantages they had gained over the Philistines:

1. The Philistines were set against one another by the power of God. They melted away like snow before the sun and *went on beating down one another* (v. 16), for (v. 20) *every man's sword was against his fellow*; they were striking each other. Now God showed them how foolish they had been in what they put their confidence in, by making their own swords and spears the instruments of their destruction, and making those weapons even more fatal in their own hands than if they had been in the hands of Israel.

2. The Israelites were then stirred up against them:

2.1. Saul's lookouts, those who stood guard at Gibeah (v. 16), soon noticed what was taking place.

2.2. Saul began to inquire of God but soon stopped. He called for the ark (v. 18), wanting to know whether it would be safe for him to attack the Philistines, considering the panic they saw they were in. Many will seek God's guidance about their safety but would never seek him about their duty. But when he learned from his scouts that the tumult in the enemy camp had increased, he commanded the priest who officiated to stop abruptly: "*Withdraw thy hand* (v. 19), don't seek any further guidance. Don't wait any longer for an answer." The reason he prohibited the priest from inquiring of God was either:

2.2.1. That he now thought he did not need an answer, as the case was clear enough. Or:

2.2.2. That he was in such a hurry to fight a losing enemy that he did not want to wait to finish his devotions.

2.3. He and his few troops vigorously attacked the enemy, and all the people "were cried together" (v. 20, margin) because they lacked silver trumpets, which God

had appointed them to use to sound the alarm on the day of battle (Nu 10:9). They summoned the people by shouting, and their number was not so great that they could not be soon gathered together.

2.4. All the Hebrews, even those from whom you would least have expected it, now turned their hands against the Philistines:

2.4.1. Those who had deserted and gone over to join the enemy side now fought against them (v. 21). Those who had been taken prisoners by them were tormenting them.

2.4.2. Those who had fled their own troops to go and hide in the mountains returned to their positions, joining the battle to pursue the Philistines (v. 22). It was not very commendable that they showed up so late, but it would have been more shameful if they had not shown up at all. And so, everyone worked together against the Philistines, but it is said (v. 23), it was *the Lord that saved Israel that day*. He used them to do it, for without him they could do nothing.

Verses 24–35

Here is an account of the trouble that the Israelites got into even on the day of their triumph.

1. Saul forbade the people, under the penalty of a curse, to taste any food that day (v. 24). We suppose Saul did it with a good intention, namely, that the people, who perhaps had been kept on short allowances for some time, would not lose time in pursuing the enemy when they found plenty of provisions in the deserted camp of the Philistines; they might eat too much and become unfit for any further service that day. But his issue of such a strict order was unwise, for if it gained time, it sapped the troops of the energy they needed to pursue the Philistines. It was ungodly to enforce this prohibition with a curse and an oath. Had he no lesser penalty than a curse with which to support his military discipline?

2. The people observed his order, but it was extremely inconvenient and unfortunate.

2.1. The soldiers were tantalized: when they pursued the enemy, they happened to go through a wood so full of wild honey that it oozed out of the trees onto the ground, but for fear of the curse, they did not so much as taste the honey (vv. 25–26).

2.2. Jonathan fell under the curse through ignorance. He had not heard of the command his father had given, for having boldly forced a way through enemy lines, he was then hotly pursuing the Philistines. Not knowing there was any danger in it, he put a piece of honeycomb on the end of his stick and sucked it (v. 27) and was very refreshed by it. He meant no harm, and did not fear any until one of the people told him about the command, and then he found himself trapped. Many good children have become distressed because of the rashness of an inconsiderate father. Jonathan, for his part, lost the crown he was heir to by his father's foolishness.

2.3. The soldiers were faint, and grew weak, as they pursued the Philistines. Jonathan foresaw that this would be the effect of the prohibition; their spirits would flag and their strength would fail for lack of food.

2.4. The worst effect of all was that in the evening, when the restraint was removed and they ate again, they were so greedy and eager to eat that they ate flesh with the blood, which was explicitly forbidden in the Law of God (v. 32). The old proverb says, "Two hungry meals make the third a gluttonous one," and this is what happened here. After Saul had been told about it, he rebuked them for the sin (v. 33). To put an end to this irregularity, he ordered that they should set up a large stone before him, and that all who had cattle to kill for their present use should bring them there and kill them under his eye on that stone (v. 33). The people did this (v. 34), and they were easily restrained and reformed when their ruler faithfully played his part.

3. On this occasion Saul built an altar (v. 35) so that he might offer a sacrifice, either to acknowledge the victory or to atone for the sin. *The same was the first altar that he built.* Saul was turning away from God, but he was now beginning to build altars, because he was zealous, as many are, for the form of godliness while denying its power. See Hos 8:14: *Israel has forgotten his Maker, and buildeth temples.*

Verses 36–46

Here is:

1. Saul's boasting against the Philistines. He proposed to pursue them all night, and *not leave a man of them*, not leave one of them alive (v. 36). Here he was showing much zeal but little wisdom, because his soldiers were so exhausted that they could not go without a good night's sleep any more than they could go without a good meal. Only the priest thought it right to go on with the devotions which had been broken off so abruptly (v. 19) and to inquire of God: *Let us draw near hither unto God* (v. 36). Rulers and great people need those around them who will remind them to take God along with them, wherever they go. And when the priest suggested it, Saul could not, for fear of shame, reject the proposal, but *asked counsel of God* (v. 37).

2. Saul's clash with his son Jonathan. The rest of this section is wholly about him, for while he is examined and judged, the Philistines make their escape.

2.1. God showed his displeasure and caused Saul to search for what had caused the curse. Saul swore by his Maker that whoever was the Achan who troubled the camp by eating the forbidden fruit would surely die, even if it was Jonathan himself.

2.2. Jonathan was found out by lot to be the offender. Saul wanted to have lots cast between himself and Jonathan on the one side and the people on the other side, perhaps because he was as confident of Jonathan's innocence in this matter as of his own (v. 40). Jonathan was finally chosen (v. 42), and Providence intended in this to support a lawful authority, reserving another way to acquit one who had done nothing to deserve death.

2.3. Jonathan frankly confessed the fact, and Saul passed sentence on him with an angry curse. Jonathan did not deny the truth, but he thought it hard that he must *die for it* (v. 43). He might very fairly have pleaded his ignorance of the law, but he submitted to the necessity with a great and noble mind: "May God's will and my father's will be done." In some cases, it is as brave to give in, as it is to fight in other cases. Saul was not pacified by his son's submission or the difficulty of his case, but expressed judgment on Jonathan with another oath (v. 44): "*God do so and more also* to me if I do not carry out the law on you, *for thou shalt surely die, Jonathan.*"

2.3.1. Saul passed this sentence too rashly, without inquiring of God. Jonathan had a very good reason to stay proceedings. What he had done was not bad in itself, and as for its prohibition, he was ignorant of that, and so he could not be accused of rebellion or disobedience.

2.3.2. Saul passed sentence in anger. If Jonathan had been worthy of death, it would have been consistent for a judge, and much more for a father, to pass sentence with tenderness and compassion. Justice is devalued when it is administered angrily and bitterly.

2.3.3. Saul backed up the sentence with a curse on himself, so that if he did not see to it that the sentence was carried out, the curse would be carried out on him; and this curse later returned on his own head. Jonathan escaped, but God rejected Saul and made him a curse. Let no one on any occasion dare to use such oaths as these, so that God does not say "Amen" to them and *make their own tongues to fall upon them* (Ps 64:8). But we have reason to think that Saul still had an affection for Jonathan, so that in reality he was punishing himself, and justly so, when he seemed so severe toward Jonathan. God used all these troublesome incidents to correct Saul for his arrogance in offering a sacrifice without Samuel.

2.4. The people rescued Jonathan from his father's hands (v. 45). Up to now they had expressed themselves very respectfully toward Saul. They accepted what seemed good to him (vv. 36, 40). But when Jonathan's life was in danger, what Saul said no longer held sway as the final word, and they opposed the execution of his sentence with the greatest zeal: "*Shall Jonathan die*, that favorite, the one who has blessed his country? Will that life be sacrificed because of a strict observance of a minute point of law and honor? He gave his life bravely in his service to the whole community, and we owe our lives and triumphs to him. No; we cannot stand by and see him treated in this way. He is the one whom God delights to honor." It is good to see Israelites zealous to protect those whom God has made instruments of the public good. "*As the Lord liveth there shall not* only not his head, but not even *a hair of his head fall to the ground*" (v. 45). They did not use any force to rescue him, but only reason and determination. Josephus says they prayed to God that Jonathan might be loosed from the curse. They supported their plea for him by saying that *he has wrought with God this day* (v. 45), that is, "he has acknowledged God's cause, and God has acknowledged his endeavors, and so his life is too precious to be thrown away because of a minute detail."

2.5. The intentions against the Philistines were quashed by this incident (v. 46): *Saul went up from following them*, and so an opportunity to complete the victory was lost.

Verses 47–52

Here is a general account of Saul's court and camp:

1. His court and family, the names of his sons and daughters (v. 49), and of his wife and his cousin, who was the general of his army (v. 50). In 2Sa 21:8 there is mention of another wife of Saul's, Rizpah, a secondary wife, and of the children he had by her.

2. His camp and military actions:

2.1. How he raised his army: *When he saw any strong valiant man*, a man who was mighty and brave, particularly suitable for service, *he took him unto him* (v. 52), as Samuel had told the people a king would do (8:11).

2.2. How he employed his army. He guarded his country against the insults of its enemies on every side and retaliated against their attacks and raids (vv. 47–48). But the enemies he struggled most with were the Philistines, with whom he had *sore* (bitter) *war all his days* (v. 52).

CHAPTER 15

In this chapter we have the final rejection of Saul as king. Here is: 1. The commission God gave him to destroy the Amalekites, with a command to do it completely (vv. 1–3). Saul's preparation for this mission (vv. 4–6);

his partial fulfillment of this commission (vv. 7–9). 2. His examination before Samuel, and sentence passed on him, despite the many feeble excuses he gave (vv. 10–31). 3. The killing of Agag (vv. 32–33); Samuel's final farewell to Saul (vv. 34–35).

Verses 1–9

Here:

1. Samuel, in God's name, solemnly commands Saul to obey the command of God. This clearly shows that God was now about to use one particular situation as a test, to see whether Saul would be obedient or not (v. 1).

1.1. Samuel reminds him of what God had done for him: *"The Lord sent me to anoint thee to be a king* (v. 1). God gave you your power, and so he expects you to use your power for him." Human advancement does not release people from obedience to God but obliges them to obey him more closely.

1.2. He tells him, in general, that because of this relationship with God, he is bound to do whatever God commands him to do: *Now therefore hearken to the voice of the Lord* (v. 1).

2. Samuel directs him to undertake a particular task, in which he must show his obedience to God more than in anything he had done before. He also gives him a reason for the command so that the severity he must use will not seem hard: *I remember that which Amalek did to Israel* (v. 2). God had a long-standing quarrel with the Amalekites for the wrongs they had done to his people Israel (Ex 17:8–16), and the crime is emphasized in Dt 25:18. This is the work that Saul is now appointed to do (v. 3): *"Go and smite* (attack) *Amalek.* Since Israel is now strong, now go and totally destroy that nation."

3. Saul then gathers his forces and descends on the country of Amalek. Saul numbered his troops in *Telaim,* which means "lambs." He numbered them "like lambs," according to the Vulgate, numbered them "by the paschal lambs," according to the Aramaic, allowing ten to a lamb, a way of numbering used by the Jews in the later times of their nation. Saul drew all his forces to the *city of Amalek.*

4. Saul gave friendly advice to the Kenites to separate themselves from the Amalekites among whom they lived. The Kenites came from the family of Jethro, Moses' father-in-law, and were a people who lived in tents, which made it easy for them to move at any time to other lands which had not yet been taken. Many of them lived among the Amalekites at this time, in a place fortified by nature, for *they put their nest in a rock,* being hardy people who could live anywhere and who were attracted to fortresslike rocky outcrops (Nu 24:21). Saul must not destroy them. Rather:

4.1. He acknowledges the kindness their ancestors showed to Israel when Israel came out of Egypt. Jethro and his family had been very helpful and useful to them in their journey through the desert, had been their eyes (Nu 10:31), and this is remembered to future generations many years later. In this way, good people leave God's blessing as an inheritance to their children's children. Those who come after us may reap the benefits of our good works when we are in our graves.

4.2. He wants them to move their tents from among the Amalekites.

5. Saul prevailed against the Amalekites, for it was more like an execution of condemned evildoers than a war against enemies. They were idolaters and were guilty of many other sins, for which they deserved to come under

the wrath of God. But when God held them accountable, he seized on the sin of their ancestors in mistreating his Israel as the reason for his quarrel.

6. But Saul did his work only partly (v. 9).

6.1. He *spared Agag* because he was a king like himself; perhaps he hoped to gain a great ransom for him.

6.2. He spared the best of the cattle and destroyed only the weak animals, which were of little use. It is probable that many of the people made their escape and took their belongings with them to other countries and that this is why we read of the Amalekites again later.

Verses 10–23

Saul is held responsible by Samuel for carrying out his commission against the Amalekites. We are told:

1. What took place between God and Samuel in secret on this occasion (vv. 10–11):

1.1. God decides to reject Saul and tells Samuel about it: *It repenteth me that I have set up Saul to be king* (v. 11). Repentance in God is not, as it is in us, a change of mind, but a change of his ways. He does not change his will, but wills a change. The change was in Saul: *He has turned back from following me* (v. 11). This is how God interpreted Saul's partial obedience and his pervasive greed. He himself had made God his enemy.

1.2. Samuel mourns and prays to God about it. *It grieved Samuel* (v. 11), Samuel was troubled that Saul had forfeited God's favor and that God had decided to reject him, and he *cried unto the Lord all night* (v. 11). The rejection of sinners is the sorrow of good people. God does not delight in their death, and neither should we.

2. What took place between Samuel and Saul in public. Samuel was sent by God to take this heavy news to Saul. He went, like Ezekiel, in *bitterness of spirit* (Eze 3:14) to meet him. But Samuel was told that Saul had already gone and had set up a triumphal arch, or some monument to his victory, at Carmel, a town in the hill country of Judah, seeking his own honor more than God's honor; Samuel was told also that he had marched to Gilgal in great pomp, for this seems to be indicated in the wording of the expression: *He has gone about, and passed on, and gone down* (v. 12), with a great deal of ceremony and pageant. Samuel met him at Gilgal, and:

2.1. Saul boasted to Samuel about his obedience: *"Blessed be thou of the Lord,* for you have sent me on a good mission, which I have had great success in, and *I have performed the commandment of the Lord."* It is very likely that if his conscience had not charged him with disobedience, he would not have been so forward in declaring his obedience; but since he did feel so charged, he did so declare it, for he hoped he would avoid being rebuked by Samuel. So also in general, sinners think that by justifying themselves they can escape being *judged by the Lord* (1Co 11:32), whereas the only way to do that is by *judging ourselves* (1Co 11:31).

2.2. Samuel convicts him by a plain demonstration of his disobedience. "Have you carried out the commandment of the Lord? *What means then the bleating of the sheep?"* (v. 14). Samuel appeals to the cattle as witnesses against him, and to their noise as their testimony against him.

2.3. Saul insists on justifying himself against this accusation (v. 15). He cannot deny the facts; the sheep and oxen were brought from the Amalekites. But:

2.3.1. It was not his fault, for *the people spared them*—as if they would dare do this without the explicit orders of Saul, when they already knew it was against the explicit orders of Samuel. Sin is a wretch that no one wants to have placed at their door. To put the blame for a sin on those who merely suggested it, were a party to it, or only followed orders in committing it is a poor excuse for not wishing to admit one's own guilt.

2.3.2. It had been done with good intentions: "It was *to sacrifice to the Lord thy God*" (v. 15). This was a false plea, for both Saul and the people intended to profit from sparing the cattle. But if it had been true, it would still have been foolish, for *God hates robbery for burnt offering* (Isa 61:8).

2.4. Samuel disallows, or rather disregards, his plea, and proceeds to declare judgment against him in God's name.

2.4.1. He reminds Saul of the honor God had given him by making him king (v. 17) *when he was little in his own sight*. Those who are advanced to honor and wealth ought often to remember their lowly beginnings, so that they may never think highly of themselves but always work hard to do great things for the God who has advanced them.

2.4.2. He puts before Saul the plainness of the orders he had to carry out (v. 18): *The Lord sent thee on a journey*. Such service was relatively easy, and its success was so certain that it was called *a journey* rather than a *war*. Had he denied himself and set aside the consideration of his own profit so completely that he had actually destroyed everything that belonged to Amalek, he would finally have been no loser by it, nor would he have undertaken this *warfare on his own charges* (1Co 9:7), at his own expense. And so:

2.4.3. He shows Saul how inexcusable it was for him to aim to profit from this mission and enrich himself by it (v. 19): "*Wherefore then didst thou fly upon* (pounce on) *the spoil* and put to your own use what should have been destroyed for God's honor?" *Thou didst not obey the voice of the Lord* (v. 19).

2.5. Saul repeats his justification of himself, determined to hold on to it in defiance of the conviction (vv. 20–21). He denies the accusation (v. 20): "*Yea, I have obeyed*, I have done all I should do," for he has done everything he thought he needed to do, being wiser, in his own eyes, than God himself. As for the plunder, he acknowledges that it should have been *utterly destroyed*. But he thought that that would be an awful waste; the cattle of the Midianites were taken as plunder in Moses' time (Nu 31:32–34), so why not the cattle of the Amalekites now? It would be better for the animals to be prey for the Israelites than for the birds and wild animals, and so he turned a blind eye to the people's taking them away for *sacrifice to the Lord* (v. 21) here at Gilgal, where they were now bringing them to.

2.6. Samuel gives a full answer to Saul's defense, since he insisted on it (vv. 22–23). Samuel appeals to Saul's conscience: *Has the Lord as great delight in sacrifices as in obedience?* Saul must have known:

2.6.1. That a humble, sincere, and conscientious obedience to the will of God is more pleasing and acceptable to him than *all burnt offerings and sacrifices* (v. 22). Carefully conforming to God's moral precepts commends us to God more than all ceremonial observances (Mic 6:6–8; Hos 6:6). Obedience was the law of innocence, but sacrifice assumes the presence of sin in the world and is a weak attempt to take away what obedience would have prevented. It is much easier to bring a young bull or lamb to be burned on the altar than to bring *every high thought into obedience* to God (2Co 10:5) and to make our will subject to his will.

2.6.2. That nothing is so offensive to God as disobedience, setting up our wills in competition with his. This is called *rebellion* and *stubbornness*, and it is said to be as bad as *witchcraft* and *idolatry* (v. 23). It is as bad to live in disobedience to the true God as to set up other gods. It was disobedience which made us all sinners (Ro 5:19), and this is the evil of sin, that it is the *transgression of the law* (1Jn 3:4) and is therefore *enmity to God* (Ro 8:7).

2.7. Samuel reads out his condemnation; in short, "*Because thou hast rejected the word of the Lord*"—you have "despised it," according to the Aramaic, you have "made nothing of it," according to the Septuagint (a Greek version of the Old Testament)—"he also has *rejected thee*, despised and made nothing of you, and rejected you *from being king*." Those who are not willing to have God rule over them are not qualified or worthy to rule over other people.

Verses 24–31

Saul is finally led to wear the clothes of someone who has repented, but it is clear that he is only playing a part and has not repented truly. Notice:

1. How poorly he expressed his repentance. He had been made aware of his fault only with a great deal of trouble, and not until he was threatened with being deposed. Then he began to relent, and not until then. This touched him at a tender spot.

1.1. He turned only to Samuel, not God, and seemed most concerned to put himself in the right in Samuel's opinion in order to keep his reputation with the people, because they all knew that Samuel was a prophet and that he had been the one used by God to advance Saul. Thinking that it would please Samuel and act as a kind of bribe to him, Saul expressed this attitude in his confession: *I have transgressed the commandment of the Lord and thy word*—as if Samuel had taken God's place (v. 24). He also turned to Samuel for forgiveness (v. 25): *I pray thee, pardon my sin*—as if anyone could forgive sin except God. The most charitable way we can interpret Saul's action is to think that he looked on Samuel as a sort of mediator between him and God and intended to speak to God when he turned to Samuel.

1.2. Saul excused his fault even in confessing it, and that is never the way of one who truly repents (v. 24): I did it *because I feared the people, and obeyed their voice*.

1.3. His only concern was to save his reputation and to keep in favor with the people; without Samuel's pardon, he thought, the people would rebel against him, or at least despise him. And so he did his best to court Samuel (v. 25).

2. How little he gained by this thin show of repentance.

2.1. Samuel repeated the sentence passed on him and did not raise any hope of it being repealed (v. 23 and again v. 26).

2.2. He illustrated the punishment by a sign. When Samuel was turning away from him, Saul tore his clothes in trying to detain him (v. 27). Samuel interpreted this incident in a way that only a prophet could. He made it represent the *rending of the kingdom* from Saul (v. 28), and that loss, like this tearing of the garment, was Saul's own doing. "He has torn the kingdom from you and *given it to a neighbour better than thou*," that is, to David, who on a later occasion cut off a corner of Saul's robe (24:4), at which Saul said (24:20), *I know that thou shalt surely be king*, perhaps remembering the sign of the tearing of the hem of Samuel's robe.

2.3. Samuel confirmed the punishment by a solemn declaration that it was irreversible (v. 29): *The Strength of Israel will not lie.*

Verses 32–35

As a prophet, Samuel is appointed over kings (Jer 1:10).

1. He destroys King Agag. He *hewed Agag in pieces* (v. 34). Notice in this:

1.1. How Agag's present worthless hopes were frustrated: he *came delicately* (v. 32), in a confident manner, to show he was a king. Having escaped the sword of that warrior Saul, he thought he was no longer in any danger from Samuel, an old prophet and a man of peace.

1.2. How his former evil ways were punished. Samuel holds him responsible not only for the sins of his ancestors but also for his own sins: *Thy sword has made women childless* (v. 33).

2. He abandons King Saul and takes his leave of him (v. 34) and *never came any more to see him* (v. 35). Samuel looked on him as rejected by God and so left him. But Samuel *mourned for Saul* (v. 35), thinking it very sad that someone who was in such a favorable position to do great things should destroy himself so foolishly.

CHAPTER 16

The story of David begins in this chapter. Here: 1. Samuel is appointed and commissioned to anoint a king from among the sons of Jesse at Bethlehem (vv. 1–5). 2. All Jesse's elder sons are passed by, and David, the youngest, is chosen and anointed (vv. 6–13). 3. Saul becomes depressed or mentally deranged, and David is chosen to bring relief to him by music (vv. 14–23).

Verses 1–5

Samuel had withdrawn to his own house in Ramah, and was determined never to return again to matters of public business, but to devote himself fully to instructing and training the sons of the prophets, whom he led, as we find in 19:20.

1. God rebukes Samuel for continuing so long to mourn for Saul's rejection. "Do not mourn for Saul, for I *have provided* (chosen) *me a king* (v. 1). The people chose a king for themselves, but he turned out to be bad. Now, I myself will choose one, *a man after my own heart*" (13:14).

2. God sends Samuel to Bethlehem to anoint one of the sons of Jesse, a person probably not unknown to Samuel. *Fill thy horn with oil* (v. 1).

3. Samuel raises an objection: it would be dangerous to go on this mission (v. 2): *If Saul hear it, he will kill me.* This shows us:

3.1. That Saul had become evil and violent since his rejection, or else Samuel would not have mentioned this. Is there any ungodly act that he would not be guilty of if he dared kill Samuel?

3.2. That Samuel's faith was not as strong as you would have expected, or else he would not have feared the rage of Saul in this way.

4. God orders Samuel to disguise his intention with a sacrifice: *Say, I have come to sacrifice* (v. 2). This was true, and it was proper that he should sacrifice when he came to anoint a king (11:15). He must give notice of a sacrifice, God said, and invite Jesse—who probably was the most important person in town—and his family to come to feast on the sacrifice. God said, *I will show thee*

what thou shalt do (v. 3). Those who go about God's work in God's way will be directed step by step.

5. And so Samuel went to Bethlehem, not in great pomp or with any large following but only with a servant to lead the heifer which he was to sacrifice; yet *the elders of Bethlehem trembled at his coming* (v. 4). They were afraid that his coming showed God's displeasure against them. They feared that he came to declare some judgment for the sins of the place. They asked him, "*Comest thou peaceably?*" (v. 4). "*I come peaceably*, for *I come to sacrifice*, not with a message of wrath against you, but with the way of peace and reconciliation. You may welcome me. You need not be afraid of my coming. And so, *sanctify yourselves*. Prepare to join with me in bringing the sacrifice, so that you may benefit from it."

6. Samuel showed a special regard for Jesse and his sons, because his private business lay with them; he probably told Jesse about that business when he first arrived and then stayed at his house. Samuel helped them in their family preparations for the public sacrifice and probably chose David and anointed him at the family ceremonies, before the sacrifice was offered or the holy feast was celebrated. Perhaps he offered private sacrifices, like Job, *according to the number of them all* (Job 1:5), and under that pretext called all Jesse's sons to appear before him.

Verses 6–13

Here we are told:

1. How all the elder sons, who seemed most likely to be chosen for advancement, were passed over:

1.1. Eliab, the eldest, was the first one to be privately presented to Samuel, probably with no one else present except Jesse, and Samuel thought he must be the man: *Surely this is the Lord's anointed* (v. 6). When God wanted to please the people with a king, he chose a handsome man, but when he wanted to have one after his own heart, he was not to be chosen according to his outward appearance. *The Lord looks on the heart* (v. 7), that is:

1.1.1. He knows the heart. We can tell what people look like, but he can tell what they are. God looks on the heart and sees its thoughts and intentions.

1.1.2. He judges people according to their hearts. May we consider true beauty to consist of what is within us, and so discern people, as far as we can, by what they are, not how they look.

1.2. When Eliab was set aside, Abinadab and Shammah, and after them, four more of the sons of Jesse, seven in all, were presented to Samuel, each one likely for the purpose, but Samuel—who now waited more carefully than he did at first for God's direction—rejected them all: *The Lord has not chosen these* (vv. 8, 10).

2. How David was finally chosen. He was the youngest of all Jesse's sons. His name means "beloved," for he was a type of the beloved Son. Notice:

2.1. How he was in the fields, *keeping the sheep* (v. 11). He was left there even though a sacrifice and a feast were going on at his father's house. David was taken *from following the ewes to feed Jacob* (Ps 78:71), just as Moses was taken from keeping the flock of Jethro. We may think that a military life would be the best preparation for the power of a king, but God saw that a pastoral life was a better preparation, at least for those graces of the Spirit which are necessary to fulfill rightly the trust of that great office. The pastoral life has the advantages of contemplation and fellowship with heaven.

2.2. How earnestly Samuel wanted him to be sent for: "*We will not sit down* to eat *till he come hither* (v. 11), for if all the rest are rejected, this must be the one."

2.3. How he looked when he did come. No notice is taken of his clothing. No doubt he was dressed according to his work, in lowly, rough clothes, as shepherds' coats usually are, but he had very honorable looks, not grand like Saul's, but sweet and attractive: *He was ruddy, of a beautiful countenance, and goodly to look to* (v. 12). He was so far from using any unnatural way to enhance his good looks that his work actually exposed them to the sun and wind, and yet the winsomeness of his expression gave clear signs of a pleasant disposition. Perhaps his modest blush when he was brought before Samuel made him appear even more good-looking.

2.4. His anointing. The Lord revealed to Samuel—as he had done in 9:15 regarding Saul—that this was the one he had to anoint (v. 12), so showing:

2.4.1. A divine appointment to the government, given to him as an inheritance that would be passed on to him in due time.

2.4.2. A divine communication of gifts and graces to qualify him for the government and to make him a type of the One who was to be the Messiah, the Anointed One, who received the Spirit, not with any restrictions, but without limit. David is said to be anointed *in the midst* (presence) *of his brethren* (v. 13). Bishop Patrick reads it, "He anointed him from the midst of his brethren" (v. 13), that is, Samuel singled him out from the others and anointed him privately, telling him to keep it a secret and not let his own brothers know; and it does seem, from what we find later (17:28), that Eliab, at least, did not know.

2.5. The advantageous effects of this anointing: the Spirit of the Lord came upon David from that day forward (v. 13). The anointing of him was not an empty ceremony but an instituted sign accompanied by divine power, and he found himself inwardly equipped with wisdom, courage, and concern for the community, although not advanced at all in his outward circumstances. Some think that his courage, by which he killed the lion and the bear, and his extraordinary musical skills were the effects and signs of the Spirit's coming on him. Samuel, having anointed David, safely went to Ramah, and we read of him only once more (19:18) before we read about his death. He now withdrew in peace, since his eyes had seen the scepter brought into the tribe of Judah.

Verses 14–23

Here we have Saul falling and David rising:

1. Saul is made a terror to himself (v. 14): *The Spirit of the Lord departed from him.* He lost all his good qualities. This was the effect of his rejection of God and a clear sign of his being rejected by him. The result was that *an evil spirit from God troubled him* (v. 14). Those who reject the Spirit become prey to evil spirits. He grew anxious, self-willed, discontented, fearful, and suspicious, every now and then flinching and shaking.

2. David is made Saul's doctor, and this is how he was brought to the king's court. He was to be a doctor who would help Saul cope with the worst of diseases when no one else could. Notice:

2.1. The means they all advised Saul to use to bring relief was music (v. 16): "Let us have a *cunning* (skillful) *player on the harp* come to you." Saul's servants would not have done wrong in sending for music to help cheer his spirits if they had also sent for a prophet to give him wise advice.

2.2. One of his servants recommended David to him as a person who could bring him relief through music, little imagining that David was the man whom Samuel

meant when he told Saul of a neighbor of his who was better than he and who would have the kingdom (15:28). Though David, after he was anointed, returned to his country business, the activity of the Spirit—represented by the oil—could not be hidden but made him shine out even from his obscurity, so that all his neighbors were amazed when they saw the great and sudden progress of his mental abilities. Even in his shepherd's clothes, David had become a person noted for wisdom and everything great. He had become a champion. Word of his fame soon reached the court, for Saul wanted to know about such people (14:52). When the Spirit of God comes on a person, the Spirit makes that person's face shine.

2.3. David is then sent for from the king's court. And it seems:

2.3.1. His father was very willing to part with him; he readily sent him with a present to Saul (v. 20). The present was, according to the custom of those times, bread and wine (see also 10:3–4), and so it was acceptable because it expressed the homage and allegiance of the one who sent it.

2.3.2. Saul was very kind to him (v. 21), *loved him greatly*, and wanted to *make him his armourbearer*, and asked his father's permission to keep him in his service (v. 22): *Let David, I pray thee, stand before me.* David's music was Saul's medicine. Music has a natural tendency to compose and cheer the mind when the mind is disturbed and saddened. It has a greater effect on some people than on others, and Saul was probably one of those on whom it had a beneficial effect. It calmed his spirit and subdued those wild fits by which the Devil controlled him. Music cannot influence the Devil, but it may close up the passages which he uses to gain access to the mind. Saul found, even after he had become David's enemy, that no one else could do the same service for him (19:9–10).

CHAPTER 17

David is the man whom God now delights to honor, for he is a man after his own heart. In the king's court he was only Saul's doctor; but in the camp he is Israel's bravest warrior. He fought a fair battle and beat Goliath of Gath. Notice in the story: 1. How great Goliath was and how he defied the armies of Israel (vv. 1–11). 2. How lowly David was when Providence led him to the army (vv. 12–30). 3. The unparalleled bravery which David had in his encounter with this Philistine (vv. 31–39). 4. The godly determination with which he attacked him (vv. 40–47). 5. The glorious victory he gained over him with a sling and a stone, and the advantage which the Israelites gained over the Philistines by that victory (vv. 48–54); the great notice which was then taken of David at the king's court (vv. 55–58).

Verses 1–11

It had not been a long time since the Philistines had been soundly beaten, but here we see them advancing again. Notice:

1. How they gathered together their armies to battle (v. 1). They attacked the Israelites' land and possessed, it seems, some part of it, for they camped in a place which belonged to Judah (v. 1). The Philistines had probably heard that Samuel had fallen out with Saul and left him and that Saul had become depressed or mentally deranged and unfit for work. Saul gathered his forces and drew up their battle lines (vv. 2–3). We must notice here that the evil spirit had, for the time being, left Saul (16:23).

David's harp had given him some relief, and perhaps the fears and matters of war prevented the return of the illness. Work is a good antidote to melancholy. David had returned to Bethlehem to keep his father's sheep. It was rare to see, in a young man who was about to be advanced as David was, such a fine example of humility and affection toward one's parents.

2. How they defied Israel with their champion Goliath, hoping to use him to recover their reputation and power. Perhaps the army of the Israelites was greater in numbers and strength than that of the Philistines, so that the Philistines refused a battle and stayed at a distance (v. 3), wanting to see the outcome decided in a single combat. With such a champion, then, they hoped to gain the victory. Notice what is said about this champion:

2.1. His enormous height. He was descended from the sons of Anak, who held onto their land at Gath in Joshua's time (Jos 11:22). He was in height *six cubits and a span* (v. 4). Bishop Cumberland calculates that a biblical cubit was more than twenty-one inches and a span was half a cubit, and so by that reckoning Goliath was eleven feet and four inches tall (that is, nearly three and a half meters), a colossal height.

2.2. His armor. *A helmet of brass* (bronze) *on his head, a coat of mail* (armor), made of bronze plates placed one over another like the scales of a fish. Because his legs were within reach of an ordinary soldier, he wore bronze boots. He also had a large bronze *target* (shield) around his neck (NIV: javelin slung over his back). The coat of armor is said to have weighed 5,000 shekels, that is, about 125 pounds (about fifty-seven kilograms), although some think the expression should be translated as referring not to the *weight* of the armor but to its *value*: it cost 5,000 shekels. His offensive weapons were extraordinary, though only his spear is described (v. 7). It was like a weaver's rod. His arm could manage what an ordinary man could scarcely lift. Only his shield was carried before him by his armor-bearer, probably for show, because, since he was wearing bronze, he hardly needed a shield.

2.3. His challenge. The Philistines had chosen him as their champion, and because they wanted to save themselves from the dangers of battle, Goliath threw down a challenge and defied the armies of Israel (vv. 8–10). He came into the valley situated between the two camps, and because his voice—like his strength—was probably much more powerful than other people's, he cried out so they could all hear him, *Choose a man, that we may fight together* (v. 8). He marveled at his own height and strength. He defied them to find one among them who would be bold enough to join battle with him.

2.3.1. He rebukes them for foolishly drawing up an army.

2.3.2. He offers to make the result of the battle rest entirely on the outcome of the duel he proposes: "If your bravest warrior kills me, we will become your servants. If I kill him, you will be ours." According to Bishop Patrick, this was sheer bravado. The Aramaic paraphrase has him boasting that he was the one who had killed Hophni and Phinehas and had taken the ark captive.

2.4. The terror this struck in Israel: *Saul and all his army were greatly afraid* (v. 11). The people would not have been dismayed except that they noticed that Saul's courage failed him. If a leader is a coward, it can hardly be expected that the followers will be bold. Jonathan must now sit still, because the honor of engaging Goliath is reserved for David.

Verses 12–30

The two armies lay camped facing one another for forty days. Perhaps there were frequent skirmishes between small detached parties. All this time, morning and evening, the defiant champion appeared on the field and repeated his challenge. All this time David looked after his father's sheep, but at the end of forty days Providence brought him to the field to gain and wear the laurel which no other Israelite dared risk his life for. We have in these verses:

1. The present state of his family. His father was old (v. 12). David's three elder brothers, who perhaps were jealous of his place at the king's court, got their father to call him back home and let them go to the camp, where they hoped to distinguish themselves and eclipse him (vv. 13–14). David himself returned to the care, hard work, and—as it turned out in v. 34—the peril of *keeping his father's sheep*.

2. The orders his father gave him to go and visit his brothers in the camp. He must take some bread and cheese to his brothers, ten loaves with some roasted grain for themselves (v. 17) and ten pieces of cheese as a present to their commander (v. 18). David must still be the one who would do the family's menial work, even though he was to be the family's greatest decoration. He did not even have so much as a donkey at his disposal to carry his load but had to take it all on his back and hurry to the camp. He must see how his brothers were doing, what news they had, and whether they were running out of supplies. He also had to see whom they associated with and what sort of life they led.

3. David's dutiful obedience. He had learned to obey before he claimed to command. God's providence brought him to the camp at just the right time, when both sides had drawn up their battle lines facing each other (v. 21). Both sides were now preparing to fight. Notice here:

3.1. How quick and lively David was (v. 22). Although he had come a long way on his journey and had carried a great load, he *ran into the army*, to see what was going on there and to pay his respects to his brothers.

3.2. How bold and daring the Philistine was (v. 23). Now that the armies had drawn themselves out into a line of battle, he came to renew his challenge.

3.3. How fearful and fainthearted the Israelites were. On his approach, they *fled from him and were sore* (greatly) *afraid* (v. 24).

3.4. How much Saul wanted a brave warrior. Whoever would accept the Philistine's challenge would be greatly rewarded (v. 25).

3.5. How much David was concerned to declare the honor of God and Israel against the defiant challenges of the Philistine. It seems that there were two considerations which fired David with holy indignation:

3.5.1. That the challenger was one who was uncircumcised, a stranger to God and out of covenant with him.

3.5.2. That the challenged were the armies of the living God, dedicated to him, employed by him and for him, so that the insults hurled at them reflected badly on the living God himself. It was this that David could not bear. When therefore some people told him what was put forward as a reward for killing the Philistine (v. 27), he asked others (v. 30), with the same righteous anger, expecting that news of his reaction would eventually reach Saul.

3.6. How David was bullied by his eldest brother Eliab and how Eliab tried to discourage him (v. 28). This can be considered as:

3.6.1. The result of Eliab's jealousy. He was the eldest brother, and David was the youngest. Eliab was now burning with anger that his younger brother would speak out such bold words against the Philistine, which he himself had not dared say. He would prefer Goliath to triumph over Israel rather than David to be the one to triumph over Goliath. Eliab intended by what he said to see that David was presented to those around him as an idle, proud young man. He gave them to understand that David's business was merely to keep sheep, and he falsely insinuated that he was a careless, unfaithful shepherd. David could not escape this hardhearted description of his qualities from his own brother.

3.6.2. As a test of David's humility, patience, and faithfulness. It was only a short test, and he passed it with flying colors, for:

3.6.2.1. He bore the provocation with a surprisingly even temper (v. 29): *"What have I now done?"* Right and reason were on his side, and he knew it. He turned away his brother's wrath with a gentle answer. This conquest of his own passion was in some ways more honorable than his conquest of Goliath.

3.6.2.2. He broke through the attempt to discourage him with a surprising determination. His brother's ill will would not divert him from his thoughts of engaging with the Philistine.

Verses 31–39

David is finally presented to Saul as his warrior, and he bravely offers to fight the Philistine (vv. 31–32). A little shepherd who only that morning came from looking after sheep had more courage than all the powerful Israelites, and he encouraged them. David had to do two things while with Saul:

1. He had to get out from under the objection Saul made to his undertaking. Saul said, "I'm sorry; you have a good heart, but you're just not up to it. There's no way you're an equal match for this Philistine." But David reasoned with him, arguing from experience: even though he was only a youth and had never fought in a war, perhaps he had achieved about as much as killing Goliath would amount to, for God had helped him to be bold enough to subdue a lion once, and another time a bear that had robbed him of his lambs (vv. 34–36). He compared the uncircumcised Philistine to these; he considered him as voracious an animal as either of them, and so he did not doubt that he could deal with him as easily. He led Saul to understand that he was not as inexperienced in dangerous fights as Saul thought.

1.1. He tells his story with boldness. When David kept sheep:

1.1.1. He showed that he had a great and tender care for his flock. When he saw a lamb in distress, he would risk his own life in trying to rescue it. This attitude qualified him to be a king. The lives of subjects should be dear to a king, and their blood precious to him (Ps 72:14). David was a type of Christ, the Good Shepherd, who *gathers the lambs in his arms and carries them in his bosom* (Isa 40:11), and who not only risked his life, but *laid down his life for his sheep* (Jn 10:15).

1.1.2. He showed that he was very bold and brave in defending his flock. "Your servant *slew both the lion and the bear*" (v. 36).

1.2. He applies his story with faith. He acknowledges (v. 37) that it was *the Lord that delivered him from the lion and the bear*. He gives God the praise for that great achievement, and so he reasons, *He will deliver me out of*

the hand of this Philistine. In this way, David takes away Saul's objection to his undertaking and gains a commission to fight the Philistine.

2. He had to get out of wearing the armor Saul wanted to make sure he wore when he went out on this great action (v. 38). David, not yet sure how best to attack his enemy, *girded on his sword* (v. 39); but he found that the armor and helmet restricted his movements too much and were a burden to him rather than a defense, and so he wanted Saul to let him take them off again. "I have never been used to such equipment as this."

Verses 40–47

We read here about:

1. The preparations made on both sides for the encounter. The Philistine was already established, as he had been every day for the previous forty days. He could move about well in his armor, for he had gotten sufficiently used to it. But what arms and ammunition does David have? Only what he brought with him as a shepherd; no breastplate or other armor, but only his shepherd's clothes; no spear, but only his staff; no sword or bow, but only his sling; no quiver, only the pouch of his shepherd's bag; no arrows, but instead, five smooth stones picked up out of the stream (v. 40). This showed that his confidence was only in the power of God.

2. The conversation which came before the encounter. Notice in this conversation:

2.1. How arrogant Goliath was:

2.1.1. How he despised his adversary (v. 42). He noticed what David was like: only a youth, not a fully strong man, *ruddy and of a fair countenance*, handsome, one more suited to accompany the Israelite girls in their dances than to lead the Israelites in their battles. He noticed what David was wearing and what weapons he used (v. 43): *Am I a dog, that thou comest to me with staves* (sticks).

2.1.2. How confident he was that he would succeed. He cursed David by his gods (v. 44): *"Come unto me, and I will give thy flesh to the fowls of the air*, and it will be a tender and delicate feast for them."

2.2. How godly David was. His speech is not showy in the slightest, but God is shown as all-powerful in it (vv. 45–47):

2.2.1. He acknowledges that he derives his authority from God: *"I come to thee in the name of the Lord*, who is *the God of the armies of Israel* by the special grace of his covenant" (v. 45). David relies on the name of God, just as Goliath relies on his sword and spear.

2.2.2. He depends for success on God (v. 46). David speaks with as much assurance as Goliath spoke with, but on a more secure basis. It is his faith that says, *"This day will the Lord deliver thee into my hand*, and not only your carcass, but also the carcasses of the armies of the Philistines, will be given to the wild birds and animals."

2.2.3. He gives the praise and glory for everything to God:

2.2.3.1. All the world would be made to know that there is a God, and that the God of Israel is the one and only living and true God, and all other gods, so-called, are worthless frauds.

2.2.3.2. All Israel will *know that the Lord saveth not with sword and spear* (v. 47) but can, when he pleases, save without either and against both (Ps 46:9). David goes into battle as a priest going to offer a sacrifice to the justice of God rather than as a soldier going to fight an enemy of his country.

Verses 48–58

Here is:

1. The encounter of the two warriors (v. 48). The Philistine advanced to this encounter with a great deal of pomp and solemnity; if he had to encounter such a lowly person, then he would do it like an arrogant mountain, covered with bronze and iron. David advanced no less actively or cheerfully, as one who aimed at simply doing the job he had to do rather than being an imposing figure: he *hasted, and ran*, not wearing heavy armor, to *meet the Philistine*. We may imagine with what tenderness and compassion the Israelites saw such a pleasant youth throwing himself into the jaws of death, but he knew whom he had believed and for whom he acted.

2. The fall of Goliath in this encounter. He was in no hurry, because he had no fear. He was confident that he would at one stroke cut off his enemy's head, but while he was preparing to do this deed grandly, David carried out his work powerfully, but without any fuss: he slung a stone, which hit him on the forehead and, in the twinkling of an eye, felled him to the ground (v. 49). Goliath knew there were famous slingers in Israel (Jdg 20:16) but was either so forgetful or presumptuous as to leave open the lower part of his helmet. To complete his task, David drew Goliath's own sword, a two-handed weapon, and used it to *cut off his head* (v. 51). David's victory over Goliath was a type of the triumphs of the Son of David over Satan and all the powers of darkness: he *spoiled* (disarmed) them *and made a show of them openly* (Col 2:15), and we are *more than conquerors* through him (Ro 8:37).

3. The defeat of the Philistines' army after the death of Goliath. They relied wholly on the strength of their champion, and so when they saw that he had been killed, they did not, as Goliath had offered, throw down their arms and surrender themselves as servants to Israel (v. 9), but took to their heels, being completely discouraged and thinking it served no purpose to oppose one before whom such a mighty man had fallen: *They fled* (v. 51). This inspired the Israelites, who *shouted and pursued them*. When they returned, they seized all the baggage, plundered the tents (v. 53), and enriched themselves with the spoils.

4. David's disposal of Goliath's head (v. 54). He took the head of the Philistine to Jerusalem to torment the Jebusites, who held the stronghold of Zion. Goliath's *armour he laid up in his tent*, but the sword was kept behind the ephod in the tabernacle, as consecrated to God (21:9).

5. The notice that was taken of David. Saul had forgotten him, being depressed and mentally deranged, little thinking that his musician would be bold enough to become his bravest warrior. Abner was a stranger to David but brought him to Saul (v. 57), and David gave a modest account of himself (v. 58). He was now introduced to the court with much greater advantages than before, and he acknowledged God's hand in performing for him everything that had gained him those advantages.

CHAPTER 18

In this chapter we see: 1. How David made the most of his triumph. He soon became Saul's constant attendant (v. 2). He became Jonathan's covenant friend (vv. 1, 3–4). 2. How he became the favorite of his country (vv. 5, 7, 16). But we also see how his triumph was diminished. Saul hated him and tried to kill him himself (vv. 8–11). 3. How Saul feared David and tried to find out how he might cause trouble for him (vv. 12–17). He proposed to give his daughter in marriage to him, but he cheated him

out of the elder daughter to provoke him (v. 19) and gave him the younger, on conditions which would put his life in danger (vv. 20–25). But David courageously fulfilled the conditions (vv. 26–27) and came to be respected more and more (vv. 28–30).

Verses 1–5

David was anointed to be king so that he would take the crown out of Saul's hand and over Jonathan's head, but we find:

1. That Saul, who now possessed the crown, put confidence in him, since God so arranged matters that his advancement at court might prepare him for future service. Saul now took David home with him and would not allow him to withdraw again to his father's house (v. 2). *Saul set him over the men of war* (v. 5), not that he made him general—Abner held that post—but he gave him a high-ranking position, perhaps commander of the bodyguard. He employed him in affairs of state and government, and *David went out whithersoever Saul sent him* (v. 5). Those who hope to rule must first learn to obey.

2. That Jonathan, who was heir to the crown, entered into a covenant with him, since God so arranged matters that David's way would be opened because his rival was his friend.

2.1. Jonathan had an extraordinary kindness and affection for him (v. 1): *The soul of Jonathan was* immediately *knit* to *the soul of David*; Jonathan became one in spirit with David. Jonathan had formerly attacked a Philistine army with the same faith and bravery with which David had attacked a Philistine giant, so they had similar inclinations. No one had so much reason to dislike David as Jonathan had because David was to take the crown away from Jonathan, but no one had a deeper affection and respect for him.

2.2. Jonathan showed his love for David by the generous present he gave him (v. 4). He was uneasy at seeing David still disguised in the lowly clothes of a poor shepherd. He therefore took care to quickly give him the clothes of a courtier—for he gave him a robe—and the outfit of a soldier—for he gave him, instead of his staff and sling, a sword and bow, and instead of his shepherd's pouch, a girdle, either a belt or a sash. Jonathan himself had worn these articles, and he now stripped himself of them to give them to David to wear. Saul's clothes would not fit him, but Jonathan's did. Their bodies were of a similar size, a circumstance which fitted in well with the harmony of their minds. David was seen in Jonathan's clothes, so that everyone could see that he was Jonathan's second self. Our Lord Jesus has shown his love to us in such a way that he stripped himself to clothe us, and he emptied himself to enrich us. In fact, he did more than Jonathan: he clothed himself with our rags, whereas Jonathan did not put on David's.

2.3. Jonathan tried to make his friendship with David last forever. They made a covenant with each other (v. 3).

3. That court and country agree in blessing him. God's grace worked so powerfully in David that he was able to bear all the respect and honor that suddenly came on him without becoming boastful. Those who quickly climb up the ladder of success need to have clear heads and tender hearts.

Verses 6–11

Now David's troubles really began, and they not only quickly followed his triumphs but arose from them.

1. He was exalted too much by ordinary people. Some time after the victory, Saul went on a triumphant

procession through the towns of Israel. When he publicly entered any place, the women sang a song, the chorus of which was, *Saul hath slain his thousands, and David his ten thousands* (v. 7).

2. This greatly displeased Saul and made him jealous of David (vv. 8–9). He should have realized they were referring only to recent events and did not in any way intend to diminish Saul's former exploits. When David killed Goliath, he had in effect killed all the Philistines who were killed that day and had defeated the whole army, so they were giving David only what was due to him. But Saul became very angry and immediately suspected that some intentions of treason lay at its root: *What can he have more but the kingdom?* (v. 8).

3. He was so angry that he wanted to kill David (vv. 10–11).

3.1. His mental derangement returned. Those who indulge in envy and hatred *give place* (a foothold) *to the devil* (Eph 4:27) and prepare for the reentry of the unclean spirit with seven others more evil (Mt 12:45). Saul claimed a religious ecstatic experience: *He prophesied in the midst of the house* (v. 10), that is, he went through the motions of being a prophet, and played the role well enough that David would be off his guard and so could be trapped. Perhaps Saul intended, if he could only kill David, to claim that he had been led to do so by God's prompting, but in reality it was diabolical anger that drove him to do this.

3.2. David returned to his harp: *He played with his hand as at other times* (v. 10).

3.3. Saul took this opportunity to try to kill David. He had a javelin or spear in his hand, which he hurled at David to kill him, and he did it not in the heat of the moment but deliberately. You would have thought he would have considered the kindness David was now showing him, in relieving him—as no one else could—in the worst of his troubles. Just look at the contrast! David has his harp in his hand and wants to serve Saul, but Saul has his spear in his hand and wants to kill David. We see here the humility and usefulness of God's persecuted people and the cruelty and barbarity of their persecutors.

3.4. David fortunately avoided the blow twice, now and again later (19:10). He did not throw the spear back at Saul, even though he had enough strength and courage to offer resistance and knew right was on his side, but he got out of Saul's way, wanting only to keep himself safe.

Verses 12–30

Saul began to be openly hostile when he threw the spear at him. His enmity continued and David received its attacks.

1. Notice how Saul expressed his hatred toward David:

1.1. He was *afraid of him* (v. 12). He stood in awe of David, just as Herod feared John (Mk 6:20). Saul was aware that he himself had lost the favorable presence of God and that David had this presence, and that is why he feared him. The way to be both feared and loved—feared by those whom we wish to overcome and loved by those whom we wish to please—is to *behave ourselves wisely* (v. 15).

1.2. Saul removed David from the court and gave him a regiment in the country (v. 13) so that he might not influence the courtiers. But Saul acted unwisely, for David's new position gave him an opportunity to seek the favor of the people, who, when he did so, *loved him* (v. 16) because he *went out and came in before them*.

1.3. Saul tried to incite David to quarrel with the Philistines at every opportunity (v. 17), insinuating that if he did so, he would be doing a good service to both his king and his God and would qualify himself for the honor Saul intended for him, which was to give his elder daughter to him in marriage.

1.4. Saul did what he could to provoke him by breaking his promise to him and giving his daughter to another man.

1.5. When Saul was thwarted in this, he offered him his other daughter.

1.5.1. Perhaps he hoped that, even after her marriage to David, she would take her father's part against her husband.

1.5.2. The conditions of the marriage must be that David would kill 100 Philistines, and as proof that those he had killed were uncircumcised, he must bring their foreskins. When David did this, he would make them want to take revenge on him, which was what Saul wanted, *for Saul thought to make David fall by the Philistines* (v. 25).

1.5.2.1. Saul's conscience would not allow him to aim at destroying David's life himself, but he thought there was nothing wrong in deliberately exposing him to the Philistines: *Let not my hand be upon him, but the hand of the Philistines* (v. 17).

1.5.2.2. Saul pretended to be especially kind toward David even when he was really trying to destroy him: *Thou shalt be my son-in-law*, he says (v. 21).

2. Notice how David behaved when the forces of Saul's displeasure ran so high against him:

2.1. *He behaved himself wisely in all his ways* (v. 14). He did not complain about how harshly he had been treated or make himself the leader of a rival faction, but managed all the affairs he was entrusted with as one who was concerned to truly serve his king and country. Then *the Lord was with him* (v. 14) and made him successful in all his undertakings.

2.2. When it was suggested to him that he would be the king's son-in-law, he again received the proposal very humbly and modestly. Notice:

2.2.1. How highly he speaks of the honor offered him: *To be son-in-law to the king* (v. 23). Religion does not teach us to be rude and impolite. We must *render honour to whom honour is due* (Ro 13:7).

2.2.2. How humbly he speaks of himself: *Who am I?* (v. 18). *Who am I, a poor man, and lightly esteemed?* (v. 23). It is good for us, however far God has advanced us, always to have a low opinion of ourselves.

2.3. When the killing of 100 Philistines was made the condition of David's marriage to Saul's daughter, he readily accepted the terms (v. 26). He did not seem to suspect that Saul intended to harm him by it. He knew God was with him, and so whatever Saul hoped, David did not fear being killed by the Philistines, although he knew he was making himself vulnerable in such an undertaking. Even after he was married, David continued to serve Israel well. When the Philistine commanders began to move toward another war, David was ready to oppose them and *behaved himself more wisely than all the servants of Saul* (v. 30). The Law exempted men from going to war in the first year of their marriage (Dt 24:5), but David loved his country too much to make use of that privilege.

3. Notice how God brought good to David out of Saul's plan against him.

3.1. Saul gave him his daughter to trap him, but in making him Saul's son-in-law that marriage was actually a favor to him: now, when he succeeded Saul, he was much less likely to provoke envy among those loyal to him.

3.2. Saul thought that by exposing him to dangerous services he would cause his death, but the more he acted against the Philistines, the more his people loved him, so that *his name was much set by* (v. 30), his fame became very great, and this rise in his reputation would make his coming to the throne easier.

CHAPTER 19

Immediately after David's marriage, his death was decreed. Four escapes from the harmful sword of Saul are described in this chapter: 1. The first, by the wise mediation of Jonathan (vv. 1–7). 2. The second, by his own quickness (vv. 8–10). 3. The third, by Michal's faithfulness (vv. 11–17). 4. The fourth, by Samuel's protection and by a temporary change in Saul (vv. 18–24).

Verses 1–7

Here we see the different characters of Saul and Jonathan in their attitudes toward David:

1. Never was an enemy so unreasonably cruel as Saul. His own plans to remove David had failed, and so he declared him an outlaw and told his son and all the royal attendants to show their loyalty to the king by killing David at the first opportunity. It was strange that he who knew how much Jonathan loved David should expect him to kill him, but Saul thought that because Jonathan was heir to the crown, he must be as jealous of David as he himself was.

2. Never was a friend so surprisingly generous as Jonathan. He not only continued to be very fond of David, even though David's glory put his in the shadows, but also bravely appeared for him now that the forces of Saul's anger were in full flood against him.

2.1. He made sure of David's present security by letting him know the danger he was in (v. 2).

2.2. He made a great effort to pacify his father and reconcile him to David. The next morning he ventured to speak to him about David (v. 3).

2.2.1. His intercession for David was very wise. In support of it he pleaded:

2.2.1.1. The service David had done for the nation and in particular for Saul. He cited as an example the relief David had given him with his harp when he had been ill; also the memorable action of his bold encounter with Goliath, which had in effect saved Saul's life and kingdom.

2.2.1.2. His innocence. If he were killed, it would be unjustified. Jonathan could not bring anything on his family more fatal than the guilt of shedding innocent blood.

2.2.2. Because his intercession was wise, it was successful. God inclined Saul's heart to listen to Jonathan.

2.2.2.1. He revoked the order for David to be killed (v. 6): *As the Lord liveth, he shall not be slain.* We suppose that he spoke as he thought for the present, but the convictions soon wore off, and his corrupt ways soon prevailed and triumphed over them.

2.2.2.2. He renewed the privilege of David's position at court. Jonathan brought him to Saul, and *he was in his presence as in times past* (v. 7), hoping that the storm was now over.

Verses 8–10

Here:

1. David continues to serve his king and country well. We find him:

1.1. Boldly using his sword to serve his country (v. 8). The war with the Philistines broke out again, which gave David a further opportunity to distinguish himself.

1.2. Gladly using his harp to serve the king. When Saul was again disturbed with fits of mental derangement, *David played with his hand* (v. 9). He had learned to repay good for evil and to trust God with his safety as he followed his duty.

2. Saul continues to hate David. He who only the other day had sworn by his Maker that David *should not be slain* (v. 6) now tried to kill him himself. Saul's fear and jealousy made him torment himself, so that he could not sit in his house without a spear in his hand, pretending it was to save his own life, but actually intending to use it to destroy David, for he tried to pin him to the wall, running at him so violently that he struck the *javelin into the wall* (v. 10).

3. God continues to take care of David and watch over him for good. Saul's attack missed its target. David was too quick for him and fled, and by a kind providence he escaped that night. David often refers to these times of preservation in the Psalms, when he speaks of God's being his shield and buckler, his rock and fortress, and delivering his *soul from death* (Ps 33:19).

Verses 11–17

Here we read about:

1. Saul's further intentions of causing trouble for David. When David had escaped the spear, Saul sent some of his guards after him to lie in wait at the door of his house and kill him in the morning as soon as he stirred (v. 11).

2. David's wonderful rescue from this danger. Michal was instrumental in it; Saul had given her to him to trap him, but she proved his protector and helper. Michal knew how angry her father was with David, quickly suspected what was going on, and so stirred herself to make sure of her husband's safety.

2.1. She removed David from the danger. She told him how imminent the danger was (v. 11): *Tomorrow thou wilt be slain*. David himself knew more of the art of fighting than of fleeing, but *Michal let him down through a window* (v. 12), and so he *fled and escaped*.

2.2. She deceived Saul and those whom he used as the instruments of his cruelty. When the doors of the house were opened in the morning and David did not appear, the messengers would want to search the house for him, and that is what they did. But Michal told them he was ill in bed (v. 14), and if they did not believe her, they could see for themselves. She had put a wooden idol in the bed and wrapped it up snugly and warmly as if it were David asleep, so ill that he could not be spoken to. She put some goats' hair around the idol to make it resemble David's hair in order to deceive them (v. 13). When Saul heard about it, he gave explicit orders: *Bring him to me in the bed, that I may slay him* (v. 15). When the messengers were sent in again, the deception was discovered (v. 16). But by this time David was safe, and Michal was not very concerned at the discovery. Yet when Saul rebuked her for helping David escape (v. 17), her answer showed less concern for his reputation than she had shown for his person: she excused herself by suggesting that David had threatened to kill her. So David suffered from both his friends and his foes, as did the Son of David.

Verses 18–24

Here is:

1. David's place of refuge. Having gotten away at night from his own house, he did not flee to Bethlehem but ran

straight to Samuel and *told him all that Saul had done to him* (v. 18). He went to him:

1.1. Because Samuel was the man who had given him assurance of the crown. In fleeing to Samuel, David made God his refuge, trusting in the *shadow of his wings* (Ps 57:1). Where else can good people turn to and be safe?

1.2. Because Samuel, as a prophet, was the best person he could have to advise him what to do at this distressing time.

1.3. Because there was a school of prophets with Samuel whom he could join in praising God, and the delight he would gain from doing this would bring him the greatest possible relief in his present distress. He enjoyed little rest or satisfaction in Saul's court, and so he went to seek it in Samuel's church.

2. David's protection in this place: *He and Samuel went and dwelt* (stayed) *in Naioth* (v. 18), where the school of the prophets was, in Ramah. But when Saul was informed about it by some of his spies (v. 19), he sent men to seize David (v. 20). When they did not bring him, he sent more; when they did not return, he sent a third group (v. 21); and when he did not receive any news from these, he went himself (v. 22). How did God rescue David, now that he was about to fall—like his own lamb had—into the mouth of the lions? Not, as David rescued his lamb, by killing the lion, nor, as God had rescued Elijah, by consuming the messengers with *fire from heaven* (2Ki 1:10), but by turning the lions into lambs:

2.1. When the messengers came to the congregation where David was among the prophets, *the Spirit of God* came on them (v. 20), and they joined with the others in praising God. Instead of overwhelming David, they themselves were overwhelmed. And so:

2.1.1. God kept David safe, for either they were put into such an ecstasy by the spirit of prophecy that they could not think of anything else and forgot why they had come and did not bother David, or else this spirit put them—for the time being at least—in such good frame of mind that they could not even imagine doing something so evil.

2.1.2. He honored the sons of the prophets and the communion of saints and showed how he can strike awe in even the worst people by the signs of his presence in the assemblies. We see here also the benefit of religious societies.

2.1.3. He exalted his power over people's spirits.

2.2. Saul himself was also overwhelmed by the spirit of prophecy. You would have thought that such a bad person was in no danger of being turned into a prophet, but he prophesied just as his messengers did (v. 23). He stripped off his royal robes and military garments, because they were either too fine or too heavy for this occasion, and it seems he fell into a trance or rapture, which continued all that day and night. Now the saying comes again, *Is Saul among the prophets?* See 10:12.

CHAPTER 20

After narrowly escaping Saul's furious attacks on several occasions, David eventually begins to consider whether he should withdraw to the country and take up arms to defend himself. But he will not do such a daring thing without first consulting his faithful friend Jonathan. 1. David complains to Jonathan about his present distress and enlists his help (vv. 1–8). 2. Jonathan faithfully promises to get and give him information on how his father is disposed toward him, and he renews the covenant of friendship with him (vv. 9–23). 3. Jonathan

carries out his test and finds, to his grief, that his father is irrevocably angry with David (vv. 24–34). 4. He tells David about this in the way they had decided (vv. 35–42).

Verses 1–8

Here:

1. While Saul was still in his trance at Naioth, David escaped to the royal court and got to speak to Jonathan. It was fortunate for him that he had such a friend at court when he had such an enemy on the throne. If there are those who hate and despise us, let us not be disturbed by that, for there are also those who love and respect us. Now:

1.1. David appeals to Jonathan himself concerning his innocence. *What have I done?* (v. 1).

1.2. He tries to convince him that despite his innocence Saul is seeking his life. Jonathan, as befitted a respectful son, tried to cover up his father's shame as far as was consistent with justice and with his loyalty to David (v. 2). David therefore gave him the assurance of an oath about his danger: "*As the Lord liveth, and as thy soul liveth, there is but a step between me and death*" (v. 3).

2. Jonathan generously offers to help him (v. 4): *Whatsoever thou desirest I will even do it for thee.*

3. David only wants Jonathan to find out to his own satisfaction, and then show his friend to his satisfaction, that Saul either really did or did not want to kill him.

3.1. The test he suggested was a very natural one. Saul was to dine publicly on the next two days in observance of the New Moon festival, when special sacrifices would be offered and feasts made of the sacrifices. At these festivals, Saul had either all his children sit with him, and David seated as one of them, or all his great officers, and David seated as one of them. Whichever it was, David decided that his seat would stay empty. If Saul allowed and accepted an excuse for his absence, David would conclude that he had changed his mind and was reconciled to him, but if he became angry and lost his temper at it, it was easy to conclude he intended to harm David.

3.2. The excuse he wanted Jonathan to give for his absence was that he was invited by his elder brother to Bethlehem, his hometown, to celebrate the festival with his relatives there, because, besides these monthly ceremonies, they now also had an annual sacrifice and a holy festival for *all the family* (v. 6). They kept a day of thanksgiving in their clan for all the comforts they enjoyed, and they prayed that those comforts would continue.

3.3. The arguments he used with Jonathan to persuade him to do this kind act for him were very bold (v. 8):

3.3.1. He had entered into a contract of friendship with Jonathan.

3.3.2. He would by no means urge Jonathan to take up his cause if he were not sure it was a righteous one. No honest person will urge a friend to do something dishonest for their sake.

Verses 9–23

Here:

1. Jonathan affirms his loyalty to David in his distress. He faithfully promised him that when the test came, he would let him know how he found his father to be disposed toward him: "If there is *good toward thee, I will show it thee*, that you may be at rest (v. 12); if evil, I will *send thee away*, that you may be safe" (v. 13). This was how he would help rescue him from the evil if it was real and from the fear of evil if it was only imaginary. Jonathan adds his wholehearted prayers to his affirmations:

"The Lord be with thee (v. 13) to protect you and give you success, *as he has been* formerly *with my father*, even though he has now withdrawn from him."

2. Jonathan provides for this covenant of friendship with David to be passed on to his descendants as an inheritance (vv. 14–16). He committed David to be a friend to his family when he was gone (v. 15). And after David's death, his family must also be bound to the family of Jonathan from generation to generation, to be kind to them; he *made a covenant* (v. 16) *with the house of David.* This kindness:

2.1. Jonathan calls *the kindness of the Lord* (v. 14), because it is such kindness as God shows.

2.2. He seals with an oath (v. 16): *The Lord require it at the hand of David's seed* if they prove to be David's enemies and deal wrongfully with the descendants of Jonathan, David's friend. Having himself sworn to David, he made David to swear to him, and David agreed to swear by his love to him, which Jonathan looked on as something sacred. Jonathan's heart was so set on this oath that when they parted this time, he concluded with a solemn appeal to God: *The Lord be between me and thee for ever* (v. 23). David remembered this covenant when he was kind to Mephibosheth (2Sa 9:7; 21:7).

3. Jonathan decides what signs he will give David to tell him how his father is disposed toward him. David would be missed and would be asked after (v. 18). On the third day—by which time he would have returned from Bethlehem—he must be at a certain place (v. 19), and Jonathan would come toward that place with his bow and arrows to shoot for recreation (v. 20). He would send a boy to fetch his arrows, and if they fell short of the boy, David must take that as a signal of safety and not be afraid to show his head (v. 21), but if he shot the arrows beyond the boy, it was a signal of danger, and he must move away for his safety (v. 22).

Verses 24–34

Jonathan is here overwhelmingly convinced of what he was so reluctant to believe, that his father had an implacable hatred toward David and would certainly kill him if he could.

1. David was missing from the festival on the first day, but nothing was said about him. *The king sat upon his seat as at other times* (v. 25), but his heart was full of jealousy and hatred toward David. When the king came to take his seat, Jonathan got up in reverence to him both as his father and as his sovereign; everyone was in their place, but David's was empty. On that day, Saul paid no attention to David's absence except that he said to himself, *"Surely he is not clean* (v. 26). He must have incurred some ceremonial defilement."

2. David is asked for on the second day (v. 27). Saul asked Jonathan, who he knew was his confidant, *Wherefore cometh not the son of Jesse to meat* (the meal)*?*

3. Jonathan makes his excuse (vv. 28–29):

3.1. That David was observing the festival somewhere else and that he had gone to pay his respects to his relatives. And in support of this reason Jonathan pleads:

3.2. That David did not go without permission, which had been humbly asked for and given by Jonathan, as his superior officer.

4. Saul then exploded into the wildest temper and raged like a lion thwarted from taking his prey. David was beyond his reach, but he attacks Jonathan for David's sake (vv. 30–31). He calls him, in effect:

4.1. An illegitimate child: *Thou son of the perverse rebellious woman* (v. 30).

4.2. A traitor: *Thou son of perverse rebellion*, that is, "you perverse rebel" (v. 30, margin).

4.3. A fool: *Thou hast chosen the son of Jesse* as your friend *to thy own confusion* (shame) (v. 30), for while he lives, *thou shalt never be established* (v. 31).

5. Jonathan is very distressed and upset by his father's cruel passion, especially because he hoped for better things (v. 2). He did not respond to his father's words about himself. As the proverb expresses it, "When you are the anvil, lie still." But he could not bear Saul's condemning David to death, and so he replied (v. 32), *Wherefore shall he be slain? What has he done?* Generous spirits can much more easily bear abuse of themselves than hear their friends abused. Saul was now so enraged that he threw his spear at Jonathan (v. 33). Jonathan *rose from table* (v. 34), thinking that the time had come to make a move now that his own life was in danger, and *would eat no meat* (food) (v. 34).

Verses 35–42

Here is:

1. Jonathan going at the time and to the place appointed (v. 35), within sight of which he knew David had hidden himself. He sent the boy to fetch his arrows, which he shot randomly (v. 36), and gave David the fateful signal by shooting an arrow beyond the boy (v. 37). Finding the coast clear and no danger of discovery, he claimed a minute's personal conversation with David after he had told him to flee for his life.

2. The saddest parting of these two friends, who, it seems, only met together once more, secretly *in a wood* (23:16). They took their leave of each other with the greatest possible affection. They embraced each other with kisses and tears. The separation of two such faithful friends was equally painful to each, but David's case was the more unfortunate, for whereas Jonathan was returning to his family and friends, David was leaving all his comforts, even those of God's sanctuary.

CHAPTER 21

David has now said good-by to Saul's court, and so from this time on to the end of this book he is looked on and treated as an outlaw and declared a traitor. His troubles are a key to the Psalms. We find David fleeing and: 1. Deceiving Ahimelech the priest to gain from him both food and weapons (vv. 1–9). 2. Deceiving Achish king of Gath by pretending to be mad (vv. 10–15). Troubles are rightly called temptations, for many people are drawn into sin by them.

Verses 1–9

Here:

1. David, in distress, flees to the tabernacle of God, now set up at Nob, a priestly town in the tribe of Benjamin. Since Shiloh was forsaken by the Lord, the tabernacle had often been moved, though the ark still remained at Kiriath Jearim. Fleeing from Saul's fury (v. 1), David came to Nob and requested help from Ahimelech the priest. Samuel the prophet could not protect him, nor could Jonathan the prince, and so he turned to Ahimelech the priest. He foresaw that he must now be an exile, so he came to the tabernacle:

1.1. To take his heartfelt leave of it, for he did not know when he would see it again.

1.2. To inquire of the Lord there and ask for direction from him as to which way would be responsible and safe.

2. Ahimelech, having heard that David has fallen into disgrace at court, looks at him with suspicion and distrust, as most people look on their friends when the world frowns on them. He was afraid of incurring Saul's displeasure by receiving him: *Why art thou alone?* (v. 1). The one who had been suddenly advanced from the solitude of a shepherd's life to the crowded and busy life of the camp was now just as quickly reduced to the desolate condition of an exile.

3. David pretends that he has been sent by Saul on public service and asks Ahimelech to supply his present needs (vv. 2–3).

3.1. Here David did not behave as he should have. He told Ahimelech a blatant lie: that Saul had given him business to attend to, that his servants had been sent away to a certain place, and that he had been charged with secrecy. This was all false. He did wrong, and it turned out to have disastrous results, for it *occasioned the death of all the persons of thy father's house* (22:22; the house of *Abiathar's* father, that is, Ahimelech's own house), as David later reflected with regret. David had great faith and courage, but now both failed him; he fell into sin through fear and cowardice, and both of these weaknesses were due to the weakness of his faith.

3.2. David begged two things from Ahimelech, *bread* and *a sword*:

3.2.1. He needed bread: *Five loaves* (v. 3). The priest objected that he had nothing except some consecrated bread, or shewbread, which had stood for a week on the golden table in the sanctuary and had been taken from there for the use of the priests and their families (v. 4). David pleaded that he and those who were with him could lawfully eat the consecrated bread in such a case of necessity, for not only were they able to fulfill the priest's condition of having abstained from sexual relations with women for the previous three days, but also *the vessels* (that is, the bodies) *of the young men were holy* (v. 5), being *possessed in sanctification and honour at all times* (1Th 4:4–5). He pleaded that the bread was in a way ordinary, now that its primary religious use has been completed, especially since, as the margin reads, "there [was] other [bread of the Presence] sanctified this day in the vessel" (v. 5), and put in its place on the table. This was David's plea, and the Son of David approved of it, so showing that mercy is to be preferred to sacrifice, that ritual observance must give way to moral duties, and that things may be done in cases of urgent providential necessity which may not be done on other occasions. Jesus used David's action to justify his disciples in picking some heads of grain on the Sabbath, for which the Pharisees criticized them (Mt 12:3–4). Ahimelech supplied David with bread: *He gave him hallowed bread* (v. 6). The shewbread consisted of only twelve loaves, and he gave David five of these (v. 3) even though they had no more in the house. But Ahimelech trusted Providence.

3.2.2. He needed a sword. He now had no weapons with him because, he pretended, he had been called away urgently (v. 8). The only sword that could be found in the tabernacle was Goliath's sword, which was stored behind the ephod. Probably David had that in mind when he asked the priest to help him with a sword, for when it was mentioned, he said, *there is none like that, give it to me* (v. 9). We may observe two things about this sword:

• Whenever he looked at it, it would greatly support his faith by reminding him of that great example of the special care of God's providence for him and its endorsement of him. Experiences are great encouragements.

• He had gratefully given it back to God, dedicating it to him and to his honor as a sign of his thankfulness. What we devote to God's praise and serve him with is very likely to be turned to our own benefit, strength, and encouragement.

4. And so David was given both weapons and food, but it was very unfortunate that one of Saul's servants who was with them before the Lord, a man named Doeg, turned out to be an evil traitor to both David and Ahimelech. By birth he was an Edomite (v. 7), and although he had converted to the Jewish religion under Saul, he still retained the old hereditary hostility of Edom toward Israel. He was a head shepherd. He was there for some reason or other to wait on the priest; it is said that he was *detained before the Lord* (v. 7). He would rather have been anywhere else than before the Lord, and so instead of taking care of the business he had come for, he planned to cause trouble for David and take revenge on Ahimelech for detaining him.

Verses 10–15

Although David is king-elect, here he is an exile. God's providences sometimes seem to be the opposite of his promises. Here is:

1. David's flight into the land of the Philistines, where he hoped to remain undiscovered in the camp of Achish king of Gath (v. 10). David went to him directly, as to one he could confide in, as in fact he later did (27:2–3). God's persecuted people have often found better treatment from Philistines than from Israelites, in Gentile theaters than in Jewish synagogues. The king of Judah imprisoned Jeremiah, and the king of Babylon set him free.

2. The disgust which the servants of Achish had at his presence, and their complaint about it to Achish (v. 11): "*Is not this David?* Is not this the one who triumphed over the Philistines? As such, he must be an enemy of our country, and how could it possibly be safe or right for us to protect or even receive such a man?" Achish perhaps had suggested to them that it would be wise to receive David because he was now Saul's enemy, and so he might later be useful to them as their friend. It is common for outlaws of a nation to be sheltered by the enemies of that nation.

3. The shock which this caused David. Although he had some reason to put his confidence in Achish, yet when he became aware that Achish's servants were anxious about him, he began to be afraid that Achish would be forced to hand him over to them; he was in fact *sorely afraid* (v. 12).

4. The method David used to escape their hands: *He feigned himself mad* (v. 13). He may to some extent be excused for this deception, for it was like a military tactic, by which he deceived his enemies to save his own life.

5. David's escape (vv. 14–15). I am inclined to think that Achish was aware that the delirium was counterfeit but that, because he wanted to protect David—as we later find he did, being very kind to him even when the rulers of the Philistines did not approve of him (28:1–2; 29:6)—he pretended to his servants that he really thought he was mad. "I will not be kind toward him, but then you also are not to harm him in any way, for if he really is mad, he is to be pitied." He therefore *drove him away*, as it says in the title of Ps 34.

CHAPTER 22

Driven away from Achish, David returns to the land of Israel to be hunted by Saul. 1. David raises his flag in the cave of Adullam, receives his relatives (v. 1), and enlists soldiers (v. 2), but moves his elderly parents to somewhere quieter (vv. 3–4) and has the prophet Gad as his counselor (v. 5). 2. Saul decides to pursue him and find him. He complains about his servants and Jonathan (vv. 6–8), and, finding out from Doeg that Ahimelech has been kind to David, he orders that Ahimelech and all the priests who are with him, eighty-five in all, be put to death, and that everything that belongs to them be destroyed (vv. 9–19). 3. Abiathar escapes this cruel execution and goes to join David (vv. 20–23).

Verses 1–5

Here:

1. David shelters in the cave of Adullam (v. 1). Whether it was a natural or artificial stronghold is not noted; access to it was probably so difficult that David thought himself able, with Goliath's sword, to guard it against all Saul's forces while he was waiting to see what God wanted to do with him (v. 3). The promise of the kingdom implied a promise of being kept for it, but David used lawful means to keep himself safe, for otherwise he would have tested God. He did not do anything that aimed at destroying Saul, but only wanted to keep himself safe. It was at this time that David wrote Ps 142, which is entitled, *A prayer when David was in the cave.*

2. David's relatives flocked to him there, *his brethren and all his father's house* (v. 1), including Joab and Abishai. They came to be protected by him, to help him, and to take up their lot with him. They were willing to suffer and risk everything with him.

3. David began to raise up forces in his own defense there (v. 2). His recent experiences had taught him that he could not save himself by fleeing, and so now he had to do so by force. He never used force offensively, however, never threatened any violence to his ruler or disturbed the peace of the kingdom in any way, but only used his forces to protect his own person. Yet this regiment was no great credit to him, for it was made up not of men who were great, rich, bold, or even good, but of those *in distress, in debt, and discontented,* men of broken fortunes and restless spirits, those who were at their wits' end and did not know what to do with themselves. When David had set up his headquarters in Adullam's cave, about 400 of these came and enlisted themselves under him.

4. David took care to settle his parents in a safe place. He could not find anywhere that was safe in all the land of Israel while Saul was so bitterly angry with him and all who belonged to him, and so he took them to the king of Moab and put them under his protection (vv. 3–4). The first thing he did was to find them a place to live that would be quiet, no matter what happened to him. With what humble faith he awaits the outcome of his present distresses: *Till I know what God will do for me* (v. 3).

5. David had the advice and help of the prophet Gad, who probably was one of the sons of the prophets who had been brought up under Samuel, and who probably had been commended by him to David as his chaplain or spiritual guide. The prophet advised him to go into the land of Judah (v. 5), as one who was confident of his own innocence, had an assurance of divine protection, and wanted, even in his present difficult circumstances, still to serve his tribe and country.

Verses 6–19

Here we read about the progress of Saul's evil. He seems to have set aside every thought of any other business and to have given himself wholly to pursuing David.

He heard eventually on the grapevine that David *was discovered* (v. 6). He then called all his officials to him and sat down under a tamarisk tree on the hill at Gibeah, with his spear in his hand as a scepter, showing the present disposition of his spirit, or rather its disorder, which made him want to kill anything and everything that stood in his way. In this bloodthirsty court of inquisition:

1. Saul was looking for information to use against David and Jonathan (vv. 7–8). There were two things that he was inclined to suspect:

1.1. That his servant David *lay in wait* (v. 8) for him, wanting to take his life, which was completely untrue. It was Saul who was seeking to kill David, not the other way around.

1.2. That his son Jonathan had incited David to set this ambush and had joined with him in plotting the death of the king. This also was obviously false. Yet Saul assumed that Jonathan and David were plotting against him, his crown, and his honor and was angry with his officials that they had not told him about it. He told them:

1.2.1. That they were very unwise, for David would never be able to give them such rewards as he had in store for them.

1.2.2. That they were unfaithful: *You have conspired against me* (v. 8).

1.2.3. That they were very unkind. He thought he would manipulate them, that he would play on their good nature by saying, "*There is none of you that is* so much as *sorry for me,* or concerned about me (v. 8)."

2. Though Saul could not find out anything against David or Jonathan from his officials, he did obtain information from Doeg against Ahimelech the priest:

2.1. An accusation is brought against Ahimelech by Doeg, and Doeg himself brings evidence against him (vv. 9–10), telling Saul what kindness Ahimelech had shown to David. He had *inquired of God for him* (v. 10)—which the priest did not do except for people of national importance and not unless the inquiry was about public affairs—and he had provided him with *bread and a sword* (v. 10). All this was true, but it was not the whole truth. He ought to have told Saul also that David had made Ahimelech believe that he was then acting on the king's behalf, so that whatever service Ahimelech did for him, however it turned out, was intended to honor Saul. If Doeg had said this, he would have put Ahimelech in the clear.

2.2. Ahimelech is summoned to appear before the king and to answer to this charge. The king sent for him and all the priests who then attended the sanctuary, whom he supposed to have aided and abetted him. Saul interrogated Ahimelech himself with the greatest disdain and anger (v. 12): *Hear now, thou son of Ahitub.* He did not even call him by name, much less give him his special title. Ahimelech held up his hand in court with the words: "*Here I am, my lord* (v. 12). I am ready to listen to what I am accused of. I know I have done no wrong."

2.3. His accusation is read out to him (v. 13), that he has been a traitor and has joined the son of Jesse in a plot to depose and murder the king. "His intention," Saul says, "was to *rise up against me,* and you helped him by giving him food and weapons." Here we see how even the most innocent actions may be open to misinterpretation. How unsafe are those who live under tyrannical governments. How thankful we should be for the favorable constitution and administration of the government we are under.

2.4. He pleads "Not guilty" to this charge (vv. 14–15). He acknowledges the facts but denies that he acted traitorously or maliciously or with any intention against the king. He insists on the established reputation which David had as Saul's most faithful servant, and he reminds the king that he himself had honored David by giving his daughter in marriage to him, that he had often found him useful, and that he had placed his trust in him. He pleads that he was used to *inquiring of God for him* (v. 15) when he was sent by Saul on any mission, and he did it now as innocently as he had ever done it.

2.5. Saul himself declares the verdict against him, as well as the sentence (v. 16): *Thou shalt surely die, Ahimelech*, as a rebel, *thou and all thy father's house*. What could be more unjust? It was unjust:

2.5.1. That Saul should declare the judgment by himself in his own cause.

2.5.2. That such a reasonable plea should be overruled and rejected without any reason given.

2.5.3. That sentence should be passed so hastily and rashly.

2.5.4. That the sentence should be passed not only on Ahimelech himself, who was the only person accused by Doeg, but also on *all his father's house* (v. 16), against whom nothing was alleged.

2.5.5. That the sentence should be pronounced not to support justice but to satisfy his brutal anger.

2.6. He issues a warrant for the immediate execution of this bloody sentence.

2.6.1. He ordered his guards to execute this sentence, but they refused (v. 17).

2.6.1.1. Never was the command of a ruler more cruelly given: *Turn and slay the priests of the Lord* (v. 17). He seems pleased to take this opportunity to get revenge on the priests of the Lord, since God himself is beyond his reach.

2.6.1.2. Never was the command of a ruler more honorably disobeyed. The guards had more sense and grace than their master. Even though they could expect to be punished, they would not dare kill the priests of the Lord. Such reverence they had for the priests' office, and so convinced they were of their innocence.

2.6.2. He ordered Doeg, the accuser, to be the executioner, and he obeyed. The most bloodthirsty tyrants have found instruments of their cruelty as barbarous as themselves. Doeg was no sooner commanded to kill the priests than he did it very willingly, and meeting with no resistance, he killed with his own hand—or so it appears—on that day eighty-five priests. They must all have been of the age of ministry, between twenty and fifty, for it is said that they *wore a linen ephod* (v. 18); and this phrase may mean that they appeared before Saul in those garments and were actually killed in them. Then, having murdered the priests, Doeg went, no doubt under orders from Saul, to their town of Nob and killed everyone there (v. 19), *men, women, and children,* and also the cattle. How deplorable was the state of religious faith at this time in Israel! To see their priests wallowing in their own blood, and the heirs of the priesthood too; to see their town of the priests devastated so that the altar of God must be neglected for lack of those who attended it—and all this by the unjust and cruel order of their own king to satisfy his barbaric rage—must have penetrated right through to the heart of all godly Israelites and have made them wish a thousand times that they had been satisfied with the government of Samuel and his sons.

Verses 20–23

Here is:

1. The escape of Abiathar, the son of Ahimelech, out of the devastation of the priests' town. It is probable that when his father went to appear before Saul to comply with his summons, Abiathar was left at home to serve at the altar, and so he escaped the first execution; then, before Doeg and his bloodthirsty men came to Nob, Abiathar probably heard in advance about the danger and had time to provide for his own safety. And where else should he go but to David (v. 20)?

2. David's indignation at the sad news he brought. David greatly mourned the calamity; he grieved not only that the deed was done but also, and especially, that he was an accessory to it: *I have occasioned* (I am responsible for) *the death of all the persons of thy father's house* (v. 22).

3. The protection David gave to Abiathar. *With me thou shalt be in safeguard* (v. 23); you will be safe with me. Now that he had time to collect his thoughts, David spoke with assurance about his own safety and promised that Abiathar would receive the full benefits of his protection. David now had not only a prophet, but also a priest, a high priest, with him, to whom he was a blessing, and they to him, and both blessings were a favorable sign of his future success. But it appears that Saul had a high priest too (28:6), for he had a Urim to consult; it is supposed that he promoted Ahitub the father of Zadok, of the family of Eleazar (1Ch 6:8). Even those who hate the power of godliness still do not want to be without its form (2Ti 3:5).

CHAPTER 23

In this chapter Saul, having made himself drunk with the blood of the Lord's priests, is seeking David's life. We see David, on the other hand, doing good but also suffering evil. Here is: 1. The good service he did for his king and country in rescuing the town of Keilah from the hands of the Philistines (vv. 1–6). 2. The danger which that brought him into and his rescue, by divine direction, from that danger (vv. 7–13). 3. David in a wood and his friend Jonathan visiting him there and encouraging him (vv. 14–18). 4. The information which the Ziphites brought to Saul about David's haunts, and the expedition Saul made to pursue him (vv. 19–25); David's narrow escape from falling into his hands (vv. 26–29).

Verses 1–6

The prophet Gad had ordered David to go into the land of Judah (22:5). Since Saul had neglected the public security, David would take care of it, even though he had been treated badly.

1. News is brought to David that the Philistines had descended on the town of Keilah and plundered the country around it (v. 1). The way for any country to be peaceful is to allow God's church to be peaceful in it. If Saul fights against David, then the Philistines will fight against his country.

2. David is willing to come to help them and relieve them. This shows:

2.1. David's generosity and public-spiritedness. He was still concerned for the security of his country and could not sit back and see it ravaged. Even though Saul, whose business it was to guard the land's borders, hated him and sought his life, David was willing to use all his powers to serve Saul and his interests against the common enemy.

2.2. David's godliness and consideration of God. He inquired of the Lord by the prophet Gad, *Shall I go and smite* (attack) *these Philistines?* (v. 2).

3. God appointed him once again to go against the Philistines and promised him success: *Go, and smite the Philistines* (v. 2). His men opposed it (v. 3). To satisfy

them he therefore *inquired of the Lord again* (v. 4), and now he received not only a full commission, which authorized him to fight even without orders from Saul—*Arise, go down to Keilah*—but also a full assurance of victory: *I will deliver the Philistines into thy hand* (v. 4).

4. And so David went against the Philistines, routed them, and saved Keilah (v. 5). It seems he also made a raid into the country of the Philistines, for he carried off their livestock as a reprisal for the wrong they had done to the men of Keilah in looting their threshing floors.

Verses 7–13

Here is:

1. Saul plotting the destruction of David (vv. 7–8). Was he not told about how David had boldly saved Keilah and rescued it from the hands of the Philistines? This should have made Saul consider what honor should be given to David, but instead he saw it as an opportunity to cause trouble for him. Notice:

1.1. How Saul maligned the God of Israel. *God hath delivered him into my hand* (v. 7). He spoke as if he, the one who had been rejected by God, had been favored by him in this situation. He is so ungodly as to link God with his cause just because he thought he had gained one advantage: David was trapped inside a town.

1.2. How Saul abused the Israel of God by making them serve his hatred for David. He called all the people together to march to Keilah, pretending to oppose the Philistines but really intending to besiege David and his men.

2. David consulting God about his own preservation. No sooner is the ephod brought to him than he uses it: *Bring hither the ephod*. We have the living words of the Scriptures in our hands, and so let us take advice from them when we are uncertain what to do. "Bring the Bible here."

2.1. David's prayer to God on this occasion is very serious and reverent. He calls God the *Lord God of Israel* twice and calls himself his *servant* three times (vv. 10–11). "Lord, direct me in this matter, about which I do not know what to do." If he had asked the men—the judges or elders—of Keilah themselves what they would do in that situation, they could not have told him, because they had not made up their own minds. On the other hand, perhaps they could have told him: perhaps they would have promised to protect him but then later would have betrayed him. God, however, could tell him infallibly: "When Saul besieges their city and demands from them that they surrender you to him, they will surrender you rather than experience the full onslaught of Saul's fury."

2.2. After David was informed of the danger he was in, he left Keilah (v. 13). His followers had now increased in number to 600. He went out with these, not knowing where he went but deciding to follow Providence. This frustrated Saul's plans. He thought God had surrendered David into his hands, but it turned out that God had rescued him from his hands, just as a bird is snatched out of the snare of the fowler (Pr 6:5).

Verses 14–18

Here is:

1. David hiding. He stayed in a *wilderness, in a mountain* (v. 14), *in a wood* (v 15). He did not draw up his forces against Saul, surprise him by some strategy, and so take revenge for his own quarrel and put an end to the disasters the country was suffering under Saul's tyrannical rule. He kept to God's way, waited for God's timing, and was content to keep himself safe in woods and deserts.

What can we say about this? Let it help even great and active people come to terms with isolation and restraint. Let it also make us long for that kingdom where goodness will forever be glorious and holiness will be held in honor.

2. Saul hunting him as his implacable enemy. His hatred was so intense that he sought him every day (v. 14).

3. God, as his powerful protector, defending him. God did not surrender him into Saul's hand, as Saul had hoped (v. 7).

4. Jonathan comforting him as his faithful and constant friend. True friendship will not shrink from danger but will readily launch out into the unknown. It will not shrink from humbling itself to serve a friend, and can easily stoop and exchange a palace for a wood. The very sight of Jonathan revived David's spirit. He spoke:

4.1. As a godly friend. He *strengthened his hand in God* (v. 16). Even though David was a strong believer, he needed the help of his friends to supply what was lacking in his faith (1Th 3:10). Jonathan helped him do this by reminding him of the promise of God. Jonathan was not able to do anything to strengthen him, but he assured him that God would.

4.2. As a self-denying friend. He took pleasure in the prospect of David's advancement to the honor which was his own birthright (v. 17). "You will live to be king, and I will think I have been advanced enough if I am next to you, second to you, near you, even though I am your subordinate. I will never claim to be your rival."

4.3. As a constant friend. He renewed his covenant of friendship with him (v. 18). True love takes delight in repeating its commitment. Our covenant with God should often be renewed, so maintaining our fellowship with him. David and Jonathan now parted, and they never saw each other again in this world.

Verses 19–29

Here:

1. The Ziphites offered their service to Saul to betray David to him (vv. 19–20). David was sheltering in the Desert of Ziph (vv. 14–15), putting greater confidence in the people of that country because they came from his own tribe. But they wanted to get in with Saul, and so they went to him. They not only told him where David was hiding (v. 19) but also invited him to come into their country. They promised to hand David over to him (v. 20).

2. Saul received their information thankfully, and gladly grasped the opportunity of hunting down David in their desert. In thanking them, he also insinuated that most of his people had shown him little concern: "You have compassion on me, which others did not have." It was strange that Saul did not go down with them immediately, but the Ziphites had set their spies in every place where he was likely to be discovered, and so Saul thought he was sure of catching his prey.

3. David was now brought into imminent danger. When he found out that the Ziphites had betrayed him, he withdrew from the hill of Hakilah to the Desert of Maon (v. 24). He wrote Ps 54 at this time, as can be seen from the title, and in this psalm he refers to the Ziphites as *strangers* (v. 3) even though they were Israelites, because they abused him barbarically. But David puts himself under divine protection: "*Behold, God is my helper* (Ps 54:4), and then all will be well." Saul pursued him closely (v. 25), until he came so near him that there was only a mountain between them (v. 26). David and his men were on one side of the mountain fleeing, and Saul and his men were on the other

side pursuing them. But this mountain was a sign of divine Providence coming between David and the destroyer, like the pillar of cloud between the Israelites and the Egyptians. David was hidden by this mountain and Saul was confounded by it. Saul hoped to surround David with his numerous forces, but the land was not suitable for what he had planned, and so he failed. The place was given a new name in memory of this (v. 28): *Selah-hammahlekoth*, "the rock of parting," because it parted Saul and David.

4. The rescue of David from this danger. Providence diverted Saul just as he was ready to lay hold of David. He received information that the Philistines were *invading the land* (v. 27). He found himself having to *go against the Philistines* (v. 28), and David was rescued by this means. Just as this Saul was distracted, so another Saul was converted, when he was *breathing out threatenings and slaughter against the saints of the Lord* (Ac 9:1).

5. David escaped in this way and took shelter in a natural stronghold, which he found in the Desert of En Gedi (v. 29).

CHAPTER 24

David had a fair opportunity to destroy Saul, and to his honor, he did not take advantage of it. The preserving of David's own life had been a great example of God's providence toward him, and now David's sparing of Saul's life was just as great an example of God's grace in him. Notice: 1. How maliciously Saul sought David's life (vv. 1–2); how generously David saved Saul's life, when he obtained an advantage over him and only cut off a piece of his robe (vv. 3–8). 2. How emotionally he reasoned with Saul after this, to try to change his attitude toward him for good (vv. 9–15). 3. The beneficial effect which this had on Saul at that time (vv. 16–22).

Verses 1–8

Here:

1. Saul renews his pursuit of David (vv. 1–2). Hearing that he is *in the wilderness of En-gedi* (v. 1), he takes 3,000 chosen men and goes in pursuit of him *upon the rocks of the wild goats* (v. 2).

2. Providence brings Saul alone into the same cave in which David and his men have hidden themselves (v. 3). In those countries there were very large caves in the sides of the rocks or mountains. They were originally natural caves but had probably been enlarged so that sheep could shelter from the heat of the sun, and so we read of places where the flocks rested at midday (SS 1:7). This cave is described as one of the sheep pens. Saul, passing that way, turned aside and entered the cave alone, to *cover his feet* (v. 3), that is, to sleep awhile or relieve himself.

3. David's servants urge him to kill Saul now that he has such a good opportunity to do so (v. 4). Saul now lay at his mercy. How apt we are to misunderstand:

- The promises of God. God had assured David that he would rescue him from Saul, and his men interpret this as authority to destroy Saul.
- The providences of God. Because it was now in his power to kill him, they concluded he could lawfully do it.

4. David *cut off the skirt of his robe* (v. 4), but he soon repented that he had done so because it was an insult to Saul's royal honor.

5. David reasons strongly both with himself and with his servants against harming Saul in any way:

5.1. He reasons with himself (v. 6): *The Lord forbid that I should do this thing*. He considered Saul now not as his enemy but as God's anointed—that is, the person whom God had appointed to reign as long as he lived, and who as such was under the special protection of God's law.

5.2. He reasons with his servants: *He suffered them not* (did not allow them) *to rise against Saul* (v. 7). In this way, he repaid good for evil and so was both a type of Christ, who saved his persecutors, and an example to all Christians.

6. David followed Saul out of the cave, and although he would not take the opportunity to kill him, he wisely took the opportunity if possible to kill his hostility, to try to convince Saul that he was not such a person as Saul thought he was. Even in showing himself now, he showed that he had an honorable opinion of Saul. His behavior was very respectful: he *stooped with his face to the earth, and bowed himself* (v. 8).

Verses 9–15

Here is David's warm and emotional speech to Saul to try to persuade him to be reconciled:

1. He calls him *father* (v. 11), for as king he was not only the father of his country but also, in particular, his father-in-law.

2. He places the blame for Saul's rage against him on Saul's evil counselors: *Wherefore hearest thou men's words?* (v. 9).

3. He solemnly declares his own innocence and denies that he intends to hurt or trouble Saul in any way: *There is neither evil nor transgression in my hand* (v. 11). Perhaps it was about this time that David wrote Ps 7, about the words of Cush the Benjamite, who some think is Saul.

4. He produces indisputable evidence to prove the falsehood of the charge against him which was the basis of Saul's hatred toward him. David was accused of seeking to hurt Saul, and yet, "*See,*" he says, "*yea, see the skirt of thy robe*" (v. 11). If what I am accused of were true, I would be standing here with your head in my hand. *The Lord delivered thee*, very surprisingly, *today into my hand. Some bade me kill thee* (v. 10)." It was for a good reason that he had refused to do it: he feared God. He was so well favored with self-control that he could not go against his heart even under the greatest provocation.

5. He declares that he is determined never to be his own avenger: "*The Lord avenge me of thee*, that is, deliver me from your hand, but whatever happens, *my hand shall not be upon thee*" (v. 12). "From evildoers come evil deeds"; people will act according to the motives and dispositions within them.

6. He tries to convince Saul that it is wrong and evil for him to pursue someone as insignificant as he (v. 14): *Whom does the king of Israel pursue* with such care and force? *A dead dog; a flea.* The Hebrew has "one flea." It was beneath the dignity of such a great king to fight against one who was an unequal match for him, one of his own servants who was brought up as a poor shepherd but was now an exile, who was neither able nor willing to offer any resistance. What credit would it be to Saul if he trampled on a dead dog? What pleasure could it give him to hunt a single flea, which, some have noted, if it is sought, is not easily found, and if it is found, is not easily caught, and if it is caught, is an inferior prize, especially for a ruler.

7. He twice appeals to God as the righteous Judge (v. 12 and again v. 15): *The Lord judge between me and thee.*

Verses 16–22

Here is:

1. Saul's contrite reply to David's words.

1.1. He melted into tears. He spoke as one quite overcome with David's kindness: *Is this thy voice, my son David? He lifted up his voice and wept* (v. 16).

1.2. He nobly acknowledges David's integrity and his own sin (v. 17): *Thou art more righteous than I.* This fair confession was enough to prove that David was innocent—it was the judgment of his enemy himself—but not enough to prove that Saul had truly repented.

1.3. He prays that God will reward David for his generous kindness toward him. *The Lord reward thee good* (v. 19).

1.4. He prophesies David's advancement to the throne (v. 20): *I know well that thou shalt surely be king.* He knew it before, because Samuel had said: *The Lord hath rent the kingdom of Israel from thee this day, and hath given it to a neighbour of thine, that is better than thou* (15:28), so it was a sinful and foolish thing to persecute David. This acknowledgment which Saul made of David's incontrovertible title to the crown was a great encouragement to David himself and also a support to his faith and hope.

1.5. He commits David with an oath to show the same tenderness to his descendants and to his name as he had now shown to his person (v. 21). He later religiously observed this oath; he supported Mephibosheth and executed as traitors those who killed Ish-Bosheth.

2. The parting of Saul and David in peace:

2.1. Saul, for the time being, stopped persecuting David. Saul went home convinced, but he was not converted. He was ashamed of his jealousy toward David but kept that root of bitterness in his heart. He was annoyed that when he had finally found David, he could not at that time find it in his heart to destroy him, as he had wanted.

2.2. David continued to provide for his own safety. He knew Saul too well to trust him, and so he went up to a stronghold (v. 22).

CHAPTER 25

Here we have a break in David's troubles with Saul; Providence gave him a breathing space. And yet now he faced other troubles. If one trouble seems to be over, we must not sit back; a storm may rise up from some other point, which is what happened to David here. 1. News of the death of Samuel could only trouble him (v. 1). But: 2. The contemptuous way in which Nabal treated him is dealt with more fully in this chapter: the character of Nabal (vv. 2–3); the humble request sent to him (vv. 4–9); his churlish response (vv. 10–12). 3. David's anger at it (vv. 13, 21–22). 4. Abigail's wise carefulness to prevent the trouble that was likely to come on her family (vv. 14–20); her speech to David to pacify him (vv. 23–31). 5. David's favorable reception of her (vv. 32–35). 6. The death of Nabal (vv. 36–38). Abigail's marriage to David (vv. 39–44).

Verse 1

Here is a short account of Samuel's death and burial:

1. Although he was a great man, he spent his final days in retirement and obscurity, because Israel had rejected him, for which God justly rebuked them.

2. In spite of his close friendship with David, for which Saul hated him, he still died in peace in the worst time of Saul's tyranny. Although Saul did not love him, he still feared him, as Herod did John, and he feared the people, for all knew that Samuel was a prophet (see Mk 11:32).

3. All Israel mourned for him. His personal character commanded this honor to be given to him when he died. The people were justly indebted to him for his service to the community in judging Israel, and they were right to show respect for his name and memory. The sons of the prophets had lost the founder of their school, but all the people had lost one who was a constant intercessor for Israel (12:23). If he went, they would lose the best friend they ever had.

4. They buried him not in the school of the prophets at Naioth but in his own house at Ramah, where he was born.

5. David then went down to the Desert of Paran, withdrawing perhaps to mourn for Samuel. Also, now that he had lost such a good friend, he knew that he was in an even more dangerous position than ever, and so he withdrew to a desert, and now it was that he *dwelt in the tents of Kedar* (Ps 120:5).

Verses 2–11

The story of Nabal begins here. We have:

1. A short account of a man we would never have heard of if he had not had dealings with David. Notice:

1.1. His name: *Nabal*, which means "a fool."

1.2. His family: he came from the house of Caleb. He inherited Caleb's lands, for Maon and Carmel were situated near Hebron, which was given to Caleb (Jos 14:14; 15:54–55), but he was far from inheriting his virtues. The Septuagint (a Greek version of the Old Testament) and some other ancient versions say he was harsh, quarrelsome, mean-spirited, churlish, and surly.

1.3. His wealth: he was *very great* (v. 2), that is, very wealthy, for riches make people look significant in the eyes of the world, but otherwise, to those who form their opinions correctly, he really looked very mean.

1.4. His wife, Abigail, a woman of great understanding. Her name means, "the joy of her father," but her father could not promise himself much joy in her when he married her to such a husband, because in so doing he showed that he was more concerned with wealth than wisdom. Many children have thrown their lives away on the garbage heap of worldly wealth; they have gotten married to that and to nothing else that is commendable. Many an Abigail is married to a Nabal.

1.5. His character. He had no sense either of honor or honesty. He had no sense of honor, for he was churlish and ill tempered; he had no sense of honesty, for he was mean in his dealings, hard and oppressive.

2. David's humble request to him, that he would send him some food for himself and his servants:

2.1. David, it seems, was in such distress that he was willing to be under obligation to him, and in effect came begging at his door.

2.2. David chose a good time to go to Nabal, when he had many people employed by him to shear his sheep, for whom he would make festive entertainment, so that they would be greatly encouraged. It was usual to hold festivals at sheepshearing times, as can be seen from Absalom's feast on that occasion (2Sa 13:24).

2.3. David ordered his men to deliver their message to Nabal with a great deal of courtesy and respect: *Go to Nabal, and greet him in my name* (v. 5). *Thus shall you say to him that liveth,* "*Peace be to thee.* Long life to you, in body and soul! *Peace be to thy house and to all that thou hast*" (v. 6). He tells them to call him his *son David* (v. 8), suggesting that David honored him as a father.

2.4. David pleaded the kindness which Nabal's shepherds had received from David and his men.

2.4.1. They did not harm the shepherds themselves; they did not terrorize them or take any of their lambs from the flock. But when we consider the condition of David's men — distressed, in debt, and discontented — and the scarcity of provisions in his camp, it must have taken a good deal of care and management to prevent them from plundering.

2.4.2. They protected them from being harmed by others. Nabal's servants, to whom David appealed, went further than David (v. 16): *They were a wall unto us, both by night and day.* David's soldiers had guarded Nabal's shepherds when the bands of the *Philistines robbed the threshing-floors* (23:1) and wanted to rob the sheepfolds. Nabal's flocks had been protected from those plunderers by David's care, and so he says, *Let us find favour in thy eyes* (v. 8).

2.5. David was very modest in his request. "Give whatever is available, and we will be thankful for it." David does not demand what he needs as a debt, either as a tax to a king, or as a levy to a general, but asks for it as a gift to a friend, who considered himself Nabal's humble servant.

3. Nabal's churlish answer to this modest request (vv. 10–11). Nabal not only denied him but also insulted him:

3.1. He speaks scornfully of David as someone insignificant, who was not worth taking notice of. The Philistines could describe him as *This is David the king of the land*, who *slew his ten thousands* (21:11), but his close neighbor Nabal, who came from the same tribe, pretends not to know him, or at least not to know him as a man of any worth or distinction: *Who is David? And who is the son of Jesse?* (v. 10).

3.2. He rebukes David for being the cause of his own present distress and uses the occasion to describe him as evil, as more suitable to be put in the stocks as a vagrant than to have any kindness shown him. How naturally does he speak the churlish, ignorant language of those who hate to help the needy! David was reduced to this distress not because of any fault of his own but purely because of the good he had done for his country and the honor which his God had put on him, and yet he was portrayed as a fugitive and runaway.

3.3. He insists that the food and drink on his table belong to him and refuses to share them with anyone. We make a mistake if we think we are absolute lords of everything we have and that we may do as we please with it. No; we are only stewards of these things, and we must use everything as we are directed, remembering that it is not our own but belongs to God, who has entrusted it to us.

Verses 12–17

Here is:

1. The report made to David of how Nabal had insulted his messengers (v. 12): *They turned their way.* They showed their displeasure by breaking away abruptly from such a churlish man. When Christ's servants are insulted in this way, they must leave it to him to plead his own cause and wait until he sorts it out.

2. David's hasty decision. He put on his sword and ordered his men to do so too:

2.1. He regretted the kindness he had done for Nabal and looked on it as if it had been wasted on him. He said, "*Surely in vain have I kept* (it's been useless keeping) *all that this fellow hath in the wilderness* (v. 21)."

2.2. He determined to destroy Nabal and everyone who belonged to him (v. 22). Here David was not acting like himself. He wanted to kill all the males of Nabal's house. He confirmed his decision passionately: *So, and more also do God* (this, and more also, may God do) *to the enemies of David* (v. 22). *Is this thy voice, O David?* (24:16). Only the other day he spared the one who was trying to take his life; and now will he not spare anything that belongs to the one who has merely insulted his messengers? He who at other times used to be calm and considerate is now made very angry by a few hard words, so that nothing can pay for them but the blood of a whole family. What good are even the best people, when God leaves them to their own devices? David expected kindness from Nabal, and so he was surprised by the insult he received. He was off his guard when he received this sudden and unexpected attack, and it unnerved him completely. How much we should pray, *Lord, lead us not into temptation* (Mt 6:13)!

3. The account given of this matter to Abigail by one of the servants, who was more thoughtful than the others (v. 14). Because Abigail was an understanding woman, she took notice of the matter, even from her servant, who:

3.1. Did David justice in commending him and his men for their respect for Nabal's shepherds (vv. 15–16). "The men were very good to us, and although they made themselves vulnerable, they still protected us and formed a wall around us."

3.2. Did Nabal no wrong in condemning him for his rudeness to David's messengers: *He railed on them* (v. 14) — literally, "he flew on them" — with an intolerable rage, and "this is what he is usually like (v. 17)."

3.3. Did Abigail and the whole family a kindness by making her aware of the likely consequences. Something must be done to pacify David.

Verses 18–31

Here is a record of Abigail's wise peacemaking to prevent her husband and family from the destruction that was about to come on them. Wisdom in such a case as this was better than weapons of war. She was wise in that:

- She acted quickly and without delay. Those who want conditions of peace must send a delegation while the enemy is still a long way away (Lk 14:32).
- She herself did what had to be done, being a woman of prudence and tact.

Abigail must try to make up for Nabal's faults.

1. By a most generous present, Abigail makes up for Nabal's denial of their request. She prepared the very best her house could afford. There was plenty of it (v. 18), not only *bread* and *flesh*, but also *raisins* and *figs*. Nabal begrudged them *water*, but she took *two bottles* (skins) *of wine*, loaded her donkeys with these supplies, and sent them on ahead. It was not only lawful but also commendable that Abigail disposed of all these goods of her husband's without his knowledge, because she did it to provide a necessary defense for him and his family, which otherwise would inevitably have been ruined. Husbands and wives have a joint interest in their worldly possessions for their common good, but if either spends wastefully or excessively in any way, it is robbing the other.

2. By her very obliging manner and winsome words, she makes up for the insulting language with which Nabal spoke to the messengers. She met David on the way; he was very indignant and was thinking how he could destroy Nabal (v. 20), but Abigail humbly, politely, and respectfully begged his favor and asked him to ignore the offense.

2.1. She speaks to him throughout with respect and courtesy. She does not criticize him for his vehemence, but she tries to bring him into a better frame of mind.

2.2. She takes responsibility for the maltreatment of his messengers: *Upon me, my lord, upon me, let this iniquity be* (v. 24). Abigail here revealed the sincerity and strength of her marital affection and concern for her family: whatever Nabal was like, he was still her husband.

2.3. She excuses her husband's faults by attributing them to his natural weaknesses and lack of understanding (v. 25). "He is simple, but not spiteful. Forgive him, for he does not know what he is doing."

2.4. She pleads her own ignorance of the matter: "*I saw not the young men* (v. 25), or else they would have received a better answer."

2.5. She assumes that she has won her point already (v. 26): *Seeing the Lord hath withholden thee.* She does not depend on her own reasoning to soften him, but on God's grace. And in fact the very mention of what he was about to do, to shed blood and take revenge, was enough to work on such a tender and gracious spirit as David. It seems from his reply (v. 33) that it affected him deeply.

2.6. She applauds David for the good services he has done against the common enemies of his country: "*My lord fighteth the battles of the Lord* against the Philistines, and so he will leave it to God to fight his battles against those who insult him" (v. 28).

2.7. She foretells the glorious outcome of his present troubles. She tells him with assurance:

2.7.1. That God will keep him safe: *The soul of my lord shall be bound in the bundle of life with the Lord thy God* (v. 29), that is, God will hold thy soul in life — as the expression is in Ps 66:9 — as we hold those things which are bundled up or which are precious to us (Ps 116:15). The Jews understand this to refer not only to the present life but also to the life to come, and so it is commonly used as an inscription on their gravestones. "Here we have laid the body, but trust that *the soul is bound up in the bundle of life, with the Lord our God*" (v. 29).

2.7.2. That God will make him victorious over his enemies. "*The Lord will certainly make my lord a sure house* (v. 28); therefore *forgive this trespass*" (v. 28). She is confident that if he overlooks the offense he will not be sorry later, but on the contrary, it will give him the unspeakable satisfaction of knowing that his wisdom and grace got the better of his temper.

Verses 32–35

As an earring of gold, and an ornament of fine gold, so is a wise reprover (person who rebukes) *upon an obedient ear* (Pr 25:12). Abigail had wisely rebuked David's temper, and he had listened to the rebuke, according to his own principles (Ps 141:5): *Let the righteous smite* (strike) *me, it shall be a kindness.*

1. David gives God thanks for sending him this fortunate restraint for his sinful ways (v. 32): *Blessed be the Lord God of Israel, who sent thee this day to meet me.* God is to be acknowledged in all the kindnesses that our friends do for us in either our soul or our body.

2. David gives Abigail thanks for coming at just the right time between him and the harm he was about to do: *Blessed be thy advice, and blessed be thou* (v. 33).

3. He seems very aware of the great danger he was in, and his awareness makes the blessing of being rescued seem even greater. He speaks of the sin as very great. He was coming to shed blood, a sin which, when he was in his right mind, he considered horrific, as can be seen in his prayer, *Deliver me from bloodguiltiness* (Ps 51:14).

4. David sent her away with a peaceful reply (v. 35). He, in effect, admits that he is overcome by her eloquence: "*I have hearkened to thy voice* and will not pursue the revenge I intended, for I *have accepted thy person*, I am pleased with you and what you have said."

Verses 36–44

Here we attend Nabal's funeral and Abigail's wedding:

1. Nabal's funeral. Here is:

1.1. *Nabal dead drunk* (v. 36). Abigail came home, and it seems he had so many people and such abundant provision around him that he missed neither her nor the supplies she took to David. *He was very drunk* (v. 36), a sign that he was *Nabal*, "a fool," who could not use his plenty without abusing it. He could not enjoy the company of his friends without making a pig of himself. There is no more certain sign that a man has only a little wisdom, and there is no more certain way to destroy the little he has, than by drinking excessively. Nabal never thought he could give too little in charity, and he also never thought he could give himself too much to his self-indulgence.

1.2. Nabal again dead with sadness (v. 37). When he had recovered a little the next morning, his wife told him how close to destruction he had brought himself and his family because of his rudeness, and with what difficulty she had intervened to prevent it. When he heard this, *his heart died within him and he became as a stone.* He became sullen and said little, because he was ashamed of his own foolishness.

1.3. Nabal, at last, really dead: *About ten days after,* when he had been kept that long under stress and pain, *the Lord smote* (struck) *him that he died* (v. 38).

2. Abigail's wedding. David was greatly charmed by the beauty of her person and the unusual wisdom of her manner and speech. He wooed her by proxy, perhaps because all his work did not allow him to come himself. She received his message with great modesty and humility (v. 41), counting herself unworthy of the honor. She agreed to the proposal, went with his messengers, took her five maids with her, and *she became his wife* (v. 42). She married him in faith, not doubting that, even though he now did not have a house of his own, God's promise to him would eventually be fulfilled.

3. The chapter concludes with a short account of David's wives:

3.1. One whom he had lost before he married Abigail: Michal, Saul's daughter, his first, and the wife of his youth, to whom he would have been faithful if she had been faithful to him, but whom Saul had given to another (v. 44) to show his displeasure toward David and renounce the relationship of father-in-law to him.

3.2. Another whom he married besides Abigail (v. 43) and, it seems, before her, for she is named first (27:3). David was carried away by the corrupt custom of those times. When he could not keep his first wife, he thought that would excuse him from keeping to his second. But we deceive ourselves if we think we can make others' faults an excuse for our own sin.

CHAPTER 26

David's troubles from Saul begin again. 1. The Ziphites informed him where David was (v. 1), and he then marched out with a considerable force to search for him (vv. 2–3). David obtained information about his movements (v. 4) and saw his camp (v. 5). 2. David and one of his men ventured into his camp at night and found him and all his guards fast asleep (vv. 6–7). Although David was strongly urged by his companion to take Saul's life, he refused to do so but only carried away his spear and his jug of water (vv. 8–12). 3. He produced these as further evidence that he had no intention of causing Saul any harm and reasoned with him about his behavior (vv. 13–20). 4. Saul was then convinced of his error, and once more stopped persecuting David (vv. 21–25).

Verses 1–5

Here:

1. Saul obtains information about David's movements and takes offensive action. The Ziphites came to him and told him where David was, at the same place where he had been when they had betrayed him earlier (23:19). For all we know, Saul would have continued in the same good spirits he was in (24:17) and would not have caused David this fresh trouble if the Ziphites had not put him up to it. But now, Saul readily seized hold of the information and went down with an army to the place where David hid himself (v. 2).

2. David obtains information about Saul's movements and takes defensive action. He was only concerned for his own safety, not Saul's destruction, and so he *abode in the wilderness* (v. 3), restraining his bold spirit by withdrawing silently, showing more true courage than he could have done by lawless opposition.

2.1. He sent out scouts, who informed him of Saul's approach, for he would not believe that Saul would deal in such an evil way with him until he received clear evidence.

2.2. He saw with his own eyes where Saul was camped (v. 5).

Verses 6–12

Here is:

1. David's bold venture into Saul's camp at night, accompanied only by his nephew, Abishai, the son of Zeruiah. Like Gideon, he dared to go past the guards, having a special assurance of divine protection.

2. The position David found the camp in: *Saul lay sleeping in the trench* or, as some read it, "in his chariot, and in the midst of his carriages," with his spear stuck in the ground near his head, and all the soldiers, including those appointed to stand guard, were *fast asleep* (v. 12). It was extraordinary that they should all be asleep at the same time, and so fast asleep that David and Abishai walked and talked among them, but not one of them stirred. Saul and all his forces lay helpless. They were all, in effect, disarmed and chained. But nothing was done to them; they were only rocked into a deep sleep.

3. Abishai's request to David for authority to kill Saul with the spear that was in the ground near his head. It was a special providence which gave David this opportunity, his nephew argued, and so he ought not to let it slip.

4. David's generous refusal to allow any harm to be done to Saul, showing a determination to hold firmly to his principles of loyalty (v. 9). No one could kill the Lord's anointed and be innocent. The thing he feared was guilt, and he was more concerned for his innocence than for his safety. He decided to wait till God thought fit to take revenge on Saul, and he would by no means take revenge himself (v. 10). He bravely put his conscience before his own personal interests and trusted God with the outcome of events. He and Abishai took the spear and jug of water which were near Saul's head (v. 12).

Verses 13–20

David then got safely away from Saul's camp—having brought with him sufficient proof that he had been there—placed himself conveniently so that Saul's men could hear him but not reach him (v. 13), and began to reason with them on what had happened.

1. David reasons ironically with Abner and taunts him scornfully. Abner got up and asked who it was who was calling and disturbing the king's rest. "It is I," David said, and then rebuked Abner for sleeping when he should have been on his guard. To confound him even more, David told him that he had lost his honor (v. 15) and that he deserved to lose his head (v. 16): "*You are all worthy to die*, by martial law, for not being on your guard when you had the king himself asleep in your presence. The signs are here in front of you. Take a look at where the king's spear is: it's in the hands of the one whom the king himself counts his enemy. Those who took that away might just as easily and surely have taken away his life. So who really are the king's best friends? Is it you who neglected him and left him exposed or is it I who protected him when he was exposed?"

2. David reasons seriously and affectionately with Saul. By this time Saul was awake enough to hear what was said and make out who was speaking (v. 17): *Is this thy voice, my son David?* He had given David's wife to another but now still called him *son*; he had been so thirsty for his blood but was still so glad to hear his voice. And now David had as good an opportunity of reaching Saul's conscience as he had just before had of taking his life.

2.1. He complains about the sad condition he has been brought into by Saul's enmity toward him. He mourns two things:

2.1.1. That he has been driven away from his master and his business: "*My lord pursues after his servant* (v. 18). Instead of being recognized as a servant, I am pursued as a rebel."

2.1.2. That he has been driven away from his God and from his religious faith. He had to live among the worshipers of foreign gods and so was tempted to join them in their idolatrous worship. If David had not been someone with extraordinary grace, who held firmly to his religious faith, then the harsh treatment he received from his own king and people, who were Israelites and worshipers of the true God, would have made him prejudiced against the religion they professed and would have driven him to seek fellowship with idolaters.

2.2. He insists on his own innocence: *What have I done or what evil is in my hand?* (v. 18).

2.3. He tries to convince Saul that his pursuit of him is not only wrong but also contemptible and beneath him. He compares himself to a partridge, a very innocent, harmless bird, which, when attempts are made on its life, flies away if it can, but offers no resistance. And would Saul bring the best of his soldiers onto the battlefield only to hunt one poor partridge? "Let us join in making our peace with God, reconciling ourselves to him, which may be done by sacrifice. I will then hope that the sin will be forgiven, whatever it is, and that the difficulty, which is causing so much trouble to both you and me, will come to an end." This is the right way to make peace; let us first make God our friend by Christ the great Sacrifice, and then all other hostilities will be put to death (Eph 2:16; Pr 16:7). He properly lays the blame on the evil counselors who advised the king to do what was dishonorable and dishonest, and he insists that they be removed from being with him and be forbidden from his presence, as those cursed before the Lord.

Verses 21–25

Here is:

1. Saul's penitent confession of his fault and foolishness in persecuting David and his promise to stop doing so. He acknowledges that he has been very wrong in persecuting him, that he has acted against God's Law (*I have sinned*) and against his own interests (*I have played the fool*) (v. 21) in pursuing as an enemy the one who could have been one of his best friends. He invites him to return to his court again: *Return, my son David* (v. 21). He promises him that he will not persecute him as he has done, but protect him: *I will no more do thee harm* (v. 21).

2. David making the most of Saul's convictions and confessions. Here is the evidence David produced of his own sincerity. He wanted one of Saul's foot soldiers to fetch the spear (v. 22), and then (v. 23):

2.1. He appeals to God as judge of the conflict: *The Lord render to every man his righteousness.*

2.2. He reminds Saul again of the proof he has now given of the respect he showed for Saul out of loyalty to him: *I would not stretch forth my hand against the Lord's anointed* (v. 23). In this he suggests to Saul that he was protected by the anointing oil, for which Saul was indebted to the Lord and ought to express his gratitude to him.

2.3. He puts himself under God's protection, not relying on Saul's promises. He begs God's favor (v. 24): "*Let my life be much set by* (valued) *in the eyes of the Lord,* however lightly you consider it."

3. Saul's prediction of David's advancement. He commends him (v. 25): *Blessed be thou, my son David.* He foretells his victories and his eventual advancement: *Thou shalt do great things* (v. 25). The royal qualities which have appeared in David—his generosity in sparing Saul, his military authority in rebuking Abner for sleeping, his care for the public welfare, and the special signs of God's presence with him—have convinced Saul that he will certainly and finally be advanced to the throne, according to the prophecies concerning him.

4. A temporary cure provided for the wound, and so they parted as friends. Saul returned to Gibeah. *David went on his way* (v. 25). After this parting, it does not appear that Saul and David ever saw each other again.

CHAPTER 27

David was a man after God's own heart, but he still had his faults, which are recorded not to be imitated but to warn us. We find that David commendably and wisely looked after the safety of himself and his family (vv. 2–4) and boldly fought Israel's battles against the Canaanites (vv. 8–9). But we find to his dishonor: 1. That he began to despair of ever being rescued (v. 1) and that he left his own country and went to live in the land of the Philistines (vv. 5–7). 2. That he deceived Achish with a prevarication, if not a lie, concerning his expedition (vv. 10–12).

Verses 1–7

Here is:

1. The triumph of David's fear, which was the effect of his weak faith (v. 1). In a depressed mood, he drew the tragic conclusion, *I shall one day perish by the hand of Saul* (v. 1). But *O thou of little faith, wherefore dost thou doubt?* (Mt 14:31). Although he had no reason to trust Saul's promises, did he not have every reason in the world

to trust the promises of God? Unbelief is a sin that easily entangles even good people. *Lord, increase our faith* (Lk 17:5)!

2. The decision David came to. Now that Saul had for the time being returned to his palace, he determined to use this opportunity to withdraw into the Philistines' country. David was no friend to himself in taking this course. God had appointed him to raise his banner *in the land of Judah* (22:5). How could he expect to remain under the protection of the God of Israel if he went out of the borders of the land of Israel?

3. The kind reception David had at Gath. Achish made him welcome, partly from a generous spirit, being proud to receive someone so brave, and partly from a political point of view, hoping that David would commit himself forever to his service, and that his example would make many others desert and come over to his side. No doubt he gave David a solemn promise of protection, which he could rely on when he could not trust Saul's promises.

4. Saul stopped pursing him (v. 4). Saul did not try again to pursue David; he was satisfied that he was in exile.

5. David's move from Gath to Ziklag:

5.1. David's request for permission to move was wise and modest (v. 5):

5.1.1. It was wise. David knew what it was to be eyed jealously in Saul's court, and he would have even more reason to fear in the court of Achish, and so he refused to be honored there. In a town of his own he could more freely exercise his religious faith and ensure that his men kept to it. His righteous soul would not be troubled there, as it had been at Gath, by the idolatries of the Philistines.

5.1.2. As it was presented to Achish, it was modest. He did not dictate terms and conditions to Achish regarding the place Achish should assign him. "*Why should thy servant dwell in the royal city* (v. 5), to crowd you out and to displease those around you?"

5.2. The gift which Achish made to David, at his request, was very generous and kind (vv. 6–7): *Achish gave him Ziklag.* In this:

5.2.1. Israel recovered their ancient right, for Ziklag was in the allotment of the tribe of Judah (Jos 15:31) and was later assigned out of that allotment, along with some other towns, to Simeon (Jos 19:5). But either it was never subdued, or the Philistines had conquered it in some struggle with Israel.

5.2.2. David gained an advantageous settlement, not only at a distance from Gath but also bordering on Israel. Although we do not find that he added to his forces at all while Saul lived—for he had only his *six hundred* men (30:10)—yet immediately after Saul's death, Ziklag was where he and his friends met up.

Verses 8–12

Here is an account of David's actions while he was in the land of the Philistines: a fierce attack he made, his success in it, and what he told Achish about it:

1. We may declare him innocent of injustice and cruelty in this action because those people whom he destroyed were those whom heaven had long before condemned to destruction. The Amalekites were to be all destroyed. Probably the Geshurites and Girzites (*Gezrites*) were branches of Amalek. Saul was rejected because he had spared them, and David made up for what was lacking in Saul's obedience before he succeeded him.

2. But we cannot excuse him for his pretense with Achish in the account he gave him of this expedition:

2.1. It seems David was not willing for Achish to know the whole truth, and so he did not spare anyone to take the news to Gath (v. 11), not because he was ashamed of what he had done as something bad, but because he was afraid that if the Philistines found out, they would be apprehensive of danger to themselves or their allies because they harbored him among them, and that they would therefore expel him from their territory.

2.2. David hid it from Achish with a prevarication that was inconsistent with his character. When asked which way he had made his raid, he answered, *Against the south of Judah* (v. 10). It was true that he had invaded those countries that lay south of Judah, but he made Achish believe he had invaded those that lay south in Judah, for example the Ziphites, who had more than once betrayed him. This is what Achish understood him to mean, and so he deduced that David *had made his people Israel to abhor him* (v. 12) and had thereby attached himself to the interests of Achish.

CHAPTER 28

Preparations are made here for that war which will put an end to the life and reign of Saul and so make way for David to come to the throne. In this war: 1. The Philistines are the aggressors and Achish their king makes David his confidant (vv. 1–2). 2. The Israelites prepare to receive them, and Saul their king consults the Devil as his privy counselor, so reaching the limit of his sins. Notice 2.1. The desperate condition Saul was in (vv. 3–6). 2.2. His turning to a medium, to bring up Samuel for him (vv. 7–14). 2.3. His conversation with the apparition (vv. 15–19) and the depression it brought him into (vv. 20–25).

Verses 1–6

We read here about:

1. The intentions of the Philistines against Israel. They decided to *fight them* (v. 1).

2. The expectation Achish had of help from David in this war. In requiring David to join him he implied, "If I protect you, I may demand service from you," and he would be glad to have such a man as David on his side. David gave him an ambiguous answer: "We will see what will be done; there will be enough time to talk about that later, but *surely thou shalt know what thy servant can do*" (v. 2). In this way, he kept himself free from making a promise to serve Achish but at the same time kept Achish expecting his service.

3. The drawing of the armies, on both sides, onto the field (v. 4): *The Philistines pitched in Shunem*, which was in the tribe of Issachar, a long way north from their own country. Saul gathered his forces on some of the nearby mountains of Gilboa and prepared to engage the Philistines.

4. The terror Saul was in: he *saw the host* (army) *of the Philistines* (v. 5), more numerous, better armed, and in better spirits than his own forces were. If he had kept close to God, he would have had no need to be afraid at the sight of a Philistine army, but since God had abandoned him, he had lost his advantage, his armies had dwindled and looked contemptible, and what was worse, his spirits failed him. He now remembered the guilty blood of the Amalekites which he had spared, and the innocent blood of the priests which he had spilled. His sins were set before him, which robbed him of all his courage. In his distress, *Saul inquired of the Lord* (v. 6).

He inquired in such a manner that it was as if he had *not inquired at all*. And so it is said (1Ch 10:14), *He inquired not of the Lord*, for he did it weakly and coldly and with the secret intention that if God did not answer him, he would consult the Devil. He did not inquire in faith but with a wavering, unstable mind. Could the one who hated and persecuted Samuel and David, who were both prophets, expect to be answered by prophets? Could the one who had killed the high priest expect to be answered by the Urim? Could the one who had sinned away the Spirit of grace expect to be answered by dreams?

5. The mention of some things that had happened some time before, to introduce the following story (v. 3):

5.1. The death of Samuel. Samuel was dead, which made the Philistines bolder and Saul more afraid.

5.2. Saul's decree against witchcraft. He had enforced the laws against *those that had familiar spirits* (v. 3), the mediums, who must not be allowed to live (Ex 22:18). Some think that he did this while he was still under Samuel's influence. Perhaps when Saul was himself troubled by an evil spirit, he suspected that he was under the influence of witchcraft, and for that reason, he destroyed all the mediums. Many seem zealous against sin when they themselves are in any way hurt by it—they will inform against swearers if they swear at them, or against drunkards if they abuse them when they are drunk—but otherwise have no concern for the glory of God or any hatred of sin as sin.

Verses 7–14

Here:

1. Saul seeks a medium or witch (v. 7). When God answered him not (v. 6), if he had humbled himself by repentance and persevered in seeking God, who knows but that God might have finally been persuaded to have dealings with him? But since he could discern no comfort from either heaven or earth (Isa 8:21–22), he decided to knock at the gates of hell, and to see if anyone there would befriend him and give him advice: *Seek me a woman that has a familiar spirit*, a woman who is a medium (v. 7). His servants immediately recommended one to him at Endor. He decided to turn to her. In this he was to blame for contempt of the God of Israel and contradiction within himself.

2. Saul goes quickly to her, but by night and in disguise, with only two servants, and probably on foot (v. 8). Those who are taken captive by Satan are forced:

2.1. To discredit themselves. Never did Saul look so contemptible as when he sneaked off to a wretched medium to find out his fortune.

2.2. To deceive others. Here we see the power of natural conscience: even those who do evil are embarrassed by it and are ashamed to do it.

3. Saul tells her why he has come and promises her exemption from any punishment.

3.1. All he wants her to do is to bring up one person from the dead. What he was hoping would serve his purpose, then, was necromancy, consulting the dead. This was expressly forbidden by the law (Dt 18:11). *Bring me up him whom I shall name* (v. 8). It was generally assumed that souls continue to exist after death and are then given great knowledge. But to think that any good souls would come up at the call of an evil spirit, or that God would allow people to gain any real advantage from a cursed satanic scheme, was absurd.

3.2. She shows her fear of the law and her suspicion that this stranger came to lure her into a trap (v. 9): *Thou knowest what Saul has done.* Notice how aware she is of the danger she is in from Saul's decree, and how careful she is to guard against it, but she is not at all apprehensive of the requirements of God's law and the terrors of his wrath. She considers what *Saul* has done, not what *God* has done, against such practices, and she fears a trap set for her life more than a trap set for her soul.

3.3. Saul promises on oath not to betray her (v. 10). But he promised more than he could deliver when he said, *There shall no punishment happen to thee,* for he who could not keep himself safe could much less keep her safe from divine vengeance.

4. Samuel, who had recently died, is the person whom Saul wanted to talk to.

4.1. As soon as Saul had given the medium the assurance she wanted, she began her sorcery and asked, *Whom shall I bring up to thee?* (v. 11).

4.2. Saul wants to speak to Samuel: *Bring me up Samuel* (v. 11). Samuel had anointed Saul to the kingdom and had formerly been his faithful friend and counselor. While Samuel was living at Ramah, not far from Gibeah of Saul, and led a school of prophets there, we never read of Saul's going to consult him. It would have been good for him if he had. But now that Samuel was dead, Saul said, *Bring me up Samuel* (v. 11), and the very next words are, *When the woman saw Samuel* (v. 12).

4.2.1. When the medium saw the apparition, she was aware that her client was Saul (v. 12): *"Why hast thou deceived me* with a disguise, for you are Saul, the very man that I am afraid of more than anyone else?" If she believed it really was Samuel whom she saw, she would have had more reason to be afraid of him, a good prophet, than of Saul, an evil king. Saul told her not to be afraid of him and inquired *what she saw* (v. 13). She said, *I saw gods* (a spirit) *ascending out of the earth.* Poor gods that come up *out of the earth*! But she speaks the language of the followers of other religions, who had their hellish gods and worshiped them.

4.2.2. If Saul had thought it necessary for his conversation with Samuel that the body of Samuel should be called up out of the grave, he would have taken the medium with him to Ramah, where his grave was, but he intended only to commune with his soul, which, if it became visible, was expected to appear in its usual physical form. God allowed the Devil to fulfill the intention, so that those who would not *receive the love of the truth* might be *given up to strong delusions and believe a lie* (2Th 2:10–11).

4.2.3. It seems that Saul was not allowed to see any kind of form himself but must take the woman's word for it that she saw *an old man covered with a mantle* (v. 14), or robe, the clothes of a judge, which Samuel had sometimes worn. Saul realized from the woman's description that it was Samuel, and he *stooped with his face to the ground* (v. 14) in reverence to Samuel, even though he did not see him.

Verses 15–19

We have here the conversation between Saul and Satan. Saul came in disguise (v. 8), but Satan soon recognized him (v. 12). Satan comes in disguise, in Samuel's robe, but Saul cannot recognize him. This is the disadvantage we labor under, in struggling against *the rulers of the darkness of this world* (Eph 6:12): they know us, while we are ignorant of their schemes.

1. The apparition impersonating Samuel asks why he has been sent for (v. 15): *Why hast thou disquieted me to bring me up?*

2. Saul complains to this false Samuel, mistaking him for the true one. His complaint is very gloomy: "*I am sorely distressed.* I do not know what to do, *for the Philistines make war against me* (v. 15). But, sadly, *God has departed from me*" (v. 15). He does not, like one who is truly repentant, acknowledge God's righteousness in refusing to answer, but like one who is enraged, he rushes at God as unkind and then runs away from him: *Therefore I have called thee* (v. 15). Saul's thoughts are so perverse that he thinks Samuel, a servant of God, would favor those whom God frowned on, as if a dead prophet could help him more than the living ones.

3. It is cold comfort which this evil spirit, clothed in Samuel's robe, gives to Saul, and it is clearly intended to drive him to despair and suicide. If it had been the true Samuel, he would have told him to repent and make his peace with God, and recall David from exile, so that he might hope to find mercy with God, but instead he described his case as helpless and hopeless, which was as useful to Saul as it later was to Judas, to whom Satan was first a tempter and then a tormentor, persuading him first to sell his master and then to hang himself.

3.1. Satan humiliates him by pointing to his present distress (v. 16).

3.2. He humiliates him by reminding him of the anointing of David to the kingdom (v. 17). But to make him believe that he was Samuel, the apparition confirmed that it was God who was speaking through him. The Devil knows how to speak with a pretense of religion and can teach *false apostles to transform themselves into the apostles of Christ* (2Co 11:13) and imitate their language.

3.3. He rebukes him for his disobedience to the command of God in not destroying the Amalekites (v. 18). Satan had helped him mitigate and excuse that sin when Samuel had dealt with him to bring him to repentance, but now he makes the sin worse, to make him despair of God's mercy.

3.4. He foretells his coming destruction (v. 19):

• That his army would be routed by the Philistines.
• That he and his sons would be killed in battle: *Tomorrow thou and thy sons shall be with me* (v. 19), that is, disembodied and in the realm of the dead.

Verses 20–25

Here we are told how Saul received this terrible message from the spirit he consulted. He wanted to be told *what he should do* (v. 15) but was only told what he had not done and what would be done to him. Notice:

1. How Saul sank under the burden (v. 20). He really was unfit to bear it, having *eaten nothing all the day before*, nor *that night*. He had been fasting when he came from the camp, and he continued to fast, not for lack of food but for lack of an appetite. *He fell all along* (full length) *on the earth* (v. 20), as if the archers of the Philistines had already struck him, *and there was no strength in him* (v. 20) to sustain him when he heard this dreadful news. He had finished consulting mediums and had found them miserable comforters.

2. With what difficulty Saul was persuaded to eat so that he would not faint on the way back to his position in the camp. The medium boldly offered him some refreshment so that he could get away from her house, fearing that if he should fall ill, especially if he were to die there, she would be punished for it as a traitor, although she had escaped punishment as a medium.

2.1. She showed herself very bold toward him in offering him some refreshment. She had a fattened calf at her house—the word refers to one that was used in treading out the grain and so could not really be spared—and so she prepared this for him (v. 24).

2.2. He showed himself very unwilling to eat: *He refused, and said, I will not eat* (v. 23). If he had labored only under a physical defect, food might have helped him, but he was in such a sad condition that his case was beyond the reach of such help. What can tasty food do for a wounded conscience?

2.3. The woman eventually, with the help of his servants, persuaded him, against his own inclination and resolution, to take some refreshment. Saul was somewhat revived, and so he and his servants *rose up and went away* before it was light (v. 25), so that they might go about their business quickly. Josephus here wonders at Saul's courage and generosity, that although he was assured he would lose both his life and his honor, he still did not desert his army but firmly returned to the camp and was ready to wage war.

CHAPTER 29

In this chapter, we see how David, who kept close to God, was removed and drawn away from his difficulties by God's providence, without any scheming on his part. We have him: 1. Marching with the Philistines (vv. 1–2); objected to by the Philistine commanders (vv. 3–5). 2. Fortunately dismissed by Achish from that service which was so unsuitable for him and which he did not know how to refuse (vv. 6–11).

Verses 1–5

Here is:

1. The great difficulty David was in. The two armies of the Philistines and the Israelites were camped and ready to encounter each other (v. 1). Achish, who had been kind to David, had obliged him to come himself and bring the forces he had into Achish's service. And so David came, and when the army was reviewed, he was with Achish in the position assigned him at the rear (v. 2). Now:

1.1. If, when the armies engaged, he were to withdraw, he would be accused not only of cowardice and treachery but also of intense ingratitude to Achish.

1.2. If, as was expected from him, he were to fight for the Philistines against Israel, he would be thought of as an enemy of the Israel of God and as a traitor to his country. This would make his own people hate him and unanimously oppose his coming to the crown. If Saul were to be killed in this encounter, as it turned out he was, David would be held responsible as if he had killed him. The result was that in either choice there seemed to be both sin and scandal. He had brought this difficulty on himself by his own ill-advised action in leaving the land of Judah. And so although God might justly have left him in this difficulty to rebuke him for his foolishness, yet because his heart was upright with him, God would *not suffer* (allow) *him to be tempted above what he was able, but with the temptation made a way for him to escape* (1Co 10:13).

2. A way provided to rescue him from this difficulty. God inclined the hearts of the Philistine commanders to oppose his fighting in the battle and insist that he be dismissed.

2.1. It was a proper question which they asked when the forces gathered: *What do these Hebrews here?* (v. 3). It was an honorable testimony which Achish gave to David on this occasion. He looked on David as a refugee,

as one who had fled from unjust persecution in his own country and had put himself under his protection, whom he was therefore justly obliged to take care of, and so he thought he would be wise to employ him.

2.2. But the commanders are dogmatic about what they want. He must be sent home:

2.2.1. Because he had been an old enemy of the Philistines, as can be seen from what was sung in honor of his triumphs over them: *Saul slew his thousands, and David his ten thousands* (v. 5).

2.2.2. Because he might be a most dangerous enemy to them and cause them more trouble than all Saul's army could (v. 4): "He may *in the battle be an adversary to us* and surprise us with an attack at the rear."

Verses 6–11

Achish was still only one of five, although he was the chief one and the only one with the title of king, and so in a council of war held on this occasion, he was outvoted and forced to dismiss David, even though he liked him very much.

1. The discharge Achish gave him was very honorable, and he did not dismiss him finally but only from the present service:

1.1. He shows the great pleasure and satisfaction he has taken in him and in dealing with him: *Thou art good in my sight as an angel of God* (v. 9).

1.2. He gives him a testimonial of his good behavior (v. 6). It is detailed and gratifying: "*Thou hast been upright.* You have been reliable, and all your behavior has been *good in my sight*, and *I have not found evil in thee.*"

1.3. He puts all the blame for his dismissal on the commanders, who would not allow him in any way to continue in the camp.

1.4. He orders him to go early, as soon as it is light (v. 10).

2. David's reception of these kind words is courteous but, we fear, not without some degree of hypocrisy. He seemed anxious to serve Achish when really he was now anxious to leave him.

3. God's providence ordered things wisely and graciously for him. The trap was released. Things turned out fortunately so that he could relieve his own town, which needed him desperately, even though he did not know it. And so the disgrace which the Philistine commanders laid on him turned out to be an advantage to him in more ways than one. *The steps of a good man are ordered by the Lord, and he delighteth in his way* (Ps 37:23). We do not now know what God is doing with us, but we will know later, and we will see that everything worked for good.

CHAPTER 30

When David was dismissed from the army of the Philistines, he did not go over to the camp of Israel, but having been expelled by Saul, he observed a clearly neutral position and silently withdrew to his own town of Ziklag, leaving the armies ready to do battle. We are told here: 1. What a sad position he found the town in, devastated by the Amalekites, and what distress it gave him and his men (vv. 1–6). 2. How he inquired of God and received a commission from him (vv. 7–8), pursued the enemy (vv. 9–10), gained information from a straggler (vv. 11–15), attacked and defeated the plunderers (vv. 16–17), and recovered all that they had taken away (vv. 18–20). 3. How he distributed the plunder (vv. 21–31).

Verses 1 – 6

Here we have:

1. The descent which the Amalekites made on Ziklag in David's absence. They surprised the town when it had been left unguarded; they plundered it, burned it, and took all the women and children prisoner and carried them off (vv. 1 – 2). They intended this to be revenge for the similar havoc that David had just brought on them and their country (27:8). Notice in this how wonderfully God inclined the hearts of these Amalekites to carry the women and children away as captives and not to kill them.

2. The confusion and fear David and his men were in when they found their houses in ashes and their wives and children taken into captivity. It had been three days' march from the camp of the Philistines to Ziklag, and when they arrived there tired, they had hoped to find rest in their houses and joy in their families. But instead, they saw a black and dismal scene (v. 3), which made them all, including David, weep, even though they were warriors, *till they had no more power to weep* (v. 4).

3. The complaints and rebellion of David's men against him (v. 6): *David was greatly distressed*, for in the midst of all his losses, his own people spoke of stoning him:

3.1. Because they looked on him as the cause of the disastrous things that had happened, by the way he had provoked the Amalekites and by his indiscretion in leaving Ziklag without a garrison.

3.2. Because they now began to despair of that advancement which they had promised themselves in following David. Before this, they had all hoped to be rulers, and now they found themselves all beggars. Saul had driven David out of his country, the Philistines had driven him out of their camp, the Amalekites had plundered his city, his wives had been taken prisoner, and now to complete his anguish, his own close friends — in whom he trusted, whom he had sheltered, and who had shared his bread — *lifted up the heel against him* (Ps 41:9) and threatened to stone him. Instead, they should have sympathized with him. Great faith must expect to be tested in such extreme ways. Things are sometimes at their worst for the church and people of God just before they begin to turn the corner and get better.

4. David's godly confidence in divine Providence and grace in this distress: *But David encouraged himself in the Lord his God* (v. 6). His men were anxious about their loss. *The soul of all the people was grieved*; the word means "bitter" (v. 6). Their own discontent and impatience added *wormwood and gall* (La 3:19) to the affliction and misery and made their case twice as bitter. But David bore it better, although he had more reason than any of them to mourn it; they gave free rein to their passions, but he set his graces to work and encouraged himself, or found strength, in God. While they discouraged one another, he kept his spirit calm and composed. It was David's practice — and he drew comfort from it — to say, *What time I am afraid I will trust in thee* (Ps 56:3). When he came to the end of his reasoning, he had not come to the end of his faith.

Verses 7 – 20

1. David inquired of the Lord both about his duty — *Shall I pursue after this troop?* — and also about the outcome — *Shall I overtake them?* (v. 8). David did not doubt in the slightest that his war against the Amalekites was just, and his inclination to attack them was strong enough — since his purpose was to recover what was dearest to him in this world — but he still would not go about it without first asking for God's guidance, so acknowledging his dependence on God and his submission to him.

2. David himself went in person and took with him all his forces to pursue the Amalekites (vv. 9 – 10). Notice how quickly the rebellion among the soldiers was quelled by his patience and faith. When they *spoke of stoning him* (v. 6), he could have spoken of hanging them or have ordered the ringleaders of the faction to be immediately beheaded; but although this would have been just, it might have had harmful effects on his interests at this critical point. All his men were willing to go along with him in pursuit of the Amalekites, and he needed them all, but he was forced to exclude a third of them on the way; 200 out of 600 were so weary after their long march that they could not cross the Besor Ravine. This was:

2.1. A great test for David's faith, whether he could go on in dependence on the word of God when so many of his men failed him. When we are disappointed and discouraged in our expectations from circumstances, but go on cheerfully, trusting in divine power, then this gives glory to God, because in so doing we continue to believe in hope against all hope.

2.2. A great example of David's tenderness to his men, that he would not push them beyond their strength, even though the matter was very urgent. The Son of David also knows what his followers are like, that we are not all strong and vigorous in our spiritual activities and conflicts, but where we are weak, he is kind; in fact, even more than that, he is strong (2Co 12:9 – 10).

3. Providence put a person in their way who gave them information about the enemy's movements and guided theirs: a poor Egyptian lad, half dead. Notice:

3.1. His master's cruelty to him. The master had used him for all the service he could, and when the lad fell sick, he cruelly left him to die in the field. Providence was just in making this poor servant, who had been so cruelly treated, instrumental in destroying a whole army of Amalekites, including his master.

3.2. David's compassion on him. Although he had reason to think that the lad was one of those who had helped destroy Ziklag, when he finds him in distress, he still generously gives him some relief, not only with *bread and water* (v. 11) but also with *figs and raisins* (v. 12). Although the Israelites wanted to move quickly and did not have plenty for themselves, they still *delivered one that was drawn unto death*; they would not say that they knew nothing about it (Pr 24:11 – 12).

3.3. The information David received from this poor Egyptian when he had recovered. He gave David an account about his raiding party:

3.3.1. What they had done (v. 14): *We made an invasion . . . .*

3.3.2. Where they had now gone (v. 15). He promised David that he would tell him on the condition that David would spare his life and protect him from his master, who, if he heard from him again, so he thought, would be doubly cruel. This poor Egyptian had such a high opinion of the obligations of an oath that he wanted no greater security for his life than this: *Swear unto me by God*, not by the gods of Egypt or Amalek, but by the one supreme God.

4. David was directed to the place where they were, securely celebrating their triumphs, and he attacked them; and, in accordance with the prayer that he was accustomed to praying, he *saw his desire* (he looked in triumph) *upon his enemies* (Ps 54:7).

4.1. Those who took the plunder were destroyed. The Amalekites had found the plunder to be rich and were celebrating with it (v. 16). David surprised them in the midst of all their revelry, which made the conquest of them and the shock he gave them easier for him and worse for them.

4.2. The plunder was recovered and taken away. Nothing was lost, but a great deal was gained:

4.2.1. They recovered all their own (vv. 18–19): *David rescued his two wives*; this is mentioned particularly, because it pleased David more than all his other achievements.

4.2.2. They also took everything that belonged to the Amalekites (v. 20): *Flocks and herds.* Those who had just spoken of stoning him now praised him, because thanks to him they now gained more than they had earlier lost. This is what makes the world go round.

Verses 21–31

Here is an account of the distribution of the plunder which was taken from the Amalekites. David disposed of the plunder as one who knew that justice and love must rule in the way we use whatever we have in this world. In the distribution of the plunder:

1. David was just and kind to those who stayed with the supplies. He greeted them (v. 21)—literally, "he asked them of peace"—encouraged them to be cheerful, assuring them that they would not lose out by having stayed behind, because it seemed to him, from their faces, that they were afraid of this.

1.1. There were those who opposed giving a share of the plunder to the men who had stayed behind. Some of David's soldiers—probably the same ones who spoke of stoning him—now spoke about defrauding their brothers; they are called *wicked men and men of Belial* (v. 22). These suggested that the 200 men who had stayed with the supplies should be given only their wives and children, but none of the plunder.

1.2. David would not allow this, but ordered that each of those who stayed behind should receive the same amount of plunder as each of those who went into battle (vv. 23–24). God's mercy to us should make us merciful to one another. It was true they had stayed behind, but:

1.2.1. It was not for lack of goodwill to the cause or to their brothers, but because they did not have the strength to keep up with them.

1.2.2. Though they stayed behind on this occasion, they had formerly taken part in many battles and done their part as well as the best of their brothers.

1.2.3. Even now they had done well, for they guarded the supplies, which otherwise might have fallen into the hands of some other enemy. Every position of service does not bring the same honor as every other, but those who are in any way useful to the common interests—even though they have a lowlier position—should share in the common advantages, just as each part of the natural body has its use and so receives its share of nourishment.

2. Having overruled the evil men and troublemakers on this occasion, David also settled the matter for the future. He made it a statute of his kingdom—a statute of distribution in the first year of David's reign, an ordinance of war (v. 25)—that *as his part* (share) *is that goes down to the battle* (v. 24), and risks his life on the battlefield, so will be the share of the one who guards the equipment.

3. David was generous and kind to all his friends. When he had given everyone their own with added interest, there was a considerable amount left over. Probably the plunder of the tents of the Amalekites consisted of much gold and jewels (Jdg 8:24, 26), and he thought it right to make presents of these to his friends, that is, the *elders of Judah* (v. 26). Several places are named here to which he sent these presents, all of them in or near the tribe of Judah. The first place named is *Beth-el*. David sent the first and best there, to those who served the Lord there, for the sake of the One who is first and best. *Hebron* is named last (v. 31), probably because he sent there the last and largest share, considering that place the best for his headquarters (2Sa 2:1). In David's sending these presents, notice:

3.1. His generosity. He did not want to make himself rich but to serve his country. Gracious souls should be generous.

3.2. His gratitude. He sent presents to *all the places where he and his men were wont to haunt* (v. 31), where they roamed. He sent them to everyone he had received kindness from, who had sheltered him and given him information or supplies.

3.3. His godliness. He calls his present *a blessing*, for no present we give to our friends will bring comfort to them except as it is made to do so by the blessing of God. The word suggests that his prayers for them accompanied his presents.

3.4. His good sense. He sent these presents among his compatriots to engage them to be ready to appear for him on his accession to the throne, which he now saw was near.

CHAPTER 31

In this chapter we read about Saul conquered and being worse off than a captive. The very same day, perhaps, that David was triumphing over the Amalekites, the Philistines were triumphing over Saul. One is set against the other, so that we may see what comes of trusting in God and what comes of abandoning him. We left Saul ready to take on the Philistines, with a shaking hand and an aching heart, having had his condemnation read out to him from hell, which he would not consider when it was read out to him from heaven. Let us now see what becomes of him. Here is: 1. His army defeated (v. 1); his three sons killed (v. 2); he himself wounded (v. 3) and killed by his own hand (v. 4). The death of his armor-bearer (v. 5) and all his men (v. 6). His country possessed by the Philistines (v. 7). 2. His camp plundered, and his dead body abandoned (v. 8); his fall triumphed in (v. 9); his body publicly exposed (v. 10) and with difficulty rescued by the men of Jabesh Gilead (vv. 11–13). This concludes the account of the fall of the man who was rejected by God. The first book of Samuel begins with the birth of Samuel, but it ends with the burial of Saul. The comparison of the two teaches us to put the honor that comes from God before any of the honors which this world pretends to have at its disposal.

Verses 1–7

The day of reckoning has now come, in which Saul will go into battle and die (26:10).

1. Saul sees his soldiers fall around him (v. 1). The best of the troops were put into disarray, and many were killed.

2. Saul sees his sons fall before him. The victorious Philistines pressed most forcibly on the king of Israel and those around him. His sons were nearest to him and all three were killed before his eyes. Jonathan—wise, courageous, and good Jonathan—who was as much David's friend as Saul was his enemy, fell with the others. His duty to his father would not allow him to stay at home, or to

withdraw when the armies engaged in battle. If the family must fall, Jonathan, who belonged to it, must also fall with it. God would open up David's way to the crown more clearly. For although Jonathan himself would have gladly resigned all his entitlements, it is still very probable that many of the people would have used his name to support the house of Saul, or at least would only have come round slowly to accept David. If Ish-Bosheth, who was now left at home as one unfit for action, and so escaped, had so many friends, what would Jonathan have been left with, who had been the people's favorite and had never forfeited their favor? This would have made it awkward for David.

3. Saul is badly wounded by the Philistines and then killed by his own hand. The archers struck him (v. 3), so that he could neither fight nor flee, and so he must inevitably fall into their hands.

3.1. He wanted to die at the hands of his own servant rather than at the hands of the Philistines, so they could not abuse him as they had abused Samson. He died as he lived, proud and jealous, and a terror to himself and all around him. Those are really in a deplorable condition who leap into a hell before them to escape a hell within them.

3.2. When his armor-bearer refused to kill him, he became his own executioner. His armor-bearer, having a deep reverence for the king his master, would not run him through, nor could he hurt him in any way.

4. Though he refused to kill his master, Saul's armor-bearer did not refuse to die with him, but *fell likewise upon his sword* (v. 5). The Jews say that Saul's armor-bearer was Doeg.

5. The country was put into such a state of confusion by the defeat of Saul's army that the inhabitants of the neighboring towns "on that side of Jordan," as it might read, left them, and the Philistines possessed the towns for a while, until things settled down in Israel (v. 7).

Verses 8–13

Scripture makes no mention of the souls of Saul and his sons, but only of their bodies. Notice:

1. How the bodies of Saul and his sons were despicably abused by the Philistines. The day after the battle, when they had recovered from their tiredness, they came to take what they wanted from the dead bodies. They found among the rest the bodies of Saul and his three sons (v. 8). Saul might have saved himself the fatal blow and have escaped, for the pursuers, for fear of whom he killed himself, did not come to the place where he was until the next day. When they found Saul's body:

1.1. They cut off his head. They meant it as a general reproach to Israel, who promised themselves that a crowned and an anointed head would save them from the Philistines, and as a special reproach to Saul, who was a head taller than other men—which perhaps he liked to boast of—but was now a head shorter.

1.2. They stripped him of his armor (v. 9), and sent that as a trophy of their victory to be set in the temple of Ashtaroth their goddess (v. 10). We are also told in 1Ch 10:10 that they hung up his head in the temple of Dagon.

1.3. They sent messengers throughout their country and ordered that notice should be publicly given in the temples of their idols of the victory they had gained (v. 9), that public rejoicings might be made and thanks given to their gods.

1.4. They fastened his body and the bodies of his sons (as appears in v. 12) to the wall of *Beth Shan*, a city that lay not far from Gilboa and was very near the River Jordan. The dead bodies were dragged there and hung up in chains, to be consumed by the birds of prey.

2. How the bodies of Saul and his sons were bravely rescued by the men of Jabesh Gilead. Little more than the River Jordan lay between Beth Shan and Jabesh Gilead, and there the Jordan could be crossed by fords. The brave men of that city boldly ventured at night to cross the river, took down the dead bodies, and gave them a decent burial (vv. 11, 13). They did this:

2.1. Out of a common concern for the honor of Israel, or the honor of the land of Israel, which was not to be defiled by the exposing of any dead bodies, and especially the honor of the crown of Israel, which was dishonored in this way by the uncircumcised.

2.2. Out of a particular sense of gratitude to Saul, for his zeal and forwardness in rescuing them from the Ammonites when he first came to the throne (11:1–15). We do not find any general mourning made for the death of Saul; we know only that those Gileadites of Jabesh honored him at his death, for:

2.2.1. They *burnt them*. This may mean that they made a fire around the bodies and added spices, to sweeten them, or it may mean that they actually burned them.

2.2.2. Then they buried the bodies—or if they had actually burned them, then they buried the bones and ashes—under a tamarisk tree, which served as a gravestone and monument.

2.2.3. They *fasted seven days* (v. 13). They mourned the death of Saul and the troubled state of Israel. They may have also added prayers to their fasting for the reestablishment of their ruined state.

A PRACTICAL AND DEVOTIONAL EXPOSITION OF THE BOOK OF

2 Samuel

This book is the history of the reign of King David. In the previous book we had an account of his appointment to the government and his struggles with Saul, which finally ended with the death of his persecutor. This book begins with his accession to the throne and is completely taken up with the matters of his government during the forty years he reigned, and is therefore entitled by the Septuagint (a Greek version of the Old Testament), *The Second Book of the Kings*. It gives us an account of David's triumphs and his troubles. We read of his triumphs over the house of Saul (chs. 1–4), over the Jebusites and Philistines (ch. 5; 21:15–22), at the bringing up of the ark (chs. 6–7), and over the neighboring nations that opposed him (chs. 8–10). Up to now the history fits what we would expect from David's character. But his cloud has a dark side. We read about the cause of his troubles, his sin, in the matter of Uriah (chs. 11–12); and we read of the troubles themselves: those that arose from the sin of Amnon (ch. 13), from the rebellion of Absalom (ch. 14) and of Sheba (ch. 20), from the plague that came on Israel because David counted the people (ch. 24), and from the famine that came on them because of the Gibeonites Saul had killed (21:1–14). We also have David's song (22:1–51), his last words (23:1–7), and a list of his mighty warriors (23:8–39). Many things in this history are very instructive, but regarding the hero it must be confessed that his honor shines brighter in his Psalms than in these historical narratives.

CHAPTER 1

We now look toward the rising sun and ask where David is and what he is doing. In this chapter, we have: 1. News brought to him at Ziklag of the death of Saul and Jonathan; an Amalekite brings it, with details (vv. 1–10). 2. David's sad reception of this news (vv. 11–12); justice done to the messenger, who boasted that he had helped Saul kill himself (vv. 13–16). 3. An elegy which David wrote on this occasion (vv. 17–27).

Verses 1–10

Here is:

1. David settling in again at Ziklag, his own town, after rescuing his family and friends from the hands of the Amalekites (v. 1): he *abode in Ziklag.* There he was ready to receive those who came to share his interests. These were not men in distress and debt, as his first followers were, but people of high caliber in their country, *mighty men, men of war,* and *captains of thousands* (as we find in 1Ch 12:1, 8, 20); such people came to him day by day.

2. Information brought to him there of the death of Saul. It was strange that he did not leave some scouts around Saul's camp to bring him early notice of the outcome of the battle, but the fact that he did not was a sign that he did not want to see the awful day of Saul's destruction, and that he was not impatient to come to the throne.

2.1. The messenger presents himself to David as a runner, acting like one who mourns a deceased ruler and is subject to his successor. He came with his clothes torn and fell to the ground to honor David (v. 2), pleasing himself with the thought that he had the honor of being the first one to respect him as his sovereign in this way, but it turned out he was the first to receive a sentence of death from him as his judge.

2.2. The messenger gives David a general account of the outcome of the battle. He told him very clearly that the army of Israel had been defeated and many had been killed, including Saul and Jonathan (v. 4). He named only Saul and Jonathan because he knew David would be most concerned for their fate, because Saul was the man whom he feared most and Jonathan the man whom he loved most.

2.3. The messenger gives David a more detailed account of the death of Saul. David wants to have a more definite report about Saul and Jonathan than of the battle in general, and so he asks, *How knowest thou that Saul and Jonathan are dead?* (v. 4). In reply to this, the young man tells him the full story, putting it beyond doubt that Saul is dead, for he himself was not only an eyewitness to his death but also instrumental in it. He says nothing in his story about the death of Jonathan, but describes only Saul, thinking—as David understands well enough (4:10)—that he will be made welcome for that and rewarded as one who brings good news.

2.3.1. The account he gives of this matter is very detailed. He said that he happened to go where Saul was (v. 6) and had found him trying to run himself through with his own spear because none of his attendants were willing to do this for him. But Saul's hand and heart both failed him in this attempt, and so he called this stranger over to him (v. 7). When he learned that the stranger was an Amalekite—that he was not one of his subjects or one of his enemies—Saul begged this favor from him (v. 9): *Stand upon me, and slay me.* "Then," the young man said, "*I stood upon him, and slew him*" (v. 10). At this word, he perhaps noticed that David looked at him with some displeasure, and so he excused himself in the next words: "*For I was sure he could not live.*"

2.3.2. It is doubtful whether this story was true. Most interpreters think that it was false, and that although the Amalekite might have happened to be there, he had not assisted in the death of Saul, but rather had given himself that role in his account because he expected that David would reward him for his actions, as one who had served him well.

2.3.3. However, the Amalekite did produce sufficient proof of the death of Saul, the crown from his head and the *bracelet* (band) from his arm. The tradition of the Jews is that this Amalekite was the son of Doeg and that Doeg, who they suppose was Saul's armor-bearer. Before Doeg killed himself, according to this tradition, he gave Saul's symbols of his royalty, his crown and band, to his son and told him to take them to David, to try to gain his favor.

Verses 11–16

Here is:

1. David's reception of this news. Far from being ecstatic, as the Amalekite expected, David was so grieved that he *rent* (tore) *his clothes* (v. 11), *mourned and fasted* (v. 12), not only for his people Israel and his friend Jonathan, but also for his enemy Saul. He did this not only as a man of honor but also as a good man and a man of conscience, who had forgiven the wrongs Saul had done him and who did not hold anything against him. He knew, before his son wrote it (Pr 24:17–18), that if we *rejoice when our enemy falls, the Lord sees it, and it displeases him,* and that *he who is glad at calamities shall not go unpunished* (Pr 17:5). From what he did when he heard about Saul's death, we see that he was by nature very sensitive and that he was kind and tender even toward those who hated him.

2. The reward David gave to the one who brought the news. Instead of promoting him, he put him to death: he judged him by the word of his own mouth, as a murderer of his ruler, and ordered him to be immediately executed as such. David did not act unjustly in this. The man was an Amalekite. So that he would not be mistaken in his story, David made him acknowledge this a second time (v. 13). Moreover, he himself confessed to the crime, so that the evidence was sufficient to convict him according to all laws, for it is assumed that all people give the best impression of themselves that they can. If he had done as he said, he deserved to die for treason (v. 14), having done what he had probably heard Saul's own armor-bearer refuse to do. If he had not done it, then by boasting about it to David he showed what he thought of David: that David was similar in character to him and would himself have gladly committed such an act. This boast was therefore an intolerable insult to the one who had again and again refused to *stretch forth his hand against the Lord's anointed* (1Sa 26:9; etc.).

Verses 17–27

When David had torn his clothes, mourned, wept, and fasted for the death of Saul, one would have thought he would count that as full repayment of the debt of honor he owed to Saul's memory. And yet he did not: here is a poem he wrote on that occasion. He intended by this elegy both to express his own sorrow at this great disaster and to move others to sorrow, since it was fitting that all should take it to heart. Further, those who did not read history could gain information from poems. We have here:

1. The orders David gave with this elegy (v. 18): *He bade them teach the children of Judah the use of the bow.* This may refer to:

1.1. The bow used in war. If so, then in this command David showed his authority over and concern for the armies of Israel and began to put right the errors of the reign of their former ruler, who had recently allowed them to make greater use of slings than of bows. And yet we find that the troops that now came to David at Ziklag were armed with bows (1Ch 12:2).

1.2. A musical instrument called *a bow,* to which the mournful songs were sung, or the elegy itself: "He ordered them to teach the children of Judah *qeshet,* 'The Bow'" (v. 18), that is, this song, which was given that title for the sake of Jonathan's bow, the achievements of which are celebrated here. It is *written in the book of Jasher* (v. 18), kept on record there, and transcribed from there into this history. That book was probably a collection of state poems. What is said elsewhere (Jos 10:13) to be written in that book is also poetic, a fragment of an historical poem.

2. The elegy itself. It is not a divine hymn; it is not given by inspiration of God to be used in his service, nor is God mentioned in it, but it is a human composition, and so was included not in the book of Psalms but in the Book of Jasher, which, because it was only a collection of ordinary poems, has long since been lost. This elegy shows David to have been:

2.1. A man of an excellent spirit, in four things:

2.1.1. He was very generous to Saul, his sworn enemy.

2.1.1.1. He conceals his faults, and although they could not be prevented from appearing in the story of his life, they are not included in this elegy. Love teaches us that in our speech, we should put everyone in the best possible light, and say nothing of those about whom we can say nothing good, especially when they have died. As the Latin puts it, *De mortuis nil nisi bonum,* "Only say good things about the dead."

2.1.1.2. He celebrates what was commendable in him: that he was *anointed with oil* (v. 21), the sacred oil, which was a sign of his advancement to, and qualification for, the government; that he was a man of war, a *mighty man* (vv. 19–21); and that he had often been victorious over the enemies of Israel and *vexed them whithersoever he turned* (1Sa 14:47). Although his sunset was under a cloud, there was a time when his sun had shone brightly. David also noted that with Jonathan, Saul was a man of a gracious disposition, who commended himself to the affections of his subjects (v. 23): *Saul and Jonathan were lovely and pleasant.* Jonathan was always so, and Saul was so as long as they worked together. If you took the two of them together, in pursuit of the enemy, there never were bolder or braver men; they were *swifter than eagles and stronger than lions* (v. 23). They were loving and gracious to each other, Jonathan a dutiful son, Saul an affectionate father, and therefore precious to each other in their lives, and *in their death they were not divided* (v. 23), but kept close together in the stand they made against the Philistines and fell together in the same cause.

2.1.2. He was very grateful to Jonathan. He mourned for what he had been: "*Very pleasant hast thou been unto me* (v. 26), but that closeness has now passed, and *I am distressed for thee*" (v. 26). He had reason to say that Jonathan's love for him was wonderful. There has surely never been anything like it, for a man to love one whom he knew would displace him, and to be so faithful to his rival: Jonathan loved David even though he knew the crown would pass over his head and rest on David's. Notice:

2.1.2.1. That nothing is more delightful in this world than a true friend, who is wise and good, who kindly receives and returns our affection and is faithful to us in what is truly good for us.

2.1.2.2. That nothing is more distressing than the loss of such a friend. It is like having to give up a part of our own selves. The more we love, the more we grieve.

2.1.3. He was deeply concerned for the honor of God. This is what he considers when he fears that *the daughters of the uncircumcised*, those who are not in covenant with God, may exult in their victory over Israel and—they thought—over the God of Israel (v. 20). Good people are touched significantly by those insults that insult God.

2.1.4. He was deeply concerned for the good of the community. It was the glory of Israel that had been killed (v. 19) and the honor of the public that had been disgraced. David hoped God would make him instrumental in recovering those losses, and yet he mourned them.

2.2. A man of a vivid imagination, as well as a wise and holy man.

2.2.1. He wishes he could prohibit the spread of the sad news, and he expresses this wish elegantly: *Tell it not in Gath*. It grieved him deeply to think that it would be made known in the cities of the Philistines.

2.2.2. He curses the mountains of Gilboa, the place where this tragedy has happened: *Let there be no dew upon you, nor fields of offerings* (v. 21). This is the disgrace David brings on the mountains of Gilboa, which having been stained with royal blood lost every right to heavenly dew.

CHAPTER 2

Saul is dead and so now David arises. 1. God directed him to go up to Hebron, and he was anointed king there (vv. 1–4). He gave thanks to the men of Jabesh Gilead for burying Saul (vv. 5–7). 2. Ish-Bosheth, the son of Saul, was set up in opposition to him (vv. 8–11). Hostilities began between David's side and Ish-Bosheth's, in which twelve of each side engaged in hand-to-hand fighting and all were killed (vv. 12–16), and Saul's side was beaten (v. 17). 3. Asahel, on David's side, was killed by Abner (vv. 18–23). 4. Joab, at Abner's request, announced a retreat (vv. 24–28). Abner returned to Mahanaim (v. 29), and the losses on both sides were added up (vv. 30–32). In summary, here is an account of civil war in Israel, which in the course of time ended in the complete settlement of David on the throne.

Verses 1–7

When Saul and Jonathan had died, although David knew he would be anointed as king, he still did not immediately send messengers throughout the territory of Israel to summon all the people to come and swear allegiance to him. Many had come from several tribes to help him while he remained at Ziklag, as we find in 1Ch 12:1–22, and he could have come to the throne and conquered with such a force. But the one who will rule with humility is the one who will not rise with violence. Notice here:

1. The direction David sought and received from God at this critical time (v. 1). He did not doubt he would be

successful, but he still used the right means, both divine and human.

1.1. Acting according to the command, David *acknowledged God in his ways* (Pr 3:6). He inquired of the Lord by the breastpiece, which Abiathar brought him. We must turn to God not only when we are in distress but also when the fortunes of the world are smiling on us and circumstances are working in our favor. He asked, *Shall I go up to any of the cities of Judah?* (v. 1). Although Ziklag lay in ruins, he would not leave it without direction from God. "If I move from here, *shall I go to one of the cities of Judah?*"

1.2. God directed his path, according to the promise (Pr 3:6). He told him to go up to Hebron, a priests' town and one of the cities of refuge. It became a refuge also for David, and God's choice of it suggested that God himself would be a kind of sanctuary for him.

2. The care David took of his family and friends in his move to Hebron:

2.1. He took his wives with him (v. 2), so that just as they had been his companions in difficult times, now too they might be with him in the kingdom. It does not appear that he had any children yet; his first was born in Hebron (3:2).

2.2. He took his friends and followers with him (v. 3). They had accompanied him in his wanderings, and so when he settled, they settled down with him.

3. The honor done for David by the men of Judah: they *anointed him king over the house of Judah* (v. 4). The tribe of Judah had often stood by itself, more often, in fact, than any other of the tribes. In Saul's time it was counted by itself as a distinct body (1Sa 15:4), and the people of this tribe had been used to acting separately. They did so now, but they did it only for themselves; they did not pretend to anoint him king *over all Israel* (as in Jdg 9:22) but only *over the house of Judah* (v. 4). David rose gradually. He was first anointed king, according to God's promise that was still to be fulfilled, which David understood would only be fulfilled when Saul died; then, when he really became king, he at first ruled over only one tribe; and finally he ruled all the tribes. In the same way, the kingdom of the Messiah, the Son of David, is set up gradually. He is Lord of all by divine appointment, but *we see not yet all things put under him* (Heb 2:8).

4. The respectful message David sent to the men of Jabesh Gilead, to express his thanks for their kindness to Saul. He still worked hard to honor the memory of his predecessor, thereby showing that he was far from aiming at the crown from any motives of ambition or enmity toward Saul, and desired it purely because he was called by God to it. "Saul was your lord," David says, "and so you did well to show him this kindness and honor." He prays to God to bless them and reward them for it: *Blessed are you. The Lord show kindness and truth to you* (v. 6). He promises to match their generosity: *I also will requite you* (v. 6). He does not turn them over to God for their reward so that he may excuse himself from rewarding them. Good wishes are good things, and examples of gratitude, but to settle for good wishes when one can do more is cheap.

Verses 8–17

Here is:

1. A rivalry between two kings—David, whom God made king, and Ish-Bosheth, whom Abner made king. One would have thought that David would have come to the throne without any opposition, since all Israel knew how clearly God had appointed him, but there is in the human heart such a spirit of perverseness and of

opposition to the counsels of God, that such a weak and unsuitable person as Ish-Bosheth, who was not thought fit to go with his father to the battle, could be thought fit to succeed him in the government, and so David was not allowed to take over peaceably.

1.1. Abner was the person who set Ish-Bosheth in competition with David. Perhaps he did this out of zeal for the family succession; more likely, he did it out of affection for his own family and relatives—for he was Saul's uncle—and because he had no other way of securing for himself his present position of honor as commander of the army. Ish-Bosheth would never have set himself up if Abner had not set him up, to make him serve his own purposes.

1.2. Mahanaim, the place where Ish-Bosheth first made his claim, was on the other side of the Jordan, where it was thought David had the least influence; because it was far away from his forces, Abner and Ish-Bosheth could take time to strengthen themselves. But they did not need much time: as soon as Ish-Bosheth raised his banner there, the unthinking people of all the tribes of Israel—or most of them—submitted to him (v. 9), and only Judah was wholly on David's side.

2. An encounter between their two armies:

2.1. It does not appear that either side brought all its forces onto the field, for the number of those killed was small (v. 30). It is likely that David would not allow them to act offensively, choosing rather to wait for the obedience of Israel to come by itself, or rather for God to bring it to him, without the shedding of the blood of the Israelites. For now, however, the men of Israel stood neutral and submitted weakly to Ish-Bosheth. They were *wise men, mighty men, men of valour, expert in war*, not doubleminded, and yet for seven straight years most of them seemed not to care who was running the country.

2.2. Abner was the aggressor in this battle. David stayed where he was to see what would happen, but the house of Saul, with Abner at its head, issued the challenge. The battle took place at Gibeon. Abner chose that place because it was in the allotted territory of Benjamin, where Saul had the most friends; yet since Abner issued the challenge, Joab, David's general, would not refuse it, but accepted it and met him *by the pool of Gibeon* (v. 13). Because David's cause was built on God's promise, he did not fear the disadvantages of the ground. The pool between them gave both sides time to think things through. Abner suggested that the encounter be between twelve from one side and twelve from the other, and Joab accepted.

2.2.1. It seems that this began as a sporting trial of skill, as a kind of tournament or duel. Abner made the suggestion (v. 14), *Let the young men arise and play before us*. However, what he really meant was that they should "play" as gladiators. When he said, "Let them *play* before us," he meant, "Let them *fight* before us." Joab, brought up under David, had enough wisdom not to make such a suggestion but not enough determination to resist and contradict it when it was made by someone else; for he stood on a point of honor, thinking it would stain his reputation to refuse a challenge, and so he said, *Let them arise* (v. 14). Twelve from each side were therefore called out as champions to join the battle, a double jury of life and death, and the champions on Abner's side seem to have been most forward, for they took to the field first (v. 15). But:

2.2.2. However it began, it ended in bloodshed (v. 16): they thrust *every man his sword into his fellow's side*, spurred on by honor, not enmity, so they *fell down together*, that is, all twenty-four were killed. The extreme stubbornness on both sides was remembered in the name given to the place: *Helkath-hazzurim*, "the field of rocky men"

(NIV: "field of daggers" or "field of hostilities"), men who were not only strong in body but completely unflinching at the sight of death. The whole army finally became involved, and Abner's forces were defeated (v. 17).

Verses 18–24

We have here the contest between Abner and Asahel. Asahel, the brother of Joab and cousin of David, was one of the main commanders of David's forces and was famous for his swiftness in running: he was *as light of foot as a wild roe* (v. 18). He gained this reputation from his fast running in pursuit, not fast running away. And yet he could not be compared to Abner as a skillful, experienced soldier. Notice:

1. How rash Asahel was in aiming to take Abner prisoner. He pursued him, not anyone else (v. 19). Proud of his relationship with David and Joab, of his own speed, and of the success of his side, the young warrior would not be satisfied with anything less, as a trophy of victory, than Abner himself, either killed or bound. He thought that would put an end to the war and effectively open up the way for David to come to the throne.

2. How generous Abner was in warning him of the danger he was exposing himself to, advising him not to *meddle to his own hurt* (2Ch 25:19).

2.1. He told him to content himself with a lesser target (v. 21).

2.2. He begged him not to make him kill him in his own defense, which he was very reluctant to do, but would do if he had to (v. 22).

3. How fatal Asahel's rashness was to him. He refused to turn aside, thinking that Abner spoke so politely because he feared him, but what happened? As soon as he caught up with Abner, Abner killed him with a backward thrust: *he smote him with the hinder end of his spear*, the butt of his spear (v. 23), which Asahel was not afraid of. When Joab and Abishai came to Asahel, they were infuriated, and they pursued Abner with even greater fury (v. 24) and eventually overtook him about sunset, when they would have had to suspend their pursuit.

Verses 25–32

Here:

1. Abner, conquered, begs for the war to end. He rallied the remainder of his forces at the top of a hill (v. 25), as if he might advance again, but humbly asked Joab for a little breathing space (v. 26). The one who had been most forward in fighting was the first to have enough of it. The one who had joked about bloodshed (*Let the young men arise and play before us*, v. 14) was now shocked to find himself on the losing side. Earlier he had spoken only of playing around with the sword; now he asked, *Shall the sword devour for ever?* (v. 26). Now he appealed to Joab himself concerning the wretched effects of civil war: *Knowest thou not that it will be bitterness in the latter end?* (v. 26). Now he begged Joab to announce a retreat and pleaded that they were brothers who should not be attacking one another. How easy it is for people to use reason when it is to their benefit even though they would not do so if it were to their harm. If Abner had been the conqueror, we would not have seen him complaining about the greed of the sword and the miseries of civil war, nor pleading that both sides were brothers.

2. Although Joab is a conqueror, he generously grants and announces a retreat, knowing very well his master's mind and how averse he is to shedding blood.

3. After the armies had separated, both sides withdrew to the places from which they had come, and both

marched at night, Abner to Mahanaim, on the other side of the Jordan (v. 29), and Joab to Hebron, where David was (v. 32). Asahel's funeral is mentioned here; they buried the others on the battlefield, but he was taken to Bethlehem and buried in the tomb of his father (v. 32).

CHAPTER 3

Here is: 1. The gradual advance of David's interests (v. 1) and the building up of his family (vv. 2–5). 2. Abner's quarrel with Ish-Bosheth and his agreement with David (vv. 6–12); the preliminaries settled (vv. 13–16); Abner's decision and attempt to bring Israel over to David's side (vv. 17–21). 3. The treacherous murder of Abner by Joab while Abner was carrying this out (vv. 22–27); David's great concern and trouble at the death of Abner (vv. 28–39).

Verses 1–6

Here is:

1. The struggle that David had with the house of Saul before his settlement on the throne was complete (v. 1). The length of this war tested the faith and patience of David. The house of Saul became weaker and weaker, lost places, lost soldiers, sank in its reputation, and was defeated in every battle. But the house of David grew stronger. Many deserted the declining cause of Saul's house. The contest between grace and corruption in the hearts of believers, who are only partly sanctified, may well be compared to the struggle recorded here. There is a long war between them, for the flesh desires what is contrary to the Spirit, and the Spirit desires what is contrary to the flesh, but as the work of sanctification goes on, corruption, like the house of Saul, becomes weaker and weaker, while grace, like the house of David, grows stronger and stronger, until we become fully mature, and judgment comes out as victory.

2. The growth of his own house. Here is an account of six sons he had by six different wives in the seven years he reigned at Hebron. David was wrong in having many wives; he acted contrary to the Law (Dt 17:17), and it was a bad example to his successors. We do not read that any of these sons became famous—three of them were infamous, Amnon, Absalom, and Adonijah. His son by Abigail is called *Chileab* (Kileab) (v. 3), whereas in 1Ch 3:1 he is called *Daniel*. The Hebrew teachers explain that his first name was Daniel, meaning "God has judged me," namely, against Nabal, but that David's enemies criticized him and said, "It is Nabal's son, and not David's"; then, they say, as he grew up, he became in his face and features extremely like David, and so he was given the name *Kileab*, which may mean "like his father," or, "his father's picture." Absalom's mother is said to be the daughter of Talmai, king of Geshur, a ruler who followed another religion. Perhaps David had hoped to strengthen his interests in this, but the child of that marriage was one who caused him grief and shame. The last is called *David's wife* (v. 5), and so some think she was Michal, his first and most rightful wife, called here by another name, and although she had no child after she mocked David, she might have had one before.

Verses 7–21

Here:

1. Abner breaks with Ish-Bosheth over a small, ill-advised provocation by Ish-Bosheth.

1.1. Ish-Bosheth accused Abner of no less a crime than sleeping with one of his father's concubines (v. 7).

1.2. Abner resented the accusation very strongly. He let Ish-Bosheth know:

1.2.1. That he despised being rebuked for it by him and would not take criticism from him. Proud people cannot bear being rebuked, especially by those whom they think they have pleased.

1.2.2. That he would certainly take his revenge on him (vv. 9–10). With the greatest arrogance and defiance he let him know that, just as he had raised him up, so he could pull him down again and also that he would do it. Abner's ambition made him zealous for Ish-Bosheth, and now his revenge made him as zealous for David. If he had had a sincere regard for God's promise to David and had acted with that in mind, he would have been steady and constant in his ways.

1.3. If Ish-Bosheth had had the spirit of someone with real strength, especially of a ruler, he might have replied that Abner's faults outweighed his merits and that he would not be served by such an evil man. But he was conscious in himself of his own weakness, and so he did not say a word.

2. Abner negotiates with David. We suppose he began to become tired of Ish-Bosheth's cause and sought an opportunity to desert it. He *sent messengers to David* to tell him that he was at his service. This shows us God can find ways to make useful to the kingdom of Christ those who have no sincere affection for it and who have vigorously set themselves against it. Enemies are sometimes made a footstool, not only to be trodden on but also to rise by. *The earth helped the woman, and the earth opened her mouth, and swallowed up the flood which the dragon cast out of his mouth* (Rev 12:16).

3. David enters into an agreement with Abner on condition that he will gain for him the return of Michal his wife (v. 13). In this:

3.1. David showed the sincerity of his marital affection for his first and most rightful wife, and that neither her marrying another man nor his marrying another woman had lessened his feelings for her. Many waters could not quench that love (SS 8:7).

3.2. David showed his respect for the house of Saul. He could not be pleased with the honors of the throne unless he had Michal, Saul's daughter, to share them with him. This was how far he was from having hate in his heart toward the family of his enemy. Abner sent him word that he must turn to Ish-Bosheth, which he did (v. 14), arguing that he had bought her at a high price and she had been wrongfully taken from him. Ish-Bosheth did not dare deny his demand, but took her from Paltiel, to whom Saul had married her (v. 15), and Abner led her to David, not doubting that he would be doubly welcome when he brought him a wife in one hand and a crown in the other. Her second husband was reluctant to part with her, but there was no way out: he must blame himself, for when he took her he knew that another man had a right to her. In the event that a disagreement has separated husband and wife, if they expect the blessing of God, they should be reconciled and come together again. All previous quarrels should be forgotten and they should live together in love, according to God's holy ordinance for marriage.

4. Abner uses his influence with the elders of Israel to bring them over to David, knowing that whichever way they go, the ordinary people will of course follow. No one can claim greater personal merit than David or claim less merit than Ish-Bosheth. "You have tested both, and the crown should be given to the one who deserves it best. Let David be your king. Since God has promised to save Israel by David's hand, you should submit to him both

from duty and from self-interest: from duty because it is God's will, and from self-interest because through David God will give you victories over your enemies. It would be the most foolish thing in the world to oppose him."

5. David concluded the treaty with Abner. Abner reported to David the feelings of the people and the success of his dealings with them (v. 19). He came now with a retinue of twenty men, and David entertained them with *a feast* (v. 20) as a sign of reconciliation and joy and as a pledge of the agreement between them. It was a feast on a covenant, like that in Ge 26:30.

Verses 22–39

We have here an account of the murder of Abner by Joab, and David's deep anger at it:

1. Joab defiantly clashed with David for negotiating with Abner. Joab was told that Abner had just left (vv. 22–23) and that a great many friendly words and deeds had passed between David and him (vv. 24–25): *What hast thou done?*—as if David was accountable to Joab for what he did—"*Why hast thou sent him away*," when you could have taken him prisoner? He came as a spy and will certainly betray you." We find no record that David answered Joab; if not, then it was not because he feared him, as Ish-Bosheth did Abner (v. 11), but because he scorned his opinion.

2. Joab very treacherously sent for Abner to come back, pretended he wanted to speak with him privately, and cruelly killed him with his own hands. In the phrase, *but David knew it not* (v. 26), there seems to be a hint that Joab used David's name under pretense of giving him some further instructions. Abner innocently returned to Hebron, and when he found Joab waiting for him at the gate, turned aside to him to speak with him, and Joab murdered him there (v. 27). It is intimated (v. 30) that Abishai knew about the plan and aided and abetted in it. Now in this:

2.1. It is certain that God was righteous. Abner had maliciously, and against the convictions of his conscience, opposed David. He had now done evil in deserting and betraying Ish-Bosheth, pretending to show respect to God and Israel while actually motivated by pride, revenge, and eagerness to control.

2.2. It is just as certain, however, that Joab was unrighteous and that he committed evil in what he did. Abner had indeed killed his brother Asahel, and Joab and Abishai pretended that the avenging of his blood was their reason for killing Abner (vv. 27, 30); yet Abner killed Asahel in an open war. Also, Abner had acted in his own defense and not till he had given Asahel fair warning, but Joab here shed *the blood of war in peace* (1Ki 2:5). What made Joab's enmity toward Abner much worse was the motive that lay at the root of it. Joab was now general of David's forces, but if Abner came to have greater influence, he might be promoted above Joab, being a senior officer and more experienced in warfare. Moreover, Joab murdered Abner treacherously, under the pretense of speaking peaceably to him (Dt 27:24). If he had challenged Abner, he would have acted as a soldier, but to assassinate him was villainous and cowardly. Abner was now actually in his master's service, so that in stabbing Abner, he struck at David himself. Finally, by committing the murder at the gate he made it even worse, by declaring it openly to all, as one who was not ashamed.

3. David took the matter deeply to heart and in many ways expressed his loathing at this awful, villainous act:

3.1. He washed his hands from the guilt of Abner's blood. *I and my kingdom are guiltless before the Lord for ever* (v. 28).

3.2. He placed the curse for it on Joab and his family (v. 29): "*Let it rest on the head of Joab.*" A resolute punishment of the murderer himself would have been more consistent with David's character than this passionate invoking of God's judgments on his descendants.

3.3. He called on all around him, even Joab himself, to mourn the death of Abner (v. 31). He did not refer to the times when he could not call him a saint or a good man, but he praised him for what was true, even though he had been his enemy, that he was *a prince and a great man.*

3.3.1. Let them all mourn it. A loss to the community must be a source of grief to everyone, for everyone shares in it. In this way David took care that honor should be done to the memory of a good man, to encourage others.

3.3.2. Let Joab especially mourn it, for though he has less willingness to do it, he has more reason to do it than any of them.

3.4. David himself followed the corpse as chief mourner and made a funeral speech at the grave. He walked behind the bier (v. 31) *and wept at the grave* (v. 32). Because he had been a brave man in the battlefield and might have done great service in guiding the community at this critical time, all former quarrels were forgotten, and David was a true mourner at his death. What he said over the grave brought tears from the eyes of all who were present (vv. 33–34): *Died Abner as a fool dieth?*

3.4.1. He speaks as one who is troubled that Abner was fooled out of his life, deceived by a pretense of friendship, and killed by surprise. Even the wisest and boldest people have no defense against treachery. To see Abner, who thought of himself as the turning point of the great affairs of Israel, made a fool of by an evil rival and suddenly falling as a sacrifice to that rival's ambition and jealousy—this stains the pride of all glory and should make us think less of worldly grandeur. Or:

3.4.2. He speaks as one boasting that Abner did not fool himself out of his life: "*Died Abner as a fool dies?* (v. 33). No; he did not die as a criminal or a traitor." "Died Abner as Nabal died?" This is the rendering of the Septuagint (a Greek version of the Old Testament). Nabal died as he lived, like himself, like a fool, but Abner's fate was such as might have been the fate of the wisest and best person in the world.

3.5. He fasted all that day and would not be persuaded to eat anything until night (v. 35).

3.6. He lamented the fact that he could not safely act justly toward the murderers (v. 39). He was weak, his kingdom had only just been settled, and a little disturbance could overthrow it. Joab's family had great influence and was bold and daring, and to make them his enemies now might have adverse effects. David is content as an individual to leave them to the judgment of God: *The Lord shall reward the doer of evil according to his wickedness* (v. 39). Now this is a lessening of David's greatness and his goodness. He ought to have done his duty and trusted God with the outcome. As the Latin expression puts it, *Fiat justitia, ruat caelum,* "Let justice be done, even though the heavens should fall." If the law had taken its course against Joab, perhaps the murder of Ish-Bosheth, Amnon, and others would have been prevented. It was worldly politics and cruel pity that spared Joab.

CHAPTER 4

Here we see the removal of Ish-Bosheth. 1. Two of his own servants killed him and brought his head to David

(vv. 1–8). 2. David, instead of rewarding them, put them to death for what they had done (vv. 9–12).

Verses 1–8

Here is:

1. The weakness of Saul's house.

1.1. As for Ish-Bosheth, his hands became weak (v. 1). All the strength they ever had came from Abner's support, and now that he was dead, Ish-Bosheth had no courage left in him. He saw himself abandoned by his friends and at the mercy of his enemies.

1.2. As for Mephibosheth, who because of the right of his father Jonathan had a prior entitlement to the throne, his feet were lame and maimed, and he was unfit for any service (v. 4). He was only five years old when his father and grandfather had been killed. When his nurse heard of the Philistines' victory, she was apprehensive that they would immediately aim at her young master, who was now the heir to the crown. She fled with the child in her arms, and because of the truth of the proverb "The more haste, the less speed," she fell with the child. One of his bones was broken or put out of joint in the fall. The bone did not set well, so he was lame for as long as he lived.

2. The murder of Saul's son. We are told here:

2.1. Who the murderers were: *Baanah* and *Rechab* (vv. 2–3). They were brothers, Ish-Bosheth's own servants, employed by him, and this made it even more evil and treacherous that they could cause him such trouble. They were Benjamites, of his own tribe. They were of the city of Beeroth, whose inhabitants, on some occasion or other, perhaps on the death of Saul, withdrew to Gittaim. The Beerothites were there when this was written.

2.2. How the murder was committed (vv. 5–7). Notice:

- Ish-Bosheth was a lazy man. He loved his ease and hated work. When he should have been at the head of his forces on the battlefield at this critical point, or taking the lead as head negotiator in an agreement with David, he was lying on his bed asleep, for his hands were weak (v. 1), and so were his head and heart.
- The treachery of Baanah and Recab. They came into the house pretending to collect supplies of wheat for their troops. The king's granary and his bedroom were close together, and so when they were getting wheat, it was easy to murder him as he lay on his bed.

2.3. The murderers triumphed in what they had done. It was as if they had performed some glorious action: they made a present of Ish-Bosheth's head to David (v. 8). They had no respect either for God or for David's honor. They aimed at nothing except making their own fortunes and gaining advancement at David's court.

Verses 9–12

Here we see justice done on the murderers of Ish-Bosheth:

1. Sentence is passed on them.

1.1. No evidence was needed, because their own tongues witnessed against them. Far from denying the facts, they gloried in them. David therefore showed them that their crime was detestable. Ish-Bosheth was a righteous person; he had neither done them any wrong nor planned to do any. As for himself, David was satisfied that Ish-Bosheth's opposition had arisen from the mistaken idea that he was entitled to the crown and from the influence of others; and so he acknowledged Ish-Bosheth as an honorable person even though he unjustly created a great deal of trouble for him.

1.2. How the crime happened made it worse. To kill him in his own house and on his bed, when he could not offer any opposition, was cruel and treacherous.

1.3. In sentencing them David quoted a precedent (v. 10): he had put to death the one who had brought him the news of the death of Saul, because that messenger thought it would be good news to David.

1.4. Then he confirmed the sentence with an oath (v. 9): *As the Lord liveth, who hath redeemed my soul out of all adversity*. He expressed himself with strong determination, to prevent anyone around him from interceding for the criminals, to show in a godly way that he depended on God to put him in possession of the promised throne, and to show that he would not be indebted to anyone to help him to it by any indirect or unlawful means.

1.5. Finally, he then signed a warrant for the execution of these men (v. 12). If evil men struck Ish-Bosheth, they deserved to die for taking God's work out of his hand.

2. Execution is carried out. The murderers were put to death according to the law, to be a memorial to David's justice. Thus the two murderers were confounded and horridly disappointed. This will also be the fate of those who think they serve the interests of the Son of David by undertaking any immoral practices—war and persecution, fraud and robbery—those who, under the cloak of religion, murder rulers, break solemn contracts, devastate countries, *hate their brethren, and cast them out, and say, Let the Lord be glorified* (Isa 66:5), those who kill their brothers and think they are doing God a good service. However much people may bless such methods of "serving" the church and the Christian cause, Christ will let them know on the great day that true Christianity was not intended to destroy humanity, and that those who think they will deserve a place in heaven for that will not escape the condemnation of hell.

CHAPTER 5

Here: 1. David is anointed king by all the tribes (vv. 1–5). 2. David makes himself master of the stronghold of Zion (vv. 6–10). 3. David builds himself a palace and strengthens himself in his kingdom (vv. 11–12). His children are born after this (vv. 13–16). 4. David is victorious over the Philistines (vv. 17–25).

Verses 1–5

Here is:

1. The humble speech of all the tribes to David, asking him to take on the government and acknowledging him as their king. Judah had submitted to David as their king more than seven years before, and their comfort and happiness under his leadership encouraged the other tribes to ask to join him. We have a full account in 1Ch 12:23–40 of what happened when Israel was unanimous that he should be its king: how many came from each tribe, with what zeal and sincerity they came, and how they were received for three days at Hebron. Here we have the reasons they had for making David king.

1.1. Their relationship to him was some motivation: "*We are thy bone and thy flesh* (v. 1); not only are you our flesh and blood—not a foreigner unqualified by the Law to be king (Dt 17:15)—but also we are yours. You will be as glad as we will be to put an end to this long civil war. You will take pity on us, protect us, and do your best for our welfare." Those who take Christ as their king may also plead in these terms with him: *We are thy bone and thy flesh*, you have made yourself in all things *like unto thy brethren* (Heb 2:17), and so be our ruler and take charge of this heap of ruins" (Isa 3:6).

1.2. His former good services to the community were a further motivation (v. 2).

1.3. The divine appointment was the greatest motivation of all.

2. The public and solemn inauguration of David (v. 3). A general assembly was called; all the elders of Israel came to him; the compact or contract was agreed to and the covenants sworn to, and both sides gave their assent. David committed himself to protect them as their judge in peace and as their commander in war, and they committed themselves to obey him. He *made a league* with them to which God was a witness: it was *before the Lord* (v. 3); and then, for the third time, he was anointed king. His advances had been gradual, so that his faith might be tried and tested and that he might gain experience. His kingdom was therefore a type of the kingdom of the Messiah, which is to gradually reach its culmination, for *we see not yet all things put under him* (Heb 2:8), but we will see it (1Co 15:25).

3. A general account of his reign and age. He was thirty years old when he began to reign upon the death of Saul (v. 4). At that age the Levites were first appointed to begin their service (Nu 4:3). It was at about that age that the Son of David embarked on his public ministry (Lk 3:23). It is then that people reach their full maturity of strength and judgment. He reigned, in all, for forty years and six months, of which seven and a half years were in Hebron and thirty-three years in Jerusalem (v. 5). Hebron had been famous (Jos 14:15). It was a priest's town. But Jerusalem was more so; it was to be the Holy City.

Verses 6–10

If Salem, the place where Melchizedek was king, was Jerusalem—as seems probable from Ps 76:2—it was famous in Abraham's time. Joshua, in his time, found it the chief city of the south part of Canaan (Jos 10:1–3). It came into Benjamin's allotted territory (Jos 18:28) but bordered Judah's (Jos 15:8). The children of Judah had taken it (Jdg 1:8), but the children of Benjamin allowed the Jebusites to live among them (Jdg 1:21), and to multiply so much among them that it became a *city of Jebusites* (Jdg 19:11). Now the very first thing that David did, after he had been anointed king over all Israel, was to take Jerusalem out of the hand of the Jebusites; and because the city belonged to Benjamin, he could not attempt this until that tribe—which had long remained loyal to Saul's house (1Ch 12:29)—submitted to him. Here we have:

1. The Jebusites' defiance of David and his forces. They said, *Except thou take away the blind and the lame, thou shalt not come in hither* (v. 6). They sent David this provocative message because they could not believe that *ever an enemy would enter into the gates of Jerusalem* (La 4:12). They trusted either:

1.1. In the protection of their gods, which David had contemptuously called *the blind and the lame* (v. 6), for *they have eyes and see not* (Jer 5:21), *feet and walk not* (Ps 115:7). Or:

1.2. In the strength of their fortifications, which they thought were naturally or artificially—or both—so impregnable that even the blind and the lame could defend them against the most powerful attacks. They depended especially on the stronghold of Zion, as something that could not be stormed.

2. David's success against the Jebusites. Their pride and arrogance, instead of daunting him, spurred him on, and when he made a general attack, he gave this order to his soldiers: "*He that smiteth the Jebusites, let him also throw down into the gutter* (v. 8), ditch or water shaft, *the lame and the blind*, who are set on the wall to defy us and our God." The Jebusites had said that if their idols did not protect them, they would never again trust or pay homage to those idols. Now David, similarly, after he had captured the fort, said that these idols, which could not protect their worshipers, would not have a place there anymore.

3. David's establishment of his royal seat in Zion. He himself lived in the fort, and around it, from *Millo and inward—Millo* refers to the town hall, statehouse, or supporting terraces—he built houses for his attendants and guards (v. 9). He succeeded in everything he set his hand to, became great in honor, strength, and wealth, more and more honorable in the eyes of his subjects and more and more formidable in the eyes of his enemies, for *the Lord God of hosts was with him* (v. 10).

Verses 11–16

Here:

1. David's royal palace is built, a fitting place for him to receive his court and to be paid homage (v. 11). When Hiram, king of Tyre, a wealthy ruler, sent congratulations to David on his accession to the throne, he offered him carpenters to build a house for him. David gratefully accepted the offer, and Hiram's workers built a house for David to his design. Many have excelled in arts and sciences who have been strangers to the covenants of promise. But David's house was never worse nor less fit to be dedicated to God because it was built by foreigners. It is prophesied of the Gospel church, *The sons of the strangers shall build up thy walls, and their kings shall minister unto thee* (Isa 60:10).

2. David's government is settled and built up (v. 12):

2.1. His kingdom was established; there was nothing to shake it. The One who made him king established him, because he was to be a type of Christ, whom God's hand would sustain.

2.2. His kingdom was exalted in the eyes of both its friends and its enemies. Never had the nation of Israel looked so great or distinguished as it began to look now. God did not make Israel his subjects for his sake, so that he might be great, rich, and authoritarian, but made him their king for their sake, so that he might lead, guide, and protect them.

3. David's family is multiplied and increased. All the sons who were born to him after he came to Jerusalem are mentioned here together, eleven in all, besides the six who had been born to him earlier in Hebron (vv. 2, 5). It is said that he *took more concubines and wives* (v. 13). Shall we praise him for this? No; we cannot praise him or justify his actions, nor can we excuse him. The bad example of the patriarchs may have made him think that there was no harm in it, that he might hope it would strengthen his interests by multiplying his alliances and increasing the royal family. But one vine by the side of the house, with the blessing of God, is enough to send out boughs to the sea and branches to the rivers. Although David had many wives, that did not keep him from coveting his neighbor's wife and dishonoring her, for men who have once broken through that fence will wander endlessly.

Verses 17–25

The particular service for which David was raised up was to *save Israel out of the hand of the Philistines* (3:18). We have here an account of two great victories that David gained over the Philistines, by which he not only made up for the disgrace and recovered the loss Israel had sustained in the battle in which Saul had been killed, but also went a long way toward totally subduing those troublesome neighbors.

1. The Philistines were the aggressors in both of these actions:

1.1. In the first attack they *came up to seek David* (v. 17) because they *heard that he was anointed king over Israel.* They therefore tried to crush his government in its early stages, before it became well established. They gathered together, but were *broken in pieces* (Isa 8:9–10).

1.2. In the second attack they *came up yet again,* hoping to regain what they had lost in the first battle, with their hearts being hardened to their destruction (v. 22).

1.3. In both they *spread themselves in the valley of Rephaim* (v. 22), which lay very near Jerusalem. They hoped to conquer that city before David had completed its fortifications. Their spreading themselves out suggests that they were very numerous.

2. In both actions, although David was willing enough to go out against them, he did not start the action until he had *inquired of the Lord* by the breastpiece (v. 19 and again v. 23). He inquired about two matters:

2.1. His duty: *Shall I go up?* (v. 19). Achish had been kind to him in his distress and had protected him. "Now," David says, "shouldn't I remember that and make peace with them rather than make war with them?" "No," God says, "they are Israel's enemies—*go up.*"

2.2. His success. His conscience asked the former question, *Shall I go up?* His wisdom asked this question, *Wilt thou deliver them into my hand?* (v. 19). He acknowledged here his dependence on God for victory. Yes, God said, *I will doubtless do it* (v. 19). If God sends us, he will support us and stand by us. The assurance God has given us of victory over our spiritual enemies, that he will soon crush Satan under our feet, should encourage us in our spiritual conflicts. David now had a great army at his command, and he was in good heart, but he still relied more on God's promise than on his own forces.

3. In the first of these battles David defeated the army of the Philistines with the sword (v. 20): he *smote them,* and when he had finished:

3.1. He gave his God the glory. He called the place *Baal-perazim,* "the lord who breaks out," because after God had broken in on their forces, he was soon in control.

3.2. He put their gods to shame. They brought the images of their gods onto the battlefield to protect them. They wanted to imitate the Israelites, who brought the ark into their camp. But when they were forced to flee, they could not stay long enough to take their idols away, for they were a *burden to the weary beasts* (Isa 46:1), and so they left them to go with the rest of their possessions into the hands of the conqueror. David and his forces used the rest of the plunder for themselves, but they burned the idols, as God had commanded (Dt 7:5). Bishop Patrick is right to notice here that when the ark fell into the Philistines' hands, it caused destruction, but when these idols fell into the hands of Israel, they could not save themselves from being destroyed.

4. In the second attack, God gave David some physical signs of his presence with him, and he told him not to attack them directly, as he had done before, but to *fetch a compass* (circle around) *behind them* (v. 23).

4.1. God ordered him to draw back, as *Israel stood still to see the salvation of the Lord* (Ex 14:13).

4.2. He promised to attack the enemy himself, by an invisible army of angels (v. 24). "You will hear the *sound of a going,* like the marching of an army in the air, *upon the tops of the mulberry* (NIV: balsam) *trees.*" God's grace

must energize us in our undertakings. The sound of the marching was:

4.2.1. A signal to David to move. It is good to march out when God goes before us. And:

4.2.2. Perhaps a warning call to battle for the enemy, which would confound them. When they heard an army marching toward their front, they quickly retreated and fell into David's army, which lay behind them at their rear.

4.3. The success of this is briefly recorded (v. 25). David observed his orders, waited for God, and then moved, but not until he had heard from God. He struck down the Philistines, even to the borders of their own country. When the kingdom of the Messiah was to be set up, the apostles who were to defeat Satan's kingdom must not attempt anything until they had received the promise of the Spirit, who *came with a sound from heaven as of a rushing mighty wind* (Ac 2:2). The sound of marching in the tops of the trees was a type of the sound of the promised Spirit's coming, and when they heard that, they must move quickly, as they did. They went out conquering and to conquer (Rev 6:2).

CHAPTER 6

Having humbled the Philistines, David here brings the ark to his own city so that it may be near him, to strengthen and adorn his newly founded government. Here is: 1. An attempt to bring the ark. The attempt failed because, although the intention was good (vv. 1–2), the Israelites were guilty of an irreverent act in carrying it on a cart (vv. 3–5). 2. They were punished for that act by the sudden death of Uzzah (vv. 6–7), which brought great fear upon David (vv. 8–9) and put an end to what he was doing (vv. 10–11). 3. The great joy and satisfaction with which the ark was eventually brought into Jerusalem (vv. 12–15); the good understanding between David and his people (vv. 17–19). 4. The uneasiness between David and his wife on that occasion (vv. 16, 20–23). And when we consider that the ark was both the sign of God's presence and a type of Christ, we will see that this story has much to teach us.

Verses 1–5

The ark was kept at Kiriath Jearim immediately after its return from being held captive among the Philistines (1Sa 7:1–2). Once Saul called for it (1Sa 14:18), but otherwise, what in former days had been so significant was neglected for many years. Yet perpetual visibility is not a mark of the true church. God is graciously present with the souls of his people even when they lack the outward signs of his presence. But now that David is settled on the throne, the honor of the ark begins to revive.

1. Honorable mention is here made of the ark. Because it had not been spoken about for a great while, now it is described as *the ark of God whose name is called by the name of the Lord of hosts that dwelleth between the cherubim* (v. 2). Let us learn from this:

1.1. To think and speak highly of God. He is the name above every name, *the Lord of hosts,* the Lord Almighty. He has all creatures in heaven and earth at his command, but he also wishes to sit on his throne between the cherubim, over the atonement cover, graciously revealing himself to his people—who are reconciled to him in a Mediator—and ready to do them good.

1.2. To think and speak honorably of holy ceremonies, which are to us as the ark was to Israel, the sign of God's presence (Mt 28:2) and the means of our fellowship with him (Ps 27:4). Christ is our ark.

2. The movement of the ark is honorably attended. Neglected for many years, now, at David's suggestion, it was sought after (1Ch 13:1–3). All the chosen men of Israel were called together to grace the ceremony, to pay their respects to the ark, and to show their joy at its restoration. Such a noble procession would have helped arouse in the young people of the nation, who perhaps had scarcely heard of the ark, a great respect for it.

3. Here are great expressions of joy at the moving of the ark (v. 5). As secret worship is better the more secret it is, so public worship is better the more public it is. We have reason to be glad when restraints are shaken off and the ark of God is made welcome in the City of David, where it has not only the protection and support, but also the encouragement, of the civil authorities. They joyfully *played before the Lord*. Dr. Lightfoot supposes that David wrote Ps 68 on this occasion, because it begins with that old prayer of Moses at the removal of the ark, *Let God arise, and let his enemies be scattered* (Ps 68:1). Notice is also taken there (Ps 68:25) *of the singers and players on instruments* who attended, and of the princes of several of the tribes (Ps 68:27). Perhaps those words in Ps 68:35, *O God, thou art terrible out of thy holy places*, were added when Uzzah died.

4. Here was an error that they were guilty of, that they carried the ark on a cart or carriage, whereas the priests should have carried it on their shoulders (v. 3). The Kohathites, who had responsibility for the ark, had no carriages assigned to them, because *their service was to bear it upon their shoulders* (Nu 7:9). The ark was not too a heavy load for them to carry between them on their shoulders as far as Mount Zion. They should not have put it on a cart as if it were something ordinary. It was no excuse for them that the Philistines had done this and had not been punished for it. The Philistines did not know any better. Philistines may use a cart to transport the ark and be exempt, but if Israelites do so, they do so at their peril. It did not change matters that it was a new cart. Old or new, it was not what God had appointed.

Verses 6–11

We have here Uzzah struck dead for touching the ark when it was on its journey toward the City of David. This was a very sad event, which dampened their spirits, stopped the progress of the ark, and for the present, dispersed the great assembly, which had come together to accompany it. The event sent them home in shock.

1. Uzzah's offense seems very small. He and his brother Ahio, the sons of Abinadab, in whose house the ark had been kept for a long time, had gotten used to being with it, and they undertook to lead the oxen that pulled the cart in which the ark was carried. This, they perhaps thought, might be the last service they would do for it, for others would be employed with it when it came to the City of David. Ahio went ahead, to clear the way, and if needed, to lead the oxen. Uzzah followed close by the side of the cart. It happened that the oxen shook the ark (v. 6). The commentators do not agree on the meaning of the original word: they "stumbled" is the reading of the margin; they "kicked," according to others, perhaps against the goad with which Uzzah drove them; they "stuck in the mud" is how others understand it. By some accident or other, the ark was in danger of being overthrown. And so Uzzah reached out his hand and took hold of it to prevent it from falling. Uzzah was a Levite, but only priests were allowed to touch the ark. Even the Kohathites, who were to carry the ark by the poles, were explicitly commanded in the

Law that *they must not touch any holy thing, lest they die* (Nu 4:15).

2. Uzzah's punishment for this offense seems very great (v. 7). He was struck dead on the spot. He had sinned there, and so it was there that he died, *by the ark of God*. Even the atonement cover could not save him. Why was God so severe with him?

2.1. The touching of the ark was forbidden to the Levites expressly under pain of death—*lest they die* (Nu 4:15).

2.2. God saw the presumption and irreverence of Uzzah's heart. Perhaps he made a great show before the great assembly. He wanted to show everyone how bold he could be with the ark, having been on familiar terms with it for such a long time.

2.3. David afterward acknowledged that Uzzah died for an irreverent act that they were all guilty of, which was carrying the ark on a cart. But Uzzah was singled out as an example, perhaps because he had been most forward in advising how the ark should be carried.

2.4. By doing this, God would strike awe in the thousands of Israel. He would convince them that the ark was still just as venerable even though it had long been in lowly surroundings. He wanted to teach them to rejoice with trembling (Ps 2:11), and always to treat holy things with reverence and holy fear.

3. David's feelings on the suffering of this blow were intense and perhaps not altogether as they should have been.

3.1. *David was displeased* (v. 8). Literally, "David's anger was kindled." The expression is the same one used for God's displeasure in v. 7. Because God was angry, David was angry and upset. The death of Uzzah did indeed cast a shadow over the glory of the ceremony, but David ought nevertheless to have seen the righteousness and wisdom of God in it, and not to have been angry about it. When we come under God's anger, we must keep our own anger under control.

3.2. He was afraid (v. 9). It seems he was afraid with dismay, for he said, *How shall the ark of the Lord come to me?* He spoke as if God took such extreme care of his ark that there was no dealing with it; and so it would be better for him to keep it far away. He should rather have said, "Let the ark come to me, and I will learn from the warning to treat it more reverently." David therefore would not take the ark into his own city till he was better prepared for its reception (v. 10).

3.3. He took care to mark the remembrance of this blow by a new name he gave to the place: *Perez-uzzah*, "the outbreak against Uzzah" (v. 8). He had just been triumphing over the assault or "outbreak" made on his enemies, and called the place *Baal-perazim*, "a place of outbreaks." But here is an outbreak on his friends. The memory of this blow would serve as a warning to future generations to beware of all rashness and irreverence in dealing with holy things.

3.4. He placed the ark in a good house, the house of Obed-Edom, a Levite, which happened to be near the place where this disaster happened, and there:

3.4.1. It was kindly received and welcomed. It stayed there *three months* (vv. 10–11). Obed-Edom knew what killings the ark had caused among the Philistines and the Bethshemites. He saw Uzzah struck dead for touching it and noticed that David himself was afraid of interfering with it. Nevertheless, he still opened his doors to it without fear, knowing it was *a savour of death unto death* (2Co 2:16) only to those that treated it wrongly.

3.4.2. It paid well the one who showed it hospitality: *The Lord blessed Obed-edom and all his household*

(v. 11). The same hand that had punished Uzzah's proud presumption rewarded Obed-Edom's humble boldness and made the ark to him *a savour of life unto life* (2Co 2:16). No one will suffer loss by receiving the ark as a guest. It is good to live in a family that receives the ark, for all around it will lead better lives because of it.

Verses 12–19

We have here the second attempt to take the ark home to the City of David. This time the attempt was successful, even though the first attempt had failed:

1. The blessing with which the house of Obed-Edom was blessed was evidence that God was reconciled to the people and that his anger was turned away. If God was at peace with them, they could cheerfully continue with their plan. The blessing was also evidence that the ark was not such a burdensome load as it was thought to be, but that, on the contrary, blessed was the person who was near it. Christ is indeed *a stone of stumbling, and a rock of offence* to those who are disobedient, but to those who believe he is a *cornerstone, elect, precious* (1Pe 2:6–8).

2. Let us see how David organized matters now:

2.1. He ordered that those whose business it was to carry the ark on their shoulders should do so. This is implied here (v. 13) and expressed in 1Ch 15:15.

2.2. When they first set out, he offered sacrifices to God (v. 13) to atone for their former errors.

2.3. He himself attended the ceremony with the most intense expressions of joy possible (v. 14): *He danced before the Lord with all his might*; he leaped for joy. His dancing was not artificial, following any particular pattern or rhythm. It was a natural expression of his great joy and delight.

2.4. All the people celebrated as the ark was carried along (v. 15): *They brought it up* into the royal city *with shouting*, and *with sound of trumpet.*

2.5. The ark was safely brought to, and honorably placed in, the tent that had been specially prepared for it (v. 17). They set it in *the midst of the tabernacle*, or tent, which David had pitched for it. As soon as it was placed safely there, he offered burnt offerings and peace offerings (fellowship offerings), in thankfulness to God and to ask God to continue to show his favor to them.

2.6. The people were then sent away with great assurance. He sent them away:

- With a gracious prayer: *He blessed them in the name of the Lord of hosts* (v. 18). By this prayer he showed his concern for their welfare and let them know they had a king who loved them.
- With a generous treat, for this is what the food he gave them was, rather than a distribution of alms to the needy.

Verses 20–23

After David had dismissed the congregation with a blessing, he *returned to bless his household* (v. 20), to offer his family thanksgiving for this national mercy. Never did David return to his house with so much joy and assurance as he did now that the ark was near him, but even this happy day ended with some uneasiness, caused by his wife. Michal was not pleased when he danced before the ark. When he came home, she scolded him. She thought he was degrading himself when he danced before the ark.

1. When Michal saw David in the street, dancing before the Lord, she *despised him in her heart* (v. 16). She thought his great zeal for the ark and the raptures of joy he felt when it came home did not befit such a great soldier, statesman, and monarch as he was.

2. When David came home most joyfully, Michal went out to meet him with her reprimands. Notice:

2.1. How she taunted him (v. 20): "*How glorious was the king of Israel today!* How distinguished you were today in the middle of the crowd!" What made her bitter was his devotion to the ark, but she meanly represented his behavior, in dancing before the ark, as immodest and immoral. We have no reason to think that this was in fact true. David no doubt was proper and controlled his zeal with discretion. To accuse anyone for their godly zeal would have been dishonorable, but to disparage one who had shown such affection for her that he would only accept the crown if she was restored to him (3:13) was evil, and it showed her to be more Saul's daughter than David's wife or Jonathan's sister.

2.2. How he replied to her criticism:

2.2.1. He intended to honor God (v. 21): *It was before the Lord*, and looking to him. However invidiously she had misinterpreted what he had done, his conscience was clear: he sincerely aimed at the glory of God. He reminded her here of the setting aside of her father's house to open up the way for him to come to the throne, so that she might not think herself the best judge of his propriety: "*God chose me before thy father, and appointed me to be ruler over Israel* (v. 21), and even if the expressions of a warm devotion to God were looked on as contemptible and out of place in your father's court, *I will* still *play* (celebrate) *before the Lord* (v. 21), and so restore the respect for such worship in my court.

- If God approves of us in what we do in our religious faith, and we do it as before the Lord, we need not worry about the criticism of other people.
- The more we are attacked for well-doing, the more determined we should be to continue in it, and the more closely we should hold to our faith.

2.2.2. He wanted to humble himself: "I *will be base* (humiliated) *in my own sight* (v. 22). Nothing will be too lowly for me to stoop to do for God's honor."

2.2.3. He did not doubt that his reputation would be enhanced among those whose bad opinion Michal pretended to fear: *Of the maidservants shall I be had in honour* (v. 22). God punished Michal for her bitterness, making her childless forever from that time on. She unjustly rebuked David for his devotion, and so God justly gave her the perpetual rebuke of barrenness. *Those that honour God he will honour*, but those who despise him, his servants, and his service *shall be lightly esteemed* (disdained) (1Sa 2:30).

CHAPTER 7

The ark is still David's concern as well as his joy. Here is: 1. David's consultation with Nathan about building a house for the ark. He disclosed his reason for it (vv. 1–2), which Nathan approved of (v. 3). 2. David's fellowship with God in this. God sent him a gracious message about it (vv. 4–17). 3. The humble prayer which David offered to God in response to that gracious message, thankfully accepting God's promises to him and fervently praying for their fulfillment (vv. 18–29).

Verses 1–3

Here is:

1. David at peace. *He sat in his house* (v. 1), quiet and undisturbed, having no occasion to go to the battlefield.

He had not been long at rest, nor would it be long before he again engaged in war, but for now he enjoyed calm. He enjoyed simply sitting in his house, meditating on the law of God.

2. David's thought of building a temple for the honor of God. He had built a palace for himself and a city for his servants, and now he thought of building a dwelling place for the ark.

2.1. He sees this as a way of expressing his gratitude for the honors God put on him. *What shall I render unto the Lord?* (Ps 116:12).

2.2. He wanted to make the most of the present calm state of affairs and make good use of the rest God had given him. David considered (v. 2) the impressiveness of his own home (*I dwell in a house of cedar*) and compared that with the lowliness of the dwelling place of the ark (*the ark dwells within curtains*). He thought it inconsistent that he should live in a palace while the ark was in a tent. David had been troubled until he found *a place for the ark* (Ps 132:4–5), and now he was troubled because he wanted to find a better place. Gracious, grateful souls cannot enjoy their own homes while they see the church of God in distress and overshadowed. David can take little pleasure in a house of cedar for himself unless the ark is properly housed.

3. David expressing this thought to Nathan the prophet. David discussed the matter with Nathan so that he might know the mind of God through him. There was no doubt that it was a good work, but it was uncertain whether it was the will of God that David should be doing it or not.

4. Nathan's approval of it: *Go, do all that is in thy heart; for the Lord is with thee* (v. 3). Nathan easily understood what was on his heart and told him to go ahead and do what was on his mind. We should do all we can to encourage and further the good plans and intentions of other people. Where we can, we should put in a good word to advance a good work. Nathan spoke this, however, not in God's name but as from himself; not as a prophet but as a wise and good man.

Verses 4–17

Here is a full revelation of God's favor to David, of which God sent him notification and assurance by Nathan the prophet. The intention of the revelation was to dissuade him from building the temple. It was therefore sent:

- By the hand of the same person who had encouraged him to do it, for if it had been sent by any other person, Nathan might have been despised and insulted, and David perplexed.
- The same night, so that Nathan would not continue for long in error nor David have his head filled anymore with thoughts of what he must never bring to pass.

Now in this message:

1. David's intention to build God a house is overruled. God knew about that intention, for he knows what is in human beings, and he was pleased with it, as appears in 1Ki 8:18: *Thou didst well that it was in thy heart.* Nevertheless, he stopped him from continuing with his intention (v. 5): "*Shalt thou build me a house?* No, *thou shalt not* (as it is explained in the parallel reference, 1Ch 17:4). There is another work appointed for you to do, which must be done first." David was a warrior, and he must enlarge the borders of Israel by continuing to make conquests. David was a sweet psalmist, and he must prepare psalms to be used in the temple when it was built, and decide on the shifts of the Levites, but his son's genius

will be more suited to building the house, and he will have more treasure to bear its cost. Let it therefore be reserved for him to do. *As every man hath received the gift, so let him minister* (1Pe 4:10). The building of a temple was to be a work of time, and preparations must be made for it, but it was something that had never been spoken about until now. God tells him:

1.1. That up to that time he had never had a house built for him (v. 6). A tabernacle had been sufficient so far, and it would serve a while longer. God does not consider outward show in his service; his presence was as surely with his people when the ark was in a tent as when it was in a temple. When Christ, like the ark, walked on earth in a tent or tabernacle, he *went about doing good* (Ac 10:38). He did not live in any house of his own until he ascended to heaven above, to his Father's house, and he sat down there. The church, like the ark, has no fixed home in this world. The church remains in a tent because its present state is both pastoral and military; its enduring city is to come. In his psalms David often calls the tabernacle a temple (e.g., Ps 5:7; 27:4; 29:9; 65:4; 138:2), because it fulfilled the intentions of a temple even though it was made only of curtains.

1.2. That he had never given any orders or directions, or the slightest suggestion, to any of the rulers or scepters of Israel, that is, to any of the judges (1Ch 17:6)—for rulers are called *sceptres* (Eze 19:14), and the great Ruler is called this (Nu 24:17)—concerning the building of the temple (v. 7).

2. David is reminded of the great things God has done for him:

2.1. He had raised him from humble and lowly conditions: *He took him from the sheepcote* (pasture) (v. 8).

2.2. He had given him success and victory over his enemies (v. 9): "*I was with thee whithersoever thou wentest,* to protect you when you were pursued, to give you success when you pursued others."

2.3. He had crowned him not only with power and authority in Israel but also with honor and reputation among the nations all around him: *I have made thee a great name* (v. 9).

3. A secure establishment is promised to God's Israel (vv. 10–11). God included this in parenthesis, before the promises he made to David himself, so that David could understand that what God intended to do for him was for Israel's sake, so that they might be happy under his leadership; God also wanted to give him the satisfaction of foreseeing peace for Israel by promising him that he would *see his children's children* (Ps 128:6). Two things are promised:

3.1. A quiet place: they would clearly possess Canaan and not be driven out or attacked.

3.2. A quiet enjoyment of that place: *The children of wickedness*—referring especially to the Philistines, who had for so long caused them so much trouble and oppression—*shall not afflict them any more* (v. 11).

4. Blessings are passed on to the family and descendants of David. David had in mind to build God a house, and in response, God promises to *build him a house* (v. 11).

4.1. Some of these promises relate to Solomon, his immediate successor, and to the royal line of Judah:

4.1.1. That God would advance him to the throne.

4.1.2. That he would settle him on the throne: *I will establish his kingdom* (v. 12), *the throne of his kingdom* (v. 13).

4.1.3. That he would use him in the good work of building the temple, which David had only the satisfaction of wanting: *He shall build a house for my name* (v. 13).

4.1.4. That he would take him into the covenant of adoption (vv. 14–15): *I will be his father, and he shall be my son.* We need nothing more to make us and our families happy than to have God as a Father to us and them. The promise here speaks *as unto sons*:

4.1.4.1. That his Father would correct him when there was occasion, for *what son is he whom the father chasteneth not?* (Heb 12:7). He *will chasten him* with *the stripes* (floggings; literally, "touches") *of the children of men* (v. 14); not a stroke, or wound, but a gentle touch.

4.1.4.2. That he would still not disinherit him (v. 15). The rebellion of the ten tribes from the house of David was a correction for the sin of that house, but the faithfulness of the other two tribes made the mercy of God to David's offspring last forever. Although that family was cut short, it was still not cut off, as the house of Saul was.

4.2. Other promises relate to Christ, who is often called *David* and the *Son of David*, that Son of David to whom these promises pointed and in whom they were fulfilled. He was of the *seed of David* (Ac 13:23). That promise, *I will be his Father, and he shall be my Son,* is explicitly applied to Christ by the writer to the Hebrews (Heb 1:5). The establishing of his house, his throne, and his kingdom *for ever* (v. 13 and twice in v. 16) can be applied to no one except Christ and his kingdom. David's house and kingdom have long since come to an end; it is only the Messiah's kingdom that is everlasting, and *of the increase of his government and peace there shall be no end* (Isa 9:7). Now:

4.2.1. This message Nathan faithfully delivered to David (v. 17), although in forbidding him to build the temple, he contradicted his original response to David (v. 3)

4.2.2. God faithfully fulfilled these promises to David and his offspring in due time.

Verses 18–29

We have here the solemn address David made to God, in response to the gracious message God had sent him. Notice:

1. The place he withdrew to: he *went in before the Lord* (v. 18), that is, into the tabernacle where the ark was, which was the sign of God's presence. He presented himself before that.

2. The position he put himself into: he *sat before the Lord* (v. 18).

2.1. This shows us his posture. Kneeling or standing, however, is certainly the most proper gesture in prayer. We may read the verse as saying, "David went in and took his place before the Lord," assuming that when he prayed, he stood up as was the usual custom. Or he "went in and continued before the Lord": he spent some time silently meditating before he began his prayer, and then remained longer than usual in the tabernacle. Or:

2.2. It may refer to his spiritual attitude at that time: he composed himself before the Lord.

3. The prayer itself, which is full of godly and devout affection toward God:

3.1. He speaks very humbly about himself and his own goodness. So he begins with wonder: *Who am I, O Lord God; and what is my house?* (v. 18). He had lowly thoughts:

3.1.1. Of his personal goodness: *Who am I?* By all accounts, he was a significant and worthy person. His physical and mental endowments were extraordinary. But when he came to speak of himself before God, he said, "*Who am I?* I am a man not worth taking any notice of."

3.1.2. Of the goodness of his family: *What is my house?* His house came from the royal tribe and was descended

from the leader of that tribe, but like Gideon, he thought of his family as poor in Judah and of himself as *the least in his father's house* (Jdg 6:15). All our achievements must be looked on as God's condescensions.

3.2. He speaks very highly and honorably of God's favors to him:

3.2.1. In what he had done for him: "*Thou hast brought me hitherto* (this far) (v. 18), to this place of great dignity and honor. You have helped me so far."

3.2.2. In what he had promised him still further. God had done great things for him already, and yet, as if those had been nothing, he had promised to do much more (v. 19). As God's people in Christ, we must acknowledge concerning this, as David did here:

3.2.2.1. That it is far beyond what we could expect: *Is this the manner of men?* Is this your usual way of dealing with man (v. 19)? That is:

- Can people expect to be dealt with in this way by their Maker? They are brought near to God, bought at a high price, taken into covenant and fellowship with God; could anything so wonderful have ever been thought of?
- Do people usually deal in this way with one another? No; the ways of our God are far above the way in which people usually deal with one another. Although God is high, he has respect for the lowly, and is this what people are like? Although he is offended by us, he pleads with us to be reconciled, is patient to be gracious to us, and multiplies his pardons: is this what people do?

3.2.2.2. That beyond this there is nothing we can want: "*And what can David say more unto thee?*" (v. 20). What more can I ask or wish for? *Thou, Lord, knowest thy servant.* You know what will make me happy. What you have promised is enough to make me happy." The promise of Christ includes everything. What more can we say for ourselves in our prayers than he has said for us in his promises?

3.3. He attributes everything to the free grace of God (v. 21), both the great things he has done for him and the great things he has made known to him.

3.4. He adores the greatness and glory of God (v. 22): *Thou art great, O Lord God! for there is none like thee.* God's gracious condescension to him and the honor he had given him did not in any way lessen his fearful worship for the divine Majesty. The nearer people come to God, the more they see of his glory. The more precious we are in his eyes, the greater he should be in ours.

3.5. He expresses a great respect for the Israel of God (vv. 23–24). As there was none among the gods to be compared with Jehovah, so there was none among the nations that could be compared with Israel, considering:

3.5.1. The works God had done for them. He went to redeem them, turned to do it as something great and fearful. The redemption of Israel, as described here, was a type of our redemption by Christ in that:

- They were redeemed from the nations and their gods, just as we are redeemed from all sin and all conformity to this present world. Christ came to save his people from their sins.
- They were redeemed to be a special people for God, purified and taken to himself, so that he might make a great name for himself and do great things for them.

3.5.2. The covenant he had made with them (v. 24). It was:

- Mutual: "They are to be your people, and you are to be a God to them. All their interests are consecrated to you, and every aspect of your character is committed to them."
- Immutable: "You have confirmed them." The One who makes the covenant makes it sure and will make it good.

3.6. He concludes with humble petitions to God:

3.6.1. He bases his petitions on the message which God has sent him (v. 27). "You have of your own good-will given me the promise that you will build a house for me, or else I could never have found it in my heart to pray such a prayer as this. These things are too great for me to beg, but not too great for you to give."

3.6.2. He rests his faith and hopes for success on the faithfulness of God's promise (v. 28): "*Thou art that God*—you are the One, *that God*, the *Lord of hosts*, the Sovereign Lord and *God of Israel*, the God whose words are true, the God who may be depended on—and *thou hast promised this goodness unto thy servant*, which I am therefore bold to pray for."

3.6.3. He makes that promise the content of his prayer and refers to it as the guide of his prayers:

3.6.3.1. He prays for the fulfilling of God's promise (v. 25). "I desire no more, and I expect no less." This is how we must turn God's promises into prayers, and then they will be fulfilled, for with God, saying and doing are not two things, as they often are with us.

3.6.3.2. He prays for the glorifying of God's name (v. 26): *Let thy name be magnified for ever*. This ought to be the summary and center of all our prayers, the Alpha and the Omega of them. We should begin with *Hallowed be thy name* (Mt 6:9) and end with *Thine is the glory for ever* (Mt 6:13). "Whether I am exalted or not, *let thy name be magnified*."

3.6.3.3. He prays for his house, for the promise has special reference to that:

- That it may be happy (v. 29): *Let it please thee to bless the house of thy servant*.
- That its happiness may last: "May it be *established before thee* (v. 26); let it *continue for ever before thee*" (v. 29). He prayed that none of his family would ever lose the right to the crown, but that they might walk before God, which would mean they would be fully established. He also prayed that his kingdom might reach its perfection in the eternal kingdom of the Messiah. When Christ once and for all sat down at the right hand of God (Heb 10:12) and received every possible assurance that his descendants and throne would be as the days of heaven, this prayer of David the son of Jesse for his offspring was abundantly answered, that it would *continue before God for ever* (v. 29).

CHAPTER 8

David had first sought the kingdom of God (Mt 6:33), establishing the ark as soon as he himself was well established. Now we are given an account: 1. Of his conquests. He triumphed over the Philistines (v. 1), the Moabites (v. 2), the king of Zobah (vv. 3–4), the Arameans (Syrians) (vv. 5–8, 13), and the Edomites (v. 14). 2. Of the gifts that were brought to him and the wealth he gained from the nations he subdued, which he dedicated to God (vv. 9–12). 3. Of his court, the administration of his government (v. 15), and his chief officers (vv. 16–18).

This gives us a general idea of the success and prosperity of David's reign.

Verses 1–8

David now received a commission to make war in order to gain revenge for Israel's grievances against its enemies and recover what was rightfully theirs, for as yet they were not in full possession of the country which the promise of God had entitled them to.

1. David totally subdued the Philistines (v. 1). They had long been oppressive and troublesome to Israel. Saul had gained no ground against them, but David completed Israel's rescue from their hands, which Samson had begun long before (Jdg 13:5). *Metheg-ammah* referred to *Gath*, the chief and royal city of the Philistines, and the towns belonging to it, among which there was a constant garrison kept by the Philistines on the hill of Ammah (2:24), which was *Metheg*, meaning "a bridle" or "curb"—on the people of Israel. David took this out of their hands and used it to gain control over them.

2. David defeated the Moabites, and he subjected them and made them bring tribute to Israel (v. 2). He divided the country into three parts, two of which he destroyed. He spared the third part, however, with its people, so that they might cultivate the ground and become subject to Israel. Balaam's prophecy was now fulfilled, *A sceptre shall arise out of Israel, and shall smite the corners of Moab*. The Moabites continued to bring tribute to Israel until after the death of Ahab (2Ki 3:4–5). They then rebelled and were never conquered again.

3. David struck the Arameans (*Syrians*). They were two separate kingdoms, as we find them described in the title of Ps 60: *Aram-naharaim*, "Syria of the rivers," whose head city was Damascus, which was famous for its rivers (2Ki 5:12); and *Aram-zobah*, which adjoined it but reached to the Euphrates. These were the two northern crowns. David began with the Arameans of Zobah (vv. 3–4). As he went to establish his border at the Euphrates River—for the land granted by divine gift to Abraham and his descendants extended that far (Ge 15:18)—the king of Zobah opposed him, because he was in possession of those countries which by right belonged to Israel, but David defeated his forces and captured his chariots and charioteers.

4. In all these wars:

4.1. David was protected: *The Lord preserved him whithersoever he went* (v. 6).

4.2. David was enriched. He took the gold shields which the servants of Hadadezer had in their custody (v. 7) and a great quantity of bronze from several towns of the Arameans (v. 8), which he was entitled to by the ancient right that the descendants of Abraham had to these countries as an inheritance.

Verses 9–14

Here is:

1. The homage paid to David by the king of Hamath, who it seems was at war with the king of Zobah at that time. When he heard of David's success against his enemy, he sent his own son as ambassador to him (vv. 9–10) to beg his friendship. David lost nothing by taking this insignificant ruler under his protection, for this country gave him, as gifts or gratuities, the same kind of wealth he took as plunder from the countries he conquered: *vessels* (articles) *of silver and gold* (v. 10). It is better to make gains harmoniously than to demand gifts or gratuities under threat.

2. The offering David made to God of the plunder of the nations. He dedicated everything to the Lord (vv. 11–12). This crowned all his victories and made them far surpass Alexander's or Caesar's. They sought their own glory, but David aimed at the glory of God. All the precious things he was master of were dedicated things, that is, they were intended to be used in building the temple. David burned their gold idols (5:21), but he dedicated their gold articles. In the same way, when a soul is conquered by the grace of the Son of David, what stands in opposition to God must be destroyed—every sinful desire must be crucified and put to death—but what may glorify him must be dedicated and its qualities changed.

3. The reputation David gained in a special way from his victory over the Arameans and their allies the Edomites: *He got himself a name.* There was probably something extraordinary in this victory, which honored him very much, but he was careful to give the honor to God.

4. David's success against the Edomites. They all became subject to David (v. 14). The Edomites continued to be subject to the kings of Judah for a long time—as the Moabites were to the kings of Israel—until they rebelled in Jehoram's time (2Ch 21:8), just as Isaac had foretold that Esau would in the course of time throw the oppression from his neck. We see that by his conquests, David:

4.1. Gained peace for his son, so that he might have time to build the temple. And:

4.2. Gained wealth for his son, so that he might have the resources to build the temple. God uses his servants in various ways, some in spiritual battles, others in spiritual buildings. One prepares work for the other, so that God may receive the glory from everything. All David's victories were a type of the success of the Gospel over the kingdom of Satan, in which the Son of David rode out conquering and to conquer (Rev 6:2).

Verses 15–18

David was not so preoccupied in his wars away from home that he neglected the administration of government at home. We see here:

1. That his care reached every part of his dominion: *He reigned over all Israel* (v. 15).

2. That he acted justly, with an unbiased and unshaken hand: *He executed judgment unto all his people* (v. 15). This shows:

2.1. His great diligence in his work and his accessibility—his willingness to be addressed and appealed to by all.

2.2. His impartiality and the fairness of his proceedings in administering justice. See also Ps 72:1–2.

3. That he kept good order and good officers in his court. Because David was the first king to have an established government—for Saul's reign had been short and unsettled—he had to make his administration a model for those to come. In Saul's time we read of no great officer except Abner, who was commander of the army. But David appointed more officers:

3.1. Two military officers: Joab, who was general of the forces on the battlefield, and Benaiah, who was over the Kerethites and Pelethites, who were either the trained company of citizen soldiery ("archers and slingers," according to the Aramaic), or, more likely, the bodyguard of soldiers or the standing force that served the king's person, the praetorian band, the militia. They were ready to do service at home, to help administer justice, and to preserve the peace.

3.2. Two ecclesiastical officers: *Zadok and Ahimelech were priests* (v. 17), that is, they were mainly employed in the priests' work under Abiathar, the high priest.

3.3. Two civil officers. One was the recorder, who reminded the king of business at the proper time. He was prime minister of state, yet not entrusted with the custody of the king's conscience (as they say of our Lord Chancellor) but only of the king's memory. The other officer was the *scribe*, or secretary of state, who drew up public orders and dispatches and recorded the judgments that were given.

3.4. David's sons, who, as they grew up to be qualified for business, were made chief rulers. They were the chief officials who worked at the king's side, as it is explained in 1Ch 18:17, so that they might come under his direction. David made his sons chief rulers, but all believers—Christ's spiritual descendants—are promoted to even higher positions, for they are *made to our God kings and priests* (Rev 1:6).

CHAPTER 9

The only thing recorded in this chapter is the kindness David showed to Jonathan's offspring for his sake. We have here: 1. David's kind inquiry into the welfare of the remnant of Saul's house and his discovery of Mephibosheth (vv. 1–4); David's kind reception of Mephibosheth when he was brought to him (vv. 5–8). 2. David's kind provision for him and his son (vv. 9–13).

Verses 1–8

Here:

1. David asks after the remnants of the ruined house of Saul (v. 1). This was a great while after his accession to the throne, for it seems that Mephibosheth, who was only five years old when Saul died, had now had a son born to him (v. 12). David had forgotten his obligations to Jonathan for too long, but now finally they come to his mind. Notice:

1.1. That he sought an opportunity to do good. *Is there any yet left of the house of Saul, that I may show him kindness?* (v. 3). "Is there anyone to whom I may not only do justice (1Ki 10:9) but also show kindness?" It is the most needy who shout the least.

1.2. That those he inquired after were the remnants of the house of Saul, to whom he wanted to show kindness for Jonathan's sake. He wanted to show kindness to the house of Saul, not only because he trusted God and did not fear what they could do to him, but also because he had a loving character and forgave what they had done to him. We must not be reluctant to show love or goodwill to those who have wronged us much. *But, contrariwise* (on the contrary), *blessing* (1Pe 3:9). This is the way to overcome evil, and to find mercy for ourselves and ours when we or they need it. Jonathan was David's sworn friend, and so he wanted to show kindness to his house. We must conscientiously perform the kindness we have promised even if we are not reminded to do it. God is faithful to us, and so let us not be unfaithful to one another. Although there is not a formal contract of friendship binding us to be faithful in love, there is still a sacred law of friendship that is no less obliging. Compassion and devotion should be shown by a friend to the one who is in misery (Job 6:14). *A brother is born for adversity* (Pr 17:17). Friendship obliges us to remember the families and surviving relatives of those we have loved.

1.3. That he calls the kindness he promises to show them the *kindness of God* (v. 3); not only great kindness, but:

1.3.1. Kindness following from the covenant between him and Jonathan, to which God was witness. See 1Sa 20:42.

1.3.2. Kindness that follows God's example, for we must be merciful as he is merciful. Jonathan's request to David was (1Sa 20:14–15), *"Show me the kindness of the Lord, that I die not,* and do the same to my descendants."

2. Information is given him concerning Mephibosheth, the son of Jonathan. Ziba was an old servant of Saul's family, and he knew the family's circumstances. He told the king that Jonathan's son was living but was *lame* or crippled, and that he lived in obscurity, probably among his mother's relatives in Lo Debar in Gilead on the other side of the Jordan, where he was *forgotten, as a dead man out of mind* (Ps 31:12). We read before about how he came to be lame (4:4).

3. Mephibosheth is brought to court. The king probably sent Ziba to bring him to Jerusalem as quickly as possible (v. 5). In this way, he relieved Makir of his trouble, and perhaps he rewarded him for what he had spent on Mephibosheth's account. This Makir appears to have been a very generous and open-handed person, one who looked after Mephibosheth not out of any disaffection for David or his government but out of compassion for the lowly son of a prince. Later we find him kind to David himself when he fled from Absalom. He is named among those who provided the king with what he wanted at Mahanaim (17:27).

3.1. Mephibosheth presented himself to David. Even though he was lame, *he fell on his face, and did reverence* (v. 6). David had given honor to Mephibosheth's father, Jonathan, when he was heir to the throne (1Sa 20:41, *he bowed himself to him three times*), and now Mephibosheth speaks to him in the same way when the situation is reversed.

3.2. David received him with every possible kindness:

3.2.1. He spoke to him as one surprised, but pleased to see him.

3.2.2. He told him not be afraid: *Fear not* (v. 7). He assured him that he had not sent for him with any bad intentions for him but to show him kindness.

3.2.3. He gives him, by gift from the crown, *all the land of Saul his father,* that is, his paternal estate, which was forfeited by Ish-Bosheth's rebellion and added to his own income. True friendship is generous.

3.2.4. Although he had given him a good estate that was sufficient to maintain him, yet for Jonathan's sake — whom perhaps he saw some resemblance of in Mephibosheth's face — he still wanted to make him a constant guest at his own table, where he would be comfortably fed. Although Mephibosheth was lame and unsightly, and did not appear to have been especially qualified for work, David still took him to be one of his family for his father's sake.

3.3. Mephibosheth accepts this kindness with great humility and self-denial. Notice how he praises David's kindness. It would have been easy to think little of it if he had wanted to.

Verses 9–13

Matters are here settled concerning Mephibosheth:

1. The gift of his father's lands is confirmed to him, and Ziba is called to witness it (v. 9). It seems that Saul had a very substantial estate, fields and vineyards to give (1Sa 22:7). However big it was, Mephibosheth is now master of it all.

2. The management of the estate is committed to Ziba. We will see later how unfaithful Ziba was to

Mephibosheth (16:3). Because David was a type of Christ, his Lord and son, his root and offspring, let his kindness to Mephibosheth serve to demonstrate the kindness and love of God our Savior toward fallen humanity, which he was under no obligation to, as David was to Jonathan. Human beings have been convicted of rebellion against God and, like Saul's house, are under a sentence of rejection from him. We have not only been brought low and made poor but also been made lame and impotent by the Fall. The Son of God inquires about the welfare of this degenerate race and comes to seek and save them. To those who humble themselves before him and commit themselves to him, he restores their lost inheritance; indeed he entitles them to a better paradise than the one that Adam lost. He also takes them into fellowship with himself, sets them with his children at his table, and gives them the feasts of heaven to enjoy.

CHAPTER 10

This chapter gives us an account of a war David had with the Ammonites and their allies the Arameans (Syrians). 1. David sent a friendly delegation to Hanun king of the Ammonites (vv. 1–2). Hanun was evil enough to think that the delegation came with ulterior and base motives, and he mistreated them (vv. 3–4). David was indignant at this (v. 5). 2. The Ammonites prepared for war against him (v. 6). David carried the war into their country and sent Joab and Abishai against them, who applied themselves to the war with a great deal of skill and bravery (vv. 7–12). Both the Ammonites and the Arameans were completely defeated (vv. 13–14). 3. The Aramean forces, which regrouped, were defeated a second time (vv. 15–19).

Verses 1–5

Here is:

1. The great respect David showed his neighbor, the king of the Ammonites (vv. 1–2).

1.1. His motivation for doing this was some kindness he had formerly received from Nahash, the deceased king. He *showed kindness to me,* David said (v. 2). In accordance with his character, when David received kindness, he decided to gratefully repay it.

1.2. The particular way he showed his respect was by sending a delegation to express condolences on the death of the king's father: *David sent to comfort him* (v. 2). It is a comfort to children, when their parents have died, to find that their parents' friends are theirs and that they intend to keep up a friendship with them.

2. The great insult which Hanun king of the Ammonites showed to David's delegation:

2.1. He listened to his nobles' spiteful suggestion that David's ambassadors were only pretending to bring their sympathy and comfort and were actually sent as spies (v. 3). Deceitful people are ready to think others as deceitful as themselves. Bishop Patrick's comment on this is that there is nothing so well intentioned that it could not be misinterpreted, and that those who love no one except themselves are in fact likely to do this.

2.2. Harboring this evil suggestion, he abused the members of David's delegation. He was a man with a corrupt and vicious spirit, one who was more suited to clean out a kennel than wear a crown. They and their reputations were under the special protection of the law of nations; they trusted the Ammonites and came among them without arms, but Hanun treated them like rogues and vagabonds, and worse, *shaved off the one half of their beards, and cut off their garments in the midst* (v. 4), to expose them to the contempt and ridicule of his servants.

3. David's tender concern for his servants who had been mistreated in this way. He sent messengers to meet them. He told them to stay at Jericho, a secluded place, where they would not come into the company of others, until the half of their beards that had been shaved off had grown to such a length that the other half might be trimmed to match (v. 5). The Jews wore their beards long; they considered it honorable to appear more mature and serious. Let us learn not to take unjust insults too much to heart. After a while they will wear off by themselves, and they will shame those who have perpetrated them, while the wronged reputation grows again in a little time, as these beards did. God will *bring forth thy righteousness as the light*, and so *wait patiently for him* (Ps 37:6–7).

Verses 6–14

Here we have:

1. The preparation which the Ammonites made for war (v. 6). They found themselves an unequal match and were forced to hire forces from other nations into their service.

2. The quick descent which David's forces made on them (v. 7). When David heard of their military preparations, he sent Joab with a great army to attack them (v. 7). David was wise enough to take the war into their country and fight them at the entrance to the gate of their capital city, *Rabbah*, as some think, or *Medeba*, a city in their borders, in front of which they had camped to guard their territory (1Ch 19:7).

3. Preparations made on both sides for a battle:

3.1. The enemy was drawn up into two groups, one of Ammonites, who, since the city belonged to them, were positioned at its gate, and the other of Arameans (Syrians), whom they had hired and who were therefore positioned at a distance in the open field. They were to attack the forces of Israel at the side or rear, while the Ammonites attacked them at the front (v. 8).

3.2. As a wise general, Joab divided his forces. He took the best soldiers under his own command to fight the Arameans. He put the rest of the forces under the command of Abishai his brother to fight the Ammonites (v. 10).

4. Joab's speech before the battle (vv. 11–12):

4.1. He wisely arranges matters with Abishai his brother. He supposed the worst, that one of them would be obliged to retreat, and so the two agreed that in that case the division that was retreating would give a signal and the other would send a detachment to relieve it. Christ's soldiers should strengthen one another's hands in their spiritual warfare. The strong must help the weak. Those who through grace are conquerors over temptation must advise, comfort, and pray for those who are tempted. *When thou art converted, strengthen thy brethren* (Lk 22:32).

4.2. He bravely encourages himself, his brother, and the rest of the officers and soldiers. When Joab saw that the vanguard of the battle was facing him both in front and behind, then instead of giving orders to make an honorable retreat, he encouraged his forces to attack even more furiously: *Be of good courage and let us play the men*, let us fight bravely (v. 12), not for pay, promotion, honor, or fame, but *for our people, and for the cities of our God* (v. 12), for the public security and good, in which the glory of God is so concerned. *God and our country* was the watchword.

4.3. He devoutly leaves the outcome to God. When we conscientiously do our duty, we may rest assured and leave the outcome of events with God.

5. The victory Joab gained over the joint forces of the Arameans and the Ammonites (vv. 13–14). First the Arameans were defeated by Joab, and then the Ammonites by Abishai. The Ammonites seem not to have fought at all, but to have fled into the city as soon as the Arameans retreated.

Verses 15–19

Here is:

1. A new attempt by the Arameans to regain their lost honor and to halt the progress of David's victorious army.

2. The defeat of this attempt by the boldness and watchfulness of David. In a pitched battle, he defeated the Arameans (v. 18). Their general was killed in the battle, and David came home triumphantly.

3. The consequences of this victory over the Arameans:

3.1. David gained several vassals. When *the kings*, or secondary rulers, who had been subject to Hadadezer, saw how powerful David was, they wisely *made peace with Israel*, whom they found they could not win a war against, *and served them*, since Israel was able to protect them. In this way, the promise made to Abraham (Ge 15:18) and repeated to Joshua (Jos 1:4), that the borders of Israel would extend to the River Euphrates, was eventually fulfilled.

3.2. The Ammonites lost their old allies: *The Syrians* (Arameans) *feared to help the children of Ammon* (v. 19).

CHAPTER 11

Scripture is faithful in recording the faults even of those people whom it praises most, which is an example of the sincerity of the authors and evidence that it was not written to serve any party. Even such stories as these were written for our learning *(Ro 15:4), so that* he that thinks he stands may take heed lest he fall *(1Co 10:12) and the harm that has come to others may serve as warnings to us. Those sins which we find David guilty of here are very great, and their enormity is emphasized. 1. He committed adultery with Bathsheba, Uriah's wife (vv. 1–5). 2. He tried to get Uriah to seem to be the father of the offspring (vv. 6–13). 3. When that plan failed, he plotted Uriah's death by the sword of the Ammonites and put the plan into effect (vv. 14–25). He married Bathsheba (vv. 26–27). Is this David? Let us who read this account understand what even the best people are when God leaves them to themselves.*

Verses 1–5

Here is:

1. David's glory in following up the war against the Ammonites (v. 1). Their city, Rabbah, made a stand and held out for a long time. Joab laid close siege to this city, and it was at the time of this siege that David fell into sin.

2. David's shame, when he himself was conquered and taken captive by his own sinful lust. The sin he was guilty of was adultery, the violation of the seventh commandment. Notice:

2.1. The conditions which led to this sin:

2.1.1. The neglect of his work. When he should have been far away with his army on the battlefield, fighting the battles of the Lord, he delegated that responsibility to others, and he himself *tarried* (remained) *still at Jerusalem* (v. 1). If he had now been at his position as head of his forces, he would not have been in the place of this temptation. When we are not in the right place to fulfill our responsibilities, we are on the path of temptation.

2.1.2. A love of ease and the indulgence of laziness: *He came off his bed at eveningtide* (v. 2). Idleness gives a great advantage to the tempter. Still waters collect filth. The bed of laziness often turns out to be the bed of lust.

2.1.3. A wandering eye: *He saw a woman washing herself* (v. 2), probably from some ceremonial defilement, according to the Law.

2.2. The steps of the sin. When he saw her, his evil desire of lust was immediately born, and:

2.2.1. He asked who she was (v. 3), perhaps intending only, if she was unmarried, to take her as his wife.

2.2.2. When the sinful desire grew more intense, then even though he was told she was already married, and whose wife she was, he sent messengers for her. Even then, maybe he wanted only to please himself with her company and conversation. But:

2.2.3. When she came, *he lay* (slept) *with her* (v. 4). She agreed all too readily, because he was a great man who was famous for his goodness.

2.3. How he made the sin even worse:

2.3.1. He was now fifty years old at least and he had many wives and concubines of his own (12:8).

2.3.2. Uriah, whom he wronged, was one of his own worthy men. He was risking his life on the battlefield for the honor and security of the king and his kingdom, where the king himself should have been.

2.3.3. Bathsheba, whom he seduced, was a woman of good reputation. A man who commits adultery wrongs and ruins not only his own soul but, as much as he can, another's soul too.

2.3.4. David was a king, whom God had entrusted with the sword of justice and the execution of the law on other criminals, particularly on adulterers. I can think of only one possible mitigating aspect: that it was done only once. It was far from being his practice; he was drawn into it by the surprise of temptation. He was not one of those of whom the prophet complains that *they were as fed horses, neighing every one after his neighbour's wife* (Jer 5:8), but God left him to himself this once. This sin teaches us that we need to pray every day, *Father, in heaven, lead us not into temptation* (Mt 6:13), and that we must watch that we do not enter into it.

Verses 6–13

Uriah had now probably been absent from his wife for some weeks. The situation of his wife would *bring to light the hidden works of darkness* (1Co 4:5), and when he came back, he would find out how he had been abused, and by whom. It might well have been expected that:

- He would prosecute his wife according to the law and have her stoned to death. Bathsheba was apprehensive about this when she sent word to David to let him know she was pregnant, suggesting that he was obligated to protect her.
- Since by law Uriah could not prosecute David for such an offense, he would take revenge another way and raise a rebellion against him. To prevent such double trouble, David sent Uriah home to spend a night or two with his wife, to make it seem that Uriah was the father of the child. Notice:

1. How the plot was made. David called Uriah home from the war under the pretense of wanting an account of *how the war prospered* and how they were getting along in the siege of Rabbah (v. 7). After David had spent as much time with Uriah as he thought necessary to cover up his intentions, he sent him to his home. When that plan failed on the first night—tired from his journey, Uriah preferred sleep to food and spent all night in the guardroom—the next night *he made him drunk* (v. 13). To make a person drunk is very evil, for any reason whatsoever. Robbing a person of their reason is worse than robbing them of their money.

2. How this plot was defeated by Uriah's determination not to sleep in his own bed. "Joab and all of Israel's soldiers are having to rough it out in the open in all sorts of weather, exposed to the enemy. How then can I go home and take things easy and enjoy my wife?" No; he declares he will not do it. Now:

2.1. This was in itself a generous resolution and one which showed Uriah to be a man who was concerned for the whole community. He was bold and strong, and his desire for physical pleasure was under control.

2.2. It could have served to awaken David's conscience and cut him to the heart by making him realize the enormity of what he had done.

Verses 14–27

When David's plan to make it appear that Uriah was the father of the child failed, making it certain that Uriah would eventually find out the wrong that had been done to him, Satan put it into David's heart to remove him. That innocent, brave, and gallant man, who was ready to die for his king's honor, must die by his king's hand. We see here how immoral desires fight against the soul and what devastation they cause in that battle. They blind the eyes, harden the heart, burn the conscience, and deprive people of all sense of honor and justice. After Satan, as a poisonous serpent, had put it into David's heart to murder Uriah, he acted as a subtle serpent to put into his head how to do it.

1. Orders are sent to Joab to put Uriah at the front of the fiercest battle and then to abandon him to the enemy (vv. 14–15). This murder has many terrible aspects.

1.1. It was deliberate.

1.2. He sent the letter by Uriah himself, and surely nothing could be more evil or cruel than this: to make him an accessory to his own death.

1.3. He thought he must take unfair advantage of Uriah's own courage and zeal for his king and country—which deserved the greatest praise and reward—to more easily cause his fate.

1.4. Many had to be involved in the guilt. Joab, the general, together with everyone who withdrew from Uriah when they should rightly have supported him, became guilty of his death.

1.5. Uriah cannot die alone; the soldiers he commands are also in danger of being killed off with him.

1.6. It would be the triumph and joy of the Ammonites, the sworn enemies of God and Israel.

2. Joab carries out these orders. Uriah had the most dangerous position assigned to him in the next attack made on the city, and he was killed in it (vv. 16–17). It was strange that Joab would do such a thing merely because of a letter, without knowing the reason why he should do this. But:

2.1. Perhaps he supposed Uriah had been guilty of a great crime.

2.2. Joab had been guilty of bloodshed, and he was probably pleased to see David himself coming under the same guilt.

3. Joab sends an account of the battle to David. A messenger is immediately sent off with a report of the latest

misfortune and the loss which they had sustained (v. 18). He slyly orders the messenger to soften the blow of the bad news by telling David that Uriah the Hittite is also dead. The messenger delivers this message in the way he has been ordered to (vv. 22–24). His account has the besieged coming out first on the besiegers (*they came out unto us into the field*, v. 23) and then the besiegers boldly doing their part (*we were upon them even to the entering of the gate*, v. 23, we forced them to withdraw hurriedly into the city), and he concludes with the mere mention of the killings of those who were shot at by arrows from the wall: *Some of the king's servants are dead*, particularly *Uriah the Hittite* (v. 24), a noted officer, who was first in the list of those who had been killed.

4. David receives the account with a secret satisfaction (v. 25).

5. David marries Uriah's widow within a short time. She submitted to the ceremony of mourning for her husband for as brief a period as custom would allow (v. 26), and then David took her to his house as his wife, and she bore him a son. The whole *matter of Uriah* (as it is called 1Ki 15:5)—the adultery, deceit, murder, and finally, this marriage—was all displeasing to the Lord. God sees and hates sin in his own people. In fact, the closer people are to God in professing their religious faith, the more displeasing their sins are to him. Let no one therefore encourage themselves in sin from this example of David, for those who sin as he did will also come under God's displeasure as he did.

CHAPTER 12

The previous chapter gave us the account of David's sin; this chapter gives us the account of his repentance. Although he sinned, he was not completely struck down but, by the grace of God, regained his honor and found mercy with God. Here is: 1. His conviction by a message Nathan brought him from God, which was a parable that made him condemn himself (vv. 1–6), and by the application of the parable, in which Nathan accused him of the sin (vv. 7–9) and declared sentence on him (vv. 10–12); his repentance and forgiveness, but with a condition (vv. 13–14). 2. The sickness and death of the child and David's behavior when the child was sick and when he died (vv. 15–23), in both of which David gave evidence of his repentance; the birth of Solomon, and God's gracious message concerning him, in which God showed his reconciliation with David (vv. 24–25). 3. The capture of Rabbah (vv. 26–31), which is mentioned as a further example of the fact that God did not deal with David according to his sins.

Verses 1–14

It seems to have been a great while after David became guilty of adultery with Bathsheba that he was brought to repent of it. When Nathan was sent to him, the child was born (v. 14). What are we to think about David's condition all this time? We may well suppose that his inner peace and worship activities lapsed and his fellowship with God was interrupted. During all that time, it is certain that he wrote no psalms, his harp was out of tune, and his soul was like a tree in winter which has life only in its roots. Let us notice:

1. The messenger God sent to him. He sent a prophet, Nathan, his faithful friend and confidant, to teach and guide him (v. 1). Although God may allow his people to fall into sin, he will not allow them to remain in it. He comes after us before we seek him, or else we would certainly be lost. Nathan was the prophet by whom God had sent him notice of his kind intentions toward him (7:4), and now he sent him this message of wrath by the same hand.

2. The message Nathan gave him:

2.1. Nathan follows a roundabout route and tells a parable, which seems to David to be a complaint made to him against one of his subjects who had wronged his poor neighbor.

2.1.1. Nathan described to David a terrible wrong which a rich man had done to an honest neighbor who was not able to contend with him: *The rich man had many flocks and herds* (v. 2). This poor man had only one lamb, a little ewe lamb, not having the means to buy or keep more. But it was a pet lamb; *it grew up with his children* (v. 3). He was fond of it, and it was with him at all times. The rich man needed a lamb to entertain a friend with, and so he took the poor man's lamb away from him by force and used that (v. 4), either out of greed, because he grudged using his own, or more probably out of indulgence, because he thought the lamb had been so well kept, because it ate and drank like a child. He thought it would surely be more dainty than any of his own and have a better flavor.

2.1.2. In this, Nathan showed David the evil of the sin David had been guilty of in defiling Bathsheba. He had many wives and concubines, whom he kept far away, as rich men keep their flocks in their fields. Marriage is a remedy for sexual immorality, but marrying many is not, for when the law of unity has been broken once, the indulged sinful desire will hardly limit itself. Observe that this evil attitude is called a traveler, for at first this is what it is, but in time, it becomes a guest, and in the end it is lord of the house.

2.1.3. Nathan used this parable to draw from David a sentence against himself. For David thought it was a true story, not doubting its truth when he heard it from Nathan himself, and so immediately declared his judgment against the offender and confirmed it with an oath (vv. 5–6):

2.1.3.1. Because of the rich man's injustice in taking away the lamb, he should pay for the lamb four times over, according to the law (Ex 22:1), *four sheep for a lamb*.

2.1.3.2. Because of the rich man's tyranny and cruelty, and the pleasure he took in mistreating the poor man, he should be put to death.

2.2. Nathan clinches matters with him finally as he applies the parable. In plain terms, "*Thou art the man* (v. 7). You are the one who has done this wrong, and much greater, to your neighbor. Did the one who took his neighbor's lamb deserve to die? And did you not take your neighbor's wife?" He is now speaking directly from God, not as one speaking up for a poor man, but as an ambassador of the great God, who shows no favoritism.

2.2.1. God, through Nathan, reminds David of the great things he has done and has intended for him. He anointed him to be king and preserved the kingdom for him (v. 7). He gave him the house of Israel and Judah. The wealth of the kingdom was at his service, and everybody was willing to please him.

2.2.2. Nathan accuses David of contempt for divine authority in the sins he has been guilty of: *Wherefore hast thou*—taking liberties with your royal dignity and power—*despised the commandment of the Lord?* (v. 9).

2.2.2.1. The murder of Uriah is mentioned twice: "*Thou hast killed Uriah with the sword* (v. 9). *Thou hast slain him with the sword of the children of Ammon* (v. 9), those uncircumcised enemies of God and Israel."

2.2.2.2. His marriage to Bathsheba is similarly mentioned twice, because he thought there was no harm in it (v. 9): *Thou hast taken his wife to be thy wife*; and again in v. 10. In marrying the woman whom he had seduced, and whose husband he had killed, he had insulted the ordinance of marriage by using it to minimize and even in a way sanctify such an evil act.

2.2.3. He informs David that an inheritance of judgment will be passed on to his descendants for this sin (v. 10): *"The sword shall never depart from thy house*, not in your time or later, but for the most part, you and your descendants will be engaged in war." Can mercy and the sword be present next to each other? Yes; people may suffer great and long afflictions but still not be excluded from the grace of the covenant. The reason given is, *Because thou hast despised me* (v. 10). It is threatened particularly:

2.2.3.1. That his children would cause him sorrow: *I will raise up evil against thee out of thy own house* (v. 11).

2.2.3.2. That his wives would be a disgrace to him, that by unparalleled immorality they would be publicly defiled in front of all Israel (vv. 11–12).

2.3. David penitently confesses his sin at this: *I have sinned against the Lord* (v. 13).

2.4. David's pardon is declared after he has repented, but with a condition. When David said *I have sinned* and Nathan realized he had truly repented:

2.4.1. Nathan assured him in God's name that his sin was forgiven: *"The Lord also has put away thy sin* beyond his punishment; *thou shalt not die"* (v. 13), that is, "not die eternally, or be driven away forever from God, as you would have been if you had not put away your sin. *The sword shall not depart from thy house* (v. 10), but:

• "It will not cut you off; you will go to your grave in peace.
• "Although you will be *chastened of the Lord* for all your days, you *shall not be condemned with the world"* (1Co 11:32).

2.4.2. But Nathan declares a sentence of death on the child (v. 14). This is the sovereignty of God; the guilty parent lives, but the guiltless infant dies.

2.4.2.1. By his sin, David had wronged God in his honor; he had *given occasion to the enemies of the Lord to blaspheme* (v. 14), he had made the enemies of the Lord show utter contempt. There is this evil in the scandalous sins of those who profess a religious faith and a relationship with God: they provide the enemies of God and religion with reasons for criticism, contempt, and blasphemy (Ro 2:24).

2.4.2.2. God will vindicate his honor by showing his displeasure against David for this sin and letting the world see that although he loves David, he still hates his sin, and he chooses to show this by the *death of the child* (v. 14).

Verses 15–25

After Nathan had delivered his message, he did not stay at court but went home, probably to pray for David, whom he had preached to. David named one of his sons by Bathsheba *Nathan*, in honor of this prophet (1Ch 3:5), and it was through this son that Christ, the great Prophet, was descended (Lk 3:31). When Nathan withdrew, David probably also withdrew and wrote Ps 51, in which—although he had been assured that his sin was pardoned—he earnestly prayed for forgiveness and mourned his sin deeply, for the time when those who truly repent are ashamed of what they have done is when God is *pacified towards them* (Eze 16:63). Here is:

1. The child's illness: *The Lord struck the child, and it was very sick.*

2. David's humiliation under this sign of God's displeasure and the intercession he made with God for the life of the child (vv. 16–17): *He fasted, and lay all night upon the earth.* This was evidence of the truth of his repentance. For:

2.1. It showed he was willing to bear the shame of his sin. If the child lived, he would be a continual reminder of that sin. Far from wanting the child to die, as most babies do in such circumstances, David prayed earnestly for the child to survive.

2.2. It brought out a more sensitive, compassionate spirit than men usually have toward little children, even their own. This was another sign of a broken and contrite spirit. Those who turn from their sin will be sensitive.

2.3. He revealed in this a great concern for another world. Nathan had told him that the child would definitely die, but while the child was still within the reach of prayer, he fervently interceded with God for him; it may be that his chief prayer was that the child's soul would be safe and blessed in another world, that is, that he would not be worse off in the future state because his father's sin was held against him.

3. The death of the child: it *died on the seventh day* (v. 18), when it was seven days old, and so not circumcised, which David might perhaps interpret as a further sign of God's displeasure—that the child died before it could be brought under the seal of the covenant. But he did not therefore doubt that the child was blessed, for the benefits of the covenant do not depend on the seals.

4. David's wonderful calmness and peace of mind when he understood the child had died. Notice:

4.1. What he did:

4.1.1. He set aside all expressions of sorrow, washed, put on lotions, and called for clean clothes, so that he might come properly before God in his house.

4.1.2. *He went up to the house of the Lord, and worshipped*, as Job did when he heard about the death of his children.

4.1.3. *Then he went to his own house* (v. 20) and ate. He was one who had benefited from his religious faith on the day of suffering.

4.2. The reason he gave for what he did. His servants thought it strange that he should afflict himself so much when the child was ill but take the child's death so easily, and so they asked him why (v. 21). He gave the following reply in answer to their question to explain his behavior:

4.2.1. That while the child was alive he thought it was his responsibility to boldly seek God's favor for the child (v. 22). When our relatives and friends are ill, the prayer of faith has been effective. While there is life there is hope, and while there is hope, there is opportunity for prayer.

4.2.2. That now the child had died, he thought it was his duty to be satisfied with God's decision concerning the child (v. 23): *Now, wherefore* (why) *should I fast?* Two things restrained his grief:

4.2.2.1. *I cannot bring him back again* (v. 23), and again, *He shall not return to me* (v. 23). Those who are dead are beyond the reach of prayer, nor can our tears benefit them.

4.2.2.2. *I shall go to him* (v. 23):

• "I shall go to the grave to him." Consideration of our own death should lessen our sorrow at the death of our relatives.
• "I shall go to heaven to him, to a state of blessedness," which even the Old Testament saints had some

expectation of. This may comfort us when our children are taken from us by death. They are better provided for, both in work and in wealth, than they could have been in this world. We will be with them soon, to be with them forever.

5. The birth of Solomon. Although David's marriage to Bathsheba had displeased the Lord, he was not therefore commanded to divorce her. Bathsheba, no doubt, suffered greatly with a sense of sin and the signs of God's displeasure. But after God had restored to David the joys of his salvation, David comforted her with the same comforts with which he himself had been comforted by God (v. 24).

5.1. In his providence, God gave them a son. They called him *Solomon*, "peaceful," because his birth was a sign of God's being at peace with them, because of the prosperity which was passed on to him by inheritance, and because he was to be a type of Christ, the Prince of Peace. David had very patiently submitted to the will of God in the death of the first child, and now God made up that loss, greatly to his advantage, in the birth of this second child.

5.2. In his grace, he especially acknowledged and favored that son: *The Lord loved him* (vv. 24 and 25) and ordered him, through the prophet Nathan, to be called *Jedidiah*, which means "loved by the Lord."

Verses 26–31

We have here an account of the conquest of Rabbah and other cities of the Ammonites. Although this is included here after the birth of David's child, it is probable that it was carried out some time before, soon after the death of Uriah, perhaps during the days of Bathsheba's mourning for him. Notice:

1. That God was very gracious in giving David this great success against his enemies. It would have been just if the sword of his enemies had been a scourge to David and his kingdom from that time on, but God broke the Ammonites' power and made David's sword victorious, even before he repented, so that this *goodness of God might lead him to repentance* (Ro 2:4).

2. That Joab acted very honestly and honorably, for when he had taken *the city of waters* (v. 27), the royal city where the palace was, and from which the rest of the city was supplied with water—so if that were cut off, the city would be quickly forced to surrender—he sent messengers to David asking him to come himself and complete this great action, so that he, instead of Joab, might be commended for it (vv. 26–28).

3. That David was both too proud and too harsh on this occasion, nor as humble or as tender as he should have been.

3.1. He seems to have been too fond of the crown of the king of Ammon (v. 30). Because it was set with precious stones, it was unusually valuable, and David wanted to place it on his head, although it would have been better to lay it at God's feet, and then put his own mouth in the dust because of his guilt.

3.2. He seems to have been too harsh with his prisoners of war (v. 31). When he took the city by storm after it had stubbornly held out against a long and expensive siege, if he had killed all whom he found bearing arms in the heat of battle, it would have been harsh enough; but to kill them afterward in cold blood, and by cruel torture, tearing them to pieces with saws and iron picks, did not befit one who, when he began to rule, promised to sing of mercy as well as judgment (Ps 101:1).*

CHAPTER 13

The righteous God had just told David through Nathan the prophet that in order to discipline him for his sin in the incident with Uriah, he would raise up evil *(calamity)* against him out of his own house *(12:11). And here we find the calamity beginning. From now on he was pursued by one trouble after another. David's sins were adultery and murder, and those sins among his children—Amnon raping his sister Tamar, and Absalom murdering his brother Amnon—were the beginnings of his punishment. We have in this chapter: 1. Amnon outrageously raping Tamar, helped in this plot by Jonadab his relative (vv. 1–20). 2. Absalom murdering Amnon for it (vv. 21–39). Both caused great sorrow for David, even more so because he was unwittingly made an accessory in both, by sending Tamar to Amnon and Amnon to Absalom.*

Verses 1–20

Here is a detailed account of Amnon's detestable evil in raping his sister. We have reason to think that Amnon's character was bad in other things. If he had not abandoned God, he would never have given in to these sinful desires.

1. Satan, as an unclean spirit, put it into his heart to lust after his sister Tamar. Beauty is a trap to many, and it proved so to her. Amnon's lust was:

1.1. Unnatural in itself. Even a natural, unregenerate conscience is shocked at the thought of such a sin; yet there is such a perverse spirit in corrupt human nature that it still desires forbidden fruit, and the more strongly it is forbidden, the more intensely it is desired.

1.2. Frustrating for him. He was so obsessed because he could not find an opportunity to seduce her that he *fell sick* (v. 2).

2. Satan, as a subtle serpent, put it into his head how to devise this evil plan. Amnon had a friend, a crafty man, who was cunning in carrying out an intrigue like this (v. 3).

2.1. This "friend" saw that Amnon looked ill and, being crafty, concluded that he was lovesick (v. 4). And so he asked him, "*Why art thou, being the king's son, lean* (so haggard)? *Being the king's son,* you have the power of a prince to command what you want and wish for. Go on, then, and use that power to satisfy your desires."

2.2. Amnon had the audacity to acknowledge his sinful lust, wrongly calling it *love* (*I love Tamar,* v. 4), and Jonadab suggested a plan to him (v. 5). Amnon was already lovesick, but he could move around. He must pretend to be so ill that he could not even get up. The best dishes from the king's table could not please him, but if he were to eat anything, then it must come from his sister Tamar's fair hand.

2.3. Amnon follows these directions and so brings Tamar within his reach. David was always fond of his children and became concerned when anything upset them. No sooner does he hear that Amnon is sick than he himself comes to visit him. When he leaves, the indulgent father asks, "Is there anything you want, that I can get for you?" "Yes, there is," says the deceiving son. "My stomach is weak, and I can't eat anything I can eat except for the special bread that my sister Tamar makes. If only I could watch her make it, then I know that would help me get better, and it will do me more good if I can eat it from her hand." David sees no reason to suspect that any trouble has been planned. He therefore immediately orders Tamar to go to be with her sick brother (v. 7).

---

*It is now generally accepted that the text does not imply that the people were tortured but that they were consigned to forced labor. [Ed.]

2.4. Having gotten her to be with him, Amnon manages to have her alone. Tamar does not have the slightest idea of what his defiled heart is full of, and so she does not hesitate to be alone with him *in the inner chamber* (v. 10). The mask is now thrown off, the food is thrown aside, and the evil wretch calls her *my sister*, but shamelessly cajoles her to *come and lie* (come to bed) *with him* (v. 11).

3. Satan, as a strong tempter, deafens his ear to all the reasons with which she resists his attacks and tries to persuade him to stop.

3.1. She calls him *my brother*, reminding him of the closeness of their relationship, which made it illegal for him to marry her, much less rape her. It was expressly forbidden (Lev 18:9) under a severe penalty (Lev 20:17).

3.2. She begs him not to rape her, which shows she never would agree to it under any circumstances.

3.3. She tells him how evil it would be.

3.4. She describes to him the disgrace of such an act: "*Whither shall I cause my shame to go* (v. 13), where could I get rid of my disgrace?"

3.5. To divert him from his dishonorable intentions, she suggests to him that the king would probably set aside the divine law and allow him to marry her, rather than see him die for love of her. It was not as if she thought David had such powers, or would pretend to have them, but she was confident that if Amnon himself told the king of his evil intentions, the king would take effective measures to protect her from him. But all her skill and all her arguments have no effect. His proud spirit cannot bear a refusal, and her honor, and all that was dear to her, must be sacrificed to his outrageous lust (v. 14). It is to be feared that although Amnon was only young, he had lived a lewd life for a long time, for a man could not suddenly come to such an extreme intensity of evil.

4. Satan, as a tormentor and betrayer, immediately turns her love of her into hatred (v. 15).

4.1. Amnon cruelly and forcefully turned her out of doors. To dismiss her so hurriedly and rudely, as if *she* had done something evil, left her no time to compose herself and thus forced her to defend herself and declare the wrong. We may learn from this the troublesome effects of sin: it bites like a snake. Sins which are sweet when committed become disgusting and painful later, and the sinner's own conscience makes them so. But to hate the person he had defiled showed that his conscience was terrified, but his heart was not humbled at all.

4.2. What becomes of the poor victim?

4.2.1. She bitterly mourned the injury she had received, as it was a stain on her honor, although her morality was not at fault. She tore her fine clothes as a sign of her sorrow and put ashes on her head, loathing her own beauty and splendor, because they had caused Amnon's unlawful love; and she went away crying because of the sin of another (v. 19).

4.2.2. She withdrew to her brother Absalom's house, because he was her own brother, and she lived there in solitude and sorrow, as a sign of her modesty and her loathing of her uncleanness. Absalom spoke kindly to her, told her to try not to take the matter to heart for the present, intending that he himself would avenge it (v. 20).

Verses 21–29

What Solomon says of the *beginning of strife* is as true of the beginning of all sin: it is like *the letting forth of water*. One trouble causes another. We are told:

1. How David was angry at the news of Amnon's sin. But was it enough that he was angry? He should have punished his son for it and disgraced him openly.

2. How Absalom was angry at it. He decided he would begin already now to play the part of judge in Israel, and since his father would not punish Amnon, he would, though from a motive of justice or zeal for virtue, but of revenge, because he reckoned himself insulted by the abuse of his sister. Here is:

2.1. The plan conceived: *Absalom hated Amnon* (v. 22). Absalom's hatred of his brother's crime would have been commendable, and he might justly have accused him of it by the due process of law, as an example to others, and have sought to gain some compensation for his wronged sister, but to hate his person and to want to assassinate him was an outrageous attack on God. He was offering to repair a violation of the seventh commandment by breaking the sixth, as if they were not all to the same extent sacred. *But he that said, Do not commit adultery, said also, Do not kill* (Jas 2:11).

2.2. The plan concealed. He said nothing to Amnon. If Absalom had reasoned the matter out with Amnon, he might have convinced him of his sin and brought him to repentance. Instead Absalom harbored this root of bitterness for two full years (v. 24). Perhaps at first he did not want to kill his brother, and was only waiting for an occasion to shame him or cause him some other trouble, but in time his hatred developed, and he wanted nothing less than his death.

2.3. The plan set up:

2.3.1. Absalom holds a feast at his house in the country, as Nabal did, on the occasion of his sheepshearing (v. 23).

2.3.2. He invites the king his father and all the officials to this feast (v. 24) so that he may make himself more respected among his neighbors. The king himself would not go, because he did not want to put Absalom to the expense of entertaining him (v. 25). However, Absalom gained permission for Amnon, and all the rest of the king's sons, to come and grace his table in the country (vv. 26–27). Absalom had been so successful in hiding his enmity toward Amnon that David saw no reason to suspect that there was any malicious plan against him behind that particular invitation.

2.4. The plan put into action (vv. 28–29):

2.4.1. Absalom's entertainment was lavish, for he decided that they would all get into high spirits with wine. But:

2.4.2. The orders he gave to his servants about Amnon, that they should mix his blood with his wine, were very cruel. He wanted Amnon to be killed *when his heart was merry with wine* (v. 28), not giving him time to say, *Lord, have mercy upon me.* His servants must commit the act and so be involved in the guilt. He was to give the word of command, *Smite Amnon*, and then they must *kill him.* He did it in the presence of *all the king's sons*, of whom it is said (8:18) that they were *chief rulers* (royal advisers), so that it was an attack on the justice of the community and also an attack on the king his father, whom they represented. There is reason to suspect that Absalom did this not only to take revenge on Amnon for raping his sister, but also to make the way clear for him to come to the throne, which he was ambitious to do and which he would be in a favorable position to do if Amnon, the eldest son, was removed. When the command was given, Absalom's servants did not fail to execute it, being buoyed up by a confidence that because their master was next in line to the throne after Amnon, he would save them from danger. The sword God had threatened had now been wielded in David's family and would not leave it.

• His eldest son falls by the sword.

• All his sons flee from the sword and come home in terror, not knowing how far their brother Absalom's bloody intentions might reach.

Verses 30–39

Here is:

1. The shock which gripped David because of the false report that was brought to Jerusalem that Absalom had *slain all the king's sons* (v. 30). This false news troubled David as much, when it first came, as if it had been true.

2. The mistake put right in two ways:

2.1. By the report of the crafty Jonadab, David's nephew, who told him, *Amnon only is dead*, not all the king's sons (vv. 32–33). He also told him that the killing had been authorized by Absalom and that this had been Absalom's intention since the day Amnon had raped his sister Tamar. At least Jonadab was not as guilty of Amnon's death as he was of Amnon's sin. This is what happens if we listen to the evil advice of so-called friends. The one who would not try to prevent Amnon's sin would not try to prevent his death, even though it seems he could have done both.

2.2. By the safe return of all the king's sons except Amnon. They confirmed the sad news that Absalom had murdered their brother Amnon. The fact that Amnon was dead, treacherously and cruelly killed by his own brother, was enough to put the king and court, the king and kingdom, into a state of real mourning. Sorrow is an especially fitting response when sin is involved.

3. Absalom running away from justice. He was now as afraid of the king's sons as they were of him. They ran from his hatred; he ran from their justice. No part of the land of Israel would shelter him. He therefore decided the best thing to do was to go to his mother's relatives, and he was received by his grandfather *Talmai, king of Geshur* (v. 37). He was protected there for *three years* (v. 38).

4. David's unease at Absalom's absence. He mourned for Amnon a good while (v. 37), but time wore off his loathing of Absalom's sin. Instead of hating him as a murderer, *he longed to go* to him (v. 39).

CHAPTER 14

We read in the previous chapter how Absalom disqualified himself from his royal father's protection and favor. In this chapter we read of how he and his father were eventually brought together again, which is recorded here to show David's foolishness in sparing him and indulging him in his evil, a foolishness for which David was soon after severely rebuked by Absalom's unusual conspiracy. 1. Joab brings before David for trial a spurious case involving a poor widow from Tekoa. In gaining from David the judgment he wants, he gets David to concede that in certain cases the death penalty against a murderer may be set aside (vv. 1–20). 2. When this case is applied, he gains from him an order to bring Absalom back to Jerusalem, though David forbids him from coming to court (vv. 21–24). 3. Absalom was finally introduced by Joab into the king's presence, and the king was completely reconciled to him (vv. 25–33).

Verses 1–20

Here is:

1. Joab's intention to get Absalom recalled from exile. Joab was active in this:

1.1. As a courtier. Joab saw how David felt and undertook to do this work.

1.2. As a friend of Absalom. He clearly foresaw that Absalom's father would eventually be reconciled to him, and so he wanted to make both of them his friends; and he thought he would be able to do that if he could be instrumental in bringing that reconciliation about.

1.3. As a statesman and one concerned for the good of the whole country. He knew how much Absalom was the people's favorite, and that if David should die while Absalom was in exile, it might cause a civil war, for although all Israel probably loved him as a person, they were still very much divided in their views about what he had done.

1.4. As one who had himself offended by murdering Abner. If he could gain Absalom's goodwill, it would help his return to a high position.

2. Joab's plan to do this by placing something rather like a parallel case before the king so skillfully that the king thought it was a real case and gave his verdict on it, as he had done with Nathan's parable.

2.1. The person he used is not named, but she is said to be *a woman of Tekoah* (v. 4). It is said that she was *a wise woman*, one with a keener understanding and a readier tongue than most of her neighbors (v. 2). The truth of the story would be less suspicious if it came, as was supposed, from the person's own mouth.

2.2. The role she assumed was that of a sad widow (v. 2). Joab knew that such a person would have easy access to the king. He was always ready to comfort mourners.

2.3. It was a case for compassion which she had to present to the king, since the judgment of all subordinate courts was against her. She told the king that she had buried her husband (v. 5)—that she had two sons who supported and comforted her in her widowed state—that these two had fallen out and fought, and that one of them had unfortunately killed the other (v. 6). For her part, she wanted to protect the manslayer, but the other relatives still insisted that the surviving brother should be put to death according to the law, so that by destroying the heir, they might receive the inheritance (v. 7). If that happened, they would destroy:

2.3.1. Her comfort: *"They shall quench my coal*, put out the only burning coal I have left (v. 7), deprive me of my only means of support in old age, and put an end to all my joy in this world."

2.3.2. Her husband's memory: "His family will die out, and they will *leave* him *neither name nor remainder* (descendant)" (v. 7).

2.4. The king promised her his favor and protection for her son:

2.4.1. On the basis of her testimony he promised to consider her case and give orders about it (v. 8).

2.4.2. The woman was not content with this, but begged that he would immediately give a judgment in her favor.

2.4.3. When he was further pressed, he made an additional promise that she would not be injured or wronged by her adversaries, but he would protect her from all harm (v. 10).

2.4.4. But she still refused to be satisfied unless she could gain her son's pardon, and protection for him also. Parents are never at ease unless their children are safe in both worlds: "*Let not the avenger of blood destroy my son* (v. 11), for I am ruined if I lose him. You might as well take my life as his. *Remember* how *the Lord thy God* (v. 11) spared Cain, and forgave you for the killing of Uriah; and let the king, who has found mercy, also show mercy."

2.4.5. When this bold widow pressed the matter even more closely, she finally gained a full pardon for her son, confirmed with an oath as she wanted. I cannot say whether David did well here by undertaking to protect a murderer, whom the cities of refuge would not protect. But there was enough latitude under the law to give a favorable judgment: he had killed his brother, but he *hated him not in time past* (Dt 19:6). The killing had been committed because of a sudden provocation, and as far as we can tell, it might have been done in his own defense.

2.5. Because the case has been judged in favor of her son, it is now time to apply it to the king's son, Absalom. The mask is here thrown off, and another scene begun. The king is surprised, but not at all displeased, to see his humble petitioner become an advocate for the prince his son. She begs his pardon and his patience for what she has further to say (v. 12).

2.5.1. She considered Absalom's case to be, in effect, the same as the one she had described as her son's. And so, if the king would protect her son even though he had killed his brother, much more should he protect his own son, and *fetch home his banished* (v. 13). It was true that Absalom's case was very different from the one she first gave. Absalom did not kill his brother in a fit of anger. Absalom was not an only son, as hers was; David had many more. But David was too emotionally involved to make critical remarks about the difference between the cases. He desired even more than she to bring the same favorable judgment on his own son as he had given her son.

2.5.2. She reasons with the king, to persuade him to recall Absalom from exile, to give him his pardon, and take him back into his favor:

2.5.2.1. She pleads the interests which the people of Israel have in him.

2.5.2.2. She pleads general human mortality (v. 14): "*We must needs die.* Amnon would have had to die at some time even if Absalom had not killed him, and so if Absalom is now to be put to death for killing him, that will not bring him back to life again."

2.5.2.3. She pleads God's mercy and his pity toward poor, guilty sinners (v. 14). Here are two great instances of the mercy of God to sinners:

• The patience he exercises toward them. When his law is broken, he does not immediately take away the life of those who break it.

• The provision he has made for their restoration to his favor, so that although they have banished themselves from him because of their sin, they still need not be rejected forever. Poor, banished sinners are likely to be rejected forever from God unless some action is taken to prevent it. It is not God's desire that they should be, for he is not willing that any should perish (2Pe 3:9).

2.6. She concludes her address with great compliments to the king and strong expressions of her assurance that he will do what is just and kind in both cases (vv. 15–17).

2.6.1. She would not have troubled the king in this way were it not for the fact that the people made her afraid (v. 15). She gave the king to understand—and he did not know it before—that the nation was disgusted at his severity toward Absalom to such an extent that she was very afraid it would lead to a general rebellion or insurrection.

2.6.2. She turned to him, confident of his wisdom and mercy. What this woman says as a compliment the prophet says as a promise (Zec 12:8), that when *the weak*

shall be as David, the house of David shall be as the angel of the Lord.

2.7. The hand of Joab is suspected by the king, and acknowledged by the woman, to be in all this (vv. 18–20). The king eventually suspected it, and then the woman very honestly owned up to it: "Your servant Joab instructed me to do this." She spoke the truth as she saw it, and in this she gave us an example to do likewise: never to tell a lie to cover up a well-managed scheme. Dare to be true; nothing needs a lie.

Verses 21–27

Notice here:

1. Orders are given for Absalom to be brought back. After Joab had received these orders:

1.1. He gave thanks to the king for honoring him by using him in an affair that was so agreeable in every way (v. 22).

1.2. He did not delay in carrying out David's orders; he brought Absalom to Jerusalem (v. 23). I do not see how David could be justified in suspending the old law (Ge 9:6), *Whoso sheds man's blood, by man shall his blood be shed.* God's laws were never intended to be like spiderwebs, which catch small flies but allow larger ones to get through. But although he allowed Absalom to return to his own house, he refused to let him come to the king's court and would not see him himself (v. 24). He made this ban in order to:

• Support his own honor, so that he might not seem to forgive him too easily.
• Humiliate Absalom further. Perhaps he thought that Absalom had not truly repented.

2. Opportunity is now taken to give an account of Absalom. Nothing is said about his wisdom and godliness or about his own devotion. All that is said about him here is:

2.1. That he was a very handsome man (v. 25). This was a poor commendation, and a fitting one for a man who had nothing else valuable to commend him. People should be valued for their good deeds, not their good looks. Many a defiled, deformed soul lives in an attractive body, and such was the soul of Absalom: defiled by blood and deformed by an unnatural hatred for his father and ruler. His body had no blemish, but his mind contained nothing but wounds and bruises.

2.2. That he had a very fine head of hair, not as the hair of a Nazarite—he was far from being that strict—but as the hair of an Adonis. He let it grow until it became a burden to him and was heavy on him. He would not cut it until he could not bear the weight any longer. As pride feels no cold, so also it feels no heat, and what feeds and satisfies it is not complained about even if it is very disagreeable. When he did finally cut it, he weighed it, to show how superior it was to that of other men, and it weighed 200 shekels, about five pounds (about 2.3 kilograms). With the oil and powder, especially if this was powdered with gold dust—as Josephus says the fashion then was—it is quite possible that it would have weighed that much. But later this fine hair proved his noose (18:9).

2.3. That his family began to be built up. It was probably some time before he had a child, and it was probably during this time of waiting that, despairing of ever having one, he set up the pillar which is mentioned in 18:18, so that his name would be remembered. Later, however, he had three sons and one daughter (v. 27).

Verses 28–33

Absalom had been an exile from his father for three years, and it was now two years that he had been a prisoner who was free to roam in his own house. In both, he was better dealt with than he deserved, but his spirit was still not humbled. He thought himself treated harshly and wronged greatly by not being restored to his position at court. He longed to see the king's face, pretending it was because he loved him, but really it was because he wanted an opportunity to take his place. He could not cause any trouble for his father until he was reconciled to him, and so this was the first part of his plan. This snake could not sting again until his father warmly accepted him back. He won this point, not by promises of reformation, but by insults and injuries:

1. By his rude behavior toward Joab, Absalom made Joab mediate for him. First, he sent for Joab to come to him, and twice Joab refused. At this point one would think that a person in Absalom's circumstances would have sent a kind message to Joab, with a large gift, but instead of this, he told his servants to set Joab's grainfields on fire (v. 30). It is strange that Absalom would think that by causing trouble for Joab he would persuade him to do him a favor. Nevertheless, this is how he brings Joab to him (v. 31). Joab was perhaps frightened at the surprising boldness and fury of Absalom, and also apprehensive that Absalom had gained a strong enough influence with the people to support him. So Joab not only puts up with this wrong but even goes on Absalom's mission to the king.

2. By his impertinent message to the king, he regained his place at court, the privilege of seeing the king's face, that is, of becoming a privy councilor (Est 1:14).

2.1. His message was proud and haughty, and inconsistent with the style of either a son or a subject (v. 32). He undervalued the favor that had been shown him in recalling him from exile and restoring him to his own house — and a house in Jerusalem at that. He defied the king's justice: "Let him kill me, if he can find it in his heart."

2.2. But he won his point with this message (v. 33). David's strong affection for him interpreted all this as the language of a great respect for his father and of a heartfelt desire for his favor, when tragically it was very different. The posture of Absalom's body seemed to show his submission to his father: *He bowed himself on his* face to the ground; and David sealed his pardon with a kiss.

CHAPTER 15

Absalom's name means "the peace of his father," but he proves David's greatest trouble. The sword that had been imposed on David's house had up to now fallen among his children, but now it begins to be drawn against him. If he had brought the murderer to justice, he would have stopped the traitor. The story of Absalom's rebellion begins with this chapter, in which we have: 1. The devious ways Absalom used to worm himself into the people's affections (vv. 1–6). 2. The open confession of his claim to the crown at Hebron—where he went pretending to fulfill a vow—and the strong group that appeared for him there (vv. 7–12). 3. Notice brought of this to David and his escape from Jerusalem (vv. 13–18). In the account of his flight we are told what took place between him and Ittai (vv. 19–22) and how concerned the country was for him (v. 23). 4. His conversation with Zadok (vv. 24–29) and his tears and prayers on this occasion (vv. 30–31). 5. Matters arranged between him and Hushai (vv. 32–37).

Verses 1–6

Absalom is no sooner restored to his place at court than he is ambitious to become king. If he had had any sense of gratitude, he would have worked hard to see how he could please his father and put him at his ease. But on the contrary, he is now thinking about how he can undermine him by stealing the hearts of the people from him. Two things commend a person to popular esteem—greatness and goodness:

1. Absalom appears great (v. 1). He had learned from the king of Geshur how to gain many horses, which the kings of Israel were not allowed to do. This made him look desirable while his father looked contemptible on his mule. The people wanted a king like the nations. Samuel had foretold that this would be *the manner of the king*: he will *have chariots and horsemen, and some shall run before his chariots* (1Sa 8:11), and this was Absalom's style. He provided himself with fifty servants running before him, and this would greatly satisfy his pride and the people's foolish whims. David thought that this show was intended only to grace his court, and so he turned a blind eye to it.

2. Absalom wishes to seem very good too, but for an evil purpose. If he had proved to be a good son and a good subject, he would have shown himself worthy of future honors after his father's death. Those who know how to obey well know how to rule well. Those who are truly good are good where they are in their own place, rather than pretending that they would be good in other people's places.

2.1. He wishes he could be a judge in Israel (v. 4). The one who should himself have been condemned to death for murder is outrageous enough to want to judge others. We do not read about Absalom's wisdom, goodness, or learning in the law, but he still wants to be a judge. Often those who are most ambitious to be promoted are those who are least fit for it. The best qualified are the most modest and self-effacing.

2.2. He follows a very bad way of achieving his wish. Thinking it beneath him to work hard to qualify for the next judge's position that came up, he has to be supreme or nothing. He wants to be the kind of judge to whom everyone who has any cause will come: he wants to take the lead in every cause. To gain the power he aims at, he tries to instill into the people's minds:

2.2.1. A bad opinion of the present leadership, as if the affairs of the kingdom were altogether neglected and no one was bothered with them. "*There is no man deputed* (representative) *of the king to hear thee* (v. 3). The king is himself old, and getting past doing the work, or else he is so taken up with his devotions that he never has time for work. His sons are so devoted to their pleasures that although they are called the king's advisers, they are not concerned about the affairs committed to them." Everyone who makes a legal appeal is made to believe that they will never have justice done for them unless Absalom is made viceroy or chief justice. It is the style of undisciplined, divisive, ambitious people to scorn an existing leadership.

2.2.2. A good opinion of his own fitness to rule. He wants the people to say, "If only Absalom were judge!" and so he commends himself to them as someone who is diligent, interested in everyone's case, and friendly and humble. If any Israelite offered to pay him homage, he allowed them to do so and embraced them as a friend. No one's style of leadership could have been more gracious and humble, while in reality his heart was as proud as Lucifer's.

Verses 7–12

Here we have the breaking out of Absalom's rebellion, which he had been planning for a long time. *Forty years* (v. 7) after David's first anointing by Samuel—for this is the interpretation I give to this number—the same restless spirit was still at work in the people, and they were still as fickle. They were as fond of a new leader now as they had been then. Absalom's conspiracy was now ready to be put into operation:

1. The place Absalom chose for his people to meet was Hebron, where he was born, and where his father began his reign and continued for several years. Everyone knew Hebron was a royal city. It was situated at the heart of the allotted territory of Judah, the tribe in which he probably thought his influence was the strongest.

2. Absalom's pretense was to go there and to invite his friends to come to him. He claimed he was going to offer a sacrifice to God, to fulfill a vow he had made during his time of exile (vv. 7–8). Under this pretense:

2.1. He gained permission from his father to go to Hebron. David would have been pleased to hear that when his son had come back to the city of God, he had remembered his vow to God and decided to fulfill it. David was overjoyed to hear that Absalom inclined to *serve the Lord* (v. 8), and so he readily allowed him to go to Hebron, and to go there with a show of reverence.

2.2. He got a good number of solid citizens to go along with him (v. 11). He knew that it would be futile to tempt them to join his conspiracy; they staunchly supported David. But he drew them along to accompany him so that the ordinary people might think that they were on his side and that David had been abandoned by some of his best friends. When religion becomes a cover, and sacrifice becomes something that makes way for conspiracy and the overthrow of the government, it is hardly surprising if some who are well disposed to religious faith—as these followers of Absalom were—are taken in by the deceit and are drawn in to support with their names something that—not having learned Satan's so-called deep secrets (Rev 2:24)—they loathe in their hearts.

3. The plan Absalom made was to get himself declared king throughout all the tribes of Israel on a given signal (v. 10). Secret messengers were sent out, to be ready in every part of the country to receive the notice with great assurance and joy. Some would conclude that David had died, others that he had resigned. Many would have loathed the mere thought of what they were doing if they had rightly understood the matter.

4. The person Absalom especially wooed and relied on in this matter was Ahithophel, a shrewd, thinking man, who had been David's counselor. It seems there was some quarrel between David and him, and he was banished and lived privately in the country. Absalom could not have found anyone more suitable in all the kingdom than one who was such a great statesman and at the same time was discontented with the present leadership. While Absalom was offering his sacrifices and pretending to fulfill his vow, he sent for this man.

5. Significant numbers of people came to join him. The people continued to come to Absalom, which made his conspiracy strong and formidable. Everyone whom he had complimented and embraced came to him; and they not only came themselves but also tried to influence as many others as they could, so that he did not lack support.

Verses 13–23

Here is:

1. Notice brought to David of Absalom's rebellion (v. 13). The matter was bad enough, but it seems to have been made to feel even worse for him than it really was, for he was told that *the hearts of the men of Israel*—that is, most of them, at least the leading men—were *after Absalom*. It is wise of rulers to make sure of the hearts of their subjects, for if they have those, they have their money, arms, and everything at their disposal.

2. The fear this put David in, and the decisions he then made. We may well imagine that he was dumbfounded when he heard that the son he had dearly loved had so unnaturally and ungratefully taken up arms against him. David did not call a council meeting, but consulted only God and his own heart and determined to leave Jerusalem immediately (v. 14). He made this strange decision either:

2.1. As one who was repenting and submitting to discipline from God's hand. Or:

2.2. As a politician. Jerusalem was a great city but could not be successfully defended. It was too large to be garrisoned by such a small force as David now had with him. He had reason to fear that most of the inhabitants were too well disposed toward Absalom to be true to his father. And he had such a love for Jerusalem that he was unwilling to turn it into a theater of war and make it vulnerable to a disastrous siege.

3. David's speedy exit from Jerusalem.

3.1. He went out of Jerusalem himself on foot, while his son Absalom had chariots and horses.

3.2. He took his household with him, his wives and children, so that he might protect them in these days of danger, and so that they might comfort him in these days of sorrow.

3.3. He took his bodyguards with him, the Kerethites and Pelethites, who were under the command of Benaiah, and the Gittites, who were under the command of Ittai (v. 18). These Gittites seem to have been by birth Philistines in David's service, having known him at Gath, having come to love him for his goodness and godliness, and having embraced the Jews' religion. David made them his bodyguard, and they remained loyal to him in his distress.

3.4. He took with him as many as he could of the people of Jerusalem and stopped some distance from the city to draw them together (v. 17). He did not force anyone to join him. Christ calls only volunteers.

4. David's conversation with Ittai the Gittite, who commanded the Philistine converts.

4.1. David dissuaded him from going along with him (vv. 19–20).

4.1.1. He wanted to test whether Ittai was sincerely on his side and not inclined to follow Absalom. He therefore told him to return to his position at Jerusalem and serve the new king.

4.1.2. If he was faithful to David, David still did not want him to be exposed to the dangers he now expected. "*Should I make thee go up and down* (wander about) *with us?* (v. 20). No; return with your compatriots." Generous souls are more concerned about the share others have in their troubles than about their own. Ittai was therefore sent away with a blessing: *Mercy and truth be with thee* (v. 20). David depended on the mercy and truth of God as the source of his comfort and happiness, both for himself and his friends; see Ps 61:7.

4.2. Ittai bravely decided not to leave him (v. 21). This faithful friend of his wanted to be wherever David was, *whether in life or death*, in a place of safety or danger. He confirmed this decision with an oath so that he might not be tempted to break it. In the same way, we should cling to the Son of David with an undivided heart so that *neither life nor death shall separate us from his love* (Ro 8:38–39).

5. The common people's sympathy with David in his affliction. When he and those with him *passed over the brook Kidron*—the very same valley that Christ crossed when he entered on his sufferings (Jn 18:1)—*toward the way of the wilderness*, which was situated between Jerusalem and Jericho, *all the country wept with a loud voice* (v. 23). And well might they weep when they saw a ruler reduced to such difficulties, forced out of his palace and in fear of his life, with a small number of people seeking shelter in a desert—when they saw the city of David, which he himself won, built, and fortified, made an unsafe home for David himself.

Verses 24–30

We have here:

1. The faithfulness of the priests and Levites and their staunch loyalty to David and his interests. If David had to go, then Zadok, Abiathar, and all the Levites wanted to accompany him and take the ark with them, so that they might use it to ask for God's guidance for him (v. 24).

2. David's sending them back into the city (vv. 25–26). Abiathar was high priest (1Ki 2:35), but Zadok was his assistant and looked after the ark most closely, while Abiathar was more active in public business (v. 24). David therefore addressed his speech to Zadok.

2.1. He is very concerned about the safety of the ark: "By all means *carry the ark back into the city* (v. 25). Surely Absalom, bad though he is, will do it no harm."

2.2. He very much wants to return to enjoying the privileges of God's house.

2.3. He is very submissive to the holy will of God concerning the outcome of these dark events. Notice that he here patiently waits for what will happen: "*Behold, here am I* as a servant expecting orders"; and notice that he is willing to commit himself to God about it: "*Let him do to me as seemeth good to him* (v. 26). I have nothing to object to. Everything that God does is good. *Let him do what he will.*" So that we may not complain about what is, let us see God's hand in every event, and so that we may not be afraid of what will be, let us see every event as being in God's hand.

3. The confidence David put in the priests that they would serve his interests to the best of their ability while he was away from them. He called Zadok *a seer* (v. 27). At such a critical time as this, one friend who was a seer was worth more than twenty who were not so discerning. David instructed Zadok and Abiathar as to:

3.1. Whom they should send to him—their two sons, Ahimaaz and Jonathan.

3.2. Where they should send them. He would camp *in the plain of the wilderness* (at the fords in the desert) until he heard from them (v. 28), and he would then move according to the information and advice they sent them.

4. The attitude of dejection that David and his men assumed when, at the beginning of their march, they went up the Mount of Olives (v. 30).

4.1. David, to mortify himself, went barefoot like a prisoner or a slave, and wept. He could not help but weep when he remembered that it was his own son, one who

had so often lain in his arms, who had turned against him so violently. And it befitted him to weep when he recognized how much of the displeasure of his God appeared in it. His sin was *ever before him* (Ps 51:3), but it was never so plain, apparent, or black as it was now. He had never wept when Saul hunted him: but his guilty conscience is overwhelming in its intensity (Ps 38:4).

4.2. When David wept, all those with him also wept, because they were affected very much by his grief and wanted to share in it.

Verses 31–37

It seems that there was nothing in Absalom's conspiracy which appeared more threatening to David than the fact that Ahithophel was in it, for in such a plan, one good head is worth a thousand good hands. Absalom was himself no politician, but he had gained one wholly on his side who was. If Ahithophel's plans could therefore be frustrated, Absalom would be as good as defeated and the head that guided the conspiracy would be cut off. This is what David tries to do:

1. By prayer. When he heard that Ahithophel had joined in the conspiracy, he lifted up his heart to God in this short prayer: *Lord, turn the counsel of Ahithophel into foolishness* (v. 31). David prayed not against Ahithophel's person but against his advice.

2. By action. We must back up our prayers with action, or else we tempt God. It was now that he wrote Ps 3:1–8, as can be seen from the title of that psalm. Some think that his singing this Psalm was the worship he now gave to God. Just then God's providence brought Hushai, the person who would be instrumental in fooling Ahithophel. He came to comfort David in his present troubles, with his coat torn and with dust on his head, but David decided to use him to spy on Absalom, and he sent him to Jerusalem to wait for Absalom's arrival, pose as a deserter from David, and offer Absalom his service (v. 34). However, I do not see how this gross pretense which David asked Hushai to make can be justified as a strategy in war. Seeing it in the best light, we might say that if Absalom had decided to rebel against his father, then it was fitting that he must be on his guard against the whole human race, and if Absalom was willing to be deceived, then let him be deceived. David commended Hushai to Zadok, and after Hushai had been given these instructions, he came to Jerusalem (v. 37), where Absalom soon came with his forces.

CHAPTER 16

In this chapter: 1. We follow David in his sad escape. We find him cheated by Ziba (vv. 1–4). 2. He is cursed by Shimei (vv. 5–14). 3. We meet Absalom in his triumphant entry, and we find him cheated there by Hushai (vv. 15–19) and counseled by Ahithophel to have sex with his father's concubines (vv. 20–23).

Verses 1–4

We read before how kind David was to Mephibosheth the son of Jonathan, wisely entrusting Mephibosheth's servant Ziba with the management of his master's estate while he generously received Mephibosheth at his own table (9:10). It seems, however, that Ziba was not content to be manager of the estate but longed to be master of it, and he thought that now was the time to get it for himself. If he could obtain it as a gift from the crown, then whether David or Absalom won did not matter to him; he was only concerned with getting what he wanted.

1. He made David a generous present of supplies, which was all the more welcome because it came at the right time (v. 1). David inferred from this that Ziba was a very discreet and generous man, one who was well disposed toward him, when all along what he really wanted was to make a bargain for himself and to see Mephibosheth's estate settled on himself. Whatever Ziba intended in this present, God's providence sent it to David to support him graciously. God makes use of bad people to fulfill his good purposes for his people, and sends them food by ravens (1Ki 17:6).

2. Having gained David's favor by way of his gift, he must next make him angry with Mephibosheth, which he does by a false accusation, suggesting that he is ungratefully intending to regain the crown for his own head, now that David and his son are fighting for it. David asks about Mephibosheth as one of his family, and his inquiry gives Ziba occasion to tell this false story about him (v. 3). David believes the slander without asking any further, convicts Mephibosheth of treason, confiscates his lands, and gives them to Ziba. This was a rash judgment, and one which he later was ashamed of, when the truth came to light (19:29). After Ziba had tricked David and won, he secretly laughed at the gullibility of the king.

Verses 5–14

Here we see how David bore up under Shimei's curses much better than he had under Ziba's flattery. The latter made him declare a wrong judgment on someone else; the former brought him to a right judgment about himself. The world's smiles are sometimes more dangerous than its frowns. Notice here:

1. How arrogant and angry Shimei was, and how he used David's present distress to make his hatred become even more outrageous. In fleeing, David had come to Bahurim, a town of Benjamin in or near which this Shimei lived. Belonging to the house of Saul, Shimei had seen all his hopes of advancement come to nothing with the fall of that house, and so he had an implacable hostility toward David, unjustly looking on him as having caused the ruin of Saul and his family only because he had succeeded Saul by divine appointment. Notice:

1.1. Why he took this opportunity to express his hatred:

1.1.1. Because he now thought he could do it safely.

1.1.2. Because now it would be most painful for David; it would add further suffering to his grief. It would be like pouring vinegar onto his wounds.

1.1.3. Because now he thought that Providence justified his scorn, and that David's present troubles showed that he deserved to be denounced by him. Job's friends condemned him on this false principle.

1.2. How his hatred was expressed:

1.2.1. *He cast stones at David* (v. 6), as if his king was a dog. *He cast* (showered him with) *dust* (v. 13), which probably would blow back into his own eyes, like the curses he threw, which because they were without foundation would return on his own head. And so while his hatred made him repugnant, its powerlessness made him ridiculous and contemptible.

1.2.2. What he said. As he threw stones, he also shot arrows, that is, bitter words (vv. 7–8). What had been done long ago to the house of Saul was the only thing he could remember. He rebuked David for this because it was the thing that he himself had lost out by. No one could have been more innocent of the blood of the house of Saul than David was. Time and again he spared Saul's life, while Saul sought to take his. Yet his supposed guilt in this matter was said to be:

1.2.2.1. What gave him his character and earned him the name of *a bloody man* (man of blood) *and a man of Belial* (scoundrel) (v. 7).

1.2.2.2. What brought the present trouble on him: *The Lord has returned upon thee the blood of the house of Saul* (v. 8). We see here how eager malicious people are to make God's judgments serve their own rage and revenge.

1.2.2.3. What would now lead to his complete destruction—for Shimei tries to make David despair of ever regaining the throne.

2. How patient and submissive David was under this abuse. The sons of Zeruiah, especially Abishai, were very angry at this attack, as well they might be: *Why should this dead dog* be allowed to *curse the king?* (v. 9). If David would only allow them, they would silence these lying, cursing lips and cut off Shimei's head. But the king would not allow it in any way: *What have I to do with you? So let him curse* (v. 10). This is how Christ rebuked the disciples who out of zeal for his honor would have commanded fire from heaven on the town that snubbed him (Lk 9:55). Let us see how David remained quiet:

2.1. The chief thing that kept him quiet was that he had deserved this trouble.

2.2. He sees the hand of God in it: *The Lord hath said unto him, Curse David* (v. 10), and again, *So let him curse, for the Lord hath bidden him* (v. 11). Insofar as it was Shimei's sin, it did not come from God, but from Satan and his own evil heart. David, however, looked beyond the instrument of his troubles to the supreme director, just as Job acknowledged, when the plunderers stripped him, *The Lord hath taken away* (Job 1:21). Nothing can better calm a gracious soul in trouble than to see the hand of God in it.

2.3. He remains quiet under the lesser affliction by considering the greater (v. 11): *My son seeks my life, much more may this Benjamite.*

2.4. He comforts himself with the hope that God would somehow bring good to him out of his trouble: *The Lord will requite me good for his cursing* (v. 12). We may depend on God to reward us not only for our services, but also for our sufferings. David finally finds accommodation at Bahurim (v. 14), where he is refreshed and is hidden from this battle of words.

Verses 15–23

Some of Absalom's friends at Jerusalem quickly told him that David had withdrawn and that he had gone with only a small following, and so Absalom could possess Jerusalem when he wanted. He therefore came without delay (v. 15), no doubt greatly encouraged by this initial success. The most famous politicians at that time were Ahithophel and Hushai. Absalom brought Ahithophel with him to Jerusalem (v. 15), and Hushai met him there (v. 16), and so he thought he must succeed. But these two men proved to be miserable counselors, for:

1. Hushai would never counsel him to act wisely. He was really his enemy. He intended to betray him.

1.1. Hushai complimented him on his accession to the throne, as if he had been completely happy with the situation and pleased that Absalom now possessed the throne (v. 16).

1.2. Absalom was surprised to find support from one who was known as David's intimate friend and confidant. Yet he easily believed what he wanted to be true, and Hushai strengthened him in his belief that he was sincere about being on his side: it was true, he had loved Absalom's father; but his day was now over, and why should he not love his successor just as well? This is how he pretended to give reasons for a decision which in reality he hated the thought of.

2. Ahithophel counseled him to commit evil, and so betrayed him as effectively as the one who was deliberately false to him, for those who advise people to sin certainly advise them to do things that will harm or hurt them. The government which is built on sin is built on sand.

2.1. It seems that Ahithophel was noted as such a deep politician that his advice was like that of one who inquires at the oracle of God (v. 23). Let us notice from this account of Ahithophel's fame as a politician:

2.1.1. That many excel in worldly wisdom who are completely devoid of heavenly grace, because those who set themselves up as the fount of all wisdom tend to despise the wisdom from God.

2.1.2. That frequently the greatest politicians act very foolishly in their own behalf. Ahithophel was praised for his wisdom, but he very unwisely took the same side as Absalom.

2.2. In this case, his politics defeated its own aim. Notice:

2.2.1. The evil guidance Ahithophel gave to Absalom. Finding that David had left his concubines to keep the house, he advised him to commit evil and *lie with them* (v. 21), because it would give assurance to all Israel:

2.2.1.1. That he was serious about his claims. There would be no doubt that he had decided to rule over everything that belonged to his predecessor if he began with his concubines.

2.2.1.2. That he was determined never to make peace with his father on any terms. Having drawn the sword in rebellion, with this provocation he threw away the scabbard — which would strengthen the hands of his people and keep them close to him. This was Ahithophel's evil plan, which showed him to be an oracle of the Devil rather than *an oracle of God*.

2.2.2. Absalom's agreement with this advice. It entirely suited his immoral and evil mind, and he did not delay in putting the plan into action (v. 22). In this, however, the word of God was fulfilled to the letter: God had threatened through Nathan that because he violated Bathsheba, David would have his own wives publicly raped (12:11–12), and some think that when Ahithophel advised it, he planned to get revenge on David for the wrong done to Bathsheba, who was his granddaughter, for she was the daughter of Eliam (11:3), who was the son of Ahithophel (23:34).

CHAPTER 17

The conflict between David and Absalom is now moving fast toward a crisis. It must be resolved by the sword. 1. Absalom calls a council of war, in which Ahithophel urges speed (vv. 1–4) but Hushai urges caution (vv. 5–13). Hushai's counsel is agreed to (v. 14), which causes Ahithophel to hang himself (v. 23). 2. Secret information is sent to David about their discussions but only with great difficulty (vv. 15–21). 3. David marches to the other side of the Jordan (vv. 22–24), where his camp is supplied by some of his friends in that country (vv. 27–29). Absalom and his forces march after him into the land of Gilead on the other side of the Jordan (vv. 25–26).

Verses 1–14

Absalom now peacefully possesses Jerusalem; the royal palace is his own. His good father reigned in Hebron, but

only over the tribe of Judah, for more than seven years. He was not quick to destroy his rival; his government was built on a promise of God, and so he waited patiently in the meantime. But the young man Absalom not only goes quickly from Hebron to Jerusalem, but is also impatient there until he has destroyed his father. He cannot be content with his throne till he has also taken his life. David and all who were loyal to him must be destroyed. No one dares oppose this decision by mentioning David's personal merits or the great service he has done for his country. No one dares suggest that banishing him would be sufficient. That David must be destroyed is, Absalom thinks, beyond dispute; the only question is how he may be destroyed.

1. Ahithophel advises that he should be pursued immediately, that very night, by a rapid-deployment force, and that only the king should be struck down, so that his forces will scatter. The result would be that the people who were now on his side would of course go over to Absalom. Nothing could be more fatal for David than the use of these measures. It was probable enough that a fierce attack, especially at night, would throw David's small force into confusion and turmoil, and that it would be easy to strike down only the king (v. 2). Compare this with the plot of that second Ahithophel, Caiaphas, against the Son of David, to crush his influence by destroying him. Let that *one man die for the people* (Jn 11:50).

2. Hushai, on the other hand, advises that they should not be too hasty in pursuing David, but should take their time to draw up all their forces against him and to overpower him by sheer numbers. When Hushai gave this guidance, he really intended to serve David and his interests, by giving himself time to warn David of his discussions, so that David might gain time to gather an army and move to those countries beyond the Jordan in which, because they were more remote, Absalom probably had least influence.

2.1. Absalom gave Hushai a reasonable invitation to advise him. All the elders of Israel approved of Ahithophel's counsel, but God overruled the heart of Absalom so that he would not act on it until he had consulted Hushai (v. 5): *Let us hear what he saith.*

2.2. Hushai gave very plausible reasons for what he said:

2.2.1. He argued against Ahithophel's advice and undertook to show the danger of following it.

2.2.1.1. He insisted very much that David was a great soldier, a man of great leadership, courage, and experience, and not so weary and weak as Ahithophel imagined. He had withdrawn from Jerusalem not because he was a coward but because he was wise.

2.2.1.2. It was true that his attendants were few in number, but they were fighters (v. 8), very brave (v. 10), and well known for their courage and experience in warfare.

2.2.1.3. David's men were all angry with Absalom, who had caused all this trouble. They were bitter and would fight with the greatest fierceness. Nothing would stand against them, especially such raw soldiers as Absalom's generally were.

2.2.1.4. He suggested that probably David and some of his men would lie in wait in a cave or some other enclosed place, and that they would attack Absalom's soldiers and put them to flight. This defeat, though over such a small party, would discourage all the others, who would not only be troubled by the defeat but also accused by their own consciences of treason against the one who they were sure was not only God's anointed, *but a man after his own heart* (1Sa 13:14) (v. 9).

2.2.2. He offered his own advice and gave his reasons:

2.2.2.1. He advised what he knew would gratify Absalom's proud and boastful temperament, although it would not really serve his interests:

- He advised that all Israel, that is, the militia of all the tribes, should gather together.
- He advised that Absalom should go to battle in person, as if he looked on him as a better soldier than Ahithophel.

2.2.2.2. He advised what seemed to make the ultimate success of the venture totally certain and free of risk. For if they could raise such vast numbers as they promised themselves, wherever they found David they would not fail to crush him:

- If it was on the battlefield, they would destroy all those with him (v. 12). Perhaps Absalom had a particular hatred toward some of David's friends and was therefore more pleased with this plan to destroy all those who were with him than with Ahithophel's plan to strike down only the king. In this way, Hushai won his point by pandering to Absalom's desire for revenge as well as to his pride.
- If it was in a city, they need not be afraid to conquer him, for they would have enough people, if need be, to drag the city itself into its river using ropes (v. 13).

2.2.3. Hushai used all these means to gain not only Absalom's approval of his advice, but also the unanimous agreement of this great council of war. They all agreed that the Hushai's advice was better than Ahithophel's (v. 14).

Verses 15–21

Hushai told the priests what had taken place in the council (v. 15). But it seems he feared that Ahithophel's advice might still be followed, and was therefore concerned that if the king did not move quickly, he might be *swallowed up* (destroyed), *and all the people that were with him* (v. 16). Absalom set such strict guards on every approach to Jerusalem that it took them a lot of effort to make sure David received the necessary information.

1. The young priests who were to be the messengers were forced to withdraw secretly from the city by En Rogel.

2. Instructions were sent to them by a poor and simple servant girl, who probably went to the well pretending to fetch water (v. 17).

3. However, because Absalom's spies were watchful, the messengers were discovered, and information was brought to Absalom about their movements: *A lad saw them and told him* (v. 18).

4. They realized they had been discovered, and they sheltered themselves in a friend's house in Bahurim, where David had refreshed himself only recently (16:14). Fortunately they were hidden in a well there, which now was perhaps dry because it was summer (v. 18). The woman of the house cleverly covered up the opening of the well with a cloth, over which she scattered grain to dry, so that the pursuers did not know it was a well, or else they would have searched it (v. 19). Being preserved in this way, they brought their information faithfully to David (v. 21), with the advice of his friends that he should not delay in passing over the Jordan, which it seems he was near.

Verses 22–29

Here is:

1. The transporting of David and his forces over the Jordan. He and all who were with him went over at night,

and not one of them deserted him. Having crossed the Jordan, he marched on many miles to Mahanaim, a Levites' city in the tribe of Gad. David now made his headquarters in this city (v. 24), which Ish-Bosheth had made his royal city (2:8). And now he had time to raise an army with which he could oppose the rebels and give them a spirited reception.

2. The death of Ahithophel (v. 23). He committed suicide. He hanged himself because he was devastated when his advice was not followed. He thought:

2.1. That he had been snubbed and that an intolerable slur had been put on his reputation for wisdom.

2.2. That his life was in danger because he had exposed himself. He concluded that because his advice was not followed, Absalom's cause would certainly fail, and then he would be the least likely to be forgiven by David, because he was the one who had specifically advised Absalom to have sex with his father's concubines. Just as David had prayed, Ahithophel's advice was now *turned into foolishness to himself* (15:31).

3. Absalom's pursuit of his father. He was not content with having driven his good father to the farthest corner of his kingdom; he decided to chase him out of the world. Absalom made a man named Amasa his general (v. 25). By birth the father of Amasa was called Jether and was an Ishmaelite (1Ch 2:17), but by religion he was called *Ithra*—a Hebrew variant—and was an Israelite. Amasa, like Joab, was David's nephew.

4. The friends David met with in this distant country. Even Shobi, a younger brother of the royal family of the Ammonites, was kind to him (v. 27). We should, as we have opportunity, *do good to all men, for he that watereth shall be watered also himself* (Gal 6:10; Pr 11:25). Makir, the son of Ammiel, was the one who had looked after Mephibosheth (9:4) until David relieved him of that responsibility. For that favor David is now repaid by this generous man, who, it seems, was the common patron of distressed rulers. We will hear about Barzillai again. These people who took pity on David and his followers when they were weary after a long march brought him furnishings for his house, *beds and basins*, and supplies for his table, *wheat and barley* (vv. 28–29). As a sign of their dutiful affection to him they brought plenty of all that he needed. Let us learn from this to be generous and open-handed, according to our abilities, to everyone in distress. God sometimes uses strangers to provide his people with the comfort which they are disappointed not to receive from their own families.

CHAPTER 18

This chapter brings to an end Absalom's rebellion and life, and so makes way for David to return to his throne. 1. David's preparations to engage the rebels (vv. 1–5); the total defeat of Absalom's party (vv. 6–8). 2. The death of Absalom and his burial (vv. 9–18). 3. News of this brought to David, who stayed at Mahanaim (vv. 19–32); his bitter mourning for Absalom (v. 33).

Verses 1–8

David raised an army, and reinforcements were sent to him from throughout Israel, at least from the neighboring tribes. We have here:

1. David's army mustered and counted (vv. 1–2). Josephus says they totaled about 4,000. He divided these into regiments and divisions, to each of which he appointed officers, and then marshaled them as he normally did,

into a right wing, left wing, and center, two of which he committed to his two old, experienced generals, Joab and Abishai, and the third to his new friend Ittai. Good order and good leadership may sometimes be as useful to an army as great numbers.

2. David himself persuaded not to go in person to the battle. David's true friends would not let him go, remembering what they had been told about Ahithophel's intention to *smite the king only* (17:2). David showed his affection for them by being daring to go with them (v. 2), and they showed their affection for him by opposing it. He might be more useful to them by waiting in the city with troop reinforcements. A place which is not yet at risk may still be a position of real service.

3. The command David gave concerning Absalom (v. 5). When the army was drawn up in their rank and file, Josephus says, David encouraged them and prayed for them, but he also told them all to beware hurting Absalom in any way. Absalom would have struck down only David. David would have spared only Absalom. Each went to the extreme. They showed how bad a child can be to the best of fathers and how good a father can be to the worst of children. It is as if the contrast were intended to make us think of the contrast between human evil toward God and God's mercy toward human beings. Bishop Hall, commenting on this passage, asks whether they should indeed be gentle with a traitor, and of all traitors, with a son. Must David's men capture him to make him accept mercy? But was not this done, the bishop concludes, as a type of that immeasurable mercy of the true King and Redeemer of Israel, who prayed for his persecutors, for his murderers, *Father, forgive them* (Lk 23:34). *Deal gently with them for my sake?* When God sends an affliction to discipline his children, it is with the command, "Deal gently with them for my sake," for he knows what we are like (Ps 103:14).

4. A complete victory gained over Absalom's forces. The battle was fought *in the wood of Ephraim* (v. 6), so called from some memorable action of the Ephraimites there, although it was situated in the tribe of Gad. David thought it right to meet the enemy with his forces some distance away, before they came to Mahanaim, so that he would not endanger that city, which had sheltered him so kindly. The cause would be decided by a pitched battle. Josephus describes the fight as being persistent, but in the end the rebels were totally defeated and 20,000 of them were killed (v. 7). They now saw what it meant to take their stand *against the Lord and his anointed* and to think *of breaking his bands asunder* (Ps 2:2–3). And so that they could see that God fought against them:

4.1. They were conquered by a few, probably by an army far fewer in number than theirs.

4.2. By fleeing, they destroyed themselves rather than saving themselves. The pits and bogs, the stumps and thickets, and as the Aramaic paraphrase understands it, the wild animals of the forest, probably caused the death of many of the scattered and confused Israelites.

Verses 9–18

Here Absalom is quite at a loss as to what to do. He is first at his wits' end, and then at his life's end. Although David's men are forbidden to lay a finger on him, he dare not look them in the face; when he finds they are near him, he spurs his mule on and flees as best he can, riding headlong through thick and thin to his own destruction.

1. He is hanged by the neck. He was riding furiously, determined and ready for anything, *under the thick boughs*

of a great oak (v. 9) which hung low and had never been cut. Either the twisted branches or a single, forked bough caught hold of his head, perhaps by his long hair, which he had been so proud of but which now justly became a noose for him. He hung there. His *mule went away* from *under him* (v. 9), as if it was glad to get clear of such a burden. He hung *between heaven and earth* (v. 9), as unworthy of either and abandoned by both.

2. He is caught alive by one of David's servants, who goes directly and tells Joab how he found that rebel (v. 10). Joab criticized the messenger for not striking him to the ground (v. 11). But although the man was zealous enough against Absalom, he did not think he was justified in doing this. "And," he said, "you yourself were a witness to the king's command about him (v. 12). Despite what you say, I know you would accuse me if I had done so" (v. 13). Those who love treason hate the traitor. Joab could not deny this, nor could he blame the man for his caution.

3. He hangs there and is pitifully hacked. Death comes to him in such a way that he feels all its terrible pain.

3.1. Joab throws three javelins into his body. While he broke the order of a too indulgent father, he performed a real service for both his king and his country, and would have endangered the welfare of both if he had not done it.

3.2. Ten of Joab's armor-bearers strike him before he is killed (v. 15). Joab then sounds the trumpet (v. 16). Now that Absalom has been killed the danger is over. The people will soon go back to their former allegiance to David, and so no more blood will be spilled.

4. His body is disposed of shamefully (vv. 17–18): they *cast it into a great pit in the wood*. They would not bring it to his father—for that would only have added to his sorrow—nor would they preserve it to be buried, but they angrily threw it into the nearest pit in the forest. Where now was the beauty he had been so proud of and for which he had been so much admired? Where were the plans he dreamed of, the castles he had built in the air? His thoughts perished, and he perished with them. To make the ignominy of Absalom's burial even worse, the writer refers to a pillar he had erected in the Kidron Valley, near Jerusalem, as a monument to himself (v. 18), at the foot of which he probably wanted to be buried. What care many people take about the disposal of their bodies when they are dead, though they care not at all about what will become of their precious souls! Absalom had had three sons (14:27), but it seems now he had none. He wanted his name to be remembered forever, and this is what happened, to his eternal dishonor.

Verses 19–33

The matter regarding Absalom is over, and we are now told:

1. How David was informed about it. He stayed behind at the city of Mahanaim. Absalom's scattered forces all made their way home toward the Jordan, which was the opposite way from Mahanaim, so that David's sentry could not see how the battle went, until a messenger deliberately came with news of the outcome, which the king sat at the gates waiting for (v. 24).

1.1. Cushi was the man whom Joab ordered to take the news (v. 21). His name means "an Ethiopian." Some think that he waited on Joab.

1.2. Ahimaaz, the young priest, one of those who brought David information about Absalom's movements (17:17), was very keen to be the messenger. He wanted this because he loved the king, and would therefore take pleasure and satisfaction in bringing him good news. Joab knew David better than Ahimaaz did, and he knew that the news of Absalom's death would spoil the acceptableness of everything else, and he loved Ahimaaz too much to let him be the messenger of this news (v. 20). However, when Cushi was gone, Ahimaaz begged permission to run after him, and he obtained that after great persistence (vv. 22–23). Perhaps it was out of tenderness to the king that he wanted to do it. He knew he could get there before Cushi, and so he wanted to give the king a vague and general report to prepare him for the plain truth that Cushi was ordered to tell him. If bad news has to come, it is best that it be given gradually, and then it will be better received.

1.3. They are both seen by the sentry on the gate of Mahanaim: Ahimaaz first (v. 24)—for although Cushi led the way, Ahimaaz soon outran him—and Cushi soon after (v. 26). When the king heard that the messenger was Ahimaaz, he concluded that he was coming with good news (v. 27). It seems that Ahimaaz was so famous for running that he was known for it from far away; and he was so well known as a good man that it was assumed that if he was the messenger, then the news must be good.

1.4. Ahimaaz cries from far away, "Peace. It is peace." And when he comes near, he tells him the news in more detail. "They are all cut off *that lifted up their hand against the king,*" and, as is right for a priest, while he gives the king the joyful good news, he gives God the glory for it at the same time. *"Blessed be the Lord thy God"* (v. 28). He has done this for you. He is your God. He is now fulfilling the promises made to maintain your throne" (7:16). When he said this, *he fell down upon his face* (v. 28), not only out of reverence for the king, but also in humble adoration of God, whose name he praised for this success. When he directed David to give God thanks for his victory, he was preparing him. The more our hearts are set on and released in giving thanks to God for our mercies, the better disposed we will be to bear the suffering and trouble that are mixed with them. Poor David was so much a father that he forgot he was a king, and so he could not be glad at the news of a victory until he knew whether the *young man Absalom be safe* (v. 29). Ahimaaz soon realized what Joab had tried to suggest to him, that the death of the king's son would make the day's news most unwelcome. "When Joab sent the king's servant, namely, Cushi, *and me thy servant,* to bring the news, *I saw a great tumult* (v. 29), but I am not saying anything about it. Cushi is more able to tell you than I can. I will not be the messenger of bad news, nor will I pretend to know what I cannot give a full account of."

1.5. Cushi is slower but surer, and besides the confirmation of the news of the victory which Ahimaaz had brought—The *Lord has avenged thee of all those that rose up against thee* (v. 31)—he also satisfies the king's questioning about Absalom (v. 32). *Is he safe?* says David. "Yes," Cushi says, "he is safe in his grave," but he is so discreet about telling him the news that however unwelcome the message is, the messenger cannot be blamed. *"The enemies of my lord the king, whoever they are, and all that rise against thee to do thee hurt, be as that young man is."*

2. How David received the news. He forgot all the joy of his deliverance and was completely overwhelmed at the sad news of Absalom's death (v. 33). *O my son Absalom! my son, my son Absalom! Would God I had died for thee. O Absalom! my son, my son!*

CHAPTER 19

At the end of the previous chapter we left David's army in triumph but David himself in tears. Here: 1. David returns to himself, because of Joab's persuasion (vv. 1–8). 2. He returns to his kingdom from exile: the men of Israel were eager to bring him back (vv. 9–10); the men of Judah had to be encouraged by David's agents to do it (vv. 11–14) and did it (v. 15). 3. At the king's coming over the Jordan, Shimei's treason is pardoned (vv. 16–23). 4. Mephibosheth's absence is excused (vv. 24–30). 5. Barzillai's kindness is recognized thankfully, and his son is rewarded (vv. 31–39). 6. The men of Israel quarrel with the men of Judah for not calling them to the ceremony of the king's restoration (vv. 40–43).

Verses 1–8

Soon after the messengers had brought news of the defeat and death of Absalom, Joab and his victorious army followed. We are told:

1. What a disappointment it was to them to find the king weeping for Absalom's death, which they saw as a sign of his displeasure against them for what they had done. What they had expected was that he would meet them with joy and thankfulness for their good services. *It was told Joab* (v. 1). The report of it ran throughout the army (v. 2), *how the king was grieved for his son.* They were reluctant to blame the king, for *whatever he did used to please them* (3:36), but they took it as a great humiliation. Their *victory was turned into mourning* (v. 2). They *stole into the city as men ashamed* (v. 3). As a compliment to their sovereign, they would not be glad about what they saw made him suffer so much.

2. How clearly and strongly Joab rebuked David for his poor judgment and lack of self-control at this critical moment. Never had David needed the hearts of his subjects more than now. Joab exalted the services of David's soldiers: *"This day they have saved thy life* (v. 5). *Thou hast shamed their faces* (v. 5)." What can be more ridiculous than loving your enemies and hating your friends? He advised him to show himself immediately to his troops, to show them his favor, to welcome them home and congratulate them on their success, and to express his thankfulness for their service.

3. How wisely and humbly David took the rebuke and advice he was given (v. 8). He shook off his grief, anointed his head, and washed his face, so that he might not show that he had been mourning. He then appeared in public in the gateway, which was like the town hall. The people flocked to him there to celebrate his and their safety, and so everything turned out well.

Verses 9–15

It is strange that David did not immediately march back to Jerusalem. Could not he himself go back with the victorious army he had with him in Gilead? He could, but he wanted to go back as a prince, with the unanimous approval of the people, and not as a conqueror forcing his way back. He wanted to go back in honor, and as his normal self, not at the head of his forces but in the arms of his subjects, for the ruler who is wise and good enough to make himself, without doubt, his people's favorite looks greater and makes himself appear much more important than the ruler who is overpowering and makes himself a terror to his people.

1. The men of Israel, that is, the ten tribes, were the first to talk about it (vv. 9–10). It was the subject of intense debate throughout the country. David had formerly helped

them, had fought their battles, subdued their enemies, and served them well. It was therefore a shame that he should continue to be banished from their country when he had been such a great benefactor to it. Absalom had now disappointed them. "We were foolishly sick of the tree, and chose the branch to reign over us. But now we have had enough of him. He has been destroyed, and we narrowly escaped being destroyed with him. Let us therefore return to our former allegiance and think about bringing the king back." Perhaps the disagreement was not about whether the king should be brought back or not—all agreed that it should be done—but about whose fault it was that it had not yet been done.

2. The men of Judah were not as forward as the others. David knew that all the others were well disposed toward him, but he knew nothing about Judah's position. David did not want to return until he knew what his own tribe was thinking. So that his way home might be clearer:

2.1. He employed Zadok and Abiathar, the two chief priests, to negotiate with the elders of Judah and to encourage them to give the king an invitation to come back to his house, which was the glory of their tribe (vv. 11–12). Perhaps they were so aware of how much they had offended David when they joined Absalom, that they were afraid to bring him back because they despaired of receiving his favor. He therefore authorized his agents to assure them of his favor with this reason: "*You are my brethren, my bone and my flesh*, my own flesh and blood (v. 12), and so I cannot be harsh with you."

2.2. He took a particular interest in Amasa, who had been Absalom's general, but who, like Joab, was his own nephew (v. 13). He acknowledged him as his relative and promised him that if he would now stand at his side before the people, he would make him commander of all his forces in place of Joab. But although David was wise in naming Amasa for this post—Joab now having become intolerably proud—he did him a bad turn by making his plans public, for it led to Amasa's death by Joab's hand (20:10).

2.3. The point was then won. He won the heart of the men of Judah so that they voted unanimously to recall the king (v. 14). God's providence brought them to this decision through the priests' persuasion and Amasa's influence. David did not make a move until he received this invitation, and then he went back to the Jordan, where they were to meet him (v. 15).

Verses 16–23

In his flight David remembered God particularly *from the land of Jordan* (Ps 42:6), and now that land, more than any other, was graced with the glories of his return. David's soldiers provided themselves with the means to cross the river, but for his own family, *a ferry boat* was deliberately sent (v. 18). Two remarkable people met him on the banks of the Jordan, both of whom had mistreated him wretchedly when he was on the run:

1. Ziba, who by accusing his master had gained from the king a gift of his master's estate (16:4). He had taken advantage of the king's gullibility and had drawn him into doing something very unkind to the son of his friend Jonathan. Ziba comes now to meet the king (v. 17), so that he may obtain the king's favor and thereby put himself in a better position for the moment when—soon—Mephibosheth tells David the truth and clears himself (v. 26).

2. Shimei, who had hurled insults at him and cursed him (16:5), but now thinks it in his interests to make peace with him. To commend himself to the king, Shimei came

in good company, with the men of Judah, and brought a regiment of the men of Benjamin with him, offering his own service and theirs to the king. What he did he did quickly and publicly. The offense was public, and so the submission should be also. He acknowledged his crime: *Thy servant doth know that I have sinned*. He begged the king's pardon: *Let not the king impute iniquity to thy servant*, that is, "Let the king not deal with me as I deserve." A suggestion that justice be carried out against him (v. 21) was made by Abishai, who would have risked his life to kill Shimei when he was cursing (16:9). David rejected Abishai's proposal with displeasure: *What have I to do with you, you sons of Zeruiah?* The less we have to do with those who have an angry, vengeful spirit, and who try to make us do what is harsh and severe, the better. It is the glory of kings to forgive those who humble and surrender themselves: "It is enough for the lion that it has its victim at its mercy." His joy disposed him to forgive. But this was not all; his experience of God's mercy in restoring him to his kingdom, his exclusion from which he attributed to his sin, also disposed him to show mercy to Shimei. Shimei then had his pardon signed and sealed with an oath.

Verses 24–30

The day of David's return was a day of remembrance. Among other things, after the case of Shimei, that of Mephibosheth came to be asked about, and he himself brought it forward:

1. He went down in the crowd *to meet the king* (v. 24), and as a proof of the sincerity of his joy at the king's return, we are told what a true mourner he was for the king's exile. He never trimmed his beard or mustache and never put on clean clothes, but completely neglected himself, as one given up to grief for the king's suffering and the kingdom's troubles.

2. When the king came to Jerusalem, Mephibosheth appeared before him (v. 25). When the king asked him why he, as one of his family, had stayed behind and had not accompanied him in his exile, he opened up fully to the king:

2.1. He complained about his servant Ziba, who should have been his friend. Ziba had been his enemy in two ways:

- He had stopped him from going along with the king, by taking for himself the donkey which was ordered to make ready for his master (v. 26), meanly taking advantage of his lameness and his inability to help himself, and:
- He had slandered him to David by accusing him of planning to usurp the government (v. 27).

2.2. He gratefully acknowledged the king's great kindness to him when he and all his father's house were at the king's mercy (v. 28).

2.3. He committed his cause to the king's pleasure, depending on the king's wisdom and his ability to discern between truth and falsehood, and giving up any claims to his own goodness.

3. David then recalls the removal of Mephibosheth's estate. He had been deceived into making a gift of it to Ziba, and now he revoked that grant and confirmed his former settlement of it: "*I have said, thou and Ziba divide the land* (v. 29), that is, let it be as I originally ordered it (9:10). The property will still be vested in you, but Ziba will be allowed to occupy it. He will cultivate the land and pay you a rent." In this way, Mephibosheth was back

in his original position; no harm was done, except that Ziba went away unpunished for giving false and malicious information against his master.

4. Mephibosheth is so joyful at the king's return that he brushes aside all his concern for his estate (v. 30): "*Yea, let him take all*; I would rather have the presence and favor of the king than any possessions."

Verses 31–39

Barzillai, the Gileadite, who had a noble seat at Rogelim, not far from Mahanaim, was the man who out of all the nobility and gentry of that country had been kindest to David in his distress. If Absalom had won, it is likely that Barzillai would have suffered for his loyalty, but now he and his family will not be losers by it. Here is:

1. Barzillai's great respect for David as his rightful sovereign: he *provided the king with much sustenance*, for himself and his family, *while he lay at Mahanaim* (v. 32). God had given him a large estate, *for he was a very great man*, and it seems he was generous in doing good with it. What else are great possessions good for?

2. The kind invitation David gave him to come to the royal court (v. 33): *Come thou over with me*. He invited him:

2.1. So that he might have the pleasure of his company and the benefit of his advice.

2.2. So that he might have an opportunity of returning his kindness: *I will feed thee with me* (v. 33).

3. Barzillai's reply to this invitation, in which:

3.1. He wonders at the king's generosity in making him this offer, minimizing his own service and exalting what the king offers in return.

3.2. He declines the invitation. He begs his majesty's forgiveness for refusing such a generous offer. But:

• He is old and unfit to move at all, especially to the royal court.

• He is dying and so must begin to think about his long journey, his move from the world (v. 37).

3.3. He wants the king to be kind to his son Kimham: "*Let him go over with my lord the king* (v. 37) and be advanced at the royal court." Whatever favors are shown to him, Barzillai will take as being done to himself.

4. David's farewell to Barzillai:

4.1. He sends him back to his country with a kiss and a blessing (v. 39), showing that he is thankful for his kindness and that he will love him and pray for him. He also promises that whatever he asks at any time, he will be ready to do for him (v. 38): *Whatsoever thou shalt think of*, when you come home, to *ask of me*, that *will I do for thee*.

4.2. He continues homeward with Kimham and leaves it to Barzillai to choose his son's advancement for him: "I will *do to him what shall seem good to thee* (v. 38)." And it seems that Barzillai asked for a country residence for him near Jerusalem, for much later we read about a place near Bethlehem, David's city, which is called *the habitation of Chimham* (Jer 41:17), which was probably allotted to him not out of the crown lands or confiscated estates, but out of David's paternal estate.

Verses 40–43

David came over the Jordan accompanied and helped only by the men of Judah, but when he had advanced as far as Gilgal, the first resting place on this side of the Jordan, *half the people of Israel* (v. 40), that is, half the troops of Israel or half of their elders and leaders, were

there to kiss his hand. They found, however, that they had come too late to witness the grandeur of his first entrance. This led to a quarrel between them and the men of Judah and was the beginning of further trouble. Here is:

1. The complaint which the men of Israel brought to the king against the men of Judah (v. 41), that the men of Judah had performed the ceremony of bringing the king over the Jordan and had not given them notice, seeming to imply that the men of Israel were not so well disposed toward the king, whereas the king himself knew that they had spoken about bringing him back before the men of Judah had even thought about it (v. 11).

2. The excuse which the men of Judah gave for their action (v. 42):

2.1. They plead their close relationship with the king: "*He is near of kin to us*, and so in a matter of ceremony, as this was, we should have priority."

2.2. They deny the implied accusation of self-seeking in what they have done: "*Have we eaten at all of the king's cost* (provisions)? (v. 42). No; we have all borne our own expenses. *Hath he given us any gift?* (v. 42). No; we have no intention of monopolizing the advantages of his return. There will be time enough for you to share in them."

3. The men of Israel's justification of their charge (v. 43). They pleaded, "*We have ten parts* (shares) *in the king*"—Judah being joined only by Simeon, whose allotted territory lay within Judah's—"and so we are offended that our advice was not asked about *bringing back the king*."

CHAPTER 20

No sooner is one of David's troubles over than another arises. 1. Before David reaches Jerusalem, a new rebellion is started by Sheba (vv. 1–2). When he comes to Jerusalem, his first work is to condemn his concubines to imprisonment until they died (v. 3). 2. Amasa, with whom he entrusts the raising of an army against Sheba, is too slow in his actions, which alarms David (vv. 4–6). One of David's generals cruelly murders the other when they are taking the field (vv. 7–13). 3. Sheba is eventually confined in the city of Abel Beth Maacah (vv. 14–15), but the citizens hand him over to Joab, and so his rebellion is crushed (vv. 16–22). 4. The chapter concludes with a short account of David's officials (vv. 23–26).

Verses 1–3

In the midst of his triumphs, David has to see his kingdom disturbed and his family disgraced:

1. His subjects rebelled from him at the instigation of a *man of Belial*, a troublemaker (v. 1), whom they followed when they forsook the *man after God's own heart* (1Sa 13:14). We must not think it strange, while we are in this world, if the end of one trouble is only the beginning of another. A broken bone, when it is set, must have time to heal. The ringleader of this rebellion was Sheba, a Benjamite by birth (v. 1), who came from the hill country of Ephraim (v. 21). Shimei and he both came from Saul's tribe, and both harbored the old grudge of Saul's house. The occasion of the rebellion was that foolish quarrel which we read about at the end of the previous chapter, between the elders of Israel and the elders of Judah, about bringing the king back. "If the king will allow himself to be monopolized by the men of Judah, let him and them do the best they can together, and we will set up a king for ourselves." This was declared by Sheba (v. 1), who probably was a well-known man and had been active in

Absalom's conspiracy. The offended Israelites took the hint and *went up from after David to follow Sheba* (v. 2). Perverting words is subverting peace, and a lot of trouble is caused by forcing invidious interpretations onto what is said and written and drawing conclusions that were never intended. The men of Judah said, *The king is near of kin to us* (19:42). "By this," the men of Israel say, "you mean that *we have no part in him*" (v. 1), whereas they meant no such thing.

2. His concubines were imprisoned for life. He was forced to confine them because they had been defiled by Absalom (v. 3). Those whom he had loved must now be hated.

Verses 4–13

Here is Amasa's fall just as he was beginning to rise. He had been Absalom's general and came over to David's side on a promise that he would be general of his forces instead of Joab.

1. Amasa has a commission to raise forces to suppress Sheba's rebellion. He is ordered to raise them as quickly as possible (v. 4), all the men of Judah within three days, but he finds them so unwilling and unready that he cannot do it within the appointed time (v. 5).

2. When Amasa was delayed, Abishai, the brother of Joab, was ordered to take the guards and standing forces and go with them to pursue Sheba (vv. 6–7), for nothing would have more dangerous consequences than to give him time. David gave these orders to Abishai because he had decided to humiliate Joab. Joab, without orders, and although disgraced, went along with his brother.

3. Joab meets Amasa near Gibeon and cruelly murders him (vv. 8–10).

3.1. He did it craftily and ingeniously, not on a sudden provocation. He drew his tunic close so that it would not hang in his way. Strapped over the tunic at his waist was his belt with a dagger in its sheath, so that the dagger would be readily available to him. His dagger was in a sheath too big for it, so that whenever he wanted, it could fall out when shaken a little, as if it fell out by accident, and then he could take it into his hand, unsuspected, as if he were going to return it into the sheath.

3.2. He did it treacherously, pretending to be Amasa's friend so that he would not be on his guard. He called him *brother*.

3.3. He did it brazenly, not in a quiet corner but at the head of Amasa's troops. He acted in contempt and defiance of David and the commission he had given to Amasa.

4. Joab immediately resumes his place as general and is careful to lead the army on in pursuit of Sheba. He knew how many favored him rather than Amasa, who had been a traitor. What man of Judah would not support his old king and his old general? But one wonders how a murderer could have the presumption to pursue a traitor. Care is taken to move the dead body out of the way and cover it with a garment (vv. 12–13). Evildoers think they are safe in their evil if they can only hide it from the eyes of the world. They think that if it is hidden, it is as if it had never been done.

Verses 14–22

Here is the conclusion of Sheba's attempt:

1. When this rebel had passed through all the tribes of Israel and found them not as willing, on second thoughts, to follow him, he finally entered Abel Beth Maacah, a strong city in the north. His followers were mostly Berites, of Beeroth in Benjamin (v. 14).

2. Joab drew up all his forces against the city, besieged it, battered the wall, and made it almost ready to be generally stormed (v. 15).

3. A shrewd woman of the city of Abel brings the matter to a satisfactory outcome, one that satisfies Joab and still saves the city. Here is:

3.1. Her agreement with Joab, by which he is engaged to lift the siege on condition that Sheba is handed over. It seems that none of the men of Abel offered to negotiate with Joab, but the wisdom of this one woman saved the city. Souls know no difference of sex. Although man is the head, it does not therefore follow that he has the monopoly of brains, and so he should not have a monopoly of the crown. Many male qualities have been found within women, and the treasure of wisdom is no less valuable for its residing in women. In the negotiation between this nameless hero and Joab:

3.1.1. She gains his attention and hearing (vv. 16–17).

3.1.2. She skillfully reasons with him on behalf of her city:

- That it was a city "famous for wisdom" (v. 18).
- That the inhabitants were generally peaceful and faithful in Israel (v. 19).
- That it was a mother in Israel, a guide and nurse to the surrounding towns and country, and that it was a part of *the inheritance of the Lord* (v. 19).
- That they had expected him to offer them peace before he attacked them, according to that known law of war set forth in Dt 20:10.

3.1.3. Joab and Abel's advocate soon agree that Sheba's head will be the price for redeeming the city. "Our quarrel is not with your city. Our quarrel is only with the traitor who is harbored among you. Hand him over, and we will be finished." A great deal of trouble would be prevented if conflicting parties would only understand each other. The single condition of peace for Abel is the surrender of the traitor. It is like this in God's dealings with the soul when it is besieged by conviction and distress. Sin is the traitor; cherished sinful desires are the rebels. If we give those up and drive away the sin, everything will be well.

3.2. Her agreement with the citizens. She went to them in her wisdom and persuaded them to cut off Sheba's head. Joab then lifted the siege and marched back to Jerusalem, with the trophies of peace rather than victory.

Verses 23–26

Here is an account of the state of David's court after his restoration to the throne. Joab kept the position of general. Benaiah, as before, was captain of the guards. Here a new office was set up, that of *treasurer* or one *over the tribute*, in charge of forced labor (v. 24), for it was not until toward the end of his reign that David began to raise taxes.

CHAPTER 21

The date of the events of this chapter is uncertain. I tend to think that they happened as they are placed here, after Absalom's and Sheba's rebellions and toward the end of David's reign. The people were counted just after the three years' famine for the Gibeonites, for what is threatened as three years' famine in 1Ch 21:12 is called seven years in 2Sa 24:12–13, three more, plus the current year, added to those three. We have here: 1. The Gibeonites avenged by a famine in the land (v. 1) and by the putting of seven of Saul's descendants to death (vv. 2–9). 2. Care taken, however, of their dead bodies, and of the bones of Saul (vv. 10–14). 3. The giants of the Philistines killed in several battles (vv. 15–22).

Verses 1–9

Here:

1. We are told of the wrong which Saul had done to the Gibeonites long before this. The Gibeonites were survivors of the Amorites (v. 2) who by trickery had made peace with Israel and had gotten Joshua to publicly promise that they would be protected. It was agreed at that time (Jos 9:23) that their lives would be spared but that they would be deprived of their lands and liberty and that they and their families would be tenants serving Israel. Saul, pretending to be zealous for the honor of Israel—so that it might not be said that any of the natives were among them—aimed to root them out, and in order to do that, killed many of them. He may have intended to be harsh toward the Gibeonites to show that he wanted to make up for his leniency toward the Amalekites. What made this a very shameful sin was that he not only shed innocent blood but also, when he did so, violated the solemn oath by which the nation was bound to protect them.

2. We find the nation of Israel disciplined with a severe famine, much later, because of this sin of Saul. Notice:

2.1. There was a famine even in the fruitful land of Israel and during the glorious reign of David: great drought and scarcity of provisions, which lasted for three consecutive years.

2.2. David inquired of God about it. Although he himself was a prophet, he must still inquire of God and seek and know God's mind in God's own way.

2.3. God was ready to answer even though David was slow in asking: *It is for* (on account of) *Saul* (v. 1). Time does not bring an end to the guilt of sin, nor can we build up hopes of being exempt just because the judgment is delayed.

3. We see vengeance taken on the house of Saul in order to take away God's wrath from the land, which was then suffering because of his sin.

3.1. David, probably by divine direction, asked the Gibeonites themselves how they should be compensated for the wrong that had been done them (v. 3).

3.2. They wanted seven of Saul's descendants to be put to death, and David granted their wish.

3.2.1. They required no *silver, nor gold* (v. 4). Nor did they take advantage of this good opportunity to be freed from their bondage under the law that says (Ex 21:26), *If a man strike out his servant's eye, he shall let him go free for his eye's sake.* They did not insist on this; although the covenant was broken on the other side, it would not also be broken on theirs. They were *Nethinim,* given to God and his people Israel, and they did not want to appear weary of the service.

3.2.2. They required no lives except those of Saul's family.

3.2.3. They would not impose on David to carry out this execution: *"Thou shalt not for us kill any man* (v. 4); we will do it ourselves, *we will hang them up unto* (expose them before) *the Lord"* (v. 6), so that if any hardship resulted from it, they would bear the blame, and not David or his house.

3.2.4. They did not require this out of hatred for Saul or his family—if they had been vengeful, they would have done something long before—but out of love for the people of Israel, whom they saw suffering because of the wrong done to them.

3.2.5. They left the naming of the people to David, who took care to keep Mephibosheth safe for Jonathan's sake, so that while he was avenging the breaking of one oath, he himself would not break another (v. 7).

3.2.6. The place, time, and manner of their execution all added to the awesomeness of their sacrifice to divine justice.

3.2.6.1. They were exposed, as under a curse, under the awful mark of God's displeasure, for the Law said, *He that is hanged is accursed of God* (Dt 21:23).

3.2.6.2. They were exposed at Gibeah of Saul (v. 6), to show that it was for his sin that they died.

Verses 10–14

We have here:

1. Saul's sons not only hanged, but also hanged in chains, their dead bodies left hanging and exposed, until the judgment which their death was to turn away had been brought to an end by the sending of rain to the land. They died as sacrifices, and so they were, in a way, offered up, not consumed all at once by fire, but gradually by the air.

2. Their dead bodies watched by Rizpah, the mother of two of them (v. 10). It was a great suffering for her, now in her old age, that she should see her two sons, who had probably comforted her and were likely to support her in her declining years, cut off so terribly. None of us knows what suffering may be in store for them. She was prohibited from seeing them decently buried, but she would make sure that they were decently watched. She did not try to change the sentence passed on them, that they should hang there until God sent rain. She did not try to forcefully take away their dead bodies, although divine law might have been quoted to support her, but she patiently submitted, pitched a tent of sackcloth near the gallows, and there with her servants and friends protected the dead bodies from birds and wild animals. In this way, she let the world know that her sons had not died because of any sin of their own and not as stubborn and rebellious sons. But they had died because of their father's sin, and so her mind could not be taken off them because of their hard fate. Although there was no way out and they must die, nevertheless they would die pitied and mourned.

3. The solemn burial of their dead bodies, with the bones of Saul and Jonathan, in the burial place of their family. Far from being displeased at what Rizpah had done, David himself was stirred by it to honor the house of Saul, and these branches of it among the rest. In this way it was made apparent that it was not out of any personal dislike for the family that he handed them over, but that he had to do it for the public good.

3.1. David now thought he would move the bodies of Saul and Jonathan from the place where the men of Jabesh Gilead had decently, but in private and in obscurity, buried them *under a tree* (1Sa 31:12–13).

3.2. With them he buried the bodies *of those that were hanged,* for when God's anger had been turned away, they were no longer looked on as a curse (vv. 13–14). When *water dropped upon them out of heaven* (v. 10), that is, when God sent rain to water the earth, they were taken down, for then it appeared *that God was entreated* (answered prayer) *for the land* (v. 14).

Verses 15–22

We have here the story of some conflicts with the Philistines, which it seems took place toward the end of David's reign. Although he had subdued them so that they could not bring any great numbers onto the battlefield, as long as there were any giants among them to be their champions, they took every opportunity to disturb the peace of Israel.

1. David himself fought one of the giants. The Philistines began the war once again (v. 15). Although David was old, he did not want to be discharged from serving the nation, but *went down* in person to fight *against the Philistines*. But age had cut his hair, as Delilah had cut Samson's hair, and after a little toil he *waxed faint*, he became exhausted (v. 15). His body could not keep up with his mind. The champion of the Philistines soon became aware of his advantage, realized that David's strength was failing him, and being himself strong and well armed, *thought to slay David* (v. 16). But because God was not in his thoughts, he and all his compatriots perished on that very day. David was promptly rescued by Abishai (v. 17). When *Abishai succoured him*, came to his rescue (v. 17), he may have given him something to drink to relieve his fainting spirits, or offered to act as his deputy; and then *he smote the Philistine and killed him* (v. 17), that is, as I understand it, David did this, for v. 22 says that David had a hand in the slaying of the giants. If David did do it, then this verse shows that he was exhausted but did not run away, that although his strength failed him, he bravely kept his ground, and then God sent him this help in his time of need. In his agonies, Christ was strengthened by an angel. Even strong saints sometimes become exhausted in spiritual conflicts. Satan attacks them furiously, but those who stand their ground and resist him will be helped and rescued, and they will be more than conquerors.

2. The other giants fell at the hands of David's men:

2.1. Saph was killed by Sibbecai, one of David's warriors (v. 18; 1Ch 11:29).

2.2. Another, who was a brother of Goliath, was killed by Elhanan, who is mentioned in 23:24.

2.3. Another, who had an unusually large build, more fingers and toes than other people (v. 20), and such an unparalleled defiance that although he had seen the fall of other giants he still defied Israel, was killed by *Jonathan the son of Shimea* (v. 21). Shimeah had one son named *Jonadab* (13:3), who I would have thought was the same person as this Jonathan except that the former was noted for his craftiness, the latter for his courage. These giants were probably the remnants of the sons of Anak. Long feared, now finally they fell. It is foolish for the strong person to *glory in his strength* (Jer 9:23). David's servants were no greater or stronger than others, but with God's help, they defeated one giant after another. The most powerful enemies are often reserved for the last conflict. David began his glory with the conquest of one giant, and here he concludes his glory with the conquest of four. Death is a Christian's last enemy, and a descendant of Anak, but we hope finally to be more than conquerors through Christ who has triumphed for us, even over that enemy.

CHAPTER 22

This chapter is a psalm of praise. We find it later included among David's psalms (Ps 18) with a few variations. We have it here as it was first composed for his own harp; in the book of Psalms we have it as it was later presented to the chief musician (Ps 18 title), for the service of the church. After the inspired writer had related David's deliverances in detail in this and the previous book, especially after the one at the close of the previous chapter, he thought it fit to record this sacred poem as a memorial of all that had been related before. Some think that David wrote this psalm when he was old, that he was generally looking back on the mercies of his life and the many wonderful preservations God had blessed him with, from first to last. If so, then this psalm shows us that in our praises we should look as far back as we can and not allow time to wear down the sense of God's favors. Here is: 1. The title of the psalm (v. 1). 2. The psalm itself, in which he gives glory to God and takes comfort in him. He writes at some length of the causes he has both for praising God and for taking comfort in him, namely, the experiences he has had of God's former favors and the expectations he has of his further favors.

Verse 1

Notice here:

1. God's people have often had many enemies and have been in imminent danger of falling into their hands. David was a man after God's own heart, but not after the people's heart: there were many who hated him and sought to destroy him. Those whom God loves should not be surprised if the world hates them.

2. Those who trust God as they follow their duty will find him always ready to help them in their greatest dangers. We will never be fully rescued from all our enemies until we reach heaven, and God will bring all his own people to that heavenly kingdom (2Ti 4:18).

3. Those who have received many special mercies from God should give him the glory for them. Each new mercy in our hands should put a new song of praise to God into our mouth.

4. We ought to be quick in giving our thanks to God: *In the day that God delivered him he sang this song* (v. 1).

Verses 2–51

Let us notice in this song of praise:

1. How David adores God and gives him glory for his infinite, perfect qualities. There is none like him, nor can any be compared with him (v. 32): *Who is God, save the Lord?* All others who are worshiped as gods are counterfeits and pretenders. *Who is a rock, save our God?* They are all dead, but *the Lord liveth* (v. 47). God is different; he completes his work, and his word is tested and is something that we may trust.

2. How David glories in the privileges he has in his relationship with this God, which he lays down as the foundation of all the benefits he has received from him: *He is my God* (v. 3). He cries to him as such (v. 7) and remains faithful to him (v. 22). David argues, "If he is *my God*, then he is also *my rock* (v. 2), that is, he is my strength and my power (v. 33), the stronghold in which I can shelter and the rock on which I build my hope (v. 3). Whatever is my strength and support, he is *the God of the rock of my salvation* (v. 47)." David often hid himself in a rock (1Sa 24:2), but God was his main hiding place. "He is my fortress, in which I am safe and secure. He is *my high tower* (v. 3), my stronghold, in which I am beyond the reach of real evils. He is *the tower of salvation* (v. 51), which can never be scaled, battered down, or undermined. God, my Savior, saves me." Christ is spoken of as the *horn of salvation* in the house of David (Lk 1:69). "Am I carrying heavy burdens? Am I ready to sink? *The Lord is my stay* (v. 19). He is the One who supports me. Am I in the dark? Is everything like night around me? Am I at a loss to know which way to go? *Thou art my lamp, O Lord!* You will show me my way, and you will dispel *my darkness*"

(v. 29). If we sincerely take the Lord as our God, he will be all this and much more to us. We will find him to be all we need and can desire.

3. How he makes the most of his privileges in this relationship with God. "If he is mine:

• *In him will I trust*" (v. 3).
• *On him I will call* (v. 4), for *he is worthy to be praised.*"
• To him will I give thanks (v. 50), and give it publicly."

4. The full account he gives to others of the great things God has done for him. This takes up most of the song. He gives God glory for both his rescues and his successes.

4.1. He glorifies the great acts of salvation God has worked for him. To glorify God's salvation, he notes:

4.1.1. That the danger from which he was rescued was very great and threatening. People *rose up against him* (v. 40 and again v. 49) who *hated him* (v. 41), including *a violent man* (v. 49), namely Saul, who had maliciously and strongly pursued him. This is expressed figuratively in vv. 5–6. The waves of death beat on him so violently, the cords and snares of death took hold of him so strongly, that he could not help himself, any more than a dead body in a grave can.

4.1.2. That his rescue was an answer to prayer (v. 7). He has left us a good example in this, that when we are in distress, we should boldly cry out to God, as children do to their parents when they are frightened.

4.1.3. That God appeared in a special way for him and against his enemies. The expressions are taken from the descent of the divine Majesty on Mount Sinai (vv. 8–9).

4.1.4. That God showed his special favor and kindness to him in these rescues (v. 20): *He delivered me, because he delighted in me.* The rescue came not because of "ordinary" providence, but because of covenant love. In this he was a type of Christ, whom God upheld because he *delighted in him* (Isa 42:1–2).

4.2. He glorifies the great successes God has crowned him with. He has not only preserved but also prospered him. He was blessed:

4.2.1. With liberty and release. He was *brought into a large* (spacious) *place* (v. 20).

4.2.2. With military skill, strength, and speed. Although he had been brought up to be a shepherd, he was also well taught in the art of warfare and well qualified for its rigors and dangers. When God called him to fight his battles, he qualified him for service.

4.2.3. With victory over his enemies, not only Saul and Absalom, but also the Philistines, Moabites, Ammonites, Syrians, and other neighboring nations, whom he subdued and made subject to Israel. His wonderful victories are described (vv. 38–43).

4.2.4. With advancement to honor and power. God *made his way perfect* (v. 33), gave him success in all his undertakings, *set him upon his high places* (v. 34), showing a position of both security and dignity. God's gentleness, his grace and tender mercy, *made him great* (v. 36).

5. The comforting reflections he gives on his own integrity, which God has graciously witnessed to and acknowledged by those wonderful rescues (vv. 21–25). He is referring especially to his integrity toward Saul and Ish-Bosheth, Absalom and Sheba, and those who either opposed his coming to the crown or tried to dethrone him. They falsely accused him and misrepresented him, but he had the testimony of his conscience for him that he was not ambitious or aspiring, not a false man of blood, as they called him. His conscience bore witness:

5.1. That he had made the word of God his rule and had kept to it (v. 23). Wherever he was, God's judgments were his guide in front of him; wherever he went, he took his religious faith along with him.

5.2. That he had carefully avoided the byways of sin. He had not willfully departed from his God. He had to admit that he had taken some false steps, but he had not abandoned God or left his ways. He could not keep himself from sins of weakness, but the grace of God had kept him from presumptuous sins. David reflected with more satisfaction on his victories over his own sin than on his conquest of Goliath and all the powers of the uncircumcised Philistines. If a great man is a good man, his goodness will be much more satisfying than his greatness.

6. The comforting prospects he has of God's further favor. He looks back just as he looks forward: with pleasure. He assures himself of the kindness God has in store for all the saints, for himself, and also for his descendants:

6.1. For all good people (vv. 26–28). He uses the occasion to lay down how God deals with people:

6.1.1. That he will do good to those who are blameless in their hearts.

6.1.1.1. God's mercy and grace will be the joy of those who are merciful and gracious.

6.1.1.2. God's uprightness, justice, and faithfulness will be the joy of those who are upright, just, and faithful, both toward God and other people.

6.1.1.3. God's purity and holiness will be the joy of those who are pure and holy. On the other hand:

6.1.2. Those who *turn aside to crooked ways* he *will lead forth with the workers of iniquity* (Ps 125:5), as he says in another psalm.

6.2. For himself. He foresaw that his conquests and kingdom would be further enlarged (vv. 45–46).

6.3. For his descendants: he *showeth mercy to his anointed* (Messiah) (v. 51), not only to David himself but also to his descendants forever. David was himself anointed by God. He therefore did not doubt that God would show mercy to him, that mercy which he had promised not to take from him or his descendants (7:15–16). He depended on that promise with an eye to Christ, who alone is his *seed for evermore* (v. 51), whose throne and kingdom still continue and will continue to the end. In this way, all his joys and all his hopes meet, as ours should, in the great Redeemer.

CHAPTER 23

The writer is now drawing toward the conclusion of David's reign and gives an account. 1. Of some of his last words, which seem to refer to his descendants, who were spoken of in the previous chapter (vv. 1–7). 2. Of the great men who were employed under him, the first three (vv. 8–17), two of the next three (vv. 18–23), and then the thirty (vv. 24–39).

Verses 1–7

Here is the last will and testament of King David, after he had settled the crown on Solomon and his treasures on the temple which was to be built.

1. The maker of the will is described:

1.1. By the lowliness of his origins: he was *the son of Jesse* (v. 1).

1.2. By the height of his advancement: he *was raised up on high* (v. 1), as one favored by God and intended for something great. He was exalted as a ruler, to sit higher, and as a prophet, to see further, because:

1.2.1. He was *the anointed of the God of Jacob* (v. 1), and so was useful to the people of God in their civil interests, to protect their country and to administer justice among them.

1.2.2. He was *the sweet psalmist of Israel* (v. 1), and so was useful to them in their religious devotions.

2. The will is an account of his fellowship with God. Notice:

2.1. What God said to him, both to direct and encourage him as king, and also to help his successors in the same way.

2.1.1. Who spoke: *The Spirit of the Lord* (v. 2), *the God of Israel* (v. 3), and *the Rock of Israel* (v. 3), which some think is an indication of the Trinity of persons in the Godhead: the Father *the God of Israel*, the Son *the Rock of Israel*, and *the Spirit* proceeding from the Father and the Son, *who spoke by the prophets* (Heb 1:1), particularly by David. David here affirms his divine inspiration, stating that in his psalms and in this composition, *the Spirit of God spoke by him* (v. 2). This honors the book of Psalms and commends the Psalms to be used by us in our devotions, because they are words which the Holy Spirit teaches.

2.1.2. What was spoken. Here a distinction seems to be made between what the Spirit of God spoke *by* David, which includes all his psalms, and what the Rock of Israel spoke *to* David, which concerned himself and his family. Those whose office it is to teach others their duty must also be sure to learn and do their own duty. Now what is said here (vv. 3–4) may be considered:

2.1.2.1. With application to David and his royal family. And so here is the duty of magistrates given to them. When a king was spoken to by God, he was not to be complimented with the honor of his position and the extent of his power, but to be told his duty: *He that ruleth over men must be just, ruling in the fear of God* (v. 3), and so must all subordinate magistrates in their positions. Let rulers remember that they rule over people, not over wild animals. They rule over people who have their foolish and weak ways and so must be dealt with patiently. They rule over people but under God, and for him; and therefore they must be just. Nor is it enough that they do no wrong; they must also not allow wrong to be done. They must also rule in the fear of God and try to further the fear of God, that is, the practice of religious faith, among those whom they rule over. *He that* rules *in the fear of God shall be as the light of the morning* (v. 4). Light is sweet and pleasant, and those who do their duty will receive strength and encouragement from it. Their joy will be the testimony of their conscience. Light is bright, and a good ruler is illustrious; their justice and godliness will be their honor. Light is a blessing, nor are there any greater or more extensive blessings to the community than rulers who *rule in the fear of God* (v. 3). *As the light of the morning* (v. 4), which is most welcome after the darkness of the night, increases and shines more and more until the perfect day (Pr 4:18), such is the growing brightness of a good government. See also Ps 72:6, 16, which were also some of the last words of David, and seem to refer to those recorded here.

2.1.2.2. With application to Christ, the Son of David, and then it must all be taken as a prophecy. The original supports this: "There shall be a ruler among men [or: over men], who will be just and will rule in the fear of God," that is, he will order the affairs of religion and divine worship according to his Father's will. He will be as *the light of the morning* (v. 4), for he is the light of the world (Jn 8:12; 9:5), and he will be as *the tender grass* (v. 4), for he is the *branch of the Lord*, and the *fruit of the earth* (Isa 4:2). See also Ps 72:2; Isa 11:1–5; 32:1–2. God gave David foresight of this by the Spirit, to comfort him under the many troubles of his family and the sad prospects he had of his degenerate descendants.

2.2. What comforting use he made of what God spoke to him, and what were his devout meditations on it in response (v. 5).

2.2.1. Trouble considered: *Although my house be not so with God* (v. 5), and *although he make it not to grow* (v. 5). David's family did not have the relationship with God that is described in vv. 3–4, the relationship he wished it had. It had not been so good or so happy. It had not been so while he lived, and he foresaw that it would not be so when he was gone. His house would be neither so godly nor so prosperous as one might have expected the descendants of such a father to be. This was what David's heart was set on concerning his children, that they might be right with God, faithful to him and zealous for him.

2.2.2. Comfort ensured: *Yet he hath made with me an everlasting covenant* (v. 5). Whatever trouble children of God may undergo in the future, they will still have some kind of comfort to balance it out (2Co 4:8–9). God has made a covenant of grace with us in Jesus Christ, and we are here told:

- That it is an *everlasting* covenant, eternal in its origin and conception, and eternal in its continuance and consequences.
- That it is *ordered*, very well arranged in every aspect, to advance the glory of God and the honor of the Mediator, together with the holiness and strengthening of believers.
- That the promised mercies are secure when the conditions are fulfilled.
- That it is *all our salvation*. Nothing except this will save us, and this is sufficient. It is only this on which our salvation depends.
- That it must therefore be *all our desire*.

2.3. The condemnation of *the sons of Belial*, evil men, read out (vv. 6–7). They will be thrust away as thorns—rejected and abandoned. This is intended:

- As a direction to magistrates to use their power to punish and suppress evil. Let them *thrust away the sons of Belial* (v. 6); see also Ps 101:8. Or:
- As a warning to magistrates, and particularly to David's sons and successors, to see that they themselves are not evildoers, as too many of them were, for then neither the dignity of their position nor their relationship with David would keep them secure from being rejected by the righteous judgments of God.

Verses 8–38

1. The list which the writer has left on record here of the great soldiers who were in David's time is intended:

1.1. To honor David, who trained them up in the arts and exercises of war and set them an example of leadership and courage.

1.2. To honor those bold warriors themselves, who were instrumental in bringing David to the throne, in settling and protecting him on the throne, and in extending his conquests.

1.3. To stir those who come later to imitate them enthusiastically.

1.4. To show how much religious faith contributes to the inspiration of people with true courage. David, both by his psalms and by his offerings for the service of the temple, greatly promoted godliness among the eminent leaders of the kingdom (1Ch 29:6), and when they became famous for their godliness, they became famous for bravery.

2. These mighty warriors are divided here into three ranks:

2.1. The first three, who had done the greatest exploits and so gained the greatest reputation: Josheb-Basshebeth (*Adino*) (v. 8), Eleazar (vv. 9–10), and Shammah (vv. 11–12). The exploits of these three brave warriors are recorded here. They distinguished themselves in the wars of Israel against their enemies, especially the Philistines:

2.1.1. Josheb-Basshebeth (v. 8) killed 800 with his spear at one encounter.

2.1.2. Eleazar defied the Philistines as they had defied Israel by Goliath, but with more success and greater bravery, for when the Israelites had gone away, he not only kept his ground, but *arose, and smote* (struck down) *the Philistines* (v. 10), on whom God struck a terror equal to the courage with which this great hero was inspired. His hand was tired, but it still clung to his sword. As long as he had any strength remaining, he held his weapon and followed through with his blow. We, likewise, in the service of God, should keep up our willingness and spiritual resolution, despite any physical weakness and tiredness: *faint, yet pursuing* (Jdg 8:4), the hand exhausted, but not leaving the sword.

2.1.3. Shammah met with some enemy troops who were foraging, and he defeated them (vv. 11–12). But notice, concerning both this exploit and that of Eleazar it is said, The Lord wrought a great victory.

2.2. The next three were distinguished from, and dignified above, the thirty, but did not equal the first three (v. 23). Of this second group of three warriors only two are named, Abishai and Benaiah, whom we have often met with in the story of David. Here is:

2.2.1. A brave action of these three working together. They accompanied David in his troubles to the cave of Adullam (v. 13), suffered with him, and so were later promoted by him. When David and his brave warriors— who had fought so well against the Philistines—were driven to protect themselves in caves and strongholds, the Philistines set a garrison in Bethlehem itself (vv. 13–14). We are told:

2.2.1.1. How fervently David longed for water from the well near the gate of Bethlehem. It was harvest time; the weather was hot; he was thirsty; perhaps good water was scarce; and so he fervently wished, "Oh that I could have just one drink from the water of the well of Bethlehem!" He had often refreshed himself with the water of that well when he was a youth. Other water could quench his thirst just as well, but he wanted water from Bethlehem more than any other.

2.2.1.2. How bravely his three mighty warriors, Abishai, Benaiah, and another unnamed, went through the camp of the Philistines, into the very jaws of danger, and took water from the well of Bethlehem without David's knowledge (v. 16). This shows:

• How much they respected their ruler, and with what pleasure they could suffer the greatest dangers and undergo the greatest hardships in his service. Will we not want to show ourselves to our Lord Jesus as ready to obey every sign of his will given to us by his word, Spirit, or providence?

• How little they feared the Philistines.

2.2.1.3. How self-denyingly David, when he had this water that had been brought from far away, *poured it out before the Lord* (v. 16). This showed he would deny his own foolish desire and punish himself for harboring and indulging such a thought. It also showed he wanted to honor God and give glory to him. He thought the water bought in this way was too precious for him to drink and was fit only to be poured out to God as a drink offering. Bishop Patrick speaks about some who think that David showed in this that it was not physical water that he longed for, but the Messiah, who had the water of life and who he knew would be born at Bethlehem, which the Philistines therefore would not be able to destroy.

2.2.2. The brave actions of two of them on other occasions. Abishai killed 300 men on one occasion (vv. 18–19). Benaiah did many great things:

2.2.2.1. He killed two Moabites who were *lion-like men* (v. 20): they were very bold, strong, fierce, and ferocious.

2.2.2.2. He killed a lion in a pit, either in self-defense, as Samson did, or perhaps out of kindness to the country, a lion that had caused a lot of trouble. Because it was a snowy day in winter, he was stiffer and the lion was fiercer and more ravenous, yet he still defeated him.

2.2.2.3. He struck down an Egyptian. The text does not say when this took place; the Egyptian was well armed, but Benaiah attacked him with no other weapon than a club, and skillfully snatched his spear out of his hand and killed him with it (v. 21). For these and similar exploits David promoted him to the position of commander in charge of his bodyguard or standing forces (v. 23).

2.3. Less great than the second three, but still notable, were the thirty-one mentioned here by name (vv. 24–39). The surnames given them here are taken, it seems, from the places where they were born or where they lived, as many of our surnames originally were. The most wise and valiant were chosen from all parts of the nation to serve the king. Several of those who are named here are listed as commanders of the twelve divisions which David appointed, one for each month of the year (1Ch 27:1–5).

3. Christ, the Son of David, has his brave warriors too, who like David's are influenced by his example. They fight his battles against the spiritual enemies of his kingdom. They are more than conquerors in his strength. Christ's apostles were his immediate attendants. They performed many great things for him, suffered much, and finally came to reign with him. They are mentioned with honor in the New Testament, as these in the Old, especially in Rev 21:14. In fact, all the good soldiers of Jesus Christ have their names better preserved than even these brave warriors have, for their names are written in heaven.

CHAPTER 24

The last words of David were good, but in this chapter we read about some of his last works, which were not his best. Nevertheless, he repented and finished well. We have here: 1. His sin, which was taking a census of the people because he had pride in his heart (vv. 1–9). 2. His conviction of sin and his repentance of it (v. 10); the punishment inflicted on him because of his sin (vv. 11–15); the withdrawal of the judgment (vv. 16–17). 3. The erecting of an altar as a sign of God's reconciliation to him and his people (vv. 18–25).

Verses 1–9

Here we have:

1. The orders which David gave to Joab to count the people of Israel and Judah (vv. 1–2). Two things here seem strange:

1.1. The sinfulness of this. What harm was there in it?

1.1.1. Some think the fault was that he counted those who were under twenty years old if they were of sufficient height and strength to bear arms, and that this was the reason why this numbering was not recorded, because it was illegal (1Ch 27:23–24).

1.1.2. Others think the fault was that he did not ask for the half shekel, which was to be paid for the service of the sanctuary whenever the people were counted, as *a ransom for their souls* (Ex 30:12).

1.1.3. Others think that he did it with the intention of imposing a tax on them for himself, to be put into his treasury. But nothing of this appears in the text, nor did David ever raise taxes.

1.1.4. Others think that the fault lay in the fact that he had no orders from God to do it.

1.1.5. Some think that it was an insult to the ancient promise which God made to Abraham, that his descendants would be as innumerable as the dust of the earth. To count them smacked of distrust in that promise.

1.1.6. The worst thing in counting the people was that David did it out of pride in his heart, which was Hezekiah's sin in showing his treasures to the ambassadors.

1.1.6.1. It was a proud thought of his own greatness in having command of such a numerous people.

1.1.6.2. It was a proud confidence in his own strength. He thought that by making known the number of his people among the nations, he would appear more formidable.

1.2. The spring from which it is said here to arise is even more strange (v. 1). It is not strange that *the anger of the Lord should be kindled against Israel*. But the fact that in this displeasure God should incite David to take a census of the people is very strange. We are sure that God is not the author of sin; he tempts no one. We are told in 1Ch 21:1 that *Satan provoked* (incited) *David to number Israel*. As an enemy, Satan suggested it as a sin, just as he put it into the heart of Judas to betray Christ. As righteous Judge, God permitted it, with the intention that he would use the sin of David so that rulers might learn from these examples, that when God's judgments are at work, they should look to see whether their sins are the cause of the trouble. If so, they should repent and mend their ways.

2. The opposition which Joab brought to these orders. Even he was aware of David's foolishness and idle boasting in this plan. There was no need to tax them, enroll them, or divide them into parts. They were all at ease and happy. Joab wanted both for their numbers to increase and for the king, even though he was old, to live to see that growth in numbers and have the satisfaction of seeing it. *"But why doth my lord the king delight in this thing?"* (v. 3). Why does he want to do such a thing? What need is there to do it?" It is only poor people who count their flocks. Joab was aware of David's pride in this, but David himself was not.

3. The orders executed nevertheless. *The king's word prevailed* (v. 4). Joab followed orders: he applied himself with some reluctance to this unpleasant task and took the army commanders to help him. The grand total was finally brought to the king at Jerusalem (v. 9). We are not told whether the numbers met David's expectation or not, nor whether the account fed his pride or humbled it.

Verses 10–17

Here David repents of the sin and is punished for it, God is grieved because of the calamity, and David, in response to God, repents even more deeply. Here is:

1. David's penitent reflection on and confession of his sin in counting the people. When the total record was finished and laid before him, his conscience was awakened that very night.

1.1. He was convicted of his sin: *His heart smote him* (v. 10) before the prophet came to him. We think it should not be read *for* (v. 11), but *"and" when David was up*, which is how it reads in the original. His conscience showed him the evil of what he had done.

1.2. He confessed it to God and fervently begged for it to be forgiven. He acknowledged that he had *done very foolishly* (v. 10) because he had done it out of pride in his heart.

2. The just and necessary correction which he suffered for this sin. David had been tossing and turning all night under a deep sense of sin, and he got up in the morning (v. 11) wanting to speak with Gad, his seer, about it. God told Gad what to say to him (v. 11).

2.1. Three things are taken for granted:

2.1.1. That David must be corrected for his fault. Pride is the first of the seven things that God hates (Pr 6:17).

2.1.2. The punishment must correspond to the sin.

2.1.3. It must be a punishment that the people have a large share in, *for God's anger was kindled against Israel* (v. 1). Although it was David's sin that directly opened the sluice gates, the sins of the people had all contributed to the flood before the sluice gates were opened.

2.2. As to the punishment that must be inflicted:

2.2.1. David is told to choose what form of discipline he should suffer (vv. 12–13). His heavenly Father must correct him, but to show that he does not do it willingly and to help David bear it more patiently, he allows David to choose whether it will be by war, famine, or plague. The prophet directs him to think it over and then tell him what answer he should give *to him that sent him* (v. 13).

2.2.2. David objects only to judgment by the sword, and as for the other two, he leaves the matter with God but indicates that his choice rests with the plague (v. 14).

2.2.2.1. He begs that he may not fall into human hands.

2.2.2.2. He gives himself to God. *Let us fall now into the hand of the Lord, for his mercies are great* (v. 14). David refers to God the decision as to which of these will be the scourge he will send. God chooses the shortest, so that he may sooner show he is reconciled with David. But some think that these words show that David indicates his choice of the plague. That is a judgment to which David and his own family are exposed as much as the lowliest subject, which is not so either in famine or in war, and so David, tenderly conscious of his own guilt, chooses that. But David has repented and dares throw himself into God's hands, knowing he will find that his mercies are great. Good people, even when they suffer under God's disapproval, will still have nothing other than good thoughts about him. *Though he slay me, yet will I trust in him* (Job 13:15).

2.2.3. A plague was then sent (v. 15), which lasted from that morning to the third day, according to Mr. Matthew Poole. Or according to Bishop Patrick and others, it lasted only to the evening of the first day, the time appointed for the evening sacrifice.

3. God's gracious relaxing of the judgment when it began to be inflicted on Jerusalem (v. 16): *The angel*

stretched out his hand upon Jerusalem. Perhaps there was more evil in Jerusalem—especially more pride, and that was the sin which was now being punished—than elsewhere, and so the hand of the destroyer was stretched out on that city. But then *the Lord repented him of the evil* (v. 16). God was grieved because of the calamity. He said to the destroying angel, *It is enough: stay now* (withdraw) *thy hand* (v. 16), and *let mercy rejoice against* (triumph over) *judgment* (Jas 2:13). This was on Mount Moriah. Dr. Lightfoot observes that this is the very place where Abraham, by a command from heaven, was stopped from killing his son, and this angel, by a similar command, was stopped from destroying Jerusalem.

4. David's renewed repentance for his sin on this occasion (v. 17). God opened his eyes and he saw the angel: saw his flaming sword stretched out to destroy and saw the angel himself ready to put it back into its sheath on the orders given him to stop the destruction. Seeing all this, David spoke to the *Lord, and said, Lo, I have sinned* (v. 17). See how he blamed himself, as if he could never speak badly enough about his own fault: "*I have sinned, and I have done wickedly* (v. 17). I have committed the crime, and so the punishment should fall on me." See how he interceded for the people, whose bitter mourning made his heart ache and his ears burn: *These sheep, what have they done?* (v. 17). Let this remind us of the grace of our Lord Jesus, who gave himself for our sins and was willing for God's hand to be against him so that we might go free. The shepherd was struck so that the sheep might be spared.

Verses 18–25

Here is:

1. A command sent to David to set up an altar in the place where he saw the angel (v. 18). This was to show to David:

1.1. That God was now completely reconciled with him, for *if the Lord had been pleased to kill him, he would not have accepted an offering* (Jdg 13:23), and so would not have ordered him to *build an altar* (v. 21). God's encouragement to us to offer him spiritual sacrifices is a sign of his reconciliation of us to himself.

1.2. That peace is made between God and sinners by sacrifice. Christ is the great atoning sacrifice, of whom all the legal sacrifices were types.

1.3. That when God's judgments are graciously withdrawn, we should acknowledge it with thankfulness to his praise.

2. The purchase which David made of the land. It seems the owner was a Jebusite named Araunah. Although by birth a Gentile, no doubt he had been converted to the Jewish religion, and was therefore allowed not only to live among the Israelites but also to possess his own house in a city (Lev 25:29–30). The piece of ground was a threshing floor, a lowly place, but dignified, a place of work, and therefore honored.

2.1. David went in person to the owner to negotiate with him. Notice how he acted justly, that he would not even use this place for the present need until he had bought it and paid for it, even though the proprietor was a foreigner and he himself was king, and even though he had explicit instructions from God to set up an altar there. God *hates robbery for burnt offering* (Isa 61:8). Notice, too, how humbly he acted. Although he was king, he went himself (v. 19) and lost no honor by it. When Araunah saw him, he *bowed himself to the ground before him* (v. 20). Great people will never be less respected for their humility, but more so.

2.2. When Araunah understood his business (v. 21), he generously offered him not only the ground to build his altar on but also *oxen for sacrifices,* and other things that might be useful for him in the service (v. 22), and all this for free. He also spoke a good prayer into the bargain: *The Lord thy God accept thee* (v. 23). This he did:

2.2.1. Because he had a generous spirit with many possessions. *He gave as a king* (v. 23). Even though he was an ordinary subject, he had the spirit of a monarch. The Hebrew says, "He gave, even the king to the king" (v. 23), from which it is supposed that Araunah had been king of the Jebusites in that place.

2.2.2. Because he highly respected David, even though David was the one who had conquered him.

2.2.3. Because he had an affection for Israel and fervently desired that *the plague might be stayed* (v. 25), and because to him the honor of having the plague stopped at his threshing floor (v. 24) was quite sufficient to pay for all he now gave to David.

2.3. David decided to pay the full value of it and did so (v. 24). He did not want to offer something to God which cost him nothing. He thanked the Jebusite, but also paid him *fifty shekels of silver* (v. 24) for the floor and for the oxen that were to be used in the present service, and later 600 shekels of gold (1Ch 21:25–27) for the adjoining land, to build the temple on.

3. The building of the altar and the offering of the proper sacrifices on it (v. 25), burnt offerings to the glory of God's justice and peace offerings (fellowship offerings) to the glory of his mercy.

A Practical and Devotional Exposition of the Book of

1 Kings

The Bible began with the story of patriarchs, prophets, and judges, people whose dealings with heaven were more direct; the record of these interactions strengthens our faith, but it is not so easily applied to our own lives, now that we do not expect visions, since the history of lives like ours is under the direction of common providence. Here, though we do not find as many types and figures of the Messiah as in those earlier books, nevertheless, we do find great expectations of him, for not only prophets but also kings wanted to see the great mysteries of the Gospel (Lk 10:24).

The two books of Samuel are introductions to the books of Kings, as they record the origins of the royal government of Saul and the royal family of David. These two books give us an account of David's successor, Solomon, the division of his kingdom, and the succession of several kings both of Judah and of Israel, with a summary of their history up to the Exile. And just as we could gather from the book of Genesis excellent rules of home management in order to lead our families well, so also we may gather from these books rules of politics, in order to direct public affairs wisely. These books give special attention to the house and family of David, from which Christ came. Some of his sons followed in his steps; others did not. The characters of the kings of Judah may be briefly given: David the godly, Solomon the wise, Rehoboam the simple, Abijah the courageous, Asa the blameless, Jehoshaphat the religious, Jehoram the evil, Ahaziah the worldly, Joash the backslider, Amaziah the rash, Uzziah the powerful, Jotham the peaceful, Ahaz the idolater, Hezekiah the reformer, Manasseh the penitent, Amon the obscure, and Josiah the tenderhearted; Jehoahaz, Jehoiakim, Jehoiachin, and Zedekiah were all evil, the kind of kings who brought ruin quickly on themselves and their kingdom. The number of the good and that of the bad come to about the same, but the reigns of the good were generally long and the reigns of the bad generally short. In 1 Kings we have: 1. The death of David (chs. 1–2). 2. The glorious reign of Solomon and his building of the temple (chs. 3–10), but also the cloud his sun set under (ch. 11). 3. The division of the kingdoms under Rehoboam, and his reign and Jeroboam's (chs. 12–14). 4. The reigns of Abijah and Asa over Judah, and Baasha and Omri over Israel (chs. 15–16). 5. Elijah's miracles (chs. 17–19). 6. Ahab's success against Ben-Hadad, his evil, and his fall (chs. 20–22). In all this history it appears that kings, though like gods to us, are only people before God, mortal and accountable.

CHAPTER 1

In this chapter we have: 1. David declining in health (vv. 1–4). 2. Adonijah aspiring to the kingdom (vv. 5–10). 3. Nathan and Bathsheba working together to secure the succession of Solomon, and obtaining an order from David for that purpose (vv. 11–31). 4. The anointing of Solomon accordingly, and the people's joy in that (vv. 32–40). 5. The effective crushing of Adonijah's uprising, and the dispersion of his faction (vv. 41–49); Solomon's sending Adonijah away on the condition that he behaves well (vv. 50–53).

Verses 1–4

Here we have David sinking under the weaknesses of old age.

1. It would have been troubling to see David so weak. He was old, and his natural temperature was so low that no clothes could keep him warm (v. 1).

2. It would have been troubling to see his doctors so unable and unskillful that they did not know any way of relieving him except by covering him. *They covered him with clothes* (v. 1), which, where there is any inner heat, will keep it in, and so increase it, but where there was no inner heat, not even royal clothing could supply warmth. Then they foolishly prescribed a young woman. His prophets should have been consulted as well as his doctors in a matter of this nature. That Abishag was married to David before she lay close to him, and was his secondary wife, is suggested by the fact that it was considered a great crime of Adonijah's that he wanted to marry her (2:22) after his father's death.

Verses 5–10

David suffered much because of his children. Amnon and Absalom had both caused him grief; the one was his firstborn, the other his third (2Sa 3:2–3). We suppose he

417

found comfort in his second, whom he had by Abigail; his fourth was Adonijah (2Sa 3:4), born in Hebron. We learn here that Adonijah was very handsome and that he was closest in age to Absalom (v. 6; and closest in temper, as it turned out). We learn, further, that in his father's eyes he had been a jewel but was now a thorn.

1. His father had spoiled him (v. 6). His father had never done anything to upset him; he had never even said to him, *Why has thou done so?* (v. 6), because he saw that that was upsetting for Adonijah. It was the son's fault that he was upset when he was rebuked and so never learned to benefit from it. It was the father's fault that because he saw that being rebuked upset him, he did not do it. And now he was justly suffering for giving in to him so much.

2. In return, he made a fool of his father. Because his father was old and confined to his bed, he *exalted himself* and said, *I will be king* (v. 5).

2.1. He considered the days of mourning for his father to be near and so made preparations to succeed him, even though he knew that both God and David had named Solomon to be the man (1Ch 22:9; 23:1).

2.2. He considered his father incapacitated by age and good for nothing, and so he immediately took possession of the throne. His father is not fit to govern, for he is old and past ruling, nor is Solomon ready, for he is young and not yet able to rule, and so Adonijah wants to govern.

2.3. To pursue this ambitious plan:

2.3.1. He got a great retinue (v. 5), *chariots and horsemen*, both for show and for strength, to wait on him and fight for him.

2.3.2. He gained strong support from no less a person than Joab, the general of the army, and from Abiathar the high priest (v. 7). They were old men, who had been faithful to David in the most difficult and troublesome of times; they had a lot of good sense and experience, and one would have thought that they would not easily have been cajoled into helping him. But God left them to themselves in this matter, perhaps to correct them for some former misbehavior with a scourge of their own making. We are told in v. 8 about those who had such a tested loyalty to David that Adonijah did not have the confidence so much as to propose his plan to them: Zadok, Benaiah, and Nathan.

2.3.3. He prepared a great entertainment (v. 9) at En Rogel, not far from Jerusalem; his guests were the king's sons and servants, whom he feasted and favored to bring them over to his side. However, Solomon was not invited, either because Adonijah despised him or because he despaired of winning him over (v. 10). Some think that Adonijah killed these sheep and oxen—even fat ones—as a sacrifice, and that he made a religious feast, beginning his attempt to gain the crown with a show of devotion, which he could do more plausibly now that the high priest himself was on his side.

Verses 11–31

We have here the effective endeavors used by Nathan and Bathsheba to obtain from David confirmation of Solomon's succession, to crush Adonijah's uprising. David himself did not know what was happening. Bathsheba lived in seclusion and knew nothing about it either until Nathan told her. Solomon probably knew about it, but he acted as if he had not heard, as if he were deaf. Although he was old enough and had wisdom beyond his years, we do not find that he moved to oppose Adonijah, but are left to suppose that he quietly composed himself and left matters to God and his friends to arrange. How is the plan brought about?

1. Nathan the prophet alerted Bathsheba to what had been happening and put her in a position to obtain an order from the king to confirm Solomon's entitlement to the throne. The matter was a concern of Nathan's because he knew God's mind, and also David's and Israel's rights. It was through Nathan that God had named Solomon *Jedidiah* (2Sa 12:25), and so he could not just sit back and see the throne usurped, which he knew was rightfully Solomon's by the will of the One from whom advancement comes. Nathan turned to Bathsheba because she had the greatest concern for Solomon and would have the freest access to David. He told her about Adonijah's attempt (v. 11), and that Adonijah was acting without David's agreement or knowledge. He suggested to her that not only was Solomon in danger of losing the crown, but also he and she would be in danger of losing their lives if Adonijah succeeded. Now, Nathan says, let me *give thee counsel how to save thy own life and the life of thy son* (v. 12). He directs her (v. 13) to go to the king, to remind him of his word and oath that Solomon would be his successor, and to ask him most humbly, *Why doth Adonijah reign?* He thought David was not so cold but that this must warm him. Conscience, as well as a sense of honor, would put life into him on such an occasion, and Nathan promised (v. 14) that while she was reasoning with the king in this way, he would come and back her up. It would be as if he came in accidentally.

2. Bathsheba, following Nathan's advice and instructions, loses no time, but immediately goes to the king to intercede for her own life. She knows she will be welcome at any time. Her address to the king on this occasion is very discreet:

2.1. She reminded him of his promise made to her, which was confirmed by a solemn oath, that Solomon would succeed him (v. 17). She knew how firmly this would grip such a conscientious man as David.

2.2. She told him about Adonijah's attempt to usurp the throne, which he knew nothing about (v. 18). She told him who Adonijah's guests were, and which people were on his side, and added that *Solomon thy servant has he not called*, which plainly showed that Adonijah looked on him as his rival and aimed to undermine him (v. 19).

2.3. She pleaded that it was very much in his power to confront this trouble and remove it (v. 20): *The eyes of all Israel are upon thee*, not only as *a king*, but also as a *prophet*. All Israel knew that not only was David himself *the anointed of the God of Jacob*, but also the *Spirit of the Lord spoke by him* (2Sa 23:1–2), and so, having waited in dependency for a divine appointment in such an important matter, they would receive David's word as an inspired word and a law to them.

2.4. She suggested the imminent danger she and her son would be in if this matter was not settled in David's lifetime (v. 21).

3. Nathan the prophet acts according to his promise and promptly steps in, to back her up while she is still speaking, even before the king has given his answer. The king was told that Nathan the prophet had come, and he was sure to be always welcome to the king. He *bowed himself with his face to the ground* (v. 23). He spoke a little more plainly to the king than Bathsheba did.

3.1. He makes the same representation of Adonijah's attempt as Bathsheba made (vv. 25–26), adding that Adonijah's side has already come to such a degree of assurance as to shout *God save king Adonijah*—as if King David had already died—and he observes, further, that they have not invited him to their feast (*Me thy servant has he not called*), so showing that they have decided not to consult either God or David in the matter.

3.2. He makes David aware of how much he should be concerned to clear himself from having a hand in it: *Hast thou said, Adonijah shall reign after me?* (v. 24), and again (v. 27), "*Is this thing done by my lord the king?* If it is so, he is not as faithful to God's word or his own word as we all thought he was. If it is not so, it is high time that we speak out against Adonijah's seizing the throne and declare Solomon the king's successor." In this way, he tries to rouse David against the usurpers so that he will act more vigorously to support Solomon's interests.

4. David then made a solemn declaration that he was firmly standing by his former decision, that Solomon would succeed him as king. Bathsheba was called in (v. 28), and the king gave these fresh assurances to her, since she was acting for and on behalf of her son:

4.1. He repeats his former promise and oath and acknowledges that he has *sworn unto her by the Lord God of Israel that Solomon shall reign after him* (v. 30).

4.2. He confirms his first oath with another, because the occasion called for it: *As the Lord liveth, that hath redeemed my soul out of all distress, even so will I certainly do this day* (vv. 29–30), unquestionably and without delay. His form of oath seems to be what he normally used on solemn occasions, for we find it in 2Sa 4:9. It carries with it a grateful acknowledgment of the goodness of God to him. Perhaps he speaks in this way on this occasion to encourage his son and successor to trust in God in the difficulties he also might meet.

5. Bathsheba receives these assurances (v. 31) with sincere good wishes for the king's health: *Let him live*. Far from thinking that he lived too long, she prayed he might live forever, if possible, to adorn the crown he wore and to be a blessing to his people.

Verses 32–40

We have here the care David took both to secure Solomon's right and to preserve the public peace, by nipping Adonijah's plan in the bud. Notice:

1. The explicit orders he gave to proclaim Solomon king. The people he entrusted with this matter were Zadok, Nathan, and Benaiah, men of power and influence whom David had always found faithful to him. David ordered them to proclaim Solomon king immediately and with all possible solemnity. They must take with them *the servants of their lord* (v. 33), the bodyguards, and all the servants of the household. They must set Solomon on the mule that David used to ride.

1.1. Zadok and Nathan, the two religious officials, must anoint him king, in God's name.

1.2. The great civil and military officers are ordered to give public notice of this, and to express the public joy on this occasion by sounding the trumpet, which the Law of Moses directed to adorn great ceremonies. The acclamations of the people must be added: *Let king Solomon live*.

1.3. They must then bring him with great pomp and solemnity into the City of David, and he must sit on the throne of his father, as his viceroy, to deal with public business during his weakness and to be his successor after his death: *He shall be king in my stead* (place) (v. 35). It would be very satisfying for David himself, and for all the parties concerned, to have this done immediately, so that after the king died there would be no dispute or disruption in public affairs.

2. The great assurance which Benaiah, in the name of the others, professes to have in these orders. The king said, "Solomon will reign for me and reign after me." Benaiah says heartily, "Amen. As the king says, so we also say. Since we can bring nothing to pass without the agree-

ment of gracious Providence, *The Lord God of my lord the king say so too*" (v. 36). This is the language of his faith in the promise of God on which Solomon's government was founded. Benaiah adds a prayer for Solomon to this (v. 37), that God will be with him as he has been with David and make his throne even greater. He knows David is not one of those who envy their children's greatness, and that he will therefore not be upset at this prayer or take offense at it, but will say a hearty *Amen* to it.

3. The immediate execution of these orders (vv. 38–40). No time was lost, and Solomon was brought with great pomp and solemnity to the place appointed. There Zadok anointed him at the direction of Nathan the prophet and David the king (v. 39). Among other sacred things, holy oil for religious services was kept in the tabernacle, where the ark was kept, and Zadok took *a horn of oil* from there and anointed Solomon with it. The horn of oil represents power and plenty. The people then expressed their great joy and satisfaction at the exaltation of Solomon. They surrounded him with their hosannas — *God save king Solomon* — and ministered to him with their music and shouts of joy (v. 40).

Verses 41–53

We have here:

1. The news of Solomon's induction being brought to Adonijah and his associates in the midst of their merrymaking: *They had made an end of eating* (v. 41). It seems it was a great while before they finished their feast, for the matter of Solomon's anointing was all ordered and finished while they were still feasting and overeating. When *they made an end of eating*, and were preparing themselves to declare their king and bring him triumphantly into the city, they *heard the sound of the trumpet* (v. 41). Joab was an old man and was alarmed by it, but Adonijah was very confident that the messenger, being a worthy man, *brought good tidings* (v. 42). "*Verily*, the best news I can bring you is that *Solomon is made king*, so that your claims are all quashed." The messenger relates to them:

1.1. With what great ceremony *Solomon* was *made king* (vv. 44–45), and that he was now *sitting on the throne of the kingdom* (v. 46).

1.2. With what general satisfaction Solomon was received as king. The people were happy, and the courtiers were happy: *The king's servants* came to him with a speech of congratulation on this occasion (v. 47). They *blessed king David*. They also prayed for Solomon, that God would make his name better than his father's, which it might well be, since he had his father's foundation to build on. A child who stands on the shoulders of a giant is higher than the giant himself. The king himself was happy: he *bowed himself upon the bed* (v. 47), not only to show his acceptance of his officials' address, but also to offer his worship to God (v. 48).

2. The effective crushing of Adonijah's uprising because of this news. It spoiled the merrymaking and made everyone get up, leave, and fend for themselves.

3. The terror Adonijah himself was in and how he tried to keep himself safe. He had despised Solomon as not worthy enough to be his guest (v. 10), but now he dreaded him as his judge. He *feared because of Solomon* (v. 50). Adonijah took hold of the horns of the altar, which was always looked on as a sanctuary or place of refuge (Ex 21:14), so showing that he dared not stand trial. He threw himself on the mercy of his ruler, and in pleading for that, he relied on nothing except the mercy of God, which was shown in the institution and acceptance of the sacrifices offered on that altar and the resulting forgiveness of sin.

4. Adonijah's humble address to Solomon for mercy. He sends a request for his life by those who are bringing Solomon news of where he is (v. 51): *Let king Solomon swear to me that he will not slay* (kill) *his servant.*

5. The orders Solomon gave concerning him. He discharged him, granting him an amnesty as long as he behaved honorably (vv. 52–53). He considered that Adonijah was his brother, and that it was his first offense. In the same way, the Son of David is merciful toward those who have been rebellious. If they will return to their former allegiance and become faithful to their Sovereign, their former crimes will not be mentioned against them, but if they continue to side with the world and the flesh, this will lead to their ruin.

CHAPTER 2

We have here: 1. The conclusion of David's reign and life: 1.1. The general command he gives to Solomon from his deathbed, to serve God (vv. 1–4), and his particular command concerning Joab, Barzillai, and Shimei (vv. 5–9). 1.2. His death and burial, and the years of his reign (vv. 10–11). 2. The beginning of Solomon's reign (v. 12). Although he was to be a prince of peace, he began his reign with some significant acts of justice: 2.1. On Adonijah, whom he put to death for his claims to the throne (vv. 13–25). 2.2. On Abiathar, whom he deposed from the high priesthood for siding with Adonijah (vv. 26–27). 2.3. On Joab, whom he put to death for his treason and previous murders (vv. 28–35). 2.4. On Shimei, whom he confined to Jerusalem for cursing David (vv. 36–38), and three years later put to death for breaking the rules (vv. 39–46).

Verses 1–11

David, that great and good man, is here a dying man (v. 1) and then a dead man (v. 10). It is good that there is another life after this, for death stains all the glory of this life and lays it in the dust. We have here:

1. The commands and instructions which David, when he was dying, gave to Solomon, his son and declared successor. He feels himself in decline and is not unwilling to acknowledge it. *I go the way of all the earth* (v. 2). Death is a way. It is not only a period of this life but also a passage to a better life. Even the sons and heirs of heaven must *go the way of all the earth*, must die, but they walk with joy along this way *through the valley of the shadow of death* (Ps 23:4). Prophets, and even kings, must go this way to a light and honor that are brighter than prophecy or sovereignty. David is going this way, and so he gives Solomon directions as to what to do.

1.1. He charges him, in general, to keep God's commandments and to be conscientious about doing his duty (vv. 2–4). He commends to him:

1.1.1. A good rule to act by—the divine will: "Govern yourself by that." David's command to him is to *keep the charge of the Lord* his God (v. 3).

1.1.2. A good spirit to act with: *Be strong and show thyself a man* (v. 2)—even though he is young in years.

1.1.3. Good reasons for all this. *That the Lord may continue* and so confirm *his word which he spoke concerning me* (v. 4). Let each successively in their own age keep God's commands, and then God will be sure to continue speaking his word. We never lose the promise until we neglect the precept. God had promised David that the Messiah would come from his body, and that promise was absolute, but the promise that there would not fail to be *a*

man from his family *on the throne of Israel* (v. 4) was conditional: it depended on his descendants' behaving themselves as they should. If Solomon fulfills the condition in his day, he does his part toward making the promise last forever. The condition is that he lives before God in all his ways, in sincerity and zeal, and with determination.

1.2. He gives him directions concerning some particular individuals, telling him what to do with them:

1.2.1. Toward Joab (v. 5). David was now aware that he had not done well in sparing Joab when he had made himself again and again offensive to the law, by murdering first Abner (2Sa 3:30) and then Amasa (2Sa 20:10), both of them great men, commanders of Israel's armies (v. 5). He killed them treacherously (*shed the blood of war in peace*, shed their blood in peacetime, v. 5) and wronged David: *Thou knowest what* he *did to me* in that. It made Joab's crime even worse that he was neither ashamed of the sin nor afraid of the punishment, but brazenly wore the belt and shoes stained by innocent blood, in defiance of the justice of both God and the king. David refers him to Solomon's wisdom (v. 6), with a sign that he was also leaving Joab to his justice.

1.2.2. Toward Barzillai's family, to whom he orders him to be kind for the sake of Barzillai, who was probably dead by this time (v. 7). The kindnesses we have received from our friends must not be buried either in their graves or ours, but our children must repay them to their family.

1.2.3. Toward Shimei (vv. 8–9). *He cursed me with a grievous curse.* The curses were more bitter because Shimei insulted him when he was in misery; it was like pouring vinegar onto his wounds. His case is left with Solomon as one who knew what was right to be done and would do as he saw fit. "His wild spirit will soon give you cause, which you should not fail to take, to bring his *hoary* (gray) *head to the grave with blood* (v. 9)." This command came not from a desire for personal revenge but from a wise zeal for the honor of the government and the covenant God had made with his family, contempt of which should not go unpunished.

2. David's death and burial (v. 10): he *was buried in the city of David*, not in the burial place of his father, as Saul was, but in his own city, which he had founded. The thrones of the house of David were set there, and so were the tombs. His epitaph may be taken from 2Sa 23:1. Here lies *David the son of Jesse, the man who was raised up on high, the anointed of the God of Jacob, and the sweet psalmist of Israel*, adding his own words (Ps 16:9), *My flesh also shall rest in hope.*

Verses 12–25

Here is:

1. Solomon's accession to the throne (v. 12). He came to it much more easily and peacefully than David did, and he saw his government established much more quickly. It is fortunate for a kingdom when the end of one good reign is the beginning of another, as happened here.

2. Solomon's just and necessary removal of Adonijah his rival, in order to see his throne established. Notice:

2.1. Adonijah's plan of treason, which was to marry Abishag, David's concubine, not because he was in love with her, but because through her he hoped to renew his claim to the throne—and marrying her might indeed help him to that end. Absalom had thought his claims would be greatly supported by having intimate relations with his father's concubines. Adonijah flattered himself that if he could succeed David in his bed, especially with the best of his wives, he could use that means as a step to succeed him on the throne.

2.2. The means Adonijah used to gain this. He dared not woo Abishag directly; instead he engaged Bathsheba to be his friend in this matter. She would be willing to believe it was a matter of love and would not be inclined to suspect it as a trick. Bathsheba was surprised to see Adonijah in her room and asked him if he came intending to cause trouble for her, because she had been instrumental in crushing his recent attempt to gain the crown. "No," he said, "I come *peaceably* (v. 13), and to beg a favor" (v. 14), that she would use her influence with her son to gain his approval, so that he might marry Abishag (vv. 16–17). He presented himself as an object of compassion, as one who had been deprived of the crown and so might be satisfied to gain a wife. He pretended in this way to be pleased with Solomon's accession to the throne, when in reality he was doing all he could to cause him trouble. *His words were smoother than butter, but war was in his heart* (Ps 55:21).

2.3. Bathsheba's words to Solomon on his behalf. She promised to speak to the king for him (v. 18) and did so (v. 19). Solomon received her with all the respect that was due to a mother, though he himself was a king: he *rose up to meet her, bowed himself to her,* and caused her *to sit on his right hand,* according to the law of the fifth commandment. She finally told him why she had come (v. 21): *Let Abishag be given to Adonijah thy brother.* It was strange that she did not suspect treason, but even more strange that she did not loathe the incest in the suggestion. But either she did not take Abishag as David's wife, because the marriage had not been consummated, or she thought the marriage could be ignored in order to please Adonijah, because of his humble submission to Solomon.

2.4. Solomon's just and wise rejection of the request. Solomon convinces his mother of the unreasonableness of the request and shows her where it would lead to, which she had not been aware of before. His reply is somewhat sharp: *"Ask for him the kingdom also* (v. 22). To ask that he might succeed the king in his bed is, in effect, asking that he might succeed him on his throne, for that is what he is aiming at." He convicts and condemns Adonijah for his claims and does so with an oath. He convicts him out of his own mouth (v. 23). He condemns him to die immediately: *He shall be put to death this day* (v. 24). It was clear enough that Adonijah aimed at the throne, and Solomon could not be safe as long as he lived. Ambitious and wild spirits usually prepare instruments of death for themselves. Many a head has been lost by trying to seize the crown.

Verses 26–34

Abiathar and Joab had both aided and abetted in Adonijah's rebellion, and they probably also lay at the root of this latest move made by Adonijah for Abishag, and it seems that Solomon knew this (v. 22). By these actions, both of the men greatly insulted God and the government, and it was even worse because of their high positions and the great influence their examples might have on many others. They were both equally guilty of treason, but in the judgment passed on them, a distinction was made, and with good reason:

1. Abiathar, in consideration of his former services, is only degraded (vv. 26–27):

1.1. Solomon convicts him; by his great wisdom he finds him guilty.

1.2. He remembers the respect Abiathar had formerly shown to David his father, and that he had both ministered to him in holy things (*had borne before him the ark of the Lord*) and tenderly sympathized with him in his sufferings.

1.3. For this reason he spares Abiathar's life, but he deposes him from his office and confines him to his country home at Anathoth. He forbids him from coming to the royal court, the city, the tabernacle, and the altar and from taking part in any public affairs.

1.4. The exclusion of Abiathar from the priesthood was the fulfillment of the sentence declared against the house of Eli (1Sa 2:30), for he was the last high priest of that family.

2. Joab, in consideration of his former sins, is put to death:

2.1. His guilty conscience sent him to the horns of the altar. He heard that Adonijah had been executed and Abiathar had been deposed, and so fearing that he would be next, he fled for refuge to the altar.

2.2. Solomon ordered him to be put to death there for the murder of Abner and Amasa, for these were the crimes on which he thought fit to base the sentence, rather than on his treason and commitment to Adonijah. He based the sentence on this: that he *fell upon two men more righteous and better than he,* who had neither done him any wrong nor meant to and who, if they had lived, probably could have given David better service than Joab did. For these crimes:

2.2.1. He must die, and it must be by the sword of public justice.

2.2.2. He must die at the altar rather than be allowed to escape. Joab decided not to move from the altar (v. 30). Benaiah hesitated to kill him there or drag him away from there, but Solomon knew the law, that the altar of God must give no protection to deliberate murderers. The altar was a refuge for those whose sins could be atoned for by the blood of animals, but not for one such as Joab. Solomon therefore ordered him to be executed there. The holiness of any place should never support the evil of any person. Those who have a living faith and firmly take hold of Christ and his righteousness—who resolve that if they must die, they will die holding on to him—will find in him a more powerful protection than Joab found at the horns of the altar. Benaiah killed him (v. 34), no doubt with all the solemnity of a public execution.

2.3. Solomon was satisfied with this act of justice, not because it satisfied any desire for personal revenge, but because it fulfilled his father's orders and was advantageous for him and his government. Peace was secured (v. 33) *upon David:* on *his seed* (descendants)*, his house, and his throne* there would be *peace for ever from the Lord.* Now that such a wild man as Joab had been removed from the scene, there would be peace. In this blessing of peace on his house and throne, Solomon devoutly looked up to God as its author and looked forward to eternity as its perfection. "It will be peace from the Lord, and peace forever from the Lord." May the Lord of peace himself give us that eternal peace.

Verses 35–46

Here is:

1. The advancement of Benaiah and Zadok, two faithful friends of Solomon and his government (v. 35). After Joab had been put to death, Benaiah was promoted to be general of the forces instead of him; and after Abiathar had been deposed, Zadok was made high priest in place of him, and

so came the fulfillment of God's sentence on the house of Eli, that it would be destroyed (1Sa 2:35): *I will raise me up a faithful priest, and will build him a sure house.*

2. What happened to Shimei. He was sent for, by a messenger, from his house at Bahurim, and expected perhaps nothing better than Adonijah's condemnation, being aware that he was still regarded as an enemy by the house of David. Solomon, however, knew how to differentiate between crimes and criminals. David had promised that he would not put Shimei to death. Solomon was not bound by that promise, but he would not go directly against it.

2.1. He confines him to Jerusalem and forbids him from going out of the city any farther than the Kidron Valley (vv. 36–37), on any pretense whatever. He would not allow him to continue to live at his country home, so that he could not cause trouble among his neighbors; instead he took him to Jerusalem, where he kept him as a prisoner who was free to roam within that city. Shimei kept his life on comfortable terms: he would live only if he was content to live in Jerusalem.

2.2. Shimei submits to this confinement and gratefully accepts his life on those terms. However, he breaks his agreement when two of his slaves run away from him to the land of the Philistines (v. 39). He goes there to search for them and brings them back from there to Jerusalem (v. 40), and Solomon finds out (v. 41). If he had told Solomon about the urgency of the occasion and begged permission to go, perhaps Solomon might have allowed him to go, but to presume either that the king would not know of his violation or that he would overlook it was an act of great defiance. Solomon condemns him for his former crime, cursing David and throwing stones at him when he was suffering. He gives orders for Shimei to be immediately executed (v. 46).

CHAPTER 3

In the previous chapter Solomon's reign seemed to involve a lot of bloodshed, but the necessary acts of justice must not be called cruelty. In this chapter Solomon's reign is seen from a different angle. We must not think the worse of God's mercy to his subjects because of his judgments on rebels. We have here: 1. Solomon's marriage to Pharaoh's daughter (v. 1); a general view of his religion (vv. 2–4). 2. A particular account of his prayer to God for wisdom, and the answer to that prayer (vv. 5–15). 3. A specific example of his wisdom, in deciding the dispute between the two prostitutes (vv. 16–28). He looks very great here, both at the altar and in the law court, and therefore it is because he looks great at the altar that he looks great in the law court.

Verses 1–4

We are told here about Solomon:

1. Something that was undeniably good, for which he is to be praised and in which he is to be imitated:

1.1. He *loved the Lord* (v. 3). Special notice was taken of God's love for him (2Sa 12:24). His name came from it: *Jedidiah,* meaning "loved by the Lord." We find that he returned that love, just as John the beloved disciple was overflowing in love. Solomon was a wise, rich, and great man, but the most eloquent commendation of him is one that describes the character of all the saints, even the poorest: that he *loved the Lord.* "He loved the worship of the Lord," reads the Aramaic. All who love God love his worship; they love to hear from him and speak to him, and so have fellowship with him.

1.2. He *walked in the statutes of David his father* (v. 3), that is, in the statutes that David gave him (2:2–3; 1Ch 28:9–10), or in God's statutes, which David his father walked in before him. He kept closely to God's ordinances. Those who truly *love God* will conscientiously *walk in his statutes* (v. 3).

1.3. He was very free and generous in what he did for the honor of God. We must never think that what is spent in the service of God is wasted.

2. Something about which it may be doubted whether it was good or not:

2.1. His marriage to Pharaoh's daughter (v. 1). We suppose she had converted to the Jewish religion, for otherwise the marriage would not have been lawful, but if so, it was surely not advisable. Some think that he did this on the advice of his friends, that she was a sincere convert—for the gods of the Egyptians are not counted among the foreign gods which his foreign wives drew him into worshiping (11:5–6)—and that the book of the Song of Songs and Ps 45:1–17 were written on this occasion. This marriage was a type of the mystical betrothal of the church to Christ, especially the Gentile church.

2.2. His worshiping on the high places, thereby tempting the people to do likewise (vv. 2–3). Abraham built his altars on hills and mountains (Ge 12:8; 22:2) and worshiped at a *grove* (Ge 21:33; NIV: tamarisk tree). The custom originated from that, and was proper, until the divine law confined them to one place (Dt 12:5–6). David kept to the ark and did not care for the high places, but Solomon, though he *walked in the statutes of his father* (v. 3) in other things, came short of him in this respect. He showed a great zeal for offering sacrifices, but to obey would have been better.

Verses 5–15

Here is an account of God's gracious appearance to Solomon and of the fellowship Solomon had with God:

1. The circumstances of God's appearance (v. 5):

1.1. The place. It was at Gibeon; that was the most important high place because the tabernacle and the bronze altar were there (2Ch 1:3). Solomon offered his great sacrifices there, and it was there that God acknowledged him. The closer we come to observing God's ways in our worship, the more reason we have to expect the signs of God's presence.

1.2. The time. It was at night, the night after he had offered that generous sacrifice (v. 4). The more we are involved in God's work, the more strength and encouragement we may expect to receive from him. If the day has been busy for Solomon, the night will be rest for him. Silence and withdrawal are friends of our fellowship with God.

1.3. The manner. It was in a dream, when he was asleep. His senses had closed down while he slept, so that God's access to his mind was clearer and more direct. In this way God used to speak to the prophets (Nu 12:6) and to individual people for their own benefit (Job 33:15–16). These divine dreams were clearly distinguishable from those in which meaningless things take place (Ecc 5:7).

2. The gracious offer God made him (v. 5). He saw the glory of God shine around him and heard a voice saying, *Ask what I shall give thee.*

3. The godly request Solomon then made to God. He readily took hold of this offer. Solomon prayed in his sleep; God's grace helped him, but it was still a real and living prayer. The grace of God brought about these gracious desires in him.

3.1. He acknowledges God's great goodness to his father David (v. 6). God's favors are doubly sweet when we see them passed on to us by the hands of those who have gone before us.

3.2. He acknowledges his own inadequacy to fulfill that great responsibility to which he is called (vv. 7–8). Here is a double plea to back up his request for wisdom:

3.2.1. That his position requires it, as he is David's successor.

3.2.2. That he wants it. As one who has a humble sense of his own weakness, he pleads, "*Lord, I am but a little child: I know not how to go out or come in* (v. 7) as I should. I do not know how to carry out my duties in the ordinary daily business of the government." Paul's question, *Who is sufficient for these things?* (2Co 2:16), is much like Solomon's here, *Who is able to judge this thy so great a people?* (v. 9). Absalom, who was foolish, wanted to be a judge; Solomon, who is wise, trembles at the undertaking and questions his own fitness to do it.

3.3. He begs God to give him wisdom (v. 9): *Give therefore thy servant an understanding heart*. This is how his good father prayed and pleaded (Ps 119:125): *I am thy servant; give me understanding*. An understanding and discerning heart is God's gift (Pr 2:6). We must pray for it (Jas 1:5), applying our prayer to our own particular calling.

3.4. God answered his request with favor. It was a pleasing prayer (v. 10): *The speech pleased the Lord*. God accepts those who put spiritual blessings before physical ones. But that was not all; his prayer was successful, and he had more success than he asked for:

3.4.1. God gave him wisdom (v. 12). No other ruler had ever been blessed with such insight and foresight.

3.4.2. Over and above that, God gave him riches and honor into the bargain (v. 13). These too are God's gifts and, as far as is good for them, are promised to all who *seek first the kingdom of God and the righteousness thereof* (Mt 6:33). Let young people learn to put grace before gold in all they choose, because *godliness has the promise of the life that now is, and of that which is to come* (1Ti 4:8), but *the life that now is* has *the promise of godliness* only if we seek God. But if we make sure of wisdom and grace, these will either bring outward prosperity with them or sweeten the lack of it. God promised Solomon riches and honor absolutely, but the promise of long life was conditional (v. 14). *If thou wilt walk in my ways, as David did, then I will lengthen thy days*. He failed to meet this condition, and so although he had riches and honor, he did not live as long to enjoy them as he naturally might have.

3.4.2.1. The way to obtain spiritual blessings is to be bold for them, to wrestle with God in prayer for them, as Solomon did for wisdom, asking only for that, as the *one thing needful* (Lk 10:42).

3.4.2.2. The way to obtain physical blessings is to be indifferent to them and to turn to God for them. Solomon had wisdom given him because he asked for it, and he had wealth given him because he did not ask for it.

3.5. Solomon responded gratefully to the appearance God was pleased to give him (v. 15). He awoke, probably in great joy. He was satisfied by God's favor, and he began to think *what he should render to the Lord* (Ps 116:12). He had made his prayer at the high place at Gibeon, and God had graciously met him there. Now he came to Jerusalem to give thanks *before the ark of the covenant* (v. 15), blaming himself, as it were, for not praying there — since the ark was the sign of God's presence — and surprised that God had been willing to meet him anywhere else. God's overlooking our mistakes should persuade us to put them right. There he offered a great sacrifice to God

and made a great feast to accompany the sacrifice, so that those around him might join him in responding with joy to the grace of God.

Verses 16–28

An example is given here of Solomon's wisdom. The proof is taken not from the mysterious ways of government, although no doubt he excelled there, but from the trial of a case between two people. Notice:

1. That the case was opened up not by lawyers but by the two parties themselves, although they were women. These two women were prostitutes. It is probable that the case had been heard in the lower courts before it was brought to Solomon, and that the judges had been unable to decide it. These two women, who lived together in a house, each gave birth to a son within three days of each other (vv. 17–18). One of them lay on her child and suffocated it and, during the same night, exchanged it for the child of the other (vv. 19–20), who was soon aware of the deception and appealed to public justice for it to be put right (v. 21).

2. The difficulty of the case. The question was, Who was the mother of this living child? Both mothers were vehement in their claim and showed a passionate concern about the matter. Neither wanted to accept the dead child as hers, although it would be cheaper to bury that dead boy than provide for the other; it was the living one they argued over. Although some of the neighbors had probably been present at the birth and circumcision of the children, they had not taken so much notice of them as to be able to distinguish between them.

3. Its resolution. Solomon listened patiently to what both sides had to say and summed up the evidence (v. 23). He called for a sword and gave orders to divide the living child between the two women. It proved an effective way of finding out the real truth. Some think that before he made this experiment, Solomon himself had noticed who was telling the truth and who was lying from the faces of the two women and how they spoke; whether he did or not, by this experiment he satisfied everyone and silenced the pretender. To find out the true mother, he could not test which mother the child loved more, and so he must test which mother loved the child the more. Both claimed to have a maternal affection, but their sincerity would be tested when the child was put in danger.

3.1. The woman who knew the child was not her own, but who stood on a point of honor in fighting for it, was content to have the baby cut into two.

3.2. The woman who knows the child is her own would rather give it up to the other woman than see it butchered. She cries out with great feeling, *O, my lord! give her the living child* (v. 26). "Let me see him given to her, rather than not see him at all." This tenderness toward the child showed that she was not the careless mother of the dead child, who had lain on him, but was the true mother of the living one, who could not bear to see him die, having compassion on the son of her womb.

4. What a great reputation Solomon gained among his people by this and other examples of his wisdom, which would have a great influence on the smooth running of his government: *They feared the king* (v. 28), *for they saw that the wisdom of God was in him*, that is, that wisdom with which God had promised to endow him.

CHAPTER 4

We had an example of the wisdom God gave to Solomon at the end of the previous chapter. In this chapter we have an account of his wealth and prosperity. We have here: 1. The splendor of his court, his ministers of state (vv. 1–6), and the district governors who supplied provisions for his household (vv. 7–19) and their work (vv. 27–28). 2. The provisions for his table (vv. 22–23); the extent of his dominion (vv. 21–24); the numbers, circumstances, and peace of his subjects (vv. 20–25); his stables (v. 26). 3. His great reputation for wisdom and learning (vv. 29–34).

Verses 1–19

We have here:

1. Solomon on his throne (v. 1): *So king Solomon was king,* that is, he was confirmed and established as king *over all Israel.*

2. The great officials of his court. Notice:

2.1. That several of them are the same as in his father's time. Zadok and Abiathar were still priests (2Sa 20:25), Jehoshaphat was recorder, and Benaiah, who in the time of Solomon's father was significant in military affairs, continued to be so now.

2.2. That others were priests' sons. His prime minister of state was *Azariah the son of Zadok the priest* (v. 2). Two others of great importance were the sons of Nathan the prophet (v. 5).

3. The district governors who supplied provisions from different parts of the country so that:

3.1. His house might always be provided for in the best way.

3.2. He himself, and those who were immediately with him, might more closely apply themselves to the work of the state, not being preoccupied and troubled with a great deal of household preparations.

3.3. Every part of the kingdom might benefit equally from the commodities that were produced by their country and from the circulation of the financial resources. Trade would be encouraged, and so wealth would increase, even in those tribes that were situated farthest away from the royal court.

3.4. The dividing of this trust into so many hands was a wise move and would prevent any one person from being continually burdened with the care of the kingdom or becoming too rich from its profits.

Verses 20–28

Surely no ruler ever had such a kingdom and such a court as Solomon's:

1. Such a kingdom. The account given here of it fulfills the prophecies which we have of it in Ps 72:1–20, which is a psalm for Solomon but also contains references to Christ.

1.1. The territories of his kingdom were large, and its subject countries many; it was foretold that he would *have dominion from sea to sea* (Ps 72:8–11). Solomon reigned over all the neighboring kingdoms, who were his subjects by force. All the rulers from the river Euphrates in the northeast to the border of Egypt southwest added to his wealth by serving him and bringing him tribute (v. 21). He had *peace on all sides* (v. 24).

1.2. The subjects of his kingdom and its inhabitants were many and happy:

1.2.1. They were numerous, and the country was well populated (v. 20): *Judah and Israel were many,* and that land was sufficient to maintain them all.

1.2.2. They were at ease; they lived in security. Every man lived *under his vine and fig tree* (v. 25). Solomon invaded no one's property; what they had they could call their own. He protected everyone in possessing and enjoying their own property.

1.2.3. They were happy in using the plenty they had, *eating and drinking, and making merry* (v. 20). Wherever you went, you would have seen all the marks of plenty, peace, and happiness. This was a type of the spiritual peace, joy, and holy security of all the faithful subjects of the Lord Jesus. *The kingdom of God is not,* as Solomon's was, *meat* (food) *and drink,* but what is infinitely better, *righteousness, and peace, and joy in the Holy Ghost* (Ro 14:17).

2. Such a court as Solomon kept can scarcely be paralleled. Once in the reign of King Xerxes, he made a *great feast* to *show the riches of his kingdom* (Est 1:3–4). But it was much more to the honor of Solomon that he kept a constant table, a table not of delicacies but of substantial food, to receive well those who came to hear his wisdom. In the same way, Christ fed those whom he taught, 5,000 at a time, more than Solomon's table could ever receive on one occasion, and all believers continually feast on him. He is far greater than Solomon in this respect. He feeds all his subjects, not with the bread that perishes, but *with that which endureth unto everlasting life* (Jn 6:27).

Verses 29–34

Solomon's wisdom was more glorious than his wealth:

1. The fountain of his wisdom: *God gave it him* (v. 29).

2. The fullness of his wisdom: *He had wisdom and understanding, exceeding much* (v. 29). It is called *largeness of heart* (v. 29), for the heart is often used in Scripture as a metaphor for the intellectual powers. He was very free and communicative, had the gift of speech as well as wisdom, was as free with his learning as he was with his food, and did not grudge giving to anyone around him. The greatness of Solomon's wisdom is illustrated by comparison. Babylonia and Egypt were countries that were famous for their learning, and from them the Greeks borrowed their learning, but the greatest scholars of those nations came short of Solomon (v. 30). *Solomon excelled them all* (v. 30), he outdid them and made them as nothing in comparison; his advice was much more valuable.

3. The fame of his wisdom. It was talked of *in all nations round about* (v. 31).

4. The fruits of his wisdom. A tree is known by its fruits. He did not bury his talent, but showed his wisdom:

4.1. In his compositions. It appears from what he spoke, or dictated to be written:

4.1.1. That he taught right and wrong. He was a man of great wisdom, for he spoke 3,000 proverbs, wise sayings, which are wonderfully useful in showing how to live. Whether those proverbs of Solomon that we have in Scripture were part of the 3,000 is uncertain.

4.1.2. That he was a poet and a man of great understanding: his songs numbered 1,005 (v. 32), of which only one still exists, because that was the only one divinely inspired, and it is therefore called his *Song of Songs.*

4.1.3. That he was a scientist, a man of great learning and insight into the mysteries of nature. From his own and others' observations and experience, he wrote about plants and animals (v. 33).

4.2. In his conversation. People of all nations came to *hear the wisdom of Solomon* (v. 34). But:

5. Solomon was a type of Christ in this, *in whom are hidden all the treasures of wisdom and knowledge* (Col 2:3), and hidden to be used, for he is *made of God to us wisdom* (1Co 1:30).

CHAPTER 5

The great work which Solomon was raised up to do was the building of the temple. In this chapter we have an account of the preparations he made for that and his other buildings. His thoughtful father had prepared plenty of gold and silver, but he must get ready wood and stone. It is about these that we see him negotiating with Hiram king of Tyre. 1. Hiram congratulated him on his accession to the throne (v. 1). Solomon told him about his intention to build the temple and asked him to provide him with workers (vv. 2–6). Hiram agreed to do this (vv. 7–9). 2. Solomon's work was well done, and Hiram's workers were well paid (vv. 10–18).

Verses 1–9

We have here an account of the friendly correspondence between Solomon and Hiram king of Tyre. Tyre was a famous trading city that was situated close to the sea and on the border of Israel. Hiram the king is described here as being *ever a lover of David* (v. 1), always on friendly terms with David. We have reason to think he was a worshiper of the true God and had himself given up the idolatry of his city, although he could not reform it. Here is:

1. Hiram's envoy bringing compliments to Solomon (v. 1).

2. Solomon's message of business to Hiram, probably sent by messengers of his own. Solomon, in his letter to Hiram, told him about:

2.1. His intention to build a temple to the honor of God. Solomon told Hiram, who was himself no stranger to the matter:

2.1.1. That David's wars had been an obstruction to him, so that he could not build this temple, even though he wanted to (v. 3).

2.1.2. That peace gave him, Solomon, an opportunity to build it, and so he decided to set about it immediately: "*God has given me rest* both at home and abroad, and there is no enemy (v. 4), no *Satan* (the Hebrew word here), no instrument of Satan to oppose it or to divert us from it."

2.2. His desire that Hiram would help him in this. The place from which wood must be obtained was Lebanon, an excellent forest in the north of Canaan, specifically referred to in the gift of that land to Israel: *all Lebanon* (Jos 13:5). Solomon was owner of all its products. Yet he acknowledged that although the trees were his, the Israelites did not have the *skill* of the Sidonians *to hew* (cut down) *timber* (v. 6), and the Sidonians were Hiram's subjects. Solomon asked Hiram to send him workers, and he promised (v. 6) both to help them (*my servants shall be with thy servants*, to work under them) and to pay them (*unto thee will I give hire for thy servants*), for the laborer, even in church work, and even though it is indeed its own wages, *is worthy of his hire* (Lk 10:7). The evangelical prophet seems to allude to this episode (Isa 60:1–22) when he prophesies:

2.2.1. That the *sons of strangers*, foreigners — such were the Tyrians and Sidonians — will *build up the wall* of the Gospel temple (Isa 60:10).

2.2.2. That *the glory of Lebanon* will be brought to it to *beautify it* (Isa 60:13).

3. Hiram's reception of, and response to, this message:

3.1. He received it with great satisfaction to himself: he *rejoiced greatly* (v. 7) that Solomon followed in his father's steps. Hiram's generous spirit rejoiced in this. Notice with what pleasure Hiram speaks about Solomon's wisdom and the extent of his dominion. Let us learn from this not to envy others either those secular advantages or those endowments of the mind in which they are better than we.

3.2. He answered it with great satisfaction to Solomon, giving him what he wanted and showing himself very

eager to help him in this great project to which he was putting his hands. We have here the articles of his agreement with Solomon, in which we may notice Hiram's wisdom:

3.2.1. He thought about the proposal before he replied (v. 8). Those who take time to consider are not wasting time.

3.2.2. He got down to details in the agreement. Solomon has spoken of cutting down trees (v. 6), and Hiram agrees to what he wants in that (v. 8), but nothing has been said about transporting the logs. He therefore undertakes to bring all the wood down from Lebanon by sea, a journey along the coast. Solomon must specify the place where the wood is to be delivered to, and Hiram will undertake to bring it to that place and be responsible for its safety. As the Sidonians were better than the Israelites at woodwork, so also they were in sailing, for Tyre and Sidon were situated at the gateway to the sea (Eze 27:3). They therefore were the most suitable people to take care of the sea transport. And:

3.2.3. If Hiram is to undertake the work, he justly expects that Solomon will undertake to pay the wages: "*Thou shalt accomplish my desire in giving food for my household* (v. 9), not only for the workers, but also for my own family." If Tyre supplies Israel with skilled workers, Israel will supply Tyre with wheat (Eze 27:17). And so we see by the wise arrangement of Providence that one country needs another.

Verses 10–18

Here is:

1. The fulfillment of the agreement between Solomon and Hiram.

1.1. Hiram delivered the wood to Solomon, according to what had been agreed to (v. 10).

1.2. Solomon transferred to Hiram the wheat he had promised him (v. 11).

2. The confirmation of the friendship that was made between them. It is wise to strengthen our friendship with those whom we find to be honest and fair, in case new friends do not turn out to be so firm or kind as old ones.

3. The laborers whom Solomon employed in preparing materials for the temple:

3.1. Some were Israelites, who were employed in felling trees and helping to square them, together with Hiram's workers. He appointed 30,000 for this work, but employed only 10,000 at a time, so that after one month's work they had two months' vacation, both for rest and to settle their own affairs at home (vv. 13–14). It was temple service, but Solomon still took care that they were not overworked.

3.2. Others were forced labor from other nations, who were to carry loads and cut stone (v. 15).

3.3. Some were employed as directors and overseers (v. 16), 3,300 who supervised the people, for preparation was now to be made, not only for the temple, but also for all the rest of Solomon's buildings at Jerusalem, here in the forest of Lebanon, and in other places of his dominion, for which see 9:17–19.

4. The laying of the foundation of the temple, for that was the building that his heart was especially set on, and so he began with that (vv. 17–18). It seems Solomon himself was present, and president, at the founding of the temple, and that the first stone was laid with great ceremony. *Solomon commanded and they brought costly stones* (v. 17) for the foundation, although because they were out of sight, poorer ones could have been used. That sincerity which is an aspect of life under the Gospel makes us lay a firm

foundation and give the most effort to that part of our religious faith which is out of the sight of other people.

CHAPTER 6

Great and long preparation had been made for the building of the temple, and here, finally, comes the account of its building. It was a magnificent work and, in its spiritual significance, one of the glories of the church. Here is: 1. The time when it was built (v. 1) and how long the building took (vv. 37–38); the silence with which it was built (v. 7); its dimensions (vv. 2–3); the message God sent to Solomon when it was being built (vv. 11–13). 2. The details: windows (v. 4), rooms (vv. 5–6, 8–10), the walls and floor (vv. 15–18), the inner sanctuary (vv. 19–22), the cherubim (vv. 23–30), the doors (vv. 31–35), and the inner courtyard (v. 36).

Verses 1–10

Here:

1. The temple is called *the house of the Lord* (v. 1), because it was:

1.1. Directed and modeled by him. Infinite Wisdom was the architect, and he gave David the plan or pattern through the Spirit.

1.2. Dedicated and devoted to him and to his honor, to be used in his service, for he revealed his glory in it in a way that corresponded to the Old Testament era. Its *beauty of holiness* (1Ch 16:29) was in its being *the house of the Lord* (v. 1), and this beauty far exceeded all its other beauties.

2. The time when it began to be built is set down precisely:

2.1. It was just 480 years after the bringing of the children of Israel out of Egypt. Allowing forty years for Moses, seventeen for Joshua, 299 for the judges, forty for Eli, forty for Samuel and Saul, forty for David, and four for Solomon before he began the work, we have the total of 480. David's tent, which was clean and convenient, though it was neither stately nor rich, is called the *house of the Lord* (2Sa 12:20), and it served as well as Solomon's temple. But when God gave Solomon great wealth, he put it into his heart to use it in this way, and graciously allowed him to, mainly because it was to be a shadow of good things to come (Heb 9:9).

2.2. It was in the fourth year of Solomon's reign, the first three years being taken up with settling the affairs of his kingdom so that they might not hinder this work in any way. Time is not wasted which is spent in composing ourselves to do the work of God and disentangling ourselves from everything that might distract or divert us.

3. The materials are brought in, ready to be put in their place (v. 7). They are so ready that there was *neither hammer nor axe heard in the house while it was in building*. It was to be the temple of the God of peace, and so no iron tool must be heard in it. Quietness and silence both befit and further religious undertakings: God's work should be done with as much care and as little noise as possible. The temple was torn down with axes and hammers, and those who destroyed it *roared in the midst of the congregation* (Ps 74:4, 6), but it was built in silence. Clamor and violence often hinder the work of God, but never further it.

4. The dimensions are set down (vv. 2–3) according to the rules of proportion. Some notice that the length and breadth were just double those of the tabernacle.

5. An account of the windows is given (v. 4): they were "broad within, and narrow without" (v. 4, margin). This is how the eyes of our mind should be, reflecting more closely on ourselves than on other people, looking much inside ourselves in self-examination, but only a little outside in criticizing others.

6. The side rooms, which served as vestries, are described (vv. 5–6); in them, the utensils of the tabernacle were carefully stored and the priests dressed. Care was taken not to insert the beams into the walls, which would weaken them (v. 6). Let not the church's strength be reduced under the pretense of adding to its beauty or advantages.

Verses 11–14

Here is:

1. The word God sent to Solomon when he was engaged in building the temple. God assured Solomon that if he proceeded and persevered in obedience to the divine law and observed the way of duty and the true worship of God, then divine loving-kindness would be drawn out both to himself—*I will perform* (fulfill) *my word with thee* (v. 12)—and to his kingdom. God probably sent him this word through a prophet:

1.1. So that by the promise he might be encouraged and strengthened in his work. Keeping an eye on God's promises will carry us happily through our work, and those who have the welfare of the community at heart will think nothing is too difficult if it will ensure signs of God's continuing presence.

1.2. So that by the condition attached to the promise, he might be alert to remember that although he built the temple so strongly, its glory would soon depart unless he and his people continued to *walk in God's statutes* (v. 12).

2. The work Solomon did for God: *So he built the house* (v. 14). Thus energized by the message God had sent him, and thus warned not to expect that God would recognize his building unless he was obedient to his laws, he was eager to proceed on God's terms. The strictness of God's government will never drive good people away from his service, but will quicken them to do it. Solomon built and finished, he went on with the work, and God went along with him until it was completed.

Verses 15–38

Here:

1. We have a particular account of the details of the building:

1.1. The paneling of the temple. It was of cedar (v. 15), which was strong and durable and had a very sweet smell. The paneling was skillfully carved with *knops* (gourds) and open flowers (v. 18).

1.2. The gilding. It was not like ours, painted over, but *the whole house*, all the inside of the temple (v. 22), even the floor (v. 30), he *overlaid with gold*, and the Most Holy Place with *pure gold* (v. 21).

1.3. The *oracle*, inner sanctuary or "speaking place," *the holy of holies*, the Most Holy Place, is so called because that is where God spoke to Moses, and perhaps to the high priest. In this place *the ark of the covenant was to be set* (v. 19). Solomon made everything new except for the ark, which was still the same one that Moses made, with its atonement cover and cherubim. That was the sign of God's presence, which is always the same with his people, whether they meet in tent or temple, and does not change with their condition.

1.4. The cherubim. Besides those at the ends of the atonement cover, which covered the ark:

1.4.1. Solomon set up two more, very large ones, with wings made of olive wood, all overlaid with gold (vv. 23–28).

1.4.2. He carved cherubim on all the walls of the house (v. 29). The followers of other religions set up idols of their gods and worshiped them, but these were intended to represent the servants of the God of Israel, the holy angels, not to be worshiped themselves.

1.5. The doors. The folding doors that led into the inner sanctuary were *a fifth part of the wall* (v. 31), those into the temple were *a fourth part* (v. 33), but both were made beautiful with cherubim carved on them (vv. 32, 35).

1.6. The inner courtyard, in which was the bronze altar at which the priests ministered. This was separated from the court where the people were by a low wall, three rows of dressed stone topped with a cornice of cedar (v. 36), so that over it the people would be able to see what was done and hear what the priests said to them.

1.7. The time spent in building. It was only seven and a half years from its foundation until it was finished (v. 38).

2. Let us now see what this temple was a type of:

2.1. Christ is the true temple; he himself spoke of the temple of his body (Jn 2:21). God himself prepared his body for him (Heb 10:5). *In him dwelt the fulness of the Godhead* (Col 2:9), as the *Shechinah* in the temple. In him all the people of God's spiritual Israel meet. Through him we have access to come with confidence to God.

2.2. Every believer is a living temple, in whom the Spirit of God lives (1Co 3:16). Even the body is a temple of the Holy Spirit who is in every believer (1Co 6:19). We are not only wonderfully made by divine Providence, but also more wonderfully made new by divine grace. This living temple is built on Christ as its foundation and will be perfected at the right time.

2.3. The Gospel church is the mystical temple; it grows to a *holy temple in the Lord* (Eph 2:21), enriched and made beautiful with the gifts and graces of the Spirit, as Solomon's temple was with gold and precious stones. Only Jews built the tabernacle, but Gentiles joined them in building the temple. Even foreigners and strangers are built together to become a *habitation* (dwelling) *of God* (Eph 2:19, 22). The temple was divided into the Holy Place and the Most Holy Place, into outer and inner courtyards, and so there is the visible and the invisible church. The door into the temple was wider than that into the inner sanctuary. Many come into a professed faith but come short of salvation. The top stone of the Gospel church will eventually be brought out with shouting, and it is a pity that there should be the noise of axes and hammers in the building. Angels are ministering spirits, serving the church on every side and all its members.

2.4. Heaven is the eternal temple. There the church will be fixed, and no longer movable. The streets of the New Jerusalem, in allusion to the floor of the temple, are said to be *of pure gold* (Rev 21:21). There the cherubim always worship at the throne of glory. The temple was uniform, and in heaven there is the perfection of beauty and harmony. In Solomon's temple there was no noise of axes and hammers. Everything is quiet and serene in heaven. Everyone who wants to be a stone in that building must be made fit and ready for it in the time of present trials and preparation. They must be cut and squared by divine grace and so made fit for a place there.

CHAPTER 7

In this chapter we have: 1. Solomon setting up several buildings for himself and his own use (vv. 1–12). 2. His furnishing of the temple which he had built for God: 2.1. With two columns (vv. 13–22). 2.2. With the Sea of cast metal *(vv. 23–26). 2.3. With ten stands of bronze (vv. 27–37), and ten basins on them (vv. 38–39). 2.4. With all the other utensils of the temple (vv. 40–50). 2.5. With the things that his father had dedicated (v. 51). The particular description of these things was not unnecessary when it was written, nor is it useless now.*

Verses 1–12

There was never anyone who had so much of the spirit of building as Solomon, nor was there anyone who wanted to build for any better purpose. He began with the temple—he built for God first—and then all his other buildings also gave satisfaction.

1. He built a house for himself (v. 1), *where he dwelt* (v. 8). His father had built a good house, but it was no reflection on his father for him to build a better one. Much of the comfort of this life is connected with pleasant housing. He spent thirteen years building this house, whereas he built the temple in a little more than seven years. He was in no hurry to build his own palace, but was impatient to see the temple finished and fit for use.

2. He built the Palace of the Forest of Lebanon (v. 2), which it is supposed was a country house, and which received its name from trees that surrounded it. Explicit mention is made not only of his buildings in Jerusalem but also of those in Lebanon (9:19), and we read of the tower of Lebanon, which looked toward Damascus (SS 7:4) and may have been part of this house. A detailed record is given of this house. Maybe it was built in Lebanon, a place famous for cedars, for the columns, beams, and roof were all cedar (vv. 2–3). Because it was intended to have pleasant views or prospects, there were three tiers of windows on each side, *light against light* (vv. 4–5), or as it may be read, "prospect against prospect."

3. He built a portico, a colonnade (v. 6), before one of his houses—either the one at Jerusalem or the one at Lebanon—which was very famous. He himself speaks of Wisdom's building her house, and *hewing out her seven pillars* (Pr 9:1).

4. At his house where he lived in Jerusalem he built a *porch of judgment*, the Hall of Justice, where the throne, or king's bench, was set, to try cases, in which he himself was appealed to, and this was richly lined with cedar, from the floor to the roof (v. 7). There he also had *another court within the porch*, a palace set farther back, of similar design, for his servants (v. 8).

5. He built a house for his wife, where she kept her court (v. 8). It is said to be *like the porch*, because like it, it was built of cedar.

Verses 13–47

Here is an account of the bronze work around the temple. There was no iron around the temple, although we find David preparing for the temple *iron for things of iron* (1Ch 29:2).

1. The skilled worker whom Solomon employed to lead this part of the work was Hiram, or Huram (2Ch 4:11), who was an Israelite on his mother's side, of the tribe of Naphtali, and whose father was a man of Tyre (v. 14). If he had the skill of one from Tyre and the affection of an Israelite for the house of God, it was fortunate that the blood of the two nations mixed in him, for that qualified him for the work he was intended to fulfill. As the tabernacle was built with the wealth of Egypt, so the temple was built with the skill of Tyre.

2. All the bronze vessels were of *bright brass* (burnished bronze) (v. 45), "good" bronze, according to the Aramaic, what was strongest and looked finest.

3. The place where all the bronze vessels were cast was the plain of Jordan, because the ground there was stiff and clayey, fit to make molds out of for the casting of the bronze (v. 46), and Solomon did not want to have this dirty, smoky work done in or near Jerusalem.

4. The quantity was not recorded. The vessels *were exceedingly many*, and it would have been an endless work to keep a record of them; *neither was the weight of the brass* recorded when it was delivered to the workers. The workers were so honest, and they had so much bronze, that there was no danger of them not having enough.

5. Some details of the bronze work are described:

5.1. Two bronze pillars that were set up *in the porch* (portico) *of the temple* (v. 21) between the temple and the courtyard of the priests, purely for decoration.

5.1.1. The fact that they were a decoration may be gathered from the account given of the intricate work that was around them, a network of interwoven chains, lilies, and pomegranates in rows, and all of burnished bronze.

5.1.2. Their significance is suggested in the names given them (v. 21): *Jachin*, "he establishes," and *Boaz*, "in him is strength." Some think they were intended to be memorials of the pillar of cloud and fire which led Israel through the desert; I prefer to think they were intended as reminders to the priests and others who came to worship at God's door:

5.1.2.1. To depend only on God to strengthen them or establish them in all their religious exercises. When we come to wait on God, and find our hearts wandering and unsteadfast, then let us by faith take this help from heaven: *Jachin*, "God will secure my wandering thoughts." When we find ourselves weak and unable to fulfill our holy duties, let this encourage us: *Boaz*, "our strength is in him," who works in us both to will and to do according to his good purpose (Php 2:13). *I will go in the strength of the Lord God* (Ps 71:16). Spiritual strength and stability should be received at the door of God's temple, where we must wait for the gifts of grace to use the means of grace.

5.1.2.2. To remember that the temple of God was strongly established among them. But when this temple was destroyed, particular notice was taken of the destruction of these pillars (2Ki 25:13, 17), which had been the signs of its establishment, and would have remained so if the people had not forsaken God.

5.2. A bronze Sea, a very large basin, more than ten cubits, that is, about fifteen feet (about 4.5 meters), in diameter, and which contained 2,000 baths, that is, about 11,500 gallons (about forty-four kiloliters), of water for the priests' use, in washing themselves and the sacrifices and in keeping the courts of the temple clean (vv. 23–26). It stood raised on the figures of twelve bronze bulls. The Gibeonites, or temple servants, who were to draw water for the house of God, had the task of filling it. Some think Solomon made the idols of bulls support this great basin in contempt of the golden calf which Israel had worshiped, so that—as Bishop Patrick expresses it—the people might see that there was nothing worthy of adoration in those figures; they were more suitable as posts than as gods.

5.3. Ten *bases*, stands, of bronze (v. 27), on which were put ten *lavers*, basins, to be filled with water for the service of the temple, because there would not be room at the Sea of cast metal for all who needed to wash there. The stands on which the basins were fixed are described in detail (vv. 27–30). They were intricately decorated and set on wheels, so that the stands and basins might be mobile and be moved around as need arose, but usually they stood in two rows, five on one side of the courtyard and five on the other (v. 39). Each basin contained forty baths, that is, about 230 gallons (about 880 liters) (v. 38).

5.4. Besides these, there was a vast number of bronze pots made to boil the flesh of the peace offerings (fellowship offerings) in, which the priests and offerers were to feast on before the Lord (see 1Sa 2:14), and there were shovels, with which they took the ashes from the altar. Some think the word refers to "fleshhooks," with which they took meat out of the pot. The basins for receiving the blood of the sacrifices were also made of bronze.

Verses 48–51

Here is:

1. The making of the gold work of the temple, which it seems was done last, for this concluded the work of the house of God. Everything within the doors was gold, and all was new—except the ark, with its atonement cover and cherubim—the old being either melted down or stored away: the golden altar, table, and lampstand with all their furnishings. The altar of incense was still *one*, for Christ and his intercession are one, but Hiram made ten golden tables (2Ch 4:8) and *ten golden candlesticks* (v. 49), suggesting how much greater is the abundance of both spiritual food and heavenly light which the Gospel blesses us with than that which the Law of Moses provided or could provide. Even the *hinges* (sockets) of the door were of gold (v. 50).

2. The bringing in of the dedicated things, things acquired as spoils of war or received as tribute, which David had devoted to the honor of God (v. 51). What was not spent on the building and furniture was stored in the treasury, for repairs, emergencies, and the general overheads of the temple service. What parents have dedicated to God, children should not give away to others or recall, but should cheerfully devote to God what was intended for godly and charitable uses, so that they may, with their possessions, inherit the blessing.

CHAPTER 8

The building and furnishings of the temple were very magnificent, but its dedication exceeded those things in glory as much as prayer and praise exceed the casting of metal and the carving of stones. The purpose of the temple was to maintain the relationship between God and his people, and here is an account of the ceremony of their first meeting there. 1. The representatives of all Israel were called together (vv. 1–2) to hold a festival to honor God for fourteen days (v. 65). The priests brought the ark into the Most Holy Place and placed it there (vv. 3–9). God took possession of it with a cloud (vv. 10–11). 2. Solomon expressed thankful acknowledgments to God and told the people the reason for their meeting (vv. 12–21). 3. In a long prayer he commended to God's gracious acceptance all the prayers that would be made in or toward this place (vv. 22–53). 4. He sent the assembly away with a blessing and an exhortation (vv. 54–61). 5. He offered many sacrifices, on which he and his people feasted, and so parted, greatly encouraged (vv. 62–66). These were Israel's golden days, types of the days of the Son of Man.

Verses 1–11

Although the temple was rich and beautiful, while it did not have the ark in it, it was like a body without a soul, or a lampstand without a light, or a house without someone living in it. All the cost and effort spent on this stately structure are lost if God does not accept them. When therefore *all the work* is ended (7:51), the *one thing needful* (Lk 10:42) is the bringing in of the ark. This must crown the work.

1. Solomon took the lead in this service, as David did in bringing the ark to Jerusalem. He summons this great assembly (v. 1) *at the feast in the seventh month* (v. 2), namely, the Feast of Tabernacles, which was set to begin on the fifteenth day of that month (Lev 23:34). David, as a very *good* man, brings the ark to a *convenient* place, near him; and Solomon, as a very *great* man, brings it to a *magnificent* place. Let children continue in God's service where their parents have left off.

2. All the people of Israel were present at the service: their judges and the chiefs of their tribes and families, all their officers, civil and military, and the heads of their clans. They all came together on this occasion:

2.1. To honor Solomon, and to express the thanks of the nation to him for all the good service he had done.

2.2. To honor the ark. National mercies call for national acknowledgments. Those who appeared before the Lord did not appear empty-handed, for they all sacrificed sheep and cattle (v. 5), and the sum of them was innumerable.

3. The priests did their part in the service. In the desert, the Levites were to carry the ark, but here—it being the last time that the ark was to be carried—the priests themselves did it, as they were ordered to do when it went around Jericho. We are told:

3.1. What was in the ark: nothing but the two stone tablets (v. 9), a treasure far exceeding all the dedicated things both of David and of Solomon. The jar of manna and Aaron's staff were *by* the ark, but not *in* it.

3.2. What was brought up with the ark (v. 4): *The tabernacle of the congregation*, the Tent of Meeting. It is probable that both what Moses set up in the desert, which was in Gibeon, and what David pitched in Zion were brought to the temple, to which they surrendered, as it were, all their holiness, integrating it into the holiness of the temple, which must from that time on be the place where God was to be sought. In this way, all the church's holy things on earth, which are so much its joy and glory, will be swallowed up in the perfection of holiness above.

3.3. Where the ark was settled, the place appointed for its rest after all its wanderings (v. 6): *In the oracle of the house*, in the inner sanctuary of the temple, from which they expected God to speak to them, the Most Holy Place, which was made so by the presence of the ark, *under the wings of the* great *cherubim* which Solomon set up (6:27), showing the special protection of angels, under which God's ordinances and the assemblies of his people are made.

4. God graciously acknowledged what was done and showed his acceptance of it (vv. 10–11). The priests could come into the Most Holy Place until God revealed his glory there, but from that time on, no one could, except at their peril, approach the ark, apart from the high priest on the Day of Atonement. And so it was not until the priests had come out of the Most Holy Place that the *Shechinah* took possession of it in a cloud, which filled not only the Most Holy Place, but also the whole temple, so that the priests who burned incense at the golden altar could not bear it. This visible revelation of God's glory:

4.1. Showed that God honored the ark and acknowledged it as a sign of his presence. Its glory had been long diminished and overshadowed by its frequent moves, the lowliness of the place where it was kept, and its being exposed too much to common view, but God now showed that it was as precious to him as ever. He wanted it looked on with as much respect as it was when Moses first brought it into his tabernacle.

4.2. Showed God's acceptance of the building and furnishings of the temple as a good service for his name and his kingdom.

4.3. Struck awe on this great assembly. What they saw confirmed their belief in what they had read in the books of Moses about the glory of God's appearances to their fathers.

4.4. Showed that God was ready to hear the prayer Solomon was now about to speak. But the glory of God appeared in a dark cloud to show:

- The darkness of that era in comparison with the light of the Gospel.
- The darkness of our present state in comparison with the vision of God, which will be the happiness of heaven, where God's glory is unveiled.

Verses 12–21

Here:

1. Solomon encourages the priests. The disciples of Christ *feared when they entered into the cloud*, though it was *a bright cloud* (Lk 9:34), and so did the priests when they found themselves wrapped in a thick cloud. To silence their fears:

1.1. He reminds them that this is a sign of God's presence (v. 12). It is a sign of his favor, for he said, *I will appear in a cloud* (Lev 16:2). Where God lives in light, faith is swallowed up in vision, and fear is swallowed up in love.

1.2. He himself welcomes it, as deserving of full acceptance (v. 13): "*Surely I come,*" God says. "*Amen,*" says Solomon. "*Even so, come, Lord* (Rev 22:20). The house is your own, completely your own; *I have surely built it for thee* (v. 13)." It is Solomon's joy that God has taken possession of his house, and it is his desire that he would keep possession of it. Let not the priests therefore dread what Solomon triumphs in so much.

2. Solomon instructs the people. He spoke briefly to the priests but *turned his face about* (v. 14) from them *to the congregation*, who stood in the outer courtyard, and addressed himself to them particularly:

2.1. He blessed them. When they saw the dark cloud enter the temple, they blessed themselves, being stunned by it and afraid that the thick darkness might be an ominous sign for them. Solomon *blessed them*, that is, he quieted them and released them from any anguish they had.

2.2. He told them about this house which he had built and was now dedicating:

2.2.1. He began his account with a thankful acknowledgment of the good hand of his God on him up to that time: *Blessed be the Lord God of Israel* (v. 15). What we delight in, God must be praised for. In this way, he had the congregation lift up their hearts in thanksgiving to God. Solomon here blessed God:

2.2.1.1. For the promise which he *spoke with his mouth to David* (v. 15).

2.2.1.2. For keeping it: he had now *fulfilled it with his hand* (v. 15). We have the best sense of God's mercies when we compare what God has done with what he said.

2.2.2. Solomon now makes a solemn surrender or dedication of this house to God. Here is a record of the special causes and considerations that moved Solomon to build this house. He records:

2.2.2.1. The lack of such a place. God had said, *I chose no city to build a house in for my name* (v. 16), and so that is the reason for building this temple.

2.2.2.2. David's intention to build such a place. God first chose the person who would rule his people—*I chose David* (v. 16)—and then put it into *his heart to build a house* for God's name (v. 17).

2.2.2.3. God's promise about him, Solomon. God approved of his father's intention (v. 18): *Thou didst well, that it was in thy heart.* What Solomon has done did not, therefore, come from his own head, and was not for his own glory; the work itself was according to his father's plans, and his doing it was according to God's appointment.

2.2.2.4. What he himself has done and with what purpose: *I have built a house*, not for my own name but *for the name of the Lord God of Israel* (v. 20), and *set there a place for the ark* (v. 21). The more we do for God, the more we are indebted to him, for the resources we have come from him, not ourselves.

Verses 22–53

After Solomon has generally surrendered this house to God, and after God has shown his acceptance of it by taking possession of it, Solomon prays. In this prayer, it is his request that this temple may be designated not only as a house of sacrifice but also as a *house of prayer for all people*. In this respect it was a type of the Gospel church; see Isa 56:7 and compare with Mt 21:13.

1. Solomon did not appoint one of the priests to offer this prayer, or one of the prophets, but did it himself, *in the presence of all the congregation of Israel* (v. 22).

1.1. It was good that he was able to do it, a sign that he had learned to pray well, and knew how to express himself to God in a suitable way as occasions arose, without using a set form of words.

1.2. It was good that he did not shy away from performing divine service in the presence of such a large congregation. Not in all his other glory, even on his ivory throne, did Solomon look so great as he did now.

2. The position in which he prayed was very reverent. It expressed his humility, seriousness, and fervency in prayer:

2.1. He *kneeled down*, as can be seen from v. 54, where he is said to *rise from his knees*; see 2Ch 6:13. Kneeling is the most fitting posture for prayer (Eph 3:14). Mr. George Herbert says, "Kneeling never spoiled silk stockings."

2.2. *He spread forth his hands towards heaven* and, so it seems from v. 54, continued to do so to the end of the prayer, showing his desire toward and expectations from God, as *a Father in heaven*. He spread out his hands, as it were to offer up the prayer from an open and released heart and to present it to heaven, and also to receive from there, with both arms, the mercy he prayed for.

3. The prayer itself was very long, and perhaps much longer than is recorded here. It is not making long prayers, but making them as a pretense, that Christ condemns. In this prayer Solomon:

3.1. Gives glory to God. He begins with this, as the most proper act of adoration.

3.1.1. He gives him the praise of what he is, the best of rulers of his people: "*Who keepest covenant and mercy with thy servants* (v. 23). You even do for them what you have not explicitly promised, provided they *walk before thee with all their heart* (v. 23)."

3.1.2. He gives him thanks for what he has done, in particular, for his family (v. 24): "*Thou hast kept with thy servant David*, as with your other servants, *that which thou promisedst him.*"

3.2. Appeals for grace and favor from God:

3.2.1. That God would give him and his family the mercy he has promised (vv. 25–26). God has helped us up to this time (2Co 1:10). Solomon repeats the promise (v. 25), *There shall not fail thee a man to sit on the throne*, not excluding the condition, *so that* (so long as) *thy children take heed to their way*, for we can only expect God to fulfill the promise if we fulfill the condition. And then he humbly begs this outcome (v. 26): *Now, O God of Israel, let thy word be verified.*

3.2.2. That God would have respect for this temple, that he would graciously acknowledge it. To this purpose:

3.2.2.1. He begins with:

- A humble expression of wonder at God's gracious condescension (v. 27): "*But will God indeed dwell on the earth?* Can we imagine that a Being infinitely high, holy, and content will stoop so low as to let it be said of him that he *dwells upon the earth?*"
- A humble acknowledgment of the fact that the house he has built, even though it is very spacious, cannot possibly contain God: "*The heaven of heavens cannot contain thee* (v. 27); this house is too small, too lowly to be the home of One who is infinite in being and glory."

3.2.2.2. After these initial thoughts, he prays in general:

- That God would graciously hear and answer the prayer he is now praying (v. 28). It is a humble prayer, a prayer from the heart, a prayer made in faith: "Lord, *hearken to it*, have respect to it, not as the prayer of Israel's king but as the prayer of your servant."
- That God would in the same way hear and answer all the prayers that would, at any time in the future, be made in or toward this house which he had now built, "*Hear it in heaven, that* (which) is indeed *thy dwelling place*, and *when thou hearest, forgive.*"

3.2.2.3. He shows in this prayer that he wants them to consider in their prayers that place where God desired to reveal his glory as he did nowhere else on earth. Only priests could come into that place, the Most Holy Place, but when the people worshiped in the courts of the temple, they must look toward the Most Holy Place as an instituted channel for their worship, to help the weakness of their faith and to be a type of the mediation of Jesus Christ, who is the true temple.

3.2.2.4. More particularly, he here gives the different cases:

3.2.2.4.*1*. If God was appealed to by an oath to determine any disputed right between people, and the oath was taken before this altar, he prayed that God would in some way or other reveal the truth and judge between the contending parties (vv. 31–32). He prayed that, in difficult matters, this throne of grace might be a throne of justice.

3.2.2.4.*2*. If the people of Israel groaned under any national disaster, or any individual Israelite under any personal calamity, he wanted the prayers made in or toward this house to be heard and answered:

3.2.2.4.*2*.*1*. In case of public judgments. He could not and would not ask that their prayer might be answered unless they also *turned from their sin* (v. 35) and *turn again to God* (v. 33), that is, unless they truly repented and reformed their ways. But if they qualified for mercy in this way, he prays:

- That God would hear from heaven.
- That he would forgive their sin.

- That he would *teach them the good way wherein they should walk*, teach them the right way to live (v. 36), by his Spirit, with his word and prophets. In this way they could learn from their troubles and be prepared for rescue, for rescue comes in love when we come back to the right way of following God and our duty.
- That he would then grant the mercy prayed for, removing the punishment and putting right the grievance.

3.2.2.4.*2.2*. In case of personal afflictions (vv. 38–40). He does not mention any individual case, as our human difficulties are so many and varied. He supposes that those bringing their requests will be very aware of their own burden: they *shall know every man the plague* (afflictions) *of his own heart* (v. 38); and he supposes that they will spread out their hands, that is, spread out their case in prayer toward this house, as Hezekiah spread the letter before the Lord (2Ki 19:14). Whether the trouble is physical or mental, they will present it to God. He refers to God all cases of this kind which may be brought here. He refers them:

- To God's knowledge of everything.
- To his justice: *Give to every man according to his ways* (v 39); and God will not fail to impart justice according to his grace, not the law, for if his justice were according to the law, we would all be ruined.
- To his mercy: *Hear, and forgive, and do* (v. 39), *that they may fear thee all their days* (v. 40).

3.2.2.4.*2.3*. In the case of the foreigner, the stranger who is not an Israelite, a convert who comes to the temple to pray to the God of Israel, being convinced of how foolish and evil it is to worship the gods of their country. He begged that God would accept and answer the convert's prayer (v. 43): *Do according to all that the stranger calleth to thee for*, do whatever the foreigner asks of you. It was in such early and old times that the signs of God's favor toward the *sinners of the Gentiles* (Gal 2:15) were seen. As there was then *one law for the native and for the stranger* (Ex 12:49), so also there was one Gospel for both.

3.2.2.4.*2.4*. In the case of an army going out to battle. In commending this case to God's favor, Solomon supposes that the army is camped at a distance, somewhere far away, and is sent by divine order *against the enemy* (v. 44).

3.2.2.4.*2.5*. Lastly, in the case of poor prisoners. In praying for divine compassion to be shown to these:

- He supposes that Israel will sin. He knew them, himself, and all human nature.
- He supposes that if Israel rebels from God, God will be *angry with them* and *deliver them into the hand of their enemies*, to be taken prisoner into a foreign country (v. 46).
- He then supposes that they will have a change of heart; that they will repent and humble themselves, saying, *We have sinned and have done perversely* (v. 47); and that *in the land of their enemies they will return to God* (v. 48), whom they abandoned in their own land.
- He supposes that in their prayers they will look toward their own land, the Holy Land, Jerusalem, the Holy City, and the temple, the holy house, and directs them to do so (v. 48).
- He prays that then God would *hear their prayers, forgive their sins, maintain* (uphold) *their cause*, and incline their *enemies to have compassion on them* (vv. 49–50).

3.2.2.5. Nowadays, under the Gospel, there is no place or building on earth that needs to be prayed in or toward to make our prayers acceptable. That was a shadow; the reality is Christ. Whatever we ask in his name will be given to us.

Verses 54–61

After Solomon's sermon in Ecclesiastes, he gives the conclusion of the whole matter, and so he does here, after this long prayer. It is called his *blessing the people* (v. 55).

1. He gives God the glory for the great things he has done for Israel (v. 56). He stands up to *bless the congregation* (v. 55) but begins by blessing God. He blesses God, who has given—he does not say honor, power, and victory to Israel, but *rest*, as if that was a blessing that was more valuable than any of those.

1.1. He refers to the *promises given by the hand of Moses* (v. 56), as he did (vv. 15, 24) to those which were made to David. There were promises given through Moses, as well as commands.

1.2. He, as it were, acknowledges full receipt of God's pledges: *There has not failed one word of all his good promises* (v. 56).

2. He blesses himself and the congregation, expressing his fervent desire and hope of four things:

2.1. The presence of God with them. This great assembly is now soon to be scattered, and it is not likely that they will ever be all together again in this world. Solomon therefore dismisses them with this blessing: "*The Lord be present with us* (v. 57), and that will be enough comfort when we are absent from each other. *The Lord our God be with us, as he was with our fathers* (v. 57). *Let him not leave us*, may he be to us today, and to ours forever, what he was to those who went before us."

2.2. The power of his grace on them: "*Let him be with us*, and continue to be with us, not that he may enlarge our lands and increase our wealth, but *that he may incline our hearts to himself, to walk in all his ways and to keep his commandments*" (v. 58).

2.3. An answer to the prayer he has now made: "*Let these my words be nigh unto the Lord our God day and night* (v. 59). May a gracious reply be received to every prayer that will be made here, and that will be a continual answer to this prayer." What Solomon asks for in this prayer is still given according to the intercession of Christ.

2.4. The glorifying of God in the widening of his kingdom among the human race. May Israel be blessed and favored in this way.

3. He solemnly commands his people to continue and persevere in their duty to God. Having spoken *to God for* them, he here speaks *from God to* them, and it would be only those who were made better by his preaching who would fare better because of his prayers.

Verses 62–66

We read before that Judah and Israel were very happy under their own vines and fig trees (4:25). Here they are so in God's courts.

1. They had great joy and encouragement when they were present at God's house, for there:

1.1. Solomon offered a great sacrifice, 22,000 cattle and 120,000 sheep, enough to have emptied the country of cattle if it had not been a very fruitful land. All these sacrifices could not be offered in one day, but had to be offered during the several days of the feast.

1.2. He kept a feast, the Feast of Tabernacles, it seems, after the Feast of Dedication, and both together lasted fourteen days (v. 65).

2. They carried this joy and encouragement with them to their own homes. The basis of their joy was God's goodness, as it should be of ours at all times.

CHAPTER 9

In this chapter we have: 1. The answer which God, in a vision, gave to Solomon's prayer, and the terms he settled with him (vv. 1–9). 2. The giving and receiving of grateful kindness between Solomon and Hiram (vv. 10–14). 3. Solomon's workers and buildings (vv. 15–24), his devotion (v. 25), and his merchant navy (vv. 26–28).

Verses 1–9

God had given a real answer to Solomon's prayer, and signs of his acceptance of it, immediately, by the *fire from heaven* which consumed the sacrifices (as we find in 2Ch 7:1), but here we have a more explicit and distinct answer to it. Notice:

1. In what way God gave him this answer. He appeared to him, as he had at Gibeon at the beginning of his reign, in a dream or vision (v. 2). The writer's comparing of this vision with that earlier one suggests that, like the earlier one (2Ch 1:6–7), this one came on the very night after he had finished ceremonies to the Lord.

2. The thrust of this answer.

2.1. He assures Solomon of his special presence in the temple Solomon had built, in answer to the prayer he had made (v. 3): *I have hallowed this house.* Solomon had dedicated it, but it was God's right to sanctify or consecrate it.

2.2. He shows him that for the future he and his people are required to be on their best behavior. Let them not rest on their laurels, thinking they can live as they please now that they have the *temple of the Lord* among them (Jer 7:4). "*If thou wilt walk before me as David did, in integrity of heart and uprightness, then I will establish the throne of thy kingdom,* but not otherwise," for that was the condition on which the promise was made (Ps 132:12). "But know, and let your family and kingdom also know, and be warned by it, that if you turn completely away from following me, Israel, even though it is a holy nation, will be cut off (v. 7), by one judgment after another. The temple, even though it is a holy house, which God himself has *hallowed for his name* (v. 7), will be abandoned and become desolate (vv. 8–9): *This house which is high* (imposing)." Those who *now pass by it are astonished* (v. 8) at its bulk and beauty; but if you abandon God, its height will make its fall so much the more amazing. God gave Solomon fair warning of this, now that he had just built and dedicated it, so that he and his people might not become proud, but fear God.

Verses 10–14

Here is an account of Solomon and Hiram and their fair and friendly parting when the work was finished:

1. Hiram fulfilled his part of the agreement completely. Far from envying Solomon's growing greatness and reputation, he helped exalt him.

2. Solomon, no doubt, fulfilled his part of the agreement and gave Hiram *food for his household,* as was agreed (5:9). But we are also told here that he gave him twenty towns—small *cities,* like those mentioned here in v. 19—*in the land of Galilee* (v. 11). Hiram came to see these towns but did not like them (v. 12): *They pleased him not.* He called the country the land of *Cabul,* a Phoenician word, according to Josephus, which means "displeasing"

or "good-for-nothing" (v. 13). He therefore returned them to Solomon, as we find in 2Ch 8:2, who rebuilt them and then settled the children of Israel there. The country was truly valuable, and so were its towns, but they did not suit Hiram's character. The Tyrians were merchants or traders who lived in fine houses. They had become rich by navigation, but did not know how to value a country that was fit for growing crops or using as pastureland. Hiram wanted Solomon to please him by becoming his partner in trade, as we find Solomon did (v. 27). Some delight in farming, and wonder what pleasure sailors can have on a rough sea. Others take as much delight in sailing, and wonder what pleasure farmers can take in a muddy country like Cabul.

Verses 15–28

We have here a further account of Solomon's greatness:

1. His buildings. He conscripted many people into forced labor and raised a great amount of money through taxes, because he planned a great deal of building work, which would both employ many hands and put him to vast expense (v. 15). He did not levy taxes to spend on war, as other rulers did, which would waste the blood of his subjects, but to spend on building, which would require only their labor and wallets. Perhaps David observed that Solomon's skills lay in building, and perhaps he foresaw that he would have his head and hands full of it, when he wrote that song of ascents for Solomon which begins, *Except the Lord build the house, those labour in vain that build it* (Ps 127:1). Solomon truly began his work at the right end, for he built God's house first, and finished that before he began his own. God blessed him then, and he prospered in all his other buildings. The further order in which Solomon built buildings is significant. God's house came first for religious worship, and then his own came for his own convenience, then a house for his wife, to which she moved as soon as it was ready for her (v. 24), then Millo—the town hall, guildhall, or supporting terraces—then the wall of Jerusalem, the royal city, then some notable and strong cities in the country, which were dilapidated and unfortified, Hazor, Megiddo, and others.

2. His workers and servants. In doing such great works, he needed to employ many workers.

2.1. Solomon employed those who remained of the conquered nations in all the slave work (vv. 20–21).

2.2. He employed Israelites in the more respectable services (vv. 22–23): *Of them he made no bondmen;* they were not slaves but God's free people, and he honored their relationship with God as a kingdom of priests.

3. His godliness and devotion (v. 25): *Three times in a year* he offered notable burnt offerings—namely, at the three annual feasts, Passover, Pentecost, and the Feast of Tabernacles—in honor of the divine institution. It is said that he offered *on the altar which he* himself *built.* He took care to build it, and then:

3.1. He himself made use of it. Many will help in the devotions of others but neglect their own.

3.2. He himself received its benefit and encouragement.

4. His merchandise. He built a fleet of trading ships at Ezion Geber (v. 26), a port on the coast of the Red Sea, the farthest stage the Israelites wandered to in the desert (Nu 33:35). The fleet traded with Ophir, perhaps in the East Indies or what is now called Sri Lanka. Gold was the commodity traded in, which meant substantial wealth. It seems that Solomon had before been Hiram's partner, or had risked money on his ships, which gave him

a rich return of 120 talents (v. 14) and encouraged him to build a fleet of his own. Solomon sent his own servants as agents, merchants, and superintendents of the cargo during the voyage, but hired Tyrians as sailors, for they had *knowledge of the sea* (v. 27). This shows us how one nation needs another, since Providence has ordered the world in this way so that there may be an interdependence in trade and commerce; for not only as Christians, but also as human beings, we are all *members one of another* (Ro 12:5). The fleet brought home to Solomon *420 talents of gold* (v. 28). Solomon gained much by his merchandise, but it seems that David gained much more by his conquests. What were Solomon's *420 talents* compared to David's *100,000 talents of gold* (1Ch 22:14; 29:4)? Solomon gained much by his trading, but he has directed us to a better calling, within reach of the poorest, having assured us from his experience of both that the *merchandise of wisdom is better than the merchandise of silver and the gain thereof than fine gold* (Pr 3:14).

CHAPTER 10

Solomon still appears great, and everything in this chapter adds to his magnificence. In fact, we read nothing about his acts of charity, for he made his kingdom so rich that it did not need them; yet many poor were undoubtedly helped by the wealth at his table. He had built a church that was never to be equaled; he did not need to build any schools or colleges, because his own palace was an academy. 1. What abundant wisdom there was at his court is seen by the fact that the queen of Sheba went to see him and was wonderfully satisfied by his hospitality (vv. 1–13), and others likewise (v. 24). 2. What abundance of wealth there was is also seen by the gold imported, with other things, every year (vv. 14–15), and in the return every three years of trading ships (v. 22). Gold was presented (v. 25), and gold was used in shields (vv. 16–17) and goblets (v. 21). A stately throne was made (vv. 18–20). He accumulated chariots and charioteers (v. 26). He traded with Egypt (vv. 28–29). Silver and cedars were abundant among his people (v. 27). Putting all these together, king Solomon exceeded all the kings of the earth for riches and for wisdom. *But what was he in comparison with the King of Kings? Where Christ is, by his word and Spirit,* Behold, a greater than Solomon is here *(Mt 12:42).*

Verses 1–13

Here is an account of the visit which the queen of Sheba made to Solomon, no doubt when he was at the height of his godliness and prosperity. Our Savior calls her *the queen of the south* (Mt 12:42), for Sheba lay south of Canaan. The common opinion is that it was in Africa, and to this day the Christians in Ethiopia are confident that she came from their country, and that Candace, who is mentioned in Ac 8:27, was her successor. But it is more probable that she came from the south part of Arabia. Notice:

1. Why the queen of Sheba came: not to engage in trade or commerce, but:

1.1. To satisfy her curiosity, for she had heard of Solomon's fame, especially his wisdom.

1.2. To receive instruction from him. She came to *hear his wisdom* and so improve her own (Mt 12:42), so that she might be more able to govern her own kingdom by his wise political principles. But what she chiefly aimed at was to be instructed in the things of God.

2. What she came with: a very great retinue, as befitted her position, intending to test Solomon's hospitality as well as his wisdom. Yet she did not come as a beggar, but brought enough to reward Solomon abundantly for his attention to her. She brought nothing lowly or common, but gold, precious stones, and spices, because she came to trade for wisdom.

3. How Solomon received her. He did not despise the weakness of her sex, but made her and all her retinue welcome. He gave her freedom to ask all her questions, to *commune with him of all that was in her heart* (v. 2). He gave her a satisfactory answer to *all her questions* (v. 3), whether natural, moral, political, or divine. But he informed her no doubt with particular care concerning God, his Law, and instituted worship.

4. How she was affected by what she saw and heard at Solomon's court. Various things are mentioned here which she wondered at; the palace buildings and furnishings, provisions every day at his table, the orderly seating of his servants, each one in their place, and the ready attendance of his ministers. But above all, the first thing that is be mentioned is his wisdom (v. 4). And the last thing to be mentioned, which crowned everything, is his godliness, the *ascent* (or stairway) *by which he went up to the house of the Lord* (v. 5)—his seriousness and devotion when he went there.

5. How she expressed herself on this occasion:

5.1. She acknowledged that her expectations had been far surpassed, although her expectations had been high from the report she had heard (vv. 6–7). She is far from thinking her journey has been a waste of time or that she has been foolish in undertaking it, but acknowledges that it has been well worth her while to come so far to see for herself what she could not believe the reports of. Those who through grace are brought to experience the delights of fellowship with God will say that not even half has been told them of the pleasures of Wisdom's ways and the benefits of its presence. And much more will glorified saints say that it was a true report which they heard of the happiness of heaven, that a thousandth part had not been told them (1Co 2:9).

5.2. She declared blessed those who constantly served him and waited on him at table: "*Happy are thy men, happy are these thy servants* (v. 8). They may improve their own wisdom by hearing yours."

5.3. She blessed God, the giver of Solomon's wisdom and wealth, and the One who had brought about his advancement, who had made him king. "He has made you king, not so that you may live in pomp and pleasure, and do what you want, but *to do judgment and justice*, to maintain justice and righteousness" (v. 9).

6. How they parted:

6.1. She made a noble present to Solomon *of gold and spices* (v. 10). The present of gold and spices which the wise men from the east brought to Christ was represented by this (Mt 2:11). In this way she paid for the wisdom she had learned, and she did not think she had paid too high a price for it. Let those who are taught by God give him their hearts, and that present will be more acceptable than this present of gold and spices. Almugwood is spoken of here (vv. 11–12) as something extraordinary, perhaps because it was much admired by the queen of Sheba.

6.2. Solomon was not backward in giving to her: *He gave her whatsoever she asked*, patterns, we may suppose, of intricate things she saw, which she could use to make similar things. Or perhaps he gave her written statements of his wisdom and godliness, *besides that which he gave her of his royal bounty* (v. 13).

Verses 14–29

Here is a further record of Solomon's prosperity:

1. How he increased in wealth.

1.1. Besides the gold that came from Ophir (9:28), he brought so much into his country from other places that the total amounted every year to *666 talents* (v. 14).

1.2. He received a great deal of revenue from the merchants, and in land taxes from the countries his father had conquered and made subject to Israel (v. 15).

1.3. He was Hiram's partner in a fleet of ships of Tarshish that traveled to and from Tyre, which imported once every three years not only gold, silver, and ivory—substantial and useful goods—but also apes and peacocks (v. 22).

1.4. He had presents given him, every year, from the neighboring rulers and great people, because they often needed to consult his great wisdom. They sent him these presents as a reward for his advice in politics.

1.5. He traded with Egypt for horses and *linen yarn*—or as some read it, "linen cloth"—the staple commodities of that country, and had his own merchants or agents whom he employed in this trade and who were responsible to him (vv. 28–29).

2. What use he made of his wealth.

2.1. He used his gold on fine things for himself, which would be more acceptable for him to do now that he had already spent so much on fine things for the house of God:

2.1.1. He made *200 targets* (large shields) and 300 small shields of hammered gold (vv. 16–17), not for service but for show, to be carried in front of him when he appeared in pomp. Solomon had *shields* and *targets* carried before him to show that he took more pleasure in using his power to defend and protect the good than in using it to correct and punish the evil, and those who benefited from his power in this way would commend him for that.

2.1.2. He made a stately throne, on which he sat, to give laws to his subjects, hear ambassadors, and give judgment on appeals (vv. 18–20). It was made of ivory, or elephants' teeth, which was very rich, but as if he had so much gold that he did not know what to do with it, he *overlaid that with gold*, the best gold.

2.1.3. He made all his goblets, and all the table furnishings, even at his country home, out of pure gold (v. 21).

2.2. He circulated his wealth among his subjects, so that the kingdom was as rich as the king. He need not consider any separate interests of his own but sought the welfare of his people. Solomon was instrumental in bringing so much gold into the country, and dispersing it, that *silver was nothing accounted of* (v. 21). If *gold in abundance* (2Ch 9:1) would make silver seem so contemptible, will not wisdom, grace, and the foretastes of heaven—which are far better than gold—make earthly wealth seem much more contemptible?

3. Let us remember:

• That this was the one who, when he was setting out in the world, did not ask for its wealth and honor, but asked for *a wise and understanding heart* (3:12).

• That this was the one who, having tasted all these enjoyments, wrote a whole book to show the *vanity* (meaninglessness) of all worldly things (Ecc 1:14) and the foolishness of setting our hearts on them, and to commend to us the practice of serious godliness. This will do infinitely more toward helping us lead lives that are happy and at ease than all the wealth and power that Solomon controlled, or than all of

such things that we ourselves, through the grace of God, may acquire—especially considering that the thousandth part of Solomon's greatness is a thousand times more than we can ever be so foolish as to promise ourselves in this world.

CHAPTER 11

Up to this time we have read only great and good things about Solomon, but the luster of both his goodness and his greatness is here tainted and overshadowed, and his sun sets under a cloud. 1. The glory of his godliness is stained by his turning away from God and his duty in his later days, marrying foreign wives and worshiping foreign gods (vv. 1–8). 2. The glory of his prosperity is stained by God's displeasure against him and the fruits of that displeasure. God sent him an angry message (vv. 9–13). 3. He raised up enemies, who unsettled Solomon, Hadad (vv. 14–22) and Rezon (vv. 23–25). 4. He took away from Solomon's descendants after him ten tribes out of his twelve and gave them to Jeroboam, whom Solomon therefore tried in vain to kill (vv. 26–40). 5. And this is all that remains to be told about Solomon, except for his death and burial (vv. 41–43), for there is nothing perfect under the sun, although everything is perfect above the sun.

Verses 1–8

This is a sad and very surprising story of Solomon's turning away from God and of his degenerate condition:

1. Let us consider its occurrences and details. *There was no king like Solomon who was beloved of his God, yet even him did outlandish* (foreign) *women cause to sin* (Ne 13:26). This is the summary of his turning away from God.

1.1. He was infatuated with *many strange* (foreign) *women* (v. 1).

1.1.1. He gave himself to women, which his mother had particularly warned him against when she said, *Give not thy strength unto women* (Pr 31:3)—perhaps alluding to Samson, who lost his strength by giving information about it to a woman. The fall of David, his father, began with the lustful desires of the flesh. The love of women has *cast down many wounded* (Pr 7:26), and according to Bishop Hall, "Many have had their head broken by their own rib."

1.1.2. He took many women, so many that they finally amounted to *700 wives and 300 concubines* (v. 3), 1,000 in all. Divine wisdom has appointed one woman for one man, and those who do not think one is enough will not think two or three enough.

1.1.3. They were foreign women, Moabites, Ammonites, and others, from the nations which God had particularly forbidden them to marry into (v. 2). Some think he married these foreigners as a political act, to gain information about the state of those countries from them.

1.1.4. To complete the trouble, *Solomon clave* (held fast) *unto these in love* (v. 2). Solomon had mastered many areas of knowledge, but what was the purpose of all that knowledge if he could not even control his own appetites?

1.2. He was drawn by them to the worship of foreign gods, as Israel was to Baal of Peor by the Moabite women. *His wives turned away his heart after other gods* (vv. 3–4).

1.2.1. He became cool and indifferent to his own religious faith and neglected the service of the God of Israel: *His heart was not perfect with* (not fully devoted to) *the*

Lord his God (v. 4), nor did he *follow him fully* (v. 6), like David. It is said that *he was not perfect* (v. 4), because he was not faithful.

1.2.2. He tolerated and maintained his wives in their idolatry and did not hesitate to join them. He built chapels for their gods (vv. 7–8), supported their priests, and occasionally attended their altars, making a joke of it, by asking, "What harm can it do? Aren't all religions the same?" According to Bishop Patrick, this has been the disease of some of our great thinkers. These high places remained here undisturbed until Josiah's time, when they were completely demolished (2Ki 23:13). This is the account given of Solomon's apostasy.

2. Let us now pause a while and mourn Solomon's fall. It is right that we stand in dismay at it.

2.1. How strange:

2.1.1. That Solomon, in his old age, should be trapped by youthful lust.

2.1.2. That such a wise man as Solomon, who was so famous for his quick understanding and sound judgment, should allow himself to be made such a fool of by these foolish women.

2.1.3. That one who had so often and so plainly warned others of the danger of the love of women should himself be so miserably captivated by it. It is easier to be trouble and make others aware of it than to avoid it ourselves.

2.1.4. That such a good man, so zealous for the worship of God, should do these sinful things.

2.2. What are we to say about all this?

2.2.1. If we think we are standing firm, we must be careful that we do not fall. We see how weak we are in ourselves, without the grace of God, and so let us live in constant dependence on his grace (1Co 10:12–13).

2.2.2. Notice the danger of being prosperous, and how hard it is to defeat the temptations that attend that condition. Solomon, like Jeshurun, grew fat and then kicked (Dt 32:15).

2.2.3. Notice that those who have made a great profession of faith need to stand on their guard; they need to be zealous in their devotion because the Devil will violently attack them, and if they behave improperly, their disgrace is greater. It is the evening that commends the day, and so let us be careful so that, having run well, we will not fail before we reach the end.

Verses 9–13

Here is:

1. God's anger against Solomon for his sin. What he did displeased the Lord, for in his sin there was:

1.1. The greatest possible ingratitude. God's appearances to Solomon were such real confirmations of his faith as should have prevented him forever from worshiping *any other god* (v. 10).

1.2. The most willful disobedience. This was the very thing concerning which *God had commanded him—that he should not go after other gods*—but he had not been restrained even by such an explicit warning (v. 10).

2. The message God then sent him (v. 11): *The Lord said unto Solomon*, probably through a prophet, that he must expect to suffer because he had turned away from God. And here:

2.1. The sentence is just: that because he had rebelled against God, part of his kingdom would rebel against his family. Sin brings ruin on families, cuts off inheritances, transfers estates, and puts human honor in the dust.

2.2. But the ways in which God mitigates it are very kind, for David's sake (vv. 12–13), that is, for the sake

of the promise made to David. The kingdom will be torn from Solomon's house, but:

2.2.1. Not immediately. Solomon will not live to see it done; instead it will be torn *out of the hand of his son* (v. 12), a son who was born to him by one of his foreign wives, for his mother was an Ammonite (14:31).

2.2.2. Not wholly. One tribe, that of Judah, the strongest and most numerous, will remain with the house of David (v. 13), for the sake of Jerusalem, which David built, and for the sake of the temple there, which Solomon built; these will not pass into other hands.

3. God graciously sending this message to Solomon to awaken his conscience and bring him to repentance. We have reason to hope that he humbled himself before God, confessed his sin, prayed for forgiveness, and returned to his duty, and that he then declared his repentance in the book of Ecclesiastes. That sermon of repentance was as true an indication of a heart which had been broken for sin and had turned away from it as David's penitential psalms were, although it was different. God's grace works differently in different people. So although Solomon fell, *he was not utterly cast down* (Ps 37:24). What God had said to David concerning him was fulfilled: *I will chasten him with the rod of men, but my mercy shall not depart from him* (2Sa 7:14–15). Although God may allow those he loves to fall into sin, he will not allow them to remain in it.

Verses 14–25

Here we have an account of two enemies who appeared against him, insignificant ones, who could not have done anything worth taking notice of if Solomon had not first made God his enemy. What harm could Hadad or Rezon have done to such a great and powerful king as Solomon, unless he had, by sin, made himself lowly and weak? And then these insignificant people turn up and menace and insult him!

1. Both these adversaries were raised up by God (vv. 14, 23). Although they themselves were moved by motives of ambition or revenge, God made use of them to serve his purposes to correct Solomon.

2. The origin of the enmity of both these adversaries toward Solomon and Israel was set in David's time, and in his conquests of their respective countries (vv. 15, 24). Solomon had the benefit of his father's successes in both the widening of his kingdom and the increase of his treasure, and would never have known anything but their benefits if only he had kept close to God, but now Solomon experiences evil that counterbalances the benefits.

2.1. Hadad, an Edomite, was Solomon's enemy. We are told:

2.1.1. What made him bear a grudge against Solomon. David had conquered Edom (2Sa 8:14). Joab had killed all the men (vv. 15–16). His revenge on Edom for their old enmity toward Israel was extreme. While Joab was burying those he had killed, Hadad, a branch of the royal family, and then only a little child, was rescued from this general killing by some of the king's servants and taken to Egypt (v. 17). They stopped on the way, first in Midian, and then in Paran, where they provided themselves with men to serve them, so that their young master might go into Egypt with a retinue consistent with his rank. He was kindly sheltered there as a distressed prince by Pharaoh, and he so commended himself that he married the queen's sister (v. 19) and had a child by her, whom the queen herself grew so fond of that she brought him up in Pharaoh's house, among the king's children.

2.1.2. What enabled him to cause trouble for Solomon. On the deaths of David and Joab, he returned to his own country, in which, it seems, he settled down and remained quiet while Solomon continued to be wise and watchful for the good of the public. But he had the opportunity of making inroads on Israel when Solomon sinned away his wisdom—just as Samson did his strength—and lost the right to divine protection. What trouble Hadad caused Solomon we are not told, but only how reluctant Pharaoh was to part with him and how fervently he wanted him to stay (v. 22): *What hast thou lacked with me?* "Nothing," Hadad says, "but let me go to my own country, my native air and soil."

2.2. Rezon, an Aramean (Syrian), was another of Solomon's enemies. When David conquered the Arameans, Rezon headed up the remnant and lived freely by plundering and robbery until Solomon became negligent, and then he gained possession of Damascus, reigned there (v. 24) and over the surrounding country (v. 25), and created trouble for Israel, probably together with Hadad, *all the days of* Solomon, that is, for the rest of his reign after his apostasy.

Verses 26–40

Here is the first mention of that infamous name of *Jeroboam the son of Nebat* (v. 26), *that made Israel to sin* (14:16), one of Solomon's enemies. God had expressly said (v. 11) that he would give the greatest part of his kingdom to *his servant*, his subordinate, and Jeroboam was the man. We have here an account:

1. Of his background (v. 26). He came from the tribe of Ephraim, next in honor to Judah. His mother was a widow.

2. Of his promotion. Solomon was wise enough, when he had work to do, to delegate work to the right people. Jeroboam was ruler of the tribute, that is, of the taxes or militia, of the house of Joseph. Notice a difference between David on the one hand, and both his predecessor and his successor on the other: when Saul saw *a valiant man he took him to himself* (1Sa 14:52); when Solomon saw an *industrious* man he promoted him; but when David saw a *godly* man, he promoted him, because David's *eyes were upon the faithful in the land* (Ps 101:6).

3. Of his appointment to govern the ten tribes after the death of Solomon. The Jews say that when he was employed by Solomon in building Millo, the supporting terraces, he took the opportunity to discredit Solomon by suggesting that he oppressed his people, hoping that this would make them dissatisfied with Solomon's rule. Solomon made him ruler over the tribes of Joseph, and as he was going to take possession of Solomon's government, he was told by a prophet in God's name that he would be king, which emboldened him to aim high, and in some instances to oppose the king.

3.1. The prophet by whom this message was sent was *Ahijah of Shiloh*; we will read about him later (14:2). It seems that Shiloh was not so completely abandoned and forgotten by God that it was not blessed with a prophet; in remembrance of the former days, God raised up Ahijah.

3.2. The sign by which it was presented to him was the tearing of a cloak into twelve pieces, and giving him ten (vv. 30–31). The prophets, both true and false, used such signs, even in New Testament times, e.g., Agabus (Ac 21:10–11).

3.3. The message itself was very detailed:

3.3.1. Ahijah assures Jeroboam that he will be king over ten of the twelve tribes of Israel (v. 31).

3.3.2. He tells him the reason: not because of his good character or because he deserves it, but to rebuke Solomon for turning away from God: "Because he, his family, and many of his people with him *have forsaken me, and worshipped other gods*" (v. 33). Jeroboam does not deserve such a good position, but Israel deserves such a bad ruler.

3.3.3. He limits Jeroboam's expectations to only the ten tribes, and to them only after the death of Solomon, so that he will not aim at all the tribes and want to trouble Solomon's government immediately. He is told:

3.3.3.1. That two tribes—called here *one tribe*, because little Benjamin was in a way lost in the thousands of Judah—would endure with the house of David, and he must never make any attempt to take them away. He must not think that David was rejected, as Saul was. The dynasty of David must be sustained and honored, in spite of all the sins of Solomon and Israel, because the Messiah must come from it. *Destroy it not*, for that *blessing is in it* (Isa 65:8).

3.3.3.2. That Solomon must keep possession of the whole government during his lifetime (vv. 34–35). Jeroboam must therefore not try to dethrone him, but wait patiently until his day dawns. Children who do not follow in their parents' steps still often get along better in this world because of their parents' godliness.

3.3.4. He gives him to understand that he will keep the crown as long as he behaves himself well. "If *thou wilt do what is right in my sight, I will build thee a sure house*, but not otherwise" (v. 38).

4. Of Jeroboam's flight into Egypt (v. 40). In some way or other Solomon came to know about all this, probably from Jeroboam's own mouth. Solomon foolishly sought to kill his successor, but Jeroboam wisely withdrew to Egypt.

Verses 41–43

Here is the conclusion of Solomon's life, and in it:

1. Reference is made to another history then in existence, but since lost, *the book of the acts of Solomon* (v. 41). Probably this book was written by a chronologer whom Solomon employed to write his official records, out of which the sacred writer took what God saw fit to communicate to the church.

2. A summary is given of the years of his reign (v. 42). His reign was as long as his father's, but not his life. Sin shortened his days.

3. His death and burial are recorded, and his successor named (v. 43).

3.1. He followed his fathers to the grave, rested with them, and was buried in David's burial place.

3.2. His son followed him to the throne.

CHAPTER 12

The glory of the kingdom of Israel was at its height and perfection in Solomon. It took a long time to reach it, but it declined quickly, and began to sink and wither in the very next reign. Here is: 1. Rehoboam's accession to the throne and Jeroboam's return from Egypt (vv. 1–2); the people's request to Rehoboam to put right their grievances, and the harsh answer he gave, at the advice of his young counselors (vv. 3–15). 2. The rebellion of the ten tribes and their setting up Jeroboam as king over them (vv. 16–20); Rehoboam's attempt to defeat them and the prohibition God gave to that attempt (vv. 21–24). 3. Jeroboam's establishment of his government on idolatry (vv. 25–33).

And so Judah became weak, being deserted by the other tribes, and Israel became weak because it deserted the house of the Lord.

Verses 1–15

Solomon had 1,000 wives and concubines, but we read about only one son he had to bear his name, and he was a fool. Sin is a bad way to build up a family. Rehoboam was the son of the wisest person on earth, yet he did not inherit his father's wisdom. Neither wisdom nor grace runs in the blood. Solomon's court was a market of wisdom and the meeting place for learned people, and Rehoboam was the court's favorite, yet all that was not enough to make him wise.

1. The people wanted to make a treaty with him at Shechem, and he condescended to meet them there.

1.1. They pretended to want to make him king, but their true purpose was to depose him. They wanted, so it appeared, to publicly install him as king in a different place from the City of David, so that he did not seem to be only king of Judah.

1.2. The place was ominous: at *Shechem*, where Abimelech set up himself as king (Jdg 9:1–57); yet it had been famous for the assembly of the representatives of the tribes there (Jos 24:1). Rehoboam knew about the threat that the kingdom would be torn away from him, and hoped to prevent it by going to Shechem and negotiating with the ten tribes there. It turned out, however, to be the most unwise thing he could have done, and only hastened the breaking away of the ten tribes.

2. The representatives of the tribes addressed him, praying to be relieved of the taxes they were burdened with. Having arranged the meeting, they sent for Jeroboam to come from Egypt to be their speaker. In their address:

2.1. They complain of the last reign: *Thy father made our yoke grievous* (v. 4). They do not complain about his father's idolatry, because they were so careless and indifferent in matters of religion. It was as if God and Molech were one and the same to them, as long as they could lead comfortable lives and not have to pay any taxes. But the complaint was unjust and without foundation. Never did a people live more comfortably than they had, nor in such great plenty. Did they pay taxes? Well, it was to advance the power and splendor of their kingdom. If Solomon's buildings cost them money, they did not cost him any blood, as war would. Divisive spirits will always find something to complain about. I cannot see anything in Solomon's administration that could make the people's burden heavy, unless perhaps he turned a blind eye to some oppression caused by the women he was obsessed by.

2.2. They demand relief from him, and if that condition is fulfilled, they will continue to be loyal to the house of David.

3. Rehoboam consulted with those around him concerning the answer he should give to what the people had said.

3.1. The serious and experienced elders of his council advised him by all means to give the petitioners a kind answer, to promise that he would put right their grievances. The way to rule is to serve, to do good and stoop down to do it, to become all things to all people and so win their hearts (1Co 9:22).

3.2. The young men of his council were angry and proud, and they advised him to respond to the people's demands with a severe and threatening answer. It showed Rehoboam's weakness that:

3.2.1. He did not prefer the advice of the elders, but thought more highly of the young men he had grown up

with and whom he knew well (v. 8). It is very important for young people setting out in the world that they depend on the right people for advice. If they reckon as their best friends those who feed their pride and further them in their pleasures, then they are already marked out for ruin.

3.2.2. He did not want to listen to moderate advice, but was pleased with those who advised him to double the taxes. These young counselors thought their elders expressed themselves in dull terms (v. 7); they, in contrast, wanted to seem witty. The elders did not undertake to put words into Rehoboam's mouth, but the young men supplied him with a pretty and ready-made proverb: *My little finger shall be thicker than my father's loins* (waist) (v. 10). The most polished-sounding words do not always make the most sense.

4. Rehoboam replied to the people according to the advice of the young men (vv. 14–15). He pretended to be proud and imperious, and thought that by this high-handed approach he could win over all who were before him. Notice:

4.1. How Rehoboam was captivated by the plan he had chosen.

4.1.1. He acknowledged their reflections on his father's government to be true: *My father made your yoke heavy* (v. 10). In this, he was unjust to his father's memory.

4.1.2. He thought he could lead them and impose himself on them more ably than his father had.

4.1.3. He threatened not only to make them feel the pinch by raising taxes, but also to rebuke them by cruel laws.

4.1.4. He spoke these provocative words to a people who had been made wealthy, strong, and proud by years of ease and prosperity, to a people who were already disposed to rebel and who already had one ready to lead them.

4.2. How God's plans were fulfilled in all this. This turn of events was *from the Lord* (v. 15). He left Rehoboam to his own foolish ways, and *hid from his eyes* the *things which belonged to his peace* (Lk 19:42). Those who lose the kingdom of heaven throw it away, as Rehoboam did his, by their own foolish willfulness.

Verses 16–24

We have here the tearing away of the kingdom of the ten tribes from the house of David. In order to bring this about:

1. The people were bold and resolute in their rebellion. *What portion* (share) *have we in David?* (v. 16). If they had asked who gave Rehoboam this advice, and had removed those evil counselors from around him, the rift might have been prevented. But to rebel in this way against the seed of David, whom God had advanced to the kingdom—passing on the inheritance to his descendants—and to set up another king in opposition to that family was a great sin; see 2Ch 13:5–8. And it is here mentioned to the praise of the tribe of Judah that they *followed the house of David* (vv. 17, 20) and found Rehoboam better than his word, and he did not rule with the rigor which he threatened at first.

2. Rehoboam was unwise in the way he continued to manage this matter.

2.1. He was very ill-advised in sending Adoniram, who was *over the tribute*, in charge of forced labor, to negotiate with them (v. 18). The very sight of him, a person whose name was hateful among them, made them angry and violent.

2.2. Some think he was also ill-advised in leaving and going so quickly to Jerusalem, for when he did that, he

deserted his friends and gave the advantage to his enemies, who had gone to their tents (v. 16) in disgust but
did not offer to make Jeroboam king until Rehoboam had
gone (v. 20).

3. God stopped his attempt to recover by the sword
what he had lost (v. 24). Things must rest as they are, and
so God forbade the battle.

3.1. It was brave of Rehoboam to want to defeat the
rebellion by force. His courage came to him when he came
to Jerusalem (v. 21). Judah and Benjamin—who feared
the Lord and the king and did not join in the troublemaking of those who wanted change—immediately raised an
army of 180,000 soldiers to recover their king's right to
the ten tribes. They were determined to stand by him.

3.2. It was more brave of Rehoboam to stop when God,
through a prophet, ordered him to lay down his arms. To
proceed in this war would be not only to *fight against
their brethren* (v. 24), whom they should love, but also
to fight against their God, to whom they should submit.
Rehoboam and his people *hearkened to* (obeyed) *the word
of the Lord*, disbanded the army, and accepted what God
had said.

3.2.1. They paid attention to the command of God,
even though it was sent by a poor prophet.

3.2.2. They considered their own interests, concluding
that although they had all the advantages, including right,
on their side, they still could not succeed if they fought in
disobedience to God.

Verses 25–33

Here is the beginning of the reign of Jeroboam. He
built Shechem first and then Peniel; he made them beautiful and strengthened them. But he formed another plan to
establish his kingdom which was fatal to the interests of
its religious life.

1. What Jeroboam wanted was to find an effective
means of securing the loyalty of those people who had
now chosen him as their king, to prevent their return to the
house of David (vv. 26–27). It seems:

1.1. He was anxious about the people, afraid that at
some time or other they would kill him and return to
Rehoboam. Jeroboam could not put any confidence in the
affections of his people, for what is gained by usurpation
cannot be enjoyed nor kept with any security.

1.2. He distrusted the promise of God and wanted to
come up with his own ways and means, and sinful ones
too, to make sure of his own safety. A practical disbelief
in God's all-sufficiency is at the root of all our treacherous
departures from him.

2. The strategy Jeroboam used in order to achieve this
was to keep the people from going up to Jerusalem to
worship.

2.1. Jeroboam realized that if the people continued to
do this, they would in time return to the house of David,
taken in by the splendor of both the court and the temple.
If they held on to their old religion, they would go back
to their old king.

2.2. He therefore dissuaded them from going up to
Jerusalem, pretending to think about what would be comfortable for them: "*It is too much for you* to go so far to
worship God (v. 28). Why should we now be tied to one
place anymore than we were in Samuel's time?"

2.3. He provided the means to help their devotion at
home. He consulted some of his politicians and set up two
golden calves as signs of God's presence. Some interpreters are charitable enough to think the calves were made
to represent the atonement cover and the cherubim over
the ark. But I think it more probable that he adopted the

idolatry of the Egyptians, in whose land he had stayed for
some time and who worshiped their god Apis, which had
a human body and head of a bull. He intended, no doubt,
just as he declares (v. 28), that these calves would represent, or rather would make present, not any false god such
as Molech or Chemosh, but only the true God, the God of
Israel, the God who brought them up out of the land of
Egypt. So he did not break the first commandment but the
second. He set up two, to gradually break the people away
from their belief in the unity of the Godhead and thereby
pave the way to the polytheism of other religions.

2.4. The people went along with what he had done and
were fond of the novelty. They *went to worship before
the one, even unto Dan* (v. 30). Those who thought it too
much to go to Jerusalem, to worship God according to the
way he had appointed, had no difficulty in going twice as
far, to Dan, to worship him according to their own inclinations. God had sometimes dispensed with the law concerning worship in one place, but he had never allowed
the worship of him through idols.

2.5. Having set up the gods, he set up facilities for
them.

2.5.1. He made *a house of high places* or of altars,
shrines on high places, probably one temple at Dan and
another at Bethel (v. 31); and he made many altars in
each.

2.5.2. He took some of the lowest of the people and
made them priests, and the lowest of the people were good
enough to be priests to his calves—indeed they were too
good. He made priests from every corner of the country.
Thus they were dispersed just as the Levites were, but
were not of the sons of Levi (v. 31). But he ordered the
priests of the high places, or altars, to live in Bethel, to
attend the public services (v. 32), just as the priests of
Judah resided at Jerusalem for the same purpose.

2.5.3. He delayed the Feast of Tabernacles, which
God had appointed on the fifteenth day of the seventh
month, to the fifteenth day of the eighth month (v. 32),
the month which he devised of his own heart, a month
of his own choosing, to show his power in ecclesiastical
matters (v. 33).

2.5.4. Because he himself assumed a power to make
priests, it is no wonder that he undertook to do the
priests' work with his own hands: *He offered upon the
altar*. He did it himself to gain the reputation of being
devout. And so:

- Jeroboam himself sinned, but perhaps he excused himself by saying that he did not commit such a wrong as
  Solomon had, who worshiped other gods.
- He *made Israel to sin* (14:16); he drew the people
  away from the worship of God and passed on an
  inheritance of idolatry to their descendants.

CHAPTER 13

*At the end of the last chapter we left Jeroboam at his altar
at Bethel. At the beginning of this chapter he received a
testimony from God against his idolatry and apostasy.
This was sent to him by a prophet, a man of God who
lived in Judah, who is the main character in the story
of this chapter, in which we are told: 1. What took place
between him and the new king: the prophet threatened
Jeroboam's altar (vv. 1–2) and gave him a sign (v. 3),
which immediately appeared (v. 5); the king threatened
the prophet and was himself made another sign, by the
shriveling up of his hand (v. 4); the hand was restored*

upon his submission and the prophet's intercession (v. 6); the prophet refused the kindness that was then offered to him (vv. 7–10). 2. What took place between this prophet and an old prophet: the old prophet deceived him with a lie and took him back to his house (vv. 11–19). Because he accepted the invitation, in disobedience to God's command, he was sentenced to death (vv. 20–22). 3. The sentence was carried out, and he was killed by a lion (vv. 23–24) and buried at Bethel (vv. 25–32). Jeroboam was then hardened in his idolatry (vv. 33–34). Thy judgments, Lord, are a great deep (Ps 36:6).

Verses 1–10

Here is:

1. A messenger sent to Jeroboam to show him God's displeasure against his idolatry (v. 1). The army of Judah that aimed to destroy him was recalled and was not allowed to draw a sword against him (12:24), but a prophet of Judah is sent to bring him back from his evil ways. He is sent before his heart is hardened, while he is only dedicating his altar, for God does not delight in the death of sinners, but would rather see them turn back to him and live.

2. The message delivered in God's name, which was not whispered but cried out with a loud voice, showing both the prophet's courage and his seriousness. It was directed not to Jeroboam or to the people but to the altar. But in condemning the altar, God condemned the founder and worshipers, who might well conclude, "If God's wrath is directed to the lifeless, guiltless altar, how will we escape?" What was foretold concerning the altar (v. 2) was that, in the course of time, a ruler of the house of David, *Josiah* by name, would defile this altar by sacrificing the idolatrous priests themselves on it, and burning human bones. Let Jeroboam know and be sure:

2.1. That the altar he now consecrated would be desecrated.

2.2. That the *priests of the high places* (v. 2) whom he had just appointed would themselves be made a sacrifice to the justice of God.

2.3. That this would be done by a branch *of the house of David* (v. 2). It was about 356 years before this prediction was fulfilled, but it was spoken of as certain and close at hand, for a thousand years with God are as one day (2Pe 3:8).

3. A sign given to confirm the truth of this prediction: that the altar would be shaken to pieces by an invisible power and the ashes of the sacrifice scattered (v. 3), which happened immediately (v. 5). This was:

3.1. Proof that the prophet had been sent by God, *who confirmed the word with this sign following* (Mk 16:20).

3.2. A sign of God's displeasure against these idolatrous sacrifices.

3.3. A disgrace to the people, whose hearts were harder than these stones and whose hearts were not split apart by the word of the Lord.

3.4. An example of what would be done to the altar by Josiah in the fulfillment of this prophecy; it was now split apart, as a sign that it would later be ruined.

4. Jeroboam's hand shriveled up when he stretched it out to seize or strike the man of God with it (v. 4). Jeroboam's inability to pull back his hand made him a spectacle to all around him, so that they might see and fear. If God in his justice hardens the hearts of sinners, so that the hand they have stretched out in sin cannot be pulled back again in repentance, then that is a spiritual judgment, which is represented by this punishment of Jeroboam and is much more terrible.

5. The quick healing of the hand that had suddenly shriveled up, when he submitted (v. 6). That word of God which should have touched his conscience did not humble him, but this one which *touched his bone and his flesh* (Job 2:5) humbles his proud spirit. He looks for help now:

5.1. Not from his calves, but only from God, from his power and his favor.

5.2. Not by his own sacrifice or incense, but by the prayer and intercession of the prophet, whom he has just threatened and wanted to destroy. But notice he does not want the prophet to pray that his sin may be forgiven, and his heart changed, only that *his hand might be restored* (v. 6). The prophet immediately turns to God for him, and God honors him by revoking the punishment at his word: he works another miracle and heals the shriveled hand, so that in the goodness of God Jeroboam may be led to repentance, and so that if he is not broken by the judgment, he may still be melted by the mercy. For now, he seems moved by both the judgment and the mercy, but this good effect will soon wear off.

6. The prophet's refusal of Jeroboam's kind invitation. Notice in this:

6.1. That God forbade his messenger to eat or drink in Bethel (v. 9), to show his complete hatred of their detestable idolatry and apostasy from God.

6.2. That Jeroboam was so moved by the healing of his hand that he was willing to express his gratitude to the prophet and pay him for his prayers (v. 7).

6.3. That the prophet, though hungry and weary, and perhaps poor, in obedience to the divine command refused both the hospitality and the reward offered him.

Verses 11–22

The man of God had honestly and firmly refused the king's invitation, even though he promised him a reward, but he was persuaded against his better judgment by an old prophet to come back with him, and dine at Bethel, contrary to the command given him. Here we find how dearly his dinner cost him. Notice:

1. The old prophet's evil. I have to call him a false prophet. Perhaps he was trained among the sons of the prophets, in one of Samuel's colleges not far away, and therefore he kept the name of a prophet, but because he had become worldly and ungodly, the spirit of prophecy had left him. If he had been a good prophet, he would have rebuked Jeroboam's idolatry.

1.1. Whether he had any good intention in taking the man of God back is not certain. One may hope that he did it out of compassion for him, concluding that he needed refreshment. Yet I suppose it was done with a bad intention, for false prophets have always been the worst enemies of the true prophets. They usually aim to destroy them, but sometimes, as here, to corrupt them and draw them away from their duty. But:

1.2. It is certain that he acted very wrongly in bringing him back. When the man of God had told him, "I may not, and so I will not, return to eat bread with you," the old prophet was evil enough to pretend that he had an order from heaven to take him back.

2. The good prophet's weakness, in allowing himself to be deceived in this way: *He went back with him* (v. 19). He was strong enough to refuse the invitation of the king, who promised him a reward, but could not resist the insinuations of one who pretended to be a prophet.

3. The actions of divine justice that then came. The message delivered to the man of God was strange. His crime is repeated (vv. 21–22), and judgment is declared

on it: "You will never reach your own house, but will quickly become a corpse, and your dead body will not be brought to *the place of thy father's sepulchres* to be buried." But it was even stranger that the old prophet himself should be the messenger. The message must have affected him all the more because he was the one who delivered it, and it made such a strong impression on his spirit that he cried out, as one in agony (v. 21). Perhaps it had a good effect on him. Those who preach God's wrath to others have truly hard hearts if they do not also fear it themselves.

Verses 23–34

Here is:

1. The death of the deceived and disobedient prophet. The old prophet who had deluded him provided him with a donkey to ride home on. But on the road, a lion attacked him and killed him (vv. 23–24). Did he think this old prophet's house safer to eat in than other houses at Bethel, when God had forbidden him to eat in any of them? That would have been "improving on" the command, as if he could make himself wiser than God. Nothing is more offensive to God than disobedience to a clear command. God is displeased with the sins of his own people, and no one who disobeys him will be protected by the sanctity of their profession, the dignity of their office, their closeness to God, or any good services they have done for God.

2. The wonderful preservation of his dead body, which was a sign of God's mercy that he remembered in the midst of wrath. The lion that gently mauled him did not devour his dead body, nor did it maul the donkey (vv. 24–26). In fact, what was more, the lion did not even attack the old prophet when he came to take away the corpse.

3. The care which the old prophet took in burying him. The case was very sad indeed: that such a good man—and such a faithful prophet who led such a bold life for God—should die as a criminal for one offense, while an old lying prophet leads a life of ease and an idolatrous ruler lives in pomp and power. We cannot judge people by looking at their sufferings, nor can we judge sins by looking at present punishments. With some people, the body is destroyed so that the spirit may be saved.

4. The command which the old prophet gave his sons concerning his own burial, that they should be sure to bury him in the same grave as the one in which the man of God was buried (v. 31): "*Lay my bones beside his bones.*" Although he was a lying prophet, he still desired to die *the death of a* true prophet (Nu 23:10). "Do not gather my soul with the sinners of Bethel, but with the man of God." He honors the deceased prophet as one whose *word* would not fall to the ground, even though *he* did. It was foretold that human bones would be burned on Jeroboam's altar. He says, "Lay mine close to his, and then they will not be disturbed," and so that was their security, as we read in 2Ki 23:18. No mention is made here of the inscription on the prophet's tomb, but it is spoken of in 2Ki 23:17, where Josiah asks, *What title is that?* and is told, *It is the sepulchre of the man of God that came from Judah, who proclaimed these things which thou hast done.*

5. The obstinacy of Jeroboam in his idolatry (v. 33): *He returned not* (did not change) *from his evil way.* Someone was found who dared repair the altar God had split apart, and then Jeroboam offered sacrifices on it again. Various methods had been used to encourage him to change his ways, but neither threats nor signs, and neither judgments nor mercies, had any effect on him, so mistakenly was he attached to his calves.

CHAPTER 14

Now that the kingdom has been divided into that of Judah and that of Israel, in this chapter we have: 1. The prophecy of the overthrow of Jeroboam's house (vv. 7–16). The illness of his child was the occasion of the prophecy (vv. 1–6), and the death of his child, together with the conclusion of his reign (vv. 19–20), was the pledge that it would come true (vv. 17–18). 2. The history of the decline of Rehoboam's house and kingdom (vv. 21–28) and the conclusion of his reign (vv. 29–31).

Verses 1–6

We read at the end of the previous chapter how Jeroboam continued to show contempt for God and religious faith. We are told here how God continued his dispute with him.

1. His child became ill (v. 1). He was probably his eldest son, and heir to the throne, for at his death all the kingdom mourned for him (v. 13). *At that time* (v. 1), when Jeroboam defiled the priesthood (13:33), his child became ill.

2. He sent his wife in disguise to ask of Ahijah the prophet *what should become of the child* (vv. 2–3).

2.1. Jeroboam's great desire, under this affliction, is to know *what shall become of the child* (v. 3), whether he will live or die.

2.1.1. It would have been wiser if he had wanted to know how they could help the child recover, but this example—as well as those of Ahaziah (2Ki 1:2) and Ben-Hadad (2Ki 8:8)—seems to show that they then had such a foolish concept of fatality that they were not interested in using anything to help someone get better. It seems that if they were sure the patient would live, they thought that to use any means to help the patient get better was unnecessary. Similarly, if the patient was going to die, they thought that such means were useless, since they were going to die anyway.

2.1.2. It would have been more godly if he had begged the prophet's prayers and driven away his idols from him. Then the child might have been restored to him, as his hand was. But most people would rather be told their fortune than their faults or their duty.

2.2. So that he might know what would happen to the child, he sent his wife to Ahijah the prophet, who lived in obscurity and neglect in Shiloh. He was now blind through age, but he was still blessed with visions of the Almighty, which do not need physical eyes but, rather, are favored by the lack of them, since the eyes of the mind are then most intent and least distracted. Jeroboam had not sent to him to get advice about setting up his calves, or about consecrating his priests, but turned to him in his time of distress, when the gods he served could not help him in any way. He sent to Ahijah because he was the one who had *told him he should be king* (v. 2). "He was once the messenger of good news, and surely he will be so again." Those who by sin disqualify themselves from comfort, but who still expect their ministers, because they are good people, to speak peace and encouragement to them, greatly wrong both themselves and their ministers.

2.3. He sent his wife to consult the prophet because she would be the best person to ask the question without stating names or describing the situation except to say, "Sir, I have a son who is ill. Will he recover or not?" It would have been much more suitable for her to stay at home to look after him than to go to Shiloh to ask what would become of him. If she goes, she must go incognito, not only to conceal herself from her own court and the country through which she passed, but also to conceal herself from the prophet himself, so that he would only answer her question about her son, and not bring up the disagreeable subject of her husband's turning away from God.

3. God gave Ahijah notice of the approach of Jeroboam's wife, and that she came in disguise, and he gave him full instructions what to say to her (v. 5), which enabled him, as she came in at the door, to call her by her name, to her great surprise, and so to reveal who she was to everyone around him (v. 6): *Come in, thou wife of Jeroboam, why feignest thou thyself to be another?*

Verses 7–20

1. The prophet anticipates the inquiry concerning the child and predicts the overthrow of Jeroboam's house because of its evil.

1.1. God calls himself the *Lord God of Israel* (v. 7). Although Israel had abandoned God, God had not rejected them. He is Israel's God, and so he will take vengeance on the one who caused them the greatest trouble he could, who defiled them and drew them away from God.

1.2. He rebukes Jeroboam with a reminder of the great favor he gave him by making him king over God's chosen Israel, taking the kingdom *from the house of David* (v. 8) to give it to him.

1.3. He accuses him of ungodliness and apostasy, and especially idolatry: *Thou hast done evil above all that were before thee* (v. 9). Although Jeroboam's calves had been claimed to have been set up in honor of the God of Israel, they are still here called *other gods* (v. 9), or foreign gods, because by them he *changed the truth of God into a lie* (Ro 1:25) and represented him as altogether different from what he really is, and because many of the ignorant worshipers ended up worshiping only the idol and were not at all led to worship the God of Israel.

1.4. He foretells the complete overthrow of Jeroboam's house (vv. 10–11). We see this fulfilled in 15:29.

1.5. He foretells the immediate death of the sick child (vv. 12–13). He foretells it:

1.5.1. In mercy to the child, for if he were to live, he might be infected with the sin of his father's house and thereby involved in its overthrow. Notice how he is characterized: *In him was found some good thing towards the Lord God of Israel, in the house of Jeroboam* (v. 13). The divine image in miniature has a special beauty in its luster. He only, out of all Jeroboam's family, will die in honor; he will be buried and will be mourned as he would have wanted. This promising child dies first in all the family, for it seems God often takes those who are close to him sooner. Heaven is the most suitable place for them; this earth is not worthy of them.

1.5.2. In anger to the family. It was a sign that the family would be ruined when *he* was taken away—he was the one who might have helped reform the family.

1.6. He foretells the setting up of another family to rule over Israel (v. 14). This was fulfilled in Baasha of Issachar, who conspired against Nadab the son of Jeroboam in the second year of his reign and murdered him and all his family.

1.7. He foretells the judgments which will come on the people of Israel because they conformed to the worship which Jeroboam had established. It is here foretold (v. 15):

1.7.1. That they would never be at ease, never fully settled in their land, but continually *shaken* (swaying) *like a reed in the water.* After they left the house of David, the government never continued long in one family; one king undermined and destroyed another.

1.7.2. That they would, before long, be totally expelled from their land. This was fulfilled in the captivity of the ten tribes under the king of Assyria.

2. Jeroboam's wife has nothing to say against the word of the Lord, but goes home with a heavy heart to their house in *Tirzah*, "a sweet, delightful place"—which is what the name means—famed for its beauty (SS 6:4).

2.1. *The child died* (v. 17), and all Israel justly mourned for the loss of such a promising prince.

2.2. Jeroboam himself died soon afterward (v. 20). When he had reigned twenty-two years, he left his crown to a son who lost it, and his life too, and all the lives of his family, within two years.

Verses 21–31

The stories of Judah and Israel are interwoven throughout this book. Jeroboam outlived Rehoboam by a few years, but his history is finished first so that the account of Rehoboam's reign may be put alongside it, and it is a sad account.

1. Nothing good is said about Rehoboam. The only record we have of him is:

1.1. That he was forty-one years old when he began to reign.

1.2. That he reigned seventeen years in Jerusalem, *the city where God put his name* (v. 21), where Rehoboam had enough opportunity to know his duty, if only he had the heart to do it.

1.3. That his mother was Naamah, an Ammonite; this is mentioned twice (vv. 21, 31). Perhaps she was a daughter of Shobi the Ammonite, who was kind to David (2Sa 17:27), and David was too willing to repay him by marrying his son into Shobi's family.

1.4. That he was continually at war with Jeroboam (v. 30), which must have been a constant cause of unease for him.

1.5. That when he had reigned only seventeen years, he died and left his throne to his son.

2. Much evil is said about the subjects, both about their character and their condition:

2.1. A most sad account is given here of their turning away from God (vv. 22–24). Judah, the only professing people God had in the world, *did evil in his sight.* Their ancestors had been bad enough, especially in the times of the judges, but they did detestable things, *above all that their fathers had done.* Nothing less than the *pouring out of the Spirit from on high* (Isa 32:15) will keep God's Israel faithful to him.

2.1.1. They became *vain in their imaginations*, futile in their thoughts about God (Ro 1:21), and *changed his glory into an image* (Ro 1:23), for they built themselves *high places, images, and groves* (v. 23), dishonoring God's name by attaching to it their idols and sacred stones, and dishonoring the ceremonies God had ordained for the worship of himself by serving their idols with them.

2.1.2. They were given up to shameful lusts—as those idolaters were in Ro 1:26–27—for there were *sodomites* (NIV: male shrine prostitutes) *in the land* (v. 24), *men with men working that which is unseemly*, men committing indecent acts with other men (Ro 1:27), acts that were not to be thought of, much less mentioned, without detestation and indignation. They dishonored God by one sin, and then God left them to dishonor themselves by another.

2.2. Notice how weak and poor they were. This was the effect of their sinful lusts. Shishak king of Egypt came against them and, either by force or by the people's surrender, made himself master of Jerusalem to such an extent that he took away the treasures both of the temple and of the treasury, of the house of the Lord and of the king's house, which David and Solomon had amassed (vv. 25–26). He also took away the golden shields that had been made only recently, in his father's time (v. 26). The king of Egypt carried these off as trophies of his victory. In their place, Rehoboam made bronze shields. This was a sign of the lessening of his glory. Sin makes gold become dim and turns the finest gold into bronze.

CHAPTER 15

In this chapter we have the history of: 1. Two of the kings of Judah: Abijah, the days of whose reign were few and evil (vv. 1–8), and Asa, who reigned long and well (vv. 9–24). 2. Two of the kings of Israel, Nadab, the son of Jeroboam, and Baasha, the destroyer of Jeroboam's family (vv. 25–34).

Verses 1–8

Here is a brief account of the short reign of *Abijam* (Abijah), the son of Rehoboam, king of Judah. He is seen as a better king in 2Ch 13:1–22, where we have an account of his war with Jeroboam. There he is called *Abijah*, "My father is the Lord," because no evil is laid to his charge. But here, where we are told of his faults, *Jah*, the name of God, is taken away from his name, and he is called *Abijam*.

1. Few details are given about Abijah:

1.1. His reign started at the beginning of Jeroboam's eighteenth year, for Rehoboam reigned only seventeen (14:21). Jeroboam indeed survived Rehoboam, but Rehoboam's Abijah lived to succeed him and to be a terror to Jeroboam, while Jeroboam's son Abijah, whom we read of in 14:1, died before him.

1.2. He reigned scarcely three years; we know this because he died before the end of Jeroboam's twentieth year (v. 9). When he became proud and felt secure in his own strength because of his great victory over Jeroboam (2Ch 13:21), God cut him off, to make way for his son Asa, who would be a better man.

1.3. *His mother's name was Maachah* (Maacah)*, the daughter of Abishalom* (v. 2), that is, perhaps, Absalom, David's son.

1.4. He carried on his father's wars with Jeroboam. As there was continual war between Rehoboam and Jeroboam—not set battles but frequent skirmishes, especially on the borders—so also there was continual war between Abijah and Jeroboam (v. 7), until Jeroboam invaded him with a great army, and then Abijah, not being forbidden from acting in his own defense, defeated Jeroboam, compelling him to be restrained during the rest of his reign (2Ch 13:20).

2. But, in general, we are told:

2.1. That he was not like David. He was not loyal to God's ordinances, although to serve his purposes against Jeroboam, he pleaded his possession of the temple and priesthood as the basis for his pride (2Ch 13:10–12). He seemed to have zeal, but he lacked sincerity; he began quite well, but he fell away and *walked in all the sins of his father* (v. 3).

2.2. That, even so, it was for David's sake that he had been advanced and that he continued on the throne. It was *for his sake* (vv. 4–5) that God *set up his son after him*; not for his own sake, nor for the sake of his father, in whose steps he trod, *but for the sake of David*, whose example he would not follow. It makes the sin of degener-

ate offspring worse that they get along better because of the godliness of their ancestors, and that they owe their blessings to it yet will not imitate it.

Verses 9–24

Here is a short account of the reign of Asa; we will find a more detailed history in 2Ch 14:1–16:14. Here is:

1. The length of his reign: *He reigned forty-one years in Jerusalem* (v. 10). In the account we have of the kings of Judah we find the number of the good kings and the bad ones nearly equal, but then we may notice, to our satisfaction, that the reign of the good kings was generally long, but that of the bad kings short.

2. The general good character of his reign (v. 11): *Asa did that which was right in the eyes of the Lord*. What is right in God's eyes is truly right. He did *as did David his father*; he kept close to God, although he was not a prophet or a psalmist, as David was. If we reach the graces of those who have gone before us, we will be commended by God even if we come short of their gifts.

3. The particular examples of Asa's godliness. His times were times of reformation.

3.1. He removed what was evil. He first struck at immorality: *He took away the sodomites out of the land*, expelled the homosexual men (NIV: male shrine prostitutes) (v. 12); he suppressed the brothels, for how can either ruler or people prosper when those cages of unclean and filthy birds, more dangerous than hospitals that care for those suffering from the plague, are allowed to remain? He then proceeded to act against idolatry: *He removed all the idols*, even those *that his father had made* (v. 12). Even when it appeared that Maacah his mother, or rather his grandmother—but called his *mother* because she had looked after educating him in his childhood— *had made an idol in a grove*, had made a repulsive Asherah pole, he would nevertheless not turn a blind eye to her idolatry. Reformation must begin at home. Asa, in everything else, wanted to honor and respect his mother. He loved her very much, but he loved God even more and—like the Levite in Dt 33:9—readily forgot the relationship when it competed with doing his duty. If she is an idolater:

3.1.1. Her idol (Asherah pole) will be destroyed or cut down, publicly exposed to contempt, defaced, and burned to ashes *by the brook Kidron*, in the Kidron Valley (v. 13).

3.1.2. She will be deposed. *He removed her from being queen* (v. 13), that is, from her position as queen mother, or else *from the queen*, that is, from influencing his wife; he banished her from the royal court and confined her to an obscure and private life.

3.2. He reestablished what was good (v. 15): he *brought into the house of God the dedicated things* which he himself had set apart, with a vow, from the spoils of the Ethiopians he had conquered. When those who in their infancy were set apart to God by baptism make a personal decision to join themselves to him and vigorously employ themselves in his service, this is bringing in the dedicated things which they and their fathers have dedicated.

4. The achievements of his reign. On the one hand, he built cities himself, to encourage the increase of his people (v. 23) and to invite others to join him because of the advantages of living there. On the other hand, he was very zealous to stop Baasha from building Ramah.

5. The faults of his reign. In both of the things for which he was praised he was found to have faults. The fairest characters still have some *but* or other in them.

5.1. Did he take away the idols? That was good, *but the high places were not removed* (v. 14), and in that respect his reformation came short of what God wanted. It was not right that when he was zealously removing idols, he did not remove these. *Nevertheless his heart was perfect with* (fully committed to) *the Lord* (v. 14). This encourages us by showing us that people may be found upright with God and be accepted by him even if they come short of doing the good that they can and should do in some aspects of their lives. The perfection which is the necessary condition of the new covenant is not to be understood as sinlessness—if it were that, we would all be ruined—but sincerity.

5.2. Did he bring in the dedicated things? That was good, but afterward he transferred possession of the dedicated things: he took the gold and silver out of the house of God and sent them as a bribe to Ben-Hadad, so that he would break his treaty with Baasha and distract Baasha from building Ramah by making inroads into his country (vv. 18–19). Asa sinned in this:

5.2.1. In tempting Ben-Hadad to break his treaty and so violate public trust. If Ben-Hadad did wrong in breaking it, as he certainly did, Asa was wrong in persuading him to break it.

5.2.2. In that he could not trust God—who had done so much for him—to free him from this difficulty, but thought he must use such indirect means as this bribe to help himself.

5.2.3. In taking the gold from the treasury of the temple, which was not to be used except on extraordinary occasions. The plan succeeded, however. Ben-Hadad attacked the towns of Israel, which made Baasha withdraw his whole force from Ramah (vv. 20–21), and this gave Asa the opportunity to demolish what Baasha had built there and take the timber and stones to build some towns of his own (v. 22). But although the plan succeeded, we find it was displeasing to God. Although Asa was proud of how skillfully he had handled matters, and although he promised himself that it would secure his peace effectively, he was told by the prophet that he had acted foolishly and that *thenceforth he should have wars*; see 2Ch 16:7–9.

6. The troubles of his reign. For the most part he prospered, but:

6.1. Baasha king of Israel was a very troublesome neighbor to him. This was the effect of the division of the kingdoms: they were continually troubling one another, which made them both easier prey to the common enemy.

6.2. In his old age he was *diseased in his feet*.

7. The conclusion of his reign. He reigned long, finished with honors, and left his throne to a successor who was in no way inferior to him.

Verses 25–34

We now come to look at the miserable state Israel was in while the kingdom of Judah was happy under Asa's good government. It was declared that they would be as *a reed shaken* (swaying) *in the water* (14:15), and that is what happened. During the single reign of Asa, the government of Israel was in the hands of six or seven different kings. Jeroboam was on the throne of Israel at the beginning of his reign and Ahab at the end of it, and between them were Nadab, Baasha, Elah, Zimri, Tibni, and Omri, undermining and destroying one another. This happened to the people of Israel because they deserted both the house of God and the house of David. Here we have:

1. The ruin and destruction of the family of Jeroboam, according to the word of the Lord through Ahijah. Jeroboam's son Nadab succeeded him. If the death of his brother Abijah had had a proper influence on him and made him religious, and if the honor given Abijah at his death had motivated Nadab to follow his good example, Nadab's reign might have been long and glorious, but he *walked in the way of his father* (v. 26). He kept the worship of his father's calves and forbade his subjects from going to Jerusalem to worship. He *sinned and made Israel to sin*, and so God brought ruin on him quickly, in the second year of his reign. Nadab was besieging Gibbethon, a town which the Philistines had taken from the Danites, and there Baasha and others plotted against him and killed him (v. 27). He had so little influence on the affections of his people that his army chose his murderer as his successor. Baasha *slew* (killed) *him* and *reigned in his stead* (v. 28). The first thing Baasha did when he came to the crown was to *cut off all the house of Jeroboam* (v. 29).

2. The advancement of Baasha. He will be tested shortly, as Jeroboam was. He reigned twenty-four years (v. 33), but he *walked in the way of Jeroboam* (v. 34), even though he had seen the results of that way.

CHAPTER 16

This chapter is concerned wholly with the kingdom of Israel, and the changes in that kingdom. In this chapter we have: 1. The destruction of Baasha's family foretold by a prophet after it had been a royal family for only twenty-six years, (vv. 1–7), and then that destruction carried out by Zimri, one of his officials (vv. 8–14). 2. The seven-day reign of Zimri and his sudden fall (vv. 15–20); the struggle between Omri and Tibni, and Omri's victory and his reign (vv. 21–28). 3. The beginning of the reign of Ahab (vv. 29–33); the rebuilding of Jericho (v. 34). All this time, in Judah things were going well.

Verses 1–14

Here is:

1. The ruin of the family of Baasha foretold. He was a man who would probably have raised and established his family. He was active, skillful, and daring, but he was also an idolater, and this brought destruction on his family.

1.1. God sent him warning of it in advance:

1.1.1. So that if the warning brought him to repent and reform his ways, the ruin might be prevented.

1.1.2. So that if he did not repent and reform his ways, it would be clear when the destruction did come that, whoever might be its instrument, it was the punishment of sin.

1.2. The warning was sent by *Jehu the son of Hanani* (v. 1). His father was a seer, or prophet, at the same time (2Ch 16:7), and had been sent to Asa king of Judah, but the son, who was young and more active, was sent on this longer and more dangerous expedition to Baasha king of Israel. Jehu continued to be useful for a long time, for we find him rebuking Jehoshaphat (2Ch 19:2) more than forty years later, and writing the records of that ruler (2Ch 20:34).

1.2.1. He reminds Baasha of the great things God has done for him (v. 2). God puts power into the hands of bad people, and he makes it serve his good purposes despite the bad use they make of it.

1.2.2. He accuses him of great crimes and wrongs:

1.2.2.1. That he had caused *Israel to sin* (v. 2) and brought them to give to foreign gods the homage due only to him.

1.2.2.2. That he had himself *provoked God to anger with the work of his hands* (v. 7), that is, by worshiping idols, the *work of men's hands*.

1.2.2.3. That he had *destroyed the house of Jeroboam* (v. 7), *because he killed him*, namely, Jeroboam's son and all his family. He was justly punished for the hatred and ambition which drove and controlled him.

1.2.3. He foretells the same destruction to come on his family which he himself had been employed to bring on the family of Jeroboam (vv. 3–4).

2. A reprieve granted for some time, so long in fact that Baasha himself dies in peace and is buried with honor in his own royal town (v. 6). He was far from being a prey either to the dogs or to the birds, which nevertheless was the judgment declared against his house (v. 4).

3. Execution finally carried out. Baasha's son Elah, like Jeroboam's son, Nadab, reigned two years and was then killed; he was killed by Zimri, one of his own soldiers, as Nadab was by Baasha. His family was punished in the same way as Jeroboam's, as had been foretold (v. 3).

3.1. As then, so now, the king himself was killed first, but Elah fell more shamefully than Nadab. Nadab was killed on the field of action and honor, when he and his army were besieging Gibbethon (15:27). When Elah's army had renewed the attempt to take Gibbethon, he should have, like Nadab, been with them as commander in chief, but he loved his own ease, and so he stayed behind to enjoy himself. When he was *drinking himself drunk in his servant's house*, Zimri killed him (vv. 9–10). Death comes easily on people when they are drunk. Besides the chronic diseases which people frequently bring on themselves by hard drinking, and which cut them off in the prime of life, people in that condition are more easily overcome by an enemy, as Amnon was by Absalom, and are more liable to suffer bad accidents, being unable to help themselves.

3.2. As then, so now, the whole family was cut off and uprooted. The first thing Zimri did was to *slay* (kill) *all the house of Baasha*. Thus he held by cruelty what he gained by treason.

Verses 15–28

Zimri, Tibni, and Omri are here all fighting for the crown. Those who are proud or ambitious destroy one another, and they involve others in the general destruction. This turmoil ends in Omri being settled as king. We are told:

1. How he was chosen, as the Roman emperors often were, by the army in the field, now camped in front of Gibbethon, so that they might immediately take revenge on Zimri for the death of Elah. The siege of Gibbethon was abandoned—Philistines are sure to gain when Israelites are quarreling—and Zimri was pursued.

2. How he conquered Zimri, who is said to have reigned seven days (v. 15), the time before Omri was declared king and was himself declared traitor. Tirzah was a beautiful city, but not fortified, so Omri soon conquered it (v. 17) and forced Zimri into the palace, which, because he was unable to defend it—but was still unwilling to surrender it—Zimri burned, with himself in it (v. 18).

3. How he struggled with Tibni and finally got clear of him: *Half of the people followed this Tibni* (v. 21). This half probably included both those who were on Zimri's side and others, who did not want a king to be chosen in the camp but in an assembly of the people. The contest between these two must have lasted some years, for it was in the twenty-seventh year of Asa that Omri was first elected (v. 15), but it was not until the thirty-first year of Asa that he began to reign without a rival. Then Tibni died, probably in battle, *and Omri reigned* (v. 22).

4. How he reigned when he was finally settled on the throne:

4.1. He made himself famous by building Samaria, which, ever after, was the royal city of the kings of Israel. He bought the ground for *two talents of silver* (v. 24). It was called *Samaria*, or "Shemeren," as it is in the Hebrew, from *Shemer*, the former owner (v. 24). The kings of Israel changed their royal seats: Shechem first, then Tirzah, now Samaria; but the kings of Judah kept constantly with Jerusalem, the city of God.

4.2. He made himself notorious for his evil, for *he did worse than all that were before him* (v. 25). He went even farther than they had in *establishing iniquity by a law* (Ps 94:20). Jeroboam caused Israel to sin by temptation, example, and appeal, but Omri did it by force.

Verses 29–34

Here is the beginning of the reign of Ahab, of whom we have more details recorded than of any of the kings of Israel.

1. He exceeded all his predecessors in evil. He *did evil above all that were before him* (v. 30), and as if it was done with a particular hostility toward both God and Israel, to defy him and ruin them, it is said, *He did more to provoke the Lord God of Israel to anger than all the kings of Israel that were before him* (v. 33).

2. He married an evil woman, Jezebel (v. 31), a zealous idolater, who had an extremely imperious and hateful personality. She was addicted to witchcraft and idolatry (2Ki 9:22) and was evil in every way. We will read in the following story what trouble she caused, and also what trouble finally happened to her (2Ki 9:33).

3. He set up the worship of Baal and served the god of the Sidonians, which may have been a sun-god or a deified hero of the Phoenicians. In honor of this false deity, whom they called *Baal*, "lord":

3.1. Ahab built a temple in Samaria, the royal city, because the temple of God was in Jerusalem, the royal city of the other kingdom.

3.2. He set up an altar in that temple, on which sacrifices to Baal were offered.

3.3. He made *a grove* around his temple; or perhaps the word refers to an Asherah pole beside his temple.

4. One of his subjects, imitating his presumption, dared rebuild Jericho, in defiance of the curse Joshua had long before declared on the one who would attempt such building (v. 34). He built for his children, but his eldest son died when he began the work, and the youngest died when he finished it, and all the rest probably between. No one ever hardened their heart against God and prospered.

CHAPTER 17

Never was Israel so blessed with a good prophet as when it was so plagued with a bad king. Never was a king so bold in sinning as Ahab; never was a prophet so bold in rebuking and threatening as Elijah, whose story begins in this chapter and is full of miracles. Scarcely any part of the Old Testament history shines more brightly than this history of the spirit and power of Elijah. He only, out of all the prophets, had the honor of Enoch, the first prophet, to be taken away from this life, so that he would not experience death, and the honor of Moses, the great prophet, to be with our Savior in his transfiguration. Whereas other prophets prophesied and wrote, he prophesied and acted without writing anything, and yet his actions give more distinction to his name than their writings did to theirs. In this chapter we have: 1. Elijah's prediction of a famine in Israel, because of a lack of rain (v. 1). 2. The provision made for him in that famine, first by the ravens at the Kerith Ravine (vv. 2–7) and then, when that brook dried up, by the widow at Zarephath, who received him because he was a prophet and gained a prophet's reward (Mt 10:41), for he multiplied her flour and oil (vv. 8–16) and raised her dead son to life (vv. 17–24). Thus his story begins with judgments and miracles, designed to awaken that foolish generation of people who had corrupted themselves so much.

Verses 1–7

The history of Elijah begins somewhat abruptly. Elijah drops, as it were, straight out of the skies, as if, like Melchizedek, he had no father or mother and no family tree, which made some of the Jews think he was an angel sent from heaven. James, however, assures us that *he was a man subject to like passions as we are* (Jas 5:17). Notice:

• The prophet's name. *Elijah* means "Jehovah is my God." "He is the One who sends me and I will acknowledge me and support me. It is he whom I want to bring Israel back to. It is he alone who can bring about that great work."
• His country: he was *of the inhabitants of Gilead* (v. 1), on the other side of the Jordan, either from the tribe of Gad or from the half tribe of Manasseh, for Gilead was divided between them. We do not need to ask about where people come from, but what they are like. If something is good, it does not matter that it comes from Nazareth (Jn 1:46). He is called *a Tishbite*, which means he came from Tishbe. The beginning of his story:

1. How he foretold a famine, which would be used to punish Israel for their sins. He declared it to the king, who had authority to reform the land and so prevent the judgment. Unless he repented and reformed his ways, this judgment would be brought on his land. There would be *neither dew nor rain for some years*. Elijah prayed earnestly *that it might not rain*; according to his prayers, the skies became as hard as stone until he *prayed again that it might rain* (Jas 5:17). Elijah lets Ahab know:
    1.1. That *the Lord is the God of Israel* (v. 1), whom Ahab has abandoned.
    1.2. That he is a *living God* (v. 1), not like the gods Ahab worships, which are dead, mute idols.
    1.3. That he himself is God's servant in office, and a messenger sent from him.
    1.4. That despite the present peace and prosperity of the kingdom of Israel, God is displeased with them for their idolatry and will rebuke them for it by withholding rain. The lack of rain will effectively prove the powerlessness of the idols the people have been worshiping and how foolish they had been to leave the living God, to worship idols that could not do good or evil.
    1.5. What privileges he has in heaven: it will be *according to my word* (v. 1).
2. How he himself was taken care of in the famine:
    2.1. How he was hidden. God told him to go *and hide himself by the brook Cherith* (v. 3). For the present, in

obedience to the divine command, he went and lived all alone in some obscure place off the beaten track, probably among the reeds of the ravine. If Providence calls us to solitude and withdrawal, we should accept that. When we cannot be useful, we must be patient, and when we cannot work for God, we must quietly wait for him.
    2.2. How he was fed. When the woman, the church, is *driven into the wilderness*, care is taken that she is fed and nourished there, *time, times, and half a time*, that is, three and a half years, which was just the time of Elijah's concealment. See Rev 12:6, 14. Elijah must drink from the brook, and the ravens were appointed to bring him food (v. 4) and did so (v. 6). Here:
        2.2.1. The provision was plentiful, good, and constant—bread and meat twice a day, daily bread and *food convenient* (Pr 30:8), neither too much nor too little. It is not good for God's servants, especially his servants the prophets, to be fussy about their food and to want a wide range of delicacies. Instead of envying those who have finer food, we should think how many there are who are better than us but who have to live contentedly on worse food and would be glad to have our leftovers.
        2.2.2. The caterers were very unlikely; it was *ravens* that brought it to him. Obadiah would gladly have received Elijah, but he was a man in a class by himself. Elijah prefigured John the Baptist, whose food was locusts and wild honey. If it is asked from where the ravens obtained this provision, and how and where it was cooked, and whether they came honestly by it, we must answer, as Jacob did (Ge 27:20), *The Lord our God brought it to them*. But why ravens?
            2.2.2.1. Ravens are birds of prey, more likely to have taken his food from him, or to have pecked out his eyes (Pr 30:17), but Samson's riddle is again solved, *Out of the eater comes forth meat* (Jdg 14:14).
            2.2.2.2. Ravens are unclean creatures. *Every raven after his kind* was, by the Law, forbidden from being eaten (Lev 11:15), yet Elijah did not think the food they brought ever to have been the worse for that reason, but ate and gave thanks, asking no questions for conscience's sake.
            2.2.2.3. Ravens feed on insects and carrion themselves, but they brought the prophet wholesome food of bread and meat.
            2.2.2.4. Ravens could bring only a little, and broken pieces, but Elijah was thankful that he received something to eat, though not a feast.
            2.2.2.5. Ravens neglect their own young ones and do not feed them, but when God pleases, they will feed his prophet.
            2.2.2.6. Ravens are themselves fed by special providence (Job 38:41; Ps 147:9), and now they fed the prophet.
    2.3. How Elijah eats his food alone for a long time, and then his provision of water, which he has received from the brook in an ordinary way, fails before what he has gained miraculously. The powers of nature are limited, but not the powers of the God of nature. Elijah's brook dried up (v. 7), *because there was no rain*.

Verses 8–16

Here is an account of the further protection Elijah received. When the brook dried up, the river Jordan did not. Why did God not send him there? Surely it was because he wanted to show that he has a variety of ways of providing for his people and is not restricted to any one way. Notice:
1. The place he is sent to, to *Zarephath*, or *Sarepta*, a town of Sidon, beyond the borders of the land of Israel

(v. 9). Our Savior notes this as an early and ancient sign of the favor of God to the lowly Gentiles in the fullness of time (Lk 4:25–26). *Many widows were in Israel in the days of Elias*, but he is sent to honor and bless with his presence a town of Sidon, a Gentile town, and so he becomes—according to Dr. Lightfoot—the first prophet to the Gentiles. Elijah was hated and driven out by his compatriots, and so he turned to the Gentiles, as the apostles were later ordered to do (Ac 18:6). But why to a town of Sidon? Perhaps because the worship of Baal had just come from there with Jezebel, who was a Sidonian (16:31). Jezebel is Elijah's greatest enemy, but to show her that her hatred is ineffective, God will find a hiding place for him even in her country.

2. The person who is appointed to receive him, a poor widow who is destitute and desolate. It is God's way, and it is his glory, to make use of the *weak and foolish things of the world* (1Co 1:27) and to honor them.

3. The provision made for him there. Providence brought the widow to meet him at just the right time at the gate of the town (v. 10):

3.1. Her circumstances and character:

3.1.1. She had nothing to live on except a handful of flour and a little oil. As far as she could see, when she had eaten the little she had, she and her son must die because she had nothing more to live on (v. 12). She had no fuel except the sticks she gathered in the streets. To her Elijah was sent, so that he might still live on Providence as much as he had when the ravens fed him. It was also out of compassion for the *low estate of his handmaiden* (Lk 1:48) that God sent the prophet to her, and he sent him not to beg from her but to lodge with her, and he would pay well for his food.

3.1.2. She was very humble and diligent. He found her gathering sticks and preparing to bake her own bread (vv. 10, 12).

3.1.3. She was very charitable and generous. When this stranger wanted her to fetch him some water to drink, she went readily, at his first word (vv. 10–11). She did not raise the objection that it was then scarce. She did not ask him what he would give her. She did not hint that he was a stranger, an Israelite, but stopped gathering sticks for herself to fetch water for him.

3.1.4. She faced a great test for her faith and obedience when, being told how low her stock of food and oil was and that she had only just enough for herself and her son, the prophet told her *make a cake for him*, and make *his* first, and then *prepare for herself and her son* (v. 13). It is true that Elijah made mention *of the God of Israel* (v. 14), but what was that to one from Sidon? Or if she had a respect for the name *Jehovah* and valued the God of Israel as the true God, what assurance had she that this stranger was his prophet or had authority to speak in his name? It was easy for a hungry beggar to impose himself on her. But she overcame all these objections and obeyed the command because she depended on the promise. Those who deal with God must deal with trust. They must seek first his kingdom, and then other things will be added. But surely the increase of this widow's faith so much as to enable her to deny herself in this way and to depend on God's promise was as great a miracle in the kingdom of grace as the increase of her oil was in the kingdom of Providence.

3.2. The care God took of her guest: *The barrel of meal wasted not, nor did the cruse of oil fail*, the jar of flour was not used up and the jug of oil did not run dry, but as they used more, more was added to them by God's

power (v. 16). Never did grain or olive increase so much in growing, says Bishop Hall, as these did in being used; and yet the *multiplying of the seed sown* (2Co 9:10) in the ordinary course of Providence is an example of the power and goodness of God that should not be overlooked just because it is ordinary. The flour and oil multiplied not by being saved but by being spent.

3.2.1. This was adequate sustenance for the prophet. Miracles continued to be his daily bread. Up to that time he had been fed with bread and meat, and now he was fed with bread and oil, which they used as we use butter.

3.2.2. This was adequate sustenance for the poor widow and her son, and also a reward to her for receiving the prophet. Christ has promised to those who open their doors to him that he will come in to them, and *sup with them*, and *they with him* (Rev 3:20). It is promised to those who trust in God that they *shall not be ashamed in the evil time, but in the days of famine they shall be satisfied* (Ps 37:19).

Verses 17–24

Here is a further reward given to the widow for her kindness to the prophet. When her son dies, he is restored to life. Notice:

1. The sickness and death of the child. It seems that he was her only son, the comfort of her widowed estate. This trouble was like a thorn in the flesh to her, so that she would not become proud because of the favors and honors given her (2Co 12:7).

1.1. She was a nurse to a great prophet. She was used in sustaining him and had strong reason to think the Lord would do her good, but now she loses her child.

1.2. She herself was nursed by a miracle. In the midst of all these fulfilling times she was afflicted in this way.

2. Her emotional complaint to the prophet about this trouble.

2.1. She expresses herself passionately: *What have I to do with thee, O thou man of God?* (v. 18). The death of her child now came as a shock to her, and it is hard to keep our spirits calm when troubles come on us suddenly and unexpectedly, when we are at peace and everything is going well. She calls him *a man of God*, but she quarrels with him as if he had caused the death of her child. How have I offended you, or been lacking in my duty? What do you have against me? *Show me wherefore thou contendest with* (what charges you have against) *me*" (Job 10:2).

2.2. Yet she expresses herself penitently: "*Hast thou come to call my sin to* your *remembrance* (v. 18), as the cause of this affliction?" Perhaps she knew about Elijah's intercession against Israel, and being aware of her former worship of Baal, the god of the Sidonians, she thought he had made intercession against her.

3. The prophet's going to God on this occasion. He gave no answer to her protest but brought matters to God, and spread out the case before him, not knowing himself what to say about it. He took the dead child from his mother's arms and laid him on his own bed (v. 19). He had probably become particularly fond of the child. He withdrew to his room, and:

3.1. He humbly reasoned with God about the death of the child (v. 20).

3.2. He fervently begged God to restore the child to life (v. 21). We do not read before this about anyone dead being raised to life, but Elijah, by divine prompting, prayed for the resurrection of this child. However, this does not give us authority to do the same. David did not expect, even in his fasting and prayer, to bring his child back to life (2Sa 12:23), but Elijah had power to work miracles, which David did not have. He *stretched himself upon the child* (v. 21), to show how much he wanted the child to be restored—if it were possible, he would put life back into him with own breath and warmth. He is very detailed in his prayer: *I pray thee let this child's soul come into him again* (v. 21), which clearly implied the existence of the soul in a separate state from the body, and consequently its immortality, which Hugo Grotius, the Dutch jurist and theologian, thinks God intended this miracle to show, to encourage his suffering people.

4. The resurrection of the child, and the great delight this gave the mother: *he revived* (v. 22). Notice the power of prayer and the power of the One who hears prayer, who *kills and makes alive* (1Sa 2:6). Elijah brought him to his mother, who probably could scarcely believe her eyes. The good woman then cried out, *Now I know that thou art a man of God* (v. 24). Even though she knew it before, when her food increased, her child's death seemed such a great unkindness that she began to question whether Elijah was indeed a man of God, but now she was abundantly satisfied that he had both the power and goodness of a man of God. In this way the death of the child was for the glory of God and the honor of his prophet.

CHAPTER 18

It does not appear that either the miraculous increase of flour and oil or the raising of the child to life had caused Elijah to be taken notice of at Zarephath. After the days set for his hiding have been completed, he is now commanded to show himself to Ahab and to expect rain on the earth (v. 1). We have: 1. His meeting with Obadiah, one of Ahab's servants, by whom he sends notice to Ahab of his coming (vv. 2–16). 2. His meeting with Ahab himself (vv. 17–20). 3. His meeting with all Israel on Mount Carmel, for a public trial of assertion of rights between the Lord and Baal. This was a most distinguished ceremony, in which Baal and his prophets were confounded and God and Elijah were honored (vv. 21–39). 4. The execution he carried out on the prophets of Baal (v. 40). 5. The merciful return of the rain at the word of Elijah (vv. 41–46).

Verses 1–16

In these verses we find:

1. The sad state of Israel at this time, in two respects:

1.1. *Jezebel cut off the prophets of the Lord* (v. 4); she *slew* (killed) *them* (v. 13). Being an idolater, she was a persecutor, and she also made Ahab one. Even in those bad times there were still some good people who feared God and served him, and some good prophets who helped them in their devotions. The priests and the Levites had all gone to Judah and Jerusalem (2Ch 11:13–14), but in their place God raised up these prophets, who read and explained the Law in private meetings, or in the families that kept their integrity. The prophets did not have the spirit of prophecy that Elijah had, nor did they offer sacrifices or burn incense, but they taught the people to live rightly and to keep close to the God of Israel. Jezebel aimed to destroy these and to put many of them to death, which was as much a public disaster as a public sin and threatened to completely destroy the meager remains of religious faith in Israel. Those few who escaped the sword were forced to run away and hide in caves, where they were buried alive and cut off, if not from life, then from usefulness, which is the purpose and satisfaction of life.

1.1.1. There was one very good man, who was a great man at the royal court, *Obadiah*, whose character corresponded to his name, "a servant of the Lord"; he feared God and was faithful to him, and yet he was in charge of Ahab's palace. He *feared the Lord greatly* (v. 3). He *feared the Lord from his youth* (v. 12).

1.1.1.1. It was strange that such an evil man as Ahab would promote him. Certainly it was because he was a man of noted honesty, diligence, and skill, and one in whom Ahab could put his confidence, whose eyes he could trust as much as his own, as is seen here (v. 5).

1.1.1.2. It was strange that such a good man as Obadiah would accept advancement in a court that was so devoted to idolatry and every kind of evil. Obadiah would not have accepted the position if he could not have had it without submitting to Baal. Obadiah could therefore enjoy with a good conscience the position he had. Those who fear God need not leave the world, bad as it is.

1.1.2. This great and good man used his power to protect God's prophets. He hid 100 of them in two caves when the persecution was intense, and he *fed them with bread and water* (v. 4). Notice how wonderfully God raises up friends for his ministers and people, to protect them in difficult times, even where one would least expect such friends.

1.2. When Jezebel cut off God's prophets, God cut off the necessary provisions by the severity of the drought. Perhaps Jezebel claimed she was persecuting God's prophets because they were the cause of the judgment: Elijah had foretold it, and he was a prophet. But God made them know that the opposite was in fact true, for the famine continued until Baal's prophets were sacrificed, and there was such a great scarcity of water that the king himself and Obadiah went in person throughout the land to look for grass for the cattle (vv. 5–6). Ahab was concerned not to *lose all the beasts* (v. 5), since many already had died, but he was not concerned about losing his soul. He took a deal of effort to look for grass, but none to look for God's favor. He worked hard to gain protection from the effects of judgment, but he did not ask how its causes could be removed. The land of Judah was situated close to the land of Israel, and there we find no complaint there of the lack of rain, *for Judah yet ruled with God*.

2. The steps taken toward putting right this offense, by Elijah's appearing again on the stage, to act as *a Tishbite*, "a converter" or "reformer" of Israel, for that is what some think his title means. Bring them back to almighty God, from whom they have rebelled, and all will quickly be well. This is what Elijah must do: see Lk 1:16–17.

2.1. Ahab had diligently searched for Elijah (v. 10). He had offered a reward to anyone who would find him. It seems his purpose in searching so diligently for him was not so much to punish him for what he had done in pronouncing the judgment as to make him undo it by revoking the punishment.

2.2. God finally ordered Elijah to present himself to Ahab, because the time had now come when he would *send rain upon the earth* (v. 1), or rather upon the land. He had been in hiding for more than one year by the Kerith Ravine and then for more than two years with the widow at Zarephath, so the third year of his staying there, referred to in v. 1, was the fourth year of the famine, which lasted in all three and a half years, as we find in Lk 4:25 and Jas 5:17.

2.3. Elijah first surrendered himself, or rather made himself known, to Obadiah. He knew, by the Spirit, where to meet him.

2.3.1. Obadiah greeted him with great respect, bowed down to the ground, and humbly asked, *Art thou that my lord Elijah?* (v. 7). As he had shown the tenderness of a father to the sons of the prophets, so he now showed the reverence of a son to this father of the prophets. This showed that he really did *fear God greatly.*

2.3.2. Elijah answers him and:

2.3.2.1. Transfers the title of honor Obadiah gave him to Ahab: "Call him your lord, not me." That is a better title for a ruler than a prophet, *who seeks not honour from men* (Jn 5:41). Prophets should be called "seers" and "shepherds" and "watchmen" and "ministers" rather than "lords," as those who are more concerned to do their duty than to exercise power.

2.3.2.2. Tells Obadiah to go and say to the king that he is there to speak with him: *Tell thy lord, Behold, Elijah is here;* he is ready to appear (v. 8).

2.3.3. Obadiah asks to be excused from carrying this message to Ahab, for it might prove as much as his life was worth. He thought that Elijah was not being serious when he told him to tell Ahab where he was, but that he intended by his request only to reveal how ineffective Ahab's hatred was, for Obadiah knew that Ahab did not deserve kindness from the prophet and that Elijah did not deserve any trouble from Ahab. He was certain that Ahab would be so enraged that he would put him to death for making a fool of him, or for not seizing Elijah himself, when he had him within his reach (v. 12). He pleaded that he did not deserve to be exposed to such a danger and have his own life put at risk: *"What have I sinned?* What have I done wrong? (v. 9). In fact (v. 13), *Was it not told my lord how I hid the prophets?* Haven't you heard, my lord, how I hid the prophets?" He mentioned this to convince Elijah that although he was Ahab's servant, he was not on his side. He who had protected so many prophets would not, he hoped, have his own life put in danger by such a great prophet.

2.3.4. Elijah satisfied him that he could safely deliver this message to Ahab. This very day, he assured him on oath, he would present himself to Ahab (v. 15).

2.3.5. News is therefore soon brought to Ahab that Elijah sent him a challenge to meet him immediately at such and such a place, and Ahab accepts the challenge: *He went to meet Elijah* (v. 16). Presumably it was a great surprise to Ahab to hear that Elijah, whom he had looked for so vigorously and had not found, had now been found without looking. He went looking for grass, and found the one from whose word, at God's mouth, he must expect rain. His guilty conscience gave him little reason to hope for it, but good reason to fear some more terrible judgment.

Verses 17–20

Here is the meeting between Ahab and Elijah, as bad a king as ever the world has been plagued with and as good a prophet as ever the church has been blessed with.

1. Ahab was true to himself and wrongly accused Elijah. He dared not strike him, remembering that Jeroboam's hand had shriveled up when it was stretched out against a prophet, but he spoke to him using bad language, which was no less an insult to God. *Art thou he that troubleth Israel?* Is that you, you troubler of Israel? (v. 17). How different this was from the words with which his servant Obadiah greeted Elijah (v. 7): *Art thou that my lord Elijah?* Obadiah feared God greatly; Ahab had sold himself to do evil, and both revealed their character by how they spoke to the prophet. It has been the fate of the best and most useful people to be called and counted as *the troublers of the land* (v. 17) and to be maligned as public nuisances. Even Christ and his apostles were misrepresented in this way (Ac 17:6).

2. Elijah was true to himself; he boldly turned the charge back on the king and asserted that the accusation was true about *him,* that he, Ahab, was *the troubler of Israel* (v. 18). Those who suffer God's judgments are those who cause the trouble, not the one who merely foretells the judgments and warns of them so that the nation may repent and prevent them. I *would have healed Israel* (Hos 7:1), but they do not want to be healed. Ahab is the troubler, the one who follows the Baals, those cursed things.

3. As one with direct authority from the King of kings, Elijah ordered an assembly of the people from all over Israel to be immediately summoned to meet on Mount Carmel, where an altar had been built to God (v. 30). All Israel must come there, to meet with Elijah, and the prophets of Baal who were dispersed throughout the country, along with the priests of the Asherahs who were Jezebel's domestic chaplains, must also be personally present there.

4. Ahab, accordingly, issued summonses to convene this great assembly (v. 20), either because he feared Elijah and dared not oppose him or because he hoped that Elijah would bless the land and speak the word so that they might have rain; and on those terms they would all be at Elijah's beck and call.

Verses 21–40

Ahab and the people expected that Elijah would, in this solemn assembly, *bless the land* and pray for rain, but he had another job to do first. The people must be brought to repent and reform their ways; then, and only then, could they look for the judgment to be removed. Those who have abandoned God must not look for his favor until they return to their former allegiance. Elijah might have looked for rain seventy times seven times and not have seen it if he had not begun his work in the right way. God's cause is so incontestably right that it need not fear having the evidence of its fairness examined and weighed.

1. Elijah rebuked the people for mixing the worship of God and the worship of Baal. Not only were there some Israelites who worshiped God and others who worshiped Baal, but also the same Israelites sometimes worshiped one and sometimes the other. This he calls (v. 21) *halting* (wavering) *between two opinions.* They worshiped God to please the prophets but also worshiped Baal to please Jezebel and to try to gain favor at court. "There can be only one God, only one infinite and supreme Being. There need be only one God, one all-powerful, all-sufficient God. How can you add to something that is already perfect? Now if we hold a trial, and if it appears that Baal is the one infinite, all-powerful Being, the one supreme Lord and all-sufficient benefactor, you should renounce Jehovah and remain faithful only to Baal, but if Jehovah is that one God, Baal is a fraud, and you must have nothing more to do with him." We can learn from this that those who waver are those who are undecided in their convictions, unstable and unsteady in their purposes, who say all the right promises but do not keep them. They begin well but do not last; they are inconsistent within themselves, or indifferent and lukewarm toward what is good. *Their heart is divided* (Hos 10:2), whereas God wants all or nothing. We are rightly given the choice *whom we will serve* (Jos 24:15). The people did not know how to respond to this reasonable proposal which Elijah has made: *They answered him not a word* (v. 21).

2. Elijah proposed to bring the matter to a fair trial, and Baal had all the external advantages on his side. The king and court were all for Baal, and so were the main body of the people. The overseers of Baal's cause were 450 men (v. 22), besides 400 more, their supporters or seconds (v. 19). The overseer of God's cause was only one man, who had just been in exile and hardly kept from starving to death, so God's cause had nothing to support it except its own right. However, the experiment was made: "Let each side prepare a sacrifice and pray to its God, and *the God that answereth by fire, let him be God* (v. 24). If neither answers in this way, then let the people become atheists. If both answer, then let them continue to *halt between two*" (v. 21). It shows Elijah's courage that he dared stand alone in the cause of God against such powers and numbers, and this matter encourages all God's witnesses and supporters never to fear human beings.

3. The people accept Elijah's proposal: it *is well spoken* (v. 24). Ahab and the prophets of Baal dared not raise any opposition for fear of the people. If they could only make this trial to come to a draw, their other advantages would give them the final victory. Let the matter therefore go to trial.

4. The prophets of Baal try first with their god, but in vain. Elijah allows them to do this (v. 25); he lets them begin, to cause them more shame. Notice:

4.1. How bold and noisy the prophets of Baal were when they turned to him. They got their sacrifices ready. They cried out as one, and with all their strength, *O Baal, hear us* (v. 26). O Baal, "answer" us (v. 26, margin). How stupid and foolish they were in their cries to Baal!

4.1.1. Like fools, *they leaped upon the altar* (v. 26), as if they could themselves become sacrifices with their bulls. *They leaped up and down* (v. 26) to please their deity.

4.1.2. Like mad people they *cut themselves in pieces with knives and lancets* (swords and spears) (v. 28), exasperated that they were not being answered, or in a kind of prophetic fury, hoping to win the favor of their god by offering their own blood to him. God expressly forbade his worshipers from cutting themselves (Dt 14:1).

4.2. How sharply Elijah spoke to them (v. 27). He stood by them and patiently heard them for many hours praying to an idol. He listened with secret indignation and disdain, and at noon taunted them: "*Cry aloud, for he is a god*, a good god that cannot be made to listen except with all this clamor." Far from being convinced and ashamed by the just rebuke Elijah gave them, Baal's prophets became even more violent, and the rebuke led them to act even more absurdly.

4.3. How deaf Baal was to them. Elijah did not stop them, but let them go on until they were tired and had completely despaired of success, which was not *till the time of the evening sacrifice* (v. 29).

5. Elijah soon gains an answer by fire from his God.

5.1. He prepared an altar. He would not use theirs, which had been defiled by their prayers to Baal, but finding on the mountain the ruins of an altar that had formerly been used in the service of the Lord, he chose to repair that (v. 30). This would suggest to them that he was not about to introduce any new religion, but to revive the faith and worship of their ancestors' God. He repaired this altar with *twelve stones, according to the number of the twelve tribes* (v. 31). Although ten of the tribes had rebelled and turned to Baal, he looked on them as still belonging to God, because of the ancient covenant with their ancestors.

5.2. Having built his altar *in the name of the Lord* (v. 32), he prepared his sacrifice (v. 33). *Behold the bullock and the wood; but where is the fire? God will provide himself* fire (Ge 22:7–8). If we sincerely offer our hearts to God, he will by his grace kindle a holy fire within them. Elijah was not a priest, nor were his attendants Levites; Mount Carmel did not have either a tabernacle or a temple. But there never was a sacrifice more acceptable to God than this.

5.3. He ordered an abundance of water to be poured on his altar, for which he had prepared a trench to hold it (v. 32). He poured twelve barrels of water—probably seawater, for the sea was near, and so much fresh water at this time of drought would have been too precious for him to waste—on the sacrifice to avoid any suspicion that there was fire underneath.

5.4. He then solemnly turned to God in prayer before his altar, humbly asking him to *turn to ashes his burnt offering* and to show his acceptance of it. His prayer was not long; it was very serious and calm and showed his mind to be composed and at rest, far different from the passion and confusion of Baal's prophets (vv. 36–37). He addressed God as *the God of Abraham, Isaac, and Israel* (v. 36), reminding the people of their relationship with God and the patriarchs. He begged that the offering would be accepted:

5.4.1. For the glory of God: "Lord, hear me and answer me, *that it may be known that thou art God in Israel*" (v. 36).

5.4.2. For the edification of the people: "*That they may know that thou art the Lord, turning their heart back again to thee*" (v. 37), so that you may return in mercy to them."

5.5. God immediately answered him by fire (v. 38). While he was still speaking, *the fire of the Lord fell, consumed the sacrifice and the wood, licked up all the water in the trench.* But this was not all; to complete the miracle, the fire consumed the *stones of the altar, and the very dust* (soil) (v. 38). Moses' altar and Solomon's were consecrated by fire from heaven, but this one was destroyed because it was not to be used anymore. We may well imagine what terror the fire struck on guilty Ahab and all the worshipers of Baal.

6. What was the result of this fair trial? The prophets of Baal had failed. Elijah, however, by the most convincing and undeniable evidence, had proved his claims on behalf of the God of Israel. And now:

6.1. The people, as the jury, gave their verdict in the trial, and they were all agreed: *They fell on their faces* and, all as one, said, "*Jehovah, he is the God*, and not Baal; *Jehovah, he is the God*" (v. 39). One would have thought they would have then inferred from this, "If he is God, he will be our God, and we will serve only him." We hope that the hearts of some of them were turned back, but most of them were only convinced, not converted. They submitted to the truth of God, that he is the only God, but did not give their personal agreement to his covenant, that he would be *their* God.

6.2. The prophets of Baal, as criminals, are seized, condemned, and executed, according to the Law (v. 40). Elijah orders them all to be killed immediately as the troublers of the land. Elijah is still acting according to an extraordinary commission from God, which is not to be used as a precedent. Those who were killed were the 450 prophets of Baal; the 400 prophets of Asherah—who some think were Sidonians—though summoned (v. 19), seem not to have attended, and so to have escaped this execution. It turned out, however, that they were reserved to be instruments of Ahab's destruction some time later, when they encouraged him to go up to Ramoth Gilead (22:6).

Verses 41–46

The people of Israel had been reformed to the extent that they had acknowledged the Lord as God. God then opened the bottles of heaven and poured out blessings on his land that very evening.

1. Elijah sent Ahab to *eat and drink*. Ahab had continued to fast all day, either religiously, since it was a day of prayer, or because he was too busy, since it was a day of great expectation, but now he may *eat and drink*, for although others perceive no sign of it, Elijah by faith hears *the sound of abundance of rain* (v. 41).

2. Elijah himself withdrew to pray. He wanted to give thanks for God's answer by fire as he now hoped for an answer by water.

2.1. He withdrew to a strange place, to the *top of Carmel*, which was very high and very private. We read therefore of those who *hide themselves in the top of Carmel* (Am 9:3). He could be alone there. Those who are called to appear and act in public for God must still find time to be private with him and keep up their relationship with him in solitude.

2.2. He put himself into a strange posture. He went down on his knees to the earth, as a sign of humility, and *put his face between his knees* (v. 42).

3. Elijah ordered his servant to tell him as soon as he discerned a cloud rising out of the sea, the Mediterranean Sea, which he had a wide view of from the top of Carmel. The sailors now call it *Cape Carmel*. His servant went to the point of the hill six times and saw nothing; he brought no good news to his master. Yet Elijah still went on praying. He continued to send his servant to see if he could discern any promising cloud, while he kept his mind set on God in prayer. He was faithful in prayer, as one who had taken up his father Jacob's determination, *I will not let thee go except thou bless me* (Ge 32:26).

4. A little cloud finally came into view, no bigger than a human hand, which soon spread over the heavens and watered the earth (vv. 44–45). Great blessings often come from small beginnings, and showers of plenty from a tiny cloud.

5. Elijah then made Ahab go home quickly, and accompanied him himself. Ahab rode in his chariot, at ease and in state (v. 45). Elijah ran on foot ahead of him. If Ahab had paid the respect to Elijah that he deserved, he would have taken him into his chariot, as the eunuch did with Philip, so that he might honor him before the elders of Israel and discuss with him more about the reformation of the kingdom. But his corruptions got the better of his convictions, and he was glad to get rid of him, as Felix was of Paul, when he sent him away and put off his meeting with him to a more convenient time.

CHAPTER 19

We left Elijah at Jezreel, still appearing in public, with all the people's eyes on him. In this chapter we have him running away again and driven into obscurity, at a time when he could hardly be spared. When people will not learn, God is just in removing their teachers from them. Notice: 1. How Elijah was driven into exile by the malice of Jezebel, his sworn enemy (vv. 1–3) 2. How he was met in his exile by the favor of God, his covenant friend. 2.1. How God fed him (vv. 4–8). 2.2. How God met with him and revealed himself to him (vv. 9, 11–13), heard his complaint (vv. 10–14), told him what to do (vv. 15–17), and encouraged him (v. 18). 3. How his hands were strengthened, at his return from exile, by Elisha's joining with him (vv. 19–21).

Verses 1–8

One would have expected, after such a public and clear revelation of the glory of God, that now they would all as one return to the worship of the God of Israel and take Elijah as their guide and prophet. But he whom God honored is neglected; no respect is given to him, no care is taken of him, no use is made of him; on the contrary, the land of Israel is now made too dangerous for him.

1. Ahab aroused Jezebel's anger against him. That queen consort, it seems, was in fact the power behind the throne controlling both the king and kingdom and doing what she wanted, until her death. Ahab's conscience would not let him persecute Elijah, but he told Jezebel all that Elijah had done (v. 1), and in telling her he meant not to convince her but to exasperate her. It is said that he told her not what *God* had done but what *Elijah* had done, as if he, by some spell or charm, had brought down fire from heaven, and the hand of the Lord had not been in it. He told her particularly that Elijah had killed the prophets.

2. Jezebel sent him a threatening message (v. 2), that she had vowed and sworn that she would ensure that he died within twenty-four hours. But why did she send him word of her intentions, and so give him an opportunity of making his escape? I tend to think that although there was nothing she wanted more than his blood, yet at this time she dared not interfere too much with him *for fear of the people*, all counting him a prophet (Mt 21:26), a great prophet. She therefore sent this message to him simply to frighten him and get him out of the way.

3. Elijah was then deeply afraid and fled for his life, probably at night, and went to Beersheba (v. 3). Where was the courage with which he had just confronted Ahab and all the prophets of Baal? He must have known that he could be very useful to Israel at this time, and he had every reason in the world to depend on God's protection while he was doing God's work; yet he fled. In his former danger, God had told him to hide himself (17:3), and so he supposed he could do so now.

4. From Beersheba he went forward into the desert, that barren, howling desert through which the Israelites had wandered. Beersheba was far away from Jezreel, and within the land of Jehoshaphat, a good king, so he thought he would be safe there. However, as if his fears haunted him even when he was out of the reach of danger, he could not rest there, but went a day's journey into desert. Perhaps he withdrew there not so much to be safe as to withdraw wholly from the world, in order to enjoy more free and intimate fellowship with God. *He left his servant at Beer-sheba* (v. 3), perhaps because he did not want to expose his servant, who was young and tender, to the hardships of the desert.

5. Being tired out by his journey, he became irritable — as children do when they are sleepy — and *wished he might die* (v. 4). Those who are as anxious as this to die are not most ready to die. Jezebel has sworn his death, and so he becomes worried and prays for death; he runs from death to death, but with this difference: he wants to die by the hand of the Lord. He would rather die in the desert than as the prophets of Baal died, as Jezebel threatened (v. 2), so that the worshipers of Baal will not gloat over and blaspheme the God of Israel. He pleads, "It is enough. I have done all I can. I have suffered enough. I am fed up with living." He pleads, *I am not better than my fathers* (ancestors) (v. 4). But is this Elijah? (18:7). Can that brave and bold spirit shrink back like this? God left him to himself like this to show that when he was bold and strong it was *in the Lord and the power of his might*

(Eph 6:10); in himself he was *no better than his fathers* (ancestors) (v. 4) or relatives.

6. God, by an angel, fed him in that desert, with its dangers and scarcities which he had deliberately thrown himself into. Elijah sulked and wanted to die; God, though he did not need him, still wanted to use him further and honor him, and so he sent an angel to *keep him alive.* Our lives would sometimes be bad if God took us at our word and gave us our foolish, passionate requests. Having prayed that he might die, he *laid him down and slept* (v. 5), perhaps wanting to die in his sleep. But he is woken up and finds himself not only well provided for with bread and water (v. 6), but even served by an angel, who guarded him when he slept, and twice called him to his food when it was ready for him (vv. 5, 7). Wherever God's children are, just as they remain on their Father's ground, so they remain under their Father's eyes and care. They may lose themselves in a desert, but God has not lost them.

7. He was taken, in the strength of this food, to Horeb, *the mount of God* (v. 8). The Spirit of the Lord led him there, probably beyond his own intentions, so that he might have fellowship with God at the same place where Moses did. The angel told him to eat a second time, because of the greatness *of the journey* that was *before him* (v. 7). This shows us that God knows what he wants us for. He makes sure we are provided with *grace sufficient* (2Co 12:9). The One who appoints what the voyage of our lives will be supplies the ship accordingly. Notice how many different ways God used to keep Elijah alive: he fed him by ravens, with multiplied meals, then by an angel, and now, to show that *man lives not by bread alone* (Dt 8:3, quoted in Mt 4:4), he kept him alive forty days without food, continually crossing the mazes of the desert, one day for each year of Israel's wanderings, yet he neither needed food nor craved it.

Verses 9–18

Here is:

1. Elijah sheltered in a cave at Mount Horeb, which is called *the mount of God* (v. 8) because God had formerly revealed his glory on it. Perhaps this was the same cave, or cleft in a rock, where Moses had hidden when the Lord *passed by before him and proclaimed his name* (Ex 33:22).

2. The appearance God made to him there and the questions God put to him: *The word of the Lord came to him* (v. 9). We cannot go anywhere beyond the reach of God's sight, his arm, and his word. John saw visions of the Almighty when he was in exile on the island of Patmos (Rev 1:9). The question God puts to the prophet is, *What doest* thou *here, Elijah?* (v. 9 and again v. 13). This is a rebuke:

2.1. For his fleeing there. "What has brought you so far away from home? Are you running away from Jezebel?" Put the emphasis on the *you.* "*You!* Such a great man, such a great prophet, so famous for being determined—are you running away from your country, abandoning who you are?"

2.2. For his staying there. "What are you doing here, in this cave? Is this a place where a prophet of the Lord should be? Is this a time for prophets to withdraw, when the public needs them so much?"

3. The account that he gives of himself in answer to the question put to him (v. 10), an account that he repeats in answer to the same question (v. 14).

3.1. He excuses his retreat. God knew, and his own conscience witnessed to him, that as long as there was

any hope of doing good, he had been *very jealous* (zealous) *for the Lord God of hosts* (vv. 10, 14). Now that he *laboured in vain*, and all his endeavors were ineffective, he thought it was time to give up the cause.

3.2. He complains about the people, their obstinacy in sin: "*The children of Israel have forsaken thy covenant* (vv. 10, 14), and that is the reason I have rejected them. Who can stay among them, to see everything sacred ruined and destroyed?" He has often been, by choice, their advocate, but now he has to be their accuser before God. He accuses them of:

3.2.1. Having rejected God's covenant. Although they kept circumcision, the sign and seal of the covenant, they had abandoned his worship and service, which was the purpose of the covenant.

3.2.2. Having *thrown down his altars* (v. 10, 14), having not only abandoned them and allowed them to decay, but in their zeal for the worship of Baal, deliberately demolished them. Although these separate altars broke in on the unity of the church, yet because they were set up and attended by those who sincerely aimed at the glory of God, God acknowledged them as his altars, as well as the one at Jerusalem, and so the breaking down of them is one of the charges brought against Israel and is called an outrageous sin.

3.2.3. *Having slain* (killed) *thy prophets with the sword* (vv. 10, 14), who probably ministered at those altars. Jezebel, a foreigner, killed them (18:4), but the accusation is made against the body of the people because most of them were *consenting to their death* (Ac 8:1), and pleased with it.

3.3. He gives the reasons why he withdrew to the desert and is living in this cave:

3.3.1. It was because he did not think there was any point in appearing publicly: "*I only am left* (vv. 10, 14). What can one do against thousands?"

3.3.2. It was because he could not appear safely: "*They seek my life to take it away* (vv. 10, 14). They are trying to kill me too. It would be better for me to spend my life in useless solitude than to give up my life in fruitless endeavors trying to reform those who hate to be reformed."

4. God's revelation of himself to him. Did he go there to meet God? God will not fail to meet him. Moses was put into the cave when God's glory passed by him, but Elijah was called out of it: *Stand upon the mount before the Lord* (v. 11). He *saw no manner of similitude*, no form of any kind, anymore than Israel did when God *talked to them in Horeb* (Dt 4:15). But:

4.1. He heard a strong wind and saw its terrible effects, for it tore the mountains apart and shattered the rocks.

4.2. He felt the magnitude of an earthquake.

4.3. He saw an outbreak of fire (v. 12). But:

4.4. Finally, he perceived *a still small voice*, a gentle whisper (v. 12), in which *the Lord was*, that is, by which he spoke to him. He did not speak out of the wind, the earthquake, or the fire. Those struck Elijah with awe, but God chose to make known his mind to him in a gentle, soft whisper, not in those terrible noises. When Elijah perceived this:

4.4.1. *He wrapped his face in his mantle*, he pulled his cloak over his face (v. 13), as one afraid to look on the glory of God. Elijah hid his face as a sign of shame for having been such a coward as to run away from his duty when he had such a powerful God to stand by him in it. The wind, earthquake, and fire did not make him cover his face, but the still, quiet voice did. Gracious souls are more affected by the tender mercies of the Lord than by his terrors.

4.4.2. He stood at the entrance of the cave, ready to hear what God had to say to him. In the revelations God formerly made of himself at this place to Moses, the Law was given to Israel. Now Elijah is called on to revive that law, especially the first two commandments, and he is told here how it is to be done. He must not only awaken and terrify the people with wonderful signs, like the earthquake and fire, but he must also try, with a still, small voice, to convince and persuade them. Faith comes by hearing the word of God (Ro 10:17); miracles only make way for it.

5. The orders God gives him to carry out. He repeats the question he put to him before, "*What doest thou here?*" (v. 13). This is not now the place where you should be." Elijah gives the same answer (v. 14), complaining that Israel has rejected God and that religious faith has been destroyed among them. God gives him a reply to this. He sends him back with directions to appoint Hazael to be king of Aram (*Syria*) (v. 15), Jehu to be king of Israel, and Elisha to be his successor in the distinguished office of prophet (v. 16), which is intended as a prediction that through these God would rebuke the corrupt Israelites, plead his own cause among them, and *avenge the quarrel* (breaking) *of his covenant* (Lev 26:25) (v. 17). Elisha will have the *sword of the Spirit* (Eph 6:17) and will terrify and wound the consciences of those who escape Hazael's sword of war and Jehu's sword of justice.

6. The encouraging information God gives him of the number of Israelites who kept their integrity, even though he thought he was all alone (v. 18): *I have left 7,000 in Israel* (besides Judea) *who have not bowed the knee to Baal*. In times of the greatest decadence and apostasy God always has had, and always will have, a remnant who are faithful to him, some who keep their integrity and do not go with the flow. It is God's work to preserve that remnant and to set them apart from the rest, for without his grace they could not have distinguished themselves. God's faithful ones are often his hidden ones, those he cherishes (Ps 83:3), and the visible church is scarcely visible—the wheat is lost in the chaff and the gold in the dross—until the day of sifting, refining, and separating comes. *The Lord knows those that are his* (2Ti 2:19), even though we do not; he sees in secret. There are more good people in the world than some wise and holy people think there are. When we reach heaven, just as we will miss many whom we thought we would meet there, so also we will meet many whom we little thought to find there. God's love often proves wider and more extensive than human love.

Verses 19–21

Elisha was named last in the orders God gave to Elijah, but he was the first to be called, for the other two were to be called by Elisha. He must take Elijah's place, yet Elijah is happy to think that he will leave the work of God in such capable hands. Notice concerning the call of Elisha:

1. That it was a surprising and unexpected call. Elijah found him *in the field*, not reading, praying, or sacrificing, but *ploughing* (v. 19). Although he was a great man, as can be seen from his feast (v. 21)—master of the ground, oxen, and servants—he still did not think it beneath him to put his hand to the plough. An honest calling in the world does not exclude us from our heavenly calling, anymore than it did Elisha, who was taken from following the plow to feed Israel and to sow the *seed of the word* (Lk 8:11), just as the apostles were taken from fishing to catch people.

2. That it was a powerful call. For now, Elijah only *cast his mantle upon him*, only threw his cloak around him (v. 19) as a sign: a sign of friendship, a sign that he would take him under his care and teaching just as he took him under his mantle. Or perhaps it was a sign of Elisha's being clothed with the spirit of Elijah—Elijah was putting some of his honor and authority on him, as Moses did on Joshua (Nu 27:20). Later, however, when Elijah went to heaven, the cloak became Elisha's own (2Ki 2:13). Immediately he *left the oxen* to go their own way, and he *ran after Elijah*. An invisible hand touched his heart and inexplicably inclined him by a secret power, without any external persuasion, to give up his farming and give himself to the ministry. Elisha came to a decision immediately, but asked for a little time, not to *ask* leave, but only to *take* leave, of his parents. Elijah told him to go back and do it; he would not force him or take him against his will. Let him sit down, count the cost, and make following God's call his own decision. The effectiveness of God's grace preserves the inborn freedom of the human will, so that those who are good are good by choice and not by constraint; they are not conscripts but volunteers.

3. That it was a pleasant and acceptable call. This can be seen from the farewell feast he held for his family (v. 21). It was a discouraging time for prophets to set out in. If he had consulted other people, he would not have been fond of Elijah's cloak, or willing to wear his coat, but Elisha cheerfully, and with a great deal of satisfaction, leaves all to go with him.

4. That it was an effective call. Elijah did not wait for him, so that he would not seem to compel him, and Elisha soon got up and went after him. He not only associated with him but also *ministered to him* as his attendant, *poured water on his hands* (2Ki 3:11). Those who want to teach must first make time to learn. Those who hope to rise and rule later must first be willing to stoop and serve.

CHAPTER 20

This chapter records the history of a war between Ben-Hadad king of Aram (Syria) and Ahab king of Israel, in which Ahab was victorious. We read nothing about Elijah or Elisha in this story. Jezebel's rage had probably died down, and the persecution of the prophets had begun to cool off, and Elijah did not want to jeopardize this fragile peace. He did not appear at court but, being told how many more thousands of good people there were in Israel than he thought, probably employed himself in founding schools of prophets in different parts of the country. These institutions could then nurture religious faith and thereby help reform the nation, since the throne and court would not be reformed. While Elijah was occupied with such tasks, God favored the nation with the successes we read about here, which were the more significant because they were gained against Ben-Hadad king of Aram, whose successor, Hazael, was ordained to be a scourge to Israel. Israel must soon suffer at the hands of the Arameans (Syrians), but now Israel triumphed over them, so that they might possibly be led to repentance by the goodness of God. Here is: 1. Ben-Hadad's attack on Israel, and his arrogant demand (vv. 1–11). 2. The defeat of Ben-Hadad by Ahab, encouraged and directed by a prophet (vv. 12–21). 3. The Arameans rallying again, and their second defeat by Ahab (vv. 22–30). 4. The peace treaty Ahab made with Ben-Hadad when he had him at his mercy (vv. 31–34), for which he is rebuked and threatened by a prophet (vv. 35–43).

Verses 1–11

Here is:

1. The threatening approach of Ben-Hadad toward Ahab's kingdom, and the siege he laid to Samaria, his royal city (v. 1). David in his time had completely subdued the Arameans (*Syrians*) and made them subject to Israel, but now they became formidable again because Israel had turned away from God. Asa had tempted the Arameans to invade Israel once (15:18–20), and now they did it of their own accord. It is dangerous to bring a foreign force into a country: future generations may pay dearly for it.

2. The treaty between these two kings.

2.1. Ben-Hadad's proud spirit sends Ahab a very arrogant demand (vv. 2–3). A conference is called to let Ahab know that Ben-Hadad will lift the siege on the condition that Ahab becomes his vassal and not only pays him a tax but also transfers all he has to Ben-Hadad, even his wives and children.

2.2. Ahab's low spirit sends Ben-Hadad a very disgraceful submission. *I am thine, and all that I have* (v. 4). Notice the effects of sin:

2.2.1. If Ahab had not by his sin provoked God to depart from him, Ben-Hadad could not have made such a demand. If we refuse to be ruled by God, we will be ruled by our enemies. A rebel toward God is a slave to all.

2.2.2. If he had not by sin wronged his own conscience and set that against him, he could not have made such a lowly surrender. Guilt discourages people and makes them cowards.

2.3. Ben-Hadad's proud spirit rises upon receiving Ahab's submission, and becomes even more arrogant, defiant, and imperious (vv. 5–6).

2.3.1. Ben-Hadad is as covetous as he is proud, and cannot go away unless he has actual possession as well as control.

2.3.2. He is as spiteful as he is haughty. If he himself had come to choose what he wanted, it would have shown some respect to a crowned head, but he sends his servants to insult the prince: *Whatsoever is pleasant in thy eyes they shall take away* (v. 6).

2.3.3. He is as unreasonable as he is unjust, and will interpret the surrender Ahab made for himself as made by all his subjects too.

2.4. Ahab's low spirit begins to rise too, at this growing arrogance, and if it does not become bold, nevertheless it becomes desperate, and he would rather risk his life than give up all he has.

2.4.1 He now takes advice from his privy council, which encourages him to stand his ground.

2.4.2. But he expresses himself very modestly in his denial (v. 9).

2.5. Ben-Hadad proudly swears the ruin of Samaria.

2.6. Ahab sends him a good enough rebuke to his assurance; he dare not defy his threats, but only reminds him of the uncertain events of war (v. 11).

Verses 12–21

After the treaty between the besiegers and the besieged has been abruptly broken off, we read an account of the battle that followed:

1. The Arameans, the besiegers, received their directions from a king who was drunk, who gave orders as he was *drinking* (v. 12), *drinking himself drunk* (v. 16) *with the kings in the pavilions* (tents)—and in the middle of the day, at that. If he had not felt secure, he would not have sat down to drink, and if he had not been drunk, he would not have felt so secure. Security and physical pleasure went together in the old world, as they did in Sodom (Lk

17:26–29). Ben-Hadad's drunkenness came before his fall, as Belshazzar's did (Da 5:1–31). In his drinking:

1.1. He orders that the city be besieged.

1.2. When the besieged launched an attack, he gave orders to take them alive (v. 18): not to kill them, which might have been done more easily and safely, but to seize them, which gave them an opportunity to kill the aggressors.

2. The Israelites, the besieged, received their directions from an inspired prophet, one of the prophets of the Lord, whom Ahab had hated and persecuted.

2.1. Look in wonder that God should send a prophet with a kind and gracious message to such an evil king as Ahab, but he did it:

2.1.1. For his people Israel's sake.

2.1.2. So that he might exalt his mercy, by doing good to a king who was so evil and unthankful, and thereby either bringing him to repentance or leaving him in a more inexcusable position.

2.1.3. So that he might mortify the pride of Ben-Hadad and restrain his defiance. He did not ask for a prophet of the Lord, but God sent one to him unasked, for he *waits* (longs) *to be gracious* (Isa 30:18).

2.2. The prophet does two things:

2.2.1. He encourages Ahab with an assurance of victory, which is more than all the elders of Israel can give him (v. 8), although they have promised to stand by him. He is told how he should make the best of this fortunate change in events: "*Thou shalt know that I am Jehovah* (v. 13), the sovereign Lord of all."

2.2.2. He instructs him what to do to gain this victory:

2.2.2.1. He must not wait for the enemy to attack him but must attack them first and surprise them in their trenches.

2.2.2.2. The people he uses must be the *young men of the princes of the provinces*, the young officers of the provincial commanders (v. 14), who were few in number, only 232, completely unfamiliar with warfare, and the most unlikely soldiers you could think of for such a bold attempt.

2.2.2.3. Ahab must himself show how great is his confidence in the word of God by taking command in person, although from the point of view of reason, in so doing he was exposing himself to the greatest danger. But:

2.2.2.4. He is allowed to make use of whatever other forces he has available, to follow up the attack when these young officers have begun the work. All he had in Samaria, or within call, were only 7,000 men (v. 15). It is significant that this is the same number as those who had not *bowed the knee to Baal* (19:18), although they were probably not the same people.

3. What happened was the following: the proud Arameans were beaten, and the poor, despised Israelites were more than conquerors. Notice how God *cuts off* (breaks) *the spirit of princes* (rulers) and makes himself *terrible to the kings of the earth* (Ps 76:12). Now where are the silver and gold he demanded from Ahab? Where are the handfuls of Samaria's dust?

Verses 22–30

Here is an account of another successful campaign which Ahab, with God's help, made against the Arameans, in which he defeated them even more soundly than he had before. How strange this is! Ahab is idolatrous but victorious, a persecutor but still a conqueror! God has wise and holy purposes in allowing evil people to succeed.

1. Ahab is advised by a prophet to prepare for another war (v. 22). The prophet told him they would renew

their attempt the next spring, hoping to regain the honor they had lost and to take revenge for the defeat they had received. He therefore told him to strengthen himself. We should always expect attacks from our spiritual enemies and should therefore keep watch over what we do.

2. Ben-Hadad is advised by those around him about the operations of the next campaign:

2.1. They advised Ben-Hadad to change his battlefield (v. 23). They assumed that it was not Israel, but Israel's gods, that had beaten them, but they spoke very ignorantly about the Lord—as *many*, whereas he is one and his name is one—as only *their* God, a local deity, exclusive to that nation, whereas he is the Creator and ruler of all the world.

2.2. They advised Ben-Hadad to change his officers (vv. 24–25), not to use the kings, who were commanders by birth, but replace them with officers, who were commanders by merit, who were used to war.

3. Both armies take to the field. Ben-Hadad, with his Arameans, pitches camp near Aphek, in the tribe of Asher. Ahab, with his forces, positioned himself some distance away opposite them (v. 27). The disproportion in their numbers was very remarkable. *The children of Israel*, who were divided in two battalions, looked like *two little flocks of kids* (goats): their numbers were small, their equipment was poor, and they looked contemptible; *but the Syrians filled the country* with their numbers, their noise, their chariots, their goods, and their equipment.

4. Ahab is encouraged to fight the Arameans, despite their advantages and confidence. A man of God is sent to him to tell him that this numerous army will *all be delivered into his hand* (v. 28), but not for his sake. He must know that the person for whom God will do this is completely unworthy.

5. After the armies had faced one another seven days, the battle began, and the Arameans were totally defeated. When Ben-Hadad, who thought his city Aphek would hold out against the conquerors, found it unfortified, and saw that the remnant of his forces were discouraged and scattered, he had nothing but concealment to rely on for safety, and so he hid himself in an inner room, "a chamber within a chamber" (v. 30, margin), so that the pursuers could not capture him. Notice how the greatest confidence often ends in the greatest cowardice.

Verses 31–43

Here is an account of what followed on from the victory which Israel gained over the Arameans:

1. Ben-Hadad's weak and pitiful submission. His servants, realizing they were all at the end of their resources, advise that they should surrender themselves unconditionally, make themselves prisoners, and ask Ahab to spare their lives (v. 31). The servants take their lives in their hands and venture out first. They have heard that the God of Israel declared his name as *gracious and merciful*, and they conclude that its kings will be like its God. This is the encouragement poor sinners should act on as they repent and humble themselves before God. "Have we not heard that the God of Israel is a merciful God? Have we not found him to be like that? Let us therefore return to him, and let our hearts be broken" (Joel 2:13). That is the repentance of the Gospel which flows from knowing the mercy of God in Christ; *there is forgiveness with him* (Ps 130:4). Ben-Hadad's servants undertake to present two things to Ahab:

1.1. Their master coming in repentance, for they *girded sackcloth on their loins* (waists) as mourners, and

put ropes on (around) *their heads* (v. 31) as condemned criminals going to be executed. There are many who pretend to repent of their wrongdoing when their wrongs do not succeed, but who would have justified it and gloried in it if they had prospered in it.

1.2. Their master coming as a beggar, begging for his life: *Thy servant Ben-hadad saith, I pray thee, let me live* (v. 32). Notice what a great change there is:

1.2.1. In his condition. He has fallen from the heights of power and prosperity to the depths of disgrace and distress.

1.2.2. In his attitude. At the beginning of the chapter we saw him bullying, swearing, threatening, and no one making higher demands than he, but here we see him crouching and whining, and no one making lower requests than he!

2. Ahab's foolish acceptance of his submission, and the treaty he suddenly made with him on that basis. He was proud to have been courted in this way by the one whom he had feared: *Is he yet alive? He is my brother* (v. 32), brother king, not brother-Israelite, and Ahab valued himself more on his royalty than on his religion. "*Is he thy brother, Ahab?* Did he treat you as a brother when he sent you that cruel message? (vv. 5–6). Would he have called you brother if he had won? Would he now have called himself *thy servant* if he had not been reduced to the most dire difficulties? Can you allow yourself to be deceived by such a false and forced submission?" Ben-Hadad, in his submission, will not only be transported honorably—he *took him up into the chariot* (v. 33)—but also be treated as an ally (v. 34): he *made a covenant with him*, not consulting God's prophets or the elders of the land. Ahab could now have demanded some of Ben-Hadad's cities, but he was content with the restoration of his own. He could now have demanded the stores, treasures, and arsenals of Damascus, but was content with a poor return, to have a Jewish quarter there where at his own expense he could build streets. He sent Ben-Hadad away with this covenant, without so much as a rebuke for his blasphemous actions toward the God of Israel, for whose honor Ahab had no concern.

3. The rebuke given to Ahab for his mercy to Ben-Hadad and his covenant with him. It was given him by a prophet, in the name of the Lord, the Jews say by Micaiah, which is not unlikely, because Ahab complains about him (22:8) that he used to *prophesy evil concerning him*. This prophet wanted to rebuke Ahab with a parable. To make his parable the more plausible, he found it necessary to put himself into the position of a wounded soldier:

3.1. With some difficulty he gets himself wounded, for he will not wound himself with his own hands. He commands one of his brother prophets, in God's name, to strike him (v. 35), but does not find the other as willing to give the blow as he is to receive it. We can only think that he declined it from a good motive. Good people can much more easily receive a wrongful attack than give one. Yet because he disobeyed a clear command of God—which was even worse if he himself was a prophet—therefore, like that other disobedient prophet (13:24), he was immediately *slain* (killed) *by a lion* (v. 36). This was intended also to show Ahab that if a good prophet was punished in this way for sparing his friend and God's when God said, *Smite*, an evil king would be worthy of a more severe punishment if he spared his enemy and God's when God said, *Smite*. The next man the prophet met with had no difficulty in striking him, and did it so that he *wounded him* (v. 37). He brought out blood with the blow, probably on his face.

3.2. Wounded as he was, and disguised with *ashes* (or with a headband) so that he would not be recognized as a prophet, he made his appeal to the king in a story in which he accused himself of the same crime as the king was now guilty of in sparing Ben-Hadad, and waited for the king's judgment on it. In short, the case is this: a prisoner taken in the battle was committed into his custody by a man with the command, *If he be missing, thy life shall be for his life* (v. 39). In the parable the prisoner has escaped through the guard's carelessness. Can the justice of the king spare him the judgment of his officer, who demands his life instead of the prisoner's? "By no means," the king says, "you should either not have undertaken the trust or have been more careful and faithful in fulfilling it; there is no way out; you have gone back on your word, and execution must be carried out: *So shall thy judgment be, thou thyself hast decided it*" (v. 40). Now the prophet has the result he wants, and so he takes off his disguise and, recognized by Ahab himself to be a prophet (v. 41), clearly tells him, "*Thou art the man.* You are being judged by the words of your own mouth. God handed into your hands one clearly marked for destruction both by his own pride and God's providence, and you have knowingly and deliberately dismissed him, and so you have been false to your trust."

3.3. We are told how Ahab resented this rebuke. He *went to his house heavy and displeased*, sullen and angry (v. 43), angry with the prophet, infuriated with God and also angry with himself.

CHAPTER 21

Ahab is still the unhappy subject of the sacred history. We move from the great affairs of his camp and kingdom to his garden. This chapter gives us an account of some things that went wrong in his domestic life. 1. Ahab is desperate to own Naboth's vineyard (vv. 1–4). 2. Naboth dies by Jezebel's plot so that the vineyard may pass to Ahab (vv. 5–14). Ahab goes to take possession of it (vv. 15–16). 3. Elijah meets him and declares the judgments of God against him for what he has unjustly done (vv. 17–24). When he humbles himself, a reprieve is granted (vv. 25–29).

Verses 1–4

Here is:

1. Ahab coveting his neighbor's vineyard, which unfortunately lay near his palace and was convenient for taking as a vegetable garden. Ahab sets his eye and his heart on this vineyard (v. 2). It will be an attractive addition to his lands. There is nothing else to do; he has to have it. Yet he is not such a tyrant that he will take it by force. He fairly suggests giving Naboth either its full value in money or a better vineyard in exchange for it. To desire property that was conveniently near his estate was not wrong, but to desire anything excessively is a fruit of selfishness.

2. The rebuff he met with in this desire. Naboth did not want to part with it at all (v. 3): *The Lord forbid it me.* Canaan was God's land in a special way; the Israelites were his tenants; and it was one of the conditions of their leases that they should not transfer any part of what came into their allotted land except in cases of extreme necessity, and then only until the Year of Jubilee (Lev 25:28). Now Naboth foresaw that if his vineyard was sold to the crown, it would never revert to his heirs, not even in the Year of Jubilee. He would gladly please the king, but he must obey God rather than people, and so he wanted to

be excused in this matter. Some think that Naboth looked on his earthly inheritance as a pledge of his inheritance in the heavenly Canaan, and that he refused to part with the former in order to avoid forfeiting his right to the latter.

3. Ahab's great discontent and disquiet as a result of Naboth's refusal. He was, as before (20:43), *heavy and displeased*, sullen and angry (v. 4); he became morose, threw himself on his bed in a sulk, and would not eat or allow others to come to him. He cursed the scrupulousness of Naboth's conscience. Nor could he bear the disappointment. It cut him to the heart to be thwarted in his wishes, and he became perfectly sick from vexation. He had all the delights of the pleasant land of Canaan at his command—the wealth of a kingdom, the pleasures of a court, and the honors and powers of a throne—but all this is not enough for him without Naboth's vineyard.

Verses 5–16

Nothing but trouble is to be expected when Jezebel, that *cursed woman* (2Ki 9:34), enters the story.

1. Pretending to comfort her afflicted husband, she feeds his pride and passion, and fans the fires of his corruption. He told her what troubled him (v. 6), but unfairly concealed Naboth's reason for his refusal, representing the refusal as obstinate when it was actually conscientious—telling her Naboth had said, *I will not give it thee*, whereas he had said, *I may not.* "What!" Jezebel said (v. 7). "*Dost thou govern Israel?* Is this how you act as king over Israel? *Arise, and eat bread.* Will any subject of yours deny you anything you want? If you do not know how to act according to the position of a king, then leave it to me to do. Just let me use your name, and I will soon *give thee the vineyard of Naboth* (v. 7). Rightly or wrongly, it will soon be yours, and see, it will have cost you nothing."

2. In order to please him, she plans and plots the death of Naboth.

2.1. If she had aimed only at getting his land, her false witnesses might have sworn him out of that by a forged deed, but Naboth must die.

2.1.1. Never were more evil orders given by any ruler than those which Jezebel sent to the judges of Jezreel (vv. 8–10). She borrowed the king's seal, although he knew nothing about what she was doing; and she used the king's name. Supported by these, she commanded the judges to show their loyalty by putting Naboth to death. She must have looked on the elders of Jezreel as those who were dead to everything honest and honorable, if she expected these orders to be obeyed.

2.1.1.1. It must be done in the name of religion: "*Proclaim a fast* (v. 9). Pretend to be afraid that there is some great offender among you who is undiscovered, for whose sake God is angry with your city. Eventually, let Naboth be singled out as the suspect." She probably chose him because he did not join with his neighbors in their worship.

2.1.1.2. It must be done in the name of justice, too, and with the formalities of a legal process. The crime they must charge him with was *blaspheming* (cursing) *God and the king* (v. 10)—a complex blasphemy.

2.1.2. Never were evil orders more corruptly obeyed than these were by the judges of Jezreel. They did *as it was written in the letters* (vv. 11–12). They did not see, or encounter, any difficulties in it, but scrupulously carried out the wicked act. They stoned Naboth to death (v. 13), and, it seems, his sons with him, or after him.

2.2. Let us pause and think about this sad story:

2.2.1. To be stunned by the evil of evildoers and by the power of Satan in the children of disobedience.

2.2.2. To mourn the hard case of oppressed innocence.

2.2.3. To commit the keeping of our lives and comforts to God, for innocence itself will not always be our security.

2.2.4. To be joyful in the belief in a judgment to come, in which such wrong judgments will be put right.

3. After Naboth has been removed, Ahab takes possession of his vineyard:

3.1. The elders of Jezreel sent notice to Jezebel without any remorse; they sent it to her as a piece of good news: *Naboth is stoned and is dead* (v. 14).

3.2. Jezebel is happy that her plot has succeeded so well and brings news to Ahab that *Naboth is not alive, but dead*. She therefore says, *Arise, take possession of his vineyard* (v. 15). He might have taken possession of it through one of his officers, but he is so pleased with this accession to Naboth's estate that he will make a special journey to Jezreel himself to receive it. It seems he came on a state visit too, as if he had won a mighty victory, for Jehu remembers long afterward that he and Bidkar accompanied Ahab at this time (2Ki 9:25).

Verses 17–29

In these verses we may notice:

1. The very unfavorable characterization of Ahab (vv. 25–26), which is included here to justify God in the harsh sentence passed on him, and to show that although it was passed on the occasion of his sin in the incident involving Naboth, God still would not have punished him so severely if he had not been guilty of many other sins, especially idolatry. He was wholly given over to sin and to its pleasures. He would take its wages, which is death (Ro 6:23). It did not excuse his crimes that *Jezebel his wife stirred him up*, that she urged him to act in such an evil way (v. 25), and that she made him, in many respects, worse than he would have been otherwise.

2. The message with which Elijah was sent to him when he went to take possession of Naboth's vineyard (vv. 17–19).

2.1. Up to that time God had kept silent; but now Ahab is rebuked and his sin set in order *before his eyes* (Ps 36:1).

2.1.1. The person sent is Elijah.

2.1.2. The place is Naboth's vineyard, and the time is just as he is taking possession of it. Then, and there, must his condemnation be read him. Now that he is pleasing himself with his ill-gotten wealth and giving directions for turning this vineyard into a vegetable garden, his food will turn sour in his stomach, for *God shall cast the fury of his wrath upon him* (Job 20:14, 20, 23).

2.2. Let us see what took place between him and the prophet:

2.2.1. Ahab expressed his wrath against Elijah, lost his temper when he saw him, and instead of humbling himself before the prophet, as he should have done (2Ch 36:12), was ready to attack him. *Hast thou found me, O my enemy?* (v. 20). This shows:

2.2.1.1. That he hated him. The last time we found them together they parted as good friends (18:46). At that time Ahab had supported the reformation, and so all was well between them, but now he had gone back to his old, sinful ways, and was worse than ever. His conscience told him he had made God his enemy, and so he could not expect Elijah to be his friend.

2.2.1.2. That he feared him: *Hast thou found me?* (v. 20). Never was a poor debtor or criminal so confounded at the sight of the officer who came to arrest him.

2.2.2. Elijah declared God's wrath against Ahab: *I have found thee, because thou hast sold thyself to work evil* (v. 20).

2.2.2.1. Elijah raises the accusation against him and convicts him on the clear and terrible evidence of the facts (v. 19): *Hast thou killed, and also taken possession?*

2.2.2.2. He passes judgment on him. He told him from God that his family would be destroyed and uprooted (v. 21) and all his descendants cut off. "*Thy blood, even thine*—even though it is royal blood, although it swells your veins with pride and boils in your heart with anger—will before long be entertainment for the dogs"; this prophecy was fulfilled in 22:38.

3. Ahab's humiliation at the sentence passed on him, and the favorable message then sent to him.

3.1. Ahab repented to some extent. The message Elijah communicated to him in God's name put him into a state of shock for the present, so that he *rent* (tore) *his clothes* and *put on sackcloth* (v. 27). Ahab put on the clothes of someone repenting, but his heart was not humbled or changed.

3.2. He then obtained a reprieve, which we may call a kind of pardon. Although it was only an external repentance—in that he mourned only the punishment, not the sin—although he did not leave his idols and did not restore the vineyard to Naboth's heirs, yet because he did give some glory to God, God took notice of it and he told Elijah to take notice of it, too: *Seest thou how Ahab humbles himself?* (v. 29). This teaches us to take notice of what is good even in those who are not so good as they should be: let the goodness be commended as far as it goes.

3.3. This gives a reason why evildoers sometimes succeed for a long time; God is rewarding their external service with external mercies. This encourages all those who truly repent and genuinely believe the holy Gospel. If a sinner who has only partially repented, and only pretended to repent, goes back home with a reprieve, there is no doubt that someone who sincerely repents will *go to his house justified* (Lk 18:14).

CHAPTER 22

It was promised at the end of the previous chapter that the overthrow of Ahab's house would not come in his days, but his days soon came to an end. We read an account of his war with the Arameans (Syrians) at Ramoth Gilead in this chapter: 1. His preparations for that war: he consulted his privy council (vv. 1–3), Jehoshaphat (v. 4), and his prophets. He consulted his own prophets, who encouraged him to go on this expedition (vv. 5–6), particularly Zedekiah (vv. 11–12); and he consulted a prophet of the Lord, Micaiah, whom Jehoshaphat wanted to come (vv. 7–8), and who was therefore brought to them (vv. 9–14). 2. Micaiah rebuked Ahab for his confidence in the false prophets (v. 15), foretold that he would fall in this expedition (vv. 16–18), and gave him an account of how he came to be deceived by his prophets (vv. 19–23). Micaiah was abused by Zedekiah (vv. 24–25) and imprisoned by Ahab (vv. 26–28). 2. The battle itself, in which Jehoshaphat was exposed but Ahab was killed (vv. 29–40). 3. At the close of the chapter we have a short account of the good reign of Jehoshaphat king of Judah (vv. 41–50) and of the evil reign of Ahaziah king of Israel (vv. 51–53).

Verses 1–14

Here we see that as a reward for Ahab's profession of repentance and humiliation—although the time is drawing near when he will fall in battle and die—he is blessed with three years' peace (v. 1), and an honorable visit is made to him by Jehoshaphat king of Judah (v. 2). The Jews have a legend that when Ahab humbled himself for his sin and lay in sackcloth, he sent for Jehoshaphat to come to him to rebuke him, and Jehoshaphat is said to have stayed with him for some time and to have given him a certain number of lashes with a scourge every day. This is a tradition without basis. Jehoshaphat probably came now to consult him about the affairs of their kingdoms. The Arameans (*Syrians*) dared not disturb Ahab in any way, but:

1. Ahab here contemplates a war against the Arameans and discusses it with those around him (v. 3). The king of Aram (*Syria*) had given him the provocation; when he lay at Ahab's mercy, he had promised to return his cities to him (20:34), and Ahab foolishly took him at his word. Ben-Hadad was one of those rulers who think they are no longer bound by their word when it is no longer in their interests to keep it. We do not know whether any other cities were returned, but Ramoth Gilead was not. It was a significant city in the tribe of Gad, on the other side of the Jordan, a Levite city, and one of the cities of refuge. Ahab blamed himself and his people for not making any move to regain it from the hands of the Arameans and rebuke Ben-Hadad's breach of their treaty.

2. Ahab engages Jehoshaphat, and draws him in to join with him in this expedition to retake Ramoth Gilead (v. 4). It is strange that Jehoshaphat goes over to Ahab's side so completely as to say, *I am as thou art, and my people as thy people* (v. 4). I hope that was not really so; Jehoshaphat and his people were not so evil and corrupt as Ahab and his people. Too much deference to evildoers has caught many good people unawares and led them into dangerous fellowship with *the unfruitful works of darkness* (Eph 5:11). Jehoshaphat came near to paying too dearly for his compliment when, in battle, he was thought to be Ahab. But some commentators notice that in joining with Israel against Aram he made up for his father's wrong in joining with Aram against Israel (15:19–20).

3. At the special urging and request of Jehoshaphat, Ahab asks for guidance from the prophets about this expedition. Ahab thought it enough to consult with his political advisers, but Jehoshaphat suggests they should *inquire of the word of the Lord* (v. 5). We can learn from this that wherever good people go, they should take their religious faith along with them, and not be ashamed to acknowledge it, not even when they are with those who are not inclined that way.

4. Ahab's 400 prophets—they called them *prophets of the groves* (Asherah) (18:19)—agreed to encourage him in this expedition and to assure him of success (v. 6). He put the question to them: *Shall I go or shall I forbear* (not go)? But they knew which way he was inclined to follow and wanted only to humor the two kings. To please Jehoshaphat, they made use of the name of God: *the LORD* (the older name sometimes used is Jehovah) *shall deliver it into the hand of the king* (v. 6). To please Ahab they said, *Go up* (v. 6). "You will certainly retake Ramoth Gilead." Zedekiah, a leading man among these prophets, illustrated his false prophecy with a sign (v. 11). He made himself a pair of iron horns, representing the two kings, with their honor and power—for both exaltation and force were represented by horns—and with these the Arameans would

without doubt be *pushed* or driven back (v. 11). All the prophets agreed, as one, that Ahab would return from this expedition as conqueror (v. 12).

5. Jehoshaphat cannot take delight in this sort of preaching; it is not what he is used to. The false prophets cannot mimic the truth so well that their fallacy will not be discerned by one who has his spiritual senses, and so he asks for *a prophet of the Lord besides* (v. 7).

6. Ahab has another prophet, but one he hates, Micaiah by name, a true prophet, and one who knew God's mind. But:

6.1. He hated him and was not ashamed to acknowledge to the king of Judah that he did. He gave this as a reason: he *doth not prophesy good concerning me, but evil* (v. 8). And whose fault was that? If Ahab had done well, he would have heard nothing but good from heaven. Those who hate God's ministers because they speak plainly to them are miserably hardened in sin and quickly heading for destruction.

6.2. He had imprisoned him. We suppose that this prophet was the one who rebuked him for his mercy to Ben-Hadad (20:38–43) and that for doing so he had been thrown into prison, where he had been for three years. This was why Ahab knew where to find him so quickly (v. 9). The prophet was bound, but *the word of the Lord was not bound* (2Ti 2:9). Jehoshaphat gave too gentle a rebuke to Ahab for expressing his indignation against a faithful prophet: *Let not the king say* so (v. 8). Sinners like Ahab must be rebuked sharply. However, he submitted to the rebuke to the extent that for fear of provoking Jehoshaphat to break off from his alliance with him, he ordered Micaiah to be sent for as quickly as possible (v. 9). Each of the two kings sat in his robes and on a throne at the entrance to the gate of Samaria, ready to receive this poor prophet and hear what he had to say. They were accompanied by a crowd of flattering prophets, who could not think of prophesying anything except what was sweet and smooth to two such glorious rulers, who were now in league with each other.

7. Micaiah is pressed by the officer who brings him to say what Ahab's false prophets said (v. 13). But Micaiah, who knows better, protests, and he backs up his protest with an oath, that he will faithfully communicate his message from God whether it is pleasing or displeasing to his ruler (v. 14): *What the Lord saith to me, that will I speak.*

Verses 15–28

Here Micaiah does well, but, as is usual, suffers wrong for doing so:

1. We are told how he faithfully communicated his message. He communicated his message in three ways, all of which displeased Ahab:

1.1. He spoke as the rest of the prophets had spoken, but ironically: *Go, and prosper* (v. 15). Ahab put the same question to him that he had put to his own prophets, seemingly wanting to know God's mind, when, like Balaam, he was strongly intent on doing as he wanted. In his answer Micaiah clearly showed that he recognized this; he told Ahab to go, but he spoke mockingly. It was as if he had said, "So go then, and accept what happens." In answer to this, Ahab made him swear to tell him the truth, and not to joke around with him (v. 16).

1.2. Being pressed in this way, he plainly foretold that the king would die in this expedition, and that his army would be scattered (v. 17). He saw them in a vision, dispersed on the mountains, as sheep with no one to guide them. This shows:

1.2.1. That Israel would be deprived of its king, who was its shepherd.

1.2.2. That they would make a dishonorable retreat. Yet *Let them return every man to his house in peace* (v. 17), no great losers by the death of their king. Micaiah testified in his prophecy what he had seen and heard. Now Ahab is offended; he turns to Jehoshaphat and appeals to him to judge whether Micaiah has not clearly shown that he has a grudge against him (v. 18).

1.3. He informed the king how it was that all his prophets encouraged him to proceed: that God had allowed Satan through them to deceive him into his destruction, and he, Micaiah, knew it by a vision. God is a great King above all kings and has a throne above all the thrones of earthly rulers. The rise and fall of rulers, the outcomes of war, and all the great affairs of state, which are the subject of discussions of great and wise people, are no more above God's direction than the lowliest concerns of people who live in the poorest cottages are beneath his notice. It is not without divine permission that the Devil deceives people; even there God serves his own purposes. Micaiah gave Ahab a fair warning, not only of the danger of proceeding in this war, but also of the danger of believing those who had encouraged him to proceed.

2. We are told how he was abused for communicating his message so faithfully.

2.1. Zedekiah, an evil prophet, arrogantly insulted him at this royal court, *smote* (slapped) *him on the cheek* (v. 24) to silence him. To strike a person within the precincts of the court, especially in the king's presence, is looked on by our law as a grave misdemeanor, but this evil prophet abuses a prophet of the Lord. Although Micaiah does not return Zedekiah's blow, he leaves him to be convinced of his error by the outcome of events. *Thou shalt know when thou hidest thyself in an inner chamber* (v. 25). It is likely that Zedekiah went with Ahab to the battle and took his horns of iron with him, to encourage the soldiers, to enjoy the pleasure of seeing his prophecy fulfilled, and to return in triumph with the king; but when the army was defeated, he fled among the rest from the sword of the enemy and sheltered himself, as Ben-Hadad had, in *an inner chamber* (20:30), so that he would not die.

2.2. Ahab, that evil king, committed Micaiah to prison (v. 27), to be fed with bread and water, rough bread and puddle water, until Ahab returned, not doubting that he would return as conqueror, and then he would put him to death for being a false prophet (v. 27). This is harsh treatment for one who wanted to prevent Ahab's downfall! Micaiah brought matters to a decisive point and called all the people to witness that he did so: *"If thou return in peace, the Lord has not spoken by me* (v. 28). May I bear the disgrace and punishment of a false prophet, if the king comes home alive."

Verses 29 – 40

The contest between God's prophet and Ahab's prophets is soon decided, and it is clear who is in the right. Here:

1. The two kings march with their forces to Ramoth Gilead (v. 29). It is amazing that Jehoshaphat, that godly ruler who had wanted to inquire by *a prophet of the Lord* (v. 7) because he did not believe Ahab's prophets, would still proceed after such a strong warning. But because of his easygoing nature, he was carried away with the delusion of his friends. He gave too much attention to Ahab's prophets, because he thought the odds were 400 to one that they would succeed.

2. Ahab adopts an ingenious plan which he hopes will keep him safe and expose his friend (v. 30): *"I will disguise myself,* and go in the clothes of a common soldier, but let *Jehoshaphat put on his robes,* to appear in the clothes of a general." He pretended to honor Jehoshaphat by doing this, but he really intended:

2.1. To make a liar out of a good prophet. He hoped in this way to avoid the danger.

2.2. To make a fool out of a good king, whom he did not sincerely love. How could it be expected that he would be true to his friend when he had been false to his God?

3. Jehoshaphat, having more godliness than discernment, put himself into a position of honor, even though it was a position of danger, and so put his life at risk, but God graciously rescued him. The king of Aram ordered his captains to direct their force not against the king of Judah — for he had no quarrel with him — but only against the king of Israel (v. 31). Some think that Ben-Hadad only wanted to have Ahab taken prisoner. Whatever the reason, when the officers saw Jehoshaphat in his royal robes, they thought he was the king of Israel and surrounded him.

3.1. In this danger, God let him know that he was displeased with him for joining in alliance with Ahab.

3.2. In his rescue, God let him know that although he was displeased with him, he still had not deserted him. Some of the commanders who knew him noticed their mistake and so stopped pursuing him.

4. Ahab receives his mortal wound in the battle. Let no one think they can hide from God's judgment. The Aramean who shot him *drew a bow at a venture,* at random (v. 34), not aiming at anyone in particular, but God so directed the arrow that:

4.1. He hit the right person.

4.2. He hit him in the right place, *between the joints of the harness,* between the sections of his armor (v. 34), the only place on him where this fatal arrow could enter.

5. The army is scattered by the enemy and sent home by the king. Ahab himself lived long enough to see that part of Micaiah's prophecy fulfilled that foretold that all Israel would be *scattered upon the hills* of Gilead (v. 17).

6. Ahab's dead body is brought to Samaria and buried there (v. 37). Now Naboth's blood was avenged (21:19), and that word of David which he wrote in Ps 68:23 was fulfilled: *That thy foot may be dipped in the blood of thy enemies, and the tongue of thy dogs in the same.*

7. The story of Ahab concludes in the usual form (vv. 39 – 40). Among other facts, an *ivory house* is mentioned, so called because many parts of it were inlaid with ivory. Perhaps it was intended to rival the stately palace of the kings of Judah, which Solomon built.

Verses 41 – 53

Here is:

1. A short account of the reign of Jehoshaphat king of Judah — of which we have a much fuller record in 2 Chronicles — and of the greatness and goodness of that ruler, neither of which was spoiled by anything except his association with the house of Ahab. We have already found that his alliance with Ahab in war was a danger to him, and his alliance with Ahaziah his son in business met no better success. He offered to be a partner with Ahaziah in a fleet of merchant ships, which would take gold from Ophir. But while they were preparing to set sail, they were wrecked by a storm, *broken at Ezion-geber* (v. 48). When Ahaziah asked to be a partner with him a second time, *Jehoshaphat would not* (v. 49). The rod of God's discipline, as explained by the word of God, had powerfully broken him away from his alliance with that ungodly, unhappy ruler. Jehoshaphat's reign appears here not to have been the longest, but one of the best.

1.1. It was not the longest, because he reigned only twenty-five years (v. 42), but these twenty-five, added to his father's favorable forty-one years, give us a pleasant idea of the flourishing condition of the kingdom of Judah and of religious faith in it.

1.2. But it was one of the best, as regards both godliness and prosperity:

1.2.1. He did well: he *did that which was right in the eyes of the Lord* (v. 43). However, the *high places were not taken away* (v. 43 — no, not even out of Judah and Benjamin, although those tribes lay so near Jerusalem that the people could not pretend, like some of the other tribes, that temple worship was inconvenient because they were far away.

1.2.2. He was successful. He prevented a repetition of the troubles that had accompanied their wars with the kingdom of Israel, establishing a lasting peace (v. 44). He put a deputy, or viceroy, in Edom, so that the kingdom was subject to him (v. 47), and in that the prophecy concerning Esau and Jacob was fulfilled, that *the elder should serve the younger* (Ge 25:23). He pleased God, and God blessed him with strength and success.

2. The beginning of the story of Ahaziah the son of Ahab (vv. 51–53). His reign was very short, not even two years. God makes quick work of some sinners. He is described as having a very bad character. He kept up not only Jeroboam's idolatry but also the worship of Baal. Although he had heard of the downfall of Jeroboam's family and had seen his own father drawn into destruction by the prophets of Baal, who had often been proved to be false prophets, he still followed the example of his evil father and the advice of his more evil mother, Jezebel, who was still living.

A PRACTICAL AND DEVOTIONAL EXPOSITION OF THE BOOK OF

2 Kings

◆━━━━◆

This second book of Kings, which the Septuagint (a Greek version of the Old Testament), numbering from Samuel, called *The Fourth Book of the Kings*, is a continuation of the former book. Some think the book might have begun better at 1Ki 22:51, where the reign of Ahaziah begins. The previous book had a distinguished beginning, with the glories of the kingdom of Israel when it was still intact, but it had a sad conclusion, with the desolation of the kingdom of Israel and then of the kingdom of Judah. But as Elijah's powerful works were very much the glory of the end of the previous book, so were Elisha's the glory of the beginning of this book. These prophets outshone their rulers, and so, as far as they go, the history will be recorded with them in mind. Here we find: 1. Elijah calling fire from heaven and ascending in fire to heaven (chs. 1–2). 2. Elisha working many miracles, both for his ruler and for the people, both for Israelites and for foreigners (chs. 3–7). 3. Hazael and Jehu anointed, the former to discipline Israel, the latter to destroy the house of Ahab and the worship of Baal (chs. 8–10). 4. The reign of several kings, both of Judah and of Israel (chs. 11–16). 5. The exile of the ten tribes (ch. 17). 6. The good and glorious reign of Hezekiah (chs. 18–20). 7. Manasseh's evil reign and Josiah's good reign (chs. 21–23). 8. The destruction of Jerusalem by the king of Babylon (chs. 24–25). Several passages of this history confirm the observation of Solomon that *righteousness exalts a nation, but sin is the reproach of any people* (Pr 14:34).

CHAPTER 1

We here find Ahaziah, the genuine son and successor of Ahab, on the throne of Israel. His reign did not last even two years; he died from a fall in his own house. 1. The message which he sent to the god of Ekron (v. 2); the message he received from the God of Israel (vv. 3–8). 2. Twice, the destruction of the messengers he sent to seize the prophet (vv. 9–12); the prophet's compassion on and compliance with the third messenger upon the messenger's submission, and the prophet's delivery of the message to the king in person (vv. 13–16). The death of Ahaziah (vv. 17–18). In the story we may observe how significant the prophet looks and how insignificant the ruler looks.

Verses 1–8

Here is Ahaziah, the evil king of Israel, suffering God's rebukes both by his providence and by his prophet, by his discipline and by his word:

1. He is thwarted in the business of ruling. How can those expect to prosper who *do evil in the sight of the Lord* and *provoke him to anger*? When he rebelled against God and turned away from his allegiance to him, Moab rebelled against Israel and against the subjection they had long accepted under the kings of Israel (v. 1).

2. He is seized with sickness in his body, not from any inward cause but from a severe accident. *He fell down through a lattice*. Ahaziah would not attempt to defeat the Moabites, fearing he might die on the battlefield, but would not be safe even if he stayed at home. Royal palaces do not always offer a firm security.

3. In his distress he sends messengers to inquire of the god of Ekron whether he will recover or not (v. 2). Here:

3.1. His inquiry was very foolish: *Shall I recover?* Even a person with ordinary common sense—and how much more a wise king?—would sooner have asked, "What treatment ought I to use so that I will recover?"

3.2. His sending of messengers to consult Baal-Zebub was evil. *Baalzebub*, which means "the lord of the flies," was one of their Baals which perhaps "replied," either by the power of the demons or by the trickery of the priests, with a humming noise, like that of a great fly, or which had, so they thought, rid their country of the swarms of flies with which it had been infested, or of some plague which flies had given to them. In the New Testament *the prince of the devils* is called *Beelzebub* (Mt 12:24).

4. Elijah is directed by God to meet the messengers, and he turns them back with an answer that will save them the work of going to Ekron.

4.1. Elijah faithfully rebukes Ahaziah's sin (v. 3): "*Is it not because there is not*—that is, because you think there is not—*a God in Israel, that you go to inquire of Baal-zebub, the god of Ekron*, a contemptible town of the Philistines (Zec 9:7), long since defeated by Israel?" Here:

4.1.1. The sin was bad enough, giving that honor to the Devil which is due only to God.

4.1.2. The interpretation which Elijah, in God's name, puts on it, makes it much worse: "It is because you think not merely that the God of Israel is not able to tell you but that there is no God at all in Israel, or else you would not send to so far away for a divine answer."

4.2. He plainly reads Ahaziah's condemnation: go, tell him *he shall surely die* (v. 4).

5. After the message has been given to Ahaziah by his servants, he asks them who sent it, and he concludes, from their description of him, that it must be Elijah (vv. 7–8). His garment was the same as Ahaziah had seen Elijah wearing in the court of Ahab his father. He was clothed in a garment of hair and had a leather belt around his waist. He was plain and unadorned in what he was wearing.

Verses 9–18

Here:

1. The king issues a warrant to apprehend Elijah. If the god of Ekron had told him he would die, he would probably have taken it quietly; but now that a prophet of the Lord tells him so, rebuking him for his sin and reminding him of the God of Israel, he cannot bear it.

2. The captain who was sent with his fifty soldiers found Elijah at the top of a hill, which some think was Carmel, and commanded him in the king's name to surrender himself (v. 9). Elijah was now far from running away, as he had done before, into the close recesses of a cave, and he boldly appeared at the top of a hill. His experience of God's protection made him bolder. The captain called him *a man of God* (v. 10). If he really had looked on him as a prophet, he would not have attempted to make him his prisoner, and if he had thought he was entrusted with the word of God, he would not have tried to command him with the word of a king.

3. Elijah, to prove that he is sent by God, calls for fire from heaven to consume this arrogant, defiant sinner. It had not been long since Elijah had brought fire from heaven to consume the sacrifice (1Ki 18:38), but because the people had defied that, the fire now fell not on the sacrifice but on the sinners themselves (v. 10). Notice here:

3.1. What an influence the prophets had in heaven; what the Spirit of God in them demanded, the power of God effected. Elijah had only to speak, and it was done.

3.2. What an influence heaven had on the prophets! God was always ready to plead their cause and avenge the wrongs done to them. No doubt Elijah did this by a divine prompting, but our Savior would not allow the disciples to use it as a precedent (Lk 9:54). "No," Christ says, "by no means, *you know not what manner of spirit you are of*" (Lk 9:55) that is:

3.2.1. "You do not consider *what manner of spirit* you are called to as disciples, and how that is different from that of the Old Testament era. It was part of that dispensation of terror for Elijah to call down fire, but the dispensation of the Spirit and of grace will in no way allow it.

3.2.2. "You are not aware what kind of spirit you are motivated by on this occasion, and how different from that of Elijah. He acted in holy zeal, but you are acting in passion. He was concerned for God's glory, but you are concerned only for your own reputation."

4. Ahaziah sends a captain a second time to apprehend Elijah (v. 11), as if he has made up his mind not to be confounded by almighty God himself. Ready with his fifty men, this captain addresses Elijah as arrogantly and defiantly as the last, and he is in a greater hurry: "*Come down quickly* (v. 11). Do not waste any time. The king's business requires speed." Elijah does not give in but calls for another flash of lightning, which immediately puts this captain and his fifty soldiers to death on the spot.

5. The third captain humbles himself and throws himself on the mercy of God and Elijah. He takes warning from the fate of his predecessors and, instead of summoning the prophet, falls down before him and begs for his life and the lives of his soldiers, acknowledging that they

have done evil and deserve punishment and also acknowledging the prophet's power (vv. 13–14): *Let my life be precious in thy sight.*

6. Elijah does more than grant the request of this third captain. God is ready to show mercy to those who repent and submit to him. Never has anyone thrown themselves on the mercy of God in vain. This captain not only has his life spared but also is allowed to escort Elijah to Ahaziah: Elijah is commanded by the angel and *goes down with him to the king* (v. 15). He comes boldly to the king and tells him to his face the message he sent to him before (v. 16), that he will soon surely die. He does not reduce the sentence either out of fear of the king's displeasure or out of pity for his misery. The God of Israel has condemned him, so he can send messengers to see whether the god of Ekron will rescue him if he likes. Ahaziah is so thunderstruck by this message when it comes from the prophet's own mouth, that neither he nor any of those around him dare harm him. They do not even insult him in any way; he comes out of that lion's den unhurt, like Daniel.

7. The prediction is fulfilled in a few days. Ahaziah died (v. 17), and because he died childless, he left his kingdom to his brother Joram.

CHAPTER 2

In this chapter we have the taking up of Elijah into heaven. At the end of the previous chapter we had an evil king leaving the world in disgrace, and here we have a holy prophet leaving the world in honor. Here is: 1. Elijah taking leave of his friends, the company of the prophets, especially Elisha, who kept close to him and walked with him across the Jordan (vv. 1–10). 2. Elijah taken into heaven by the ministry of angels (v. 11) and Elisha's mourning this earth's loss of him (v. 12). 3. Elisha revealed to be a prophet in Elijah's place: 3.1. By the dividing of the Jordan (vv. 13–14). 3.2. By the respect which the company of the prophets showed him (vv. 15–18). 3.3. By the healing of the bad waters of Jericho (vv. 19–22). 3.4. By the destruction of the children of Bethel who jeered at him (vv. 23–25).

Verses 1–8

Elijah's times and the events of his life are dated as little as those of any great person in Scripture. We are not told his age, or in what year of Ahab's reign he first appeared, or in what year of Joram's he disappeared, and so we cannot work out how long he flourished. It is probably between twenty and thirty years in all. Here we are told:

1. That God had determined to take him up into heaven by a whirlwind (v. 1). It is not for us to say why God in this way honored Elijah more than any other prophet. He was a man *subject to like passions as we are*, he was a man just like us (Jas 5:17); he knew sin, yet he never tasted death. We may suppose that in this:

1.1. God looked back on his past services, which were notable and extraordinary, and he wanted to reward those services and to encourage the companies of the prophets to follow him in the steps of his zeal and faithfulness and to witness against the corruptions of the age they lived in.

1.2. God looked down on the present dark and corrupt state of the church, and he wanted to give a tangible proof of another life after this one and draw the hearts of the faithful few upward toward himself and that other life.

1.3. God looked forward to the Gospel era, and in the taking up of Elijah he gave a type of and prefigured the ascension of Christ and the opening of the kingdom of heaven to all believers. Elijah, by faith and prayer, had had intimate dealings with heaven, and now he was taken there, to assure us that if we have our citizenship in heaven while we are here on earth, we will soon be there, and the soul—and that is our true self—will be happy there forever.

2. That Elisha had determined that, as long as Elijah remained on earth, he would remain faithful to him and not leave him. Elijah seemed keen to shake him off and wanted him to stay behind at Gilgal, at Bethel, and at Jericho (vv. 2, 4, 6). Some think he did this out of humility. He knew what glory God intended for him but did not want to appear to glory in it. But in vain Elijah asked him to stay here or there; Elisha decided to stay nowhere except behind his master until Elijah went to heaven and left him behind on earth. "Whatever comes of it, *I will not leave thee.*" But why was this so?

2.1. Because he wanted to be edified by Elijah's holy and heavenly conduct as long as he stayed on earth.

2.2. Because he wanted to see Elijah's departure for himself, actually see him when he was taken up, so that his faith might be confirmed and he might come to know more about the invisible world.

3. That Elijah, before his departure, visited the schools of the prophets and took his leave of them. It seems there were such schools in many cities in Israel, probably even in Samaria itself. Here we find *sons of the prophets* (vv. 3, 5) in considerable numbers, even at Bethel, where one of the calves had been set up, and at Jericho, which had just been rebuilt in defiance of a divine curse. At Jerusalem and in the kingdom of Judah they had priests and Levites and the temple service, the lack of which in the kingdom of Israel God graciously made up for by these colleges, where prophets were trained and where they exercised religious faith and devotion.

4. That the sons of the prophets knew that he was soon to be taken away, and:

4.1. They told Elisha about it, both at Bethel (v. 3) and at Jericho (v. 5): *Knowest thou that the Lord will take away thy master from thy head today?* Elisha knew it all too well, and *sorrow had filled his heart* for this reason—as happened with the disciples in a similar case (Jn 16:6)—and so he did not need to be told about it. He did not really want to listen to it. *I know it; hold you your peace* (vv. 3, 5). He speaks with a reverent silence in expectation of the event: "I know it; *be silent*" (Zec 2:13).

4.2. They went themselves to be witnesses of it at a distance, although they could not come closer (v. 7): *Fifty of them stood to view afar off,* wanting to satisfy their curiosity, but God so ordered it that they could be eyewitnesses of the honor heaven gave that prophet, who was *despised and rejected of men* (Isa 53:3).

5. That the miraculous dividing of the River Jordan introduced Elijah's being taken up into the heavenly Canaan, just as it had introduced the entrance of Israel into the earthly Canaan (v. 8). He must go onto the other side of the Jordan to be taken up into heaven, because his native country of Gilead was there, and so that he might be near the place where Moses died, and so that honor might be given to that part of the country which was most despised. God wanted to exalt Elijah in his departure, as he did Joshua in his entrance, by dividing this river (Jos 3:7). When God takes up his faithful ones to heaven, death is the Jordan which they must pass through immediately before they are taken up. They find a safe and encouraging way through it, for the death of Christ has divided those waters so that the redeemed of the Lord may pass over.

Verses 9–12

Here:

1. Elijah makes his will, and leaves Elisha his heir, anointing him—more than when he *cast his mantle upon him* (1Ki 19:19)—to be prophet in his place.

1.1. Elijah was very pleased with the loyalty of Elisha's affection and attendance and told him to ask what he should do for him, what blessing he should leave him at their parting.

1.2. Elisha, who has this great opportunity of enriching himself with the best riches, prays for *a double portion of his spirit* (v. 9). He does not ask for wealth, honor, or exemption from trouble, but to be qualified to serve God and his generation. He asks:

1.2.1. For the Spirit. He does not imply that the gifts and graces of the Spirit are in Elijah's power to give, and so he does not say, "Give me the Spirit"—he knows very well that is God's gift—but, "Let the Spirit be upon me—intercede with God for this for me."

1.2.2. For *his* spirit, because he was to be a prophet in the place of Elijah, to carry on his work, to nurture the companies of the prophets and face their enemies, and because he had the same difficulties to encounter.

1.2.3. For *a double portion of his spirit* (v. 9); he does not mean double what Elijah had, but double what the rest of the prophets had, from whom so much would not be expected as from Elisha, who had been brought up under Elijah.

1.3. Elijah promised him what he asked, but with two provisos (v. 10):

1.3.1. Provided he put a proper value on it and esteemed it highly. He taught Elisha to do this by calling it *a hard thing* (v. 10), not too difficult for God to do but too great for him to expect.

1.3.2. Provided he kept close to his master, even to the final moments, and saw him: *If thou see me when I am taken from thee, it shall be* (v. 10) so, but not otherwise.

2. Elijah is taken up to heaven in a fiery chariot (v. 11). Like Enoch, he was taken up into heaven so *that he should not see death* and was, as the poet Abraham Cowley expresses it, "the second man that leaped the ditch / where all the rest of mankind fell, / and went not downward to the sky." Let us not ask many curious questions about this matter; let it be enough that we are told:

2.1. What his Lord, when he came, found him doing. He was talking with Elisha, instructing and encouraging him, directing him in his work and urging him to do it, for the good of those he left behind. He was not meditating or praying, as one wholly taken up with the world he was going to, but was busy talking to build others up, as one concerned about the kingdom of God among his fellows.

2.2. What means of transport his Lord sent for him—a *chariot of fire and horses of fire* (v. 11), so that he might ride in state and in triumph, like a ruler and conqueror, in fact, *more than a conqueror* (Ro 8:37). In Scripture, the angels are called *cherubim* and *seraphim,* and their appearance here, although it may seem beneath their dignity, corresponds to both those names, for:

2.2.1. *Seraphim* means "burning ones," and God is said to make them *a flame of fire* (Ps 104:4).

2.2.2. *Cherubim* may mean "chariots," and they are called *the chariots of God* (Ps 68:17). The chariot and horses appeared like fire, not in burning but in brightness, not to torture or consume him but to make his ascension conspicuous and distinguished in the eyes of those who stood far away to view it. Elijah had burned with holy zeal for God and his honor, and now he was refined and taken up into heaven with a heavenly fire.

2.3. How he was separated from Elisha: this chariot parted them.

2.4. Where he was taken. He *went up by a whirlwind into heaven* (v. 11). Elijah had once, in a passion, wanted to die, but God was so gracious to him as to honor him with this special privilege, that he would never see death; and by this instance and that of Enoch:

2.4.1. God showed how human beings would have left the world if they had not sinned: not by death but by being directly taken up into heaven.

2.4.2. God gave a glimpse of that life and immortality which are brought to light by the Gospel, and of the opening of the kingdom of heaven to all believers, just as it was opened here to Elijah. The event also prefigured Christ's ascension.

3. Elisha passionately mourns the loss of that great prophet.

3.1. He saw Elijah taken and was thus assured of the granting of his request for a double portion of Elijah's spirit. He looked steadfastly toward heaven, from which he was to expect that gift, as the disciples did (Ac 1:10). He saw it for a while, but the vision soon went out of his sight, and *he saw him no more* (v. 12).

3.2. He tore his own clothes as a sign of the sense he had of his own and the public loss. Although Elijah had gone triumphantly to heaven, this world could hardly spare him. Surely their hearts are hard whose eyes are dry when God takes away faithful and useful people and, in so doing, calls for weeping and mourning. Though Elijah's departure made way for Elisha's advancement, Elisha still mourned his loss, for he loved him and could have served him forever.

3.3. He ascribed to him a very honorable character. He himself had lost the guide of his youth: *My father, my father* (v. 12). The whole community had lost its best guard; he was *the chariot of Israel, and the horsemen thereof* (v. 12). He would have brought them all to heaven, as in this chariot, if it had not been their own fault.

Verses 13–18

Here is an account of what followed immediately after Elijah was taken up into heaven:

1. The signs of God's presence with Elisha and the marks of his advancement into Elijah's place.

1.1. He possessed Elijah's cloak, the badge of his office, which he probably put on and wore for his master's sake (v. 13). When Elijah went up to heaven, he left his cloak as a legacy for Elisha, and it was still a sign of the descent of the Spirit on him. It meant more to Elisha than if Elijah had bequeathed to him thousands in gold and silver. Elisha took it up as a significant piece of clothing to be worn. He who had so cheerfully obeyed the summons issued by means of the cloak and had then become Elijah's servant (1Ki 19:19) is now honored with it and becomes his successor.

1.2. He possessed Elijah's power to divide the Jordan (v. 14). Having parted with his father, he returns to his followers in the companies of the prophets. The river Jordan is between him and them; it was divided to make way for Elijah to go to his glory. Elisha will see whether it will divide to make way for him to do his work. Elijah's last miracle will be Elisha's first. In dividing the waters:

1.2.1. He makes use of Elijah's cloak, as Elijah himself did (v. 8), to show that he intends to keep to his master's methods.

1.2.2. He turns to Elijah's God: *Where is the Lord God of Elijah?* (v. 14). He does not ask, "Where is Elijah?" but,

"The God who acknowledged, protected, and provided for Elijah, and honored him in many ways, especially now at his end, where is he? Lord, am I not promised Elijah's spirit? Fulfill that promise now." The words which come next in the original, *aph-hu*, "even he" or "also he," which we join to the following clause, *when he also had smitten the waters*, are interpreted by some as an answer to this question, *Where is Elijah's God?* (v. 14). "He continues to remain close at hand even now. We have lost Elijah, but we have not lost Elijah's God. He *has* not *forsaken the earth* (Eze 9:9); even he is still with me." We can learn from this that those who walk in the spirit and steps of their godly and faithful predecessors will certainly experience the same grace they experienced. Elijah's God will be Elisha's too. The Lord God of the holy prophets is the same yesterday, today, and forever. What use will it be to us if we have the cloaks of those who have gone, their places, their books, if we do not also have their spirit and their God?

1.3. He possessed Elijah's influence in the company of the prophets (v. 15). Some, who had placed themselves conveniently near the Jordan to see what took place, were surprised to see the Jordan divided before Elisha on his return, and took that as a convincing sign that *the spirit of Elijah did rest upon him*. And so they went to meet him, to congratulate him on his safe passage through fire and water and on the honor God had given him, and they *bowed themselves to the ground before him* (v. 15). They were trained up in the schools, whereas Elisha had been taken from the plow, but when they realized God was with him and that this was *the man whom he delighted to honour* (Est 6:6), they readily submitted to him as their leader and father, as the people did to Joshua when Moses had died (Jos 1:17). We must honor those whom God honors, whoever they are.

2. The unnecessary search which the company of the prophets made for Elijah:

2.1. They suggested that he had possibly been set down, either dead or alive, on some mountain or in some valley (v. 16). Some of them perhaps raised this question because they objected to the choice of Elisha: "Let us first be sure that Elijah has definitely gone."

2.2. Elisha did not agree to their suggestion until they persisted and he had to give in to their badgering (v. 17). They urged him until he was too ashamed to oppose it anymore; he yielded so that he would not be thought lacking in respect for his old master or unwilling to give him back his role.

2.3. The outcome made them ashamed of their proposal. After their messengers had tired themselves out with searching in vain, they returned and gave Elisha an opportunity to rebuke his friends for being so foolish: *Did I not say unto you, Go not?* (v. 18). Crossing hills and valleys will never bring us to Elijah, but imitating his holy faith and zeal will, in due time.

Verses 19–25

Elisha worked more miracles than Elijah. Some reckon them to be double in number. Two are recorded in these verses—a miracle of mercy in Jericho and a miracle of judgment in Bethel (Ps 101:1). Here is:

1. A blessing on the waters of Jericho, which was powerful enough to make them wholesome. Jericho was built in disobedience to a command, yet even within those walls that were built by sin we find the beginnings of godliness. Elisha went there to satisfy the disciples with a more detailed account of Elijah's being taken up to heaven than their witnesses, who saw at a distance, could give

them. He stayed there while the fifty men were searching for Elijah. And:

1.1. The people of Jericho told him their complaint (v. 19). They had not turned to Elijah about this matter, perhaps because he was not so accessible as Elisha. The town was well situated and gave good views, but they did not have wholesome water to drink or fruitful soil to provide food for them. Some think that not all the ground around Jericho was unproductive and had bad water, but only a part.

1.2. He soon remedied their problem. Prophets should try to make every place they come to, in some way or other, better for the people who live there, trying to sweeten bitter spirits and to make fruitful any unproductive souls by applying the word of God. Elisha will make their waters wholesome, but:

1.2.1. They must provide him with salt in a new bowl (v. 20). Even if salt had been the right thing to season the water with, what could such a small quantity do toward it, and how would it be better if it was in a new bowl? Those who want to be helped must have their faith and obedience tested in this way, however. God's works of grace are carried out not by any activity of ourselves but by observing his institutions.

1.2.2. He threw the salt *into into the spring of the waters* (v. 21) and so healed the streams and the ground they watered. This shows us that the way to reform the lives of people is to renew their hearts. Let those be seasoned with the salt of grace, for *out of them are the issues of life,* for they are the wellspring of life (Pr 4:23). Purify the heart, and that will cleanse the hands.

1.2.3. He did not pretend to do this by his own power but did it in God's name: *Thus saith the Lord, I have healed these waters* (v. 21). By helping them with a *Thus saith the Lord* (v. 21), he would prepare them to be more willing later to receive a rebuke, warning, or command from him when it was introduced in the same way.

1.2.4. The cure was permanent, not only for that time: *The waters were healed unto this day* (v. 22).

2. A curse on the children of Bethel. At Bethel there was another school of prophets. Elisha went there next, and the scholars welcomed him with every respect, but the people of the town were abusive to him. One of Jeroboam's calves was at Bethel; they were proud of this and hated those who rebuked them. We presume it was their usual practice to jeer at the prophets as they went along the streets, to call them by some nickname or other, and if possible to drive them out of their town. If the abuse done to Elisha had been the first offense of that kind, it would probably have not been so severely punished. But *mocking the messengers of the Lord* and *misusing the prophets* was one of the *crying sins of Israel,* as we find in 2Ch 36:16. Now here we have:

2.1. An instance of that sin. The *children of Bethel* (v. 23), the boys and girls who were playing in the streets, went out to meet him, and they gathered around him and jeered at him as if he were a fool: *Go up, thou bald head, go up, thou bald head* (v. 23). It was his character as a prophet that they wanted to abuse. The honor God had crowned him with should have been enough to cover his bald head and protect him from their jeering. These children spoke as they were taught; they had learned from their idolatrous parents to call prophets by foul names and to use bad language. As the proverb expresses it, "As the old cock crows, so crows the young."

2.2. An example of that ruin which ultimately came on Israel for misusing God's prophets, a ruin of which this was intended to give them fair warning. Elisha

heard their taunts for a good while with patience, but at length he *turned and looked upon them* (v. 24), to see if a grave and severe look would disconcert them, but they *were not ashamed, neither could they blush* (Jer 6:15). He therefore *cursed them in the name of the Lord* (v. 24), to punish the dishonor given to God. His summons was immediately obeyed; two *she bears* came out of an adjacent wood and immediately killed forty-two of the young people (v. 24). Now in this the prophet was justified, for he did it by divine prompting. He also wanted to punish the parents and so make them afraid of God's judgments. Let parents, who want to be encouraged by their children, train them well, for as Bishop Hall says, "In vain do we look for good from those children whose education we have neglected; and in vain do we grieve for those miscarriages (mistakes) which our care might have prevented."

CHAPTER 3

We are now called to consider the national affairs of Israel, in which we find Elisha concerned. Here is: 1. The general character of Joram, king of Israel (vv. 1–3). 2. A war with Moab, in which Joram and his allies were engaged (vv. 4–8); the difficulties which the confederate army was reduced to in its expedition against Moab, its leaders' turning to Elisha in their distress, and the answer of peace he gave them (vv. 9–19). 3. The glorious outcome of this campaign (vv. 20–25) and the cruel method the king of Moab took to make the confederate army withdraw (vv. 26–27). The house of Ahab had been condemned to be destroyed, and its ruin was now not far away.

Verses 1–5

Jehoram (Joram), the son of Ahab and brother of Ahaziah, was now on the throne of Israel, and although he was a bad man, two commendable things are recorded about him:

1. That he removed his father's idols. He did evil in many things, but not like his father Ahab or his mother Jezebel (v. 2). Perhaps Jehoshaphat, who by his alliance with the house of Ahab made his own family worse, did something toward making Ahab's better. Joram *put away the image* (sacred stone) *of Baal* (v. 2), deciding to worship only the God of Israel and to consult only his prophets. So far, so good, but it did not prevent the destruction of Ahab's family.

1.1. He only put away the sacred stone of Baal *which his father had made* (v. 2). He did not destroy the worship of Baal among the people, for Jehu found it prevalent (10:19). Reforming his family was good, but he should have used his power also to reform his kingdom.

1.2. When he put away the sacred stone of Baal, he clung to the worship of the calves, that shrewd sin of Jeroboam (v. 3). *He departed not therefrom,* because that was the instrument by which the division between the two tribes was maintained, making it unnecessary for the people to go to Jerusalem to worship. Those who part only with the sins that they lose by, and continue to indulge in the sins they gain from, do not truly reform their ways.

1.3. He only *put away* the sacred stone of Baal; he did not break it into pieces as he should have.

2. That he did what he could to regain his brother's losses. As he had something more of the religion of an Israelite than his father, so also he had something more of the spirit of a king than his brother. Moab rebelled against

Israel immediately on the death of Ahab (1:1). We do not find that Ahaziah made any attempt to rebuke or subdue them. The tribute which the king of Moab paid was a very considerable part of the income of the crown of Israel: *100,000 lambs, and 100,000 rams* (v. 4). Taxes in those days were paid not so much in money as in the goods of the country. The rebellion of Moab was a great loss to Israel, but Ahaziah sat back and did nothing. An upper room in his house, however, proved as fatal to him as the high places of the field could have been (1:2), and the breaking of his lattice let onto his throne a man of more active disposition.

Verses 6–19

Joram has no sooner gotten the scepter into his hand than he takes the sword to regain control of Moab. Here we have:

1. The agreement between Joram king of Israel and Jehoshaphat king of Judah to undertake this expedition. Joram mobilized an army (v. 6), and he had such an opinion of the godly king of Judah that:

1.1. He courted him as his confederate: *Wilt thou go with me against Moab?* And he gained him. Although Judah and Israel are unhappily divided from each other, they can still unite against Moab, their common enemy. Jehoshaphat negotiates with Israel as a fellow kingdom. Those who can never find it in their hearts to forgive and forget old wrongs are a menace to their own peace and strength.

1.2. He consulted him as his confidant (v. 8). He took advice from Jehoshaphat, who was wiser and more experienced than himself, about which way they should attack the country of Moab. Jehoshaphat advised that they should not march against it by the most direct route, over the Jordan, but go around *through the wilderness of Edom*, so that they might take the king of Edom, who was subject to him, and his forces along with them.

2. The great difficulties that the army of the confederates came into in this expedition. Before they saw the face of the enemy, they were all in danger of dying for lack of water (v. 9). The king of Israel sadly mourned the present distress and the imminent danger. It was he who had *called these kings together*, but he blamed Providence and called it unkind: the Lord, he said, has *called them together*.

3. Jehoshaphat's good suggestion to ask advice from God in this crisis (v. 11). The place they were now in must have reminded them of the *wonders of which their fathers told them*, the waters brought out of the rock. The thought of this probably encouraged Jehoshaphat to ask, *Is there not here a prophet of the Lord* (v. 11), like Moses? It was good that Jehoshaphat inquired of the Lord now, but it would have been much better if he had done it sooner, before he directed this course, so that the distress might have been prevented.

4. The recommendation of Elisha as a suitable person for them to consult (v. 11). Maybe it was by special direction from heaven that Elisha accompanied them, as *the chariot of Israel and the horsemen thereof* (2:12). A servant of the king of Israel knew of his being there while the king himself did not. Probably it was such a servant as Obadiah was to Joram's father Ahab, one who *feared the Lord* (1Ki 18:3); to such a person Elisha made himself known, not to the kings.

5. The turning of the kings to Elisha. They went down to him in his quarters (v. 12). The one who humbled himself was exalted in this way; he appeared great when three kings came to knock at his door and beg his assistance.

6. The reception Elisha gave them:

6.1. He was direct with the evil king of Israel (v. 13): *"What have I to do with thee? Get thee to the prophets of thy father and mother*, whom you have supported and maintained in your prosperity, and let them help you now in your distress. The world and the flesh have ruled you, so let them help you. Why should God be *inquired of by* you?"* (Eze 14:3). Elisha told him to his face, in righteous indignation at his evil, that he could scarcely find it in his heart to *look towards him* or to *see him* (v. 14). Joram was to be respected as a ruler, and Elisha, as a subject, would honor him; but as a prophet he would also declare his sin to him. Joram had so much self-control as to patiently accept this plain speaking. He had no interest in listening to the prophets of Baal, but had come humbly to ask for help from the God of Israel and his prophet, presenting the situation of his alliance as disastrous and humbly commending it to the prophet's compassionate consideration. In effect, he acknowledged himself as unworthy but asked that the other kings not be destroyed for his sake.

6.2. He showed a great respect for the godly king of Judah, *regarded his presence* (v. 14), and, for his sake, would *inquire of the Lord* (v. 11) for them all.

6.3. He composed himself to receive instructions from God. His zeal at the present time meant that he was not in the right frame of mind for prayer and the activity of the Spirit, which required a very calm and composed spirit. He therefore called for a musician (v. 15), a godly musician, one accustomed to playing on the harp and singing psalms. After Elisha had been refreshed in this way, and the tumult of his spirits had been calmed by this divine music, *the hand of the Lord came upon him* (v. 15), and the presence of God gave him more honor than that of the three kings.

6.4. God, by him, gives them the assurance that the outcome of the present distress will be encouraging and glorious.

6.4.1. They will quickly be supplied with water (vv. 16–17). To test their faith and obedience, he tells them to *make the valley full of ditches* to receive the water. Elijah, by prayer, gained water from the clouds, but Elisha gains it from … nobody knows. The spring of these waters will be as secret as the head of the Nile. God is not restricted by ordinary circumstances. It is usually by plentiful rain that God *confirms his inheritance* (Ps 68:9), but here it is done without rain, at least without rain in that place.

6.4.2. That supply will be a promise of later victory (v. 18): *"This is but a light* (is an easy) *thing in the sight of the Lord*. You will not only be saved from dying but also return in triumph." It is promised that they will defeat the rebellious country.

Verses 20–27

1. Here we read about the divine gift of both things God had promised through Elisha—water and victory, and the former not only a promise of the latter but also a means to it.

1.1. It relieved their armies, which were about to die (v. 20). And this relief came just at the time of the *offering of the morning sacrifice* on the altar at Jerusalem. We now cannot decide that one hour is more acceptable than another, because our High Priest is always appearing for us, to present and plead his sacrifice. God chose that time as the hour of mercy to honor the daily sacrifice, which had been despised. God answered Daniel's prayer just at the *time of the evening oblation* (sacrifice) (Da 9:21).

1.2. It deceived their enemies, who were ready to triumph, promising themselves that it would be easy to deal with an army so worn out from such a long march through the Desert of Edom. Notice:

1.2.1. How easily they were deceived by their own delusions.

1.2.1.1. They saw the water in the valley where the army of Israel lay camped, and they thought it was blood (v. 22), because they knew the valley to be dry, and they could not imagine that it would be filled with water. The sun shone on it, and probably the sky was red and lowering, making the water appear red, and they were willing to believe, *This is blood* (v. 23).

1.2.1.2. If their enemies' camp was so full of blood, the Moabites concluded, "The kings must have fallen out with one another, and they have *smitten* (killed) *one another. Now therefore, Moab, to the spoil*" (v. 23).

1.2.2. How fatally they then destroyed themselves. They rushed carelessly into the camp of Israel to plunder it, but saw the truth when it was too late. The Israelites were encouraged by the assurances Elisha had given them of victory, and so they fell on the Moabites with the greatest fury, conquered them, and pursued them to their own country (v. 24), which they devastated (v. 25), destroying the towns, covering every good field with stones, stopping up the springs, and cutting down every good tree. They left only the royal city standing, the walls of which they made great breaches in with their battering rams.

2. At the close of this chapter we are told what the king of Moab did when he found himself utterly at the besiegers' mercy.

2.1. He attempted something bold and brave. He got together 700 of his best soldiers and used them to try to break through the king of Edom's sector. Since the Edomite soldiers were only mercenaries, he thought that that would be the most vulnerable section and that he was more likely to make his escape that way. But it did not work; even the king of Edom proved too hard for him and forced him to withdraw (v. 26).

2.2. When this failed, he did something wild and cruel; he took his own son, his eldest son who was to succeed him—no one could have been more dear to himself and his people—and *offered him for a burnt offering upon the wall* (v. 27). He did this:

2.2.1. To try to gain the favor of Chemosh his god, which, being a devil, delighted in blood, murder, and the destruction of humans.

2.2.2. To terrify the besiegers and make them withdraw. He therefore did it *upon the wall*, in their view, so that they could see what desperate measures he would take rather than surrender, and how dearly he would sell his city and life.

CHAPTER 4

Elisha had done great service for the three kings. They owed their lives and triumphs to his prayers and prophecies. One would then have expected that this chapter would tell us what honors were given to Elisha because of this. No; the wise man rescued the army, but no one remembered him (Ecc 9:15). Or, if he had promotion offered to him, he refused it: he preferred the honor of doing good in the companies of the prophets to the honor of being great in the courts of rulers. God exalted him, and that was enough for him, for here we have him employed in working no fewer than five miracles. 1. He multiplied the poor widow's oil (vv. 1–7). 2. He gained

for the good Shunammite the blessing of a son in her old age (vv. 8–17). 3. He raised that boy to life when he had died (vv. 18–37). 4. He healed the poisonous stew (vv. 38–41). 5. He fed 100 men with twenty small loaves (vv. 42–44).

Verses 1–7

Elisha's miracles were to be used; they were not for show. The one recorded here was an act of real love. The miracles of Christ were similar; they were not only great wonders but also great favors to those for whom they were done.

1. Elisha readily receives a poor widow's complaint. She was the widow of a prophet. It seems that the prophets had wives just as the priests did. Marriage is honorable to all and not inconsistent with the most sacred professions. Now, from the complaint of this poor woman (v. 1), we are given to understand:

1.1. That her husband, being *one of the sons of the prophets*, was well known to Elisha.

1.2. That he had the reputation of being godly. He was one who kept his integrity at a time of general apostasy, one of the 7,000 who had not bowed the knee to Baal.

1.3. That he was dead. As with all the prophets, being clothed with the spirit of prophecy did not mean that he was armed against the stroke of death.

1.4. That he had died poor and owed in debt more than he was worth. He did not get into debt because he was wasteful or because he had an immoderate, self-indulgent lifestyle, for he revered the Lord. But it may be the lot of those who fear God to be in debt, and insolvent, through circumstances that have brought suffering, losses at sea, bad debts, or their own foolishness, for the *children of light* are not always *wise for this world* (Lk 16:8). Perhaps this prophet was made poor by persecution: when Jezebel ruled, prophets had much trouble eking out a living, especially if they had families.

1.5. That the creditors were very harsh with her. She had two sons who could support her widowed state, and their labor was reckoned to be her assets, which therefore must be used, and they must be slaves for seven years (Ex 21:2) to work off this debt. In this distress the poor widow goes to Elisha, depending on the promise that the *seed of the righteous* will not be forsaken (Pr 11:21).

2. Elisha effectively relieves this poor widow's distress and puts her in a position both to pay off her debts and to maintain herself and her family. He did not merely give her something small to provide for her now but set her up in the world to sell oil, and he put a stock into her hand to begin with.

2.1. He instructed her what to do. He considered her case: *What shall I do for thee?* (v. 2). God is able to supply all her needs, and if she has a little in the way of possessions, her needs must be supplied by his blessing and increasing that little. Elisha therefore asked what she had that she could make money from, and found she had nothing to sell except one pot of oil (v. 2). If she had not had this pot of oil, divine power could have supplied her, but because she had this, divine power would make use of it, so teaching us to make the best of what we have. The prophet knew she had a good reputation among her neighbors and told her to borrow from them *empty vessels* (jars) (v. 3). He instructed her to shut the door on herself and her sons while she filled all those jars from that one. The oil was multiplied as it was poured, as the other widow's flour was as it was used. The way to increase what we have is to use it; *to him that hath will be given.*

2.2. She did it in obedience to his word, firmly believing in divine power and goodness. She and her sons were all amazed to find their pot, like a fountain of living water, always flowing and yet always full.

2.3. The oil continued to flow for as long as she had any empty jars to receive it. God gives more than we ask. If there had been more jars, there is enough in God to fill them—enough for all, enough for each.

2.4. The prophet instructed her what to do with the oil she had (v. 7).

2.4.1. She must sell the oil to those who were rich and could afford to provide it to themselves.

2.4.2. She must pay her debts with the money she received for her oil. It is one of the basic laws of our religious faith that we give to everyone their due, for conscience's sake.

2.4.3. The rest must not be stored away; rather, she and her children must live on the money received from the sale of it, with which they must maintain an honest way of life.

• Let those who are poor and in distress be encouraged to trust God. *Verily thou shalt be fed* (Ps 37:3), though not feasted. It is true that we cannot now expect miracles, but we may expect mercies if we wait on God and seek him.

• Let those whom God has blessed with plenty use it for the glory of God and under the direction of his word.

Verses 8 – 17

The giving of a son to those who were old and had been childless for a long time was an ancient sign of divine power and favor. We find it here also among the miracles worked by Elisha. Notice:

1. The kindness of the Shunammite woman to Elisha. Shunem lay on the road between Samaria and Carmel, a road which Elisha often traveled along, as we find in 2:25. *There* lived *a great* (well-to-do) *woman* (v. 8) who was very hospitable. Such a famous man as Elisha could not keep passing backward and forward unobserved. This godly woman had probably noticed his presence and boldly urged him to stay for a meal (v. 8). He was modest and did not want to be a trouble to anyone. It was therefore not without difficulty that he was first drawn into getting to know her and her husband, but later, whenever he went that way, he called there. She suggests to her husband:

1.1. That the stranger she would invite was *a holy man of God*, who therefore would do good to their family.

1.2. That the kindness she wanted to show him would not cost them much; she would make a small room for him on the roof of their house. The furniture would be very plain: only a bed, table, chair, and lampstand, all that was necessary for his convenience. Elisha seemed very pleased with this accommodation.

2. Elisha's gratitude for this kindness.

2.1. He offered to use his influence for her in the king's court (v. 13) "*Wouldst thou be spoken for to the king, or the captain of the host* (v. 13), can we speak on your behalf to the king or the commander of the army, for a civil or military position for your husband? How can I be of service to you?" But she does not need any good offices of this kind to be done for her. She says: *I dwell among my own people* (v. 13), that is, "I have a home among my own people. We are already well off just as we are and have no need to advance ourselves." Some years after this we find that this Shunammite had occasion to be spoken for to the king, although she did not need it now (8:3 – 4).

2.2. He did use his influence for her in the court of heaven. Elisha asked his servant Gehazi what favor he should do for her. Gehazi reminded him that she was childless, had great possessions but no son to leave them to, and was past hope of having any children because her husband was old. If Elisha could gain this favor from God for her, it would remove from her what was then her only grievance. He sent for her immediately. She very humbly and respectfully stood in the doorway (v. 15), according to her usual modesty, and then he assured her that within a year she would give birth to a son (v. 16). The fulfillment confirmed the truth of the promise, and within the time stated: *She bore a son* at the season that Elisha spoke of (v. 17).

Verses 18 – 37

Undoubtedly, after the birth of this son, the prophet's visits were doubly welcome to the helpful Shunammite. He had thought himself indebted to her, but from this time on, as long as she lived, she would think herself indebted to him, and think that she could never do too much for him. We may also suppose that the child was very dear to the prophet, as the son of his prayers, and very dear to the parents, as the son of their old age. But here is:

1. The sudden death of the child. A child of promise, a child of prayer, and given in love, but so harshly taken away. But how wonderfully does the wise and godly mother guard her lips under this surprising affliction! She had heard of the raising of the widow's son of Zarephath; she knew that the spirit of Elijah rested on Elisha. She had such confidence in God's goodness that she was very ready to believe that the One who had so quickly taken away what he had given would restore what he had now taken away. In this faith she makes preparation not for the burial of her dead child but for his resurrection, for she *lays him on the prophet's bed* (v. 21), expecting that the prophet will support his friend. *O woman! great is thy faith* (Mt 15:28).

2. The sad mother's turning to the prophet on this sad occasion, for it took place when he happened to be at the college on Mount Carmel, not far away.

2.1. She asked permission from her husband to go to the prophet but did not tell him why she was going, fearing that he did not have enough faith to let her go (v. 22). Notice how this husband and wife showed mutual respect for each other. She was so dutiful to him that she would not go until she had told him about her journey, and he was so kind to her that he would not oppose it, although she did not think it right to tell him about why she was going.

2.2. She went as quickly as she could to the prophet (v. 24), and he saw her at a distance and sent his servant to ask whether anything was wrong (vv. 25 – 26). The answer was general: *It is well.* Gehazi was not the one she came to complain to, and so she put him off with this. This shows us that when God calls away our dearest relatives by death, we should quietly say, "Everything is fine both with us and them." Things are *well*, for everything that God does is well; all is well with those who have gone, if they have gone to heaven, and all is well with us who stay behind if by the suffering we are furthered on our way there.

2.3. When she came to the prophet, she humbly reasoned with him about her present trouble. Elisha waited to hear from her, since he did not know directly from God what was the cause of her trouble. What she said was very passionate. She appealed to the prophet:

2.3.1. About how indifferent she had been to the offer of this mercy which was now taken away from her: "*Did I desire a son of my lord?* Did I ask you for a son, my lord? (v. 28). *No;* you know I did not; it was your own proposal, not mine. I was not anxious about the lack of a son, as Hannah was, nor did I beg, like Rachel, *Give me children or else I die*" (Ge 30:1).

2.3.2. About her entire dependence on the prophet's word, pleading with the prophet for the child to be raised to life again: "*I said, Do not deceive me,* and I know you will not."

3. The raising of the child back to life. The woman probably gave Elisha a fuller account of the child's death, and he gave her a fuller promise of his resurrection, than is related here, where we are told briefly:

3.1. That Elisha sent Gehazi to go quickly to the dead child, gave him his staff, and told him to lay that on the boy's face (v. 29). Bishop Hall suggests that it was done out of human pride, not by divine prompting, and so it failed in its effect. God will not have such great favors given too cheaply, nor will they be too easily come by, so that they are not undervalued.

3.2. That the woman decided not to go back without the prophet himself (v. 30): *I will not leave thee.* She had no great expectations of the staff; she wanted its owner. And she was right in thinking this way, for she knew he would come with the power of God.

3.3. That the prophet, by fervent prayer, obtained from God the restoration of this dead child to life. He found the child dead on his own bed (v. 32) *and shut the door upon them twain* (on the two of them) (v. 33).

3.3.1. How closely the prophet applied himself to this great work. Perhaps he was aware that he had tempted God too much in expecting to carry it out by means of the staff in Gehazi's hand. Notice:

3.3.1.1. He *prayed unto the Lord* (v. 33), probably as Elijah had done, *Let this child's soul come into him again,* let this boy's life return to him (1Ki 17:21). Christ raised the dead to life as one having authority—*Damsel, arise* (Mt 5:41)—*Young man, I say unto thee, Arise* (Lk 7:14)—*Lazarus, come forth* (Jn 11:43), for he was powerful and faithful as a Son, the Lord of life, but Elijah and Elisha did it by requests, as servants.

3.3.1.2. He *lay upon the child* (v. 34), as if he would give him some of his life-giving warmth or spirit. He first *put his mouth to the child's mouth,* as if, in God's name, he would breathe into him the breath of life; then *his eyes to the child's eyes,* to open them again to the light of life; then *his hands to the child's hands,* to put strength into them. He then *returned, and walked in the house* (v. 35), as one full of care and concern, and wholly intent on what he was doing. Then he went upstairs again and *stretched himself upon the child* a second time (v. 35).

3.3.2. How gradually the restoration was performed. When he first stretched himself out on the boy, *the flesh of the child waxed* (grew) *warm* (v. 34), which gave the prophet encouragement to continue to be bold in prayer. After a while, *the child sneezed seven times* (v. 35), which was a sign not only of life but also of liveliness.

3.3.3. How joyfully the child was restored alive to his mother (vv. 36–37), and all parties concerned *were not a little comforted* (Ac 20:12).

Verses 38–44

Here is Elisha in his place, in his element, among the company of the prophets, teaching them and, as a father, providing for them. There was a famine in that region because of the evil of those who lived there, the same as we read of in 8:1. It continued seven years, twice as long as the famine in Elijah's time.

1. He made harmful food become safe and wholesome.

1.1. While all the prophets were meeting with him, he ordered his servant to provide food for their bodies while he was breaking the bread of life for their souls. He ordered only that stew should be cooked for them from herbs (v. 38). The company of the prophets should be examples of moderation and putting to death excessive desires.

1.2. One of the servants, who was sent to gather herbs, by mistake brought in something harmful and mixed it into the pottage; the herbs are called *wild gourds* (v. 39). Some think the harmful herb was bitter colocynth, a strongly laxative herb, and dangerous.

1.3. The guests complained to Elisha of the unwholesomeness of their food. They cried out, *There is death in the pot* (v. 40).

1.4. Elisha immediately cured the bad taste and prevented the bad effects of this unwholesome stew. As he had earlier healed the bitter waters with salt, he now heals the bitter soup with flour (v. 41). Now all was well: there was not only no death in the pot but also no harm in it.

2. He made a little food go a long way:

2.1. Elisha had a present brought to him of twenty loaves of barley bread and some heads of grain (v. 42), an especially valuable present when there was a famine in the land.

2.2. Having freely received, he freely gave, ordering it all to be set before the company of the prophets, reserving none for himself, none for later. It befits the fathers of the prophets to be liberal to the sons of the prophets.

2.3. Although the loaves were small, he satisfied 100 men with twenty loaves (vv. 43–44). His servant thought that setting so little food before so many people would bring shame on his master, but Elisha, in God's name, declared it to be a full meal for them, and that is how it turned out. They ate, and there was food left over, not because they were not hungry but because the bread increased as they ate it.

CHAPTER 5

Two more of Elisha's miracles are recorded in this chapter. 1. The cleansing of Naaman, a Syrian, a foreigner, from his leprosy. Here we learn of 1.1. The severity of his illness (v. 1). 1.2. The providence that brought him to Elisha, which was the information given him by a captive young girl (vv. 2–4); a letter from the king of Aram (Syria) to the king of Israel, to introduce Naaman (vv. 5–7); and the invitation Elisha sent him (v. 8). 1.3. The treatment prescribed to heal him, his submission to that treatment, and his healing (vv. 9–14). 1.4. The grateful acknowledgment he then made to Elisha (vv. 15–19). 2. The striking of Gehazi, his own servant, with that leprosy. Here we are told of: 2.1. Gehazi's sins, which were lying about his master to Naaman (vv. 20–24) and then lying to his master when his master questioned him (v. 25). 2.2. His punishment for these sins. Naaman's leprosy was passed on to his family (vv. 26–27). If the healing of Naaman was a type of the calling of the Gentiles, as our Savior seems to make it (Lk 4:27), this blow to Gehazi may be looked on as a type of the blinding and rejecting of the Jews, who envied God's grace to the Gentiles as Gehazi envied Elisha's favor to Naaman.

Verses 1–8

Our Savior's miracles were intended for the lost sheep of the house of Israel, but one, like a crumb, fell from the table to a woman of Canaan. Similarly, Elisha worked one miracle for Naaman, an Aramean (*Syrian*), for God does good to all, and wants everyone to be saved. Here is:

1. The great distress Naaman was in, in the midst of all his honors (v. 1). He was very acceptable to his king; he was his favorite and his prime minister of state. He was also a bold man. But he was a burden to himself because he had a skin disease. Everyone has some *but* or other in their character, something that is a blemish and diminishes them. Naaman was as great as the world could make him, yet—as Bishop Hall expresses it—the lowest slave in Aram (*Syria*) would not change skins with him.

2. The information given him about Elisha's power by a young girl who served his wife (vv. 2–3). This girl was by birth an Israelite, taken captive providentially into Aram and then promoted into Naaman's family, where she made known Elisha's fame to the honor of Israel and Israel's God. The unhappy scattering of the people of God has sometimes proved the happy occasion for spreading the knowledge of God (Ac 8:4). This young girl acted as befitted a trueborn Israelite: she considered the honor of her country, and even though she was only young, she could speak about the famous prophet among them. And as befitted a good servant, she wanted the health and welfare of her master. *Elisha* had *not cleansed any leper in Israel* (Lk 4:27), but this young girl reasoned that he *could* heal her master, and that he *would* do it, even though her master was an Aramean.

3. The appeal which the king of Aram then made to the king of Israel on Naaman's behalf. Notice what Naaman did when he received this modest suggestion:

3.1. He would not send for the prophet to come to him but would go to him himself; he wanted to pay fitting honor to one who was able to heal diseases under divine power.

3.2. He would not go in disguise, even though his errand proclaimed his terrible disease, but went on a state visit, and with a great retinue, to give more honor to the prophet.

3.3. He would not go empty-handed, but took with him gold, silver, and clothing to present to his doctor.

3.4. He would not go without a letter to the king of Israel from the king his master, who himself fervently wanted Naaman to recover.

4. The shock this gave to the king of Israel (v. 7). He thought that the letter was:

4.1. An act of great defiance toward God, and so he tore his clothes, according to the custom of the Jews when they heard or read something they thought blasphemous. What else could the letter mean but to attribute to him a divine power? "*Am I a God, to kill* (v. 7) whom I will, and *make alive* whom I will? No; I do not claim to have such authority."

4.2. A threat against himself. He appeals to those around him to confirm this: "*See how he seeketh a quarrel against me* (v. 7); he wants me to heal this leper, and if I do not—even though I cannot—he will use that as an excuse to wage war against me"; he suspects this all the more because Naaman is the king of Aram's general. If he had remembered Elisha and his power, he would easily have understood the letter and have known what he had to do.

5. The offer which Elisha made of his services. Hearing of the occasion on which the king had torn his clothes, he sent a message to him to let him know that if his patient would come to him, his labor would not be in vain (v. 8): "*He shall know that there is a prophet in Israel*, who can do what the king of Israel does not dare attempt and what the prophets of Aram cannot claim to do."

Verses 9–14

Here we have the healing of Naaman's leprosy:

1. The short and clear direction which the prophet gave him, with an assurance of success. Naaman with all his retinue came to Elisha's door as a beggar asking for gifts. Naaman expected to have his compliment returned, but Elisha gave him his answer without any formality. He would not go to the door to meet him personally, wanting not to seem too pleased with the honor given him, but sent a messenger to Naaman, saying, *Go wash in Jordan seven times* (v. 10), promising him that if he did this, his disease would be healed. The promise was clear: *Thou shalt be clean* (v. 10). The treatment prescribed was direct: *Go wash in Jordan* (v. 10). It was intended as a sign of the healing and a test of his obedience. Those who want to be helped by God must do as they are told.

2. Naaman's disgust at the prescribed treatment because it was not what he expected. Two things disgusted him:

2.1. That Elisha, he thought, was insulting him by sending him orders through a servant and not coming to him himself (v. 11). Having big expectations of healing, he had been working out how the healing would happen: "*He will surely come out to me*, that is the least he can do to me, a lord of Aram, to me, one who has so often been victorious over Israel. *He will stand* and *call on the name of his God.* He will name me in his prayer, and then he will *wave his hand over the place*, and so bring about the healing." And because the thing was not done just like that, he lost his temper. He scorned to be healed unless he was humored as well.

2.2. That Elisha, he thought, was insulting his country. He took it hard that he must be sent to wash in the Jordan, a river of Israel, when he thought *Abana and Pharpar, rivers of Damascus, better than all the waters of Israel* (v. 12). *May I not wash in them and be clean?* (v. 12). He could wash in them and be clean from dirt, but not wash in them and be clean from leprosy. Jordan was the appointed river, and if he expected healing by divine power, he should accept the divine will without asking why. Naaman talked himself into such a temper—as angry people often do—that he turned away from the prophet's door in a rage, ready to swear he would never have anything more to say to Elisha. But who then would be the loser?

3. The modest advice which his servants gave him—with an implicit rebuke to his anger—to observe the prophet's prescription (v. 13). "*If the prophet had bidden thee* (told you to) *do some great thing* (v. 13), if he had prescribed some difficult medical treatment, *Wouldst thou not have done it?* (v. 13). No doubt you would have. And will you not submit to such a simple way as this, *Wash and be clean?* (v. 13)." The rebuke was modest, respectful, rational, and considerate. If the servants had stirred up their master's angry resentment and offered to avenge his quarrel on the prophet, how troublesome would the consequences have been! They reasoned with him:

3.1. From his fervent wish to be healed: *Wouldst thou not do* (v. 13) anything? When diseased sinners come to the point at which they are content to do anything, to submit to anything, to part with anything, in order to be healed, then—and not until then—there begins to be some hope for them. They will take Christ on his own terms when they are made willing to have Christ on any terms.

3.2. From the simplicity of the prescribed treatment: *Wash and be clean* (v. 13). The prescribed treatment to heal the leprosy of sin is so clear that we are completely inexcusable if we do not observe it. It is only, "Believe and be saved"—"Repent, and be forgiven"—"Wash, and be clean."

4. The healing that was brought about by using the treatment prescribed (v. 14). Naaman had second thoughts and tried the experiment. *His flesh came again, like the flesh of a child*, to his great surprise and joy.

Verses 15–19

Of the ten lepers that our Savior cleansed, the only one who *returned to give thanks* was *a Samaritan* (Lk 17:16). This Aramean did so also, and he here reveals himself to be:

1. Convinced of the power of the God of Israel, convinced not merely that he is God but that he alone is God, and that *there is no God in all the earth but in Israel* (v. 15). If he had seen other lepers cleansed, perhaps the sight would not have convinced him, but the mercy of the healing affected him even more than the miracle itself. Those are best able to speak of the power of divine grace who themselves have experienced it.

2. Grateful to Elisha the prophet: "And so, for the sake of him whose servant you are, I have a present for you: silver, gold, and clothing; be pleased to accept whatever you want." But Elisha generously refused the fee, not because he did not need it—for he was poor enough—but because he did not want to be indebted to this Aramean. It would honor God very much to show this new convert that the servants of the God of Israel were taught to look on the wealth of this world with a holy contempt, for seeing this would confirm him in his belief that *there was no God but in Israel* (v. 15). See 1Co 9:18; 2Co 11:9.

3. Converted to the worship of the God of Israel. Not only will he offer a sacrifice to the Lord to give thanks for his healing; he also decides he will never offer sacrifices to any other gods (v. 17). It was indeed a fortunate healing of his leprosy, since it healed him of the more dangerous disease of his idolatry. But:

3.1. In one instance he overdid things: he wanted not only to worship the God of Israel but also to take clods of earth from the prophet's garden to *make an altar of* (v. 17). He who had just spoken disparagingly of the waters of Israel (v. 12) now went to the other extreme and overvalued the earth of Israel, supposing that an altar of that earth would be most acceptable to him.

3.2. In another instance he underdid things: he reserved for himself the freedom to bow in the temple of Rimmon, out of politeness to his master the king and according to the duty of his place at court (v. 18); *in this thing* he must be excused. If in making a covenant with God we keep back any known sin and continue to indulge ourselves in it, holding onto that sin makes our covenant null and void. We must reject all our sins and not use any temple of Rimmon as an exception. If we ask for a dispensation to continue in any sin for the future, we are mocking God and deceiving ourselves.

Verses 20–27

Elisha, a holy prophet, a man of God, has only one servant, and he proves to be an evil fellow. One would have expected that Elisha's servant would be a saint—even Ahab's servant Obadiah was—but even Christ himself had a Judas among his followers. Here is:

1. Gehazi's sin.

1.1. The love of money, that root of all evil, lay at its root. His master scorned Naaman's treasures, but he coveted them (v. 20). His heart, according to Bishop Hall, was packed up in Naaman's chests, and he must run after him to fetch it.

1.2. He blamed his master for refusing Naaman's present, envied and grudged his kindness and generosity to this stranger.

1.3. When Naaman got down from his chariot to meet him (v. 21), Gehazi told him a deliberate lie, that his master had sent him to Naaman.

1.4. He was evil enough to misrepresent his master to Naaman as one who had soon changed his mind about his generosity. His story about two young men from the company of the prophets was foolish and false. If he was begging something for two young scholars, surely less than a talent of silver would have been enough for them.

1.5. There was danger that he would take Naaman away from that holy religious faith which he had embraced, and lower his high opinion of it.

1.6. His trying to hide what he had unjustly gained added much to his sin. He hid it to keep it secure until he would have the opportunity of making use of it (v. 24), and then he denied his deed: *he went in, and stood before his master* (v. 25), ready to receive his orders. His master asked him where he had been. He replied, with pretended innocence, "Your servant didn't go anywhere."

2. The punishment of this sin. Elisha immediately judged him for it, and notice:

2.1. How he was convinced. He thought he could deceive the prophet, but he was soon given to understand that the Spirit of prophecy could not be deceived and that it was futile to lie to the Holy Spirit. Elisha could tell him:

2.1.1. What he had done, even though he had denied it. "You say you went nowhere, but *went not my heart with thee?*" (v. 26).

2.1.2. What he intended, even though he kept that in his own heart. He could tell him the very thoughts and intentions of his heart (Heb 4:12), that he was planning to buy ground and cattle now that he had gained these two talents. He wanted to leave Elisha's service and set up a life for himself. "*Is it a time to receive money?* (v. 26). Is this now the opportunity to make money for yourself and make yourself rich? Couldn't you find a better way of making money than by lying about your master and putting a stumbling block before a young convert?"

2.2. How he was punished for it: *The leprosy of Naaman shall cleave* (cling) *to thee* (v. 27). *He went out from his presence a leper as white as snow* (v. 27). He was stigmatized in this way and given notoriety, carrying the mark of his shame wherever he went. What did Gehazi gain, even though he "gained" two talents, when that meant he lost his health, his honor, his peace, and his service, and, if he did not repent, his soul forever? See Job 20:12–14.

CHAPTER 6

In this chapter we have: 1. A further account of the wonderful works of Elisha: 1.1. His making iron float (vv. 1–7). 1.2. His disclosing to the king of Israel the secret directions of the king of Aram (Syria) (vv. 8–12). 1.3. His saving himself from the hands of those who were sent to capture him (vv. 13–23). 2. The besieging of Samaria by the Arameans (Syrians) and the great distress the city was reduced to (vv. 24–33).

Verses 1–7

Several things may be noticed here:

1. Concerning the company of the prophets: their condition and character. The college here spoken of seems to be that at Gilgal, and it was near the Jordan. Wherever Elisha stayed, as many as possible of the company would

probably have flocked to him to benefit from his teaching, advice, and prayers. Everyone wanted to live with him and be near him.

1.1. Their number increased so that they needed more room: *The place is too strait* (too small) *for us* (v. 1). This was good to hear, for it was a sign that many were being added to their number. Elisha's miracles doubtless drew many.

1.2. They were humble. It is right that the company of the prophets, who profess to look for great things in the other world, should be content with lowly things in this world.

1.3. They were poor. Poverty is no bar to prophecy.

1.4. They were hardworking and also willing to make great efforts. Let no one think an honest employment either a burden or a disparagement.

1.5. They had a very high opinion of Elisha. They would not set about building at all without his permission (v. 2). They would not willingly go to cut down timber without his presence: *Go with thy servants* (v. 3). Good disciples always want to be under good discipline.

1.6. They were honest and were careful to give everyone what belonged to them. When one of them accidentally struck too hard, his axhead fell off into the water, and he cried out with a deep concern, *Alas, master! For it was borrowed* (v. 5). This prophet probably was poor and did not have the resources to pay for the ax, which made its loss even more troublesome.

2. Concerning the father of the prophets, Elisha:

2.1. That he was a man of great humility and compassion. He went with the company of the prophets to the woods when they wanted him to go with them (v. 3).

2.2. That he was a man of great power. He could make iron float, contrary to its nature (v. 6). In this way, God's grace can raise the stony iron heart which has sunk into the mud of this world, and raise our naturally worldly minds to things above.

Verses 8–12

Here we have Elisha, with his spirit of prophecy, serving the king, as earlier he had helped the company of the prophets. Notice:

1. How the king of Israel was told by Elisha about all the intentions of his enemy, the king of Aram (*Syria*).

1.1. The enemies of God's Israel are shrewd in their plans against God and restless in their attempts against him.

1.2. All those plans, even the deepest, are known to God. He knows not only what people do but also what they intend to do, and has many ways of frustrating them.

1.3. It is a great advantage to us if we are warned of our danger, so that we may stand on our guard against it. The work of God's prophets is to give us warning. The king of Israel took notice of the warnings Elisha gave him of his danger from the Arameans, but not the warnings he gave him of his danger by his sins.

2. How the king of Aram resented this. He suspected treachery among his servants; he thought that his directions were being betrayed (v. 11). But one of his servants, who had heard from Naaman and others of Elisha's wonderful works, worked out that it must be Elisha who was giving this information to the king of Israel (v. 12).

Verses 13–23

Here is:

1. The great force which the king of Aram sent to capture Elisha. He found out where he was, at Dothan (v. 13), which was not far from Samaria, and he sent there a strong

force, which was to attack him by night and take him back dead or alive (v. 14). He hoped that such a strong force would be sure to capture him, especially because they would be taking him by surprise.

2. The severe state of shock which the prophet's servant was in when he noticed the city surrounded by the Arameans, and the effective means the prophet used to pacify him and free him from his fears.

2.1. How afraid he was. He ran straight to Elisha to tell him about it: "*Alas, master! What shall we do?* (v. 15). We are ruined! It is futile to think of either fighting or fleeing. There is no way to avoid falling into their hands." If only he had considered that he was involved with his master, by whom God had done great things and whom God would not now leave to *fall into the hands of the uncircumcised*, he would not have been so much at a loss. If he had only said, "What shall *I* do?" (v. 15), it would have been more excusable.

2.2. How his master quieted him:

2.2.1. By word. What he said to him (v. 16) is spoken to all the faithful servants of God, when *without are fightings and within are fears*, when there are conflicts on the outside and fears within (2Co 7:5): "*Fear not* with that fear which has torment and dismay, *for those that are with us*, to protect us, *are more than those that are against us*, to destroy us — unspeakably more numerous angels — and God, who is infinitely more powerful." When we are emphasizing the causes of our fears, we should make sure we have clear, great, and high thoughts of God and the invisible world. *If God be for us*, we know what follows (Ro 8:31).

2.2.2. By vision (v. 17).

2.2.2.1. It seems Elisha was very concerned to see his servant satisfied; he had just come into Elisha's service and did not have the advantage of experience.

2.2.2.2. Elisha saw himself as safe and wanted nothing more than that his servant might see what he saw, a guard of angels around him.

2.2.2.3. To be satisfied, his servant needed nothing more than to have his eyes opened. Elisha therefore prayed for that, and he gained it for him: *Lord, open his eyes that he may see* (v. 17). His physical eyes were open, and with them he saw the danger. "Lord, open his eyes of faith, so that with them he may see the protection we are under." The opening of our eyes will mean the silencing of our fears. We tend to be most frightened in the dark. The clearer sight we have of the sovereignty and power of heaven, the less we will fear disasters on earth.

3. The shameful defeat which Elisha caused the Aramean forces who came to capture him.

3.1. He prayed to God to strike them with blindness, and they were all immediately struck blind, not completely blind, but in such a way that they could not recognize the people and places they had known before (v. 18). They were so confused that those among them whom they depended on for information did not recognize that place as Dothan or the person before them as Elisha, but *groped at noonday as in the night*.

3.2. When they were bewildered and confused, he led them to Samaria (v. 19), promising that he would show them the man they were looking for, and he did so. He did not lie to them when he told them, *This is not the way, nor is this the city* where Elisha is, for he had now come out of the city.

3.3. When he had taken them to Samaria, he prayed that God would so open their eyes that they might recognize where they were (v. 20), *and behold*, to their great terror, *they were in the midst of Samaria*, where there was probably a standing force that was able to destroy them all or make them prisoners of war.

3.4. When he had them at his mercy, he showed that he was influenced by divine goodness as well as divine power:

3.4.1. He took care to protect them from the danger into which he had brought them, and was content to show them what he could have done. The sword of the king of Israel was at his service: *My father, shall I smite* (kill) *them?* And again, as if he longed for the attack, *Shall I smite* (kill) *them?* The prophet, however, would by no means allow him to touch them; they were brought there to be convinced and shamed, not to be killed (v. 22). They were not the king's prisoners; they were God's prisoners and the prophet's, and so he must not harm them.

3.4.2. He took care to provide for them; he ordered the king to treat them generously and then dismiss them fairly, which he did (v. 23).

3.4.2.1. The king was to be commended for being so submissive to the prophet, contrary to both his inclinations and, it seemed, his interests (1Sa 24:19). He was so willing to oblige Elisha that he *prepared great provision* (a great feast) (v. 23) for them, to the credit of his court, the country, and Elisha.

3.4.2.2. The prophet was to be commended for being so generous to his enemies. The great duty of loving our enemies and doing good to those who hate us was both commanded — *If thy enemy hunger, feed him* (Pr 25:21–22; see also Ex 23:4–5) — and practiced in the Old Testament; Elisha's actions here are an example.

4. The good effect this had, for the present, on the Arameans. They *came no more into the land of Israel* (v. 23). The most glorious victory over an enemy is to turn him into a friend.

Verses 24–33

This last paragraph of this chapter begins a new story. Here is:

1. The siege which the king of Aram laid against Samaria. The Arameans had soon forgotten the kindnesses they had just received in Samaria, and now, without any provocation, sought to destroy it (v. 24). The country had probably been plundered and devastated by the time this capital city was brought into the dire straits described in v. 25. The recent famine in the land was probably the reason that their stores were empty, so that while the sword devoured those outside the city, the famine inside was more severe, for the Arameans had not wanted to storm the city but to starve it. The famine was so great that a donkey's head was sold for eighty shekels of silver, and a small quantity of seed pods, then called *dove's dung* (v. 25) — no more than the weight of six eggs — sold for five shekels. How worthless money is in times of famine, when it is so freely parted with for anything that can be eaten.

2. The sad complaint which a poor woman had to make to the king, in the awful predicament of the famine. He was *passing by upon the wall* (v. 26) to give orders for the mounting of the guard, when a woman of the city cried out to him, *Help, my lord, O king!* (v. 26). He replied sadly (v. 27): *If the Lord do not help thee, whence shall I?* Some think it was a *quarreling* word, but it seems more likely that it was a *quieting* word: "Let us be content, and make the best of our affliction, looking up to God, for until he helps us, I cannot help you."

2.1. He mourns the emptiness of the threshing floor and the winepress.

2.2. He acknowledges himself to be unable to help unless God helps them. However, although he cannot help her, he is willing to listen to her (v. 28): "*What ails thee?* What's the matter? Is there anything unique in your situation? Are you getting along worse than your neighbors?" Yes; in fact, she and one of her neighbors had come to a barbaric agreement, that because all their supplies were failing, they would boil and eat first her son and then her neighbor's. Hers had been eaten — and now her neighbor hid hers (vv. 28–29).

3. The king's indignation against Elisha on this occasion. He mourned the disaster, *rent* (tore) *his clothes, and had sackcloth upon his flesh* (v. 30), as one sincerely concerned about the misery of his people and his inability to help them. He did not mourn his own sins, however, or the sins of his people. Instead of vowing to pull down the calves at Dan and Bethel, he swore *the death of Elisha* (v. 31). Why? What had Elisha done? His head was the most innocent and valuable in all Israel. And so it was in the days of the persecuting emperors: when the empire was suffering any extraordinary disaster, the blame was put on the Christians, and they were doomed to destruction. "Throw the Christians to the lions."

4. The foreknowledge Elisha had of the king's plans against him (v. 32). He sat composed in his house, and the elders with him. He told the elders that there was an official coming from the king to cut off his head and that they must stop him at the door, for the king his master was following him, to revoke the order.

5. The king's emotional speech, when he came to prevent the carrying out of his decree for Elisha to be beheaded. He seems to have been in a struggle between his convictions and his corruptions.

CHAPTER 7

Relief is here brought to Samaria and its king. 1. It is foretold by Elisha, and an unbelieving officer is excluded from its benefits (vv. 1–2). 2. It is brought about by an inexplicable shock that God gave the Arameans (Syrians) (v. 6), which made them hurriedly withdraw (v. 7); by the timely discovery which four lepers made of this (vv. 3–5), and the account which they gave of it to the court (vv. 8–11); and by the cautious investigation which the king made to determine the truth of it (vv. 12–15). The outcome corresponded to the prediction as regards both the sudden plenty (v. 16) and the death of the unbelieving officer (vv. 17–20).

Verses 1–2

Here:

1. Elisha foretells that within twenty-four hours the city will have plenty (v. 1).

1.1. The king of Israel despaired of it and grew weary of waiting. Elisha foretold it when things were at the worst. Human extremity is God's opportunity to exalt his own power. His time to appear for his people is when *their power is gone* (Dt 32:36). The king said, *Why shall I wait for the Lord any longer?* (6:33). "Well," Elisha said, "*now hear you the word of the Lord* (v. 1); listen to what he is saying. Tomorrow, grain will be sold at the usual price at the gate of Samaria."

1.2. The result of that would be great plenty. Of course, this would happen anyway, after a time, but that grain would be so cheap in such a short time was inconceivable.

2. An officer of Israel who happened to be present openly declared his disbelief in this prediction (v. 2).

He was a courtier whom the king liked, on whom he depended, and the king trusted him greatly.

3. A just condemnation was passed on him for his unfaithfulness: that he would see this great plenty so that he would be convicted, but not eat it and be comforted by it.

Verses 3–11

We are here told:

1. How the siege of Samaria was lifted in the evening, at dusk (vv. 6–7), not by might or power, but by the Spirit of the Lord Almighty (Zec 4:6), striking terror on the spirits of those laying siege. Here not a sword was drawn against them. Rather:

1.1. *The Lord made them to hear a noise of chariots and horses* (v. 6). The Arameans (*Syrians*) who besieged Dothan had their *sight* deceived (6:18), but these people had their *hearing* deceived. Whether the noise was really made in the air by the ministry of angels, or whether it was only a sound in their ears, is not certain, but whatever it was, it came from God, who both *brings the wind out of his treasures* (storehouses) (Jer 10:13) and *forms the spirit of man within him* (Zec 12:1). Signs from the invisible world are either comforting or terrible, according to whether people are at peace with God or at war with him.

1.2. Hearing this noise, they concluded that the king of Israel must have received help from some foreign power: *He has hired against us the kings of the Hittites and the kings of the Egyptians* (v. 6).

1.3. Then they all fled for their lives with incredible speed; they left their camp as it was. They did not even stay to take their horses, which might have helped them escape more quickly (v. 7). God can make those who will not fear him fear at the shaking of a leaf.

2. How the Arameans' escape was discovered by four men with leprosy. [Ed. note: The KJV translates the Hebrew word *sara'* as "leprous," although the Hebrew word referred to various diseases affecting the skin, not necessarily leprosy.] Samaria was rescued, but its people did not know that it was. The watchmen on the walls were not aware of the retreat of their enemies, because they stole away so silently. But Providence employed four lepers, who lived outside the gate, to be the messengers because they were excluded from the city as ceremonially unclean. The Jews say they were Gehazi and his three sons. Notice:

2.1. How these lepers reasoned themselves into deciding to make a visit at night to the Aramean camp (vv. 3–4). They were about to die for hunger; no one passed through the gate to relieve them. They therefore decided to go over to the enemy and throw themselves at their mercy. Perhaps the Arameans would have compassion on them and keep them alive. They made this decision, and as night fell they went to the Aramean camp and to their great surprise found it completely deserted, with no one to be seen or heard (v. 5).

2.2. How these lepers reasoned themselves into bringing news of this to the city. They ate and drank in the first tent they came to (v. 8) and began to think of enriching themselves with the plunder. But then they corrected themselves (v. 9): "*We do not well* to hide this good news from the rest of our community, so let us tell them the news. Even though it will wake them up from sleep, it will be *life from the dead* (Ro 11:15) to them." When they had reached this decision, they returned to the city gate and told the gatekeepers what they had discovered (v. 10).

The gatekeepers immediately took the news to the king's palace (v. 11), and it was no less acceptable for having come from lepers.

Verses 12–20

We have here:

1. The king's suspicion of a trick in the Arameans' retreat (v. 12). He feared that they had withdrawn to set an ambush, to draw out the besieged, so that they might gain an advantage and attack them.

2. The course the king and his servants took to avoid falling into a trap. They sent spies to see what had happened to the Arameans and found that they really had all fled, commanders as well as ordinary soldiers. They could track them by their clothing, which they had thrown off and left along the way in their headlong rush (v. 15). The one who advised them to make this search seems to have been very aware of the desperate plight the people of the city were in (v. 13). He advised sending five horses, but it seems there were only two horses fit to be sent, and those were chariot horses (v. 14).

3. The plenty that was in Samaria from the plunder of the Aramean camp (v. 16). God decided that the besieging of Samaria, which was intended to bring about its destruction, should be turned to its advantage, and that Israel would now be enriched with the plunder of the Arameans, just as they had been with that of the Egyptians. The word of Elisha was fulfilled to the smallest detail: *A measure of fine flour was sold for a shekel* (v. 16). Those who plundered the camp had not only enough to supply themselves with, but also excess to sell at a low price to benefit others, and so even *those that tarried* (remained) *at home did divide the spoil* (Ps 68:12; Isa 33:23).

4. The death of the unbelieving officer who questioned the truth of Elisha's word. This officer:

4.1. Was promoted by the king to be in *charge of the gate* (v. 17), to keep the peace and to see that there was no tumult or disorder in distributing and disposing of the plunder.

4.2. Was trampled to death by people in the gateway, either by accident, because the crowd was so great and he was in the thickest part of it, or perhaps intentionally, because he misused his power. However it happened, God's justice was glorified in it, and the word of Elisha was fulfilled. He saw the plenty: grain was cheap without *opening windows in heaven* (v. 19); and then he saw his own foolishness in dictating to God; but he did not eat from the plenty he saw. This is compared with the prediction (vv. 18–20), so that we may take special notice of it and learn:

- How deeply God is grieved by our distrust of him and of his power, providence, and promises.
- How uncertain life and its enjoyments are. Honor and power cannot keep people from sudden and inglorious deaths. The one on whom the king depended was trampled on by the people.

CHAPTER 8

The passages recorded in this chapter make us look back. 1. We read before of a Shunammite woman who had been kind to Elisha; now we are told how she later got along better because of it: Elisha gave her helpful advice, and the king showed her favor for Elisha's sake (vv. 1–6). 2. We read before of the appointment of Hazael as king over Aram (Syria) (1Ki 19:15), and here we have an account of his accession to that throne by killing his master (vv. 7–15). 3. We read before of Jehoram's reigning over Judah in his father Jehoshaphat's place (1Ki 22:50), and now here we have a short and sad history of his short and evil reign (vv. 16–24) and the beginning of the history of the reign of his son Ahaziah (vv. 25–29).

Verses 1–6

Here we see that:

1. The evil of Israel was punished by a long famine, one of God's severe judgments often threatened in the Law. The famine in Samaria was soon relieved by the lifting of the siege, but neither that judgment nor that mercy had a beneficial influence on them. If lesser judgments do not bring people to repentance, the Lord will send greater and longer ones. This famine continued for seven years, twice as long as that in Elijah's time, for if people walk contrary to his ways, he will make the furnace even hotter.

2. The kindness of the good Shunammite to the prophet was rewarded by the care that was taken of her in that famine.

2.1. She was warned in advance about this famine so that she might make provision for it. She was directed to move to another country; she would find plenty anywhere except in Israel.

2.2. Providence gave her a comfortable settlement in *the land of the Philistines* (v. 2), who, although subdued by David, had not been completely uprooted. It seems the famine was only in the land of Israel, and other countries which were close to them had plenty at the same time. This clearly showed the direct hand of God in it.

3. The request that the Shunammite brought to the king when she returned was favored. She presented it to him at an opportune time.

3.1. When the famine was over, she *returned out of the land of the Philistines* (v. 3).

3.2. At her return, she found herself unable to take possession of her own estate, since it had been confiscated by an office of the king or taken in her absence by some neighbors.

3.3. She turned to the king himself to put matters right.

3.4. She found the king talking with Gehazi about Elisha's miracles (v. 4). The Law did not forbid all dealings with lepers, but only living with them. Because there were then no priests in Israel, perhaps the king or someone appointed by him had the task of inspecting lepers and passing judgment on them, which might have been how he came to know Gehazi.

3.5. This fortunate coincidence supported both Gehazi's story and her request.

3.5.1. It made the king ready to believe Gehazi's story when it was confirmed by the people most closely concerned: *"This is the woman, and this her son*; let them speak for themselves"* (v. 5).

3.5.2. It made him ready to grant her request, for who would not be ready to favor one whom heaven had favored in this way, and to support a life which had been given once and again by a miracle? In consideration of this, the king gave orders that her land should be given back to her together with all the profits that had been made from it in her absence. It is not enough for those in authority that they themselves do not do wrong; they must also support the rights of those who have been wronged.

Verses 7–15

Here:

1. We may ask what took Elisha to Damascus, the chief city of Aram (*Syria*). Perhaps he went to visit Naaman, his convert, and to strengthen him in his choice of the true religion, which was more necessary now because he had left his position—for Hazael is presumed to be commander of the army—he either resigned it or was turned out of it, because he would not bow heartily in the temple of Rimmon. Some think Elisha went to Damascus because of the famine; more likely, he went there in obedience to the orders God gave Elijah (1Ki 19:15): "Go *to Damascus to anoint Hazael*, you, or your successor."

2. We notice that Ben-Hadad, that great, rich, and powerful king, was sick. No honor, wealth, or power will keep people from the ordinary diseases and disasters of human life. Palaces and thrones are as vulnerable to sickness and death as the lowliest cottage.

3. We are amazed that the king of Aram, in his sickness, would make Elisha his oracle.

3.1. News was soon brought to him that *the man of God*—for he was well known by that title in Aram since he had healed Naaman—had come to Damascus (v. 7). "Never at a better time," Ben-Hadad said. "*Go, and inquire of the Lord by him*" (v. 8). In his health he *bowed down in the house* (temple) *of Rimmon* (5:18), but now that he was ill, he distrusted his idol and wanted to inquire of the God of Israel. This is all the more significant:

3.1.1. Because it was not long since a king of Israel had, in his sickness, sent messengers to inquire of the god of Ekron (1:2), as if there had been no God in Israel.

3.1.2. Because it was not long since this Ben-Hadad had sent a great force to deal with Elisha as an enemy (6:14), but now he is courting him as a prophet.

3.2. To honor the prophet:

3.2.1. He sends *to* him, not *for* him. Like the centurion (Mt 8:8), he thought himself unworthy that the man of God should come under his roof.

3.2.2. He sends Hazael, his prime minister of state, not an ordinary messenger, to him.

3.2.3. He sends him a noble present *of every good thing of Damascus*, forty camel-loads (v. 9), welcoming him to Damascus. Elisha probably accepted it, although he refused Naaman's.

3.2.4. He orders Hazael to call his master *his son Ben-hadad* (v. 9), conforming to the language of Israel, whose people called the prophets *fathers*.

3.2.5. He inquires of him, *Shall I recover?* (v. 9), and so honors him as one who knew the secrets of heaven.

4. We see that what took place between Hazael and Elisha is especially significant.

4.1. Elisha answered Hazael's inquiry concerning the king, telling him that he would recover, that the disease was not fatal, but that he would die another way (v. 10), not a natural but a violent death.

4.2. Elisha looked Hazael in the face with an unusual concern, until he made Hazael feel ashamed and blush, and made himself weep (v. 11).

4.3. When Hazael asked Elisha why he wept, he told him what a great deal of trouble he foresaw that Hazael would do to the Israel of God (v. 12). Elisha wept to think that Israelites would ever be so mistreated. Notice what havoc war makes, what havoc sin makes, and how human nature was changed by the Fall and robbed even of humanity itself.

4.4. Hazael was greatly surprised at this prediction (v. 13): *What*, he says, *Is thy servant a dog, that he* should do this great thing? He looks on this great thing as being:

- An act of great power, only to be done by a crowned head.
- An act of great cruelty, which could only be done by one dead to all honor and goodness. It is possible for someone evil to express great hatred at sin when under the convictions and restraints of natural conscience, but later to be reconciled to it.

4.5. In answer to this, Elisha told him only that he should be king over Syria (Aram) (v. 13). He would then have power to do it, and he would then find it in his heart to do it.

5. We see what trouble Hazael then caused to his master.

5.1. He cheated his master in an evil way and misrepresented the prophet (v. 14): He told me thou shouldst certainly recover. By withholding Elisha's prediction of the king's death, Hazael wronged the king, who lost the benefits of this warning to prepare for death, and it also wronged Elisha, who would be considered a false prophet.

5.2. He cruelly murdered his master and so fulfilled the prophet's word (v. 15). He soaked a thick cloth in cold water and spread it on the king's face, and it suffocated him immediately. Hazael, who was Ben-Hadad's confidant, was his murderer, and some think he was not suspected of murdering him, nor did the truth ever come out except by the pen of this inspired writer.

Verses 16–24

Here is a brief account of the life and reign of Joram (Jehoram), one of the worst of the kings of Judah, but the son and successor of Jehoshaphat, one of the best. A nation is sometimes justly punished with the miseries of a bad reign for not making the most of the blessings and advantages of a good one.

Concerning Jehoram, notice:

1. The general idea here given of his evil (v. 18): He did as the house of Ahab, and he could not have done worse. Jehoram chose to model himself on the house of Ahab rather than that of his father, and this choice destroyed him.

2. The occasions of his evildoing. His father was a very good man and no doubt took care to have him taught the sound knowledge of the Lord, but:

2.1. It is certain that Jehoshaphat did wrong in marrying his son to the daughter of Ahab. Those who are ill matched are already half-ruined.

2.2. He did not do well in making Jehoram king in his own lifetime. It is said here (v. 16) that he began to reign, Jehoshaphat being then king. The father gratified his son's pride in this. Jehoshaphat had once made this evil son his viceroy, when he went with Ahab to Ramoth Gilead—from this information we conclude that Jehoshaphat's seventeenth year (1Ki 22:51) was the second of Joram king of Israel (1:17)—but later, in his twenty-second year, he made him a partner in his government. It has been harmful to many young people to come too soon into their estates. Samuel gained nothing by making his sons judges (1Sa 8:1).

3. The rebukes of Providence which he was under for his evil:

3.1. The Edomites rebelled. They had been under the government of the kings of Judah ever since David's time, about 150 years (v. 20). Jehoram attempted to subdue

them, and he did defeat them (v. 21), but he could not regain power over them: Yet Edom revolted (v. 22), and the Edomites were, after this, bitter enemies of the Jews, as appears by the prophecy of Obadiah and Ps 137:7.

3.2. Libnah rebelled. This was a town in Judah, in the heart of his country, a priests' town. The inhabitants of this town shook off his government because he had forsaken God and would have compelled them to do so too (2Ch 21:10–11). In order that they might preserve their religion, they set up a free state.

3.3. His reign was short. God destroyed him in midlife, when he was only forty years old and had reigned only eight years.

4. The gracious care of Providence to keep the kingdom of Judah and the house of David, despite the apostasies and disasters of Jehoram's reign (v. 19): Yet the Lord would not destroy Judah.

5. The conclusion of this ungodly and inglorious reign (vv. 23–24). No details about him are given here, but we are told elsewhere (2Ch 21:19–20) that he died of sore diseases and died without being desired.

Verses 25–29

Just as among ordinary people there are some we call little, who are not significant—they are little regarded and valued—so also there are among kings some whom, in comparison with others, we may call little kings. Ahaziah was one of these. He looks lowly in history, and in God's account he was downright detestable, because he was evil. Jehoshaphat and Ahab had the same names in their families at the same time; by sharing names in this way, they wanted to compliment each other. Ahab had two sons, Ahaziah and Joram, who reigned successively; Jehoshaphat had a son and grandson named Jehoram and Ahaziah, who likewise reigned successively. Ahaziah king of Israel had reigned only two years; Ahaziah king of Judah reigned only one. We are told here that his relationship with Ahab's family was the occasion:

1. Of his evil (v. 27): He walked in the way of the house of Ahab, that idolatrous, bloodthirsty house, for his mother was Ahab's daughter (v. 26). When men choose wives for themselves, they must remember that they are choosing mothers for their children, and be concerned to choose properly.

2. Of his fall. Joram, his mother's brother, courted him to join with him to recover Ramoth Gilead, an undertaking that had been fatal to Ahab. It was fatal also for Joram, his son, for he was wounded in that expedition (v. 28) and returned to Jezreel to be healed, leaving his army there in possession of the place. Ahaziah likewise returned, but went to Jezreel to see Joram (v. 29).

CHAPTER 9

Hazael and Jehu were intended to be the instruments of God's justice in destroying the house of Ahab. Elijah was told to appoint them to this service, but when Ahab was humbled, a reprieve was granted, and so it was left to Elisha to appoint them. We read of Hazael's elevation to the throne of Aram in the previous chapter. Now we must consider Jehu coming to the throne of Israel, for anyone who escaped the sword of Hazael, as Joram and Ahaziah did, must be killed by Jehu. 1. A commission is sent to Jehu by the hand of one of the prophets, appointing him to take over the government and destroy the house of Ahab (vv. 1–10). 2. He quickly fulfills this commission: 2.1. He communicates it to his officials (vv. 11–15). 2.2.

He marches directly to Jezreel (vv. 16–20) and there kills Joram king of Israel (vv. 21–26) and Ahaziah king of Judah (vv. 27–29). 2.3. He kills Jezebel (vv. 30–37).

Verses 1–10

We have here the anointing of Jehu as king of Israel. It does not appear that Jehu aimed at leading the government. Some think that he had been anointed before by Elijah, whom God ordered to do it, but only privately, and with a sign that he must not act until he received further orders, as Samuel anointed David long before he was to come to the throne; but that is unlikely, for then we must suppose that Elijah had anointed Hazael too.

1. The commission is sent.

1.1. Elisha did not himself go to anoint Jehu, because he was old and unfit for such a journey and so well known that he could not do it privately, and so he sent *one of the sons of the prophets* to do it (v. 1).

1.2. When he sent him:

1.2.1. He put into his hands the oil with which he must anoint Jehu: *Take this box* (flask) *of oil* (vv. 1, 3). Solomon was anointed with *oil out of the tabernacle* (1Ki 1:39). That was not now available, but oil from a prophet's hand was equivalent to oil from God's house.

1.2.2. He put into his mouth the words which he must say (v. 3): *I have anointed thee king* (vv. 7–10).

1.2.3. He also ordered him:

- To do it privately, to single out Jehu from the rest of the army officers and anoint him *in an inner chamber* (v. 2).
- To do it quickly. When he had done it, he must *flee and not tarry*, run and not delay (v. 3).

2. The commission is delivered. The young prophet set off quickly to do his work and immediately came to Ramoth Gilead (v. 4). There he found the army officers in a council of war (v. 5). With the assurance that befitted a messenger from God, and as one having authority, he called Jehu out from the others: *I have an errand to thee, O captain*, I have a message for you, commander (v. 5). Perhaps Jehu had some idea about what was about to happen, and so, in order that he might not seem too eager to accept the honor, he asked, *To which of all us, for which of us?* (v. 5). When the prophet had him alone, he anointed him (v. 6).

2.1. He invests him with the royal dignity: *Thus saith the Lord God of Israel* (v. 6), whose messenger I am; in his name *I have anointed thee king over the people of the Lord* (v. 6). He reminds him that he has been made king:

2.1.1. *By the God of Israel* (v. 6). It is he that Jehu must see his power as coming from; he must use it for him. He must be accountable to him.

2.1.2. *Over the Israel of God* (v. 6). Even though the people of Israel have forfeited all the honor of their relationship with God, they are still here called the *people of the Lord* (v. 6), for he has rights in them. Jehu must look on the people he has been made king of as the *people of the Lord* (v. 6), God's free people, not to be misused or tyrannized, *God's people*, and so to be ruled for him and according to his laws.

2.2. He instructs him in his present duties, which are to destroy all the house of Ahab (v. 7), not so that he may clear his own way to the throne but so that he may carry out the judgments of God on that guilty and offensive family. He calls Ahab Jehu's *master* but reminds him, "You are under a higher obligation to your Master in heaven than to your master Ahab. He has determined

that *the whole house of Ahab shall perish* (v. 8), and *by thy hand*. Do not be afraid of danger; his command will keep you safe and make you successful." So that Jehu may intelligently carry out this act on the house of Ahab, the prophet tells him:

2.2.1. What their crime was. It was bad enough that they were idolaters, but that is not mentioned here; the only conflict God had with them was not as persecutors, not so much their *throwing down God's altars* as their *slaying* (putting to death) *his prophets with the sword* (1Ki 19:10). This was the sin that brought on Jerusalem its first destruction (2Ch 36:16) and its final one (Mt 23:37–38). Jezebel's idolatry and witchcraft were not so offensive as her persecution of the prophets, killing some and driving the rest into caves (1Ki 18:4).

2.2.2. What their condemnation was. They were sentenced to complete destruction, and Jehu was particularly directed to throw Jezebel to the dogs (v. 10).

Verses 11–15

After a pause Jehu returned to his place with his fellow officers, making no comment on what had happened, since he wanted, it seems, to keep matters to himself for the present. Notice:

1. With what contempt the officers speak of the young prophet (v. 11): "*Wherefore came this mad fellow to thee?* What business did he have with you?" They thought that the prophets were fools and that the *spiritual men were mad* (Hos 9:7). Those who have no religious faith commonly speak with disdain about those who do have it, and look on them as mad. They said of our Savior, *He is beside himself* (Mk 3:21); of John the Baptist, *He has a devil* (Mt 11:18); and of the apostle Paul, *Much learning has made him mad* (Ac 26:24). The highest wisdom is presented as foolishness, and those who understand themselves the best are considered out of their mind. Perhaps Jehu intended it as a rebuke to his friends when he said, "*You know the man* (v. 11) to be a prophet, and so you can guess what his business is: to show me my faults and to teach me my duty. I don't need to tell you about it." He tried to put them off in this way, but they urged him to tell them. "That's not true," they said, "we can't work out why he came, and so tell us." When Jehu was pressed to do this, he told them that the prophet had *anointed him king*, and he probably showed them the oil on his head (v. 12).

2. With what respect they congratulated the new king when they were first told of his advancement (v. 13). As a sign of their subjection and allegiance to him, they put their cloaks under him so that he might stand on the bare steps (v. 13), in full view of the soldiers, who, when they first received the news of his accession to be king, came to grace the occasion.

3. With what caution Jehu proceeded. He had the army with him. Joram had left it and had gone home badly wounded. Jehu's good leadership was apparent in two things:

- He complimented the officers and would do nothing without their advice and agreement.
- He planned to surprise Joram, and in order to do this, he planned to attack him quickly. The suddenness of an attack may sometimes be as much of an advantage as its actual force.

Verses 16–29

From Ramoth Gilead to Jezreel was more than one day's journey. About midway between them, the river

Jordan had to be crossed. Finally he had the cursed king within sight, and then within reach.

1. Joram's lookout sees Jehu and his retinue in the distance and warns the king that some troops are approaching, but he cannot see whether they are friends or foes. But the king first sends one messenger, and then another, to bring him news (vv. 17–19). Each messenger asks the same question: *"Is it peace?* Are you for us or for our enemy?" Each gets the same answer: *What hast thou to do with peace? Turn thee behind me* (vv. 18–19). The lookout reports that the messengers have been taken prisoner and eventually observes that the leader of these troops is driving like Jehu, who it seems was noted for his *furious*, wild driving. A man of such a forceful temperament was most suitable for the service for which Jehu was intended.

2. Joram himself goes out to meet him and takes Ahaziah king of Judah along with him. Neither of them was equipped for war, because they did not expect an enemy to be approaching, but they went out quickly to satisfy their curiosity.

2.1. The place where Joram met Jehu was ominous: *In the portion of* (ground of) *Naboth the Jezreelite* (v. 21). The very sight of that plot of ground was enough to make Joram tremble and Jehu expect triumph, for Joram had the guilt of Naboth's blood fighting against him, and Jehu had the force of Elijah's curse fighting for him.

2.2. Joram's demand was still the same: *"Is it peace, Jehu?* Have you come in peace, Jehu (v. 22)? Is everything fine? Are you coming home fleeing from the Arameans or as a conqueror over them?"

2.3. Jehu's reply was very striking. He answered Joram with a question: *What peace* can you expect, *so long as the whoredoms* (idolatry) *of thy mother Jezebel and her witchcrafts are so many?* (v. 22). Notice:

2.3.1. He charges him with his mother's evil. She stands impeached for idolatry, both spiritual and physical, and also for witchcraft, sorcery, and divination, used in honor of her idols. These were many and increased, for those who abandon themselves to evil ways do not know where they will end.

2.3.2. For that reason he removes any chance of peace for him. "What peace can come to a house in which there is so much evil which has not been repented of ?" The way of sin can never be the way of peace (Isa 57:21). Sinners can have no peace so long as they persist in sin, but as soon as it is repented of and abandoned, then there is peace.

2.4. The execution was carried out immediately. When Joram heard his mother's crimes mentioned, his heart failed him. He immediately concluded that the long-threatened day of judgment had come and cried out, *"There is treachery, O Ahaziah!* (v. 23). Jehu is our enemy, and it is time for us to flee for our safety." Both fled and:

2.4.1. Joram king of Israel was killed immediately (v. 24). Jehu killed him with his own hands. He died as a criminal, under the sentence of the law, and Jehu, the executioner, disposed of the dead body according to the same sentence. Naboth's vineyard was close by, which reminded him of the circumstances of the condemnation Elijah had passed on Ahab: *"I will requite thee in this plat* (plot of ground), *said the Lord* (vv. 25–26), *for the blood of Naboth* himself, and *for the blood of his sons*. That very piece of ground which he had made himself master of with so much pride and pleasure and at the expense of the guilt of innocent blood now became the place where his son's dead body lay exposed and for the whole world to see.

2.4.2. Ahaziah king of Judah was chased and killed a little later and not far away (vv. 27–28). Although he was now in Joram's company, he would not have been killed if he had not joined with the house of Ahab both in relationship and in sin.

Verses 30–37

The greatest offender in the house of Ahab was Jezebel. It was she who introduced Baal, killed the Lord's prophets, planned the murder of Naboth, and stirred up first her husband and then her sons to commit evil. She is here called *a cursed woman* (v. 34). Her reign had survived the reigns of three kings, but now, finally, her day of destruction had come. Jezebel's destruction may be looked on as a type of the destruction of idolaters and persecutors. We have here:

1. Jezebel challenging the judgment. She heard that Jehu had killed her son for her idolatry and witchcraft and thrown his dead body onto the plot of ground that had belonged to Naboth, and that he was now coming to Jezreel. Now she set herself at a window at the entrance of the city gate to defy Jehu.

1.1. Instead of hiding herself, as one who was afraid of divine vengeance, she exposed herself to it and did not deign to flee.

1.2. Instead of humbling herself and mourning her son, she *painted her face, and tired her head* (arranged her hair) (v. 30), so that she might make herself appear, so she thought, great and majestic, hoping to intimidate Jehu. There is no surer sign of ruin than an unhumbled heart under humbling circumstances.

1.3. Instead of trembling before Jehu, the instrument of God's vengeance, she thought she would make him tremble by asking a threatening question: *Had Zimri peace, who slew his master?* Did Zimri have peace, who murdered his master (v. 31)? Notice:

1.3.1. She took no notice of the hand of God against her family, but defied the one who was only acting as the sword in God's hand.

1.3.2. She pleased herself with the thought that what Jehu was now doing would certainly end in his own destruction, and that he would have no peace.

1.3.3. She quoted a precedent to deter him from pursuing this undertaking: *"Had Zimri peace?* (v. 31). No, he had not; he came to the throne by blood and treachery, and within seven days was forced to burn the palace around him with himself in it, and can you expect to fare any better?" Zimri had no authority for what he did, but was incited to do it merely by his own ambition and cruelty, whereas Jehu was anointed by one of the sons of the prophets, and acted by order from heaven, which would support him.

2. Jehu demanding help to act against her. He looks up to the window, unafraid at the threats of her bold — but weak — rage and cries out, *Who is on my side? Who?* (v. 32). When the work of reformation is under way, it is time to ask, "Who will help?"

3. Her own attendants giving her up to his just revenge. Two or three officials looked out on Jehu so as to give him encouragement to believe they were on his side. He called to them to immediately throw her down. This was one way of stoning evildoers, throwing them down from some steep place. This was how vengeance was taken on her for the stoning of Naboth. They threw her down (v. 33). She was put to death with great dishonor, dashed against the wall and the pavement.

4. The very dogs completing her shame and ruin, according to the prophecy. Jehu thought he would show

some respect to Jezebel's person and bury her. Bad though she was, she was still a daughter, a king's daughter, a king's wife, and a king's mother: *Go and bury her* (v. 34). But while Jehu was eating and drinking, the dogs had devoured her dead body. The hungry dogs had no respect for the dignity of her background: a king's daughter was no more to them than a common person. When news was brought of this to Jehu, he remembered the threat (1Ki 21:23), *The dogs shall eat Jezebel by the wall of Jezreel.* Jezebel's name remained nowhere, except for being stigmatized in Holy Scripture. They could not even say, "This is Jezebel's dust. This is Jezebel's grave."

CHAPTER 10

We have in this chapter: 1. A further account of Jehu's carrying out his commission. He destroyed: 1.1. All Ahab's sons (vv. 1–10) and all Ahab's relatives (vv. 11–14, 17). 1.2. Ahab's idolatry. Jehu took Jehonadab to see his zeal for the Lord in dealing with it (vv. 15–16), summoned all the worshipers of Baal to attend (vv. 18–23), killed them all (vv. 24–25), and abolished that idolatry (vv. 26–28). 2. A short account of the administration of his government. The old idolatry of Israel, the worship of the calves, was retained (vv. 29–31). This brought God's judgment on them through Hazael, and it is with this judgment that Jehu's reign concludes (vv. 32–36).

Verses 1–14

Jehu knew the whole house of Ahab must be destroyed.

1. He got the heads of all the sons of Ahab cut off by their own guardians at Samaria. These sons of Ahab were now in Samaria, a strong city. Perhaps they had been brought there for safety on the occasion of the war with Aram or when Jehu's insurrection took place. With them were the rulers of Jezreel, the great officers of the court, who went to Samaria to keep themselves safe or to consider what to do. Jehu did not think it right to take his forces to Samaria to destroy the sons, but so that the hand of God might appear more remarkably in it, he made their guardians their murderers.

1.1. He sent a challenge to their friends to stand by them (vv. 2–3). It was not as if he wanted them to do this or expected they would; rather, he was rebuking them for their cowardice and complete inability to fight against God's will.

1.2. He gained from them a submission. They wisely reasoned with themselves: "*Behold, two kings stood not before him* but fell as sacrifices to his rage; *how then shall we stand?* If two kings could not resist him, how can we?" (v. 4). So they sent him their surrender: "*We are thy servants,* your subjects, and we *will do all that thou shalt bid us* (v. 5)."

1.3. He profited by their submission so far as to make them the executioners of those whom they taught (v. 6). These elders of Jezreel had been evil and had obeyed Jezebel's order to murder Naboth (1Ki 21:11). She probably gloried in the power she had over them, and now the same evil spirit makes them as pliable to Jehu and as ready to obey his orders for the murder of Ahab's sons. When the heads were presented to Jehu, he rebuked those who were the executioners, but he also acknowledged the hand of God in it.

1.3.1. He seems to blame those who have executed this vengeance. "I killed only one; they have killed all these. Let not the people of Samaria, or any friends of the house

of Ahab, ever condemn me for what I have done, when their own elders and the very guardians of the orphans have done this." But:

1.3.2. He sees the righteous judgment of God behind it all (v. 10): *The Lord hath done that which he spoke by Elijah.*

2. He proceeded to destroy all who remained in the house of Ahab, not only those who were descended from him but also those who were related to him. Having done this in Jezreel, he did the same in Samaria (v. 17): he killed *all that remained to Ahab in Samaria.* This was awful bloodshed, and it is not now to be used as a precedent. Let the guilty suffer, but not the innocent for their sakes.

3. Providence brought the relatives of Ahaziah across his path as he was carrying out his commission, and he killed them likewise (vv. 12–14).

3.1. They were branches of Ahab's house, being descended from Athaliah, and so came within his commission.

3.2. They were tainted with the evil of the house of Ahab.

3.3. They were now going to court the leaders of the house of Ahab, to greet the children of the king and the queen, Joram and Jezebel, which showed that they were linked to them in affection as well as by blood relationship.

Verses 15–28

Jehu presses on with his work, and here:

1. He seeks the friendship of a good man, *Jehonadab the son of Rechab* (vv. 15–16). *This* Jehonadab, although dead to the world and having little to do with its business—as can be seen by his command to his descendants, which they religiously observed until 250 to 300 years later, not to drink wine or live in cities (Jer 35:6–11)—went on this occasion to meet Jehu, so that he might encourage him in the work to which God had called him. Jehonadab, though not a prophet, priest, or Levite, was respected for the life of self-denial and devotion that he lived. And Jehu, though a soldier, knew him and honored him. When he met him—even though it is likely he drove now as furiously as ever—he stopped to speak to him:

1.1. Jehu greeted him; he "blessed him"—which is the meaning of the word—he paid him respect.

1.2. Jehu professed that *his heart was right with him* (v. 15), that he had a true affection for him and a respect for the crown of his Nazariteship; and he wanted to know whether Jehonadab had the same affection for him: *Is thy heart right?* Jehonadab gave him his word (*It is*), and gave him his hand as a pledge of his heart.

1.3. Jehu took him up into his chariot and took him along with him to Samaria. All serious people would think the better of Jehu when they saw Jehonadab in the chariot with him. This was not the only time in which the godliness of some has been made to serve others' politics, or in which scheming people have strengthened themselves by drawing good people onto their side. Jehonadab is a stranger to the ways of worldly wisdom, and so if Jehu is a servant of God and an enemy of Baal, Jehonadab will be his faithful friend. "Come then," Jehu says, "come with me, *and see my zeal for the Lord*" (v. 16). This is commonly taken as giving cause to suspect that the zeal he pretended for the Lord was really a zeal for himself and his own advancement. For:

1.3.1. He boasted about it and spoke as if God and the people around him were greatly indebted to him for it.

1.3.2. He wanted it to be seen and taken notice of, like the Pharisees, who did everything to be seen by others. Jehonadab went with him, however, and probably encouraged him and helped him carry out his commission (v. 17), destroying all Ahab's friends in Samaria. A person may hate cruelty but love justice.

2. He plans the destruction of all the worshipers of Baal. Jehu's plan is to destroy them all together.

2.1. He brought them all together into the temple of Baal by a trick. He pretended he would worship Baal more than Ahab had ever done (v. 18). He issued a declaration requiring the attendance of all the worshipers of Baal with him at the offering of a sacrifice to Baal (vv. 19–20).

2.2. He was careful that none of the servants of the Lord would be among them (v. 23).

2.3. He gave orders to destroy them all, and Jehonadab joined him in that task (v. 23). Then the guards were sent in to put them all to death

2.4. When the idolaters had been destroyed in this way, the idolatry itself was totally abolished. The buildings around the house of Baal were destroyed. All the little idols, statues, pictures, or shrines which decorated Baal's temple, with the great sacred stone of Baal itself, were brought out and burned (vv. 26–27), and the temple of Baal was broken down. This was how the worship of Baal was completely destroyed. This is how God will destroy all the gods of the nations, and sooner or later, he will triumph over them all.

Verses 29–36

Here is the complete account of the reign of Jehu:

1. God's approval of what Jehu had done.

1.1. God declared what he had done to be right. The destruction of idolaters and idolatry was something right in God's eyes.

1.2. God promised him a reward, that his children of the fourth generation from him would *sit upon the throne of Israel*.

2. Jehu's carelessness in carrying out his next duties. This shows that his heart was not right with God, that he only partially reformed his ways.

2.1. He did not put away every evil. He abandoned the sins of Ahab but not the sins of Jeroboam. He rejected Baal but remained loyal to Jeroboam's golden calves, the worship of which was a form of political idolatry. It had been begun and kept up for political reasons, to prevent the return of the ten tribes to the house of David, and so Jehu clung to that. True conversion is not only from those sins which destroy worldly interest but also from those which support and befriend it. To abandon those is the greatest test to see whether we can deny ourselves and trust God.

2.2. He put away evil, but he did not follow what was good (v. 31): *He took no heed to walk in the law of the Lord God of Israel*. He had shown great care and zeal to root out false religion, but for true religious faith he was not at all concerned. He showed no zeal for pleasing God. It seems he was a man who had little religious faith within himself, and yet God used him as an instrument of reformation in Israel.

3. The judgment that came on Israel in his reign. There was a general decay in godliness and an increase in worldliness, and so it is not strange that the next news we hear is, *In those days the Lord began to cut Israel short*, to reduce the size of Israel (v. 32). Their neighbors encroached on them on every side. King Hazael of Aram (*Syria*) was, more than any other, a source of trouble to them: he *smote* (defeated) *them in all the coasts* (territory) *of Israel* (v. 32).

4. The conclusion of Jehu's reign (vv. 34–36). Because he was not careful to serve God, the memorials of his mighty enterprises and achievements are justly buried in oblivion.

CHAPTER 11

Now we must consider the affairs of the kingdom of Judah. 1. Athaliah usurps the government and destroys all the royal family (v. 1). Joash, a child one year old, is wonderfully preserved (vv. 2–3). 2. After six years he is brought forward and, through the agency of Jehoiada, made king (vv. 4–12). 3. Athaliah is killed (vv. 13–16). 4. Both the civil and religious interests of the kingdom are well established in the hands of Joash (vv. 17–21).

Verses 1–3

God had assured David that his family would continue, which is called his *ordaining a lamp for his anointed* (Ps 132:17). Here we have David's promised lamp almost extinguished but still wonderfully preserved.

1. It was almost extinguished by the cruel hatred of Athaliah, the queen mother, who, when she heard that her son Ahaziah had been killed by Jehu, *arose and destroyed all the seed royal* (all the royal family) (v. 1), all whom she knew to be related to the crown. She did it:

1.1. From a spirit of ambition. She thirsted after the power to rule and thought she could not gain it any other way.

1.2. From a spirit of revenge and anger against God. Because the house of Ahab had been completely destroyed, she decided, as it were, to pay back the house of David by destroying it. She is rightly called *Athaliah, that wicked woman* (2Ch 24:7), Jezebel's own daughter.

2. It was wonderfully preserved by the godly care of one of Jehoram's daughters (who was the wife of Jehoiada the priest), who stole away one of the king's sons, Joash, and hid him (vv. 2–3). The place of his safety was the temple of the Lord, one of the rooms belonging to the temple, a place Athaliah seldom bothered with. When his aunt took him there, she was putting him under God's special protection, and so hid him by faith, just as Moses had been hidden. Now David's words to one of his offspring were fulfilled (Ps 27:5): *In the secret of his tabernacle shall he hide me*. It was with good reason that this Joash, when he grew up, set himself to repair the temple of the Lord, for it had been a safe place for him. Notice the wisdom and care of Providence and how it prepares for what it intends to bring about. Notice, too, what blessings people lay up in store for their families when they marry their children to people who are wise and good.

Verses 4–12

Queen Athaliah was dictator for six years. While Jehu was destroying the worship of Baal in Israel, she was establishing it in Judah, as can be seen from 2Ch 24:7. All this time Joash lay hidden, entitled to a crown and intended for it, but buried alive in obscurity. Then, in his seventh year, he was ready to be shown, as one having served his first apprenticeship in life and arrived at his first critical year. By that time the people had become tired of Athaliah's tyranny and were ready for change. How that change came about we are told here:

1. The one who arranged this great matter was Jehoiada the priest, probably the high priest. He was a man of

authority by his birth and office. He was related to the
royal family, and if all the royal family was destroyed,
his wife, as daughter of Jehoram, would be more entitled to the crown than Athaliah was. By his eminent
gifts and graces he was qualified to serve his country,
and he could not do a better service than to free it from
Athaliah's usurpation.

2. The way he went about things was very discreet, and
befitting for someone as wise and good as Jehoiada.

2.1. He arranged matters with the *rulers* (commanders)
of hundreds and the captains (v. 19); these latter were the
holders of ecclesiastical, civil, and military office. He got
them to come to him in the temple, discussed matters with
them, made them swear an oath of secrecy, and *showed
them the king's son* (v. 4). What a pleasant surprise it was
to these leaders, who feared that the house and family of
David had been completely destroyed, to find such a spark
as this among the embers.

2.2. He stationed the priests and Levites, who were
more immediately under his direction, along the different access routes to the temple, to keep guard. David had
divided the priests into groups. Every Sabbath morning a
new group came to serve, but the group of the previous
week did not stop serving until the evening of the Sabbath,
so that on the Sabbath, when double service had to be
undertaken, there were double numbers to do it. Jehoiada
employed these to serve on this great occasion. He armed
them from the temple armory with David's spears and
shields. They were ordered to do two things:

2.2.1. To protect the young king from being attacked.

2.2.2. To preserve the holy temple from being defiled
by the crowd of people who would come together on this
occasion (v. 6).

2.3. When the guards were at their posts, the king was
brought out (v. 12). Jehoiada, without delay, proceeded
to crown this young king. This was done with great ceremony (v. 12).

2.3.1. As a sign that Joash was being invested with
kingly power, Jehoiada *put the crown upon him.*

2.3.2. As a sign of his obligation to govern by the Law
and to make the word of God his rule, he presented him
with a copy of the covenant (Dt 17:18–19).

2.3.3. As a sign of his receiving the Spirit, to qualify
him for this great work to which he had been called, he
anointed him.

2.3.4. As a sign of the people's acceptance of him and
subjection to his government, they clapped their hands
with joy and expressed their sincere good wishes to him:
God save the king, long live the king (v. 12). They made
him their king and agreed with the divine appointment.
They had reason to welcome to the crown the one whose
right it was, and they had reason to pray, *Let him live,* concerning the one who came to them as life from the dead
and in whom the house of David was to live. With such
expressions of joy and assurance the kingdom of Christ
must also be welcomed into our hearts when his throne is
set up there and Satan the usurper is deposed.

Verses 13–16

It was probably the original intention that when they finished the ceremony of the king's inauguration, they would
visit Athaliah and call her to account for her murders, usurpation, and tyranny, but like her mother Jezebel, she went
out to meet them and hastened her own destruction.

1. Hearing the noise, she was shocked to see what
the reason was (v. 13). Jehoiada and his friends declared
what they were doing. It was strange that she acted so

ill-advisedly as to come out herself, and it appears she
came out alone.

2. Seeing what had been done, she cried out for help.
She saw the king's position by the pillar occupied by one
to whom the officers and the people were paying homage.
This made her tear her clothes and cry, "Treason! Treason! Come and help me against the traitors!"

3. Jehoiada gave orders to put her to death as an idolater,
a usurper, and an enemy of the community. Care was taken
that she would not be killed in the temple and that whoever
appeared for her would die with her. She tried to make her
escape via the back way to the palace, through the stalls,
but they pursued her and killed her there (v. 16).

Verses 17–21

Jehoiada had completed the hardest part of his work,
now that he had made the young prince's way to the throne
free from all opposition by putting Athaliah to death. We
have an account of two things:

1. The good foundations he laid by having all those who
were present make a contract with one another in person
(v. 17). Now that the prince and people were together in
God's house, Jehoiada took care that they should jointly
make a covenant with God, and mutually covenant with
each other, so that they might rightly understand their
duty both to God and to one another.

1.1. He tried to establish and secure the interests of
religious faith among them by making a covenant between
them and God. In this covenant, the king stands on the
same level as his subjects and is as committed as any of
them to serve the Lord. This commitment meant they
renounced Baal, whom many of them had worshiped,
and submitted themselves to God's rule. By our commitment to God the commitments of every relationship are
strengthened. They *first gave themselves to the Lord,* and
then *to us* (2Co 8:5).

1.2. He then established both the coronation oath and
the oath of allegiance, the compact or covenant between
the king and the people, by which the king was obliged to
govern according to law and protect his subjects, and they
were obliged, while he did so, to obey him and to trust in
him and be truly loyal to him.

2. The good beginnings he built on those foundations:

2.1. In accordance with their covenant with God, they
immediately abolished idolatry. Everyone, now that they
had such a good leader, helped to tear down Baal's temple,
with its altars and sacred stones. All the worshipers of
Baal, it seems, deserted him; only his priest Mattan stood
by the altar. Though everyone abandoned Baal, Mattan
did not, and so he was killed there. Having destroyed
Baal's temple, they appointed *officers over the house of
God* (v. 18), to see that the service of God was regularly
performed by the proper people, at the due times, and
according to the ways God had instituted.

2.2. In accordance with their covenant with one
another:

2.2.1. The king was brought in state to the royal palace
and sat there on the throne of judgment, *the thrones of
the house of David* (v. 19), ready to receive petitions and
appeals, which he would refer to Jehoiada to give answers
to and judgment on.

2.2.2. The people rejoiced and Jerusalem was quiet
(v. 20).

CHAPTER 12

*This chapter gives us the history of the reign of Joash,
which does not fulfill its glorious beginnings which*

we read about in the previous chapter. He was not so illustrious at forty years old as he was at seven. Yet his reign is to be reckoned as one of the better; it appears much worse in 2Ch 24:1–27 than it does here. Here we are only told: 1. That he did well while Jehoiada lived (vv. 1–3). 2. That he was careful and active in repairing the temple (vv. 4–16). 3. That after a contemptible agreement with Hazael (vv. 17–18) he died in obscurity (vv. 19–21).

Verses 1–3

A general account is given of Joash, that:

1. He reigned forty years.

2. He did what was right as long as Jehoiada lived to instruct him (v. 2).

3. The high places were not taken away (v. 3). Up and down the country they had altars for both sacrifice and incense, to the honor of only the God of Israel, but in competition with God's altar at Jerusalem. These private altars, perhaps, had been used more in the recent bad reigns than they had been used formerly, because it was not safe to go up to Jerusalem, nor was the temple service performed as it should have been. It may be that Jehoiada turned a blind eye to them because he hoped that the reforming of the temple and the putting of things into a good shape there would gradually draw people away from their high places, so that they would fade away by themselves.

Verses 4–16

Here is an account of the repairing of the temple in the reign of Joash:

1. Although Solomon had built it and it was made from the best materials and in the best way, in time it still began to decay, and there were breaches (damage) found in it (v. 5). Even temples themselves become worse for wear, but the heavenly temple will never become old. Yet it was not only the teeth of time that had caused this damage; the sons of Athaliah had also broken up the house of God (2Ch 24:7).

2. The king himself was the first and the most eager in his concern to repair the temple:

2.1. Because he was king, and God expects and requires from those who have power that they use it to maintain and support religious faith, to redress grievances, and to repair decay.

2.2. Because the temple had been both his nursery and his sanctuary when he was a child, in grateful remembrance of which he now showed himself to be zealous to honor it. Those who have experienced the comfort and benefit of religious meetings will make the support of them their care and the prosperity of them their chief joy.

3. The priests were ordered to collect money for these repairs and to make sure that the work was done. He gave them orders to levy the money. They must not wait until it was paid in but must demand it from the respective districts where they knew it was due, either as redemption money, as required in the Law in Ex 30:12, or as "estimation money," as required in the Law in Lev 27:2–3, or as a freewill offering (v. 4).

4. This method did not fulfill the intention, however (v. 6). Little money was raised. Either the priests were negligent and did not call on the people to pay their dues, or the people had so little trust in the priests' management that they were reluctant to put money into their hands. But whatever money was raised was not put to the proper use: The breaches of the house were not repaired.

5. Another method was therefore used. The king had set his heart firmly on having the breaches (damages) of the house repaired (v. 7). His eventual apostasy gives us cause to question whether he had as good an affection for the service of the temple as he had for its structure. Many have been zealous to see churches built and nicely decorated and been zealous for other forms of godliness but have not known its power (2Ti 3:5). However, we commend his zeal. Another course was taken:

5.1. To raise money (vv. 9–10). The money was put into a public chest, and then people brought it in readily and in great abundance. The high priest and the royal secretary counted the money and set it aside in bags.

5.1.1. The money that was dropped into the chest through a hole in the lid, beyond recall, to show that once something has been given to God, it must never be taken back.

5.1.2. The chest was put on the right-hand side as they went in, which some think is alluded to in the rule of kindness which our Savior gives, Let not thy left hand know what thy right hand doeth (Mt 6:3). But while the high priest and the royal secretary were receiving all they could for the repair of the temple, they did not break in on what was the stated maintenance of the priests (v. 16). Let us not make the cost of repairing the temple an excuse for starving the servants of the temple.

5.2. To spend the money that was raised:

5.2.1. They did not put it into the hands of the priests, who were not experienced in such matters because they had other work to take care of, but into the hands of those that did the work, or at least had the oversight of it (v. 11). Those who were entrusted did the business:

5.2.1.1. Carefully, purchasing the materials and paying the workers (v. 12).

5.2.1.2. Faithfully; the workers had such a reputation for honesty that there was no need to inspect their bills or audit their accounts. Those who think it is not sinful to cheat the government, cheat the country, or cheat the church will be made to think differently when God sets their sins in order before them.

5.2.2. They did not spend it on decorations for the temple, on gold or silver vessels, but first on necessary repairs (v. 13).

Verses 17–21

When Joash had rebelled from God and become both an idolater and a persecutor, the hand of the Lord was against him, and his last state was worse than his first (Mt 12:45).

1. His wealth and honor made him an easy target for his neighbors. When Hazael had overpowered Israel (10:32), he threatened Judah and Jerusalem likewise; he took Gath, a strong city (v. 17), and then intended to march with his forces against Jerusalem. Joash had neither the courage nor the strength to fight against him, but gave him all the dedicated things and all the gold that was found both in his treasury and in the treasuries of the temple (v. 18) to bribe him to march another way. If he had not abandoned God and lost his protection, his affairs would not have been brought to such a critical state. He lost the honor of a ruler and a soldier. He made himself and his kingdom poor. By showing Hazael that he could take home such a great plunder without lifting a finger, he tempted him to come again. And the next year the army of Aram came up against Jerusalem, destroyed the leaders, and plundered the city (2Ch 24:23–24).

2. His life became an easy target for his own servants. They plotted against him and killed him (vv. 20–21), to

get revenge on him for murdering a prophet, Jehoiada's son. This is how Joash fell. He began in the spirit but ended in the flesh.

CHAPTER 13

This chapter brings us again to the history of the kings of Israel, and particularly the family of Jehu. We have here an account of: 1. The reign of his son Jehoahaz, which continued for seventeen years. We are told of his bad character in general (vv. 1–2), the trouble he was brought into (v. 3 and again v. 22), and the dwindling of his responsibilities (v. 7). 2. His humiliation before God and God's compassion toward him (vv. 4–5 and again v. 23); his continuation in his idolatry, nevertheless (v. 6); and his death (vv. 8–9). 3. The reign of Jehu's grandson Jehoash, which continued for sixteen years. Here is a general account of his reign (vv. 10–13), but a particular account of the death of Elisha. The king paid him a kind visit (v. 14), and he encouraged the king in his wars with Aram (vv. 15–19). 4. Elisha's death and burial (v. 20), and a miracle worked by his bones (v. 21). And, lastly, we learn of the advantages Jehoash gained against the Arameans (Syrians), according to Elisha's predictions (vv. 24–25).

Verses 1–9

This general account of the reign of Jehoahaz, and of the state of Israel during his seventeen years reign, lets us see:

1. The glory of Israel turned to shame (Ps 4:2). How its crown has been disgraced and its honor laid in the dust!

1.1. It was to the honor of Israel that they worshiped the only living and true God, who is a Spirit, an eternal mind, who had appointed rules by which the people were to worship him, but by *changing the glory of their incorruptible God into the similitude* (image) *of an ox, the truth of God into a lie* (Ps 106:20; Ro 1:25), they lost this honor and put themselves on the same level as the nations who worshiped what their own hands had made. We find here that the king *followed the sins of Jeroboam* (v. 2), and the people departed *not from them, but walked therein* (v. 6).

1.2. It was to the honor of Israel that they were taken under the special protection of heaven. God himself was their defense. But here, as often before, we find them robbed of this glory and exposed to the defiance of all their neighbors. By their sins they provoked God to anger, and then he *delivered them into the hands of Hazael and Ben-hadad* (v. 3). *Hazael oppressed Israel* (v. 22). Surely never was any nation so often picked at and pillaged by its neighbors as Israel.

2. Some sparks of Israel's ancient honor appearing in these ashes. For:

2.1. It was the ancient honor of Israel that they were a praying people, and here we find something of that honor revived, for Jehoahaz their king, in his distress, *besought the Lord* (v. 4). He sought the Lord's favor and turned to him for help. He did not turn to the calves—what help could they give him?—but to the Lord.

2.2. It was the ancient honor of Israel that they had *God nigh unto them in all that which they called upon him for* (Dt 4:7), and this was the case here. Although God might justly have rejected the prayer as something detestable to him, *the Lord* still *hearkened unto Jehoahaz*, and to his prayer for himself and for his people (v. 4), and *he gave Israel a saviour* (v. 5). The deliverer he gave was not Jehoahaz himself—for during his days Hazael oppressed

Israel (v. 22)—but his son, to whom, in answer to his father's prayers, God gave success against the Arameans, so that he recaptured the towns they had taken from his father (v. 25). God gave this gracious answer to the prayer of Jehoahaz in remembrance of his covenant with Abraham (v. 23). Notice how swift God is to show mercy, how willing he is to find a reason to be gracious, or else he would not have looked so far back as to that ancient covenant.

Verses 10–19

We have here Jehoash, or *Joash*, the son of Jehoahaz and grandson of Jehu, on the throne of Israel. Probably the house of Jehu intended to give some respect to the house of David when they gave this heir apparent to the crown the same name as the one who was then king of Judah.

1. He was not the worst, but because he kept that ancient and shrewd idolatry of the house of Jeroboam, it is said, *He did that which was evil in the sight of the Lord.*

2. The detailed account of what took place between him and Elisha contains several remarkable things:

2.1. Elisha became ill (v. 14).

2.1.1. It was now about sixty years since he had been first called to be a prophet. It was a great mercy to Israel, and especially to the company of the prophets, that he had continued to be a burning and shining light (Jn 5:35) for so long.

2.1.2. For all of the later part of his life, from the time Jehu was anointed, which was forty-five years before Jehoash began his reign, we find no mention made of him or of anything he did until we find him here on his deathbed.

2.2. King Jehoash visited him in his sickness and *wept over him* (v. 14). This was evidence of some good in him, that he valued and had affection for a faithful prophet. When the king heard of Elisha's sickness, he came to visit him and to receive his dying counsel and blessing. He mourned him with the same words with which Elisha had himself mourned the removal of Elijah: *My father, my father* (v. 14).

2.3. Elisha gave the king great assurances of his success against the Arameans, Israel's present oppressors, and encouraged him to vigorously pursue war against them. "*I die, but God will surely visit you* (Ge 50:24). He has the remnant of the Spirit (Mal 2:15) and can raise up other prophets to pray for you." He gives him a sign. He orders him to *take bow and arrows* (v. 15). God will be the agent, but Jehoash must be the instrument, and to show that he will be successful, Elisha gives him a sign, by instructing him:

2.3.1. To shoot an arrow toward Aram (vv. 16–17). Because of the arrow's significance, the king received the words of command from the prophet: *Put thy hand upon the bow—Open the window—Shoot.* It was as if he were a child who had never drawn a bow before: *Elisha put his hands upon the king's hands*, to show that in all his expeditions against the Arameans he must look to God for direction and strength. The trembling hands of a dying prophet, when they showed the support and transfer of the power of God, gave this arrow more force than the hands of the king in his full strength. The Arameans had themselves controlled the country to the east (10:33). It was in that direction therefore that the arrow was aimed, and the prophet gave to the shooting of this arrow such an interpretation as made it a commission to the king to attack the Arameans and a promise of success in that commission.

It is the *arrow of the Lord's deliverance* (victory), *even the arrow of deliverance from Syria*, the arrow of victory over Aram (v. 17).

2.3.2. To *smite upon the ground* with the arrows (vv. 18–19). Having in God's name assured the king of victory over the Arameans, the prophet will now test him and see whether he will make the most of his victories, whether he will follow them up with more zeal than Ahab showed when Ben-Hadad lay at his mercy. To test this, Elisha tells him to strike the arrows on the ground. "Now show me what you will do to them when you have them down." The king did not show that eagerness and ardor which one might have expected on this occasion, but struck only three times, and no more. Perhaps he thought that it was a silly thing to do, that three times was often enough for him to play the fool simply to please the prophet. But by condemning the sign, he lost the thing that the sign stood for, greatly to the grief of the dying prophet, who told him he should have struck the ground five or six times. Not being restricted in the power and promises of God, why should he be restricted in his own expectations and endeavors?

Verses 20–25

Here:

1. We go to the grave of Elisha. He died at a good old age, and they buried him. What follows shows what power there was in his life to keep away judgments. As soon as he was dead, the Moabite raiders invaded the land. They were roving, skulking bands, who murdered and plundered by surprise. The king was apprehensive of danger only from the Arameans, but it was the Moabites who invaded him. There was also power in Elisha's dead body: it communicated life to another dead body (v. 21). This great miracle was a clear indication of another life after this. The neighbors were carrying the dead body of a man to the grave, and fearing that it would fall into the hands of the Moabites—a group of whom they saw at a distance near the place where the body was to be interred—they laid the corpse in the nearest convenient place, which proved to be Elisha's grave. When the dead man touched Elisha's bones, he revived and, it is likely, went home again with his friends. Elijah was honored *in* his departure. Elisha was honored *after* his departure. God allocates honors as he pleases, but one way or another, the rest for all his saints will be glorious (Isa 11:10).

2. We see the sword of Jehoash king of Israel used successfully against the Arameans.

2.1. The cause of his success was God's favor (v. 23): *The Lord was gracious to them, had compassion on them* in their miseries, and showed concern for them. It was because of the Lord's great love that they were not consumed (La 3:22); he showed them mercy because he wanted to give them an opportunity to repent.

2.2. The effect of his success. He recaptured from the hands of Ben-Hadad the towns of Israel which the Arameans had taken possession of (v. 25). Jehoash defeated the Arameans three times, just as often as he had struck the ground with the arrows, and then his victories came to an end.

CHAPTER 14

This chapter continues the history of the succession of kings in both Judah and Israel. 1. In the kingdom of Judah, here is the complete history of Amaziah's reign: his good character (vv. 1–4), the justice he carried out

on the murderers of his father (vv. 5–6), his victory over the Edomites (v. 7), his war with Jehoash and his defeat in that war (vv. 8–14), and his eventual fall by a conspiracy against him (vv. 17–20). We have also the beginning of the history of Azariah (vv. 21–22). 2. In the kingdom of Israel, we see the conclusion of the reign of Jehoash (vv. 15–16) and the complete history of Jeroboam II, his son (vv. 23–29).

Verses 1–7

Amaziah was the son and successor of Joash. Let us see him:

1. In the temple. He acted well there, to some extent, like Joash, but not like David (v. 3). He began well but did not persevere. It is not enough to do what our godly predecessors did, simply to keep up their practices; we must also do *as* they did, from the same springs of faith and devotion and with the same sincerity and determination. It is here commented on, as before, that *the high places were not taken away* (v. 4).

2. In the court of law. We have him there exercising justice on the traitors who murdered his father; he did not do it as soon as he came to the crown, when it might cause some disturbance, but wisely deferred it until the kingdom was firmly in his grasp (v. 5). He did not kill the children of the murderers, because the Law of Moses had expressly provided that the children should not be put to death for the fathers (v. 6).

3. On the battlefield. There we find him triumphing over the Edomites (v. 7). Edom rebelled from under the rule of Judah in Jehoram's time (8:22). Now Amaziah makes war on them to bring them back to their allegiance. We will find a more detailed account of this expedition in 2Ch 25:5–13.

Verses 8–14

For several successive generations after the division of the kingdoms, Judah suffered much from the *enmity* of Israel. After Asa's time, for several successive generations, it suffered more from *the friendship* of Israel, and by the alliance and relationships made with them. But now we meet with hostility between them again.

1. Amaziah, without any provocation, and without showing any reason for the quarrel, challenged Jehoash onto the battlefield (v. 8): "*Come, let us look one another in the face.* Let us try our strength in battle." This showed he was proud, presumptuous, and wasteful of blood. Some think that he had the vanity to imagine that he would subdue the kingdom of Israel and reunite it with Judah.

2. Jehoash gravely rebuked him for his challenge and advised him to withdraw (vv. 9–10).

2.1. He humbles Amaziah's pride by comparing himself to a cedar, a stately tree, and Amaziah to a thistle, a lowly weed, telling him that, far from fearing him, he despised him and scorned having anything to do with him or making any alliance with him, just as the cedar would scorn any proposal to marry his daughter to a thistle. He thinks the ancient house of David is not worthy of being named in the same breath as the house of Jehu, even though Jehu was an upstart.

2.2. He foretells his fall: *A wild beast trode down the thistle*, trampled the thistle underfoot (v. 9), and so put an end to his negotiation with the cedar. Jehoash thinks his forces can crush Amaziah just as easily.

2.3. He shows him how foolish his challenge is. "You are proud that you have defeated Edom, as if that had made you formidable to the whole human race."

2.4. He advises him to be content with the honor he has already gained and not risk losing that by grasping at more that is beyond his reach.

3. Amaziah persisted in his decision, and the outcome was disastrous.

3.1. His army was defeated and dispersed (v. 12). Josephus says that when they were about to engage, they were struck with such terror that they did not strike any blows but ran away immediately, everyone as fast as he could.

3.2. He himself was taken prisoner by the king of Israel, and then had enough of *looking him in the face* (v. 11).

3.3. The conqueror entered Jerusalem. It tamely opened itself to him, but he still broke down its wall — and according to Josephus, drove his chariot triumphantly through the breach — to disgrace the people.

4. Jehoash plundered Jerusalem, took away all that was valuable, and returned to Samaria loaded with plunder (v. 14).

Verses 15 – 22

Here are three kings brought to their graves in these few verses:

1. Jehoash king of Israel (vv. 15 – 16).

2. Amaziah king of Judah. For fifteen years he survived his conqueror the king of Israel (v. 17). He was killed by his own subjects, who hated him for his improper management of public affairs (v. 19). They made Jerusalem too unsafe for him — the ignominious breach in their walls had been caused by his foolish presumption — and he fled to Lachish. We are not told how long he continued to be concealed or sheltered there, but eventually he was murdered there (v. 19).

3. Azariah succeeded Amaziah, but not until twelve years after his father's death, for Amaziah died in the fifteenth year of Jeroboam (as appears by comparing v. 23 with v. 2), but Azariah did not begin his reign till the twenty-seventh year of Jeroboam (15:1), and so he must have been only four years old at the death of his father, so that for twelve years until he came to be sixteen, the government was in the hands of protectors. He reigned for a very long time (15:2), but the account of his reign is here diligently hushed up and broken off abruptly (v. 22): *He built Elath* — which had belonged to the Edomites.

Verses 23 – 29

Here is an account of the reign of Jeroboam II:

1. His reign was long, the longest of all the reigns of the kings of Israel: *He reigned forty-one years* (v. 23); but his contemporary, Azariah, the king of Judah, reigned even longer, fifty-two years. This Jeroboam reigned as long as Asa had (1Ki 15:10), but one did what was good and the other what was evil. We cannot measure human character by the length of a person's life or by their outward prosperity.

2. His character was the same as that of the rest of those kings: *He did that which was evil* (v. 24), for *he departed not from the sins of Jeroboam.* He kept the worship of the calves, thinking it was not harmful because it had been the practice of his predecessors. But a sin is no less evil in God's sight just because it has been a long-standing practice.

3. But he prospered more than most of them, for although he did evil in the sight of the Lord in that one thing, it is probable that in other respects there was some good found in him, and so God acknowledged him:

3.1. By prophecy. He raised up Jonah, the son of Amittai, a Galilean. It is a sign that God has not rejected his people if he continues to have faithful ministers among

them. When Elisha, who strengthened the hands of Jehoash, was removed, Jonah was sent to encourage his son. It is probable that he was a young man when God sent him to Nineveh, and that he knew only a little about the visions of God when he flew off in a rage as he did. If so, God's using him as a messenger of mercy to Israel is clear evidence of the forgiveness of his faults and foolish ways. A commission amounts to a pardon.

3.2. By Providence. The event was *according to the word of the Lord* (v. 25): he was successful. He *restored the coast* (territory) *of Israel* (v. 25), recaptured those frontier towns and countries that were situated from Hamath in the north to the Sea of the Arabah (v. 25). Two reasons are given why God blessed them with those victories:

3.2.1. Because their distress was very great, which made them the objects of his compassion (v. 26). Those who lived in the countries which the enemies had conquered were miserably oppressed and enslaved. The rest were probably made much poorer because of the frequent raids made by the enemy to plunder them. Let those whose case is pitiable take comfort from divine pity. We read of God's tender compassion (Isa 63:15; Jer 31:20) and that he is full of compassion (Ps 86:15).

3.2.2. Because he had not as yet said *he would blot out the name of Israel* (v. 27). If *blot out the name of Israel* refers to the dispersion of the ten tribes, he did say it and do it not long afterward. If it refers to the complete destruction of the name of Israel, he never said it, nor will he ever do it, for that name still remains under heaven in the *gospel Israel* and will to the end of time.

4. Here is the conclusion of his reign. We read of Jeroboam's powerful military achievements (v. 28). There had been many prophets in Israel, but none had left any of their prophecies in writing till those of this age began to do so, and their prophecies are part of the canon of Scripture. It was in the reign of this Jeroboam that Hosea began to prophesy, and he was the first who wrote his prophecies. The word of the Lord through him is therefore called *the beginning of the word of the Lord* (Hos 1:2). At the same time Amos prophesied, and wrote his prophecy, soon afterward Micah, and then Isaiah, in the days of Ahaz and Hezekiah. God never left himself without a witness.

CHAPTER 15

1. The history of two of the kings of Judah is briefly recorded: Azariah, or Uzziah (vv. 1 – 7), and Jotham his son (vv. 32 – 38). 2. The history of many of the kings of Israel who reigned at the same time is also given briefly, five kings in succession. Zechariah, the last of the house of Jehu, reigned six months, and then was killed and succeeded by Shallum (vv. 8 – 12). Shallum reigned one month and then was killed and succeeded by Menahem (vv. 13 – 15). Menahem reigned, or rather tyrannized, for ten years and then died in his bed; he left his son to succeed him and then suffer for him (vv. 16 – 22). Pekahiah reigned two years and then was killed and succeeded by Pekah (vv. 23 – 36). Pekah reigned twenty years and then was killed and succeeded by Hoshea, the last of all the kings of Israel (vv. 27 – 31), for things were now moving quickly toward the final destruction of that kingdom.

Verses 1 – 7

This is a short account of the reign of Azariah:

1. Most of the account is general. He began to reign when he was young and reigned for a long time (v. 2).

For the most part, he did what was right (v. 3), but he was not zealous or courageous enough to take away the high places (v. 4).

2. What is special (v. 5)—that God struck him with leprosy (see note on 5:1)—is related in more detail together with its cause in 2Ch 26:16–21, where we also have a fuller account of the glories of the earlier part of his reign, as well as of the disgraces of its later part. We are told here that:

2.1. He suffered from a skin disease.

2.2. God struck him with this skin disease to rebuke him for his presumptuous encroaching on the priests' office.

2.3. He suffered this skin disease *to the day of his death* (v. 5). Although we have reason to think that he repented and the sin was forgiven, nevertheless, to warn others, he continued to bear this mark of God's displeasure.

2.4. He *dwelt in a several* (separate) *house* (v. 5) as one who was made ceremonially unclean according to the Law; he had to submit to the discipline of the Law even though he was king.

2.5. His son was his viceroy in charge of both the affairs of his court—for *he was over the house* (v. 5)—and of his kingdom—he was *judging the people of the land* (v. 5). It was both a comfort to him and a blessing to his kingdom that he had such a son to take his place.

Verses 8–31

The best days of the kingdom of Israel were during the time when the government was in Jehu's family. During his reign and the next three reigns, although there were many detestable corruptions and severe afflictions in Israel, the crown still continued in succession, the kings died in their beds, and some care was taken of public affairs; but those days had come to an end, and the history of about thirty-three years which we have in these verses represents the affairs of that kingdom in the most intense confusion possible.

1. Let us consider these unhappy changes in leadership. These were truly bad times.

1.1. God had tested the people of Israel by giving judgments and mercies that had been explained and enforced by his servants the prophets, but the people had persisted in not repenting and reforming their ways. God was therefore just in bringing these miseries on them.

1.2. God fulfilled his promise to Jehu, that his sons to the fourth generation after him would sit on the throne of Israel, which was a greater favor than was shown to any of the royal families either before or afterward. This was how God rewarded Jehu for his zeal in destroying the worship of Baal and the house of Ahab, but when the limit of the sins of the house of Jehu had been reached, God administered justice on it for the blood that had been shed, called *the blood of Jezreel* (Hos 1:4).

1.3. All these kings did that *which* was *evil in the sight of the Lord, for they walked in the sins of Jeroboam the son of Nebat* (v. 9). Although they differed from one another, they all had this in common: they kept their idolatry, and the people loved to have it that way.

1.4. Each of these except one conspired against his predecessor and killed him—*Shallum, Menahem, Pekah*, and *Hoshea*, all traitors and murderers, yet each one of them a king for a while. One evil person is often made a scourge to another, and all evil people eventually bring ruin on themselves.

1.5. The ambition of these great kings made the nation miserable. Here Tiphsah, a city of Israel, is cruelly

destroyed, with all its surroundings, by one of these pretenders (v. 16).

1.6. While the nation was shattered by divisions at home in this way, the kings of Assyria, first one (v. 19) and then another (v. 29), came against it and did what they pleased.

1.7. This was the condition of Israel just before it was completely destroyed and taken into exile, for that was in the ninth year of Hoshea, the last of these usurpers. If the people had humbled themselves before God and sought his face during these confusing and bewildering times, that final destruction might have been prevented.

2. Let us now take a brief view of the individual reigns:

2.1. Zechariah, the son of Jeroboam, began to reign in the thirty-eighth year of Azariah, or Uzziah, king of Judah (v. 8). Some chronologers reckon that, because of the disturbances and conflicts in the kingdom, between Jeroboam and his son Zechariah the throne was vacant for twenty-two years. Zechariah was deposed before he was well established on the throne. He reigned for only six months, and then Shallum *slew* (killed) *him before the people* (v. 10), with the approval of the people, whom Zechariah had somehow made himself hated by; so ended the line of Jehu.

2.2. But did Shallum have peace, the one who assassinated his master? No; he did not (v. 13). He was king for only one month, and then he was cut off. Menahem, either provoked by Shallum's crime or spurred on by his example, soon served him as he had served his master—he assassinated *him and reigned in his stead* (v. 14).

2.3. Menahem held the kingdom for ten years (v. 17). He was so outrageously cruel to those of his own nation who hesitated a little to submit to him that he not only destroyed a city but also *ripped up* (ripped open) *all the women with child* (v. 16). He hoped that these cruel methods would frighten everyone else into joining him, but when the king of Assyria came against him:

2.3.1. He had so little confidence in his people that he dared not meet him as an enemy, but was obliged, at vast expense, to buy peace with him.

2.3.2. He needed such help *to confirm the kingdom in his hand* (v. 19) that he made it part of his bargain with the king of Assyria that he would help Menahem against his own subjects who were discontented with him. In this way he got clear of the king of Assyria at this time, but the invader's army now gained so much booty with such little trouble that it was encouraged to come again, not long after, and at that time the Assyrians devastated everything.

2.4. Pekahiah, the son of Menahem, succeeded his father but reigned only two years, and then was treacherously killed by Pekah.

2.5. Although Pekah gained the kingdom by treason, he kept it for twenty years (v. 27). It was that long before his violent dealings eventually returned on his own head. This Pekah, son of Remaliah:

2.5.1. Made himself more significant abroad than any of these usurpers, for he was a great terror to the kingdom of Judah, as we find in Isa 7:1–25.

2.5.2. Lost a great part of his kingdom to the king of Assyria. By this judgment God punished him for his attempt on Judah and Jerusalem.

2.5.3. Forfeited his life soon after this to the hostility of his compatriots. They were probably disgusted at him for leaving them exposed to a foreign enemy while he was invading Judah, and Hoshea took advantage of their resentment and, to gain his crown, attacked him, *slew (killed) him, and reigned in his stead* (v. 30). He must have wanted a crown very much to risk his life as a traitor at this time. It was a crown which a wise man would not have picked up in the street—it had lately been fatal to all the heads that had worn it—but Hoshea risked his life for it, and it cost him dearly.

Verses 32–38

Here is a short account of the reign of Jotham king of Judah, about whom we are told:

1. That he reigned very well, that he *did that which was right in the sight of the Lord* (v. 34). Josephus has a very high opinion of him, describing him as devout toward God and just toward others, and as one who gave himself for the public good. Although the high places were not taken away, nevertheless, to draw people away from them and keep them close to God's Holy Place, he showed great respect for the temple and rebuilt the *higher gate*, the Upper Gate to the temple. If judges cannot do all they would like to to suppress evil and worldliness, then let them do all they can to support and advance godliness and virtue. If they cannot tear down the high places of sin, let them build and adorn the high gates of God's house.

2. That he died in midlife (v. 33). From these accounts it appears that none of all the kings of Judah reached David's age, seventy, the usual age of human beings. We do not find Asa's age. Uzziah lived to be sixty-eight, Manasseh sixty-seven, and Jehoshaphat sixty, and these were the three oldest. Many of those who were notable did not reach fifty. This Jotham died at forty-one.

3. That in his days a confederacy was formed against Judah by Rezin and Remaliah's son, the king of Aram and the king of Israel, which appeared so formidable at the beginning of the reign of Ahaz that when he and the people were informed of it, their hearts were shaken: *the heart of the people, as the trees of the wood, are moved with the wind* (Isa 7:2).

CHAPTER 16

This chapter considers the reign of Ahaz. 1. He was a notorious idolater (vv. 1–4). 2. He used the treasuries of the temple as well as his own to hire the king of Assyria to invade Aram (Syria) and Israel (vv. 5–9). 3. He took a copy of the idol's altar which he saw at Damascus to make a new altar for God's temple (vv. 10–16). 4. He abused and removed the temple furnishings (vv. 17–18). And so his story ends (vv. 19–20).

Verses 1–4

Here we have the general character of the reign of Ahaz.

1. He *did not that which was right like David* (v. 2). He had no love for the temple, was not conscientious in doing his duty to God, and had no regard for God's Law. He was a disgrace to that honorable name and family, which was therefore really a disgrace to him.

2. He walked *in the way of the kings of Israel* (v. 3), who all worshiped the calves. The kings of Israel pleaded political reasons for their idolatry, but Ahaz offered no such pretense. They were his enemies as well as their own worst enemies because of their idolatry, but he walked in their ways.

3. He *made his sons to pass through the fire*, to the honor of his false gods. He *burnt his children in the fire* (2Ch 28:3); he sacrificed some of them and perhaps

forced others to pass between two fires, or to be drawn through flames, as a sign of their dedication to the idol.

4. He did *according to the abominations of the heathen whom the Lord had cast out*, followed the detestable ways of the nations the Lord had driven out (v. 3).

5. He *sacrificed in the high places* (v. 4). If his father had been zealous enough to remove them, the defiling of his sons might have been prevented, but those who turn a blind eye to sin do not know what dangerous traps they are setting for those who come after them.

Verses 5–9

Here is:

1. The attempt of his confederate neighbors, the kings of Aram and Israel, to attack him. They wanted to defeat Jerusalem and set their own king there (Isa 7:6). They did not do this, but the king of Aram regained Elath, a significant port on the Red Sea, which Amaziah had taken from the Arameans (14:22).

2. Ahaz' plan to get himself clear of them. Having abandoned God, he had neither the courage nor the strength to advance against his enemies, nor could he, with any boldness, ask God to help, but he asked the king of Assyria for help and got him to come to his relief. The sin itself was its own punishment, for though he achieved his aim, nevertheless, all things considered, he made a bad bargain. The king of Assyria did comply and, to serve his own purposes, attacked Damascus, which was a strong diversion for the king of Aram (v. 9) and made him drop his plans against Ahaz; the Assyrians also took the Arameans captive to Kir. Yet to achieve this aim:

2.1. Ahaz made himself a slave (v. 7): *I am thy servant and thy son* (vassal).

2.2. Ahaz made himself poor, for he took the silver and gold that were stored in the treasuries both of the temple and of the royal palace and sent them to the king of Assyria (v. 8). We do not know what authority he had to dispose of the public revenues, but it is common for those who get themselves into difficulty by one sin to try to help themselves get out of it by another.

Verses 10–16

Though Ahaz had himself offered sacrifices at high places (v. 4), God's altar had up to that time remained in its place and continued to be used, but here we have it taken away by evil King Ahaz, and another altar, an idolatrous one, put in its place. We have here:

1. The sketch and plans of this new altar taken from one at Damascus by the king himself (v. 10). After the king of Assyria had captured Damascus, Ahaz went there to congratulate him and to receive his commands. At Damascus he saw an altar that took his fancy, and he just had to have an altar like that one. A copy of it must be made immediately.

2. The making of the new altar by Uriah the priest (v. 11). Whatever pretense he had, it was most evil for him as a chief priest to make this altar in compliance with an idolatrous ruler, for in doing this he betrayed his trust, dishonored his authority, and defiled the crown of his priesthood, making himself a servant to sinful human desires.

3. The dedication of the new altar. Uriah set it near the bronze altar. The king was extremely pleased with it and presented his burnt offering on it (vv. 12–13). His sacrifices were not presented to the God of Israel but to the gods of Damascus.

4. The removal of God's altar to make room for it. Ahaz removes God's altar to an obscure corner on the north side

of the court and puts his own in front of the sanctuary in its place. His superstitious innovation first jostles *with* God's sacred institution, but soon jostles it *out*. We can learn from this that those who are not content to make God their all will soon disregard him altogether. Ahaz dare not totally demolish the bronze altar; now, he says, it will be for him to seek guidance at (v. 15). He pretends to give it a more noble use than the one for which it was originally instituted. The altar was never intended to give guidance, but Ahaz wants to put it to that use. The Jews say that afterward he used its bronze to make the famous *dial of Ahaz* (20:11).

Verses 17–20

Here is:

1. Ahaz abusing the temple, not the building itself but some of its furnishings:

1.1. He removed the basins from the movable stands (1Ki 7:28–29) and removed the Sea (v. 17). The priests used these for washing parts of the sacrifices or maybe themselves.

1.2. He removed the Sabbath canopy (v. 18), set up either in honor of the Sabbath or for the convenience of the priests, when they officiated in greater numbers on the Sabbath than on other days.

1.3. He turned the royal entryway another way, to show that he did not intend to frequent the house of the Lord anymore. This was the entryway which led to the house of the Lord for the convenience of the royal family; perhaps it was that stairway which Solomon had made and which the queen of Sheba admired (1Ki 10:5).

2. Ahaz giving up his life in midlife, thirty-six years old (v. 19), and leaving his kingdom to a better man, Hezekiah his son (v. 20), who turned out to be as much a friend to the temple as his father had been its enemy.

CHAPTER 17

This chapter gives us an account of the exile of the ten tribes, and so finishes the history of that kingdom, which lasted about 200 years from the accession to the throne of Jeroboam the son of Nebat. Here is: 1. A short narrative of this destruction (vv. 1–6). 2. Remarks about it and its causes (vv. 7–23). 3. An account of the nations which succeeded them in possession of their land, and the hybrid religion they set up among them (vv. 24–41).

Verses 1–6

We have here the reign and ruin of Hoshea, the last king of Israel, about whom notice:

1. That although he forced his way to the crown by treason and murder—as we read in 15:30—he still did not gain possession of the crown until seven or eight years after those crimes.

2. That although he was bad, he was not so bad as the kings of Israel before him (v. 2), nor was he so devoted to the calves as they had been. Some say that this Hoshea lifted the prohibition against going up to Jerusalem to worship, a prohibition that the former kings had put their subjects under. But what are we to make of this ordering of events by Providence that led to the destruction of the kingdom of Israel in the reign of one of the best of its kings? If Hoshea was not so bad as the former kings, the people were still as bad as those who had gone before them. Their king let them do better, but they acted as badly as ever, and so the blame for their sin and downfall lay wholly on them.

3. That the destruction came gradually.

4. That they brought it on themselves by the indirect course they took to shake off the tyranny of the king of Assyria (v. 4). If the king and the people of Israel had turned to God, made their peace with him, and offered their prayers to him, they might have regained their liberty, relief, and honor. But they withheld their tribute and trusted the king of Egypt to help them in their rebellion, which, if they had undertaken it with his help, would have meant only a change of oppressor. But Egypt became to them like the splintered reed of a staff (18:21; Isa 36:6).

5. That complete destruction came on them.

5.1. The king of Israel was taken prisoner.

5.2. The land of Israel became a target for attack. The army of the king of Assyria treated the people as traitors to be punished with the sword of justice rather than as enemies.

5.3. The royal city of Israel was besieged and eventually captured. It held out for three years after the country was conquered.

5.4. The people of Israel were deported to Assyria (v. 6). Most of the people, those who were of any significance, were forcibly taken away into the conqueror's country, to be slaves and beggars there. Those who forgot God were themselves forgotten. Many of the lowlier people were left behind, many from every tribe, and they either went over to Judah or became subject to the Assyrian colonies; their descendants were *Galileans* or *Samaritans*. But this was the end of Israel as a nation. Now they became *Lo-ammi*, "not a people" (Hos 1:9), and *Lo-ruhamah*, "unpitied" (Hos 1:6). James writes to the twelve tribes scattered among the nations (Jas 1:1), and Paul speaks of the twelve tribes which *instantly* (earnestly) *served God day and night* (Ac 26:7), so that although we never read about those who were exiled, a remnant of them did escape, to preserve the name of Israel until it came to be taken up by the Gospel church, the spiritual Israel, in which it will always remain (Gal 6:16).

Verses 7–23

The reasons for the destruction of the kingdom of the ten tribes are given here:

• It was *the Lord that removed Israel out of his sight* (v. 18). Whoever the instruments were, he was the author of this disaster. It was *destruction from the Almighty* (Isa 13:6); the Assyrian was but the *rod of his anger* (Isa 10:5). But why would God destroy a people that was raised up and joined together, as Israel was, by God's miracles and direction? Was it purely an act of sovereignty? No; it was an act of necessary justice. For:

• They provoked him to do this by their evil. Was it God's doing? No; it was their own; it was their own conduct and actions that brought this punishment on them (Jer 4:18). It was their own evil that corrected them, and this is here very movingly opened up as the root cause of all the desolations of Israel. The writer shows:

1. What God had done for the people of Israel, to commit them to serve him:

1.1. He gave them their freedom (v. 7). This meant they were bound in duty and gratitude to be his servants, for he had loosed their chains. Nor would the One who rescued them from the hand of the king of Egypt have contradicted himself so far as to hand them over to the hands of the king of Assyria, as he did, if they had not by their sin first abandoned their liberty and sold themselves.

1.2. He gave them their Law and was himself their king. They could not plead ignorance of good and evil, sin and duty.

1.3. He gave them *their land*, for he *cast out the heathen* (drove out the nations) *from before them* (v. 8) to make room for them. The driving out of the nations because of their idolatry was as fair a warning as could be given to Israel not to follow them.

2. What they had done against God, despite these commitments which he had placed on them:

2.1. They *sinned against the Lord their God* (v. 7). They *did those things that were not right* (v. 9), but *secretly*. They *sold themselves to do evil in the sight of the Lord* (v. 17), that is, they devoted themselves to sin, as slaves to the service of those to whom they gave themselves, and by obstinately persisting in sin, they hardened their hearts so much that eventually it became impossible for them to recover themselves.

2.2. Although they were guilty of much immorality and broke all the commands of the second table of the Ten Commandments, nothing is mentioned here except their idolatry. This was their besetting sin. This was, of all their sins, the one that was most offensive to God. It was the spiritual unfaithfulness that broke the marriage covenant and allowed in all other evils. They feared other gods (v. 7), that is, they worshiped them and paid homage to them as if they feared their displeasure. They *built themselves high places in all their cities* (v. 9). If in any place there was only a watchtower—a country town with no walls but only a tower to shelter the guards in times of danger—or if there was only a lodge for shepherds, even such a site as that must be honored with a high place, and that with an altar. If it was a fenced city, it must be further fortified with a high place. They *set them up images and groves*, "Asherim"—wooden idols or Asherah poles, as some think the term means; we translate it as *groves* or "Ashtaroth"—directly contrary to the second commandment (v. 10). They served idols (v. 12), the works of their own hands. They *burnt incense in all the high places*, to the honor of foreign gods—for it was to the dishonor of the true God (v. 11). Besides the idols cast in the shape of calves, they *worshiped all the host of heaven*—the sun, moon, and stars. They also used divination and sorcery so that they might receive directions from the gods.

3. The ways God used with them to bring them away from their idolatry, and to what little purpose. Although they had abandoned God's family of priests, he did not leave them without a succession of prophets, who made it their work to teach them the knowledge of the Lord, but all was in vain (v. 14).

4. How God punished them for their sins. He *was very angry with them* (v. 18). He afflicted them (v. 20) and *delivered them into the hand of spoilers*, plunderers, in the days of the judges and of Saul, and afterward in the days of most of their kings, to see if they could be woken up by the judgments of God to consider and mend their ways. But when all these forms of correction were not enough to drive out their folly (Pr 22:15), God first *rent* (tore) *Israel from the house of David* (v. 21), under which they might have been happy.

5. A complaint against Judah in the middle of all this about Israel (v. 19): *Also Judah kept not the commandments of God.* Although they were not quite so bad as Israel, they still *walked in the statutes of Israel.*

Verses 24–41

When the children of Israel were displaced and turned out of Canaan, the king of Assyria soon transplanted

there the people he could spare from his own country, who would be servants to him and masters to the Israelites who remained. Here we have an account of these new inhabitants.

1. We are told about the Assyrians who were brought into the land of Israel:

1.1. They possessed Samaria and *dwelt in the cities* (towns) *thereof* (v. 24).

1.2. When they first came, God *sent lions among them* (vv. 25–26). The people were probably insufficient to populate the country, and so *the beasts of the field multiplied against them* (Ex 23:29). Besides the natural cause, there was also the clear hand of God in it. God arranged for them to have this rough welcome to restrain their pride.

1.3. They sent a complaint of this trouble to their master the king, probably describing the loss their new colony had sustained from the lions and the continual fear they were in because of them, and stating that they looked on it as a judgment on them for not worshiping the God of the land, which they could not do, because they did not know how to worship him (v. 26). In this matter, they shamed the Israelites, who were not so ready to listen to the voice of God's judgments as they were. Assyrians begged to be taught what Israelites hated to be taught.

1.4. The king of Assyria took care to have them taught *the manner of the God of the land*, how to worship the Lord (vv. 27–28), not out of any affection for that God, but to rescue his subjects from the lions. He sent back one of the priests of the calves, and he came and lived among them to teach them how they should *fear* (worship) the Lord (v. 28). Being taught in this way, they made a hybrid religion. They worshiped the God of Israel out of fear and their own idols out of love (v. 33): *They feared the Lord* but they *served their own gods*. If we may believe the traditions of the Jewish teachers, Succoth Benoth was worshiped as a hen and chick, Nergal as a cock, Ashima as a smooth goat, Nibhaz as a dog, Tartak as a donkey, Adrammelech as a peacock, and Anammelech as a pheasant. Our own teachers tell us—and their view is more probable—that Succoth Benoth, meaning "the tents of the daughters," was Venus. Nergal, being worshiped by the Cuthites, or Persians, was "the fire." Adrammelech and Anammelech were different aspects of Molech. This mixed superstition is here said to *continue unto this day* (v. 41), until the time that this book was written; and it continued long after, more than 350 years in all, until the time of Alexander the Great, when Manasseh went over to the Samaritans, drawing many of the Jews over to him, and succeeded in persuading the Samaritans to throw away all their idols and worship only the God of Israel.

2. We are also told about the Israelites who were taken into the land of Assyria. When the two tribes were later taken into Babylon, they were healed of their idolatry, and so, after seventy years, they were brought back with joy, but the ten tribes were hardened in the furnace and so were justly lost in it and left to perish. When they were in the hand of their enemies and stood in need of being rescued, they were so stupid that they persisted in their former practices (v. 40). They served both the true God and false gods, as if they could not tell the difference between them. *Ephraim is joined to idols, let him alone* (Hos 4:17). This is how they lived, and so did the nations that succeeded them.

CHAPTER 18

When the prophet had condemned Ephraim for lies and deceit, he comforted himself with the thought that Judah still *"ruled with God and was faithful with the Most Holy"(Hos 11:12, margin). This chapter shows us the affairs of Judah in a good state, so that it may be seen that God has not totally rejected the descendants of Abraham (Ro 11:1). 1. Hezekiah is here on the throne reforming his kingdom (vv. 1–6) and succeeding in all his undertakings (vv. 7–8), at the same time as the ten tribes are taken into exile (vv. 9–12). 2. Judah is invaded by Sennacherib, the king of Assyria (v. 13), and is made to pay tribute (vv. 14–16). 3. Jerusalem is besieged (v. 17), God is blasphemed and reviled, and his people are urged to rebel in a powerful speech by the* Rab-shakeh *(the field commander) (vv. 18–37). In the next chapter we will see how matters ended well and to the honor and comfort of the great reformer.*

Verses 1–8

We have here a general account of the reign of Hezekiah.

1. His great godliness, which was more wonderful because his father was one of the worst of the kings, but Hezekiah was one of the best. Whatever good there is in anyone comes not from nature but from grace, which, contrary to nature, is grafted into the cultivated olive tree that was wild by nature (Ro 11:24). Moreover, grace surmounts the greatest difficulties and disadvantages. Ahaz probably gave his son a bad education as well as a bad example. Uriah his priest perhaps taught him, and his attendants and companions were probably those who were devoted to idolatry, but nevertheless Hezekiah became well known for his goodness. When God's grace is at work, what can stop it?

1.1. He was a genuine son of David (v. 3): *He did that which was right, according to all that David his* father did. Hezekiah was a second David. He had the kind of love for God's word and God's house that David had. Let us not be frightened into thinking that when times and people are bad, they must necessarily and naturally become even worse. That does not follow, for after many bad kings, God raised up one who was like David himself.

1.2. He was a zealous reformer of his kingdom (2Ch 29:3). He found his kingdom very corrupt and the people very superstitious in everything. They had always been so, but in the last reign they had become worse than ever. Idolatry had spread throughout the land. Hezekiah's spirit was stirred up against this idolatry, and so, as soon as he had power in his hands, he set himself to abolish it (v. 4).

1.2.1. The sacred stones and the Asherah poles were idolatrous. He smashed and destroyed these.

1.2.2. The high places—although they had sometimes been used by the prophets on special occasions and had been ignored by the good kings up to that time—nevertheless defied the temple and gave an opportunity for idolatrous customs to be introduced. Hezekiah chose to be ruled by God's word rather than the example of his predecessors, and so he removed the high places. He made it a law that they should be removed, and it was carried out vigorously.

1.2.3. The bronze snake was originally instituted by God, but because it had been abused in idolatry, Hezekiah broke it into pieces. It seems that it had been carefully preserved as a memorial of God's goodness to their ancestors in the desert (Nu 21:9). But when they began to worship the created things more than the Creator, those who refused to worship sacred stones from other nations were nevertheless drawn by the tempter to burn incense to the bronze snake, because that was made by order from God

himself and had been an instrument for good to them. And so Hezekiah, in his godly zeal for God's honor, not only forbade the people to worship it but, so that it might never be misused in that way anymore, showed the people that it was *Nehushtan*, nothing else but "a piece of bronze," and so it was worthless and evil to burn incense to it. He then broke it into pieces. If anyone thinks that the just honor of the bronze snake was diminished by this incident, they have only to look at Jn 3:14, where our Savior makes it a type of himself.

1.3. He was famous for two things in his reformation:

1.3.1. Confidence in God. In abolishing idolatry, he was in danger of displeasing his subjects and causing them to rebel, but *he trusted in the Lord God of Israel* (v. 5) to boldly support him in what he did and to keep him from harm.

1.3.2. Faithfulness in his duty.

2. His great prosperity (vv. 7–8). He was with God, and then God was with him. Finding himself successful:

2.1. He sought independence from the king of Assyria, whom his father had submitted to. When he had rejected the idolatry of the nations, he might as well reject their oppression too.

2.2. He made a strong attack on the Philistines and defeated them as far as Gaza.

Verses 9–16

The kingdom of Assyria had now become a significant power. We have here an account:

1. Of the success of Shalmaneser, king of Assyria, against Israel, his besieging Samaria (v. 9), capturing it (v. 10), and taking the people into exile (v. 11), with the reason why God brought this judgment on them (v. 12): *Because they obeyed not the voice of the Lord their God.* This was related in the previous chapter, but it is repeated here:

1.1. Because it was something that stirred Hezekiah and his people to zealously remove the idolatry, because they saw the destruction which it brought on Israel.

1.2. Because it was something that Hezekiah mourned greatly but did not have the strength to prevent. Although ten tribes had rebelled from the house of David, nevertheless, because they too were descendents of Israel (Jacob, Ge 32:28), he could not have been happy to see the disaster that came on them.

1.3. Because it was something which exposed Hezekiah and his kingdom to the king of Assyria and made it much easier for him to invade the land.

2. Of the attempt of Sennacherib, the next king of Assyria, against Judah. The attack he made on Judah was a disaster for that kingdom. God would use it to test the faith of Hezekiah and rebuke the people, because they did not willingly part with their idols but kept them in their hearts. Even times of reformation may prove troublesome times, and then the blame is placed on the reformers. This disaster appears terrible for Hezekiah when we consider:

2.1. How much he lost of his country (v. 13). The king of Assyria took all or most of the fortified cities of Judah, the frontier towns and the garrisons.

2.2. How dearly he paid for his peace. He saw Jerusalem itself in danger of falling into enemy hands, and he was willing to buy its safety at the expense:

2.2.1. Of a lowly submission (v. 14). Where was Hezekiah's courage? Where was his confidence in God?

2.2.2. Of a vast sum of money, 300 talents of silver, more than eleven tons (about ten metric tons), and thirty talents of gold, more than one ton (about one metric ton), to be paid as a present redemption. To raise this sum, he was forced not only to empty the public treasuries (v. 15) but also to strip the gold from the doors and doorposts of the temple (v. 16). Though *the temple sanctified the gold*, nevertheless, because the necessity was urgent, he thought he could be as bold with that as his father David was with the consecrated bread. His father Ahaz had plundered the temple, showing contempt for it (2Ch 28:24). He had repaid with interest what his father took, and now with all due reverence, he was only seeking permission to borrow it in an emergency and for a greater good.

Verses 17–37

Here:

1. Jerusalem is besieged by Sennacherib's army (v. 17). He sent three of his generals with a large army against Jerusalem. Is this the *great king*, the king of Assyria? Let him never be named with honor, since he could do something so dishonorable as this: to take Hezekiah's money, which he gave him on condition that he would withdraw his army, and then to advance against his capital city.

2. Hezekiah, and his leaders and the people, are railed on by the *Rab-shakeh*, the field commander and chief speaker of the three generals, a person with the most satirical disposition. He was instructed what to say by Sennacherib, who intended to pick a new quarrel with Hezekiah. Sennacherib had promised that upon receipt of Hezekiah's money he would withdraw his army, and so it would be shameful to launch a forcible attack on Jerusalem immediately, but he sent the field commander to persuade Hezekiah to surrender and told him that if Hezekiah refused, he should lay siege to the city and then, if it held out, take it by storm. The field commander had the boldness to want an audience with the king himself at the aqueduct of the Upper Pool, outside the walls of the city, but Hezekiah was wise enough to decline a personal meeting and sent three commissioners to hear what he had to say. They interrupted him only once during his speech, which was only to ask him to speak Aramaic; they would consider what he said and report it to the king, and if they did not bring back to him a satisfactory answer, then he could appeal to the people, by speaking *in the Jews' language*, Hebrew (v. 26). Hilkiah did not consider, however, what an unreasonable man he was dealing with, or else he would not have made this request, for it only exasperated the field commander (v. 27). Against all rules of decency and honor, he threatened the soldiers, tried to persuade them to desert or mutiny, and threatened that if they held out, he would reduce them to the last extremities of famine. He then tried to persuade Hezekiah, and his leaders and people, to surrender the city.

2.1. He exalts his master the king of Assyria. Twice he calls him *That great king, the king of Assyria* (v. 19 and again v. 28). But to those who by faith see the King of kings in all his power and glory, even the king of Assyria looks lowly and little (Ps 82:6–7).

2.2. He tries to make them believe that it will be to their advantage if they surrender. If they surrender, seek his favor by paying a tribute, and throw themselves on his mercy, he will treat them very well (v. 31). If they surrender themselves to his mercy, then even though they must expect to be prisoners, it will in reality be fortunate for them to be in that condition.

2.2.1. Their imprisonment will be to their advantage, for they will *eat every man of his own vine* (v. 31). Although the property of their estates will pass to the conquerors, they will still have free use of them.

2.2.2. Their captivity will be to their advantage: *I will take you away to a land like your own land* (v. 32). Yet how would they be any better off for that, when they had nothing in that foreign land to call their own?

2.3. What he aims at especially is to convince them that it is futile for them to hold out: *What confidence is this wherein thou trustest?* (v. 19). He says to the people (v. 29), "*Let not Hezekiah deceive you* to your own destruction, for *he shall not be able to deliver you*. You will either bend or break." He supposes Hezekiah might trust in three things, and he tries to show that these are inadequate:

2.3.1. His own military preparations: *Thou sayest, I have counsel* (strategy) *and strength for the war* (v. 20), and we find that he had these (2Ch 32:3). But the field commander ridicules this. With the greatest possible arrogance he challenges Hezekiah to produce 2,000 riders who know how to manage a horse, and if Hezekiah can do this, Sennacherib will risk giving him 2,000 horses. The field commander falsely insinuates that Hezekiah has no horsemen fit to be soldiers (v. 23).

2.3.2. His alliance with Egypt. He supposes that Hezekiah is trusting in Egypt for chariots and horsemen (v. 24), because the king of Israel did so, and he says truly of this object of confidence that it is *a bruised reed*, a splintered reed of a staff (v. 21). It will not only fail a man when he leans on it but *will* also *go into his hand and pierce it* (Eze 29:6–7). This is what the king of Egypt is like, says the field commander.

2.3.3. His privileges with God (v. 22). He supported himself by depending on the power and promise of God. He encouraged himself and his people with this (v. 30 and again v. 32): *The Lord will surely deliver us*. The field commander was aware that this was their great support, and so he attempted to shake this, as did David's enemies, who used all the skill they could to drive him away from his confidence in God (Ps 3:2; 11:1), and this is how Christ's enemies also acted (Mt 27:43). The field commander suggested three things to discourage their confidence in God:

2.3.3.1. That Hezekiah had lost the right to God's protection, that he had removed himself from it, by *destroying the high places and the altars* (v. 22). Here he took foreign gods as a standard and compared them with the God of Israel. The gods of other nations delighted in having many altars and temples. He concluded that Hezekiah had caused great offense to the God of Israel by confining his people to one altar.

2.3.3.2. That God had given orders to destroy Jerusalem at this time (v. 25): *Have I now come up without the Lord?* This is all mockery and extravagant boasting. He made this claim to terrify the *people that were on the wall* (v. 26).

2.3.3.3. That if Jehovah, the God of Israel, should undertake to protect them from the king of Assyria, he would not be able to do it. He concluded his speech with this blasphemy (vv. 33–35). Notice here:

- His pride. When he conquered a city, he reckoned he had also conquered its gods, and he rated himself highly for having done so.
- His ungodliness. The God of Israel was not a local god but the God of the whole earth. The tradition of the Jews is that the field commander was an apostate Jew, which was why he was so fluent in speaking Hebrew. If this is so, his ignorance of the God of Israel was less excusable and his enmity less strange, for apostates are commonly the most bitter and spiteful enemies; take, for example, Julian, "the Apostate."

3. The commissioners acted as Hezekiah's representatives:

3.1. They held their peace, but not for lack of something to say both on God's behalf and on Hezekiah's. The king had commanded them not to answer him, and they observed their instructions.

3.2. They tore their clothes in loathing at his blasphemy and in grief at the despised and afflicted condition of Jerusalem, the shame of which was a burden to them.

3.3. They faithfully reported the matter to the king, their master, and *told him the words of* the *Rab-shakeh* (the field commander) (v. 37).

CHAPTER 19

Jerusalem was about to be swallowed up by the Assyrian army. In this chapter we have an account of its glorious rescue, not by sword or bow but by prayer and prophecy, and by the hand of an angel. 1. Hezekiah was greatly concerned, and he sent for the prophet Isaiah to ask him to pray (vv. 1–5). Hezekiah received from Isaiah an answer of peace (vv. 6–7). 2. Sennacherib sent a letter to Hezekiah to frighten him into surrendering (vv. 8–13). Hezekiah then, in an earnest prayer, commended his case to God, the righteous Judge, and begged him to help (vv. 14–19). 3. God, through Isaiah, sent him a very comforting message, assuring that him he would be rescued (vv. 20–34). 4. The army of the Assyrians were all killed by an angel, and Sennacherib himself was killed by his own sons (vv. 35–37). And so God glorified himself and saved his people.

Verses 1–7

After the contents of the speech by the Rab-shakeh (the field commander) had been brought to Hezekiah:

1. Hezekiah disclosed a deep concern at the dishonor given to God by the field commander's blasphemy. When he heard it, he *rent* (tore) *his clothes and covered himself with sackcloth* (v. 1). Royal robes are not too good to be torn, and royal flesh is not too good to be clothed with sackcloth, as a sign of humiliation because of the indignity done to God and the dangers and terrors of his Jerusalem. The king put on sackcloth, but many of his subjects still wore fine clothing.

2. He *went up to the house of the Lord* (v. 1) to meditate and pray. He did not consider what answer he would give to the field commander but referred the matter to God. "You will answer, Lord, for me" (George Herbert).

3. He sent for the prophet Isaiah by honorable messengers to ask for his prayers (vv. 2–4). Eliakim and Shebna were two of those who had heard the words of the field commander and were therefore well suited to tell Isaiah what had taken place. The messengers were to go in sackcloth, because they were to represent the king, who also was wearing sackcloth.

3.1. Their mission to Isaiah was to ask, "*Lift up thy prayer for the remnant that is left* (v. 4), that is, for Judah, which is only a remnant, now that the ten tribes have gone—for Jerusalem, which is only a remnant now that the fortified cities of Judah have been taken." Note here that when we want the prayers of others for us, we must not think that that excuses us from praying. When Hezekiah sent for Isaiah to pray for him, he himself *went into the house of the Lord* (v. 1) to offer his own prayers. When the interests of God's church are brought very low, so that there is only a remnant left, then it is time to *lift up our prayer for that remnant* (v. 4).

3.2. Two things are urged on Isaiah in order to engage his prayers for them:

3.2.1. Their fear of the enemy (v. 3). "We are ready to die; *if thou canst do anything, have compassion upon us and help us*" (Mk 9:22).

3.2.2. Their hope in God. They look to him and depend on him to appear for them. "He has heard and known the blasphemous words of the field commander, and so perhaps he will hear and rebuke them. We hope he will. Help us with your prayers to bring our cause before him, and then we are content to leave matters with him."

4. God, by Isaiah, sent word to Hezekiah to assure him that he would glorify himself in the destruction of the Assyrians. Though dismayed, Hezekiah sent to Isaiah not to ask about the outcome but to ask for help in doing his duty. And so God encouraged Hezekiah: "*Be not afraid of the words which thou hast heard* (v. 6); they are only words, even though they are proud and fiery words, and words are only air." He promised to frighten the king of Assyria more than the field commander had frightened him: *I will send a blast* (spirit) *upon him* (v. 7)—that plague which killed his army.

Verses 8–19

After the field commander had delivered his message and received no answer, he left his army in front of Jerusalem under the command of the other generals and went to the king to await further orders. He found him besieging Libnah, a town that had rebelled from Judah (8:22). However, the king was now alarmed by the rumor that the king of the Cushites, who bordered on the Arabians, was coming out against him with a great army (v. 9). This made him want to gain Jerusalem as quickly as possible. To take it by force would cost him more time and troops than he could spare, and so he renewed his verbal attack on Hezekiah to persuade him to weakly surrender.

1. Sennacherib sent a letter to Hezekiah, an abusive and blasphemous letter, to persuade him to surrender Jerusalem: *Let not thy God deceive thee* (v. 10). To terrify Hezekiah and drive him from his firm stand, he exalts himself and his own achievements. Notice how proudly he boasts:

1.1. Of the lands he has conquered (v. 11): *All lands*, and completely destroyed! So far was he from destroying every land, that at this time the land of Cush, and Tirhakah its king, were a terror to him.

1.2. Of the gods he has conquered (v. 12).

1.3. Of the kings he has conquered (v. 13), the *king of Hamath and the king of Arpad*. Whether he means the prince or the idol, his intention is to make himself appear greater than either.

2. Hezekiah was not so proud as not to receive the letter. When he had read it, he was not in such a passion as to write an answer to it in the same provocative tones; instead he immediately went up to the temple, presented himself, and then *spread the letter before the Lord* (v. 14). It was not as if God needed to have the letter shown to him, but by doing this Hezekiah showed that he acknowledged God in all his ways. In the prayer which Hezekiah prayed over this letter:

2.1. He adores the God whom Sennacherib has blasphemed (v. 15). He calls him *the God of Israel*, because Israel is his special people, and *the God that dwellest between the cherubim*, because the special dwelling place of his glory on earth is there, but he gives glory to him as *the God of the whole earth*, not as Sennacherib thought him to be, *the God of Israel only*, confined to the temple.

2.2. He appeals to God concerning the arrogance and godlessness of Sennacherib (v. 16).

2.3. He acknowledges Sennacherib's triumphs over the gods of the nations but distinguishes between them and the God of Israel (vv. 17–18): he has indeed *cast their gods into the fire*, for *they were no gods*.

2.4. He prays that God will now glorify himself in the defeat of Sennacherib and in rescuing Jerusalem from his hands (v. 19): "*Now therefore save us*. Let all the world know, and be made to acknowledge, that *thou art the Lord God*, the self-existent and sovereign God, *even thou only*, and that all pretenders are worthless."

Verses 20–34

Here is the gracious answer that God gave to Hezekiah's prayer. In general, God assured him that his prayer concerning Sennacherib was heard (v. 20). This message speaks of two things:

1. Confusion and shame for Sennacherib and his forces. It is foretold here that he will be humbled and broken. Sennacherib is presented:

1.1. As the target of Jerusalem's mocking (v. 21). He thought that he himself was the terror of the Daughter of Zion, that pure and beautiful virgin, and that by his threats he could force her to submit to him: "But because she is a virgin in her Father's house and under his protection, she defies and despises you; she mocks you. Your hatred is both powerless and absurd; the One who sits in heaven is laughing at you (Ps 2:4), as do those who are under his protection." God wanted to use this word to silence the fears of Hezekiah and his people.

1.2. As God's enemy. Hezekiah pleaded this: "Lord, he has insulted you" (v. 16). "He has," God says (v. 22), "and I do indeed take the insult as against myself: *Whom hast thou reproached?* Who is it you have insulted? Is it not the Holy One of Israel, whose honor is dear to him, and who has power to vindicate his honor, which the gods of the nations do not have?"

1.3. As a proud fool who spoke empty, boastful words and *boasted of a false gift* (Pr 25:14). His boasts, as well as his threats, insulted the Lord. For:

1.3.1. He exalted his own achievements far too much (vv. 23–24): *Thou hast said* so and so. Sennacherib thinks he is so great and significant! Just because he drives his chariots to the tops of the highest mountains and forces his way through woods and rivers, breaking through all difficulties, he thinks he is master of everything he turns to.

1.3.2. He took to himself the glory of doing these great things, whereas they were all *the Lord's doing* (vv. 25–26). "And as for how you laid waste the earth, particularly in Judah, you are only the instrument in God's hand, a mere tool: it is *I that have brought it to pass*" (v. 25). Sennacherib's boasts are explained in Isa 10:13–14: *By the strength of my hand I have done it, and by my wisdom*; and they are answered (Isa 10:15), *Shall the axe boast itself against him that heweth therewith* (swings it)?

1.4. As under the restraint and rebuke of the God whom he blasphemed.

1.4.1. God knew all his actions (v. 27): "*I know* where you are staying and what you are secretly planning, the noise and bluster you are making: I know all about it."

1.4.2. God controlled all his actions (v. 28): "*I will put my hook in* (my cord through) *thy nose*, you great Leviathan (Job 41:1–2), my bridle in your jaws, you great Behemoth. I will restrain you, direct you, turn you where I please, and send you home as a fool, just as you came."

2. Salvation and joy for Hezekiah and his people. This will be a sign to them that God's favor has returned, that he is reconciled to them, and that his anger is turned away (Isa 12:1): the outcome of their present distress will be good in every respect.

2.1. Supplies were scarce and expensive, and what should they do for food? The fruits of the earth were consumed by the Assyrian army (Isa 32:9–10). Why, they will not only live in the land, but *verily they shall be fed* (Ps 37:3). "Eat this year what has grown by itself, and you will reap what you did not sow." But the next year was the sabbatical year, when the land was to rest, and so they must neither sow nor reap. What must they do that year? Why, *Jehovah-jireh*, "The Lord will provide" (Ge 22:8). And then, the third year, their farming would return to its former ways, and they would sow and reap as they used to do.

2.2. The country was laid waste, families were broken up and scattered, and everything was in a state of confusion. How could it be otherwise when it was overrun by such an army? As to this, it is promised that the remnant of the house of Judah will again be established in their own homes and they will increase and grow rich (v. 30). Notice how their prosperity is described: it is taking root downward and bearing fruit upward. Such is the prosperity of the soul. It is taking root downward by faith in Christ, and then being outwardly productive in fruits of righteousness.

2.3. The city was shut up; no one went out or came in. Now, however, the remnant in Jerusalem and Zion will go out freely, and no one will be able to prevent them, and no one will make them afraid (v. 31). There had been great destruction both in city and country, but in both a remnant escaped, which was a type of the saved remnant of true Israelites — as can be seen by comparing Isa 10:22–23, which speaks of this event, with Ro 9:27–28 — and they will go out into the glorious liberty of the children of God (Ro 8:21).

2.4. The Assyrians were advancing toward Jerusalem and would shortly besiege it in a set form, and it was in grave danger of falling into their hands. But it was promised that although their enemies had now camped in front of the city, they would never *come into the city*, no, not even *shoot an arrow* into it (vv. 32–33) — that Sennacherib would be forced to withdraw with shame.

2.5. The honor and truth of God are committed to do all this. These are great things, but how will they be put into practice? Why, *the zeal of the Lord of hosts shall do this* (v. 31). God's zeal is:

2.5.1. For his own honor (v. 34): "I will do it for my own sake, to give myself an eternal name." God's reasons of mercy are taken from within himself.

2.5.2. For his own truth: "I will do it for my servant David's sake, not because he deserves it but because of the promise made to him and the covenant made with him, those sure mercies of David."

Verses 35–37

The word was no sooner spoken than the work was done.

1. The army of Assyria was completely defeated. Hezekiah did not have sufficient forces to march out on them and attack their camp, nor would God do it by sword or bow. It was *not by the sword of a mighty man or of a mean man*, that is, it was not by any human being at all, but by an angel, that the Assyrian army was to fall (Isa 31:8). Josephus says it was done by a plague, which meant instant

death to them. The number of those who were killed was very great, 185,000, with the field commander probably among them. When the besieged *arose, early in the morning, behold they were all dead corpses* (v. 35), scarcely anyone living among them. Some think Ps 76:1–12 was written on this occasion, where we read that the *stout-hearted were spoiled* (valiant men lay plundered) *and slept their sleep*, their final long sleep (Ps 76:5).

2. The king of Assyria was totally overwhelmed. He was ashamed to see himself defeated in this way after all his proud boasting. *He departed, and went, and returned.* The expression suggests his great mental disorder and distraction (v. 36). And it was not long before God killed him too, by the hands of *two of his own sons* (v. 37). The God of Israel had done enough to convince him that he, the Lord, was the only true God, whom Sennacherib therefore should worship, but he persisted in his idolatry. He tried to go to his false god to protect him against a God of irresistible power. His sons who murdered him were allowed to escape, and would be looked on all the more leniently for what they had done if it is true, as Bishop Patrick suggests, that he was now vowing to sacrifice them to his god. His successor was another son, *Esarhaddon*, who did not aim, like his father, to widen his conquests but rather to consolidate them, for it was he who first sent colonies of Assyrians to inhabit the country of Samaria, as it would seem from Ezr 4:2, where the Samaritans say it was *Esarhaddon that brought them thither.*

CHAPTER 20

In this chapter we have: 1. Hezekiah's illness, and his recovery in answer to prayer, in fulfillment of a promise, by the use of means, and with confirmation by a sign (vv. 1–11). 2. Hezekiah's sin and his recovery from that (vv. 12–19). In both of these, Isaiah was God's messenger to him. Finally, we have the conclusion of his reign (vv. 20–21).

Verses 1–11

After the writer has shown us blasphemous Sennacherib destroyed at the point of gaining victory, we read here how prayerful Hezekiah was rescued at the point of death. Here is:

1. Hezekiah's illness. *In those days was Hezekiah sick* (v. 1), that is, in the same year in which the king of Assyria besieged Jerusalem. Some think it was at the time that the Assyrian army was besieging the city or preparing to do so. Others think it was soon after Sennacherib's defeat. In the middle of his triumphs, Hezekiah was overtaken by illness. It seems he was suffering from the plague, for we read of *a boil* or a sore such as those caused by the plague (v. 7). The same disease which killed the Assyrians was testing him. Hezekiah, so recently favored by heaven above most people, was dangerously ill.

2. Warning brought to him to prepare for death. It is brought by Isaiah. The prophet tells him:

2.1. That his illness is fatal, and if he does not recover by a miraculous blessing, the illness will certainly prove fatal: *Thou shalt die, and not live* (v. 1).

2.2. That he must therefore quickly get ready to die: *Set thy house in order* (v. 1). We are called to put our own heart in order by renewed acts of repentance, faith, and submission to God, with cheerful good-bys to this world and welcomes to the other. Put your house in order, make your will, settle your estate, put your affairs in the best possible order, to help those who will come after you.

3. His prayer: *He prayed unto the Lord* (v. 2). Is any one of you sick? Let them be prayed for, let them be prayed with, and let them pray (Jas 5:14). Hezekiah had found that prayers of faith lead to answers of peace. His body had now received the sentence of death, and if it was reversible, it would have to be reversed by prayer. If the sentence was irreversible, prayer is still one of the best ways to prepare for death, because this is how we call on strength and grace from God to enable us to finish well. Notice:

3.1. The circumstances of this prayer:

3.1.1. He *turned his face to the wall* (v. 2), probably as he lay in his bed. He did this perhaps to gain privacy: he could not withdraw to his room as he used to do, but he turned from those who were around him to converse with God. Or, as some think, he turned his face toward the temple, to show how willingly he would have gone there to present this prayer—as he had in 19:1, 14—if he had been able.

3.1.2. He *wept sorely* (bitterly) (v. 3). Some understand this to mean that he was unwilling to die. It is in human nature to dread the separation of soul and body. There was also something special about Hezekiah's case. He was now in the middle of his time of usefulness; he had begun a good work of reformation, and he feared that if he were to die, it would collapse because of the corruption of the people. Let Hezekiah's prayer interpret his tears, and in *that* we find nothing that suggests that he was actually afraid of dying.

3.2. The prayer itself: "*Remember now, O Lord! how I have walked before thee in truth* (v. 3). Either spare my life so that I may continue to walk in these ways, or if my work is finished, receive me to the glory which you have prepared for those who have walked as I have." Hezekiah does not pray, "Lord, spare me," or "Lord, take me; God's will be done," but, *Lord, remember me* (v. 3). "Whether I live or die, let me be yours."

4. The answer God immediately gave to Hezekiah's prayer. The prophet had reached only as far as the middle court when he was sent back with another message to Hezekiah (vv. 4–5), to tell him that he would recover. In response to Hezekiah's prayer God did something for him which he would not have done otherwise. God here calls Hezekiah *the captain* (leader) *of his people* (v. 5), to show that he would reprieve him for his people's sake. He calls himself the God of David, to show that he would reprieve him out of a consideration for the covenant made with David. In this answer:

4.1. God honors his prayers: *I have heard thy prayer; I have seen thy tears.*

4.2. God does more than answer his prayers. Hezekiah asked only that God would remember his integrity, but God here promises:

4.2.1. To restore him from his illness: *I will heal thee.*

4.2.2. To restore him to such a degree of health that on the third day he would go up to give thanks to the house of the Lord.

4.2.3. To add fifteen years to his life.

4.2.4. To rescue Jerusalem from the king of Assyria (v. 6). This was the thing which Hezekiah's heart was set on as much as his own recovery, and so the promise of this is repeated here.

5. The means to be used for his recovery (v. 7). Isaiah was his doctor. He ordered an external application, something very cheap and ordinary: "Apply a *lump* (poultice) *of figs to the boil*, to bring it to a head, so that the fluid may be discharged that way." It is our duty when we are ill to

make use of such means as are proper to help nature, or else we are not trusting God but putting him to the test. Plain and ordinary medicines must not be looked down on, for God has graciously made many of these useful to us.

6. The sign which was given to encourage his faith:

6.1. He begged for it not out of any distrust in the power or promise of God but because he looked on the things promised as great and worthy of being confirmed in this way. Hezekiah asked not, *"What is the sign* (v. 8) that I will go up to the thrones of judgment or up to the gate?" but, *"What is the sign* that I will go *up to the house of the Lord?"* (v. 8). He wanted to recover so that he might glorify God *in the gates of the daughter of Zion* (Ps 9:14). It is not worth living for any other purpose than to serve God.

6.2. He was given the choice whether the sun should go back or go forward. It is supposed that the degrees were half hours, and that it was just noon when the suggestion was made, and the question is, "Will the sun go back to its place at seven in the morning or forward to its place at five in the evening?" He humbly wanted the sun to go back ten degrees, because although either would be a great miracle, it was the natural course of the sun to go forward, and its going back would seem more unusual and would point more clearly to Hezekiah's *returning to the days of his youth* (Job 33:25) and the lengthening of the days of his life. It was done accordingly upon the prayer of Isaiah (v. 11). God brought the sun back ten degrees, which Hezekiah recognized when he saw the shadow go back on *the dial of Ahaz* (v.11), which he could probably see through the window of his room. The same was observed to have happened on all other dials, even in Babylon (2Ch 32:31). Whether this backward movement of the sun was gradual — which would make the day ten hours longer than usual — or whether it darted back suddenly, and after continuing a little while was restored again to its usual place — so that no change was made in the state of the heavenly bodies, as Bishop Patrick thinks — we are not told.

Verses 12–21

We read here of:

1. A delegation of envoys sent by the king of Babylon to Hezekiah to congratulate him on his recovery (v. 12). The kings of Babylon had up to that time been subjects to the kings of Assyria, and Nineveh was the royal city. We read of Babylon being subject to the king of Assyria in 17:24. But gradually things changed so much that Assyria became subject to the kings of Babylon. This king of Babylon sent his compliments to Hezekiah for two reasons:

1.1. Because of religion. The Babylonians worshiped the sun, and when they noticed what honor their god had given Hezekiah by going back for his sake, they thought themselves also obliged to honor him.

1.2. Because of civil interests. If the king of Babylon was now thinking of rebelling against the king of Assyria, it would be wise to get Hezekiah on his side. He found himself indebted to Hezekiah and his God for the weakening of the Assyrian forces, and he had reason to think he could not have a more powerful and useful ally than one who had so much influence in heaven.

2. The kind reception Hezekiah gave these envoys (v. 13):

• He was too obliging to them. He *hearkened unto them*. Although they were idolaters, he was too eager to make an alliance with their master the king.

• He was too generous in showing them his palace, his treasures, and his armory, so that they might see, and might report to their master, what a great king he was.

3. The examination of Hezekiah about this matter (vv. 14–15). Isaiah, who had often comforted him, now had to convict him. "Who are these people? What do they want?" Hezekiah not only submitted to the examination but openly confessed: *There is nothing among my treasures that I have not shown them* (v. 15). Why then did he not bring them to Isaiah, and show them the one who was the best treasure and who by his prayers had been instrumental in working all those wonders which these envoys had come to ask about?

4. The sentence passed on Hezekiah for his pride and vanity. The sentence is (vv. 17–18):

4.1. That the treasures he was so proud of would later become plundered.

4.2. That the king of Babylon, with whom he so desired an alliance, would be the enemy who would take them as plunder. The sins of Manasseh, his idolatries and murders, were the cause of that disaster, but it is foretold to Hezekiah now to convict him of his pride. Hezekiah had enjoyed helping the king of Babylon rise to greater power and reduce the excessive power of the kings of Assyria, but now he was told that his royal offspring would become the king of Babylon's slave. Babylon will be the destruction of those who are fond of Babylon.

5. Hezekiah's humble and patient submission to this sentence (v. 19). "It is not only just but also good, for he will bring good out of it and do me good by letting me know of it."

6. The conclusion of Hezekiah's life and story (vv. 20–21). In 2Ch 29:1–32:33 much more is recorded of Hezekiah's work of reformation. It also seems that in the civil chronicles there were many things recorded of his power and good deeds for Jerusalem, particularly his bringing water by pipes into the city. But this writer leaves him *asleep with his fathers* (v. 21), and a son on his throne who will prove perverse. Evil Ahaz was the son of a godly father and the father of a godly son; holy Hezekiah was the son of an evil father and the father of an evil son.

CHAPTER 21

In this chapter we have the short but sad account of the reigns of two of the kings of Judah, Manasseh and Amon. Concerning Manasseh, the only record we have of him here is: 1. That he devoted himself to sin, to every kind of evil, idolatry, and murder (vv. 1–9, 16). 2. That therefore God gave him, and also Jerusalem for his sake, over to destruction (vv. 10–18). In the book of Chronicles we have a record of his troubles and of his repentance. 3. Concerning Amon we are told only that he lived in sin (vv. 19–22), died quickly by the sword, and left good Josiah as his successor (vv. 23–26). Jerusalem was very much defiled and weakened by these two reigns.

Verses 1–9

The beauty of Jerusalem is stained, and all its glory and joy sunk and gone. These verses give such an account of this reign as makes it, in all respects, the reverse of the last, and, in a way, its ruin.

1. Manasseh began young. He was only *twelve years old* when he began to reign (v. 1), born when his father was about forty-two years old, three years after his illness. Being young:

1.1. He was full of his own honor. He thought himself very wise, prided himself on undoing what his father had done.

1.2. He was easily led astray by those who *lay in wait to deceive* him (Eph 4:14). They were those who were enemies of Hezekiah's reforms. They kept an affection for the old idolatry, flattered him, and used his power for their own purposes.

2. He reigned for a long time, the longest of any of the kings of Judah, fifty-five years. This was the only very bad reign that was a long one. We hope that at the beginning of his reign for some time affairs continued to move in the same way that his father had left them and that at the end of his reign, after he repented, religious faith made progress again. Though he reigned for a long time, some of this time he was a prisoner in Babylon.

3. He reigned very badly.

3.1. In general, *He did that which was evil in the sight of the Lord*, and *He did after the abominations of the heathen* (v. 2) and as did Ahab (v. 3). In fact (v. 9), he *did more evil than did the nations whom the Lord destroyed*.

3.2. More particularly:

3.2.1. He rebuilt the high places which his father had destroyed (v. 3).

3.2.2. He set up other gods: altars to Baal, *a grove* (NIV: an Asherah pole), and all the starry hosts — the sun, the moon, other planets, and the constellations (v. 3). He worshiped and served all these and gave their names to the idols he made, then paid homage to them. He built altars to them (v. 5), and no doubt he offered sacrifices on these altars.

3.2.3. He made his son pass through the fire, thereby dedicating him as a worshiper of Molech in contempt of the seal of circumcision by which he had been dedicated to God.

3.2.4. He sought guidance from the Devil, practiced sorcery and divination and had dealings with mediums (v. 6), as Saul did. He closely associated with conjurers and fortune-tellers, who claimed to predict the future by means of the stars or the clouds, lucky and unlucky days, good and bad omens, the flight of birds or the entrails of wild animals.

3.2.5. We find later (v. 16) that he shed innocent blood. *The blood of the prophets* is a particular charge brought against Jerusalem, and he probably put to death many of them. The tradition of the Jews is that he had the prophet Isaiah sawed in two, and many think the writer to the Hebrews refers to this in Heb 11:37.

3.3. Three things are mentioned here as worsening Manasseh's idolatry:

• That he set up his idols and altars *in the house of the Lord* (v. 4), in the two courts of the temple (v. 5), in the very place about which God had said to Solomon, *Here will I put my name* (v. 7),

• That he gravely insulted the word of God and his covenant with Israel.

• That he led the people of God astray.

Verses 10–18

Here we read of the judgment of Judah and Jerusalem. The prophets were sent, in the first place, to teach the people the knowledge of God, to remind them of their duty. If they were not successful in that, their next work was to rebuke them for their sins so that they might repent. If they did not succeed in this, and the sinners continued in their perverse ways, the prophets' next task was to prophesy God's judgment, so that, by the terror of it, those who had ignored their obligations to his love might be woken up to their need of repentance. We have here:

1. A statement of the crime. The accusation on which the judgment is based is read out (v. 11).

2. A prophecy of the judgment God would bring on them for this: *They have done that which was evil*, and so *I am bringing evil upon them* (v. 12). It would speak loudly to the world and cause people to think deeply. When God made judgment the plumb line, it would be *the plummet of* (plumb line used against) *the house of Ahab*, marking out Jerusalem for the same destruction that came on that wretched family. See Isa 28:17. *I will wipe it as a man wipes a dish* (v. 13). The city would be emptied of its inhabitants, who had been its filth, as a dish is emptied when it is wiped: "They will all be taken captive; the *land shall enjoy her sabbaths* (Lev 26:34) and be set aside as a dish is when it is wiped." This would be to purify, not destroy, Jerusalem. The dish will not be dropped, broken into pieces, or melted down, but only wiped. Sin is spoken of here as the beginning and end of the reason for their suffering.

3. Manasseh convicted and condemned. This is all we have about him, but in the book of Chronicles we read of his repentance and his acceptance with God. He was buried, probably by his own orders, *in the garden of his own house* (v. 18). He did this because he was truly humbled for his sins and because he considered himself *no more worthy to be called a son* (Lk 15:19), a son of David, and so not worthy even to have his dead body buried *in the sepulchres of his fathers*. It is better and more honorable for a sinner to die repenting and be buried in a garden than to die unrepentant and be buried in an abbey.

Verses 19–26

Here is a short account of the short and inglorious reign of Amon, the son of Manasseh, a son who was not born until Manasseh was forty-five years old.

1. His reign was evil: *He forsook the God of his fathers* (v. 22). He disobeyed the commands given to his fathers. He followed in the steps of his father's idolatry, and he revived what his father had put down at the end of his days.

2. His end was tragic. Since he had rebelled against God, his own servants *conspired against him and slew* (killed) *him* when he had reigned only two years (v. 23). The people of the land did two things by their representatives.

2.1. They carried out justice against the traitors who had killed the king: they put them to death, for although he was *a bad* king, he was *their* king, and it was a part of the loyalty they owed him to avenge his death.

2.2. They did themselves a kindness by *making Josiah his son king in his stead* (place) (v. 24), encouraged perhaps by the promising signs, evident even when he was young, that he would be a good king. Now they were making the favorable change from one of the worst to one of the best kings of Judah.

CHAPTER 22

This chapter begins the story of the reign of good King Josiah. Here, after his general character is stated (vv. 1–2), we have a detailed account of the respect he gave to: 1. God's house, which he repaired (vv. 3–7). 2. God's book, which he was greatly affected by when it was read (vv. 8–11). 3. God's messengers, whom he then consulted (vv. 12–14), and through whom he received an answer foretelling Jerusalem's destruction (vv. 15–17) but promising favor to him (vv. 18–20). Upon receiving this answer, he set about the glorious work of reformation which we have an account of in the next chapter.

Verses 1–10

We are told about Josiah:

1. That he was very young when he began to reign (v. 1), only eight years old. England once had a king who was a child, Edward VI, who was only ten years old when he became king. Josiah, being young, had not been influenced badly by the example of his father and grandfather, but soon saw their errors, and God gave him grace to take warning from them. See Eze 18:14–22.

2. That he *did that which was right in the sight of the Lord* (v. 2). Notice the sovereignty of divine grace: the father is passed over and left to die in his sin; the son is a chosen instrument. Nothing is too hard for divine grace to do. There are errors on both sides, but God kept him on the right path. He did not fall into either superstition or worldliness.

3. That he took care to repair the temple. He did this in the eighteenth year of his reign (v. 3). Compare 2Ch 34:8. He began much sooner to *seek the Lord*, as can be seen in 2Ch 34:3, but it is to be feared that the work of reformation went slowly and met with a great deal of opposition. He sent Shaphan, the secretary of state, to Hilkiah, the high priest, to reckon up the money that had been collected for this use by the doorkeepers (v. 4), for it seems they used much the same way of raising money as Joash did (12:9). He ordered that the money which had been collected in this way be spent on repairing the temple (vv. 5–6). And now, it seems, the workers—as happened in the days of Joash—acquitted themselves so well that *there was no reckoning made with them*, they did not need to account for the money entrusted to them (v. 7); this is certainly mentioned to the praise of the workers.

4. That in repairing the temple, the Book of the Law was fortunately found and brought to the king (vv. 8, 10). Some think this book was the original manuscript of the five books of Moses, written in his own hand. Others think it was an ancient and authentic copy.

4.1. It seems that this Book of the Law had been lost or had gone missing. Perhaps it had been carelessly mislaid or neglected, thrown into a corner—as some people cast aside their Bibles—by those who did not know its value, and it lay forgotten there. Or maybe it was maliciously hidden by some of the idolatrous kings, buried in the hope that it would never see the light of day again. Some think that it was carefully stored by some of its supporters so that it would not fall into the hands of its enemies. Whoever the instruments of its preservation were, we should acknowledge the hand of God in it. If this was the only authentic copy of the Pentateuch then in being, we now have reason to thank God, on our knees, for that fortunate providence by which Hilkiah found this book at that time, that he found it when *he sought it not* (Isa 65:1). God's care of the Bible is a clear sign of his involvement in it.

4.2. Whether this was the only authentic copy in existence or not, it seems the things contained in it were new both to the king himself and also to the high priest, for when the king read it, he tore his clothes. If the Book of the Law had been lost, it seems difficult to work out what rule *Josiah* followed in doing what was *right in the sight of the Lord* (v. 2), and how the priests and people maintained their religious ceremonies. I am inclined to

think that the people generally used abstracts of the Law, like our shortened summaries of laws, a sort of manual of religious services instructing them to observe their religion but leaving out what the priests thought fit, particularly the promises and threats (Lev 26:1–14 and Dt 28:1–68). These were the parts of the Law which Josiah was so much affected by (v. 13), for they were new to him. No summaries, extracts, or anthologies of the Bible, even though they may have their use, can effectively communicate and preserve the knowledge of God and his will as much as the complete Bible itself.

4.3. It greatly showed God's favor, and was a good sign for Josiah and his people, that the Book of the Law was brought to light at this time, to direct and speed up the great reformation that Josiah had begun. The translation of the Scriptures into common languages was the glory, strength, and joy of the Protestant Reformation. It is significant that they were doing something good, repairing the temple, when they found the Book of the Law. Those who do their duty according to their knowledge will have their knowledge increased.

4.4. Hilkiah the priest was very pleased at the discovery. He said to Shaphan, "Rejoice with me, for *I have found the book of the law* (v. 8)"; *eureka*, "I have found" that jewel of inestimable value. "Here, take it to the king; it is the richest jewel of his crown. Read it to him. He walks in *the way of David his father*" (v. 2).

Verses 11–20

The Book of the Law is not stored up in the king's cabinet as an old relic, a rarity to be admired, but is read out to the king. Those who respect their Bibles the most are those who study them and have daily dealings with the Scriptures, who feed on that bread and walk by that light.

1. The impressions which the reading of the Law made on Josiah. He had long thought his kingdom to be in a bad condition because of the idolatry and ungodliness among them, but he never thought it so bad as he realized it was from the Book of the Law now read to him. The tearing of his clothes showed the breaking of his heart.

2. His turning to God: *Go, inquire of the Lord for me* (v. 13).

2.1. We may presume that he wanted to know two things:

2.1.1. "Inquire what we are to do. What should we do to turn away God's wrath and prevent the judgments which our sins have deserved?"

2.1.2. "Inquire what will happen and how we should prepare." He acknowledges, "*Our fathers have not hearkened to* (obeyed) *the words of this book* (v. 13). If this is the rule which shows us what is right, then certainly our ancestors have been very much in the wrong. Certainly *great is the wrath that is kindled against us* (v. 13). If this is the word of God, as no doubt it is, and if he is going to be true to his word, as no doubt he will be, we are all ruined."

2.2. Josiah sent this inquiry:

2.2.1. By some of his great men, who are named in v. 12 and again in v. 14.

2.2.2. To Huldah the prophetess (v. 14). The spirit of prophecy was sometimes put not only into *earthen* (2Co 4:7) vessels but also into *weaker* (1Pe 3:7) vessels. Miriam helped lead Israel out of Egypt (Mic 6:4), Deborah judged them, and now Huldah instructed them in the mind of God, and her being a married woman was no reason why she should not also be a prophetess; *marriage is honourable in all* (Heb 13:4). It was a mercy to Jerusalem that when Bibles were scarce, they had prophets, just as it was a mercy later that, when prophecy ceased, they had more Bibles. The reason the king's messengers made Huldah their oracle was probably that her husband had a place at court, for he was keeper of the wardrobe. They had probably consulted her on other occasions and had found that the *word of God in her mouth was truth* (1Ki 17:24). She was near, for she lived at Jerusalem, in the Second District. The Jews say that she prophesied among the women, the ladies at court, who probably had their apartments there.

3. The answer he received from God to his inquiry. Huldah replied in the words of a prophet, speaking from the One before whom all stand on the same level: *Tell the man that sent you to me* (v. 15).

3.1. She let him know what judgments God had in store for Judah and Jerusalem (vv. 16–17): *My wrath shall be kindled against this place.*

3.2. She let him know what mercy God had in store for him:

3.2.1. Notice is taken of his great tenderness and concern (v. 19): *Thy heart was tender* and responsive. He received the impressions of God's word, trembled at it, and submitted to it. This is having a sensitive, responsive heart, and this is how he *humbled himself before the Lord* (v. 19). Those who most fear God's wrath are least likely to feel it.

3.2.2. A reprieve is granted till after his death (v. 20): *I will gather thee to thy fathers.* God promised him he would not live to see it, which would have been only a small reward for his great godliness if there had not been another world in which he would be abundantly rewarded (Heb 11:16). He died in the love and favor of God, which protects such a peace as the circumstances of death, including even dying on the battlefield, could not change or break in on.

CHAPTER 23

We have here: 1. The beneficial continuance of the good things of Josiah's reign and the progress of the reformation he began: reading the law (vv. 1–2), renewing the covenant (v. 3), cleansing the temple (v. 4), removing idols and idolatry—with all their relics in every place, as far as his power reached (vv. 5–20)—keeping a sacred Passover (vv. 21–23), and clearing the country of mediums and spiritists (v. 24). In all this he acted with extraordinary energy (v. 25). 2. The sad conclusion of his reign in his untimely death, as a sign of the continuance of God's wrath against Jerusalem (vv. 26–30). 3. The even more unfortunate results of his death, in the evil reigns of his two sons Jehoahaz and Jehoiakim, who came after him (vv. 31–37).

Verses 1–3

Josiah had received a message from God that the destruction of Jerusalem could not be prevented, but he did not therefore sit down in despair. Here we have the preparations for reformation:

1. He called a general assembly of the people—the elders, the judges or representatives of Judah and Jerusalem—to meet him *in the house of the Lord* (v. 2), along with the priests and prophets—both God's ordinary ministers and his extraordinary ones—so that their act might be a national act.

2. Instead of making a speech to this assembly, he ordered the Book of the Law to be read to them. In fact, it seems he read it himself (v. 2), as one who was greatly affected by it and who wanted them to be so too. Besides the assembly of the great people, he had a congregation of the *men of Judah and the inhabitants of Jerusalem* to hear the Law being read. If only the people would be as firmly determined to obey the law as he was to govern by the law, the kingdom would be happy.

3. Instead of proposing laws to confirm them in their duty, he proposed that they should all join together in committing themselves to God (v. 3). The Book of the Law was the Book of the Covenant, the covenant that said that if they wanted to be God's people, he would be their God. They here commit themselves to do their part, not doubting that then God would do his. Those who made the covenant were both the king himself and all the people. The king stood by his pillar (11:14) and publicly declared his agreement with this covenant. *All the people* likewise *stood to the covenant* (v. 3)

Verses 4–24

We have here an account of such a reformation as we have not met with in all the history of the kings of Judah, such a thorough purging of all the detestable things and the laying of foundations for such a glorious good work. Even Josiah's reformation did not save Jerusalem, however, for most of the people, after all, hated being reformed. Let us notice:

1. What great evil there was, and had been, in Judah and Jerusalem.

1.1. Even in the house of the Lord, that sacred temple which Solomon built, which was dedicated to the honor and for the worship of the God of Israel, there were found vessels and all kinds of articles for the worship of Baal *and of the grove* (Asherah) and *of all the host of heaven* (v. 4). Even though Josiah had suppressed the worship of idols, the articles made for that worship were still all carefully preserved, even in the temple itself.

1.2. Just *at the entering in* (entrance) *of the house of the Lord* was a stable for horses that were kept for religious use. They were holy horses, *given to the sun* (v. 11)—as if he who *rejoiceth as a strong man to run a race* (Ps 19:5) needed them—making their religion conform to the poetic fictions of the sun's chariot. Some say that those horses were to be led out in pomp every morning to meet the rising sun; others say that the worshipers of the sun rode out on them to praise the rising sun. It seems that they drew *the chariots of the sun*, chariots dedicated to the sun, which the people worshiped.

1.3. Close *by the house of the Lord* there were *houses of the sodomites* (v. 7), where every kind of sexual immorality and lewdness, even what was most unnatural, was practiced under the pretense of religion in honor of their unholy gods. Those who dishonored their God were justly left to dishonor themselves (Ro 1:24–32). There were women who *wove hangings for the grove* (v. 7), tents which surrounded the idol of Venus, where the worshipers committed all kind of immorality *in the house of the Lord* (v. 7).

1.4. Many idolatrous altars were found (v. 12), some in the palace, *on the top of the upper chamber of Ahaz.* Because the roofs of their houses were flat, they made them their high places and set up domestic altars on them (Jer 19:13; Zep 1:5).

1.5. There was *Tophet, in the valley of the children of Hinnom* (v. 10), very near Jerusalem, where the image of Molech—that god of unnatural cruelty, as others were gods of unnatural immorality—was kept. Some sacrificed their children to this god, burning them in the fire. Others dedicated their children, making them pass through the fire (v. 10), *labouring in the very fire* (Hab 2:13). It is supposed to have been called *Tophet* from *toph*, "a drum or tambourine," because they beat drums during the burning of the children so that their cries might not be heard.

1.6. There were *high places before Jerusalem*, which *Solomon had built* (v. 13). There were also high places all over the kingdom, from *Geba to Beer-sheba* (v. 8), and *high places of the gates, in the entering in* (entrance) *of the gate of the governor*.

1.7. There were idolatrous priests—*Chemarim*, men who wore black clothing—who officiated at all those idolatrous altars (v. 5). See Zep 1:4. Those who sacrificed to Osiris, who wept for Tammuz (Eze 8:14), or who worshiped the hellish deities put on black garments as mourners.

1.8. There were conjurers and wizards and those who *dealt with familiar spirits* (mediums) (v. 24).

2. How completely good Josiah destroyed all those relics of idolatry.

2.1. He ordered Hilkiah and the other priests to clear the temple. All the vessels that had been made for Baal must be removed. They must all be burned, and the ashes of them taken to Bethel. That place had been the common source of idolatry, for one of the calves had been set up there.

2.2. The idolatrous priests were all killed. He put to death, according to the Law, those of them who did not come from the house of Aaron or who had sacrificed to Baal or other false gods (v. 20). He killed them on their own altars, the most acceptable sacrifice that had ever been offered on them. He also prohibited those who were descendants of Aaron and yet had burned incense on the high places, but only to the true God, from ever approaching the altar of the Lord. He allowed them, however, to eat the unleavened bread with their fellow priests, with whom they were to live. Unleavened bread, heavy and unpleasant though it was, was better than they deserved, and that would have been enough to keep them alive.

2.3. All the sacred stones were broken into pieces and burned. The Asherah pole (*the grove*) (v. 6), some goddess or other, was reduced to ashes, and the ashes thrown on the graves of the common people (v. 6), the ordinary burial place in the city. According to the Law, ceremonial uncleanness was contracted by contact with a grave, so that in throwing the ashes there Josiah declared them to be impure. He *filled the places of the groves with the bones of men* (v. 14); as he carried the ashes of the sacred stones to the graves, to mix them with dead human bones, so also he carried dead human bones to the places where the sacred stones had once been, and put them in their place, so that in both ways he might make idolatry detestable. The people would then be kept clean both of the dust of the sacred stones and also of the ruins of the places where they had been worshiped.

2.4. All the evil houses were suppressed, those dens of immorality that kept idolaters, the quarters of the male shrine prostitutes (v. 7). The high places were broken down in the same way and leveled to the ground (v. 8). Tophet, which was in a valley, in contrast to other places of idolatry, which were on hills or high places, was also desecrated (v. 10). It was made the burial place for the city. We have a whole sermon about this (Jer 19:1–15), where it is said, *They will bury in Tophet* (Jer 19:11), and the whole city is threatened to be made like Tophet.

2.5. The horses that had been dedicated to the sun were taken away and put to common use, and he burned *the chariots of the sun* with fire.

2.6. He got rid of the mediums and spiritists (v. 24).

3. How Josiah's zeal extended to the cities of Israel that were within his reach. The ten tribes had been taken into exile, and the Assyrian colonies did not fully populate the country, so many towns had probably put themselves under the protection of the kings of Judah (2Ch 30:1; 34:6). He visited these towns to continue his reformation.

3.1. He desecrated and demolished Jeroboam's altar at Bethel, with the high place and the Asherah pole which belonged to it (vv. 15–16). The golden calf, it seems, was gone—*Thy calf, O Samaria, has cast thee off* (Hos 8:5)—but the altar was there. This was:

3.1.1. Defiled (v. 16). As Josiah, in his godly zeal, was ransacking the old idolatrous places, he noticed the tombs on the hillside, in which the idolatrous priests were probably buried. He had these tombs opened, took out the bones, and *burnt them upon the altar* (v. 20). In this way, he defiled the altar, desecrated it, and made it detestable.

3.1.2. Demolished. He broke down the altar and all its accessories (v. 15). He burned down what could be burned, *stamped it small to powder*, and made it *as dust before the wind*.

3.2. He destroyed all the shrines at the high places, all those synagogues of Satan which were in the towns of Samaria (v. 19).

3.3. He carefully preserved the tombstone of that man of God who came from Judah to foretell this. This was that good prophet who declared these things against the altar of Bethel but who was himself killed by a lion. To show that God's displeasure against him went no farther than his death, God so ordered things that when all the graves around his were disturbed, his remained safe (vv. 17–18), and no one moved his bones.

4. What a sacred Passover Josiah and his people kept after all this. When they had cleared the country of the old yeast, they then turned to keeping the feast. We do not have such a detailed account of this Passover as we had of the one in Hezekiah's time (2Ch 30:1–27). But generally, we are told that no such Passover had been held in any of the previous reigns, not *from the days of the judges* (v. 22). It seems that this Passover was extraordinary for the number and devotion of those who participated in it, their sacrifices and offerings, and their careful observance of the laws of the feast. God was pleased to reward their zeal in destroying idolatry with unusual signs of his presence and favor. All this went together to make it a special Passover.

Verses 25–30

1. It is here acknowledged that Josiah was one of the best kings who ever occupied the throne of David (v. 25). As Hezekiah was unrivaled for his faith and dependence on God in difficult times (18:5), so Josiah was unrivaled for his sincerity and zeal in carrying out his work of reformation.

- He *turned to the Lord* (v. 25), from whom his ancestors had rebelled. He did what he could to turn his kingdom also to the Lord.
- He did this *with his heart and soul* (v. 25).
- He did it with *all his heart*, and *all his soul*, and *all his might* (v. 25)—with energy, courage, and determination.
- He did this *according to all the law of Moses* (v. 25). In everything he did, he walked according to God's rule.

2. Despite all this, he was destroyed by a violent death in midlife, and his kingdom was overthrown a few years later. One would have expected that nothing but prosperity

and glory in both king and kingdom would follow such a reformation as this, but in fact we find quite the opposite, and both are under a cloud.

2.1. Even the reformed kingdom continues to be marked out for destruction. *Notwithstanding, the Lord turned not from the fierceness of his great wrath* (v. 26). What God spoke by the prophet (Jer 18:7–8) is certainly true, that if a nation destined for destruction *turns from the evil* of sin, God will *repent of the evil* of punishment. We must therefore conclude that even though Josiah's people submitted to Josiah's power, they did not fully take on Josiah's motives. They were turned by force; they did not voluntarily *turn from their evil way* but still continued to have an affection for their idols. And so the One who knows the human heart would not revoke the sentence, which was that Judah would be removed, as Israel had been, and Jerusalem itself rejected (v. 27). But even this destruction was intended to lead to their effective reformation, and so we must say that the sickness had come to a head, and they were ready to be healed.

2.2. As evidence of this, even the reforming king was destroyed in the middle of his usefulness, out of mercy to him, so that he might not see the evil which was going to come on his kingdom. The king of Egypt waged war with *the king of Assyria*: this is what the king of Babylon is now called. Josiah's kingdom lay between them. He therefore thought it necessary to oppose the king of Egypt and restrain the increasing threat of his power. Therefore *Josiah went against him*, and he was killed in the first engagement (vv. 29–30). We must praise God's righteousness for taking such a jewel away from an unthankful people who did not know how to value it. They mourned his death greatly (2Ch 35:25), urged on by Jeremiah, who told them its meaning and what a bad omen it was.

Verses 31–37

Jerusalem did not see a good day after Josiah was laid in his grave; one trouble came after another, till within twenty-two years it was totally destroyed. Here is a short account of the reign of two of his sons; the former we find a prisoner, and the latter a vassal, of the king of Egypt. After this king of Egypt had killed Josiah, he sent all his force against his family and kingdom.

1. Jehoahaz, a younger son, was first made king by *the people of the land* (v. 30), probably because he was of a more warlike disposition than his elder brother and so was more likely to advance against the king of Egypt and to avenge his father's death. He did evil (v. 32). He did *according to all that his* evil *fathers had done*. Although he did not have time to do much, he had chosen his role models. He was only king for three months, and he was then made a prisoner, and lived and died as such.

2. Eliakim, another son of Josiah, was made king by the king of Egypt. The crown of Judah had up to that time always descended from father to son, and never, until now, from one brother to another. The king of Egypt used his power in making him king and showed it further in changing his name. He called him *Jehoiakim*, a name that refers to Jehovah, for he had no intention of making him renounce or forget the religious faith of his country. We are told concerning Jehoiakim that the king of Egypt made him poor. He exacted from him a vast levy of *100 talents of silver and a talent of gold* (v. 33), which, with much difficulty, he squeezed out of his subjects and gave to Pharaoh (v. 35). Despite the rebukes of Providence that he was under, by which he should have been convinced, humbled, and reformed, he *did that which was evil in the sight of the Lord* (v. 37).

CHAPTER 24

Things are moving quickly toward the complete destruction of Jerusalem. We left Jehoiakim on the throne, put there by the king of Egypt. We have here: 1. The troubles of his reign: how he was brought into subjection by the king of Babylon (vv. 1–6), and how Egypt, too, was conquered by Nebuchadnezzar (v. 7). 2. The desolations of his son's reign, which lasted only three months. Then he and all his leaders were forced to surrender unconditionally and were taken into exile in Babylon (vv. 8–16). 3. The preparations made during the next reign, which was the last of all, for the complete destruction of Jerusalem (vv. 17–20).

Verses 1–7

Here is the first mention of *Nebuchadnezzar*, king of Babylon (v. 1), that head of gold (Da 2:38). He was a powerful ruler, and one who was the terror of the mighty (Eze 32:27). His name would not have been known in sacred Scripture, however, if he had not been used in the destruction of Jerusalem and the exile of the Jews.

1. He made Jehoiakim his vassal and kept him in subjection for three years (v. 1). Nebuchadnezzar began his reign in the fourth year of Jehoiakim. In his eighth year he took Jehoiakim prisoner, but he restored him to his throne upon his promise to be faithful to him. Jehoiakim kept that promise for about three years, but then he rebelled, probably in the hope of getting help from the king of Egypt.

2. When Jehoiakim rebelled, Nebuchadnezzar sent his forces against him to destroy his country: raiding bands of Babylonians, Arameans, Moabites, and Ammonites, who were all now serving and paying tribute to the king of Babylon (v. 2). They had also kept, and now showed, their old hostility toward God's Israel. God intended two things in allowing Judah to be harassed in this way:

2.1. The punishment of the sins of Manasseh, which God now inflicted on *the third and fourth generation*. The reason he waited such a long time before he punished them was to see if the nation would repent, but they continued without repenting.

2.2. Especially, punishment for *the innocent blood* Manasseh *shed*. Although Manasseh repented, and although we have reason to think that even the persecutions and murders he was guilty of were forgiven, nevertheless, because they were national sins, they still lay charged against the land, and national judgment was demanded. Perhaps some people were now living who had aided and abetted in shedding innocent blood. Notice that nations must mourn the sins of their ancestors so that they do not suffer for them.

3. The king of Egypt, too, was subdued by the king of Babylon, and a great part of his country was taken away from him (v. 7). He dared not *come any more out of his land* (v. 7). Afterward he attempted to relieve Zedekiah, but he was obliged to withdraw (Jer 37:7).

4. Jehoiakim saw his country devastated and himself ready to fall into enemy hands, and it seems he died of a broken heart, in midlife (v. 6).

Verses 8–20

This should have been the history of King Jehoiachin's *reign*, but regrettably it is only the history of King Jehoiachin's *captivity*, as it is called (Eze 1:2). He came to the crown not to have the honor of wearing it but to have the shame of losing it.

1. His reign was short and insignificant. He reigned only three months and was then removed and taken

captive to Babylon. This young king reigned long enough, however, to show that he justly suffered for his ancestors' sins, for he followed in their steps (v. 9).

2. The disasters that came on him, his family, and his people at the beginning of his reign were very severe:

2.1. Jerusalem was besieged by the king of Babylon (vv. 10–11).

2.2. Jehoiachin immediately surrendered, because he lacked the faith and godliness of an Israelite and therefore did not have the strong determination of a soldier or ruler. He and his royal family gave themselves up as prisoners of war.

2.3. Nebuchadnezzar rifled the treasuries of both the church and the state and took away the silver and gold from both (v. 13). Now was fulfilled the word of God through Isaiah (20:17), *All that is in thy house shall be carried to Babylon.*

2.4. He took a large part of Jerusalem away into exile. Some had been taken away eight years before this, in the first year of Nebuchadnezzar and the third of Jehoiakim, among whom were Daniel and his fellows. See Da 1:1, 6. Now he took away:

2.4.1. The young king himself and his family (v. 15), and we find (25:27–29) that for thirty-seven years he continued to be confined a prisoner.

2.4.2. All the leaders, the officials and warriors.

2.4.3. All the warriors, the *mighty men of valour* (v. 14), *the mighty of the land* (v. 15), *the men of might, even all that were strong and apt for war* (v. 16).

2.4.4. All the skilled workers and artisans who made weapons of war. In this exile Ezekiel the prophet was taken away (Eze 1:1–2).

3. The successor whom the king of Babylon appointed in place of Jehoiachin. The king of Babylon made Mattaniah king, the son of Josiah, and to let all the world know that he was his puppet, he changed his name and called him *Zedekiah* (v. 17). This Zedekiah was the last king of Judah. The name which the king of Babylon gave him means "the justice of the Lord." *He rebelled against the king of Babylon* (v. 20). This was the most foolish thing he could do, and it hastened the ruin of his kingdom.

CHAPTER 25

In this chapter we have: 1. The complete destruction of Jerusalem by the Babylonians: the city besieged and taken (vv. 1–4), the houses burned down (vv. 8–9), the walls broken down (v. 10), and the inhabitants taken away into exile (vv. 11–12). The glory of Jerusalem was that it was the Royal City, where the thrones of the house of David stood (Ps 122:5), but that glory now departed, for the ruler was made a most miserable prisoner, and the royal seed was destroyed (vv. 5–7). 2. The principal officers being put to death (vv. 18–21). It was the Holy City, where the testimony of Israel was, but that glory now departed, for Solomon's temple was burned to the ground (v. 9), and the sacred articles which remained were taken away to Babylon (vv. 13–17). 3. The dispersion of the remnant in Judah under Gedaliah (vv. 22–26) and the support which, after thirty-seven years' imprisonment, was given to Jehoiachin, the captive king of Judah (vv. 27–30).

Verses 1–7

We left King Zedekiah rebelling against the king of Babylon (24:20), trying to shake off his oppression.

1. The king of Babylon's army laid siege to Jerusalem (v. 1). The siege lasted two years; at first the army withdrew for fear of the king of Egypt (Jer 37:11), but finding him not so powerful as they had thought, they soon returned.

2. During this siege the famine continued (v. 3).

3. Finally the city was taken by storm: it was *broken up* (v. 4). The besiegers broke through the city walls and forced their way into the city.

4. The king, his family, and all his leaders escaped at night, by some secret passages. The Babylonians were told about the king's escape, and they quickly overtook him (v. 5).

4.1. He was brought to the king of Babylon and tried by a council of war for rebelling against the one to whom he had sworn allegiance.

4.2. His *sons were slain before his eyes* (v. 7).

4.3. His eyes were put out. By this he was deprived of the light of the sun. Jeremiah prophesied that Zedekiah would be brought to Babylon (Jer 32:5; 34:3). Ezekiel prophesied that he would not see Babylon (Eze 12:13). He was brought there, but because his eyes had been put out, he did not see it. In this way he ended his days before he ended his life.

4.4. He was *bound in fetters of brass* (bronze shackles) and so *carried to Babylon* (v. 7). To increase his disgrace, they led him bound.

Verses 8–21

About a month later (compare v. 8 with v. 3) Nebuzaradan was sent with orders to complete the destruction of Jerusalem. God gave them this space to repent, after all the previous days of his patience, but in vain.

1. The city and temple are burned down (v. 9). The temple was that holy and beautiful house (Isa 64:11) that David prepared for and that Solomon built at such vast expense—that house which God had his eye and heart set on forever (1Ki 9:3)—and yet it must be turned to ashes with the rest of the city. By the burning of the temple God showed how little he cares for the external pomp of his worship when the life and power of religious life are neglected. The people trusted in the temple as if it would protect them in their sins (Jer 7:4). It is significant that the second temple was burned down by the Romans in the same month, and on the same day of the month, that the first temple was burned down by the Babylonians, which, Josephus says, was the tenth of August.

2. The walls of Jerusalem are broken down (v. 10), as if the victorious army wanted to get their revenge on them for having kept them out so long. These walls were never repaired until Nehemiah's time.

3. The remaining people are taken captive to Babylon (v. 11). Only the poor of the land were left behind (v. 12), to cultivate the ground and trim the vineyards for the Babylonians. Sometimes poverty acts as a protection, for those who have nothing have nothing to lose.

4. The bronze articles and other accessories of the temple are taken away, those of silver and gold having already been taken. Those two famous bronze columns, Jakin and Boaz, which stood for the strength and stability of the temple of God, were broken into pieces, and their bronze was taken to Babylon (v. 13).

5. Several of the great men are cold-bloodedly killed. This meant that this disaster was complete: *So Judah was carried away out of their land* (v. 21), about 820 years after they were given possession of it by Joshua. Sin kept their fathers forty years out of Canaan, and now turned *them* out.

Verses 22–30

In these verses we have:

1. The dispersion of the remaining people. The city of Jerusalem was completely devastated, but there were some people in the land of Judah (v. 22) who had weathered the storm and escaped with their lives (Jer 45:5). The king of Babylon appointed one of their own, Gedaliah, as their governor and protector under him. He was a very good man, and one who would make the best of the bad situation they were in (v. 22). His father Ahikam was one who supported and protected Jeremiah when the officials had vowed his death (Jer 26:24). This Gedaliah had probably, on the advice of Jeremiah, gone over to the Babylonians and behaved so well that the king of Babylon entrusted him with the government. He did not live in Jerusalem but in Mizpah, in the land of Benjamin, a place famous in Samuel's time. Those who had fled from Zedekiah went there (v. 4) and put themselves under his protection (v. 23). Although Gedaliah did not have the pomp and power of a sovereign ruler, he could still have been a greater blessing to them than many of their kings had been. Yet this promising settlement was dashed to pieces, and not by the Babylonians but by some of their own number. Ishmael, who was of the royal family, envied Gedaliah's advancement and the happy settlement of the people under him, and so he killed him and all his friends, both Jews and Babylonians. The Babylonians had reason enough to be offended at the murder of Gedaliah, but if those who remained had humbly raised an objection, alleging that it was only the act of Ishmael and his party, those who were innocent would not have been punished for it. However, contrary to the counsel of Jeremiah, they all went to Egypt, where they probably gradually mixed with the Egyptians and were never heard of again as Israelites. And so their end came because of their foolishness and disobedience, and Egypt was their end, so that the last verse of that chapter of threats might be fulfilled (Dt 28:68): *The Lord shall bring thee into Egypt again.* These events are related in more detail by the prophet Jeremiah (Jer 40:1–45:5).

2. The reviving of the captive ruler. We hear no more about Zedekiah, but about Jehoiachin, or Jeconiah, who surrendered himself (24:12), we are told here that as soon as Evil-Merodach came to the throne, on the death of his father, Nebuchadnezzar, he released him from prison—where he had been confined for thirty-seven years, and was now fifty-five years old—*spoke kindly to him* (v. 28), gave him royal clothes instead of his prison garments, kept him in his own palace (v. 29), and gave an allowance to him and his family which in some measure corresponded to his rank, *a daily rate for every day as long as he lived* (v. 30). Consider this:

2.1. As a very happy change in Jehoiachin's condition. To have honor and liberty after he had been so long held in confinement and disgrace was like the coming of morning after a very dark, long night. Let no one say that they will never see good again because they have long seen little except evil. The most miserable people do not know what blessed turn of events Providence may still bring them (Ps 90:15). However, death to saints who have suffered is a change similar to this one that came to Jehoiachin: it will release them from their prison. It will shake off their outer prison garments, and it will send them to the throne, to the table of the King of kings, and to the glorious liberty of God's children (Ro 8:21).

2.2. As a very generous act of Evil-Merodach's. He thought his father had made the oppression of his captives too hard to bear, and so with human tenderness and the honor of a ruler, he made it lighter. The Jews say that this Evil-Merodach had himself been imprisoned by his own father when his father was restored from his madness—that he had been punished in this way for some mismanagement during the time of his father's incapacity—and that in prison he had contracted a friendship with Jehoiachin, as a result of which, as soon as he had it in his power, he showed him this kindness as a fellow sufferer. Some suggest that Evil-Merodach had learned from Daniel and his fellows the principles of true religion.

2.3. As a kind act of Providence. Thirty-six of the seventy years of their exile had then past, and now to see their king advanced in this way would be an encouraging sign to the captive people that their own release would come at the set time. In times when we are perplexed, let us therefore not despair.

A PRACTICAL AND DEVOTIONAL EXPOSITION OF
THE BOOK OF

1 Chronicles

In ordinary things repetition is thought unnecessary and tiresome, but in sacred things *precept must be upon precept and line upon line* (Isa 28:10). The apostle Paul wrote: *To me, to write the same things is not grievous* (is no trouble), *but for you it is safe* (Php 3:1). These books of Chronicles are to a great extent repetition, as is much of the second and third of the four Gospels, but there is no tautology either here or there, no *vain repetitions* (Mt 6:7). We may be ready to think that of all the books of Holy Scripture, the two we could most easily do without are the two books of Chronicles. Perhaps we could. But no, we could not *easily* do without them, for there are many excellent and helpful things in them which we do not find elsewhere. And as for what we find here that we have already met with: 1. It might have been very useful to those who lived when these books were first published, before the canon of the Old Testament was completed and its parts put together, for it would have reminded them of what was related in more detail in the other books. Summaries, abridgments, and references are useful in theology as well as law. What has already been said may perhaps not be said in vain. 2. It is still useful, because with it, *out of the mouth of two witnesses every word may be established* (Mt 18:16) and, being instilled, may be remembered.

The writer of these books is thought to be Ezra, that *ready scribe* (a teacher well versed) *in the law of the Lord* (Ezr 7:6). The story of the apocryphal writer—which says that because all the law had been burned, Ezra was divinely inspired to write it all over again (2 Esd 14:21-44)—is without basis; yet this story might have its origin in the books of Chronicles, where, though we do not find all the same story repeated, we do find the names of all those who were the subjects of that story. In the Hebrew these books are called "words of days," journals or annals, because, under divine direction, they were collected from some public and authentic records. The collection was made after the Exile, but it sometimes kept the language of the original that had been written earlier, as where it contains the phrase (2Ch 5:9) *there it is unto this day*, which must have been written before the destruction of the temple. The Septuagint (a Greek version of the Old Testament) calls it a book *Paraleipomenôn*, "of things omitted" (i.e., a book of things omitted [in the Kings account]) by the preceding historians, and there are several such things in it. It is the rear guard, the mobilized force of this sacred camp, that gathers up the leftovers so that nothing is lost.

In this first book we have: 1. A collection of sacred genealogies from Adam to David. They are not those which the apostle Paul calls *endless genealogies* (1Ti 1:4), but have their use and purpose in Christ (chs. 1–9). Various short passages of the history are included here which we have not had before. 2. A repetition of the history of the transfer of the kingdom from Saul to David, and of the triumph of David's reign, with many additions (chs. 10–21). 3. An original account of David's establishment of ecclesiastical affairs and his preparation for building the temple (chs. 22–29).

CHAPTER 1

These genealogies: 1. Were of great use when they were preserved and put into the hands of the Jews after their return from Babylon, because the Exile had confused everything, and in that dispersion they would have been in danger of losing the distinctions of their tribes and families. This therefore revives the ancient landmarks (Pr 22:28) of even some of the tribes who were deported to Assyria. 2. Are still useful to illustrate the story of Scripture, and especially to give the background of the family line of the Messiah, so that it might be clear that

our blessed Savior was, according to the prophecies which went before of him, the son of David, the son of Judah, the son of Abraham, the son of Adam.

In this chapter we have a summary of all the genealogies of the book of Genesis, until we come to Jacob: 1. The descendants from Adam to Noah and his sons (vv. 1–4); the descendants of Noah's sons, by which the earth was repopulated (vv. 5–23); the descendants from Shem to Abraham (vv. 24–28). 2. The descendants of Ishmael, and of Abraham's sons by Keturah (vv. 29–35); the descendants of Esau (vv. 36–54).

Verses 1–27

This section has *Adam* as its first word and *Abraham* as its last. Adam was the common father of our flesh, our humanity, Abraham the common father of the faithful. Because Adam broke the covenant of innocence before the Fall, we were all made miserable; because of the covenant of grace made with Abraham, we all are, or may be, made happy. We all are, by nature, the seed of Adam, branches of that wild olive (Ro 11:24). Let us see to it that by faith we become the seed of Abraham (Ro 4:11–12), that we are grafted into the good olive and share in the nourishing sap from the olive root.

1. The first four verses of this section and the last four, which are linked together by Shem (vv. 4, 24), contain Christ's sacred line of descent from Adam to Abraham, and are included in the same order in the genealogy of him given in Lk 3:34–38, except that there the names are listed in ascending order, whereas here they are in descending order.

2. All the verses in between repeat the account of the repopulating of the earth by the sons of Noah after the Flood. The writer begins with those who were strangers to the church, the sons of Japheth, who were planted in the *isles of the Gentiles* (Ge 10:5), those western parts of the world, the countries of Europe. The sons of Ham moved southward toward Africa and those parts of Asia in southern latitudes. The descendants of Shem (vv. 17–23) populated Asia and spread eastward. The Assyrians, Syrians, Babylonians, Persians, and Arabians descended from these. At first, the origins of these respective nations were known, but the nations have mixed with one another so much—by the development of trade, commerce, and conquest and by the planting of colonies, the taking of captives, and many other circumstances—that no one nation, or the greatest part of any, is completely descended from any one of these sources. We can be sure only of this: that God has made all the nations from one man (Ac 17:26). The great promise of the Messiah was, according to Bishop Patrick, transferred from Adam to Seth, from him to Shem, from him to Eber, and so to the Hebrew nation, which was entrusted above all nations with that sacred treasure until the promise was fulfilled and the Messiah had come.

Verses 28–54

All nations except the descendants of Abraham have already been taken away from this genealogy: they do not share in this matter. *The Lord's portion is his people* (Dt 32:9). Not that we can conclude from this that therefore no particular people from any other nation except the descendants of Abraham found favor with God. There were very many good people in the world who were outside the scope of God's unique covenant with Abraham, whose names were in the Book of Life even though they were not descended from any of the following families written in this book. *The Lord knows those who are his* (2Ti 2:19). But Israel was a chosen nation, elect as a type, and no other nation, as a nation, was so honored and privileged as the Jewish nation was. This is the holy nation which is the subject of the sacred story, and so next we take away all the descendants of Abraham except the descendants of Jacob.

1. We will have little to say of the *Ishmaelites*. They were the sons of the slave woman, who were to be gotten rid of and not to be heirs with the child of the promise. Ishmael's twelve sons are just named here (vv. 29–31), to show the fulfillment of the promise God made to Abraham

that Ishmael would become a great nation, and especially that he would be the father of twelve rulers (Ge 17:20).

2. We will have little to say of the *Midianites*, who descended from Abraham's children by Keturah. They were *children of the east* (Jdg 6:3; 7:12; etc.) and were separated from Isaac, the heir of the promise (Ge 25:6), and so they are only named here (v. 32).

3. We do not have much to say about the *Edomites*. They had a long-standing hostility toward God's Israel, but because they descended from Esau, the son of Isaac, we have an account of their families, and the names of some of their famous men (vv. 35–54).

CHAPTER 2

We have now come to the main purpose of the book, the register of the children of Israel, that special people, who were to dwell alone, and not be reckoned among the nations *(Nu 23:9). We have here: 1. The names of the twelve sons of Israel (vv. 1–2); an account of the tribe of Judah, which takes priority, not so much for the sake of David as for the sake of the Son of David, our Lord, who was descended from Judah (Heb 7:14); the first descendants from Judah, down to Jesse (vv. 3–12); the children of Jesse (vv. 13–17). 2. The descendants of Hezron, not only through Ram, from whom David came, but also through Caleb (vv. 18–20), Segub (vv. 21–24), Jerahmeel (vv. 25–41), and more by Caleb (vv. 42–49), along with the family of Caleb the son of Hur (vv. 50–55).*

Verses 1–17

Here is:

1. The family of Jacob. His twelve sons are named here, that well-known number so often celebrated throughout almost the whole Bible. At every turn we meet the twelve tribes who are descended from these twelve patriarchs. The personal character of several of them was not the best—the first four were very tarnished—yet the covenant was still passed on to their descendants, for it was of free grace that it was said, *Jacob have I loved* (Ro 9:13)—*not of works, lest any man should boast* (Eph 2:9).

2. The family of Judah. That tribe was the most commended and most numerous of all the tribes. Its genealogy is therefore the first and most detailed of them all. In the account of the first branches of that famous tree, of which Christ was to be the top branch, we meet with:

2.1. Some who were evil. Here is Er, Judah's eldest son, who was *evil in the sight of the Lord* and was destroyed at the beginning of his days (v. 3). His brother nearest in age, Onan, fared no better. Here is Tamar, with whom Judah, her father-in-law, committed incest (v. 4). And here is Achan, called *Achar*, "a troubler," who troubled Israel by taking the devoted things (v. 7).

2.2. Some who were wise and good, such as Heman and Ethan, Calcol and Darda. Perhaps these were not directly the sons of Zerah but his descendants, and are named because they were the glory of their father's house (1Ki 4:31).

2.3. Some who were great, such as Nahshon, who was leader of Judah when the camp of Israel was formed in the desert, and so led the vanguard on that glorious journey, and *Salma*, or Salmon, who was in that position of honor when they entered Canaan (vv. 10–11).

3. The family of Jesse, of which a particular record is kept for the sake of David and of the Son of David, who *is a rod out of the stem of Jesse* (Isa 11:1). From this it can be seen that David was a seventh son, and that his three

great commanders, Joab, Abishai, and Asahel, were the sons of one of his sisters, and Amasa of another.

Verses 18–55

Very few of those mentioned in this section are mentioned anywhere else.

1. Here we find Bezalel, who was the leading skilled craft worker in building the tabernacle (Ex 31:2).

2. Hezron was one of the seventy who went down with Jacob to Egypt (Ge 46:12). The achievements of Jair, mentioned in vv. 22–23, took place long after the conquest of Canaan. The genealogy of several of these individuals ends in with a person but with a place or country: one is said to be *the father of Kirjath-jearim* (v. 50), another of Bethlehem (v. 51), which was afterward David's city. They were referred to in this way because these places fell to their allotted territory in the division of the land. Among all these great families we are glad to find some who were *families of scribes. Would to God that all the Lord's people were prophets* (Nu 11:29): all the families of Israel families of scribes, well instructed in the kingdom of heaven.

CHAPTER 3

Of all the families of Israel none was so famous as the family of David. That is the family which was mentioned in v. 15 of the previous chapter. Here we have a full account of it: 1. David's sons (vv. 1–9). 2. His successors on the throne as long as the kingdom continued (vv. 10–16); the remnant of his family during and after the Exile (vv. 17–24). From this family, as concerning the flesh, Christ came (Ro 9:5).

Verses 1–9

We had an account of David's sons in 2Sa 3:2–5; 5:14–16. Some of them were a grief to him, such as Amnon, Absalom, and Adonijah. None imitated his godliness or devotion except Solomon, and he fell far short of it. One of them, whom Bathsheba gave birth to, he called Nathan, probably in honor of Nathan the prophet, who rebuked him for his sin in that matter and was instrumental in bringing him to repentance. It seems he loved Nathan all the better for it as long as he lived. It is wise to consider those who deal faithfully with us to be our best friends. Our Lord Jesus descended from this son of David (Lk 3:31). Here are two Elishamas (although one was also known as Elishua) and two Eliphelets (vv. 6–8). Probably the two former were dead, and so David called two more by their names.

Verses 10–24

Because David had nineteen sons, we may suppose that they raised many noble families in Israel whom we never read about in the history. But Scripture gives us an account only of the descendants of Solomon here, and of Nathan in Lk 3:31. We have here:

1. The great and celebrated names by which the line of David is drawn down to the Exile, the kings of Judah in direct succession. Seldom has a crown gone in direct line from father to son for a total of seventeen generations, as here. This was the reward of David's godliness. About the time of the Exile, the direct line of descent was interrupted, and the crown went from one brother to another and from a nephew to an uncle.

2. The less famous—and most of them very obscure—names in which the house of David existed after the Exile. The only famous man of that house that we meet with at their return from captivity is Zerubbabel, the grandson of Shealtiel (vv. 17–19). Shealtiel is said to be *the son of*

Jeconiah (Jehoiachin) because he was adopted by him and because, as some think, he succeeded him in the position to which he was restored by Evil-Merodach. Otherwise Jehoiachin was recorded as childless (Jer 22:30): he was *the signet God plucked from his right hand* (Jer 22:24), and Zerubbabel took his place, and so God said to him (Hag 2:23), *I will make thee as a signet* (my signet ring). The descendants of Zerubbabel here do not have the same names as they do in the genealogies of Mt 1:1–17 and Lk 3:23–38, but those no doubt were taken from the public registers which the priests kept of all the families of Judah, especially that of David.

CHAPTER 4

In this chapter we have: 1. A further account of the genealogies of the tribe of Judah, the most famous and most numerous of all the tribes: the descendants of Shobal the son of Hur (vv. 1–4), and of Ashhur, the posthumous son of Hezron, who was mentioned in 2:24; some details concerning Jabez (vv. 5–10); the descendants of Kelub and others (vv. 11–20) and those of Shelah (vv. 21–23). 2. An account of the descendants and towns of Simeon, and an account of their conquest of Gedor and of the Amalekites in the hill country of Seir (vv. 24–43).

Verses 1–10

One reason, no doubt, why Ezra, the writer, gives such great detail in the register of the tribe of Judah is that together with the tribes of Simeon, Benjamin, and Levi, it made up the kingdom of Judah, which had returned from the Exile when this was written, whereas most of the other tribes were lost in the kingdom of Assyria. The most remarkable person in this paragraph is Jabez, the founder of one of the families of Aharhel, mentioned in v. 8. Here is:

1. The reason for his name: his mother gave him the name *Because I bore him with sorrow* (v. 9). *Jabez* sounds like the Hebrew word for "pain." Usually the sorrow of childbirth is forgotten afterward *for joy that the child is born* (Jn 16:21), but here it seems it was remembered when the child came to be circumcised, and care was taken to remember it for as long as he lived:

1.1. So that it might be a continual reminder to her to be thankful to God as long as she lived for bringing her through that time of sorrow.

1.2. So that it might likewise remind him of what this world is into which she gave birth to him, a vale of tears, in which he must expect *few days and full of trouble* (Job 14:1). It might also remind him to love and honor his mother, to try hard in everything to comfort the one who had brought him into the world with so much sorrow.

2. His great character: *He was more honourable than his brethren* (v. 9). Why he was more honorable we do not know, but we have most reason to think it was because of his learning and godliness:

- His learning, because we find that *the families of the scribes dwelt at Jabez* (2:55), a city which, it is likely, took its name from him.
- His godliness, because we read here that he was a man of prayer.

3. The prayer he prayed, just as he was setting out in the world. He set himself to acknowledge God in all his ways, and he put himself under God's blessing and protection, and so he prospered. Notice:

3.1. To whom he prayed: he *called on the God of Israel* (v. 10), a God in covenant with his people, the God with whom Jacob had wrestled and prevailed and by whom he was therefore called Israel (Ge 32:28).

3.2. What was the nature of his prayer:

3.2.1. As the margin reads, it was a solemn vow: "If thou wilt" *bless me indeed,* and then the sense is incomplete, but it may easily be filled out from Jacob's vow with something like "then you will be my God." He, as it were, gives God a blank check for him to write what he pleases: "Lord, if you will bless me and keep me, do what you will with me. I will be at your command and at your disposal forever."

3.2.2. As the main text reads, it was the language of a most fervent and affectionate desire: *O that thou wouldst bless me* (v. 10)*!*

3.3. What was the subject of his prayer? He prayed four things:

3.3.1. That God would really bless him: "That *thou wilt bless me* (v. 10), bless me greatly with abundant blessings."

3.3.2. That God would enlarge his territory, make him prosper in his undertakings in such a way that, whether by work or by war, the property that had been given him would increase.

3.3.3. That God's hand would be with him. God's hand with us is truly a hand sufficient for us; his hand to lead us, protect us, and strengthen us, and to work all our works in us and for us, is all-sufficient.

3.3.4. That God would keep him from evil, the evil of sin, the evil of trouble, and all the evil intentions of his enemies, so that they might not hurt him or grieve him.

3.4. *God granted him that which he requested* (v. 10). He prospered him remarkably and gave him success in his undertakings, in his studies, in his worldly business, and in his conflicts with the Canaanites.

Verses 11–23

We may notice in these verses:

1. Here is a whole clan of skilled craft workers who applied themselves to manufacturing all sorts of things, a kind of work in which they were more skilled and diligent than their neighbors (v. 14). There was a valley where they lived which was named after them, *the valley of craftsmen.*

2. One of these married the daughter of Pharaoh king of Egypt (v. 18)—*Pharaoh* was the ordinary name for all kings of Egypt.

3. Another is said to be the *father of the house of those that wrought fine linen,* of the clans of the linen workers (v. 21). They were the best weavers in the kingdom, and they brought up their children to do the same business from one generation to the next. His descendants lived in the city of Mareshah, whose product or staple commodity was linen cloth, which their kings and priests wore.

4. The people of another clan had had *dominion in Moab* but were now in slavery in Babylon (vv. 22–23).

4.1. It was found among the ancient records that they ruled in Moab (v. 22). They settled there probably in David's time, when that country was conquered.

4.2. Their descendants were now potters and gardeners in Babylon, where they *dwelt with the king for his work* (v. 23), gained a good livelihood, and so did not want to return to their own land, after the years of Exile.

Verses 24–43

Here are some of the genealogies of the tribe of Simeon. It is said of this tribe that they *increased greatly,* but *not like the children of Judah* (v. 27). Notice:

1. The towns allotted them (v. 28), about which compare Jos 19:1–9. When it is said that these towns were theirs *unto the reign of David* (v. 31), the suggestion is given that when the ten tribes rebelled from the house of David, many of the Simeonites left these towns, because they lay within Judah, and established themselves elsewhere.

2. The ground they gained elsewhere. In the days of Hezekiah a generation of Simeonites, whose tribe had long lain low and submitted, found the courage to act boldly and extend their territories.

2.1. Some of them attacked a place in Arabia called *the entrance of Gedor* (v. 39); they conquered it and lived there. This adds to the glory of Hezekiah's godly reign: as his kingdom in general prospered, so also did individual families.

2.2. Others of them, 500 in number, under the command of four brothers named here, launched an invasion on the hill country of Seir, struck the Amalekites, and took possession of their country (vv. 42–43).

CHAPTER 5

This chapter gives us some account of the two and a half tribes that were positioned on the other side of the Jordan. 1. Of Reuben (vv. 1–10); of Gad (vv. 11–17). 2. Of the half tribe of Manasseh (vv. 23–24). Concerning all three acting together we are told how they conquered the Hagrites (vv. 18–22) and how they themselves were eventually conquered and taken captive by the king of Assyria, because they abandoned God (vv. 25–26).

Verses 1–17

Here is an extract from the genealogies:

1. Of the tribe of Reuben, where we have:

1.1. The reason why this tribe was made subordinate. Reuben, the firstborn of Israel, forfeited his birthright by defiling his father's concubine. The advantages of the birthright were power and a double share of the inheritance. Because Reuben had forfeited these, it was thought too much that both should be transferred to any one person, and so they were divided.

1.1.1. Joseph had the double share of the inheritance, for two tribes descended from him, Ephraim and Manasseh, each of whom had a son's portion—for this is how Jacob by faith blessed them (Heb 11:21; Ge 48:15, 22)—and each of those tribes was as significant as any one of the twelve, except Judah. But:

1.1.2. Judah had the power. It was on him that the dying patriarch had passed on the scepter (Ge 49:10). From him came the chief ruler: first David, and in the fullness of time the Messiah, the Ruler referred to in Mic 5:2.

1.2. The genealogy of the leaders of this tribe down to Beerah, who was their head when the king of Assyria took them into exile (vv. 4–6).

1.3. The enlargement of the territories of this tribe. Because they increased and their cattle multiplied, they crowded out their neighbors the Hagrites and extended their conquests.

2. Of the tribe of Gad. Some great families of that tribe are named here (v. 12), including seven who were the children of Abihail, whose genealogy is taken upward from son to father (vv. 14–15) just as that of vv. 4–5 was listed downward from father to son.

Verses 18–26

The heads of the half tribe of Manasseh, a tribe that, like Reuben and Gad, was positioned on the other side of the Jordan, are named here (vv. 23–24). Their allotted territory was originally only Bashan, but afterward they increased so much in wealth and power that they spread far north, even to Hermon. Two things are recorded here about these tribes on the other side of the Jordan, things in which they were all involved. They all shared:

1. In a glorious victory over the Hagrites. This is what the Ishmaelites were now called, to remind them that they were *the sons of the bondwoman* Hagar, who was *cast out* (Gal 4:30). Notice:

1.1. What a bold army these frontier tribes took onto the battlefield against the Hagrites, more than 44,000 soldiers, all strong, brave, and ready for military service.

1.2. What course they took to engage God for them: they *cried to God* and *put their trust in him* (v. 20). Although they had a powerful army, they did not depend on that but relied on the power of God. For something similar, see 2Ch 13:14. In our spiritual conflicts, we must look to heaven for strength, and it is believing prayer that will be effective. If the battle is the Lord's, there is reason to hope it will be successful.

2. In an inglorious captivity. If they had kept close to God and their duty, they would have continued to enjoy both their ancient territory and their new conquests, but they *transgressed against the God of their fathers* (v. 25). They lived on the borders of the nation's territory, and of all the tribes they had the closest dealings with the neighboring nations, which meant they learned their idolatrous customs and defiled the other tribes. These tribes were the first to be placed, and they were also the first to be displaced. They wanted to have the best land and did not consider that it lay most exposed to other nations. Those who are controlled in their choices more by feelings than by reason or faith may expect to bear the corresponding consequences.

CHAPTER 6

Although Joseph and Judah shared between them the forfeited honors of the birthright, Levi was still the first of all the tribes, and it was given an honor more valuable than either the superiority in rank or the double share of the inheritance, and that was the priesthood. God set that tribe apart for himself. It was Moses' tribe, and perhaps the tribe was especially favored for his sake. We have an account of that tribe in this chapter: 1. Their genealogy: the first fathers of the tribe (vv. 1–3), the line of the priests from Aaron to the Exile (vv. 4–15), and the line of some of their other families (vv. 16–30). 2. Their work: the work of the Levites (vv. 31–48) and of the priests (vv. 49–53). 3. The towns appointed for them in the land of Canaan (vv. 54–81).

Verses 1–30

The priests and Levites were more concerned than any other Israelites to keep their line of descent clear and to be able to show that it was so, because all the honors and privileges of their office depended on their genealogy. Very little is recorded here of the genealogies of this sacred tribe:

1. The tribe's first fathers are named twice here (vv. 1, 16): Gershon, Kohath, and Merari, three names which we read very much about in the book of Numbers. Aaron, Moses, and Miriam are also mentioned, and we know much more than their names, remembering that these were the Moses and Aaron whom God honored by using them as instruments of Israel's rescue and settlement (Ex 6:26–27). They prefigured the One who was to come, Moses as a

prophet and Aaron as a priest. The mention of Nadab and Abihu must remind us of the terrors of divine justice.

2. The line of Eleazar, the successor of Aaron, is here drawn down to the time of the Exile (vv. 4–15). It begins with Eleazar, who came out of slavery in Egypt, and ends with Jehozadak, who was taken captive to Babylon. Not all the ones named here were high priests, for during the time of the judges, that honor was on some occasion or other given to the family of Ithamar, from which Eli came. In Zadok, however (v. 8; see also 2Sa 8:17; 1Ki 1:44–45), it returned to the right line. It is said here of Azariah (v. 10), *He it is that executed the priest's office in the temple that Solomon built.* It is supposed that this was that Azariah who boldly opposed the presumption of King Uzziah when he took over the priest's role (2Ch 26:17–18). This befitted a priest, who should be truly zealous for his God. One of the families of Gershon (that of Libni) is here taken as far back as Samuel, who had the honor of a prophet added to that of a Levite. One of the families of Merari (that of Mahli) is similarly taken forward several generations (vv. 29–30).

Verses 31–53

When the Levites were first ordained in the desert, much of the work that they were appointed to do was carrying and taking care of the tabernacle and its accessories while they journeyed through the desert. In David's time their numbers increased, and although most of them were dispersed throughout the nation to teach the people the good knowledge of the Lord, those who served in the house of God were so numerous that there was not constant work for all of them. And so David received a special commission and instructions from God to reorganize the Levites, as we will find later in this book. We are told here what work he assigned them:

1. Singing (v. 31). David was exalted as *the sweet psalmist of Israel* (2Sa 23:1) not only to write psalms but also to appoint the singing of them in the house of the Lord, and he did this after the ark came to rest (v. 31). While the ark was captive, obscure, and unsettled, the harps were hung on the willow trees (Ps 137:2); it was thought that the time was not right to sing. But once the harps were taken up again and the songs revived when the ark had been brought up to Jerusalem, the playing and singing was to continue. Now that their previous responsibilities for the ark had ended because it came to rest in Jerusalem, they had other work assigned to them — for Levites should never be lazy — and were used in the ministry of singing. These singers kept that service in the tabernacle until the temple was built, and then they *waited on* (served in) *their office* there (v. 32). Here we have an account of the three great masters who were employed in the ministry of sacred singing, with their respective families, for they served *with their children*, that is, with those who were descended from them or were allied to them (v. 33). Heman, Asaph, and Ethan were the three who were appointed to this service, one from each of the three clans of the Levites.

1.1. Heman and his family came from the clan of Kohath (v. 33). He was a man of a sad spirit — if it is the same Heman who wrote Ps 88 — and yet he was a singer. He was the grandson of Samuel the prophet, the son of Joel, of whom it is said that *he walked not in the ways of Samuel* (1Sa 8:2–3), but it seems that although the son did not, the grandson did. Perhaps when David made Heman the chief, he was showing respect for his old friend Samuel.

1.2. Asaph came from the clan of Gershon and was called Heman's *brother* or associate, because he held the same office and came from the same tribe, although he came from a different clan. He was positioned at Heman's right hand in the choir (v. 39). Several of the psalms bear his name. It is clear that he was the author of some psalms, for we read of those people who praised the Lord in the words of David and of Asaph (2Ch 29:30). He was a seer as well as a singer (2Ch 29:30). His genealogy is traced upward here, through names completely unknown, as far back as Levi (vv. 39–43).

1.3. Ethan came from the clan of Merari (v. 44). He was appointed to serve at Heman's left hand. His genealogy is also traced back up to Levi (v. 47).

2. Serving. There was a great deal of service to be done *in the tabernacle of the house of God* (v. 48): to provide water and fuel; to wash, sweep, and carry out ashes; to kill, flay, and boil the sacrifices. To all such services Levites were appointed—those from other families, or perhaps those who were not fit to be singers, who did not have a good voice or a good ear for music. *As every man has received the gift, so let him minister* (1Pe 4:10).

3. Sacrificing. The offering of sacrifices was to be done only by the priests (v. 49). Only they were to sprinkle the blood and burn the incense. As for the work of the Most Holy Place, that was to be done only by the high priest. Each had his work, and they all needed one another and helped one another to do it. We are told here about the work of the priests. They were to make atonement for Israel, to mediate between the people and God. They were not to exalt and enrich themselves but to serve the community. They presided in God's house, but they must observe all that God commanded.

Verses 54–81

Here is an account of the Levites' towns. They and their possessions were under the special care of divine Providence. Just as God was their inheritance, so also God was their protection. A cottage will be like a castle to those who take refuge in the shadow of the Almighty. It will not discredit Holy Scripture if the names of some of the places are not spelled exactly the same here as in Jos 21:1–45. It is common for towns and cities to have several names: for example, in England, *Sarum* and *Salisbury*, *Salop* and *Shropshire*. These are more unlike than *Hilen* (v. 58) and *Holon* (Jos 21:15), *Ashan* (v. 59) and *Ain* (Jos 21:16), *Alemeth* (v. 60) and *Almon* (Jos 21:18), for names change over time. In this appointment of towns for the Levites, God took care:

1. To fulfill Jacob's prophecy for this tribe, that it would be *scattered in Israel* (Ge 49:7).

2. To spread the knowledge of himself and his law to all parts of the land of Israel. Every tribe had Levites' towns in it.

3. To comfortably maintain those who ministered in holy things. Some of the most significant towns of Israel fell to the Levites' lot.

CHAPTER 7

In this chapter we have some account of the genealogies: 1. Of Issachar (vv. 1–5); of Benjamin (vv. 6–12); of Naphtali (v. 13); of Manasseh (vv. 14–19). 2. Of Ephraim (vv. 20–29); of Asher (vv. 30–40).

Verses 1–19

We have here a brief account:

1. Of the tribe of Issachar, whom Jacob had compared to a *strong ass, couching between two burdens,*

a rawboned donkey lying down between two saddlebags (Ge 49:14), a diligent tribe whose people looked after their country business very closely and *rejoiced in their tents* (Dt 33:18). Their country was so fruitful that they saw no danger of overstocking the pasture, and the people were so clever that they could find work for everyone. People should not complain about their numbers, provided they allow no one to be idle. The number of fighting men in each clan is set down here; the tribe had a total of more than 145,000.

2. Of the tribe of Benjamin. Some account is given of this tribe, but a more detailed one comes in the next chapter. The militia of this tribe scarcely reached 60,000, but they are said to be fighting men ready to go out to war (vv. 7, 9, 11). It was to the honor of this tribe that it produced Saul, the first king, and even more to its honor that it remained faithful to the rightful kings of the house of David when the other tribes rebelled.

3. Of the tribe of Naphtali (v. 13). Only the first fathers of that tribe are named, the very same that we find in Ge 46:24, except that the one called *Shillem* there is called *Shallum* here. None of their descendants are named, perhaps because their genealogies were lost.

4. Of the tribe of Manasseh, that part of it which was placed on the west side of the Jordan, for we had some account of the other part before (5:23–26). One of them married an Aramean, that is, a Syrian (v. 14). This was during their slavery in Egypt—it was already then that they began to mix with other nations. The father married an Aramean; Makir, the son of that marriage, married a daughter of Benjamin (v. 15).

Verses 20–40

We have an account here:

1. Of the tribe of Ephraim. We read that that tribe did great things when it reached maturity. Here we have the disasters that befell it in its early stages, while it was in Egypt.

1.1. The men of Gath, Philistines, giants, killed many of the sons of that family of Ephraim, *because they came down to take away their cattle* (v. 21). It is uncertain who the aggressors were. Some consider the men of Gath to have been the aggressors, supposing that they came down to the land of Goshen to drive away the Ephraimites' cattle, and then killed the owners because they stood up to them. Others think that the Ephraimites attacked the men of Gath to plunder them. I tend toward thinking that the men of Gath attacked the Ephraimites, because the Israelites in Egypt were shepherds, not soldiers. They had many cattle of their own, and so were not likely to risk their lives for their neighbors' cattle: and the words of v. 21 may read, "The men of Gath killed them, for they came down to take away their cattle."

1.2. *Ephraim mourned many days* (v. 22). Nothing takes the elderly to the grave with greater sorrow than to see the young who have descended from them going to the grave first, especially if they are strong and healthy. It was a friendly task that his relatives undertook when *they came to comfort him* (v. 22).

1.3. The repair of this damage, to some extent, by the addition of another son to his family in his old age (v. 23), like Seth, *another seed instead of that of Abel whom Cain slew* (killed) (Ge 4:25). When God gives comfort to his mourners, *makes glad according to the days wherein he afflicted* (Ps 90:15), showing his mercy and setting it opposite the crosses he requires us to bear, we should take notice of the kindness and tenderness of divine Providence. It is as if *it repented God concerning his servants* (Ps 90:13). But Ephraim's joy in having another son born into his family could not make him forget his grief, for he gave a sad name to this son, *Beriah*, "in trouble," for he was born when the family was in mourning, when *it went evil with his house*, when there had been misfortune in his family (v. 23). It is added as a further honor to the house of Ephraim that a son of that tribe was employed in the conquest of Canaan, *Jehoshua* (Joshua) *the son of Nun* (v. 27).

2. Of the tribe of Asher. Some significant men of that tribe are named here. Their militia was not as numerous as that of some other tribes, only 26,000 men in all, but its leaders were outstanding, and its warriors fine and brave (v. 40). Perhaps they were wise in wanting not to make their trained bands numerous but to have a few who were useful and ready for battle.

CHAPTER 8

We had some account given us of Benjamin in the previous chapter. Here we have a longer listing of the great people of that tribe, because from that tribe came Saul, the first king of Israel (10:1), and also because that tribe stayed with Judah, inhabited much of Jerusalem, and was one of the two tribes that went into exile and came back (9:1). We have here: 1. Some of the leaders of that tribe named (vv. 1–32). 2. A more detailed account of the family of Saul (vv. 33–40).

Verses 1–32

There is little or nothing of history in all these verses.

1. We presume that the writer, Ezra, took the genealogies we have here as he found them, in the form in which they were handed in by the different tribes. Here, as before, some genealogies are in ascending order, others in descending order. Some have numbers attached, others places. Some have historical remarks intermingled, others do not. Some are shorter, others longer. Some agree with other records, others differ. Probably, some were torn, erased, and blotted, while others were more legible. Those of Dan and Reuben have been lost completely. Many things in these genealogies which seem to us complex, brief, and confusing were clear and easily understood by them then, because they knew how to make up any deficiencies.

2. There were now many great and powerful nations on earth, and many eminent people in them, whose names are buried and forgotten forever, while the names of many of the Israel of God are carefully preserved here and remembered eternally. They are *Jasher, Jeshurun*, "just ones," and "the memory of the just is blessed."

3. This tribe of Benjamin was once brought to a very low ebb, during the time of the judges, on the occasion of the sin of Gibeah, when only 600 men escaped the sword of justice (Jdg 19–20), but in these genealogies it is considered to be as significant as almost any of the tribes.

4. Here is mention of one Ehud (v. 6), of one Gera (v. 5), and (v. 8) of one who descended from him, who *begat* (was the father of) *children in the country of Moab*, which leads us to think the Ehud named here was the second judge of Israel, for he too is said to *be the son of Gera* and *a Benjamite* (Jdg 3:15), and he rescued Israel from the oppression of the Moabites by killing the king of Moab.

5. Here are mentioned some of the Benjamites that *drove away the inhabitants of Gath* (v. 13)—perhaps those who had killed the Ephraimites (7:21). One of those who carried out this act of justice was named *Beriah*, that name which reminded them of the wrong done to them (7:23).

6. Particular notice is taken of those who had *dwelt in Jerusalem* (v. 28 and again v. 32), so that those whose ancestors had lived there might be motivated to settle there when they returned from the Exile. And so we find (Ne 11:2) that *the people blessed those that willingly offered themselves to dwell at Jerusalem*.

Verses 33–40

Among all the genealogies of the tribes there is no mention of any of the kings of Israel after their defection from the house of David, much less of their families. Not a word is written about Jeroboam's family or Baasha's, Omri's or Jehu's, for they were all idolaters. But we have a detailed account of the family of Saul, which was the royal family before David was promoted:

1. Before Saul, only Kish and Ner are named, his father and grandfather (v. 33). 1Sa 9:1 says Kish was the son of Abiel, but he was in fact the son of Ner and the grandson of Abiel, as appears in 1Sa 14:51. In many languages, including Hebrew, it is common to use *son* for grandsons and other descendants.

2. After Saul, several of his sons are named, but none of their descendants, except those of Jonathan, for the sake of his sincere kindness to David. This genealogy ends with Ulam, whose family became famous in the tribe of Benjamin for the number of its brave warriors. There were at one time 150 archers who were all that one man's descendants.

CHAPTER 9

This chapter suggests to us that one purpose in recording all these genealogies was to direct the Jews, now that they had returned from the Exile, as to which families they should live with and where they should live, for here we have an account of those who first took possession of Jerusalem after their return from Babylon and began to rebuild it on the old foundations. 1. The Israelites (vv. 2–9). 2. The priests (vv. 10–13). 3. The Levites and other temple servants (vv. 14–26; v. 2: Levites and Nethinims). 4. The particular responsibilities given to some of the priests and Levites (vv. 27–34). 5. A repetition of the genealogy of King Saul (vv. 35–44).

Verses 1–13

The first verse tells us about *the books of the kings of Israel and Judah* (v. 1). Mentioning Israel and Judah, the writer takes note of their being *carried away to Babylon for their transgression*, because of their unfaithfulness (v. 1). Then comes an account of those who were the first to return from exile and begin living in their towns again, especially in Jerusalem.

1. The Israelites. That general name is used (v. 2) because along with those of Judah and Benjamin there were many from Ephraim and Manasseh and the rest of the ten tribes (v. 3). Some had escaped to Judah when the main group of the ten tribes had been taken into exile; others had returned to Judah following the changes in Assyria. These would all have gone into exile with Judah and Benjamin. It was foretold that the *children of Judah and of Israel* would be *gathered together and come up out of the land* (Hos 1:11), and that they would again be one nation (Eze 37:22). Pieces of metal which have been separate will come together again when melted in the same crucible. Many both from Judah and from Israel stayed behind in exile.

2. The priests (v. 10). They were to be commended for coming with the first group.

2.1. It is said of one of them that he was *the ruler of the house of God* (v. 11), not the chief ruler, for Joshua was then the high priest, but his deputy.

2.2. It is said of many of them that they were *very able men for the service of the house of God* (v. 13). In the house of God there is always a ministry to be done, and it is good for the church when those who are employed in that ministry are qualified to do it, *able ministers of the new testament* (2Co 3:6). The duties of the temple required great courage and mental strength as well as physical strength, and so the priests are praised as *mighty men of valour*.

Verses 14–34

We have here a further account of the good state of affairs effected in religious faith immediately after the return of the people from Babylon. The recent lack of worship made them very eager to set up the worship of God among them, and so they began their worship of God in the right way.

1. Before the house of the Lord was built, they had the tabernacle, a plain and movable tent. Those who cannot yet reach as far as a temple must not be without a tabernacle. They should be thankful for that and make the best of it. We should never let God's work be left undone just because of a lack of a place to do it in.

2. In allotting to the priests and Levites their respective employments, the people had the model that had been drawn up by David and Samuel the seer (v. 22). Samuel, in his time, had drawn up the outline of this model and laid the foundations for it, even though the ark was then in obscurity, and David later finished it. Both acted under the immediate direction of God.

3. Most of them lived at Jerusalem (v. 34), but some lived in villages (vv. 16, 22), perhaps because there was not yet room for them in Jerusalem. They were employed in the service of the tabernacle (v. 25).

4. Many of the Levites were employed as *porters*, gatekeepers of the house of God, four chief gatekeepers (v. 26) and others under them, a total of 212 (v. 22). They were in charge of the gates (v. 23), were keepers of the "thresholds," as the margin of v. 19 reads, and keepers of the entrance to the dwelling place of the Lord. This seemed a lowly office, but David would rather have it than *dwell in the tents of wickedness* (Ps 84:10). Their role was:

- To open the doors of God's house every morning (v. 27) and shut them at night.
- To keep away the unclean and prevent entry by those who were forbidden by law.
- To direct and introduce into the courts of the Lord those who came there to worship. Ministers have a work of this kind to do.

5. Here is one Phinehas, a son of Eleazar, who is said to have been *a ruler over them in time past* (v. 20), not the famous high priest of that name but a famous Levite, of whom it is said here that *the Lord was with him* (v. 20), or, as the Aramaic reads, "the Word of the Lord was his helper."

6. It is said of some of them that *they lodged* (were stationed) *round about the house of God* (v. 27). The Levites were positioned around the tabernacle when they marched through the desert. They were *porters* then in one sense, bearing the burdens of the sanctuary; they were *porters* now in a different sense, serving the gates and the doors. In both cases, they kept charge of the sanctuary.

7. Everyone knew their responsibility. Some were entrusted with the articles used in the temple services, to count them in and out (v. 28). Others were appointed to prepare the fine flour, wine, and oil (v. 29). Others, who were priests, had the task of mixing the spices (v. 30). Others took care of the grain offerings (v. 31). Others looked after the shewbread (v. 32). God is the God of order, but what everyone thinks someone else will do ends up being done by no one.

8. The singers *were employed in that work day and night* (v. 33). They were the *chief fathers of the Levites* (the heads of Levite families [v. 34]) who made it a life's work, not ordinary musicians for whom it was only a trade. They remained in the temple rooms so that they might closely and constantly serve there, and so they were excused from all other services. It seems some groups sang continually, at least at stated hours, both day and night. God was continually praised in this way.

Verses 35–44

These verses are the same as 8:29–38, giving an account of the ancestors of Saul and the descendants of Jonathan. *There* it is the conclusion of the genealogy of Benjamin; *here* it is an introduction to the story of Saul.

CHAPTER 10

In this chapter we have: 1. The fatal defeat of Saul's army by the Philistines, and the fatal stroke which Saul gave himself (vv. 1–7). 2. The Philistines' triumph (vv. 8–10). 3. The respect which the people of Jabesh Gilead showed the royal corpse (vv. 11–12). 4. The reason for Saul's rejection (vv. 13–14).

Verses 1–7

This account of Saul's death is the same as the one in 1Sa 31:1-13. But let us notice:

1. Rulers sin and the people suffer for it.

2. Parents sin and the children suffer for it. When the limit of Saul's sins had been reached (compare Ge 15:16), and his day came to fall, which David foresaw (1Sa 26:10), he went into battle, and not only he himself died, but also all his sons with him, except Ish-Bosheth. That included Jonathan, that gracious and generous man, for *all things come alike to all* (Ecc 9:2).

Verses 8–14

Here:

1. From the triumph of the Philistines over Saul we may learn:

1.1. That the greater the honor that people are advanced to, the greater shame they are in danger of falling into.

1.2. That if we do not give God the glory for our successes, even the Philistines will rise up in judgment against us and condemn us, for when they had gained their victory over Saul, they *sent tidings to their idols*, sent messengers to declare the news among their idols (v. 9). Pathetic idols: they did not know what took place just a few miles away until the news was given them, and when they were told it, they were still none the wiser! The Philistines also put Saul's armor *in the house of their gods* (v. 10).

2. From the triumph of the people of Jabesh Gilead in rescuing the bodies of Saul and his sons, we may learn that respect is due to the remains of the deceased. We must treat the dead body with respect, remembering that it once had an immortal soul and will one day be joined to it again.

3. From the triumphs of divine justice in the destruction of Saul, we may learn:

- That the sin of sinners will certainly find them out.
- That no one's greatness can exempt them from the judgments of God.

CHAPTER 11

In this chapter there is repeated the account of: 1. The advancement of David to the throne by common approval, immediately after the death of Saul (vv. 1–3). 2. His gaining of the fortress of Zion from the hands of the Jebusites (vv. 4–9). 3. The catalog of the mighty warriors of his kingdom (vv. 10–47).

Verses 1–9

David is here brought to possess:

1. The throne of Israel, after he had reigned only over Judah for seven years in Hebron. The people anointed him their king because of his relationship with them (v. 1), his former good services, and especially God's appointment (v. 2). He made a covenant with them to protect them, and they agreed to be faithful and loyal to him (v. 3).

2. The stronghold of Zion, which was held by the Jebusites until David's time. We are not sure whether David had this in view as a place fit to make a royal city, or whether he received the promise of it from God, but it seems one of his first exploits was to make himself master of that fort, and when he gained possession of it, he called it the *city of David* (v. 7). Reference is made to this in Ps 2:6: *I have set my king upon my holy hill of Zion.*

Verses 10–47

We have here an account of David's worthy warriors, the great men who served him and were promoted by him. We read the first edition of this catalog in 2Sa 23:8–39. This is much the same, except that those named here from vv. 41–47 to the end are added. Notice:

1. The connection of this catalog with what is said about David (v. 9). *The Lord of hosts was with him, and these were the mighty men which he had* (vv. 9-10). God was with him and worked for him, but he used people, means, and situations.

2. The heading of this list (v. 10): *These are the men who strengthened themselves with him.* In strengthening him, they strengthened themselves and their own interests, for his advancement was theirs.

3. What made all these warriors honorable was the good service they did for their king and country. They helped make David king (v. 10), which was a good work. They killed the Philistines and other enemies of Israel and were instrumental in saving Israel. The honors of Christ's kingdom are prepared for those who *fight the good fight of faith* (1Ti 6:12), who work hard and suffer, who are willing to risk all, even life itself, for Christ and a good conscience.

4. Among all the great exploits of David's mighty warriors, there is nothing great mentioned about David himself except his *pouring out before the Lord* the *water* which he had *longed for* (vv. 18–19). David showed four honorable attitudes in that action:

4.1. Repentance for his own weakness.

4.2. Denial of his own appetite. He longed for the water of the well of Bethlehem, but when he had it, he would not drink it, because he would not satisfy himself in this way to please a foolish fancy.

4.3. Devotion toward God. That water which he thought too good and too precious for him to drink himself, he *poured out to the Lord* (v. 18) as *a drink offering.*

4.4. Tenderness toward his servants. It confounded him very much to think that three brave men would risk their lives to get water for him.

5. The power of God must be acknowledged in the wonderful achievements of these heroes.

6. One of these worthies is said to be *an Ammonite* (v. 39), another *a Moabite* (v. 46), although the Law stated that an *Ammonite* and *a Moabite should not enter into the congregation of the Lord* (Dt 23:3). These warriors had probably shown such sincere support for the interests of Israel that in their case it was thought fit to dispense with that law. This decision also showed that the Son of David would take some of his worthy people from among the Gentiles.

CHAPTER 12

It was not immediately, but gradually, that David came to the throne. His kingdom was to last, and so, like fruits that keep the longest, it matured slowly. We are told here: 1. What help he received at Ziklag to make him king of Judah (vv. 1–22). 2. What help he received at Hebron to make him king over all Israel more than seven years later (vv. 23–40).

Verses 1–22

We have here an account of those who appeared and acted as David's friends on the death of Saul, to bring about the change of government. While he was being persecuted, all the forces he had came to only 600 warriors, but when the time came for him to begin to take the offensive, Providence brought more to help him. Even *while he kept himself close* (while he was banished)*, because of Saul* (v. 1), even while he did not show himself in order to invite or encourage his friends and well-wishers to join him — not foreseeing that the death of Saul was so close — even then, God was inclining and preparing others to come over to him. Those who trust God to do his work for them in his own way and his own time will find that his providence surpasses all their own forecasts and careful management.

1. Some of Saul's relatives from the tribe of Benjamin came over to David (v. 2). These Benjamites are described as being very skillful, trained in shooting arrows and slinging stones, and able to use both hands — clever, active people. See also Jdg 20:16.

2. Some of the tribe of Gad, although they were settled on the other side of the Jordan, were so convinced of David's entitlement and qualifications that they defected to David, even though he was *in the hold* (stronghold) *in the wilderness* (v. 8). Only a few, eleven in all, are named here, but they added great support to David's strength. Up to that time those who had come had been mostly those with broken fortunes, those who were distressed or discontented, and mercenaries, who came to him for protection rather than to give him any service (1Sa 22:2). But these Gadites were brave warriors, *men of war, and fit for the battle* (v. 8). They were disciplined in their own tribe (v. 14). We are not told what enemies they met in the valleys when they had crossed over the Jordan, but they chased them with their lionlike faces and pursued them with intense fierceness *towards the east and towards the west* (v. 15).

3. Some of Judah and Benjamin came to him (v. 16). Their leader was Amasai, although whether he was the same man as the Amasa who was later on Absalom's side (2Sa 17:25) is not stated.

3.1. David's wise negotiation with them (v. 17). He was surprised to see them, because he had so often been in danger from the treachery of the people of Ziph and the people of Keilah, even though they were all people of Judah. It is hardly surprising that he was cautious when he met these people of Judah. Notice:

3.1.1. How fairly he deals with them.

3.1.1.1. If they are faithful and honorable, he will reward them. But:

3.1.1.2. If they are false and have come to betray him into the hands of Saul, claiming friendship, he leaves them to God, for him to take vengeance on. Never was anyone more violently attacked than David—except the Son of David—but he still had the testimony of his conscience that he had done nothing wrong.

3.1.2. Notice in this appeal:

3.1.2.1. He calls God the *God of our fathers* (v. 17), both his fathers and theirs. In this way, he was reminding them not to deal wrongly with him, for they both descended from the same patriarchs, and both depended on the same God.

3.1.2.2. He does not invoke any terrible judgment on them.

3.2. Their sincere commitment to David (v. 18). Their spokesman was Amasai, on whom the *Spirit of the Lord came*. Nothing could have been said more finely, in a livelier way, or more relevantly for this occasion. *Thine are we, David, and on thy side, thou son of Jesse* (v. 18). In calling him *son of Jesse* (v. 18), they reminded themselves that he was descended by line from Nahshon and Salmon, who in their days were leaders of the tribe of Judah. Saul called him that in disdain (1Sa 20:27; 22:7), but they looked on it as his honor. "*Peace, peace, be unto thee* (v. 18), all the good your heart wants, and *peace be to thy helpers* (v. 18), among whom we desire to be placed, so that peace may be on us." He assured him of help from heaven: *For thy God helpeth thee* (v. 18). From these expressions of Amasai we may learn how to show our affection for and allegiance to the Lord Jesus.

3.3. David's cheerful acceptance of them onto his side and into his friendship. *David received them* (v. 18) and made them leaders of his raiding bands (v. 18).

4. Some of the men of Manasseh likewise joined him (v. 19). Providence gave them a fair opportunity to do so when he and his men marched through their country on this occasion. We have the story in 1Sa 29:1–11. When he returned, some great men of Manasseh fell in with David to help him *against the band of Amalekites* (1Ch 12:19–21) who had plundered Ziklag.

Verses 23–40

Here is an account of those who were active in establishing David on the throne after the death of Ish-Bosheth, those whom every tribe brought *ready armed to the war*, in case there was any opposition (v. 23):

1. Those tribes that lived nearest brought the fewest: Judah only 6,800 (v. 24), Simeon only 7,100 (v. 25), whereas Zebulun, which lay far away, brought 50,000, Asher 40,000, and the two and a half tribes east of the Jordan 120,000. It was not as if the closest tribes were uncommitted to the cause; they showed wisdom in bringing few, since all the others were within call.

2. The Levites themselves, and the priests—here called the family of Aaron—appeared sincere in this cause, and were ready, if need be, to fight for David as well as pray for him, because they knew he was called by God to rule (vv. 26–28).

3. Even some of Saul's relatives came over to David (v. 29).

4. It is said of most of these that they were *mighty men of valour* (vv. 25, 28, 30), of others that they were *expert in war* (vv. 35–36), and of them all that they *could keep rank*, could serve in the ranks (v. 38).

5. Some were so considerate as to bring arms with them.

6. The warriors from Issachar were the fewest in all, only 200, but were still as useful to David's interests as those who came in the greatest numbers, since these few were in effect the whole tribe—for *they had understanding of the times* (v. 32). It may be that they understood *the times* of nature, that they were skilled at forecasting the weather, for example. Or perhaps they *knew the times* politically (Est 1:13), understood public affairs, the mood and attitudes of the nation, and the trends of present events. They were also men of great influence, who had *all their brethren at their commandment*. And so we find them referred to as *the princes of Issachar* (Jdg 5:15). They knew how to rule, and the rest knew how to obey.

7. It is said of them all that they engaged in this undertaking *with a perfect heart*, with one mind (v. 38).

8. The men of Judah, and others of the adjacent tribes, prepared to supply food to the respective camps of the more distant tribes when they came to Hebron (vv. 39–40).

CHAPTER 13

In this chapter the religious faith of the people is attended to. 1. David confers with the representatives of the people about bringing the ark up out of obscurity into a public place (vv. 1–4). 2. With a great deal of sacredness and joy, it is carried from Kiriath Jearim (vv. 5–8). 3. Uzzah is struck dead for touching it (vv. 9–14).

Verses 1–8

Here is:

1. David's godly suggestion to bring the ark of God to Jerusalem, so that the royal city might be the Holy City (vv. 1–3).

1.1. As soon as David was established on the throne, he had thoughts about the ark of God: *Let us bring the ark to us* (v. 3). He aimed:

1.1.1. To honor God by showing respect for his ark, the sign of his presence.

1.1.2. To have the comfort and benefit of that sacred oracle. "Let us bring it to us, not only so that we may be a credit to it but also so that it may be a blessing to us." It is wise of those who are setting out in the world to take God's ark with them, to make his oracles their counselors and his laws their rule.

1.2. He conferred with the leaders of the people about it (v. 1). He did this:

1.2.1. So that he might show respect and honor to the officers and leaders of the kingdom. No ruler who is wise will want to be autocratic.

1.2.2. So that he might be advised by them as to how to go about doing it.

1.3. He wanted all the people to be summoned to attend on this occasion, both to honor the ark and also to satisfy and build up the people (v. 2). Notice:

1.3.1. He calls the ordinary people *brethren*, which speaks of his humility and condescension.

1.3.2. He speaks of the people as a remnant who had escaped: *Our brethren that are left in all the land of Israel* (v. 2). Under Providence they had been scattered.

1.3.3. He takes care that the priests and Levites especially should be summoned to attend the ark.

1.4. All this assumes that it is *of the Lord their God* (v. 2). Whatever we undertake, we must ask, "Is it of the Lord? Can we gain his approval for us to do it?"

1.5. They needed to put right what had gone wrong in the last reign: "For *we inquired not at it in the days of Saul* (v. 3)." David makes no irritated reflections on Saul but, speaking generally, says, *We inquired not at it* (v. 3), making himself guilty of this neglect along with others.

2. The people's ready agreement to this proposal (v. 4): *The thing was right in the eyes of all the people.*

3. The sacredness of bringing up the ark (vv. 5–8), which we read of before in 2Sa 6:1–3.

Verses 9–14

We read earlier of the Lord's wrath breaking out on Uzzah, which meant that all their joy came to an end (2Sa 6:6–8). Let the sin of Uzzah warn us all to beware of presumption, rashness, and irreverence in dealing with holy things (v. 9), and not to think that a good intention will justify a bad action.

CHAPTER 14

In this chapter we have: 1. David's kingdom established (vv. 1–2). 2. His family built up (vv. 3–7). 3. His enemies, the Philistines, defeated in two campaigns (vv. 8–17). This is repeated here from 2Sa 5:11–25.

Verses 1–7

We may notice here:

1. No one is sufficient within themselves; everyone needs their neighbors and should be thankful for their help. David had a very large kingdom, King Hiram of Tyre a very small one, but David could not build himself a house in the way he had in mind unless Hiram provided him with both workers and materials (v. 1).

2. It is very satisfying to a wise person to be settled, and to a good person to see the special providence of God in their establishment. The people had made David king, but he could not be at ease until he knew that *the Lord had confirmed him king over Israel* (v. 2).

3. We must look on all our advancements as intended to make us useful. We are blessed so that we may be a blessing to others. See Ge 12:2.

Verses 8–17

This narrative of David's triumph over the Philistines is much the same as we had in 2Sa 5:17–25. Let the attack which the Philistines made on David forbid us from feeling secure in any settlement or advancement. When we are most at ease, something or other may come to terrorize or trouble us. Christ's kingdom is defied by the Serpent's descendants, especially when it makes any advances. Let David's thankful acknowledgment of the hand of God in his successes direct us to bring all our sacrifices of praise to God's altar. *Not unto us, O Lord! not unto us, but to thy name give glory* (Ps 115:1).

CHAPTER 15

It was good to bring the ark into the City of David. This task had been attempted but not completed—the ark lay in the house of Obed-Edom—and this chapter gives us an account its completion: 1. How it was done more properly than before: a place was prepared for the ark (v. 1); the priests were ordered to carry it (vv. 2–15); the Levites had their work assigned to them in accompanying it (vv. 16–24). 2. How it was done more successfully than before (v. 25): the Levites made no mistake in their work (v. 26); David and the people met with nothing to dampen their joy (vv. 27–28).

Verses 1–24

Preparations are made for the ark to be brought home to the City of David from the house of Obed-Edom.

1. David prepared a place for the ark to be received before he brought it to him. He had no time to *build a house*, but he *pitched a tent* for it (v. 1)—probably according to the pattern shown to Moses on the mountain, or as close to that pattern as possible—of curtains and frames. Wherever we build for ourselves, we must also make sure we give space to God's ark, to a church in our house.

2. David ordered the Levites or priests to carry the ark on their shoulders. The Kohathites carried it on the people's ordinary journeys, and so had no carts allocated to them, because their work was to *bear upon their shoulders* (Nu 7:9). But on extraordinary occasions, such as when they crossed the Jordan and surrounded Jericho, the priests carried it. This rule was clear, but David himself had forgotten it and had placed the ark on a cart. David was now careful not only to summon the Levites to the ceremony, as he did all Israel (v. 3) and as he had done before (13:2), but also to see to it that they assembled (v. 4), especially the sons of Aaron (v. 11). He gave them the sacred responsibility (v. 12): "*You are the chief of the fathers of the Levites,* you are the heads of the Levitical families, and so *you* are to *bring up the ark of the Lord.*"

3. The Levites and priests consecrated themselves (v. 14) and were ready to carry the ark on their shoulders, according to the Law (v. 15).

4. Leaders were appointed to make the ark welcome with every possible joy (v. 16). Heman, Asaph, and Ethan were now appointed (v. 17). They undertook to sound the bronze cymbals (v. 19), others were to play the lyres (v. 20), others harps, on the *Sheminith,* or "eighth," eight notes higher or lower than the rest, according to the rules of playing music together (v. 21). Some who were priests blew trumpets (v. 24), as was usual when the ark was moved (Nu 10:8) and at feasts (Ps 81:3). And one was put in charge of the singing (v. 22), for *he was skillful*—he could both sing well himself and teach others.

Verses 25–29

All things had now been prepared for carrying the ark to the City of David and for its reception there, and here we have an account of its sacred transfer to that city from the house of Obed-Edom.

1. *God helped the Levites* who carried it. If God did not help us, we could not move a step. Because the Levites remembered the outbreak of the Lord's anger against Uzzah, they were probably ready to tremble when they took up the ark, but God *helped* them, silenced their fears and strengthened their faith. God's ministers, who carry the vessels of the Lord (Isa 52:11), especially need divine help in their service, so that God may be glorified in them and his church built up.

2. When the Levites experienced the signs of God's presence with them, they offered sacrifices of praise to him (v. 26).

3. There were great expressions of joy: the sacred music was played, David danced, the singers sang, and the people shouted (vv. 27–28). We had this before (2Sa 6:14–15).

CHAPTER 16

This chapter concludes the establishment of public worship of God in David's reign. Here is: 1. The ceremony with which the ark was established (vv. 1–6). 2. The psalm David sang on this occasion (vv. 7–36). 3. The establishment of public worship of God from that time onward (vv. 37–43).

Verses 1–6

It was a glorious day when the ark of God was safely put in the tent David had pitched for it.

1. The ark had been placed in obscurity in a country town, *in the fields of the wood* (Ps 132:6), and it had now been moved to a public place, to the royal city. It had been neglected as something despised and broken; now it was marked by respect, and it was used in inquiring of God. This was only a tent, a humble and lowly dwelling place, but it was also the tabernacle, the temple, which David often speaks about in his psalms with so much affection. David, who pitched a tent for the ark and continued to be loyal to it, did far better than Solomon, who built a temple for it but turned his back on it in his later years. The church's poorest times were its purest.

2. Now David was at peace within himself: the ark was established, and it was established near him. He takes care:

2.1. That God will receive glory for it:

2.1.1. By sacrifices (v. 1): burnt offerings in adoration of his perfect nature and peace offerings (fellowship offerings) to acknowledge his favors.

2.1.2. By songs. He appointed Levites to record this story in song for the benefit of others.

2.2. That the people will enjoy it. They will get along better because of this day's ceremony, because he gives them all not only a royal treat but also *a blessing in the name of the Lord*, as a father and as a prophet (v. 2).

Verses 7–36

We have here the psalm of thanksgiving which David wrote by the Spirit, and which he passed on to the director of music, to be sung on the occasion of the public entrance of the ark into the tent prepared for it. It is collected from several psalms: vv. 8–23 are taken from Ps 105:1–15; vv. 23–34 are the whole of Ps 96, with a few changes; v. 34 is taken from Ps 136:1 and several others; and vv. 35–36 are taken from the close of Ps 106, vv. 47–48. Some think this collection by David warrants us to do likewise, to make up hymns from David's psalms, part from one and part from another, put together so as to express and stir the devotion of Christians. In the midst of our praises we must not forget to pray for the help and relief of those saints and servants of God who are in distress (v. 35): *Save us, gather us, deliver us from the heathen*, the nations, those who are scattered and oppressed. When we are expressing our joy at God's favors to us, we must also remember our afflicted brothers and sisters and pray for their salvation and rescue as we pray for our own. We are members of one another (Ro 12:5), and so when we say, "Lord, save *them*," it is not wrong to add, "Lord, also save *us*." Let us make God the Alpha and Omega of our praises (Rev 1:8). David begins (v. 8) with *Give thanks to the Lord*; he concludes (v. 36), *Blessed be the Lord*. And whereas in the passage from which this doxology is taken (Ps 106:48) it is added, *Let all the people say, Amen, Praise ye the Lord*, here we find they acted according to that instruction: *All the people said, Amen, and praised the Lord* (v. 36).

Verses 37–43

The worship of God is to be not only the work of an occasional feast day, brought in to grace a triumph, but also the work of every day. David therefore establishes it here as something constant.

1. At Jerusalem, where the ark was, Asaph and his associates were appointed to *minister before the ark continually* with songs of praise, *as every day's work required*

(v. 37). No sacrifices were offered there, and no incense was burned, because the altars were not there, but David's prayers were *directed as incense, and the lifting up of his hands as the evening sacrifice* (Ps 141:2). Here we see how early on spiritual worship took the place of ceremonial worship.

2. At Gibeon there were altars where the priests served, because the ceremonial worship had been divinely instituted and must by no means be excluded. Their work was to offer sacrifices and burn incense, which they did *continually, morning and evening, according to the law of Moses* (vv. 39–40). These must be maintained, because however inferior they were in their own nature to the moral services of prayer and praise, they were still types of the mediation of Christ. They were greatly honored, and their observance was significant. At Gibeon, where the altars were, David also appointed *singers to give thanks to the Lord*, and the chorus of all their songs must be *For his mercy endureth for ever* (v. 41).

- The people were satisfied and went home pleased.
- David returned to bless his house. He decided to keep up his family worship, which public worship must not replace.

CHAPTER 17

This chapter is the same as 2Sa 7:1–29. It would be worthwhile to look back at the commentary on that earlier chapter. We have in general two things here: 1. God's gracious acceptance of David's purpose to build him a house, and the promise he then made (vv. 1–15). 2. David's gracious acceptance of God's good promise to build him a house, and the prayer he then made (vv. 16–27).

Verses 1–15

Let us notice here:

1. David felt awkward living in a palace of cedar while the ark stayed under a tent (v. 1). Those who think about where they can invest the fruit of their labors would do well to ask what condition the ark is in, and consider whether their resources could be put to better use by supporting it.

2. How ready God's prophets should be to encourage every good purpose (v. 2).

3. How little God is moved by outward show and splendor in his service. His ark was content in a tabernacle (v. 5). He commanded the judges to *feed his people*, but never told them to *build him a house* (v. 6).

4. How graciously God accepts his people's good purposes, even though he himself prevents them from being carried out. David must not build this house (v. 4). He must prepare for it but not actually do it, just as Moses had to lead Israel within sight of Canaan but then leave it to Joshua to give them possession of it. Yet although David was not allowed to build the temple:

4.1. He must not think that his advancement had been futile. No; "It was indeed for a position of honor that *I took thee from the sheepcote*, the pasture, yet it was not for the honor of being the builder of the temple but for that of being *ruler over my people Israel*."

4.2. He must not think that his good purpose was futile and that he would lose his reward. He would be rewarded as fully as if he had done it; *"The Lord will build thee a house* and attach the crown of Israel to it" (v. 10). If there is a willing mind, it will be not only accepted but also rewarded.

4.3. He must not think that this good work would never be done, and that it was futile even to think about it. No; *I will raise up thy seed, and he will build me a house* (vv. 11–12).

4.4. He must not confine his thoughts to the physical success of his family, but must also have thoughts about the kingdom of the Messiah, who would descend from his body, and whose throne would be *established for evermore* (v. 14).

Verses 16–27

Here is David's reverent prayer to God in answer to the gracious message he has just received from him. By faith he has received the promises, and now he welcomes them and is persuaded by them, as the patriarchs were (Heb 11:13). What an example of humble, believing, and fervent prayer this is for us! Notice only those few expressions in which the prayer in this account differs from that earlier record of it.

1. What is expressed by way of question in 2 Samuel (*Is this the manner of men, O Lord God?* 2Sa 7:19) is an acknowledgment here: "*Thou hast regarded me according to the estate of a man of high degree*, you have looked on me as though I were the most exalted of men" (v. 17). In view of the covenant relationship that God has with believers, he places a very high regard on them, even though they are lowly and evil.

2. After the words *What can David say more unto thee*, there is added *for the honour of thy servant?* (v. 18). This shows us the honor God puts on his servants by taking them into covenant and fellowship with himself. These privileges are so great that his servants need not and cannot want to be honored more highly.

3. It is significant that what in Samuel is said to be *for thy word's sake* (2Sa 7:21) is here said to be *for thy servant's sake* (v. 19). Jesus Christ is both *the Word of God* (Rev 19:13) and *the servant of God* (Isa 42:1), and it is for his sake, because of his mediation, that the promises are both made and fulfilled to all believers.

4. In Samuel, the Lord Almighty is said to be the *God over Israel* (2Sa 7:26); here he is said to be *the God of Israel, even a God to Israel* (v. 24). There were those who were called *gods* of such and such nations, gods of Assyria and Egypt, gods of Hamad and Arpad, but they were not gods to them, for they did them no good at all. They were mere nothings, simply names. But *the God of Israel is a God to Israel* (v. 24). All his attributes and qualities give them real benefits and advantages.

5. The closing words in Samuel are, *With thy blessing let the house of thy servant be blessed for ever* (2Sa 7:29). This is the language of holy desire. But the closing words here are the language of a most holy faith: *For thou blessest, O Lord! and it shall be blessed for ever* (v. 27). David's prayer concludes as God's promise did (v. 14), with what is *forever*. God's word looks at eternal things, and so should our desires and hopes.

CHAPTER 18

Those who seek first the kingdom of God and his righteousness, as David did, will have other things added to them (Mt 6:33). Here is: 1. His success abroad. He conquered the Philistines (v. 1), the Moabites (v. 2), the king of Zobah (vv. 3–4), and the Arameans (Syrians) (vv. 5–8). He made the king of Hamath his subject (vv. 9–11) and also the Edomites (vv. 12–13). 2. His success at home. His court and kingdom flourished (vv. 14–17). We have had an account of all this before (2Sa 8:1–14).

Verses 1–8

After this (v. 1), David did great exploits. After the sweet fellowship he had had with God by the word and prayer, he went on in his work with great strength and courage, *conquering and to conquer* (Rev 6:2). For several generations the Philistines had caused trouble for Israel, but now *David subdued them* (v. 1). Such is the uncertainty of this world that frequently people lose their wealth and power when they think they can establish it. Hadadezer was struck *as he went to establish his dominion* (control) (v. 3). The Arameans of Damascus were struck down when they came to help Hadadezer.

Verses 9–17

What God blesses us with we must honor him with. It was said before (v. 6), and it is repeated here (v. 13), that *the Lord preserved David whithersoever he went*. God gives power to people not so that they may look great with it but so that they may do good with it.

CHAPTER 19

Here is repeated the story of David's war with the Ammonites and the Arameans (Syrians), their allies, which we read before in 2Sa 10:1–19. Here is: 1. David's politeness to the king of Ammon, in sending a delegation expressing condolences to him on the occasion of his father's death (vv. 1–2); the Ammonite king's great rudeness to David in the evil way he treated his delegation (vv. 3–4). 2. David's concern for his servants (v. 5), his righteous anger at the Ammonite king's rudeness, and the war which ensued, in which the Ammonites acted prudently in bringing the Arameans to help them (vv. 6–7), Joab acted boldly (vv. 8–13), and Israel was again and again victorious (vv. 14–19).

Verses 1–5

It is excellent for good people to be neighborly, and especially to be grateful. David wants to pay his respects to Hanun because he is his neighbor, and religion teaches us to be polite and to be ready to act kindly toward those we live among, nor must any differences in religion obstruct this. But besides this, David also remembered the kindness which Hanun's father, Nahash, showed to him. Yet those who are corrupt and have evil intentions tend to be jealous and to suspect others wrongly, without proper reason; and so Hanun's servants suggested that David's delegation came as spies—as if such a great and powerful man as David needed to do something so contemptible. And so Hanun, against international law, treated David's delegation disgracefully.

Verses 6–19

We may see here:

1. The hearts of sinners are hardened to their destruction. The children of Ammon saw that *they had made themselves odious to David* (v. 6), and they would have been wise to seek conditions of peace, to humble themselves, and to offer any satisfaction for the wrong they had done him. But instead of this, they prepared for war, and so brought on themselves, by David's hand, those devastations which he never intended for them.

2. The courage of brave people is heightened and strengthened by difficulties. When Joab saw that the battle lines were set against him in front and behind (v. 10) instead of thinking he would withdraw, he redoubled his efforts, and not only spoke, but also acted, boldly and had

great presence of mind when he saw he was surrounded. He engaged the help of his brother Abishai so they could support each other (v. 12), encouraged himself and the rest of the officers to be forceful in their respective positions, and then left the outcome of events to God: *Let the Lord do that which is right in his sight* (Ex 15:26).

3. The Ammonites did as much as they could to make the best of their position: they brought as good a force as they could onto the battlefield; but because their cause was bad, they were defeated. Right will prevail and triumph at last.

4. Although the Arameans (*Syrians*) were not in any way concerned with the merits of the cause, but served only as mercenaries to the Ammonites, when the Ammonites were beaten, the Arameans were concerned to regain their honor and therefore called on the assistance of the Arameans on the other side of the Euphrates. But this was in vain, for they still *fled before Israel* (v. 18). When the Arameans found that Israel was the conqueror, they not only broke off their alliance with the Ammonites and decided they would not help them anymore (v. 19), *but also made peace with David and became his servants* (subject to him).

CHAPTER 20

Here is a repetition of the story of David's wars: 1. His war with the Ammonites and the capture of Rabbah (vv. 1–3). 2. His wars with the giants of the Philistines (vv. 4–8).

Verses 1–3

Here we have Rabbah, the capital of the Ammonite kingdom, destroyed (v. 1); its king's crown put on David's head (v. 2); and David's great harshness toward the people (v. 3). We had a fuller account of this in 2Sa 11:1–12:31. While Joab was besieging Rabbah, David fell into that great sin in the incident with Uriah.

Verses 4–8

The Philistines were nearly, but not completely, subdued earlier (18:1); some of their giants remained. But they too were finally defeated. In the conflicts between grace and corruption there are some sins which, like these giants, are not defeated without much difficulty and a long struggle. Notice:

1. We never read of giants among the Israelites, as we do of giants among the Philistines; there were giants of Gath but not giants of Jerusalem. The growth of God's plants is in usefulness, not in size.

2. Although David's servants were of ordinary height, they were too strong for the giants of Gath in every battle, because they had God on their side. We need not fear those who are great and against us when we have the great God on our side. What can a mere finger more on each hand do, or one more toe on each foot, to fight against almighty God?

CHAPTER 21

David's sin in counting the people is told here because in the atonement made for that sin, a suggestion was given of the plot of ground on which the temple would be built. Here is: 1. How David sinned by forcing Joab to count the people (vv. 1–6). 2. How David was sorry for what he had done as soon as he realized its sinfulness (vv. 7–8); the sad dilemma (or rather, trilemma) he

faced when he was given the option of choosing how he would be punished for this sin, what rod of discipline he would be beaten with (vv. 9–13); the terrible ravages made by the plague in the country, and the narrow escape which Jerusalem had from being devastated by it (vv. 14–17). 3. How David repented and offered sacrifices on this occasion, and how the plague was withdrawn (vv. 18–30). We read and meditated on this terrible story in 2Sa 24:1–25.

Verses 1–6

Taking a census of the people, one would think, was no bad thing. Why should the shepherd not know the number of the flock? But David acted out of pride in his heart. There is no sin that contains more denial of God's sovereignty, and so is more offensive to God, than pride. The sin was David's, and notice:

1. How active the tempter was in it (v. 1): *Satan stood up against Israel, and provoked David* to do it. It is said in 2Sa 24:1 that *the anger of the Lord was kindled against Israel, and he moved David* to do it. This earlier account must be explained by what is suggested here: that God allowed the Devil to do it for wise and holy purposes. When Satan intended to cause trouble for Israel, what course did he take? He did not *move God against them to destroy them*, incite God against them to ruin them (Job 2:3), but incited David, the best friend the people had, to take a census of them, and so David offended God and set him against them. This shows us that the Devil causes more trouble for us by tempting us to sin against our God than he does by accusing us before our God.

2. How passive the instrument was. Joab, the person whom David used, was an active man in public business, but to undertake this task, he had to be forced, and he did it with the greatest possible reluctance. There was no one more eager than he to do anything for the honor of the king or the welfare of the kingdom, but he wanted to be excused in this matter. It was unnecessary. There was no need at all for it. It was also dangerous. In doing it, he might be the cause of sin in Israel, and might provoke God against them. There was a general displeasure at these orders, which confirmed Joab in his dislike of them. He left out two tribes in the numbering (vv. 5–6), two considerable ones, Levi and Benjamin, and perhaps was not very exact in counting the others, because he did not do it with any delight, which might perhaps be one reason for the difference between the totals here and those in 2Sa 24:9.

Verses 7–17

David is here under the rod of discipline for counting the people, that rod of correction which drives out the foolishness of pride bound up in the heart (Pr 22:15). Let us notice:

1. How he was corrected. God takes notice of, and is displeased with, the sins of his people; and no sin is more displeasing to him than pride in the human heart. David must have the people counted: *Bring me the number of them*, he says, *that I may know it* (v. 2). But now God counts them differently, and so David has another number of the people brought to him, a number that causes him more bewilderment than his census gave him satisfaction, namely, a black list of deaths. He sees the destroying angel with his sword drawn against Jerusalem (v. 16). Plagues make the greatest devastations in the most populous places.

2. How he responded to the correction: he acknowledged that he had sinned, that he had acted foolishly, and

he begged that, however he might be corrected, its guilt might be taken away. "I submit to the discipline, but let only me suffer because of it, for I am the one who has sinned."

2.1. He threw himself on the mercy of God, even though he knew God was angry with him, and he did not harbor any angry thoughts about God. Whatever state we are in, *Let us fall into the hands of the Lord, for his mercies are great* (v. 13). Even when God expresses his disapproval of good people, they think good of him. *Though he slay me, yet will I trust in him* (Job 13:15).

2.2. He expressed a very tender concern for the people, and it went to his heart to see them have to suffer the plague because of his sin: *These sheep, what have they done?* (v. 17).

Verses 18–30

When David repented, his peace was made with God. When David repented of the sin, God relented from his punishment and ordered the destroying angel to *stay his hand* and *sheath his sword* (v. 27). Directions were given to David to build an altar on the threshing floor of *Ornan,* Araunah (v. 18). The commanding of David to build an altar was a happy sign of reconciliation. David immediately made a bargain with Araunah for the threshing floor, for though Araunah generously offered it to him for free, he would not serve God at other people's expense. God showed his acceptance of David's offerings on this altar: he *answered him from heaven by fire* (v. 26). And David continued to offer his sacrifices on this altar. The bronze altar which Moses made was at Gibeon (v. 29), and all the sacrifices of Israel were offered there, but David was so terrified at the sight of the sword of the angel that he could not go there (v. 30). The business required speed now that the plague had begun. And so God was kind to him and told him to build an altar in that place. The symbols of unity were not so much insisted on as unity itself. When the present distress was over, as long as he lived, David sacrificed there, even though the altar at Gibeon was still maintained. "God has graciously met me here, and so I will still expect to meet with him."

CHAPTER 22

Out of the eater comes forth meat *(Jdg 14:14). It was on the occasion of the terrible judgment on Israel for the sin of David that God indicated that he wanted another altar set up, and it was also then that he indicated the place where he wanted to have the temple built. These signs of God's favor: 1. Directed him to the place (v. 1). 2. Encouraged him to do the work. 2.1. He set about preparing for the building (vv. 2–5). 2.2. He instructed Solomon and told him about this work (vv. 6–16). 2.3. He commanded the leaders to help Solomon do it (vv. 17–19). There is a great deal of difference between the attitude of David's spirit at the beginning of the previous chapter and his attitude at the beginning of this one. There we saw pride in his heart in counting the people; here we see his humility in preparing for the service of God.*

Verses 1–5

Here:

1. The place for the building of the temple is settled on (v. 1). The ground was a threshing floor, for the church of the living God is his floor, his threshing, and *the corn of his floor* (Isa 21:10). Christ's *fan is in his hand, to thoroughly purge his floor,* his winnowing fork is in his hand,

and he will clear his threshing floor (Mt 3:12). This is to be the house because this is the altar. The temple was built for the sake of the altar. There were altars long before there were temples.

2. Preparation is made for that building. David must not build it, but he would do all he could toward it: he *prepared abundantly before his death* (v. 5).

2.1. What led him to make such preparations.

2.1.1. Solomon was young and inexperienced, and unlikely to apply himself vigorously to this task at first, so that unless David set the wheels in motion, Solomon would be in danger of losing a great deal of time to begin with.

2.1.2. The house must be very splendid and lavish, strong and beautiful, everything about it being the best of its kind, because it was intended to honor the Lord of the whole earth. It was also to be a type of Christ, in whom all fullness dwells and in whom all treasures are hidden (Col 1:19; 2:3). The grandeur of the house would help give the worshipers a sense of holy awe and reverence for God, and would invite strangers to come to see it as one of the wonders of the world. They would then come to know the true God.

2.2. What preparations he made. In general, he prepared an abundance of cedar and stone, iron and bronze (vv. 2–4). He had cedar from the Tyrians and the Sidonians. He also got workers together, *the strangers that were in the land of Israel* (v. 2).

Verses 6–16

Solomon was *to build a house for the Lord God of Israel* (v. 6).

1. David tells him why he did not do it himself. It was in his mind to do it (v. 7), but God forbade him from doing it, because *he had shed much blood* (v. 8). Some think this refers to the blood of Uriah, but that honor was forbidden him before he had shed that blood, and so the reference must be to the blood he shed in his wars.

2. David gives him the reasons why he is assigning this task to him:

2.1. Because God has named him as the man who will do it: "*A son shall be born to thee,* who will be called *Solomon,* and *he shall build a house for my name*" (vv. 9–10).

2.2. Because he will have the time and opportunity to do it. He will have rest from his enemies abroad, and he will have peace and quiet at home. Let him therefore build the house.

3. David gives him an account of the vast preparations he has made for this building (v. 14) as an encouragement to Solomon to undertake cheerfully the work for which such a solid foundation has been laid. The treasure mentioned here, 100,000 talents of gold and 1,000,000 talents of silver, is such an incredible sum that most interpreters think this is an error in the text or that the talent is here no more than a plate, piece, or ingot.

4. David instructs him to keep God's commandments (v. 13). He must not think that by building the temple he can buy a special dispensation to sin.

5. David encourages him to go about this great work and to continue to do it (v. 13). It is God's work, and it will come to perfection.

6. David encourages Solomon not to rest in the preparations his father has made. He prays for him: *The Lord give thee wisdom and understanding, and give thee charge concerning* (put you in command of) *Israel* (v. 12). He concludes (v. 16), *Arise and be doing* (now begin the work)*, and the Lord be with thee.*

Verses 17–19

David here engages the leaders of Israel to help Solomon do the great work he has to do. God has given them victory, rest, and a good land as an inheritance. He impresses on them what should make them eager to do it (v. 19): *Set your heart and soul to seek God*. If only the heart is sincerely committed to God, then the head and hand, the possessions and interests, will all be used to serve him cheerfully.

CHAPTER 23

Having given commands for building the temple, David now establishes the services of the temple, together with its offices and officials. In the recent evil days, and during the wars at the beginning of his reign, although the Levitical services were maintained, things were not properly in order, nor did they have the desirable beauty and exactness. Because David was a prophet as well as a leader, he set in order the things that were wanting (Tit 1:5). He declared Solomon as his successor (v. 1). 2. He counted the Levites and appointed them to their respective offices (vv. 2–5). 3. He took an account of the various families of the Levites (vv. 6–23). 4. He took a new count of them, counting all who were twenty years old or more, and appointed work for them (vv. 24–32).

Verses 1–23

We have here:

1. David making Solomon king, not to reign with him, or reign under him, but only to reign after him. He did this in a sacred assembly of all the leaders of Israel, which made Adonijah's attempt to take Solomon's entitlement to the throne very arrogant and absurd.

2. The Levites being counted, according to the rule in Moses' time, from thirty years old to fifty (Nu 4:2–3). Their number in Moses' time, according to this rule, was 8,580 (Nu 4:47–48), but the useful men in Levi's tribe now came to 38,000.

3. The Levites being distributed to their respective positions (vv. 4–5), so that everyone might be employed, for, of all people, a lazy Levite is most absurd. The work assigned to the Levites had four aspects:

3.1. Some, in fact by far the greatest number, were to set in motion the work of the house of the Lord: 24,000, almost two-thirds, were appointed to this service, to help the priests in killing the sacrifices, washing them, and burning them; to have the meat offerings and drink offerings ready; and to keep all the articles of the temple clean and everything in its place. One thousand Levites served each week, making twenty-four rotating divisions. Perhaps while the temple was being built some of these were employed to help the builders hasten that work.

3.2. Others were officers and judges, not in the affairs of the temple but in the country. They were magistrates, to administer justice according to the laws of God, to settle difficulties, and to determine any conflicts. There were 6,000 of these, in the different parts of the kingdom, who helped the leaders and elders of every tribe in administering justice.

3.3. Others were gatekeepers who guarded all the entrances to the house of God, to examine those who wanted to come in and to bar those who wanted to force their way in.

3.4. Others were singers and players on musical instruments, whose task it was to maintain that part of the service. This was a new office.

4. The Levites being gathered in their respective families and clans, so that an account of them might more easily be kept by having a roll call, which each family could do for itself. In this account of the families of the Levites the descendants of Moses stood on the same level as the ordinary Levites, while the descendants of Aaron were promoted to the priest's office, to *sanctify the most holy things* (v. 13). The leveling of Moses' family with the rest shows his self-denial. He was no self-seeking man, as appears from his leaving to his children no special marks of distinction, which was a sign that he had the Spirit of God and not the spirit of the world. The elevation of Aaron's family above the rest was a reward for his self-denial. When his younger brother Moses was *made a god to Pharaoh* (Ex 7:1), and he was only Moses' prophet, who must speak for Moses, observe his orders, and do as he was instructed, Aaron never disputed it. Because he personally submitted to his junior, in accordance with the will of God, God highly exalted his family (Php 2:9).

Verses 24–32

Here is:

1. An alteration made in how the number of the Levite men fit for service was to be reckoned: whereas in Moses' time they were not enlisted or taken into service until they were thirty years old, or admitted as probationers until twenty-five (Nu 8:24), David ordered under God's direction that they should be numbered *for the service of the house of the Lord* from the age of twenty years old and upward (v. 24). Perhaps many of the young Levites, because they had no work appointed for them until they were twenty-five years old, had developed lazy habits, and to prevent this unseemly behavior they were set to work and brought under discipline at twenty years old. There was now no need to carry the tabernacle and its articles. The service was now much easier, and it would not overwork them or overload them if they took it on at twenty years old. The people of Israel had multiplied, and so they needed more hands for the temple service, so that every Israelite who brought an offering might find a Levite ready to help.

2. The work of the priests was (v. 13) to *sanctify the most holy things, to burn incense before the Lord*, and to *bless in his name*. The Levites were not to interfere with that work, but they had enough work to do, according to the positions to which they were assigned (vv. 4–5):

2.1. Those who were to *set forward* (supervise) *the work of the house of God* (v. 4) were to *wait on the sons of Aaron* (v. 28). They were to do the drudgery of the house of God, to keep the courtyards and side rooms clean, to set things in their places. They must prepare the consecrated bread which the priests were to set on the table, and they must provide the flour and wafers for the meat offerings, so that the priests might have everything readily available.

2.2. The standard weights and measures were all kept in the sanctuary, and the Levites took care of them, to see that they were exact and to test other weights and measures by them when an appeal was made.

2.3. The work of the singers was to *thank* and *praise the Lord* (v. 30) at the offering of the morning and evening sacrifices and of other sacrifices on the Sabbaths, New Moon festivals, and so on (v. 31). Moses appointed that the priests should blow trumpets over the burnt offerings and other sacrifices, and at the appointed feasts (Nu 10:10). The sound of the trumpet was awe-inspiring, and it would affect the worshipers, but it was not a voice, nor was it such a reasonable service (Ro 12:1) as the one which David appointed, of singing psalms on those occasions. As the Jewish church grew from its infancy, it became more and more intelligent in its devotions.

2.4. The work of the gatekeepers (v. 5) was to keep *the charge of the tabernacle and of the holy place*, so that no one might come near except those who were allowed to (v. 32).

CHAPTER 24

This chapter gives us a more detailed account of the grouping of the priests and Levites into different divisions, to fulfill the normal duties of their offices according to their families. Here are the divisions: 1. Of the priests (vv. 1–19). 2. Of the Levites (vv. 20–31).

Verses 1–19

The particular account of the arrangement of the priestly divisions when Ezra wrote it was very useful in directing their church affairs after they returned from exile. The title of this record is given in v. 1: *These are the divisions of the sons of Aaron.* Their distribution was for the purpose of dividing the work among themselves.

1. This distribution was made so that the duties of their office could be properly fulfilled. In the mystical body, every member has a use for the good of the whole (Ro 12:4–5; 1Co 12:12).

2. The arrangement was made by drawing lots, so that the decisions might come from the Lord (Pr 16:33), to prevent any quarreling or arguing. As God is the God of order, so he is also the God of peace (1Co 16:33).

3. The lots were drawn in public and with great ceremony, in the presence of the king, leaders, and priests, so that there could be no possible opportunity for any fraudulent practices or even any suspicion of them.

4. The task that the priests were chosen to undertake was presiding in the affairs of the sanctuary (v. 5), in their different divisions and turns. What was to be determined by drawing lots was only the order of service; they were choosing not who would serve but who would serve first, and who next. Of the twenty-four leading priests, sixteen came from the house of Eleazar and eight from that of Ithamar. The way in which lots were drawn is suggested in v. 6: one family was taken from Eleazar and one from Ithamar. The names of the sixteen leaders from Eleazar were put in one container, the eight from Ithamar in another, and they drew them out alternately, as long as those for Ithamar lasted, and then out of those from Eleazar only; or maybe they drew two for Eleazar and then one for Ithamar throughout.

5. Among these twenty-four divisions the eighth is that of Abijah or Abia (v. 10), which is mentioned in Lk 1:5 as the priestly division which Zechariah the father of John the Baptist belonged to. It therefore appears that these priestly divisions which David now arranged continued until the destruction of the second temple by the Romans, even though they were interrupted perhaps in the reigns of bad kings and broken off for a long time by the Exile.

Verses 20–31

Most of the Levites named here have been mentioned before (23:16–23). But they are mentioned here as leaders of the twenty-four divisions of Levites, each division of which was to serve one of the twenty-four divisions of the priests every time those priests took their turn ministering

in the temple. The families of the oldest brother drew lots just as those of their younger brothers did. Those who were from the older families came down to the same level as those of the younger families, and all took their places as God directed by the drawing of lots, not according to seniority. If the younger brothers are faithful and sincere, they will be no less accepted by Christ than the oldest brothers.

CHAPTER 25

Having arranged the divisions of the Levites who were to help the priests in their service, David proceeds in this chapter to organize those who were appointed as singers and musicians in the temple. Here: 1. The people who were to be employed are listed: Asaph, Heman, and Jeduthun (v. 1), their sons (vv. 2–6), and other skilled people (v. 7). 2. We are told that the order in which they were to serve was decided by the drawing of lots (vv. 8–31).

Verses 1–7

Notice:

1. Singing the praises of God is here called *prophesying* (vv. 1–3). It was not that all those who were used in this service were honored with visions of God. Heman is actually said to be the *king's seer in the words of God* (v. 5), but the psalms they sang were composed by prophets, and many of them were prophetic. In Samuel's time, too, singing God's praises was called *prophesying* (1Sa 10:5; 19:20).

2. This is here called *a service*, and the persons involved in it *workmen* (v. 1). In our present weak and corrupt state, the singing of God's praises will not be done as it should be without labor and struggle.

3. Here a great variety of musical instruments was used: *harps, psalteries* (lyres)*, and cymbals* (vv. 1, 6); and there was one who *lifted up the horn* (v. 5), that is, played a wind instrument.

4. The main aim of all this temple music, whether vocal or instrumental, was to give glory and honor to God. The intention of continuing to sing Psalms in the Gospel church is *to make melody with the heart*, together with the voice, *to the Lord* (Eph 5:19).

5. The supervision of the king is similarly taken notice of (v. 2 and again v. 6). His responsibility for the proper and regular observance of divine institutions, both ancient and modern, is an example to everyone in authority to use their power to further religious faith and to support the laws of Christ.

6. The fathers presided in this service, Asaph, Heman, and Jeduthun (v. 1), and the children were *under the hands* (supervision) *of their father* (vv. 2–3, 6). Heman, Asaph, and Jeduthun probably had been brought up under Samuel and had received their education in the schools of the prophets which he had founded and led. They were then pupils, but now they had become masters. Just as Solomon completed what David began, so David completed what Samuel began.

7. There were others also, besides the sons of these three leaders, who are called their *brethren*, who were *instructed in the songs of the Lord* and were trained and skilled in music (v. 7). They were all Levites and numbered 288. But these were a small number compared with the 4,000 whom David appointed to *praise the Lord* (v. 3). The 4,000 were probably distributed throughout the kingdom to lead the country congregations in this good work, for although the sacrifices instituted by the hand of Moses

could be offered only at one place, the psalms written by David could be sung everywhere (1Ti 2:8).

Verses 8–31

Twenty-four people are named at the beginning of this chapter as sons of those three leaders, Asaph, Heman, and Jeduthun. Ethan was the third (6:44), but probably he was dead before the arrangement was completed, and Jeduthun came instead of him. (It is also possible that Ethan and Jeduthun were two names for the same person.) All twenty-four, who were named in vv. 2–4, were qualified for the service and called to it. In what order must they serve? This was determined by drawing lots.

1. The lots were drawn impartially. The 288 Levites were placed in twenty-four groups, twelve in a group, in two rows, twelve groups in a row, and so they cast lots, *ward against ward*, young and old alike, teacher and student, all on the same level.

2. God decided the matter as he pleased. The respective merits of the people are much more important than seniority of age or priority of birth.

3. Probably each ensemble had twelve, some for singing and others for instrumental music. Let us learn to glorify God with one mind and one mouth, and that will be the best combination.

CHAPTER 26

Here is an account of the work of the Levites. That tribe had not been significant during all the time of the judges, until Eli and Samuel appeared. But when David revived religious faith, the Levites were, of all men, held in the highest regard. It was fortunate that Israel had Levites who were sensible and qualified to support the honor of their tribe. Here is an account: 1. Of the Levites who were appointed to be gatekeepers (vv. 1–19). 2. Of those who were appointed to be treasurers and storekeepers (vv. 20–28). 3. Of those who were assigned to be officials and judges in the country and were entrusted with the administration of public affairs (vv. 29–32).

Verses 1–19

Notice:

1. Gatekeepers were appointed to be present at the temple. They guarded all the roads that led to it, and they opened and shut all the outer doors. They were to direct those who were going to worship in the courts of the sanctuary, to instruct worshipers in the reverence they were to observe, to encourage those who were afraid, to send away foreigners and those who were unclean, and to guard against enemies of the temple. In allusion to this office, ministers are said to have *the keys of the kingdom of heaven* committed to them (Mt 16:19), so that they may admit and exclude people according to the law of Christ.

2. It is noted of several who were called to this service that they were *mighty men of valour* (v. 6), *strong men* (v. 7), *able men* (v. 8), capable men, and that one of them was *a wise counsellor* (v. 14). Whatever service God calls people to, he either finds them qualified for it or makes them so.

3. The sons of Obed-Edom were employed in this office, sixty-two from that family. This was the one who received the ark with reverence and happiness, and notice how he was rewarded for it:

3.1. He had eight *sons* (v. 5), *for God blessed him*.

3.2. His sons were promoted to positions of trust in the sanctuary. They had faithfully looked after the ark in their own house, and now they were called to look after it in God's house. Those who keep God's ordinances in their own tent are fit to take care of them in God's tabernacle (1Ti 3:4–5).

4. It is said of one here that *though he was not the firstborn, his father made him the chief* (v. 10), either because he was very good or because the elder son was very weak.

5. The gatekeepers, like the singers, had their positions assigned them by the drawing of lots, so many at such a gate, and so many at another gate, so that everyone might know his position and perform his allotted task (v. 13).

Verses 20–28

Notice:

1. There were *treasures* (treasuries) *of the house of God* (v. 20). A great house cannot be well kept without stores of all different provisions. These treasuries were a type of the plenty there is in our heavenly Father's house, enough and to spare. In Christ, the true temple, are hidden *treasures of wisdom and knowledge* (Col 2:3) and *unsearchable riches* (Eph 3:8).

2. There were *treasures of* (treasuries for) *dedicated things* (v. 20) as a grateful acknowledgment of God's protection. Abraham gave Melchizedek the *tenth of the spoils* (Heb 7:4). In Moses' time, when the army officers returned victorious, they brought their plunder as an *oblation* (offering) *to the Lord* (Nu 31:50). Recently, this godly custom had been revived. Not only Samuel and David, but also Saul, Abner, and Joab had dedicated their plunder to the honor and support of the house of God (v. 28).

Verses 29–32

The judiciary is an ordinance of God for the good of the church as much as the ministry is. We are told here:

1. The Levites were employed in administering justice together with the leaders and elders of the different tribes, who could not be supposed to understand the Law so well as the Levites, who made it their business to study it. None of those Levites who were employed in the service of the sanctuary, none of the singers or gatekeepers, were concerned with these external matters. Either it was thought that one kind of work was enough to fully occupy a person, or it was considered presumptuous to undertake both.

2. Their responsibility was both *in all business of the Lord* and *in the service of kings* (v. 30 and again v. 32). They managed the affairs of the country, civil as well as ecclesiastical, took care of both God's tithes and the king's taxes, punished offenses committed directly against God and his honor and also those against the government and the public peace, guarded against both idolatry and injustice, and took care to see that laws against both were enforced.

3. There were more Levites employed as judges for the two and a half tribes on the other side of the Jordan than for all the rest of the tribes. There were 2,700 for that region, while on the west side of the Jordan there were 1,700 (vv. 30, 32). Either those distant tribes were not so well provided for as the rest with judges of their own, or because they lay farthest from Jerusalem and were on the borders of neighboring nations, they were most in danger of being defiled by idolatry, and were most in need of the help of Levites to prevent it.

CHAPTER 27

In this chapter we have the civil or administrative government of the state, including the military: 1. The twelve commanders, one for each month of the year (vv. 1–15). 2. The officers over the different tribes (vv. 16–24). 3. The king's overseers (vv. 25–34).

Verses 1–15

Here is an account of the regulation of the militia of the kingdom. David himself was a warrior. He planned to keep a constant force, but it was not a standing army.

1. He kept 24,000 constantly equipped. This was a sufficient strength to secure the public peace and security.

2. He changed them every month. This meant that the total number of the militia came to 288,000, perhaps about a fifth of the able men of the kingdom.

3. Every division had a commander in charge of it. All these twelve leading commanders are mentioned among David's mighty warriors (2Sa 23:8–39; 1Ch 11:10–47). Benaiah is here called a chief priest (v. 5). Because kohen may mean "a priest" or "a leader," it might be better translated here as "a chief ruler" or, as in the margin, "a principal officer." When David's wars were over, he revived this method for the peaceful reign of his son Solomon.

Verses 16–34

Here is an account:

1. Of the officers over the tribes. Something of the ancient order instituted by Moses in the desert was still maintained, that every tribe should have its own chief or leader. Whether these officers were like lord-lieutenants who guided them in their military affairs, or chief justices who presided in their courts of law, is not clear. Their power was probably much less now that all the tribes were united under one king than it had been when they had generally acted separately.

2. Of the counting of the people (vv. 23–24). It is here said:

2.1. That when David ordered the people to be counted, he forbade the counting of those under twenty years old.

2.2. That the count which David took of the people, in the pride of his heart, was not used to good effect, because it was never completed or done with precision, nor was it ever registered as an authentic record. Joab was disgusted at it, and he fulfilled it incompletely; David was ashamed of it and wanted it to be forgotten, because God sent his wrath for it against Israel.

3. Of the king's overseers:

3.1. The rulers of the king's substance (property) (v. 31) had oversight and charge of the king's farming, his vineyards, his olive groves, his herds, his camels, his donkeys, and his flocks. Here are overseers all engaged in such necessary service as was consistent with the simplicity and plainness of those times. David was a great soldier, a great scholar, and a great leader, but he was also a great manager of his estate.

3.2. The attendants on the king's person were those who were noted for their wisdom. His uncle was a wise man and a scribe. He was not only skilled in politics, but also well read in the Scriptures, and was his counselor (v. 32). Hushai, an honorable man, was his companion and confidant.

CHAPTER 28

The account of David's departure at the beginning of the first book of Kings does not make his sun shine nearly so brightly as that given in this and the following chapter, where we have his solemn farewell both to his son and to his subjects. In this chapter we have: 1. The calling of a general assembly of the people (v. 1); a solemn declaration that Solomon was to receive the divine inheritance of both the crown and the honor of building the temple (vv. 2–7); an encouragement to the people and to Solomon to give themselves wholeheartedly to their religious faith (vv. 8–10). 2. The plans and materials delivered to Solomon for building the temple (vv. 11–19) and the encouragement given him to undertake it and proceed with it (vv. 20–21).

Verses 1–10

David has served his generation by the will of God (Ac 13:36). But the time is now drawing near for him to die, and as a type of the Son of David, the nearer he comes to his end, the busier he is.

1. He summoned all the leaders to come to him, so that he might take leave of them all together (v. 1). Moses did this (Dt 31:28), as did Joshua (Jos 23:2; 24:1).

2. He spoke to them with a great deal of respect and tenderness. He not only exerted himself to get up from his bed but also got up out of his chair and stood up upon his feet (v. 2), in reverence to God. He wanted also to show due reverence to this solemn assembly of the Israel of God, as if, though greater than any individual among them, he knew that he was less great than this whole assembly. It had been a great delight to him that they were all his servants (21:3), but now he called them his brothers, whom he loved, his people, whom he took care of, not his servants, whom he ordered about: Hear me, my brethren, and my people (v. 2).

3. He declared the desire he had had to build a temple for God, and how God had not allowed him to fulfill that desire (vv. 2–3). He must serve the public with the sword; a different person must serve with the measuring line and the plumb line. Times of peace are times to build (Ac 9:31).

4. He gave evidence of his own right to the crown, and then Solomon's; both were undoubtedly of divine origin. No right of being the firstborn is claimed; the honor came by worth, not age.

4.1. Judah was not the eldest son of Jacob, but God still chose that tribe as the ruling tribe; Jacob passed the scepter on to Judah (Ge 49:10).

4.2. It does not appear that the family of Jesse was the senior house of that tribe.

4.3. David was the youngest son of Jesse, but it seemed good to God to make him king.

4.4. Solomon was one of the youngest sons of David, but God still chose him to sit on the throne, because he was the likeliest of all of them to build the temple; he was the wisest and most inclined to do so.

5. He opened up to them God's gracious purposes concerning Solomon (vv. 6–7): I have chosen him to be my son. God said about him, prefiguring One who was to come:

5.1. He shall build my house. Christ is both the founder and the foundation of the Gospel temple.

5.2. I will establish his kingdom forever. This is to be fulfilled in the kingdom of the Messiah, which will continue in his hands throughout all ages (Isa 9:7; Lk 1:33) and will then be delivered to God, the Father, perhaps to be delivered back to the Redeemer forever. As for Solomon, the promise of the establishment of his kingdom is made conditional here: If he be constant (if he is unswerving) to do my commandments, as at this day (v. 7).

6. He commanded them to remain faithful to God and their duty (v. 8). Notice:

6.1. The substance of this command: Keep, and seek for all the commandments of the Lord your God. The Lord was their God; his commandments must be their rule; they must be concerned to know their duty, search the Scriptures, take advice, seek the law from those whose lips were to keep this knowledge, and pray to God to teach and direct them. God's commandments will not be kept without great care.

6.2. The seriousness of this command. He commanded them in the sight of all Israel, thinking, "God bears witness, and this congregation bears witness, that they have been given good advice and have received fair warning. If they do not accept it, it is their fault, and God and the people will be witnesses against them." See 1Ti 5:21; 2Ti 4:1.

6.3. The motive to observe this command. This was the way to be happy, to enjoy peaceful possession of this good land, and to be able to pass it on to their children as an inheritance.

7. He concluded with a command to Solomon himself (vv. 9–10). He was very concerned that Solomon should have a religious faith. Notice:

7.1. The command David gives Solomon. He had been born in God's house and so was bound to be his by duty; he had been brought up in his house and so was bound to him by gratitude. *Thy own friend, and thy father's friend, forsake not* (Pr 27:10).

7.2. The arguments to support this command:

7.2.1. Two arguments of general motivation:

7.2.1.1. That the secrets of our souls are open before God. He searches all hearts, even the hearts of monarchs, which are unsearchable to us (Pr 25:3).

7.2.1.2. That we are happy or miserable here, and forever, according to whether we serve God or not. *If we seek him diligently, he will be found of us* (v. 9; Heb 11:6; cf. Jer 29:13–14), and that is enough to make us happy. God never rejects anyone until they have first rejected him.

7.2.2. One argument particular to Solomon (v. 10): *"Thou art to build a house for the sanctuary*; seek and serve God, therefore, so that that work may be done from good motives, rightly, and may be accepted by him."

7.3. The means prescribed, and they are prescribed for us also:

- Caution: *Take heed* (v. 10); beware of and consider everything that looks like, or leads to, evil.
- Courage: *Be strong, and do it* (v. 10). We cannot do our work as we should unless we are determined to do it and receive strength from God's grace to do it.

Verses 11–21

As to the general command that David gave his son to seek God and serve him, the Book of the Law was his only rule in that, and there needed to be no other. In building the temple, however, David was now to give him three things:

1. A plan of the building, because it was to be such a building as neither he nor his architects had ever seen before. Moses had a pattern of the tabernacle shown him on the mountain (Heb 8:5), and so did David of the temple, by the immediate hand of God on him (v. 19). *He had this pattern by the Spirit*, the Spirit had put these plans in his mind (v. 12). No ingenious design springing from either David's devotion or Solomon's wisdom must be trusted in such a matter. The temple must be a sacred thing and a type of Christ. It was a kind of sacrament, and so must not be left to mere human skill or creativity to be planned, but must be framed by God himself. David gave these plans to Solomon so that he might know what

to supply and might follow these rules. Particular parts of the plan are mentioned here: a plan of the portico, of the chambers, of the courts, and of the rooms around the courts, in which the dedicated things were stored. He gave him a schedule of the divisions of the priests, plans for the articles to be used in the services (v. 13), and a *pattern of the chariot of the cherubims* (v. 18; NIV: the plan for the chariot, that is, the cherubim). Besides the two cherubim over the *mercy seat* (v. 11; NIV: place of atonement), there were two much larger cherubim, whose wings reached from wall to wall (1Ki 6:23–28), and David here gave Solomon the plan for these, called *a chariot*, because the angels are the chariots of God (Ps 68:17).

2. Materials for the most costly articles to be used in the temple. So that these articles might not be made any less than the plans, he weighed out the exact quantity for each article of both gold and silver (v. 14). In the tabernacle there was only one golden lampstand; in the temple there were ten (1Ki 7:49), besides silver ones, which may have been handheld candlesticks (v. 15). In the tabernacle there was only one table, but in the temple, besides the one on which the consecrated bread was placed, there were ten others for different uses (2Ch 4:8), besides silver tables, for because this house was much larger than the tabernacle, it would look bare if it did not have a correspondingly larger amount of furniture. The gold for the altar of incense is particularly said to be *refined gold* (v. 18), purer than any other, for that was a type of the intercession of Christ, than which nothing is more pure and perfect.

3. Directions as to which way to look for help in this great undertaking. "God will help you, and you must look to him in the first place (v. 20). *The Lord God, even my God*, whom I have chosen and served, who has all along been present with me and prospered me, and to whom, from my own experience of his power and goodness, I commend you—he will be with you, to direct, strengthen, and prosper you. He will not fail you or abandon you." We may be sure that God, who acknowledged our ancestors and carried them through the services of their day, will also continue to be with us in our day if we remain faithful to him. He will never leave us while he has any work to do in us or by us. Furthermore, "good men will help you (v. 21). The priests and Levites will advise you, and you may discuss matters with them. You have good workers, who are both willing and skillful." These are two very good qualities in workers, especially in those who work on the temple. "The leaders and the people will not slow down or oppose the work. They will be wholly at your command, everyone in their place and ready to move the work on."

CHAPTER 29

David had said what he had to say to Solomon. But he had something more to say to the assembly before he left them. 1. He pressed them to contribute, according to their ability, toward the building and furnishing of the temple (vv. 1–5). They then made their gifts with great generosity (vv. 6–9). 2. David offered sacred prayers and praises to God on that occasion (vv. 10–20), with sacrifices (vv. 21–22). 3. Solomon was then enthroned as king with great joy and splendor (vv. 23–25). Soon after this, David came to the end of his days (vv. 26–30). And it is hard to say which shines more brightly here, the setting sun or the rising sun.

Verses 1–9

Notice here:

1. David spoke to the assembly to persuade them to contribute toward the building of the temple. Though David would not force them to give by means of a tax, he would recommend that then was a good time for a freewill offering, because what is done in works of kindness and godliness should be done willingly and not under coercion. God loves a cheerful giver (2Co 9:7).

1.1. David wanted them to remember that Solomon was young and needed help, but he was the person whom God had chosen to do this work.

1.2. The work was great, and everyone should contribute to carrying it out.

1.3. David tells them what great preparations have been made for this work. He did not want them to bear the whole burden of the cost, but he wanted them to show their goodwill by adding to what had already been done (v. 2): *I have prepared with all my might.*

1.4. David sets them a good example. He had generously offered 3,000 talents of gold and 7,000 talents of silver of his own to make the house rich and beautiful (vv. 4–5). He had done this because he had *set his affection on* the house of his God (Col 3:2).

1.5. David stirs them up to do as he has done (v. 5): *And who then is willing to consecrate his service this day unto the Lord?* We must make the service of God our work, must "fill our hands to the Lord," as the Hebrew of v. 5 reads. The filling of our hands with the service of God suggests that we should serve only him, serve him generously, and serve him in the strength of the grace that comes from him.

2. How generously they all contributed toward building the temple when they were encouraged to do so. How generous they were can be seen from the total of the contributions (vv. 7–8). They gave as befitted leaders of Israel. *The people rejoiced* (v. 9): they were glad to have the opportunity to honor God with their resources and glad to have the prospect of completing this good work. *David rejoiced with great joy* (v. 9) that his son and successor would have people around him who were so well disposed toward the house of God, and that this work, on which his heart was so much set, was likely to continue.

Verses 10–22

Here is:

1. The sacred address which David made to God: *Wherefore David blessed the Lord before all the congregation.* David's psalms in 1 Chronicles, which appear toward the end of the book, are mostly psalms of praise. The nearer we come to the world of eternal praise, the more we should speak the language of that world and do its work. In this address:

1.1. He adores God and gives glory to him as the God of Israel, *blessed for ever and ever* (v. 10). The Lord's Prayer ends with a doxology similar to the one David begins with here — *for thine is the kingdom, the power, and the glory* (Mt 6:13). This is proper praise to God — an expression of holy awe and reverence, acknowledging:

1.1.1. His infinite qualities. He is the fountain and center of everything that is glorious and blessed. His is the *greatness*: his greatness is immense and incomprehensible. His is the *power*, and it is almighty and irresistible. His is the *glory*, for his glory is his own majestic purpose and the purpose of the whole creation. His is the *victory*; he transcends and surpasses all and is able to conquer and subdue all things to himself. His is the *majesty*, real and personal, inexpressible, and inconceivable.

1.1.2. His sovereign authority, as rightful owner and possessor of all: "*All that is in heaven, and in the earth, is thine* (v. 11): *thine is the kingdom* (v. 11), and all monarchs are your subjects, for you are the head and are to be exalted and worshiped as head over all."

1.1.3. His universal influence and power. All rich and honorable people receive their riches and honors from God. What they had given back to him was only a small part of what they had received from him.

1.2. He acknowledges with thankfulness the grace of God that enabled them to contribute so cheerfully toward the building of the temple (vv. 13–14): *Now therefore, our God, we thank thee.* It is a great example of the power of God's grace in us to be able to do the work of God willingly.

1.3. He speaks very humbly of himself, his people, and the offerings they had now presented to God:

1.3.1. For himself, and those who joined him, although they were leaders, he was amazed that God would take such notice of them and do so much for them (v. 14): *Who am I, O Lord?* for (v. 15) we *are strangers before thee, and sojourners,* poor contemptible creatures. *Our days on the earth are as a shadow.* This image suggests that our life is empty, dark, and brief; it is a life that will end either in perfect light or perfect darkness. The next words explain it: *There is no abiding* (v. 15), no hope or expectation. We cannot expect any great matters from our life, nor can we expect it to continue for long, which forbids us to boast of the service we do for God — it is the service of such a short life, and so what can we pretend to earn by it?

1.3.2. As for their offerings, *Lord,* he says, *of thy own have we given thee* (v. 14), and again (v. 16), *It cometh of thy hand, and is all thy own. Let him that glories glory in the Lord* (1Co 1:31).

1.4. He appeals to God concerning his own sincerity in what he did (v. 17). It gives good people great assurance to think that God *tries the heart* and *has pleasure in uprightness.* It was encouraging for David that God knew the pleasure with which he both presented his own offering and saw the people's offering. He was neither proud of his own good work nor envious of the good works of others.

1.5. He prays to God for the people and for Solomon, that both may continue as they have begun. In this prayer he addresses God as *the God of Abraham, Isaac, and Jacob* (v. 18), a God in covenant with those patriarchs and, for their sakes, still with his people now.

1.5.1. For the people he prays (v. 18) that what God in his goodness has put into their minds he will always keep there, that they may always have the same thoughts about things as they now seem to have. Great results depend on what is innermost, and what is uppermost, in the desires of our heart, what we aim at and what we love to think about. If any good has taken possession of our hearts or the hearts of our friends, then it is good to commit it in prayer to the keeping of God's grace: "Lord, keep it there, keep it there forever. Strengthen their resolutions. They are in a good frame of mind now; keep them loyal to you when I am gone, them and theirs forever."

1.5.2. For Solomon he prays (v. 19), *Give him a perfect heart.* He does not pray, "Lord, make him a rich man, a great man, and a learned man," but, "Lord, make him an honorable man," for that is better than all. But his building the house would not prove that he served with a whole-hearted devotion unless he also conscientiously kept

God's commandments. We are not helping build churches that will save us if we lead lives that disobey God's law.

2. The cheerful cooperation of this great assembly in this ceremony:

2.1. They joined with David in adoring God. *Now bless the Lord your God* (v. 20), he said; and they did, by *bowing down their heads*, as a gesture of adoration. When someone prays for the congregation, the only people who will receive a blessing are those who agree with the prayer, not so much by *bowing down the head* as by *lifting up the soul*.

2.2. They paid their respects to the king. They looked on him as an instrument in God's hand of much good to them, and in honoring him, they honored God.

2.3. The next day they offered many sacrifices to God (v. 21).

2.4. They feasted with great joy before God (v. 22).

2.5. They made Solomon king a second time. Before, he had been hurriedly anointed, on the occasion of Adonijah's rebellion, and it was thought right to repeat the ceremony, to give the people a deeper assurance. They *anointed him to the Lord*.

Verses 23–30

These verses see King Solomon come to his throne and King David go to his grave.

1. Here is Solomon rising (v. 23): *Solomon sat on the throne of the Lord*. The throne of Israel is called *the throne of the Lord* because God is not only the King of all nations, with all monarchs ruling under him, but also, especially, King of Israel (1Sa 12:12). Solomon's kingdom was a type of the kingdom of the Messiah, and the Messiah's throne really is *the throne of the Lord*. Solomon was successful because:

1.1. His people honored him, as one to whom honor is due (Ro 13:7): *All Israel obeyed him*, that is, they were ready to swear allegiance to him (v. 23). God inclined their hearts to do so, so that his reign might be peaceful from the start. His father was a better man than he was, but his father came to the crown with much difficulty, after long delay, and by many slow steps. David had more faith, and so he was tested more. *They submitted themselves*; the Hebrew says, "They gave the hand under Solomon," that is, they committed themselves under oath to be true to him—putting the hand under the thigh was an old ceremony used in pledging an oath.

1.2. God honored him, for he will honor those who honor him (1Sa 2:30): *The Lord magnified Solomon exceedingly* (v. 25). None of all the previous judges or kings of Israel were so distinguished as he was, or lived in such splendor.

2. Here is David setting, that great man leaving the stage of life. The writer here brings him to the end of his days, leaves him asleep, and draws the curtains around him.

2.1. The writer gives a summary account of the years of his reign (vv. 26–27).

2.2. The writer gives a short account of his death (v. 28), that he died *full of days, riches, and honour*, honored both by God and by people. He had been a warrior since his youth, but was preserved through all the dangers of a military life, lived to a good old age, and died in peace, in his bed—in bed rather than on the battlefield, and yet in the bed of honor. For a fuller account of David's life and reign the writer refers to the histories or records of those times, which were written by Samuel while he lived, and were continued, after his death, by Nathan and Gad (v. 29).

A PRACTICAL AND DEVOTIONAL EXPOSITION OF
THE BOOK OF

2 Chronicles

❧━━━━━◆

This book begins with the reign of Solomon and the building of the temple and continues the history of the kings of Judah from then to the Exile. It ends with the fall of the monarchy and the destruction of the temple. As that monarchy of the house of David was prior in time to all those four celebrated ones of which Nebuchadnezzar dreamed (Da 2:29–43), so also it was superior to them all in honor and dignity. The succession was kept in a lineal descent throughout the whole monarchy, which continued between 400 and 500 years, and, after a long eclipse, shone out again in the kingdom of the Messiah, *of the increase of whose government and peace there shall be no end* (Isa 9:7).

The story of the house of David as we had it before, in the first and second books of Kings, was mixed with the story of the kings of Israel, which *there* took up more space than the story of Judah, but *here* the history of the kings of Judah is complete. Much is repeated here, but many of the passages from Kings are enlarged on, and several different ones are added, especially relating to religious faith, for it is a history of the church. All the good kings prospered, and the evil kings suffered. We have here the peaceful reign of Solomon (chs. 1–9), the blemished reign of Rehoboam (chs. 10–12), the short but busy reign of Abijah (ch. 13), the long and happy reign of Asa (chs. 14–16), the godly and prosperous reign of Jehoshaphat (chs. 17–20), the ungodly and notorious reigns of Jehoram and Ahaziah (chs. 21–22), the unsteady reigns of Joash and Amaziah (chs. 23–25), the long and prosperous reign of Uzziah (Azariah) (ch. 26), the regular reign of Jotham (ch. 27), the ungodly and evil reign of Ahaz (ch. 28), the gracious and glorious reign of Hezekiah (chs. 29–32), the evil reigns of Manasseh and Amon (ch. 33), the reforming reign of Josiah (chs. 34–35), and the destructive reigns of his sons (ch. 36). If we put all these together, the truth of that word of God in 1Sa 2:30 will appear: *Those that honour me I will honour, but those that despise me shall be lightly esteemed.*

CHAPTER 1

At the end of the previous book we read how God exalted Solomon and how Israel obeyed him. Now here we have an account of: 1. How Solomon honored God by sacrifice (vv. 1–6) and by prayer (vv. 7–12). 2. How he honored Israel by increasing its power, wealth, and trade (vv. 13–17).

Verses 1–12

Here is:

1. Solomon's great prosperity (v. 1). God was with him, and he was *strengthened in his kingdom.*

2. Solomon's great godliness and devotion.

2.1. All those in his court who were important must also be good, at least to the extent that they joined him in worshiping God. He asked the commanders and judges, leaders, and heads of families to go with him to Gibeon (vv. 2–3). Solomon began his reign with this public and godly visit to God's altar, and it was a very good sign for the future. Judges are likely to do well for themselves and their people when they take God along with them early on in their careers.

2.2. He offered very many sacrifices to God there (v. 6). His father, David, had left him many flocks and

herds (1Ch 27:29, 31), and so he gave God what was due to him from them. The ark was at Jerusalem (v. 4), but the altar was at Gibeon (v. 5), and he took his sacrifices there.

2.3. He prayed well to God. We had this prayer, with its answer, in 1Ki 3:5–15.

2.3.1. God said Solomon could ask for whatever he wanted. God did this not only so that Solomon might be led to the right way of obtaining the favors that were intended for him—prayer—but also so that he might find out what was in Solomon's heart. Human character can be seen in our choices and desires. "What do you want to *have?*" tests us as much as, "What do you want to *do?*"

2.3.2. As a genuine son of David, he chooses spiritual blessings rather than physical. His request is, *Give me wisdom and knowledge* (v. 10). God gives the faculty of understanding, and we must turn to him to furnish that gift. Solomon pleads on the basis of two things which we did not have in Kings:

2.3.2.1. *Thou hast made me reign in my father's stead* (v. 8). "If I must reign instead of my father, Lord, then give me my father's spirit."

2.3.2.2. *Let thy promise to David my father be established* (v. 9). The promise was, *He shall build a house for* my name, *I will establish* his throne, *he shall be my son,* and *my mercy shall not depart from him.* "Now, Lord, unless you give me wisdom, your house will not be built, nor will my throne be established. *Lord, give me wisdom, therefore*" (v. 10).

2.4. He received a gracious answer to this prayer (vv. 11–12):

2.4.1. God gave him the wisdom that he asked for because he asked for it. Those who sincerely desire to know and do their duty will never lack God's grace.

2.4.2. God gave him the wealth and honor which he did not ask for, because he did not ask for them. Those who make this world their aim and purpose in life come short of the other world and are disappointed in this world too, but those who make the other world their aim and purpose will not only obtain that, and full satisfaction from it, but also enjoy many of this world's advantages along the way.

Verses 13–17

Here is:

1. Solomon's entry into government (v. 13): he came from before the tabernacle, and reigned over Israel. He would not carry out any acts of government until he had completed his acts of devotion. He would not take honor onto himself until he had first given honor to God—first the Tent of Meeting, and then the throne.

2. The splendor of his court (v. 14): *He gathered chariots and horsemen.* He made silver and gold very cheap and common (v. 15). An increase in gold lowers its value, but an increase in grace advances its price. The more people enjoy grace, the more they value it. *How much better is it* therefore *to get wisdom than gold!* (Pr 16:16). He also opened up trade with Egypt, from where he imported horses and *linen yarn,* which he exported again to the kings of Aram (*Syria*), no doubt at great profit (vv. 16–17). We had this before in 1Ki 10:28–29.

CHAPTER 2

Solomon's trading and the encouragement he gave both to trade and to manufacturers, which we read about at the end of the previous chapter, were very commendable. But building was the work he was intended to do, and so he turns to that work here. Here is: 1. Solomon's determination to build the temple and a royal palace, and his appointing of laborers to be employed in that work (vv. 1–2, 17–18); his request to Hiram king of Tyre to provide him both with skilled workers and with materials (vv. 3–10). 2. Hiram's willing reply to, and compliance with, his request (vv. 11–16).

Verses 1–10

Solomon's wisdom was given him not merely for speculation or for conversation to entertain his friends, but for action, and so he immediately got down to the task before him. Notice:

1. His determination for the task (v. 1): *He determined to build,* in the first place, *a house for the name of the Lord.* It is right that God, who is first, should be served first: first a temple and then a palace. Moreover, the palace itself was to be a house not so much for his own convenience and greatness as for the kingdom, for its honor among its neighbors and for receiving the people in an appropriate building whenever they wanted to turn to their leader. He aimed at the good of the community in both projects. We are not born for ourselves but for God and our country.

2. His message to Hiram king of Tyre. The thrust of his message to him is represented here in much the same way as it was in 1Ki 5:2–6.

2.1. The reasons why he turns to Hiram are more fully represented here:

2.1.1. He pleads his father's influence with Hiram and the kindness his father had received from him (v. 3): *As thou didst deal with David, so deal with me.*

2.1.2. He presents his plans in building the temple. He intended it as a place of religious worship (v. 4). The house was built so that it might be dedicated to God and used in his service. He mentions various detailed services that were to be performed there, to inform Hiram.

2.1.3. He tries to inspire Hiram with high thoughts about the God of Israel, by expressing the great respect he had for his holy name: *Great is our God above all gods* (v. 5), above all idols, above all leaders. So:

2.1.3.1. "The house must be great; not in proportion to the greatness of the God to whom it is to be dedicated—for there is no proportion between finite things and the infinite—but in some proportion to the great value and respect we have for this God.

2.1.3.2. "But even if it is so great, it cannot be a dwelling place for our great God. Let Hiram not think that the God of Israel, like the gods of the nations, *dwells in temples made with hands* (Ac 17:24). *No;* the *heaven of heavens cannot contain him* (v. 6). It is intended only as a convenient place for his priests and worshipers, so that they may have a proper place for offering sacrifices in his presence."

2.1.3.3. He looked on himself, even though he was a powerful leader, as unworthy of the honor of being employed in this great work: *Who am I that I should build him a house?* (v. 6).

2.2. The requests he makes to him are set down here in more detail than we had before. He wanted Hiram to provide him with:

2.2.1. A good worker (v. 7): *Send me a man.* "There are skilled workers in Jerusalem, but not such engravers as there are in Tyre. And since temple work must be the best of its kind, let me have the best workers that there are."

2.2.2. Good materials to work with (v. 8), much cedar and other kinds of wood (vv. 8–9), for the house must be *wonderful* and *great.*

3. Solomon's agreement to maintain the workers (v. 10), to give them so much wheat and barley, so much wine and oil. He did not feed his workers with bread and water but with plenty, and with everything that was the best.

Verses 11–18

Here we have:

1. The response which Hiram gave to Solomon's message, in which he shows a great respect for Solomon and a readiness to serve him.

1.1. He congratulates Israel on having such a king as Solomon (v. 11): *Because the Lord loved his people, he has made thee king.*

1.2. He blesses God for raising up such a successor to David (v. 12). Hiram not only was very well disposed toward the Jewish nation, and pleased with their prosperity, but also worshiped Jehovah, *the God of Israel,* who was now known by that name in the neighboring nations. Now that the people of Israel kept close to the Law and worship of God, and so preserved their honor, the willingness of the neighboring nations to be taught the true religious faith by Israel was as great as Israel's willingness, later, when it turned away from God, to be defiled by the idolatries and superstitions of its neighbors.

1.3. He sent him a very skilled worker who would not fail to fulfill his expectations in everything, one who had both Jewish and Gentile blood in him, for his mother was an Israelite but his father came from Tyre.

1.4. He promised him as much wood as he needed, and undertook to deliver it to Joppa, and also confirmed that he would rely on Solomon to look after the workers as he had promised (vv. 15–16).

2. The orders which Solomon gave about the workers. He would not employ the freeborn Israelites in the servile work of the temple itself, not even as overseers of it. He employed the foreigners who had converted to the Jewish religion for this work. There were vast numbers of them in the land at this time (v. 17); if any of them came from the devoted nations, those that were to be given to the Lord by destruction, perhaps they came under the law of the Gibeonites and others (Jos 9:21), which provided that they would be to be woodcutters for the people. The total number of them is given in v. 2 and again in v. 18: 150,000.

CHAPTER 3

In this chapter we have: 1. The place and time of building the temple (vv. 1–2); its dimensions and rich decorations (vv. 3–9). 2. The cherubim in the Most Holy Place (vv. 10–13); the curtain (v. 14); the two pillars (vv. 15–17). We have already had an account of all this in 1Ki chapters 6 and 7.

Verses 1–9

Here we learn of:

1. The place where the temple was built. It had already been decided (1Ch 22:1).

1.1. It must be at Jerusalem, for that was the place God had chosen. The royal city must be the Holy City.

1.2. It must be on Mount Moriah, which some think was the place in the land of Moriah where Abraham had offered Isaac (Ge 22:2).

1.3. It must be *where the Lord appeared to David*, and *answered him by fire* (1Ch 21:18, 26). Atonement had once been made there, and so in remembrance of that, atonement must still be made there.

1.4. It must be in the place which David had prepared, that is, the place which he had not only bought with his money but also chosen by divine direction.

1.5. It must be on the threshing floor of Araunah.

2. The time when it was begun: not until the fourth year of Solomon's reign (v. 2). The first three years were employed in making necessary preparations for it. Three years would pass quickly, considering how many people were to join together and be put to work.

3. The dimensions of the temple, about which Solomon was instructed (v. 3)—as he was in other things—by his father. V. 3 may be read, "This was the foundation which Solomon laid for the building of the house"; that is, this was the rule he went by. And the rule was that the building should be so many cubits in length and breadth *after the first measure*, that is, according to the cubit of the old standard, for its dimensions were given by God's wisdom.

4. The decorations of the temple. The woodwork was very fine, but it was *overlaid with pure gold* (v. 4), with *fine gold* (v. 5), and that in turn was embossed with *palm trees* and chain designs. It was gold *of Parvaim* (v. 6), the best gold. The *beams* and *posts*, the *walls* and *doors*, were *overlaid with gold* (v. 7). The Most Holy Place, which was twenty cubits square, that is, about thirty feet (about nine meters) square, was all *overlaid with fine gold* (v. 8), even

the *upper chambers* (v. 9), or rather the upper floor or roof—top, bottom, and sides were all overlaid with gold. Every one of the nails, screws, or pins with which the golden plates were fastened to the walls that were overlaid with them weighed fifty shekels, or was worth so much, with all its skilled creativity. A great many precious stones were dedicated to God (1Ch 29:2, 8), and these were set here and there, where they would be seen to their best advantage.

Verses 10–17

Here is an account of:

1. The two cherubim which were set up in the Most Holy Place. There were two already over the ark, which covered the place of atonement with their wings; those were small ones. Although those remained—because they belonged to the ark, which was not to be remade, as all the other furnishings of the temple were—now that the Most Holy Place was enlarged, these two large ones were added. These cherubim are said to be of *image work* (v. 10), to represent the angels who serve the divine Majesty. Each wing extended five cubits, that is, about 7.5 feet (about 2.3 meters), so that the whole was twenty cubits, that is, about thirty feet (about nine meters) (vv. 12–13), which was just the width of the Most Holy Place (v. 8). They stood on their feet, as servants, facing inwardly toward the ark (v. 13), so that it might be clear that they were not set there to be adored—for then they would have been made to be seated, as on a throne, and their faces would have been toward their worshipers—but rather that they themselves served the invisible God. We must not worship angels, but we must worship *with* angels, because we have come into fellowship with them (Heb 12:22) and must do the will of God as the angels do. Compare 1Co 11:10 with Isa 6:2.

2. The curtain that separated the Holy Place and the Most Holy Place (v. 14). This represented the darkness of that era and the distance which the worshipers were kept at, but at the death of Christ, this curtain was torn, for through him we are brought near, and have boldness (Eph 2:13; 3:12) not only to look, but even to enter, into the Most Holy Place (Heb 10:19–20). Solomon had cherubim embroidered on it; the Hebrew reads literally, "he caused them to ascend," that is, they were embossed, in raised work.

3. The two pillars which were set up before the temple. End to end, they would have measured somewhat more than thirty-five cubits, that is, about fifty-two feet (about sixteen meters) (v. 15), each by itself being about eighteen cubits high, that is, about twenty-seven feet (about 8.2 meters) high. See 1Ki 7:15–22, where we looked at those pillars, *Jachin* and *Boaz*.

CHAPTER 4

Here is a further account of the furnishings of God's house. 1. Those things that were of bronze: the altar for burnt offerings (v. 1), the Sea and basins to hold water (vv. 2–6), the bronze with which the doors of the court were overlaid (v. 9), the furnishings of the altar, and other things (vv. 10–18). 2. Those that were of gold: the lampstands and tables (vv. 7–8), the altar of incense (v. 19), and the accessories for each of these (vv. 20–22). All these, except the bronze altar (v. 1), were described in more detail in 1Ki 7:23–50.

Verses 1–10

David often speaks with much affection both of the *house of the Lord* and of the *courts of our God* (Ps 92:13).

1. There were the things in the open court, in the view of all the people, which were very significant:

1.1. There was the bronze altar (v. 1). All the sacrifices were offered on this, and it consecrated the gift. This altar was much larger than the one Moses made in the tabernacle. That one was five cubits square, that is, about seven and a half feet (about 2.3 meters) square; this one was twenty cubits square, that is, about thirty feet (about nine meters) square. God had greatly expanded his people's borders, and so it was right that they should expand his altars. Our response should be in proportion to what we have received. It was ten cubits high, that is, about fifteen feet (about 4.5 meters) high, so that the people who worshiped in the courts could see the sacrifices being burned, and so that their eye might affect their heart with their sorrow for sin. And with the smoke of the sacrifices their hearts could rise to heaven in holy longing toward God and his favor. In all our devotions we must keep our eye of faith fixed on Christ, the great sacrifice of atonement.

1.2. There was the cast-metal Sea, a very large bronze reservoir, in which they put water for the priests to wash in (vv. 2, 6). The Holy Spirit showed by this:

1.2.1. The fullness of merit that is in Jesus Christ for all those who by faith turn to him for the cleansing of their consciences, so that they may serve the *living God* (Heb 9:14).

1.2.2. Our great Gospel duty, which is to cleanse ourselves by true repentance. Our hearts must be consecrated, or else we cannot consecrate the name of God. Those who draw near to God must *cleanse their hands, and purify their hearts* (Jas 4:8).

1.3. There were ten basins of bronze, in which they washed the things that they offered as burnt offerings (v. 6). Just as the priests were washed, so must the sacrifices be washed too. We must not only cleanse ourselves in preparation for our religious services, but also carefully put away all those idle thoughts which cling to our services themselves and defile them.

1.4. The doors of the court were overlaid with bronze (v. 9), to give them both strength and beauty, and so that they might not rot with the weather.

2. There were the things in the house of the Lord, into which only the priests went to minister, which also were very significant. All was gold there. The nearer we come to God, the purer we must be, and the purer we will be.

2.1. There were ten golden lampstands, according to the design of the one which was in the tabernacle (v. 7). The written word is a lamp and a light (Ps 119:105), shining in a dark place. In Moses' time they had only one lampstand, the Pentateuch, but the addition of other books of Scripture in the course of time could be represented by the increase of the number of the lampstands. Light increased. In Revelation, the lampstands are the churches (Rev 1:20). Moses set up only one, the church of the Jews, but in the Gospel temple, not only believers, but also churches, are multiplied.

2.2. There were ten golden tables (v. 8), tables on which the *showbread was set* (v. 19). One hundred golden sprinkling bowls belonged to those tables.

2.3. There was a golden altar (v. 19), on which they burned incense.

Verses 11–22

Here is a summary both of the bronze work and of the gold work of the temple:

1. Huram the worker was very exact: *He finished all that he was to make* (v. 11). *Huram his father*, he is called (v. 16). Probably it was a sort of nickname, for the king of

Tyre called him *Huram-Abi*, "Huram my father," Huram-Abi being a great artist and like a father to the skilled craft workers in bronze and iron.

2. Solomon was very generous. He made *all the vessels in great abundance* (v. 18), so that some might be stored up for use when others had become worn out.

CHAPTER 5

After the temple had been built and furnished for God, we have here: 1. Possession of it given to God, by bringing in the dedicated things (v. 1), but especially the ark, the sign of his presence (vv. 2–10). 2. Possession taken by him, in a cloud (vv. 11–14).

Verses 1–10

This corresponds to what we read in 1Ki 8:2–10, where an account was given of the solemn introduction of the ark into the newly erected temple.

1. There needed to be no great ceremony to bring in the dedicated things (v. 1). They added to the wealth of the temple, and perhaps to its beauty, but they could not add to its holiness, for it was the *temple that sanctified the gold* (Mt 23:17). See how righteous Solomon was toward both God and his father. Whatever David had dedicated to God, Solomon put among the treasures of the temple. When Solomon had made so many furnishings for the temple (4:18), many materials were left over, which he would not convert to any other use, but stored up in the treasury for when they might be needed.

2. But it was right that the ark should be brought in with great ceremony, and this is what happened. All the other furnishings were new, and larger — in proportion to the temple — than they had been in the tabernacle. But the ark, with the atonement cover and the cherubim, was the same, for the presence and the grace of God are the same in small gatherings as they are in large ones. Wherever two or three are gathered together in Christ's name, he is as truly present as if there were 2,000 or 3,000 (Mt 18:20). The ark was brought in, accompanied by a very large assembly of the elders of Israel, who came to grace the ceremony (vv. 2–4). The ark was carried by the priests (v. 7), brought into the Most Holy Place, and put under the wings of the great cherubim which Solomon had set up there (vv. 7–8). *There they are unto this day* (v. 9), not the day when this book was written after the Exile, but the day when the first account of these events was written, the account from which this story is transcribed. The ark was a type of Christ and, as such, a sign of the presence of God. The temple itself, if Christ leaves it, is a desolate place (Mt 23:38).

3. With the ark they brought up the Tent of Meeting and all the *holy vessels that were in the tabernacle* (v. 5).

4. This was done with great joy. They held a holy festival on the occasion (v. 3), during which they *sacrificed sheep and oxen without number* (v. 6). When Christ is formed in a soul (Gal 4:19), when the law is written on the heart (Jer 31:33), when the ark of the covenant is established there, so that the soul becomes the temple of the Holy Spirit (1Co 6:19), that soul is truly satisfied.

Verses 11–14

Solomon and the elders of Israel had done what they could to grace the ceremony of bringing in the ark, but God showed his acceptance of what they did by putting the greatest honor on it. The cloud of glory that filled the house made it more beautiful than all the gold with which it was overlaid or the precious stones with which it was decorated. And yet that was no glory in comparison with the glory of the Gospel era (2Co 3:8–10). Notice:

1. How God took possession of the temple: he *filled it with a cloud* (v. 13).

1.1. This was how he showed that he accepted this temple as meaning the same thing to him that the tabernacle of Moses had meant (Ex 40:34).

1.2. This was how he showed consideration for the weakness of those to whom he revealed himself, who could not bear the dazzling luster of divine light. Christ revealed things to his disciples as they were able to bear them, and in parables (Mk 4:33–34), which wrapped up divine things as in a cloud.

2. When God took possession of it.

2.1. *When the priests had come out of the holy place* (v. 11). This is how to give possession. All must come out, so that the rightful owner may go in. Do we want God to live in our hearts? We must give him room by letting everything else give way.

2.2. When the singers and musicians praised God, then the house was filled with a cloud. This is significant; it was not when they offered sacrifices, but when they sang the praises of God, that God gave them this sign of his favor, for the sacrifice of praise *pleaseth the Lord* better than that of *an ox or bullock* (Ps 69:31). Where unity is, the Lord commands the blessing (Ps 133). God's goodness is his glory (Ex 33:18–19; 34:6–7), and he is pleased when we give him the glory of it.

3. What its effects were. The *priests themselves could not stand to minister, by reason of the cloud* (v. 14). The Word was made flesh, and when he comes to his temple, like a refiner's fire, *who may abide the day of his coming? And who shall stand when he appeareth?* (Mal 3:1–2).

CHAPTER 6

Now that the glory of the Lord, as a thick cloud, has filled the temple, Solomon immediately makes the most of the opportunity and speaks to God. 1. He makes a sacred declaration of his intention in building this temple, to please the people and to honor God, both of whom he blesses (vv. 1–11). 2. He makes a sacred prayer to God that he would graciously accept and answer all the prayers that would be made in the temple (vv. 12–42). We had this whole chapter before, with very little variation, in 1Ki 8:12–53, which it would be useful to refer to.

Verses 1–11

In all our religious activities it is very important that our intentions are good and that we are single-minded. If Solomon had built this temple out of pride, it would not have turned at all to his advantage.

1. He did it for the glory and honor of God; this was his highest and ultimate purpose. The temple was *for the name of the Lord God of Israel* (v. 10), to be a *house of habitation for him*, a magnificent temple for him (v. 2).

2. He did it according to God's choice of Jerusalem as the city in which he would be pleased to have his name rest (v. 6): *I have chosen Jerusalem*.

3. He did it according to the good intentions of his father, who never had an opportunity to put them into effect: *It was in the heart of David my father to build a house for God*; the plan was his, and this is to be known to his honor (v. 7). God approved of it, even though he did not allow David to carry it out (v. 8): *Thou didst well that it was in thy heart* (1Ki 8:18). Temple work is often

done in this way: one person sows and another reaps (Jn 4:37–38); one generation begins something which the next generation completes. Every good deed does not have to be an original.

4. He did it to fulfill the word which God had spoken. God had said, *Thy son shall build the house for my name*, and now he had done it (vv. 9–10).

Verses 12–42

In the previous verses Solomon had, as it were, signed and sealed the deed of dedication by which the temple was given to the honor and service of God. Here he speaks the prayer of consecration, by which the temple prefigured Christ, the great Mediator, through whom we are to offer all our prayers.

1. Here are some doctrinal truths set down:

1.1. That the God of Israel is a Being of incomparable perfection. We cannot describe him, but we know there is *none like him in heaven or in earth* (v. 14).

1.2. That he is, and will be, true to every word that he has spoken; and everyone who serves him sincerely will definitely find him both faithful and kind.

1.3. That he is a Being who is infinite and vast, whom heaven, and the highest heaven, cannot contain, and we can add nothing to his happiness by the best we can do for him (v. 18). He is infinitely beyond the bounds of creation and infinitely above the praises of all intelligent creatures.

1.4. That he, and *he only, knows the hearts of the children of men* (v. 30). All human thoughts, aims, and attitudes lie open before him. The thoughts and intentions of our hearts cannot be hidden from God (Heb 4:12), who knows not only what is in the heart, but also the heart itself and its every beat.

1.5. That there is no such thing as sinless perfection to be found in this life (v. 36).

2. Here are some points for consideration:

2.1. He supposed that if doubts and conflicts arose between people, both sides would agree to turn to God, and would require the person whose testimony would decide the matter to take an oath (v. 22).

2.2. He supposed that although Israel enjoyed a deep peace and tranquility, troublesome times would come.

2.3. He supposed that those who had not called on God at other times would still seek him promptly and seriously in times of trouble. Trouble will drive those to God who have said to him, "Go away" (vv. 24, 26, 28).

2.4. He supposed that foreigners would come from far away to respect and worship the God of Israel.

3. Here are appropriate petitions:

3.1. That God would acknowledge and recognize this temple.

3.2. That God would hear and accept the prayers which would be made in or toward that place (v. 21). He prayed that God would hear from his dwelling place, from heaven. Heaven is still his dwelling place, not this temple, and so help must come from there. *When thou hearest, forgive* (v. 21). This shows us that the forgiveness of our sins makes way for all the other answers to our prayers:

3.3. That God would give judgment according to his justice for every appeal made to him (vv. 23, 30).

3.4. That God would respond in mercy to his people when they repented, reformed their ways, and sought him (vv. 25, 27, 38–39).

3.5. That God would make foreigners welcome to this house and answer their prayers (v. 33).

3.6. That God would, on every occasion, own and plead the cause of his people Israel against all who oppose it (v. 35 and again v. 39): *Maintain* (uphold) *their cause*.

3.7. He concludes this prayer with some expressions which he had learned from his godly father and borrowed from one of his psalms. We did not have them in the parallel passage in 1Ki 8, but we have them here (vv. 41–42). He prayed:

- That God would take possession of the temple and keep possession of it, that he would make it his resting place: *Thou and the ark* (v. 41). What will the ark do without the God of the ark—ordinance without the God of the ordinances?
- That he would make the ministers of the temple a blessing to the community: *Clothe them with salvation* (v. 41), that is, not only save them, but also make them instruments that save others by offering the sacrifices of righteousness.
- That the service of the temple might give all the Lord's people great joy and assurance.

CHAPTER 7

In this chapter we have God's answer to Solomon's prayer. 1. His public answer by fire from heaven, which consumed the sacrifices (v. 1) and deeply moved the priests and people (vv. 2–3). That sign of God's acceptance encouraged them to continue the ceremonies of the festival for fourteen days, and Solomon was encouraged to continue carrying out all his plans for the honor of God (vv. 4–11). 2. His private answer by word of mouth, in a dream or vision of the night (vv. 12–22). Most of these things we had before (1Ki 8:1–9:9).

Verses 1–11

Here is:

1. The gracious answer which God immediately gave to Solomon's prayer: the *fire came down from heaven and consumed the sacrifice* (v. 1). This was how God showed his acceptance of Moses (Lev 9:24), Gideon (Jdg 6:21), David (1Ch 21:26), and Elijah (1Ki 18:38); in general, to accept the burnt sacrifice is, in Hebrew (see also Ps 20:3), to turn it to ashes. Let us apply this:

1.1. To the suffering of Christ. When it was the Lord's will to crush him and cause him to suffer because he had laid on him the iniquity of us all (Isa 53:6, 10), he showed his goodwill toward human beings. His death was our life, and he was made sin (2Co 5:21) and a curse that we might inherit righteousness and a blessing.

1.2. To the sanctification of the Spirit, who descends like fire, burning up our sinful and corrupt desires. Those animals must be sacrificed, or we are ruined. The fire kindles in our souls a holy zeal of godly and devout affections, to burn constantly on the altar of our heart.

2. The grateful response made to God for this gracious sign of his favor.

2.1. The people *worshipped and praised God* (v. 3) with reverence, adoring the glory of God: *They bowed their faces to the ground and worshipped* (v. 3). They expressed their deep reverence for God's majesty, their glad submission to his authority, and the sense they had of their own unworthiness to come into God's presence. When the fire of the Lord came down, they praised him, saying, *He is good, for his mercy endureth for ever* (v. 3). This is a song that is always timely and one for which our hearts and tongues should always be in tune.

2.2. The king and all the people offered many sacrifices (vv. 4–5).

2.3. The priests fulfilled their part; they took their positions. The singers and musicians also took theirs (v. 6), with the instruments *David had made to praise the Lord, when David praised by their ministry.* Some read this part of the verse as saying, "with the instruments that David had made and the hymn that David had put into their hand" (see also 1Ch 16:7).

2.4. The whole congregation expressed the greatest possible joy and assurance. They kept the festival of dedicating the altar for seven days, from the second to the ninth; the tenth day was the Day of Atonement, when they were to humble their souls for sin, and that was not out of place amid their joy. On the fifteenth day, the Feast of Tabernacles began, and this continued until the twenty-second, and they did not go their own ways until the twenty-third.

Verses 12–22

God appeared to Solomon in the night, as he had once before (1:7)—and now, as then, it was after a day of sacrifice—and gave him a special answer to his prayer. We had the main part of it before (1Ki 9:2–9).

1. He promised to acknowledge and recognize this temple as *a house of sacrifice to Israel* and *a house of prayer for all people* (Isa 56:7): *My name shall be there for ever* (vv. 12–16).

2. He promised to answer the prayers of his people that would be offered in that place at any time (vv. 13–15).

2.1. National judgments are thought of here (v. 13): famine, plague, and perhaps war, for *locusts to devour the land* may refer to enemies who are as greedy as locusts ravaging all in their path.

2.2. National repentance, prayer, and reformation are required (v. 14).

2.3. National mercy is then promised, that God will forgive their sin, which brought the judgment on them, and then heal their land and put right all their grievances. Forgiving mercy makes way for healing mercy (Ps 103:3; Mt 9:2).

3. He promised to make Solomon's kingdom last, on condition that he persevered in doing his duty (vv. 17–18). But he set before Solomon death as well as life (Dt 30:15), the curse as well as the blessing (Dt 11:26–28).

3.1. He thought it possible that even though they had built this temple to the honor of God, they might still be drawn away to worship other gods (v. 19).

3.2. He threatened it as certain that, if they did so, it would mean the ruin of both state and church.

CHAPTER 8

In this chapter we are told: 1. What towns and cities Solomon built (vv. 1–6); what workers Solomon employed (vv. 7–10); how carefully he looked after a proper settlement for his wife (v. 11). 2. What a good system he established in the temple worship (vv. 12–16); what trade he had with foreign countries (vv. 17–18).

Verses 1–11

There is a similar account in 1Ki 9:10–24.

1. Although Solomon was a man of great learning and knowledge, he spent his days not in contemplation but in action, in building cities and fortifying them.

2. He employed a great many people and kept them working. A great many foreigners lived in Israel, many of whom remained from the Canaanites. They were welcome to live in Israel, but not to live and do nothing.

3. When Solomon had begun his work by building the house of God, and had done that work well and quickly, he was successful in all his undertakings, so that *he built all that he desired to build* (v. 6). Yet he knew how to set boundaries to his desires. He finished all he wanted, and then he did not want anything more.

4. One reason why Solomon deliberately built a palace for the queen, and moved her and her court to it, was that he thought it was not right that she should *dwell in the house of David* (v. 11). She had probably converted to the Jewish religion, but it is questionable whether all her servants had. Perhaps they had the idols of Egypt among them. Now although Solomon did not have enough zeal and courage to suppress and punish what was wrong there, he considered the honor of his father's memory important enough to justify preventing dishonor from coming to the place where the ark of God had been and where godly David had offered many good prayers and sung many sweet psalms.

Verses 12–18

Here is:

1. Solomon's devotion. The purpose of building the temple was to worship in the temple. Whatever it cost him to build that structure, if he had neglected the worship that was to be performed there, it would all have been futile. When Solomon had built the temple:

1.1. He kept up the holy sacrifices there, according to the Law of Moses (vv. 12–13). Spiritual sacrifices are now required of us (1Pe 2:5); we are to bring them daily and weekly, and it is good to have a settled pattern of devotion.

1.2. He kept up holy songs there, according to the order of David, who is called here *the man of God* (v. 14), as Moses was, because he was both instructed and authorized by God to make these requirements; Solomon made sure these requirements were observed *as the duty of every day required* (v. 14). *None departed from the commandment of the king concerning any matter* (v. 15). When the temple worship was put into this good order, *The house of the Lord was perfected* (v. 16).

2. Solomon's trading. He himself in person visited the seaport towns of Elath and Ezion Geber. Canaan was a rich country, but he still had to send to Ophir for gold. The Israelites were a wise and understanding people (Dt 4:6), but he still had to be indebted to the king of Tyre for officers who knew the sea (v. 18). Canaan was God's special land, however, and Israel God's special people. This teaches us that grace, not gold, is the best wealth, and knowledge of God and his Law is the best kind of knowledge.

CHAPTER 9

Solomon here continues to appear great both at home and abroad (see also 1Ki 10). Nothing is added here; but his apostasy near the time of his death, which was recorded there (1Ki 11), is omitted here, and the close of this chapter brings him to the grave with an unstained reputation. Here we see: 1. The honor which the queen of Sheba gave to Solomon when she visited him to hear his wisdom (vv. 1–12). 2. Many examples of the riches and splendor of Solomon's court (vv. 13–28); the conclusion of his reign (vv. 29–31).

Verses 1–12

This passage of story has been considered in detail in 1Ki 10, but because our Savior has given it as an example for us in seeking him (Mt 12:42), let us observe briefly:

1. *Those who honour God he will honour* (1Sa 2:30). Solomon had greatly honored God by building, beautifying, and dedicating the temple. All his wisdom and his wealth had been used to make that building a perfect work, and now God made his wisdom and wealth contribute greatly to his reputation.

2. Those who know the worth of true wisdom will not grudge any pains or expense to gain it. The queen of Sheba put herself to a great deal of trouble and expense to hear the wisdom of Solomon, yet when she had learned from him to serve God and do her duty, she thought it had all been worthwhile. Heavenly wisdom is that *pearl of great price* (Mt 13:46) which is a good bargain if we buy it by leaving everything we have.

3. Everyone should use whatever gift they have received to build up and serve others (1Pet 4:10), as the opportunity arises. Solomon was generous in sharing his wisdom and willing to teach others what he knew himself.

4. The queen of Sheba was deeply moved to see the respect with which Solomon's servants attended him and with which both he and they attended the house of God.

5. Those who have the opportunity to deal constantly with those who are knowledgeable, wise, and good are happy. The queen of Sheba thought Solomon's servants happy because they continually *heard his wisdom*. It is significant that the descendants of those who had places at his court thought themselves sufficiently distinguished and honored by being called the *children of Solomon's servants* (Ezr 2:55; Ne 7:57). It is right for those who are wise and good to be generous according to their position and power. The queen of Sheba was generous toward Solomon, and so Solomon was the same toward her (vv. 9, 12). They both knew how to value wisdom, and so neither of them coveted money, and both of them cultivated and confirmed their friendship by giving and receiving presents.

Verses 13–31

1. Here is Solomon reigning in wealth and power, at ease and enjoying abundance such as has never since been paralleled by any other king. The most distinguished were famous for their wars, but Solomon reigned for forty years in lasting peace. Some of those who might be thought to rival Solomon withdrew and kept people in awe of them by keeping them at a distance, but Solomon traveled abroad much and appeared on public business. So the promise was fulfilled that God would give him riches, wealth, and honor, such as no kings *have had, or shall have* (1:12).

1.1. Never had any ruler appeared in public with greater splendor than Solomon did, which to those who judge by physical sight, as most do, would commend him very much. He had 200 *targets* (large shields) and 300 small shields, all of hammered gold, carried in front of him (vv. 15–16), and he sat on a most imposing throne (vv. 17–19). *There was not the like in any kingdom*.

1.2. Never had any ruler more gold and silver, even though there were no gold or silver mines in his own kingdom.

1.3. Never had any ruler had such presents brought to him by all his neighbors as Solomon had: *All the kings of Arabia, and governors of the country, brought him gold and silver* (v. 14), not as tributes which he extorted from them, but as freewill offerings to seek his favor or by way of exchange for agricultural products such as grain or cattle. In this he was a type of Christ, to whom, as soon as he was born, the wise men of the east brought presents, *gold, frankincense, and myrrh* (Mt 2:11), and to whom all who are around him must bring gifts (Ps 76:11; Ro 12:1).

1.4. Never was any ruler so famous for wisdom, so courted, consulted, or marveled at (v. 23).

2. Here is Solomon dying, stripped of all his pomp. He is leaving all his wealth and power, not to one concerning whom he does not know *whether he would be a wise man or a fool* (Ecc 2:19), but to one who he knows will be a fool. This was all meaningless, a chasing after the wind (vv. 29–31; Ecc 2:17). Yet it is significant that no mention is made here of Solomon's departure from God in his final days. This is omitted because, though he fell, he was not completely rejected. His sin is not recorded again because it was repented of and forgiven, and so became as if it had never been. The silence of Scripture sometimes speaks. I am willing to believe that its silence here about the sin of Solomon is a sign that none of the sins he committed were remembered against him (Eze 33:16). When God forgives sin, he *casts it behind his back and remembers it no more* (Isa 38:17).

CHAPTER 10

This chapter is copied almost word for word from 1Ki 12:1–19. Solomon's turning away from God was not repeated, but the turning away of the ten tribes from his family is repeated in this chapter, where we find: 1. How foolish Rehoboam was in negotiating with them (vv. 5–14). 2. How evil the people were in complaining about Solomon (vv. 2–4) and abandoning Rehoboam (vv. 16–19). 3. How just and righteous God was in all this (v. 15). His plan was fulfilled in this.

Verses 1–11

We may notice here:

1. The wisest and best cannot make everybody happy. Solomon made his kingdom rich and moved it forward. He did everything that could have been done to make them happy and at ease, but perhaps he had shown poor judgment in imposing taxes and services on them. No one is completely wise. It is probable that when Solomon turned away from God and his duty, his wisdom failed him, and God left him to himself to act in this unwise manner. Even Solomon's treasures were exhausted by his love of women, and it was probably to maintain them, together with their pride, luxury, and idolatry, that he burdened his subjects.

2. Turbulent and ungrateful spirits will find fault with the government and complain of grievances. Had they not had peace in Solomon's time? They were never plundered by invaders, as they had been formerly. They had never become fearful because of the threat of war or been forced to risk their lives on the battlefield. Did they not have plenty — enough food and money? But they complained that Solomon gave them a heavy load to bear.

3. Many destroy themselves and their interests by trampling on and provoking their subordinates. Rehoboam thought that because he was king he could assume as much authority as his father had. But although he wore his father's crown, he lacked his father's brains. Such a wise man as Solomon may do as he wants, but such a fool as Rehoboam must do as he can. Rehoboam paid dearly for his threats and his big words, and for thinking he could get anything he wanted. A tender consideration of those who are subordinates, and an eagerness to put them at their ease, will commend all in authority, in the church, in the nation, and in families.

4. Moderate counsels are generally the wisest and best. Gentleness will do what violence will not do. Rehoboam's old, experienced counselors advised him to use this method (v. 7): "*Be kind to this people, and please them, and speak good words to them*, and you will keep them on your side forever." Good words cost nothing except a little self-denial, but they buy what is good.

Verses 12–19

We may learn here:

1. When public affairs are in turmoil, violence only makes bad things even worse. Rough answers, such as Rehoboam gave here, only stir up anger and add fuel to the fire.

2. Whatever human plans and intentions are, God is doing his own work through them. He is fulfilling the word he has spoken, not a jot or tittle of which will fall empty to the ground (Mt 5:18).

3. Worldly wealth, honor, and power are very uncertain. *Solomon reigned over all Israel* (9:30), and one would have thought he had done enough to keep the monarchy safely in his family for many years. But he is scarcely cold in his grave before ten of the twelve tribes finally rebel from his son. All the good service he has done for Israel is now forgotten.

4. God often punishes the children for the sins of their fathers (Ex 20:5). Solomon abandons God, and so his son after him is abandoned by most of his people. In the same way, God makes the punitive consequences of sin last for a long time and continue visibly after the sinner's death, wanting to show how terrible sin is, and perhaps also to give some hint that its punishment lasts forever. The one who sins against God not only wrongs their soul, but perhaps also wrongs their descendants more than they think.

5. When God is fulfilling his threats, he will take care that, at the same time, his promises do not fall empty to the ground. When Solomon's sin is remembered, and because of it his son loses ten tribes, David's godliness is not forgotten, nor is the promise that was made to him. For David's sake, his grandson retains a kingdom of two tribes.

CHAPTER 11

Here we continue the story of Rehoboam. We have here: 1. His attempt to regain the ten tribes he had lost, and the abandoning of that attempt in obedience to God's command (vv. 1–4); his successful attempts to keep the two tribes that remained (vv. 5–12). 2. The turning of the priests and Levites to him (vv. 13–17) and an account of his wives and children (vv. 18–23).

Verses 1–12

In the previous chapter we read about how the ten tribes deserted the house of David. They had formerly moved away from that family (2Sa 20:1–2), and now they totally rejected it, not considering how much it would weaken their common interests. But in this way the *kingdom*, as well as the *house*, of David must be corrected.

1. Finally, Rehoboam boldly raises an army with the intention of defeating the rebels (v. 1). Judah and Benjamin were ready to help him as best they could to regain what was rightfully his. Judah was his own tribe, and they had acknowledged him some years before the others did; Benjamin was the tribe in which Jerusalem, or the greatest part of it, stood.

2. But as someone who was conscientious, when God forbade him from pursuing this plan, he obeyed him and abandoned it, either because he had a reverence for divine

authority or because he knew he would not succeed if he went against God's command. He and his army *obeyed the words of the Lord* (v. 4), and although it looked weak and would mean they would be shamed by their neighbors, nevertheless, because it was God's will, they laid down their arms.

3. Rehoboam wisely fortified his own country. Now, his older and experienced counselors were listened to, and they advised him to submit to the will of God about what was lost and to see that he kept what he had. It was probably on their advice that:

- He fortified his frontiers and many of the principal towns of his kingdom.
- He provided them with a good store of food and arms (vv. 11–12). He did not sit down sullenly and say that he would do nothing for the public security if he could not fight; instead he wisely provided against an attack. Those who are prevented from being conquerors may still be builders.

Verses 13–23

Notice here:

1. Rehoboam was strengthened by the priests and Levites and all the devout and godly Israelites.

1.1. Jeroboam set up such a form of worship as made them withdraw from his altar, and he would not allow them to go to Jerusalem to worship at the altar there. So he totally *cast them off from executing the priest's office* (v. 14). He was very willing to make room for contemptible people whom he *ordained priests for the high places* (v. 15). Compare 1Ki 12:31.

1.2. They then *left their suburbs and possessions*, their pasturelands and property (v. 14). They were driven out of all their cities except those in Judah and Benjamin. But why did they leave their possessions?

1.2.1. Because they saw that they could do no good among their neighbors, in whom the old tendency to idolatry had been revived now that Jeroboam had set up his calves.

1.2.2. Because they themselves would be continually tempted.

1.2.3. Because they had reason to expect persecution from Jeroboam and his sons.

1.3. They *came to Judah and Jerusalem* (v. 14) and "presented themselves to him" (v. 13, margin), to Rehoboam.

1.3.1. It was a mercy that when Jeroboam rejected them, there were those living so close who would make them welcome.

1.3.2. Their coming was evidence that they loved their work better than the support that was due them, in that they *left their suburbs* (their pasturelands) because they were restrained from serving God there. They threw themselves on God's providence and the kindness of their relatives. It is better to live on gifts, or die in a prison, with a good conscience, than be rolling in wealth and pleasure with a corrupt conscience.

1.3.3. It was wise and praiseworthy of Rehoboam and his people to make the priests and Levites welcome. Conscientious refugees will bring a blessing with them to the countries that receive them, just as they leave a curse behind them with those that have expelled them.

1.4. When the priests and Levites came to Jerusalem, all the godly and devout Israelites of every tribe followed them.

1.5. They *strengthened the kingdom of Judah* (v. 17) by their godliness and prayers. See Zec 12:5. They made

Rehoboam and his people *strong three years*. This is how long the people *walked in the way of David and Solomon* (v. 17). But when they abandoned that way, the best friends they had could no longer help and strengthen them.

2. Rehoboam was weakened by indulging in pleasure. He *desired many wives*, as his father did (v. 23). However:

2.1. In *this* he was wiser than his father: he does not appear to have married foreign wives. The wives mentioned here were daughters of Israel, from the family of David.

2.2. In *this* he was more fortunate than his father: he had many sons and daughters, whereas we do not read of more than one son of his father. Several of Rehoboam's sons are named here (vv. 19–20) as notable and active men whom he thought it wise to *disperse throughout the countries of Judah and Benjamin* (v. 23). He could be confident that they would preserve the public peace, and he could trust them with fortified cities, which might stand him in good stead in case of invasion.

CHAPTER 12

This chapter gives us a more detailed account of the reign of Rehoboam than we had in Kings, and it is a very sad account. 1. Rehoboam and his people did evil in the sight of the Lord (v. 1). God then handed them over into the hands of Shishak king of Egypt, who oppressed them greatly (vv. 2–4). God sent a prophet to them to explain the judgment to them and call them to repentance (v. 5). They then humbled themselves (v. 6). When they repented, God turned from his anger (vv. 7, 12) but still left them under his displeasure (vv. 8–11). 2. Here is the general character of Rehoboam and his reign, with its conclusion (vv. 13–16).

Verses 1–12

Israel was disgraced and weakened by being divided into two kingdoms, but because the kingdom of Judah had both the temple and the royal city, its people might have done well if they had continued to be faithful to their duty.

1. Rehoboam and his people left God (v. 1). For three happy years he walked in the way of David and Solomon (11:17), but it ended, and he became lax in his worship of God. As long as he thought his throne was unstable, he kept close to his duty, so that he might have God as his friend, but when his position as king was firm, he thought he no longer needed his religious faith—he was safe without it.

2. God quickly brought troubles on them to lead them to repentance before their hearts became hard. It was in the fourth year of Rehoboam's reign that they began to become corrupt, and in the fifth year the king of Egypt came up against them with a vast army, took *the fenced cities of Judah, and came against Jerusalem* (vv. 2–4). The fact that this disaster came on them so soon after they began to abandon the worship of God showed clearly that it was from the Lord, because they had sinned against him. They had little reason to expect the attack, because they had had friendly relations with Egypt in the previous reign.

3. So that they would rightly understand the meaning of this providence, God explains the discipline by word (v. 5). When the leaders of Judah all met in Jerusalem at a council of war, God sent the prophet Shemaiah to them, the same one who had brought them an order from God not to fight against the ten tribes (11:2). He told them

clearly that the reason why Shishak prevailed against them was that they had abandoned God.

4. When the rebukes of both word and punishment were connected, the king and leaders humbled themselves before God for their sin, and patiently accepted its punishment, saying, *The Lord is righteous* (v. 6).

5. Upon their profession of repentance, God saved them from destruction, but he still left them under some remaining anxiety about judgment, to prevent their further rebellion.

5.1. Now that Shishak's army had gained control of all the fortified cities, what could be expected of such a vast and victorious army but that the whole country, including even Jerusalem itself, would shortly be theirs? But when God says, *Here shall the proud waves be stayed* (halt) (Job 38:11), the most threatening force strangely dwindles and becomes powerless. When the destroying angel came to Jerusalem, he was forbidden to destroy it: *My wrath shall not be poured out upon Jerusalem* (vv. 7, 12). The God of mercy is ready to take the first opportunity to be merciful.

5.2. He gave them some measure of deliverance, not complete, but partial. They partially reformed their ways, and for "a little while" (v. 7. margin), but they soon relapsed, and just as their reformation was, so was their deliverance. But it is said (v. 12), *In Judah things went well:*

5.2.1. With respect to godliness. "In Judah there were good things" (v. 12, margin), good ministers, good people, good families.

5.2.2. With respect to prosperity. In Judah things went badly when all the fortified cities were captured (v. 4), but when they repented, their affairs changed, and things went well.

5.3. But God left them to suffer severely at the hands of Shishak, as regards both their liberty and their wealth:

5.3.1. Their liberty (v. 8): *They shall be his servants; that they may know my service, and the service of the kingdoms of the countries.* They perhaps complained about the strictness of their religion. "Let them better themselves if they can; let the neighboring leaders rule over them for a while." The more God's service is compared with other services, the more reasonable and easy God's service will appear. Are the laws of temperance thought to be hard? The effects of intemperance are much harder. The service of virtue is perfect liberty, but the service of sinful desires is perfect slavery.

5.3.2. Their wealth. The king of Egypt plundered both the temple and the royal palace, the treasuries of both of which Solomon had left very full. He *took them away;* in fact, he *took all* he could lay his hands on (v. 9). This was why he came.

Verses 13–16

The story of Rehoboam's reign concludes here. Two things are especially significant:

1. That he was finally well established in his kingdom (v. 13). He *strengthened himself in Jerusalem* (v. 13), and he reigned there seventeen years. He had his royal seat in the Holy City, which made his ungodliness less tolerable—near the temple, but far from God. Frequent skirmishes took place between his subjects and Jeroboam's, such as amounted to *continual wars* (v. 15), but he held his own and did not so grossly *forsake the law of God* as he had done (v. 1) in his fourth year.

2. That he was never rightly established in his religious faith (v. 14). He did not serve the Lord because he did not seek the Lord. He did not pray, as Solomon did, for

wisdom and grace. If we prayed better, we would be better in every way. He did evil because he was never determined to do what is good.

CHAPTER 13

Here is a much more detailed account of the reign of Abijah, the son of Rehoboam, than there was in 1 Kings. Here we find him more brave and successful in war than his father was. He reigned only three years, and was famous mainly for a glorious victory he won over the forces of Jeroboam (vv. 1–2). Here we have: 1. Both armies brought onto the field (v. 3); the appeal Abijah made before the battle, setting out the justice of his cause (vv. 4–12). 2. The distress caused to Judah by the tactics of Jeroboam (vv. 13–14); the victory they nevertheless gained, by the power of God (vv. 15–20); the conclusion of Abijah's reign (vv. 21–22).

Verses 1–12

Abijah's mother was earlier called *Maachah*, the daughter of Absalom (11:20); here she is called *Michaiah*, the daughter of Uriel. She was probably a granddaughter of Absalom, by his daughter Tamar (2Sa 14:27), and her immediate father was probably this Uriel.

1. God gave Abijah permission to engage with Jeroboam, and was on his side in the conflict. Probably Jeroboam was now the aggressor, and what Abijah did was for his own necessary defense. Perhaps Jeroboam claimed the crown of Judah. It was brave of Abijah to take up arms against these defiant claims, and God stood by him. Abijah is allowed to rebuke them.

2. Jeroboam's army was double the number of Abijah's army (v. 3), for he had ten tribes, while Abijah had only two. The smaller number proved victorious, however.

3. Before Abijah fought them, he reasoned with them to stop fighting the house of David. It is good to try to use reason before we use force. We must never turn to violence until all other forms of persuasion have been tried in vain. War must be the last resort. Fair reasoning may do a great deal of good and prevent a great deal of trouble. With his army Abijah had reached the heart of their country, for he made this speech in the hill country of Ephraim. Abijah undertakes to prove two things:

3.1. That he has divine right on his side: "You know that *God gave the kingdom to David and his sons for ever*" (v. 5) by a covenant of salt, a lasting covenant, a covenant made by sacrifice, which was always salted, according to Bishop Patrick. All Israel had acknowledged that David was a king of God's choice, and that God had passed on the crown by inheritance to his family. In the first place, therefore, Jeroboam's taking the crown of Israel was not justifiable. His attempt to disturb the peace and possession of the king of Judah, however, was not in any way excusable. Abijah shows:

3.1.1. That there was a great deal of dishonesty when Jeroboam first set himself up: he *rebelled against his lord* (v. 6), who had advanced him (1Ki 11:28); he corruptly took advantage of Rehoboam's weakness. Those who supported him are here called *vain men*, worthless scoundrels (see Jdg 11:3).

3.1.2. That there was a great deal of ungodliness in Jeroboam's present attempt, for in fighting against the house of David, he fought *against the kingdom of the Lord* (v. 8).

3.2. That he has God on his side. He emphasized this point, that the religion of Jeroboam and his army was false and idolatrous, but that he and his people, the men of Judah, had the pure worship of the true and living God among them. It appears from the description of Abijah's character in 1Ki 15:3 that he himself was not truly committed to his religious faith, and yet he founded his hope of success in this war chiefly on the religion of his kingdom. Whatever he was otherwise, it seems he was no idolater. Whatever corruptions there were in the kingdom of Judah, the state of religion among them was better than in the kingdom of Israel, with which they were now fighting. It was the cause of his kingdom that he was pleading, and though he was not himself as good as he should have been, he still hoped that, for the sake of the good people and good things that were in Judah, God would now come and show that he was on their side. "We *keep his charge* (vv. 10–11). We observe his requirements. We do not worship sacred stones; we have no priests except those he has ordained, no ceremonies of worship except what he has prescribed. He is our commander, and so we may be sure that he is with us, because we are with him (v. 12). And in the day of battle we will be *remembered before the Lord our God* and *saved from our enemies.*" He concludes with a fair warning to his enemies. *Fight not against the God of your fathers* (v. 12).

Verses 13–22

Jeroboam decided not to pay any attention to Abijah's speech, and so he heard it, but he was not really listening to it. He came to fight, not to argue. The longest sword, he thought, would decide the matter, not the better cause.

1. Jeroboam, who trusted in his politics, was beaten. He was so far from engaging in fair reasoning that he did not want to fight a fair battle. Terms of negotiation were probably agreed on, but Jeroboam corruptly took advantage of the situation and, while he was negotiating, *laid his ambushment* (ambush) *behind Judah* (v. 13), against all recognized customs of professional soldiers.

2. Abijah and his people, who trusted in their God, came off as conquerors, despite the disproportionate weakness in their numbers.

2.1. They were exposed to great difficulties and put into a state of great shock, for *the battle was before and behind,* they were being attacked at both front and rear (v. 14). A good cause may be involved in difficulties and distress for a time.

2.2. In this distress, when danger was on every side, which way should they look for rescue except upwards? It is an unspeakable comfort that no enemy, no plan or ambush, can cut off our communication with heaven. Our channel there is always open.

2.2.1. *They cried unto the Lord* (v. 14).

2.2.2. They *relied on the God of their fathers* and committed themselves to him (v. 18). The prayer of faith is effective prayer, and this is the means by which we overcome the world, *even our faith* (1Jn 5:4).

2.2.3. The *priests sounded the trumpets* (v. 14) to put life into their faith.

2.2.4. They shouted in confidence of victory: "The day is our own, for God is with us." They added the shout of faith to the cry of prayer and so became more than conquerors (Ro 8:37).

2.3. They therefore gained a complete victory: *As the men of Judah shouted* for joy in God's salvation, *God smote* (struck) *Jeroboam* (v. 15) and his army with such terror that they fled as quickly as possible. Their conquerors were not merciful, but the battle was the Lord's. He wanted to rebuke the idolatry of Israel and recognize the house of David.

2.4. The result of this was that although the children of Israel were not brought back to the house of David, they were subdued on that occasion (v. 18). Many towns were taken, especially Bethel, and they remained in the possession of the kings of Judah (v. 19).

3. Both the conquered and the conqueror died not long after:

3.1. Jeroboam never recovered from this defeat, although he survived for two or three years. He could not gain his *strength again* (v. 20).

3.2. Abijah became powerful after his victory. But soon after his triumphs, death conquered the conqueror.

CHAPTER 14

In this and the two following chapters we have the history of the reign of Asa, a good and long reign. In this chapter we have: 1. His godliness (vv. 1–5) and his wisdom (vv. 6–8). 2. His success, particularly in the glorious victory he obtained over a great army of Ethiopians (Cushites) that came out against him (vv. 9–15).

Verses 1–8

Here is:

1. Asa's general character (v. 2): he did *that which was good and right in the eyes of the Lord his God.*

1.1. He aimed at pleasing God. He did his best to present himself to God as one approved by him (2Ti 2:15).

1.2. He knew that God was always looking on him, and that helped him very much in keeping to what was good and right.

2. A blessed work of reformation which Asa put into effect as soon as he came to the throne.

2.1. He removed and abolished idolatry. Since Solomon allowed idolatry at the end of his reign, nothing had been done to suppress it. Foreign gods were worshiped, and they had their altars, sacred stones, and Asherah poles, and although the temple service was kept by the priests (13:10), it was neglected by many of the people. As soon as Asa had power in his hands, he made it his business to destroy all those idolatrous altars and sacred stones (vv. 3, 5). He hoped that by destroying the idols, he would reform the idolaters, so that they themselves would not be destroyed.

2.2. He revived and established the pure worship of God, and since the priests played their part in serving at God's altars, he made the people play theirs (v. 4): *He commanded Judah to seek the Lord God of their fathers,* and not the gods of the nations, and *to do the law and the commandments.* In doing this, *the kingdom was quiet before him* (v. 5).

3. The tranquility of Asa's kingdom, after constant fear of war during the previous two reigns: *In his days the land was quiet ten years* (v. 1). There was no war with the kingdom of Israel. Abijah's victory laid the foundation for Asa's peace, which was the reward of his godliness and reformation. Although Abijah had little religious faith himself, he was instrumental in preparing the way for one who had much.

4. The advantage Asa took of that tranquility: *The land had rest, for the Lord had given him rest* (v. 6).

4.1. Asa takes notice of the rest the people have received. He regards it as the gift of God and as the reward of the reformation he has begun: *Because we have sought the Lord our God, he has given us rest* (v. 7). We find by experience that it is good to *seek the Lord*; it gives us rest.

4.2. He discusses with his people, by their representatives, how to make good use of the peace they enjoy and finishes by saying:

4.2.1. That they must not be lazy, but busy. In the years when he had no war he said, "Let us build; let us still be active." When the *churches had rest*, they were *built up* (Ac 9:31). When the sword is sheathed, it is good to take up the trowel and work.

4.2.2. That they must not feel secure, but prepare for wars. In times of peace we must get ready for trouble.

4.2.2.1. He fortified his main towns with *walls, towers, gates, and bars* (v. 7). He speaks as if he expected that trouble would arise, and then it would be too late to fortify, and they would wish they had done it. *So they built and prospered* (v. 7).

4.2.2.2. He had a good army ready to bring onto the field (v. 8). Judah and Benjamin were mustered individually, and Benjamin had almost as many soldiers as Judah. These two tribes were armed in different ways, both offensively and defensively. The soldiers of Judah guarded themselves with large shields, the soldiers of Benjamin with small shields (1Ki 10:16–17). The soldiers of Judah fought with spears; the soldiers of Benjamin drew bows, to reach the enemy at a distance.

Verses 9–15

Here is:

1. The peace of Asa's kingdom disturbed by a formidable army of *Ethiopians* (Cushites) who invaded it (vv. 9–10).

2. The appeal Asa made to God on occasion of the threatening cloud which now hung over his head (v. 11). He who sought God in the day of prosperity could cry out with holy boldness to God in the day of trouble, and call him *his God*. His prayer is short, but contains much:

2.1. He gives to God the glory of his infinite power and sovereignty: *It is nothing with thee to help* and save by many or few (1Sa 14:6). God works in his own strength, not in the strength of the instruments. "We do not say, Lord, take our part, for we have a good army for you to use; but take our part, for without you we have no power."

2.2. He lays hold of their covenant relationship, in which God was theirs. *O Lord, our God!*

2.3. He pleads on the basis of their dependence on God. Though well prepared for war, he did not trust in his preparations, but said, "Lord, *we rest on thee, and in thy name we go against this multitude* (v. 11). We have authority from you. We are aiming only at your glory and are trusting in your strength."

2.4. He involves God in their cause: "*Let not man* (literally, "mortal man") *prevail against thee* (v. 11). The enemy is mortal. Make it clear what an unequal match they are for the immortal God."

3. The glorious victory God gave Asa over his enemies:

3.1. God defeated the enemy and confounded their forces (v. 12): *The Lord smote the Ethiopians*, he struck down the Cushites with terror, so that they fled but did not know why or where.

3.2. Asa and his soldiers took advantage of the victory God gave them against the enemy. They destroyed them, took the plunder of their camp, and destroyed all the villages that were in league with them, to which they had fled for shelter (v. 14). They then took away vast numbers of cattle from enemy country (v. 15).

CHAPTER 15

Asa and his army were now returning in triumph from the battle, loaded with plunder and trophies of victory. He knew that the work of reformation which he had begun in his kingdom had not been completed; his enemies abroad were subdued, but there were more dangerous enemies at home—idols in Judah and Benjamin. Here we have: 1. The message which God sent to him, by a prophet, to encourage him in the work of reformation (vv. 1–7). 2. The strength which this message put into that cause, and their proceeding to undertake it. Idols were removed (v. 8); the plunder was dedicated to God (vv. 9–11); a covenant was made with God, and a law was enforced to punish idolaters (vv. 12–15); the court was reformed (v. 16). Dedicated things were brought into the house of God (v. 18).

Verses 1–7

Here a prophet was sent to Asa and his army when they returned triumphantly from the battle with the Cushites, not to congratulate them on their success but to encourage them to do their duty. This is the proper business of God's ministers. The *Spirit of God came* on the prophet (v. 1), both to instruct him what he should say and to enable him to say it clearly and boldly.

1. He told them plainly on what terms they stood with God. Let them not think that because they had obtained this victory, all was theirs forever. If they do well, things will go well with them, but not otherwise.

• *The Lord is with you while you are with him* (v. 2).
• *If you seek him, he will be found of you* (v. 2).
• If you abandon him and his service, he is not bound to you, and he will certainly leave you.

2. He set before them the consequences of abandoning God and his service, that the only way to have their trouble removed would be by repenting and returning to God. When Israel abandoned their duty, they were overrun by a flood of atheism, ungodliness, irreligion, and every kind of wrong (v. 3). They were continually troubled by wars, both at home and abroad (vv. 5–6). But when their troubles made them turn to God, they found that they did not seek him in vain (v. 4). But the question is, to what time does this refer?

2.1. Some think it looks as far back as the days of the judges. These were sad times, when they were frequently oppressed by one enemy or another and severely troubled by Moabites, Midianites, Ammonites, and other nations. When they turned to God in their confusion and repented, prayed, and reformed their ways, he raised up deliverers for them.

2.2. Others think it describes the state of the ten tribes—who were now properly called *Israel*—in the days of Asa. In those times there was no peace (v. 5). Because of its war with Judah, Israel had frequent disturbances; the recent insurrection of Baasha had similar effects. The people of Israel provoked God with all their sin, and then he *vexed them with all adversity*, troubled them with every kind of distress (v. 6). *When they turned to God* (v. 4), however, he answered their prayer.

2.3. Others think that the whole passage may refer to the future: in later times *Israel will be without the true God and a teaching priest* (v. 3), and they will be destroyed by one judgment after another until they *return to God* and *seek him*. See Hos 3:4.

3. He used this as the basis for his encouragement to them to pursue vigorously the work of reformation (v. 7): *Be strong, for your work shall be rewarded.*

Verses 8–19

1. We are here told about the good effects the previous sermon had on Asa:

1.1. He became bolder for God than he had been. He now took courage. He realized how vital it was that there should be further reformation, and he had a great assurance of God's presence with him to undertake it. Now he was bold enough to destroy all the detestable idols. He also *renewed the altar of the Lord* (v. 8).

1.2. He extended his influence further than before (v. 9). He called a general assembly, and brought *strangers*, people from the ten tribes who had settled among them. Their coming was a great encouragement to him. They came because *they saw that the Lord his God was with him.* The invitation he gave them to the general assembly was a great encouragement to them. This meeting was held in the third month, probably at the Feast of Pentecost, which was in that month.

1.3. He and his people offered sacrifices to God, as his share of the plunder they had gained (v. 11). These sacrifices were intended as a form of thanksgiving for the favors they had received and as a prayer for further favors. Prayers and praises are now our spiritual sacrifices (1Pe 2:5). *He brought into the house of God all the dedicated things* (v. 18). It is honorable to give back to God the things that are his.

1.4. *They entered into covenant with God* (v. 12). They repented that they had broken their commitments to him and resolved to do better in the future. It is right that those who are repenting—being converted—should renew their covenants. Notice:

1.4.1. What this covenant was. Its substance was the same as that of the one they had been obliged to keep before. But to renew it would help increase their sense of obligation, strengthen them against temptations, and be a testimony to the justice and goodness of God's command that they keep it. And by all joining together in this covenant, they strengthened one another. They committed themselves to do two things:

1.4.1.1. Diligently seek God themselves, seek his commands and his favor. What is religious faith but seeking God, inquiring after him, and turning to him on every occasion?

1.4.1.2. Oblige others to seek him as far as they could (v. 13). They agreed that *whosoever would not seek the Lord God of Israel*—that is, obstinate idolaters or stubborn atheists—would be put to death.

1.4.2. How they made this covenant:

1.4.2.1. Very gladly, and with every possible expression of joy: *They swore* (took an oath) *unto the Lord* (v. 14). They did this loudly; they all rejoiced about the oath (vv. 14–15). All honorable Israelites were pleased with their own commitment to God, and they were all pleased with one another's. They rejoiced in it as a promising way of preventing them from turning away from God and as a good sign of God's presence with them. It is an honor and happiness to be committed to God.

1.4.2.2. Very sincerely and zealously, and with great determination: *They swore to God with all their hearts,* and *sought him with their whole desire* (v. 15). If God has the heart, we have the joy.

2. We are told what the effects were of their sacred covenanting with God:

2.1. God acted with favor toward them: *He* was *found of them, and gave them rest round about* (v. 15), so that there was no war for a long time after (v. 19), though there was constant bickering between Judah and Israel on their border (1Ki 15:16).

2.2. Generally, they did well for him. They carried on the reformation to such an extent that Maacah, the queen mother, was deposed for idolatry and her Asherah pole was destroyed (v. 16). Asa knew he must honor God more than he honored his grandmother. He dared not leave an idol in a room in his palace while he was destroying idols in the cities of his kingdom. We may suppose that Maacah was convinced of her sin, and so she was not put to death. But because she had been an idolater, Asa thought fit to deprive her of the dignity and authority she had. But the reformation was not complete; the high places were not all taken away, even though many of them were (vv. 3, 5). There may be defects in some particular duties even when our heart is generally committed to God. Sincerity is less than sinless perfection.

CHAPTER 16

This chapter concludes the history of the reign of Asa. Here is: 1. A foolish treaty with Ben-Hadad king of Aram (Syria) (vv. 1–6). 2. The rebuke for it which God sent to him through a prophet (vv. 7–9); Asa's anger at the prophet for his faithfulness (v. 10); the sickness, death, and burial of Asa (vv. 11–14).

Verses 1–6

We had this passage before (1Ki 15:17–24), and in the events related here Asa made several mistakes.

1. He did not do right in making a treaty with Ben-Hadad king of Aram (v. 3). If he had relied more on his covenant, and his father's covenant, with God, he would not have boasted so much of his treaty, and his father's, with the royal family of Aram.

2. If he had had due regard to the honor of Israel in general, he would have found some other way of deflecting Baasha than by calling in a foreign force, and inviting into the country a common enemy of Israel and Judah, who in the course of time might cause trouble for Judah too.

3. It was undoubtedly sinful of Ben-Hadad to break his treaty with Baasha without any provocation, merely through the influence of a bribe, and if that was a sin for him, then it was certainly a sin for Asa to prompt him to do it, especially to employ him to do it.

4. To take silver and gold from the house of the Lord for this purpose only made his sin even worse (v. 2).

5. It is good for Asa that he did not have to answer for all Ben-Hadad's bloodshed and plundering in the cities of Israel. Perhaps Asa had not intended that the Arameans (*Syrians*) would take matters that far. Be that as it may, the project succeeded. Ben-Hadad well and truly diverted Baasha's attention and made him stop building Ramah and go to defend his own country in the north, which gave Asa the opportunity not only to demolish Baasha's fortifications but also to seize the materials and put them to his own use.

Verses 7–14

Here is:

1. A clear and faithful rebuke given to Asa by a prophet of the Lord because Asa made this treaty with Ben-Hadad. The one who brought the rebuke was Hanani the seer, the father of Jehu, another prophet, whom we read of in 1Ki

16:1; 2Ch 19:2. What the prophet here accuses him of as his greatest fault is his *relying on the king of Syria and not on the Lord his God* (v. 7). He clearly tells the king that he has acted foolishly in this (v. 9). It is foolish to lean on a *broken reed* (Isa 36:6) when we can depend on the Rock of ages (Isa 26:4). To convince Asa how foolish he is, the prophet shows him:

1.1. That he acted against his experience (v. 8). Asa of all people had no reason to distrust God. He had found God to be a very present and powerful helper (Ps 46:1). "What!" said the prophet. *"Were not the Ethiopians and the Lubims a huge host,* were not the Cushites and Libyans a mighty army (v. 8), enough to swallow up a kingdom? And yet, *because thou didst rely on the Lord, he delivered them into thy hand* (v. 8). And wasn't he also sufficient to help you against Baasha?" But how deceitful our hearts are! We trust in God when we have nothing else to trust in, but the moment we have other things to depend on, we tend to rely too much on them.

1.2. That he acted against his knowledge of God and his providence (v. 9). Asa could not trust God, and so he paid homage to Ben-Hadad.

1.3. That he acted against his own interests.

1.3.1. He has lost an opportunity to restrain the increasing power of the king of Aram (v. 7): his *host* (army) *has escaped out of thy hand*, which otherwise would have joined with Baasha's and fallen with it.

1.3.2. He has incurred God's displeasure, and so from then on he must expect no peace, only the constant threat of war (v. 9).

2. Asa's anger at this rebuke. Although it came from God through one who was known to be his messenger, he was still angry with the seer for telling him how foolish he was. *He was in a rage with him* (v. 10).

2.1. In his rage he committed the prophet to jail, *put him in a prison house* (v. 10) as an evildoer, or, as some read it, "into the stocks."

2.2. Having proceeded this far, *he oppressed some of the people* (v. 10), probably those who supported the prophet in his sufferings or were known to be his special friends.

3. Asa's sickness. Two years before he died *he was diseased in his feet* (v. 12), afflicted with an intensely painful gout. He had put the prophet in the stocks, and now God put him in the stocks; his punishment corresponded to his sin. His making use of physicians was his duty, but to trust them, to expect something from them which could be received only from God, was his sin and foolishness.

4. Asa's death and burial. His funeral had something extraordinarily grand about it (v. 14). They arranged a very magnificent burial for him. This funeral pomp was an expression of the great respect his people had for him, despite the failings and weaknesses of his final days. The great godliness and usefulness of good people should be remembered to their praise, even though they have had their blemishes. Let their faults be buried in their graves, while their services are remembered over their graves.

CHAPTER 17

Here begin the life and reign of Jehoshaphat, who was one of the best who wielded the scepter of Judah after David died. He was the good son of a good father; this time grace ran in the blood. In this chapter we have: 1. His accession to, and establishment on, the throne (vv. 1–2, 5); his personal godliness (vv. 3–4, 6); the measures he took to promote religious faith in his kingdom (vv. 7–9).

2. *The powerful influence he had among the neighbors (vv. 10–11); the great strength of his kingdom, both in its garrisons and in its standing forces (vv. 12–19).*

Verses 1–9

Here we read about Jehoshaphat:

1. How wise he was. As soon as he came to the crown, he *strengthened himself against Israel* (v. 1). Ahab, an active, warlike leader, had then been three years on the throne of Israel. The first thing Jehoshaphat had to do was to restrain the growing power of the king of Israel. He did this effectively and without bloodshed, and Ahab soon sought an alliance. Jehoshaphat strengthened himself not in order to act offensively against Israel or to invade it, but only to maintain his own ground, which he did by fortifying the towns on his frontiers and putting garrisons, stronger ones than there had been, in the towns of Ephraim.

2. How good he was.

2.1. He *walked in the ways of his father David* (v. 3). In the characterizations of the kings, David's ways are often made the standard, as in 1Ki 15:3, 11; 2Ki 14:3; 18:3. Jehoshaphat followed David insofar as David followed God but no further. The words here allow another reading: "He walked in the ways of David his father" (*hareshonim*), "the early ways" (v. 3), or those "ancient ways." He proposed to take as his example the early times of the royal family, those purest times, before the corruptions of later reigns came in. It is good to be cautious even in following the best people, so that we do not copy them when they sin.

2.2. He *sought not to Baalim, but sought to the Lord God of his father* (vv. 3–4).

2.3. He *walked in God's commandments*. He not only worshiped the true God but also worshiped him according to his own appointed ways, *and not after the doings* (practices) *of Israel* (v. 4).

2.4. *His heart was lifted up in the ways of the Lord* (v. 6), or "he lifted up his heart." He had a living and warm faith. He was *fervent in spirit, serving the Lord* (Ro 12:11). He went about his work cheerfully, pleasantly, and enthusiastically, like Jacob, who, after his vision of God at Bethel, "lifted up his feet" (Ge 29:1, margin).

3. How useful he was. He was not only a good man but also a good king. He not only was good himself but also did good.

3.1. He took away the teachers of lies, for this is what idols are called (Hab 2:18), the *high places* and *the groves* (v. 6). This is meant to describe those in which idols were worshiped, not those that were dedicated only to the true God.

3.2. He sent out teachers of truth. When he inquired into the state of religious faith in his kingdom, he found his people to be generally very ignorant: they *knew not that they did evil*. Jehoshaphat decided to begin his work in the right way. He did not lead them blindfold into a reformation but tried to see to it that they were well taught, knowing that that would lead to wholeness. In this good work he used:

3.2.1. His *princes* (officials). He ordered them to administer justice, and in so doing they must not only correct the people when they did wrong but also teach them how to do better; they must give the people a reason for what they were doing.

3.2.2. The *Levites* and *priests*, who went with the officials and *taught in Judah, having the book of the law with them* (vv. 8–9). They had the role of teacher (Dt 33:10).

3.3. Notice how much good may be done when Moses and Aaron work together, when officials, with their power, and priests and Levites, with their knowledge of Scripture, agree to teach the people the good knowledge of God and their duty. These itinerant judges and preachers were together instrumental in spreading a bright light throughout the towns of Judah. *They had the book of the law of the Lord with them* (v. 9) to convince the people, so that they might see that these teachers had divine authority for what they said and that they passed on to them only what they had received from the Lord (1Co 11:23).

4. How happy he was: *The Lord was with him* (v. 3); "the word of the Lord was his helper," is the Aramaic paraphrase; *the Lord established the kingdom in his hand* (v. 5). *All Judah brought him presents*, acknowledging his kindness in sending preachers among them. The more true religious faith there is among a people, the more conscientious loyalty there will be. Great riches and honor may hinder the ways of the Lord, and can be a source of pride, but they had quite the opposite effect on Jehoshaphat. His abundance was like oil on the wheels of his obedience, and the more he had of the wealth of this world, the more his heart was *lifted up in the ways of the Lord*.

Verses 10–19

Here is a further account of Jehoshaphat's great prosperity and the flourishing state of his kingdom.

1. He had good influence on the neighboring leaders and nations. Although he was perhaps not such a great soldier as David or such a great a scholar as Solomon, yet *the fear of the Lord fell so upon* his neighbors that they all had a reverence for him (v. 10). *None of them made war against him*. Many of them brought gifts to him (v. 11) to gain his friendship.

2. He had very considerable stores laid up in the cities of Judah.

3. He got the militia in good order. Five commanders, perhaps like *lord lieutenants*, are named here, with the numbers of those under their command. It is said of one of these great commanders, *Amasiah*, that *he willingly offered himself unto the Lord* (v. 16): not only to the king, to serve him in this post, but also to the Lord, to glorify him in it. It was usual in those days for great generals to offer their plunder to the Lord (1Ch 26:26). But this good man offered himself first and then his dedicated things to the Lord. The armies were probably dispersed all over the country, and each person generally lived on their own land, but they often came together to be trained, and were ready to be called up whenever occasion arose.

4. Notice that it was not Jehoshaphat's formidable army that struck terror on the neighboring nations, but the fear of God which fell on them when Jehoshaphat reformed his country and set up a preaching ministry in it (v. 10).

CHAPTER 18

We had the story of this chapter previously, just as it is related here, in the story of the reign of Ahab king of Israel (2Ki 22:41–50). Here is: 1. The alliance Jehoshaphat contracted with Ahab (v. 1); his agreement to join with Ahab in his mission to regain Ramoth Gilead from the hands of the Arameans (Syrians) (vv. 2–3). 2. Their consultation with false and true prophets before they went (vv. 4–27). 3. The success of their mission. Jehoshaphat just barely escaped (vv. 28–32), but Ahab received his fatal wound (vv. 33–34).

Verses 1–3

Here is:

1. Jehoshaphat growing greater.

2. Jehoshaphat not growing wiser, or else he would not have joined with that corrupt Israelite, Ahab, who had surrendered himself to evil. He allied himself in marriage with Ahab, that is, he married his son Jehoram to Ahab's daughter Athaliah.

2.1. This was the worst match that had ever been made by anyone of the house of David.

2.1.1. Perhaps pride made the match. His religion forbade him to marry his son to a daughter of any of the leaders of the nations around him, and because he had a great deal of riches and honor, he thought it beneath him to marry him to a commoner. She must be a king's daughter, and that meant Ahab's, he thought, hardly considering that Jezebel was her mother.

2.1.2. Some think he did it as a cunning political act, hoping that it would unite the kingdoms in his son.

2.2. This match brought Jehoshaphat:

2.2.1. Into very close association with Ahab. He paid him a visit at Samaria, and Ahab, proud of the honor which Jehoshaphat gave him, honored him with entertainment, according to the splendor of those times—with *sheep and oxen*, simple food.

2.2.2. Into a treaty with Ahab against the Arameans. Ahab persuaded him to join forces with him in a mission to recapture Ramoth Gilead, a city in the tribe of Gad, on the other side of the Jordan. Did Ahab not know that that city, and all the other towns and cities of Israel, rightfully belonged to Jehoshaphat, as heir of the house of David? The feast Ahab held for Jehoshaphat was intended only to persuade him to join the expedition.

Verses 4–27

This is almost word for word the same as 1Ki 22:41–50. Here we may think:

1. Of the great duty of acknowledging God in all our ways *and inquiring at his word*, whatever we undertake. Jehoshaphat was not willing to proceed till he had done this (v. 4).

2. Of the great danger of bad company even to good people. Here, Jehoshaphat wants to please Ahab, sits in his robes, and dares not rebuke that false prophet who corruptly abused the faithful seer. Nor does he dare oppose Ahab when he commits the true prophet to prison.

3. Of the unhappiness of those who are surrounded by people who flatter them, especially flattering prophets, who proclaim peace to them and prophesy nothing but smooth words. It was in this way that Ahab was cheated and justly brought to his destruction, for he listened to such false prophets. He preferred those who humored him rather than a good prophet who gave him fair warning of the danger he was in.

4. Of the power of Satan, by divine permission, *in the children of disobedience* (Eph 2:2). One lying spirit can make 400 lying prophets and can use them to deceive Ahab (v. 21).

5. Of the justice of God toward those who will not receive the love of the truth, but rebel against it (v. 21): he gives them up to strong delusions so that they will believe the lie (2Th 2:11).

6. Of the difficult position of faithful ministers, whose lot it has often been to be hated, persecuted, and ill treated for being true to their God and just and kind to human souls. For having a good conscience, Micaiah was struck, imprisoned, and condemned to suffer. But he could appeal to God to vindicate his right, and he could be sure that God would decide in his favor, as all those who are persecuted for their faithfulness may do (v. 27).

Verses 28–34

We have here:

1. Good Jehoshaphat showing himself in his robes, thereby endangering himself, but nevertheless rescued. We have reason to think that while Ahab claimed friendship, he was really aiming to take Jehoshaphat's life; otherwise he would never have advised him to enter into the battle with his robes on, which would surely make him an easy target for the enemy. The enemy soon saw the robes and strongly attacked the unwary king, who now, when it was too late, wished he were wearing the ordinary clothes of the lowliest soldier rather than his royal robes. But *the Lord helped him out* of his distress, *by moving the captains* (commanders) *to depart from him* (v. 31). God has every human heart in his hand, and he directs them as he pleases (Pr 21:1), to serve his purposes contrary to their own original intentions. Many are moved to action by an invisible power that neither they nor others understand.

2. Evil Ahab disguising himself, and therefore thinking himself safe, but nevertheless killed (v. 33). Jehoshaphat is safe in his robes, and Ahab is killed in his armor.

CHAPTER 19

Here is a further account of the good reign of Jehoshaphat: 1. His return in peace to Jerusalem (v. 1); the rebuke given himself for siding himself with Ahab and acting with him (vv. 2–3); the great concern he then took to reform his kingdom (v. 4). 2. The instructions he gave to his judges, both those in the country towns that held lower courts (vv. 5–7) and those in Jerusalem who sat as the supreme court of the kingdom (vv. 8–11).

Verses 1–4

Here is:

1. The great favor God showed to Jehoshaphat:

1.1. In bringing him back safely from his dangerous mission with Ahab, which could have cost him dearly (v. 1): *He returned to his house in peace.* Whenever we return in peace to our houses, we should acknowledge God's providence in preserving our going out and our coming in (Ps 121:8). He fared better than he deserved.

1.2. In sending him a rebuke for his alliance with Ahab. It is a great mercy to be told in time where we have gone wrong, so that we may repent of and put right our errors before it is too late. The prophet by whom the rebuke was sent was Jehu the son of Hanani. The father had been a distinguished prophet in the previous reign, as appeared by Asa's putting him in the stocks for his plain dealings, but the son was not afraid to rebuke another king. The prophet told him plainly that he had done wrong in joining with Ahab: *Shouldst thou love those that hate the Lord?* (v. 2). God was displeased with him for doing this: *"There is wrath upon thee from before the Lord* (v. 2). You must repent and make your peace with him, or things will go wrong for you."* He did this, and God's anger was turned away. But the prophet took notice of what was commendable, as it is proper for us to do when we give a rebuke (v. 3): *"There are good things found in thee,* and so although God is displeased with you, he does not, and will not, reject you."*

2. Jehoshaphat took the rebuke well, was not angry with the seer as his father was, but accepted it. He *dwelt at Jerusalem* (v. 4). He was concerned with his own business at home and would not expose himself to danger by making any further visits to Ahab. To make up for the visit he had made to Ahab, he made a godly tour of his own kingdom:

he personally *went out through the people* from Beersheba in the south to the hill country of Ephraim in the north, and *brought them back to the Lord God of their fathers* (v. 4), that is, he did all he could toward restoring their worship of God. His recent alliance with the idolatrous house of Ahab had had a bad influence on his own kingdom. Many were encouraged to rebel against God and follow idols when they saw even their reforming king on such intimate terms with idolaters, and so he thought himself doubly obliged to do everything he could to restore them.

Verses 5–11

Having done what he could to make his people good, Jehoshaphat here makes sure, if possible, to keep them in such a state by the influence of a settled judiciary. He had sent preachers among them to instruct them (17:7–9), but now he saw that it was also necessary to send judges among them to see that the laws were carried out and that they deterred evildoers. Here is:

1. He set up lower law courts in several cities of the kingdom (v. 5). The judges of these courts were to keep the people worshiping God, to punish offenses against the law, and to decide disputes between them. Here is the charge he gave them (v. 6): *Take heed what you do* (v. 6). And again, *"Take heed and do it* (v. 7). Mind your business; make sure you do not make any mistakes." Judges, of all people, need to be careful, because so much depends on the correctness of their verdict. *"Let the fear of the Lord be upon you* (v. 7), and that will restrain you, keep you from doing wrong, and make you committed to doing your duty." *The powers that be are ordained by God* (Ro 13:1), and for him: *"You judge not for man, but for the Lord* (v. 6). Your task is to glorify him and serve the interests of his kingdom among the human race. He is *with you in the judgment* (v. 6), to notice what you do and to call you to account if you do wrong."

2. He set up a supreme court in Jerusalem, which was turned to in all the difficult cases that came to the lesser courts. This court sat at Jerusalem, for *there were set the thrones of judgment* (Ps 122:5). There they would be under the inspection of the king himself. Notice:

2.1. The cases within the jurisdiction of this court were of two kinds:

2.1.1. Criminal cases, brought by the crown but here called *the judgment of the Lord* (v. 8), because the law of God was the law of the country. All criminals were accused of breaking some part of his law and were said to break his peace, to offend his crown and honor.

2.1.2. Controversies between different parties, called here *controversies* (disputes) (v. 8) and *causes of their brethren* (v. 10), disputes *between blood and blood* (see Dt 17:8), between the family of the person killed and that of the person who committed the homicide. In such a case, the courts of the temple or the horns of the altar were probably the places most often used as sanctuaries—for since the rebellion of the ten tribes, all the cities of refuge except Hebron belonged to the kingdom of Israel—and so the trial of homicides was reserved for the court at Jerusalem.

2.2. The judges of this court were of two kinds: some of *the Levites and priests* who were most learned in the law, noted for their great wisdom, men of proven integrity; and some of *the chief of the fathers of Israel* (v. 8), heads of Israelite families or people of age and experience.

2.3. The two chiefs, or presidents, of this court. Amariah, the high priest, was to lead in ecclesiastical cases. Zebadiah, the chief justice of the civil branch of the court, was to preside in all civil cases (v. 11).

2.4. The subordinate officers of the court. "Some of *the Levites shall be officers before you*" (v. 11). They must see to it that they acted out of good motives. They must do everything in the *fear of the Lord*, and *with a perfect upright heart*, wholeheartedly (v. 9). They must act boldly. "Act with courage, and do not fear other people; be bold and daring in fulfilling your duty. God will protect you, no matter who is against you."

CHAPTER 20

We have here: 1. The great danger and distress that Jehoshaphat and his kingdom were in from a foreign invasion (vv. 1–2); the godly path he followed to achieve security: fasting, praying, and seeking God (vv. 3–13). 2. The assurance which God, by a prophet, immediately gave them of victory (vv. 14–17); their thankful and trusting reception of that assurance (vv. 18–21). 3. The defeat which God then gave to their enemies (vv. 22–25); a sacred thanksgiving which they held for their victory and for its good results (vv. 26–30). 4. The conclusion of the reign of Jehoshaphat (vv. 31–37).

Verses 1–13

Here we see Jehoshaphat in distress. This was followed, however, by a glorious rescue that abundantly rewarded his godliness. We have here:

1. A formidable invasion of Jehoshaphat's kingdom by the Moabites and Ammonites (v. 1). Jehoshaphat was surprised when the enemy entered his country (v. 2). We are not told what quarrel they pretended to have with Jehoshaphat. They are said to come *from beyond the sea,* that is, the Dead Sea, where Sodom had stood. The neighboring nations had feared Jehoshaphat (17:10), but perhaps his alliance with Ahab had lowered him in their esteem.

2. The preparation Jehoshaphat made against the invaders. No mention is made of his gathering of his forces, but he probably did this; his main concern, however, was to gain the favor of God. He had the same mind as his father David. If we must be corrected, let us *not fall into the hands of man* but *into the hand of the Lord, for his mercies are great* (2Sa 24:14).

2.1. He feared. His awareness of his guilt made him afraid.

2.2. *He set himself to seek the Lord* (v. 3) and, in the first place, to make him his friend. 2.3. He *proclaimed a fast throughout all Judah* (v. 3). He appointed a day of national humility and prayer, so that they might join together in confessing their sins and *asking help of the Lord* (v. 4).

2.4. The people gathered readily out of all the towns of Judah in the court of the temple to join in prayer (v. 4).

2.5. Jehoshaphat himself spoke for the congregation to God. The prayer Jehoshaphat prayed is recorded. He acknowledges the sovereign power of God's providence. He gives the glory of it to God and is himself assured of its comfort (v. 6): "*Art not thou God in heaven?* Rule these nations; set bounds on their daring, defiant threats." He takes hold of their covenant relationship with God. "You who are *God in heaven* are the *God of our fathers* (v. 6) and *our God* (v. 7). Whom should we seek, whom should we trust in, to help us, except the God we have chosen and served? We hold this land as a gift from you. Do not allow us to be *cast out of thy possession* (v. 11)." He mentions the temple they built for God's name (v. 8), not as something that deserved any merit from God—they gave him what was his own, *for all that is in the heaven and*

in the earth is thine (1Ch 29:11)—but as a sign of God's favor toward them (vv. 8–9). "Lord, when it was built, it was intended to encourage our faith at such a time as this. Your name is here; we are here. Lord, help us, for the glory of your name." He professes his entire dependence on God to be rescued. Although he had a great army of well-disciplined foot soldiers, he still said, "*We have no might against this great company* (v. 12). Our only hope is that *our eyes are upon thee* (v. 12). O God! We are trusting in you; our souls are waiting for you."

Verses 14–19

Here is God's gracious answer to Jehoshaphat's prayer. *While he was yet speaking, God heard* (Isa 65:24). Before the assembly was dismissed, they had assurance given them that they would be victorious, for we never seek God in vain.

1. The spirit of prophecy came on a Levite *in the midst of the congregation* (v. 14). He was a descendant of Asaph and so was one of the singers; God honored that office. There needed to be no sign; the thing itself was to be fulfilled the very next day, and that would be enough confirmation of his prophecy.

2. He encouraged them to trust in God, although the danger was very threatening (v. 15): *Be not afraid. The battle is not yours; the battle is God's.*

3. He tells them about the enemy's movements and orders them to march toward them, with particular directions as to where they will find them. *Tomorrow,* the day after the fast, *go you down against them* (vv. 16–17).

4. He assures them that they will be not the glorious instruments, but the joyful spectators, of the complete defeat of the enemy: "You will not need even to strike a blow; the work will be done for you; only stand still and watch it" (v. 17). If Christian soldiers will only go out against their spiritual enemies, the God of peace will *tread the enemies under his feet* (La 1:15) and make his soldiers *more than conquerors* (Ro 8:37).

5. Jehoshaphat and his people received these assurances with faith, reverence, and thankfulness. They *bowed their heads.* Jehoshaphat first, and then all the people, *fell before the Lord, and worshipped* (v. 18). They lifted up their voices in praise to God (v. 19).

Verses 20–30

Here we see the prayer answered and the previous promise fulfilled in the total defeat of the enemies' forces and the triumph of Jehoshaphat's forces over them.

1. Never was an army arrayed on the battlefield as Jehoshaphat's was. He had soldiers *ready prepared for war* (17:18), but no comment is made of their military equipment, their swords, spears, shields, or bows. But Jehoshaphat took care:

1.1. That faith should be their armor. As they went out, instead of calling them to wield their weapons, he commanded them to *believe in the Lord God* and to trust in his word by the mouth of his prophets. He assured them that if they did that, they would *prosper* and *be established* (v. 20).

1.2. That praise and thanksgiving should be their vanguard (v. 21). Jehoshaphat called a council of war, and it was decided to appoint *singers to go out before the army* to praise God, with that ancient and good doxology which eternity itself will not wear out: *Praise the Lord; for his mercy endureth for ever* (v. 21). By making this unusual advance toward the battlefield, Jehoshaphat intended to express his firm reliance on the word of God.

2. Never was an army so inexplicably destroyed as that enemy. It was not by thunder, hail, or the sword of an angel, not by the force of the sword, but by ambushes that the Lord himself set against them, which Bishop Patrick thinks were the enemies themselves, whom God struck with such confusion that they fell on their own friends as if they were enemies, and *every one helped to destroy another*, so that *none escaped* (vv. 23–24). God did this *when his people began to sing and to praise* (v. 22). When they began the work of praise, God completed their rescue.

3. Never was plunder so cheerfully collected, for Jehoshaphat's army had nothing to do apart from that; the rest was done for them. The plunder *was more than they could carry away* at once, and they were *three days in gathering it* (v. 25).

4. Never was a victory celebrated with deeper and freer thanksgiving. They held a day of praise in the camp before they withdrew their forces from the battlefield. On the fourth day they assembled in a valley, where they blessed God with so much zeal and fervency that that day's activities gave a name to the place, the valley of *Berachah*, that is, "blessing" or "praise" (v. 26). But they did not think this enough, and so they came in a sacred procession, with Jehoshaphat at their head, to Jerusalem, so that the country they passed through might join them in their praises. They could then give thanks for the mercy at the place where they had obtained it by prayer, *in the house of the Lord* (vv. 27–28). Public mercies call for public acknowledgments *in the courts of the Lord's house* (Ps 116:19).

5. Never was a victory put to a better advantage than this, for:

5.1. Jehoshaphat's kingdom was made to look great and significant abroad (v. 29). It brought upon the neighboring countries a reverence for God and a careful fear of doing any wrong to his people.

5.2. Things were peaceful and quiet at home (v. 30). They were at peace among themselves; and they had peace at their borders, free from the fear of being defied by their neighbors, because God had given them rest on every side. If he gives them rest, who can disturb them?

Verses 31–37

We are now drawing toward the close of the story of Jehoshaphat's reign. This was the general character of his reign: he did what was right in the sight of the Lord (v. 32), kept close to the worship of God, and did what he could to keep his people close to it. But two sad facts are recorded about his reign:

1. The people still retained a fondness for the high places (v. 33). Those that had been set up in honor of foreign gods were taken away (17:6), but those where the true God was worshiped were less reprehensible and so were thought permissible.

2. Jehoshaphat himself still retained a fondness for the house of Ahab because he had married his son to a daughter of that family; he retained this fondness even though he had been clearly rebuked for it and had come near to suffering for it. He collaborated with that son, Ahaziah, not in war, as with his father, but in trade, to become his partner in a fleet bound for Tarshish. God spoke to him, to show him the error of his ways and to bring him to repentance:

2.1. By a prophet, who foretold the failure of his project (v. 37). And:

2.2. By a storm, which wrecked the ships in the port before they set sail, by which he was warned to break off

his alliance with Ahaziah. It seems he took the warning, for when Ahaziah afterward pressed him to work together with him again, he *would not* (1Ki 22:49).

CHAPTER 21

Jehoram, one of the most evil kings, succeeded Jehoshaphat, one of the best. In this way the people were punished for not making better use of Jehoshaphat's good government and his reformation (20:33). Here is: 1. Jehoram's advancement to the throne (vv. 1–3); the evil method he used to establish himself on it, by murdering his brothers (v. 4); the idolatry and other evils he was guilty of (vv. 5–6, 11). 2. The prophecy of Elijah against him (vv. 12–15); the judgments of God on him, in the rebellion of his subjects from him (vv. 8–10) and the success of his enemies against him (vv. 16–17); his miserable sickness and humiliating death (vv. 18–20); the preservation, nevertheless, of the house of David (v. 7).

Verses 1–11

We find here:

1. Jehoshaphat was a very anxious and indulgent father to Jehoram. He had many other sons, who are named here (v. 2), and it is said (v. 13) that they were better than Jehoram, and any of them would have been more fit for the crown than he was, but because he was the oldest (v. 3), his father gave him the kingdom. His birthright entitled him to a double share of his father's estate (Dt 21:17), but if he appeared completely unqualified for government—the purpose of which is the welfare of the people—and likely to undo all his father had done, it would perhaps have been better to set him aside and take the next son who was promising and did not show his tendency to idolatry.

2. Jehoram was a most cruel brother to his father's sons. As soon as he had established himself on the throne, he killed all his brothers with the sword, either by false accusation, under the pretext of law, or by assassination. With them he killed some of the *princes*, officials, of Israel who were faithful to them, or who were likely to avenge their death.

3. Jehoram was a most evil king, who corrupted and defiled his kingdom and destroyed the reformation that his righteous father and grandfather had carried out: he *walked in the way of the house of Ahab* (v. 6). He made high places and did his best to set up idolatry again (v. 11).

3.1. As for the inhabitants of Jerusalem, where he kept his court, he easily drew them into his spiritual adultery.

3.2. The country people seem to have been brought back to idolatry with more difficulty, but those who would not be corrupted by flattery were forced to share in his detestable idolatrous practices.

4. When he abandoned God and his worship, his subjects withdrew from their allegiance to him.

4.1. Some of the provinces abroad that were subject to him did so. The Edomites rebelled (v. 8), and although he rebuked them (v. 9), he could not subdue them (v. 10).

4.2. One of the towns of his own kingdom did so. Libnah rebelled (v. 10) and set itself up as a free state, so that it became as it had been before the conquest, when it had a king of its own (Jos 12:15).

5. God nevertheless cherished his covenant with the house of David, and so he would not destroy the royal family, even though it had corrupted itself so degenerately (v. 7).

Verses 12–20

We have here:

1. A warning from God sent to Jehoram by a letter from Elijah the prophet. By this it appears that Jehoram came to the throne and showed his character before Elijah went to heaven. We will presume that the time of his departure was at hand, so that he could not go in person to Jehoram, but that when he heard of Jehoram's great evil in murdering his brothers, he left this letter with Elisha, to be sent to him at the first opportunity. It might therefore have been either a means to reclaim Jehoram or a witness against him.

1.1. His crimes are plainly declared to him—his departure from the honorable ways of God, in which he had been educated (v. 12)—his conformity to the ways of the house of Ahab—his setting up and enforcing idolatry in his kingdom—and his murdering his brothers.

1.2. Judgment is given against him for these crimes. He is clearly told that his sin will certainly be the destruction:

1.2.1. Of his kingdom and family (v. 14). His people justly suffer because they went along with his idolatry, and his wives because they drew him into it.

1.2.2. Of his health and life. If he had learned to humble himself when he received this threatening message from Elijah, who knows but he might eventually have obtained a reprieve? But it does not appear that he took any notice of it; Elijah seemed to him *as one that mocked* (Ge 19:14).

2. The threatened judgments brought on him because he defied the warning.

2.1. Notice Jehoram stripped of all his comforts. God *stirred up the spirit of his neighbours* (v. 16) against him. They found some occasion or other to quarrel with him and invaded his country. It seems, however, that they fought only against the king's palace; they made directly for that place and *carried away all the substance* (goods) *found in it*. They also *carried away* his sons, and we find later (22:1) that they *slew* (killed) *them all*. Now all his sons were killed except one. If he had not come from the house of David, that one would not have escaped.

2.2. His disease was very severe. He was ill for two years and could gain no relief. This severe disease overtook him just after his palace had been plundered and his wives and children carried off. Perhaps his grief and mental anguish because of that disaster led to his sickness. To be sick and poor, sick and solitary, but especially to be sick and in sin, sick and deprived of grace to bear the suffering, and deprived of comfort to offset it, is very sad indeed.

2.3. He reigned only eight years and then *departed without being desired* (v. 20). To show what little affection or respect they had for him, they would not *bury him in the sepulchres of the kings* (v. 20), thinking him unworthy. They put this further disgrace on him: they *made no burning for him* (no fire in his honor), *like the burning of his fathers* (v. 19). They did not honor him with any sweet blended perfumes or precious spices.

CHAPTER 22

In the last chapter we read of the carrying away of Jehoram's sons and his wives; but here we find one of his sons and one of his wives left to be the disgrace and death of his family: 1. Ahaziah was its disgrace because he shared in the sin, and the destruction, of the house of Ahab (vv. 1–9). 2. Athaliah was its death, for she destroyed all the royal descendants and usurped the throne (vv. 10–12).

Verses 1–9

We have here an account of the reign of Ahaziah, a short reign of only one year. He was called *Jehoahaz* in 21:17; here he is called *Ahaziah*, a variant of the same name. He is here said to be *forty-two years old* when he began to reign (v. 2); it is said in 2Ki 8:26 that he was twenty-two years old. Some understand this forty-two to be the age of his mother Athaliah, for in the original it is, "he was the son of forty-two years." The history of Ahaziah's reign is briefly summed up in two verses (vv. 3–4).

1. He did evil; he *walked in the way of the house of Ahab, did evil in the sight of the Lord* like the people of that house (vv. 3–4). He worshiped the same false gods that they worshiped, the Baals and the Ashtoreths. These Baals encouraged in their worshipers all kinds of immoral and sinful practices that the God of Israel had strictly forbidden.

2. He was counseled by his mother and her relatives to do so. *She was his counsellor* (v. 3), and so were *they*, after the death of his father (v. 4). The counsel of evildoers is the destruction of many young people when they are setting out in the world. This young prince might have received better advice from the princes and the judges, the priests and the Levites, who had been famous in his grandfather's time for teaching the knowledge of God, but the house of Ahab flattered him, and *he walked after their counsel* (v. 5).

3. He was counseled by them to his destruction. It was bad enough that they exposed him to the sword of the Arameans (*Syrians*), drawing him to join with Joram king of Israel in a mission to Ramoth Gilead, where Joram was wounded, a mission that was not for his honor. But that was not all: by engaging Ahaziah in very close dealings with Joram king of Israel, they involved him in the overall downfall of the house of Ahab. He came on a visit to Joram (v. 6) just at the time that Jehu was executing the judgment of God on that idolatrous family, and so he was destroyed with them (vv. 7–9).

Verses 10–12

We have here what we had before in 2Ki 11:1–16:

1. An evil woman trying to destroy the house of David so that she might set up a throne for herself on its ruins. Athaliah cruelly destroyed all the royal descendants (v. 10), perhaps intending that, when she herself was ready to give up the crown of Judah, she would transfer it to some of her own relatives.

2. A good woman effectively preserving it from being completely annihilated. One of the late king's sons, a child of a year old, was rescued from among the dead, saved by the care of Jehoiada's wife (vv. 11–12).

CHAPTER 23

Athaliah had been a tyrant for six years; in this chapter we have her deposed and killed, and Joash, the rightful heir, enthroned. The story was related before in 2Ki 11:4–21. 1. Jehoiada prepared the people for the king: told them his intentions, armed them, and appointed them to their positions (vv. 1–10). He then revealed the king to the people, crowned him, and anointed him (v. 11). 2. He killed the usurper (vv. 12–15); he reformed the kingdom, reestablished religious faith, and restored civil government (vv. 16–21).

Verses 1–11

Imagine the bad state of affairs in Jerusalem during Athaliah's six years of usurping the throne. But now, after such a long, dark night, the new day in this revolution was all the brighter and more welcome. The continuation of David's descendants and throne was what God had sworn in his holiness (Ps 89:35), and so now the flow of government was running again in the right channel. The instrument and chief manager of the restoration is Jehoiada:

1. A man of great wisdom, who kept the young prince for many years until he was fit to appear in public. He prepared his work beforehand, and then carried it out with wonderful secrecy and speed.

2. A man of great influence. The commanders joined him (v. 1). The Levites and the heads of Israelite families came to Jerusalem when he called (v. 2). *The Levites and all Judah did as Jehoiada commanded* (v. 8).

3. A man of great faith. *The king's son shall reign*, must reign, *as the Lord hath said*.

4. A man of great religion. He gave special orders that none of the people should come into the temple of the Lord except the priests and Levites, who were holy, on penalty of death (vv. 6–7). Sacred things should never be profaned, not even to support civil rights.

5. A man of great determination. When he had begun the task, he went through with it: he *brought out the king, crowned him, and gave him the Testimony*, a copy of the covenant (v. 11).

Verses 12–21

We have here:

1. The people pleased (vv. 12–13). When the king was standing by his pillar, where it was his exclusive right to stand, *all the people of the land rejoiced to see a rod sprung out of the stem of Jesse* (Isa 11:1).

2. Athaliah killed. She ventured *into the house of the Lord* at that time, and cried, *Treason, treason!* (v. 13). But nobody supported her or took her side. Jehoiada, acting as protector while the king was still a minor, ordered her to be killed (v. 14), and the order was carried out immediately (v. 15).

3. The original contract agreed to (v. 16). In 2 Kings it is said that Jehoiada made a covenant between the *Lord*, the people, and the king (2Ki 11:17). Here it is said to be between *himself*, the people, and the king, for he as God's priest was God's representative in this transaction, or a kind of mediator, as Moses was. Let us look on ourselves and one another as *the Lord's people* (v. 16), and this will have a powerful effect on us as we fulfill all our duties to both God and people.

4. Baal destroyed (v. 17). The people would have completed only half their work if they had destroyed only the usurper of the *king's* right, and not the usurper of *God's* right — if they had protected the honor of the throne but not that of the altar. Baal's temple, its altars, and its idols must all be torn down; they must all be destroyed (Dt 13:5–6).

5. The temple worship revived (vv. 18–19). Jehoiada restored *the offices of the house of the Lord*.

- He appointed the priests to their divisions, to offer the sacrifices properly.
- He appointed assignments to singers, as David had appointed.
- The doorkeepers were put into their respective positions as David had ordered (v. 19), to take care that no one who was ceremonially unclean would be admitted into the courts of the temple.

6. The civil government reestablished (v. 20). They brought the king in state to his own palace, and set him *upon the throne of the kingdom*, to administer law and

judgment, either personally or by Jehoiada, his tutor. In this way, this good revolution was completed.

CHAPTER 24

We have here the history of the reign of Joash. We read before how wonderfully he was preserved for the throne and placed on it, and here we are told how he began in the Spirit but ended in the flesh. 1. He did well at the beginning of his time, while Jehoiada lived. In particular, he took care to put the temple into a state of good repair (vv. 1–14). 2. But he turned away from God at the end of his life, after Jehoiada's death, and his apostasy was his ruin. He set up the worship of Baals again (vv. 15–18), even though he was warned against it (v. 19); he put Zechariah the prophet to death because he rebuked him for what he had done (vv. 20–22). The judgments of God came on him for it. The Arameans invaded him (vv. 23–24). He was struck with severe diseases; his own servants plotted against him and killed him (vv. 25–27).

Verses 1–14

This is an account of Joash's good beginnings.

1. It is a fortunate thing for young people, when they are setting out in the world, to be under the direction of those who are wise, good, and faithful to them, as Joash was under the influence of Jehoiada, during whose time he *did that which was right* (v. 2). Let those who are young consider it a blessing to have those who will warn them against what is evil and encourage them to do what is good. Let them not consider it a mark of weakness to listen to such people. The person who will not take advice cannot be helped. It is especially wise for young people to take advice concerning whom they will marry.

2. People may go far in the outward performances of religion merely by the power of their education and the influence of their friends, even when they are not prompted by the living reality of grace in their hearts.

3. In the outward expressions of devotion it is possible that those who have only the form of godliness may excel those who have its power (compare 2Ti 3:5). Joash is more concerned and more zealous to repair the temple than Jehoiada himself, whom he rebukes for his negligence in that matter (v. 6). It is easier to *build* temples than to *be* temples for God.

4. The repairing of churches is a good work. When Joash found that one way of raising money did not work as he expected, he tried another. The dropping of money into a chest, through a hole in its lid, was a way that had not been used before, and perhaps its very novelty made it successful in raising money. A great deal of money was dropped in, and with a great deal of cheerfulness: they all rejoiced (v. 10).

Verses 15–27

We have here a sad account of the corruption and apostasy of Joash. God had done great things for him; he had done something for God, but now he proved ungrateful to his God. We find here:

1. The time of his apostasy. He was never sincere, he never acted from good motives, but only to please Jehoiada, who had helped him gain the crown, and because he had been protected in the temple and had risen up from the ruins of idolatry. When the wind turned, he turned with it.

1.1. His good counselor left him; he was removed from him by death. *They buried him among the kings* (v. 16), with this honorable eulogy: that *he had done good in Israel* (v. 16). Judah is called *Israel* because, the other tribes having rebelled from God, only they were true Israelites. Jehoiada finished his course with honor, but the little religious faith that Joash had was all buried in his grave, and after his death both king and kingdom degenerated miserably. How necessary it is that, as our Savior said, we *have salt in ourselves* (Mk 9:50), that we live out our religious faith from inner and real motivations that will take us through every change. Then the loss of a parent, minister, or friend will not lead us to lose our faith.

1.2. Bad counselors got close to him, wormed their way into his affections, and, instead of offering their condolences, congratulated him on the death of his old tutor as something that had freed him from discipline. They told him he must no longer be controlled by the priests, that he could do as he pleased. It was the *princes* (officials) *of Judah* who were keen on corrupting him (v. 17). His father and grandfather were corrupted by the house of *Ahab*, from whom nothing better could have been expected. But that the officials of Judah should entice their king was very sad. And he listened to them: their kind words pleased him and were more agreeable than Jehoiada's orders had been.

2. The apostasy itself: *They left the house of God, and served groves and idols*, they abandoned the temple of the Lord and worshiped Asherah poles and idols (v. 18). The officials had a request to make to the king. They wanted to set up again the Asherah poles and idols, which had been thrown down at the beginning of his reign, for they hated—so they said—to be always confined to the "dull and old-fashioned" services of the temple. And he not only allowed them to do it themselves, but even joined them.

3. What made this apostasy worse. God *sent prophets to them* (v. 19) to rebuke them. It is the work of ministers to bring people not to themselves but to God—to bring back to him those who have been unfaithful to him. But Joash and his counselors condemned all the prophets and killed one of the most distinguished, *Zechariah the son of Jehoiada* (v. 20).

3.1. The people had gathered in the courtyard of the temple, when this Zechariah, filled with the Spirit of prophecy, stood up and clearly told the people of their sin and what its consequences would be. He did not accuse any particular individuals, but reminded them of what was written in the Law. "*You transgress the commandments of the Lord* (v. 20). You know that you are doing this when you serve Asherah poles and idols. Why will you offend God in this way and wrong yourselves?"

3.2. The officials, or some of them, plotted, *and by order of the king* they stoned him to death immediately, not under pretense of the Law, accusing him as a blasphemer, traitor, or false prophet, but in a popular disturbance, *in the court of the house of the Lord*. The *person* was sacred—a priest; the *place* was sacred—the courtyard of the temple, the inner court, *between the porch and the altar*; the *message* was even more sacred. The rebuke had been just, the warning fair, both backed up by Scripture, and the delivery very gentle and tender. The Jews say there were seven sins in this: they killed a priest, a prophet, a judge; they shed innocent blood, and defiled the courtyard of the temple, the Sabbath, and the Day of Atonement—for their tradition says this happened on that day.

3.3. This Zechariah, who suffered martyrdom for his faithfulness to God and his country, was the son of Jehoiada, who had done so much good in Israel, and particularly had been as a father to Joash (v. 22).

3.4. The dying martyr prophetically invoked vengeance on his murderers: *The Lord look upon it, and require it*, call you to account (v. 22). This came not from a spirit of revenge, but from a spirit of prophecy: *He will require it* (v. 22). This precious blood was quickly accounted for in the judgments that came on this apostate king. It came to be reckoned afterward in the destruction of Jerusalem by the Babylonians (36:16). In fact, our Savior calls the persecutors of him and his Gospel responsible for the blood of this Zechariah. So loud and so long does the blood of the martyrs cry out. See Mt 23:35.

4. The judgments of God which came on Joash for his awful evil:

4.1. A small army of Arameans (*Syrians*) invaded Jerusalem, destroyed the leaders, plundered the city, and sent its plunder to Damascus (vv. 23–24).

4.2. God struck him with great diseases, physical or mental, or both.

4.3. His own officials conspired against him. They killed him in his bed *for the blood of the sons of Jehoiada* (v. 25), which seems to imply that he killed not only Zechariah but also other sons of Jehoiada for his sake.

4.4. His people would not bury him in the tombs of the kings because he had stained his honor by his evil administration.

CHAPTER 25

Amaziah's reign, recorded in this chapter, was not one of the worst, but it was far from good. Most of the passages in this chapter were more briefly related in 2Ki 14:1–22. Here we find Amaziah: 1. A just revenger for his father's death (vv. 1–4), an obedient observer of the command of God (vv. 5–10), and a cruel conqueror of the Edomites (vv. 11–13). 2. A foolish worshiper of the gods of Edom and intolerant when he is rebuked for it (vv. 14–16). 3. Rashly challenging the king of Israel, suffering because of his rashness (vv. 17–24), and lastly, ending his days dishonorably (vv. 25–28).

Verses 1–13

Here is:

1. The general character of Amaziah: *He did that which was right in the eyes of the Lord.* He worshiped the true God, kept the temple worship going, and supported religion in his kingdom; but he did not do it *with a perfect heart* (v. 2), that is, he did not do it wholeheartedly. He was not a man of serious godliness or devotion. He was not against it, but he was cool and indifferent toward it. Such is the character of too many in this Laodicean age: they do what is good, but not wholeheartedly.

2. A necessary act of justice toward the traitors who murdered his father: he put them to death (v. 3). Although they intended to avenge the death of the prophet on their king, they presumptuously took God's work out of his hands. Amaziah therefore did what was right in holding them responsible (v. 4).

3. Amaziah's mission against the Edomites:

3.1. The great preparation he made for this expedition:

3.1.1. He mustered his own forces (v. 5). He found in Judah and Benjamin 300,000 ready for military service, whereas in Jehoshaphat's time there had been four times as many. Sin weakens a people, diminishes them, discourages them, and reduces their numbers.

3.1.2. He hired auxiliary troops from the kingdom of Israel (v. 6).

3.2. The command which God sent him by a prophet to dismiss the forces of Israel (vv. 7–8). If he made sure of God's presence, the army he had of his own people would be adequate. But in particular, he must not take in *their* assistance: *For the Lord is not with the children of Ephraim, because they are not with him*, but worship the calves.

3.3. The objection which Amaziah made to this command, and the satisfactory answer which the prophet gave to that objection (v. 9). The king had paid 100 talents of silver, that is, about 3.75 tons (about 3.4 metric tons) of silver, to the Israelite warriors as advance payment. "Now," he says, "if I send them back, I will lose that: *But what shall we do for the 100 talents?*" This is an objection people often make against their duty: they are afraid of losing by it. "Don't pay any attention to that," the prophet said. "*The Lord is able to give thee much more than this*, and you may depend on it, he will make sure you do not lose by him." What does it mean to trust in God, but to be willing to risk the loss of anything for him? We can have such willingness because we are confident that the security he gives us, to assure us that we will not lose by him, is good, and that whatever we give up for his sake will be made up to us in kind or in kindness. He is just and good, and he is also solvent. The king lost 100 talents by his obedience, and we find just that sum given to his grandson Jotham as a present (27:5). The principal was then repaid with interest, 10,000 measures (cors) of wheat and as many of barley.

3.4. His obedience to the command of God, which is recorded to his honor. He *separated the army of Ephraim, to go home again* (v. 10). But they went home very angry.

3.5. His triumphs over the Edomites (vv. 11–12). He left 10,000 soldiers dead there on the battlefield; he took 10,000 more as prisoners and brutally killed them all by throwing them off some steep and craggy cliff. We are not told what caused him to act so cruelly toward them.

3.6. The trouble which the disbanded soldiers of Israel caused to the towns of Judah, either on their return or soon after (v. 13). They were so angry at being sent home that they thought if they could not share with Judah in the plunder from Edom, they would attack Judah. They plundered several towns on the borders, killing 3,000 who put up resistance. But why did God allow this to be done? He no doubt intended to use this to rebuke those towns of Judah for their idolatry, which was found mainly in those parts of the country nearest to Israel.

Verses 14–16

Here is:

1. The rebellion of Amaziah, his turning from the God of Israel to the gods of the Edomites. How outrageously foolish could he be? Ahaz worshiped the gods of those who had conquered him, and for this he had some little excuse (28:23). But for Amaziah to worship the gods of those whom he had conquered, who could not protect their own worshipers, was the greatest possible absurdity. If he had thrown the idols down from the rock and broken them to pieces instead of the prisoners, he would have shown more of the godliness as well as more of the compassion of an Israelite, but perhaps because of his barbaric cruelty he was given up to this absurd idolatry.

2. The rebuke which God sent him through a prophet for this sin. The prophet reasoned with him mildly and fairly: *Why hast thou sought* the favor of those gods *which could not deliver their own people?* (v. 15).

3. The manner of reply Amaziah gave to the one who rebuked him (v. 16). He could say nothing to excuse his own foolishness, but he lost his temper.

3.1. He taunted the prophet as interfering in things that were not his business: *Art thou made of the king's counsel, have we appointed you as an adviser to the king?*

3.2. He silenced him, forbade him to say another word to him. *He said to the seer, See not* (Isa 30:10).

3.3. He threatened him. He seems to remind him of the fate, in the last reign, of Zechariah, who was put to death for being outspoken with the king, and he tells him to take that warning.

4. The condemnation which the prophet pronounced on him for this. He had more to say to him by way of instruction and advice, but because he found him stubbornly holding to his sin, he stopped. The condition of those with whom the Holy Spirit *forbears to strive*, with whom he no longer contends by ministers and conscience (Ge 6:3), is wretched. If the rebukes of others and of the conscience are constantly snubbed and confounded, they will eventually stop. So *I gave them up to their own hearts' lusts* (Ro 1:24).

Verses 17–28

Here we have this corrupt king humbled by his neighbor and murdered by his own subjects:

1. Never was a proud king more completely humbled than Amaziah was by Jehoash king of Israel.

1.1. This part of the story, which was as fully related in 2Ki 14:8–22 as it is here, includes the foolish challenge which Amaziah sent to Jehoash (v. 17), Jehoash's proud and scornful answer to it (v. 18) and the friendly advice he gave him to sit still and know when he was well off (v. 19), Amaziah's deliberate persistence in his challenge (vv. 20–21), his defeat (v. 22), and the disaster he brought on himself and his city (vv. 23–24). It verifies two of Solomon's proverbs:

• That *a man's pride will* bring him low (Pr 29:23).
• That the one who goes out quickly to fight will probably not know what to do in the end, when his neighbor has put *him to shame* (Pr 25:8).

1.2. But there are two passages in this story that we do not have in 2 Kings.

1.2.1. That *Amaziah took advice* before he challenged the king of Israel (v. 17). But from whom? Not the prophet, but from his own advisers, who would have flattered him and told him to go up and succeed (1Ki 22:12, 15).

1.2.2. Amaziah's lack of wisdom is made to punish his lack of godliness (v. 20).

2. Never was a poor king more violently pursued by his own subjects. "From the time" that he departed from the Lord, as v. 27 may be read, the hearts of his subjects departed from him, and they began to plot against him in Jerusalem. Eventually the unrest reached such a high pitch—and he realized the roots of the plot were very deep—that he thought it right to leave his royal city and flee to Lachish. But they sent assassins to track him down, and they killed him there.

CHAPTER 26

This chapter gives us an account of the reign of Uzziah, or Azariah, as he was called in Kings (2Ki 14:21; 15:1–7). Here is: 1. His good character in general (vv. 1–5); his great prosperity in his battles, his buildings, and all the affairs of his kingdom (vv. 6–15). 2. His presumption in intruding on the priests' role, for which he was struck with leprosy, and confined by it (vv. 16–21) even to his death (vv. 22–23).

Verses 1–15

We have here an account of two things concerning Uzziah:

1. His godliness. He was not particularly distinguished or zealous in this respect, but *he did that which was right in the sight of the Lord* (v. 4). He maintained the pure worship of the true God *as his father* did, and was better than his father, inasmuch as he never worshiped idols as his father did. It is said (v. 5), he *sought God in the days of Zechariah*, who some think was the son of that Zechariah whom his grandfather Joash killed. This Zechariah was one who *had understanding in the visions of God* and had a great influence on Uzziah.

2. His prosperity:

2.1. In general, *as long as he sought the Lord* and was concerned for his religious faith, *God made him to prosper* (v. 5).

2.2. Here are several particular examples of his prosperity:

2.2.1. His success in his wars: *God helped him* (v. 7), and then he triumphed over the Philistines. He demolished the fortifications of their towns and set up his own garrisons among them (v. 6). He made the Ammonites pay him tribute (v. 8).

2.2.2. The greatness of his fame and reputation. His name was celebrated throughout all the neighboring countries (v. 8). It was a good name, the name of one known for having a good relationship with God and with good people.

2.2.3. His buildings. While he acted offensively abroad, he did not neglect the defense of his kingdom at home, but *built towers in Jerusalem* and fortified them (v. 9). Much of the wall of Jerusalem was broken down in his father's time, and so Uzziah, to prevent similar trouble from happening again in the future, fortified it and *built a tower at the corner gate* (25:23). But the best way he strengthened Jerusalem was his faithfulness to the worship of God. While he fortified the city, he did not forget the country, and he also *built towers in the desert* (v. 10), to protect the country people from invasions by plunderers (21:16).

2.2.4. His farming. He dealt much in cattle and grain. He *loved husbandry*, loved the soil (v. 10).

2.2.5. His standing armies. He had, it seems, two military establishments:

2.2.5.1. A *host of fighting men*, a well-trained army that was ready to go out to war abroad. These *went out to war by bands*, in divisions (v. 11). They brought in plunder from the neighboring countries by way of reprisal for their pillaging of Judah.

2.2.5.2. Another army for guards and garrisons, who were ready to defend the country in case of invasion (vv. 12–13). Uzziah provided himself with a great armory (v. 14), spears, bows, and slingstones, shields, helmets, and coats of armor. Swords are not mentioned, probably because every soldier had a sword of his own. *Engines* of war, machines, were invented in his time, to shoot arrows and hurl large stones onto besiegers from the towers and corner defenses (v. 15). It is terrible to think that the fights and quarrels which come from sinful desires have made it necessary for people to use their skill and expertise to invent instruments of death.

Verses 16–23

The only blemish we find on the character of King Uzziah:

1. His sin was that he intruded on the priest's role. The sin of his predecessors was that they abandoned the temple of the Lord (v. 18) and burned incense on idolatrous altars (25:14). His was that he encroached on the temple of the Lord, went into it farther than he was allowed, and attempted on his own to *burn incense upon the altar* of God.

1.1. What lay at the root of his sin was pride in his heart (v. 16): *When he was strong*—and he was wonderfully helped by the good providence of God *till he was so* (v. 15)—when he became important in wealth and power, instead of lifting up the name of God in gratitude, his *heart was lifted up to his destruction* (v. 16).

1.2. His sin was *going into the temple of the Lord to burn incense* (v. 16), probably when he himself had some special occasion to seek God's favor.

1.2.1. Perhaps he thought that the priests did not do their work so devoutly as they ought, or that he could do it better. Or:

1.2.2. He noticed that the idolatrous kings had themselves burned incense at the altars of their gods. His father had done so, as had Jeroboam (1Ki 13:1), but because he had decided to remain faithful to God's altar, he thought he would try to come as near to it as the idolatrous kings did to their altars. But it is called a *transgression against the Lord his God* (v. 16).

1.3. He was opposed in this attempt by the chief priest and other priests who were with him and helped him (vv. 17–18). They were ready to burn incense for the king, according to the duty of their place, but when he offered to do it himself, they plainly let him know that he was interfering in things that were forbidden to him, and that he did so at his peril. "*It appertaineth not to thee, O Uzziah*, but *to the priests*. It is not right for you, Uzziah, to burn incense. That is for the priests (v. 18). It is their birthright, as sons of Aaron, and they are consecrated to the service." Aaron and his descendants were appointed by the Law to burn incense (Ex 30:7). See also Dt 33:10; 1Ch 23:13. David had blessed the people, and Solomon and Jehoshaphat had prayed with them and preached to them. Uzziah could have done these things, and he would have been commended for it, but burning incense was a service to be performed only by the priests. Even though Korah and his accomplices were Levites, they paid dearly for offering to burn incense, because it was the work of priests only (Nu 16:35). We, in faith, are to bring the incense of our prayers through the name of our Lord Jesus, the great High Priest of our profession (Heb 3:1), or else we cannot expect them to be accepted by God (Rev 8:3).

1.4. He lost his temper with the priests who rebuked him (v. 19): *Uzziah was wroth*, he became angry and would not part with the censer in his hand.

2. His punishment was an incurable leprosy, which broke out on his forehead while he was arguing with the priests. [Ed. note: The KJV translates the Hebrew word *ṣara'at* as "leprosy," although this word refers to various skin conditions, not necessarily leprosy.]

2.1. When the leprosy appeared, they were bold enough to throw him out of the temple. In fact, he himself *hasted to go out*, he himself was eager to leave, *because the Lord had smitten* (afflicted) *him* (v. 20) with a disease which was a particular sign of his anger, and which he knew would separate him from ordinary dealings with people, and much more from the altar of God.

2.2. It remained a lasting punishment of his sin, for he continued to be a *leper to the day of his death* (v. 21),

2.3. It was a punishment that corresponded to the sin, as an image does to a face in a mirror.

2.3.1. Pride lay at the root of his sin, and God humbled him and dishonored him.

2.3.2. He intruded on the role of the priests in contempt of them, and God struck him with a disease which made him a special subject of inspection and sentence by the priests, for the *judgment of the leprosy* belonged to them (Dt 24:8).

2.3.3. He went into the temple of God, into which only the priests were allowed to go, and he was therefore thrown out of the very courts of the temple, which the lowliest of his subjects who was ceremonially clean could freely enter.

CHAPTER 27

Here is a very short account of the reign of Jotham, a godly and prosperous king, of whom we would wish to have known more. The account we do have, however, describes: 1. The date and length of his reign (vv. 1, 8). 2. Its general good character (vv. 2, 6). 3. Its prosperity (vv. 3–5). 4. Its scope and end (vv. 7, 9).

Verses 1–9

There is not much more related here concerning Jotham than we had before (2Ki 15:32–38).

1. He reigned well. He *did that which was right in the sight of the Lord* (v. 2). He *prepared his ways before the Lord his God* (v. 6). He walked steadfastly in the path of his God-given duty, not like some of those who had gone before him, who, although they had some good in them, lost their trustworthiness by their unfaithfulness and lack of integrity. Two things are observed here about his character:

- What was wrong in his father he put right in himself (v. 2).
- What was wrong in his people he was not successful in putting right: *The people did yet corruptly*, they continued their corrupt practices (v. 2).

2. He prospered.

2.1. He built. He began with *the gate of the house of the Lord* (v. 3), which he repaired beautifully and raised. He then *fortified the wall of Ophel, and built cities in the mountains of Judah* (vv. 3–4).

2.2. He conquered. He conquered the Ammonites, who had invaded Judah in Jehoshaphat's time (20:1). He *became mighty* (v. 6) in wealth, power, and influence with the neighboring nations, who courted his friendship and feared his anger. He gained this by *preparing his ways before the Lord his God.*

3. He finished his course too soon, but he finished it with honor. He died when he was only forty-one years of age (v. 8), but *his wars and his ways*, his wars abroad and his ways at home, were so glorious that they were recorded in the book of the kings of Israel as well as that of the kings of Judah (v. 7).

CHAPTER 28

This chapter is the history of the bad reign of Ahaz the son of Jotham. We have here: 1. His great evil (vv. 1–4). 2.

The trouble he brought by it (vv. 5–8); the rebuke which God sent by a prophet to the army of Israel for crushing their brothers and sisters of Judah, and their obedience following that rebuke (vv. 9–15). 3. The many disasters that followed for Ahaz and his people (vv. 16–21); the continuance of his idolatry despite this (vv. 22–25), and the end of his life (vv. 26–27).

Verses 1–5

Surely no one ever had a better opportunity to do good than Ahaz, but in these few verses we see him:

1. Wretchedly corrupted and defiled. He had had a good education, but *he did not that which was right in the sight of the Lord* (v. 1); in fact, he did a great deal of wrong, wrong to God, to his own soul, and to his people. He walked in the way of the rebellious Israelites and the Canaanites. He made cast idols and worshiped them. He abandoned the temple of the Lord and sacrificed and burned incense on the hilltops, as if they would bring him nearer heaven, and under every spreading tree, as if they would represent the protection and influence of heaven in their shade and overhanging cover. To complete his evil, as one completely devoid of all natural affection as well as religious faith, he *burnt his children in the fire to Moloch* (v. 3).

2. Wretchedly plundered.

2.1. The Arameans (*Syrians*) abused him and gloated over him. They defeated him on the battlefield and took away a great many of his people into captivity.

2.2. Even though the king of Israel was an idolater too, he was made a scourge to Ahaz and *smote him with a great slaughter*, inflicted heavy casualties on him (v. 5).

Verses 6–15

We have here:

1. Treacherous Judah under the rebukes of God's providence. Never since they were a kingdom had there been such bloodshed among them—and by Israelites, too. It is just of God to cause the people whom we follow in sin, or those who are our partners in sin, to make trouble for us. A war broke out between Judah and Israel, in which Judah was defeated.

1.1. There were heavy casualties on the battlefield. Vast numbers were killed (v. 6), and some of those were of high rank, for example, the king's son. The kingdom of Israel was not strong at this time, but it was strong enough to bring such a great destruction on Judah.

1.2. There was a great captivity of *women and children* (v. 8).

2. Even victorious Israel under the rebuke of God's word. Here is:

2.1. The message which God sent the Israelites by a prophet, who went out to meet them. He went not to praise their bravery but to tell them, in God's name, of their faults.

2.1.1. He told them how they had won this victory which they were so proud of. *Not for your righteousness*, you are to know, but *for their wickedness* (Dt 9:5) *they are broken off*; and therefore, *be not you highminded* (arrogant), *but fear lest God also spare not you* (Ro 11:20–21).

2.1.2. He accused them of abusing the power God had given them over their brothers and sisters. The conquerors are here rebuked:

2.1.2.1. For the cruelty of their killings on the battlefield. They had indeed *shed the blood of war in war* (compare 1Ki 2:5), and so we may think it to have been lawful, but they did it from the bad motive of hatred toward their brothers and sisters and in a bad manner—with a barbaric fury: *The wrath of man worketh not the righteousness of God* (Jas 1:20).

2.1.2.2. For the arrogance with which they dealt with their prisoners. "*You now purpose* (intend) *to keep them under* (v. 10), to use them or sell them as slaves, even though they are your brothers and sisters and freeborn Israelites."

2.1.3. He reminded them of their own sins, by which they too were liable to suffer the wrath of God: *Are there not with you, even with you, sins against the Lord your God?* (v. 10). This is intended as a restraint on:

2.1.3.1. Their triumph in their success. "You are sinners, and sinners, of all people, ought not to be proud, for if judgment begins like this with those who have *the house of God* among them, what will be the conclusion of those who worship the calves?"

2.1.3.2. Their harshness toward their brothers and sisters. Sinners, of all people, ought not to be cruel. "You have enough sins to answer for already, and so you need not add this to the others."

2.1.4. He commanded them to release the prisoners and send them home again quickly (v. 11): "because you sinned, *the fierce wrath of God is upon you*, and there is no other way of escaping it than by showing mercy."

2.2. The decision of the leaders not to detain the prisoners. They *stood up against those that came from the war*, flushed with victory, and told them plainly that they must not bring their captives into Samaria (vv. 12–13). The armed men accepted the decision and left their captives and the plunder to the disposal of the officials (v. 14). In doing this they showed more truly heroic bravery than they had shown in taking them. It is very honorable for people to submit to the authority of reason and religion above their own interests. The officials generously sent home the poor captives, after providing well for them (v. 15).

Verses 16–27

Here is:

1. The great distress which the kingdom of Ahaz was reduced to because of his sin. In general:

1.1. *The Lord brought Judah low* (v. 19). They had just been high in wealth and power; but God found a way of humbling them and making them as contemptible as previously they had been formidable.

1.2. Ahaz made Judah naked. Just as his sin corrupted them, so also it exposed them. It made them naked by putting them to shame, for it left them exposed to contempt, just as we are when we are naked. It made them naked by putting them in danger, for it exposed them to attacks, like someone who is unarmed (Ex 32:25). Sin strips people. The Edomites, in particular, wanting to gain revenge for Amaziah's cruel treatment of them (25:12), attacked Judah and took away many prisoners (v. 17). The Philistines also raided them, took and kept possession of several towns and villages that lay near them (v. 18), and so they too gained revenge, for Uzziah had invaded their land (26:6).

2. The addition which Ahaz made both to the national distress and to the national guilt.

2.1. He added to the distress by ingratiating himself with foreign kings, in the hope that they would relieve him. When the Edomites and Philistines were troubling him, *he sent to the kings of Assyria to help him* (v. 16). He pillaged the house of God and the royal palace and squeezed money out of the princes to hire these foreign

forces into his service (v. 21). But what did Ahaz gain from the king of Assyria? Why, he *came to him*, but he *distressed him*, and *strengthened him not* (v. 20), *helped him not* (v. 21). The forces of the Assyrian were imposed on his country, and so made it poor and weak.

2.2. He added to the guilt by worshiping foreign gods, in the hope that they would help him.

2.2.1. He abused the temple of God, for he *cut in pieces the vessels*, its utensils (v. 24), so that the priests could not perform the temple services, because they lacked the proper utensils. And finally, he *shut up the doors*, so that the people could not attend the temple (v. 24).

2.2.2. He defied the altar of God, for he *made himself altars in every corner of Jerusalem* (v. 24), so that, as the prophet Hosea says (Hos 12:11), they were like *heaps in the furrows* (piles of stones) *of the fields*. And he set up high places in the towns of Judah for the people to burn incense to the idols of their choice, as if to deliberately *provoke the God of his fathers* (v. 25).

2.2.3. He rejected God himself, for he *sacrificed to the gods of Damascus* (v. 23), because he feared them, thinking that they had helped his enemies, and that if he could bring them onto his side, they would help him. And what came of it? The gods of Aram (*Syria*) befriended Ahaz no more than the kings of Assyria did; they were *the ruin* (downfall) *of him and of all Israel* (v. 23). This sin defiled the people so that the reformation of the next reign could not be effective in healing them of their tendency toward idolatry, and they retained that root of bitterness (Dt 29:18; Heb 12:15) until the Exile in Babylon uprooted it.

3. The conclusion of the reign of Ahaz. It seems that he died without having repented, and so he died a shameful death, for he was not buried *in the sepulchres* (tombs) *of the kings* (v. 27).

CHAPTER 29

We are here entering on a pleasant scene, the good and glorious reign of Hezekiah, in which we will find more of God and religious faith than perhaps in any of the good reigns we have so far read about, for he was a very zealous, devout, and good man; there was no one like him. In this chapter we have an account of the work of reformation which he set about enthusiastically immediately after he became king. Here is: 1. His encouragement to the priests and Levites, when he gave them possession of the house of God again (vv. 1–11). 2. The care and effort which the Levites took to purify the temple, and to put things in order there (vv. 12–19). 3. A revival of God's ordinances—which had been neglected—in which atonement was made for the sins of the previous reign, and the ordained pattern of temple worship was reestablished, to the great satisfaction of king and people (vv. 20–36).

Verses 1–11

Here is:

1. Hezekiah coming to the throne when he is *twenty-five years old* (v. 1). Joash, who came to the crown after two bad reigns, was only seven years old; Josiah, who came after two bad reigns, was only eight; in each case the young age of the new king meant a delay in the work of reformation. But Hezekiah had come to maturity, and so he applied himself immediately to that task.

2. His general character. He *did that which was right like David* (v. 2). Of several of his predecessors it had been said that they did what was right, *but not like David*,

not with David's integrity and zeal. But here was one who had as genuine a devotion to the ark and the Law of God as David had.

3. His prompt application to the great work of restoring religious faith. The first thing he did was to *open the doors of the house of the Lord* (v. 3). He found Judah in low spirits and exposed, but he did not start by reviving the civil interests of his kingdom. No; he started by restoring religious faith. Those who begin with God are beginning at the right end of their work.

4. His speech to the priests and Levites. Hezekiah's encouragement to the Levites is full of feeling:

4.1. He placed before them the low and deplorable state to which religious faith had come among them (vv. 6–7): *Our fathers have trespassed*, they have been unfaithful. He complained:

4.1.1. That the house of God had been abandoned: *They have forsaken God, and turned their backs upon his habitation* (dwelling place) (v. 6).

4.1.2. That the instituted worship of God there had fallen into neglect. The lamps had not been lit, and incense was not burned. There are still similar acts of negligence, and they are no less reprehensible: when the word is not opened and read as it should be—for the *lighting of the lamps* was a type for the opening and reading of Scripture—and when prayers and praises are not appropriately offered—for the *burning of incense* was a type for the offering of prayers and praises (v. 7).

4.2. He showed the sad effects of the neglect and decay of religious faith among them (vv. 8–9).

4.3. He declared his own complete purpose and determination to revive religious faith and to make it his business to further it (v. 10): "*It is in my heart to make a covenant with the Lord God of Israel*. I intend to worship only him, and in the way in which he has appointed." Not only would he himself make this covenant; he would ensure that his people joined to accept its demands and promises.

4.4. He engaged and encouraged the Levites and priests to do their duty on this occasion. He began with this (v. 5), and he ended with this (v. 11). He called them *Levites* to remind them of their obligation to God, and he called them his *sons* to remind them of their relationship with himself, to remind them that he expected that, *as a son with the father, they should serve with him* in the work of reforming the land.

4.4.1. He told them what their duty was, to consecrate *themselves* first—by repenting of what they had neglected and renewing their covenants with God—and then to *sanctify the house of God* (v. 5). As his servants, they should make it clean and establish it for the purposes for which it had originally been set up.

4.4.2. He encouraged them to do it (v. 11). "Be not now deceived," is the reading of the margin. Those who, by neglecting God's service, mock him and think they are cheating him are only cheating themselves. God expected them to work. They were not chosen to laze around, to enjoy the honor of their positions, just to let others do the work. No; they were to serve him and minister to him.

Verses 12–19

Here is busy work, good work, and necessary work, to purify the temple of the Lord:

1. The people who did this work were the priests and Levites, who should have kept the temple pure. Several of the Levites are named here, two from each of the three main families, Kohath, Gershon, and Merari (v. 12), and

two from each of the three families of singers, Asaph, Heman, and Jeduthun (vv. 13–14); these particular Levites were chosen because they were more zealous and active than the rest. When God has a work to do, he will raise up leaders to organize it. And it is not always those who are first in position or rank who are most qualified for service or who are most eager to do it.

2. The work was *cleansing the house of God*, purifying the temple of the Lord (v. 15):

2.1. From the ordinary dirt it had picked up while it was closed: dust, cobwebs, and rust on the utensils.

2.2. From the idols and idolatrous altars that had been set up in it, which although they may have been neat and tidy, were a greater defilement than if the temple had become the main sewer of the city. The priests were not mentioned as leaders in this work, but only they dared go *into the inner part of the house* (sanctuary of the temple) *to cleanse it* (v. 16); and so they did, with perhaps the high priest entering the Most Holy Place, to purify that. Whatever filth the priests brought into the court the Levites carried out to the Kidron Valley.

3. The speed with which they did this work was remarkable. They began on the first day of the first month, a happy beginning of the New Year, and one that promised to be a good year. This is how every year should begin: with a reformation of what has been wrong, and the purifying, by true repentance, of all the defilements that have been picked up during the previous year. They cleared and cleansed the temple in eight days, and in eight days more the courtyards of the temple (v. 17).

4. The report they gave of it to Hezekiah was very pleasing (vv. 18–19). They knew the good king had set his heart on God's altar and that he longed to attend it, and so they made a point of telling him that it was now ready for use; the utensils for the altar had been scoured and brightened up. They gathered together those utensils which Ahaz had sinfully taken away; they consecrated them and put them in their place *before the altar*.

Verses 20–36

An assembly was called to meet the king in the temple the very next day (v. 20). All the good people in Jerusalem were no doubt very glad when it was said, *Let us go up to the house of the Lord* (Ps 122:1). As soon as Hezekiah heard that the temple was ready for him, he lost no time, and was ready for it. He rose early to go up to the house of the Lord, earlier that day than other days, to show that his heart was set on his work there.

1. The people must look back and make atonement for the sins of the previous reign. They thought it not enough to mourn and leave those sins; they also brought a sin offering. Even our repentance and reformation will not obtain forgiveness except in and through Christ, who was made *sin* (that is, a sin offering) for us (2Co 5:21). The only way for those who repent to find peace is through his blood. Notice:

1.1. The sin offering was *for the kingdom, for the sanctuary*, and *for Judah* (v. 21), that is, to make atonement for the sins of the official leaders, the priests, and the people, for all their lives had been corrupt. The Law of Moses appointed sacrifices to make atonement for the sins of the whole community (Lev 4:13–14; Nu 15:24–25), so that the national judgments which their national sins deserved might be averted. For this purpose we must now look to Christ as the great sacrifice of atonement, while also looking to him for the forgiveness and salvation of particular individuals.

1.2. The Law appointed only one goat as a sin offering, as on the Day of Atonement (Lev 16:15) and on such extraordinary occasions as this (Nu 15:24). But here they offered seven (v. 21), because the sins of the community had been great and had gone on for a long time. Seven is a perfect number. Our great sin offering is only one, but that one *perfects* forever *those that are sanctified* (Heb 10:14).

1.3. The king and the *congregation*—that is, the representatives of the community—*laid their hands on the heads of the goats* that were presented as the *sin offering* (v. 23). They did this to acknowledge that they were guilty before God and to show that they wanted the guilt of the sinner to be transferred onto the sacrifice. By faith we lay our hands on the Lord Jesus and so *receive the atonement* (Ro 5:11).

1.4. Burnt offerings were offered with the sin offerings, *seven bullocks*, *seven rams*, and *seven lambs* (v. 21). The intention of the burnt offerings was to give glory to the God of Israel, whom they recognized as the only true God, which it was right to do at the same time as they brought the sin offering to make atonement for their offenses. The blood of the burnt offerings, as well as of the sin offering, was *sprinkled upon the altar* (v. 22), to make reconciliation *for all Israel* (v. 24), and not only for Judah. Christ is a sacrifice of atonement not only for the sins of Israel, but for those *of the whole world* (1Jn 2:1–2).

1.5. While the offerings were burning on the altar, the *Levites* sang *the song of the Lord* (v. 27), the Psalms composed by David and Asaph (v. 30), accompanied by the musical instruments which God had by his prophets commanded them to use (v. 25), and which had been neglected for a long time. Even sorrow for sin must not put us out of step with praising God.

1.6. The king and all the congregation showed their agreement to and approval of everything that had been done, by *bowing their heads* and *worshipping*. This is noted in vv. 28–30.

2. They must also look forward. The temple worship was to be reestablished, so that it might be continually maintained, and Hezekiah called them to do this (v. 31). "Now that you have *consecrated yourselves to the Lord*—now that you have dedicated yourselves to him, have made atonement and a covenant by sacrifice, and are solemnly reconciled and committed to him—now *come near, and bring sacrifices*." Having first dedicated ourselves to the Lord, we must then bring the sacrifices of prayer, praise, and gifts to his house. In this work, it was found:

2.1. That the people were free. Being called to do this by the king, they brought their offerings, although not in such abundance as in the glorious days of Solomon, but according to what they had, and as much as one could expect considering their poverty and their former godlessness.

2.1.1. Some were so generous as to bring burnt offerings, which were wholly consumed to the honor of God, and of which the one bringing the offering had no part.

2.1.2. Others brought peace offerings (fellowship offerings) and thank offerings, the fat of which was burned on the altar, and the flesh divided between the priests and those bringing the offering (v. 35).

2.2. That *the priests were few*, too few for the service (v. 34).

2.3. That the Levites were eager to do the work. They had been *more upright in heart to sanctify themselves* (more conscientious in consecrating themselves) *than the priests* (v. 34). They were better disposed to the work and

better prepared and qualified for it. They were to be commended for this, and as a reward, they had the honor of being employed in what was the priests' work: they *helped them to flay* (skin) *the offerings*. This was not according to the Law (Lev 1:5–6), but the irregularity was disregarded in cases of necessity, and so encouragement was given to the faithful and zealous Levites, and the careless priests were justly disgraced.

2.4. That everyone was pleased. The king and all the people rejoiced at this good turn of events and the new face of religious faith the kingdom had now put on (v. 36). Two things in this matter pleased them:

2.4.1. That it happened quickly: *The thing was done suddenly*, in a short time, with a great deal of ease, and without any opposition.

2.4.2. That the hand of God was clearly in it: *God had prepared the people* (v. 34) by the hidden influences of his grace, so that many of those who were devoted to the idolatrous altars in the last reign were now adoring God's altar just as much.

CHAPTER 30

In this chapter we have an account of the Passover which Hezekiah celebrated in the first year of his reign. 1. The discussion about it, and the decision he and his people reached to observe it (vv. 2–5); the invitation he sent to Judah and Israel to come and celebrate it (vv. 6–12). 2. Its joyful celebration (vv. 13–27). This meant that the reformation which had been set in motion in the previous chapter was now greatly advanced and established.

Verses 1–12

Here is:

1. A Passover decided on. "How are we to revive it?" Hezekiah said. "The regular time has passed for this year; the priests are not prepared" (v. 3). Probably many of them wanted to delay it, but Hezekiah found a provision in the Law of Moses that particular individuals who were unclean in the first month could keep the Passover on the fourteenth day of the second month (Nu 9:11), and he did not doubt that that could be extended to the whole community. They therefore decided to celebrate the Passover *in the second month* (v. 2).

2. A proclamation issued to give notice of this Passover and to call the people to come to it.

2.1. An invitation was sent to the ten tribes that had rebelled, to encourage them to come and attend this ceremony. Letters were written to Ephraim and Manasseh to invite them to Jerusalem to celebrate this Passover (v. 1), with the godly intention of bringing them back to the Lord God of Israel. "Let them have whom they want as their king," Hezekiah said, "as long as they take God as their God." We have here:

2.1.1. The contents of the letters sent on this occasion, in which Hezekiah shows great concern both for the honor of God and for the welfare of the neighboring kingdom of Israel. "*Yield yourselves unto the Lord*. Before you can come into fellowship with him, you must come into covenant with him." "Give the hand to the Lord; submit to him," is the meaning; "agree to take him as your God." "The doors of the sanctuary are now open, and you are free to enter. The temple worship is now revived, and you are welcome to join in it. You are the people of Israel. The God you are called to return to is the God of Abraham, Isaac, and Jacob, a God in covenant with your first fathers. Your forebears who abandoned him and sinned against him have been made an object of horror; their apostasy and idolatry have been their downfall, as you see (v. 7). You yourselves are only a *remnant* who have narrowly *escaped out of the hands of the kings of Assyria* (v. 6). If you return to God in your duty, he will return to you in his mercy." He begins with this (v. 6) and ends with it too (v. 9). Could anything be expressed with greater feeling? Could there be a better cause, or could it have been pleaded in better terms?

2.1.2. The reception which Hezekiah's messengers and message met with. It does not appear that Hoshea, who was now king of Israel, forbade his subjects to accept the invitation. They could go to Jerusalem to worship if they wanted to, for although he did evil, he was *not like the kings of Israel that were before him* (2Ki 17:2). Yet most of his subjects showed contempt at the call and turned a deaf ear to it. The messengers went from town to town, but the people *laughed them to scorn, and mocked them* (v. 10). The destruction of the kingdom of the ten tribes was now close. It was only a few years after this that the king of Assyria laid siege to Samaria, which ended in the exile of those tribes. But there were a few who accepted the invitation. Even in the worst of times, God has kept his remnant. He had a few here. Some from Asher, Manasseh, and Zebulun—there is no mention of any from Ephraim, although some of that tribe are mentioned in v. 18—*humbled themselves, and came to Jerusalem* (v. 11).

2.2. A command was given to the men of Judah to attend this ceremony, and they universally obeyed it (v. 12). They did it with one heart and were of one mind in it, and *the hand of God gave* them that *one heart*.

Verses 13–20

The time appointed for the Passover arrived, and a great assembly came together on that occasion (v. 13). We have here:

1. The good preparations the people made for the Passover: *They took away* all *the* idolatrous *altars* that were found, not only in the temple, but also *in Jerusalem* (v. 14). The best preparation we can make for the Gospel Passover is to get rid of our sins, any forms of spiritual idolatry.

2. The celebration of the Passover. The people were so eager and zealous to do this that the priests and Levites were embarrassed; the ordinary people were more ready to bring sacrifices than they, the priests and Levites, were to offer them. This made them consecrate themselves (v. 15).

3. The irregularities the people were guilty of in this ceremony.

3.1. The *Levites killed the passover*, which should have been done only by the priests (v. 17).

3.2. Many who were not purified according to the strictness of the Law were allowed to eat the Passover (v. 18). The Dutch jurist and theologian Hugo Grotius observes from this that ritual institutions must give way not only to public necessity but also to public benefits.

4. Hezekiah's prayer to God for the forgiveness of this irregularity. His prayer was:

4.1. Short, but to the point: *The good Lord pardon every one* (v. 18) in the assembly who has *prepared his heart* (v. 19) for those services, even though the ceremonial preparations are lacking. For *this is* the *one thing needful*, that we *seek God* (Ps 14:2; Lk 10:42), his favor, his honor, and that we set our hearts to do it. Yet even where the heart is settled and sincere, there may still be many defects and weaknesses. These defects need pardoning and healing

grace, for omissions in duty are sins as well as omissions of duty. The way to obtain pardon for our deficiencies in duty is to seek it from God in prayer.

4.2. Successful: *The Lord hearkened to Hezekiah*, and in answer to his prayer, he *healed the people* (v. 20); not only did he not count their sin against them, but he also graciously accepted their services. Healing shows not only forgiveness (Isa 6:10; Ps 103:3) but also comfort and peace (Isa 57:18; Mal 4:2).

Verses 21–27

After the Passover came the Feast of Unleavened Bread, which continued for seven days.

1. Many sacrifices were offered to God in peace offerings (fellowship offerings), by which they both acknowledged and sought the favor of God.

2. Many good prayers were offered to God with the fellowship offerings (v. 22). They *made confession to the Lord God of their fathers*, in which the intention and meaning of the fellowship offerings were directed and explained.

3. There was a great deal of good preaching. The Levites, whose task it was (Dt 33:10), *taught the people the good knowledge of the Lord* (v. 22). Hezekiah himself did not preach, but he *spoke comfortably to the Levites* (v. 22) who did; he attended their preaching, commended their diligence, and assured them with encouraging words of his protection and support.

4. They sang psalms every day (v. 21): *The Levites and priests praised the Lord day by day.*

5. Having celebrated the seven days of the feast in this way, they were so encouraged by the worship that they *kept other seven days* (v. 23). The case was extraordinary: they had been without the ordinance for a long time; they had become guilty because of its neglect; a very great assembly was now together, and they all had a godly attitude. They did not know when they might have another such opportunity, and so they could not now find it in their hearts to separate until they had doubled the time. How unlike those who contemptuously sniffed at God's service and said, *What a weariness is it!* (Mal 1:13), or those who asked, *When will the sabbath be gone?* (Am 8:5).

6. They did all this *with gladness* (v. 23). They all rejoiced, especially *the strangers* (v. 25). *So there was great joy in Jerusalem* (v. 26). There had never been anything like this since the dedication of the temple in Solomon's time.

7. The assembly was finally dismissed with a blessing (v. 27):

7.1. The priests declared it, for it was part of their work to *bless the people* (Nu 6:22–23), in which they were both the people's mouthpiece to God by prayer and God's mouthpiece to the people by promise, for their blessing included both. What a comfort it is to a congregation to be sent home crowned in this way!

7.2. God said *Amen* to it, for the prayer that goes *unto heaven* (v. 27) will come down again to this earth in showers of blessings.

CHAPTER 31

We have here a further account of the good reformation which Hezekiah was instrumental in carrying out, and the good progress he made. 1. All the remnants of idolatry were destroyed and abolished (v. 1). The priests and Levites were set to work again, each one in his place (v. 2). Care was taken that they should be maintained properly. The royal gifts to the clergy, and for the support of the temple service, were duly paid (v. 3). Orders were given for the collecting of the people's quota (v. 4). The people brought in their dues in abundance (vv. 5–10). 2. Commissioners were appointed for the proper distribution of what was brought in (vv. 11–19). The chapter concludes with a general commendation of Hezekiah's sincerity in all his undertakings (vv. 20–21).

Verses 1–10

We have here an account of what was done after the Passover. What had been lacking in preparatory ceremony before the Passover, the people made up for in a very good way afterward.

1. They vigorously applied themselves to destroying all remnants of idolatry (v. 1).

1.1. This was done immediately after the Passover. If our hearts have burned within us at a religious service (Lk 24:32), that spirit of burning will consume the remnants of corruption. Perhaps, because Hoshea the king of Israel did not forbid it, the people's zeal took them to destroy idolatry in many parts of his kingdom; at least those who came out of Ephraim and Manasseh to keep the Passover—as many did (30:18)—destroyed all their own sacred stones and Asherah poles, and many more as well.

1.2. They destroyed everything. Although these objects were very old, worth a lot of money, very beautiful, and very well patronized, they must nevertheless all be destroyed.

2. Hezekiah revived and restored the divisions of the priests and Levites, which David had appointed and which had not been regularly followed recently (v. 2). And all this took place in the *gates* or courts of *the tents of the Lord* (v. 2), his dwelling place. The temple is here called a tent because the temple privileges are movable and this temple was soon to be removed.

3. He used part of the revenue of the crown to maintain and support the altar. It was a generous and godly act, in which he considered both God's honor and his people's needs, as a faithful servant to God and a kind father to the people.

4. He issued a declaration, first to the inhabitants of Jerusalem (v. 4) but later to the *cities of Judah* as well (v. 6), that they must conscientiously pay their dues to the priests and Levites, according to the Law.

5. The people then very readily brought in their tithes. What the priests needed, for themselves and their families, they used, and the surplus was *laid in heaps* (v. 6). The heaps increased throughout the harvest, as the fruits of the earth were gathered in, for God was to have what was due to him out of everything. When the harvest had ended, they finished their heaps (v. 7). Hezekiah *questioned the priests and Levites* about them, why they did not use what was paid in, but had stored it up (v. 9), to which it was replied that they had made use of all they needed to maintain themselves and their families and to store up for winter, and that this was what was left over (v. 10). They did not store these heaps out of greed, but to show what plentiful provision God had made for them. Notice the response which the king and his officials gave to it (v. 8). They gave thanks to God for his good providence, which gave them something to bring, and for his good grace, which gave them hearts to bring it with.

Verses 11–21

We have here:

1. Two particular examples of the care of Hezekiah concerning church matters. After the tithes and other holy gifts had been brought in, he made sure:

1.1. That they were carefully stored, not left in exposed heaps and thus liable to be wasted and stolen. He ordered storehouses to be prepared in some courts of the temple (v. 11), and the offerings were taken into them.

1.2. That they were faithfully spent on the uses they were intended for. Church monies are not to be stored up any longer than necessary. Distribution was made out of the offerings of the Lord:

1.2.1. To the priests in the towns (v. 15), who stayed at home while their brothers went to Jerusalem, and who did good in the towns by *teaching the good knowledge of the Lord* (30:22).

1.2.2. To those who *entered into the house of the Lord,* all the *males from three years old and upwards,* for it seems that the boys of even that young age were allowed to come into the temple with their parents, and shared with them in this distribution (v. 16).

1.2.3. To the Levites from twenty years old and upwards (v. 17).

1.2.4. To the wives and children of the priests and Levites. They were comfortably maintained out of those offerings (v. 18). In maintaining ministers, consideration must be given to their families.

2. A description of Hezekiah's services to support religious faith (vv. 20–21).

- His godly zeal reached to every part of his kingdom: *Thus he did throughout all Judah.*

- He sincerely wanted to please God, and he proved himself to God in all he did: he *wrought that which was good before the Lord his God.*

CHAPTER 32

This chapter concludes the history of the reign of Hezekiah. 1. The attack which Sennacherib mounted on him, and the care Hezekiah took to fortify himself, his city, and the minds of his people against that enemy (vv. 1–8). 2. The insulting and blasphemous letters and messages which Sennacherib sent him (vv. 9–19); the real answer God gave to Sennacherib's blasphemies, and to Hezekiah's prayers, in the total defeat of the Assyrian army, to the shame of Sennacherib and the honor of Hezekiah (vv. 20–23). 3. Hezekiah's illness and his recovery from it, and his sin and his recovery from that, with the honors that came to him alive and dead (vv. 24–33).

Verses 1–8

We read here of:

1. The frightening plans Sennacherib had for Hezekiah's kingdom. Sennacherib was now, as Nebuchadnezzar was later, the terror and curse of that part of the world. He aimed to set up a despotic monarchy for himself on the ruins of all his neighbors. His predecessor Shalmaneser had just begun to rule over the kingdom of Israel and had taken captive the ten tribes. Sennacherib thought that he would similarly gain Judah for himself. It is significant that at just about this time, Rome—a city which later came to reign more than any other had done *over the kings of the earth*—was built by Romulus. Sennacherib invaded Judah immediately after the reestablishment of religious faith there: *After these things he entered into Judah* (v. 1). Perhaps Sennacherib intended to rebuke Hezekiah for destroying that idolatry to which he himself was devoted. One would have expected now to hear of nothing but perfect peace, and that no one would dare interfere with a people so qualified by divine favor, but

the next news we hear is of the threat of a destructive army entering the country and ready to devastate everything. The little opposition which Sennacherib met with on entering Judah led him to think that everything was his own. He expected to *win all the fenced* (fortified) *cities* (v. 1) and intended to make war on Jerusalem (v. 2). See 2Ki 18:7, 13.

2. The preparation which Hezekiah made against this threatening storm: *He took counsel with his princes,* he consulted with his officials (v. 3). With their advice he provided:

2.1. That the country would give Sennacherib a cold reception, for he made sure the enemy would not find any water there. All hands were immediately set to work to *stop up the fountains* (block all the springs) and *the brook that ran through the midst of the land* (v. 4). This is similar to the policy commonly practiced nowadays of destroying forage in the face of an invading army.

2.2. That the city would give him a warm reception. For this purpose he repaired the wall, built towers, made many "weapons" (v. 5, margin) and shields (v. 5), and appointed military officers (v. 6).

3. The encouragement which he gave to his people to depend on God at this time of distress. He gathered them together in the square at the city gate and *spoke comfortably to them* (v. 6). He put life into his people, especially his officers, by what he said, as he spoke to their hearts and encouraged them.

3.1. He tried to keep down their fears: *"Be strong and courageous* (v. 7); do not think of surrendering the city or giving yourselves up, but decide to hold the city to the last person." The prophet had encouraged them in this way from God (Isa 10:24): *Be not afraid of the Assyrians;* and now here the king was encouraging them.

3.2. He tried to keep up their faith in order to silence and suppress their fears. "Sennacherib has *a multitude with him* (v. 7), but there are *more with us than with him* (v. 7), for we have God with us, and how many does he count as? The only thing our enemy has is human strength to trust in, but *with us is the Lord* (v. 8), whose power is irresistible, our God, whose promise cannot be broken, a God in covenant with us, *to help us, and to fight our battles* (v. 8)." God will lift us above any powerful fear of people. He that *feareth the fury of the oppressor forgetteth the Lord his Maker* (Isa 51:12–13). Hezekiah probably said more about the presence of God with them and his power to help them. Let those who serve Jesus Christ as his soldiers rest in this way on his word, and boldly say, *Since God is for us, who can be against us?* (Ro 8:31).

Verses 9–23

We had the story of the fury and blasphemy of Sennacherib, Hezekiah's prayer, and the rescue of Jerusalem by the destruction of the Assyrian army more fully in 2Ki 18:1–19:37. These verses show us:

1. The ungodliness and hatred of the church's enemies. Sennacherib has his hands full in besieging Lachish (v. 9), but he hears that Hezekiah is fortifying Jerusalem and encouraging his people to hold out, and so before he comes in person to besiege it, he sends messengers and writes letters to frighten Hezekiah and his people into surrendering the city. He does not deal with Hezekiah as a man of honor, but uses underhand ways to terrify the ordinary people and to try to persuade them to desert him. He represents Hezekiah as one who wants to betray them *to famine and thirst* (v. 11), as one who has exposed them already to divine displeasure by taking away the high places and altars (v. 12). This proud blasphemer compares the great Jehovah, the Maker of heaven and earth, to the false gods of other nations, the work of human hands, and thinks him no more able to rescue his worshipers than those other gods were able to rescue theirs (v. 19), as if an infinite and eternal Spirit had no more wisdom and power than a stone or the trunk of a tree. He boasts of his triumphs over the gods of the nations, that none of them could protect their people (vv. 13–15), and so he infers, as if the God of Israel were inferior to them all, *How much less shall your God deliver you?* (v. 15). All this was intended to frighten the people away from their hope in God. The Assyrians hoped in this way to take the city by weakening the hands of those who must defend it. When Satan tempts us, he aims to destroy our faith in God's all-sufficiency, knowing that he will win if he can do that. We will keep our ground if our *faith fail not* (Lk 22:32).

2. The duty to pray and cry out to heaven in times of distress. Hezekiah did this, and the prophet Isaiah joined him (v. 20). It was a good time when the king and the prophet joined together in prayer in this way.

3. The power and goodness of God. He is able both to control his enemies, even if they are very powerful, and also to relieve his friends, even if they are very weak.

3.1. As the blasphemies of his enemies set him against them (Dt 32:27), so the prayers of his people gain his help for them. The army of the Assyrians was destroyed by the sword of an angel, which triumphed in killing the mighty warriors. After the king of the Assyrians had been disgraced in this way, he was cut down with the sword of his own sons.

3.2. By this miracle God was glorified as the protector of his people. He saved Jerusalem not only from the hands of Sennacherib but also from the hand *of all others* (v. 22). Such a rescue as this was a pledge of further mercy to come, and he *guided them,* that is, he took care of them in every way.

Verses 24–33

Here we conclude the story of Hezekiah with an account of three things concerning him:

1. His illness and his recovery from it (v. 24). The account of his illness is only briefly mentioned here; we had a detailed account of it in 2Ki 20:1–11. His illness seemed likely to prove fatal. He prayed at his most critical point. God answered him and gave him a sign that he would recover, the going back of the sun by ten steps.

2. His sin and his repentance for it, which were also previously related in more detail (2Ki 20:12–21). The occasion of it was the king of Babylon's sending an envoy to him to honor him and congratulate him on his recovery. But it is added that they came to inquire of *the wonder that was done in the land* (v. 31), either the destruction of the Assyrian army or the going back of the sun. The Assyrians were their enemies; they came to inquire concerning the Assyrians' fall, so that they might rejoice in it. The sun was their god; they came to inquire concerning the favor their god had shown to Hezekiah, so that they might honor the one whom their god honored (v. 31). His sin was that *his heart was lifted up* (v. 25). He was proud of the honor God had given him in so many ways and of the honor his neighbors had given him by bringing him presents, and now he was proud that the king of Babylon would send an envoy to treat him kindly and seek his friendship: it made him conceited (2Co 12:7). When Hezekiah had destroyed other idolatries, he began to idolize himself. Although we

cannot ever adequately repay God's goodness to us, we must thankfully respond to it. His repentance for this sin: *He humbled himself for the pride of his heart* (v. 26).

3. The honor given to Hezekiah both while he lived and when he died. He had very great riches and honor (v. 27). Among his great achievements, his blocking the Gihon spring is mentioned (v. 30), which was done on the occasion of Sennacherib's invasion (vv. 3–4). The water had come into what is called the Old Pool (Isa 22:11) and the Upper Pool (Isa 7:3); but he gathered water into a new place, for the greater convenience of the city, called the Lower Pool (Isa 22:9). And, in general, he prospered in all his works, for they were good. The prophet Isaiah wrote about his life and reign (v. 32), his acts and his goodness and godliness. The people *did him honor at his death* (v. 33), burying him where the tombs of David's descendants are. They honored him also, perhaps, by making as great a fire for him as for Asa, or—what was even more honorable—by mourning greatly for him, as the people had for Josiah.

CHAPTER 33

In this chapter we have the history of the reigns: 1. Of Manasseh, who had a long reign. 1.1. His wretched apostasy from God and his rebellion to idolatry and evil (vv. 1–10). 1.2. His happy return to God in his affliction: his repentance (vv. 11–13), reformation (vv. 15–17), and prosperity (v. 14); the conclusion of his reign (vv. 18–20). 2. Of Amon, who reigned corruptly (vv. 21–23) and soon ended his days unhappily (vv. 24–25).

Verses 1–10

We have here an account of the great evil of Manasseh. It is almost the same, word for word, as what we read in 2Ki 21:1–9. This foolish young king acted against the good example and good education his father had given him. Manasseh gave himself to all ungodliness, copied the detestable practices of the followers of other religions (v. 2), ruined the established religion, undid his father's glorious reformation (v. 3), dishonored the temple of God with his idolatry (vv. 4–5), sacrificed his children to Molech, and made the Devil's lying sorcerers his guides and his counselors (v. 6). What made the sin of Manasseh worse was that God *spoke to him and his people* by the prophets, *but they would not hearken* (v. 10). We marvel here at the grace of God in speaking to them, and their stubbornness in turning a deaf ear to him—that either their evil did not completely bring to an end his goodness, but he still longed to be gracious (Isa 30:18), or his goodness did not turn them from their evil, but they still hated to be reformed. Corruption in worship is such a weakness of the church that the church will easily tend to fall back into it again even when it seems to have been healed. The god of this world has strangely blinded people's minds (2Co 4:4) and has a great power over those who are held captive by him; otherwise he would not be able to draw them away from God, their best friend, to depend on their sworn enemy.

Verses 11–20

We have seen how Manasseh in his evil undid the good works his father had done; here we have him repenting and undoing the evil he himself had done. It is a memorable instance of the riches of God's pardoning mercy and the power of his renewing grace. Here is:

1. The occasion of Manasseh's repentance: his affliction. God brought a foreign enemy on him. Manasseh's father had faithfully served God, and the king of Babylon had curried favor with him; now that Manasseh had treacherously departed from God, the same king invaded him. The king of Babylon is here called the *king of Assyria* because he had now gained power over Assyria, which he could do more easily because of the defeat of Sennacherib's army and its destruction at Jerusalem. The commander took *Manasseh among the thorns* (v. 11), in some bush or other, perhaps in his garden, where he had hidden himself. Or perhaps it is spoken figuratively: he was confused in his ways and did not know which way to turn. He was in great difficulties and did not know how to get out of them and so became an easy target to the Assyrian commanders, who no doubt plundered his house and took away what they wanted, as Isaiah had foretold (2Ki 20:17–18). What was Hezekiah's pride was their prey. They bound Manasseh, who had been held before with the cords of his own sin, and took him prisoner to Babylon.

2. The expressions of his repentance (vv. 12–13): *When he was in affliction*, he had time to come to himself—and good reason to do so.

2.1. He was convinced that Jehovah is the only living and true God. If he had been a prince in the palace of Babylon, he would probably have been confirmed in his idolatry, but because he was held captive in the prisons of Babylon, he was convinced of it and reclaimed from it.

2.2. He turned to God as his God, renouncing every other god and resolving to remain faithful only to God, the God of his ancestors and a God in covenant with him.

2.3. He humbled himself greatly before him.

2.4. He prayed to God to forgive his sin and to return his favor. The prayer that we find among the apocryphal books entitled "The Prayer of Manasseh," which is supposed to have been written when he was taken captive in Babylon, is a good prayer, and very relevant in this case.

3. God's gracious acceptance of his repentance: God answered his prayer. Although it may be only by affliction that we are driven to God, he will not therefore reject us if we sincerely seek him, for afflictions are sent on purpose to lead us to him. Let not great sinners despair, since Manasseh himself repented and found favor with God; in him God *showed forth a pattern of longsuffering*, an example of his patience (1Ti 1:16; Isa 1:18).

4. The fruits in keeping with repentance (Mt 3:8) which he produced after his return to his own land (vv. 15–16). He got rid of the foreign gods, their idols, and that image, whatever it was, which he had set up with so much ceremony in the temple of the Lord. He returned to his duty, for he repaired the altar of the Lord. He then sacrificed peace offerings (fellowship offerings) to seek God's favor, and thank offerings to praise him for rescuing him.

5. His prosperity, to some extent, after his repentance. When he returned to God in his duty, God returned to him in mercy. Josephus says that all the rest of his time he was so changed for the better that he was looked on as a very happy man.

Verses 21–25

Little is recorded about Amon, but since it is bad, it is enough. Here is:

1. His great evil. He did as *Manasseh had done* in the days of his apostasy (v. 22). When Manasseh *cast* (threw) *out the images*, he did not completely destroy them, according to the law which required Israel to *burn the images with fire* (Dt 7:5). This example shows how necessary that law was, for because the *carved images* were only thrown aside and not burned, Amon knew where

to find them, soon set them up again, and sacrificed to them. It is added, *He trespassed more and more* (v. 23). He *humbled not himself before the Lord, as his father had humbled himself* (v. 23). He fell like him, but did not get up again like him. It is not so much sin as impenitence in sin that ruins people.

2. His prompt destruction. He reigned only two years, and then his servants *conspired against him* and *slew* (assassinated) *him* (v. 24).

CHAPTER 34

In this chapter we have: 1. A general account of Josiah's character (vv. 1–2). 2. His zeal to uproot idolatry (vv. 3–7). 3. His concern to repair the temple (vv. 8–13). 4. The finding of the Book of the Law and the good use made of it (vv. 14–28). 5. The public reading of the Law to the people and their renewal of their covenant with God (vv. 29–33). Much of this we had in 2Ki 22.

Verses 1–7

Josiah came to the throne when he was very young, only eight years old, and he reigned *thirty-one years* (v. 1). At the beginning of his reign things went much as they had in his father's time, because, being a child, he must have left the management of them to others, so that it was not until his twelfth year that the reformation began (v. 3). He reigned very well (v. 2), approved himself to God, followed in the steps of David, and did not turn aside either *to the right hand or to the left*. While he was young, about sixteen years old, he *began to seek after God* (v. 3). In the twelfth year of his reign, when he probably took the work of the administration of government entirely into his own hands, he began to purge his kingdom of the remnants of idolatry. He destroyed the high places, Asherah poles, carved idols, cast images, altars, and all forms of idolatry (vv. 3–4). He not only got rid of them, as Manasseh did, but also broke them to pieces, crushing them to powder. This destruction of idolatry is here said to be in his twelfth year, but it was said in 2Ki 23:23 to have been in his eighteenth year. Something was probably done toward it in his twelfth year; it was then that he began to purge the idolatry, but that good work met with opposition, so it was not completed until they found the Book of the Law six years later.

Verses 8–13

Orders are given by the king for the temple to be repaired (v. 8). When he had purged the temple of its corruptions, he began to fit it out for the services that were to be performed in it. Those who truly love God will *love the habitation of his house* (Ps 26:8). The Levites went about the country and collected money toward it, which was returned to the three trustees mentioned (v. 8). They brought it to Hilkiah the high priest (v. 9), and he and they put it into the hands of workers, both overseers and laborers (vv. 10–11). It is noticed that the workers were industrious and honest: they *did the work faithfully* (v. 12). It is also suggested that the overseers were capable people, for it is said that those employed to inspect this work were skillful in *instruments of music*. It was not that their skill in music was of any use in architecture, but it was evidence that they were people of good sense and skill. They all needed one another, and the work needed both. The overseers of the work should not despise the laborers, and those who do the physical hard labor should not begrudge those whose work is to direct. Each should respect the other in love,

and from the different gifts and dispositions of both, God should receive the glory, and the church the benefits.

Verses 14–28

We had this whole paragraph in 2Ki 22:8–20 just as it is related here, and we have nothing to add here to the observations we made there. We take the opportunity to bless God that we have plenty of Bibles, and that they are, or may be, in the hands of everyone, that the Book of the Law and Gospel is not lost or scarce. Bibles are jewels, but we thank God that they are not rarities. If the things in Scripture were new to us, as they were to Josiah, surely they would make deeper impressions on us than they usually do, but they are not less significant—and so we should not spend any less time considering them—just because they are well known. We are here instructed that when we are under conviction of sin and we fear divine wrath, we should inquire of the Lord. This is what Josiah did (v. 21). We should ask, as they did (Ac 2:37), *Men and brethren, what shall we do?* and especially, like the jailor, *What must I do to be saved?* (Ac 16:30). Praise God, we have the living words to which to turn with these inquiries. We are here encouraged to humble ourselves before God and to seek him, as Josiah did.

Verses 29–33

Here is an account of the further advances which Josiah made toward reforming his kingdom when he heard the Law read and received the message God sent him through the prophetess Huldah (vv 23–28). Happy are the people who have such a king. They were well taught. He did not make them do their duty until he had first instructed them in it. He called all the people together, great and small, young and old, rich and poor, high and low. *He that hath ears to hear, let him hear* (Mt 11:15) the words of *the book of the covenant* (v. 30). The king himself read the book to the people (v. 30). After the articles of agreement between God and Israel had been read, so that they might make an intelligent covenant with God, both king and people signed their names to it, as it were, with great seriousness. He caused *all that were present to stand to it*, to pledge themselves to it (v. 32), and made them all *to serve, even to serve the Lord their God* (v. 33). *All his days they departed not from following the Lord* (v. 33). Josiah kept them, with much trouble, from turning to idolatry again. *All his days* were days of restraining them, but this suggested that there was in them *a bent to backslide* (Hos 11:7), a strong inclination to idolatry. Josiah was sincere in what he did, but most of the people were unwilling to go along with it and still longed for their idols. God saw this, and so from that time, when one would have thought the foundations had been laid for a long-lasting security and peace, the decree was declared for their destruction.

CHAPTER 35

Here we accompany Josiah: 1. To the temple, where we see his religious care for the proper observance of the ordinance of the Passover according to the Law (vv. 1–19). 2. To the battlefield, where we see his rashness in engaging with the king of Egypt, and how dearly it cost him (vv. 20–23). 3. To the grave, where we see him bitterly mourned (vv. 24–27).

Verses 1–19

Josiah's destruction of idols and idolatry was related at length in 2 Kings and only mentioned here in 2 Chronicles, in the previous chapter (34:33), but his celebration of the

Passover, only touched on in 2 Kings (23:21), is related in detail here. Many feasts and festivals of the Lord were appointed by the ceremonial law, but the Passover was the main one. When the two great reformers Hezekiah and Josiah celebrated it, they revived religious life in their day. The ordinance of the Lord's Supper is like the Passover; and the proper observance of that sacrament is an example and a means of both the growth in purity and beauty of churches and the growth in godliness and devotion of individual Christians. In the account of Hezekiah's Passover the great zeal of the people and their deep devotion were significant, but little of the same spirit appears here. It was more out of compliance to the king's wishes that they all celebrated the Passover (vv. 17–18) than from any great inclination on their part. They took some pride in this form of godliness, but little pleasure in its power (2Ti 3:5).

1. The king directed and encouraged the priests and Levites to do their part in this ceremony. Let us see how this good king managed his clergy on this occasion:

1.1. He led them back to the duties they were appointed to fulfill according to the Law of Moses (v. 6) and the directions written by David and Solomon (v. 4).

1.2. He ordered the ark to be set in its place.

1.3. He told them to *serve God and his people Israel* (v. 3).

1.4. He told them to *sanctify themselves*, and *prepare their brethren* (v. 6). Ministers' work must begin at home, but it must not end there. They must do what they can to *prepare their brethren* by warning, instructing, encouraging, strengthening, and comforting them.

1.5. He *encouraged them to the service* (v. 2). He spoke encouragingly to them, as Hezekiah had (30:22).

2. The king and his officials, influenced by his example, gave generously to bear the costs of this Passover. At his own cost, Josiah provided the assembly with Passover lambs and other sacrifices to be offered during the seven days of the feast. The leading priests contributed toward the priests' expenses, as Josiah did toward the people's.

3. The priests and Levites performed their work very eagerly (v. 10); they also took care to honor God *by eating of the passover* themselves (v. 14).

4. The singers expressed the joy of the congregation, and the gatekeepers made sure that no one broke in to defile anything or disturb the assembly, and that no one left the assembly before the service was finished.

5. The whole ceremony was performed according to the Law (vv. 16–17); there had been none like it since Samuel's time (v. 18).

Verses 20–27

It was thirteen years from Josiah's famous Passover to his death. During this time things went well in his kingdom, and religious faith flourished. The next news we hear of Josiah is that he dies in midlife and in the midst of his usefulness, before he is even forty years old. We had this sad story in 2Ki 23:29–30.

1. Josiah was a very good king, but he was very much to be blamed for his rashness in going out to war against the king of Egypt without any reason. It was bad enough that, as we learned in 2 Kings, he meddled in a quarrel which had nothing to do with him (Pr 26:17). But here it looks worse, for the king of Egypt sent messengers to warn him against this enterprise (v. 21).

1.1. The king of Egypt argued with Josiah:

1.1.1. From principles of justice. If even a *righteous man* engages in an *unrighteous cause*, he should not expect to prosper (Eze 3:20; Pr 3:30).

1.1.2. From principles of religion: "*God is with me*; in fact, *he commanded me to make haste* (v. 21), and so, if you slow down my movements, you are arguing with God." It cannot be that the king of Egypt only pretended this, hoping to stop Josiah, for it is said here (v. 22) that the words of Neco were from the mouth of God. Either by a dream, or by a strong prompting which he had reason to think was from God, or by Jeremiah or some other prophet, God had ordered him to make war on the king of Assyria.

1.1.3. From principles of political prudence: "*That he destroy thee not* (v. 21); if you engage against one who has not only a better army and a better cause, but also God on his side, you do so at your peril."

1.2. For the punishment of a hypocritical nation, Josiah, whose own heart was upright with the Lord his God, was allowed to become so obsessed that he took no notice of these fair reasonings and refused to give up his enterprise. He *would not turn his face from him*, but went in person and fought the Egyptian army in the *valley of Megiddo* (v. 22). In this matter he did not walk in the ways of David his father, for if David had faced such a situation, he would have inquired of the Lord, *Shall I go up? Wilt thou deliver them into my hands?* (2Sa 5:19).

2. The people were evil, but they were to be commended for mourning the death of Josiah as they did. All Judah and Jerusalem, that foolish, irrational people, *mourned for him* (v. 24). Elegies were inserted into the collections of state poems and may have been written in Lamentations. This showed:

2.1. That they had some respect for their good king, and that although they did not warmly go along with him in all his good intentions, they still greatly honored him.

2.2. That they had some sense of their own danger now that he was gone. They mourned the death of the one who was their defense against God's judgment. Many will shed tears for their troubles but not be persuaded to part with their sins.

CHAPTER 36

Here we have: 1. A short but sad account of the complete destruction of Judah and Jerusalem within a few years after Josiah's death. 1.1. The history of it in the unhappy reigns of Jehoahaz for three months (vv. 1–4), Jehoiakim for eleven years (vv. 5–8), Jehoiachin for three months (vv. 9–10), and Zedekiah for eleven years (v. 11). The destruction was finally completed in the killing of very many people (v. 17), the plundering and burning of the temple and all the palaces, the desolation of the city (vv. 18–19), and the exile of the people who remained (v. 20). 1.2. Some remarks on it concerning the punishment of sin that came through it, Zedekiah's evil (vv. 12–13), the idolatry the people were guilty of (v. 14), and their mocking of God's prophets (vv. 15–16). The word of God was fulfilled in this (v. 21). 2. The dawning of the day of their rescue in Cyrus' proclamation (vv. 22–23).

Verses 1–10

The destruction of Judah and Jerusalem comes about gradually. God gives them both time and encouragement to repent and waits to be gracious (Isa 30:18). The history of these reigns was more fully recorded in the last three chapters of 2 Kings.

1. Jehoahaz was made king by the people (v. 1) but soon deposed by Pharaoh Neco and taken prisoner to Egypt (vv. 2–4). We hear no more about this young prince.

2. Jehoiakim was set up by the king of Egypt and reigned eleven years. How low was Judah brought when the king of Egypt, an old enemy of their land, gave what king he pleased to the kingdom and what name he pleased to the king (v. 4)! He made Eliakim king, and he called him *Jehoiakim* as a sign of his authority over him. *Jehoiakim did that which was evil* (v. 5); we read elsewhere of the *abominations which he did* (v. 8; see 2Ki 23:37; Jer 22:13–19; 26:20–24). We hear no more of the king of Egypt, but the king of Babylon attacked Jehoiakim (v. 6), seized him, and bound him, with the intention of taking him away to Babylon; it seems, however, that either he allowed Jehoiakim to reign as his vassal, or death released the prisoner before he was taken away. However, the best and most valuable articles from the temple were now taken away and made use of in Nebuchadnezzar's temple in Babylon (v. 7). As the taking away of these things to Babylon began the destruction of Jerusalem, so Belshazzar's daring desecration of them there meant that the limit of the sins of Babylon was reached, for when he drank wine in them to the honor of his gods, the writing on the wall presented him with his condemnation (Da 5:3–6). In the reference to the book of the Kings about Jehoiakim, mention is made of *that which was found in him* (v. 8), which seems to refer to his treachery toward the king of Babylon. Some of the Jewish writers, however, understand it as referring to certain distinctive marks found on his dead body, in honor of his idol, cuttings such as God had forbidden (Lev 19:28).

3. Jehoiachin, or Jeconiah, the son of Jehoiakim, attempted to reign in his place, and he reigned long enough to show his evil inclinations, but after three months and ten days, the king of Babylon sent for him and took him away captive, with more of the articles of value from the temple.

Verses 11–21

Here is an account of the destruction of the kingdom of Judah and the city of Jerusalem by the *Chaldeans*, the Babylonians. Abraham, God's friend (2Ch 10:7; Isa 41:8; Jas 2:23), was called out of that country, from Ur of the Chaldeans, when God took him into covenant and fellowship with himself. Now his corrupt descendants were taken into that country again, as a sign that they had forfeited all that kindness with which they had been regarded for the father's sake.

1. The sins that brought about this desolation.

1.1. Zedekiah, the king in whose days it came, brought it on himself by his own foolishness.

1.1.1. If only he had made God his friend, that would have prevented the fall of Jerusalem. Jeremiah brought him messages from God, but the accusation against him here is that he *humbled not himself before Jeremiah* (v. 12). Because he would not make himself a servant to God in this way, he was made a slave to his enemies.

1.1.2. If only he had been true to his covenant with the king of Babylon, that would have prevented his downfall, but he *rebelled against him*, even though he had taken an oath to be his faithful vassal (v. 13). It was this that provoked the king of Babylon to deal so harshly with him as he did. The thing that ruined Zedekiah was that he not only *turned not to the Lord God of Israel* but also *stiffened his neck and hardened his heart from turning to him* (v. 13), and so, in effect, he *would not be healed*, he *would not live*, that is, he chose not to be healed or to live (Eze 33:11).

1.2. The great sin that brought this destruction was idolatry. The priests, even the leaders of the priests, who should have opposed idolatry, were its ringleaders.

1.3. What made their sin even worse was their mocking of God's prophets, who were sent to call them to repentance (vv. 15–16).

1.3.1. God showed tender compassion toward them in sending prophets to them. The reason given why God by his prophets contended with them in this way is that he had compassion on his people and on his dwelling place, and wanted to use these ways of preventing their ruin. The methods God takes to bring back sinners by his word, by ministers, by conscience, and by providences all show his compassion and pity toward them and his unwillingness *that any should perish* (2Pe 3:9).

1.3.2. *They mocked the messengers of God, despised his word in their mouths, and also misused the prophets*, treating them as their enemies. Their terrible treatment of Jeremiah—who lived at this time—about which we read much in the book of his prophecy, is an example of this. This brought wrath on them with no way of escape, for it was sinning against the way of escape itself. Nothing is more offensive to God than mistreatment of his faithful ministers, for what is done against them he takes as done against himself. *Saul, Saul, why persecutest thou me?* (Ac 9:4). Persecution was the sin that brought on Jerusalem its final destruction by the Romans. See Mt 23:34–37.

2. The desolation itself, and some few of its details, which we had more fully in 2Ki 25.

2.1. Very many were killed, even *in the house of their sanctuary* (v. 17), to where they fled for refuge, hoping that the holiness of the place would protect them. The Babylonians not only paid no reverence to the sanctuary but also showed no natural pity either to the tender sex or to revered old age.

2.2. All the remaining articles of the temple, great and small, and all the treasures, sacred and secular, the treasures of God's house and of the king and his officials, were seized and taken to Babylon (v. 18).

2.3. The temple was burned, the walls of Jerusalem were demolished, the houses—called here the *palaces* (Ps 48:3), as they were so rich and lavish—reduced to ashes, and all the furnishings, here called *the goodly vessels thereof*, everything of value, destroyed (v. 19).

2.4. The remainder of the people who escaped the sword were taken into exile in Babylon (v. 20), impoverished, enslaved, insulted, and exposed to all the miseries of a strange and cruel land. Now *they sat down by the rivers of Babylon* and mingled their tears with those streams (Ps 137:1). And though it seems that there they were healed of idolatry, it appears from the prophet Ezekiel that they were still not healed of mocking the prophets.

2.5. The land lay desolate while they were in exile in Babylon (v. 21). Now this may be considered:

2.5.1. As being the just punishment of their former abuse of it. They had served Baal with its fruits, and so *cursed is the ground for their sakes* (Ge 3:17). Now the land *enjoyed her Sabbaths*, its Sabbath rests (v. 21), as God had threatened by Moses (Lev 26:34).

2.5.2. As giving some encouragement to their hopes that they would, in due time, return to it. If others had come and taken possession of it, they might have despaired of ever recovering it, but while it lay desolate, it lay, as it were, waiting for them again.

Verses 22–23

These last two verses of this book look in two directions:

1. They look back to the prophecy of Jeremiah and show how it was fulfilled (v. 22). By him God had promised the restoration of the captives and the rebuilding of

Jerusalem at the end of seventy years, and the set time to favor Zion eventually came. After a long and dark night, *the dayspring from on high visited them*, the rising sun came to those captives from heaven (Lk 1:78).

2. They look forward to the history of Ezra, which begins with the repetition of vv. 22–23 (Ezr 1:1–3). In Ezra the verses are the introduction to a pleasant story; here they are the conclusion of a very sad one. We learn from them that although God's church may be struck down, it is not rejected, although his people are corrected, they are not abandoned, although they are thrown into the furnace, they are not lost there (Da 3:26–27), or left there any longer than until the dross has been separated out (Isa 1:25). It may be a long time coming, but the vision awaits an appointed time, and *at the end it will speak* and will not prove false, and so although it lingers, wait for it, for it will certainly come and will not delay (Hab 2:3).

A Practical and Devotional Exposition of the Book of

Ezra

The story of this book is the fulfillment of Jeremiah's prophecy concerning the return of the Jews from Babylon at the end of seventy years, and it is a type of the fulfillment of the prophecies of Revelation concerning the rescue of the Gospel church from the New Testament Babylon. In this book, Ezra kept the records of that great change and communicated them to the church. His name means "a helper," and he was a true helper to the people. We will have a detailed account about him in ch. 7, where he himself enters onto the stage. The book gives us an account of: 1. The Jews' return from exile (chs. 1–2). 2. The building of the temple, the opposition it met with, and its final completion despite the opposition (chs. 3–6). 3. Ezra's coming to Jerusalem (chs. 7–8). 4. The cleansing work he did there in making the men with foreign wives divorce them (chs. 9–10).

CHAPTER 1

In this chapter we have: 1. The proclamation which Cyrus king of Persia issued for the release of all the Jews whom he found captive in Babylon and for the building of their temple in Jerusalem (vv. 1–4). 2. The return of many (vv. 5–6). 3. Orders given for the restoring of the articles of the temple (vv. 7–11). This is the dawn of the day of rescue.

Verses 1–4

It is right for us here to consider:

1. What was the state of the Jews exiled in Babylon. They were under the power of those who hated them; they had nothing they could call their own, no temple and no altar; if they sang psalms, their enemies ridiculed them; and yet they still had prophets among them. Some of them were promoted at court, others were comfortably settled in the country, and they were all carried along by the hope that they would return to their own land again in due time, in expectation of which they preserved among them a separateness of their families, the knowledge of their religious faith, and an aversion to idolatry.

2. What was the state of the government under which they lived. Nebuchadnezzar took many of them into exile in the first year of his reign, which was the fourth year of Jehoiakim; he reigned forty-five years, his son Evil-Merodach twenty-three, and his grandson Belshazzar three years, which make up the seventy years. A charge is brought against Nebuchadnezzar that he *opened not the house of his prisoners* (Isa 14:17). And Daniel told him that if he had shown mercy to the poor Jews, it would have been the *lengthening of his tranquillity* (Da 4:27). But the limit of the sins of Babylon was eventually reached, and then destruction was brought on it by Darius the Mede and Cyrus the Persian, which we read of in Da 5:31. Darius, when he grew old, left the government to Cyrus, and he was employed as the instrument to rescue the Jews as soon as he controlled the kingdom of Babylon. Perhaps he did this out of godly respect to the prophecy of Isaiah. In this prophecy, Cyrus was expressly named as the one who would do this work for God, and for whom God would do great things (Isa 44:28; 45:1). Some say that Cyrus's name in Persian means "the sun," noting he brought light and healing to the church of God and was a distinguished type of Christ, the *Sun of righteousness* (Mal 4:2).

3. From where this proclamation arose. *The Lord stirred up the spirit* (moved the heart) *of Cyrus* (v. 1). It is said of Cyrus that he neither acknowledged God nor knew how to serve him, but God knew him and knew how to use him for his own ends (Isa 45:4). God rules the world by his influence on people's spirits, and whatever good is done at any time, it is God who moves the heart to do it, puts thoughts into the mind, gives to the understanding the ability to form a right judgment, and directs the will in whichever way he pleases.

4. The reference this proclamation had to the prophecy of Jeremiah, by whom God had not only promised that they would return, but also fixed the time. What Cyrus now did has long since been said to have been the *confirming of the word of God's servants* (Isa 44:26). While Jeremiah lived, he was hated and despised, but Providence honored him in this way much later, that a mighty monarch was influenced to act according to the word of the Lord that had come by his mouth.

5. The date of this proclamation. It was in his first year, not the first of his reign over Persia, the kingdom he was born to, but the first of his reign over Babylon, the kingdom he had conquered.

6. The declaring of this proclamation, both by word of mouth and in writing, so that it might be more acceptable and might be sent to those distant provinces where the ten tribes were scattered in Assyria and Media (2Ki 17:6).

7. The purpose of this proclamation of liberty:

7.1. The preamble shows the causes and considerations by which he was influenced (v. 2). His mind was enlightened by the knowledge of Jehovah, the God of Israel, as the only *living and true God*, the *God of heaven*, who is the sovereign Lord and the One who controls all *the kingdoms of the earth*. He says of him (v. 3), *He is the God*, God alone, God above all. He professes that he does this service to God in gratitude to him for the favors he has given him: *The God of heaven has given me all the kingdoms of the earth* (v. 2). He means that God has given him all that was given to Nebuchadnezzar, whose rule, Daniel says, was *to the end of the earth* (Da 4:22; 5:19).

7.2. He gives free permission to all the Jews who were in his kingdoms to go to Jerusalem and *build the temple of the Lord* there (v. 3).

7.3. He adds instructions for a collection to be taken for the expenses of those who are poor and not able to bear their own costs (v. 4). "Whoever remains because he does not have the means to pay his expenses to go to Jerusalem, *let the men of his place help him*." Cyrus not only gave his good wishes to those who went—*Their God be with them* (v. 3)—but also took care to provide them with the things they needed.

Verses 5–11

We are told here:

1. How Cyrus's proclamation was successful in motivating other people.

1.1. After he had given permission to the Jews to go to Jerusalem, many of them went up (v. 5). The same God who had raised up the spirit of Cyrus to proclaim this liberty raised up their spirits to receive its benefits, for it was done *not by might, nor by power, but by the Spirit of the Lord of hosts* (Zec 4:6). Now:

1.1.1. The temptation was perhaps too strong for some of them to stay in Babylon. The discouragements of their return were many and great: the journey would be long, their wives and children were not fit for traveling, their own land was foreign to them, and the road there was completely unknown. Go up to Jerusalem! What would they do there? It was all in ruins, and in the midst of enemies for whom they would be easy prey. Such thoughts made many of them stay in Babylon, or at least not go up with the first group of people.

1.1.2. But there were some who overcame these difficulties. These were the ones *whose spirits God raised* (v. 5), whose hearts God moved. By his Spirit and grace, he filled them with a generous desire for liberty, a gracious affection for their own land, and a longing for the free and public exercise of their religious faith.

1.1.3. The call and offer of the Gospel are like Cyrus's proclamation. *Deliverance is preached to the captives* (Lk 4:18). Those who are bound by the unrighteous rule of sin, and bound over to the righteous judgment of God, may be set free by Jesus Christ. Whoever returns to God in repentance and faith, Jesus Christ has opened the way for them. Let them go out of the slavery of sin to come into the *glorious liberty of the children of God* (Ro 8:21). The offer is open to all. Christ makes this offer according to the Father's gift to him of *all power both in heaven and in earth* (Mt 28:18) and according to his command to him to *build God a house* (v. 2), to set up for him a church in the world, a kingdom on earth. Many who hear this joyful sound choose to sit still in Babylon; they are in love with their sins and will not venture out to face the difficulties of a holy life. But there are some who break through the discouragements, who decide to build the temple of God, to make heaven of their religion, whatever it may cost them. This is how the heavenly Canaan will be populated, even though many perish in Babylon. The Gospel offer will not be made in vain.

1.2. After Cyrus had given the order that their neighbors should help them, they did so (v. 6). All those around them provided them with gold, silver, and goods to pay the costs of their journey, and to help them in building and furnishing both their own houses and God's temple. As the tabernacle was made of the plunder from Egypt, and the first temple built by the labors of foreigners, so the second temple was built by the contributions of the Babylonians. All this foreshadows the admission of Gentiles into the church in due time.

2. How this proclamation was supported by Cyrus himself. To prove the sincerity of his fondness for the house of God, he not only released the people of God but also restored the articles of the temple (vv. 7–8). Notice here that Judah had a prince, even in exile. Sheshbazzar, perhaps the same person as Zerubbabel, is here called *prince of Judah* (v. 8). The Babylonians called him *Sheshbazzar*, which means "joy in tribulation," but among his own people he went by the name of *Zerubbabel*, "a stranger in Babylon." This is how he looked on himself; he considered Jerusalem his home, although, as Josephus says, he was leader of the bodyguard of the king of Babylon. He looked after the interests of the Jews. The sacred articles were counted out to him (v. 8), and he took care that they were taken safely to Jerusalem (v. 11).

CHAPTER 2

We were told in the previous chapter that many returned from Babylon upon receiving Cyrus's proclamation. Here we have a list (v. 1) of the different families that returned: 1. The leaders (v. 2). 2. The people (vv. 3–35). 3. The priests, Levites, and servants of the temple (vv. 36–63). 4. The grand total, with an account of their servants and followers (vv. 64–67). 5. Their offerings for the service of the temple (vv. 68–70).

Verses 1–35

We may notice here that:

1. A written account was kept of the families who came out of exile, and the numbers of each family. This was done for their honor, as part of their reward for their faith and courage, and their affection for their own land, and also to motivate others to follow their good example. The names of all those true Israelites who accept the offer of salvation through Christ will be found, to their honor, in a more sacred record than this, even in *the Lamb's book of life* (Rev 21:27). The account that was kept of the families who came out of exile was also intended for the benefit of future generations, so that they might know from whom they had descended and to whom they were allied.

2. They are called *children of the province* (v. 1). Judah had been a distinguished kingdom, to which other kingdoms had been made provinces, subject to it and dependent on it, but it was now itself made a province, to receive laws and commissions from the king of Persia and to be accountable to him.

3. They are said to come *every one to his city* (v. 1), that is, each returned to the town assigned to them, and in this assignment, no doubt, consideration was given to the settlements assigned to them by Joshua, and it was to those, as closely as possible, that they returned.

4. The leaders are mentioned first (v. 2). Zerubbabel and Jeshua were their Moses and Aaron, the former their chief prince, the latter their chief priest.

5. Some of these different families are named after the persons who were their ancestors, and others after the places in which they had formerly lived. Here are two

families that are called *the children of Elam* (one, v. 7; another, v. 31), and the number of both is the same, 1,254, which is strange. The children of Bethlehem (v. 21) were only 123, although it was David's city, for Bethlehem was *little among the thousands of Judah*, but the Messiah must come from there (Mic 5:2). Anathoth had been a famous place in the tribe of Benjamin, but here it numbered only 128 (v. 23), which must be because of the divine curse which the people of Anathoth brought on themselves by persecuting Jeremiah, who came from their town (Jer 11:21, 23).

Verses 36–63

Here is an account:

1. Of the priests who returned. They were a considerable number and made up about a tenth of the whole group. The total was more than 42,000 (v. 64), and four families of priests made up more than 4,200 (vv. 36–39).

2. Of the Levites. I cannot help wondering at the small number of them, for including both the singers and the gatekeepers (vv. 40–42), they did not come to 350.

3. Of the *Nethinim*, the temple servants, the Gibeonites, "given"—for that may be the meaning of their name—by Joshua first (Jos 9:27), and again by David (8:20), when Saul had expelled them, to be employed by the Levites in the work of God's house as *hewers of wood and drawers of water*.

4. Of some who were looked on as Israelites by birth but could not prove a clear title to the honor, and others who were looked on as priests but had the same problem.

4.1. Some who could not prove themselves Israelites (vv. 59–60), a considerable number, who presumed they were descended from Jacob but could not produce their family record. They would still go up to Jerusalem, because they had an affection for the house and people of God.

4.2. Others who could not prove they were priests, but were thought to have been descended from Aaron.

Verses 64–70

Here is:

1. The grand total of the whole company who returned from Babylon (v. 64). The total of the numbers mentioned before was fewer than 30,000 (29,818), which means that there were more than 12,000 who probably came not from Judah and Benjamin but from the rest of the tribes of Israel. This was more than double the number that had been taken into exile in Babylon by Nebuchadnezzar, so that, as in Egypt, the time of their affliction was a time of their increase.

2. Their retinue. Their servants were comparatively few (v. 65), and their donkeys, horses, camels, and mules were about as many (vv. 66–67). But notice is taken of 200 *singing men and women* who were among them, who were intended (as those referred to in 2Ch 35:25) to arouse *their mourning*.

3. Their offerings. It is said (vv. 68–69):

3.1. That they *came to the house of the Lord at Jerusalem*, but that holy and beautiful house was now in ruins.

3.2. That they offered freely toward the *setting of it up in its place*, they gave freewill offerings toward the rebuilding of the house of God on its site (v. 68). That, it seems, was the first house they talked about setting up. Their offering was nothing in comparison with the offerings of the leaders in David's time; then they offered in talents (1Ch 29:7), and now by *drams* (drachmas), but because these gifts had been given according to their

ability, they were as acceptable to God as the talents, like the widow's mite.

3.3. That they settled in their own towns (v. 70). Although their towns had fallen into disrepair, nevertheless, because they were still their towns, those that God had assigned them, they were content to settle in them. Their poverty was bad, but their unity and unanimity were its good effects.

CHAPTER 3

The ground uncultivated, their towns in ruins, all in chaos; but here we have an account of the care the people quickly took to reestablish religious faith among them. They laid a good foundation and began their work at the right end. 1. They set up an altar and offered sacrifices on it, celebrated the feasts, and contributed toward rebuilding the temple (vv. 1–7). 2. They laid the foundation of the temple with a mixture of joy and sorrow (vv. 8–13).

Verses 1–7

Here we see:

1. A general assembly of the returned Israelites at Jerusalem in the *seventh month* (v. 1). We may suppose that they came from Babylon in the spring and traveled four months. The seventh month therefore soon came, in which many of the feasts of the Lord were to be celebrated. Such was their zeal for religious observances that they left all their business in the country to attend God's altar. They came *as one man* (v. 1). If worldly business is deferred to give way to the works of religious faith, it will prosper the better.

2. The care which their leaders took to have an altar ready for them to serve at.

2.1. Jeshua and his fellow priests, and Zerubbabel and his associates, built *the altar of the God of Israel* (v. 2), probably in the same place where it had stood before (v. 3). They could not have a temple immediately, but they did not want to be without an altar. Wherever Abraham went, he *built an altar* (Ge 12:7; 13:18); and wherever we go, even though we may perhaps lack the benefit of the lampstand of preaching and the consecrated bread of Communion, if we do not bring the sacrifices of prayer and praise, we are lacking in our duty, for we have an altar always available that sanctifies the gift.

2.2. The reason given why they set up the altar quickly: *Fear was upon them, because of the people of the land* (v. 3). They were in the midst of enemies who hated them and their religion. Because they were afraid, they set up the altar. Apprehension of danger should stir us to do our duty. We should put our fears to good use in this way: they should drive us to our knees.

3. The sacrifices they offered on the altar. Let not those who have an altar never use it.

3.1. They began *on the first day of the seventh month* (v. 6).

3.2. Having begun, they kept up the *continual burnt offering* (v. 5), *morning and evening* (v. 3). They had known from sad experience what it was to lack the assurance and encouragement of being able to refer to the daily sacrifice in their daily prayers.

3.3. They observed all the *set feasts of the Lord* and offered the sacrifices appointed for each, particularly for the Feast of Tabernacles (vv. 4–5). Now that they were beginning to settle in their towns, this feast could serve as a good reminder to them of how their ancestors had lived in tents in the desert.

3.4. They offered freewill offerings (v. 5). The Law required much, but they brought more, for although they had little wealth to support the expense of their sacrifices, they were very enthusiastic and probably denied themselves at their own tables so that they might give a plentiful supply to God's altar.

4. The preparation they made to build the temple (v. 7). Tyre and Sidon must now, as before, provide them with workers, and Lebanon with timber, orders for both of which they had had from Cyrus.

Verses 8-13

There was no dispute among the returned Jews whether they should build the temple or not. Here we therefore have an account of the beginning of that admirable work. Notice:

1. When the work was begun: as soon as the season of the year allowed (v. 8), and when they had ended the Passover ceremonies. They took little more than half a year to prepare the ground and materials.

2. Who began the work: Zerubbabel and Jeshua and their brothers. The work of God is likely to go well when judges, ministers, and people all work together sincerely.

3. They appointed the *Levites to set forward the work* (v. 8), and they did it by *setting forward the workmen* (v. 9) and strengthening their hands with good and encouraging words.

4. How God was praised at the laying of the foundation of the temple (vv. 10–11); the priests with the trumpets appointed by Moses, and the Levites with the cymbals appointed by David, played together to help the singing of the eternal hymn that will never go out of date, and to which our tongues should never be out of tune: *God is good, and his mercy endureth for ever* (v. 11). Let all the streams of mercy be traced back to the fountain. Whatever things are like, *God is good to Israel* (Ps 73:1), good to us. Let the reviving of the church's interests, when they seemed dead, be attributed to the continuation of God's mercy forever, for that is how the church continues.

5. How the people were affected. There were different feelings among the people of God, and they all expressed themselves according to their own feelings, but there was no disagreement among them.

5.1. Those who knew only the misery of having no temple at all praised the Lord with shouts of joy when they saw only the foundation of one temple laid (v. 11). To them even this foundation seemed great, and was as life from the dead. They shouted, so that *the noise was heard afar off* (v. 13).

5.2. Those who remembered the glory of the first temple which Solomon built, and considered how inferior this was likely to be to that—perhaps in dimensions and certainly in magnificence and lavishness—*wept with a loud voice* (v. 12). If we date the destruction of the first temple 586 BC, and the return from Babylon 537 BC, the foundation of the new temple was laid in 536 BC, fifty years after the temple was burned down. Many now alive might remember the first temple standing. These people mourned the disproportions between this temple and the former. And:

5.2.1. There was some reason for it; and if they channeled their tears in the right way, and mourned the sin that was the cause of this sad change, they did well.

5.2.2. Yet they were weak to mix those tears with the general joy of the people and so dampen it. In the harmony of public joys, let us not be dissonant strings. They were priests and Levites, who should have known

and taught others how to be properly moved by various circumstances. They should not have let the memory of former afflictions drown out the sense of present mercies. This mixture of sorrow and joy is a representation of this world. We can scarcely distinguish *the shouts of joy from the noise of the weeping* (v. 13).

CHAPTER 4

The work of rebuilding the temple had no sooner begun than it met with opposition; the Samaritans were enemies of the Jews and their religion, and they set themselves to obstruct it. 1. They offered to be partners in the building work, but only so they might be able to slow it down. Their offer, however, was refused (vv. 1–3); they discouraged the Jews in their work and tried to dissuade them from doing it (vv. 4–5). 2. They corruptly misrepresented, by a letter to the king of Persia, both the project and those who undertook it (vv. 6–16). 3. They obtained from him an order to stop the building (vv. 17–22), which was immediately carried out (vv. 23–24).

Verses 1-5

Here is an example of the old enmity between the seed of the woman and the seed of the Serpent. God's temple cannot be built without Satan raging, but the *gates of hell shall not prevail against it* (Mt 16:18). The Gospel kingdom was similarly set up with much struggling and contention.

1. Those who undertook this work were *children of the captivity*, the exiles (v. 1), who had just come out of exile, were born in exile, and still had the marks of exile on them. Although they were not now captives, they remained under the control of those whose captives they had just been. Israel was God's son, his firstborn, but by their sin the people sold and enslaved themselves, and so became children of exile.

2. Those who opposed this work are here said to be *the adversaries of Judah and Benjamin* (v. 1), not the Babylonians or Persians, but the leftovers of the ten tribes and the foreigners who had joined them and who had patched together the hybrid religion described in 2Ki 17:33: *They feared the Lord, and served their own gods too*. They are called *the people of the land* (v. 4).

3. Their opposition contained much of the subtlety of the old Serpent. When they heard that the temple was being built, they were immediately aware that it would be a fatal blow to their superstitious ways and set themselves to oppose it.

3.1. They offered their services to build alongside the Israelites only so that it would give them an opportunity to slow the work down while they pretended to help. Their offer was plausible enough and looked kind: "*We will build with you*. We'll help you to plan and we'll contribute toward the cost, *for we seek your God as you do*" (v. 2). This was false, for although they sought the same God, they did not seek only him, nor did they seek him in the way he appointed. *The chief of the fathers* (heads of the families) *of Israel* were soon aware that they did not mean kindness, whatever they pretended, but that their real intention was to cause trouble, and so these leaders told them plainly, "*You have nothing to do with us*. You have *no part or lot* with us *in this matter* (Ac 8:21). You are not true Israelites or faithful worshipers of God; *you worship you know not what* (Jn 4:22). We dare not be in fellowship with you, and so we ourselves will build it."

3.2. When this plot failed, they did what they could to distract the Jews from the work and discourage them in it. Those who were cool and indifferent were drawn away from the work by this troublesome scheming, though the work needed their help (v. 4). We should therefore not be surprised at the unceasing attempts of the church's enemies to stop the building of God's temple. He whom they serve, and whose work they are doing, is *unwearied* in *walking to and fro through the earth* (Zec 1:11) to cause trouble.

Verses 6–16

Cyrus remained steadfastly faithful to the Jews' side. His successor was *Ahasuerus*, Xerxes (v. 6), possibly the same person whom writers of other religions called *Cambyses*, who had never taken such notice of the despised Jews as to concern himself with them. To him these Samaritans appealed by letter for an order to stop the building of the temple. They did it at the beginning of his reign, having decided to lose no time when they thought they had a king who would suit their purposes. Notice how watchful the church's enemies are to seize the first opportunity to cause trouble—let its friends be no less careful in showing it kind acts. Here we see:

1. The general purpose of the letter which they sent to the king to inform him of this matter. It is called (v. 6) *an accusation against the inhabitants of Judah and Jerusalem.*

2. The people involved in the writing of this letter. The conspirators who plotted it are named (v. 7), as well as the writers (v. 8) who formulated it, and those who signed it (v. 9)—those who agreed with it and joined with them. The *rulers take counsel together against the Lord* (Ps 2:2) and his temple. The building of the temple would do them no harm, but they came forward to oppose it with the greatest concern and vehemence, perhaps because the prophets of the God of Israel had foretold the *famishing* and *perishing* of all the *gods of the heathen* (Zep 2:11; Jer 10:11). The people agreed with them in their futile plotting (Ps 2:1). All the different colonies of the settlement around Jerusalem—from Assyria, Babylonia, Persia, and other lands—set their hands, by their representatives, to this letter.

3. A copy of the letter itself, which Ezra inserts here from the records of the kingdom of Persia.

3.1. They describe themselves as very loyal to the government and greatly concerned for its honor and interests. "Because we are salted with the salt of the palace" (v. 14, margin)—that is, "Because we have our salary from the court, and could no more live without it than flesh could be preserved without salt"—"Because of this, *it is not meet* (proper) *for us to see the king's dishonour*" (v. 14), and so they urge him to stop the building of the temple.

3.2. They describe the Jews as disloyal, and as dangerous to the government, asserting that Jerusalem was *the rebellious and bad city* (v. 12), *hurtful to kings and provinces* (v. 15).

3.2.1. Their history of what was past was invidious: *within this city sedition was moved of old time*; the city had been a place of rebellion from ancient times, and that was why it was destroyed (v. 15). There was some truth in this, because of the attempts of Jehoiakim and Zedekiah to shake off the oppression of the king of Babylon. Yet their efforts to recover their rights would have been justifiable if they had used the right method and first made their peace with God. Furthermore, though these Jews and their rulers had been guilty of rebellion, it was still unjust to mark this indelibly against the whole city. In exile, the behavior of the Jews had been so good as to be sufficient, with any reasonable people, to take away that shame.

3.2.2. Their information concerning what was now going on was grossly false as regards fact. They were very careful to inform the king that the Jews had *set up the walls of this city* (v. 12). They had only begun to build the temple, which Cyrus commanded them to do, but as for the walls, nothing had been done, nor were there any plans to repair them, as appears from the ruined condition they were in many years later (Ne 1:3).

3.2.3. Their assessment of the consequences was totally without basis and absurd. They were very confident that if this city were to be built, not only would the Jews *pay no toll, tribute, or custom* (duty) (v. 13), but all the countries in Trans-Euphrates would immediately rebel, being drawn to do so by the Jews' example, and if the reigning king should turn a blind eye to this, he would wrong not only himself but also his successors: *Thou shalt endamage the revenue of the kings*, the royal revenues will suffer (v. 13). Notice how every line of this letter breathes out both the subtlety and evil of the old Serpent.

Verses 17–24

We have here:

1. The orders which the king of Persia gave in answer to the information sent him by the Samaritans against the Jews. He allowed himself to be deceived by their falsehood and was very willing to satisfy them with an order to stop the building. He consulted the records concerning Jerusalem, and found that it had indeed rebelled against the king of Babylon, that it was, therefore, as they called it, *a bad city* (vv. 12, 19), and that in former times kings had reigned there, to whom all the countries on that side of the river had paid tribute (v. 20). He appointed these Samaritans to immediately stop the building of the city (vv. 21–22). Neither they, in their letter, nor he, in his order, makes any mention of the temple, and the building of that, because both they and he knew that they had a command from Cyrus to rebuild that. They spoke only of the *city*: "Let not *that* be built," that is, as a city with walls and gates.

2. The use which the enemies of the Jews made of these orders, so fraudulently obtained. The order was only to prevent the walling of the *city*, but having compulsion and power on their side, they interpreted it as relating to the *temple*, for it was that which they were ill disposed toward.

3. A return to the chronological account following Ezra's general summary of the opposition experienced over the years, as set out in vv. 6–23. The consequence was that *the work of the house of God ceased* (v. 24) for a time because of the power and arrogant defiance of its enemies.

CHAPTER 5

At the end of the previous chapter we left the temple work at a halt, but because it is God's work, it will be revived, and here we have an account of its revival. The Holy Spirit: 1. Warmed its coolhearted friends and encouraged them to build (vv. 1–2). 2. Cooled its hotheaded enemies and caused them to have a better attitude, for although they secretly disliked the work as much as those in the previous chapter, nevertheless, they were milder toward the builders (vv. 3–5). They were also fairer in their representation of the matter to the king, which we have an account of (vv. 6–17).

Verses 1–2

During this time the Jews had an altar and a tabernacle. But the counselors who had been hired to hinder the work

(4:5) told them that the time had not come for the building of the temple (Hag 1:2), urging that it had been long before the right time came for the building of Solomon's temple; and so the Jews were comfortable in their own *ceiled* (paneled) *houses*, while *God's house lay waste* (Hag 1:4). However:

1. They had two good ministers, who fervently persuaded them in God's name to set the wheels of business in motion again. Haggai and Zechariah both began to prophesy in the second year of Darius, as appears in Hag 1:1; Zec 1:1. The temple of God is to be built not by secular force but *by the word of God*. Like the *weapons of our warfare*, the instruments of our building *are not carnal* (worldly) but *spiritual* (2Co 10:4). It is the business of God's prophets to stir God's people up to do what is good, and to help them in it, to *strengthen their hands* (Ne 2:18), and, by suitable thoughts drawn from the word of God, to inspire them to do their duty and encourage them in it. They prophesied *in the name*, or, as some read it, "in the cause," or "for the sake," *of the God of Israel* (v. 1); they spoke by commission from him and argued from his authority.

2. They had two good judges, who were eager and active to do this work: Zerubbabel, their chief ruler or governor, and Jeshua, their chief priest (v. 2). These great men thought it not beneath them to be given orders and taught by the prophets of the Lord, but were happy to be so ordered and taught. They were glad to be able to help revive this good work. Read Hag 1:1–15 here—for that is the best commentary on these two verses—and see what great things God does by his word, which he *exalts above all his name* (Ps 138:2), and by his Spirit working with it.

Verses 3–17

We have here:

1. The notice which their neighbors soon took of the revival of this good work. No sooner did the Spirit of God encourage the friends of the temple to come forward to support it than the evil spirit stirred up its enemies to come forward to oppose it. While the people built and paneled their own homes, their enemies did not trouble them in any way (Hag 1:4), but when they began to work again on the temple, a warning was sounded, and everyone worked together to try to stop them (vv. 3–4). The opponents are named: *Tatnai* (Tattenai) and *Shethar-boznai* (Shethar-Bozenai). Although these people were real enemies of building the temple, they made some attempt to tell the truth. If *all men have not faith* (2Th 3:2), it is good that some do have faith, together with a sense of honor. The church's enemies are not all equally evil and unreasonable.

2. The care which Providence took of this good work (v. 5): *The eye of their God was upon the elders of the Jews.* God was watching over those who were active in the work, so that their enemies could not, as they wanted to, cause them to stop until the matter came to Darius. These enemies asked them to stop only till they had instructions from the king about the matter, but the elders would not yield even that much, for *the eye of God was upon them.* The elders of the Jews saw *the eye of God upon them* (v. 5), to notice what they did and acknowledge them as his own when they did well. They were then encouraged to face their enemies and to continue vigorously with their work, despite all the opposition they met with.

3. The account they sent to the king of this matter. Notice:

3.1. How fully the elders of the Jews gave the Samaritans an account of what was going on. The Samaritans put these questions to them: "By what authority are you doing these things. Who gave you that authority (Mt 21:23)?" They replied, *"We are the servants of the God of heaven and earth* (v. 11). The God we worship is not some local god, and so we cannot be accused of setting up some breakaway faction or sect in building this temple to his honor. The God we submit to is the God on whom the whole creation depends. We should therefore be protected and helped by everyone and hindered by no one. It was to punish us for our sins that we were, for a time, excluded from possession of this temple. It was not because the gods of the nations had prevailed against our God, but because we had offended him (v. 12), for which he handed us over, along with our temple, to the king of Babylon. We have the royal decree of Cyrus to justify us."

3.2. That they give this account of their proceedings without asking what authority the Samaritans had to examine them, or rebuking them for their idolatry, superstitions, or mixed religion. Let us learn from this to be humble and reverent in *giving a reason of the hope that is in us* (1Pe 3:15), to understand rightly, and then to declare readily, what we do in God's service and why we are doing it.

3.3. How fairly the Samaritans presented this to the king. They called the temple at Jerusalem the *house of the great God* (v. 8), for although the Samaritans had many gods and lords, they acknowledged the God of Israel to be the *great God*, who is above all gods. They told him truly what had been done, not stating that the Jews were fortifying the city as if they intended to make war, but only that they were setting up the temple as those who intended to offer worship (v. 8). God's people are less likely to be persecuted if they are not misrepresented; they are less likely to be attacked if they do not appear to be in the wrong. If the cause of God and truth is fairly stated, and fairly heard, it will hold its ground.

CHAPTER 6

We read in ch. 3 of how solemnly the foundation of the temple had been laid. In chs. 4–5 we read how slowly the building went, and with how much difficulty. But in this chapter we read how gloriously, and with what shouts, the top stone was finally brought out. As for God, his work is perfect (Dt 32:4; 2Sa 22:31); it may be slow work, but it will be a sure work. Here we have: 1. An account of the decree of Cyrus for building the temple (vv. 1–5); the enforcing of that decree by a new order from Darius to complete that work (vv. 6–12). 2. The completion of the building of the temple (vv. 13–15); its solemn dedication (vv. 16–18) and its inauguration with the celebration of the Passover (vv. 19–22).

Verses 1–12

Here:

1. The decree of Cyrus for building the temple is repeated. A search was ordered to be made for it among the archives. It was looked for in Babylon (v. 1), but it was not found there. Finally it was found at *Achmetha* (Ecbatana), in the province of Media (v. 2) (vv. 3–5). Here is:

1.1. An order for the temple to be built: *Let the house of God at Jerusalem be builded*—"let *that* house be built," as it may be read—within such and such dimensions, and with such and such materials.

1.2. An order for paying the expenses of the building from the king's revenue (v. 4). We do not find that they had received what was ordered for them here, because the disposition of things at court had changed.

1.3. An order for restoring the articles and utensils of the temple that Nebuchadnezzar had taken away (v. 5), along with an order that the priests, the Lord's ministers, should return them all to their places in the house of God.

2. Cyrus's decree is confirmed by a decree of Darius, based on it and in pursuance of it.

2.1. The decree of Darius is explicit and satisfying:

2.1.1. He forbids his officers to do anything to oppose the building of the temple. The expression suggests he knew they wanted to hinder it: *Be you far hence,* stay away from there (v. 6); *let the work of this house of God alone* (v. 7).

2.1.2. He orders them to help the builders with money from his own royal treasury, so that the Jews may:

2.1.2.1. Carry out the work of building (v. 8). He follows the example of Cyrus in this (v. 4).

2.1.2.2. Maintain the sacrifices there once the temple is built (v. 9). Notice how he honors:

- Israel's God, whom he calls once and again the *God of heaven.*
- God's ministers, by ordering his commissioners to give supplies for the temple service at the request of the priests.
- Prayer: *That they may pray for the life of the king* (v. 10).

2.1.3. He enforces his decree with a penalty (v. 11).

2.1.4. He passes a divine curse to all those rulers and people who would ever have any hand in destroying this house (v. 12).

2.2. The heart of kings is in the hand of God, and he turns it whichever way he pleases (Pr 21:1). He makes them what they are, for he is *King of Kings* (Rev 19:16). When God's time has come to accomplish his gracious purposes concerning his church, he will further those purposes by raising up instruments from among those from whom such good service was not expected. *The earth sometimes helps the woman* (Rev 12:16), and those who have little religion in themselves are sometimes used to defend religious faith. When the enemies of the Jews appealed to Darius, they hoped to obtain an order to suppress them, but instead they received an order to supply them.

Verses 13–22

Here we have:

1. The Jews' enemies made their friends. When these enemies received this order from the king, they came as quickly to encourage and help the work as their predecessors had come to try to stop it (4:23).

2. The building of the temple carried out and finished in a short time (vv. 14–15). Now the *elders of the Jews built* with cheerfulness. They found themselves bound to do it *by the commandment of the God of Israel* (v. 14). They found themselves shamed into it by the commandment of the Gentile kings, formerly Cyrus, now Darius, and some time later, Artaxerxes. They found themselves encouraged in doing it by the prophesying of Haggai and Zechariah. The work went on so prosperously that it was completed within four years. The Gospel church, that spiritual temple, is taking a long time to be built, but it will eventually be finished, when the mystical body is completed. Every believer is *a living temple, building up himself in his most holy faith* (Jude 20). Much opposition is given to this work by Satan and our own sin. We tend to be idle, and so the work proceeds with many stops and starts, but he that has *begun the good work* (Php 1:6) will see that it is completed, and will *bring forth judgment unto victory* (Mt 12:20).

3. The dedication of the temple. When it was built, because it was designed only for sacred uses, they showed by example how it should be used, which according to Bishop Patrick is the proper sense of the word *dedicate.* They celebrated with great ceremony and probably with a public declaration of its being set apart from ordinary uses and being given over to the honor of God, to be used in his worship.

3.1. The people employed in this service were not only *the priests and Levites* who officiated but also *the children of Israel,* some of each of the *twelve tribes* — although Judah and Benjamin were the chief — and *the rest of the children of the captivity* (v. 16).

3.2. The sacrifices offered on this occasion were *bullocks, rams, and lambs* (v. 17), as burnt offerings and peace offerings (fellowship offerings); they are not to be compared in number with those that had been offered at the dedication of Solomon's temple, but because they were according to the Jews' present ability, they were accepted. These hundreds meant more to them than Solomon's thousands did to him.

3.3. This service was performed with joy.

3.4. When they dedicated the house, they established the temple services. Although the temple service could not now be performed with so much style and plenty as before, because of their poverty, nevertheless, perhaps it was still performed with as much purity and faithfulness to the divine institution, which was its true glory. There is no beauty like the beauty of holiness.

4. The celebration of the Passover in the newly erected temple. Now that they had just been brought out of exile in Babylon, it was the right time to remember their rescue from slavery in Egypt. Fresh blessings should remind us of former blessings. Now they made a joyful festival of it, for it came in the month after the temple had been completed and dedicated (v. 19). Notice is here taken:

4.1. Of the purity of the priests and Levites that *killed the Passover* (v. 20). They joined together in their preparations, so they could help one another and each one of them would be pure. The purity of ministers adds much to the beauty of their ministry, as does their unity.

4.2. Of the converts who shared with them in this ceremony: *All such as had separated themselves unto them* (v. 21), all who had left their country with their superstitions and thrown in their lot with the Israel of God. They had *turned from the filthiness of the heathen of the land,* from the unclean practices of their Gentile neighbors (v. 21), both their idolatry and immorality, *to seek the Lord God of Israel* (v. 21) as their God, and now they ate the Passover.

4.3. Of the great pleasure and satisfaction with which they all celebrated the Feast of Unleavened Bread (v. 22). *The Lord had made them joyful.* He had given them both cause to rejoice and hearts to rejoice.

CHAPTER 7

Ezra's precious name greeted us initially in the title of the book, but this chapter introduces him to public activity in another reign, that of Artaxerxes. Zerubbabel and Jeshua had probably grown old by this time, if they had not passed away, nor do we hear any more about Haggai and Zechariah; they have completed their testimony. What will become of the cause of God and Israel when these useful instruments are set aside? We may trust God, who has the residue of the Spirit (Mal 2:15), to raise up others in their place. Ezra here, and Nehemiah in the next book, are as useful in their days as those others were in theirs. Here is: 1. *An account, in general, of Ezra himself, and of his mission to Jerusalem for the public good (vv. 1–10). 2. A copy of the commission which Artaxerxes gave him (vv. 11–26). 3 His thankfulness to God for it (vv. 27–28).*

Verses 1–10

Here is:

1. Ezra's background. He was one of the sons of Aaron, a priest. God chose him to be an instrument to do good in Israel so that he might honor the priesthood, the glory of which had been to a large extent eclipsed by the exile. He is said to be *the son of Seraiah* (v. 1), that Seraiah, maybe, whom the king of Babylon put to death when he devastated Jerusalem (2Ki 25:18, 21). The shortest length of time it could have been since Seraiah died would have been about seventy-five years, and many consider it to be much longer. Because they think Ezra had been called in the prime of life to engage in public service, they therefore think that Seraiah was not his immediate parent but his grandfather or great-grandfather.

2. Ezra's character. Although he came from the younger branch of the family, his personal qualifications made him very distinguished.

2.1. He was a man of great learning, *a ready scribe, in the law of Moses* (v. 6). He was very conversant with the Scriptures, especially the writings of Moses. He had a ready and skilled grasp of the words and was well versed in their sense and meaning. It is to be feared that the state of learning had been low among the Jews in Babylon, but Ezra was instrumental in reviving it. The Jews say that he collected and collated all the copies of the Law he could find, and published an accurate edition of it, with all the prophetic books, historical and poetic, that were given by divine inspiration, and so made up the canon of the Old Testament, with the addition of the prophecies and histories of his own time. Now that prophecy was about to cease, it was time to promote the knowledge of Scripture (Mal 4:4).

2.2. He was a man of great godliness and holy zeal (v. 10): *He had prepared his heart* (devoted himself) *to seek the law of the Lord.* The Babylonians, among whom he was born and bred, were famous for literature, especially the study of the stars, which, because he was a studious man, Ezra may have been tempted to turn to. But he overcame such temptation; the law of his God meant more to him than all the writings of their magicians and astrologers. He *sought the law of the Lord*, that is, he searched the Scriptures and sought the knowledge of God, of his mind and will. He made it his rule for life. He set himself *to teach Israel the statutes and judgments* (v. 10) of that Law. He first learned and did, and then taught. He *prepared his heart* (v. 10) to do all this, he devoted himself to do it.

3. Ezra's journey to Jerusalem for the good of his country: *He went up from Babylon* (v. 6) and four months later arrived in Jerusalem (v. 8). Notice:

3.1. How kind the king was to him. He *granted him all his request* (v. 6), whatever he desired to enable him to serve his country.

3.2. How kind his people were to him. When he went, many more went with him, because once he had gone to Jerusalem, they themselves would dare to live there.

3.3. How kind his God was to him. He obtained this favor from his king and country by *the good hand of the Lord that was upon him* (vv. 6, 9).

Verses 11–26

Here is the commission which the Persian emperor gave to Ezra, giving him authority to act for the good of the Jews. The commission begins, *Artaxerxes, king of kings* (v. 12). This is, however, too high a title for any mortal to assume. It is true that he was king of some kings, but to speak as if he were king of all kings was to usurp the right of the One who has *all power both in heaven and in earth* (Mt 28:18). He sends greetings to his trusty and well-beloved Ezra, whom he calls *a scribe of the law of the God of heaven* (v. 12). Ezra reckoned it more his honor to be *a scribe of God's law* than to be a peer or leader of the empire.

1. Artaxerxes gives Ezra permission to go to Jerusalem, and gives the same permission to as many of his compatriots as want to go with him (v. 13).

2. He gives him authority to inquire into the affairs of Judah and Jerusalem (v. 14). The rule of Ezra's inquiry was to be *the law of his God, which was in his hand.* He must ask whether the Jews, in their religion, had acted and were acting according to that Law — whether the temple was built, the priesthood was established, and the sacrifices were offered according to divine appointment. If he found anything not right, he must see that it was amended, and like Titus in Crete, he must *set in order the things that were wanting* (left unfinished) (Tit 1:5). And so the Jews were restored to their ancient privilege of governing themselves by that law.

3. He entrusts him with the money that was freely given by the king himself and his counselors, and collected among his subjects, for the service of the house of God (vv. 15–16). Ezra was entrusted:

- With receiving this money and carrying it to Jerusalem.
- With spending this money in the best way, on sacrifices to be offered on the altar of God (v. 17), and on whatever else he or his fellow Israelites thought fit (v. 18), the only restriction being that it should be *after the will of their God.*

4. He draws up an order for Ezra requiring the *treasurers on that side the river* (the Trans-Euphrates) (v. 21) to provide him with what he needed from the king's revenues, and to charge it to the king's account (vv. 20, 22). This was done with thought, because Ezra had not yet inquired into the state of things and did not know what he would need, and so he was modest in his demands.

5. He commands him to let nothing be lacking that needs to be done in or around the temple for the honor of the God of Israel. Notice in this command (v. 23):

5.1. How honorably he speaks of God. Before, he called him *the God of Jerusalem*; but here, so that it will not be thought that he looks on the Lord as a local god, he twice calls him, with great respect, the *God of heaven.*

5.2. How strictly he would have the Jews follow the word and Law of God, which he had probably read and admired: "Whatsoever is *commanded by your God*, let it be done diligently and with due care and speed."

6. He exempts all the ministers of the temple from paying taxes to the government. From the greatest of the priests to the lowliest of the temple servants, *it shall not be lawful* for the king's officers *to impose* that *toll, tribute, or custom* (duty) *upon them*, which the rest of the king's subjects paid (v. 24).

7. He empowers Ezra to appoint and name judges and magistrates for all the Jews of Trans-Euphrates (vv. 25–26). It was a great favor to them to have Jewish nobles, and especially to have them appointed by Ezra.

7.1. All who *knew the laws of Ezra's God*, that is, all who professed the Jewish religion, were to come under the jurisdiction of these judges, which suggests they were exempt from the jurisdiction of the pagan magistrates.

7.2. These judges were allowed and encouraged to make converts: let them *teach the laws of God* to *those that do not know them* (v. 25). They were not allowed to make new laws but must see that the laws of God were duly implemented, and they were entrusted with the sword in order that they might be *a terror to evildoers* (Ro 13:3).

Verses 27–28

Ezra blessed God for two things:

1. His commission. He says, *Blessed be God that put such a thing as this into the king's heart* (v. 27). God can put things into people's hearts which would not come there by themselves, and into their minds too, both by his providence and by his grace, in things concerning *both life and godliness* (2Pe 1:3). If there appears to be any good either in our own hearts or in the hearts of others, we must acknowledge that it was God who put it there and bless him for it. When leaders and magistrates act to suppress vice and encourage religious faith, we must thank God, who *put it into their hearts* to do so.

2. The encouragement he had in pursuance of his commission (v. 28): *He has extended mercy to me.* Ezra himself was a man of courage, yet he attributed his encouragement not to his own heart but to God's hand: "I was strengthened to undertake the services, *as the hand of the Lord my God was upon me* to direct and support me."

CHAPTER 8

This chapter gives us a more detailed account of Ezra's journey to Jerusalem. We have here: 1. The people who went with him (vv. 1–20). 2. The sacred fast which he held with his people, to pray for God's presence with them on the journey (vv. 21–23). 3. The care he took of the treasure he had with him and the responsibility for it that he gave to the priests, into whose custody he committed it (vv. 24–30). 4. The care God took of him and his people on the way (v. 31); their safe arrival at Jerusalem, where they delivered their treasure to the priests (vv. 32–34) and their commissions to the royal satraps (v. 36), and offered sacrifices to God (v. 35).

Verses 1–20

After Ezra had received his commission from the king, he called for volunteers, as it were. *He set up an ensign to assemble the outcasts of Israel and the dispersed of Judah* (Isa 11:12). "Whoever of the children of Zion, who *dwell with the daughters of Babylon* (Zec 2:7), is disposed to go to Jerusalem, now that the temple there is finished and the temple worship set up, now is their time."

1. Some offered to go with Ezra willingly. The heads of several families are named here, for their honor, and the numbers of the males that each brought totaled 1,496. Several of their families, or clans, named here were mentioned before (2:3–20).

2. The Levites who went in this group were, in a way, pressed into service. Ezra appointed a general assembly of all his company at a certain place on New Year's Day, the first day of the first month (7:9). There he mustered them, and he *found there none of the sons of Levi* (v. 15). There were some priests, but no others who were Levites. Where was the spirit of that sacred tribe? Ezra had enough money for the worship of the temple, but he lacked the men. He therefore chose from his group eleven men of learning to be employed to fill this deplorable vacancy.

He sent them to the appropriate place, where there was a college of Levites, *the place Casiphia* (v. 17), probably a street or square in Babylon for that purpose—"Silver Street" we might call it, for *ceseph* means "silver." He sent them to the appropriate person, Iddo, the president of the college, to urge him to send some of the younger men, *ministers for the house of our God* (v. 17). Though it was short notice, they brought about forty Levites to serve Ezra. More of the *Nethinim*, or temple servants—the "lowest order" of the temple ministers—appeared eager to go than of the Levites themselves. Of these *Nethinim*, 220 enlisted themselves on this hasty summons and had the honor to be referred to by name in Ezra's roll call (v. 20).

Verses 21–23

Ezra has gained Levites, but what good will that be unless he also has God with him? Notice:

1. The steadfast confidence he had in God and in his gracious protection. God's servants have his power engaged for them; his enemies have it engaged against them. Ezra believed this with his heart, and he confessed it with his mouth (Ro 10:9) before the king. He was therefore ashamed to ask the king for a convoy, for in so doing he might make the king and those around him doubt either God's power to help his people or Ezra's confidence in that power. Not that those who depend on God should not use proper means for their preservation, but when the honor of God is concerned, one would rather make oneself vulnerable than do anything to harm that honor.

2. The solemn appeal he made to God in that confidence: he *proclaimed a fast* (v. 21). Public prayers must be made for public mercies. Their fasting was:

2.1. To express their humbling of themselves. He declares this to be the meaning of it: "*that we might afflict* (humble) *ourselves before our God* (v. 21) for our sins, and so be qualified to receive pardon for them."

2.2. To stir up their prayer for God's favor. Prayer was always joined with fasting. Their mission to come to the throne of grace was *to seek of God the right way* (v. 21), that is, to commit themselves to the guidance of divine Providence, to put themselves under divine protection, and to beg God to guide and keep them on their journey and bring them safely to their destination.

3. The success of their appeal (v. 23): *We besought* (petitioned) *our God* by joint prayer, *and he was entreated of us*, answered our prayer.

Verses 24–30

Here is an account of the special care which Ezra took of the treasure he had with him, which belonged to God's sanctuary. Notice:

1. Having committed its keeping to God, he committed its keeping to trustworthy people, whose business it was to guard it, although without God they would have watched in vain (Ps 127:1).

2. Having prayed to God to preserve all the resources they had with them, he shows himself to be especially concerned for the part which belonged to the house of God and was an offering to him. He appointed this trust to twelve leading priests, and as many Levites (vv. 24, 30). Ezra told them why he had put those things into their hands (v. 28): *You are holy unto the Lord, the vessels* (articles) *are holy also*, and who is so qualified to take care of holy things as holy people? He *weighed to them the silver, the gold, and the vessels* (v. 25), because he expected to receive it back from them by being weighed out. He gave them responsibility for these treasures (v. 29): "*Watch you, and keep them*, so that they are not lost, stolen, or

mixed with other articles. Keep them together, keep them by themselves, and keep them safe until you weigh them out in the temple, in front of the leaders there."

Verses 31–36

We now accompany Ezra as he goes to Jerusalem. The great number of people who went with him made his journey slow and the stages of his journey short. We are told that his God was good, and that he acknowledged his goodness: *The hand of our God was upon us* (v. 31). Even the common dangers of journeys should make us consecrate our departure with prayer and our peaceful and safe return with praise and thanksgiving; how much more should God be looked to in such a dangerous expedition as this? They were brought safely to their destination (v. 32). We are also told that his companions were devout. As soon as they came close to the altar, they thought they ought to offer a sacrifice, regardless of what they had done in Babylon (v. 35). Among their sacrifices they included a sin offering, for it is the atonement that sweetens and secures every blessing to us. The number of their offerings related to the number of the tribes, twelve bulls, twelve male goats, and ninety-six rams, showing the union of the two kingdoms, according to what had been foretold (Eze 37:22). Now no longer did two tribes go one way and ten another, but all twelve met by their representatives at the same altar. Even the enemies of the Jews became their friends; they submitted to Ezra's commission, and instead of hindering the people of God, they helped them (v. 36).

CHAPTER 9

Now that Ezra led them, their enemies had either their hearts turned or at least their hands tied; their neighbors were civil, and we hear of no wars or rumors of wars (Mt 24:6). Everything was as good as it could be, considering that they were few, poor, and subject to a foreign ruler. Look at home; we hear nothing of Baal, Ashtoreths, or Molech, no idols, Asherah images, or golden calves, not even high places—the temple was duly respected and the temple service carefully kept up. Yet all was not well. We have here: 1. A complaint brought to Ezra of the many marriages that had been made with foreign wives (vv. 1–2); how greatly troubled he, and others influenced by his example, were when they were told this (vv. 3–4). 2. The solemn confession which he made of this sin to God (vv. 5–15).

Verses 1–4

Ezra sees nothing wrong, but information is brought him that many of the people, in fact even some of the officials, have married wives from the families of the nations, have joined themselves in marriage to foreigners. Notice:

1. What the sin was: *mingling with the people of those lands* (v. 2), associating with them both in trade and in life, and taking *their daughters in marriages* to their sons. They disobeyed the explicit command of God, which forbade all close relationships, particularly marriage, with people from the nations (Dt 7:3). They made themselves, especially their children, vulnerable to the dangers of idolatry, the very sin that had once been the ruin of their nation.

2. The people who were guilty of this sin, not only some of the unthinking people of Israel, who knew no better, but *many of the priests and Levites* (3:12), whose

responsibility it was to teach the Law. A nation is wretched when it has leaders who defile it and cause its people to go astray.

3. The information that was given to Ezra. It was given by those of the leaders who had kept their integrity and their honor. They turned to Ezra, hoping that his wisdom, authority, and influence would succeed.

4. The impression this made on Ezra (v. 3): *he rent* (tore) *his clothes, plucked off his hair,* and *sat down astonied* (appalled). It grieved him very much to think that a people called by God's name should break his Law so blatantly. Sorrow for sin must be great sorrow, as Ezra's was, *as for an only son or a firstborn* (Jer 6:26).

5. The influence which Ezra's grief had on others. People soon noticed it, and all the devout and godly people nearby gathered around him. All good people should acknowledge those who come forward and act in the cause of God against evil and worldliness, to stand by them and do what they can to encourage them.

Verses 5–15

It is a most moving address Ezra makes to heaven on this occasion. Notice:

1. He made this address at *the evening sacrifice* (v. 5). It was probably then that devout people were accustomed to come into the courts of the temple to offer their own prayers. Ezra chose to make this confession within their hearing so that they might be made duly aware of the sins of their people. The sacrifice, especially the evening sacrifice, was a type of the great atoning sacrifice. Ezra looked to this with the eye of faith in his address of repentance to God. He makes confession with his hand, as it were, on the head of that great sacrifice, through whom *we receive the atonement* (Ro 5:11).

2. His preparation for this address:

2.1. He *rose up from his heaviness* (his humiliation) (v. 5) and shook off the burden of his grief as far as was necessary to lift up his heart to God.

2.2. He *fell upon his knees* (v. 5), put himself into the position of someone humbly repenting, representing the people for whom he was now an intercessor.

2.3. He *spread out his hands* (v. 5), as one moved by what he was going to say, offering it to God.

3. The address itself. It should not properly be called a prayer, for there is not a word of petition in it, but if we give prayer its full scope, it is the offering of godly devotion to God, and the devotion which Ezra expresses here is very devout and pious. His address is a confession of repentance for sin, not his own, but the sin of his people. Notice in this address:

3.1. The confession he makes of the sin and the punishments that have come from it in the past. Although he himself is wholly clear from this guilt, he still includes himself with the sinners, because he is a member of the same community—*our iniquities and our trespass* (v. 6).

3.1.1. He acknowledges their sins to have been very great: *"Our iniquities are increased over our heads"* (v. 6). We are ready to perish in them as if we were in deep water." But let this be the comfort of those who truly repent: that though their sins reach to the heavens, God's mercy is *in the heavens* (Ps 36:5).

3.1.2. The recent mercies God had given them made their sins worse—streams of mercy: that they were *not forsaken in their bondage* (v. 9), had not been deserted by God in their bondage, but even in Babylon had the signs of God's presence; that they were a remnant of Israelites left, a few out of many, and those few having narrowly escaped the hands of their enemies because of the favor of the kings of Persia; and, especially, that they had *a nail in his holy place* (v. 8), that is, they had been given a firm place in his sanctuary — as it is explained in v. 9: they had set up the *house of God.* They had their religious faith established and the worship of the temple set up as a regular routine. All this mercy had enlightened their eyes and revived their hearts (Ps 19:8); it was life from the dead to them. "Now," Ezra says, "how ungrateful are we to have offended a God who has been so kind to us!"

3.1.3. Their sin was against an explicit command: *We have forsaken thy commandments* (v. 10). God had strictly forbidden intermarriage with the nations. Ezra repeats the command (vv. 11–12). Nothing could be clearer: *Give not your daughters to their sons, nor take their daughters to your sons.* The reason given is that if they intermarried with those nations, they would defile themselves. It was an unclean land, and they were a holy people. Ezra realized the awfulness of their sin and acknowledged that although the punishment was very great, it was less than they deserved.

3.2. His godly devotion in making this confession.

3.2.1. He speaks as one who is very much ashamed. He begins with this (v. 6): *O my God! I am ashamed and blush, O my God! to lift up my face unto thee.* Sin is shameful. Holy shame is as necessary a part of true and frank repentance as holy sorrow. The sins of others should be our shame, and we should be embarrassed for those who are not embarrassed for themselves.

3.2.2. He speaks as one who is dismayed (v. 10): Those who truly repent are at a loss what to say. Are we to say, "We have *not sinned,* or, *God will not require it.* Surely he won't call me to account" (Ps 10:13)? If we do, *we deceive ourselves, and the truth is not in us* (1Jn 1:8). Are we to say, "Have patience with us, and we will pay you everything (Mt 18:26), *thousands of rams, or our firstborn for our transgression*" (Mic 6:7)? God will not be mocked like this: he knows we are spiritually bankrupt. Are we to say, "*There is no hope* (Isa 57:10), and *let come on us what will*" (Job 13:13)? That is only making bad things worse. Those who truly repent should, with Ezra, beg God to teach them. What are we to say? Say, "I have sinned. I have acted foolishly. God be merciful to me, a sinner," and similar words. See Hos 14:2.

3.2.3. He speaks as one who has a deep assurance of the righteousness of God. "*Thou art righteous* (v. 15), wise, just, and good; you will neither do us wrong nor be hard on us, and so see *we are before thee.* We lie at your feet, waiting our condemnation; *we cannot stand before thee* insisting on any righteousness of our own (Eze 33:13; Php 3:9), having no plea to support us, and so we fall down before you, knowing our sin. We can only throw ourselves on your mercy. *Do unto us whatsoever seemeth good unto thee* (Jdg 10:15). We have nothing to say or do, except *make supplication to our judge*" (Job 9:15). This is how good people should lay their grief before God and then leave it with him.

CHAPTER 10

Here we have that wrong put right which was complained of and mourned in the previous chapter. Notice: 1. How the people's hearts were prepared for it to be put right (v. 1); how the putting right of it was proposed to Ezra by Shecaniah (vv. 2–4); and how the proposal was put into effect. The leaders were sworn to stand by it (v. 5). 2. Ezra was the first to come forward in support of it (v. 6); a general assembly was called (vv. 7–9). They

all, in accordance with Ezra's encouragement, agreed to the reformation (vv. 10–14). 3. Commissioners were appointed to inquire who had married foreign wives and to oblige them to divorce them, which was done accordingly (vv. 15–17), and a list of the names of those who were found guilty is handed in (vv. 18–44).

Verses 1–5

We are told here:

1. What good effects Ezra's humiliation and confession of sin had on the people. No sooner was it rumored in the city that their new governor, in whom they rejoiced, was himself so grief-stricken for them and their sin, than immediately there *assembled to him a very great congregation,* to mix their tears with his (v. 1). Notice what a good influence the examples of great people may have on their subordinates. When Ezra, a scribe, a scholar, and a man in authority under the king, mourned the national immorality so deeply, they concluded that they were indeed very guilty.

2. What a good suggestion Shecaniah made on this occasion. The place was *Bochim,* "a place of weepers" (Jdg 2:1), but it seems there was profound silence among the people till Shecaniah, one of Ezra's companions from Babylon (8:3, 5), stood up and made a speech to Ezra, in which he acknowledged the national guilt, briefly summed up all Ezra's confession, and confirmed that it was true: *We have trespassed against our God, and have taken strange* (foreign) *wives* (v. 2). It does not appear that Shecaniah was himself to blame in this matter, but his father was guilty, as were several of his father's house (as appears from v. 26), and so he reckoned himself among the guilty. *Now there is hope;* now that the disease had been discovered, it was half-cured. The sin that truly troubles us will not ruin us. The case was clear; what had been done wrong must be put right as far as possible. *Let us put* (send) *away all the wives, and such as are born of them* (v. 3). Ezra despaired of ever bringing the people to do it, but Shecaniah, who had more dealings with the people than he did, assured him it was practicable if they went about it wisely. As to the case of being *unequally yoked with unbelievers* (2Co 6:14), Shecaniah's counsel is not binding now. It is certain that such marriages are sinful and should not be made, but they are not invalid. "What should not have been done must, when it has been done, remain in force." Our rule under the Gospel is, *If a brother has a wife that believeth not,* and *she be pleased to dwell with him, let him not put her away* (1Co 7:12–13). Shecaniah said to Ezra and the people: "Let us covenant not only that if we have foreign wives ourselves, we will divorce them, but also that if we do not have such wives, we will do what we can to make others divorce theirs."

Verses 6–14

Here is an account of the proceedings about the foreign wives. Ezra sent orders to all the exiles to come to him at Jerusalem *within three days* (vv. 7–8). Within the set time, most of the people met at Jerusalem and made their appearance *in the street of the house of God,* in the square before the house of God (v. 9). Ezra issued the command at these proceedings. He had called them together, he said, because he found that since their return from exile, they had *increased the trespass of Israel* by *marrying strange wives,* they had added to Israel's guilt by marrying foreign women (v. 10), which would certainly be a way of reintroducing idolatry. They must now *confess their sin to God* and set themselves apart from all idolaters, especially idolatrous wives (vv. 10–11). The people submitted not only to Ezra's jurisdiction in general but also to his investigation and decision in this matter: *As thou hast said, so must we do* (v. 12).

Verses 15–44

The assembly had been dismissed, so that each might give and receive information to facilitate the matter. Commissioners sat as judges. Ezra was president, and the other commissioners were *certain chief* men *of the fathers* (men who were family heads) who were qualified with wisdom and zeal above others for this service (v. 16). They began

the first day of the tenth month to examine the matter (v. 16), which was only ten days after this method was first proposed (v. 9), and they finished in three months (v. 17). About 113 in total are named here who had married foreign wives; some of them, it is said (v. 44), had children by them, which implies that not many of them had, for God had not crowned those marriages with that blessing. Whether the children were turned out with the mothers, as Shecaniah proposed, is not stated, but it seems not. However, the wives who were divorced were probably well provided for, according to their rank.

A PRACTICAL AND DEVOTIONAL EXPOSITION OF THE BOOK OF

Nehemiah

This book continues the history of the *children of the captivity* (Ezr 10:16), the exiles, the poor Jews who had just returned from Babylon to their own land. At this time not only the Persian monarchy flourished in great pomp and power, but also Greece and Rome began to be significant. We have authentic accounts in existence of the affairs of those powerful states, but the sacred and inspired history takes notice only of the state of the Jews. Although neither Ezra the scribe nor Nehemiah the governor ever wore a crown, commanded an army, conquered any country, or was famous as a philosopher or great orator, both of them, because they were godly and praying men and were very useful in their day to the interests of religious faith, were really greater and more honorable than any of the Roman consuls or dictators, or even any of the bright stars of Greece, such as Xenophon, Demosthenes, or Plato himself, who lived at the same time. We have a full account in this book of how Nehemiah advanced the establishment of Israel. He records not only the works of his hands in managing public affairs, but also the workings of his heart in it. He was governor of Judea under Artaxerxes king of Persia for twelve years, from the twentieth (1:1) to the thirty-second year (13:6) of the reign of that king, whom Dr. Lightfoot thinks is the same Artaxerxes as Ezra received his commission from.

This book relates: 1. Nehemiah's concern for Jerusalem and the commission he obtained from the king to go there (chs. 1–2). 2. His building the wall of Jerusalem despite the opposition he met with (chs. 3–4). 3. His dealing with the people's complaints (ch. 5). 4. His finishing the wall (ch. 6). 5. The list of the exiles who returned (ch. 7). 6. The religious ceremonies of reading the Law, fasting, and praying, and the renewing of their covenants, to which he called the people (chs. 8–10). 7. The care he took to repopulate the Holy City and establish the holy tribe (chs. 11–12). 8. His zeal in reforming various abuses (ch. 13). Some call this "The second book of Ezra," not because he was its author, but because it is a continuation of the history of the previous book, with which it is connected (v. 1). This was the last *historical* book of the Old Testament that was written, as Malachi was the last *prophetic* book.

CHAPTER 1

Here we first meet with Nehemiah at the Persian court: 1. Inquiring into the state of the Jews and Jerusalem (vv. 1–2); informed of their deplorable condition (v. 3); fasting and praying for them (v. 4). 2. In deep and heartfelt prayer (vv. 5–11).

Verses 1–4

Notice:

1. Nehemiah's position at the court of Persia. He was *in Shushan the palace*, or royal city, of the king of Persia (NIV: in the citadel of Susa), where the court was ordinarily kept (v. 1), and he was *the king's cupbearer* (v. 11). After holding this position at court, he would be better qualified for the service to his country for which God had intended him, as Moses was better qualified to govern because he was brought up in Pharaoh's court, and David because he was brought up in Saul's. Nehemiah would also have had a better opportunity to serve his country by his influence on the king and those around him. God has his remnant in all places; we read of Obadiah in the house of Ahab, saints in Caesar's household, and a godly Nehemiah in the citadel of Susa. God can make the courts of monarchs sometimes be nurseries to the friends and patrons of the church's cause, and other times sanctuaries for them.

2. Nehemiah's sensitive and compassionate inquiry into the state of the Jews in their own land (v. 2). It happened that a friend and relative of his came to court, with some others, through whom he had the opportunity of being fully informed about how things were going with the exiles and what position Jerusalem, the beloved city, was in. Nehemiah himself lived in ease, honor, and fullness, but he could not forget that he was still an Israelite, nor could he shake off the thoughts of his brothers and sisters suffering. In spirit, like Moses (Ac 7:23) he visited them and looked on their burdens. Although he was a great man, he still did not think it beneath him to be aware of his brothers and sisters who were lowly and despised, nor was he ashamed to acknowledge his relationship with them and his concern for them. Although he himself did not go to settle at Jerusalem, he still did not judge or despise those who had returned.

3. The sad account which is given Nehemiah of the present state of the Jews and Jerusalem (v. 3). Hanani, the person he asked, is described as one who *feared God above many* (7:2), and so he would not only speak the truth but also, when he spoke of the desolations of Jerusalem, speak tenderly. His mission to the court at this time was probably to ask some favor, some relief or other, that they needed. The account he gives is:

3.1. That the holy descendants were miserably trampled on and abused, *in great affliction and reproach*, that they were in great trouble and disgrace (v. 3), insulted at every opportunity by their neighbors, and *filled with the scorning of those that were at ease* (Ps 123:4).

3.2. That the holy city was exposed and in ruins. The wall of Jerusalem was still broken down, and the gates (v. 3) were in ruins, as the Babylonians had left them. This made the condition of the inhabitants both despicable under the lasting marks of poverty and slavery, and also very dangerous, for their enemies could launch an attack on them whenever they pleased. The temple was built, the government settled, and the work of reformation had made some headway, but here was one good work still undone; this was still lacking.

4. The great distress this caused Nehemiah and the deep concern it gave him (v. 4). He *wept and mourned* (v. 4). He *fasted and prayed* (v. 4).

Verses 5–11

We have here Nehemiah's prayer, a prayer that referred to all the prayers he had for some time previously been offering to God day and night, while he continued to be distressed at the desolation of Jerusalem. It also refers to the petition he was now intending to present to the king his master for his favor to Jerusalem. We may notice in this prayer:

1. His humble and reverent address to God. It teaches us to draw near to God:

1.1. With holy reverence of his majesty and glory, remembering that he is the God of heaven, infinitely above us and infinitely greater than all the principalities and powers of both the upper and the lower worlds, angels and kings.

1.2. With a holy confidence in his grace and truth, for he *keepeth covenant and mercy for those that love him* (v. 5), not only the mercy that is promised, but even more than he promised.

2. His general request for the hearing and acceptance of all the prayers and confessions he now made to God (v. 6): "*Let thy ear be attentive to the prayer, which I pray before thee.*"

3. His penitent confession of sin. Not only Israel has sinned—but also *I and my father's house have sinned* (v. 6).

4. The pleas he urged for mercy for his people Israel:

4.1. He pleaded what God had formerly said to them. He had truly said that if they broke covenant with him, he would *scatter them among the nations*, and that threat had been fulfilled in their exile. Never had a people been so widely dispersed as Israel was at that time, even though at first they had been so closely united. He had also said that if they *turned to him*, as now they began to do, having renounced idolatry and kept to the temple worship, he would *gather them again*. He quotes this from Dt 30:1–5 and asks God to remember it—although the eternal Mind needs no reminding—as what he guided his desires by and based his faith and hope on, when he prayed this prayer. If God did not remember his promises more than we remember his precepts, we would be ruined. Our best

pleas in prayer are therefore those that are taken from the promises of God, the *word on which he has caused us to hope* (Ps 119:49).

4.2. He pleads the relationship in which they stand with God: "These are your servants and your people (v. 10), whom you have set apart for yourself and have taken into covenant with you. Will you allow your sworn enemies to trample on and oppress your sworn servants? If you will not appear for your people, whom will you appear for?" See Isa 63:19. As evidence of their being God's servants, he describes them by saying (v. 11), "They desire to fear your name; they not only are called by your name, but really have reverence for your name. They now worship you, and only you, according to your will. They are in awe of all the revelations you are pleased to make of yourself. They have a desire to do this."

4.3. He pleads the great things God has formerly done for them (v. 10): "*Whom thou hast redeemed by thy great power*, in former days. Your power is still the same; will you not therefore still redeem them and complete their redemption? Let not those who have a God of infinite power on their side be overpowered by the enemy."

5. His conclusion with a particular petition, that God will prosper him in his undertaking and give him favor with the king: *this man*, he calls him, for the greatest people are still merely human before God. They must recognize themselves as such (Ps 9:20), and others must recognize that too. *Who art thou that thou shouldst be afraid of a man?* (Isa 51:12). *Mercy in the sight of this man* (v. 11) is what he prays for, meaning not the king's mercy, but mercy from God while he addresses the king. Favor with other people gives us strength and encouragement when we see it as coming from the mercy of God.

CHAPTER 2

We read in the previous chapter how Nehemiah wrestled with God and prevailed (Ge 32:24, 28), and here we are told how, like Jacob, he prevailed also with people, and so found that his prayers were heard and answered. 1. He prevailed with the king so that he sent him to Jerusalem with a commission to build a wall around it and granted him what was necessary to do it (vv. 1–8). 2. He prevailed against his enemies who wanted to obstruct him on his journey (vv. 9–11) and mocked him in his undertaking (vv. 19–20). He prevailed on his own people to join with him in this good work: he viewed the desolations of the walls (vv. 12–16) and then persuaded all of them to lend a hand toward rebuilding the walls (vv. 17–18).

Verses 1–8

Nehemiah had prayed for the relief of his compatriots and then set himself to plan what he could do toward it. Nearly four months passed, however, from Kislev to Nisan—November to March—before Nehemiah made his request to the king for leave to go to Jerusalem, either because the winter was not a proper time for such a journey or because it was that long before his time of waiting had passed, and he could not come into the king's presence without being called for (Est 4:11). Now that he attended the king's table, he hoped to have his ear. Now here is:

1. The cause Nehemiah gave the king to inquire into his cares and griefs: he appeared sad in his presence. He took the wine and gave it to the king when he called for it, expecting him then to look him in the face. He was not usually sad in the king's presence, but conformed to

the rules of the court—as courtiers must—which would allow no sorrowful expression (Est 4:2). Good people should, by their cheerfulness, do what they can to try to convince the world of the pleasantness of the ways of religion and to take away the shame attached to them as people who are said to be always going about with long faces, but there is a time and a place for everything (Ecc 3:4). Nehemiah now saw cause both to be sad and to appear so. The miseries of Jerusalem gave him cause to be sad, and his display of grief would cause the king to ask why he was sad.

2. The kind notice which the king took of Nehemiah's sadness and the inquiry he made into the reasons for it (v. 2): *Why is thy countenance sad, seeing thou art not sick?*

3. The account Nehemiah gives the king of the reason for his sadness. He gives it with fear and humility. He modestly asks, *"Why should not my countenance be as sad as it is when the city, the place of my fathers' sepulchres, lieth waste?"* (v. 3). He says that the true cause of his grief is that Jerusalem lies in ruins.

4. The encouragement which the king gave Nehemiah to say what was on his mind, and how Nehemiah then turned in his heart to God (v. 4). The king liked him and was not pleased to see him sad. It is also probable that he had a kindness for the Jews' religion; he had shown it before in the commission he had given to Ezra, who was a man of the church, and he showed it now again by the position into which he put Nehemiah, who was a statesman. Wanting, therefore, only to know how he might be useful to Jerusalem, the king asked his worried friend, *"For what dost thou make request? What is it you want?"* Nehemiah immediately *prayed to the God of heaven* (v. 4) that he would give him wisdom to ask properly and that he would incline the king's heart to grant him his request. It was a secret, sudden, exclamatory prayer darted up to God; he lifted up his heart to the God, who understands the language of the heart: *Lord, give me a mouth and wisdom* (Lk 21:15); *Lord, give me mercy in the sight of this man* (1:11).

5. Nehemiah's humble petition to the king. He asked for a commission to go as governor to Judah, to build the wall of Jerusalem. He also asked for an escort (v. 7), and letters to the governors, not only to allow him to pass through their respective provinces, but also to supply him with what he needed; and he asked for another letter requiring the keeper of the forest of Lebanon to give him timber for the work that he planned.

6. The king's great favor to Nehemiah in asking him *when he would return* (v. 6). He showed that he was reluctant to lose him. Yet he would spare him for a while and would let him have inserted into his commission the words he wanted (v. 8). Here was an immediate answer to his prayer. In the account he gives of the success of his petition, notice:

- The presence of the queen, who sat beside the king (v. 6), which apparently was unusual in the Persian court (Est 1:11).
- The power and grace of God. Nehemiah won the point *according to the good hand of his God upon him* (Ezr 7:9).

Verses 9–20

We are told here:

1. How Nehemiah was dismissed by the court he was sent from. The king appointed *captains of the army* (army officers) and *horsemen* to go *with him* (v. 9), both to

guard him and to show that he was a man whom the king delighted to honor (Est 6:6–11), so that all the king's servants might respect him accordingly.

2. How Nehemiah was received by the country he was sent to:

2.1. By the Jews and their friends at Jerusalem. We are told:

2.1.1. While he hid the nature of his mission, they took little notice of him. He was at *Jerusalem three days* (v. 11), and it does not appear that any of the leaders of the city were waiting for him to congratulate him on his arrival; he remained unknown.

2.1.2. Although they took little notice of him, he took great notice of them and their state. He got up at night and viewed the ruins of the walls, probably by moonlight (v. 13), so that he might see what had to be done and how they would have to go about it, whether the old foundations were adequate, and which old materials could be used. Those who want to build up the church's walls must first take notice of the ruins of those walls. Those who want to know how to put things right must first ask what is wrong, what needs to be reformed, and what may remain as it is.

2.1.3. When he disclosed his intentions to the rulers and people, they cheerfully agreed with him in it. He did not tell them, to begin with, why he came (v. 16), because he did not want it to seem that he was doing it for show, and because if he found it impracticable, he could withdraw more honorably if he had not revealed his purpose. But when he had viewed and considered the matters and probably sensed the thoughts and feelings of the rulers and people, he told them *what God had put into his heart* (v. 12), namely, to *build up the wall of Jerusalem* (v. 17). *Come, therefore, and let us build up the wall* (v. 17). He did not undertake to do the work without them—it could not be done by only one person—nor did he issue commands imperiously, even though he had the king's commission. No; he encouraged them in a friendly and kind way to join him in this work. To encourage them in this, he speaks of his plan:

- As owing its origin to the special grace of God. He does not commend himself in it, claiming that it was a good thought of his own, but acknowledges that *God put it into his heart* (v. 12).
- As owing its progress up to that time to the special providence of God. He produced the king's commission and told them how readily it had been granted and how eager the king was to support his plan, in which Nehemiah saw *the hand of his God good upon him* (v. 18). They all immediately decided to agree with him: *Let us rise up and build* (v. 18). *So they strengthened their hands* (v. 18), their own and one another's, *for this good work* (v. 18). Many more good works would be undertaken if there were only a good leader to head them up.

2.2. By those that wished harm on the Jews. When Sanballat and Tobiah, two of the Samaritans—but by birth the former a Moabite and the latter an Ammonite—saw someone coming with a commission from the king to benefit Israel, they *were exceedingly grieved*, they were very much disturbed (v. 10) that all their paltry little efforts to weaken Israel had been frustrated by a fair, noble, and generous plan to strengthen them. When they saw someone coming in that way, who professedly *sought the welfare of the children of Israel* (v. 10), it troubled them deeply. When Nehemiah began to act, they set out to stop him, but their efforts were futile (vv. 19–20). Notice with what good reasoning the Jews dealt with these discouragements. They encouraged themselves with the thought that they were the *servants of the God of heaven* (v. 20), the only true and living God, that they were acting for him in what they did, and that therefore he would support them and prosper them, even though the nations conspired (Ps 2:1).

CHAPTER 3

Saying and doing are often two different things: many are ready to say, "Let us get up and build," but sit back and do nothing, like that smooth-tongued son who said, I go, Sir, but went not (Mt 21:30). Those who undertook this work were not like such people. As soon as they had decided to build the wall around Jerusalem, they lost no time, but immediately set about the work. This chapter gives an account of two things: 1. The names of the builders, which are recorded here to their honor, for they were those who showed a great zeal for God and their country. 2. The order of the building; they started where they were and worked their way around to where they began. They repaired the section from the Sheep Gate to the Fish Gate (vv. 1–2); from there to the old gate (Jeshanah Gate) (vv. 3–5); from there to the Valley Gate (vv. 6–12); from there to the Dung Gate (vv. 13–14); from there to the Fountain Gate (v. 15); from there to the Water Gate (vv. 16–26); and from there by the Horse Gate to the Sheep Gate again, where they began (vv. 27–32). And so they completed their work around the city.

Verses 1–32

Several things are significant in the account given of the building of the wall around Jerusalem:

1. Eliashib the high priest and his fellow priests took the lead in this group of builders (v. 1). If there was work to do, who was so qualified as they to do it? If there was danger ahead, who was so qualified as they to take the risk? The Sheep Gate, so called because through it the sheep were brought to be sacrificed in the temple, was repaired by the priests, because *the offerings of the Lord made by fire* were their inheritance (Dt 18:1). And it is only of this gate that it is said *they sanctified it* with the word and prayer.

2. Those who undertook this work were very many, each taking their share in the work according to their ability, some more and some less.

3. Many who were active in the work were not themselves inhabitants of Jerusalem, and therefore did it purely for the public welfare, not for any personal or private interest or advantage. Here are the men from Jericho (v. 2), from Gibeon and Mizpah (v. 7), and from Zanoah (v. 13). Every Israelite should lend a hand toward building up Jerusalem.

4. Several leaders, both from Jerusalem and from other towns, were active in this work, thinking themselves bound by honor to do all they could and all that their wealth and power enabled them to do to further this good work.

5. Here the nobles of Tekoa are justly rebuked because they *put not their necks* (would not put their shoulders) *to the work of their Lord* (v. 5), that is, they would not come under the discipline of being obliged to perform this service. They thought the dignity and liberty of their rank exempted them from "getting their hands dirty" and serving God and doing good.

6. Two people joined together in repairing *the old gate* (the Jeshanah Gate) (v. 6), and so were cofounders, and shared the honor of doing it between them. We must be thankful that the good work we cannot ourselves achieve individually may be shared with those who will come with us as partners. Some think that this is called the *old gate* because it belonged to the ancient Salem, which was said to have been originally built by Melchizedek.

7. Several good and honest businesspeople, as well as priests and rulers, were active in this work—*goldsmiths, apothecaries* (perfume-makers), *merchants* (vv. 8, 32). They did not think their callings excused them, nor did they plead that they could not leave their shops to attend to public business, knowing that what they lost would certainly be made up for by the blessing of God on their callings.

8. Some women are spoken of as helping in this *work—Shallum and his daughters* (v. 12)—who, although they could not help physically, still, having their inheritance in their own hands, or being rich widows, contributed money to buy materials and pay the workers. The apostle Paul speaks of some good women who *laboured with him in the gospel* (Php 4:3).

9. Some are described as those who repaired *over against* (opposite or in front of) *their houses* (vv. 10, 23, 28–29), and one who was probably only a lodger repaired *over against* (opposite) *his chamber* (v. 30). When a good work is to be done, everyone should apply themselves to do that which is nearest to themselves and is within their reach. If everyone swept their own front door, the street would be clean; if everyone did their part, then things would be more satisfactory. If the one who has only a room will help in their neighborhood, they are doing their part.

10. One is described as *earnestly* repairing what came to his share (v. 20). It is good to be thus *zealously affected in a good thing* (Gal 4:18), and this good man's zeal probably caused many others to make a greater effort and work more quickly.

11. One of these builders is described as being *the sixth son* of his father (v. 30). His five elder brothers, it seems, did not turn out to do this work, but he did. In doing what is good we need not wait for our elders to go before us; if they refuse, it does not therefore follow that we must also. And so the younger brother, if he does better than the others, does God and his generation a better service, and is indeed a better person. Those who are most useful are honored the most.

12. Some of those who had finished their section helped their fellow builders; they undertook another share where they saw there was most need. Meremoth repaired in v. 4 and again in v. 21. And the men of Tekoa, besides the section they repaired (v. 5), undertook to repair another section (v. 27), which is especially remarkable because their nobles set them a bad example by withdrawing from the work; perhaps this bad example, instead of giving them an excuse to sit back and do nothing, made them so much more eager to do the work that they decided to do twice as much, so that their zeal might either shame or make up for the greed and carelessness of their nobles.

13. No mention is made of any particular share that Nehemiah himself had in this work. A namesake of his is mentioned (v. 16). But did he do nothing? Yes, yet although he did not repair any particular section of the wall, he did more than any of them, for he had oversight of the whole project. Half of his servants worked where they were most needed, and the other half stood guard, as we find later (4:16), while he himself personally did the rounds, directing and encouraging the builders as he walked round, putting his hand to the work where needed, and keeping a watchful eye on the movements of the enemy, as we will see in the next chapter. A ship's captain need not run the engine; it is enough for them to steer the vessel.

CHAPTER 4

We left all hands at work in the previous chapter in building the wall around Jerusalem. But such good work is not usually carried out without opposition, and in this chapter we are told what opposition came and how Nehemiah advanced the work in spite of it. 1. Enemies mocked and ridiculed their undertaking, but they responded to their scoffing with their prayers. They simply took no notice of them and went on with their work nevertheless (vv. 1–6). 2. Enemies plotted to kill them, to stop them by force (vv. 7–8, 10–12). To guard against this, Nehemiah prayed (v. 9), posted guards (v. 13), and encouraged them to fight (v. 14), and so the plan was frustrated (v. 15). 3. The work therefore continued with every necessary precaution taken against a surprise attack (vv. 16–23).

Verses 1–6

Here is:

1. The spiteful ridicule of Sanballat and Tobiah toward the Jews for trying to rebuild the wall around Jerusalem. News of the rebuilding of the wall immediately rang out throughout the country; information came to Samaria, the home of the enemies to the Jews, and here we are told how they received the news:

1.1. In their hearts. They were very angry at what was being undertaken, and had *great indignation* (v. 1). They were greatly incensed that Nehemiah had come to promote the welfare of the children of Israel (2:10), but when they heard of this great undertaking for their good, they could not endure it.

1.2. In their words. They despised it and ridiculed it. "*These feeble Jews*: what will they use for materials (v. 2)? *Will they revive* (bring back to life) *the stones out of the rubbish?* And why are they working so fast? Do they think they can rebuild the wall of a whole city in one day, and then celebrate a feast of dedication with sacrifices the next day? How foolish can you get? How ridiculous could they be? If a fox go up"—not with its subtlety but with its weight—"it will break down their stone wall."

2. Nehemiah's humble and devout address to God when he heard of these abusive remarks. He did not answer these fools according to their folly (Pr 26:4). He did not rebuke them for their weakness, but only looked to God in prayer.

2.1. He begs God to take notice of the indignity shown to them (v. 4), and we are to imitate him in this: *Hear, O our God! for we are despised.*

2.2. He begs God to avenge their cause and turn their insults back on the enemies themselves (vv. 4–5). This was spoken by a spirit of prophecy rather than by a spirit of prayer, and is not to be imitated by us, who are taught by Christ to *pray for* those who *despitefully use and persecute us* (Mt 5:44). Christ himself prayed for those who insulted him: *Father, forgive them* (Lk 23:34).

3. The energy of the builders, despite these thoughts (v. 6). They worked so quickly that in a short time they had built the wall to half its height, for the people worked at it with all their hearts.

Verses 7–15

We have here:

1. The conspiracy the Jews' enemies formed against them, to stop the building by killing the builders. The plotters were not only Sanballat and Tobiah but also other neighboring people whom they had drawn into the conspiracy. *They were very wroth. Cursed be their anger, for it was fierce, and their wrath, for it was cruel* (Ge 49:7).

There was nothing to do now but *fight against Jerusalem* (v. 8). But why? What quarrel did they have with the Jews? They hated the Jews' godliness and were therefore angry at their prosperity and wanted to destroy them. The prevention of good work is what evildoers aim at and promise themselves, but good work is God's work, and it will surely succeed.

2. The discouragements the builders themselves labored under. At the very time when the enemies said, let us *cause the work to cease* (v. 11), Judah said, "Let us give up, for we are not able to carry on with it" (v. 10). They represented the laborers as being too tired, and the remaining difficulties—even that first part of the work, the removing of the rubbish—as insuperable, and so they thought it best that they stop for the moment. On many occasions, active leaders have to use as much energy in grappling with the fears of their friends as they do in facing the terrors of their enemies.

3. The information brought to Nehemiah of the enemies' plans (v. 12). It came from *Jews that dwelt by them*, in the country. These compatriots of theirs were not zealous enough to come to Jerusalem to help their brothers in building the wall, but having the opportunity—because of where they were—to find out what the enemy was thinking, they had enough honesty and care for their brothers to tell them about it. In fact, they themselves came to tell them, so the intelligence might be believed all the more. They told them ten times, repeating it in earnest, and with a great concern, with the report being confirmed by many witnesses: "Whatever place you turn to, they are against us, so you must be on your guard on all sides."

4. The godly and wise methods which Nehemiah then used to frustrate their plots and to keep his work and workers safe.

4.1. It is said (v. 14) that he *looked*.

4.1.1. He looked up, called on God to be on his side, and put himself and his cause under divine protection (v. 9): *We made our prayer unto our God.* That was what this good man did, and it should also be what we do. He spread out before God all his cares, griefs, and fears, so putting himself at ease. This was the first thing he did; before he did anything practical, he offered his prayer to God, for we must always begin with him.

4.1.2. He looked around him. Having prayed, he *set a watch* (posted a guard) *against them* (v. 9). The instructions Christ has given us in our spiritual warfare correspond to this example (Mt 26:41): *Watch and pray.* If we think we can keep ourselves safe only by prayer, without needing to be watchful, then we are lazy and we tempt God. If we are watchful but do not pray, then we are proud and insult God, and either way we lose his protection.

4.2. Notice:

4.2.1. How he posted the guards (v. 13). *In the lower places* he set them *behind the wall*, so that they might trouble the enemy over it, using it as a parapet, but in *the higher places*, where the wall had been built to its full height, he set them on it, so that they might be able to throw down from the top of it stones or arrows onto the heads of the attackers. He posted them *after* (by) *their families*, so that mutual relationships might commit them to help one another.

4.2.2. How he encouraged the people (v. 14). "Come," he says, "*be not afraid of them*," but be bold, considering whom you are fighting under. You cannot have a better commander: *Remember the Lord, who is great and terrible* (awesome) (v. 14). You think your enemies are *great and terrible*, but what are they compared with God, especially in opposition to him? He is far above them and has control over them. He will be awesome to them when he comes to judge them." An ever-present fear of God is the best antidote to the ensnaring fear of people.

5. The disappointment this gave the enemies (v. 15). When they found that their plot had been discovered and that the Jews were on their guard, they concluded that it was useless to attempt anything and that *God had brought their counsel to nought*. They knew they could not win unless they launched a surprise attack, and if their plot was known, it had been quashed. The Jews then *returned everyone to his work*, much more cheerfully because they clearly saw that God acknowledged it and acknowledged them in doing it.

Verses 16–23

When the builders felt secure enough *to return to their work*, concluding that the plotting of their enemies had been frustrated, they were still not so confident as to lay down their arms.

1. While one half worked, the other half carried arms, holding *spears, and shields, and bows*, not only for themselves but also for the laborers, who would immediately stop work and take up their weapons on the first sign of any movement by the enemy (v. 16). Dividing their time in this way between their trowels and their spears, they are said to *work with one hand* and hold their weapons *with the other* (v. 17), which cannot be understood literally, for the work would require both hands, but it suggests they were equally employed in both tasks.

2. All the builders wore a sword at their sides (v. 18), which they could carry without hindering their work. The word of God is the sword of the Spirit (Eph 6:17), which we should always have at hand and never need to search for, both in our work and in our spiritual conflict.

3. Care was taken both to get and to give early notice of the approach of the enemy, in case they should try to surprise them. Nehemiah kept a trumpeter always by him to sound the alarm at the first suspicion of danger. The work was extensive, and the builders were widely separated, for they were working on all parts of the wall at the same time. Nehemiah continually walked around the walls to oversee the work and encourage the workers. When they acted as workers, they had to be dispersed to wherever there was work to do. When they acted as soldiers, however, they had to come close together and be grouped as one body. Similarly, the laborers in Christ's building should be ready to unite against a common foe.

4. The inhabitants of the villages were ordered to stay within Jerusalem, with their helpers, not only so they might be nearer their work in the morning, but also so they might be ready to help in case of an attack at night (v. 22).

5. Both Nehemiah himself and all those with him got on with their work. The spears were held up, and the sight of them terrified the enemy, not only from sunrise to sunset but also from dusk to sunrise (v. 21).

CHAPTER 5

We read in the previous chapter how bravely Nehemiah, as a wise and faithful governor, stood on his guard against the attacks of external enemies. Here we see him no less bold and active in putting right domestic grievances, and having kept the people from being destroyed by their enemies, he now keeps them from destroying one another. Here is: 1. The complaint which the poor made to him of the great hardships which the rich, from whom they had been forced to borrow money, had

imposed on them (vv. 1–5). 2. The effective ways Nehemiah took both to reform the oppressors and to relieve the oppressed (vv. 6–13). 3. The good example of compassion and kindness which he set for them as governor (vv. 14–19).

Verses 1–5

Hard times and hard hearts made the poor miserable.

1. The times they lived in were hard. There was a famine of grain (v. 3), probably because of a lack of rain. When the market prices are high because provisions are scarce, the poor soon feel the pinch. What made the scarcity that is here complained of even more severe was the fact that their *sons and their daughters were many* (v. 2). The families who were most needy had the most children. As grain was expensive, so also the taxes on the king's tax on their fields and vineyards had to be paid (v. 4). This mark of their captivity still remained on them. Now it seems they did not have the necessary means of their own to buy grain and pay taxes, but had to borrow. Their families had left Babylon poor; they had had to go to great expense to build houses for themselves, and they had not yet recovered when these additional burdens came on them.

2. The people they dealt with were hard. Money must be found from somewhere, and it had to be borrowed. Those who lent them money took advantage of their state of necessity and were very hard on them.

2.1. The lenders exacted interest from them at twelve percent, *the hundredth part* every month (v. 11). If the poor have to borrow merely to maintain their families, and we are able to help them, it is certain we should either lend freely what they need or, if they are unlikely to be able to repay it, freely give them something toward it.

2.2. They forced them to mortgage to them their lands and houses as a security for the loan (v. 3), and not only so, but also took the profits of the mortgaged properties as interest (v. 5, compare v. 11), so that gradually they might gain control of all they had. But this was not the worst of it.

2.3. They subjected their children to slavery to be sold at pleasure (v. 5). "Our heirs must be their slaves, and *it is not in our power* (we are powerless) *to redeem them*" (v. 5). This was their humble protest to Nehemiah, because they saw that he was not only a great man who could relieve them but also a good man who would do all he could. Let us mourn the hardships which many in the world groan under. Let us put ourselves into their shoes and remember in our prayers those who are burdened, help them, and be burdened with them. But let those who show no mercy expect *judgment without mercy* (Jas 2:13). It aggravated the sin of these oppressing Jews that they themselves had been so recently rescued from slavery, which should have made them *undo the heavy burdens* (Isa 58:6) out of gratitude.

Verses 6–13

It seems the complaint described above was made to Nehemiah at the time when he had his head and hands as full as possible with the public business of building the wall, but he realized that the protest was just, and so he did not reject it. The case called for prompt intervention, and so he immediately considered it, knowing that even if he built Jerusalem's walls very high, thick, and strong, the city would not be safe while such abuses were tolerated.

1. He was very angry (v. 6).

2. He *consulted with himself*, he pondered what he should do (v. 7). This shows that he did not say or do

anything unwise. Before he rebuked the nobles, he thought about what he should say and when and how he should say it.

3. He *rebuked the nobles and rulers* (officials) (v. 7), who were the ones with the money, and whose power perhaps made them bolder in their oppression. Let no one imagine that their position of honor places them beyond correction.

4. He set up a great assembly against them. He called the people together to support their testimony—which the people will generally be eager to do—against the oppressions and extortions (v. 12). Ezra and Nehemiah were both very wise, good, and useful leaders, but in not dissimilar cases, there was a great deal of difference in the way they handled things. When Ezra was told about the sin of the officials in marrying foreign wives, he tore his clothes, wept, and prayed, and was hardly persuaded to attempt a reformation, fearing it would be impracticable, for he was a man of a mild, sensitive spirit. When Nehemiah was told about something just as bad, his anger was immediately aroused; he rebuked the offenders, stirred up the people against them, and did not rest until he had used all the harsh methods he could, forcing them to reform, for he was a man of passionate and eager spirit.

4.1. Holy people may differ very much from each other in their natural temperament.

4.2. God's work may be done equally well by more than one method, which is a good reason why we should neither accuse someone about the way they are doing something nor consider our own way of doing things the only possible way.

5. He reasoned the case with them and showed them the evil of what they had done. The ordinary way of reforming people's behavior is to try in the first place to convince their consciences. He lays before them the following facts:

5.1. That those whom they oppressed were their own people.

5.2. That the oppressed had only just been redeemed *out of the hand of the heathen* (Gentiles) (v. 8) by the wonderful providence of God. "We have made all this effort to gain their liberty from the hands of the Gentiles," he said, "and now will their own rulers enslave them?"

5.3. That it was a great sin to oppress the poor in this way (v. 9).

5.4. That it was a disgrace to the faith that they all professed. "Consider *the reproach of the heathen our* (our Gentile) *enemies* (v. 9). They will say, 'These Jews, who profess to be so devoted to God: see how cruel they are to one another!'" Nothing exposes religious faith more to the taunts of its enemies than the worldliness and hardheartedness of those who profess it.

6. He earnestly pressed them not only not to deal so harshly with their poor neighbors, but also to restore what they had gained (v. 11). Notice how familiarly he speaks to them: *Let us leave off this usury*, let the exacting of usury stop (v. 10). He includes himself, as is right for those who rebuke, although he is far from being in any way guilty of the crime. They must stop charging too much interest. Though he has authority to command, *yet, for love's sake, he rather beseeches* (Phm 9).

7. He gained a promise from them (v. 12): *We will restore them.* He sent for the priests to make the nobles and officials give their oath that they would fulfill this promise. *So let God shake out every man that performeth*

not this promise (v. 13). This was a threat to which the people said *Amen.* With this *Amen* the people *praised the Lord* (v. 13). This cheerful promising was good, but what follows was even better: *They did according to this promise* (v. 12), and were faithful to what they had done.

Verses 14–19

Nehemiah relates in more detail what his practice was, not in pride or boasting, but to encourage both his successors and the lesser judges to be as kind as possible to the people.

1. He states how his predecessors had acted (v. 15). He did not name them, because what he had to say about them did not commend them, and in such cases it is good to omit names. The government took *forty shekels of silver* from them—probably this much a day—but besides that they made the people provide them with *bread and wine*, and they also allowed their servants to squeeze all they could out of the people.

2. He tells us what had been his own practice.

2.1. In general, he had not done as the former governors did. The fear of God restrained him from oppressing the people. He was generous purely for conscience's sake. He gained nothing except the satisfaction of doing good: *Neither bought we any land* (v. 16).

2.2. More particularly, notice:

2.2.1. How little Nehemiah received of what was allotted to him as governor. So far was he from extorting more than his due that he never demanded even what was his due, but lived on what he had gained in the court of the king of Persia and his own estate in Judea. The reason he gives for this self-denial is, *Because the bondage was heavy upon the people*, because the demands were heavy on these people (v. 18). In thinking about our own demands, we must consider not only the justice of such demands but also the ability of those on whom we make them.

2.2.2. How much he gave of his servants' work (v. 16) and his own food (vv. 17–18), any of which he might have withheld.

3. He concludes with a prayer (v. 19): *Think upon me, my God, for good*, remember me with favor, O my God.

3.1. Nehemiah here mentions what he has *done for this people* (v. 19), to shame the officials out of their oppression.

3.2. He mentions it to God in prayer, not as if he thought that he deserved any favor from God or that God was indebted to him. "If God do but *think upon me for good* (v. 19), then I will have enough."

CHAPTER 6

Now that the cries of oppressed poverty have been stilled, the building of the wall is progressing, and in this chapter we find it finished with joy. We read before how the Jews' enemies were frustrated in their plans to bring it to an end by force (ch. 4). Here we see how their attempts to drive Nehemiah away from it were frustrated: 1. When they tried to get him to come to a meeting, with the intention of causing him trouble, he would not move (vv. 1–4); when they wanted to make him believe his undertaking represented sedition and treason (vv. 5–9), he paid no attention. 2. When they hired false prophets to advise him to withdraw (vv. 10–14), he still kept his ground. 3. Despite the secret association maintained between these enemies and some false and treacherous Jews, the work was finished (vv. 15–19).

Verses 1–9

Here is an account of two plots on Nehemiah's life:

1. A plot to lure him into a trap. The enemies heard that all the gaps in the wall had been filled in, so that they considered it as good as done, even though the *doors of the gates* had still not been set in place (v. 1); it must therefore be "now or never" that they boldly remove Nehemiah.

1.1. With subtlety they tried to woo him to meet them in a village in the allotted territory of Benjamin: "*Come, let us meet together* (v. 2) to discuss the common interests of our provinces." *But they thought to do him a mischief*, they were scheming to harm him (v. 2).

1.2. He refused the suggestion. He did not want the work to stop; he knew it would if he left it for even a short time, and *why should it cease while I come down to you?* Four times *I answered them*, he says, *after the same manner* (v. 4).

2. A plot to terrify him away from his work. This is Sanballat's attempt, but it is futile.

2.1. He tries to fill Nehemiah with the apprehension that his undertaking to build the walls of Jerusalem is generally seen as divisive and seditious (vv. 5–7). This is written to him in an open letter, as something generally known and talked about—"*Gashmu* (Geshem) will confirm it is true"—that Nehemiah is aiming to make himself king and to shake off the Persian oppression. Sanballat pretends to inform Nehemiah of this as his friend—"*Let us take counsel together* (v. 7) how to quell the report." He hopes, like Judas, to kiss and kill. Nehemiah denies not only that such things are true but also that they were ever said; he knows his own reputation better than to believe he is suspected in this way.

2.2. Nehemiah therefore escaped the trap and stood his ground. While we conscientiously do our duty, let us trust God with our good name. Nehemiah lifts up his heart to heaven in this short prayer: *Now therefore, O God! strengthen my hands* (v. 9). When we are entering on any particular service or conflict in our Christian work and warfare, this is a good prayer: *Now therefore, O God! strengthen my hands* (v. 9).

Verses 10–14

The Jews' enemies leave no stone unturned in trying to take Nehemiah away from building the wall around Jerusalem. Now they try to drive him into the temple for his own safety; they want him to be anywhere except at his work. Notice:

1. The enemies' evil in organizing this temptation:

1.1. What they wanted was to make Nehemiah do something foolish, so that they might intimidate him, laugh at him—*That I should be afraid* (v. 13)—and so that they might have *matter for an evil report* and *might reproach me*, give him a bad name to discredit him.

1.2. The tools they used were a false prophet and prophetess, whom they hired to persuade Nehemiah to leave his work and withdraw for his own safety. The false prophet was Shemaiah, of whom it is said that he shut in at his own home, claiming to withdraw for meditation. Nehemiah went to his house to discuss things with him (v. 10). Other prophets were there, and one prophetess, Noadiah (v. 14), who were on the side of the Jews' enemies.

1.3. The claims were plausible. These prophets suggested to Nehemiah that the enemies would come and kill him at night. They pretended to be very concerned for his safety. They very gravely advised him to hide himself in the temple until the danger was over. If Nehemiah had

been persuaded to do this, the people would immediately have stopped their work and thrown down their arms, and everyone would have fled for their own safety; and then the enemies might easily, and without opposition, have broken down the wall again.

2. The courage of Nehemiah in overcoming this temptation. He emerges as conqueror.

2.1. He immediately decided not to give in to it (v. 11). "*Should such a man as I flee?* I will not go in. I will rather die at my work than live in humiliating retreat from it."

2.2. He was immediately aware of what was its cause (v. 12): "*I perceived that God had not sent him,* that Shemaiah gave this advice not by any divine direction but as a plot against me." Nehemiah says he dreaded two things—that he might:

2.2.1. Offend God: *That I should be afraid, and do so, and sin* (v. 13). Sin is what we should dread above anything, and it is a good protection against sin to be afraid of nothing but sin.

2.2.2. Shame himself: *That they might reproach* (discredit) *me* (v. 13).

2.3. He humbly begs God to deal with them for their evil scheming against him (v. 14): *My God, think thou upon Tobiah,* and the rest of them, *according to their works.*

Verses 15–19

Nehemiah here finishes the wall of Jerusalem, but still has trouble created by his enemies.

1. Tobiah and the other adversaries of the Jews were humiliated to see the wall built despite all their attempts to prevent it. The wall was finished *in fifty-two days,* and we have reason to believe they rested on the Sabbaths (v. 15). Many were employed, and what they did they did cheerfully, because they loved it. When the enemies heard that the wall had been finished before they thought it had even been properly begun, they were *much cast down in their own eyes,* they lost their self-confidence (v. 16): they envied the prosperity and success of the Jews. They were grieved to see the walls of Jerusalem built. If it was of God, it would be futile to think of opposing it; it would certainly prevail and be victorious.

2. Nehemiah had the trouble, despite this, of seeing some of his own people treacherously deal with Tobiah. Many in Judah were established in a secret alliance with him to advance the interests of his country, even though it would certainly mean the ruin of their own. They were *sworn unto* (under oath to) *him,* not as their ruler but as their friend and ally, because both he and his son had married daughters of Israel (v. 18). Notice the trouble caused by intermarrying with foreigners, for one Gentile who was converted by this practice probably meant that ten Jews were perverted. They had the cheek to try to woo Nehemiah himself into a friendship with Tobiah. They were so false as to betray Nehemiah's words of advice to him. All their thoughts against Nehemiah were for evil, but God thought about him for good (Ge 50:20).

CHAPTER 7

Nehemiah, having fortified Jerusalem with gates and walls, is next concerned: 1. To see the city strengthened (vv. 1–4). 2. To see it populated, and in order to do this, he reviews the register of the exiles—the families who first returned—uses it to call the roll, and records it (vv. 5–73). We will see later what use he made of it, when he brought one out of every ten to live in Jerusalem (11:1).

Verses 1–4

God says about his church (Isa 62:6), *I have set watchmen upon thy walls, O Jerusalem!* This is Nehemiah's responsibility, for dead walls, without living people to guard them, are a poor defense for a city.

1. He appointed *the porters* (gatekeepers), *singers, and Levites* (v. 1) in their places to do their work. God's worship is the defense of a place, and his ministers, when they keep to their duty, are those who guard the walls.

2. He appointed two governors or consuls, to whom he committed the care of the city and gave the responsibility to provide for public peace and security. Hanani, Nehemiah's brother, who came to him with the news of the devastation of Jerusalem, was one, a man of approved integrity and devotion for his country; the other was Hananiah, who had been ruler of the palace. Of this Hananiah it is said that he was a *faithful man and one that feared God above many*, a man of integrity who feared God more than most people do (v. 2).

3. He gave orders about the shutting of the gates and the guarding of the walls (vv. 3–4). The city was large in circumference. The walls enclosed the same ground as before, but much of it lay waste, because the houses were not built, so Nehemiah walled the city in faith, looking to the promise of repopulating it which God had recently made by the prophet (Zec 8:3–8). Although the people were now few, he believed they would be multiplied, and so he built the walls to make room for them. Notice the protection Nehemiah commanded for it. He ordered the rulers of the city themselves:

- To stand by and see that the city gates were shut up and barred every night.
- To take care that the gates were not opened in the morning until they could see that everything was clear and quiet.
- To set guards who would give prompt notice of danger if the enemy approached. As their turn to watch came, the members of each guard must post themselves *over against* (near) *their own houses* (v. 3), because then they would be particularly watchful. Public security depends on everyone's special care to guard themselves and their own family against the common enemy of sin. They became aware that *except the Lord kept the city the watchman waked but in vain* (Ps 127:1).

Verses 5–73

Here is another good project of Nehemiah's. He knew very well that the security of a city, under God, depends more on the number and courage of its inhabitants than on the height or strength of its walls. He thought it right to count the people so that he might find out which families had formerly been settled in Jerusalem and might bring them back, and so that he might find out which other families could be influenced by their religion or by their business to come and rebuild the houses in Jerusalem and live in them. The rulers of a nation are wise if they can keep a balance between the city and the country, so that its cities do not become so large that they drain and impoverish the country, nor so weak that they cannot protect it. Notice:

1. From where this good plan of Nehemiah's came. He acknowledges, *My God put it into my heart* (v. 5).

2. What method he took to pursue this plan.

2.1. He called the rulers together, and the people, so that he might receive an account of the present state of their families—their number and strength and where they had settled.

2.2. He reviewed the old *register of the genealogy of those who came up at the first,* the genealogical record of those who had been the first to return (v. 5), and compared the present list with that. We have here the repetition of the list from Ezr 2. There are many differences between the numbers in this list and those in the list in Ezra. What differences there are probably came about because of either mistakes made by transcribers or the diversity of the copies from which the numbers were taken. Alternatively, one list may have accounted for these families when they set out from Babylon with Zerubbabel, the other for the same families when they actually arrived in Jerusalem. The grand totals are all just the same in Ezra and Nehemiah, except for the singers, who are 200 in Ezra and 245 here. Here is also an account of the offerings given toward the work of God (vv. 70–72), which is so different from that in Ezr 2:68–69 that it may be questioned whether it refers to the same contribution. Here the chief governor, who was not mentioned in Ezra, begins the offering; and the single sum mentioned in Ezra exceeds all those put together here. It is still, however, probable that it was the same offering, but that the account in Ezra followed one copy of the lists, and this account another, for v. 73 is the same as Ezr 2:70 and Ezr 3:1. We bless God that our faith and hope are not built on the fine details of names and numbers, genealogies, and chronologies, but on the great things of the Law (Mt 23:23) and Gospel.

CHAPTER 8

Ezra came from Babylon about thirteen years before Nehemiah came, yet here we read of a good work by Nehemiah that could have been done before but was not done until he came, for he was a man of an active and vital spirit. Nehemiah's zeal set Ezra's learning to work, and then great things were done, as we find here. 1. The public and sacred reading and explaining of the Law (vv. 1–8). 2. The joy which the people were ordered to express on that occasion (vv. 9–12). 3. The celebration of the Feast of Tabernacles according to the Law (vv. 13–18).

Verses 1–8

Here is an account of a sacred religious assembly and the good work done there.

1. The time of the assembly was the *first day of the seventh month* (v. 2). That was the day of the Feast of Trumpets, which was a Sabbath, and on that day they were to have a *holy convocation* (assembly) (Lev 23:24; Nu 29:1). But that was not all: it was on that day that they had set up the altar and begun to offer their burnt offerings after their return from exile (Ezr 3:1–6). This was a recent mercy in the memory of many then still alive.

2. The place was in the *street that was before the water gate* (v. 1), a spacious square capable of holding many people, which the courtyard of the temple could not do, for probably it was not now built nearly as large as it had been in Solomon's time. Sacrifices were to be offered only at the entrance of the temple, but praying, praising, and preaching were and are religious services which may acceptably be performed anywhere. When this congregation met in the city square, no doubt God was with them.

3. The persons who met were all the people; they were not forced to come, but willingly gathered by common agreement, as one. Not only men came, but also women

and children. As children come to exercise reason, they must be trained in exercises of religious faith.

4. The leader of this assembly and service was Ezra the priest.

4.1. His calling to the service was very clear; he held the office of a priest and was qualified as a teacher, and so the *people spoke to him to bring the book of the law* and read it to them (v. 1).

4.2. His position was advantageous. He stood on a pulpit or high wooden platform, "which they made for the word," as the original reads, for the preaching of the word, so that what he said might be more gracefully communicated and better heard, and so that those listening might be able to see him (Lk 4:20).

4.3. He had several helpers. Some of these stood beside him (v. 4), six on his right hand and seven on his left. Others who are mentioned (v. 7) seem to have been employed at the same time in other places close by, to read and explain to those who could not come within Ezra's hearing.

5. The religious exercises performed in this assembly were not ceremonial but moral: praying and preaching. Ezra, as leader of the assembly, was:

5.1. The people's mouthpiece to God, and they warmly joined him (v. 6). He blessed the Lord as the great God. The people said, *Amen, Amen*, and *lifted up their hands*. They also *bowed their heads* as a sign of reverence.

5.2. God's mouthpiece to the people, and they listened to him attentively. *Ezra brought the law before the congregation* (v. 2). When ministers go into the pulpit, they should take their Bibles with them. Ezra did so. It is from there they must take their knowledge. See 2Ch 17:9. He opened the book with great reverence and solemnity, *in the sight of all the people* (v. 5). He and others read aloud the Book of the Law, *from morning till noon* (v. 3), and they read *distinctly* (v. 8). Let people who read and preach the word also learn to communicate clearly, as those who understand what they say and are moved by it themselves, and who therefore want their listeners to understand it, retain it, and be similarly affected by it. *It is a snare for a man to devour that which is holy* (Pr 20:25). They explained what they read. It is necessary that those who hear the word should understand it. It is therefore necessary that those whose role is teaching should explain the word and make it clear. When Ezra opened the book, *all the people stood up* (v. 5), so showing respect for both Ezra and the word he was about to read.

Verses 9–12

We may notice:

1. The people were hurt by the words of the Law read out to them. The Law shows people their sins, and their misery and danger because of sin. When they heard it, they therefore *all wept* (v. 9): it was a good sign that their hearts were sensitive and tender, like Josiah's when he heard the words of the Law. They wept to think how they had offended God.

2. The people were healed and comforted with the words of peace spoken to them. It was one of the sacred festivals, during which it was their duty to rejoice, and even sorrow for sin must not prevent us from being joyful in God, but must rather lead us to be joyful. Ezra was pleased to see them so affected by the word, but Nehemiah pointed out to him—and Ezra agreed with the thought—that now was not the right time. This day was holy—and so was to be celebrated with joy and praise, not as if it were *a day to afflict* (humble) *their souls*. They forbade the people to *mourn and weep* (v. 9): *Be not sorry* (v. 10); *hold your peace, neither be you grieved* (v. 11). They

commanded them to show their joy, to put *on the garments of praise instead of the spirit of heaviness* (despair) (Isa 61:3). They allowed them, as a sign of their joy, to feast. But then it must be:

- With kindness to the poor: "*Send portions to those for whom nothing is prepared* (v. 10), so that your abundance may supply what they lack, so that they may rejoice with you."
- With godliness and devotion: *The joy of the Lord is your strength* (v. 10). Holy joy will act as oil to the wheels of our obedience.

3. The assembly complied with the directions given them. Their weeping was *stilled* (v. 11), and they *made great mirth*, celebrated with great joy (v. 12). Those who *sow in tears shall reap in joy* (Ps 126:5). Those who tremble at the convictions of the word may triumph in its encouragements. They were joyful not because they enjoyed choice food and sweet drinks, and had many people around them who did the same, but because they had *understood the words that were declared to them*. The darkness of trouble comes from the darkness of ignorance and failure. When the words were first declared to them, they wept, but when they understood them, they were joyful. They discovered the precious promises made to those who had repented and reformed their ways, and so there was hope in Israel.

Verses 13–18

We have here:

1. The people's renewed attention to the word. The next day, although it was not a festival, their leaders came together again to hear Ezra explain the words of the Law (v. 13). Now the priests and the Levites themselves came with the *chief of the fathers of all the people* (the heads of all the families) *to Ezra* (v. 13), "so that," as the margin reads, "they might instruct in the words of the law." They came to be taught themselves, in order to be trained to teach others. Because they had been tested and made more aware than ever of their own deficiencies and his greatness, on the second day their humility set them at Ezra's feet, as learners of him.

2. The people's ready obedience to the word as soon as they were made aware of their duty. It is probable that Ezra, *after the wisdom of his God that was in his hand* (Ezr 7:25), when they turned to him for instruction from the Law on the second day of the seventh month, read to them those laws which concerned the feasts of that month, including that of the Feast of Tabernacles (Lev 23:34; Dt 16:13).

2.1. The divine appointment of the Feast of Tabernacles was reviewed (vv. 14–15). *They found written in the law* a commandment about it. This Feast of Tabernacles reminded them of their living in tents in the desert, which is a representation of our tabernacle state in this world. The feast prefigures the conversion of the nations to trust in Christ (Zec 14:16); they will come to *keep the feast of tabernacles*, as those who have no enduring city here (Heb 13:14). The people themselves were to bring back branches of trees—those in Jerusalem took them from the Mount of Olives—to make booths, or shelters, with them, in which they were to stay.

2.2. This feast was religiously observed, just as it had been appointed (vv. 16–17).

2.2.1. They observed the ceremony: *They sat in booths*, which the priests and Levites set up in the courtyards of the temple. Those with houses of their own set up booths on the roofs of their houses or in their courtyards. Those who did not have a house set them up in the streets. All their holy festivals, especially this one, were to be celebrated with joy.

2.2.2. They attended the reading and explaining of the word of God during all the days of the feast (v. 18).

CHAPTER 9

Here is an account of a fast that was kept on a day of humiliation. We have here an account of: 1. How this fast was observed (vv. 1–3). 2. What were the main subjects of the prayer made to God on that occasion, concluding with a sacred commitment of fresh obedience (vv. 4–38).

Verses 1–3

Here is a general account of a national fast which the children of Israel held, probably by order from Nehemiah. It was a human fast, but such *a fast as God had chosen*, for:

1. It was a day *to afflict* (humble) *the soul* (Isa 58:5). They probably gathered in the temple courtyards as mourners, in sackcloth and ashes, with dust on their heads (v. 1). They were restrained from *weeping* in 8:9, but now they were directed to weep.

2. It was a day *to loose the bands of wickedness*, and that is the fast that God has chosen (Isa 58:6). Without this, wearing sackcloth and ashes is meaningless.

3. It was a day of fellowship with God. *They fasted to him, even to him* (Zec 7:5), for:

3.1. They spoke to him in prayer. Fasting without prayer is a body without a soul, a worthless carcass.

3.2. They heard him speaking to them by his word, for they read in the Book of the Law. By looking into the mirror of the Law, we may see where we are weak and defiled, and we may know what to acknowledge and what to put right. The time was equally divided between these two. Three hours — a quarter of the daytime hours — were spent in reading, explaining, and applying the Scriptures, and three hours in confessing sin and praying, so that altogether they stayed six hours and spent all the time in the sacred acts of religious faith, not for one moment saying, *Behold, what a weariness is it!* (Mal 1:13).

Verses 4–38

Here is:

1. An account of how this day of fasting was carried out:

1.1. The names of the ministers who were employed. They are named twice (vv. 4–5). Either they prayed successively, or, as some think, there were eight different congregations some way from one another, and each had a Levite to lead it.

1.2. How they served God. They prayed to God to forgive the sins of Israel and show his favor toward them. They praised God, for praise is not out of place on a day of fasting. In every act of devotion we must aim at this, *to give unto God the glory due to his name* (1Ch 16:29). We have a summary of their prayers recorded here.

2. A fearful adoration of God, as a perfect and glorious Being and the fountain of all beings (vv. 5–6). Those in the assembly are called on to show their agreement with this by standing up, and then the minister addresses himself to God: *Blessed be thy glorious name*. God is adored here:

2.1. As the only living and true God: *Thou art Jehovah alone* (v. 6).

2.2. As the Creator of all things: *Thou hast made heaven, earth, and seas* (v. 6) and all that is in them.

2.3. As the great Protector of the whole creation: "You preserve in being all the creatures you have given existence to."

2.4. As the object of the creatures' praises: "*The host of heaven*, the world of holy angels, *worshippeth thee* (v. 6). But your *name is exalted above all blessing and praise* (v. 5)."

3. A thankful acknowledgment of God's favors to Israel.

3.1. Many are listed here before him.

3.2. Particular examples of God's goodness to Israel are remembered here:

3.2.1. The call of Abraham (v. 7).

3.2.2. The covenant God made with Abraham to give the land of Canaan to him and his descendants, a type of the better country (Heb 11:16) (v. 8).

3.2.3. The rescue of Israel from Egypt (vv. 9–11). It was the right time to remember this, now that these ministers were interceding for the completion of the people's deliverance from Babylon.

3.2.4. The leading of them through the desert by the pillar of cloud and fire, which showed them the way to go, directing all their stages and all their steps (v. 12). They were guided as to when they should move and when and where they should rest. The pillar was also a visible sign of God's presence with them to guide and guard them.

3.2.5. The plentiful provision made for them in the desert, so that they might not die of hunger: *Thou gavest them bread from heaven*, and *water out of the rock* (v. 15), and to encourage them, a promise that they would go and possess the land of Canaan. They had enough food and drink on the way and the good land as their destination; what more could they want? This reference is repeated (v. 20) in order to emphasize that the mercy was continued despite their sins and blasphemies: *Forty years didst thou sustain them* (v. 21).

3.2.6. The giving of the Law on Mount Sinai. The Lawgiver was glorious (v. 13). "You not only sent, but even came down yourself, and *didst speak with them*" (Dt 4:33). No nation on earth had such *right judgments, true laws*, and *good statutes* (Dt 4:8). And with *the law* and *the sabbath*, he *gave his good Spirit to instruct them* (v. 20). Besides the Law given on Mount Sinai, the five books of Moses, which he wrote *as he was moved by the Holy Ghost* (2Pe 1:21), served as constant instructions to them.

3.2.7. The giving to them of possession of the land of Canaan, *kingdoms and nations* (v. 22). They were made so numerous as to populate it (v. 23) and so victorious that they ruled it (v. 24).

3.2.8. God's great readiness to forgive their sins and bring about their rescue when they had brought his judgment on themselves because of their blasphemies. Later, when they had settled down in Canaan and delivered themselves by their sins into the hands of their enemies, but then submitted to him and humbly cried out, he *gave them saviours* (v. 27), the judges, by whom God rescued them many times when they were on the brink of destruction.

3.2.9. The fair warnings God gave them through his servants the prophets. When he rescued them from their troubles, he *testified* (warned them) *against their sins* (vv. 28–29), so that they might not misinterpret their being rescued as his turning a blind eye to their evil. The testimony of the prophets was the testimony of the Spirit in the prophets, and it was the Spirit of Christ in them (1Pe 1:10–11). They *spoke as they were moved by the Holy Ghost* (2Pe 1:21), and what they said is to be received accordingly.

3.2.10. The extension of God's patience and the moderating of his rebukes: *Many years did he forbear* (he was patient with) *them* (v. 30), reluctant to punish them and waiting to see if they would repent. And when he did punish them, he did not *utterly consume them nor forsake them* (v. 31).

4. A penitent confession of sin, both their own sins and the sins of their ancestors.

4.1. They begin with the sins of Israel in the desert: "They, even our ancestors," *dealt proudly and hardened their necks* (v. 16). Pride is at the root of human obstinacy and disobedience. When people do not make proper use of either God's ordinances or his providences, what can be expected of them? Two great sins are mentioned here, which they were guilty of in the desert—thinking of a return:

4.1.1. To slavery in Egypt, which for the sake of the garlic and onions, they preferred to the glorious liberty of the Israel of God (Ro 8:21), which had a few difficulties and disadvantages.

4.1.2. To the idolatry of Egypt: *They made a molten calf* and were so foolish as to say, *This is thy God* (v. 18).

4.2. They next mourned the blasphemies of their ancestors after they had been given possession of Canaan.

4.3. They finally come nearer to their own times and mourn the sins which brought those judgments on them which they have long been groaning under and are now only partly rescued from. They see two things as the cause of the troubles of themselves and their ancestors:

4.3.1. Contempt for the good law God had given them: they *sinned against thy judgments* (v. 29), the dictates of divine wisdom and the demands of divine sovereignty.

4.3.2. Contempt for the good land God had given them (v. 35). Those who did not want to serve God in their own land were made to serve their enemies in a foreign land, as had been threatened (Dt 28:47–48).

5. A humble description of the judgments of God, which they had been and were now under.

5.1. Former judgments are remembered, which they had not heeded. In the days of the judges their *enemies vexed* (oppressed) *them* (v. 27), and when they committed evil again, God again *left them in* (abandoned them to) *the hand of their enemies*.

5.2. Their present troubled state is laid before the Lord (vv. 36–37): *We are servants this day*. Freeborn Israelites are now slaves to the kings of Persia. They freely acknowledge that this came as a result of their sins. Poverty and slavery are the *fruits* of sin; it is sin that brings us into all our misery.

6. Their address to God in these troubles:

6.1. By way of request, that their troubles might not *seem little* (trifling) (v. 32). It is the only request in all this prayer. The trouble was universal; it had come on their *kings, princes, priests, prophets, fathers, and all their people*; they had all shared in the sin (v. 34), and now all shared in the judgment. It had continued for a long time: *From the time of the kings of Assyria* (v. 32), who took the ten tribes into exile, *unto this day*. "Lord, let it not all seem as nothing to you and not worthy of consideration, or as not needing to be relieved." They do not tell God what he should do for them, but leave it to him.

6.2. By way of acknowledgment, despite this, that these troubles really were less than they deserved (v. 33). They acknowledged the justice of God in all their troubles.

7. The result and conclusion of this whole matter. After this long statement of their case, they finally came to the decision. "Because of all this, we make a binding covenant with God. Because we have often abandoned God, we will now more firmly than ever commit ourselves to him. Because we have suffered so much for sin, we will

now steadfastly turn away from it, so that we may not defy him anymore." A certain number of the leaders, priests, and Levites were chosen as the representatives of the assembly, to sign and seal it in the name of them all.

CHAPTER 10

In this chapter we have a particular account of the covenant which had been decided on at the end of the previous chapter. We have here: 1. The names of those who set their names and seals to the covenant (vv. 1–27); an account of those who gave it their agreement and approval (vv. 28–29). 2. The covenant itself and its articles: 2.1. In general, that they would observe and do all God's commandments (v. 29). 2.2. In particular, that they would not intermarry with the peoples around them (v. 30), dishonor the Sabbath, or be harsh with their debtors (v. 31), and that they would carefully pay their church dues for the maintenance of temple worship (vv. 32–39).

Verses 1–31

When Israel was first brought into covenant with God, the covenant was confirmed by sacrifice and the sprinkling of blood (Ex 24:1–8). But here it was done by the more natural and usual way of sealing and signing the written articles of the covenant.

1. The names of those official people who, as the representatives and leaders of the assembly, set their hands and seals to this covenant. Nehemiah, who was the governor, signed first. After him, twenty-two priests signed. After the priests, seventeen Levites signed this covenant, among whom we find all or most of those who were the spokesmen of the assembly in prayer (9:4–5). Those who lead in prayer should also lead in every other good work. After the Levites, forty-four of the leaders of the people signed for themselves and all the rest.

2. The agreement of the rest of the people with them, and the rest of the priests and Levites, who showed their approval of what their leaders did. With them joined:

2.1. Their wives and children, for they had sinned, and they, too, must reform their ways.

2.2. The converts of neighboring nations, all that had separated themselves from the people of the lands, their gods and their worship, *unto* (for the sake of) *the law of God* (v. 28) and the observance of that law. Notice what conversion is; it is separating ourselves from the ways of this world and devoting ourselves to the direction of the word of God. And just as there is one law, so also there is only one covenant and one baptism for foreigners and for those born in the land. Notice how the agreement of the people is expressed (v. 29): *They* (all) *clave to their brethren* (joined their fellow Israelites).

3. The general purpose of this covenant. They placed on themselves no other burden than this necessary thing (Ac 15:28), which they were already obliged to keep by every other commitment of duty, right, and gratitude: to *walk in God's law, and to do all his commandments* (v. 29).

4. Some of the particular articles of this covenant, which were relevant to their present temptations:

4.1. That they would not intermarry with the peoples around them (v. 30).

4.2. That they would not trade on the Sabbath, or on any other day about which the Law had said, *You shall do no work therein* (Lev 23:3). The Sabbath is a market day for our souls, not for our bodies.

4.3. That they would not be harsh in demanding repayment of their debts, but would observe the seventh year as a year of canceling debts, according to the Law (v. 31).

Verses 32-39

1. It was decided, in general, that the temple worship would be carefully maintained and that the work of the house of their God would be done at the right times, according to the Law (v. 33). It is likely to go well with our families when care is taken that the work of God's house goes well. It was likewise decided that they would never *forsake the house of their God* (v. 39) for the temple of any other god or for the high places, as the idolaters had done, nor would they abandon it for their farms and trading, as those did who were ungodly or godless. Those who abandon the worship of God abandon God.

2. It was decided, in accordance with this, that they would be generous in maintaining the temple service, and not starve it. The priests were ready to do their part if the people would do theirs, which was to provide them materials to work with. Now here it was agreed and decided:

2.1. That a stock would be raised to plentifully supply God's table and altar. Each of the people therefore agreed to contribute yearly a third of a shekel, that is, about one-eighth of an ounce (about four grams), for the cost of these expenses. When everyone acts together, and everyone gives toward a good work, even though each one gives only a small amount, the whole amount will be considerable. The governor did not impose this tax; the people assumed responsibility for it themselves (vv. 32-33).

2.2. That particular care would be taken to provide wood for the altar, to keep the fire constantly burning.

2.3. That all those things which God's Law had appointed for the maintenance of the priests and Levites would be duly paid, so that they might not be under any temptation to neglect it to make necessary provision for their families. Firstfruits and tithes were then the main sources of the minister's revenues, and they here decide to bring in the firstfruits honestly and to bring in their tithes similarly. This was the law (Nu 18:21-28), but these dues had been withheld, as a result of which God, by the prophet, accused them of *robbing him* (Mal 3:8-9), at the same time encouraging them to be more just to him and those who received these gifts and offerings, with the promise that if they brought the *tithes into the storehouse*, he would *pour out blessings upon them* (Mal 3:10). They therefore decided to do this, so that there might be food in God's house. They said, "We will do it *in all the cities of our tillage* (in all the towns in which we work)" (v. 37). The Septuagint, the Greek version of the Old Testament, reads, "in all the cities of our servitude," for they were servants in their own land (v. 36). Though they paid great taxes to the kings of Persia, and much hardship was put on them, they would not use that as an excuse for not paying their tithes, but wanted to give God what was his as well as give Caesar what was his (Mt 22:21).

CHAPTER 11

Jerusalem was walled around, but it was not yet fully inhabited. Nehemiah's next concern is to bring people into it. 1. The methods taken to repopulate it (vv. 1-2); the main people who lived there, from Judah and Benjamin (vv. 3-9) and from the priests and Levites (vv. 10-19). 2. The different towns and villages of Judah and Benjamin that were populated by the rest of their families (vv. 20-36).

Verses 1-19

Jerusalem is called here *the holy city* (v. 1), because the temple was there and God had chosen to put his name there. The holy seed should all have chosen to live there, but on the contrary:

1. They did not want to live there:

1.1. Because a greater strictness was expected from the inhabitants of Jerusalem than from others. Those who do not want to be holy themselves shy away from living in a holy city. Or:

1.2. Because Jerusalem, of all places, was most hated by the neighboring peoples, which made it a dangerous place—as a position of honor often is—and therefore many were not willing to expose themselves. Fear of persecution and mocking keeps many out of the Holy City and makes them unwilling to support God and religious faith, for they do not consider that just as Jerusalem is threatened and insulted by its enemies, so also it is especially protected by its God and made a *quiet habitation* (Isa 33:20; Ps 46:4-5). Or:

1.3. Because it was more to their worldly advantage to live in the country. Jerusalem was no city of trade, and so there was not so much money to be gained there in commerce as there was in the country with its grain and cattle.

2. How it was repopulated:

2.1. The leaders lived there (v. 1). That was the proper place for them to live, because *there were set the thrones of judgment* (Ps 122:5). Their living in Jerusalem would invite and encourage others too. "The mighty draw others in like magnets."

2.2. There were some who willingly offered to live in Jerusalem, nobly forgoing their own secular interest for the public welfare (v. 2). They *sought the good of Jerusalem, because of the house of the Lord their God.*

2.3. After reviewing their whole number, those already living in Jerusalem concluded that there was room to bring one in ten who were still outside to live there. Who this should be was determined by lot, *the disposal of which*, all knew, *was of the Lord* (Pr 16:33).

3. By whom it was repopulated:

3.1. Many of the descendants of Judah and Benjamin lived there, for originally a part of the city lay in the allotted territory of one of those tribes and part in that of the other. The larger part was in the allotted territory of Benjamin, and so we find here only 468 families from the descendants of Judah in Jerusalem (vv. 7-8), but 928 from Benjamin. Though the Benjamites were more in number, it is said of the descendants of Judah (v. 6) that they were valiant, ready to serve, and able to defend the city in case of an attack. Judah has not lost its ancient character of a lion's cub (Ge 49:9): bold and daring. Of the Benjamites who lived in Jerusalem we are told here who was *overseer* (chief officer) and who was second (v. 9).

3.2. Many of the priests and Levites settled in Jerusalem. Of the priests who undertook the work of the temple in their divisions, there were 822 from one family, 242 from another, and 128 from another (vv. 12-14). It is said of some of them that they were *mighty men of valour* (able men) (v. 14). Some of the Levites also came and lived in Jerusalem, but few in comparison, 284 in all (v. 18), with 172 gatekeepers (v. 19), for much of their work was to *teach the good knowledge of God* (2Ch 30:22) throughout the country, which is why they were scattered throughout Israel.

3.2.1. It is said of one of the Levites that he had *the oversight of the outward business* (outside work) *of the house of God* (v. 16). The priests were the chief managers of the work within the temple gates, but this Levite was entrusted with the secular concerns of God's house, the collecting of the contributions, the providing of materials for the temple worship, and the like. Those who take care of the outward concerns of the church, such as the serving at tables, are as necessary in their place as those who take care of its inner concerns, who give themselves to the word and prayer (Ac 6:2, 4).

3.2.2. It is said of another that he was *the principal to begin the thanksgiving in prayer*, the director who led in thanksgiving and prayer (v. 17). He probably had a good ear and a good voice, and was a skilled singer, and so was chosen to lead the psalm. He was precentor in the temple.

Verses 20–36

Here is an account of the other towns, in which *the residue* (rest) *of Israel* lived (v. 20). It was necessary that Jerusalem should be repopulated, yet not in such a way that it would drain the country.

1. The temple servants, the descendants of the Gibeonites, lived in Ophel, which was near the wall of Jerusalem (3:26)

2. Although the Levites were dispersed throughout the towns of Judah, they still had an overseer who lived in Jerusalem, who was in charge of their order and was their provincial leader.

3. Some of the singers were appointed to look after the necessary repairs of the temple. They were *over the business of the house of God* (v. 22). The king of Persia allotted a special living allowance for them, besides what belonged to them as Levites (v. 23).

4. Here is one who was the king's commissioner in Jerusalem. He is said to be at the king's hand, to be the king's agent, in all matters concerning the people (v. 24), to determine disputes that arose between the king's officers and his subjects, and to make sure that what was due to the king from the people was duly paid in and what was allowed by the king for the temple worship was duly paid out. The Jews were fortunate that one of their number held this post.

5. Here is an account of the villages, or country towns, which were inhabited by the rest of Israel—the villages in which the descendants of Judah lived (vv. 25–30), those that were inhabited by the descendants of Benjamin (vv. 31–35), and divisions for the Levites among both (v. 36).

CHAPTER 12

In this chapter there are preserved on record: 1. The names of the leaders of the priests and the Levites who came up with Zerubbabel (vv. 1–9); the succession of the high priests (vv. 10–11); the names of the next generation of the other leading priests (vv. 12–21); the distinguished Levites in Nehemiah's time (vv. 22–26). 2. The ceremony of dedicating the wall of Jerusalem (vv. 27–43). 3. The establishment of the services of the priests and Levites in the temple (vv. 44–47).

Verses 1–26

Here are the names of very many priests and Levites who were famous in their day among the Jews who returned from exile. Perhaps the list is intended to encourage future generations, who came after them as priests and inherited their honor and promotion, to imitate their courage and faithfulness. We have here:

1. The names of the priests and Levites who came up with the people who left Babylon first.

2. The succession of high priests during the Persian monarchy, from Jeshua, who was high priest at the time of the restoration, to Jaddua (or Jaddus), who was high

priest when Alexander the Great came to Jerusalem after conquering Tyre. Alexander gave great respect to that Jaddus, who met him in his high-priestly garments and showed him the prophecy of Daniel, which foretold his conquests.

3. The next generation of priests, who were the leaders and were active in the days of Joiakim, and were sons of the first group. Of those who are mentioned in vv. 1–11 as famous in their generation, all but two are mentioned again in vv. 12–24—although with some variation in their names—as having sons who were similarly famous in their generation. It was rare that twenty good fathers should leave behind them twenty good sons.

4. The next generation of Levites, or rather a later generation; for those priests who are mentioned flourished in the days of Joiakim the high priest, and these Levites in the days of Eliashib (v. 22). A generation of Levites was *raised up*, who were *recorded* as *chief of the fathers* (family heads) (v. 22) and were extremely useful to the interests of the church, and their service was no less acceptable because they were only Levites. Because Eliashib the high priest was closely associated with Tobiah (13:4), the other priests grew negligent, but then the Levites appeared more enthusiastic. Those who were now employed in teaching (8:7) and praying (9:4–5) were all Levites, not priests, consideration being given to their personal qualifications more than their order.

Verses 27–43

The dedication of the wall of Jerusalem.

1. We must ask what was the meaning of this dedication of the wall. It was not done until the city had been pretty much repopulated (11:1). It was a sacred thanksgiving to God for his great mercy. They dedicated the city in a special way to God and his honor, and took possession of it for him and in his name. This city was *a holy city*, like no other, the *city of the great King* (Ps 48:2; Mt 5:35). They put the city and its walls under God's protection, acknowledging that *unless the Lord kept the city* the walls were *built in vain* (Ps 127:1).

2. We must notice with what ceremony it was performed under the direction of Nehemiah. The Levites from all parts of the country were called on to attend (vv. 28–29). They purified themselves, the people, the gates, and the wall. This purification was probably carried out by sprinkling the *water of purifying* (Nu 8:7)—or of *separation* (cleansing), as it is called in Nu 19:9—on themselves and the people, the walls, and the gates. This was a type of the blood of Christ, with which our consciences are cleansed from dead works, and so we are fit to serve the living God (Heb 9:14). The leaders, priests, and Levites walked around the top of the wall in two large choirs, with musical instruments, to show the dedication of it all to God (v. 36). They met at one place, where they divided into two choirs. Half of the leaders, with several priests and Levites, went to the right, Ezra leading the way (v. 36). The other half of the leaders and priests, who also gave thanks, went to the left, Nehemiah bringing up the rear (v. 38). Eventually both groups met in the temple, where they joined their thanksgivings (v. 40). The crowd of people probably walked on the ground, some within the wall and others outside it. The people greatly rejoiced (v. 43). Their shouts came from their genuine joy, and so they are noted here, for God graciously accepts honest, zealous services, even if they come from lowly and unskilled people. The women and children rejoiced, and their hosannas were not despised.

Verses 44–47

When the ceremonies of a thanksgiving day leave such impressions on ministers and people that both are more careful and cheerful in doing their duty afterward, then such ceremonies are indeed acceptable to God. This is what happened here.

1. The ministers were more careful than they had been in doing their work (v. 45). *The singers kept the ward* (service) *of their God*, attending in due time to the duty of their office; *the porters* (gatekeepers), *too, kept the ward* (service) *of the purification*, that is, they took care to preserve the purity of the temple.

2. The people were more careful than they had been in maintaining their ministers.

2.1. Care is here taken to collect their dues. The ministers were modest people and would rather lose their rights than demand them for themselves. Many of the people were careless and would not bring their dues unless they were called on to do so. *Some* people *were* therefore *appointed* whose service it would be to gather into the treasuries, *out of the fields of the cities, the portions* (shares) *of the law for the priests and Levites* (v. 44).

2.2. Care is taken that, being *gathered in*, the dues would be duly *paid out* (v. 47). They gave the singers and gatekeepers their daily share, over and above what was due to them as Levites, for we suppose that when David and Solomon appointed them to do their work (vv. 45–46), above what was required from them as Levites, they established a fund for their further encouragement. For the other Levites, the tithes, here called *the holy things* (portions) (v. 47), were duly set apart for them, out of which they paid the priests their tithe according to the Law.

CHAPTER 13

After Nehemiah had completed what he had undertaken to fence and fill the Holy City, he returned to the king his master, who was not willing to be without him for a long time, as appears from v. 6. But after some time, he obtained permission to go back to Jerusalem, to put right grievances and cleanse some corruptions which had crept in while he had been absent. 1. He turned out from Israel those of foreign descent, especially the Moabites and Ammonites (vv. 1–3). With a particular anger, he expelled Tobiah from the lodgings he had gained in the court of the temple (vv. 4–9). 2. He provided for the priests and Levites to have a firmer and more secure maintenance than before (vv. 10–14). 3. He restrained the desecration of the Sabbath (vv. 15–22). 4. He restrained the growing trouble of the people's marrying foreign wives (vv. 23–31).

Verses 1–9

Israelites were not to associate closely with the nations or allow any of their own people to have intimate dealings with the nations.

1. The law to this effect happened to be read *on that day, in the audience of the people* (v. 1), on the day the wall was dedicated. They found a law that the Ammonites and Moabites must not settle as naturalized people among them and must not unite with them (v. 1). The reason given is that they had wronged and been ill natured toward the Israel of God (v. 2); they had not shown them common civility, but had sought their destruction. We have this law in Dt 23:3–5.

2. The people readily complied with this law (v. 3). We see here the benefit of the public reading of the word of God. It reveals to us our sin and our responsibilities, good and evil, and it shows us where we have gone wrong. They *separated from Israel all the mixed multitude* (all who were of foreign descent) (v. 3), who in old times had been a trap for them, for it was written that the *mixed multitude fell a lusting*, the rabble began to crave other food (Nu 11:4). They expelled these dangerous usurpers.

3. We read of the particular case of Tobiah, who was an Ammonite. He had the same enmity toward Israel that his ancestors had, the spirit of an Ammonite, as can be seen from his anger toward Nehemiah (2:10). Notice:

3.1. How Eliashib, the high priest, corruptly took this Tobiah in to a lodger—even worse: in the courts of the temple. He was closely associated with Tobiah (v. 4), first by marriage and then by friendship. His grandson had married the daughter of Sanballat (v. 28), Tobiah's ally in opposing Nehemiah (2:10; 4:7–8). Probably some other person in his family had married into Tobiah's family. It was expressly provided by the Law that the high priest must marry *one of his own people*, or else he *profanes his seed* (defiles his offspring) *among his people* (Lev 21:14–15). In the courts of the temple he tried to make one large room for Tobiah by using several smaller rooms that had formerly been storerooms (v. 5). That Tobiah the Ammonite should be received with respect in Israel, and even in the courts of God's house, as if to defy God himself, was almost as bad as setting up an idol there. An Ammonite must not *come into the congregation* (v. 1); and will one of the worst and most evil Ammonites be wooed to come into the temple itself? Well might Nehemiah add (v. 6), *But all this time was not I at Jerusalem.* If he had been there, the high priest would not have dared do such a thing.

3.2. How boldly Nehemiah, the chief governor, throws him out, and everything that belongs to him, and restores the chambers to their proper use. When he comes to Jerusalem and is informed by the people who are troubled at the intimate relationship that has developed between their chief priest and their chief enemy, it grieved him sorely (vv. 7–8). Nehemiah has power and he uses it for God. Tobiah will be expelled. Nehemiah is not afraid of his anger, or Eliashib's, but expels the intruder by throwing out all his household goods. Our Savior cleansed the temple in the same way so that the *house of prayer* might not be a *den of thieves* (Mt 21:13). Similarly, those who want to throw sin out of their hearts, those living temples, must throw out all those things which sinful desires feed and fuel on. The temple stores will be brought in again, and the *vessels of the house of God* (temple articles) *put in their places* (v. 9), but the chambers must first be sprinkled with the water of purification and so cleansed. Similarly, when sin is thrown out of the heart by repentance, let the blood of Christ be applied to it by faith, and then let it be given the graces of God's Spirit for every good work.

Verses 10–14

Here is another grievance put right by Nehemiah:

1. The Levites had been wronged. Their *portions had not been given them* (v. 10). The Levites were so modest that they did not seek them: *for the Levites and singers fled every one to his field* (v. 10). This is included as a reason either:

1.1. Why their payments were withheld. The Levites were nonresidents: when they should have been doing their work around the temple, they were on their farms in the country, and so the people were not very much inclined to give them their maintenance. Or rather:

1.2. Why Nehemiah soon realized that their dues had been denied them: he missed them from their posts. "Every one of them has gone to gain a livelihood for himself and his family from the land, for his work would not support him." If you pay ministers poorly, you should not complain if you get a poor ministry.

2. Nehemiah began with the rulers, placing the blame on them and calling them to account: *"Why is the house of God forsaken* (neglected)*?* (v. 11). Why are the Levites starved out of it?"

3. He did not delay in bringing the dispersed Levites back to *their places* and setting them at their posts (v. 11).

4. He made the people bring in their tithes (v. 12).

5. He provided that the Levites should be paid justly and promptly. Commissioners were appointed to see that this was done (v. 13).

6. Having no reward from those for whom he did these good services, Nehemiah looks to God as the One who will reward him (v. 14): *Remember me, O my God, concerning this.* He was a man much given to godly exclamatory prayers. He prays simply, *Remember me* (v. 14); he does not pray, "Reward me."

Verses 15–22

Here is another example of the reformation in which Nehemiah was so active. He revived consecration of the Sabbath and so kept the authority of the fourth commandment.

1. The Law of the Sabbath was very strict and was insisted on, and with good reason too, for religious faith is never on the throne while Sabbaths are trodden underfoot. But Nehemiah discovered that even in Judah this law was being wretchedly broken.

1.1. The farmers trod their winepresses and brought home their grain on that day (v. 15), although there was a clear command that in *earing* (plowing) *time, and in harvest time, they should rest* on the Sabbaths (Ex 34:21).

1.2. The carriers *loaded their asses with all manner of burdens* (loads) (v. 15) and had no scruples in doing so, although there was a particular condition in the Law that cattle should rest (Dt 5:14) and that they should *bear no burden on the sabbath day* (Jer 17:21).

1.3. The merchants and sellers of the famous trading city of Tyre *sold all manner of wares* (merchandise) on the Sabbath day (v. 16).

2. Nehemiah reformed the abuse.

2.1. *He testified against those* who desecrated the Sabbath (v. 15 and again v. 21).

2.2. He reasoned with the rulers about the offense; he took the nobles of Judah to task (v. 17). He accused them: *You do it.* They did not carry grain or sell fish, but they turned a blind eye to those who did, and they did not use their power to restrain the offenders, and so made themselves guilty, like those judges who bear the sword in vain (Ro 13:4). They also set a bad example in other things. If the nobles allowed themselves sport, recreation, idle visits, and idle talk on the Sabbath, then businesspeople, both in city and in country, would consider it more justifiable to desecrate it by their worldly employments. He reasoned the case with them (v. 18). If they did not accept the warning, but returned to the same sins again, they had reason to expect further judgments: *You bring more wrath upon Israel by profaning the sabbath.*

2.3. He took care to prevent the desecration of the Sabbath, as one who aimed only at reformation. If he could reform them, he would not punish them, and if he had to punish them, it was only so that he might reform them. This is an example to judges to be those who restrain others, who wisely guide and warn to try to prevent the need for punishment. He ordered the gates of Jerusalem to be kept shut from the evening before the Sabbath until the morning after, and he set his own servants to watch them, so that no loads were brought in on the Sabbath, late the night before, or early the morning after, so that the Sabbath time would not be encroached on (v. 19). He threatened those who came with goods to the gates, telling them that if they came again, he would certainly lay hands on them (v. 21). He commanded the Levites to take care to rightly consecrate the Sabbath, that they should cleanse themselves in the first place, and so set a good example to the people, and that some of them should come and guard the gates (v. 22). There is likely to be a reformation in this and other respects when judges and ministers work together. The healing he brought about lasted, for in our Savior's time we find the Jews going to the other extreme, and being overscrupulous about the ceremonial aspects of Sabbath consecration.

2.4. He concludes this passage with a prayer (v. 22).

Verses 23–31

Here is one further example of Nehemiah's godly zeal in purifying his compatriots as a special people for God. Notice here:

1. How they had corrupted themselves by marrying foreign wives. This had been complained about in Ezra's time, and much was done toward reformation (Ezr 9:1–10:44). As a good governor, Nehemiah inquired into the state of the families of those who were his responsibility, so that he might reform what was wrong in them, and so heal the streams by healing the springs. He found that many of the Jews had *married wives of Ashdod, of Ammon, and of Moab* (v. 23). He talked with the children and found they were children of foreigners, for their *speech betrayed them* (Mt 26:73). The children had been brought up with their mothers, and learned to talk from them, their nurses, and their servants, so that they could not speak the Jews' language, or not purely, but *half in the speech of Ashdod* (v. 24), or Ammon, or Moab, according to the mother's native language.

2. What action Nehemiah took to cleanse this corruption:

2.1. He showed them how evil it was, and the obligation he was under to witness against it. He quotes a command, to prove that it was in itself a great sin, and he makes them take an oath on that command, *You shall not give your daughters unto their sons,* which is taken from Dt 7:3. He also quotes a precedent, to show them its harmful consequences, which made it necessary for the rulers to censure it (v. 26): *Did not Solomon king of Israel sin by these things?*

2.2. He showed that he was highly displeased with it, so that he might wake them up to a due sense of its evil. He *contended with* (rebuked) *them* (v. 25). He showed them how empty their excuses were, and he argued intensely with them. When he had silenced them, he cursed them, that is, he declared the judgments of God against them and showed them what their sin deserved. Ezra, in the same circumstances, had pulled out his own hair, in holy sorrow for the sin (Ezr 9:3); Nehemiah pulled out their hair, in holy indignation at the sinners.

2.3. He required them not to take any more such wives, and separated those whom they had taken: he cleansed them from all foreigners, both men and women (v. 30), and made them promise on oath that they would never take foreign wives again (v. 25).

2.4. He took particular care of the priests' families, so that they might not come under this guilt. He found, on inquiry, that a branch of the high priest's own family, one of his grandsons, had married a daughter of Sanballat, that notorious enemy of the Jews (2:10; 4:1), and so had, in effect, entangled his interests with those of the Samaritans (v. 28). It seems this young priest would not divorce his wife, and so Nehemiah drove him away from him, deprived him, degraded him, and made him forever incapable of being part of the priesthood. Josephus says that this expelled priest was Manasseh, and that when Nehemiah drove him away, he went to his father-in-law Sanballat, who built him a temple on Mount Gerizim, like that at Jerusalem, and promised him he would be high priest in it, and that that was then laid as the foundation of the Samaritans' claims, which were still alive in our Savior's time. Here are Nehemiah's prayers on this occasion:

- He prays, *Remember them, O my God* (v. 29). "Lord, persuade them; convince and convert them; remind them what they should be like and what they should do, so they may come to themselves."
- He prays, *Remember me, O my God* (v. 31).

A PRACTICAL AND DEVOTIONAL EXPOSITION OF THE BOOK OF

Esther

God does not deal with us according to our foolishness and weakness. Those Jews who were scattered in the provinces of the nations were taken care of, just as those who gathered in the land of Judea were. They were wonderfully preserved when doomed to destruction and appointed as sheep to be slaughtered (Ps 44:22). It is not certain who wrote this book. Mordecai was as able as anyone to write about several passages in it from his own knowledge. We are told (9:20) that he wrote such an account of them as was necessary to inform his people of the basis of their observing the Feast of Purim: *Mordecai wrote these things* and sent them enclosed in letters to all the Jews.

It is the record of a plot against the Jews to destroy them all. The name of God is not found in this book, but the apocryphal addition to it—which is not in the Hebrew, and was never received by the Jews into the canon of Scripture—has, *Then Mordecai said, God hath done these things* (Rest of Est 10:4). But although the name of God is not found here, the finger of God is, directing many minute events to bring about the rescue of his people. In such ways as God acted to defeat Haman's plot he will still protect his people. We are told: 1. How Esther came to be queen and Mordecai came to be great at court; they were to be the instruments of the intended rescue (chs. 1–2). 2. For what reason, and by what cunning method, Haman the Amalekite gained an order for the destruction of all the Jews (ch. 3). 3. The great distress the Jews were then in (ch. 4). 4. The defeating of Haman's plot on Mordecai's life (chs. 5–7). 5. The defeating of his general plot against the Jews (ch. 8). 6. The care that was taken to remember this forever (chs. 9–10).

CHAPTER 1

The purpose of recording the story of this chapter is to show how a way was made for Esther to come to the throne so that she could be instrumental in defeating Haman's plot. This took place long before the plot was hatched, so that we may look with wonder at the foresight and vast reaches of Providence. Xerxes the king: 1. In his prime gives banquets (vv. 1–9). 2. In his temper divorces his queen, because she would not come to him when he sent for her (vv. 10–22). This shows how God serves his own purposes even by our sins and foolish ways.

Verses 1–9

The commentators are not agreed which of the kings of Persia this *Ahasuerus* (Xerxes) was. Mordecai is said to have been one of those who were taken into exile from Jerusalem (2:5–6), from which it would seem this Ahasuerus was one of the first kings of that empire. Dr. Lightfoot thinks that he was that Artaxerxes who hindered the building of the temple, who is also called *Ahasuerus* (Ezr 4:6–7), after his great-grandfather, who was a Mede by descent (Da 9:1). We have here an account:

1. Of the vast extent of his dominion. In the time of Darius and Cyrus there were only 120 *princes* (satraps or royal rulers) (Da 6:1); now there were 127, *from India to Ethiopia* (Cush) (v. 1). It had become an overextended kingdom, which in time would sink under its own weight.

2. Of the great splendor and magnificence of his court. He held a most extravagant feast to show the riches of his glorious kingdom and the honour of his excellent majesty (v. 4). This was boasting glory, for no purpose at all. If he had shown the riches of his kingdom, as some of his successors did, by contributing toward the building of the temple (Ezr 6:8; 7:22), it would have been put to a better use. Xerxes gave two feasts:

2.1. One for his nobles and princes, which lasted a hundred and eighty days (vv. 3–4).

2.2. Another for all the people, both great and small (v. 5), which lasted seven days (v. 5) in the court of the garden (v. 5). The tents or pavilions which were pitched there for all the people were very fine and rich, as were the couches and the pavement under their feet (v. 6).

3. Of the good order which in some respects was kept there nevertheless. The Aramaic paraphrase says that the goblets of the temple were used in this feast, to the great sorrow of the godly Jews. Yet we observe in the account given here two things which were commendable in these feasts:

3.1. The drinking was *according to the law* (v. 8), probably some law just passed; *none did compel*, no one was compelled to drink—*none did compel* by constantly bringing them wine, as Josephus explains it. This warning of an unbelieving prince, even when he was showing his generosity, may shame many who are called Christians, who think they have not made their friends properly welcome unless they have made them drunk, and who, under pretense of offering a toast to different people, pass around sin, and then death.

3.2. There was no mixed dancing. Queen Vashti gave a banquet for the women in her own apartment, *in the royal house* (v. 9). While the king showed the honor of his majesty, she and her ladies showed the honor of their modesty, which is the true glory of the fair sex.

Verses 10–22

Xerxes' feast ended in sorrow because of his own foolishness. There was an unhappy disagreement between the king and queen, which abruptly broke off the feast, and sent the guests away silent and ashamed.

1. It was certainly the king's weakness to send for Vashti to come into his presence when he was drunk and in company with many men in the same condition. When *his heart was merry* (in high spirits) *with wine* (v. 10), Vashti must come, well dressed as she was, with *the crown on her head*, so that the princes and people might see how beautiful she was (vv. 10–11). By this:

1.1. He dishonored himself as her husband, who should not expose her but be to her *a covering of the eyes* (Ge 20:16).

1.2. He diminished himself as a king. It was against the custom of the Persians for the women to appear in public, and he put her into great difficulties when he commanded—not courteously asked, but commanded—her to do something so unladylike and make a show of herself.

2. Perhaps it was not wise of her to deny him. *She refused to come* (v. 12), although he sent his command by seven honorable messengers. If she had come, as long as it was clear that she did it out of simple obedience, it would have been no reflection on her modesty. Perhaps she refused in a haughty manner, and then it was certainly evil; she scorned to come at the king's command. This humiliated him intensely!

3. The king then became furious. He who ruled over 127 provinces could not control his own spirit; his *anger burned in him* (v. 12) (Pr 16:32).

4. Although he was very angry, the king would not do anything until he had first discussed it with his privy councilors. These experts are described as being learned—they *knew law* and *judgment*, were experts in matters of law and justice—and wise—they *knew the times*, knew the right course to follow. The king had great confidence in them and honored them: they *saw the kings face and sat first in the kingdom*, they had special access to the king and were highest in the kingdom (vv. 13–14).

4.1. The question proposed to this cabinet council (v. 15): *What shall we do to the queen Vashti according to the law?*

4.2. The proposal which Memucan made, that Vashti should be divorced for her disobedience.

4.2.1. He shows what would be the adverse effects of the queen's disobedience to her husband if it was ignored.

4.2.2. He shows what would be the good effects of a decree against Vashti that she should be divorced: *the wives would give to their husbands honour*, and every man would therefore be ruler over his own household, as he should be. They therefore gave this judgment against her, that she should never again come into the king's presence, and this judgment was confirmed in such a way that it could never be reversed (v. 19).

4.3. The edict that was passed according to this proposal, declaring that the queen was divorced for willful disobedience, according to the law, and that if other wives were similarly undutiful to their husbands, they must expect to be disgraced in the same way (vv. 21–22), for, after all, were they any better than the queen?

CHAPTER 2

Two things were working toward the rescue of the Jews from Haman's conspiracy: 1. The advancement of Esther to be queen instead of Vashti. Many others were candidates for the honor (vv. 1–4), but Esther, an orphan and a captive Jew (vv. 5–7), commended herself first to the eunuch in charge of the king's harem (vv. 8–11) and then to the king (vv. 12–17), who made her queen (vv. 18–20). 2. The good service that Mordecai did for the king in discovering a plot against his life (vv. 21–23).

Verses 1–20

Vashti was humbled for her haughtiness; Esther is advanced for her humility. Notice:

1. The extravagant process that was followed to please the king with another wife instead of Vashti. Josephus says that when Xerxes' anger subsided, he wanted to be reconciled to Vashti except for the fact that, according to the constitution of the government, the judgment was irrevocable. Therefore, to make him forget her, his servants devised a plan to first entertain him with a great variety of concubines, and then lead him to choose the one he liked most of all to be his wife. All the provinces of his kingdom must be searched for beautiful girls, and commissioners must be appointed to choose them (v. 3). After the king had taken them once to his bed, they were looked on as secondary wives or concubines, were maintained by the king accordingly, and were not allowed to marry. This shows us what absurd practices those who were destitute of divine revelation embarked on, those who, as a punishment for their idolatry, were given up to sinful desires (Ro 1:26). Having broken that law of creation which resulted from God's making human beings, that is, the law against idolatry, they broke another law, which was founded on his making one man and one woman. What a great need there was of the Gospel of Christ to purify people from the lustful desires of the flesh and to bring them back to the original institution.

2. The overruling providence of God in bringing Esther to be queen. She came in her turn, after several others, and it was found that she surpassed them all. Concerning Esther we notice:

2.1. Her origin and character.

2.1.1. She was one of the exiles, a Jew and one who shared with her people in their captivity.

2.1.2. She was an orphan; her father and mother were both dead (v. 7), but when they had left her, the Lord took care of her (Ps 27:10).

2.1.3. She was fair and beautiful, lovely in form and features (v. 7), "fair of form, and good of countenance" (v. 7, margin). Her wisdom and virtue were her greatest beauty, but it is an advantage to a diamond to be well set.

2.1.4. Mordecai, her cousin, was her guardian; he *brought her up, and took her for his own daughter* (v. 7). Let God be acknowledged for raising up friends for orphans; let it be an encouragement to the godliness of kindness and love that many who have taken care of the education of orphans have lived to see abundant fruit from their care and effort, to their great encouragement. Because Mordecai was Esther's guardian, we are told:

2.1.4.1. How tenderly he looked after her, as if she had been his own child (v. 11).

2.1.4.2. How respectful she was to him. Though she was his equal by blood relation, nevertheless, because she was his subordinate in age and dependence, she honored him as her father—*did his commandment* (v. 20). She did not *show her people nor her kindred*, she did not reveal her nationality and family background, because Mordecai had told her not to (v. 10). He did not tell her tell a lie to hide her background; he told her only not to volunteer her nationality. Because she was born in Susa, and her parents were both dead, everyone assumed her to be of Persian extraction.

2.2. Her advancement. Who would have thought that a Jew, a captive, and an orphan was born to be a queen and empress? Hegai, who was in charge of the king's harem, honored her (vv. 8–9) and was ready to serve her. The king himself fell in love with her. The more natural the beauty is, the more pleasant it is. *The king loved Esther above all the women* (v. 17). Now he need not take time to deliberate; he quickly decided to *set the royal crown upon her head, and make her queen* (v. 17). This was done in his seventh year (v. 16). He graced the ceremony of her coronation with *a royal feast* (v. 18). He also granted *a release to the provinces* (v. 18), a remission of overdue taxes or an act of grace for criminals, or perhaps a general holiday throughout the provinces. Esther still *did the commandment of Mordecai, as when she was brought up with him* (v. 20). Mordecai sat *in the king's gate* (v. 19), which was the height of his promotion. He was one of the doorkeepers of the court, the gate being the place where justice was dispensed.

Verses 21–23

The good service which Mordecai did for the government by uncovering a plot against the life of the king is recorded here, because it will be mentioned again later to his advantage. No step is now taken toward Haman's plan to destroy the Jews, but several steps are taken toward God's plan to rescue them. God now gives Mordecai an opportunity of doing a good deed for the king, so that he may have a better opportunity later to do a good turn for the Jews.

1. A plot was hatched against the king by two of his own officers, who sought *to lay hands on him*, not only to make him a prisoner but also to take his life (v. 21).

2. Mordecai found out about their treason and told Esther, who then told the king, and in this way he confirmed her in and commended himself to the king's favor.

3. The traitors were hanged, as they deserved to be, but not until their treason had been investigated and found to be true (v. 23). The whole matter was recorded in the king's journals, with a particular note that Mordecai was the man who uncovered the treason.

CHAPTER 3

A very black and mournful scene begins here, which threatens the destruction of all the people of God. 1. Haman is made the king's favorite (v. 1); Mordecai refuses to give him the honor he demands (vv. 2–4); Haman vows to take revenge on all the Jews for Mordecai's offense (vv. 5–6). 2. Haman, on the basis of a malicious misrepresentation of the Jews, obtains an order from the king to have them all massacred on a certain day (vv. 7–13). This order is published throughout the kingdom (vv. 14–15).

Verses 1–6

Here we have:

1. Haman promoted by the king and adored by the people. Haman was an Agagite—an Amalekite, according to Josephus—probably from the descendants of someone named Agag, a common name of the kings of Amalek, as appears in Nu 24:7. The king liked him—rulers do not have to give reasons for their favors—made him his favorite, his confidant, and his prime minister of state. It is clear that he was not a man of honor, justice, true courage, or stable character; on the contrary, he was proud, passionate, and vengeful. Yet he was promoted and treated with kindness, and there was no one so great as he.

2. Mordecai remaining faithful to his principles with a bold and daring determination, and refusing to give honor to Haman as the rest of the king's servants did (v. 2). He was urged to do so by his friends; they *spoke daily to him* (v. 4) to persuade him to conform. But it was all in vain. He did not listen to them, but told them plainly that he was a Jew and could not conscientiously honor Haman. It does not appear that anyone had any scruples about conforming to it except Mordecai; but his refusal was still godly, conscientious, and pleasing to God, because:

2.1. The religion of the Jews forbade them to give such extravagant honor to any mortal, especially to such an evildoer as Haman. In the apocryphal chapters of this book (13:12–14) Mordecai is seen appealing to God about this: *Thou knowest, Lord, that it was neither in contempt nor pride, nor for any desire of glory, that I did not bow down to proud Haman, for I could have been content with good will, for the salvation of Israel, to kiss the soles of his feet; but I did this that I might not prefer the glory of man above the glory of God, neither will I worship any but thee.*

2.2. He especially thought it an act of injustice to his nation to give such honor to an Amalekite, a member of a nation which God had sworn that he would be at war against forever (Ex 17:16) and concerning which he had given that solemn command (Dt 25:17), *Remember what Amalek did.*

3. Haman meditating revenge. Some who hoped to gain favor with Haman told him about Mordecai's rudeness, waiting to see whether Mordecai would bend or break (v. 4). Haman then noticed it himself and was *full of wrath*, he became very angry (v. 5). It was soon decided that Mordecai must die. To Haman, Mordecai's life counted for nothing toward satisfaction for the supposed insult; thousands of innocent and valuable lives must be sacrificed to his anger, and so he vows that all the people of Mordecai shall be destroyed for his offense, because his being a Jew was the reason he gave for not submitting to Haman.

Verses 7–15

Haman does not doubt he can find those who are desperate and bloodthirsty enough to cut all the Jews' throats if only the king gives him permission. He obtains permission and a commission to do it.

1. Haman makes a false and malicious representation of the Jews and their character to the king (v. 8). He wanted the king to believe:

1.1. That the Jews were a contemptible people and that it would not do him any good if he protected them: "*A certain people there is scattered abroad and dispersed in all the provinces* (v. 8) as restless wanderers on earth, and inhabitants of all countries, the burden and scandal of the places they live in."

1.2. That they were a dangerous people. "They have laws of their own; they do not conform to the statutes of the kingdom and may be looked on as dissatisfied with the government and likely to cause a rebellion."

2. Haman aims for permission to destroy them all (v. 9). He knew many people who hated the Jews. *Let it be written*, therefore, *that they may be destroyed.* Just give the order for a general massacre of all the Jews. If the king will please him in this matter, Haman will give him a present of *ten thousand talents*, which will be *paid into the king's treasuries* (v. 9). He thought this would get around the strongest objection to his proposal, that the government would sustain a loss in its revenues by the destruction of so many of its subjects. No doubt Haman knew how to reimburse himself from the plunder of the Jews—which his soldiers would seize for him (v. 13)—and expected in this way to make them bear the cost of their own destruction.

3. Haman obtains what he desires, a full commission to do what he wants with the Jews (vv. 10–11). The king was so captivated by Haman that he was willing to believe the worst about the Jews, and he handed them into his hands, as lambs to the lion: *The people are thine, do with them as it seemeth good unto thee* (v. 11). So little did he consider how much Haman would gain in plunder that he also let him keep the ten thousand talents: *The silver is thine* (v. 11).

4. Haman then consults his soothsayers to find out what day would be lucky for the intended massacre (v. 7). The decision was made in the first month, in the twelfth year of the king, when Esther had been his wife about five years. The lot fell on the twelfth month, so that Mordecai and Esther had eleven months to frustrate the plan. Although Haman was eager to see all the Jews destroyed, he still submitted to his superstitious rules. God's wisdom serves its own purposes by human foolishness. Haman has appealed to the lot, and to the lot he shall go; and the lot, by delaying the execution, renders judgment against him and breaks the neck of the plot.

5. The bloody decree is drawn up, signed, and declared, giving orders to the militia of every province to be ready for *the thirteenth day of the twelfth month*, and on that day to murder all the Jews, men, women, and children, and seize their goods (vv. 12–14). The Jews are not accused of any crime; yet they must die, with no mercy shown to them.

6. The different moods of the court and the city:

- The court was very happy with it: *The king and Haman sat down to drink* (v. 15). Haman was afraid that the king's conscience might strike him for what he had done, and so to prevent that, he kept him drinking. Many use this detestable way of drowning their convictions; they harden their own hearts and the hearts of others in sin.
- The city was very sad about it: *The city Shushan was perplexed* (v. 15), not only the Jews themselves but also all their neighbors who had any principles of justice and compassion. It grieved them to see people who lived at peace treated so barbarically, but the king and Haman were not in the slightest concerned about such things.

CHAPTER 4

Things here begin to work toward a rescue, and they begin at the right end. 1. The Jews' friends take to heart the danger and mourn it (vv. 1–4). 2. Matters are agreed on between Mordecai and Esther to prevent it: Esther inquires into this case and receives a particular account

of it (vv. 5–7); Mordecai urges her to intercede with the king for the edict to be revoked (vv. 8–9); Esther responds with the objection of the danger of addressing the king without being called (vv. 10–12); Mordecai urges her to dare to go (vv. 13–14); Esther, after a religious fast of three days, promises to do so (vv. 15–17), and we will find later that she was successful.*

Verses 1–4

Here is an account of the general sorrow among the Jews when Haman's bloodthirsty edict was declared against them.

1. Mordecai cried bitterly, *rent* (tore) *his clothes, and put on sackcloth* (vv. 1–2). In this way he not only expressed his grief but also proclaimed it, so that everyone might notice he was not ashamed to acknowledge he was a friend of the Jews and a fellow sufferer with them. It was noble of him to publicly take up what he knew to be a righteous cause, and the cause of God, even when it seemed a desperate and lost cause. Mordecai knew that Haman's spite was directed against him primarily and that it was for his sake that all the other Jews were being attacked, and so it troubled him greatly that his people should suffer because of his principles. But because he could appeal to God that what he did came from his sense of right and wrong, he could with assurance commit his own cause and that of his people to the One who judges righteously (1Pe 2:23). Attention is drawn here to a law that *none might enter into the king's gate clothed with sackcloth* (v. 2); none must come near the king wearing mourning clothes, because the king was not willing to hear the complaints of such people. Nothing except what was bright and pleasant must be seen at court. This made Mordecai keep his distance; he came before the gate but did not take his place *in the gate.*

2. All the Jews in every province took it very much to heart (v. 3). They denied themselves the physical delights of their tables—they fasted and mixed tears with their food and drink (Ps 102:9)—and *they lay in sackcloth and ashes.*

3. When Queen Esther became aware of how troubled Mordecai was, she *was exceedingly grieved*, she was in great distress (v. 4). Mordecai's grief was hers, and the Jews' danger was her distress. Esther sent a change of clothes to Mordecai, but because he wanted to make her aware how great his grief was, and then tell her its cause, *he received it not*, he would not accept them (v. 4), but was like one who refused to be comforted.

Verses 5–17

The laws of Persia confined the wives, especially the king's wives, so it was not possible for Mordecai to meet Esther, but various messages are here carried between them by Hathach, whom the king had assigned to take care of her.

1. Esther sent Hathach to Mordecai to know more fully what the trouble was which he was now mourning about (v. 5) and why he would not take off his sackcloth.

2. Mordecai sent her an authentic account of the whole matter, with the instruction that she should go and intercede with the king: *Mordecai told him all that had happened unto him* (v. 7), how angry Haman had become with him for not submitting to him and how he had obtained this decree. He also sent her an exact copy of the edict, so that she might see what imminent danger she and her people were in. He urged her that if she had any respect for him or any kindness for the Jewish nation, she would set right the misinformation with which the king had been deceived.

3. Esther presented her case to Mordecai, that she could not, except by putting her life in danger, address the king.

3.1. The law was explicit, and everyone knew it: whoever came to the king without being called must be put to death unless he was pleased to *hold out the golden sceptre to them*. This made the royal palace little better than a royal prison, and the kings found themselves becoming morose. It was also bad for their subjects, for what good could they have from a king when they never had the freedom to turn to him to put right their grievances? It is not like this in the court of the King of kings; we may *come boldly* at any time to the footstool of his throne of grace (Heb 4:16) and may be sure of a response of peace to the prayer of faith. It was particularly uncomfortable for their wives, for there was no condition in the law to make an exception for them.

3.2. Her case was very discouraging at that time. Providence so ordered things that at just this time she was under a cloud, and the king's affections were cooled toward her, for she had been *kept from his presence thirty days* (v. 11).

4. Mordecai still insisted that whatever risks she might have to take, she must turn to the king in this important matter (vv. 13–14). He suggested to her:

4.1. That it was her own cause, for the decree to *destroy all the Jews* did not exclude her: "*Think not*, therefore, that *thou shalt escape in the king's house*, that you alone of all the Jews will escape (v. 13), that the palace will protect you and the crown will save your head. No; you are a Jew, and if the others are destroyed, you will be too."

4.2. That it was a cause which, one way or another, would certainly be taken up, and which she therefore could safely commit herself to. "If you decline to serve in this way, *enlargement* (relief) *and deliverance will arise to the Jews from another place*" (v. 14). This was the language of strong faith, which did not waver through unbelief with regard to the promise when the danger was most threatening, but *against hope believed in hope* (Ro 4:18, 20).

4.3. That if she now deserted her friends because of her cowardice and unbelief, she would have reason to fear that some judgment from heaven would destroy her and her family: "*Thou and thy father's house shall be destroyed* (v. 14), while the rest of the families of the Jews will be preserved."

4.4. That divine Providence had this in view in bringing her to be queen: *Who knows whether thou hast come to the kingdom for such a time as this?* (v. 14). Every one of us should consider why God has put us where we are, and when any particular opportunity to serve God and our generation offers itself, we must take care that we do not let it slip. Mordecai urged these things to Esther, and some of the Jewish writers who delight in making up stories add another thing which had *happened to him* (v. 7) which he wanted her to be told: that going home in great heaviness of spirit, the night before when he knew about Haman's plot, he met three Jewish children coming from school, whom he asked what they had learned that day. One of them told him his lesson was, *Be not afraid of sudden fear* (Pr 3:25–26); the second told him his was, *Take counsel together, and it shall come to nought* (Isa 8:10); the third told him his was, *I have made, and I will bear, even I will carry and will deliver you* (Isa 46:4).

5. Esther then decided, whatever it might cost her, to turn to the king, but not until she and her friends had first turned to God. Let them first fast and pray to obtain God's favor, and then she could hope to find favor with the king (vv. 15–16). She spoke:

5.1. With the godliness and devotion of an Israelite, for she believed that God's favor could be gained by prayer. She knew it was the practice of good people, in extraordinary cases, to add fasting to prayer. She therefore:

5.1.1. Asked that Mordecai direct the Jews who were in Susa to *sanctify a fast* and *call a solemn assembly* (Joel 1:14), that is, to meet in the synagogues to which they belonged, and to pray for her and keep a sacred fast.

5.1.2. Promised that she and her family would declare this fast in her apartment of the palace, for she could not come to their assemblies. Those who are confined to privacy may join their prayers with those of the sacred assemblies of God's people; those who are absent in body may still be present in spirit (1Co 5:3).

5.2. With the courage and determination of a queen. "When we have sought God in this matter, *I will go in unto the king* to intercede for my people. *I know it is not according to the king's law* (v. 16), but it is according to God's Law, and so I will dare to go, and *if I perish, I perish* (v. 16). I cannot lose my life in a better cause. It is better for me to do my duty and die with them." She does not say this in despair or anger, but as a holy decision to do her duty and trust God as to how events would turn out.

CHAPTER 5

The last we heard of Haman was that he was drinking (3:15). The last we heard of Queen Esther was that she was in tears, fasting and praying. Now this chapter sees: 1. Esther being joyful, smiled on by the king and honored with his company at the banquet when they were drinking wine (vv. 1–8). 2. Haman being worried because he did not have Mordecai bowing and scraping to him, and very angrily setting up a gallows for him (vv. 9–14).

Verses 1–8

Here is:

1. Esther's bold approach to the king (v. 1). When the time appointed for the fast had been completed, she lost no time, and on the third day she addressed the king while the impressions of her devotions were still fresh on her spirit. Now she *put on her royal apparel* (robes) (v. 1) so that she might commend herself better to the king, and she put aside her clothes of fasting. In the Apocrypha (Rest of Est 14:15–16), she appeals to God: *Thou knowest, Lord, I abhor the sign of my high estate* (high position) *which is upon my head, in the days wherein I show myself.* She stood *in the inner court over against* (in front of) *the king*, expecting to be condemned, caught between hope and fear.

2. The favorable reception which the king gave Esther. When he *saw her*, she *obtained favour in his sight* (v. 2). The apocryphal author and Josephus say that she took two maids with her, on one of whom she leaned for support, while the other followed carrying the train of her robe; that she looked happy, but her heart was fearful and in anguish; that the king, lifting up his face, which shone with splendor, at first looked very fiercely at her, upon which she grew pale, fainted, and collapsed onto the head of the maid who went in front of her. Then God changed the spirit of the king, and in alarm he leaped from his throne, took her in his arms until she came to herself, and comforted her with loving, soothing words (Rest of Est 15:5–8). Here we are told only:

2.1. That he protected her from the law and assured her of safety by *holding out to her the golden sceptre* (v. 2), which she thankfully *touched the top of*, so presenting herself to him as a humble petitioner.

2.2. That he encouraged her address (v. 3): *What wilt thou, queen Esther, and what is thy request?* Esther feared that she would die, but was promised that she would have whatever she might ask for, even up to *half of the kingdom*. Let us infer from this story, as our Savior does from the parable of the unjust judge, an encouragement to *pray always* to our God, *and not faint* (Lk 18:1–8). Esther came to a proud, arrogant man; we come to the God of love and grace. She was not called; we are: the Spirit says, *Come*, and the bride says, *Come* (Rev 22:17). She had a law against her; we have a promise, in fact many promises, in favor of us: *Ask, and it shall be given you* (Mt 7:7). She had no friend to introduce her or intercede for her, while on the contrary he who was then the king's favorite was her enemy; but we have an Advocate with the Father, with whom he is pleased. *Let us therefore come boldly to the throne of grace* (Heb 4:16).

2.3. That the only request she had to make to him, at this time, was that he would come to a banquet which she had prepared for him, and bring Haman along with him (vv. 4–5). She would try to get him into a pleasant mood and soften his spirit, so that he might respond favorably when listening to the complaint she had to make to him. She would please him also by giving attention to Haman, his favorite—by inviting the one whose company she knew the king loved and whom she wanted to have present when she made her complaint.

2.4. That he readily came and ordered Haman to come along with him (v. 5). He renewed his kind inquiry there (*What is thy petition?*) and his generous promise, that it would be granted, even up to half of the kingdom (v. 6), a proverbial expression by which he assured her that he would deny her nothing reasonable.

2.5. That then Esther thought fit to ask no more than a promise that he would accept another banquet, the next day, in her apartment, and Haman with him (vv. 7–8), suggesting to him that she would then let him know what her business was. She knew that putting it off in this way would probably be taken as an expression of the great reverence she had for the king and of her unwillingness to be too insistent toward him.

Verses 9–14

Here we see Haman, in whom pride and anger were supreme:

1. Puffed up with the honor of being invited to Esther's feast. He was *joyful and glad of heart* at it (v. 9). He thought it was because she had been so very much charmed by his conversation that she had invited him also to accompany the king the next day. But Mordecai was as determined as ever: *He stood not up, nor moved for him*, he neither rose nor showed fear in his presence (v. 9). Haman could hardly bear it; in fact, the higher Haman was lifted up, the more impatient he was with the contempt shown toward him and the more angry he became at it. He would have gladly drawn his sword and used it to kill Mordecai for defying him, but because he hoped he would soon see him fall with all the Jews, he restrained himself from stabbing him.

2. Meditating revenge, assisted by his wife and his friends (v. 14). To satisfy his fancy they advise him to get *a gallows ready* (v. 14) and have it set up by his own house, so that as soon as he can get the warrant signed, there may be no delay in carrying out the execution. This pleases Haman very much, and he has the gallows made

and set up immediately. It must be fifty cubits, that is, about seventy-five feet (about twenty-three meters) high, to give greater disgrace to Mordecai and make him a spectacle to everyone who passed by. They advised him to go early the next morning to the king and obtain an order from him for Mordecai to be hanged.

CHAPTER 6

This chapter opens with a very surprising scene. When Haman hoped to be Mordecai's judge, he was made his servant, to his great confusion and humiliation, and so the way was made for the defeat of Haman's plot and the rescue of the Jews. 1. The providence of God commends Mordecai in the night to the king's favor (vv. 1–3). 2. Haman, who came to make the king angry against Mordecai, is employed as an instrument of showing the king's favor to him (vv. 4–11). 3. Haman's friends interpret these events for him as signs of his condemnation, which is carried out in the next chapter (vv. 12–14).

Verses 1–3

When Satan put it into the heart of Haman to plan Mordecai's death, God put it into the heart of the king to plan Mordecai's honor. The steps which Providence took toward the advancement of Mordecai:

1. *On that night could not the king sleep* (v. 1). "His sleep fled away," is the literal sense; perhaps, like a shadow, the more he pursued it, the farther it went from him.

2. When he could not sleep, he called to have the book of the chronicles of his reign read to him (v. 1). It was God who put it into his heart to call for that rather than for music or songs, which would have been more likely to give him rest.

3. The servant who read to him came to the article about Mordecai. Among other things it was found written that Mordecai had uncovered a plot against the life of the king and in so doing had prevented it from being carried out (v. 2). We read in 2:23 how Mordecai's good service was recorded, and here it is found on record.

4. The king inquired *what honour and dignity* (recognition) *had been done to Mordecai* (v. 3) for this, suspecting this good service to have gone unrewarded.

5. The servants informed him that Mordecai had not been honored in any way for that outstanding service. He used to sit at the king's gate, and he sat there still. Although humility, modesty, and self-denial are very valuable in God's sight, they often hinder human promotion in this world. Mordecai rises no higher than the king's gate, while proud and ambitious Haman gets the king's ear and heart, but although the ambitious rise fast, the humble are steadfast. Mordecai is at this time, by the king's edict, condemned to destruction with all the Jews, though it is acknowledged that he deserves recognition.

Verses 4–11

It is now morning, and the people begin to stir.

1. Haman is so impatient to get Mordecai hanged that he comes to the royal court early, before any other business is brought, to obtain a warrant for Mordecai's execution (v. 4), which he is sure he will get without any problem. He can tell the king that he is so confident of the justice of his request and of the king's favorable response to it that he has already prepared a gallows: one word from the king will complete his satisfaction.

2. The king is so impatient to have Mordecai honored that he wants to know who is in the court that is fit to

be employed in it. Word is brought him that Haman is in the court (v. 5). "*Let him come in*," the king says; "he is the best man to be used both in directing and in dispensing the king's favor." (The king knew nothing about any quarrel Haman had with Mordecai.) Haman is brought in immediately, proud of the honor given to him in being admitted into the king's bedroom before he is up. Now Haman thinks he has the best opportunity he could wish for to denounce Mordecai, but the king's heart is as full as his, and it is right he should speak first.

3. The king asks Haman how he should express his favor to one whom he has marked out as a favorite: *What shall be done to the man whom the king delights to honour?* (v. 6).

4. Haman concludes that he himself is the intended favorite and so prescribes the highest expressions of honor that could be given to a subject. Now Haman thinks he is carving out honor for himself, and so he is very liberal in his generosity (vv. 8–9).

5. The king confounds him with the positive order that he must immediately go himself and give all this honor to Mordecai the Jew (v. 10). If only the king had said, as Haman expected, *Thou art the man* (2Sa 12:7)! But he is thunderstruck when the king tells him not to order someone else to do all this, but to do it himself for Mordecai the Jew, the very man he hates above all others and whose destruction he is now plotting!

6. Haman dares not dispute nor even appear to dislike the king's order, and so, with the greatest reluctance, he brings it to Mordecai, who now cringes no more before Haman than he did before, valuing his pretended respect no more than he earlier feared his hidden hatred. The royal robes are brought and Mordecai is dressed. He rides in state through the city, recognized as the king's favorite (v. 11).

Verses 12–14

We may notice here:

1. How unassuming Mordecai was toward his advancement. He *came again to the king's gate* (v. 12); he returned to his place and its duty immediately and took care of his business as diligently as he had before.

2. How depressed Haman was because of his disappointment. To wait on any man, but especially Mordecai, and at that time, when he had hoped to see him hanged, was enough to break such a proud heart.

3. How this event was recognized by his wife and his friends as a sign of his condemnation: "If Mordecai is, as they say he is, *of the seed of the Jews, before whom thou hast begun to fall*, never expect to *prevail against him*, for *thou shalt surely fall before him*" (v. 13). This Mordecai was *of the seed of the Jews*, he was of Jewish origin (v. 13). Their enemies sometimes called them *feeble Jews* (Ne 4:2), but they sometimes found them to be formidable. They are a holy offspring, a praying offspring, in covenant with God, and an offspring that the Lord has blessed all along, and so let their enemies not expect to triumph over them.

4. He was now sent for to go to the banquet that Esther had prepared (v. 14). He thought this was opportune, hoping it would revive his drooping spirits and save his sinking honor.

CHAPTER 7

We are now to attend the second banquet to which the king and Haman were invited, and there: 1. Esther presents her request to the king for her life and the life of her people (vv. 1–4). She plainly tells the king that Haman is the man who wants to destroy her and all her friends (vv. 5–6). 2. The king then gives orders for Haman to be hanged on the gallows Haman himself has prepared for Mordecai, and the orders are carried out (vv. 7–10).

Verses 1–6

The king, in a good mood, and Haman, in a bad mood, meet at Esther's table.

1. The king urged Esther a third time to tell him what her request was, for he longed to know, and he repeated his promise that whatever it was, it would be granted (v. 2).

2. Esther finally surprises the king with her request for the preservation of herself and her compatriots from death and destruction (vv. 3–4). That a friend, a wife, should have occasion to present such a request was very moving: *Let my life be given me at my petition, and my people at my request* (v. 3). To move the king even more, she suggests she and her people were bought and sold. They had not sold themselves by any offense against the government, but were sold to satisfy the pride and revenge of one man. Moreover, it was not only their liberty but also their lives that were sold. "Had we been sold," she says, "into slavery, I would not have complained, for we might have regained our liberty in time, though the king would have suffered a loss. Whatever might have been paid for us, the loss of so many hard workers from his kingdom would have been a greater loss to the king than the price would have made up for." *We are sold*, she says, *to be destroyed, to be slain* (killed)*, and to perish* (v. 4). She refers to the words of the decree (3:13), which aimed at nothing short of their destruction.

3. The king is stunned at the appeal and asks (v. 5), *Who is he, and where is he, that durst* (dared) *presume in his heart to do so?* We are sometimes surprised at the mention of that evil which we ourselves are accused of. Xerxes is amazed at that evil which he himself is guilty of, for he agreed to that edict decreeing bloodshed for the Jews. *Thou art the man* (2Sa 12:7), Esther might have truly said.

4. Esther charges Haman with the crime directly and in the presence of the king: "He is here; let him speak for himself, for that is why he was invited: *The adversary and enemy is this wicked Haman* (v. 6). He is the one who has wanted to murder us."

5. Haman is concerned for his safety: *He was afraid before the king and queen* (v. 6). It was time for him to fear when the queen was his prosecutor, the king his judge, and his own conscience a witness against him.

Verses 7–10

Here:

1. The king withdraws in anger. He got up from the table in a great rage and *went into the palace garden* to cool down and consider what was to be done (v. 7). He blames himself for being so foolish as to condemn an innocent nation to destruction, including his own queen, on the evil accusations of a self-seeking man, without examining the truth of the allegations. He condemns Haman, whom he had become so fond of, for being so vile as to draw him in to agree to such an evil action.

2. Haman makes a humble request to the queen for his life. He might have easily realized by the king's hastily leaving the room that *there was evil determined against him* (v. 7). How lowly Haman looks, first standing up and then falling down at Esther's feet, begging her to save his life and accept all he had. How great Esther looks, who has recently been neglected and condemned. Now her sworn enemy acknowledges that he is at her mercy, and

he begs his life from her. The day is coming when those who hate and persecute God's chosen ones would gladly become indebted to them.

3. The king returns, even angrier with Haman.

4. Those around him were ready to be the instruments of his wrath. The courtiers who revered Haman when he was the upcoming favorite now set themselves as much against him when he was falling in disgrace. As soon as the king spoke an angry word, *they covered Haman's face* (v. 8), as that of a condemned man. His condemnation was sealed, and they marked him out for execution. Those who are hanged commonly have their faces covered. One of those who had just been sent to Haman's house to fetch him for the banquet told the king about the gallows Haman had prepared for Mordecai (v. 9).

5. The king gave orders that he should be hanged on his own gallows, and the orders were carried out.

CHAPTER 8

1. Haman's plot was to raise an estate for himself, but since all his estate was confiscated because of his treason, it is given to Esther and Mordecai (vv. 1–2). 2. His plot was to destroy the Jews, and Esther deals with that by fervently interceding for the reversal of the edict against them (vv. 3–6). It is in effect refersed by the declaring of another edict, published here, authorizing the Jews to stand up in their own defense against their enemies (vv. 7–14). 3. This leads to great joy among the Jews and all their friends (vv. 15–17).

Verses 1–2

Here is:

1. Esther enriched. Haman was hanged as a traitor, and so his estate was forfeited to the crown, and the king gave it all to Esther.

2. Mordecai promoted. His procession that morning through the streets of the city was only a sudden blaze of honor; but here we have a more long-lasting promotion to which he was elevated. He was acknowledged as the queen's cousin; it seems that until now the king did not know this, though Esther had been queen for four years. Mordecai was such a humble and modest man and was so far from being ambitious to seek a place at court that he had hidden the fact that he was related to the queen and that she had obligations to him as her guardian. Now, finally, *Esther had told what he was to her* (v. 1), one who was closely related to her, who took care of her when she was an orphan, and whom she still respected as a father. All the trust that the king had rested in Haman and all the power he had given him were here transferred to Mordecai, for he gave Mordecai the ring he had taken from Haman. He made this humble, trustworthy man his confidant. The queen made him her steward, to manage Haman's estate: *She set Mordecai over the house of Haman* (v. 2).

Verses 3–14

Haman, the chief enemy of the Jews, was hanged, and Mordecai and Esther, their chief friends, were adequately protected, but there were many others in the king's dominions who hated the Jews and wanted their destruction. All the rest of that people were exposed to the rage and hatred of these other enemies, for the edict against the Jews was still in force.

1. The queen here makes intercession very boldly and movingly. She comes uncalled a second time into the king's presence (v. 3) and is, as before, encouraged

to present her request by the king's holding out the gold scepter to her (v. 4). Her request is that the king, having put away Haman, would also put away the trouble Haman devised against the Jews. Esther presents this request with much affection: she *fell down at the king's feet and besought* (pleaded with) *him with tears* (v. 3), every tear as precious as any of the pearls which she wore as jewelry. *If it please the king and if I have found favour in his sight*—and again, "If what I am asking seems right and reasonable before the king, and if I who ask it *be pleasing in his eyes*, let the edict be overruled." She supports her request with a moving plea: "*For how can I endure to see the evil that shall come* (how can I bear to see disaster fall) *upon my people?* (v. 6)."

2. The king here acts to prevent the trouble Haman planned. The king knew, and he told the queen, that according to the constitution of the Persian government, the former edict could not be revoked (v. 8): what was *written in the king's name, and sealed with the king's ring, might* not, for any reason whatever, be reversed. But he found a way of undoing what Haman had devised and thwarting his intentions, by signing and publishing another decree to authorize the Jews to act in their own defense, to oppose force by force and destroy the attackers. This would be effective security for them. "*Write for the Jews as it liketh you* (v. 8), saving only the honor of our constitution. Let the difficulty be dealt with as effectively as possible without reversing the letters." This edict was to be drawn up and published in the respective languages of all the provinces. The purpose of this decree was to commission the Jews, on the day which was appointed for their destruction, to draw together as a body for their own defense. And:

2.1. They were authorized to stand up for their lives, so that whoever attacked them would do so at their peril.

2.2. They were permitted not only to act defensively but also to *destroy, slay* (kill), *and cause to perish, all the power of the people that would assault them.* Now:

2.2.1. This showed his kindness to the Jews and was a sufficient condition for their safety, for the latter decree would be looked on as a tacit overruling of the former. But:

2.2.2. It also shows the absurdity of that branch of their constitution that said that none of the king's edicts could be repealed, for it made the king wage a civil war in his own kingdom, between the Jews and their enemies, so that both sides took up arms by his authority, and yet *against his authority.*

Verses 15–17

Here is a blessed change, Mordecai in royal colors and all the Jews joyful.

1. Mordecai in royal colors (v. 15). Having obtained an order for the relief of all the Jews, he was at ease: he put on the *royal apparel.* His robes were rich, *blue and white, of fine linen and purple*; so was his crown: it was *of gold.* These things were marks of the king's favor and the fruit of God's favor to his church. The city of Susa was aware of its advantage in the promotion of Mordecai and so *rejoiced and was glad* (v. 15)

2. The Jews joyful (vv. 16–17). The Jews, who only recently were under a dark cloud, dejected and disgraced, now had *light and gladness, joy and honour, a feast and a good day.* One good effect of this rescue was that *many of the people of the land*, many people of other nationalities (v. 17), who were thoughtful, sober, and well disposed, became Jews; they converted to the Jewish religion, renounced idolatry, and worshiped only the true God. *We will go with you, for we have heard*, we have seen, *that*

God is with you (Zec 8:23), *the shield of your help, and the sword of your excellency* (your glorious sword) (Dt 33:29).

CHAPTER 9

We left two royal edicts in force, both given at the court of Susa, one bearing the date of the thirteenth day of the first month and appointing that on the next thirteenth day of the twelfth month all the Jews were to be killed, another bearing the date of the twenty-third day of the third month and authorizing the Jews, on the day appointed for them to be killed, to draw the sword in their own defense. The Jews' cause was to be tried by battle, and the day was fixed by authority. Their enemies decided not to lose the advantages given them by the first edict, in the hope of defeating them by numbers; the Jews relied on the goodness of their God and the justice of their cause. 1. What a glorious day it was, that year, for the Jews, along with the two following days—a day of victory and triumph, both in the city of Susa and in all the king's other provinces (vv. 1–19). 2. What a memorable day it was made for future generations, by an annual feast in commemoration of this great deliverance, called the Feast of Purim (vv. 20–32).

Verses 1–19

Here a decisive battle is fought between the Jews and their enemies, which the Jews won. Neither side could call the other *rebels*, for they were both supported by royal authority.

1. The enemies of the Jews were those who attacked.

2. But the Jews were the conquerors. That very day when the king's decree for their destruction was to be carried out, the day that their enemies thought would be *their* day, proved *God's day* (Ps 37:13).

2.1. *They gathered themselves together in their cities*, marshaled together and standing in their own defense, offering violence to none, but defying everyone. If they had not had an edict to authorize them, they would not have dared to do it, but because they had such support, they were fighting legally. If they had acted separately, each family individually, they would have been an easy target for their enemies, but acting together, and gathering together in their cities, they strengthened one another and dared to face their enemies.

2.2. All the king's officers, who were ordered by the first edict to further the Jews' destruction (3:12–13), conformed to the later edict and *helped the Jews*, which tipped the scales in their favor (v. 3). The provinces would generally do as the rulers of the provinces inclined, and so their favoring the Jews would greatly help them. But why did they help them? Not because they had any sympathy for them, but because *the fear of Mordecai fell upon them* (v. 3), since he clearly had the support of both God and the king.

2.3. *No man could withstand them* (v. 2), and so *they did what they would to those that hated them* (v. 5). The Jews were made so strangely strong and encouraged, and their enemies so weak and discouraged, that none of those who had marked themselves out for destruction escaped. On the thirteenth day of the month Adar, in the city of Susa they killed 500 men (v. 6) and the ten sons of *Haman* (v. 10). On the fourteenth day in Susa they killed 300 more, who had escaped the sword on the previous day of execution (v. 15). Esther obtained permission from the king for them to do this, in order to terrorize their

enemies and completely crush that dangerous faction that sympathized with Haman. What justifies them in killing so many is that they did it in their own just and necessary defense; they *stood for* (defended) *their lives* (v. 16), authorized to do so by the law of self-preservation as well as by the king's decree. The king's commission had authorized them to *take the spoil* of their enemies *for a prey* (8:11), and they had a fair opportunity of enriching themselves with it. But the Jews would not do this:

2.3.1. So that they might, to the honor of their religion, show a holy and generous contempt of worldly wealth, like their father Abraham, who scorned the thought of enriching himself with Sodom's plunder (Ge 14:23).

2.3.2. So that they might make it clear that they aimed at nothing but their own preservation, using their influence at court to save their lives, not increase their estates.

2.3.3. Their commission authorized them to destroy the families of their enemies, even the *little ones and the women* (8:11). But their humanity forbade them to do that. They killed none except those they found carrying weapons, and so they did not take the plunder, but left it for the women and children. They acted with a consideration and compassion which are worth imitating.

Verses 20–32

To make sure it would be remembered for future generations:

1. The history was written, and copies of it were spread throughout all the Jews in every province of the empire, *both nigh* (near) *and far* (v. 20). Mordecai *wrote all these things* (v. 20). And if this book is the same as the one he wrote—as many think it is—what a difference there is between Mordecai's style and Nehemiah's. At every turn, Nehemiah notes divine Providence and the *good hand of his God* on him (Ne 2:8), which is very good to encourage godly devotion in the minds of his readers, but Mordecai never even mentions the name of God in the whole story. Nehemiah wrote his book at Jerusalem, where religion was in fashion; Mordecai wrote his at the citadel of Susa, where politics was more in evidence than godliness, and he wrote according to the spirit of the place. Because there is so little of the language of Canaan in this book, many think it was not written by Mordecai, but was an extract from the journals of the kings of Persia.

2. A festival was instituted, to be observed yearly from generation to generation by the Jews, to remember this wonderful miracle which God worked for them, that the *children who should be born* might know it, and *declare it to their children, that they might set their hope in God* (Ps 78:6–7). Future generations would reap the benefits of this rescue and therefore ought to celebrate its commemoration. Concerning this festival we are here told:

2.1. It was observed every year on *the fourteenth and fifteenth days of the twelfth month*, just a month before the Passover (v. 21). They observed two days together as days of thanksgiving, and did not think them too long to be spent in praising God. On the fourteenth day country Jews rested, and on the fifteenth those in Susa, and they observed both those days.

2.2. It was called the *feast of Purim* (v. 26), from *Pur*, a Persian word which means "the lot," because Haman had used a lot to determine this to be the time of the Jews' destruction. Every decision of the lot comes from the Lord, however (Pr 16:33), who had determined it to be the time of their triumph.

2.3. It was not a divine institution—and therefore not called *a holy day*—but a day of human appointing, by which it was made *a good day*, a day of joy (vv. 19, 22).

2.3.1. The Jews ordained it and took it on themselves (v. 27); they voluntarily *undertook to do as they had begin* (v. 23).

2.3.2. Mordecai and Esther confirmed their decision, so that it might be more binding on future generations, and might be well commended, having been signed with those great names. They *wrote*:

- *With all authority* (v. 29), Esther being queen and Mordecai prime minister of state.
- *With words of peace and truth*, words of goodwill and assurance (v. 30). Although they wrote with authority, they wrote with sensitivity.

2.4. By whom it was to be observed—by *all the Jews*, and by *their seed*, and by all those who *joined themselves to them* (v. 27). A joint expression of joy and praise is one aspect of the fellowship of saints.

2.5. Why it was to be observed—so that the remembrance of the great things God had done for his church might never *perish from their seed* (v. 28). When Esther was in danger of her life, she *came before the king*, and he repealed the edict (v. 25). Good deeds done for the Israel of God should be remembered, to encourage others to act similarly. The more cries we have offered up in our troubles, and the more prayers for our rescue, the more we should be thankful to God when he does rescue us.

2.6. How it was to be observed. They should make it:

2.6.1. A day of joyfulness, *a day of feasting and joy* (v. 22).

2.6.2. A day of generosity, *sending portions* (presents of food) *one to another* (v. 22), as a sign of mutual respect, and being joined so much more closely to each other in love by this and other public common dangers and rescues.

2.6.3. A day of kindness, sending *gifts to the poor* (v. 22). Those who have received mercy must also show mercy as a sign of their gratitude. Giving thanks and giving to the needy should go together, so that when we are rejoicing and blessing God, the heart of the poor may rejoice with us. At the feast they always read the whole story in the synagogue each day, and offer three prayers to God. In the first they praise God for counting them worthy to attend this divine service; in the second they thank him for the miraculous preservation of their ancestors; and in the third they praise him that they have lived to observe another festival in memory of it.

CHAPTER 10

This is only part of a chapter; the rest of it, beginning at v. 4, and six further chapters are found only in the Greek and are considered part of the Apocrypha. In these three verses we have only some brief signs: 1. Of the greatness of Xerxes on the throne (vv. 1–2). 2. Of the great blessing that Mordecai, his favorite, was to his people (vv. 2–3).

Verses 1–3

We are told here:

1. How great and powerful King Xerxes was. He had a vast kingdom, including islands as well as continental lands, and he raised from it a vast revenue. Besides the usual taxes which the kings of Persia exacted (Ezr 4:13), he imposed an additional tax on his subjects (v. 1): *The king laid a tribute*. Besides this example of the greatness of Xerxes, there might be given many more that were *acts of his power and of his might* (v. 2). These, however, are not recorded here in the sacred story, which is confined to the Jews and tells the affairs of other nations only where they involved the Jews.

2. How great and good Mordecai was. Mordecai had long sat contentedly at the king's gate, but now he was finally advanced. The declaration of the greatness to which the king advanced Mordecai was *written in the chronicles of the kingdom* (v. 2) as a significant contribution to the great achievements of the king. He was *great among the Jews* (v. 3), not only great above them, but also very close to them, dear to them, and very much respected by them. He was good, for he did good. He did not disown his people, even though they were foreigners and captives, dispersed and despised. He still described himself as *Mordecai the Jew* (v. 3). He did not seek his own wealth or try to raise an estate for himself and his family. He used his power, wealth, and influence with the king and queen for the public good. He did not side with any one group of people against another but, whatever differences there were among them, was a father to them all.

A Practical and Devotional Exposition of the Book of

Job

The book of Job stands by itself, unconnected with any other book of the Bible, and so it should be considered by itself. Many copies of the Hebrew Bible place it after the book of Psalms, and some after Proverbs, which perhaps has caused some experts to think it was written by Isaiah or one of the later prophets. Yet it is most appropriately placed first in this collection of divine morality. Being doctrinal, it properly precedes and introduces the book of Psalms, which is devotional, and the book of Proverbs, which is practical, for how can we worship or obey a God whom we do not know? As to this book:

1. We are sure that it is given by inspiration of God, even though we are not certain who wrote it. Although the Jews were not friends of Job, because he was excluded from the citizenship of Israel, they still faithfully kept the *oracles of God* entrusted to them (Ro 3:2), always including this book in their sacred canon. The history is referred to by one New Testament writer (Jas 5:11), and one passage (5:13) is quoted by the apostle Paul, with the usual form of quoting Scripture, *It is written* (1Co 3:19). It seems most probable to me that Elihu wrote it, or at least the discourses, because in 32:15–16 he mixes the words of a historian with those of a debater. If we suppose that Job wrote it himself, we may observe that some of the Jewish writers themselves acknowledge him to be a prophet among the Gentiles. If we suppose that Elihu wrote it, we may note that he had a spirit of prophecy which *filled him with matter* (words) *and constrained him* (32:18).

2. It is, in substance, a true story, and not fiction, although the dialogues are poetic. No doubt there was such a man as Job; the prophet Ezekiel names him alongside Noah and Daniel (Eze 14:14). We have here the story of his prosperity and godliness, his unusual suffering and exemplary patience, the substance of his talks with his friends, and God's discourse with him out of the storm, with his eventual return to a very prosperous condition. No doubt it is exactly true, though the inspired writer is allowed the usual liberty of putting the subject which Job and his friends talked about into his own words.

3. It is very old, although we cannot set the precise time either when Job lived or when the book was written. So many, and so evident, are its "gray hairs," the marks of its antiquity, that we have reason to think that holy Job was a contemporary of Isaac and Jacob. Although he was not a coheir with them of the promise of the earthly Canaan, he still lived in expectation with them of the *better country, that is, the heavenly* (Heb 11:16). He was probably one of the descendants of Nahor, Abraham's brother, whose firstborn was Uz (Ge 22:21), and in whose family religious faith was maintained for some time, as can be seen from Ge 31:53, where God is called not only the *God of Abraham*, but also *the God of Nahor.* He lived before the time when people's lives were shortened to seventy or eighty years, as they were in Moses' time, before sacrifices were confined to one altar, before the general apostasy of the nations from the knowledge and worship of the true God, and while there was still no other idolatry known except the worship of the sun and moon, which was punished by the judges (31:26–28). He lived while God was known by the name of *God Almighty* more than by the name of *Jehovah*, for he is called *Shaddai*, "the Almighty," more than thirty times in this book. He lived while divine knowledge was communicated not by writing but by tradition, for appeals are made to that here (5:1; 8:8; 15:18; 21:29). We therefore have reason to think that he lived before Moses, because there is no mention at all of the rescue of Israel from Egypt or of the giving of the Law. We conclude that we are here taken back to the age of the patriarchs, and we receive this book with respect not only for its authority but also for its antiquity.

4. We are sure that it is very useful to the church and to every true Christian, even though many passages in it are dark and difficult to understand. It is a book that makes a great deal of work for the commentators, but enough is clear to make the whole profitable, and it was all written for our learning (Ro 15:4).

4.1. This noble poem presents to us, in very clear and lively way, five things among others.

4.1.1. It is *a monument of early theology.* The first and great principles of the light of nature, on which natural religion is founded, are here, in a heated, long, and learned dispute; they are not only taken for granted, but also by common agreement clearly set down as eternal truths. Have the being of God, his glorious character and qualities, his unsearchable wisdom, his irresistible power, his inconceivable glory, his unwavering justice, and his incontestable sovereignty ever been discussed more clearly, fully, reverently, and eloquently than in this book? The creation of the world and its government are wonderfully described here, not so that we can speculate about its minute details, but so that we may feel powerfully obligated to fear and serve, to submit to and trust in, our Creator. Moral good and evil, virtue and vice, have never come more to life — the beauty of the one and the deformity of the other — than in this book, nor has the inviolable rule of God's judgment ever been more clearly set down. These are not questions to be kept for theological seminaries. This book speaks of them as sacred truths of undoubted certainty.

4.1.2. It presents us with *an example of Gentile godliness.* This great saint was from outside the covenant, not an Israelite, not even a proselyte, yet there is no one like him for religious faith, nor has there ever been such a favorite of heaven on earth. It was true, therefore, before the apostle Peter realized it, that *in every nation he that fears God and works righteousness* (does what is right) *is accepted of him* (Ac 10:35). There were *children of God scattered abroad* (Jn 11:52), who were not joined to the *children of the kingdom* (Mt 8:11–12).

4.1.3. It presents us with *an exposition of the book of Providence.* The prosperity of evildoers and the suffering of the righteous have always been reckoned to be two chapters that are as hard as any in that book, but here they are explained, and reconciled with divine wisdom, purity, and goodness.

4.1.4. It presents us with *a great example of patience* and close faithfulness to God in the midst of the most severe disasters. Sir Richard Blackmore, a most skillful writer, in the excellent preface to his paraphrase of this book, considers Job a hero suitable for an epic poem, for, he writes, "He appears brave in distress and valiant in affliction, maintains his virtue, and with that his character, under the most exasperating provocations that the malice of hell could invent, and thereby gives a most noble example of passive fortitude, a character no way inferior to that of the active hero."

4.1.5. It presents us with *an illustrious type of Christ,* the details of which we will try to note as we go along. In general, Job was a great sufferer; he was emptied and humbled, but for the purpose of his greater glory (Php 2:6–11). Christ abased himself in the same way, so that we might be exalted. Bishop Patrick quotes St. Jerome speaking of Job more than once as a type of Christ, who *for the joy that was set before him endured the cross* (Heb 12:2), who was persecuted for a time by people and devils, who also seemed to have been abandoned by God, but was raised up as an intercessor for his friends who had added affliction to his misery. When James speaks of the *patience of Job,* he immediately takes notice of *the end of the Lord,* that is, of the Lord Jesus (as some understand it), of whom Job was a type (Jas 5:11).

4.2. In this book we have:

4.2.1. The story of Job's sufferings and his patience under them (chs. 1–2), not without a mixture of human weakness (ch. 3).

4.2.2. A dispute between him and his friends, in which:

4.2.2.1. The opponents were Eliphaz, Bildad, and Zophar.

4.2.2.2. The respondent was Job.

4.2.2.3. The moderators were, first, Elihu (chs. 32–37), and second, God himself (chs. 38–41).

4.2.3. The outcome of everything in Job's honor and prosperity (ch. 42). On the whole, we learn that *many are the afflictions of the righteous, but* that when the Lord *delivers them out of them all* (Ps 34:19), the *trial of their faith will be found to praise, and honour, and glory* (1Pe 1:7).

CHAPTER 1

The story of Job begins here with an account: 1. Of his great godliness in general (v. 1) and in particular (v. 5). 2. Of his great prosperity (vv. 2–4). 3. Of the hatred of Satan against him and the permission Satan gained to test his faithfulness (vv. 6–12). 4. Of the surprising troubles that came on him, the ruin of his possessions (vv. 13–17) and the death of his children (vv. 18–19). 5. Of his outstanding patience and godliness in these troubles (vv. 20–22). In all this, he is shown to us as an example of how to suffer affliction, from which no prosperity can protect us, but through which integrity and uprightness will preserve us.

Verses 1–3

We are told here about Job:

1. He was a man, and so *subject to like passions as we are,* having the same nature as we have (Jas 5:17). He was *ish,* a man in authority. The country he lived in was the land of Uz, in the eastern part of Arabia, near the Euphrates. God has his remnant everywhere. It was the privilege of the land of Uz to have such a good man as Job in it; the worse others were round about him, the better he was. His name *Job,* or *Jjob* according to some, means "one hated and counted as an enemy." Others think it means "one that grieves or groans."

2. He was a very good man, especially devout and better than his neighbors: *He was perfect and upright* (v. 1).

It is the judgment of God concerning him, and we are sure that is true.

2.1. Job was a religious man, *one that feared God* (v. 1), that is, he worshiped him.

2.2. He was sincere in his religion. He was *perfect*, that is, blameless, though not sinless, as he himself acknowledges (9:20): *If I say I am perfect, I shall be proved perverse*. With respect to all God's commandments, he aimed at perfection, and was really as good as he seemed to be. He was wholehearted and single-minded in his devotion.

2.3. He was upright in his dealings both with God and with other people. He was faithful to his promises, steady in his advice, and completely trustworthy.

2.4. The fear of God reigning in his heart was the motive that governed his whole life.

2.5. He dreaded the thought of doing what was wrong. He *eschewed* (shunned) *evil* (v. 1) with the greatest abhorrence. *The fear of the Lord is to hate evil* (Pr 8:13), and then *by the fear of the Lord men depart from evil* (Pr 16:6).

3. He was prosperous but also godly. Although it is hard and rare, it is not impossible for *a rich man to enter into the kingdom of heaven* (Mt 19:23). He was prosperous, and his prosperity gave a luster to his godliness, and gave the one who was so good even greater opportunities to do good.

3.1. He had a large family. He was distinguished for his religious faith, but he was no hermit or recluse. He was the father and master of a family.

3.2. He had a good estate to support his family; his *substance* was considerable; he owned very much (v. 3). Riches are called *substance*, though to the soul and the other world, they are mere shadows, *things that are not* (Pr 23:5). Job's possessions are described not by the acres of land he was lord of, but:

3.2.1. By his cattle—*sheep and camels, oxen and asses* (v. 3). As soon as God made human beings and provided for their maintenance by fruits and plants, he made them rich and great by giving them *dominion over the creatures* (Ge 1:28).

3.2.2. By his servants. He had a very good household, and so he both had honor and did good. Job's wealth and wisdom entitled him to the honor and power he had in his country, which he describes in ch. 29. Job was upright and *therefore* grew rich, for honesty is the best policy, and godliness and love are ordinarily the surest ways to succeed. The account of Job's godliness and prosperity comes before the story of his great suffering to show that neither will keep us safe from the disasters of human life. Godliness will not keep us safe, as Job's mistaken friends thought, for *all things come alike to all* (Ecc 9:2); nor will success keep us safe, as a careless world thinks (Isa 47:8).

Verses 4–5

We have here a further account of Job's prosperity and his godliness.

1. Job's great comfort in his children is taken notice of as an example of his prosperity, for our temporary comforts are borrowed, depend on others, and are as susceptible to change as the people around us are. It was a comfort to this good man:

1.1. To see his children grown up and settled in the world. All his sons had houses of their own and probably were married.

1.2. To see them successful in their affairs, able to hold feasts for one another as well as feed themselves.

1.3. To see them in health.

1.4. Especially to see them live in love, unity, and mutual good affection, with no discord or quarrels among them.

1.5. To see the brothers so kind to their sisters that they invited them to eat and drink with them.

1.6. That they feasted in their own houses.

2. Job's great care for his children is noted as an example of his godliness (v. 5). Notice Job's godly concern for the spiritual welfare of his children.

2.1. He protected them with a godly jealousy. We should regard ourselves and those who are dearest to us with a similar godly jealousy, as far as is necessary to our care and efforts for their good.

2.2. As soon as a period of feasting had run its course, he called them to take part in religious ceremonies.

2.3. He sent to them to prepare for a reverent service of worship; he *sent and sanctified them* (had them purified) (v. 5). He ordered them to examine their own consciences and repent of what they had done wrong in their feasting. He kept his authority over them in this way for their own good, and they submitted to it, even though they lived in their own houses. He was still the priest of the family, and they all came to his altar, valuing their share of his prayers more than their share of his possessions. Parents cannot give grace to their children—it is God who sanctifies (Ex 31:13; Lev 20:8; etc.)—but they can still give advice and warnings at the right time to further their sanctification.

2.4. He offered sacrifices for them. Job, like Abraham, had an altar for his family, on which he probably offered daily sacrifices. On this extraordinary occasion, however, he offered more sacrifices than usual, *according to the number of them all* (v. 5), one for each child. "I prayed for this child, according to their particular temper, mind, and condition"; our prayers, as well as our actions, must reflect our knowledge of such particulars. He got up early, as one whose heart was set on his work. He required his children to attend the sacrifice.

2.5. He did this *continually*. The acts of repentance and faith must be renewed often, because we often repeat our sins. Those who serve God uprightly will serve him continually.

Verses 6–12

Job was not only so rich and great, but also so wise and good, that one would have thought the mountain of his prosperity stood so firmly that it could not be moved. Here, however, we see a dark cloud gathering over his head. The Devil, having a great hostility toward Job because of his distinguished godliness, begged and obtained permission to torment him. It does not in any way detract from the credibility of Job's story in general for this conversation between God and Satan to be considered as a parable, like that of Micaiah (1Ki 22:19), an allegory representing the hatred of the Devil against good people and the divine restraint which that hatred is under. We have here:

1. Satan among the angels, *the sons of God* (v. 6). *Satan* means "an adversary," of God, people, and everything good. He forced his way into a meeting of the *sons of God* who came to *present themselves before the Lord*. This means either:

1.1. A meeting of the saints on earth. Those who professed religion in the patriarchal age were called *sons of God* (Ge 6:2). Even then they had religious meetings and regular times for them. But there was a Satan among the sons of God. When they came together, he was among them, to distract and disturb them. Or:

1.2. A meeting of the angels in heaven. They are *the sons of God* in 38:7. Satan was originally one of them.

2. The examination of Satan concerning how he came to be there (v. 7): *The Lord said unto Satan, Whence*

comest thou? He knew very well from where he came, and with what intentions he came there—that as the good angels came to do good, he came to obtain permission to cause harm—but by calling him to account God wanted to show him that he was under control and restraint.

3. The account Satan gives of himself and of the tour he has made. He says, "I have come *from going to and fro in the earth*, from roaming through the earth and going back and forth in it" (v. 7).

3.1. He could not pretend he had been doing any good.

3.2. He would not acknowledge he had been doing any harm. While we are on this earth, we are within his reach, and he penetrates every corner of it with so much subtlety, swiftness, and diligence that we cannot be safe anywhere from his temptations.

3.3. Yet he seems to give some description of his own character. Perhaps it was spoken proudly; perhaps it was spoken with anxiety and discontent. He had been roaming back and forth and could find no rest, but was as much a restless wanderer as Cain was in the land of Nod. Perhaps it was spoken carefully: "I have been working hard, going back and forth," looking for an opportunity to cause trouble.

4. The question God puts to him concerning Job (v. 8): *Hast thou considered my servant Job?* How honorably God speaks of Job and how lovingly he declares to Satan Job's good character: "There is *my servant Job*; I have *none like him* (v. 8)." *Hast thou considered my servant Job?* He intends by this to answer the Devil's apparent boast of the influence he has on this earth. God says, "Job is my faithful servant." Satan may boast, but he will not triumph. It is as if God had said, "Satan, I know why you have come; you have come to accuse Job. But *hast thou considered him?* (v. 8)."

5. The Devil's evil insinuation against Job in answer to God's praise of him. He could not deny that Job feared God, but suggested that he was mercenary in his religious faith and therefore a hypocrite (v. 9): *Doth Job fear God for nought?* Notice how impatient the Devil became when hearing Job praised, even though it was God himself who praised him. Those who cannot tolerate hearing anyone praised but themselves are like the Devil. How slyly he censured him as a hypocrite, not asserting that he was so, but only asking, "Is he not so?" This is the common way of slanderers, whisperers, and backbiters, to suggest by way of a question something which they have no reason to think is true. How unjustly he accused him of being mercenary, to prove he was a hypocrite. It was very true that Job did not fear God for nothing; he gained much by it, for godliness is great gain (1Ti 6:6); but it was false that he would not have feared God if he had not gained material wealth by it, as events proved. Job's friends accused him of hypocrisy because he was greatly afflicted; Satan accused him because he greatly prospered.

6. The complaint Satan made about Job's prosperity (v. 10). Notice that God's special people are taken under his special protection, they and all who belong to them. God's grace guards their spiritual life, and divine Providence their natural life. God had prospered Job not for idleness or injustice, but for following the path of honest diligence: *Thou hast blessed the work of his hands* (v. 10). The Devil speaks about it in distress. "I see you have *made a hedge about him, round about.*" The wicked one *saw it and was grieved* (Ps 112:10), and he argued against Job that the only reason why he served God was that God prospered him.

7. The proof Satan proposes to give of the hypocrisy and mercenariness of Job's religion, if only he might have permission to rob him of his wealth. "Let this be put to the test," he says (v. 11); "make him poor, express your disapproval of him, turn your hand against him, and then we'll see where his religion is; strike what he has, and then his true character will be seen." How spitefully he speaks of the impression it would make on Job: "He will not only let his devotion fall away but will *even curse thee to thy face*" (v. 11). God declared Job to be the best person then alive. If Satan can prove him a hypocrite, it will follow that God does not have one faithful servant on earth and that there is no such thing as true and sincere godliness in the world, and that religious faith is all sham and Satan is the real king over the whole human race.

8. The permission God gave Satan to afflict Job to test his sincerity.

8.1. It is something to wonder at that God should give Satan such permission as this, but he did it for his own glory, for the honor of Job, to explain providence, and to encourage his suffering people in all ages. He allowed Job to be tested, as he allowed Peter to be sifted, but he took care that *his faith should not fail* (Lk 22:31–32).

8.2. It is a matter of comfort that God has the Devil *on a chain*. He could not afflict Job without first having asked and received permission from God, and even then he could not test him any further than he had permission for: "*Only upon himself put not forth thy hand*" (v. 12); do not harm his body, but you can strike what belongs to him." The Devil has limited power.

9. Satan's departure from this meeting of the angels. He went out now not to roam back and forth throughout the earth but to fall directly on poor Job, who was carefully going about his duties, knowing nothing about the matter.

Verses 13–19

Here is a detailed account of Job's troubles:

1. Satan brought them on him the very day that his children began their period of feasting at their *eldest brother's house* (v. 13).

2. They all came on Job at once; while one messenger was still speaking bad news, another came, and before he had told his story, a third and a fourth followed immediately. Satan ordered it in this way:

2.1. So that it might appear, through Job's troubles, that God was extraordinarily displeased with him.

2.2. So that he might not have an opportunity to consider, and reason himself into gracious submission, but might instead be overwhelmed by a combination of calamities.

3. They took from him all that he had and brought all his enjoyment to an end.

3.1. He had 500 *yoke of oxen* and 500 *she asses*, and an adequate number of servants to look after them; and all these he lost at once (vv. 14–15). His neighbors the Sabeans carried off the oxen and donkeys and killed the servants who faithfully and bravely did all they could to defend them, *and one only escaped* (v. 15). When Satan has God's permission to cause trouble, he will not lack evildoers to be his instruments in making things happen.

3.2. He had 7,000 *sheep*, and shepherds who looked after them, and he lost all those at the same time by lightning (v. 16). Job was perhaps ready to rebuke the Sabeans and strike out against them for their injustice and cruelty, when the next news immediately directed him to look upwards: *The fire of God has fallen from heaven.* All his sheep and shepherds were not only killed, but burned up by lighting at once, and only one shepherd was left alive to take the news to poor Job. This would tempt Job to say, *It is in vain to serve God* (Mal 3:14). The messenger called the lightning the *fire of God* (v. 16). How terrible then was the news of this destruction, which came directly from the hand of God!

3.3. He had 3,000 *camels*, and servants taking care of them, and he lost them all at the same time through the Chaldeans, who came in three raiding parties, drove them away, and killed the servants (v. 17). When the way of evildoers prospers, and they carry off their plunder, while just and good people are suddenly destroyed, God's righteousness is like the great deep, the bottom of which we cannot measure (Ps 36:6).

3.4. His dearest and most valuable possessions were his ten children, and to conclude the tragedy, news was brought him, at the same time, that they had been killed in the house in which they were feasting and buried in its ruins, with all the servants who waited on them, except one who had come quickly with news of it (vv. 18–19). This was the greatest of Job's losses, and so the Devil reserved it for last, so that if the other provocations failed, this might make him curse God. Our children are part of ourselves; it is very hard to lose them, and it affects good people in as sensitive an area as any. But to give them all up at once, to see those who had been his cares and hopes for so many years all destroyed in a moment, truly cut him to the quick. They all died together; not one was left. They died suddenly; he could not prepare for it. They died when they were feasting and making merry; if they had died suddenly when they were praying, he might have been able to accept it better. And they were taken away when he needed them most to comfort him in all his other losses.

Verses 20–22

The Devil had done all he wanted permission to do against Job to provoke him to curse God. The one who in the morning had been the richest person in the east was proverbially poor by nightfall. If his riches had been, as Satan insinuated, the only motive for his religious faith, then now that he had lost his riches, he would certainly have lost his religious faith, but the account in these verses of his godly behavior in his suffering sufficiently proved the Devil a liar and Job an honest man.

1. Job behaved bravely in his troubles (v. 20): he *arose, and rent his mantle* (tore his robe), *and shaved his head*—which were the usual expressions of great sorrow—to show that he was aware that the hand of the Lord had gone out against him, but he did not break out into wild passion. He kept his temper and boldly maintained a calm self-control within his own soul, even during all these provocations. He did not even begin to show his feelings until he heard of the death of his children, and then he got up and tore his robe. A worldly, unbelieving heart would have said, "Now that the food is gone, it is good that the mouths have also gone." But Job knew better and would have been thankful if Providence had spared his children, even though he had little or nothing for them, for *Jehovah-jireh*, "the Lord will provide."

2. Job behaved wisely in his troubles, like *one that feared God and eschewed* (shunned) the *evil* (v. 8) of sin more than that of outward trouble.

2.1. He humbled himself under the hand of God and came to terms with the circumstances he was now under, as one who knew how to be in want as well as how to have plenty (Php 4:12).

2.2. He composed himself with quiet thoughts, so that he might not be disturbed from his calm self-control by these events. He reasons from the common state of human life, which he describes by applying it to himself: *Naked came I*—like others—*out of my mother's womb, and naked shall I return thither* (v. 21). The apostle Paul alludes to this passage from Job (1Ti 6:7): *We brought nothing* of this world's goods *into the world*, but have them from others, and *it is certain that we can carry nothing out*, but must leave them to others. This consideration silences Job in all his losses. He is only where he was originally. He looks on himself as only naked, not maimed or wounded. He is himself still his own person, even though nothing else is his own; he is simply reduced to his original condition. He is only where he would have been finally. He is only unclothed, or rather unburdened, a little sooner than he expected. We expect to take off our clothes when it is near bedtime, though it is a nuisance to have to do so a long time before.

2.3. We are happy to see Job in such a good attitude, because whether his attitude toward God would change was the very test to which his integrity was being put. The Devil said that he would curse God in his adversity, but he blessed him and so proved himself honorable.

2.3.1. He acknowledged the hand of God both in the mercies he had formerly enjoyed and in the adversities he was now suffering: *The Lord gave, and the Lord has taken away* (v. 21). The same One who gave has taken away, and may he not do what he wills with his own people? Notice how Job looks beyond the instruments and keeps his eye on the primary cause.

2.3.2. He adored God in both. When all was gone, he fell down and worshiped. Adversities must not distract us from exercising our religious faith, but stimulate us to do it. Weeping must not stop the work of sowing, nor must it hinder worshiping. Job gives God thanks for the good intended for him by his adversities, for graciously supporting him in those adversities, and for the confident hope he has of a good final outcome.

3. Job receives an honorable testimony from the Holy Spirit to his faithfulness and good behavior in his adversities. He passed his test with acclaim (v. 22).

CHAPTER 2

At the end of the previous chapter we left Job acquitting himself very well in a fair test between God and Satan. One would have thought that this would be the end of the matter, and that Job would never have his reputation called into question again, but Job is tested a second time. 1. Satan wants a further test, to strike his flesh and bones (vv. 1–5); God, for his holy purposes, permits it (v. 6). 2. Satan strikes him with a very painful and detestable disease (vv. 7–8); his wife tempts him to curse God, but he resists the temptation (vv. 9–10). 3. His friends come to sympathize with him and comfort him (vv. 11–13). In this, he is held up as an example of patient suffering in adversity and affliction.

Verses 1–6

Satan wants to have Job's cause recalled. Here is:

1. The court set, and the prosecutor making his appearance (vv. 1–2) as before (1:6–7). The angels served God's throne, and Satan was among them. He is asked the same question as before, *Whence comest thou?* (v. 2), and he answers as before, *From going to and fro in the earth* (v. 2), as if he has been doing no harm.

2. The judge himself pleading for Job (v. 3): "*Hast thou considered my servant Job* better than you did before, *a perfect and an upright man?* For you see he *still holds fast his integrity.*" Satan is condemned for his allegations against Job: "*Thou movedst* (incited) *me against him*, as an accuser, *to destroy him without cause*" (v. 3). How good it is for us that we are not to be judged by people or devils, for perhaps they would destroy us, rightly or

wrongly, but our judgment comes from the Lord, whose judgment is never wrong or biased. Job is commended for his faithfulness despite the attacks made on him: "*Still he holds fast his integrity* (v. 3), as his weapon, and you cannot disarm him. It is his treasure, and you cannot rob him of that. In fact, all your attempts to do so only make him maintain his integrity even more firmly." Faithfulness is the crown of integrity.

3. The accusation further pursued (v. 4). *Skin for skin, and all that a man has, will he give for his life.* People will not only risk, but also give, what belongs to them to save their lives. Satan uses this as the basis for an accusation against Job, slyly presenting him:

3.1. As unnatural to those around him, and one who has not taken to heart the death of his children and servants.

3.2. As completely selfish, and being concerned only for his own ease and safety.

4. A challenge given to make a further test of Job's integrity (v. 5): "*Put forth thy hand now and touch his bone and his flesh,* and then *he will curse thee to thy face* (v. 5) and let go of his integrity." Nothing is more likely to disturb the thoughts and disorder the mind than acute pain and physical illness. The apostle Paul himself was very concerned about enduring a thorn in the flesh, nor could he have borne it without special grace from Christ (2Co 12:7–9).

5. Permission granted for Satan to make this test (v. 6). "*He is in thy hand,* do your worst with him, *only save his life* (v. 6), or his soul. Afflict him, but not to death." "Save his soul," that is, "his reason," according to some; "keep that for him to use, for otherwise it will be no fair test. If he should curse God in his insanity, that would not disprove his integrity. It would be the language not of his heart but of his illness."

Verses 7–10

Having gained permission to tear apart the life of poor Job and torment him, Satan immediately got down to work with him, first as a tormentor and then as a tempter. The temptation was managed with all the cunning and subtlety of the old Serpent, who was here playing the same game against Job that he played against our first parents (Ge 3:1–24).

1. The Devil provokes Job to curse God by striking him with painful sores, so making him a burden to himself (vv. 7–8).

1.1. The disease that came on Job was severe: Satan *smote him with sore boils,* afflicted him with painful sores (v. 7), all over him, from head to foot, perhaps a severe case of erysipelas.

1.2. The way he looked after himself in this illness was very strange (v. 8).

1.2.1. Instead of applying healing ointment, *he took a potsherd,* a piece of broken pottery, *to scrape himself* with it. This poor man had come to a very sorry state indeed. Even Lazarus was given some relief by the tongues of the dogs that came and *licked his sores* (Lk 16:21), but poor Job had no one to help him. None of those he had formerly been kind to had the gratitude to minister to him in his time of need, either because the disease was offensive and loathsome or because they thought it was infectious.

1.2.2. Instead of resting in a soft, warm bed, he *sat down among the ashes* (v. 8). He did this to humble himself under the mighty hand of God, and to remind himself of his lowly and poor condition. In the Septuagint rendering of this sentence, Job sits down on a rubbish heap outside the city (the Septuagint is a Greek version of the Old Testament); but the original says no more than that he sat "in the midst of the ashes" (v. 8).

2. The Devil urges Job, by the persuasions of his own wife, to curse God (v. 9). She was spared to him, when the rest of his comforts were taken away, for this purpose, to be one who troubled and tempted him. If Satan leaves anything that he has permission to take away, it is with the intention of causing trouble. She ridicules Job for his faithfulness in his religious faith: "*Dost thou still retain thy integrity?* (v. 9). Are you so weak and foolish as to submit to a God who, far from rewarding your services with marks of his favor, strips and scourges you without provocation? Is this a God that you should still be loving, blessing, and serving?" She urges him to give up his religion, to blaspheme God, and to dare him to do his worst: "*Curse God and die* (v. 9); save yourself by becoming your own executioner. Put an end to your troubles by putting an end to your life." These are two of the blackest and most terrible of all Satan's temptations. Nothing is more against natural conscience than blaspheming God, and nothing goes against natural sense so much as committing suicide.

3. Job bravely resists and overcomes the temptation (v. 10).

3.1. He was very indignant at having such a thing mentioned to him: "What! Curse God? I hate even the thought of it. *Get thee behind me, Satan*" (Mt 16:23). In other cases Job reasoned with his wife very mildly, even when she was unkind to him (19:17): *I entreated her for the children's sake of my own body.* But when she tried to persuade him to curse God, he was very displeased and showed her the evil of what she said. In such a godly household as Job's, his wife was one who had been well disposed toward religious faith, but now that all their possessions and comforts were gone, she could not bear the loss with the same frame of mind that Job had. When Peter was a Satan to Christ, Christ told him plainly, *Thou art an offence* (stumbling block) *to me* (Mt 16:23). If those whom we think wise and good at any time speak what is foolish and bad, we should rebuke them faithfully.

3.2. He reasoned against the temptation: *Shall we receive good at the hand of God, and shall we not receive evil* (trouble) *also?* (v. 10). We must try to convince those whom we rebuke. Job argues for not only coping with evil but also receiving it: *Shall we not receive evil* (v. 10), that is: "Shall we not expect to receive it? If God gives us so many good things, shall we be surprised, or think it strange, if he sometimes afflicts us, when he has told us that prosperity and adversity are set opposite each other as a pair?" (1Pe 4:12; Ecc 7:14). "Shall we not set ourselves to receive it rightly?" The word means "to receive it as a gift," and refers to a godly affection and spiritual attitude in our adversities, counting them as gifts (Php 1:29), accepting them as punishments of our sin (Lev 26:41), accepting the will of God in them—"Let him do to me as seems good to him." "Shall we receive so much good as has come to us from the hand of God during all those years of peace and prosperity, and shall we not now receive evil, when God thinks fit to lay it on us?" If we receive so much good physically, shall we not also receive some good spiritually, something which, by making our faces sadder, will make our hearts better?

4. And so Job kept his integrity, and Satan's intentions against him were defeated: *In all this did not Job sin with his lips* (v. 10). Grace gained the upper hand, and he took care that no bitter root might grow up to trouble him (Heb 12:15).

Verses 11–13

Here is an account of the kind visit Job's three friends paid him in his suffering. Some people, who were his enemies, gloated over him in his adversities (16:10; 19:18; 30:1). But his friends were concerned for him and tried to comfort him. Three of them are named (v. 11): Eliphaz, Bildad, and Zophar. These three were renowned for their wisdom and goodness, as can be seen from their speeches. They were very old men and had a great reputation for knowledge. They were well respected for their judgment (32:6).

1. Job, in his prosperity, had become friends with them. Much of the comfort of this life lies in the friendship we have with those who are wise and good; and those who have a few such friends should value them highly. It is supposed that Job's three friends were all descendants of Abraham. Eliphaz descended from Teman, the grandson of Esau (Ge 36:11), Bildad probably descended from Shuah, Abraham's son by Keturah (Ge 25:2). Zophar is thought by some to be the same as Zepho, a descendant of Esau (Ge 36:11). The preservation of so much wisdom and godliness among those who were foreigners to the covenants of promise was a happy sign of the grace God would give to the Gentiles in the future, when the wall of hostility would be taken down (Eph 2:14). Esau was rejected, but many who came from him inherited some of the best blessings.

2. They continued their friendship with Job even in his adversities, when most of his friends had abandoned him (19:14). They showed their friendship in two ways:

2.1. By kindly visiting him in his affliction, to sympathize with him and comfort him (v. 11). They came to share with him in his grief, as formerly they had come to share with him in his comforts. Visiting those in distress, if done from good motives, will soon be greatly rewarded (Mt 25:36). By visiting those who are suffering we may contribute to our own graces, for many good lessons can be learned from the troubles of others. We may also contribute to the comforts of those we visit, for by showing them respect, we encourage them, and some good word may be spoken to them which may help relieve their sorrow. Job's friends came to sympathize with him, to mix their tears with his, and so to comfort him. It is much more pleasant to visit suffering persons for whom comfort is appropriate than to visit those whom we must first rebuke. They were not sent for, but came of their own accord (6:22). They came with the intention of comforting him, but they turned out to be miserable comforters (16:2) through the poor way they handled the situation. When they saw him from a distance, he was so disfigured and deformed with his sores that *they knew him not*, they could hardly recognize him (v. 12). Notice what changes a painful disease, or oppressive care and grief, makes on the face in such a brief time! *Is this Job?* Seeing him so miserably changed, they did not leave him in a state of shock or loathing, but expressed much more their tenderness toward him.

2.2. By showing their tender sympathy and concern for him in his suffering. *They wept* aloud (v. 12). Seeing them renewed Job's grief and set him weeping again, which brought floods of tears from their eyes. *They rent* (tore) *their clothes, and sprinkled dust upon their heads* (v. 12), as those who would strip themselves and humble themselves to sympathize with their friend who was stripped and humbled. They had probably often sat with him on his couches or at his table in his days of prosperity and were therefore willing to share with him in his grief and poverty because they had shared with him in his joy and plenty. Though he was not now able to provide hospitality, they decided to stay with him until they saw him get better or die, and so they stayed in lodgings near him. They came and sat with him every day, for seven days in all. They

came as his companions in adversity. They sat with him, but *none spoke a word* (v. 13) to him; they only listened to the detailed accounts he gave of his troubles. By such a long silence they would suggest that what they said later had been well thought through and digested and was the result of much consideration. We should think twice before we speak once, especially in such a case as this. We should think for a long time, and we will be better able to speak briefly and to the point.

CHAPTER 3

You have heard of the patience of Job, *says James (Jas 5:11). We have heard of that, and of his impatience, too. In this chapter we find him cursing his day: 1. Complaining that he was born (vv. 1–10). 2. Complaining that he did not die as soon as he was born (vv. 11–19). 3. Complaining that his life was now continuing when he was in misery (vv. 20–26).*

Verses 1–10

Job's heart was deeply troubled for a long time, and while he was meditating, *the fire burned* (Ps 39:3), and all the more so because he bottled up his emotions. Job and his friends sat thinking for a long time, but they said nothing. The friends were afraid to say what they thought because they did not want to make him feel even worse, and he dared not express his thoughts because he did not want to offend them. Job is the first to express his thoughts. In short, he cursed the day of his birth and he wished he had never been born.

1. The extremity of his trouble and the anguish within his spirit may excuse it in part, but he cannot be justified in it. He has now forgotten the good he was born to, the good years have been overtaken by the bad years, he is filled with thoughts only of trouble, and he wishes he had never been born. The prophet Jeremiah himself expressed his painful sense of his adversities in language not unlike this: *Woe is me, my mother, that thou hast borne me!* (Jer 15:10). *Cursed be the day wherein I was born* (Jer 20:14). There is no circumstance of life in this world in which we cannot—unless it is our own fault—honor God, work out our own salvation (Php 2:12), and make sure we will have happiness in the better world to come. There is no reason at all to wish we had never been born, but a great deal of sense in saying that we have had our life for good reasons. Yet it must be acknowledged that, if there were not another life after this, there are so many sorrows and troubles in this world that we might sometimes be tempted to say that we were *made in vain* (Ps 89:47) and to wish we had never existed. However, let us note, in acclaiming the spiritual life above the natural, that though many have cursed the day of their first birth, never has anyone cursed the day of their new birth, or wished they had never received grace, and the Spirit of grace.

2. Job cursed his day, but he did not curse his God. He was weary of his life, and would gladly have parted with that, but he was not weary of his religious faith. He held fast to that with determination, and he would never let it go. The dispute between God and Satan concerning Job was not over whether Job had his weaknesses and whether he *was subject to like passions as we are* (Jas 5:17)—that was assumed—but whether he was a hypocrite who secretly hated God and who, if he were provoked, would openly show his hatred. But when the test came, it turned out that he was no such person.

2.1. The particular expressions which Job used in cursing his day are full of poetic imagination, fire, and emotion. We need not be too detailed in our comments on them. When he wants to express his passionate wish that he had never existed, he attacks the day and wishes:

2.1.1. That earth might forget it.

2.1.2. That heaven might disapprove of it: *Let not God regard it from above* (v. 4). Let the gloominess of the day represent the condition of Job, whose sun went down at noon.

2.1.3. That all joy might abandon it: *Let no joyful voice come therein* (v. 7); may it be a long night, and not "see the eyelids of the morning" (v. 9, margin), which bring joy with them.

2.1.4. That all curses might follow it (v. 8): "Let no one ever want to see it, but on the contrary, *let those curse it that curse the day*. Whatever day anyone is tempted to curse, may they at the same time curse my birthday.

2.2. But how foolish it was to wish that his eyes had never seen the light so that they might not have seen sorrow, which he still might hope to live through, and beyond which he might see joy!

Verses 11–19

Job perhaps now reflects and thinks about how foolish he has been in wishing he had never been born. He now follows up that wish with another, with which he thinks he can put it right: the wish that he had died as soon as he was born; but this is little better. Job here complains about life as a curse, and he considers death and the grave the greatest and most desirable happiness. Surely Satan was deceived in Job when he applied that saying to him, *All that a man hath will he give for his life* (2:4), for there was never anyone who valued life less than he did.

1. He ungratefully quarrels with life and how angry he is that it was not taken from him as soon as it was given him (vv. 11–12): *Why died not I from the womb?* Notice here how weak and helpless we human beings are when we come into the world, and how slender the thread of life is when it is first drawn. How mercifully and lovingly God's providence took care of us when we first entered this world. How much futility and trouble in our spirits is part of human life. If we did not have a God to serve in this world, and have better things to hope for in another world, considering the faculties we are endowed with and the troubles we are surrounded by, we would be strongly tempted to wish that we had *died from the womb* (v. 11). Yet however bitter life is, we must say, "It was because of the Lord's mercies that we did not die at birth, that we were not consumed" (La 3:22). Hatred of life contradicts the common sense, thoughts, and feelings of the human race, and our own at any other time. When the old man in the fable was tired with his burden, and he threw it down in discontent and called for Death, and Death came to him and asked him what he wanted him to do, his answer was, "Nothing, except to help me up with my burden."

2. He passionately praises death and the grave and seems to have fallen in love with death. To want to die so that we may be with Christ, so that we may be free from sin, and so that we may be *clothed upon with our house which is from heaven*, with our heavenly dwelling (2Co 5:2), is the effect and a sign of grace; but to desire to die only so that we may rest quietly in the grave and be rescued from the troubles of this life smacks of evil. Job here worries himself into thinking that if only he had died as soon as he was born:

2.1. He would have been (v. 14) "*with kings and counsellors of the earth*, whose pomp, power, and politics cannot put them beyond the reach of death, nor protect them from the grave, nor distinguish their dust from common dust in the grave." Though they filled their houses with silver, they were still forced to leave it all behind them, never to return to it. Some understand the *desolate places* which the kings and counselors are here said *to build for themselves* (v. 14) as referring to the tombs or monuments they prepared for themselves in their lifetime. Some understand the *gold* which the rulers had, and the silver with which they *filled their houses*, to refer to the treasures which, they say, were usually deposited in the graves of such great leaders. Such ways have been used to preserve their dignity, if possible, on the other side of death, and to keep them from lying with those of lesser rank, but people cannot do this for themselves. Death is, and always will be, an irresistible leveler. "Death mixes scepters with spades." In the grave, *a hidden untimely birth* (v. 16), a child that either never saw the light of day or only just opened their eyes and peeped into the world and, not liking it, closed them again and left it quickly, lies as quietly at rest, as high and as safe, as kings, counselors, and rulers who had gold. "And so," Job says, "I wish I had lain there in the dust rather than lived to lie here in these ashes!"

2.2. His condition would have been much better than it was now (v. 13): "*Then should I have lain still, and been quiet*, which now I cannot do. I cannot be at peace; I am tossing about and disturbed. Then *I should have slept*, whereas now I cannot sleep at all; *then had I been at rest*, whereas now I am restless." Now that life and immortality have been brought to a much clearer light by the Gospel than before, true Christians can give a better account than this of the gains of death. But all that poor Job dreamed of was rest and quietness in the grave and rest from the fear of bad news and the feeling of painful sores. *Then should I have been quiet.* How finely he describes the peace of the grave. Those who now are troubled will be beyond the reach of trouble there (v. 17): *There the wicked cease from troubling* (turmoil). Those who are now worn out will see the end of their tiredness. *There the weary are at rest* (v. 17). Those who were enslaved here are at liberty there. Death is the prisoner's discharge, the relief of the oppressed, and the servant's release (v. 18).

Verses 20–26

Job complains here that his life has been continued and not cut off.

1. He thinks it hard, in general, that miserable lives should be prolonged (vv. 20–22): *Wherefore is light in life given to those that are bitter in soul?* Life is called *light* because it is pleasant and useful for walking and working. It is candlelight; the longer it burns, the shorter it is, and the nearer it comes to the base. This light is said to be given us. Job reckons that to those who are in misery it is a gift but not a gift, since it only serves to help them see their own misery. He here speaks of those who long for death when they have outlived their comforts and usefulness and are burdened with old age and weaknesses, or are in pain or sickness, poverty or disgrace, but to whom it does not yet come, while at the same time it comes to many who dread it and want to put it far away from them. The continuance and length of life must be according to God's will, not according to ours. It is not right that we should be consulted as to how long we want to live and when we would like to die; our times are in the hand of One better than ourselves (Ps 31:15). *Some dig for it as for hidden treasures* (v. 21), that is, they would give anything

to be sent out of this world. It may be a sin to long for death, but we are sure it is no sin to long for heaven.

2. He thinks himself, in particular, to have been harshly dealt with, that he could not be relieved of his pain and misery by death. To be so impatient with life because of the troubles we meet is not only unnatural in itself, but also ungrateful to the giver of life. Grace teaches us to be willing, in the middle of life's greatest comforts, to die, and to be willing, in the middle of its greatest crosses, to live. He had no comfort from his life: *My sighing comes before I eat* (v. 24). His griefs returned as regularly as his mealtimes, and suffering was his daily bread. He had no prospect of seeing his condition get better: *His way was hidden*, and God had *hedged him in* (v. 23). What made his grief now even more painful was that in the times of his prosperity he had not been conscious either of negligence or false security, which might have caused God to rebuke him in this way. He had maintained such a fear of trouble as was necessary to keep up his guard. He was afraid for his children when they were feasting, that they might offend God (1:5), *and* afraid for his servants, that they might offend his neighbors. He took every possible care he could of his own health, but all that was not enough. He had not let himself feel secure, nor had he indulged in a life of ease and luxury, but trouble came. And so his way was hidden, for he did not know why God was contending with him.

CHAPTER 4

Now that Job has expressed his feelings, his friends here seriously express their judgment on his case. The dispute begins, and it soon becomes fierce. The opponents are Job's three friends. Job himself is the defendant. Then Elihu appears, as moderator, and finally God himself gives judgment on the dispute. The question in dispute is whether Job is an honorable person or not. Satan dare not pretend that Job's cursing his day constitutes cursing his God; he cannot deny that Job still maintains his integrity. But Job's friends want to have it that, if Job were honorable, he would not have been so severely afflicted, and so they urge him to confess himself to be hypocritical in the profession he has made of his religious faith. "No," Job says, "I will never do this; I have offended God, but my heart has nevertheless been upright with him"; and he still keeps the assurance of his integrity. Eliphaz, who probably was the oldest, begins with him in this chapter, in which: 1. He asks for a patient hearing (v. 2); he compliments Job by acknowledging his great and useful practice of his religious faith (vv. 3–4); he charges him with being hypocritical in putting it into effect, basing his charge on Job's present troubles and his behavior in them (vv. 5–6). 2. To complete his reasoning, he maintains that human evil always brings God's judgments (vv. 7–11). 3. He backs up his assertion by a vision which he had, in which he was reminded of the incontrovertible purity and justice of God and the lowliness, weakness, and sinfulness of human beings (vv. 12–21). In all this he aims to humble Job's spirit and to make him both penitent and patient in his suffering.

Verses 1–6

In these verses:

1. Eliphaz excuses the distress he is now about to cause Job by his speech (v. 2): "*If we assay a word with thee*, if someone ventures a word with you, offering a word of rebuke and advice, will you become impatient and take it

the wrong way? We have reason to fear you will, but there is no other way: 'Who can refrain from words?'" (v. 2, margin). Notice how tenderly he speaks about Job and his present suffering: "If we tell you our mind, *wilt thou be grieved?* (v. 2)." We should be backward in saying what we foresee will be painful, even though it is necessary. How confidently he speaks of the truth of what he is about to say: *Who can withhold himself from speaking?* (v. 2). When our friends, even our friends who are suffering, say or do wrong, it is foolish not to rebuke them because we fear offending them.

2. Eliphaz brings a twofold charge against Job:

2.1. A charge as to his particular behavior in his suffering. He accuses him of being weak and fainthearted.

2.1.1. He takes notice of Job's former usefulness in comforting others. He acknowledges that Job has instructed many people, not only his own children and servants. He *strengthened the weak hands* (v. 3) with suitable advice and comfort for work, service, and spiritual warfare. Those who have an abundance of spiritual riches should abound in spiritual love. But why does Eliphaz mention this here? Perhaps he is praising Job for the good he has done so that he may make the intended rebuke more acceptable to him. He also remembers how Job has comforted others and recognizes that as a reason why Job might justly expect himself to be comforted. Perhaps he says this by way of pity, mourning that through the intensity of his suffering Job cannot apply those comforts to himself which he has formerly given to others. Most think that Eliphaz intends to rebuke Job by reminding him of his knowledge and the good support he has given others. It is as if he had said, "You have taught others; why do you not teach yourself?"

2.1.2. He rebukes him for his present low spirits (v. 5). "*Now* that *it has come upon thee*, now that *it touches thee, thou faintest, thou art troubled.*" He makes too light of Job's afflictions: "It *touches* (strikes) you." This was the very word that Satan himself had used (1:11; 2:5). If Eliphaz had felt one half of Job's suffering, he would have said, "It strikes me; it wounds me," but in speaking of Job's suffering, he makes very light of it. He also makes too much of Job's anger. We must make allowances for people in deep distress, and we should put a favorable interpretation on what they say.

2.2. A charge as to his general character before his suffering. He accuses him of being evil and falsehearted, and this aspect of the accusation is unjust and completely without foundation. He ridicules him very unkindly, rebukes him concerning the great profession of faith he has made, as if it had all now come to nothing and proved to be all show (v. 6): "*Is not this thy fear, thy confidence, thy hope, and the uprightness of thy ways*—isn't this all that your faith amounts to, this weakness you have shown in the face of suffering? Does not everything now appear to be mere pretense? If you had been sincere in your profession, God would not have afflicted you in this way, nor would you have behaved like this in the suffering." This was the very thing Satan aimed at: to prove Job a hypocrite. When he could not himself prove to God that Job was a hypocrite, Satan tried, through his friends, to prove it to Job himself, to persuade Job to confess himself to be a hypocrite. But by the grace of God, Job was enabled to maintain his integrity, and would not bear false witness against himself. Those who rashly and uncharitably criticize their brothers and sisters and condemn them as hypocrites are doing Satan's work. This verse is translated differently in several editions of our English Bibles. One of the first, in 1612, inverts the last two items: "Is not this thy fear, thy confidence, the uprightness of thy ways, and thy hope?" A 1660 edition reads, "Is not thy fear thy confidence, and the uprightness of thy ways thy hope?" That is, "Is it not now clear that all your religious faith, as expressed in both your devotion and your life, was only for what you thought you could get out of it? If it had been sincere, would it not have kept you from this despair? It is true, *if thou faint in the day of adversity, thy strength* and grace *is small* (Pr 24:10), but it does not therefore follow that you have no grace and no strength at all." A person's character cannot be seen from one single act.

Verses 7–11

Eliphaz here presents another argument to prove Job to be a hypocrite; he cites not only his impatience under his afflictions as evidence against him, but also even his suffering itself. He lays down two principles:

1. Good people have never been ruined in this way. To prove this, he appeals to Job's own observation (v. 7): "*Remember, I pray thee*; and give me one example of anyone who was righteous but who was destroyed as you are." If we understand "destroyed" to refer to a final destruction, his principle is true. No one who is righteous perishes forever (2Th 2:3). But if we understand it to refer to any temporal disaster, his principle is not true.

2. Evil people are often ruined in this way. For the proof of this he brings his own observation (v. 8): "*Even as I have seen*, many times, *those that plough iniquity, and sow wickedness, reap accordingly; by the blast of God they perish*, at the blast of his anger they perish (v. 9). We have reason to think that, whatever profession of faith you have made, you have sown trouble and evil."

2.1. He speaks of sinners in general, sinners who sow seeds of trouble, expecting to gain from their sin. Some understand *iniquity and wickedness* (v. 8) to refer to wrong and injury done to others. They will be paid in their own coin. Those who are troublesome will be paid back with trouble (2Th 1:6; Jos 7:25). He further describes their destruction (v. 9): *By the blast* (breath) *of God they perish*. Some think that in attributing the destruction of sinners to the blast of God and *the breath of his nostrils* (v. 9), Eliphaz refers to the wind which blew the house down on Job's children.

2.2. He speaks particularly of tyrants and cruel oppressors, using the metaphor of lions (vv. 10–11). The Hebrew language has five different names for lions, and they are all used here to set out the terrible tearing power, fierceness, and cruelty of proud oppressors. The voice of their roaring will be stopped. God will take away their power to cause harm: *The teeth of the young lions are broken* (v. 10). They will not enrich themselves with the spoil of their neighbors. Even *the old lion* is famished and *perishes for lack of prey* (v. 11). Furthermore, they will not leave behind offspring to succeed them: *The stout lion's whelps* (the cubs of the lioness) *are scattered abroad* (v. 11) to seek food for themselves, which the old ones used to get for them (Na 2:12). Perhaps Eliphaz intended this to reflect on Job, as if he, being the *greatest of all the men of the east* (1:3), had gained his possessions from plunder, but now his power and possessions had gone, and his family were scattered. If this was Eliphaz's meaning, it was a pity that a man whom God commended should be abused in this way.

Verses 12–21

Eliphaz has undertaken to convince Job of the sin and foolishness of his discontent and impatience, and he here appeals to a vision, which he relates to Job. It would have been good if he had kept to the purpose of this vision, which would have served as grounds on which to rebuke Job for his grumbling but not to condemn him as a hypocrite. The people of God did not then have any written word to quote, and so God sometimes told them common truths by extraordinary ways of revelation. We can be thankful that we who have Bibles have a more certain word there to depend on than even visions and voices (2Pe 1:19). Notice:

1. This message was sent to Eliphaz *secretly* (v. 12). Some of the sweetest fellowship that gracious souls have with God is in secret, where no eye sees except the eye of him who is all-seeing. God has ways of bringing conviction, counsel, and comfort to his people unobserved by the world, in private whispers, which come as powerfully and effectively as the public ministry. *He received a little thereof* (v. 12). We know a tiny amount in comparison with what there is to be known and what we will know when we reach heaven. It was brought to him in the *visions of the night* (v.13), when he had withdrawn from the world and its business and everything around him was peaceful and quiet. It was introduced by terrors: *Fear came upon him, and trembling* (v. 14). A holy awe and reverence of God and his majestic being struck his spirit, and this prepared him for a divine vision.

2. The vision was real, not a dream (vv. 15–16). If some have been so foolish as to impose false visions on others, and some are so foolish as to have been deceived by them, it does not therefore follow that there cannot have been visions of spirits, both good and bad. He *could not discern the form thereof* (v. 16); he could not exactly tell in his own mind what it was, much less give an accurate description of it. His conscience was to be awakened and informed, not his curiosity aroused.

3. The message was delivered in a still, small voice (1Ki 19:12). The message was (v. 17), "*Shall mortal man be more just than God*, the immortal God? *Shall a man be* thought to be, or pretend to be, *more pure than his Maker?*" It is a rebuke of Job's complaints and discontent: "Will a mere mortal pretend to be more just and pure than God? Will a mortal more truly understand, and more strictly observe, the rules and laws of justice than God?"

4. Eliphaz comments on this:

4.1. He shows how small the angels themselves are in comparison with God (v. 18). Angels are God's servants, servants who wait on him and work for him. If the world were left to the government of the angels, and they were trusted with the sole management of affairs, they would take false steps, and everything would not be done for the best, as it now is. Angels are intelligent beings, but they are only finite.

4.2. He reasons from this how much lower human beings are and how much less they are to be trusted or gloried in. If there is such a distance between God and angels, how much more distance there is between God and human beings!

4.2.1. Look at human beings in their life, and they are very lowly (v. 19). If we consider human beings in their best state, they are contemptible in comparison with the holy angels, even though honorable compared with the wild animals. Angels are pure spirits; the souls of human beings *dwell in houses of clay*: such are human bodies. Angels are free; the human soul is housed, and the body is a cloud around it, an impediment, like a piece of wood tied to the leg which stops it from moving; it is the soul's cage or prison. Angels are settled, but the very *foundation of* that house of clay in which human beings live *is in the dust* (v. 19). We stand only on dust; some stand on a higher heap of dust than others, but it is still the earth that supports us and will soon swallow us up. Angels are immortal, but human beings are soon *crushed like a moth* (v. 19) between the fingers. A little thing will destroy human life. Human beings are "crushed before the face of the moth" is the meaning. Is such a creature as this to be trusted in, or can any service be expected from human beings by the God who does not trust angels themselves?

4.2.2. In their death they appear even more contemptible and unfit to be trusted. People are mortal and dying (vv. 20–21). They are dying every day (1Co 15:31) and are continually wasting away: they are *destroyed from morning to evening*, between dawn and dusk they are broken to pieces (v. 20). In death all their excellence passes away. Beauty, strength, and learning not only cannot protect them from death but also must die with them. Their pomp, wealth, or power will not follow them. Their wisdom cannot save them from death. Will such a lowly, weak, foolish, sinful, and dying creature as this pretend to be *more just than God and more pure than his Maker?* (v. 17). No; instead of quarreling with his afflictions, let him wonder that he has escaped hell.

CHAPTER 5

Eliphaz has supported his charge against Job with an appeal to a word from heaven that has been sent him in a vision. In this chapter, he appeals to those who give testimony on earth, the faithful witnesses of God's truth in all ages (v. 1). They will testify: 1. That the sin of sinners leads to their destruction (vv. 2–5). 2. That suffering is still the common experience of the human race (vv. 6–7); that when we are suffering, our wise duty is to turn to God, for he is able and ready to help us (vv. 8–16). 3. That the afflictions which are endured well will end well, and if Job were in a better frame of mind, he would be convinced that God had great mercy in store for him (vv. 17–27). He then concludes his speech in a somewhat better spirit than he began it.

Verses 1–5

Eliphaz is so convinced of the rightness of his own cause that he suggests that Job himself choose the arbitrators (v. 1): "*Call now, if there be any that will* answer you. Can you produce an example of anyone who was really *a saint* (a holy one) who was reduced to such extremities as you are now reduced to? God never dealt with anyone who loved his name as he is dealing with you, and so surely you are not holy. Did ever any good man curse his day as you did?" *To which of the saints wilt thou turn?* (v. 1). Good people are called *saints* even in the Old Testament, and so we do not know why we should not give them the same title as the good people of the New Testament, saying "St. Abraham," "St. Moses," and "St. Isaiah" as well as "St. Matthew" and "St. Mark," and "St. David the psalmist" as well as "St. David the British bishop." There are two things which Eliphaz maintains here, and on which he does not doubt that all the saints agree with him:

1. That the sin of sinners directly leads to their own ruin (v. 2): *Wrath kills the foolish man*, his own wrath, and so he is foolish for indulging in it. *Envy rots the bones and so kills the silly one*, the simple one who is worn down by it. "This is what it is like with you," says Eliphaz. "While you are quarreling with God, you are causing the greatest trouble for yourself." Job has told his wife she spoke like

the foolish women; now Eliphaz tells him he is acting like simple fools.

2. That their prosperity is short and their destruction certain (vv. 3–5). He seems here to parallel Job's case with what is commonly the case of evildoers. Job's prosperity has now come to an end, and so has the prosperity of other evildoers. Eliphaz foresaw their ruin. Those who looked only at present things blessed the home of these evildoers and thought them content. But Eliphaz *cursed it suddenly*, that is, he plainly saw and foretold their ruin. And eventually he saw what he had foreseen. Their families and possessions were ruined. He clearly and invidiously reflects on Job's calamities in these details. His children were crushed (v. 4), *and there was none to deliver them*. This language is commonly used to refer to the destruction of the families of evildoers, to make them give back their ill-gotten gains. They leave it to their children, but that will not prevent the rightful owners from defeating their children by proving their title invalid by the due course of law. Job's possessions were plundered (v. 5), like those of evildoers. The hungry robbers, the Sabeans and Chaldeans, ran off with them and devoured them, and Eliphaz says, "I have often noticed this in others." What has been gained by plunder and pillage has been lost in the same way. The careful owner protected it all around with thorns and thought it was safe, but the fence proved insignificant against the greed of the plunderers, which will go through the thorns and briers and *burn them together* (Isa 27:4).

Verses 6–16

When Eliphaz mentioned the loss of Job's possessions and the death of his children as the just punishment of his sin, he touched him at a very sensitive spot, but so that he may not drive him to despair, he here begins to encourage him. Now he speaks with kind tones, as if he wants to make up for the harsh words he has spoken to him.

1. He reminds him that no suffering comes about by chance or can be attributed to secondary causes: it *doth not come forth of the dust*, nor *spring out of the ground*, as the grass does (v. 6). If people are evil, they must not pin the blame on the soil, the climate, or the stars, but on themselves.

2. He reminds him that trouble and affliction are what we have every reason to expect in this world: *Man is brought to trouble* (v. 7), not merely as human beings, but as sinful human beings. And such is the weakness of our bodies and the worthlessness of our enjoyments that from there, too, our troubles arise as naturally *as the sparks fly upwards* (v. 7). Why should we then be surprised and consider our suffering to be strange? Why should we argue against them as being hard?

3. He instructs him how he should behave in his suffering (v. 8): *I would seek unto God*; "surely I would" is the sense. It is easy to say what we would do if we were in another person's position, but when it comes to the actual test, perhaps it would not be found so easy to do as we think or say. And yet it is good and opportune advice that Eliphaz gives: "For my part, the best thing I think I could do if I were you would be to turn to God." We must by prayer call on God's mercy and grace even when he contends with us. We must seek his favor when we have lost everything we have in the world. *Is any afflicted? Let him pray* (Jas 5:13). This will relieve the heart and soothe every hurt. *To God would I commit my cause*, I would appeal to him (v. 8). Having laid it at his feet, I would leave it in his hands.

4. He encourages him to seek God in this way, to commit his cause to him.

4.1. He commends to his consideration God's almighty power and sovereign rule. In general, he *doeth great things* (v. 9), truly great, for he can do anything. He does everything according to the counsel of his own will. The works of nature are mysterious, and the wisest philosophers have acknowledged themselves at a loss. The intentions of Providence are much deeper and more inexplicable (Ro 11:33). He does great *things without number* (v. 9); his power is never exhausted, nor will all his purposes ever be fulfilled until the end of time. Now, by the consideration of this, Eliphaz intends to convince Job of his fault and foolishness in quarreling with God.

4.2. He gives some examples of God's rule and power. God does great things in the kingdom of nature: *He gives rain upon the earth* (v. 10), which stands here for all the gifts of common providence, all the *fruitful seasons* by which he *filleth our hearts with food and gladness* (Ac 14:17). He also does great things in the lives of people. He not only enriches the poor and comforts the needy by the rain he sends (v. 10), but also, in order to advance those who are low, *disappoints the devices of the crafty*, thwarts the plans of the crafty, for v. 11 is to be joined to v. 12. God can defeat all the intentions of his enemies and also of his people's enemies. The plots of Ahithophel, Sanballat, and Haman were thwarted. The hostilities of Aram (*Syria*) and Ephraim against Judah, of Gebal and Ammon and Amalek against God's Israel, of the kings of the earth and the leaders against the Lord and against his anointed (Ps 2:2), were all crushed. The learned people of the nations were deceived by their own worthless philosophies (Col 2:8). When God brings people to nothing, they are perplexed and at a loss, even in those things that seem the clearest and simplest (v. 14): *They meet with darkness* even *in the daytime*: in fact (as in v. 14, margin), "they run into darkness" by the violence and haste of their own counsels. See 12:20, 24–25. He exalts the humble (v. 11). The lowly in heart and those who mourn are advanced by him, comforted and caused to *dwell on high*, in the *munitions* (fortress) *of rocks* (Isa 33:16). *So the poor*, who began to despair, *have hope.* The experiences of some encourage others to hope the best in the most difficult times, for it is the glory of God to send help to the helpless and hope to the hopeless.

Verses 17–27

Eliphaz gives Job a comforting view of the way his suffering will end if only he will regain his temper and come to terms with his suffering. Notice:

1. The timely word of warning and exhortation that he gives him (v. 17): "*Despise not thou the chastening of the Almighty.* Call it discipline; it comes from the father's love and is intended for the child's good. Let grace conquer the hatred which nature has against suffering, and reconcile yourself to the will of God in it." We must never think it beneath us to come under his discipline, but consider, on the contrary, that God really exalts a person when he *visits and tries him* (7:17–18). Do not overlook and disregard it, as if it were only an accident and the product of secondary causes, but take great notice of it as the voice of God and a messenger from heaven.

2. The comforting words of encouragement which he gives him.

2.1. *Happy is the man whom God correcteth* (v. 17), if he makes the most of the correction. To good people, correction is evidence of their adoption as God's children and a means of their sanctification; it puts to death the corrupt sinful desires, gradually draws their heart away from a worldly life, draws them nearer to God, brings them to their Bibles, brings them to their knees, and so is achieving for them an eternal glory that far outweighs all their suffering (2Co 4:17). And so, if Job would bear his affliction as the Lord's discipline, the results and effects of it would be very good (v. 18). When God wounds by the rebukes of providence, he binds up by encouragements of his Spirit.

2.2. In the following verses Eliphaz speaks directly to Job and gives him many precious promises of the great and kind things which God would do for him if only he would humble himself under his hand. And although Job's friends spoke some things that were not right both about God and about Job, the general teachings they laid down expressed the godly sense of the patriarchal age; and given that the apostle Paul quoted v. 13 in 1Co 1:19 as canonical Scripture, and that the command in v. 17, referred to in Heb 12:5, is no doubt binding on us, these promises too must be received and applied as divine promises, and through endurance and the encouragement of this part of the Scriptures we may have hope (Ro 15:4). It is here promised that:

2.2.1 As afflictions and troubles come, help will also graciously come, as often as necessary: *In six troubles he shall* be ready to *deliver thee; yea, and in seven* (v. 19).

2.2.2. Whatever troubles good people may be in, *there shall no evil touch them*, no harm will befall you (v. 19); they will do them no real harm. They may hiss, but they cannot hurt (Ps 91:10).

2.2.3. When devastating judgments come, God's people will be taken under special protection (v. 20).

2.2.4. Of all the hateful things that may be said against God's people, none will affect them so as to hurt them (v. 21). The best people, even the most inoffensive, cannot protect themselves from misrepresentation, criticism, and false accusation. People cannot hide themselves from these, but God can protect them from them, so that even the most malicious slander will not disturb their peace or blemish their reputation.

2.2.5. They will have a holy security and peace of mind arising from their hope and confidence in God. When dangers are most threatening, they will *not be afraid of destruction*, not even when they see it coming (v. 21). They will not be afraid *of the beasts of the field* when they attack them, or of people who are as cruel as wild animals. In fact, *at destruction and famine thou shalt laugh* (v. 22). Blessed Paul laughed at destruction when he said, *O death! where is thy sting?* (1Co 15:55), when, in the name of all the saints, he defied all the calamities of this present time to *separate us from the love of God*, concluding that *in all these things we are more than conquerors* (Ro 8:35–39).

2.2.6. Being at peace with God, they will have a covenant of friendship with the whole creation (v. 23). "When you walk over your land, you will not need to fear stumbling, for *thou shalt be at league* (in covenant) *with the stones of the field*, not to dash your foot against any of them, nor will you be in danger from *the beasts of the field*, for they will all be at peace with you."

2.2.7. Their houses and families will encourage them and make them strong (v. 24). "That your tent is secure" is the meaning; where people live in God and are at home in him, their house is secure. "*Thou shalt visit*"—that is, take stock of—"*thy habitation* (your property) and review it *and shalt not sin.*" God will provide a settlement for his people, perhaps lowly and movable, a cottage or a tent, but nevertheless a settled and quiet home. "*Thou shalt* not sin," or "wander," as some understand it: "you will not be a restless wanderer." They will have wisdom to lead their families in the right way, to manage their affairs with discretion, which is here called *visiting their habitation*. Godliness in a family crowns its peace and prosperity.

2.2.8. Their descendants will be numerous and prosperous. Job has lost all his children; "but," Eliphaz says, "if you return to God, he will again build up your family." It gives parents great encouragement to see the prosperity—especially the spiritual prosperity—of their children. If they are truly good, they are truly great, however insignificant they may appear in the world.

2.2.9. Their death will occur at the right time, and they will eventually finish their course (1Ti 4:7) with joy and honor (v. 26). If the providence of God does not give us long life, but the grace of God gives us satisfaction with the time allotted to us, we may well be said to have come to a full age. Our times are in God's hands (Ps 31:15); it is right that they are, for he will make sure that his people die at the best time. Even if their death may seem untimely to us, it will be found not to have been at the wrong time.

2.3. In v. 27 he commends these promises to Job as trustworthy sayings (1Ti 1:15), which he can be confident of the truth of: "*Lo, this we have searched, and so it is* (v. 27). We have indeed received these things by tradition from our ancestors, but we have diligently studied them, and have been confirmed in our belief from our own observations and experience, and we all agree that it is true." *Hear it, and know thou it for thy good* (v. 27). It is not enough to hear and know the truth; we must also apply it and become wiser and better by it. Apply it to yourself; say not only, "This is true," but also, "This is true for me." A sermon is indeed good when we apply it to ourselves and it does us good.

CHAPTER 6

Eliphaz finished his speech with an air of assurance, but Job is not convinced by everything he has said; he still justifies himself in his complaints and condemns Eliphaz for the weakness of his argument. 1. He shows that he was right to complain about his troubles as he did, and that this would be clear to any impartial judge (vv. 1–7). 2. He maintains his passionate desire that he may be quickly destroyed and so be relieved of all his misery (vv. 8–13). 3. He rebukes his friends for their unkind criticism of him and the unkind way they have treated him (vv. 14–30). It must be acknowledged that Job, in all this, spoke much that was reasonable, but also that he spoke with a mixture of intense emotion and human weakness. And in this contest, as indeed in most contests, there were faults on both sides.

Verses 1–7

At the beginning of his speech, Eliphaz was very sharp with Job, yet it does not appear that Job interrupted him at all, and when Eliphaz has finished his speech, Job gives his reply, in which he speaks with great emotion:

1. He presents his *calamity* in general as having been much heavier than either his expression of it or their estimation of it (vv. 2–3). He would gladly appeal to a third person, one who had just weights and balances with which to weigh his grief and calamity. He wishes they would set his anguish and all its expressions in one scale and his calamity and all its details in the other; they would find, as he says in 23:2, that *his stroke was heavier than his groaning*, for whatever his grief is, his calamity is *heavier than the sand*

of the sea (v. 3). Therefore, he says, *my words are swallowed up* (v. 3), that is, "You must therefore excuse the rashness and the bitterness of my expressions." Now, in saying this, he is doing three things. First, he is complaining that his friends undertook to give him spiritual medicine before they had thoroughly understood his condition. Second, he is excusing the passionate expressions he used when he cursed his day. Though he cannot himself justify all he has said, he still thinks his friends should not have condemned it so violently. Third, he is requesting the charitable and compassionate sympathy of his friends with him.

2. He complains about the trouble and terror of mind he is in as the most painful part of his misery (v. 4). In this he was a type of Christ, who, in his sufferings, complained most about the sufferings of his soul. Now *is my soul troubled* (Jn 12:27). *My soul is exceedingly sorrowful* (Mt 26:38). *My God, my God, why hast thou forsaken me?* (Mt 27:46). Poor Job sadly complains: *The arrows of the Almighty are within me* (v. 4). What cut him to the heart was to think that the God he loved and served had placed him under these marks of his displeasure. Trouble of mind is the most painful trouble to have to experience. *A wounded spirit who can bear* (Pr 18:14)? The poison or heat of these arrows is said to drink up his spirit, because it disturbed his reason, shook his determination, exhausted his strength, and threatened his life. He saw himself charged by *the terrors of God* (v. 4) as by an army marshaled in battle array, and surrounded by them.

3. He reflects on his friends' severe criticism of his complaints. Their rebukes were without basis. He complained, it is true, now that he was suffering this affliction, but he never used to complain. He did not *bray* (cry out) *when he had grass*, or *low* (call out) *over his fodder* (v. 5). But now that he had been completely deprived of all his comforts, he would be like a stick or stone—without even the sense of an ox or a wild donkey—if he did not somehow express his grief. He was forced to eat tasteless food and was so poor that he did not even have a grain of salt with which to season it, or to give a little taste to the white of an egg, which was now the tastiest dish on his table (v. 6). Food which once he would have scorned to touch was his *sorrowful meat* (v. 7).

Verses 8–13

The troubled sea rages most when it dashes against the rocks. Instead of withdrawing what he has said, Job here repeats it more strongly than before:

1. He still most passionately wants to die. He can see no end to his troubles except death and does not even have the patience to await the set time for that. He has a request to make; there is something he longs for (v. 8): *that it would please God to destroy me* (v. 9). Observe that although Job very much wanted to die and was angry that his death was delayed, he still did not attempt to destroy himself, to take away his own life; he only begged *that it would please God to destroy him* (v. 9).

2. He expresses this desire in a prayer, that God would grant him this request.

3. He promises himself effective relief and the redress of all his grievances by the stroke of death (v. 10): *Then should I yet have comfort*. If Job had not had a good conscience, he could not have spoken with this assurance of the comfort on the other side of death.

4. He challenges death to do its worst. If he could not die without first suffering severe pains, nevertheless, knowing that he would eventually die, he would make nothing of the pains of dying: "I *would harden myself in sorrow* (v. 10).

Let him not spare (v. 10); I want no lessening of that pain which will put a happy end to all my pain."

5. He bases his comfort on the testimony of his conscience that he has been faithful and firm in professing his religious faith: *I have not concealed the words of the Holy One* (v. 10).

6. He uses the miserable condition he is now in to justify himself in this extreme desire for death (vv. 11–12). Very cleverly, but perversely, he argues against the encouragements that have been given him. "*What is my strength, that I should hope?* (v. 11). You see how I am weak and low, and so what reason have I to hope that I will see better days? *Is my strength the strength of stones?* (v. 12). Are my muscles made of bronze and my sinews of steel? No; they are not, and so I cannot keep going in this pain and misery, but must sink under the load." *What is our strength?* It is a dependent strength. We have no more strength than God gives us, for we live and move in him. "*What is my end, that I should desire to prolong my life?* (v. 11). What comfort can I promise myself in life that is comparable to the comfort I promise myself in death?"

7. He forestalls the suspicion that he is delirious (v. 13): "*Is not my help in me?* Do you think wisdom has been driven completely away from me, and that I have gone mad? No; I am not insane, most excellent Eliphaz, but *speak the words of truth and soberness*" (Ac 26:25).

Verses 14–21

Eliphaz has been very harsh in his criticism of Job, and his companions have indicated their agreement with him. Poor Job here complains about their unkindness, as making his misery even worse and giving him a further excuse for his wish to die, for what satisfaction could he expect in this world when those who should have been his comforters proved to be his tormentors?

1. He shows what reason he had to expect kindness from them. His expectation was based on the ordinary principles of humanity (v. 14): "*To him that is afflicted pity should be shown from his friend*; and he that does not show that pity *forsakes the fear of the Almighty*." Inhumanity is ungodly and irreligious. The Aramaic reads, "He who withholds compassion from his friend forsakes the fear of the Almighty." When a person is afflicted, they will see who their true friends are and who merely pretend to be friends.

2. He shows how miserably he was disappointed in his expectations of them (v. 15): "*My brethren, who should have helped me, have dealt deceitfully as a brook.*" No one questioned but that the drift of their speeches would be to comfort Job by reminding him of his former godliness, the assurance of God's favor to him, and the prospect of a glorious outcome of events, but instead of this, they attacked him with their rebukes and criticism, condemned him as a hypocrite, and poured vinegar instead of oil on his wounds. We cannot expect too little from our fellow human beings or too much from our Creator. God will surpass our hopes as much as people come short of them. To illustrate this disappointment which he met with, Job here refers to the failing of streams in summer:

2.1. He compares his expectations of them, which they had raised by coming to comfort him with such gravity, to the expectation that weary, thirsty travelers have of finding water in summer where they have often seen it in great abundance in winter (v. 19). *The troops of Tema and Sheba*, the caravans of the merchants of those countries, whose road lay through the deserts of Arabia, looked and waited for a supply of water from those streams. "Near here," one of them said. "A little farther," another said. "When I last traveled this way, there was enough water for us to be refreshed." The disappointment of Job's expectation is here compared to the confusion which seized the poor travelers when they found heaps of sand in the places where they had expected floods of water. In winter, when they were not thirsty, there was enough water. Everyone will praise and admire those who are full and in prosperity. But in the heat of summer, when they needed water, it was then that it failed them; it had vanished (v. 17) when they turned aside to find it (v. 18).

2.2. When Job was successful, his friends meant something to him, but "*now you are nothing*, now I can find no comfort in you; my only comfort is in God. You are not what you have been, what you should be, what you pretend to be, what I thought you would have been, *for you see my casting down and are afraid* (v. 21). You are afraid that, if you acknowledge me, you will be obliged look after and provide for me."

Verses 22–30

Poor Job goes on here to rebuke his friends for their unkindness. If only they would think impartially, and speak as they thought, they would have to acknowledge:

1. That although he was in need, he still was not begging, nor was he a burden to his friends. Job was be glad to see his friends, but he would not say, *Bring unto me* (v. 22), or, *Deliver me* (v. 23). He did not desire to put them to any expense; "Did I send for you to *deliver me out of the hand of the mighty?* (v. 23). No; I never expected you either to expose yourselves to any danger or to put yourselves to any expense on my account." Job's not asking for their help did not excuse them from offering it when he needed it and when it was in their power to give it. It often happens that from people, even when we expect a little, we receive less, but from God, even when we expect much, we receive more (Eph 3:20).

2. That although he differed with them, he was not stubborn, but ready to submit to conviction: "*Teach me, and I will hold my tongue* (v. 24), for I have often found, with pleasure and wonder, *how forcible right words are.* But the method you use will never convert anyone: *What doth your arguing reprove*, what do your arguments prove? Your hypothesis is false, your assumptions are without basis, the way you deal with people is weak, and your application is harsh and uncharitable."

3. That although he had indeed been at fault, they still should not have treated him so harshly (vv. 26–27): "*Do you imagine*, do you mean, *to reprove words*, to correct what I say, these passionate expressions of mine in this desperate condition, as if they were certain signs that I was an ungodly unbeliever? A little kindness would have excused my words and would have interpreted them more favorably. Will a person's spiritual state be judged by some rash and hasty words, which an extraordinary problem draws out of them? Is it kind or just to criticize someone in such a situation?" They took advantage of his weakness and the helpless condition he was in: *You overwhelm the fatherless* (v. 27), he said, using a proverbial expression that denotes the depths of cruelty and inhumanness. They only pretended to be kind: "*You dig a pit for your friend* (v. 27). You not only are unkind to me, as your friend, but also, claiming to be friends, take advantage of me." When they came to see him, he thought he could speak his mind freely with them. But this freedom of speech, which their professions of concern for him led him to have, exposed him to their criticism, and so they could be said to have dug a pit for him.

4. That although he had spoken in a very passionate way, he was still mainly in the right, and that his suffering, although highly unusual, did not prove he was a hypocrite or evil. "*Be content*, and *look upon me*; what do you see in me that shows me to be either mad or evil? Let the appearance of my face prove that although I have cursed my day, I do not curse my God. You hear what I have to say: *Is there iniquity in my tongue?* Is there evil on my lips? Do you have wrong you can charge me with? Have I blasphemed God or renounced him? *Return, I pray you*; reconsider what is going on here, but this time do it without prejudice. You will find *my righteousness is in it*," that is, "I am in the right in this matter, and although I cannot keep my temper as I should, I have kept my integrity."

CHAPTER 7

Job continues to express the bitter feelings he has over his adversities, and he tries to justify his desire to die. 1. He complains to himself and his friends about his troubles and the constant distress he is in (vv. 1–6). 2. He turns to God and complains to him for the rest of the chapter (vv. 7–21), in which: 2.1. He pleads for death, which puts to an end our troubles in this world (vv. 7–10), and he passionately complains about the miserable condition he is now in (vv. 11–16). 2.2. He is amazed that God will contend with him, and he begs that his sins will be forgiven and he will be quickly released from his misery (vv. 17–21).

Verses 1–6

Job here excuses what he himself could not justify, namely, his excessive desire to die.

1. Everyone must die soon. "Please do not mistake my desire to die, as if I thought I could die before the time set by God. No; I know very well that that time has been fixed. I am simply expressing myself in such language to freely air my present distress: *Is there not an appointed time*"—meaning, "a warfare," as in v. 1, margin—"to *man upon earth, and are not his days* here *like the days of a hireling?*" (v. 1). Certainly there is, and it is easy to say by whom the decision is made: by the One who made us and who has placed us here. We are not to think that we are governed by the blind fate of the Stoics or the blind fortune of the Epicureans, but by the wise, holy, and sovereign counsel of God. Our life is "a warfare" (v. 1, margin) and *as the days of a hireling* (v. 1). We are, each one of us, to look on ourselves in this world:

1.1. As soldiers, exposed to hardship and surrounded by enemies. We must serve under a commanding officer. When the days of our warfare are completed (Isa 40:2), we must be disbanded.

1.2. As laborers who take work for the day, who do the work of the day in its day and must give an account for it at night.

2. He had as much reason, he thought, to wish to die as poor servants or hirelings who are tired of their work desperately wish for the evening shadows to come, when they will receive their pay and go to rest (v. 2). The comparison is clear, even if the application is somewhat obscure. Exactness of language is not to be expected from someone in Job's condition. "*As a servant earnestly desires the shadow* (v. 2), *so* also, and for the same reason, I fervently desire death, for *I am made to possess months of vanity* (futility)" (v. 3). Listen to his complaint:

2.1. His days were futile and had been so for a long while. Every day was a burden to him, because he was unable to do good or spend it in any meaningful way. But when we

are prevented from working for God, if we will only sit still quietly for him, it is all the same; we will still be accepted.

2.2. His nights were restless (vv. 3–4). The night relieves the work and weariness of the day, not only for those who work but also for those who suffer. But poor Job could not gain this relief. This made him dread the night as much as the servant desires it.

2.3. His body was unwholesome (v. 5).

2.4. His life was moving quickly toward its end (v. 6). He thought he had no reason to expect a long life, for he found himself declining fast (v. 6): *My days are swifter than a weaver's shuttle*; and so he no longer hoped to be restored to his former prosperous state.

Verses 7–16

Job is here begging God either to bring him some relief or to bring his life to an end. He presents himself to God:

1. As a dying man, surely and speedily dying (v. 7): *O remember that my life is wind*, but a breath. He commends himself to God as an object of his pity and compassion, with this thought: that he is a frail creature and that his time in this world is uncertain. *The eye of him that hath* here *seen me shall see me no more* there (v. 8). Dying is something that is done only once. This is illustrated by the blotting out and scattering of a cloud. It vanishes and is gone; it resolves itself into air and is never formed again. Other clouds come, but the same cloud never returns. It is like that with a new generation of people (v. 10): *He shall return no more to his house*. He might have drawn a better conclusion from these reasons than this (v. 11): *Therefore I will not refrain my mouth; I will speak; I will complain*. It is better to die praying and praising than to die complaining and quarreling.

2. As a diseased man, in intense pain, both physically and mentally. In this part of his speech he is beside himself: "*Am I a sea, or a whale* (v. 12), a raging sea that must be kept within limits, or an unruly whale, which must be forcefully restrained from consuming all the fish of the sea?" His bed, instead of comforting him, terrifies him, and his couch, instead of relieving his suffering, only makes it worse. Although Job's dreams may partly have arisen from his illness, we have reason to think Satan also had a hand in them, for he delights in terrifying those whom he cannot destroy; but Job looks up to God and mistakes Satan's actions for the *terrors of God setting themselves in array* (marshaled) *against him* (6:4). We should therefore pray to God that our dreams may neither defile nor distress us. Job wants to have rest in his grave, where he may lie in peace with no further tossing backward and forward, nor any frightening dreams (vv. 15–16). He is fond of death: *his soul chose strangling and death rather than life* (v. 15); any death rather than such a life as this. No doubt this was the voice of Job's weakness, for although a good man would not wish to live always in this world and would prefer strangling and death to sin, as the martyrs did, he would still be content to live as long as God wants and would not choose death rather than life, because life is our opportunity to glorify God and prepare for heaven.

Verses 17–21

Job here reasons with God:

1. Concerning his dealings with human beings in general (vv. 17–18): *What is man, that thou shouldst magnify him?* We are making a mistake about God and the nature of his providence if we think it belittles him to take notice of the lowliest of his creatures. Job acknowledges God's favor to human beings in general, even when he is complaining about his own particular troubles. "*What is man*, a poor, weak, and lowly creature, *that thou*, the great and

glorious God, should have dealings with him as you do? *What is man*:

1.1. "That you should give him such honor, *shouldst magnify him* (v. 17), by taking him into covenant and fellowship with yourself?

1.2. "That *thou shouldst set thy heart upon him* (v. 17), giving him so much attention as one who is precious to you?

1.3. "*That thou shouldst visit him* with your compassions *every morning* (v. 18)?"

2. Concerning his dealings with him in particular:

2.1. That he is the target for God's arrows: "*Thou hast set me as a mark against thee*" (v. 20). "My case is special; no one has been shot at as I have been."

2.2. That he is *a burden to himself* (v. 20), ready to sink under the load of his own life.

2.3. That he has no respite from his griefs (v. 19): "*How long* will it be before you cause your discipline to *depart from me*, or before you lessen the harshness of your correction, at least long enough for me *swallow down my spittle?*" It seems Job's illness lay in his throat and almost choked him, so that he could not even swallow his spittle. He later complained (30:18) that it *bound him about like the collar of his coat.* "Lord," he says, "will you not give me some respite, some time to regain my breath?" (9:18).

2.4. That he is in distress about his sins. He freely acknowledges himself guilty before God: *I have sinned* (v. 20). God has described him as a *perfect* (blameless) *and an upright man* (1:8), but when he describes himself, he says, *I have sinned.* People may be upright even though, as human beings, they are not sinless; and those who have sincerely repented are accepted, through a Mediator, as blameless according to the Gospel. Job maintained, in opposition to his friends, that he was not a hypocrite, that he was not evil, but nevertheless he readily acknowledged to his God that he had sinned. When we are suffering, it is the right time to confess our sin as the cause of our affliction. Penitent confessions would drown out and silence passionate complaints. He seriously asks how he may make his peace with God: "*What shall I do unto thee*, what shall I do for you (v. 20), having done so much against you?" In our repentance we must keep good thoughts of God, as One who does not delight in destroying his creatures, but rather wants them to return to him and live. "You are the Savior of the world; be my Savior, for I throw myself on your mercy." He fervently begs for the forgiveness of his sins (v. 21). Just as the passion in his spirit made his complaints more bitter, so on the other hand, it also made his prayers more real and persistent, as here: *Why dost thou not pardon my transgression?* When the mercy of God pardons the offenses that are committed by us, the grace of God takes away the sin that reigns in us. Wherever God removes the guilt of sin, he breaks the power of sin.

CHAPTER 8

Job's friends are like Job's messengers; they closely followed on another's heels: the messengers with bad news and the friends with harsh criticism. Both unintentionally served Satan's plans: the messengers to drive him from his integrity, the friends to drive him from the enjoyment of it. Eliphaz did not reply to what Job had said in answer to him, but left it to Bildad. Eliphaz had undertaken to show that because Job was painfully afflicted, he was certainly evil; Bildad is of much the same mind and will conclude that Job is an evildoer unless God quickly comes to help him. In this chapter, he tries to convince

Job that: 1. He has spoken too emotionally (v. 2); he and his children have suffered justly (vv. 3–4); if he has truly repented, God will soon reverse his circumstances (vv. 5–7). 2. It is a usual thing for Providence to extinguish the joys and hopes of evildoers as his have been extinguished, and the friends therefore have reason to suspect him of being a hypocrite (vv. 8–19). 3. Their suspicions will be substantially confirmed unless God quickly comes to help him (vv. 20–22).

Verses 1–7

Here:

1. Bildad rebukes Job for what he has said (v. 2), criticizes his emotions, but as is too common, does so with even more emotion. Job spoke a great deal of good sense, but Bildad rebuts what Job has said with this: *How long wilt thou speak these things?* Bildad compares Job's speech to *a strong wind.*

2. Bildad justifies God in what he has done. He had no occasion to do this at this time, for Job had not condemned God, as Bildad would have it thought; if Bildad must justify God, he could at least have done it without reflecting badly on Job's children, as he did here.

2.1. He is right in general, that God does not pervert what is right, that he never acts against any settled rule of justice (v. 3).

2.2. But he takes it for granted that Job's children—the death of whom was one of his greatest sufferings—had been guilty of some outrageous evil (v. 4). Job readily acknowledged that God did not pervert justice, but it did not therefore follow that his children died for some great offense. It is true that we and our children have sinned against God, but extraordinary suffering is not always the punishment of extraordinary sins. It is sometimes the testing of extraordinary graces, and in our judgment of another person's situation we should take the more favorable view, as our Savior says in Lk 13:2–4.

3. Bildad led Job to hope that if he was indeed upright, as he said he was, he would still see a good outcome of his present troubles: "Although your children have sinned against him and have been rejected because of their offense, if you are pure and upright yourself, and if, as evidence of that, you will now seek God and submit to him, then everything will still be well" (vv. 5–7). This may be taken in one of two ways, either:

3.1. As intending to prove that Job was a hypocrite and an evildoer by pointing to the continuation of his afflictions. Bildad was wrong here, for a good person may be afflicted in their time of testing not only very painfully but also for a very long time, and yet even if it lasts for life, it is only for a moment in comparison with eternity. Or:

3.2. As intending to direct and encourage Job, so that he might not despair completely. There might still be hope if only he would take the right course. He gives him hope that he will still see good days, secretly suspecting, however, that he is not qualified to see them. Let Job not object that he has so little left to begin living with in the world that it is impossible he should ever prosper as in the past. No; "Although your beginnings are very humble, a handful of flour in a jar and a little oil in a jug (1Ki 17:12), God's blessing will multiply that to produce great prosperity." This is God's way of enriching the souls of his people with grace and comfort, not with one giant step, but gradually.

Verses 8–19

Bildad will not be so bold as to say, with Eliphaz, that no one who was upright was ever destroyed in this way (4:7), but he takes it for granted that God ordinarily does bring on evildoers shame and ruin in this world, and that by making their prosperity short, he shows their godliness to be false. Whether this definitely proves that all who are destroyed in this way have been hypocrites, he will not say.

1. He proves the certain destruction of all the hopes and joys of hypocrites by appealing to previous ages. He does not insist on his own judgment and that of his companions: *We are but of yesterday, and know nothing* (v. 9). He refers to the testimony of the elders (v. 8). *They will teach thee*, and tell you (v. 10), that from the beginning of their time to the end, the judgments of God pursued evildoers. Bishop Patrick suggests that because Bildad was a Shuhite, descended from Shuah, one of Abraham's sons by Keturah (Ge 25:2), in this historical reference he is particularly remarking, on the one hand, on the rewards gained by the descendants of faithful Abraham from the blessing of God, and on the other, on the uprooting of those eastern people in whose country Abraham's descendants had settled.

2. He illustrates this truth by some comparisons:

2.1. The hopes and joys of the hypocrite are compared to *flag*, a reed (vv. 11–13). It grows up out of the swamp and water. Hypocrites cannot gain their hope without some false, rotten ground or other from which that hope can grow, and which supports and keeps it alive, any more than reeds can grow up without swampy ground. Hypocrites build on worldly prosperity, the plausible profession they make of religion, the good opinion of their neighbors, and their own favorable view of themselves, which are no solid foundation on which to rest their confidence. They may look green and bright for a while—the reeds growing higher than the grass—but they are light, hollow, and empty. They soon wither, *before any other herb*, more quickly than grass (v. 12). Even *while it is in its greenness*, it is dried up and gone in a little time. *So are the paths of all that forget God* (v. 13); they take the same way that the reeds do, *for the hypocrite's hope shall perish*.

2.2. The hope of hypocrites is compared to a spider's web, or a spider's house (as the margin of v. 14 reads), a cobweb (vv. 14–15). Like the spider's web, the hope of hypocrites comes from within themselves; it is the figment of their own imagination and arises merely from the notion of their own goodness and adequacy. There is a great deal of difference between the work of the bee and that of the spider. Diligent Christians, like hardworking bees, derive all their comfort from the heavenly dews of God's word, but hypocrites, like subtle spiders, weave theirs out of their own false claims about God, as if he were a hypocrite too. The hope of hypocrites is something they are very fond of, as the spider is of its web. The spider wraps itself in it, calls it its house, *leans upon it, and holds it fast* (clings to it) (v. 15). It is said of the spider that *she takes hold with her hands, and is in kings' palaces* (Pr 30:28). Similarly, worldly people hug themselves in the greatness and strength of their outward prosperity. They pride themselves on their houses as their palaces, but they will be swept away, as the cobweb is swept away by a broom, when God comes to clean his house.

2.3. The hypocrite is here compared to a flourishing and well-rooted tree, which, although it does not itself wither, will still be easily cut down *and its place know it no more* (Ps 103:16). Notice this tree when it is fair and flourishing (v. 16) under the protection of the garden wall and with the benefit of the garden soil; because it takes deep root, it is never likely to be struck down by stormy winds, for its roots are entwined around a pile of rocks (v. 17). It grows on firm ground, not, like reeds, in swampy water. This is how evildoers, when they prosper in the world, think they

are secure. Notice this tree when it is felled and forgotten, nevertheless, *destroyed from his place* (v. 18).

Verses 20–22

Bildad sums up what he has to say in a few words:

1. On the one hand, if Job was blameless and upright, God would not *cast him away* (reject him) (v. 20). Although he now seemed to have been forsaken by God, God would still return to him, and his *mouth* would be *filled with laughing* (v. 21). Those who loved him would be glad with him, but those who hated him and had triumphed at his downfall would be ashamed of their arrogance. Now it is true that *God will not cast away a perfect* (upright) *man* (v. 20); he may be downcast for a short time, but he will not be rejected forever (Ps 37:24). It is true, if not in this world, then in the next. But it did not therefore follow that if Job was not perfectly restored to his former prosperity, he would forfeit the characterization of being blameless.

2. On the other hand, if he was an evildoer, God would not help him but would leave him to perish in his present distresses (v. 20), and his *dwelling place* would *come to nought* (v. 22). It is true that *the dwelling place of the wicked*, sooner or later, *will come to nought* (v. 22). Only those *who make God their dwelling place* are safe forever (Ps 90:1; 91:1). Sin brings destruction on people and families. But to argue, as Bildad cunningly does, that because Job's family was lost, and he himself at present seemed helpless, he therefore certainly was ungodly and evil, was neither just nor charitable.

CHAPTER 9

In this and the next chapter we have Job's answer to Bildad's speech, in which he speaks honorably of God, humbly of himself, and emotionally about his troubles, but without one word of criticism against his friends. In this chapter we have: 1. The doctrine of God's justice established (v. 2); proof of it, from his wisdom, power, and sovereign rule (vv. 3–13). 2. The application of this teaching, in which Job condemns himself as unable to contend with God (vv. 14–21). 3. Job maintaining his point that we cannot judge people's character from their outward condition (vv. 22–24). 4. Job complaining about the greatness of his troubles, the confusion he is in, and how he is at a loss for what to say or do (vv. 25–35).

Verses 1–13

Bildad began with a rebuke to Job for talking so much (8:2). Job does not respond to that, but on Bildad's next point, that God never perverts justice, Job agrees with him: I *know it is so of a truth* (v. 2). *How should man be just with God?* (How can a mortal be righteous before God?) (v. 2). Some understand this as an emotional complaint that God is strict and harsh, and it cannot be denied that this chapter contains some ill-tempered statements. But we prefer to take this as a godly confession of human sinfulness, and especially his own, that if God should deal with any of us according to what our sins deserve, we would certainly be ruined.

1. Job establishes it as a truth that mortals are an unequal match for their Maker:

1.1. In a dispute (v. 3): *If he will contend with him*, either at law or in any argument, *he cannot answer him one* (one time out) *of a thousand*. When God spoke to Job out of the storm, he asked him a great many questions—*Dost thou know* this? *Canst thou do* that?—none of which could Job give an answer to (chs. 38–39). God can accuse us of a thousand offenses, and we cannot answer him so as to be acquitted of any of his charges.

1.2. In combat (v. 4): *Who hath hardened himself against him and hath prospered*, who has resisted him and come out unscathed? You cannot come up with any example of rebellion in which a daring sinner who *hardened himself against God* did not find God too hard for him and then pay dearly for being so foolish.

2. He proves it by showing what sort of a God is the God with whom we have to do (Heb 4:13): *He is wise in heart*, his wisdom is profound, and so we cannot answer him adequately in law; he is *mighty in strength*, his power is vast (v. 4), and so we cannot fight with him and win. The Devil promised himself that Job would curse God and speak evil of him in the day of his suffering, but instead of that, he sets himself to honor God and speak highly of him.

2.1. As the God of nature, he acts with an uncontrollable power and does what he pleases, for all the order and all the powers of nature come from him and depend on him.

2.1.1. When he pleases, he can change the course of nature and turn back its flow (vv. 5–7). For instance, nothing is firmer than the mountains, and when we speak of moving mountains, we are referring to something impossible; but God's power can make them change where they rest. He can level them and overturn them. People have to take great efforts to pass over them, but when God pleases, he can make them pass away. And nothing is more fixed than the earth turning on its axis, but God can, when he pleases, *shake the earth out of its place*, move it from its center, and make even *its pillars to tremble* (v. 6). God has enough power to shake the earth from under the guilty human race, which makes it groan under the burden of sin (Ro 8:22), and so to *shake the wicked out of it* (38:13). But he maintains the earth, with human beings on it, and he does not make it, as he did once, swallow up the rebels (Nu 16:32). Nothing is more constant than the rising sun. It never misses its appointed time to rise. But when God pleases, he can stop it. This is how great God's power is; and how great then is his goodness, which causes his sun to shine even on those who are evil and unthankful (Lk 6:35), even though he could withhold it! Job is here speaking about what God can do; if we understand it to refer to what he has actually done, all these verses may perhaps be applied to Noah's flood.

2.1.2. As long as he pleases, he keeps the settled course and order of nature, and this is a continued creation. He himself alone, by his own power, and without the help of any other, *spreads out the heaven* (v. 8); not only did he stretch them out in the beginning, but he still stretches them out. *He treads upon the waves of the sea* (v. 8), that is, he restrains them and keeps them down, so that they do not come to deluge the earth (Ps 104:9), which is given as a reason why we should all fear God and stand in awe of him (Jer 5:22). God makes the constellations; three are named for all the rest (v. 9), *Arcturus* (the Bear), *Orion*, and *Pleiades*, and in general *the chambers* (constellations) *of the south*. He not only makes the stars, but also makes them what they are for people, and he inclines human hearts to observe them, which animals cannot do. Divine direction and rule are over not only those stars which we see and have named, but also those in the other hemisphere, around the South Pole, which never come into our sight, called here *the chambers* (constellations) *of the south*.

2.2. In the kingdom of providence, too, God does many great things, many that can be wondered at (v. 10). God is a great God, and *doeth great things*, he works miracles; his works of wonder are so many that we cannot number them. They are so mysterious that we cannot fathom them. He acts invisibly and in ways we cannot discern (v. 11). "*He goes by me* in his activities, *and I see him not, I perceive him not. His way is in the sea*" (Ps 77:19). Our finite understandings cannot fathom his counsels, understand his movements, or comprehend the ways he takes. We are therefore incompetent to judge how God acts, because we do not know what he does or what he plans. The secrets of his rule are beyond us, and therefore we cannot pretend to explain them. He acts with incontrovertible sovereignty (v. 12). What action can be brought against him in court? Or *who will say unto him, What doest thou?* God is not obliged to give us a reason for what he does. We do not understand the meaning of his ways; there will be enough time in the next world to know, when it will become clear that what now seemed to be done according to divine right was done in infinite Wisdom and for the best. He acts with irresistible power, which no creature can resist (v. 13). *If God will not withdraw his anger, the proud helpers do stoop under him*; that is, he certainly breaks and crushes those who proudly help one another against him.

Verses 14–21

What Job has said of the utter inability of human beings to contend with God he here applies to himself, and in effect he despairs of gaining his favor. This response arises from the dark and cloudy apprehensions which he now has of God's displeasure against him.

1. He dared not argue with God (v. 14): "*If the proud helpers do stoop under him, how much less shall* I, a poor weak creature, who, far from being a helper, am so helpless, *answer him?* What can I say against what God does?"

2. He dared not insist on his own justification before God. Although he justified his own integrity to his friends and would not admit that he was a hypocrite and an evildoer, as they suggested, he still would never plead this integrity as his righteousness before God.

2.1. He knew so much of God that he dare not stand trial against him (vv. 15–19).

2.1.1. God knew him better than he knew himself, and so (v. 15), "*Though I were righteous* in my own apprehension, and my own heart did not condemn me, *yet God is greater than my heart* and knows those secret faults and errors of mine which I do not and cannot understand. He can charge me with them, and so *I would not answer.*" Job therefore would plead with God for mercy and not think he could get off according to any goodness in himself.

2.1.2. He had no reason to think that there was anything in his prayers to commend them. God answers before we call and not because we call. He gives gracious answers to our prayers, but not because of our prayers (v. 16): "*If I had called, and he had answered*, given me what I asked for, yet because I am so weak and my best prayers imperfect, *I would not believe he had hearkened* (listened) *to my voice*. I could not say that he had *saved with his right hand and answered me* (Ps 60:5), but must say that he did it purely for his own name's sake."

2.1.3. His present miseries made him all too aware that in this life, God in his sovereignty reserves the full and exact distribution of rewards and punishments for the future state. Job was not aware in himself of any extraordinary guilt, but he still experienced extraordinary suffering

(vv. 17–18). He was *broken with a tempest*, crushed by a storm. His troubles came on him so thick and fast that he had no breathing space, and he was filled with bitterness. And he presumed to say that all this was *without cause*, without any great provocation given. Here, no doubt, *he spoke unadvisedly with his lips* (Ps 106:33); he reflected badly on God's goodness in rashly saying that he was not allowed *to take his breath*, while he still had such good use of his reason and speech as to be able to talk in this way. He also reflected badly on God's justice in saying that his suffering was without cause. There is no disputing, as someone said to Caesar, with the one who commands legions. Much less is it possible to argue with the One who has legions of angels at his command.

2.2. He knew so much of himself that he dared not stand a trial (vv. 20–21). "*If I go* about to *justify myself*, to plead a righteousness of my own, my defense will be my offense, and *my own mouth shall condemn me* even when it tries to acquit me." Good people, who know the deceitfulness of their own heart, are suspicious of more evil in themselves than they are really conscious of, and so will by no means think of justifying themselves before God. "Even if I were free from gross sin, even if my conscience would not accuse me of any terrible crime, I still would not believe my own heart so far as to insist on my own innocence. Nor would I think my life worth striving for with God."

Verses 22–24

Here Job touches briefly on the main point now being argued between him and his friends. They maintained that those who are righteous and good always prosper in this world, and none but evildoers are in misery and distress. He asserted, on the contrary, that it is a common thing for evildoers to prosper and for the righteous to be greatly afflicted. "I said it, and say it again, that all things come alike to all" (Ecc 9:2). It must be acknowledged that there is much truth in what Job means here, that when temporal judgments are sent, they come on both good and bad people. Let this help God's children come to terms with their troubles; they are times of testing and refinement, designed for their honor and benefit, and if God desires to use troubles in this way, let his children not be displeased. On the other hand, evildoers are so far from being made the marks of God's judgments that *the earth is given into their hand* (v. 24), *into the hand of the wicked one*; in the original, the word is singular. Evildoers have the earth given to them. Yet the righteous have heaven given to them, and which is better: heaven without earth or earth without heaven? Job therefore ought not to have said, concerning the trial of the innocent, *He laughs at it*, for God does not afflict willingly (La 3:33). When we become impassioned, either in debate or in vexation, we need to set a watch over the door of our lips (Ps 141:3).

Verses 25–35

Job here grows more hot tempered. When we are in trouble, we are allowed to complain to God, as the psalmist does here, but we must by no means complain about God, as Job does here:

1. His complaint that his prosperous days had gone is fair enough (vv. 25–26): "*My days*, that is, all my good days, have gone, never to return. They have suddenly gone, before I knew it."

2. His complaint about his present uneasiness is excusable (vv. 27–28). He did all he could to compose himself as his friends advised him to. He would try to *forget his*

complaints and praise God. But he found he could not do it: "*I am afraid of all my sorrows*, I still dread all my sufferings" (v. 28).

3. His complaint toward God, calling him merciless and inescapable, cannot be excused. He knew better, and at another time he would have been far from harboring such harsh thoughts of God. Good people do not always speak according to their true nature, but God, who knows how they are formed (Ps 103:14) and the strength of their temptations, allows them to later withdraw what they have wrongly said by repenting, and then he will not hold them responsible for it.

3.1. Job seems to speak here:

3.1.1. As if he despaired of ever obtaining any relief or redress of his grievances from God: "*I know that thou wilt not hold me innocent*" (v. 28). My afflictions have continued for such a long time. *Why then do I labour* in vain to clear myself and maintain my own integrity?" (v. 29). With human beings it is often hopeless (Mk 10:27) to try to clear the name of the most innocent people. But it is not so in our dealings with God, to whom it has never been futile to commit a righteous cause (vv. 30–31). Yet in Job's view, "Even *if I wash myself with snow water*, no matter how evident I make my integrity, it will be all in vain; judgment must surely go against me. *Thou shalt plunge me in the ditch*"—the pit of destruction, according to some, or rather a slime pit, the filthy gutter, or the sewer—"which will make me so foul smelling to everyone around me that *my own clothes shall abhor me*, and I will even hate to touch myself." He saw his suffering as coming from God. But these words may also be interpreted in a better sense. He may not be speaking of God disrespectfully but saying that even if we keep our hands clean from the defilements of gross sin which come under the eyes of the world, yet God, who knows our hearts, can still accuse us of so many secret sins as will forever take away every claim to purity and innocence and make us see ourselves as repugnant in the sight of the holy God. While Paul was a Pharisee, he made his hands very clean, but when the commandment came and revealed to him the sins of his heart, he became aware of sinful desires that *plunged him in the ditch*.

3.1.2. As if he despaired of ever receiving a fair hearing from God. He complains that he is not on fair terms with God (v. 32): "*He is not a man, as I am*. I could dare argue with a man like myself. *Neither is there any daysman* (someone to arbitrate) *between us*." This complaint that there was not such an arbitrator is in effect a wish that there were one, and so the Septuagint (a Greek version of the Old Testament) reads: "Oh that there were a mediator between us!" Job would gladly refer the matter to such a person, but no creature could be a referee, and so he must refer the matter to God himself and simply accept his judgment. Our Lord Jesus is the blessed Mediator, who has mediated between heaven and earth. The Gospel leaves us no justification for such a complaint as Job's. Job did not know how to speak to God with the confidence with which he used to approach him (vv. 34–35). *Let him take his rod away from me.* He is not referring so much to his outward adversities as to *his fear* (i.e., God's fear, the fear of God), which *terrified him* (v. 34).

3.2. From all this may we learn to pity those who are wounded in spirit. We must learn also to keep good thoughts of God in our minds, for harsh thoughts of him allow much trouble to come in.

CHAPTER 10

Job acknowledges that he is full of confusion and shame (v. 15), and indeed he does not know what to say, and perhaps sometimes scarcely knows what he is saying. In this chapter: 1. He complains about the hardships he is suffering (vv. 1–7). He then comforts himself with the knowledge that he is in the hand of the God who made him (vv. 8–13). 3. He complains again about how harshly God has dealt with him (vv. 14–17), and then he comforts himself with the knowledge that death will put an end to his troubles (vv. 18–22).

Verses 1–7

Here is:

1. An emotional decision to persist in his complaint (v. 1). He decides to give himself some relief by expressing his anger. *My soul is weary of my life.* He will express the bitterness of his soul by speaking out violent words. Job's corruption is speaking here, but grace still adds a word.

1.1. He will complain, but he will *leave his complaint upon himself,* he will direct his complaint at himself (v. 1).

1.2. He will speak, but he will express the *bitterness of his soul* (v. 1), not his settled judgment. If I speak wrongly, it is *not I, but sin that dwells in me* (Ro 7:17), not my soul, but its bitterness.

2. A humble petition to God. He will speak, but the first word will be a prayer (v. 2):

2.1. That he may be rescued from the sting of his afflictions, which is sin (1Co 15:56). "You are correcting me; I will bear that as well as I can, but do not condemn me!" It is the comfort of those who are in Christ Jesus that although they suffer, there is still *no condemnation to them* (Ro 8:1). They may therefore pray, "Lord, do not condemn me; my friends condemn me, but please, not you."

2.2. That he may know the true cause of his suffering, and that is sin too: Lord, *show me wherefore thou contendest with me,* tell me what charges you have against me (v. 2). When God afflicts us, he contends with us, and when he contends with us, there is always a reason.

3. A petulant complaint against God for his dealings with him.

3.1. He thinks it is not consistent with the goodness of God and the mercifulness of his nature to deal so harshly with his creature as to put more on him than he can bear (v. 3): *Is it good unto thee that thou shouldst oppress?* "This cannot give you pleasure; it cannot honor you. And so, *What profit is there in my blood,* what gain is there in my destruction?" (Ps 30:9). Far be it from Job to think that God is treating him wrongly, but he is quite at a loss for how to reconcile God's providences with his justice, as good people have often been, and we must wait until the Day comes that will fully explain it.

3.2. He thinks it is not consistent with the infinite knowledge of God to torture his prisoner, as it were, to draw out a confession from him (vv. 4–6). Many things are hidden from human eyes, the hidden and complex; *there is a path which* even *the vulture's eye has not seen* (28:7): but nothing is, or can be, hidden from the eye of God, to which all things are exposed and open. Human eyes see only the outward appearance (1Sa 16:7), but God sees everything as it truly is. Human eyes see things gradually, but God sees everything all at once. Human eyes soon become tired, but the keeper of Israel neither slumbers nor sleeps (Ps 121:3–4), and his sight never wears out. *God sees not as man sees* (1Sa 16:7), that is, he does not judge as we human beings judge; no, *we are sure that the judgment of God is according to truth* (Ro 2:2). As God is not shortsighted—as human beings are—so also he is not short-lived (v. 5): "*Are thy days as the days*

of man, few and evil?" People grow wiser by experience and must take time to conduct their searches. But it is not so with God; to him nothing is past, nothing is future, everything is present.

3.3. He thinks it looks like an abuse of his almighty power to keep in custody a poor prisoner whom he knows to be innocent, only because there is no one who can rescue him from his hand (v. 7): *Thou knowest that I am not wicked.* He has already acknowledged he is a sinner, but he here states that he is not given to sin and is not an enemy of God. "I cannot say that I am not lacking or that I am not weak, but through grace I can say, *I am not wicked*: you know I am not, for *thou knowest I love thee* (Jn 21:15)."

Verses 8–13

In these verses we may notice:

1. Job sees God as his Creator and preserver and describes his dependence on him as the author and upholder of his being.

1.1. God made us, he, and not our parents, who were only the instruments of his power and providence in bringing us forth. *He made us, and not we ourselves* (Ps 100:3). The soul also, which gives life to the body, is his gift. Job notices both here.

1.1.1. The body *is made as the clay* (v. 9), molded into shape as the clay is formed into a piece of pottery according to the skill and will of the potter. The formation of human bodies in the womb is described by a beautiful comparison (v. 10)—*Thou hast poured me out like milk, and curdled me like cheese*—and by introducing some further details (v. 11). Although we come naked into this world, the body itself is both clothed and armed. The skin and flesh are its clothing; the bones and sinews are its armor, which is not, however, offensive, but defensive. The vital organs, the heart and lungs, are thus clothed and not to be seen, knit together and not to be hurt. The wonderful structure of human bodies is an outstanding example of the wisdom, power, and goodness of the Creator. What a pity it is that these bodies, which are capable of being temples of the Holy Spirit (1Co 6:19), should be instruments of unrighteousness (Ro 6:13)!

1.1.2. The soul is the life, the soul is the person, and this is the gift of God: "*Thou hast granted me life* (v. 12), breathed into me the breath of life (Ge 2:7), without which the body would be only a worthless carcass." God is the Father of spirits (Heb 12:9): he made us living souls and endowed us with the power of reason; he gave us *life and favour* (v. 12), and life is a favor. Now Job was in a better frame of mind than he was when he quarreled with life as a burden and asked, *Why died I not from the womb?* (3:11).

1.2. God sustains us. Having lit the lamp of life, he does not leave it to burn on its own, but continually supplies it with fresh oil: "Your coming to me has preserved my spirit, kept me alive, and protected me from the adversaries of life. You have blessed me with its daily supplies."

2. He pleads this with God (v. 9): *Remember, I beseech thee, that thou hast made me.*

2.1. "You have made me, and so you do not need to test me to see what I am made of, by punishing me.

2.2. "You have made me, like clay, by an act of your sovereign will, and will you undo that work by a similar act of sovereign will?

2.3. "Will you destroy the work of your own hands? Will you not spare and help me, will you not stand by the work of your own hands (Ps 138:8)?" Job did not know how to reconcile God's former favors and his present frowns, but nevertheless he concludes (v. 13), "You have hidden these things in your heart."

Verses 14–22

We have here:

1. Job's emotional complaints. He continues to strike this harsh and unpleasant note, in which, although he cannot be justified, he may be excused. If we think it reflects badly on him, let it be a warning to us to keep our tempers better.

1.1. He complains about the strictness of God's judgment and the harshness of his proceedings against him. He thinks of it is as *summum jus*, "justice bordering on severity." He complains:

1.1.1. That God has taken every opportunity against him: "*If I sin, then thou markest me*, you are watching me (v. 14)."

1.1.2. That God has pursued those advantages to the utmost: "*Thou wilt not acquit me from my iniquity*, you will not let my offense go unpunished (v. 14)." While his troubles continue, he cannot receive an assurance of forgiveness or hear that voice of joy and gladness (Jer 33:11). It is very hard to see love in God's heart when we see frowns on his face and his rod of discipline in his hand.

1.1.3. That as for himself, whatever his character is like, his case is very uncomfortable (v. 15).

1.1.3.1. If he is evil, he is most certainly ruined in the next world: *If I be wicked, woe to me* (v. 15).

1.1.3.2. If he is *righteous*, he still dare not *lift up his head*. He dare not answer as he did before (v. 15). He is so oppressed and overwhelmed by his troubles that he cannot look up with any comfort or confidence.

1.2. He complains about the severity of the punishment. He thought God was not only punishing him for every failure, but also punishing him intensely (vv. 16–17). God *hunted him* as a lion. God not only was a stranger to him but also *showed himself marvellous upon* (displayed his awesome power against) *him* (v. 16), by bringing extraordinary troubles on him and so making him a wonder to many. What made his afflictions even more severe was that he felt God's *indignation*, his anger, in them. And they continually grew worse. He insisted very much on this. When he hoped the tide of his pain would soon turn and begin to recede, it flowed still higher and higher.

1.3. He complains about his life, that he was ever born to all this trouble and misery (vv. 18–19): "If this was intended as my destiny, *why was I brought out of the womb* and not suffocated there or stifled at birth?" Mr. Joseph Caryl interprets this question in Job's favor. We may charitably suppose, according to Mr. Caryl, that what troubled Job was that he was in a condition of life which, so he thought, hindered the main purpose of his life, which was to glorify God. He feared that his troubles might reflect dishonor on God and cause his enemies to blaspheme, and so he wishes, *O that I had given up the ghost*, I wish I had died (v. 18). A godly man, Mr. Caryl observes, reckons that his life is without meaning if he does not live to the praise and glory of God. Yet if that was Job's meaning, it was based on a mistake, for we *may glorify the Lord in the fires* (Isa 24:15).

2. Job's humble requests. He prays that God would *see his affliction* (v. 15) and that he would grant him some relief.

CHAPTER 11

The wounds of poor Job were still bleeding, and his sores were still painful, but not one of his friends brought him any oil or balm to comfort him. Zophar, his third friend, pours as much vinegar onto his wounds as the other two friends who had addressed him. 1. He brings an arrogant accusation against Job, of being proud and false in justifying himself (vv. 1–4). 2. He appeals to God for Job's conviction (v. 5), and he begs that Job may be made aware of: 2.1. God's unfailing wisdom and his incontrovertible justice (v. 6). 2.2. His unsearchable attributes (vv. 7–9). 2.3. His absolute sovereignty and uncontrollable power (v. 10). 2.4. His knowledge of the human race (vv. 11–12). 3. He assures Job that if he repents and reforms his ways (vv. 13–14), God will restore him to his former prosperity and security (vv. 15–19), but that if he is evil, then to expect God to do that for him is futile (v. 20).

Verses 1–6

It is sad to see what excessive emotions even wise and good people sometimes fall into in the heat of an argument, and Zophar is an example of this. Eliphaz began with a very modest introduction (4:2). Bildad was a little rougher with Job (8:2). But Zophar falls on him without mercy. *Should a man full of talk be justified*, is this talker to be vindicated? *And should thy lies make men hold their peace*, shall your idle talk reduce men to silence (vv. 2–3)? Is this the way to comfort Job? Is this appropriate language for one who appears as an advocate for God and his justice?

1. He describes Job in different terms from what he really is (vv. 2–3). He would have Job thought of as one who loves to hear himself talk, so that it might be looked on as an act of justice to correct him. We have read and considered Job's speeches in the previous chapters and have found them to be full of good sense, and we have found that his motives are right and his reasoning strong, and that what there is in them of anger and excessive emotion a little love will excuse and overlook, but here Zophar invidiously portrays him:

1.1. As someone who never considers what he says: *Should not the multitude of words be answered*, are all these words to go unanswered? (v. 2). Sometimes it is not important whether they are answered or not. *Should a man full of talk*—margin, "a man of lips," one who is all words and only a voice—*be justified?* (v. 2). Should he be justified in his talkativeness, as in effect he is if he is not rebuked for it? No; for *in the multitude of words there wanteth not sin*, when words are many, sin is not absent (Pr 10:19).

1.2. As someone who has no scruples about what he says. He made Job out to be a liar and one who hoped that by lying arrogantly he would silence his enemies: *should thy lies make men hold their peace*, will your idle talk reduce men to silence? He also made him out to be one who ridiculed other people. Job was not mad, but spoke words of truth and soberness, and yet he was misrepresented in this way.

2. He charges Job with saying what he has not said (v. 4): *Thou hast said, My doctrine is pure*, my beliefs are flawless. Job spoke more wisely about God than his friends did. If he had expressed himself unwarily, it did not therefore follow that his doctrine was not true. But Zophar accused him of saying, *I am clean in thy eyes*, I am pure in your sight (v. 4). Job had not said this. It is true that he had said, *Thou knowest that I am not wicked* (10:7), but he had also said, *I have sinned* (7:20). It is also true that he had maintained he was not a hypocrite as they had accused him of being, but to argue that he would therefore not acknowledge himself to be a sinner was an unfair insinuation.

3. He appeals to God and wants him to appear against Job. He will not be satisfied unless God immediately appears to silence and condemn him. We are commonly too ready to involve God in our quarrels, unduly confident, like Zophar here, that if only he would speak, he would speak for us: *O that God would speak*, for he would certainly *open his lips against thee* (v. 5); yet when God did speak, he opened his lips for Job and spoke against his three friends. Zophar despairs of convincing Job himself, and so he wants God to convince him of two things:

3.1. The unsearchable depths of God's wisdom. Zophar wants God himself to show Job as much of the secrets of divine wisdom as might convince him *that they are* at least *double to that which is* (v. 6). What we know of God is nothing compared with what we cannot know. What is hidden is more than double what appears (Eph 3:9). Some understand this as referring to the fact that God knows a great deal more evil about us than we know about ourselves.

3.2. The unobjectionable justice of his proceedings. *"God exacteth of thee less than thy iniquity deserves,* God has even forgotten some of your sin" (v. 6), or, as some read it, "he forgives part of your sin."

Verses 7–12

Zophar here speaks about God and his greatness and glory, about human beings and how senseless and foolish they are.

1. God is described as:

1.1. An incomprehensible Being. We who know so little of God's nature are not competent to judge divine Providence, and so when we criticize its actions, we are talking about things we do not understand. Zophar here shows that God's nature infinitely exceeds the capacities of our understanding: *"Canst thou find out God, find him out to perfection?* Can you fathom the mysteries of God? Can you probe the limits of the Almighty?" We may seek and find God (Ac 17:27), and we may believe in him, but we cannot understand him. We may know that he is, but we cannot know what he is. This is a good reason why we should always speak of God with humility and caution and never quarrel with him. This is also why we should be thankful to him for what he has revealed of himself and should long to be where we will see him as he is (1Co 13:9–10). We cannot fathom God's intentions or work out the reasons why he acts as he does. His judgments are profound (Ps 36:6). Paul attributes to divine love the immeasurable dimensions that Zophar here attributes to divine wisdom, and he commends that love to us so that we will know it fully: *That you may know the breadth, and length, and depth, and height, of the love of Christ* (Eph 3:18–19).

1.2. A sovereign Lord (v. 10): *If he cut off* by death— margin, "If he make a change," for death is a change; if he makes changes in nations, in families, in our own lives—or *if he gather to himself man's spirit, then who can hinder* (oppose) *him?* (v. 10). God is also a strict and just observer of individual people (v. 11): *He knows vain* (deceitful) *men.* He takes note of human deceitfulness—or as some understand it, "their little sins," their worthless thoughts and words and their inconsistency in doing what is good. He observes people who are evil: *He sees* gross *wickedness also* (v. 11). *Will he not then consider it?* (v. 11).

2. Notice here how human beings are described, and let them be humbled (v. 12). God sees that the one who is without sense wants to be wise, and wants to be thought so, *though he is born like a wild ass's colt,* so foolish, unteachable and untamable. Human beings are without sense; "empty" is the meaning of the word. God made

human beings full, but they have emptied themselves, and now they are hollow; they have nothing in them. They are *like the beasts that perish* (Ps 49:20; 73:22), idiots, born like stupid donkeys, like wild donkey's colts that have not yet been brought into service. If people ever come to be good for anything, it is only because of the grace of Christ, who once, on the day of his triumphant entry into Jerusalem, used a donkey's colt. They are willful and uncontrollable. A donkey's colt may be put to good use, but the wild donkey's colt will never be reclaimed, and it does not hear a driver's shout. See 39:5–7. But they are also proud and conceited. Now are such creatures fit to argue with God or call him to account?

Verses 13–20

Like his two other friends, Zophar here encourages Job to hope for better times if he would only come into a better frame of mind.

1. He gives Job good advice (vv. 13–14), as did Eliphaz (5:8) and Bildad (8:5). Job must look within; his mind must be changed and the tree made good. He must *prepare his heart* (v. 13). The work of conversion and reformation must begin there. He must also look up and *stretch out his hands towards God* (v. 13), that is, he must pray to him fervently and boldly. To *give the hand to the Lord* means to submit ourselves to him and covenant with him (2Ch 30:8). Job had prayed, but Zophar wanted him to pray in a better way, not as if he were presenting a challenge, but as one who came to make a humble request. He must put right what was wrong (v. 14): *"If iniquity be in thy hand*—if there is any sin which you are still making a practice of—*put it far away."* The guilt of sin is not removed unless the gains of sin are restored. He must do all he can to reform his family too: *"Let not wickedness dwell in thy tabernacles,* allow no evil to stay in your tent (v. 14). Let your house not shelter any evildoers, any evil practices, or any wealth gained by evil."

2. He assures him that he will receive comfort if he takes this advice (vv. 15–20). *"Then shalt thou lift up thy face towards heaven* (v. 15) without shame. You may come to the throne of grace boldly (Heb 4:16), and not with that terror and dismay that you had expressed before" (9:34). *Thou shalt be steadfast, and shalt not fear* (v. 15). Job is full of shame and confusion (10:15) as long as he looks on God as his enemy and quarrels with him, but Zophar assures him that if he will submit and humble himself, his mind will be composed: *"Thou shalt forget thy misery.* You will be completely freed from the influences your misery has on you, and *thou shalt remember it as waters that pass away* or are poured out of a container, which leave no taste or stain behind them as other liquids do." Job has tried to forget his complaint (9:27) and has found he cannot. But if he will sincerely turn to God, Zophar says, then though his light is now overshadowed, it will shine again, and this time more brightly than ever (v. 17). Although now he is in a continual fear and terror, he will live in a holy peace and security and find himself continually at rest and at peace (v. 18): *Thou shalt be secure, because there is hope. Thou shalt dig about thee* (v. 18), that is, "You will be as safe as an army in its entrenchment." Those who submit to God's rule are safe both day and night: *"Thou shalt dig in safety* (v. 18), you and your servants for you. You will not again be attacked by plunderers, who set on your servants in the fields" (vv. 14–15). It is not a part of promised prosperity that he will live an idle life; he must have a calling and follow it, and when he is doing his work, he will be under divine protection. *"Thou shalt lie down* (v. 19). You will not be

forced to wander where there is no place to rest your head; you will go to bed at bedtime, and not only will no one hurt you, but also no one will make you afraid or even give you any reason to fear." Although he is now treated with disdain, his favor will be courted: "*Many shall make suit to thee*, many will court your favor (v. 19), and think it is in their interests to gain your friendship."

3. Zophar concludes with a brief account of the condemnation of evildoers (v. 20): *But the eyes of the wicked shall fail*. He suspects that Job will not accept his advice, and he tells him what would then come of it, putting death as well as life before him (Dt 30:15, 19). *When a wicked man dies, his expectation perishes* (Pr 11:7). *Their hope shall be as a puff of breath* (v. 20, margin), vanished and past recall. Those who will not flee to God will realize it is futile to think of fleeing from him.

CHAPTER 12

In this and the two following chapters we have Job's reply to Zophar's speech, in which, as before, he first reasons with his friends (see 13:19) and then turns to his God. In this chapter he addresses his friends, and: 1. He condemns the judgment they have given of his character (vv. 1–5). 2. He contradicts what they have said about the destruction of evildoers in this world, showing that they often prosper (vv. 6–11). 3. He agrees with what they have said about the wisdom, power, and sovereignty of God and speaks about it at length (vv. 12–25).

Verses 1–5

The rebukes Job here gives his friends may serve to rebuke all who are proud and scornful.

1. He criticizes them for their conceit and the high opinion they seem to have of their own wisdom.

1.1. He says that they claimed a monopoly of wisdom (v. 2). He speaks ironically: *"No doubt you are the people*; you think yourselves fit to dictate and give laws to the whole human race. You therefore think everyone must bow down to you, and rightly or wrongly, we must all speak just as you do. So you think you three must be the voice of the people, the majority, and have the deciding vote. You think not only that there is no one, but also that there will be no one, as wise as you, and that therefore *wisdom shall die with you* (v. 2), that all the world will be foolish when you have gone and that everyone will be in the dark when your sun has set." It is foolish for us to think there will be any great lasting loss when we are gone, since God can raise up others who are more qualified than we to do his work.

1.2. He does himself the justice of submitting his claim as one who shares in the gifts of wisdom (v. 3): *But I have understanding* (margin, "a heart") *as well as you*; in fact, "I fall not lower than you" (v. 3, margin). "I am as well able to judge the methods and meanings of divine Providence, and to read its difficult chapters, as you." He does not say this to exalt himself. *"Yea, who knows not such things as these?* (v. 3). The things you have said are true are plain and clear to everyone, themes which many people can talk about as excellently as you or I." He says this, rather, to humble them, and to restrain the high opinion they have of themselves as being like university professors.

2. He complains of the great contempt with which they have treated him (v. 4): *I am as one mocked*. We tend to consider rebukes as expressions of scorn and to think ourselves mocked when we are only advised and warned. However, there was some reason for this accusation; they came to comfort him, but they troubled him, and so he thought they were mocking him. It made his suffering worse that they were his *neighbours*, his friends, his companions, people who professed religion, who *called upon God* and said that he *answered them* (v. 4). Yet Job, too, could turn to God and appeal to him. Here we see the common fate of those who fall into adversity: the mockers were themselves rich and at ease, and so they despised him who had fallen into poverty.

Verses 6–11

All Job's friends followed the principle that evildoers cannot prosper for long in this world: *the eyes of the wicked shall fail* (11:20). Job here opposes this principle, and maintains that when God directs outward human affairs, he acts according to his sovereignty, reserving the exact distribution of rewards and punishments for the future state.

1. He asserts as an undoubted truth that evildoers may, and often do, prosper long in this world (v. 6). He describes them: they are *robbers*, and as such provoke God. They are the worst kind of sinners, blasphemers and persecutors. Perhaps he is referring to the Sabeans and Chaldeans, who robbed him and had always lived from pillage and plunder. Such sinners prosper in spite of their sins. Even *their tabernacles* (tents) *prosper* (v. 6), those who live with them and those who come after them and descend from them. It seems as if a blessing were passed on as an inheritance to their families, and what has been gained by fraud is sometimes passed on to succeeding generations. This shows us we cannot judge people's godliness by their plenty, nor can we discern what is in people's hearts from what they have in their hands.

2. He appeals even to the lower creatures for proof of this—the animals and birds, the trees, even the earth itself. Look at these, and they will tell you (vv. 7–8). Even among the wild animals the greater devour the less and the stronger prey on the weaker, and people are like fish in the sea (Hab 1:14). If sin had not come into the world, we may suppose there would have been no such disorder among the creatures, but that the wolf and the lamb would have lain down together (Isa 11:6). Zophar had made God's sovereignty an utterly incomprehensible mystery (11:7). "Far from that," Job says, "we may learn what we need to know even from the lower creatures, for *who knows not from all these?* (v. 9). Anyone may easily gather by looking at creation that *the hand of the Lord has wrought* (done) *this*." A wise Providence guides and governs all these things by rules. We should learn from God's sovereign rule over the lower creatures and come to accept all the ways he arranges human life.

3. He sees everything as being determined by the absolute ownership that God has over all creatures (v. 10): *In whose hand is the soul of every living thing*. All the creatures, especially human beings, derive their being from him. *All* souls are his; and may he not do what he wants with his own? The name *Jehovah* is used here (v. 9), and it is the only time we meet with it in all the speeches between Job and his friends, for God was then more usually known by the name of *Shaddai*, "the Almighty."

4. The words of v. 11, *Doth not the ear try words, as the mouth tastes meat?* may be taken either as the conclusion of the previous speech or as the introduction to what follows. The human mind has as good a faculty of discerning between truth and error, when duly stated, as the palate has of discerning between sweet and bitter foods. Job seems to appeal to anyone's impartial judgment in this argument.

Verses 12–25

This is a noble speech of Job's about the wisdom, power, and sovereignty of God. It would be good if wise and good people who differ on minor things would think most about those great things on which they are agreed. On this subject Job speaks as one true to himself. Here are no emotional complaints, no ill-tempered reflections, but only what is bold and great.

1. He asserts the unsearchable wisdom and irresistible power of God. He concedes that among people there is *wisdom and understanding* (v. 12), but notes that it is to be found only with *the ancient*, who gain it by long and constant experience. When they have gained wisdom, however, they have lost their strength. But *with God there are* both *wisdom and strength* (v. 13), wisdom to intend the best and strength to accomplish what is intended. He does not gain counsel or understanding, as we do, by observation, but has it essentially and eternally in himself (v. 13). Happy are those who have this God as their God, for they have infinite Wisdom and strength on their side. All human attempts to challenge him are foolish and fruitless (v. 14): *He breaketh down, and it cannot be built again.*

2. He gives an example from nature to prove this teaching (v. 15). God has the command of *the waters, binds them as in a garment* (Pr 30:4), holds them *in the hollow of his hand* (Isa 40:12).

2.1. Great droughts are sometimes great judgments: *He withholds the waters, and they dry up* (v. 15). If the skies are like bronze, the earth is like iron (Dt 28:23).

2.2. Great flooding is sometimes a great judgment. He raises the waters and *overturns the earth* (v. 15), the products from it and the buildings on it.

3. He gives many examples of this teaching in God's powerful direction of human beings.

3.1. In general (v. 16): "With him are strength and reason" is how some translate it; strength and consistency are within him. It is a pleasing word in the original. With him are the very essence and extract of wisdom. "With him are power and all that is" is how some understand it. He is complete within himself, and by him and in him all things exist. Having this strength and wisdom, he knows how to make use not only of those who are wise and good, but also even of those who are foolish and evil, who one would think could not in any way be useful to the purposes of his providence. *The deceived and the deceiver are his* (v. 16); the simplest and lowliest people who are deceived are not beneath his notice; even the subtlety of the subtlest deceivers cannot escape his notice.

3.2. He next gives individual examples of the wisdom and power of God in the changes of states and kingdoms. Some think that Job is here referring to the destruction of those powerful nations, the Rephaites, the Zuzites, the Emites, and the Horites, mentioned in Ge 14:5–6; Dt 2:10, 20, in which perhaps it was particularly noticed how strangely they were confounded and enfeebled. If so, the reference is intended to show that whenever something like that is done in the affairs of nations, it is God who does it, and we must notice in it his sovereign rule even over those who think they are the most powerful, wise, and absolute. Compare these statements with those of Eliphaz in 5:12–14.

3.2.1. Those who are wise are sometimes strangely confounded, and the hand of God must be acknowledged in this (v. 17): *He leadeth counsellors away spoiled.* His counsel stands, while all their purposes are confounded. *He maketh the judges fools* (v. 17). He works in such a way on their minds that he deprives them of

their qualifications for business, and so they become real fools. Let not wise people therefore boast in their wisdom (Jer 9:23), and let the most able counselors and judges not become proud of their positions, but let them humbly depend on God for their abilities to continue. Even older people, who may think they have a right to their wisdom because it has been theirs for such a long time, may still be deprived of it by the weaknesses of age, which brings them into their second childhood: he *taketh away the understanding of the aged* (v. 20).

3.2.2. Those who were high and in authority are strangely humbled, impoverished, and made slaves, and it is God who humbles them (v. 18): *He looseth the bond of kings*, takes from them the power with which they ruled their subjects; he unbuckles their belts, so that the sword drops from their side, and then it is not surprising that the crown quickly drops from their head, immediately after which follows the *girding of their loins with a girdle*, the tying of another kind of belt around their waist (v. 18), a badge of slavery.

3.2.3. Those who were strong are strangely weakened, and it is God who weakens them (v. 21), who *overthrows the mighty* (v. 19). Those who were famed for eloquence and entrusted with public business are strangely silenced and have nothing to say (v. 20): *He removeth away the speech of the trusty*, so that they cannot speak as they intended and as they used to, with freedom and clearness. Instead, they blunder and falter, and their words come to nothing. Those who were honored and marveled at will strangely fall into disgrace (v. 21): *He poureth contempt upon princes* (nobles). What was secret and lay hidden is strangely brought to light and exposed (Mk 4:22) (v. 22): *He discovers deep things out of darkness*. Plans secretly dreamed up are discovered and defeated; evil committed in secret and cunningly hidden is found out. Kingdoms ebb and flow, wax and wane, and both come from God (v. 23). *He taketh away the heart of the chief of the people*: their leaders most well known for their martial capabilities are disheartened and ready to flee at the shaking of a leaf (Ps 76:5). Those who were pressing home their plans at full speed are strangely bewildered and at a loss, wandering around as if they were in a desert (v. 24), groping in the dark and staggering as drunkards (v. 25; Isa 59:10). Heaven and earth are shaken, but the Lord sits enthroned as king forever (Ps 29:10), and with him we look for *a kingdom that cannot be shaken* (Heb 12:28).

CHAPTER 13

Job here comes to apply what he has said. 1. He is very bold with his friends, comparing himself with them despite the humbled state he is in (vv. 1–2), condemning them for their falsehood and partiality (vv. 4–8), threatening them with the judgments of God for these wrongs (vv. 9–12), asking them to be silent (vv. 5, 13, 17), and turning from them to God (v. 3). 2. He is very bold with his God. In some expressions his faith is very bold, but not more bold than is acceptable (vv. 15–16, 18). In other expressions his emotions get the better of him as he protests to God about his deplorable condition (vv. 14–19), complaining about his confusion (vv. 20–22) and his perplexity over not knowing what sin of his has caused God to afflict him (vv. 23–28).

Verses 1–12

Job heatedly expresses his anger at the unkindness of his friends:

1. He appears to be even with them in understanding, not needing to be taught by them (vv. 1–2). They compelled him, as the Corinthians did Paul, to commend himself and his own knowledge, yet not by way of self-applause, but of self-justification. Those are fortunate who not only see and hear, but also understand the greatness, glory, and sovereignty of God. He thinks this will justify what he said before (12:3), which he repeats here (v. 2): "*What you know, the same do I know also*, so that I do not need to come to you to be taught; *I am not inferior unto you* in wisdom."

2. He turns from them to God (v. 3): *Surely I would speak to the Almighty*. Job would rather argue with God himself than with his friends.

3. He condemns them for their unjust and unkind treatment of him (v. 4). They falsely accused him, and that was unjust: *You are forgers* (inventors) *of lies*. They held wrong thoughts about divine Providence as if it noticeably afflicted only evildoers in this world, and so they drew a false judgment from that about Job, that he was therefore definitely ungodly. They said they were going to heal him and try to be his doctors, but they were all *physicians of no value* (v. 4), worthless physicians, who could do no more good than an idol can.

4. He begs that they would be silent and listen to him patiently (vv. 5–6). "*Hold your peace, and it shall be your wisdom*, for you will hide your ignorance and evil nature. *Hear now my reasoning*" (v. 6). Perhaps although they did not interrupt him in his speech, they still seemed uninterested and did not pay much attention to what he said. He therefore begged that they would not only hear but also listen.

5. He tries to convince them of the wrong they are doing to God's honor as long as they pretend to plead for him (vv. 7–8). God and his cause do not need such advocates: "*Will you* think to *contend for God* (v. 8), as if his justice were clouded over and needed to be cleared up, or as if he were at a loss what to say and needed you to speak for him?" If we were forever silent, the heavens would declare his righteousness. Under the pretense of justifying God in afflicting Job, they condemned Job imperiously as a hypocrite and an evildoer. "This," he says, "is *speaking wickedly*" (v. 7), for a lack of love and a spirit of criticism are great evils. God's truth does not need us to lie for him, nor does God's cause need our sinful ways or passions.

6. He tries to instill in them a fear of God's judgment, and so improve their attitude. Let them consider whether they can give him a good account of what they have done (v. 9): *Is it good that he should search you out?* For those who have integrity, who live honorably, it is good that God should search their lives. But for those who look one way but go another, it is bad, because he will put them to shame. Let them consider the severity of his rebukes and displeasure against them (v. 10): "*If you do accept persons*, if you secretly show partiality, even if in secret and in your heart, *he will surely reprove you*. You who have a great knowledge of God and profess fear of him, how dare you talk like this, and so freely?" There is a fearful splendor in God. His splendor in itself is precious, but considering how different human beings are from God by nature, and how we have fallen away and been degraded by sin, God's splendor is awesome. Let them consider themselves, and what an unequal match they are for this great God (v. 12): "*Your remembrances* — all that is in you for which you hope to be remembered when you are gone — *are like unto ashes*, worthless and weak and easily trampled on and blown away. *Your bodies are like bodies of clay*. Your

representations for God are no better than dust, and the arguments you amass are only like heaps of dirt."

Verses 13–22

Job here takes a fresh and firm hold of his integrity, as one who is determined not to let it go or allow it to be taken from him.

1. He begs his friends and all those with him to leave him alone, not to interrupt him in what he is about to say (v. 13) but to diligently listen to it (v. 17). He wants his own declaration to be decisive, for no one except God and himself knows his heart. "Be silent therefore, and let me hear no more from you, but listen closely to what I am saying, and let what I swear on oath lead to a confirmation and an end to the conflict."

2. He decides to be faithful to the testimony his own conscience gives of his integrity: "I will speak in my own defense, and *let come on me what will*, come what may (v. 13). I hope God will not think, as you do, that I commit an offense by defending my cause. He will vindicate me (v. 18). I know that I'll be proved right and that nothing adverse will happen to me." He decides (v. 15) he *will maintain his own ways*. "*If I hold my tongue* and do not speak for myself, my silence now will silence me forever, for *I shall* certainly *give up the ghost*, I will die" (v. 19).

3. He complains of the extreme pain and misery he is in (v. 14): *Wherefore do I take my flesh in my teeth?* That is "Why am I suffering such agony? I can only wonder that God should place so much upon me when he knows I am not evil." Even the most patient person would be troubled if, having lost everything but their good conscience and a well-deserved good name, they were denied the comfort of those too.

4. He still depends on God for justification and salvation, the two great things we hope for in Christ (v. 18): *I have ordered my cause, and*, in the whole matter, *I know that I shall be justified*. Those whose hearts are upright with God, who do not walk according to the flesh but according to the Spirit (Gal 5:16, 25), may be sure that in Christ there will be no condemnation for them (Ro 8:1–4), but that, no matter who accuses them of anything, they will be justified. *He also shall be my salvation* (v. 16). He is not referring here to temporal salvation — he hardly expected that — but he is very confident concerning his eternal salvation. He knew he was not a hypocrite, and so he concluded he would not be rejected. Sincerity is an important aspect of life under the Gospel; nothing will ruin us except the lack of that. *Though he slay me, yet will I trust in him* (v. 15). This is a very high expression of faith. We must still rejoice in God even when we have nothing else to rejoice in. We are to remain faithful to him at all costs, even when we cannot at present find encouragement in him.

5. He wishes to argue the case even with God himself, if only he might gain permission to settle the preliminaries of the negotiation (vv. 20–22). "*Withdraw thy hand far from me* (v. 21), for while I am in this extreme agony, I am fit for nothing. *Let not thy dread make me afraid*, stop frightening me with your terrors" (v. 21). "Lord," Job says, "let me not be put into such a frightened dread in my spirit, together with this physical suffering, for then I must certainly give up and will make nothing of it." However can good people, and much less bad people, reason with God so as to be justified before him, when they are in intense pain?

Verses 23–28

Here:

1. Job asks about his sins and begs that they will be revealed to him. *Make me to know my transgressions*

(v. 23). His friends are ready to tell him how numerous and how offensive they are (22:5). "But Lord," he says, "let me know them from you, *for thy judgment is according to truth* (Ro 2:2), but theirs is not." *That which I see not, teach thou me* (34:32). Those who truly repent are willing to know the worst about themselves. We should all want to know what our offenses are, so that we may be specific in confessing them and on our guard against them in the future.

2. He bitterly complains that God has withdrawn from him (v. 24): *Wherefore hidest thou thy face?* This must be meant to refer to something more than his outward suffering; *his soul was also sorely vexed* (was in anguish) (Ps 6:3). God had hidden his face as one who was a stranger to him, who was displeased with him. The Holy Spirit sometimes denies his favors to the best and dearest saints and servants in this world. Signs of heaven are blotted out, a sense of assurance is broken, and the return of delighting in God is despaired of for the present (Ps 77:7–9; 88:7, 15–16). These are severe burdens for a gracious soul that values God's loving-kindness as better than life (Ps 63:3). *A wounded spirit who can bear?* (Pr 18:14). By asking, *Why hidest thou thy face?* (v. 24) Job teaches us that when at any time we have a sense of the withdrawal of God's presence, we should ask why that has happened—what is the sin for which he is correcting us, and what is the good he is intending to grant us? Job's sufferings were a type of the sufferings of Christ, from whom not only human beings hid their faces (Isa 53:3), but also God hid his, as can be seen from the darkness which surrounded him on the cross when he cried out, *My God, my God, why hast thou forsaken me?* (Mt 27:46).

3. He humbly pleads with God his own complete inability to stand before him (v. 25): "*Wilt thou break a leaf, pursue the dry stubble,* will you torment a wind-blown leaf ? Will you chase after dry chaff? We should have such an understanding of the goodness and compassion of God as to believe that he will not *break the bruised reed* (Mt 12:20).

4. He sadly complains about how harshly God has dealt with him. He acknowledges that it was because of his sins that God had contended with him, but he still thinks it hard (v. 26): *Thou writest bitter things against me.* Afflictions are bitter. "In these *thou makest me to possess* (inherit) *the iniquities of my youth*" (v. 26), that is, "you are punishing me for them and thereby reminding me of them and obliging me to renew my repentance for them." Time does not wear out the guilt of sin. God writes down bitter things against us, to bring forgotten sins to mind and make us have godly sorrow for them so that we break away from them. "*Thou puttest my feet also in the stocks* (shackles) to correct every false step I take. *Thou settest a print upon the heels of my feet.* No sooner have I taken a wrong step, even a very small one, than I immediately suffer for it. The punishment follows on the heels of the sin. Now:

• It was not true that God was seeking to take advantage of him. He is so far from doing this that he does not deal with us according to what we deserve (Ps 103:10) even for our open sins. This therefore was Job's sadness speaking; in his sober thoughts, he never presented God as a hard Master in this way.

• But we should keep such a strict and watchful eye as this on ourselves and our own steps, both to reveal past sins and to prevent them in the future.

5. He finds himself quickly wasting away under the heavy hand of God (v. 28). *He*—that is, human

beings—*as a rotten thing*, the principle of whose corruption is in itself, *consumes* (wastes away) *even like a moth-eaten garment*, which continually becomes worse and worse. Where there is little health in the soul, it is not surprising there is little health in the flesh (Ps 38:3).

CHAPTER 14

Job goes on to speak to God and himself. He has reminded his friends of their frailty and mortality (13:12); here he reminds himself of his own and pleads these conditions with God as grounds for alleviating his misery. Here we have an account: 1. Of human life, that it is short (vv. 1–3), sorrowful (v. 1), sinful (v. 4), and set (vv. 5, 14). 2. Of human death, that it brings an end to our present life, to which we will not return (vv. 7–12), and that it hides us from the calamities of life (v. 13), destroys the hopes of life (vv. 18–19), sends us away from the business of life (v. 20), and keeps us in the dark concerning our relatives in this life, however much we have formerly cared about them (vv. 21–22). 3. Of the use Job makes of all this. He pleads it with God—who, he thinks, has been too strict and harsh with him (vv. 16–17)—begging that, out of consideration for his weakness, God would not contend with him (v. 3), but grant him some respite (v. 6). He undertakes to prepare for death (v. 14) and encourages himself to hope that it will be comfortable to him (v. 15). This chapter is suitable for funeral ceremonies.

Verses 1–6

We are here led to think:

1. About the origins of human life. The origin of life lies in God, for he *breathed into man the breath of life* (Ge 2:7), and we live in him, but we date our own origin from our birth, and it is from then that we date both its frailty and its corruption.

1.1. Its frailty: *Man, that is born of a woman*, is therefore *of few days* (v. 1). This may refer to the first woman, who was called *Eve*, or it may refer to everyone's immediate mother.

1.2. Its corruption (v. 4): *Who can bring a clean thing out of an unclean?* We are not only condemned by a legal conviction but also corrupted by a hereditary disease. Our Lord Jesus, being made sin for us, is said to be *made of a woman* (Gal 4:4).

2. About the nature of human life: it is *a flower*, it is *a shadow* (v. 2). The flower is fading, and all its beauty soon withers and is gone (Isa 4:7–8). The shadow is fleeting, and its very being will soon be lost and drowned in the shadows of the night.

3. About the shortness and uncertainty of human life: *Man is of few days* (v. 1). Life is here calculated not according to months or years but days, for we cannot be sure of any day. Human beings are sometimes no sooner born than they are *cut down* (v. 2). As soon as they come into the world and enter its business, they are rushed away just when they have put their hand to the plow. If not cut down immediately, still, *he flees as a shadow* (v. 2); his condition and shape never continue for long.

4. About the calamitous state of human life. Human beings live only for a short time, and the days we live are sad ones. During these few days, our lives are full of trouble, not only troubled but *full of trouble* (v. 1), either working or worrying, being sad or scared. When we reach heaven, our days will be many and perfectly free from all trouble, and in the meantime faith, hope, and love balance out our present suffering (1Co 13:13).

5. About the sinfulness of human life, arising from the sinfulness of human nature. This is how some understand that question (v. 4), *Who can bring a clean thing out of an unclean?* He intends it as a plea with God for compassion: "Lord, do not be so harsh as to keep a record of my sins of human frailty and infirmity, for you know my weakness. *O remember that I am flesh!*" The Aramaic paraphrase has a significant reading of this verse: "Who can make a man clean that is defiled by sin? Cannot One, that is, God?"

6. About the determined end of human life (v. 5). Nothing takes place by chance, not even the operation of a bow drawn at random (1Ki 22:34). We are no more governed by the Stoic's blind fate than by the Epicurean's blind fortune. The consideration of our own inability to contend with God, of our own sinfulness and weakness, should lead us to pray, *Lord, enter not into judgment with thy servant* (Ps 143:2). This is how we may find some relief in our extreme troubles: by commending ourselves to the compassion of the God who knows how we are formed (Ps 103:14) and will take that into account even when we are in poor form.

Verses 7–15

Job here shows:

1. That death is a departure from this world forever. A person who has been destroyed by death will not be revived, as a tree that is cut down will be. He excellently describes the hope for such a tree (vv. 7–9). If the trunk of the tree is cut down and only the stump is left in the ground, even though it seems dead and dry, it will still send out new shoots again, as if it had only just been planted. But human beings have no such prospect of a return to life. Vegetable life is cheap and easy: the scent of water will reclaim it. Animal life, in some insects and birds, is so also: the heat of the sun revives it. But when the rational soul is once withdrawn, it is too great and too noble to be recalled by any of the powers of nature. It is beyond the reach of the sun or rain and cannot be restored except by the direct workings of almighty God himself, for (v. 10) *man dieth and wasteth away, yea, man giveth up the ghost, and where is he?* Two words are used here for *man: Geber,* "a mighty man," who, although mighty, still dies, and *Adam,* "a man of the earth," who, because earthy, gives up his spirit. After death, *Where is he?* (v. 10). Human beings are not where they were; their place does not know them anymore (Ps 103:16); but "is he nowhere?" This is how some understand it. Human beings are somewhere, and it is a terrible consideration to think where those who have breathed their last are, and where we will be when we breathe our last. Our soul has gone to the world of spirits, into eternity, never to return to this world.

2. That human beings will return to life again in another world, at the end of time, when *the heavens* are *no more.* Then *they shall awake and be raised out of their sleep* (v. 12). The resurrection of the dead was no doubt part of what Job believed, as is evident from 19:26. On the basis of that belief, we have three things:

2.1. A humble petition for a hiding place in the grave (v. 13). It was not only out of a passionate weariness of this life that he wanted to die, but also out of a godly assurance of a better life, to which he would ultimately rise.

2.2. A holy determination to wait patiently for the will of God both in his death and in his resurrection (v. 14): *If a man die, shall he live again? All the days of my appointed time will I wait until my change come.* Because Job's friends proved to be such miserable comforters (16:2), he set himself to be his own comforter. His case

was now bad, but he pleased himself with the expectation that it would change.

2.3. A joyful expectation of bliss and satisfaction (v. 15): then *thou shalt call, and I will answer thee.* He was now under such a cloud that he could not, and dared not, answer (9:15, 35; 13:22), but he comforted himself with the thought that a time would come when God would call and he would answer. "*Thou wilt have a desire to the work of thy hands* (v. 15), you will long for the creature your hands have made. You have mercy in store for me, not only as one who has been made by your providence, but also as one renewed by your grace"; otherwise *he that made them will not save* them (Isa 27:11). Grace in the soul is the work of God's own hands, and so he will not abandon it in this world (Ps 138:8), but will have a longing for it, to perfect it in the other and crown it with endless glory.

Verses 16–22

Job returns to his complaints, and although he is not without hope of future bliss, he finds it very hard to get over his present grievances.

1. He complains of the particular hardships he thinks he is suffering because of the strictness of God's justice (vv. 16–17). As a child who is severely disciplined longs to grow up, he longed to go from here to that world where God's wrath will be a thing of the past, because he was now under continual signs of God's anger. "When will that change come for me? *For now thou* seem to me to *number my steps,* and *watch over my sin,* and *seal it up in a bag,* as legal accusations are kept in a secure place, to be produced against the prisoner." See Dt 32:34.

1.1. He gives due respect to divine justice by acknowledging that he is suffering for his sins and offenses, that he has done enough to deserve all that has been placed on him. But:

1.2. He wrongs divine goodness in suggesting that God is harsh enough to keep a record of what he has done wrong (Ps 130:3) and put the worst interpretation on everything. He spoke to this effect also in 13:27. But we are punished less than our sins deserve. God does indeed *seal up* and *sew* for the day of wrath the disobedience of those who do not repent, but he blots out the sins of his people like a cloud (Isa 44:22).

2. He complains about the lowly condition of the human race in general. We live in a dying world.

2.1. We see the decays of the earth itself:

2.1.1. Of its strongest parts (v. 18). Nothing will last forever, for we see even mountains decay and come to nothing. They wither and fall like leaves; rocks become old and pass away by the continual beating of the sea against them. *The waters wear* away *the stones* (v. 19) with their constant lapping, not by force but by the constancy with which they come. Everything on earth is the worse for wear. Time wears away everything.

2.1.2. Of its natural products. The things which grow out of the earth and seem to be firmly rooted in it are sometimes washed away by too much rain (v. 19).

2.2. It is no wonder then if we see human beings decay on earth, for we are of the earth. Job begins to think that his case is not special and that he should therefore come to terms with the common lot of humanity. How futile it is to expect much from the enjoyments of life: "*Thou destroyest the hope of man* (v.19)," that is, "you put an end to all the plans he has made and all the prospects of satisfaction he has flattered himself with." Death will destroy all those hopes built on worldly confidence and limited to mere worldly comforts. But death will bring to full perfection, not destroy, hope in Christ and hope in heaven. Considering this should moderate our cares concerning our children and families. God will know what comes of them when we are gone. Let us therefore commit them to him. Let us leave them with him and not burden ourselves with unnecessary and unproductive worries about them. It is true wisdom to make our peace with God in Christ and keep a good conscience, in order to treasure up comforts which will support and relieve us in readiness for the pains and sorrows of the time of our death.

CHAPTER 15

Perhaps Job thought that even if he had not convinced his three friends, he had at least silenced them, but it seems he had not. In this chapter they launch a second attack on him. Eliphaz here keeps close to the principles on which he has condemned Job, and: 1. He rebukes Job for vindicating himself and unfairly reasons from the supposed wrongness of Job's self-vindication that Job is also guilty of many other evil things (vv. 1–13); he tries to persuade him to humble himself before God and bear shame himself (vv. 14–16). 2. He gives him a long lecture about the miserable condition of evildoers, who harden their hearts against God and the judgments prepared for them (vv. 17–35). Good use may be made both of his rebukes, because they are clear, and of his teaching, for it is sound, although both are wrongly applied to Job.

Verses 1–16

Eliphaz here clashes with Job because Job contradicted what he and his colleagues had said. He accuses Job of several crimes, only because he would not acknowledge himself to be a hypocrite.

1. He accuses him of being foolish and absurd (vv. 2–3) and claims that although he has had the reputation of being wise, he has now completely lost that reputation. It is common for those who are angrily engaged in an argument to describe one another's reasons as extremely arrogant and ridiculous. There is a great deal of empty knowledge and so-called learning, which is useless and therefore worthless. This is the kind of knowledge that puffs up (2Co 8:1), which causes people to swell up with pride at their own achievements. Worthless knowledge or unprofitable talk ought to be rebuked and restrained, especially in wise people, because by their example they, of all people, do the most harm by it.

2. He accuses him of being ungodly and irreligious (v. 4): "*Thou castest off fear*," that is, "the fear of God, the reverence for God which you should have, and then *thou restrainest prayer*, you hinder devotion to God." Notice how religious faith is summed up, fearing God and praying to him, the former the most necessary principle, the latter the most necessary practice. Those who are prayerless are also fearless and graceless. Those who either omit prayer or restrict themselves in it, quenching the spirit of adoption (1Th 5:19; Ro 8:15) and denying themselves the liberty they might have in the duty, *restrain prayer*. This is bad enough, but it is even worse to restrain others from praying, to prohibit and discourage prayer, as Darius did (Da 6:7).

2.1. Perhaps Eliphaz accused Job of this because he thought that Job talked about God so freely—as if he were his equal—that he must have completely rejected every religious respect for him. This accusation was totally untrue, yet not totally unreasonable. We should not only take care that we continue to pray and fear God, but also be careful that we never make any imprudent comments which may give an opportunity to those who want to take advantage of us and question our sincerity and faithfulness in our religious faith.

2.2. Or perhaps he was concerned about what others would reason from the teaching Job held to: "If what Job says is true, that a man may suffer so much and still be a good man, then we may as well say good-by to all religious faith, prayer, and the fear of God." And so he says, *Thy mouth utters thy iniquity*—"teaches it" is the meaning. "You are teaching others to have the same harsh thoughts of God and religion that you yourself have." And *thou choosest* (you adopt) *the tongue of the crafty* (v. 5), that is, "You speak out your sin with a show and pretense of godliness, mixing some good words with the bad, as traders do when trying to sell their goods." In his first speech, Eliphaz had spoken against Job on mere supposition (4:6–7), but now he had obtained proof against him from his own words (v. 6): *Thy own mouth condemns thee, and not I*. Yet he should have considered that he and his fellows had provoked Job to say what they were now making use of, and that was not fair.

3. He accuses him of intolerable arrogance and pride. Job made a just, reasonable, and modest demand when he said (12:3), "Allow me that *I have understanding as well as you*," but notice how his friends try to take advantage of him. His words are misinterpreted, as if he pretended to be wiser than anyone else. Perhaps the friends are referring to how long he has known the world: "*Art thou the first man that was born* (v. 7)? *Wast thou made before the hills* (v. 7), as Wisdom herself was (Pr 8:23)? Do you know more about the world than any of us? No; you were only born yesterday like us" (8:9). Or perhaps they are referring to how long he has known God (v. 8): *Hast thou heard the secret of God?* Eliphaz also describes Job:

3.1. As claiming to have knowledge that no one else has: "*Dost thou restrain* (limit) *wisdom to thyself* (v. 8), as if no one were wise except you?" Job had said (13:2), *What you know, the same do I know also* (I also know).

3.2. As opposing the stream of the wisdom of old age, which all who argue with each other claim to have on their side: "*With us are the grayheaded and very aged men* (v. 10). We have the fathers on our side."

4. He accuses him of showing contempt for the counsel and comfort given him by his friends (v. 11): *Are the consolations of God small with thee?* Eliphaz is offended that Job does not value the comfort he and his friends have shown him more than it seems he does. He describes this as an insult shown to divine consolations in general, as if they were insignificant to him, whereas in reality they were not. If he had not valued them highly, he could not have endured as he had in his suffering.

5. He accuses him of opposition to God himself and to religion (vv. 12–13): "*Why doth thy heart carry thee away* into such indecent, irreligious expressions?" He thought Job's spirit was bitter toward God, and thus changed from what it had been and angry at God's dealings with him. Eliphaz lacked honesty and kindness, or else he would not have interpreted so harshly the speeches of one who had such a settled reputation for godliness and who was now being tempted.

6. He accuses him of justifying himself to such a degree as even to deny his share in the common corruption and defilement of human nature (v. 14): *What is man, that he should be clean*, that is, that he should pretend to be so, or that anyone should expect to find him so? What is *he that is born of a woman, a sinful woman, that he should be righteous?* Eliphaz thinks he can persuade Job by these

plain truths, whereas Job just now said the same (14:4): *Who can bring a clean thing out of an unclean?* But does it therefore follow that Job is a hypocrite and an evildoer, which is all that he denied? Not at all. Although a human being, as one born of a woman, is not pure, nevertheless, as one born again of the Spirit, they are pure (Jn 3:5, 7). To show this further Eliphaz here adds:

6.1. That the brightest creatures are imperfect and impure before God (v. 15). He takes no pleasure in the heavens in and of themselves. However pure they seem to us, they have many flaws and blemishes to his eye: *The heavens are not clean in his sight* (v. 15). If the stars have no light in the sight of the sun, what light has the sun in the sight of God? See Isa 24:23.

6.2. That human beings are much more so (v. 16): *How much more abominable and filthy is man!* If saints are not to be trusted, then much less are sinners. If the heavens are not pure, which are as God made them, then much less human beings, who have become degenerate. In fact, human beings are vile and corrupt in God's sight, and if they repent, they see themselves as such in their own sight, and so detest themselves for their sin.

Verses 17–35

Eliphaz here comes to maintain his own thesis, on which he based his criticism of Job. Since those who are evil are certainly miserable, those who are miserable are certainly evil, and therefore Job must be evil.

1. His solemn introduction (v. 17): "*I will show thee what is worth hearing and will not reason, as you do, unprofitably.*" He promises to teach him:

1.1. From his own experience and observation: "*That which I have* myself *seen, in different situations, I will declare.*"

1.2. From the wisdom of the elders (v. 18): *which wise men have told from their fathers.* Contemporary wisdom and learning come very much from those of former generations. Good children learn a good deal from their good parents, and what we have learned from our ancestors we must pass on to future generations.

2. The speech itself.

2.1. Those who are wise and good usually succeed in this world. This he only hints at (v. 19), saying that those with whose wisdom he agrees were such as had land given only to them. They fully and peacefully enjoyed it. Job said, *The earth is given into the hand of* evildoers (9:24). "No," Eliphaz says, "it is given into the hands of the saints, and they are not robbed or plundered by foreigners attacking them, as you have been by the Sabeans and Chaldeans."

2.2. Evildoers, particularly tyrannical rulers, are subject to continual terror and die miserably. This he talks more about, showing that even those who defy God's judgments will suffer under them in the end. He speaks in the singular — *the wicked man* — meaning perhaps Job himself. In 22:9–10 he expressly accuses Job both of the tyranny and of the faintheartedness described here; here, however, he thinks that the application of what he is saying is very easy, so that Job can see his own face in this description.

2.2.1. He describes the sinner who lives in such a miserable state (vv. 25–28). It is no ordinary sinner who defies God (v. 25). If you tell them about God's law and its obligations, they tear off those chains (Ps 2:3). If you tell him about divine wrath, he tells almighty God to do his worst, for he will not be controlled by law or conscience. *He stretches out his hand against God,* to show that if it were in his power, he would stop him from being God.

This sort of evildoer *strengthens himself* (vaunts himself) *against the Almighty.* It is wild madness on the part of arrogant sinners that they think they can fight against almighty God. *He runs upon him,* rushes at God himself, rushes headlong against him in desperation. When he finds himself an unequal match for him, he flies in his face, although at the same time he falls on the point of his sword or the sharp spike of his shield. He wraps himself up in his own security, worldliness, and sensuality (v. 27): *He covers his face with his fatness.* This shows both the indulgence of the flesh with daily delicious food and drink and also the hardening of the heart against the judgments of God. The fat that covers the arrogant sinner's face gives a look of boldness and pride, and what covers his waist allows them to lie easy, be comfortable, and feel little, but this will turn out to be slight protection from the arrows of God's wrath. He enriches himself with the plunder around him (v. 28). *They conceive mischief* (trouble), and then they put it into effect by *preparing deceit,* fashioning deceit in their womb, pretending to protect those whom they want to defeat and making alliances of peace so as to carry on their war more effectively.

2.2.2. The miserable condition of this *wicked man* (v. 20), as regards both spiritual and temporal judgments.

2.2.2.1. His inner peace is continually disturbed. His own conscience accuses him, and he suffers torment throughout life (v. 20). His sins stare him in the face everywhere he turns. He is troubled by not knowing how long his wealth and power will last: *The number of years is hidden to the oppressor* (v. 20). He is under a certain and fearful expectation of judgment. A terrible sound rings in his ears (v. 21). He knows that God is angry with him and that all the world hates him. He has done nothing to make his peace with either. *He knows that the day of darkness* (v. 23) (or rather the night of darkness) *is ready at his hand,* that it is appointed for him and cannot be set aside. What follows is therefore not surprising (v. 24): *Trouble and anguish* will make him afraid of worse to come. If at any time he is in trouble, he despairs of getting out of it (v. 22). He has such a dread of poverty and is so fearful of any loss of his possessions that in his own imagination he is already wandering around looking for bread.

2.2.2.2. His outward prosperity will soon come to an end. How can he prosper when God *runs upon him*? This is how some understand v. 26. God will certainly tread down those whom he triumphs over. Many who gain much by fraud and injustice still do not become rich: it goes out as it comes in; it is gained by one sin and spent on another sin. The evildoer is concerned to leave what he has gained and kept for his children after him. But the branches of his family will perish. *They shall not be green* (v. 32). *The flame shall dry them up* (v. 30). He will shake off his offspring like blossoms that never form or like the *unripe grape* (v. 33). Many families have been ruined by the sin of a parent. When he is in trouble, he is concerned about how to get out of it — not how to gain good from it — but he is also thwarted in this (v. 30): *He shall not depart out of darkness.* He is concerned to protect his partners, but that is in vain (vv. 34–35). *The congregation* of them, all his associates, they and all their tabernacles, *shall be desolate.*

2.2.3. Will the prosperity of arrogant sinners end so miserably? If so, then (v. 31) *let not him that is deceived trust in vanity* (what is worthless). Those who are trusting their sinful ways to gain wealth *trust in vanity* (what is worthless), and *vanity will be their recompence,* they will get nothing in return (v. 31). Those who trust their wealth when they have gained it—especially the wealth they have gained dishonestly—trust in what is worthless, for it will give them no satisfaction. They will acknowledge at length, with the greatest perplexity, that *a deceived* (deluded) *heart turned them aside*, and that they deceived themselves with *a lie in their right hand* (Isa 44:20).

CHAPTER 16

This chapter begins Job's reply to the speech of Eliphaz in the previous chapter. It is the second part of the same song of mourning which he had wept before, and it is set to the same sad tune. 1. He rebukes his friends for their unkind treatment of him (vv. 1–5). 2. He describes his own situation as deplorable (vv. 6–16). 3. He still holds to his integrity, and on the basis of it he appeals to God's righteous judgment for the correction of his friends' unrighteous criticisms (vv. 17–22).

Verses 1–5

Both Job and his friends undervalue one another's good sense, wisdom, and anxiety. The more long-drawn-out the dispute, the more intense it becomes. Eliphaz had described Job's speeches as worthless and unprofitable, and Job here describes Eliphaz' speeches in a similar way. Job here rebukes Eliphaz:

1. For unnecessary repetition (v. 2): *I have heard many such things.*

2. For incompetent application. "*Miserable comforters are you all* (v. 2). Instead of offering anything to relieve my suffering, you are adding further suffering to it and making it even more painful for me to bear." Patients are in a very bad way when their medicine turns out to be poison and their doctors are in fact their worst disease.

3. For endless arrogance. Job wishes that *vain* (empty) *words might have an end* (v. 3).

4. For ill-founded obstinacy. *What emboldeneth thee, that thou answerest* (v. 3)*?* It is an act of great and inexplicable presumption to accuse people of those crimes which we cannot prove they have committed, to pass judgment on the spiritual state of others simply by looking at their outward condition, and to keep on stating those objections which have been answered again and again, as Eliphaz did.

5. For breaking the sacred laws of friendship. This is a cutting rebuke (vv. 4–5). He wants his friends, in their imagination, to suppose that they are going through the misery he is going through and that he is at peace as they are. He describes the unkindness of their behavior toward him by showing what he could do to them if they were in his place: *I could speak as you do* (v. 4). He then shows them what they should do, by telling them what he would do in such a situation (v. 5): "*I would strengthen you.* I would say all I could to relieve your grief and would do nothing to make it worse." What is the duty we owe our brothers and sisters in their affliction? We should say and do all we can to strengthen them, to encourage their confidence in God, support their sinking spirits, and relieve their sorrow—the causes of their sorrow, if possible, or at least their anger at those causes. Good words cost nothing, but they may be useful to those who are sorrowful, not only because it is some comfort for them to see their friends concerned for them, but also so that they may be reminded of what they may have forgotten through overwhelming grief. Though hard words break no bones, kind words may still help broken bones to become glad (Ps 51:8).

Verses 6–16

Job complains here as bitterly as anywhere in all his speeches. Sometimes expressing grief brings relief, but "*Though I speak*," Job says, "*my grief is not assuaged* (v. 5), what I say is misinterpreted so that it makes my grief even worse." At other times, keeping silence makes the trouble easier and sooner forgotten, but Job says, "*Though I forbear, what am I eased?* If I refrain, it does not go away (v. 6)." If he complained, he was criticized for yielding to passion; if he did not complain, he was criticized for being uncommunicative. If he insisted on his integrity, that was his crime; if he did not respond to the accusations of his friends, his silence was taken as a confession of guilt.

1. His family was scattered (v. 7). It was true that he had company, but he really would have preferred to be without his so-called friends, for they seemed to gloat over his calamities.

2. His body was worn away with disease and pains (v. 8). His face was furrowed, not with age but with sickness: *Thou hast filled me with wrinkles.* These are called *witnesses against him*, but it may also be read, "They are witnesses *for* me, that my complaint is not without reason."

3. His enemy threatened him (v. 9): *He tears me in his wrath.* But who is this enemy? Who could it be?

3.1. Eliphaz, who showed himself to be very angry with him; what he said tore apart Job's good name and thundered out nothing but terror to him. Or:

3.2. Satan. He was his enemy who hated him and aimed to make him curse God. It is not improbable that this is the enemy he is referring to. Or:

3.3. God himself. If we understand it to refer to him, the expressions are as rash as any he used. God hates none of his creatures, but in Job's depression it seemed to him to be almighty God who was bringing terror on him.

4. Everyone around him was abusive toward him (v. 10). Job was a type of Christ in this, in the view of early commentators: these same expressions are used in the prophecies of his sufferings: *They gaped upon me with their mouths* (Ps 22:13), and, *They shall smite the Judge of Israel with a rod upon the cheek* (Mic 5:1), which was literally fulfilled in Mt 26:67.

5. God, instead of rescuing him from their hands, as he hoped, gave him into their hands (v. 11): *He hath turned me over into the hands of the wicked.* Job was also a type of Christ in that he was delivered into the hands of evil-doers. Through evildoers Jesus Christ was crucified and killed by the *determinate counsel and foreknowledge of God* (Ac 2:23).

6. God not only gave him over to evildoers, but also took him into his own hands (v. 12): "*I was at ease,* comfortably enjoying the gifts of God's goodness, but *he has broken me asunder,* has shattered me, made me suffer this agonizing pain, and torn me limb from limb. *He has set me up for his mark* (v. 12), the target at which he is pleased to shoot all his arrows." When God set him up as a target, *his archers* immediately *compassed him round*, surrounded him (v. 13). Whoever our enemies are, we must look on them as God's archers and see him directing the arrows. *It is the Lord; let him do what seemeth him good* (1Sa 3:18). As if he had no mercy in reserve for him, he neither spared or lessened the extreme pain. "*He breaketh me with breach upon breach,* he bursts on me with one wound after another." He thought that God was attacking him *like a giant* (warrior) (v. 14), whom he could not possibly stand against or confront. Even good people, when

they are in great and extraordinary troubles, find it very hard not to harbor harsh thoughts against God.

7. Job has deprived himself of all his honor and comfort. As one who truly and patiently repented, Job humbled himself under the mighty hand of God (vv. 15–16). In dressing himself, he placed no value on either his ease or his style, but sewed sackcloth over his skin. He thought such clothing good enough for such a defiled and diseased body as his. He did not insist on any points of honor, but debased himself under humbling providences: *He defiled his horn* (buried his brow) *in the dust* (v. 15) and refused the respect that had once been given to his status. *"My face is foul* (red) *with weeping* so constantly for my sins, for God's displeasure against me, and for my friends' unkindness. This has brought a *shadow of death upon my eyelids,* deep shadows ring my eyes."

Verses 17–22

Job's condition was very miserable, but:

1. He had the testimony of his conscience that he had walked uprightly and had never allowed himself to commit any gross sin. No one was ever more ready than he to acknowledge his sins of weakness, but he could not accuse himself of any grave crime, any for which he should be made more miserable than others (v. 17). Eliphaz had described him as a tyrant and oppressor. "No," he said, "my hands have been free of violence. I never did any wrong to anyone, but always despised getting things by oppression." Eliphaz had accused him of being hypocritical in his religious faith, but when he described prayer, that great act of religious faith, he professed that he was pure in it, although not free from all weakness. His prayer was not like the prayers of the Pharisees, who only wanted to be seen by others (Mt 6:5) and used their prayers to serve their own purposes. He supported the assertion of his own integrity with a sacred oath, calling for shame and confusion to come on him if it was not true (v. 18). If there was any violence on his hands, he wanted it to be revealed: *O earth! cover thou not my blood* (v. 18), that is, "the innocent blood of others, which I am suspected to have shed." If there was any impurity in my prayers, he wanted them not to be accepted: *Let my cry have no place.*

2. He could appeal to God's knowledge of everything about his integrity (v. 19). The positive witness within us will do us little good if we do not also have a witness in heaven for us, for *God is greater than our hearts* (1Jn 3:20), and we are not to be our own judges. This is therefore what Job can rejoice in: *My witness is in heaven* (v. 19). It brings unspeakable comfort to good people, when they are criticized by their brothers or sisters, that they remember there is a God in heaven who knows their integrity and will clear it sooner or later.

3. He had a God whom he could turn to and before whom he could disclose his true thoughts (vv. 20–21). "My so-called friends scorn me; they have not only set themselves to resist me, but also are using all their skill and eloquence to criticize me." Yet he did not doubt that God was now aware of his sorrow: *My eye pours out tears to God* (v. 20). Even tears, when consecrated to God, relieve troubled spirits, and if people pay no attention to our grief, let us still be comforted by knowing that God sees our tears. If only he could now have the same freedom to argue his case in God's court that people usually have in human courts, he did not doubt that he would win his case, for the Judge himself was a witness of his integrity. The language of this wish is like that in Isa 50:7–8: *I know that I shall not be ashamed, for he is near that justifies me.*

4. He had a hope of death which would put an end to all his troubles. He had such confidence toward God that he could take pleasure in thinking of the approach of death, when his everlasting state would be determined, as one who did not doubt that it would go well for him then: *When a few years have come,* those years which have been determined and appointed for me, *then I shall go the way whence I shall not return* (v. 22). To die is to *go the way whence we shall not return* (v. 22). It is to go on a journey from the physical world to the spiritual world. It is a journey to our permanent home. All of us must certainly go on this journey. Thinking about it gives strength and encouragement to those who keep a good conscience, for it is the crown of their integrity.

CHAPTER 17

In this chapter: 1. Job reflects on the harsh criticisms his friends have expressed to him, and looking on himself as dying (v. 1), he appeals to God and begs him to appear quickly for him and vindicate him, because they have wronged him and he does not know how to vindicate himself (vv. 2–7). But he hopes that although it will be surprising for good people to see him mistreated in this way, it will not be a stumbling block to them (vv. 8–9). 2. He responds to the worthless hopes his friends have fed to him (vv. 10–16).

Verses 1–9

Job's speech is broken, and he moves suddenly from one topic to another, as is usual with people who are troubled. Here is:

1. Job's terrible condition, which he describes to justify his own complaints.

1.1. He was a dying man (v. 1). He has said (16:22), *"When a few years have come,* I will go on that long journey." But here he corrects himself. "Why do I talk of years to come? *My breath is* already *corrupt,* I am finished." Our life is going, for the breath of our lives is going. We should therefore be concerned to carefully redeem our time (Eph 5:16), to spend our days preparing for eternity. We are expected in our final home: *The graves are ready for me.* He speaks of the *sepulchres of his fathers,* to which he must be gathered.

1.2. He was a despised man (v. 6): *"He"*—that is, Eliphaz, according to some, or God—*"has made me a byword of the people,* a laughingstock to many, and *aforetime* (previously) *I was as a tabret* (tambourine)." They made up songs about him; his name became proverbially well known: "As poor as Job." *"He has* now *made me a byword,* a reproach among people, whereas before, in my prosperity, I was the favorite of the human race."

1.3. He was a man of sorrows (Isa 53:3). He wept so much that he had almost lost his sight: *My eye is dim by reason of sorrow* (v. 7). See also 16:16. He had become a complete skeleton: *"All my members are* (my whole frame is) *as a shadow* (v. 7). I am not to be called a man, but am only the *shadow of a man."*

2. The hurtful use which his friends made of his miseries. They condemned him as a hypocrite because he was suffering so terribly.

2.1. Job looks on himself as having being cruelly abused by them. "They are *mockers* who are laughing at my misfortune because I have been brought so low." They had all promised him that he would be happy if he would take their advice. He looked on all this as mere flattery and as something intended only to trouble him all the more. He called this their *provocation,* their hostility.

2.2. He condemns it: it was a sign that *God had hidden their heart from understanding* (v. 4). Those who are empty of compassion are also lacking in understanding. Where there is not tenderness in a person, one may question whether there is understanding in them. *Therefore shalt thou not exalt them*, therefore you will not let them triumph (v. 4). Those whose minds have been closed from understanding are certainly kept back from honor. The one who breaks the sacred laws of friendship loses the right to benefit from them, not only for themselves but also for their descendants: "*Even the eyes of his children shall fail*, and when they look for help and comfort from their own and their father's friends, they will look in vain as I have done. They will be as gravely disappointed as I am with you." Those who wrong their neighbors may, in the end, wrong their own children.

2.3. He appeals to God to correct them (v. 3): *Lay down now, put me in a surety with thee*, give me, O God, the pledge you demand." Those whose hearts do not condemn them have confidence toward God, and they can come with humble and confident boldness and beg him to search and test them (Ps 139:23). Mr. Poole's *English Annotations* gives this reading of the verse: "Appoint, I pray thee, my surety with thee, namely, Christ who is with thee in heaven." "Who dare then contend with me? Who shall bring any charge if Christ is my Advocate?" (Ro 8:32–33).

3. The good use which the righteous should make of Job's suffering from God, from his enemies, and from his friends (vv. 8–9).

3.1. These righteous are *upright men*, honest and sincere, who act from firm and wholehearted motives. This was Job's own character—he was blameless and upright (1:1)—and he probably speaks especially of those upright people who have been his friends and associates. They are *the innocent* (v. 8), not perfectly so, but innocence is what they aim at and press toward. Sincerity is a key aspect of the believer's life under the Gospel. They have *clean hands*, hands that are kept clean from gross defilements of sin and, when stained by weakness, are *washed with innocency* (Ps 26:6).

3.2. How would these good people respond to Job's suffering?

3.2.1. It will dismay them: *Upright men shall be astonished* (appalled) *at this* (v. 8); they will be stunned to hear that such a good man as Job should be so sorely afflicted in his body, reputation, and possessions, that God should lay his hand so heavily on him, and that his friends, who should have comforted him, should have added to his grief.

3.2.2. Yet the righteous will also be encouraged to confront the corrupt and harmful inferences which evildoers will draw from Job's sufferings, such as that God has abandoned the earth, that it is futile to serve him, and the like. The boldness of the attacks ungodly people make on religion should sharpen the courage and determination of its friends and advocates. When evil is rampant, it is not a time for virtue to hide itself in fear. *The righteous*, instead of drawing back at this frightful prospect, *shall* with much more faithfulness and determination *hold on* (hold to) *his way* (v. 9) and press forward. Those who keep their eye on heaven as their final destination will keep their feet firmly on the path of religious faith as their way of life, whatever difficulties and discouragements they come across. By observing the testing of other good people, as well as experiencing their own tests, they will be made stronger and more active in their own duty, more warm

and affectionate, more resolute and undaunted. The gusts of wind make travelers gather their cloaks more closely and firmly around them.

Verses 10–16

Job's friends had pretended to comfort him with the hope of his return to a prosperous condition.

1. They were foolish to talk like that (v. 10): "*Return, and come now*, be convinced that you are wrong. Let me persuade you to share my opinion, *for I cannot find one wise man among you*, not one who knows how to explain the difficulties of God's providence or how to apply the encouragement of his promises." When we suffer, it is unwise to draw comfort from the possibility of recovery in this world. Such a recovery is at best uncertain. We would therefore be wiser to comfort ourselves and others in times of distress with what will not fail, that is, the promise of God, his love and grace, and a well-founded hope of eternal life.

2. It would be much more foolish for him to take any notice of them, because:

2.1. All his plans had already been frustrated, and he was totally confused (vv. 11–12). He had had thoughts about enlarging his territory (Ex 34:24; Dt 12:20), increasing his livestock, and seeing his children settled down. He also probably had had many godly thoughts of developing religious faith in his country. He concluded, however, that all these thoughts had now come to an end and that he would never have the satisfaction of seeing his plans put into operation. The end of our days will mean the end of all our plans and hopes for this world, but if we wholeheartedly remain faithful to the Lord, death will not end our relationship with him. Job was in a state of constant unease (v. 12). Because *the thoughts of his heart* were broken, they *changed the night into day and shortened the light*.

2.2. All his expectations from this world would very soon be buried in the grave with him. It was therefore absurd for him to think about such noble things as they had flattered him with the hope of (5:19; 8:21; 11:17). "Unfortunately you are only making a fool of me." He tries not only to reconcile himself to the grave, but also to commend it to himself: "It is my home." The grave is a home; it is like a prison to evildoers (24:19–20), but to the godly it is a Bethany, a passageway to their way home. "There," he said, "I have made my bed." The grave is a bed, for we will rest on it in the evening of our days on earth and rise from it on the morning of our eternal day (Isa 57:2). Let this make good people willing to die. It is only like going to bed. They are weary and sleepy, and it is time they were in their beds. Why should they not go willingly when their father calls? He saw all his hopes from this world falling into the grave with him (vv. 15–16): "Since I must soon leave this world, where is my hope? How can I expect to prosper when I do not expect to live?" He is not without hope, but his hope is not in what they want it to be. "No, that hope which I comfort myself with is something beyond sight, not things that are visible and temporal, but things which are invisible and eternal."

CHAPTER 18

In this chapter Bildad makes a second attack on Job. In his first speech (ch. 8) he gave him encouragement to hope that all would still go well with him. He has grown more perverse, and far from being convinced by Job's reasons, he is now even more exasperated. 1. He sharply rebukes Job for being proud, overwrought, and stubborn in his opinions (vv. 1–4). 2. He develops the teaching he maintained earlier concerning the misery of evildoers *(vv. 5–21)*. In this he seems to have in mind Job's complaints about the miserable condition he was in. Bildad says, "This is the condition of an evildoer, and so you are one."

Verses 1–4

Bildad shoots his arrows, his bitter words, against poor Job, little thinking that although he is a wise and good man, he is here fulfilling Satan's intentions of adding to Job's suffering. He accuses him of:

1. Making endless and worthless speeches, as Eliphaz has accused him (15:2–3): *How long will it be ere* (before) *you make an end of words?* (v. 2). Bildad is tired of having to listen to others. He is impatient for his turn to speak. Everyone can see how inconsistent this behavior is in other people, but few who are guilty of it can see it in themselves. There had been a time when Job had had the last word in every argument (29:22): *After my words they spoke not again.* He was then in a position of power and prosperity, but now that he had become poor and humbled, he was scarcely allowed to speak at all.

2. Paying no attention to what has been said to him, as suggested by the words, *Mark* (Pay attention)*, and afterwards we will speak* (v. 2).

3. Having a proud contempt and disdain of his friends and of what they offered (v. 3): *Wherefore are we counted as beasts*, why are we regarded as cattle? It is true that Job called them *mockers*. He also described them as unwise and unkind. But he did not regard them as cattle. Bildad, however, presents the matter in this way. His fiery spirit is willing to find an excuse for being hard on Job. Those who want to treat others severely will have it thought that others have first treated them so.

4. Having excessive emotion: *He teareth himself in his anger* (v. 4). Here he seems to respond to what Job said in 13:14: *Wherefore do I take my flesh in my teeth?*

5. Proudly and arrogantly expecting to dictate even to providence itself: *"Shall the earth be forsaken for thee*, is the earth to be abandoned for your sake? (v. 4). There is no reason for the course of nature to be changed and the established rules of government to be broken simply to satisfy one human being. Job, do you really think the world cannot stand without you, that if you are ruined, all the world will be ruined and abandoned with you?" To expect that God's counsels should change, his method alter, and his word fail merely to please us is as absurd and unreasonable as to think that *the earth should be forsaken for us and the rock removed out of its place* (v. 4).

Verses 5–10

The rest of Bildad's speech is entirely taken up with a well-balanced description of the miserable condition of evildoers, in which there is a great deal of truth. But it is not true that all evildoers are made miserable in this world, nor is it true that all who are brought into great distress are *therefore* to be thought of as evildoers. And so although Bildad thought it was easy to simply apply this description to Job, it was neither safe nor just to do so.

1. The destruction of evildoers is foreseen and foretold, using the image of darkness (vv. 5–6): *Yea, the light of the wicked shall be put out.* "*Yea*," Bildad says, "so it is; you are clouded over and weakened. You are made miserable, and nothing better could be expected, for *the light of the wicked shall be put out*, and so your lamp will be also."

2. The preparations for that destruction are described, using the image of an animal or a bird caught in a trap,

or a criminal arrested and taken into custody to receive punishment (vv. 7–10).

2.1. Satan is preparing for the destruction of the evildoer. He is *the robber that shall prevail against him* (v. 9). He *hunts for the precious life* (Pr 6:26).

2.2. The evildoer is preparing for his own destruction by continuing in sin and *so treasuring up wrath against the day of wrath* (Ro 2:5). *His own counsels* (schemes) *cast* (throw) *him down* (v. 7). He is *cast* (thrust) *into a net by his own feet* (v. 8).

2.3. God is preparing for his destruction. The sinner is confused so that he falls into the trap. *The steps of his strength*, his high and mighty projects, *shall be straitened* (are weakened) (v. 7), so that he will not fulfill his intentions, and the more he tries to extricate himself, the more he will become entangled. *The gin* (trap) *shall take* (seize) *him by the heel* (v. 9). He can no more escape the divine wrath that is pursuing him than a fugitive once seized can escape from a pursuer.

Verses 11–21

Bildad describes the destruction itself.

1. He will be weakened by the dread of God's wrath (vv. 11–12): *Terror shall make him afraid on every side.* The terrors of the sinner's conscience will haunt him, so that he will never be at peace. His feet will do him no good; they are held tight in the trap (v. 9). He sees his ruin coming. He feels himself completely unable to fight against it, either to escape it or to cope with it.

2. Miserable is the death of the evildoer, however merry and secure his life has been.

2.1. Notice the evildoer dying, arrested by *the firstborn of death* (v. 13)—*some* disease, or some stroke that has in it a more than usual likeness to death itself. The heralds of death *devour the strength* (eat away parts) *of his skin* (v. 13) and bring rottenness to his bones and consume them. *His confidence shall then be rooted out of his tabernacle* (v. 14), that is, everything he trusted in for his support will be taken away from him.

2.2. Notice him dead:

2.2.1. He is then brought to *the king of terrors* (v. 14). Death is terrible to nature; our Savior himself prayed, *Father, save me from this hour* (Jn 12:27). But for the evildoer it is especially *the king of terrors* (v. 14). How happy, then, are the saints, and how much are they indebted to the Lord Jesus, by whom death is abolished, and its power changed, to such an extent that this king of terrors has become a friend and servant!

2.2.2. He is then *driven from light into darkness* (v. 18), from the light of this world, and his prosperous condition in it, into darkness.

2.2.3. He is then *chased out of the world* (v. 18), hurried and dragged away by the messengers of death, greatly against his will, chased like Adam out of Paradise, for the world is his paradise. The whole world is weary of him and is glad to get rid of him. This is death to the evildoer.

3. His family will decline and be destroyed (v. 15). Even his home will be ruined for the sake of its owner: *Brimstone shall be scattered upon his habitation* (v. 15), burning sulfur rained on it as on Sodom, to the destruction of which this seems to refer. Some think Bildad is here rebuking Job by reminding him of the burning of his sheep and servants by fire from heaven. The reason is given: *Because it is none of his* (v. 15), that is, it was unjustly gained. The evildoer's children will die, either with him or after him (v. 16). Those who consider the true honor of their family and the welfare of its branches will be afraid of seeing them wither because of sin. The

destruction of the sinner's family is mentioned again (v. 19): *He shall neither have son nor nephew.* Sin passes an inheritance of a curse on to descendants. It is probable that Bildad is thinking about the death of Job's children and servants as further proof of his being evil.

4. The memory of the evildoer will be buried with him or made detestable; he will either be forgotten or spoken of with dishonor (v. 17): *His remembrance shall perish from the earth.* All his honor will be lost in the dust, so that *he shall have no name in the street* (v. 17); he will die to no one's regret (2Ch 21:20).

5. Notice the universal dismay at his fall (v. 20). Those who see it are appalled. Terrible sins bring awful punishments. Ignorance of God is a willful ignorance, for there is a general revelation that can be known of him which is sufficient to leave evildoers without excuse forever (Ro 2:1). They do not know God, and then they commit all sin.

CHAPTER 19

This chapter is Job's answer to Bildad's speech. Although his spirit was distressed and Bildad was perverse, Job still allowed him to say all he wanted to say, but when Bildad had finished, Job gave him a good answer, in which: 1. He complains of being treated unkindly. And he takes it as very unfair that: 1.1. His comforters have added to his affliction (vv. 2–7). 1.2. His God is the author of his suffering (vv. 8–12). 1.3. His relatives and friends treat him as a stranger and are suspicious of him in his suffering (vv. 13–19). 1.4. No compassion has been shown to him in his affliction (vv. 20–22). 2. He comforts himself, however, with a confident hope of happiness in the other world—even though he has so little comfort in this world—by making a sacred confession of faith, with the wish that it may be recorded as evidence of his sincerity (vv. 23–27); and he concludes with a warning to his friends not to continue in their harsh criticism of him (vv. 28–29). His cheerful views of the future state may shame us as Christians and silence our complaints, or at least balance them out.

Verses 1–7

Bildad twice began with a *How long* (8:2; 18:2), and so now Job also begins with *How long* (v. 2). Job had more cause to think they had taken a long time criticizing him than they had cause to think he had taken a long time trying to justify himself. Notice here:

1. They *vexed* (tormented) *his soul* (v. 2). They were his friends and came to comfort him, but in fact they had done quite differently. They had come with their seriousness and claimed wisdom and godliness, but in fact they had set themselves to rob him of the only comfort he had left in a good God, a good conscience, and a good name, and this tormented him to his heart. They *broke him in pieces with words* (v. 2). They *reproached him* (v. 3). They gave him a bad name and *made themselves strange to him* (v. 3). They regarded him with distrust and suspicion now that he was in trouble. It seemed as if they hardly recognized him. They *magnified* (exalted) *themselves against him* (v. 5). They not only regarded him with suspicion, but also gloated over him in his misfortune and exalted themselves to make him look small. *They pleaded against him his reproach* (v. 5), that is, they wanted to use his suffering as an argument to prove he was evil.

2. They had abused him often in this way (v. 3): *These ten times you have reproached me. Ten times,* that is, very often. They were not ashamed of what they did (v. 3).

They had reason to be ashamed of their hardheartedness, uncharitableness, and deceitfulness, which were inconsistent with being friends.

3. He answers their harsh criticism by showing them that what they condemned could be excused, which they should have considered. The errors of his judgment were excusable (v. 4): *"Be it indeed that I have erred,* suppose that I have indeed gone astray and done wrong through ignorance or mistake," Job said. "Even if it is so, *my error remaineth with myself,"* that is, "I speak according to the best of my judgment, with all sincerity; my words are not primarily directed toward you, to contradict you." *Hast thou faith? Have it to thyself* (Ro 14:22). Some give this sense to these words: "If I am in error, it is I who must suffer for it, and so you do not need to concern yourselves." The outbreaks of his emotion, although not justifiable, were still excusable, considering the immensity of his grief and the intensity of his misery. *Know then that God has overthrown* (wronged) *me* (v. 6). He wanted them to consider three things:

3.1. His trouble was very great. He had been defeated; he was enclosed as in a net and could not get out.

3.2. God was the author of it, and he was fighting against God in it. "I have enough on my hands grappling with God's displeasure; don't show me yours as well!"

3.3. He could not gain any hope of putting right his grievances (v. 7). *I cry out of wrong, but I am not heard,* even though I cry, "I've been wronged!" I get no response (v. 7).

Verses 8–22

Bildad has perverted Job's complaints by making them a description of the miserable condition of an evildoer, but Job repeats them to arouse the pity of his friends, if there was any left in them.

1. Job complains about the signs of God's displeasure: *"He hath kindled his wrath against me,* which burns me and gives me pain" (v. 11). Enlightened consciences fear it now, but will not feel it later. Job's present fear was that *God counted him as one of his enemies* (v. 11); yet at the same time, God loved him as his faithful friend. It is a gross mistake, but a very common one, to think that those whom God afflicts he is treating as his enemies. The truth, however, is the opposite: *For as many as he loves he rebukes and chastens* (disciplines) (Rev 3:19). "*He has stripped me of my glory,* my wealth, honor, power, and every opportunity I had to do good. My children were my honor, but I have lost them, and he has taken away from me whatever was a crown to my head. He has laid all my honor in the dust." If he looked at his present troubles, he saw God giving them their commission, and their orders were to attack him. They were *his troops,* which acted at his direction and *encamped against him* (v. 12). It did not so much trouble him that his miseries came on him in troops as that they were *God's* troops: it seemed from this as if God was fighting against him and intended to destroy him. There had been a time when God's armies encamped around him for safety. Now they surrounded him and *destroyed him on every side* (v. 10). He saw the hand of God cutting off every hope (v. 8): "*He hath fenced* (blocked) *up my way, that I cannot pass.* There is now no way open for me to help myself." Hope in this life is something perishable, but when the hope of good people is cut off from this world, it is only removed like a tree that is transplanted from this nursery to the garden of the Lord (Isa 51:3). We will have no reason to complain if God moves our hopes from sand to rock, from temporal things to eternal things (Eph 4:18).

2. Job complains about the unkindness of his relatives and all his former acquaintances. He also acknowledges the hand of God in this (v. 13): *He has put my brethren far from me,* that is, "He has laid those afflictions on me which frighten them away from me and make them stand far away from me and my suffering." But this does not excuse Job's relatives and friends from the guilt of being extremely ungrateful and unjust toward him. His relatives and friends, his neighbors, and those he had formerly known well, who were bound by the laws of friendship and politeness, were *estranged from him* (v. 13). Poor Job was treated badly by his own family, and some of his worst enemies were those in his own home. His own servants showed him no respect. His maidservants did not attend him in his illness, but *counted him for a stranger and an alien* (v. 15). Although he was now ill, he was not cross and imperious, but begged his servants, though he had authority to command, and yet they would not be polite to him; they were neither kind nor just. But one would have thought that when everyone else abandoned him, his dear wife would have been sensitive toward him. But no; because he would not curse God and die, as she had tried to get him to do, she did not want to go near him, nor did she take any notice of what he said (v. 17). Even the little children who were born in his house, the children of his own servants, despised him (v. 18); they let him know that they did not respect or love him.

3. Job complains that his body is wasting away; all its good looks and strength have gone (v. 20): *My bone cleaves now to my skin.*

4. For all these reasons Job commends himself to the compassion of his friends: "*Have pity upon me, have pity upon me, O you my friends! Have pity upon me, for the hand of God hath touched* (struck) *me."* Yet if they would not relieve his suffering by showing pity, they must still not be so cruel as to add to it by their criticism and scorn (v. 22): "*Why do you persecute me as God does?"* If they showed delight in his adversity, let them be content that his flesh had wasted away and was all but gone. Let them not wound his spirit. Great tenderness is due to those who are suffering, especially to those who are troubled in mind.

Verses 23 – 29

There is much both of Christ and of heaven in these verses, and the one who said such things as these *declared plainly that he sought the better country, that is, the heavenly,* as the patriarchs of that age did (Heb 11:14 – 16). We have here Job's creed or confession of faith. He had often professed his belief in God the Father Almighty, the Maker of heaven and earth, and in the principles of natural religion, but here we see that he was not unfamiliar with revealed religion. Although the revelation of the promised Seed and the promised inheritance was then discerned only as the dawning of the day, nevertheless, Job had been taught by God to believe in a living Redeemer and to look for the resurrection of the dead and the life of the world to come, for there is no doubt that he must be understood to be speaking about such matters. These were the things he comforted himself with the expectation of, not a rescue from his troubles or a revival of his happiness in this world, as some would understand him. The expressions he uses here—of the Redeemer's *standing at the latter day upon the earth* (v. 25), of his seeing God, and *seeing him for himself* (v. 27)—are wretchedly forced if they are understood as referring to any temporal rescue. Job was at this time under an extraordinary prompting of the Holy Spirit. He was raised above himself, given light and utterance. And some notice that after this we do not

find in Job's speeches such passionate complaints about God and his providence as before. This hope quieted his spirit, stilled the storm; and having here dropped anchor *within the veil* (Heb 6:19), his mind was kept firm from this time on. Notice:

1. For what purpose Job here makes this confession of his faith. Never was anything said more relevantly, or to a better purpose: his friends rebuked him for being a hypocrite, but he appeals to his creed, to his confession of faith, to his hope, and to his own conscience. These comfort him with the expectation of a blessed resurrection. *These are not the words of him that has a devil,* of a person possessed by a demon (Jn 10:21). He appeals to the coming of the Redeemer. As if in court, he leaves the dispute at the bar, as it were, to appeal to the judgment of the bench. Job is now afflicted, and this is his medicine. Having been pushed too far, he is kept from fainting by this—he believes that he will *see the goodness of the Lord in the land of the living* (Ps 27:13), not in this world, for that is the land of the dying.

2. How solemnly he introduces his confession (vv. 23 – 24). He breaks off abruptly from complaining and triumphs in his comforts. And so that his words might be recorded for generations to come, he wishes, *O that my words were now written* (v. 23). God graciously granted Job what he here somewhat passionately wished for. His words are printed in God's book, so that wherever that book is read, this will be told in memory of Job.

3. His confession itself is written in vv. 25 – 27. What does he believe in?

3.1. Job believes in the glory of the Redeemer (v. 25): *I know that my Redeemer liveth,* that he exists and is my life, *and that he shall stand at the latter day upon the earth* (v. 25). There is a Redeemer provided for fallen humanity, and Jesus Christ is that Redeemer. The word is *go'el,* which is used for the next of kin, the closest relative, to whom, by the Law of Moses, the right of redeeming a mortgaged estate belonged (Lev 25:25). Our heavenly inheritance was mortgaged by sin; we are ourselves completely unable to redeem it. Christ is our closest relative, the next of kin, who is able to redeem it. He has paid our debt, satisfied God's justice for sin, and so has taken away the mortgage and made a new settlement of the inheritance on us. Not only our inheritance, but also we ourselves need a Redeemer. We are sold under sin, sold as slaves to sin. Our Lord Jesus has brought about a redemption for us and declares redemption to us, and so he is truly the Redeemer. *Because he lives we shall live also* (Jn 14:19). When Job had lost all his wealth and all his friends, he was still not separate from Christ or cut off from his relationship with him: "He is still my Redeemer." That closest relative remained faithful to him when all his other relatives had abandoned him, and he gained comfort from that. *I know*—notice with what assurance he speaks, as one confident of this very thing—*I know that my Redeemer lives* (v. 25).

3.2. He believes in the happiness of the redeemed and his own entitlement to that happiness. He knows his body will decay in the grave, and he speaks about it with a holy unconcern: *Though after my skin* (v. 26) *they destroy this body.* Job mentions this so that the glory of the resurrection he believes in and hopes for may shine more brightly. The same power that made the human body originally out of common dust can raise it out of its own dust. He comforts himself with the hope of happiness on the other side of death and the grave: "After I shall awake, though this body be destroyed, yet out of my flesh shall I see God" (v. 26, margin). But soul and body will come together again. That body which must be destroyed in the grave will be raised again as a glorious body. "*Yet in my flesh* (v. 26) I will see God." Job speaks of seeing him with eyes of flesh: "*in my flesh*, with my eyes." The same body that died will rise again, a glorified body, *a spiritual body* (1Co 15:44). And Job and God, too, will come together again: *In my flesh shall I see God* (v. 26). *My eyes shall behold him, and not another* (v. 27).

4. His confession of faith gave strength and encouragement to him, but it spoke warning and terror to those who set themselves against him: it was a word of warning to them not to persist in their unkind treatment of him (v. 28). They should ask themselves, "*Why persecute we him, seeing the root of the matter*, or the root of the word, *is found in him?*" A strong and vital activity of grace in the heart is the root of the matter, and it is as necessary to our religious faith as a root is to the tree. Love for God and our brothers and sisters, faith in Christ, and hatred of sin—these too are the root of the matter. Other things are only leaves in comparison with these. Serious godliness is what is most needed (Lk 10:42). We are to believe that many have the root of the matter in them who do not agree with us in everything—who have their foolish ways, weaknesses, and mistakes—and to conclude that if we persecute any such people, then we do so at our peril. Job and his friends differed in some of their understandings of the ways of providence, but they agreed on the root of the matter, the belief in another world. Good people need to be frightened away from sin by the terrors of the Almighty, particularly from the sin of rashly judging their brothers or sisters (Mt 7:1; Jas 3:1).

CHAPTER 20

One would have thought that such an excellent confession of faith as Job just made would have satisfied his friends, but they do not seem to have taken any notice of it, and so Zophar attacks him as vehemently as before. 1. His introduction is brief, but intense (vv. 1–3); his speech is long and all about one subject, the certain misery of evildoers and the ruin that awaits them. He asserts, in general, that the prosperity of the evildoer is short, and his ruin sure (vv. 4–9). 2. He proves the misery of the evildoer's condition by many instances—that he will have a diseased body, a troubled conscience, ruined possessions, a poor family, and a notorious name, and that he himself will perish under the weight of divine wrath (vv. 10–29). But the great mistake was that Zophar thought that God never varied from this method and that Job was therefore, without doubt, an evildoer.

Verses 1–9

Here:

1. Zophar begins very emotionally (v. 2): *Therefore do my thoughts cause me to answer*, my troubled thoughts prompt me to answer. He takes no notice of what Job has said to arouse his friends' pity. He excuses his haste for two reasons:

1.1. That Job has provoked him so strongly (v. 3): "*I have heard the check of my reproach*, I have heard a rebuke that dishonors me." Job's friends, I think, were too proud to deal with someone in such a humble condition; arrogant spirits are impatient when being contradicted. They cannot bear to be rebuked.

1.2. That his own heart causes him to reply (v. 2)— his *thoughts*—for *out of the abundance of the heart the mouth speaks* (Mt 12:34); yet he attributes the authorship of these thoughts (v. 3) to *the spirit of his understanding*.

2. Zophar proceeds to show the destruction of evildoers, insinuating that because Job is ruined, he is therefore certainly an evildoer. Notice:

2.1. He introduces his doctrine with an appeal to Job's own knowledge and conviction: *Knowest thou not this?* He also appeals to the experience of all ages: it has been known from ancient times that the sin of sinners will be their ruin.

2.2. He states his doctrine (v. 5): *The triumphing of the wicked is short, and the joy of the hypocrite but for a moment.* Notice: Job's friends were reluctant at first to acknowledge that evildoers could prosper at all (4:9), until Job proved it clearly (9:24; 12:6), and now Zophar accepts it, but he asserts that they will not prosper for long.

2.3. He illustrates it (vv. 6–9). He supposes the prosperity of the evildoer to be very great, as great as you can imagine (v. 6). He is also confident that the ruin of the evildoer will therefore be very great, and his fall the more terrible because he has risen so high: *He shall perish for ever* (v. 7).

Verses 10–22

The instances of the miserable condition of the evildoer in this world are expressed here with great fullness:

1. What the evil is for which he is punished.

1.1. Sinful desires, called here *the sins of his youth* (v. 11). The forbidden physical pleasures are said to be *sweet in his mouth* (v. 12); he indulges himself in gratifying all his sinful desires. His delight in them is the satisfaction *he hides under his tongue* (v. 12) as the tastiest thing possible. *He keeps it still within his mouth* (v. 13). If he has that, he desires no more. Or perhaps his hiding it and keeping it under his tongue shows his diligent concealment of his beloved sinful desires.

1.2. The love of the world and its wealth. He has swallowed down riches as eagerly as a hungry man swallows down food. It is what he desired (v. 20). It is what he labored for (v. 18), any and every way, legal or illegal, simply to get rich. We must labor *not to be rich* (Pr 23:4) but to be loving, *that we may have to give* (Eph 4:28), not to spend. He expected rivers of worldly delights.

1.3. Violence, oppression, and injustice toward his poor neighbors (v. 19). This evildoer is accused of having abandoned the poor, oppressed them, and forcibly taken away their houses.

2. His punishment for this evil: he will never see the rivers, the floods, the brooks flowing with honey and cream with which he had hoped to satiate himself. The enjoyment falls far below his high expectations. He will become ill in his body, and how little comfort do people have in riches if they are not healthy! *His bones are full of the sins of his youth* (v. 11), that is, of the effects of those sins. The sins of his youth will therefore lie down with him in the dust. He will also be disturbed and troubled in mind: *Surely he will not feel quietness in his belly* (v. 20). Let no one expect to enjoy comfortably what they have gained unjustly. Even that evil which was sweet in the doing, rolled under the tongue as a tasty morsel, becomes bitter on reflection and, when looked back on, fills him with horror and distress. Sin is like this: it is turned into *the gall of asps*, than which nothing is more bitter, the poison of serpents (v. 16), than which nothing is more fatal; and so it will be to him. In the fullness of his plenty, when he thinks he cannot become happier, distress will overtake him. Many anxieties will perplex his mind. He will be dispossessed of his property, which will sink and dwindle away to nothing, so that *he shall not rejoice therein* (v. 18). *His children shall seek to please the poor*, while his own hands will restore their

goods to them with shame (v. 18). And so *he shall not save of that which he desired* (v. 20); not only will he not save it all, but in fact he will save none of it. In all this, Zophar is referring to Job, who has lost everything and is reduced to extreme wretchedness.

Verses 23–29

Zophar here comes to show the final and total ruin of the evildoer:

1. His ruin will arise from God's wrath and vengeance (v. 23). *God shall cast* (vent) *the fury of his wrath upon him and rain it upon him* (v. 23). Every word here speaks of terror. There is no protection against this except in Christ, who is the only shelter from the wind and the storm (Isa 32:2). Perhaps Zophar is here thinking about the death of Job's children when they were eating and drinking.

2. His ruin will be inevitable (v. 24): *He shall flee from the iron weapon*, but if he escapes the sword, *the bow of steel* (NIV: a bronze-tipped arrow) *shall strike him through.*

3. His ruin will be complete and terrible. See what *terrors are upon him* (v. 25)!

4. Sometimes it is a ruin that comes on him which he is unaware of (v. 26). The darkness in which he is wrapped up in is a hidden darkness, and it is *hid in his secret place*, to which he has withdrawn in hope of shelter. He never withdraws into his own conscience without finding himself totally at a loss and in the dark. He is wasted away by a soft, gentle fire. When the fuel is very combustible, the fire needs no blowing, and that is what he is like; he is ripe for ruin.

5. It is a ruin not only of himself but also of his family: *It shall go ill with him that is left in his tabernacle* (v. 26), for the curse will reach him too, and he will be destroyed. *His goods shall flow away* (v. 28) from his family as fast as they flowed into it.

6. It is a ruin that will clearly be shown to be just and righteous and to have been brought on him by himself, by his own evil acts, for (v. 27) *the heaven shall reveal his iniquity.*

7. Zophar concludes like an orator (v. 29): *This is the portion of a wicked man from God*. Never was any teaching better explained, or worse applied, than this one by Zophar, who intended all this to prove Job a hypocrite. Let us receive the good explanation, and apply it better.

CHAPTER 21

This is Job's reply to Zophar's speech, in which he complains less about his own adversities and misery than he did in his previous speeches and moves closer to the general question disputed between them: whether outward prosperity and its continuation are a mark of the true church and its true members, so that the ruin of a person's prosperity is enough to prove that person is a hypocrite, even though there is no other evidence. They asserted this, but Job denied it.

1. His introduction is aimed at influencing their emotions so that he may gain their attention (vv. 1–6). 2. His speech is aimed at leading them to correct judgments and putting right their mistakes. He acknowledges that God does sometimes put an evildoer in chains, as it were, as a terror to others, but he denies that he always does so. In fact, he maintains that God usually acts otherwise, allowing even the worst sinners to live all their days in prosperity and to leave the world without any visible mark of his wrath on them. 3. He describes the great prosperity of evildoers (vv. 7–13); he shows their great ungodliness, in which they are hardened in their prosperity (vv. 14–16).

4. He foretells their eventual ruin, but after a long reprieve (vv. 17–21); he notices a great variety in the ways of God's providence toward people, even bad people (vv. 22–26). 5. He undermines the basis of his friends' severe criticism of him by showing that the destruction of evildoers is reserved for the other world, and that they often escape to the end in this world (vv. 27–34), and Job was clearly right in this.

Verses 1–6

Job here commends himself to the compassionate consideration of his friends.

1. What he asks of them is very fair, that they would allow him to speak (v. 3) and not interrupt him. They came to comfort him. "Now," he says, "*let this be your consolations* (v. 2). If you have no other comforts to give me, just listen to me patiently. After I have spoken, you may go on with what you have to say, and I will not stop you even if you continue to mock me. If you will only give me a fair hearing, I believe what I will say will change your mind and make you pity me rather than mock me." Yet they were not his judges (v. 4): "*Is my complaint to man?* No; if it were directed at people, I would see that there is little purpose in complaining. But my complaint is directed toward God, and it is to him that I appeal. Let him be Judge between you and me."

2. He urges them, reasonably, to recognize that his was not a common case, but an extraordinary one. He himself was amazed: "*When I remember* that terrible day in which I was suddenly stripped of all my comforts, that day on which I was struck by painful sores—when I remember all the harsh speeches which you have grieved me with—I confess *I am afraid, and trembling takes hold of my flesh*, especially when I compare my situation with that of the many evildoers who pass through the world in prosperity and with the praise of their neighbors."

Verses 7–16

In their last speeches, all Job's three friends had spoken at length describing the miserable conditions of evildoers in this world. "It is true," Job says, "remarkable judgments are sometimes brought on notorious sinners, but not always, for there are many examples of great and long prosperity among those who are openly evil. Even though they are hardened in their evil by their prosperity, they are still allowed to prosper."

1. He here describes their prosperity in its height, breadth, and length. They live and are not suddenly destroyed by strikes of divine vengeance. Not only do they live, but they also *live in prosperity* (1Sa 25:6). They are *mighty in power*; they are promoted to places of authority and trust. This is the day of God's patience, and in one way or another, he makes use of their prosperity to serve his own purposes, while their impunity prepares them for their ruin. *Their seed is* (their children are) *established in their sight*. They are at ease and quiet (v. 9). Whereas Zophar has spoken of their continual frights and terrors, Job says, *Their houses are safe* both from danger and from the fear of it (v. 9). They are rich and are successful in their material wealth. He gives only one example of this (v. 10). They are happy and live cheerful lives (vv. 11–12).

2. He shows how they abuse their prosperity and are confirmed and hardened by it in their ungodliness (vv. 14–15). God allows them to prosper; but let us not wonder at it, for *the prosperity of fools destroys them*, by hardening them in sin (Pr 1:32; Ps 73:7–9). How disrespectful these prosperous sinners are toward God and religion. It is as if because they have so much of this

world, they have no need to look out for another. How ill disposed they are toward God and religion. They abandon both and reject any thoughts of either.

3. The world is what they have chosen. That is what they are preoccupied with; that is what they think they are happy with. As long as they have that, they think they can live without God. *We desire not the knowledge of thy ways* (v. 14). The two great bonds by which we are drawn and held to religious faith are those of duty and benefit. Yet they will not believe it is their duty to be religious: *What is the Almighty, that we should serve him?* (v. 15). How disrespectfully they speak of God: *What is the Almighty?* (v. 15). They speak about him as if he were a mere name. How harshly they speak of religion. They call it a *service*, meaning that they look on it as a chore and drudgery. Notice how highly they speak of themselves: *"That we should serve him* (v. 15). We who are rich and powerful— will we be subject and accountable to him? No; we are lords" (Jer 2:31). Nor will they believe it is to their benefit to have a living religious faith: *What profit shall we have if we pray unto him?* (v. 15). Is nothing to be called gain except the physical wealth and honor of this world? If we gain the favor of God and blessings that are spiritual and eternal, we have no reason to complain that we are incurring a loss because of our religious faith.

4. He shows their foolishness in this and totally denies any agreement with them (v. 16): *Lo, their good is not in their hand*, that is, they did not gain it without God; their prosperity did not come from their own hands, and so they are very ungrateful to show such disrespect to God. It was *not their might, nor the power of their hand* (Zec 4:6) that gained them this wealth, and so they should remember the God who gave it to them. Nor can they keep their prosperity without God, and so they are very unwise to lose their involvement with him and tell him to leave them. Some think it means: "Their *good*, their wealth, rests in their barns and their bags. It is stored up there. It is not in their hands, to do good to others with it, and so what good does it do them?" "Therefore," Job says, "*the counsel of the wicked is far from me* (v. 16). Far be it from me that I should think like them, that I should speak as they speak, do as they do, and follow them. Their *posterity approve their sayings*, though *their way* be *their folly* (Ps 49:13); but I know better than to walk in their ways."

Verses 17–26

Job has described the prosperity of evildoers, and now:

1. He sets this in opposition to what his friends have maintained concerning the certain destruction of evildoers in this life. "Tell me, *how often* do you see *the candle of the wicked put out?* Do you not as often see it burned down to the base, until it goes out by itself (v. 17)? How often do you see *their destruction come upon them* or *God distributing sorrows in his anger* among them? Do you not as often see their happiness and prosperity continuing to the end?"

2. He reconciles this to the holiness and justice of God. Although evildoers prosper all their days, they are *as stubble and chaff before the stormy wind* (v. 18). They are light and worthless, of no account either with God or with wise and good people. They are ready for destruction and continually exposed to it, and at the height of all their success and power there is only one step between them and ruin. Although they prosper in this world, they will still be reckoned with in the next world. For now, perhaps, the evildoer may not be made to fear the wrath to come, but when it comes, he will know it (v. 20): *His eyes shall see his destruction*, though earlier he could not be

persuaded to believe it would come. They *will not see, but they shall see* (Isa 26:11). The eyes that have been willfully shut against the grace of God will be opened to see their destruction. *What pleasure has he in his house after him?* (v. 21). The gain of the world will be little for sinners who have lost their soul.

3. To account for the distinction which Providence makes between one evildoer and another, he refers to the wisdom and sovereignty of God (v. 22): *Shall any pretend to teach God knowledge?* Shall we presume to tell God how he should rule the world, which sinners he should spare and which he should punish? So vast is the disproportion between time and eternity that if hell is eventually the fate of every sinner, it makes little difference if one goes there singing and another sighing. One person dies suddenly, *in his full strength*, in full vigor, not weakened by age or sickness (v. 23), *being wholly at ease and quiet*, under no apprehension at all of the approach of death, and in no fear of it; because *his breasts are full of milk and his bones moistened with marrow* (v. 24)—that is, his body is well nourished, healthy, and vigorous, like that of a cow that is fat and in good health—he counts on nothing but a long life full of happiness and pleasure. Yet he is cut off in a moment by the stroke of death. Another person dies slowly and only after a great deal of pain and misery (v. 25), *in the bitterness of his soul*, such as poor Job was himself now in, *and never eats with pleasure*, through sickness, age, or depression. Yet how indiscernible this difference is in the grave.

Verses 27–34

In these verses:

1. Job opposes the opinion of his friends, on the basis of which they have condemned him as an evildoer: that evildoers are sure to fall into such visible ruin as Job has now fallen into. *"I know your thoughts,"* Job says (v. 27), *"and the devices* (schemes) *which you wrongfully imagine against* my comfort and honor, and how can such people be convinced?" His friends were ready to say, "Where is *the house of the prince* (great man)? (v. 28). Where is Job's house, or the house of his eldest son, in which his children were holding a feast? Look at the circumstances of Job's house and family, and then ask, *Where are the dwelling places of the wicked?* and you will soon see that Job's house is in the same predicament as the houses of tyrants and oppressors."

2. Job sets down his own judgment to the contrary. He is willing to refer the cause to the next person who passes by (v. 29): *"Have you not asked those that go by the way?* Turn to whomever you will, and you will find they all agree with me, that the punishment of sinners is intended more for the other world than for this. *Do you not know the tokens* (signs) (v. 29) of this truth?"

2.1. What is it that Job is here asserting? Two things:

2.1.1. That impenitent sinners will certainly be punished in the next world.

2.1.2. That we are therefore not to think it strange if they prosper greatly in this world. They are spared now because they are to be punished then. The sinner is here thought to be the terror of the wise and good, whom he keeps in such awe that none dare *declare his way to his face* (v. 31). No one will be free enough to rebuke such a sinner. And if no one dare declare his way to his face, much less dare anyone repay him for what he has done and make him give back what he has obtained by injustice. But there is a day coming when such people will be told of their faults, when those who would not make restitution for the wrongs they had done will themselves be repaid for them. The sinner is also thought to die and be buried with a great deal of show (vv. 32–33). He must die; but everything you can think of will be done to take away the shame of death. He will have a magnificent funeral—a poor thing for anyone to be proud of the prospect of, yet to some it seems very significant. Well, *he shall be brought to the grave* (v. 32) in state. He will have an imposing, stately monument set up over the tomb. *He shall remain in the tomb* (v. 32) with a great "Here lies" inscription over it, and no doubt a long eulogy, too. *The clods* (soil) *of the valley shall be sweet to him* (v. 33); there will be as much done as possible to take away the offensiveness of the grave. But this is all a joke; what is the light, or what is the perfume, to someone who is dead? It will be alleged, to try to reduce the disgrace of death, that it is the common fate: that sinner has only yielded to fate, *and every man shall draw after him, as there are innumerable before him* (v. 33).

2.2. From all this Job reasons the irrelevance of their speeches (v. 34). They were based on a wrong premise: *In your answers there remains falsehood. You comfort me in vain* (v. 34). Where there is no truth, little comfort can be expected.

CHAPTER 22

Eliphaz here begins a third attack on poor Job, in which Bildad follows but Zophar draws back and no longer participates. In this chapter: 1. Eliphaz reprimands Job for his complaints about God and God's dealings with him, from which he infers that Job thinks God has done him wrong (vv. 1–4). 2. He accuses him of many grave crimes and misdemeanors, for which he supposes God is now punishing him: oppression and injustice (vv. 5–11), unbelief and unfaithfulness (vv. 12–14). 3. He compares Job's case to that of the old world (vv. 15–20). 4. He gives him very good advice, assuring him that if he would accept it, God would return in mercy to him and he would return to his former prosperity (vv. 21–30).

Verses 1–4

What Eliphaz says here is unjustly applied to Job, but in itself it is very true and good:

1. That when God does us good, it is not because he is indebted to us. Eliphaz here shows that the righteousness and blameless ways of the best person in the world are of no real benefit or advantage to God, and so cannot be thought of as deserving anything from him. For us, the benefits of religious faith infinitely outweigh its losses. But can anyone be of any value to God? No; God is such that he cannot receive any benefit or advantage from mere humans; what can be added to what is infinite? *Is it any gain to him* (v. 3), any real addition to his glory or wealth, *if we make our way perfect* (blameless)? (v. 3). God has indeed said in his word that he is pleased with the righteous. He sees them, and his delight is in them and their prayers. But all that adds nothing to the infinite satisfaction which the eternal Mind has in itself.

2. That when God restrains or rebukes us, it is not because he is apprehensive of any danger from us (v. 4): "*Will he reprove thee for fear of thee?*" Satan indeed suggested to our first parents that God forbade them the tree of knowledge for fear of them, so that they would not become gods and thereby become rivals with him, but it was an evil insinuation. God rebukes good people because he loves them, but he never rebukes great people because he fears them.

Verses 5–14

Eliphaz and his companions have only generally condemned Job as an evildoer and a hypocrite, but Eliphaz here positively and explicitly charges him with many grave crimes and misdemeanors. "Come," Eliphaz says, "we have been beating around the bush for too long. We've been too kind to Job. It is about time we were direct with him. We must plainly tell him, *Thou art the man* (2Sa 12:7), the tyrant, oppressor, and unbeliever we have been speaking about all this time. *Is not thy wickedness great?* (v. 5). It most certainly is, or else your troubles would not be so great." For all we know, when Eliphaz accused Job falsely, as he did here, he was guilty of as great a sin and as great a wrong to Job as the Sabeans and Chaldeans who robbed him were, for a person's good name is more precious and valuable than their wealth. Eliphaz could produce no actual examples of Job's guilt in any of the details that come here, but it seems he was determined to make bold but general slanderous statements, to sling all the mud he possibly could at Job, not doubting that some would stick to him. Job, whom God himself praised as the best man in the world, is here described by one of his friends, who himself was a wise and good man, as one of the greatest villains on the earth. Let us consider the details of this accusation:

1. Eliphaz accused Job of oppression and injustice, alleging that when he was prosperous, he not only did not use his wealth and power to do good, but on the contrary did a great deal of harm with them. This was completely untrue, as appears from the account Job gives of himself in 29:12–17 and the description God gave of him in 1:1–3, and yet Eliphaz tells him:

1.1. That he has been cruel and unmerciful to the poor. *Thou hast taken a pledge from thy brother for nought*, or, as the Septuagint (the Greek version of the Old Testament) reads, "Thou hast taken thy brethren for pledges," and that for no reason. He imprisoned them and enslaved them because they could not pay. He has taken the very clothes of his bankrupt tenants and debtors, so that he has *stripped them naked* (v. 6). He has not been kind to the poor: "*Thou hast not given* so much as a cup of cold *water to the weary to drink*; in fact, *thou hast withholden bread from the hungry* in their dire need. Poor widows have been sent away empty-handed and sad from your doors (v. 9). Those who came to you for justice, you sent away without even listening to them or helping them in any way. Worst of all, *the arms of the fatherless have been broken*; the strength of those who could help themselves only a little has been broken." This, the most extreme aspect of the charge, is only insinuated: *The arms of the fatherless have been broken.* "They have been broken by those under you, and you have turned a blind eye to it, which makes you guilty."

1.2. That he has been biased in favor of the rich and powerful (v. 8): "The poor were not fed at your door, while the rich feasted at your table." He attributes all Job's present troubles to these supposed sins (vv. 10–11): "*Snares are round about thee* (v. 10), and others are as harsh toward you as you have been toward the poor. No sin cries out more loudly than unmercifulness, and so *sudden fear troubles* (peril terrifies) *thee* (v. 10)." Those who have not shown mercy may justly be denied the assurance that they will receive mercy, and then what can they expect except snares, darkness, and continual terror?

2. Eliphaz accused Job of unbelief, unfaithfulness, and gross ungodliness; he who did not fear God did not respect people. He would have it thought that Job was an

Epicurean, one who acknowledged the existence of God but denied his providence.

2.1. Eliphaz referred to an important truth, which he thought, if Job had duly considered it, would have prevented him from becoming so distraught in his complaints and so bold in justifying himself (v. 12): *Is not God in the height of heaven?* He reveals himself in a special way to the upper world, and from there he reveals himself in a way suited to this lower world. When we *behold the height of the stars, how high they are* (v. 12), we should at the same time also consider the transcendent majesty of God, who is above the stars, and how lofty he is.

2.2. He accused Job of having made bad use of this teaching, which he might have made good use of (v. 13). "This is *holding* (suppressing) *the truth in unrighteousness* (Ro 1:18); you are willing to acknowledge that *God is in the height of heaven* (v. 12), but you reason from that, *How doth God know?*" (v. 13). Eliphaz suspects that Job thinks that because God is in the heights of heaven it is therefore impossible for him to see and hear what is done so far away on earth, especially since there is a *dark cloud* (v. 13), many *thick clouds* (v. 14), that come between him and us and *are a covering to him*—as if God had *eyes of flesh* (10:4). Distances of space create no difficulty to the One who fills everything, any more than the span of time does to the One who is eternal. Or: *He walks in the circuit of heaven*, he goes about in the vaulted heavens (v. 14), and is occupied delighting in the glorious perfection in that bright and peaceful world; why should he trouble himself with us? This is an absurd, as well as very ungodly, thought which Eliphaz here ascribes to Job, for it supposes that the administration of government is a burden and disparagement to the supreme Governor and that the acts of justice and mercy are a burden to One who is infinitely wise, holy, and good. If the sun, a mere inanimate creation, can reach every part of this earth (Ps 19:6) with its light and influence, even from that vast height of the visible heavens in which it is, and in the vault about which it goes, and through many thick and dark clouds too, who are we to question the Creator?

Verses 15–20

Eliphaz, having tried to convict Job, here tries to wake him up to sense his danger because of his sin, and he does this by comparing his situation with that of sinners in the old world, *who were overflown with* (washed away by) *a flood* (v. 16), and the *remnant of whom the fire consumed* (v. 20), namely, the Sodomites, who, in comparison to the old world, were only a remnant. Eliphaz wanted Job to *mark the old way which wicked men have trodden* (v. 15). According to one interpretation, they said to God, *Depart from us*, and then *what could the Almighty do with them* but destroy them? (v. 17). Those who will not submit to God's golden scepter must expect to be broken to pieces by his iron rod (Ps 2:9). Others believe it means, "What has he done to oblige us? *What can the Almighty do* by way of wrath to make us miserable, or by way of favor to make us happy?" *The Lord will not do good, neither will he do evil* (Zep 1:12). Eliphaz shows how absurd this is by calling God *the Almighty*, for if he is almighty, what is there that he cannot do? *Yet he had filled their houses with good things* (v. 18). Many have their houses full of goods but their hearts empty of grace, and so are marked out for ruin. *But the counsel of the wicked is far from me* (v. 18). Job said this of himself (21:16), and Eliphaz is not slow to adopt the same attitude. If they cannot agree on their principles about God, they can still agree to renounce the

principles of those who live without God in the world (Eph 2:12). The righteous will take pleasure and satisfaction in this, because in it God is glorified. They will use the occasion to expose the foolishness of sinners and show how ridiculous their principles are. "*Our substance is not cut down*," says Eliphaz, "as theirs was, and as yours is. We continue to prosper, which is a sign that we are the favorites of heaven and in the right." He used the same rule that condemned Job to exalt himself and his companions. *Job's* substance is cut down, and so he is an evildoer; *ours* is not, and so we are righteous.

Verses 21–30

Eliphaz earlier set before Job the miserable condition of an evildoer, so that he might frighten him into repentance. Here, on the other hand, he shows him the happiness which certainly comes to those who do repent, so that he may draw and encourage him to it. Ministers must try both ways to deal with people. They must speak to them from Mount Sinai with the terrors of the law and also from Mount Zion with the comforts of the Gospel. They must set before them both life and death, good and evil, the blessing and the curse (Dt 30:15, 19). Notice here:

1. The good advice which Eliphaz gave Job; but it was based on the false supposition that he was an evildoer.

1.1. "*Acquaint now thyself with God* (v. 21). Don't be such a stranger to him, as you once were when you rejected reverence of him and were not concerned to pray to him." It is our honor that we are made capable of this friendship, our misery that we have lost it by sin, and our privilege that through Christ we are invited to return to it.

1.2. "*Be at peace* (v. 21), at peace with yourself. And be at peace with your God; be reconciled to him."

1.3. *Receive the law from his mouth* (v. 22). "Having made your peace with God, submit to his rule, be determined that your life will be controlled by him, so that you may keep yourself in his love."

1.4. *Lay up his word in thy heart.* It is not enough to receive it; we must also lay hold of it (Pr 3:18).

1.5. *Return to the Almighty* (v. 23). "Do not only turn away from sin, but also turn to God and your duty. Do not only turn toward the Almighty with good feelings and good beginnings, but *return to him*. Return home to him, quite to him," according to Mr. Matthew Poole.

1.6. *Put away iniquity far from thy tabernacle* (v. 23). This was the advice Zophar gave him (11:14). "*Let not wickedness dwell in thy tabernacle.* Put sin far away—in fact, the farther away the better, not only from your heart and hand, but also from your house."

2. The encouragement which Eliphaz gives Job, that he will be very happy if only he will accept this good advice. In general, "*Thereby good shall come unto thee* (v. 21). You are now ruined and humbled, but *if thou return to God, thou shalt be built up* (v. 23) again, and your present ruins will be restored and repaired. Your family will be built up in children, your possessions in wealth, and your soul in holiness and comfort."

2.1. Temporal blessings would be given him in abundance. It is promised that he would be very rich (v. 24): "*Thou shalt lay up gold as dust*, that is, in such great abundance, and *shalt have plenty of silver* (v. 25), whereas now you are poor and robbed of everything." "You will have silver of strength" (v. 25, margin), which, being gained honestly, will wear well—silver like steel. Wealth is a true blessing when we are not ensnared with the love of it. But also, "You will *lay up gold as dust* and *as the stones of the brooks* (v. 24), that is, so little will you value it or expect from it that you will lay it at your feet (Ac 4:35), not treasure it in your heart." He would still be very safe, for *the Almighty shall be thy defender*. In fact, he will be *thy defence* (v. 25). He "shall be thy gold," (v. 25, margin), and it is the same word that is used for gold in v. 24, but it also means a stronghold, because *money is a defence* (Ecc 7:12). Worldly people make gold their god, but saints make God their gold, and those who are enriched with his favor and grace may truly be said *to have abundance of the best gold*, and to have it stored in the best way possible.

2.2. He would be enriched with spiritual blessings "*For then shalt thou have thy delight in the Almighty*, and so it is that the Almighty comes to be your gold—by your delighting in him, just as worldly people delight in their money. Then, when you want to draw near to him, *thou shalt lift up thy face to God* (v. 26) with boldness, and not fear, as you have done just now. "You will send letters by prayer to God: *Thou shalt make thy prayer*"—the meaning is, "You will multiply your prayers"—"to him, and he will not think your letters a nuisance, even though they are many and long. *He shall hear thee* (v. 27), and he will make it clear he does so by what he does for you and in you." He would have an inner assurance in managing all his outward undertakings (v. 28): "*Thou shalt decree a thing, and it shall be established unto thee*," that is, "You will make decisions in all your plans with so much wisdom, grace, and submission to the will of God that the outcome of them will be to your heart's content. "*Thou shalt commit thy works unto the Lord* by faith and prayer, and then *thy thoughts shall be established*. You will be at peace and pleased, whatever occurs (Pr 16:3)." And, "Whereas you are now complaining about the darkness around you, then *the light shall shine on thy ways*" (v. 28), that is, "God will guide and direct you." Even in times of general calamity and danger he would have great joy and hope (v. 29): "*When men are cast down* (brought low) around you and are despondent, *then shalt thou say, There is lifting up*."

2.3. He would be a blessing to his country and an instrument of good to many (v. 30): *God shall*, in answer to your prayers, *deliver the island of the innocent*, and in doing so he will show respect for *the pureness of thy hands*. Or, "He will deliver those who are not innocent, and they are delivered by the pureness of your hands," as it more probably should read. Good people do much for the public good. Sinners get along better because of saints, whether they are aware of it or not. Eliphaz and his two friends were delivered by the *pureness of Job's hands* (v. 30) (42:8).

CHAPTER 23

Job's reply to Eliphaz begins in this chapter. In this reply he appeals to God, begs him to listen to his case, and does not doubt that he will fulfill his plan, having the testimony of his own conscience in favor of his integrity. There seems to be a struggle between flesh and spirit, fear and faith, throughout this chapter. 1. He complains about his terrible condition, and especially God's withdrawal from him, which meant that he could not have his appeal heard (vv. 1–5) or discern the meaning of God's dealings with him (vv. 8–9) or gain any hope of relief (vv. 13–14). This made a deep impression of trouble and terror on him (vv. 15–17). But: 2. In the midst of these complaints he comforts himself with the assurance of God's mercy (vv. 6–7) and his own integrity, which God himself was a witness to (vv. 10–12).

Verses 1–7

Job is confident that he has been wronged by his friends, and so, ill as he is, he will not give up the cause or let them have the final word. Here:

1. He justifies his own resentments and his descriptions of his trouble (v. 2): "*Even today*, I acknowledge, *my complaint is bitter. Even today* is my complaint counted as 'rebellion,'"—as some understand it—"but I do not complain more than there is just cause to, *for my stroke is heavier than my groaning* (v. 2). The pains of my body and the wounds of my spirit are such that I have just reason to complain."

2. He appeals to the just judgment of God for relief from the criticism of his friends, and he thinks this is evidence for him that he is not a hypocrite, for if he were one, he would not dare make such an appeal as this.

2.1. He is so sure of the justice of God's tribunal that he longs to appear before it (v. 3): *O that I knew where I might find him!* This may properly express the cry of longing from a soul convinced that it has lost God by sin and is forever ruined if it does not recover its share in his favor.

2.2. He is so sure of the goodness of his own case that he longs for it to be laid open at God's court of law (v. 4): "I *would order my cause before him* and set it in its true light." We may apply this to our duty of prayer, in which we have *boldness to enter into the holiest* (Heb 10:19) and to come even to the footstool of the throne of grace. We have not only freedom of access but also freedom of speech. We are allowed to *order our cause before God* (v. 4). We dare not be so free with earthly leaders as a humble, holy soul may be with God. We are allowed not only to pray but also to plead, not only to ask but also to argue, in fact, to *fill our mouths with arguments* (v. 4), not to move God—he is perfectly well aware of the goodness of our cause without our having to show it—but to move ourselves, to stir our fervency and encourage our faith in prayer.

2.3. He is so sure of a sentence in favor of him that he even longs to hear it (v. 5): *I would know the words which he would answer me*. It is right in every argument to let the word of God determine it. Let us know what he answers and understand what he says.

3. He assures himself with the hope that God will deal favorably with him in this matter (vv. 6–7). The same power that is engaged against proud sinners is engaged for humble saints, who live effectively for God with the strength gained from him, as Jacob did (Hos 12:3). See also Ps 68:35. There in the court of heaven, when the final sentence is to be given, *the righteous* person *might dispute with him* and come away with his righteousness upheld. Now, even the upright are often *chastened of the Lord* (1Co 11:32), and they cannot argue against it; integrity by itself is no protection against either misrepresentation or misfortune. But in the day of judgment *you shall discern between the righteous and the wicked*, whereas now we can scarcely distinguish them, there is such a little difference between them in their outward condition. Then *I shall be delivered for ever from my judge*. Those who are handed over to God as their owner and ruler will be forever rescued from him as their judge and avenger, and there is no fleeing from his justice except by fleeing to his mercy.

Verses 8–12

Here:
1. Job complains that he cannot understand the meaning of the ways of God's providence concerning him

(vv. 8–9): *I go forward, but he is not there.* He had a great desire to appear before God and gain a hearing of his case, but the Judge was not to be found. Job believed, no doubt, that God is present everywhere, but because of the disorder and tumult his spirit was in, he could not fix his attention on what he knew of God. He could not see how he had sinned more than others, nor could he discern what other purpose God had in mind in making him suffer in this way. He was completely at a loss to know what God intended to do with him.

2. He satisfies himself with the knowledge that God himself is a witness to his integrity, and he therefore does not doubt that things will turn out well.

2.1. Having almost lost himself in the labyrinth of divine deliberations, he sits down contentedly with this thought: "Although I do not know the way that he takes— yet *he knows the way that I take*" (v. 10). It is a great comfort to those with upright motives that God understands those motives even if people do not, cannot, or will not. "He knows that, however much I may sometimes have taken a false step, I have still *taken a good way*, have *chosen the way of truth* (Ps 119:30), and so *he knows my way*," that is, he accepts it and is pleased with it, as he is said to *know the way of the righteous* (Ps 1:6). Job reasons, *When he hath tried me, I shall come forth as gold* (v. 10). The trial will have an end. *God will not contend for ever* (Isa 57:16). Those who *keep the way of the Lord* may comfort themselves with the knowledge that they will come out as gold, approved and improved, found to be good and made to be better.

2.2. Now what encouraged Job to hope that his present troubles would end well was the testimony of his conscience. God's way was the way he walked in (v. 11): "*My foot hath held his steps*," that is, "my feet have followed his steps closely." God's word was the rule he walked by (v. 12). He conducted himself by *the commandment of God's lips.* Job kept closely to the law of God. *I have esteemed the words of his mouth more than my necessary food*, I have treasured the words of his mouth more than my daily bread (v. 12); that is, he could as well have lived without his daily bread as without the word of God. "I have laid it up," is the meaning, as those who store provisions for a siege, or as Joseph stored grain before the famine. The word of God is to our souls what our daily bread is to our bodies. It sustains our spiritual life and strengthens us for the activities of life.

Verses 13–17

Some believe Job is here complaining that God dealt unjustly and unfairly with him. His complaint here is indeed bitter and perverse, and he reasons himself into a kind of forced patience, which he cannot do without concluding that God has dealt harshly with him. Yet the worst he says is that he cannot explain why God has dealt with him as he has.

1. He establishes good truths (vv. 13–14).

1.1. That God's ways are unchangeable: *He is in one mind, and who can turn him?* "He is one," as some read it, or "in one"; he has no counselors who try to persuade him to change his plans. Prayer can effectively change God's way and his providence, but never has his will or purpose changed, for *known unto God are all his works* (Ac 15:18).

1.2. That God's power is irresistible: *What his soul desires* or intends, *even that he does* (v. 13). *None can stay his hand* (Da 4:35). *Whatever the Lord pleased that did he* (Ps 135:6), and always will, because it is always best. *He performs the thing that is appointed for me. Many such

things are with him* (v. 14), that is, there are many things in his providence which we cannot explain, but must see in the light of his absolute sovereignty.

2. But he applies these good truths badly. He said, *Therefore am I troubled at his presence*, I am terrified before him (v. 15). What confusion poor Job was now in, for he contradicted himself. He had only just been troubled because of God's absence (vv. 8–9); now he is troubled at his presence. *When I consider, I am afraid of him* (v. 15). *The Almighty troubled him* and so *made his heart soft* (faint), made it painfully sensitive, so that everything in the present seemed pressing and everything in the future a threat. He quarreled with God *because I was not cut off before the darkness* (v. 17).

CHAPTER 24

Having expressed his emotion through his complaints recorded in the previous chapter, and so gained some relief, Job breaks off from them abruptly and now turns to a further discussion of the doctrinal controversy between him and his friends concerning the prosperity of evildoers. He has shown that many live in ease even though they are ungodly and worldly and despise all religious practices (ch. 21). He here goes further and shows that many who are troublesome to others, who openly defy all the laws of justice and common honesty, still thrive and succeed in their unrighteous practices in this world. What he said before (12:6), The tabernacles of robbers prosper, he here enlarges on. 1. Those who openly do wrong to their poor neighbors are not called to account, nor are the injured put right (vv. 2–12), even though those who do wrong are very cruel (vv. 21–22). 2. Those who secretly practice evil often go undiscovered and unpunished (vv. 13–17). 3. God punishes such people by secret judgments and reserves them for future judgments (vv. 18–20 and vv. 23–25), so that, generally, we cannot say all who are in trouble are evil, for it is also certainly true that not all who are prosperous are righteous.

Verses 1–12

Job's friends were very definite in saying that they would soon see the fall of evildoers, however much they might prosper for a while. Not at all, Job says; *though times are not hidden from the Almighty, yet those that know him do not presently see his day* (v. 1). God rules the world. Bad times are not hidden from him, even though evildoers who make the times bad say to one another, he has *forsaken the earth* (Eze 8:12; Ps 94:6–7). Before Job asks the reasons why evildoers prosper, he asserts God's knowledge of everything. But he asserts that those who know him—wise and good people who are acquainted with him, and whom he confides in—*do not see his day*, the day of his judging in their favor. We will soon know why the judgment is delayed. Even the wisest people, and those who know God best, do not see it yet. God will exercise their faith and patience and encourage their prayers for the coming of his kingdom, for which they are to *cry day and night to him* (Lk 18:7). Job mentions two kinds of unrighteous people, whom all the world sees thriving in their sin:

1. Tyrants and those who do wrong under pretense of law and authority.

1.1. They *remove the landmarks*, move the boundary stones, claiming the stones have been misplaced (v. 2); they think they can effectively take and secure for their descendants what they have gained wrongfully. This was forbidden by the Law of Moses (Dt 19:14), and whoever did it came under a curse (Dt 27:17).

1.2. *They violently take away flocks*, pretending that the rightful owners have lost the right to them, and they also take *the feed thereof* (v. 2). If a poor, fatherless child has only a donkey of his own to gain a little money with, they find some excuse or other to take it away. It does not matter if a widow has only an ox to work her small farm; claiming the repayment of some small debt, or arrears of rent, they seize this ox as a pledge, even though perhaps it is all the widow has. God has chosen one of the titles of his honor to be *a Father of the fatherless and a judge of the widows* (Ps 68:5), and so those who do not do all they can to protect orphans and widows will not be considered his friends, and he will call to account those who trouble and oppress them.

1.3. In their hearts, they love to ridicule people and gloat over poor people, whom they prevent from gaining relief. They threaten to punish them as vagabonds and so force them to flee. *They pluck the fatherless from the breast*, that is, having made poor infants fatherless, they then make them motherless as well. Having taken away the father's life, they break the mother's heart and so starve the children and leave them to perish. People who show no mercy to those who are at their mercy will themselves receive judgment without mercy. These powerful oppressors squeeze the poor so hard with their extortion that they *cause them to go naked without clothing* (v. 10).

1.4. They oppress the laborers they employ in their service. "Those who carry their sheaves are hungry" (v. 10); see also v. 11: those who *make oil within their walls*, who work hard and crush olives among the terraces, still go thirsty.

1.5. In cities, too, we see the tears of the oppressed (v. 12): *Men groan from out of the city*, the groans of the dying rise from the city, where the rich merchants and traders are as cruel toward their poor debtors as the landlords in the country are toward their poor tenants.

2. Robbers and those who commit wrong by sheer force, like the raiding parties of the Sabeans and Chaldeans which had recently plundered him. They are characterized as *wild asses in the desert* (v. 5), untamed, uncontrollable, and unreasonable. They choose the deserts to live in. The desert is indeed the most suitable place for such evildoers (39:6). But no desert can put people out of the reach of God's eye and hand. Their trade is to steal, and they attack everyone around them. They are diligent and take pains at it: they *rise betimes* (early) *for a prey* (v. 5). They not only rob travelers but also raid their neighbors, *reaping every one his corn in the field* (v. 6), that is, they invade other people's ground, cut their fodder, and take it away just as freely as if it were their own. *They cause the naked*, whom they have stripped, not leaving them any clothes even on their backs, *to lodge*, in the cold nights, *without clothing*, so that *they are wet with the showers of the mountains* (drenched by mountain rains) *and, for want of a* better *shelter, embrace* (hug) *the rock*, glad to have a cave to protect them from the perils of the weather. The impunity of these oppressors and destroyers is expressed concisely (v. 12): *Yet God layeth not folly to them*, God charges no one with wrongdoing; he does not prosecute them with his judgments until he says, *Thou fool, this night thy soul shall be required of thee* (Lk 12:20).

Verses 13–17

These verses describe another kind of sinner who goes unpunished because they are undiscovered. *They rebel against the light* (v. 13). Some understand it figuratively,

as referring to their own consciences. They profess to know God, but they rebel against the knowledge they have of him. Others understand it literally: they have the daylight but choose the night as the best time for their evil. In this paragraph Job mentions three kinds of sinners who avoid the light: murderers (v. 14), adulterers (v. 15), and housebreakers (v. 16). Job observes that they are in a state of continual terror for fear of being discovered (v. 17): *The morning is to them even as the shadow of death.* The light of the day, which is welcome to upright people, is a terror to evildoers. They curse the sun because it exposes them.

Verses 18–25

Job at the end of his speech:

1. Gives some further examples of the wickedness of these cruel, bloody evildoers.

1.1. Some are pirates and robbers at sea. This is how some interpreters apply the expressions in v. 18: *He is swift "upon" the waters.* Privateers choose those ships that sail the best. Their *portion is cursed in the earth*, and they *behold not the way of the vineyards*, that is, they despise as poor and useless the work of those who farm the ground and plant vineyards. But others see this as a further description of the behavior of those sinners who are afraid of the light: if they are discovered, they get away as fast as possible, choosing to lurk not in the vineyards, for fear of being discovered, but in some cursed, lonely, desolate place, which no one looks after and where no one will look for them.

1.2. Some abuse those who are in trouble, adding further suffering to the afflicted. Barrenness was looked on as a great shame, and those who came under that affliction were rebuked for it. This is what is meant by *evil entreating* (wronging) *the barren that beareth not* (v. 21); it is wronging those who are childless.

1.3. There are those who by hardening themselves to cruelty finally come to be *the terror of the mighty in the land of the living* (Eze 32:27) (v. 22): *He draws the mighty into a trap by his power. He rises up* in his anger, and lashes out at all around him so furiously that *no man is sure of his life*.

2. Shows that these daring sinners prosper, that for a while they live an easy life; in fact, they often end their days in peace and seem to have a feeling of security (v. 23). They are exalted for a while. At length, they are taken out of the world very silently and gently. "They go down to the grave as easily as snow-water sinks into the dry ground when it is melted by the sun," as Bishop Patrick explains v. 19. He paraphrases v. 20: "God sets no such mark of his displeasure upon him but that his mother may soon forget him. Neither he nor his wickedness is any more remembered than a tree which is broken to shivers." And of v. 24, *They are taken out of the way as all others*, he says, "they are shut up in their graves like all other men; nay, they die as easily as an ear of corn is cropped with your hand."

3. Foresees their fall, however. God's *eyes are upon their ways* (v. 23). Although now he keeps silent, he will soon show that their most secret sins, which they thought *no eye should see* (v. 15), were seen by him and will be recalled. The *grave shall consume* (snatch away) *those that have sinned*; that land of darkness will be the destiny of those who *love darkness rather than light* (Jn 3:19). Their pride will be brought down and laid in the dust (v. 24). Job acknowledges that evildoers will be completely miserable on the other side of death, but completely denies what his friends asserted, that they are usually miserable in this life.

4. Concludes with a bold challenge to all who are present to disprove what he has said (v. 25): "*If it be not so now*, as I have declared, and if it does not follow from this that I have been unjustly condemned and criticized, then let those who can do it undertake to prove me a liar."

CHAPTER 25

Bildad gives a short reply to Job's last speech. He drops the main question concerning the prosperity of evildoers, but because he thinks Job has been too bold with respect to the divine Majesty in his appeals to the divine tribunal (ch. 23), he shows in a few words the infinite distance between God and human beings, teaching us: 1. To have high and honorable thoughts of God (vv. 1–3, 5). 2. To have lowly thoughts of ourselves (vv. 4, 6). These are two good lessons for us all to learn, however misapplied they were to Job.

Verses 1–6

Bildad is to be commended for speaking no further on the subject on which Job and he differed and for speaking so well on the matter about which Job and he were agreed. Bildad uses two ways to exalt God and to humble humanity:

1. He shows how glorious God is, and from that he reasons how guilty and impure human beings are before him (vv. 2–4). God is the sovereign Lord of all, and *with him is terrible* (awesome) *majesty* (37:22). *Dominion and fear* (awe) *are with him* (v. 2). He who gave existence to all has an incontrovertible authority to give laws and can enforce the laws he gives. His having dominion— his being Lord—shows he is both owner and ruler of all creatures. They are all his, they are all under his direction and at his disposal, and he is therefore to be feared by all his creatures. Yet *He* also *maketh peace in his high places*, he establishes order in the heights of heaven (v. 2). The holy angels never quarrel with him or with one another, but rest completely in his will and carry it out without murmuring or complaining. The high places are *his* high places, for *the heaven, even the heavens, are the Lord's* (Ps 115:16). Peace is God's work. Where there is such peace, it is he who makes it (Isa 57:19). There is perfect peace in heaven, for perfect holiness is there, and God is there, who is love. Finally, he is a God of irresistible power: *Is there any number of his armies*, can his forces be numbered (v. 3)? His providence extends to all: *Upon whom does not his light arise?* (v. 3). *How then can man be justified with God? Or how can he be clean?* Human beings are not only lowly but also evil, not only earthly but also corrupt. We cannot be justified; we cannot be pure:

- In comparison with God.
- In debate with God.
- In the sight of God. If God is so great and glorious, how can human beings, who are so guilty and impure, appear before him?

2. He shows how dark and deficient even the heavenly bodies are in the sight of God, and in comparison with him, and from that he reasons how little, lowly, and worthless human beings are. The lights of heaven have no glory, because God's glory surpasses everything. They are like a candle, which even though it burns, does not shine when it is set in the clear light of the sun. The *moon shall be confounded, and the sun ashamed, when the Lord of hosts shall reign in Mount Sion.* How dare Job appeal so confidently to God, who would reveal in him the wrong

which he was not aware of in himself? Although human beings are noble creatures, in comparison with God they are mere worms of the earth (v. 6): *How much less* does *man* shine in honor, how much less is he pure in righteousness *that is a worm?* What little reason have human beings to be proud, and what great reason to be humble! Will human beings be so foolish as to argue with their Maker?

CHAPTER 26

This is Job's short reply to Bildad's short speech, in which he confirms what Bildad said and surpasses him in exalting God, to show what reason he still has to say, as he did in 13:2, What you know, the same do I know also. He shows: 1. That Bildad's speech was true and good, but not to the point (vv. 1–4). 2. That it was unnecessary, for he knew it, believed it, and could speak about it as well as Bildad could (vv. 5–13). This he did in the rest of his speech, concluding that everything came short of what the subject deserved (v. 14).

Verses 1–4

Bildad thinks that he has made a fine speech, but Job perversely shows that his performance was not so valuable as he thought it was:

1. There was no great substance to be found in the speech (v. 3): *How hast thou plentifully declared the thing as it is*, and what great insight have you displayed? This was spoken ironically, rebuking Bildad.

1.1. Bildad thought he had spoken very clearly, had *declared the thing as it is.*

1.2. He thought he had spoken very fully, but he had declared it poorly and scantily in comparison with the vast extent of the subject.

2. There was no great use to be made of it. "What good have you achieved by all that you have said? *How hast thou*, with all this mighty flourish, *helped him that is without power?* (v. 2). Job wanted to convince Bildad:

- That he had done God no service by his speech.
- That he had done his cause no service by it.
- That he had done him, Job, no service by it. Bildad pretended to convince, instruct, and comfort Job, but what he had said was unfortunately pointless. "*To whom hast thou uttered words?* (v. 4). Was it to me that you directed your speech? And do you take me to be such a child that I need this instruction?" Not everything that is true and good is always suitable and well timed. To one who was humbled and broken, as Job was, Bildad should have preached the grace and mercy of God, rather than his greatness and majesty. Job asks him, *Whose spirit came from thee?* (v. 4), that is, "What troubled soul would ever have been revived, relieved, and brought to itself by such words as yours?"

Verses 5–14

Now they were talking about a subject on which they were all agreed: the infinite glory and power of God.

1. Many examples are given here of the wisdom and power of God in the creation and sustaining of the world:

1.1. If we look around us to the earth and waters beneath, we will see striking signs of God's almighty power:

1.1.1. *He hangs the earth upon nothing* (v. 7). We cannot even hang a feather on nothing, but divine wisdom hangs the whole earth in this way.

1.1.2. He *sets bounds to the waters of the sea* and marks them off (v. 10), so that they may not *return to cover the earth.*

1.1.3. He *forms dead things under the waters* (v. 5). *Rephaim,* "giants," *are formed under the waters* (v. 5), that is, vast, bulky creatures, like whales. [Ed. note: The KJV translates *Rephaim* as "dead things"; this is usually nowadays translated as "the dead," "departed spirits," or "spirits of the dead."]

1.1.4. By mighty storms he shakes the mountains, which are here called *the pillars of heaven* (v. 11), and even *divides the sea, and smites* (cuts) *through its proud waves* (v. 12).

1.2. We can even imagine examples of God's power in hell. We may understand "hell and destruction" (v. 6) to refer to the grave and those who are buried in it, and then we may recognize that they are under the eye of God, even though they are out of our sight, which may strengthen our belief in the resurrection of the dead. We may also consider these words as referring to the place of the damned.

1.3. If we look to heaven above, we see examples of God's sovereignty and power: *He stretches out the north over the empty place,* he spreads out the northern skies over empty space (v. 7). This is what he did at first, when *he stretched out the heavens like a curtain* (Ps 104:2), and *he* still *binds up the waters in his thick clouds,* as if they were tied closely in a bag, and despite the immense weight of water that is raised and stored, *the cloud is not rent* (torn) *under them*; instead the waters distill, as it were, through the cloud, and so come drop by drop, in mercy to the earth, in light or heavy rain, according to his will. *He holds back the face of his throne,* that light in which he lives, *and spreads a cloud upon it,* through which *he judges* (22:13). *By his Spirit,* the eternal Spirit that moved on the face of the waters (Ge 1:2), *he has garnished the heavens* (v. 13). He not only made the heavens, but also made them beautiful. He has wonderfully graced them with stars by night and painted them with the light of the sun by day. "If the pavement is so richly inlaid, then what must the palace be like? If the visible skies are so glorious, then what can the invisible heaven be like?" It is uncertain what is meant by *the crooked serpent* (v. 13), referring to another thing his hands have formed. Some consider it to be part of the decoration of the skies, the Milky Way; others think it refers to some particular constellation by that name. It is the same word that is used for *leviathan* (Isa 27:1) and probably refers to the crocodile or whale, in which is seen much of the power of the Creator, and why may Job not conclude with that example, when God himself does so (ch. 41)?

2. Job concludes (v. 14): *Lo, these are parts of his ways,* the outer fringes of his works, by which he makes himself known to mere mortals. Here he acknowledges, with adoration, the revelations that have been made about God. These things which he himself has said, and which Bildad has said, are God's ways, and they know something of God. But he wonders at the depths of what has not been revealed. What we know about God is nothing in comparison with what is in God and what God is. He is infinite and incomprehensible. Our understanding and ability is weak and shallow. The full revelation of divine glory is reserved for the future state.

CHAPTER 27

Job had sometimes complained that his friends would scarcely allow him to speak. But now they left him the opportunity to say what he wanted. What Job had said in ch. 26 was a sufficient answer to Bildad's speech, but now Job went on and said all he wanted to say on this matter. 1. He begins with a solemn declaration of his integrity and of his determination to be faithful to it (vv. 1–6). 2. He expresses the dread he has of that hypocrisy which they accused him of (vv. 7–10). 3. He shows the wretched end that comes to evildoers despite their long prosperity, and the curse that comes on them and is passed on to their families (vv. 11–23).*

Verses 1–6

Job's speech is called *a parable* (*mashal*), the title of Solomon's proverbs, because it was instructive, and he spoke as one with authority (Mk 1:22). The word comes from another that means "to rule or have authority," and some think the use of it shows that Job now triumphed over his opponents. We say of excellent preachers that they know how to command their hearers. Job here supports all he has said in maintaining his own integrity by taking a solemn oath, to silence any contradiction and take the blame completely on himself if he goes astray. Notice:

1. The form of his oath (v. 2): *As God liveth, who hath taken away my judgment.* Here he speaks highly of God in calling him "the living God"—the ever-living, eternal God, who has life in himself. But he speaks harshly and unfittingly about God when he says that God has *taken away his judgment*—denied him justice in this dispute and not appeared to defend him—and that by continuing his troubles, on which his friends based their criticism of him, God has taken from him the opportunity he had hoped to have before now to clear himself. He also accuses God of *vexing his soul,* making him taste bitterness of soul (v. 2; compare 7:11), by placing such great affliction on him. But notice Job's confidence in the goodness both of his cause and of his God, that although at that time God seemed angry with him and seemed to act against him, he could still cheerfully commit his cause to him.

2. The substance of his oath (vv. 3–4):

2.1. That he would not *speak wickedness, or utter deceit,* that, as all along in this argument he had spoken his mind, so he would never go against and wrong his conscience by speaking otherwise. He would never maintain any teaching or assert any fact except what he believed to be true. Nor would he deny the truth, however much it might act against him. He would not be brought by their unjust criticism to falsely accuse himself.

2.2. That he would stand by this decision as long as he lived (v. 3): *All the while my breath is in me.* With things that are doubtful and indifferent, it is not safe to be too decisive. We do not know what reason we may have to change our mind. But with something so plain and clear as this, we cannot be too definite in affirming that we will never speak evil.

3. The explanation of his oath (vv. 5–6): "*God forbid that I should justify you* in your uncharitable criticism of me, by acknowledging myself to be a hypocrite. No; *until I die I will not remove my integrity from me; my righteousness I hold fast, and will not let it go.*" Job complained much about the reproaches of his friends, but now he said, *My heart shall not reproach me* (v. 6), that is, "I will never give my heart cause to blame myself, but will keep my conscience clear of offense, and as long as I do, I will not allow my heart to shame me."

Verses 7–10

Job here expresses the dread he has of being found to be a hypocrite:

1. He looked on the hypocrite's condition as the most miserable that anyone could ever be in (v. 7): *Let my enemy be as the wicked*—a proverbial expression. If he could wish the greatest evil on his worst enemy, he would wish them the fate of an evildoer, knowing that he could not wish them any worse.

2. The reasons why he is shocked at this thought:

2.1. Because the hypocrite's hopes will not be crowned (v. 8): *For what is the hope of the hypocrite?* Job's friends had tried to persuade him that all his hope was only the hope of the hypocrite (4:6). "No," he said, "I would not, for all the world, be so foolish as to build on such a corrupt foundation, for *what is the hope of the hypocrite?*" (v. 8). It is certain that true hypocrites, with all their gains and hopes, will be miserable in death.

2.2. Because the hypocrite's prayer will not be heard (v. 9): *Will God hear his cry when trouble comes upon him?* If true repentance comes to such a hypocrite, God will hear his cry and accept him (Isa 1:18); but if he continues unchanged without repenting, he should not think he will find favor with God. Notice:

2.3. The hypocrite's religion is neither strengthening nor constant (v. 10): *Will he delight himself in the Almighty? Will he always call upon God?* No; in times of prosperity he will not call on God, but insult him. In times of adversity he will not call on God, but curse him. The reason why hypocrites do not persevere in their religious faith is that they have no pleasure in it.

Verses 11–23

Now that the heat of the battle was nearly over, Job was willing to acknowledge how much he agreed with his friends and where the difference between his opinion and theirs lay.

- He agreed with them that evildoers are miserable, that God will surely call cruel oppressors to account and retaliate against them for all the ways they have shown disrespect to God and all the wrongs they have done to their neighbors. This truth is greatly confirmed by the complete agreement of even these angry debaters. But:
- They differed in *this*: the friends held that these deserved judgments are immediately and visibly brought on evil oppressors, but Job held that in many cases judgments do not fall on them quickly but are delayed for some time.

1. Job here undertakes to set this matter in its true light (vv. 11–12): *I will teach you.*

1.1. What he would teach them: "*that which is with the Almighty*," that is, "the ways and purposes of God concerning evildoers." This, Job says, *will I not conceal. For the things revealed belong to us and our children* (Dt 29:29).

1.2. How he would teach them: *By the hand of God* (v. 11). Those whom God teaches with his strong power are most able to teach others (Isa 8:11).

1.3. What reason they had to learn those things which he was about to teach them (v. 12): "*You yourselves have seen it. Why then are you thus altogether vain,* why then all this meaningless talk, to condemn me as an evildoer because I am afflicted?" He offers now to set before them *the portion* (fate) *of a wicked man with God,* particularly *of oppressors* (v. 13). Compare 20:29. Their fate in the world may be wealth and promotion, but their fate with God is ruin and misery.

2. He does it by showing that evildoers may in some instances prosper, but that ruin follows them and that is their heritage, their fate.

2.1. They may prosper in their children, but ruin will come on them. *His children* perhaps *are multiplied* (v. 14), or "exalted," according to some; they are numerous and are raised to great honor and material wealth. But the arrows of God's justice will justly be directed at them: *sword, famine, and pestilence* (2Sa 24:13).

2.1.1. Some of them will die by the sword of war, by the sword of justice for their crimes, or the sword of the murderer for their wealth.

2.1.2. Others will die of famine (v. 14): *His offspring shall not be satisfied with bread.*

2.1.3. Those who *remain shall be buried in death* (v. 15), that is, they will die from the plague, which is called *death* (Rev 6:8), and be buried privately and quickly, without any ceremony, *buried with the burial of an ass* (Jer 22:19); and even their *widows shall not weep* (v. 15).

2.2. They may prosper in their property and possessions, but ruin awaits *them* too (vv. 16–18). *They heap up silver* in abundance *as the dust* and *prepare raiment as the clay.* They have heaps of clothes around them, as plentiful as piles of clay. But what comes of it? God will so order it that *the just shall wear his raiment and the innocent shall divide his silver* (v. 17). Good people will honestly gain the wealth that evildoers have gained dishonestly, and they will do good with it. The innocent will not hoard the silver, but will distribute it among the poor. Money is like manure, good for nothing if it is not spread. Evildoers will probably have built strong and stately houses for themselves, but they are like the cocoon which the moth makes for itself in old clothes, out of which it will soon be shaken (v. 18). They feel very secure in their house, like moths, and have no sense of danger, but it will prove as short-lived as *a booth* (hut) *which the keeper* (watchman) *makes,* which will quickly be taken down.

2.3. Destruction comes to them, although they lived in good health and at ease for a long time (v. 19): *The rich man shall lie down to sleep, but he shall not be gathered,* that is, his mind will not be composed, gathered in to enjoy his wealth. He does not sleep so contentedly as people think he does. *His abundance will not suffer* (allow) *him to sleep* so sweetly as the *labouring man* (Ecc 5:12). His cares increase his fears, and both together make him uneasy. He is miserable in death. It is the greatest terror to him (vv. 20–21). *Terrors take hold of him as waters,* as if he were surrounded by flowing tides. He trembles to think of leaving this world, much more of moving to another. The storm of death may be said *to steal* (snatch) *him away in the night* (v. 20). He is said *to be carried away* (v. 21) and hurled out of his place as by a storm, by an east wind that is terrible, violent, and noisy. To godly people, death is an acceptable gust of wind to carry them to the heavenly country. But the evildoer is miserable after death. His soul falls under the just anger of God, *For God shall cast* (hurl) *upon him and not spare.* Those who will not be persuaded now to flee to the arms of divine grace, which are stretched out to receive them, will not be able to flee from the arms of divine wrath. And his memory falls under the just anger of the whole human race (v. 23): *Men shall clap their hands at him,* that is, they will be pleased at his demise.

CHAPTER 28

Here Job forgets his sores and sorrows and talks as a philosopher. The knowledge of the reasons of God's rule over the world is kept from us, and we must neither claim it nor reach after it. Zophar had wished that

God would show Job the secrets of wisdom *(11:6). No, Job says,* the secret things belong not to us, but things revealed *(Dt 29:29). And here he talks: 1. About worldly wealth, how diligently it is sought for by human beings, and what dangers they fall into to gain it (vv. 1–11). 2. About wisdom (v. 12). In general, its value is very great; it is of inestimable worth (vv. 13, 15–19). Its place is secret (vv. 14, 20–22). 3. In particular, there is a wisdom which is hidden in God (vv. 23–27), and there is a wisdom which is revealed to the human race (v. 28). Our inquiries into the former must be restrained, but those into the latter encouraged.*

Verses 1–11

Job shows here:

- How far human knowledge may go to dig into the depths of nature and seize its riches. But does it therefore follow that people may use that knowledge to understand why some evildoers prosper and others are punished? By no means. The caves of the earth may be explored, but not the counsels of heaven.
- How much effort worldly people take to gain riches. He describes the source of that silver that rich evildoers *heaped up* (27:16) and how it was obtained, to show what little reason they have to be proud of their wealth and to be showing it all off. Notice here:

1. The wealth of this world is hidden in the earth. The silver and the gold, which people refine later, are mined from it (v. 1). Iron and less valuable, but more useful, metals are *taken out of the earth* (v. 2) and are found there in plentiful supply, which lowers their price but is a great kindness to people, who could do much better without gold than without iron. In fact, *out of the earth comes bread,* that is, food, necessary to support life (v. 5). Our sustenance is taken from there to remind us of our own origin. We are from the earth. *Under it is turned up as it were fire:* precious stones, which sparkle as fire, and coal, which is fuel for the fire. The wisdom of the Creator has placed these things:

1.1. Out of our sight, to teach us not to set our eyes on them (Pr 23:5).

1.2. Under our feet, to teach us to trample on them with a holy contempt.

2. The wealth that is hidden in the earth cannot be obtained except by a great deal of difficulty:

2.1. It is hard to find wealth: only randomly is there *a vein* (mine) *for the silver* (v. 1).

2.2. When found, wealth is mined with difficulty. If one way fails, the miners must try another, till they have *searched out all perfection* and turned every stone to get what they want (v. 3). They must fight against underground water (vv. 4, 10–11) and force their way through rocks which are, as it were, the roots of the mountains (v. 9). God has made the mining of gold, silver, and precious stones so difficult:

2.2.1. To stir people to hard work. If valuable things were too easily obtained, people would never learn to make an effort.

2.2.2. To restrain a display of luxury. What is necessary is gained with comparatively little hard work from the surface of the earth, but what serves as decoration must be dug out with a great deal of effort from deep down. To be fed is cheap, but to be fine is expensive.

3. Although underground wealth is hard to obtain, people still want it. They *search out all perfection* (v. 3). They have ways and means, machines to dry up the water and carry it away when the water floods the mines and

threatens to drown the work (v. 4). They have pumps, pipes, and channels to clear their way, and when the obstacles have been removed, they tread *the path which no fowl knoweth* (vv. 7–8), unseen by the falcon's eye, which is piercing and quick sighted, and untrodden by the *lion's whelps,* which cross all the paths of the desert. They work their way through the rocks and mine under the mountains (v. 10). Those who dig in the mines put their lives at risk, for they are obliged to *bind* (dam up) *the floods from overflowing* (v. 11). They are in continual danger of being suffocated by harmful gases or crushed or buried alive by the fall of earth onto them. *Their eye sees every precious thing* (v. 10). With the prospect of taking hold of them, they make light of all these difficulties. "Go to the miners then, you sluggard in your religious faith. Consider their ways, and be wise" (compare Pr 6:6). Let their courage, diligence, and faithfulness in seeking the wealth that perishes shame us out of our laziness and faintheartedness in working for true riches.

Verses 12–19

Job here comes to speak of another, more valuable jewel, *wisdom and understanding* (v. 12), knowing and enjoying God and ourselves. There is more true knowledge, satisfaction, and happiness in sound theology, which shows us the way to the joys of heaven, than in science or mathematics, which explain how we can find a way to the depths of the earth. Two things cannot be discovered about this wisdom:

1. Its worth, for that cannot be reckoned. It is infinitely more valuable than all the riches in this world: *Man knows not the price thereof* (v. 13). That is, few people put a proper value on it. The value of an object depends on who is looking at it, as in Aesop's fable of the rooster who found a precious jewel while scratching in the farmyard and said he would rather have one grain of delicious barley than all the jewels in the world. People do not know the value of grace and so will take no effort to gain it. But the verse also has another sense: No one can possibly give anything of equal value in exchange for wisdom. Job enlarges on this in vv. 15–19, where he makes a list of the most valuable treasures of this world. Wisdom cannot be bought with these. It is a gift of *the Holy Spirit,* which *cannot be bought with money* (Ac 8:20). Spiritual gifts are given without money and without price (Isa 55:1), because they cannot be bought with money. It is *better to get wisdom than gold* (Pr 16:16). Gold belongs to another, wisdom to us; gold is for the body and time, wisdom for the soul and eternity.

2. Its place, for that cannot be found. *Where shall wisdom be found?* (v. 12). This is a question we should all ask. While most people ask, "Where can money be found?" we should ask, *Where may wisdom be found?* We are not to seek futile philosophy (Col 2:8) or godless politics, but true religious faith, for that is the only true wisdom. Job completely despairs of finding it anywhere but in God: *It is not found in* this *land of the living* (v. 13). We cannot reach a right understanding of God and his will, or of ourselves and our duty and our best interests, by reading any book but God's book, nor by consulting any people but the people of God. The corruption of human nature is such that no true wisdom is to be found with any except those who are born again and who, through grace, share in the divine nature. Ask the miners, and through them *the depth* (deep) *will say, It is not in me* (v. 14). Ask the mariners, and through them *the sea will say, It is not in me* (v. 14). It can never be gained by trading on the seas or diving into them. It can never be *sucked from the*

abundance of the seas or the treasures hidden in the sand (Dt 33:19).

Verses 20–28

There is a twofold wisdom, one *hidden in God*, which is secret and *belongs not to us*, the other made known by him and revealed to us, which *belongs to us and to our children* (Dt 29:29).

1. The knowledge of God's secret will, the will of his providence, is beyond our reach. It *belongs to the Lord our God* (Dt 29:29). To know what God will do later and the reasons for what he is doing now is the knowledge that Job speaks of first:

1.1. This knowledge is hidden from us. It is high; we cannot reach it (vv. 21–22): *It is hid from the eyes of all living*, even of philosophers, politicians, and saints; it is *kept close from the fowls of the air* (concealed even from the birds of the air), although their eyes see far away (39:29). Even those who soar to the highest and dizziest heights in their thinking, above the heads of other people, cannot claim to have this knowledge. "What fools we are," Job says, "to be fighting in the dark like this, to be arguing about what we do not understand!" The plumb line of human reason can never fathom the depths of divine counsels. Yet there is a world on the other side of death and the grave, and we will clearly see there what we are now in the dark about. When *the mystery of God shall be finished* (Rev 10:7), it will be laid open, and we will know as we are known (1Co 13:12). When the curtain of humanity is torn, and the intervening clouds are dispersed, we will know what God does, although we do not know now (Jn 13:7).

1.2. This knowledge is hidden in God, as the apostle Paul writes in Eph 3:9. People sometimes do what they cannot give a good reason for, but there is a reason in every aspect of the will of God. He knows both what he is doing and why he is doing it. Two reasons are given why God, and only he, must understand his own way:

1.2.1. Because all events are now directed by an all-seeing and almighty Providence (vv. 24–25). He who governs the world knows everything. One day's events, and one person's affairs, have such reference to, and such dependence on, another's, that only God, the One to whom all events and all affairs are open and laid bare, and who sees the whole at one complete and certain view, is a competent Judge of every part. He is also all-powerful. To prove this, Job mentions the winds and waters (v. 25). What is lighter than the wind? But God has ways of establishing its force. He both weighs and measures the waters of the sea and the rain, allotting the proportion of every tide and every shower. There is a great and constant communication between clouds and seas, the waters above the sky and those under it. Vapors go up, rain comes down, air is condensed into water, water evaporates into air, but the great God keeps an exact record of all the stock with which this trade is carried out for the public benefit. Now if Providence is so exact in these things, then much more will he be in dispensing frowns and favors, rewards and punishments, to people, according to the rules of his justice.

1.2.2. Because all events were planned and determined from eternity by his infallible knowledge and unchangeable decree (vv. 26–27). He settled the course of nature. Job mentions particularly a decree for the rain and a way for the thunder and lightning. God's purposes appointed both the general method and the particular uses of these strange actions, both their causes and their effects. Some think that in the first part of v. 27 Job is speaking of

wisdom as a person, and so they render it, "Then he saw her and showed her...."

2. The knowledge of God's revealed will is within our reach. It is on the same level as we are and will do us good (v. 28): *Unto man he said, Behold, the fear of the Lord, that is wisdom.* Let it not be said that when God hid his ways from human beings, it was because he begrudged them anything that would lead to their real happiness and satisfaction. He let them know as much as is necessary and fit for them as subjects, but they must not think they are qualified to advise him what to do. No less wisdom, according to Archbishop John Tillotson, than what made the world can thoroughly understand the order by which it is governed. But let people look on this as their wisdom: to fear the Lord and avoid evil. When God forbade Adam and Eve to eat from the tree of knowledge, he allowed them to eat from the tree of life, and this wisdom is that tree (Pr 2:6). We cannot reach true wisdom except by divine revelation. *The fear of the Lord, that is the wisdom* (v. 28). Pure and undefiled religion is to *fear the Lord and depart from evil* (Pr 3:7), which corresponds to God's description of Job (1:1). The *fear of the Lord* (v. 28) is the source and summary of all religion. There is a servile fear of God that springs from harsh thoughts of him, but this is the opposite of true religion (Mt 25:24). There is a selfish fear of God that springs from a terror of him, which may be a good step toward religious faith (Ac 9:5). But there is a childlike fear of God that springs from great and high thoughts of him, which is the life and soul of all true religious faith. Wherever this wisdom reigns in the heart, it will work itself out as a constant concern to *depart from evil* (Pr 16:6). This is essential to religious faith.

CHAPTER 29

Job here describes the height of the prosperity from which he has fallen and the depth of the adversity into which he has come. He does this to move the pity of his friends and to justify his own complaints. But then to avoid his friends' criticism of him, he makes a declaration of his own integrity. In this chapter he looks back to the days of his prosperity and shows: 1. What comfort he had in his house and family (vv. 1–6). 2. What honor he had in his country (vv. 7–10); what a large amount of good he did as a judge (vv. 11–17). 3. What prospect he had of the continuation of his comforts at home (vv. 18–20) and of his interests away from home (vv. 21–25).

Verses 1–6

Job begins here with a wish (v. 2): *O that I were as in months past!* how I long for the months gone by; and so he gives this account of his prosperity. "O that I might be restored to my former prosperous condition, and then the criticisms and reproaches of my friends would be properly silenced, even on their own principles, and set aside forever!" He wishes his spirit were as much encouraged in the service of God as it had been, and that he would have as much freedom and fellowship with him. This was *in the days of his youth* (v. 4), when he was in his prime. Two things made the past months pleasant to Job:

1. That he had comfort in his God. This was the main thing he rejoiced in during his prosperity, as its spring and sweetness, that he enjoyed the favor of God and the signs of that favor. They were *the days when God preserved me* (v. 2). *God's candle shone upon his head*, that is, God turned his face toward him. That guided him through his doubts, encouraged him in his griefs, supported him under

his burdens, and helped him through all his difficulties. *The secret of God was upon my tabernacle*, that is, God spoke freely with him, as one intimate friend with another. He knew God's mind and was not in the dark about it, as he recently had been. *The Almighty was yet with me. Now* he thought God had departed from him, but in those days he was *with him*, and that meant everything to him. If God's presence is with someone in their home, even if that home is only a cottage, it makes it both a castle and a palace.

2. That he had comfort in his family. Everything was pleasant there: he had both mouths for his food and food for his mouths; the lack of either is a great affliction. Job speaks very feelingly of this comfort now that he has been deprived of it. Yet we think wrongly if, when we have lost our children, we cannot comfort ourselves with the knowledge that even so, we have not lost our God. He had plentiful material wealth to support this numerous family (v. 6). His dairy abounded to such a degree that he could, if he had wanted to, *wash his steps with butter*, and his olive groves were so fruitful that it seemed as if the *rock poured him out rivers of oil*. He reckoned his wealth not by his silver and gold, which were to be stored away, but by his butter and oil, which were to be used, for what are possessions for but to make good use of them for ourselves and do good with them for others?

Verses 7–17

Here we see Job in a position of honor and power. Justice was administered at the gate, in the public square, in the places where people met and to which they all could have free access, so that everyone who wanted to could be a witness to everything that was said and done. Because Job was a judge, we are told here:

1. What a profound respect was shown to him, not only because of the honor of his position but also because of his personal merit. The people honored him and stood in awe of him (v. 8). *The young men*, who were perhaps conscious of something wrong in themselves, *hid themselves*, stepped aside, when he came by. Although *the aged* kept their ground, they would not keep their seats: they *arose and stood up* to show him respect. The chief men and nobles showed him great respect (vv. 9–10). When he came into court, *the princes* (chief men) *refrained talking, the nobles held their peace* (vv. 9–10), so that they might listen more diligently to what he said.

2. What a great deal of good he did in his position. Job respected himself not because of the honor of his family, the great possessions he had, and the attention that was given to him, but for his usefulness.

2.1. All who heard what he said, and saw how he put himself out for the public good with all the fatherly authority and tender affection a good lord has for his land and those who live on it, blessed him and spoke well of him (v. 11). Such was the blessing of the one who was dying (v. 13) and who by Job's actions was rescued from death.

2.2. If the poor were injured or oppressed, they could cry out to Job, and if he found the allegations of their requests true, he *delivered the poor that cried* (v. 12) and would not allow them to be trampled on. He was *a father to the poor*, not only a judge to protect them and see that they were not wronged, but also a father to provide for them and see that they were not in want, to advise and direct them. Those who were about to die he saved from dying, taking care of those who were sick, those who were outcasts, those who were falsely accused, and those who were in danger of being turned out of their houses. When widows were sighing in their grief and trembling for fear,

he made them sing for joy. Those who were for any reason at a loss Job helped suitably and promptly (v. 15): *I was eyes to the blind* and *feet to the lame*.

2.3. He devoted himself to administering justice (v. 14): *I put on righteousness and it clothed me*, that is, administering justice was like putting on his clothes. He always appeared in it, as in his clothing, and was never without it. *My judgment was as a robe and a diadem* (NIV: turban) (v. 14). If judges fulfill the duties of their position, that is an honor for them far beyond their fine clothes. If they do not conscientiously fulfill their responsibilities, then their robe and diadem, their gown and cap, are a disgrace. As clothes on a dead body will never make the person warm, so robes on evildoers will never make them honorable. *The cause which I knew not I searched out*. He diligently investigated matters of fact, listened patiently and impartially to both sides.

2.4. He respected himself for the restraint he put on the violence of proud evildoers (v. 17): *I broke the jaws of the wicked*. He does not say that he broke their necks. He did not take away their lives, but he broke their jaws, took away their power to cause trouble. Good judges must be like this: a terror and restraint to evildoers and a protection to the innocent. A judge on the bench needs to be as bold and brave as a commander on the battlefield.

Verses 18–25

1. Job's thoughts in his prosperity (v. 18): *Then I said, I shall die in my nest*. He saw no storm arising to shake his home, and so he concluded, *Tomorrow shall be as this day* (Isa 56:12). In the midst of his prosperity he thought about death, and the thought did not disturb him. But he also flattered himself with the vain hope that he would *multiply his days as the sand* (v. 18). He was thinking of the grains of sand on the seashore, but it would be better if we reckoned our days by the sand in the hourglass, which will soon run out.

2. The basis of these thoughts. He was aware of no physical illness in his body; his land was not under a mortgage or any other liability, nor was he aware of any underlying rot setting in. He was like a tree whose roots not only extended a long way, which kept the tree firm, so that it was in no danger of falling down, but also *spread out by the waters*, which fed it. Blessed with the richness of the earth, he thought he was blessed by the kind influences of heaven, for the *dew lay all* night on his branches. His *bow was renewed in his hand*, that is, his power to protect himself continually increased, so that he had little reason to fear the insults of the Sabeans and Chaldeans. Nor did he have any reason to distrust the loyalty of his friends. Surely nothing could be done against him when really nothing was done without him. He was consulted as an oracle (v. 21). When others were not listened to, everyone *gave ear* to him *and kept silence at his counsel*, knowing that as nothing could be said against it, so nothing need be added to it. And so, *after his words, they spoke not again* (v. 22). He had the hearts and affections of all his neighbors. Those whom he spoke to were considered honored, and they felt honored. His words fell like the showers of rain on them, and they waited for them as for the rain (vv. 22–23) "*If I laughed on them*, intending to show that I was pleased with them or that I wished to be pleasant with them, it was such a favor that *they believed it not* for joy," or because it was something rare to see this serious man smile. He *chose out their way*, he was their leader: he sat at the helm and steered for them. He *dwelt as a king in the army* (v. 25), giving orders which were not to be disputed. Not everyone who has the spirit of wisdom

has the spirit of government, but Job had both. Yet he also had the tenderness of a comforter. Our Lord Jesus is such a King as Job was, the poor man's King.

CHAPTER 30

It is a sad "But now" with which this chapter begins. 1. Job had held a position of great honor, but he had now fallen into disgrace; and he was as much vilified now, even by the lowliest, as he had been exalted by the greatest before (vv. 1–14). 2. He had received much inward comfort, but now he was a burden to himself (vv. 15–16) and overwhelmed by sorrow (vv. 28–31). He had long enjoyed good health, but now he was sick and in pain (vv. 17–19, 29–30). There was a time when he had an intimate friendship with God, but now his communication with heaven was cut off (vv. 20–22). He had promised himself a long life, but now he saw death at his door (v. 23). But two things brought him some relief: that his troubles would not follow him to the grave (v. 24) and that his conscience testified to him that in his prosperity he had sympathized with those who were in misery (v. 25).

Verses 1–14

Here Job complains about the great disgrace he has descended to from the heights of honor and reputation. He insists on two things as making his affliction even worse:

1. The lowliness of the people who insulted him. He was spurned by the lowliest and most contemptible people.

1.1. They were young, younger than he was (v. 1), *the youth* (v. 12), who ought to have behaved themselves respectfully toward him because of his age and importance.

1.2. Their fathers were so contemptible that such a person as Job would have disdained to take them into the lowest service in his house, such as looking after the sheep and accompanying the shepherds with sheep dogs (v. 1). Job himself, with all his patience and wisdom, could make nothing of them (v. 2). The young ones were not fit for work because they were so lazy: *Whereto might the strength of their hands profit me?* The old ones were not fit to be trusted with the smallest matters, for their *old age was perished*—they were in their second childhood.

1.3. They were extremely poor (v. 3). Their own laziness and wastefulness had brought them into difficulties, and nobody was eager to come forward and help them. And so they were forced to flee to the deserts both for shelter and for sustenance, and they were reduced to a sorry state indeed when they *cut up mallows by the bushes* (NIV: in the brush they gathered salt herb) and were glad to eat them for lack of proper food (v. 4). This needy world is full of Satan's poor.

1.4. *They were driven forth* (banished) *from among men* (v. 5). Idle people are a public nuisance, but it may be better to put such people into a home established to provide work for the unemployed poor than, as here, into a desert, which will punish them but never reform them. They were forced to live in *caves of the earth*, and *they brayed* like asses *among the bushes* (vv. 6–7). Mr. Broughton renders v. 7, "They groan among the trees and smart among the nettles"; they are stung and scratched where they hoped to find shelter and protection.

1.5. Such people as these were abusive to Job in revenge: when he, as a good judge, was in prosperity and power, he carried out laws which were in force against

vagabonds, rogues, and rough beggars, and these evildoers now remembered his judgments and held them against him. They also did it in triumph: they thought that in his distress he had now become like one of them.

2. The greatness of the insults that were directed at him. *I am their song and their byword.* They shunned him as a detestable object, hated him, and kept their distance from him (v. 10), as an ugly monster or as one suffering from an infectious illness. They tripped him up, set traps for him (v. 12), and kicked him, either in wrath or in jest. *They raise up against me the ways of their destruction* (v. 12), or as some understand this, "They threw on me the cause of their woe," that is, they put onto him the blame for their being driven out. It is common for criminals to hate the judges and laws by which they are punished. They misrepresented his former way of life, which is here called *marring his path* (v. 13). They considered him a tyrant because he acted justly toward them. Perhaps Job's friends based their unkind criticism of him (22:6–10) on the cries of these despicable people. They were fools in other things, but wise enough to cause trouble, and needed no help in plotting evil schemes. Some read it, "They hold my heaviness as a profit, though they are never the better." *They came upon me as a wide breaking in of waters*, when the dam is broken, or, "They came as soldiers come into a gaping breach which they have made in the wall of a besieged city, pouring in on me with the greatest fury." *They rolled themselves in the desolation* as people roll themselves in a soft and easy bed, and they rolled themselves on the ruins of his life with all the weight of their hatred.

3. All this contempt shown to him was caused by the troubles he was in (v. 11): *"Because he has loosed my cord*, because God has taken away the honor and power with which I was clothed (12:18), because he has afflicted me, therefore *they have let loose the bridle before me"* (v. 11), that is, "they have thrown off restraints and given themselves the liberty to say and do what they please against me." "Because God hath loosed *his* cord, has taken off his bridle of restraint from their hatred, they take away the bridle from me," that is, "they take no account of my authority and do not stand in awe of me." Those who today cry, *Hosanna*, may tomorrow cry, *Crucify.* But there is an honor which comes from God which, if we keep it secure, we will find does not change and cannot be lost.

Verses 15–31

This second part of Job's complaint is very bitter.

1. In general, it was a day of great suffering and sorrow:

1.1. Suffering seized him and surprised him. *The days of affliction have taken hold upon me.* They have gripped me; *they have arrested me*, as sheriffs arrest debtors. It surprised him (v. 27): *"The days of affliction prevented me,"* that is, "they confronted me when they came on me without giving me any prior warning. I did not make any provision for such an evil day."

1.2. He was in great sorrow because of it. His *bowels boiled* with grief *and rested not*, the churning inside him never stopped (v. 27). The sense of his adversities was continually and relentlessly preying on his mind and spirit. He *went mourning* from day to day, and such a cloud was constantly on his mind that he went, in effect, *without the sun*, blackened (v. 28). He was *a brother to dragons* (NIV: of jackals) *and owls* (v. 29), both in choosing solitude and withdrawal, as they do (Isa 34:13), and in making a fearful, hideous noise as they do.

2. The terror and trouble that seized his soul were the most painful parts of his adversity (vv. 15–16). In his

second discourse he complained of the *terrors of God setting themselves in array against him* (6:4). And still, whichever way he looked, they turned on him; whichever way he fled, they pursued him, pursued *his soul*. The soul is the main part of a human being, and so what pursues the soul, and threatens that, should be dreaded most of all. *My welfare* and dignity *pass away*, as suddenly, quickly, and irrecoverably *as a cloud* (v. 15). If he looked within, he found his spirit not only wounded, but even *poured out upon him*, ebbing away (v. 16).

3. His physical diseases went to all his bones (v. 17). It was like a sword in his bones, which *pierced him in the night season*. His *sinews took no rest*. Because of his pain, sleep departed from his eyes. *His bones were burnt with heat* (v. 30). He had a constant fever; he was full of boils. His *skin was black upon him* (v. 30). Some think it was this which bound him like a collar. He was *cast into the mire* (thrown into the mud) (v. 19), or "compared with mud," as some understand it: his body looked more like a heap of dirt than anything else.

4. What afflicted him most of all was that God seemed to be his enemy and to be fighting against him. "*I cry unto thee*, as one who is serious, *I stand up* and cry out, as one who is waiting for an answer, but you do not hear, *thou regardest not*, as far as I can see." What he says about God is one of the worst sentences Job ever spoke (v. 21): *Thou hast become cruel to me*, you turn on me ruthlessly. Job was unjust and ungrateful when he said this about him. He thought God was fighting against him and had stirred up his whole strength to ruin him: *With thy strong hand thou opposest thyself against me* (v. 21), like an enemy. He thought God triumphed over him (v. 22): *Thou liftest me up to the wind*, as a feather or the chaff which the wind plays with.

5. He expected now that God would soon destroy him completely: "*I know that thou wilt bring me*, with even more terror, *to death*, although I might have been brought there without all this trouble, for it is *the house appointed for all living*" (v. 23).

6. Two things made his trouble even worse. First, it had been a very great disappointment to his expectations (v. 26): "*When I looked for* good, for more good, or at least for the continuation of what I had, then evil came." All our worldly enjoyments are very uncertain. Second, it had been a very great change in his condition (v. 31): "*My harp is turned* to (tuned to) *mourning*, and my *organ* (flute) to the voice of those who weep." In his prosperity, Job had taken the *timbrel* (tambourine) and harp and had rejoiced at the sound of the flute (21:12).

7. In the midst of all this he comforts himself, but only a little. He foresees that death will bring all his adversities to an end (v. 24): although God now opposes him, Job says, "*he will not stretch out his hand to the grave*." And he reflects with satisfaction on the concern he always had for the adversities of others when he himself was at peace (v. 25): *Did not I weep for him that was in trouble?* His conscience testifies to him that he always sympathized with people in misery and that he did what he could to help them, and so he has reason to expect that both God and his friends will eventually pity him. "Did not my soul burn for the poor?" is how some read it, comparing this with the words of the apostle Paul (2Co 11:29), *Who is offended, and I burn not?*

CHAPTER 31

Here Job protests his integrity with particular examples, to clear himself of those crimes with which his friends

have falsely charged him. Job's friends have been detailed in declaring their charges against him, and so he responds in similar detail in his declaration, which seems to refer especially to what Eliphaz accused him of (22:6–9). The sins from which he here acquits himself are: 1. Lustfulness and sexual immorality in his heart (vv. 1–4). 2. Fraud and injustice in business (vv. 4–8). 3. Adultery (vv. 9–12). 4. Arrogance and harshness toward his servants (vv. 13–15). 5. A lack of mercy to the poor, the widows, and the fatherless (vv. 16–23). 6. Confidence in his worldly wealth (vv. 24–25). 7. Idolatry (vv. 26–28). 8. Revenge (vv. 29–31). 9. Neglect of poor strangers (v. 32). 10. Hypocrisy in concealing his own sins and cowardice in ignoring the sins of others (vv. 33–34). 11. Oppression and the violent invasion of other people's rights (vv. 38–40). And toward the end, he appeals to God's judgment about his integrity (vv. 35–37). In all this we may see, on the one hand, how the patriarchal age understood good and evil and what it condemned as sinful even in those ancient times, and on the other, a noble pattern of godliness and goodness for us to imitate.

Verses 1–8

The lusts of the flesh and the love of the world are two fatal rocks on which many have been shipwrecked. Job protests he was always careful to stand guard against these.

1. He stood on his guard against the lusts of the flesh (Gal 5:16). He kept himself pure not only from adultery, from defiling his neighbors' wives (v. 9), but also from all immorality with any women whatever. *I made a covenant with my eyes*, that is, "I watched and guarded against every possible opportunity of sin; *why then should I think upon a maid?*" that is, "by that means, through the grace of God, I kept myself from the very first step toward it." He would not so much as allow a lustful look. Those who want to keep their hearts pure must guard their eyes, which are both the outlets and inlets of immorality. He would not even allow an immoral thought. It was not for fear of shame among other people, even though that is to be considered (Pr 6:33), but for fear of the wrath and curse of God. Sexual immorality is a sin that forfeits all good and excludes us from the hope of it (v. 2): *What portion of God is there from above*, what is our lot from God above? *Is not destruction*, a quick and sure destruction, *to those wicked* people, *and a strange punishment to the workers of* this *iniquity?* Is there not ruin for this kind of evildoer, disaster for those who do this kind of wrong? Some read it, "Is there not separation for the workers of iniquity?" *This is* the sinfulness of the sin: that it separates the mind from God (Eph 4:18–19). *Doth not he see my ways?* (v. 4). O God! thou hast searched me and known me (Ps 139:1). God sees what rules we walk by, what company we walk with, what destination we walk toward, and therefore what ways we walk in. Job acknowledges, He *counts all my steps* (v. 4), all my false steps in my duty and all my wrong steps into the way of sin. God takes a more exact notice of us than we do of ourselves, for who of us has ever counted their own steps? But God counts them.

2. He stood on his guard against the love of the world and carefully avoided all sinful means of gaining wealth. He dreaded all forbidden profit as much as all forbidden pleasure. He never *walked with vanity* (v. 5), that is, he had never dared tell a lie to gain a good bargain. He never rushed to become rich by using deceitful means, but always acted carefully so as to avoid doing something unjust through any lack of thought. His *steps never turned*

out of the way of justice or fair dealing; he never deviated from that (v. 7). His heart did not *walk after* (was not led by) *his eyes* (v. 7), that is, he did not covet what he saw that belonged to another, nor did he wish it were his own. Covetousness is called the *lust of the eye* (1Jn 2:16). *No blot had cleaved to his hands*, his hands had not been defiled (v. 7), that is, he could not be accused either of gaining anything dishonestly or of keeping what belonged to another. Injustice is a stain both on the possessions gained by it and on the owner; it spoils the beauty of both. Job confirms this declaration of his integrity with a further declaration that he is willing to have his goods searched (v. 6): *Let me be weighed in an even balance* (on honest scales), that is, "Let what I have gained be investigated, and it will be found to have a just weight." Furthermore, he is willing to forfeit the whole cargo if any prohibited or contraband goods are found in it, anything but what he has gained honestly (v. 8): "*Let me sow, and let another eat,*" which was already agreed to be the fate of oppressors (5:5), "and *let my offspring*, all the trees that I have planted, *be rooted out.*" He still knows he is innocent, and he will risk all he has left on the outcome of the test.

Verses 9 – 15

We have here two more examples of Job's integrity:

1. He had a very great loathing for the sin of adultery. He was careful not to threaten any wrong to his neighbor's marriage. He did not even covet his neighbor's wife, for *his heart was not deceived by a woman*. He never *laid wait* (lurked) *at his neighbour's door* (v. 9) to gain an opportunity to defile his wife in her husband's absence. "If I am guilty of that shameful sin," he says, "*Let my wife grind to another*"—"may she be a slave," according to some, "a prostitute," according to others. God often punishes the sins of one with the sin of another, the adultery of the husband with the adultery of the wife. Those who are not just and faithful to their relatives must not think it strange if their relatives are unjust and unfaithful to them. *For it is an iniquity to be punished by the judges* (v. 11). Adultery is a crime which the civil magistrate should take notice of and punish. *It is a fire.* Lust is a fire in the soul: those who give in to it are said to burn.

2. He had a very great tenderness toward his servants and ruled them compassionately. He did not *despise the cause of his manservant* or of his *maidservant, when they contended with him.* If they had offended him or if someone had brought him a complaint about them, or if, on the other hand, they complained of any hardship he had put on them, he allowed them to tell their story, and he put right their grievances to the extent that they appeared to be in the right. He considered, "If I should be imperious and severe with my servants, *what then shall I do when God riseth up,* what shall I do when God confronts me?" (v. 14). When he was tempted to be harsh with his servants, this thought came very promptly into his mind: "*Did not he that made me in the womb make him?* I am a creature as much as they are, and my being came from and is dependent on him as much as theirs. My servants share the same nature as I do, and we are all the work of the same hand."

Verses 16 – 23

Eliphaz had especially accused Job of being unmerciful toward the poor (22:6–9). It appears from Job's protest that it was completely false and without foundation. Notice here:

1. He had always been compassionate to the poor and concerned for them, especially the widows and fatherless, and was always ready to grant their desires and fulfill their

expectations (v. 16). If he simply noticed from a widow's mournful, craving look that she expected gifts from him, he had enough compassion to give it, and he *never caused the eyes of the widow to fail.* He was a father to the fatherless, took care of orphans. He provided good food for them; they ate the same food as he did (v. 17). They did not eat up after him the leftover crumbs that had fallen from his table, but ate the best dishes on his table with him. He took particular care to clothe those who were without clothing, which would have been more expensive to him than giving them food (v. 19). If Job knew of any people who were in such distress, he deliberately had good, warm, strong clothes made for them from *the fleece of his sheep* (v. 20). He never so much as *lifted up his hand against the fatherless* (v. 21). He never used his power to crush those who stood in his way, even though he *saw his help in the gate,* that is, though he had enough influence, both with the people and the judges, both to enable him to get as much out of them as possible and to support him when he had done it.

2. The curse with which he confirms this declaration (v. 22): "If I have been oppressive toward the poor, *let my arm fall from my shoulder blade and my arm be broken from the bone,*" that is, "may the flesh rot off from the bone and may one bone become out of joint and broken off from another."

3. The principles by which Job was restrained from all acts of unkindness and lack of mercy. "*Destruction from God was a terror to me* whenever I was tempted to commit this sin, and *by reason of his highness* (for fear of his splendor) *I could not endure* the thought of making him my enemy." He thought of the infinite distance between him and God. Those who oppress the poor and pervert the course of justice forget that *he who is higher than the highest regardeth,* and *there is a higher than they,* who is able to deal with them (Ecc 5:8), but Job considered this.

Verses 24 – 32

In these verses we have four further articles of Job's declaration, which not only assure us about what he was like and did, but also teach us what we should be like and do:

1. He declares that he never set his heart on the wealth of this world. Job's *wealth was great,* and he *had gotten much* (v. 25), yet he put no great confidence in it: he did not *make gold his hope* (v. 24). It is hard to have riches and not to trust in them, and it is this which makes it so difficult for *a rich man to enter into the kingdom of God* (Mt 19:23; Mk 10:23).

2. He declares that he never gave to the creation the worship and glory which are due only to God; he was never guilty of idolatry (vv. 26–28). He not only never bowed the knee to Baal (1Ki 19:18)—some think Baal was intended to represent the sun, and so if he never fell down and worshiped the sun, then he also did not bow the knee to Baal—but also kept his eye, heart, and lips pure from this sin. This was his covenant: that whenever he looked at the lights of heaven, he would by faith look through them and beyond them to the Father of lights (Jas 1:17). He did not give them the least act of adoration: *His mouth did not kiss his hand* (v. 27), which, it is likely, was a ceremony then commonly used even by some who would still not wish to be thought idolaters. In giving divine honors to the sun and moon, they could not reach out to kiss them, but to show their goodwill they kissed their hand, thus revering as their masters those things which God has made servants to this lower world, to give us our light. He looked on it as an insult to the civil magistrate: it *were*

an iniquity to be punished by the judge, as a public nuisance. He looked on it as an even greater insult to the God of heaven, and nothing less than high treason against his crown and dignity. Idolatry is, in effect, atheism.

3. He declares that, far from causing or planning trouble for anyone, he has neither desired nor delighted in the hurt of his worst enemy. He did not even rejoice when any trouble happened to them (v. 29). He did not even wish in his own mind that evil might come to them (v. 30). He was very strongly urged to take revenge, but nevertheless he kept himself clear from it (v. 31): The men of his tabernacle, the domestic servants in his household and those around him, were enraged at Job's enemy: "O that we had of his flesh! Our master is satisfied to forgive him, but we cannot be so satisfied."

4. He declares that he was never unkind or inhospitable to strangers (v. 32): The stranger lodged not in the street. Job's door was always open to travelers, so that he could see who passed by and invite them in, as Abraham did (Ge 18:1).

Verses 33–40

Job's declaration that he was innocent of three more sins:

1. Of pretense and hypocrisy. The general crime of which his friends accused him was that under the cloak of a profession of religious faith he had maintained secret habits of sin; in reality he was as bad as other people, they said, but he was skillful enough to hide it. Zophar suggested (20:12) that he hid his iniquity under his tongue. "No," Job says, "I have never done so (v. 33); I never covered my transgression as Adam, never tried to lessen my sin by making frivolous excuses. I have never hid my iniquity in my bosom."

2. Of cowardice and fear. He points to his courage in doing good as evidence of his sincerity in it (v. 34): Did I fear a great multitude, that I kept silence? No; everyone who knew Job knew he was a person with a fearless determination to do good, and that he did not fear the face of crowds, but set his face like flint (Isa 50:7). He did not, he dared not, keep silent when he knew he had to speak up in an honest cause. Nor did he stay indoors when he knew he had to go out and do good. He placed no value on the shouts of the crowd, he did not fear what the mob was thinking, and he did not set great store by the threats of those in power: The contempt of families never terrified him.

3. Of oppression and violence, and doing wrong to his poor neighbors. Notice here:

3.1. What his declaration is—that the property that was his he had gained and used honestly, so that his land could not cry out against him nor the furrows thereof complain (v. 38), as they do against those who gain possession of land by fraud and extortion (Hab 2:9–11). He could safely say two things about his property. First, he never ate the fruits of it without money (v. 39). What he bought, he had paid for. The workers he employed duly received their pay in wages. Second, he never brought about the death of the owners of property he wanted to buy; he never obtained property, as Ahab gained Naboth's vineyard, by killing the heir and seizing the inheritance (compare Mt 21:38). Nor did he ever starve those who rented his lands or kill them by driving hard bargains with them or treating them harshly.

3.2. How he confirms his declaration, with a suitable oath (v. 40): "If I have gained my estate unjustly, let thistles grow instead of wheat, the worst weeds instead of the best grains." Toward the end of his declaration, Job

appeals to the judgment seat of God concerning the truth of what he is saying (vv. 35–37): O that he would hear me, even that the Almighty would answer me!

3.2.1. A trial is moved for. "O that one," anyone, would hear me." An upright heart does not fear being scrutinized. The one with honest motives wishes there were a window into their inner self, so that everyone might see the intentions of their heart. But an upright heart particularly wants to see everything determined by the judgment of God, which we are sure is according to the truth (Ro 2:2).

3.2.2. The prosecutor is called, and the plaintiff is summoned and ordered to read out his complaint against the prisoner: "O that my adversary had written a book (v. 35): that my friends, who accuse me of hypocrisy, would set down their charge in writing, so that it might be made certain and we might argue about it." If he was shown to have been guilty of any sin, which he was not yet aware of, he would be glad to know about it, so that he might repent of it and receive pardon for it. If he was falsely accused, he did not doubt he would be able to disprove the allegations.

3.2.3. The defendant is ready to appear and give his accusers all the justice they want. He will declare unto them the number of his steps (v. 37). He will reveal to them the story of his life. He is so confident of his integrity that he will go near to him as a prince to be crowned rather than as a prisoner to be tried. Near to him: near his accuser to listen to the charge and near his judge to listen to the judgment. He has now said all he will say in answer to his friends. He will later say something by way of self-reproach and self-condemnation (40:4–5; 42:2–6), but here he ends what he has to say by way of self-defense and self-vindication.

CHAPTER 32

The stage is clear. The time is right for a moderator to intervene, and Elihu is the one. In this chapter we have: 1. An account of him, his parentage, his presence in this argument, and his thoughts about it (vv. 1–5). 2. The defense he made of his boldly undertaking to speak about a matter which had been so fully and learnedly argued by those older than he. He pleaded that: 2.1. Although he did not have the experience of one who is old, he still had the understanding of one who is human (vv. 6–10). 2.2. He had patiently listened to all they had had to say (vv. 11–13). 2.3. He had something new to offer (vv. 14–17). 2.4. His mind was full of words, and it would be a relief for him to express them (vv. 18–20). 2.5. He was determined to speak impartially (vv. 21–22). And he spoke so well that Job made no reply to him, and God did not rebuke him.

Verses 1–5

When the ones who were arguing were old men, as a rebuke to them for their undignified anger, a young man was raised up to be the moderator. We have here:

1. The reason why Job's three friends were silent. They ceased to answer him and allowed him to have his say because he was righteous in his own eyes (v. 1). It was futile to argue with someone who was so opinionated (v. 1). Yet they had not evaluated Job fairly: he really was righteous before God, not merely righteous in his own eyes.

2. The reasons why Elihu, the fourth one, now spoke up. Elihu means "My God is he." He is said to be a Buzite, descended from Buz, Nahor's second son (Ge 22:21), and of the kindred of Ram, that is, "Aram," according to

some, from whom the Arameans or Syrians descended and were named (Ge 22:21). "Of the kindred of Abram," says the Aramaic paraphrase, supposing him to be first called *Ram*, "high," then *Abram*, "a high father," and lastly *Abraham*, "the high father of many."

2.1. Elihu spoke because he was angry and thought he had good reason to be. He was angry with Job because he thought Job had not spoken as reverently of God as he should have, and that was true (v. 2): *He justified himself more than God*, that is, he was more careful and took more effort to clear himself from the implication that he was unrighteous because he had been afflicted than to clear God from the accusation that he was unrighteous in afflicting him. Elihu acknowledged Job to be a good man, but he knew that it is too great a compliment to our friends not to tell them their faults. He was angry with Job's friends, on the other hand, because he thought they had not behaved so kindly toward Job as they should have (v. 3): *They had found no answer, and yet had condemned Job.* When a quarrel is carried on to the extent that this one was, there is almost always fault on both sides. Elihu, as was right for a moderator, took neither side.

2.2. He spoke because he thought that it was time to speak. Elihu observed Job and patiently listened to Job's speeches, until the words of Job were ended (31:40).

Verses 6–14

Elihu here appears to have been:

1. A man of great modesty and humility. "*I am young, and therefore I was afraid, and durst* (dared) *not show you my opinion*, for fear I should either prove mistaken or do what was unbecoming for me." We should be quick to hear the opinions of others and slow to speak our own (Jas 1:19), especially when we go against the judgment of those whom, on the basis of their learning and godliness, we justly respect. *I said, Days* (age) *should speak.* Age and experience give a person a great advantage in evaluating matters, both by providing them with much more food for thought and by maturing their faculties. It is good *lodging with an old disciple* (Ac 21:16; Tit 2:4). Elihu's modesty appeared in the patient attention he gave to what his seniors said (vv. 11–12). He gave them diligent and careful attention. Although they often needed to search for what to say and consider how to say it, although they kept on pausing and hesitating, he listened to their reasons. We must often be willing to listen to what we do not like, or else we cannot test all things (1Th 5:21). Those who have listened may speak, and those who have learned may teach.

2. A man of great sense and courage, and one who knew when and how to speak as well as when and how to remain silent (Ecc 3:7). Although he had so much respect for his friends as not to interrupt them by his speaking, he still had so much regard for truth and justice—his better friends—as not to betray them by his silence. He boldly pleads:

2.1. That human beings are rational creatures and so have some insight and should be allowed to speak freely in turn. He means the same as Job—*But I have understanding as well as you* (12:3)—when he says (v. 8), *But there is a spirit in man*, but he expresses it a little more modestly, saying that one person has as much understanding as another, and no one can pretend to have a monopoly of reason. The soul is a spirit, neither material itself nor dependent on matter. It is an understanding spirit and is able to discover and receive truth, to think about and reason with it, and to direct others and to render judgment accordingly. This understanding spirit is in every human

being; it is the light *that lighteth every man* (Jn 1:9). It is the inspiration of the Almighty that gives us this understanding spirit.

2.2. That those who are advanced above others in grandness and seriousness do not always go beyond them proportionately in knowledge and wisdom (v. 9): *Great men are not always wise*; it is unfortunate that they are not, for then they would never do harm with their greatness and would do so much more good with their wisdom. *The aged do not* always *understand judgment*, do not always understand what is right; even *they* may be mistaken, and they must not take it as an insult if they are contradicted, but rather take it as a kindness that they are being taught by younger people: *Therefore I said, hearken to me* (v. 10). Those who have good eyesight can see further on level ground than those who are shortsighted can see from the top of the highest mountain. *Better is a poor and wise child than an old and foolish king* (Ecc 4:13).

2.3. That it is necessary for something to be said to set this argument in its true light. "I must speak, *lest you should say, We have found out wisdom*, I must speak so that you will not think that your argument against Job is conclusive and that he cannot be convinced and humbled by any other argument except this of yours: *that God casteth him down and not man*, that his extraordinary suffering shows that God is his enemy and that he is therefore certainly an evildoer. I must show you that this is a false hypothesis and that Job may be convinced of his hypocrisy without holding to that hypothesis."

2.4. That he has something new to offer. He will not reply to Job's declarations of his integrity, but will allow the truth of them, and so he does not intervene as his enemy: *He hath not directed his words against me* (v. 14). He will not repeat their arguments or make us of their principles: "*Neither will I answer him with your speeches* (arguments) (v. 14). Not with the same words—for if I only said what has already been said, I might justly be silenced as being rude—nor in the same way. I do not want to be guilty myself of that perversity toward him which I dislike in you."

Verses 15–22

Three things justify Elihu in adding his thoughts on this subject which had already been so thoroughly discussed by such learned debaters:

1. The stage was clear, and he was not interrupting any of the speakers on either side: *They were amazed* (dismayed) (v. 15); *they stood still, and answered no more* (v. 16). And so *I said* (v. 17), "*I will answer also my part.* The judgment is the Lord's, and it must be determined by him; he alone knows who is right and who is wrong. But since you each have your own opinion, I will also give mine, and let it be received along with the rest."

2. He was uneasy, and even in pain, in his desire to be unburdened of his thoughts on this matter. "*I am full of matter* (full of words) (v. 18), having carefully listened to all that has been said up to now and having thought about it myself. *The spirit within me* (v. 18) not only teaches me what to say, but also compels me to say it, so that if I do not give expression, I will *burst like bottles of new wine* when it is fermenting (v. 19). *I will speak, that I may be refreshed* (v. 20), not only so that I may be relieved of the pain of bottling up my thoughts, but also so that I may have the pleasure of trying, according to my place and abilities, to do good."

3. He was determined to speak, with sincerity, what he thought was true, not what he thought would please others (vv. 21–22): "*Let me not accept any man's person*, as

biased judges do, who aim to make themselves rich rather than to administer justice. I am determined not to flatter anyone." He who made us hates all pretense and flattery, and he will soon *put lying lips to silence* (Ps 31:18) and *cut off flattering lips* (Ps 12:3).

CHAPTER 33

Elihu's speech here does not disappoint the expectations which his introduction raised. It is substantial, vibrant, and very much to the point. 1. He requests Job's favorable acceptance of what he is about to say (vv. 1–7). 2. In God's name, he brings an action against Job for words he spoke in the heat of the argument which reflected on God as dealing harshly with him (vv. 8–11); he tries to convince him of his fault and foolishness in this by showing him God's sovereign rule over humanity (vv. 12–13). 3. He also shows him the care God takes of human beings when he puts physical afflictions on them (v. 14). Job has sometimes complained of frightening dreams (7:14). "Why," Elihu says, "God sometimes cautions and instructs people by such dreams" (vv. 15–18). 4. Job has complained especially about his sicknesses and pains, and as for these, Elihu shows in detail that, far from being signs of God's wrath, as Job takes them, or evidence of Job's hypocrisy, as his friends take them, they are really wise and gracious ways that divine grace uses to help him come to know God more and to bring about patience, a deeper experience, and hope (vv. 19–30). 5. And lastly, he concludes with a request to Job either to answer him or to allow him to continue (vv. 31–33).

Verses 1–7

Elihu here uses several arguments to persuade Job to receive the instructions he is now about to give him. Let Job consider that Elihu does not join with his three friends against him. In the previous chapter he declared his dislike of their ways, rejected their hypothesis, and completely set aside the method they adopted in order to heal Job. *"Wherefore, Job, I pray thee, hear my speech* (v. 1). *I am trying a new way; therefore hearken to all my words."* Furthermore, he intends to take the matter seriously: he *opened his mouth* (v. 2), with deliberation and intention. And he will speak as he thinks: *"My words shall be of the uprightness of my heart,* the sincere product of my convictions and feelings." What he says will be simple, and not difficult or obscure: my *lips shall utter knowledge clearly* (v. 3). He will make the best use he can of the reason and understanding God has given him. He acknowledges himself unfit to engage in an argument with his elders, but he wants them not to despise his youth (1Ti 4:12). He would be very willing to hear what Job can raise as an objection against what he has to say (v. 5): *"If thou canst, answer me."* He reminds Job that he has often wished for a person who would appear for God, with whom he could be free to argue and to whom he could refer the matter as arbitrator, and he tells Job that he will be such a person (v. 6): "I am, according *to thy wish, in God's stead."* Yet he is not an unequal match for Job: *"I also am formed out of the clay* (v. 6), I also as well as you." In urging God not to be harsh toward him, Job has given the reason (10:9), *Remember that thou hast made me as the clay.* "*I,*" Elihu says, "am *formed out of the clay* as well as you," or as some read it, "formed of the same clay." *My terror shall not make thee afraid.* If we want to rightly persuade people, it must be by reason, not by terror, by thoughtful arguments, not by a heavy hand.

Verses 8–13

In these verses:

1. Elihu accuses Job in detail of some expressions that have come from him, dishonoring the justice and goodness of God in his dealings with him. *"Thou hast spoken it in mine hearing* and in the hearing of all this company." When we hear anything said that tends to dishonor God, we should publicly bear testimony against it. What is said wrongly in our hearing we should be concerned to rebuke, for *you are my witnesses, saith the Lord* (Isa 43:12), to confront the person who dishonors God. First, Job has presented himself as innocent (v. 9): *I am clean without transgression.* Job has not said this in so many words; he has acknowledged he has sinned and is impure before God. But he has indeed said, *Thou knowest that I am not wicked* (10:7), *my righteousness I hold fast* (27:6). Elihu did not deal fairly in accusing Job of saying he was pure and innocent from all transgression, since Job had only pleaded that he was upright and innocent from great transgressions. Second, Job has presented God as harsh in noting what he has done wrong (vv. 10–11), as if God had sought opportunity to pick quarrels with him. *He findeth occasions against me.*

2. Elihu tries to convince him that he has spoken wrongly by speaking in this way, and that he should humble himself before God for it and withdraw this complaint with repentance (v. 12): *Behold, in this thou art not just.* Notice the difference between the charge which Elihu brought against Job and what was brought against him by his other friends: they would not acknowledge he was just at all, but Elihu only says, "In saying this, you are not just." Job himself said a great deal concerning the greatness of God, his irresistible power and incontrovertible sovereignty, his awesome majesty and unsearchable vastness; and he had said it very well. "Now," Elihu says, "only consider what you yourself have said about the greatness of God, and apply it to yourself. If he is greater than human beings, he is greater than you, and you will have enough reason to repent of these ill-natured reflections on him and tremble to think of your own presumption." There is enough in this one plain truth, *that God is greater than man* (v. 12), to forever silence all our complaints about his providence and our objections to his dealings with us. He is not only more wise and powerful than we, but also more holy, just, and good, for these are the transcendent, glorious, and magnificent qualities of his divine nature. God is greater than human beings in these ways, and so it is absurd and unreasonable to find fault with him. God is not accountable to us (v. 13): *Why dost thou strive against him?* It is unreasonable for us weak, foolish, sinful creatures to argue or contend with a God of infinite wisdom, power, and goodness. Some read it, "He gives not account of all his matters"; he reveals as much as he thinks fit for us to know, as follows (v. 14).

Verses 14–18

Job had complained that God had kept him completely in the dark about the meaning of his dealings with him, and he therefore concluded that God was dealing with him as his enemy. "No," Elihu says, "he is speaking to you, but you do not perceive him. The fault is therefore yours, not his. He intends good for you even in those ways which you interpret harshly." Notice in general:

- What a friend God is to our well-being: *He speaketh to us once, yea, twice* (v. 14). When one warning is neglected, he gives another.

• What enemies we are to our own well-being: *Man perceives it not* (v. 14). None of us is aware that it is the voice of God. We stop up our ears (Zec 7:11; Ac 7:57), cut ourselves off from God, and reject the counsel of God. God teaches and warns people by their own consciences. Notice:

1. The right time and opportunity for these warnings (v. 15): *In a dream, in slumberings upon the bed,* when people have withdrawn from the world and all its busyness and work. He made known his mind to the prophets by visions and dreams (Nu 12:6). When he stirred up conscience, his usual deputy, in the soul of a person to do its work, he took either that opportunity which arose when deep sleep had come on them — for although dreams mostly come from imagination, some may come from conscience — or that which arose during their *slumberings,* those times between sleeping and waking, when they reflect at night on what has happened in the past day or think in the morning about what is to happen in the coming day. Then is the right time for their hearts to rebuke them for what they have done wrong and to guide them as to what they should do.

2. The power and force with which those warnings come (v. 16). *Then he opens the ears of men,* which before were closed. He opens their hearts, as he opened Lydia's (Ac 16:14), and so he opens their ears. He *sealeth their instruction* (v. 16), that is, the instruction that is intended for them and is suited for them. He makes their souls receive the deep and lasting impression of his teaching, as the wax receives the deep and lasting impression of the seal.

3. The purposes of these warnings that are sent:

3.1. To keep people from sin, especially the sin of pride (v. 17): *that he may withdraw man from his purpose,* that is, turn people away from wrong. Many people have been stopped in their tracks from pursuing sin by the timely restraints of their own conscience, saying, *Do not this abominable thing which the Lord hates* (Jer 44:4). God especially uses these warnings to *hide pride from man,* to keep people from pride (v. 17). Some read it that God sends these messages in order to "take away pride from people," to pluck out that root of bitterness (Dt 29:18; Heb 12:15) which is the cause of so much sin.

3.2. To keep people from ruin (v. 18). When God speaks by the warnings of conscience to turn them away from sin, he *keeps back* their souls *from the pit,* so that sin will not destroy them. What a mercy it is to be under the restraints of an awakened conscience. Faithful are the wounds, and kind is the discipline, of that friend (Pr 27:6).

Verses 19–28

God speaks a second time, tries another way to convince and reclaim sinners, and that is by providences — both those that afflict and those that are merciful (and so in providence itself he speaks twice) — and by the timely instructions of good ministers. Job complained much about his illnesses and concluded from them that God was angry with him, but Elihu shows that God often afflicts the body in love, and with gracious intentions for the good of the soul. This part of Elihu's speech will be of great use to us to help us learn from sickness, by which God speaks to people. Here is:

1. The results sickness brings (vv. 19–21) when God sends it by his commission.

1.1. The sick man is full of pain all over his body (v. 19): *He is chastened with pain upon his bed.* Pain and illness turn a soft bed into a thorny bed. It is frequently true that the stronger the patient is, the more intense the pain is. It is not the suffering of flesh that is complained about, but the aching of bones. It is an inward, rooted pain, and not only the bones of one limb, but *the multitude of his bones* (v. 19) are disciplined in this way. Yet by the grace of God, the pain of the body is often used to do good to the soul.

1.2. He has completely lost his appetite, the common effect of sickness (v. 20): *His life abhorreth bread,* the most necessary food.

1.3. He has become a complete skeleton, nothing but skin and bones (v. 21).

1.4. *His soul draws near to the grave,* and everyone around him — and the patient himself — thinks he is dying. The messengers of death, here called *the destroyers,* are ready to seize him.

2. Provision is made for the patient's guidance so that when God speaks in this way to him, he may be heard and understood (v. 23). The patient is fortunate *if there be a messenger* (an angel) *with him, an interpreter* (a mediator) to explain God's providence and help him understand its meaning, *a man of wisdom* (Mic 6:9) who knows the voice of the rod of discipline and its interpretation. The advice and help of a good minister are as necessary and timely, and should be as acceptable, in sickness as those of a good doctor, especially if the minister is skilled in explaining and learning from providence. Their work at such a time is *to show his uprightness* (v. 23), that is, to show God's uprightness to him, to show that God is afflicting him in faithfulness. If it appears that the patient is truly godly, the interpreter will not do as Job's friends did and make it his business to prove that the patient is a hypocrite because he is afflicted, but will show the patient's own uprightness, despite his suffering, so that he may be put at rest.

3. God graciously accepts the patient upon his repentance (v. 24). Wherever God finds a gracious heart, he will be found to be a gracious God, and:

3.1. He will give a gracious order for the patient's discharge from that death which is the wages of sin (Ro 6:23).

3.2. He will give a gracious reason for this order: *I have found a ransom* (v. 24), or sacrifice of atonement; Jesus Christ is that ransom; Elihu calls him a ransom, and Job has called him his Redeemer (19:25), for he is both the purchaser and the price, the priest and the sacrifice. God glories in what has been found: "I have found the ransom; I, even I, am the One who has done it" (Isa 51:12).

4. The patient recovers. When he repents, notice what a blessed change takes place:

4.1. His body recovers health (v. 25). This is not always the result of a sick person's repentance and return to God, but it sometimes is, and recovery from sickness is a true mercy when it arises from the forgiveness of sin. Persuade the patient to claim the ransom, Elihu says, and then *his flesh shall be fresher than* (renewed like) *a child's* (v. 25), and there will be nothing left of the illness; *he shall return to the days of his youth* (v. 25), to his former good looks and strength.

4.2. His soul regains peace (v. 26). Having repented, he has been bringing requests to God, and so he has learned to pray. And when he prays, his prayers are accepted. All those who truly repent have greater joy at the return of God's favor than at any example whatsoever of prosperity or pleasure (Ps 4:6–7).

5. The general rule which God will go by in dealing with people is inferred from this example (vv. 27–28). As sick people who submit to God are restored, so all others who truly repent of their sins will also find mercy with God. Do we want to know the nature of sin and its evil?

It is the perversion of what is right; it is most unjust and unreasonable; it is the rebellion of the creation against the Creator, the usurped rule of the flesh over the spirit. Do we want to know what is to be gained by sin? *It profiteth us not* (v. 27). What is repentance, and why should we repent? We must confess the fact of sin—*I have sinned*; we must confess the error of our sin, its iniquity and dishonesty—*I have perverted that which was right* (v. 27); and we must confess the foolishness of sin—"I have been so foolish and ignorant, for *it profited me not* (v. 27)." God looks on sinners with his compassion, wanting to hear this from them, for he takes no pleasure in their destruction. If anyone humbles himself in this way, he will have the benefit of everlasting life and joy: *His life shall see the light* (v. 28), that is, all good, in the vision and fullness of God.

Verses 29–33

Elihu briefly sums up what he has said, showing that God's great and gracious intention, in all the ways of providence toward people, is to save them from being miserable forever and to make them happy forever (vv. 29–30). He deals with them by their conscience, by providences, by ministers, by mercies, and by suffering. He makes them ill, and he makes them well again. All providences are to be looked on as God's activities with people, his strivings with people. Why does he take all this effort with man? It *is to bring back his soul from the pit* (v. 30). Job is welcome to make what objections he can (v. 32): *If thou hast any thing to say* for yourself, to vindicate yourself, *answer me. Speak, for I desire to justify thee.* Yet Elihu also lets him know that he has something more to say, which he wants him to pay patient attention to (v. 33): *Hold thy peace, and I will teach thee wisdom.*

CHAPTER 34

Elihu probably paused for a while to see if Job had anything to say, but because Job sat silently, Elihu proceeded. 1. He asks not only for the attention but also for the help of the company gathered (vv. 1–4, 16); he charges Job with some more expressions that have come from him (vv. 5–9). 2. He undertakes to persuade him that he has spoken wrongly, by showing very fully: 2.1. God's incontrovertible justice (vv. 10–12, 17–19, 23). 2.2. His sovereign rule (vv. 13–15). 2.3. His almighty power (vv. 20, 24). 2.4. His omniscience (vv. 21–22, 25). 2.5. His severity against sinners (vv. 26–28). 2.6. His overruling providence (vv. 29–30). 3. He instructs him in what he should say (vv. 31–32). And then, lastly, he leaves the matter to Job's own conscience and concludes with a sharp rebuke for his discontent (vv. 33–37). Job not only bore all this patiently but also accepted it kindly, because whereas his other friends had accused him of things from which his own conscience acquitted him, Elihu charged him only with that for which probably his own heart now on reflection began to condemn him.

Verses 1–9

Here:

1. Elihu addresses himself to those who are listening, and he tries to gain their goodwill and attention.

1.1. He calls them *wise men*, those who *have knowledge* (v. 2). It is good to deal with those who understand reason. Elihu differs with them in his opinion, but he still calls them wise and understanding.

1.2. He appeals to their judgment and so submits to their testing (v. 3). *The ear of* the wise *tries words*, to

discern whether what is said is true or false, right or wrong, and those who speak must submit their words to be tested by intelligent people.

1.3. He takes them into partnership with him in examining and discussing this matter (v. 4). He does not pretend to be the sole dictator. "Let us agree to set aside all hostility and prejudices, and *let us choose to ourselves judgment. Let us know among ourselves,* by comparing notes and discussing our reasons, *what is good* and what is not."

2. Elihu forcefully accuses Job for some of the emotional words he has spoken, which reflected badly on God's rule.

2.1. He repeats the words Job has spoken as closely as he can remember. Job has said, *I am righteous* (v. 5), and when urged to confess his guilt, has adamantly maintained his plea, *Not guilty: Should I lie against my right?* (v. 6). *My wound is incurable* and likely to be fatal, and yet *without transgression,* although I am guiltless (v. 6); *not for any injustice in my hand* (16:16–17). He has, in effect, said that there is nothing to be gained in the service of God and that no one will in the long run be better because they are his (v. 9). Elihu gathers this as Job's opinion by an inference from what he said in 9:22: *He destroys the perfect and the wicked;* this indeed contains some truth—for all share a common destiny (Ecc 9:2)—but it was badly expressed. Job sits down silently under this charge and does not attempt to justify himself. From this Mr. Joseph Caryl rightly observes that good people sometimes speak worse than they intend, and that good people will prefer to bear more blame than they deserve rather than stand and excuse themselves when they have deserved some blame.

2.2. He charges Job: *What man is like Job?* (v. 7). "Is there anyone like Job, or did you ever hear anyone talk so extravagantly? He sits in the seat of mockers (Ps 1:1): he *drinketh up scorning like water* by these foolish pronouncements of his: he makes himself the object of scorn; he lays himself open to rebuke and gives opportunity for others to laugh at him." He also walks in the way of the ungodly and stands in the way of sinners (Ps 1:1): he *goes in company with the workers of iniquity* (v. 8)—not that he associates with them in his life, but he favors and supports them in his opinion, to strengthen them.

Verses 10–15

The scope of Elihu's speech is to reconcile Job to his suffering. He has shown (ch. 33) that God meant him no harm in afflicting him, but intended it for his spiritual benefit. Now he shows that God did him no wrong in afflicting him, nor had he punished him more than he deserved. He directs his speech to all the listeners: "*Hearken to me, you men of understanding* (v. 10)." The righteous God, says Elihu, never did, and never will do, any wrong to any of his creatures; his ways are just, and ours are unjust.

1. This truth is set down both negatively and positively: *God cannot do wickedness,* nor can *the Almighty commit iniquity* (v. 10). It is inconsistent with his perfect nature, and so it is also inconsistent with his pure will (v. 12): *God will not do wickedly, neither will the Almighty* pervert the course of justice. He will never either do wrong to anyone or deny right to anyone, but *the heavens will* shortly *declare his righteousness* (Ps 50:6). Although he is almighty, he never uses his power to support injustice. He is *Shaddai,* "the almighty God," and he therefore cannot be *tempted with evil* (Jas 1:13). On the contrary, he does right to all (v. 11): *The work of a man shall he render unto him.*

2. This truth is vehemently asserted with an assurance of its truth—*Yea, surely* (v. 12)—and with a loathing of

the very thought of the contrary (v. 10)—*Far be it from God that he should do wickedness*, and from us that we should imagine such a thing.

3. This truth is clearly proved by two arguments:

- God's independent, absolute sovereignty and rule (v. 13): *Who has given him a charge over the earth?* He has the sole administration of human kingdoms and has taken it on himself.
- His irresistible power (v. 14): *If he set his heart upon man*, to contend with him—much more if, as some read it, "he set his heart against man," to destroy him—if he dealt with people either by strict sovereignty or by strict justice, no one would stand before him; human spirit and breath would soon all be gone, and *all flesh would perish together* (v. 15).

Verses 16–30

Elihu here speaks more directly to Job.

1. God is not to be argued with for anything he does. *Shall even he that hates right govern?* (v. 17). The righteous Lord loves righteousness so much that, in comparison to him, even Job himself, although blameless and upright, might be said to hate justice—and will he govern? Will he pretend to direct God or correct what he does? *Wilt thou condemn him that is most just* (v. 17) and is not able to be anything but just? *He regardeth not the rich more than the poor*, he does not favor the rich over the poor, and so it is right he should rule, and it is not right that we should find fault with him (v. 19). Great people will fare no better, nor will they find any favor because of their wealth or greatness. The poor will fare none the worse because of their poverty, nor will an honorable cause be denied.

2. God is to be acknowledged and submitted to in all that he does. Elihu here suggests several considerations to Job to engender in him great and high thoughts of God, and so to persuade him to submit and proceed no farther in his argument with him.

2.1. God is almighty, and so is able to deal with the strongest people when he enters into judgment with them (v. 20). Even *the people*, the body of a nation, although they are numerous, *shall be troubled*, disturbed and confused when God so wishes. Even *the mighty* people, the princes, *shall*, if God speaks the word, *be taken away* from their throne. Nor is it only one single mighty person that he can overpower in this way, but even many of them (v. 24).

2.2. God is omniscient and can find out what is most secret. As the strongest person cannot oppose his strength, so the most subtle cannot escape his eye. If, therefore, some people are punished either more or less than we think they should be, instead of arguing with God, we should realize that it is because of some hidden cause known only to God. For everything is open before him (v. 21): *His eyes are upon the ways of man. There is no darkness nor shadow of death* so secret, so far from light or sight, that *the workers of iniquity may hide themselves* in it from the all-seeing eye of the righteous God. Evildoers may find ways and means to hide themselves from others, but not from God: *He knows their works* (v. 25), both what they do and what they plan to do.

2.3. God is righteous. *He will not lay upon man more than right* (v. 23). Just as he will not punish the innocent, so he will not exact from those who are guilty more than their sins deserve, and infinite Wisdom will judge the relationship between sin and punishment. Job was

therefore to be blamed for his complaints about God. To prove that God does not *lay upon* the wicked *more than right* (v. 23), Elihu shows what their evil was (vv. 27–28). These unjust judges were rebels against God: They *turned back from him*, rejected the fear of him; and they abandoned the very thoughts of him, for *they would not consider any of his ways* (v. 27). They could not be bothered with either his commands or his providences, but lived without God in the world (Eph 2:12). They were tyrants to everyone (v. 28).

2.4. God rules incontrovertibly over all the lives of people. He guides and rules over the lives of both communities and individual people, so his plans cannot be hindered and what he does cannot be changed (v. 29). The frowns of all the world cannot trouble those whom God calms with his smiles. *When he gives quietness*, who then *can make trouble?* (v. 29). If God gives outward peace to a nation, he can secure what he gives. If God gives inward peace to an individual, neither the accusations of Satan nor the suffering of this present time, and not even the arrests of death itself, can cause trouble. If God in displeasure *hides his face* and withholds the assurance of his favor, *who then can behold him?* (v. 29).

2.5. God is wise, and he takes care of the well-being of the community and so ensures that *the hypocrite reign not, lest the people be ensnared* (v. 30). Notice here:

- The pride of hypocrites. Their aim is to reign; they want to receive the reward of praise from the people and power in the world.
- The practice of tyrants. When they aim to set themselves up, they sometimes use religion as a cover for their ambitious ways.
- The perilous position the people are in when hypocrites reign. They are likely to be ensnared in sin, trouble, or both.

Verses 31–37

In these verses:

1. Elihu advises Job what he should say in his suffering (vv. 31–32). In general, he wants him to repent of his misbehavior and immoderate expressions in his suffering. Job's other friends wanted him to acknowledge he was an evildoer, and by going too far they nullified any good effect. Elihu asks him only to acknowledge that he has, in the way he has handled the argument, *spoken unadvisedly with his lips* (Ps 106:33). He advises Job:

1.1. To humble himself before God for his sins and accept the punishment of them, to say, "*I have borne chastisement*; I am guilty (v. 31)." Many who are punished do not bear their punishment well and so, in effect, do not bear it at all. If people sincerely repent, they will accept well what God does and will bear their punishment as a surgical operation intended for good.

1.2. To pray to God to reveal his sins to him (v. 32).

1.3. To promise reformation (v. 31), to say, "*I will not offend any more. If I have done iniquity* (or *seeing I have*), *I will do so no more*; whatever you show me that I have done wrong, I will put it right by your grace in the future."

2. Elihu reasons with him concerning his discontent and uneasiness in his suffering (v. 33). We are ready to think everything that concerns us should be just as we want it, but Elihu shows here it is absurd and unreasonable to expect this: "*Should it be according to thy mind*, should God then reward you on your terms? No; why should he do that?"

3. Elihu appeals to all intelligent and unbiased people to judge whether there is not sin and foolishness in what Job has said. "*My desire is that Job may be tried unto the end*, that Job may be tested to the utmost. May he continue to be tested until the purpose of his testing is fulfilled." He appeals both to God and to people and desires the judgment of both on it. Some read v. 36 as an appeal to God: "My Father, let Job be tried" (v. 36, margin), for the same word means "my desire" and "my father," and some suppose he lifted up his eyes when he said this, meaning, "*O my Father who art in heaven!* May Job be tested until he is humbled."

CHAPTER 35

Because Job still remains silent, Elihu undertakes a third time to show him that he has spoken wrongly and should take back his words. 1. Job has presented religious faith as something unimportant and unprofitable; Elihu shows the opposite is true (vv. 1–8). 2. He has complained about God as being deaf to the pleas of the oppressed, and Elihu here justifies God against this charge (vv. 9–13). 3. He has despaired of God's favor ever returning to him, because it was delayed for so long, but Elihu shows him the true cause of the delay (vv. 14–16).

Verses 1–8

We have here:

1. The sinful words which Elihu charges Job with (vv. 2–3). *Thinkest thou this to be right?* he asks him (v. 2). This suggests his good opinion of Job, that Job thought better than he spoke, and that when he realizes his mistake, he will not stand by it. "You have in effect said, *My righteousness is more than God's*," Elihu charges (v. 2), for this was what Job implied when he said, *What profit shall I have, if I be cleansed from my sin?* If he gained nothing from his religious faith, God was more indebted to him than he was to God. But although there might be apparent grounds for charging Job with saying these words, it was still not fair, since he himself had made them the evil words of prospering sinners—*What profit shall we have if we pray to him?* (21:15)—and had immediately disowned them (21:16).

2. The good answer which Elihu gives to this (v. 4): "*I will undertake to answer thee, and thy companions with thee*," that is, "I will silence all those who approve what you have said." To do this he turns to his old saying (33:12) that God is greater than any mortal. Elihu has no need to prove that God is above mortals; it is already agreed by everyone. But he wants Job, and us, to be affected by this truth, through a visible demonstration of the height of the heavens and the clouds (v. 5). They are far above us, and God is far above them—how much then is he beyond the reach of either our sins or our services! Look to the heavens, and see the clouds. Elihu utterly denies that God can be either prejudiced or advantaged by what anyone, even the greatest person on earth, does or can do. Sin is said to be against God because this is what the sinner intends it to be, and so God takes it as such. It wrongs his honor, but it cannot *do* anything *against him*, cannot affect him. Job therefore spoke wrongly by saying, *What profit is it that I am cleansed from my sin?* God did not gain from his reformation, and who then would gain if Job himself did not? The services of the best saints do not benefit him (v. 7): *If thou be righteous, what givest thou to him?*

Verses 9–13

Elihu returns an answer to another comment that Job made, which, he thought, dishonored the justice and goodness of God.

1. Job complained that God did not regard the pleas of the oppressed against their oppressors (v. 9): "*By reason of the multitude of oppressions they make the oppressed to cry*, but it is futile: God does not come to put them right." This seems to refer to those words of Job in 24:12: *Men groan from out of the city, and the soul of the wounded cries out* against the oppressors, *yet God lays not folly to them*. Is there a righteous God, and can it be that he hears and sees so slowly?

2. Elihu solves the difficulty. If the pleas of the oppressed are not heard, the fault is in themselves; they *ask and have not, because they ask amiss* (with wrong motives) (Jas 4:3). *They cry out by reason of the arm of the mighty* (v. 9), but it is not a penitent and praying cry; it is the cry of nature and passion, not of grace.

2.1. They do not inquire after God or seek to come to know him in their suffering (v. 10): *But none saith, Where is God my Maker?* God is our Maker, the author of our being. It is our duty, therefore, to inquire of him. Where is he, that we may show him our respect? Everyone asks: how can I be happy? How can I be rich? How can I get along in life? But no one asks, *Where is God my Maker?* (v. 10).

2.2. They do not take notice of the mercies they enjoy in their suffering.

2.2.1. He provides for our inward comfort and joy in our outward troubles. He *gives songs in the night* (v. 10), that is, when our condition is very dark and sad. There is something in God, in his providence and promise, which is sufficient not only to support us but also to fill us with joy and comfort (Phm 7) and to enable us even to rejoice in our troubles (Ro 12:12; 2Co 7:4). When we neglect the comforts of God which are stored up for us, it is just of God to reject our prayers.

2.2.2. He preserves our reason and understanding (v. 11): *Who teaches us more than the beasts of the earth*, that is, who has endowed us with more noble powers and faculties than they are endowed with and has made us capable of greater pleasures and work here and forever? Now this is something to give thanks for, even under the heaviest burdens of suffering. Whatever we are deprived of, we still have our immortal souls; even those who kill the body cannot harm them. This is the finest aspect of reason, that it makes us capable of religious faith, and it is especially in that that we are *taught more than the beasts and the fowls* (v. 11). They have wonderful instincts and abilities to seek out food, healing, and shelter, but none of them can ask, *Where is God my Maker?* (v. 10). Something like logic, science, and politics has been observed among the animals, but never anything of theology or religious faith; these are exclusive to human beings. If, therefore, the oppressed only *cry by reason of the arm of the mighty* (v. 9) and do not look to God, they are doing no more than the animals, who complain when they are hurt. God relieves the animals because they cry out to him according to the best of their ability (38:41; Ps 104:21). But why should relief be expected by human beings who are capable of seeking God as their Maker but still cry out to him no differently from animals?

2.3. They are proud and unhumbled in their suffering. *There they cry but none gives answer.* God does not rescue them, *because of the pride of evil men*; those who cry are evildoers. They *regard iniquity in their hearts* (cherish sin in their hearts), and so God will not hear their prayers (Ps 66:18; Isa 1:15). The case is clear then: if we cry out to God to take away the oppression and affliction we are suffering, and they are not removed, the reason is not that the Lord is too weak or that his ear is deaf, but that the affliction has not yet done its work. We have not yet been sufficiently humbled, and so must be thankful that it continues.

Verses 14–16

Here is:

1. Another sinful comment for which Elihu rebukes Job (v. 14): *Thou sayest thou shalt not see him*, that is: "You complain that you do not understand the meaning of his harsh dealings with you." Just as in times of prosperity we are ready to think our mountain will never be brought low (Isa 40:4), so in times of adversity we are ready to think our valley will never be filled (2Ki 3:17), but in both experiences, to conclude that *tomorrow must be as this day* (Isa 56:12) is as absurd as to think that the weather will always be the same as it is now, whether good or bad, and that the tide will always be coming in, or that the tide will always be going out.

2. The answer which Elihu gives: when Job looks up to God, he has no just reason to speak so despairingly: *Judgment is before him*, your case is before him (v. 14), that is, "He knows what he is doing. He will do everything in his infinite wisdom and justice; he has the entire plan and model of providence before him. *Therefore trust in him*, depend on him, wait for him, and believe that things will finally turn out well." He is a God of justice (Isa 30:18); we will see no reason to despair of obtaining relief from him, but every reason in the world to hope in him. Yet "*because it is not so*, because you did not trust in him, the affliction which at first came from love now has displeasure mixed in with it. Now God *has visited* (punished) you *in his anger*." Elihu concludes, therefore, that *Job opens his mouth in vain* (v. 16) because he does not trust in God and wait for him. Let not those who distrust God *think that they shall receive anything from him* (Jas 1:7). Elihu does not, like Job's other friends, condemn him for being a hypocrite, but charges him only with Moses' sin, *speaking unadvisedly with his lips* (Ps 106:33) when his spirit was provoked.

CHAPTER 36

Having rebuked Job in detail for some of his rash words, Elihu urges many reasons why Job should submit to the hand of God. His reasons are taken from a consideration of the wisdom and righteousness of God, his care of his people, and especially his greatness and almighty power. 1. His introduction (vv. 2–4). 2. The account he gives of the ways of God's providence toward people, which are according to how they conduct themselves (vv. 5–15). 3. The just warning and good counsel he gives Job (vv. 16–21). 4. His demonstration of God's sovereignty and almighty power, which is a reason why we should all submit to him in his dealings with us (vv. 22–33).

Verses 1–4

Once more Elihu begs the patience of those listening, especially Job. To gain this, he pleads:

1. That he has a good cause and a noble and fruitful subject: *I have yet to speak on God's behalf*, there is more to be said in God's behalf (v. 2).

2. That he has something unusual to offer: *I will fetch my knowledge from afar* (v. 3), that is, we will have to

go back to first principles. It is worthwhile to go far in seeking this knowledge of God, to dig it out, to travel for it. Our efforts will be rewarded, and even if it comes from far away, it will not have been bought at too high a price. "*My words shall not be false*. He who is blameless or upright in knowledge is now reasoning with you, and so let his speech not only have a fair hearing but also be well received, because it is meant well."

Verses 5–14

Elihu speaks on God's behalf and shows that the actions of divine Providence are all according to the eternal rules of justice. God acts as a righteous ruler, for:

1. He does not think it beneath him to take notice of the lowliest of his subjects; *God is mighty*, infinitely so, and yet he despises no one (v. 5). Job thought himself and his cause had been discredited because God had not immediately appeared for him. "No," Elihu says, *God despises not any*, which is a good reason why we should honor everyone.

2. He gives no support to the greatest if they are evil (v. 6): *He preserves not the life of the wicked*. Although their lives may be prolonged, they are not under any special care of divine Providence, but only its general, common protection.

3. He is always ready to set right those who have been wronged in any way and to plead their cause (v. 6). If people will not set right the poor who have been wronged, God will.

4. He takes particular care to protect his good subjects (v. 7). He not only looks on them, but never looks away from them: *He withdraws not his eyes from the righteous.* Although they may sometimes seem neglected and forgotten, the tender, careful eye of their heavenly Father never withdraws from them.

4.1. Sometimes he promotes good people to places of trust and honor (v. 7): *With kings are they on the throne*, and every sheaf is made to bow to theirs (Ge 37:7). When righteous people are advanced to positions of honor and power, it is a mercy to them. It is also a blessing to those over whom they are put: *When the righteous bear rule the city rejoices* (Pr 29:2).

4.2. If at any time he subjects them to affliction, it is for the good of their souls (vv. 8–10). *If they be bound in fetters* (chains), put in prison as Joseph was, or *holden* (held firm) *in the cords of* any other *affliction*, confined by pain and sickness, confined by poverty, it is for the good of their souls, the consideration of which should help us come to terms with the affliction. God intends three things when he afflicts us:

- To reveal past sins to us: *He shows them their work*, what they have done (v. 9). Sin is our own work.
- To open up our hearts to receive instructions now: then *he opens their ear to discipline* (v. 10). God teaches those whom he disciplines (Ps 94:12), and the affliction makes people willing to learn, softens the wax so that it may receive the impression of the seal. It does not do this by itself, however; the grace of God works with it and by it.
- To deter and draw us away from sin in the future.

4.3. If the affliction does its work and accomplishes what he sent it to do (Isa 55:11), he will strengthen and encourage them again, according to the time that he has afflicted them (v. 11; compare Ps 90:15). If we faithfully serve God:

4.3.1. We have the promise of outward prosperity, the promise of the life that now is (1Ti 4:8) and its benefits, as far as they are for God's glory and our good, and who would want them to go any farther?

4.3.2. We have the possession of inward delights, the encouragement of fellowship with God and a good conscience, and that great peace possessed by those who love God's law.

4.4. If the affliction does not do its work, let them expect to be destroyed. The consuming fire will be effective if the refining fire is not, for when God judges he will prevail (Ro 3:4).

5. He brings ruin on hypocrites, the secret enemies of his kingdom, such as those whom Elihu described in v. 12, who, though numbered among the righteous, did not obey God. *They cry not when he binds them* (v. 13), that is, when they are suffering, tied with the cords of trouble, their hearts are hardened; they are stubborn and unhumbled and will not cry out to God or ask him to help them. They *die in youth, and their life is among the unclean* (v. 14).

Verses 15–23

Elihu here turns his attention more to Job, and:

1. He tells him what God would have done for him before this if he had been properly humbled under his affliction (v. 15). God looks with tenderness on the poor in spirit, those who have a broken and contrite heart (Ps 51:17), and when they are suffering, he is ready to help them. He *opens their ears* and makes them hear joy and gladness (Ps 51:8), even *in* their *oppressions*. "If you had submitted to the will of God, your liberty and plenty would have been restored to you to your benefit.

1.1. "You would have been released, not confined by your sickness and disgrace: *He would have removed thee into a broad place where is no straitness*, he would have moved you into a spacious place free from restriction (v. 16), and you would no longer have been cramped like this and have had all your plans frustrated.

1.2. "You would have been enriched, and would not have been left in this poor condition; you would have had your table richly spread, not only with good food but also with the finest kernels of wheat."

2. He charges him with harming his own interests and causing the continuation of his own trouble (v. 17): "*But thou hast fulfilled the judgment of the wicked*," that is, "Whatever is your true character, in this you have behaved as an evildoer, and *that is why* judgment and justice have taken hold of you."

3. He cautions him not to persist in his perverseness.

3.1. Let him not think he is secure. "*Because there is wrath*—that is, because God is a righteous ruler, because you have reason to fear you are under God's displeasure—therefore *beware lest he take thee away* suddenly *with his stroke*, and be wise to make your peace with him quickly and see his anger turned away from you" (Ps 2:10). Arguers are all too ready to threaten one another with God's wrath, but this was a friendly warning to Job, and a necessary one.

3.2. Let him not promise himself that if God's wrath is kindled against him, he can find ways to escape its blows. There is no escape by using money, no buying pardon with silver, gold, or such corruptible things: "Even *a great ransom cannot deliver thee* (v. 18) when God judges you. If *all the forces of strength* (v. 19) were at your command, if you could muster very many servants to appear for you, it would all be in vain. There is *none that can deliver out of his hand*" (Da 8:4). There is no escape by fleeing and hiding (v. 20): "*Desire not the night*, which often favors the retreat of a conquered army and gives it cover. Do not think you can escape the righteous judgment of God

in that way, for the *darkness hideth not from him*" (Ps 139:11–12).

3.3. Let him not continue his unjust quarrel with God. "*Take heed*, look to your own spirit, and *regard not iniquity*, do not return to it, for you will be in danger if you do." Let him not dare give orders to God or tell him what to do (vv. 22–23): "*Behold, God exalteth by his power*," that is, "He does, may, and can set up and pull down whom he pleases, and so it is not for you or me to argue with him." He is an incomparable teacher: *Who teaches like him?* (v. 22). It is absurd for us to teach him, the One who is himself the fountain of light, truth, knowledge, and instruction. *He that teaches man knowledge*, as none else can, *shall not he know?* (Ps 94:0–10). Shall we light a candle and show it to the sun? When Elihu wants to give glory to God as a ruler, he praises him as a teacher, for rulers must teach. He teaches by the Bible, and that is the best book; he teaches by his Son, and he is the best Master.

Verses 24–33

Elihu is here trying to give Job great and high thoughts of God, and so to persuade him to cheerfully submit to his providence.

1. He describes the work of God in general (v. 24). God does nothing halfheartedly. His visible works, those of nature, are those we marvel at and commend, and we observe in them the Creator's wisdom, power, and goodness. Shall we then find fault with his ways toward us? Whichever way we look, we say, "This is *the work of God*," the finger of God; it is the Lord's doing (Ps 118:23; Mt 21:42). Everyone can see, from far away, that the heavens and all the lights in the heavens, the earth and all its fruits, are the work of almighty God. Look at the tiniest works of nature through a microscope; do they not appear intricately made? The eternal power and Godhead of the Creator are *clearly seen and understood* by the *things that are made* (Ro 1:20). We should wonder at these works of his when we look at them. The beauty and excellence of the work of God and the harmony of all its parts are things that we must remember to exalt and praise him greatly for.

2. He describes God, their author, as infinite and unsearchable (v. 26). The streams of existence, power, and perfection should lead us to the fountain. *God is great*, infinitely great, and therefore greatly to be praised (Ps 145:1). He is great, and so *we know him not*. We know that he is, but not what he is. We know what he is not, but not what he is. We know in part (1Co 13:12), but not perfectly. *The number of his years cannot* possibly *be searched out* (v. 26), for he is eternal; they are past finding out. He is a Being without beginning, succession, or end, who always was, and always will be, and always the same, the great *I AM*. This is a good reason why we should not dictate to him or quarrel with him.

3. He gives some examples of God's wisdom, power, and sovereign rule, beginning in this chapter with the clouds and the rain that comes from them. We do not need to be too critical in examining either the exact words in or the science behind this noble speech. Its general scope is to show that God is infinitely great, and the Lord of all, the first cause and supreme director of all creatures, who *has all power in heaven and earth* (Mt 28:18)—and whom we should, therefore, with all humility and reverence, adore, speak well of, and honor—and that it is presumptuous for us to give him orders for the rules and methods of his special providence toward the human race. In order to try to give Job a sense of God's greatness and sovereignty, Elihu has already directed him (35:5) to look at the clouds. Now, consider the clouds:

3.1. As springs for this lower world, the source and storehouse of its moisture. The clouds above distill water on the earth below. If the heavens become bronze, the earth becomes iron (Dt 28:23), and so the promise of plenty runs, *I will hear* (respond to) *the heavens and they shall hear* (respond to) *the earth* (Hos 2:21). Every good gift comes from above, from him who is both Father of lights (Jas 1:17) and Father of the rain. The clouds are here said to *distil upon man* (v. 28), for though God truly *causes it to rain in the wilderness where no man is* (38:26; Ps 104:11), yet people are mentioned particularly, as those for whom the animals were made useful and from whom the praise and thanks are required directly. With people, he *causes his rain to fall upon the just and upon the unjust* (Mt 5:45). The clouds are said to distill the water in *small drops*, not in gushes, as when the *windows of heaven were opened* (Ge 7:11). God waters the earth with what he once drowned it with. Although it comes down in drops, it distills on the human race *abundantly* (v. 28) and is therefore called *the river of God which is full of water* (Ps 65:9). The clouds *pour down according to the vapour* they draw up (v. 27). The heavens are fair to the earth, but the earth is not fair in the return it makes.

3.2. As shadows for the upper world (v. 29): *Can any understand the spreading of the clouds?* Shall we then pretend to understand the reasons and methods of God's judicial ways with people, whose characters and cases are so different? We are favored by the intervention of the clouds between us and the sun, for they serve as an umbrella to shelter us from the violent heat of the sun. *A cloud of dew in the heat of harvest* is spoken of as very great refreshment (Isa 18:4). Yet we are sometimes frowned on by them, for they make the earth dark at noon and eclipse the light of the sun. Sin is compared to a cloud (Isa 44:22), because it comes between us and the light of God's face and obstructs that light. But although the clouds darken the sun for a time and pour down rain, yet after he has exhausted the cloud, *he spreads his light upon it* (v. 30). There is *a clear shining after rain* (2Sa 23:4).

CHAPTER 37

Elihu here goes on to praise the wonderful power of God in the atmosphere and in all the changes of the weather. If we submit to the will of God in those changes, take the weather as it is and make the best of it, why then should we not also submit to other changes in our condition? 1. He observes the hand of God: 1.1. In thunder and lightning (vv. 1–5). 1.2. In ice and snow, rains and wind (vv. 6–13). 2. He applies it to Job and challenges him to explain the occurrences of these works of nature, so that in confessing his ignorance of them, he may acknowledge himself to be an incompetent judge of the ways of divine Providence (vv. 14–22). 3. He concludes with his principle that God is great and greatly to be feared (vv. 23–24).

Verses 1–5

Thunder and lightning are signs of the glory and majesty of almighty God. And so he has not left himself without witness of his greatness—since he has provided these signs of it—just as he has not left himself without witness of his goodness, but has sent the rain from heaven and fruitful seasons (Ac 14:17). It is very probable that at this time, when Elihu was speaking, there was thunder and lightning, for he speaks of the phenomena as being present; and because God was about to speak

(38:1), these were, as on Mount Sinai, the proper introductions to command the attention and awe of those present. Notice here:

1. How Elihu himself was moved, and how he wanted to move Job, with the appearance of God's glory in thunder and lightning (vv. 1–2). "For my part," Elihu says, "*my heart trembles* (pounds) at it; it is still terrible to me and makes my heart beat as if it is about to leap *out of its place.*" He also calls on Job to give his attention to it (v. 2): *Hear attentively the noise of his voice.* To understand the instructions God wants to give us through thunder, we should listen with great attention and concentration. Thunder is called *the voice of the Lord* (Ps 29:3–9), because God uses it to call the human race to fear him.

2. How he describes thunder and lightning. God directs the thunder, and it is *his* lightning (v. 3). Their production and movements do not come about by chance, although they may seem to us to be accidental and uncontrollable. The thunderclaps roll *under the whole heaven* and are heard far and near, as the flashes of lightning dart to *the ends of the earth.* The lightning is directed first, and *after it a voice roars* (v. 4). The thunder is here called *the voice of God's excellency* (majesty), because he declares his transcendent power and greatness by it. *He will not stay* (restrain) the rain and showers that usually follow the thunder, but will pour them out on the earth *when his voice is heard* (v. 4). Does God thunder out in such marvelous ways with his voice? Then we must conclude that his other works are great and incomprehensible. From this one example we may argue more generally, that in the ways of providence, there are things that are too great and too strong for us to oppose, resist, or strive against.

Verses 6–13

The changes and extremes of weather, wet or dry, hot or cold, are the subject of a great deal of our ordinary talk, but how rarely do we think and speak of these things, as Elihu does here, with a fearful respect for God! We must take notice of the glory of God not only in thunder and lightning but also in the more ordinary changes in the weather.

1. The snow and rain (v. 6). Then *he saith to the snow, Be thou* (fall) *on the earth.* He speaks, and it is done: as in the creation of the world, *Let there be light* (Ge 1:3), so also in the works of common providence, *Snow, be thou on the earth.* Saying and doing are not different things with God, although they are with us. When he speaks the word, *the small rain* distills and *the great rain* pours down as he pleases—"the winter rain." The providence of God is to be acknowledged both by farmers in the fields and travelers on the road, in every shower of rain, whether it does them a kindness or unkindness. It is sinful and foolish to argue with God's providence in the weather. The effect of extreme winter weather makes both every person and every animal withdraw. *He seals up the hand of every man.* In frost and snow, farmers cannot do their work, nor can some traders or travelers. The plow is set aside, ships are docked, and people are taken away from their work so that they all *may know his work,* so that they may contemplate that and give him the glory. When we are confined to our houses, we should be driven to our Bibles and our knees. The animals also withdraw *to their dens and remain in their* secret *places* (v. 8). Wild animals must seek shelter for themselves, to which they are led by their instinct, while the tame animals, which are useful to people, are housed and protected by their care (Ex 9:20).

2. The winds, which blow from different quarters and produce different effects (v. 9): "Out of the hidden place,"

so it may read, *comes the whirlwind*; it turns around, and so it is hard to say from which point it comes, but it comes, literally, from "the hidden chamber," which I prefer to the *south*, because he says here (v. 17) that the wind from the south is not a whirlwind but a warming, soothing wind.

3. The *frost* (ice) (v. 10). Notice its cause: it is *given by the breath of God*, that is, by the word of his power and the command of his will, or as some understand it, by the wind, which is the breath of God, as the thunder is his voice. It is caused by the cold, freezing wind from the north. Notice its effect: *The breadth of the waters is straitened*, that is, the waters are restricted, numbed, and bound up in frozen crystals. This is such an example of the power of God that if it were not usual, it would be close to miraculous.

4. The clouds. He speaks about three different kinds of cloud:

4.1. Dense, black, thick clouds, full of showers, and *he wearies* these with watering (v. 11), that is, they spend themselves and are exhausted by the rain into which they melt and are dissolved, pouring out water until they are empty and can pour out no more. The clouds water the earth until they are exhausted; they are spent for our benefit.

4.2. Bright, thin clouds, clouds without water; and these *he scattereth*; they are dispersed by themselves.

4.3. Scudding clouds, which do not dissolve, like the thick cloud, into heavy rain, but are taken on the wings of the wind from place to place, releasing showers as they go. These are said to be *turned round about* by his counsels (v. 12).

Verses 14–20

Elihu here focuses himself directly on Job, wanting him to apply to himself what he has said up to this time. He begs him to listen to his words (v. 14), to pause a little: *Stand still, and consider the wondrous works of God.* In order to humble Job, Elihu shows him:

1. That Job has no insight into natural causes, that he can neither see their origins nor foresee their effects (vv. 15–17): *Dost thou know* this and know what are *the wondrous works of him who is perfect in knowledge?* We are taught here:

1.1. The perfection of God's knowledge. It is one of the most glorious attributes of God that he is perfect in knowledge; he knows everything. His knowledge is intuitive, intimate, and whole: he *sees*. Nothing is far away in his knowledge; everything is close. Nothing is future; everything is present. Nothing hidden; everything open.

1.2. The imperfection of our knowledge. The greatest scientists are very much in the dark about the power and works of nature. We are a paradox to ourselves, and everything about us is a mystery. It is good for us to be made aware of how little we know. Some have confessed their ignorance, and those who refuse to do so have betrayed it. But what incompetent judges we are of God's ways, since we understand so little of how he works. We may foresee changes in the weather a few hours before, by ordinary observation, or we may notice from looking at the barometer that the weather is about to change, but how little do these changes show us about the purposes of God! We do not know how the clouds are suspended in the air, how they are *balanced*, which is one of the wonders of God. They are suspended in such a way that they do not fall in a deluge or cloudburst. *He quiets the earth by the south wind* (v. 17) when spring comes. As he has a blustering, freezing north wind, so also he has a thawing, restful south wind; the Spirit is compared to both, because he both convicts and comforts (SS 4:16).

2. That Job had no share at all in the original creation of the world (v. 18): *Hast thou with him spread out the sky?* The creation of the sky is a glorious example of God's power. It is *strong*, deriving its name, *firmament*, from its stability. It still is what it was, and allows no decay, nor will the laws of heaven be changed until the lease expires with time. It is *a molten looking glass*, a mirror of cast bronze (v. 18), smooth and polished, and without the slightest flaw or crack. In this, as in a mirror, we *may behold the glory of God* and the wisdom of *his handywork* (Ps 19:1).

3. That neither Job nor the others who are present are able to speak of the glory of God to the vast extent that the subject deserves (vv. 19–20). He challenges Job ironically: "*Teach us*, if you can, *what we shall say unto him* (v. 19). You want to reason with God and want us to argue with him on your behalf. Go on, then, teach us what we should say." Elihu acknowledges his own inadequacy: *We cannot order our speech* (draw up our case) *by reason of darkness* (v. 19). Those who through grace know much of God still know little compared with what can be known, and what will be known when what is perfect comes and the curtain is torn and we see him face to face (1Co 3:16; 13:10, 12). Elihu is even ashamed of what he has said—not of the position he took but of the way he has handled it: "*Shall it be told him that I speak*, should he be told that I want to speak? (v. 20). Shall it be reported to him as a service, worthy of his notice? By no means; let it never be spoken of in that way"—for he fears that the subject has suffered in his attempt to try to talk about it, just as an attractive face is spoiled by a bad painter.

Verses 21–24

Elihu here concludes his speech with some short but great sayings concerning the glory of God:

1. God has said that he will *dwell in the thick darkness* and *make that his pavilion* (2Ch 6:1; Ps 18:11). Elihu saw the cloud, with a whirlwind within it, coming from the south, but now it hung so thick and black over their heads that none of them could *see the bright light which* just before *was in the clouds* (v. 21). But he looked to the north and saw it clear that way, which gave him hope that the clouds were not gathering to bring a downpour; he and his listeners were covered, but not surrounded, by them. He expected that "the wind will pass" (v. 21) *and cleanse them*, and then *fair weather would come out of the north* (v. 22) and all would be well. God will not always frown, nor will he contend forever (Isa 57:16).

2. Elihu is quick to draw matters to a conclusion now that God is about to speak. He comments:

2.1. That *with God is terrible majesty.* He is a God of glory and transcendent perfection.

2.2. That when we speak about the Almighty, we must acknowledge that we *cannot find him out*; our finite understanding cannot comprehend his infinite, perfect nature (v. 23). Can we put the ocean into a bottle?

2.3. That *God is excellent* (exalted) *in power* (v. 23).

2.4. That God is no less excellent in wisdom and righteousness, *in judgment and plenty of justice*, in his justice and great righteousness (v. 23), or else there would be little splendor in his power.

2.5. That *God will not afflict* (oppress) (v. 23), that is, that he will not afflict willingly. It gives him no pleasure to *grieve the children of men* (La 3:33), much less his own children. Some read it, "The Almighty, whom we cannot fathom, is great in power, but he will not oppress in judgment, and with him is great righteousness (v. 23), nor is he so strict as to record what we do wrong" (Ps 130:3).

2.6. That God does not value the criticism of those who think they are wise: *He respecteth them not* (he does not regard them) (v. 24).

CHAPTER 38

In most arguments, the real battle is to see who will have the last word. In this dispute, Job's friends had tamely given it to Job, and then he to Elihu. But after all the quarrels of the lawyers, the judge must have the final word, as God did here, and as he will have in every argument. Job had often appealed to God and had talked boldly, but when God took up the throne, Job had nothing to say in his own defense and was silent before him. Job's friends had sometimes appealed to God too: O that God would speak (11:5). Now, finally, God does speak, when Job, by Elihu's clear and meticulous arguments, has been softened a little and is humbled. It is the responsibility of ministers to prepare the way of the Lord (Isa 40:3; Mt 3:3).

The intention of God in his greatness is to humble Job and to bring him to repent of and recant his emotional and immoderate outbursts concerning God's providential dealings. He does this by calling on Job to compare God's eternity with his own time, God's knowledge of everything with his own ignorance, and God's almighty power with his own lack of power. 1. He begins by issuing a rousing challenge and general demand (vv. 1–3). 2. He then goes on to use various detailed examples and proofs to show Job's complete inability to argue with God: for he knows nothing about the founding of the earth (vv. 4–7); nothing about the limiting of the sea (vv. 8–11); nothing about the morning light (vv. 12–15); nothing about the dark recesses of the sea and earth (vv. 16–21); nothing about the springs in the clouds (vv. 22–27) or the secret counsels by which they are directed. He can do nothing toward producing the rain, ice, or lightning (vv. 28–30, 34–35, 37–38), nothing toward directing the stars and their influences (vv. 31–33), nothing toward making his own soul (v. 36). And, lastly, he cannot provide for the lions or the ravens (vv. 39–41). If Job is puzzled by these ordinary works of nature, how dare he pretend to delve into the counsels of God's rule and judge them?

Verses 1–3

Let us notice here:

1. Who speaks—the *Lord*, Jehovah, not a created angel but the eternal Word himself, the second person of the blessed Trinity, for it is he by whom the worlds were made, and he was no other One than the Son of God. He begins with the creation of the world. Elihu had said, *God speaks to men and they do not perceive it* (33:14), but they must have perceived this.

2. When he spoke—*Then*. When they had all had their say, it was *then* time for God to step in, whose judgment is based on truth (Ro 2:2). Job had silenced his three friends, but he could not convince them of his general integrity. Elihu had silenced Job, but could not bring him to acknowledge that he had handled this argument badly. But now God comes and does both. First he convinces Job that his speech was ill-advised and makes him cry, "I have done wrong." And having humbled him, he honors him, by convincing his three friends that they have done him wrong.

3. How he spoke—*Out of the whirlwind*, the rolling and enveloping storm. A whirlwind introduced Ezekiel's vision (Eze 1:4) and Elijah's (1Ki 19:11). God is said to have *his way in the whirlwind* (Na 1:3), and here, to show that even the stormy wind fulfills his word (Ps 148:8), it was made the means which brought that word.

4. To whom he spoke: he *answered Job*, directed his speech to him, to convince him of what was wrong before he cleared him of the unjust slander he had received.

5. What he said. The introduction is very searching:

5.1. God charges Job with ignorance and presumption in what he has said (v. 2): "*Who is this* that talks like this? Is this Job? What, my servant Job, a blameless and upright man? Can he forget himself to such an extent, and act so unlike himself? Who and where is he *that darkens counsel thus by words without knowledge?* Let him show his face if he dare and stand by what he has said." A humble faith and sincere obedience will see farther and better into the secrets of the Lord than all the philosophy of universities and the investigations of science. This first word which God spoke is all the more significant because Job, in his repentance, focused on it as what silenced and humbled him (42:3). He repeated this and echoed it as the arrow that stuck fast on him: "I am the fool that has obscured your purposes."

5.2. God challenges Job to give such proofs of his knowledge as will serve to justify his inquiries into divine purposes (v. 3): "*Gird up now thy loins like a* bold *man; I will demand of thee*, I will put some questions to you, *and answer me* if you can, before I answer yours."

Verses 4–11

To humble Job, God here shows him his ignorance about even the earth and the sea.

1. Concerning the founding of the earth.

1.1. Let him say where he was when this world was made (v. 4): "*Where wast thou when I laid the foundations of the earth?* Were you present when the world was made?" Notice here:

1.1.1. The greatness and glory of God: *I laid the foundations of the earth.*

1.1.2. The lowliness of human beings: *Where wast thou* (v. 4) then? We were so far from having any hand in the creation of the world, which might entitle us to rule it, so far from even being witnesses to it, by which we might have gained insight into it, that we were not then in existence. The first people were not then in existence; much less were we. It was Christ's honor to be present when this was done (Pr 8:22–31; Jn 1:1–2), but *we are of yesterday and know nothing* (8:9). Let us not, therefore, find fault with the works of God.

1.2. Let him describe how this world was made: "*Declare, if thou hast* so much *understanding* (v. 4), how that work has advanced. Step forward, and *tell who laid the measures thereof* (who marked off its dimensions) and *stretched out the line upon it*, who stretched a measuring line across it? Were you the architect who built the model and then marked off its dimensions?" The vast bulk of the earth is molded as exactly as if it had been determined by a measuring line, but who can describe how it was shaped into this form and how it came to be established so firmly? Although it is suspended on nothing, it is still fixed in space, but who can tell *upon what the foundations of it are fastened*, on what its footings are set, so that it may not sink under its own weight, or *who laid the corner stone thereof*, so that it may not fall apart (v. 6)?

1.3. Let him repeat, if he can, the songs of praise which were sung at that ceremony (v. 7), *when the morning stars sang together*, the blessed angels who in the early morning of time shone as brightly as the morning star, going immediately before the light which God commanded to shine out of darkness on earth, which was formless and empty. They were *the sons of God*, who *shouted for joy* when they saw the foundations of the earth being laid. The angels are called *the sons of God* because they bear much of his image, are with him in his home above, and serve him as a son serves his father.

2. Concerning the limiting of the sea to the place set for it (v. 8). This refers to the third day's work, when God said (Ge 1:9), *Let the waters under the heaven be gathered together unto one place, and it was so.*

2.1. Out of the great deep or chaos, in which earth and water were mixed, in obedience to the divine command, the waters *broke forth like a child out of the womb* (v. 8).

2.2. This newborn babe is clothed and wrapped (v. 9). *The cloud* is made *the garment thereof*, with which it is covered, and *thick darkness*—that is, shores far removed from one another and completely in the dark about one another—*is a swaddlingband for it.* It is not said that he made *rocks and mountains* its swaddling bands, but *clouds and darkness*, something that we are not aware of and would think least likely for such a purpose.

2.3. There is also a cradle provided for this baby: I *broke up for it my decreed place*, set limits on it (v. 10). Valleys were sunk for it in the earth, spacious enough to receive it, and there it was laid to sleep, and if it is sometimes tossed about by the wind, that, as Bishop Patrick observes, is only the rocking of the cradle, which makes it go to sleep more quickly. As for the sea, so for each one of us, there are fixed limits, for the One who marked out their set times also set the boundaries of our lands.

2.4. Because this baby became unruly and dangerous through human sin—which was the origin of all unrest and danger in this lower world—a prison was also provided for it: *bars and doors are set* (v. 10). It is also said to it, by way of restraining its arrogance, *Hitherto shalt thou come, but no further.* The sea is God's, for he made it; he restrains it. He says to it, *Here shall thy proud waves be stayed* (halt) (v. 11). This may be considered as an act of God's power over the sea. Although the sea is so vast, and although its movement is sometimes extremely violent, God still has it under his control. Its waves rise no higher, its tides roll no further, than God allows; and this is mentioned as a reason why we should stand in awe of God (Jer 5:22), and also why we should encourage ourselves in him, for the One who halts the noise of the sea, even the noise of its waves, can, when he pleases, still the turmoil of the people (Ps 65:7).

Verses 12–24

The Lord here proceeds to ask Job many puzzling questions, to convince him of his ignorance and so shame him for his foolishness in giving orders to God. Job is here challenged to give an account of six things:

1. The springs of the morning, the dawn, the rising sun (vv. 12–15).

1.1. It was not we or any other human being who commanded the morning light originally, nor was it any human being who appointed the place where it was to spring up and shine, or its timing. The constant and regular succession of day and night was nothing we contrived; it shows the glory of God, and the work of his hands, not ours (Ps 19:1–2).

1.2. It is quite beyond our power to change this course: "*Hast thou commanded the morning since thy days?* (v. 12). No; never. Why then will you pretend to direct God's purposes, or expect to have the ways of providence changed in your favor?"

1.3. It is God who has appointed the dawn to come to the world, and he spreads the morning light through the air, which receives it as readily as the clay does the seal (v. 14), immediately allowing an impression of it to be made, so that the air is suddenly enlightened all over by it, as the wax is stamped with the image on the seal; *and they stand as a garment*, the earth's features stand out like those of a garment. The earth puts on a new face every morning; it dresses itself as we do; it puts on light as clothing, and is then to be seen.

1.4. This is made a terror to evildoers. God makes the light a minister of his justice as well as of his mercy. It is designed *to shake the wicked out of the earth*, and for that purpose *it takes hold of the ends of it*, as we take hold of the ends of a cloth to shake the dust and moths out of it. Job has observed what a terror morning light is to criminals, because it reveals them (24:13–16), and God here asks him whether the world is indebted to him for that kindness. No; the great Judge of the world sends out the rays of the morning light as his messengers to detect criminals (v. 15), so that their light may be *withholden* (denied) from them, their upraised arm—which they have lifted up against God and other people—may be *broken*, and they may be deprived of their power to cause trouble. They will lose their comfort, confidence, liberty, and lives. Here we are reminded of the "Benedictus" (Lk 1:78–79): By the *tender mercy of our God the dayspring from on high has visited us*, the rising sun has come to us from heaven, *to give light to those that sit in darkness* (2Co 4:6); we are also reminded of the "Magnificat," which shows that God, in his Gospel, has *shown strength with his arm, scattered the proud, and put down the mighty* (Lk 1:51) by that light by which he intended to shake evildoers, to shake evil itself from the earth and break its power.

2. The springs of the sea (v. 16): "*Hast thou entered into* them, or *hast thou walked in the search of the depth?* God's way in ruling the world is said to be *in the sea*, and *in the great waters* (Ps 77:19), showing that it is hidden from us and not to be looked into by us.

3. The gates of death: *Have* these *been open to thee?* (v. 17). Death is a great secret. *Man knows not his time* (Ecc 9:12). We cannot describe what death is. Let us make sure that the gates of heaven will be opened to us on the other side of death, and then we do not need to fear the opening of the gates of death, even though it is a way we are to go only once. While we are here, in this physical world, we speak of the world of spirits in the same way that blind people speak about colors.

4. The breadth of the earth (v. 18): *Hast thou perceived* that? The knowledge of this might seem to be most at his level and within his reach, but he is challenged to declare it if he can. The earth is only a point in the universe, yet small as it is, we cannot be exact in declaring its dimensions. Job had never sailed around the world, and neither had anyone before him. People knew so little about the extent of the earth that, as I write, the discovery of the vast continent of America, after it had long lain hidden from human memory, is still recent. It is presumptuous for us, who do not know the extent of the earth, to try to fathom the depths of God's purposes.

5. The place and way of light and darkness. He spoke before of the dawn (v. 12), and he returns to speak of it again (v. 19): *Where is the way where light dwells*, where does light come from? And again (v. 24): *By what way is the light parted?* When in the beginning God first spread darkness over the face of the deep, and afterward commanded the light to shine out of darkness by the mighty word, *Let there be light* (Ge 1:3), did Job witness this

order and action? Although we long very much either for the shining of the morning or for the shadows of the evening, we do not know where to send or go to obtain them, nor can we tell *the paths to the house thereof* (v. 20). We were not born then, and the number of our days has not been so great that we can describe the birth of that first-born of the visible creation (v. 21). Will we then undertake to speak about God's purposes, which were from eternity, or to know the paths to their dwellings, and to ask for them to be changed? It is not our orders that are carried out by the dawn and the darkness of the night. We cannot even say where they come from or where they go (v. 24): *By what way is the light parted* in the morning, when, in an instant, it shoots into all parts of the air above the horizon? It is a marvelous change that comes every morning with the return of the light, and every evening by the return of the darkness, but we expect them, and so they do not surprise or disturb us. If we reckoned similarly with changes in our outward condition, we would neither at the brightest noon expect daylight to last forever nor at the darkest midnight despair of the morning ever returning. God has set the one opposite the other, like the day and night, and so must we (Ecc 7:14).

6. The *treasures of the snow and hail* (vv. 22–23): *"Hast thou entered* into these and taken a view of them?" The snow and hail are generated in the clouds, and they come from there in such abundance that one would think there were vast amounts of them stored up there, whereas indeed they are produced suddenly, just as they are about to fall. How foolish it is to fight against God, who is prepared for battle and war, and how much it is in our interests to make our peace with him and keep ourselves in his love.

Verses 25–41

Up to now God has put questions to Job to convince him of his ignorance. Now he proceeds to show his weakness. Just as Job knows very little and therefore should not argue with divine purposes, so also he can do very little and therefore should not oppose the ways of providence. Let him consider what great things God does, and see whether he can do the same.

1. God has thunder, lightning, rain, and ice at his command, but Job does not, and so let him not dare compare himself with God or argue with him.

1.1. God has sovereign rule over the waters, even when they seem to overflow and to come away from his restraint (v. 25). He has *divided a watercourse*, cut a channel for the torrents of rain. The hearts of kings are therefore said to be *in God's hand*; and he directs them, as he directs the rains, those rivers of God, wherever he wishes (Pr 21:1). The lightning and the thunder are not blind bullets, but go the way God himself directs, and he means no harm by them. In directing the course of the rain, he does not neglect the desert (vv. 26–27), *where no man is.* God's providence reaches farther than human diligence. If God did not have more kindness for many of the lower creatures than humans have, things would go badly for them. When *there was not a man to till the ground*, a mist came up and watered it. But we cannot make it fruitful without God, for it is he who gives the growth (1Co 3:6–7). God has enough for all, and he wonderfully provides even for those creatures that humans neither need to serve them nor make provision for. He is, in a sense, *the Father of the rain* (v. 28). Even the small drops of dew he distills on the earth, as the God of nature. As the God of grace, he rains righteousness on us and is himself like dew to Israel. See Hos 14:5; Mic 5:5–7. The ice and the frost, by

which the waters are frozen, are produced by his providence (vv. 29–30). These are very common things, and this fact lessens their strangeness. But considering what a vast change is made by them in a very short time, we may well ask, *"Out of whose womb came the ice?* (v. 29). What created power could produce such a wonderful work?" No power except that of the Creator himself.

1.2. Job cannot command one shower of rain: "*Canst thou lift up thy voice to the clouds*, those containers of heaven, *that abundance of waters may cover thee* (v. 34), to water your fields when they are dry and parched?" Nor can he commission one flash of lightning, if he wants to use it to bring terror on his enemies (v. 35): "*Canst thou send lightnings, that they may go* on your mission? Will they come at your call and say to you, *Here we are?*" No; the ministers of God's wrath will not be our ministers.

2. God has the stars of heaven under his command and awareness. God especially mentions the fixed stars. It is thought that they have an influence on this earth despite their vast distance—not on the human mind or the events of providence, for human destinies are not determined by stars, but on the ordinary course of nature. And if the stars rule in such a way over this earth (v. 33), although they are only matter, much more does the One who is their Maker and ours, and who is an eternal Mind. *Canst thou bind the sweet influences of Pleiades? Canst thou loose the bands* (cords) *of Orion?* Both summer and winter have their courses. God can change them when he pleases. He can make the spring cold, and so bind the sweet influences of Pleiades, and make the winter warm, and so loose the cords of Orion, but we cannot. God, who *calls the stars by their names* (Ps 147:4), calls them out at their respective seasons, setting times for their rising and setting. But this is not our realm; we cannot *bring forth Mazzaroth*, the stars in the southern signs, or *guide Arcturus* (lead out the Bear), those in the northern sky (v. 32). We *know not the ordinances* (laws) *of heaven* (v. 33). We are so far from being able to change them that we cannot explain them; they are a secret to us. Will we then pretend to know God's purposes? Will we then teach God how to rule the world?

3. God is the author and giver, the father and fountain, of all wisdom and understanding (v. 36). Human souls are nobler and more excellent beings than the stars of heaven and shine more brightly. The powers and faculties of reason with which human beings are endowed bring them into some alliance with the blessed angels, and where does this light come from, except from the Father of lights (Jas 1:17)? *Who* else *has put wisdom into the inner parts of* man and *given understanding to the heart?* (v. 36). Both the rational soul itself and its powers come from him as the God of nature, for he forms the human spirit. We did not make our own souls, nor can we describe how they act or how they are united with our bodies. Only the One who made them knows them. Will we claim to be wiser than God, when all our wisdom comes from him?

4. God has the clouds under his watchful eye and government (v. 37). Can anyone, with all their wisdom, undertake to *number the clouds*? And when the clouds have poured down plenty of rain, so that *the dust grows into hardness*—solid mud—and *the clods cleave fast* (stick) *together* (v. 38), *who can stay the bottles* (water jars) *of heaven?* (v. 37). As we cannot command a shower of rain without God (1Ki 17:1; 18:42–46; Jas 5:17), so we cannot command a fine day without him.

5. God provides food for the lower creatures. The following chapter is completely taken up with examples of God's power and goodness toward animals, and so some commentators transfer to the next chapter the last

three verses of this chapter, which speak of the provision made for:

5.1. The lions (vv. 39–40). "Let us put that to the test, then: *Wilt thou hunt the prey for the lion?* You value yourself on the basis of the cattle you once owned, the oxen, donkeys, and camels that fed at your manger, but will you undertake to take care of the lions, and *the young lions, when they couch* (crouch) *in their dens*, waiting for their prey? No; they can fend for themselves without you. But I do it." The all-sufficiency of divine Providence has the resources to satisfy the desire of every living thing. Notice the goodness of divine Providence, that wherever it has given life, it will also give the livelihood.

5.2. The young ravens (v. 41). It is the same with ravenous birds: they are fed by divine Providence. *Who* but God *provides for the raven his food?* They cry, and this is interpreted as crying out to God. Because it is the cry of nature, it is looked on as being directed to the God of nature. He provides for them in some way or other, so that they grow up and reach maturity. And the One who takes this care of the young ravens will certainly not see his people lack anything they need.

CHAPTER 39

God here proceeds to show Job what little reason he has to accuse him of being unkind, since he is so compassionate toward the lower creatures and takes such tender care of them. Further, he shows him what great reason he has to be humble, since he knows so little about the creatures around him and has so little influence on them, and what great reason to submit to the God on whom they all depend. He speaks particularly: 1. About the wild goat and the doe (vv. 1–4); the wild donkey (vv. 5–8); the wild ox (vv. 9–12). 2. The peacock (v. 13) and the ostrich (vv. 13–18). 3. The horse (vv. 19–25). 4. The hawk and the eagle (vv. 26–30).

Verses 1–12

God shows Job here how little he knows about the wild creatures, which run about the deserts but are under the care of divine providence.

1. The *wild goats* and the *hinds* (does). Although they give birth to their young with much difficulty and sorrow and receive no help from humans, their young ones are safely born by the good providence of God (v. 3). Concerning the growth of their young (v. 4), God notes, *They are in good liking*, they grow strong and healthy. After their mothers have suckled them for a while, they fend for themselves in the wild and are no longer a burden to them, which is an example to children that when they have grown up, they must not always rely on their parents.

2. The *wild ass*, a creature we frequently read about in Scripture, which is according to some not tamable. *Who* but God *has sent out the wild ass free?* He has made him inclined toward liberty, and so he has given him liberty. Freedom from service, and liberty to wander at pleasure, are the privileges of only a wild donkey. It is a pity that any person should want such liberty. It is better to work and be good at something than wander around and be good for nothing. Yet to the wild ass Providence has assigned an unenclosed home (v. 6): *Whose house I have made the wilderness*, where he has enough space to move around. The tame donkey that works and is useful to people has its master's manger to go to for both shelter and food, and it lives in a fruitful land. The wild donkey, however, who wants his liberty, must have it in a barren land. He has no owner, nor will he submit to anyone: *He scorns the*

multitude (tumult) *of the city*, and *the crying* (shout) *of the driver is nothing to him. The range of the mountains is his pasture* (v. 8), and that pasture is bare. He *searches after here and there a* (any) *green thing* (v. 8), something he can find and pick up, whereas the donkeys that work have plenty of green things to eat, without searching for them. We may reason from the uncontrollability of this and other creatures how unqualified we are to command Providence, since we cannot even impose our will on a wild donkey's colt.

3. The wild ox or *unicorn* (Hebrew: *rem*), a strong (Nu 23:22), stately, proud creature (Ps 92:10). He is able to serve, but not willing, and God here challenges Job to force him to serve. "Since you are trying," God says, "to bring everything beneath your control, begin with the wild ox; try out your skill on that animal. Now that your oxen and donkeys are all gone, see whether the wild ox will be willing to serve you instead (v. 9) and whether he will be content with the provision you used to make for them: *Will he abide by thy crib*, will he stay by your manger at night? No; you can neither tame him nor hold him to the furrow with a harness" (v. 10). Although the wild ox will not serve us or submit with a harness to work a furrow, there are still tame oxen that will. "You dare not rely on him, even though his *strength is great*; you will not *leave thy labour to him* (v. 11), as you did with your donkeys or oxen. You will never depend on the wild ox, which is unlikely to come to your harvest work, much less finish it, to *bring home thy seed and gather it into thy barn*" (vv. 11–12).

Verses 13–18

The ostrich is a very large bird, but it never flies. Some have even called it "a winged camel." Notice:

1. Something that it has in common with the peacock, that is, beautiful feathers (v. 13): "Did you give proud wings to the peacocks?" Fine feathers make proud birds. The peacock is an emblem of pride; the ostrich also has beautiful feathers, but it is a foolish bird. God gives his gifts variously, and those gifts that appear the finest are not always the most valuable. Who would not rather have the voice of the nightingale than the tail of the peacock, or would not rather have the eye of the eagle and its soaring wings, and the natural affection of the stork, than the beautiful wings and feathers of the ostrich, which can never rise above the earth and is without natural affection?

2. Something that is peculiar to itself. Most birds, as well as other animals, are strangely guided by their natural instinct to provide for the preservation of their young. But the ostrich is unnatural, for the mother drops her eggs anywhere on the ground and does not care for them until they hatch. If the sand and the sun will hatch them, all well and good, for she will not warm them (v. 14). *The foot* of a traveler *may crush them*, and *the wild beast break them* (v. 15). *She is hardened against her young ones.* Her work in laying her eggs is futile, because she does not have that tender concern for them that she should have. *God has deprived her of wisdom.* This suggests that the ability which other animals have to nourish and preserve their young is a gift from God, and that, where it is not given, God has denied it, so that we may learn to make use of this care for them, as well as of the preservation of the ostrich as well as by the wisdom of the ant (Pr 6:6). Many parents are as negligent of their children: some are negligent of their children's bodies, not providing for their own household, and so are as bad as the ostrich; but many more are as negligent of their children's souls, taking no care of their education, sending them out into the world untaught and unprepared, and

forgetting what corruption there is in the world through its sinful desires (2Pe 1:4). The mother ostrich leaves her eggs in danger, but if she herself is in danger, she then lifts up her wings, and using them runs so fast that a horse rider could not overtake her at full speed: *She scorneth the horse and his rider.* Those who are least under the law of natural affection often fight most for the law of self-preservation.

Verses 19–25

Having displayed his power in those creatures that despise humans, God here shows it in one creature that is useful to humans, and that is the horse, especially *the horse that is prepared against* (made ready for) *the day of battle* (Pr 21:31). It seems there was a noble breed of horses in Job's country. The great horse has a great deal of strength and spirit (v. 19): *Hast thou given the horse strength?* Horses use their strength for humans, but God gave it to them. He is the fountain of all the powers of nature. It is a mercy to humans that we have such a servant, which although very strong, still submits to the direction of a child and does not rebel against its owner. His neck is *clothed with thunder* (v. 19), with a large and flowing mane. In snorting, *the glory of his nostrils*, he flings up his head and throws foam about, and *is terrible* (v. 20). Notice how he prances (v. 21): *He paws in the valley. He goes on to meet the armed men* (v. 21), excited only by *the sound of the trumpet, the thunder of the captains, and the shouting* (vv. 24–25) of the soldiers (v. 25). Notice how fearless he is (v. 22): *He mocks at fear* and laughs it off. High spirits are commended in horses rather than in human beings, who are not suited to being fierce or angry. This description of the war horse will help explain the characterization given to presumptuous sinners in Jer 8:6.

Verses 26–30

The birds are proof of the wonderful power and providences of God.

1. The *hawk* is a noble bird of great strength and wisdom, but still a bird of prey (v. 26). This bird is here commented on because of its flight, which is swift and strong, and especially for the course it steers *towards the south*, to which it follows the sun in winter. This is its wise instinct, but it was God, not humans, who gave it this wisdom.

2. The *eagle*, a royal bird, is here noted:

2.1. For the height of her flight. No bird soars so high, has such a strong wing, or can bear sunlight so well. Now, "*Doth she mount at thy command?* (v. 27). No; it is by the natural power and instinct God has given her."

2.2. For the strength of her nest. Her house is a castle and a stronghold; (v. 28); she makes it *on high* and *on the rock, the crag of the rock* (v. 28), so that she and her young are out of the reach of danger.

2.3. For her quicksightedness (v. 29): *Her eyes behold afar off*, not upwards, but downwards, in search of her prey. In this she is a symbol of a hypocrite, who while professing religious faith seems to rise toward heaven, but keeps their eyes and heart on their prey on earth: some physical advantage, some widow's house or other they hope to devour under pretense of devotion (Mt 23:14).

2.4. For the way she has of maintaining herself and her young. She preys on living animals, which she seizes, tears to pieces, and then carries to her young ones, which are taught to *suck up* (feast on) *blood* (v. 30). They do this by instinct and know no better. Our Savior refers to this instinct of the eagle (Mt 24:28): *Wheresoever the carcase is, there will the eagles be gathered together.*

CHAPTER 40

In the previous chapter, God put many humbling questions to Job, but now in this chapter: 1. He demands an answer to them (vv. 1–2); Job submits in humble silence (vv. 3–5). 2. In order to convict him, God proceeds to reason with him concerning the infinite distance and imbalance between him and God, showing that he is by no means an equal match for God. He challenges him (vv. 6–7) to rival him, if he dare, in justice (v. 8), power (v. 9), majesty (v. 10), and rule over the proud (vv. 11–14). 3. He gives an example of his power in one particular animal, here called the behemoth *(vv. 15–24).*

Verses 1–5

Here is:

1. A humbling challenge which God gave to Job. Job remained silent, and so God demanded his reply (vv. 1–2). Some think God spoke in a still, small voice, which had a more powerful effect on Job than the storm had, as it had on Elijah (1Ki 19:12–13).

1.1. God puts a convincing question to him: "*Shall he that contendeth with the Almighty instruct him*, will the one who argues with God correct him? (v. 2)." Those who quarrel with God are, in effect, trying to teach him how to do his work. Some read it, "Is it any wisdom to contend with the Almighty?"

1.2. God demands a quick reply to it: "*He that reproaches God let him answer*, let the one who accuses God answer (v. 2) this question according to his own conscience, and let his answer be, 'Far be it from me to argue with the Almighty or to try to teach him.'"

2. Job's humble submission. Job now came to himself (Lk 15:17) and began to soften into godly sorrow. When his friends reasoned with him, he did not yield. They had condemned him as an evildoer; Elihu himself had been very sharp with him (34:7–8, 37); but God had not spoken to him in such harsh words. We may expect better treatment from God than we receive from our friends. The good man is overcome by this here and submits himself as a conquered captive to the grace of God.

2.1. He acknowledges himself to be an offender (v. 4): "*Behold, I am vile,* I am unworthy and contemptible in my own eyes." Repentance changes our opinion of ourselves. When God talks with him, he has nothing to say: *What will I answer thee?* He here gives the reason for his silence; it is not because he is sullen, but because he is convinced he has been wrong.

2.2. He promises not to offend anymore. He imposes silence on himself (v. 4): "I will put my hand over my mouth; I will use it as a bridle, to restrain all emotional thoughts which may arise in my mind, and keep them from breaking out in immoderate speech." Job has allowed his evil thoughts to be expressed: "*Once have I spoken* wrongly, *yea, twice*, at different times, in one speech and another, but I have finished. I will not answer; I will not stand by what I have said or say it again; I will proceed no farther."

Verses 6–14

Job is greatly humbled by what God has already said, but not sufficiently humbled; God here proceeds to reason with him as he did before (v. 6). He begins with a challenge (v. 7; see also 38:3): "*Gird up thy loins now like a man*; if you have the courage and confidence you have claimed to have, then show them now." We must acknowledge:

1. We cannot rival God for justice. The Lord is righteous and holy in his dealings with us, but we behave in an unrighteous and unholy way toward him; we have much to blame ourselves for, but nothing to blame him for (v. 8): *"Wilt thou disannul my judgment,* would you discredit my justice?" *"Wilt thou,"* says God, *"condemn me, that thou mayest be righteous,* would you condemn me to justify yourself (v. 8)? Must my honor suffer to support your reputation?"

2. We cannot rival God for power, and so just as arguing with him is an act of great ungodliness, so also it is very arrogant: *"Hast thou an arm like God,* equal to his in length and strength? *Or canst thou thunder with a voice like him,* as he did earlier (37:1–2), or as he does now out of the storm?" Human beings cannot speak so convincingly, powerfully, or with such a commanding, conquering force as God can, who *speaks, and it is done.* His creative voice is called his *thunder* (Ps 104:7), as is his voice with which he terrifies and shatters his enemies. *Out of heaven shall he thunder upon them* (1Sa 2:10).

3. We cannot rival God for beauty or majesty (v. 10). "If you want to be compared to him, and if for that purpose you want to appear more attractive, then put on your best clothes: *Deck thyself now with majesty and excellency.* Appear in all your military splendor and all the royal pageantry that you have; make the best of everything that will make you look good. *Array thyself with glory and beauty,* such as may make your enemies reverence you and may charm your friends. But what is all that compared to divine majesty and beauty? It is nothing more than the light of a glowworm compared with the light of the sun in its power."

4. We cannot rival God for his rule over the proud (vv. 11–14). If Job can humble proud tyrants and oppressors as easily and effectively as God can, then it will be acknowledged that he has some reason to compete with God. Notice here:

4.1. The justice Job is here challenged to administer is to bring proud people low by a look.

4.1.1. It is supposed here that God can do it and will do it himself, or else he would not have suggested Job try to do it. In this, God proves himself to be God: he opposes the proud (Jas 4:6), sits as judge over them, and is able to destroy them. Proud people are evildoers, and pride lies at the root of much evil in this world. Proud people will certainly be brought low, for *pride goes before destruction* (Pr 16:18). When the wrath of God is scattered among the proud, it will humble them, break them, and bring them down. *Who knows the power of his anger?* (Ps 90:11). God can and does easily humble proud tyrants; he can *look upon them, and bring them low* by one angry look, just as he can, by one gracious look, revive the hearts of those who are contrite. He can not only bring them down to the dust, from which they might hope to arise, but also *hide them in the dust,* like the proud Egyptian whom Moses killed and *hid in the sand* (Ex 2:12). They were proud of how great they looked, but they will be buried and forgotten as those who are hidden in the dust. They were linked by alliances to cause trouble, but are now bound in bundles ready for burning (Mt 13:30). They are hidden *together* (17:16). He *binds their faces in secret* (v. 13), or as dead men. God will gain final victory over proud sinners who set themselves in opposition to him.

4.1.2. It is here proposed that Job do it. He has been passionately quarreling with God and his providence. "Come," God says, "first try your hand on proud people, and you will soon see how little they esteem your anger. Will I then regard it or be moved by it?" If God, and he

only, has enough power to humble proud people, no doubt he has enough wisdom to know when and how to do it, and it is not for us to give orders to him or to teach him how to rule the world.

4.2. The justice which is here promised to be done to him if he can perform such mighty works (v. 14): *"Then will I also confess unto thee that thy right hand* is sufficient to save you, although, in the end, it would be too weak to contend with me."

Verses 15–24

To further prove his own power, God concludes his speech with the description of two strong animals, far exceeding human beings in bulk and strength, one of which he calls the *behemoth,* the other the *leviathan.* In these verses we have the former described. *"Behold now behemoth* (v. 15), and consider whether you are able to argue with the One who made that animal and gave it all its power, and whether you would not be wiser to submit to him and make your peace with him." *Behemoth* may refer to animals in general, but here it must refer to one particular species. Some understand it to refer to the elephant; others to an amphibious animal, the hippopotamus (the "river horse"), which lives in the Nile River. But I tend to agree with the ancient opinion, that it is a description of the elephant. Notice:

1. The description here given of the *behemoth.*

1.1. His body is very strong and well built. *His strength is in his loins* (v. 16). His bones, compared with those of other creatures, *are like bars of iron* (v. 18). His backbone is so strong that although his tail is not large, he still moves it like a cedar, with commanding force (v. 17).

1.2. He feeds on the crops of the earth and does not prey on other animals: he *eats grass as an ox* (v. 15), and the *mountains bring him forth food* (v. 20). The animals of the field do not tremble before elephants or flee from them, as they do from a lion, but play around them, knowing they are safe.

1.3. He *lodges under the shady trees* (v. 21), which *cover him with their shadow* (v. 22), where he has a free and open air to breathe in, while lions, which live on their prey, when they want to rest, have to withdraw into a close and dark den, to live or stay in thickets (38:40). Those who are a terror to others must also at times be a terror to themselves, but those who let others roam at ease around them will be at ease themselves. Although the reeds and fens and the poplars by the stream are a very weak and slender fortification, they are still sufficient as defense and security for those who dread no harm because they intend none.

1.4. He is a very great and greedy drinker. His size is huge, and so he must be supplied accordingly (v. 23). His eyes are bigger than his stomach, for when he is very thirsty, *he trusts that he can drink up Jordan in his mouth* (v. 23), and even *takes it with his eyes* (v. 24). His nose has great strength, for when he goes greedily to drink, he *pierces through snares* (v. 24), or nets.

2. This description of this immense animal is an argument to humble ourselves before God in his greatness. He made this vast animal; he is the *behemoth which I made* (v. 15). He is here rightly called the *chief,* in his kind, *of the ways of God* (v. 19), ranking first among the distinguished examples of the Creator's power and wisdom. "It is the *behemoth, which I made with thee* (v. 15); I made that animal as much as I made you, and he does not quarrel with me, so why do you?" *He that made him can make his sword to approach to him* (v. 19), that is, the same hand that made him can, despite his great bulk and strength, unmake him again at pleasure, can kill an elephant as

easily as a worm or a fly, without any difficulty. God, who gave existence to all creatures, may take away what he gave, for may he not do what he wishes with his own? The *behemoth* perhaps is here intended—as well as the *leviathan* later—to represent those proud tyrants and oppressors whom God has just challenged Job to humble and bring down. The One who designed the engine and put all of its parts together knows how to take it to pieces.

CHAPTER 41

The description given here of the leviathan, *a very large, strong, formidable fish or sea animal, is intended to further convince Job of his own powerlessness and of God's almighty power. 1. To convince Job of his own weakness, he is here challenged to subdue and tame this* leviathan *(vv. 1–10). 2. To convince Job of God's power and awesome majesty, several detailed aspects of the strength and terror of the* leviathan *are described, a strength which is no more than what God has given him, or more than God has under his control (vv. 11–12). The face of the* leviathan *is said to be fearsome (vv. 13–14), his scales tightly sealed (vv. 15–17), his breath and snortings sparkling (vv. 18–21), his flesh firm (vv. 22–24), his strength and spirit insuperable when he is attacked (vv. 25–30), his movement turbulent (vv. 31–32), so that he is generally a terrible creature, and human beings are no match for him (vv. 33–34).*

Verses 1–10

Whether the *leviathan* is a crocodile or a whale is much disputed by commentators. The whale is much larger and a nobler animal, and the creation of whales was generally looked on as a most noble proof of the eternal power of the Creator. Here in these verses:

1. God showed how unable Job is to control the *leviathan.*

1.1. He could not catch him by fishing (vv. 1–2). He had no bait with which he could trick him, no fishhook with which to catch him, no fishing line with which to pull him out of the water, and no thorn to run through his gills, on which he could take him home.

1.2. He could not force him to cry out for mercy (vv. 3–4). "He knows his own strength too well to *make many supplications to thee,* and to *make a covenant with thee* to be your servant on the condition that you will save its life."

1.3. He could not entice him into a cage, to be kept there as a pet for children to play with (v. 5).

1.4. He could not have him served up to his table; he and his companions could not make a banquet of him.

1.5. They could not enrich themselves with spoil from him: *Shall they part him among the merchants* (v. 6), the bones to one, the oil to another? If they could catch him, they would, but the art of fishing for whales had probably not been perfected then, as it has been since.

1.6. They could not destroy him; they could not *fill his head with fish spears* (v. 7).

1.7. It was futile to try to subdue him: *The hope of taking him is in vain* (v. 9). *Shall not one be cast down even at the sight of him?* "Touch *leviathan* if you dare; *remember the battle,* how unable you are to counter such force." In this way, Job is also warned not to proceed in his argument with God, but to make his peace with him.

2. He reasons from this how unable Job is to argue with the Almighty. *None is so fierce,* none so foolhardy, *that he dares* to *stir up* the *leviathan* (v. 10). *Who then is able to stand before God?*

Verses 11–34

In the previous verses God had shown Job how unable he was to deal with the *leviathan,* and he here sets out his own power over that massive, mighty creature. Here is:

1. God's sovereign rule and independence established (v. 11).

1.1. That God is indebted to none of his creatures. "*Who has prevented me?*" that is, "Who has any claim against me that I must pay; who has placed any obligations on me by any services they have done to me?"

1.2. That God is the rightful Lord and owner of all creatures: "*Whatsoever is under the whole heaven* (v. 11), animate or inanimate, is *mine.*"

2. The proof and illustration of this, from the wonderful structure of the *leviathan* (v. 12).

2.1. The parts of his body and the power he wields are things that God will not fail to mention. Although *leviathan* is a creature of monstrous bulk, he has a *comely proportion,* a graceful form (v. 12).

2.1.1. On first impression, the *leviathan* appears formidable and unapproachable (vv. 13–14). Who dares, while he is alive, to come near enough to him to see or examine *the face of his garment,* the skin with which he is clothed, or to bridle him like a horse, or to come within reach of his jaws, which are like a *double bridle*? Who will dare to look into his mouth, as we do into a horse's mouth? If we were to *open the doors of his face,* we would see *his teeth terrible round about.*

2.1.2. *His scales are* his beauty and strength, and therefore *his pride* (vv. 15–17). The crocodile is indeed remarkable for its scales; if, on the other hand, we understand this to refer to the whale, we must understand these "shields," which are what the word literally refers to, to be the various layers of his skin.

2.1.3. The *leviathan* scatters terror with his very breath; if he spouts up water, it is as if flashes of light are being thrown out, either with the froth itself or with the light of the sun shining through it (v. 18). The eyes of the whale are reported to shine at night *like the eyelids of the morning*; some say the same of the crocodile. Probably these hyperbolical expressions are used of the *leviathan* to suggest how fearful the wrath of God is.

2.1.4. The *leviathan* is of invincible strength, so that he frightens everything that comes his way but is himself not frightened by anyone. Looking at his neck, one sees that strength resides there (v. 22). *Sorrow rejoices* (or "rides in triumph") *before him,* for he causes havoc wherever he goes. His flesh is of *brass,* which Job complained his was not (6:12). *His heart is as firm as a stone* (v. 24). He has spirit equal to his physical strength. *When he raises up himself,* like a moving mountain in the great waters, even *the mighty are afraid* that he may overturn their ships.

2.1.5. All the instruments of slaughter that are used against him do him no harm and are therefore no terror to him (vv. 26–29).

2.1.6. His very movement disturbs the water and puts it into a state of ferment (vv. 31–32).

2.2. God concludes with four general thoughts concerning this animal:

2.2.1. *Upon earth there is not his like* (v. 33). No creature in this world can compare with him for strength. It is good for human beings that he is confined to the waters and there has *a watch set upon him* (7:12).

2.2.2. He *is made without fear* (v. 33). The creatures are as they are made; the *leviathan* has courage in his constitution.

2.2.3. He is very proud. Although lodged in the deep, *he beholds all high things* (v. 34).

2.2.4. *He is a king over all the children of pride.*
Whatever physical achievements people are proud of
and puffed up with, the *leviathan* surpasses them and is
a king over them. Some read this as referring to God: "He
who beholds all high things, even he, is King over all the
children of pride"; he can tame the *behemoth* (40:15) and
the *leviathan.* This speech about those two animals was
included to prove that it is only God who can *look upon
proud men and abase them.* He is *King over all the children of pride* (v. 34), whether wild or tame, and can make
them all either bend or break before him (Isa 2:11).

CHAPTER 42

Solomon says, Better is the end of a thing than the beginning thereof *(Ecc 7:8). This was true in the story of Job;
in the evening, it was light. We have come across three
things in this book which, I confess, have troubled me
very much, but we find all three grievances put right in
this chapter. 1. It has greatly troubled us to see such a
holy man as Job so anxious, and especially to hear him
quarrel with God. Here he recovers his temper and is
sorry for the wrong he has said; he takes it back and
humbles himself before God (vv. 1–6). 2. It has also
greatly troubled us to see Job and his friends being at
such variance, even though they were all very wise and
good people. Here, however, we have this conflict also
set right, the differences between them satisfactorily
dealt with, and all joining together in sacrifices and
prayers, mutually accepted by God (vv. 7–9). 3. It has
also troubled us to see a man of such distinguished godliness and usefulness as Job suffering so intensely, in so
much pain, so poor, so dishonored, and made the very
center of all the adversities of human life, but here we
have this grievance also put right. Job is healed of all
his ailments, more honored and loved than ever, enriched
with double the possessions he had before, surrounded
by all the comforts of life, and as great an example of
prosperity as he had ever been of affliction and perseverance (vv. 10–17). All this is written to teach us, so
that we, under these and similar discouragements, may
have hope through endurance and the encouragement we
receive from these Scriptures (Ro 15:4).*

Verses 1–6

The words of Job to justify himself have come to an
end (31:40). The words of Job to judge and condemn himself have begun (40:4–5), and with these he here continues. Although his patience has not finished its work, his
repentance at his impatience has. He is here thoroughly
humbled for his foolish and rash speaking, and he is
forgiven. When God had said everything to him about
his own greatness and power in the creatures, *then Job
answered the Lord* (v. 1) in submission.

1. Job submits to the truth of God's unlimited power,
knowledge, and authority. This was the purpose of God's
speech out of the storm (v. 2).

1.1. He acknowledges that God can do everything.
What can be too hard for the One who made the *behemoth*
and *leviathan* and directs both as he pleases? He knew
this before and spoke very well on the subject himself,
but now he knows it more fully and is better able to apply
it. *"Thou canst do everything"* (v. 2), and so you can lift
me up out of this low condition, though I have so often
foolishly despaired of being rescued; I now believe you
are able to do this."

1.2. He acknowledges that *no thought can be withholden from him* (v. 2). God is aware of every anxious,

discontented, or unfaithful thought in our minds. *Whatever the Lord pleased, that did he* (Ps 135:6). Job has
said this emotionally, complaining about it (23:13): *What
his soul desireth even that he doeth*; now he says, with
delight and satisfaction, that God's *counsels shall stand*
(Isa 46:10). If God's thoughts about us are *thoughts of
good, to give us* even *an* un*expected end* (Jer 29:11), he
cannot be stopped from fulfilling his gracious purposes.

2. Job acknowledges he is guilty of what God charged
him with at the beginning of his speech (v. 3). "Lord, the
first word you said was, *Who is this that hideth counsel
by words without knowledge?* That word convinced me.
I acknowledge *I am the man* who has been so foolish.
That word struck my conscience and showed me my sin. I
have ignorantly overlooked the counsels and purposes of
God in afflicting me, and so have quarreled with God and
insisted too much on justifying myself: *Therefore I uttered
that which I understood not"* (v. 3), that is, "I spoke about
things I did not understand. I have judged the ways of
Providence, even though I was a complete stranger to the
reasons why you act as you do." He acknowledges himself to be ignorant of divine counsels, as we all are. We
see what God does, but we do not know why he does it
or what he will lead everything to. The reason why we
quarrel with Providence is that we do not understand it.
He acknowledges himself to be presumptuous in undertaking to speak about what he did not understand and to
make accusations about what he could not judge. *He that
answereth a matter before he heareth it, it is folly and
shame to him* (Pr 18:13).

3. Job will not answer, but he will *make supplication to
his Judge*, as he has said (9:15). "*Hear, I beseech thee, and
I will speak* (v. 4), not speak as a plaintiff or defendant
(13:22), but as a humble petitioner."

4. Job puts himself into the posture of one who is
repenting. In true repentance there must be not only conviction of sin, but also contrition and godly sorrow for it,
sorrow *after a godly manner* (2Co 7:9).

4.1. Job looked to God in his repentance. "*I have heard
of thee by the hearing of the ear.* I have known something of your greatness, power, and sovereign authority.
But now you have shown me yourself in your glorious
majesty by direct revelation. *Now my eyes see thee*, and
so I now repent and take back what I said foolishly." It
is a great mercy to have a good education, and to know
the things of God *by hearing* (Ro 10:17) the teaching
of his word and ministers. Yet when the understanding
is enlightened by the Spirit of grace, our knowledge of
divine things exceeds what we had before by as much as
the knowledge we have of a thing by seeing it for ourselves exceeds that which we have of it only by hearing
reports or rumors. God reveals his Son to us by the teachings of other people, but he reveals his Son in us by the
teachings of his Spirit (Gal 1:16), and so *changes us into
the same image* (2Co 3:18). God sometimes reveals himself most fully to his people by the rebukes of his word
and providence. *Blessed is the man whom thou chastenest
and teachest* (Ps 94:12).

4.2. Job thought hard thoughts about himself (v. 6):
Wherefore I abhor myself, and repent in dust and ashes.
Even good people, who have no blatant and outrageous
sins to repent of, must be greatly afflicted in their soul for
the activity and outbreaks of pride, passion, perversity,
and discontent, and for all their rash words. The more we
see of the glory and majesty of God, and the more we
see of the evil and repugnance of sin, and of ourselves
because of sin, the more we will humble and despise our-

selves for it. Let us leave it to God to rule the world, and be concerned, in the strength of his grace, to govern ourselves and our own hearts well.

Verses 7–9

While God was teaching Job out of the storm, one would have thought that only he was in the wrong, and that the case would certainly go against him, but here we find the sentence is given in Job's favor. Judge nothing, therefore, before the appointed time (1Co 4:5). Those who are truly righteous before God may have their righteousness clouded and eclipsed by great and uncommon adversities, by the severe criticism of their fellows, and by the sharp rebukes of conscience. But in due time, all these clouds will blow over, and God will *bring forth their righteousness as the light and their judgment as the noonday* (Ps 37:6). We have here:

1. Judgment given against Job's three friends, on the dispute between them and Job. Elihu is not criticized here, for he did not take sides in the argument, but acted as moderator. Job is exalted and his three friends are humbled. There is some truth on each side, and it is right that the judgment is the Lord's.

1.1. Job is greatly exalted and comes away with honor. Notice:

1.1.1. When God appeared for him: *After the Lord had spoken these words unto Job* (v. 7). After the Lord brought him to repentance for what he had said wrongly, then he acknowledged him in what he had said rightly. Those who truly repent will find favor with God, and what they have said and done wrongly will not be mentioned against them anymore.

1.1.2. How he appeared for him.

1.1.2.1. God calls him again and again *his servant Job*, four times in vv. 7–8, and he seems to take pleasure in calling him so, as he did before his troubles (1:8): "*Hast thou considered my servant Job?* Although he is poor and despised, he is my servant nevertheless, and he is as dear to me as when he was prosperous. Although he has his faults, and has appeared to be as human as anyone else, although he has argued with me, has set about discrediting my justice, and has obscured my counsel by words spoken without knowledge, he has now seen the errors of his ways and is sorry for them, and so he is still my servant Job." If God says, *Well done, good and faithful servant* (Mt 25:21), it is of little consequence who says otherwise.

1.1.2.2. He acknowledges that Job has *spoken of him the thing that was right* (vv. 7–8), beyond what his opponents have done. Job has given a much better and truer account of divine Providence than they have. They have wronged God by making prosperity a mark of the true church and affliction a sure sign of God's wrath. Job has referred things to the future judgment and the future state more than his friends have, and so he has spoken what is right about God better than his friends have. Although he has spoken some things wrongly, even about God, he is still commended for what he has spoken that was right. Job has been in the right, and his friends in the wrong, but it was he who was in pain, and they who were at peace — clear evidence that we cannot judge people by looking at their faces or purses. It is only God who can judge infallibly, because he sees our hearts.

1.1.2.3. He will promise on behalf of Job that despite all the wrong his friends have done him, Job is such a good person, and with such a humble, tender, and forgiving spirit, that he will very readily pray for them: *My servant Job will pray for you* (v. 8). Those who truly repent will not only find favor as petitioners for themselves, but

also be accepted as intercessors for others. And just as Job prayed and offered sacrifice for those who had grieved and wounded his spirit, so also Christ prayed and died for his persecutors, and always lives *making intercession for the transgressors* (Isa 53:12; Heb 7:25).

1.2. Job's friends are greatly humbled and come away disgraced. They were good people and belonged to God, and so God would not let them remain undisturbed in their mistakes any more than Job, but having humbled Job by a speech out of the storm, he used another way to humble them. In most disputes and arguments there is some wrong on both sides, either in the merits of the case or in the way in which the quarrel has been handled, if not in both, and it is right that both sides should be told about it and made to see their errors.

1.2.1. God tells them plainly that they have *not spoken of him the thing that was right, like Job* (v. 8), that is, they have criticized and condemned Job on a false basis, they have presented God as fighting against Job as an enemy when really he was only testing him as a friend. People are not speaking well of God if they present his fatherly discipline of his own children as judicial punishments. It is dangerous to judge uncharitably the spiritual and eternal state of others, for in so doing we may perhaps condemn those whom God has accepted.

1.2.2. He assures them he is angry with them: *My wrath is kindled against thee and thy two friends* (v. 7). He requires from them a sacrifice to make atonement for what they have said wrongly. Each of them must bring *seven bullocks, and* each of them *seven rams*, to be offered to God as a *burnt offering* (v. 8). He orders them to go to Job and beg him to offer their sacrifices and pray for them, or else they will not be accepted. They thought that they were the only favorites of heaven and that Job had no influence there, but God gives them to understand that Job has a greater influence there than they. Job and his friends have differed in their opinion about many things, but now they are to become friends. They must agree on a sacrifice and a prayer, and that must bring them together. Those who differ in thoughts about minor things are still one in Christ, the great sacrifice, and meet at the same throne of grace, and therefore should love and bear with one another. Our quarrels with God always begin with us, but reconciliation begins with him.

2. The judgment against Job's friends accepted by them (v. 9). They were good people, and as soon as they understood what the will of the Lord was, they did as he commanded them. Peace with God is to be obtained only in his own way and on his own terms, and they will never seem hard to those who know how to value that privilege. Job's friends had all joined together to accuse Job, and now they joined together in begging his forgiveness. Those who have sinned together should repent together.

Verses 10–17

You have heard of the patience (perseverance) *of Job,* says James (Jas 5:11), *and have seen the end of the Lord,* that is, what the Lord finally brought about with his troubles. At the beginning of this book, we read about Job's perseverance in his troubles, as an example. Here, at the close, to encourage us to follow that example, we have the fortunate outcome of his troubles and the prosperous condition to which he was restored. Perhaps, too, the extraordinary prosperity which Job was crowned with after his adversities was intended to give us as Christians a type and figure of the glory and happiness of heaven, which the adversities of this present time are achieving for us (Ro 8:18). Those who, when they are tested, rightly endure temptation will receive a *crown of life* (Jas 1:12).

1. God returned in mercy to Job. This gave a new outlook to his life immediately, and everything now appeared as pleasant and promising as before it had looked gloomy and terrible. God *turned his captivity* (v. 10), that is, he restored his fortunes and took away all causes of his complaints. He loosed him from the bonds with which Satan had restrained him for a long time. What was more, he felt a very great change in his mind. The mental turmoil was all over, and the comforts of God were now as much the delight of his soul as his terrors had been its burden. The tide had turned; his troubles began to go out as fast as they had come in, just *when he was praying for his friends* (v. 10). We are really doing a good work when we pray for our friends, if we pray rightly, for in those prayers there is not only faith but also love. Christ has taught us to pray with and for others in teaching us to say, *Our Father,* and in seeking mercy for others, we may find mercy ourselves. God doubled his possessions: *Also the Lord gave Job twice as much as he had before* (v. 10). He suffered for the glory of God, and so God made it up to him with interest, even more than compound interest. God will take care that no one is a loser because of him. Job's friends had often said, "*If thou wert pure and upright, surely now he would awake* (rouse himself) *for thee* (8:6). But he does not rouse himself for you, and so you are not upright." "Well," God says, "although your argument is not conclusive, I will use even that argument to show the integrity of my servant Job; the latter part of his life will be very prosperous."

2. Job's old acquaintances, neighbors, and relatives were very kind to him (v. 11). They wept with his grief, rejoiced with his joys, and did not turn out to be such miserable comforters as his three friends (16:2), who at first had been so eager and intrusive in visiting him. These were not so great or learned and eloquent as his three friends, but they proved much more skillful and kind in comforting Job. They took up a collection among themselves to make up his losses and to reestablish him. *Every one gave him a piece of money and every one an earring of gold* (v. 11), which would be as good as money to him. When God was friendly to him, they were all willing to be friendly too (Ps 119:74, 79). Others perhaps withdrew because he was poor, hard up, and a sad spectacle, but now that he began to recover, they were willing to renew their friendship with him. Fair-weather friends, who disappear in winter, will return in the spring, even though their friendship is of little value. Job *prayed for his friends* (v. 10), and then they flocked around him, overcome by his kindness, and everyone wanted to share in his prayers.

3. Job's possessions strangely increased, by the blessing of God on the little that his friends gave him. He received their courtesy with thankfulness and did not think it beneath him to have his estate restored by the contributions of others. God gave him what was far better than their money and earrings, and that was his blessing (v. 12). The Lord comforted him now for as many days as he had afflicted him (Ps 90:15), and *blessed his latter end more than his beginning.* The last days of good people sometimes prove their best days, their last works their best works, their last encouragements their best encouragements, for their path, like that of the morning light, shines more and more till the full light of day (Pr 4:18). We do not know what good times we may be reserved for in the latter part of our lives.

4. Job's family was built up again, and he had great comfort in his children (vv. 13–15). The number of his children was the same as before, *seven sons and three daughters* (v. 13). Some say the reason why they were not doubled, as his cattle were, was that his children who were dead were not lost, but had gone before him to a better world, and so he had two "flocks" of children, as we may put it, *mahanaim,* "two camps" (Ge 32:2), one in heaven, the other on earth. The names of his daughters are recorded here (v. 14), because their meanings seem intended to perpetuate the remembrance of God's great goodness to him in the surprising change of his condition. He called the first *Jemima,* which may mean "the day," because of the shining out of his prosperity after the dark night of affliction. The name of the next, *Kezia,* refers to cinnamon, a spice of very fragrant smell. The third he called *Keren-happuch,* that is, "plenty restored," or "a container of antimony" (a highly prized eye shadow), because, he said, God had wiped away the tears which had made his face offensive (16:16). We are told that God gave these daughters great beauty: *no women so fair as the daughters of Job* (v. 15). He made them coheirs with their brothers.

5. Job's life was long. He lived to enjoy much of the comfort of this life, for he saw his descendants to the fourth generation (v. 16). Although his children were not doubled to him, nevertheless, in his children's children—and those are the crown of the aged—they were more than doubled. God has ways of restoring the losses of life of those who are childless, and of balancing out their sorrows, as happened to Job when he had buried all his children. He died full of days, satisfied with life in this world and willing to leave it; not in an angry manner, as he was in during the days of his suffering, but devoutly, and so, as Eliphaz had encouraged him to hope, he *came to his grave like a shock of corn* (sheaves gathered) *in his season* (5:26).

A PRACTICAL AND DEVOTIONAL EXPOSITION OF THE BOOK OF

Psalms

We have before us one of the finest and most excellent parts of all the Old Testament; there is so much in it of Christ and his Gospel, as well as of God and his Law, that it has in fact been called *the abstract, or summary, of both Testaments*. The history of Israel, which we dealt with at length, led us to camps and councils, and there we received and were instructed in the knowledge of God. The book of Job took us to school, and we considered profitable and controversial matters for discussion about God and providence. But this book brings us into the sanctuary, leads us away from dealings with our fellow human beings, with politicians, philosophers, or debaters in this world, and directs us to enter into fellowship with God, by encouraging and resting our souls in him, lifting up and releasing our hearts toward him. Here we may be on the mountain with God, and we do not understand what is good for us if we do not say, *It is good to be here* (Lk 9:33). Let us consider:

1. The title of this book. 1.1. It is called the *Psalms*; under that title it is referred to in Lk 24:44. The Hebrew calls it *Tehillim*, which properly means "Psalms of praise," because many of them are such, but *Psalms* is a more general word, referring to all metrical compositions fit to be sung, which may well relate to history, doctrine, or supplication, as well as praise. Although singing is especially the voice of joy, the intention of songs is to help the memory, and to express and excite all the other emotions as well as joy. The priests made mournful meditations as well as joyful ones, and the divine institution of singing psalms has this largely in mind, for we are directed not only to praise God, but also to teach and admonish ourselves and one another *in psalms, and hymns, and spiritual songs* (Col 3:16). 1.2. It is called the *Book of Psalms*; it is quoted in that way by the apostle Peter (Ac 1:20). It is a collection of psalms, of all the psalms that were divinely inspired.

2. The author of this book. It is, of course, derived originally from the blessed Holy Spirit. The psalms are spiritual songs, words that the Holy Sprit taught. The author of most of them was David, the son of Jesse, who is therefore called the *sweet psalmist of Israel* (2Sa 23:1). Some psalms that do not have his name in their titles are still expressly ascribed to him elsewhere, such as Pss 2 (Ac 4:25) and 96 and 105 (1Ch 16). One psalm is expressly said to be *the prayer of Moses* (90); and the fact that some of the psalms were written by Asaph is suggested in 2Ch 29:30, where the people are said to *praise the Lord in the words of David and Asaph*, who is there called *a seer* or prophet. Some of the psalms seem to have been written much later, such as Ps 137, which was written at the time of the Exile in Babylon, but the great majority of them were certainly written by David himself.

3. The scope of this book. It is clearly intended: 3.1. To help the exercises of religious faith and to kindle in the human soul the godly devotion which we are to give to God as our Creator, owner, ruler, and benefactor. The book of Job helps show the basic principles of divine attributes and providence, but this book helps us build on them and turn that knowledge into prayers and praises and expressions of dependence on him. Other parts of Scripture show that God is infinitely above us, and our sovereign Lord, but this book shows us that there are ways in which we may maintain our fellowship with him in all the changing scenes of human life. 3.2. To promote the excellencies of revealed religious faith, and in the most pleasant and powerful way to commend it to the world. There is indeed little or nothing of the ceremonial law in the book of *Psalms*. Although sacrifice and offering were still to continue for a long time, they are nevertheless here presented as things which God did not desire (40:6; 51:16), as things that are comparatively insignificant and which in time were to disappear. But those parts of the word and law of God which are moral and are binding on us forever are exalted and made honorable here. And Christ, the crown and center of revealed religion, the foundation, cornerstone, and capstone of that blessed building, is here clearly spoken of in type and prophecy; so also are his sufferings and the glory that would follow, and the kingdom that he would set up in the world.

4. The use of this book. Because all Scripture is inspired by God, it is profitable to shed divine light onto our understanding (2Ti 3:16), but this book is of special use to communicate divine life and power, and a holy warmth, to our inner life. 4.1. It is useful for singing. Even the experts are not certain what the rules of Hebrew meter are. But these psalms should be rendered according to the meter of every language, at least so that they may be sung to build up the church. These divine poems are so rich and so well constructed that they can never be exhausted; they can never be worn threadbare. 4.2. It is useful for being read by the ministers of Christ, as containing excellent truths and rules concerning good and evil. 4.3. It is useful for being read and meditated on by all good people. The psalmist's experiences are of great use to direct, warn, and encourage us. In telling us, as he often does, what took place between God and his soul, he lets us know what we may expect from God, and what God will expect, require, and graciously accept from us. Even the psalmist's expressions are of great use, and by them the Spirit helps our weaknesses in prayer (Ro 8:26). If we become familiar with David's psalms, then whatever mission we have at the throne of grace, we may find in the Psalms apt expressions with which to convey it, sound words that cannot be condemned (Tit 2:8). We may sometimes use one special psalm and sometimes another, and pray it over, that is, enlarge on each verse in our own thoughts and offer up our meditations to God as they arise from the expressions we find there. Nor is it only our devotion that the book of Psalms helps, teaching us how to offer praise so as to glorify God; it is also a guidebook for the actions of our lives and teaches us how to *order our conversation aright, so that*, in the end, *we may see the salvation of God* (50:23). The Psalms were therefore useful to the Old Testament church, but to us Christians they may be more useful than they were to those who lived before Christ, for just as Moses' sacrifices, so also David's songs, are explained and made more intelligible by the Gospel of Christ, which allows us to come behind the curtain (Heb 6:19), so that if we add the apostle Paul's prayers in his letters and the new songs in Revelation to David's prayers and praises, we will be thoroughly equipped for this good work (2Ti 3:17).

As to the division of this book, we need not be very concerned; there is no connection (or only rarely) between one psalm and another, nor is there any discernible reason for placing them in the order in which we here find them. Some have tried to classify the psalms under headings, according to their subject matter, but there is often such a variety in one and the same psalm that this cannot be done with any conviction. The seven penitential Psalms have been especially singled out by the devotions of many. They are reckoned to be 6, 32, 38, 51, 102, 130, and 143. The Psalms were divided into five books, each concluding with *Amen, Amen*, or *Hallelujah*; the first ending with 41, the second with 72, the third with 89, the fourth with 106, the fifth with 150. Let true Christians divide them for themselves in whatever way enables them to get to know them better, so that they may have them near them on every occasion and may sing them in the spirit and with the understanding (Eph 6:18; Ps 47:7).

PSALM 1

This is a psalm of instruction concerning good and evil, setting before us life and death, the blessing and the curse (Dt 30:19), so that we may follow the right way, which leads to happiness, and avoid what will certainly end in our misery and ruin. This psalm shows us: 1. The holiness and happiness of godly people (vv. 1–3). 2. The sinfulness and misery of evildoers (vv. 4–5). 3. The basis and reasons for the conditions of both (v. 6).

Verses 1–3

The psalmist begins with the character and condition of godly people, so that those to whom the comfort of godliness belongs may first take comfort in it. Here is:

1. A description of the spirit and way of godly people, which we are to use to test ourselves. The Lord knows those who are his by name (Jn 10:3), but we must know them by their character. The character of good people is shown here in the rules they choose to walk by.

1.1. A godly person (v. 1) *walks not in the council of the ungodly.* This aspect of character is put first because departing from evil is the point at which wisdom begins. The godly person sees evildoers all around him; the world is full of them. They are here described by three names: *ungodly, sinners,* and *scornful.* They are *ungodly* at first, rejecting the fear of God. When the practices of religious

faith are set aside, they come to be *sinners*, that is, they break out into open rebellion against God. Sins of omission make way for sins of commission, and the heart is so hardened by these that finally they come to be *scorners*, that is, they openly defy all that is sacred, mock and scoff at religious faith, and make jokes about sin. The word which we translate *ungodly* refers to those who are evil and unsettled, having no certain end to aim at; they walk by no certain rule, but are at the command of every sinful desire and at the beck and call of every temptation. The good person looks at this with a sad heart. He does not follow their ways. He does *not walk in the counsel of the ungodly* (v. 1): he does not take his standards from their principles or act according to the advice they give and take. He *stands not in the way of sinners* (v. 1): he avoids doing as they do; he will not follow the way of sinners. He *sits not in the seat of the scornful* (v. 1): he does not associate with those who plot ways and means to support and advance the Devil's kingdom.

1.2. A godly person submits to the guidance of the word of God and comes to know his word in order that he may do what is good and remain faithful to it (v. 2). All who are pleased there is a God must also be pleased there is a Bible, a revelation of God, his will, and the only way to happiness in him. *In that law doth he meditate day and night* (v. 2). To meditate on God's word is to discuss with ourselves the great things it contains, with concentration of mind and devoted attention, until we are appropriately affected by those things and experience their savor and power in our hearts.

2. An assurance given of the happiness of the godly person. God blesses him, and that blessing will make him happy. Goodness and holiness not only lead to happiness (Rev 22:14) but are happiness itself. Even if there were not another life after this, those people who kept to the path of their duty would be those who were happy. *He shall be like a tree*, fruitful and flourishing. God's blessing produces real effects. The good person is planted by the grace of God. The trees the psalmist had in mind were by nature wild olives and would continue to be until they were grafted afresh and planted by a power from above (Ro 11:17–24). No good tree ever grew by itself; every tree is *the planting of the Lord*, and so he must be glorified in it, to display his splendor (Isa 61:3). The godly person is placed near the means of grace, here called *the rivers of water* (v. 3). It is from these that he receives supplies of strength and vigor, but in secret, undiscerned ways. It is expected from those who enjoy the mercies of grace that, both in the attitude of their minds and in the constant progress of their lives, they will comply with the intentions of that grace and produce fruit. *His leaf also shall not wither* (v. 3). As to those who produce only the leaves of faith, without any good fruit, even their leaves will wither, but if the word of God rules in the heart, that will keep the faith fresh; laurels won in this way will never wither.

Verses 4–6

Here:

1. The description of the ungodly is given (v. 4). In general, they are the reverse of the righteous, both in character and in condition. They yield no fruit but grapes of Sodom; they burden the ground (Lk 13:7). In particular, whereas the righteous are like valuable, useful fruitful trees, *they are like the chaff which the wind drives away* (v. 4), the very lightest of the chaff, the dust which the owner of the floor wants to have driven away, as incapable of being put to any use.

2. The fate of the ungodly is read (v. 5). *They shall not stand in the judgment*, that is, they will be found guilty. They will not stand *in the congregation of the righteous* (v. 5). Evildoers will have no place in that congregation. No one unclean or unsanctified will enter into the New Jerusalem (Rev 21:27). Hypocrites in this world, who made a plausible profession, may put themselves into the assembly of the righteous and remain undisturbed and undiscovered there, but Christ cannot be deceived, even though his ministers may.

3. The reason is given for this different state of the godly and evildoers (v. 6). The Lord approves of and is pleased with the way of the righteous, and so, under the influence of his gracious smiles, it will prosper and end well. But he is angry at the way of evildoers; all they do is offensive to him, and so their way will perish, and they in it.

In praying over and singing these verses, let us develop a holy dread of the fate of evildoers, and with a righteous concern present ourselves approved to God in everything (2Ti 2:15), seeking his favor with our whole hearts.

PSALM 2

As the previous psalm was moral and showed us our duty, so this one is evangelical and shows us our Savior. Using David's kingdom as a type—for that kingdom was divinely appointed, met with much opposition, but prevailed at last—the kingdom of the Messiah, the Son of David, is prophesied. It is interpreted as referring to Christ in Ac 4:25–26; 13:33; Heb 1:5. The Holy Spirit foretells here: 1. The opposition that will be raised against the kingdom of the Messiah (vv. 1–3); the frustrating and rebuking of that opposition (vv. 4–5); the setting up of the kingdom of Christ, despite that opposition (v. 6). 2. The confirmation and establishment of the kingdom (v. 7); a promise of the enlargement and success of the kingdom (vv. 8–9). 3. A call and exhortation that will be given to kings and rulers to submit themselves as willing subjects of this kingdom (vv. 10–12). Or, we have here threats declared against the enemies of Christ's kingdom (vv. 1–6); promises made to Christ himself, the head of this kingdom (vv. 7–9); counsel given to all to embrace the interests of this kingdom (vv. 10–12).*

Verses 1–6

We have here a very great struggle for the kingdom of Christ, with hell and heaven contesting it. The arena of this battle is this earth. Notice:

1. The mighty opposition that would be raised against the Messiah and his kingdom (vv. 1–3). One would have expected that such a great blessing to this world would be universally welcomed and taken up. Yet never were the ideas of any group of philosophers, or the powers of any ruler, opposed with so much violence as the teaching and rule of Christ. We are told:

1.1. Who will oppose Christ's kingdom. Princes and people, court and country, sometimes have separate interests, but here they are all united against Christ. Though Christ's kingdom is not of this world (Jn 18:36) and is not in the slightest way calculated to weaken their interests, the kings of the earth and rulers are immediately up in arms. As the Philistines and their lords, Saul and his courtiers, the disaffected party and their ringleaders, opposed David's coming to the crown, so also Herod and Pilate, the Gentiles and the Jews, did all they could against Christ and his growing relationship with people (Ac 4:27).

1.2. Who it is that they quarrel with. They quarrel *against the Lord and against his anointed* (v. 2), that is, against all religion in general and the Christian religion in particular. The great author of our holy faith (Heb 12:2) is here called *the Lord's anointed*, or the Anointed one, *Messiah* or *Christ*, in allusion to the anointing of David as king. It is spiteful and evil.

1.3. The opposition they give. They *rage* and conspire; they gnash their teeth in anger at the setting up of Christ's kingdom, and their opposition is deliberate and cunning. They *imagine*; they plot or contrive ways of suppressing the advance of Christ's kingdom. It is resolute and obstinate; they *set themselves* to defy reason. They combine and ally themselves with one another; they *take counsel together* (v. 2) to enliven and encourage one another. They will be content to retain such ideas of the kingdom of God and the Messiah as will support their own rule. If the Lord and his Anointed One will make them rich and great in the world, then they will make them welcome. But if they are going to restrain their corrupt appetites and passions, *they will not have this man to reign over them* (Lk 19:14). Christ has *bands and cords*, chains and fetters (v. 3), for us, but they are *cords of a man*, conforming to reason, and *bands of love*, conducive to our best interests (Hos 11:4). Why do people oppose religion except because they do not want to be under its restraints and obligations? They want to break in pieces the bonds of conscience they are under and the ties of God's commandments.

1.4. They are here reasoned with about it (v. 1). Why do they do this? They can show no good reason for opposing such a just, holy, and gracious rule. They can hope for no success in opposing such a powerful kingdom. It is *a vain thing*. When they have done their worst, Christ will have a church in the world, and that church will be glorious and triumphant. It is *built upon a rock, and the gates of hell shall not prevail against it* (Mt 16:18).

2. The mighty conquest gained over all this threatening opposition. The perfect rest of the eternal Mind may be our comfort whenever our minds are disturbed. We are tossed about on earth and on the sea, but he sits in heaven, where he has prepared his throne for judgment.

2.1. The attempts of Christ's enemies are easily ridiculed. God *laughs at* them. They are all fools.

2.2. They are justly punished (v. 5). Although God despises them as powerless, he is justly displeased with them. The enemies conspire, but they cannot disturb God. His setting up of the kingdom of his Son, despite them, is the greatest possible frustration to them.

2.3. They are certainly defeated, and all their plans turned upside down (v. 6): *Yet have I set my king upon my holy hill of Zion*. Jesus Christ is King, and God is pleased to call him *his* King, because he is appointed by him and entrusted by him with the sole administration of rule and justice. He is his King, for he is precious to the Father, and One in whom he is well pleased (Mk 1:11). Christ did not take this honor on himself, but was called to it. Being called to this honor, he was confirmed in it. "*I have set him* (v. 6), I have settled him."

We are to sing vv. 1–6 with holy joy, triumphing in Jesus Christ as the One to whom power is entrusted. We are to pray in the firm belief of the assurance given here, "Father in heaven, *Thy kingdom come* (Mt 6:10); let your Son's kingdom come."

Verses 7–9

Let us now hear what the Messiah himself has to say for his kingdom.

1. The kingdom of the Messiah is founded on an eternal decree of God the Father. It was not a sudden decision, not a mere test or experiment, but the result of the plans of divine wisdom.

2. There is a declaration of that decree, as far as is necessary to satisfy all those who are called and commanded to yield themselves as subjects to this king, and as far as is necessary to leave those without excuse (Ro 2:1) who will not have him reign over them. Christ here claims a twofold entitlement to his kingdom:

2.1. An entitlement by inheritance (v. 7): *Thou art my Son, this day have I begotten thee*. The writer to the Hebrews quotes this Scripture (Heb 1:5) to prove that Christ has a name superior to that of the angels, but that he *obtained it by inheritance* (Heb 1:4). He is the Son of God and so is of the same nature as the Father. He has in him all the fullness of the Godhead (Col 2:9), infinite Wisdom, power, and holiness. It is for this reason we are to receive him as a King, for because the *Father loveth the Son he hath given all things into his hand* (Jn 3:35; 5:20). Being a Son, he is heir of all things (Heb 1:2), and because the Father has made the worlds by him, it is easy to reason from this that he also rules them by him, for he is the eternal Wisdom and the eternal Word. Immediately after his resurrection, he entered on the ministry of his kingdom as mediator; it was then that he said, *All power is given unto me* (Mt 28:18).

2.2. An entitlement by agreement (vv. 8–9). The agreement is, in short, this: the Son must undertake the *office* of an intercessor, and, on that condition, he will have the honor and power of a universal monarch. The Father will grant more than half of the kingdom (Est 5:3; Mk 6:23), even the kingdom itself. The Son's rule will be universal: it is here promised him that he will have *the heathen* (the nations) as his inheritance, not only the Jews but also the Gentiles. A great part of the Gentile world received the Gospel when it was first preached, but it still has to be accomplished further, when *the kingdoms of this world shall become the kingdoms of the Lord and of his Christ* (Rev 11:15). The Son's rule will also be victorious: *Thou shalt break them*—those of them who oppose your kingdom—*with a rod of iron* (v. 9). This was in part fulfilled when the nation of the Jews, those who persisted in unbelief and enmity to Christ's Gospel, were destroyed by the Roman power. It was fulfilled further in the destruction of the powers of nations, when the Christian faith was established. But it will not be completely fulfilled until all opposing rule, principality, and powers are finally destroyed (110:5–6; 1Co 15:24).

In praying over and singing these verses, we must give glory to Christ as the eternal Son of God and our rightful Lord, and must take comfort from this promise, and plead it with God: that the kingdom of Christ will be enlarged and established and will triumph over all opposition.

Verses 10–12

Here is the practical application of this Gospel teaching about the kingdom of the Messiah, by way of exhortation to the kings and rulers of the earth. They hear that it is futile to oppose Christ's rule, and so they should be wise enough to submit to it. The One who has power to destroy them shows that he has no pleasure in their destruction, for he puts them into a position to make themselves happy (v. 10). What is said to them is said to everyone. We are exhorted:

1. To fear God and stand in awe of him (v. 11). This is the great duty of religious faith. We must serve God in every service of worship, with a holy fear. We must rejoice in God, but with holy trembling. Our salvation must be worked out *with fear and trembling* (Php 2:12).

2. To welcome Jesus Christ and submit to him (v. 12). This is the great duty of the Christian faith.

2.1. The command given to this effect: *Kiss the Son* (v. 12). Christ is called the *Son* because this was what he was declared to be (v. 7): *Thou art my Son*. He is the Son of God by eternal generation, and for that reason he is to be adored by us. Our duty to Christ is here expressed figuratively: *Kiss the Son* (v. 12), not with a betraying kiss, as Judas kissed him, but with a believing kiss. And it must be a kiss of affection and sincere love: "*Kiss the Son* (v. 12); enter into a covenant of friendship with him, and let him be very dear and precious to you. Love him above all others, love him sincerely, love him very much, as the woman did who was forgiven much and kissed his feet as a sign of it" (Lk 7:38). We are to give him a kiss of our allegiance and loyalty, submit to his rule, and take on his yoke.

2.2. The reasons given to add force to this command:

2.2.1. The certain ruin we are destined for if we refuse and reject Christ: "*Kiss the Son* (v. 12), for your lives are in danger if you do not. Do it, *lest he be angry*" (v. 12).

2.2.2. The happiness we are sure of if we submit to Christ. In the day of wrath, blessed will those be who by trusting in Christ have made him their refuge and guardian. When the hearts of others fail them for fear, they will lift up their heads with joy.

In praying over and singing these verses, we should have our hearts filled with a holy awe of God, but at the same time lifted up with a cheerful confidence in Christ, in whose mediation we may gain strength and encouragement for ourselves and one another.

PSALM 3

As the previous psalm showed us the royal dignity of the Redeemer, with David put forward as a type of him, so this psalm shows us, by the example of David in distress but under divine protection, the peace and holy security of the redeemed. David, driven from his palace, from the royal city, from the Holy City, by his rebellious son Absalom: 1. Complains to God about his enemies (vv. 1–2); confides in God and encourages himself in him as his God, nevertheless (v. 3). 2. Recollects the assurance he had in the gracious answers God gave his prayers and remembers his experience of God's goodness to him (vv. 4–5); triumphs over his fears (v. 6) and over his enemies (v. 7); gives God the glory and encourages himself with the divine blessing and salvation which are certain for all the people of God (v. 8).

Title

1. The title of this psalm and those of many others are each like a key hanging ready at the door, to open it so that we may go in and partake of the good things inside. When we know on what occasion a psalm was written, we are in a better position to explain it.

2. David was very sad. As he fled, he went up the Mount of Olives, and he wept greatly, with his head covered, going barefoot. It was *then* that he wrote this encouraging psalm. He wept and prayed, wept and sang, wept and believed. Is anyone in trouble with undutiful and disobedient children? David was, but that did not lessen his joy in God or put him out of tune to sing holy songs.

3. He was in great danger. The plot against him had been skillfully planned. Those who sought to destroy him were formidable, with his own son as their leader, and so his life seemed to be in danger. But it was *then* that he remembered and kept hold of the privileges of his relationship with God. Dangers and shocks should drive us to God, not away from him.

4. He had now received a great deal of provocation from those he had reason to expect better things of: from his son, whom he had spoiled, and from his subjects, whom he had been such a great blessing to.

5. He was suffering for his sin in the incident with Uriah. This was the evil which, for that sin, God threatened to *raise up against him out of his own house* (2Sa 12:11). But all these reasons did not make him reject his confidence in God's power and goodness or make him despair of help. Even our sorrow for sin must not prevent either our joy in God or our hope in God.

6. He seemed cowardly in fleeing from Absalom, leaving his royal city without even fighting for it, but this psalm shows he was full of true courage arising from his faith in God.

Verses 1–3

In these three verses David turns to God. When anything grieves us or frightens us, where else should we go except to him (Jn 6:68)? He comes to his God:

1. With a description of his distress (vv. 1–2). He looks around and takes a view of his enemies' camp, as it were. David was in the hearts of his subjects as much as any king ever was, but now he had suddenly lost them. They rose up against him. Their aim was to cause him trouble, but that was not all. They said about him, *There*

is no help for him in God (v. 2). They put a spiteful and invidious interpretation on his troubles, as Job's friends did on his, concluding that because his servants and subjects had abandoned him and did not help him, God had deserted him and his cause, and he was therefore to be looked on as a hypocrite and an evildoer. They tried to shake his confidence in God and drive him to despair of ever receiving relief from him: "They have said it to my soul," it may be read; compare 11:1; 42:10. David comes to God and tells him what his enemies said of him. "They say, *There is no help for me in thee,* but Lord, if it is so, I am ruined. They say to my soul, 'There is no salvation,'"—for the word translated "help" also means "salvation"—"*for him in God*; but Lord, say to my soul, *I am thy salvation* (35:3), and that will give me assurance and silence them in due time." He adds *Selah* to this complaint. Some think this word refers to the music with which, in David's time, the psalms were sung; others think it refers to the sense and that it is a note commanding a solemn pause. *Selah,* "Mark that," or, "Stop and consider this a little." So when it is written here that they say, *There is no help for him in God, Selah* (v. 2), it is as if to say, "Take time for such a thought as this. *Get thee behind me, Satan* (Mt 16:23)."

2. With a profession of his dependence on God (v. 3). David took hold of God all the more firmly when his enemies said, *There is no help for him in God* (v. 2). He cried out with great assurance, "*But thou, O Lord! art a shield for me* (v. 3). *Thou art a shield for me,* or a shield 'around me,' to keep me safe on every side, since my enemies have surrounded me." *Thou art my glory. Thou art the lifter up of my head* (v. 3). If God's people can lift up their heads with joy in the worst of times, knowing that in all things God works for the good of those who love him (Ro 8:28), they will acknowledge it is God who lifts up their head, who gives them both cause to rejoice and hearts to rejoice.

Verses 4–8

David has used the provocation of his enemies to stir himself up to take hold of God as his God, and in this way he has gained assurance by looking upward when, if he looked around him, he could see only what was discouraging. He here looks back with pleasant reflections and forward with pleasant expectations of a happy conclusion to which the dark times he is now in will soon be brought.

1. David had been exercised by many difficulties, often oppressed and brought very low, but he still found God to be all-sufficient.

1.1. His troubles had always brought him to his knees, and in all his difficulties and dangers he had been enabled to acknowledge God and lift up his heart to him, and his voice too: *I cried unto God with my voice* (v. 4).

1.2. He had always found God ready to answer his prayers: *He heard me out of his holy hill* (v. 4), that is, from heaven, the high and holy place, and from the ark on Mount Zion, from which it was his practice to answer those who sought him. Christ was *set King upon the holy hill of Zion* (2:6), and it is through him, whom the Father always hears, that our prayers are heard.

1.3. He had always been very safe and at peace under divine protection (v. 5): "*I laid myself down and slept,* composed and quiet; *and awaked* refreshed, *for the Lord sustained me.*"

1.3.1. We can apply this to the common mercies of every night, which we should give thanks for every morning when we are by ourselves and with our families.

1.3.2. It seems here to refer to the wonderful quietness and calmness of David's spirit in the midst of dangers. Having in prayer committed himself and his cause to God, and being sure of his protection, his heart was settled, and he was at peace.

1.4. God had often broken the power and restrained the hatred of his enemies, had *smitten them upon the cheek bone* (v. 7), had silenced them and defeated their words.

2. Notice with what confidence he looks ahead to the dangers he must still face.

2.1. His fears are all stilled and silenced (v. 6). *"I will not be afraid of ten thousands of people,* who either in a foreign invasion or in an internal rebellion *set themselves,* or camp, *against me round about."* When David was fleeing from Absalom, he told Zadok to take the ark back, spoke doubtfully about how his present troubles would be resolved, and concluded, like a humble penitent, *Here I am; let him do to me what seemeth to him good* (2Sa 15:26). But now he speaks confidently like a strong believer and is not afraid about how events will turn out.

2.2. His prayers are encouraged (v. 7). He believes God is his Savior, but he still prays; in fact, this is why he prays: *Arise, O Lord; save me, O my God!*

2.3. His faith becomes triumphant. He began the psalm with complaints about the power and hatred of his enemies, but he concludes it with an expression of joy at the power and grace of his God, and now he sees that the One who is with him is more than those who are against him (1Ki 6:16–17) (v. 8). He here rests his confidence on two great truths:

- That *salvation belongeth unto the Lord* (v. 8). He has the power to save, even if the danger is very great.
- That his blessing is on his people. He not only has power to save them, but also has assured them of his gracious intentions. In his word, he has declared a blessing on his people, and they must believe that such a blessing rests on them, even though its effects may not be visible.

PSALM 4

David was a preacher, and many of his psalms are doctrinal and practical as well as devotional. The greatest part of this psalm is doctrinal and practical. Here: 1. David begins with a short prayer (v. 1), and that prayer is a sermon. He directs his speech to the sons of men *and in God's name rebukes them for the dishonor they give to God and the harm they do their own souls (v. 2); he sets before them the happiness of godly people, to encourage them to be religious (v. 3); he calls on them to consider their ways (v. 4); he encourages them to serve God and trust in him (v. 5). 2. He gives an account of his own experiences of the grace of God working in him (vv. 6–8).*

Title

The title of the psalm tells us that David, having written it under divine inspiration for the use of the church, passed it to the *chief musician.* In 1Ch 25 we have a particular account of how this ministry was provided for: the arranging of the different groups of singers, each with a leader, and the share each had in the work.

Verses 1–5

1. David speaks to God (v. 1): *Have mercy upon me, and hear me.* All the notice God wishes to take of our prayers, and all the response he is willing to make to

them, must be ascribed not to anything we deserve, but purely to his mercy. "Hear me for the sake of your mercy" is our best plea. David here pleads two more things as the basis for his request:

1.1. "You are the *God of my righteousness* (v. 1). You are not only a righteous God yourself, but also the author of my righteous ways. By your grace you have worked good in me; you have made me righteous. *Hear me* for that reason.

1.2. *"Thou hast* formerly *enlarged me when I was in distress* (v. 1), enlarged my heart in holy joy and comfort in my distress; I am now at large, freed by you from my distress. *Now Lord,* have mercy on me and listen to me. *Thou hast; wilt thou not?* For you are God, and you do not change; your work is perfect."

2. David speaks to the *sons of men,* to convict and convert those who still do not know God, and who do not want the Messiah, the Son of David, to reign over them.

2.1. He tries to convince them that their ungodly ways are foolish (v. 2).

2.1.1. "You are corrupting yourselves, for you are *sons of men"* — the thought is that human beings are noble — "consider the dignity of your nature, and do not act so irrationally and in a way that does not give you your real honor.

2.1.2. "You are dishonoring your Maker, *turning his glory into shame"* (v. 2). Those who dishonor God's holy name, ridicule his word and ordinances, and deny him by their deeds while they profess to know him are *turning his glory into shame* (v. 2). *"You love vanity* (delusions) and *seek after leasing* (v. 2), seek false gods, *lying,* or what is *a lie.* You set your hearts on what will finally turn out to be a mere delusion and a lie." Those who love the world and seek the things of this world love delusion and seek false gods.

2.2. He shows them the special favor God has for his people, the special protection they are under and the special privileges to which they are entitled (v. 3). Those who *offend one of these little ones* (Mt 18:6), those whom God has *set apart for himself* (v. 3), will find their lives in danger. God regards that those who lay a finger on them as touching the apple of his eye (Zec 2:10), and he will make their persecutors know it, sooner or later. They *shall be mine, saith the Lord, in that day when I make up my jewels* (Mal 3:17). *Know this;* let godly people know it, and let evildoers know it and beware how they are hurting those whom God protects.

2.3. He warns them against sin and encourages them both to be afraid and to reason themselves out of sinning (v. 4): *Stand in awe and sin not*—"be angry and do not sin" is the reading of the Septuagint (a Greek version of the Old Testament). One good way to prevent sin and preserve a holy awe is to be frequent and serious in *communing with our own hearts* (v. 4): "Talk with your hearts; you have a great deal to say to them; they may be spoken to at any time; do not leave unsaid anything that you ought to say to them." If we are thoughtful, there is every possibility we will be wise and good. "Choose a time when you can be by yourself. Do it when you lie awake *upon your beds* (v. 4). Before you go to sleep at night"—as even some teachers who do not know God suggest—"examine your consciences for what you have done that day, especially what you have done wrong, so that you may repent of it. When you wake at night, meditate on God and the things concerning your peace" (Lk 19:42).

2.4. He advises them to conscientiously do their duty (v. 5): *Offer to God the sacrifice of righteousness.* We must not only stop doing evil, but also learn to do good (Isa 1:16–17). "*Offer sacrifices to him*, your own selves first, your best sacrifices. Let all your devotions come from an upright heart; let all your gifts to the needy be sacrifices of righteousness." Honor him, by trusting only in him, not in your wealth or in an arm of flesh (2Ch 32:8). Trust in his providence, and lean not on your own understanding (Pr 3:5). Trust in his grace, and do not set about trying to establish your own righteousness or adequacy (Ro 10:3).

Verses 6–8

We have here:

1. The foolish desire of worldly people: *There be many that say, Who will show us any good?* (v. 6). "Who will make us see good?" What good they meant is suggested in v. 7. It was the increase of their grain and new wine. All they wanted was to have plenty of worldly wealth, so that they might enjoy an abundance of worldly delights. They asked about the good that may be seen, and they showed no concern for the good things that are invisible and are the objects only of faith. As we must be taught to worship an invisible God, so we should seek an unseen good (2Co 4:18). With the eye of faith we can see farther than with our physical eyes. All that worldly people want is outward good, present good, partial good, good food, good drink, good business, and good possessions. But what are all these worth without a good God and a good heart? Any good will be enough for most people, but a gracious soul will not be satisfied that way.

2. The wise choice which godly people make. David, and the godly few who are faithful to him, join in this prayer: *Lord lift thou up the light of thy countenance upon us*, let the light of your face shine upon us (v. 6). He and his friends agree in their choice of God's favor as where their happiness lies. It is this that they consider better than life (63:3) and all its comforts. Although David speaks only about himself in vv. 7–8, in this prayer he speaks for others also—"*upon us*," just as Christ taught us to pray, *Our Father*. All the saints come to the throne of grace on the same mission, and they are one in this: they all want God's favor as their chief good. We should ask it for others as well as for ourselves, for in God's favor there is enough for us all, and we will never receive less because others share in what we have. This is what, above anything, they are joyful about (v. 7): "*Thou hast often put gladness into my heart.*" When God puts grace into the heart, he puts joy in the heart too, inward, solid, and substantial joy. "*I will lay myself down*, with the assurance of your favor, *in peace* (v. 8), *for thou only makest me to dwell in safety* (v. 8)." When he comes to sleep the sleep of death, he will then, with good old Simeon, *depart in peace* (Lk 2:29), being assured that God will receive his soul. He commits all his life to God and contentedly leaves his future with him.

PSALM 5

This psalm is a prayer, a sacred address to God, at a time when the psalmist was brought into distress by the hatred of his enemies. 1. David establishes a strong fellowship between his soul and God, promising God that he will pray and promising himself that God will certainly listen to him (vv. 1–3); he gives the glory to God and is assured of God's holiness (vv. 4–6). 2. He declares his determination to keep close to the public worship of God (v. 7). He prays for himself, that God will guide him (v. 8); against his enemies, that God will destroy them (*vv. 9–10*); *for all the people of God, that God will give them joy and keep them safe* (*vv. 11–12*).

Verses 1–6

In these verses David prays to God:

1. As a God who hears prayer. He has always been such a God, ever since people began to call on the name of the Lord (Ge 4:26), and he is still as ready to listen to our prayers. David describes him here: *O Lord* (vv. 1, 3), *Jehovah*, a self-existent, self-sufficient Being, whom we are bound to adore, and, "*my King and my God* (v. 2), to whom I have sworn allegiance, and under the protection of whom, as my King, I have put myself." We believe that the God we pray to is *a* King and *a* God, King of kings and God of gods; but the most powerful plea in prayer is an acknowledgment of him as *our* King and *our* God. Notice:

1.1. What David here prays for, which may encourage our faith and hope as we speak to God. *Give ear to my words, O Lord!* (v. 1). With other people, things are sometimes different. Some people perhaps will not or cannot hear us; our enemies are so proud that they will not, and our friends may be so far away that they cannot; but although God is high above us in heaven, he can and will listen to us. *Consider my meditation* (v. 1). David's prayers were made up not only of his words, but also of his meditation. Meditation and prayer should go together (19:14).

1.2. David here promises four things, and so must we:

1.2.1. That he will pray carefully. The assurances God has given us of his readiness to hear prayer should confirm our determination to live and die praying.

1.2.2. That he will pray *in the morning* (v. 3). Morning prayer is our duty; we are at our fittest to pray when we are freshest, liveliest, and in our most composed state of mind, when we are clear of the sleepiness of the night and have been revived, but are not yet filled with the business of the day. That is the time when we have our greatest need of prayer.

1.2.3. That he will be wholehearted: *I will direct my prayer* (v. 3), just as an archer aims at a target; we should turn to God with such a firmness and determination. And we must aim at his honor and glory as the highest purpose in all our prayers. Let our first petition be, *Hallowed, be thy name*, and then we may be sure of the same gracious answer to it that was given to Christ himself: *I have glorified it, and I will glorify it yet again* (Jn 12:28).

1.2.4. That he will patiently wait for a favorable answer: "*I will look up*, I will look after my prayers, and hear what God the Lord will speak (85:8; Hab 2:1), so that if he gives what I have asked, I may be thankful; so that if he denies my request, I may be patient; and so that if he delays in answering, I may continue to pray and wait and not give up."

2. As a God who hates sin (vv. 4–6). David takes notice of this. As the God with whom we have to do (Heb 4:13) is gracious and merciful, so also he is pure and holy. Although he is ready to hear prayer, he will not listen to our prayers if we harbor sin in our heart (66:18). God takes no pleasure in evil, even if it is covered by a veneer of religion. Let those who delight in sin know, therefore, that God takes no delight in them. "You will destroy those whom you hate," especially two kinds of sinners, who are here marked out for destruction, those who tell lies and are deceitful and those who are cruel: *Thou wilt abhor the bloody* (bloodthirsty) *man* (v. 6), for to the God of mercy, whom mercy pleases, inhumanity is no less perverse, no less hateful, than deceit.

Verses 7–12

In these verses David describes three kinds of people: himself, his enemies, and all the people of God, and he adds a prayer to each description.

1. He describes himself and prays for himself (vv. 7–8).

1.1. He is firmly decided to remain close to God and his worship:

1.1.1. To worship God, to give him his loyalty, and to give him the glory due to his name (29:2; 96:8).

1.1.2. To worship him publicly: "*I will come into thy house* (v. 7), the courts of your house, to worship there with other faithful worshipers." David often prayed alone (vv. 2–3), but he was also very faithful and devout in attending the sanctuary.

1.1.3. To worship him reverently and with a due sense of the infinite distance between God and people.

1.1.4. To take his encouragement in worship only from God himself. The mercy of God should always be both the foundation of our hopes and the fountain of our joy in everything we have to do with him.

1.2. He fervently prays that God by his grace will guide and preserve him always in the path of his duty (v. 8): "*Lead me in thy righteousness, because of my enemies*; the Hebrew reads literally, "Because of those who observe me," that is, "those who watch for me to stumble and seek to take unfair advantage of me."

2. He describes his enemies and prays against them (vv. 9–10). He has spoken (v. 6) of God's hating those who are bloodthirsty and deceitful. "Now, Lord," he says, "that is what my enemies are like: they are deceitful. Their words cannot be trusted. They do not speak reliably. Because of their sins, they have deserved destruction; there is enough to justify God in their being completely rejected: *Cast them out in the multitude of their transgressions* (v. 10), by which they have reached the measure of their sins and are ready to be destroyed." He pleads, "*They have rebelled against thee* (v. 10). If they had only been my enemies, I could safely have forgiven them, but they are rebels against God, his crown and honor. They oppose his government and will not repent to give him the glory. I therefore plainly foresee their ruin." His prayer for their destruction does not come from a spirit of revenge, but from a spirit of prophecy, by which he foretells that all who rebel against God will certainly be destroyed by their own plans and intrigues.

3. He describes the people of God and prays for them, concluding with an assurance of their happiness. They are the righteous (v. 12), for they *put their trust in God* (v. 11). They are assured of his power and all-sufficiency, they dare to risk everything on his promises, and they are confident of his protection. "*Let them rejoice* (v. 11); may they have cause to rejoice and hearts that rejoice. Fill them with a great and unspeakable joy." Let all who are entitled to God's promises share in our prayers; may grace be with all those who sincerely love Christ. "They are safe under the protection of your favor." *With favour wilt thou crown him*, as some understand it; and *with favour wilt thou compass him as with a shield*. In war, a shield guards only one side, but the favor of God toward the saints is a defense on every side. It is like the hedge around Job (Job 1:1): as long as they keep themselves under God's protection, they are completely safe and should be completely assured.

PSALM 6

David, as well as Jeremiah, was a weeping prophet, and this psalm is one of his lamentations. It was written at

a time of great trouble, both outer and inner. Is anyone troubled? Is anyone sick (Jas 5:13)? Let them sing this psalm. He begins with sorrowful complaints, but ends with joyful praises. The psalmist complains about three things: sickness of body, trouble of mind, and the insults of his enemies occasioned by both. 1. He pours out his complaints before God, prays to be saved from his wrath, and begs fervently for the return of his favor (vv. 1–7). 2. He assures himself of a favorable answer, soon, to his full satisfaction (vv. 8–10). This psalm is like the book of Job.

Verses 1–7

These verses are the language of a heart truly humbled under humbling providences, of a broken and contrite spirit (51:17) under great afflictions. Notice:

1. The description he gives God of his grievances. He pours out his complaint before him. To where else should children go with their complaints except to their father? He complains about physical pain and sickness (v. 2): *My bones are vexed*. His bones and his flesh, like Job's, have been struck. He complains about inner trouble: *My soul is also sorely vexed*, in anguish (v. 3), and that is much more painful than physical pain. It is sad when someone has their bones and their soul in agony at the same time. David not only suffered in both of these ways, but suffered for a long time: *Thou, O Lord! how long?* At such times, we must turn and speak to the living God—who is the only doctor of both body and mind—and not to the Assyrians (2Ki 19:4, 14–19) or the god of Ekron (2Ki 1:2).

2. The impression which his troubles made on him. They lay very heavily on him; he *groaned till he was weary*. David had more courage and wisdom than to mourn like this because of any outward suffering, but when sin sat heavily on his conscience, he grieved and mourned in secret, and even his soul refused to be comforted (77:2). Those who truly repent withdraw by themselves in order to weep. David mourned at night on the bed, where he lay searching his own heart (4:4), and no eye saw his grief except the eye of the One who sees everything. Peter went out, covered his face, and wept (Mt 26:75). David's eyes grew weak and old because of his enemies, who rejoiced in his suffering and misinterpreted his tears.

3. The requests which he offers to God in this sad and distressed state. What he fears as the greatest evil is the anger of God. He therefore prays (v. 1), *O Lord! rebuke me not in thy anger*, even though I have deserved it, *neither chasten me in thy hot displeasure*. He can bear the rebuke and discipline well enough if at the same time God lets the light of his face shine on him (4:6) and enables him to hear by his Spirit the joy and gladness of his loving-kindness (51:8). The affliction of his body will be tolerable if only he has comfort in his soul. What he wants as the greatest good, and what would restore all well-being to him, is the favor and friendship of God. He prays that God would pity him and look on him with compassion; that God would forgive his sins; that God would show his power to relieve him: *Lord, heal me* (v. 2), *save me* (v. 4); that he would be at peace with him: "*Return, O Lord!* (v. 4) take me back into your favor, and be reconciled to me"; and that he would especially preserve his inner being and its interests, whatever might happen to his body: *O Lord! deliver my soul* (v. 4).

4. The pleas with which he supports his requests, not to move God but to move himself. He pleads his own misery: "*I am sorely troubled. O Lord! How long* will I be so?" And he pleads God's mercy and glory (v. 5): "*For in death there is no remembrance of thee.*"

Verses 8–10

Here comes a sudden change for the better. The one who was groaning, weeping, and giving up everything as hopeless (vv. 6–7) here looks very happy and speaks very cheerfully.

1. He sets himself apart from the ungodly evildoers and strengthens himself against their insults (v. 8): *Depart from me, all you workers of iniquity.* The evildoers had harassed him, taunted him, and asked him, "Where is your God?" triumphing over his despondency and despair, but now he had the means to answer those who mocked him, for God had now assured his spirit and would soon complete his rescue. Perhaps they had tempted him, but now he said, "*Depart from me*; I will never listen to your advice; you wanted me to curse God and die (Job 2:9), but I will bless him and live." When God has done great things for us, this should make us seek diligently to discover what we can do for him.

2. He assures himself that God is, and will be, gracious to him, despite the present signs of wrath which he feels. He is confident of a gracious answer to this prayer which he is now offering. While he is still speaking, he is aware that God hears, and so he speaks of it with an air of triumph: *The Lord hath heard* (v. 8 and again v. 9), *The Lord hath heard.* He reasons from this that all his other prayers have been favorably listened to: "He *has heard the voice of my supplication* (v. 9), and so he *will receive my prayer* (v. 9)."

3. He either prays for the conversion or prophesies the destruction of his enemies and persecutors (v. 10).

3.1. It may very well be taken as a prayer for their conversion: "May they all be ashamed of their criticism of me. May they be distressed at their own foolish ways as all those who truly repent are. May they return to have a better attitude and frame of mind."

3.2. If they are not converted, it is a prediction of their confusion and ruin. "They shall be ashamed and greatly dismayed"—as v. 10 may be read—and justly so. They rejoiced that David was dismayed (vv. 2–3), and so, as usually happens, the evil recoils on them; they also will be greatly dismayed.

PSALM 7

It appears from the title of this psalm that it was written with a particular reference to the malicious accusations unjustly made against David by some of his enemies. When he was wronged: 1. He turned to God for his favor (vv. 1–2); he appealed to God concerning his innocence (vv. 3–5); he prayed to God to plead his cause and judge in favor of him against his persecutors (vv. 6–9). 2. He expressed his confidence that God would judge in his favor (vv. 10–17); he promised to give God the glory for rescuing him (v. 17).

Title

Shiggaion is "a song" or "psalm" (the word is used in this way only here and in Hab 3:1)—"a wandering song," according to some, the content and composition of its several parts being different, but artificially put together to be "a delightful song," according to others. David not only wrote it, but also devoutly sang it to the Lord himself, *concerning the words* or life *of Cush the Benjamite,* that is, possibly of some relative of Saul named *Cush,* who was a hardened enemy of David and caused trouble between him and Saul. When David was mistreated in this way, he turned to the Lord. His spirit was not disturbed by it; there

were no conflicting notes from his harp. And so let the wrongs we receive from others not kindle and arouse our anger, but rather kindle and arouse our devotion to God.

Verses 1–9

In these verses:

1. David puts himself under God's protection (v. 1): "*Lord, save me, and deliver me* from the power and hatred of *all those that persecute me,* so that they may not have their will against me." He pleads:

1.1. His relationship with God. "You are *my God,* and so where else should I go to except to you?"

1.2. His confidence in God: "Lord, save me, for I depend on you: *In thee do I put my trust* (v. 1), and not in any arm of flesh" (2Ch 32:8).

1.3. The hatred and rage of his enemies and the imminent danger he is in of being devoured by them: "Lord, save me, or I will die; they will *tear my soul like a lion* (v. 2) ripping its prey to pieces."

1.4. The failure of all other helpers: "*Lord,* be willing to rescue me, for otherwise *there is none to deliver*" (v. 2).

2. David makes a sacred declaration of his innocence in those matters in which he has been accused, and he makes a fearful oath about this as he appeals to God, the searcher of hearts (vv. 3–5). David has no earthly court he can appeal to, but he has the heavenly court, and a righteous Judge there, whom he can call *his God.* He is charged with traitorous intentions against Saul's crown and life. He completely denies this. *I have delivered him that without cause is my enemy* (v. 4). David had no intentions of taking Saul's life: Providence so ordered matters that Saul lay at his mercy, and there were those around him who would have quickly killed Saul, but David prevented it, when he cut off a corner of his robe (1Sa 24:4) and afterward when he took away his spear (1Sa 26:12), to show him what he could have done. If he is guilty, he says (v. 5), then *Let the enemy persecute my soul* to the death, and my good name when I am gone: let him *lay my honour in the dust.* David here confirms his declaration of his innocence with an oath or curse.

3. Having this testimony of his conscience declaring his innocence, David humbly prays to God to show himself against his persecutors. He supports every petition with a good plea.

3.1. He prays that God would reveal his wrath against his enemies: "Lord, they are unjustly angry with me. But I am praying that you will be justly angry with them and let them know that you are (v. 6). *In thy anger lift up thyself* to the seat of judgment, *because of the rage of my enemies.*"

3.2. He prays that God would plead his cause. *Awake for me to judgment*—let my cause receive a hearing—to *the judgment which thou hast commanded* (v. 6). He prays (v. 7), "*Return thou on high* so that it may be universally acknowledged that heaven itself recognizes and pleads David's cause." He prays again (v. 8), "*Judge me,* judge for me, give sentence in my favor." *The Lord shall judge the people* (v. 8). It is his place; it is his promise. *God is the judge* (75:7); "Therefore, Lord, judge me." It would be for the glory of God and the building up and comfort of his people if God would appear for him: "*So shall the congregation of the people compass thee about* (gather around you) (v. 7). Do it for their sakes, therefore, so that they may serve you with their praises and services in the courts of your house."

3.3. He prays, in general, for the conversion of sinners and the establishment of saints (v. 9): "*O let the wickedness,* not only of my evil enemies but also *of all* the wicked, come to an end, but establish the just." His plea to back up this request is, *For the righteous God trieth the hearts and the reins* (searches minds and hearts) (v. 9); and therefore he knows the secret evil of evildoers and knows how to bring it to an end. Here are two things which each one of us must want and may hope for:

- The destruction of sin, that it may be brought to an end in ourselves and others. And this is what all who love God, and who hate evil for his sake, want and pray for.
- The making secure of righteousness: *But establish the just* (v. 9). Just as we pray that the evil may be made good, so also we pray that the good may be made better.

Verses 10–17

Having submitted his appeal to God by prayer and by this sacred profession of his integrity, David now, as it were, claims judgment for himself on the appeal. He bases his claim on his faith in the word of God and on the assurance it gives of the happiness and security of the righteous and the certain destruction of evildoers who do not repent.

1. David is confident that he will find God to be his powerful protector and Savior and that God will support his oppressed innocence (v. 10): *My defence is of God.* "My shield is on God," some read it; there is something in God which gives the assurance of protection to all who are his. David rests this confidence on two things:

1.1. The particular favor God has for all who are sincere: *He saves the upright in heart* (v. 10) and will therefore *preserve them to his heavenly kingdom* (2Ti 4:18). He rescues them from their present troubles as far as is good for them.

1.2. The general respect he has for justice and equity: *God judgeth the righteous* (v. 11); he acknowledges every righteous cause, and he will maintain it in all who are righteous and will protect them. "God is a righteous Judge" is how some understand this. He not only acts according to righteousness himself, but also takes care that righteousness is acted on by people, and he will avenge and punish all unrighteousness.

2. David is no less confident of the destruction of all his persecutors, those who would not *repent, to give glory to God.* He reads out their condemnation here for their good, so that if possible, they might turn from their enmity; whether or not they turn, he reads it for his own comfort, so that he may not be afraid of them or distressed at their temporary prosperity and success. He realizes:

2.1. That God is angry with evildoers even when they are at their happiest and most prosperous. If they are allowed to prosper, it is in wrath, and if they pray, even their prayers are detestable. The wrath of God remains on them (Jn 3:36).

2.2. The destruction of sinners may be prevented by their conversion, for the threat is given with a condition: *If he turn not* from his evil way, if he does not drop his enmity against the people of God, then he may expect to be ruined, but if he turns, it is implied that his sin will be forgiven and all will be well. In this way, even the threats of wrath are introduced with a gracious implication of mercy. While God is preparing his instruments of death, he warns sinners of their danger and gives them opportunity to repent and prevent their destruction. He is slow to punish, and patient with us, *not willing that any should perish* (2Pe 3:9).

2.3. Sinners will destroy themselves (vv. 14–16). The sinner is described here as taking a great deal of effort to ruin himself. His behavior is compared to the pains of a pregnant woman who has a miscarriage (v. 14). In the head, the sinner conceives trouble. He sits there dreaming up his deep plots and secret schemes. In the heart, the sinner is pregnant with evil and is in labor pains, longing to give birth to the evil project he is hatching against the people of God. But what does it come to when it is born? Falsehood, self-deception, a lie in his right hand that he does not recognize (Isa 44:20). His behavior is also like the pains taken by a man who works hard to dig a pit and then falls into it and dies in it. This is true, in a sense, for all sinners. They are preparing destruction for themselves by preparing themselves for destruction.

PSALM 8

This psalm is a solemn meditation on the glory and greatness of God. It begins and ends with the same acknowledgment of the transcendent majesty of God's name. To prove God's glory, the psalmist gives examples of his goodness to human beings, for God's goodness is his glory (Ex 33:18–19, 22). God is to be glorified: 1. For making himself and his great name known to us (v. 1); for making use of the weakest people to serve his own purposes (v. 2). 2. For making even the heavenly bodies useful to human beings (vv. 3–4); for making human beings rule over the creatures in this lower world, so placing them a little lower than the angels (vv. 5–8). In the New Testament, this psalm is applied to Christ and the redemption he brought, the honor given by people to him (v. 2; compare with Mt 21:16), and the honor put on people by him, both in his humiliation, when he was made a little lower than the angels, and in his exaltation, when he was crowned with glory and honor (vv. 5–6); see also Heb 2:6–8; 1Co 15:27.

Title

The psalmist here sets himself to give God the glory due to his name (29:2; 96:8).

Verses 1–2

Here David wonders at two things:

1. How plainly God displays his glory himself (v. 1). He speaks to God with all humility and reverence, as the Lord and his people's Lord: *O Lord our Lord!* If we believe that God is the Lord, we must confess and acknowledge him as our Lord.

1.1. How brightly God's glory shines even in this lower world: *How excellent is thy name in all the earth!* (v. 1). The works of creation and providence show and declare to all the world that there is an infinite Being. In every speech and language the voice of God's name is heard, or at least can be heard (19:3).

1.2. How much more brightly it shines in the upper world: *Who hast set thy glory above the heavens* (v. 1).

1.2.1. God is infinitely more glorious and majestic than the most noble creatures and those that shine most brightly.

1.2.2. Whereas on earth we only hear God's majestic name, and praise that, the angels and blessed spirits above see his glory, and praise that. However, he is exalted far above even their blessing and praise (Ne 9:5).

1.2.3. In the exaltation of the Lord Jesus to the right hand of God—for Jesus is the radiance of his Father's glory and the exact representation of his being (Heb 1:3)—God set his glory above the heavens, far above all principalities and powers (Eph 1:21).

2. How powerfully God declares his glory by the weakest of his creatures (v. 2): *Out of the mouth of babes and sucklings hast thou ordained strength*, or ordained praise, the praise of your strength (Mt 21:16). This expresses the glory of God:

2.1. In the realm of nature. The care God takes of little children—when they first enter the world as the most helpless beings—the special protection they are under, and the provision nature has made for them should be acknowledged by each one of us, to the glory of God, as showing his power and goodness. We should do so all the more because we have all received this benefit.

2.2. In the realm of providence. In the government of this lower world God makes use of human beings.

2.3. In the realm of grace, the kingdom of the Messiah. It is foretold here that by the apostles, who were looked on as mere babes, *unlearned and ignorant men* (Ac 4:13), lowly and contemptible, and *by the foolishness of their preaching* (1Co 1:21), the Devil's kingdom would be demolished, as Jericho's walls were by the sound of rams' horns. The Gospel is called "the arm of the Lord" and "the rod of his strength," and it was ordained to work wonders not from the lips of philosophers, great orators, or wise politicians, but from the lips of a group of poor fishermen. We hear children shouting, *Hosanna to the Son of David* (Mt 21:9), when the chief priests and Pharisees will not acknowledge him. Sometimes the grace of God appears wonderfully in young children, and he *teaches* those *knowledge and makes* those *to understand doctrine, who are* but *newly weaned from the milk and drawn from the breasts* (Isa 28:9). Sometimes the power of God brings about great things in his church by using weak and unlikely instruments.

Verses 3–9

David here goes on to exalt the honor of God by describing the honors he has put on human beings, especially Jesus Christ. The condescension of divine grace calls for our praise as much as the elevations of divine glory. Notice here:

1. What it is that leads the psalmist to wonder at God's condescending favor toward human beings. It is his consideration of the luster and influence of the heavenly bodies, which are within our sight (v. 3): *I consider thy heavens*, particularly, *the moon and the stars*. It is our duty to consider the heavens. We see them; we have to see them. This is one of the marks that distinguish human beings from the animals, that while *they* are so framed as to look down to the earth, human beings are made erect to look up toward heaven. *The heavens, even the heavens, are the Lord's* (115:16), because they are the work of his fingers. He made them, and he made them easily. The stretching out of the heavens did not need any outstretched arm; it was done with a word; it was only *the work of his fingers* (v. 3). Even the lesser lights, the moon and stars, show the glory and power of the Father of lights (Jas 1:17) and provide us with something to praise him for. God not only made them but *ordained* them, and the ordinances of heaven can never be changed. When we consider how the glory of God shines in the higher world, we may well wonder that he should take notice of such lowly creatures as human beings. When we consider how very useful the heavens are to human beings on earth, we may well say, "Lord, what are mere mortals, that in enacting the ordinances of heaven you should consider us and the benefits that we will receive, and that our comfort and advantage should be considered in making the lights of heaven and in directing their movements?"

2. How the psalmist expresses this wonder (v. 4): "*Lord, what is man—enosh*, sinful, weak, miserable mortals, creatures who neglect you and their duty to you—*that thou art mindful of him?* The psalmist is amazed that God should notice mere mortals and their actions and lives, that in making the world he considered human beings! What is the *son of man, that thou visitest him* as one friend visits another, that you talk with them and concern yourself with them! This refers:

2.1. To the human race in general. Although human beings are as worms (Job 25:6), God still respects them and is very kind to them. Above all creatures in this lower world, man is the favorite and darling of Providence. We may be sure that he takes precedence over all the inhabitants of this lower world, for he is made *a little lower than the angels* (v. 5), lower indeed, because by his body he is related to the earth and to the animals that perish, but by his soul, which is spiritual and immortal, he is so closely related to the holy angels that he may be truly said to be only *a little lower than they*, and he is in fact next in order to them. He is for a little while lower than the angels, while his great soul is cooped up in a house of clay, but the children of the resurrection will be "like the angels" (Lk 20:36), and no longer lower than they. He is endowed with noble faculties and abilities: *Thou hast crowned him with glory and honour* (v. 5). Reason is man's crown of glory; let him not dishonor that crown by disturbing the use of it, nor lose that crown by going against its dictates. God has put all things under his feet, so that he might be served not only by the labor, but also by the products and lives, of the lower creatures. These creatures have all been given into man's hands, or rather, have all been *put under his feet* (v. 6). Some of the lower animals are mentioned (vv. 7–8), not only *sheep and oxen*, which people take care of and provide for, but also the wild animals saved at the Flood and those creatures which are most distant from human beings, like the birds of the air and the fish of the sea, which live in another element and pass unseen through the seas. Human beings are able to catch these, although many of them are much stronger and many of them are much swifter than they are.

2.2. Especially to Jesus Christ. We are taught to understand it with reference to him in Heb 2:6–8, where, to prove the sovereign rule of Christ both in heaven and on earth, the writer to the Hebrews shows that he is the *man*, that *son of man*, spoken of here. He is the One whom God *has crowned with glory and honour* and made to *have dominion over the works of his hands*. We have reason to humbly evaluate ourselves against this truth and thankfully wonder at the grace of God in it, acknowledging:

2.2.1. That Jesus Christ took on human nature and humbled himself in that nature. He was made a little lower than the angels for a while when he took on himself the form of a servant and made himself nothing.

2.2.2. That in that nature, he is exalted to be Lord of all. God the Father exalted him, because he had humbled himself; he *crowned him with glory and honour*, the glory which he had with him before the worlds were (Jn 17:5). All the creatures are put under his feet, and even in the days of his humanity, he showed his power over them, as when he commanded the winds and the seas (Mt 8:26; 14:32).

PSALM 9

In this psalm: 1. David praises God for pleading his cause and giving him victory over the enemies of his country (vv. 1–6), and he calls on others to join him in his songs of praise (vv. 11–12). 2. He prays to God that he might have a further occasion to praise him (vv. 13–14, 19–20). He triumphs in the assurance he has of God's judging the world (vv. 7–8), protecting his oppressed people (vv. 9–10, 18), and destroying his and their implacable enemies (vv. 15–17).

Title

The title of this psalm gives a very uncertain note concerning when it was written. It is *upon Muth-labben*, which some believe refers to the death of Goliath, others of Nabal, others of Absalom; but I tend to think it refers to a tune or musical instrument which this psalm was intended to be sung to. I suspect the enemies are the Philistines and other neighboring nations (2Sa 5:8).

Verses 1–10

In these verses:

1. David praises God for his mercies and the great things he has just done for him and his rule (vv. 1–2). Holy joy is the life of thankful praise, just as thankful praise is the language of holy joy: *I will be glad and rejoice in thee* (v. 2). The triumphs of the Redeemer should be the triumphs of the redeemed; see Rev 12:10; 15:3–4; 19:5.

2. David acknowledges the almighty power of God as what the strongest and boldest of his enemies are unable to fight against or resist (v. 3). They are forced to turn back. Once they have turned back, they fall and perish; even their withdrawal means they will be destroyed. They will no more save themselves by fleeing than by fighting. The presence of the Lord and the glory of his power are sufficient to destroy the enemies of God and his people. This was fulfilled when our Lord Jesus, with his words, *I am he*, made his enemies *fall back* at his presence (Jn 18:6).

3. David gives God the glory of his righteousness, shown when he appeared on David's behalf (v. 4): "*Thou hast maintained my right and my cause*, that is, my righteous cause. When that was put to the test, *thou satest* (you sat) *in the throne, judging right*" (v. 4).

4. David records with joy the triumphs of the God of heaven over all the powers of hell, and he accompanies those triumphs with his praises (v. 5): "*Thou hast rebuked the heathen* (the nations). You have given them real proofs of your displeasure against them." *Thou hast destroyed the wicked.* He had buried them in oblivion.

5. David triumphs over the enemy whom God has appeared against (v. 6): *Thou hast destroyed cities.* Either: "You, O enemy, have destroyed our cities, at least in your intention and imagination," or: "You, O God, have destroyed their cities by the desolation brought on their country." It may be taken either way.

6. David encourages himself and others in God and enjoys thinking about him. He occupies his mind:

6.1. With thoughts of God's eternity. We see nothing durable on this earth; even well-built cities are buried in rubbish and forgotten. But the Lord will reign forever (v. 7).

6.2. With thoughts of God's sovereignty both in government and in judgment: *He has prepared his throne*, has established it in his infinite Wisdom and settled it by his unchangeable counsels.

6.3. With thoughts of God's justice and righteousness in all the workings of his government. He *shall judge the world*, all people and all disputes, *shall minister judgment to the people*—will determine their fate both in this and in the future state—in righteousness and *in uprightness*, in complete and perfect justice.

6.4. With thoughts of that special favor which God shows to his own people and the special protection which he takes them under. *He will be a refuge for the oppressed*, a safe, strong place for the oppressed, *in times of trouble.*

6.5. With thoughts of that sweet assurance and peace of mind which those have who make God their refuge (v. 10): "*Those that know thy name will put their trust in thee*, as I have done, and then they will find, as I have found, that you do not abandon those who seek you." The better God is known, the more he is trusted. Those who know him to be a God of infinite Wisdom will trust him even when they cannot see him (Job 35:14). Those who know him to be a God of almighty power will trust him when confidence in people fails and they have no one else, and nothing else, to put their trust in (2Ch 20:12). Those who know him to be a God of infinite grace and goodness will trust him even *though he slay them* (Job 13:15). Those who know him to be a God of unbreakable truth and faithfulness will be joyful at his word of promise, and rest on that. Those who know him to be the Father of spirits (Heb 12:9), and an eternal Father, will trust him with their souls even to the end.

Verses 11–20

In these verses:

1. After David has himself praised God, he calls on and invites others to praise him also (v. 11). *Sing praises to the Lord who dwelleth* (is enthroned) *in Zion.* As the special home of his glory is in heaven, so the special home of his grace is in his church, of which Zion was a type. Let those whom he calls particularly notice the justice of God in avenging the blood of his people Israel on the Philistines and their other evil neighbors, who, when they had made war on them, had treated them cruelly and shown them no mercy (v. 12).

2. Having praised God for former blessings and rescues, David fervently prays that God would still appear for him, for he does not yet see everything put under him. "*Have mercy upon me*, for I have only trouble and no assets to help my case; I must depend on mercy for help. *Lord, consider my trouble* (v. 13), and do for me as you think fit." In support of this prayer, he pleads the experience he has had of divine help and the expectation he now has of it continuing: "*O thou that liftest me up* (v. 13), you who can do it, you who have done it, you who will do it, whose divine right it is to lift up your people *from the gates of death*" (v. 13). We are never brought to such a low position, and so close to death, that God cannot raise us up from it. If he has saved us from spiritual and eternal death, we may take encouragement from that to hope that he will be an ever-present help to us in all our troubles (46:1). David also pleads his sincere intention to praise God when his victories are complete (v. 14): "Lord, save me, *that I may show forth all thy praise.*"

3. By faith David foresees and foretells the certain destruction of all evildoers, both in this world and in the one to come. God acts in judgment on them when the limit of their sins is reached (Ge 15:16), and he makes their fall dishonorable, for they fall into the pit they themselves have dug (7:15). Drunkards kill themselves; prodigals make beggars of themselves; the argumentative bring

trouble on themselves. In these judgments the wrath of God is revealed from heaven against all godlessness and evil (Ro 1:18). The *wicked shall be turned into hell, all the nations that forget God*, as captives go to prison. Neglect of God is the cause of all the evil of evildoers.

4. David encourages the people of God to wait for his salvation, even though it might be delayed for a long time (v. 18). Needy people may think themselves, and others may think them, forgotten for a while, and their expectation of help from God may seem to have gone. But whoever believes does not act hastily (Isa 28:16); the revelation awaits an appointed time, and it will be revealed at the end (Hab 2:3). We may rest our lives on the undoubted truth that God's people will not always be forgotten, nor will they always be disappointed in their hopes of the promise.

5. David concludes with prayer that God would humble the pride, break the power, and bring to nothing the schemes of all the evil enemies of his church: "*Arise, O Lord!* (v. 19). Stir yourself, exert your power, take your judgment seat, and deal with all these arrogant and defiant enemies of your name, your cause, and your people. *Let not man prevail* (v. 19); consider your own honor, and let not weak mortals triumph against the kingdom and interests of the almighty and immortal God. *Shall mortal man be too hard for God, too strong for his Maker?*" (Job 4:17). It is very desirable, and does much for the glory of God and the peace and welfare of the universe, for people to know and consider themselves to be human, dependent creatures, changeable, mortal, and accountable.

PSALM 10

The Septuagint (a Greek version of the Old Testament) joins this psalm with the ninth and makes them one, but the Hebrew makes it a separate psalm, and the scope and style are certainly different. In this psalm: 1. David complains of the evil of evildoers and notices the delay of God's appearing against them (vv. 1–11). 2. He prays to God to appear against them to relieve his people, and he comforts himself with the hope that God will do so in due time (vv. 12–18).

Verses 1–11

In these verses, David shows:

1. A very great devotion for God and his favor, for in the time of trouble, what he complains about most strongly is God's withdrawal of his gracious presence (v. 1): "*Why standest thou afar off*, as one unconcerned by the dishonor shown to your name and the wrongs done to the people?" When outward rescue is hidden from us, we think that God is far away and that that is the reason we lack inner assurance. But really it is because we judge things by outward appearance; we stand far away from God in our unbelief, and then we complain that God is standing far away from us.

2. A very great anger against sin. He looks at the sinners and is grieved and dismayed, and brings to his heavenly Father the report of their evil. Vehement and sarcastic denunciations against evildoers do more harm than good. If we want to speak about their evil, let it be to God in prayer, for he alone can make them better. This long description of the evil of evildoers is summed up here in its first words (v. 2), *The wicked in his pride doth persecute the poor*, where evildoers are accused of two things: pride and persecution, the former the cause of the latter. Tyranny, both in state and in church, owes its

origin to pride. Having begun this description, the psalmist immediately inserts a short prayer in parenthesis: *Let them be taken*, as proud people often are, *in the devices* (schemes) *that they have imagined* (devised) (v. 2). These two headings are enlarged on:

2.1. Evildoers are proud, conceited, and arrogant.

2.1.1. The sinner proudly boasts of his power and success. He *boasts of his heart's desire* (v. 3), boasts that he can do what he pleases.

2.1.2. He proudly contradicts the judgment of God, which, we are sure, is based on truth (Ro 2:2), for he *blesses the covetous, whom the Lord abhors* (v. 3). See how God and people differ in their attitudes: God detests greedy, worldly people who make money their God and idol; he looks on them as his enemies and will have no fellowship with them. *The friendship of the world is enmity to God* (Jas 4:4). But arrogant persecutors bless them and agree with what they say (49:13).

2.1.3. The sinner arrogantly rejects thoughts of God (v. 4). *God is not in all his thoughts* (v. 4), there is no room for God in his thoughts. All the thoughts he has are that there is no God. The cause of this ungodliness and hostility toward religious faith is pride. People will not seek after God because they think they do not need him; they are self-sufficient.

2.1.4. The sinner proudly makes light of God's commandments and judgments (v. 5): *His ways are always grievous*. If you tell him about God's judgments that are to be carried out on those who continue in their sins, he will not be convinced there is any reality in them. Those judgments are *far above out of his sight* (v. 5), and so he thinks they are only imaginary.

2.1.5. He proudly defies trouble and is confident his own prosperity will continue (v. 6): *He hath said in his heart*, and pleased himself with the thought, *I shall not be moved*, my goods are laid up for many years, and *I shall never be in adversity*—like Babylon, which said, *I shall be a lady for ever* (Isa 47:7; Rev 18:7). But those who think destruction is farthest from them are in reality closest to it.

2.2. They are cruel persecutors. To gratify their pride and greed, and to oppose God and religion, they oppress everyone within their reach. They are bitter and malicious (v. 7): *His mouth is full of cursing*. He is false and treacherous. Like Esau, that skillful hunter, *he sits in the lurking places, in the secret places*, and *his eyes are privily* (in secret) *set* to cause trouble (v. 8), not because he is ashamed of what he does—if he were ashamed, there would be some hope he would repent—or because he is afraid of the wrath of God—for he thinks God will never call him to account (v. 11)—but because he is afraid that his plans may be discovered and therefore not carried out. Those who have power should protect the innocent and provide for the poor, but if they do not, the poor, whose guardians they should be, will destroy them. And what do they aim at? It is to *catch the poor*, and *draw them into their net* (v. 9), that is, to get them into their power, not only to strip them, but also to *murder them.* They *hunt for the precious life* (Pr 6:26). It is God's poor people they are persecuting, whom they hate because they belong to and resemble God. *He lies in wait as a lion* (v. 9) that is thirsting after blood, and he enjoys consuming his prey. *He crouches and humbles himself,* as wild animals do, so that they may get their prey within their reach. This suggests that the corrupt spirits of persecutors and oppressors will stoop to anything, however mean, to fulfill their evil schemes. They could not break all the laws of justice and goodness toward people unless they had first shaken off all sense of religious faith and risen in rebellion against the light of its most sacred and self-evident principles: *He hath said in his heart, God has forgotten.*

Verses 12–18

David now turns to speak to God, basing his address to him on the foregoing description of the inhumanity and ungodliness of the oppressors. Notice:

1. What he prays for:

1.1. That God would himself appear (v. 12): "*Arise, O Lord; O God, lift up thy hand;* reveal your presence and providence in the affairs of this world. *Arise, O Lord* to confound those who say you are hiding your face."

1.2. That God would appear for his people: "*Forget not the humble,* those who are suffering, those who are poor, who have been made poorer, and who are poor in spirit. Their oppressors have been presumptuous enough to say that you have forgotten them; and in their despair, they are ready to say the same. Lord, make it clear that they are both mistaken."

1.3. That God would appear against their persecutors (v. 15). *Break thou the arm of the wicked,* take away their power, *that the hypocrite reign not, lest the people be ensnared* (Job 34:30).

2. What he pleads in support of these requests, to encourage his own faith as he presents them:

2.1. He pleads the great contempt which these arrogant oppressors have shown toward God himself (v. 13): "*Wherefore do the wicked contemn* (revile) *God?*" That is what they are doing, for they are saying, "*Thou wilt not require it;* you will never call us to account for what we do." In this they are very mistaken; they could not have put greater dishonor on God and his righteousness. *Wherefore do the wicked thus contemn* (revile) *God?* (v. 13). It is because they do not know him. Why are they allowed to revile God in this way? It is because the Day of Judgment is still to come.

2.2. He pleads the notice God took of the ungodliness and sin of these oppressors (v. 14).

2.3. He pleads the dependence of the oppressed on God: "*The poor* victim *commits himself unto thee* (v. 14); each of them does so, including me." "They leave themselves with you," some read it, "not giving you orders, but submitting to your orders, to your wisdom and will. They are your willing subjects and put themselves under your protection, and so protect them."

2.4. He pleads the relationship in which God stands with us:

2.4.1. As a great God. He *is King for ever and ever* (v. 16). "Lord, may all who give you their loyalty and tribute as their King receive the benefit of your rule and find their refuge in you."

2.4.2. As a good God. He is the helper of the fatherless (v. 14), of those who have no one else who can help them and who have many who wrong them.

2.5. He pleads the experience which God's church and people have had of God's readiness to support them. "*The heathen* (nations) *have perished out of his land;* the remnants of the Canaanites, the seven devoted nations, which have for a long time been thorns in the flesh of Israel, have now been finally and completely uprooted. This is an encouragement to us to hope that God will similarly break the power of the oppressive Israelites, who are in some respects worse than the nations." He has heard and answered their prayers (v. 17): "*Lord, thou hast* many times *heard the desire of the humble;* you never said to one who came to you in distress, *Seek in vain* (Isa 45:19). Why may not we hope that the wonders and favors which

our fathers told us about will continue and be repeated? You are the same, and your power, promise, and relationship with your people are the same. The activity and effect of grace are the same in them. Why may we not hope, therefore, that the One who has been will still be, and will always be, a God who hears prayer?" God prepares the heart for prayer by kindling holy desires, strengthening our most holy faith, settling our thoughts, and lifting our affections, and then he graciously accepts the prayer. And when he accepts it, he will answer it, and when he answers the prayer of the persecuted, he will plead their cause. He will defend the fatherless and oppressed, he will clear their innocence, restore their comforts, and reward them for all the loss and damage. He will put an end to the terror of the persecutors. Notice how the psalmist now makes light of the power of the proud persecutor whom he earlier described in this psalm: he is but *a man of the earth* (v. 18), "a man out of the earth," a mere mortal who has sprung from the earth, and so is weak and lowly. He is but *a man that shall die, a son of man that shall be as grass* (Isa 51:12). The One who protects us is the Lord of heaven; those who persecute us are mere mortals.

PSALM 11

In this psalm we have David's struggle with and triumph over a strong temptation to distrust God. It is thought to have been written when he began to feel the outpouring of Saul's jealousy and had had the spear thrown at him twice. He was then advised to run away. "No," he says, "I am trusting in God, and so I will stand my ground." Notice: 1. How he describes the temptation and perhaps debates within himself (vv. 1–3). 2. How he answers his temptation and silences it by considering God's rule and providence (v. 4), his favor to the righteous, and the wrath which is reserved for evildoers (vv. 5–7). It will be useful to meditate on this psalm in times of national fear, when the abuse of the church's enemies is bold and threatening.

Verses 1–3

Here is:

1. David's settled determination to make God his confidence: *In the Lord put I my trust* (v. 1). Before the psalmist gives an account of the temptation he was faced with to distrust God, he records his determination to trust in him, as what he had decided to live and die by.

2. David's anger with the temptation not to trust in God: "*How say you to my soul, Flee as a bird to your mountain* (v. 1), to be secure there beyond the reach of the fowler?" This may be taken either:

2.1. As the serious advice of his timid friends. Some who heartily wished David well urged him to flee when they saw how maliciously Saul sought his life:

2.1.1. Because he would not be safe where he was (v. 2). "Notice," they say, "how *the wicked bend their bow;* Saul and his instruments are aiming to take your life, and the integrity of your heart will not be your security."

2.1.2. Because he could no longer be useful where he was. "For," they say, "*if the foundations be destroyed*" (v. 3) — as they were by Saul's maladministration — "if the civil state and government become unstable and shaken (75:3; 82:5), what can you do with your righteousness to put right the grievances?"

2.2. As a taunt which his enemies mocked him with, harassing him for the profession of confidence in God that he frequently made, and scornfully telling him to see what good that would do him now. "You say, God is your mountain. Go on, then, flee to him now, and see if that helps you." If we take it in this way, vv. 2–3 are David's response to this sarcasm, in which:

2.2.1. He complains of the evil of those who abuse him (v. 2): *They bend their bow and make ready their arrows.* We are told in 64:3 what their arrows are, namely, bitter words, which they speak to try to discourage hope in God.

2.2.2. He resists the temptation with a gracious abhorrence (v. 3). The principles of religion are the foundations on which the faith and hope of the righteous are built.

Verses 4–7

It is said that if a tree is shaken, its roots become deeper and firmer. The attempt of David's enemies to discourage his confidence in God makes him cling even more closely to his most basic principles. What shocked his faith, and has shocked the faith of many people, was the prosperity of evildoers and the adversities and distress which the best people sometimes find themselves in. From such a shock there was likely to arise the evil thought, *Surely it is vain to serve God* (Mal 3:14). But in order to silence and shame all such thoughts, David here calls on us to consider that:

1. There is a God in heaven: *The Lord is in his holy temple* above (v. 4), where, although he is out of our sight, we are not out of his. Or: he is in his holy temple, that is, in his church. He is a God in covenant and fellowship with his people.

2. This God rules the world. The Lord has not only his home, but also his throne, in heaven, and he has *set the dominion thereof in the earth* (Job 38:33). Let us by faith see God on his throne of glory: on his throne of government, giving law, movement, and purpose to all his creatures; on his throne of judgment; and on his throne of grace, to which his people may come boldly to receive mercy and grace (Heb 4:16). We will then have no reason to be discouraged by the pride and power of oppressors, or by any of the suffering that comes to the righteous.

3. This God knows perfectly everyone's true character: *His eyes behold, his eyelids try* (his eyes examine), *the children of men* (v. 4). He not only sees them but examines them. He knows not only all they say and do but also what they think, what they plan.

4. If God afflicts good people, it is to test them and is therefore for their good (v. 5). The Lord examines everyone so that he may *do them good in their latter end* (Dt 8:16).

5. However much persecutors and oppressors may prosper for a while, they are now under, and will perish forever under, the wrath of God. *The wicked and him that loveth violence, his soul hateth* (v. 5). Their prosperity is so far from being evidence of God's love that their abuse of it certainly makes them the object of his hatred. The One who hates nothing that he has made still hates those who have wronged themselves. *Upon the wicked he shall rain snares.* Here is a double metaphor, to show that the punishment of evildoers is unavoidable. It will surprise them just as a sudden shower sometimes surprises travelers on a summer's day. It will be like a trap for them, to hold them firmly and keep them prisoners, until the Day of Judgment comes. It is *fire, and brimstone, and a horrible tempest* (v. 6), which is a clear allusion to the destruction of Sodom and Gomorrah.

6. Although honest, good people may be oppressed, God does and will acknowledge them and favor them. That is why God will severely judge persecutors and oppressors, because those whom they oppress and persecute are precious to him: *Whosoever toucheth them toucheth the*

apple of his eye (Zec 2:8) (v. 7). He looks graciously on them: *His countenance doth behold the upright* (v. 7). He is like a tender father and looks on them with pleasure. Like dutiful children, they are pleased and deeply satisfied with his favor. They walk in the light of the Lord.

PSALM 12

It is thought that David wrote this psalm in Saul's reign, when there was a general decay of godliness, which he complains about to God here, and with deep emotion, for he himself suffered from the treachery of his false friends and his sworn enemies. 1. He begs help from God, because there is no one whom he dares to trust (vv. 1–2). 2. He foretells the destruction of his proud and threatening enemies (vv. 3–4). 3. He assures himself and others that however badly things are going now (v. 8), God will preserve his own people and keep them securely in his care (vv. 5, 7) and will certainly fulfill his promises for them (v. 6).

Verses 1–8

This psalm provides us with good thoughts for bad times.

1. Let us see what it is that makes the times bad, and when they may be said to be so. The world thinks that scarcity of money, a lack of business, and the devastations of war make the times bad. But Scripture attributes the badness of the times to causes of a different kind. *Perilous times shall come* (2Ti 3:1), for sin will increase, and that is what David is complaining about here. Times are bad:

1.1. When there is a general decay in godliness and integrity among people (v. 1): *when the godly man ceases and the faithful fail.* Notice how these two characteristics are put together here, godliness and faithfulness. As there is no true wisdom, so there is no true godliness, without integrity. Godly people are faithful and loyal. They are scrupulous about being faithful both to God and to other people. They are said to *cease and fail* here. Those who were godly and faithful had been taken away, and those who were left had sadly degenerated and were not what they once were.

1.2. When people are so spiteful that they plan evil and trouble against their neighbors, but so corrupt that they cover up their schemes with plausible professions of friendship. Thus *they speak vanity*—that is, lies—*every one to his neighbour, with flattering lips and a double* (deceptive) *heart* (v. 2). They will kiss and kill. This makes the Devil's image complete, a web of evil, lies, and deception. The times are truly bad when it is impossible to come across sincere people.

1.3. When proud sinners have arrived at such a level of ungodliness as to say, *"With our tongue will we prevail* against the cause of good. *Our lips are our own*, and we can say what we want. *Who is lord over us*, either to restrain us or to hold us responsible?" (v. 4). *Our lips are our own* (v. 4)—an unjust claim, for who made the human mouth, in whose hand is our breath, and whose is the air we breathe in? They speak as if he had no authority either to command or to judge them: *Who is lord over us?* (v. 4). These are like Pharaoh's words (Ex 5:2).

1.4. When the poor and needy are oppressed, abused, and held in contempt. This is implied in v. 5, where God himself takes notice of *the oppression of the poor* and *the sighing of the needy.*

1.5. When evil increases and is made known openly and shamelessly with the protection and support of those in authority (v. 8). *When the vilest men are exalted to* places of trust and power—then *the wicked walk on every side.* See also Pr 29:2: *When the wicked bear rule the people mourn.*

2. When times are so bad, it is encouraging to think:

2.1. We have a God to turn to, whom we may ask and expect to put right all our grievances. He begins with this (v. 1): "*Help, Lord; for the godly man ceaseth. It is time for thee, Lord, to work* (act)" (119:126).

2.2. God will certainly judge false and proud people. He will punish and restrain their arrogance. People cannot uncover the falsehood of flatterers or humble the pride of those who say proud things, but God in his righteousness will *cut off all flattering lips* (v. 3). Some translate it as a prayer: "May God silence those false and spiteful lips."

2.3. God will, in due time, rescue his oppressed people and protect them from the evil schemes of their persecutors (v. 5): *Now, will I arise, saith the Lord.* When the oppressors are at the height of their pride and arrogance—when they say, *Who is lord over us?*—then it is God's time to let them know, to their cost, that he is above them. When the oppressed are in the depths of their distress and depression, then it is God's time to reveal himself for them, as he did for Israel when they were most dejected and Pharaoh's power was at its height. *Now will I arise. I will set him in safety* (v. 5), or in salvation, not only protect him, but also restore him to his former prosperity. I will bring him out into a place of abundance (66:12), so that, on the whole, he will lose nothing from his sufferings.

2.4. Although people are false, God remains faithful. *The words of the Lord are pure* and flawless (v. 6); not only are they all true, but they are also pure, like silver refined in a furnace of clay.

2.5. God will protect his chosen remnant for himself, however bad the times (v. 7): *Thou shalt preserve them from this generation for ever.* The Lord knows those who are his (2Ti 2:19) in times of general apostasy, and they will be enabled to keep their integrity.

PSALM 13

This psalm considers the deserted soul's state and cure. Whether it was written on any particular occasion is not stated, but in general: 1. David complains sadly that God has withdrawn from him for a long time and has delayed in bringing him relief (vv. 1–2). 2. He prays to God fervently to consider his situation and comfort him (vv. 3–4). He assures himself of a favorable reply, and so concludes the psalm with joy and triumph, because he concludes that his restoration is as good as done (vv. 5–6).

Verses 1–6

In this psalm we see David pouring out his soul to God during a time of suffering:

1. It is some relief to a troubled spirit to be able to express its griefs, especially to bring them to the throne of grace, where we are sure to find One who is distressed in the distress of his people (Isa 63:9). We may go there by faith and speak freely with boldness (Eph 3:12). David thought God had forgotten him. Not that any good person can doubt the omniscience, goodness, and faithfulness of God, but this is a perverse expression of prevalent fear, which, when it arises from a high regard and sincere desire of God's favor, will be passed over and forgiven even though it is wrong, for second thoughts will withdraw it and repent of it. He was racked with cares, which filled his mind: *I take counsel in my soul*; "I am wrestling with my thoughts. I am at a loss and do not have a friend I can put my confidence in. *I have sorrow in my heart daily.*" The bread of sorrow is sometimes the daily bread saints must eat (127:2). Our Master himself was a man of sorrows (Isa 53:3). David complained about his enemies' arrogance, which added to his grief. He protested to God, "*How long* will things be like this?" and, "Will things be like this *for ever?*" When trouble lasts a long time, it is a common temptation to think it will last forever. Despondency then turns into despair, and those who have been without joy for a long time begin eventually to be without hope.

2. His complaints stir up his prayers (vv. 3–4). We should never allow ourselves to make any complaints except those we can offer to God and those that drive us to our knees. "*Consider* my case, *hear* my complaints, and *lighten my eyes.* Strengthen my faith," for faith is the eye of the soul, with which it sees above, and sees beyond merely physical things. "Lord, enable me to look beyond my present troubles and foresee their beneficial outcome." He concludes that if his eyes are not enlightened quickly, he will die: "I will *sleep the sleep of death* (v. 3); I cannot continue to live under the burden of all these cares and grief." It will satisfy the pride of his enemy, who will say, "*I have prevailed* (v. 4), I have triumphed. I have succeeded; I have proved too hard for him and his God."

3. His prayer is soon turned into praise (vv. 5–6): but *my heart shall rejoice and I will sing to the Lord.* What a surprising change there is in a few lines! At the beginning of the psalm we saw him drooping, trembling, and ready to sink into depression and despair, but by the end of the psalm he is rejoicing in God, lifted up and released in his praises. Notice the power of faith and the power of prayer, and how good it is to draw near to God. "In former distresses *I have trusted in the mercy of God* (v. 5), and I never found that it failed me. Even in the depths of this distress, when God hid his face from me, when conflicts were on the outside and there were fears within (2Co 7:5), *I still trusted in the mercy of God* (v. 5). That was like an anchor in a storm. This helped me, so that although I was tossed about, I was not overwhelmed. I continue to trust in your mercy." His faith in God's mercy fills his heart with joy in his salvation, for joy and peace come *by believing* (Ro 15:13). *Believing, you rejoice* (1Pe 1:8). "*I will sing unto the Lord*, sing when I remember what he has done in the past. Even though I may never recover the peace I once had, I will die blessing God that I once had it. He has been good to me in the past, and he will have the glory for that, however he may deal with me now. I will sing in the hope of what he will finally do for me, being confident that everything will end well in eternity."

PSALM 14

It is not stated on what occasion this psalm was written. Some say David wrote it when Saul persecuted him; others, when Absalom rebelled against him. But these are mere conjectures, which are not definite enough for us to legitimately explain the psalm by. The apostle Paul quotes part of this psalm (Ro 3:10) to prove that Jews and Gentiles are all under sin (Ro 3:9) and that all the world is guilty before God (Ro 3:19). He leads us to understand it, in general, as a description of the depravity of human nature. In all the psalms from Ps 3 to this one, except Ps 8, David complained about those who hated and persecuted him, insulted him and abused him; here he traces all those bitter streams back to the fountain, the general corruption of human nature, and sees that not only his enemies, but in fact the whole human race, have been corrupted in this way. Here is: 1. An accusation brought against an evil world (v. 1); the proof of the accusation (vv. 2–3). 2. A serious pleading with sinners, especially persecutors, regarding this accusation (vv. 4–6); a believing prayer for the salvation of Israel and joyful expectation of it (v. 7).

Verses 1–3

Sin is the disease of the human race, and it appears here to be malignant and epidemic.

1. Notice how malignant it is (v. 1), in two things:

1.1. The contempt it shows for the honor of God, for some practical atheism lies at the root of all sin. *The fool hath said in his heart, There is no God.* We are sometimes tempted to think, "Surely there never was so much atheism and hostility to religion as there is in our own times," but we see that the past was no better. Sinners are those who say in their hearts, *There is no God* (v. 1); they are atheists. They cannot be sure there is a God, and so they are willing to think there might not be one. They are fools. They are simple and unwise, and this thought is evidence for it; they are evil and ungodly, and this thought is the cause of it.

1.2. The corruption and disgrace it puts on the nature of human beings. Sinners are corrupt, completely degenerated from what human beings were in their original state of innocence: *They have become filthy* (v. 3), putrid and rotten. *They are* truly *corrupt*, for they do God no service, bring him no honor, and do themselves no real favor. They do a great deal of harm. *They have done abominable works* (v. 1), for all sinful works are like that. This follows from their saying, *There is no God* (v. 1), for those who *profess they know God, but in works deny him, are abominable, and to every good work reprobate*, unfit for doing anything good (Tit 1:16).

2. Notice how epidemic this disease is. It has infected the whole human race. God himself is here brought in as a witness (vv. 2–3). *The Lord looked down from heaven* (v. 2). God looks at all *the children of men* (v. 2). The question was *whether there were any* among them *that did understand* (v. 2) themselves rightly, their duty and interests, any who sought God and put him first. Notice the result of this inquiry (v. 3). On his search, it appeared, *They have all gone aside*, they have all turned away from God. *There is none that doeth good, no, not one*, until the free and powerful grace of God has brought about a change. When God made the world, he looked on his own work, and *all was very good* (Ge 1:31), but when he looked on human work some time later, he saw that all was very bad (Ge 6:5).

Verses 4–7

In these verses the psalmist tries:

1. To convince sinners of the evil and danger of their ways, however secure they are in those ways. He shows them three things, which they may not be very willing to see — their evil, their foolishness, and their danger.

1.1. Their evil. This is described in four ways:

1.1.1. They themselves are *workers of iniquity* (v. 4) and take as much pleasure in it as anyone ever did in their work.

1.1.2. They *eat up* (devour) *God's people* with as much greediness *as they eat bread* (v. 4); the real reason they hate God's people is that they hate God. It is food and drink to persecutors to be causing trouble.

1.1.3. They *call not upon the Lord* (v. 4). What good can be expected from those who live without prayer?

1.1.4. They *shame the counsel of the poor* (v. 6) and criticize them for making God their refuge, just as David's enemies rebuked him in 11:1.

1.2. Their foolishness: *They have no knowledge* (v. 4). If they had any knowledge of God, if they rightly understood themselves, they would not be so cruel or abusive.

1.3. Their danger (v. 5): *There were they in great fear.* There have been many examples of proud and cruel persecutors who have been made "terrors to themselves" and to all around them (Jer 20:1–4).

2. To comfort the people of God. They have God's presence (v. 5): he *is in the generation* (company) *of the righteous.* They have his protection (v. 6): *The Lord is their refuge.* When David was driven out by Absalom and his rebellious accomplices, he comforted himself with the assurance that God would in due time *turn again his captivity* (126:1), restore his fortunes. But surely this pleasant prospect looks farther. At the beginning of the psalm, he mourned the general corruption of the human race, and in the sad prospect of that, he now wished for the salvation which in the fullness of time would come out of Zion — that great salvation from sin which would be brought about by the Redeemer, who was expected *to come to Zion*, to *turn away ungodliness from Jacob* (Ro 11:26).

PSALM 15

The scope of this short but outstanding psalm is to show us the way to heaven and to convince us that if we want to be happy, we must be holy and blameless. Christ, who is himself the way (Jn 14:6), and in whom we must walk, has also shown us the same way prescribed here (Mt 19:17): If thou wilt enter into life, keep the commandments. *In this psalm: 1. By the question (v. 1), we are instructed and stirred to ask the way. 2. By the answer to that question, in the rest of the psalm, we are instructed to walk in that way (vv. 2–5). 3. By the assurance, at the close of the psalm, of the security and happiness of those who fulfill these characteristics, we are encouraged to walk in that way (v. 5).*

Verses 1–5

Here is:

1. A very serious and significant question concerning the character of a citizen of Zion (v. 1): "*Lord, who will abide in thy tabernacle* (your sanctuary)*?* Let me know who will go to heaven." It is not that the psalmist wants to know the name of such people — only the Lord knows those who are his (2Ti 2:19) — but he wants a description of them: "What kind of people are those whom you will acknowledge and crown with special and eternal favors?" We should all be concerned to ask ourselves the question, "Lord, what shall I be, and do, that I may *abide in thy tabernacle?*" (v. 1). See also Lk 18:18; Ac 16:30.

1.1. Notice to whom this inquiry is addressed — God himself.

1.2. Notice how this inquiry is expressed in Old Testament language.

1.2.1. By the *tabernacle* we may understand the church militant, of which Moses' tabernacle was a type: lowly, portable, and suited to the desert. God reveals himself there, and he meets his people there, as he did once in the tabernacle of the Testimony, the Tent of Meeting.

1.2.2. The *holy hill*, which alludes to Mount Zion, on which the temple was to be built by Solomon, may be understood to refer to the church triumphant. It is our concern to know who will live there, so that we may make sure we will have a place among them.

2. A very direct and detailed answer to this question, describing the particular characteristics of a citizen of Zion:

2.1. He is sincere and wholehearted in his religious faith: he *walketh uprightly* (blamelessly) (v. 2), according to the condition of the covenant set forth in Ge 17:1: *"Walk before me, and be thou perfect"* — the word there translated *perfect* is the same word here translated *uprightly* — "and then you will find me to be an all-sufficient God." The citizen of Zion really is what he professes to be, sound in heart, and leads a life of integrity before God in all he does. His eyes may be weak, but they are fixed on one thing. He has his spots, but he does not paint. He is an *Israelite indeed in whom is no guile* (Jn 1:47; 2Co 1:12). True religion is sincere.

2.2. He is scrupulously honest and just in all his dealings, faithful and fair toward everyone with whom he has to do: he *worketh righteousness* (v. 2). In his reckoning, agreements based on lies cannot be good or desirable. He strongly believes that anyone who wrongs their neighbor, even convincingly, will ultimately prove to have done the greatest wrong to themselves.

2.3. He is one who tries to do all the good he can to his neighbors. He is very careful not to harm anyone and is especially concerned to protect his neighbor's reputation (v. 3). He thinks the best of everyone and the worst of no one. If a wrong description of a neighbor is given to him, or an unkind story is told to him, he will disprove it if he can; if not, it will end with him and go no farther. His *charity* (love) *will cover a multitude of sins* (1Pe 4:8).

2.4. He values other people by their goodness and godliness and not by how they look in the world (v. 5). He thinks no worse of a godly person because they are poor or lowly, *but he knows those that fear the Lord* (v. 4). In his reckoning, sincere godliness, wherever that is found, honors a person, and makes their face shine (Ecc 8:1), more than wealth, cleverness, or a great reputation can or does. He honors such people.

2.5. He is one who always puts a good conscience before any secular interest or advantage. If he has promised on oath to do something, he will remain faithful to it and *change not* (v. 4), even though it turns out later to harm him or be detrimental to his worldly interests or possessions.

2.6. He will not increase his wealth by unjust practices (v. 5). *He putteth not out his money to usury*, so that he may live a life of ease off the labors of others. There is no reason why the lender should not share in the profit which the borrower makes of their money, any more than for the owner of land to demand rent from its occupant, because money is, like ability and work, as useful as land. But citizens of Zion will freely lend to the poor, according to their ability, and not be rigorous or harsh in recovering their rights from those who are poor because of no fault of their own. *He will not take a reward against the innocent* (v. 5). If he is in any way employed in the administration of public justice, he will not, for any personal gain or hope of personal gain, do anything to harm a righteous cause.

3. A confirmation of this characterization of the citizen of Zion as a conclusion to the psalm. He is like the hill of Zion itself, which cannot be shaken. Every true living member of the church, like the church itself, is built on a rock, which the gates of hell cannot overcome (Mt 16:18): *He that doeth these things shall never be moved* (v. 5).

PSALM 16

This psalm has something of David in it, but much more of Christ. It begins with such expressions of devotion as may be applied to Christ, but concludes with such confidence of a resurrection as must be applied to Christ, and only to him, and cannot be understood to refer to David, as both the apostle Peter and the apostle Paul observed (Ac 2:24; 13:36). 1. David speaks the language of all true Christians, professing his confidence in God (v. 1), his submission to him (v. 2), his devotion to the people of God (v. 3), and his faithfulness to the true worship of God (vv. 4–7). 2. He speaks of himself as a type of Christ, and so he speaks the language of Christ himself, to whom all the rest of the psalm is applied explicitly and in detail in Ac 2:25–28. 3. He speaks of the special presence of God with the Redeemer in his work and his sufferings (v. 8) and of the prospect which the Redeemer will have of his own resurrection and the glory that will follow, which will take him cheerfully through his work (vv. 9–11).

Title

This psalm is entitled *Michtam*, which some translate as "a golden psalm," more to be valued than much pure gold (19:10), because it speaks so clearly of Christ and his resurrection; and Christ is the true treasure hidden in the field of the Old Testament (Mt 13:44).

Verses 1–7

1. David here flees to God's protection (v. 1): *"Preserve me, O God!* Preserve me from the death, and especially from the sins, to which I am continually exposed, *for in thee,* and only in you, *do I put my trust."* This applies to Christ, who prayed, *Father, save me from this hour* (Jn 12:27), and trusted in God that he would rescue him.

2. David recognizes his solemn dedication of himself to God as his God (v. 2): *"O my soul! thou hast said unto the Lord, Thou art my Lord,* and so you may dare to trust him. *Thou art my Lord.* I submit to your authority and leadership and rest in you. You are the strength of my heart."

3. David devotes himself to the honor of God in the service of the saints (vv. 2–3): *My goodness extends not to thee, but to the saints.* If God is ours, we must, for his sake, extend our goodness to those who are his, to the saints in the land, for he takes what is done to them as being done to himself, having made them his receivers. Those who are renewed by the grace of God and devoted to the glory of God are saints on earth. Christ delights even in the saints in the land, despite their many weaknesses, which is a good reason why we should too.

4. David disowns the worship of all false gods and all fellowship with their worshipers (v. 4). He delivers a condemnation of idolaters: *Their sorrows shall be multiplied,* both by the judgments they bring on themselves from the true God, whom they abandon, and by the disappointment they meet with in the false gods they follow. *"Their drink offerings of blood will I not offer,* I will not pour out their libations of blood (v. 4), not only because the gods they are offered to are a lie, but also because the offerings themselves are cruel." At God's altar, because the blood made atonement, drinking of it was strictly prohibited, and the drink offerings were of wine, but the Devil ordered his worshipers to drink the blood of the sacrifices, to teach them cruelty. Some commentators also apply this to Christ and his work, showing the nature of the sacrifice he offered. It was not the blood of bulls and goats, which was offered according to the law — he never referred to that by name, nor did he ever mention it in any other way — but his own blood.

5. David repeats the sacred choice he has made of God as his inheritance and as the one in whom his happiness

lies (v. 5); he encourages himself about the choice (v. 6) and gives God the glory for it (v. 7). Heaven is our inheritance. We must take that as our home, our rest, and our eternal good, and look on this world as no more ours than a country we pass through on a journey. This means confiding in the Lord to secure this portion: "*Thou maintainest my lot*, you have made my lot secure (v. 5). By your promise you have set yourself as mine. You will graciously fulfill what you have promised: *The lines have fallen to me in pleasant places.*" Those who have God as their inheritance have reason to say this. What more could they want? "*Return unto thy rest, O my soul!* (116:7) and look no farther." Those whose inheritance lies, as David's did, in a land of light and a valley of vision (Isa 22:1), where God is known and worshiped, have good reason to say, *The lines have fallen to me in pleasant places* (v. 6); much more those who have Immanuel's land and Immanuel's love. "*I will bless the Lord who has given me counsel*, this counsel, to take him as my inheritance and happiness." If we have received pleasure from it, let God receive the praise of it. After God had counseled him by his word and Spirit, his own *reins* (his own thoughts) also instructed him during the night (v. 7). When he was silent and solitary and had withdrawn from the world, then his own conscience—*the reins* (mind) of Jer 17:10—not only reflected with contentment on the choice he had made, but also instructed and warned him about the duties arising from this choice.

All this may be applied to Christ, who made the Lord his inheritance and was pleased with that inheritance and made his Father's glory his highest aim. We may also apply it to ourselves, in singing it, renewing our choice of God as ours, with holy delight and assurance.

Verses 8–11

All these verses are quoted by the apostle Peter in his first sermon, after the Holy Spirit has been poured out on the Day of Pentecost (Ac 2:25–28), and he tells us explicitly that in them David is speaking about Christ, and especially his resurrection. We may allow something of the activity of David's own godly devotion toward God, but in these high and holy thoughts toward God and heaven he was carried by the spirit of prophecy beyond consideration of himself and his own situation to foretell the glory of the Messiah. The New Testament provides us with the key to let us in on the mystery of these lines.

1. These verses must certainly be applied to Christ. It is about him that prophet is speaking; many Old Testament prophets *testified beforehand the sufferings of Christ and the glory that should follow* (1Pe 1:11), and that is the subject of this prophecy. It is foretold:

1.1. That he would suffer and die. When David says, *My flesh shall rest* (v. 9), it is implied that Christ must take off his body, that he would not only die but also be buried, and remain for some time under the power of death.

1.2. That he would be wonderfully supported by divine power in suffering and dying and that he would not be shaken until he could say, *It is finished* (Jn 19:30). His heart would rejoice and his glory be joyful; he would continue with his work not only with determination, but also with joy. By his glory is meant his *tongue*, as is seen in Ac 2:26. There were three things which carried him joyfully through it:

1.2.1. The respect he had for his Father's will and glory in what he did: *I have set the Lord always before me* (v. 8).

1.2.2. The assurance he had of his Father's presence with him in his sufferings: *He is at my right hand* (v. 8), an ever-present help, close at hand in times of need.

1.2.3. The prospect he had of the glorious outcome to his sufferings. It was *for the joy set before him* that *he endured the cross* (Heb 12:2). He rested in hope, and that made his place of rest glorious (Isa 11:10). See Jn 13:31–32.

1.3. That he would be brought through his sufferings and taken from the power of death by a glorious resurrection.

1.4. That he would be greatly rewarded for his sufferings, with the joy set before him (v. 11). "*Thou wilt show me the path of life*, and lead me to that life through this dark valley." Being confident of this, when he gave up his spirit, he said, *Father, into thy hands I commit my spirit* (Lk 23:46), and a little before, *Father, glorify me with thy own self* (Jn 17:5).

2. Because Christ is the head of the body, the church (Col 1:18), these verses may also generally be applied to all true Christians, those guided and quickened by the Spirit of Christ. In singing them, when we have first given glory to Christ, we may then encourage and build up ourselves and one another with them. Dying Christians, as well as a dying Christ, may cheerfully take off the body in the confident hope of a joyful resurrection: *My flesh also shall rest in hope* (v. 9).

PSALM 17

David was in great distress and danger because of the hatred of his enemies, and in this psalm he turns in prayer to God, his tried and tested refuge, and seeks shelter in him. 1. He appeals to God concerning his integrity (vv. 1–4); he prays to God that he will continue to be upheld in his integrity and preserved from the hatred of his enemies (vv. 5–8, 13). 2. He describes his enemies, using the description as a plea with God for his preservation (vv. 9–12, 14); he comforts himself with the hope of his future happiness (v. 15).

Verses 1–7

This psalm is a prayer. There is a time for praise and a time for prayer. David was now being persecuted, probably by Saul. He speaks to God in these verses by making an appeal—"*Hear the right, O Lord!* (v. 1), may my righteous cause be heard before your tribunal and may you declare your judgment on it"—and by making a request—*Give ear unto my prayer* (v. 1 and again v. 6), *Incline thy ear unto me and hear my speech.* He is sincere and is not pretending with God in his prayer: *It goeth not out of feigned* (deceitful) *lips* (v. 1). Deceitful prayers are fruitless. He has prayed at other times: "*I have called upon thee* formerly (v. 6), and so, Lord, listen to me now." It will be a great encouragement to us when trouble comes that the wheels of our prayer life are already moving, for then we may come with greater boldness to the throne of grace (Heb 4:16). He is encouraged by his faith to expect that God will act on his prayers: "*I know thou wilt hear me*, and so, O God, *incline thy ear to me*" (v. 6).

1. David brings his appeal to the court of heaven. "Lord, do right by me, for Saul is so vehement and prejudiced that he will not hear me. Lord, *let my sentence come forth from thy presence*, may my vindication come from you (v. 2). People condemn me to be pursued and destroyed as an evildoer. Lord, I turn from them to you with this appeal." Sincerity fears no scrutiny, not even by God himself, according to the basis of the covenant of grace: *Let thy eyes behold the things that are equal* (see what is right) (v. 2).

1.1. The evidence by which he hopes to be successful in his appeal is that God has tested him: *Thou hast proved my heart* (v. 3). He knew God had tested him by his own conscience, which is God's deputy in the soul. *The spirit of a man is the candle of the Lord* (Pr 20:27). God had searched him with this, and had come to him at night, when he *communed with his own heart on his bed* (4:4). God had also tested him by the opportunities he had had to kill Saul.

1.2. Although God could witness to its integrity, he himself noted two things about which his conscience bore witness. First, he had a settled determination to avoid all sins of the tongue: "I have fully purposed and resolved, with the strength of God's grace, that my mouth will not disobey God." Second, he had been as careful to refrain from sinful actions as from sinful words (v. 4): "*Concerning the* common *works of men*, the actions of human life, I have, by the direction of your word, *kept myself from the paths of the destroyer*, from the ways of the violent." Some understand this to refer to the fact that he himself had not destroyed Saul when it lay within his power. It may also be taken more generally. He kept himself from all evil, and tried, according to the duty of his position, to keep others from it too.

2. David's request is that he might experience the good work of God in him as evidence of and qualification for the goodwill of God toward him: this is grace and peace from God the Father (Ro 1:7; 1Co 1:3; 2Co 1:2; etc.).

2.1. He prays for the work of God's grace in him (v. 5): "*Hold up my goings in thy paths.* Lord, by your grace, I have kept myself from the paths of the destroyer. By the same grace may I be kept on your paths."

2.2. He prays for the signs of God's favor to him (v. 7): *O thou that savest by thy right hand*—by your own power, for you do not need to use any other agency—*those who put their trust in thee from those that rise up against them.* Those who trust in God have many enemies, but they have one friend who is able to deal with them all. The margin of v. 7 reads, "Thou that savest those who trust in thee from those that rise up against thy right hand." Those who are the enemies of the saints are rebels against God and his right hand. *Show thy marvellous loving-kindness* (v. 7). "Set apart your great love for me; do not give me merely common mercies, but be gracious to me, *as thou usest to do* (as you always do) *to those who love thy name*" (119:132).

Verses 8–15

We may notice in these verses:

1. What David prays for. This prayer is both a prediction of the preservation of Christ through all the hardships and difficulties of his humiliation, and a pattern for Christians, showing them how to commit the keeping of their souls to God, trusting him to *preserve them to his heavenly kingdom* (2Ti 4:18). He prays:

1.1. That he himself might be protected (v. 8): "Keep me safe, hide me close to you, where I cannot be found, where I cannot be reached. Rescue my soul, not only my mortal life from death, but also my immortal spirit from sin." He prays that God would keep him as someone keeps the apple of their eye, its pupil, which nature has wonderfully protected and teaches us to guard. If we keep God's law as the *apple of our eye* (Pr 7:2), we may expect that God will keep us in the same way, for it is said concerning his people that whoever *touches them touches the apple of his eye* (Zec 2:8). He prays that God would keep him with as much tenderness as a mother hen gathers her young ones under her wings; Christ, too, uses the comparison (Mt 23:37). "*Hide me under the shadow of thy wings* (v. 8), where I may be both safe and warm." Or it may allude to the wings of the cherubim shielding the atonement cover:

"May I be taken under the protection of that glorious grace which belongs to God's Israel." David prays further, "Lord, keep me from the evildoers of the world."

1.2. That all the intentions of his enemies to bring him either to sin or to trouble might be defeated (v. 13): "*Arise, O Lord!* Appear for me, confront them, confound them. *They have set their eyes bowing down to the earth,* lying in wait for me; now *cast them down*, make them look low in their own eyes." While Saul persecuted David, how often did he miss his target when he was confident he would succeed! And how Christ's enemies were disappointed by his resurrection, when they thought they had triumphed by putting him to death!

2. What David pleads, to encourage his own faith in these requests. He pleads:

2.1. The evil of his enemies: They are *my deadly enemies* (v. 9), literally, "enemies against the soul." They are worldly, proud, and arrogant (v. 10): *They are enclosed in their own fat*, wrapped up in themselves; their callous hearts are closed, absorbed in their own honor, power, and abundance. They make light of God and defy his judgments (73:7; Job 15:27). They *compass me about* (surround me) (v. 9). "They *set their eyes bowing down to the earth* (v. 11): they are watchful and set on causing us trouble; they look down out of guilt, because they never let slip any opportunity of accomplishing their purpose." "Their ringleader, Saul, is especially bloodthirsty and cruel (v. 12), *like a lion* that lives off its prey and so is greedy for it." This is appropriately applied to Saul, who sought David *on the rocks of the wild goats* (1Sa 24:2) and in *the wilderness of Ziph* (1Sa 26:2), where lions used to crouch, ready to attack their prey.

2.2. The power God has over them, to control and restrain them. "Lord, they are *thy sword*," God's sword, which he can wield as he pleases, which cannot move without him, and which he will sheathe when he has completed his work with it. "They are *thy hand*, by which you rebuke your people and make them sense your displeasure." He expects to be rescued by God's hand because the trouble came from God's hand.

2.3. Their outward prosperity (v. 14). They are *men of the world*, driven by the spirit of the world, in love with its wealth and pleasures. They *have their portion* (reward) *in this life* (v. 14). They have abundance from this world. *Their bellies thou fillest with thy hidden treasures* (v. 14). The things of this world are called *treasures* because that is how they view them. Otherwise, compared with spiritual and eternal blessings, these treasures are mere trash. Those who eat sumptuously every day have their *bellies filled with these hidden treasures* (v. 14), and such treasures will *fill* only *the belly* (1Co 6:13), not the soul. David's enemies have numerous families and a great deal to leave to them: *They are full of children* (v. 14), but they have enough for them all, and *leave the rest of their substance to their babes* (v. 14), to their grandchildren.

2.4. His own dependence on God as his inheritance and basis for happiness. "They have their reward in this life, but as for me (v. 15), I am not one of them; I have only a little of this world." When the soul awakes, at death, out of its slumber in the body, and when the body awakes, at the resurrection, out of its slumber in the grave, blessedness will consist of three things:

- The immediate sight of God and his glory: *I will behold thy face* (v. 15), not, as in this world, through a glass darkly (1Co 13:12).
- Participation in his likeness. When he shall appear we shall be like him, for we shall see him as he is.

• A complete and full assurance resulting from all this: *I shall be satisfied* (v. 15), fully satisfied with it.

PSALM 18

We met with this psalm before, in the story of David's life (2Sa 22). That was its first edition; here it is revived, changed a little, and fitted for the service of the church. It is David's thanksgiving for the many times God had rescued him. The poetry is fine, the images are bold, and the expressions are noble, and every word is appropriate and significant, but the godliness surpasses the poetry. Holy faith, love, joy, praise, and hope are living, moving, and active here. 1. David triumphs in God (vv. 1–3); he exalts God for rescuing him (vv. 4–19). 2. He takes comfort from his integrity, which God has cleared (vv. 20–28). 3. He gives God the glory for all his achievements (vv. 29–42); he encourages himself with the expectation of what God will further do for him and his descendants (vv. 43–50).

Title

We had this title before in 2Sa 22:1, except that here are we told that the psalm was delivered *to the chief musician*, the director of temple music or precentor. David is here called *the servant of the Lord*, as Moses was. It was more his honor that he was a servant of the Lord than that he was king of a great kingdom, and this is how he himself considered it (116:16): *O Lord! truly I am thy servant.*

Verses 1–19

In these verses:

1. David triumphs in God and his relationship with him. The first words of the psalm, *I will love thee, O Lord! my strength*, are the introduction to the scope and contents of the whole psalm. A relationship with the person loved is the lover's delight. This, therefore, is the string he now touches, the note he plays with much pleasure (v. 2): "*The* Lord *Jehovah is my God*, and so he is my rock, *my fortress*, all that I need and want in my present distress."

2. David sets himself to exalt the rescues God has brought about for him, so that he may be all the more moved in his response of praise. It is good for us to observe all the circumstances of a blessing, which exalt the power of God and his goodness to us in it.

2.1. The more imminent and threatening the danger was from which we were rescued, the greater is the mercy that has been shown. David now remembers how the forces of his enemies poured in on him, which he calls the *floods of ungodly men*.

2.2. The more fervent we have been in praying to God to be rescued, and the more directly the rescue answers our prayers, the more we are obliged to be thankful. David's rescues were like this (v. 6). David was found to be one who prayed, and God was found to be a God who listens to prayer.

2.3. The more wonderful God's appearances are in any rescue, the greater it is: such were the ways David was rescued. God's revelation of his presence and glory is described in splendid terms (vv. 7–15). There was little of human beings in these rescues, but much of God. God moved even the *foundations of the hills* (v. 7), as he had done at Mount Sinai. He showed his anger and displeasure against the enemies and persecutors of his people: *He was wroth* (angry) (v. 7). His anger smoked (v. 8), and *coals were kindled by it.* He showed his readiness to plead

his people's cause and bring about their rescue, for he *rode upon a cherub and did fly*, to uphold righteousness and to relieve his distressed servants (v. 10). No opposition or obstruction can be raised against him *who rides on the wings of the wind* (v. 10), *who rides on the heavens* (68:33) in his majesty to help his people. He showed his condescension in taking notice of David's case: *He bowed* (parted) *the heavens and came down* (v. 9). He did not send an angel, but came himself, as One suffering with the suffering of his people (Isa 63:9). He enclosed himself in darkness (Isa 45:15), but commanded light to shine out of darkness for his people. He *made darkness his pavilion* (covering) (v. 11). His glory is invisible. We do not know the way he takes, even when he is coming toward us in ways of mercy, but when his intentions are secret, they are kind, for although he hides himself, he is still the God of Israel, the Savior. And *at his brightness, the thick clouds pass* (v. 12).

2.4. The greater the difficulties that lie in the path of rescue, the more glorious the rescue. To rescue David, the waters were to be divided until the very channels were seen. The earth was to be split until its very foundations were laid bare (v. 15). There were many waters, deep waters, and he was to be drawn out of these (v. 16). As Moses was drawn out of the water literally, and took his name from that experience, so also David was drawn out of the water figuratively. His enemies were too quick for him, for *they prevented* (confronted) *him in the day of his calamity* (v. 18). But in the midst of his troubles, the Lord was his strong support, so he did not sink. God will not only rescue his people from their troubles in due time, but also sustain them and support them in their troubles in the meantime.

2.5. What especially exalted the rescue was that his well-being was its fruit. "*He brought me forth also* out of my distress *into a large place*, where I had room not only to turn but also to thrive. *He delivered me because he delighted in me*, not because I deserved it but because of his own grace and goodwill."

In praying over and singing these verses, we may apply them to Christ, the Son of David. The sorrows of death surrounded him; he prayed in his distress (Heb 5:7); God made the earth shake and tremble, and the rocks split, and brought him out in his resurrection into a spacious place, because he delighted in him and in his work.

Verses 20–28

Here:

1. David reflects with contentment on his own integrity and rejoices in the testimony of his conscience that he has led a life of integrity and godly sincerity, not in accordance with worldly wisdom (2Co 1:12). His rescues were evidence of this, and this was the great encouragement of his rescues. His rescues showed other people his innocence and acquitted him from those crimes which he was falsely accused of. He calls this *rewarding him according to his righteousness* (v. 20 and again v. 24). His rescues confirmed the testimony of his own conscience for him, which he here reviews with a great deal of pleasure (vv. 21–23). Although we are conscious that we often fall and take many false steps, if we come back to God in repentance and continue to follow our duty, it will not be considered a departure from our God, for it is not an evil departure from him. David had kept his eye on the rule of God's commands (v. 22): *All his judgments were before me.*

2. David uses this occasion to lay down the rules of God's government and judgment, so that we may know not only what God expects from us, but also what we may expect from him (vv. 25–26). Those who show mercy

to others will find mercy with God (Mt 5:7). Wherever God finds an upright person, God will be found to be irreproachable.

3. David takes these truths about God as a source of comfort for the humble — *Thou wilt save the afflicted people* (v. 27), those who are wronged and bear it patiently; as a source of terror to the proud — *Thou wilt bring down high looks*, bring low those whose eyes are haughty, who expect great things for themselves and look down on the poor and godly with scorn and disdain; and as a source of encouragement for himself — "*Thou wilt light my candle*, you keep my lamp burning (v. 28), that is, you will revive and comfort my sorrowful spirit, and not leave me sad. You will light my candle so that I may work by it; you will give me an opportunity to serve you and the interests of your kingdom."

Verses 29–50

In these verses:

1. David looks back with thankfulness on the great things God has done for him. When we set ourselves to praise God for one blessing, we must be led by that to observe the many more which he has shown us every day of our lives. Many things have contributed to David's advancement, and he acknowledges the hand of God in all of them, to teach us to do likewise.

1.1. God has given him all his skill and understanding in military affairs, which he was not brought up with or intended for by his parents, his natural skills tending more toward music, poetry, and a contemplative life: *He teaches my hands to war*, he trains my hands for battle (v. 34).

1.2. God has given him physical strength to go through the work and hardships of war: God *girded him with strength* (v. 32 and again v. 39) to such an extent that he could break even a bow of steel (NIV: bronze) (v. 34). God is sure to equip his people for the service he intends for them.

1.3. Similarly, God has given him great speed, not to rush away from his enemies but to rush on them (v. 33): *He makes my feet like hinds' feet* (v. 36); "*Thou hast enlarged my steps under me*, but" — whereas those who take long steps tend to make missteps — "my feet did not slip."

1.4. God has made him very bold. If troops stood in his way, he thought nothing of running through them; if the obstacle was a wall, he thought nothing of scaling it (v. 29); if ramparts and bulwarks, he soon mounted them, and with God's help stood on the enemy's heights (v. 33).

1.5. God had protected him and kept him safe in great dangers. "*Thou hast given me the shield of thy salvation*" (v. 35), and that has surrounded me. That has rescued me from the attacks of the people who aimed to destroy me (v. 43), particularly from the violent people" (v. 48), that is, especially from Saul, who threw a spear at him more than once.

1.6. God has given him success in his plans; it is he who has made his way perfect (v. 32) and it is his right hand that has sustained him (v. 35).

1.7. God has given him victory over his enemies, the Philistines, Moabites, Ammonites, and all who fought against Israel. Those whom God has abandoned are easily defeated: *Then did I beat them small as the dust* (v. 42). But he avenges those whose cause is just (v. 47), and those whom he favors will certainly be *lifted up above those that rise up against them* (v. 48).

1.8. God has raised him to the throne; he has not only rescued him and kept him alive but also honored him and

made him great (v. 35): *Thy gentleness* — "your discipline and instruction," according to some — *has made me great*. The good lessons David learned in his affliction prepared him for the honor and power intended for him, and his being humbled helped increase his greatness very much.

2. David looks up with humble and reverent adoration at God's glory and perfection. He tries to praise, magnify, bless, and exalt God (v. 46). He honors him:

2.1. As a living God: *The Lord liveth* (v. 46). The gods of the nations were dead. But God lives forever, and he will not fail those who trust in him; and because he lives, they also will live, for he is their life.

2.2. As a completing God: *As for God*, not only is he himself perfect, but *his way is perfect* (v. 30). God is able to complete what he has begun to build (Php 1:6).

2.3. As a faithful God: *The word of the Lord is tried* (proven) (v. 30). "I have tested it," David says, "and it has not failed me." David observes that in God's providences for him, he has kept his promises to him. And when he makes this observation, the providences are sweetened for him and the promises honored by him.

2.4. As the protector and defender of his people. David had found him to be so: "*He is the God of my salvation* (v. 46), by whose power and grace I am and hope to be saved; but he is not only the God of *my* salvation: he is a *buckler* (shield) *to all those that trust in him* (v. 30). He shelters and protects them all: he is both able and ready to do so."

3. David looks forward with a confident hope that God will still do him good. He is sure that his enemies will be completely subdued and that his government will extend so far that even a people whom he has not known will serve him (v. 43). *As soon as they hear of me they shall obey me* (v. 44). His descendants will continue forever in the Messiah, who, he foresees, will come from his body (v. 50). He *shows mercy to his anointed*, his Messiah, *to David* himself — who was a type of the Anointed of the God of Jacob (2Sa 23:1) — *and to his seed for evermore*.

PSALM 19

There are two excellent books which God has in his greatness published to instruct and build up human beings. This psalm deals with both of them and commends them both to our diligent study. 1. The book of the creation, in which we may easily read of the power and Godhead of the Creator (Ro 1:20) (vv. 1–6). 2. The book of the Scriptures, which declares God's will for our duty. He shows the splendor and usefulness of that book (vv. 7–11) and then teaches us how to make the most of it (vv. 12–14).

Verses 1–6

In these verses, the psalmist takes the things that are seen every day by all the world, and he leads us to consider the invisible things of God (Ro 1:20). His glory shines transcendently bright in the visible heavens, both in their structure and beauty and in the order and influence of the heavenly bodies. This example of divine power shows up not only the foolishness of atheists — who see there is a heaven but say, "There is no God," who see the effects but say, "There is no cause" — but also the foolishness of idolaters and the futility of their thinking (Ro 1:21). Such people give to the lights of heaven the glory which those lights themselves direct them to give only to the Father of lights (Jas 1:17), God, whose glory is declared by the heavens. Notice:

1. What it is that creation informs us about. Creation serves us in many ways, but above all by proclaiming the work of God's hands and thereby declaring his glory (v. 1). It speak clearly that it is God's handiwork. Every process and movement must have its beginning. The heavens could not have made themselves; to think that is a contradiction in terms. It could not have been produced by an accidental collision of atoms; that is absurd, fit to be ridiculed rather than reasoned. It must, therefore, have a Creator, who can be no other than an eternal Mind, infinitely wise, powerful, and good. From the magnificence of the work we may easily deduce the infinite perfection of its great author. From the brightness of the heavens we may reason that the Creator is light. The vastness of their extent speaks of his immensity, and their height speaks of his transcendence and sovereignty. Their influence on this earth speaks of his rule, providence, and universal generosity. Taken all together, they declare his almighty power.

2. What are some of those things which declare this.

2.1. The heavens and the skies—the vast expanse of air and space and the spheres of the planets and stars. Human beings have an advantage over the animals in the structure of their body: whereas the animals are made to look downward, which is where their spirits must go, human beings are made go erect, to look upward, because their spirit must soon go upward, and it is there that their thoughts must now rise.

2.2. The constant and regular succession of day and night (v. 2): *Day unto day, and night unto night* speak of the glory of the God who first divided light and darkness. By this constant revolution God not only glorifies himself but also satisfies us, for as the light of the morning is the friend of the business of the day, so the shadows of the evening are the friend to the rest of the night. Every day and night speak of the goodness of God, and when they have finished their declaration, they leave it to the next day, and the next night, to declare the same.

2.3. The light and influence of the sun especially declare the glory of God, for this is the one out of all the heavenly bodies that is the most conspicuous and the most useful to this lower world, which would be all a dungeon, all a desert, without it. In the heavens God has *set a tabernacle* (pitched a tent) *for the sun* (v. 4). The heavenly bodies are called *hosts of heaven* and so are rightly said to *dwell in tents*, like soldiers in their camps. That glorious creation was not made to be idle; *his going forth*—at least what is apparent to our eyes—*is from one point of the heavens, and his circuit* (v. 6) from there to the opposite point, and so it returns to the same point again to complete its daily revolution. It follows its course with such constancy and regularity that we can know the hour and minute at which the sun will rise at a certain place on any given day. Notice the brightness with which it appears. It is *as a bridegroom coming out of his chamber* (v. 5), splendidly dressed and arrayed, as finely as possible, looking joyful himself and making all around him joyful. Notice, too, the cheerfulness with which it makes this tour: for the service of human beings, it *rejoices as a strong man to run a race* (v. 5).

3. To whom this declaration is made of the glory of God. It is made to every part of the world (vv. 3–4): *There is no speech nor language* where heaven's voice is not heard. *Their line has gone through all the earth* (probably, the equator), and with it *their words to the end of the world*, declaring the eternal power of the God of nature (v. 4). "They have no speech or language," some read it, "and yet their voice is heard." Every person may hear these natural,

immortal preachers communicate to them the wonders of God in their own native language (Ac 2:11).

Verses 7–14

God's glory—that is, his goodness to the human race (Ex 33:18–19)—appears much in the works of creation, but much more in and by divine revelation. The Holy Scriptures, as they are a rule both of our duty to God and of our expectation from him, are of much greater use and benefit to us than day or night, the air we breathe, or the light of the sun.

1. The psalmist gives an account of the excellent qualities and uses of the word of God, in six sentences (vv. 7–9), in each of which the name *Jehovah* is repeated. Here are six distinct titles given to the word of God, to include the whole of God's revelation, both its precepts and its promises, and especially those of the Gospel.

1.1. *The law of the Lord is perfect* (v. 7). It is perfectly free from any defect. It is perfectly filled with all good and perfectly fitted for the purpose for which it is intended, so that God's people may be thoroughly equipped (2Ti 3:17). Nothing is to be added to it or taken away from it (Rev 22:18–19). It is of use to *convert* (revive) *the soul* (v. 7), to bring us back to ourselves (Lk 15:17), our God, and our duty.

1.2. *The testimony of the Lord is sure* (v. 7). It is a solid foundation of strength and encouragement and a solid foundation of lasting hope. It will make even *the simple* wise for their souls and eternity. Those who are humbly simple, who are aware of their own foolish ways but willing to be taught, will be made wise by the word of God (25:9).

1.3. *The statutes of the Lord are right* (v. 8), conforming exactly to the eternal rules and principles of good and evil. Because they are right, they *rejoice the heart* (v. 8). The law, as we see it in the hands of Christ, gives cause for joy, and when it is written on our hearts (Jer 31:33), it lays a foundation for eternal joy, by restoring us to our right mind (Mk 5:15).

1.4. *The commandment of the Lord is pure* (v. 8). It is the ordinary means which the Spirit uses to *enlighten the eyes* (v. 8); it brings us to a sight and sense of our sin and misery and directs us to follow our duty.

1.5. *The fear of the Lord is clean* (v. 9); it will cleanse our way (119:9). It also *endureth for ever* (v. 9). The ceremonial law has long since been abolished, but the law concerning the fear of God remains the same. Time will not change the nature of moral good and evil.

1.6. *The judgments of the Lord*—all his precepts, which are framed in infinite Wisdom—*are true* (v. 9) *altogether*. They are all in harmony with one another.

2. The psalmist expresses the great value he places on the word of God and the great advantage he has, and hopes to have, from it (vv. 10–11). He prizes the commandments of God, preferring them to all the wealth of this world. Gold comes from the earth and is worldly, but grace is the image of the heavenly realm. Gold serves only the body and the concerns of time, but grace serves the soul and the concerns of eternity. The word of God, received by faith, is sweet to the soul, *sweeter than honey and the honeycomb* (v. 10). Worldly pleasures are deceitful, will soon become excessive, and never satisfy. The delights of religious faith, however, are solid and satisfying, and there is no danger of having too much of them. *By them is thy servant warned, and in keeping them there is great reward* (v. 11). The word of God is a word of warning to the human race. It warns us of the duty we have to

do and the dangers we are to avoid. There is a reward not only later, *for* keeping God's commandments, but now, *in* keeping them, for obedience is its own *great reward.*

3. The psalmist draws some good conclusions from his meditation on the splendor of the word of God.

3.1. He uses this occasion to make a repentant reflection on his own sins, for *by the law is the knowledge of sin* (Ro 3:20). "Is the commandment holy, just, and good? Then *who can understand his errors?* (v. 12). I cannot, whoever can." From the rightness of the divine law, the psalmist learns to call his sins his *errors.* Every act of disobedience against the commandment is an error, a deviation from the rule we are to live by. God knows a great deal more evil of us than we do of ourselves.

3.2. He uses this occasion to pray against sin. Finding himself unable to specify all the details of his sins, he cries out, *Lord, cleanse me from my secret faults* (v. 12). He refers not to sins that are hidden from God, since none are, nor only to sins that are hidden from the world, but to those that are hidden from his own observation of himself. Then, having prayed that his sins of weakness might be forgiven, he prays that *presumptuous* (willful) *sins* might be prevented (v. 13). His plea: "*So shall I be upright* (blameless), and I *shall be innocent from the great transgression*" (v. 13). He calls a presumptuous sin a *great transgression,* because no sacrifice was accepted for it (Nu 15:28–30).

3.3. He uses the occasion to humbly beg divine acceptance of his thoughts and devotions (v. 14). Having prayed to God to keep him from sin, he begs God to accept his actions. His actions are services to God, the *words of his mouth and the meditations of his heart* (v. 14), his holy devotions offered to God. His concern is that they might be acceptable to God, for if our services are not acceptable to God, what good do they do us?

PSALM 20

This psalm is a prayer for the king, and the next a thanksgiving for him. In this psalm we may notice: 1. What it is they ask of God for the king (vv. 1–5). 2. With what assurance they ask it. The people triumph (v. 5), then the ruler (v. 6), then both together (vv. 7–8), and in this assurance David concludes with a prayer to God to hear him (v. 9).

Title

This prayer for David is entitled *a psalm of David.* It is right for those who want the prayers of their friends to tell them in detail what they want them to ask God for them. Paul often asked his friends to pray for him.

Verses 1–5

Notice here:

1. What it is that they are taught to ask God for the king. *The Lord hear thee in the day of trouble* (v. 1), and *the Lord fulfil all thy petitions* (v. 5). David himself knew many days of trouble, days of disappointment or distress, days of being crushed or confused. Neither the crown on his head nor the grace in his heart would exempt him from trouble. The prayers of others for us must be wanted for the support of, but not to take the place of, our own prayers for ourselves. "*The name of the God of Jacob defend thee* (v. 1) and put you beyond reach of your enemies." Mercies out of the sanctuary are the sweetest mercies. *The Lord remember all thy offerings and accept thy burnt sacrifice* (v. 3), or "turn them to ashes," that is, "May the Lord give

you the victory and success which you asked for from him by your prayer with sacrifices, thereby making his acceptance of the sacrifice as abundantly clear as he ever did by kindling it with fire from heaven." We may know that God accepts our spiritual sacrifices if by his Spirit he kindles in our souls a holy fire of godly and divine love and by it makes our hearts burn within us (Lk 24:32). *The Lord grant thee according to thy own heart.* They could pray in faith for this, because they knew David was a man after God's own heart (1Sa 13:14), and would want nothing except what was pleasing to God.

2. What confidence they had of a favorable answer to these requests for themselves and their good king (v. 5): "*We will rejoice in thy salvation.* We who are subjects will rejoice in the preservation and prosperity of our ruler." *In the name of our God will we set* (lift) *up our banners* (v. 5).

These prayers for David are prophecies of Christ, the Son of David, and they were greatly answered in him. He completed the work of our redemption and made war on the powers of darkness (Eph 6:12). In the day of trouble, when his soul was exceedingly sorrowful (Mt 26:38), the Lord heard him *in that he feared,* heard him in his reverent submission (Heb 5:7), and *sent him help out of the sanctuary* (v. 2).

Verses 6–9

Here is:

1. David himself triumphing in the share he has in the prayers of good people (v. 6): "*Now know I that the Lord saveth his anointed,* because he has stirred up the hearts of the descendants of Jacob to pray for him." *He will hear him from his holy heaven* (v. 6), of which the sanctuary was a type (Heb 9:23), and from the throne he has prepared in heaven, of which the atonement cover was a type. He will hear him *with the saving strength of his right hand* (v. 6), not by letter or by word of mouth, but by his right hand, by the saving power of his right hand. He will make it clear that he hears him by what he does for him.

2. His people triumphing in God, in their relationship with him and his revelation of himself to them. The children of this world trust in circumstances, and they think everything is going well if those are smiling on them. They trust *in chariots and in horses* (v. 7). The more of those they can bring onto the field, the more certain they are of success in their wars. "But," the Israelites say, "we have neither chariots nor horses to trust in, nor do we want them. And if we did have them, we would not build our hopes of success on that, *but we will remember,* and rely on, *the name of the Lord our God* (v. 7). Those who trusted in their chariots and horses are brought to their knees and fall, and, far from saving them, their chariots and horses actually helped sink them and made them easier and more valuable prey for the conqueror (2Sa 8:4). But we who trust in the name of the Lord our God not only stand firm and keep our ground, but also have risen, gained ground from the enemy, and defeated them."

3. The concluding of their prayer for the king with a hosanna: "*Save,* now, we beseech thee, O *Lord!*" (v. 9). As we read this verse, it may be taken as a prayer that God would not only bless the king—"Save, Lord, and give him success"—but also that he would make him a blessing to them—"*Let the king hear us* (v. 9) when we call to him for justice and mercy." Those who want to receive good from their magistrates must pray for them in this way, for they, like all other creatures, are to us what God makes them to be, and no more.

PSALM 21

As the previous psalm was a prayer that God would protect and prosper the king, so this psalm is a prayer of thanksgiving for the success God had blessed him with. Those whom we have prayed for we should also give thanks for, especially for rulers in whose prosperity we share. The people are taught here: 1. To congratulate the king on his victories and the honor he has achieved (vv. 1–6). 2. To have confidence in the power of God to complete the destruction of the enemies of his kingdom (vv. 7–13).

Verses 1–6

David here speaks about himself in the first place, professing that his joy is in God's strength and in his salvation, not in the strength or success of his armies. He also tells his subjects to be joyful with him, and to give God all the glory for the victories he has gained.

1. They congratulate the king on his joys and join him in them (v. 1): "*The king rejoices. He is joyful in thy strength*, and so are we. What pleases the king pleases us" (2Sa 3:36).

2. They give God all the praise for those things which are the subject of their king's joy.

2.1. God has heard his prayers (v. 2): *Thou hast given him his heart's desire.*

2.2. God has surprised him with favors and far surpassed his expectations (v. 3): *Thou preventest* (you come before) *him with the blessings of goodness.* The psalmist here considers it especially kind that these blessings were given in advance. When God's blessings come sooner and prove richer than we have imagined, when they are given before we have even prayed for them, before we were ready for them, in fact, when we feared the contrary, then it may be truly said that he has come before us with them.

2.3. God has advanced him to the highest honor and the most extensive power: "*Thou hast set a crown of pure gold upon his head* (v. 3) and kept it there, when his enemies attempted to reject it."

2.4. God has assured him his kingdom will last forever. "When he went out on a dangerous expedition, *he asked* his *life of thee*—and in that expedition he was taking his life into his own hands—*and thou* not only *gavest him that* but also gave him *length of days for ever and ever* (v. 4). Not only did you prolong his life far beyond his expectations, but you also assured him of a blessed immortality in a future state and of the continuation of his kingdom in the Messiah, who will come from his body."

2.5. God has advanced him to the highest honor and dignity (v. 5): "*His glory is great*, far beyond that of all the neighboring rulers, in the salvation you have brought about for him and by him." The glory which every good person is ambitious to see is the salvation of the Lord.

2.6. God has given him the satisfaction of being the channel for all happiness to the human race (v. 6): "Thou hast set him to be blessings for ever," reads the margin. "You have made him a universal blessing to the world, in whom the families of the earth are, and will be, blessed (Ge 12:3). You have also *made him exceeding glad with the countenance*, the favor, you have given to his undertaking and to him in the carrying out of it." Notice how the spirit of prophecy gradually rises here to what especially concerns Christ, for no one besides him is blessed forever; much less is anyone blessed forever and exalted to the preeminence that this expression signifies.

Verses 7–13

The psalmist, having taught his people to look back with joy and praise on what God has done for him and them, here teaches them to look forward with faith, hope, and prayer to what God will further do for them: "*The king rejoices in God* (v. 1), and so we will be thankful; the *king trusteth in the Lord* (v. 7), and so we will be encouraged." The joy and confidence of Christ our King is the basis for all our joy and confidence.

1. They are confident of the stability of David's kingdom. *Through the mercy of the Most High*, not through his own merit or strength, *he shall not be moved* (shaken) (v. 7).

2. They are confident of the destruction of all the impenitent and implacable enemies of David's kingdom. The success with which God had blessed David's battles up to that time was a pledge of the rest God would give him from all his enemies around him. They hated David because God had set him apart for himself (4:3). They hated Christ because they hated the light, but both were hated for no just cause, and God was hated in both (Jn 15:23, 25). *They intended evil against thee* and devised evil schemes. They claimed to fight only against David, but their enmity was in fact against God himself. Those who aimed at deposing King David were aiming, in effect, at deposing Jehovah from being God. "They devise what they are *not able to perform* (succeed in)" (v. 11). Their hatred is powerless, and they *imagine a vain thing* (plot in vain) (2:1). They will be found out (v. 8): "*Thy hand shall find them out.* Although they are very cunningly disguised by the pretense and profession of friendship, although mixed with the faithful subjects of this kingdom and hardly distinguishable from them, although they flee from justice and run off to their own secret hideouts, your hand will still find them out wherever they are." *Their fruit and their seed shall be destroyed* (v. 10).

3. They therefore have confidence to ask God that he would still appear for his anointed (v. 13), that he would act for him in his own strength, by the direct activity of his power as almighty God and Father of spirits (Heb 12:9).

PSALM 22

The Spirit of Christ, which was in the prophets, testifies in this psalm, as clearly and fully as anywhere in the whole Old Testament, to the sufferings of Christ and the glory that should follow (1Pe 1:11). There is no doubt that David is speaking about Jesus Christ here, not of himself or any other person. Much of this psalm is explicitly applied to Christ in the New Testament, all of it may be applied to him, and some of it must be understood as referring only to him. In this psalm David speaks: 1. Of the humiliation of Christ (vv. 1–21), when, as a type of Christ, he complains about the calamitous condition which for many reasons he is now in. 1.1. He complains, and mixes encouragement in with his complaints: he complains (vv. 1–2), but encourages himself (vv. 3–5), complains again (vv. 6–8), but encourages himself again (vv. 9–10). 1.2. He complains, but mixes prayers with his complaints: he complains of the power and rage of his enemies (vv. 12–13, 16, 18) and of his own physical weakness and decline (vv. 14–15, 17), but he prays that God would not be far from him (vv. 11, 19) and that God would save and rescue him (vv. 19–21). 2. Of the exaltation of Christ, foretelling that his undertaking would be for the glory of God (vv. 22–25), for the salvation and joy of his people (vv. 26–29), and for making his own kingdom last forever (vv. 30–31).

Verses 1–10

In these verses we have:

1. A sad complaint of God's withdrawal (vv. 1–2).

1.1. This may be applied to David or any other child of God who lacks a sense of his favor and is pressed with, and groaning under, the burdens of his displeasure, as one overwhelmed by grief and terror, crying out desperately for relief. He here considers himself abandoned by God, not heard or helped, but calling out to him again and again, *My God*, continuing to cry out day and night to him and fervently desiring to experience his gracious presence. Spiritual desertions are the saints' most severe form of suffering. To cry out, "My God, why am I sick? Why am I poor?" would give reason to suspect discontent and worldliness. But to cry out, *Why hast thou forsaken me?* (v. 1), is to speak the language of a heart that has committed its happiness to God's favor. When we lack the faith of assurance, we must live by the faith of allegiance. "Whatever things are like, God is still good, and he is mine; *though he slay me, yet will I trust in him* (Job 13:15).

1.2. But it must be applied to Christ, for he used the first words of this complaint to pour out his soul before God when he was on the cross (Mt 27:46). He probably proceeded to speak out the following words, and, some think, repeated the whole psalm, if not aloud—because those on the ground objected to the first words—then to himself. In his sufferings, Christ cried out from his heart to his Father for his favor and presence with him. He cried *in the daytime*, on the cross, *and in the night season* (v. 2), when he was in agony in the garden. *He offered up strong crying and tears to him that was able to save him*—and with fear, too (Heb 5:7). But because Christ was himself made sin for us (2Co 5:21), the Father subjected him to the effects of his wrath and displeasure against sin. *It pleased the Lord to bruise him and put him to grief* (Isa 53:10).

2. Encouragement taken, in the midst of these circumstances (vv. 3–5). "*But thou art holy*, not unjust, untrue, or unkind in any of your ways. Although you do not come immediately to relieve your people who are suffering, you still love them. You are faithful to your covenant with them, and you cannot tolerate the sin and evil of their persecutors (Hab 1:13). *Thou inhabitest the praises of Israel* (v. 3). You reveal your glory, grace, and special presence to your people in the sanctuary, where they worship you with their praise. You are always ready to receive their homage, and you have said about the tent of meeting, *This is my rest for ever*" (132:14). Although God seems to turn a deaf ear to them for a while, he is still very pleased with his people's praises, and he will, in due time, give them reason to change their tone: *Hope in God, for I shall yet praise him* (43:5). The psalmist will take comfort from the experiences which the saints in former ages had of the benefits of faith and prayer (vv. 4–5): "*Our fathers trusted in thee, cried unto thee, and thou didst deliver them*, and so, in due time, you will also save me, for never was anyone who hoped in you made ashamed of their hope. Never did anyone seek you in vain (Isa 45:19). And you are still the same in yourself and the same to your people that you always have been."

3. The complaint renewed about another form of suffering, and that is human contempt and scorn. This complaint is by no means as bitter as the earlier one about God's withdrawal, but just as that withdrawal strikes a gracious soul, so this contempt touches a generous soul—and on a tender spot (vv. 6–8). Human beings, at best, are worms, but Christ became *a worm, and no man* (v. 6). If he had not made himself a worm, he could not have been trampled on as he was. He was condemned as a bad man, a blasphemer

(Mt 9:3), a Sabbath-breaker (Mt 12:2), a drunkard (Mt 11:19), a false prophet (Lk 7:39), an enemy of Caesar (Jn 19:12), an ally of the prince of demons (Mt 12:24). He was despised by the people as contemptible, not worth taking notice of, and from a country having no reputation (Php 2:7), his relatives being poor manual laborers and his followers being not of the rulers or Pharisees, but of the common people. He was ridiculed as foolish, as one who deceived not only others but also himself. David was sometimes taunted for his confidence in God, but in the sufferings of Christ this was literally and exactly fulfilled. (Mt 27:43): *He trusted in God; let him deliver him.*

4. Encouragement taken in the midst of these circumstances also (vv. 9–10): "People despise me, *but thou art he that took me out of the womb.*" David and other good people have often, for our guidance, encouraged themselves with the thought that God not only was the God of their ancestors, as David wrote earlier in the psalm (v. 4), but also is the God of their infancy, who began to take care of them at an early age, as soon as they had being, and who therefore will never, they hope, reject them. He who looked after us so much in that helpless and inadequate state will not leave us when he has brought us up and nursed us to be able to serve him. Notice the early examples of God's providential care for us:

4.1. At birth: *He took us also out of the womb* (v. 9), or else we would have died there or been suffocated at birth.

4.2. At the breast: "*Thou didst make me hope* when I was upon my mother's breasts (v. 9); you provided for me to be sustained and protected from the dangers to which I was exposed. This therefore encourages me to hope in you all my days." The blessings of the breasts crown the blessings of the womb and so are the pledges of the blessings of our whole lives: surely the One who fed us will never starve us (Job 3:12).

4.3. In our early dedication to him: *I was cast* (thrust) *upon thee from the womb* (v. 10), which perhaps refers to his circumcision on the eighth day. His parents then committed him and gave him to God, the God of the covenant, for circumcision was a seal of the covenant. This encouraged him to trust in God.

4.4. In the experience we have had of God's goodness to us all ever since, as shown in extended and uninterrupted preservation and in unfailing and constant supplies: *Thou art my God*, providing for me and watching over me for good, *from my mother's belly* (womb) (v. 10), that is, from my coming into the world to this day. This applies to our Lord Jesus, over whose incarnation and birth Providence watched with a special care, when he was born in a stable, laid in a manger, and immediately exposed to the hatred of Herod, and forced to flee to Egypt.

Verses 11–21

1. Here is Christ suffering. David was often in trouble and surrounded by enemies, but many of the details mentioned here are those that were never true of David and therefore must be taken as referring to Christ in the depths of his humiliation.

1.1. He is deserted by his friends: *Trouble* and distress are *near*, and *there is none to help*, no one to uphold him (v. 11). He trod the winepress alone (Isa 63:3), for all his disciples abandoned him and fled.

1.2. He is insulted and surrounded by his enemies—those of a higher rank, who are compared to bulls because of their strength and fury: *strong bulls of Bashan* (v. 12). The chief priests and elders who persecuted Christ were like this, as were others of a lower rank, who are compared to dogs (v. 16)—filthy, greedy, and untiring in hunting him down. An *assembly of the wicked* plotted against him (v. 16), for the chief priests sat in council to consider how they could seize Christ. These enemies were numerous and unanimous: "Many—and those of different and conflicting interests among themselves, such as Herod and Pilate—have agreed to surround me. They have carried their plot a long way, and seem to have won, for they have *beset me round* (v. 12). They have surrounded me (v. 16). They are formidable and threatening (v. 13): *They gaped upon me with their mouths*, to show me that they were going to swallow me up."

1.3. He is crucified. The method of his death itself is described, although it was never used among the Jews: *They pierced my hands and my feet* (v. 16), which were nailed to the cursed tree, from which the whole body was left to hang.

1.4. He is dying (vv. 14–15), dying in pain and anguish, because he was to make atonement for sin. "*I am poured out like water. My heart is like wax. My strength is dried up. My tongue cleaveth to my jaws. Thou hast brought me to the dust of death* (vv. 14–15); I am ready to fall into the grave," for nothing less would satisfy divine justice. The life of the sinner was forfeited, and so the life of the sacrifice must be the price of its ransom. The sentence of death passed on Adam was expressed in this way: *Unto dust thou shalt return* (Ge 3:19). And so Christ, considering that punishment in his obedience to death (Php 2:8), uses a similar expression here: *Thou hast brought me to* (you lay me in) *the dust of death* (v. 15).

1.5. He was stripped. The shame of nakedness was the immediate result of sin, and so our Lord Jesus was stripped of his clothes when he was crucified, to clothe us with the robe of his righteousness, so that the shame of our nakedness might not be apparent. We are told here:

1.5.1. How his body looked when it was stripped: *I may tell* (count) *all my bones* (v. 17). *They look and stare upon me* (v. 17); "the bystanders and passersby are stunned to see my bones stand out in this way, and instead of pitying me, they are pleased at such a dismal sight."

1.5.2. What they did with his clothes, which they took from him (v. 18): *They parted my garments among them*, giving a part to every soldier, and *upon my vesture*, the seamless garment, *do they cast lots*. This particular circumstance was fulfilled precisely (Jn 19:23–24). And although it was not an important aspect of Christ's suffering, it is still a great example of the fulfillment of Scripture in him. *Thus it was written, and* therefore *thus it behoved* (was necessary for) *Christ to suffer* (Lk 24:46).

2. Here is Christ praying earnestly; he prayed that the cup might pass from him. David's prayer here was a type of Christ's praying. He calls God his *strength* (v. 19). He prays: *Be not thou far from me* (v. 11 and again v. 19). "Whoever stands aloof from my suffering, Lord, please let it not be you." And the Father *heard him in that* (because) *he feared* (Heb 5:7), and he enabled him to go through with his undertaking. The psalmist here calls his soul his *darling*, his "only one": "*My soul* is my only one. I have only one soul to take care of, and so my shame will be greater if I neglect it, and my loss will be greater if I let it perish. Because it is my only one, it should be precious to me, and I should be deeply concerned for its eternal welfare." Notice what the danger is from which he prays to be rescued: *from the sword* (v. 20), the flaming sword of divine wrath, which flashes back and forth (Ge 3:24). "Oh save my soul from that. Lord, although I lose my life, let me not lose your love. Save me from *the power of the dog* and *from the lion's mouth*" (v. 21). This seems to refer to

Satan, the enemy who bruised the heel of the seed of the woman (Ge 3:15). "Lord, save me from being defeated by his terrors." He pleads, "You have formerly *heard me from the horns of the unicorn* (wild oxen)" (v. 21), that is, "you have saved me from them in answer to my prayer." Has God rescued us from the horns of the wild oxen (v. 21), so that we are not tossed about? Let that encourage us to trust we will be rescued from the lion's mouth, so that we will not be torn apart. He who has rescued us in the past will do so again. This prayer of Christ was, no doubt, answered, for the Father always heard him (Jn 11:42). And although he did not save him from death, he did not allow him to see decay (16:11), but raised him up on the third day from the dust of death. This was a greater demonstration of God's favor to him than if he had helped him down from the cross, for that would have prevented him from completing the work he came to do, whereas his resurrection crowned that work.

Verses 22–31

As the first words of complaint were used by Christ himself on the cross, so the first words of the triumph are expressly applied to him (Heb 2:12) and are made his own words: *I will declare thy name unto my brethren, in the midst of the church will I sing praise unto thee*. Here there are spoken of five thoughts which gave Jesus a great sense of satisfaction and triumph when he was suffering:

1. That he would have a church in the world. This is implied here; similarly, Isaiah later said that Christ would *see his seed* (Isa 53:10). It pleased him to think that by the declaring of God's name, by the preaching of the eternal Gospel in its clarity and purity, many would be powerfully called to him and to God by him. Ministers would be employed in declaring this teaching to the world to accomplish this. Those who were called in this way would be brought into a very close and precious relationship with him as his brothers and sisters; not only believing Jews, his compatriots, but also those of the Gentiles who became fellow heirs and came from the same body (Heb 2:11). These brothers and sisters would be incorporated into a great assembly. This is the universal church, the whole family that is named from him (Eph 3:15), to which all the *children of God that were scattered abroad are collected*, and in which they are united (Jn 11:52; Eph 1:10). And it pleased Christ that they would also be incorporated into smaller assemblies, members of that great body. These would be counted as the seed of Jacob and Israel (v. 23), so that the blessing of Abraham might come on them even though they were Gentiles (Gal 3:14). The Gospel church is called *the Israel of God* (Gal 6:16).

2. That God would be greatly honored and glorified in him by that church. He foresaw with pleasure:

- That God would be glorified by the church which would be gathered to him. All who fear the Lord will praise him (v. 23), every true Israelite (Jn 1:47). See 118:2–4; 135:19–20.
- That God would be glorified in the Redeemer and in his work. Christ is said to praise God in the church. All our praises must center on the work of redemption.

3. That all humble, gracious souls would enjoy full satisfaction and happiness in God (v. 26). Those who pray much will give thanks much: *Those shall praise the Lord that seek him* (v. 26), because they are sure of finding him through Christ, in the hope of which they have reason to praise him even while they are seeking him. The souls that are devoted to him will be happy with him forever: *Your heart shall live for ever* (v. 26).

4. That the church of Christ, and with it the kingdom of God on earth, would reach all the corners of the world and would include all kinds of people. Whereas the Jews had long been the only professing people of God, now all the ends of the world would come into the church, and with the partition wall being brought down (Eph 2:14), the Gentiles would also be included. It is here prophesied that they would be converted: they *shall remember, and turn to the Lord.* Serious reflection is the first step, and it is a good step, toward true conversion. We must consider and turn. The prodigal son first came to himself (Lk 15:17) and then returned to his father. They would then be admitted into fellowship with God and the assemblies that serve him: *They shall worship before thee,* for *in every place incense shall be offered to God* (Mal 1:11; Isa 66:23). There is good reason why all the families of the nations should bow down to God, for (v. 28) *the kingdom is the Lord's.*

4.1. The kingdom of nature is the Lord Jehovah's, and his providence rules among the nations.

4.2. The kingdom of grace is the Lord Christ's, and he, as Mediator, is the One who rules over the nations. He is head over all things for his church (Eph 1:22). High and low, rich and poor, slave and free all meet together in Christ. Christ will receive the worship of many great ones. *Those that are fat upon the earth,* who live in all their pomp and power, *shall eat and worship.* The poor will also receive his Gospel: *Those that go down to the dust* (v. 29), who sit in the dust (113:7), who can scarcely keep life and soul together, *shall bow before him* (v. 29), before the Lord Jesus, who considers it his special honor to be the king of the poor and needy (72:12). Seeing we cannot keep alive our own souls, we will be wise to have an obedient faith and commit our souls to Jesus Christ, who is able to save them and keep them alive forever.

5. That the church of Christ, and with it the kingdom of God on earth, would continue to the end, throughout all time. *A seed shall serve him* (v. 30); there will be a remnant, greater or smaller, enough to preserve the inheritance. *They shall be accounted to him for a generation* (v. 30); he will be the same to them as he was to those who went before them. *They shall come* (v. 31). They will rise up in their day, not only to maintain the goodness of the previous generation and do the work of their own generation, but also to serve the honor of Christ and the good of souls in generations to come. They will pass on to them the sacred deposit of the Gospel of Christ.

In praying over and singing these verses we must keep our thoughts fixed on Christ. We must triumph in the name of Christ as being above every name (Php 2:9). We must honor him ourselves, rejoice in the honors others give him, and rejoice in the assurance we have that there will be a people praising him on earth when we are praising him in heaven.

PSALM 23

This is a psalm which has been sung by true Christians with a great deal of joy and assurance and which will be so sung as long as this world exists. 1. The psalmist here claims to know God as his shepherd (v. 1). 2. He recalls his experience of the good things God has done for him as his shepherd (vv. 2–3, 5). 3. He reasons from this that he will lack no good thing (v. 1), that he need not fear any evil (v. 4), and that God will never leave or forsake him with his mercy; and so he decides never to leave God by leaving the path of duty (v. 6). As in the previous psalm he described Christ dying for his sheep,

so here he describes Christians as receiving the benefits of all the care and tenderness of God, our good and great shepherd.

Verses 1–6

1. From God's being his shepherd he reasons that he will not lack anything good for him (v. 1). There was a time when David himself was a shepherd. He was taken from tending the sheep (78:70–71), and so he knows from his experience the cares and tender feelings that a good shepherd has toward his flock. He remembers how much they need a shepherd; he once risked his life to rescue a lamb (1Sa 17:34–35). He therefore uses this illustration to show God's care for his people. It is also to this that our Savior seems to refer when he says, *I am the shepherd of the sheep; the good shepherd* (Jn 10:11). See also Isa 40:11. He gathers them into his fold and provides for them. We must know the shepherd's voice and follow him. When David considers that God is his shepherd, he can boldly say, *I shall not want* (v. 1). More is implied than is expressed, not only, *I shall not want* (v. 1), but also, "I will be supplied with whatever I need, and if I do not have everything I want, then I may conclude it is either not right for me or not good for me, or that I will have it in due time."

2. From God's fulfilling the role of a good shepherd to him he reasons that he need not fear any evil in the greatest dangers and difficulties he could be in (vv. 2–4).

2.1. Notice the contentment of the saints as the sheep of God's pasture.

2.1.1. They are well placed: *He maketh me to lie down in green pastures* (v. 2). We have the encouragements of this life from God's good hand; we receive our daily bread from him as our Father. The greatest abundance is only dry pasture to evildoers, who enjoy only what pleases their senses. Those who are godly, however, who taste the goodness of God in everything they enjoy, know the world to be a green pasture even though they have only a little of it (37:16; Pr 15:16–17). God makes his saints lie down; he gives them peace and contentment in their own minds, whatever their lot is. Their souls live at peace in him, and that makes every pasture green.

2.1.2. They are well guided. *He leadeth me beside the still waters* (v. 2). Those who feed on God's goodness must also follow his direction. He directs their eyes, their ways, and their heart toward his love. God provides for his people not only food and rest but also refreshment and delight. God leads his people not to the stagnant waters, which are dirty and gather filth, nor to the raging and troubled sea or the rapid, rolling floods, but to the silent, flowing waters, for the quiet but running waters correspond best to those spirits that flow out toward God but do so silently. "*He leadeth me in the paths of righteousness,* as I do my duty. He instructs me in that by his word, and he directs me in it by conscience and providence." The path of duty is true and pleasant. We cannot walk in these paths unless God both leads us to them and leads us in them.

2.1.3. They are well helped when anything harms them: *He restoreth my soul* (v. 3). When, after one sin, David's heart struck him, and after another, Nathan was sent to tell him, *Thou art the man* (2Sa 12:7), God restored his soul. Although God may allow his people to fall into sin, he will not allow them to lie still in it.

2.2. Notice the courage of a dying saint (v. 4): "Having had such an experience of God's goodness to me all my life time after time, I will never distrust him, not even in the final crisis of death. *Though I walk through the valley of the shadow of death* (v. 4), that is, although I am in danger of death, although I am in the middle of many dangers, deep as a valley, I will still be at peace." The word *death* does indeed sound terrible. But even as David imagines the distress of death, he uses four words which reduce its terror. It is only the *shadow* of death; there is no substantial evil in it. The shadow of a snake cannot bite, nor can the shadow of a sword kill. It is the *valley* of the shadow, deep, dark, and dirty, but the valleys are fruitful, and death itself has many fruits of encouragement to God's people. It is only a *walk* in this valley: a gentle, pleasant walk. It is a walk *through* this valley; they will not lose their way in this valley, but will safely reach the mountain of spices on its other side (SS 8:14). Death contains no evil for the child of God. It cannot separate us from the love of God (Ro 8:38–39). It kills the body but cannot harm the soul (Mt 10:28). The good shepherd will not only lead, but also take, his sheep through this valley. His presence will give them strength and encouragement: *Thou art with me* (v. 4). His word and Spirit will give them strength and encouragement—his *rod and staff* (v. 4); the phrase alludes to the shepherd's crook, or the rod under which the sheep passed when they were counted (Lev 27:32), or the staff with which the shepherds drove away the dogs that tried to tear the sheep to pieces.

3. From the good gifts of God's goodness to him he now reasons the faithfulness and eternity of his mercy (vv. 5–6). "*Thou preparest a table before me*; you have provided for me everything I have needed, all that I have needed both for body and for soul, for time and eternity." He has enough food, a table that is spread and a cup that is filled, food to satisfy his hunger and drink to quench his thirst. "*My cup runs over* (v. 5), enough for myself and my friends too." *Thou anointest my head with oil* (v. 5). He has said (v. 1), *I shall not want*, but now he speaks more positively: *Surely goodness and mercy shall follow me all the days of my life* (v. 6). His hope rises, and his faith is strengthened, by being exercised. "It will *follow* me, as that water from the rock, Christ, followed the camp of Israel through the desert (1Co 10:4). It will follow me all my life long, even to the end," for those whom God loves he loves to the end. *Surely* it will. "Because goodness and mercy have followed me all the days of my life on earth, when those days come to an end, I will move to a better world, to *dwell in the house of the Lord for ever* (v. 6), in our Father's house above, where there are many rooms" (Jn 14:2).

PSALM 24

This psalm mainly concerns the kingdom of Jesus Christ: 1. His providential kingdom, by which he rules the world (vv. 1–2). 2. The kingdom of his grace, by which he rules his church: 2.1. Concerning the subjects of the kingdom: their character (vv. 4, 6) and their charter (v. 5). 2.2. Concerning the King of that kingdom, and a summons to everyone to give him access (vv. 7–10).

Verses 1–2

1. We are not to think that only the heavens are the Lord's, that this earth—because it is such a small and insignificant part of creation—is neglected, and that he claims no interest in it. No; even the earth is his.

1.1. When God gave the earth to human beings, he still reserved title to it for himself, only letting it out to them as tenants (Mt 21:33–34): *The earth is the Lord's and the fulness thereof* (v. 1). The mines, the fruits the earth produces, all the animals of the forest and the cattle on a thousand hills (50:10), our lands and houses, and every use that this earth is put to by human skill and diligence, are all his. In the kingdom of grace, these are rightly

looked on as empty and meaningless, because they are nothing to a soul, but in the kingdom of providence, they are fullness. *The earth is full of God's riches, so is the great and wide sea also* (104:24–25).

1.2. The inhabited part of this earth (Pr 8:31) is his in a special way—the *world and those that dwell therein* (v. 1). We ourselves are not our own: our bodies and our souls do not belong to us.

2. The earth belongs to the Lord by his indisputable title, *for he hath founded it upon the seas* and *established it upon the floods* (v. 2). He made it and fitted it for people to use. Matter is his, for he made it from nothing. The form is his, for he made it according to his own eternal counsels and plans. He continues it; he has *established* and fixed it, so that although one generation passes away and another comes, the earth remains forever (Ecc 1:4). His providence, too, is a continued creation (119:90).

Verses 3–6

From this world and its fullness, the psalmist's meditations suddenly turn to the great things of another world, the foundation of which is not on the seas or waters (Heb 11:10). And so, here is:

1. A question about better things (Heb 11:40; 12:24) (v. 3). This earth is God's footstool (Isa 66:1; Mt 5:35), but we must be here only for a while and soon leave this world, and *Who then shall ascend into the hill of the Lord?* Who will go to heaven later, and, as a pledge of that, have fellowship with God in his holy ordinances now? When a soul that knows and considers its own nature, origin, and immortality has viewed the earth and its fullness, it will sit down unsatisfied. "What will I do to rise to that hill, that high place, where the Lord lives, that I may stay in that happy and holy place where he meets his people?"

2. An answer to this question, in which we see both the nature and the privileges of God's own people, who will have fellowship with him in grace and glory.

2.1. Their nature: they are those who keep themselves from all gross acts of sin. They have *clean hands*. Hands lifted up in prayer must be pure, without any blemish of unjust gain clinging to them, or anything else that defiles and is offensive to the holy God. God's people are also those who make it a matter of conscience to be inwardly as good as they outwardly seem. They have *pure hearts*. A pure heart is one that is sincere, purified by faith, and conformed to the image and will of God; see Mt 5:8. They are those who do not set their desires on the things of this world (Col 3:2), who do not *lift up their souls unto vanity* (v. 4). They are those who deal honestly both with God and with other people. They are a praying people (v. 6): *This is the generation of those that seek him.* In every age there is a remnant of such people, those who are like this, who are *accounted to the Lord for a generation* (22:30). It is to the hill of the Lord that we must ascend, considering acceptance by him to be the summit of our happiness, and because the way is uphill, we need to exert ourselves as much as we can, as those who seek him diligently. God's people unite themselves with other people of God, seeking God with them. They seek God's face as Jacob did, who was named *Israel* because he wrestled with God and prevailed; he sought him and found him. As soon as Paul was converted, he *joined himself to the disciples* (Ac 9:26). "Thy face, O God of Jacob" is the reading of the margin and is a good translation.

2.2. Their privileges: they will be made truly and forever happy. They will be justified and sanctified. These are the spiritual blessings in heavenly things (Eph 1:3) which they will receive, and they are righteousness indeed, the very thing they hunger and thirst for (Mt 5:6). They will be saved, for God himself will be the God of their salvation.

Verses 7–10

What is spoken once is spoken a second time in these verses; such repetitions are usual in songs. Entrance is demanded, then demanded again, for the King of glory; the doors and gates are to be thrown open. *Who is this King of glory?* (v. 8). *It is the Lord, strong and mighty, the Lord, mighty in battle, the Lord of hosts* (vv. 8, 10).

1. This magnificent entrance probably refers to the sacred bringing in of the ark into the tent David pitched for it; or perhaps it was for the bringing of the ark into the temple Solomon built for it, for as David prepared materials for the building of the temple, it was right for him to prepare a psalm for its dedication. The doors are called *everlasting* (ancient) *doors* (v. 9), because they will last much longer than the door of the tabernacle, which was only a curtain. In his word and ordinances for worship, God is to be welcomed by us. The doors and gates must be thrown open to him.

2. No doubt this entrance also points to Christ, of whom the ark, with its atonement cover, was a type. We may apply it to the ascension of Christ to heaven and the welcome given him there. The gates of heaven must then be opened to him—those doors that may be truly called *everlasting*. Our Redeemer found them closed, but after he had made atonement for sin by his blood and gained the right to *enter into the holy place* (Heb 9:12), as one with authority, he demanded access not only for himself but also for us, for as the forerunner, he has entered for us and *opened the kingdom of heaven to all believers*. We may apply these verses to Christ's entering into human souls by his word and Spirit so that they may be his temples. Christ's presence in them is like the presence of the ark in the temple; it consecrates them. *Behold, he stands at the door and knocks* (Rev 3:20). The gates and doors of the heart must be opened to him not only as access is given to a guest but also as possession is given to the rightful owner. This is the Gospel call and demand, that we let Jesus Christ, the King of glory, come into our souls and welcome him with hosannas: *Blessed is he that cometh* (Mt 21:9).

PSALM 25

This psalm is full of devotion to God: the expressions of holy desires toward his favor and grace and the actions that proceed from faith in his promises. We may learn from it: 1. What it is to pray (vv. 1, 15). 2. What we must pray for: the forgiveness of sins (vv. 6–7, 11, 18), direction for our duty (vv. 4–5), the favor of God (v. 16), rescue from our troubles (vv. 17–18), preservation from our enemies (vv. 20–21), and the salvation of the church of God (v. 22). 3. What we may plead in prayer: our confidence in God (vv. 2–3, 5, 20–21), our desire for his glory (v. 11), our distress and the hatred of our enemies (vv. 17, 19), and our integrity (v. 21). 4. What precious promises we have to encourage us in prayer: promises of guidance and instruction (vv. 8–9, 12), the benefits of the covenant (v. 10), and the delight of fellowship with God (vv. 13–14).

Verses 1–7

Here is David's profession of his desire toward God and his dependence on him. He often begins his psalms with such professions, not to influence God but to motivate himself.

1. He professes his desire toward God: *Unto thee, O Lord! do I lift up my soul* (v. 1). When we worship God,

we must lift up our souls to him. Prayer is the ascent of the soul to God. *Sursum corda,* "Lift up your hearts," was an ancient call to devotion.

2. He professes his dependence on God (v. 2): *O my God, I trust in thee.* His conscience witnesses to him that he has no confidence in himself or in any other creature. He satisfies himself with this profession of faith in God. *"Let me not be ashamed* (v. 2) of my confidence in you; let me not be shaken from it by any terrible fears. And in the end, let me not be prevented from gaining what I am depending on you for; Lord, *keep what I have committed unto thee"* (2Ti 1:12). *Let those be ashamed that transgress without cause* (v. 3)—literally, "transgress in vain." The weaker the temptation by which people are drawn to sin, the stronger have been the corruption by which they were driven to it. Those who sin for the sake of sinning are the worst transgressors.

3. He asks direction from God in order to fulfill his duty (vv. 4–5). He prays, and prays again, that God will teach him. *Teach me* not fine words or fine ideas, but *thy ways, thy paths, thy truth,* the ways in which you walk toward me, which are *all mercy and truth* (v. 10), and the ways in which you want me to walk toward you. *Show me thy way,* and so *teach me"* (v. 5). When we are uncertain about which way to follow, we should pray fervently that God would make it clear to us what he wants us to do. *"Lead me,* and so *teach me." Thou art the God of my salvation* (v. 5). If God is saving us, he will also teach us and lead us. He who gives salvation will also give instruction. *On thee do I wait all the day* (v. 5). From where should servants expect direction except from their own master, on whom they wait all the day?

4. He appeals to God's infinite mercy, not claiming to have any goodness in himself (v. 6): *"Remember, O Lord! thy tender mercies,* and for the sake of those mercies, lead me and teach me, for they *have been ever of old."*

5. He is fervent in asking for the forgiveness of his sins (v. 7): *"O remember not the sins of my youth.* Lord, remember your mercies (v. 6), which speak for me, and not my sins, which speak against me." When God forgives sin, he is said to *remember it no more,* which shows absolute remission: he forgives and forgets.

Verses 8–14

God's promises are mixed here with David's prayers. There were many requests in the earlier part of the psalm, and we will find many in the final part, and here, in the middle of the psalm, he meditates on the promises. The promises of God are not only the best foundation of prayer, telling us what to pray for, but also a present answer to prayer. Let our prayers be made according to the promises, and then the promises may be read as responses to the prayer. We are to believe that prayer is heard because the promises will be fulfilled. But in the middle of the promises, we find one request which seems to have been included somewhat abruptly, and should have followed on v. 7. It is v. 11, *Pardon my iniquity.* He backs up this request with a double plea. *"For thy name's sake pardon my iniquity,* and, *Pardon my iniquity, for it is great* (v. 11), and so I am ruined, unless infinite mercy intervenes to forgive it."

Let us now consider the great and precious promises in these verses and notice:

1. To whom these promises refer and who may expect to benefit from them: sinners. These promises are trustworthy to those who, although they have been sinners, now keep God's word. Although through the weakness of the flesh they sometimes break the commands, they

sincerely repent when they do wrong, they are constantly loyal by faith to God as their God, and they keep the covenant, not breaking it. They are those who fear him (v. 12 and again v. 14), who stand in awe of his majesty and worship him with reverence, who submit to his authority and obey him cheerfully.

2. Two things which confirm all the promises:

2.1. The perfections of God's nature confirm his promises. We value a promise in proportion to our esteem for the character of the one who makes it. We may therefore depend on God's promises, for *good and upright is the Lord* (v. 8), as good as his word, and so he will be upright in fulfilling them.

2.2. All he says and does conforms with those perfections (v. 10): *All the paths of the Lord*—all his promises and all his providences—*are mercy and truth*; they are, like himself, good and upright, loving and faithful.

3. What these promises are:

3.1. That God will tell them what their duty is and instruct them how to carry it out. This is insisted on the most, because it is an answer to David's prayers (vv. 4–5), *Show me thy ways and lead me.* We should fix our thoughts on those promises which suit our present situation.

3.1.1. He *will teach sinners in the way* (v. 8), because they are sinners and so need teaching. When they want to be taught, then he will teach them the way to be reconciled to God, the way to a well-founded peace in their conscience, and the way to receive eternal life.

3.1.2. *The meek will he guide* (v. 9), that is, those who are humble and lowly in their own eyes, who distrust themselves. They want to be taught; they have honestly decided to follow divine guidance. He will guide such people *in judgment*, that is, in what is right, by the rule of the written word.

3.1.3. *Him that feareth the Lord he will teach in the way that he shall choose* (v. 12), either in the way that God will choose or the way that the good person will choose. It comes to the same thing, for those who fear the Lord choose the things that please him.

3.2. That God will make them at peace (v. 13): *His soul shall dwell at ease,* "shall lodge in goodness" (v. 13, margin). Those who devote themselves to the fear of God, who give themselves to be taught by God, will find things go well with them.

3.3. That God will give to them and their descendants as much of this world as is good for them: *His seed shall inherit the earth* (v. 13). Their children will get along better when they go on because of their prayers.

3.4. That God will take them into his confidence and into fellowship with himself (v. 14): *The secret of the Lord is with those that fear him.* They understand his word, for *if any man do his will, he shall know of the doctrine whether it be of God* (Jn 7:17).

Verses 15–22

Encouraged by the promises he has been meditating on, David concludes the psalm, as he began, with professions of dependence on God and love toward him.

1. He lays before God the terrible situation he is in. His feet are held fast and entangled in a net or trap, so he cannot extricate himself from his difficulties (v. 15). He is *desolate and afflicted* (v. 16). David calls himself *desolate and solitary* because he does not depend on his servants and soldiers, but relies entirely and only on God as if he had no prospect at all of help from any other creature. *The troubles of his heart are enlarged* (v. 17); he grows more and more sad and depressed.

2. He expresses his dependence on God in these troubles (v. 15): *My eyes are ever towards the Lord.* Those who always have their eyes toward God will find that their feet do not remain long in the snare. He repeats his profession of dependence on God (v. 20)—*Let me not be ashamed, for I put my trust in thee*—and of his expectation from him—*I wait on thee* (v. 21).

3. He prays fervently to God for help and relief: *Forgive all my sins.* Lord, *forgive all, take away all iniquity.* It is significant that, as for his suffering, he asks no more than for God to consider it. "*Look upon my affliction and my pain* (v. 18), and do with it as you please." But as regards his sin, he asks for nothing less than a full pardon: *Forgive all my sins* (v. 18). Yet he does pray for the putting right of his grievances: *Turn thou unto me* (v. 16). His condition is troubled, and with reference to that, he prays, "*O bring thou me out of my distresses* (v. 17). I see no way of being rescued, but you can either find one or make one." He pleads God's mercy: *Have mercy upon me* (v. 16). Even people with the greatest merits would be ruined if they did not have a God of infinite mercies. He pleads his own misery, which makes him the proper object of divine mercy. He pleads the sin of his enemies: "Lord, consider them, how cruel they are, and rescue me from them." He pleads his own integrity (v. 21). Although he has acknowledged himself guilty before God, yet as for his enemies, he has the testimony of his conscience that he has done them no wrong. Sincerity is our best form of security in the worst times. *Redeem Israel, O God! out of all his troubles.* David's troubles were great, and he was serious in asking God to rescue him, but he did not forget the distresses of God's church.

PSALM 26

In this psalm, David puts himself under a sacred test by God and his own conscience, both of which he appeals to concerning his integrity (vv. 1–2). To prove his integrity he asserts: 1. His faithful consideration of God and his grace (v. 3) and his deep loathing of sin and sinners (vv. 4–5). 2. His sincere devotion to the services of the worship of God, and his concern for them (vv. 6–8). Having proved his integrity, he prays to be rescued from the condemnation of evildoers (vv. 9–10); he throws himself on the mercy and grace of God, with a determination to maintain his integrity and his confidence in God (vv. 11–12).

Verses 1–5

David probably wrote this psalm when he was being persecuted by Saul, who described him as an evildoer and falsely accused him of many crimes. In this he was a type of Christ, who was made an object of scorn. Notice what David does in this situation:

1. He appeals to God's righteous sentence (v. 1): "*Judge me, O Lord,* vindicate me before my accusers." He cannot justify himself against the charge of sin. He acknowledges that his sin is great and he is ruined unless God, in his infinite mercy, forgives him, but he can justify himself against the charge of hypocrisy. It is an encouragement to everyone who is sincere in their religious faith that God himself is a witness to their sincerity.

2. He submits to God's unerring search (v. 2): *Examine me, O Lord, and prove me,* as gold is tested to see if it meets the required standard. He was so sincere in his devotion to his God that he wished he had a window onto his inner self, so that whoever wanted to might look into his heart.

3. He solemnly declares his sincerity (v. 1): "*I have walked in my integrity*; I have led a blameless life; my

actual way of life corresponds to my profession, and one part of it is in harmony with another." Proofs of his integrity encouraged him to trust in the Lord as his righteous Judge; *therefore I shall not slide* (waver) (v. 1). Those who are sincere in their religious faith may trust in God to keep them from wavering, that is, to keep them from turning their backs on their faith.

3.1. He constantly considered God and his grace (v. 3): *Thy loving-kindness is before my eyes.* And he governed himself by the word of God as his rule: "*I have walked in thy truth* (v. 3), that is, according to your law, for your law is truth."

3.2. He had no fellowship with the unfruitful works of darkness (Eph 5:11) or with those who do such works (vv. 4–5). Great care to avoid bad company is both a good sign of our integrity and a good way of keeping it. "*I have not sat with them*, and I *will not go in with them*" (v. 4). The company of hypocrites is as dangerous company as any, and as much to be avoided. Evildoers claim friendship to those whom they would try to draw into their snares, but they are trying to deceive them. *When they speak fair, believe them not* (Jer 12:6). Though sometimes he could not avoid being in the company of bad people, he still would not *go in with them* (v. 4); he would not choose such people as his friends. "I have hated *ecclesiam malignantium*," "the church of the malignant," in the words of the Vulgate (a Latin translation of the Bible). Just as good people in a group make one another better, and are enabled to do much more good, evildoers together make one another worse and cause much more trouble.

Verses 6–12

In these verses:

1. As a further sign of his integrity, David mentions his sincere devotion for the services of the worship of God.

1.1. He was very careful in his preparation for worship: *I will wash my hands in innocency* (v. 6). In our preparation for worship, we must not only clear ourselves from the charge of hypocrisy, and declare our innocence of that—which was represented by *washing the hands* (Dt 21:6)—but also take pains to cleanse ourselves by renewing our repentance.

1.2. He was very diligent and sincere in observing the ordinances of worship: *I will compass* (go around) *thy altar* (v. 6); here he alludes to the custom of the priests, who, while the sacrifice was being offered, walked around the altar, and probably those offering the sacrifice did the same at some distance, showing a diligent regard for what was being done and a dutiful attention to it.

1.3. In all his observance of these ordinances, he aimed at the glory of God.

1.4. He did this with delight: "*Lord*, you know how dearly *I have loved the habitation of thy house* (v. 8), the tabernacle where you are pleased to live among your people and receive their homage, *the place where thy honour dwells.*"

2. Having given proofs of his integrity, he prays fervently that he may not suffer the condemnation of evildoers (vv. 9–10). *Gather not my soul with sinners* (v. 9). "They are bloodthirsty; they thirst after blood and are guilty of shedding innocent blood. They are always causing trouble. Although they make gains from their evil—their right hand is full of bribes which they have taken to pervert the course of justice—that will never make their case any better, for *what is a man profited if he gain the whole world and lose his soul?*" (Mt 16:26). He dreads sharing with them.

3. With a holy, humble confidence, David commits himself to the grace of God (vv. 11–12). "As for me, whatever others do, I will walk in my integrity; I will lead a blameless life." He prays for divine grace both to enable him to do so and to give him assurance because of it: "Redeem me from the hands of my enemies, and be merciful to me, living and dying." He is pleased with his steadiness: "*My foot stands in an even place*, where I will not stumble and from where I will not fall." He promises himself that though he is now perhaps banished from public worship, he will again have an opportunity to bless God in the assembly of his people.

PSALM 27

Some think David wrote this psalm before he came to the throne, when he was in the midst of his troubles, perhaps on the occasion of the death of his parents, but the Jews think he wrote it when he was old, on the occasion when Abishai wonderfully rescued him from the sword of a Philistine giant (2Sa 21:16–17). Perhaps it was not written on any particular occasion; it expresses very well the godly devotion with which gracious souls are carried toward God at all times, especially in times of trouble. Here is: 1. The courage and holy bravery of his faith (vv. 1–3); the delight he took in fellowship with God and the benefits he experienced from it (vv. 4–6). 2. His desire for God, and for his favor and grace (vv. 7–9, 11–12); his expectations from God, and the encouragement he gave others to hope in him (vv. 10, 13–14).

Verses 1–6

We may notice here:

1. With what a living faith David triumphs in God and glories in his holy name (105:3).

1.1. *The Lord is my light* (v. 1). David's subjects called him *the light of Israel* (2Sa 21:17). He was indeed a burning and a shining light (Jn 5:35), but he acknowledges that he shines, like the moon, with a borrowed light. The light God casts on him reflects on them: *The Lord is my light* (v. 1).

1.2. "He is *my salvation* (v. 1), in whom I am safe and by whom I will be saved."

1.3. "He is *the strength of my life* (v. 1), not only the One who is a stronghold to protect my exposed life, but also the strength of my weak life."

2. With what a fearless courage he triumphs over his enemies. There is no bravery like that which comes by faith. If God is for him, who can be against him (Ro 8:31)? *Whom shall I fear? Of whom shall I be afraid?* (v. 1). His enemies attacked him, *to eat up his flesh*. They aimed at nothing less and were certain they would be successful, but they fell. It is not, "He struck them and they fell," but, "They *stumbled and fell.*" They were so confounded and weakened that they could not continue with their plans. "Although there are a large number of them, *a host* (an army) of them, although they *encamp against me*, an army against one person, *my heart* still *shall not fear*" (v. 3). Armies cannot harm us if God Almighty protects us. "Indeed, in this assurance that God is for me, *I will be confident*" (v. 3). "*He shall hide me*, not in the *strongholds of* En-gedi (1Sa 23:29), but *in the secret* (shelter) *of his tabernacle*" (v. 5). *Now shall my head be lifted up above my enemies*, not only so they cannot reach it with their arrows, but also so that I will be exalted to rule over them."

3. With what a gracious fervency he prays for constant fellowship with God in holy worship (v. 4).

3.1. What it is he desires—to *dwell in the house of the Lord* (v. 4). The priests have their lodgings in the courts of God's house, and David wishes he were one of them. All God's children want to live in God's house; where else should they live? Do we hope that praising God will be the blessed inheritance of our eternity? If so, we should surely make it the business of our present time.

3.2. How fervently he desires this: "This is the *one thing I have desired of the Lord* (v. 4) and which I will seek after." If he could ask only one thing from God, it would be this, for this was on his heart more than anything else. He would live in God's house *to behold the beauty of the Lord and to inquire in his temple* (v. 4). He knew something of the beauty of the Lord; his holiness is his beauty (110:3); his goodness is his beauty (Zec 9:17). The harmony of all his attributes is the beauty of his nature. In God's house troubles would not find him. Joash, one of David's descendants, was hidden for six years in the house of the Lord, and he was not only kept from being killed there, but also reserved for the crown (2Ki 11:3). The temple was thought to be a safe place for Nehemiah to go to (Ne 6:10). The safety of believers, however, is not in the walls of the temple but in the God of the temple, and their strength and encouragement are in fellowship with him.

Verses 7–14

In these verses, David expresses:

1. His desire toward God, in many requests. If he cannot go to the house of the Lord now, then wherever he can, he will find a way to go to the throne of grace in prayer.

1.1. He humbly requests a gracious hearing. "*Hear, O Lord, when I cry*, not only with my heart but, as one who is in earnest, *with my voice* too." If we pray and believe, God will graciously hear and answer.

1.2. He lays hold of the kind invitation God has given him to do this duty (v. 8). He directs his thoughts to the call God has given him to the throne of his grace. *My heart said unto thee*, or *of thee*—in the original, the verse begins with this phrase—*Seek you my face* (v. 8). He first meditated on that, and preached it over and over again to himself—and that is the best preaching: it is hearing twice what God speaks once. "My heart said to me that *thou saidst, Seek ye my face.*" Then he returns what he has meditated on, to give this godly decision: *Thy face, Lord, will I seek* (v. 8). The opening of God's hand will satisfy the desire of living things (145:16), but it is only the shining of his face that will satisfy the desire of a living soul (4:6–7).

1.3. He makes several specific requests. He acknowledges that he has deserved God's anger, but he begs that however God might correct him, he would not reject him from his presence: "*O leave me not, neither forsake me* (v. 9); do not withdraw the activity of your power from me, for then I would be helpless. Do not withdraw the signs of your goodwill to me, for then I would be discouraged." He asks for the benefit of divine guidance (v. 11): "*Teach me thy way, O Lord!* Give me understanding of what your providences toward me mean, so that I may not go astray, but walk in right paths, and so that I may not hesitate, but walk with certain steps." He begs to be guided *in a plain* (straight) *path, because of his enemies*, or (as the margin reads it) "those which observe me." He asks for the benefit of divine protection (v. 12): "*Deliver me not over to the will of my enemies.* Lord, let them not defeat me, for they are aiming at my life, and I have no protection from them except your power over their consciences. *False witnesses have risen up against me*, who aim at more than taking away my reputation, for they *breathe out cruelty* (violence). It is blood they are thirsting for."

2. His dependence on God: "*When my father and my mother forsake me*, the nearest and dearest friends I have in the world, from whom I may expect most relief and with most reason, when they die, or are far away from me, or are unable to help me in time of need, or are unkind to me or do not remember me and will not help me, when I am as helpless as a poor orphan, then I know *the Lord will take me up.*" He believed he would *see the goodness of the Lord in the land of the living*, and if he had not done so, he would *have fainted* under his afflictions. Those who walk by faith in the goodness of the Lord will in due time walk in the sight of that goodness. He took encouragement not so much from the knowledge that he would see the land of the living as from knowing that he would see the goodness of God in it, for to a gracious soul, that is where the real comfort of all creature comforts lies. Heaven is that land that may truly be called *the land of the living* (v. 13). This earth is the land of the dying. There is nothing like the believing hope of eternal life to keep us from despair in all our present adversities. In the meantime he says to himself, or to his friends, *He shall strengthen thy heart*, he will sustain your spirit. *Wait on the Lord* in that strength by faith, prayer, and a humble submission to his will: *wait, I say* (v. 14), on the Lord. Whatever you do, do not neglect your regular worship of God. Those who wait on the Lord have good reason to be very courageous.

PSALM 28

The first part of this psalm is the prayer of a saint at war and in distress (vv. 1–3), to which is added the sentence against God's implacable enemies (vv. 4–5). The second part of the psalm expresses the thanksgiving of a saint in triumph, who has been rescued from his troubles (vv. 6–8), to which is added a prophetic prayer for all God's faithful loyal subjects (v. 9).

Verses 1–5

In these verses David prays in a heartfelt way:

1. He prays that God will graciously hear and answer him, now that he is calling on him in his distress (vv. 1–2). "O Lord, my rock," he prays, showing his belief in God's power. "*To thee will I cry*, as one who is in earnest. I am about to fall, and I will unless you come to help me soon. *If thou be silent to me* and I do not have the signs of your favor, I am *like those that go down into the pit* (v. 1)—I am dead, lost, and ruined. If God is not my friend, my hope and my help have perished. *I lift up my hands towards thy holy oracle*" (v. 2). Here he shows an earnest expectation that he will receive the answer he desires. The Most Holy Place within the veil is here, as elsewhere, called the *oracle*. The ark and the atonement cover were there; it was there that God was said to *dwell between the cherubim*, and from there he spoke to his people (Nu 7:89). This was a type of Christ, and it is to him that we must lift our eyes and hands, for it is through him that all good comes to us from God.

2. He prays to be saved from the condemnation of evildoers: "Lord, I am present in the Most Holy Place; *draw me not away* from that *with the wicked, and with the workers of iniquity*" (v. 3). "Lord, never leave me to myself, to use such deceitful or disloyal means for my safety as they are using to try to destroy me."

3. He invokes the just judgments of God on evildoers (v. 4): *Give* (repay) *them according to their deeds.* This is not the language of passion or revenge, nor is it inconsistent with the duty of praying for our enemies. But he wanted to show how far he was from following the practices of

evildoers. The verse is also a prophecy that God will, sooner or later, repay all impenitent sinners according to what they deserve. If what has been done wrong is not undone by repentance, the day of reckoning will certainly come, when God will repay everyone who persists in their evil deeds. It is a prophecy especially about the destruction of destroyers: *"They speak peace to their neighbours, but mischief* (trouble) *is in their hearts* (v. 3). Lord, *give* (repay) *them according to their deeds* (v. 4)."

4. He foretells their destruction for their contempt toward God and what his hands have done (v. 5): *"Because they regard not the works of the Lord and the operations of his hands*, by which he reveals himself and speaks to human beings, *he will destroy them* in this world and in the next, *and not build them up."* Why do people question the Being or attributes of God, except because they do not properly regard the works of his hands, which declare his glory and clearly reveal his invisible qualities (Ro 1:20)?

Verses 6–9

In these verses:

1. David gives God thanks. David prayed in faith (v. 2), *Hear the voice of my supplications*, and it is by the same faith that he now gives thanks (v. 6) that *God has heard the voice of his supplications*. Those who pray in faith may rejoice in hope (Ro 5:2). What we gain by prayer we must declare in praise.

2. David encourages himself to hope in God for the fulfilling of everything that concerns him. This is the way to attain peace: let us begin by praising God that it is attainable. Notice his experience of the benefits of his dependence on God: *"My heart trusted in him* (v. 7), and in his power and promises. I have not done so in vain, for *I am helped* (v. 7). I have often been helped. Not only has God given me, in his appropriate time, the help I trusted him for, but also my very trust in him has helped me in the meantime and kept me from despair" (27:13). *Therefore my heart greatly rejoices* (v. 7).

3. David pleases himself with the privileges all good people share through Christ in God (v. 8): *"The Lord is their strength*; not only mine, but also the strength of every believer." This is our fellowship with all the saints, that God is their strength and ours, Christ their Lord and ours (1Co 1:2).

4. David concludes with a short but comprehensive prayer for the church of God (v. 9). He prays for Israel, not as his people — "Save my people, and bless my inheritance" — even though they are so, but as *thy people. The Lord's portion is his people* (Dt 32:9). What he begs God for them is:

• That he would save them from their enemies.
• That he would bless them with all good.
• That he would *feed them.* "Direct their counsels and actions rightly, and overrule their affairs for good. Feed them, rule them, shepherd them. Set pastors and teachers over them, who will do their work with wisdom and understanding."
• That he would *lift them up for ever* (v. 9), *lift* them up out of their troubles, and that he would do this not only for those of that time but also for his people in every age to come, even to the end of time.

PSALM 29

It is thought that David probably wrote this psalm at the time of a great storm of thunder, lightning, and rain, just *as Ps 8 was his meditation on a moonlit night and Ps 19 on a sunny morning. 1. He calls on the powerful ones in the world to give glory to God (vv. 1–2). 2. To convince them of the goodness of the God they are to adore, he takes notice of God's power in the thunder, lightning, and rain (vv. 3–9), his sovereign rule over the world (v. 10), and his special favor to his church (v. 11).*

Verses 1–11

In this psalm we have:

1. A call to the great people on earth to give their allegiance to the great God. David interpreted every clap of thunder as a call to himself and other rulers to give glory to God in his greatness. *"O you mighty* ones (v. 1), who have power, *Give unto the Lord*, and again, and a third time, *Give unto the Lord* (vv. 1–2)." He is willing to interpret the recognition of his glory and his rule over us as a gift to him: *"Give unto the Lord* first yourselves, and then your service. *Give unto the Lord glory and strength* (v. 1). Acknowledge his glory and strength, and whatever glory or strength he has entrusted you with, offer it to him, to be used for his honor and in his service. Give him your crowns; let them be laid at his feet. Give him your scepters, your swords, and your keys. Put everything into his hand, so that you, in using them, may give him honor and praise." What is said here to the powerful is said to everyone: *Worship the Lord* (v. 2); it is the essence of the eternal Gospel (Rev 14:6–7). Religious worship is *giving to the Lord the glory due to his name* (v. 2). *Worship the Lord in the beauty of holiness* (v. 2). Adore him not only as one who is infinitely fearful and therefore to be revered above all, but also as one who is infinitely lovely and therefore to be loved and enjoyed above all. We must especially consider the beauty of his holiness. There is a beauty in holiness, and it is this that gives an acceptable beauty to every act of worship.

2. Good reason given for this command.

2.1. His sufficiency in himself, as shown in his name, Jehovah, "I AM THAT I AM," which is repeated here no fewer than eighteen times in this short psalm, twice in every verse but three, and once in two of those three.

2.2. His sovereignty over all things. The psalmist here declares God's rule:

2.2.1. In the kingdom of nature: in the wonderful effects and activities of nature. It is the God of glory that thunders. Everyone who hears thunder will acknowledge that *the voice of the Lord is full of majesty* (v. 4). If his voice is so terrible, what is his power like? *The voice of the Lord is* indeed *powerful* (v. 4), as can be seen from the wonders it works. *The voice of the Lord*, in thunder, often *broke the cedars*, including the strong and grand cedars of Lebanon. Some understand *the voice of the Lord* to refer to the violent winds which shook the cedars and tore off their tops. But earthquakes also shook the ground itself on which the trees grew and made *Lebanon and Sirion* dance, and *the wilderness of Kadesh* was similarly shaken (v. 8). So the trees were shaken by winds, the ground by earthquakes, and both by thunder, and I therefore tend to think *the voice of the Lord* refers to all three of these forces. Dr. Henry Hammond understands these verses to refer to God's terrifying and conquering of the neighboring kingdoms that were at war against Israel and that opposed David, such as the Arameans (*Syrians*), whose country lay near the forest of Lebanon; the Amorites, who bordered on Mount Hermon; and the Moabites and Ammonites, who lived around the Desert of Kadesh. Fires have been caused by lightning. The voice of the Lord, in thunder, is therefore said to *divide the flames of fire* (v. 7), to scatter them on the earth. The terror of thunder makes deer give birth earlier, and some think more easily, than they would have otherwise. The thunder is said here to *discover the forest*, that is, to so terrify the wild animals of the forest that they leave their dens and thickets in which they have hidden themselves and so are exposed.

2.2.2. In the kingdom of providence (v. 10). God is to be praised as the ruler of the human race. He *sits on* (sits enthroned over) *the flood; he sits* (sits enthroned as) *King for ever.* The ebbing and flowing of this lower world, with its many disturbances and changes, do not disturb in the slightest the rest or the purposes of the Eternal Mind. *He sits King for ever* (v. 10). No end can, or will, be put to his rule. His administration of his kingdom is in harmony with the thoughts he has had from eternity and the purposes he has for eternity.

2.2.3. In the kingdom of grace. Here his glory shines most brightly. *In his temple*, where his people respond to his revelations of himself and his mind and bring him their praises, *every one speaks of his glory. All his works do praise him*, but it is only his saints who bless him and speak of the glory of his works (145:10). *He will give strength to his people*, to protect them from every evil and equip them for every good work (2Ti 3:17). *He will bless his people with peace.* Peace is a blessing of immeasurable value, which God intends for all his people.

PSALM 30

This is a psalm of thanksgiving for the great ways in which God had rescued David, written for the occasion of the dedication of his house of cedar. 1. He praises God for the ways in which God has rescued him (vv. 1–3); he calls on others to praise him too (vv. 4–5). 2. He blames himself for his former, false sense of security (vv. 6–7); he recollects the prayers and complaints he has made in his distress (vv. 8–10). He uses them to stir himself to be very thankful to God for the present change (vv. 11–12).

Title

It was the commendable practice of the devout Jews—a practice allowed and accepted, though not explicitly appointed—that when they had built a new house, they *dedicated it to God* (Dt 20:5). David did so when his house was built and he was taking possession of it (2Sa 5:11). The houses we live in should, when we first come into them, be dedicated to God, as little sanctuaries. We must solemnly commit ourselves, our families, and the life of every member of our family, to God's guidance and pray for his presence and blessing.

Verses 1–5

In these verses:

1. David himself gives God thanks for the great ways in which he has rescued him (v. 1): "*I will extol thee, O Lord!* I will exalt your name. I will praise you as One who is high and lifted up. *I cried to thee, and thou hast* not only heard me but also *healed me.* You healed my illness; you healed my disturbed and restless mind; you healed the disordered and troubled affairs of the kingdom." He was brought to the point of death, falling into the grave and ready *to go down into the pit*, but was still rescued and kept alive (v. 3). A life received back from the dead should be spent in exalting the God of our life.

2. David calls on others to join with him in praising God: "*Sing unto the Lord, O you saints of his!* Let them give thanks at the remembrance of his holiness" (v. 4). Let them praise his holy name, for his holiness is remembered throughout all generations." It is a good sign that we to some extent share in his holiness if we can heartily rejoice and give thanks when we remember it. We have found his frowns, the times of his displeasure, to be very short. Although we have deserved that they be eternal, and that he should be angry with us till he had destroyed us (Ezr 9:14), and that we should never be reconciled, yet *his anger endureth but for a moment* (v. 5). If *weeping endureth for a night* (v. 5), as surely as the light of the morning returns, so surely will joy and comfort soon return to the people of God. This is because the covenant of grace is as firm and secure as the covenant of the day. *In his favour is life* (v. 5), that is, all good. It is the life of the soul, spiritual life, the pledge of eternal life.

Verses 6–12

In these verses we have an account of three different states David was in, one after the other, and of the activity of his heart toward God in each of these states.

1. "*In my prosperity*, when I felt secure in good physical health and God had *given me rest from all my enemies, I said, I shall never be moved.* I had no apprehensions of danger for any reason." He thought his prosperity was as fixed as a mountain: *Thou, through thy favour, hast made my mountain to stand strong* (v. 7). He does not look on his prosperity as his *heaven*—as worldly people do, who make their prosperity their joy—only as his *mountain*. It is still earth, only raised a little higher than the ordinary level.

2. Suddenly he fell into trouble, and then he prayed to God and pleaded fervently for God to help and relieve him. His mountain was shaken, and he along with it. It turned out that the time when he felt secure was the time when he was least safe: *Thou didst hide thy face and I was troubled* (v. 7)—in mind, body, or wealth. If God hides his face, a good person is certainly dismayed, even though no other adversity happens to them; when the sun sets, night certainly follows, and the moon and all the stars cannot make daylight. When his mountain was shaken, he lifted up his eyes above the hills (compare 121:1). Is anyone in trouble? *Let him pray* (Jas 5:13). *I cried to thee, O Lord!* It seems God's withdrawal made his prayers even more powerful. *What profit is there in my blood?* (What gain is there in my destruction?) Thus he implied he would willingly die if by it he could do any real service to God or his country (Php 2:17), but that he could not see what good would be done by his dying on his sickbed when he might have died on the bed of honor. *Shall the dust praise thee?* (v. 9). The sanctified spirit that returns to God will continue to praise him, but the dust, which returns to the earth, will not praise him or declare his truth.

3. In due time God rescued him from his troubles and restored him to his former prosperity. His prayers were answered, and his *mourning was turned into dancing* (v. 11). But what frame of mind was he in at this happy change of affairs? What does he say now? He tells us (v. 12): his complaints were turned to praise. *I will give thanks unto thee for ever* (v. 12). This is how we must learn to adjust our lives to the various providences of God.

PSALM 31

David probably wrote this psalm when he was being persecuted by Saul. Some passages in it correspond particularly to the narrow escapes he had, at Keilah (1Sa 23:13); in the Desert of Maon, when Saul marched on one side of the mountain and he on the other (1Sa 23:24–28); and soon afterward, in the cave in the Desert of En Gedi (1Sa 24). It is a mixture of prayer, praise, and professions of confidence in God. 1. David professes his great confidence in God, and with that confidence he prays to be saved from his present troubles (vv. 1–8). 2. He complains of the miserable condition he is in and prays that God would graciously support him against his persecutors (vv. 9–18). 3. He concludes the psalm with praise and triumph, giving glory to God and encouraging himself and others to trust in him (vv. 19–24).

Verses 1–8

Faith and prayer must go together.

1. In his distress, David prays fervently for God to help and relieve him. He prays that God, not only in mercy but also in righteousness, would rescue him, as a righteous Judge would come between him and his unrighteous persecutors. He prays also that God would rescue him quickly, for if the rescue is delayed for a long time, he fears his faith might fail. "*Be thou my strong rock*, as immovable and impregnable as a natural stronghold, and my *house of defence*, a strongly built fortress, and all *to save me*" (v. 2). *Lord, lead me and guide me*" (v. 3). Those who decide to follow God's direction may in faith pray for it.

2. In this prayer, David gives glory to God by repeatedly declaring his confidence in him and his dependence on him. "*In thee, O Lord, do I put my trust*, not in myself, or in any sufficiency of my own, or in any other creature. *Let me never be ashamed*, let me not fail to receive any of the good you have promised me."

2.1. He had chosen God as his protector, and God had undertaken to be so (v. 3): "*Thou art my rock and my fortress*, by your covenant with me and my faithful agreement with that covenant; therefore, *be my strong rock*" (v. 2). If God is our strength, we may trust that he will both put his strength in us and declare his strength for us.

2.2. He gave up his soul in a special way to him (v. 5): *Into thy hands I commit my spirit*. David is here looked on as a man in distress and trouble. His great care is for his soul, his spirit, his better part. Our outward afflictions should increase our concern for our souls. Many think that while they are confused about their worldly affairs, they may be excused if they neglect their souls. The truth is, however, that the greater danger our lives and worldly interests are in, the more we should be concerned to look to our souls, so that we may keep possession of our souls when we can keep possession of nothing else (Lk 21:19). He thinks the best he can do for his soul is to commit it into the hands of God. He has prayed (v. 4) to be taken out of the trap of outward trouble, but because he does not insist on that, but wants God's will to be done, he immediately drops that request and commits his spirit, his inner being, into God's hand. "Lord, whatever happens to me physically, may it go well with my soul."

3. He rejected any alliance with those who put their confidence in an arm of flesh (2Ch 32:8) (v. 6): "*I have hated those that regard lying vanities*, those who cling to worthless idols, who expect to receive help from false gods, which are worthless and a lie." This could also refer to astrologers and those who pay attention to them.

4. He comforted himself with his hope in God, and he made himself not only at peace but also joyful in it (v. 7).

5. He encouraged himself in this hope by remembering the experiences he had had of God's goodness to him: "*Thou hast considered my trouble* (v. 7), wisely giving the appropriate answer to it; in condescension and compassion you have considered the humble state of your servant (Lk 1:48). *Thou hast known my soul in adversities* (v. 7), and you have shown a tender concern and care for it. *Thou hast not shut me up into the hand of the enemy*, but have set me free, in *a large room*, a spacious place, to which I may escape for my own safety" (v. 8).

Verses 9–18

In vv. 1–8, David appealed to God's righteousness. In vv. 9–18, he appeals to his mercy and pleads the greatness of his own misery, which made it right that he be the object of that mercy. Notice:

1. The complaint he makes of his trouble and distress (v. 9): "*Have mercy upon me, O Lord, for I am in trouble* and need your mercy." His troubles had made him a man of sorrows (Isa 53:3). We may guess from David's complexion, which was ruddy and cheerful, by his musical skills, and by his ventures in his early days, that his natural disposition was happy and secure, that he did not take troubles to heart, but we see here that he had come almost to a state in which he could weep no more tears, and his breath was sighed away. His body was affected by the sorrows of his mind (v. 10): *My strength fails, my bones are consumed*, and all *because of my iniquity*. His friends were unkind and looked at him with distrust and suspicion. He was *a fear to his acquaintance*; when they saw him, they *fled from him* (v. 11). He was forgotten by them, *as a dead man out of mind* (v. 12), and looked on with contempt *as a broken vessel*, like a piece of broken pottery. The world is full of such fair-weather friends, who disappear in winter. His enemies were unjust in their criticism of him. He was an object of *reproach among all his enemies, but especially among his neighbours* (v. 11). And so he *heard the slander of many* (v. 13); everyone had a stone to throw at him, because *fear was on every side* (v. 13).

2. His confidence in God in the midst of these troubles. Everything around him looked black and dismal and threatened to drive him to despair: "*But I trusted in thee, O Lord* (v. 14), and so was kept from sinking." His enemies robbed him of his good reputation among people, but they could not rob him of his strength in God, because they could not drive him away from his confidence in God. "*Thou art my God*; I have chosen you as mine, and you have promised to be mine." *My times are in thy hand* (v. 15). If we add this plea to the first one, it makes the contentment complete. If God has our times in his hand, he can help us, and if he is our God, he will help us — what then can discourage us?

3. His requests to God, in this faith and confidence. "Our opportunities are in God's hand," as some read it, and so he knows how to choose the best time to rescue us, and we must be willing to wait for that time to come. When David had Saul at his mercy in the cave, those around him said, "*This is the time* in which God will free you from Saul" (1Sa 24:4). "*No*," David said, "the time has not yet come for me to be set free until it can be brought about without sin. I will wait for that time, for it is God's time, and that is the best time." He particularly prays for the silencing of those who show contempt for and slander the people of God (v. 18): *Let lying lips be put to silence, that speak grievous things proudly and contemptuously against the righteous*. It seems they thought it was not a sin to deliberately lie if it might expose a good person to either hatred or contempt. *Hear, O our God! for we are despised* (Ne 4:4).

Verses 19 – 24

We have three things in these verses:

1. The acknowledgment David makes of God's goodness to his people in general (vv. 19 – 20). God is good to everyone, but he is especially good to Israel. Those who have a share in this goodness are described as those who fear God and trust in him, who stand in awe of his greatness and depend on his grace. This goodness is said to be *laid up for them* and *wrought for them* (v. 19). There is enough in the bank and also enough in hand. This goodness is stored up in his promise for all who fear God, but this promise is fulfilled for those who trust in him. If what is stored up for us in the treasures of the eternal covenant is not given to us, it is our own fault, because we do not believe. God preserves human beings and animals, but he especially protects his own people (v. 20): *Thou shalt hide them.* The saints are God's hidden ones. Notice the defense the saints are under: *Thou shalt hide them in the secret* (shelter) *of thy presence, in a pavilion* (v. 20). God's providence will keep them safe from the hatred of their enemies. He has many ways of sheltering them. When Baruch and Jeremiah were searched for, *the Lord hid them* (Jer 36:26).

2. The thankful response David makes for God's goodness to him in particular (vv. 21 – 22). *"He has shown me his marvellous kindness,* beyond what I could possibly have expected." Acts of special preservation call for special thanksgiving. He had fear within himself, but God was better to him than his fears (v. 22). Although his faith had failed, God's promise did not: *Thou heardest the voice of my supplication* (v. 22), despite this. He mentions his own unbelief in contrast to God's faithfulness, which makes God's unfailing love more amazing and wonderful.

3. The encouragement David then gives to all the saints (vv. 23 – 24). *O love the Lord! all you his saints.* It is the character of the saints that they love God, but they must be called on to love him even more, to love him better, and to give proofs of their love. David wants them to set their hope on God (v. 24): *"Be of good courage;* be strong and take heart; whatever difficulties or dangers you may face, do not give up. The God you trust in will strengthen your heart as you trust in him."

PSALM 32

Although this psalm does not speak of Christ, it still has a great deal of the Gospel in it. We have here a summary: 1. Of the Gospel grace in the pardon of sin (vv. 1 – 2), divine protection (v. 7), and divine guidance (v. 8). 2. Of the Gospel duty: to confess sin (vv. 3 – 5), to pray (v. 6), to manage our lives well (vv. 9 – 10), and to rejoice in God (v. 11).

Title

This psalm is entitled *Maschil,* which some take to be only the name of the tune to which it was set and was to be sung. But others think it is significant; the margin reads, "A psalm of David giving instruction," and there is nothing in which we need more instruction than the nature of true blessing — what we must do so we may be happy.

Verses 1 – 6

In general our happiness consists in receiving the favor of God, not in having the wealth of this world — it consists in spiritual blessings. When it is said here, *Blessed is the man whose iniquity is forgiven,* the meaning is, "This is the basis of such blessedness. This is the fundamental

privilege from which all the other aspects of blessedness flow." We are instructed here:

1. About the nature of the pardon of sin.

1.1. It is the forgiving of transgression. *Sin is the transgression of the law* (1Jn 3:4). When we repent, the transgression — our disobedience — is forgiven, that is, the necessity of being punished which we were under is canceled. It is lifted or removed, so when our sin is pardoned, we are relieved of a heavy burden.

1.2. It is the covering of sin, so that our shameful nakedness is covered (Rev 3:18). When sin is pardoned, it is covered with the robe of Christ's righteousness.

1.3. It is the not imputing of iniquity, not laying it to the sinner's charge. Because the righteousness of Christ has been imputed to us and we have been made *the righteousness of God in him* (2Co 5:21), our iniquity is not imputed, God having *laid upon him the iniquity of us all* (Isa 53:6) and made him *sin for us.*

2. About the character of those whose sins are pardoned: *in whose spirit there is no guile* (v. 2). He does not say, "there is no guilt," for where is there who lives and does not sin (1Ki 8:46)? — but no *guile,* deceit. The pardoned sinner is one who does not pretend with God in professing repentance and faith. *While I kept silence my bones waxed* (grew) *old.* Those who stifle their convictions may be said to keep silent; they are those who, when they cannot avoid seeing the evil of sin and the danger they are in because of it, try to put their minds at rest by not thinking about it, by distracting their minds with something else, who will not relieve their consciences by repentance and confession, and who choose rather to waste away in their sins than to follow the way God has appointed to find rest for their souls (Jer 6:16; Mt 11:29).

3. About the true and only way to peace of conscience. We are here taught to confess our sins so that they may be forgiven, to declare them so that we may be justified. David did this: *I acknowledged my sin unto thee,* and no longer *hid my iniquity* (v. 5).

4. About God's readiness to pardon sin in those who truly repent of it: *"I said, I will confess, and* immediately *thou forgavest the iniquity of my sin* (v. 5) and gave me the assurance of pardon in my own conscience. I immediately found rest in my own soul." In the same way, the father of the prodigal son saw his son returning *when he was yet afar off* (Lk 15:20) and ran to meet him with the kiss that sealed his pardon. *For this shall every one that is godly pray unto thee.* All godly people are praying people. As soon as Paul was converted, *Behold, he prays* (Ac 9:11). Those who are sincere in prayer and devote themselves much to it will discover its benefits when they are in trouble: *Surely in the floods of great waters* (v. 6), which threaten very much, *they shall not come nigh them* (v. 6).

Verses 7 – 11

1. David speaks to God, professing his confidence in him and expectation from him (v. 7). *"Thou art my hiding place* (v. 7). When I turn to you in faith, I see every reason in the world to be at peace and to think myself beyond the reach of any real evil. *Thou shalt preserve me from trouble* (v. 7), from its sting and from its attacks, as far as is good for me. *Thou shalt preserve me from* such trouble as I was in *while I kept silence"* (v. 3). When God has forgiven our sins, if he leaves us to ourselves, we will soon get into debt again as much as we ever were. When we have received the assurance of forgiveness of our sins, we must therefore flee to the grace of God to be kept from returning to our previous foolish ways. "You will not only save me, but *compass me about* (surround me) *with songs*

of deliverance (v. 7). As *every one that is godly shall pray with me* (v. 6), so they will also give thanks with me."

2. David turns his speech to other people. Having himself been converted, he does what he can to *strengthen his brethren* (Lk 22:32): *I will instruct thee*, whoever you are who want to be taught, *and teach thee in the way which thou shalt go* (v. 8). When Solomon repented, he immediately became a teacher (Ecc 1:1). *I will guide thee with my eye* (v. 8). Some apply this to God's leadership and direction. But it should probably be interpreted as referring to David's promise to those who sat under his instruction, especially his own children and family: "I will counsel thee; my eye shall be upon thee," the margin reads; "I will give you the best possible advice and then observe whether you take it or not." Spiritual guides must be overseers. Here is a word of caution to sinners, not to be unruly and uncontrollable: *Be you not as the horse and the mule, which have no understanding* (v. 9). It is our honor and good fortune that we have understanding, that we are capable of being ruled by reason and of reasoning with ourselves. Where there is renewing grace, there is no need for the bit and bridle of restraining grace. The reason for this caution is that the way of sin will certainly end in sorrow (v. 10). Here is also a word of comfort to saints: they are assured that if they will only trust in the Lord and keep close to him, *mercy shall compass* (surround) *them* on every side (v. 10).

The Dutch jurist and theologian Hugo Grotius thinks this psalm was intended to be sung on the Day of Atonement.

PSALM 33

This is a psalm of praise. The psalmist: 1. Calls on the righteous to praise God (vv. 1–3). 2. Provides us with subjects for praise. We must praise God for his justice, goodness, and truth, in his word and in all his works (vv. 4–5); for his power in the work of creation (vv. 6–9); for the sovereignty of his providence in ruling over the world (vv. 10–11 and again vv. 13–17); for the special favor he has toward his own chosen people (v. 12 and again vv. 18–22).

Verses 1–11

The psalmist expresses four things in these verses:

1. The great desire that God might be praised. Holy joy is the heart and soul of praise (v. 1): *Rejoice in the Lord, you righteous.* This is how the previous psalm concluded and how this psalm begins. Thankful praise is the breath and language of holy joy (v. 2): *"Praise the Lord.* Speak well of him and give him the glory due to his name" (29:2). Religious songs are the proper expressions of thankful praise (v. 3): *"Sing unto him a new song,* the best you have." Instrumental music now accompanied the temple songs (v. 2): *Sing unto him with the psaltery and an instrument of ten strings* (the ten-stringed lyre). Here is a good rule for this duty: "Do it *skilfully,* and *with a loud noise* (v. 3). Let it have the best both of our minds and our hearts. Let it be done intelligently, with a clear head and with a warm heart." Here is also a good reason for this duty: *For praise is comely* (fitting) *for the upright* (v. 1).

2. The high thoughts he had of God and his infinite qualities (vv. 4–5). God makes himself known to us:

2.1. In his *word,* which here stands for all divine revelation, everything that God has at many times and in various ways spoken to human beings (Heb 1:1).

2.2. In his *works,* and those are all *done in truth* (v. 4). The copy of all God's works agrees exactly with the great original, the plan in the eternal Mind, and does not vary in the least. God reveals in his works that he is a God of firm justice: *He loveth righteousness and judgment* (v. 5). He is a God of inexhaustible goodness: *The earth is full of his goodness* (v. 5), that is, of its proofs and demonstrations. The benevolent influences which the earth receives from above, the fruits it is enabled to produce, the provision that is made both for humans and animals, and the common blessings with which all the nations of the earth are blessed all clearly show that *the earth is full of his goodness* (v. 5)—even including the darkest, coldest, hottest, and driest parts. What a pity it is that this earth, which is so full of God's goodness, should be so empty of his praises, and that out of the many who enjoy his goodness so few live for his glory!

3. The conviction he was under of the almighty power of God, as seen in the creation of the world. We "believe in God," and so we praise him as "the Father Almighty, maker of heaven and earth," and this is how we are taught to praise him. Notice:

3.1. How God made the world and brought all things into being. It was done:

- Easily: all things were made *by the word of the Lord and by the breath of his mouth* (v. 6). Christ is the Word, the Spirit is the breath, so that God the Father made the world, just as he rules it and redeems it, by his Son and Spirit. *He spoke,* and he commanded (v. 9), and that was enough; there needed to be nothing more. With human beings, saying and doing are two different things, but this is not so with God.
- Effectively: *And it stood fast* (firm) (v. 9). What God does he does according to his purposes; he does it and it stands firm.

3.2. What he made. He made everything, but notice is taken here:

3.2.1. Of *the heavens, and the host of them* (v. 6). The visible skies, the sun, moon, and stars; heaven, the angels, and their powers.

3.2.2. Of the waters and their treasures (v. 7). The earth was originally covered with water, and *he gathered the waters together as a heap,* so that the dry land might appear. He did not leave them to continue as a heap, however, but *laid up the depth in storehouses.*

3.3. What use is to be made of this (v. 8): *Let all the earth fear the Lord, and stand in awe of him*; that is, let every human being worship him and give glory to him (95:5–6).

4. The assurance he had of God's rule and sovereignty (vv. 10–11). Come and use the eye of faith to see God on his throne:

- Frustrating the plans of his enemies: *He bringeth the counsel of the heathen to nought,* he foils the plans of the nations.
- Fulfilling his own decrees: *The counsel of the Lord standeth forever* (v. 11). Through every change God has never changed his plans, but in every event, the eternal purpose of God is fulfilled, even what is most surprising to us.

Verses 12–22

Give God the glory:

1. For his common providence toward all the human race.

1.1. The whole human race is under his eye, including the heart of each person. He knows better than people themselves all the activity and work of the souls, which no one else knows but them (vv. 13–14). He not only sees them, but *looks upon them*; he watches them closely.

1.2. *He fashions their hearts* (v. 15). He formed the spirit of each person within them. He is therefore called *the Father of spirits* (Heb 12:9). The artist who makes clocks can explain the movement of every wheel. David uses this argument in applying it to himself (139:1, 14). He "fashions them together," as some understand it; just as the wheels in a watch, although they come in different shapes, sizes, and movements, are all put together to serve one and the same purpose, so also human hearts and their dispositions, however much they vary from one another and seem to contradict one another, are nevertheless all overruled to serve the divine purpose, which is one.

1.3. All the powers of creation depend on him, and they have no use or significance without him (vv. 16–17). The strength of an army is nothing without God. *The multitude of a host*, the size of an army (v. 16), cannot protect those under a commander unless God himself protects them. The strength of a great warrior is nothing without God. *A mighty man*, for example, Goliath, *is not delivered by much strength* (v. 16) when his day of destruction comes. *Let not the strong man* then *glory in his strength* (Jer 9:24), but let us all strengthen ourselves in the Lord our God. The strength of a horse is nothing without God (v. 17): *A horse is a vain thing for safety*. Although a horse is very strong, it cannot save people. In war, horses were very highly regarded and very much depended on, so that God forbade the kings of Israel to *multiply horses* (Dt 17:16), because if they did, they might be tempted to trust in them and take their confidence away from God. David hamstrung the Aramean horses (2Sa 8:4); here he hamstrings all the horses in the world by declaring that a horse cannot save people in battle.

2. For his special grace. *Blessed is the nation whose God is the Lord*, namely Israel. It is wise of them to take the Lord as their God. It is their joy that they are the people whom God has chosen as his own inheritance, whom he protects and cultivates and uses as someone does their inheritance (Dt 32:9). God looks closely at the whole human race, but his special favor and delight are with those who fear him. While those who depend on arms and armies, on chariots and horses, die when their expectations are disappointed, God's people are safe under his protection, for he will save their soul from death when there seems to be only a step between them and it (1Sa 20:3). If he does not save the body from physical death, he will still save the soul from spiritual and eternal death. Whatever happens, their souls will live and praise him, either in this world or in the better one. He will *keep them alive in famine* (v. 19). When visible means fail, God will find some way or other to supply them. We must consider the events of his providence and adjust ourselves to them. Our souls must wait in hope for him (v. 20). We must rely on God, *hoping in his mercy* (v. 18). *This is trusting in his holy name* (v. 21). We must have hearts that are full of joy because of God (v. 21). Our expectations from God are not to replace, but are to encourage, our turning to him. The psalm therefore concludes with a short but comprehensive prayer: "*Let thy mercy, O Lord, be upon us*; let us always receive its benefits and encouragement, not according to what we deserve, but *according as we hope in thee*, that is, according to the promise which you have given us in your word and according to the faith which you have given us by your Spirit and grace."

PSALM 34

This psalm was written on a specific occasion, as can be seen from the title. 1. David praises God for the experience which he and others have had of his goodness (vv. 1–6); he encourages all good people to trust in God (vv. 7–10). 2. David gives good advice to us all, to take care to do our duty both to God and to others (vv. 11–14). To support this good advice, he sets before us good and evil, the blessing and the curse (Dt 30:15, 19) (vv. 15–22).

Title

Because David was forced to flee his country, which had been made too dangerous for him by Saul's anger, he sought shelter as close to it as he could, in the land of the Philistines. It was soon discovered who he was, and he was brought before the king, Achish, here called *Abimelech* (his title). So that he would not be treated as a spy, he pretended to be insane, so that Achish might dismiss him as someone who was contemptible rather than know him as someone who was dangerous. And this plan meant he escaped being roughly treated by Achish. Even when he was in danger, his heart was so fixed in his trust in God that he was able to write this excellent psalm, which has as many marks of a calm and composed spirit as any other psalm.

Verses 1–10

There is something intricate in the composition of this psalm, for it is what is called an acrostic psalm, that is, a psalm in which the first verse begins with the first letter in the Hebrew alphabet, the second with the second letter, and so on, each verse beginning with the letter that follows that which began the previous verse.

1. David engages and excites himself to praise God. "*I will bless the Lord at all times*, on all occasions. *His praise shall continually be in my mouth*" (v. 1). He will praise him heartily: "*My soul shall make her boast in the Lord*, in my relationship with him, my share in him, and my expectations from him" (v. 2).

2. David calls on others to join with him in this activity. He expects they will (v. 2): "*The humble shall hear thereof*, both of my rescue and my thankfulness, *and be glad*." He wants us all to join him:

2.1. In great and high thoughts of God. We cannot make God greater or higher than he is, but if we adore him as infinitely great, and higher than the highest, he is willing to accept this exaltation of him. We must do this together. God's praises sound best when many people offer them. We must join in thanksgiving to God for his readiness to hear prayer. David has found him to be a God who answers prayer (v. 4): "*I sought the Lord*, in my distress. I asked for his favor, begged his help, *and he heard me*. He answered my request immediately *and delivered me from all my fears*, both from the death I feared and from the unrest and disturbance caused by my fears of it." God rescues us from the former by his providence working for us, and from the latter by his grace working in us, to silence our fears and to quiet the tumult of our spirits. Many besides David have *looked unto God* in faith and prayer *and have been lightened by it* (v. 5). Prayer has wonderfully revived and comforted them. One example is Hannah, who, when she had prayed, *went her way, and did eat, and her countenance was no more sad* (1Sa 1:18). These people spoken of here had their expectations raised, and events did not prove them wrong: *Their faces were not ashamed* (v. 5) of their confidence. *This poor man cried* (v. 6), one single, lowly, and insignificant person, one whom nobody looked on with any respect or any concern, but he was as welcome to the throne of grace as David or anyone else: *The Lord heard him,* took notice of his circumstances and his prayers, *and saved him out of all his troubles* (v. 6). *The angel of the Lord,* or "a guard of angels," according to some, *encamps round about those that fear God,* like a bodyguard guarding a ruler, *and delivers them.*

2.2. In kind and good thoughts of God (v. 8): *O taste and see that the Lord is good.* The goodness of God includes both the beauty and loveliness of his being and the goodness of his providence and grace.

2.3. In being determined to seek God and serve him and continue to fear him (v. 9): *O fear the Lord, you his saints. Fear the Lord*; that is, worship him, and take care to do your duty to him in everything. Do not fear him and avoid him, but fear him and seek him (v. 10). To encourage us to fear God and seek him, it is here promised for those who do so, even in this world of lack, that they *shall want no good thing.* They will have sufficient grace to support the spiritual life (84:11; 2Co 12:9), and as for this life, they will have what is necessary to support it from the hand of God. As a Father, he will feed them with the food they need. They will have what further comforts they need, as far as infinite Wisdom sees good, and what they lack in one thing will be made up for in another. What God denies them he will give them grace to be content not to have, and then they will not lack it (Dt 3:26). Paul had ample, and he was content (Php 4:11, 18).

Verses 11–22

In the second part of this psalm, David undertakes to teach children. We do not know if he had any children of his own at that time, but he wishes to instruct the children of his people, and so he calls an assembly of them (v. 11): *"Come, you children, Hearken unto me* (v. 11), leave your playing, set aside your toys, and listen to what I have to say to you. Do not only hear what I am going to say, but also heed and obey me." He undertakes to teach *them the fear of the Lord* (v. 11), including all the duties of religious faith.

1. He presumes that everyone wants to be happy (v. 12): *What man is he that desireth life?*

2. He shows the true and only way to happiness both in this world and the world to come (vv. 13–14).

2.1. We must learn to keep a tight rein on our tongues (Jas 1:26), to be careful about what we say, so that we never speak wrongly, to God's dishonor or our neighbor's harm: *Keep thy tongue from evil speaking, lying, and slandering.*

2.2. We must be upright and sincere in everything we say, not double-tongued.

2.3. We must *depart from evil* (v. 14), from evil works and evildoers.

2.4. It is not enough that we do no harm in this world; we must also try to lead useful and purposeful lives.

2.5. We must *seek peace and pursue it* (v. 14). *Follow peace with all men* (Heb 12:14), be willing to deny ourselves a great deal, both in honor and interest, for the sake of peace.

3. Here life and death, good and evil, the blessing and the curse are plainly set before us, so that we may choose life and live (Dt 30:15, 19). See Isa 3:10–11.

3.1. *Woe to the wicked, it shall be ill with them* (Isa 3:11), however much they bless themselves in their own way. *The face of the Lord is against those that do evil* (v. 16). *Evil shall slay the wicked* (v. 21). Their death will

be miserable. It will certainly be so, even if they die on a soft feather bed or on the bed of honor. The word used here for the *evil* which kills evildoers is the singular form of the same word that is used in v. 19 to refer to the afflictions of the righteous. This shows that godly people have many troubles, and yet they do them no harm, for God will rescue them from them all, whereas evildoers have fewer troubles, perhaps only one, but that one may lead to their complete destruction. One trouble with a curse in it kills, but many troubles with a blessing in them are harmless; in fact, they are profitable.

3.2. But *say to the righteous, It shall be well with them* (Isa 3:10). All good people receive God's special favor and protection. *The eyes of the Lord are upon the righteous* (v. 15), to direct and guide them, to protect and keep them. Parents who are very fond of a child will not let that child go out of their sight. None of God's children are ever outside his sight: *They cry, and the Lord hears them.* He is always ready to hear them, listening to them as a tender mother listens to the cry of her child, which another woman would not notice. He not only takes notice of what we say, but also is ready to come with help and relief (v. 18): *He is nigh to those that are of a broken heart, and saves them.* He is close to them for his good purposes. *He keepeth all his bones*—not only his soul, but also his body, not only his body in general, but also every bone in it: *Not one of them is broken.* The one who has a broken heart will not have a broken bone, for David himself had found that, when he had a contrite heart, the *broken bones* were *made to rejoice* (51:8, 17). *Many are the afflictions of the righteous*; David, for example, suffered many hardships (132:1). God acts to rescue and save them: *He delivers them out of all their troubles* (vv. 17, 19). He saves them (v. 18), so that although they fall into trouble, it will not destroy them.

PSALM 35

In this psalm, David appeals to the righteous Judge of heaven and earth against his enemies who hate and persecute him. It is thought that Saul and his party are the people he is referring to, for David had the greatest struggles with them. 1. He complains to God about the wrongs they did him. 2. He pleads his own innocence, that he never provoked them (vv. 7, 19), but, on the contrary, had tried to please them (vv. 12–14). 3. He prays to God to protect and rescue him. 4. He prophesies the destruction of his persecutors (vv. 4–6, 8); he promises himself that he will still see better days (vv. 9–10) and promises God that he will then serve him with his praises (vv. 18, 28).

Verses 1–10

In these verses we have:

1. David's presentation of his case to God, describing the restless rage and hatred of his persecutors. They persecuted him with tireless hatred; they *sought after his soul* (v. 4), that is, his life. Nothing less would satisfy their bloodthirstiness.

2. David's appeal to God concerning his integrity and the justice of his cause. If a fellow subject had wronged him, he might have appealed to his ruler, as the apostle Paul did to Caesar; but when his ruler wronged him, he appealed to his God, who is prince and Judge of the kings of the earth, to contend for him: *Plead my cause, O Lord!* (v. 1).

3. David's prayer to God to reveal himself both for him and to him in this test. He prays that God would *fight*

for him *against his* enemies, to disable them and prevent them from harming him and to defeat their plans against him. He prays that God would reveal himself to him: "*Say unto my soul, I am thy salvation* (v. 3). Let me have an inner strength in all these outward troubles." If God is our friend, it does not matter who is our enemy.

4. David's prospect of the destruction of his enemies, which he prays for, though not out of hatred or revenge: *Let them be confounded and put to shame* (v. 4). Dr. Henry Hammond understands it to mean, "They shall be confounded; they shall be turned back." This may be taken as a prayer for their repentance, for all penitents are made ashamed of their sins and turned back from them. *They shall be as chaff before the wind* (v. 5; see also 1:4). Evildoers will be unable to stand before the judgments of God (1:5). Their way will be *dark and slippery*, or as the margin reads, "darkness and slipperiness."

5. David's prospect of his own rescue, which, having committed his cause to God, he did not doubt would be brought about (vv. 9–10). He trusted that God would encourage him in this way: "*My soul shall be joyful*, not in my own peace and security but *in the Lord* and in his favor, in his promise and *in his salvation* according to the promise." He promised that then God would receive the glory of it (v. 10): *All my bones shall say, Lord, who is like unto thee?*

Verses 11–16

Here David accuses his enemies of two great evils: perjury and ingratitude.

1. Perjury (v. 11). When Saul wanted to condemn David for treason in order to get him exiled, *False witnesses did rise up*, who would swear anything; *they laid to my charge things that I knew not.* This example of the wrong done to David was a type of the wrongs done to the Son of David, against whom also false witnesses came (Mt 26:60).

2. Ingratitude. There is scarcely anything worse than calling someone ungrateful. This was the character of David's enemies (v. 12): *They rewarded me evil for good.* He had deserved good not only from the public in general, but also from those particular people who were now most bitter against him. Probably it was then well known whom he meant; it may have been Saul himself. David here shows:

2.1. How tenderly, and with what a warm affection, he had behaved toward them in their suffering (vv. 13–14). He prayed for them. To his prayers he added humility and self-denial, both as regards what he ate — he fasted, at least from pleasant food — and also in the clothes he wore. He put on sackcloth to express his grief, not only for their suffering but also for their sin, for this was how a penitent looked and acted. His fasting also gave an edge to his praying. He was so intent in his devotions that he had no appetite to eat, nor would he allow himself time to eat: "*My prayer returned into my own bosom* (v. 13); I had the encouragement of having done my duty and of having proved myself to be a loving neighbor."

2.2. How arrogantly and with what a cruel hatred — in fact, worse than cruel — they had behaved toward him (vv. 15–16): *In my adversity they rejoiced. They gnashed upon me with their teeth.* David was the fool of their play, and his defeat was the talk of the town as these hypocritical mockers sat down to their feasts; it was the song of the drunkards (69:12). This has often been the hard fate of the best people. The apostles were made a spectacle to the world (1Co 4:9).

Verses 17–28

In these verses, as before:

1. David describes the great injustice, hatred, and arrogance of his persecutors, pleading this with God as a reason why he should protect him from them. *They hated him without a cause* (v. 19); indeed, they hated him for those very actions of good service that should have prompted them to love and honor him. This is quoted with application to Christ and is said to be fulfilled in him: *They hated me without cause* (Jn 15:25). *They speak not peace* (v. 20). If they met him, they did not have the good manners to give him the time of day. They were like Joseph's brothers, who would not *speak peaceably to him* (Ge 37:4). *They opened their mouth wide against me.* They set themselves against all the serious, good people who were loyal to David (v. 20): *They devised deceitful matters* (false accusations) to trap and destroy *those that were quiet in the land.*

2. David appeals to God against them, the *God to whom vengeance belongs* (94:1). He appeals to his knowledge (v. 22): *This thou hast seen.* He appeals to God's justice: "*Awake to my judgment, even to my cause,* rise to my defense, and let it be heard in your court" (v. 23). "*Judge me, O Lord my God!* Vindicate me in your righteousness, pass sentence on this appeal, *according to the righteousness of* your nature and rule" (v. 24).

3. David prays fervently to God to graciously support him and his friends, to act for him, not stand by as a spectator (v. 17): "*Lord, how long wilt thou look on? Rescue my soul from the destructions* they are plotting against it; rescue *my darling*, my precious life, *from the lions.* My soul, my precious life, is the only life I have, and therefore the shame is the greater if I neglect it and the loss is the greater if I lose it. It is my only one, and therefore should be precious to me. It should be carefully protected and provided for. It is my soul that is in danger; Lord, rescue it." He wants his innocence to be cleared in such a way that they may be ashamed of the slander which they have been guilty of against him, and he wants his position to be strengthened in such a way that they may be ashamed of plotting against him and of their expectations of his destruction, so that they may either be brought to the sort of shame that will be a step toward their reformation or may receive as their inheritance that which will be their eternal misery. Despite the methods that have been used to defame David, make him repugnant, and frighten people from acknowledging him, there are still some who support his righteous cause, who delight in his vindication, and he prays for them: *Let them say continually, The Lord be magnified*, by us and others, *who hath pleasure in the prosperity of his servant* (v. 27).

4. David promises to respond with praise to the mercy he hopes to gain by prayer: "*I will give thee thanks*, as the One who has rescued me (v. 18), *and my tongue shall speak of thy righteousness* (v. 28), the justice of your judgments and all your ways."

PSALM 36

We see here: 1. The sinfulness of sin, and how troublesome it is (vv. 1–4). 2. The goodness of God, and how gracious he is to all his creatures in general (vv. 5–6) and especially to his own people (vv. 7–9). By this the psalmist is encouraged to pray for all the saints (v. 10), and for himself and his own preservation in particular (v. 11), and to triumph in the certain fall of his enemies (v. 12).

Title

In the title of this psalm, David is called *the servant of the Lord.* Why he is called this here and not in any other psalm, except in the title of Ps 18, cannot be explained, but he was here a servant not only as every good person is God's servant, but also as a king and a prophet.

Verses 1–4

In these verses, David describes the evil of evildoers, sin in its causes and sin in its colors, in its root and in its branches.

1. Here is the root of bitterness (Heb 12:15), from which all the evil of evildoers comes. *"The transgression of the wicked* (as it is described afterward in vv. 3–4) *saith within my heart*—makes me conclude within myself—*that there is no fear of God before his eyes,* for if there were, if he had any awe of his majesty or fear of his wrath, he would not dare break the laws of God and disobey his covenants with him." *He flattereth himself in his own eyes;* that is, while he continues in sin, he thinks he is acting wisely and doing rather well for himself. He either does not see or will not acknowledge the evil and danger of his evil practices. He calls evil good and good evil (Isa 5:20). He claims that his immorality is simply "pushing back the boundaries of freedom" and that his deception has a clever wisdom about it, and he even suggests to himself that the persecution of the people of God is an act of necessary justice. But the day is coming when sinners will be exposed as such, when their *iniquity shall be found to be hateful* (v. 2).

2. Here are the cursed branches which spring from this root of bitterness. Sinners defy God. *The words of his mouth are iniquity and deceit,* his words are evil and deceitful; he plans wrong but tries to cover it up with plausible excuses. The sparks of virtue are extinguished, his principles thwarted, his good beginnings come to nothing: he has ceased *to be wise and to do good* (v. 3). *He devises mischief* (plots evil) *upon his bed.* Those who stop doing good begin to do evil. Because they do evil themselves, they have no dislike of it in others at all: *He abhors not evil,* he does not reject what is wrong (v. 4), but on the contrary, takes pleasure in it and is glad to see others as bad as himself.

Verses 5–12

Having looked around sadly on the evil of evildoers, David here looks up with assurance to the goodness of God. Notice:

1. His meditations on the grace of God. He acknowledges:

1.1. The transcendent perfections of the divine nature. *Thy mercy, O Lord, is in the heavens,* your love, O Lord, reaches to the heavens (v. 5). However bad the world is, let us never think worse of God or of his rule; let us not take the presence of evil as a reflection on God's purity, as if he supported sin, but wonder at his patience, that he is so patient with those who provoke him so arrogantly, even causing his sun to shine and his rain to fall on them (Mt 5:45). He is a God of unbreakable truth: *Thy faithfulness reaches unto the clouds* (skies) (v. 5). God's faithfulness reaches so high that it does not change with the weather, as human faithfulness does, for it reaches to the skies, above the clouds and all the changes of this world. He is a God of incontrovertible justice: *Thy righteousness is like the great mountains* (v. 6). He is a God of unsearchable wisdom: *Thy judgments are a great deep* (v. 6) that cannot be fathomed with the plumb line of any finite understanding."

1.2. The extensive care and generosity of divine Providence: *"Thou preservest man and beast* (v. 6). You not only protect people and animals from trouble, but also supply them with what they need to support their life."

1.3. The special favor of God to the saints. Notice:

1.3.1. Their character (v. 7). They are those who are drawn by the *excellency of God's loving-kindness to put their trust under the shadow of his wings.*

1.3.2. Their privilege. "They will be greatly satisfied with the riches of your house; their needs will be supplied, their cravings satisfied, and all their resources filled." They will find in God all they need, everything that an enlightened and liberated soul can want to receive. Although gracious souls continually want more of God, they never desire more than God. *I have all, and abound* (Php 4:18). Their joys will be constant: *Thou shalt make them drink of the river of thy pleasures* (delights). There are delights that are truly divine. "They are your pleasures, which not only come from you because you give them, but also are traced back to you because you are the substance and center of them." There is a river of these delights, which is always full and fresh and always flowing. The pleasures of this world are merely foul puddle water, but the delights of faith are pure and pleasant, and as clear as crystal (Rev 22:1). Because they have God himself as their happiness, they have a fountain of life, from which those rivers of delight flow (v. 8). In him they have light in perfection—wisdom, knowledge, and joy, all included in this light: *In thy light we will see light.* "In the knowledge of you in grace, and the vision of you in glory, we will have what will abundantly satisfy our understanding." That divine light which shines in the Scriptures, and especially in the face of Christ, the light of the world (Jn 8:12), has all truth in it. "In our fellowship with you now, by the flow of your grace toward us and the return of our devotion to you, and in the future fullness of you in heaven, we will have all the good we can desire."

2. His prayers, intercessions, and holy triumphs based on his meditation.

2.1. He intercedes for all the saints (v. 10).

2.1.1. The people he prays for are those who know God: the upright in heart, those who make a sincere profession of their faith and are faithful toward both God and other people.

2.1.2. The blessing he begs for them is God's unfailing love, that is, the signs of his favor toward them, and his righteousness, that is, the workings of his grace in them.

2.2. He prays for himself, that he may be preserved in his integrity and assurance (v. 11): *"Let not the foot of pride come against me,* to trip me up or trample all over me; *and let not the hand of the wicked,* which is stretched out against me, prevail to *remove me,* either from my purity and integrity, by any temptation, or from my peace and strength, by any trouble."

If in praying over and singing this psalm, our hearts are duly affected by the hatred of sin and an assurance of God's unfailing love, then we are singing it with grace and understanding.

PSALM 37

This psalm is a sermon, and it is an excellent and useful sermon, not intended—like most of the psalms—for our devotions, but for our way of life. It contains no prayer or praise, but is all instruction; it is Maschil, *"a teaching psalm." It is an explanation of some of the hardest lessons of the book of providence, the advancement of evildoers and the disgrace of the righteous. 1. David forbids us to fret at the prosperity of evildoers in their evil (vv. 1, 7–8). 2. He gives very good reasons why we should not fret at it: because the character of evildoers is shameful (vv. 12, 14, 21, 32), despite their prosperity, and the character of the righteous is honorable (vv. 21, 26, 30–31); because evildoers are close to destruction and ruin (vv. 2, 9–10, 20, 35–36, 38), whereas the righteous are certain of salvation and protection from all the harmful intentions of evildoers (vv. 13, 15, 17, 28, 33, 39–40); and because God has special mercy and favor in store for all good people (vv. 11, 16, 18–19, 22–25, 28–29, 37). 3. He prescribes very good remedies for this sin of envying the prosperity of evildoers, and great encouragement to use those remedies (vv. 3–6, 27, 34).*

Verses 1–6

1. We are warned here against being discontented at the prosperity and success of evildoers (vv. 1–2): *Fret not thyself, neither be thou envious.* David is probably speaking these words first to himself. What is to be preached to others is most likely to succeed in its aim if first preached to ourselves. When we look out, we see the world full of *evildoers* and *workers of iniquity* who are flourishing and prospering. When we look within our spirits, we find ourselves tempted to fret and be envious. We tend to fret against God, as if he were being unkind to the world and unkind to his church in allowing such people to live, prosper, and succeed. We tend to envy them the ease they have in gaining wealth, perhaps unlawfully, and in gratifying their desires, and we wish that we could shake off the restraints of conscience and become like them. Yet when we look forward with the eye of faith, we see no reason to envy evildoers for their prosperity, for their ruin is close and they are moving quickly toward it (v. 2). They flourish, but only like the grass (v. 2; 103:15), like the green plants, which nobody bothers about. They will soon wither in themselves. Outward prosperity fades, and so does the life itself to which it is confined.

2. We are advised here to lead a life of confidence in God, and that will keep us from fretting at the success of evildoers. If we take good care of our own souls, we will see little reason to envy those who do not look after theirs. Here are three excellent commands, and to support them there are three precious promises that we may rely on:

2.1. We must make God our hope, and then we will be able to subsist comfortably in this world (v. 3). It is required that we *trust in the Lord and do good.* We must not think we can trust in God and then do as we want, but if we trust in him, it is promised that we will be well provided for in this world: *So shalt thou dwell in the land, and verily thou shalt be fed* (v. 3). "You will be peacefully settled, and you will receive a comfortable maintenance: *Verily thou shalt be fed* " (v. 3). Some read it, "Thou shalt be fed by faith," as the just are said to live by faith (Ro 1:17), and it is good life. It is good to feed on the promises of God.

2.2. We must make God our heart's delight, and then we will have our heart's desire (v. 4). We were commanded (v. 3) to do good, and then follows this command to delight in God, which is as much our privilege as our duty. And this pleasant duty has a promise attached to it: *He shall give thee the desires of thy heart* (v. 4). He has not promised to satisfy all physical appetites, but to give us all the desires of the heart, all the desires of the soul. What is the desire of the heart of a good person? It is to know God, to love him, and to live for him, to please him and to be pleased in him.

2.3. We must make God our guide, and submit in everything to his guidance and his ordering of our circumstances, and then all our affairs, even those that seem most intricate and confusing, will work out well (vv. 5–6). The responsibility is simple, and if we follow it rightly, it will put us at our ease: *Commit thy way unto the Lord* (v. 5); the margin reads, "roll thy way upon the Lord." See also 55:22; Pr 16:3. *Cast thy burden upon the Lord*, the burden of your cares (1Pe 5:7). "Reveal thy way unto the Lord" is the reading of the Septuagint (a Greek version of the Old Testament), that is, "Spread out your case, and all your cares about it, in prayer before the Lord, and then trust in him to work things out well, in the full assurance that everything God does is good." We must follow Providence, not force it; we must submit to infinite Wisdom and not give God orders.

3. The promises are very sweet. "*He shall bring that to pass* (v. 5), whatever it is, which you have committed to him; you will be content even if it is not according to your plans. He will find ways to take you out of the difficulties you find yourself in, to still your fears and to bring about your purposes to your great satisfaction." *He shall bring forth thy righteousness as the light and thy judgment as the noonday* (v. 6), that is, "he will make it clear that you are honorable, and that is honor enough." If we are careful to keep a good conscience, we may leave it to God to take care of our reputation.

Verses 7–20

In these verses we have:

1. The previous commands instilled.

1.1. Let us calm ourselves by believing in God: "*Rest in the Lord, and wait patiently for him*" (v. 7), that is, come to terms with all he does and rest in that. Be satisfied that he will make everything work for our good (Ro 8:28), even though we do not know how. "Be silent before the Lord" is the literal meaning, but in a submissive — not sullen! — silence.

1.2. Let us not become disturbed by what we see in this world: "*Fret not thyself because of him who prospers in his wicked way* (v. 7), who although he is bad still prospers and grows rich and great in the world. If your heart begins to rise at this thought, knock down such a thought, and *cease from anger* (v. 8). *Fret not thyself in any wise to do evil* (v. 8). Do not envy evildoers' prosperity, for then you may be tempted to fall in with them and follow the same evil ways they take to enrich and advance themselves, or you may be tempted to take some reckless action to avoid them and their power."

2. The foregoing reasons repeated.

2.1. Good people have no reason to envy the worldly prosperity of evildoers. *Evildoers shall be cut off* by some sudden stroke of divine justice in the middle of their prosperity. The condition of the righteous, on the other hand, even in this life, is better in every way and more desirable than that of evildoers (v. 16). A godly person's little is very much better than an evildoer's wealth. It comes from a better hand, from the hand of special love, not simply from the hand of common providence. *Those that wait upon the Lord*, who depend on him in a life of expectancy, who seek him, *shall inherit the earth*, as a sign of his present favor to them and a pledge of better things for them in the other world. *The meek shall inherit the earth.* Our Savior has made this a Gospel promise, and he declared a confirmation of the blessing on the meek (Mt 5:5). They *shall delight themselves in the abundance of peace* (v. 11), that peace which the world cannot give (Jn 14:27). They will delight themselves in this. God *knows their days* (v. 18). He notices them particularly, all they do and everything that happens to them. He keeps a record of the days of their service, and not one day's work will go unrewarded. *Their inheritance shall be for ever.* Their time on earth is calculated by days, which will soon be numbered (Da 5:26). God observes them, and he gives them, each day, the blessings appropriate to that day. But he never intended their inheritance to be confined within the limits of those days. No; such an inheritance must be the portion of an immortal soul and therefore must last as long as that soul lasts, and the course of its life will run parallel with that longest line of all: eternity itself: *Their inheritance shall be for ever* (v. 18); not their inheritance on earth, but that incorruptible inheritance that cannot be lost and is stored for them in heaven (1Pe 1:4).

2.2. Good people have no reason to fret at the occasional success of the plans of evildoers against the just.

2.2.1. Their plots will be their shame (vv. 12–13). It is true that *the wicked plotteth against the just*; they are proud and arrogant. But God despises all their attempts as worthless and ineffective. People have their day now. God's day will give a decisive judgment.

2.2.2. Their attempts will be their destruction (vv. 14–15). Notice how cruel they are: they *have drawn the sword, and bent the bow,* and these military preparations are made against the helpless, *the poor and needy*—and against the guiltless, *such as are of upright conversation,* those whose ways are upright. But notice how justly their hatred turns back on them: *Their sword shall turn into their own heart* (v. 15).

2.2.3. Those who are not suddenly destroyed will still be prevented from causing any further trouble: *Their bows shall be broken* (v. 15); the instruments of their cruelty will fail them. And even *their arms shall be broken,* so they will not be able to continue their enterprises (v. 17).

Verses 21–33

Notice here:

1. What is required of us for the way to our happiness. If we want to be blessed by God:

1.1. We must make sure we give everybody what belongs to them, for *the wicked borrows and pays not again* (v. 21). It is the first thing which the Lord our God requires of us, that we lead just lives (Mic 6:8), rendering to everyone their due.

1.2. We must be ready to do all acts of kindness and generosity, for it is an example of God's goodness to the righteous that he puts it into their power to be kind and to do good. It is also an example of the goodness of the righteous that they have hearts in proportion to their wealth: *He shows mercy, and gives* (v. 21). *He is ever merciful and lends* (v. 26), and sometimes there is as true kindness in lending as in giving.

1.3. We must leave our sins and engage in the practice of serious godliness (v. 27): *Depart from evil and do good.*

1.4. We must speak many good words, and we must use our tongues to glorify God and build up others. It is one of the characteristics of a righteous person (v. 30) that their *mouth speaketh wisdom.* The mouth will speak out of the abundance of a good heart (Mt 12:34) what is good and helpful to build others up (Eph 4:29).

1.5. We must have our wills brought into complete submission to the will and word of God (v. 31): *The law of God,* of his God, *is in his heart*; and we are only pretending that God is our God if we do not receive his law into our hearts and submit to his rule.

2. The things that are assured to us, on these conditions, as examples of our happiness and comfort:

2.1. That we will receive a blessing from God, and that blessing will be the spring, sweetness, and security of all our physical comforts and enjoyments (v. 22): *Such as are blessed of God,* as all the righteous are, with a Father's blessing, *shall,* because of that, *inherit the earth,* or "the land"—for this is how the same word is translated in v. 29—the land of Canaan, that glory of all lands.

2.2. That God will plan and direct our actions and lives so that they may give him the greatest possible glory (v. 23): *The steps of a good man are ordered by the Lord.* God directs the steps of good people; not only their ways in general, by his written word, but also their particular steps, by the whispers of conscience, saying, *This is the way, walk in it* (Isa 30:21). He does not always show them their way from far off, but leads them step by step, as children are led, and so keeps them continually depending on his guidance.

2.3. That God will keep us from being destroyed by our falls either into sin or into trouble (v. 24): *Though he fall, he shall not be utterly cast down.* Good people may sin, but the grace of God will restore them to repentance, so that although they may be caught in a sin (Gal 6:1), they will not fall completely. Although they may, for a time, lose the joys of God's salvation, such joys will be restored to them, for God will uphold them with his hand and with his free Spirit (51:12). The roots will be kept alive even though the leaves wither, and spring will come after winter. And although good people may be in distress, their lives in difficulties, their spirits low, they will not fall down completely; God will be the strength of their hearts when their flesh and heart fail (73:26).

2.4. That we will not lack what we need to support this life (v. 25): "*I have been young and now am old,* and, among all the changes I have seen in people's outward condition and the observations I have made of them, *I never saw the righteous forsaken* by God or others." There are very few examples of good people, or their families, who are reduced to such extreme poverty as many evildoers bring on themselves by their evil. Some believe that this promise relates especially to those who are kind and generous to the poor, and that it shows that David never observed any who brought poverty on themselves by their kindness.

2.5. That God will not desert us, but will graciously protect us in our difficulties (v. 28): *The Lord loves judgment*; he delights in doing justice himself, and he delights in those who do justice. He therefore will not abandon his saints when they face adversities.

2.6. That we will be comfortably settled in this world, and be even more comfortably settled when we leave this world; that we will *dwell for evermore* (v. 27) and not be *cut off as the seed of the wicked* (v. 28); that we *shall inherit the land* which the Lord our God gives us (Ex 20:12; Dt 5:16; etc.) *and dwell therein for ever* (v. 29). But we will not live on this earth forever; there is no continuing city here (Heb 13:14). It is only in heaven, that city which has foundations (Heb 11:10), that the righteous will live forever. That will be their eternal dwelling place.

2.7. That we will not be hunted by our enemies, those who seek to destroy us (vv. 32–33).

Verses 34–40

Here is the psalmist's conclusion of this sermon.

1. The duty here impressed on us is still the same (v. 34): *Wait on the Lord and keep his way.* If we make sure we *keep God's way,* we may cheerfully wait on him and commit our way to him, and we will find him a good Master both to his working servants and to his waiting servants.

2. The reasons to support this duty are much the same too, taken from the certain destruction of evildoers and the certain salvation of the righteous. Notice:

2.1. The final misery of evildoers, however much they may prosper in the meantime: *The end of the wicked shall be cut off* (v. 38), and their life cannot be considered good if it undoubtedly ends so terribly. *Transgressors shall be destroyed together* (v. 38). In this world, God singles out one sinner here and another there, out of many, to be made an example and a warning, but on the Day of Judgment there will be a general destruction of all evildoers, and not one will escape.

2.2. The final blessedness of the righteous. Those who keep God's way may be assured that in due time he will *exalt them to inherit the land* (v. 34). He will advance them to a place in the heavenly mansions, to a position of dignity, honor, and true wealth in the New Jerusalem, to inherit that good land, that land of promise, of which Canaan was a type. He will exalt them above all contempt and danger. Let all people *mark the perfect* (blameless) *man, and behold the upright*; take notice of him to observe what comes of him, and you will find that *the end of that man is peace. The salvation of the righteous is of the Lord*; it will be the Lord's doing. He will *save them*, not only keep them safe but also make them happy, *because they trust in him* (v. 40).

PSALM 38

This is one of the penitential psalms. It is full of grief and complaints from beginning to end. David's sins and his suffering are the cause of his grief and the subject of his complaints. 1. He complains of God's displeasure, and of his own sin which provoked God to be against him (vv. 1–5); of his physical sickness (vv. 6–10); and of the unkindness of his friends (v. 11). 2. He complains of the wrongs his enemies do to him, pleading his good behavior toward them, but at the same time confessing his sins to God (vv. 12–20). Lastly, he concludes the psalm with fervent prayers to God for his gracious presence and help (vv. 21–22).

Title

The title of this psalm is significant: it is *a psalm to bring to remembrance* (title). Ps 70, which was also written in a time of suffering, contains the same title.

Verses 1–11

1. David prays to be saved from the wrath of God and from the displeasure God is showing him in his suffering (v. 1): *O Lord, rebuke me not in thy wrath.* We should pray, like David, that however God rebukes and chastens us, it may not be in his wrath and displeasure, for that will add bitterness to our suffering and misery. Those who want to escape the wrath of God must pray against that more than they pray against any outward affliction. They should be content to bear any outward affliction while it comes from, and is consistent with, the love of God.

2. David mourns bitterly the impressions of God's displeasure on his soul (v. 2): *Thy arrows stick fast* (have pierced) *in me.* He complains of God's wrath as the cause of the physical illness he is suffering (v. 3): *There is no soundness in my flesh because of thy anger.* Its bitterness, instilled in his mind, affects his body, but that is not the worst of it. It has also caused anxiety in his heart, so that he has forgotten the courage of a soldier, the honor of a ruler, and all the cheerfulness of the sweet psalmist of Israel (2Sa 23:1), and groans in anguish (v. 8).

3. David acknowledges his sin to be the cause of all his troubles, and he groans more under the burden of guilt than under any other burden (v. 3). He complains that his flesh has no health. "It is *because of thy anger*; your anger kindles the fire which burns so fiercely within me." But in the next words he justifies God in this and takes all the blame onto himself: "It is *because of my sin.* I have deserved it, and so I have brought it on myself. My own sin corrects me." It is therefore sin that this good man complains most of. Sin is a heavy burden (v. 4): "My iniquities have *gone over my head.* My own guilt overwhelms me as raging waters overwhelm one who is sinking and drowning, or like a heavy burden on my head, pressing down on me more than I can bear or support." Sin keeps people from soaring upward and pressing onward. "*My wounds stink and are corrupt*, as physical wounds rankle, fester, and become putrid because they are not dressed or looked after. This is because of my own *foolishness.*" Sins are painful, mortal wounds (Ge 4:23). A slight sore that is neglected may prove to have fatal consequences, and so may a slight sin not dealt with and left unrepented of.

4. David groans within himself because of his afflictions and tries to relieve his grief by expressing it and pouring out his complaint before the Lord.

4.1. He was troubled in mind, his conscience was in pain, and he had no rest in his own spirit, and who can bear a wounded spirit (Pr 18:14)? He was *troubled*, or bent over, *bowed down greatly*, and went *mourning all the day long* (v. 6).

4.2. He was sick and weak in body; his back was suffering from some terrible illness, some swelling, ulcer, or inflammation. (Some think it was a sore caused by the plague, such as Hezekiah's boil [2Ki 20:7].) There was *no soundness in his flesh* (v. 7); like Job, he was ill all over his body. Sickness subdues the strongest body and the bravest spirit. David was famous for his courage and great exploits, but when God contended with him by physical sickness and the impressions of his wrath on his mind, his heart failed him, and he became as weak as water.

4.3. His friends were unkind to him (v. 11): "*My lovers*—my friends, who were with me in happier days—now *stand aloof from my sore.*" Even *his kinsmen*, his relatives who were related to him by blood or marriage, *stood afar off* (v. 11).

5. In the midst of his complaints, David comforts himself with the notice God graciously takes of both his sorrows and his prayers (v. 9): "*Lord, all my desire is before thee.* You know what I lack and what I wish to have: *My groaning is not hidden from thee.* You know the burdens I am groaning under and the blessings I groan for."

Verses 12–22

In these verses:

1. David complains about the power and hatred of his enemies, who it seems took his physical weakness and mental trouble as an opportunity not only to gloat over him, but also to cause him further trouble. He has a great deal to say against them, which he humbly offers—as he did before in 25:19: *Consider my enemies*—as a reason why God should support him. "They are very cunning and subtle. They restlessly *lay snares*; they *imagine deceits* (plot deceptions) *all the day long* (v. 12). They are very arrogant and insolent: *When my foot slips* (v. 16), when I make a mistake or take a false step, they exalt themselves over me; they are pleased with it and gloat over my misfortune. They are not only unjust but also very ungrateful: they *hate me wrongfully* (v. 19). I never did them any wrong, but they *render evil for good* (v. 20). I have done

many kind acts for them—and so I would have expected them to be kind to me now—but *for my love they are my adversaries*, in return for my friendship they accuse me (109:4). *They are my adversaries* merely *because I follow the thing that good is*" (v. 20). They hated him not only because of his kindness to them but also because of his devotion and obedience to God. They hated him because they hated God and all who bear his image.

2. David reflects, with encouragement, on his own peaceful and devout behavior in the middle of all the wrongs done to him and all the dishonor shown him. If we continue to maintain our integrity and our peace, who can harm us? David did this here. He kept his temper; he was not shaken or disturbed by any of the troublesome things said or done against him (vv. 13–14): *I, as a deaf man, heard not.* Here David was a type of Christ, who was like a sheep that is silent before its shearer (Isa 53:7), and when insults were hurled against him, he did not retaliate. Both Christ and David are examples teaching us not to repay insults with insults. He kept close to his God by faith and prayer. His friends should have acknowledged him, stood by him, and appeared as witnesses for him, but they withdrew from him (v. 10). But God is a friend who will never fail us if we hope in him. "You will answer, O Lord, for me."

3. David laments his own weakness and foolishness. *I am ready to halt* (v. 17). This is best explained by a similar thought which the psalmist remembered in a similar case (73:2): *My feet were almost gone, when I saw the prosperity of the wicked.* It is similar here: *I was ready to halt*, ready to fall and say, I have *cleansed my hands in vain* (73:13). When good people have thought only of their sorrow, they have been about to fall, but when they have set their heart on God, they have kept standing. Although he could justify himself before other people, he would judge and condemn himself before God (v. 18): "*I will declare my iniquity* and not cover it up. *I will be sorry for my sin*, and not make light of it." This self-condemnation helped make him silent under the rebukes of Providence and the criticism of people.

4. David concludes with fervent prayers to God for his gracious presence (vv. 21–22): "*Forsake me not, O Lord*, even though my friends have abandoned me and I deserve to be abandoned by you. Do not be far from me, as my unfaithful heart is ready to fear that you are."

PSALM 39

When he wrote this psalm, David seems to have been remembering a time of great difficulty, for it is with some difficulty that he composes his spirit to take the good counsel he gave others (Ps 37), to rest in the Lord and wait patiently for him (37:7), without fretting. 1. He relates the struggle within him between grace and corruption, and between passion and patience (vv. 1–3); he recalls how he meditated on the doctrine of human frailty and mortality and prayed to God to instruct him in it (vv. 4–6). 2. He remembers how he turned to God for his sins to be forgiven, for his suffering to be removed, and for his life to be extended till he was ready to die (vv. 7–13).

Verses 1–6

David recalls here, and leaves on record, the thoughts he had in his heart during his suffering. He remembers:

1. That he made covenants with God. When at any time we are tempted to sin, we must call to mind the solemn vows we have made against the specific sin we are on the brink of.

1.1. He remembers that he decided to be careful in the way he lived (v. 1): *I said, I will take heed to my ways.* Having decided to watch our ways, we must, on every occasion, remind ourselves of that resolution.

1.2. He remembers that he especially covenanted against sins of the tongue. It is not so easy as we wish not to sin in thought; but David decided that if an evil thought were to come to him, he would put his hand over his mouth and suppress it, so that it went no farther. "*I will keep a bridle*, or muzzle, *upon my mouth*" (v. 1). Watchfulness in habits is like a bridle on the head; watchfulness in the act and exercise is the hand on the bridle. David would keep a muzzle on his mouth, as we do on a wild dog that is fierce and causes trouble. It takes special and steadfast resolution to restrain evil from breaking out on our lips, and this is how sinful words are muzzled. When he was in the company of evildoers, he would make sure he did not say anything that might harden them or give them cause to blaspheme.

2. In accordance with these covenants, he made a great effort to bridle his tongue (v. 2): *I was dumb with silence*; *I held my peace even from good.* But what are we to say about his keeping silence *even from good*? I tend to think he was weak in this. Because he had resolved not to say just anything that came to his mind, he wanted to say nothing, going to the extreme.

3. The less he spoke, the more he thought, and with all the more passion. Binding up the infected part only increased his anguish: *My sorrow was stirred* (v. 2), *my heart was hot within me* (v. 3). He could bridle his tongue, but he could not restrain his emotions. This shows us that those who are of an anxious and discontented spirit should not reflect too much, for while they allow their thoughts to dwell on the causes of the adversity, the fire of their discontent is fueled and burns even more furiously. If, therefore, we want to prevent the trouble caused by uncontrolled passions, we must put right the grievance of uncontrolled thoughts.

4. When he finally did say something, it was to the point: *At the last I spoke with my tongue* (v. 3). I take this to be not a breaking of his good resolve but a putting right of his mistake in taking it too far. He had kept silence *even from good* (v. 2), but now he would remain silent no longer.

4.1. He prayed to God to make him aware of the shortness and uncertainty of life and the near approach of death (v. 4): *Lord, make me to know my end and the measure of my days.* He did not mean, "Lord, let me know how long I will live and when I will die." Rather, *Lord, make me to know my end* means, "Lord, give me wisdom and grace to consider it (Dt 32:29) and to make good use of what I do know about it. Lord, make me consider the end of my life." Death brings to an end the probationary period of this present life. To evildoers it is the end of all joys; to the godly it is the end of all sorrows. When we look on death as something far away, we are tempted to put off making necessary preparations for it, but when we consider how short life is, we will make sure we do what we ought to do, not only with all our strength but also with all possible speed.

4.2. He meditated on the brevity and meaninglessness of life, pleading them with God so that God might relieve him of the burdens of life and pleading them with himself to encourage himself to do the work of this life. *Behold, thou hast made my days as a handbreadth*, the breadth of four fingers, a small, definite measurement, always before our eyes. We need not be skilled at arithmetic to add up the number of our days. No; we have the extent of them at our fingertips, and it is a total of one short handbreadth. Our time is short, and God has made it so, for *the number of our months is with him* (Job 14:5). It is short, and God knows it is: it *is as nothing before thee* (v. 5). All time is nothing compared with God's eternity; much less our personal share of time. Human life on earth is meaningless and worthless, and so it is wise to make sure of a better life. "All man is all vanity," as it may be understood; everything about human beings is uncertain; nothing is substantial and durable except what concerns the new humanity (Eph 2:15). *Selah* is added, as a note commanding observation. "Stop here, and pause for a while, so that you may take time to consider and apply this truth, that each person's life *is vanity*, a mere breath." To prove the meaningless mortality of human beings, he mentions three things here (v. 6):

- The meaninglessness of our joys and honors: *Surely every man walks*—even for an occasion of great dignity, or even for pleasure—*in a vain show*, in a shadow, as a mere phantom.
- The meaninglessness of our griefs and fears. *Surely they are disquieted in vain* (v. 6). Our troubles are often a figment of our imagination. They are always fruitless.
- The meaninglessness of our cares and toils. Human beings take a great deal of effort to *heap up riches* (v. 6), and yet they are like heaps of manure in a field, good for nothing unless they are spread.

Verses 7–13

The psalmist recalls, further, that he turned his eyes and heart heavenward. When there is no solid satisfaction to be found in creation, it is to be found in God and in fellowship with him. Our disappointments in the world should drive us to him. David here recalls expressing:

1. His dependence on God (v. 7). He despaired of ever finding happiness in the things of this world, and he gave up any expectation of it: "*Now, Lord, what wait I* (what do I look) *for?* There's nothing to be gained from this world; there's nothing to wish for, nothing to hope for from this earth." We cannot expect to be constantly healthy or successful, or to be always on good terms with everyone we know, for everything is as uncertain as our continuing to live here. He took hold of happiness and satisfaction in God: *My hope is in thee* (v. 7).

2. His submission to God and his cheerful acceptance of his holy will (v. 9). "*Because thou didst it* (v. 9); I knew it did not come about by chance, but according to what you appointed." We may say about every event, "This is the finger of God; it is the Lord's doing," no matter who was instrumental in doing it.

3. His desire toward God, and the prayers he offered to him. He prayed:

3.1. For his sin to be forgiven and his shame to be prevented (v. 8). Before he prayed (v. 10), *Remove thy stroke* (scourge) *from me*, he prayed (v. 8), "*Deliver me from all my offences*, from my guilt, from the punishment I have deserved." He pleaded, *Make me not a reproach to the foolish*, do not make me the scorn of fools. Evildoers are foolish, and they show their foolishness most when they think they show their great knowledge by mocking God's people.

3.2. For his suffering to be taken away, for quick relief from his present burdens (v. 10): *Remove thy stroke* (scourge) *away from me*.

3.2.1. He pleaded the crisis he had been reduced to by his suffering, which made him the proper object of God's compassion: *I am consumed* (overcome) *by the blow of thy hand* (v. 10). His sickness was so intense that his spirits failed, his strength had wasted away, and his body was emaciated. Our own actions provoke trouble onto us, and we are beaten with the rod of our own making. It is the *yoke of our transgressions*, even though it is *bound with his hand* (La 1:14). God's rebukes make human *beauty* (wealth) *to consume away like a moth* (v. 11). Some believe the moth represents human beings, who are as easily crushed as a moth by the mere touch of a finger (Job 4:19). Others believe it represents divine rebukes, which silently and imperceptibly devastate and devour us, as moths do clothes.

3.2.2. He pleaded the good effects made on him by his suffering. He hoped that the purpose had been fulfilled for which it had been sent (Isa 55:11), and that therefore it would be removed in mercy. It had set him weeping, and he hoped God would take notice of that. *Lord, hold not thy peace at my tears* (v. 12). God does not willingly afflict and grieve *the children of men* (La 3:33), much less his own children, and he will not ignore their tears. He will either speak words to rescue them or in the meantime speak comfort to them. David's suffering had set him praying, and adversities are sent to encourage us to pray. It had helped wean him from the world and take his affections away from it. He began now more than ever to look on himself as *a stranger and sojourner* (v. 12) here, like all his ancestors, not at home in this world, but traveling through it to another and better world (Heb 11:13–14). He would never consider himself to be at home until he reached heaven.

3.3. For a reprieve for a little longer (v. 13): "*O spare me*, relieve me, raise me up from this illness, so that I may regain my strength both physically and mentally, and my spirits may become calmer, more composed, and more ready for the next world, *before I go hence* by death, *and* will *be no more* in this world." *Let my soul live, and it shall praise thee* (119:175).

PSALM 40

It seems David wrote this psalm when he was rescued by the power and goodness of God from some great and pressing trouble, which he was in danger of being overwhelmed by. It was probably some trouble of mind arising from a sense of sin and God's displeasure toward him for it. In this psalm: 1. David records with thankfulness and praise God's favor to him in rescuing him from his deep distress (vv. 1–5). 2. He then uses the occasion to speak about the work of our redemption by Christ (vv. 6–10). 3. That encourages him to pray to God for mercy and grace both for himself and for his friends (vv. 11–17).

Verses 1–5

We have in these verses:

1. The great distress and trouble that the psalmist had been in.

2. His humble waiting on God and his faithful expectations from him in the depths of his cries: *I waited patiently for the Lord* (v. 1). Literally, *Waiting, I waited.* He expected relief from no other source than God. The same hand which tears apart must also bring healing; the hand that injures must also bind up the wound (Hos 6:1), or else it will never be done. But he waited patiently, which suggests that help did not come quickly. Nevertheless, he did not doubt that

it would definitely come, and he decided to continue to believe, hope, and pray until it eventually came. We can apply this to Christ. His agony, both in the garden and on the cross, was also a slimy pit and mud and mire. His soul was then, like David's here, troubled and overwhelmed with sorrow, but he, like David, also prayed, *Father, glorify thy name; Father, save me* (Jn 12:27–28); and he, like David, kept hold of his relationship with his Father—"My God, my God"—and so waited patiently for him.

3. His heartening experience of God's goodness to him in his distress, which he records for the honor of God and also for his own and others' encouragement. *He inclined unto me and heard my cry* (v. 1). Those who have suffered a deep sense of spiritual depression and have been relieved of it by the grace of God may apply this very appropriately to themselves. They have been brought up out of a slimy pit. The mercy is completed by their being given a firm place, a rock, on which to stand. They have been lifted up with the hopes of heaven as far as, earlier, they were depressed by the fears of hell. *"He has put a new song in my mouth* (v. 3); he has given me reason to rejoice and a heart to rejoice." David was brought, as it were, into a new world, and that filled his mouth with a new song, *even praise to our God* (v. 3).

4. David's experience should encourage many to hope in God, and for that purpose, he records it here: *Many shall see, and fear, and trust in the Lord* (v. 3). There is a holy, reverent fear of God which is not only consistent with, but also the foundation of, our hope in him. They will not fear him and avoid him, but fear him and trust in him in their greatest difficulties. They will not doubt that they will find him as able and ready to help them as David found him to be in his distress. The psalmist invites others to put their hope and trust in God, as he did, by declaring those happy who do so (v. 4): *"Blessed is the man that makes the Lord his trust,* and him only, who *respects not* (does not look to) *the proud,* that is, who neither does as those who trust in themselves nor depends on those who proudly encourage others to trust in them, for both the one and the other turn aside to falsehood, as indeed all those do who turn away from God." This can be especially applied to our faith in Christ. Blessed are those who trust in him and in his righteousness. The joyful sense David had of this mercy led him to note, with thankfulness, the many other favors he had received from God (v. 5). *"Many, O Lord my God, are thy wonderful works which thou hast done,* both for me and for others; this is only one of many." All his wonders and miracles are the result of his thoughts toward us. These are the plans of infinite Wisdom, the intentions of eternal love (1Co 2:7; Jer 31:3), *thoughts of good and not of evil* (Jer 29:11). Yet how the links of the golden chain are joined is a mystery to us; we will not be able to explain it until the veil is torn and the mystery of God accomplished. When we have said all we can about the miracles of divine love toward us, we must conclude with an "and so on," adoring the depths of it but completely unable to fathom its full extent.

Verses 6–10

The psalmist is lost in wonder, love, and praise at the miracles God has worked for his people, and he remarkably prophesies here the miracle which surpasses all others and is the foundation and fountain of them all, that of our redemption by our Lord Jesus Christ. This paragraph is quoted by the writer to the Hebrews (Heb 10:5–7) and applied to Christ and his work for us. Notice:

1. The complete inadequacy of the legal sacrifices to atone for sin in order to bring about our peace with God and our joy in him: *"Sacrifice and offering thou didst not desire* (v. 6); you did not want the Redeemer to offer them." He must offer something, but not these (Heb 8:3). Even while the law concerning them was fully effective, it could be said that God did not desire them, or accept them, for their own sake. They could not take away the guilt of sin by satisfying God's justice. The life of a sheep, which is so much less valuable than that of a human being (Mt 12:12), could not be offered as an equivalent for a human life, much less as a way of preserving the honor of God's rule and laws and repairing the damage done to that honor by human sin. These sacrifices could not take away the terror of sin by pacifying the conscience or take away the power of sin by sanctifying the nature; it was impossible (Heb 9:9; 10:1–4). What there was in them that was valuable resulted from their reference to Jesus Christ, of whom they were types—shadows of good things to come (Col 2:17) and tests of the faith and obedience of God's people, tests of their obedience to the Law and their faith in the Gospel. But the reality must come, which is Christ, who must bring that glory to God and that grace to human beings which it was impossible for those sacrifices ever to bring.

2. The appointment of our Lord Jesus to the work of Mediator: *My ears hast thou opened* (v. 6). God the Father disposed him to do this (Isa 50:5–6) and then made him go through with it. The sentence reads literally, "My ears you have dug." This is thought to allude to the law and custom of binding servants to serve forever by piercing their ear to the doorpost; see Ex 21:6.

3. Christ's own voluntary agreement to do this work: *"Then said I, Lo, I come* (v. 7); *then,* when sacrifice and offering would not be sufficient, rather than let the work go undone, I said, 'Here I am, to enter the arena against the powers of darkness and advance the interests of God's glory and kingdom.'" He freely offered himself for this service. He firmly committed himself to do it: "I come; I promise to come in the fullness of time." He freely acknowledged himself to be committed to this work: he said, *Lo, I come* (v. 7); he said it throughout the Old Testament to the saints, who therefore knew him by the title *ho erchomenos,* "the One who would come."

4. The reason why Christ came in pursuit of his undertaking—because in the scroll of the book it was written about him. In the secret records of divine decrees and counsels, it was written that his ear was opened and that he said, *Lo, I come.* There the covenant of redemption was recorded. Moses and all the prophets also testified about him.

5. The pleasure Christ took in his undertaking. Having freely offered himself to it, he did not fail, nor was he discouraged, but proceeded with every possible assurance within himself (vv. 8–9): *I delight to do thy will, O my God.*

6. The declaring of the Gospel to people, even *in the great congregation* (vv. 9–10). The same person who as a priest brought about redemption for us, was also a prophet who makes it known to us, first by his own preaching, then by his apostles, and still by his word and Spirit. The *great salvation began to be spoken by the Lord* (Heb 2:3). What is preached is *righteousness* (v. 9), God's righteousness (v. 10), God's *faithfulness* to his promise, God's *loving-kindness* and his *truth,* his unfailing love according to his word. It is preached *to the great congregation* (v. 9 and again v. 10). The Gospel was preached to great assemblies of both Jews and Gentiles. It is preached freely and openly: *I have not refrained my lips; I have not hid it; I have not concealed it* (vv. 9–10).

Verses 11–17

Having assumed the role of the Messiah in order to meditate on and speak about the work of redemption, the psalmist now speaks in his own voice in order to apply this teaching to himself.

1. This may encourage us to pray for the mercy of God and put ourselves under the protection of that mercy (v. 11). "Lord, you have not spared your Son; you have not withheld even him. And so *withhold not thou thy tender mercies*, which you have stored up for us in him, for will you not *with him also freely give us all things* (Ro 8:32)? *Let thy loving-kindness and thy truth continually preserve me*" (v. 11).

2. This may encourage us concerning the guilt of sin, that Jesus Christ has done what sacrifice and offering could not do toward acquitting us from it. The psalmist saw his sins to be evil, the worst of evil; he saw that they surrounded him *more than the hairs of his head* (v. 12). The sight of sin oppressed him so much that he could not hold up his head—*I am not able to look up*; much less could he keep up his *heart*—*therefore my heart fails me* (v. 12). He cried out with a holy passion, "*Be pleased, O Lord, to deliver me* (v. 13). In such cases, where the fate of an immortal soul is concerned, delays are dangerous. Therefore, *O Lord, make haste to help me.*"

3. This may encourage us to hope for victory over our spiritual enemies, who seek to destroy our souls (v. 14). If Christ has triumphed over them, we will be more than conquerors through him (Ro 8:37). Believing this, we may pray with humble boldness, *Let them be ashamed and confounded together*, and *driven backward* (v. 14). *Let them be desolate* (v. 15). When a child of God is brought into that slimy pit, and the mud and mire, Satan cries out, *Aha! aha!* thinking he has won, but he will rage when he sees the burning stick snatched out of the fire (Zec 3:2), and will be *desolate, for a reward of his shame* (appalled at his own shame) (v. 15).

4. This may encourage all who seek God and love his salvation to be joyful in him and praise him (v. 16).

5. This may encourage the saints, in suffering and distress, to trust in God and encourage themselves in him (v. 17). David himself did this: *I am poor and needy, yet the Lord thinketh upon me* in and through the Mediator, by whom we are accepted.

PSALM 41

God's kindness and truth have often been the strength and support of the saints when they have had experiences of people's unkindness and treachery. David found his enemies very cruel, but also his God very gracious. 1. He here encourages himself in his fellowship with God in his sickness, by faith receiving and taking hold of God's promises (vv. 1–3) and lifting up his heart in prayer (v. 4). 2. He describes the hatred of his enemies toward him (vv. 5–9); he leaves his case with God (vv. 10–12), and so the psalm concludes with a doxology (v. 13).

Verses 1–4

In these verses we have:

1. God's promises of help, strength, and encouragement to those who care about weak people.

1.1. In mentioning these, David is thinking either of:

1.1.1. His friends, who were kind to him: *Blessed is he that considers* (has regard for) (v. 1) poor David. The provocations which his enemies gave him only endeared his friends much more to him. Or:

1.1.2. Himself. He had considered the poor and had helped them, and so he was sure God would, according to his promise, strengthen and encourage him in his sickness.

1.2. We must regard them more generally, as applying to us. *Blessed are the merciful, for they shall obtain mercy* (Mt 5:7). The mercy which is required of us is to care for those who are poor or afflicted, whether in mind, body, or possessions. We must take notice of their suffering and ask about their condition. We must sympathize with them and act kindly toward them. Those who care about the poor *shall be blessed upon the earth* (v. 2). This branch of godliness, as much as any, contains the promise of the life that now is (1Ti 4:8) and is usually rewarded with material blessings. Those who separate themselves from those who have hard hearts will be separated by God from those who are treated harshly. "*They shall be preserved and kept alive* (v. 2) when the arrows of death are flying thick and fast around them." The goodwill of a God who loves us is enough to protect us from the ill will of all who hate us, whether they are people or demons, and we may promise ourselves that goodwill if we have cared about the poor and helped relieve and rescue them. In sickness (v. 3), *The Lord will strengthen him*, both in body and in mind, *upon the bed of languishing*, on the sickbed on which he has lain sick for a long time, and *he will make all his bed*—a very gracious phrase, alluding to the care of those who nurse and tend sick people, and especially mothers who take care of their children when they are sick, making their beds comfortable for them. God will make all his bed from head to foot, so that no part will be uncomfortable. He will, literally, "turn" his bed, shake it up and make it very comfortable; or he will turn it into a bed of health. He has not promised that those who are merciful will never be ill, or that their sickness will not end in death, but he has promised to enable them to bear their suffering with patience and await the outcome cheerfully. The soul will be made peaceful by his grace even when the body is in pain.

2. David's prayer, directed and encouraged by these promises (v. 4): *I said, heal my soul.* Sin is the sickness of the soul; forgiving mercy and renewing grace heals it. We should desire to receive this spiritual healing more than our physical health.

Verses 5–13

David often complained about the arrogant behavior of his enemies toward him when he was ill: *my enemies speak evil of me.* They wanted to grieve his spirit, to destroy his reputation.

1. What was the behavior of his enemies toward him?

1.1. They longed for his death: *When shall he die, and his name perish* with him? They envied him his reputation and the honor he had gained, and they did not doubt that if he were dead, his honor would not accompany him to the dust. But in fact his name lives and flourishes to this day in the sacred writings, and will continue to do so to the end of time, for *the memory of the just is*, and will be, *blessed* (Pr 10:7).

1.2. They made use of everything they could to criticize him (v. 6): "*If he come to see me*"—as it has always been reckoned an act of neighborly kindness to visit the sick—"*he speaks vanity* (falsehood) (v. 6). He pretends to be a friend, but it is all only flattery and falsehood." We complain, and justly so, of the insincerity of our times, and that there are hardly any true friends to be found among people, but it seems this shows us that former days were no better than now. David's friends made invidious remarks about everything he said or did: *His heart gathereth iniquity* (gathers slander) *to itself* (v. 6), misinterprets everything. If David prayed or gave them good advice, they would ridicule it, calling it hypocritical. If he did not say anything good when evildoers visited him (39:1, 2), they would say that he had forgotten his religious faith now that he was ill.

1.3. They *whispered together against him* (v. 7), speaking secretly into one another's ears things which they were too ashamed to speak out (Eph 5:12), and which, if they had, they knew would be proved wrong. Gossips and backbiters are included among the worst sinners (Ro 1:29–30). "The disease he is now suffering from will certainly be his end," they said, "for it is the punishment for some terrible crime, which he will not be brought to repent of, and it shows that he is, whatever his appearance, an evildoer."

1.4. There was one person particularly in whom he had placed a great deal of confidence, who took his enemies' side (v. 9): *My own familiar friend*. He is probably referring to Ahithophel, who had been his close friend and prime minister of state, in whom he had trusted, and who *did eat of his bread*, that is, with whom he had been on very close terms. But this evil and treacherous confidant of David's forgot all the bread he had eaten, and he *lifted up his heel against him* (v. 9) who had promoted him. Let us not think it strange if we are abused by such people: David was, as was the Son of David; for it is of Judas that David, inspired by the Holy Spirit, here spoke. And this is how our Savior himself interpreted the verse: he gave Judas the piece of bread *so that the Scripture might be fulfilled, He that eats bread with me has lifted up his heel against me* (Jn 13:18, 26). In fact, have not we ourselves behaved so treacherously and insincerely toward God? We *eat of his bread* daily, and yet *lift up the heel against him* (v. 9).

2. How did David bear this arrogant, ill-natured behavior of his enemies toward him? He said nothing to them, but turned to God: "*O Lord, be thou merciful to me*, for they are unmerciful (v. 10). Lift me up *that I may requite them*" (v. 10). Some read it, "that I may repay them good for evil"—for that was David's practice (7:4; 35:13). They hoped for his death, but he found himself recovering because of God's mercy, and this would add to the strength and encouragement he gained in his recovery. "Because by your grace you uphold me in my integrity, I know that you will, in your glory, set me forever in your presence." The best people in the world maintain their integrity no longer than God upholds them in it, for by his grace we are what we are. If we are left to ourselves, we will not only fall, but also fall away. The psalm concludes with a sacred doxology or adoration of God as *the Lord God of Israel* (v. 13). It is not certain whether this verse belongs to this particular psalm. It may have been added as the conclusion of the first book of Psalms, which is reckoned to end here; similar doxologies appear at 72:19; 89:52; and 106:48. If this is its significance, it teaches us to make God, who is the Alpha, also to be the Omega (Rev 1:8): to make him who is the beginning of every good work also its end.

Is anyone troubled by sickness (Jas 5:13)? Let them sing the beginning of this psalm. Is anyone persecuted by enemies? Let them sing the end of this psalm.

PSALM 42

If the book of Psalms is a mirror of godly and devout feelings, as some have named it, this particular psalm
certainly deserves such a title. Gracious desires are strong and fervent here; gracious hopes and fears, joys and sorrows, are struggling, but the good, acceptable emotions emerge victorious. Or we may take it as a conflict between sense and faith, sense raising the objections and faith responding to them. 1. Faith begins with holy desires toward God and fellowship with him (vv. 1–2); sense complains about the darkness and obscurity of the present, made worse by the memory of former enjoyments (vv. 3–4); faith silences the complaint with the assurance of a final good outcome (v. 5). 2. Sense renews its complaints of the present dark and sad state (vv. 6–7); faith upholds the heart, nevertheless, with the hope that the day will dawn (v. 8); sense repeats its mourning (vv. 9–10) and raises the same objection it had earlier raised concerning its grievances. Faith has the last word (v. 11), to silence the complaints of sense.

Title

The title does not tell us who wrote this psalm, but it was most probably David, and we think it was written by him at a time when, either by Saul's persecution or by Absalom's rebellion, he was driven out of the sanctuary and cut off from the privileges of waiting on God in public worship.

Verses 1–5

Holy love toward God is the very life and soul of religious faith. Here we have some of the expressions of that love.

1. Holy love thirsting. Here is love on the move, soaring in holy desire toward the Lord and toward remembering his name (vv. 1–2): "*My soul panteth, thirsteth, for God*, for nothing more than God, but only for more and more of him." Notice:

1.1. When it was that David expressed his passionate desire toward God: when he was prevented from taking part in outward opportunities to worship God, when he was banished to the land of Jordan, far from the courts of God's house. Sometimes God teaches us to know the worth of mercies by withdrawing them. He may whet our appetite for the means of grace by interrupting those means. David now went about mourning, but he longed for God.

1.2. What is the object of his desire and what it is he thirsts after. He longs and thirsts for God, not for worship itself, but the God who is worshiped. Living souls can never find their rest anywhere except in the living God. He longs to *come and appear before God* (v. 2): to meet with God, to make himself known to him, as one who knows himself to be sincere; to wait on him, as a servant appears before his master; and to give an account to him, as one who knows that God will judge him. To come and meet with God is as much the desire of the upright as it is the fear of the hypocrite.

1.3. How much he desires to come. His longing for the water of the well of Bethlehem was nothing compared with this. He likens it to the *panting of a hart* (v. 1)—a deer, or especially a hunted buck, which is naturally hot and thirsty—for *the water brooks* (v. 1). Gracious souls fervently desire fellowship with God.

2. Holy love mourning God's absence (v. 3): "*My tears have been my meat* (food) *day and night* during this enforced absence from God's house." Even the royal prophet was a weeping prophet when he lacked the assurance of God's house. His tears mixed with his food; in fact, they were *his meat day and night*. He fed and feasted on his own tears. Two things made his grief even more intense:

2.1. His enemies harassed him: *They continually say unto me, Where is thy God?* (v. 3). Because he was absent from the ark, the sign of God's presence, they concluded that he had lost his God. Those people are mistaken who think that when they have deprived us of our Bibles, our ministers, and our sacred meetings, they have deprived us of our God, for although God has bound us to attend to those people and things when they are available, he has not bound himself to them. We know where our God is, and where to find him, even when we do not know where his ark is, or where to find it. Wherever we are, a way is open toward heaven. Because God did not immediately come to David's rescue, his enemies concluded that God had abandoned him, but they were deceived here also. It does not follow that the saints have lost their God because they have lost all their other friends. However, with this evil thought concerning God and his people, they added further suffering to the one who was already suffering, and that was what they wanted to do. Nothing is more painful to a gracious soul than what is intended to shake its hope and confidence in God.

2.2. He remembered his former freedom and enjoyments (v. 4). David remembered the *days of old*, and then *his soul was poured out in him.* When he had these thoughts, he was overwhelmed, and the thought almost broke his heart. He poured out his soul within him in sorrow, and then poured out his soul before God in prayer. What afflicted him was not the remembrance of the pleasures at court or the hospitality in his own house, from which he had now been banished, but the memory of the free access he had formerly had to God's house. He *went to the house of God* (v. 4), even though it was only a tent in his time; when he was being persecuted by Saul, the ark was in a private house (2Sa 6:3). But the lowliness of the place did not lessen his respect for that sacred sign of God's presence. He *went with the multitude* (v. 4), and did not think it beneath his dignity to lead the crowd in waiting on God. In fact, it added to its delight that he was accompanied by a multitude, and so it is mentioned twice, as what he now greatly mourned and missed. He went *with the voice of joy and praise* (v. 4), not only with joy and praise in his heart, but also with its outward expressions. He went to keep festive *holydays*, not to keep them in vain, worthless merriment and play, but in religious exercises.

3. Holy love hoping (v. 5): *Why art thou cast down, O my soul?* He feels sorrow for a very good reason, but it must not exceed its proper limits or actually depress his spirits. He therefore communes with his own heart (4:4), to help himself. "You are disturbed, discouraged, and confused. Now why are you like this?" Many of our discouragements would disappear if we looked closely into the reasons for them. "*Why am I cast down?*" (v. 5). Is there a real cause for it? Are there not others who have a more just cause, but who are not making such a fuss? Do we not, at the same time, have cause to be encouraged?" A faithful confidence in God is a sovereign antidote against general depression and spiritual discouragement. And so, when we rebuke ourselves for our dejection, we must speak a command to ourselves to hope in God. When the soul is wrapped up in itself, it sinks, but if it takes hold of the power and promises of God, it keeps its head above water. *Hope thou in God* (v. 5) *for I shall yet praise him* (v. 5); I will experience such a change in my spirit that I will have a heart to praise him. We will praise him *for the help of his countenance* (v. 5), for his favor, the support we receive from it, and the assurance we gain from it.

Verses 6–11

Complaints and comforts here take their turn, like day and night in the natural course of life:

1. He complains about his spiritual dejection, but he comforts himself with the thoughts of God (v. 6). His soul is downcast, and he goes to God and tells him so: *O my God, my soul is cast down within me.* In his devotions, his soul is lifted up. He has often remembered God and been strengthened, and so he follows that course now. He has been driven to the farthest borders of the land of Canaan, to shelter there from the rage of his persecutors—sometimes to *the country about Jordan*, and when discovered there, to *the land of the Hermonites* (v. 6), or to Mount Mizar, "the little hill." Wherever he has gone, he has taken his religious faith along with him. In all these places, he remembered God, lifted his heart to him, and kept up his personal fellowship with him. This is the comfort of the banished, the wanderers, the travelers, those who are strangers in a strange land: that wherever they are, there is a way open toward heaven. Distance and time could not make him forget what his heart was set so much on and what was so close to his heart.

2. He complains of the signs of God's displeasure against him, but also encourages himself with the hope of the return of his favor in due time.

2.1. He saw his troubles as coming from God's wrath, and that discouraged him (v. 7): "*Deep calls unto deep*, one affliction comes on the back of another, as if it were called to follow it quickly. Your waterfalls sound the signal and alarm for war." Whatever waves and breakers of suffering go over us at any time, we must call them God's waves and his breakers, so that we may be humbled and may have hope that although we are threatened, we will not be destroyed, for the waves and breakers are under his divine restraint. Let not good people think it strange if they have to experience many times of testing which follow one another closely. God knows what he is doing, and so will they shortly.

2.2. He expected his rescue to come from God's favor (v. 8): *Yet the Lord will command his loving-kindness.* After the storm will come calm. The prospect of this supported him when deep called to deep. He considered the favor of God to be the fountain of all the good he looked for. God's giving his favor is called his *commanding* it. This suggests he gives it freely. We cannot pretend to have deserved it; it is given by his sovereignty. He directs it as a king. By directing his unfailing love, he directs the waves and the breakers, and they will obey him (Mt 8:27). He will do this *in the daytime* (v. 8), for God's unfailing love will bring daylight to the soul at any time. If God would direct his unfailing love toward him, he would receive and welcome it with great love and devotion. He would rejoice in God: *In the night his song shall be with me. My prayer shall be to the God of my life* (v. 8). God is the God of our lives, in whom we live and move (Ac 17:28), the author and giver of all our comforts, and so to whom should we turn in prayer, except to him?

3. He complains about the arrogance of his enemies, but he still encourages himself in God as his friend (vv. 9–11). He has not lost his temper, but weeps silently in grief, and we cannot blame him for this. It must grieve someone who truly loves his country to see himself persecuted as if he were the country's enemy. But David should not have concluded from this that God had forgotten him and rejected him, saying, "Why must I go around mourning? *Why hast thou forgotten me?*" (v. 9). We may complain to God, but we should not complain about him in this

way. *They say daily unto me, Where is thy God?* — a taunt which was intended to discourage his hope in God. Yet his strength is that God is his rock (v. 9) — a rock to build on, a rock to take shelter in. He can say what he has to say to God his rock and can be sure he will be graciously heard. He therefore repeats what he said before (v. 5) and concludes with this (v. 11): *Why art thou cast down, O my soul?* And here, finally, his faith wins the victory and forces his enemies to leave the field. He wins this victory by repeating what he said before, rebuking himself, as he had before, for his dejection and disquiet, and encouraging himself to trust in the name of the Lord and to rest in his God. It may be very useful to us to think our good thoughts over again, and if we do not gain a victory with them at first, then perhaps we may the second time.

PSALM 43

This psalm was probably written on the same occasion as the previous one and, having no title, may be looked on as an appendix to it. Because the depression soon returned, he immediately applied the same remedy, because he had entered the remedy in his book with a probatum est, "it has been proved." When it was necessary, Christ himself prayed a second and third time saying the same words (Mt 26:44). In this psalm: 1. David appeals to God concerning the wrongs done to him by his enemies (vv. 1–2). 2. He prays to God to restore to him the freedom to enjoy public worship again, and he promises to make good use of the opportunities (vv. 3–4). 3. He tries to still the turmoil in his own spirit with a living hope and confidence in God (v. 5).

Verses 1–5

David here turns in faith and prayer to God, as his judge, his strength, his guide, his joy, and his hope. He considers God:

1. As his Judge (v. 1): *Judge* (vindicate) *me, O God, and plead my cause.* There were those who accused him; he was the defendant against them. And there were those who had wronged him; he was the plaintiff against them. Here was a sinful body of people, whom he calls an *ungodly* or unmerciful *nation.* And here was one bad leader, who was deceitful and unjust, probably Saul, who not only showed no kindness to David, but also dealt dishonestly and treacherously with him. Or if Absalom was the man he was referring to, his character was no better. As to the quarrel God had with him for sin, he prays, "*Enter not into judgment with me* (143:2), for then I will be condemned," but as to the quarrel his enemies had with him, he prays, "Lord, *judge me*, vindicate me, for I know I will be justified; *plead my cause against them* (v. 1). Take my side, and in your providence support me."

2. As his all-sufficient strength. This is how he considers God (v. 2): "*Thou art the God of my strength, my God, my strength*, from whom all my strength is derived, in whom I strengthen myself. You have often strengthened me. Without you I am as weak as water and completely unable to do or suffer anything for you." David now went around mourning (v. 2; 42:9), devoid of spiritual joy, but he found God to be his stronghold. If we cannot rejoice in God, we may still support ourselves in him; we may have spiritual support even when we lack spiritual delight. "You are the God on whom I depend as my strength; why then are you rejecting me?" This was a mistake, for God never rejected anyone who trusted in him, whatever sad thoughts they may have had about their own state.

3. As his faithful guide (v. 3): *Lead me, bring me to thy holy hill.* His heart is set on *the holy hill and the tabernacles* (v. 3), not on his family comforts, his advancement at court, or his recreation. He is keen to see God's dwelling place again. Therefore, he prays, "*Send out thy light and thy truth* (v. 3); let me have these as a fruit of your favor, which is light, and as the fulfillment of your promise, which is truth." We are still to pray for God's light and truth, the Spirit of light and truth, who makes up for the lack of Christ's physical presence, to lead us into the mystery of godliness (1Ti 3:16) and to guide us on our way to heaven.

4. As his joy and delight. If God guides him to his dwelling place, if he restores his former freedom to him, he knows very well what he has to do: *Then will I go unto the altar of God* (v. 4). He will get as close as he possibly can to God, his joy and delight. Those who come to God must come to him as their joy and delight, not only as their future happiness but also as their present joy. Such joy is no ordinary happiness, but a delight and joy, far surpassing all the joys of sense and time. In the original, the phrase is emphatic: "unto God the gladness of my joy," or of my triumph.

5. As his never-failing hope (v. 5). Here as before, David quarrels with himself for his dejection and discouragement: *Why art thou cast down, O my soul?* He then calms himself in the confident expectation he has of giving glory to God — *Hope in* God, for I will still praise him — and of enjoying glory with God: he is the *health* (help) *of my countenance and my God.*

PSALM 44

We are not told who wrote this psalm or when and on what occasion it was written. It is a psalm intended for a day of fasting and humbling on the occasion of some public disaster, either actual or threatened. Here, the church is taught: 1. To acknowledge with thankfulness, to the glory of God, the great things God has done for their ancestors (vv. 1–8). 2. To set forth words of remembrance concerning the disastrous days they are now in (vv. 9–16). 3. To declare their integrity and loyalty to God nevertheless (vv. 17–22), and to submit a request at the throne of grace for help and relief (vv. 22–26).

Verses 1–8

In these verses, the church, although now trampled on, remembers the days of its victory. This is mentioned here:

- To emphasize the church's present distress. The burden of slavery must have lain very heavily on those who used to wear the crown of victory, and the signs of God's displeasure must have been very painful to those who had long been used to the signs of his favor.
- To encourage the hope of God's people that God would restore them. The psalmist therefore mixes prayers and confident expectations with the record of former mercies.

Notice:

1. Their commemoration of the great things God has formerly done for them.

1.1. In general: *Our fathers have told us what work thou didst in their days.* "They have told us the *work* which you did," for there is a wonderful harmony and uniformity in all that God does, and its many wheels all make one movement (Eze 10:13): many works make only one work. It is a debt which every age owes to future generations to keep a record of God's wonders and pass on their knowledge to the next generation. Children must listen to what their parents tell them about the wonders of God.

1.2. In particular, they have learned how wonderfully God originally planted Israel in Canaan (vv. 2–3). This was not because of the Israelites' own merit, but only because of God's favor and free grace: it was *through the light of your countenance* (face), *because thou hadst a favor to* (for you loved) *them*. It was not by their own sword that they came into possession of the land, although they had many powerful warriors. Nor did their own strength save them from being driven back by the Canaanites and put to shame. It was God who planted Israel in that good land, as a careful farmer plants a tree, from which they promise themselves fruit. This can be applied to the planting of the Christian church in the world by the preaching of the Gospel. The nations, such as the Canaanites, were not driven out all at once, but little by little, not by any human skill or power—for God chose to do it by the weak and foolish things of the world (1Co 1:27)—but by the wisdom and power of God. Christ by his Spirit went out conquering and to conquer (Rev 6:2), and remembering his conquests is a great support and encouragement to those who are now groaning under the yoke of anti-Christian tyranny. *Thou hast*, many times, *saved us from our enemies*, and have made *those that hated us* flee, and so put them to shame"; for example, he gave many successes to the judges against the nations who oppressed Israel. The persecutors of the Christian church and those who hate it have many times been put to shame by the power of truth (Ac 6:10).

2. The good use they make of this record of the great things God did for their ancestors. They take God as their sovereign Lord (v. 4): *Thou art my King, O God!* The psalmist speaks for himself here: "Lord, *Thou art my King*; where can I go with my requests, except to you? The favor I ask is not for myself, but for your church." They turn to him in prayer, as they always have done, asking him to rescue his people when they are in trouble at any time: *Command deliverances for Jacob.* "Command it, as one with authority (Mt 7:29), whose command will be obeyed." Just as they acknowledged it was not their own sword and bow that had saved them in the past (v. 3), so neither did they trust in their own sword or bow to save them for the future (v. 6): "I will not trust in my bow, or in any of my military preparations, as if those would stand me in good stead without God. *Through thy name*—because of your wisdom directing us, your power strengthening us and working for us, and your promises securing success for us—we will trample on those who rise up against us. We have boasted in God. We will do so every day, and all day long."

Verses 9–16

The people of God here complain to him about the lowly and afflicted condition they are now in, under the dominant power of their enemies and oppressors.

1. They lacked the usual signs of God's favor to them and presence with them (v. 9): "*Thou hast cast off*; you seem to have rejected us and our cause and so have *put us to shame*." When God's people are downcast, they are tempted to think they have been rejected and abandoned by God, but they are mistaken.

2. They were overcome by their enemies on the battlefield (v. 10): *Thou makest us to turn back from the enemy*, as Joshua complained when they were routed at Ai (Jos 7:8): "We are discouraged. Attempts to shake off the

bondage of the Babylonians have failed, and we have in fact lost ground to them."

3. They were doomed to the sword and to captivity (v. 11): "*Thou hast given us like sheep appointed for meat.* Our enemies hesitate to kill an Israelite no more than to kill a sheep." They looked on themselves as bought and sold, and they blamed God for it—*Thou sellest thy people* (v. 12)—when they should have seen their own sin as the reason for their being sold. *Thou dost not increase thy wealth by their price* (v. 12); they suggest that they would have happily suffered this if they had been sure it was for God's glory.

4. They were burdened with contempt, and every possible shame was put on them. They also acknowledge God in this: *Thou makest us a reproach* (v. 13). The nations, the people who were strangers to the citizenship of Israel and strangers to the covenants of promise, made them a byword. The reproach was constant (v. 15): *My confusion is continually before me. The shame of my face has covered me.* And it reflected badly on God himself. The reproach by the enemy and those intent on getting revenge on them was in fact downright blasphemy against God (v. 16 and 2Ki 19:3).

Verses 17–26

Greatly troubled and oppressed, the people of God turn to him:

1. To make an appeal concerning their integrity. Although they have suffered these hard things, they have still kept close to God and their duty (v. 17): "*All this has come upon us*, and it is perhaps as bad as it can get, *yet have we not forgotten thee.* We have neither forgotten you nor stopped worshiping you, for although we cannot deny that we have dealt foolishly, yet we have not *dealt falsely in thy covenant*, so as to reject you and go after foreign gods. Although idolaters were our conquerors, we have not therefore abandoned you." The trouble they have long been in is very great: "We have been *sorely broken in the place of dragons*, among people as fierce, furious, and cruel as jackals. We have been *covered with the shadow of death* (v. 19), that is, we have been deeply depressed, and what we fear is nothing short of death. Although you have killed us, we have continued to trust in you: *Our heart has not turned back* (v. 18); we have not secretly withdrawn our affections from you, nor have our steps *declined from thy way* (v. 18), the way which you have appointed for us to walk in." As long as our troubles do not drive us from our duty to God, we should not allow them to drive us from our assurance in God, for he will not leave us if we do not leave him. "*If we have forgotten the name of our God*, under the pretext that he has forgotten us, or in our distress have *stretched out our hands to a strange god*, as more likely to help us, *shall not God search this out?* Will he not judge it and hold us responsible for it?" They suffered these hard things because they kept close to God and did what they knew was right (v. 22): "It is *for thy sake that we are killed all the day long*, because we are in a relationship with you, are called by your name, call on your name, and will not worship other gods."

2. To make their requests concerning their present distress, that God would rescue them. *Awake, arise* (v. 23). *Arise for our help; redeem us* (v. 26). They have complained (v. 12) that God has sold them; they pray here (v. 26) that God would redeem them, because we can appeal only to God, for he is our only hope. They earlier complained (v. 9), *Thou hast cast us off*, but here they pray (v. 23), "*Cast us not off for ever*; let us not be permanently abandoned by God." Their demands are moving: *Why*

sleepest thou? (v. 23). The expression is figurative—as in 78:65: *Then the Lord awaked as one out of sleep*—but it was applied to Christ literally (Mt 8:24). He was asleep when his disciples were in a storm, and they awoke him, saying, *Lord, save us, we perish* (Mt 8:25). They plead the poor sinner's pleas: "*Our soul is bowed down to the dust* under the general grief and fear. We have become like contemptible creatures moving along the ground: *Our belly cleaves unto the earth*; we cannot lift ourselves up, nor can we revive our own flagging spirits or get ourselves out of our low and sad condition. We lie exposed to being trodden on by every enemy who comes along wanting to insult us. *O redeem us for they mercies' sake*" (v. 26).

PSALM 45

This psalm is an eminent prophecy of Messiah the Prince. It contains the Gospel throughout. It points only to Christ, as a bridegroom taking the church to himself in marriage and as a king ruling in it and ruling for it. Our Savior was probably referring to this psalm when he compared the kingdom of heaven, more than once, to a wedding ceremony, even a royal one (Mt 22:2; 25:1). The introduction speaks of the splendor of the song (v. 1). The psalm speaks of: 1. The royal bridegroom, who is Christ: 1.1. The surpassing magnificence of his person (v. 2). 1.2. The glory of his victories (vv. 3–5). 1.3. The righteousness of his rule (vv. 6–7). 1.4. The splendor of his court (vv. 8–9). 2. The royal bride, which is the church: 2.1. Her agreement gained (vv. 10–11). 2.2. The marriage solemnized (vv. 12–15). 2.3. The offspring of this marriage (vv. 16–17).

Title

Some consider *Shoshannim* to refer to a six-stringed musical instrument; others believe it refers to lilies or roses, which probably were scattered, with other flowers, at marriage ceremonies. It is *a Song of loves* (title), concerning the holy love between Christ and his church. It is also a song of those who are loved, the virgin companions of the bride (v. 14), a song prepared in order to be sung by them.

Verses 1–5

1. The introduction (v. 1) speaks about:

1.1. The dignity of the theme. It is *a good matter*. It concerns *the King*, King Jesus, his kingdom, and his rule.

1.2. The magnificent way in which the psalm is composed. This song was a confession with the mouth of faith in the heart concerning Christ and his church (Ro 10:8–10). *My heart is inditing* (dictating) *it* (v. 1). We speak best of Christ and divine things when we are speaking about what has warmed and affected our own hearts. The theme was well expressed: *I will speak of the things which I have made* (v. 1). Not: "I will speak secondhand about things I have heard from others," that is, speak mechanically without understanding, but, "I will speak of the things which I myself have studied and worked through. *My tongue is as the pen of a ready writer*" (v. 1). I will be guided by my heart in every word just as a pen is guided by the hand." We call the prophets the writers of Scripture, whereas in reality they were only the pens. The tongue of the most fluent arguer or the most eloquent orator is only the pen with which God writes what he pleases.

2. In these verses the Lord Jesus is described:

2.1. As most beautiful and precious in himself. It is a marriage song, and so the all-surpassing splendor of

Christ is described as the beauty of the royal bridegroom (v. 2): *Thou art fairer than the children of men*, than any of them. In v. 1, the psalmist wanted to speak *about* the King, but immediately he directs his speech *to* him. Those who feel wonder and devotion toward Christ love to go to him and tell him so. *Thou art fair*, you are *fairer than the children of men*.

2.2. As the great favorite of heaven. He is *fairer than the children of men*. He has grace, and he has this grace for us: *Grace is poured into thy lips* (v. 2). By his word, his promise, and his Gospel, the goodwill of God is made known to us and the good work of God is begun and carried out in us. The Gospel of grace is poured into his lips, for it *began to be spoken by the Lord* (Heb 2:3), and we receive it from him. He has the words of eternal life (Jn 6:68). The Aramaic reads, "The spirit of prophecy is put into thy lips." "And so, because you are the great trustee of divine grace for the benefit of people, *therefore God has blessed thee for ever* (v. 2). He has made you an eternal blessing, so that in you all the nations of the earth will be blessed" (Ge 18:18; 22:18; 26:4).

2.3. As victorious over all his enemies. The royal bridegroom is to rescue his bride from her slavery by the sword; he is to conquer her, and to conquer for her, and then to marry her.

2.3.1. His preparations for war (v. 3): *Gird thy sword upon thy thigh, O most mighty*. The word of God is the sword of the Spirit (Eph 6:17; Isa 49:2). By the promises of that word and the grace contained in those promises, souls are made willing to submit to Jesus Christ and become his loyal subjects. Many Jews and Gentiles were converted by the Gospel of Christ.

2.3.2. His going out to this holy war: he goes out *with his glory and his majesty* (v. 3), as a great king takes to the field with much display of splendor—his sword, glory, and majesty. In his Gospel, he appears surpassingly great and magnificent, glorious and blessed, in the honor and majesty which the Father has laid on him. Both in his person and his Gospel, Christ had no external glory or majesty, nothing to attract us, for he had no beauty or majesty (Isa 53:2), nothing to inspire reverence when he *took upon him the form of a servant* (Php 2:7). It was all his spiritual glory and majesty. *In thy majesty ride prosperously* (v. 4). "*Thy kingdom come*" (Mt 6:10); go on and triumph."

2.3.3. The glorious cause in which he is engaged— *because of truth, and meekness, and righteousness* (v. 4). These had to some extent sunk and become lost, and Christ came to retrieve and rescue them. The Gospel itself is *truth, meekness, and righteousness* (v. 4). It directs by the power of truth and righteousness, for Christianity has these incontrovertibly on its side, although it is to be declared with humility and gentleness (1Co 4:12–13; 2Ti 2:25). Christ appears in it in his *truth, meekness, and righteousness*, and these are his glory and majesty, and he will triumph because of these. People are brought to believe in him because he is true. They are brought to learn from him because he is humble (Mt 11:29): the gentleness of Christ is very powerful (2Co 10:1). They are brought to submit to him because he is righteous and rules with justice.

2.3.4. The success of his mission: *Thy right hand shall teach thee terrible things* (NIV: display awesome deeds) (v. 4). In order to bring about the conversion and submission of souls to him, awesome things need to be done; the heart must be pierced, conscience must be shocked, and the terrors of the Lord must make way for his comfort. The next verse describes these terrible things (v. 5): *Thy arrows are sharp in the heart of the king's enemies*. Those who were by nature enemies are wounded in this way, so that they may be subdued and reconciled. Convictions are like the arrows drawn by the bow, which pierce the heart to which they are directed and bring people to submit to Christ, in obedience to his laws and government.

Verses 6–9

We have here the royal bridegroom filling his throne with righteousness and keeping his court with splendor.

1. He here fills his throne with righteousness. It is God the Father who says to the Son, *Thy throne, O God, is for ever and ever* (v. 6), as appears in Heb 1:8–9, where this is quoted to prove that he is God and has *a more excellent name than the angels* (Heb 1:4). Notice what is said about his rule:

1.1. Its eternity: it is *for ever and ever*. It will continue on earth throughout all time. Even when the kingdom will be *delivered up to God even the Father* (1Co 15:24), the throne of the Redeemer will continue.

1.2. Its equity: *The sceptre of thy kingdom* (v. 6), the administration of your rule, *is right* and just, exactly according to the eternal counsel and will of God, which is the eternal basis and reason of good and evil.

1.3. Its establishment and elevation: *Therefore God, even thy God has anointed thee with the oil of gladness* (v. 7). Christ, as Mediator, called God *his God* (Jn 20:17), since he is commissioned by God and is the head of those who are taken into covenant with him. "As a reward for what you have done and suffered for the advancement of righteousness and the destruction of sin, God has anointed you with the oil of joy and has brought you all the honors and all the joys of your exalted state." *Because he humbled himself, God has highly exalted him* (Php 2:8–9). God's anointing him shows the power and glory to which he is exalted. He is given all the honor and authority of the Messiah.

2. He keeps his court with splendor and magnificence.

2.1. His robes of state, in which he appears, are taken notice of, not because of their pomp, which might strike awe on spectators, but because of the pleasant scents with which they are perfumed (v. 8): *They smell of myrrh, aloes, and cassia,* the *oil of gladness* with which he and his clothes are anointed. These were some of the ingredients of the holy anointing oil which God appointed, which was not to be put to any common use (Ex 30:23–24) and which was a type of the anointing of the Spirit which Christ, the great High Priest of our profession (Heb 3:1), received, and to which this therefore seems to refer.

2.2. His royal palaces are said to be *ivory* ones, which in those days were considered most magnificent. The rooms of light in heaven are the *ivory palaces* meant here; it is from heaven that all the joys both of Christ and of believers come, and it is there that those joys will be perfect forever.

2.3. The beautiful women of his court shine very brightly. Individual believers are here compared to the finely dressed ladies at court: *Kings' daughters are among thy honourable women.* All true believers are born from above (Jn 3:3); they are the children of the King of Kings. The church in general is compared here to the queen herself—the queen-consort, the wife of the king, whom, by an eternal covenant, he pledged to be married to. She stands *at his right hand in gold of Ophir* (v. 9). This is *the bride, the Lamb's wife* (Rev 21:9); her graces, which are her jewels, are compared to *fine linen, clean and white* (Rev 19:8), for their purity. Here they are compared to *gold of Ophir* (v. 9) for their costliness. For just as we

owe our redemption, so also we owe our adorning, not to corruptible things but to *the precious blood of the Son of God* (1Pe 1:19).

Verses 10–17

This final part of the psalm is addressed to the royal bride, standing on the right-hand side of the royal bridegroom. God, who said to the Son, *Thy throne is for ever and ever* (v. 6), speaks these words to the church.

1. He tells her of the duties expected of her, which should be considered by all those who come to know the Lord Jesus Christ: "*Hearken,* therefore, *and consider* this, *and incline thy ear* (v. 10), that is, submit to these conditions of your marriage and bring your will in line with them."

1.1. She must renounce all others. This is the law of marriage: *Forget thy own people and thy father's house* (v. 10). This shows:

1.1.1. How necessary it was for those who had converted from Judaism or paganism to the faith of Christ to completely get rid of the old yeast (1Co 5:7–8) and not to bring into their Christian profession either the Jewish ceremonies or foreign idolatries, for these would make Christianity into a hybrid religion, like that of the Samaritans.

1.1.2. How necessary it is for us all, when we come to follow Jesus Christ, to *hate* — in comparison — *father and mother* (Lk 14:26) and all that is dear to us in this world. This means we are to love them less than we love Christ. *So shall the king greatly desire thy beauty* (v. 11), which suggests that the mixing of her old rites and customs, whether Jewish or Gentile, with her religion, would spoil her beauty. The beauty of holiness, both in the church and individual believers, is very precious in the sight of Christ.

1.2. She must revere, love, honor, and obey him: *He is thy Lord, and worship thou him* (v. 11). We must worship him as God and our Lord, for this is the will of God, that *all men should honour the Son even as they honour the Father* (Jn 5:23).

2. He tells her of the honors intended for her:

2.1. People will pay great homage to her and give her rich presents (v. 12): "*The daughter of Tyre*" — a rich and splendid city — "the *daughter of the King of Tyre* will be *there with a gift*; every royal family around will send one of its members, as a representative of the whole family, to seek your favor and gain influence with you. *Even the rich among the people* will seek your favor, for the sake of the groom you are marrying, so that through you they may make him their friend."

2.2. She will be very splendid and highly respected in the eyes of all (v. 13): *The king's daughter is all glorious within.* The glory of the church is spiritual, and that is truly all glory. It is the glory of the soul, and that is within us as human beings; it is glory in God's sight, and it is a pledge of eternal glory. Although all her glory is within, *her clothing* also *is of wrought* (is interwoven with) *gold* (v. 13); the way of life of Christians, in which they live in the world, must be enriched by good works, like interwoven gold, which is worked with great care.

2.3. Her wedding will be celebrated with great honor and joy (vv. 14–15): *She shall be brought to the king.* No one is brought to Christ except those whom the Father brings, and he has undertaken to do this work. No one else is brought *to the king* in this way (v. 14) to *enter into the king's palace* (v. 15).

2.4. The offspring of this marriage will be distinguished (v. 16): *Instead of thy fathers shall be thy children.* Instead of the Old Testament church, the plan of which had become old and was ready to *vanish away* (Heb 8:13), as the ancestors were who were dying, there will be a New Testament church, grafted into the same olive (Ro 11:17).

2.5. The praise of this marriage will last forever in the praises of the royal bridegroom (v. 17): *I will make thy name to be remembered.* His Father has given him *a name above every name* (Php 2:9), and he here promises to make it last forever, by keeping up a succession of ministers and Christians in every age, who will lift his name high, and in this way it will therefore *endure for ever* (72:17).

PSALM 46

This psalm encourages us: 1. To take comfort in God when things look black and threatening (vv. 1–5). 2. To mention, to his praise, the great things he has worked for his church against its enemies (vv. 6–9); to assure ourselves that the God who has glorified his own name will glorify it again (Jn 12:28) (vv. 10–11).

Verses 1–5

The psalmist teaches us by his own example:

1. To triumph in God and in his presence with us, especially when we have had some fresh experiences of his appearing on our behalf (v. 1): *God is our refuge and strength.* Are we in distress? He is our help, an ever-present help, One whom we have found to be so, a tried-and-tested help, just as Christ is called a *tried stone* (Isa 28:16).

2. To triumph over the greatest dangers: *God is our strength and our help,* a God who is all-sufficient to us, and *therefore will not we fear* (v. 2). It is our duty, in fact our privilege, to be without fear in this way. It is a sign of a clear conscience, an honorable heart, and a living faith in God, his providence, and his promises. Notice here:

2.1. How threatening the danger is. Imagine the earth giving way and being thrown into the sea; the mountains, the strongest and firmest parts of the earth, lying buried in the uncharted depths of the ocean; the sea roaring and foaming so as even to *shake the mountains* (v. 3). Even if kingdoms and states are in confusion, caught up in wars, tossed about by tumults—even if their powers conspire to act together against the church and people of God—even if all these things happen, we will not be afraid, knowing that all these troubles will end well for the church.

2.2. How well founded the defiance of this danger is. It is not any private, individual concern of ours that we take pains for. It is the city of God, *the holy place of the tabernacles of the Most High,* the holy place where the Most High dwells (v. 4); it is the ark of God for which our hearts tremble (1Sa 4:13). But when we consider what God has provided for the strength and security of his church, we see every reason for our hearts to be settled and to be set above the fear of bad news. *There is a river the streams whereof shall make it glad,* even when the waters of the sea roar and threaten it. The covenant of grace is the river, the promises of which are the streams; or the Spirit of grace is the river (Jn 7:38–39), the comforts of whom are *the streams that make glad the city of our God* (v. 4). Although heaven and earth are shaken, yet *God is in the midst of her, she shall not be moved* (v. 5). The church will survive the world and will be happy when it is in ruins. God will help the church out of her troubles, *and that right early* (v. 5)—at the break of day, when morning comes, that is, very quickly, for he is *a present help* (v. 1). He will come promptly, when things are at their most critical point and when the relief is most welcome.

Verses 6–11

These verses give glory to God both as King of nations and as King of saints.

1. As King of nations. He restrains the rage and breaks the power of the nations who oppose him and his interests in the world (v. 6): *The heathen raged* (nations were in uproar) both at David's coming to the throne and at the setting up of the kingdom of the Son of David; compare 2:1–2. *The kingdoms were moved* (v. 6) with indignation and rose furiously and violently to oppose it, but God *uttered* (lifted) *his voice* (v. 6) and spoke to them in his wrath. They were then moved in a different sense: they were confounded and struck by terror. Such a melting of the spirits of the enemies is described in Jdg 5:4–5; see also Lk 21:25–26. When he wishes, he can cause havoc among the nations and devastate everything (v. 8): *Come, behold the works of the Lord;* they are to be observed (66:5) and pondered (111:2). War is a tragedy which commonly destroys the stage it is acted on; David took the war into the enemies' country, and it brought great desolation there. Stand in awe of God. Say, *How terrible art thou in thy works!* (66:3). When he wishes to put his sword back into the sheath, he brings to an end the wars of the nations and crowns them with peace (v. 9). *He makes wars to cease unto the end of the earth* (v. 9), sometimes out of compassion for the nations, that they may have a breathing space, when they have run out of breath because of long wars with each other. The total destruction of Gog and Magog is prophetically described by the burning of their weapons of war (Eze 39:9–10), which also suggests the church's perfect security and assurance of lasting peace, which made it unnecessary to store those weapons of war for their own use. The bringing of a long war to a peaceful outcome is a work of the Lord, which we should look at with thankfulness and wonder.

2. As King of saints, and because he is, we must acknowledge that *great and marvellous are his works* (Rev 15:3). He does and will do great things. Let his enemies be still and make no more threats, but know that God is God, that he is infinitely above them. Let them stop their raging, for it is all in vain: *he that sits in heaven laughs at them* (2:4), and in spite of all their powerless hatred he will be exalted in the earth, not merely in the church. People set themselves up, but let them know that God will be exalted. He will glorify his own name, and *wherein they deal proudly* (arrogantly) *he will be above them* (Ex 18:11), and he will make them know that he is so. Let his own people be still as well, and no longer tremble. Let them know, to their assurance, that the Lord is God. When we pray, *Father, glorify thy name,* we should have faith that the answer will be the same as that given to Christ when he himself prayed that prayer: *I have both glorified it and I will glorify it yet again* (Jn 12:28). Amen. Lord, so be it. Let all believers triumph in this. We have the presence of an almighty God: *The Lord of hosts is with us* (v. 11). This sovereign Lord is with us, he is on our side, and he acts with us and has promised he will never leave us. Armies may rise up against us, but we need not fear them if God Almighty is with us. We are under the protection of a God in covenant with his people, who not only is able to help them but also is committed to helping them in honor and faithfulness. He is the God of Jacob, not only Jacob the person but also Jacob the people.

In praying over and singing this psalm we may apply it either to our spiritual enemies and the encouragement we have to hope that through Christ we will be more than conquerors over them (Ro 8:37), or to the public enemies of Christ's kingdom in the world. It is said of Luther that when he heard any discouraging news, he would say, "Come let us sing Psalm 46."

PSALM 47

The scope of this psalm is to stir us up to praise God, and: 1. We are instructed how to do it: publicly, cheerfully, and intelligently (vv. 1, 6–7). 2. We are given great reasons for praise: God's majesty (v. 2); his sovereign and universal authority (vv. 7–9); the great things he has done, and will do, for his people (vv. 3–5). Many suppose that this psalm was written when the ark was brought up to Mount Zion, which v. 5 seems to refer to (God has gone up with a shout), but it looks farther, to the ascension of Christ to the heavenly Zion after he had completed his work on earth, and to the setting up of his kingdom in the world.

Verses 1–4

His own heart being filled with great and good thoughts of God, the psalmist tries to commit all those around him to celebrate who God is by praising him. Notice:

1. Who the people are who are called on to praise God: "*All you people* (v. 1), all you people of Israel"; so it may be taken as a prophecy of the conversion of the Gentiles and the bringing of them into the church; see Ro 15:11.

2. What they are called on to do: "*Clap your hands* (v. 1), as those who cannot contain themselves; *shout unto God* (v. 1), not to make him hear, but to make everyone around you hear. Shout *with the voice of triumph* (v. 1) in him, his power, and his goodness, so that others may join with you in such joy."

3. What is suggested to us as what we should praise God for. *The Lord most high is terrible, a King over all the earth* (v. 2). He takes special care of his people and their concerns, has done so, and will always do so. God had done this for Israel: he had planted them in Canaan, and they had continued there to this day. The kingdom of the Messiah was to be set over all the earth, and not confined to the Jewish nation. Jesus Christ will subdue the Gentiles; he will bring them in "as sheep into the fold"; this is the significance of v. 3: not that he will slaughter them, but that he will preserve them. *He shall choose our inheritance for us.* God had chosen the land of Canaan as an inheritance for Israel. It was the land which the Lord their God sought out for them; see Dt 32:8. And the setting up of God's sanctuary in it made it *the excellency, the pride and honor, of Jacob* (Am 6:8). We may apply this spiritually to:

- The happiness of the saints, that God himself has chosen their inheritance for them, and that he has stored up for them an imperishable inheritance in the next world (1Pe 1:4).
- The faith and submission of the saints to God. This is the language of every gracious soul: "God will choose my inheritance for me. He knows what is good for me better than I do myself, and so I will have no will of my own except what is submitted to his."

Verses 5–9

Should not subjects praise their king? God is our God, our King, and so we must praise him. But here is a necessary guideline added (v. 7): *Sing you praises with understanding,* "with *maskil.*"

- "Intelligently; as those who understand why they are praising God and what the meaning of the service is." This is the Gospel rule (1Co 14:15).
- "Instructively, as those who want to make others understand God's glorious nature, and to teach them to praise him."

1. We must praise God as One who has *gone up* (v. 5): *God has gone up with a shout.* This may refer:

1.1. To the carrying up of the ark to the hill of Zion. Because the ark was the instituted sign of God's special presence with them, when that was brought up by his authority he could be said to *go up.*

1.2. To the ascension of our Lord Jesus into heaven when he had completed his work on earth (Ac 1:9). Then *God went up with a shout* (v. 5), the shout of a King and conqueror.

2. We must praise God as One who *reigns* (vv. 7–8). *He sits upon the throne of his holiness* (v. 8), which he has prepared in the heavens, and he rules over all. Notice here the extent of God's government; all are born within his lordship; even the nations that serve other gods are ruled by the true God, our God, whether they want to be or not. Notice the justice of his government; it is a throne of holiness on which he sits, from which he issues warrants, orders, and judgments, and in which we are sure there is no sin. Jesus Christ, who is God, and whose *throne is for ever and ever* (Heb 1:8), *reigns over* the nations (v. 8). Not only is he entrusted with the government of the kingdom of providence, but he will also set up the kingdom of his grace in the Gentile world and rule in the hearts of many who were foreigners to the covenant of promise (Eph 2:12–13).

3. We must praise God as One who is served and honored by *the princes of the people* (v. 9).

3.1. It was the honor of Israel that they were *the people of the God of Abraham* (v. 9). They were fortunate to have a settled government, *princes of their people,* who were the *shields of their land* (v. 9). The judiciary is the shield of a nation, and it is a great blessing to any people to have a judiciary that *belongs unto the Lord,* is devoted to his honor and service. And it is to the honor of God that the *shields of the earth do belong to him,* in another sense (v. 9): the judiciary is his institution, and he serves his own purposes by it in ruling the world. The unanimous agreement of the leaders of a nation in matters concerning peace is a very good sign, which promises many blessings.

3.2. It may also be applied to the calling of the Gentiles into the church of Christ, and taken as a prophecy that the kings of the earth and their people would join the church in the days of the Messiah. When the *shields of the earth* (v. 9), the emblems of royal dignity (1Ki 14:27–28), are surrendered to the Lord Jesus—as the keys of a city are presented to its conqueror or sovereign—when nobles use their power to advance the interests of religious faith, then Christ is greatly exalted.

PSALM 48

This psalm, like the two previous psalms, is a song of triumph. Some think it was written on the occasion of Jehoshaphat's victory (2Ch 20); others think it was written at Sennacherib's defeat, when his army laid siege to Jerusalem in Hezekiah's time. Jerusalem is praised here: 1. For its relationship with God (vv. 1–2). 2. For God's care of it (v. 3). 3. For the terror it strikes on its enemies (vv. 4–7). 4. For the delight it gives its friends, who enjoy thinking about: 4.1. What God has done, does, and will do for it (v. 8). 4.2. The gracious revelations he makes of himself in and for that holy city (vv. 9–10). 4.3. The effective provision made for its security (vv. 11–13). 4.4. The assurance we have of the eternal nature of God's covenant with the children of Zion (v. 14).

Verses 1–7

What is said to the honor of Jerusalem is:

1. That he said kinder things about Zion than he ever said about any other place on earth. *This is my rest for ever; here will I dwell, for I have desired it* (132:13–14). It is *the city of the great King* (v. 2), the King of all the earth, who is pleased to declare himself present there in a special way. *In Judah God is known, and his name is great* (76:1), but especially in Jerusalem *God is great* (v. 1). It is therefore called *the mountain of his holiness* (v. 1), for *holiness to the Lord* is written on it and all its furnishings (Zec 14:20). God was known as a refuge not only in the streets of Jerusalem but even in its citadels. On all these accounts, Jerusalem, and especially Mount Zion, on which the temple was built, were universally beloved and *admired—beautiful for situation*, and *the joy of the whole earth* (v. 2). The situation of a city must be pleasing in every way when infinite Wisdom has chosen it as the place of the sanctuary. What made it beautiful was that it was his holy mountain, for there is beauty in holiness (29:2; 96:9; 2Ch 20:21). Mount Zion was on the north side of Jerusalem and so was a shelter to the city from the cold and bleak winds which blew from that region.

2. That the kings of the earth were afraid of it. The Israelites had had a great many reasons to fear their enemies, for *the kings were assembled* (v. 4). They advanced and marched together, not doubting they would soon control that city which could have brought joy to the whole earth, but which instead provoked the earth to envy. But the very sight of Jerusalem struck them with great apprehension and restrained their fury, just as the sight of the tents of Jacob frightened Balaam from his purposes in cursing Israel (Nu 24:2): *They saw it and marvelled, and hasted away* (v. 5). It was not that there was anything visible in Jerusalem that was so formidable, but the sight of it brought to mind what they had heard about the special presence of God in that city and the divine protection it was under. They still knew they were an unequal match for almighty God, and so *fear came upon them, and pain* (v. 6). The shock they were in when they saw Jerusalem is here compared to the pangs of a woman in labor. The defeat of their intentions against Jerusalem here is compared to the terrible destruction of a fleet of ships in a violent storm, when some are split, others shattered, and all are dispersed (v. 7).

Verses 8–14

1. Let our faith in the word of God be confirmed by this. "What we have heard was accomplished in former providences, in the days of old, we have seen accomplished now, in our own days. We have heard that God is God Almighty, that Jerusalem is the city of our God, and that it is dear to him and is under his special care, and now we have seen it. We have seen the power of our God, his goodness, and his care and concern for us, and he is a *wall of fire round about Jerusalem and the glory in the midst of her*" (Zec 2:5).

2. Let our hope for the stability and eternity of the church be encouraged by this. "From what we have seen in the city of our God, and from comparing what we have seen with what we have heard, we conclude that God will

establish it forever." This was not fulfilled in Jerusalem—that city has long since been destroyed, and all its glory laid in the dust—but is fulfilled in the Gospel church.

3. Let our minds be filled with good thoughts of God from this. "From what we have heard and seen and what we hope for, let us think very much about God's unfailing love whenever we meet in the midst of his temple" (v. 9).

4. Let us give God the glory for the great things he has done for us and talk about them to his honor (v. 10): "*According to thy name, O God, so is thy praise*, not only in Jerusalem but also to the ends of the earth." As far as his name goes, so far will his praise go—at least, so far it should go; and finally it will go so far, when all the ends of the world will praise him (22:27; Rev 11:15). Some understand *his name* to refer especially to that glorious name of his, *the Lord of hosts* (v. 8). According to that name, so is his praise, for all the creatures are under his command, even to the ends of the earth.

5. Let all the members of the church especially be strengthened and encouraged by what God does for his church in general (v. 11): "*Let Mount Zion rejoice*, let the priests and Levites who serve in the sanctuary, and then let all *the daughters of Judah*, the country towns, and their inhabitants, be glad. Let the women sing and dance, as they usually do on occasions of public joy, and celebrate with thankfulness the great salvation which God has worked for us."

6. Let us diligently observe the examples and signs of the church's beauty, strength, and security, and let us faithfully pass on our observations to those who come after us (vv. 12–13): *Walk about Zion.* Some think this refers to the ceremony of a triumphant procession: Let those who are involved in that ceremony walk around the walls, as the people did in Ne 12:31, singing and praising God. In doing this, let them *tell* (count) *the towers and mark well the bulwarks* (ramparts) and exalt the way that God has recently and wonderfully rescued them. Let them notice, with wonder, that the towers and ramparts are strong in all respects and undamaged by the kings who had gathered against the city. *Tell this to the generation following* (v. 13) as a wonderful example of God's care for his holy city. *Mark ye well her bulwarks* (v. 13). This sentence may also be read, *Set your hearts on her bulwarks*, which suggests that the main ramparts of Zion were not physical objects, which the people could set their eyes on, but the objects of faith, which they must set their hearts on. Calvin observes here that when the people are directed to pass on to future generations a particular account of the towers, ramparts, and citadels of Jerusalem, it is implied that in the course of time these will all be destroyed and no longer remain visible, for otherwise, why was there a need to preserve their description and history? When the disciples were wondering at the buildings of the temple, their Master told them that in a little time one stone there would not be *left upon another* (Mt 24:1–2). This verse must therefore certainly be applied to the Gospel church. See it founded on Christ, the rock strengthened by divine power, guarded by the One who neither slumbers nor sleeps (121:4).

7. Let us triumph in God and in the assurances we have of his eternal, unfailing love (v. 14). Speak about this to the next generation: that *this God*, who has now done such great things for us, *is our God for ever and ever*. If he is our God, *he will be our guide*, our faithful and constant guide. He will be our guide "above death," as some understand this; he will guide us in such a way as to set us above the reach of death. He will be our guide "beyond death,"

according to others. He will lead us safely to happiness on the other side of death, to a life in which there will be no more death.

PSALM 49

This psalm is a sermon, and so is the next. In most of the psalms we have the writer praying or praising; in these we have him preaching. 1. In the introduction, the psalmist proposes to wake worldly people up from their false security (vv. 1–3) and to comfort himself and other godly people in the day of trouble (vv. 4–5). 2. In the rest of the psalm: 2.1. He tries to convince sinners how foolish they are in devoting themselves to the wealth of this world, by showing them that they cannot, with all their wealth, save their friends from death (vv. 6–9); they cannot save themselves from death (v. 10); they cannot assure themselves of happiness in this world (vv. 11–12); and much less can they assure themselves of happiness in the other world (v. 14). 2.2. He tries to encourage himself and other good people against the fear of death (v. 15) and against the fear of the prospering power of evildoers (vv. 16–20).

Verses 1–5

This is the psalmist's introduction to his speech about the worthlessness of the world and its inability to make us happy.

1. He demands the attention of others (vv. 1–2): *Hear, all you people, and give ear* (listen), *all you inhabitants of the world* (v. 1), for this teaching is not exclusive to those who are blessed with divine revelation; even the light of nature bears witness to it to all people. Everyone may know, and so let everyone consider, that their riches will not profit them in the day of death. Poor people are in as much danger from an excessive desire for the wealth of the world as rich people are from excessively delighting in it. *My mouth shall speak of wisdom.* What he has to say is wisdom and insight; it will make those who receive it wise and understanding. It is what he himself has well digested.

2. He engages his own attention (v. 4): *I will incline my ear to a parable.* It is called *a parable* not because it is figurative and obscure but because it is wise and instructive (Pr 1:2). It is the same word that is used for Solomon's proverbs. Those who undertake to teach others must first learn themselves.

3. He promises to make the matter as clear and moving as possible: *I will open my dark saying upon the harp,* I will expound my riddle with the harp (v. 4). Some did not understand it; it was a puzzle to them. If you tell such people about the worthlessness of visible things and of the reality and importance of invisible things, they say, *Ah Lord God! doth he not speak parables?* (Eze 20:49). Others understood it well enough, but they were not moved by it. It never affected them, and he would open it up on the harp for their sake, and try that method to see if it would work on them and win them. As the poet George Herbert wrote, "A verse may find him who a sermon flies."

4. He begins by applying it to himself: *Wherefore* (Why) *should I fear?* (v. 5); he means, *Wherefore should I fear their fear* (Isa 8:12), the fears of worldly people? "Why should I be afraid *of* them? Why should I fear when days of evil and persecution come, *when the iniquity of my heels shall compass me about* (v. 5), when my enemies who surround me try to trip me up with all their attempts to deceive me? Why should I be afraid of all those whose power lies in their wealth? I will not fear

their power, for it cannot help them destroy me." But also, "Why should I be afraid *like* them?" In the Day of Judgment the *iniquity of our heels* (v. 5)—or of our steps, our past sins—will surround us, and it will be set out before us. In these days, worldly evildoers will be afraid; there will be nothing more terrible to those who have set their hearts on the world than to think of leaving it. Why should good people fear death, however, when they have God with them (23:4)?

Verses 6–14

In these verses we have:

1. A description of the spirit and ways of worldly people, whose reward is in this life (17:14). People may have great worldly wealth and be made better by it, their hearts may be released in love, thankfulness, and obedience, and they may do good with it which will be credited to their account. It is not, therefore, because people have riches that they are called worldly, but because they set their hearts on them as what is best. These worldly people are here described: *They trust in their wealth* (v. 6); they depend on it as their reward and basis for happiness. They put their security in gold (Job 31:24), and so it becomes their god. This is why our Savior explains the difficulty of the salvation of rich people (Mk 10:24): *How hard is it for those that trust in riches to enter into the kingdom of God!* See also 1Ti 6:17. *They* therefore *call their lands after their own names* (v. 11), hoping that will make them remembered forever, and if their lands do keep the names by which they called them, it is a poor honor; but the name of a property is often changed with the change of owner. *Their inward thought is that their houses shall continue for ever,* and they please themselves with this thought.

2. A demonstration of their foolishness in these matters. In general (v. 13), *This their way is their folly.* To the one who thought his goods were laid up for many years and that they would be an inheritance for his soul, God himself declared, *Thou fool* (Lk 12:19–20). The love of this world is a disease that runs in the blood; people have it naturally, and they will keep it until the grace of God heals it.

2.1. With all their wealth worldly people cannot save the life of the dearest friend they have in the world, nor can they "buy time" for someone who is arrested by death (vv. 7–9). But this looks further, to the eternal redemption that was to be brought by the Messiah. Eternal life is a jewel of too great a value to be bought by the wealth of this world. We are *not redeemed with corruptible things, such as silver and gold* (1Pe 1:18–19). Christ achieved something for us which all the riches of the world could not do; it is therefore right that he be dearer to us than any worldly thing. Christ achieved something for us which a brother, sister, or friend could not do for us, in fact, which no one with the greatest wealth or influence could do, and so those who *love father or brother more than him are not worthy of him* (Mt 10:37).

2.2. With all their wealth they cannot protect themselves from the attack of death. Some rich people are wise politicians, but even they cannot use all their skill to outwit death or evade its stroke. Others are *fools and brutish* (senseless) (v. 10); although such people do no good, perhaps they also do no great harm in the world. That, however, will not excuse them. They will perish and be taken away by death just as certainly as the wise were who caused trouble with all their deceit.

2.3. As their wealth will not help them in their hour of death, so neither will their honor (v. 12): *Man, being in honour, abides not.* Imagine someone promoted to the highest rung on the career ladder, who is as great and happy as the world can make them, someone magnificent; they will not endure. Their honor does not last; it is a mere fleeting shadow.

2.4. Their condition on the other side of death will be very miserable. While saints can ask proud death, *Where is thy sting?* (1Co 15:55), death will ask proud sinners, "Where is your wealth, your pomp?" The beauty of holiness is something that the grave, which consumes every other beauty, cannot touch or damage in any way.

Verses 15–20

Here are good reasons given to good people as to:

1. Why they should not be afraid of death. There is no reason for that fear if they have such an encouraging prospect as David had here of a happy state on the other side of death (v. 15). The confident hope of the soul's redemption from the grave and reception to glory are the great support and joy of the children of God in the hour of death. They are confident:

1.1. That God will redeem their souls from the power of the grave, which includes:

1.1.1. The preserving of the soul from going to the grave with the body. The grave has power over the body because of the sentence in Ge 3:19, and it is unyielding enough in carrying out that power (SS 8:6), but it has no such power over the soul. It has power to silence, imprison, and consume the body, but the soul then moves, acts, and converses more freely than ever (Rev 6:9–10); it is immaterial and immortal. When death breaks the dark lantern, it cannot extinguish the flame that was confined in it.

1.1.2. The reuniting of the soul and body at the resurrection. *God shall redeem my soul from the sheol of hell* (v. 15), and so the first death has no sting and the grave has no victory.

1.2. That God will receive them to himself. He redeems their souls so that he may receive them. *Into thy hands I commit my spirit, for thou hast redeemed it* (31:5). He will receive them into his favor, and he will admit them into his kingdom, into the rooms (Jn 14:2–3), the eternal dwellings (Lk 16:9), prepared for them.

2. Why they should not be afraid of the prosperity and power of evildoers in this world.

2.1. He supposes the temptation to be very strong to envy the prosperity of sinners, for he supposes they are made rich, and so are enabled to be the law to everyone around them and have everything at their command. They are at ease and secure in themselves and in their own minds (v. 18): *In his lifetime he blessed his soul,* that is, he thought he was very happy because he was successful in the world. Believers *bless themselves in the God of truth* (Isa 65:16) and think they are happy if he is theirs; worldly people bless themselves with the wealth of the world and think they are happy if they have great riches. They applaud in themselves that which God condemns and speak peace to themselves when God declares war against them. Yet the second half of the verse may refer to the good man, not the evildoer, for it is in the second person: "Worldly people exalted themselves; but you do not, like them, *speak* well of yourself. Instead, you *do* well for yourself, by making sure of your eternal welfare. You will be praised, if not by other people, then by God, which will be to your eternal honor."

2.2. He suggests what is sufficient to take away the strength of the temptation, by directing us to look forward to the final destiny of prosperous sinners (v. 17; see

also 73:17). *When he dies*, it is assumed that he goes into another world himself, but *he shall carry nothing away with him* of all what he has been accumulating for so long. Grace is glory that will ascend with us, but no earthly glory will descend with us. *The soul shall go to the generation of his fathers,* his worldly, corrupt ancestors, whose sayings he approved of and whose steps he followed in, his ancestors who would not listen to the word of God (Zec 1:4). A fool—an evildoer—with riches, is really as contemptible an animal as any under the sun; such people are *like the beasts that perish* (v. 20). In fact, it is better to be an animal than to be a human being who makes himself or herself like an animal.

In praying over and singing this psalm, let us receive these instructions and be wise (2:10).

PSALM 50

This psalm, like the previous one, is a psalm of instruction, not of prayer or praise. God by his prophet deals in this psalm with those who are, in profession, the church's children, to convict them of their sin and foolishness in putting their trust in ritual services while they have neglected practical godliness. It is a proof to worldly Jews, both those who based their religious faith on the external ceremonies and neglected the superior duties of prayer and praise, and those who explained the law to others, but themselves led evil lives. It is also a prediction of the abolition of the ceremonial law and the introduction of a spiritual way of worship, in and through the kingdom of the Messiah (Jn 4:23–24). Finally, it is a representation of the Day of Judgment, in which God will call people to give an account of how they have observed those things which they have been taught. People will be judged according to those things which are written in the books (Rev 20:12), and so when Christ speaks as a Lawgiver, he is appropriately described as speaking as a Judge.

Here is: 1. The glorious appearance of the Prince who gives law and judgment (vv. 1–6). 2. Instruction given to his worshipers to turn their sacrifices into prayers (vv. 7–15). 3. A rebuke given to those who claim to worship God but lead lives of disobedience to his commands (vv. 16–20), their condemnation read (vv. 21–22), and warning given to all to attend to their lives as well as their devotions (v. 23).

Title

It is probable that Asaph was not only the chief musician, who put a tune to this psalm, but also the author of it; in Hezekiah's time the people praised God *in the words of David and of Asaph the seer* (2Ch 29:30).

Verses 1–6

Here is:

1. The court called in the name of the King of kings (v. 1): *The mighty God, even the Lord, hath spoken*—El, Elohim, Jehovah, the God of infinite power, justice, and mercy, Father, Son, and Holy Spirit. God is the Judge, the Son of God came into this world for judgment (Jn 9:39), and the Holy Spirit is the Spirit of judgment (Isa 4:4; 26:4). All the earth is called to attend.

2. The judgment set and the Judge taking his seat. Just as when God gave the Law to Israel in the desert, it was said, *He came from Sinai, and rose up from Seir; and shone forth from Mount Paran, and came with ten thousands of his saints, and then from his right hand went a fiery law* (Dt 33:2), so also, with allusion to that, when

God comes to rebuke them for their hypocrisy and declare his Gospel to take the place of the legal institutions, it is said here:

2.1. That *he shall shine out of Zion*, as on that earlier occasion he shone from the top of Sinai (v. 2). Because his sanctuary was now established in Zion, it would be from there that his judgments would be declared against that offensive people, and from there that orders would be issued to carry them out (Joel 2:1): *Blow you the trumpet in Zion*. The Gospel, which set up spiritual worship, was to *go forth from Mount Zion* (Isa 2:3; Mic 4:2), and its preachers were to *begin at Jerusalem* (Lk 24:47). Zion is here called *the perfection of beauty* (v. 2), because it was the holy hill, and holiness is indeed perfect beauty.

2.2. That he *shall come, and not keep silence* (v. 3). He will no longer seem to ignore human sins, as he had (v. 21), but will show his displeasure at them and declare that the barrier of the ceremonial law is to be taken down (Eph 2:14); this will now no longer be concealed. In the great day *our God shall come and shall not keep silence* (v. 3), but will make those who would not listen to his law hear his judgment.

2.3. That his appearance will be majestic and terrible: *A fire shall devour before him* (v. 3). The fire of his judgments will make way for the rebukes of his word, in order to awaken the hypocritical people of the Jews, so that sinners in Zion may become afraid of that devouring fire (Isa 33:14) and be shocked out of their sins. When his Gospel kingdom was to be set up, Christ *came to send fire on the earth* (Lk 12:49). The Spirit was given in what seemed to be tongues of fire, introduced by a sound like the blowing of a violent wind (Ac 2:2–3). And in the Last Judgment Christ will come in blazing fire (2Th 1:7–8).

2.4. That just as on Mount Sinai he came with thousands upon thousands of his saints (Dt 33:2; Jude 14), so now he will *call to the heavens from above*, to take notice of this sacred trial (v. 4).

3. The parties summoned (v. 5): *Gather my saints together unto me*. This may be understood as referring to either:

3.1. True saints. When God rejects the services of those who only offered sacrifices, trusting in their external actions, he will graciously accept those who in sacrificing *make a covenant with him*, and thereby serve and fulfill the purpose of the institution of sacrifices. It is only by sacrifice — by Christ the great sacrifice, from whom all the legal sacrifices derived what value they had — that we poor sinners can enter into the covenant relationship with God and be accepted by him. Or:

3.2. Professing saints, such as the people of Israel, who are called *a kingdom of priests* and *a holy nation* (Ex 19:6).

4. The outcome of this sacred trial foretold (v. 6): *The heavens shall declare his righteousness*, those heavens that were called to be witnesses to the trial (v. 4). The *people in heaven shall say, Hallelujah. As the heavens declare the glory*, wisdom, and power of God the Creator (19:1), so also, and no less, they will openly declare the glory, justice, and righteousness of God the *Judge*. They will declare both so loudly that *there is no speech nor language where their voice is not heard* (19:3).

Verses 7–15

God here deals with those who have put all their trust in the observances of the ceremonial law and think those are sufficient.

1. He lays down the original contract between him and Israel.

2. He spurns the legal sacrifices (vv. 8–13). Now:

2.1. This may be considered as looking back to their use under the Law. God had a dispute with the Jews, but what was the basic reason for this conflict? They thought God was greatly indebted to them for the many sacrifices they had brought to his altar, but God here showed them he did not need their sacrifices. What need did he have for their bulls and goats when he has command of all *the beasts of the forest*, and the *cattle upon a thousand hills* (vv. 9–10)? God's infinite self-sufficiency proves our complete insufficiency to add anything to him. He could not gain any benefit from their sacrifices. *Will I eat the flesh of bulls?* It is as absurd to think that their sacrifices could, in themselves, and because of any innate goodness in them, give God any more delight, as it would be to imagine that an infinite Spirit could be supported by food and drink, as our bodies are. No; *to obey is better than sacrifice* (1Sa 15:22), and to love God and our neighbor *better than all burnt offerings* (Mk 12:33).

2.2. This may be considered as looking forward to the abolishing of the old sacrificial ways of worship by the Gospel of Christ. When God sets up the kingdom of the Messiah, he will abolish the old ways of worship by sacrifice and offerings; he will no more need these to be *continually before him* (v. 8). He will no more require his worshipers to bring him their bulls and their goats, to be burned on his altar (v. 9).

3. He points to the best sacrifices of prayer and praise as those offerings which, under the law, were preferred to all burnt offerings and sacrifices; even then, it was on these better sacrifices that the greatest emphasis was laid, and now, under the Gospel, they come in place of those worldly ordinances which were imposed until the times of reformation. He shows us here (vv. 14–15) what is good, and what the Lord our God requires of us and will accept (Mic 6:8), when sacrifices have been superseded.

3.1. We must come in repentance and acknowledge our sins: "Offer to God confession." *A broken and contrite heart* is the sacrifice which *God will not despise* (51:17). If the sin was not abandoned, the sin offering was not accepted.

3.2. We must give God thanks for his mercies to us: *Offer to God thanksgiving* (v. 14) every day, and often every day — *seven times a day will I praise thee* (119:164). *This shall please the Lord*, if it comes from a humble, thankful heart, full of love for him and joy in him, *better than an ox or bullock that has horns and hoofs* (69:30–31).

3.3. We must be careful to fulfill our covenants with him: *Pay thy vows to the Most High* (v. 14). Leave your sins, and do your duty better. Dr. Henry Hammond applies this to the great Gospel ordinance of the Eucharist, in which we are to give thanks to God for his great love in sending his Son to save us. Instead of all the Old Testament types of a Christ to come, we have that blessed memorial of a Christ already come.

3.4. In times of trouble we must turn to God in faithful and fervent prayer (v. 15): *Call upon me in the day of trouble*.

Verses 16–23

Having instructed his people through the psalmist in the right way to worship him, God here speaks to evildoers and hypocrites.

1. The charge brought against them.

1.1. They are charged with invading and usurping the honors and privileges of religion (v. 16): *What hast thou to do*, O evildoer, *to declare my statutes*, what right have you to recite my laws? This is a challenge to those who appear godly but who are really worldly, to show what entitlement or authority they have to wear the cloak of religion. Some think it points prophetically to the scribes and Pharisees who were the teachers and leaders of the Jewish church at the time when the kingdom of the Messiah and the Gospel way of worship spoken of in vv. 7–15 were to be set up. They violently opposed that great change and used all the power and influence which they had from sitting in Moses' seat (Mt 23:2–3) to prevent it; the account which our blessed Savior gives of them (Mt 23), and the apostle Paul (Ro 2:21–22), makes this remonstration fit them very well. They took it on themselves to recite God's laws, but they hated Christ's teaching; and so how could they explain the law, when they rejected the Gospel? But the verse also applies to all those who practice iniquity but profess godliness, especially if they also preach it.

1.2. They are charged with breaking and disobeying the laws and commands of religious faith. They are charged with:

1.2.1. A defiant contempt for the word of God (v. 17): *Thou hatest instruction.* They loved to give instruction, to tell others what they should do, as this fed their pride, but they hated to receive instruction from God himself, for that would humble them. *Thou castest my words behind thee* (v. 17).

1.2.2. A close alliance with the worst of sinners (v. 18): "*When thou sawest a thief,* instead of rebuking him, *thou consentedst with him,* you approved of his practices and even wanted to share in the profits of his cursed trade. *Thou hast* also *been partaker with adulterers.*"

1.2.3. A constant persistence in the worst sins of the tongue (v. 19): "*Thou givest thy mouth to evil.* You not only allow yourself to engage in, but also completely devote yourself to, speaking all kinds of evil." They lie: *Thy tongue frames deceit* (v. 19). They slander (v. 20): "*Thou sittest, and speakest against thy brother*; you corruptly abuse and misrepresent him. *Thou sittest* and do this, as a judge on the bench, who has authority. You sit in the seat of the scornful (1:1), to deride and slander those whom you should respect and be kind to."

2. The proof of this charge (v. 21): "*These things thou hast done.* The facts are too clear to be denied; the fault is too bad to be excused. God knows these things, and your own heart also knows what you have done."

3. The Judge's patience and the sinner's abuse of that patience: "*I kept silence* (v. 21), I did not disturb you in your sinful ways, but left you alone to take your course. Sentence against your evil works was delayed and not carried out quickly." His patience is even more wonderful because sinners make such wrong use of it. Sinners take God's silence as his agreement, and they take his patience as his "turning a blind eye" to their sin, and so the longer the delay in the coming of their punishment, the more their hearts are hardened.

4. The fair warning given of the dreadful fate of hypocrites (v. 22): "*Now consider this, you that forget God*; consider that God knows and keeps account of all your sins. Patience abused will turn to greater wrath, for if these things are not considered, and the consideration of them not made the most of, he will *tear you in pieces, and there will be none to deliver*" (v. 22).

5. Full instructions given to us all about how to prevent this fearful condemnation.

5.1. The chief purpose of human beings is to glorify God, and we are told here that *whoso offers praise glorifies him*; whether they are Jew or Gentile, those spiritual sacrifices will be accepted from them. We must praise God, direct our sacrifice of praise to God (Heb 13:15), as every sacrifice was directed. We must see to it that the sacrifice is made by sacred fire, that it is kindled with the flame of holy and devout affection.

5.2. The chief purpose of human beings, in conjunction with this, is to enjoy God, and we are told here that those who *order their conversation aright* (consider their ways) *shall see his salvation* (v. 23). Thanksgiving is good, but "thanksliving" is even better.

PSALM 51

This psalm is the most outstanding of the penitential psalms, and the most expressive of the cares and desires of a repenting sinner. In this psalm: 1. David confesses his sin (vv. 3–6). 2. He prays fervently for his sin to be pardoned (vv. 1–2, 7, 9); for peace of conscience (vv. 8, 12); for grace to go and sin no more (Jn 8:11) (vv. 10–11, 14); and for free access to God (v. 15). 3. He promises to do what he can for the good of the souls of others (v. 13) and for the glory of God (vv. 16–17, 19). He concludes with a prayer for Zion and Jerusalem (v. 18).

Title

The title refers to a very sad story, that of David's fall.

1. The sin which he mourns in this psalm is the foolishness and wickedness he committed with his neighbor's wife. This sin of David's is recorded as a warning to us all, that those who think they are standing should be careful that they do not fall (1Co 10:12).

2. He was brought to the repentance he expresses in this psalm through the ministry of Nathan, who was sent by God to convict him of his sin. But those who have been overtaken in any sin (Gal 6:1) should regard a faithful rebuke as the greatest kindness that can be shown them, and they should regard a wise rebuker as their best friend (Pr 27:6). *Let the righteous smite* (strike) *me, and it shall be excellent oil* (141:5).

3. Because David had been convicted of his sin, he poured out his soul to God in prayer for mercy and grace.

4. By divine inspiration he wrote about the activity of his heart toward God in a psalm on this occasion.

Verses 1–6

In these verses we have:

1. David's humble petition (vv. 1–2). His prayer is much the same as what our Savior puts into the mouth of the penitent tax collector in the parable: *God be merciful to me a sinner* (Lk 18:13). David does not balance out the evil he has done with the good he has done, nor does he think his services will atone for his offenses. No; he flees to God's infinite mercy and depends only on that for pardon and peace: *Have mercy upon me, O God!* (v. 1). Notice:

1.1. What his plea is for this mercy: "Have mercy on me, O God! Have mercy on me for mercy's sake. I have nothing to plead with you except:

- "The freeness of your mercy according to your unfailing love, your great compassion, and the goodness of your nature, which makes you pity those in great need.
- "The fullness of your mercy."

1.2. What is the particular mercy that he begs—the pardon of sin. *Blot out my transgressions,* as a debt is blotted or crossed out in an accounts book, when either the debtor has paid the amount owed or the creditor has canceled it. *"Wash me thoroughly from my iniquity.* Cleanse me from my sin."* Nathan has assured David, when he first professed repentance, that his sin is pardoned. *The Lord has put away thy sin; thou shalt not die* (2Sa 12:13). But he still prays, *Wash me, cleanse me, blot out my transgressions.* God has forgiven him, but he cannot forgive himself, and so he boldly seeks pardon.

2. David's penitential confessions (vv. 3–5).

2.1. He was very free in acknowledging his guilt before God: *I acknowledge my transgressions* (v. 3). He had formerly found this to be the only way to relieve his conscience (32:4–5). Nathan said, *Thou art the man* (2Sa 12:7) *I am,* said David; *I have sinned* (v. 4).

2.2. He had such a deep sense of his sin that he was thinking about it continually with sorrow and shame. *"My sin is ever before me* (v. 3). It is always against me."

2.2.1. He confesses his actual transgressions (v. 4): *Against thee, thee only, have I sinned.* If the best people sin, they should set the best examples of repentance. David declared his confession of sin publicly so that when he came into trouble later, no one could say God had committed any wrong against him, for he acknowledged that the Lord is righteous. All true penitents will, like David, justify God by condemning themselves. *Thou art just in all that is brought upon us* (Ne 9:33).

2.2.2. He confesses his original corruption (v. 5): *Behold, I was shapen in iniquity.* David elsewhere speaks of the marvelous structure of his body (139:14–15); it was *curiously wrought* (woven together), he says. But here he says it was sinful at birth, that sin was twisted in with it. This was not as it came out of God's hands. It is to be sadly mourned by each of us that we have brought into this world a corrupt nature with us, wretchedly degenerated from its original purity and rightness. This is what we call "original sin," because it is as ancient as our origin and because it is the origin of all our actual sins. It is a bias to turn away from God.

3. David's acknowledgment of the grace of God (v. 6), both his goodwill toward us and his good work in us. His goodwill toward us: *"thou desirest truth in the inward parts,* you want us to be completely upright and sincere, and true to our profession." His good work in us: *"In the hidden part thou havest made me to know wisdom,"* or, as our text reads, *"shalt make me to know wisdom"* (v. 6). Truth and wisdom will go a long way toward making someone good. God himself works in us what God requires of us, and he does so in the normal way, by enlightening the mind and thereby gaining the will. David was conscious of the uprightness of his heart toward God in his repentance, and so he did not doubt that God would accept him. He hoped that God would enable him to live up to his decision, that in the hidden part, in his inner self, the *hidden man of the heart* (1Pe 3:4), he would teach him wisdom so that he could discern and avoid the intentions of the tempter another time.

Verses 7–13

1. Notice what David prays for. He here offers many requests, which, if we only add to them, "for Christ's sake," are as much according to the Gospel as any other requests.

1.1. He prays that God would cleanse him from his sins and from the defilement of them that he had become infected with (v. 7): *Purge me with hyssop.* The expression here alludes to a ceremonial separation of a person with an infectious skin disease, or of those who had

become unclean by touching a dead body; such persons were cleansed by a sprinkling on them of water or blood, or both, with a bunch of hyssop; and by this cleansing they were finally discharged from the restraints they were placed under because of their defilement. "Lord, let me be as well assured of my restoration to your favor, and to the privileges of fellowship with you, as such persons are assured of their readmission to their former privileges." But the expression is based on the grace of the Gospel: *Purge me with hyssop,* that is, "with the blood of Christ applied to my soul by a living faith," as the blood of purification was sprinkled with a bunch of hyssop. It is the blood of Christ—which is therefore called *the blood of sprinkling* (Heb 12:24)—that purges the conscience from dead works, from the guilt of sin and fear of God which exclude us from fellowship with him, just as, under the Law, coming into contact with a dead body excluded a man from the courts of God's house.

1.2. He prays that because his sins have been pardoned, he might have the assurance of that pardon. He does not ask to be comforted until he is first cleansed, but if the bitter root of sin is taken away (Dt 29:18; Heb 12:15), he can pray in faith, *"Make me to hear joy and gladness* (v. 8), that is, let me have a well-founded peace that you have created and spoken, *so that the bones which thou has broken* by your conviction and threats *may rejoice."* The pain of a heart that has been truly crushed because of sin may well be compared with the pain of a broken bone. The same Spirit who as a Spirit of slavery strikes and wounds is also as a Spirit of adoption (Ro 8:15) who heals and binds up (Hos 6:1).

1.3. He prays for complete and effective pardon. This is what he seeks most fervently as the basis of his assurance (v. 9): *"Hide thy face from my sins,* that is, do not be provoked by them to deal with me as I deserve. They are always before me, but let them be put behind your back. *Blot out all my iniquities* from your accounts book; blot them out, just as a cloud is blotted out and dispelled by the rays of the sun" (Isa 44:22).

1.4. He prays for sanctifying grace. His great concern is to get his corrupt nature changed, and so he prays, *"Create in me a clean heart, O God! Lord, renew a right spirit within me* (v. 10); repair the decay of spiritual strength. Renew a constant and steadfast spirit within me." He has discovered much inconsistency and unfaithfulness within himself in this matter, and so he prays, "Lord, establish me in the future, so that I may never depart from you in the same way again."

1.5. He prays for the continuation of God's goodwill toward him and the progress of his good work in him (v. 11). *"Cast me not away from thy presence,* as one whom you despise and cannot bear to look at. *Take not thy Holy Spirit from me."* (v. 11). We are ruined if God takes away his Holy Spirit from us. Saul was a sad example of this. How completely sinful and miserable he was when the Spirit of the Lord departed from him! David knows it, and so he begs fervently: "Lord, whatever you take away from me, my children, my crown, or my life, *take not thy Holy Spirit from me"* (v. 11).

1.6. He prays for the restoration of divine assurance and the constant flow of divine grace (v. 12). *Restore unto me the joy of thy salvation.* A child of God knows no true or solid joy except the joy of God's salvation, and joy in God their Savior and in the hope of eternal life. *"Uphold me with thy free Spirit* (v. 12): I am ready to fall, either into sin or into despair, but Lord, sustain me. My own spirit is not sufficient. If I am left to myself, I will certainly sink."

2. Notice what David promises (v. 13): *I will teach transgressors thy ways.* He himself has broken God's law, and so he can speak from experience to others who have. Because he has found mercy with God through repentance, he can teach other people God's ways. Penitents should be preachers. *Sinners shall be converted unto thee,* will turn back to you (v. 13).

Verses 14–19

1. David prays against the guilt of sin and prays for the grace of God. He supports both requests with a plea taken from the glory of God, which he promises to declare with thankfulness. The specific sin he prays against is blood-guilt, the sin he has now been guilty of, having killed Uriah with the sword of the children of Ammon. He promises that if God would save him, *his tongue would sing aloud of his righteousness* (v. 14); God would have the glory both of pardoning mercy and of preventing grace. He prays for the grace of God and promises to use that grace to his glory (v. 15): *"O Lord, open thou my lips,* not only so I may teach and instruct sinners but also so *that my mouth may show forth thy praise,* so that I may have a heart released in praise." Guilt had closed up his lips, and so he had little confidence toward God. To those who are tongue-tied because of their guilt the assurance of forgiveness says effectively, *Ephphatha,* "Be opened" (Mk 7:34). When the lips are opened, what should they speak but the praises of God?

2. David offers the sacrifice of a penitent and contrite heart. He knew that the sacrifices of animals were in themselves not significant with God (v. 16). As they cannot make atonement for sin, so God cannot take any satisfaction in them, except that the offering of them shows love and duty toward him. David also knew how acceptable true repentance is to God (v. 17): *The sacrifices of God are a broken spirit.* It is a painful work that is done there, nothing less than breaking the heart, not in despair but in necessary humiliation and sorrow for sin. It is a sensitive heart that responds to the word of God, a heart subdued and brought into obedience. It is a tender heart, like Josiah's (2Ki 22:19), that trembles at God's word. The breaking of Christ's body for sin is the only sacrifice of atonement, for no sacrifice except that could take away sin, but the breaking of our hearts for sin is a sacrifice of acknowledgment.

3. David intercedes for Zion and Jerusalem:

3.1. For the good of the church of God (v. 18): *Do good in thy good pleasure unto Zion,* that is, "to all the worshipers in Zion, to all who love and fear your name. Keep them from falling into such terrible and devastating sins; defend and help all who fear your name." Those who have been in spiritual troubles themselves know how to pity and pray for others who have been afflicted in a similar way. Even when we are at our busiest in our lives, and have important matters of our own to bring to the throne of grace, we must not forget to pray for the church of God; in fact, our Master taught us to begin our daily prayers with that: *Hallowed be thy name, Thy kingdom come* (Lk 11:2).

3.2. For the honor of the churches of God (v. 19). They would come to his tabernacle with whole burnt offerings, which were intended purely for the glory of God, and they would offer not only lambs and rams but also bulls, the costliest sacrifices, on his altar. *"Thou shalt be pleased with them* (v. 19), that is, we will have reason to hope our worship is acceptable when we see the sin taken away which threatened to prevent your acceptance." It is a great encouragement to think of the fellowship that is between God and his people in their public meetings, how he is honored by their humble service and they are made happy by his gracious acceptance of it.

Those whose consciences accuse them with any gross sin should pray over this psalm again and again, looking confidently to Jesus Christ the Mediator.

PSALM 52

David was very sad when he said to Abiathar (1Sa 22:22), I have occasioned the death of all the persons of thy father's house, *who were put to death on Doeg's malicious information. He wrote this psalm to bring some relief to his mind: 1. He calls Doeg to account for what he has done (v. 1); he accuses him (vv. 2–4); he passes sentence on him (v. 5). 2. He foretells how the righteous will triumph when they see the sentence carried out (vv. 6–7); he comforts himself in the mercy of God (vv. 8–9).*

Title

The title is a brief account of the story to which the psalm refers.

Verses 1–5

1. David accurately argues the case against this proud and *mighty man,* Doeg (v. 1). Doeg was by his office a *mighty man,* for he was set over the servants of Saul; he was in charge of the management of the household. He boasted not only of the power he had to do harm but also of the harm he actually did. It is uncertain how the following words come in: *The goodness of God endures continually* (v. 1). Some consider it the evil man's answer to this question. The patience and forbearance of God—those great proofs of his goodness—are abused by sinners, with the result that their hearts are hardened in their evil ways. Because God is continually doing them good, they boast in their troublemaking. But their prosperity is to be taken as showing the sinfulness of their sin: "God is continually doing good, and those who follow God's example and do good have reason to delight in being like him, but you are continually causing trouble, are completely unlike him in that respect, are in conflict with him, and even glory in being so."

2. David draws up a very serious accusation against Doeg in the court of heaven (vv. 2–4). He accuses him of evil on his tongue and evil in his heart. Specifically, he accuses him of four things:

2.1. Malice. His tongue plots destruction, not only pricking like a needle but also cutting *like a sharp razor* (v. 2).

2.2. Falsehood. It was *a deceitful tongue* that he caused this trouble with (v. 4). He loved to lie (v. 3), and this sharpened razor practiced deceit (v. 2). He told the truth but not the whole truth. It will not save us from the guilt of lying to be able to say, "There was some truth in what we said," if we pervert it and make it appear different from what it was.

2.3. Subtlety in sin: *"Thy tongue devises mischiefs* (v. 2), that is, it plots the destruction which your heart is dreaming up."

2.4. Desire for sin: *"Thou lovest evil more than good* (v. 3), that is, you love evil. You would rather please Saul by telling a lie than please God by speaking the truth." Doeg's spirit is shared by those who, instead of being pleased to have an opportunity to do someone a kind act, are glad when they have a good occasion to cause trouble for them.

3. David reads his condemnation and declares the judgments of God against him for his evil (v. 5): "You have destroyed the priests of the Lord, and so *God shall likewise destroy thee for ever*" (v. 5). Doeg is here condemned:

3.1. To be driven out of the church: *He shall pluck* (tear) *thee out of the tabernacle* (v. 5), not Doeg's own dwelling place, but God's. He was justly deprived of all the privileges of God's house, since he had caused so much trouble to God's servants.

3.2. To be driven out of the world: "*He shall root thee out of the land of the living* (v. 5), in which you thought you were so deeply rooted."

Verses 6–9

David was at this time in great distress; the trouble Doeg had caused him was only the beginning of his sorrows. And yet here we see him triumphing in trouble.

1. In the fall of Doeg. He speaks the language all righteous people use in such a case. The righteous will observe God's judgments on Doeg and speak about them:

1.1. To the glory of God: *They shall see and fear* (v. 6), that is, they will have reverence for the justice of God.

1.2. To the shame of Doeg. They will laugh at him, not in jest but with a rational, serious laughter, as *he that sits in heaven shall laugh at him* (2:4). Doeg will appear ridiculous and worthy to be laughed at. *Lo, this is the man that made not God his strength*; who did not make God his stronghold. Now what destroyed Doeg's prosperity was:

1.2.1. That he did not build it on a rock (Mt 7:24): *He made not God his strength* (v. 7). Those who think they can support themselves in their power and wealth without God and religious faith are deceiving themselves miserably.

1.2.2. That he built it on the sand (Mt 7:26). He thought his wealth would support itself: *He trusted in the abundance of his riches* (v. 7), which, he imagined, were *laid up for many years* (Lk 12:19).

2. In his own stability (vv. 8–9). "This mighty man is snatched away by the roots, *but I am like a green olive tree*, planted and rooted, firmly established and flourishing. He has been turned out of God's dwelling place, but I am established in it." Now what must we do so that we may be like flourishing olive trees?

2.1. We must live a life of faith and holy confidence in God and his grace. *I trust in the mercy of God for ever and ever* (v. 8).

2.2. We must live a life of thankfulness and holy joy in God (v. 9): "*I will praise thee for ever, because thou hast done it*, you have fulfilled your promise to me."

2.3. We must live a life of expectation and humble dependence on God: "*I will wait on thy name* (v. 9); I will wait on you in all those ways in which you have made yourself known, hoping that you will reveal your favor to me and willingly waiting for the time you have appointed for revealing it, *for it is good before thy saints*" (v. 9).

PSALM 53

In this psalm, God speaks twice, for this is almost word for word the same as Ps 14. The scope of it is to convict us of our sins. The word, as a convicting word, is compared to a hammer (Jer 23:29), the blows of which must be frequently repeated. Through the psalmist here, God: 1. Shows us how bad we are (v. 1). 2. Proves it to us by his own certain knowledge (vv. 2–3). 3. Speaks terror to persecutors, the worst of sinners (vv. 4–5). 4. Speaks encouragement to God's persecuted people (v. 6).

Verses 1–6

1. The fact of sin. Is that proved? Yes; God is a witness to it. All the sinfulness of their hearts and lives is exposed and open before him.

2. The fault of sin. It is what makes this world such an evil world; it is turning away from God (v. 3).

3. The fountain of sin. How is it that people are so bad? Surely it is because *there is no fear of God before their eyes* (36:1). Evil human practices flow from bad motives.

4. The foolishness of sin. People who harbor corrupt thoughts are fools. Atheists, whether in opinion or practice, are the greatest fools in the world. Those who do not seek God do not understand. They are like animals (32:9). For human beings are distinguished from animals not so much by the powers of reason as by a capacity for religious faith. *The workers of iniquity have no knowledge*; those who do not know God (v. 4) may truly be said to know nothing.

5. The filthiness of sin. Sinners are corrupt (v. 1); their nature is perverted and spoiled, and the more noble the nature, the more evil it is when it is depraved.

6. The fruit of sin. Notice to what level of cruelty it finally brings people. When human hearts are hardened through the deceitfulness of sin (Heb 3:13), notice their cruelty to their brothers and sisters, those who are bone of their bone: because their brothers and sisters will not plunge with them into the same flood of dissipation (1Pe 4:4), they *eat them up as they eat bread* (v. 4), as if they had become not only animals, but animals that prey on people.

7. The fear and shame that accompany sin (v. 5): *There were those in great fear* who had made God their enemy. *The wicked flees when none pursues* (Lev 26:17). Notice the reason for this fear; it is that God has formerly *scattered the bones of those that encamped against* (attacked) his people (v. 5), not only broken their power and dispersed their forces, but also killed them.

8. The faith of the saints, and their hope and power concerning the remedy for this great evil (v. 6). There will come a Savior, a great salvation, a salvation from sin!

PSALM 54

The key of this psalm hangs at the door, for its title tells us when it was written—when the inhabitants of Ziph, men of Judah (types of Judas the traitor), betrayed David to Saul, by informing Saul where David was and putting him in a position to seize him. They did this twice (1Sa 23:19; 26:1), and it is recorded to their eternal shame. The psalm is sweet; the former part of it, perhaps, was meditated on when he was in his distress and put into writing when the danger was over, with the addition of the last two verses, which express his thankfulness for the rescue. And yet this conclusion could also have been written in faith, when he was in the midst of his terrible experience. Here: 1. He complains to God about the hatred of his enemies and prays for help against them (vv. 1–3). 2. He encourages himself with an assurance that he will receive divine favor and protection and that in due time his enemies will be confounded and he will be rescued (vv. 4–7).

Title

Here we see the great distress that David was now in. The Ziphites came of their own free will and told Saul where David was, with a promise to hand him over to him. Never may good people expect to be completely safe and secure until they reach heaven. How treacherous and meddlesome these Ziphites were!

Verses 1–3

Notice:

1. David's prayer for God to help and rescue him (vv. 1–2). David had no plea to depend on but God's name, and he had no power to depend on but God's strength, and he made those his refuge and confidence. Even when he fled, when he had no opportunity to address God formally, he was continually lifting up prayers to heaven: "*Hear my prayer*, which comes from my heart, and *give ear to the words of my mouth*" (v. 2).

2. David's plea, which is based on the character of his enemies (v. 3). They are *strangers*. These were the Ziphites, unworthy of the name of Israelites. "They have treated me more corruptly and cruelly than the Philistines themselves would have." They are *oppressors*. Saul was like this. As king, he should have used his power to protect all his good subjects, but he abused it for their destruction. The Ziphites were formidable and threatening. They not only hated David and wished him evil but also rose up against him as a body, joining their powers together to cause trouble for him. They were spiteful and malicious: *They seek after my soul* (v. 3). *They have not set God before them* (v. 3), that is, they have totally rejected all thoughts of God. They have no regard for him; they do not consider that when they fight against his people, they are fighting against him.

Verses 4–7

We have here the living actions of David's faith in his prayer.

1. He is sure that he has God on his side: *Behold, God is my helper*. Although people and devils aim to destroy us, they will not succeed as long as God is our helper: *The Lord is with those that uphold my soul*. Compare 118:7: "*The Lord taketh my part with those that help me.*"

2. Because God has joined with him, David does not doubt that his enemies will fall before him (v. 5): "*He shall reward evil unto my enemies that observe me*. God in his righteousness will return the evil they intended against me on their own heads." David would not repay evil to them, but he knows God will: *I as a deaf man heard not, for thou wilt hear* (38:13, 15). We must not take revenge ourselves, because God has said, *Vengeance is mine* (Ro 12:19). But he prays, *Cut them off in thy truth* (v. 5). This is not a prayer of malice but a prayer of faith, for it considers the word of God and wants only that to be fulfilled.

3. He promises to give thanks to God for all the experiences he has had of his goodness to him (v. 6): *I will sacrifice unto thee. I will praise thy name*. A thankful heart, and *the calves* (NIV: fruit) *of our lips* (Hos 14:2) giving thanks to his name, are the sacrifices God will accept.

4. He speaks of his being saved as something already done (v. 7): "I will praise your name and say, '*He has delivered me*'; this will therefore be my song." *My eye has seen its desire upon my enemies*, my eyes have looked in triumph on my foes; his eyes had seen them not destroyed and ruined but forced to retreat, news being brought to Saul that the Philistines were attacking him (1Sa 23:27–28). All David desired was for himself to be safe; when he saw Saul draw away his forces, he received his desire. This may perhaps point to Christ, of whom David was a type; God would rescue him from all the troubles of his state of humiliation, and he was completely sure of it. All things are said to be put under his feet (110:1; Mt

22:44; Heb 1:13; etc.), for although we do not yet see all things put under him, we are still sure that he will reign until all his enemies are made his footstool and that he will ultimately triumph over them.

PSALM 55

Many commentators think that David wrote this psalm on the occasion of Absalom's conspiracy, and that the particular enemy he here speaks about, who dealt treacherously with him, was Ahithophel. Some people therefore consider David's troubles here a type of Christ's sufferings, and Ahithophel's treachery a figure of Judas's, because they both hanged themselves. There is nothing in it, however, that is particularly applied to Christ in the New Testament. David was in great distress when he wrote this psalm. 1. He prays that God would reveal his favor to him and pleads his own sorrow and fear (vv. 1–8). 2. He prays that God would reveal his displeasure against his enemies and pleads their great evil and treachery (vv. 9–15, 20–21). 3. He assures himself that God will, in due time, support him against his enemies, comforts himself with the hope of it, and encourages others to trust in God (vv. 16–19, 22–23).

Verses 1–8

In these verses we have:

1. David praying. Prayer is a relief for every wound and a comfort to the spirit under every burden: *Give ear to my prayer, O God* (vv. 1–2). *Hide not thyself from my supplication*, pay attention to my cry for help. If we, in our prayers, sincerely lay ourselves, our case, and our hearts open to God, we have reason to hope he will not hide himself, his favor, and his comfort from us.

2. David weeping, for here he was a type of Christ, who was a man of sorrows (Isa 53:3) and often in tears (v. 2): "*I mourn in my complaint*" — or "in my meditation, my sad musings" — "and I *make a noise*; I cannot cope with the sighs, groans, and other expressions of grief that reveal it to those around me." He mourns *because of the voice of the enemy*, the threats and insults of Absalom's party, which grew and which intimidated and stirred up the people to cry out against David and shout him out of his palace and capital city, as later the chief priests stirred the mob to cry out against the Son of David, *Away with him — Crucify him* (Jn 19:15). *They cast iniquity upon me*, they bring down suffering upon me (v. 3). They themselves hated him. They therefore deliberately set out to make him repugnant, so others also might hate him. This made him very sad, all the more so because he could remember the time when he was the favorite of the people and was referred to as *David*, "a beloved one" — for that is the meaning of his name.

3. David trembling and in great fear. We may suppose that he was fearful at the outbreak of Absalom's conspiracy and the general defection of the people. David was a very bold man, and he distinguished himself by his courage in some very famous situations, but when the danger was unexpected and imminent, his heart failed him. Now David's *heart was sorely pained within him; the terrors of death had fallen upon him* (v. 4). *Fearfulness of mind and trembling of body came upon him*, and horror covered and overwhelmed him (v. 5). Sometimes David's faith made him fearless, and he could boldly say, when surrounded by enemies, *I will not be afraid what man can do unto me* (56:11). But at other times his fears got the better of him and even controlled him, for even the best people are not

always strong in faith. He wanted so much, in this terrible experience, to withdraw to a desert, anywhere that was far enough away that he could not hear the voice of the enemy or see their oppression. He said (v. 6), to God in prayer, to himself in meditation, to his friends in complaint: *O that I had wings like a dove.* He was so surrounded by enemies that he did not see how he could escape except by flying away, and so he wished, *O that I had wings!* (v. 6), not those of a hawk that flies strongly, *but like a dove* that flies swiftly. He wanted to have wings not to fly and attack prey but to fly from birds of prey, for his enemies were like this. The dove flies low and takes shelter as soon as it can, and this is how David would fly. He wanted to make his escape *from the wind, storm, and tempest,* the tumult and ferment that the city was now in, and the danger to which he was exposed. "*I would fly away and be at rest* (v. 6). I would fly anywhere, even far away to a barren and terrible desert, just so I might be quiet" (v. 7).

Verses 9–15

David complains here about his enemies, whose evil plots have brought him to his wits' end, though not to the end of his faith:

1. He describes the character of his enemies. They were the worst kind of people, and his description of them accords very well with the character of Absalom and his accomplices.

1.1. He complains about the city of Jerusalem, which strangely fell in with Absalom and fell away from David: *How has that faithful city become a harlot!* (Isa 1:21). David saw nothing but *violence and strife in the city* (v. 9). He saw that violence and strife were present day and night; they were, so to speak, constant watchmen (v. 10). There was *wickedness,* all kinds of destructive forces, *in the midst thereof.* Deception and falsehood and all kinds of treachery *departed not from her streets* (v. 11). Is Jerusalem, the headquarters of God's priests, being so wrongly taught? Can Jerusalem be so ungrateful to David himself, its own illustrious founder, and be made too dangerous for him, so that he cannot live there?

1.2. He complains about one of the ringleaders of the conspiracy, who has worked hard to stir up jealousy, to misrepresent him and his government, and to enrage the city against him. Who was most active in doing this? "Not a sworn enemy, not Shimei, or any of those who refused to take an oath of allegiance to me, for then I could have coped with it, for I would not have expected better from them." *But it was thou, a man my equal* (v. 13). The Aramaic paraphrase names Ahithophel as the person referred to here. "*We took counsel together,* spent many hours together, with much pleasure, talking about religious matters"; or as Dr. Henry Hammond reads it, "We jointly attended the assembly of the people; I gave him the right hand of fellowship (Gal 2:9) in holy worship, and then we walked together to the house of God, to attend the public worship service." There always has been and always will be a mixture of good and bad people, sound and unsound, in the visible church. We must not be surprised if we are sadly deceived and disappointed by some people who have made great claims to two sacred things, religious faith and friendship. Although David himself was very wise, he himself was deceived, which may make similar disappointments more tolerable to us.

2. His prayers against them. He prays:

2.1. That God would disperse them, as he did the Babel builders (v. 9): "*Destroy* (confuse), *O Lord, and divide their tongues,* by making them disagree among themselves and clash with one another." God often destroys the church's

enemies by confusing or dividing them, and there is no more certain way to destroy a people than by dividing them.

2.2. That God would destroy them, as he did Dathan and Abiram: "*Let death seize upon them* by divine warrant, and *let them go down quickly into hell.* May they die and be buried, and so be completely destroyed in a moment, for evil is wherever they are; it is in their midst."

Verses 16–23

In these verses:

1. David perseveres in his determination to call on God, because he is assured he will not seek him in vain (Isa 45:19) (v. 16): "*As for me,* let them take whatever course they please to protect themselves; let violence and strife guard them; prayer will be my defense; I have found comfort in this, and so I will continue with it: *I will call upon God* and commit myself to him, and the *Lord shall save me.*" *I will pray and cry aloud* (v. 17). "I will meditate" is the meaning of the first verb. "I will pray frequently, every day, and three times a day: *evening, and morning, and at noon* (v. 17). Those who think three meals a day little enough for the body should think much more that three set times of prayer a day are little enough for the soul, and they should count prayer as a pleasure, not a chore. It was Daniel's practice to pray three times a day (Da 6:10), and noon was one of Peter's hours of prayer (Ac 10:9).

2. David assures himself that God will in due time answer his prayers as he desires.

2.1. That he himself will be rescued and that his fears will be prevented. He begins to rejoice in hope (Ro 5:2) (v. 18): *God has delivered my soul in peace,* that is, he will rescue it; David is as sure of the rescue as if it had already happened. With the eye of faith he now sees himself surrounded, as Elisha was, by chariots of fire and horses of fire, and so he is triumphant: *There are many with me,* more *with me than against me* (2Ki 6:16–17).

2.2. That his enemies will be judged and brought down.

2.2.1. David here gives their character as the reason he expects God to bring them down. They have no awe of God (v. 19): "*Because they have no changes*—no afflictions, nothing to interrupt their constant course of prosperity, no problems in life to weaken them, *therefore they fear not God.*" They are treacherous and false and will not be held by the most sacred and solemn commitments (v. 20). They are evil and hypocritical, claiming friendship while they intend to cause trouble (v. 21): *The words of his mouth*—he is probably referring especially to Ahithophel—*were smoother than butter and softer than oil.* At the same time, *war was in his heart.* Those very words had such a troublesome intention behind them that they were like *drawn swords* designed to stab someone.

2.2.2. David here foretells their ruin. *God shall hear and afflict them;* God will *bring them down.* They are bloodythirsty people who have destroyed others, and so God will justly destroy them; they are deceitful people, and they have defrauded others of perhaps half what they were due, and so now God will cut short their lives.

3. David encourages himself and all good people to commit themselves to God, with confidence in him. "*I will trust in thee,* in your providence, power, and mercy, not in my own wisdom, strength, or goodness. When the bloodthirsty and deceitful are destroyed in the middle of their lives, I will still live by faith in you." And he wants others to do this (v. 22): *Cast thy burden upon the Lord,* whoever you are who are burdened, and whatever the burden is. *Cast thy care* (anxiety) *upon the Lord* is the

rendering of the Septuagint (a Greek version of the Old Testament), to which the apostle Peter refers (1Pe 5:7). Anxiety is a burden; it weighs the heart down (Pr 12:25). To give our burdens to God is to rest on his providence and promises. If we do so, it is promised:

3.1. That he will sustain us. He has not promised to free us immediately from the troubles which cause our anxieties and fears, but he will provide that we are not tempted beyond what we are able to resist (1Co 10:13).

3.2. That he will never *suffer* (allow) *the righteous to be moved* (v. 22), to be so shaken by any troubles as to make them give up either their duty to God or their assurance in him.

PSALM 56

It seems from this and many other psalms that even in times of the greatest trouble and distress David never hung his harp on the willow trees (137:2); even when his dangers and fears were greatest, he was still tunefully singing God's praises. He was in imminent danger when he wrote this psalm. 1. He complains about the hatred of his enemies and begs mercy for himself and justice against them (vv. 1–2, 5–7). 2. He confides in God, being assured that God is on his side and that while he lives he will praise God (vv. 3–4, 8–13).

Title

In this psalm, David confidently throws himself into the hands of God, even when, by his fear and foolishness, he has thrown himself into the hands of the Philistines (1Sa 21:10–11). This is called *Michtam*, "a golden psalm." Some other psalms have this same title, but this one has something special in the title; it is on *Jonath-elem-rechokim*, which means "a dove on distant oaks." Some apply this to David himself, who wished to fly away on the wings of a dove (55:6). He was forced to wander far away, to seek shelter in distant countries. There he was like the doves of the valleys, sad and mourning, but silent, neither murmuring against God nor railing at the instruments of his trouble.

Verses 1–7

1. David complains to God about the hatred of his enemies, to show what reason he has to fear them (v. 1): *Be merciful unto me, O God.* That request includes all the good we come to the throne of grace for. He prays that he might find mercy with God, for he can find no mercy with people. When he fled from the cruel hands of Saul, he fell into the cruel hands of the Philistines. So he says, "Lord, be merciful to me now, or I am ruined. *They are many that fight against me*, and they think they can defeat me by their sheer force of numbers. Notice this, *O thou Most High*, and make it obvious that *wherein* (in the matter in which) *they deal proudly thou art above them*" (Ex 18:11). They are very cruel: they want to *swallow him up* (v. 1 and again v. 2). They are unanimous (v. 6): *They gather themselves together*; even though they are many and have different interests among themselves, they are still united and act together against David, as Herod and Pilate were against the Son of David. David's enemies are very powerful, too much for him unless God helps him: "*They fight against me* (v. 2); *they oppress me* (v. 1). I am almost overcome and defeated by them, and reduced to the point of death." They are very subtle and crafty (v. 6): "*They hide themselves*; they cover up their intentions so that they may pursue them more effectively. They hide

themselves like a lion in its den so that they may watch my steps," that is, "they observe everything I say and do with a critical eye on me, so they may have something to accuse me of." They are very spiteful and malicious. "*They wrest my words*, they twist them, to draw something out of them which was never intended." They are very tireless and restless. They continually wait for his soul; it is his precious life they hunt for (Pr 6:26); it is his death they long for (v. 6).

2. David encourages himself in God, and in his promises, power, and providence (vv. 3–4). "*What time I am afraid* (v. 3), in the day of my fear, when I am most terrified on the outside and most afraid within, then *I will trust in thee* (v. 3), and so my fears will be silenced." He decides to make God's promises the matter of his praises: *In God I will praise*, not only his work which he has done, but also his word which he has spoken. Some understand *his word* to refer to his providences, every event that he orders and appoints: "When I speak well of God, I will also speak well of everything he does." Supported in this way, he will defy every adverse power: "*When in God I have put my trust*, I am secure and at peace, and *I will not fear what flesh* (mere mortals) *can do unto me*" (v. 4). Just as we must not trust human strength when it is committed to act for us, so we must not be afraid of human strength when it is engaged against us.

3. David foresees and foretells the fall of those who fight against him (v. 7): *Shall they escape by iniquity?* They hope to escape God's judgments, just as they escape those of people, by violence, fraud, injustice, and treachery; but will they escape? No; they certainly will not. The sin of sinners will never be their security.

Verses 8–13

David here comforts himself with several things in the days of distress and fear:

1. That God takes particular notice of all his grievances and all his griefs (v. 8). *Thou tellest* (you number) *my wanderings*, my flights. David was now only a young man—under thirty—yet he had moved many times; he had moved from his father's house to the court and from there to the camp, and now he was hunted like a partridge on the mountains (1Sa 26:20), but he was comforted by knowing that God kept a detailed account of all his movements and numbered all the weary steps he took, by day or night. When he was wandering, he often wept, and so he prayed, "*Put thou my tears into thy bottle*, to be preserved and looked on; in fact, I know they are *in thy book* (v. 8), the book of your remembrance." God has a bottle and a book for his people's tears, both those for their sins and those for their sufferings. He observes them with compassion and tender concern; he is afflicted in their afflictions and knows when their souls are suffering. Paul recalled Timothy's tears (2Ti 1:4), and God will not forget the sorrows of his people. God will comfort his people for as long a time as he has afflicted them (90:15), and he will enable those who sowed with tears to reap with joy (126:5). What was sown as tears will come up as pearls.

2. That his prayers will be powerful enough to defeat and confuse his enemies, as well as to support and encourage himself (v. 9): "*When I cry unto thee, then shall my enemies turn back*; I need no other weapons than prayers and tears; *this I know, for God is for me*, to plead my cause, to protect and rescue me. If God is for me, who can be against me so as to overcome me?" (Ro 8:31). We fight best on our knees (Eph 6:18).

3. That his faith in God will set him above the fear of mere human beings (vv. 10–11). He repeats here, with

strong emotion, what he said in v. 4: "*In God will I praise his word*; that is, I will firmly depend on the promise for the sake of the One who made it. *In God have I put my trust*, and only in him, and so *I will not be afraid what man can do unto me* (v. 11), although I know very well what he would do if he could" (vv. 1–2).

4. That he is committed to God (v. 12): "*Thy vows are upon me, O God*—not on me as a burden which I am loaded down with, but as a badge which I glory in. It should be a matter of consideration and joy that *the vows of God are upon* us—that we are bound to live for our God under our baptismal vows renewed at the Lord's table, under the vows we make when we feel convicted of sin, or under those we have made when being punished.

5. That he will still have more and more reason to praise him: *I will render praises unto thee* (v. 12). This is part of the fulfillment of his vows, for vows of thankfulness— thank offerings presented to him—rightly accompany prayers for mercy and must be fulfilled when the mercy is received. "*Thou hast delivered my soul*, my life, *from death*, which was about to seize me." If God has rescued us from sin, either rescued us from committing it by his preventing grace or rescued us from the punishment of it by his forgiving mercy, we have reason to acknowledge that he has also rescued our souls from death, which is the wages of sin (Ro 6:23). "You will *deliver my feet from falling* (stumbling) (v. 13); you have done the greater, and so you will also do the less; you have begun a good work, and so you will continue it and complete it" (Php 1:6) Those who think they are standing must be careful they do not fall (1Co 10:12), because even the best people stand for no longer than God upholds them. God never brought his people out of Egypt to kill them in the desert. He who in conversion rescues the soul from such a great death as sin will not fail *to preserve it to his heavenly kingdom* (2Ti 4:18).

PSALM 57

This psalm is very much like the previous one; it was written on a similar occasion, when David was both in danger of trouble and tempted to sin. It begins as that one did: Be merciful to me; *the method is also the same. 1. He begins with prayer and complaint, but not without some assurance of being successful in his request (vv. 1–6). 2. He concludes with joy and praise (vv. 7–11).*

Title

The title of this psalm has one new word in it, *Al-taschith*, "Do not destroy." Some consider it to be some known tune to which this psalm was set; others think it refers to the occasion and subject matter of this psalm. "Do not destroy," that is, David would not allow Saul to be destroyed even when, in the cave, there was a fair opportunity of killing him and David's own servants wanted to do so. "No," David says, "do not destroy him" (1Sa 24:4, 6). Or rather God would not allow David to be destroyed by Saul; he allowed Saul to persecute David, but still under this restraint, "Do not destroy him."

Verses 1–6

Here we see:

1. David supporting himself with faith and hope in God, and prayer to him (vv. 1–2). *Be merciful to me, O Lord*; this was the tax collector's prayer (Lk 18:13). To commend himself to God's mercy, he here professes:

1.1. That all his dependence is on God: *My soul trusteth in thee* (v. 1). At the footstool of the throne of God's

grace, David humbly professed his confidence in him: *In the shadow of thy wings will I make my refuge*, as chicks take shelter under the wings of the hen when the birds of prey are about to attack them, *until these calamities be overpast*, until the disaster has passed. He was confident his troubles would end well in due time; these disasters would pass. He encouraged himself in the goodness of God's nature, by which he helps and protects his people, as a hen instinctively shelters its young ones.

1.2. That all his desire is toward God (v. 2): "*I will cry unto God Most High* for help and relief; I will lift up my soul to the Most High God and pray fervently to him, *to God that performs all things for me*."

1.3. That all his expectation is from God (v. 3): *He shall send from heaven, and save me*. Those who make God their only refuge and flee to him in faith and prayer may be sure of salvation in his way and his time. Whichever way David looks on this earth, there is no refuge or help, but he looks for it from heaven. Those who lift up their hearts to things above may expect all good to come from there. *God shall send forth his mercy and truth* (v. 3). We need nothing more to make us happy than to have the benefit of the mercy and truth of God (25:10).

2. David describing the power and hatred of his enemies (v. 4): *My soul is among lions*. He describes their hateful plans against him (v. 6) and shows their outcome: "*They have prepared a net for my steps*, in which to capture me, so that I may not escape from their hands again. *They have digged a pit before me*, so that I may, before I know it, run headlong into it." But let us see what comes of it.

- It is indeed disturbing to David: *My soul is bowed down* (v. 6). But:
  - It was destruction to them; they dug a pit for David, *into the midst whereof they have fallen* (v. 6).

3. David praying to God to glorify himself and his own great name (v. 5): "Whatever becomes of me and my interests, *be thou exalted, O God, above the heavens. Let thy glory be above* or over *all the earth*; may all those who live on earth come to know and praise you." Here we see how God's glory should lie nearer our hearts than any particular interests of our own, and how we should be more concerned for it than for our own interests. When David was in his greatest distress and disgrace, he did not pray, "Lord, exalt me," but, *Lord, exalt thy own name*. In the same way, when the Son of David was troubled, he prayed, *Father, save me from this hour*, and he immediately withdrew that request and presented this instead: *For this cause came I to this hour; Father, glorify thy name* (Jn 12:27–28).

Verses 7–11

How strangely has the tune changed here! By his living and active faith, David's prayer and complaints are suddenly here turned into praises and thanksgivings. Notice:

1. How he prepares himself for the duty of praise (v. 7): "*My heart is fixed, O God, my heart is fixed*. My heart is steadfast, upright, or lifted up, whereas before it was bowed down (v. 6). *My heart is fixed*: my heart is ready for every event, being *stayed upon God* (112:7; Isa 26:3). *My heart is fixed* to *sing and give praise* (v. 7), *attending on the Lord without distraction*, with undivided devotion" (1Co 7:35).

2. How he stirs himself to the duty of praise (v. 8): *Awake up my glory*, that is, "my tongue"—our tongue is our glory, and never more so than when it is praising God—or "my soul," which must first be awakened; dull and sleepy devotions will never be acceptable to God.

3. How he pleases himself and even prides himself in the work of praise. He resolves to *praise him among the people* and to *sing unto him among the nations* (v. 9). This suggests:

3.1. That he would even make the earth ring with his sacred songs, so that everyone might take notice of how much he thought himself indebted to the goodness of God.

3.2. That he wanted to bring others to join with him in praising God. He would declare God's praises *among the people*. In his psalms, which fill the universal church and will do so until the end of time, David may be said to be still *praising God among the people* and *singing to him among the nations* (v. 9), for all good people make use of his words in praising God.

4. How he provides himself with subject matter for praise (v. 10). *Thy mercy is great unto the heavens*, great beyond what can be conceived or expected, and *thy truth unto the clouds* (v. 10), great beyond what can be discovered, for what eye can reach what is enveloped in the clouds?

5. How he finally leaves it to God to glorify his own name (v. 11): *Be thou exalted, O God.*

PSALM 58

Some commentators think that before Saul began to persecute David by the use of troops, he brought a legal case against him, on which David was condemned unheard and convicted as a traitor by the great council and then declared an outlaw, one whom anyone could kill and no one could protect. It is thought that David wrote this psalm after the leaders had passed this conviction in order to gain favor with Saul. 1. He describes their sin (vv. 1–5). 2. He invokes and foretells their ruin (vv. 6–9), which will lead to the encouragement of the saints (v. 10) and the glory of God (v. 11).

Title

We have reason to think that this psalm refers to the hatred of Saul against David.

Verses 1–5

In these verses David speaks not as a king, for he has not yet come to the throne, but as a prophet, and in God's name he calls to account and convicts his judges. He accuses them of two things:

1. The corruption of their government. They were an assembly or group of judges. One would not have thought that an assembly of such people could be bribed or influenced by payment, but it seems they were, because the son of Kish could do for them what the son of Jesse could not (1Sa 22:7). On the one hand, the judges would not act rightly. They would not protect or vindicate oppressed innocence (v. 1): *"Do you indeed speak righteousness, or judge uprightly?* No; your own consciences must tell you that you are not discharging the trust vested in you as magistrates, by which you are bound to be *a terror to evildoers and a praise to those that do well* (1Pe 2:14). Remember that you are mortal human beings and that you stand on the same level before God as the lowliest of those you trample on. You yourselves will be called to account and judged." On the other hand, they did a great deal of wrong: *In heart you work wickedness.* The more thought that has gone into any act of evil, the worse it is (Ecc 8:11). And what was their evil? *"You weigh the violence of your hands in the earth,* your hands mete out violence on the earth" (v. 2)—or "in the land"—"the peace of

which you have been appointed to preserve." They did all the violence and wrong they could, either to enrich or to avenge themselves, and they *weighed* it out. They acted with a great deal of scheming and care: literally, "You frame it with a straightedge and lines." They did it in the name of justice.

2. The corruption of their nature. This was the root from which their bitterness sprang (v. 3): *The wicked*, who work evil in their hearts, *are estranged from the womb*; they go astray from God and all good, *alienated from the life of God* (Eph 4:18) and from its motivations, powers, and delights. They are called *transgressors from the womb*, and it is not a mistaken name. One can therefore expect nothing else except that they *will deal very treacherously* (Isa 48:8). They go astray from God and their duty as soon as they are born, that is, as soon as they possibly can. The foolishness bound up in their hearts (Pr 22:15) appears with the first acts of reason. Three instances are given here of the corruption of their nature:

2.1. Falsehood. They soon learn to speak lies, and they *bend their tongues, like their bows*, for that purpose (Jer 9:3).

2.2. Malice. *Their poison*—that is, their hatred or ill will, and the spite they bore toward goodness and all good people, especially David—was *like the poison of a serpent* (v. 4), innate, venomous, very troublesome, and something they could never be healed of.

2.3. Stubbornness. They are malicious, and nothing will have any effect on them. No reason or kindness will soften them or change them. *They are like the deaf adder that stops her ear* (vv. 4–5). David compares them to the deaf adder or cobra, concerning which there was then the tradition that whereas, in general, music or some other art had a way of charming snakes, so that they were destroyed or at least rendered powerless to cause any further trouble, this deaf cobra would place one ear to the ground and stop up the other with its tail, so that it could not hear the voice of the charm, and would thereby defeat the charmer's intention and keep itself safe.

Verses 6–11

In these verses we have:

1. David's prayers against his enemies, and all the enemies of God's church and people.

1.1. He prays that they might be disabled from causing any further trouble (v. 6): *Break their teeth, O God!* Not so much that they might not feed themselves as that they might not be able to attack others (3:7). He does not say, "Break their necks"—no; let them live to repent; *slay them not, lest my people forget* (59:11)—but, "Break their teeth, for they are lions. They are like young lions that live by pillaging."

1.2. He prays that they might be frustrated in the plots they have already set and might not be successful: *"When he bends his bow* and takes aim *to shoot his arrows* at the upright in heart, *let them be as cut in pieces* (v. 7). Let them fall at his feet and never come near the target."

1.3. He prays that they and others on their side might be devastated and come to nothing, that they might *melt away as waters that run continually* (v. 7); that is, that they may be like *water spilt upon the ground, which cannot be gathered up again* (2Sa 14:14), but gradually dries away and disappears. He prays (v. 8) that they might *melt as a snail* (slug), which wastes away as it moves along; with every stretch it leaves some of its moisture behind and gradually destroys itself, although it makes the path shine after it (Job 41:32). And the psalmist prays that they might be *like the untimely birth of a woman*, a stillborn child (v. 8), which dies as soon as it begins to live and never *sees the sun.*

2. David's prediction of his enemies' ruin (v. 9): "Before your pots can feel the heat of a fire of thorns beneath them."

2.1. The proverbial expressions are a little difficult, but the sense is clear: that the judgments of God often catch evildoers by surprise in the middle of their merrymaking and sweep them away unexpectedly.

2.2. There are two things which the psalmist promises himself as the effects of sinners' destruction:

2.2.1. That saints will be encouraged and comforted by it (v. 10): *The righteous will rejoice when he sees the vengeance.* The prosperity and success of evildoers are a discouragement to the righteous; they sadden their hearts and are sometimes a strong temptation to them to question their foundations (73:2, 13). But when they see the judgments of God, they are glad that their faith in God's providence, justice, and righteousness in governing the world has been confirmed.

2.2.2. That sinners will be convicted and converted by it (v. 11). The vengeance God sometimes brings on evildoers in this world will make people say, *Verily, there is a reward for the righteous.* Some will have their minds so changed that they will willingly confess, with great assurance, *that God is,* and:

- *That he is the* generous *rewarder* of his saints and servants (Heb 11:6): *Verily* (surely) *there is a reward* — or *a fruit* — *to the righteous.* Even in this world there are rewards for the righteous.
- That he is the righteous ruler of the world and will surely judge the enemies of his kingdom. *He is a God,* not a weak mortal, not an angel, not a mere name, not — as atheists suggest — a figment of human fear or imagination, not a deified hero, not the sun and moon — as idolaters imagine — but a God, a self-existent and perfect Being. It is he who judges the earth.

PSALM 59

This psalm is of the same kind and scope as the six or seven previous psalms. They are all filled with David's complaints about the hatred of his enemies and their cruel and troublesome intentions against him, his prayers and prophecies against them, and his encouragement and confidence in God as his God. The complaints consist of words spoken naturally, and we may allow ourselves to speak the same language here as David; the prayers and prophecies proceed from a prophetic spirit and look forward to Christ and the enemies of his kingdom, and so should not be used as a precedent; the encouragement and confidence he has come from grace and a most holy faith, and should be imitated by each one of us. In this psalm: 1. David prays to God to defend and rescue him from his enemies (vv. 1–7). 2. He foresees and foretells the destruction of his enemies (vv. 8–17).

Title

Saul sent a party of his guards to surround David's house at night so that they might seize him and kill him; we have the story in 1Sa 19:11–18. It was when hostilities against David had just begun and he had just narrowly escaped Saul's spear. These first outbreaks of Saul's hatred must have disturbed David and have been both painful and terrifying, but he nevertheless maintained his

fellowship with God, as well as such calmness that he was never unable to pray to God and praise him.

Verses 1–7

1. David prays to be rescued from the hands of his enemies: "*Deliver me from my enemies, O my God.* You are *God,* and you can rescue me, *my* God, under whose protection I have put myself. Set me high up beyond the reach of the power and hatred of those who rise up against me. Rescue me and save me." He prays (v. 4), "*Awake to help me,* take notice of my situation, look on it with compassion, and exert your power to help me." In the same way, the disciples in the storm awoke Christ, saying, *Master, save us, we perish* (Mt 8:25). And we should pray just as fervently to be defended and rescued from our spiritual enemies, the temptations of Satan and the impurity of our own hearts, which wage war against our spiritual life.

2. David pleads to be rescued. Our God allows us not only to pray but also to plead, to fill our mouths with arguments (Job 23:4), not to move him but to move ourselves. David does so here.

2.1. He pleads the bad character of his enemies. They are *workers of iniquity,* and so they are not only his enemies but also God's enemies; they are *bloody men,* those who thirst for blood (v. 2), and so they are not only his enemies but also enemies of the whole human race.

2.2. He pleads their hatred against him and the imminent danger he is in from them (v. 3). "*They lie in wait* (v. 3), conspiring to find an opportunity to cause me trouble. They are united in an alliance, and have actually *gathered* together *against me.* They are very clever in their scheming, and *they run and prepare themselves* (v. 4), with the greatest speed and fury, to cause me trouble." He takes particular notice of the wild behavior of the messengers Saul sent to capture him (v. 6): "*They return at evening* from the positions assigned them during the day, to apply themselves to their evil works, and then *they make a noise like a dog* pursuing a hare." *They belch* (spew) *out with their mouth* the hatred that is boiling in their hearts (v. 7). *Swords are in their lips;* that is, "they speak daggers that wound my heart with grief (42:10), and slander which stabs and wounds my reputation."

2.3. He pleads his own innocence, not toward God — he was never backward in acknowledging he was guilty before him — but toward his persecutors. "*Not for my transgression, nor for my sin, O Lord,* you who know all things." And again (v. 4): *without my fault,* I have done no wrong. The innocence of the godly will not protect them from the hatred of evildoers. Yet although our innocence will not protect us from troubles, it will greatly support and strengthen us in our troubles. If we are conscious of our own innocence, we may with humble confidence appeal to God and beg him to plead our wronged cause.

2.4. He pleads that his enemies are ungodly and godless, and that they use defiance of God to prop themselves up in their hatred toward David: *For who,* they say, *doth hear,* who can hear us? (v. 7). Not God himself (10:11; 94:7).

3. David refers himself and his case to the just judgment of God (v. 5). *Be not merciful to any wicked transgressors. Selah,* "Mark that." Though he had transgressed, he had repented, and did not obstinately persist in wrongdoing, and so he was not a *wicked* transgressor and could appeal to God in this way.

Verses 8–17

By a godly decision to wait on God, David here encourages himself regarding the powerful threats of his enemies.

1. He decides to wait on God (v. 9): *Because of his strength.* In times of danger and difficulty, we are wise and responsible if we wait on God, for he is our defense. David hopes:

1.1. That God will be a God of mercy to him (v. 10): *"The God of my mercy shall prevent* (go before) *me* with the blessings of his goodness and the gifts of his mercy and be better to me than my own expectations." Whatever mercy there is in God, it is stored up for us and is ready to be given to us.

1.2. That God will be a God of vengeance to his persecutors. Here are several things which he foretells concerning his enemies.

1.2.1. He foresees that God will expose them to scorn; indeed, they have made themselves look ridiculous (v. 8). "They think God *does not hear them, but thou, O Lord, shalt laugh at them* for their foolishness, their thinking that he who made the ear will not hear (94:9), and *thou shalt have in derision* (scoff at) all other such people who live without God in the world" (Eph 2:12).

1.2.2. He hopes that God will make them constant memorials to his justice (v. 11): *"Slay them not;* let them not be killed outright, *lest my people forget."* Similarly, Cain himself, although a murderer, was not killed, so that vengeance would not be forgotten, but was sentenced to be *a fugitive and a vagabond,* a restless wanderer (Ge 4:12). "Scatter them in such a way that they may never again unite to cause trouble; *bring them down, O Lord, our shield!"* (v. 11).

1.2.3. He hopes that they will be dealt with according to what they deserve (v. 12): *"For the sin of their mouth, even for the words of their lips, let them* for this *be taken* (caught) *in their pride,* because they lied and cursed others and themselves," which was a sin Saul was subject to (1Sa 14:28, 44). Saul and his party think they can rule and get away with anything, but they will be made to know that there is One who is higher than they are, that there is One who does and will overrule them. He *rules in Jacob,* for it is there he keeps court; it is there that he is known and that his name is great. But he *rules to the end of the earth,* for all nations are within the territories of his kingdom.

1.2.4. He hopes that God will make their sin their punishment (v. 14; compare v. 6). Their sin was their hunting for David to attack him; their punishment will be that they will be reduced to such extreme poverty that they will hunt for meat to satisfy their hunger. They will therefore not be destroyed at once, but scattered (v. 11). He foretells that they will be forced to beg for their bread from door to door. *Let them make*—or, since it is both a petition and a prediction, *They shall make*—*a noise like a dog* (v. 14). When they were seeking David, they made a noise like an angry dog snarling and barking, and now when they are seeking food, they make a noise like a hungry dog howling and wailing. Those who repent of their sins *mourn,* when in trouble, *like doves;* those whose hearts are hardened make a noise, when in trouble, like dogs, *like a wild bull in a net, full of the fury of the Lord* (Isa 51:20). If they are not satisfied, they will stay all night—so that what people give them is not given with goodwill, but only to get rid of them, so that they will not eventually wear them out (Lk 18:5). It is not poverty but discontent that makes people unhappy.

2. He expects to praise God, that God's providence will find him things to praise him for and that God's grace will produce in him a heart to praise him (vv. 16–17).

2.1. He will praise God for his power and his mercy; his song will be about both. Power without mercy is to

be dreaded; and mercy without power is not something people can expect much benefit from. However, God's power, by which he is able to help us, and his mercy, by which he is inclined to help us, will justly be the eternal subject of praise by all the saints. David will praise God because at many times he has found him his defense and refuge in trouble (v. 16).

2.2. He will *sing aloud* (v. 16), as one who is very moved by the glory of God, is not ashamed to acknowledge it, and wants to move others with it.

PSALM 60

After many psalms which David wrote in times of distress, this was intended for a day of victory. It was written after he was established on the throne, on the occasion of a famous victory which God blessed his forces with over the Arameans (Syrians) and Edomites. It was when David was at his most successful, and the affairs of his kingdom seem to have been in a better position then than they ever were either before or after. See 2Sa 8:3, 13; 1Ch 18:3, 12. David was as godly in his success as he was in times of adversity. In this psalm: 1. He reflects on the bad state the interests of the community have been in for many years (vv. 1–3); he takes notice of the recent change for the better in their affairs (v. 4); he prays for God's Israel to be rescued from their enemies (v. 5). 2. He triumphs in the hope of their victories (vv. 6–12).

Title

The title tells us the general intention of the psalm. It is a *Michtam,* or "jewel,"of David, and it is *to teach.* The Levites must teach it to the people, and through it teach them both to trust in God and to triumph in him. David was at war with the Arameans and was still in conflict with them, both those of Mesopotamia and those of Zobah. He had gained a great victory over the Edomites by his forces under the command of Joab, who had left 12,000 of the enemy dead. He is concerned about his conflict with the Assyrians, and he prays about that.

Verses 1–5

In these verses we have:

1. A sad record of the many disgraces and disappointments which God had put the people under for some years before.

1.1. He complains about the *hard things* they have seen, that is, the desperate times they have experienced, while the Philistines and other ill-disposed neighbors have been taking every advantage against them (v. 3).

1.2. He acknowledges God's displeasure as the cause of all the hardships they have gone through: *"Thou hast been displeased* by us, displeased with us (v. 1), and in your displeasure you have rejected us and scattered us, or else our enemies could not have defeated us."

1.3. He mourns the adverse effects and results of the failures of the recent years. The whole nation has been in turmoil: *Thou hast made the earth* (or the land) *to tremble* (v. 2). The good people themselves are in a state of desperate shock: *"Thou hast made us to drink the wine of astonishment* (wine that makes us stagger) (v. 3); we were like people who were drunk, and at our wits' end, not knowing how to reconcile these ways with God's promises. We can do nothing, nor do we know what to do." When God is moving in our favor, it is good for us to remember our former adversities. Our adversities contrast with our joys.

2. A thankful recognition of the encouragement God has given them to hope that although things have long been bad, they will now soon begin to mend (v. 4): *"Thou hast given a banner to those that fear thee*—for bad though the times are, there is a remnant who desire to fear your name, for whom you have a tender concern—so *that it may be displayed* by you, *because of the truth* of your promise which you will fulfill, and so that it may be unfurled by them as well, to defend truth and justice" (45:4). This banner was David's rule and its establishment and enlargement over all Israel. His rule united them, as soldiers are gathered together under their flag. It encouraged them and put life into them. It struck terror on their enemies, to whom they could now hang out the flag of defiance. Christ, the Son of David, is given as *an ensign of the people* (Isa 11:10), as a banner for those who fear God. He is the center of their unity; they glory and take courage in him. His love is the banner over them (SS 2:4); they wage war with the powers of darkness (Eph 6:12) in his name and strength, and under him the church becomes as fearful as an army with banners (SS 6:4).

3. A humble request that they would receive mercy soon. *"O turn thyself to us again* (v. 1); smile on us, be at peace with us, and we will have peace in that peace." Also, *"Heal the breaches of our land* (v. 2), not only the cracks and fractures made by our enemies, but also those made among ourselves by our unhappy divisions." And he prayed that God, by reconciling his people to himself and to each other, would preserve them from the hands of their enemies (v. 5): *"That thy beloved may be delivered, save with thy right hand,* and by such instruments as you wish to use, *and hear me."* God's praying people may take the general acts of salvation of the church as answers to their specific prayers.

Verses 6–12

David here rejoices in hope and prays in hope (v. 6): *"God has spoken in his holiness*—that is, he has given me his word of promise, has *sworn by his holiness, and he will not lie unto David* (89:35), and so *I will rejoice* (v. 6) with the hopes of the fulfillment of the promise, which was intended as more than merely a pleasant promise."

1. David here rejoices as he looks forward to two things:

1.1. The completion of the revolution in his own kingdom. Since God has *spoken in his holiness* that David will be king, he does not doubt that the kingdom is all his; it is as sure as if it were already in his hand: *"I will divide Shechem* (a pleasant town in the hill country of Ephraim) *and mete out the valley of Succoth* (v. 6) as my own. *Gilead is mine, and Manasseh is mine,* and both have been completely subdued" (v. 7). Ephraim will supply him with soldiers as his bodyguards and his regular army; Judah will supply him with capable judges for his courts of justice; and so Ephraim will be *the strength of his head,* and Judah *his lawgiver.* Active believers may similarly triumph in the promises, for they are all yes and amen in Christ (2Co 1:20). *"God has spoken in his holiness* (v. 6), and so pardon is mine, peace is mine, grace is mine, Christ is mine, heaven is mine, God himself is mine." *All is yours, for you are Christ's* (1Co 3:22–23).

1.2. The conquering of the neighboring nations, which have troubled Israel, which are still dangerous, and which oppose David (v. 8). Moab will be enslaved and set to do the lowliest drudgery. *The Moabites became David's servants* (2Sa 8:2). Edom will be made a rubbish heap to throw old sandals on (v. 8); at least David will take possession of it as his own, which was represented by

drawing off his shoe over it (Ru 4:7). As for the Philistines, let them, if they dare, gloat over him as they have done; he will soon force them to change their tune. But the war is not yet over; there is *a strong city,* perhaps Rabbah of the Ammonites, which still holds out; Edom has not yet been subdued. Now David is here inquiring for help to carry on the war: *"Who will bring me into the strong city?* (v. 9). *Wilt not thou, O God?* For you have *spoken in thy holiness* (v. 10), and will you not be as good as your word?" He takes notice of the frowns of Providence that the Israelites have been under: *Thou hadst* seemed to have *cast us off* (rejected us); *thou didst not go forth with our armies* (v. 10). At the same time that they recognize God's justice in what is past, they hope in his mercy for what is to come.

2. David prays in hope. His prayer is, *Give us help from trouble* (v. 11). Even in the day of their triumph they see themselves in trouble, because they are still at war, which is troublesome even to the winning side. Although they are now conquerors, nevertheless, because the outcome of war is so uncertain, unless God helps them in their next battle, they might be defeated, and so, *Lord, send us help from the sanctuary* (20:2). *Help from trouble* (v. 11) is rest from war, which they pray for as those who seek justice, not victory. *"Through God we shall do valiantly,* and so we will win, for *he it is,* and only he, *that shall tread down our enemies,* and he will receive the praise for doing it." Although *it is God that performs all things for us* (57:2), there is still something to be done by us. Hope in God is the best motivation for true courage. Those who do their duty under his leadership can afford to do it valiantly, for what do those who have God on their side need to fear?

PSALM 61

In this psalm, as in many others, David begins with prayers and tears, but ends with songs of praise. When a soul is lifted up to God, it becomes contented again. It seems David was driven out when he wrote this psalm, although whether he has banished by Saul or by Absalom is uncertain. 1. He will call on God because God has protected him (vv. 1–3). 2. He will call on God because God has provided well for him (vv. 4–5); he will praise God because he has the assurance of the continuation of God's favor to him (vv. 6–8).

Verses 1–4

In these verses we may notice:

1. David's attentive faithfulness and diligence toward God in prayer in times of distress or trouble: "Whatever comes, *I will cry unto thee* (v. 2), as one who will not let you go unless you bless him" (Ge 32:26). He will do this despite his distance from the sanctuary: *"from the end of the earth,* or of the land, from the most remote and obscure corner of the country, *will I cry unto thee* (v. 2). Though *my heart is overwhelmed* (v. 2), it has not sunk so low, it is not so burdened, that it cannot be lifted up to God in prayer. In fact, because my heart is about to be overwhelmed, that is why *I will cry unto thee* (v. 2), for when I cry out to you, I know you will bring me support and relief." Weeping must encourage our prayer, not stifle it.

2. The specific request David offered to God when his heart was overwhelmed and he was about to sink: *Lead me to the rock that is higher than I* (v. 2), that is "to the rock which is too high for me to reach unless you help me up to it, to the rock on the top of which I will be set further beyond reach of my troubles, and nearer the more

serene and quiet region, than I can reach by any power or wisdom of my own." This rock is Christ (1Co 10:4); those in him are secure.

3. David's desire for and expectation of a favorable reply. He begs in faith (v. 1): "*Hear my cry, O God, attend unto my prayer;* that is, let me have the encouragement now of knowing I am heard (20:6), and in due time let me receive what I am praying for."

4. The reason for this expectation, which is the plea David uses to support his request (v. 3): "*Thou hast been a shelter for me;* I have found in you a rock higher than I, and so I trust you will continue to lead me to that rock."

5. David's determination to continue on the path of duty to God and of continual dependence on him (v. 4). David has been banished from the tabernacle, which is his greatest grievance, but he is assured that God by his providence will bring him back. He speaks of remaining in it *for ever* because that tabernacle was a type and figure of heaven (Heb 9:8–9, 24). Those who live in God's tabernacle on earth—which is a house of duty—during their short *ever* on earth, will live in that tabernacle which is the house of glory for an endless *ever. I will trust in the covert of thy wings* (v. 4), as chicks seek both warmth and security under the wings of the hen.

Verses 5–8

In these verses we may notice:

1. With what delight David looks back to what God has done for him formerly (v. 5): *Thou, O God, hast heard my vows.* God witnesses all our vows, all our good plans, and all our solemn promises of fresh obedience. "The prayers you have graciously heard and answered" encouraged him now to pray, *O God, hear my cry* (v. 1). "You have heard my vows and given a real answer to them, for *thou hast given me a heritage of those that fear thy name*" (v. 5). We need desire no better heritage than the heritage of those who fear God.

2. With what assurance David looks forward to the continuation of his life (v. 6): *Thou shalt prolong the king's life.* He had decided firmly to remain in God's tabernacle forever (v. 4), doing his duty; and now his hope was that he would remain in God's presence forever as an encouragement.

3. With what boldness David begs God to take him and keep him always under his protection: *O prepare mercy and truth which may preserve him* (v. 7). David is certain that God will prolong his life, and so he prays that he would preserve it, not that he would prepare for him a strong bodyguard, or a well-fortified castle, but that he would prepare *mercy and truth* (love and faithfulness) to keep him. We need not want to be more secure than we are under the protection of God's love and faithfulness.

4. With what joy David vows the grateful response of doing his duty toward God (v. 8): *So will I sing praise unto thy name for ever, that I may daily perform my vows* (v. 8). His praising God was itself the fulfillment of his vows.

PSALM 62

This psalm has nothing in it that is specifically either prayer or praise, nor is it stated on which occasion it was written, or whether for any particular occasion, whether sad or joyful. But in it: 1. David professes his own confidence in God and dependence on him with much delight (vv. 1–7). 2. He fervently stirs and encourages others to similarly trust in God, and not in any creature (vv. 8–12).

Verses 1–7

In these verses we have:

1. David's profession of dependence on God, and only on him, for all good (v. 1): *Truly my soul waiteth upon God.* "Whatever difficulties or dangers I may meet, even if God frowns on me and I face discouragements as I serve him, my soul will still wait on God"—or, literally, "my soul is silent toward God; it says nothing against what he is doing, but quietly hopes and expectantly waits for what he will do. I know my salvation will come from him, and so I will wait patiently on him until it does come, for his time is the best time."

2. The reasons for this dependence (v. 2): *He only is my rock and my salvation; he is my defence.* Other people are not enough; they are nothing without him, and so I will look beyond them to him.

3. The use David makes of his confidence in God.

3.1. His heart is steadfast (57:7). "If God is my strength and mighty deliverer, *I shall not be greatly moved*, I will not be shaken or ruined. I may be shocked, but I will not sink."

3.2. His enemies are scorned, and all their attempts against him looked on by him with contempt (vv. 3–4). "*How long will you* do it? Will you never be convinced of the error of your ways? Will your hatred never exhaust itself?" Envy lies at the root of their malice; they are grieved at David's advancement, and so they plot to blacken his character and make him look small—and that was indeed *casting him down from his excellency*—in order to prevent his promotion. *They delight in lies. They bless with their mouth*; they compliment David to his face—*but they curse inwardly*; in their hearts they wish him all kinds of trouble, and privately they carry out some evil plan or other in the hope of destroying him. It is dangerous to put our trust in people who are false like this, but God is faithful. *You shall be slain all of you*, by the righteous judgments of God. Saul and his servants were killed by the Philistines on Mount Gilboa in accordance with this prediction. God's church is built on a rock which will stand (Mt 16:18), but those who fight against it will be *as a bowing* (leaning) *wall and a tottering fence*, which, because it has a rotten foundation, collapses suddenly and buries in ruins those who put themselves in its shadow and shelter.

3.3. David himself is encouraged to continue to wait on God (vv. 5–7). "If God will save my soul, then as for everything else, let him do what he pleases with me, and I will accept his plans, knowing they will *all turn* out *to my salvation*" (Php 1:19). He repeats (v. 6) what he earlier said concerning God (v. 2), as one who has meditated much about it in his thoughts: "*He only is my rock and my salvation; he is my defence;* I know he is." The first time he said these words, he added, *I shall not be greatly moved*; here he says, *I shall not be moved* at all. And just as David's faith in God progresses to an unshaken state of relying on him, so also his joy in God turns itself into a holy triumph (v. 7): *In God is my salvation and my glory.*

Verses 8–12

Here we have David's encouragement to others to trust in God and wait for him.

1. He advises everyone to wait on God, as he has done (v. 8). *You people,* he says; that is, all people; all are welcome to trust in God, for he is *the confidence of all the ends of the earth* (65:5). "*Trust in him;* depend on him to fulfill everything for you. Depend on his wisdom and goodness, his power and promises, his providence and

grace. Do this *at all times*" (v. 8). *Pour out your heart before him* (v. 8). The expression seems to allude to the pouring out of drink offerings before the Lord. When we repent and confess our sin, our hearts are *poured out before God* (1Sa 7:6). But here it is used to describe prayer, which, if it is as it should be, is the pouring out of the heart before God. We must lay our grievances before him, offer our desires to him with all humility and freedom, patiently submitting our wills to his: this is pouring out our hearts. *God is a refuge for us*, not only my refuge (v. 7), but also a refuge for us all, for as many as will flee to him and take shelter in him.

2. He cautions us to be careful that we do not misplace our confidence. Let us not trust the people of this world, for they are broken reeds (2Ki 18:21) (v. 9): *Surely men of low degree are vanity*, completely unable to help us, and *men of high degree are a lie*; they will deceive us if we trust in them. One would have thought people who are highborn could be depended on for their wisdom, power, or influence. But if you put them *in the balance*, the balance of Scripture, or rather test them, to see what they are really like, whether they will fulfill your expectations from them or not, you will write *Tekel* on them: "You have been weighed on the scales and found wanting" (Da 5:27); together they are *lighter than vanity*, only a breath (v. 9). Let us not trust in the wealth of this world; let that not be made our strong city (v. 10): *Trust not in oppression*; that is, in riches gained fraudulently or violently. In fact, because it is hard to have riches and not trust in them, we must be careful not to value them too much if they increase, even if lawfully and honestly: "*Set not your heart upon them* (v. 10); do not be eager for them." We are most in danger of doing this when riches increase.

3. He gives a very good reason why we should make God our confidence: that he is a God of infinite power, mercy, and righteousness (vv. 11–12). "God has spoken it, and I have heard it once, in fact, twice—that is, many times—by the events that have especially concerned me. He has spoken it and I have heard it by revelation, by dreams and visions (Job 4:15), by the glorious revelation of himself on Mount Sinai"—to which, some think, this especially refers—"and by the written word." God speaks twice to some people and they will not hear him even once, but he speaks to other people only once and they hear twice. Compare Job 33:14. Now what is it that is spoken and heard? *Power belongs to God* (v. 11); he is almighty and can do everything; with him nothing is impossible (Lk 1:37). He is a God of infinite goodness. Here the psalmist turns his speech to God himself, wanting to give him the glory of his goodness, which is his glory (Ex 33:18–19): *Also unto thee, O Lord, belongeth mercy* (v. 12). He is merciful in a way that is unique to himself; he is the *Father of mercies* (2Co 1:3). He never did, nor ever will do, any wrong to any of his creatures: *For thou renderest to every man according to his work* (v. 12).

PSALM 63

This psalm expresses as much warmth and living devotion as any of David's psalms of so few words. As the sweetest of Paul's letters were those written in prison, so some of the sweetest of David's psalms were those written, as this one was, in a desert. Here is:1. His desire toward God (vv. 1–2). 2. His respect for and worship of God (vv. 3–4); his satisfaction in God (v. 5); his personal fellowship with God (v. 6). 3. His joyful dependence on God (vv. 7–8); his holy triumph in God over his enemies and in the assurance of his own safety (vv. 9–11).

Title

The title tells us when the psalm was written, when David was *in the wilderness of Judah*; that is, *in the forest of Hareth* (1Sa 22:5) or in *the wilderness of Ziph* (1Sa 23:15). Even though Canaan was a fruitful land and was occupied by many people, there were still deserts, places less fruitful and less inhabited than others. It will be like this in the world and in the church, but not in heaven. There *the wilderness shall blossom as the rose* (Isa 35:1). The best and dearest of God's saints and servants may sometimes find their lot cast in a desert. There are psalms that are right for a desert, and we have reason to thank God that it is the Desert of Judah we are in, not the Desert of Sin (Ex 16:1).

Verses 1–2

In these verses David stirs up himself to take hold of God:

1. By a living and active faith: *O God, thou art my God* (v. 1). We must acknowledge that God is real, that we speak to One who truly exists and who is present with us, when we say, *O God*. These are serious words; it is very sad that the name of God should ever be used as a swear word.

2. By godly, heartfelt devotion.

2.1. He decides to seek God, his favor, and his grace: *Thou art my God* (v. 1), and so *I will seek thee* (v. 1): *should not a people seek unto their God?* (Isa 8:19). *Early will I seek thee* (v. 1). "*My soul thirsteth for thee* and *my flesh longeth for thee*—that is, my whole being is moved by this activity—here *in a dry and thirsty land*" (v. 1).

2.2. He longs to enjoy God. What is it that he wishes for so passionately? What is his request? It is this (v. 2): "*To see thy power and thy glory*, as I have seen you in the sanctuary. That is, to see it here in this desert as I have seen it in the tabernacle, to see it in secret as I have seen it in the sacred assembly." But he also longs to be taken out of the desert, not so that he may see his friends again and be restored to the delights and merriment of court, but so that he may have access to the sanctuary; he longs not to see the priests there and be involved in the ceremony of worship, but *to see thy power and glory*. He does not say, "as I have seen them," but *as I have seen thee*. We cannot see the essence of God, but we see him in seeing by faith his attributes and qualities. Those minutes David spent in fellowship with God were precious minutes; he loved to think back over them again and again.

Verses 3–6

Here we see how quickly David's complaints and prayers turn to praises and thanksgivings! David was now in a desert, but he had his heart released because he praised God. Notice:

1. What David will praise God for (v. 3): *Because thy loving-kindness is better than life*. It is our spiritual life, and that is better than physical life (30:5). We have better provisions and better possessions than the wealth of this world can give us, and in the service of God, and in fellowship with him, we have better employment and better enjoyment than we can have in the work and ways of the world.

2. How David will praise God, and for how long (v. 4). "*Thus will I bless* (glorify) *thee*, as I have begun to; the present godly devotion will not pass away like the morning mist (Hos 6:4), but shine more and more brightly, like the morning sun" (Pr 4:18). *I will bless thee while I live* (v. 4). Praising God must be the work of our whole lives.

I will lift up my hands in thy name (v. 4). We must look to God's name in all our prayers and praises; in all of them we are taught to begin with *Hallowed be thy name* (Mt 6:9) and to conclude with *Thine is the glory* (Mt 6:13).

3. With what pleasure and delight David will praise God (v. 5). *My soul shall be satisfied as with marrow and fatness*, not only as with bread, which is nourishing, but as with rich food, which is enjoyable and delicious (Isa 25:6). There is something in a gracious God, and in fellowship with him, that gives deep assurance to a gracious soul (36:8; 65:4). And there is something in a gracious soul which takes great delight in God and fellowship with him. He will praise God *with joyful lips*. When someone believes with the heart and is thankful, confession must be made with the mouth of praise and thanksgiving (Ro 10:9), to the glory of God. It is not that the expressions of the mouth are accepted without the heart (Mt 15:8), but the mouth must speak out of the overflow of the heart (Mt 12:34; Ps 45:1). Praising lips must be joyful ones.

4. How David will meditate on God when he is most isolated (v. 6): "I will praise you *when I remember thee upon my bed.*" God was in all his thoughts, which is the reverse of the evildoer's character (10:4). The thoughts of God were close to him: "*I remember thee* (v. 6); that is, when I go to think, I find you at my right hand, present in my mind." And his thoughts were fixed on him: *I meditate on thee* (v. 6). Thoughts of God must not be short-lived, passing through the mind, but long-lasting, enduring in the mind. David was now wandering about and unsettled, but wherever he went, he took his religious faith with him. When we cannot sleep because of pain, sickness of body, or any disturbing thoughts, our souls should remember God, and they may then be at peace and find rest. Perhaps an hour's devout meditation will do us more good than an hour's sleep would have done. See also 4:4; 16:7; 17:3; 119:62.

Verses 7–11

David here expresses his confidence in God and his joyful hope in him (v. 7): *In the shadow of thy wings I will rejoice.* He alludes here either to the wings of the cherubim stretched out over the ark of the covenant, between which God's presence is said to be, or to the wings of a bird, under which helpless young ones shelter. If we understand the reference to be to the wings of a bird, then they might be either those of the eagle (Ex 19:4; Dt 32:11), which would speak of divine power, or those of the hen (Mt 23:37), which would speak more of divine tenderness. It is a phrase often used in the psalms (17:8; 36:7; 57:1; 61:4; 91:4), and nowhere else in this sense except Ru 2:12, where, when Ruth became a convert, she was said to *trust under the wings of the God of Israel.* It is our duty to *rejoice in the shadow of God's wings* (v. 7), which shows we are to turn to him in faith and prayer as naturally as chicks, when they are cold or frightened, run under the wings of the hen. Let us see:

1. What were the supports and encouragements of David's confidence in God.

1.1. His former experiences of God's power in helping him: "*Because thou hast been my help* when other helps and helpers failed me, I will continue to rejoice in your salvation. I will trust in you for the future and will do so with delight and holy joy."

1.2. The present sense he had of God's grace taking him through these times (v. 8): *My soul follows hard after* (clings to) *thee.* This speaks of a fervent wish and a serious and vigorous desire to maintain fellowship with God.

David acknowledged, to the glory of God, *Thy right hand upholds me* (v. 8).

2. What it was that David triumphed in the hope of:

2.1. That his enemies would be destroyed (vv. 9–10). There were those who *sought his soul to destroy it*, not only his life, which they attacked, both to prevent his coming to the throne and because they envied and hated him for his wisdom, godliness, and usefulness, but also his soul, which they sought to destroy by banishing him from God's public worship services. But they would *go into the lower parts of the earth* (v. 9), to the grave, to hell; their enmity toward David would be their death. *They shall be a portion for foxes*, food for jackals (v. 10); either their dead bodies would be prey for ravenous wild animals, or their houses and estates would be lived in by wild animals (Isa 34:14).

2.2. That he himself would finally win the battle (v. 11), that he would be advanced to the throne to which he had been anointed: *The king shall rejoice in God.* David's advancement will bring encouragement to his friends. *Every one that swears* to *him*, that is, to David, everyone who comes onto his side and takes an oath of allegiance to him, *shall glory* in his success. *Those that fear thee will be glad when they see me* (119:74). Those who wholeheartedly support the cause of Christ will glory in its ultimate victory. *If we suffer with him, we shall also reign with him* (2Ti 2:12). David's advancement would confound his enemies: *The mouth of those that speak lies* (v. 11), of Saul, Doeg, and others who misrepresented David, *shall be* completely *stopped* (silenced).

PSALM 64

This whole psalm refers to David's enemies, persecutors, and slanderers. 1. He prays to God to keep him safe from their malicious intentions against him (vv. 1–2); he describes them in very bad terms (vv. 3–6). 2. By the spirit of prophecy he foretells their destruction (vv. 7–10).

Verses 1–6

In these verses, David lays before God a description of his own danger and of his enemies' character.

1. He fervently begs God to preserve him (vv. 1–2): *Hear my voice, O God, in my prayer*; grant me the thing I pray for. *Lord, preserve my life from fear of the enemy.* He prays, "*Hide me from the secret counsel* (conspiracy) *of the wicked* (v. 2), from the trouble they secretly plot among themselves against me, and *from the insurrection of the workers of iniquity* (v. 2), who join together in their plans to cause trouble for me."

2. He complains of the great hatred and evil of his enemies.

2.1. They are very spiteful in their slander and insults (vv. 3–4). They are described as warriors, with their swords and bows, archers who take aim exactly, secretly, and suddenly, and shoot at harmless birds that are not aware of any danger. Their tongues are their swords. The tongue is a small part of the body, but like the sword, it is a dangerous weapon. *Bitter words* are *their* arrows — defamatory words, vitriolic descriptions, false representations, poisonous slander. They are aiming at those who are upright. The better people are, the more they are envied by those who are evil, and the more evil is said about them. They *shoot in secret* (v. 4), so that those they shoot at may not see them and so avoid the danger, for *in vain* is the net spread in the sight of any bird (Pr 1:17). And suddenly do they shoot (v. 4), without giving any lawful warning or any opportunity for those they attack to defend themselves. They fear not (v. 4), that is, they are confident of their success.

2.2. They are very secretive and determined in their evil plans (v. 5). They discuss among themselves how they can cause the most trouble: They commune of laying snares privily, they talk about hiding their snares (v. 5). All their fellowship is in sin, and all they talk about is how to sin safely, how they can get away with their sinful ways. They say, Who shall see them? (v. 5). A practical disbelief in God's complete knowledge of everything lies at the root of all the evil of evildoers.

2.3. They work very hard at putting their plans into action (v. 6): "They search out iniquity; they take a great deal of effort to plot some injustice to accuse me of; they dig deep, look far back, and go to the greatest lengths to devise something to accuse me of." Half the effort many people take to condemn their souls would be enough to save them.

Verses 7–10

We may notice here:

1. The judgments of God on these evil persecutors of David. The punishment corresponds to the sin.

1.1. They shot at David secretly and suddenly, to wound him; but God will shoot at them, for he ordains his arrows against the persecutors (7:13). See also 21:12. God's arrows will hit more surely, fly more quickly, and pierce more deeply than theirs do or can.

1.2. Their tongues were against him, but God will make their tongues to fall upon (go against) themselves. Those who love to curse will find that their curses come back on them. Furthermore, sometimes people's secret evil is brought to light by their own confession, and then their own tongue goes against them.

2. The influence which these judgments will have on others.

2.1. The neighbors of these evildoers will avoid them and run for their lives. They shall flee away (v. 8) for fear of being involved in their destruction.

2.2. Those people who look on will have reverence for the providence of God in this (v. 9). They shall wisely consider his doing. They will be moved by a holy awe of God when they consider his ways. They will speak to one another and to everyone around them about the justice of God in punishing persecutors. This is the finger of God (Ex 8:19).

2.3. Good people will especially take notice of it (v. 10). The righteous shall be glad in the Lord, not glad to see the misery and destruction of their fellow creatures, but glad that God is glorified, and his word fulfilled, and that the cause of wronged innocence has been successfully pleaded. It will encourage their faith.

PSALM 65

In this psalm we are directed to give God the glory for his power and goodness, which appear: 1. In the kingdom of grace (v. 1), in his hearing prayer (v. 2), pardoning sin (v. 3), satisfying the souls of the people (v. 4), and protecting and supporting them (v. 5). 2. In the kingdom of providence, in his forming the mountains (v. 6), calming the sea (v. 7), preserving the regular succession of day and night (v. 8), and making the earth fruitful (vv. 9–13).

Verses 1–5

As the mouthpiece of a congregation, the psalmist here has no particular concern of his own at the throne of grace, but begins with an address to God. Notice:

1. How he gives glory to God (v. 1).

1.1. By humble thankfulness: Praise waiteth for thee, O God, in Zion, waits in hope of the desired mercy, waits until it arrives, so that it may be received with thankfulness when it comes. "Praise awaits you, O God, with a complete assurance of your holy will and a complete dependence on your mercy." "Praise is silent to you" is the meaning—being struck in silent wonder and lacking words to express the great goodness of God. Just as there are holy groanings which cannot be uttered (Ro 8:26), so also there is holy adoration which cannot be spoken.

1.2. By sincere faithfulness: Unto thee will the vow be performed, that is, the sacrifice that was vowed will be offered. Better not to vow than to make a vow and then not fulfill it (Ecc 5:5).

2. What he gives him glory for.

2.1. For hearing prayer (v. 2): Praise waits for thee (v. 1), and why is it so ready?

2.1.1. "Because you are ready to grant our requests. O thou that hearest prayer! (v. 2), you can answer every prayer, for you are able to do for us more than we can ask or even imagine (Eph 3:20), and you will answer every prayer of faith, either in kind or in kindness."

2.1.2. Because, for that reason, we are ready to run to him when we are in difficulties. "Therefore, because you are a God who hears prayer, unto thee shall all flesh come (v. 2)."

2.2. For pardoning sin. In this respect, who is a God like him (Mic 7:18)? "Our sins reach the heavens (Ezr 9:6), iniquities prevail against us, we are overwhelmed by sins; our own consciences accuse us, and we can make no reply, and yet as for our transgressions, thou shalt purge them away, so that we will not be condemned for them."

2.3. For welcoming those who wait on him and for the encouragement they have in fellowship with him. Sins must first be forgiven (v. 3), and then we are welcome to approach God's altars (v. 4).

2.3.1. They are blessed. Not only is the nation blessed (33:12), but also blessed is the man, the particular person, however lowly, whom thou choosest, and causest to approach unto thee, that he may dwell in thy courts (v. 4). To come into fellowship with God is to be with him as One we love and esteem. It is to live in his courts, as the priests and Levites did, who were at home in God's house; it is to be faithful in the exercises of religious faith. We come into fellowship with God not commended by any goodness in ourselves, but only because of God's free choice: "Blessed is the man whom thou choosest (v. 4), and whom you thereby set apart from others who are left to themselves."

2.3.2. They will have assurance. Here the psalmist changes the person; not "He will be satisfied"—the man whom God chooses—but We will be satisfied, which teaches us to apply the promises to ourselves: We shall be satisfied (are filled) with the goodness of thy house, even of thy holy temple (v. 4). God maintains a good house. There is much goodness in his house, much righteousness, much grace, and all the encouragements of the eternal covenant. There is enough for all and enough for each. It is ready and always ready. It is all freely available and can be bought without money and without cost (Isa 55:1).

2.4. For the activity of his power on their behalf (v. 5): By terrible (awesome) things in righteousness wilt thou *answer us, O God of our salvation!* This may be understood to refer to the rebukes that God in his providence sometimes gives his own people. He often answers them by awesome deeds, to awaken and quicken them, but he always acts in righteousness. He neither does them any wrong nor means them any harm, for even then he is the God of their salvation. See Isa 45:15.

2.5. For the care he takes of all his people. He is *the confidence* (hope) *of all the ends of the earth* (v. 5), that is, of all the saints throughout the world, not only those of the descendants of Israel, for he is the God of the Gentiles as well as the Jews.

Verses 6–13

Notice his power and sovereignty as the God of nature.

1. He establishes the earth, and it endures (119:90). *By his* own *strength he setteth fast* (formed) *the mountains* (v. 6); they are called *everlasting mountains* (Hab 3:6). But God's covenant with his people is said to stand more firmly than they do (Isa 54:10).

2. He stills the sea, and it is quiet (v. 7). The stormy sea makes a great noise, but when it is God's will, he commands silence among the waves and puts them to sleep. He quickly turns the storm into a calm (107:29). By the sea, as well as by the unchangeableness of the earth, it appears that the One whom the sea and the dry land belong to is *girded with power*, wears a belt of strength (v. 6). Similarly, our Lord Jesus proved his divine power when he *commanded the winds and waves, and they obeyed him* (Mt 8:27). To this quieting of the sea David adds, as something similar, that God stills *the tumult of the people* (v. 7).

3. He renews morning and evening (v. 8). This regular succession of day and night may be considered:

3.1. As an example of God's great power, and so it strikes awe in everyone: *Those that dwell in the uttermost parts of the earth are afraid at thy tokens* (signs or wonders) (v. 8). They are convinced by them that there is a Supreme Being, a sovereign ruler, before whom they should fear and tremble.

3.2. As an example of God's great goodness, and so it brings encouragement to everyone: *Thou makest the outgoings of the morning*, before the sun rises, *and of the evening*, before the sun sets, *to rejoice* (v. 8). Just as it is God who scatters the light of the morning and draws the curtains of the evening, so also he gives us reason to be glad for both. We are to look on our daily worship alone and with our families as both the most important of our daily occupations and the most delightful of our daily encouragements.

4. He waters the earth and makes it fruitful. How much the fruitfulness of this lower part of creation depends on the influence of the upper is easy to observe. If the heavens are as hard as bronze, the earth is like iron (Dt 28:23), which is a physical sign to a weary world that every good and perfect gift is from above (Jas 1:17). All God's blessings, even spiritual ones, are expressed by saying that he *rains his righteousness on us* (Hos 10:12). The common blessing of rain from heaven and fruitful seasons is described:

4.1. It contains much of the power and goodness of God. God, who made the earth, comes to it, takes care of it, and shows his care toward it (v. 9). God, who made it dry land, waters it so that it will become fruitful. Although the plants of the earth flourished before God caused it to rain, even then there was a mist which fulfilled the intention and *watered the whole face of the*

ground (Ge 2:5–6). Our hearts are dry and barren unless God himself comes as the dew to us and waters us (Hos 14:5). He will water the plants of his own planting and make them grow. Rain is *the river of God, which is full of water* (v. 9). This river of God enriches the earth, and without it the earth would quickly be poor. The riches of the earth's surface are much more useful to human beings than those hidden in its depths. We could live well enough without silver and gold, but we cannot live without grain and grass.

4.2. A great deal of benefit comes from it to the earth and to human beings on it.

4.2.1. To the earth itself. The rain in season gives it a new face. Even *the ridges* of the earth, from which the rain seems to slide, are watered *abundantly*, for they drink in the rain which drenches them; the earth's *furrows*, which are turned up by the plow, are settled by the rain and made fit to receive the seed (v. 10). They are settled by being made soft. What makes the soil of the heart tender settles it, for the heart is established by grace. In the same way, spring is a pledge of blessing on the whole year, which God is therefore said to *crown with his goodness* (v. 11). *His paths* are said to *drop fatness* (richness). These expressions of God's goodness to this lower world are extensive (v. 12): *They drop upon the pastures of the wilderness*, not merely on the pastures of inhabited land. The wild areas, which people take little care of and receive no crops from, are under the care of divine Providence, and we should be thankful not only for what serves us but also for what serves any part of the creation. The gifts of God's goodness are so extensive that in them the hills, *the little hills, rejoice on every side*, even on the north side, which lies farthest from the sun. Hills are not beyond the needs of God's providence; little hills are not beneath his notice.

4.2.2. To human beings on earth. *As for the earth, out of it comes bread* (Job 28:5), for out of it comes grain, but God himself prepared every grain that comes from it. He provides rain for the earth so that he may prepare grain for people, under whose feet he has put the rest of the creatures (8:6–8) and for whose use he has fitted them. The yearly produce of grain is not only a work of the same power that raises the dead, but also an example of that power that is not dissimilar to the raising of the dead—as can be seen by what our Savior said (Jn 12:24)—and the constant benefit we have from it is an example of the goodness that endures forever. Grain and cattle are the two staple commodities produced by the earth, and both are the result of God's goodness in watering the earth (v. 13). The valleys are so fruitful they seem to be *covered over with corn* at harvest time. The lowest parts of the earth are commonly the most fruitful, and one acre of the humble valleys is worth five acres on the mountain slopes. But both arable land and pastureland fulfill the purposes of their creation and are said to *shout for joy and sing* (v. 13), because both are useful to the honor of God and the strength of human beings.

PSALM 66

This is a psalm of thanksgiving. All people are called on to praise God here: 1. For his general sovereign power over the whole creation (vv. 1–7). 2. For the special signs of his favor to the church, his own people (vv. 8–12). And then: 3. The psalmist praises God for his own experiences of his goodness to him in particular, especially in answering his prayers (vv. 13–20).

Verses 1–7

1. In these verses the psalmist calls on all people to praise God, *all you lands, all the earth* (v. 1). This speaks of:

1.1. The glory of God, for he is good to every person.

1.2. The duty of human beings, that everyone is to praise God; it is part of the law of creation and so is required of every creature.

1.3. A prophecy of the conversion of the Gentiles to faith in Christ. The time would come when every land would praise God.

1.4. A sincere goodwill which the psalmist has for this good work of praising God. He wishes that God received tribute from every nation on earth, not only from the land of Israel. We must be sincere and zealous, open and public, as those who are not ashamed of their Master. And both these are implied in *making a joyful noise*. When we praise God, we are to glorify him. "Consider it your greatest glory to praise God" is how some understand this.

2. He has called on all lands to praise God (v. 1), and he now foretells (v. 4) that they will do so: *All the earth shall worship thee*. They will *sing to God*, that is, *sing to his name* (v. 4), for it is only to his revealed glory, by which he has made himself known, not his essential glory, that we can contribute anything by our praises.

3. We are called on here *to come and see the works of God* (v. 5), for *his own works praise him*, whether we do so or not. The reason we do not praise him more and better is that we do not take careful note of his works as we should. Let us therefore see God's works (v. 5). Then let us speak of them, and speak of them to him (v. 3): *Say unto God, How terrible* (awesome) *art thou in thy works.*

3.1. God's works are wonderful in themselves. God *is terrible* (awesome) in his works. In all his actions toward human beings he is awesome and to be considered with great reverence. Much religious faith lies in reverence toward God's providence.

3.2. God's works are formidable to his enemies and have forced and frightened them into a feigned submission many times (v. 3): *Through the greatness of thy power*, before which no one can stand, *shall thy enemies submit themselves unto thee.* "They will bow down to you" is the meaning; that is, "they will be compelled, very much against their wills, to make their peace with you on any terms."

3.3. God's works are encouraging and beneficial to his people (v. 6). When Israel came out of Egypt, *he turned the sea into dry land* before them, which encouraged them to follow God's guidance through the desert. When they were to enter Canaan, the Jordan River parted before them to encourage them in their wars, and *they went through that flood on foot.* The joys of our ancestors were our joys, and we should look on ourselves as sharing in them.

3.4. God's works have a commanding effect on everyone. By his works God maintains his sovereignty over the world (v. 7): *He rules by his power for ever; his eyes behold the nations.* He has a commanding arm. *Strong is his hand, and high is his right hand* (89:13). David reasons from this, *Let not the rebellious exalt themselves* (v. 7); let not those who have rebellious hearts dare to rise up in any acts of rebellion against God.

Verses 8–12

We have reason to bless God for two things:

1. His general protection (v. 9): *He holdeth our soul in life.* "He puts our soul in life" is the meaning. He gave us our being and upholds our existence by his constant renewed acts; his providence is a continued creation. As a Latin proverb puts it, "It is not mere existence, but happiness, which deserves the name of life." He *suffers not* (does not allow) *our feet to be moved* (v. 9). He prevents many unforeseen evils.

2. His particular acts by which he rescues his people from great distress. Notice:

2.1. How painful the distresses and dangers were (vv. 11–12). It is not clear which particular trouble of the church these verses are referring to; they might be the troubles of some private individuals or families. But whatever they were, the people were oppressed by problems and kept under them as with a load *upon their loins*, a burden on their backs (v. 11). Is anything more dangerous than fire and water? *We went through fire and water*, that is, afflictions of different kinds. *When men rose up against us*, that was fire and water (124:2–4), and this was the case here: "*Thou hast caused men to ride over our heads*" (v. 12), to trample all over us and gloat over us, to intimidate and abuse us, in fact, to try to make complete slaves of us. They have said to our souls, *Bow down* (fall prostrate), *that we may go over*" (Isa 51:23).

2.2. How gracious God's intentions were in bringing them into this distress and danger. Notice what the meaning of it is (v. 10): *Thou, O God, hast proved us, and tried us.* Suffering refines us, as silver is refined in the fire. Our graces are exercised in this way so that they may become stronger and more active and so that we may become better people, as silver is made better when it is refined by fire and its dross is removed. This will be for our inexpressible benefit, for this is how we come to share in God's holiness (Heb 12:10).

2.3. How glorious the final outcome was. The troubles of the church will certainly end well. God's people were in fire and water, but they came through them: "*We went through fire and water* (v. 12), and we did not die in the flames or floods." Whatever the troubles of the saints are, we bless God that there is a way through them. *Thou broughtest us out into a wealthy place* (v. 12), literally, "into a well-watered place," *like the gardens of the Lord* (Ge 13:10), and one that is therefore fruitful.

Verses 13–20

Having stirred up all people to bless the Lord, the psalmist here stirs himself:

1. In his devotions to his God (vv. 13–15).

1.1. By offering costly sacrifices (v. 13): *I will go into thy house with burnt offerings.* His sacrifices would be offered publicly, in the place which God had chosen: "I will go into your house with them." Christ is our temple, to whom we must bring our spiritual gifts and by whom they are sanctified. David's sacrifices will be the best of their kind—*burnt sacrifices*, which were completely burned up on the altar. He will *offer bullocks with goats* (v. 15) and *with the incense of rams* (v. 15), or "rams with incense." The incense was a type of Christ's intercession, without which our best sacrifices will not be accepted.

1.2. By a conscientious fulfillment of his vows. The psalmist had decided to do this (vv. 13–14): *I will pay thee my vows, which my lips have uttered when I was in trouble.*

2. In his declarations to his friends (v. 16). He calls an assembly of good people to hear his thankful account of God's favors toward him: *Come and hear, all you who fear God.* God's people should share their experiences with each other. We should use every opportunity to tell one another about the great things God has done for our souls,

the spiritual blessings with which he has blessed us (Eph 1:3). Now what was it that God had done for his soul?

2.1. He had created in him a love for the duty of prayer and had by his grace released his heart for that duty (v. 17): *I cried unto him with my mouth, and he was extolled with my tongue.* God allows us to pray, gives commands and encouragements to pray, and to crown everything, gives us a heart to pray. By crying out to him we do indeed praise him. He is willing to consider himself honored by the humble and confident prayers of the upright. He has been willing to unite his interests with ours to such an extent that in seeking our own welfare, we seek his glory. Another way to read the second half of the verse is, "His exaltation was under my tongue," that is, "I was considering in my mind how I might exalt his name." When prayers are in our mouths, praises must be in our hearts.

2.2. He had created in him a dread of sin as an enemy of prayer (v. 18): *If I regard iniquity in my heart,* I know very well *the Lord will not hear me.* The sense is plain: *If I regard iniquity in my heart,* that is, "If I cherish it, if I have favorable thoughts of it, if I love it, indulge it, and allow myself to consider it, God will not hear my prayer, nor can I expect a favorable answer to it."

2.3. He had graciously granted him the reply he desired to his prayers (v. 19). God did this for his soul: by answering his prayer, he gave him a sign of his favor. And so he concluded (v. 20), *Blessed be God.* What we gain by prayer we must respond to in praise. So that it would not be thought that the rescue was granted for the sake of some worthiness of his prayer, he ascribed it to God's love. "It was not my prayer that brought the rescue, but his love that sent it."

PSALM 67

Here is: 1. A prayer for the success of the church of Israel (v. 1). 2. A prayer that the Gentiles will be converted and that they will be brought into the church (vv. 2 – 5). 3. A prospect of happy and glorious times when God will do this (vv. 6 – 7).

Verses 1 – 7

The psalmist was honored with the spirit of prophecy so that he might foretell the enlargement of God's kingdom.

1. He begins with a prayer for the well-being and prosperity of the church as it then was (v. 1). When our Savior taught us to say, *Our Father,* he showed we should pray with and for others. The psalmist therefore does not pray, "God be merciful to me, and bless me," but *God be merciful to us, and bless us.* We are taught here:

1.1. That all our happiness comes from God's love, and so the first thing prayed for is, *God be merciful to us* (v. 1), to us sinners.

1.2. That our happiness is imparted and protected by God's blessing: *God bless us* (v. 1); that is, may he give us the privilege of sharing in his promises and give to us all the good contained in them. *God bless us* is a comprehensive prayer.

1.3. That our happiness is completed by the light of his face (Nu 6:24 – 26): *God cause his face to shine upon us* (v. 1), that is, "May God by his grace qualify us for his favor and then give us the signs of his favor." "To shine with us" is the margin reading: "May God cause his face to shine with us, working with us, and may the light of his face crown that work with success."

2. He moves from this to a prayer for the conversion of the Gentiles (v. 2): *That thy way may be known upon earth.* We too should be concerned for the whole earth in our prayers. *Father in heaven, hallowed be thy name, thy kingdom come* (Lk 11:2).

2.1. These verses, which point to the conversion of the Gentiles, may be taken:

2.1.1. As a prayer, and so it speaks of the desire of the Old Testament saints. There was nothing they wanted more than the dismantling of the dividing wall (Eph 2:14) and the releasing of the benefits of God's salvation. Notice then how the spirit of the Jews in the days of Christ and his apostles differed from the spirit of their ancestors. The true Israelites in former times wanted God's name to be known among the Gentiles, but those false Jews were angry at the preaching of the Gospel to the Gentiles.

2.1.2. As a prophecy that it will be as he prays here.

2.2. Three things are prayed for with reference to the Gentiles:

2.2.1. That divine revelation might be sent among them (v. 2). "May they all know, as well as we do, *what is good and what the Lord our God requires of them* (Mic 6:8); may they be blessed and honored with the same righteous statutes and judgments that are so much the praise of our nation and the envy of all its neighbors" (Dt 4:8). If God makes known his ways to us, and we walk in them, he will show us his salvation (50:23). Those who themselves have experienced the pleasantness of God's ways and the assurance of his salvation must want and pray that those things may be declared to others, in fact, to all nations.

2.2.2. That divine worship may be set up among them, as it will be wherever divine revelation is received and embraced (v. 3): "*Let the people praise thee, O God.* May they have reasons to praise you; may they have hearts that praise you; in fact, may not only some, but *all the people, praise thee.*" It is a prayer:

- That the Gospel might be preached to them, and then they would have good reason to praise God, as one praises him for the coming of the dawn after a long and dark night (Lk 1:78).
- That they might be converted and brought into the church, and then they would have a new nature in them that would praise God.
- That they might be joined into sacred assemblies, that they might praise him altogether with one mind and one mouth (Ro 15:6).

2.2.3. That divine government may be acknowledged (v. 4): *O let the nations be glad, and sing for joy!* The joy he wishes to the nations is holy joy, for it is joy that *God has taken to himself his great power and has reigned.* May they be glad that *thou shalt judge the people righteously* (v. 4). Let us all be glad that we are not to judge one another, but that the One who judges us is the Lord, whose judgment we are sure is based on truth (Ro 2:2).

3. He concludes with the joyful prospect of nothing but good when God does this, when the nations will be converted and brought to praise God.

3.1. The lower world will smile on them, and they will enjoy its fruits (v. 6): *Then shall the earth yield her increase.* This is not to say that God did not give rain from heaven and fruitful seasons to the nations when they *sat in darkness* (Mt 4:16; Ac 14:17); but when they were converted, the earth produced a harvest for God. Then it was fruitful for a good purpose. It then yielded a greater harvest than before, and this would bring great encouragement to people who through Christ acquired the covenant entitlement to its fruits and had a sanctified use of it.

3.2. The upper world will smile on them, and they will have its favors, which is much better: *God, even our own God, shall bless us* (v. 6). And again (v. 7), *God shall bless us.* We receive the products of the earth as a true mercy when our own God gives us his blessing with it.

3.3. All the world will be brought to do as they do: *The ends of the earth shall fear him* (v. 7), that is, they will worship him, and they will do so with a godly fear.

PSALM 68

The title of this psalm does not say on what occasion David wrote it, but it was probably when he brought the ark from the house of Obed-Edom to the tent he had pitched for it in Zion, for the psalm's first words are the prayer which Moses used at the moving of the ark (Nu 10:35). 1. He begins with prayer, both against God's enemies (vv. 1–2) and for his people (v. 3). 2. He proceeds to praise, which takes up the rest of the psalm, and he suggests as subjects for praise: 2.1. The greatness and goodness of God (vv. 4–6). 2.2. The wonderful works God has worked for his people in ages past, leading them through the desert (vv. 7–8), settling them in Canaan (vv. 9–10), giving them victory over their enemies (vv. 11–12), and rescuing them from the hands of their oppressors (vv. 13–14). 2.3. The special presence of God in his church (vv. 15–17). 2.4. The ascension of Christ (v. 18) and the salvation of God's people through Christ (vv. 19–20). 2.5. The victories which Christ will gain over his enemies and the favors he will give his church (vv. 21–28). 2.6. The enlargement of the church by the coming of the Gentiles into it (vv. 29–31). 3. And so he concludes the psalm with an awesome acknowledgment of the glory and grace of God (vv. 32–35).

Verses 1–6

In these verses:

1. David prays that God would appear in his glory:

1.1. To confound his enemies (vv. 1–2): "*Let God arise*, as a judge to pass sentence on them, as a general to take to the field and act against them, *and let them be scattered.* May God arise, as the sun does when it shines brightly at full strength, and may the children of darkness be scattered, as the shadows of the evening flee before the rising sun." In praying this way David comments on Moses' prayer (Nu 10:35), not only repeating it with application to himself and his own times, but also enlarging on it to show us how to use the prayers of Scripture. Although we are to pray for our enemies as such, we are still to pray against God's enemies as such, against their enmity toward him and all their attempts to destroy his kingdom.

1.2. To give assurance and joy to his own people (v. 3): "*Let the righteous be glad*, those who are now sorrowful; *let them rejoice before God*, may they be happy and joyful."

2. David praises God for his glorious appearances.

2.1. As a great God, infinitely great (v. 4): he *rides upon the heavens, by his name JAH.* He is the cause of all the movements of the heavenly bodies, just as one who rides in a chariot sets it in motion; he has supreme command over the influences of heaven. He rules these by his name, *Jah*, or *Jehovah*, the Lord, by his self-existent and self-sufficient being, the fountain of all existence, power, movement, and perfection; this is his name forever.

2.2. As a gracious God, a God of mercy and tender compassion. He is great, but because he is a God of great power, he uses his power to help those who are distressed (vv. 5–6). The fatherless, the widows, and the lonely find him to be a God who is all they need. He who *rides on the heavens* is *a Father of the fatherless* (v. 5). *Though God be high, yet has he respect unto the lowly* (138:6). He is *a Father of the fatherless* (v. 5), to have compassion on them, to bless them, to teach them, to provide for them, and to give them what they need. They are free to call him Father and to plead their relationship with him as their guardian (10:14, 18; 146:9). He is a patron of the widows, to advise them and to see that they are rightly dealt with, to acknowledge them and take up their cause (Pr 22:23). He listens to all their complaints and is generous in providing for all their needs. He is so *in his holy habitation* (dwelling place) (v. 5). Let them go to his holy dwelling place, to his word, and to his services of worship, and there they will find him, and find comfort in him. When families are to be built up, he establishes them: *God sets the solitary in families* (v. 6). He gives family or good friends to those who were lonely. He *makes those dwell at home that were* forced "to seek help abroad" (Dr. Henry Hammond's comment), putting those who were destitute into a position to gain their livelihood.

2.3. As a righteous God:

• In relieving the oppressed. He *brings out those that are bound with chains* (v. 6) and sets free those who have been unjustly imprisoned and enslaved. No chains can hold those whom God sets free.

• In dealing with oppressors: *The rebellious dwell in a dry land* (v. 6) and find no comfort in what they have gained fraudulently or by harming others.

Verses 7–14

Fresh blessings should remind us of former blessings and revive our sense of gratitude for them. Let them always remember:

1. That God himself guided Israel through the desert (v. 7). It was not so much a journey as a march, for they went as soldiers, as an army with banners.

2. That God revealed his glorious presence with them at Mount Sinai (v. 8). Never did any people see the glory of God or hear his voice as Israel did (Dt 4:32–33). Never had any people had such an excellent law given them, explained, and enforced in such a way. *Sinai itself*, that vast and long mountain range, *was moved at the presence of God* (v. 8); see also Jdg 5:4–5; Dt 33:2; Hab 3:3. Just as this terrible appearance of the divine Majesty would possess them with a fear of him, so also it would encourage their faith in him and their dependence on him. Whatever mountains of difficulty lay in the way of their being happily settled, the One who could move Sinai itself could move them.

3. That God provided very comfortably for them both in the desert and in Canaan (vv. 9–10): *Thou didst send a plentiful rain and hast prepared of thy goodness for the poor.* This may refer:

3.1. To the provision of their camp in the desert with manna, which was rained down on them, as were the quails (78:24, 27). Or:

3.2. To the timely supplies given them in Canaan, that land *flowing with milk and honey*, which is said to *drink water of the rain of heaven* (Dt 11:11). This also looks further, to the spiritual provision made for God's Israel; the Spirit of grace and the Gospel of grace are the plentiful rain with which God confirms his inheritance, and from which the fruit of that inheritance grows (Isa 45:8).

4. That God often gave them victory over their enemies. *The Lord gave the word* (v. 11), as the general of their armies. He raised up judges for them, gave them their commissions and instructions, and assured them of success. God gave them his word—*the word of the Lord came* to them (Jer 1:2; Eze 1:3; Hos 1:1; etc.)—and then *great was the company of those that published it*, of preachers and prophets, both male and female (the word here is feminine) (v. 11). *Kings of armies did flee*; they withdrew without striking a blow; they fled quickly and never rallied again. *She that tarried at home divided the spoil* (v. 12). Not only the men, the soldiers who stayed with the supplies, who were to share the plunder (1Sa 30:24), but even the women who stayed at home had a share, which shows the abundance of plunder that was to be taken. *When the Almighty scattered kings for her* (the church), *she was white as snow in Salmon*, purified and refined by the mercies of God; *when the host went forth against the enemy, they kept themselves from every wicked thing* (Dt 23:9), and so the army returned victorious, and the victory confirmed Israel in their purity and godliness. By the resurrection of Christ our spiritual enemies were made to flee; they were disabled forever from harming any of God's people.

5. That from a low and despised condition they had been advanced to one of splendor and prosperity. When they were slaves in Egypt, and later when they were oppressed sometimes by one powerful neighbor and sometimes by another, they did, as it were, *lie among the pots* (v. 13), or rubbish, as despised, broken vessels. But God finally *delivered them from the pots* (81:6), and in David's time they were set to be one of the most prosperous kingdoms in the world, *like the wings of a dove covered with silver* (v. 13). "And so," comments Dr. Henry Hammond, "under Christ's kingdom, the idolaters who had been worshiping wood and stone and been given up to their sinful desires would leave that detestable condition and be advanced to the service of Christ and the practice of all Christian virtues, the greatest inner beauties in the world."

Verses 15–21

Having praised God as the God of Israel in general, David comes here to give him praise as Zion's God in a special way; compare 9:11: *Sing praises to the Lord who dwelleth in Zion*, which is why Zion is called *the hill of God*.

1. He compares *the hill of God* with the mountains of Bashan and other high and fruitful hills, and he prefers it to them (vv. 15–16). It is true that Zion is only small and low in comparison with them, but it is preeminent above them all: it is the hill of God. "Why do you gloat over poor Zion and boast of your own significance? This is the hill that God has chosen." Zion was especially honorable because it was a type of the Gospel church, which is therefore called Mount Zion (Heb 12:22), and this is suggested here when he says, *The Lord will dwell in it for ever*.

2. He compares it with Mount Sinai, of which he has spoken already (v. 8), and he shows that Zion has the *Shechinah*, or divine presence, in it as really, although not as perceptibly, as Sinai itself had (v. 17). Angels are the chariots of God. They are very numerous: *Twenty thousands*, very many thousands. An innumerable company of angels lives in the heavenly Jerusalem (Heb 12:22). Some read the last words of the verse, "Sinai is in the sanctuary," that is, the sanctuary was to take the place, for Israel, of Mount Sinai, from where they received the divine words.

3. The glory of Mount Zion was the King whom God *set on that holy hill* (2:6). The psalmist speaks here about the ascension of that King, and his words are explicitly applied to this in Eph 4:8: *Thou hast ascended on high* (v. 18); compare 47:5–6. Christ's ascension is spoken of to his honor.

3.1. It was then that he triumphed over the gates of hell. He led *captivity captive* (v. 18), that is, he led his captives in triumph, as great conquerors used to do (Col 2:15). He led captive those who had led us captive and who, if he had not intervened, would have held us captive forever. In fact, he *led captivity itself captive* (v. 18), having completely broken the power of sin and Satan. This suggests the complete victory which Jesus Christ gained over our spiritual enemies, which was such that through him *we also are more than conquerors*, that is, victors (Ro 8:37).

3.2. It was then that he opened the gates of heaven to all believers: *Thou hast received gifts for men* (v. 18). He *gave gifts to men* is how the apostle Paul reads it (Eph 4:8). And he gave what he had received; having received power to give eternal life, he gives it to *as many as were given him* (Jn 17:2). The margin reads: "Thou hast received gifts in the man," that is, in the human nature with which Christ was willing to clothe himself so that he might be *a merciful and faithful high priest in things pertaining to God* (Heb 2:17). To exalt the kindness and love of Christ to us in receiving these gifts for us, the psalmist remarks that he received them even for *the rebellious* (v. 18), for those who had been rebellious. Perhaps it is especially meant to refer to the Gentiles, who had been *enemies in their minds by wicked works* (Col 1:21). It greatly exalts the grace of Christ that through him, when rebels submit, they are not only pardoned but also promoted. Christ came to a rebellious world not to condemn it, but so that it might be saved through him (Jn 3:17). He *received gifts for the rebellious* so that *the Lord God might dwell among them* (v. 18), so that he might set up a church in a rebellious world.

4. The glory of Zion's King is that he is a Savior and generous giver to all his willing people and a consuming fire to all those who persist in rebelling against him (vv. 19–21). We have here set before us good and evil, life and death, and the blessing and the curse (Dt 30:15, 19; Mk 16:16). So many, so extensive, are the gifts of God's goodness that he may be truly said to *load us* with them; he *pours out blessings till there is no room to receive them* (Mal 3:10). *He is our God* (95:7), and so he will be the God of eternal salvation to us, for only that will correspond to the vast depths of his covenant relationship with us as his people. Those who persist in being his enemies will certainly be destroyed (v. 21): *God shall wound the head of his enemies*, of Satan, the old Serpent, of whom it was foretold by the first promise that *the seed of the woman* would *break his head* (Ge 3:15). He will *wound* (crush) *the hairy scalp* (crowns) *of such a one as goeth on still in his trespasses* (v. 21). In calling the head *the hairy scalp* the psalmist may be alluding to Absalom, whose flowing hair was his restraint and led to his death. Or it may refer to the fiercest and cruelest of his enemies, who let their hair grow to make themselves look more frightful.

Verses 22–31

We have three things in these verses:

1. The gracious promise which God makes that he will redeem his people and give them victory over his and their enemies (vv. 22–23): *The Lord said, "I will* do great things for my people, as the God of their salvation." *I will*

again bring them from the depths of the sea (v. 22)—as he did with Israel when he brought them out of the slavery of Egypt into the peace and freedom of the desert—and *I will again bring them from Bashan* (v. 22)—as he did with Israel when he delivered them from their shortages and wanderings in the desert into the fullness and settlement of the land of Canaan, for the land of Bashan was on the other side of the Jordan, where they had wars with Sihon and Og, and from where their next move was into Canaan. But this is not all. He will also make them victorious over their enemies (v. 23): *That thy feet may be dipped*, as you pass along, *in the blood of thy enemies*, and so that the *tongue of thy dogs* may lap *in the same*. Dogs licked the blood of Ahab, and in the account of the destruction of the anti-Christian generation, we read of blood up *to the horses' bridles* (Rev 14:20).

2. The welcome that God's own people will give to these glorious revelations of his grace.

2.1. "*They have seen*, your people have seen, *thy goings* (your procession), *O God!* While others pay no attention to the work of the Lord, they have seen the procession of my God, my King, in the sanctuary." An active faith lays hold of God; he is God and King, but that is not all: he is *my* God and King. God's most remarkable activities in and by his word and ordinances take place in the sanctuary, and especially among his people in the Gospel church.

2.2. When we see his procession in his sanctuary, those of us who are most directly employed in the service of the temple praise him (v. 25). It was expected that the Levites would lead in his praises. And because it was a day of extraordinary triumph, there were among them young women playing tambourines. "Similarly," according to Dr. Henry Hammond, "when Christ has gone up to heaven, the apostles will celebrate and declare it to all the world, and even the women who witnessed it will warmly join with them in making it known." Let all the people of Israel in their sacred religious assembly give glory to God: *Bless God*, not only in temples but also in synagogues, or in the schools of the prophets, or wherever there is a congregation of those who *come forth from the fountain of Israel* (v. 26). Public mercies that we jointly share in call for public thanksgivings, which everyone should join in. Let those among them who are the most eminent go before the others in praising God (v. 27). There was *little Benjamin*, which was the royal tribe in Saul's time, *with their rulers*, and there were *the princes of Judah*, which was the royal tribe in David's time, and *their council*, their leaders.

2.3. We depend on him to complete what he has begun (v. 28). In the first part of the verse, the psalmist speaks to Israel: "*Thy God has commanded thy strength*; that is, whatever is done for you, or whatever strength you have to help yourself, comes from God, his power, his grace, and the word which he has summoned." In the second part of this verse, he speaks to God, encouraged by his experiences: "*Strengthen, O God, that which thou hast wrought for us* (v. 28). Lord, confirm what you have summoned, fulfill what you have promised, and bring to a favorable conclusion the good work you have so gloriously begun" (Php 1:6).

3. The powerful invitation and motivation which will be given those who are outside to come and join the church (vv. 29–31). This was partly fulfilled by the coming of many converts to the Jewish religion in the days of David and Solomon. It was to have its complete fulfillment, however, in the conversion of the Gentile nations to the faith of Christ (Eph 3:6).

3.1. Some will submit for fear (v. 30): "*The company of spearmen*, who stand out against Christ and his

Gospel, who are enraged and violent like a herd of bulls, fat and rebellious as *the calves of the people*"—which is a description of those Jews and Gentiles who opposed the Gospel of Christ and did what they could to prevent the setting up of his kingdom in the world. "Lord, rebuke them, humble their pride and confound their evil, until they are conquered by the convictions of their consciences and each one of them is brought to *submit themselves with pieces of silver*, glad to make their peace with the church on any terms." Many people have been happily saved from destruction by being rebuked. But as for those who will not submit, he prays for their dispersion, which amounts to a prophecy of it: *Scatter thou the people that delight in war* (v. 30). This may refer to the unbelieving Jews, who delighted in making war on the holy race and would not submit, and so were scattered over the face of the earth. David had himself been a warrior, but he could appeal to God that he never delighted in war and bloodshed for its own sake.

3.2. Others will submit willingly (vv. 29, 31): *Because of thy temple at Jerusalem*—David speaks about this in faith, for the temple of Jerusalem had not yet been built in his time; only the materials and model had been prepared—*Because of thy temple at Jerusalem, kings shall bring presents unto thee.* He mentions Egypt and Cush (Ethiopia), two countries out of which subjects and petitioners were least to be expected (v. 31): *Princes shall come out of Egypt* as envoys to seek God's favor and to submit to him. They will be accepted, for the *Lord of hosts shall* then *bless them, saying, Blessed be Egypt my people* (Isa 19:25). Even Cush, which had stretched out its hands against God's Israel (2Ch 14:9), would now *stretch out her hands unto God* (v. 31), in prayer, in presents, and to take hold of him, and would do that soon.

Verses 32–35

Having prayed for the Gentiles, the psalmist here invites them to come and join the devout Israelites in praising God, suggesting that their accession to the church would make them joyful and would therefore be the subject of their praise (v. 32): let the *kingdoms of the earth sing praises to the Lord*:

1. Because of his supreme and sovereign rule: *He rides on the heavens of heavens which were of old* (v. 33); compare v. 4. From the beginning, in fact, from before all time, he has prepared his throne. He sits in the vault of heaven and directs the influences of his power and goodness to this world.

2. Because of his awesome majesty: *He sends out his voice*, and that voice is mighty. This may refer either generally to the thunder, which is called the voice of the Lord and is said to be powerful and majestic (29:3–4), or in particular to the thunder in which God spoke to Israel at Mount Sinai.

3. Because of his mighty power: *Ascribe you strength unto God. Thine is the kingdom and power*, and therefore *thine is the glory.* We must acknowledge his power:

- In the kingdom of grace: *His excellency* (majesty) *is over Israel*; he shows his sovereign care in protecting and governing his church.
- In the kingdom of providence: *His strength is in the clouds*, from where the thunder of his power, the light and great rains of his strength, come.

4. Because of the glory of his sanctuary and the wonders worked there (v. 35): *O God, thou art terrible* (awesome) *out of thy holy places.* God is to be wondered at and adored with reverence and godly fear by all those

who serve him in his sanctuary, who receive his word. No quality of God is to be more feared by sinners than his holiness.

5. Because of the grace given to his people: *The God of Israel is he that gives strength and power to his people*, which the gods of the nations, who were worthless and deceitful, could not give their worshipers; how could they help them, when they could not even help themselves? If it is the God of Israel who gives strength and power to his people, they should say, *Blessed be God*. If everything comes from him, let all the praise for it go back to him.

PSALM 69

David wrote this psalm when he was suffering. 1. He complains about the great distress and trouble he is in, and he passionately begs God to relieve and help him (vv. 1–21). 2. He invokes the judgments of God on his persecutors (vv. 22–29). 3. He concludes with the voice of joy and praise, with the assurance that God will help him and will work things out well for the church (vv. 30–36). Several passages in this psalm are applied to Christ in the New Testament and are said to be fulfilled in him (vv. 4, 9, 21), and v. 22 refers to the enemies of Christ. It is like Ps 22: it begins with the humiliation of Christ and ends with his exaltation.

Verses 1–12

In these verses David complains about his troubles:

1. His complaints are very sad, and he pours them out before the Lord as one who hopes to relieve himself of a burden which lies very heavily on him.

1.1. He complains about the deep effects his troubles have on his spirit (vv. 1–2): "The *waters of affliction*, those bitter waters, *have come unto my soul*. They not only threaten my life but also disturb my mind, so that I cannot enjoy God and my own life as I once did." *The spirit of a man will sustain his infirmity* (Pr 18:14), but what will we do when the spirit has been wounded? That was David's situation. This points to the suffering Christ experienced in his own soul, and the inner agony he was in when he said, *Now is my soul troubled* (Jn 12:27), and, *My soul is exceedingly sorrowful* (overwhelmed with sorrow) (Mt 26:38), for it was his soul that he made an offering for sin (Isa 53:10).

1.2. He complains that his troubles have continued for a long time (v. 3): *I am weary of my crying*. He cried out to his God, and the more death was in his sight, the more life there was in his prayers. He did not receive an immediate favorable answer. *My eyes fail while I wait for my God* (v. 3). But his pleading with God was a sign that he had decided not to give up believing and praying. His throat was parched, but his heart was not; his eyes failed, but his faith did not. In the same way, our Lord Jesus cried out on the cross, *Why hast thou forsaken me?* but at the same time, he kept hold of his relationship with God: *My God, my God* (Mt 27:46).

1.3. He complains about how much his many enemies hate him, how unjust and cruel they are, and the hardships they put on him (v. 4). "*They hate me without a cause* (v. 4); I never did them the slightest wrong, that they should bear me such ill will." Our Savior applies this to himself (Jn 15:25): *They hated me without a cause*. These enemies were not to be disregarded; their number was formidable—*They are more than the hairs of my head* (v. 4)—and also their strength—they *are mighty* in authority and power. *Then I restored that which I took*

not away (what I did not steal) (v. 4). If we apply this to David, it was what his enemies compelled him to do, and it was what he agreed to so that if possible he might pacify them and make them at peace with him. But if we apply it to Christ, it is a significant description of the atonement he made to God for our sin by his blood: *Then he restored what he took not away*; he experienced the punishment that was due to us; he paid our debt and suffered for our offenses. Some instances of God's glory were taken away by human sin; human honor, peace, and happiness were also taken away; neither of these did he take away, and yet he restored them by the power of his death.

1.4. He complains about the unkindness of his friends and relatives (v. 8): "*I have become a stranger to my brethren*, a foreigner to my own family; they shamelessly attack me, are embarrassed to talk to me, and are ashamed to acknowledge me." This was fulfilled in Christ, whose *brethren did not believe on him* (Jn 7:5), who *came to his own and his own received him not* (Jn 1:11), and who was abandoned by his disciples.

1.5. He complains about the contempt put on him and the scorn which he continually has to endure. It is especially here that his complaint points to Christ, who for our sakes submitted to the greatest disgrace and made himself nothing. David here takes notice of the indignities done him. They ridiculed him for the things he did by which he both humbled himself and honored God. When David acted out of devotion to God and to show his respect toward him, *wept and chastened his soul with fasting* (v. 10), and *made sackcloth his garment* (v. 11), as humble penitents used to do, then instead of commending his devotion, they did all they could to prevent others from following his good example, for it is said that *that was to his reproach* (scorn) (v. 10). They laughed at him for being so foolish as to humble himself in such a way, and even for this he *became a proverb to them* (v. 11). Even the gravest and the most honorable mocked him, from whom better should have been expected: *Those that sit in the gate speak against me*. He was also the song of the drunkards. They made fun of him and caused their companions to do so too. Notice what is the common lot of the best people: those who are commended by the wise are the song of fools. But it is easy for those who rightly judge things (Lk 7:43) to despise being despised in this way.

2. His confessions of sin are very serious (v. 5): "*O God, thou knowest my foolishness*, both what I have done and what I have not done, and so you know how innocent I am of those crimes which they accuse me of." This is the genuine confession of someone who is repenting, who knows that he cannot prosper if he pretends he has not sinned and that he is therefore wise to acknowledge his sin, because it is exposed and lies open before God. God knows the corruption of our nature: "*Thou knowest the foolishness* (v. 5) that is bound up in my heart" (Pr 22:15). He also knows the sins of our lives, even those committed most secretly. They are all done in his sight, and are never put behind his back until they are repented of and pardoned.

3. His requests are passionate. "*Save me, O God*, save me from sinking and despairing." *Let not those that wait on thee, O Lord God of hosts, and that seek thee, O God of Israel, be ashamed and confounded for my sake!* This suggests his fear that if God did not support him, it would be a discouragement to all other good people and would give their enemies reason to triumph over them. If Jesus Christ had not been acknowledged and accepted by his Father in his suffering, all who seek God and hope in him would have been ashamed and confounded, but they have

confidence toward God and may come boldly in Christ's name to the throne of grace (Heb 4:16).

4. His plea is very powerful (vv. 7, 9). "Lord, take away the scorn and plead my cause. *For thy sake I have borne reproach* (I have endured scorn)." Those who are spoken about wrongly for doing well may leave it to God in humble confidence to *bring forth their righteousness as the light* (37:6). "*The zeal of thy house has eaten me up* (consumes me) (v. 9). Those who hate you and your house hate me for that reason, because they know how zealous I am for it. It is this that has devoured all the love and respect they might have had for me." Or the verse may be interpreted as showing David's zeal for God's house, showing that he was as indignant at all the dishonor shown to God's name as if it had been shown to his own name. He took to heart all the contempt given to religious faith. Both parts of v. 9 apply to Christ.

4.1. It showed his love for his Father that *the zeal of his house did even eat him up* when he drove the buyers and sellers out of the temple, which reminded his disciples of this text (Jn 2:17).

4.2. It showed his self-denial, and that he did not live to please himself, that the *reproaches of those that reproached God fell upon him* (Ro 15:3), and he set us an example in this.

Verses 13–21

David's enemies have spoken evil about him for his fasting and praying, and he has been sung about by the drunkards, but nevertheless he is determined to continue praying. Although we may be jeered at for doing good, we must never be jeered out of it. *As for me, my prayer is unto thee, O Lord!* Notice:

1. What his requests are: *Hear me* (v. 13), and again, *Hear me, O Lord!* (v. 16), "*Hear me speedily* (v. 17), not only listen to what I am saying, but also give what I ask. *Deliver me out of the mire* (v. 14); let me not sink in it, but help me out and *set my feet on a rock* (40:2). *Let me be delivered from those that hate me*, as a lamb from the paw of a lion (v. 14). Although I have come into deep water (v. 2), do not let the waters overwhelm me (v. 15). Do not let me fall into the gulf of despair; do not let the deep swallow me up. Do not let the pit close its mouth over me, for if that were to happen, I would surely be done for." He prayed that God would turn to him (v. 16), that he would smile on him and not hide his face from him (v. 17).

2. What his pleas are to support these requests:

2.1. He pleads God's mercy, love, and truth (v. 13): *In the multitude of thy mercy hear me.* He repeats his argument taken from the mercy of God: *Hear me,* for *thy loving-kindness is good* (v. 16). His love is rich, plentiful, and abundant. "Turn to me, *according to the multitude of thy tender mercies*" (v. 16).

2.2. He pleads his own distress and affliction: "*Hide not thy face* from me, *for I am in trouble* (v. 17), and so I need your favor. Since I am in trouble, your favor will be coming at the right time and I will know how to value it." *Thou hast known my reproach, my shame, and my dishonour.* The psalmist speaks the language of a noble nature when he says (v. 20), *Reproach* (scorn) *has broken my heart; I am full of heaviness* (I am left helpless), for it is hard on one who knows the worth of a good name to be given a bad reputation. When we consider what an honor it is to be dishonored for the sake of God, however, and to be counted worthy to suffer disgrace for his name, as the apostles considered it in Ac 5:41, we will see there is no reason at all why it should be heartbreaking to us.

2.3. He pleads the arrogance and cruelty of his enemies (v. 18). "*My adversaries are all before thee* (v. 19); you know what danger I am in from them, what enemies they are to you, and how much dishonor is brought on you in what they do and intend against me." One example of their cruelty is given (v. 21): *They gave me gall for my meat*—the word *gall* stands for a bitter herb and is often linked with *wormwood*—*and in my thirst they gave me vinegar to drink.* This was literally fulfilled in Christ, and pointed so directly to him that he did not say *It is finished* until this was fulfilled (Jn 19:28–29).

2.4. He pleads the unkindness of his friends and his disappointment in them (v. 20): *I looked for some to take pity, but there was none*; they all failed him like summer streams. This was fulfilled in Christ, for in his sufferings all his disciples forsook him and fled.

Verses 22–29

These imprecations are not David's prayers against his enemies, but prophecies of the destruction of Christ's persecutors, especially the Jewish nation, which our Lord himself foretold with tears, and which was fulfilled about forty years after the death of Christ. The first two verses of this paragraph are expressly applied to the judgments of God on the unbelieving Jews by the apostle Paul (vv. 22–23; Ro 11:9–10), and so the whole must be considered that way. Notice:

1. The judgments which would come on those who crucified Christ. These judgments would not come on all of them, for there were those who had a hand in his death but repented and found mercy (Ac 2:23; 3:14–15); but they would come on those who justified it by a stubborn infidelity and rejection of his Gospel and by a hardened enmity toward his disciples and followers; and they would come on their successors. See 1Th 2:15–16. It is here foretold:

1.1. That their sacrifices and offerings would be trouble and harm to them (v. 22): *Let their table become a snare.* This may be understood to refer to the altar of the Lord, which is called *his table* (Eze 39:20; Mal 1:7, 12) *and theirs* (Ro 11:9) because in feasting on the sacrifices they shared in the altar. Or it may be understood to refer to their ordinary creature comforts, even their necessary food. They gave Christ gall and vinegar, and so it is right that their food and drink will be made gall and vinegar to them.

1.2. That they would never have the assurance of either the knowledge or the peace which believers are blessed with in the Gospel of Christ (v. 23). *Let their eyes be darkened*, so that they will not see the glory of God in the face of Christ (2Co 4:6). Their sin was that they would not see, but shut their eyes to the light. "May they be driven to despair and filled with constant confusion." This was fulfilled in the desperate counsels of the Jews when the Romans attacked them.

1.3. That they would fall and lie under God's anger and fiery indignation (v. 24): *Pour out thy indignation upon them.*

1.4. That their place and nation would be completely taken away, the very thing that they were afraid of and that they were trying to prevent, as they claimed, when they persecuted Christ (Jn 11:48): *Let their habitation be desolate*, may their place be deserted (v. 25), which was fulfilled when their country was devastated by the Romans and when *Zion, for their sakes, was ploughed as a field* (Mic 3:12). The temple was the house which they were especially proud of, but this was *left unto them desolate* (Mt 23:38). *Let none dwell in their tents* (v. 25), which was remarkably fulfilled in Judah and Jerusalem, for after the destruction of the Jews it was a long time before the country was inhabited and prospered again.

1.5. That their way to ruin would be downhill, and nothing would stop them (v. 27): "Lord, leave them to themselves, to *add iniquity to iniquity.*" *Let them not come into thy righteousness* (v. 27). It is not that God excludes any from that righteousness, for the Gospel excludes no one except those who exclude themselves by their unbelief.

1.6. That they would be cut off from all hopes of happiness (v. 28): "*Let them be blotted out of the book of the living.* May they not be allowed to live any longer, because the longer they live, the more trouble they will cause." Many unbelieving Jews were killed by the sword or famine. The nation was blotted out as a nation and did not become a people.

2. What the sin is for which these terrible judgments would come on these persecutors of Christ (v. 26): *They persecute him whom thou hast smitten, and talk to the grief of thy wounded.* Christ was the One whom God had struck, for *it pleased the Lord to bruise him,* and he was considered *stricken, smitten of God, and afflicted,* and so people *hid their faces from him* (Isa 53:3–4, 10). They persecuted him with such a rage that it reached heaven; they cried out, *Crucify him, crucify him* (Lk 23:21).

3. What the psalmist thinks about himself in the middle of all this (v. 29): "*But I am poor and sorrowful; that is the worst of my situation. I am suffering under outward affliction, although I am written among* (listed with) *the righteous* (v. 28) and am not under God's wrath as they are."

Verses 30–36

Here the psalmist, as both a type of Christ and an example to Christians, takes up holy joy and praise to conclude the psalm that he began with complaints and expressions of his sorrows.

1. He decides he himself will praise God (vv. 30–31): "*I will praise the name of God* not only with my heart but also with my song, and *magnify him with thanksgiving.*" And *this shall please the Lord* through Christ, who is the Mediator of our praises as well as of our prayers, more than the most valuable legal sacrifices, *an ox or bullock* (v. 31), would please him. This is a plain indication that in the days of the Messiah an end would be put not only to the sacrifices instituted by the ceremonial law, not only the sacrifices of atonement but also those of praise and acknowledgment, and that instead of them spiritual sacrifices of praise and thanksgiving would be accepted. It is a great encouragement to us that humble and thankful praises are more pleasing to God than the most costly, showy sacrifices are or ever were.

2. He encourages other good people to rejoice in God and continue to seek him (vv. 32–33): *The humble shall see this and be glad.* They will see:

• How ready God is to listen to the poor when they cry out to him, and to give them what they call on him for.
• The exaltation of the Savior, for the psalmist has been speaking of him, and he has been speaking about himself as a type of him.

3. He calls on every creature, the heaven and earth and sea and the inhabitants of each, to praise God (v. 34). The praises of the world must be offered for God's favors to his church (vv. 35–36), for God will save Zion, the holy mountain, where his service was maintained. *The cities of Judah shall be built:* individual churches will be formed and added according to the Gospel pattern, so that there

may be a remnant to *dwell there* and to possess it. Those who love his name, who are kindly disposed to religious faith in general, will take up the Christian religion and take their place in the Christian church. They will dwell there as citizens of the household of God (Eph 2:19). David will never lack someone to stand before him. The Redeemer will see his offspring, and prolong his days in them (Isa 53:10), until the mystery of God is accomplished (Rev 10:7) and the mystical body completed.

PSALM 70

This psalm is adapted to a state of suffering; it is copied almost word for word from Ps 40:13–17, and some think that is why it is entitled a psalm to bring to remembrance. *David here prays that God would send: 1. Help to him (vv. 1, 5). 2. Shame on his enemies (vv. 2–3). 3. Joy to his friends (v. 4).*

Title

The title tells us that this psalm was intended *to bring to remembrance,* that is, to remind God of his mercy and promises. In prayer, we may use the words we have often used before: in his agony our Savior prayed three times, repeating the same words (Mt 26:44). David here uses words he has used before.

Verses 1–5

1. David here prays that God would come quickly to relieve and help him (vv. 1, 5): "*I am poor and needy,* in want and in distress, and much at a loss within myself. *Make haste unto me* (v. 1), for the longing desire of my soul is toward you. I will perish if I am not helped quickly. I have no one else I can expect relief from: *Thou art my help and my deliverer* (v. 5). You have committed yourself to be so to all who seek you. I depend on you to be so to me; I have often found you to be so. You are all I need; therefore come quickly to me."

2. David prays that God would cover the faces of his enemies with shame (vv. 2–3). "*Let them be ashamed* (v. 2); may they be brought to repentance and put to shame so that they seek your name (83:16). May they see their foolishness in fighting against those whom you protect. However, may their intentions against me be thwarted, and then they will be put to shame and confusion, and *much cast down in their own eyes*" (Ne 6:16).

3. David prays that God would fill the hearts of his friends with joy (v. 4). Let us make the service of God our great work and the favor of God our great delight and pleasure, for that is seeking him and loving his salvation. Let us then be assured that the joy of the Lord will fill our minds and the praises of the Lord will fill our mouths. If it is not so, then we have only ourselves to blame. All who have good wishes for the strength and encouragement of the saints, and who desire the glory of God, must surely say a hearty *amen* to this prayer, that those who love God's salvation may say continually, *Let God be magnified* (v. 4).

PSALM 71

David wrote this psalm in his old age. But he was not detailed in presenting his case, because he intended it for the general use of God's people in their suffering, especially by those who face their declining years, for this psalm, above any other, is fitted for the use of older disciples of Jesus Christ. 1. He begins the psalm with confident prayers that God would rescue and save him (vv. 2, 4), that he would not reject him (v. 9) or be far from him (v. 12), but would enable him to praise him (v. 8), and that his enemies might be put to shame (v. 13). He pleads his confidence in God (vv. 1, 3, 5, 7), the experience he has had of help from God (vv. 6, 17), and the hatred of his enemies toward him (vv. 10–11). 2. He concludes the psalm with confident praises (v. 14). His hope was never more established (vv. 16, 18, 20–21). His joys and thanksgiving were never more released (vv. 15, 19, 22–24). He is in ecstasy with joyful praise.

Verses 1–13

David prays here for two things in general, that he might not be put to shame and that his enemies and persecutors might be put to shame:

1. He prays that he might never become ashamed of his dependence on God or disappointed in his confident expectations of him. Every true believer may come boldly to the throne of grace (Heb 4:16) with this request.

1.1. David professes his confidence in God, and he repeats his profession of that confidence, describing it to God and pleading it with him. We praise God by telling him, if it is true, that our complete confidence is in him (v. 1): "*In thee, O Lord! and only in you, do I put my trust.* Whatever others may do, I choose the God of Jacob as my help." *Thou art my rock and my fortress* (v. 3); and again, *Thou art my refuge, my strong refuge* (v. 7), that is, "I flee to you and am sure to be safe in you and under your protection. If you protect me, no one or nothing can harm me. *Thou art my hope and my trust*" (v. 5); that is, "you have said to me in your word that you are the proper object of my hope and trust. I have hoped in you and have never found it in vain to do so."

1.2. His confidence in God is supported and encouraged by his experiences (vv. 5–6): "*Thou hast been my trust from my youth*; ever since I was capable of discerning between my right hand and my left, I have rested on you, for *by thee have I been holden up* (held up) *from the womb.*" The One who has helped us from birth should be our hope from our youth. If we received so much mercy from God before we were capable of serving him in any way, we should lose no time in serving him when we are capable of doing so. "You are the One who took me into the arms of your grace, under the shadow of your wings (17:8; 36:7; etc.), into the bond of your covenant. I have reason to hope that you will protect me; you who have upheld me up to this time will not let me fall now. You who helped me when I could not help myself will not abandon me now that I am as helpless as I was then. *My praise shall therefore be continually of thee* (v. 6)."

1.3. His requests to God are:

1.3.1. That he might *never be put to confusion* (v. 1), that he might not be disappointed because he does not receive the mercy he expected and so become ashamed of his expectation.

1.3.2. That he might be rescued from the hands of his enemies (v. 2): "*Deliver me in thy righteousness.* As you are the righteous Judge of the world, pleading the cause of the wronged, cause me in some way or other to escape. *Incline thy ear unto my prayers* (v. 2), respond to them and save me from my troubles" (v. 4). *Thou hast given commandment to save me* (v. 3), that is, "you have promised to do it," and there is such effectiveness in God's promises that they are often spoken of as commands. Many eyes are on the psalmist (v. 7): "*I am as a wonder* (portent) *unto many*; everyone is waiting to see what will be the outcome of the extraordinary troubles I have fallen into and the

extraordinary confidence I profess to have in God." Or, "I am looked on as a freak, I am avoided by everyone, and so am ruined unless the Lord is my refuge. People abandon me, but God will not."

1.3.3. That he might always find rest and safety in God (v. 3): *Be thou my strong habitation*; be to me *a rock of repose, whereto I may continually resort*, a rock of refuge to which I can always go. Those who are at home with God, who live a life of fellowship with him and confidence in him, who continually turn to him in faith and prayer, may promise themselves a strong refuge, one that will never fall by itself and can never be broken through by any invading power. "*Let my mouth be filled with thy praise*, as it now is with my complaints, and then I will not be ashamed of my hope, but my enemies will be ashamed of their arrogance."

1.3.4. That he might not be neglected now in his declining years (v. 9): *Cast me not off* now *in the time of my old age; forsake me not when my strength fails.* Notice:

1.3.4.1. The weaknesses of old age: *My strength fails.* Whereas there was once a strong physical body and a vigorous mind, strong eyesight, a strong voice, and strong limbs, unfortunately they have failed in old age.

1.3.4.2. The desire he had for the continuation of God's presence with him in these weaknesses: *Lord, cast me not off; do not then forsake me* (v. 9). Rejection and abandonment by God is to be dreaded at any time, especially in old age and when our strength fails us, for God is the strength of our heart (73:26). But the faithful servants of God may be well assured that he will not reject them in old age or abandon them when their strength fails. He is a Master who does not reject old servants. David again prays in confidence (v. 12): "*O God, be not far from me; O my God, make haste for my help*, so that I will not perish before help comes."

2. He prays that his enemies might be made ashamed of their plots against him. "*They lay wait for my soul* (v. 10), and they want to harm me (v. 13). *They take counsel together.* They say, *God has forsaken him: persecute and take* (pursue and seize) *him* (v. 11)." The premises of David's enemies are completely false here. All are not forsaken by God who think they are or who are thought by others to have been. And just as their premises were false, so also was their deduction cruel. But *rejoice not against me, O my enemy: though I fall, I shall rise* (Mic 7:8). The One who seems to forsake for a few moments will come with kindness forever. "*Let them be confounded and consumed that are adversaries to my soul.* If they are not put to shame by repentance, and thereby saved, may they be confounded with everlasting disgrace, and so be ruined."

Verses 14–24

David is here in a holy rapture of joy and praise, arising from his faith and hope in God. We have both together in v. 14, where there is a sudden and significant change in his voice. His fears are all silenced, his hopes raised, and his prayers turned to thanksgiving. "Let my enemies say whatever they want in order to drive me to despair; *I will hope continually*, hope in every condition, even on the cloudiest and darkest day. I will continue to hope to the end."

1. His heart is established in faith and hope.

1.1. What he hopes in are God's power and promises. "*I will go in the strength of the Lord God*, not sit down in despair, but stir myself; I will go out and go on not in any strength of my own but in God's strength and in the strength of his grace. *I will make mention of thy righteousness* (v. 16), that is, your faithfulness to every word which you have spoken, the justice of your ways, and your kindness to your people who trust in you. I will mention this as my plea in prayer for your mercy."

1.2. What he hopes for:

1.2.1. That God will not leave him in his old age, but will be the same to him to the end that he has been to him throughout his life (vv. 17–18). *Thou hast taught me from my youth.* He acknowledges he is obliged to give God thanks for the great favor of the good education and good instructions which his parents gave him when he was young. When he was middle-aged, he had *declared all God's wondrous works* (v. 17). Those who have gained goodness when they were young must continue to do good when they are grown up and must continue to share what they have received. *Now that I am old and gray-headed* (v. 18), dying to this world and moving quickly to another, *O God, forsake me not* (v. 18). Those who have been taught by God from their youth, and who have made it the business of their lives to honor him, may be sure that he will not leave them when they are old and gray, but will make the evil days of old age their best days. "I will not only *show thy strength*, by my own experience of it, *to this generation* (v. 18), but also leave my observations on record for the benefit of future generations, and so show it *to every one that is to come*" (v. 18). This is a debt which the old disciples of Christ owe to succeeding generations: they should leave behind a sacred testimony of the power, delights, and benefits of religious faith, and the truth of God's promises.

1.2.2. That God will revive him and raise him up from his present low and unhappy condition (v. 20): *Thou who hast made me to see and feel great and sore* (many and bitter) *troubles*, above most people, *shalt quicken me again.* He does not say, "You have burdened me with those troubles," but "you have shown them to me," as a tender father shows his child the rod of discipline to maintain the child's respect. If we have a due consideration of the hand of God in our troubles, we may promise ourselves, in due time, to be rescued from them.

1.2.3. He hopes that God will advance his honor and joy more than ever (v. 21): "You will not only restore me to *my greatness* again but also *increase* it and give me greater honor after this unpleasant experience than before. You will not only comfort me but also *comfort me on every side*, so that I will see nothing black or threatening around me anywhere." Sometimes God makes his people's troubles lead to an increase in their honor, and their sun shines even more brightly because it has been under a cloud.

1.2.4. He hopes that all his enemies will be put to shame (v. 24). *They are confounded, they are brought to shame* (they are put to shame and confusion) *that seek my hurt.*

2. Let us now see how his heart is released in joy and praise, how he rejoices and sings in hope, for we are saved by hope:

2.1. He will speak about God's righteousness and his salvation: *My mouth shall show forth thy righteousness and thy salvation*; and again (v. 24), *My tongue shall talk of thy righteousness*, and this *all the day.* God's righteousness, which David seems to be especially moved by here, has many aspects: the uprightness of his nature, the justice of his ways in providence, the righteous laws he has given us to be ruled by, the righteous promises he has given us to depend on, and the eternal righteousness which his Son has brought for our justification. God's righteousness and his salvation are here linked together.

2.2. He will speak about them with wonder: "*I know not the numbers* (measure) *thereof* (v. 15). Although I cannot give a detailed record of your favors to me because they are so many, nevertheless, knowing they are without number, I will still continue to speak about them, for I will find in them new subjects for praise" (v. 19). This is praising God, acknowledging his qualities and actions to be so high that we cannot apprehend them and so great that we cannot comprehend them. *O God, who is like unto thee?* (v. 19). None in heaven, none on earth; no angel, no king. God is incomparable; we do not rightly praise him if we do not acknowledge him to be so. *I will praise thee, even thy truth.* God is made known by his word; if we praise that and its truth, we praise him. It is God's honor that he is the Holy One; it is his people's honor that he is *the Holy One of Israel.*

2.3. He will express his joy and delight in sacred music—*with the psaltery* (harp) (v. 22); he excelled in playing the harp, and he would use his best skill to declare God's praises to such advantage as might affect others. "*Unto thee will I sing* (v. 22), to your honor, and with a desire to be accepted by you. *My lips shall greatly rejoice when I sing unto thee* (v. 23), knowing they cannot be put to better use. *My soul* will rejoice, *which thou hast redeemed*" (v. 23). We do not make music to the Lord by singing his praises (Eph 5:19) if we do not do this with our hearts. My lips may rejoice, but that is nothing. It is mere lip service, even though it is a service, but if that is all, it is lost labor in serving God. The soul must also be at work, and we must give all that is within us to bless his holy name (103:1).

PSALM 72

The previous psalm was written by David when he was old, and it seems this one was too, for Solomon was now in a favorable position to receive the crown. The previous psalm was David's prayer for himself, this one is for his son and successor, and the prayers of David the son of Jesse end with these two, as we find at the close of this psalm. This is entitled a Psalm for Solomon; *it is probable that David dictated it, or rather, that it was dictated to him by the blessed Spirit, and that this happened a short time before he died, when, by divine direction, he settled the succession and gave orders to proclaim Solomon king (1Ki 1:30). But although Solomon's name is used here, Christ's kingdom is prophesied about by using Solomon's kingdom as a type and figure of it. In the spirit, David: 1. Begins with a short prayer for his successor (v. 1). 2. Passes immediately on to a long prediction of the glories of his reign (vv. 2–17). 3. Concludes with praise to the God of Israel (vv. 18–20).*

Verse 1

This verse is a prayer for the king's son:

1. We may apply it to Solomon: *Give him thy judgments, O God, and thy righteousness* (v. 1); make him a man and king; make him a good man and a good king.

1.1. It is the prayer of a father for his child, a dying blessing, such as the patriarchs passed on to their children. Solomon learned to pray for himself as his father had prayed for him, not that God would give him riches and honor, but that God would give him a wise and understanding heart (1Ki 3:9). Parents cannot give grace to their children, but they may bring them in prayer to the God of grace.

1.2. It is the prayer of a king for his successor. David had maintained justice during his reign, and now he prayed that his son might do so too. We should have such a concern as this for future generations.

1.3. It is the prayer of subjects for their king. It seems David wrote this psalm for the people to use, so that when they sang it, they might pray for Solomon. Those who want to live quiet and peaceful lives must pray for kings and all in authority (1Ti 2:1–2), that God would give them his justice and righteousness.

2. We may apply it to Christ; not that he who intercedes for us (Heb 7:25) needs us to intercede for him, but:

2.1. It is a prayer of the Old Testament church for the Messiah to be sent.

2.2. It is an expression of the assurance which all true believers have in the authority which the Lord Jesus has received from the Father: "May he have all power both in heaven and on earth (Mt 28:18), and be the Lord our righteousness (Jer 23:6); may he be the great trustee of divine grace for all who are his."

Verses 2–17

Using the reign of Solomon as a type or shadow (Heb 8:5; 10:1), the psalmist here prophesies the prosperity and perpetuity of the kingdom of Christ. It comes as a plea to support the prayer. His plea is, "Lord, *give him thy judgments and thy righteousness* (v. 1), and then your people, who are committed to his charge, will enjoy the benefits of it." The prophecy is also itself a favorable answer to the prayer, bringing promises of mercy. That this prophecy must refer to the kingdom of the Messiah is clear, because it contains many passages that cannot be applied to the reign of Solomon. The kingdom here spoken of is to last as long as the sun, but Solomon's soon died out. Therefore even the Jewish expositors understand it to refer to the kingdom of the Messiah.

1. It would be *a righteous government* (v. 2): *He shall judge thy people with righteousness.* Compare Isa 11:4. All the laws of Christ's kingdom are consistent with the eternal rules of justice. The peace of his kingdom will be supported by righteousness (v. 3).

2. It would be a peaceful government: *The mountains shall bring peace, and the little hills* (v. 3), that is, according to Dr. Henry Hammond, both the higher and lower courts of justice in Solomon's kingdom. There will be *abundance of peace* (v. 7). Solomon's name signifies "peaceful," and his reign was peaceful. But peace is especially the glory of Christ's kingdom, for wherever that kingdom prevails, it reconciles people to God, to themselves, and to one another, and removes all enmities, for he is our peace (Eph 2:14).

3. The poor and needy would especially be taken under the protection of this government: *He shall judge thy poor* (v. 2). This King will be sure to judge so as to save *the poor of the people* and *the children of the needy* (v. 4). This is insisted on again in vv. 12–13, showing that Christ would be sure to support his poor and afflicted people who had been wronged. *He will deliver the needy* who lie at the mercy of their oppressors. *He will spare the needy* who throw themselves on his mercy. He *will save their souls* (v. 13), and that is all they want. *Blessed are the poor in spirit, for theirs is the kingdom of heaven* (Mt 5:3). Christ is the King of the poor and afflicted.

4. Proud oppressors will be judged: *He shall break them in pieces* (v. 4). The Devil is the great oppressor, whom Christ will break in pieces and whose kingdom he will destroy. *So precious shall their blood be unto him* (v. 14) that not a drop of it will be shed by the deceit or violence of Satan or his instruments without being judged.

Christ is a King who, although he sometimes calls his subjects to resist to the point of shedding their blood for him (Heb 12:4), does not waste their blood.

5. Religious faith will flourish under Christ's government (v. 5): *They shall fear thee as long as the sun and moon endure.* Solomon indeed built the temple, but it did not last long. This therefore must point to Christ's kingdom. Faith in Christ will set up, and keep up, the fear of God, and so this is the eternal Gospel that is preached. And just as Christ's government promotes devotion toward God, so also it promotes both justice and love among people (v. 7): *In his days shall the righteous flourish.* When the law of Christ is written on the heart (Jer 31:33; 2Co 3:3), it disposes people to be upright and just and to give everyone their due. It also disposes people to lead lives of love and so produces great peace and beats swords into plowshares (Isa 2:4; Mic 4:3). Both holiness and love will last forever in Christ's kingdom and will never decay, for the subjects of the kingdom will *fear God as long as the sun and moon endure* (v. 7). Christianity has gained a foothold in the world, and it will keep its ground until the end of time, and once its power has gained a foothold in the heart, it will continue there until, by death, the sun, the moon, and the stars—that is, the physical senses—are darkened.

6. Christ's government will give great assurance to all his faithful, loving subjects (v. 6): *He shall*, by the grace and encouragement of his Spirit, *come down like rain upon the mown grass*; not on what is cut down but on what is left growing, so that it may spring up again even though it was cut off.

7. Christ's kingdom will be greatly enlarged, considering:

7.1. The extent of his territories (v. 8): *He shall have dominion from sea to sea*, from the South Sea to the North, or from the Red Sea to the Mediterranean, *and from the river*, Euphrates or Nile, *to the ends of the earth.* Solomon's kingdom was very large (1Ki 4:21), according to the promise (Ge 15:18). But no sea or river is named here, so that the use of these proverbial expressions might suggest the universal monarchy of the Lord Jesus. His Gospel has been, or will be, preached *to all nations* (Mt 24:14). His territories will be extended to those countries:

• That were foreigners to him: *Those that dwell in the wilderness* (v. 9), that seldom hear news, will hear the good news of the Redeemer, *shall bow before him* (v. 9), will believe in him, worship him, and take his yoke on them (Mt 11:29).

• That were enemies to him and had fought against him: *They shall lick the dust* (v. 9).

7.2. The status of those who are subject to him. He will reign not only over those who live in the desert, the peasants and poor people, but also over those who live in palaces (v. 10): *The kings of Tarshish, and of the isles*, those that are farthest from Israel and are *the isles of the Gentiles* (Ge 10:5), *shall bring presents* to him as their sovereign Lord. This was literally fulfilled in Solomon, for *all the kings of the earth sought the wisdom of Solomon, and brought every man his present* (2Ch 9:23–24). It was also fulfilled in Christ, when the wise men from the east came to worship him and *brought him presents* (Mt 2:11).

8. The king will be honored and loved by all his subjects (v. 15): *He shall live*; his subjects will desire his life—*O king, live for ever*—and with good reason, for he has said, *Because I live, you shall live also* (Jn 14:19).

Presents will be given to him. Although he can live without them—for he does not need either the gifts or the services of anyone—yet to him *shall be given of the gold of Sheba* (v. 15). He who is the best must be served with the best. Prayers will be made for him, and they will be made continually. The people prayed for Solomon, and that helped make him and his reign such a great blessing to them. But how does this apply to Christ? He does not need our prayers, nor can he receive any benefit from them. But the Old Testament saints prayed for his coming; they prayed continually for it, for they called him *He that should come* (Mt 11:3). And now that he has come, we must pray for the success of his Gospel and the advancement of his kingdom, which he calls praying for him (Mt 21:9). Praises will be made to him: *Daily shall he be praised* (v. 15).

9. Under the king's rule there will be a wonderful increase both of food and of mouths. The country will grow rich. If only a handful of grain is sown on the top of the mountains—where one would expect only a little to grow—its fruit will flourish like Lebanon; it will come up as thick, tall, and strong as the cedars of Lebanon. This can be applied to the wonderful products of the seed of the Gospel in the days of the Messiah. When a handful of that seed was sown on the mountainous and barren soil of the Gentile world, it produced a wonderful harvest gathered in for Christ. The fields were white for harvest (Jn 4:35; Mt 9:37). The towns in this kingdom will grow populous: *Those of the city will flourish like grass*, thrive in great numbers.

10. The King's government will last forever, both to his honor and to the happiness of his subjects. The Lord Jesus will reign forever: this may be understood to refer only to him, not at all to Solomon. It is only Christ who will be feared throughout all generations (v. 5) as long as the sun and moon last (v. 7).

10.1. The honor of the prince is immortal and will never be corrupted (v. 17): his name will endure forever. As the names of earthly princes live by being handed down to future generations, so also Christ's name lives because he himself lives.

10.2. The happiness of the people is universal, too: *Men shall be blessed*, truly and forever blessed, *in him* (v. 17).

Verses 18–20

1. The psalmist is released in thanksgiving for the prophecy and promise here (vv. 18–19). Every word of God is so certain that we have great reasons to give thanks for what he has said even though it has not yet been accomplished. We must acknowledge that God is worthy to be praised for all the great things he has done for the world. *Blessed be the Lord*, that is, *blessed be his glorious name*. We are here taught to bless the name of Christ, and to bless God in Christ:

1.1. As the Lord God, as a self-existent, self-sufficient Being and our sovereign Lord.

1.2. As the God of Israel, in covenant relationship with his people and worshiped by them.

1.3. As the God *who only* (who alone) *does wondrous things* (v. 18), in creation and providence, and especially in redemption, which surpasses all his other works.

2. The psalmist is passionate in prayer for the fulfillment of this prophecy and promise: *Let the whole earth be filled with his glory* (v. 19). David closes the prayer with a double seal: *Amen and amen* (v. 19). He even closes his life with this prayer (v. 20). This was the last psalm that he ever wrote, although it is not placed last in this collection. He breathed his last with these words: "May God be

glorified, may the kingdom of the Messiah be set up, and there is nothing further I desire. With this may *the prayers of David the son of Jesse* be *ended. Even so, come, Lord Jesus, come quickly*" (Rev 22: 20).

PSALM 73

This psalm and the ten that follow it bear the name of Asaph in their titles. If he was their author, as many think, we rightly call them the psalms of Asaph. If he was only the director of music, to whom they were given, the reading of the margin is correct, which calls them "Psalms for Asaph." Although the Spirit of prophecy through sacred songs came mainly on David—who is therefore called the sweet psalmist of Israel (2 Sa 23:1)—God also gave some of the Spirit to those around him. This psalm gives us an account of the conflict which the psalmist had with a strong temptation to envy the prosperity of evildoers. He begins his account with a sacred principle that helped him keep his ground (v. 1). He then tells us: 1. How he fell into the temptation (vv. 2–14). 2. How he got out of the temptation (vv. 15–20). 3. What he gained from the temptation and how he was a better person because of it (vv. 21–28).

Verses 1–14

This psalm begins somewhat abruptly: "Yet God is good to Israel" (v. 1, margin). Although evildoers receive many gifts from his providential goodness, we must still acknowledge that he is especially good to Israel. The psalmist records a temptation to envy the prosperity of the evildoers:

1. He first sets down that great principle which he decided to abide by while he was thinking about this temptation (v. 1). When Job entered into such a temptation, he set as his principle the complete knowledge of God: *Times are not hidden from the Almighty* (Job 24:1). Jeremiah's principle is the justice of God: *Righteous art thou, O God! when I plead with thee* (Jer 12:1). Habakkuk's principle is the holiness of God: *Thou art of purer eyes than to behold iniquity* (Hab 1:13). The psalmist's, here, is the goodness of God. He had had many thoughts in his mind about the providences of God, but this word finally settled him: "For all this, God is good, *good to Israel, even to those that are of a clean heart*" (v. 1). Those who are pure in heart (Mt 5:8) are the Israel of God. God, who is good to all, is especially good to his church and people, as he was to Israel in ancient times.

2. He comes now to relate the jolt that was given to his faith in God's special goodness to Israel by the strong temptation to think that the Israel of God is no happier than other peoples and that God is no kinder to his people than he is to others.

2.1. He speaks of having had a very narrow escape from being completely overthrown by this temptation (v. 2): "*But as for me*, although I was so assured of the goodness of God to Israel, yet *my feet were almost gone*—the tempter had almost tripped me up; *my steps had well nigh slipped, for I was envious at the foolish*" (v. 3). Storms come which will test even the firmest anchors. Many precious souls, who will live forever, have narrowly escaped death.

2.2. This is the psalmist's temptation.

2.2.1. He *saw*, with sadness, *the prosperity of the wicked* (v. 3). They seem to have the least share of the troubles and adversities of this life (v. 5): *They are not in the troubles of other men*, even of wise and good people, *neither are they plagued like other men.* They seem to have some special privilege that makes them exempt from the ordinary destiny of bearing sorrows. They also seem to have the greatest share of the comforts of this life. They live in peace so that *their eyes stand out with fatness* (v. 7). There are many who have a great deal of this life in their hands, but nothing of the other life in their hearts. These evildoers are ungodly, but they prosper and *increase in riches* (v. 12). "They are the prosperous of the age," as some read it. Furthermore, their end seems to be peaceful. This is mentioned first, as what is strangest of all (v. 4): *There are no bands* (pains) *in their death.* They are not taken from this world by a violent death. In fact, they are not bound by the terrors of conscience in their dying moments. We cannot discern people's state on the other side of death. People may die like lambs but still have their place with the goats.

2.2.2. They made very bad use of their outward prosperity and were hardened by it in their sin.

2.2.2.1. It made them very proud and arrogant. Because they live in peace, *pride compasses them as a chain* (is their necklace) (v. 6). "Pride ties on their chain," or "necklace," is how Dr. Henry Hammond reads it. It does no harm to wear a chain or necklace, but when it is worn to gratify a conceited mind, it stops being merely decorative. Just as the pride of sinners appears in their dress, so also it is expressed in their words: *They speak loftily* (v. 8); they make a pretense of *great swelling words of vanity* (2Pe 2:18).

2.2.2.2. It made them oppressive to their poor neighbors (v. 6): *Violence covers them as a garment. They speak wickedly concerning oppression* (v. 8); they oppress others and justify themselves in it. *They are corrupt* (v. 8), that is, they are given up to pleasures and everything excessive and self-indulgent.

2.2.2.3. It made them very arrogant in their behavior toward both God and people (v. 9): *They set their mouth against the heavens,* showing contempt toward God himself. They cannot reach the heavens with their hands, to shake God's throne, but they can show their hatred toward it by speaking out against the heavens. *Their tongue* also *walks through the earth,* and they take the liberty of abusing all who get in their way. They could not have been so evil if they had not learned to say (v. 11), *How doth God know? And is there knowledge in the Most High?* What an insult it is to the God of infinite knowledge, from whom all knowledge comes, to ask, *Is there knowledge in him?* (v. 11). Well may the psalmist say (v. 12), *Behold, these are the ungodly.*

2.2.3. He noticed that while evildoers prospered in their ungodliness, good people were suffering great affliction, and he himself in particular. He looked out and saw many of God's people greatly at a loss (v. 10): "Because evildoers are so arrogant and defiant, *therefore his people return hither.* They do not know what to say about it any more than I do, all the more because *waters of a full cup are wrung out to them;* they are forced not only to drink of the bitter cup of affliction, but to drink it all. Care is taken that they do not lose a drop of that unpleasant drink; the waters are wrung out to them, or for them, so they may have the dregs of the cup." They also shed abundant tears at the blasphemies of evildoers, and in this way, too, waters are wrung out to them, or rather wrung out of them. "For my part," he said, "*all the day long have I been plagued* with one affliction or another, *and chastened every morning,* as regularly as morning comes."

2.2.4. From all this arose a very strong temptation to reject his religious faith. Even among God's professing people, there are those who say, "*How does God know? Surely all things are left to blind chance, not directed by an all-seeing God.*" Although the psalmist's feet had not gone quite as far along the path of temptation as to question God's complete knowledge, he was still tempted to question the benefits of religious faith and to say (v. 13), *Verily, I have cleansed my heart in vain,* and have *washed my hands in innocency* to no purpose. But when the pure in heart, those blessed ones, see God (Mt 5:8), they will not say that they cleansed their hearts in vain.

Verses 15–20

Here we are told how the psalmist kept his foothold and gained the victory.

1. He kept up his respect for God's people, and he used that to restrain himself from speaking out his wrong thoughts (v. 15). He gained the victory gradually, and this was the first point he gained. He was ready to say, *Verily, I have cleansed my heart in vain* (v. 13), but he was able to keep silent by considering, "*If I say, I will speak thus, behold, I should* give the greatest possible offense to *the generation of thy children*" (v. 15). Notice that although he thought wrongly, he took care not to speak out the evil thought he had conceived. If you have been so foolish as to think evil, *lay thy hand upon thy mouth* and let it go no further (Pr 30:32). We must think twice before we speak, because some things may be thought which should not be spoken and because second thoughts may correct mistakes we may make with our first. There is nothing that can give more general offense to the generation of God's children than to say that *we have cleansed our heart in vain* (v. 13) or that it is pointless to serve God.

2. He foresaw the ruin of evildoers. "I tried to understand the meaning of this unaccountable way of Providence, but *it was too painful for me.* I could not defeat it by the strength of my own reasoning." If there were not another life after this, we could not fully reconcile the prosperity of evildoers with the justice of God. But *he went into the sanctuary of God* (v. 17); he consulted the Scriptures, and he prayed to God to make this matter clear to him. And he finally understood that evildoers should be pitied rather than envied, for they were heading for destruction. The sanctuary must be where tempted souls turn. All is well that ends well, eternally well, but nothing is well that ends badly, eternally badly. The prosperity of evildoers is short and uncertain. The high places in which Providence sets them are *slippery places* (v. 18). Their destruction is sure, sudden, and very great. They flourish for a time, but are ruined forever. He speaks of it as being done by God, and so it cannot be resisted: *Thou castest them down* (v. 18). Their ruin is swift, for *how are they brought into desolation as in a moment!* (v. 19). It is a total and final destruction: *They are utterly consumed with terrors* (v. 19). Their prosperity is therefore not to be envied at all, but rather despised. *As a dream when one awaketh, so, O Lord! when thou awakest*—or "when they awake," as some understand it—*thou shalt despise their image,* their shadow, *and make it to vanish.* "In the day of the great judgment" is the reading of the Aramaic paraphrase: "On that day *they shall rise to shame and everlasting contempt*" (Da 12:2). Notice that they will be made to wake up from the sleep of their ungodly security, and then God will despise their dreams. Notice how God despised a rich man's dreams when he said, *Thou fool, this night thy soul shall be required of thee!* (Lk 12:19–20).

Verses 21–28

Here is an account of the good use the psalmist made of that severe temptation with which he had been attacked and which had almost defeated him.

1. He learned to think low thoughts of himself and to humble and accuse himself before God (vv. 21–22). *My heart was grieved, and I was pricked in my reins.* Temptation was like a thorn in the flesh to Paul (2Co 12:7). This particular temptation, the working of envy and discontent, is as painful as any. The psalmist acknowledges he has been ignorant to trouble himself in this way: "I was so ignorant of what I might have known. *I was as a beast before thee* (v. 22). Animals are concerned only with the present and never look ahead to what is to come, and that is how I acted. To be ready to wish I was one of them, and to think of changing places with them! *So foolish was I.*"

2. He used the occasion to acknowledge his dependence on the grace of God (v. 23): "*Nevertheless,* although I am foolish, *I am continually with thee* and in your favor; *thou hast holden* (held) *me by my right hand.*" He said in the hour of temptation (v. 14), *All the day long have I been plagued,* but here he corrects himself for that passionate complaint: "Although God has disciplined me, he has not rejected me. Despite all the burdens of my life, *I have been continually* with you (v. 23). Although God has sometimes written bitter things against me (Job 13:26), he has still *holden me by my right hand* (v. 23), to prevent my losing my way in the desert through which I have been walking." If he has maintained in us the spiritual life, the pledge of eternal life, we should not complain. "*My feet were almost gone* (v. 2), and they would have gone completely, beyond recovery, except that you have held me by my right hand and so kept me from falling."

3. He encouraged himself to hope that the same God who had rescued him from this evil work would *preserve him to his heavenly kingdom,* as the apostle Paul also prays (2Ti 4:18): "I am now upheld by you, and so *thou shalt guide me with thy counsel* (v. 24), leading me, as you have done up to this time, and *thou shalt afterwards receive me to glory*" (v. 24). The psalmist had narrowly missed paying dearly for following his own counsels in this temptation, and so he decided that in the future he would take God's advice. If God directs us to do our duty, he will afterward reconcile us to all the dark providences that now puzzle and perplex us, and it will relieve us of the anguish we may suffer from some threatening temptations.

4. He was encouraged to cling more closely to God, and very much confirmed and comforted in having chosen him (vv. 25–26). He had complained about his afflictions (v. 14), but this makes them very light and easy: *All will be well* if God is mine (Dt 5:29). We have here the longings of a consecrated soul toward God, and its rest in him: *Whom have I in heaven but thee?* (v. 25). There is scarcely a verse in all the psalms more expressive than this of the godly and devout affections that a soul may have toward God. God alone, who made the soul, can make it happy. If God is our happiness, we must have him— *Whom have I but thee?* (v. 25)—we must choose him. Our desires must not only be offered to God; they must also all end in him; we must desire nothing more than God, but still more and more of him. "*There is none in heaven but thee. I desire none on earth besides thee* (v. 25), not only no one in heaven, which we know little about, but also no one on earth, where we have many friends and where many of our present interests and concerns are." *My flesh and my heart fail* (v. 26). Others have experienced, and we must expect, the failing of both flesh and heart. The body will fail because of sickness, age, and death. *But God is the strength of my heart and my portion for ever* (v. 26). The psalmist speaks as one not concerned about the body—let

that fail, there is no way out—but as one concerned about the soul, to be *strengthened in the inner man* (Eph 3:16).

5. He was fully convinced of the miserable condition of all evildoers. He learned this in the sanctuary on this occasion, and he would never forget it (v. 27): "For those who are far from you, far by distance and by estrangement, who desire the Almighty to depart from them, will certainly perish."

6. He was greatly encouraged to cling to God and confide in him (v. 28). Our drawing near to God arises from his drawing near to us, and it is this happy meeting that makes for happiness. Here a great truth is set down, that it is good to draw near to God; but its living reality lies in the application, *It is good for me.* If evildoers, despite all their prosperity, will perish and be destroyed, then let us trust in the Lord God, in him, not in them (see 146:3–5), in him, not in our worldly prosperity. Let us trust in God, and neither fret about them (37:1) nor be afraid of them.

PSALM 74

This psalm describes in great detail the destruction of Jerusalem and the temple by Nebuchadnezzar. Some interpreters tend to think it was written by David, or Asaph in David's time, or that it was written by another Asaph, who lived at the time of the exile. Others tend to think it was written by Jeremiah and, after the return from exile, handed to the sons of Asaph—who were called by that name—for the public service of the church. This was the most well-known family of the singers in Ezra's time. See Ezr 2:41; 3:10; Ne 11:17, 22; 12:35, 46. The terrible situation of the people of God at that time is here spread out before the Lord and left with him (2Ki 19:14). The prophet, in the name of the church: 1. Expresses complaints about the miseries they are suffering, to encourage their prayers (vv. 1–11). 2. Expresses pleas to encourage their faith in prayer (vv. 12–17). 3. Concludes with various requests to God for him to rescue them (vv. 18–23).

Title

This psalm is entitled *Maschil,* "a psalm to give instruction," for it was written on a day of disaster. It is intended to give instruction.

Verses 1–11

The people of God complain about three things:

1. They complain of the displeasure of God against them, as the cause and bitterness of all their calamities. They complain to God (v. 1). Christ himself cried out on the cross, *My God, my God, why hast thou forsaken me?* (Mt 27:46). This is the plea of the church here: *O God, why hast thou forsaken us for ever?* Here we must understand them to be speaking from their present dark and sad fears. The people of God must not think that because they are downcast, they have therefore been rejected, that because people reject them, God also has. This complaint, however, seems to suggest they dreaded God's rejection of them more than anything. *Why does thy anger smoke* (smolder)? (v. 1), that is, why does it rise up so much that everyone around us notices it? They plead:

1.1. Their relationship with him: "We are *the sheep of thy pasture* (v. 1). That the wolves attack the sheep is nothing unusual, but has any shepherd ever been so displeased with their own sheep? *Remember,* we are *thy congregation* (v. 2), joined and devoted to your praise. We are *the rod,* or tribe, *of thy inheritance,* from whom you have received praise and worship more than from the neighboring nations. We are pleading for *Mount Zion, wherein thou hast dwelt* (v. 2), which has been the place of your special delight and residence, your possession and home."

1.2. The great things God has done for them. "It is *thy congregation*, which you have *purchased of old* by many miracles of mercy when they were first formed into a people. It is *thy inheritance, which thou hast redeemed* (v. 2) when they were sold into slavery. Now, Lord, will you now abandon a people that cost you so much, those who have been so precious to you?" How much more reason have we to hope that God will not reject anyone whom Christ has redeemed with his own blood.

1.3. The disastrous state they are in (v. 3): "*Lift up thy feet*, that is, turn your steps and come quickly to repair the destruction of your sanctuary, which otherwise will be irreparable forever."

2. They complain about the outrage and cruelty of their enemies, but only about what they have done against the sanctuary and the synagogue. The temple at Jerusalem was the *dwelling place of God's name* and was therefore the *sanctuary* or *holy place* (v. 7). Here, the enemies acted wickedly (v. 3), for they destroyed it out of downright disrespect and contempt for God. They *roared in the midst of God's congregations* (v. 4), where God's faithful people were in his presence in humble, reverent silence. *They set up their ensigns for signs* (v. 4). They set up the banners of their army in the temple. This arrogant defiance of God and his power touched his people at a tender spot. The enemies took pride in destroying *the carved work* (paneling) (v. 6) of the temple. Some read it, "They show themselves, as one who lifts up axes on high in a thicket of trees," for this is how they smashed the carved paneling in the temple. They had no more scruples about smashing down the rich paneling in the temple than woodcutters have about cutting down trees in the forest. They set fire to it and so violated it or *destroyed it to the ground* (v. 7). The Babylonians burned down the house of God (2Ch 36:19). And the Romans *left not there one stone upon another* (Mt 24:2), until Zion, the holy mountain, was *plowed as a field* (Jer 26:18–20; Mic 3:12) by Titus Vespasian. The psalmist also complains about the destruction of the synagogues, or schools of the prophets. *Let us destroy them together*; they destroyed not only the temple but all the places where God was worshiped. They *burnt up all the synagogues of God in the land* and devastated them all.

3. What made all these disasters even worse was that God's people had no prospect at all of any relief, nor could they see an end of them (v. 9): "We see our enemy's sign set up in the sanctuary, but *we see not our signs. There is no more any prophet* to tell us how long the trouble will last and when these terrible things will come to an end, so that hope may support us in our troubles." *How long shall the adversary reproach and blaspheme thy name?* Not "How long will these troubles last?" but "How long will God be blasphemed? *Why withdrawest thou thy hand?* Why do you not stretch it out, to rescue your people and destroy your enemies?"

Verses 12–17

Two things quiet the minds of those who are grieving for the sacred assembly:

1. That God is the God of Israel, a God in covenant with his people (v. 12): *God is my King of old*. This comes as both a plea in prayer to God and a support for their own faith and hope, to encourage themselves to expect to be rescued, considering the *days of old* (77:5). Several things

are mentioned here which God had done for his people as their King since ancient times, which encouraged them to commit themselves to him and depend on him.

1.1. He had divided the sea before them when they came out of Egypt, not by the strength of Moses or his rod but by his own strength. The One who could do that could do anything.

1.2. He had destroyed Pharaoh and the Egyptians. Pharaoh was the *leviathan*; the Egyptians were the fierce and cruel *dragons*. God crushed their powers, even though they were many, and he finally drowned them all in the Red Sea. This was a type of Christ's victory over Satan and his kingdom, according to the first promise, that the seed of the woman would break the serpent's head (Ge 3:15). This providence was food for their faith and hope, to encourage them in the other difficulties they were likely to meet in the desert.

1.3. God had twice changed the course of nature, both by bringing streams out of the rock and by turning streams into rock (v. 15). He had dissolved the rock into waters: "Thou didst bring out the fountain and the flood" out of the flinty rock (Dt 32:13). Let it never be forgotten, but especially remembered, that the rock was Christ (1Co 10:4), and the waters from it were spiritual drink. He had also congealed the waters into rock: *Thou driedst up mighty* rapid *rivers* (v. 15), the Jordan, especially at the time when it overflowed all its banks (Jos 3:15). He who did these things could now rescue his oppressed people.

2. That the God of Israel is the God of nature (vv. 16–17). It is he who directs the regular succession and cycle of creation: day and night. He is the Lord of all time. It is he who opens the eyelids of morning light; it is he who draws the curtains of the evening shadows. He has prepared, or established, the moon and the sun. "Thou hast *appointed all the bounds of the earth*, and the different climates of its various regions, for *thou hast made summer and winter* (v. 17), the frigid and the torrid zones, or rather, the constant cycles of the year and its different seasons." He who originally had power to settle, and still had power to preserve, this course of nature by the daily and annual movements of the heavenly bodies surely also has all power to save and to destroy. He who is faithful to his covenant with the day and with the night will certainly fulfill his promises to his people. His covenant with Abraham and his descendants is as firm as the covenant with Noah and his sons (Ge 8:21).

Verses 18–23

Here, the psalmist begs most fervently in the name of the church that God would act for them against their enemies, and that he would put an end to their present troubles. *Arise, O God, plead thy own cause.*

1. The persecutors are God's sworn enemies: "Lord, they have not only abused us; they have also directly and immediately *blasphemed* (reviled) *thy name*" (v. 18). The psalmist insists very much on this: "We dare not respond to their mocking; Lord, you respond to them. Remember that the *foolish people have blasphemed thy name* (v. 18) and that still *the foolish man reproaches thee daily*" (v. 22). Those who mock God are foolish. Just as unbelief is foolish (14:1), ungodliness and blasphemy are no less so. Those who pour scorn on religious faith and sacred things may be praised as being the world's cleverest people, but the reality is that they are the greatest fools! These enemies do not keep their blasphemous thoughts to themselves, but declare them loudly—*forget not the voice of thy enemies* (v. 23). God does not need to be reminded by us of what he has to do, but we must

show our concern for his honor in this way and believe he will vindicate us.

2. The persecuted are his covenant people. They have fallen into the hands of *the multitude of the wicked* (v. 19). *The dark places of the earth are full of the habitations of cruelty* (v. 20). The land of the Babylonians—where there was none of the light of the knowledge of the true God, although it was otherwise well known for its learning and arts—was indeed a dark place. Its inhabitants were *alienated from the life of God through the ignorance that was in them* (Eph 4:18), and so they were cruel: where there was no true knowledge of God, there could scarcely be any humanity. The psalmist pleads with God: "It is *thy turtledove* (your dove) that is ready to be swallowed up by many evildoers" (v. 19). In its harmlessness and mildness, the church is a dove; it is a dove, too, in its mourning in days of distress; it is a turtledove in its faithfulness and in the loyalty of its love. "Will your dove, which is true to you and devoted to your honor, be handed over to the *hand of the multitude of the wicked*? Lord, it will be your honor to help the weak, especially your own people. Will you not fulfill the promises you have made in your covenant with them? Rise up, Lord, for those who will praise your name, rise up against those who blaspheme it."

PSALM 75

Although this psalm is attributed to Asaph in its title, it fits in so exactly with David's circumstances at his coming to the crown after the death of Saul that most interpreters apply it to that time, supposing that either Asaph wrote it in the person of David, as his poet laureate, or David himself wrote it and then passed it on to Asaph as precentor of the temple. In this psalm: 1. David gives God thanks for bringing him to the throne (vv. 1, 9). 2. He promises to give himself for the public good by using the power God has given him (vv. 2–3, 10). 3. He restrains the arrogance of those who oppose his coming to the throne (vv. 4–5). 4. He draws a reason for all this from God's sovereignty over human affairs (vv. 6–8).

Verses 1–5

In these verses:

1. The psalmist gives God the praise for the great things he has done for him and his people Israel (v. 1): *Unto thee, O God, do we give thanks.* Moreover, "not only do *I* give thanks, but also *we* do, I and all my friends." There are many works which God does for his people that may truly be called *wondrous works.* They are beyond the ordinary course of providence. These wonderful deeds declare the nearness of his name.

2. He places himself under an obligation to use his power well (v. 2): *When I shall receive the congregation I will judge uprightly.* He takes it for granted that God will in due time fulfill what he has promised concerning him. "When I am a judge, I will judge, and *judge uprightly*; not as those who went before me, who either neglected judgment or perverted the course of justice." Positions of public trust are to be undertaken with great integrity. Those who judge must judge uprightly, according to the rules of justice, without showing favoritism.

3. He promises himself that his government will be a public blessing to Israel (v. 3). The present state of the kingdom was very bad: *The earth and all the inhabitants thereof are dissolved* (quake). This is hardly surprising, since the former reign was so dissolute that everything went to rack and ruin. The people were all split, two

against three and three against two, crumbled into various factions and parties, which was likely to lead to their destruction, but *I bear up the pillars of it,* I hold its pillars firm. The whole fabric of society would have sunk if David had not held up its pillars. This may be well applied to Christ and his rule.

4. He restrains those who oppose his government, who are against his accession to the throne and obstruct his administration. *I said unto the fools, Deal not foolishly,* "Boast no more." As soon as he came to the throne, he issued a proclamation against evil and ungodliness, and here we have the contents of this declaration.

4.1. To the simple, contemptible sinners, the fools in Israel, who corrupted themselves, he said, "*Deal not foolishly,* boast no more, do not go so directly against your reason and your interests."

4.2. To the proud, daring sinners, *the wicked,* who defy God, he said, "*Lift not up the horn*; do not boast of your power and rights. *Lift not up your horn on high,* as though you have the power to have what you want and do what you want. *Speak not with a stiff neck* (v. 5), in which there is a hardened arrogance that will never bend to the will of God in his government, for those who will not bend will break."

Verses 6–10

1. Here two great truths are set down concerning God's rule of the world.

1.1. That it is only from God that kings receive their power (vv. 6–7), and so David would give only God the praise for his advancement. We see strange changes in states and kingdoms, and we are surprised at the sudden shame of some and the elevation of others. We are directed here to look to their author. We are told negatively: *Promotion comes not from the east, nor from the west, nor from the desert.* People cannot gain promotion either by the wisdom or wealth of the children of the east, or by the numerous forces of *the isles of the Gentiles,* which lay westward, or those of Egypt or Arabia, which lay south. No agreeing smiles of secondary causes will advance people to higher positions without the primary cause: God himself. The learned Bishop Lloyd gives this interpretation: all people took the origin of power to be in the heavens, but many did not know from what in heaven it came. The eastern nations, who were generally given to astrology, took it to have come from their stars, especially the sun, their god. David's response here, the bishop says, is, "No; it comes neither from the east nor from the west, neither from the rising nor from the setting of such and such a planet or constellation, nor from the south nor from the exaltation of the sun or any star in mid heaven." David does not mention the north, because the same word that signifies the north refers to the secret place, and it does come from the secret of God's counsel, or from the sanctuary in Zion, which lay on the north side of Jerusalem. We are told positively: *God is the judge,* the governor or ruler. When parties contend for the prize, it is he who *puts down one and sets up another* (v. 7) as he sees fit, so as to serve his own purposes and see his own ways fulfilled. He who is infinitely wise, holy, and good has power to set up and put down those whom he pleases, when he pleases, however he pleases.

1.2. That all must receive their destiny only from God (v. 8): *In the hand of the Lord there is a cup,* which he puts into the hands of human beings, a cup of providence, made up of many ingredients. The sufferings of Christ are called *a cup* (Mt 20:22; Jn 18:11). *The wine is red* (v. 8), showing the wrath of God, which is instilled into the judgments carried out on sinners. It is red as fire, for it burns. It is *full of mixture* (v. 8). There is a mixture of mercy and grace in the cup of affliction when it is put into the hands of God's own people, a mixture of the curse when it is put into the hands of evildoers; it is wine mixed with gall. Some drops of this wrath may fall on good people; they have their share in common adversities, but the dregs of the cup are reserved for evildoers. The disaster itself is only the agent into which the curse is infused; the top of the agent has a little of the infusion, but the sediment is pure wrath, and these dregs will become the portion of sinners. They will *wring them out* (v. 8), so that not a drop of the wrath will be left behind.

2. Here are two practical conclusions:

2.1. He will praise God and give him glory for the power to which he has advanced him (v. 9): *I will declare for ever* what *thy wondrous works declare* (v. 1). He will give glory to God also as the God of Jacob, knowing it was for Jacob his servant's sake, and because he loved his people Israel, that he made him king over them.

2.2. He will, as he promised earlier (vv. 2, 4), use the power with which he is entrusted for the great purposes for which it was put into his hands (v. 10). "Although not all the heads, yet *all the horns, of the wicked will I cut off* (v. 10), with which they exercise power over their poor neighbors; I will disable them from causing trouble."

PSALM 76

This psalm seems to have been written on the occasion of some great victory. The Septuagint (a Greek version of the Old Testament) calls it "A song on the Assyrians," and for that reason many interpreters have thought that it was written in Hezekiah's time, when Sennacherib's army, then besieging Jerusalem, was annihilated by an angel of the Lord (2Ki 19:35). Or it might have been written by Asaph, who lived in David's time, to celebrate the many triumphs with which God delighted to honor that reign. 1. The psalmist congratulates the church as happy because it has God so near (vv. 1–3). He celebrates the glory of God's power (vv. 4–6). 2. He gives reasons why this should cause everyone to fear him (vv. 7–9) and should cause his people to trust in him and pay their vows to him (vv. 10–12). It is a psalm suitable for a thanksgiving day.

Verses 1–6

The psalmist triumphs in God, who is the center of all our triumphs. He triumphs:

1. In the revelation God has made of himself to them (v. 1). It is the honor and privilege of Judah and Israel that *God is known* among them, and where he is known, *his name will* be *great*.

2. In the signs of God's special presence with them in his services of public worship (v. 2). God was known in the whole land of Judah and Israel, but his tabernacle and his dwelling place were in Salem, in Zion (v. 2). It was there that he kept court; there he received the praise of his people from their sacrifices. They turned to him there, and it was about that place that he said, here will I dwell, for I have desired it (132:14).

3. In the victories they have gained over their enemies (v. 3): *There broke he the arrows of the bow.*

3.1. Here are bows and arrows, shields and swords, all ready for battle, but all are broken and rendered useless. In the tabernacle and dwelling place in Zion, he broke the flashing arrows; it was done on the battlefield, but it is said to have been done in the sanctuary because it is in

answer to the prayers God's people made to him. Public successes owe as much to what is done in the church as to what is done in the camp. Now:

3.2. This victory led very much to the immortal honor of Israel's God (v. 4): "*Thou art,* and have revealed yourself to be, *more glorious and excellent than the mountains of prey* (NIV: mountains rich with game), more majestic than the great and mighty ones who think they are as secure as mountains, but really are *mountains of prey,* of preying, oppressive to all around them. It is their glory to destroy; it is yours to rescue." The victory also led to the immortal shame of Israel's enemies (vv. 5–6). "The stouthearted have despoiled and disarmed themselves" is how some read v. 5; when God pleases, he can make his enemies weaken and destroy themselves. *They have slept,* not the sleep of the righteous, but *their sleep,* the sleep of sinners, who will awake to eternal shame. The warriors can no more *find their hands* (v. 5) than the valiant can their spirit. As the bold are deprived of courage, so the strong are made lame and cannot even find their hands, to save their own heads, much less harm their enemies.

Verses 7–12

This victory communicates three things here:

1. Terror to God's enemies (vv. 7–9): *Thou, even thou, art to be feared.* Let all the world learn from this event to stand in awe of the great God. *Who may stand in thy sight from the minute that thou art angry?* (v. 7). God's people are the *meek of the earth* (v. 9) (Zep 2:3), who can bear any wrong, but who themselves do no one any wrong. Yet, although those who are humble expose themselves to wrong because of their humility, God will sooner or later come to save them. When God comes to save *all the meek of the earth* (v. 9), he will *cause judgment to be heard from heaven* (v. 8). The righteous God seems to keep silence for a long time, but sooner or later he will make his judgment heard. When God is pronouncing judgment from heaven, it is time for earth itself to wait in a fearful and reverent silence: *The earth feared and was still* (v. 8).

2. Comfort to God's people (v. 10). *Surely the wrath of man will praise thee,* not only by the restraints put on it, forcing it to confess its own lack of power, but also by the freedom given to it for a time. The more the nations rage and plot against the Lord and his anointed, the more will God be praised for setting *his King on his holy hill of Zion* in spite of them (2:1, 6). What will not turn to his praise will not be allowed to break out: *The remainder of wrath shalt thou restrain.*

3. Duty to all (vv. 11–12). Let all submit to this great God and become his loyal subjects. Each one of us is commanded to do homage to the King of kings: *Vow and pay,* that is, make vows of allegiance to him and be careful to keep them. And having taken him as our King, let us bring presents to him. It is not that God needs any present we can bring, but prayers and praises, especially our hearts, are the presents we should bring to the Lord our God. He should be feared: *He is the fear* (Ge 31:42, 53; Isa 8:13); his name is glorious, and with him is terrible majesty. *He will cut off the spirit of princes,* he breaks the spirit of rulers; he will snip off the spirit as easily as we snip off a flower from the stalk or a bunch of grapes from the vine; this is the meaning of the word.

PSALM 77

This psalm begins with sorrowful complaints but ends with strengthening encouragements. The complaints seem to be about personal grievances, but the encouragements relate to the public concerns of the church. One of the Jewish authorities says that this psalm is spoken in the dialect of the captives, and so some think it was written during the Exile in Babylon. 1. The psalmist recalls here how he complained about the deep impressions which his troubles made on his spirits (vv. 1–10). 2. He recalls how he encouraged himself to hope that things would ultimately turn out well, by remembering the former occasions on which God came to the rescue of his people (vv. 11–20).

Verses 1–10

We have here a real description of a good man in the grip of depression. Saints whose spirits are sagging may see themselves in a mirror here. The griefs and fears seem to have been finished with when he wrote this psalm, for he says (v. 1), *I cried unto God, and he gave ear unto me.* Though he found this assurance only later, he mentions it at the beginning of his account to show that his trouble did not end in despair. Notice:

1. His sorrowful prayers. *My voice was unto God, and I cried, even with my voice unto God.* This is how he expressed his grief and gained some relief. This was indeed the right way to gain relief (v. 2): *In the day of my trouble I sought the Lord.* Those who suffer troubles of the mind must not think of drinking them away or laughing them away, but must pray them away.

2. His sorrowful grief. *My sore,* or wound, *ran in the night* (v. 2) and bled inwardly. It did not stop, even during the time appointed for rest and sleep. *My soul refused to be comforted* (v. 2); he was not in the mood to listen to those who tried to encourage him. If those who are in a state of deep sorrow completely refuse to be comforted, they not only harm themselves but also show disrespect for God.

3. His sorrowful thoughts. When he remembered God, his thoughts focused only on his justice, wrath, and fearful majesty, and so God himself became a terror to him. He could not enjoy sleep, which, if it is quiet and refreshing, brings rest from our griefs and cares: *"Thou holdest my eyes waking* with your terrors, which make me full of tossings to and fro until the dawning of the day"* (Job 7:4). He could not speak, because of the confusion of thoughts; he was so troubled that he could not speak and restore himself. Grief never preys so much on the spirits as when it is stifled and bottled up.

4. His sorrowful reflections (vv. 5–6): *"I have considered the days of old* and compared them with the present. Our former prosperity makes our present calamities seem worse, for we cannot see the wonders our ancestors told us about." But *say not thou* that *the former days were better than these* (Ecc 7:10), for you do not know whether they were or not. Further, we should not let the memory of the comforts we have lost make us unthankful for those that are left. He especially *called to remembrance his song in the night* (v. 6), but he was out of harmony with it, and the memory meant he only *poured out his soul in him* (42:4). See also Job 35:10.

5. His sorrowful fears: *"I communed with my own heart* (v. 6). Come, my soul, how will these things turn out? And so I began to reason, *Will the Lord cast off* (reject) *for ever* (v. 7), as he is doing at the moment? His *tender mercies* have been withheld, but *are they shut up,* have they come to an end *in anger?"* (vv. 7–9). This is the language of a depressed and abandoned soul, not uncommon even with those who *fear the Lord* (Isa 50:10).

5.1. He was groaning under a severe trouble. Of all troubles, spiritual trouble is the most painful to a gracious soul; nothing wounds and pierces it like the dread of God's anger.

5.2. He was grappling with strong temptations. On cloudy and dark days, God's own people may be tempted to draw desperate conclusions about their own spiritual state and the condition of God's church and kingdom in the world, and they may even give up everything as lost. But we must not give way to such suggestions.

5.2.1. Let faith answer them from the Scripture: *Will the Lord cast off for ever?* (v. 7). Not at all (Ro 11:1)! *Is his mercy clean gone for ever?* (v. 8). No; his *mercy endures for ever* (1Ch16:34); as it is *from everlasting,* it is *to everlasting* (103:17). *Doth his promise fail for evermore?* (v. 8). No; *it is impossible for God to lie* (Heb 6:18). *Has he in anger shut up his tender mercies?* (v. 9). No; they are *new every morning* (La 3:23), and so, *How shall I give thee up, Ephraim?* (Hos 11:8–9).

5.2.2. He suddenly restrained himself with the word *Selah:* "Stop there; go no farther." He then chided himself (v. 10): *I said, This is my infirmity.* He was soon aware that had not spoken rightly, and so, *Why art thou cast down, O my soul?* (42:5). "I said, 'this is my affliction,'" as some understand the verse. "Everyone has their affliction, their thorn in the flesh. This is mine, the cross I must bear." Depression in spirit and distrust of God in adversity and suffering are too often the weaknesses of good people. When such thoughts arise in us at any time, we must stop them from rising farther. We must argue down the rebellion of unbelief: *But I will remember the years of the right hand of the Most High* (v. 10). He had been considering the *years of ancient times* (v. 5), the blessings he enjoyed previously, and the memory of them had only added to his grief, but now he considered them as *the years of the right hand of the Most High* (v. 10); he recalled that those blessings of ancient times came from the sovereign command of the right hand of the One who is *over all, God blessed for ever* (Ro 9:5), and this gave him assurance.

Verses 11–20

The psalmist here recovered himself. He tried again, and this second time he found it was not in vain. *"I will remember, surely I will,* what God has done for his people of old, until I can reason a favorable way out of these present dark paths"* (vv. 11–12). Due remembrance of the works of God is a powerful antidote to distrusting his promises, for he is a God who does not change.

Two things, in general, satisfied him:

1. That *God's way is in the sanctuary* (v. 13). "His ways are holy" is how some understand this. He has holy purposes in everything he does. He acts according to his promises, which he has made known in the sanctuary. All he does is intended for the good of his church.

2. That God's *way is in the sea* (v. 19). Although God is holy, just, and good, we still cannot explain why he acts as he does. *His path is in the great waters and his footsteps are not known* (v. 19). God's ways are like deep waters that cannot be fathomed (36:6), like the way of a ship on the high seas, which cannot be traced (Pr 30:18–19).

2.1. No god can be compared with the God of Israel. *Who is so great a God as our God?* Let us first give God the glory for the great things he has done for his people. Let us acknowledge him in these. He is far above all comparison.

2.2. He is a God of almighty power (v. 14): *"Thou alone doest wonders* (compare 72:18), above the powers of any creature. *Thou hast* visibly, and beyond any contradiction, *declared thy strength among the people."* God brought Israel out of Egypt (v. 15). This was the beginning of his mercy to them. Although they were rescued powerfully, they were still said to have been redeemed, as if it had been done by paying a price, because it was a type of the great redemption, which was to be brought about in the fullness of time both by price and by power. He divided the Red Sea before them (v. 16): *The waters gave way, and a path was made through them.* Not only the surface of the waters, but also *the depths, were troubled,* and opened up to the right and the left. He destroyed the Egyptians (v. 17): *The skies sent out a sound; thy arrows also went abroad,* which is explained in v. 18: *The voice of thy thunder was heard in the heaven*—that was the sound which the skies sent out—*the lightnings lightened the* world—those were the arrows which went out, by which the Egyptian forces were overcome. When the waters returned to their place, *his footsteps were not known* (v. 19); there were no footprints to be seen. He took his people Israel under his own guidance and protection (v. 20): *Thou leadest thy people like a flock.* He went in front of them with all the care and tenderness of a shepherd. Moses and Aaron led them, but they could not have done this without God, and God did it with and through them. Moses was their governor, Aaron their high priest. The judiciary and the ministry, those two great institutions, are still as great a mercy to any people as the pillar of cloud and fire was to Israel in the desert, even though they are not as great a miracle as that pillar was.

PSALM 78

This psalm is historical. Here is: 1. The introduction to this church history, commending it to the study of generations to come (vv. 1–8). 2. The history itself from Moses to David: it is put into a psalm or song because the singing of the things related here would move the people more than the telling of a simple narrative would. The general scope of this psalm is in vv. 9–11. As to the details, we are told: 2.1. What wonderful deeds God had worked for them (vv. 12–16). 2.2. How ungrateful they were to God for his favors: how they murmured against God and distrusted him (vv. 17–20), and only insincerely repented and submitted when he punished them (vv. 34–37), and how they showed their disrespect toward God by their idolatry after they came into Canaan (vv. 56–58). 2.3. How God justly punished them for their sins (vv. 21–22) in the desert (vv. 29–33), and punished them now, more recently, allowing the ark to be captured by the Philistines (vv. 59–64). 2.4. How graciously God had spared them and returned in mercy to them, despite their offenses, and settled them happily in both church and state (vv. 65–72). These things happened to them for examples (1Co 10:11; Heb 4:11).

Verses 1–8

These verses contain the introduction to this narrative. It is indeed a *Maschil,* "a psalm to give instruction."

1. The psalmist demands attention (v. 1): *Give ear, O my people, to my law.* Some consider these to be the words of the psalmist. He calls his instructions his *law* or edict; such was their commanding force in themselves. But David was a king, and in issuing this command he would introduce his royal power to build up his people. Or perhaps the psalmist says *Give ear* because he is a prophet and speaks as God's mouthpiece, and so he calls them *my people* and demands submission to what he says as submission to a law.

2. Several reasons are given why we should give diligent attention.

2.1. The things discussed are significant (v. 2): *I will open my mouth in a parable, I will utter dark sayings* (hidden things), which demand your most serious attention. Yet they are called *dark sayings* not because they are difficult to understand but because they are to be carefully looked into.

2.2. They are the memorials to antiquity—*dark sayings of old which our fathers have told us* (v. 3). They are certain and undisputed matters. The honor we owe to our parents and ancestors makes us listen to what our ancestors have told us.

2.3. They are to be passed on to future generations, and this places a responsibility on us to carefully hand them down (v. 4): because our ancestors told them to us *we will not hide them from their children.* We must be concerned for future generations in general. What we are to pass on to our children is not only the knowledge of languages, arts, and sciences, freedom and possessions, but especially the praises of the Lord and his wonderful deeds. We must take great care to deposit our religious faith purely and completely into the hands of those who come after us.

2.3.1. The Law of God was given with a particular command that those to whom it was given must teach it diligently to their children (v. 5): *He established a testimony* or covenant, and enacted law, in Jacob and Israel, which he *commanded them to make known to their children* (Dt 6:7, 20). The church of God, like the Roman commonwealth as described by one historian, was not to be "a thing of one age," but was to be maintained from one generation to another.

2.3.2. We must also fully and clearly pass on the knowledge of the providences of God concerning his people. God gave orders that his laws should be made known to future generations; it is also necessary that his works should be made known. Let these be told to our children and our children's children so *that, not forgetting the works of God* done in former days, *they* may *set their hope in God and keep his commandments.* Only those who carefully seek to do his commandments may confidently hope for God's salvation. And let the children be told of God's works so that they may be warned (v. 8): So *that they might not be as their fathers, a stubborn and rebellious generation.* Although they were the descendants of Abraham and had been taken into covenant with God, their *spirit was not stedfast* (faithful) *with him* (v. 8), but took every occasion to desert him.

Verses 9–39

In these verses:

1. The psalmist observes the rebukes that the people of Israel have brought on themselves because they rebelled against God (vv. 9–11). *The children of Ephraim,* the tribe in which Shiloh was, although they were well armed with bows, still *turned back in the day of battle.* This seems to refer to the shameful defeat they suffered from the Philistines in Eli's time, when the Philistines captured the ark (1Sa 4:10–11). Well might that event be so fresh in David's mind more than forty years later, for the ark was not brought out of obscurity until David brought it from Kiriath Jearim to his own city, although it was quickly retrieved after that memorable battle in which it was seized by the Philistines. Note the shameful cowardice of the descendants of Ephraim. Sin discourages people and takes away their heart. The people of Ephraim were evil and treacherous, for *they kept not the covenant of God.* They *forgot his works and* his *wonders* (v. 11).

Our forgetfulness of God's works lies at the root of our disobedience to his laws.

2. He uses the occasion here to consider precedents. The narrative in these verses is significant, for it relates a kind of struggle between God's goodness and human evil, with mercy ultimately triumphing over judgment (Jas 2:13).

2.1. God did great things for his people Israel when he first formed them into a people: *Marvellous things did he in the sight of their fathers* (v. 12). He made a path for them through the Red Sea and gave them courage to pass through it, although the waters stood higher than their heads, like a wall (v. 13). He provided a guide for them through the uncharted paths of the desert (v. 14); he led them step by step, *in the day time by a cloud*, which also protected them from the heat, and *all the night with a light of fire*, which made the darkness of night less fearful, and perhaps kept away wild animals (Zec 2:5). He supplied their camp with fresh water in a dry and thirsty land (63:1) by splitting a rock (vv. 15–16): *He clave* (split) *the rocks in the wilderness.* He gave them water to drink from the dry and hard rock, not distilled out of a retort, drop by drop, but in streams *running down like rivers*, from the great depths. God gives an abundance of water: he is rich in mercy.

2.2. When God began to bless them in this way, they began to rebel against him (v. 17): *They sinned yet more against him.* They endured the misery of their slavery better than the difficulties of their rescue; they never complained against their taskmasters as much as they did against Moses and Aaron. *They provoked the Most High* (v. 17). In the desert they said and did what they knew would offend him: *They tempted God in their heart* (v. 18). They tempted him:

2.2.1. By desiring, or rather demanding, those things he had not thought fit to give them: *They asked meat for their lust*, demanded the food they craved. God had given them manna, wholesome, pleasant food, and a lot of it. But this was not enough for them; they had to have the food they craved, rich delicacies.

2.2.2. By distrusting his power to give them what they needed. They challenged him to give them meat, and if he did not, they would say it was because he could not (v. 19): *They spoke against God.* It was as offensive a remark as could be made against God to say, *Can God furnish a table in the wilderness?* Self-indulgence is unreasonable and insatiable! These gluttons, who enjoyed the good life, thought the provision of a well-spread table such a great feat that it was more than God could provide for them in the desert. Which is easier, to provide a well-spread table in the desert, which someone rich can do, or to bring water out of a rock, which the greatest power on earth cannot do? Even if we are asking for something very great, we should acknowledge, *Lord, if thou wilt, thou canst* (Mt 8:2).

2.3. God was justly angry at the rebellion of the people and was very displeased with them (v. 21): *The Lord heard this, and was wroth.*

2.3.1. God was very angry at their rebellion (v. 22) because it showed that *they believed not in God. They trusted not in the salvation* he had begun to work for them, for if they had trusted him, they would not have questioned the progress of that salvation as they did. He *commanded the clouds from above.* The usual way in which this worked was by showers leading to the earth's production of grain, but now, when God commanded them, they showered down grain itself, which is therefore called here *the corn* (grain) *of heaven.* Everyone, even the

least child in Israel, "ate the bread of the mighty" (v. 25, margin), but it was also strong meat for the strong. They did not find they lacked, for *he sent them meat to the full* (v. 25). The daily provision God makes for us has no less of God's mercy.

2.3.2. He expressed his anger at their rebellion not by denying them what they craved so inordinately, but by granting it to them. *He caused an east wind to blow and a south wind*, either a southeast wind, or an east wind first to bring in quail from that direction and then a south wind to bring in more from that direction; and in this way *he rained flesh upon them.* There was an abundance of it, *as dust, as the sand of the sea* (v. 27), so that the lowliest Israelite would have enough. It cost them nothing as well—not even the hard work of taking it from the mountains, for *he let it fall in the midst of their camp, round about their habitation* (all around their tents) (v. 28). We have the account in Nu 11:31–32. He made them pay dearly for the quail, for although *he gave them their own desire, they were not estranged from their lust* (vv. 29–30). Their appetite was insatiable; they were well filled, but they were still not satisfied. Such is the nature of desire; the more it is indulged the more indulgent it grows. There were some contented Israelites, who ate moderately of the quail and were not harmed, for it was not the food that poisoned them, but their own desires.

2.4. The judgments of God on them did not reform them any more than his mercies had (v. 32): *For all this, they sinned still*; they murmured and quarreled with God and Moses as much as ever. Those who will be never melted by the mercies of God nor broken by his judgments have truly hard hearts.

2.5. They persisted in their sins, and God continued in his judgments, but they were judgments of another kind, which did not come suddenly, but slowly. *Therefore their days did he consume in vanity* (futility) in the desert, and *their years in trouble* (terror). They were condemned to spend thirty-eight tedious years in the desert, which were spent in sheer futility, for in all those years not one step was taken toward Canaan; they turned back again and again and wandered to and fro as in a maze. Those who continue to sin must continue to expect trouble and terror. And the reason why we spend our days in so much futility and terror, why we live with so little comfort and to so little purpose, is that we do not live by faith.

2.6. They professed repentance under these rebukes, but they were not genuine in this profession. Their profession was plausible (vv. 34–35): *When he slew them*, or condemned them to be killed, *then they sought him.* They were so frightened that they cried out to God for mercy and promised they would reform and be very good; then *they returned to God, and inquired early after him.* Yet they were not sincere in this profession (vv. 36–37): *They did but flatter him with their mouth*, as if they thought that by persuasive speech they could prevail upon him to withdraw the sentence. They thawed out in the sun but froze again in the shade. They *lied to God with their tongues, for their heart was not with him* (vv. 36–37)

2.7. God then had pity on them and put an end to the judgments which had been threatened and had been partly executed (vv. 38–39): *But he, being full of compassion, forgave their iniquity.* He spared their lives until they had brought up another generation, which would enter the Promised Land. Because he was *full of compassion* and merciful (v. 38), he said, *How shall I give thee up, Ephraim? How shall I deliver thee, Israel?* (Hos 11:8). Although they did not rightly remember that he was their rock, he *remembered that they were but flesh* (they were

only human) (v. 39). He considered how easy it would
have been to crush them: *They are as a wind that passeth away and cometh not again* (v. 39). It would be easy
to argue that they should be justly destroyed, but God
argues, on the contrary, that he will not destroy them, for
the reasoning that is true to his nature is, *He, being full of
compassion* (merciful), *forgave* (v. 38).

Verses 40–72

The matter and scope of these verses are the same as
those of the previous verses, to show what great mercies
God had given to Israel, how offensive the people had
been, what judgments he had brought on them for their
sins, and yet how, in judgment, he finally remembered
mercy (Hab 3:2). Notice:

1. The sins of Israel in the desert, mentioned again
(vv. 40–41): *How often did they provoke him in the wilderness!* God kept an account (Nu 14:22): *They have
tempted me these ten times.* By rebelling against him so
much, they did not so much anger him as sadden him, for
he looked on them as his children—*Israel is my son, my
firstborn* (Ex 4:22). They grieved him because they made
him afflict them, which he did not do willingly (La 3:33).
After they had humbled themselves before him, they
turned back and tempted God (put him to the test), *and
limited the Holy One of Israel* (v. 41), prescribing to him
what proofs he should give of his power and presence with
them and how he should lead them and provide for them.
It is presumptuous for us to limit *the Holy One of Israel*
(v. 41), for because he is *the Holy One of Israel* (v. 41), he
will do what is best for our good. What led to their limiting God was their forgetting his favors in the past (v. 42).
There are some days which become significant because
they are days of special acts of rescue, and they should
never be forgotten.

2. The mercies of God to Israel. The catalog of the miracles God did for them begins farther back, and is carried
farther forward, than the one we had before (vv. 12–37).

2.1. This account begins with their rescue from Egypt
by means of the plagues God used to compel the Egyptians to release them.

2.1.1. Several of the plagues of Egypt are mentioned
here, which speak loudly of the power of God and his
favor to Israel.

2.1.1.1. The waters were turned into blood; the Egyptians had made themselves drunk with the blood of God's
people, including the infants, and now God gave them
blood to drink, *for they were worthy* (for that was what they
deserved; Rev 16:6) (v. 44). The flies and frogs infested
them (v. 45). The plague of locusts ate their crops, which
they had worked for (v. 46). The *hail destroyed* their trees,
especially *their vines,* the weakest of trees (v. 47), and
their cattle, especially *their flocks* of sheep, the weakest
of their cattle (v. 48); and the *frost,* or sleet, was so violent
that it destroyed even the *sycamore trees.*

2.1.1.2. The death of the firstborn was the last and
most severe plague of Egypt, and it brought about Israel's
rescue. It was the first to be intended (Ex 4:23), but last to
be carried out, for if gentler methods had done their work,
this would have been prevented. So often had Pharaoh's
heart become hardened again after lesser judgments had
softened it that God now *stirred up all his wrath. He made
a way to* (prepared a path for) *his anger* (v. 50). He did
not unleash it on them indecisively, but forcefully. His
anger was weighed out with the greatest precision in the
balances of justice, for even in his greatest displeasure,
he never did, and never will do, any wrong to any of his
creatures: the path of his anger is always weighed out

with the utmost care. *He sent evil* (destroying) *angels
among them* (v. 49), not evil in their own nature, but evil
with respect to the destructive mission they were sent on.
They were destroying angels, or angels of punishment.
The punishment itself was very severe: *He smote* (struck
down) *all the firstborn in Egypt* (v. 51), *the chief of their
strength,* the hopes of their respective families, the firstfruits of manhood.

2.1.2. By these plagues God made a way for *his own
people to go forth like sheep* (v. 52) that did not know
where they were going, and *guided them in the wilderness,* as a shepherd guides their flock, with every possible
care and tenderness (v. 52). *He led them on safely,* through
dangerous paths, so that *they feared not,* that is, they did
not need to fear. *But the sea overwhelmed their enemies,*
who dared pursue them into it (v. 53). It was a path to the
Israelites, but a grave to their persecutors.

2.2. It is carried down as far as their settlement in
Canaan (v. 54): *He brought them to the border of his
sanctuary,* to the land in the middle of which he set up
his sanctuary. The land that is the border of God's sanctuary is a happy land. The whole land in general, and Zion
in particular, was *the mountain which his right hand had
purchased* (v. 54). He *made them to ride on the high
places of the earth* (Isa 58:14; Dt 32:13). They found the
Canaanites in full possession of that land, but God made
his people *Israel tread upon their high places, dividing*
(allotting) each tribe *an inheritance* (v. 55).

3. The sins of Israel after they had settled in Canaan
(vv. 56–58). The children were *like their fathers,* and
brought their old sins into their new homes. They seemed
at times to be devoted to God, but they quickly turned aside
and rebelled against him with their high places and their
idols, so arousing God's anger. Idolatry was the sin that
entangled them most (Heb 12:1), and although they often
professed repentance for it, they also often turned back
to it again.

4. The judgments God brought on them for these sins.
Idolatry is condoned among the Gentiles, but not in Israel
(v. 59): *When God heard this,* when he heard the outcry of
their sins, which came before him (Ge 18:20–21), he was
very angry. He abandoned his tabernacle among them,
removing the defense which it brought (v. 60). God never
leaves us until we leave him. The *tabernacle at Shiloh* was
the tent God had placed among men, in which God would
in very deed dwell with men upon the earth (2Ch 6:18),
but when his people acted treacherously, he justly abandoned it, and then all its glory departed (1Sa 4:21–22).
He gave up everything into the hands of the enemy. Those
whom God abandons become easy prey to the destroyer.
God allowed the Philistines to capture the ark and take it
away as a trophy of their victory, to show that he had abandoned not only the tabernacle but also even the ark itself
(v. 61): *He delivered his strength into captivity,* as if it had
been weakened and overcome, *and his glory* fell under the
disgrace of being abandoned *into the enemy's hand.* We
have the story in 1Sa 4:11. He allowed the armies of Israel
to be defeated by the Philistines (vv. 62–63): *He gave his
people over unto the sword,* for he was very angry with
his inheritance. His wrath was the *fire which consumed
their young men* in the prime of their lives, and devastated them so much that *their maidens were not given to*
(in) *marriage* because there were no young men for them
to be given to. Even *their priests,* who attended the ark,
fell by the sword (v. 64), Hophni and Phinehas. They died
because they became evil and were very corrupt sinners
in the sight of the Lord. When the priests fell, *their widows made no lamentation* (could not weep) (v. 64). The

widow of Phinehas, instead of mourning her husband's death, died herself, after she had called her son *Ichabod* (1Sa 4:19).

5. God's return to them in mercy and his gracious support for them after this. God was *grieved for the miseries of Israel* (Jdg 10:16). And so *then the Lord awaked as one out of sleep* (v. 65), *and like a mighty man that shouteth by reason of wine*, like one who is refreshed from sleep, and who has a happy heart because of the sober and moderate use of wine, and is therefore vigorous.

5.1. He sent a plague on the Philistines who held the ark captive (v. 66). He struck them with tumors *in the hinder parts*. Sooner or later God will glorify himself by putting disgrace on his enemies, even when they are most exalted by their successes.

5.2. He provided a new place for his ark to settle after it had been in captivity for some months and in obscurity for some years. He did *refuse* (rejected) *the tabernacle of Joseph*; he never sent the ark back to Shiloh, in the tribe of Ephraim (v. 67). The ruins of that place were a constant memorial to divine justice. *Go, see what I did to Shiloh* (Jer 7:12). But he did not completely take away the glory from Israel; the ark was moved but not removed. Shiloh had lost it, but Israel had not. God will keep a church in the world, and a kingdom among people, even though this or that place may have its lampstand removed (Rev 2:5). When God *chose not the tribe of Ephraim* (v. 67), the tribe from which Joshua came, he *chose the tribe of Judah* (v. 68), because from that tribe would come Jesus, who is greater than Joshua. Kiriath Jearim, the place to which the ark was brought after its rescue from the hands of the Philistines, was in the tribe of Judah. From there it was moved to Zion, *the Mount Zion which he loved* (v. 68), which *was beautiful for situation, the joy of the whole earth* (48:2). It was there that he *built his sanctuary like high palaces* and *like the earth* (v. 69). David indeed set up only a tent for the ark, but a temple was then designed and prepared for, and finished by his son. Solomon built it, but it is said here that *God built it*, for his father had taught him, perhaps with reference to this undertaking, that *except the Lord build the house, those labour in vain* who build it (127:1). It was not finally destroyed until the Gospel temple was set up, which is to continue *as long as the sun and moon endure* (89:36–37), and against which the *gates of hell shall not prevail* (Mt 16:18).

5.3. He set a good government over his people, a monarchy, and a monarch after his own heart (1Sa 13:14): *He chose David his servant* out of all the thousands of Israel; into his hand he put the scepter, out of his body Christ was to come, and he was to be a type of Christ (v. 70). Notice that although David descended from the ruler of the tribe of Judah (Nu 2:3; 7:11–12; Ru 4:12, 18–20), his education was poor. He was not brought up as a scholar or a soldier, but as a shepherd. He was *taken from the sheepfolds* (v. 70), as Moses was, for God delights to honor the humble and diligent. Sometimes he finds those who have spent their early days in solitude and contemplation most qualified for public action. The Son of David was rebuked for the obscurity of his origins: *Is not this the carpenter?* (Mk 6:3). David does not say he was taken from leading the rams, but *from following the ewes*, especially those *great with young* (v. 71), which suggests that of all the good qualities of a shepherd, the one he was noted most for was his tenderness and compassion to those of his flock that most needed his care. It was a great honor that God put on him in advancing him to be a king, especially to be king over Jacob and Israel, God's own people, who are near and dear to him. It also showed the great trust

that rested on David. Because David had such a great trust put into his hands, he obtained mercy from the Lord and was found to be both skillful and faithful in discharging this responsibility (v. 72): *So he fed them*; he ruled them and taught them, guided and protected them *according to the integrity of his heart* (v. 72), aiming at nothing but the glory of God and the good of the people committed to his charge. He was not only very sincere in what he intended but also very wise in what he did. Fortunate are the people under such a government! The psalmist has good reason to make this the finishing and crowning example of God's favor to Israel, for David was a type of Christ, the great and good Shepherd.

PSALM 79

This psalm most probably refers to the destruction of Jerusalem and the temple. It is set to the same tune, as we may put it, as the Lamentations of Jeremiah, and that weeping prophet uses two verses from it (vv. 6–7) in his prayer (Jer 10:25). Some think it was written long before such a time by the spirit of prophecy and was prepared for the use of the church on that dark day. Whatever the particular occasion was, we have here: 1. A description of the deplorable condition the people of God were in at this time (vv. 1–5). 2. A request to God for help and relief (vv. 6–7, 10, 12), that their sins might be forgiven (vv. 8–9), and that they might be rescued (v. 11); a plea taken from the readiness of his people to praise him (v. 13).

Verses 1–5

Here is a sad complaint brought to the court of heaven.

1. They complain here about the outrageous fury of the oppressors, which was exerted:

1.1. Against places (v. 1). They caused all the trouble they could:

1.1.1. To the Holy Land. They invaded that and made inroads into it: "*The heathen* (nations) *have come into thy inheritance* to plunder and ravage it." Canaan was precious to the godly Israelites more because it was God's inheritance than because it belonged to them. Wrongs done to religious faith should grieve us even more than those done to rights that all have in common, or even those done to our own rights. In the previous psalm the psalmist had spoken of it as an example of God's great favor to Israel that he had *cast out the heathen* (driven out the nations) *before them* (78:55). But notice what a change sin has made now; the nations are allowed to invade them.

1.1.2. To the Holy City: *They have laid Jerusalem on heaps* (v. 1). The inhabitants were buried in the ruins of their own houses. The sanctuary that God had built, and which was thought to be as durable as the earth, had now been leveled to the ground: *Thy holy temple have they defiled* (v. 1), by entering it and devastating it. God's own people had defiled it by their sins, and so God allowed their enemies to defile it by their arrogance.

1.2. Against God's people. They wasted blood and killed without mercy (v. 3): *Their blood have they shed like water*, wherever they were, *round about Jerusalem*, in all the roads to the city. The sword waited for whoever went out or came in. And when they had killed them, they would not let anyone bury them. They even dug up their dead bodies, *the flesh of God's saints*, whose names and memories they had a deep hatred for, and *gave them to be meat to the fowls of the heaven and to the beasts of the earth* (v. 2). They hung them in chains, which was painful for the Jews, because God had given them an explicit law against this, as something cruel (Dt 21:23).

1.3. Against their names (v. 4): *"We that survive have become a reproach to our neighbours*; they all try to mistreat us and load us down with contempt. The result is that we have become *a scorn and derision to those that are round about us."* If God's professing people turn away from what they and their ancestors were, then they must expect to be told about it.

2. They wonder at God's anger (v. 5). They discern this in the anger of their neighbors: *How long, Lord, wilt thou be angry?* Will it be *for ever?* This shows that they wanted nothing more than that God would be reconciled to them, and then the remnants of human wrath would be restrained (76:10).

Verses 6 – 13

The requests made here to God are very suitable for the present troubles of the church.

1. They pray that God would turn away his anger from them so as to turn it onto those who persecute and mistreat them (v. 6). This prayer is in effect a prophecy, in which the *wrath of God is revealed from heaven against all ungodliness and unrighteousness of men* (Ro 1:18). The reason why people do not call on God is that they do not know him or realize how able and willing he is to help them. Those who persist in their ignorance of God and neglect prayer are ungodly. They live *without God in the world* (Eph 2:12). The persecutors *have devoured Jacob* (v. 7). They have not only disturbed him but also devoured him. They have not only encroached on his dwelling place, the land of Canaan, but also laid it waste by plundering and depopulating it. *"Pour out thy wrath* (v. 6) on them; not only restrain them from causing further trouble, but also judge them for the trouble they have already caused."

2. They pray for the pardon of sin, which they acknowledge to be the cause of all their adversities. "Do not hold against us our first sins," which some believe goes back as far as the golden calf. If the children by repentance cut off the inheritance of their parents' sin, they may in faith pray that God will not hold that sin against them (v. 8). When God pardons sin, he blots it out and remembers it no more (Jer 31:34). *Deliver us, and purge away our sins* (v. 9). When we have been rescued through forgiveness of sin, and our rescue flows from that, then we have been rescued in love, and such a rescue is a true mercy.

3. They pray that God would quickly bring their troubles to a good conclusion: *Let thy tender mercies speedily prevent* (come quickly to meet) *us* (v. 8). Unless divine mercy quickly intervened to prevent their destruction, they would be ruined. This encouraged their boldness: *"Lord, help us; Lord, deliver us* (v. 9); help us in our troubles, so that we may cope with them well. Save us from sinking under the weight of our sin. *We are brought very low* (v. 8); we are in desperate need and are lost unless you help us." Those who make God the God of their salvation will find him to be so. The people plead no goodness in themselves; they do not claim to have any, but, *"Help us for the glory of thy name* (v. 9); pardon us for your name's sake. *Wherefore* (why) *should the heathen* (nations) *say, 'Where is their God?* He has abandoned them and forgotten them. This is the result of worshiping a God whom they cannot see'?" "Lord," they say, "make it clear that you are with us by showing them that you are indeed with us and for us, so that when we are asked, *Where is your God?* (v. 10), we may be able to say, 'He is near us, and you can see he is by what he does for us.'"

4. They pray that God would take revenge on their adversaries: "Let the avenging of our blood," according to the ancient law (Ge 9:6), "be known among the nations; and *let God be known among the heathen* as *the God to whom vengeance belongs* (94:1) and the God who embraces his people's cause." We may in faith pray that God would pay back onto sinners' own shoulders the insults with which they have blasphemed him, and that he would humble them and bring them to repentance.

5. They pray that God would find a way to rescue his poor prisoners (v. 11; 69:33). Their brothers and sisters who had fallen into the hands of the enemy were closely guarded prisoners, and because they dared not be heard to complain, they expressed their grief in deep and quiet *sighing* (groans). *"Let their sighs come up before thee* (v. 11), and be willing to take notice of their groans." They promised a response of praise to the answers of prayer (v. 13): *So we will give thee thanks for ever.* They committed themselves not only to give God thanks at present but also to *show forth his praise unto all generations* (v. 13).

PSALM 80

This psalm has much the same purpose as the previous one. Some think it was written on the occasion of the destruction and exile of the ten tribes. But the problems of the Israel of God were many; perhaps many are not recorded in the sacred history, and perhaps some of those not recorded gave rise to this psalm. 1. The psalmist begs for the signs of God's presence with them and favor to them (vv. 1 – 3); he complains about the present rebukes they are under (vv. 4 – 7). 2. He illustrates the present desolation of the church by comparing it to a vine and a vineyard, which has flourished but has now been destroyed (vv. 8 – 16); he concludes by praying to God for the preparing of mercy for them (61:7) and the preparing of them for mercy (vv. 17 – 19).

Verses 1 – 7

The psalmist here turns to God in prayer concerning the present afflicted state of Israel.

1. He begs God's favor for them (vv. 1 – 2), as the Shepherd of Israel, under whose guidance and care Israel was. He *leads Joseph like a flock* (v. 1), to the best pastures and out of danger. He *dwells between the cherubim* (v. 1), where he is ready to receive requests and to give directions. The mercy seat (atonement cover) was between the cherubim, and it is a great encouragement in prayer to look up to God as sitting on the throne of grace. The psalmist wants God to listen to the cries of their misery and their prayers, to *stir up his strength* (v. 2). His power seems to have fallen asleep: "Lord, awaken it. Lord, be a powerful and present help to your people. Lord, do this *before Ephraim, Benjamin, and Manasseh"* (v. 2). Perhaps these three tribes are named because they were the tribes which formed the division of the camp of Israel that in their journey through the desert followed immediately after the tabernacle, so that before them the ark of God's strength rose to scatter their enemies (Nu 10:35; Ps 68:1; 2Ch 6:41).

2. He complains about God's displeasure. God was angry, and he feared that more than anything (v. 4). He sensed that God was *angry against the prayer of his people.* That God should be angry at the sins of his people and at the prayers of his enemies is not strange, but that he should be angry at the prayers of his people is very strange. If he is really angry at the prayers of his people,

we may be sure it is because they are asking in the wrong way or with wrong motives (Jas 4:3). But perhaps it is only in their own thoughts; he seems to be angry with their prayers when really he is not, for this is how he is testing their perseverance in prayer, as Christ tested the woman of Canaan when he said, *It is not meet to take the children's bread and cast it to dogs* (Mt 15:26). Now the signs of God's displeasure that Israel had suffered under for a long time were both their sorrow and shame. Their sorrow: *Thou feedest them with the bread of tears*; they eat their food from day to day in tears; this was the vinegar in which they *dipped their morsel* (42:3). Many who spend their time in sorrow will spend their eternity in joy. Their shame (v. 6): their enemies laughed among themselves to see the frightful state they were falling into and the disappointments they met.

3. He prays fervently for converting grace for them so that they may be saved: *Turn* (restore) *us again, O God!* (v. 3). *Turn* (restore) *us again, O God of hosts!* (v. 7), and then *cause thy face to shine and we shall be saved.* It is the chorus of this song, for we have it again (v. 19). "Lord, turn us back to you in repentance and reformation, and no doubt you will then return to us in mercy and deliverance." Notice:

- There is no salvation apart from God's favor.
- There is no receiving favor from God unless we are turned to him.
- There is no conversion to God except by his own grace. *Turn thou me, and I shall be turned*, restore me, and I will return (Jer 31:18). The prayer here is for a national conversion: national holiness would lead to national happiness.

Verses 8–19

Here, the psalmist presents his appeal before the Israel of God. He presses it home at the throne of grace. The church is here represented as a vine (vv. 8, 14) and a vineyard (v. 15). The root of this vine is Christ (Ro 11:18). The branches are believers (Jn 15:5). The church is like a vine, weak and needing support, unsightly and having an unpromising exterior, but spreading and fruitful, and its fruit is excellent. The church is a fine and noble vine; we have reason to acknowledge the goodness of God for planting such a vine in the desert of this world and preserving it to this day. Notice:

1. How the vine of the Old Testament church was originally planted. It was *brought out of Egypt* (v. 8) boldly; *the heathen* (nations) *were cast* (driven) *out* (v. 8) of Canaan to make space for it, seven nations to make space for that one.

2. How the vine spread and flourished.

2.1. The land of Canaan itself was fully populated. At first the Israelites were not numerous enough to repopulate it (Ex 23:29). But in Solomon's time *Judah and Israel were many as the sand of the sea* (1Ki 4:20). Israel had not only many men, but also those *mighty men of valour*, the best fighting men (Jos 10:7).

2.2. They extended their conquests and rule to the neighboring countries (v. 11): *She sent out her boughs to the sea*, which probably refers to the Mediterranean, and *her branches to the river*, to the river of Egypt southward, the river of Damascus northward, or rather the Euphrates River eastward (Ge 15:18). What is significant here about this vine is that it is praised for its *shadow*, its *boughs*, and its *branches*, but not a word is mentioned about its fruit, for *Israel was an empty vine* (Hos 10:1). God came

looking for grapes, but saw bad fruit (Isa 5:2). No tree is so useless or worthless as a vine that does not produce fruit (Eze 15:2, 6).

3. How the vine was wasted and ruined: "Lord, you have done great things for this vine, and why should it all be undone? Will God abandon and why himself gave existence to?" (v. 12). *Why hast thou then broken down her hedges?* There was a good reason. This noble vine had become *the degenerate plant of a strange vine* (Jer 2:21). As soon as God *broke down its hedges* (v. 12) and left it exposed, troops of enemies immediately broke in. Those who passed by picked its grapes; the *boar out of the wood* and the *wild beast of the field* were ready to ravage it (v. 13). Yet these cruel enemies were under a restraint, for till God had *broken down its hedges* (v. 12), they could not pick a leaf from this vine. The deplorable state of Israel is described (v. 16): *It is burnt with fire; it is cut down*; the people were treated like thorns and briers, which are close to being cursed and which end up being burned, and they were no longer like vines that were protected and cherished.

4. Their requests to God.

4.1. That God would help the vine (vv. 14–15) "*Look down from heaven*, that place of power, from where you can send effective relief, and come and help this vine. Lord, it is formed by you and for you, and so it may with humble confidence be committed to you and to your own care." What we see as the *branch* is the *son* (*Ben*) in Hebrew, "the son whom you have raised up for yourself in your wisdom." That branch was to come out of the stock of Israel—*my servant the branch* (Zec 3:8)—and so until he came, Israel in general, and the house of David in particular, must be preserved. *He is the true vine* (Jn 15:1; Isa 11:1).

4.2. "*Let thy hand be upon the man of thy right hand*," that king, whoever it was, of the house of David who was now to go in and out before them (1Sa 8:20; 12:2; 2Sa 5:20); "may your hand be on him not only to protect and cover him but also to acknowledge him, strengthen him, and give him success." *So will not we go back from thee* (v. 18). This prayer is also added: "*Quicken us*, put life into us, and then *we will call upon thy name*" (v. 18). We cannot call on God's name rightly unless he revives us. Many interpreters, both Jewish and Christian, apply this to the Messiah, the Son of David, the protector and Savior of the church and the keeper of the vineyard. He is the man of God's right hand, to whom he has "sworn by his right hand," as the Aramaic reads, whom he has exalted to his right hand, and who is indeed his right-hand man, the arm of the Lord, for all power is given to him. Believers are stable and faithful because of the resources—the grace and strength—which are available for us in Jesus Christ (68:28).

PSALM 81

This psalm was written, it is thought, for the ceremony of a particular ordinance, either that of the New Moon festival in general or that of the Feast of Trumpets on the New Moon of the seventh month (Lev 23:24; Nu 29:1). When David, by the Spirit, introduced the singing of psalms into the temple service, this psalm was intended for that day. In this psalm, the two great intentions of our religious meetings are answered: to give glory to God and to receive instruction from God, to behold the beauty of the Lord and to inquire in his temple (Ps 27:4). This psalm helps us on our sacred feast days: 1. In praising

God for what he is to his people (vv. 1–3) and has done for them (vv. 4–7). 2. In teaching and admonishing one another (Col 3:16) about the obligations we are under to God (vv. 8–10), the dangers of rebelling against him (vv. 11–12), and the happiness we would have if only we kept close to him (vv. 13–16).

Verses 1–7

When the people of God were gathered on *the solemn day, the day of the feast of the Lord*, they must be told they had work to do, for we do not go to church to sleep or to be lazy.

1. By hearing this psalm, the worshipers of God are encouraged to do their work, and in singing it, they are taught to stir up both themselves and one another to do the work (vv. 1–3). In doing this we must consider God as *our strength*, and as *the God of Jacob* (v. 1). It is to him, as our strength, that we must pray, and we must sing praises to him as the God of all the wrestling offspring of Jacob, with whom we have spiritual fellowship. We must do this using every expression of holy joy and triumph. In those days this was to be done by musical instruments, the *timbrel, harp, and psaltery*, tambourine, harp, and lyre; and by blowing *the trumpet* (v. 2), to remember, some think, the sound of the trumpet on Mount Sinai, which became louder and louder. Singing aloud suggests we must be warm and adoring when we praise God. No time is wrong to praise God, but some times are appointed, not for God to meet us, because he is always ready to do so, but for us to meet one another, so that we may join together in praising God.

2. They are here instructed in their work. *This was a statute for Israel*, to maintain religious faith among them; it was a *law of the God of Jacob*, which all the descendants of Jacob were committed to and must be subject to. This sacred service was *ordained for a testimony* (v. 5), a constant traditional sign, so that they might know and remember what God had done for their ancestors. When God went out against the land of Egypt, to force Pharaoh to release Israel, he ordained sacred feast days to be observed by statute forever in their generations (Ex 12:17; 27:21; etc.) as a memorial of this rescue; he especially ordained the Passover, which perhaps *the solemn feast day* refers to (v. 3). Here he changes the point of view (v. 6). God speaks by him, saying, *I removed the shoulder from the burden*, I removed the burden from their shoulders. Let God's people remember on the feast day that God had brought them out of the house of slavery; he had removed from their shoulders the burden of oppression under which they were about to sink. He *had delivered their hands from the pots* (v. 6), or baskets, in which they carried clay or bricks. God had also rescued them at the Red Sea. He responded to them then with a real answer, out of *the secret place of thunder* (v. 7). This may refer to the giving of the Law on Mount Sinai, which was the secret place, for to look at it too closely meant death (Ex 19:21), and it was in a thundercloud that God spoke then. God had endured their behavior in the desert: "*I proved thee at the waters of Meribah* (v. 7); it was there that you showed what you were really like, what an unfaithful, murmuring people you were, but I still continued my favor toward you." Now if they were to remember their redemption from Egypt on their sacred feast days, how much more should we, on the Christian Sabbath, remember an even more glorious redemption brought for us by Jesus Christ, and from a worse state than slavery in Egypt.

Verses 8–16

Here, God speaks to Israel through the psalmist, and through them to us:

1. He commands their diligent and serious attention to what he is about to say (v. 8): "*Hear, O my people!* Listen with the greatest seriousness to what is being said, for it is what *I will testify unto* (I am warning) *thee*. Do not only give me a hearing, but *hearken unto me*, that is, listen to me, be advised and warned by me, be ruled by me."

2. He reminds them of their obligation to him because he is the Lord their God and Redeemer (v. 10): *I am the Lord thy God, who brought thee out of the land of Egypt*. This is the introduction to the Ten Commandments, and it is a powerful reason why we should keep them.

3. He gives them a summary of both the commands and the promises he gave them, as the Lord and their God, when they left Egypt. The great command was that they must have no other gods before him (v. 9): *There shall no strange* (foreign) *god be in thee*, none besides your own true God. The great promise was that God himself, as an all-sufficient God, would be near them (Dt 4:7), that if they remained faithful to him as their powerful protector and ruler, they would always find him to be their generous benefactor: "*Open thy mouth wide and I will fill it* (v. 10), as the young ravens that cry open their mouths wide and the old ones fill them." We cannot look for too little from creatures or too much from the Creator. Mere worldly pleasures may sate but will never satisfy (Isa 55:2); divine pleasures will satisfy and never sate.

4. He accuses them of having great contempt for his authority (v. 11). He had done much for them and wanted to do more, but all was in vain: "*My people would not hearken to my voice* but turned a deaf ear to all I said." *They would* have *none of me*. "They did not accept my word" is the Aramaic reading; God was willing to be God to them, but they were not willing to be his people. "Israel, the offspring of Jacob my friend, defied me, and *would* have *none of me*." All the evil in this evil world comes from the willfulness of the sinful will.

5. In this way, he justifies himself in the spiritual judgments he has brought on them (v. 12): *So I gave them up unto their own hearts' lusts*, their stubborn hearts, which would be more dangerous enemies and more troublesome oppressors to them than any of the neighboring nations ever were. God withdrew his Spirit from them, took away the bridle of restraining grace, and left them to their own devices. *Ephraim is joined to idols; let him alone* (Hos 4:17). Let them follow their own course. Notice what follows: *They walked in their own counsels* (v. 12). "I left them to do what they wanted, and then they did everything that was wrong."

6. He testifies his goodwill to them. He saw how desperate their situation was, and how certain their destruction, when they were handed over to follow their own desires. God here looks on them with compassion and shows that it was with reluctance that he had abandoned them to their foolish fate. *O that my people had hearkened*, if only my people had listened (v. 13). See also Isa 48:18. This was Christ's lament at the obstinacy of Jerusalem: *If thou hadst known* (Lk 19:42). The expressions here are very moving (vv. 13–16) and are intended to show how unwilling God is that anyone should perish (2Pe 3:9) and that he wants everyone to reach repentance. Notice:

6.1. The great mercy God had in store for his people, which he would have brought to them if they had been obedient. *I should* (would) *have subdued their enemies*; and it is only God who is to be depended on to subdue our enemies. He would have done it *soon* (quickly); if he simply turns his hand, the *haters of the Lord will submit themselves to him* (v. 15). In spite of all the attempts of their enemies against them, *their time should have endured for ever* (v. 15), and they would never have been hindered in possessing the good land God had given them. He would have given them a great abundance of all good things (v. 16): *He should have fed them with the finest of the wheat*, with the best wheat. Wheat was the staple commodity of Canaan. He would have provided for them not only the finest bread, but also *with honey out of the rock would he have satisfied them* (v. 16). In short, God intended to make them at peace and happy in every way.

6.2. The duty God required from them as the condition of all this mercy. He expected nothing more than that they would *hearken to him* (v. 13), as students listen to their teachers to receive instructions and as servants listen to their master to receive commands, and that they would *walk in his ways* (v. 13).

6.3. The reason for withholding mercy is said to be their neglect of the duty: if they had *hearkened to me, I would soon have subdued their enemies* (vv. 13–14). National sin or disobedience is the great and only thing that slows down and obstructs national rescue. It is sin that makes our troubles last a long time and makes salvation slow in coming.

PSALM 82

A suitable setting for this psalm is rulers' courts and courts of justice, not only in Israel but also in other nations, to instruct the judges of the earth *(2:10),* to tell them their duty, as in 2Sa 23:3, and also to tell them their faults, as in 58:1. We have here: 1. The honor of the judiciary and its dependence on God (v. 1); the duty of judges (vv. 3–4); the corruption of bad judges and the trouble they cause (vv. 2, 5). 2. Their condemnation read out (vv. 6–7); the desire and prayer of all good people that the kingdom of God may be increasingly set up (v. 8).*

Verses 1–5

We have here:

1. God's supreme presidency and authority in every council and court (v. 1): *God stands*, as chief director, *in the congregation of the mighty*, the mighty One, "in the councils of the ruler," the supreme judge. He judges among the "gods," the lesser judges; both the legislative and the executive powers of rulers are under his eye and his hand. The judges are the *mighty* ones. They are powerful in their authority for the sake of the public good. They are, in Hebrew, called "gods"; the same word is used for these subordinate rulers that is used for the sovereign ruler of the world. They are *elohim*. Angels are called this because God uses their service in ruling this lower world. Judges in a lesser capacity are also his ministers, ministers of his providence in general, to maintain order and peace, and of his justice in particular, punishing evildoers and protecting those who do right. Good judges are God's vice-regents and are a great blessing to a people. In a mixed monarchy, here is the sovereign, and here is his assembly, his privy council, his parliament, his judges, who are called *gods. God stands*; he *judges among them* (v. 1). They receive their power from him and are responsible to him. *By him kings reign* (Pr 8:15). God has their hearts in his hands, and his purposes will stand, whatever is going on in human hearts. Let judges consider this and stand in awe at it; God is with them

in giving judgments (2Ch 19:6; Dt 1:17). Let subjects consider this and be encouraged by it, for good rulers and good judges are under divine direction, and bad ones are under divine restraint.

2. A command given to all judges to do good with their power, as they will answer for it to the One who has entrusted this responsibility to them (vv. 3–4). *Defend the poor*, who have no money with which to pay for legal advice, *and the fatherless*, who, while they are still young and unable to help themselves, have lost those who would normally have guided them in their youth. Judges must be fathers to their country. They are to administer justice impartially and do *right to the* afflicted and needy. They must also rescue those who have already fallen into the hands of oppressors. *Rid* (deliver) *them out of the hand of the wicked* (v. 4). These are the clients who are not profitable to an attorney, yet judges must embrace their cause.

3. An accusation drawn up against bad judges. They *judge unjustly*, against the laws of justice and the dictates of conscience. To do unjustly is bad, but to judge unjustly is far worse, because it is doing wrong in the name of right. They were told clearly enough that it was their office and duty to protect and rescue the poor, but they judge unjustly, for *they know not, neither will they understand* (v. 5). They have thwarted their own consciences and so continue to walk in darkness. The result of this sin is that *all the foundations of the earth* (or the land) *are out of course* (shaken) (v. 5). The failure of people who are in positions of public trust brings trouble on the whole nation.

Verses 6–8

We have here:

1. Earthly gods diminished and brought down (vv. 6–7). The dignity of the character of earthly gods is acknowledged (v. 6): *I have said, You are gods.* He called them *gods* because they received a commission from God and were delegated and appointed by him to keep the public peace. God has put some of his honor on them, and he uses them in ruling the world by his providence. When people have so much honor put on them by the hand of God, and so much honor given them by others—as indeed they should have because of their offices—it is hard for them not to become proud of it and puffed up by it (1Co 4:6). But a mortifying thought follows: *You shall die like men* (v. 7). This may be taken as referring to either:

1.1. The punishment of bad judges, those who judged unjustly and by their misrule shook the foundations of the earth. They will die like other evildoers, *fall like one of the* pagan *princes* (v. 7). Or:

1.2. The period of the glory of all judges in this world. "You are called 'gods,' but you do not have a license to live forever; *you shall die like men* (v. 7), like ordinary mortals, and *like one of them, you, O princes! shall fall*, you will fall like every other ruler" (v. 7). Death mixes scepters with spades.

2. The God of heaven exalted (v. 8). The psalmist finds it useless to reason with these proud oppressors. He therefore looks up to God and begs him *to take unto himself his great power; Arise, O God! Judge the earth.* And he believes that he will do it: *Thou shalt inherit all nations.* We must pray in faith, *"Arise, O God, judge the earth* (v. 8), deal with those who judge unjustly, and set shepherds over your people who are after your own heart." It is a prayer that Christ would come, who is to judge the earth, that God would *give him the heathen* (nations) *for his inheritance.*

PSALM 83

This psalm is the last of those that bear the name of Asaph. Some think it was written when the Moabites and Ammonites, those children of Lot spoken about here (v. 8), descended with their allies on the land of Judah in Jehoshaphat's time (2Ch 20:1). Others think it was written with reference to all the alliances of the neighboring nations against Israel, from beginning to end. The psalmist appeals here to: 1. God's knowledge, by a description of the intentions and attempts of Israel's enemies to destroy Israel (vv. 1–8). 2. God's justice, by a fervent prayer for the defeating of their attempt (vv. 9–18).

Title

The Israel of God was in danger and great distress.

Verses 1–8

1. The psalmist here begs God to act on behalf of his threatened people (v. 1): "*Keep not thou silence, O God,* but give judgment for us against those who are doing us an obvious wrong." Sometimes God is silent, as if he is going to observe absolute neutrality and let others fight it out. Then he allows us to call on him, as here, "*Keep not thou silence, O God!*" (v. 1). Lord, speak to us by the prophets to encourage us against our fears. Lord, speak for us by providence and speak against our enemies; speak rescue to us and disappointment to them."

2. Here is an account of the grand alliance of the neighboring nations against Israel, which the psalmist begs God to break.

2.1. This alliance is formed against the Israel of God, and so is, in effect, against the God of Israel. They hated the religious worshipers of God because they hated God's holy religion and the worship of him. *They are confederate against thee* (v. 5). "Lord," the psalmist says, "they are your enemies, for they are conspiring against *thy hidden ones,* those you cherish." God's people are *his hidden ones.* Their life is *hid with Christ in God* (Col 3:3). God takes them under his special protection; he hides them in the hollow of his hand. But their enemies decide to destroy those whom God decides to preserve. *Thy enemies make a tumult* (v. 2).

2.2. The alliance is carried on with a great deal of passion and violence. The enemies are noisy in their outcries. This is included as a reason that God should not remain silent: "The enemies talk big words and go on talking a lot; Lord, may they not be the only ones to talk; *speak to them in thy wrath*" (2:5). *They have lifted up the head* (v. 2). In their confidence they have so elevated themselves that it seems they think they can overpower the Almighty. They have *taken crafty counsel* (v. 3). Whatever separate clashing interests they have among themselves, when they act against the people of God, they *consult with one consent,* they plot together with one mind (v. 5).

2.3. What they aim at in their alliance is nothing less than the complete destruction and annihilation of Israel (v. 4): "*Come, let us cut them off from being a nation, that the name of Israel may be no more in remembrance,* not ever again in history." It is the secret wish of many evildoers that the church of God might be swept out of existence in this world, that there might be no such thing as religious faith among the human race. Having banished its sense from their own hearts, they would gladly also see the whole earth rid of it, but *he that sits in heaven shall laugh at them* (2:4).

2.4. The nations that entered this alliance are named here (vv. 6–8); the Edomites and Ishmaelites, both

descendants of Abraham, are in the vanguard. These were allied to Israel in blood and yet in alliance with each other against Israel. The spirit of persecution has broken through even the strongest bonds of nature. *The brother shall betray the brother to death* (Mk 13:12). The Philistines had long been a thorn in Israel's side and caused a great deal of trouble. *Assur* (Assyria) *also is joined with them* (v. 8).

Verses 9–18

The psalmist prays for the destruction of those combined forces and foretells it in God's name. This prophecy reaches all the enemies of the Gospel church.

1. The defeat of former alliances may be pleaded in prayer to God, because God is still the same to his people and the same against his and their enemies; there is no change in him. "*Do to them as to the Midianites;* may they be defeated by their own fears, for the Midianites were defeated in this way, more than by Gideon's 300 men. Rout them as you did the army of Jabin, king of Canaan, which was under Sisera's command (Jdg 4:15). *They became as dung for the earth,* like refuse on the ground (v. 10); their dead bodies were thrown like dung in heaps by Barak's small but victorious army." *So let all thy enemies perish, O Lord!* (Jdg 5:31), that is, "So they will perish." He prays that their leaders might be destroyed as they had been formerly (vv. 11–12). They said, *Let us take to ourselves the houses of God in possession* (v. 12), the *pleasant places* of God, which we may understand to refer to the land of Canaan, which was a pleasant land and was Emmanuel's land (Isa 8:8), or the temple, which was indeed God's pleasant and treasured place (Isa 64:11), or, as Dr. Henry Hammond suggests, the pleasant pastures, which these Arabians, who traded in cattle, especially looked for. They will be made *like Oreb and Zeeb* (Jdg 7:25) and *like Zeba and Zalmunna* (Jdg 8:21).

2. He prays that God would *make them like a wheel* (v. 13), that they might be in continual movement, unsettled and off balance in all their conspiracies, that they might roll down easily and quickly to their own destruction. Or, as some think, he prayed that they might be broken by the judgments of God, as grain is broken, or beaten out, by the wheel which was then used in threshing. "Although the wheel continually turns round, it is fixed on its own axis, but may they be no more fixed than light stubble, which the wind quickly blows away." When the stubble is driven away by the wind, it will finally come to rest under some hedge, or in some ditch, but he prays that they might be not only driven away as stubble but also burned up as stubble. We have the application of these comparisons in v. 15: *So persecute* (pursue) *them with thy tempest,* pursue them to their complete destruction, and make *them afraid with thy storm.*

3. He illustrates it by the good results of their confusion (vv. 16–18). They did what they could to make God's people ashamed, but the shame will ultimately turn back on them. The beginning of this shame might be a means of their conversion: "May they be broken and thwarted in their attempts, so *that they may seek thy name, O Lord!*" (v. 16). What we should fervently want and beg God for our enemies and persecutors is that God would bring them to repentance, and we should desire that they will not be shamed any more than will lead toward their conversion. If they will not become ashamed and repent, which would end their troubles, may they be put to shame so that other people may know and acknowledge, even if they themselves will not, *that thou, whose name alone is JEHOVAH,*

a name that we may speak but may not give to any other, *art the Most High over all the earth.*

PSALM 84

It is thought that David wrote this psalm when he was forced by Absalom's conspiracy to leave his city, which he mourned his absence from because it was the Holy City. This psalm contains the godly longings of a gracious soul for God and for fellowship with him. Even though it is not entitled as such, it may be rightly looked on as a psalm or song for the Sabbath day. The psalmist here expresses his feelings with great devotion: 1. For the services of public worship of God. He shows the value he sets on them (v. 1), his desire toward them (vv. 2–3), his conviction of the happiness of those who enjoy them (vv. 4–7), and his locating his own happiness in the enjoying of them (v. 10). 2. To the God of the services of worship: his desire toward him (vv. 8–9), his faith in him (v. 11), and the happiness of those who put their confidence in him (v. 12).

Verses 1–7

Because the psalmist has been forcefully restrained from waiting on God in the public services of worship, his absence has increased his conviction of their value more than ever. Notice:

1. The wonderful beauty he sees in holy institutions (v. 1): *How amiable are thy tabernacles* (how lovely is your dwelling place)*, O Lord of hosts!* The tabernacle or dwelling place is spoken of as more than one (*thy tabernacles*) because there were several courts which the people attended, and because the tabernacle itself consisted of a Holy Place and a Most Holy Place. How lovely is the sanctuary in the eyes of all who are truly consecrated! Gracious souls see a wonderful and inexpressible beauty in holiness, and in holy work. A tabernacle was a lowly dwelling place, but the beauty of holiness is spiritual, and the glory of the ordinances of worship is within the tabernacle.

2. The deep desire he had to return to the enjoyment of public worship, or rather, of God himself (v. 2). It was a complete desire: body, soul, and spirit. It was an intense desire. He longed, fainted, and cried out. Yet it was not so much the courts of the Lord that he coveted; it was *for the living God* himself that he cried out in prayer. Services of worship are empty if we do not meet with God in them.

3. His grudging the happiness of the little birds that made their nests in the buildings next to God's altars (v. 3). *The sparrow has found a house and the swallow a nest for herself.*

3.1. These little birds, by natural instinct, provided homes for themselves in houses, as other birds do in the woods. David imagines there are some such sparrows in the buildings around the courts of God's house, and wishes he himself were with them. He would rather live in a bird's nest near God's altars than in a palace far away from them. He sometimes wished for *the wings of a dove*, on which to *fly into the wilderness* (55:6), but here he wants the wings of a sparrow, so that he might fly undiscovered into God's courts. The word for *sparrow* refers to any little bird, and, if I may offer a suggestion, perhaps in David's time, when music was introduced so much into sacred services, songbirds in cages were hung around the courts of the tabernacle to complete the harmony, for we find the singing of birds mentioned to the glory of God (104:12); perhaps it is these birds, then, whose happiness David envies and with which he would gladly change places.

3.2. David envies the happiness not of those birds that fly over the altars, but of those that have their nests there. David will not think it enough to stop over in God's house *as a wayfaring man to tarry for a night* (Jer 14:8); let this be his rest and his home; he wants to live there. He says these birds not only have nests for themselves there but also lay their young there, for those who have a place in God's courts themselves must want their children also to have *a place and a name* (Isa 56:5) in God's house. Notice how he considers God in this address: you are the *Lord of hosts, my King and my God* (v. 3). Where should a poor, distressed subject seek for protection except with his king? *And should not a people seek unto their God?* (Isa 8:19). My King, my God, is the Lord Almighty; by him and his altars may I live and die.

4. His acknowledgment of the happiness both of the ministers and of the people who can freely attend God's altars.

4.1. Blessed are the ministers, the priests and Levites, who have their homes around the tabernacle and who are employed in its service (v. 4). *They will be still praising thee*, and if there is a heaven on earth, it consists in praising God, continually praising him. If we apply this to his house above, then we can see that those angels and glorified saints who live there are blessed, for they *rest not day nor night from praising God* (Rev 4:8).

4.2. Blessed are the people, those who live in the country, who, although they do not constantly live in God's house as the priests do, still have free access to it. *"Blessed is the man whose strength is in thee*, who makes you his strength and strongly rests on you."

4.2.1. They are those who love holy public worship, *in whose heart are the ways of them* (v. 5), that is, those who, having placed their happiness in God as their destiny, rejoice in all the ways that lead to him.

4.2.2. They are those who will overcome difficulties and discouragements in order to worship the Lord (v. 6). When they leave the country to worship at the feasts, their way lies through many dry and sandy valleys, in which they may be about to die of thirst, but they dig little pits to receive and keep the rainwater to refresh themselves. Their way lies through many weeping valleys, which is what *Baca* means, that is, many watery valleys, which are impassable when *the rain filleth the pools* in wet weather (v. 6). But by draining the pools, they make a road for the benefit of those who go up to Jerusalem. Care should be taken to keep in good repair those roads that lead to the church as well as those that lead to the market. But all this is intended to show that they really want to make the journey. Our way to heaven lies through a valley of Baca, but even that may be made a source of refreshment if we make good use of the comforts God has provided for pilgrims on their way to the heavenly city.

4.2.3. They are those who continue to press forward until they finally come to their journey's end; *they go from strength to strength* (v. 7). Instead of being tired out by the tediousness of their journey and the difficulties they meet, they become more lively and cheerful as they come closer to Jerusalem. Those who press forward in their Christian lives will find God adding further grace to grace (Jn 1:16).

Verses 8–12

Here:

1. The psalmist prays for God to hear and accept him. He prays (vv. 8–9) only that God would hear his prayer and listen to him, not mentioning his particular request. He calls himself, in the opinion of many, *God's anointed,*

for David was anointed by God and anointed for him. In this request he looks to God using several of his glorious titles: *the Lord God of hosts* (Lord God Almighty) (v. 8), who has all creatures at his command; the *God of Jacob* (v. 8), a God in covenant with his own people; and *God our shield* (v. 9), the One who protects his people in a special way.

2. He pleads his love for God's public services of worship and his dependence on God himself.

2.1. God's courts were his choice (v. 10). "*A day spent in thy courts*, in attending the services of worship, wholly removed from all worldly affairs, *is better than a thousand* anywhere else in the world. *I would rather be a doorkeeper*, I would rather be in the lowliest position and office, *in the house of my God, than dwell* as master of ceremonies *in the tents of wickedness* (v. 10). I would rather be a porter in God's house than a ruler in those tents where evil reigns, rather lie at the threshold. That was the beggar's place (Ac 3:2), but "it does not matter," David says; "let that be my place rather than none."

2.2. God himself was his hope, and joy, and all. *The Lord God is a sun and shield*. On earth we lead our lives in darkness, but if God is our God, he will be our sun, to enlighten and enliven us, to guide and direct us. We are in danger here, but he will be our shield to protect us: *The Lord will give grace and glory* (v. 11). *Grace* refers to both the goodwill of God toward us and the good work of God in us; *glory* refers to both the honor which he now puts on us, in adopting us as his children, and what he has prepared for us as the inheritance of children. God will give his people grace in this world in preparation for glory, and glory in the other world will be the perfection of grace. Both are God's free gifts. *No good thing will be withheld from those that walk uprightly* (blamelessly) (v. 11). This is a comprehensive promise and is such an assurance of the present comfort of saints that, whatever they desire and think they need, they may be sure that either infinite Wisdom sees that it is not good for them or infinite Goodness will give it to them in due time. Those who enjoy the privileges of God's house are blessed. If we cannot go to the house of the Lord, we may still go by faith to the Lord of the house, and we will be happy and may be at peace in him.

PSALM 85

Interpreters generally think this psalm was written after the return of the Jews from their exile in Babylon, when they still remained under some signs of God's displeasure. The church was suffering from a flood here: clouds were above, waves were underneath; everything was dark and dismal. The church is like Noah in the ark, between life and death, between hope and fear, and so we may say that: 1. Here the dove is sent out in prayer. The requests are against sin and wrath (v. 4) and for mercy and grace (v. 7). The pleas are taken from former favors (vv. 1–3) and present troubles (vv. 5–6). 2. The dove returns with an olive branch of peace and good news; the psalmist expresses his expectation of its return (v. 8) and then recounts the favors to God's Israel which, by the spirit of prophecy, he wants others to take assurance from and which, by the spirit of faith, he himself takes assurance from (vv. 9–13).

Verses 1–7

The people of God are in a very low and weak condition but are shown here how to speak to God.

1. They are to acknowledge with thankfulness the great things God has done for them (vv. 1–3). God has been gracious toward their land and has smiled on it as his own: "*Thou hast been favourable to thy land*, showing by special favors that you regard it as yours." He has not dealt with them according to what their offenses have deserved (v. 2): "*Thou hast forgiven the iniquity of thy people* and not punished them as you might justly have done. *Thou hast covered all their sin.*" Their restoration from exile was indeed an example of God's favor to them, since it was accompanied by the forgiveness of their sins. "Having *covered all their sin* (v. 2), you have *taken away all thy wrath*," for when sin is set aside, God's anger ceases. God is pacified if we are purified.

2. They are told to pray to God for grace and mercy with reference to their present distress. This is inferred from *Thou hast forgiven the iniquity of thy people* (v. 2). "You have done good to our ancestors; do good to us, too, for we are the children of the same covenant."

2.1. They pray for converting grace: "*Turn* (restore) *us, O God of our salvation!*" (v. 4).

2.2. They pray for the removal of the signs of God's displeasure: "*Cause thine anger towards us to cease*" (v. 4). Notice the method: "First turn us to yourself, and then cause your anger to turn from us."

2.3. They pray for the revelation of God's goodwill to them (v. 7): "*Show us thy mercy, O Lord!* Let us know that you have mercy on us and also mercy in store for us."

2.4. They pray that God would appear on their behalf: "*Grant us thy salvation* (v. 7); grant it by your promise, and then, no doubt, you will work by it your providence."

3. They are told to plead humbly with God about their present troubles (vv. 5–6). "*Wilt thou be angry with us for ever? Wilt thou draw out thy anger unto all generations?* You were not angry with our ancestors forever, but soon turned from the fierceness of your wrath; why then will you be angry with us forever? *Wilt thou not revive us again* (v. 6), revive us by rescuing us?" God had given the children of the captivity *some reviving in their bondage* (Ezr 9:8). Their return from Babylon was as *life from the dead* (Eze 37:11–12). "Now, Lord," they say, "*wilt thou not revive us again*, and *put thy hand again the second time* (Isa 11:11) to gather us in (126:1, 4)? *Revive thy work in the midst of the years* (Hab 3:2). Revive us again." If God is the fountain of all our mercies, he must be the center of all our joys.

Verses 8–13

Here is an answer to the prayers and pleas.

1. In general, it is the response they desire. The psalmist is soon aware of this (v. 8), for he *stands upon his watchtower to hear what God will say unto him*. "Compose yourself, O my soul. Wait on God in humble silence and wait for him to act. I have spoken enough; now I will listen to what God has to say and will welcome his holy will. *What saith my Lord unto his servant?*" (Jos 5:14). *He will speak peace to his people, and to his saints* (v. 8). Sooner or later, God will give them peace. If he does not command outward peace, he will still evoke inner peace, speaking to their hearts by his Spirit what he has spoken to their ears by his word and ministers, making them hear joy and gladness (51:8). The psalmist takes encouragement from this, and so must we: "*I will hear what God the Lord will speak* (v. 8), listen to the assurances he gives of peace, in response to prayer." *But let them not turn again to folly* (v. 8), for it is only on these terms that peace is to be expected.

2. Here are the details of this favorable response. He gives us the pleasant prospect of the flourishing state of the church in the last five verses of the psalm, which describe the peace and prosperity God blessed the children of the exile with when they resettled in their own land. But it may also be taken both as a promise to all who fear God and act righteously, that they will be at peace and happy, and as a prophecy of the kingdom of the Messiah and of the blessings with which that kingdom would be enriched. Here is:

2.1. Help at hand (v. 9): "*Surely his salvation is nigh.*" When the number of bricks is doubled, then Moses comes (Ex 5). When trouble is near, salvation is also near, for God is an ever-present help to all his people in times of trouble (46:1).

2.2. Honor secured: "*That glory may dwell in our land*" (v. 9), that we may have the worship of God settled and established among us, for that is the glory of a land. When that goes, *Ichabod*, 'the glory has departed' (1Sa 4:21); when that stays, glory dwells."

2.3. Graces meeting, and happily embracing each other (vv. 10–11): *Mercy and truth, righteousness and peace, kiss each other.* This may be understood to refer:

2.3.1. To the reformation of the people and of the government. When mercy and truth are prevalent in every meeting, when righteousness and peace kiss in every embrace, and when ordinary honesty is indeed the usual practice, then glory lives in a land.

2.3.2. To the return of God's favor. When the people of a nation return to God, he will return to them and remain with them by way of mercy. This is how some understand this, human truth and God's mercy, human righteousness and God's peace, meeting together. If *truth spring out of the earth*, that is, as Dr. Henry Hammond explains it, out of the human heart, the proper soil for it to grow in, then righteousness, that is, God's mercy, will look down from heaven, as the sun does on the world when it sheds its influence on the crops of the earth and nurtures them.

2.3.3. To the harmony of the divine attributes in the Messiah's undertaking. Our salvation is so well worked out, so well arranged, that God may have mercy on poor sinners, and be at peace with them, without any injustice being done to his truth and righteousness.

2.4. Great plenty of everything desirable (v. 12): *The Lord shall give that which is good*, everything that he sees to be good for us. When the glory of the Gospel has its home in our land, then it will give its harvest.

2.5. Reliable guidance in the life of faith (v. 13): *The righteousness* of his promise to us, assuring us of happiness, and the righteousness of sanctification, his good work in us, will go before him. These will be our guide to *set us in the way of his steps*, so that we may go out to meet him when he is coming toward us in mercy.

PSALM 86

This psalm is entitled a prayer of David; it was probably a prayer he often used himself and commended to the use of others, especially in times of trouble. In this prayer, David: 1. Gives glory to God (vv. 8–10, 12–13). 2. Seeks grace that God would hear his prayers (vv. 1, 6–7), preserve and save him, and be merciful to him (vv. 2–3, 16); that he would give him joy, grace, and strength; and also that he would honor him (vv. 4, 11, 17). He pleads God's goodness (vv. 5, 15) and the hatred of his enemies (v. 14).

Title

This psalm was made known under the title of *a prayer of David.*

Verses 1–7

Notice here:

1. The requests he brings to God. *Unto thee, O Lord, do I lift up my soul*, as he said in 25:1. In every aspect of prayer, the soul must rise on the wings of faith and holy desire.

1.1. He begs God to graciously listen to his prayers (v. 1): *Bow down thy ear, O Lord, hear me.* When God hears our prayers, it is rightly said that he *bows down his ear* to them, for it is amazing that God condescends to accept such lowly creatures as we are and such defective prayers as ours.

1.2. He begs God to take him under his special protection (v. 2): "*Preserve my soul; save thy servant.* Keep my soul from sin, which is an evil and dangerous thing to my soul. Guard my soul, and so save me." God guards and keeps all those whom he saves, and he will guard them for his heavenly kingdom.

1.3. He begs God to look on him with pity and compassion (v. 3): *Be merciful to me, O Lord!* "People show no mercy; we ourselves deserve no mercy, but Lord, for the sake of your mercy, be *merciful unto me.*"

1.4. He begs God to fill his inner being with encouragement and strength (v. 4): *Rejoice the soul of thy servant.* It is God only who can *put gladness into the heart* (4:7) and who makes the soul rejoice. Just as it is the duty of those who are God's servants to *serve him with gladness* (100:2), so also it is their privilege to be *filled with joy and peace in believing* (Ro 15:13). Prayer nurtures spiritual joy.

2. The pleas with which he supports these requests:

2.1. He pleads his relationship with God: "You are my God, to whom I have devoted myself, and on whom I depend, and I am your servant (v. 2)."

2.2. He pleads his distress: "*Hear me, for I am poor and needy*" (v. 1).

2.3. He pleads God's goodwill toward all who seek him (v. 5): "To you do I *lift up my soul* in desire and expectation, *for thou, Lord, art good.*"

2.4. He pleads God's good work in him, by which he has qualified him to receive the signs of his favor. "*I am holy*, and so guard my soul." He does not say this out of pride or boasting, but with a humble thankfulness to God. "I am one whom you favor" is the reading of the margin, one whom you have *set apart for thyself. I am holy* (v. 2), but also needy, *poor in the world, but rich in faith* (Jas 2:5). *I cry unto thee daily, and all the day* (v. 3). We will be encouraged if a problem finds the wheels of prayer already in motion, so that they do not then need to be set in motion. "*In the day of my trouble*, whatever others do, *I will call upon thee*, and commit my situation to you, for you will hear and answer me."

Verses 8–17

David here continues in prayer.

1. He gives glory to God. *Among the gods*, the false gods, whom the nations worshiped, the angels, the kings of the earth, among them all, *there is none like unto thee, O Lord!* There is none so wise, mighty, or good. *Neither are there any works like unto thy works*, which is an undeniable proof that there is no one like him. He is the fountain of all being and the center of all praise (v. 9): "*Thou hast made all nations*, made them from one man. They all derive their existence from you and constantly depend on

you, and so *they shall come and worship before thee and glorify thy name.*" This was to have its complete fulfillment in the days of the Messiah. "All nations will worship before you, because as King of nations *thou art great*; your sovereignty is absolute, and to prove this, *thou doest wondrous things.* Only you are God, and not only is there none like you, but also there is no one besides you." Human beings are bad and evil (v. 14); no mercy is to be expected from them, *but thou, O Lord, art a God full of compassion, and gracious* (v. 15). Human beings are cruel, but God is gracious; people are false, but God is faithful. God is not only compassionate but *full of compassion,* and in him *mercy rejoiceth against* (triumphs over) *judgment* (Jas 2:13). It is some assurance to upright people to think that others will praise and glorify God, but it is their greatest concern and delight to do it themselves. "Whatever others do," David says, "*I will praise thee, O Lord my God!* (v. 12). I will praise you not only as the Lord but also as my God. I will do it as long as I live, and I hope to do it in eternity." He had good reason to decide to praise God in this way: *For great is thy mercy towards me* (v. 13). *Thou hast delivered my soul from the lowest hell* (v. 13).

2. He prays from the heart for mercy and grace from God. He complains about the restless and implacable hatred of his enemies toward him (v. 14). "They are *violent men,* who think they can get away with anything by using sheer force, whether they are right or wrong. They are formidable and ruthless. They *rise up against me in* open rebellion. They want not only to depose me but also to destroy me. Lord, rise up against them, for they are your enemies as well as mine." His requests are:

2.1. For the activity of God's grace in him (v. 11). "*Teach me thy way, O Lord,* the way in which you have appointed me to walk. When I am in doubt about it, make it clear to me what I should do. Let me hear the voice saying, *This is the way*" (Isa 30:21). *Teach me thy way; I will walk in thy truth* (v. 11). One would think it should be, "Teach me your truth, and I will walk in your way," but it all comes to the same thing; it is the way of truth that God teaches, and we must choose to walk in that (119:30). Christ is the way and the truth, and we must both learn Christ (Eph 4:20) and walk in him (Col 2:6). "*Unite my heart to fear thy name* (v. 11). Give me an undivided heart. Make me sincere in my religious faith. A hypocrite has a double heart, but may my heart be wholly committed to God, not divided between him and the world or wandering from him."

2.2. For the signs of God's favor to him (vv. 16–17). He prays for three things:

• That God would speak peace and encouragement to him: "*O turn unto me,* as to the one you love."
• That God would rescue him and bring him to a safe place: "Give me *thy strength*; put strength into me, so that I may help myself. Exert your strength for me, so that I may be saved from the hands of those who want to destroy me."
• That God would honor him: "*Show me a token for good* (v. 17). Let me see some signs of your favor toward me, so *that those who hate me may see it, and be ashamed* (v. 17) of their enmity to me, as they will have reason to be when they realize that *thou, Lord, hast helped me and comforted me* (v. 17)."

PSALM 87

The previous psalm was clear, but this psalm contains things that are dark and difficult to understand (2Pe

3:16). *It is a psalm in praise of Zion, as a type and figure of the Gospel church. For the temple's sake, Zion is here preferred: 1. To the rest of the land of Canaan, as being crowned with special signs of God's favor (vv. 1–3). 2. To any other place or country, as being filled with people who were more eminent, and with more of them, and with a more plentiful supply of divine blessings (vv. 4–7). Some think this psalm was written to express the joy of God's people when Zion was flourishing; others think it was written to encourage their faith and hope when Zion was in ruins and was to be rebuilt after the Exile.*

Verses 1–3

Some consider the first words of the psalm to be part of the title; it is a psalm or song whose subject is the holy mountain — the temple built in Zion on Mount Moriah. Three things are observed here in praise of the temple:

1. That it was founded on the *holy mountains* (v. 1). It is built high. The *mountain of the Lord's house is established upon the top of the mountains* (Isa 2:2). It is built firmly on eternal mountains and perpetual hills, for it is more likely that the mountains will shake and the hills be removed (46:2) than that the covenant of God's peace will be annulled, and the church is built on that (Isa 54:10). Holiness is the strength and stability of the church: it is this that will support it and keep it from sinking. It is not so much that it is built on mountains as that it is built on *holy* mountains — on the promises of God.

2. That God had expressed a particular affection for it (v. 2): *The Lord loveth the gates of Zion,* of the temple, of "the houses of doctrine" (the Aramaic reading), *more than all the dwellings of Jacob,* whether in Jerusalem or anywhere else in the country.

3. That there was much said about it in the word of God (v. 3): *Glorious things are spoken of thee, O city of God!* God said about the temple, *My eyes and my heart shall be there perpetually; I have sanctified this house, that my name may be there for ever* (2Ch 7:16). But even more glorious things are spoken about the Gospel church. It is the bride of Christ and has been bought by his blood; it is *a peculiar people* (a people belonging to God), *a holy nation, a royal priesthood* (1Pe 2:9), and the *gates of hell shall not prevail against it* (Mt 16:18).

Verses 4–7

Zion is here compared with other places and preferred to them; the church of Christ is more glorious and excellent than all the nations of the earth.

1. It is acknowledged that other places have their glories (v. 4): "*I will make mention of Rahab*" (that is, Egypt) "*and Babylon, to those that know me; behold Philistia and Tyre, with Ethiopia,* and we will observe that *this man was born there*; here and there one famous man, well known for knowledge and virtue, may be quoted, who was a native of these countries; here and there one who becomes a convert and worshiper of the true God." Some give this another sense, supposing that it is a prophecy. God says, "I will record Egypt and Babylon with those who know me. I will record them as my people as much as Israel when they receive the Gospel of Christ, and acknowledge them as born again in Zion and admitted to the privileges of Zion as freely as trueborn Israelites." Those who were strangers and foreigners became *fellow-citizens with the saints* (Eph 2:19).

2. It is proved that the glory of Zion surpasses them all, for many reasons, for:

2.1. Zion will produce many great and good people, many prophets and kings, who will be greater favorites of heaven and greater blessings to the earth, than were ever born or brought up in Egypt or Babylon. *A man, a man was born in her,* by which some understand Christ, born in Bethlehem near Zion. The greatest honor that was ever given the Jewish nation was that from it, *as concerning the flesh, Christ came* (Ro 9:5).

2.2. Zion's interests will be strengthened and established by an almighty power. *The Highest himself shall undertake to establish her* (v. 5) on an eternal foundation. Whatever tumults and revolutions there are in states and kingdoms, and however much heaven and earth may be shaken, these are things which cannot be shaken but will certainly remain.

2.3. Zion's children will be registered with honor (v. 6): *The Lord shall count, when he writes up the people,* makes a record of his subjects, *that this man was born there,* and so is a subject by birth, by the first birth, being born in his house—and by the second birth, being born again of his Spirit.

2.4. Zion's songs will be sung with joy and triumph: *As well the singers as the players on instruments shall be there* to praise God (v. 7). It was much to the honor of Zion, and is to the honor of the Gospel church, that God is served and worshiped there with rejoicing: his work is done gladly; see 68:25. *All my springs are in thee* (v. 7), O Zion!

PSALM 88

This psalm is a lamentation, and it does not conclude, as the melancholy psalms usually do, with the slightest note of comfort or joy, but is mourning and woe from beginning to end. The psalmist here complains about personal matters, especially a troubled mind. It is placed among the penitential psalms. In this psalm we have: 1. The great spiritual pressure that the psalmist was under (vv. 3–6). 2. The wrath of God, which was the cause of that pressure (vv. 7, 15–17). 3. The evil of his friends (vv. 8, 18). 4. The prayer he offered to God (vv. 1–2, 9, 13). 5. His humble complaints and pleadings with God (vv. 10–12, 14).

Verses 1–9

The very first words are the only words of comfort in the whole psalm. Before he begins his complaint, the psalmist calls God *the God of his salvation* (v. 1), which shows that, bad though things were, he looked to God for salvation and depended on him to be its author.

1. Here we see the psalmist as a man of prayer. It was a comfort to him that he had prayed; it was his complaint that he was still suffering, despite his prayer. "*I have cried unto* you (v. 1) and have *stretched out my hands unto thee* (v. 9), as one who wants to take hold of you, and even grab at your mercy, having a holy fear of falling short and missing it." He was frequent and constant in prayer: *I have called upon thee daily* (v. 9), in fact, *day and night* (v. 1). He directed his prayer to God and expected and desired an answer from him (v. 2): "*Let my prayer come before thee,* to be accepted by you."

2. He was a man of sorrows (Isa 53:3), and so some consider him to be a type of Christ. He cries out (v. 3), *My soul is full of troubles;* similarly, Christ said, *Now is my soul troubled* (Jn 12:27); and in his agony Christ said, *My soul is exceedingly sorrowful even unto death* (Mt 26:38), like the psalmist's soul here, for he says, *My life draws nigh unto the grave.*

3. He saw himself as a dying man, whose heart was ready to break with sorrow (v. 5): "I am set apart among

the dead like those who have been killed and who lie in the grave, whom, in fact, you no longer even remember in order to protect or provide for their dead bodies. "*Thou hast laid me in the lowest pit,* put me as low as possible; my condition is low, my spirits are low, *in darkness, in the deep*" (v. 6). Good people may suffer in this way through the power of depression and the weakness of faith.

4. He complained most about God's displeasure against him (v. 7): *Thy wrath lies hard upon me.* If he could have discerned the favor and love of God in his suffering, it would have lain more lightly on him, but it lay very hard on him, so hard that he was ready to sink and faint under it.

5. It added to his affliction that his friends had deserted him. When we are in trouble, it is some encouragement to have those around us who love us and sympathize with us, but this good man had no one (v. 8): *Thou hast put away my acquaintance* (closest friends) *far from me.* "*Thou hast made me an abomination* (made me repulsive) *to them* (v. 8); they are not only shy of me but also sick of me. I am looked on by them not only with contempt but also with loathing."

6. He looked on his case as helpless and deplorable: "*I am shut up, and I cannot come forth* (out) (v. 8). I am a prisoner with no means of escape." He weeps for himself (v. 9): *My eye mourneth by reason of affliction,* my eyes are dim with grief. But weeping must not prevent us from praying; we must sow in tears (126:5): *My eye mourns, but I cry unto thee daily.*

Verses 10–18

In these verses:

1. The psalmist complains to God about the present deplorable condition he is in (vv. 10–12): "*Wilt thou show wonders to the dead,* that is, *Wilt thou do a miraculous work to the dead,* raising them to life again? Will those who are dead and buried *rise up to praise thee?* Departed souls may indeed know God's wonders and declare his faithfulness, justice, and unfailing love, but deceased bodies cannot. They can neither receive strength or encouragement from God's favors nor respond to them in praise." But he pleads with God for prompt relief: "Lord, you are good, faithful, and righteous. These aspects of your character will be made known in my rescue, but unless you come to help me quickly, it will be too late."

2. He decides to continue to be faithful in prayer, because the rescue has been delayed (v. 13) "*Unto thee have I cried* many times, and I have found encouragement in that, and so I will continue to pray; *in the morning shall my prayer prevent* (come before) *thee.*" How can he say, *My prayer shall prevent* (come before) *thee* (v. 13)? It suggests he will be up earlier than usual to pray, will *prevent* (that is, go before) his usual hour of prayer. "My prayer will not wait for the encouragement of the beginnings of mercy, but will reach out in faith and expectation even before dawn."

3. He sets down what he will say to God in prayer. He will humbly reason (v. 14): "*Lord, why castest thou off* (why do you reject) *my soul?* What is it that has caused you to treat me as one whom you have abandoned? *Show me wherefore thou contendest with me,* tell me what charges you have against me" (Job 10:2). Nothing grieves the children of God so much as God's hiding his face from them, nor is there anything they dread so much as God's rejecting them. If the sun is clouded over, the earth becomes dark, but if the sun should abandon the earth and reject it completely, think what a dungeon it would it be. *I suffer thy terrors* (v. 15). The psalmist here explains himself, telling us what he means by God's *terrors* and his

fierce wrath. "*I am* so *afflicted* with them that I am *ready to die* and," literally, "give up the ghost. *Thy terrors have cut me off*" (v. 16). They have almost taken away the use of his reason: *When I suffer thy terrors I am distracted* (v. 15). This has continued a long time: *From my youth up I suffer thy terrors* (v. 15). From childhood he has suffered from bouts of depression. Sometimes God prepares people for distinguished service by giving them exercises of this kind. No friend will encourage him (v. 18): *Lover and friend* (loved ones and companions) *hast thou put far from me.* Next to the encouragements of religious faith are those of friendship and society, and so to be without friends in this life is to be almost without any comfort.

PSALM 89

Many psalms that begin with a complaint and a prayer end in joy and praise, but this one begins with joy and praise and ends with sad complaints and requests. It is uncertain when it was written. We know only, in general, that it was at a time when the house of David was unfortunately overshadowed. 1. In the joyful and pleasant part of the psalm, the psalmist gives glory to God. He does this briefly at the beginning, mentioning God's mercy and truth in v. 1 and his covenant in vv. 2–4, but in more detail in the following verses, in which: 1.1. He adores the glory and perfect nature of God (vv. 5–14). 1.2. He takes pleasure in the happiness of those who are admitted into fellowship with him (vv. 15–18). 1.3. He builds all his hope on God's covenant with David, as a type of Christ (vv. 19–37). 2. In the sad part of the psalm, he mourns the present adverse state of the ruler and royal family (vv. 38–45), pleads with God about this (vv. 46–49), and then concludes by praying for it to be put right (vv. 50–51).

Verses 1–4

The psalmist has a very sad complaint to make of the wretched condition of the family of David at this time, but he begins the psalm with songs of praise. Let our complaints be turned into thanksgiving.

1. Whatever things are like, the eternal God is good and true (v. 1). God's mercies are inexhaustible and his truth is unbreakable, and we should use that as a basis for our joy and praise: "*I will sing of the mercies of the Lord for ever*, sing a song of praise to God's honor, an uplifting song to encourage myself, an instructive song to build up others."

2. Whatever things are happening, the eternal covenant is firm and sure (vv. 2–4). First we have the psalmist's faith and hope: "Things are looking black now, and threaten to totally destroy the house of David, but *I have said*, and I have authority from the word of God to say it, that *mercy shall be built up for ever*, that your love stands firm forever." If God's love stands firm forever, then the *tabernacle of David, which has fallen down,* will *be raised out of its ruins* and *built up as in the days of old* (Am 9:11). Then we have a summary of the covenant on which this faith and hope are built: *I have said it*, says the psalmist, for *God hath sworn it.* The psalmist brings in the words of God himself (v. 3), in which God acknowledges, to the encouragement of his people, "*I have made a covenant*, and so I will fulfill it." The covenant is made with David, representing the covenant of grace made with Christ as head of the church and with all believers as his spiritual offspring. It was promised that his family line would continue—*Thy seed* (line) *will I establish for ever*

(v. 4). *I will build up thy throne to all generations* (v. 4). This has its fulfillment only in Christ, who was of the line of David and who lives forever.

Verses 5–14

These verses are full of the praises of God. Notice:

1. Where, and by whom, God is to be praised. "The angels in *the heavens shall praise thy wonders, O Lord!*" (v. 5). The works of God are wonderful even to those who know them most intimately. The more God's works are known, the more they are wondered at and praised. God is praised also by the assemblies of his saints on earth. "Your faithfulness and the truth of your promise, that rock on which the church is built, will be praised in the assembly of the saints, who owe everything to that faithfulness, and whose constant comfort it is that there is a promise, and that the One who has promised is faithful" (Heb 10:23; 11:11). In religious meetings, God has promised the presence of his grace, but we must also look to his glorious presence in them, so that the familiarity we are admitted to may not breed the slightest contempt. A holy awe of God must fall on us, and fill us, whenever we come near to God, even in private.

2. What it is to praise God; it is to acknowledge that there is none like him: *Who in the heaven can be compared with the Lord?* (v. 6). *To whom will you liken me, or shall I be equal? saith the Holy One* (Isa 40:25). This is insisted on again (v. 8): *Who is a strong Lord like unto thee?* Among people, it is too often found that those who are most able to break their word are least careful to keep it, but God is strong, faithful, and trustworthy. He can do everything, but will never do anything unjust.

3. What we should, in our praises, give God glory for. Several things are mentioned:

3.1. The command God has of the most unruly creatures (v. 9). *Thou rulest the raging of the sea.* This is included here to show God's almighty power, and so what kind of man then was the Lord Jesus, whom the *winds and seas obeyed* (Mt 8:27)?

3.2. The victories God has gained over the enemies of his church. *Thou hast broken Rahab*—meaning many proud enemies, especially Egypt—crushed it in pieces, as one that has been killed and rendered completely unable to make any headway again. The memory of the crushing of Egypt to pieces is an encouragement to the church in reference to the present power of Babylon, for God is still the same.

3.3. The undeniable ownership he has over all creatures (vv. 11–12): "People are honored for their large possessions, but *the heavens are thine, O Lord, the earth also is thine. The world and the fulness thereof* (50:12), all its riches, all its inhabitants, both the houses and the householders, are all yours, for *thou hast founded them.*" He specifies:

3.3.1. The farthest parts of the world: "*Thou hast created them* (v. 12), and so you know them, look after them, and have received tributes of praise from them." The north is said to be *hung over the empty place* (Job 26:7), but God is the owner of what fullness it has.

3.3.2. The highest parts of the world. He mentions two of the highest hills in Canaan, *Tabor and Hermon.* "These will rejoice in your name, for they produce offerings for your altar." Tabor is commonly thought to have been that high mountain in Galilee on the top of which Christ was transfigured.

3.4. The power and justice, the mercy and truth, with which he rules the world and human lives (vv. 13–14). God is able to do everything, for he is the Lord God

Almighty. He never did, or ever will do, anything either unjust or unwise, for *righteousness and judgment are the habitation of his throne* (v. 14). He always does what is kind to his people and consistent with the word he has spoken: "*Mercy and truth shall go before thy face* (v. 14), truth in being as good as your word, mercy in being better."

Verses 15–18

Having shown in detail the blessedness of the God of Israel, the psalmist here shows the blessedness of the Israel of God. Just as *there is none like unto the God of Jeshurun, so, happy art thou, O Israel! There is none like unto thee, O people!* (Dt 33:29), especially as a type of the Gospel Israel, consisting of all true believers, whose happiness is described here.

1. Glorious revelations are made to them, and good news is brought to them. They hear, *they know, the joyful sound* (v. 15). This may refer:

1.1. To the shout of a victorious army. Israel has the signs of God's presence with it in its wars. Or:

1.2. To the sound that was made over the sacrifices on the sacred feast days (vv. 1–3). This was the happiness of Israel, that they had among them the free and open profession of God's holy religion. Or:

1.3. To the sound of the jubilee trumpet, which was a joyful sound to servants and debtors, to whom it declared release (Lev 25). The Gospel is indeed a joyful sound, a sound of victory, liberty, and fellowship with God. Blessed are the people who hear it, know it, and make it welcome.

2. Special signs of God's favor are given them: "*They shall walk, O Lord, in the light of thy countenance* (your presence) (v. 15). They will be controlled by your direction; they will be guided by your eye. They will delight in your assurance."

3. They never lack reasons to be joyful. Those who rejoice in Christ Jesus have enough to balance out their grievances and silence their griefs, and so their joy will be complete (1Jn 1:4).

4. Their relationship with God is their honor and dignity. "In *thy righteousness shall they be exalted*, and not in any righteousness of their own. In your favor, which we hope for through Christ, *our horn shall be exalted*" (v. 17). The horn stands for strength, beauty, and plenty.

5. Their relationship with God is their protection and safety (v. 18), or as the margin reads: "For our shield is of the Lord, and our king is from the Holy One of Israel." If God is our ruler, he will also be our defender, and who then can harm us?"

Verses 19–37

The covenant God had made with David and his offspring was mentioned before (vv. 3–4), but it is enlarged on in these verses. It certainly looks to Christ, and has its fulfillment in him much more than in David. The encouragements of our redemption flow from the covenant of redemption; all our springs are in that (Isa 55:3). *I will make an everlasting covenant with you, even the sure mercies of David* (Ac 13:34). Notice:

1. What assurance we have of the truth of the promise, which may encourage us to build on it. We are told here, *Thou didst speak in a vision to thy Holy One*. God's promise to David, which is referred to especially, was spoken in a vision to Nathan the prophet (2Sa 7:12–17). Then, when the *Holy One of Israel was their king* (v. 18), he appointed David to be his vice-regent. Notice how it was sworn and ratified (v. 35): *Once have I sworn by my*

holiness. His swearing once is enough; he need not swear again, as David did (1Sa 20:17), for his word and oath are unchangeable.

2. The choosing of the person to whom the promise is given (vv. 19–20). David was a king of God's own choosing, and so is Christ, and so both are called *God's kings* (2:6). David was a mighty man, chosen out of the people. God exalted him and ordered Samuel to anoint him. But this may be applied to Christ.

- He is mighty, *able to save to the uttermost* (Heb 7:25), for he is the Son of God, mighty in love.
- He is *chosen out of the people* (v. 19), one of us, bone of our bone, one who shares our flesh and blood.
- God has found him. He is a Savior of God's own provision.
- God has *laid help upon him*, given him strength (v. 19). He has exalted him, by constituting him as Prophet, Priest, and King of his church, clothing him with power, raising him from the dead, and setting him at his own right hand. He is called *Messiah*, or *Christ*, the *Anointed One*.

3. The promises made to this chosen one, to David as the type and the Son of David as the fulfillment:

3.1. With reference to himself, as king and God's servant. It is promised here:

3.1.1. That God would stand by him and strengthen him in his work (v. 21): "*With him my hand* not only will be, but *shall be established* (sustained), by promise. *My arm also shall strengthen him* to go through and endure all these difficulties."

3.1.2. That he would be victorious over his enemies, that they would not encroach on him (v. 22): *The son of wickedness shall not exact upon him* (not subject him to tribute) or afflict him further. Christ became a guarantee for our debt, and so Satan and death thought they would take advantage of him, but he satisfied the demands of God's justice, and then they could not demand more from him. *The prince of this world cometh, but he has nothing in me* (Jn 14:30). *I will beat down his foes before his face*; the prince of this world will be driven out, powers and authorities will be disarmed (Col 2:15), and he will be the death of death itself, and the destruction of the grave (Hos 13:14).

3.1.3. *My faithfulness and my mercy shall be with him*. They were with David; God continued to be merciful toward him, and so he showed himself faithful. They were with Christ; God fulfilled all his promises to him. But that is not all; God's mercy to us, and his faithfulness to us, are with Christ. It is in him that all the promises of God are Yes and Amen (2Co 1:20). So if any poor sinners hope to benefit from the faithfulness and mercy of God, let them know that it is with Christ and that they must turn to him to receive it (v. 28): *My mercy will I keep for him for evermore*. All the streams of divine goodness run in Christ's mediation forever. And just as the mercy of God flows to us through him, so the promise of God is firm to us through him: *My covenant shall stand fast with him* (v. 28), both the covenant of redemption made with him and the covenant of grace made with us in him.

3.1.4. That his kingdom would be greatly enlarged (v. 25): *I will set his hand in the sea*—he will rule over the seas and the islands of the sea—and *his right hand in the rivers*, the inland countries irrigated by rivers. David's kingdom extended to the Great Sea (the Mediterranean) and the Red Sea, to the river of Egypt and the River Euphrates. But it is in the kingdom of the Messiah that this has its complete fulfillment, and will have it increasingly, when *the kingdoms of this world shall become the kingdoms of the Lord and of his Christ* (Rev 11:15)

3.1.5. That he would acknowledge God as his Father, and God would acknowledge him as his Son, his firstborn (vv. 26–27). This is a comment on the words in Nathan's message concerning Solomon, for he as well as David was a type of Christ: *I will be his Father and he shall be my Son* (2Sa 7:14), and the relationship was acknowledged on both sides. *He shall cry unto me, Thou art my Father* (v. 26). Christ did during the days of his life on earth, when he offered up loud cries to God and taught us to address him as *our Father in heaven* (Mt 6:9). *I will make him my firstborn* (v. 27). It is Christ's right to be the *firstborn of every creature* and, as such, the *heir of all things* (Col 1:15; Heb 1:2, 6).

3.2. With reference to his descendants. God's covenants always included the descendants of those making the covenant (vv. 29, 36): *His seed shall endure for ever*, and with it his throne. This will be understood differently according to whether we apply it to Christ or David.

3.2.1. If we apply it to David, we understand *his seed* to refer to his successors, Solomon and the following kings of Judah. It is supposed that they might become corrupt. In such a case, they must expect to come under divine rebukes. But although they had been corrected, they would not be disinherited. This refers to that part of Nathan's message in which God said, *If he commit iniquity, I will chasten him*, but *my mercy shall not depart from him* (2Sa 7:14–15). David's line and throne did endure in that the family of David continued to be a distinguished family until the coming of the Son of David, whose throne would endure forever; see Lk 1:27, 32; 2:4, 11.

3.2.2. If we apply it to Christ, we understand *his seed* to refer to his subjects, all believers, his spiritual descendants, the children God has given him (Heb 2:13). These are the offspring who will live forever, and his throne will stand in the midst of them, in the church in the heart, *as the days of heaven* (v. 29). Christ will have a people in the world to serve and honor him to the end. *He shall see his seed; he shall prolong his days* (Isa 53:10). Christ's throne and kingdom will last forever. The kingdom of his grace will continue through all the ages of time, and the kingdom of his glory to the endless ages of eternity.

3.2.2.1. It is supposed here that there will be much that is wrong in the subjects of Christ's kingdom. His children may *forsake God's law* (v. 30) by sins of omission and *break his statutes* (v. 31) by sins of commission. Many corruptions exist in the church, as well as in the hearts of those who are its members. They are told here that they must suffer for it (v. 32): *I will visit their transgression with a rod*. Their relationship with Christ will not excuse them from being called to account. But notice what affliction is to God's people. It is only a rod, not an ax or a sword; it is to correct them, not destroy them. It is a rod in the hand of God—*I will visit them* (v. 32). *If they break my law, then I will visit their transgression with the rod* (vv. 31–32), but not otherwise.

3.2.2.2. The continuation of Christ's kingdom is made certain by the unbreakable promise and oath of God, despite all this (v. 33): *Nevertheless, my kindness will I not totally and finally take from him*. Adversities not only are consistent with covenant love but also flow from it to the people of God. For Christ's sake, mercy is stored up for us in him, and God says, *I will not take it from him* (v. 33). *I will not lie unto David* (v. 35). *My faithfulness shall not fail, my covenant will I not break* (vv. 33–34). What is said and sworn is that God will keep a church in the world

for as long as the sun and moon last (vv. 36–37). The *seed of Christ shall be established for ever*, as *lights of the world* (Php 2:15) as long as the world stands, to shine in it, and when it comes to an end, they will be permanent lights shining in the Father's kingdom.

Verses 38–52

In these verses we have:

1. A very sad complaint about the present miserable state of David's family, which the psalmist thinks is hard to reconcile with the covenant God made with David. "You said you would not *take away thy loving-kindness, but thou hast cast off* (rejected) *thine anointed*." It is sometimes not easy to reconcile God's providences with his promises, but God's works fulfill his word and never contradict it.

1.1. David's house seemed to have lost its share in God. God had been pleased with his anointed, but now he was *wroth* (very angry) *with him* (v. 38)

1.2. The honor of the house of David was lost and placed in the dust: *Thou hast profaned* (defiled) *his crown*, which was always looked on as sacred, by *casting* (knocking) *it to the ground*, to be trampled on (v. 39).

1.3. David's house was exposed and made vulnerable to all the neighbors (v. 40): *Thou hast broken down all his hedges*—all those walls that protected them, especially the protection they thought God's covenant and promise had given them—and "you *have made even his strong holds a ruin* (reduced your strongholds to ruin)." *He is a reproach to* (the scorn of) *his neighbours* (v. 41), who triumph over his fall from such a highly honored position. Everyone helps make his adversity even worse (v. 42): "*Thou hast set up* (exalted) *the right hand of his adversaries*, not only given them power, but also inclined them to use their power this way."

1.4. David's house was rendered unable to help itself (v. 43): "*Thou hast turned the edge of his sword* and made it blunt, so it cannot continue to kill as it has done, and what is worse, you have turned the edge of his spirit and taken away his courage, *and hast not made him to stand* as he used to do *in the battle*."

1.5. David's house was on the brink of a dishonorable departure (v. 45): *The days of his youth hast thou shortened*. This seems to suggest that the psalm was written in Rehoboam's time, when the house of David was only in the days of its youth, but had become old and had already begun to decay. When descendants become corrupt, families fall into disgrace, and sin stains their glory. We tend to locate the happiness of the church in something outward, and to think the promise fails if we fail to see what we expect. Yet our Master clearly told us his kingdom is not of this world.

2. A very emotional plea to God about this. *How long, O Lord, wilt thou hide thyself? For ever?* What grieved them most was that God himself had kept them in the dark for a long time. The time since God had withdrawn himself seemed an eternal night: *Thou hidest thyself for ever.*

2.1. He pleads the shortness and futility of life (v. 47): *Remember how short my time is*, "how transitory I am," how unable I am to bear the power of your wrath, and that I am therefore a proper object of your pity. *Wherefore hast thou made all men in vain?* Why have you created all humanity for such futility? If the former great love spoken of in v. 49 is forgotten—that love that relates to another life—human beings are indeed created for futility. Considering that human beings are mortal, if there were not a future state on the other side of death, we might be ready to think that humanity had been created for futility. Yet if we think that God has made humanity for futility because so many people have short lives, we must be corrected, for although it is true that God has made them live such lives, it is not therefore true that that they have been created for futility. For those whose days are few may still glorify God and do some good; they may maintain their fellowship with God and reach heaven. And if we think that God has made human beings for futility because most people neither serve him nor enjoy him, here too we must be corrected, for although it is true that, as to themselves, they were created for futility, it was not because of God that they were created for futility; it was because of themselves. The psalmist also pleads the universality of death (v. 48): *"What man is he that liveth* (who can live) *and shall not see death?* The king himself is not exempt. Lord, since he has to die, let not his whole life become so miserable. Let him not be handed over to the power of the grave by the miseries of a dying life until his time has come." We should make sure of happiness on the other side of death, so that *when we fail* (are gone), *we may be received into everlasting habitations* (dwellings).

2.2. He pleads the kindness God had for his servant David (v. 49): *"Lord, where are thy former loving-kindnesses,* which you showed, *nay, which thou swarest,* to *David in thy truth?* Will you fail to do what you promised?" God's unchangeableness and faithfulness assure us that he will not reject those whom he has chosen and made a covenant with.

2.3. He pleads the indignity shown to God's anointed one (vv. 50–51). "Those who are mocking us like this are your enemies, and will you not punish them for doing so?" *They have reproached the footsteps of thy anointed,* they have mocked every step of your anointed one (v. 51). They saw all the steps which the king had taken in the course of his administration, tracked down his every move, so that they might make invidious remarks about everything he had said and done. Or if we apply it to Christ, the Lord's Messiah, they mocked the Jews because of the slowness of his coming. The Jews called him *He that should come* (Mt 11:3), but because he had not yet come, their enemies told them that he would never come and they must stop looking for him.

3. Praise to God, even after this sad complaint (v. 52): *Blessed be the Lord for evermore, Amen, and Amen.* This is how he confronts the scorn of his enemies. The more others blaspheme God, the more we should praise him. This is how the psalmist corrects his own complaints. He began the psalm with thanksgiving, before he made his complaint (v. 1); and now he concludes it with a doxology.

PSALM 90

As the title states, this psalm was written by Moses, the earliest writer of the Holy Scriptures. We have on record his song of praise (Ex 15:1–21, which is alluded to in Rev 15:3), and an instructive song of his (Dt 32:1–43). But this is called a prayer. It is thought that this psalm was written on the occasion of the sentence passed on Israel in the desert for their unbelief, grumbling, and rebellion, the sentence declaring that their carcasses would fall in the desert, that they would be wasted away by a series of hardships for thirty-eight years, and that none of them who were then adults would enter Canaan. We have the story to which this psalm seems to refer in Nu 14. Moses probably wrote this prayer to be used daily by the people in their tents, or by the priests in the services of the tabernacle in the desert. In it: 1. Moses encourages himself

and his people with the eternity of God and their privileges of being his people (vv. 1–2); he humbles himself and his people with the consideration of the weakness of human beings (vv. 3–6). 2. He submits himself and his people to the righteous sentence of God passed on them (vv. 7–11). 3. He commits himself and his people to God by prayer for divine mercy and grace and for the return of God's favor (vv. 12–17).

Title

This psalm is entitled *a prayer of Moses.* Moses taught the people of Israel to pray, and he put words into their mouths which they might use in turning to the Lord.

Verses 1–6

In these verses we are taught:

1. To praise God for the care he takes of his people at all times (v. 1): *Lord, thou hast been to us a dwelling place* (a refuge or help) *in all generations.* They plead his former kindness to their ancestors. Canaan was a land of pilgrimage to their fathers the patriarchs, who had lived there in tents, but then God was their dwelling place, and wherever they went, they were at home and at rest in him. Egypt had been a land of slavery for many years, but even then God was their refuge.

2. To glorify God for his eternity (v. 2): *Before the mountains were brought forth* (*before he made the highest part of the dust of the world,* as it is expressed in Pr 8:26), *before the earth gave birth to life, or, before thou hadst formed the earth and the world*—that is, before the beginning of time—*you had being; even from everlasting to everlasting thou art God.* In all the suffering that arises from our own mortality, we may take encouragement and strength from God's immortality.

3. To acknowledge God's absolute, sovereign rule over human beings and his power to direct them as he pleases (v. 3): *Thou turnest man to destruction* (dust), you destroy the body, this earthly house, *and* you say, *Return, you children of men.* He calls people to repent of their sins and live a new life. He sometimes wonderfully restores them, saying, *Return to* (v. 3) life and salvation again. Although God turns all people to dust, he will still say, *Return, you children of men* (v. 3), at the general resurrection, when, although people die, they will live again (Jn 11:35).

4. To acknowledge the infinite difference between God and human beings (v. 4). "A thousand years is a long time to us, an age to which we cannot expect to survive, but it is, *in thy sight, as yesterday,* as one day; in fact, it is only as *a watch of the night,*" which was just three hours. Between a minute and a million years there is some proportion, but between time and eternity there is none. It might be objected regarding the teaching of the resurrection that it is a long time since it was expected and it still has not come. Let that not be a difficulty, for a thousand years, in God's sight, is as one day.

5. To see the weakness of human beings and their futility even in their best state (vv. 5–6). If we look at people, we will see that their lives are mortal: *Thou carriest them away as with a flood* (v. 5). As soon as we are born, we begin to die, and every day of our life takes us closer to death. People are taken away as with a flood, and yet *they are as a sleep,* in the sleep of death (v. 5). They do not consider their own weakness. Like people who are asleep, they imagine great things for themselves, until death wakes them up. Time passes by unobserved by us, as it does with people who are asleep. Their lives are short, like that of the grass, which springs up and flourishes and looks green and pleasant in the morning, but is cut

down in the evening, and dries up and withers and loses all its beauty. Death will change us shortly, and perhaps suddenly. Death changes us greatly and in a short time. Human beings in their prime flourish like grass.

Verses 7–11

In vv. 1–6, Moses mourned the weakness of human life in general. But here he teaches the people of Israel to confess before God the righteous sentence of death which they have brought on themselves because of their sins.

1. They are taught here to acknowledge the wrath of God as the cause of all their misery. *We are consumed, we are troubled*, and it is *by thy anger, by thy wrath* (v. 7); *our days have passed away in thy wrath* (v. 9). We tend to look on death as nothing more than a debt owing to nature, but the reality is different. If human beings had continued in their original pure state, there would have been no such debt owed by us. It is a debt to the justice of God, a debt to the law. *Sin entered into the world, and death by sin* (Ro 5:12).

2. They are taught to confess their sins (v. 8): *Thou hast set our iniquities before thee, even our secret sins.* Here God looked at their unbelief and grumbling, their distrusting of his power and their despising of the pleasant land. "*Thou hast set our secret sins*—those which go no further than the heart and which are at the root of all the overt acts—*in the light of thy countenance* (presence) (v. 8); that is, you have found these out, have brought these also to the account and made us see them when previously we overlooked them."

3. They are taught to look on themselves as dying and passing away, and not to think that their lives will be either long or pleasant (v. 9). "Although we are not totally deprived of our remaining years, we are still likely to *spend* them *as a tale that is told.*" They spent thirty-eight years wearily in the desert, for little or nothing is recorded about what happened to them from the second year to the fortieth. Their joyful prospect of a prosperous, glorious life in Canaan was turned to the sad prospect of a tedious death in the desert. This applies to the state of each one of us in the wilderness of this world: *We spend our years* (v. 9), we bring them to an end, each year, and all at last, *as a tale that is told.* Some of our years are like a pleasant story, others are more like a tragic one, most are mixed, but all are brief: what took a long time to do may be told in a short time. Each year that passes is *as a tale that is told* (v. 9); but how many of them have there been? What is their number? As they were futile, so also they were few (v. 10), seventy or eighty at most, which may be understood to refer either:

3.1. To the length of time the Israelites spent in the desert. All those who were counted when they left Egypt, who were more than twenty years old, were to die within thirty-eight years. The people counted only those who *were able to go forth to war* (Nu 1:3), most of whom were probably between twenty and forty, and so must all have died before they were eighty years old, and many before they were sixty. Notice what sin caused. Or:

3.2. To the lives of human beings in general ever since the times of Moses. It may be read in this way: "Our years are seventy, and the years of some, if they have strength, are eighty; but the span of our years, their whole extent, from infancy to old age, is only trouble and sorrow." We must eat bread by the sweat of our brow (Ge 3:19).

4. They are taught by all this to stand in awe of the wrath of God (v. 11): *Who knows the power of thy anger?* The psalmist speaks as one who is afraid of God's anger and stunned at the greatness of its power. *Who knows it* (v. 11), so as to make the most of such knowledge? Those who mock sin and make light of Christ surely do not know the power of God's anger.

Verses 12–17

These are the requests of this prayer, based on the previous meditations and acknowledgments. They were instructed to pray for four things:

1. For a consecration of the sad life they now had. "*Lord, teach us to number our days* (v. 12); Lord, give us appropriate grace to consider how few they are, how short a time we have to live in this world." We must number our days as we think about our life's work, and therefore have it diligently in mind, as those who have no time to trifle away. Those who want to learn this arithmetic must pray for divine instruction.

2. For the turning away of God's anger from them: "*Yet return, O Lord!* Be reconciled to us, and *let it repent thee concerning* (have compassion on) *thy servants* (v. 13); send us news of peace to strengthen us again after this bad news. *We are thy servants, thy people* (Isa 64:9); when will you change your ways toward us?" In response to this prayer, and on their profession of repentance in Nu 14:39–40, God, in the next chapter, proceeded with the laws concerning sacrifices (Nu 15:1–31), which was a sign that he had compassion on his servants, for *if the Lord had been pleased to kill them, he would not have shown them such things as these* (Jdg 13:23).

3. For joy and assurance at the response of God's favor to them (vv. 14–15). They pray for God's mercy, for they do not pretend to have any plea based on their own merit. *Have mercy upon us, O God!* Let us pray for God's mercy *early in the morning* of our days, when we are young and flourishing (v. 6). "*O satisfy us with thy mercy*, not only so that we may be at peace and at rest within ourselves, which we can never be while we are under your wrath, but also so that we *may rejoice and be glad*, glad not only for a time, at the first signs of your favor, but *all our days* (v. 14), even though we have to spend them in the desert. *Make us glad according to the days wherein thou hast afflicted us* (v. 15); may the days of our joy in your favor be as many as the days of our pain under your displeasure, and may the days of your favor be as pleasant as those others have been sad. Now put into our hands the cup of salvation" (116:13).

4. For the progress of the work of God among them despite all this (vv. 16–17). "*Let thy work appear upon thy servants*; may it be seen that you have worked in our lives, to bring us home to yourself and make us fit for yourself. Let your work be seen, and in it your glory will also be seen by us and those who come after us." In this prayer, they are perhaps distinguishing between themselves and their children, for this was the distinction God made in his message to them: *Your carcases shall fall in this wilderness, but your little ones I will bring into Canaan* (Nu 14:32). "Lord," they say, "may *thy work appear upon us*, to reform us and bring us into a better spirit, and then *let thy glory appear to our children* (v. 16) by fulfilling the promise to them which we have lost." *Let the beauty of the Lord our God be upon us* (v. 17); may it be clear that God favors us. "May the grace of God in us, and the light of our good works, make our faces shine, and may divine encouragement put gladness into our hearts and a glow on our faces, and that also will be the beauty of the Lord on us. *Establish thou the work of our hands upon us*" (v. 17). God's working on us (v. 16) does not release us from doing all we can to serve him and work out our

salvation (Php 2:12–13). But when we have done all we can, we must wait on God for the success.

This psalm applies very much to the frailty of human life in general, and in praying over and singing this psalm, we may apply it to our years of passage through the wilderness of this world. It also provides us with meditations and prayers very suitable for funeral services.

PSALM 91

This psalm was probably written by David; it is a document that guarantees protection to all true believers, not in the name of King David but in the name of the King of kings, and under the seal of heaven. Notice: 1. The psalmist's own firm determination to take God as his keeper (v. 2), a determination he uses to give both direction and encouragement to others (v. 9). 2. The promises which are made here, in God's name, to all those who sincerely take God as their keeper: 2.1. They will be taken under the special care of heaven (vv. 1, 4). 2.2. They will be rescued from the hatred of the powers of darkness (vv. 3, 5–6) by special preservation (vv. 7–8). 2.3. They will be the responsibility of holy angels (vv. 10–12). 2.4. They will triumph over their enemies (v. 13) 2.5. They will be the special favorites of God himself (vv. 14–16).

Verses 1–8

In these verses we have:

1. A great truth generally set down, that all those who live a life of fellowship with God are constantly safe under his protection and may therefore keep a holy calmness of mind at all times (v. 1). It is the character of true believers that they *dwell in the secret place of the Most High.* They are at home in God; they return to God and find him to be their rest. They come to know the inner life of religious faith. They make it a choice of their hearts to serve God, to worship within the veil. It is the privilege and encouragement of those who do so that they *abide under the shadow of the Almighty;* he shelters them. They are at home in God's protection.

2. The psalmist applying this to himself to give him strength and encouragement (v. 2): *I will say of the Lord,* whatever others may say about him, *He is my refuge.* Idolaters called their idols their *most strong holds* (their mightiest fortresses) (Da 11:39), but they were deceiving themselves in this, for only those who make the Lord their God and their fortress are secure. Because there is no reason to question his sufficiency, it rightly follows, *In him will I trust* (v. 2).

3. The great encouragement he gives to others to do the same, an encouragement based not only on his own experience but also on the truth of God's promise (v. 3): *Surely he shall deliver thee.* Now here it is promised:

3.1. That believers will be kept from those troubles that would be fatal to them (v. 3). This promise protects the natural life and is often fulfilled in our preservation from dangers that threaten and are very near. It also protects the spiritual life, by divine grace, from the temptations of Satan.

3.2. That God himself will protect them: *He shall cover thee with his feathers, under his wings* (v. 4), which alludes to the hen *gathering her chickens under her wings* (Mt 23:37). She not only protects them by natural instinct but also calls them under that protection when she sees them in danger. She not only keeps them safe but also nurtures them and keeps them warm. God is pleased to compare his caring for his people to the hen's care for her

chicks. And yet, although wings and feathers are spread out with the greatest tenderness, they are still weak and easily broken through, and so it is added, *His truth shall be thy shield and buckler* (rampart) (v. 4), a strong defense. God is as willing to guard his people as a hen is to guard her chicks, and as able as a warrior in armor.

3.3. That he will keep them not only from evil but also from the fear of evil (vv. 5–6). By his grace God will keep you from disturbing, distrusting fears—fears which bring torment—in the midst of the greatest dangers. Wisdom will keep you from being afraid without reason, and faith will keep you from being excessively afraid. You will not be afraid of the arrow, knowing that although it may hit you, it cannot hurt you. If it takes away your natural life, it will be so far from doing any harm to your spiritual life that it will perfect it.

3.4. That they will be preserved in common adversities in a special way (v. 7): "When *thousands and ten thousands fall* in sickness or are killed by the sword in battle, when they *fall at thy side, at thy right hand, yet it shall not come nigh thee;* neither death nor the fear of death will come near you." When many are dying around us, although that must wake us up to prepare for our own death, we must still not give way to fear (1Pe 3:6); nor may we become enslaved to fear *through fear of death* (Heb 2:15), as many do throughout their lifetime. God's people will not only be preserved but also see their enemies destroyed: *Only with thy eyes shalt thou behold and see the just reward of the wicked;* perhaps this refers to the destruction of the firstborn of Egypt by the plague.

Verses 9–16

More promises are given here, to the same effect as those in vv. 1–8:

1. The psalmist assures believers of divine protection, from his own experience. Notice:

1.1. The character of those who will enjoy the benefit and encouragement of these promises. They are those who make *the Most High their habitation* (dwelling place) (v. 9), who live in love and so live in God. It is our duty to be at home in God: to choose him, and then to live our lives in him as our dwelling place; and when we have made it our duty, it will also be our privilege. We will be as welcome to him as people are in their own home. To encourage us to make the Lord our dwelling place and to hope for safety and assurance in him, the psalmist describes the encouragement he has had in doing so: "He whom you make your *habitation* (dwelling place) *is my refuge* (v. 9); and I have found him to be firm and faithful. In him there is enough room and shelter for both you and me."

1.2. The promises are firm to all who have made *the Most High* their *habitation* (dwelling place). Whatever happens to them, nothing will hurt them (v. 10). Though trouble or affliction may come to you, there will be no real evil in it, for it will come from the love of God and will be consecrated. It will come not for your harm but for your good, and although for *the present, it be not joyous but grievous* (Heb 12:11), in the end, it will have such good effects that you yourself will acknowledge that *no evil* (harm) *befell thee* (v. 10). He who is the Lord of the angels, who gave them their being and gives laws to them, to whom they belong and whom they were made to serve, *shall give his angels a charge over thee* (v. 11), not only over the church in general but also over every individual believer. The command is *to keep thee in all thy ways;* there is a restriction on the promise: they *shall keep thee in thy ways* (v. 11), that is, "as long as you keep in the path of your duty." Wherever the saints go, the angels are given responsibility for them, as servants are with children. *Thou shalt tread upon the lion and adder.* The Devil is called *a roaring lion,* the old *serpent, the red dragon,* and it seems to be this promise that the apostle is alluding to in Ro 16:20: *The God of peace shall bruise* (crush or tread) *Satan under your feet.* Christ has broken the serpent's head, disarmed our spiritual enemies (Col 2:15). The promise may also be applied to the care of divine Providence by which we are kept from ferocious, harmful creatures—*the wild beasts of the field shall be at peace with thee* (Job 5:23)—and in fact we have ways of taming them (Jas 3:7).

2. The psalmist brings in God himself speaking words of assurance to the saints, declaring the mercy he has in store for them (vv. 14–16). Notice:

2.1. To whom these promises belong. They are characterized by three qualities:

- They are those who know God's name. We cannot fully know his nature, but he has made himself known by his name.
- They are those who have set their love on him. Those who rightly know him will love him.
- They are those who in prayer keep up a constant relationship with him.

2.2. What the promises are which God makes to the saints:

2.2.1. That God will, in due time, rescue them from trouble: *I will deliver him* (v. 14 and again v. 15). The repetition of the promise implies a double rescue, living and dying, a rescue in trouble and also a rescue out of trouble.

2.2.2. That he will, in the meantime, *be with them in trouble* (v. 15). If he does not immediately put an end to their suffering, they will still have his gracious presence with them in their troubles.

2.2.3. That he will answer their prayers: *He shall call upon me* (v. 15); I will pour on him the spirit of prayer, *and then I will answer.* He will answer by promises, by providences, and by graces that *strengthen them with strength in their souls* (138:3). Similarly, the Lord answered Paul with *grace sufficient* (2Co 12:9).

2.2.4. That he will exalt and honor them: *I will set him on high* (v. 14), beyond the reach of trouble, above the storms of life, on a *rock* (Isa 33:16) *above the waves* (93:4). The grace of God will enable them to look down on the things of this world with a holy disdain and indifference and to look up to the things of the next world with a holy ambition and concern.

2.2.5. That they will have sufficient days in this world (v. 16): *With long life will I satisfy him.* They will live long enough: they will live in this world until they have done the work they were sent here for and are ready for heaven, and that is long enough. Someone may die young, but still have died full of days (Ge 35:29), satisfied with life.

2.2.6. That they will have eternal life in the other world. This crowns the blessedness: *I will show him my salvation* (v. 16). It is probable that the word refers to the better country, that is, the heavenly one (Heb 11:16).

PSALM 92

This psalm was probably written by David, and because it is intended for use on the Sabbath day: 1. Praise, the work of the Sabbath, is commended (vv. 1–3). 2. God's works, which gave rise to the Sabbath, are celebrated as great and unsearchable in general (vv. 4–6); and in particular, with reference to the works both of providence and of redemption, the psalmist sings to God of mercy and judgment (101:1), alternating three times: 2.1. Evildoers will perish (v. 7), but God is eternal (v. 8). 2.2. God's enemies will be cut off, but David will be exalted (vv. 9–10). 2.3. David's enemies will be confounded (v. 11), but all the righteous will be fruitful and flourishing (vv. 12–15).

Title

This psalm was appointed to be sung—at least it was usually sung—in the sanctuary on the Sabbath. The Sabbath must be a day not only of holy rest but also of holy work. The proper work of the Sabbath is praising God. Every Sabbath must be a day of thanksgiving. One of the Jewish writers believes the psalm refers to the kingdom of the Messiah, and he calls it "A psalm or song for the age to come," the age that will be all Sabbath.

Verses 1–6

In these verses:

1. We are called on and encouraged to praise God (vv. 1–3): *It is a good thing to give thanks unto the Lord.* Praising God is a good work: it is good in itself and also good for us. Notice here:

1.1. How we must praise God. We must do it by *showing forth his lovingkindness and his faithfulness* (v. 2). We must declare not only his greatness and majesty, his holiness and justice, which exalt him and strike awe in us, but also his love and his faithfulness, for his goodness is his glory (Ex 33:18–19), and by these he declares his name. His mercy and truth are the great supports of our faith and hope, and the great encouragements of our love and obedience. When this psalm was written, this praise was offered not only by singing but also by accompaniment, *upon an instrument of ten strings* (a ten-stringed lyre) (v. 3).

1.2. When we must praise God—in *the morning and every night* (v. 2), not only on Sabbaths but every day; not only in public meetings but also in private and in our families. We must begin and end every day with praising God.

2. We have an example set before us in the psalmist himself: *Thou, Lord, hast made me glad through thy work. I will triumph in* (sing for joy at) *the works of thy hands* (v. 4). As we joyfully remember what God has done for us, let us sing for joy at what he will do. We cannot begin to comprehend the greatness of God's works, and so we must reverently and fearfully wonder at them. "The works of human beings are little and trifling, for their thoughts are shallow, but, Lord, *thy works are great* and cannot be measured, for *thy thoughts are very deep* and cannot be fathomed." The greatness of God's works should lead us to consider the depths of his thoughts.

3. The psalmist shows us the character of those who neglect the works of God (v. 6), and thereby warns us not to neglect them. Those who will not acquaint themselves with God's works or give him the glory for them are fools.

Verses 7–15

The psalmist has said (v. 4) that he will take the opportunity to triumph and sing for joy about the works of God, and he does so here.

1. He triumphs over God's enemies (vv. 7, 9, 11). When they are flourishing (v. 7) as *the grass* in spring—so thickly sown, so green, and growing so fast—*and all the*

workers of iniquity do flourish in all their show and power, one would have thought that it was a sure sign of God's favor. In reality it is totally different, however. The very *prosperity of fools shall slay* (kill) *them* (Pr 1:32). He triumphs over his enemies even though they are daring (v. 9). "They are your enemies, Lord"; they fight against God. They will perish, for *who ever hardened his heart against God and prospered?* (Job 9:4). Although they have particular hatred against the psalmist, he still triumphs over them (v. 11): *"My eye shall see* (the fulfillment of) *my desire on my enemies that rise up against me.* I will see them not only made unable to cause me any more trouble, but also judged for the trouble they have already done me, and brought either to repentance or to ruin."

2. He triumphs in God, in his glory and grace:

2.1. In the glory of God (v. 8).

2.2. In the grace of God, his favor, and its fruits (v. 10).

2.2.1. To him: *My horn shalt thou exalt* (v. 10) when *thy enemies perish,* for *then shall the righteous shine forth as the sun* (Mt 13:43), when evildoers will be condemned to *shame and everlasting contempt* (Da 12:2). He adds, *I shall be anointed with fresh oil* (v. 10), which shows a fresh confirmation in the office to which he has been anointed, or an abundance of plenty, so that he will have fresh oil as often as he pleases, or renewed comforts to revive him when his spirits droop. Grace is the anointing of the Spirit.

2.2.2. To all the saints, who are described here as *trees of righteousness* (1:3; Isa 61:3). They are *planted in the house of the Lord* (v. 13). The trees of righteousness do not grow by themselves; they are planted. And they are planted not in ordinary soil but in the house of the Lord. Trees are not usually planted in a house, but God's trees are said to be planted in his house because it is from his grace, by his word and Spirit, that they receive all the sap and power that keep them alive and make them fruitful.

2.2.3. It is promised here that they will grow (v. 12). Where God gives true grace, he will give more grace. God's trees will grow higher, like the tall cedars of Lebanon. They will grow closer to heaven; they will grow stronger, like cedars, and more ready for use. They will be cheerful in and respected by all around them. They will flourish like palm trees, which have elegant trunks and large branches (Lev 23:40; Jdg 4:5). Dates, their fruit, are very pleasant, but their staying green is especially alluded to here. Evildoers flourish like the grass (v. 7), which soon withers, but the righteous are like palm trees, which live a long time and do not change in winter. It has been said of palm trees that the more they are pressed down, the more they grow. The righteous are like that; they flourish under their burdens. They will be fruitful. The products of sanctification, which are all the instances of a living devotion, and good works, by which God is glorified and others are built up, are all the fruits of righteousness; to abound in these is the privilege of the righteous. It is promised that they will bear fruit in old age. When other trees are old, they stop bearing fruit, but the strength of grace in God's trees does not fail with the strength of nature. The last days of the saints are sometimes their best ones, and their last work their best. As it is by the promises that believers first share in the divine nature, so it is by the promises that that divine nature is preserved and maintained in them. Whoever has trusted in God has found him faithful and all-sufficient, and no one has ever been ashamed of their hope in him (Isa 28:16; Ro 9:33; 10:11).

PSALM 93

This short psalm sets out the honor of the kingdom of God. It relates to the kingdom of his providence, by which he governs the world, and to the kingdom of his grace, by which he protects the church. The administration of both these kingdoms is put into the hands of the Messiah, and to him, no doubt, the prophet here bears witness, and to his kingdom. Glorious things are here spoken about God's kingdom (87:3). 1. Have other kings their royal robes? So has he (v. 1). 2. Have they their thrones? So has he (v. 2). 3. Have they their enemies whom they subdue and triumph over? So has he (vv. 3–4). 4. Is it their honor to be faithful and holy? So it is his (v. 5).

Verses 1–5

The Lord reigns (v. 1). It is the song of the Gospel church, of the glorified church (Rev 19:6): *Hallelujah*; the Lord *God omnipotent reigns.* We are told how he reigns:

1. The Lord reigns gloriously: *He is clothed with majesty* (v. 1).

2. He reigns powerfully. He is not only robed in majesty, as a ruler at court, but also *clothed with strength* (v. 1), as a general in a camp. He has the resources to support his greatness and make it truly formidable. See him not only wearing robes, but also wearing armor. With this power *he has girded himself*; he wears it like a belt (v. 1). His power is not derived from any other being, nor do the operations of his power depend on any other being. The world was established by the creative power of God, when he founded it on the seas (24:2). It remains established by the providence which upholds all things and which is a continuing creation. Although God robes himself in majesty, he still condescends to take care of this lower world and to settle its affairs, and if he established the world, then much more will he establish his church, so it cannot be moved.

3. He reigns eternally (v. 2): *Thy throne is established of old.* The whole administration of his sovereignty was settled in his eternal counsels before all worlds. Because God himself is eternal, his throne and all its decrees are also, for in an eternal mind there can be only eternal thoughts.

4. He reigns triumphantly (vv. 3–4). *The floods* (seas) *have lifted up, O Lord*—the plea is made to God himself—*the floods have lifted up their voice,* which speaks of terror. This alludes to a stormy sea. The church is said to *be tossed with tempests* (Isa 54:11). We may apply this to the tumults that sometimes rage within us, but if the Lord reigns there, even the winds and seas will obey him (Mk 4:39–41). An immovable anchor is cast in this storm (v. 4): *The Lord himself is mightier.* The power of the church's enemies is only *as the noise of many waters* (v. 4); there is more to its sound than to its substance. *Pharaoh king of Egypt is but a noise* (Jer 46:17). The unlimited sovereignty and irresistible power of the great Jehovah are very encouraging to the people of God when they meet all the noise and rush in this world (46:1–2).

5. He reigns in truth and holiness (v. 5). All his promises are unbreakably faithful: *Thy testimonies are very sure.* Just as God is able to protect his church, so also he is true to the promises he has made for its security and victory. God's church is his house. Its holiness is its beauty, and it is its strength and security. It is the holiness of God's house that protects it from the thunder of the great waters. Where there is purity, there will be peace.

PSALM 94

This psalm was written when the church of God was depressed, oppressed, and persecuted. It is an appeal to God for his people against his and their enemies. This psalm speaks of two things: 1. Conviction and terror to the persecutors (vv. 1–11), showing them their danger and foolishness and arguing with them. 2. Comfort and peace to the persecuted (vv. 12–23), assuring them, both from God's promise and from the psalmist's own experience, that their troubles will end well.

Verses 1–11

In these verses we have:

1. A solemn appeal to God against the cruel oppressors of his people (vv. 1–2). Notice:

1.1. The titles God's people give to him to encourage their faith in this appeal: *O God, to whom vengeance belongeth* (v. 1); and *thou Judge of the earth* (v. 1). He is Judge, supreme judge, the only judge, from whom every human judgment comes. He who gives law judges everyone according to their works (62:12; Pr 24:12), against the standard of that law. His throne is the last refuge, the last resort, as the law puts it, of oppressed innocence. He is the *judge of the earth* (v. 2), of the whole earth. As he has authority to avenge wrong, so also it is his nature to do so. And so he is addressed, *"O God, to whom vengeance belongs* (v. 1), who will not always allow might to prevail against right."* This is a good reason why we must not take revenge ourselves; God has said, *Vengeance is mine*, and it is arrogant and presumptuous of us to usurp his prerogative and step onto his throne (Ro 12:19).

1.2. What they ask God for. "Lord," they say, "show yourself; make them know that you exist and that you are ready to *show thyself strong on the behalf of those whose hearts are upright with thee"* (2Ch 16:9). The enemies think God has been conquered because his people have been. *Render a reward to the proud* (v. 2), that is, "Judge them for all their arrogance and the wrongs they have done to your people."

2. A humble complaint to God about the pride and cruelty of the oppressors. They are evil; they are *workers of iniquity* (v. 4), and so they hate and persecute those whose goodness shames and condemns them. They are arrogant and take pleasure in exalting themselves. Those who have a high opinion of themselves, who go around boasting, tend to speak harshly about others: *"They break in pieces* (crush) *thy people, O Lord*, and do all they can to afflict your inheritance, to grieve, crush, oppress, and uproot them."* God's people are his inheritance. The oppressors are inhuman and take pleasure in wronging those who are least able to help themselves (v. 6). "Lord, *how long* will they act in this way?"

3. A charge of ungodliness made against the persecutors.

3.1. Their ungodly thoughts are here laid bare (v. 7): *Yet they say, The Lord shall not see.* They are still arrogant enough to say, *"The Lord shall not see;* he will not only ignore small faults but turn a blind eye to great ones too."

3.2. Those who say either that Jehovah the living God will not see or that the God of Jacob will not regard the wrongs done to his people are named *Nabal* (1Sa 25:25–26), and they are foolish. (v. 8): *"Understand, you brutish* (senseless) *among the people*, and let reason guide you. God sees and regards all you say and do." No one is so bad that ways cannot be used to reclaim and reform them. No one is so senseless or foolish that ways should not be tried to see whether they may still become wise;

while there is life there is hope. To prove the foolishness of those who question God, the psalmist argues:

3.2.1. From the works of creation (v. 9), specifically the formation of human bodies, which proves both that there is a God and that God has in himself, infinitely and transcendently, all those qualities that are in any part of his creation. *He that planted the ear—shall he not hear?* (v. 9). *He that formed the eye—shall he not see?* (v. 9). Could he give, would he give, that perfection to a creature which he has not in himself? By the knowledge of ourselves we may be led a long way toward knowing about God. By knowing about our own bodies, with their sensory organs, we are led to conclude that if we can see and hear, God can much more; certainly, then, by knowing that our souls are noble we may conclude that God is eminently more so. The gods of the nations had eyes but could not see, ears but could not hear (115:5–6; 135:16–17); our God has no eyes or ears, as we have, but we must conclude that he both sees and hears, because we have our sight and hearing from him.

3.2.2. From the works of Providence (v. 10): *He that chastises the heathen* (disciplines nations) for worshiping many false gods, *shall not he* much more *correct* his own people for their ungodliness and godlessness? Dr. Henry Hammond gives another very probable sense of this: "'He that instructs the nations' (that is, gives them his law), 'shall he not correct,' that is, shall he not judge them according to that law, and call them to an account for their violations of it?" The same word means "to chastise or discipline" and "to teach or instruct," because discipline is intended for instruction and instruction should go along with discipline.

3.2.3. From the works of grace: *He that teaches man knowledge, shall he not know?* (v. 10). As the God of nature, he has given the light of reason, but as the God of grace he has given the light of revelation. He has shown human beings what true wisdom and understanding is; and he who does this, will he not know all things (Job 28:23, 28)? God will take notice even of what we think (v. 11): *The Lord knows the thoughts of man, that they are vanity.* Even good thoughts contain a fickleness and inconstancy which may well be called *vanity.* Thoughts are words to God, and worthless thoughts offend him.

Verses 12–23

The psalmist speaks comfort to suffering saints from God's promises and his own experience:

1. From God's promises, which not only stop the saints from being miserable but also secure their happiness (v. 12): *Blessed is the man whom thou chastenest.* Here the psalmist looks beyond the instruments of trouble and looks to the hand of God, thus putting a totally different understanding on the trouble. The enemies crush God's people (v. 5); God, however, uses them to discipline his people, as a father does the son in whom he delights (Pr 3:12; Heb 12:6), and the persecutors are only the rod he uses. Now it is promised here:

1.1. That God's people will benefit by their sufferings. When he disciplines them, he will teach them, and blessed are those who are under his discipline, for *who teaches like God* (Job 36:22). When we are disciplined, we must pray to be taught and must look into the law as the best interpreter of Providence. It is not the discipline itself that does good, but the teaching that goes along with it and explains it.

1.2. That they will endure their sufferings (v. 13): *That thou mayest give him rest from the days of adversity.* The days of their adversities will not go on forever. God's purpose in teaching his people by their troubles is to prepare them to be rescued; he wants to give them rest from their troubles after reforming them, to remove the affliction when it has done its work.

1.3. That they will see the destruction of those who are the instruments of their sufferings.

1.4. That although they may be unhappy, they will certainly not be rejected (v. 14). Whatever their friends do, God will not reject them or drive them out of his covenant or his care. The apostle Paul comforted himself with this (Ro 11:1).

1.5. That bad as things are, they will get better (v. 15): *Judgment shall return unto* (judgment will again be founded on) *righteousness.* The seeming disorder of providence — for it was never really disordered — will be put right. Then *all the upright in heart shall be after it.* They will return to a prosperous and flourishing condition and shine out of obscurity. They will come to terms with the ways of Providence and respond with love. Dr. Henry Hammond thinks this was most famously fulfilled in the destruction of Jerusalem and, afterward, of pagan Rome, in the crucifiers of Christ and persecutors of Christians, and in the rest that the churches then enjoyed.

2. From his own experiences.

2.1. He and his friends had been oppressed by cruel and arrogant people, who had power in their hands and abused it by mistreating all good people. The oppressors were *evildoers* and *workers of iniquity* (v. 16); they abandoned themselves to all kinds of ungodliness and immorality, and then their throne was a *throne of iniquity* (v. 20). Sin is terrible enough even when human laws are against it, though they often prove too weak to effectively restrain it, but how terrible and troublesome it is when it is supported by law! These workers of iniquity *condemn the innocent blood* (v. 21) for breaking their laws. Think, for example, about Daniel's enemies; they brought on misery by a law when they obtained an ungodly decree against prayer (Da 6:7). When Daniel would not obey it, they *condemned his innocent blood* (v. 21) to the lions. Those people who have given themselves most generously to the human race have often, as here, been treated as the worst evildoers in the name of law and justice.

2.2. The oppression they were under fell very hard on them. The psalmist *had almost dwelt in silence* (v. 17). He was at his wits' end, did not know what to say or do, and was ready to fall into the grave, that land of silence. In a similar situation the apostle Paul *received a sentence of death within himself* (2Co 1:8–9). The psalmist said, "*My foot slippeth* (v. 18); I have to *fall. I shall one day perish by the hand of Saul* (1Sa 27:1). My hope is failing me; I do not find such a firm footing for my faith as I have found in the past." See 73:2. He had many confused and bewildering thoughts within him about his situation, about the course of action he should take, and about how things were likely to turn out.

2.3. In this distress they sought help and relief (v. 16): "*Who will rise up for me against the evildoers?* Have I any friend who, out of love for me, will support me?" He looked, but there was no one to save him (18:41), none to uphold righteousness (Isa 63:5). When the apostle Paul was brought before Nero's throne of sin, *no man stood by him* (2Ti 4:16). God's people here cried out, "Lord, *shall the throne of iniquity have fellowship with thee?* Will you support these tyrants in their evil? We know you will not." A throne has fellowship with God when it is a throne of justice and corresponds to the reason why it was set up, but when it becomes a *throne of iniquity*, it no longer has fellowship with God.

2.4. They found help and relief in God, and only in him. *Unless I had* made him *my help*, by putting my trust in him and expecting help from him, I could never have kept my own soul, but living by faith in him has kept my head above water and has given me breath and something to say. We are indebted for spiritual support not only to God's power but also to his love: "*Thy mercy*, the gifts of your mercy and my hope in your mercy, *held me up. In the multitude of my thoughts within me*, which are crowding and jostling for my attention in my mind, *thy comforts delight my soul*, silence my unquiet thoughts and keep my mind at peace." God's comforts will reach the depths of the soul, and not only the imagination, and they will bring with them a peace and delight that the smiles of the world cannot give and that the frowns of the world cannot take away.

2.5. God is, and will be, a righteous Judge, One who protects right and punishes wrong. The psalmist had both the assurance and the experience of this. "When no one else will, can, or dare shelter me, *the Lord is my defence*, to preserve me from the evil of my troubles, from sinking under them and being destroyed by them. He is *the rock of my refuge*, in the clefts of which I may shelter and on the top of which I may set my feet, to be beyond the reach of danger."

PSALM 95

This psalm may be significantly explained by understanding and comparing Heb 3–4, where the psalm appears both to have been written by David and to have been intended for the days of the Messiah, for there it is said explicitly (Heb 4:7) that the day spoken of here (v. 7) is to be understood as the Gospel day, in which God speaks to us by his Son and offers us a rest besides that of Canaan. In singing psalms it is intended: 1. That we should extol him with music and song (vv. 1–2) as a great God (vv. 3–5) and as the One who has graciously given us so much (vv. 6–7). 2. That we should teach and admonish ourselves and one another (Col 3:16); and we are taught and warned here to hear God's voice (v. 7) and not to harden our hearts, as the Israelites did in the desert (vv. 8–9), so that we may not fall under God's wrath and come short of his rest, as they did (vv. 10–11).

Verses 1–7

Here, the psalmist motivates himself and others to praise God. He often does this elsewhere. Notice:

1. How God is to be praised. The song of praise must be *a joyful noise* (v. 1 and again v. 2). Spiritual joy is the heart and soul of thankful praise. *Rejoice in him* as our Father and King and as a God in covenant with us. We must praise him with humble reverence and holy awe (v. 6): "*Let us worship, and bow down, and kneel before him*, as is right for those who know what an infinite distance there is between us and God, and how much we are in danger of his wrath and in need of his mercy." We must speak out his praises from the abundance of a heart (Mt 12:34) filled with love, joy, and thankfulness — *Sing to the Lord; make a noise, a joyful noise to him, with psalms* (vv. 1–2). We must praise God together in our worship services: "*Come, let us sing* (v. 1); let us join together in singing to the Lord. *Let us come* together *before his presence* (v. 2), where his people usually expect revelations from him."

2. Why God is to be praised:

2.1. Because he is *a great God* and sovereign Lord of all (v. 3).

2.1.1. He has great power: *He is a great King above all gods* (v. 3), above all those he has delegated power to, all rulers and judges—to whom he said, *You are gods* (82:6)—and above all false gods.

2.1.2. He has great possessions. This lower world is mentioned particularly. How great is that God whose *the whole earth is* (48:2), *and the fulness thereof* (24:1), in whose hand it is, since he actually directs everything (v. 4). Even *the deep places of the earth are in his hand*, and *the strength of the hills*, whatever grows or feeds on them, *is his also.* Whatever strength any creature has is derived from God and is used for him (v. 5): *The sea is his*, for *he made it.* He gathered its waters and established its shores. *The dry land* is his, for *his hands formed* it, when his word made *the dry land* appear (Ge 1:9). Because he is the Creator of everything, he is without dispute the owner of all. Since this is a Gospel psalm, we may very well think that it is the Lord Jesus whom we are here taught to praise. As Mediator, he is *a great King above all gods* (v. 3); *by him*, as the eternal Word, *all things were made* (Jn 1:3), and it was right that he who was the Creator of all should be the restorer and reconciler of all (Col 1:16, 20).

2.2. Because he is our God. He not only has rule over us, as he has over all creatures, but also stands in a special relationship with us (v. 7): *He is our God.* He is our Creator. We must *kneel before the Lord our Maker* (v. 6). Idolaters kneel before the so-called gods they themselves made; we kneel before a God who made us. He is our Savior and the author of our happiness. He is called *the rock of our salvation* (v. 1). We are indebted to him in every possible way: *We are the people of his pasture and the sheep of his hand* (v. 7). We must praise him, because he preserves and sustains us. All the church's children are especially his; Israel is *the people of his pasture and the sheep of his hand* (v. 7). He therefore demands their loyalty in a special way. The Gospel church is his flock. Christ is its great and Good Shepherd, and so *glory in the churches* must be given to him *throughout all ages* (Eph 3:21).

Verses 7–11

The second part of this psalm is an encouragement to those who sing Gospel psalms to live Gospel lives. Notice:

1. The duty required of all those who *are the people of* Christ's *pasture and the sheep of his hand* (v. 7). He expects that they *hear his voice* (v. 7), for he has said, *My sheep hear my voice* (Jn 10:27). If you call him *Master*, or *Lord*, then *do the things which he says* (Lk 6:46) and be his willing and obedient people. Listening to the voice of Christ is the same as believing.

2. The sin they are warned against is hardness of heart. *If you will* (want to) *hear his voice* (v. 7), and benefit by what you hear, then do *not harden your hearts* (v. 8), for the seed sown on rocky places never brought any fruit to maturity (Mk 4:5–6).

3. The example of the Israelites in the desert.

3.1. "Make sure you do not sin as they did, so that you will not be excluded from the eternal rest as they were excluded from Canaan." They provoked God so often by their distrust and grumblings that the whole time they remained in the desert might be called a *day of temptation*, or Massah, the other name given to that place (Ex 17:7), because they tempted and tested the Lord, saying, *Is the Lord among us or is he not?* The more experience we have had of the power and goodness of God, the greater our sin is if we distrust him.

3.2. The accusation is drawn up, in God's name, against the unbelieving Israelites (vv. 9–10). Their sin was unbelief: they *tempted* God and *proved* him (Nu 14:3–4). This is called *rebellion* (Dt 1:26, 32). What made this sin worse was that they *saw God's work* (v. 9); they saw what he had done for them in bringing them out of Egypt, in fact, what he was now doing for them every day in the bread he rained down from heaven (105:40) and the water from the rock (Ex 17:6; Nu 20:11; 1Co 10:4). They could not have had more conclusive signs of God's presence with them. *It is a people that do err in their hearts, and they have not known my ways* (v. 10). People's unbelief and distrust in God, their grumbling and quarrels with him, are the effect of their ignorance. They saw his work (v. 9), and he *made known his acts to them* (103:7), but they *did not know* the ways of his providence or the ways of his commandments. The reason why people disrespect and abandon the ways of God is that they do not know them. *They do err in their heart* (v. 10); they go astray from the path; they turn back in their hearts. The sins of God's professing people—especially their distrust of him—not only anger him but also grieve him. Notice the patience of God toward offensive sinners. He was grieved with them for forty years, but those years ended in the triumphant entrance into Canaan by the next generation.

3.3. The sentence passed on them for their sin (v. 11). He *swore solemnly in his wrath* (v. 11), his just and holy wrath. God is not subject to such unrestrained passions as we are, but he is said to be angry at sin and sinners, to show the evil of sin and the justice of God's rule. What he swore was *that they should* (would) *not enter into his rest* (v. 11), the rest which he had prepared for them, a settlement for them and theirs.

4. This case of Israel may be applied to those of their future generations who lived in David's time, when this psalm was written. But it must also be applied to us Christians, because this is how the writer to the Hebrews applies it (Heb 4:1–11). There is a spiritual and eternal rest placed in front of us and promised to us, of which Canaan was a type. Those who, like Israel, distrust God, will justly be excluded from his rest: they themselves have decided it (Heb 4:1).

PSALM 96

This psalm was sung at the transfer of the ark. It looks further, however, to the kingdom of Christ, and is intended to celebrate the glories of that kingdom, especially the accession of the Gentiles to it. Here is: 1. A call given to all people to praise God, to worship him, as a great and glorious God (vv. 1–9). 2. Notice given to all people of God's universal rule and judgment, which should be the subject of universal joy (vv. 10–13).

Verses 1–9

The call here to praise God is very strong and lively.

1. We are here required to honour God:

1.1. With songs (vv. 1–2). We are called on three times to *sing unto the Lord*; that is, "*Bless his name* (v. 2), speak well of him, and so, that you may bring others to think well of him too." *Sing a new song* (v. 1), the product of fresh devotion. A new song is a song that is responding to new favors. A new song is a New Testament song, a song of praise for the new covenant and the precious privileges of that covenant. A new song is a song that will always be new. This is a prophecy of the calling of the Gentiles. All the earth will have this *new song put into their mouths* (40:3). Let the subject of this song be *his salvation*, the great salvation which was to be brought by the Lord Jesus.

1.2. With sermons (v. 3): *Declare his glory among the heathen* (nations), even *his wonders among all people*. Salvation by Christ is spoken of here as a miraculous work. This salvation was, in the Old Testament times, as heaven's happiness is now, *a glory to be revealed*.

1.3. With religious services (vv. 7–9). Although in every nation those who feared God and worked righteousness were accepted by him up to that time (Ac 10:35), instituted acts of worship were still exclusive to the Jewish religion. All the earth is called here to tremble before the Lord, to worship him. The acts of devotion to God are described here. We must *give* (ascribe) *unto the Lord* (v. 8). It is what must be paid, and if it is not paid, it will be recovered, but if it comes from holy love, God is pleased to accept it as a gift. We must *give* (ascribe) *unto the Lord the glory due unto his name* (v. 8). We must *bring an offering into his courts* (v. 8). First, we must bring ourselves, the *offering up of the Gentiles* (Ro 15:16); then, we must offer the *sacrifices of praise continually* (Heb 13:15). We must *worship him in the beauty of holiness* (v. 9), with holy hearts, consecrated by the grace of God, devoted to the glory of God. All the acts of worship must be performed with a holy awe and fear.

2. Glorious things are here said about God. *The Lord is great, and* so is *greatly to be praised* (v. 4) and *to be feared*. Even the new song declares God to be great as well as good. He is great in his sovereignty over all who claim to be gods; he is *feared above all gods* (v. 4), *all* rulers, who were often worshiped as gods after their deaths. He is great in his claim of ownership over the creation, even the noblest part of it, for it is his own work and derives its existence from him. *Splendour and majesty are before him*, in his immediate presence above, where the angels cover their faces because they are unable to bear the dazzling brightness of his glory. *Strength and beauty are in his sanctuary*, in both the sanctuary above and this one below. If we serve him in his sanctuary, we will see his beauty, for *God is love* (1Jn 4:8), and we will experience his strength, for *he is our rock*.

Verses 10–13

We have here instructions given to those who were to preach the Gospel to the nations.

1. Let it be told *that the Lord reigns* (v. 10), the Lord Christ reigns, that King whom God determined to install on Zion, his holy hill (2:6). Notice how this was first said *among the heathen* by Peter (Ac 10:42). Some of the old commentators added a gloss to this, which gradually crept into the text, "The Lord reigneth from the tree" (this is how Justin Martyr, Augustine, and others quote it), meaning the cross, when there was written over him the title, *The King of the Jews*.

2. Let it be told that Christ's government will be the world's wonderful destiny. *The world also shall be established, that it shall not be moved* (v. 10). Sin gave it a shock and still threatens it, but Christ, as Redeemer, upholds all things (Heb 1:3) and preserves the course of nature. As far as the Christian religion is embraced, it will establish states and kingdoms and preserve good order among people.

3. Let them be told that Christ's rule will be just and righteous. He himself says, *For judgment have I come into this world* (Jn 9:39; 12:31), and he declares that all judgment was committed to him (Jn 5:22, 27). He will rule in the hearts and consciences of people by the commanding power of truth and the Spirit of righteousness

and sanctification. When Pilate asked our Savior, *Art thou a king?* he answered, *For this cause came I into the world, that I should bear witness to the truth* (Jn 18:37).

4. Let them be told that his coming draws near, that this King, this Judge, stands at the door. Between this and his first coming, many ages intervened, but he came at the appointed time, and his second coming will also be as sure.

5. Let them be called on to rejoice in the Messiah, and in this great trust to be deposited in his hands (vv. 11–12): *Let heaven and earth rejoice, the sea, the field, and all the trees of the wood*. The meaning is:

5.1. That the days of the Messiah will be joyful ones. When Samaria received the Gospel, there was great joy in that city (Ac 8:8), and when the Ethiopian eunuch was baptized, *he went on his way rejoicing* (Ac 8:39).

5.2. That it is the duty of each one of us to welcome Christ and his kingdom, for although he comes conquering and to conquer (Rev 6:2), he still comes in peace.

5.3. That the whole creation will have reason to be full of joy at the setting up of Christ's kingdom, even the sea and the field. There will, in the first place, be *joy in heaven, joy in the presence of the angels of God* (Lk 15:10), but God will graciously accept the holy joy and praises of all those who wish the kingdom of Christ well, even if they are very lowly.

PSALM 97

This psalm is set to the same tune as the previous psalm. Christ is the Alpha and the Omega of both (Rev 1:8). It is he who reigns, to the joy of the whole human race (v. 1), and his government speaks: 1. Terror to his enemies, for he is a ruler of inflexible justice and irresistible power (vv. 2–7). 2. Encouragement to his friends and loyal subjects, arising from his sovereignty, the care he takes of his people, and the provision he makes for them (vv. 8–12).

Verses 1–7

What was to be said among the nations in the previous psalm (96:10) is repeated here (v. 1) and is made the subject of this psalm and of Ps 99. *The Lord reigns* (v. 1); that is the great truth set down here. The Lord Jesus reigns:

1. *Let the earth rejoice* (v. 1), for in so doing it is *established* (96:10). Not only let the people of Israel rejoice in him as King of the Jews, and the daughter of Zion rejoice in him as her King, but let all the earth rejoice. *Let the multitude of isles*, the many distant shores, *be glad thereof* (v. 1). All have reason to be joyful about Christ's government. Sometimes indeed *clouds and darkness are round about him* (v. 2); his ways are completely inexplicable; *his way is in the sea, and his path in the great waters* (77:19). There is a depth in his counsels which we must not claim to fathom. But *righteousness and judgment are* still *the habitation* (foundation) *of his throne* (v. 2); a golden thread of justice runs all through the intricacies of his administration. This is his home, for it is his dwelling place. He rules here, for it is *the habitation* (foundation) *of his throne* (v. 2). *His commandments are*, and will be, *all righteous*. Who can contradict or dispute what *the heavens declare?* (50:6). *All the people see his glory* (v. 6), or may see it. The glory of God, in the face of Christ (2Co 4:6), was made to shine in distant countries. *Worship him, all you gods*. The words in Heb 1:6, "*Let all the angels of God worship him*," are a key to this whole psalm and show us that it must be applied to the exalted Redeemer. All power is given him both in heaven and earth (Mt 28:18),

with *angels, authorities, and powers, being made subject unto him* (1Pe 3:22).

2. Christ's rule, although it might be a matter of joy to all, would still be a matter of terror to some, and it would be their own fault it was so (vv. 3–5, 7). Just as he who reigns, to the *joy of the whole earth* (Ps 48:2), has his subjects, so also he has *his enemies* (v. 3). These enemies are here called *hills* (v. 5), because of their height, strength, and immovable obstinacy. Their persecuting the apostles and *forbidding them to speak to the Gentiles* added to their sin and brought *wrath upon them to the uttermost* (1Th 2:15–16). That wrath is compared here to consuming fire, which will not only burn the rubbish on the hills but even *melt the hills* themselves *like wax* (v. 5). The firmest and most daring opposition will be thwarted *at the presence of the Lord. The earth saw and trembled*, and the ears of all who listened were made to tingle (2Ki 21:12). This was fulfilled in the destruction of Jerusalem and the Jewish nation by the Romans, about forty years after Christ's resurrection, a destruction which, like fire and like lightning, dismayed all their neighbors (Dt 29:24). Idolaters also would be put to shame by the setting up of Christ's kingdom (v. 7): *Confounded be all those who serve graven images*, the Gentile world, who *did service to those that by nature are no gods* (Gal 4:8). This is a prayer for the conversion of the Gentiles, that those who have served mute idols for so long may be convinced of their error and ashamed of their foolishness, and may by the power of Christ's Gospel be brought to serve the only living and true God. It is also a prophecy of the destruction of those who did not want to be reformed or reclaimed from their idolatry. The prophecy was fulfilled in the destruction of paganism in the Roman Empire about 300 years after Christ.

Verses 8–12

Notice here:

1. The reasons given for Zion's joy in the Redeemer's rule. God is glorified, and whatever leads to his honor is his people's pleasure. *Thou, Lord, art high above all the earth* (v. 9). The exaltation of Christ and the advancement of God's glory are the subjects of the joy of all the saints. *He preserves the souls of the saints*, he guards the lives of his faithful ones. He protects their lives as long as he has work for them to do. But something more is meant than their lives, for those who want to be his disciples must be willing to lay down their lives. It is the *immortal soul* that Christ preserves, the inner being, which may be renewed more and more when outwardly we decay (2Co 4:16). *Light is sown for the righteous*, that is, *gladness for the upright in heart*. The subjects of Christ's kingdom are told to expect trouble in the world, but let them know to their comfort that *light is sown* for them. What is sown will sprout again in due time. Like winter seed, it may lie long underground, but it will return in a rich and plentiful crop. Christ told his disciples when he left them (Jn 16:20), *You shall be sorrowful, but your sorrow shall be turned into joy.*

2. The rules given for Zion's joy. Let it be a pure and holy joy. "You who love the Lord Jesus, who long for his coming and his kingdom, who love his word and his exaltation, see that you hate evil." A true love for God will show itself in a real hatred of all sin, as something detestable, something that he hates. Let their joy end in God (v. 12): *Rejoice in the Lord, you righteous.* All the lines of joy must meet in him, the center of everything. See Php 3:3; 4:4. And let their joy express itself in praise

and thanksgiving: *Give thanks at the remembrance of his holiness* (v. 12).

PSALM 98

This psalm is to the same effect as the two previous psalms; it is a prophecy of the kingdom of the Messiah, its being set up in the world and the bringing into it of Gentiles. The Aramaic entitles it "a prophetic psalm." It sets out: 1. The glory of the Redeemer (vv. 1–3). 2. The joy of the redeemed (vv. 4–9).

Verses 1–3

A song of praise for redeeming love is *a new song.* Converts sing *a new song*; they change the focus of their wonder and they change their joy, and so they change their tune. Let this new song be sung to the praise of God in consideration of these four things:

1. The wonders he has done: *He has done marvellous things* (v. 1). The work of our salvation by Christ is a miracle. The more it is known, the more it will be wondered at.

2. The conquests he has won: *His right hand and his holy arm have gotten him the victory* (v. 1). Our Redeemer has overcome all the difficulties that were in the way of our redemption. He gained his victory by his own power.

3. The revelations he has made to the world in the work of redemption. He has revealed to us the work he has done for us, and it is by his Son that he has both worked and revealed; the Gospel revelation is the basis on which the Gospel kingdom is founded—the *word which God sent* (Ac 10:36).

4. The fulfillment of the prophecies and promises of the Old Testament. In sending Christ, God is said to *perform the mercy promised to our fathers, and to remember the holy covenant* (Lk 1:72). It was in consideration of that, and not because of any good in them.

Verses 4–9

The setting up of the kingdom of Christ is represented here as a subject of joy and praise.

1. Let all people rejoice in it, for they all receive, or may receive, benefits from it. Again and again we are called on by every possible means to express our joy in it and give God praise for it. Let sacred songs be sung to the new King. Let their songs be accompanied by sacred music, by the soft and gentle music of *the harp*; but also—since it is a victorious King whose glory is to be celebrated—let him be proclaimed with the martial sound of the *trumpet* and *cornet* (ram's horn) (v. 6).

2. Let the lower creatures rejoice in it (vv. 7–9). This is to the same effect as what we had before, in 96:11–13: *Let the sea roar*, and let it not be called, as it used to be, *a dreadful noise*, but *a joyful noise*, for the coming of Christ and the salvation he brought have totally changed the nature of the troubles and terrors of this world, so that when the seas *lift up their voice, lift up their waves* (93:3), we must consider the sea to be not roaring against us, but rather rejoicing with us. One would have thought that Virgil had these psalms in mind, as well as the oracles of the Cumean Sibyl, in his fourth eclogue. Living in the reign of Augustus Caesar, a little before our Savior's birth, he applies to Asinius Pollio in that eclogue—either through ignorance or evil motives—the ancient prophecies which at that time were expected to be fulfilled; yet he acknowledges that those prophecies looked for the birth of a child

from heaven who would be a great blessing to the world and restore the golden age—"A new race descends from the lofty sky"—and who would take away sin—"Thy influence shall efface every stain of corruption, / And free the world from alarm." He says many other things about this long-looked-for child, which the Spaniard Ludovicus Vives thinks apply to Christ, and he concludes, as the psalmist does here, with a prospect of the rejoicing of the whole creation in this: "See how this promis'd age makes all rejoice." And if all rejoice, why should not we?

PSALM 99

More than the previous psalms, this psalm seems to dwell on the Old Testament dispensation and the revelation of God's glory and grace in that. The promises definitely belonged to Israel, and they were committed to believe them, but the giving of the Law and the temple worship also belonged to them, and they were also committed to dutifully and conscientiously attend to those things (Ro 9:4). And they are called to do this in this psalm, where there is much of Christ, for the rule of the church was in the hands of the eternal Word before his incarnation, and besides, the ceremonial services were types and figures of worship under the Gospel. The people of Israel are required here to praise and exalt God and to worship before him, taking into consideration these two things: 1. The favorable constitution of the government they are under, both in sacred and civil things (vv. 1–5). 2. Some examples of its beneficial administration (vv. 6–9).

Verses 1–5

The foundation of all religion is set down in this truth: *the Lord reigns* (v. 1). God rules the world by his providence, and he rules the church by his grace, and both by his Son. We are to believe not only that *the Lord lives* but also that *the Lord reigns* (v. 1). It is the triumph of the Christian church, and here it was the triumph of the Jewish church, that Jehovah was their King; and so it is reasoned, *Let the people* (nations) *tremble* (v. 1). The Old Testament dispensation contained much terror. But we do not now come to *that mount that burned with fire* (Heb 12:18). Now that *the Lord reigns, let the earth rejoice* (97:1). He ruled then more by the power of holy fear; now he rules by the power of holy love. *The Lord reigns, let the earth be moved* (v. 1). Those who submit to him will be established and not *moved* (96:10), but those who oppose him will be shaken. The kingdom of Christ cannot be shaken; the *things which cannot be shaken shall remain* (Heb 12:27). *In these is continuance* (Isa 64:5). God's kingdom, set up in Israel, is here the subject of the psalmist's praise.

1. The psalmist affirms two things:

1.1. God rules in matters of religion: *He sitteth between the cherubim* (v. 1), to decree law by the oracles given there. This was the honor of Israel, that they had among them the *Shechinah*, or special presence of God. *The Lord is great in Zion* (v. 2). He is known and praised there (76:1–2). *He is high* there *above all people* (v. 2). In Zion the perfect divine nature appears more glorious than anywhere else. And so *let those* who live in Zion and worship there *praise thy great and terrible name* (v. 3), *for it is holy.*

1.2. He is all in all (1Co 15:28) in their civil government (v. 4). As the statute of Israel was in Jerusalem, so also *there were set thrones of judgment* (122:4–5). Their government was a theocracy. God raised up David to rule

over them, and he is *the king* whose *strength loves judgment* (justice) (v. 4). He is strong. He has all his strength from God. The people of Israel had a good king, but they were here taught to look to God as the One by whom their king reigned (compare Pr 8:15): *Thou dost establish equity*—that is, God gave them those excellent laws by which they were governed—and *thou executest judgment and righteousness in Jacob*, in Jacob you have done what is just and right (v. 4).

2. Putting these two things together, we see that the happiness of Israel was far above that of any other people (v. 5): "*Exalt you the Lord our God, and worship at his footstool.* Give him glory for the good rule you are under, as it is now established, both in church and state."

Verses 6–9

The happiness of Israel under God's government is revealed further here by some particular examples of his rule, especially with reference to those people who were the most useful governors of that people—Moses, Aaron, and Samuel. In the first two the theocracy or divine government began, and in the last that form of government ended to a great extent. Notice about these three rulers:

1. The intimate fellowship they had with God. No other nation on earth had three people who had such fellowship with heaven and whom God *knew by name* (Ex 33:17). Although Samuel was not among his priests, he was still *among those that called on his name* (v. 6). *They called upon the Lord* (v. 6), and they were all well known for this. They honored him by their obedience: *They kept his testimonies, and the ordinances that he gave them* (v. 7). They were careful to do their duty. Moses did all according to the pattern shown him (Ex 25:9, 40); it is often repeated, *According to all that God commanded Moses, so did he* (Ex 40:16). Aaron and Samuel did likewise. They were all wonderfully effective with God in prayer; miracles were worked in response to their urgent pleas. He had *communed* with them (Ex 31:18) as one friend talks familiarly with another (Dt 34:10) (v. 7).

2. The good work they did for Israel. They interceded for the people, and they also obtained for them many favorable responses. *Moses stood in the gap* (106:23), and *Aaron between the living and the dead* (Nu 16:48), and when Israel was in distress, Samuel cried to the Lord for them (1Sa 7:9). This is referred to here (v. 8): "*Thou answeredst them, O Lord our God! Thou wast a God that forgavest* the people they prayed for." The people are again called on to praise God (v. 9): "*Exalt the Lord our God*, for what he has done for us in former days as well as recently, *and worship at his holy hill* of Zion."

PSALM 100

It is with good reason that many believers frequently sing this psalm in their meetings. The Jews say it was written to be sung with their thank offerings, but we say that just as there is nothing in it that is exclusive to their way of life, so also, since it begins with a call to all the earth to praise God, it clearly extends to the Gospel church. Here: 1. We are called on to praise God and rejoice in him (vv. 1–2, 4). 2. We are provided with subject matter for praise: his being and his relationship with us (v. 3) and his mercy and truth (v. 5).

Verses 1–5

1. The psalm corresponds to its title, *A psalm of praise.* If we take the previous psalm to be a call to the Jewish

church to rejoice in the constitution of God's kingdom, which they were under—just as the four psalms before it were intended for the days of the Messiah—then this psalm was perhaps intended for converts who came from every nation to the Jews' religion. Here is a strong invitation to worship God. In every act of religious worship, whether in private or with our families, we come into God's presence and serve him, but it is especially in public worship that we *enter into his gates and into his courts*. And we are to *serve* (worship) *the Lord with gladness*. We really do serve God when we have holy joy. Gospel worshipers should be joyful worshipers. We must *come before his presence with singing* (v. 2), not only songs of joy but also songs of praise. *Enter into his gates with thanksgiving* (v. 4). We must take it as a great favor that we are allowed to worship him, and that acts of worship have been instituted and opportunities given for us to wait on God on such occasions.

2. The subject and motives of praise are very important (vv. 3, 5). We are to know what God is in himself and what he is to us. Knowledge deepens devotion and obedience: blind sacrifices never please an all-seeing God. Let us know the following seven things concerning the Lord Jehovah.

2.1. *That the Lord he is God* (v. 3), the only living and true God—that he is a Being who is infinitely perfect, self-existent, and self-sufficient. He is the fountain of all being. He is an eternal Spirit, incomprehensible and independent, the original source and final purpose of everything.

2.2. That he is our Creator: *It is he that has made us, and not we ourselves* (v. 3). He gave us existence. He is the One who both formed our bodies and is the Father of our spirits (Heb 12:9). We did not, and could not, make ourselves.

2.3. That he is therefore our rightful owner. The Masoretes changed one letter in the Hebrew and read it, "He made us, and we are his, or we belong to him." If we put both readings together, we learn that because God *made us, and not we ourselves* (v. 3), we are therefore not our own, but his.

2.4. That he is our sovereign ruler: *We are his people* (v. 3).

2.5. That he is the One who gives generously to us. We are *the sheep of his pasture* (v. 3), whom he takes care of, "the flock of his feeding," as it may be read.

2.6. That he is a God of infinite mercy and goodness (v. 5).

2.7. That he is a God of unbreakable truth and faithfulness (v. 5).

PSALM 101

David certainly was the author of this psalm. It is a solemn vow that he made to God when he took on himself the responsibility of a family and the kingdom. It is not significant whether it was written when he entered on the government immediately after the death of Saul (as some think) or when he began to reign over all Israel and brought the ark into the City of David (as others think). Either way, it is an excellent model for the good government of a palace or the maintenance of morality and respect and, thereby, good order, but it also applies to private families; it is the householder's psalm. Here is: 1. The general scope of David's vow (vv. 1–2). 2. Its details (vv. 3–5, 7–8). He would favor and encourage those who were virtuous (v. 6).

Verses 1–8

David here gives himself and others a model of both a good judge and a good head of a family. Notice:

1. The chosen subject of the psalm (v. 1): *I will sing of mercy and judgment*. Since David was first anointed as king, he had met with many rebukes and much hardship on the one hand, but had been wonderfully rescued many times and had had favors done for him on the other hand. He would sing about these to God. God's providences with his people are usually mixed—*mercy and judgment*, love and justice (v. 1); God has set one over against the other (Ecc 7:14), appointing them to alternate like typical English weather in April: sunshine and showers. Whatever our outward condition, neither the laughter of prosperity nor the tears of suffering must put us off singing sacred songs. Or the phrase may be understood to refer to David's mercy and judgment; in this psalm he would promise to be merciful and just. Family mercies and family suffering are both calls to family faith.

2. The general decision David made to behave thoughtfully in his court (v. 2). We have here:

2.1. A good purpose concerning his way of life. He will live according to rules, particularly in his family. He describes, in particular, how he will *walk within his house* (v. 2), where he is more out of sight of the world, but where he still sees himself under the eye of God. He decides to *walk in a perfect* (blameless) *way* (v. 2), in the path of God's commandments. *I will behave myself wisely* (v. 2).

2.2. A good prayer: *O when wilt thou come unto me?* (v. 2). When a person has a house of their own, it is desirable to have God come to them and live with them in it. As he had decided, David *behaved himself wisely in all his ways; and* (v. 2), as he prayed, *the Lord was with him*.

3. His particular decision to practice no evil himself (v. 3): "*I will set no wicked thing before my eyes*; I will not want or aim at anything except what is for the glory of God and the public good."

4. His further decision not to keep bad servants or to employ around him those who are perverse. He will have nothing to do with spiteful, malicious people, who do not care what trouble they cause to those they quarrel with (v. 4): "*A froward heart*—one that delights in being cross and perverse—*shall depart from me*, as unfit for society, the bond of which is love. *I will not know* such a *wicked person. Whoso privily slanders his neighbour*, either starts or spreads false rumors to harm his neighbor's good name, *him will I cut off* from my family and court." He will also prevent the promotion of those who hope to gain favor with him in this way. "Therefore a person *that has a high look and a proud heart will I not suffer* (I will put to silence) (v. 5); I will have no patience with those who continue to grasp at any promotion they can lay their hands on, for it is certain that they are not aiming to do good, but only to make themselves and their families look great." God resists the proud (Jas 4:6; 1Pe 5:5), and so will David. "*He that worketh deceit*, though he may worm his way into my family, will, as soon as he is discovered, *not dwell within my house*." David will not use such people to act for him.

5. His decision to put honest and good people in positions of trust under him (v. 6): *My eyes shall be upon the faithful in the land*. The kingdom must be searched for honorable people to be made courtiers, and if some are better than others, they must be promoted. Saul chose servants for their *goodliness* (1Sa 8:16), but David for their goodness.

6. His decision to extend his zeal to reform the city and country as well as the court (v. 8). He would be eager and zealous in advancing the reformation of conduct and the suppression of evil. What he aimed at was not only the securing of his own government and the peace of the country but also the honor of God in the purity of his church: *That I may cut off all wicked doers from the city of the Lord* (v. 8).

PSALM 102

Some think that David wrote this psalm at the time of Absalom's rebellion; others think that Nehemiah, Daniel, or another prophet wrote it for the church to use when it was in exile in Babylon. But it is clear, from the application of vv. 25–26 to Christ (Heb 1:10–12), that the psalm refers to the days of the Messiah and speaks either of his affliction or of the afflictions of his church for his sake. In the psalm we have: 1. A sad complaint by the psalmist, either for himself or in the name of the church, concerning great afflictions (v. 1–11). 2. Prompt strength and encouragement from a consideration of the eternity of God (vv. 12, 24, 27) and from a confident prospect of the rescue that God will, in due time, bring about for his afflicted church (vv. 13–22), along with a prospect of the church's continued existence in the world (v. 28).

Title

The title of this psalm is *a prayer of the afflicted.* Here is a prayer put into the hands of the afflicted, yet let them not merely set their hands to it, as if signing a legal document, but apply their hearts to it, and only then present it to God. When our state and our spirits are overwhelmed, it is our duty to *pour out our complaints before the Lord* in prayer (title). The phrase implies that God allows us to be free with him, granting us freedom of speech with him as well as freedom of access to him; it also suggests what a relief it is to an afflicted spirit to unburden itself by humbly presenting its grievances and griefs. The psalmist here unburdens himself in this way.

Verses 1–11

1. He humbly begs God to take notice of his suffering and of his prayer in his suffering (vv. 1–2). Let us *lift up the prayer*, and our souls with it. If we bring *a prayer in faith*, we may in faith say, *Hear my prayer, O Lord!* (v. 1). "Reveal yourself to me; not only hear me but also answer me. Give me the rescue I need and am seeking. Answer me quickly, even *in the day when I call*" (v. 2).

2. He makes a sad complaint about the lowly condition he has been reduced to by his suffering. His body is emaciated. As prosperity and joy are described *by making fat* (giving health to) *the bones* (Pr 15:30), so also great trouble and grief are here described by the opposites: "*My bones are burnt as a hearth* (like glowing embers) (v. 3); they *cleave* (cling) *to my skin* (v. 5); in fact, *my heart is smitten* (blighted), *and withered like grass* (v. 4). I am *withered like grass* (v. 11), scorched by the burning heat of my troubles." He is so taken up with the thoughts of his troubles that he *forgets to eat his bread* (v. 4). He has no appetite. He has withdrawn into himself, as depressed people do. His friends have abandoned him and are reluctant to meet him (vv. 6–7): "*I am like a pelican of the wilderness*, a desert owl or a bittern, which makes a sad noise; *I am like an owl*, which likes to live in deserted, ruined buildings; *I watch, and am as a sparrow upon the house top.* I live in an attic and spend my time poring

over my troubles and groaning to myself." Now that his friends have left him, his enemies set themselves against him (v. 8). When they cannot reach him in any other way, they shoot arrows of *bitter words* at him. He is fasting and weeping under the signs of God's displeasure (vv. 9–10), yet it is not so much the trouble itself that distresses him as the wrath of God that he knows is the cause of the trouble. *My days are consumed like smoke* (v. 3), which vanishes quickly away. They are *like a shadow that declines* (goes down) (v. 11), like the evening shadow. Now all this is properly a prayer for one person who is suffering, yet it is still thought to be a description of the suffering of the church of God, with which the psalmist sympathizes, making public grievances his own.

Verses 12–22

Many very great and precious encouragements here balance out the previous complaints, for *unto the upright there arises light in the darkness* (112:4).

1. We are dying creatures, and our ventures and benefits are dying, but God is always the living and eternal God (v. 11): "*My days are like a shadow*; there is no way out; night is coming on me; but *thou, O Lord, shalt endure for ever*" (v. 12). God *endures for ever* (v. 12); he is his church's faithful protector, and so we may be confident that its interests will not be neglected.

2. Poor Zion is now in distress, but there will come a time when she will be helped (v. 13). The hope of rescue is based on the goodness of God and on the power of God—there is a time set for the church to be rescued. It is the time which infinite Wisdom has appointed, and so it is the best time; it is the time that eternal Truth has established, and so it is a definite time and will not be forgotten or delayed further. Zion was now in ruins, that is, the temple that was built in the City of David: the favoring of Zion is the rebuilding of the temple, as it is explained in v. 16. "*Thy servants take pleasure* even in *the stones* of the temple (its stones were very dear to your servants)—although they have been thrown down and scattered—and *thy servants* regard with *favour* even *the dust*, its very rubbish and ruins." When the temple was ruined, its stones were still to be used in the new building, and there were those who encouraged themselves with that. *The heathen* (nations) *shall fear the name of the Lord*; when God honors his church by his providence, the nations will have better thoughts of it than they had had. They will say, "We will go with you, for we have *seen that God is with you*" (Zec 8:23). *All* that have made his glory their main aim want it and pray for it.

3. The prayers of God's people now seem to be disrespected and ignored, but they will be listened to and greatly encouraged (v. 17): *He will regard* (respond to) *the prayer of the destitute.* They are the *destitute.* The word that is used here is well chosen, for it refers to the heath in the desert, a low shrub or bush, like the hyssop of the wall. God's people are in a low and broken state, rich with spiritual blessings but devoid of physical good things. When we consider our own lowliness, our darkness, our cold deadness, and the many defects in our prayers, we have cause to suspect that our prayers will be received with disdain in heaven, but we are assured here of the opposite, for we have an advocate with the Father (1Jn 2:1) and are written under grace, not under law (Ro 6:14). This *shall be written for the generation to come, that none may despair* even if they are destitute, nor think their prayers are forgotten because they have not received an immediate answer to them. Many who are now unborn will, by

reading the history of the church, praise the Lord for his answers to prayers.

4. The prisoners who are unjustly under condemnation seem to be sheep appointed to be slaughtered, but care will be taken that they will be released (vv. 19–20): God has *looked down from the height of his sanctuary, from heaven,* to act in grace, *to hear the groaning of the prisoners* and *to loose those that are appointed to death.* God takes notice not only of the prayers of his afflicted people, which are the language of grace, but even of their groans, which are the language of nature. An example is Peter (Ac 12:6). If God declares his name by his providences, we must acknowledge them and declare his praise, which should echo his name. God will release his people who have been prisoners and captives in Babylon so *that they may declare his name in Zion,* the place he has chosen to put his name (1Ki 11:36), *and his praise in Jerusalem,* at their return there. They will help draw in others to worship God (v. 22): *When the people of God are gathered together* at Jerusalem—as they were after their return from Babylon—many from the kingdoms joined with them *to serve* (worship) *the Lord.* But also look further, to the conversion of the Gentiles to the Christian faith in the last days. Christ has declared *liberty to the captives* and *the opening of the prison to those that were bound* (Lk 4:18), so that they may declare the name of the Lord in the Gospel church, in which Jews and Gentiles will join together as one.

Verses 23–28

We may notice here:

1. The imminent danger that the Jewish church was in of being completely destroyed by the exile in Babylon (v. 23): *He weakened my strength in the way.* The psalmist speaks about this as in his own person, and it applies very much to common afflictions of individuals of the time. Physical diseases soon *weaken our strength in the way* (v. 23). When we are in midlife, our strength is weakened, and what can we expect but that the *number of our months should be cut off in the midst?* (Job 21:21). It has often been the destiny of those who have used their strength well to have it weakened; it has often been the lot of those whom it is hard to do without to have their lives shortened.

2. A prayer that the church would be sustained (v. 24): "O my God, take me not away in the midst of my days." May this poor church not be cut off until the Messiah comes." This is a prayer for those who are suffering, and we too may pray, as individuals, that God would not *take us away in the midst of our days* (v. 24) but, if it is his will, spare us to do him further service and to be made more fit for heaven.

3. A plea to back up this prayer. The plea is taken from the eternity of the promised Messiah (vv. 25–27). The writer to the Hebrews quotes these verses (Heb 1:10–12). It is a great encouragement, when we consider all the changes that come over the church and all the dangers it is in, that *Jesus Christ is the same yesterday, today, and for ever* (Heb 13:8). *Thy years are throughout all generations* (v. 24) and cannot be shortened. It is also encouraging, when we consider the death of our own bodies and the removal of our friends from us, that God is a God who lives eternally and that, therefore, if he is ours, we may have eternal encouragement in him. Earth and heaven, the universe and its fullness, derive their existence from God by his Son (v. 25): "*Of old hast thou laid the foundation of the earth,* which is established *on the seas* and *on the floods,* and still *it abides*; much more will the church

remain, therefore, since it is *built upon a rock* (Mt 7:24)." God will unmake the world again (vv. 26–27): *They shall perish,* for *thou shalt change them* by the same almighty power that made them, and *thou shalt endure*; *thou art the same.* God and the world, Christ and the creation, are rivals for the inmost and uppermost positions in the immortal human soul.

3.1. A part of the creation is fading and dying: *They shall perish* (v. 26); they will not last as long as we will last. Heaven and earth will *wax* (grow) *old as a garment* (Isa 50:9). *As a vesture shalt thou change them, and they shall be changed* (v. 26), altered, so that they will be *new heavens and a new earth* (Isa 66:22). Notice God's sovereignty over heaven and earth. He can change them as he pleases and when he pleases. The cycles of day and night, summer and winter, are pledges of their final change, when *the heavens* and *time,* which is measured by them, *shall be no more* (Job 14:12).

3.2. An inheritance in God is perpetual and everlasting: *Thou art the same,* subject to no change, and *thy years have no end* (v. 27). Christ will be the same in the fulfillment as he was in the promise, the same to his church in exile as he was to his church at liberty. Let the church not fear that her strength is to be weakened or her days shortened as long as Christ himself is both her strength and her life. He is the same and has said, *Because I live you shall live also* (Jn 14:19).

4. An encouraging assurance of an answer to this prayer (v. 28): *The children of thy servants shall continue*; since Christ is the same, the church will continue from one generation to another. From the eternity of the head we may infer the perpetuity of the body, although it is often weak and ill and even at death's door. Those who hope to *wear out the saints of the Most High* (Da 7:25) will be mistaken.

PSALM 103

This psalm calls more for devotion than for explanation. The psalmist: 1. Motivates himself and his own soul to praise God (vv. 1–2): 1.1. For his favor to him in particular (vv. 3–5), to the church in general, and to all good people, to whom God is and will be just, kind, and faithful (vv. 6–18). 1.2. For his government of the world (v. 19). 2. Requests the help of the holy angels and all the works of God to praise him (vv. 20–22).

Verses 1–5

David *communes with his own heart* (4:4), and it is not foolish to talk to oneself in this way. Notice:

1. How he motivates himself to fulfill the duty of praise (vv. 1–2). It is the Lord who is to be blessed. It is the soul that is to be used in blessing God, *and all that is within* (v. 1) us. The work requires our inner being, the whole person, and even that is little enough.

2. How he provides himself with an abundance of subjects for praise: "Come, my soul, consider what God has done for you.

2.1. "He has pardoned your sins (v. 3); he has forgiven, and *does forgive, all thy iniquities.*" This is mentioned first because it is by the forgiveness of our sins that what kept good things from us is taken away and we are restored to God's favor, which gives good things to us. He is still forgiving, as we are still sinning and repenting.

2.2. "He has cured your sickness." Our crimes were capital offenses, but God saves our lives by forgiving them; our diseases were mortal, but God saves our lives by healing them. These two go together; as for God, his work is perfect (18:30) and is not done incompletely. If God takes away the guilt of sin by forgiving mercy, he will also break its power by renewing grace.

2.3. "He has rescued you from danger." *The redemption of the soul is precious* (49:8); we ourselves cannot achieve our redemption, and so we are all the more indebted to divine grace, which has achieved it, and to the One who has *obtained eternal redemption for us* (Heb 9:12). See also Job 33:24, 28.

2.4. "He has not only saved you from death and ruin but also made you truly and completely happy by giving you honor, pleasure, and long life." *He crowns thee with his loving-kindness and tender mercies*, and what greater position can a poor soul be given than to be advanced into the love and favor of God? "He has given you a prospect and pledge of long life: *Thy youth is renewed like the eagle's*" (v. 5). The eagle lives for a long time, and ornithologists say that when old it casts all its feathers — as in fact it changes them to a great extent every year at molting time — and fresh ones come, so that it becomes young again. When God gives the gracious assurance of his Spirit, he restores his people from decay and fills them with new life and joy, a pledge of eternal life and joy, and then they may be said to *return to the days of their youth* (Job 33:25).

Verses 6–18

1. Truly God is good to all (v. 6): he *executes righteousness and judgment for all that are oppressed*.

2. God is especially good to Israel.

2.1. He has revealed himself and his grace to us (v. 7): *He made known his ways unto Moses*, and by him *his acts to the children of Israel*. Divine revelation is one of the greatest divine favors, for God restores us to himself by revealing himself to us, and gives us all good by giving us knowledge.

2.2. He has never been exacting and severe with us, but always tender, full of compassion, and ready to forgive.

2.2.1. It is his nature to be so (v. 8): *The Lord is merciful and gracious*. He is not easily angered (v. 8). He is *slow to anger*, very patient toward those who are very provoking, and he delays in punishing so that he may give opportunity for people to repent. He does not quickly execute the sentence of his law. Although he shows his displeasure against us for our sins by the rebukes of providence and the reproaches of our own consciences, he will not always keep us in pain and terror; rather, after the spirit of slavery he will give the spirit of adoption (Ro 8:15).

2.2.2. We have found him so. *He has not dealt with us after our sins* (v. 10). He has not inflicted on us the punishment we deserved. *God's patience should lead us to repentance* (Ro 2:4).

2.3. He has forgiven our sins, not only my *iniquity* (v. 3) but also *our transgressions* (v. 12). Notice the riches of God's mercy (v. 11): *As the heaven is high above the earth* — so high that the earth is only a tiny point in such a vast expanse — so God's mercy is far above the goodness of those who fear him most, so far above and beyond them that there is no comparison at all between them. Notice also the fullness of his forgiveness as evidence of the riches of his mercy (v. 12): *As far as the east is from the west, so far has he removed our transgressions from us*, so that we will never be charged with them or condemned for them. If we thoroughly forsake them, God will thoroughly forgive them.

2.4. He has had compassion on our sorrows (vv. 13–14). God is a Father to those who fear him. He acknowledges

them as his children, and he is tender toward them as a father. A father has compassion on his children who are weak in knowledge and teaches them; he has compassion on them when they are self-willed and is patient toward them; he has compassion on them when they are sick and comforts them (Isa 66:13); he has compassion on them when they fall down and he helps them up again; he has compassion on them when they have offended and — when they submit to him — forgives them; he has compassion on them when they are wronged and puts things right for them. These are some of the ways *the Lord pities those that fear him* (v. 13). He knows how we are formed, for he formed us, and having himself made human beings from the dust, *he remembers that we are dust* (v. 14).

2.5. He has made his covenant mercy last forever, and so he has provided relief for our weakness (vv. 15–18). *As for man, his days are as grass* (v. 15), which grows out of the earth, rises only a little way above it, and soon withers. Mortals at best are *like a flower of the field* (v. 15), which, although a little different from the grass, will soon wither with it. Garden flowers are usually of a higher quality and more valuable, and although they too wither, they will last longer because they are sheltered by a garden wall and a gardener's care, but the flowers of the field, to which life is here compared, are not only withering in themselves but also exposed to the cold wind and liable to be eaten and trodden on by the animals of the field. Human life is not only wasting away by itself; its length may be shortened by a thousand accidents. God considers this and has compassion on us; let us consider it ourselves and humble ourselves. Notice how long and lasting is God's mercy to his people (vv. 17–18): it will continue longer than their lives and will survive their present state. Only those who are careful to keep God's precepts will enjoy the benefits of his promises. The continuation of his mercy belongs to such people. It will last longer than their lives on earth, and so they need not be troubled even if their lives are short, since death itself will not cut off or disturb their happiness. God's mercy is better than life (63:3), for it will survive it.

Verses 19–22

Here:

1. The doctrine of universal providence is set down (v. 19). God has secured the happiness of his own people by promise and covenant, but he keeps the whole human race, and the world in general, by common providence. *The Lord has a throne* of his own, a throne of glory, a throne of government. But although God's throne is in heaven, and he keeps his court there, and we are to direct our prayers to him there — *Our Father who art in heaven* (Mt 6:9) — *his kingdom rules over all* (v. 19). He takes notice of all the inhabitants of this lower world and all that is going on in it. *His kingdom rules over all* (v. 19).

2. The duty of universal praise is inferred from this: if everyone is under God's rule, then everyone must praise and worship him.

2.1. Let the holy angels praise him (vv. 20–21). It is not as if they needed any encouragement from us to praise God, for they do so continually; but in this way David expresses his high thoughts of God as worthy of the adoration of the holy angels.

2.2. Let *all his works* praise him (v. 22), that is, let all people in all parts of the world praise God. And yes, even the lower creatures, which are God's works also: let them praise him by fulfilling his purpose for them, even though they cannot praise him as his saints can (145:10). David began with *Bless the Lord, O my soul!* and, when he had written and sung this excellent hymn to his honor, he did not say, "Now, O my soul! You have blessed the Lord, sit down and take a rest," but, *"Bless the Lord, O my soul! still more and more."*

PSALM 104

This psalm was probably written by the same hand, and at the same time, as the previous psalm, for just as that one ended, so this one begins, with Bless the Lord, O my soul, *and concludes with it, too. Yet the style is somewhat different, because the subject is different: the scope of the previous psalm was to celebrate the goodness of God and his tender mercy and compassion, to which a soft and sweet style was most appropriate. The scope of this psalm is to celebrate his greatness, majesty, and sovereignty, which should be done with majestic and lofty poetry. God is praised there as the God of grace, and here as the God of nature. This noble poem is thought by very competent judges to greatly surpass the Greek and Latin poets on any subject of this nature, not only because of its godliness and devotion—that is beyond dispute—but also because of its imaginativeness and all its beautiful expressiveness. The psalmist here gives God the glory for many great things: 1. The splendor of his majesty in the upper world (vv. 1–4). 2. The creation of the sea and the dry land (vv. 5–9). 3. The provision he makes for sustaining all creatures according to their different needs (vv. 10–18 and again vv. 27–28). 4. The regular courses of the sun and moon (vv. 19–24). 5. The furnishing of the sea with all its creatures (vv. 25–26). 6. God's sovereign power over all the creatures (vv. 29–32). 7. He concludes with an agreeable determination to continue to praise God (vv. 33–35).*

Verses 1–9

When we turn to any religious service, we must *stir up ourselves to take hold on God* (Isa 64:7), and this is what David does here.

1. The psalmist looks up to the divine glory shining in the upper world, of which faith is the evidence, although it is one of the things that are unseen (Heb 11:1). Notice the reverence and holy awe that he begins his meditation with: *O Lord my God, thou art very great!* (v. 1). Rulers appear great:

1.1. In their robes, and what are God's robes? *Thou art clothed with honour and majesty* (v. 1). *Thou coverest thyself with light as with a garment* (v. 2). God *dwells in light* (1Ti 6:16) and clothes himself with it.

1.2. In their palaces or pavilions (or canopies), and what is God's palace and his canopy? He *stretches out the heavens like a curtain* (v. 2). He did this at the beginning when he made the *firmament,* whose name in Hebrew comes from its form as an expanse (Ge 1:7). The expanse is stretched out around the earth like a curtain to shade the dazzling light of the upper world, for although God *covers himself with light* (v. 2), out of compassion to us *he makes darkness his pavilion* (canopy) (18:11). *Thick clouds are a covering to him.* The vastness of this canopy may lead us to consider how very great is he who *fills heaven and earth.* Though air and water flow, by divine power they are kept as tightly and as firmly in the places assigned them as rooms are with their beams and rafters. How great is God, whose reception room is built and fixed in this way!

1.3. In their carriages of state, with their stately horses, which add much to the magnificence of their entries, but

God *makes the clouds his chariots* (v. 3). He descended in a cloud as in a chariot to Mount Sinai to give the Law and to Mount Tabor to declare the Gospel (Mt 17:5), and he *walks* at a truly gentle, but stately, pace *upon the wings of the wind.*

1.4. In their retinue or train of attendants; and here also God is very great, for he *makes his angels spirits* and *ministers* to him (v. 4).

2. The psalmist looks down and around to the power of God shining in this lower world.

2.1. He has founded the earth (v. 5). Though he has *hung it upon nothing* (Job 26:7), it is still as immovable as if it had been set on the most solid foundations. Although it has received a dangerous shock by human sin and although the terrible powers of hell strike at it, *it still shall not be removed for ever* (v. 5), that is, not until the end of time, when it must give way to the new earth.

2.2. He has set boundaries for the sea, for that belongs to him too.

2.2.1. He set limits on it when he created it. God said, *Let the waters under the heaven be gathered to one place, and let the dry land appear* (Ge 1:9). This command of God is called here his *rebuke* (v. 7), as if he gave it because he was displeased that the earth was unfit for people to live on. Power accompanied this word, and so it is also called here *the voice of his thunder* (v. 7). *At thy rebuke* (v. 7): as if the waters were made aware that they were out of place, *they fled.* As it is said on another occasion (77:16), *The waters saw thee, O God! the waters saw thee; they were afraid.* It is the same here; God rebuked the waters for the sake of people, to prepare room for them.

2.2.2. He keeps it within limits (v. 9). The waters are forbidden to pass beyond the boundaries set for them; they may not, and so they do not, *turn again to cover the earth.*

Verses 10–18

1. He provides fresh water for all his creatures: *He sends the springs into the valleys* (v. 10). It is God who *sends the springs into the* brooks, *which* flow by easy steps between *the hills* and are filled by the rainwater that descends from them. These *give drink* not only to people and those creatures that are immediately useful to them but also *to every beast of the field* (v. 11), for where God has given life he also provides a livelihood.

2. He provides proper food for them (Pr 30:8), for both humans and animals: *He waters the hills from his chambers* (v. 13), from those chambers spoken of in v. 3, *the beams of which he lays in the waters,* those store chambers, the clouds that distill fruitful showers. It is satisfying to the earth to bear fruit from God's works for the benefit of people, for in so doing it fulfills the purpose of its creation.

2.1. For the cattle there is grass, and the wild animals that do not live on grass feed on those that do. Humans have *herbs* (plants), *wine, and oil, and bread* (v. 15). We must depend on God for all the supports of this life. Let us also consider that we are on the same level as the animals: the same earth, the same plot of ground that gives grass for the cattle, also gives grain for humans.

2.2. In fact, divine Providence not only provides animals with their proper food but also gives plants theirs (v. 16): *The trees of the Lord are full of sap,* not only trees that belong to people, which they take care of in their orchards, parks, and other enclosures, but also God's trees, which grow in the deserts and are taken care of only by his providence. They *are full of sap* and lack no nourishment. Even *the cedars of Lebanon* have enough from the earth.

They are trees *which he has planted* and which he will therefore protect and provide for. We may apply this to the trees of righteousness (Isa 61:3), which are planted by the Lord in his vineyard. These *are full of sap*, for God waters what he plants, and those that *are planted in the house of the Lord shall flourish in the courts of our God* (92:13).

3. He takes care that they will have suitable homes to live in. God has given human beings wisdom to build for themselves and the cattle that are useful to them, but there are some creatures which God provides more immediate homes for:

3.1. The birds. Some birds instinctively make their nests in the bushes near rivers (v. 12): *By the springs* that *run among the hills* some of the *fowls of heaven have their habitation* (dwelling place), *which sing among the branches*. They sing according to their ability to the honor of their Creator and benefactor, and their singing may shame our silence. Our *heavenly Father feeds them* (Mt 6:26). Those that fly high in the sky will not lack resting places. *The stork* is mentioned particularly; *the fir* (pine) *trees* (v. 17), which are very high, *are her house* (v. 17).

3.2. The smaller kinds of animals (v. 18): *The wild goats* are instinctively guided to *the high hills*, which are a refuge for them. *The conies* (the hyraxes or rock badgers), which are also helpless animals, find shelter in *the rocks*, where they can defy the wild animals. If God provides like this for the lower creatures, will he not himself much more be a refuge and dwelling place for his own people?

Verses 19–30

We are taught here to praise and exalt God:

1. For the constant cycles and succession of day and night, and the power of the sun and moon over them. The nations worshiped the sun and moon as gods. Scripture therefore uses every occasion to show that the gods they worshiped are the creatures and servants of the true God (v. 19).

1.1. The shadows of the evening are the friends of the rest of the night (v. 20): *Thou makest darkness and it is night*, which, although black, contributes to the beauty of nature and is a contrast to daylight. Under the protection of the night *all the beasts of the forest creep forth* (prowl around) to feed, which they are afraid of doing in the day.

1.2. The light of the morning is the friend of the business of the day (vv. 22–23): *The sun arises*—just as he *knows his going down*, so also, thank God, he knows the time of sunrise—and then the wild animals go to their rest. The wild animals prowl around with terror, but people go out boldly, as those who have authority.

2. For the restocking of the ocean (vv. 25–26): *As the earth is full of God's riches, so is this great and wide sea.* It seems a useless part of the world, or at least seems not to warrant the space it occupies, yet God has appointed it to its place and made it useful to humans both for navigation and as his storehouse for fish. God did not make the sea in vain, any more than he did the earth.

3. For the prompt and plentiful provision made for all creatures (vv. 27–28). God gives generously to them: he *gives them their meat* (food); he *opens his hand and they are filled with good*. Even the lowliest creatures are not beneath his notice. They *all wait upon him* (145:15). They seek their food according to the natural instincts God has put into them and at the proper time for it.

4. For the absolute power and sovereignty he has over all creatures, by which every species is still maintained, although individual creatures in each species are dying and decaying daily. *Thou takest away their breath*, which is in

your hand, and then, and not till then, *they die and return to their dust* (v. 29), going back to their origins. The *spirit of the beast, which goes downward*, is at God's command, as well as *the spirit of a man, which goes upward* (Ecc 3:21). Although one generation passes away, another generation comes, and they are created new from time to time. New creatures rise up in place of the old ones, and this is a continual creation. And so the *face of the earth is renewed* from day to day by the light of the sun, which makes it beautifully new every morning, and from year to year by its produce, which enriches it afresh every spring and makes the land look completely different than it looked all winter.

5. In the middle of this speech, the psalmist breaks out into wonder at the works of God (v. 24): *O Lord, how manifold are thy works! In wisdom hast thou made them all.*

Verses 31–35

The psalmist concludes this meditation by expressing:

1. Praise to God: *The glory of the Lord shall endure for ever* (v. 31). It will endure to the end of time in his works of creation and providence; it will endure to eternity in the happiness and adoration of saints and angels. Human glory is fading; God's glory is eternal. *The Lord shall rejoice in his works* (v. 31). We often do things that, when we review them, we find we cannot rejoice in, but are displeased with and wish we could undo. But God always *rejoices in his works* (v. 31), because they are all done in wisdom. He is to be praised as a God of almighty power (v. 32): *He looks on the earth, and it trembles*, unable to bear his frowns; it trembles, as Sinai did, *at the presence of the Lord. He touches the hills, and they smoke.* The volcanoes, or burning mountains, such as Mount Etna, are signs of the power of God's wrath, directed toward proud, unhumbled sinners. *Who knows the power of his anger?* (90:11). Who dares to defy God? Because we have our existence from God and depend on him to support and continue our lives as long as we live, we must continue to praise God, and when we have no life or existence on earth, we hope to have a better life and existence in a better world and there be doing this work in a better way and in better company.

2. Joy to himself (v. 34): *My meditation of him shall be sweet*; it will be single-minded and attentive; it will be loving and persuasive, and so it will be sweet. "*I will be glad in the Lord*; it will be a delight for me to praise him. I will be glad to have every opportunity to make known his glory. I will *rejoice in the Lord always*, and only in him."

3. Terror to evildoers (v. 35): *Let the sinners be consumed out of the earth; and let the wicked be no more.* None can prosper who harden themselves against almighty God. "When *the wicked are no more* (v. 35), I hope to be praising God in the world without end (Eph 3:21), and so, *Praise you the Lord* (v. 35); let everyone around me join me in praising God. *Hallelujah*, sing praise to Jehovah." This is the first time that we meet with *Hallelujah*.

PSALM 105

This is a long psalm; its general scope is the same as that of most of the psalms, to make known the glory of God, but the subject matter is individual. Every time we come to the throne of grace we may, if we so please, provide ourselves with new songs from the word of God. In the previous psalm we are taught to praise God for his wonderful works of common providence with reference to the world in general. Here we are directed to praise him for his special favors to his church. We find in vv. 1–11 the beginning of the psalm which David committed to Asaph (1Ch 16:8–18) to be used, so it seems, in the daily service of the sanctuary when the ark was settled in the place he had prepared for it (1Ch 16:7–36). David intended it to be used in teaching his people the obligations they were under to be loyal and faithful to their holy faith. After an introduction (vv. 1–7) he sets forth the history itself in several sections: 1. God's covenant with the patriarchs (vv. 8–11). 2. His care of them while they were strangers (vv. 12–15). 3. His raising up Joseph to be the shepherd and rock of Israel (vv. 16–22). 4. The growth of Israel in Egypt and their rescue from Egypt (vv. 23–38). 5. The care he took of them in the desert and their settlement in Canaan (vv. 39–45).

Verses 1–7

Our devotion is here warmly stirred, and we are encouraged to praise God so that we may encourage ourselves to do so. Notice:

1. Our duty to give God the glory due to his name.

1.1. *Give thanks to him* (v. 1), as One who has always given to us generously.

1.2. *Call upon his name* (v. 1), as One on whom you depend for further favors. Praying for further mercies is an acknowledgment of former mercies.

1.3. *Make known his deeds* (v. 1) so that others may join with you in praising him. *Talk of all his wondrous works* (v. 2), as we talk about things that we are full of. We should talk about them *as we sit in the house and as we go by the way* (Dt 6:7).

1.4. *Sing psalms* (praise) *to* (v. 2) God's honor, as those who rejoice in him and want to testify about that joy and to pass it on to future generations, just as memorable things were formerly handed down in songs, when writing was rarely used.

1.5. *Glory in his holy name* (v. 3), boasting not about your own achievements but that you know God and are in a close relationship with him (Jer 9:23–24).

1.6. *Seek him*; put your happiness in him, and then pursue that happiness. *Seek his strength*, that is, his grace, the power of his Spirit to work in you what is good, which we cannot do except by the strength that comes from him. "*Seek his face evermore* (v. 4). Seek it while you live in this world, and then you will have it when you live in the next world, and even there you will be forever seeking it in infinite progression, and yet will always be satisfied by it."

1.7. *Let the hearts of those rejoice that do seek him* (v. 3), for they have chosen well. If those who *seek the Lord* have reason to rejoice, then much more have those who have *found him.*

2. Some arguments to encourage us to do these duties:

2.1. "Consider what he has said and also what he has done to commit us forever to him. Remember the miracles of his providence which he has *wrought for you* and the people who have gone before you; and remember the wonders of his law, which he has written to you and entrusted you with—*the judgments of his mouth* as well as the judgments of his hand" (v. 5).

2.2. "Consider the relationship you stand in with him (v. 6): *You are the seed of Abraham his servant; the children of Jacob his chosen, chosen* and *beloved* for the ancestors' sake and therefore obligated to follow in the steps of those whose honors you inherit. You are the children of godly parents; do not become corrupt. You are God's church on earth, and if you do not praise him, then who will?"

Verses 8–24

We are taught here that in praising God we must look back a long way, giving him the glory for what he did for his church in former ages, especially when it was being founded and formed. The accounts in the Gospels and the Acts of the Apostles, which tell of the birth of the Christian church, are also proper subjects for our praise; the psalmist here uses the stories in Genesis and Exodus, which tell of the birth of the Jewish church. He praises God for:

1. His promise to the patriarchs, that he would give to their descendants the land of Canaan as an inheritance. This was a type of the promise of eternal life made to all believers in Christ. In all the marvelous works God did for Israel *he remembered his covenant* (v. 8), and he will remember it *for ever*. In the parallel reference it is expressed as our duty (1Ch 16:15): *Be you mindful always of his covenant.* The promise is here called *a covenant* because there was something required on the part of the people as the condition of the promise. Notice to whom God *swore by himself* (Heb 6:13–14). Here is the covenant itself: *Unto thee will I give the land of Canaan* (v. 11). The patriarchs had a right to it not by providence but by promise, and their descendants would be given possession of it as *the lot of their inheritance*, an entitlement that was guaranteed because of their birth. It would come to them by the favor of God, not because of any goodness in them. Heaven is the inheritance we have obtained (Eph 1:11). And *this is the promise which God has promised us*—as Canaan was the promise he promised them—*even eternal life* (1Jn 2:25; Tit 1:2).

2. His providences for the patriarchs while they were waiting for the fulfillment of this promise, which show us the care God takes of his people in this world, while they are still on this side of the heavenly Canaan, for these things happened to them as examples (1Co 10:11) and encouragements to all the heirs of promise (Heb 6:17), who live by faith as they did (Hab 2:4; Heb 10:38).

2.1. They were wonderfully protected and sheltered, and, as the Jewish authorities express it, gathered under the wings of the divine Majesty. This is elaborated on in vv. 12–15. Here we may notice that they were exposed to injustice from human beings. God's promises to the three renowned patriarchs, Abraham, and Isaac, and Jacob, were very rich; again and again he told them he would be their God. But his acts for them in this world were few. Yet even in this world he did not desert them; but so that he might appear on their behalf and be seen doing extraordinary things for them, he troubled them with extraordinary difficulties.

2.1.1. They were very few in number. Abraham was the only one called (Isa 51:2).

2.1.2. They were strangers, and so were very likely to be mistreated. Their religious faith caused them to be looked on as strangers (1Pe 4:4) and attacked like speckled birds (Jer 12:9).

2.1.3. They were unsettled (v. 13): they went from one nation to another, from one part of the land to another; in fact, they went *from one kingdom to another people*, from Canaan to Egypt and from Egypt to the land of the Philistines, forced to do so by famine. They were guarded by the special providence of God (vv. 14–15).

2.1.4. They were not able to help themselves, but no one was allowed to oppress them; even those who hated them had their hands tied and could not do what they wanted. This may refer to Ge 35:5, where we find that the terror of God was on the cities around them, so that although those cities wanted to attack, they did not pursue the children of Jacob.

2.1.5. Even crowned heads who wanted to oppress them were controlled and thwarted: *he reproved kings for their sakes* in dreams and visions, saying, *"Touch not my anointed*; do not harm my prophets." For doing wrong to Abraham, Pharaoh king of Egypt was plagued (Ge 12:17) and Abimelech king of Gerar was sharply rebuked (Ge 20:6).

2.2. They were wonderfully provided for and supplied. To test the patriarchs' faith God cut off all their supplies even in that good land, but even then he graciously provided for them. It was in obedience to his decree and in dependence on his promise that they now lived in Canaan, and so he could not in honor allow that they should lack any good thing (34:10). As he restrained one Pharaoh from harming them, so also he raised up another to do them a kindness, by promoting and entrusting Joseph, of whose story we here have a summary. Many years before the famine began he was sent before them so that he would be able to feed them in the famine. He did not even go as an agent or a delegate, but *was sold* there as *a servant*, a slave for life, without any prospect of ever being set free. But he was brought even lower; he was made a prisoner (v. 18): *His feet they hurt with fetters.* He was unjustly charged with raping his mistress, and "the iron entered into his soul" (v. 18 in the Vulgate), that is, it was very painful to him, but all this was the way to his promotion. He continued to be a prisoner, but was neither put on trial nor given bail *until the time* appointed by God for his release (v. 19), when *his word came*, that is, when his interpretations of dreams came true. The report of it came to Pharaoh's ears through the chief cupbearer, and then *the word of the Lord cleared him*, that is, the power God gave him to foretell things took away the shame his mistress had loaded on him, for it could not be thought that God would give such a power to such a bad person as he was said to be. *God's word tried him*, tested his faith and patience, and then it powerfully came to command his release. There is a set time when God's word will come to encourage and strengthen all who trust in it (Hab 2:3). *At the end it shall speak, and not lie.* God gave the word, and then *the king sent and loosed* (released) *him* (v. 20). When Pharaoh found him to be a favorite of heaven, he *let him go free*. He advanced him to the highest position of honor (vv. 21–22), lord high chamberlain of his household and prime minister of state. In all this Joseph was intended to save the house of Israel from perishing by the famine. Because Joseph was sent on ahead in this way and put into the position of maintaining all his father's house, *Israel also came into Egypt* (v. 23), where he and all his family were comfortably provided for during the course of many years.

2.3. They multiplied wonderfully, according to the promise made to Abraham that his descendants would be as many as the grains of sand on the seashore (v. 24; Ge 22:17).

Verses 25–45

After the history of the patriarchs comes the history of the people of Israel, of their growth into a nation. We read here of:

1. Their suffering in Egypt (v. 25): *He* turned the *heart* of the Egyptians, who had protected them, *to hate* them and *deal subtilly* (craftily) with them. God's goodness to his people angered the Egyptians against them. They *dealt subtilly* with them, finding ways and means of weakening them and preventing them from growing. They made their burdens heavy and their lives bitter and killed their male children as soon as they were born.

2. Their rescue from Egypt, which is included in the introduction to the Ten Commandments, so that it might never be forgotten. Notice:

2.1. The instruments used in that rescue (v. 26): *He sent Moses his servant* on this mission and commissioned Aaron with him. Moses was intended to be their lawgiver and chief judge, Aaron to be their chief priest.

2.2. The method of bringing about that rescue: the plagues of Egypt (v. 27). "They showed the words of his signs" is how the original reads, for every plague has an explanation along with it. The plagues spoke out loud. All or most of them are mentioned here, although not in the order in which they were inflicted:

2.2.1. The plague of darkness (v. 28). This was one of the last, although it is mentioned first here. The old translation reads, "They were not obedient to his word," which may be applied to Pharaoh and the Egyptians, who *would not let the people go* despite the terror of this plague.

2.2.2. The turning of the Nile River, which they idolized, *into blood*, which *slew* (killed) *their fish* (v. 29) (Nu 11:5).

2.2.3. The frogs, of which their land produced a great multitude.

2.2.4. Swarms of flies that came in the air, and lice in their clothes (v. 31; Ex 8:17, 24).

2.2.5. Hailstones that struck their trees, even the strongest timber trees in *their coasts*, and killed their vines and other fruit trees (vv. 32–33).

2.2.6. *Locusts and caterpillars* that destroyed *all the people's vegetation* and ate the bread before it could reach their mouths (vv. 34–35).

2.2.7. Having mentioned all except the plague on the animals and the plague of boils, he concludes with what was the final stroke, and that was the death of *the firstborn* (v. 36).

2.3. The mercies that accompanied this rescue. They had been made poor, but they came out rich and wealthy. God not only brought them out but *brought them forth with silver and gold* (v. 37). Their lives had become bitter, and their bodies and spirits been broken by their slavery, but when God brought them out, *there was not one feeble person*, no one who was sick, no one who faltered, *among their tribes* (v. 37). They had been trampled on and triumphed over, but they were brought out with honor (v. 38). They had spent their days in sorrow and sighing because of their slavery, but now he brought them out *with joy and gladness* (v. 43; Isa 35:10).

2.4. The special care God took of them in the desert. He *spread a cloud for a covering* (v. 39), which was not only a screen and umbrella for them but also a stately robe. A cloud was often God's canopy (18:11), and now it was Israel's. He appointed a pillar of *fire to give light in the night* (v. 39). He fed them with both what they needed and what they enjoyed. *He opened the rock, and the waters gushed out* (v. 41).

2.5. Their eventual entry into Canaan (v. 44): *He gave them the lands of the heathen* (nations).

2.6. The reasons why God did all this for them.

2.6.1. He himself wanted to fulfill the promises of the word (v. 42). *Because he remembered the word of his holiness* (that is, his covenant) *with Abraham his servant*, he would not allow one jot or tittle of that to fall empty to the ground (Mt 5:18; 1Sa 3:19). See also Dt 7:8.

2.6.2. He wanted them to fulfill the commands of the word; to commit them to those commands was the greatest kindness he could ever give them. Because God had done them so much good, they could more cheerfully receive his law, realizing that it was intended for their good. He wanted them to be thankful to him and aware of their obligations and therefore to lead lives of obedience to him. The reason we are made, sustained, and redeemed is so that we may live in obedience to the will of God. The *Hallelujah* with which the psalm ends may be taken as a thankful acknowledgment of God's favors.

PSALM 106

We must give glory to God by confessing not only his goodness but also our own badness. The previous psalm was a history of God's goodness to Israel; this psalm is a history of their rebellions and offenses; but it begins and ends with Hallelujah, for even sorrow for sin must not put us out of tune to praise God. In this psalm we have: 1. The introduction to the narrative, giving honor to God (vv. 1–2) and encouragement to the saints (v. 3) and expressing the desire of the faithful toward God's favor (vv. 4–5). 2. The narrative itself of the sins of Israel, emphasized by the great things God did for them, a record of which is interwoven into the general account: their offenses at the Red Sea (vv. 6–12) and their cravings (vv. 13–15), mutinies (vv. 16–18), worshiping of the golden calf (vv. 19–23), grumbling (vv. 24–27), joining themselves to Baal of Peor (vv. 28–31), quarreling with Moses (vv. 32–33), and collaborating with the nations of Canaan (vv. 34–39). To this is added an account of how God rebuked them for their sins but saved them from ruin (vv. 40–46). 3. The conclusion of the psalm with prayer and praise (vv. 47–48).

Verses 1–5

We are here taught to:

1. Bless God (vv. 1–2), give him thanks for his goodness and give him the glory for his greatness, his *mighty acts.* When we have said all we possibly can about the mighty acts of the Lord, not even a small part has been told.

2. Bless the people of God and count them happy (v. 3). God's people are those whose motives are sound: *They keep judgment,* they *do righteousness,* they do what is right and are just to God and to everyone. They are faithful and constant in practicing these.

3. Bless ourselves by asking God's favor, put our happiness in it, and seek it accordingly with all seriousness. Just as there is a people in the world that is especially God's people, so also there is a special favor which God shows to that people, which all gracious souls want to share in: *"O visit me with thy salvation* (v. 4), come to my aid when you save. Let that salvation be my portion forever (73:26), so *that I may see the good of thy chosen* (v. 5) and be as happy as the saints are. I will then not want to be any happier."

Verses 6–12

Here begins a penitential confession of sin, which was especially timely now that the church was suffering distress. This is how we must vindicate God in everything he brings on us, acknowledging that he has done right because *we have done wickedly* (v. 6).

1. God's afflicted people acknowledge themselves guilty before God (v. 6): *"We have sinned with our fathers. We have committed iniquity,* what is sinful in itself, and we have sinned boldly and presumptuously."

2. They mourn the sins their ancestors committed when they were first formed into a people.

2.1. The foolish ignorance of Israel in the midst of the favors God showed them (v. 7): *They understood not thy wonders in Egypt.* They thought the plagues of Egypt were intended to rescue them, whereas they were intended also to teach and convict them, not only to force them out of their Egyptian slavery but also to heal them of their inclination to follow the Egyptian idols. We lose the benefit of providences because we do not understand them. And just as their understanding was dull, so also their memories were treacherous. *They remembered not the multitude of* God's *mercies* (v. 7) in them.

2.2. Their perversity arising from this ignorance: *They provoked him at the sea, even at the Red Sea* (v. 7). Their offense was that they despaired of being rescued; they even wished they had been left in Egypt (Ex 14:11–12). They rebelled against him, as if all that power had no mercy in it and he had brought them out of Egypt deliberately to *kill them in the wilderness* (Dt 9:28).

2.3. The great salvation God worked for them despite their offenses (vv. 8–11). He forced a passage for them through the sea. He intervened between them and their pursuers and prevented their pursuers from cutting them off as they intended. The Red Sea, which was to them a path, became a grave to the Egyptians (v. 11) (Ex 14:30). Although they did not deserve this favor, he intended it, and the fact that they did not deserve it would not change his intention or make him withdraw his promise or fail to fulfill it. Moses prays (Nu 14:17, 19), *Let the power of my Lord be great and pardon the iniquity of this people.* The power of the God of grace in forgiving sin and sparing sinners is as much to be wondered at as the power of the God of nature in separating the waters.

2.4. The good effects this had on them at that time (v. 12): *Then believed they his words* and acknowledged that God was truly with them and that he had brought them out of Egypt in his mercy, and not with any intention of killing them in the desert. *They sang his praise* (v. 12) in that song of Moses written on this great occasion (Ex 15:1–18).

Verses 13–33

This is a shortened history of Israel's rebellions in the desert, and this shorter version is shortened even further by the apostle Paul with application to us Christians (1Co 10:5).

1. The cause of their sin was disregard for the works and word of God (v. 13).

1.1. They ignored what he had done for them: *They soon forgot his works.* "They made haste": their expectations ran before God's promises; they expected to be in Canaan soon, and because they were not, they questioned whether they would ever reach them. Again (vv. 21–22): *They forgot God their Saviour.* Those who forget the works of God forget God himself, who makes himself known by his works.

1.2. They ignored what God had said to them, and they would not depend on it: *They waited not for his counsel* (v. 13). They did not have the patience to wait for God's time. The difficulties were looked on as insuperable.

2. Many of their sins are mentioned here, together with the signs of God's displeasure which they came under for those sins.

2.1. They wanted to have meat to eat but would not believe God could give it to them (v. 14). They were probably within a step of Canaan but did not have the patience to wait until they got there for delicacies. How did God show his displeasure against them for this? We are told how (v. 15): *He gave them their request,* but he gave it to them in anger and with a curse, for he *sent leanness into their soul;* he filled them with uneasiness of mind, terror of conscience, and self-reproach. Or perhaps this stands for that great plague the Lord struck them with *while the flesh was yet between their teeth*, as we read in Nu 11:33.

2.2. They quarreled with the leadership God had set over them both in church and in state (v. 16): *They envied Moses* his authority *in the camp* as supreme commander and chief justice; they envied *Aaron* his power as *saint of the Lord*, consecrated to the office of high priest. Korah wanted the position of chief priest, while Dathan and Abiram, as leaders of the tribe of Reuben, Jacob's eldest son, wanted to be chief judges. How did God show his displeasure for this? We are told how (vv. 17–18); we have the story in Nu 16:32, 35. Those who defied the face of civil authority were punished by *the earth*, which *opened and swallowed* them up. Those who wanted to usurp the ecclesiastical authority in things relating to God suffered the vengeance of heaven, and those who claimed it was their job to sacrifice were themselves sacrificed to divine justice.

2.3. They made and worshiped the golden calf, doing this in Horeb, where the Law had been given and where God had explicitly said, *Thou shalt neither make any graven image nor bow down* to it (Ex 20:4–5); they did both: *They made a calf and worshipped it* (v. 19).

2.3.1. Here they showed great disrespect for the two great lights (Ge 1:16) God has made to rule the moral world:

- The light of human reason, for they *changed their Glory* (v. 20; Ro 1:23), their God, into the likeness of Apis, one of the Egyptian idols, a bull that eats grass. Nothing could be more grossly and scandalously absurd.
- The light of divine revelation, which was shown them not only in the words God spoke to them but also in the works he did for them (vv. 21–22).

2.3.2. For these reasons, God showed his displeasure by declaring the decree that he would cut them off from being a people, just as they, as far as lay in their power, had in effect cut him off from being a God. He spoke about destroying them (v. 23), and he certainly would have done so if Moses, his chosen one, had not stood before him in the breach (v. 23). Notice the power of prayer and the privileges God's chosen ones have in heaven. Notice a type of Christ, God's chosen One, his elect, in whom his soul delights (Isa 42:1), who stood before him in the breach to turn away his wrath from a sinful world and who always lives to make intercession for this purpose (Heb 7:25).

2.4. They believed the report of the faithless spies about the land of Canaan, in contradiction to the promise of God (v. 24), and therefore wanted to choose a leader and return to Egypt, wickedly accusing God of intending to bring them there so they might be taken as prey by the Canaanites (Nu 14:2–3). And when they were reminded of God's power and promises, they were so far from obeying the voice of the Lord that they tried to stone those who spoke to them (Nu 14:10). This also was displeasing to God, and so he swore in his wrath that they would not enter his rest (95:11; Nu 14:28), and he threatened that their children also would be *overthrown and scattered* (vv. 26–27), and the whole nation dispersed, but Moses prevailed in his prayer for mercy for their descendants, that they might enter Canaan.

2.5. They were guilty of a great sin with Baal of Peor. This was the sin of the new generation, when they were within a step of Canaan (v. 28): *They joined themselves to Baal-peor*, and so got caught up in both idolatry and adultery, in physical and spiritual unfaithfulness (Nu 25:1–3). Those who had often shared at the altar of the living God now *ate the sacrifices of the dead* from the idols of Moab, which were dead idols, or dead people canonized or deified, or sacrifices to the devilish idols on behalf of their dead friends. They provoked God to anger by these evil deeds (v. 29). In a short time a plague among them swept away 24,000 of those arrogant sinners. God stirred up Phinehas to use his power as a judge to suppress the sin and restrain its contagion. In his zeal for the Lord Almighty, he *stood up and executed judgment* on Zimri and Cozbi, a service that so pleased God that the plague was then stopped (v. 30). Because Phinehas here distinguished himself, a special mark of honor was put on him, for what he did was credited to him as righteousness for all generations (v. 31; see also Ge 15:6).

2.6. Their continued grumbling to the very end of their wanderings, for in the fortieth year they angered God at the waters of Meribah (v. 32); this verse refers to the story in Nu 20:3–5. Things now went badly with Moses for their sakes, for although he was the most humble person on earth (Nu 12:3), their clamor at that time was so perverse and provocative that they made him lose his temper, and having now grown very old and off his guard, he spoke rashly (v. 33), for he said in anger, *Hear now, you rebels, must we fetch water out of this rock for you?* (Nu 20:10). God showed his displeasure against the people's sin by excluding Moses and Aaron from Canaan for their misbehavior on this occasion. If he deals so severely with Moses for one rash word, what is deserved by those who have spoken many presumptuous, evil words? God deprived them of the blessing of Moses' guidance and leadership at a time when they needed it most, so that his death was more a punishment to them than to him.

Verses 34–48

Here:

1. The narrative concludes with an account of Israel's behavior in Canaan, which was similar to that in the desert, and of God's dealings with them, in which, as all along, both justice and mercy appeared.

1.1. They provoked God very much. By the time they had just settled in Canaan they became corrupt and abandoned God. They spared the nations which God had condemned to destruction (v. 34), promising themselves that they would not join in any dangerous relationships with them. The next news we hear is that they *mingled among the heathen* (nations) (vv. 34–35), made alliances with them and contracted intimate relationships with them, so that they *learned their works* (v. 35). They never thought they would join in their worship, but they gradually adopted this too (v. 36). That sin led to many more and brought God's judgment on them. When they joined them in some of their idolatrous services, they little thought they would ever be guilty of that cruel and inhuman act of idolatry, the sacrificing of their living children to the dead gods of the nations, but they finally came to that (vv. 37–38). *They sacrificed their sons and daughters*, parts of their very selves, to demons, adding the most unnatural murder to their idolatry. They *shed innocent blood*, the most innocent, for it was the blood of infants—even the *blood of their sons and daughters*. Their sin was, in part, their own punishment, for by it they wronged both their country—*the land was polluted with* (desecrated by their) *blood* (v. 38)—and their consciences—*they went a whoring with their own inventions*, prostituted themselves with their own deeds (v. 39), and so polluted their own minds and were made repugnant in the sight of the holy God.

1.2. God brought his judgments on them, and what else could be expected?

1.2.1. He was angry with them, for he regarded their sins as more ungrateful from them than from the nations that never knew him. *He abhorred his own inheritance.* The worst thing about sin is that it makes us detestable to God, and the closer anyone professes to be to God, the more detestable it is if they rebel against him; he regards them as we regard a pile of garbage outside our front door.

1.2.2. Their enemies then fell on them, and because their defense had departed, their enemies destroyed them easily (vv. 41–42): *He gave them into the hands of the heathen* (nations). The punishment corresponded to their sin. They *mingled with the heathen and learned their works,* they mingled with the nations and adopted their customs (v. 35); and so God justly used the nations as instruments to discipline them. The nations hated them. Those who have turned their backs on God forfeit all the loving deeds on God's side and gain none on Satan's, and when those who *hated* Israel *ruled over them* (v. 41), it is no wonder that they oppressed them.

1.2.3. When God gave them some help, they still continued in their sins, and their troubles also continued (v. 43). This refers to the days of the judges, when God often raised up deliverers and rescued them but they relapsed into idolatry. Those who will not humble themselves in repentance are justly corrupted.

1.2.4. Eventually they cried out to God, and God responded in favor to them (vv. 44–46). They were disciplined for their sins, but not destroyed; they were downcast, but not rejected. God *heard their cry* with tender compassion (v. 44; compare Ex 3:7) and overlooked their offenses. Although he is not *a man that he should repent* (1Sa 15:29), so as to change his mind, he is still a gracious God, who pities us and changes his ways. Bad as they were, he would not break faith with them, because he would not break his own promises. He not only restrained the remainder of their enemies' wrath (76:10) but also put compassion into even such stony hearts as theirs and made them relent, which was more than any human being could have done.

2. The psalm concludes with prayer and praise:

2.1. Prayer at the completion of his people's rescue. Probably many who were forced into foreign countries at the times of the judges—as Naomi was (Ru 1:1)—had not returned at the beginning of David's reign, and so it was timely to pray, "Lord, gather the dispersed Israelites *from among the heathen* (nations), *to give thanks to thy holy name*" (v. 47), in the Lord's house, from which they were now exiled.

2.2. Praise for its beginning and progress (v. 48): *Blessed be the Lord God of Israel from everlasting to everlasting.* Let the priests say this, and then *let all the people say, Amen, Praise the Lord.*

PSALM 107

The psalmist here notices some examples of God's providential care of people in general, especially when they are in distress, for he is the God of the whole earth and a Father to the whole human race. There were still those who did not belong to the citizenship of Israel but who

worshiped the true God (Eph 2:12, 13), and even those who worshiped idols had some knowledge of a Supreme Being, to whom they looked above all their false gods when they were in great need. God took particular care of such people when they prayed in their distress. 1. The psalmist specifies some of the most common adversities of human life and shows how God, in answer to their prayers, helps those who suffer in them: 1.1. Exile and dispersion (vv. 2–9). 1.2. Captivity and imprisonment (vv. 10–16). 1.3. Sickness and physical illness (vv. 17–22). 1.4. Danger and distress at sea (vv. 23–32). 2. He mentions events in nations and families, in which God's hand is to be seen by his own people with a joyful acknowledgment of his goodness (vv. 33–43).*

Verses 1–9

Here is:

1. A general call to everyone to give thanks to God (v. 1).

2. A particular call to *the redeemed of the Lord* (v. 2), which may well be applied spiritually to the *children of God that were scattered abroad,* whom Christ died to *gather together in one* out of all lands (Jn 11:52; Mt 24:31). But it seems here to refer to a physical rescue brought about for them when *they cried unto the Lord* (v. 6).

2.1. They were in enemy country, but God brought about their rescue: *He redeemed them from the hand of the enemy* (v. 2), perhaps *by the Spirit of God* (Zec 4:6), working in human spirits.

2.2. They were scattered as exiles, but God gathered them out of all the countries to which they had been scattered (v. 3). God knows those who are his (2Ti 2:19) and where to find them.

2.3. They were bewildered, had no road to travel on, no dwelling place to rest in (v. 4). *They wandered in the wilderness* (v. 4). But *God led them forth by the right way* (v. 7); he directed them so *that they might go to a city of habitation,* a city in which they could settle. This may refer to poor travelers in general, especially those whose way lay through the uncultivated and uninhabited lands of Arabia, where they may often have been at a loss, or it may refer to the wanderings of the children of Israel in the desert for forty years.

2.4. They were about to die of hunger (v. 5). Israel's needs were supplied at the right time. The same God who has led us has also fed us to this day. Now those who receive mercy are called on to respond in thanks for all this (v. 8): *O that men*—it refers especially to those people God has graciously relieved—*would praise the Lord for his goodness* to them in particular, *and for his wonderful works* to others of *the children of men!*

Verses 10–16

We are to take notice of the goodness of God toward prisoners and captives. Prisoners are said to *sit in darkness* (v. 10), desolate and dejected. They sit *in the shadow of death,* which suggests great danger. They are *bound in affliction, and* many times *in iron, because they* rebelled against the words of God. They despised the counsel of the Most High God and thought they neither needed it nor would be any better off with it; and those who will not receive advice cannot be helped. This is why they are suffering in chains. The intention of this adversity is to *bring down their heart* (v. 12), to humble them because of their sin. Their duty in this adversity is to pray (v. 13). Prisoners who could not find the time to pray when they were free now find they have time; they now see their need of God's help, although formerly they thought they could get by without him. *They cried unto the Lord, and he saved them* (v. 13). *He brought them out of darkness into light*, and their freedom was like life from the dead for them (v. 14). Were they in chains? He broke through their bonds. Were they imprisoned in strong castles? *He broke the gates of brass* (v. 16), and he did not put back the *bars of iron* with which those gates were fastened, but cut through them (v. 16).

Verses 17–22

Physical illness is another of the adversities of life that give us an opportunity to experience the goodness of God.

1. If we did not sin, we would not be sick. Sinners are fools; they wrong themselves and act against all their own interests, not only their spiritual interests but also their secular ones. They harm their physical health by excess and endanger their lives by overindulging their appetites. When those who doted most on the food that perishes become sick, they are sick of that very food, and the delicacies they once loved are loathed. And when the appetite is gone, life is as good as gone: *Then they cry unto the Lord* (v. 19). Is any sick? Let them pray; let them be prayed for (Jas 5:14). Prayer is a lotion for every sore.

2. It is by the power and mercy of God that we recover from sickness, and then it is our duty to be thankful. *He sent his word and healed them* (v. 20). This may be applied to the miraculous healings Christ worked when he was on earth; he said, *Be clean, Be whole*, and the work was done. It may also be applied to the spiritual healings which the Spirit of grace works in the new birth. He sends his word and heals souls. In the common instances of recovery from sickness God in his providence has only to speak, and it is done. When those who have been ill are restored, they must respond to God in praise (vv. 21–22): *Let all men praise the Lord for his goodness*, and let those, especially, to whom God has given new life spend it in his service. *Let them sacrifice with thanksgiving*, not only bring a thank offering to the altar but also bring a thankful heart to God.

Verses 23–32

The psalmist here calls on those who have been rescued from dangers at sea to give glory to God. Although the Israelites did not engage in trade very much, their neighbors the Tyrians and Sidonians did, and perhaps this part of the psalm has them in mind especially.

1. The power of God is seen at all times in the sea (vv. 23–24). It is seen by those *that go down to the sea in ships, as* mariners, merchants, fishermen, or passengers, *that do business in great waters. These see the works of the Lord, and his wonders* (v. 24). The sea itself is a wonder: its vastness, its saltiness, all its ebbing and flowing. The great variety of living creatures in the sea is amazing. Let those who go to sea be led by all the wonders they see there to consider and adore the infinite nature of God, to whom the sea belongs because he made it and commands it.

2. The power of God is seen especially in storms at sea. Wonders begin to happen in the sea when God *commands and raises the* strong *wind*, which *fulfils his word* (148:8). A stranger who has never seen it would not think it possible for a ship to survive as it does in a storm at sea, to ride it out, but God taught people to make ships that would strangely float on the water. When the storm is very high, even those that are used to the sea can neither shake off nor disguise their fears, but are completely *at their*

wits' end (v. 27), not knowing what more they can do to preserve their lives. Those who go to sea must expect such dangers, and the best preparation for them is free access to God in prayer. We have a saying, "Let those who want to learn to pray go to sea"; I say, "Let those who want to go to sea learn to pray." Those who have the Lord as their God have a present help in every time of need, so that when they are at their wits' end, they are not at their faith's end. In answer to their prayers, God sometimes comes to the aid of those in distress at sea: *He brings them out* (v. 28) of the danger. *He makes the storm a calm* (v. 29). Sailors are put at ease. The voyage becomes prosperous and successful: *So he brings them to their desired haven* (v. 30). God takes his people safely through all the storms they meet with on their journey toward heaven, and he eventually lands them in the desired harbor.

Verses 33–43

Having given God the glory for the providential help given to people in distress, the psalmist here gives him the glory for the changes in providence, and the surprises it sometimes brings to people's lives.

1. He gives some examples of these changes:

1.1. Fruitful countries are made barren, and barren countries are made fruitful. Much of the comfort of this life depends on the land in which we live. Human sin has often spoiled the fruitfulness of the soil. The goodness of God has often put right the barrenness of the soil and turned a *wilderness*, a land of drought, *into watersprings* (v. 35).

1.2. Needy families are raised up and made rich, while prosperous families are made poor and decay. We see many people greatly prospering whose beginnings were small (vv. 36–38). Those who were *hungry* are made to *dwell* in fruitful lands; they settle there. Providence puts good land into their hands, and they build on it. But places to live in, however convenient, are useless without land where the inhabitants can *sow the fields, and plant vineyards* (v. 37). Human work must accompany God's blessing, and then God's blessing will crown human work. The fruitfulness of the soil encourages diligence, and usually *the hand of the diligent*, under the blessing of God, *makes rich* (Pr 10:4) (v. 38). We see many people who have suddenly risen suddenly sink and come to nothing (v. 39) by adverse circumstances, and they end their days as low as they began them. Or we see their descendants after them lose ground as fast as they gained it, and scatter what they gathered together. Those who were noble and great in the world are humbled, and those who were lowly and contemptible are advanced to positions of honor (vv. 40–41). God will humble those who exalt themselves; he makes *them to wander in the wilderness, where there is no way.* Those who were afflicted and trampled on are not only rescued but also lifted out of the reach of their troubles. God is to be acknowledged both in setting up families and in building them up. Let nobles not be envied nor the poor despised, for God has many ways of changing the conditions of both.

2. Such surprising changes are useful:

2.1. To encourage the saints. They notice these ways with pleasure (v. 42). It gives great encouragement and strength to good people to see how God directs human beings as the potter fashions the clay, to see despised goodness advanced and ungodly pride humbled, to see it shown that *verily there is a God that judges in the earth* (58:11).

2.2. To silence sinners. When sinners see how their punishment corresponds to their sin and how justly God deals with them in taking away from them those gifts of his which they have used wrongly, they will not have one word to say for themselves.

2.3. To satisfy everyone about God's goodness (v. 43): *Whoso is wise, and will observe these things*, these various ways of divine Providence, *even they shall understand the loving-kindness of the Lord*. A wise observance of the providences of God will lead very much to the maturing of true Christians.

PSALM 108

This psalm begins with praise and concludes with prayer, and faith is at work in both. 1. David here gives thanks to God for mercies to himself (vv. 1–5). 2. He prays to God for mercies for the land (vv. 6–13). Vv. 1–5 are taken from 57:7–11; vv. 6–13 are taken from 60:5–12. This suggests that it is not only permissible but also sometimes convenient to gather some verses from one psalm and some from another to be sung together to the glory of God.

Verses 1–5

We may here learn how to praise God from the example of one who had mastered that art.

1. We must praise God with an assured heart. Wandering and straggling thoughts must be gathered in and kept close to the work in hand.

2. We must praise God with free expression: I will praise him *with my glory*, that is, with my tongue. Our tongue is our glory, and never more so than when it is used in praising God. David's skill in music was his glory; it made him famous, and so he would consecrate it to the praise of God. We must praise God with whatever gifts we excel in.

3. We must praise God with wholehearted devotion, and we must encourage ourselves so that it may be done in a living and real way, not carelessly or halfheartedly (v. 2): *Awake, psaltery and harp*; let it not be sung with a dull and sleepy tune, but let all the music be lively. Enthusiastic devotions honor God.

4. We must praise God publicly, as those who are not ashamed to acknowledge our obligations to him.

5. We must, in our praises, exalt the mercy and truth of God (v. 4). We cannot see farther than the clouds and sky; whatever we see of God's mercy and truth, there is still more to be seen, and more reserved to be seen, in the other world.

Verses 6–13

Here we may learn how to pray as well as praise. We must be public-spirited in prayer, having on our hearts the concerns of the church of God (v. 6). It is God's *beloved*, and so it must be ours too. We must therefore pray for it to be saved. A living faith can be joyful about what God has said even though it is not yet done, for with him saying and doing are not two things, whatever they may be with us. God had promised David to give him the hearts of his subjects, and so David surveys the different parts of the country as already his own: "*Shechem* and *Succoth, Gilead* and *Manasseh, Ephraim* and *Judah*, are all my own" (v. 8). With such assurance as this we may speak of the fulfillment of what God has promised to the Son of David. God will, without fail, give him the nations as his *inheritance and the utmost parts of the earth for his possession* (2:8). David looks on *Moab* and *Edom* and *Philistia* as his own already (v. 9). We must take encouragement from the beginnings of mercy to pray and hope for mercy to be completed (vv. 10–11): "*Who will bring me into the strong cities* that are still not conquered? Who will give

me control of the country of *Edom*, which has not yet been subdued?" The question how they should subdue the Edomites was probably to be discussed in his council of war, but he brings it into his prayers: *Wilt not thou, O God?* (v. 11). We must not be discouraged in prayer or taken away from our hold on God, even though Providence has frowned on us in some situations. We must seek help from God, renouncing all confidence in created things (v. 12). *Vain is the help of man*, human help is worthless. "It really is so, and so we are ruined if you do not help us; we know it is so, and we therefore depend on you for help and have even more reason to expect it." We must do our part, but we can do nothing by ourselves; it is only *through God that we shall do valiantly* (v. 13), gain the victory.

PSALM 109

Whether David wrote this psalm when he was persecuted by Saul, or when his son Absalom rebelled against him, or on the occasion of some other trouble, is uncertain, but the curse in v. 8 is applied to Judas (Ac 1:20). The rest of the prayers here against his enemies, too, were the expressions not of passion but of the Spirit of prophecy. 1. He voices a complaint about the hatred of his enemies and with it an appeal to the righteous God (vv. 1–5). 2. He prays against his enemies (vv. 6–20). 3. He prays for himself, that God would help him in his lowly condition (vv. 21–29); he concludes with a joyful expectation that God will support him (vv. 30–31).

Verses 1–5

It is the indescribable comfort of all good people that whoever is against them, God is for them:

1. David turns to God's judgment (v. 1): "*Hold not thy peace*, but *let my sentence come forth from thy presence* (17:2). Do not delay in giving judgment about the appeal made to you." The title he gives God is "*O God of my praise* (v. 1), the God in whom *I glory*, not glorying in any wisdom or strength of my own."

2. He complains about his enemies: they are *wicked*; they delight in causing trouble (v. 2); their words are *words of hatred* (v. 3). "They are *deceitful* in their declarations and professions of kindness, while at the same time they speak against me behind my back *with a lying tongue*" (v. 2). They are restless in their plotting. They are unjust; their accusations of him and judgments against him are all without basis: "*They have fought against me without a cause* (v. 3); I never gave them any provocation." They are very ungrateful and have *rewarded him evil for good* (v. 5). *For my love they are my adversaries*. The more he tried to please them, the more they hated him.

3. He decides to be faithful to his duty and take comfort from that: *But I give myself unto prayer* (v. 4). When David's enemies falsely accused him and misrepresented him, he turned to God and committed his cause to him in prayer. Although they accused him in response to his friendship, he still continued to pray for them; if others are abusive toward us and wrong us, let us still not fail in our duty to them or *sin against the Lord in ceasing to pray for them* (1Sa 12:23). Here David was a type of Christ, who was surrounded by *words of hatred* (v. 3) but still *gave himself to prayer* (v. 4), to pray for them. *Father, forgive them* (Lk 23:34).

Verses 6–20

David here focuses on one particular person who is worse than his other enemies, and he invokes and predicts his destruction in a holy zeal for God and against sin, looking to the enemies of Christ, especially Judas, who betrayed him, foreseeing that he will be, as our Savior calls him, *a son of perdition* (Jn 17:12). Calvin speaks of a detestable sacrilege involving these verses that was common in his time among Franciscan friars and other monks: if anyone had malice against a neighbor, they could hire some of these monks to curse him every day, and the monks would do so in the words of these verses. Greater ungodliness can hardly be imagined than to express a devilish passion using the words of Holy Scripture.

1. The curses are very terrible, fully set against the implacable enemies and persecutors of God's church and people, who *will not repent, to give him glory* (Rev 16:9). It is here foretold concerning this bad man:

1.1. That he would be sentenced as a criminal (vv. 6–7): "*Set thou a wicked man over him*, to be as cruel and oppressive to him as he has been to others. Set his own evil heart over him, set his own conscience against him; may that fly in his face."

1.2. That, being condemned, he would be executed as a most notorious evildoer. He would lose his life; the length of his life would be shortened by the sword of justice. Such bloodthirsty and *deceitful men shall not live out half their days* (55:23). Consequently his home would be given to others. His family would be beheaded and beggared; *his wife* would be made *a widow* and *his children fatherless* by his untimely death (v. 9). They would be *vagabonds and would beg* (v. 10), because they were conscious in themselves that everyone had good reason to hate them because of their father. His possessions would be ruined, as the possessions of evildoers are confiscated (v. 11). Because this evildoer has never shown mercy, there will *be none to extend mercy to him*, by *favouring his fatherless children* when he is gone (v. 12). The children of evildoers often fare worse because of their parents' evil; human affection is closed to them. This should not be so, for why should children suffer for what was not their fault? However, this is often their unhappy fate. Notice here what it is that rushes some people to shameful deaths and brings the families and wealth of others to ruin, makes them and their families contemptible and repugnant, and passes on an inheritance of poverty, shame, and misery to future generations. It is sin, sin which is so troublesome and destructive.

2. The grounds stated for these curses show them to be just, even though they sound very severe.

2.1. To justify the curses of vengeance on the sinner's descendants, the sin of his ancestors is mentioned here (vv. 14–15), *the iniquity of his fathers* and *the sin of his mother*. All the innocent blood that had been shed on the earth, from that of righteous Abel, was required from that persecuting generation who, by putting Christ to death, *filled up the measure* (reached the limit of the sins) *of their fathers* (Mt 23:31–36; Ge 15:16).

2.2. To justify the curses of vengeance on the sinner himself, he is accused of his own sin, which called out for accusation. He had loved cruelty: he had persecuted the poor, whom he should have protected and relieved, and *slain* (killed) *the broken in heart*, whom he should have comforted and healed. Here is a truly cruel man, one not fit to live. He had loved cursing, and so may the curse come back on his head (vv. 17–19). May God's cursing him be his shame, as his cursing his neighbor was his pride. This points to the complete destruction of Judas and the spiritual judgments which fell on the Jews for crucifying Christ. The psalmist concludes his curses with a terrible *Amen*.

Verses 21–31

David takes God's comforts to himself, but very humbly.

1. He pours out his complaint before God. "*I am poor and needy* (v. 22) and one who needs and craves your help." He was troubled in mind (v. 22): "*My heart is wounded within me.* I am not only broken with outward troubles but also wounded by a sense of guilt; and *a wounded spirit who can bear?*" (Pr 18:14). He was unsettled, *tossed up and down like the locust* (v. 23). His mind was unsteady, and he was hunted like a partridge on the mountains (1Sa 26:20). His body had wasted away and was almost worn away (v. 24): *My knees are weak through fasting*, either enforced fasting or voluntary fasting, when he humbled his soul. But it is better to have this physical leanness and a soul prospering and in health than, like Israel, to have leanness sent into the soul (106:15) while the body is feasted. In all this David was a type of Christ, who was weakened and scorned like this in his humiliation.

2. He prays for mercy for himself. "Lord, do for me whatever you think is right for me so that it will be for my benefit in the end, although at present it does not seem so." More particularly, he prays (v. 26): "*Help me, O Lord my God: O save me.* Save me from sin, help me to do my duty." He prays (v. 28), "Though they *curse, thou shalt bless.*" If God blesses us, we need not care who curses us.

3. He prays that his enemies might *be ashamed* (v. 28), *clothed with shame* (v. 29), that they might *cover themselves with their own confusion*, that they might be left to themselves, to do what would expose them and *manifest their folly before all men* (make clear their foolishness to everyone) (2Ti 3:9). But no, he is praying that they might be brought to repentance, which is the main thing we should beg from God for our enemies.

4. He pleads God's glory, the honor of his name: "*Deliver me, because thy mercy is good*; may that be the fullness of my salvation." He concludes the psalm with the joy of faith. He promises God that he will praise him (v. 30). He promises himself that he will have reasons to praise God (v. 31). God protected David in his sufferings, and he was also present with the Lord Jesus in his; he saved his soul from those who claimed to judge it and received it into his own hands (31:5; Lk 23:46).

PSALM 110

This psalm is pure Gospel. It is only, and wholly, taken up with Christ, the Messiah promised to ancestors and expected by them. It is clear that the Jews in former times, even the worst of them, understood it in this way, for when the Lord Jesus questioned the Pharisees about the first words of this psalm, where he assumed that David, by the Spirit, called Christ his Lord though he was his son, they chose to say nothing. They did not admit that there was any question whether David was indeed speaking of the Messiah; they freely acknowledged such a clear truth, even though they foresaw that it would make them look bad (Mt 22:41–46). As our Redeemer, Christ executes the office of prophet, priest, and king, with reference both to his humiliation and to his exaltation, and each of these is described here. 1. His prophetic office (v. 2). 2. His priestly office (v. 4). 3. His kingly office (vv. 1, 3, 5–6). 4. His states of humiliation and exaltation (v. 7).

Title

Some have called this psalm "David's creed," because almost all the articles of the Christian faith are found in it.

The title calls it *a Psalm of David*, for in faithfully foreseeing the Messiah he both praised God and encouraged himself, and we, who have seen fulfilled what is foretold here, should sing praises to God and be encouraged even more.

Verses 1–4

Glorious things are spoken here about Christ (87:3):

1. He is David's Lord. We must take special notice of this because he himself does. *David, in spirit, calls him Lord* (Mt 22:43).

2. He is constituted a sovereign Lord by the counsel and decree of God himself: *The Lord*, Jehovah, *said unto him, Sit* (v. 1) as a king. He *receives of the Father* this honor and glory (2Pe 1:17).

3. He is to be advanced to the highest honor and entrusted with absolute sovereign power: *Sit thou at my right hand* (v. 1). Sitting is a resting position; after his services and sufferings, he rested. It is a ruling position; he sits to give law and justice.

4. All his enemies will in due time be made his footstool. Even Christ himself has enemies who fight against his kingdom. There are those who do not want him to reign over them (Lk 19:27), and in rejecting him they join themselves to Satan, who does not want him to reign at all. These enemies *will be made his footstool* (v. 1). Yet it will not be done immediately; the writer to the Hebrews notices this: *We see not yet all things put under him* (Heb 2:8). Christ himself will wait until it is done.

5. He will have a kingdom set up in the world, beginning at Jerusalem (v. 2). The kingdom of Christ arose from Zion, the City of David, for he was the Son of David, and was to have *the throne of his father David* (Lk 1:32). *The rod of his strength*, or "his strong rod," means his eternal Gospel and the power of the Holy Spirit. God sent out this strong rod; he poured out the Spirit and gave both commissions and qualifications to those who preached the word and *ministered the Spirit* (Gal 3:5). It was sent out of Zion, for the Spirit was given there, and there the preaching of the Gospel among all nations must begin: at Jerusalem.

6. When his kingdom has been set up, it will be maintained in the world despite all the opposition of the powers of darkness. He will rule *in the midst of his enemies* (v. 2). He sits in heaven with his friends all around him; he rules on earth *in the midst of his enemies*.

7. He will have a great number of subjects, who will give him honor and praise (v. 3).

7.1. They will be his own people, given him by the Father. *Thine they were and thou gavest them me* (Jn 17:6). They are redeemed by him (Tit 2:14). They are his by right and therefore belonged to him even before they gave their consent.

7.2. They will be *a willing people*, servants who choose their service, soldiers who are volunteers and not conscripts.

7.3. They will be so *in the day of his power* (v. 3), "in the day of your muster." "In the day of your armies," according to some; "when the first preachers of the Gospel will be sent out, as Christ's forces, then all who are *thy people shall be willing*; that will be your time to set up your kingdom."

7.4. They will be so *in the beauty of holiness*; they will be charmed into submitting to Christ by the sight given them of the beauty of the one who is the holy Jesus. They will be admitted by him into the beauty of holiness, as spiritual priests, to minister in his sanctuary, in the beautiful robes or ornaments of grace and sanctification. Holiness is the uniform of Christ's family and what *becomes*

his house for ever (93:5). Christ's soldiers all wear such robes; these are the clothes they wear.

7.5. He will have great numbers of people devoted to him. In the early days of the Gospel, in the morning of the New Testament, in the youth of the church, great numbers flocked to Christ, and there were *multitudes that believed, a remnant of Jacob* that was as *dew from the Lord* (Mic 5:7; Isa 64:4, 8). *The dew of the youth* (v. 3) is a numerous, glorious, and hopeful sign of young people flocking to Christ, which would be to the world as dew to the ground, to make it fruitful.

7.6. He will be not only a king but also a priest (v. 4). Our Lord Jesus Christ is God's minister to us and our Advocate with God, and so he is a Mediator between us and God. He is said to be *a priest for ever* (v. 4), not only because we are never to expect any other dispensation of grace except by the priesthood of Christ, but also because the blessed fruits and results of his priesthood will remain for eternity. He is a priest not of the order of Aaron but of that of Melchizedek, which, as it came before that of Aaron, was also for many reasons superior. The writer to the Hebrews comments on these words in detail (Heb 7) and uses them to develop what he writes about Christ's priestly office, which he shows was not a new idea, but built on this certain word of prophecy. For just as the New Testament explains the Old, so the Old Testament confirms the New, and Jesus Christ is the Alpha and Omega of both.

Verses 5–7

Here we have our great Redeemer:

1. Conquering his enemies (vv. 5–6). Our Lord Jesus will certainly bring to nothing all the opposition shown to his kingdom. Notice:

1.1. The conqueror: *The Lord, Adonai*, the Lord Jesus Christ, to whom all judgment is committed. He will successfully resist his enemies. Christ's sitting at the right hand of God speaks as much terror to his enemies as happiness to his people.

1.2. The time set for this victory: *In the day of his wrath* (v. 5), that is, at the time appointed for it, when the limit of their sins has been reached and they are ready for ruin (Ge 15:16; Mt 23:32).

1.3. The extent of this victory. He *shall strike through* (crush) *kings* (v. 5). Satan is the prince of this world (Jn 12:31), death is the king of terrors, and we read of kings who make war with the Lamb (Rev 19:19); but they will all be brought down and broken. The trophies of Christ's victories will be set up *among the heathen* (nations) (v. 6), and in many countries, wherever any of his enemies are.

1.4. The justice of this victory: *He shall judge among them* (v. 6). This is not a military execution, which is carried out in anger, but a judicial one.

1.5. The effect of this victory; it will be the complete destruction of all his enemies. He will *wound the heads*, crush the rulers (v. 6), which seems to refer to the first promise of the Messiah (Ge 3:15), that he would *bruise the serpent's head*. He will *fill the places with the dead bodies* (v. 6). Those killed by the Lord will be many.

2. Saving his friends and strengthening them (v. 7).

2.1. He will be humbled: *He shall drink of the brook in the way*, that bitter cup which the Father put into his hand. Christ drank from this brook when he was made a curse for us, and so, when he began his suffering, he *went over the brook Kidron* (v. 7) (Jn 18:1).

2.2. He will be exalted: *Therefore shall he lift up the head*. When he died, he *bowed the head* (Jn 19:30), but he soon lifted up his head by his own power at his resurrection. He lifted up his head as a conqueror. Because he drank from the brook beside the path, he lifted up his own head, and so lifted up the heads of all his faithful followers, who, *if they suffer with him, shall also reign with him* (2Ti 2:12).

PSALM 111

This and several of the psalms that follow it seem to have been written by David for the service of the church in its sacred festivals. This is a psalm of praise. It opens with Hallelujah—Praise the Lord—*showing that we must use this psalm with hearts that are ready to praise God. It is an acrostic poem, each line of which begins with the successive letter of the Hebrew alphabet, in exact order. The psalmist encourages praising God and: 1. Sets himself as an example (v. 1). 2. Provides us with reasons for praising him drawn from his works (vv. 2–9). 3. Commends the holy fear of God and a careful obedience to his commands as the most acceptable way of praising God (v. 10).*

Verses 1–5

Having begun with *Hallelujah*, the psalmist keeps to his text.

1. He decides to praise God himself (v. 1). We must praise God both in private and in public, in smaller and bigger meetings, in our own families and also in the Lord's house.

2. He commends to us the *works of the Lord* (v. 2) as the subject of our meditation when we are praising him—the ways of Providence toward the world, the church, and individual people. His works are:

2.1. Great like himself; there is nothing in them that is lowly or insignificant: they are the products of infinite Wisdom and power.

2.2. Interesting and stimulating to those who inquire into them—*sought out of* (pondered by) *all those that have pleasure therein* (v. 2). Those who delight in the works of God will not be satisfied by looking at them only superficially, but will carefully search into them and observe them. In studying both science and history we explore the greatness and glory of God's works.

2.3. Just and holy; *his righteousness endures for ever* (v. 3).

2.4. Memorable, fit to be remembered and recorded. Much that we do is so insignificant that the best thing we can do is to forget it. But notice is to be taken of God's works, and an account is to be kept of them (v. 4). *He has made his wonderful works to be remembered.*

2.5. Kind. In them the Lord shows that he is *gracious and full of compassion* (v. 4). *He has given meat* (food) *to those that fear him: he will be ever mindful of his covenant* (v. 5), so they can taste his covenant love even in common blessings. Some think this refers to the manna with which God fed his people in the desert.

Verses 6–10

We are here taught to give glory to God:

1. For the great things he has done for his people, for his people Israel, formerly and more recently: *He has shown his people the power of his works* (v. 6).

1.1. The possession God gave to Israel of the land of Canaan. He did this in Joshua's time, when the seven nations were subdued, and in David's time, when many of the neighboring nations became subject to David.

1.2. The many times he rescued his people when they had sold themselves into the hands of their enemies by their sins (v. 9). These redemptions were types of the great redemption which was to be brought by the Lord Jesus in the fullness of time.

2. For the stability both of his word and of his works, which assure us of the great things he will do for his people.

2.1. What God has done will never be undone. He will not undo it himself, and people and demons cannot undo it (v. 7): *The works of his hand are verity* (truth or faithfulness) *and judgment* (justice) (v. 8), that is, they are done in truth and uprightness. We may be assured at the beginning of his works that they will be completed.

2.2. What God has said will never be unsaid: *All his commandments are sure* (v. 7), all right and therefore steady.

3. For the setting up and establishing of religious faith, because the revelation of religious faith leads so much to his honor. If you look back on what he has made known of himself in his word and in his works, you will see, and say, that God is great. Because the ways of religious faith lead so much to our happiness, reverence of him and obedience to him are as much in our interests as they are our duty. People can never begin to be wise until they begin to fear God. All true wisdom arises from true religious faith and has its foundation in it. *A good understanding have all those that do his commandments* (v. 10). Where the fear of the Lord rules in the heart, there will be a constant care to keep his commandments, not simply to talk about them but also to obey them, and those who do so have a good understanding. Their obedience is clear evidence that their hearts really do fear God. We have reason to praise God, to praise him forever, because he has put people into such a good position to become happy.

PSALM 112

This psalm is composed as an acrostic, as the previous psalm is, and, also like the previous psalm, begins with Hallelujah, *even though it deals with the happiness of the saints, because their happiness leads to the glory of God. It is a comment on the last verse of the previous psalm, and shows how wise we are if we fear God and obey his commandments. We have here: 1. The character of the righteous (v. 1). 2. The blessedness of the righteous (vv. 2–9). 3. The misery of evildoers (v. 10). So good and evil are set out before us, the blessing and the curse (Dt 11:26; 30:15).*

Verses 1–5

The psalmist begins with a call to us to praise God, but immediately turns to praise the people of God. We have reason to praise the Lord that there are people in the world who fear and serve him. Such people are happy because of the grace of God. Here we have:

1. A description of those who are here declared blessed, to whom these promises are made.

1.1. Their motives are good. They are disposed to acknowledge God's rule and stand in awe of him and have constant reverence for his majesty and obedience to his will. Those who *fear the Lord* as a Father and have the nature of a child, not a slave, *delight greatly in his commandments*. The commandments are written on their hearts, and they consider them an easy and pleasant yoke (Mt 11:30). They delight not only in God's promises but also in his commands.

1.2. They are genuine and sincere in their professions and intentions. They are called *the upright* (vv. 2, 4), who really are as good as they seem to be and are faithful to both God and people. There is no true religious faith without sincerity; that is part of the life of the believer under the Gospel.

1.3. They are both just and kind in all their actions. One example is given of their kindness (v. 5): he *shows favour and lends*. Sometimes there is as much kindness in lending as there is in giving, as it obliges the borrower to be both conscientious and honest.

2. The blessedness that is here passed on as an inheritance to those who fulfill these characteristics. All happiness comes to *the man that feareth the Lord* (v. 1).

2.1. The descendants of good people will fare better because of their parents' goodness (v. 2): *His seed shall be mighty on earth*. Religious faith has lifted many families, if not to advance them highly, then to settle them firmly. When good people themselves are happy in heaven, their descendants perhaps are significant on earth and will themselves acknowledge that it is because of a blessing descending from their forebears. *The generation of the upright shall be blessed* (v. 2); if they follow in the footsteps of their parents, they will be more blessed because of their relationship with them.

2.2. Good people themselves — especially their souls — will prosper in the world (v. 3). They will be blessed with outward prosperity as far as is good for them. But what is much better is that they will be blessed with spiritual blessings (Eph 1:3), which are the true riches. Grace is better than gold, for it will outlast it. They will have wealth and riches and will also keep up their religious faith. When this endures in a family, and the heirs of the parents' estate inherit their virtues too, then that is a truly happy family.

2.3. They will be encouraged in their suffering (v. 4): *Unto the upright there arises light in the darkness*. They will have their share of the ordinary troubles of human life, but *when they sit in darkness, the Lord shall be a light to them* (Mic 7:8).

2.4. They will have wisdom to deal with all their concerns (v. 5). It is part of the character of good people that they will use their wisdom to deal rightly in business, in gaining and saving, so that they may have something they can give to others (Eph 4:28).

Verses 6–10

In these verses we have:

1. The assurance of saints and their stability. It is the joy of good people that they *shall not be moved for ever* (v. 6).

1.1. Good people will have a settled reputation. They will have a good name with God and other people: *The righteous shall be in everlasting remembrance* (v. 6). There are those who do all they can to stain their reputation and to pour scorn on them, but their integrity will survive them. Some who have been well known for their righteousness are long remembered on earth; but in heaven their remembrance will be truly eternal. Those who are forgotten and despised on earth are remembered and honored there, and their righteousness results in praise, honor, and glory (1Pe 1:7). What will especially lead to the honor of good people is their generosity to the poor: *He has dispersed, he has given to the poor*; he has not allowed his kind acts to be of only one kind, or directed them to only a few people that he feels a special kindness for, but has scattered them.

1.2. Good people will have settled spirits, for they will not be afraid; their hearts are secure (vv. 7–8). They seek to keep their minds steadfastly on God (Isa 26:3) and so keep themselves calm, and God has promised them both reason to do so and grace to do so. The security of the heart is a sovereign response to the disturbing fear of bad news. Trusting in the Lord is the best and most certain way of keeping the heart secure. *He will not be afraid, till he see his desire on his enemies*, that is, until he reaches heaven, where he will see Satan, and all his spiritual enemies, crushed under his feet. "Until he looks on his oppressors," looks boldly in their faces, now no longer under their power.

2. The vexation of sinners (v. 10). The happiness of the righteous will grieve them. They will be angry to see that those whom they hated and despised, and whose ruin they sought and hoped to see, have become the favorites of heaven and have been advanced to rule over them (49:14).

PSALM 113

This psalm begins and ends with Hallelujah, *for like many others, it is intended to further the great and good work of praising God. 1. We are urged to praise God (vv. 1–3). 2. We are provided with reasons for praising him: the elevation of his glory and greatness (vv. 4–5) and the condescension of his grace and goodness (vv. 6–9), which very much illustrate each other.*

Verses 1–9

In this psalm:

1. We are encouraged to give glory to God.

1.1. The invitation is insistent: *Praise you the Lord*, and again and again, *Praise him, praise him; blessed be his name*, for he is to be praised (vv. 1–3).

1.2. The invitation is very extensive: *Praise, O you servants of the Lord!* (v. 1). God has praise from his own people. They are the ones who have most reason to praise him. The angels, too, are the servants of the Lord; they praise God better than we can. Let God be praised throughout all generations. *Blessed be his name now and always* (v. 2). From *the rising of the sun to the going down of the same* (v. 3), that is, throughout the world, in every place where people live. It should be praised by all nations, for in every place, from east to west, appear the clear proofs and results of his wisdom, power, and goodness.

2. We are instructed what to give him the glory for here:

2.1. Let us look up with eyes of faith and see how high his glory is in the upper world, and proclaim that to his praise (vv. 4–5). If we put all the nations together, he is far above them all; they are in his presence as the *drop of the bucket and the small dust of the balance* (Isa 40:15, 17). The throne of his glory is in the highest heavens. *His glory is above the heavens* (v. 4), that is, above the angels; he is above what they are. He is also above what they do, for they are under his command, and he is above their wildest imaginations of him.

2.2. Let us look around with perceptive eyes and see how extensive his goodness is in this lower world, and proclaim that to his praise. He is a God *who exalts himself to dwell, who humbles himself, in heaven, and in earth* (v. 6). God is said to *exalt himself* and to *humble himself*; both are his own acts. God's condescending goodness appears:

2.2.1. In the notice he takes of the world below him. His glory *is above the nations* and *above the heavens*, but neither is neglected by him. *God is great, yet he despises not any* (Job 36:5). *He humbles himself* (stoops down) *to behold* (v. 6) all his creatures. Considering the infinite perfection, sufficiency, and happiness of God, it must be acknowledged as an act of great condescension that God is willing to take into the thoughts of his eternal purposes and into the hand of his universal providence both the powers of heaven and the peoples of the earth (Da 4:35); even here he humbles himself. If it is so condescending for God to look on things in heaven and on earth, what an amazing condescension was it for the Son of God to come from heaven to earth and take our nature on himself, so that he might *seek and save those that were lost* (Lk 19:10)!

2.2.2. In the special favor he sometimes shows to the least and lowest peoples. He looks not only on the great things in the earth but also on the lowliest, and does wonders for them, deeds outside the normal ways of providence and the ordinary series of causes, which show that the world is ruled not by a course of nature — for that would always run in the same channel — but by the God of nature, who delights in doing things we have not expected. He acts sometimes suddenly (vv. 7 – 8): *He raises up the poor out of the dust, that he may set him with princes.* Gideon is taken from threshing, Saul from seeking donkeys, and David from looking after the sheep; the apostles are taken from fishing to be *fishers of men* (Mt 4:19). The treasure of the Gospel is put into jars of clay (2Co 4:7), and the weak and foolish people of the world are chosen to preach it, to confound the *wise and mighty* (1Co 1:27 – 28) and to show that this all-surpassing power is from God and not from us (2Co 4:7). When Joseph's goodness was tested and revealed, he was raised from the prison dust and *set with princes* (v. 8). Those who have long been childless are sometimes, suddenly, made fruitful (v. 9). This may look back to Sarah and Rebekah, Rachel, Hannah, and Samson's mother, or forward to Elizabeth, and there have been many such examples, in which God has looked on the affliction of his female servants and taken away their disgrace. *He makes the barren woman to keep house* (v. 9), not only builds up the family but also finds the heads of the family something to do.

PSALM 114

The rescue of Israel from Egypt gave birth to its church and nation. In this psalm that miracle is celebrated in vibrant praise; it was therefore rightly made a part of the great hallelujah, or song of praise, which the Jews sang at the close of the Passover supper. It must never be forgotten: 1. That they were brought out of slavery (v. 1). 2. That God set up his tabernacle among them (v. 2). 3. That the Red Sea and the Jordan were separated in front of them (vv. 3, 5). 4. That the earth shook at the giving of the Law, when God came down on Mount Sinai (vv. 4, 6 – 7). 5. That God gave them water from the rock (v. 8).

Verses 1 – 8

The psalmist remembers here *the days of old* (143:5) and the wonders which their ancestors told them of (Jdg 6:13), for just as time does not wear out the guilt of sin, so also it should not wear out the sense of mercy. Let it never be forgotten:

1. That God brought Israel out of the house of slavery (Ex 20:2) boldly and with his outstretched arm (Dt 26:8):

Israel went out of Egypt (v. 1). They did not sneak out secretly, but marched out with all the marks of honor.

2. That God himself framed their civil and sacred constitution (v. 2): *Judah and Israel were his sanctuary, his dominion.* When he rescued them from the hand of their oppressors, it was so *that they might serve him* (Lk 1:74 – 75) in the duties of religious worship and in obedience to the moral law. He set up his sanctuary among them, in which he gave them the special signs of his presence with them and promised to receive their praise and tribute. He was himself their lawgiver and judge, and their government was a theocracy: *The Lord was their King.*

3. That the Red Sea was divided in front of them when they left Egypt, both for their rescue and for the destruction of their enemies, as was the river Jordan when they entered Canaan. The psalmist asks poetically (v. 5), *What ailed thee* (why was it), *O thou sea, that thou fleddest?* And the psalmist provides the sea with an answer: it was *at the presence of the Lord* (v. 7). This is intended to show that it was not from any natural cause, but was *at the presence of the Lord*, who gave the word (86:11). Israel triumphs over the sea. There is no sea, no Jordan, that is so deep or broad that when God's time comes for the redemption of his people, it will not be separated and driven back if it stands in the way. We can apply this:

3.1. To the planting of the Christian church in the world. Why did Satan and the powers of darkness tremble and submit as they did (Mk 1:34)? Why were the pagan oracles silenced and struck dead? Why did their idolatries and sorcery die out in the presence the Gospel? Why did those who persecuted and opposed the Gospel give up their cause and call out to the rocks and mountains to protect them? It was *at the presence of the Lord* (v. 7) and of that power which went along with the Gospel.

3.2. To the work of grace in the heart. What redirects the stream in a regenerate soul? Why do sinful and corrupt desires flee, so that prejudices are removed and the whole person becomes new (Eph 2:15)? It is at the presence of God's Spirit that arguments are demolished (2Co 10:5).

4. That the earth shook and trembled when God came down on Mount Sinai to give the Law (v. 4): *The mountains skipped like rams, and* then *the little hills* might well be excused if they skipped *like lambs*, either when they were frightened or when they played together.

5. That God supplied them with water from the rock, which followed them through the dry and sandy deserts (1Co 10:4). The same almighty power that turned waters into a rock to be a wall to Israel (Ex 14:22) turned the rock into waters to be a well to Israel. They had been protected by miracles, and by miracles they were provided for, for such was the pool, those springs of water into which the hard rock was turned, *and that rock was Christ* (1Co 10:4).

PSALM 115

Some ancient translations, such as the Septuagint and the Vulgate, attach this psalm to the previous one, but it is a separate psalm in Hebrew. Here we are taught to give glory: 1. To God, not ourselves (v. 1). 2. To God, not to idols (vv. 2 – 8). We must give God glory: 2.1. By trusting in him and in his promises and blessings (vv. 9 – 15). 2.2. By blessing him (vv. 16 – 18).

Verses 1 – 8

These verses show us a good response to the boasting of self and the scorn of idolaters:

1. Boasting is excluded here forever (v. 1; Ro 3:27). Let no good opinion of our own merits be given any place either in our prayers or in our praises, but let both center on God's glory. All the good we do is done by the power of his grace, and all the good we receive is the gift of his dear mercy, and so he must receive all the praise. All our songs must be sung to this humble tune: *Not unto us, O Lord!* and again, *Not unto us, but to thy name* (v. 1); let all the glory be given to him. This must be the highest and ultimate purpose in our prayers, and so it is made the first request in the Lord's Prayer, as what guides all the rest: *Hallowed be thy name* (Mt 6:9), and so for that to happen, *Give us our daily bread* (Mt 6:11).

2. The scorn of the nations is forever silenced here.

2.1. The psalmist complains of the scorn of the nations (v. 2): *Wherefore should they say, Where is now their God?* Do they not know that our God is everywhere by his providence and is always near to us by his promise and grace?

2.2. He gives a direct answer to their question (v. 3). "Do they ask where our God is? *Our God is in the heavens*, where the gods of the nations never were, *in the heavens*, and so out of sight, but although his majesty is unapproachable (1Ti 6:16), it does not therefore follow that his existence is in question. In the lower world is the evidence of his power. Do you ask where he is? He is at the beginning and end of everything, *and not far from any of us* (Ac 17:27).

2.3. He turns their question back onto them. He in effect asks, "What are the gods of the nations?"

2.3.1. He shows that although their gods are not shapeless, they are senseless.

2.3.1.1. Idolaters originally worshiped the sun and moon (Job 31:26), which was bad enough, but not so bad as what they now came to, which was the worship of idols (v. 4). They were made of *silver and gold*, dug from the earth—"Man found them poor and dirty in a mine" (George Herbert), proper things to make money from, but not to be used in making gods. They were made by craft workers; they are creatures of *men's vain imaginations* (Ro 1:21) and *the works of men's hands* (v. 4) and so can have no divinity in them. *The workmen made it, therefore it is not God* (Hos 8:6).

2.3.1.2. These idols are represented here (vv. 5–7) as the most ridiculous things, a mere jest, more suitable for a toy shop than a temple, better for children to play with than for people to pray to. The painter, the carver, the sculptor, all did their parts well enough; they made them with *mouths* and *eyes*, *ears* and *noses*, *hands* and *feet*. But they could put no life into them and so no sense. They would have been better off worshiping a dead carcass—for that once had life in it—than a dead idol, which neither has life nor ever can have. *They speak not* in answer to those who consult them; the crafty priest must speak for them. In Baal's idol there was *no voice, neither any that answered* (1Ki 18:26). *They see not* the worshipers prostrate before them, much less their burdens and needs. *They hear not* their prayers, even though they are loud; *they smell not* their incense, even though it is very strong and sweet; *they handle not* the gifts presented to them, much less have they any gifts to give their worshipers; they cannot *stretch forth their hands to the needy* (Pr 31:20). *They walk not* (v. 7), they cannot move a step to help those who turn to them. In fact, they cannot even so much as *breathe through their throat* (v. 7), they have not the slightest sign of life.

2.3.2. He reasons from this the foolishness of their worshipers (v. 8): *Those that make them* images show

their ingenuity and no doubt are intelligent, *but those that make them* gods show how stupid and foolish they are. *They see not* the invisible things of the true and living God in the works of creation (Ro 1:20); *they hear not* (v. 6) the voice of the day and the night, which declare his glory in every speech and language (19:2–3). By worshiping these foolish puppets, they make themselves more and more foolish like them, and put themselves farther away from everything spiritual, sinking deeper into the mire of worldliness.

Verses 9–18

In these verses:

1. All of us are fervently encouraged to put our confidence in God and not allow our confidence in him to be shaken by the insults of the nations over us because of our present distress. It is foolish to trust in dead idols, but it is wise to trust in the living God, for he is a *help and a shield* (v. 9) to those who *trust in them* (v. 8). Therefore let Israel trust in the Lord—the body of the people, as to their public interests, and every individual Israelite, as to their own private concerns. Let the priests, the Lord's ministers, and all the families of the *house of Aaron, trust in the Lord* (v. 10). They should be examples to others of a cheerful confidence in God in the worst of times. Let converts, who are not descendants of Israel but who *fear the Lord*, who worship him and are careful to follow him—let them *trust in him*, for he will not fail or forsake them (v. 11).

2. We are greatly encouraged to trust in God. *The Lord has been mindful of* (has remembered) *us*. All our strength and encouragement come from God's *thoughts to us-ward* (40:5); he *has been mindful of us* even though we have forgotten him. We may reason from what he has done for us that *he will bless us*; the One who has been our *help and our shield* will remain so; we therefore have reason to hope that he who has rescued before and does so now will also rescue us in the future. *He will bless us*; he has promised that he will. God's blessing us means not only that he speaks good to us but also that he does well for us (v. 13); *he will bless those that fear the Lord*, even though they do not come from the house of Israel or the house of Aaron, for it was true even before Peter perceived it *that in every nation he that fears God is accepted with him* and blessed (Ac 10:34–35). Both the weak in grace and the strong in grace will be blessed by God, the lambs and the sheep of his flock. It is promised (v. 14), *The Lord shall increase you*, especially with an increase in spiritual blessings (Eph 1:3), with the increase of God (Col 2:19). He will bless you with an increase in knowledge and wisdom, grace, holiness, and joy. "*He shall increase you more and more* (v. 14), so that as long as you live you will continue to increase, until you come to perfection (Eph 4:13), as the shining light" (Pr 4:18). "*You and your children* (v. 14); you in your children." For *you are blessed of the Lord* (v. 15); you and your children are blessed; *all that see them shall acknowledge them, that they are the seed which the Lord has blessed* (Isa 69:9).

3. Our praise of God is encouraged by the example of the psalmist, who concludes with a determination to persevere in praising him. God is to be praised (v. 16). Notice how imposing his palace is, and the throne he has prepared in the heavens: *The heaven, even the heavens are the Lord's. The earth he has given to the children of men* (v. 16), having made it for them to use and to supply them with food, drink, and accommodation. The dead are not able to praise him (v. 17), nor are *any that go into silence*. The dead body cannot praise God, yet the soul

indeed lives in a state of separation from the body and is able to praise God, and the souls of the faithful, after they are delivered from the burdens of the flesh, do praise God and continue to praise him, for they go to the land of perfect light and constant work. We should therefore be concerned to praise him (v. 18): *But we*, we who are alive, *will bless the Lord from this time forth* and to eternity. *Hallelujah.*

PSALM 116

This is a thanksgiving psalm. Notice: 1. The great distress and danger that the psalmist was in, which almost drove him to despair (vv. 3, 10–11); how he turned to God in that distress (v. 4); his experience of God's goodness to him in answer to prayer; how God heard him (vv. 1–2), pitied him (vv. 5–6), and rescued him (v. 8). 2. His concern for the acknowledgments he would make of the goodness of God to him (v. 12): he would love God (v. 1); he would continue to call on him (vv. 2, 13, 17); he would rest in him (v. 7); he would walk before him (v. 9); he would pay his vows of thanksgiving, acknowledging the loving care God took of him, and he would do this publicly (vv. 13–15, 17–19). Lastly, he would continue to be God's faithful servant until the end of his life (v. 16). Such sighs of a holy soul show that it is very happy.

Verses 1–9

In this part of the psalm we have:

1. A general description of David's experience and his godly decisions (vv. 1–2), which introduces the contents of the whole psalm. He has experienced God's goodness to him in answer to prayer: *He has inclined his ear to me* (v. 2). It is wonderfully condescending of God to hear prayer; it is bowing his ear. David begins the psalm somewhat abruptly with a profession of what his heart is full of: *I love the Lord* (as 18:1). It is right that he begins in this way, according to the first and great commandment (Mt 22:36–37). *Therefore I will call upon him* (v. 2). Why should we glean in any other field when we have been so well treated in this one (Ru 2:8)? In fact, *I will call upon him as long as I live* (v. 2)—Hebrew, "in my days"—every day, to the last day.

2. A more detailed account of God's gracious dealings with him. Let us look at David's experiences. He was in great distress and trouble (v. 3): *The sorrows of death compassed me* (NIV: the cords of death entangled me), that is, such sorrows as were likely to lead to death. Perhaps extreme physical pain or mental trouble is called here *the pains of hell*. In his trouble he had turned to God in faithful and fervent prayer (v. 4). He tells us that he prayed: *Then called I upon the name of the Lord.* He tells us what his prayer was; it was short but to the point: "*O Lord! I beseech thee, deliver my soul*; save me from death, and save me from sin, for that is killing my soul." He found by experience that God is gracious and merciful and that in his compassion he *preserves the simple* (v. 6). Because they are *simple*—simplehearted, sincere, and upright, and with no falsehood—God therefore preserves them, as he preserved Paul, who had conducted himself in the world *not with fleshly wisdom, but in simplicity and godly sincerity* (2Co 1:12). Let David speak from his own experience. "*I was brought low*, was plunged into the depths of misery, and then *he helped me*. He helped me both bear the worst and hope the best; he helped me to pray, or else I wouldn't have wanted to; he helped me to wait, or else I wouldn't have had the faith. I was one of the helpless ones

God kept, the poor man who *cried and the Lord heard him.*" God graciously rescued:

2.1. His *soul from death* (v. 8). It is because of God's great mercy to us that we are alive, and we are more aware of the mercy if we have been at death's door but have been spared and raised up. The rescue of the soul from spiritual death is especially to be acknowledged by all those who are now sanctified and will soon be glorified.

2.2. His *eyes from tears* (v. 8), that is, his heart from excessive grief.

2.3. His *feet from falling* (v. 8), from falling into sin and so into misery. God has done all this for him, and so he will lead a life of delight in God (v. 7): "*Return unto thy rest, O my soul!* God has dealt kindly with you, and so you need not fear that he will ever deal harshly with you." God is the soul's rest; only in him can it *dwell at ease* (25:13); it must therefore turn to him and rejoice in him. "Return to the rest that Christ gives to *the weary and heavy laden*" (Mt 11:28). He will live a life of devotion to God (v. 9): "*I will walk before the Lord in the land of the living*, that is, in this world, as long as I continue to live in it." The *land of the living* (v. 9) is a land of mercy, which we should be thankful for; it is a land of opportunity, which we should make the most of.

Verses 10–19

The Septuagint (a Greek version of the Old Testament) and some other ancient versions make these verses a separate psalm from the former; and some have called it "The Martyr's psalm" because of v. 15. David here confesses three things:

1. His faith (v. 10): *I believed, therefore have I spoken.* This is quoted by the apostle Paul with application to himself and his fellow ministers (2Co 4:13), who, although they suffered for Christ, were not ashamed to acknowledge him. David trusted the existence, providence, and promises of God, especially the assurance God had given him by Samuel that he would exchange his crook for a scepter. He went through a great deal of hardship believing this, and so he spoke to God by prayer (v. 4) and praise (v. 12).

2. His fear (v. 11): *I was greatly afflicted* (v. 10), and then *I said in my haste*—"in my dismay," according to some, "in my flight," according to others, when Saul was pursuing him—*All men are liars*, all with whom he had to do, Saul and all his courtiers; his friends, who he thought would stand by him, deserted him and disowned him when he fell into disgrace at court. When we speak wrongly in haste, we must repent and take back our words, as David did (31:22), and then we will not be held responsible for them.

3. His gratitude (v. 12–19). God has been better to him than his fears and has graciously rescued him from his troubles, and so:

3.1. He asks, *What shall I render unto the Lord for all his benefits towards me?* Here he speaks as one who is aware of the many mercies he has received from God— *all his benefits*. He knows he cannot really repay him with anything that would be in proportion to what he has received, but he wants to give back something acceptable as the acknowledgment of a grateful mind.

3.2. He will offer his praises and prayers to God in a very devout and sacred way (vv. 13, 17).

3.2.1. "*I will take the cup of salvation*, that is, I will offer as a sign of my thankfulness to God the drink offerings appointed by the Law, and I will express my joy at God's goodness to me with my friends"; this is called *the cup of deliverance* because it was drunk in memory of his deliverance. "Because God has lavished on me so many benefits, I will readily accept whatever cup he puts into my hands; I will not argue with him, but will welcome his holy will." David spoke the language of the Son of David. *The cup that my Father has given me, shall I not* take it and *drink it?* (Jn 18:11).

3.2.2. *I will offer to thee the sacrifice of thanksgiving.* We must first *give our own selves* to God as *living sacrifices* (Ro 12:1; 2Co 8:5), and then give what we have for his honor in works of godliness and kindness. Why should we offer something to God which costs us nothing?

3.3. He will always have good thoughts of God, who is very concerned for the lives and the encouragement of his people (v. 15): *Precious in the sight of the Lord is the death of his saints*, so precious that he will not encourage any of David's enemies by allowing them to kill him. David has encouraged himself with this thought in the depths of his distress and danger, and now that events have confirmed it, he comforts others with it.

3.3.1. Having asked, *What shall I render?* (v. 12), he here surrenders himself, which was *more than all burnt offerings and sacrifice* (Mk 12:33) (v. 16): "*O Lord! truly I am thy servant.* I choose to be so; I decide to be so; I will live and die in your service." He has called God's people, who are dear to him, *his saints*; but when he comes to state his own relationship to God, he does not say, *Truly I am thy saint*, but, *I am thy servant.* David is a king, but he glories in being God's servant. People came to be servants in one of two ways, by birth or by redemption. David was God's servant in both ways. By birth: "Lord, I was born in your house; I am *the son of thy handmaid* (v. 16), and so I am yours." It is a great mercy to be the children of godly parents, as it makes us aware of our duty and may be pleaded with God for mercy. By redemption: those who obtained the release of a captive took that person as their servant. "*Lord, thou hast loosed my bonds* (chains) (v. 16); and so *I am thy servant* (v. 16) and am entitled to your protection as well as obliged to do your work." Bishop Patrick reads it, "The very bonds which you have loosed will bind me faster to you."

3.3.2. He will be careful to pay his vows and fulfill what he has promised. Vows are debts that must be paid, for it is better not to vow than to make a vow and not fulfill it (Ecc 5:5). He will fulfill his vows in the tabernacle, *in the midst of Jerusalem* (v. 19), so that he may make devotion more acceptable in the wider community.

PSALM 117

This psalm is short and sweet. I think the reason that it is sung so often is its brevity, but if we rightly understood and considered it, we would sing it more often because of its sweetness. Here is: 1. A sacred call to all nations to praise God (v. 1). 2. Good reasons suggested for that praise (v. 2).

Verses 1–2

There is a great deal of the Gospel in this psalm. The apostle Paul has provided us with a key to it (Ro 15:11), quoting it as proof that the Gospel was to be preached to the Gentile nations, an assertion that was still a great stumbling block to the Jews. Why should that offend them when it is said—and they themselves had often sung it— *Praise the Lord, all you nations* (Gentiles), *praise him, all you people?* Some of the Jewish writers confess that this psalm refers to the kingdom of the Messiah; in fact, one of them thinks that it consists of two verses to show

that in the days of the Messiah God will be glorified by two kinds of people: the Jews, according to the Law of Moses, and the Gentiles, who fulfill the Seven Precepts of the Sons of Noah; together, these will make up one church, just as these two verses make up one psalm. We have here:

1. The vast extent of the Gospel church (v. 1). Here *all nations* are called to praise the Lord, which could not be applied to the Old Testament times, because unless the people of the land became Jews and were circumcised, they were not allowed to praise God with the Jews. But the Gospel of Christ is ordered to be preached to all nations, and by him the dividing wall of hostility has been taken down, and those who were *afar off* are *made nigh* (Eph 2:13–14). Note who would be admitted into the church: *All nations* and *all people* (v. 1). The original words are the same that are used for the *heathen that rage* and the *people that imagine* (who plot) against Christ (2:1); those who had been enemies to his kingdom would become his willing subjects. The Gospel of the kingdom was to be preached to *all the world, for a witness to all nations* (Mt 24:14; Mk 16:15). Because the news of the Gospel would be sent to all nations, it would give them reason to praise God; the institution of Gospel services of worship would give them opportunity to praise God, and the power of Gospel grace would give them hearts to praise him.

2. The unsearchable riches of Gospel grace, which are to be the matter of our praise (v. 2). In the Gospel, those celebrated attributes of God, his mercy and his truth (85:10; 89:2; etc.; NIV: love and faithfulness), shine most brightly in themselves and most encouragingly to us. These are the things for which the Gentiles should glorify God (Ro 15:8–9): for *the truth of God* and for *his mercy.* God's love is the fountain of all our comforts, and his faithfulness is the foundation of all our hopes, and so we must praise the Lord for both.

PSALM 118

David probably wrote this psalm when he had finally gained the victory, after he had successfully weathered many storms and gained full possession of the kingdom to which he had been anointed. He invites his friends to join him in having a confident expectation of the promised Messiah, of whose kingdom, and of whose exaltation to it, David's kingdom and exaltation were types. It is certain that the prophet is here bearing witness to him in the second part of the psalm. Christ himself applies it to himself (Mt 21:42), and the former part of the psalm may fairly, and without undue straining, be seen to harmonize with him and his undertaking. Some think it was first intended for the ceremony of bringing the ark into the City of David and was later sung at the Feast of Tabernacles. In it: 1. David calls on everyone around him to give God glory for his goodness (vv. 1–4); from his experience of God's power and compassion, he encourages himself and others to trust in God (vv. 5–18). 2. He gives thanks for his advancement to the throne, as it prefigured the exaltation of Christ (vv. 19–23); the people, the priests, and the psalmist himself triumph over the prospect of the Redeemer's kingdom (vv. 24–29).

Verses 1–18

It appears here, as it often does elsewhere, that David had his heart full of the goodness of God.

1. David celebrates God's mercy in general and calls on others to acknowledge it from their own experience (v. 1).

Priests and people, Jews and converts, must all acknowledge God's goodness and all join in the same thankful song. If they can say no more, let them say this to him, that *his mercy endures for ever*, that they experience it every day.

2. David keeps a record of God's gracious dealings with him in particular. In his time, David had gone through a great deal of difficulty, which gave him great experience of God's goodness. Let us therefore notice here:

2.1. The great distress and danger he has been in, which he reflects on to exalt God's goodness to him in his present advancement. There are many people who, when their spirits are lifted, do not want to speak about their former depression, but here David takes every opportunity to remember his own low state. He was *in distress* (v. 5); there were many who *hated him* (v. 7), and this must have been a heavy burden on one with such a sincere spirit, who wanted to gain the love of all. *All nations compassed me about* (surrounded me) (v. 10). All the nations around Israel tried to disturb David when he had just come to the throne: Philistines, Moabites, Syrians, and Ammonites. They allied themselves against him. They were dangerous and violent, and succeeded for a time in their attempts against him: *They compassed me about like bees* (v. 12), swarmed around him, attacked him with their harmful stings, but it was to their own destruction, as the bee loses its life when it stings. Trouble came to David by the wrongs people did him (v. 13): "*Thou—my enemy—hast thrust sore at me.* You pushed me back violently so that I was about to fall." Trouble also came to him by the afflictions which God laid on him (v. 18): *The Lord has chastened me sore* (severely). People pushed him back to destroy him; God rebuked him to teach him. They pushed him back with the hatred of enemies; God rebuked him with the love and tenderness of a Father.

2.2. The favor God gave David in his distress. God heard his prayer (v. 5): "*He answered me* with relief; he did more for me than I could ever ask; he released my heart in prayer and gave me more, far more than I wanted." God confounded the intentions of his enemies against him: they were *quenched as the fire of thorns* (v. 12), which burns furiously for a while, makes a loud noise and great flames, but quickly dies out and cannot do the trouble it threatened. God sustained his life when there was only a step between him and death (v. 18; 1Sa 20:3): "He has *chastened me*, but he has not *given me over unto death*, for he has not given me over to the will of my enemies."

2.3. The use David made of this favor. He can say from his own experience, *It is better*, more secure, more reasonable, *to trust in the Lord, than to put confidence in man*, even though it is *in princes* (vv. 8–9). God's favor also enabled him to be victorious in that trust. *The Lord is on my side*. If we are on God's side, then he is on ours; if we are for him and with him, he will be for us and with us (v. 7): "*The Lord takes my part* and stands up for me *with those that help me.*" And so (v. 14), "*The Lord is my strength and my song;* I depend on him as my strength, and I comfort myself in him as my song." If God is our strength, he must also be our song; if he works in us all the time, he must also receive all praise and glory from us. If he is our strength and our song, he has become not only our Savior but also our salvation. David triumphs in an assurance of the continuation of his encouragement, his victory, and his life:

2.3.1. His encouragement (v. 15): *The voice of rejoicing and salvation is in the tabernacles of the righteous*, especially in mine, in my family. The homes of righteous people in this world are only lowly and portable tabernacles; we have *no continuing city* here (Heb 13:14). But these tabernacles are more encouraging to them than the palaces of the evildoers are to them, for in the house where religious faith rules there is salvation. Where there is salvation, there is cause for rejoicing, for continual joy in God. Where there is rejoicing, there should be *the voice* of rejoicing, that is, praise and thanksgiving.

2.3.2. His victory: *The right hand of the Lord does valiantly* (v. 15) and *is exalted* (v. 16), for, as some read v. 16, "it has exalted me."

2.3.3. His life (v. 17): "*I shall not die* by the hands of my enemies who seek my life, *but live and declare the works of the Lord*; I will live as a monument to God's mercy and power; his works will be declared in me, and I will make it the work of my life to praise and exalt God, looking on that as the reason my life has been preserved."

Verses 19–29

We have here a glorious prophecy of the humiliation and exaltation of our Lord Jesus Christ, of his sufferings and the glory that would follow. Peter applies it directly to the chief priests and teachers of the law, and none of them could accuse him of misapplying it (Ac 4:11). Notice here:

1. The introduction with which this precious prophecy begins (vv. 19–21).

1.1. The psalmist wants to be admitted to the sanctuary of God to celebrate there the glory of him *that cometh in the name of the Lord* (v. 26): *Open to me the gates of righteousness* (v. 19). The temple gates are called this. And when the gates of righteousness are opened to us, we must *go into them*, we must enter the Most Holy Place (Heb 10:19), as far as we are allowed, *and praise the Lord* (v. 19).

1.2. He sees admission granted him (v. 20): *This is the gate of the Lord*, the gate he has appointed, *into which the righteous shall enter.* Some understand this gate to refer to Christ, by whom we are taken into fellowship with God and by whom our praises are accepted; he is *the way*; there is no coming to the Father except by him (Jn 14:6). The psalmist triumphs in the revelation that the gate of righteousness, which has been shut for so long and was knocked at for so long, has now finally been opened.

1.3. He promises to give thanks to God for this favor (v. 21): *I will praise thee.* Those who saw Christ's day at such a great distance saw good reasons to praise God for the prospect (Jn 8:56), for in him they saw that God had heard them, had heard the prayers of the Old Testament saints for the coming of the Messiah, and he would be their salvation.

2. The prophecy itself (vv. 22–23). This may contain some references to David's advancement; he was the stone that Saul and his courtiers rejected, but was by the wonderful providence of God advanced to be the capstone of the building. But it mainly refers to Christ, and we have here:

2.1. His humiliation. He is *the stone which the builders refused* (v. 22); he is the *stone cut out of the mountain without hands* (Da 2:34). This stone was *rejected by the builders* (v. 22), by the rulers and people of the Jews (Ac 4:8, 10–11); they refused to acknowledge him as the Messiah. They denied him in the presence of Pilate (Ac 3:13) when they said, *We have no king but Caesar* (Jn 19:15).

2.2. His exaltation. He *has become the head stone of the corner* (v. 22); he is both advanced to the highest degree of honor and given the greatest work, so that he may be both above all and all in all (Eph 1:23; Col 3:11). He is the chief cornerstone in the foundation, in whom

Jew and Gentile are united, so that they may be built up into one holy house. He is the chief capstone in the corner, in whom the building is completed, and who must be supreme in all things (Col 1:18), as the *author and finisher of our faith* (Heb 12:2).

2.3. The hand of God in all this. God's hand was with him throughout his whole undertaking, and from first to last Jesus did his Father's will. This should be *marvellous in our eyes* (v. 23). Christ's name is *Wonderful* (Isa 9:6); and the redemption he brought about is the most wonderful of all God's works.

3. The joy with which the prophecy is received, the acclamations which accompany this prediction.

3.1. Let the day be celebrated to the honor of God with great joy (v. 24): *This is the day the Lord has* made. Or it may be rightly understood to apply to the Christian Sabbath, which we make holy in remembrance of Christ's resurrection, when the rejected stone began to be exalted. Here is the doctrine of the Christian Sabbath: *It is the day which the Lord has made* (v. 24). He has made it significant, he has made it holy, he has set it apart from other days; he has *made it for man* (Mk 2:27). *We will rejoice and be glad in it* (v. 24), not only in the institution of the day but also on the occasion of it, Christ's becoming the *head of the corner.* Sabbaths must be days of rejoicing.

3.2. Let the exalted Redeemer be met, and attended, with joyful hosannas (vv. 25–26). This is like the shout, "Long live the king," and expresses a hearty joy for his accession to the crown. *Hosanna* means, "Save now, I pray you." "Lord, save me, I pray you; may this Savior be *my* Savior, and therefore my ruler; may I be taken under his protection and recognized as one of his willing subjects. May I have victory over those sinful desires *that war against my soul* (1Pe 2:11), and may divine grace remain in my heart *conquering and to conquer*" (Rev 6:2). "Lord, preserve even the Savior himself. May his name be consecrated, may his *kingdom come*, his *will be done*" (Mt 6:10). *Let prayer be made for him continually* (72:15). When we rejoice in his kingdom on the Lord's Day, we must pray for it to advance more and more. Let the priests, the Lord's ministers, do their part in this great ceremony (v. 26). Let them bless the prince with their praises: *Blessed is he that cometh in the name of the Lord.* We must welcome him into our hearts, saying, "Come in, blessed One of the Lord; come in by your grace and Spirit, and take possession of me as your own." We must pray for the relief and building up of his church, for the preparation for his second coming, and then that the One who has said, *Surely I come quickly*, would *even so come* (Rev 22:20). Christ's ministers are not only authorized but also appointed to declare a blessing in his name on all his loyal subjects who love him and his rule in sincerity (Eph 6:24).

3.3. Let sacrifices of thanksgiving be offered to the honor of him who offered for us the great atoning sacrifice (v. 27). *He has shown us light* (v. 27), that is, he has given us the knowledge of himself and his will. He has made his light shine upon us; he has given us reason for joy, which is light to the soul, by giving us a prospect of eternal light in heaven. This privilege lays a duty on us: *Bind the sacrifice with cords*, so that when it has been killed, its blood may be sprinkled *upon the horns of the altar* (v. 27), according to the Law. Or this may have some special significance here; the sacrifice we are to offer to God, in thanksgiving for redeeming love, is ourselves, not to be killed on the altar, but to be presented as *living sacrifices* (Ro 12:1), to bring spiritual sacrifices of prayer and praise.

3.4. The psalmist concludes with his own thankful acknowledgments of divine grace, in which he calls on others to join with him (vv. 28–29). He wants everyone around him to give thanks to God for this good news of great joy to all people, that there is a Redeemer, Christ the Lord (Lk 2:10–11). It is in him that God *is good* to people and that *his mercy endures for ever* (v. 29). He concludes this psalm as he began it (v. 1), for God's glory must be the Alpha and Omega, the beginning and the end, of whatever we say to him.

PSALM 119

This is a psalm in a class by itself, like none of the other psalms; it surpasses them all. It seems to me to be a collection of David's brief godly and devout prayers, the short and sudden sighs and elevations of his soul to God, which he wrote down as they occurred. There is seldom any coherence between the verses; like Solomon's proverbs, this is a chest of gold rings, not a chain of gold links. And we may learn from the psalmist's example to get used to such brief godly prayers—which are an excellent means of maintaining fellowship with God. What some have said about this psalm is true: "Those who read it thoughtfully will find it either warms them or shames them."

Its composition is extraordinary and exact. It is divided into twenty-two parts, according to the number of the letters of the Hebrew alphabet, and each part consists of eight verses, all the verses of the first part beginning with Aleph, all the verses of the second with Beth, and so on, without any errors in the whole psalm. Some have called it the saints' alphabet. Be that as it may, it would be useful to learners, a help both in committing it to memory and in calling it to mind as need be. Once the letter of the first word had been remembered, that would bring up the whole verse, and so young people would more easily learn it by heart and better remember it even to their old age.

The general scope and intention of this psalm is to exalt the Law and honor it, to set out the excellence and usefulness of divine revelation, and to commend it to us, by the psalmist's own example, as a rule for our lives. He speaks from experience about its benefit and fervently prays, from first to last, for God's grace to continue with him.

There are ten different words by which divine revelation is referred to in this psalm, each of them expressing its whole extent and the system of religious faith which is based on it and guided by it. The things contained in Scripture and drawn from it are then called: 1. God's Law, because they are enacted by him as our Sovereign. 2. His way, because they are the rule both of his providence and of our obedience. 3. His testimonies, because they are solemnly declared to the world. 4. His commandments, because they are given with authority and deposited and entrusted with us. 5. His precepts, because they are prescribed to us. 6. His word, or saying, because it is the declaration of his mind, and Christ, the eternal Word, is all in all in it (Eph 1:23; Col 3:11). 7. His judgments, because we must both judge and be judged by them. 8. His righteousness, because it is all holy, just, and good, and the rule and standard of righteousness. 9. His statutes, because they are fixed and have perpetual obligation. 10. His truth, or faithfulness, because the principles on which the divine law is built are eternal truths. I think there is only one verse (v. 122) in this psalm which does not contain one or other of these ten words; only in three or four are they used concerning God's providence or David's practice (as vv. 75, 84, 121), and in v. 132 they are called God's name.

The great respect and affection David had for the word of God is more wonderful considering how little he had of it in comparison with what we now have; he had in writing no more perhaps than the first books of Moses, which were just the dawn of this day, and this shames us, who enjoy the full divine revelation but are so cold toward it.

1. Aleph

Verses 1–3

The psalmist here shows that godly people are happy people. We are told what we must do and be like so that we may gain happiness. Those are happy:

1. Who make the will of God the rule of all their actions. God's word is a law to them; they walk in the paths of that law. This is *walking in God's ways* (v. 3), the ways which he has marked out for us.

2. Who are upright and blameless in their religious faith—*undefiled in the way* (v. 1)—who not only keep themselves *unspotted from the world* (Jas 1:27) but are consistently sincere in their intentions, *in whose spirit there is no guile* (32:2), who really are as good as they seem to be and whose actual lives have integrity and are in harmony with what they profess.

3. Who are true to the trust placed on them as God's professing people. Those who want to *walk in the law of the Lord* must *keep his testimonies* (vv. 1–2), that is, his truths. Or *his testimonies* may refer to his covenant; the ark of the covenant is called *the ark of the testimony* (Ex 25:22). Those who do not keep the commandments of God do not keep his covenant.

4. Who single-mindedly look to God as their highest good and greatest purpose in all they do in their religious faith (v. 2): they *seek him with their whole heart*.

5. Who carefully avoid all sin (v. 3): *They do no iniquity*. They are conscious of much that still hinders them from following the way of God, but not of that sin which leads them to abandon those ways.

Verses 4–6

We are taught here to acknowledge ourselves to be under the highest obligations to walk according to God's Law: "*Thou hast commanded us to keep thy precepts*, you have laid down precepts (v. 4), to make religious faith our rule." We are also taught to look to God for wisdom and grace to obey him (v. 5). "You want me to keep your precepts, and, Lord, I will gladly keep them." *This is the will of God, even our sanctification* (1Th 4:3). Every good person has *a respect to all* God's *commandments*, both those that concern us inwardly and those that concern us outwardly, both those addressed to the mind and those addressed to the heart. People who have a sincere *respect to all* God's *commandments shall not be ashamed*. They will have a blamelessness and courage in their own souls.

Verses 7–8

Here is:

1. David seeking to master his religious faith. He hopes to *learn* God's *righteous judgments* (v. 7). He knows much already, but he is still pressing onward and wants to know even more. As long as we live, we must be scholars in Christ's school and sit at his feet.

2. The use he would make of his divine learning. *I will praise thee when I have learned thy judgments* (v. 7). In this he suggests that he cannot learn unless God teaches him, and that divine instructions are special blessings.

Those who have fully resolved, in the strength of God's grace, to keep his statutes have learned them well.

3. His prayer to God not to leave him. Good people see themselves as ruined if God abandons them, for then Satan will be too powerful for them.

2. Beth

Verse 9

Here is:

1. A significant question asked. How may the next generation be made better than this one? *Wherewithal shall a young man cleanse his way?* (v. 9).

2. A satisfactory answer given to this question. Young people may effectively *cleanse their way by taking heed thereto according to* the *word of* God (v. 9). Young people must make the word of God their rule. That will do more toward purifying young people than the laws of rulers or the morals of philosophers. They must carefully apply that rule as a standard and use that chart and compass to steer their way through life.

Verse 10

Here is David's experience: "*I have sought thee* (v. 10). If I have not yet found you, *I have sought thee*, and you never said, 'Seek me in vain,' nor will you say so to me, for I *have sought thee with my whole heart* (v. 10; see also Isa 45:19). You have inclined me to seek your precepts, so do not allow me to stray from them."

Verse 11

Here is the close application which David made of the word of God to himself: *He hid it in his heart* (v. 11) so that it might be readily available to him whenever he needed it. God's word is a treasure worth storing, and the only place it can be safely stored is in our hearts. If we have it only in our minds, our memories may fail us, but if our hearts are formed into its mold and its impressions remain on our souls, then it is secure.

Verse 12

Here David gives glory to God: *Blessed art thou, O Lord!* (v. 12). He asks grace from God: "*Teach me thy statutes* (v. 12); may I know and do my duty in everything."

Verses 13–16

Here:

1. David has edified others with what he had been taught from the word of God (v. 13). He did this not only as a king, by making orders and administering justice according to the word of God, or only as a prophet, by his psalms, but also in his ordinary life.

2. He looks forward with a holy determination never to cool off in his affection for the word of God (v. 15): *I will meditate in thy precepts*. He not only spoke about them to others but also *communed with his own heart* (4:4) about them. David took more delight in God's statutes than in the pleasures of his court or the honors of his camp, more than in his sword or in his harp. When the law is written on the heart (Jer 31:33), duty becomes a delight.

3. Gimel

Verse 17

David prays, *Deal bountifully with* me, *that I may live* (v. 17). It was God's goodness that gave us this life, and the same goodness that gave it keeps it going and provides all its supports and encouragements. We should therefore spend our lives in God's service.

Verse 18

There are *wondrous things* in God's *law* (v. 18), not only unusual things, which are unexpected, but also excellent things, which are to be valued, and things which were long *hidden from the wise and prudent* but are now *revealed unto babes* (Mt 11:25). If there were wonders in the law, then much more in the Gospel. By nature we are blind to the things of God until his grace causes the scales to fall from our eyes (Ac 9:18). The more God opens our eyes, the more wonderful things we will see in the word of God.

Verse 19

Here we have:

1. The acknowledgment which David makes of his own condition: *I am a stranger in the earth* (v. 19). All good people confess themselves to be so, for heaven is their home, and the world is just where they are temporarily staying, the land of their pilgrimage (Ex 6:4). David knew as much of the world, and was as well known in it, as most people. Foreigners submitted to him, and people he had not known served him (18:43); he had a name like the names of great people (2Sa 7:9), but he still called himself a stranger. We are all strangers on earth and must consider ourselves so.

2. The request he makes to God: *Hide not thy commandments from me* (v. 19). He means more: "Lord, show your commandments to me; may I never know the lack of the word of God, and as long as I live, may I grow in knowing it more and more. I am a stranger and therefore need a guide, a guard, a companion, and an encourager; may I always have your commands in view, for they will be all this to me, everything that a poor stranger can desire. I am a stranger here and will soon be gone; may your commands prepare me for my move from here."

Verse 20

David has prayed that God would open his eyes (v. 18) and open the law (v. 19); now here he pleads with a fervent desire for knowledge and grace.

Verse 21

Here is the wretched character of evildoers. Their attitude is bad. They are *proud* and arrogant; they exalt themselves above other people. But that is not all: they exalt themselves against God and set up their wills in opposition to the will of God. There is some pride at the root of every willful sin. They *do err from thy commandments* (v. 21) and follow principles contrary to your commandments, and then it is not surprising that they stray in practice. They are certainly cursed, for *God resists the proud* (Jas 4:6); and those who reject the commands of the law put themselves under its curse (Gal 3:10).

Verse 22

Here David prays against the scorn and contempt of people, that they might be *removed*, or, literally, rolled away from him. This suggests that the people laughed at him and that neither his greatness nor his goodness could protect him from being slandered or ridiculed. Yet he was not laughed out of doing good: "Lord, take it away from me, *for I have kept thy testimonies* (v. 22) nevertheless." If we still maintain our integrity in days of testing, we may be sure things will end well for us.

Verse 23

David was mistreated even by great people, who should have been more aware of his good character and his life. Here David was a type of Christ, for it was the rulers of this world who reviled and *crucified the Lord of glory* (1Co 2:8). When mistreated in this way, David *meditated in God's statutes* (v. 23); he continued to do his duty and paid no attention to them. When they spoke against him, he found something in the word of God that encouraged and strengthened him, and then none of these things could move him.

Verse 24

Here David explains his meditation on God's statutes (v. 23), which was useful to him when rulers spoke against him. God's statutes were *his counsellors*, and they advised him to bear it patiently and commit his cause to God.

4. Daleth

Verse 25

Here is:

1. David's complaint. *My soul cleaves to* (is laid low in) *the dust* (v. 25), which is a complaint either:

1.1. Of his sin, his inclination toward the world and a lack of desire for holy duties. David's complaint here is like the apostle Paul's complaint that his body was like a body of death (Ro 7:24). Or:

1.2. Of his afflictions, trouble either in his mind or in his circumstances, and both together brought him even to the *dust of death*.

2. His request for help: "Preserve my life according to your word. By your providence put life into what I do, and by your grace put life into my devotion; heal me of my spiritual coldness and give me energy in my devotion to you."

Verses 26–27

David had opened up his life and his heart to God: "*I have declared my ways* (v. 26), acknowledging you in all of them; I have taken you along with me in all my plans and work." It is an indescribable comfort to a gracious soul to think with what tenderness all its complaints are received by a gracious God (1Jn 5:14–15). He would put this comfort to good use for the honor of God: "Let me have a good understanding of *the way of thy precepts; so shall I talk* with more assurance *of thy wondrous works*" (v. 27).

Verses 28–29

Here is:

1. David's description of his own sorrow: *My soul melteth for heaviness*, is weary with sorrow (v. 28), which is to the same effect as v. 25, *My soul cleaveth to* (is laid low in) *the dust*. Weariness in the human spirit makes it melt like a candle, drop by drop.

2. His request for God's grace: "*Strengthen thou me with strength in my soul, according to thy word*" (v. 28): *Remove from me the way of lying*. David in a difficult situation had deceived Ahimelech (1Sa 21:2) and Achish (1Sa 21:13; 27:10). It is a great temptation to lie in very difficult situations and excuse it as being for a good cause or as a necessary self-defense, and so David prays that God would prevent him from falling into this sin anymore. "*Grant me thy law graciously*; grant me that to keep me from the *way of lying*" (v. 29). David had written the law with his own hand, for the king was obliged to write a copy of it for his own use (Dt 17:18), but he prays that

he might have it written on his heart (Jer 31:33). "Grant it to me *graciously*"; he begs it as a special sign of God's favor.

Verses 30–32

Those who want to make anything significant of their religious faith must first make it their sincere and deliberate choice; this is what David did: *I have chosen the way of truth* (v. 30). This shows us:

- The way of sincere godliness is the way of truth; the principles it is founded on are principles of eternal truth, and it is the only way to true happiness.
- We must choose to walk in this way not because we know no other way but because we know no better way; in fact we know no other safe and good way. Let us choose to follow that way, to walk in it even though it is narrow (Mt 7:14). *Thy judgments have I laid before me* (v. 30), as those who are learning to write place what they have to copy in front of them so that they may follow it when writing, as workers set out a model or plan so that they may follow it exactly in their work. We must have the word in our hearts by consistently conforming to it, so that we may walk by God's rule. Those who choose to follow religious faith as their rule are likely to adhere to it faithfully: *I have stuck to thy testimonies* (v. 31). Those who are Christians by choice are likely to be steady Christians, while those who are casual Christians change their minds if the wind changes. "*Lord, put me not to shame* (v. 31); do not reject my services, which will confuse me more greatly." The more encouragement God gives us, the more homage he expects from us (v. 32). God by his Spirit *enlarges*, or sets free, the hearts of his people when he gives them wisdom—for that is called *largeness of heart* (1Ki 4:29)—when he *sheds abroad the love of God* (Ro 5:5) in the heart and puts gladness there. The joy of our Lord should oil the wheels of our obedience.

5. He

Verses 33–34

Here:

1. David begs to be taught by God himself, knowing that *none teaches like him* (Job 36:22). "Teach me to follow your statutes; teach me the path of my duty as no one else could teach: *Lord, give me understanding*" (v. 34).

2. He promises faithfully that he will be a good student. If God will teach him, he is sure he will learn well: "I will keep the Law, which I will never do unless I am taught by God."

Verses 35–36

He has prayed before for God to enlighten his understanding so that he might know his duty; here he prays to God to make him submit to his will and to quicken the active powers of his soul so that he might do his duty, for *it is God that works in us both to will and to do*, as well as to understand, what is good (Php 2:13). Notice here: "*Make me to go* (v. 35); strengthen me for every good work. *Incline my heart to thy testimonies* (v. 36), to those things which your testimonies prescribe; not only make me willing to do my duty, as what I must do, but also make me want to do my duty." Duty is done with delight when the heart is inclined to do it, and it is God's grace that inclines us. "Restrain and mortify the inclination there is in me to *covetousness*." Covetousness is a

sin which is opposed to all God's testimonies. Those who want the love of God to be rooted in them must get the love of the world rooted out of them.

Verse 37

Here David prays for grace to restrain him: *Turn away my eyes from beholding vanity* (worthless things) (v. 37). The honors, pleasures, and profits of the world are worthless things; the sight of them and the prospect of them draw many people away from the paths of godliness and religious faith. When the eyes are fixed on these, they infect the heart with the love of them, and then it is separated from God and divine things; we ought to pray that God by his providence would keep worthless things out of our sight and that by his grace he would keep us from being captivated by seeing them.

Verse 38

Good people are *God's servants*, subject to his law and employed in his work, that is, *devoted to his fear* (v. 38), given to his direction and disposal and taken up with high thoughts of him and all those acts of devotion which lead to his glory. Those who are God's servants may, in faith and with humble boldness, pray that God would *establish his word to them* (v. 38), that is, that he would fulfill his promises to them in due time. We must pray for what God has promised; we need not be so ambitious as to ask for more; we need not be so modest as to ask for less.

Verse 39

Here David prays against *reproach*, as he did before (v. 22). He has done what might give *occasion to the enemies of the Lord to blaspheme* (2Sa 12:14); now he prays that God, who has everyone's hearts and tongues in his hands (Pr 21:1), would be willing to prevent this, to *deliver him from all his transgressions* so that he *might not be the reproach of the foolish*, which he feared (39:8). "Lord, you are sitting on the throne, and *thy judgments are right and good* (v. 39), just and kind, to those who have been wronged, and so I appeal to you against the unjust and unkind criticism I am facing."

Verse 40

Here David professes the passionate devotion he has for the word of God: "*I have longed after thy precepts* (v. 40); not only have I loved them but also I have fervently desired to know them more. You have worked in me this languishing desire; put life into me so that I may pursue it; *quicken me in thy righteousness* (v. 40), in your righteous ways, according to your righteous promises."

6. Waw

Verses 41–42

Here is:

1. David's prayer for the salvation of the Lord. "Lord, you are my Savior; I am miserable in myself, and only you can make me happy; *let thy salvation come to me* (v. 41). Come quickly with salvation from my present physical distresses, and come with eternal salvation by giving me what I need to qualify for it."

2. His dependence on the grace and promise of God for that salvation. These are the two pillars on which our hope is built, and they will not fail us.

Verses 43–44

Here is David's humble request for an instructed tongue, so that he might know how to *speak a word in season* (Isa 50:4) for the glory of God: *Take not the word of truth utterly out of my mouth* (v. 43). He means, "Lord, may the word of truth be always in my mouth; may I have the necessary wisdom and courage both to use my knowledge to teach others and to clearly declare my faith whenever I am called to do so" (1Pe 3:15). He professes his commitment to his duty in the strength of God's grace: *"So shall I keep thy law continually* (v. 44). If I have your word not only in my heart but also in my mouth, I will do all I should do and stand complete in your complete will."

Verses 45–48

Notice in these verses what a fondness David had of the law of God: *"I seek thy precepts* (v. 45). I do all I can to *understand what the will of the Lord is* (Eph 5:17) and to seek his mind. *I seek thy precepts,* for *I have loved them* (vv. 47–48). I agree with them, affirming not only that they are good but also that they are good for me." He promises himself five things in the strength of God's grace:

- That he will be free and at peace in what he does: *"I will walk at liberty* (v. 45), freed from what is evil and free to do what is good, doing it not because I am forced to but because I want to."
- That he will be bold and courageous in doing his duty: *I will speak of thy testimonies before kings* (v. 46). We must never be afraid to acknowledge our faith, even though it may expose us to the wrath of kings, but speak of it as something we will live and die by, as the three young men did before Nebuchadnezzar (Da 3:16; Ac 4:20).
- That he will be cheerful and pleased to do his duty (v. 47): *"I will delight myself in thy commandments,* in all my dealings with them, in conforming to them. I will never be so pleased with myself as when I do what is pleasing to God."
- That he will be diligent and vigorous in doing his duty: *I will lift up my hands to thy commandments* (v. 48). "I will take up my hands to do the command, not only to praise it but also to practice it; in fact, I will lift up my hands to do it, that is, I will exert all my strength to do it."
- That he will be thoughtful and considerate in doing his duty (v. 48): *"I will meditate in thy statutes."*

7. Zayin

Verse 49

David here prays to God for the mercy and grace he hopes for, pleading that God has given him the promise in which he hopes: "Lord, I want nothing more than that you would *remember thy word unto thy servant* (v. 49) and *do as thou hast said"*; see 1Ch 17:23. "You are faithful, and so you will fulfill your promises and not break your word." He who by his Spirit worked faith in us will, according to our faith, work it out for us and not disappoint us.

Verse 50

Here is David's experience of benefiting from God's word. *"Thy word has quickened me.* It made me alive when I was dead in sin (Ro 4:17; Eph 2:1, 5); it has restored me many times when I was unresponsive in duty; it has quickened me to do what is good when I was backward and reluctant to do it, and it has stirred up in me what is good when I was cold and indifferent."

Verse 51

David had been laughed at for his religious faith. Although he had done significant service for his country, nevertheless, because he was devout and conscientious, *the proud have him greatly in derision.* They laughed at him for his praying and called it purely ritual, laughed at his seriousness and called it moping, and laughed at his strict observance of his faith and called it needlessly fussy. But he had not been laughed *out of* his religious faith. Travelers go on their way even though dogs bark at them. Those who cannot bear harsh words for Christ can bear very little.

Verse 52

When David was laughed at for his godliness, he not only held fast his integrity but also encouraged himself. He not only endured scorn but endured it cheerfully. It was an encouragement to him to think that it was for God's sake that he endured scorn. Those who are laughed at for their faithfulness to God's law may encourage themselves with this: that *the reproach* (disgrace) *of Christ* will prove, in the end, *greater riches* to them *than the treasures of Egypt* (Heb 11:26).

Verse 53

Here is the character of those who are openly and grossly evil: *They forsake thy law.* And here is the impression which the evil of evildoers made on David: it frightened him. He trembled to think of the dishonor it gave God, the gratification it gave Satan, and the trouble it gave human souls. He feared the consequences of it both for the sinners themselves and for the interests of God's kingdom.

Verse 54

This world is where we are simply lodging, the house in which we are pilgrims. We must confess that we are *strangers and pilgrims upon earth* (Heb 11:13), who are not at home here and will not stay here long. Even David's palace is just the house of his pilgrimage. *"Thy statutes have been my songs,* with which I occupy myself here," as travelers often distract themselves from thinking about their weariness and remove some of the tedium of their journey by occasionally singing pleasant songs. David was the sweet singer of Israel (2Sa 23:1), and here we are told where he drew material for his songs from; they were all taken from the word of God.

Verses 55–56

When others were asleep, David thought about God's name, and by repeating that thought he increased his knowledge of it. When he was suffering at night, he called this to mind. *"I remembered thy name in the night* (v. 55) and so was careful to keep your law all day. I had the comfort of keeping your law because I kept it." God's word pays its own wages. A heart to obey the will of God is a most valuable reward of obedience.

8. Heth

Verse 57

David can appeal to God about this: "Lord, you know I have chosen you as my portion and depend on you to make me content." Godly people make the law of God their rule: *"I have said that I would keep thy words;* and I will do what by your grace I have said I will do, and I will be faithful to it to the end." Those who find God to be all they need must take him as their ruler.

Verse 58

In the previous verse David reflected on his covenants with God, and he here reflects on his prayers to God and renews his request. He prays, "*Be merciful to me*, by forgiving what I have done wrong and by giving me grace to do better for the future." He prays *with his whole heart*.

Verses 59–60

David *thought on his ways* (v. 59). His thoughts were settled. Some consider this to be an allusion to embroiderers, who sew very exactly and carefully to hide the least flaw, or to those who draw up the fine details of financial accounts, who ask, "What do I owe? What am I worth?" He *turned his feet to God's testimonies* (v. 59). He determined to make the word of God the rule of his life and to walk by that rule. He did this immediately and without any hesitation (v. 60): *I made haste and delayed not*. The account David here gives of himself may refer either to his constant practice every day or to the time when he first came to know God and religious faith, when he began to throw off the worthlessness of childhood and youth and to remember his Creator (Ecc 12:1).

Verse 61

David's enemies were evildoers who hated him for his godliness and tried to take away his good name. But here are the testimonies of David's conscience that he had remained faithful to his religious faith when he had been robbed of everything else, as Job did when the bands of the Chaldeans and Sabeans had robbed him (Job 1:15–17, 22): *But I have not forgotten thy law*.

Verse 62

Though David in this psalm is very much in prayer, he still does not neglect the duty of thanksgiving, for those who pray much will also have much to give thanks for. He does not say, "*I will give thanks* because of your favors to me," but, "*because of thy righteous judgments*, all that your providence has set out in wisdom and justice." David's heart was set on giving thanks. He would *rise at midnight to give thanks* to God. Public worship will not excuse us from private devotion. He did not lie still and give thanks, but got up out of his bed, perhaps in the cold and in the dark, to do it more solemnly.

Verse 63

David often expressed the great love he had for God; here he expresses the great love he has for the people of God. He loves them not so much because they are his best friends and therefore most eager to serve him, but because they are those who *fear God* and *keep his precepts*; he is *a companion of them*. He also joins with them in holy acts of worship in the courts of the Lord, where rich and poor, prince and peasant, meet together. He sympathizes with them in their joys and sorrows (Heb 10:33).

Verse 64

Here David pleads that God would be good to all the creatures according to their needs and abilities; just as heaven is full of God's glory, so *the earth is full of his mercy*. Not only human beings on earth, but even the lower creatures, taste God's goodness. He therefore prays that God would be good to him according to his needs and abilities.

9. Teth

Verses 65–66

Here David makes a thankful acknowledgment of God's gracious dealings with him throughout his life:

Thou hast dealt well with thy servant (v. 65). However God has dealt with us, we must acknowledge he has dealt *well* with us, much better than we deserve, and all in his love and with the intention of working for our good (Ro 8:28). David bases a request for divine instruction on these experiences: *Teach me good judgment and knowledge* (v. 66). "Teach me the goodness of judgment and knowledge," a good enjoyment—"Teach me," literally, "good taste," the ability to discern different things, to distinguish between truth and falsehood, good and evil, for *the ear tries words, as the mouth tastes meat* (Job 34:3). Many people have knowledge but have little judgment. Where God has given a good heart, a good mind too may be prayed for in faith.

Verse 67

David tells:

1. Of the temptations of prosperity: "*Before I was afflicted*, while I lived in peace and plenty and knew no sorrow, *I went astray* (v. 67) from God and my duty." Prosperity is the unhappy cause of much sin; it makes people proud of themselves, indulgent of their flesh, forgetful of God, in love with the world, and deaf to the rebukes of the word. See 30:6.

2. Of the benefit of suffering: "*Now have I kept thy word*, and so have recovered from my wandering." God often uses suffering to bring back to himself those who have wandered away from him. The prodigal son's distress brought him first to himself and then to his father (Lk 15:17–20).

Verse 68

Here David praises God's goodness and gives him glory for it: *Thou art good and doest good*. "Lord, you do good to all, you are the One who gives generously to all creatures; this is the good I beg you to do to me. Instruct me in my duty, incline me to it, and enable me to do it."

Verses 69–70

Those who were proud envied David's reputation because it put them in the shade, and so they did all they could to ruin him. In their pride they persuaded themselves that they were not sinning by telling a deliberate lie if it was going to expose him to contempt. David bore it patiently; he kept that precept which forbade him from returning abuse for abuse. He did not envy their prosperity. *Their heart is as fat as grease* (NIV: is callous) (v. 70). The proud are *at ease* (123:4); they are full of the world, with its wealth and pleasures, and this makes them falsely secure and stupid; they are unfeeling. They involve themselves in the pleasures of the world. But "I would not change places with them. *I delight in thy law* (v. 70); I base my security on the promises of God's word." The children of God who know spiritual delights need not envy the children of this world their worldly pleasures.

Verse 71

Proud people and evildoers lived in all their display of pleasure while David continued to suffer even though he had kept close to God and his duty. Yet David could say from experience, *It was good for me*. He had learned many good lessons from his suffering. The suffering had contributed to his growth in knowledge and grace. The One who rebuked him taught him.

Verse 72

God's *law*, which David got to know more in his suffering, was *better* to him than all the *gold and silver* which he lost by his suffering. David had only a little of the word of God in comparison with what we now have, but notice how highly he valued it. We have the complete Old and New Testaments. He valued the law because it is *the law of God's mouth*, the revelation of his will. His riches increased, and yet he did not set his heart on them, but on the word of God.

10. Yodh

Verse 73

David here adores God as the author of his existence (Job 10:8). Everyone is as truly the work of God's hands as the first man was (139:15 – 16). "*Thy hands have* not only *made me* but also *fashioned me*, made me noble and fine, endowed with these powers and faculties." He also turns to God as the God of grace and asks him to be the author of his new and better being. "Lord, make me anew by your grace so that I may fulfill the purpose of my creation and my life may be worthwhile: *Give me understanding, that I may learn thy commandments.*"

Verse 74

Here is the confidence of this good man in the hope of God's salvation: "*I have hoped in thy word.* It is a hope that *maketh not ashamed* (Ro 5:5), a hope that is a present assurance and will end in fruitfulness." The comforts which some of God's children have in God, and the favors they have received from him, should be the subject of joy to others.

Verse 75

David is still suffering, and he acknowledges that his sin was justly corrected: *I know, O Lord, that thy judgments are right*; they are truly righteous. We know that God is holy in his nature and wise and just in every act of his rule, and so we know, in general, that his *judgments are right*, even though in some particular instances there may be difficulties which we cannot easily resolve. Troubles are in the covenant, and so they are not meant to hurt us, but are intended for our good.

Verses 76 – 77

Here is a passionate request to God for his favor. Those who acknowledge the justice of God in their suffering, as David had done (v. 75), may in faith and humble boldness ask fervently for the mercy of God, and the signs and fruits of that mercy, in their suffering. David prays for God's *merciful kindness* (his unfailing love) (v. 76), his *tender mercies* (compassion) (v. 77). "May your compassion *come to me*," that is, "its signs and effects; may it work to help and save me. That will comfort me when nothing else will; that will comfort me for whatever makes me sad."

Verses 78 – 79

Here David shows that there were those who dealt perversely with him and misinterpreted all he said and did, but he gave it no attention. He knew it was *without cause* (v. 78). Taunts that come to us without cause, like curses without cause, do not hurt us and so should not move us. He could pray in faith, "*Let* them *be ashamed*, that is, may they be brought either to repentance or to ruin." But he valued the goodwill of saints. *Let those that fear thee turn to me* (v. 79). Good people want the friendship and company of those who are good. Some think the verse suggests that when David had been guilty of that grievous sin of murdering Uriah, those who feared God cut

themselves off from him because they were ashamed of him. This troubled him, and so he prayed, "Lord, let them *turn to me* again."

Verse 80

Here David prays for sincerity and expresses his fear of the consequences of hypocrisy: "*Let my heart be sound* (v. 80), so that I may come *boldly to the throne of grace* (Heb 4:16) and may lift up my face without blemish at the great day."

11. Kaph

Verses 81 – 82

The psalmist longs *for the salvation of the Lord* and *for his word* (vv. 81 – 82), that is, salvation according to the word. He is eager not for mere figments of imagination but for the real objects of faith, salvation from the present adversities and doubts and fears. The verse may be understood to refer to the coming of the Messiah; the souls of the faithful even *fainted to see* that salvation of which the prophets testified (1Pe 1:10). They searched intently for it. Abraham saw it at a distance, and so did others (Jn 8:56; Heb 11:11 – 13), but at such a distance that they could not see it decisively. David cried out, *When wilt thou comfort me?* (v. 82). When the *eyes fail*, yet (v. 82) faith must not, for *the vision is for an appointed time, and at the end it shall speak and shall not lie* (Hab 2:3).

Verse 83

David begs God to come quickly to comfort him, *for I have become like a bottle in the smoke* (v. 83), a leather bottle, which if hung for any length of time in smoke became not only blackened with soot but also dried and shriveled up. David is wasted like this by age, sickness, and sorrow. He used to be ruddy, with a fine appearance and handsome features (1Sa 16:12; 17:42), but now he is withered, his color is all gone, and his cheeks are furrowed. When a bottle is wrinkled like this with smoke, it is thrown away and not used anymore. Similarly, David, in his low estate, is looked on *as a despised broken vessel* (31:12). Yet though his suffering has been great, it still has not driven him away from his duty, and so he is within reach of God's promise: *Yet do I not forget thy statutes* (v. 83).

Verse 84

David prays against those who are causing him trouble. He prays not for power to avenge himself—he has no hatred toward anyone—but that God would act in his vengeance. "*The days of my suffering are many*; you see, Lord, how many they are; when will you come in mercy to me? Oh may the days of my trouble be shortened."

Verses 85 – 87

Here David's severe persecution was a type and figure of the state both of Christ and of Christians. His persecutors are *proud* and unjust. *They have digged pits for him* to fall into (v. 85), which suggests that they were deliberate in their plots against him. Here they showed their enmity to God himself. The pits they *dug for him* are *not after God's law*; he means they are very much against his law, which forbids us to *devise evil to our neighbour* (Pr 14:22). The law appointed that, if someone dug a pit which led to any trouble, they must pay for the trouble caused (Ex 21:33 – 34), and much more so when it was dug with malicious intent. He begs that God would stand by him and help him: "*They persecute me; help thou me*

(v. 86); help me in my troubles, so that I may cope with them patiently, and at the right time help me out of my troubles." *God help me* is an excellent comprehensive prayer; it is a pity that it should ever be used lightly.

Verse 88

Here is David praying for divine grace: *Quicken me after thy loving-kindness; so shall I keep thy testimonies.* He has prayed before, *Quicken me in thy righteousness* (v. 40), but here it is, *Quicken me after thy loving-kindness.* The surest sign of God's goodwill toward us is his good work in us.

12. Lamedh

Verses 89–91

The psalmist here acknowledges the unchangeableness of the word of God and all God's purposes: "*For ever, O Lord! thy word is settled,* it stands firm" (v. 89). "Thou art forever thyself," some read it; "you are the same, and you do not change, and this is proof of it. *Thy word,* by which the heavens were made, is eternal in its everlasting results"; *thy faithfulness is unto all generations* (v. 90). He refers to the faithfulness of the course of nature to prove it: *Thou hast established the earth for ever and it abides* (v. 90). It is because of God's promise to Noah (Ge 8:22) that *day and night, summer and winter,* follow a steady course. All creatures are, in their places and according to their abilities, useful to their Creator, and they fulfill the purposes of their creation. Will human beings be the only ones who rebel from his allegiance, the only unprofitable burden on the earth (Lk 13:9)?

Verse 92

Here David was suffering and was ready to *perish in his affliction,* not likely to die so much as to despair; he therefore wondered at the goodness of God to him, that he had kept possession of his own soul, was enabled to keep close to his God, and was not driven away from his religious faith. God's law was his delight in his suffering; it gave him great encouragement and strength. His meditation on it gave him delight in the midst of his solitude and sorrow. The Bible is a pleasant companion at any time.

Verse 93

The best sign of our love for the word of God is never to forget it. Notice here what is the best help for bad memories, namely, good devotion.

Verse 94

Here David claims his relationship with God: "*I am thine,* devoted to you and belonging to you, yours by covenant." He proves his claim: "*I have sought thy precepts.*" This will be the best evidence that we belong to God. He uses his claim: *I am thine; save me.*

Verse 95

Here David complains about the hatred of his enemies. He comforts himself in the word of God as his protection: "While they are plotting my destruction, *I consider thy testimonies,* which protect me for my salvation."

Verse 96

David's testimony is, *I have seen an end of* (a limit to) *all perfection.* It is a poor perfection that has a limit! But all those things in this world which pass for perfection are like this. In his time, David had seen Goliath, the strongest person, overcome; Asahel, the swiftest, overtaken;

Ahithophel, the wisest, made a fool of; Absalom, the fairest, disfigured; and, in short, he had *seen an end of all perfection.* The glory of people is like the flowers of the field (40:6). *But thy commandment is exceedingly broad,* your commands are boundless. The word of God reaches into every situation, to all times.

13. Mem

Verse 97

Here is David's inexpressible love for the word of God: *O how love I thy law!* He not only loved the promises but also loved the law, delighting in it in his inner being (Eph 3:16). We love what we love to think about; David showed he loved the word of God by meditating on it.

Verses 98–100

Here is an account of David's learning. In his youth he was concerned with work in the country as a shepherd; from his youth up, he was concerned with work in the court and camp. How then could he gain a great fund of learning? He received it from God, its author: *Thou hast made me wise* (v. 98). He received it by the word of God, by *his commandments* and *his testimonies.* Wherever good people go, they carry their Bible along with them, if not in their hands, then in their heads and hearts. The best way to use knowledge is to continually live in, and be full of, sincere godliness, all its forms, for *if any man do his will, he shall know of the doctrine* of Christ, will know more and more of it (Jn 7:17). The love of the truth prepares the way to receive its light; the *pure in heart shall see God* (Mt 5:8). He got the better of his enemies; God used these means to make him wiser than they in order to enable him to frustrate the plans they devised against him. He had more insight than all his *teachers.* He may be referring to those who had been his teachers when he was young. He built so well on the foundation they had laid that, with the help of his Bible, he became able to teach all of them. It is no reflection on our teachers, but rather an honor to them, if we improve so much as to surpass them. He had more understanding than *the ancients,* either those of his day or those of former days. In short, the written word is a surer guide to heaven than all the teachers and elders of the church; and if the sacred Scriptures are kept to, they will teach us more wisdom than all these writings of *the ancients.*

Verse 101

Here is David's care to avoid the ways of sin: "*I have refrained* (kept) *my feet from the evil ways* they were ready to step aside into. I restrained myself and drew back as soon as I was aware I was entering into temptation" (Mt 26:41). His not sinning was evidence that he carefully aimed to keep God's word and had made that his rule.

Verse 102

Here is David's faithfulness in his religious faith. He had *not departed from God's judgments*; he had not chosen any rule except the word of God, nor had he deliberately deviated from that rule. "It was divine grace in my heart that enabled me to receive those instructions as coming from you."

Verses 103–104

Here is the pleasure and delight which David took in the word of God; it was *sweet to his taste, sweeter than honey* (v. 103). There is such a thing as spiritual taste, an inner savor and relish of divine things. Here also is the benefit and advantage he gained by the word of God. The word of God helped him toward a good mind: "*Through thy precepts I get understanding* (v. 104) to discern between truth and falsehood, good and evil, so as not to make mistakes either in how I live or in how I advise others." It helped him toward a good heart: "Because I have gained an understanding of the truth, *I hate every false way* (v. 104) and have firmly decided not to turn aside into it."

14. Nun

Verse 105

Notice the nature of the word of God and his great intention in giving it to the world; it is a *lamp and a light.* It reveals to us things about God and ourselves which otherwise we could not have known. The command is a lamp kept burning with the oil of the Spirit; it is like the lamps in the sanctuary (Ex 27:20) and the pillar of fire to Israel (Ex 13:21–22). It must be not only a *light to our eyes*, to satisfy them, but also a *light to our feet* and *to our path*, to direct us in choosing our way in general and also in the particular steps we take along that way.

Verse 106

Here is the idea David had about religious faith; it is *keeping God's righteous judgments.* God's commands are his judgments. It is good for us to commit ourselves with a solemn oath to be religious. We must swear to the Lord as subjects swear allegiance to their sovereign, promising loyalty, appealing to God concerning the sincerity of our promise.

Verse 107

Here we see David laboring under many discouragements. He is turning to God in this condition; he prays for God's grace: "*Quicken me, O Lord!* Give me energy, make me cheerful; revive me in my suffering to greater diligence in my work."

Verse 108

What David prays for fervently is the acceptance of the *freewill offerings*, offerings not of his money but of his *mouth*, his willing prayers and praises. Our offerings must be *freewill offerings*, for we must offer them prolifically and cheerfully, and it is this willing mind that is accepted (1Ch 28:9; 2Co 8:12).

Verses 109–110

Here David is in danger of losing his life. There is just one step between him and death (1Sa 20:3), for the *wicked have laid a snare* (v. 110) for him. Saul did so many times, because he hated him for his godliness. What they could not bring about by open force they hoped to achieve by treachery, which made him say, *My soul is continually in my hand* (v. 109). Amidst the many worries about his own safety he finds room in his head and heart for the word of God, keeping that in his mind as fresh as ever; and where that dwells richly (Col 3:16), it will be *a well of living water* (Jn 7:38).

Verses 111–112

The psalmist decides to be faithful to the word of God and to live and die by it. "*Thy testimonies*—the truths and promises of your word—*have I taken as a heritage for ever, for they are the rejoicing of my heart*" (v. 111). He expects eternal happiness in God's testimonies. The covenant God has made with him is an eternal covenant, and so he takes it as *a heritage for ever.* He decides to rule himself by it: *I have inclined my heart to do thy statutes* (v. 112). Those who want to have the blessings of God's testimonies must come under the discipline of his statutes.

15. Samekh

Verse 113

Here we have David's fear of the coming of sin and its beginnings: *I hate vain thoughts.* Although David could not say that he was free from worthless thoughts, he could still say he hated them; he did not tolerate them or accept them in any way, but did what he could to keep them out, or at least to keep them under. *But thy law do I love*, which forbids those worthless thoughts and threatens them. The more we love the law of God, the more we will control our worthless thoughts and the more hateful they will be to us.

Verse 114

When Saul pursued David, David often took himself off to a secure place for shelter; in war he guarded himself with his shield. Now God was both of these to him, a refuge to protect him from danger and a shield to protect him in danger, to protect his life from death and his soul from sin.

Verse 115

David's brave determination as a saint is like that of a soldier, for true courage consists in a steady determination against every sin and a commitment to every duty. Those who decide to keep the commands of God must have no close association with evildoers, for bad company is a great hindrance to a holy life. We must not choose evildoers as our companions (1:1; Eph 5:11).

Verses 116–117

Here David prays for sustaining grace. He seeks the Lord twice for this sufficient grace: *Uphold me* (v. 116), and again, *Hold thou me up* (v. 117). He sees himself as not only unable to go on in his duty by any strength of his own, but also in danger of falling into sin unless he is prevented from doing so by divine grace. We stand no longer than God upholds us and can go no farther than he carries us. Those who hope in God's word may be sure that the word will not fail them and that their hopes will not be dashed.

Verses 118–120

Here is God's judgment on evildoers, on those who *wander from his statutes* (v. 118), who do not want to submit to God's rule. Notice how God deals with them, so that we may neither fear them nor envy them. He *puts them all away like dross* (v. 119). Evildoers are as dross, which although it is mixed with the good metal in ore, and seems to have the same substance, must be separated from it. God rejects them because they *err from his statutes* (v. 118) and because *their deceit is falsehood* (v. 118), that is, because they deceive themselves by setting up false rules in opposition to God's decrees, and because they deceive others with their hypocritical pretense. David fears the wrath of God: *My flesh trembles for fear of thee* (v. 120). Instead of gloating over those who have fallen under God's displeasure, he humbles himself.

16. Ayin

Verses 121–122

David had not done wrong; he could truly say, "*I have done judgment and justice* (what is righteous and just)

(v. 121). I have been careful to repay everyone their due and have not by force or fraud hindered anyone from what is rightfully theirs." He is aware that he cannot successfully resist his oppressors or enemies by himself, and so he begs God to act for him. Christ is our surety with God, and if he is so, providence will be our surety against all the world.

Verse 123

Being oppressed, David waits and wishes here for the salvation of the Lord. He knows it comes slowly. He was sometimes verging on despair and thought that because the salvation did not come when he expected it, it would never come. Even though our eyes fail, God's word does not, and so those who build on it, even though they are now discouraged, will at the right time experience his salvation.

Verses 124–125

Here is David's request for divine instruction: "*Teach me thy statutes* (v. 124); let me know all my duty." In difficult times we should want more to be told what we must do than what we may expect, and we should pray more to be led into the knowledge of the commands of Scripture than into the prophecies of Scripture. He pleads his relationship with God: "*I am thy servant* (v. 125) and have work to do for you, and so *teach me* to do it and to do it well."

Verse 126

Here David complains against the daring ungodliness of evildoers and expresses a desire that God would appear to vindicate his own honor: "*It is time for thee, Lord, to work*, to act and do something to show effectively how wrong unbelievers and the unfaithful are, to silence those who speak against the heavens." Some read it — and the original will bear this reading — "It is time to work for thee, O Lord!" It is time for everyone to appear on the Lord's side in their place, against the threatening growth of ungodliness and immorality.

Verses 127–128

Here, as often in this psalm, David professes the great love he has for the word and law of God. David saw that the word of God fulfills every purpose better than money, for it enriches the soul toward God, and so he loved it more than gold, for it had done something for him which gold could not do and would stand him in good stead when the wealth of the world would fail him.

17. Pe

Verse 129

The word of God shows us amazing revelations of God, Christ, and the next world, and wonderful proofs of divine love and grace. The majesty of the style, the purity of the material, and the harmony of the parts are all wonderful. Its effects on the human conscience, both to convict and encourage, are wonderful.

Verse 130

Here is the great use for which the word of God was intended, to give light, that is, to give understanding. Even *the entrance* (unfolding) *of God's word gives light*. If we begin at the beginning and read it, we will find the very first verses of the Bible give us surprising, but satisfying, revelations of the origin of the universe. We find that we begin to see when we begin to study the word of God.

Some understand this to refer to the New Testament, which was the opening or unfolding of the Old Testament and which would shed light on life and immortality. It shows us a way to heaven so clear that the *wayfaring men, though fools, shall not err therein* (Isa 35:8).

Verse 131

When Christ is formed in the soul (Gal 4:19), there are gracious longings: *I opened my mouth and panted*, as one overcome by heat, or almost suffocated, pants for fresh air.

Verse 132

Here is David's request for God's favor to himself: "*Look* graciously *upon me; and be merciful to me*." His request is humble. He does not ask for the actions of God's hand, but only for the smiles of his face, and for that he does not plead his merit, but begs mercy. "Lord, I am one of *those that love thy name*, who love you and your word, and it is your usual way to be kind to those who do so." If people love God, he will treat them in a way with which they will be entirely satisfied (1Co 10:13).

Verse 133

In this verse David is as eager for the good work of God in him as he was in the previous verse for the goodwill of God toward him. He prays: "*Order my steps in thy word*; having led me in the right way, cause every step I take on that way to be under the guidance of your grace. *Let no iniquity have dominion over me*, let no sin rule over me so as to take me captive."

Verse 134

Here David prays that he might live a quiet and peaceful life (1Ti 2:2) and might not be harassed and disturbed by those who try to trouble him. "Let me be rescued from the hands of my enemies, so that I will keep your precepts more cheerfully."

Verse 135

Here, as often elsewhere, David describes himself as God's servant, a title he gloried in even though he was king. He is very ambitious to know his Master's favor, counting that as his happiness and as what he knows will do him the most good. "*Make thy face to shine upon thy servant*; let me be accepted by you, and let me know I am accepted. If the world frowns on me, may you still smile."

Verse 136

David is in sorrow. His sorrow is great, so great that he weeps *rivers of tears*. David has prayed that he might be able to take encouragement in knowing God's favor (v. 135); now he pleads that he is qualified for that encouragement and needs it, for he is one of those who mourn in Zion (Isa 61:3). His sorrow is godly (2Co 7:10). He does not weep because of his troubles, even though he has many, but because God is being dishonored: *because they keep not thy law*; *they* may refer either to the people around him (v. 139) or to his eyes.

18. Tsadhe

Verses 137–138

Here is the righteousness of God. He rules the world by his providence according to the principles of justice, and he never did, and never can do, any wrong to any of his creatures. As he acts like himself, so his law requires that we act like ourselves and like him, that we be just to ourselves and to all we deal with, and true to all the commitments we put ourselves under both to God and to our fellow human beings.

Verse 139

Here is the great contempt which evildoers put on religious faith: *My enemies have forgotten thy words.* David reckoned as his enemies those who forgot the words of God, because such people were enemies of religious faith; his *zeal consumed him* (wore him out) when he observed their ungodliness. Zeal against sin should constrain us to do what we can against it where we are, or at least to be more active in our religious faith.

Verse 140

All good people love the word of God, because they are his servants and because his word allows them to know their Master's will and guides them to do their Master's work.

Verse 141

God has chosen the foolish things of the world (1Co 1:27), and it has often been the fate of his people to be despised. David is poor but devout; he will not reject his religious faith even though it has exposed him to contempt, for he knows that that contempt is intended to test his faithfulness.

Verse 142

God's word is a law, and that law is truth, and so we are under a double obligation. First, we are reasonable creatures, and as such we must be ruled by truth. If the principles are true, the practices must be in accord with them; otherwise we do not act rationally. Second, we are creatures, and so subjects, and must be ruled by our Creator. Whatever he commands, we are committed to obey as a law. Here is truth brought to the understanding, to rule there and guide the activities of the whole person, but in case that authority should become weak through the flesh, here is a law to bind the will and bring that into submission.

Verses 143–144

David finds himself not only lowly but also miserable, as far as this world could make him so: *Trouble and anguish have taken hold on me* (v. 143)—trouble on the outside, anguish within. *Yet thy commandments are my delights* (v. 143). The word of God has a variety of delights, which the saints often enjoy most sweetly when they are suffering trouble and anguish (2Co 1:5). He does not say, "Give me a further revelation," but, *Give me a further understanding.*

19. Qoph

Verses 145–146

Here we have David's good prayers. He *cried with his whole heart* (v. 145). We are likely to be effective in prayer when we strive and wrestle in prayer. He cried to God. Where should children go but to their father when anything is wrong? The great thing he prayed for was salvation: *Save me* (v. 146). We need desire nothing more than God's salvation (50:23) and the *things that accompany it* (Heb 6:9).

Verses 147–148

Hope in God's word encouraged him to continue to be bold in prayer even though his prayers were not answered immediately: "*I hoped in thy word* (v. 147), which I knew would not fail me." The more intimately we know the word of God, and the more we dwell on it in our thoughts, the more able we will be to speak to God. Merely reading the word is not enough; we must also meditate on it. David began the day with God. The first thing he did in the morning, before he undertook any business, was to pray. If our first thoughts in the morning are of God, they will help keep us in his fear all day long. Even in *the night watches*, when David woke up from his first sleep, he would rather meditate and pray than turn over and go back to sleep.

Verse 149

Here David turns to God for grace and strength with great reverence. "*Lord, quicken me*; stir me up to do what is good, revive me, give me energy, and make me joyful in doing it. Enable me to put good habits into action."

Verses 150–151

David was in danger from his enemies. They followed him closely, and he was about to fall into their hands: *They draw nigh* (v. 150). They were at his heels. God sometimes allows persecutors to triumph a long way against his people, so that, as David said (1Sa 20:3), *There is but a step between them and death.* It is the joy of the saints that, when trouble is near, God is also near, and no trouble can come between them and him. He is never far to seek; he is within our call.

Verse 152

This confirms the previous verse: *All thy commandments are truth* (v. 151). He is referring to the covenant, the word which God has commanded to a thousand generations. The promises are *founded for ever*, so that even when heaven and earth pass away, every jot and tittle of the promise will stand firm (Mt 5:18; 2Co 1:20). David *knew of old* (v. 152), from the days of his youth, ever since he began to look to God, that the word of God is something you may risk everything on.

20. Resh

Verses 153–154

David looks to God's compassion and prays, "*Consider my affliction*" (v. 153). He looks to God's power and prays, "*Deliver me*" (v. 153), and again, "*Deliver me.*" He looks to God's righteousness and prays, "*Plead my cause* (v. 154) and take me as your client." He looks to God's grace and prays, "*Quicken me* (v. 154). Lord, revive and comfort me until I am rescued!"

Verse 155

How can people expect to seek God's favor effectively in adversity when they have never sought out his statutes in prosperity? Eternal salvation is far from them. They thrust it far from them by thrusting the Savior far away from them. It is so far from them that they cannot reach it, and the longer they persist in sin, the further away it is.

Verse 156

David had spoken of the misery of evildoers (v. 155), but God is good nevertheless. There was sufficient compassion in God to have saved them if they had not despised the riches of those mercies (Ro 2:4).

Verse 157

Because David was a national leader, he had many enemies, but he also had many friends, many people who loved him and wished him well; so let him set one over against the other (Ecc 7:14). Here David was a type of both Christ and his church. The enemies, the persecutors, of both are many. Even if people have many enemies, they need not fear any of them if they steadily follow their duty.

Verse 158

David *beheld the transgressors*, and it *grieved* him to see them dishonor God, serve Satan, corrupt the world, and destroy their own souls.

Verse 159

David does not say, "Consider how I fulfill your precepts"; he is aware in himself that he comes short in many things; rather, he says, "Consider how I love them." Our obedience is pleasing to God, and pleasant to ourselves, only when it comes from a motive of love.

Verse 160

David here encourages himself with the faithfulness of God's word: *It is true from the beginning*. Ever since God began to reveal himself to people, all he said was true and to be trusted. From its beginning, the church was built on this rock (Mt 16:17–18). It has not gained its validity over time. "But the beginning of God's word was true" is how some read this; his government rested on a sure foundation. It will be proved faithful to the end.

21. Sin and Shin

Verse 161

The best people have often been persecuted; and the situation is even worse if the persecutors are rulers, for they have not only the sword in their hands but also the law on their side, and can do harm with respectability and in the name of justice. It is sad that the power that judges have from God and should use for him should ever be employed against him. David never gave them provocation. "They would make me stand in awe of them and their word and do as they tell me to, but *my heart stands in awe of* (trembles at) *thy word*. I have decided to please God and be faithful to him, no matter who is displeased and falls out with me."

Verse 162

He has just said that his heart trembled at God's word, and here he declares that he rejoices in it. The more reverence we have for the word of God, the more joy we will find in it.

Verse 163

Love and hatred are the most important human emotions; if these are rightly established, the rest act as they should. In David we here see them fixed correctly:

1. He had a deep-rooted hatred toward sin; he cannot even bear to think about it: *I hate and abhor lying*, which may be taken to represent all sin. Hypocrisy is lying; false teaching is lying; breaking faith is lying. Lying, whether at work or at home, is a sin which all good people hate.

2. He had a deep-rooted devotion for the word of God: *Thy law do I love*. The reason he loved the law of God was that it is true.

Verse 164

Many think that once a week is enough, or once or twice a day, but David wanted to praise God seven times a day at least. We must praise God at every meal, giving thanks in everything (1Th 5:18). We must praise God for

his *precepts*, for his promises, and even for our suffering, if through grace we gain good from it.

Verse 165

Good people, who are ruled by a motive of love for the word of God, are at peace and have a holy serenity; none enjoy themselves more than they do. They may have great troubles outside but still enjoy great peace within, an abundance of inner light. They will make the best of the situations they find themselves in, and they will not quarrel with anything that God does.

Verse 166

Here is the whole duty of human beings (Ecc 12:13). We must keep our eye on God's favor as our aim: *Lord, I have hoped for thy salvation*. And we must keep our eye on God's word as our rule: *I have done thy commandments*. God has joined these two together, and let no one separate them (Mt 19:6). We cannot have good reasons to hope for God's salvation unless we set ourselves to follow his commands (Rev 22:14).

Verses 167–168

Our love for the word of God must be a superlative love, and it must also be a victorious love, which will subdue and mortify our sinful desires. Physical exercise does little good in matters of religious faith (1Ti 4:8); we must make it a work of our hearts or we make nothing of it.

22. Taw

Verses 169–170

We must come to God as beggars asking for gifts. The psalmist is concerned to have his prayer come before God, come *near* before him, that is, that by faith he might have grace and strength and fervency to lift up his prayers, that no guilt might come between him and God to shut out his prayers and separate him from God, and that God would graciously receive his prayers and take notice of them.

Verse 171

Here is a great favor that David expects from God, that he will teach him his *statutes*. He has often prayed for this in this psalm, and now that he is drawing toward the end of the psalm he speaks of it as something he assumes. *My lips shall utter praise when thou hast taught me*. He will then have cause to praise God. He will then know how to praise God and have a heart to do it.

Verse 172

The more we see of God's commands, the more diligent we should be to help others know them. We should always make the word of God the controller of our speech, so as never to disobey it by sinful speaking or sinful silence. We should also often make it the subject of what we speak about, so that it may feed many people and *minister grace to the hearers* (Eph 4:29).

Verses 173–174

David prays that divine grace would work for him: *Let thy hand help me* (v. 173). He looks to God in the hope that the hand that made him would help him, for if the Lord does not help us, which created thing can help us? He pleads three things:

• That he has made religious faith his serious and deliberate choice: "*I have chosen thy precepts*" (v. 173).

• That his heart is set on heaven: *"I have longed for thy salvation"* (v. 174).
• That he takes pleasure in doing his duty: *"Thy law is my delight"* (v. 174).

Verse 175

"May I live so that, as I serve my country and provide for my family, I may praise God here in this world of conflict and opposition." *Let my soul live*, that is, let me be sanctified and encouraged—for sanctification and encouragement are the life of the soul—*and* then *it shall praise thee*.

Verse 176

As unconverted sinners are like lost sheep (Lk 15:4), so weak and unsteady saints are like lost sheep (Mt 18:12–13). We tend to wander like sheep, and when we have gone astray, we are not inclined to find our way back again. "Lord, seek me, as I used to seek my sheep when they went astray," for David had himself been a kind shepherd. "Lord, acknowledge me as one of your own, for although I am a stray sheep, I have your brand on me." He therefore concludes the psalm with a penitent sense of his own sin and a confident dependence on God's grace.

PSALM 120

This psalm is thought to have been written by David on the occasion of Doeg's accusing him and the priests to Saul, because it is like Ps 52, which was written on that occasion, and because the psalmist complains of being driven out of the assembly of the Lord and forced to live among cruel people. 1. He prays to God to rescue him from the trouble intended for him by false and malicious tongues (vv. 1–2); he threatens the judgments of God against such people (vv. 3–4). 2. He complains about his evil neighbors, who are quarrelsome and troublesome (vv. 5–7).

Title

This psalm is the first of fifteen that are here put together under the title of *Songs of degrees* ("Songs of ascents"). Some think they were sung on the fifteen steps or stairs by which the people went up from the outer court of the temple to the inner court; others think there were fifteen stages, and so a progression, in the people's return journey from exile.

Verses 1–4

David was greatly distressed by *lying lips and a deceitful tongue* (v. 2). There were those who sought to destroy him, and they had almost brought it about. They flattered him so that they might without suspicion carry out their evil intentions against him. *They* smiled to his face and kissed him even when they were aiming to strike his heart. Here David was a type of Christ, who was caused pain and suffering by lying lips and deceitful tongues. Having no protection from false tongues, he appealed to the One who has the hearts of all people in his hand (Pr 21:1) and can, when he wishes, restrain their tongues. His prayer was, *Deliver my soul, O Lord! from lying lips* (v. 2). He obtained a gracious answer to this prayer. Let liars consider what they will receive: *God shall shoot at them with an arrow; suddenly shall they be wounded.* They put God far away from them, but his arrows can reach them from afar. They will strike deep into the hardest heart. His wrath is compared to burning coals of the broom tree,

which are not said to flame or crackle like thorns under a pot (Ecc 7:6), but to have an intense heat and keep the fire going for a very long time—even when it seems to have gone out.

Verses 5–7

The psalmist here complains about the bad neighborhood into which he was driven, and some connect vv. 3–4 to this: "What will deceitful tongues do to those who are exposed to them? What will people gain by living among such malicious, deceitful people? Nothing but *sharp arrows* and *coals of juniper*" (v. 4). Woe is me, David says, *that I sojourn in Mesech and Kedar* (v. 5). Not that David lived in the country of Meshech or Kedar, but he lived among ignorant and cruel people, like the inhabitants of Meshech and Kedar. While he was in exile, he looked on himself as a sojourner, one who was never at home. Good people cannot think of themselves as being at home while they are banished from the public worship of God. It is a great sadness to all who love God to be without the means of grace and fellowship with God. He *dwells in the tents of Kedar* (v. 5), where the shepherds probably had a reputation for being contentious, like the shepherds of Abraham and Lot (Ge 13:7). The people David lived with not only hated him but also hated peace. Perhaps Saul's court was the Meshech and Kedar in which David lived, and Saul was the man he was referring to who hated peace. "I peace" is the reading of the original; "I love peace and pursue it; *I am for peace* (v. 7) and have made it clear that I am so."

PSALM 121

Some call this the soldier's psalm and think it was written in the camp, when David was risking his life on the battlefield. Others call it the traveler's psalm—for it contains nothing of military dangers—and think David wrote it to be his companion on a journey. But wherever we are, at home or away, we are exposed to more dangers than we are aware of, and this psalm directs and encourages us to rest ourselves and our confidence in God. 1. David here assures himself of help from God (vv. 1–2). 2. He assures others of it (vv. 3–8).

Verses 1–8

This psalm teaches us:
1. To rest on God as a God all-sufficient for us. "Shall I lift up my eyes to the hills?" is how some read it. "Does my help come from there? Will I depend on the powers of the earth, on the strength of rulers, who hold their heads high toward heaven? No; I never expect help to come from them; my confidence is only in God." "We must lift up our eyes above the hills" is how some understand it; we must look beyond mere instruments to God, who makes them what they are to us. *"My help comes from the Lord* (v. 2), and I expect it to come from him in his own way and time." We must encourage our confidence in God with the knowledge that he *made heaven and earth* (v. 2), and the One who did that can do anything.
2. To encourage ourselves in God when our difficulties and dangers are greatest.
2.1. God himself has undertaken to watch over us: *The Lord is thy keeper* (v. 5).
2.2. The same One who protects the church in general is committed to keep every individual believer, and he does it by the same wisdom, power, and promises. *He that keepeth Israel* (v. 4) *is thy keeper* (v. 5). The shepherd of

the flock is the shepherd of every sheep, and he will take care that not one of his little ones will perish (Mt 18:14).

2.3. He is a watchful keeper: "*He that keepeth Israel,* who keeps you, O Israelite, *shall neither slumber nor sleep*" (v. 4).

2.4. He not only protects those whom he watches over but also refreshes them: he *is their shade* (v. 5). He is always near to his people to protect and refresh them. He is never far away; he *is* their *keeper* and *shade on their right hand* (v. 5), so that he is never far to seek. The right hand is the hand that works; when they turn to do their duty, they will find God ready to help them and give them success (16:8).

2.5. He will protect them from all the harmful effects of the heavenly bodies (v. 6): *The sun shall not smite thee* with its heat *by day nor the moon* with its cold and moisture *by night.* He will keep them *night and day* (Isa 27:3). It may also be understood figuratively: "You will not be hurt either by the open attacks of your enemies, which are as visible as the scorching rays of the sun, or by their secret treachery, which is like the imperceptible influence of the cold at night."

2.6. His protection will make them safe in every respect: "*The Lord shall preserve thee from all evil* (v. 7), the harm caused by sin and trouble. Even what kills will not harm you." It is the spiritual life, especially, that God will take under his protection: *He shall preserve* (watch over) *thy soul* (v. 7). He will watch over us in all our ways: "*He shall preserve thy going out and thy coming in* (v. 8). You will be under his protection as you go on your journeys and voyages and as you return. He will keep you in life and in death, in your going out and continuing on the journey of life and in your coming in when you die, your going out to your work in the morning of your days and your coming home to your rest when the evening of old age calls you in" (104:23). He will continue his care over us *from this time forth and even for evermore* (v. 8).

PSALM 122

This psalm seems to have been written by David for use by the people of Israel when they came up to Jerusalem to worship at the three sacred festivals. It was in David's time that Jerusalem was first chosen to be the city where God would record his name. Here is: 1. The joy with which they were to go up to Jerusalem (vv. 1–2); the great respect they were to have for Jerusalem (vv. 3–5). 2. The great concern they were to have for Jerusalem and the prayers they were to offer for its welfare (vv. 6–9).

Verses 1–5

We should worship God in our own homes, but that is not enough; we must also *go into the house of the Lord* (v. 1) to pay our respect to him there, and *not forsake the assembling of ourselves together* (Heb 10:25). Those who are happy in God will be happy when he calls and gives opportunities to serve him. We should want our Christian friends, when they have any good work in hand, to call for us and take us along with them. When those who came from the country found the journey long, they encouraged themselves with the thought that they would soon be in Jerusalem, and that would make up for all the tiredness they felt. It is the beautiful city, not only *for situation* (48:2) but also as regards its building. It is built in a uniform way, closely compacted together (v. 3), the houses strengthening and supporting one another. It was a type of the Gospel church, which is closely compacted together

in holy love and Christian fellowship, so that it is all as one city. It is the Holy City (v. 4), the place where all the people of Israel meet one another: *Thither the tribes go up,* from all parts of the country, for their general rendezvous, and they come together to hear what God has to say to them. It is the royal city (v. 5): *There are set thrones of judgment.* The people had reason to love Jerusalem, because justice was administered there by a man after God's own heart (1Sa 13:14).

Verses 6–9

David calls on others to wish Jerusalem well (vv. 6–7). *Pray for the peace of Jerusalem,* for its welfare, for all good things to happen to it, especially for the uniting of inhabitants among themselves. The peace and welfare of the Gospel church, particularly in our land, is to be fervently desired and prayed for by each one of us. Words are put into our mouths (v. 7): *Peace be within thy walls,* for all the inhabitants in general, all who live within the walls, from the least to the greatest. "May peace be in your fortifications; may they never be attacked, or, if they are, may they never be captured, but may they protect the city effectively." Moreover, "may *prosperity* be *in the palaces* (citadels) (v. 7) of the great people who lead and direct public affairs." He decided that whatever others did, he would say, *Peace be within thee* (v. 8). He did not say, "Let others pray for the public peace, the priests and the prophets, whose business it is, and the people who have nothing else to do, and I will fight for it and rule for it." No; he was firm: "I will pray for it too." It is *for my brethren and companions' sakes* (v. 8), that is, for the sake of all true Israelites, whom I look on as *my brethren* (as he calls them in 1Ch 28:2) and who have often been my companions in worshiping God, which has made me love them. Our concern for the good of the whole community is right when it comes from a sincere love for God's institutions and his faithful worshipers.

PSALM 123

This psalm was written at a time when the church of God was brought low; some think it was when the Jews were in exile in Babylon. The psalmist begins as if he were speaking only for himself (v. 1), but soon speaks in the name of the church. Here is: 1. Their expectation of mercy from God (vv. 1–2). 2. Their plea for mercy with God (vv. 3–4).

Verses 1–4

We have here:

1. The sacred declaration which God's people make of faith and hope in God (vv. 1–2). Notice the title given to God: *O thou that dwellest in the heavens* (v. 1). Our Lord Jesus has taught us to look to God in prayer as *our Father in heaven* (Mt 6:9). Heaven is a place of prospect and power; the One whose throne is in heaven sees from there all the tragedies that come to his people, and he can come from there to save them. In every prayer we lift up the eye of our soul to God, especially in trouble, which was the situation here. Our eyes must wait on God as *the Lord* and as *our God, until that he have mercy upon us* (v. 2). This is illustrated (v. 2) by a comparison: our eyes are to God as *the eyes of a servant* and *handmaid to the hand of their master and mistress.* The eyes of a servant are looking to his master's hand to give direction, expecting to be given his work. Servants look to their master or their mistress to receive their food at the right time

(Pr 31:15). And we must look to God for daily bread, for sufficient grace. If servants meet with opposition in their work, if they are questioned for what they are doing, who should support them and put things right but their master, who set them to work? When the people of God are persecuted, they may appeal to their Master: *We are thine; save us* (119:94; Isa 63:19). The people of God were now under his rebukes, and where else should they turn except to the One who struck them (Isa 9:13)? They submitted themselves and humbled themselves under God's mighty hand. The servant expects his wages, his *well done*, from his master. Hypocrites look to the world's hand; they receive their reward from there (Mt 6:2); but true Christians look to God as their rewarder (Heb 11:6).

2. The humble address which God's people present to him in their dreadful condition (vv. 3–4): *Have mercy upon us, O Lord, have mercy upon us.* They set out their grievances: *We are exceedingly filled with contempt* (v. 3). They are wounded and upset by the insults. Some think the words that are translated *those that are at ease* and *the proud* (v. 4) refer to the good people who are scorned and held in contempt. "Our soul is troubled to see how those who are at peace, those who are honorable, are scorned and despised." But taking the words as we read them, they were the ones who enjoyed an easy life and were worldly and irreligious (Job 12:5). They crushed God's people, thinking they exalted themselves by reviling them.

PSALM 124

We think David wrote this psalm on the occasion of some great rescue which God brought about for him and his people. Whatever it was, he seems to have been greatly moved and to have wanted to impress on others the goodness of God in making a way of escape for them. 1. He exalts the greatness of the danger they were in (vv. 1–5). 2. He gives God the glory for their escape; he takes encouragement from this to trust in God (vv. 6–8).

Verses 1–5

The people of God came to the very brink of destruction. The more desperate the disease appears to have been, the more the skill of the Physician appears in the cure. *Men rose up against us* (v. 2), human beings like us, but bent on destroying us. Nothing less would serve than the destruction of those whom they had taken a disliking to. "God was on our side; he took our part, embraced our cause, and came to our aid." God was Jehovah; that is emphasized. "If it had not been Jehovah himself, a God of infinite power and perfection, who had undertaken to rescue us, our enemies would have overpowered us." Fortunate are the people, therefore, whose God is all-sufficient (33:12).

Verses 6–8

The psalmist further exalts the great rescue God has just brought about for them. They were rescued like a lamb out of the very jaws of a beast of prey. They were rescued like *a bird*, a little bird or sparrow, *out of the snare of the fowler* (v. 7). God's people are caught up in the trap and are as unable to help themselves out as any weak and defenseless bird is. It is then that God breaks the snare and makes the enemies' plans futile. *Our help is in the name of the Lord.* David had told us (121:2) to depend on God to help us in our personal concerns; here it is the concerns of the public. It is an encouragement that Israel's God is

the one who made the world and that therefore he will have a church in the world and can protect that church in times of the greatest danger and distress.

PSALM 125

This short psalm may be summed up in those words of the prophet, Say you to the righteous, it will be well with him. Woe to the wicked, it will be ill with him *(Isa 3:10–11). It is certainly well with the people of God, for: 1. They have the promises of a good God that they will be steadfast (v. 1) and safe (v. 2) and not always depressed (v. 3). 2. They have the prayers of a good man, which will be heard for them (v. 4); disaster will certainly come to evildoers, particularly to those who turn their back on God (v. 5).*

Verses 1–3

Three very precious promises are made to the people of God. Notice:

1. The character of God's people, to whom these promises belong. They:

- Are *righteous* (v. 3), righteous before God, righteous to God, and righteous to all people.
- *Trust in the Lord* (v. 1); they depend on his care and devote themselves to his honor. The closer our expectations are confined to God, the higher may be our expectations that we will be blessed by him.

2. The promises themselves.

2.1. That their hearts will be established by faith: those minds that are fixed on God will be truly sustained. They will stand firm in their faith (Isa 7:9). *They shall be as Mount Zion* (v. 1), which is firm because it is a mountain supported by providence, and much more so because it is a holy mountain supported by God's promises.

2.2. That in committing themselves to God, they will be safe and under his protection from all the insults of their enemies, as Jerusalem was a natural fortress and fortification in the *mountains* that *were round about* it (v. 2).

2.3. That their troubles will last no longer than their strength will serve to support them (v. 3). It is promised that although the *rod of the wicked* may come on them, it will not come to *rest* on them (v. 3); it will not continue as long as the enemies intend or as long as the people of God fear. God will cut the trouble short in righteousness, so short that even *with the temptation he will make a way for them to escape* (1Co 10:13).

Verses 4–5

Here is the prayer the psalmist offers for the happiness of those who are sincere and faithful (v. 4): *Do good, O Lord, unto those that are good.* He does not say, "Do good, O Lord, to those who are perfect," to those who are sinless and spotless, but to those who are sincere and honest. God's promises should encourage our prayers. Notice the prospect he has of the destruction of hypocrites and deserters. He does not pray for it, but he predicts it. The last words, *Peace upon Israel* (v. 5), may be taken as a prayer: "May God keep his Israel in peace when his judgment is dealing with evildoers." We may also read them as a promise: *Peace shall be upon Israel* (v. 5).

PSALM 126

This psalm was written with reference to some great and surprising rescue of the people of God from slavery and distress, most likely at their return from exile in Babylon in Ezra's time. Although Babylon is not mentioned here (as it is in 137), their captivity there was most remarkable both in itself and because their return was a type of our redemption in Christ. This psalm was probably written by Ezra or some of the prophets who came with the first returning exiles. 1. Those who have returned from exile are called on to be thankful (vv. 1–3). 2. Those who remain in exile are prayed for (v. 4) and encouraged (vv. 5–6).

Verses 1–3

While the people of Israel were in exile in Babylon, their harps were hung on the poplar (*willow*) trees (137), but now that they had been brought back from exile, they picked up their harps again; Providence pipes to them, and they dance (Mt 11:17). The long lack of blessings greatly sweetens their return. Cyrus, for political reasons, declared freedom to God's exiles, but it was *the Lord's doing* (118:23), according to his word spoken many years before. God sent them into exile not as dross is put into a fire to be burned up, but as gold to be refined. It came so suddenly that at first they were confused, not knowing what to make of it or what it would lead to: "We thought ourselves *like them that dream* (v. 1). We thought it too good to be true." The surprise of it put them into such a state of ecstatic joy that they could scarcely contain themselves within the bounds of decency in expressing it: *Our mouth was filled with laughter and our tongue with singing* (v. 2). Their neighbors took notice: "*They said among the heathen* (nations), 'Jehovah, the God of Israel, *has done great things* (v. 2) for that people, such as our gods cannot do for us.'" The nations were only spectators, and they spoke of it as mere news; they did not themselves share in the matter; but the people of God spoke of it as those who were personally involved in it. It is reassuring to speak of the redemption Christ has brought as being achieved for us personally. *He loved me, and gave himself for me* (Gal 2:20).

Verses 4–6

These verses look forward to the blessings that were still lacking. Those who had come out of exile were still in distress, even in their own land (Ne 1:3), and many remained in Babylon. "*Turn again our captivity.* Restore our fortunes. May those who have returned to their own land be relieved of the burdens they still groan under. May those who remain in Babylon have their hearts stirred, as ours were, to receive all the benefits of the liberty they have received." The beginnings of mercy are encouragements to us to pray for them to be completed. All the saints may encourage themselves with the confidence that their tears will certainly finally become a harvest of joy (vv. 5–6). Weeping must not stop sowing; when we suffer ill, we must continue to do good. In fact, as the ground is prepared for the seed by the rain, there are tears which are themselves the seeds that we must sow, tears of sorrow for sin—our own sin and others' sin—tears of sympathy for the suffering church, and tears of tenderness in prayer and under the teaching of God's word. Job, Joseph, David, and many others had harvests of joy after sorrow. Those who sow in tears of godly sorrow (2Co 7:10) will reap in joy of a sealed pardon and a settled peace.

PSALM 127

This is a family psalm, different from the state poems and church poems we have read before. It is entitled A Song

of degrees for Solomon, *implying that it was dedicated to him by his father. Because Solomon had a house to build, a city to keep, and offspring to raise up for his father, David told him to look to God and to depend on his providence, without which all his wisdom, care, and diligence would not be enough. Some think it was written by Solomon himself, and they compare it with* Ecclesiastes, *as the scope of both is the same, to show the meaninglessness of worldly care and how necessary it is that we keep in favor with God. We must depend on God: 1. For wealth (vv. 1–2). 2. For heirs to leave wealth to (vv. 3–5).*

Verses 1–5

Solomon would tend to lean on his own understanding and insight (Pr 3:5), and so his father teaches him to look higher, to take God with him in all he does. We must look to God:

1. In all the affairs and business of the family. We must depend on God's blessing and not our own planning:

1.1. To raise a family: *Except the Lord build the house*, by his providence and blessing, *those labour in vain*, even though they are clever, *that build it* (v. 1). We may understand this to refer to the physical house: unless the Lord blesses the work of building, it is futile for people to build. If the model and designs are laid in pride and self-importance, or if the foundations are laid in oppression and injustice (Hab 2:11–12), God certainly does not build there; in fact, if God is not acknowledged, we have no reason to expect his blessing, and without his blessing everything comes to nothing. Or perhaps this is to be understood as referring to making a lowly family significant; people work hard to do this by advantageous marriage alliances, services, actions, and purchases, but all is in vain unless God builds up the family.

1.2. To protect a family or a city. If the guards of the city cannot protect it without God, much less can good owners of houses save their houses from being damaged.

1.3. To enrich a family. This work takes time and thought, and time and thought cannot do it without the favor of Providence. "*It is vain for you to rise up early and sit up late* (v. 2), and so deny yourselves your physical refreshment, in eagerly pursuing the wealth of this world." People do all this to gain money, but all this work is in vain unless God prospers them, for *riches are* not always *to men of understanding* (Ecc 9:11). Those who love God and are loved by him have their minds at peace and live very comfortably without all this worry. God gives us sleep as he gives it to his loved ones when with it he also gives us grace to lie down in fear of him—our souls return to him and lean on him as our rest—and when we wake up to be still with him (139:18; 3:5) and to use the refreshment we have gained from sleep to serve him. *He gives his beloved sleep* (v. 2), that is, quietness and contentment of mind, comfortable enjoyment of the present moment and an encouraging expectation of the future.

2. In the growth of families. Children are *God's gift* (v. 3), and they are to us what he makes them, comforts or crosses. *Children are a heritage* and *a reward* (v. 3) and are to be counted as such, blessings not burdens, for the One who sends mouths will also send food if we trust in him. Children are a heritage for the Lord as well as from him. The family that has many children is like a quiver full of arrows, probably of different sizes, but all useful at one time or another; children of different abilities and inclinations may be useful to the family in different ways.

PSALM 128

This psalm, like the previous one, is a psalm for families. In that psalm we were taught that the prosperity of our families depends on the blessing of God; in this psalm we are taught that the only way to obtain the blessing that will make our families comfortable is to live in the fear of God and in obedience to him. Those who do so will be blessed (vv. 1–2, 4). In particular: 1. They will be prosperous and successful in their work (v. 2). 2. Their relationships will be pleasant (v. 3). 3. They will live to see their families brought up (v. 6). 4. They will have the satisfaction of seeing the church of God flourishing (vv. 5–6).

Verses 1–6

Godliness holds promise for the present life and the life to come (1Ti 4:8).

1. It is set down that those who are truly righteous are truly happy. In every nation those who fear God and do what is right are accepted by him (Ac 10:35), and so are blessed whether they are noble or lowly, rich or poor, in the world; if religious faith rules their lives, it will protect and enrich them. *"Happy shalt thou be* if you *fear God and walk in his ways* (v. 1). *It shall be well with thee* (v. 2); whatever happens to you, good will be brought out of it; good things will come to you while you live, better things when you die, and the best of all in eternity."

2. Particular promises are made to godly people.

2.1. *Thou shalt eat the labour of thy hands* (v. 2). Here is a promise that they will have something to do—for a life of laziness is miserable and uncomfortable—and will have the ability to do it, and will not be forced to be indebted to others for the food they need to live on. The same promise assures them that they will succeed in their work and that they and their family will enjoy what they gain. As the sleep of a laborer is sweet (Ecc 5:12), so also their food.

2.2. They will also have comfort in their family relationships. As a wife and children are very much a husband's care, so also, if by the grace of God they are as they should be, they are very much a man's delight. The *wife* will be as *a vine by the sides of the house* (v. 3), not only as a spreading vine, which is decorative, but also as a fruitful vine, with the fruit of which both God and other people are honored (Jdg 9:13). The vine is a weak and tender plant and needs to be supported and nurtured, but it is very valuable. The wife's place is in her and her husband's house; her home is there, and that is her castle. *Where is Sarah thy wife? Behold, in the tent* (Ge 18:9); where else should she be? Her place is *by the sides of the house* (v. 3), not underfoot to be trampled on, or on the rooftop shouting her demands. The *children* will be *as olive plants* (v. 3), likely to become olive trees. It is satisfying to parents who have a table that is spread, even though it is only with ordinary food, to see their children around it, and not scattered or separated from their parents. Parents love to have their children at table with them, to maintain the pleasantness of table talk, to see them in good health, needing food and not medicine, to have them as *olive plants*, straight and green, nourishing the sap of their good education. "Your family will be built up and maintained, and you will have the pleasure of seeing it." *Children's children* (v. 6), if they are good children, *are the crown of old men* (Pr 17:6), who tend to be fond of their grandchildren.

2.3. "You will *see the good of Jerusalem* (v. 5) as long as you will live, even though you live a long time. You will not have your private comforts altered and made bitter by public troubles."

PSALM 129

This psalm relates to the public concerns of God's Israel. It was probably written when the Israelites were in exile in Babylon or about the time of their return. 1. They look back with thankfulness for the former times when God rescued them (vv. 1–4). 2. They look forward with a confident prayer for the destruction of all the enemies of Zion (vv. 5–8).

Verses 1–4

The church of God here speaks as one person, one who is now old and gray-haired but remembering former days.

1. The church has often been greatly troubled by its enemies on earth. God's people have always had many enemies, and the state of the church, from its infancy, has frequently been one of adversity. *The ploughers ploughed upon my back* (v. 3). The enemies of God's people have all along cruelly abused them. They lacerated them as farmers break up the ground with their plowshares. When God allowed them to plow in this way, he intended it for his people's good; he allowed it so that, their fallow ground being broken up, he might sow the seeds of his grace on them and reap a harvest of good from them, but the enemies did not intend this. *They made long their furrows* (v. 3), never knowing when to stop and aiming to destroy the church. Many commentators understand the *furrows* they made on the backs of God's people to refer to the lashes their enemies gave them. "The cutters cut upon my back" is how they read it. God's people have often *had trials of cruel scourgings*, and this was fulfilled in Christ, who *gave his back to the smiters* (Isa 50:6).

2. The church has always been graciously rescued by her friend in heaven. The enemies' plans have been defeated. Christ has built his church on a rock, and the gates of hell have not prevailed against it, and nor will they ever do so (Mt 16:18). God *has cut asunder the cords of the wicked* (v. 4); he has cut their harnesses and straps and so spoiled their plowing. He has cut their whips and so spoiled their lashing; he has cut the bands of slavery with which they held God's people.

Verses 5–8

The psalmist concludes his psalm as Deborah did her song, *So let all thy enemies perish, O Lord!* (Jdg 5:31). The confusion predicted is illustrated by a comparison; while God's people will flourish as the laden palm tree or the green and fruitful olive, their enemies will *wither as the grass upon the housetop* (v. 6). Since they are enemies of Zion, they are so certainly marked out for destruction that they may be looked on as grass on roofs, which is sparse, short, and unpleasant, and good for nothing. It *withers before it grows up* (v. 6) to any fruitfulness, because it has no root (Mt 13:6); and the higher its position, which perhaps is its pride, the more it is exposed to the scorching heat of the sun, and so the sooner it withers. Mowing the grass on the roof would be a joke, and so those who have a reverence for the name of God will not corrupt it by using it in a usual form of greeting, merely to give an impression of devotion.

PSALM 130

This psalm is wholly taken up with spiritual matters. It is reckoned as one of the seven penitential psalms, which have sometimes been used by penitents when they have become members of the church, and in praying over and singing it, we should all be concerned to apply it to ourselves. The psalmist here expresses: 1. His desire toward God (vv. 1–2); his repentance to God (vv. 3–4). 2. His waiting on God (vv. 5–6); his expectation from God (vv. 7–8).

Verses 1–4

In these verses we are taught that the best people may sometimes be in *the depths,* suffering great trouble. But in the greatest depths, it is still our privilege to cry out to God and be heard. To cry out to God is the best way to prevent ourselves from sinking lower and also to restore ourselves from the *horrible pit and miry clay* (40:1–2). *If thou, Lord, shouldst mark iniquities, O Lord, who shall stand?* His calling God *Lord* twice, in so few words, *Jah* and *Adonai,* is emphatic and suggests a fearful sense of God's glorious majesty and a dread of his wrath. We cannot justify ourselves before God or plead "Not guilty." If God deals with us according to strict justice, we are ruined. *It is because of his mercy that we are not consumed* by his wrath (La 3:22). It is an inexpressible comfort to us that whenever we approach God, he forgives, for that is what we need. He has promised to forgive the sins of those who repent. "There is atoning sacrifice with you" is how some read it. Jesus Christ is the great atoning sacrifice, and through him we hope to gain forgiveness. This encourages us to come into his service so that we will not be turned away for every misdemeanor—nor, in fact, for any, if we truly repent.

Verses 5–8

"I wait for the Lord (v. 5)—I expect relief and comfort from him, believing it will come, longing until it does come, but patiently bearing the delay until it comes, and deciding to look for it from nowhere else. *My soul doth wait. In his word do I hope"* (v. 5). We must hope only for what he has promised in his word, and not for the figments of our own imagination. "I am well assured that morning will come, and so I am assured that God will respond in mercy to me. For God's covenant is firmer than the decree of day and night; they will come to an end, but his covenant is eternal." Those who look after sick people and those who are away from home on their journey are wishing to see dawn long before it comes, but this upright man longs even more earnestly for the signs of God's favor and the coming of his grace. *Mercy is with* him in all his works and purposes. Jesus Christ *saves his people from their sins* (Mt 1:21), *redeems them from all iniquity* (Tit 2:14), and *turns away ungodliness from Jacob* (Ro 11:26). Redemption from sin includes redemption from all other evils and so is a full redemption.

PSALM 131

This psalm is David's profession of humility with thankfulness to God for his grace. David probably made this declaration as a response to Saul, who represented David as an ambitious, aspiring man who sought the kingdom out of pride in his heart while claiming to be appointed by God. David appeals to God, protesting that the opposite is in fact true: 1. He aims at nothing elevated or great (v. 1). 2. He is at peace in every condition that God has assigned him (v. 2), and so: 3. He encourages all upright people to trust in God as he does (v. 3).

Verses 1–3

It was David's joy that his heart could assure him that he had walked humbly with his God (Mic 6:8). He did

not aim at an exalted position; if God had so planned his life, he would have been content to spend all his days in the sheepfolds. His own brother, in anger, accused him of pride (1Sa 17:28), but the accusation was unjust and without basis. He had neither a scornful nor an ambitious look: *"My eyes are not lofty* (v. 1), either to look with jealousy on those who are above me or to look down on those who are below me."* He had not proudly aimed at the kingdom, and since God had appointed him to it, he had been as humble as a little child. Our Savior has taught us humility: we must *become as little children* (Mt 18:3). Our hearts want worldly things as naturally as babies want the breast. But by the grace of God, a soul that has been sanctified has been weaned from such things. Similarly, a gracious soul quiets itself under the loss of what it loved and lives comfortably on God and covenant grace.

PSALM 132

This psalm was probably written by Solomon to be sung at the dedication of the temple that he built according to the command his father gave him (1Ch 28:2–21). Having fulfilled his trust, he begs God to recognize what he has done. 1. He built this house for the honor and service of God, and when he brings into it the ark, the sign of God's presence, he wants God himself to come and possess it (vv. 8–10). Solomon concluded his prayer with these words in 2Ch 6:41–42. 2. He built it according to the orders he had received from his father, and so his plea to support these petitions refer to David. 2.1. He pleads David's godliness toward God (vv. 1–7). 2.2. He pleads God's promise to David (vv. 11–18).

Verses 1–10

Here is Solomon's address to God for his favor to him and for his acceptance of his building a house to God's name. Notice:

1. What he pleads—two things:

1.1. That what he has done has been according to the godly vow that his father David made to build a house for God. Solomon does not plead any merit of his own: "I, who am asking you to do this, am not worthy, but *Lord, remember David* (v. 1), with whom you made the covenant." He especially pleads the solemn vow that David had made as soon as he was established in his rule, before he was settled in a house of his own, that he would build a house for God. David had noticed that the Law frequently mentioned the *place that God would choose to put his name* (Dt 16:11), to which all the tribes would turn. When he came to the crown, there was no such place; Shiloh was abandoned, and no other place was chosen, for lack of which the festivals of the Lord were not kept with proper ceremony. "Well," David says, "I will find such a place where all the tribes may meet, a dwelling *for the Mighty One of Jacob* (v. 5), a place for the ark, where there will be space for both the priests and the people to attend it." The matter had long been talked about, but nothing had been done, until finally David, when he went out one morning on his public business at the beginning of his reign, vowed that before nightfall he would come to a decision—would determine, perhaps, the place where the tent would be pitched to receive the ark; or perhaps the verse refers to the place where Solomon would build the temple, which was not fixed until the end of David's reign. *Then David said, This is the house of the Lord.* In the morning it is good to establish work for the day, committing ourselves to complete it before we go to bed that night, while submitting to

God's providence, for we *know not what a day may bring forth* (Pr 27:1).

1.2. That it was according to the expectations of the people of Israel (vv. 6–7). They asked where the ark was, for they lamented its obscurity (1Sa 7:2). They *heard of it at Ephratah,* that is, at Shiloh, in the tribe of Ephraim; they were told that it had been there but had gone. They *found it,* at last, *in the fields of the wood* (v. 6), that is, in Kiriath Jearim, which means "the city of woods." It was from there that all Israel brought it, with great ceremony, at the beginning of David's reign (1Ch 13:6), and so in building this house for the ark Solomon had pleased all Israel. They decided to be present at it: "Just let us have a convenient place, and *we will go into his tabernacle* to pay our homage there; *we will worship at his footstool* (v. 7) as subjects and petitioners, which we neglected to do *in the days of Saul* for lack of such a place" (1Ch 13:3).

2. What he prays for (vv. 8–10). He prays that God would condescend not only to take possession of the temple which he had built but also to take up residence in it. *Let thy priests be clothed with righteousness* (v. 9). "They are *thy priests* and will discredit their relationship to you if they *be not clothed with righteousness.*" He also prays that the people of God might have the encouragement of the properly organized worship services among them. "*Turn not away the face of thy anointed* (v. 10), that is, do not deny me the things I have asked you for, do not send me away ashamed."

Verses 11–18

These promises relate to the establishment both of church and of state, both to the throne of the house of David and to the testimony of Israel established on Mount Zion. The promises concerning Mount Zion are as applicable to the Gospel church as these concerning David's descendants are to Christ, and so both may be pleaded by us and are very encouraging to us. Here is:

1. The choice God made of David's house and Mount Zion. Both were of divine appointment.

1.1. God chose David's family as the royal family and confirmed his choice by an oath (vv. 11–12). This promise refers to:

1.1.1. A long succession of kings that would descend from his body: *Of the fruit of thy body will I set upon thy throne* (v. 11), which was fulfilled in Solomon; David himself lived to see it with great satisfaction (1Ki 1:48). The crown was also passed on as a conditional inheritance to his heirs forever: *If thy children will keep my covenant and my testimony that I shall teach them* (v. 12). In the end they did not keep God's covenant, and so the inheritance was finally cut off and *the sceptre* gradually *departed from Judah* (Ge 49:10).

1.1.2. An eternal successor, a greater king who would descend from his body; of *the increase of his government and peace there shall be no end* (Isa 9:7; Lk 1:33). The apostle Peter applies this to Christ; in fact, he tells us that David himself understood it in this way (Ac 2:30).

1.2. God chose Zion as the holy hill, and he confirmed his choice by the delight he took in it (vv. 13–14). God said, *Here will I dwell* (v. 14), and so David said, *Here will I dwell,* for he was faithful to what he decided: *It is good for me to be near to God* (73:28). Zion must be here looked on as a type of the Gospel church, which is called *Mount Zion* (Heb 12:22), and what is here said about Zion has its complete fulfillment in the Gospel church. Zion was long ago plowed as a field, but the church of Christ *is the house of the living God* (1Ti 3:15), and it is his resting

place forever and will be always blessed with his presence, to the end of the world.

2. The blessing God has in store for David's house and Mount Zion. God blesses those whom he chooses.

2.1. God, having chosen Mount Zion, promises to bless it. The promise refers, on the one hand, to blessings of the present life, for godliness holds promises for that (v. 15; 1Ti 4:8). The earth will produce its harvest (67:6; Eze 34:27); where religious faith is set up there will be provision. God's people have a special blessing in enjoying ordinary things, and that blessing gives a special sweetness to them. The promise goes further: *I will satisfy her poor with bread* (v. 15). They will have enough. If there is a scarcity, the poor are the first who feel it, so it is a sure sign of plenty if they have enough. This may also be understood spiritually, as referring to the provision made for the soul in the word and services of worship; God will abundantly bless those services so that they nurture us in our new humanity (Eph 2:15), and in so doing he will satisfy the poor in spirit with the bread of life (Mt 5:3; Jn 6:35). The promise refers, on the other hand, to blessings of the life that is to come, things concerning godliness (v. 16; 1Ti 4:8), which is an answer to the prayer in v. 9. It was desired that the priests might be *clothed with righteousness;* it is promised here that God will *clothe them with salvation.* They will save both themselves and those that hear them and thereby *add those to the church that shall be saved* (Ac 2:47).

2.2. Having chosen David's family, God here promises to bless them also with suitable blessings. *There,* in Zion, *will I make the horn of David to bud* (grow) (v. 17). Royal honor will increase more and more, and constant additions will be made to its glory. Christ is the *horn of salvation* that God has raised up and made to grow *in the house of his servant David* (Lk 1:69). *I have ordained a lamp for my anointed* (v. 17). You will *light my candle* (18:28). The lamp that God ordains is likely to burn brightly. *Lamp* refers to a successor, for when a lamp is almost gone out, another may be lit from it; it also refers to a succession, for God's ordaining of a lamp means that David will not lack anyone to stand before God. Christ is the lamp and the light of the world (Jn 8:12; 9:5). "*His enemies,* who have plotted against him, *will I clothe with shame* (v. 18) when they will see their plans frustrated." *Upon himself shall his crown flourish* (v. 18), that is, his rule will be his honor more and more. The crowns of earthly rulers *endure not to all generations* (Pr 27:24), but Christ's crown will endure to all eternity, and the crowns reserved for his faithful subjects are those that will *not fade away* (1Pe 5:4).

PSALM 133

This psalm is a brief psalm of praise on the subject of unity and love among the people of God. Some think David wrote this psalm on the occasion of the union between the tribes when they all met unanimously to make him king. Here is: 1. The doctrine of the blessing of love among God's people (v. 1). 2. The illustration of that doctrine by two comparisons (v. 2). 3. Proof of it, in a good reason given for it (v. 3).

Verses 1–3

1. Notice what is commended—*brethren dwelling together in unity* (v. 1). Sometimes it is decided that the best way to keep the peace is for brothers and sisters to live separately and far away from one another, so that enmity

and conflict may be prevented (Ge 13:9), but the goodness and pleasantness are *for brethren to dwell together* and so *to dwell in unity*, "to live as one," as some read it, as having one heart, one soul, and one aim. The tribes of Israel had for a long time had separate interests during the rule of the judges, but now that they were united under one common leader, he wanted them to be aware how much their unity would be to their advantage, especially now that the ark was settled, and with it the place of meeting for public worship and the center of their unity. Now let them live in love.

2. See how commendable it is. It is good in itself, conforming to the will of God; it is good for us, to give us honor, strength, and encouragement. It is pleasant and pleasing to God and all good people; it constantly brings delight to those who live in unity. It is rare and wonderful.

3. See how its pleasantness is illustrated. It is as fragrant as the holy anointing oil, which was strongly perfumed. Poured so plentifully on the head of Aaron or his successor the high priest that it ran down the face, even onto the collar or binding of his robes (v. 2), it diffused its scent to the great delight of all those standing by. Our love for our brothers and sisters must be holy, pure, and devoted to God. Holy love is, in God's sight, precious. Christ's love to the human race was part of that *oil of gladness* with which he was *anointed above his fellows* (45:7). Aaron and his sons were not allowed to minister to the Lord until they had been anointed with this oil, and neither are our services acceptable to God without this holy love; if we do not have it, we are nothing (1Co 13:1–2). It is profitable as well as pleasing; it is *as the dew* (v. 3); it brings plenty of blessings along with it, blessings as numerous as dewdrops. It cools the scorching heat of human passion as the evening dews cool the air and refresh the earth. It moistens the heart and makes it tender and fit to receive the good seed of the word (Mt 13:18–23). It is *as the dew of Hermon* (v. 3), an ordinary hill—for love for one another is the beauty and benefit of people in general—*and as the dew that descended upon the mountains of Zion* (v. 3), a holy mountain, for it contributes greatly to the fruitfulness of holy communities. People who love are blessed; they are blessed by God, and so are truly blessed. The blessing that God gives to those who live in love is *life for evermore* (v. 3); that is the blessing of blessings. Those who live in love not only live in God, but already live in heaven.

PSALM 134

This is the last of the fifteen songs of ascents, and if they were at any time sung all together in the temple service, it would have made a good conclusion, for its intention was to stir up the ministers to continue with their work at night, when the ceremonies of the day had been completed. Some consider this psalm a dialogue: 1. In the first two verses the priests or Levites who sat up all night to keep watch on the house of the Lord were called on to spend that time not in idle talk but in acts of devotion. 2. In the last verse those who were called on in this way to praise God prayed for the one who gave them that encouragement, either the high priest or the commander of the guard.

Verses 1–3

This psalm instructs us about a twofold blessing:
1. Our blessing God, that is, praising him, which we are taught to do in vv. 1–2.

1.1. It is a call to the *Levites* to do it. Some of them *by night stood in the house of the Lord* (v. 1) to guard the holy things in the temple and see that they were not desecrated, and to guard the rich things of the temple and see that they were not plundered. While the ark was in a tent, there was more need for guards to protect it. They were also present to see that neither the fire on the altar nor the lamps on the lampstand went out. It was probably usual for some devout and godly Israelites to sit up with them; we read of one who departed *not from the temple night or day* (Lk 2:37). Now these are here called on to *bless the Lord* (v. 2).

1.2. It is a call to us to do it, who, as Christians, are made priests or Levites to our God (Isa 66:21; Rev 5:10). We are the *servants of the Lord* (v. 1); we have a place and a name in his house, in his sanctuary; we stand in his presence to minister to him. Let us therefore *bless the Lord* (v. 2). Let us *lift up* our *hands* in prayer, praise, and vows; let us do our work with diligence, cheerfulness, and purity of mind.

2. God's blessing us, and that is doing us good, which we are here taught to desire (v. 3). We need desire nothing more to make us happy than to be blessed by the Lord, for those whom he blesses are truly blessed.

PSALM 135

This is one of the Hallelujah psalms; Hallelujah comes at its beginning and at its end; it is its Amen, its Alpha and its Omega. 1. It begins with a call to praise God (vv. 1–3). 2. It goes on to provide us with reasons for praise. God is to be praised: 2.1. As the God of Jacob (v. 4). 2.2. As the God of gods (v. 5). 2.3. As the God of the whole world (vv. 6–7). 2.4. As a fearful God toward the enemies of Israel (vv. 8–11). 2.5. As a gracious God to Israel (vv. 12–14). 2.6. As the only living God, all other gods being worthless and a deception (vv. 15–18). It concludes with another encouragement to everyone concerned to praise God (vv. 19–21).

Verses 1–4

Notice:
1. The duty we are called to—to *praise the Lord*, to *praise his name; praise him*, and again *praise him* (v. 1). We must not only thank him for what he has done for us but also praise him for what he is in himself and what he has done for others.

2. The people who are called on to do this—the *servants of the Lord* (v. 1), the priests and Levites *that stand in his house* (v. 2) and all the devout and godly Israelites who stand *in the courts of his house* to worship there (v. 2). Who will praise him if they do not?

3. The reasons why we should praise God: He is good to all. His goodness is his glory (Ex 33:18–19), and we must mention it to his glory. The work is its own wages.

Verses 5–14

The psalmist has suggested to us the goodness of God as the proper subject of our joyful praises; he suggests here the greatness of God as the proper subject of our fearful praise.

1. He asserts the doctrine of God's greatness (v. 5): *The Lord is great*, truly great, a God who knows no limits of time or place.

2. He proves him to be a great God by pointing to the greatness of his power (v. 6). He has absolute power and may do what he wants. This absolute and almighty power

is universal in extent; he does what he wishes *in heaven, in earth, in the seas*, and in *all the deep places* (v. 6) that are at the bottom of the sea or the center of the earth.

3. He gives examples of his great power:

3.1. In the kingdom of nature (v. 7). All the powers of nature prove the greatness of the God of nature, from whom they are derived and on whom they depend. The sequence of natural causes not only was made by him at first, but also is continued by him. It is by his power that vapors are drawn up from this land-and-water globe. The heat of the sun raises them up, but that power comes from God. It is he who forms the rain from the clouds, and in the fruitful showers of rain those vapors are returned to benefit the earth. He *makes lightnings for the rain* (v. 7); by them he shakes the clouds so that they may water the earth. Here fire and water are thoroughly reconciled by God's almighty power. Winds blow where they please, from whatever direction they please, and we are so far from directing them that we cannot tell where they come from or where they are going (Jn 3:8), but God *brings them out of his treasuries* (v. 7) with precision and planning.

3.2. In the kingdom of humankind. Notice God's sovereign and irresistible power:

• In bringing Israel out of Egypt, humbling Pharaoh by many plagues and so forcing him to let them go.
• In destroying the kingdoms of Canaan in front of them (v. 10). No power of hell or earth can prevent the fulfillment of the promise of God when the set time has come.
• In settling them in the Promised Land. The One who gives kingdoms to whomever he pleases gave Canaan as an inheritance to his people Israel.

4. He exults that God's glory and grace will last forever. His glory is everlasting: *Thy name, O God, endures for ever.* This seems to refer to Ex 3:15, where, when God had called himself *the God of Abraham, Isaac, and Jacob*, he added, *This is my name for ever and this is my memorial unto all generations.* His grace will also endure forever. He will be kind to his people. He will plead their cause against others who fight against them. *He will judge his people* (v. 14), that is, he will vindicate them and will not allow them to be oppressed. Nor will he himself accuse them forever; he will *repent himself concerning* (have compassion on) *his servants* (v. 14)

Verses 15–21

These verses intend:

1. To strengthen the people of God against idolatry and all false worship by showing what kind of gods the nations worshiped, as in 115:4–8. They were gods made by human hands and so had no power except what their makers gave them. They had the form of animals but could not do anything, not even anything *animals* can do. Their worshipers were therefore as stupid and senseless as they were, both those who made them to be worshiped and those who trusted in them when they were made (v. 18).

2. To encourage the people of God to true devotion in worshiping the true God (vv. 19–21). In the parallel reference (115:9–11) the powerlessness of idols is given as a reason for our duty to *trust in the Lord*; here it is a reason to *bless him*. By putting our trust in God we give glory to him.

PSALM 136

The scope of this psalm is the same as that of the previous psalm, but the second half of each verse is the same,

repeated throughout the psalm, for his mercy endureth for ever. It is agreed that such choruses add very much to the beauty of a song and help to keep it moving. The repetition of it twenty-six times suggests that God's mercies to his people are repeated and drawn out, as it were, by continuing from beginning to end. The eternal continuation of the love of God is very much his honor. This most excellent sentence that God's mercy endureth for ever is exalted above all the truths about God, not only by its repetition here but also by the special signs of divine acceptance with which God acknowledged the singing of this psalm (2Ch 5:13; 20:21–22). We must praise God: 1. As great and good in himself (vv. 1–3); as the Creator of the world (vv. 5–9). 2. As Israel's God and Savior (vv. 10–22). 3. As our Redeemer (vv. 23–24); as the One who is generous to the whole creation, and God over all, blessed forevermore (vv. 25–26; Ro 9:5).

Verses 1–9

The duty we are here again and again called to is to give thanks, to *offer the sacrifice of praise continually*, not the fruits of our land or cattle, but *the fruit of our lips, giving thanks to his name* (Heb 13:15). We must give thanks *to the Lord*, Jehovah, Israel's God (v. 1), *the God of gods* (v. 2), the God whom angels adore, from whom judges derive their power (v. 2), *to the Lord of lords* (v. 3), the Sovereign of all sovereigns (v. 3). We must give thanks to God for his goodness and mercy (v. 1): *Give thanks to the Lord* not only because he does good but also because he is good. Not only for that mercy which is now given to us here on earth but also for what will endure forever in the glories and joys of heaven. We must give God thanks for the examples of his power and wisdom. He made the heavens and spread them out, and not only do we see in them his wisdom and power, but we also taste his mercy in their kind influence; as long as the heavens endure, the mercy of God endures in them (v. 5). *The earth hath he given to the children of men* (115:16), and all its produce. He placed the sun, moon, and stars in the expanse of the sky, to shed their light and influences on this earth (vv. 7–9).

Verses 10–22

Here are mentioned, as often elsewhere in the Psalms, the great things God did for Israel when he formed them into a people and set up his kingdom among them; they are mentioned as examples of both the power of God and the special kindness he had for Israel. He brought them out of Egypt (vv. 10–12). He forced a way for them through the Red Sea, which obstructed them when they first set out. He not only parted the sea but also gave his people courage to go through it when it had parted, which was an example of God's power over human hearts, just as the former act showed his power over the water. He led them through a vast, howling desert (v. 16); he led them and fed them there. He destroyed kings to make way for them (vv. 17–18). It is good to go into the details of God's favors and not to view them generally; it is good to notice and recognize in each example that God's *mercy endureth for ever.* He gave them possession of a good land (vv. 21–22). As he said to the Egyptians, *Let my people go,* so he said to the Canaanites, *Let my people in,* so that they may serve me. In this *God's mercy* to them *endureth for ever*, because it was a type of the heavenly Canaan, the *mercy of our Lord Jesus Christ unto eternal life* (Jude 21).

Verses 23–26

God's eternal mercy is celebrated here in the redemption of his church (vv. 23–24). In the many redemptions worked for the Jewish church, redeeming them from the hands of their oppressors, we have a great deal of reason to say, *His mercy endureth for ever.* When, in the years of their slavery, they were in a very bad state, God remembered them and raised up saviors for them, the judges, and finally, David. But how much more reason do we find in the great redemption of the universal church, of which these were types, to say, *"He remembered us in our low estate,* when things were going badly for us, *for his mercy endureth for ever.* He sent his Son to redeem us from sin, death, hell, and all our spiritual enemies, *for his mercy endureth for ever."* It is an example of the mercy of God's providence that wherever he has given life, he also gives good and sufficient food, and he who provides for such a large family is a good housekeeper. His eternal mercy is celebrated in all his glories and all his gifts (v. 26): *Give thanks to the God of heaven.* This and that particular mercy may perhaps last awhile, but the mercy that is in God *endures for ever*; it is an inexhaustible fountain.

PSALM 137

There are various psalms that are thought to have been written in the final days of the Jewish church, when prophecy came near to being concluded and the canon of the Old Testament was ready to be closed, but none of them appears so clearly to be of a late date as this psalm, which was written when the people of God were captives in Babylon. It was probably toward the end of their exile, for they then saw the destruction of Babylon advancing quickly (v. 8), which would mean they would be released. It is a mournful psalm, a lamentation. Here: 1. The sad captives cannot enjoy themselves (vv. 1–2); they cannot indulge their proud oppressors (vv. 3–4); they cannot forget Jerusalem (vv. 5–6). 2. They cannot forgive Edom and Babylon (vv. 7–9).

Verses 1–6

We have here:

1. The Daughter of Zion covered with a cloud and living with the daughter of Babylon, the people of God in tears, but nevertheless sowing in tears (126:5). They were *by the rivers of Babylon* (v. 1), in a foreign land, far away from their own country, from which they were taken as captives. The land of Babylon was now a land of slavery to that people, as Egypt had been at the beginning of their days. Their conquerors kept them *by the rivers,* intending to employ them there. In Eze 1:3 we find some of them by the *river Chebar.* By these rivers of Babylon they *sat down* to give free rein to their grief by dwelling on their miseries. Thoughts of Zion made them weep tears; but they were deliberate tears—we *sat down and wept*—we *wept when we remembered Zion* (v. 1), the holy hill on which the temple was built. Their affection for God's house was far greater than their concern for their own houses. They set aside their musical instruments (v. 2): *We hung our harps upon the willows.* They did not hide their harps in the bushes or in the hollows of the rocks, but hung them up for everyone to see, so that those who saw the harps might be moved by the deplorable change in the lives of the Israelites. But perhaps they were at fault in doing this, for praising God is never out of season.

2. The abuse their enemies subjected them to when they were in this wretched condition (v. 3). They had *carried them away captive* from their own land and then *wasted* (tormented) *them* in the land of their exile. To complete their woe their captors gloated over them: they *required* (demanded) *of us mirth and a song.* They revealed an evil and corrupt spirit when they mocked and sarcastically demanded songs of joy from their prisoners, who were already in great distress. They mocked them for their former joys and their present griefs and challenged them to be merry when they knew they were unhappy. No songs would be right for them except the *songs of Zion* (v. 3), with which God had been honored, and so in this demand their captors insulted God himself, as Belshazzar did when he drank wine from the temple goblets.

3. The patience with which they bore this abuse (v. 4). They had set aside their harps and would not pick them up again. Ungodly scoffers are not to be humored. The reason they gave was very mild and godly: *How shall we sing the Lord's song in a strange land?* (v. 4). "It is the *Lord's song*; it is sacred; it is a special song to worship God in the temple, and so we dare not sing it in a foreign land, among idolaters."

4. The constant devotion they kept for Jerusalem, the city of their ceremonies, even though they were then in Babylon. It was always in their minds; they remembered it, although many of them had never seen it. When they prayed every day, they opened their windows toward Jerusalem, and how then could they forget it? *"Let my right hand forget her cunning* (skill)"—which the hand of an expert musician never can, unless it is damaged—"in fact, *let my tongue cleave to the roof of my mouth* (vv. 5–6), if I do not have a good word to say about Jerusalem wherever I am."

Verses 7–9

Having afflicted themselves with the thoughts of the ruins of Jerusalem, the godly Jews in Babylon here please themselves with the prospect of the ruin of its impenitent and implacable enemies. This did not come from a spirit of revenge, but from a holy zeal for the glory of God and the honor of his kingdom. And all this was a result of the old enmity Esau bore against Jacob because Jacob gained the birthright and the blessing (Ge 25:29–34; 27:1–36). *Lord, remember* them, says the psalmist, which is an appeal to God's justice against them. Far be it from any of us to avenge ourselves, if it should ever be in our power; we will leave it to the One who has said, *Vengeance is mine* (Ro 12:19). *O daughter of Babylon!* Proud and secure as you are, we know well you *are to be destroyed,* or, as Dr. Henry Hammond understands it, "who are the destroyer." The destroyers will themselves be destroyed (Rev 13:10). "You will be served *as thou hast served us* (v. 8), treated as cruelly by the destroyers as we have been treated by you." Those who did not show mercy when they had power must not expect to find mercy. When Babylon is captured, all who are in it, even its little ones, will be killed. No one escapes if the little ones die. Those are the seed of another generation, so if they are cut off, the destruction will be not only total, as Jerusalem's was, but also final.

PSALM 138

It is not stated on what occasion David wrote this psalm, but in it: 1. He looks back with thankfulness on the experiences he has had of God's goodness to him (vv. 1–3). 2. He looks forward with encouragement in the hope that others will continue to praise God as he has (vv. 4–5) and that God will continue to do him good (vv. 6–8).

Verses 1–5

Notice here:

1. David wants to praise God with sincerity and zeal: *"With my whole heart* (v. 1), with all that is within me (103:1), my inner motivation agreeing with my outer expression. *Before the gods will I sing praise unto thee* (v. 1), before the rulers, judges, and leaders. *I will worship toward thy holy temple"* (v. 2). The priests alone went into the temple; the nearest that people could go was to worship toward it at a distance. Christ is our temple, and we must look toward him as the Mediator between us and God in all our praises of him. Heaven is God's holy temple, and we must lift up our eyes toward heaven in all our prayers to God. *Our Father in heaven* (Mt 6:9).

2. David wants to praise God for the fountain of his comforts—*for thy loving-kindness and for thy truth* (v. 2). *For thou hast magnified thy word*—your promise, which is truth—*above all thy name* (v. 2). God has made himself known to us in many ways in creation and providence, but most clearly by his word. Some interpreters understand this to refer to Christ, the essential Word, and his Gospel, which are exalted above all the revelations God had made of himself to Christ's ancestors. David has suffered adversities, and he remembers, *Thou strengthenedst me with strength in my soul* (v. 3). If God gives us strength in our souls to bear the burdens, resist the temptations, and do the duties belonging to a state of suffering, if he strengthens us to keep hold of him by faith, to maintain the peace of our own minds and to wait patiently for the outcome of events, then we must acknowledge that he has answered us, and we must be thankful.

3. David himself was king, and so he hoped kings would be persuaded by his own experience and example to take up his religious faith. This may refer to the kings who were David's neighbors, such as Hiram. *They will all praise thee.* When they visited David and, after his death, Solomon, as *all the kings of the earth* are explicitly said to have done (2Ch 9:23), they readily joined in worshiping the God of Israel. It may also look further, to the calling of the Gentiles and the discipling of all nations by the Gospel of Christ, of whom it is said that *all kings shall fall down before him* (72:11). They will *sing in the ways of the Lord* (v. 5), because of his providence and grace toward them.

Verses 6–8

David here encourages himself with three things:

1. The favor God shows to his humble people (v. 6): *Though the Lord be high, yet has he respect unto the lowly*; he smiles on them and is pleased with them; and, sooner or later, he will honor them, while *he knows the proud afar off* (v. 6); he knows them but disowns them.

2. The care God takes of his afflicted and oppressed people (v. 7). Although David was great and good, he expected to *walk in the midst of trouble*, but nevertheless he encouraged himself with hope. "When my spirit is about to sink and fail, *thou shalt revive me*, you will preserve my life and make me cheerful even when I am in trouble." God would protect him: "*Thou shalt stretch forth thy hand*, though not against my enemies to destroy them, yet *against the wrath of my enemies* (v. 7), to restrain it and set limits on it" (76:10). God would rescue him in due time: *Thy right hand shall save me* (v. 7). Christ is the right hand of the Lord, and that will save all those who serve him.

3. Whatever good work God has begun for his people, he will complete it (v. 8): "*The Lord will perfect that*

which concerns me, what is most necessary for me." All good people are most concerned about their duty to God and their happiness in God, that the former may be faithfully done and the latter effectively secured, and if these really are what our hearts are most set on, then a good work has begun in us, and the One who has begun it will complete it (Php 1:6). Our hopes that we will persevere must be based not on our own strength, for that will fail us, but on the mercy of God, for that will not fail. It is a good plea: *"Lord, thy mercy endures for ever* (v. 8); may I forever be a good example of it." He turns his expectation into a request: *"Forsake not, do not abandon, the work of thy own hands* (v. 8). Lord, I am the work of your own hands, as is my soul, and do not abandon me."

PSALM 139

Some Jewish teachers think this psalm is the most excellent of the psalms of David. It is a very godly and devout meditation on the doctrine of God's omniscience. 1. This doctrine is asserted (vv. 1–6). 2. It is confirmed by two arguments: God is present everywhere, and so he knows everything (vv. 7–12); he made us, and so he knows us (vv. 13–16). 3. Some deductions are made from this doctrine. It may fill us with an uplifting wonder toward God (vv. 17–18), with a holy hatred of sin and sinners (vv. 19–22), and with a holy assurance in our own integrity (vv. 23–24).

Verses 1–6

The God with whom we have to do (Heb 4:13) knows us perfectly, and all movements and actions of both our inner and our outer beings are open before him.

1. David sets down this doctrine by way of a prayer to God, acknowledging it to him and giving him the glory. When we speak to God about himself, we find ourselves concerned to speak with the greatest sincerity and reverence.

2. He sets it down by applying it to himself. He says not, *"Thou hast known* all," but, *Thou hast known me, searched me and known me* (v. 1). David was a king, and *the hearts of kings are unsearchable* to their subjects (Pr 25:3), but they are not so to their Sovereign (Pr 21:1).

3. He gets down to details: "You know me wherever I am and whatever I am doing. You know me and everything that belongs to me. *Thou knowest* me and all my movements, *my downsitting* to rest, *my uprising* (v. 2) to work. You know me when I come home, how I walk in front of my house, and when I go out, what tasks I do. You know all my thoughts. They are often unobserved by us ourselves; but *thou understandest my thought afar off"* (v. 2). Or: "*Thou understandest my thought afar off*, even before I think it, and long after I have thought it and I myself have forgotten it." Or: "*Thou understandest my thought from afar*; from the heights of heaven you see into the depths of the heart" (33:14). "*Thou compassest* every particular *path*, so as to thoroughly discern the good and evil of what I do. *Thou knowest* me when I retire; you know *my lying down* (v. 3); when I am reflecting on what has passed all day, you know what I have in my heart and with what thoughts I go to bed. *There is not a word in my tongue*, not a worthless word or a good word, *but thou knowest it altogether."* Some read it, "When there is not a word in my tongue, O Lord! you know everything"; for thoughts are words to God. *Thou hast beset me* (you hem me in) *behind and before* (v. 5). Wherever we are, we are under the eye and hand of God. God knows us as

we know ourselves, not only what we see but also what we feel and do.

4. He speaks of it with wonder (v. 6): *It is too wonderful for me; it is high* (lofty). We cannot search to find out how God searches and finds us out; nor do we know how we are known.

Verses 7–16

David is sure that God knows him and all his ways perfectly:

1. Because he is always under his eye. If God is present everywhere, he must also know everything. Heaven and earth include the whole creation, and the Creator fills both (Jer 23:24). He not only knows both and governs both but also fills both. Every part of the creation is under God's influence.

1.1. No flight can remove us from God's presence: "*Whither shall I go from thy Spirit, from thy presence* (v. 7), that is, from your spiritual presence, from yourself, who are a Spirit?" *God is a Spirit* (Jn 4:24). It is foolish to think that because we cannot see God, he cannot see us: *Whither shall I flee from thy presence?* (v. 7). "Wherever you turn, you will see God meeting you," as Seneca said. David specifies the most faraway places, and he counts on meeting God there:

1.1.1. In heaven: "*If I ascend* there, as I hope to soon, *thou art there* (v. 8), and it will be my eternal happiness to be with you there."

1.1.2. *In hell*, that is, *Sheol*, which may be understood as the depths of the earth, its very center. If we were to dig as deep as we can underground and think we could hide ourselves there, we would be mistaken. Or the phrase may be understood to refer to the world of the dead. Even when we are moved from the sight of all living beings, we are not out of sight of the living God; we cannot hide ourselves from his eye. Or it may be understood as referring to the place of the condemned: *If I make my bed in hell*—a truly uncomfortable place to make a bed in, *behold, thou art there* (v. 8), in your power and justice.

1.1.3. In the most distant corners of this world: "*If I take the wings of the morning* (v. 9), the rays of the morning light, elsewhere called the wings of the sun (Mal 4:2), than which nothing is faster, and if I flee on them to *the uttermost parts of the sea* (v. 9) or of the earth, I will find you there. If I fled to the farthest and most obscure islands—the most remote and unknown part of the world—I would still find you there; *there shall thy hand lead me*, as far as I *go, and thy right hand shall hold me* (v. 10), so I can go no further; I cannot go beyond your reach."

1.2. No curtain can hide us from God's eye (vv. 11–12). "*If I say, surely the darkness shall cover me*, when nothing else will, I find I am deceived; the curtains of the evening will do me no more good than the wings of the morning; *even the night shall be light about me.*" No hypocritical mask or disguise, however outwardly respectable it is, can save any person or action from being seen in its true light before God.

2. Because he is the work of his hands. The one who framed the mechanism knows all its movements. God made us, and so he knows us: "*Thou hast possessed my reins*, you created my inmost being. Your possession of my inmost being is rightfully yours, *for thou coveredst me* (knit me together) *in my mother's womb* (v. 13), that is, you made me in the secret place" (Job 10:11). The soul is hidden from everyone around us. It was God himself who formed us, and so he can, when he pleases, find us. "*I will praise thee* (v. 14), the author of my being; my

parents were only the instruments of it." We were his work according to the divine pattern: *In thy book all my members* (days) *were written* (v. 16). Eternal wisdom formed the plan. We are *fearfully and wonderfully made* (v. 14); we may justly be amazed at these living temples, the composition of every part, and the harmony of all the parts together. We should consider it a great mercy that all our members *in continuance were fashioned* (v. 16), according to how they were written in the book of God's wise purposes, *when as yet there was none of them* (v. 16).

Verses 17–24

Here the psalmist applies the doctrine of God's omniscience:

1. He acknowledges with wonder and thankfulness the care God has taken of him throughout his life (vv. 17–18). God, who knows him, thinks about him, and his thoughts toward him are thoughts of love. God's omniscience has watched over us to do us good (Jer 31:28). Providence has had great scope in helping us and has brought things about for our good that have been completely beyond our planning or foresight. We cannot conceive how great God's compassions are, and they are new every morning (La 3:23). "*When I awake* each morning, *I am still with thee* (v. 18), under your eye and care, safe and at peace under your protection."

2. He concludes from this teaching that ruin will finally and certainly come to sinners. God knows all the evil of evildoers, and so he will judge it. God will punish them because they defiantly offend him (v. 20): *They speak against thee wickedly*. They are his *enemies*, and they declare their enmity by *taking his name in vain*, by misusing his name (v. 20). Some consider the verse a description of hypocrites: "They speak of you to cause trouble; they talk about God, pretending to be devout, and because they are God's enemies, while they pretend friendship they are really *taking his name in vain* (v. 20) and swearing falsely." He defies them: "*Depart from me, you bloody* (bloodthirsty) *men* (v. 19); you will not defile me, for I will not believe in your friendship, nor will I have fellowship with you. You cannot destroy me." David detests them (vv. 21–22): "Lord, you know the heart and can witness for me; *do not I hate those that hate thee*, because they hate you? I hate them because I love you and hate to see such dishonor shown to your blessed name. *Am not I grieved with those that rise up against thee*, grieved to see their rebellion and to foresee their ruin, which it will certainly lead to?" All who fear God hate sin and mourn for sinners. "*I hate them*"—that is, I hate the work of them that turn aside (101:3).

3. He appeals to God concerning his sincerity (vv. 23–24): "Lord, I hope I am not evil in any way, but *see if there be any wicked way in me* (v. 24), any corrupt inclination remaining in me; let me see it; and uproot it from me, for I do not allow it." *Lead me in the way everlasting* (v. 24).

PSALM 140

This and the four following psalms belong very much together, and their theme is the same as the one we met with at the beginning and in the middle of the book of Psalms. They were written by David, it seems, when he was being persecuted by Saul. In this psalm: 1. David complains about the hatred of his enemies, and he prays to God to keep him safe from them (vv. 1–5); he encourages himself in God as his God (vv. 6–7). 2. He prays for and prophesies the destruction of his persecutors (vv. 8–11), and he assures all God's afflicted people that their troubles will end well at the proper time (vv. 12–13).

Verses 1–7

As in other things David was a type of Christ, so also in this: he suffered before he reigned, he was humbled before he was exalted, and just as there were many people who loved him, valued him, and sought to honor him, so also there were many who hated and envied him and sought to cause trouble for him.

1. He describes his enemies. There is one person who seems to have been their ringleader, whom he calls *the evil man* and *the violent man* (vv. 1, 4); he is probably referring to Saul. But there are many besides this one who have allied themselves against David. They are very subtle: they have devised evil plans in their hearts with all possible cunning (v. 2). *They have*, like strong hunters, *hidden a snare, spread a net*, and *set gins* (traps) (v. 5), so that he might fall into their hands before he knew what was happening to him. Great persecutors have often been great politicians, and this has made them more formidable, but *the Lord preserves the simple* (116:6). *They have sharpened their tongues like a serpent* (v. 3), which injects its venom with its tongue. There is so much hatred in all they say that one would think there was nothing *under their lips* but *adders' poison* (v. 3). They are all *gathered together* against me *for war* (v. 2). Those who can agree on nothing else can agree that they will persecute someone good. Herod and Pilate united in this, and here they were like Satan, who is not divided against himself, since all the demons agree in following Beelzebub (Mt 12:24–27). The pride of persecutors may still be a source of encouragement for those who are being persecuted, for the more arrogant the persecutors are, the sooner will their destruction come.

2. He prays: "Lord, *deliver me, preserve me, keep me* (vv. 1, 4); do not let them succeed in taking away my life, my reputation, my interests, and my strength, to prevent my coming to the throne. *Keep me* from behaving as they do, or as they promise themselves I will do."

3. He triumphs in God, and so, in effect, he triumphs over his persecutors (vv. 6–7). "*I said, Thou art my God* (v. 6), and if he is my God, he is also my shield and mighty protector." He takes encouragement in his access to God, in knowing that he was taken not only into covenant with God but also into fellowship with him. He had help from God and happiness in him: "*O God the Lord— Jehovah Adonai*, as *Jehovah* you are self-existent and self-sufficient, the God in covenant with me, an infinitely perfect God; as *Adonai* you are my support, my ruler, and my governor, and so you are *the strength of my salvation* (v. 7), my strong Savior. *Thou hast covered my head in the day of battle*" (v. 7).

Verses 8–13

David prays: "*Grant not, O Lord! the desires of the wicked*, but frustrate them; *hear the voice of my supplications*" (v. 6). He prays: "*O further not his wicked device* (v. 8); let not Providence favor any of his intentions, but frustrate them; allow *not his wicked device* to proceed, but restrain him, and stop him in what he is pursuing." He foretells the ruin of his enemies: "*The mischief of their own lips* will *cover* their heads (v. 9); the evil they have wished for me will come on them, their curses will be thrown back in their faces, and the very plans they have set against me will turn to their own destruction" (7:15–16). The judgments of God will *fall upon them*;

these judgments are compared to *burning coals* (v. 10), in allusion to the destruction of Sodom. *Evil speakers* must expect to be shaken, for they will never *be established in the earth*. What is gained by fraud, falsehood, slander, or unjust accusations will not succeed. "*I know that the Lord will maintain* (uphold) *the* just and wronged *cause of* his *afflicted* people and will not allow might always to succeed against right, even though it is only *the rights of the poor*." The closing words, *The upright shall dwell in thy presence* (v. 13), show both God's favor toward them— "You will allow them to live in your sight, in grace here and in glory hereafter, and it will be their security and happiness"—and their duty to God.

PSALM 141

David was in distress when he wrote this psalm. He prays: 1. For God's favorable acceptance (vv. 1–2). 2. For his powerful assistance (vv. 3–4). 3. That others may be instrumental in doing good to his soul, as he hopes to be to the souls of others (vv. 5–6). 4. That because he and his friends are now brought to the point of death, God would graciously come to help and rescue them (vv. 7–10).

Verses 1–4

David teaches us here to pray to God for two things: mercy to accept what we do right and grace to keep us from doing wrong.

1. David loved to pray, and here he asks God to hear his prayers and answer them (vv. 1–2). *David cried unto God.* His calling out shows he was fervent in prayer: "*Give ear to my voice*; graciously listen to me." Those who call out in prayer may hope to be heard in prayer not for their loudness but for the liveliness of their faith. *Make haste unto me.* Whoever believes does not act hastily (Isa 28:16), but those who pray may ask fervently that God will act hastily. His *praying* and *lifting up his hands in prayer* shows both the raising of his desire and the expression of his hope and expectation; the lifting up of the hands showed the lifting up of the heart and was used instead of lifting up the sacrifices that were waved before the Lord. Prayer is a spiritual sacrifice; it is the offering up of the soul, and of its best devotion, to God. Prayer has a sweet-smelling aroma to God, like incense, which, however, has no aroma without fire; nor has prayer any fragrance without the fire of holy love and fervor.

2. David begs that he might be kept from sin, knowing that his prayers will not be accepted unless he takes care to keep watch against sin. We must desire God's grace in us as earnestly as we desire his favor toward us. "*Set a watch, O Lord, before my mouth*, and because nature has made my lips as a door for my words, let grace guard that door, so that no word may be allowed to leave it that may in any way tend to dishonor God or hurt others. *Incline not my heart to any evil thing*; whatever inclination there is in me to sin, let it be not only restrained but also put to death by divine grace." While we live in such an evil world and carry within us such evil hearts, we need to pray that we may be neither seduced by any allurement nor driven on by any provocation. "*Let me not eat of their dainties*" (delicacies). Let me not join with them, for if I do I may become enticed into their sins." Good people will pray even against the sweetness of sin.

Verses 5–10

Here:

1. David wants to be told about his faults. *Let the righteous smite me; it shall be a kindness.* We are taught here

how to receive the rebukes of the righteous and wise. "If my own heart does not *smite me*, as it should, let my friend do it; let me never fall under that fearful judgment of being left alone in sin." We must consider it part of friendship. We must not only bear it patiently but also take it as a kindness. Although reproofs cut us, they are given in order to heal us, and so they are much more desirable than the kisses of an enemy (Pr 27:6) or the song of fools (Ecc 7:5). It *shall be as an excellent oil* to a wound, to soothe it and close it up; *it shall not break my head* (v. 5), as some think it will, who could as well cope with having their heads injured as with being told of their faults. "I do not think like that," David says; "it is my sin that has crushed my head and my bones (51:8). The rebuke is *an excellent oil*, to heal the bruises sin has caused me. It will not *break my head* (v. 5), if only it may help to break my heart."

2. David hopes his persecutors will, some time or other, bear to be told their faults, as he is willing to be told his (v. 6). Some think this refers to the change of mind that Saul had when he said with tears, *Is this thy voice, my son David?* (1Sa 24:16; 26:21).

3. David complains about the critical need to which he and his friends have been reduced (v. 7): "*Our bones are scattered at the grave's mouth*, out of which they have been thrown up, so long have we been dead; and they are as little regarded as woodchips are by woodcutters, who throw them in heaps and neglect them."

4. David throws himself on God and depends on him for rescue: "*But my eyes are unto thee* (v. 8). I expect relief from you, bad though things are, and in *thee is my trust*."

PSALM 142

This psalm is a prayer, the substance of which David offered to God when he was forced by Saul to take shelter in a cave, and which he later wrote in this form. Here is: 1. The complaint he makes to God (vv. 1–2) of the cunning, strength, and hatred of his enemies (vv. 3–6) and the coldness and indifference of his friends (v. 4). 2. The strength and encouragement he gains from knowing that God knows his situation (v. 3) and is his refuge (v. 5). 3. His expectation from God that he will hear and rescue him (vv. 6–7); his expectation from the righteous that they will join him in praise (v. 7).

Title

Whether it was in the cave of Adullam or in that of En Gedi that David prayed this prayer is not significant; it is clear he was in distress. When he dared not use his hands against his ruler, he lifted them up to his God. There is no cave so deep or dark that we may not send our souls up from it in prayer to God. He calls this prayer a *Maschil*, "a psalm of instruction," because of the good lessons he learned in the cave on his knees.

Verses 1–3

In these verses notice:
1. How David complained to God (vv. 1–2). When the danger was over, he was not ashamed to acknowledge, as great spirits sometimes are, the shock he had suffered. Let no one think it beneath them to cry out to God when they are suffering, as children cry out to their parents when anything frightens them. *He cried unto the Lord with his voice*, with an inaudible voice in his mind, as some think, for because he was hidden in the cave, he dared not speak audibly, for that might betray him, but silent

prayers uttered in the mind are heard by God. He hears the groanings that we cannot, or dare not, utter (Ro 8:26). *I showed before him my trouble* (v. 2). As one who put his confidence in God, he revealed his true feelings to him and then happily left matters with him. We tend to keep our troubles too much to ourselves, making them worse by dwelling on them, whereas by sharing them with God we could give the anxiety they cause to the One who cares for us (1Pe 5:7).

2. What he complained about: "*In the way wherein I walked*, suspecting no danger, *have they privily* (secretly) *laid a snare for me* (v. 3) to entrap me." Saul gave Michal his daughter to David with the purpose that she might be *a snare to him* (1Sa 18:21).

3. What gave him strength and encouragement in the midst of these complaints (v. 3): "*When my spirit was overwhelmed within me* and about to sink under the burden of grief and fear, *then thou knewest my path*, that is, then it gave me delight to recall that you knew it. You knew it, that is, you protected and preserved me" (31:7; Dt 2:7).

Verses 4–7

David had been disowned and deserted by his friends (v. 4). When he was made an outlaw, *no man would know him* and everybody was reluctant to have any dealings with him. He looked *on his right hand* for support (109:31), but since it would likely have cost Jonathan his life to appear for him, no one was willing to come to defend his innocence. How many good people have been deceived by such fair-weather friends, who disappear as soon as winter comes! Here he was a type of Christ, who was abandoned by everyone, even his own disciples; he had to tread the winepress alone (Isa 63:3). David tells us what he said to God in the cave: "*Thou art my refuge and my portion in the land of the living*. The cave I am in is only a poor refuge. Lord, *thy name* is the *strong tower* that *I run into* (Pr 18:10). You are *my refuge*, in whom alone I consider myself safe." Those who sincerely take the Lord as their God will find him to be all-sufficient, and they may humbly claim their privilege: "*Lord, thou art my refuge in the land of the living* (v. 5), that is, while I live and exist, whether in this world or in the better one." He addressed himself to God (vv. 5–6). "Lord, *deliver me from my persecutors*; either tie their hands or turn their hearts, break their power or blight their plans, restrain them or rescue me, *for they are stronger than I*. Lord, *bring my soul out of prison* (v. 7), not only bring me safe out of this cave, but also bring me out of all my bewilderment."

PSALM 143

This psalm, like those before, is a prayer of David, and full of complaints about the great distress and danger he was in. In this psalm: 1. He complains about his troubles (v. 3) and the weakness of his spirit (vv. 4–5); he prays fervently (v. 6) that God would listen to him (vv. 1–7), that God would not deal with him according to his sins (v. 2), and that he would not hide his face from him (v. 7), but show his favor to him (v. 8). 2. He prays that God would guide and direct him in the path of his duty (vv. 8, 10) and revive him in it (v. 11), that he would rescue him from his troubles (vv. 9, 11), and that he would in due time judge his persecutors (v. 12).

Verses 1–6

Here:
1. David comes as a petitioner to his God and a petitioner against his persecutors, and he begs that God will

administer justice on his case, in his faithfulness as the Judge of right and wrong. We have no righteousness of our own to plead, and so we must plead God's righteousness, the word of promise he has freely given us and caused us to hope in.

2. He humbly begs not to be proceeded against in strict justice (v. 2). He seems here, if not to correct, then to explain, his plea (v. 1), "Deliver me *in thy righteousness.*" "I mean," he says, "the righteous promises of the Gospel, not the righteous threats of the Law." His request is, *"Enter not into judgment with thy servant* (v. 2); do not deal with me in strict justice, as I deserve to be dealt with." Before David prays for his trouble to be removed, he prays for his sin to be forgiven, and he depends on sheer mercy for that.

3. He complains about his enemies (v. 3): "Saul, that great enemy, *has persecuted my soul,* sought my life with restless hatred. He has forced me to *dwell in darkness,* not only in dark caves but also in dark thoughts and apprehensions, in the clouds of depression, as helpless and hopeless as *those that have been long dead.* Lord, let me find mercy with you, for I find no mercy with people."

4. He complains about his mental oppression, brought about by his outward troubles (v. 4): *Therefore is my spirit* faint, overpowered, and *overwhelmed within me.*

5. He uses the right means to relieve his troubled spirit. If he can keep possession of nothing else, he will do what he can to keep possession of his own soul and to keep his inner peace. He looks back and *remembers the days of old* (v. 5), the previous occasions when God helped his suffering people and him in particular. He looks around and notices the works of God in the physical creation and the rule of Providence in the world: *I meditate on all thy works* (v. 5). *"I muse on"* — or (as some read it) "I discourse of" — *"the* activity *of thy hands,* how great and good it is!" The more we consider the power of God, the less we will fear the face or force of human beings (Isa 51:12–13). He looks up with fervent desires toward God and his favor (v. 6): *I stretch forth my hands unto thee. My soul thirsteth after thee*; "my soul is to you" is the meaning, "completely devoted to you, set on you; it is *as a thirsty land,* which, because it is parched with excessive heat, splits open for lack of rain."

Verses 7–12

David here prays for three things:

1. The revelation of God's favor toward him. He dreads God's disapproval: "Lord, *hide not thy face from me"* (v. 7). Dismayed saints have sometimes cried out at the wrath of God, as if they were condemned sinners (88:6; Job 6:4). He asks for God's favor (v. 8): *Cause me to hear thy loving-kindness in the morning.* God speaks to us by his word and by his providence, and we should both want and try to *hear his loving-kindness in both* (107:43).

2. The activity of God's grace in him. *Cause me to know the way wherein I should walk* (v. 8). Good people do not ask which is the way in which they must walk, or which is the most pleasant way, but which is the *right* way, the way in which they should walk. The psalmist pleads, *"I lift up my soul unto thee* (v. 8), to be molded and fashioned according to your will. *Teach me to do thy will* (v. 10), not only show me what your will is, but also teach me how to do it." *Lead me into the land of uprightness* (v. 10), that settled way of holy living that will lead to heaven. We cannot find the way that will take us to that land unless God shows us, nor can we go that way unless he takes us by the hand and leads us, as we lead those who are weak, lame, shy, or shortsighted. The plea

is, *"Thy Spirit is good* (v. 10) and able to make me good," good and willing to help those who do not know which way to turn. "Let your good Spirit lead me" is how some understand this. He prays that he might be revived to do his will (v. 11): *"Quicken me, O Lord!* Revive my grace, so that I may be active; revive my devotions, so that they may be revitalized."

3. The appearance of God's providence for him (v. 9): *"Deliver me, O Lord! from my enemies,* so that they may not have their will against me, *for I flee unto thee to hide me."* He prays: "Rescue me not only from my outer troubles but also from the troubles that threaten to overwhelm my soul and my spirit."

PSALM 144

The four previous psalms seem to have been written by David before his accession to the throne, when he was being persecuted by Saul; this psalm seems to have been written afterward. In this psalm: 1. He acknowledges with triumph and thankfulness the great goodness of God toward him in putting him in charge of the government (vv. 1–4); he prays to God to help him against the enemies who threaten him (vv. 5–8 and again v. 11). 2. He rejoices in the assurance of victory over them (vv. 9–10); he prays for the prosperity of his own kingdom (vv. 12–15).

Verses 1–8

Here:

1. David acknowledges his dependence on God and his obligations to him (vv. 1–2). *Blessed be the Lord my strength* (v. 1)—literally, "my rock"—*my goodness, my fortress* (v. 2). He uses many words to express the assurance he has in God. "He is *my strength,* on whom I rest, and *my goodness*; not only is he good to me, but he is the author of all the goodness that is in me, and *from whom comes every good and perfect gift"* (Jas 1:17). David had formerly sheltered in strongholds at En Gedi (1Sa 23:29), which perhaps were natural fortresses. He had just come to take control of the stronghold of Zion, which was fortified by human skill, and he *dwelt in the fort* (2Sa 5:7, 9). But he did not depend on these. "Lord," he says, "you are *my fortress* and *my high tower.* And you are not only *my fortress* at home but also *my shield* (v. 2) when I am on the battlefield." Wherever believers go, they take their protection along with them. He was brought up as a shepherd, and it seems that neither his parents nor he had any higher ambitions for his future. But God had made him a soldier. His hands had been used to the shepherd's crook and his fingers to the harp, but God *taught his hands to war and his fingers to fight* (v. 1), because God intended him to be Israel's champion. God had made him a sovereign ruler and had taught him to wield the scepter as well as the sword; he *subdueth my people under me* (v. 2).

2. He wonders at God's condescension to human beings and to himself in particular (vv. 3–4): "Lord, *what is man,* what poor, lowly creatures they are, *that thou takest knowledge of him, that thou makest account of him?"* Here is the lowliness and mortality of human beings, despite the dignity put on them (v. 4): *Man is like to vanity* (like a breath); human beings are so weak, frail, and helpless, they are surrounded by so many weaknesses, and their lives here are so short and uncertain, that they are like mere breaths.

3. He begs God to give him success against the enemies who have invaded him (vv. 5–8). He does not specify who

they are that he is afraid of, but says, *Scatter them, destroy them.* But he describes them later (vv. 7–8): "They are *strange children*, Philistines, foreigners, bad neighbors of Israel. You cannot take their word, for their *mouth speaketh vanity* (their mouths are full of lies) (v. 8); in fact, if they give their hand to back up their word, or offer their hand to help you, they cannot be trusted, for *their right hand is a right hand of falsehood*" (v. 8). David prays that God would come: "*Bow* (part) *thy heavens, O Lord,* and make it clear that they are indeed yours and that you are their Lord (Isa 66:1). *Touch the mountains* (v. 5), our strong and grand enemies, *and* let them *smoke.* Show yourself as you did on Mount Sinai."

Verses 9–15

In this latter part of the psalm as in the former, David first gives glory to God and then begs mercy from him.

1. He praises God for the experiences he has had of his goodness to him (vv. 9–10). In the midst of his complaints concerning the power and treachery of his enemies comes holy praise to his God: *I will sing a new song to thee, O God!* He will sing a song of praise for fresh mercies. He tells us what this new song will be (v. 10): *It is he that giveth salvation* (victories) *unto kings.* Kings protect their people, but it is God who is *their* protector. How much service must they render with their power, then, to him who gives them all their victories! He has committed himself to give victories to those kings who are his subjects and rule for him, as can be seen from the great things he did for *David his servant* (v. 10). This may refer to Christ the Son of David, and then it is truly a new song, in fact a New Testament song.

2. He prays for the continuation of God's favor:

2.1. That he might be rescued from the public enemies (v. 11). He here repeats his prayer and plea (vv. 7–8).

2.2. That he might see public peace and prosperity: "Lord, let us have the victory, so that we may have quietness, which we will never have while our enemies have it in their power to cause us trouble." David wanted promising offspring for his people (v. 12): "*That our sons and our daughters may be* in all respects such as we could wish." It is desirable to see *our daughters as corner stones* (v. 12), or pillars, *polished after the similitude of a palace,* carved to adorn a palace (v. 12), or temple. Families are united and connected by daughters, to their mutual strength, as the parts of a building are by the cornerstones, and when they are graceful and beautiful both in body and in mind, they are then formed to adorn a beautiful structure. When we see our daughters settled down and strong in wisdom, when we see them united to Christ in faith and purified and consecrated to God as living temples, we think we are fortunate in them. He prays for growing resources with a growing family:

• That their storehouses might be well stocked with the fruits and products of the earth: "*That our garners* (barns) *may be full* (v. 13), that having abundance, we may be thankful to God, generous to our friends, and charitable to the poor."

• That their flocks might greatly increase: "*That our sheep may bring forth thousands, and ten thousands* (v. 13), *in our* fields." Much of the wealth of their country consisted in their flocks.

• That their animals that were intended to serve them might be fit for that work: *That our oxen may be strong to labour* (v. 14) with the plow.

2.3. "Let our enemies not invade us; let us not have cause to march out against them." War brings with it

plenty of trouble, whether it is offensive or defensive. "Let there be no oppression or faction—no *complaining in our streets*, no cries of distress in our streets (v. 14), so that the people may have no cause to be distressed and complain about their government or one another." It is good to live in peaceful dwelling places (Isa 32:18). Here is his reflection on this description of the prosperity of the nation, which he wanted so much (v. 15): *Happy are the people that are in such a case*—but it is rarely so, and never for long—*yea, happy are the people whose God is the Lord.*

PSALM 145

The five previous psalms were all similar: all full of prayers; this psalm, with the five that follow it, to the end of the book, are all similar too: they are all full of praise. And it is significant that after five psalms of prayer come six psalms of praise, for those who are much in prayer will not lack reasons for praise, and those who have been effective in prayer must also abound in praise. When we have received mercy, our thanksgiving for it should even surpass the prayers we offered for it when we were pursuing it. The book of Psalms concludes with psalms of praise, all praise, for praise is the conclusion of the matter (Ecc 12:13); it is what all the psalms center on. This way of concluding the book also shows that toward the end of their lives God's people should very much abound in praise, because at the end of their lives they hope to move to the world of eternal praise, and the closer they come to heaven, the more they should get used to the work of heaven.

This is one of those psalms that are composed as acrostic poems (like Psalms 25 and 34) so that they might be more easily committed to memory and kept in mind. The Jewish writers justly extol this psalm as a star of the greatest magnitude in this bright constellation; and some of them have a fanciful saying about it, not unlike some of the Catholic superstitions, that whoever sings this psalm constantly three times a day will certainly be happy in the world to come. In this psalm: 1. David engages himself and others to praise God (vv. 1–2, 4–7, 10–12). 2. He focuses on those things that are proper subjects for praise, God's greatness (v. 3), his goodness (vv. 8–9), and the proofs of both in the ruling of his kingdom (v. 13), the kingdom of providence (vv. 14–16) and the kingdom of grace (vv. 17–20). And then he concludes with a firm decision to continue to praise God (v. 21).

Title

The entitling of this psalm as *David's psalm of praise* may suggest that he took particular pleasure in it and sang it often; it was his companion wherever he went.

Verses 1–9

In the first part of the psalm God's glorious attributes are praised, and in the second part his kingdom and its rule are praised. Notice:

1. Who will give glory to God. Whatever others do, the psalmist himself will praise God very much. It will be his duty and his delight. He wants to give glory to God not only in his sacred devotions but also in his ordinary conversation. He will be faithful in doing this work: *Every day will I bless thee* (v. 2). We must let no day pass, though it be very busy or very sad, without praising God. God blesses us every day, doing good for us; there is therefore every reason that we should bless him every day, speaking well of him. David does not doubt that others also will

want to join in this work. His zeal would cause many to join in praising God, and it has done so. They will keep it up in an uninterrupted succession (v. 4): *One generation shall praise thy works to another.*

2. What we must give God glory for: his greatness and great works, and his goodness, which is his glory. We must declare that the Lord is great. If he is great, then he is greatly to be praised with all that is within us (103:1), to the utmost of our powers. His greatness cannot be comprehended. When we cannot by searching sound out the bottom of a thing, we must sit down at the edge and adore the depths (Ro 11:33). We must see God acting and working in every aspect of life in this lower world. We must also praise him for his goodness; this is his glory (Ex 33:19). *They shall abundantly utter the memory of thy great goodness* (v. 7). His goodness can never be exhausted, for he will always be as rich in mercy as he ever was. But whenever we speak about God's great goodness, we must not forget, at the same time, to *sing of his righteousness* (v. 7), for just as he is gracious in rewarding those who serve him faithfully, so also he is righteous in punishing those who rebel against him. There is a fountain of goodness in God's nature (v. 8): *The Lord is gracious* to those who serve him; he is *full of compassion* to those who need him, *slow to anger* to those who have offended him, *and of great mercy* to all who seek him and appeal to him. He is ready to give and ready to forgive.

Verse 10–21

The greatness and goodness of God were celebrated in the first part of this psalm; in these verses we are taught to give him *the glory of his kingdom* (v. 11), in the ruling of which his greatness and goodness shine so clearly and brightly. Notice:

1. From whom praise is expected (v. 10): *All God's works shall praise* him. All God's works praise him as a beautiful building praises its builder or a well-drawn picture praises its painter, but the saints bless him as the children of wise and tender parents rise up and call them blessed (Pr 31:28).

2. For what this praise is to be given: *They shall speak of thy kingdom* (v. 11). The psalmist here exalts God's greatness and goodness by applying them to his kingdom.

2.1. His kingdom is truly great, for all the kings and kingdoms of the earth are under his control. The courts of Solomon and Xerxes were magnificent, but when compared with the glorious majesty of God's kingdom, they were just like glowworms are to the sun. When the saints *speak of the glory of* God's *kingdom* (v. 11), they must *talk of* his *power* (v. 11), and as proof of that, let them *make known his mighty acts* (v. 12). His kingdom will last forever (v. 13). The thrones of princes totter, the flowers of their crowns wither, and monarchies come and go, but Lord, *thy kingdom is an everlasting kingdom.*

2.2. His kingdom is good. His royal title is *the Lord God, gracious and merciful* (2Ch 30:9), and his rule corresponds to his title. The goodness of God is shown in what he does:

2.2.1. For all the creatures in general (vv. 15–16): he *provides food for all flesh.* All creatures live on God, and just as they had their existence from him originally, so they depend on him to continue in it. The lower creatures do not know God, nor are they capable of doing so, but they are said to *wait upon God* because they seek their food by the instinct that the God of nature has put in them: *Thou givest them their meat in due season* (v. 15).

2.2.2. For human beings in particular, whom he rules over as rational creatures. He is just in all the acts of his rule; he wrongs no one but administers justice to all. *The ways of the Lord are equal* (Eze 18:25), although ours are unequal. He supports those who are sinking, and it is his honor to help the weak (v. 14). He *upholds all that fall*, in that, although they fall, they are not completely struck down (37:24). If those who were *bowed down* by oppression and suffering are *raised up*, it was God who raised them. And with respect to all those *that are heavy laden* (Mt 11:28) under the burden of sin, if they come to Christ by faith, he will bring them relief; he will raise them up again. He is very ready to listen to and answer the prayers of his people (vv. 18–19). The grace of his kingdom is shown in that his subjects have not only freedom to bring their petitions but also every encouragement to do so. It was said (v. 16) that he *satisfies the desire of every living thing*; much more *will he fulfil the desire of those that fear him* (v. 19), for the One who feeds his birds will not starve his own children. *He will hear their call and will save them* (v. 19), and that is hearing them effectively, as he *heard* David—that is, saved him—*from the horns of the unicorns* (wild oxen) (22:21). He will hear and help us if we worship and serve him with holy awe. In all devotions, inner impressions must be answerable to outer expressions; otherwise they are not carried out in integrity. He takes under his special protection those who have confidence in him (v. 20): *The Lord preserves all those that love him.*

3. The psalmist concludes (v. 21): *My mouth shall speak the praise of the Lord.* When we have said all we can in praising God, there is still more to be said. Just as the end of one mercy marks the beginning of another, so should the end of one thanksgiving be the beginning of another. As long as we still have breath to draw, let our mouths speak God's praises. *Let all flesh*, the whole human race, *bless his holy name for ever and ever* (v. 21).

PSALM 146

This and the remaining psalms that follow begin and end with Hallelujah, a word which concisely expresses much of God's praise, for in it we praise him by his name Jah, the contraction of Jehovah. In this excellent psalm of praise: 1. The psalmist commits himself to praise God (vv. 1–2). 2. He commits others to trust in him, which is one way of praising him. He shows: 2.1. Why we should not trust in human beings (vv. 3–4). 2.2. Why we should trust in God (v. 5), namely, because of his power in the kingdom of nature (v. 6), his rule in the kingdom of providence (v. 7), and his grace in the kingdom of the Messiah (vv. 8–9), that eternal kingdom (v. 10), to which many of the Jewish writers believe this psalm refers.

Verses 1–4

David himself was a powerful prince, and yet he thought that his honor, so far from excusing him from praise, rather obliged him to take the lead in it: *Praise the Lord, O my soul!* And he decided to be faithful in it: "I will praise him with my heart, *I will sing praises* to him as *the Lord*, infinitely blessed and glorious in himself, and as *my God*, in covenant with me." It might be thought that he himself, having been such a great blessing to his country, should be adored, according to the custom of the pagan nations, who worshiped their heroes as gods; it might be thought that his people would all come and *trust in his shadow* (Jdg 9:15). "No," David says, "*Put not your trust in princes* (v. 3), not in me or in any other; do not put your confidence in them. Do not put too much trust in their faithfulness; it is possible they may change their mind and break their word." Nor can we be sure how long they will remain with us. Suppose a king has it in his power to help us as long as he is alive; he may be suddenly taken away from us when we expect most from him (v. 4). Princes are mortal, like other people, and so we cannot have the assurance of help from them that we may have from almighty God, who is immortal.

Verses 5–10

Here the psalmist encourages us to put our confidence in God: *Happy is he that has the God of Jacob for his help, whose hope is in the Lord his God* (v. 5).

1. Consider the character of those whom God will uphold. They are those:

1.1. Who take him as their God and serve and worship him accordingly.

1.2. Who have their hope in him and live a life of dependence on him. Every believer may look on him as the God of Jacob, of the church in general, and so they may expect relief from him in public difficulties; each believer may also look on him as their God in particular and so may depend on him in all their personal needs and difficulties. Dr. Henry Hammond quotes one of the rabbis, who says about v. 10 that it belongs to the days of the Messiah. Dr. Hammond thinks this can be seen by comparing vv. 7–8 with the characteristics Christ gives of the Messiah in Mt 11:5–6: *The blind receive their sight, the lame walk.* And he thinks the closing words there, *Blessed is he whosoever shall not be offended in me*, may very well refer to v. 5: *Happy is the man that hopes in the Lord his God* and does not take offense at him.

2. Consider the great encouragements given us to hope in *the Lord our God.*

2.1. He is the *Maker of the world* (v. 6) and so has all power in himself and the command of the powers of all creatures (v. 6). This can be applied very much to Christ, by whom God made the world, and *without whom was not anything made that was made* (Jn 1:3). It is a great support to faith that the Redeemer of the world is the same as its Creator and therefore has goodwill toward it.

2.2. He is a God of unbreakable faithfulness. Our Lord Jesus is the Amen, *the faithful witness*, as well as *the beginning*, the author and originator, *of the creation of God* (Rev 3:14).

2.3. He supports wronged innocence: *He pleads the cause of the oppressed*, and he *executes judgment* for them. The Messiah came to rescue people from the hands of Satan, the great oppressor, and because all judgment is committed to him, the judgment of persecutors is included among the rest (Jude 15).

2.4. He is a generous giver to those in need: *He gives food to the hungry* (v. 7). God does this in ordinary ways to fulfill natural cravings, and he sometimes does so in an extraordinary way, as when ravens fed Elijah. Christ acted extraordinarily more than once when he fed thousands miraculously. This encourages us to hope in him as the One who will nourish our souls with the bread of life (Jn 6:35, 48).

2.5. He is the author of liberty to those who were bound: *The Lord looseth* (sets free) *the prisoners* (v. 7). He brought Israel out of slavery in Egypt and afterward in Babylon. The miracles Christ worked, in making the mute speak and the deaf hear with that one word, *Ephphatha*, "Be opened" (Mk 7:34), cleansing those with infectious

skin diseases (Mt 8:2–3; 11:5) and so setting them free from confinement, and raising the dead from their graves (Jn 11:1–44), may all be included in this *loosing the prisoners.* We may take encouragement from these to hope in him for the spiritual liberty which he came to proclaim (Isa 61:1–2).

2.6. He gives sight to those who have been long deprived of it: *The Lord can open the eyes of the blind* (v. 8), and he has often made his afflicted people see that comfort which before they were not aware of, as can be seen from Hagar (Ge 21:19) and the prophet's servant (2Ki 6:17). But this refers especially to Christ, for *since the world began was it not heard that any man opened the eyes of one that was born blind* until Christ did it (Jn 9:32) and so encouraged us to hope in him for spiritual enlightenment.

2.7. He sets straight what was crooked and *raises those that are bowed down* (v. 8) by supporting them under their burdens and, in due time, taking away their burdens. This was literally carried out by Christ when he made a poor woman straight who had been *bowed together, and could in no wise lift up herself* (Lk 13:11), and he still does so by his grace, giving rest to those who were weary and burdened (Mt 11:28) and raising up with his comforts those who were humbled and cast down by a conviction of their sin.

2.8. He is constantly kind toward all good people: *The Lord loveth the righteous* (v. 8).

2.9. He has a tender concern for those who are in special need of his care: *The Lord preserves the strangers* (foreigners) (v. 9).

2.10. He will destroy all those who oppose his kingdom. It is the glory of the Messiah that he will overthrow all the purposes of hell and earth that act against his church. His kingdom will continue through all the ages of time, to the farthest reach of eternity (v. 10). Let this encourage us to trust in God at all times and believe that *the Lord shall reign for ever* in spite of all the hatred of the powers of darkness, *even thy God, O Zion! unto all generations.*

PSALM 147

This is another psalm of praise. Some think it was written after the return of the Jews from exile, but what is said in vv. 2, 13 may be applied well enough to the first building and fortifying of Jerusalem and the gathering in of those who had been exiles in Saul's time. The Septuagint (a Greek version of the Old Testament) divides it into two, but both have the same significance. 1. We are called on to praise God (vv. 1, 7, 12). 2. We are provided with reasons for praise, for God is to be glorified as the God of nature (vv. 4–5, 8–9, 15–18); as the God of grace (vv. 3, 6, 10–11); and as the God of Israel, Jerusalem, and Zion, establishing his people's civil state (vv. 2, 13–14) and, especially, establishing religious faith among them (vv. 19–20).

Verses 1–11

Here:

1. The duty of praise is commended to us. We are called to do this duty again and again: *Praise you the Lord* (v. 1 and again v. 7), *Sing to the Lord with thanksgiving, sing praise on the harp to our God*—let all our praises be directed to him and center on him—*for it is good* to do so. It is our duty and so is good in itself. It is also good for us, for in giving honor to God we greatly honor ourselves.

2. God is the proper object of our praises, for several reasons.

2.1. The care he takes of his chosen people (v. 2). Is Jerusalem to be raised up from small beginnings? Is it to be restored from ruin? The answer is yes to both: *The Lord builds up Jerusalem.* The Gospel church, the Jerusalem that is from above, is built by him. Are any of his people in exile? Have they made themselves so by their own foolishness? He gathers them by granting them repentance and bringing them into the fellowship of saints (Ac 5:31; 2Ti 2:25).

2.2. The comforts he has laid up for those who truly repent (v. 3). They are *broken in heart,* humbled and troubled because of sin, inwardly in pain when they remember it. Their very hearts are torn under the sense of dishonor they have given to God and the wrong they have done themselves by their sin. To those whom God heals with the assuring comforts of his Spirit he speaks peace.

2.3. The sovereignty he has over the lights of heaven (vv. 4–5). The stars are innumerable, but *he calleth them all by their names.* They are his servants: he musters them; they come and go at his bidding, and all their movements are under his direction. The psalmist mentions this as one example of many, to show that *great is our Lord and of great power*—he can do what he pleases—and *his understanding is infinite* (v. 5). Human knowledge is soon drained, but God's knowledge is a depth that can never be fathomed.

2.4. The pleasure he takes in humbling the proud and exalting the humble. (v. 6). *The Lord lifts up the meek,* who lower themselves before him and whom people trample on, but *the wicked,* who behave arrogantly toward God and scornfully toward other people, who lift themselves in pride and foolishness, he *casteth down to the ground.*

2.5. The provision he makes for the lower creatures (vv. 8–9). *He covereth the heaven with clouds.* Clouds look depressing, but without them we would have no rain and so no fruit. In the same way, adversities, when we are under them, look black, dark, and unpleasant, but from these clouds of adversity come the showers that make the harvest *yield the peaceable fruits of righteousness* (Heb 12:11). By the rain which distills on the earth he *makes grass to grow upon the mountains* (v. 8), even the high mountains, grass that people neither take care of nor reap the benefit of. This grass he *gives* to *the beast* for *his food,* to the wild animals that run about on the mountains and that people make no provision for. And even the *young ravens,* which, because they are abandoned by their older ones, *cry* (v. 9), are heard by him, and ways are found to feed them.

2.6. The delight he takes in his people (vv. 10–11). God will delight to honor not the strength of armies but the strength of grace. *He delighteth not in the strength of the horse,* warhorses, nor in infantry, for he *taketh no pleasure in the legs of a man* (v. 10). When one king makes war on another king and he goes to God to pray for success, it will do him no good to plead, "Lord, I have a bold army; the horses and foot soldiers are in good order." But God is pleased to acknowledge the strength of grace. The Lord accepts and *takes pleasure* in those who *fear him and that hope in his mercy* (v. 11). Our fear must save our hope from becoming presumption, and our hope must save our fear from sinking into despair.

Verses 12–20

Jerusalem, the Holy City, and Zion, the holy hill, are called on to *praise God* (v. 12). Jerusalem and Zion must praise God:

1. For the prosperity and flourishing state of their civil interests (vv. 13–14).

1.1. For their common security. They had gates and kept their gates barred in times of danger, but that would not have been an effective security for them unless God had *strengthened the bars of their gates* and made their fortifications stronger.

1.2. For the increase of their people. This strengthens the bars of the gates as much as anything.

1.3. For the public peace, that they were rescued from the terrors and devastation of war: *He makes peace in thy borders* (v. 14); he did this by putting an end to the wars that were taking place and preventing the wars that were threatened and feared.

1.4. For great plenty, the common effect of peace: he *filleth thee with the finest of the wheat* (v. 14). Canaan abounded with the finest kernels of wheat (Dt 32:14) and exported it to countries abroad, as can be seen from Eze 27:17. The land of Israel was not rich in precious stones or spices, but with *the finest of the wheat* (v. 14), with bread, which strengthens human hearts (104:15).

2. For his wonderful power in the weather. The One who protects Zion and Jerusalem is the almighty God from whom all the powers of nature are derived and on whom they depend.

2.1. In general, *He sendeth forth his commandment upon earth,* (v. 15). As the world was made originally by his word of almighty power, so it is still upheld and governed by the same word (Heb 1:3). *God speaks and it is done* (Eze 39:8).

2.2. In particular, frosts and thaws are wonderful changes, and we must acknowledge him in them. With him are the *treasures* (storehouses) *of the snow and the hail* (Job 38:22–23), and he draws from these storehouses as he pleases. Snow falls silently, making no more noise than the fall of a lock of wool; it covers the earth and keeps it warm like a woolen fleece, and so furthers its fruitfulness. God can work using opposites, bringing something to eat out of the eater (Jdg 14:14) and warming the earth with cold snow. When he wishes (v. 18), *he sends out his word and melts them;* the frost, snow, and ice all dissolve quickly, and in order to bring this about he *causes the wind,* the *south wind, to blow,* and *the waters,* which were frozen, to *flow* again as they did before. This melting word may represent the Gospel of Christ, and this melting wind the Spirit of Christ, for the Spirit is compared to the wind (Jn 3:8); both are sent to melt frozen souls. Converting grace, like a thaw, softens the heart that was hard; it moistens it and melts it into tears of repentance; it warms good devotion and makes our affections flow, which before were chilled and stopped up. It can be clearly seen, but how it is done is inexplicable: such is the change brought about in the conversion of a soul, when God's word and Spirit are sent to melt it and bring it back to him.

3. For his special favor to Israel in giving them his word and laws. Jacob and Israel had God's laws and decrees among them. They were under his special government; the municipal laws of their nation were framed and enacted by him, and their constitution was a theocracy. They had the benefit of divine revelation; the great things of God's law were written for them. They did not find out God's laws and decrees by themselves; rather, *God showed his word unto Jacob,* and by that word he made known to them his *statutes and judgments* (v. 19). Other nations had plenty of good things outwardly; some nations were very rich, others had fine and powerful princes and refined literature, but none were blessed with God's laws and

decrees as Israel was. Let *Israel* therefore *praise the Lord* in observing these laws.

PSALM 148

This psalm is a most sacred and serious call to all created things to praise their Creator according to their ability and to show his eternal power and Godhead, the invisible things of which are revealed in the things that are seen (Ro 1:20). Here the psalmist wants very much for God to be praised more, and so he does all he can to enlist all around him and all who will come after him, whose hearts must be dead and cold if they are not raised in praising God by the lofty flights of divine poetry we find in this psalm. 1. He calls on the created things in the upper world to praise the Lord, both those endowed with reason, able to do it actively (vv. 1–2), and those not so endowed and therefore able to do it only objectively, as causes of praise (vv. 3–6). 2. He calls on the creatures of this lower world, both those that can only provide themselves as subjects for praise (vv. 7–10) and those that, endowed with reason, can offer up this sacrifice (vv. 11–13), especially his own people, who have more cause to do it than any others (v. 14).

Verses 1–6

In this dark and depressed world, we know only a little of the world of light and exaltation. But we know this:

1. That above us there is a world of blessed angels by whom God is praised. There is an innumerable company of such angels. The psalmist looks (vv. 1–2) to *the heavens,* to *the heights.* The heavens are the heights, and so we must lift up our souls above the world to God in *the heavens,* and we must *set our affections on things above* (Col 3:2). It is the psalmist's delight to think that God is praised *in the heights.* When in singing this psalm we call on the angels to praise God, as we did in 103:20, we mean that we want God to be praised by the most able beings and in the best way, that we have spiritual fellowship with those who live in his house above, and that we have come by faith, hope, and holy love to the *innumerable company of angels* (Heb 12:22).

2. That there is above us not only an assembly of blessed spirits but also vast galaxies of heavenly bodies, those bright ones the stars, in which God is praised. There are the *sun, moon,* and *stars,* which continually, either day or night, present themselves to our view as a mirror in which we may see a faint shadow—we must call it that, not a likeness—of the glory of the One who is *the Father of lights* (Jas 1:17) (v. 3). *The heavens of heavens are the Lord's* (115:16), and *yet they cannot contain him* (1Ki 8:27). The Babylonian paraphrase reads, "Praise him, you heavens of heavens, and you waters that depend on the word of him who is above the heavens." *Let them praise the name of the Lord* (v. 5), that is, let us praise the name of the Lord for them and notice what constant and fresh reasons for praise may be drawn from them. *He commanded* them, great as they are, out of nothing, *and they were created* (v. 5) at the speaking of a word. He still upholds and keeps them (v. 6): *He hath established them for ever and ever,* that is, to the end of time, which is relatively short, but is all the time they are needed for.

Verses 7–14

Even in this world, dark and bad though it is, God is praised: *Praise you the Lord from the earth* (v. 7).
1. Even those creatures not honored with the powers of reason are summoned to join in this recital, because

God may be glorified in them (vv. 7–10). Let the *dragons* or great sea creatures (possibly, whales) that frolic in the mighty waters (104:26) dance in the presence of the Lord, to his glory. *All deeps* and their inhabitants praise God. *Out of the depths* God may be praised as well as prayed to. In the sky, there are igneous or fiery phenomena: lightning is fire. Aqueous or watery phenomena are there as well: *hail, snow,* and the *vapours* (clouds) from which they come. There are *stormy winds;* even though they are very strong and stormy, they *fulfil God's word,* and Christ showed he had divine power when he *commanded even the winds and the seas,* and *they obeyed him* (Mk 4:41). On the earth's surface, too, we find subjects for praise. There are *mountains and all hills.* There are plants, some outstanding for their usefulness, like the *fruitful trees,* for whose fruits God is to be praised, others outstanding for their stateliness, like *all cedars,* those *trees of the Lord.* In the animal kingdom we find God glorified by both the *beasts* that run wild *and all cattle* that are tame and serve human beings (v. 10). Even the *creeping things* (small creatures) have not sunk so low, nor the *flying fowl* (birds) soared so high, that they cannot be called on to *praise the Lord.* Much of the wisdom, power, and goodness of the Creator appears in the various abilities and instincts of animals and creatures, in the provision made for them and the use made of them. Surely we must acknowledge God in wonder and with thankfulness.

2. Much more should those creatures that are honored with the powers of reason use them to praise God: *Kings of the earth and all people* (vv. 11–12). God is to be praised for the order and constitution of kingdoms, both for the part that commands and for the part that submits to those commands: *Kings of the earth and all people* (v. 11). God is to be praised also in the constitution of families, for he has founded them; and God is to be praised for all the comfort of relatives, the comfort that parents and children, and brothers and sisters, find in each other. Let all kinds of people praise God. Those on whom God has placed honor must honor him with it, and the power they are entrusted with makes them able to bring more glory to God and give him more service than others. But the praises of the ordinary people are also expected: Christ did not despise the hosannas of the crowd. Let *young men and maidens* (v. 12) channel their enjoyment in this way. *Old men* must not think that either the dignity or the weakness of old age will excuse them from it. *Children* (v. 12) too must learn to praise God at an early age. *His glory is above* both *the earth and the heaven,* and let all the inhabitants both of earth and of heaven praise him and acknowledge that his name is to be exalted *far above all blessing and praise* (Ne 9:5).

3. Most of all his own people, who are honored with special privileges, must especially give glory to him (v. 14). They had him *nigh to them in all that which they called upon him for* (Dt 4:7). This blessing has now come on the Gentiles, through Christ, for those who *were afar off are* by *his blood made nigh* (Eph 2:13). Let those whom God honors honor him.

PSALM 149

The previous psalm was a hymn of praise to the Creator; this is a hymn of praise to the Redeemer. It is a psalm of triumph in the God of Israel and over the enemies of Israel. Some think it was written when David had captured the stronghold of Zion and settled his government there. But it also looks beyond that to the kingdom of the Messiah, who goes out conquering and to conquer (Rev 6:2). This psalm declares: 1. Great joy to all the people of God (vv. 1–5). 2. Great terror to their proudest enemies (vv. 6–9).

Verses 1–5

We have here:

1. The calls given to God's Israel to praise him. In the previous psalm all his works were encouraged to praise him, but here his saints are especially required to praise him. Israel in general, the body of the church (v. 2), especially the children of Zion, the inhabitants of that holy hill, who are closer to God than other Israelites—those who have the word and laws of God near them (Dt 30:14)—are justly expected to do more to praise God than others. All true Christians may call themselves the children of Zion, for we have come unto Mount Zion in faith and hope (Heb 12:22). Let Israel rejoice, and the children of Zion be joyful (v. 2), and the saints be joyful in glory (v. 5). The power of godliness in our hearts consists in making God our chief joy and encouraging ourselves in him, and our faith in Christ is shown by our rejoicing in him. We must sing a new song, sing with real devotion, which makes the song new even if the words have been used before. The Gospel rule for psalmody is to sing with the spirit and with the understanding (1Co 14:15; Ps 47:7). We must praise God in public, in the sacred assembly (v. 1), in the congregation of saints. This is how God's name must be acknowledged before the world. We must also praise him in private. Let the saints be so carried away with their joy in God as to sing aloud upon their beds (v. 5) when they awake at night, full of the praises of God, as David did (119:62).

2. The reason given to God's Israel for praising God. He gave us our existence as human beings, and we have reason to praise him for that, for it is a noble and excellent existence. He brought Israel into being as a people, as a church. If he made them, he is their King; he who gave them existence may without doubt also give them his law. He is a king who rules by love and so is to be praised, for the Lord takes pleasure in his people (v. 4): in their services, in their prosperity, in fellowship with them, and in sharing his favor with them. He has prepared a future glory for them: he will beautify (crown) the meek (v. 4), that is, the lowly and contrite in heart, who are patient in suffering and show all meekness toward all men (Tit 3:2). They will appear beautiful before all the world with the beauty he gives them. The righteous will be made beautiful on the day when they shine forth as the sun (Mt 13:43). In the hope of this, let them now, in the darkest day, sing a new song (v. 1).

Verses 6–9

The Israel of God is here described as triumphing over its enemies, which is both a reason for the people to praise God—let them give glory to God for these triumphs—and also the reward for their praise. Those who are truly thankful to God for their tranquility will be blessed with victory.

1. The many victories over the nations of Canaan and other nations who were set apart in a special way to be destroyed began with Moses and Joshua, who, when they taught Israel the high praises of the Lord, also put a two-edged sword in their hand (v. 6). David did so too, for besides being Israel's beloved singer (2Sa 23:1), he was also the commander of its armies and taught the children of Judah how to use the bow (2Sa 1:18). They executed (inflicted) vengeance upon the heathen—the nations of the Philistines, Moabites, Ammonites, and others (2Sa 8:1)—and punishments upon the people for all the wrong they had done to God's people (v. 7). Their kings and nobles were taken prisoner (v. 8). Some apply this to the time of the Maccabees, when the Jews gained occasional and great advantages against their oppressors.

2. If it seems strange that the humble should, despite their humility, be so severe, their justification is that they did not act from any personal hatred or revenge or any bloodthirsty political wishes that controlled them, but by commission from God, according to his direction, and in obedience to his command. But since no such special commissions can now be produced, this verse will in no way justify violence under the guise of religion, whether of subjects against their rulers, of rulers against their subjects, or of both against their neighbors, for Christ never intended his Gospel to be spread by fire and sword or for his righteousness to be ushered in by man's anger (Jas 1:20). When the high praises of God are in our mouth, we should also have an olive branch of peace in our hands.

3. Christ's victories are by the power of his Gospel and grace over spiritual enemies, in which all believers are more than conquerors (Ro 8:37). The word of God is the two-edged sword (Heb 4:12), the sword of the Spirit (Eph 6:17). The first preachers of the Gospel won a glorious victory over the powers of darkness with this two-edged sword; vengeance was inflicted on the gods of the nations by the conviction and conversion of those who had long worshiped them. The strongholds of Satan were demolished (2Co 10:4–5); rulers, such as Felix, were made to tremble at the word; Satan, the god of this world (2Co 4:4), was driven out, according to the judgment given against him. Believers fight against their own sinfulness with this two-edged sword, and, through the grace of God, subdue and mortify the corruption within them; self, which once reigned, is bound with chains and brought to submit to the yoke of Christ. This honour have all the saints (v. 9).

PSALM 150

The first and last of the psalms are each short and memorable. Their themes, however, are very different: the first psalm is a detailed instruction to explain our duty, to prepare us for the encouragement of our devotions; this final psalm is all rapture and praise and was perhaps deliberately written to be the conclusion of these sacred songs. The psalmist had himself been full of the praises of God, and here he would gladly fill all the world with them: again and again he calls out, Praise the Lord, praise him, praise him, no fewer than thirteen times in these six short verses. He shows: 1. For what God is to be praised (vv. 1–2). 2. How God is to be praised (vv. 3–5). 3. Who must praise the Lord; it is the business of everyone (v. 6).

Verses 1–6

If, as some suppose, this psalm was primarily intended to encourage the Levites to do their work in the house of the Lord as singers and players on instruments, we must still take it as also speaking to us, who are made to be spiritual priests to our God (Rev 5:10).

1. This tribute of praise comes:

• From his sanctuary (v. 1); praise him there. Let his priests, let his people, who are in his presence there serve him with their praises. Where should he be praised except in the place where he especially reveals his glory and shares his grace?

• From *the firmament of his power* (mighty heavens) (v. 1). *Praise him* because of his power and glory that appear in the expanse of the heavens, its vastness and beauty, and because of its powerful influence on this earth.

2. It is due him for:

2.1. The works of his power (v. 2): *Praise him for his mighty acts*, for "his mightinesses," for all the acts of his power: the power of his providence; the power of his grace; what he has done in creating, ruling, and redeeming the world; what he has done for people in general and for his own church and children in particular.

2.2. The glory and majesty of his being: *Praise him according to his excellent greatness* (v. 2). Not that our praises can match God's greatness in the slightest, because that is infinite; yet we must raise our conceptions and expressions to the highest possible extent. Do not be afraid of saying too much in praising God; the danger we are in is not saying too much about him, but saying too little.

3. How this tribute must be paid, with all kinds of musical instruments that were then used in the temple service (vv. 3–5). In serving God we should spare no cost or effort. The best music in God's ears is devout and godly expressions of love, not necessarily tuneful strings, but a tuneful heart. Praise God with a strong faith; praise him with holy love and delight; praise him with complete trust in Christ; praise him with a confident triumph over the powers of darkness; praise him by showing universal respect for all his commands; praise him by furthering the interests of the kingdom of his grace; praise him by having a living hope and expectation of the kingdom of his glory. Various instruments are used in praising God, but it should all be done with perfect harmony; they must not hinder, but help one another. The New Testament concert is *with one mind and one mouth to glorify God* (Ro 15:6).

4. Who must pay this tribute (v. 6): *Let everything that has breath praise the Lord*. The psalmist began this psalm with a call to those who had a place in his sanctuary and were employed in the temple service, but he concludes with a call to all people, looking to the time when the Gentiles would be taken into the church and this incense could be offered in every place as acceptably as at Jerusalem (Mal 1:11). The singing of birds is a kind of praise to God. The wild animals are in effect saying to people, "We would praise God if we could; you do it for us." Some think that *everything that has breath* refers only to human beings. In that case, now that the Gospel must be preached *to every creature* (Mk 16:15), every human creature, it is required that every human creature should praise the Lord. Prayers are called *our breathings* (La 3:56). Let everyone who breathes toward God in prayer breathe out his praises too. While we have breath let us praise the Lord, and when at our death we run out of breath, we will move to a better state to breathe God's praises in a freer and better air.

The first three of the five books of psalms according to the Hebrew division ended with *Amen and Amen*, the fourth with *Amen, Hallelujah*, but the last, and with it the whole book, concludes with only *Hallelujah*, because the last six psalms are wholly taken up in praising God and there is not a word of complaint or request in them. Let us often delight in thinking about what glorified saints are doing in heaven, about the life of those whom we have known on earth but who have gone to heaven before us, and let it encourage us to do our part of the will of God on earth as those who are in heaven do theirs (Mt 6:10). *Hallelujah* is the word there; let us echo it now, *Hallelujah, praise you the Lord* (v. 6).

A Practical and Devotional Exposition of the Book of

Proverbs

Here is:

1. A new author, used by the Holy Spirit to make known the mind of God to us, writing as moved by the *finger of God*, as the Spirit of God is called here, and that writer is Solomon. This book of Scripture came by his hand, as did the two that follow it, Ecclesiastes and Song of Songs, a sermon and a song. Some think he wrote the Song of Songs when he was very young, Proverbs in midlife, and Ecclesiastes when he was old.

1.1. He was a king and a king's son. The writers of Scripture up to this point were mostly men of rank in the world, such as Moses and Joshua, Samuel and David, and now Solomon, but after him the inspired writers were generally lowly prophets, insignificant people in the world, because the dispensation was approaching in which God would choose the *weak and foolish things of the world to confound the wise and mighty* (1Co 1:27) and in which lowly people would be used in evangelizing. Solomon was a very rich king, and his dominions were very great, but he was also a prophet and a prophet's son.

1.2. He was one whom God endowed with extraordinary wisdom and knowledge in answer to his prayers at his accession to the throne. His prayer was exemplary: *Give me a wise and an understanding heart* (1Ki 3:5–14); the answer to that prayer was encouraging: he had what he wanted and *all other things given to him as well* (Mt 6:33).

1.3. He was one who had his faults, and in his final years he turned aside from the good ways of God. But let those who are most eminently useful take warning from this not to become proud or falsely secure, and let us all learn not to think the worse of good instructions even though we receive them from those who do not themselves altogether live up to them.

2. A new way of writing, in which divine wisdom is taught to us in proverbs, or short sentences, which contain their whole meaning within themselves and are not connected with one another. We have had divine *laws*, *histories*, and *songs*, and now we have divine *proverbs*; infinite Wisdom has used a variety of methods to teach us. Teaching by proverbs was:

2.1. An old way of teaching. It was the oldest way among the Greeks; each of the seven wise men of Greece had a saying that he prided himself on and that made him famous. These sentences were inscribed on pillars and held in great respect.

2.2. A plain and easy way of teaching. A proverb, which carries both its sense and its evidence in a brief passage, is quickly apprehended and easily remembered.

2.3. A very profitable way of teaching, one that fulfilled its purpose wonderfully well. The world is ruled by proverbs. Sayings that begin, *As saith the proverb of the ancients* (1Sa 24:13), or, as we commonly express it, "As the saying goes," greatly affect the ideas people form and the decisions they make. Some think we may judge the ethos and character of a nation by what its ordinary proverbs are like. But there are also many corrupt proverbs, which tend to defile the mind and harden people in their sin. Satan has his proverbs, and the world and the flesh also have their proverbs, which reflect shame on God and religion (Eze 12:22; 18:2). These proverbs of Solomon were not simply a collection of the wise sayings that had been previously expressed, as some have thought, but were the dictates of the Spirit of God through Solomon. The very first of them (v. 7) agrees with what God said to people in the beginning: *Behold, the fear of the Lord, that is wisdom* (Job 28:28); and so although Solomon was great, and his name alone commends his writings, a *greater* one *than Solomon is here* now (Mt 12:42). It is God, through Solomon, who speaks to us here.

The first nine chapters of this book are considered an introduction, encouraging the study and practice of wisdom's rules. We then have the first volume of Solomon's proverbs (chs. 10–24); after that a second volume (chs. 25–29), and then Agur's prophecy (ch. 30) and Lemuel's (ch. 31).

CHAPTER 1

Those who read David's psalms, especially the psalms toward the end of the book, would be tempted to think that religious faith is all joy and consists of nothing but the delights of devotion. Without doubt there is a time for such pleasures, but while we are on earth we have a life to live in the flesh. We must live in the world, and it is into the world that we must now be taught to take our religious faith, which is rational and very useful for dealing with human life. Our faith is as helpful for making our faces shine before those around us because of our wise, honest, useful lives (Ps 104:15; Mt 5:16) as it is for making our hearts burn toward God in holy and godly devotion. In this chapter we have: 1. The title of the book, showing its general scope and intention (vv. 1–6). 2. Its basic principle commended to our serious consideration (vv. 7–9). 3. A necessary warning against being enticed by bad company (vv. 10–19). 4. A faithful and vital description of wisdom's reasoning with people and of the certain destruction of those who turn a deaf ear to such reasoning (vv. 20–33).

Verses 1–6

Here is an introduction to the book, which some think was attached to it by the collector, possibly Ezra, but more likely it was written by Solomon himself to suggest his purpose in writing the book.

1. They are *the proverbs of Solomon* (v. 1). His name means "peaceful," and the character both of his spirit and of his reign was peaceful. David, whose life was full of troubles, wrote a book of devotion, for *is any afflicted? Let him pray* (Jas 5:13). Solomon, who lived quietly, wrote a book of instruction, for when the *churches had rest they were edified* (Ac 9:31). In times of peace we should teach ourselves and others the things that we must practice in troublesome times. He was *the son of David* (v. 1). He had been blessed with a good education, and many prayers had been offered for him (Ps 72:1), and the effect of both appeared in his wisdom and usefulness. He was *king of Israel* (v. 1). The whole earth sought audience with Solomon *to hear his wisdom* (1Ki 4:30; 10:24). His servants had collected 3,000 of his proverbs (1Ki 4:32), but these of his own writing do not amount to a thousand. He was divinely inspired in these.

2. They were written for the use and benefit of all (vv. 2–4). This book will help us:

2.1. To form right ideas about things, to give our minds clear and distinct ideas so that we may know how to speak and act wisely.

2.2. To distinguish between truth and falsehood, good and evil — *to perceive the words of understanding* (v. 2).

2.3. To live our lives rightly (v. 3). This book will give the knowledge that will incline us to give everyone their due, to God the things that are God's, in all aspects of religious faith, and to all people what is due to them (Mt 22:21).

3. They are of use to everyone but are designed especially:

3.1. For *the simple, to give subtlety* (prudence) *to them.* The instructions here given are plain. Those who are likely to benefit by them are those who are aware of their own ignorance and their need to be taught, and even the simple, if they receive these instructions in their light and power, will be given understanding; they will become graciously crafty at knowing the sin they should avoid and the duty they should do (compare Ge 3:1, 4–5).

3.2. For young people, to give them *knowledge and discretion* (v. 4). Youth is the age at which we learn, become

more aware, and remember what is received. Young people tend to be rash, headstrong, and inconsiderate; *man is born like the wild ass's colt* (Job 11:12) and therefore needs to be trained by the restraints and disciplined by the rules found here. Solomon looked to future generations in writing this book, hoping by it to train the minds of the coming generation with the great principles of wisdom and goodness.

4. Those who are young and simple may be made wise by them and are not excluded from Solomon's school as they were from Plato's, but even wise people must listen and not think themselves too wise to learn. A wise man, by adding to his learning, benefits not only himself but also others:

4.1. As a counselor. *A man of understanding* in these precepts of wisdom *shall* gradually *attain unto wise counsels* (gain guidance) (v. 5); he will come, literally, to "sit at the helm." Those whom God has blessed with wisdom must work at doing good with it. It is more honorable to be a counselor to a ruler, but it is more loving to be a counselor to the poor.

4.2. As an interpreter (v. 6) — *to understand a proverb.* Solomon was himself famous for explaining riddles and solving hard questions, which in the past was the popular entertainment of the eastern princes. Here he undertakes to provide his readers with that talent. "They will *understand a proverb*, even *the interpretation*, without which the proverb is like an uncracked nut. When they hear a wise saying, even if it is a figure of speech, they will understand its sense and know how to use it."

Verses 7–9

Having undertaken to *teach a young man knowledge and discretion* (v. 4), Solomon here lays down two general rules: fear God, and honor your parents. Let young people:

1. Regard God as their supreme ruler.

1.1. He lays down the truth that *the fear of the Lord is the beginning of knowledge* (v. 7); it is "the principal part of knowledge," as the margin expresses it. We are not qualified to profit from the instructions given us unless our minds are possessed with a holy reverence for God and every thought within us is brought into obedience to him.

1.2. To confirm this truth, he observes that *fools* — unbelievers who have no respect for God — *despise wisdom and instruction* (v. 7). Those who do not fear God and value the Scriptures are fools, and although they may pretend to admire knowledge, they are really strangers to and enemies of wisdom.

2. Regard their parents as their superiors (vv. 8–9): *My son, hear the instruction of thy father.* He means not only that he wants his own children to heed him, nor only that he wants his pupils to look on him as their father and listen to his teaching, but also that he wants all children to be dutiful and respectful to their parents.

2.1. He takes it for granted that parents will use all their wisdom to instruct their children and will use the authority they have to give the law to them for their good. They are rational creatures, and when we tell them what they must do, we must also tell them why. But children are willful, and so the Law is needed alongside the instruction.

2.2. He tells children both to receive and to retain the good lessons and laws their parents give them. "*Hear the instruction of thy father* (v. 8), be thankful for it, and submit to it. *Forsake not their law*; do not think that when you are grown up and no longer need a teacher, you may live without any restraint. No; *the law of thy mother* (v. 8) was according to the law of your God, and so it must never be forsaken." Some observe that whereas the laws of the Persians and Romans provided only that children should pay respect to their father, God's law protects the honor of the mother also. "When you carefully observe the instructions and laws of your parents, they *shall be an ornament of grace unto thy head* (v. 9) and make you look like those who wear gold *chains about their necks.*"

Verses 10–19

Here Solomon gives another general rule to young people: Beware being enticed by bad company (v. 10): "*My son,* whom I love and have a tender concern for, *if sinners entice thee, consent thou not.*" Sinners love to have company in their sin; the angels that fell were tempters almost as soon as they were sinners. They do not threaten or argue, but entice with flattery and fine words. "*Consent thou not,* do not give in to them (v. 10), and then, although they entice you, they cannot force you to join them. Have no fellowship with them." To support this warning:

1. He describes the deceptive reasons sinners use in their temptations to beguile unstable souls. He specifies highwaymen, who do what they can to draw others into their gang (vv. 11–14). "*Come with us* (v. 11); we'd like your company." At first they pretend to ask for nothing more, but soon their wooing moves to a higher plane (v. 14): "*Cast in thy lot among us*; let's make a pact to live and die together: and *let us all have one* common *purse,* so that what we gain together we may merrily spend together." They are bloodthirsty and hate those who are innocent, because by their honesty and sheer hard work the innocent shame and condemn them: "*Let us* therefore *lay* (lie in) *wait for* their *blood* and *lurk privily* for them (waylay them) (v. 11). The innocent travel unarmed. We will therefore attack them easily. And just think how sweet it will be *to swallow them up alive!*" (v. 12). They hope to gain good plunder by it (v. 13): "We will *find all precious substance* (all sorts of valuable things) by following this trade. So what if we risk our necks by it? We are going to *fill our houses with spoil.*" They call it *precious substance* (valuable things), whereas in reality it is neither substantial nor valuable; it is a mere worthless shadow, especially if it is gained by robbery (Ps 62:10).

2. He shows how these ways are harmful (v. 15): "*My son, walk not thou in the way with them; refrain thy foot from their path*; do not follow in their footsteps, do not do as they do." Consider their way (v. 16): *Their feet run to evil,* to what is displeasing to God and harmful to people, for they *make haste to shed blood.* The way of sin is downhill; having taken that way, people cannot stop themselves; in fact, the longer they continue in it, the faster they run; they are in a hurry to do evil. They are clearly told that this evil way will certainly end in their own destruction, but they still persist in it. They are like a senseless bird that sees a net spread out to capture it but is lured in by the bait nevertheless, not taking any notice of the warning its own eyes have seen (v. 17; Hos 7:11–12). Their greed for gain rushes them into those practices which will not allow them to live out half their days (Ps 55:23).

3. Now, although Solomon specifies only the temptation to rob on highways, he nevertheless intends this as a warning against all other evils that sinners lure people into. Such are the ways of the drunkards and immoral.

Verses 20–33

Having shown how dangerous it is to listen to the temptations of Satan, Solomon here shows how dangerous it is not to listen to the calls of God. Notice:

1. By whom God calls to us—by *wisdom.* It is *wisdom* that calls aloud. The word is plural, "wisdoms," for just as there is infinite wisdom in God, so also there is the *manifold wisdom of God* (Eph 3:10). God speaks to people by all kinds of wisdom.

1.1. Human understanding is wisdom, the light and law of nature, the powers and faculties of reason, and the service of conscience (Job 38:36).

1.2. Civil government is wisdom; magistrates are God's vice-regents.

1.3. Divine revelation is wisdom; all its dictates and its laws are as wise as wisdom itself. God declares his mind to sinners by the written word, by his servants the prophets, and by all the ministers of this word (Lk 1:2).

1.4. Christ himself is Wisdom, is "Wisdoms," for *in him are hidden all the treasures of wisdom and knowledge* (Col 2:3), and he is the center of all divine revelation, not only the essential Wisdom but also the eternal Word (Jn 1:1), by whom God speaks to us and to whom he has *committed all judgment* (Jn 5:22). He calls himself *Wisdom* (Lk 7:35).

2. He calls to us:

2.1. Very publicly, so that whoever has ears to hear may hear (Mt 11:15; 13:9, 43). The rules of wisdom are declared *in the streets* (v. 20), not only in the schools or in the palaces of rulers but also among the ordinary people who pass in and out of *the opening of the gates* and *the city* (v. 21).

2.2. Very emotionally; she *cries,* she *utters her words* (v. 21) with all possible clarity and love. God wants to be heard and heeded.

3. What the call of God and Christ is.

3.1. He rebukes sinners for their foolishness and their obstinate persistence in it (v. 22). In general, those rebuked here are the *simple. Simple ones love simplicity* (v. 22). They behave foolishly and are at home when they are doing simple things, enjoying themselves in their own deceit and flattering themselves in their evil. Specifically, they are *scorners who delight in scorning* (v. 22) and make a joke of everything that comes across their paths. Scoffers at religion are meant especially. Those rebuked are also *fools* who *hate knowledge* (v. 22). It is those who do not rightly understand religious faith who are its enemies. The worst fools are those who despise being instructed. The God of heaven wants sinners to be converted and reformed and does not want them to be ruined. He is very displeased at their negligence, he longs to be gracious (Isa 30:18), and he is willing to reason with them (Isa 1:18).

3.2. He invites them to repent and become wise (v. 23). *Turn you at my reproof,* that is, return to your right mind (Mk 5:15), respond to God, turn to your duty, turn and live (Eze 18:32; 33:11). Those who love simplicity find themselves morally powerless to change their own mind and way; they cannot turn by any power of their own. God answers this, "*Behold, I will pour out my Spirit unto you* (v. 23); set yourselves to do what you can, and the grace of God will work in you both to will and to do the good that, without that grace, you could not do" (Php 2:12–13). *I will pour out my Spirit unto you* (v. 23). The means of this grace is the word. It is therefore promised, "*I will make known my words unto you* (v. 23), not only speak them to you but also make you understand them."

3.3. He reads out the condemnation of those who continue to be stubborn against all these means of grace (vv. 24–32).

3.3.1. The crime is narrated. It is, in short, rejecting Christ and the offers of his grace and refusing to submit to the terms of his Gospel, which would have saved them both from the curse of the *law of God* and from the control of the *law of sin* (Ro 7:25). Christ *stretched out his hand* (v. 24) to offer them mercy, but they refused, and no one paid attention (v. 24). Christ not only rebuked them for what they did wrong but also advised them to do better—those are *reproofs of instruction* (6:23) and signs of love and goodwill—but they *set at nought all his counsel* as not worth heeding, and *would none of* (wanted to have nothing to do with) *his reproof* (v. 25). This is repeated (v. 30): "They *would none of my counsel*, but rejected and spurned it. *They despised all my reproof* as if it were one big joke and something not worth taking any notice of." They were encouraged to submit to the government of right reason and religion, but they rebelled against both. Reason would not rule them, for *they hated knowledge* (v. 29) because it showed that their deeds were evil (Jn 3:20). Religion could not rule them, for they *did not choose the fear of the Lord* (v. 29), but chose to walk in the way of *their heart and in the sight of their eyes* (Ecc 11:9).

3.3.2. The sentence is pronounced. They would not accept the benefits of God's mercy when it was offered them, and so they will justly fall as victims to his justice (29:1). These threats will be completely fulfilled on the Day of Judgment, but there are already some pledges of the fulfillment in present judgments.

3.3.2.1. Sinners are now prosperous and secure, but their *calamity will come* (v. 26); troubles will come to their mind and their possessions, which will convince them of their foolishness in rejecting God. Their *fear shall come*—what they were afraid of will come on them—it will *come as desolation* (v. 27), like a powerful storm or flood bearing down on them. It will come *as a whirlwind* (v. 27), which suddenly and forcefully drives out all the chaff. *Distress and anguish shall come upon them* (v. 27), for they will see no way of escape (v. 27).

3.3.2.2. God pities their foolishness now, but then he will *laugh at their calamity* (v. 26). Those who mock religion are only making themselves appear ridiculous to all the world.

3.3.2.3. God is ready now to hear their prayers and meet them with mercy, if they would only seek him for it, but then the door will be closed, and they will cry in vain (v. 28): "*Then shall they call upon me* when it is too late, *Lord, Lord, open to us* (Mt 25:11), but *I will not answer* (v. 28), because when I called, they would not answer." But, usually, while there is life, there is opportunity for prayer and hope of things going right, and so this must refer to the inexorable justice of the Last Judgment.

3.3.2.4. They are now eager to follow their own ways, but then they will have had enough of them (v. 31). They will *eat the fruit of their own way* (v. 31); their wages will be according to their work.

3.3.2.5. They now pride themselves on their worldly prosperity, but then that will only make their destruction worse (v. 32). They are now proud of their own security and worldliness, but "the ease of the simple" (v. 32, margin) *shall slay them*. The more secure they feel, the more certain and the more terrible will be their destruction, *and the prosperity of fools shall* help *destroy them* by making them proud, attaching their hearts to the world, providing them with fuel for their sinful desires, and hardening their hearts in their evil ways.

3.4. He concludes with an assurance of happiness and security to all those who submit to the instructions of wisdom (v. 33): "*Whoso hearkeneth unto me* and will be ruled by me *shall dwell* under the special protection of heaven, so that nothing will do them any real harm. They will have

no disquieting apprehensions of danger; they will be not only secure from evil but *quiet from the fear of* it" (v. 33).

CHAPTER 2

Solomon turns in this chapter to those who are willing to be taught, and: 1. He shows them that if they want to use the means of knowledge and grace, they will gain from God the knowledge and grace they seek (vv. 1–9). 2. He shows them what an advantage it would be to them. It would keep them from the snares of evil men (vv. 10–15) and of evil women (vv. 16–19); it would lead them to follow, and keep them in, the ways of good people (vv. 20–22).

Verses 1–9

Solomon tells us where we may find wisdom and how we may gain it. We are told:

1. What ways we must use to obtain wisdom:

1.1. We must pay close attention to the word of God, for that is the word of wisdom, *which is able to make us wise unto salvation* (2Ti 3:15) (vv. 1–2). The words of God are the fountain and basis of wisdom and understanding. Many wise things may be found in human works, but divine revelation and the true religion built on it are completely wise.

1.2. We must be prayerful (v. 3). We must *cry after knowledge*. We must *lift our voice for understanding* (v. 3), cry out to heaven, from which we should expect these good and perfect gifts (Job 38:34; Jas 1:17). We must cry out for understanding, speak for it, seek it, and submit our tongues to wisdom's commands.

1.3. We must be willing to make an effort (v. 4); we must *seek it as silver*, preferring it to all the wealth of this world and working as hard to search for it as those who work in mines.

2. What success we may hope for when we use these means. Our hard work will be effective, not in vain, for: "*Thou shalt understand the fear of the Lord* (v. 5), that is, you will know how to worship him rightly." *Thou shalt find the knowledge of God*, which is necessary for a right reverence toward him. We will know how to behave rightly toward other people (v. 9): "*Thou shalt understand*, by the word of God, *righteousness, and judgment, and equity.* You will learn the principles of justice, kindness, and fairness that will prepare you for every relationship and for being faithful to every trust placed in you. This wisdom will give you not only a right concept of justice but also a disposition to put it into practice, giving everyone their due."

3. What basis we have to hope for this success in our pursuit of wisdom. We must take our encouragement only from God (vv. 6–8):

3.1. God has wisdom to give (v. 6). Not only is *the Lord* wise himself; he also *gives wisdom*.

3.2. He has blessed the world with a revelation of his will. *Out of his mouth*, by the Law and the Prophets, by the written word and by his ministers, *come knowledge and understanding* (v. 6). It is a revelation of truth and goodness such as will make us truly knowledgeable and wise.

3.3. He has particularly provided that good people, who genuinely want to do his will, will have that *knowledge and understanding* (vv. 7–8). *The righteous*, those who *walk uprightly*, are *his saints*, devoted to his honor and set apart for his service. The means of wisdom are given to all, but wisdom itself, *sound wisdom*, is stored *up for the righteous* (v. 7), stored up in Christ their head. The One who is the Spirit of revelation in the word is a Spirit of wisdom in the souls of those who are sanctified. Some read it, "He stores up substance for the righteous," not only substantial knowledge but also substantial happiness and comfort (8:21). Even those who *walk uprightly* may fall into danger so that their faith may be tested, but God is *a buckler* (shield) *to them* (v. 7), so that nothing that happens to them will do them any real harm. If we depend on God and seek him for wisdom, he will uphold us in our integrity. He will enable us to *keep the paths of judgment* (v. 8), for he *preserves the way of his saints* (v. 8). *Work out your salvation*, for *God works in you* (Php 2:12–13).

Verses 10–22

True wisdom will keep us from the paths of sin and thereby do us a greater kindness than if it made us rich with all the wealth of the world. This wisdom will be useful to us:

1. To keep us from the evil of sin, and so from the trouble that goes along with it.

1.1. In general (vv. 10–11), "When wisdom controls you completely, it will *keep thee*." When it *enters into the heart* (v. 10) as yeast into dough, then it is likely to do us good. "When you call the practice of goodness not a burdensome chore but *liberty* and *pleasure*, then you will enjoy its benefits."

1.2. More particularly, wisdom will keep us:

1.2.1. From men of corrupt principles, unbelieving, worldly men, who make it their business to corrupt the judgments of young men and instill into their minds prejudice against religious faith and arguments for evil: "It *will deliver thee from the way of the evil man* (v. 12), *from the way* in which he walks and in which he tries to persuade you to walk." People of this kind *speak froward* (devious) *things* (v. 12); they say all they can against religion. *They leave the paths of uprightness*, which they were trained in, *to walk in the ways of darkness*, which hate the light, in which men are led blindfold by ignorance and error, and which lead men into complete darkness. They take pleasure in sin, both in committing it themselves and in seeing others commit it (v. 14). They *rejoice* in opportunities *to do evil*. Fools find it entertaining to cause trouble, to see those who are promising drawn into the ways of sin and then see them hardened and confirmed in those ways. Their *ways are crooked*; they follow a way with many twists and turns to escape the pursuit of their convictions.

1.2.2. From women of corrupt practices, who would lead a man to *fleshly lusts*, which defile the body, that living temple, but also *war against the soul* (1Pe 2:11). The adulterous woman is here called *the strange woman* (v. 16), to be avoided by every Israelite as if she were a pagan, a foreigner to that holy community. Consider:

1.2.2.1. How false she is. She is false to the man she entices. She speaks enticing words, tells him how much she admires him above any other man, but she *flatters with her words* (v. 16); she has no true affection for him, nor any desire for his welfare, any more than Delilah had for Samson's. All she wants is to pick his pocket and satisfy her own sordid, sinful desires. She is false to her husband and breaks the sacred obligation she is under to him. She is false to God himself: she *forgets the covenant of her God*, the marriage covenant (v. 17), to which God is not only a witness but also a party, for because he instituted the ordinance, both sides vow to him to be true to each other.

1.2.2.2. How fatal it will prove to follow her (vv. 18–19). Beware of the sin of adultery. It is a sin that has a direct tendency to kill the soul and extinguish every good spiritual devotion. Let wisdom keep every man not only from

the evil woman but also from the evil house, for the *house inclines to death* (v. 18), "and her paths to Rephaim, to the giants," as some read it, the sinners of the old world, who plunged into a flood of dissipation (1Pe 4:4) and were soon destroyed, their foundation being overthrown by the Flood (Job 22:16; Ge 6:4; 7:21, 23). *None*, or next to none, *that go unto her, return again* (v. 19). It is very rare that anyone who is caught up in this snare of the Devil recovers; their hearts have become so hardened, and their mind so blinded, by the deceitfulness of this sin.

1.3. Many interpreters think that this warning against the *strange woman* (v. 16) has, besides the literal sense, a figurative one, that it is also a warning against idolatry, which is spiritual unfaithfulness. Wisdom will keep you from becoming intimate with the worshipers of idols. Wisdom will also keep you from being captivated by the fleshly mind and from submitting the spirit to the control of the flesh.

2. To guide and direct us in what is good (v. 20): *that thou mayest* walk in the way of good people. We will be wise to walk in that way, to ask for the good and old way and to walk in it (Jer 6:16; Heb 6:12; 12:1). *The paths of the righteous* (v. 20) are the paths of life. "So that you may imitate those excellent people, the patriarchs and prophets," as Bishop Patrick paraphrases it, "and be preserved in *the paths of those righteous* people who followed them." *The upright shall dwell in the land* peacefully and quietly as long as they live.

CHAPTER 3

This chapter is one of the most excellent in all this book, both as an argument to persuade us to be religious and as a set of directions for following that way. 1. We must be faithful in doing our duty because that is the way to be happy (vv. 1–4). 2. We must live a life of dependence on God because that is the way to be safe (v. 5–6). 3. We must maintain the fear of God because that is the way to be healthy (vv. 7–8). 4. We must serve God with our possessions because that is the way to be rich (vv. 9–10). 5. We must bear afflictions well because that is the way to benefit from them (vv. 11–12). 6. We must make an effort to gain wisdom because that is the way to gain wisdom (vv. 13–20). 7. We must be guided according to the rules of wisdom, right reason, and religious faith, because that is the way to be at peace (vv. 21–26). 8. We must do all the good we can to our neighbors and do them no harm (vv. 27–35).

Verses 1–6

We are here taught to lead a life of fellowship with God, which produces overwhelming benefits.

1. We must continually remember God's commands (vv. 1–2). We must take God's law and commands as our standard. Not only our heads but also our hearts must *keep God's commandments* (v. 1). To encourage us to submit ourselves to every restraint and injunction of God's law, we are assured (v. 2) that this certainly leads to long life and prosperity. Even the days of old age will not be evil, but will be days in which we still find pleasure (Ecc 12:1): *Peace shall they* continually *add to thee* (v. 2). Great and growing *peace have those that love the law* (Ps 119:165).

2. We must continually remember God's promises, which accompany his commands (v. 3): "Let not mercy and truth forsake you, God's mercy in promising and his truth in fulfilling the promises. Bind them around your neck, as the most graceful ornament." Having a share in

the mercy and truth of God is the greatest honor we are capable of in this world. "Write them on the tablet of your heart, as things that are precious to you. Take pleasure in applying them and thinking about them." To encourage us to do this, we are assured (v. 4) that this is the way to commend ourselves both to our Creator and to our fellow creatures: *So shalt thou find favour and good understanding* (v. 4). Good people seek the favor of God first. They will be acknowledged as Wisdom's children (Mt 11:19) and commended by God. Such good people want to enjoy the favor of other people too, to be held in high esteem by many of their fellows (Est 10:3); and their fellows will understand them correctly.

3. We must continually remember God's providence; we must depend on it in every aspect of our life, both in faith and in prayer. We must trust in the Lord with all our hearts (v. 5); we must believe that he is able to do what he wills, that he is wise and will therefore do what is best, and that he is good, according to his promises, and will therefore do what is best for us if we love and serve him. *In all thy ways acknowledge God* (v. 6). In prayer, we must ask what his will is and not plan anything except what we are sure is right. We must ask his advice and seek direction from him. We must ask him to give us success as those who know the race is not to the swift (Ecc 9:11). To encourage us to do this, it is promised, "He will direct your paths, so that your way will be safe and good and all will finally go well."

Verses 7–12

Here are three exhortations, each backed up by a good reason:

1. We must live in humble and dutiful submission to God and his rule (v. 7): *"Fear the Lord* as your sovereign Lord and Master; be guided in everything by your religious faith and submission to the divine *will." Be not wise in thy own eyes* (v. 7). There is no greater enemy to the power of religion and the fear of God in the heart than pride in our own wisdom. *Fear the Lord, and depart from evil* (v. 7); beware of doing anything that might offend him or forfeit his care. To encourage us to live in such a fear of God it is promised that it will be as useful to us as the food we must eat to survive (v. 8). *It shall be health to thy navel* (NIV: body). It will be strengthening: it will be *marrow to thy bones*. Wisdom and moderation, calmness of mind, and self-control of appetites and passions, which religion teaches, lead very much not only to spiritual health but also to good physical habits.

2. We must make good use of our possessions, and that is the way to see them increase (vv. 9–10). *Honour the Lord with thy substance*. Worldly wealth is comparatively poor, but such as it is, we must honor God with it, and then it may become substantial. We must honor God *with our increase* (crops) (v. 9). The reference here is to the crops of the earth, for we live off crops that come from the land, so that we may be kept constantly dependent on God. God, who is the first and best, must receive the first and best of everything. *So shall thy barns be filled with plenty* (v. 10). "God will bless you with an increase of what is for use, not for display or ostentation—for spending, not for hoarding." What we give we have.

3. We must behave rightly in times of adversity (vv. 11–12). We must not despise adversity, even if it is very light and short, as if it were something not worth taking notice of, or as if it were not sent to us on an errand and so needed no answer. We must not be hard, insensitive, and stoical in our troubles, concluding that we can easily endure them without God. We must not become weary of adversity, not become discouraged, lose our own souls, or be driven to despair. Adversity is a divine correction, *the chastening of the Lord* (v. 11). It comes from God, and so we must not become weary of it, for he knows how we are formed (Ps 103:14), both what we need (Mt 6:23) and what we can bear (1Co 10:13). It is a fatherly correction; it does not come from his vindictive justice as a Judge, but from his wise affection as a father. The father corrects *the son whom he* (v. 12) loves; in fact, he does it because he loves him and wants him to become wise and good.

Verses 13–20

Happy is the man that findeth wisdom (v. 13), the true wisdom that consists of the knowledge and love of God and a complete conformity to all the intentions of his truths, the ways of his providence, and his laws. Notice:

1. What it is to find wisdom so as to be made happy from it. Happy are those who, having found it, make it their own, who, literally, "draw out understanding." Knowing that they do not have understanding within themselves, they draw it by the bucket of prayer from the fountain of all wisdom, *who gives liberally* (Jas 1:5). They take pains in obtaining it, as miners do in extracting ore from a mine. A thing has been well gained, gained to good effect, when it has in this way been used to good effect. We read here of the merchandise of wisdom, which suggests that we must make it our business, and not a sideline, as merchants give their main attention and time to buying and selling. This is the pearl of great price that, when we have found it, we must willingly sell everything to buy (Mt 13:45–46). *Buy the truth* (23:23); it does not say at what price, because we must buy it at any price rather than miss out on the opportunity to make it our own. It is not enough to take hold of wisdom; we must also keep our hold of it, hold it fast, with a determination never to let it go and to persevere in the ways of wisdom to the end.

2. The happiness of those who find it.

2.1. It is a transcendent happiness, more than can be found in worldly wealth, even if we owned a lot of it (vv. 14–15). All the wealth in the world would not buy heavenly wisdom; it *cannot be gotten for gold* (Job 28:15). All the world's wealth would not make up for the lack of heavenly wisdom or be the price of a soul lost by its own foolishness. All of it would not make someone half so happy as those are who have true wisdom even though they have none of these things.

2.2. It is a true happiness, for it includes all the things that are supposed to make people happy (vv. 16–17). Wisdom is here represented as a bright and bountiful queen, extending gifts to her faithful and loving subjects. She offers life *in her right hand* (v. 16). Religious faith gives us the best way to prolong our lives, and if our days on earth are no more than our neighbor's, it will make safe for us eternal life in a better world. She extends riches and honor with *her left hand* (v. 16). True godliness contains the greatest true pleasure. *Her ways are ways of pleasantness* (v. 17). All the enjoyments and physical pleasures of this world cannot compare with the pleasure that gracious souls have in fellowship with God and in doing good. The way of religious faith is both the right way and a pleasant way. It is smooth, clean, and strewn with roses: *All her paths are peace* (v. 17). There is not only peace at the end but also peace along the way.

2.3. It is the happiness of paradise (v. 18): *She is a tree of life*. True grace is to the soul what the Tree of Life would have been, the tree from which our first parents were excluded because they ate from the forbidden tree. Those who feed on this heavenly wisdom will find it to be an antidote against age and death: they will *eat and live for ever* (Ge 3:22).

2.4. It is sharing in the happiness of God himself, for wisdom is his eternal glory and blessedness (vv. 19–20). *Happy is the man that finds wisdom* (v. 13), for he will be *thoroughly furnished for every good word and work* (2Ti 3:17). Christ has the resources to fulfill all the promises of long life, riches, and honor, for all the wealth of heaven, earth, and seas belongs to him.

Verses 21–26

Solomon here exhorts us to keep hold of wisdom.

1. The exhortation is to keep the rules of religious faith always in view and always in the heart (v. 21). "*My son, let them not depart from thy eyes*; do not let them out of your sight so that you wander after worthless things. Keep them always in your mind, and as long as you live, maintain and cultivate your knowledge of them." We must also keep them always in the heart, for it is in the treasury of the hidden heart that we must *keep sound wisdom and discretion*.

2. The argument to back up this exhortation is taken from the indescribable benefit that wisdom will be to us if it is kept to. "It will be *life to thy soul* (v. 22); it will inspire you to do your duty; it will revive you in times of trouble when you begin to droop and become discouraged. It will be your spiritual life and the promise of eternal life." It will be *grace to thy neck*, as a chain of gold or a jewel; "pleasant to your taste," according to some; it will "add grace to all you say," according to others; it will provide you with acceptable words, which will increase your reputation. Wisdom will also bring perfect safety and security. Good people are taken under God's special protection; they are safe and may be at rest (v. 23). If our religious faith accompanies us, it will lead us on: "*Then shalt thou walk in thy way safely*. The natural life and all that belongs to it will come under the protection of God's providence; the spiritual life and all its interests will come under the protection of his grace. You will therefore be kept from falling into sin or trouble." The way of duty is the way of safety. "We are in danger of falling, but wisdom will keep you, so that *thy foot shall not stumble* at those things that cause many to stumble; you will know how to overcome them." By night (v. 24) we are exposed to many frightful things. "But maintain your fellowship with God and keep a good conscience, and then *when thou liest down thou shalt not be afraid* of fire, thieves, ghosts, or any terror of the darkness, knowing that when we and all our friends are asleep, the One who *keeps Israel neither slumbers nor sleeps*" (Ps 121:4). The way to have a good night's rest is to keep a good conscience; and the sleep of a wise and godly person, like that of a laborer, is sweet (Ecc 5:12). Integrity and uprightness will keep us, so that we need *not be afraid of sudden fear* (v. 25). And let not wise and good people fear the *desolation of the wicked, when it comes*, that is, the trouble evildoers cause to religious faith and religious people.

Verses 27–35

Here we have various excellent commands of wisdom that relate to our neighbor.

1. We must render to everyone their due, both in justice and in kindness, and not delay in doing it (vv. 27–28): "*Withhold not good from those to whom it is due, when it is in the power of thy hand to do it.* You are greatly at fault

if by your extravagance you have disabled yourself from acting justly and showing mercy (Mic 6:8). If you have it with you today, do not say to your neighbor, *Go thy way for this time* and come back later when it is more convenient, and then I will see what I can do for you; *tomorrow I will give*. Thou art not sure thou wilt live till tomorrow, or that tomorrow thou wilt *have it by thee* (v. 28). Do not excuse yourself from a duty that must be done, and do not delight in keeping your neighbor in pain or suspense or enjoy showing the power givers have over beggars, but act readily and cheerfully, and always act from a motivation of good conscience toward God. Do good to *those to whom it is due*"; do it, literally, to the "lords and owners of it," to those who are entitled to it for any reason. This requires us:

- To pay our just debts without fraud, deceit, or delay.
- To give wages to those who have earned them.
- To provide for our relatives and others who depend on us, for it is due to them.
- To render what is due to both church and state, judges and ministers.
- To be available for all acts of friendship and humanity and to be neighborly in everything, for these are things that are due by the law of "doing as we would be done by."
- To be charitable to the poor and those in need.

2. We must never intend any hurt or harm to anybody (v. 29): "*Devise not evil against thy neighbour*, for they *dwell securely by* (live trustfully near) you and harbor no jealousy or suspicion of you, and so are off their guard."

3. We must not be quarrelsome or contentious (v. 30): "Do not accuse anyone for no reason; do not fight for what you are not entitled to; do not resent as a provocation something that may have been only an oversight. Never trouble your neighbor with frivolous complaints or accusations or troublesome lawsuits when you might be able to sort it out in a friendly way." Going to court must be the last resort.

4. We must not envy the prosperity of evildoers (v. 31). "*Envy not the oppressor*, even though he is rich and great. *Choose none of his ways*; do not imitate him. Never think of doing as he does, even though you think you will gain by it everything he has, for that would be a high price to pay." To show what little reason saints have to envy sinners, Solomon here, in vv. 32–35, compares the condition of sinners with that of saints. Saints are loved by him (v. 32). Perverse sinners, whose lives go fundamentally against his will, are an *abomination to the Lord*. God, who hates nothing that he has made (*Book of Common Prayer*, Collect for Ash Wednesday), detests those who have so spoiled their lives. The righteous therefore have no reason to envy them, for he communicates to them the secret assurance of his love (v. 32); they know his mind, including the intentions of providence, better than others. Saints are under his blessing, they and their homes (v. 33). The just have a home, a poor cottage—the word is used for a sheepfold—a very humble home, but God blesses it from the beginning of the year to the end. Those who exalt themselves will certainly be humbled (Mt 23:12): *Surely he scorns the scorners.* Those who scorn submission to the disciplines of religious faith, who laugh at all godliness and godly people, will find that God will expose them to scorn before the whole world. Those who humble themselves will be exalted (Mt 23:12), for *he gives grace to the lowly* (v. 34); he works in them that which gives them honor and for which they are *accepted*

of God and approved of men (Ro 14:18). The destiny of sinners will be their eternal shame; the destiny of saints will be their endless honor (v. 35).

CHAPTER 4

In this chapter Solomon uses a wide variety of expressions to instill the same things he urged on us in the previous chapters. Here is: 1. A positive exhortation to study wisdom, that is, true religious faith and godliness; this exhortation is taken from the good instructions his father gave him, and it is backed up by many significant arguments (vv. 1–13). 2. A necessary warning against bad company (vv. 14–19). 3. Detailed instructions for how to obtain and keep wisdom and produce its fruits (vv. 20–27).

Verses 1–13

Here we have:

1. The invitation Solomon gives to his children (vv. 1–2): *Hear, you children, the instruction of a father.* "Let my own children, in the first place, receive those instructions that I set down here, which are also for others to use." Judges and ministers should be concerned to take more than usual care to give instruction to their own families. Let all young people make an effort to gain knowledge and grace in the days of their childhood and youth, for that is the age when their minds are being formed and trained. He does not say, *My* children, but *Ye* children. Let everyone who wants to receive instruction come with a childlike attitude even though they have grown up. Let all prejudices be set aside, and the mind be as a clear sheet of paper. Let them be teachable, submissive, and self-effacing; let them accept the word as the word of a father, which comes with both authority and affection. We must see it as coming from God *our Father in heaven* (Mt 6:9), to whom we pray and from whom we expect to receive blessings, the Father of our spirits (Heb 12:9). We must look on our teachers as our fathers; they love us and seek our welfare. We are told not only that it is the *instruction of a father* but also that it is *understanding* (v. 1), and so it should be welcomed by all reasonable creatures. Religious faith has reason on its side, and we are taught it by fair reasoning. It is indeed a law (v. 2), but that law is founded on unquestionable principles of truth, on *good doctrine*, which deserves full acceptance (1Ti 1:15). If we accept the doctrine, we must also submit to the law.

2. The instructions he gives them. Notice:

2.1. He received these instructions from his parents, and he teaches his children the same things his parents taught him (vv. 3–4).

2.1.1. His parents loved him, and so they taught him: *I was my father's son.* David had many sons, but Solomon was his son *indeed*, as Isaac is called (Ge 17:19), and for the same reason, because the covenant was passed on to him as an inheritance. He was *tender, and only beloved, in the sight of his mother* (v. 3). Although he was a prince, heir to the crown, they did not allow him to live without restraint; they taught him. And perhaps David was all the stricter with Solomon in his upbringing because he had seen the adverse effects of undue indulgence in Adonijah, whom he had not rebuked for anything (1Ki 1:6).

2.1.2. What his parents taught him he teaches others. When Solomon was grown up, he not only remembered the good lessons his parents taught him when he was a child but also took pleasure in repeating them. Although Solomon himself was wise and divinely inspired,

nevertheless, when he was to teach wisdom, he did not think it beneath him to quote his father. Those who want to teach well in matters of religious faith must not look with contempt on the knowledge of those who have gone before them. If we are to keep to the good old ways, why should we despise the good old words (Jer 6:16)? Solomon backs up his exhortations with the authority of his father David, a man well known in his generation.

2.2. What these instructions were (vv. 4–13).

2.2.1. Command and exhortation. In teaching his son, David expressed himself with great warmth and boldness, inculcating the same matter again and again.

2.2.1.1. He commends to him his Bible and his catechism as the means: his father's *words* (v. 4), the *words of his mouth* (v. 5), his *sayings* (v. 10), all the good lessons he had taught him. Perhaps David is referring particularly to the book of Psalms, many of which were *maskils*, "psalms of instruction," and two of which are expressly said to be *for Solomon.* Solomon must *hear and receive them* (v. 10). He must *hold fast the form of sound words* (2Ti 1:13) that his father gave him (v. 4): *Let thy heart retain my words*; and if the word is not hidden in the heart, deposited securely in the will and affections, it will not be firmly held onto. He must live his life by them: *Keep my commandments.* He must abide by them: *"Decline not from the words of my mouth* (v. 5), fearing they will be too severe a restraint for you; instead *take fast hold of instruction* (v. 13), having decided to keep your hold and never let it go or turn away from it."

2.2.1.2. He commends to him wisdom and understanding as the end to be aimed at in using these means. A motivation of religious faith in the heart is the one thing that is needed (Lk 10:42), and so: "Get this *wisdom*, gain this *understanding*" (v. 5). And again, "*Get wisdom*, and *with all thy getting, get understanding* (v. 7). Get wisdom from experience, get it *above all thy getting* (v. 7); take more care and effort to get this than to get the wealth of this world." True wisdom is the gift of God, but God gives it to those who labor for it. *Forget her not* (v. 5), *forsake her not* (v. 6), *let her not go* (v. 6), *but keep her.* Love her (v. 6) and *embrace her* (v. 8), as worldly people love their wealth and set their hearts on it. If we cannot be very wise, let us still be true lovers of wisdom; let us embrace wisdom with a sincere affection, as those who wonder at its beauty. "*Exalt her* (v. 8). Always keep high thoughts of religious faith, and do all you can to maintain its good name among people." Let Wisdom's children not only prove her right (Mt 11:19) but also exalt her, honoring those who fear the Lord, even though they are lowly in the world, and regarding *a poor wise man* (Ecc 9:15), so exalting wisdom.

2.2.2. Motivation and inducement to seek wisdom and submit to it.

2.2.2.1. It is what is supreme (v. 7): *Wisdom is the principal thing*; other things that we are concerned to obtain and keep are nothing compared with it. It is what commends us to God, makes the soul beautiful, and enables us to live for some good purpose in the world and finally to reach heaven; and so it is what is supreme.

2.2.2.2. It has reason and justice on its side (v. 11): "*I have taught thee in the way of wisdom*, and that is what it will ultimately be found to be. *I have led thee in right paths*, which conform to the eternal rules and reasons of good and evil." David not only taught his son by good instructions but also led him by a good example and by applying general instructions to individual situations.

2.2.2.3. It would be much to Solomon's own advantage: *Keep my commandments and live* (v. 4). The word of our Savior agrees with this: *If thou wilt enter into life, keep the commandments* (Mt 19:17). "Receive wisdom's sayings, *and the years of thy life shall be many* (v. 10), as many in this world as infinite Wisdom sees fit, and in the other world you will live the years that can never be numbered. *Keep her,* therefore, whatever it costs you, *for she is thy life* (v. 13). Love wisdom and cling to her, and she will *preserve thee, she shall keep thee* (v. 6) from sin, the worst of evils. She will keep you from hurting yourself, and then no one else can hurt you." As the saying goes, "Keep your shop and your shop will keep you"; similarly, "Keep your wisdom, and your wisdom will keep you. It will be your honor and reputation (v. 8): *Exalt* wisdom and she will abundantly reward it, although she does not need your service; *she shall promote* (exalt) *thee, she shall bring thee to honour.*" He insists on this (v. 9): "*She shall give to thy head an ornament of grace* in this world, and in the other world *a crown of glory shall she deliver to thee,* a crown that will never wither" (Jas 1:9–12).

Verses 14–19

Some commentators think David's instructions to Solomon, which began at v. 4, continue to the end of the chapter, but it is more probable that Solomon begins again here. In these verses he warns us against the way of evildoers.

1. The warning itself (vv. 14–15). We must beware of falling in with sin and sinners: *Enter not into the paths of the wicked.* "If, before you were aware, you set foot on the path at the gate because it was wide, *go not on in the way of evil men* (v. 14). As soon as you become aware of your mistake, withdraw immediately, do not take any further step, do not even stay one minute longer on the path that certainly leads to destruction." The verse also suggests how far we should keep away from sin and sinners; he does not say, "Keep a proper distance," but, "Keep a great distance, the farther the better; never think you can get far enough away from it."

2. The reasons to back up this warning: "Consider the character of the people whose ways you are warned to avoid." They are troublesome (vv. 16–17). They are continually endeavoring to *cause some to fall,* to ruin them in body and soul. Trouble is rest and sleep to them; trouble is food and drink to them. *They eat the bread of wickedness and drink the wine of violence* (v. 17). All they eat and drink is gained by robbery and oppression. "Avoid the company of those who delight in causing harm and trouble, for whatever friendship they may pretend to show, they will cause trouble for you; you will harm yourself if you fall in with them (1:18), and they will harm you if you do not. The way of righteousness, on the other hand, is light (v. 18): *The path of the just,* the path they have chosen to follow, *is as light*; the *light shines on their ways* (Job 22:28). Christ is *their way,* and he is *the light.* They are guided by the word of God, and that *is a light to their feet* (Ps 119:105); they themselves are *light in the Lord* (Eph 5:8), and they *walk in the light as he is in the light* (1Jn 1:7). Their path is as the morning light, which *shines out of obscurity* (Isa 58:8, 10) and puts an end to the *works of darkness* (Ro 13:12). It is a growing light; it *shines more and more* (v. 18), not like the light of a shooting star, which soon disappears out of sight, or that of a candle, which burns dimly and burns out, but like that of the rising sun, which shines more brightly as it goes up in the sky. This path will arrive in the end at *the perfect day* (v. 18). The *way* of sin *is as darkness* (v. 19). The works Solomon has warned us not to have fellowship with are *works of darkness* (Ro 13:12). What true pleasure and satisfaction can people have if they know no pleasure and satisfaction except what they have in causing trouble?

The way of the wicked is dark and therefore dangerous, for they stumble and *know not at what they stumble* (v. 19).

Verses 20–27

Having warned us not to do wrong, Solomon here teaches us how to do right (Isa 1:16–17).

1. We must continually look to the word of God.

1.1. The sayings of wisdom must become the principles that guide our lives, the "checks and balances" of our lives to warn us about the possible dangers we face and the duties we are to undertake, so *"Incline thy ear to them* (v. 20); humbly submit to them; listen closely to them." We must keep hold of them carefully (v. 21); we must set them before us as our rule: *"Let them not depart from thy eyes*; view them, review them, and aim to conform to them in everything." We must deposit them within us as commanding principles: *"Keep them in the midst of thy heart,* as things that are precious to you and that you are afraid of losing."

1.2. The reason why we must make much of the words of wisdom is that they will be both food and medicine to us, like *the tree of life* (Rev 22:2; Eze 47:12).

- Food: *For they are life unto those that find them* (v. 22). As the spiritual life was begun by the word, so by the same word it continues to be maintained and nourished.
- Medicine. They are *health to all their flesh,* to the whole being, both body and soul; they help keep both in a good condition. They are "a medicine to all their flesh," for all their corruptions. The word of God contains a proper remedy for all our spiritual diseases.

2. We must keep a watchful eye and a strict hand on all the activities of our inward being (v. 23). *Keep thy heart with all diligence.* God, who gave us these souls, gave us a strict responsibility with them. We must set a strict guard on all the avenues of the soul; we are to keep our hearts from doing harm and being harmed, from being defiled by sin or disturbed by trouble. We are to keep out bad thoughts and keep up good thoughts. We are to keep our desires set on right objects and within proper limits. "Keep them with all keepings" is the sense; there are many ways of keeping things—care, power, or calling in help—and we must use all these to keep our hearts. A good reason is given for taking such care of the heart: because *out of it are the issues of life,* because the heart is the wellspring of life (v. 23). From a well-kept heart living streams and good crops will flow to the glory of God and the edification of others.

3. We must set a *watch before the door of our lips* (Ps 141:3), so that we do not cause offense with our tongue (v. 24): *Put away from thee a froward mouth and perverse lips.* We must develop a great detestation of all kinds of evil words, cursing, swearing, lying, slandering, contentiousness, filthiness, and foolish talking (Eph 5:4), all of which come from *a froward mouth and perverse lips* that will not be controlled by either reason or religion, but are against both, and all of which are as ugly and ill favored to God as a crooked and distorted mouth is to other people.

4. We must make a covenant with our eyes (Job 31:1): "Let them *look right on and straight before thee* (v. 25). Let your eyes be fixed and not drift and follow everything that presents itself to your sight, for then they will be diverted from good and become caught up in evil. Let your intentions be sincere and consistent; do not look furtively at any way of gaining a secret advantage." We must keep our eyes on our Master, careful to aim for his approval; we are to fix our gaze directly on him, to consider our rule of life and conform to that; we are to keep our eyes focused

on our goal, the *prize of the high calling* (Php 3:14), and direct all our attention toward that.

5. We must act considerately in all we do (v. 26): *Ponder the path of thy feet*; "weigh it; consider it"; "put the word of God in one scale and what you have done, or are about to do, in the other, and see how they balance each other out. Do nothing rashly."

6. We must act with steadiness, caution, and consistency: "*Let all thy ways be established* (v. 26) and do not be unstable in them."

CHAPTER 5

The scope of this chapter is much the same as that of chapter 2. Here is: 1. An exhortation to come to know and to submit to the laws of wisdom in general (vv. 1–2); a particular warning against the sin of adultery (vv. 3–14). 2. Remedies prescribed against that sin: marital love (vv. 15–20), a regard to God's omniscience (v. 21), and a fear of the wretched end of evildoers (vv. 22–23).

Verses 1–14

Here we have:

1. A solemn foreword to introduce the warning that follows (vv. 1–2). Solomon here addresses himself to his son, that is, to all young men as to his children. "It *is my wisdom, my understanding* (v. 1); I undertake to teach you the wisdom that is to be learned in my school." Solomon's lectures are not intended to fill our heads with subjects for idle speculation or disputable matters, but to guide us in our conduct.

2. The warning itself to abstain from sinful desires, from adultery and all sexual immorality. Some apply this figuratively, understanding the adulterous woman to refer to idolatry or false doctrine, which tend to corrupt the human mind and character, but its primary scope is clearly to warn us against seventh-commandment sins. We are warned:

2.1. Not to listen to the charm of this sin. It is true that *the lips of a strange* (adulterous) *woman drop as a honeycomb* (v. 3); the kisses and words of her mouth are *smoother than oil*, so that its poisonous pill may go down smoothly with no suspicion of harm in it. But remember that it *is bitter as wormwood* (v. 4). What tasted delicious in the mouth rises in the stomach and turns sour. Even if some people who have been guilty of this sin have repented and been saved, the direct tendency of it is still to destroy body and soul; its *feet go down to death*. How false its charm is. The adulterous woman flatters and speaks fair words of honey and oil, but she will deceive those who listen to her: *Her ways are movable* (crooked), *that thou canst not know them* (v. 6). She is like Proteus, able to put on many shapes so that she may keep in favor with those whom she has designs on. And what does she aim at with all her artful deeds? Nothing but to keep them from *pondering the path of life* (v. 6), for she knows that once they give thought to their way of life, she will certainly lose them. People are *ignorant of Satan's devices* (2Co 2:11) if they do not understand that what he aims at in all his temptations is to keep them from choosing the path of life, to prevent them from believing.

2.2. Not even to come near this sin.

2.2.1. The warning is urgent: "*Remove thy way far from her* (v. 8); if your way happens to be near hers, change your path rather than expose yourself to a possible danger. *Come not nigh the door of her house*; walk on the other side of the road; in fact, it is better to go down some other road, even though it is the long way around." Our corrupt nature is such a tinderbox that it is sheer madness, for any reason whatsoever, pretended or otherwise, to come near it with sparks.

2.2.2. The arguments are based on the many troubles that accompany this sin.

2.2.2.1. It ruins the reputation. "Thou wilt *give thy honour* (best strength) *unto others* (v. 9); you yourself will lose it. If you follow this way, you are in effect putting a stone into the hand of each of your neighbors so that they can throw it at you, for they will cry shame on you, as one who is foolish."

2.2.2.2. It spoils your life; it gives *the years* of youth, the prime of your life, *unto the cruel* (v. 9). Those years that should be given to honoring a gracious God are spent in the service of a cruel sin.

2.2.2.3. It ruins possessions (v. 10): "*Strangers* will be *filled with thy wealth*, which you are only entrusted with as a steward for your family. The fruit of *thy labours*, which should provide for the members of your own family, will be used in *the house of a stranger*, who neither has any right to it nor will ever thank you for it."

2.2.2.4. It destroys health and shortens human life: *Thy flesh and thy body* will be *consumed* by it (v. 11). The sinful desires of sexual immorality *war* not only *against the soul* (1Pe 2:11), which the sinner neglects and does not care about, but also against the body, which he so indulges and so much wants to pamper.

2.2.2.5. It will fill the mind with horror—if the sinner's conscience is ever stirred. "Although you may be merry now, *sporting thyself in thy own deceivings* (reveling in your pleasures) (2Pe 2:13), you will certainly *mourn at the last* (at the end of your life you will groan) (v. 11). Solomon represents the convicted sinner reproaching himself because he hated to be reformed and therefore hated to be informed. He could not bear either to be taught his duty or to be told his faults—My *heart despised reproof* (v. 12). He has to acknowledge that parents and ministers advised him well and gave him fair warning (v. 13). He did not, however, take their advice; he did not *obey their voice*, for indeed he *never inclined his ear to those that instructed him*. By the frequent acts of sin, habits became so deep-rooted and established that his heart was fully set on committing them (v. 14): *I was almost in all evil in the midst of the congregation and assembly.*

Verses 15–23

Having shown the great evil of adultery and sexual immorality, Solomon prescribes remedies against them.

1. Enjoy with satisfaction the comforts of lawful marriage, which was ordained for the prevention of sexual immorality. Let no one complain that God has dealt unkindly with him by forbidding him pleasures that he has a natural desire for, for God has graciously provided for that desire to be satisfied regularly. "It is true that you are not allowed to eat the fruit of every tree in the garden, but choose one that you find pleasing, and you will be allowed to eat freely from that one. Nature will be content with that, but sinful desires will not be content with anything." Let young men marry and not burn with passion (1Co 7:9). Have a *cistern, a well of thy own* (v. 15), the wife *of thy youth* (v. 18). As George Herbert wrote, "Wholly abstain, or wed." Let the man who is married take delight in his wife, and let him love her not only because she is the wife that he himself has chosen and he should be pleased with his own choice, but because she is the wife that God in his providence appointed for him. *Let thy fountain be blessed* (v. 18); you are to think yourself very fortunate in her. Look on her as a blessed wife; let

her have your blessing. Pray daily for her, and then *rejoice with her*. Mutual delight is the bond of mutual faithfulness. Let him delight in his wife and love her dearly (v. 19). If you want to be excessive in your love, let it be only toward your own wife. Let a man take delight in his own children and look on them with delight (vv. 16–17). Let him scorn the offer of forbidden pleasures when he is *always ravished with the love* (v. 19) of a good and faithful wife; let him consider how absurd it would be for him to be *ravished with* (captivated by) *a strange* (adulterous) *woman* (v. 20). If the dictates of reason are listened to, the laws of goodness will be obeyed.

2. "Realize that the eyes of God are always on you, and let his fear rule in your heart" (v. 21). *The ways of man*, all human activities, are *before the eyes of the Lord* (v. 21). However secretly or cunningly a person does a deed, God sees it in its true light and knows all about it: its causes, circumstances, and consequences. He not only sees but also *ponders all his goings*; he examines all his paths (v. 21). He judges the paths as One who will soon judge the sinner for them.

3. "Foresee the certain ruin of those who continue in their disobedience." Those who live in this sin promise themselves they will be exempt, but they are only deceiving themselves; their sin will find them out (Nu 32:23; vv. 22–23). As their own iniquities stop them in their tracks with shame and censure (Jer 7:19), so their own iniquities will stop them in their tracks and hold them tightly to the judgments of God. There need be no prison or chains; they will be *holden* (held fast) *in the cords of their own sins* (v. 22).

CHAPTER 6

In this chapter we have: 1. A warning against rashly putting up money for what your neighbor owes (vv. 1–5). 2. A rebuke to laziness (vv. 6–11). 3. The character and fate of one who is malicious and troublesome (vv. 12–15); an account of seven things that God hates (vv. 16–19). 4. An exhortation to come to know the word of God well (vv. 20–23); a repeated warning of the harmful consequences of the sin of sexual immorality (vv. 24–35).

Verses 1–5

It is one of the excellent features of the word of God that it teaches us not only divine wisdom for the next world but also human wisdom for this world, so that we may plan our affairs rightly. This is one good rule: to avoid putting up money for what your neighbor owes, because it often leads to poverty and ruin in families.

1. Putting up security for our neighbor's debts is a trap; we must regard it that way and refuse to get involved in it (vv. 1–2). "It is dangerous enough for someone to be committed in this way for a friend, even if he is well acquainted with his friend's circumstances and well assured of his good standing, but much more dangerous to *strike the hands with a stranger* (v. 1), to put up security for one whom you do not know to be either able or honest." If you have rashly entered into such a commitment, either because you were wheedled into it or because you hope to have the same kindness done to you another time, know that *thou art snared with* (you have been trapped by) *the words of thy mouth* (v. 2).

2. If we have been drawn into this trap, we will be wise to use all means to get out of it as quickly as possible (vv. 3–5). The obligation lies dormant for a short time; we hear nothing more about it. The debt is not demanded; the debtor says, "Don't worry; we'll take care of it." But

the agreement remains in force, interest is running up, and the creditor may come to you whenever he wants and may perhaps act hastily or harshly. Therefore *deliver* (free) *thyself*; do not rest until either the creditor gives up the bond or the debtor secures the debt in another way. Leave no stone unturned until you have agreed with your enemy and settled the matter (Mt 5:25), so that your obligation may not turn up again against you or your family.

3. But how are we to understand this? We are not to think it is unlawful in any case to put up money for what another person owes; it may be an act of justice or charity. Paul put up security for Onesimus (Phm 19). We may help set up a young person in business when we know him to be honest; we may give him credit by passing on a good word for him and so do him a great kindness without harming ourselves.

4. But everyone would be wise to keep out of debt as far as possible, for it is a burden. It ties you up with the cares of this world and possibly puts you into a dangerous position of doing wrong or suffering wrong. The *borrower is servant to the lender* (22:7) and makes himself indebted to this world. You should never put up more money for what someone else owed than what you yourself are both able and willing to pay, and can afford to pay without hurting your family.

Verses 6–11

In these verses Solomon addresses himself to the *sluggard* (lazy person), who loves his ease, lives a life of idleness, does not stick to anything, and especially is careless in the matter of religious faith. Solomon speaks:

1. By way of instruction (vv. 6–8). He sends him to school, for he must be trained. The sluggard is not willing to come to school to him—dreamy students never love alert teachers—and so the teacher has found another school for him, as lowly as he can desire. *Go to the ant*; "to the bee" is the reading of the Septuagint (a Greek version of the Old Testament). People are taught more than the beasts of the earth and made wiser than the birds of the air (Job 35:11), but they have become so corrupt that they may learn wisdom from the lowliest insects and be put to shame by them. When we notice the wonderful wisdom of the lower creatures, we must receive instruction for ourselves. By spiritualizing ordinary things, we may make the things of God more natural and accessible to us so that they may be part of our daily life. *Consider her ways* (v. 6). The sluggard is lazy because he does not consider. In particular, learn to *provide meat* (store provisions) *in summer* (v. 8). We must prepare for the future: we must not eat everything up and store nothing; at harvest time we are to put something aside to spend later. Save for winter, for needs and difficulties that may arise, and for old age; and much more should we do so in spiritual matters. In enjoying the means of grace, we are not to forget the times when we may lack them. In life we are to provide for death; in time we are to provide for eternity. Even *in summer*, when the weather is hot, the ant is busy *gathering food* (v. 8) and storing it. The ants do not take it easy or indulge in pleasure like grasshoppers, which sing and have fun in summer and then perish in winter. The ants help one another; if one has a grain of corn too big for it to carry home, its neighbors come to help. We would be wise to make the most of the season while that favors us. *Walk while you have the light* (Jn 12:35). The ant has *no guides* or *rulers* (v. 7), but acts by itself, following its natural instincts. We also have parents, teachers, ministers, and judges to remind us of our duty, to guide us in it.

2. By way of rebuke (vv. 9–11). In these verses:

2.1. He pleads with the sluggard: "*How long wilt thou sleep, O sluggard?* (v. 9). *When wilt thou* think it time to *arise?*" Sluggards should be roused in the duties of their particular calling as human beings and their general calling as Christians. "*How long wilt thou* waste thy time, and *when wilt thou be* a better manager? How long wilt thou* love thy ease, and *when wilt thou* learn to deny thyself, to make an effort in life? How long wilt thou* (v. 9) delay, put off, and waste opportunities, and *when wilt thou* stir thyself to do what thou hast to do, what you must do or be ruined forever?"

2.2. He exposes the frivolous excuses the sluggard makes for himself. When he awakes, he stretches himself and begs for more *sleep*, more *slumber*. He is snug and warm in bed and cannot bear to think about getting up, especially for work. He promises himself and his master that he wants only *a little* more *sleep, a little* more *slumber* (v. 10), and then he will get up and go to work. But he is deceiving himself; the more one indulges laziness, the stronger it grows. This is how great work is left undone: by being put off just a little longer from one day to the next. A little more sleep turns out to last for eternity.

2.3. He gives him fair warning of the fatal consequences of his laziness (v. 11). *Poverty and want* (v. 11) will certainly come to those who are lazy in their work. Those who leave their lives in a state of confusion will soon see them go to waste and rack and ruin. Spiritual poverty comes to those who are lazy in serving God. "It will leave you as naked as if you had been stripped by robbers on the highway," comments Bishop Patrick.

Verses 12–19

1. If lazy people are to be condemned when they do nothing, then much more are those condemned who contrive to do all the evil possible. It is a *naughty* (troublesome) *person* that is here spoken of, in Hebrew "a man of Belial." Such a man is *wicked*; he makes it his business to do evil, especially with his tongue, for he *walks* and works out his plots with a *froward* (corrupt) *mouth* (v. 12), by lying and perversity. He has the subtlety of the Serpent and carries out his conspiracies with a great deal of slyness (v. 13), *with his eyes, with his feet, with his fingers.* Those whom he uses as tools of his evil understand the corrupt meaning of a wink of the eye, a stamp of the feet, or the slightest movement of his fingers. He gives orders to do evil so that he may not be suspected. It is not so much ambition or greed that *is in his heart* as downright *frowardness* (v. 14), malice, and ill nature. He aims not so much at enriching or advancing himself as doing harm to those around him. *His calamity shall come*; disaster will overtake him, and *he shall be broken* (he will suddenly be destroyed); those who think up trouble for others will themselves see trouble come on them. *Suddenly shall he be broken*, to punish him for all the evil ways he has surprised people in the traps he has set for them.

2. Here is a list of the things that are especially offensive to God, all of which are generally to be found in people of Belial. God hates every sin, but there are some sins he hates especially, and all those mentioned here are ones that are harmful to our neighbor. We must hate in ourselves the things God hates.

2.1. Haughtiness and contempt of others—a *proud look* (v. 17). Pride is the first, because it is at the root of much sin. When it shows on the face, it testifies openly that people overvalue themselves and undervalue everyone around them, and this is especially hateful to God.

2.2. Falsehood and fraud and pretense. Next to a *proud look*, nothing is more detestable to God than *a lying tongue* (v. 17); nothing is more sacred than truth, and nothing is more necessary to good relationships than speaking the truth.

2.3. Cruelty and bloodthirstiness. The Devil was, from the beginning, a liar and a murderer (Jn 8:44), and therefore *hands that shed innocent blood* (v. 17) are, like *a lying tongue*, hateful to God, because they bear the Devil's image and serve him.

2.4. Cunning in plotting sin, *a heart* that dreams up evil plans and a mind that *devises wicked imaginations* (evil schemes) (v. 18). The more cunning and slyness in sin, the more detestable it is to God.

2.5. Vigor and diligence in pursuing sin—*feet that are swift in running to mischief* (in rushing into evil) (v. 18). The eagerness and hard work of sinners in their sinful pursuits may shame us who go about doing good so clumsily and unfeelingly.

2.6. Bearing false witness. There can be no greater insult to God, nor greater harm to our neighbor, than to knowingly give a false testimony.

2.7. Causing trouble between relatives and neighbors, using every possible evil means, not only to alienate people from one another, but also to stir up anger against one another. The God of love and peace hates *him that sows discord among brethren* (NIV: stirs up dissension among brothers) (v. 19).

Verses 20–35

Here is:

1. A general exhortation to remain loyal to the word of God and to take it as our guide in all our actions.

1.1. We must look on the word of God as both a light (v. 23) and a law (vv. 20, 23). It is a light, which our understanding must submit to; it *is a lamp* to our eyes to show us the way and give direction to our feet. The word of God reveals to us truths of eternal certainty. Scripture light is sure light. God's word is also a law, which our wills must submit to.

1.2. We must receive it as *our father's commandment* and *the law of our mother* (v. 20). It is God's command and his law. Our parents pointed us toward it and trained us to know and observe it. We do not believe God's word is true because they have said so—for we have tried it ourselves and find it comes from God—but we are indebted to them for commending it to us. The cautions, counsels, and commands our parents gave us agree with the word of God, and so we must be faithful to them.

1.3. We must keep the word of God and the good instructions our parents gave us from it. "*Keep thy father's commandment* (v. 20), keep it and never forsake it." We must never set them aside (v. 21): *Bind them continually* not only *upon thy hand*—as Moses had directed (Dt 6:8)—but also *upon thy heart*. Phylacteries tied on the hand were of no value at all excepting for prompting godly thoughts and affections in the heart. *Tie them about thy neck* (v. 21), literally, as an ornament "about your throat"; let them be a guard so that no forbidden fruit may be allowed to go in or any evil word allowed to go out through the throat. If we bind it continually on our hearts:

1.3.1. It will be our guide. We must follow its direction. "*When thou goest, it shall lead thee* (v. 22); it will lead you in the good and right way. It will say to you when you are about to turn aside, *This is the way; walk in it* (Isa 30:21). Let it be your rule, and then you will be led by the Spirit (Gal 5:18); he will be your guide and support."

1.3.2. It will be our guard: "*When thou sleepest* and art exposed to the evil powers of darkness, *it shall keep thee* (v. 22); you will be safe, and you will know you are." It will be our companion: "*When thou awakest* in the night and knowest not how to spend thy waking moments, *it shall talk with thee*, with pleasant meditations in the night watches. *When thou awakest* in the morning and art thinking over the work of the coming day, *it shall talk with thee* about it (v. 22) and help thee plan for the best" (Ps 1:2).

2. A particular warning against the sin of sexual immorality.

2.1. When we consider how prevalent this sin is, we will not be surprised that the warnings against it are repeated so often. "The corrections of discipline are *the way of life* for you because they are intended *to keep thee from the evil,* immoral *woman,* who will be certain death to you, to keep you from being lured by *the flattery of the tongue of a strange woman* (the smooth talk of a wayward woman), who pretends to love you but intends to ruin you." The greatest kindness we can do ourselves is to keep far away from this sin (v. 25): "*Lust not after her beauty,* not even *in thy heart,* for if you do, you have already *committed adultery with her there* (Mt 5:28). Don't talk about the charms of her face; *let her not take thee with her eyelids* (v. 25). Her looks are arrows and fiery darts; they call it a pleasing captivity, but it is a destructive one that is worse than slavery in Egypt."

2.2. Solomon here urges various arguments to back up this warning. It is a sin that makes men poor; it wastes their wealth and reduces them to beggars (v. 26): *By means of a whorish woman a man is brought to a piece of bread,* the prostitute reduces you to a loaf of bread. It threatens death; it kills men: *The adulteress will hunt for the precious* (prey upon your very) *life* (v. 26), perhaps intentionally, as Delilah did for Samson's. It brings guilt on the conscience. He that *touches his neighbour's wife,* with immodesty, cannot be *innocent* (v. 29). The bold and arrogant sinner says, "I may be able to sin but escape punishment." He might as well say, I will *take fire into my bosom and not burn my clothes* (v. 27). It is a much more scandalous sin than stealing (vv. 30–33). When Nathan wanted to convict David of the evil of his adultery, he did it using a parable about the most terrible theft, which in David's judgment deserved to be punished by death (2Sa 12:5), and he then showed him that his sin was *more exceedingly sinful* than that. It brings greater shame on a man's reason, for he cannot excuse it, as a thief may, by saying that it was to satisfy his hunger (v. 30). Therefore *whoever commits adultery with a woman lacks understanding* (v. 32) and deserves to be stigmatized as a downright fool. It will be *a wound* to his good name and a *dishonour* to his family, and although its guilt may be done away with by repentance, its *reproach* never will be. David's sin in the case of Uriah not only was a perpetual blemish on his own character but also gave occasion to the enemies of the Lord to blaspheme his name too. A man who touches his neighbor's wife with inappropriate familiarity gives his neighbor occasion for jealousy, and much more he who defiles her; and however well he might think he had kept it a secret, his sin could then be *discovered by the waters of jealousy* (Nu 5:17–29).

CHAPTER 7

The scope of this chapter, like that of several of the previous chapters, is to warn young men against the sinful

desires of the flesh. Solomon remembered what adverse consequences those desires had led to in his father, and perhaps he also found himself, and perceived his son, to be devoted to them, and so he thought he could never say enough to dissuade men from them. In this chapter we have: 1. A general exhortation to subject our minds to the principles and government of the word of God, as a sovereign antidote against this sin (vv. 1–5). 2. A particular presentation of the great danger (vv. 6–23). 3. A serious warning to beware of all approaches toward this sin (vv. 24–27). We should all pray, Lord, lead us not into this temptation (Mt 6:13).

Verses 1–5

These verses are an introduction to Solomon's warning against sexual immorality, much the same as that in 6:20–35, and ending (v. 5), as that earlier introduction did (6:24), "*to keep* you from the adulterous woman." He speaks in God's name, for it is God's commandments that we are to *keep,* his *words,* his *law.* We must keep his word as our life: *Keep my commandments and live* (v. 2); keep *my law as the apple of thy eye* (v. 2). A little thing can hurt the eye, and so nature has guarded it well. We pray, with David, that God would keep us as the apple of his eye (Ps 17:8), that our lives and comforts may be precious in his sight; and they will be so (Zec 2:8) if we see his law as similarly precious and are afraid of disobeying it even slightly. "*Bind them upon thy fingers*; let them be precious to you; look on them as the *signet* ring *on thy right hand* (Jer 22:24); wear them continually as your wedding ring, the badge of your engagement to God." Look on the word of God as honoring you, as a badge of your dignity. *Write them upon the table of thy heart* (v. 3), as we say that the names of the friends we dearly love are written on our hearts. "*Say unto wisdom, Thou art my sister,* whom I dearly love and delight in; *and call understanding thy kinswoman,* to whom you are closely related, and for whom you have a pure affection; call her your close friend." We must become familiar with the word of God, as our defense and armor, to keep us *from the strange* (adulterous) *woman,* from sin, particularly from the sin of sexual immorality (v. 5).

Verses 6–23

Here Solomon backs up his warning against the sin of sexual immorality by telling a story about a young man who was to all intents and purposes ruined by the enticements of an adulterous woman. Such a story would be a suitable subject for the immoral and ungodly playwrights of our time to turn into a play, and with them the prostitute would be a heroine; nothing would be so entertaining to the audience as her skill in beguiling the young man. Her conquests would be celebrated as the triumphs of wit and love, and the comedy would conclude very pleasantly; and every young man who saw it acted out would fervently want to be picked up like that. This is how *fools make a mock at sin* (14:9). But Solomon here relates it—and all who are wise and good understand it—as a very sad story. The brazenness of the adulterous woman is very justly looked on with the greatest indignation, and the weak young man with great sympathy. It is thought to be a parable, or imaginary case, but I have little doubt it was true, and is still too often true.

Solomon was a judge and, as such, scrutinized the conduct of his subjects. But here he writes as a minister, a prophet, one who is a watchman by office, to sound the warning, so that we may not be ignorant of Satan's devices, but may know where to redouble our guard.

1. The person tempted was *a young man* (v. 7). Evil desires are called *youthful lusts* (2Ti 2:22). Young people should especially strengthen their resolutions against this sin. He was a young man *void of understanding* (v. 7), who went out into the world lacking the principles of wisdom and the fear of God that he should have had. He went out to sea without ballast, without a pilot, ropes, or compass. He kept bad company. He was sauntering about with nothing to do, *passing through the street* (v. 8) as one who did not know what to do with himself. One of the sins of corrupt Sodom was *abundance of idleness* (Eze 16:49). He walked about at night. Having fellowship with the unfruitful works of darkness (Eph 5:11), he began to move *in the twilight in the evening* (v. 9). He steered his course toward the house of one who he thought would welcome him and whom he might have fun with; he went *near her corner*, the *way to her house* (v. 8), against Solomon's advice (5:8), *Come not nigh the door of her house.*

2. The person tempting was not a common prostitute but a married woman (v. 19). Among her neighbors she was not suspected of any such evil, but in the *twilight of the evening* (v. 9), when her husband was away, she was detestably brazen. She has the *attire of a harlot* (v. 10), gaudy and flaunting. She is *subtle of heart* (v. 10), knows all the tricks in the book on how to get her way, knows how to use all her caresses to serve her own evil purposes. *She is loud and stubborn* (v. 11), talkative and self-willed, noisy and troublesome, willful and headstrong, refusing to accept any advice, much less rebuke, from husband or parents, ministers or friends. She is *a daughter of Belial* (1Sa 1:16), one who cannot tolerate any discipline. She is all for gadding about, changing place and company. She is here, there, and everywhere, except where she should be. She *lies in wait at every corner* (v. 12) to pick up any man she can prey on. Virtue seems a burden to those who are not content at home.

3. She met the young flame. Perhaps she knew him; however, she knew by the way he walked that he was the kind of man she wanted. She therefore *caught him about* the neck and *kissed* him, against all rules of modesty (v. 13), and *with an impudent* (brazen) *face* invited him not only to *her house* but also to *her bed.*

3.1. She invited him to dine with her (vv. 14–15): *I have peace offerings* (fellowship offerings) *with me.* By doing this, she gives him to understand that she is surrounded by so many blessings that she can offer fellowship offerings as a sign of joy and thankfulness; so he need not fear having his pocket picked. She has gone that day to the temple and is as well respected there as anyone who worships in the courts of the Lord. She has paid her vows and, as she thinks, made everything right with God Almighty, and so she can launch out on a new set of sins. It is sad that a show of godliness should shelter iniquity. The Pharisees uttered long prayers so that they could more plausibly continue their greedy and troublesome schemes. According to the Law, the greatest part of the flesh of the fellowship offerings was returned to those bringing the offerings, to feast on with their friends (Lev 7:15). "Come," she says, "come home with me, for I have enough entertainment, and only need some good company to help me enjoy it." She pretends to have a very great devotion for him beyond her affection for any other man: "Because I have a good supper on the table, *I came forth to meet thee*, for no friend in the world will be so welcome to it as you are (v. 15).

3.2. She invited him to lie with her. They will sit down to eat and drink, and then get up to play (Ex 32:6), to behave immorally. The bed *is decked with coverings of tapestry* and *carved works* (v. 16). The sheets are of *fine linen of Egypt* (v. 16). The bed is *perfumed* with the sweetest scents (v. 17). Come, therefore, and *let us take our fill of love* (v. 18). Does she say, "Of *love*?" She means, "Of *lust*"; it is a pity that the name of love should be abused in this way. True love comes from heaven.

3.3. She anticipated the objection he might make. "Don't worry," she says, "the *good man is not at home*" (v. 19); she does not call him her *husband*, but "the *good man* of the house, whom I am tired of." But might he not return quickly? No; "he has *gone a long journey* (v. 19) and cannot return suddenly; he *appointed the day* (v. 20) of his return, and he never comes home sooner than he says. He has taken a bag of money with (v. 20) him, either to buy goods—and then he will not return until he has spent it all—or to revel." Whether justly or not, she implies he is a bad husband; this is how she represents him, because she has decided to be a bad wife and must have that as an excuse. This is often suggested without good reason, but it is never a sufficient excuse.

4. She was successful in promising the young man everything that was pleasant, and impunity in enjoying it all (v. 21). It seems that although the youth was very simple, he had no malicious intentions; otherwise a word, a call, or a wink would have been enough, and there would have been no need for all this talk. But although he did not intend any such thing as he proposed—though in fact something in his conscience opposed it—yet *with her much fair speech she caused him to yield.* His corruptions finally triumphed over his convictions. *With the flattery of her lips she forced him*; he could not close his ears against such a charmer, and surrendered. Solomon here looks on this foolish young man with compassion when he sees him follow the adulterous woman. He gives him up as ruined. Going without his breastplate (Eph 6:14; 1Th 5:8), he will receive the wound of death (v. 23). What makes his case more pitiful is that he himself is not aware of his misery and danger; he goes on laughing to his ruin.

Verses 24–27

Here is the application of the story: "*Hearken to me therefore*, and not to such seducers (v. 24); listen to a father, not to an enemy. *Let not thy heart decline to her ways* (v. 25); never leave the paths of goodness. Do not only keep your feet from those ways, but do not even let your heart incline to them. Let reason, conscience, and the fear of God rule in your heart; restrain the inclinations of your physical appetite." Thousands of victims have been ruined by this sin, and they are not only weak and simple youths, such as the one of whom Solomon speaks here; *many strong men* also *have been slain by her* (v. 26). Therefore *stand in awe and sin not* (Ps 4:4).

CHAPTER 8

The word of God has wisdom. 1. Divine revelation is the word and wisdom of God, and so is the pure and undefiled religion that is built on that revelation (Jas 1:27); Solomon here speaks about that (vv. 1–21). By it, God instructs, directs, and blesses people. 2. The Redeemer is the eternal Word and wisdom, the Logos (Jn 1:1). He is the Wisdom that speaks to the people in the first part of this chapter. All divine revelation passes through his hand and centers on him, but it is about him as the personal Wisdom, the second person of the Godhead, that Solomon speaks in the second part (vv. 22–31). He concludes with a repeated command to pay attention to the voice of God in his word (vv. 32–36).

Verses 1–11

1. The things revealed are easily known, for they *belong to us and to our children* (Dt 29:29) and are declared in some measure by the works of creation (Ps 19:1), more fully by human conscience and the eternal reasons and rules of good and evil, but most clearly by Moses and the prophets. The commands of wisdom:

1.1. Are declared aloud (v. 1): *Does not Wisdom cry?* Yes, she calls out and does not hold back (Isa 58:1). The curses and blessings were read out with a loud voice by the Levites (Dt 27:14). People's own hearts sometimes speak aloud to them; there are clamors of conscience, as well as whispers.

1.2. Are declared from the heights (v. 2): *She stands in the top* of high places; it was from the top of Mount Sinai that the Law was given, and Christ explained it in his Sermon on the Mount. Wisdom speaks openly; truth seeks no dark corners, but gladly appeals to the light.

1.3. Are declared *in the places of concourse*, in noisy streets (1:21), where many people are gathered together. Wisdom's revelations and directions are given to everyone.

1.4. Are declared where they are most needed and so are made known *in the places of the paths* (v. 2), where many roads meet. The foolish person *knows not how to go to the city* (Ecc 10:15), so Wisdom stands ready to direct them. Wisdom stands *at the gates, at the entry of the city* (v. 3), ready to tell them where the seer's house is (1Sa 9:18). In fact, wisdom follows people into their own houses and calls out to them *at the coming in at the doors* (v. 3), saying, *Peace be to this house* (Lk 10:5).

1.5. Are spoken to us: "*Unto you, O men! I call* (v. 4), not to angels—they do not need these instructions—not to demons—they are beyond the hope offered in them—not to wild animals—they cannot understand them—but 'to you, O people.'" They are intended to make people wise (v. 5); they are calculated not only for people who are capable of wisdom, but for all sinners, all fallen, foolish people who need it and are ruined without it: "*O you simple ones, understand wisdom.* Even though you are simple, Wisdom will undertake to give *you an understanding heart.*"

2. The things revealed are worthy of full acceptance (1Ti 1:15). They are *excellent things* (v. 6), literally, "princely things." Things that relate to an eternal God, an immortal soul, and an eternal state must be *excellent things*. They are *right things* (v. 6), *all in righteousness* (v. 8), and there is *nothing froward* (crooked) *or perverse in them*. They contain nothing that puts any hardship on us, nothing that puts us under any undue restraint, nothing that is inconsistent with the dignity and liberty of human nature. They are of unquestionable truth. *My mouth shall speak truth* (v. 7). Every word of God is true. His word to us is *yea, and amen* (2Co 1:20); let ours, therefore, never be *yea and nay* (2Co 1:18–20). They are all *plain*, not hard to understand. If the book is sealed, it is so to those who are willingly ignorant.

3. The right knowledge of those things is to be preferred to all the wealth of this world (vv. 10–11): *Receive my instruction, and not silver. Wisdom is* in itself—and so must be in our reckoning—*better than rubies* (v. 11). It will be of greater value to us; it will be a better ornament than jewels.

Verses 12–21

Wisdom here is Christ, *in whom are hidden all the treasures of wisdom and knowledge* (Col 2:3); it is Christ in the word and Christ in the heart, not only Christ revealed *to* us, but Christ revealed *in* us.

1. Divine wisdom gives people good minds (v. 12): *I Wisdom dwell with prudence*, not with worldly politics but with true discretion. Wisdom dwells with prudence, for prudence is both the product of religious faith and an ornament to it. More *witty inventions* (NIV: knowledge and discretion) are *found* (v. 12) with the help of Scripture, both to correctly understand God's providences and to do good in our generation, than were ever discovered by the learning of the philosophers or the politics of our leaders. We may apply the verse to Christ himself. We had *found out many witty inventions*, or plans, that would lead to our destruction; he found one to restore us.

2. Divine wisdom gives people good hearts (v. 13). True religious faith, consisting in *the fear of the Lord*, teaches people:

- To hate all sin, as displeasing to God and destructive to the soul: *The fear of the Lord is to hate evil, the evil way*.
- To particularly hate pride and passion, those two common and dangerous sins.

3. Divine wisdom has a great influence on public affairs (v. 14). Christ, as God, has strength and wisdom; as Redeemer, he is *the wisdom of God and the power of God* (1Co 1:24). He is the Wonderful Counselor (Isa 9:6) and gives grace, which is *sound wisdom*. True religious faith gives people the best counsel in all difficult cases and helps make their way plain. And so Wisdom says, *By me kings reign* (vv. 15–16). They reign by him and so should reign for him. Religious faith is very much the strength and support of civil government; it teaches subjects their duty, and *so by it kings reign* over them more easily; it teaches kings their duty, and so *by it kings reign as* they ought; they *decree justice* (v. 15) as long as they *rule in the fear of God* (2Sa 23:3). Good rulers are those in whom religious faith rules.

4. Divine wisdom will make all those who receive it happy.

4.1. They will be happy in the love of Christ, for it is he who says, *I love those that love me* (v. 17). "*Those that seek me early* (v. 17), that is, who seek me passionately, who seek me before anything else, who begin to seek me early in the days of their youth (Ecc 12:1)—such people will find what they seek." Christ will be theirs, and they will be his (SS 2:16).

4.2. They will have as much riches and honor as infinite Wisdom sees good to give them (v. 18). Those riches are *riches and righteousness* (v. 18), riches gained honestly, not by fraud and oppression but in regular ways, and they are used charitably, for alms are called *righteousness* (Mt 6:1, where the word translated "alms" is one that is elsewhere translated "righteousness"; Ps 112:9; 2Co 9:9). Therefore they are *durable* (enduring) *riches* (v. 18). That which is gained well will last well and will be left to the children's children, and what is well spent in works of godliness and kindness is invested at the best interest and so will retain its value. Those who receive wisdom will have what is infinitely better even if they do not have riches and honor in this world (v. 19): "*My fruit is better than gold* and will be used in a better way; it will be of greater value within smaller limits, and *my revenue* (what I yield) is *better than the choicest silver*, and will be more useful."

4.3. They will be happy in the grace of God now; that will be their guide in the good way they follow (v. 20). This is the fruit of wisdom that is *better than gold, than fine gold*; it *leads us in the way of righteousness*. It shows us the way and goes before us in that way, which is the way that God wants us to walk in and which will certainly bring us to our desired end.

4.4. They will be happy in the glory of God in heaven (v. 21). It is a happiness that exists by itself and stands alone, without the accidental supports of outward circumstances. Spiritual and eternal things are the only real and substantial things. Joy in God is substantial; it is solid and well grounded. The promises are the guarantees that belong to those who love God, Christ is their security, and both are substantial. This happiness is satisfying; it will not only fill their hands but also *fill their treasures* (v. 21). The things of this world may fill people's bellies (Ps 17:14), but not their treasuries, for they cannot keep *goods* secure *for many years* (Lk 12:19).

Verses 22–31

Wisdom here has personal properties and actions; and that intelligent, divine person can be none other than the Son of God himself, to whom the main things here said about wisdom are attributed in other Scriptures. We find the best explanation of these verses in the first four verses of John's Gospel. *In the beginning was the Word* (Jn 1:1). Concerning the Son of God notice:

1. His divine nature and distinct personhood, one with the Father and of the same essence, was *a person in himself*, whom *the Lord possessed* (v. 22), *who was set up* (v. 23), *was brought forth* (vv. 24–25), and *was by him* (v. 30), for he was *the express image of his person* (Heb 1:3).

2. His eternity; he was begotten by the Father, for *the Lord possessed* (v. 22) him, as his own Son, his beloved Son, took him *in his bosom* (Jn 1:18), embraced him; he was *brought forth as the only begotten of the Father* (Jn 1:14), and this *before all worlds*. The Word was eternal; it existed before the world was created, before the beginning of time, and so it must follow that the Word was from eternity. *The Lord possessed him in the beginning of his way* (v. 22), the beginning of his eternal counsels, for those were *before his works*. This way had no beginning, for God's purposes are eternal, as he is, and God speaks to us in our own language. Wisdom explains herself (v. 23): *I was set up from everlasting, before the earth was*, and before human beings were made, before the sea was (v. 24), *when there were no depths* (oceans) in which the waters were gathered together, *no fountains* from which those waters might rise, none of the waters on which the Spirit of God moved to produce the visible creation (Ge 1:2). Before the mountains existed, the eternal Word *brought forth*. He existed before the inhabited parts of the world, which people cultivate (v. 26), *the fields* in the valleys, to which the mountains are as a wall, being *the highest part of the dust of the world*. This latter expression means "the first part of the dust," according to some, the atoms that make up the different parts of the world; or it may be read, "the main part of the dust," and understood to refer to human beings, the main part of the dust, dust given life and refined. The eternal Word was in existence before human beings were made, for *in him was the life of men* (Jn 1:4).

3. His activity in making the world. He not only existed before the world but also was present—not as a spectator but as the architect—when the world was made. *By him God made the worlds* (Eph 3:9; Heb 1:2; Col 1:16). When on the first day of Creation God said, *Let there be light* (Ge 1:3), and produced it with a word, this eternal Wisdom was that almighty Word: then *I was there, when he prepared the heavens* (v. 27). He was no less active when on the second day God stretched out the vast expanse of *the firmament,*

setting that as *a compass upon the face of the depth*, when he marked out the horizon on the face of the deep (v. 27; Job 26:10), surrounded it on all sides with that canopy or curtain. He was also employed in the third day's work, when the *waters above the heavens* were gathered together by *establishing the clouds above*, and those under the heavens by *strengthening the fountains of the deep*, which send out those waters (v. 28), and by keeping the boundaries of the sea, which contains those waters (v. 29).

4. The infinite delight that the Father had in him, and he in the Father (v. 30): *I was by him, as one brought up with him*. As he was brought forth by eternal generation by the Father, so also by an eternal counsel he was brought up with him. The Son did what he saw the Father doing (Jn 5:19); he pleased his Father, did according to the commandments he received from his Father, and all this *as one brought up with him* (v. 30). He was *daily his Father's delight—my elect, in whom my soul delighteth*, says God (Isa 42:1). This may be understood to refer to the satisfaction they had in each other with reference to the great work of redemption.

5. The gracious concern he had for the human race (v. 31). Wisdom *rejoiced*, but not so much in the rich products of the earth as in the redemption and salvation of human beings living on the earth.

Verses 32–36

The application of Wisdom's speech is intended to bring us all to a complete submission to the laws of religious faith and to put right what is wrong in our hearts and lives. Here is:

1. An exhortation to listen to and obey the voice of Wisdom, to discern the voice of Christ, as the sheep know the shepherd's voice (Jn 10:3, 14, 16, 27). "*Hearken unto me, O you children!* (v. 32). Read the written word, sit under the word that is preached, bless God for both, and hear him speaking to you in both." Let Wisdom's children justify Wisdom (Mt 11:19) by listening to her. Hear Wisdom's words with a willing heart (v. 33): "*Hear instruction, and refuse it not*, either as something you think you do not need or as something you do not like; it is offered to you as a kindness, and it is at your peril if you refuse it." We must listen to Wisdom so as to *watch daily at her gates* (v. 34), as beggars receive alms, as clients and patients receive advice, and as servants wait with humble patience *at the posts of her doors* (v. 34). We must watch and wait as Christ's hearers did; they hung on his words (Lk 19:48) and *came early in the morning to hear him* (Lk 21:38).

2. An assurance of happiness to all those who do listen to and obey Wisdom. They will find what they seek (Mt 7:7). But will it change their lives for the better if they find it? Yes (v. 35): *Whoso finds me finds life*, that is, all happiness, all the good that they need or can desire. Christ is Wisdom, and those who find Christ *find life*, for Christ is life to all believers.

3. The condemnation passed on all who reject Wisdom and her proposals (v. 36). They destroy themselves, and Wisdom will not prevent them, because they have disregarded all her advice. They *sin against Christ* (1Co 8:12); they defy his authority and act against all the purposes of his life and death. Those who offend Christ do the greatest wrong to themselves; they *wrong their own souls* (v. 36). *O Israel! thou hast destroyed thyself* (Hos 13:9).

CHAPTER 9

Christ and sin are rivals for the human soul. The intention of this description is to set before us life and death, good and evil (Dt 30:15, 19); and there need be no more than a fair stating of the case to make us decide which of those we are to choose. 1. In the name of Wisdom, Christ invites us to accept his offer and so to enter into fellowship with him (vv. 1–6). Having foretold the different responses to his invitation (vv. 7–9), he briefly shows what he requires from us (v. 10) and what he intends for us (v. 11), and then leaves it to us to choose what we will do (v. 12). 2. Sin, in the character of a foolish woman, tries to persuade us to accept what she has prepared for us (vv. 13–16), pretending it is very delicious (v. 17). But Solomon tells us what the reckoning will be (v. 18).

Verses 1–12

Wisdom is here introduced as a magnificent and generous queen, very great and very generous; the Word of God is this Wisdom, in which God makes known his goodwill toward people; God the Word is this Wisdom, to whom the Father has committed all judgment (Jn 5:22). The word is plural, *Wisdoms*, for in Christ are hidden treasures of wisdom (Col 2:3). Notice:

1. The rich provision Wisdom has made to receive all those who want to be her disciples. This is presented by using the metaphor of a lavish feast.

1.1. A stately palace is provided (v. 1). Wisdom does not find a house spacious enough for all her guests and has therefore specially built one, and has *hewn out her seven pillars*. Heaven is the house Wisdom has built to receive all her guests who are called to the marriage supper of the Lamb (Rev 19:9); that is her Father's house, where there are many mansions, and to which she has gone to prepare places for us (Jn 14:2).

1.2. A wonderful feast is prepared (v. 2): *She has killed her beasts; she has mingled her wine*. The first part means literally, "She has killed her sacrifice"; it is a lavish feast, but it is also a sacred feast of sacrifice. *She has* completely *furnished her table* with all the delights a soul could desire—righteousness and grace, peace and joy, the assurances of God's love, the encouragements of the Spirit, and all the promises of eternal life.

2. The gracious invitation she has given, not to some particular friends but to everyone in general: *She has sent forth her maidens* (v. 3). The ministers of the Gospel are commissioned to give notice of the preparations God has made in the eternal covenant for all those who are willing to fulfill its terms, and those are to be absolutely pure, not corrupting themselves or the word of God, and faithfully observing their orders. They are to call on everyone they come across, even in *the highways and hedges*, to come and feast with Wisdom, for *all things are now ready* (Lk 14:23). She herself *cries upon* (calls from) *the highest places of the city* (v. 3), as one who is passionately concerned about people's welfare. The invitation is given: *Whoso is simple* and *wants* (lacks) *understanding* (v. 4). Wisdom invites such people because what she has to give is what they need most. Those who are simple are invited so they may become wise. Let those who lack, literally, "a heart," come here, and they will gain one. Her preparations are designed to heal the mind. We are invited to Wisdom's house: *Turn in hither* (v. 4). I say *we* are, for who is there among us who need not acknowledge they have the character of the invited, who are simple and lack judgment? We are invited to her table (v. 5): *Come, eat of my bread*, that is, taste the true pleasures that are to be found in the knowledge and fear of God. Acting on the promises of the Gospel in faith, we feed and feast on the provisions Christ has made for poor souls. But before coming, we must break away from all bad company: "Forsake the

foolish, do not associate with them." The first step toward goodness is to avoid evil, and so avoid evildoers. "Live not a mere animal life, but the fully human life. *Live* and you *shall live*; live spiritually, and you will live eternally" (Eph 5:14).

3. The instructions Wisdom gives to the ministers and others who are endeavoring where they are to serve her intentions. Their work must be not only to tell in general what food and medicine have been prepared for souls but also to address themselves to particular individuals, tell them their faults, *reprove, rebuke* (vv. 7–8). They must instruct them how to put right what is wrong—*teach* (v. 9). The word of God is intended—and so is the ministry of that word—*for reproof, for correction, and for instruction in righteousness* (2Ti 3:16). The ministers would meet with some *scorners* and *wicked men* who would mock the messengers of the Lord and abuse them. And although they were not forbidden to invite those simple ones to Wisdom's house, they were still advised not to pursue the invitation by rebuking them. Thus Christ said of the Pharisees, *Let them alone* (Mt 15:14). Wisdom's ministers would meet with others who were wise, good, and just; we thank God that not everyone is a mocker. We meet with some people who are wise enough to be willing and glad to be taught. If need be, we must rebuke them, for wise people are not so completely wise that there is nothing in them that does not need correction. The more wisdom a person has, the more they should want to have their weaknesses shown them. With our rebukes we must also *give instruction* and *teach* them (v. 9). It is as great an example of wisdom to receive correction as it is to give it. A wise person will be made wiser by correction; they *will increase in learning* (v. 9), grow in knowledge, and so grow in grace (2Pe 3:18).

4. The instructions Wisdom gives to those who have been invited, which her servants must instill in them.

4.1. The servants must let them know what true wisdom consists of (v. 10). The *fear of God is the beginning of wisdom*. A reverence for God's majesty and a fear of his wrath are the first steps toward true religious faith. *The knowledge of holy* things (the word is plural) *is understanding*, the things concerning the service of God—those are called *holy things*—the things that concern our own sanctification.

4.2. They must let them know what will be the benefits of this wisdom (v. 11): "*By me thy days shall be multiplied*. Wisdom will contribute to physical health, and so *the years of thy life* on earth *shall be increased*. It will bring you to heaven, and there the *years of thy life shall be increased without end*."

4.3. They must let them know what will be the consequences of their choosing or refusing this fair offer (v. 12). "If you are wise, you will be wise for yourself; you will gain from it; Wisdom will not gain from it. If you scorn Wisdom's offer, you alone will *bear it*—bear the blame and the loss."

Verses 13–18

We are told here how hard the tempter works to seduce unwary souls to follow the paths of sin. Notice:

1. Who is the tempter—a *foolish woman* (v. 13), *Folly* herself, in opposition to Wisdom. I take this *foolish woman* to refer especially to worldly, ungodly pleasure (v. 13), for that defiles the mind and deadens the conscience. This tempter is here described as ignorant: *She is simple and knows nothing* (v. 13), that is, she has no sufficient and solid reason to offer. *Whoredom* (prostitution), *and wine, and new wine, take away the heart* (Hos 4:11);

they infatuate people and make them foolish. The less she has to offer that is reasonable, the more violent and urgent she is, and she behaves in a brazen manner. She *is clamorous* and noisy (v. 13). *She sits at the door of her house* (v. 14) watching to see whom she can prey on. *She sits on a seat*—literally, "on a throne"—*in the high places of the city*, as if she had authority. Perhaps she influences more people by pretending to be fashionable than by pretending to be pleasant.

2. Who are the tempted—young people who have been well brought up. They are *passengers that go right on their ways*, those who pass by straight on their way (v. 15), who have been trained in the ways of religious faith and goodness and who set out very hopefully and well, and are not like that young man in 7:8 who was *going the way to her house*. Folly sets traps for such people and uses all her charms to corrupt them. She calls them *simple* and *wanting understanding* (lacking judgment) (v. 16), and so she encourages them to come to her school so that they might be set free from the restraints and formalities of their religious faith.

3. What the temptation is (v. 17): *Stolen waters are sweet*. She tempts them with water and bread, whereas Wisdom invites people to the animals she has killed and the wine she has mixed. Bread and water are, however, acceptable enough to those who are hungry and thirsty, and this is claimed to be more *sweet* and *pleasant* than usual, for it is *stolen water and bread eaten in secret*, with a fear of being discovered. The pleasures of prohibited, sinful desires are boasted of as more enjoyable than those of rightly ordered love, and dishonest gain is preferred to what is gained justly.

4. An effective antidote against the temptation (v. 18). Those who are drawn aside by these enticements through a lack of judgment are led on, ignorantly, to their own inevitable ruin: *He knows not that the dead are there*, that those who live in pleasure are *dead while they live, dead in trespasses and sins* (Eph 2:1). *Her guests*, who are treated with these *stolen waters* (v. 17), are taken prisoner by Satan at his will.

CHAPTER 10

Up to this point we have been standing in the porch or introduction to the proverbs; they begin in earnest here. They are short but significant sentences: most of them are couplets, two sentences in one verse, concisely illustrating each other. It is rare, however, that there is any logical link between the verses, much less any thread through the whole address, and so in these chapters we do not need to attempt to reduce the contents to their various headings. Their scope is to set before us good and evil, blessings and curses (Dt 30:15, 19). Many of the proverbs in this chapter relate to controlling the tongue.

Verse 1

Solomon speaks to us as children and observes here how much the comfort of parents—natural, political, and ecclesiastical parents—depends on the good behavior of those they are responsible for. Children are to behave wisely and live up to their good upbringing so that they may make the hearts of their parents glad. It adds to the comfort of young people that they are doing something toward rewarding their parents for all the care they have given them and that they will give pleasure to their parents in old age (Ecc 12:1). And it is the duty of parents to be glad about their children's wisdom and doing good.

Verses 2–3

These two verses have the same meaning. Wealth that people gain unjustly will do them no good, because God will blight it: *Treasures of wickedness profit nothing* (v. 2). When profit and loss come to be balanced out, the profit gained from the treasures will by no means balance out the loss sustained by the evil (Mt 16:26). They have gained no good for the soul. God *casts away the substance of the wicked* (v. 3). We often see what has been gathered together by human injustice scattered by the justice of God. What is honestly gained will be useful, for God will bless it. *Righteousness delivers from death* (v. 2), that is, wealth that is rightly gained, kept, and used fulfills the purpose of wealth, which is to keep us alive and be our defense.

Verse 4

Those *who deal with a slack hand*, with lazy hands, who are careless and negligent in their work, are likely to *become poor*. It may be read to refer to those "who deal with a deceitful hand"; those who think they can make themselves rich by fraud will in the end make themselves poor, not only by bringing the curse of God on what they have but also by forfeiting their reputation with other people. Those who are diligent and honest, who are careful about how they live, are likely to increase in what they have. This is true in spiritual matters as well as in worldly matters. Laziness and hypocrisy lead to spiritual poverty, but those who are *fervent in spirit, serving the Lord* (Ro 12:11), are likely to be *rich in faith* (Jas 2:5) and *rich in good works* (1Ti 6:18).

Verse 5

Those who make the most of the opportunities given them, who provide for later life while provision is available, *gather* crops *in summer*, which is the time of harvest. He who does so *is a wise son*. He acts wisely for his parents, whom, if need be, he should maintain. *He who sleeps*, who idles away time and neglects work, especially *who sleeps in harvest* when he should be storing up for winter, *is a son that causes shame*. He is foolish; he prepares shame for himself when winter comes. Those who gain wisdom in the days of their youth *gather in summer*, and they will enjoy the prestige from their hard work, but those who waste the days of youth will bear the shame of laziness in later years.

Verse 6

Many and various blessings will come from above and remain visibly on the heads of good people. Blessings will rest on their head as a crown to dignify them and as a helmet to protect them. *The mouth of the wicked is covered* with *violence*. Their mouths will be shut up with shame for the violence they have done.

Verse 7

When the days of both the righteous and the wicked are fulfilled, they must die. There is no visible difference between their bodies in the grave, but there is a vast difference in the spiritual world between the souls of the one and those of the other. Blessed people leave behind them blessed memories. God will honor those who honor him (Ps 112:3, 6, 9). It is also part of the duty of the survivors to give such honor: "Let the memory of the just be blessed," as the Jews read it, and it is a rule of theirs to name an eminently just man who is dead without adding, "Let his memory be blessed." Bad people are and will be forgotten, or spoken of with contempt.

Verse 8

The obedient will *receive commandments*; they will consider it a privilege to receive direction and be told their duty. They are wise in this respect; those who are teachable are *wise in heart*, and they will stand and be established. The disobedient, who do not want to be directed, who will not endure any discipline, who will not be taught, and who accept no advice, are fools, for they act against themselves and their own interests. They are commonly *prating* (chattering) *fools*, full of big words, but actually full of nonsense, boasting about themselves.

Verse 9

A person's integrity will be his security: *He that walks uprightly* toward God and other people, who is faithful in both and means what he says, *walks surely.* He is safe under divine protection. He may go his way with humble boldness, strengthened against the temptations of Satan, the troubles of the world, and the reproaches of human beings. A person's dishonesty will be his shame: *He that perverts his way*, who makes a pretense of his relationship with God and other people, though for a time he may disguise himself and be thought genuine, *shall be known* for what he is.

Verse 10

Trouble is here said to come on crafty, self-deceiving sinners: Such a person is *he that winks with the eye* as if he took no notice of you when he is really watching for an opportunity to do you harm, who makes signs to his accomplices to help carry out his evil plans, *causes sorrow* both to others and to himself. *A prating fool shall fall*, as was said before (v. 8). But his case is the less dangerous of the two. He does not create so much sorrow to others as *he that winks with his eyes.* The dog that barks is not always the dog that bites.

Verse 11

Notice how diligent a good man is in communicating his goodness: *His mouth*, the outlet of his mind, *is a well of life.* It is a constant spring from which good words come that build up others (Eph 4:29). Notice how diligent a bad man is in concealing his badness in order to do harm with it: *The mouth of the wicked covers violence*; he disguises the trouble he intends to make by professing friendship. *Violence covers the mouth of the wicked*; what he gains by violence will be violently taken away from him (Job 5:4–5).

Verse 12

The great troublemaker is hatred. Even where there is no clear occasion for conflict, *hatred* still looks for one to *stir it up.* The most spiteful, ill-natured people are those who take pleasure in setting their neighbors at war with one another by telling tales, making false allegations or misrepresentations, or blowing the sparks of a conflict into flames, over which they warm their hands with an unaccountable pleasure. The great peacemaker is *love*, which *covers all sins*, that is, the offenses in relationships where there is discord. Love does not declare the offense and make it worse, but conceals it and extenuates it as far as it can be concealed and extenuated. Love will excuse the offense; when we are able to say no ill was intended, that it was an oversight, and that we love our friend nevertheless, our love covers our own offense. Love will also overlook the offense that is given us, thus covering that, and this is how conflict is prevented.

Verse 13

Wisdom and grace are the honor of good people. It is commendable to have wisdom, but it is even more honorable to be instrumental in making others wise. Foolishness and sin are the shame of bad people: *A rod is for the back of him that is void of understanding*—"of the person who lacks a heart." Such people expose themselves to the lashes of their own conscience, to the censures of the judge, and to the righteous judgments of God.

Verse 14

Notice:

1. It is the wisdom of the wise that they treasure up useful knowledge, which will lead to their preservation. The reason *wisdom* is *found in their lips* (v. 13) is that it is stored in their hearts.

2. It is the foolishness of fools that they lay up trouble in their hearts. Their *mouth is near destruction* (v. 14), having the *sharp arrows of bitter words* (Ps 64:3) always ready to shoot about.

Verse 15

Rich people think they are happy because they are rich, but that is their mistake: *The rich man's wealth is*, in his own thinking, *his strong city*, whereas it is completely insufficient to protect him from the worst evils. Poor people think they are ruined because they are poor, but that is their mistake. Their poverty depresses their spirits, whereas a person may live very comfortably, even though they have only a little to live on, if they are content, keep a good conscience, and live by faith.

Verse 16

A righteous man eats only *the labour of his hands*, but that *labour tends to life* (v. 16). He aims at nothing but gaining an honest livelihood; he wants to simply live and maintain his family. Nor is such a man concerned only with his own life; he also wants to see what good he can do for others. He labors *that he may have to give* (Eph 4:28). A wicked man's wealth leads *to sin.* He makes it the food and fuel of his sinful desires, his pride and self-indulgence; he gets hurt by it and does not benefit from it.

Verse 17

Those who not only receive instruction but also keep it are in the right. They keep it for their own use, so that they may live their lives by it; and they keep it for the benefit of others, so that they may instruct them. Those who do not receive instruction but willfully and obstinately refuse it are in the wrong. They refuse to be taught their duty because it reveals their faults to them. Travelers who have missed their way but cannot bear to be shown the right way will continue to go astray; they certainly miss *the way of life* (v. 17).

Verse 18

Notice here that hatred is foolishness and evil when it is concealed by flattery and pretense: he who *hides hatred with lying lips is a fool*, even though he may think he is wise. *Lying lips* are bad enough in themselves, but they have an additional evil when they are made *a cloak of maliciousness*, a cover-up for evil (1Pe 2:16). Hatred is no better when expressed in spiteful language. *He that utters slander is a fool* too, for God will sooner or later show that righteousness is the light that the slanderer is trying to cover up.

Verse 19

Usually those who say much say much that is wrong, and among many words there must be many idle words. Those who love to hear themselves talk do not consider what work they are making for their repentance. It is therefore good to *keep our mouth as with a bridle* (Ps 39:1): *he that refrains his lips* (v. 19), who often restrains himself, is wise.

Verses 20–21

Value people not by their wealth and advancement in the world but by their goodness. Good people are good for something. As long as they have a mouth to speak with, that will make them both valuable and useful. *The tongue of the just is as choice silver* (v. 20); they are sincere and free from the dross of deception and evil intentions. They will enrich the people who hear them with wisdom. Their mouth also makes them useful: *The lips of the righteous feed many* (v. 21), for they are full of the word of God, which is the bread of life (Jn 6:35, 48), with which souls are nourished. Bad people are good for nothing. *The heart of the wicked is little worth* (v. 20). Their principles, ideas, thoughts, purposes, and all the things that occupy them and move them are worldly and godless and so are of no value. *He that is of the earth speaks of the earth*, and neither understands nor enjoys the things of God (Jn 3:31; 1Co 2:14).

Verse 22

Worldly wealth is what most people set their hearts very much on, but they are generally mistaken in both the nature of what they desire and the way they hope to gain it. The kind of wealth that is desirable consists not only in having abundance but also in having it *with no sorrow* (trouble) (v. 20). Such wealth is to be expected not from toiling endlessly for it (Ps 127:2), but from *the blessing of God* (v. 22). It is this that *makes rich and adds no sorrow.* What comes from the love of God has the grace of God as its companion, to keep the soul from those tumultuous desires of which the increase of riches is commonly the driving force.

Verse 23

It *is as sport* (fun) *to a fool to do mischief.* He laughs at sin. When he is warned not to sin, he makes fun of the warning. When he has sinned, he ridicules correction and laughs away the convictions of his own conscience (14:9). Wisdom has evidence of its own excellence. You need say no more in praise of *a man of understanding* than this: "He is an *understanding* man; he *has wisdom.*"

Verses 24–25

1. It will be as bad with evildoers as they can fear and as good with the righteous as they can desire. It is true that evildoers sometimes buoy themselves up in their evil with vain hopes that deceive them, but at other times they are haunted by just fears, and those *fears shall come upon them* (v. 24). It is true that the righteous sometimes have their fears, but their desire is toward the favor of God and happiness in him, and that *desire shall be granted* (v. 24). According to their faith, not according to their fear, it will be *unto them* (Ps 37:4).

2. The prosperity of evildoers will end quickly, but the happiness of the righteous will never end (v. 25).

Verse 26

Those who are lazy are not fit to be sent on an errand. Such people are therefore very unsuitable to be ministers and Christ's messengers. Lazy servants cause as much discomfort and trouble to their masters as *vinegar* does *to the teeth* and *smoke to the eyes*; they provoke their masters' anger as vinegar sets teeth on edge, and they cause them grief to see their business neglected and ruined, just as smoke makes the eyes water.

Verses 27–28

Religious faith extends people's lives and crowns their hopes. *What man is he that would see good days?* (1Pe 3:10). Let him fear God, and then his days will be not only many but also happy, for *the hope of the righteous shall be gladness* (v. 28). Evil, on the other hand, shortens people's lives and frustrates their hopes.

Verses 29–30

Strength and stability are the inheritance of those whose lives show integrity: *The way of the Lord*, the way in which he walks with us, *is strength to the upright* (v. 29); it confirms them and gives them a refuge in their uprightness. All God's dealings with them, both merciful and troublesome, encourage them to do their duty and keep them going in discouragements. *The way of the Lord*, the way of godliness that he appoints for us to walk, is also *strength to the upright.* A good conscience, kept pure from sin, gives a person boldness in times of danger. That *joy of the Lord* which is to be found only in the *way of the Lord will* be our strength (Ne 8:10), and so *the righteous shall never be removed* (uprooted) (v. 30). Ruin and destruction are the certain consequences of evil. God's judgments will uproot them.

Verses 31–32

It is both the proof and the praise of a man's wisdom and goodness that he speaks wisely and well. In his words, a good man *bringeth forth wisdom* (v. 31) to benefit others. He *knoweth what is acceptable* (fitting) (v. 32), what words will please God. It is the sin, and will be the destruction, of an evil man that he is wicked and speaks wickedly.

CHAPTER 11

Verse 1

Nothing is more offensive to God than deceit in business. *A false balance* here stands for all kinds of unjust and fraudulent practices in dealing with people, which are all detestable to the Lord. People make light of such deception and think it is not sinful if money is to be gained from it. On the other hand, nothing is more pleasing to God than fair and honest dealing, and nothing is more necessary to make us and our devotions acceptable to him: *A just weight is his delight.*

Verse 2

Pride is a shame to mere mortals, who are dependent on God, who live on the gifts of others, and who through sin have lost the right to their possessions. Those who are proud make themselves contemptible; it is a sin for which God often humbles people, as he did Nebuchadnezzar (Da 4:29–33) and Herod (Ac 12:21–23), whose humiliation came immediately after their boasting. As there is foolishness and shame with the proud, so *with the lowly there is wisdom*; that will be their honor, for a person's wisdom gains them respect and makes their face shine before other people (Ecc 8:1; Mt 5:16).

Verse 3

The integrity of honest people will itself be their guide. Their motives are settled and their rule of life sure, and so their way is plain (Ps 5:8); their sincerity keeps them steady, and they need not change direction every time the wind turns (Eph 4:14); since they have no other goal to aim at than to keep a good conscience. The sin of evildoers will itself be their ruin. The perverseness, duplicity, and trickery of sinners will be their destruction, even though they think they are very strong.

Verse 4

Riches will be of no advantage on the *day of wrath.* They will neither deflect the stroke of death nor relieve its pain, much less remove its sting. What use will this world's birthrights be then? A good conscience will ease the pain of death; it is the privilege of only the righteous not to be hurt by the second death, and not really hurt by the first.

Verses 5–6

These two verses have the same gist as v. 3. The ways of religious faith are straight and safe, and we may enjoy holy security in them. *The righteousness of the upright* (v. 6) will defend them; it will protect them from the lures of the Devil and the world and their attacks. The ways of evil are dangerous and destructive: *The wicked shall fall* into misery and ruin *by their own wickedness* (v. 5). Their sin will be their punishment.

Verse 7

It will only aggravate the misery of evildoers that their hopes will sink into despair just when they expect them to be fulfilled. When godly people die, their hopes are surpassed and all their fears vanish, but when evildoers die, their hopes *vanish.*

Verse 8

Good people are helped out of the problems they thought they had become lost in, and their feet are set in a place of abundance (Ps 34:19; 66:12). God has found a way to rescue his people even when they have despaired. Evildoers have fallen into the troubles they thought were far from them. Mordecai is saved from the gallows, Daniel from the lions' den, and Peter from prison, and their persecutors *come in their stead.* The Israelites are rescued from the Red Sea, and the Egyptians are drowned there.

Verse 9

It is not only the murderer with his sword, but also the *hypocrite with his mouth,* that *destroys his neighbour,* leading him astray into sin or trouble under the pretense of kindness or goodwill. *Death and life are in the power of the tongue* (18:21), but no tongue is more fatal than the one that flatters.

Verses 10–11

Good people are generally well loved by their neighbors. *When it goes well with the righteous* (v. 10), when they are advanced and put into positions of doing the good they want to do, it is so much the better for everyone around them, and *the city rejoices.* Evildoers may perhaps have a well-wisher here and there, but among most of their neighbors they receive ill will. They may be feared, but they are not loved, and so *when they perish there is shouting* for joy (v. 10). There is good reason for these opposite reactions: those who are good do good, but

wickedness proceeds from the wicked (1Sa 24:13). Good people are a blessing to their communities. *By the blessing of the upright* (v. 11)—the blessings with which they are blessed, which enlarge their range of usefulness—the blessings with which they bless their neighbors, their advice, examples, prayers—the blessings with which God blesses others for their sake—by all these *is the city exalted* (v. 11). But evildoers are a public nuisance.

Verses 12–13

Silence is commended as an aspect of true friendship and therefore a sign of wisdom. If *a man of understanding,* who rules his own spirit (16:32), is provoked, he holds his tongue, so that he may neither express his anger nor arouse the anger of others by any abusive or perverse language. To this wise concealment two great evils of the tongue are opposed. *He that is void of wisdom* (v. 12) reveals his own foolishness when he *despises his neighbour,* calling him *Raca* and *Thou fool* (Mt 5:22) at the least provocation. *A talebearer* (gossip) (v. 13), on the other hand, abuses a person behind his back, repeating from house to house all the stories he can pick up, whether they are true or false, in order to cause trouble and sow dissension (6:14, 19); he *reveals secrets* that he has been entrusted with. He therefore breaks the laws, and forfeits all the privileges, of friendship and good living.

Verse 14

Where no counsel is, where there is no guidance and everything is done rashly, or where there is no prudent deliberation for the common good, but only private intrigues for factions and divided interests, *the people fall;* they crumble into splinter groups and fall to pieces. Councils of war are necessary for military operations; two eyes see more than one, and mutual advice is mutual assistance. *In the multitude of counselors,* in having many advisers, who see their need of one another and act together out of joint concern for the public welfare, *there is safety,* victory is made sure.

Verse 15

Our possessions are not our own; we are merely stewards of them. There is a good management that is good divinity, part of the character of a good person (Ps 112:5). Every person must behave justly toward their own family, or else they are not true to their stewardship. In particular, we must not rashly put up security for a stranger. There is danger of bringing trouble on ourselves by it, and on our families too when we have died: *He that is surety for a stranger shall smart* (suffer) *for it;* he will sadly be crushed and broken by it and perhaps become bankrupt.

Verse 16

Strong men retain riches. Men of drive and influence are able to do well against all who stand in their way; they are likely to keep what they have and gain more. A *gracious woman* is as careful to keep her reputation for wisdom and modesty, humility and courtesy, and all those other graces that are the true ornaments of her sex, as strong men are to protect their possessions, and those women who are truly gracious will keep their honor by their good behavior.

Verse 17

A *merciful,* tender, good-humored *man does good to his own soul,* makes himself calm and keeps himself so. He takes pleasure in doing his duty and contributing to the comfort of those who are to him as *his own soul* (1Sa

18:1, 3; 20:17), for *we are members one of another* (Eph 4:25). By the *soul* we may understand the *inward man*, the inner being, as the apostle Paul calls it (Ro 7:22), and in that case this proverb teaches us that the first and great act of mercy is to provide our own souls with the necessary supports of our spiritual life. A *cruel*, perverse, ill-natured man *troubles his own flesh* (v. 17), and so his sin becomes his punishment.

Verse 18

The wicked works a deceitful work (earns deceptive wages); he builds for himself a house on the sand, which will deceive him when the storm comes (Mt 7:26–27). *Sin deceived me, and by it slew me* (Ro 7:11). Those *that sow righteousness* will gain *a sure reward* (v. 18). It will be as sure to them as eternal truth can make it.

Verse 19

True holiness is true happiness; it is a preparation for it, a pledge and promise of it. *Righteousness* inclines, disposes, and leads the soul *to life*. Those who indulge in sin are preparing themselves for destruction.

Verse 20

We should be concerned to know what God hates and what he loves, so that we may direct our lives accordingly. Nothing is more offensive to God than hypocrisy and double-dealing, for these are contained in the meaning of the word *frowardness* (perversity), referring to those who pretend to be just but actually intend wrong, walking in crooked ways to avoid being discovered. Nothing is more pleasing to God than sincerity and plain dealing.

Verse 21

Alliances in sin will certainly be broken and will not protect sinners: *Though hand join in hand.* Though there are many who agree by their practice to keep evil in favor, though they are in league to support and spread it, although evil children follow in the footsteps of their evil parents, they will not be held guiltless (Ex 20:7); it will not excuse them to say that they were doing as most other people were doing and as their friends were doing. *The seed of the righteous*, who follow the steps of their righteousness, even though they may fall into trouble, will *be delivered* in due time.

Verse 22

By *discretion* here we must understand *religious faith* and *grace*, a true enjoyment of the honors and pleasures that accompany unblemished goodness, and so *a woman without discretion* is a woman of a loose and dissolute character. Beauty or physical attractiveness is *as a jewel of gold*, and where there is wisdom and grace to guard against the temptations it brings, it is a fine adornment. A foolish and immoral woman, however, one who is frivolous, is appropriately compared to a pig, even though she may be very good-looking; she wallows in the mire of indecent, sinful desires, which defile the mind and conscience, and even though she has washed, she still returns to them. It is sad that beauty should be abused. It is completely misplaced, *as a jewel in a swine's snout*, which it uses to dig in a pile of rubbish.

Verse 23

The righteous want *good, only good*; all they desire is that it may go well with everyone around them; they wish no harm to come to anyone, but happiness for everyone. As to themselves, they want to obtain the favor of a good

God and to keep the peace of a good conscience, and they will have the good they desire (Ps 37:4). *The wicked* expect and want trouble for others; they will receive it in return: as they loved to curse, so they will be cursed in return.

Verse 24

People may become rich by wisely spending what they have, may give freely in works of godliness, kindness, and generosity but gain even more; in fact, their wealth may multiply, just as grain multiplies by being sown. But our gain is especially to be ascribed to God; he blesses the hands that give and so makes them hands that receive (2Co 9:10). People may, on the other hand, become poor by being mean with what they have, *withholding more than is meet* (withholding unduly), not paying debts, not relieving the poor, not providing what is needed for the family. This *tends to poverty* (v. 24) and forfeits the blessing of God.

Verse 25

The liberal soul, the one who prays for people who suffer and provides for them, who scatters blessings with gracious lips and generous hands, that soul *shall be made fat* (will prosper) (v. 25) with true pleasure and be made rich with more grace. *He that waters* others with the streams of his goodness *shall be also watered himself*; God will certainly return plentiful showers of his blessing. "He that waters, even he shall be as rain," as some understand it; he will be strengthened as clouds that return after the rain (Ecc 12:2), and so be made even more useful.

Verse 26

When grain is expensive and scarce, it is a sin to withhold it in the hope that its price will increase even further, to push up and keep up the market when grain is already selling at a price high enough to cause suffering to the poor. At such a time it is the duty of those who have stocks of grain to consider the poor; they should be willing to sell at the market price and be content with a moderate profit.

Verse 27

The first phrase of this verse means literally, "He who rises early to what is good," who seeks opportunities to serve his friends and relieve the poor and gives of himself to them; such a person *procures favour*. Everyone around him will love him, and, what is better than life (Ps 63:3), he has God's unfailing love. Those who are dedicated to causing trouble ruin themselves.

Verse 28

Our righteousness will stand us in good stead when our riches fail us: *The righteous shall* then *flourish as a branch* (v. 28), the branch of righteousness, like a tree whose leaf will not wither (Ps 1:3). When those who put down roots in the world wither, those who are grafted into Christ will be fruitful and flourishing.

Verse 29

Two extremes in dealing with matters of family life are here condemned:

1. Overcautious and ungodly ways, on the one hand. There are those who by their anxiety about their business and worry about their losses, and their niggardliness toward their families, *trouble their own houses*; others think that by supporting factions and conflicts in their

families they will serve some useful purpose for themselves. But they will both be disappointed; they will *inherit the wind*. All they will obtain from these schemes will be empty and worthless as the wind.

2. Carelessness and lack of good sense, on the other hand. He who is a fool in his business, who does not look after it properly, who does not make good plans, not only loses his reputation but also becomes a *servant to the wise in heart*. He becomes poor, while those who manage matters wisely advance themselves and come to rule over him.

Verse 30

The righteous are as *trees of life*; the fruits of their godliness and goodness, their instructions, corrections, examples, and prayers, their privileges in heaven and their influence on earth, are like the fruits of that tree in paradise (Ge 3:22–24; Rev 2:7), contributing to the nourishment of the spiritual life of many people; they adorn paradise, God's church on earth. The wise are something more; they are as trees of knowledge, commanded knowledge. By sharing his wisdom with others, *He that is wise wins souls*, wins them over to the interests of God's kingdom. Those who want to win souls need wisdom to know how to deal with them.

Verse 31

This is the only one of Solomon's proverbs that has a note commanding attention attached to it, *Behold!* which suggests it contains not only an evident truth, but also an eminent truth. Some understand *recompense* to mean the same thing with reference to both groups here, namely, displeasure: if *the righteous* do wrong, they will be punished for their offenses in this world; much more will evildoers be punished for theirs, which are committed not through weakness but in arrogance. Others understand it as a "recompense" of reward to the righteous and punishment to sinners. There are some *recompenses in the earth*, in this world, though many sins go unpunished in the earth, and many services unrewarded, which shows there is a judgment to come. Many times *the righteous* are *recompensed* for their righteousness here on earth (v. 31), even though that is not the only reward intended for them, but whatever the word of God has promised them, or the wisdom of God sees good to give them, they will have on earth. *The wicked* also are sometimes remarkably punished in this life: nations, families, and individual people.

CHAPTER 12

Verse 1

Those who have grace will delight in all the instructions given them by the word or providence of God; they will value being brought up well and think it is not a hardship, but fortunate, to be under a strict and wise discipline. Those who take it as an insult to be told about their faults, and an infringement of their liberty to be reminded of their duty, show themselves devoid not only of grace but also of common sense. Those who want to live in lax families and communities, where there are no restraints, are truly stupid.

Verse 2

Our Father judges his children very much by the way they behave toward one another, and so *a good man*, one who is merciful and kind and does good, *obtains the favour of the Lord* by his prayers; but God *will condemn* as unworthy of a place in his kingdom those who devise wicked schemes against their neighbors.

Verse 3

Although people may advance themselves by their sinful ways, such means will not make them settled or secure. *A man shall not be established by wickedness*; it may set him on high places, but the ground there is slippery (Ps 73:18). Although good people may have little of the things of this world, what is honestly gained will wear well.

Verse 4

The man who is blessed with a good wife is as happy as if he were a king, for she is nothing less than *a crown* to him. A noble woman is godly and wise, active in doing good for her family; she is careful to do her duty and can bear adversities without losing her composure. She is faithful to him and by her example teaches his children and servants to be so too. A bad wife is no better than *rottenness in his bones*, an incurable disease, and she also *makes him ashamed*. She who is stupid and lazy, wasteful and immoral, easily angered and liable to speak bad language, brings both discredit and discomfort to her husband.

Verse 5

We are mistaken if we imagine we can think what we like: our thoughts are noticed by God. A good person may think bad thoughts, but he does not indulge them and harbor them. It is a person's honor to have honest intentions, even though a word or action may be misplaced, mistimed, or at least misinterpreted. But it is a person's shame to act with deceit and evil intent to cheat others.

Verse 6

In the previous verse the *thoughts* of evildoers and the righteous were compared. But those whose *words lie in wait for blood* are truly evil; their tongues are as swords to those who stand in their way, to good people they hate and persecute. For an example, see Lk 20:20–21. Good people speak words that help their neighbors: the *mouth of the upright* is ready to be opened to support the cause of the oppressed, those who cannot speak up for themselves (31:8).

Verse 7

Just touch evildoers and they disappear; they stand on such slippery ground that the slightest form of trouble brings them down, like the apples of Sodom in the old English proverb, which look attractive, but if touched, turn to dust. The prosperity of the righteous, however, will endure. Death will remove them, but their *house* will *stand* firm; their families will continue.

Verse 8

The best reputation is the kind that accompanies goodness and the wise conduct of one's life: *A man shall be commended* not according to his riches or high rank in life, his skills or dexterity, but *according to his wisdom*, the honesty of his intentions. The worst shame is the kind that follows evil. He who turns aside to follow dishonest ways *shall be despised*.

Verse 9

It is the foolishness of some people to want to make themselves appear significant when they are away from home even when they lack the necessities of life at home—even when, if their debts were paid, they would not be worth a piece of bread; in fact, they may deny themselves food to buy clothes, so that they may appear to be bright and cheerful because, as the proverb expresses it, "Fine feathers make fine birds." The character of another group of people is better in every way: these people are content with their lot in a humble sphere; they may be looked down on for the plain clothing they wear, but they can afford to have in their own homes not only the necessities of life but also the things that make life a little easier. They have not only bread but also a servant.

Verse 10

A good man is merciful. He cares even for *the life of his beast*, not only because it is his servant but also because it is God's creature. The animals that are our responsibility must be provided for; they must have necessary food and rest. Balaam was rebuked for beating his donkey (Nu 22:30, 32). The Law took care of oxen (Ex 23:12; Dt 25:4). An evildoer, on the other hand, will be unmerciful; even his *tender mercies* are *cruel*; the natural compassion he had as a human being is turned into hardheartedness.

Verse 11

It is wise to take care of one's business and follow an honest calling, for that is the way, by the blessing of God, to gain a livelihood. Be busy, and that is the best way to be at peace. Keep at your work and your work will keep you. It is foolish to neglect one's business; those who do so are *void of understanding* and come to lack bread. They make themselves a burden to other people, taking bread from other people's mouths.

Verse 12

Here is the care and aim of an evil person: he *desires the net of evil men*. "Oh that I were only as cunning as he is, oh that I could cheat as well as he, if only I could take revenge on the person I hate!" A good person, however, desires to do good and be firmly established in doing good. Evildoers want only a net with which they can fish for themselves; righteous people want to flourish with fruit to benefit others and glorify God (Ro 14:6).

Verse 13

Many have had to pay dearly in this world for the sins of their lips, and have had to suffer lashes on their back because they have not restrained their tongues (Ps 64:8). The righteous escape from this trouble by their own wisdom when God in mercy comes to help them.

Verse 14

Even good words will turn to a person's good advantage: *A man* will gain strength now, inner pleasure that is truly satisfying, by the good he does with his godly words and wise advice. Good works, much more, will be abundantly rewarded.

Verse 15

A fool thinks he is right in everything he does, and *therefore* he never asks for advice. A wise person is willing to be advised; he wants other people to guide him, and he *hearkens* (listen) *to counsel*, being uncertain about his own judgment.

Verse 16

Passion is foolish: a wise person may become angry when there is just cause, but he then has his anger under control: he is lord of his anger, but the fool's anger lords it over him. Those who soon become angry, who are quickly inflamed by the slightest spark, do not have the control they should have over their own spirits (16:32). Humility is wisdom: *A prudent man covers shame*. He covers up the anger within him; he restrains his lips. We are acting kindly toward ourselves, and it will lead to calmness within us, if we mitigate and excuse the injuries and insults we receive instead of emphasizing them and making the worst of them.

Verse 17

Here is:

1. A faithful witness commended because he presents everything fairly, to the best of his knowledge, whether in a formal judgment or in the ordinary course of life, whether he is on oath or not. He makes it clear he is guided and motivated by the principles and laws of righteousness, and he promotes justice by honoring it.

2. A false witness condemned as a cheat; he *shows forth deceit*, he has a lying spirit.

Verse 18

The tongue is death or life, poison or medicine, according to how it is used. Slander, like a sword, wounds the reputation of those about whom it is spoken. Whisperings and evil allegations act like a sword and divide and tear apart the bonds of love and friendship and separate those who have been close to each other. There are also words that are curing and healing, closing up the wounds that the backbiting tongue has inflicted, restoring peace, and persuading people to be reconciled.

Verse 19

If truth is spoken, it will last. What is true will always be true; we may be faithful to it. But *a lying tongue* will be disproved. When a liar comes to be examined, he will be found telling several different stories; he will not be consistent with himself as those who speak the truth are. Truth may be eclipsed, but it *will* come to light: the truth will out.

Verse 20

Those who plot evil are deceiving themselves. Even if they plot very skillfully, deceivers will certainly be deceived. However, those who seek the things that will lead to peace (Ro 14:19) and give peaceful advice, who promote attempts at healing and further the public welfare, will enjoy not only the credit for doing so but also the comfort from doing so. *Blessed are the peacemakers* (Mt 5:9).

Verse 21

If people are sincerely righteous, God has committed himself to see that no evil will come to them. He will, by the power of his grace in them, keep them. Although they may be tempted, they will not be overcome by the temptation, and although they have troubles, those troubles will have no disastrous effects on them (Ps 91:10), for troubles will be overruled and made to work for their good (Ro 8:28). Those who live in contempt of God and their fellow human beings will be made miserable with the troubles that come on them. Those who delight in causing trouble will have enough of it.

Verse 22

Lying is detestable to the Lord not only because it is disobedience to his law but also because it is destructive to human society. However, those who *deal truly* and sincerely in all their dealings are *his delight*, and he is pleased with them.

Verse 23

He who is wise communicates his knowledge when it may build up others, but he hides it when showing it might bring praise to him. Wise people will carefully avoid everything that smacks of ostentation. But those who are foolish cannot avoid declaring their foolishness.

Verse 24

Industriousness is the way to be advanced. Solomon promoted Jeroboam because he saw he was an industrious young man who did his work well (1Ki 11:28). Those who work hard to learn when they are young will obtain what will enable them to rule, and so to rest, when they are old. Foolishness is the way to slavery. Those who, because they will not make an effort to pursue an honest calling, live according to dishonest subterfuge are worthless and poverty-stricken, and will be kept low.

Verse 25

The cause and consequence of depression is *heaviness* (anxiety) *in the heart*; it is a burden of care, fear, and sorrow on the spirits; it makes them stoop; it drains them and sinks them. A cure of depression is *a good word* from God, which, applied by faith, *makes the heart glad. Cast thy burden upon the Lord, and he shall sustain thee* (Ps 55:22). The good word of God, particularly the Gospel, is intended to gladden the hearts of those who are weary and burdened (Mt 11:28).

Verse 26

"The righteous is more abundant than his neighbour" is the reading of the margin; he is richer, not in this world's goods but in the graces and comforts of the Spirit, which are true riches. There is a true excellence in religious faith; it makes people noble; it inspires them with a generous motivation. The righteous person's neighbor may be more significant in the world, but the righteous person has intrinsic worth. Evildoers walk in a way that leads them astray. It seems to them a pleasant way, but it is all a deception.

Verse 27

Here is what may make us hate laziness and deceit, for the word here signifies both: *The slothful*, deceitful *man has* roast meat, but what he roasts is not what he himself *took in hunting.* Or if lazy, deceitful people have taken anything in hunting, they still do not roast it when they have taken it; they do not enjoy it; perhaps God will not allow them to. The *substance* (prized possession) *of a diligent man* (v. 27), even though it may not be great, *is* still *precious.* It comes from the blessing of God, and so the diligent man enjoys good from it, together with his family. It is his own daily bread, not bread from other people's mouths.

Verse 28

Religious faith is a *pathway*, a way God has formed for us (Isa 35:8); it is a highway, the king's highway, the King of kings' highway, a way that has been trodden before us by all the saints, the good old way (Jer 6:16), full of the footsteps of the flock. There is not only life at the end but life on the way. In it *there is no death*, none of the sorrows of the world that produce death.

CHAPTER 13

Verse 1

There is great hope for those who have a reverence for their parents and are willing to be advised and warned by them. There is little hope for those who will not so much as *hear rebuke*, but scorn submission to their parents' direction and scoff at those who deal faithfully with them. How can they put right their mistakes if they do not want to be told about them?

Verse 2

If what comes from the heart is good (Mt 12:34–35), inner comfort and satisfaction will be daily bread. But violence will be thrown back in the face of those who commit it: *The soul of the transgressors* who plot trouble and release it in word and action *shall eat violence*; they will have their belly full of it. Everyone will drink as they have brewed and eat as they speak, for by our words we are either acquitted or condemned (Mt 12:37).

Verse 3

Guarding the lips is guarding the soul. He who is cautious, who thinks twice before he speaks, *keeps his life* from a great deal of guilt and grief. He saves himself the trouble of many bitter reflections. Many people are ruined by an uncontrolled tongue.

Verse 4

The lazy want the gains of the diligent, but they hate the effort the diligent make; they covet everything that is to be coveted, but will not lift a finger to do anything. It therefore follows, *they have nothing*. Let those who will not work *not eat* but go hungry (2Th 3:10). The happiness and honor of the diligent will be that they will have abundance. This is especially true in spiritual matters.

Verse 5

It is the undoubted character of every righteous person that he *hates lying*—that is, all sin, for every sin is a lie, and especially all fraud and falsehood in business and in speech. Not only will he not tell a lie, but he also detests lying, because he has a deep-rooted, overriding love for truth and justice and a desire to be like God. If the evildoer's eyes were opened and his conscience awakened, he would *abhor himself and repent in dust and ashes* (Job 42:6).

Verse 6

Those who are *upright in their way*, who deal sincerely both with God and with their fellows, will find that their integrity will keep them from the temptations of Satan, which will not prevail over them. For those who are evil, even their evil will mean they will be ultimately overthrown, and they are held in its cords in the meantime.

Verse 7

The world is a great fraud. Some people who are truly poor want to be thought of as rich; they trade and spend as if they were rich, and they make a great show, when perhaps, if all their debts were paid, it would be clear they are not worth a dime. This is sin, and it will be shameful. Some people who are actually rich want to be thought of as poor, because they wrongly live below what God has given them. This shows ingratitude to God, injustice to the family and neighborhood, and a lack of charity to the poor. There are many presumptuous hypocrites, who are truly poor and devoid of grace but pretend they are rich and will not recognize their poverty. There are many timorous, trembling Christians, who are spiritually rich and full of grace but think they are poor; by their doubts and fears, their complaints and griefs, they *make themselves poor.*

Verse 8

We tend to judge people's blessedness, at least in this world, by their wealth. Solomon shows what a grave mistake this is. Those who are rich may be respected by some for their riches, yet they are envied by others, who endanger their lives, which they must therefore ransom with their riches. How little are people indebted to their wealth when it only serves to redeem a life that otherwise would not have been in danger! Those who are poor may be despised and overlooked by some who should be their friends, yet they are despised and overlooked by others who would be their enemies if they had anything.

Verse 9

The light of the righteous rejoices, that is, it shines brightly; it increases and gives them joy. Even their outward prosperity is their joy, and much more so those gifts, graces, and comforts with which their souls are illuminated. *The lamp of the wicked* burns dimly and faintly; it looks sad, like a small candle in a large urn, and it will shortly *be put out* (v. 9).

Verse 10

Foolish pride breeds quarrels. Do you want to know *whence come wars and fightings* (Jas 4:1)? They come from this root of bitterness (Heb 12:14–15). When people are proud, they have no patience for being contradicted, no patience for any rival, no patience for contempt or anything that looks like slight disrespect, and this is where quarrels among relatives and neighbors, in states and kingdoms, and in churches and Christian communities come from. People want revenge, not forgiveness, because they are proud. Those who are humble and peaceful will ask and take advice, will consult their own consciences, their Bibles, their ministers, and their friends to preserve quietness and prevent quarrels from breaking out.

Verse 11

What is gained dishonestly will never last long. What is gained by unlawful ways—ways that are unbecoming to a Christian—and what is gained by gambling may as truly be said to be *gotten by vanity* as what is gained by fraud and lying, and such gain *will be diminished.* What is gained by honest hard work will become more, rather than less; it will be a living; it will be a plentiful inheritance.

Verse 12

Nothing is more painful than the disappointment of raised expectations, even if the thing hoped for is not actually denied but only delayed. Nothing is more pleasant than to enjoy what we have long wished and waited for. It puts people into a kind of paradise, a garden of pleasure, for *it is a tree of life.* The happiness of heaven will be all the more welcome to the saints because it is what they have longed for with their hearts as the crown of all their hopes.

Verse 13

Those who prefer the rules of godless politics to divine commands, who put the attractions of this world and the flesh before God's promises and encouragements, scorn his word. They will justly *be destroyed; but he that fears*

the commandment, who fears God, has reverence for his word, and is afraid of displeasing God and incurring the penalties attached to the commandment, *shall be rewarded* for his godly fear.

Verse 14

By *the law of the wise* we may understand the principles and rules by which they govern their lives. These principles and rules will be constant springs of comfort, as *a fountain of life.* The closer we keep to those rules, the more effectively we keep our own peace. Those who follow the dictates of this law will escape *the snares of death* that those who abandon *the law of the wise* fall into.

Verse 15

Those who conduct themselves wisely, *serving Christ*, are *accepted of God and approved of men* (Ro 14:17–18). The way of sinners is rough and uneasy. It is *hard*, hard on others, who complain about it, and hard on the sinners themselves, who can take little delight in their own lives while they are doing what is displeasing to everyone around them.

Verse 16

It is wise to be cautious. *Every prudent*, discreet *man* acts with deliberation and is careful not to interfere with what he knows nothing about. It is foolish to be rash, as the *fool* is, who is eager to undertake what he is completely unfit for, so making himself appear ridiculous.

Verse 17

Here we see the adverse effects of betraying a trust. *A wicked messenger*, who, being sent to negotiate any business, is unfaithful to the one who employed him, will be discovered and punished. We see also the happy effects of faithfulness: an *ambassador* who *faithfully* discharges this trust and serves the interests of those who employ him brings healing to those by whom and for whom he is employed; he heals differences between them; he also brings healing to himself, for he is protecting his own interests. This may be applied to ministers, Christ's messengers.

Verse 18

He who is so proud that he despises being taught will certainly be humbled. He who is so humble that he takes it well to be told his faults will certainly be exalted: *He that regards a reproof* gains respect.

Verse 19

There are strong desires for happiness in human beings; God has provided for the fulfillment of those desires. *The desire* of good people for the favor of God and spiritual blessings brings what *is sweet to their souls* (Ps 4:6–7). But evildoers will not be happy, for *it is* detestable to them *to depart from evil*, which is necessary for them to become happy.

Verse 20

Those who want to be good must keep good company, which is evidence in their favor that they do indeed want to be good—people's character may be known by the company they choose. Many are brought to ruin by bad company.

Verse 21

God is sure to catch up with those he is pursuing. They may prosper for a while and think they are secure, but their condemnation is not asleep (2Pe 2:3), even though they are. *The righteous* will be abundantly rewarded for all the good they have done and all the wrong they have suffered in this world.

Verse 22

A *good man's* wealth lasts. He is to be commended for being thoughtful toward his descendants. He is especially careful, both by justice and by charity, to obtain the blessing of God on what he has and to pass on that blessing to his children as an inheritance. If he should not leave them much of this world's goods, then his prayers, instructions, and good example will be the best inheritance, and the promises of the covenant will be an inheritance to his *children's children* (Ps 103:17). In his providence, God often brings into the hands of the godly what evildoers had stored up for themselves.

Verse 23

A small estate may be improved by hard work, so that a person who makes the best of everything may live comfortably on it. The smaller the field is, the more skill and hard work the owner needs to put into it, and it will have very good results. If they dig, they will not need to beg. A great estate, on the other hand, may be ruined by indiscretion. People overreach themselves by building too much or buying too much without the resources to pay for it. They keep a better table or more servants than they can afford.

Verse 24

To teach children what is good it is necessary to correct in them what is wrong. It is the parent's rod that must be used, directed by wisdom and love and intended for good, not the rod of a servant. It is good to begin restraining before sinful habits set in. Those who do not keep their children under strict discipline show they really hate them, even though they pretend to be fond of them.

Verse 25

It is the happiness of the righteous that they will have enough and that they know when they have had enough. Those who feed on the bread of life eat and are filled (Jn 6:35, 41, 48). It is the misery of evildoers that, through the insatiableness of their desires, they always want more; their souls are not satisfied with the world and the flesh, and even their *belly shall want* (they will be hungry); their physical appetite is always craving for more.

CHAPTER 14

Verse 1

A good wife is a great blessing to a family. By a prudent wife, one who is godly, hard-working, and considerate, the affairs of the family are made to prosper: debts are paid, the children are well educated, and the family has comfort at home and a good name in the community — this is how a house is built well. Many families are ruined by the poor household management of the wife, as well as by that of the husband. *A foolish* woman, one who has no fear of God, who is stubborn, wasteful, and unreliable, who indulges in lavish meals and revelry, who loves playing cards and enjoying wild nights out, will as certainly be the ruin of her house as if she *plucked it down with her hand.*

Verse 2

When grace is reigning, it shows itself in reverence and honor toward God. When sin is reigning, it shows itself in nothing less than contempt for God.

Verse 3

Where there is pride in the heart and no wisdom in the head to suppress it, it commonly shows itself in the words that are spoken: *In the mouth there is pride*, proud boasting and scorning; this is the *rod*, or branch, *of pride*; the word is used only here and in Isa 11:1. This branch grows from that root of bitterness (Heb 12:15) that is in the heart. The root must be plucked out, or else we cannot defeat the branch. The word could also refer to a rod that beats and strikes, *a rod of pride* that strikes others. *The lips of the wise shall preserve them* from creating for others the trouble that proud people create with their tongues, and from bringing on themselves the trouble that proud and arrogant people are often involved in.

Verse 4

The neglect of good management leads to poverty: *Where no oxen are*, to cultivate the ground and tread out the grain, *the crib* (manger) is empty, *is clean*; there is no straw for the cattle, and so no bread for people to eat. *The crib* indeed *is clean* from dung, which pleases those who like everything to be neat and tidy, who cannot bear to do a good day's work because it means getting their hands dirty, and so will sell their oxen to keep the manger clean. This shows the foolishness of those who devote themselves to the pleasures of the country but do not take care of the farm, who, as we say, "own more horses than kine (cows), more dogs than swine (pigs)"; their families must suffer from their poor management. Those who work hard with their land are likely to reap benefits from it.

Verse 5

In the administration of justice much depends on witnesses, and so it is necessary for the common good that witnesses have principles. A witness who is careful will not dare give a testimony that is in the slightest untrue or deceitful. But a witness who is willing to be bribed, biased, and browbeaten *will utter lies* — with as much assurance as if what they said were all true.

Verse 6

The reason why some people seek wisdom and do not find it is that they do not seek it from a right motive. They are mockers, and they ask for instruction only so that they may mock at and ridicule what is told them. He *that understands* so as to *depart from evil* (for *that is understanding*, Job 28:28), abandon his prejudices, and set aside all corrupt thoughts and attitudes will easily take in instruction and learn its lessons.

Verse 7

An evildoer is foolish. We must stay away from such people. Sometimes the only way available to rebuke evil words is to leave the company of the speaker so you cannot hear them.

Verse 8

It is not the wisdom of the learned, which consists only of speculation, that is here commended, but *the wisdom of the prudent*, which is practical, useful to direct our actions. What is commended *is to understand our own way*, not to be critics of and busybodies in other people's lives, but to be vigilant in our lives and to understand the directions of our own way. The bad behavior of bad people deceives them. They do not rightly understand their way; they think they do, but they miss their way.

Verse 9

Evildoers are hardened in their evil: they *make a mock at sin*. They look at others' sins and laugh at them, and they make light of their own sins. Those who make light of sin make light of Christ. If good people offend in anything, they immediately repent and obtain the favor of God. They have goodwill to one another, and in their communities there is mutual love and compassion in cases of offense, with no mocking.

Verse 10

Everyone feels their own burden most, especially what weighs heavily on their spirits. We must not criticize the griefs of others, for we do not know what they are feeling; their suffering is perhaps too heavy for their groaning to express (Job 23:2). Yet many people enjoy divine comforts that others are not aware of, much less are sharers in.

Verse 11

Sin is the destruction of great families. Righteousness is the rise and stability of even lowly families: even *the tabernacle of the upright*, though portable and contemptible as a tent, *shall flourish*, if infinite Wisdom sees fit to bless it.

Verse 12

The way of ignorance and carelessness and the way of pleasing the flesh seem right to those who walk in them, and much more the way of hypocrisy in religion, external rituals, partial reformation, and blind zeal; they imagine that these will bring them to heaven. They will perish with a lie in their right hand (Isa 44:20). Self-deceivers will ultimately prove to be self-destroyers.

Verse 13

Sometimes when sinners are under conviction or some great trouble, they hide their sadness by a forced mirth, because they do not want to appear to submit to God even when he fetters them (Job 36:13). Even when people really are merry, at the same time there is something that spoils their merriment; their consciences tell them they have no reason to be happy (Hos 9:1); they must see that their mirth is meaningless (Ecc 2:1–2). Spiritual joy is fixed in the soul; the joy of the hypocrite comes only from the mouth. *The end of that mirth is heaviness.*

Verse 14

The *backslider in heart*, who for fear of suffering, or in hope of profit or pleasure, abandons God and his duty, will be *filled with his own ways*; God will give him an excess of them. *He that is filthy shall be filthy still* (Rev 22:11). *A good man shall be* abundantly *satisfied from himself*, from what God has done in him. As sinners never think they have enough sin till it takes them to hell, so saints never think they have enough grace till it takes them to heaven.

Verse 15

It is foolish to be gullible, to believe every report that is flying around, to take things on trust from mere hearsay, and to believe everyone who promises to pay promptly. *The prudent man* will rest before he trusts.

Verse 16

Holy fear is an excellent guard for every holy thing and against everything unholy. It is wise to depart *from evil*, to be afraid of approaching sin or dallying with its beginnings. Presumption is foolish. If, when warned of danger, people *rage and are confident* (hotheaded and reckless), furiously push on, persist in their rebellion, and play about on the precipice, they are foolish.

Verse 17

People who are irritable and touchy and *soon* become *angry* say and do what is ridiculous and so expose themselves to contempt. *A man of wicked devices* (a crafty man), who stifles his anger until he has an opportunity to take revenge, is hated by everyone. Angry people, surprised by temptation, disgrace themselves, but it is soon over, and they are sorry for it. But the character of a spiteful, revengeful person is repugnant; there is no protection from him and no cure for him.

Verse 18

Sin is the shame of sinners: *The simple*, who love simplicity, gain nothing by it, but *inherit folly*. What they esteem themselves for is really foolish. They will forever regret their own foolish choice. Wisdom is the honor of the wise: *The prudent crown* themselves *with knowledge*. Wise heads will be respected as if they were crowned heads. Wisdom is not only proved right, but also glorified, in all her children (Mt 11:19).

Verse 19

Evildoers are often made poor and brought low, so that they are forced to beg, because their evil has reduced them to difficulties, while good people, who enjoy the blessing of God, are made rich and enabled to give, and do give, even to evildoers, for where God gives life we must not deny a livelihood.

Verse 20

The poor, who should be pitied and relieved, are *hated*, and people keep their distance from them, even their *own neighbour*. Most people are fair-weather friends who disappear in winter. It is good to have God as our friend, for he will not abandon us when we are poor. *The rich have many friends*, many who befriend them in the hope of getting something from them.

Verse 21

People's character and condition are measured by their behavior toward their poor neighbors. *He that despises his neighbour* because his neighbor is from a lowly background, had a rural education, and looks insignificant, who thinks it beneath him to take any notice of him, *is a sinner*, and will be dealt with as a sinner. *He that has mercy on the poor*, who is ready to do all the good he can for them, does what is pleasing to God.

Verse 22

Those who not only do evil but also plot it think that by sinning with cunning and carrying out their conspiracies with more deception than others, they will come off better. But they are mistaken. God's justice cannot be outwitted. Those who plan evil against their neighbors go astray, for it will end in their own destruction. Those who are so generous as to plan ways of being generous to others, who seek opportunities to do good and plan how to make their kindness as extensive and as acceptable as possible to those who need it—*by liberal things they shall stand* (Isa 32:8).

Verse 23

Hard-working people are generally successful people. "The stirring hand gets a penny." Those who love to boast about their business and make a big noise about it and who waste time in tittle-tattle waste what they have, and the course they take *tends to penury* (poverty). This is also true in the affairs of our souls; those who make an effort to serve God, who strive fervently in prayer, will benefit from it. But if people's religion is only all talk and noise, they will be spiritually poor and come to nothing.

Verse 24

If people are wise and good, riches make them much more honorable and useful and give them more influence. Those who have wealth and the wisdom to use it will have great opportunities to honor God and do good in the world. If people are evil and corrupt, their wealth will only serve to expose them.

Verse 25

A faithful witness *delivers the souls* of the innocent, who are falsely accused, and he rescues their good reputation, which is as precious to them as their lives. A false witness forges *lies* (Job 13:4; Ps 119:69), and yet he pours them out with the greatest possible assurance. It is in the interests of a nation to detect and punish false-witness bearing, for truth is the glue that holds a community together.

Verses 26–27

The *fear of the Lord* here stands for all gracious principles, which produce gracious practices. Where the fear of the Lord reigns, it produces security and peace of mind. It enables a person to keep hold of peace and gives them boldness before God and the world. The fear of the Lord passes on an inheritance of blessing to descendants. The children of religious parents often conduct themselves better because of their parents' instruction and example and fare better because of their parents' faith and prayers. "*Our fathers trusted in thee* (Ps 22:4), and so we will." The fear of the Lord is an overflowing and ever-flowing spring of comfort and joy. It is a sovereign antidote against sin and temptation.

Verse 28

Here are two maxims in politics:

1. That it is greatly to the honor of a king to have a well-populated kingdom; it is a sign that he is ruling well, since foreigners are invited to come and settle under his protection and his own subjects live comfortably. It is therefore the wisdom of rulers to promote the increase of their people by a mild and gentle government and by encouraging trade and agriculture.

2. That when the people are fewer in numbers, the ruler is weakened: "In the lack of people is the leanness of the ruler," as some understand it; trade is dead, the ground is uncultivated, the army lacks recruits, the navy does not have enough staff, and all because there are not sufficient people.

Verse 29

Humility is wisdom. *He* who rightly understands himself and the weaknesses of human nature, who *is slow to anger* and knows how to excuse the faults of others as well as his own, so as not to be at all provoked and made to lose his own soul, *is of great understanding*. Unrestrained anger is foolish: *he that is hasty of spirit* (quick-tempered), whose heart is tinder to every spark of provocation, who is all fire and fiber, thinks that is the way to be raised up, whereas really he *exalts his own folly*.

Verse 30

Our health depends on controlling our emotions and keeping our minds calm. A healing spirit, made up of love and humility, a hearty, friendly, and cheerful disposition, is *the life of the flesh*; it contributes to a good physical constitution; people grow more content with good humor. A fretful, envious, discontented spirit makes the face look pale and is the *rottenness of the bones*.

Verse 31

Let whoever wrongs a poor person know that they are showing disrespect to their Maker. God made them and gave them being, and he is the same One who gave the poor their being. We all have one Father, one Maker. He considers himself honored in the kindnesses done the poor; he takes kindnesses done to the poor as done to himself and will therefore show that he is pleased with such deeds. *I was hungry, and you gave me meat* (food) (Mt 25:35).

Verse 32

The evildoer clings so closely to the world that he cannot find it in his heart to leave it, but is driven out of it; his soul is required (Lk 12:20); it is forced from him. He *is driven away in his wickedness*; he dies in his sins. When a godly man finishes his course, he *has hope in his death* of a happiness on the other side of death, of better things in another world than he ever had in this one.

Verse 33

Modesty is the badge of wisdom. A modest man's *wisdom rests in his heart* (v. 33); he digests what he knows; he has it readily available to him, but he does not make a big noise about it. If fools have a little smattering of knowledge, they take every occasion to show it off.

Verse 34

A nation is honored by the reign of justice. Righteous administration of government, justice between one person and another, public support given to religious faith, and kindness and compassion to foreigners all uphold the throne, elevate people's minds, and qualify a nation to receive and enjoy the favor of God. A nation is disgraced by the reign of vice: *Sin is a reproach to any* city or kingdom. The people of Israel were great when they were good, but when they abandoned God, all around them treated them with contempt and crushed them.

Verse 35

In a well-ordered court and government, smiles and favors are dispensed among those in positions of public trust according to their merits. Those who behave themselves wisely will be respected and promoted. No one's services will be neglected to please a party or a favorite. Those who are selfish and false, who betray their country, oppress the poor, and sow seeds of discord (6:14, 19), will be displaced.

CHAPTER 15

Verse 1

Peace may be kept by gentle speech. If wrath has risen like a threatening cloud, full of stormy thunder, *a soft answer* will disperse it and turn it away. If you are trying to explain your reasons or plead a righteous cause, it is better to be humble than angry; difficult arguments are best expressed with gentle words. Nothing stirs up anger and sows the seeds of discord (6:14, 19) like *grievous* (harsh) *words*, calling people mean names, rebuking them for their weaknesses, or anything that devalues and demeans them.

Verse 2

He who has knowledge must not only enjoy it, as if it were only for his own entertainment, but also use it, *use it aright*, to build up others. It is *the tongue* that must make use of it. An evil heart, on the other hand, expresses hurtful words with the tongue, for *the mouth of fools poureth out foolishness*, and this also includes filthy and foolish talk (Eph 5:4), which corrupts good character (1Co 15:33).

Verse 3

The eyes of the Lord are in every place, for he not only sees everyone from on high (Ps 33:13) but also is present everywhere. Secret sins, services, and sorrows are all under his eye. He is displeased with the evil and approves of the good. This speaks as much comfort to saints as it does terror to sinners.

Verse 4

A good tongue brings healing to sin-sick souls by convincing them of their need to repent, and brings healing to peace and love when they are broken, by reconciling opposing sides in a conflict. This is the healing of the tongue, which *is a tree of life*, the leaves of which have a healing power (Rev 22:2). Those who know how to speak well will make the place where they live into a paradise. An evil tongue brings wounding.

Verse 5

Let those in authority give instruction and correction to those they have responsibility for. They must not only teach with the light of knowledge but also rebuke with the heat of zeal. Both must be done with the authority and affection of a father and mother. It goes against the grain with good-tempered people to find fault and make those around them uneasy, but it is better to do this than to allow wrongdoers to continue along the path to destruction. Those who disrespect their good education are fools and are likely to live and to die as fools.

Verse 6

Where righteousness is, there are both riches and the encouragements riches can bring. If there is not much of this world's possessions, still, where there is grace, there is true treasure. And to those who have only a little, if they have the heart to be content with that (Php 4:11) and enjoy the comfort of the little they have, it will be enough; it is all the riches they need. Where evil is, although there may be riches, there comes trouble of spirit.

Verse 7

We use knowledge rightly when we spread it, not keeping it to ourselves or to a few of our close friends. We must exert ourselves to spread useful knowledge; we must teach some so that they may teach others.

Verse 8

God has sacrifices brought to him even by evildoers. Their sacrifices, however, though costly, are not accepted by God because they are not offered in sincerity or from good motives. God has such a love for upright and good people that their *prayer is a delight* to him.

Verse 9

The sacrifices of the wicked are an abomination to God (v. 8) not because they lack some of the finer points of ritual but because the whole course and tenor of their lives is evil.

Verse 10

This shows that those who cannot bear to be corrected must expect to be destroyed. Of all sinners, apostates resent stern discipline most, those who have turned away from God.

Verse 11

This confirms what was said earlier (v. 3) concerning God's omnipresence; he is everywhere at once, and so he can discern and judge good and evil. God knows all things, even those things that are hidden from the eyes of all other living beings (Job 28:20–24). The word here used for *destruction* is *Abaddon*, which is one of the Devil's names (Rev 9:11). That destroyer, though he deceives us, cannot evade or elude God's knowledge. God sees through all his disguises. Sheol (the state of separate souls and all their circumstances) and Abaddon (the place of the condemned and all their torments) are both alike under God's eye. If he sees through the depths and schemes of Satan himself, *much more* does he search human hearts. *God is greater than our hearts* (1Jn 3:20) and knows them better than we know them ourselves. He is therefore an infallible Judge of every person's character (Heb 4:13).

Verse 12

A mocker is a person who not only laughs at God and religious faith but also defies the ways used to convict and reform him. He cannot bear to look into his own heart and consider it seriously (Ps 4:4), or to let his own heart strike him, if he can help it. His case is sad indeed, since he is afraid of arguing with himself. He cannot bear to ask for advice or warnings from his friends.

Verse 13

Harmless mirth is commended to us as contributing to the health of the body, giving people energy and rendering them fit for business, and contributing to the acceptableness of one's behavior, making the face shine (Ps 104:15) and helping us to be pleasant to one another. A cheerful spirit, with wisdom and grace, is a beautiful ornament to religious faith, puts a further luster on the beauty of holiness (1Ch 16:29; 2Ch 20:21), and makes people more capable of doing good. Harmful heartache is what we are warned against as a great enemy. When it has control and rules us, *the spirit is broken* and crushed and becomes unfit to serve God.

Verse 14

Here are two things to be wondered at: a wise man is not satisfied with his wisdom, but seeks to increase it; the more he has, the more he wants. A fool is satisfied with his folly and does not seek a cure for it.

Verse 15

Some people suffer in oppression or affliction and are sorrowful; all their days are miserable. People who suffer in this way are not to be criticized or despised, but should be pitied and prayed for, helped and comforted. Others are of a cheerful spirit; and they have not only good days, but *a continual feast*; they enjoy a good time that never ends. And if they serve God with a cheerful heart, if their wealth oils the wheels of their obedience—all this and heaven too!—then they may indeed say that they serve a good Master.

Verses 16–17

Christian contentment and joy in God make life pleasant and comfortable. Cheerfulness of spirit will give people *a continual feast* (v. 15) even though they may have little in this world, as long as they have holiness and love. *A little*, if we keep a good conscience, serving God faithfully with the little we have, will make us more comfortable than if we had *great treasure and trouble therewith*. Those who have *great treasure* often find it brings turmoil (v. 16). If those who have great wealth would do their duty with it and then trust God with the outcome, their treasure would not bring so much turmoil. It is therefore far better to have only a little of the world, to maintain fellowship with God, enjoy him in all we have, and live by faith, than to have the greatest plenty and live without God in the world (Eph 2:12). If *brethren dwell together in unity* (Ps 133:1), if they are friendly, cheerful, and pleasant, that will make a *dinner of herbs* (vegetables) (v. 17) a feast that is sufficient in itself. Love will sweeten it, and then those gathered can be as happy as if they had all the fine things of this world. If there is mutual enmity and strife, even though the whole fattened calf has been slaughtered for a first-rate meal, there can be no comfort in it; the yeast of malice (1Co 5:8), of mutual strife, is enough to make everything sour.

Verse 18

Anger lights the fire that sets cities and churches burning: *A wrathful man*, one who burns with anger, causes other people to quarrel. *He that is slow to anger* not only *prevents* strife but also throws water on the flames if the fire has already been kindled, unites those who have fallen out, and uses gentle methods to ensure that both sides make concessions for the sake of peace.

Verse 19

Those who have no heart to do their work pretend that they cannot do their work without a great deal of hardship and danger, and they therefore go about it with as much reluctance as if they went barefoot through a thorny hedge. An honest desire and endeavor to do our duty will, by the grace of God, make our way smooth, and we will find it strewn with roses.

Verse 20

Good children are the joy of their parents, who should have joy from them, having taken so much care and effort in bringing them up. It adds much to the satisfaction of those who are good if they have reason to think they will be a comfort to their parents in their declining years. Evil children hold their parents in contempt, disrespecting their authority and poorly paying back all their kindness.

Verse 21

An evildoer sins not only without regret, but with delight. A fool walks here, there, and everywhere, according to no rules; he acts without sincerity or steadiness. In contrast, *a man of understanding*, the eyes of whose understanding are enlightened by the Spirit, *walks uprightly* (straight). He lives a consistent life; he seeks in everything to conform to the will of God.

Verse 22

If people will not take the time and trouble to consult with others, if they are so confident about their own judgment that they scorn asking others, then they are unlikely to bring about anything significant. They will be defeated by circumstances that, with a little consultation, might have been foreseen and avoided.

Verse 23

Our speech is wise when it is timely, when, as we say, it hits the nail on the head. Many a good word falls short of doing the good it might have done because it is not well timed.

Verse 24

The way of wisdom and holiness is *the way of life*, the way that leads to eternal life. Be wise and live. It is the way to escape *from hell beneath*. Good people set their *affections on things above* (Col 3:2) and consider those things. Their *conversation* (citizenship) *is in heaven* (Php 3:20); their way leads directly there; that is where their treasure is (Mt 6:21), *above*, far out of reach of enemies, above all the changes of this lower world.

Verse 25

The proud, who exalt themselves, trample on everyone around them. God *will destroy* such people, not only them but also *their houses*. God delights to support those who are dejected. *He will establish the border* that the poor widow is not herself able to defend and make good.

Verse 26

The thoughts of evildoers are, for the most part, those that God hates, those that are offensive to him who not only knows the heart and everything that goes on there but also requires that the innermost and highest place in it be given to him. The *words of the pure* may refer both to their devotions to God and also to their general conversations with other people. Both are pleasing to God when they come from a pure, and purified, heart.

Verse 27

He that is greedy of gain, and so makes himself a slave to the world, rushes about, upsetting all who are around him by making them tense, worrying about every little loss or disappointment and quarreling with everybody who gets in the way of making a profit. He is a burden and source of trouble to his children and servants. Those who are generous pass on a blessing to their families. *He that* hates all sinful, indirect ways of gaining money—who hates to be mean and mercenary and is willing, if need be, to do good without being paid for it—he will have the comfort of life; his name and family will live and endure.

Verse 28

It is the character of a righteous man that he is convinced that he must give an account of his words, and he knows they can have a good or bad influence on others. He therefore weighs up his words before he speaks, so as to speak truthfully. And it is his *heart* that *answers*; he speaks out the thoughts of his heart (Ps 15:2). He wants to speak apt and profitable words, and therefore he *studies to* (thinks about how he will) *answer* (v. 28), so that his speech may be filled with grace (Ne 2:4; 5:7). An evildoer never takes any care about what he says; his *mouth pours out evil things* (v. 28), to the dishonor of God and religion.

Verse 29

God sets himself far away from those who defy him. He will draw near in mercy to those who draw near to him in their duty (Jas 4:8).

Verse 30

It is pleasant to have a good prospect, to see the light of the sun (Ecc 11:7) and by it to see the wonderful works of God with which this lower world is beautified and enriched. Consideration of this should make us thankful for our eyesight. It is also very comforting to hear *a good report* (good news) concerning others; good people have no greater joy than to hear that their friends are walking in the truth (3Jn 4).

Verse 31

The ear that can take *the reproof* will love the person who gives it. Faithful, friendly rebukes are here called *the reproofs of life* because they are the means of giving spiritual life. Those who learn well and obey well are likely in time also to teach well and rule well.

Verse 32

Those who "refuse correction" (margin) *despise their own souls*. The fundamental error of sinners is undervaluing their own souls; undervaluing them, they harm the soul to please the body. *He that hears reproof* and puts right his faults *gets understanding*, by which his soul is kept safe from evil ways and directed to follow good ways.

Verse 33

An awe of God on our spirits will give us the wisest counsels and correct us whenever we say or do something unwise. Where there is humility, this is a happy sign of honor and a preparation for it.

CHAPTER 16

Verse 1

The reading given to this passage by most is different from that of our translation: *The preparation of the heart* is *in man* — he may plan this, that, and the other — but *the answer of the tongue*, not only the delivery of what he intended to speak but also the outcome of what he intended to do, *is of the Lord*. Man proposes, but God disposes (Thomas à Kempis, *The Imitation of Christ*, 1.19):
1. *Man proposes.* Human beings have been given freedom of thought and freedom of the will; they may make their plans and formulate their schemes as they think best, but when all has been said and done:
2. *God disposes.* Human beings cannot go about their business without the help and blessing of God, who made the human mouth and teaches us what we will say (Ex 4:12).

Verse 2

We all tend to be partial in judging ourselves. The judgment of God on us is based on truth (Ro 2:2): he *weighs the spirits* (weighs our motives) in his just and unerring scales. He knows what is in us and passes judgment on us accordingly, and we must stand or fall by his judgment.

Verse 3

The only way to have our *thoughts established is* to *commit our works to the Lord*. The great concerns of our souls must be committed to the grace of God. All our outward concerns must be committed to the providence of God, and to the sovereign, wise, and gracious direction of that providence. "Roll your works on the Lord" is the sense; roll the burden of your cares from yourself onto God.

Verse 4

God is the primary cause. Even evildoers are his creatures, although they are rebels; he gave them those powers with which they fight against him. God is the final end. Everything comes from him, and so all is for him.

Verse 5

The pride of sinners sets God against them. The power of sinners cannot protect them from God, even though they may strengthen themselves with both hands. Although they strengthen one another with their alliances, joining forces against God, they will not escape his righteous judgment.

Verse 6

The guilt of sin is taken away from us by the *mercy and truth* of God, in Jesus Christ the Mediator, and not legal sacrifices (Mic 6:7–8). By him the power of sin is broken in us and corrupt inclinations are purged. *By the fear of the Lord*, and the influence of that fear, *men depart from evil*; those who keep in their minds a holy fear and reverence of God will not dare sin against him.

Verse 7

God can turn enemies into friends when he pleases. The One who has all hearts in his hand can make *a man's enemies to be at peace with him*. He will do it for us when we please him. God made Esau to be at peace with Jacob (Ge 33:1–15), Abimelech with Isaac (Ge 26:6–31).

Verse 8

Small gains, honestly come by, with which a person is content and serves God cheerfully, putting them to a right use, are much more valuable than great wealth gained unjustly and then wrongly kept or spent. Such wealth gives much more inner satisfaction and a better reputation to all who are wise and good. It will last longer and will stand them in good stead on the great day, when people will be judged not according to what they had but according to what they did.

Verse 9

Human beings are reasonable creatures, with an ability to plan for themselves, and dependent creatures, subject to the direction and rule of their Maker. If people *devise their way* so as to make God's glory their purpose and his will their rule, they may expect that he will *direct their steps* by his Spirit and grace, so that they will not miss their way or come short of their final end. *Lord, direct my way* (1Th 3:11).

Verse 10

This may be read as a command to the kings and judges on earth to be wise and well taught. Let them be just and rule in the fear of God. It may also be taken as a promise to all good kings that if they sincerely aim at God's glory and seek direction from him, he will qualify them with wisdom and grace above others, in proportion to the eminence of their position and the trust placed in them.

Verse 11

The administration of public justice by the magistrate is a service of God; in it the scales are held and should be held by a steady and impartial hand. The observance of justice in business between persons is similarly a divine appointment.

Verse 12

A good king not only is just but also detests wrongdoing. He hates the thought of doing wrong and perverting the course of justice. The king who is careful to use his power rightly will find that that is the best security of his government, because it will gain the blessing of God, which will be a firm basis for the throne and a strong protection around it.

Verse 13

Good kings hate hangers-on and flatterers. They are not only honest themselves but also careful to employ under them those who are honest. A good king will put in power those who are conscientious and who will say what is righteous and wise.

Verses 14–15

These two verses show the power of kings, which is great everywhere but was especially so in the countries of the ancient Near East, where they had absolute and unlimited power. We have reason to bless God for the favorable constitution of the government we live under, which keeps the rights of the ruler without harming the liberty of the subjects. But here it is suggested:

1. How formidable *the wrath of a king is*: it is *as messengers of death* (v. 14); the wrath of Xerxes was so to Haman (Est 7:7–10). An angry word from an angry ruler has been *a messenger of death* to many people. A *man* must be very *wise* if he knows how to appease the wrath of a king with an aptly spoken word, as Jonathan once calmed his father's anger against David (1Sa 19:6).

2. How valuable and desirable the king's favor is to those who have incurred his displeasure, is life from the dead if the king is reconciled to them. To others it is *as a cloud of the latter rain*, like a rain cloud in spring (v. 15), which is very refreshing to the ground. People are foolish if they reject God's favor in order to escape an earthly ruler's wrath and obtain his favor.

Verse 16

Heavenly wisdom is better than worldly wealth and is to be preferred to it. Grace is more valuable than gold. Grace is the gift of God's special favor; gold is the gift of common providence. Grace is for the soul and eternity; gold is only for the body and time. Grace will stand us in good stead in our dying hour, when gold will do us no good. In getting wealth there are all the old questions about where it all leads to, but there is true joy and satisfaction of spirit in gaining wisdom. *Great peace have those that love it* (Ps 119:165).

Verse 17

It is *the way of the upright* to avoid sin, and this is a highway marked out by authority, tracked by many people who have gone before us. It is the concern of upright people to look after their souls. Those who are faithful in doing their duty protect their happiness. If we keep to our path, God will keep us.

Verse 18

Pride leads to destruction. When those who have lifted themselves up are laid low, it is the act of justice. Pharaoh (Ex 14:15–31), Sennacherib (2Ki 19:32–37), and Nebuchadnezzar (Da 4:29–33) were all examples of this. When proud people defy God's judgments, it is a sign that those judgments are just at the door, as for example in the cases of Ben-Hadad (2Ki 8:7–15) and

Herod (Ac 12:21–23). Let us therefore not fear the pride of others, but greatly fear pride in ourselves.

Verse 19

Those who are proud and put themselves forward, who constantly push forward and scramble for promotion, are those who commonly *divide the spoil* and share it among them. Humility commends us to the favor of God; it qualifies us for his gracious visits, protects us from many temptations, and keeps quiet and calmness in our souls. It is much better than arrogance, which, though it carries the honor and wealth of the world, makes God a person's enemy and the Devil their master.

Verse 20

Wisdom gains people respect and success, but it is only godliness that will secure true happiness. Some understand the first part of the verse as referring to godliness, which is true wisdom: "He that attends to the word"—the word of God (13:13)—will *find good* in it and prosper by it. And whoever *trusts in the Lord* (v. 20) is blessed.

Verse 21

Those who have solid wisdom will receive credit for it, and their judgment will be held in respect. Those who with their wisdom express their feelings easily and with good grace will *increase learning*; they spread knowledge to others, promote instruction, and do good by it, and that is how they increase their own stock of knowledge. *To him that has, and uses what he has, more shall be given* (Mk 4:25).

Verse 22

There is always some good to be gained from a wise and good person. His understanding is *a spring of life* to himself; within his own thoughts he builds himself up, if not others. There is nothing good to be gained from a fool.

Verse 23

Solomon earlier commended eloquence, or *the sweetness of the lips* (v. 21), and seemed to prefer it to wisdom, but here he corrects himself, as it were, and shows that unless there is good treasure within a person (Mt 12:35) to support that eloquence, it is worth little. Wisdom in *the heart is* what is most important. Quaint expressions may please the ear and indulge the fancy, but it is learning that is persuasive, and wisdom in the heart is necessary for this.

Verse 24

The pleasant words commended here must be those that *the heart of the wise teaches and adds learning to* (v. 23), words of timely advice, sensible instruction, and kind encouragement, words taken from God's word, for this is what Solomon learned from his father to consider *sweeter than honey and the honeycomb* (Ps 19:10). Many things are pleasant but not profitable, but these *pleasant words are health to the bones*, to the inner being (Ro 7:22), as well as *sweet to the soul*.

Verse 25

We had this before (14:12), but it is repeated here:

- As a warning to us all to be impartial in examining ourselves.
- As a threat to those whose way is not right, however right it may seem to them or others.

Verse 26

This verse is intended to make us diligent and to encourage us both in our worldly business and in the work of our religious faith, for the original reads literally, "The soul that labors labors for itself." It is a work of the heart that is being referred to here, the labor of the soul. If we make religious faith our business, God will make it a blessing to us.

Verses 27–28

There are those who are not only ungodly in themselves but also spiteful and troublesome toward others, and they are the worst kind of people: they *dig up evil* (v. 27); they work hard to find something on which to base some slanderous statement. If nothing is obvious, they dig around for it, delving into confidential matters or into the past, arousing evil suspicions and forcing innuendos. On the lips of such a slanderous scoundrel *there is as a fire* (v. 27), to brand his neighbor's reputation. *A froward* (perverse) *man*, who cannot find it in his heart to love anyone but himself, is troubled to see others live a life of love, and so he makes it his business to *sow strife* (v. 28) by telling lies and reporting ill-natured stories between *chief* (close) *friends*, so as to *separate* them from one another. Those who commit such evil deeds are evil indeed; they are doing the Devil's work.

Verses 29–30

Evildoers are described to us so that we may neither act like them nor have anything to do with them. They are *violent men* (v. 29), who pursue all their purposes by plunder and oppression, who *shut their eyes*, applying their minds closely *to devising froward things* (perversity) (v. 30), to plotting how they may cause the greatest trouble to their neighbors. Then, *moving their lips*, giving the word of command to their agents, they *bring evil to pass* (v. 30). Such people do all they can to *entice* others to join them in causing trouble, *leading them in a way that is not good* (v. 29) and is offensive to God.

Verse 31

Let mature people be mature disciples. If old people *be found in the way of righteousness*, their age will be their honor. Old age as such is honorable and commands respect, but if old people are found on a sinful path, their honor is lost and their crown is placed in the dust (Isa 65:20). Grace is the glory of old age.

Verse 32

The grace of humility is to be *slow to anger*, not easily enraged, not inclined to react quickly with resentment to provocation, so slow in our steps toward anger that we may be quickly stopped and pacified. It is to control our own spirits. Those who keep control of their passions are *better than the mighty*. See: one greater than Alexander or Caesar is here (Mt 12:42). The conquest of our own unruly passions requires more true wisdom, and a more steady management, than the gaining of a victory over an enemy. No lives or treasures are sacrificed to it. It is harder to quash an insurrection at home than to resist an invasion from abroad; humility enables us to be *more than conquerors* (Ro 8:37).

Verse 33

Nothing comes to pass by chance, nor is any event determined by blind fate; everything happens by the will and purposes of God. We must look on all the directions of Providence concerning our affairs as the directing of our lot, the answer to what we referred to God, and we must therefore accept them.

CHAPTER 17

Verse 1

These words commend family love and peace as contributing very much to the comfort of human life. Those who live in unity and quietness and seek to make themselves pleasing to one another live very comfortably, even if they work hard and live hard lives, even if they may only each have *a morsel*, and *a dry morsel* at that. There may be peace and contentment where there are not three meals a day, provided that all those living together have satisfaction in God's providence and mutual satisfaction in each other's wisdom. Holy love may be found even in a cottage. Those who live in strife, who are always shouting at each other and fighting, live uncomfortably even if they have plenty of fine things. They cannot expect the blessing of God on them. Love will sweeten *a dry morsel*, but strife will make *a house full of sacrifices* sour and bitter.

Verse 2

True merit does not go by position. Sometimes it so happens that the servant is wise and a blessing and credit to the family when the son is a fool and a disgrace to the family. True dignity will go by merit. Wise servants may come to have such privileges with their master as being included in the children's share of the estate and *having part of the inheritance among the brethren*.

Verse 3

As *the fining pot* (crucible) *is for silver*, both to test it and to purify it, so *the Lord tries* (tests) *the hearts*. He searches to see whether they meet his standard, and those that are at his standard he refines and makes even purer (Jer 17:10). God tests the heart by affliction (Ps 66:10–11), and he often tests his people in the furnace of affliction (Isa 48:10) to refine them. It is only God who *tries* (tests) *the hearts*. People have no such way of testing one another's hearts.

Verse 4

Those who commit evil support themselves by falsehood and lying: *A wicked doer gives* ear, with a great deal of pleasure, *to false lips*, lips that will justify them in the wrong they do. Sinners will strengthen one another's hands.

Verse 5

Those who trample on the poor, who laugh at them in their need, *reproach their Maker*, who acknowledges them, takes care of them, and can, when he pleases, reduce us to poverty too. *He that is glad at calamities* that come to others so that he may build himself up on the ruin of others and gossip about the judgments of God when they are away from home—let him know that he *shall not go unpunished*.

Verse 6

It is an honor to a man to live long enough to see his children's children (Ps 128:6; Ge 50:23), to see his family develop and grow through them, and to see them likely to serve their generation according to the will of God. This crowns and completes the comfort of *old men* in this world. It is an honor to children to have wise and godly parents, to have them kept alive when they have themselves grown up and established themselves in the world.

Verse 7

Fool, in Solomon's proverbs, refers to an evildoer, from whom *excellent speech* is unbefitting, because their way of life contradicts their eloquent words. If it is unbefitting for a contemptible person to presume to speak as a philosopher or politician, then it is even more unbefitting for a ruler, a person of honor, to take advantage of the confidence that is put in them to lie, pretend, and be careless about breaking their word.

Verse 8

Rich people value a little money as if it were a *precious stone*. They esteem themselves on the basis of their money as if it were not only a decoration but also a source of power over everyone and everything—including justice itself—as if all must be at their beck and call. Wherever they turn this sparkling diamond, they expect it to dazzle the eyes of everyone around them, making them do just what they want in the hope of getting that jewel for themselves.

Verse 9

The way to preserve peace among relatives and neighbors is to make the best of everything, not to tell others what has been said or done against them when it is not necessary for their safety, nor to take notice of what has been said or done against ourselves, but to excuse both and put the best interpretation on them. "It was an oversight, and so overlook it. It was done through forgetfulness, and so forget it."

Verse 10

A word is enough for a wise person, but lashes are not enough for a fool, not enough to make them aware of their errors so that they may repent of them.

Verse 11

A man is truly evil if he seeks every occasion to rebel against God and the government God has set over him, and to contradict and constantly pick quarrels with those around him. "A rebellious man seeks trouble" is how some understand it; he is looking for any opportunity to disturb the public peace. Because he will not be reclaimed by mild and gentle methods, *a cruel messenger shall be sent against him*, some terrible judgment or other, as a messenger from God.

Verse 12

A passionate man is brutish. When he loses his temper, he is a *fool in his folly*. He is dangerous; he challenges everyone who gets in his way, even if innocent. A bear robbed of her cubs attacks the first person she meets, thinking they are the robber. Anger is temporary madness. You may more easily guard against an enraged bear than against an extremely angry person.

Verse 13

A malicious, troublesome man is ungrateful to his friends. To repay evil for evil is uncivilized, but to repay evil for good is devilish. He is also unkind to his family, for he passes on a curse to it.

Verse 14

Here is the danger in *the beginning of strife*. One hot word leads to another, and so on, until it turns out like the breaching of a dam. When the water has gained a small opening, it widens the breach by itself, and then it cannot be stopped. Take note, therefore, of the first sparks of a dispute and extinguish them as soon as they appear.

Verse 15

When those entrusted with the administration of public justice either acquit the guilty or condemn those who are not guilty, they defeat the purpose of government, which is to protect the good and punish the bad.

Verse 16

We are amazed at God's great goodness to a foolish person in putting *a price* (money) *into his hand to get wisdom*. We have rational souls, the means of grace, the strivings of the Spirit (Ge 6:3), access to God in prayer (Ro 5:2; Eph 2:18; 3:12); we also have times and opportunities to gain wisdom. Good parents, relatives, ministers, and friends all help to gain wisdom. Wisdom itself is *a price*, something valuable. We have reason to wonder that God should entrust us with such advantages. Man's neglect of God's favor and his own true interests is absurd and inexplicable: *He has no heart to it.*

Verse 17

Friends must be faithful to each other *at all times*. It is not true friendship if it is not faithful. Fair-weather friends fly to you in summer but disappear for the winter. But if I love my friends because they are wise and good, even though they fall into poverty and disgrace, I will continue to love them. Christ is a friend who loves at all times (Jn 13:1; Ro 8:35), and this is how we must love him. Relatives must be especially careful and tender toward one another in times of affliction: *A brother is born* to help a brother or sister in distress. Some interpret it in this way: "A friend who loves at all times is born— that is, becomes—a brother in adversity," and is so to be valued.

Verse 18

It is wise to keep out of debt as far as possible, and especially to dread putting up security for others. Those who are *void of understanding* are commonly caught up in this trap, to the harm of their families.

Verse 19

He that loves strife, who loves to go to court in matters of worldly business, who loves disputes in religious matters and loves to fall out with others in the ordinary course of life—*he loves transgression*. He pretends to stand up for truth and right, but in reality he loves sin. Those who are ambitious expose themselves to trouble. *He that exalts his gate*, who builds a stately house, or at least a fine façade, so that his house may be higher and better than his neighbors', seeks his own destruction.

Verse 20

He that has a froward (perverse) *heart*, who sows the seeds of dissension (6:14, 19) and is full of anger, cannot take any rational satisfaction in it; he *finds no good*. *He that has a perverse* (deceitful) *tongue*, whose speech is twisted, abusive, or backbiting, loses his friends, provokes his enemies, and pulls trouble down on his own head.

Verse 21

There was *joy when a man was born into the world* (Jn 16:21), but if he turns out to be evil, his own father wishes he had never been born. Absalom's name meant his "father's peace," but he was the cause of his greatest trouble. *The father of a fool* takes it so much to heart that he *has no joy* in anything else.

Verse 22

It is healthy to be cheerful. The Lord is for the body. He has provided for it by giving not only food but also medicine. He tells us here that the best medicine *is a merry heart*. Solomon does not mean a heart devoted to futile, worldly, and godless merriment, but a heart that rejoices in God and serves him with gladness. God allows us to be cheerful and gives us many reasons to be cheerful, especially if by his grace he gives us hearts to be cheerful. This "does good to a medicine," as some understand it; it will make medicine more effective. Or "it does good as a medicine," to the body, making it ready and fit for its work. The sorrows of the mind often contribute to the weakness of the body: *A broken spirit*, depressed by the burden of afflictions, and especially a conscience wounded by the sense of guilt, *dries the bones*.

Verse 23

It *is a wicked man* who will *take a gift* in exchange for giving a false testimony, verdict, or judgment. He is ashamed of it, for he takes it, with all possible secrecy, *out of the bosom*, where he knows it is ready for him; it is well-hidden. Thus the course of justice is not only obstructed but also perverted and turned to injustice.

Verse 24

A man is intelligent if he lays his *wisdom before him*, as the map and compass with which he steers his way through life; he is constantly looking at it. One who has a roving and rambling fancy will never be fit for any solid work; he cannot fix his thoughts on one subject or pursue any one purpose with steadiness.

Verse 25

Evil children are an affliction to both of their parents. They bring anger to the father because they despise his authority, and sorrow and bitterness to the mother because they abuse her tenderness.

Verse 26

Let magistrates see to it that they never *punish the just*. When rulers become tyrants and persecutors, their thrones will be neither firm nor comfortable. Let subjects not find fault with the government for doing its duty, for it is evil *to strike princes for equity* by defaming their administration.

Verses 27–28

A gracious spirit is a precious spirit, and it makes a person amiable and *more excellent than his neighbour* (12:26). He has "a calm spirit," as some read it, not fiery from anger. A calm head and a warm heart are an admirable combination. *He that has knowledge* and aims to do good with it is careful that when he does speak, he is speaking to the point. He *spares his words* (v. 27), because words are better spared than wrongly used.

CHAPTER 18

Verse 1

The original text of this verse is difficult. Some take it as a rebuke of an affected superiority. When people take pride in *separating themselves* from the feelings and company of others, contradicting all that has been said and advancing new ideas of their own, it is to satisfy a desire of boasting, and they seek and meddle in what does not concern them, passing judgment on everyone's situation. Our translation, on the other hand, seems to take the verse as an incentive to diligence in pursuing wisdom. If we want to gain knowledge or grace, then we must desire it, we must *separate ourselves* from all those things that would slow us down in pursuing it, we must withdraw from the hustle and bustle of this world's worthless things, and then we must *seek and intermeddle with all* the means and instructions of *wisdom*, which means to get to know a range of opinions so that we may test all things and hold fast to what is good (1Th 5:21).

Verse 2

A fool may claim to have understanding and to pursue it, but he has no true delight in this pursuit. He does not love his work, his business, his Bible, or his prayers; he would rather be playing the fool with worldly pleasures. Nor does he have any good intentions in this pursuit, only *that his heart may discover itself*, that he might air his own opinions, have something to show off with, because he loves the sound of his own voice.

Verse 3

This may include two meanings:
1. Evildoers are mockers and put *contempt* on others. *When the wicked comes* into any company, comes into the colleges of wisdom or assemblies for worship, *then comes contempt* of God, his people, his ministers, and everything that is said and done.
2. Evildoers are shameful people and bring *contempt* on themselves, for God has said that those *who despise him shall be lightly esteemed* (1Sa 2:30).

Verse 4

An intelligent man has a good treasure of useful things within him (Mt 12:35), which gives him something relevant and useful to say. This is like *deep waters*, which make no noise but never run dry. The words of such a *man's mouth are as a flowing* (bubbling) *brook*. They flow naturally; they are clean and fresh.

Verse 5

This justly condemns those ministers of justice who pervert the course of justice by overlooking people's crimes because of their position or wealth. The merits of the cause must be considered, not the person.

Verses 6–7

A fool's lips enter into contention (v. 6) by putting forward foolish ideas that others oppose, starting a quarrel. The arrogant, the hot-tempered, and drunkards are all fools, whose lips *enter into contention*. The *fool's mouth*, in effect, *calls for strokes*; it invites a beating (v. 6). The fool has spoken words that deserve to be punished by a beating, and he involves himself in ruin: *A fool's mouth*, which has led, or would have led, to the destruction of others, ultimately turns out to *his own destruction* (v. 7).

Verse 8

Gossips are those who secretly tell stories from house to house with the intention of ruining reputations, breaking friendships, and causing trouble between relatives. The words of such people are here said to be "like as when men are wounded" (margin); gossips pretend that it is with the greatest possible grief and reluctance that they are speaking about the troubles of others. They look as if they themselves had been wounded by those troubles, whereas really they are fond of the story and tell it with pride and delight. Their words seem to express sympathy, but they go *down as poison into the innermost parts of the belly.* The words of the gossip wound those about whom they are spoken, their reputation and interests, and those to whom they are spoken, their love and kindness.

Verse 9

Some people waste what they own, living beyond their means, and are justly branded as fools by others. Idleness is no better. One who is lazy in his work—literally, whose "hands hang down"—who stands, as we put it, with his hands in his pockets, is the extravagant person's own brother. One scatters what he has, the other lets it run through his fingers.

Verse 10

Here we see God's sufficiency for the saints: his *name is a strong tower* for them, in which they may rest when they are tired and be protected when they are being pursued. The wealth stored in this tower is enough to make them rich. The strength of this tower is enough to protect them.

Verse 11

The rich man has his share and treasure in the things of this world (Ps 17:14; Mt 6:19). His wealth is as much his confidence as God is the confidence of the godly, and he expects as much from it as godly people do from their God. He makes his *wealth his city,* where he lives and rules with much self-satisfaction and smugness, and he defies danger, as if nothing could hurt him. *His scales are his pride* (Job 41:15); his wealth is his wall, and he thinks it is *a high wall* that cannot be scaled; he is deceiving himself. It is *a strong city* and *a high wall,* but it is so only *in his own conceit* (imagination).

Verse 12

Pride foreshadows destruction, and destruction will be the final punishment of pride. Humility leads to honor, and honor will be the final reward of humility.

Verse 13

Some take pride in being quick off the mark. They *answer a matter before they hear it.* When they have heard one side, they think the matter so clear that they need not trouble themselves to listen to the other side. Actually, however, although a ready wit is good for bantering, it is solid judgment and sound wisdom that are truly effective. It is foolish for people to give their opinion on a matter that they do not have the patience to look into more seriously.

Verse 14

Many weaknesses and adversities that we are affected by in this world, whether they concern our physical well-being, our reputation, or our possessions, may be endured as long as we have good courage. It also helps if we are able to act with reason and resolution, especially if we

have a good conscience. If the *spirit of a man will sustain the infirmity,* much more will the spirit of a Christian, or rather the Spirit of God witnessing and working with our spirits (Ro 8:16) in times of trouble.

Verse 15

The more discerning a person is, the more they will thirst for knowledge, the knowledge of God and their duty, and the way to heaven, for that is the best kind of knowledge. We must get knowledge not only into our heads but also into our hearts.

Verse 16

A man's gift, if he is in prison, may gain his release. Or if a lowly man does not know how to gain access to a famous person, he may do so by giving a fee or a present to the servants of the famous person, which will open up the way for him. His gift will enable him to sit among *great men,* in honor and power. Notice how corrupt the world is when people's gifts will do for them what their merits will not do, even though they deserve advancement for them.

Verse 17

This shows that one story sounds valid until another one is told. The person who speaks first will be sure to tell a story that will make their case look good, whether it really is or not. The defendant should then be heard and allowed to cross-examine the witnesses, which may make the matter appear quite different than it had. We must therefore remember that we have two ears to listen to both sides of an argument before we express our opinion.

Verse 18

Disputes often happen among powerful people, who are confident they can get what they want and therefore will hardly condescend to get their hands dirty by negotiating a compromise, whereas those who are poor are forced to make their peace and sit down as losers. Even the disputes of powerful people may be ended by casting lots if a compromise cannot be reached in any other way.

Verse 19

Great care must be taken to prevent quarrels from breaking out among relatives and those who are under special obligations to each other, because such quarrels are most unnatural and unseemly. Great care must be taken to reach a compromise in conflicts between relatives, and as quickly as possible, because it is a very difficult task.

Verse 20

Our satisfaction and peace depend very much on the testimony of our own consciences, whether for us or against us. The *belly* stands here for the inner being, the conscience (20:27). The testimony of our consciences will be for us or against us according to whether we have or have not controlled our tongues well. According to whether *the fruit of the mouth* is good or bad, so is the person's character, and therefore the testimony of their conscience.

Verse 21

Many have died because of their own foul words, and many have been killed by false words; on the other hand, many have saved their lives, or secured the comfort of them, by wise, gentle words, and other lives have been saved by a timely word of testimony or intercession for them.

Verse 22

A good wife is a great blessing to a man. He that *finds a wife*—that is, a true wife; a bad wife does not deserve to be called by such an honorable name—who finds a suitable helper and companion for himself (Ge 2:18)—that is a wife in the original meaning of the term—has found what will not only contribute more than anything to his comfort in this life but also lead him forward on the way to heaven. God is to be acknowledged with thankfulness for this blessing.

Verse 23

Although poverty brings many physical disadvantages, it often has a good effect on the spirit, for it makes people humble. It teaches them to *use entreaties*, to plead for mercy. It tells them they must take what is given them and be thankful. We are all poor when we come to the throne of God's grace, and so we must plead. Although a prosperous condition has many advantages, it often brings this trouble: it makes people proud, conceited, and arrogant. It is very foolish of some rich people, especially those who have risen from humble beginnings, to think they should answer roughly, whereas the best way is to be gentle and considerate (Jas 3:17).

Verse 24

If we want to have friends and keep them, we must not only not insult them, but also love them. We may promise ourselves a great deal of comfort in a true friend. Sometimes *there is a friend*, who is not related to us, the ties of whose respect and love prove stronger than natural ties. Christ is a friend to all believers who *sticks closer than a brother*.

CHAPTER 19
Verse 1

Notice here:
1. The reputation and comfort of a poor man. Let him be honest and *walk in integrity*, let his life be blameless; let him keep a good conscience. Let him speak and act with sincerity when he is strongly tempted to break his word, and then let him esteem himself on the basis of that, for all wise and good people will value such a person.
2. The shame of a rich man, despite all his pomp. If he is shallow and speaks evil words, he is a *fool*.

Verse 2

Some read this, "To be without the knowledge of the soul is not good." *He that hastes with his feet*—who does things in a rush, inconsiderately, not taking the time to ponder the path of his feet—*sins*. It is about as good not to know as not to consider what we know.

Verse 3

The foolishness of man perverts his way (ruins his life). People encounter all kinds of adversities and disappointments in life, and it is because of their own foolish ways; it is their own sin that corrects them. When they have gotten themselves into a mess, they blame God, and their hearts rage against him as if he had done them wrong, whereas in reality they have wronged themselves.

Verse 4

Wealth enables a man to send many presents and do many kind acts, and so gains him many friends, who flatter him but really love only what he has. If a person who was loved and respected while he was successful suddenly becomes poor, he becomes *separated from his neighbour*. He is not acknowledged or looked on; people keep him at a distance, and he is told he is troublesome.

Verse 5

People *teach their tongues to speak lies* (Jer 9:5). If people take the liberty of lying in conversation, then if they are ever tempted to the greater evil of false-witness bearing, they have already prepared themselves to yield to it, though they have seemed to detest it. Lying *shall not escape* the righteous judgment of God, who is jealous and will not allow his name to be dishonored.

Verses 6–7

The ruler who has power to give out the top positions has his waiting room filled with people wanting to ingratiate themselves with him and ask favors, those who are ready to adore him for what they can get out of him. This shows how fervently we should then seek the favor of God, which is far beyond that of any earthly ruler. But it seems generosity is more effective than grandness itself for gaining respect, for *every man is a friend to him that gives gifts* (v. 6). Those who are counted benefactors exercise authority, which may give them the opportunity to do good (Lk 22:25). Those who are poor and lowly are shown no respect and despised. It should not be so; we must honor everyone, even the most lowly. *All the brethren of the poor do hate him* (v. 7); even his own relatives look on him as a stain on their family's good name. Then his other friends, who were not related to him, *go far from him*, to get out of his way. *He pursues them with words* (v. 7), hoping to boldly win back their friendship and kindness, but it is futile; they want to have nothing more to do with him. Let poor people therefore make God their friend and seek him with their prayers, and they will find he will not fail to help them.

Verse 8

Get wisdom; gain knowledge, grace, and friendship with God; those who do so show that they *love their own souls*, and they will be found to have done themselves the greatest possible kindness. Those who *keep understanding* will certainly *find good* and prosper.

Verse 9

We need to be warned again and again of the danger of the sin of lying and bearing false witness. A person who commits these sins *shall perish*. His punishment will be his destruction. It is a sin that condemns and destroys.

Verse 10

Pleasure and liberty are inappropriate for fools. A person who does not have wisdom and grace has no right or entitlement to true joy, and so it is unfitting. Power and honor are inappropriate for people with a servile spirit. No one is so insolent and intolerable as a beggar on horseback, *a servant when he reigns* (30:22).

Verse 11

A wise person will observe these two rules about anger:
1. Not to be overhasty in expressing it: *Discretion* (wisdom) teaches us to *defer our anger* until we have thoroughly considered all the merits of the offense, and then to delay pursuing anger until there is no danger of its

being expressed immoderately. Plato said to his servant, "I want to beat you, except I am angry."

2. Not to be overcritical in it. It is here made a man's *glory to pass over a transgression*, to overlook an offense, or if he sees fit to take notice of it, still to forgive it.

Verse 12

Kings are not ordinary people; their frowns are terrible and their smiles encouraging, and so they should be concerned that they never by their frowns frighten off a good person from doing good, or ever by their smiles support an evildoer in doing wrong, for then they are abusing their influence (Ro 13:3). Let subjects be faithful and dutiful to their rulers, and as they do good services to the public, let them be encouraged by a hope for the favor of their rulers.

Verse 13

A foolish son brings anguish to a father and is his ruin. A son who will not apply himself to study or business, who will not take advice, who lives an immoral, promiscuous, and reckless life, who spends what he has extravagantly, bets and wastes it (1Pe 4:3–4; Lk 15:12–13), or who is proud, silly, and conceited is a grief *of his father*. An irritable, perverse wife is as great an affliction: her *contentions are continual*. Those who are used to finding fault with others never lack something or other to find fault with; it is *a continual dropping*, that is, a continual nuisance, as it is to have a roof in such disrepair that it lets in rain everywhere, so that there is nowhere to stay dry.

Verse 14

A wise and noble wife is a fine gift of God's providence to a man—a wife who *is prudent*, in contrast to one who is contentious (v. 13). *A prudent wife* makes the best of everything. If a man has such a wife, let him attribute it to the goodness of God, who made a suitable partner for him (Ge 2:18) and, perhaps by some twists and turns of providence that seemed random, brought her to him (Ge 2:22). Good possessions may be *the inheritance of fathers*, which, by the common direction of Providence, comes as a matter of course to a man, but no man has a good wife by descent or inheritance.

Verse 15

A lazy disposition numbs people and makes them careless about their own lives, as if they were *cast into a deep sleep*, dreaming much but never actually doing anything. Even their souls are idle and lulled to sleep; their rational powers have become chilled and frozen. Those who will not work cannot expect to eat (2Th 3:10), but must *suffer hunger*. One who is idle in the affairs of his soul, who takes no effort to work out his salvation (Php 2:12), will perish for lack of what is necessary for his spiritual life and happiness.

Verse 16

Those who seek to *keep the commandment* in everything, who live according to God's rules, *keep their own souls*; they protect their present peace and future happiness. If we keep God's word, God's word will keep us from everything really harmful.

Verse 17

The duty of love includes two things:

• Compassion, which is the inner motivation of love in the heart; it is to *have pity on the poor*.

• Generosity. We must not only pity the poor but also give to them according to their need and our ability (Jas 2:15–16). It is love to *do* good for the poor, as well as to give. What is either given to the poor or done for them God will credit as lent to him, literally, "lent with interest." God accepts it as if it were done to him: *He will pay him again*, in physical, spiritual, and eternal blessings.

Verse 18

As soon as a corrupt disposition appears in children, in their misbehavior, restrain it immediately, before it becomes a hardened habit. If they can change their behavior without correction, all well and good; but if you find that your forgiving them once, on a pretended repentance and promise of mending their ways, only makes them bolder in offending again, be firm in your resolve. It is better that your child should cry under your rod of discipline than under the sword of the magistrate, or of divine vengeance.

Verse 19

Angry people are never without trouble. Those who have headstrong, hot-tempered passions commonly bring themselves and their families into difficulties by troublesome lawsuits or quarrels. All these troubles and others would be prevented if they would gain control of their own spirits (16:32). It may also be read as referring to the previous verse: "He that is of great wrath," a child who is to be corrected and will not tolerate being rebuked, who cries out, "deserves to be punished"; *for, if thou deliver him*, if you let him off, then you will be forced to punish him more the next time.

Verse 20

It is well with those who are *wise in their latter end*, wise for their future state, wise for another world. Those who want to *be wise in their latter end* must be willing to be taught, advised, and corrected when they are young.

Verse 21

God knows the *many devices that are in men's hearts* (as those referred to in Ps 2:1–3; Mic 4:11). God's purposes often thwart or frustrate human plans, but their plans cannot change his purposes in the least, nor disturb their proceedings. Crafty, scheming people think they can outwit everyone else, but there is a God in heaven who laughs at them (Ps 2:4)! All God's purposes, which we are sure are right and good, will be fulfilled in due time!

Verse 22

It must be *the desire of a man*, if he has any spark of goodness in him, to be kind. It is far better to have a heart to do good and lack ability to do it than to have ability to do it and lack a heart to do it. *A poor man*, who wishes you well but can promise you nothing because he has nothing to be kind with, *is better than a liar*, who makes you believe he will do mighty things but, when it comes to starting them, does nothing at all.

Verse 23

Notice what is gained by those who live in the fear of God. They *shall not be visited with evil*, they will be untouched by trouble; illness or other forms of suffering may come on them, but there will be nothing to harm the soul, whereas all worldly satisfactions are short-lived and disappear quickly. Such people will have true and complete happiness. Serious godliness leads directly *to life*, that is, to all good, to eternal life.

Verse 24

A sluggard is here exposed as a fool. He is concerned only to save himself from work and cold. He *hides his hand in his bosom*; his hands are cold and he must warm them close to his chest; he has decided not to get involved in any work or hardship. He will not even make the effort to feed himself, not even lift his finger to put food into his own mouth.

Verse 25

The punishment of mockers will have a good effect on others. If it does not cure people who have become infected, it may prevent the spreading of the infection. The rebuke of wise people will have a good effect on them. If you *reprove one that has understanding*, he will understand himself. He accepts correction tolerantly and wisely learns from it.

Verse 26

The sin of an uncontrolled son wrongs his parents; it is sinfully ungrateful to those who brought him into the world and who took so much care of him: *He wastes his father*, wastes his wealth, which he should have had to support him in his old age, and breaks his heart. He *chases away his mother*. All his rudeness and arrogance makes her tired of her house, and she is glad to withdraw for a little peace and quiet, and when he has spent everything, he drives her out of the house.

Verse 27

There is something that seems intended for the instruction, but really leads to the destruction, of young people. Agents of evil will undertake to teach them how to think lightly of sins, how to stop up the mouth of their own consciences, and how to steer clear of restraints. Wise people will do well to turn a deaf ear to such instructions.

Verse 28

An ungodly witness is one who bears false witness against his neighbor, who will break his oath and commit perjury to cause trouble for someone else; there is great injustice and great ungodliness in such an act. If you tell him about the law and principles of justice, that the Scriptures and oaths are sacred and that a day of judgment is coming, he laughs it all off. He is greedy and glad to have any opportunity to sin.

Verse 29

Mockers are fools. Those who ridicule things that are sacred and serious only make themselves ridiculous.

CHAPTER 20

Verse 1

Wine is a mocker; strong drink is raging. At first it brings smiles, but in the end it bites like a snake (23:32). It rages on the sinner's conscience, and there is fury in the body. "When the wine is in, the wit is out," and then the person acts according to their natural temperament, either mocks like a fool or rages like a lunatic. Drunkenness, which claims to be sociable, makes people unfit for society. A drunkard is a fool and is likely to remain so.

Verse 2

Some rulers rule by wisdom and love, like God himself, but those who arrogantly rule by terror are like a lion in the forest, exerting brutal power. How unwise it is, therefore, to quarrel with such rulers. Those who do so *sin against their own lives*. Much more do those do so who provoke the King of kings to anger.

Verse 3

A person may think he is wise if he is quick to react angrily to an insulting remark, that he is wise to insist on every fine point of honor or right, but one who *meddles* in this way creates unnecessary trouble for himself. In reality *it is an honour for a man to cease from strife*, to let go of a dispute, to forgive an injury, and to be friends.

Verse 4

Laziness keeps people away from plowing and sowing in season: they always have some excuse or other up their sleeve, but the true reason is that it is *cold* weather. Some people are similarly careless about matters concerning their souls. Those who *will not plough* in seedtime cannot expect to reap at harvest time. They must beg for their bread when the diligent are bringing home their sheaves with joy (Ps 126:6).

Verse 5

A man's wisdom is here said to be useful to him for drawing out the thoughts of others like water in order to gain knowledge of them and from them. On the one hand, although a man's purposes are carefully hidden, so that they are as *deep water* that cannot be fathomed, there are those who by their sly questionings will draw out of them both what they have done and what they intend to do. On the other hand, some people are very able and qualified to advise others, but they are reserved; they have a great deal in them but are reluctant to release it. *A man of understanding will draw it out*, as one draws wine out of a container.

Verse 6

Most people will talk a great deal about their own kind acts, hospitality, and godliness. But it is hard to find those who are truly kind and generous, who have done more than they care to hear spoken about, who will be true friends to someone in a crisis.

Verse 7

A good man does right, is blameless, and keeps a good conscience; he derives comfort from his life. He is not susceptible to the awkwardness or apprehension to which the deceitful are subject. He also does well for his family. God has mercy in store for the descendants of the faithful.

Verse 8

A king is worthy of that title if he *sits on the throne* not as a throne of honor, to take his ease, making people keep their distance from him, but as a *throne of judgment*, so that he may administer justice and make amends to those who have been injured. If he inspects his affairs himself, those who are employed under him will be restrained from doing wrong. If great people are good and use their power as they should, what good will they do and what evil will they prevent!

Verse 9

This question is not only a challenge to anyone to prove themselves sinless, but also a lament for the corruption of human beings. Here, in this imperfect state, no person whatever can claim to be without sin. Those who think they are as good as they should be cannot claim to be without sin, and those who are really good dare not say this.

Verse 10

In paying and receiving money, which was then commonly done using scale balances, some people in Solomon's time had *divers* (differing) *weights*, a lesser weight for what they paid and a greater weight for what they received; they also had differing measures, a smaller measure to sell by and a larger measure to buy by. Under this heading are included all kinds of fraud and deceit in business and trade. They are all *alike an abomination to the Lord*. He hates those who break the common faith by which justice is maintained.

Verse 11

A tree is known by its fruits (Mt 12:33), even a young tree, and small children by their actions. Children show their true character. You may soon see what their temperament is like. Parents should observe their children to discover their inclinations and skills, and manage them accordingly, developing their good abilities and steering them away from the bad ones.

Verse 12

God is the God of nature, and he *formed the eye* and *planted the ear* (Ps 94:9). Hearing and seeing are sensory perceptions, and we must particularly acknowledge God's goodness in them. It is God who gives us ears to listen to his voice and eyes to see his beauty, for it is he who opens our understanding.

Verse 13

Although you have to sleep, *love not sleep*, as those do who hate to work. Do not love sleep for its own sake, but only as a preparation for further work. When you wake up, look up; do not miss any opportunities, but seize them; apply yourself closely to your work.

Verse 14

Notice what ways people use to obtain a good bargain and to buy something cheaply. They belittle and run down what they know is valuable; they cry out, "*It is naught, it is naught*; it has this and the other fault. It is too expensive; we can buy better and more cheaply elsewhere, or have previously bought better and more cheaply." However, sellers exaggerate as much in commending their goods and justifying their price as buyers do in running them down, and so there are faults on both sides. When the buyer has beaten down the price that the seller is asking for, the buyer goes on his way, boasting about what fine goods he has just bought at his own price.

Verse 15

The *lips of knowledge*—a good understanding to guide the lips and a fine eloquence in spreading their knowledge—are to be preferred to gold and rubies. They are rarer in themselves, scarcer and harder to find. They make us rich toward God, rich in good works (1Ti 2:9–10).

Verse 16

Those who will put up security for anyone who asks them, including their lazy companions, cannot last long. Those who are in relationships with wayward women will soon be beggars; never give them credit without a good pledge.

Verse 17

All the pleasures and profits of sin are *bread of deceit*, food gained by fraud. They are stolen, because they are forbidden fruit. They will deceive people, for they are not what they promise. For a time, however, they are *rolled under the tongue as a sweet morsel* (Job 20:12). Afterward, the sinner's *mouth shall be filled with gravel*. Some nations have punished evildoers by mixing gravel in with their bread.

Verse 18

Ask God's advice and seek his direction. What is done hastily and rashly may be repented of at leisure. We should be especially wise and cautious in engaging in war. Consider the matter very carefully and take advice whether the war should be begun or not, and when it has begun, consider how it may be pursued, for good management is as important as great courage.

Verse 19

Gossips are called *talebearers* because they are unprincipled people who go about carrying stories, who cause trouble among neighbors and relatives, who sow in people's minds the seeds of jealousy toward their governors, ministers, or one another, and who reveal confidential information. "Do not get to know such people; do not listen to them, for you may be sure they will betray your secrets too and tell tales about you." Flatterers are usually gossips.

Verse 20

Here is an undutiful child who gradually becomes evil. The child began by despising his father and mother, but he finally reaches the point of cursing them, in defiance of God and his Law, which has made this a capital offense (Ex 21:17; Mt 15:4). An undutiful child ultimately becomes very miserable: *His lamp shall be put out in obscure darkness*; all his honor will be laid in the dust.

Verse 21

There are those who have resolved to get rich by any means, right or wrong, who will cheat even their own parents, grudging themselves and their families food. Wealth that is suddenly accumulated is often ruined as suddenly. It proves the saying "soon ripe and soon rotten"; premature success is often short-lived.

Verse 22

We must not avenge ourselves: "*Say not thou I will recompense* (repay) *evil* for evil. Do not wish revenge. Never say that you will do something that you cannot in faith pray to God to help you in, and you cannot do that if you are plotting revenge." We must refer the matter to God, and leave him to plead our cause, to uphold our rights, and deal with those who wrong us in such a way as he thinks fit and in his own time.

Verse 23

This is to the same effect as what was said in v. 10. It is added here, *A false balance is not good*, to suggest that it is not only detestable to God but also unprofitable to sinners themselves; there is really no good to be gained by it, for a bargain made deceitfully will ultimately prove not to be a bargain at all.

Verse 24

We must constantly depend on God. All our natural actions depend on his providence, and all our spiritual actions depend on his grace. The best people are no better than God makes them. We cannot foresee future events, and so *How can a man understand his own way?* We understand so little about our own ways that we do not know what is good for us, and so we must commit our way to the Lord.

Verse 25

Sacrilege, people dedicating holy things but then putting them to their own use, is here called *devouring* them. What is devoted to the service of God should be carefully preserved for its intended purposes. Those who rush through religious services such as praying and preaching may be said to *devour that which is holy. It is a snare to a man, after* he has made *vows* to God, *to inquire* how he may avoid them or think up excuses to break them. If their subject matter was doubtful and the expressions were ambiguous, that was his own fault; he should have made them with greater care and caution.

Verse 26

Magistrates must *scatter* (winnow out) *the wicked*, who are in close relationships, and there is no way of scattering them but *by bringing the wheel* (driving the threshing wheel) *over them*, that is, enforcing the laws against them, crushing their power and quashing their projects.

Verse 27

The great human soul is a divine light; it is the *candle of the Lord*, a candle that he has lit. The noble faculty of conscience is God's deputy in the soul; it is a candle lit not only by him but also for him. With the help of conscience we come to know ourselves. The human spirit has a consciousness of itself (1Co 2:11); it searches the ways and attitudes of the soul, commends what is good, and condemns what is not good.

Verse 28

A good king must be strictly faithful to his word; he must loathe all pretense and support truth. He must also rule mercifully and be compassionate. These virtues will make him comfortable and secure, loved by his people.

Verse 29

Both young and old have their advantages, and neither of them should despise or envy the other. The young are strong and fit for action, able to break through any difficulties. The old are grave and qualified to give advice, and although they do not have the strength of young people, they have more wisdom and experience.

Verse 30

Many people need severe rebukes. Some criminals must feel the rigors of the law and public justice; gentle methods will have no effect on them; they must receive blows and wounds. Severe rebukes sometimes do a great deal of good, as caustic substances contribute to the healing of a wound, destroying the overgrown flesh.

CHAPTER 21

Verse 1

Even human *hearts* are in God's hands. God can change people's minds; he can turn them away from what they seemed most intent on, as the farmer uses irrigation channels to direct the water through the land, which does not change the nature of the water or coerce it, any more than God's providence coerces the innate freedom of the human will, but directs its course to serve his own purposes.

Verse 2

We are all inclined to have too favorable an opinion of our own character. A proud heart is very clever in making something appear right when it is far from being so, to silence the voice of conscience. God looks at the heart and judges people according to their actions, motives, and intentions.

Verse 3

Many people deceive themselves with the thought that if they offer sacrifices, those will obtain for them special exemption for unrighteousness. Living a good life—acting justly and loving mercy (Mic 6:8)—is more pleasing to God than the most ostentatious devotion. Sacrifices were a divine institution and were acceptable to God if they were offered in faith and with repentance, but not otherwise (Isa 1:11). But even then moral duties were preferred to them (1Sa 15:22).

Verse 4

Evildoers carry themselves about arrogantly and scornfully toward both God and other people and are always plotting some trouble.

Verse 5

If we want to live abundant and comfortable lives, we must be conscientious in our business and not shrink from hard work and trouble. Those who are rash and inconsiderate in their affairs, who are greedy to make gains regardless of right or wrong and want to get rich quickly by unjust practices, are on the road to poverty.

Verse 6

Those who hope to make themselves rich by following dishonest practices may perhaps store up treasures, but they will not meet with the satisfaction they expect. It is a *vanity tossed to and fro*, a fleeting vapor, disappointment and trouble of spirit to them (Ecc 2:11, 17, 26; etc.). They lay themselves open to others' envy and ill will and to the wrath of God.

Verse 7

Getting money by lying (v. 6) is no better than downright robbery or violence. Cheating is stealing. The cause of injustice is that people *refuse to do judgment*; they will not render to everyone their due, but want to withhold it, and sins of omission make way for sins of commission; they ultimately come to commit robbery or violence itself.

Verse 8

The perverse person, who is deceitful, who acts by cunning and swindles in everything he does, makes his way devious, contrary to all rules of honor and honesty. It is devious, for you do not know where to find him. People who are pure are proved to be such by their work, for it *is right*, it is just and consistent, and they are accepted by God and approved by human beings (Ro 14:18).

Verse 9

What a great affliction it is for a man to have a quarrelsome woman as his wife, who is fretful toward herself and constantly angry with her children and servants. If a man has a large house, spacious and grand, having such a wife will make his comfort bitter to him. He finds that the best way is to withdraw *into a corner of the housetop* and sit alone there, out of earshot of all her shouting and complaints.

Verse 10

An evildoer wants evil to be done so that he may take delight in having a hand in it. *His neighbours*, his friends and closest relatives, cannot receive the smallest act of kindness from him.

Verse 11

Let the law be carried out on mockers, and even those who are simple will be woken up and alarmed by it. They will discern the evil of sin. *When the wise person is instructed by* the preaching of the word, *he* — not only the wise person himself but also the simple person who is listening — *receives knowledge.*

Verse 12

The righteous man — the judge or magistrate — *examines the house of the wicked*. He searches it for arms or stolen goods, diligently inquiring about their family, so that he may *overthrow the wicked for their wickedness* and prevent their causing any further trouble.

Verse 13

An uncharitable person *stops his ears at the cry of the poor*, turns them away from his house and takes no pity on them (Ac 7:57; 1Jn 3:17). He himself will be reduced to difficulties, which will make him *cry* out. People will not listen to him, but reward him as he rewarded others. God will not listen to him, for those who *showed no mercy shall have judgment without mercy* (Jas 2:13).

Verse 14

A good present, wisely managed, will turn away some people's anger, even when it seems implacable. If a gift is a bribe to pervert the course of justice, that is so disgraceful that even those who like receiving bribes are ashamed of it.

Verse 15

Good people find pleasure and delight in seeing justice administered by the government they live under, and also in practicing it themselves. It is a terror to evildoers to see laws enacted against vice and ungodliness.

Verse 16

The sinner *wanders out of the way of understanding*, and once he has left that good way, he wanders endlessly. The way of religious faith is *the way of understanding*; those who are not truly godly are not truly intelligent; they go astray like lost sheep (Isa 53:6).

Verse 17

The epicure *loves pleasure.* God allows us to use physical delights soberly and moderately, such as *wine to make glad the heart* (Ps 104:15) and *oil to make the face to shine* (Ps 104:15) and enhance its beauty. However, people who set their heart on such pleasures and are impatient about everything that goes against them *will be poor;* they cannot live without the full range of this world's fine things. Many a man about town becomes poor.

Verse 18

The wicked, who cause trouble in a land, should be punished in order to prevent those national judgments that otherwise would be inflicted. God will leave many evildoers to be destroyed rather than abandon his own people.

Verse 19

Unrestrained anger spoils and makes bitter the good points of all relationships. Those who cannot live in peace and love cannot live in peace and happiness.

Verse 20

Those who are wise will increase what they have and live in abundance; their wisdom will teach them to balance out their expenditure and their income and to build up a good store of all necessary things, particularly of *oil*, one of the staple commodities of Canaan (Dt 8:8). It is better to have an old-fashioned house that is well furnished and well provided for than a fine modern one that is poorly managed.

Verse 21

We must act justly and love mercy (Mic 6:8), and even though we cannot reach perfection, it will be an encouragement to us if we aim at it. Those who *follow after righteousness* will *find righteousness.*

Verse 22

Those who have wisdom, even though they are very modest and do not promise much, often fulfill great things, even against those who are so confident in their strength. A well-managed strategy may effectively *scale the city of the mighty and cast down the strength* it had such confidence in. *A wise man* will gain the affections of people and conquer them by strength of reason, which is a more noble conquest than that obtained by force of arms.

Verse 23

Those who want to keep their souls must keep watch on the door of their lips (Ps 141:3); they must *keep the mouth* in moderation, to see that nothing is eaten or drunk excessively. They must *keep the tongue* also, so that no forbidden or corrupt word leaves the door of the lips. Keep your heart, and that will keep your tongue from sin; keep your tongue, and that will keep your heart from trouble.

Verse 24

Most of the wrath that sets on fire the human spirit and whole communities *is proud wrath*. People cannot bear to suffer the slightest disrespect shown them; they cannot bear being contradicted without quickly beginning to lose their temper. Pride and arrogance makes them mockers when they are angry.

Verses 25–26

Lazy people are as fit for work as other people. They are their own worst enemies, for besides being starved by their laziness, they are stabbed by their desires. Although their hands refuse to work, their hearts do not stop craving for riches, pleasures, and honors. They expect everyone to serve them. Many who must have money to spend on satisfying the things of the flesh, and who are not concerned to gain them honestly, have become robbers, and that has killed them. The righteous and hardworking have their desires satisfied, and they enjoy not only that delight but also the further satisfaction of doing good to others.

Lazy people are always eager to receive, *but the righteous are always wanting to give without sparing.*

Verse 27

Sacrifices were divinely instituted, and when they were offered in faith and accompanied by repentance and reformation, God was pleased. But they were detestable when they were brought by evildoers, who did not repent of their sins, put to death their sinful desires (Ro 8:13; Col 3:5), and put their lives right. *Much more when* they were brought with *wicked minds*, when they were made not only by evil people but also for the purpose of serving their evil. When people show off in their devotions, when holiness is mere pretense to cover up some evil, then the fulfillment is especially detestable (Isa 66:5).

Verse 28

A person may tell a lie perhaps in haste, but one who knowingly, deliberately, and solemnly gives a false testimony is guilty of sinning shamelessly. The vengeance he invoked on himself when he swore falsely will rebound on him. He *who hears*—that is, obeys—the command of God, which is to *speak every man truth with his neighbour* (Eph 4:25), testifies nothing but what he knows to be true; he *speaks constantly*—that is, consistently with himself.

Verse 29

An evildoer *hardens* (steels) *his* face—puts on a bold front so that he may not blush—so that he may bluff his way, without trembling in the slightest when he commits the greatest crimes; he defies the terrors of the law and the restraints of his own conscience. A good person does not say, "What *shall I* do?" but, "What *should I* do?" And so he *directs his way* by a safe and established rule.

Verses 30–31

There can be no success against God. Although people think they have *wisdom, understanding*, and *counsel* (v. 30) and the best politics and the best politicians on their side, nevertheless, if it is *against the Lord* (v. 30), it cannot succeed for long. There can be no success without God. Even if the cause is a good one and the means of pursuing it make success very likely, people must still acknowledge God and take him with them. Means must of course be used; *the horse* must be *prepared against the day of battle* (v. 31), and foot soldiers too. *But*, in the end, victory is *of the Lord*; he can save without armies, but armies cannot save without him.

CHAPTER 22

Verse 1

We should be more careful to do things by which we may gain and keep a good name than to do those things by which we may raise and increase our wealth. Great riches may be used to relieve the physical needs of others, but a good name may be used to commend religious faith to them. To be well loved, to have a share in the respect and love of those around us: this is better *than silver and gold*.

Verse 2

The greatest people in the world must acknowledge God to be their Maker, and they are under the same obligations to be subject to him as the lowliest people, and the poorest people have the honor of being the work of God's hands as much as the greatest people. *Rich and poor meet together* in the court of God's justice. They are all guilty before God. They all meet at the throne of God's grace; the poor are as welcome there as the rich. There is the same Christ, the same Scriptures, the same Spirit, and the same covenant of promises for them both. There is the same heaven for poor saints as there is for rich ones.

Verse 3

A prudent man will foresee an evil before it comes and be on his guard. When storm clouds are gathering, he takes notice of the warning and flees to the name of the Lord as his strong tower (18:10). *The simple*, who believe every word that flatters them, will believe no word that warns them, and so they *pass on and are punished*. For an example of both of these see Ex 9:20–21.

Verse 4

Religious faith consists very much of *humility and the fear of the Lord*, that is, walking humbly with God (Mic 6:8). We see here what is to be gained by religious faith: in this world, *riches, and honour*, and strength, *and* long *life* as far as God sees good, and at the end, the privileges of the covenant of grace *and* eternal *life*.

Verse 5

In the way of the froward (perverse), that corrupt way that is against the will and word of God, *thorns and snares are* found, thorns of grief for their past sins and traps to trip them up in further sin. *He that keeps his soul*, who watches carefully over his own heart and ways, is *far from* those *thorns and snares*, for his way is both plain and pleasant.

Verse 6

Train up children when they are still young and learning. Teach them; initiate them. *Train* them as soldiers, who are taught to handle their arms, keep rank, and follow commands. *Train* them *in the way they should go*, the way in which, if you love them, you want them to go. "Train up children according to their capabilities" is how some understand this, with a gentle hand, as nurses feed children, a little and often (Dt 6:7). Good impressions made on them when they are young will remain on them all their days.

Verse 7

The rich rule over the poor, and too often with pride and harshness, unlike God, who, although he is great, does not despise anyone. *The borrower is servant to the lender* and must sometimes beg from them, *Have patience with me* (Mt 18:26). Some sell their liberty to satisfy their self-indulgence.

Verse 8

Ill-gotten gains will not bring prosperity. *He that sows iniquity*, who acts unjustly in the hope of gaining something by it, *shall reap vanity*. If the rod of authority becomes *a rod of anger*, if people rule by anger instead of wisdom, to serve their own passions instead of the public welfare, their power will not support them (Isa 10:24–25).

Verse 9

A kind person has *a bountiful* (generous) *eye*, opposed to *the evil* (stingy) *eye* (23:6) and the same as the *single eye* (Mt 6:22), an eye that seeks out people to be kind to, an eye that moves the heart with compassion when it sees a person in need and misery, an eye that looks pleasant when making a gift, which makes the gift doubly acceptable. He is also generous: *He gives of his bread*, the food he himself was going to eat. God himself will bless him.

Verse 10

The scorner sows seeds of dissension (6:14, 19). Much of the *strife and contention* that disturb the peace is caused by "the evil interpreter," as some read it, who puts the worst interpretation on everything and takes pride in poking fun at everyone. Those who want to keep the peace must exclude mockers.

Verse 11

A person of distinction and accomplishment, one fit to be employed in public business, must be honest and *love pureness of heart*, hate all impurity, and be free from all deceit, from all selfishness and sinister intentions; he must be just, and he must delight in keeping his own conscience clean. He must also speak with good grace, not to ingratiate himself and flatter other people, but to express his feelings decently, in language as clean as his spirit. *The king will be his friend*, if the king is wise and good and understands his own and his people's interest.

Verse 12

God takes special care to *preserve knowledge*, that is, to maintain religious faith in the world by maintaining among human beings a knowledge of himself and of the difference between good and evil. He preserves and watches over *men of knowledge*, wise and good people (2Ch 16:9), particularly faithful witnesses, who speak out what they know. *He overthrows the words of the transgressor* and *preserves knowledge* in spite of them.

Verse 13

Many people frighten themselves from real duties by imaginary difficulties: *the slothful man* has work to do outside in the fields, but he thinks *there is a lion* there. He talks about *a lion without* (outside) but takes no thought about the real danger he is in from the Devil, that *roaring lion* (28:15) in bed with him, and from his own laziness, which is killing him.

Verse 14

This is intended to warn all young men against sexual immorality. As they consider the welfare of their souls, let them be careful of *the mouth of strange women*, of the kisses of their lips (7:13), their alluring charms. Dread them; have nothing to do with them. Those who abandon themselves to that sin are abandoned by God, who takes away his restraining grace.

Verse 15

Sin is *foolishness*; it is contrary both to our reason and to our true interests. It *is in the heart*; there is an inner bias to sin, to speak and act foolishly. It is not only *found* there but also *bound* there; it is attached to the heart; corrupt and evil dispositions cling closely to the soul. Correction is necessary to cure this corruption. There must be strictness and harshness, which will cause grief. Children need to be corrected and kept well disciplined by their parents; and we all need to be corrected by our heavenly Father (Heb 12:6–7), and we must submit to his rod of discipline.

Verse 16

Rich people sometimes *oppress the poor and give to the rich*. They will not relieve the poor in charity, but they will give presents *to the rich* and throw great parties for them, either in boasting, so that they may look great, or strategically, so that it may gain them some advantage. Such people *shall surely come to want* (poverty). Many people have become beggars by their foolish generosity, but never has anyone become a beggar by their wise charity. Christ tells us to invite the poor (Lk 14:12–13).

Verses 17–21

Solomon here changes his style. Since the beginning of chapter 10, he has set down certain doctrinal truths, leaving us to make the application as we went along, but from here to the end of chapter 24 he directs his speech to his son, his pupil, his reader, his hearer, speaking as to one particular person. Up to this point, for the most part, the sense he was expressing was contained in one verse, but here it is usually drawn out further. We have here:

1. A heartfelt exhortation to obtain wisdom and grace by paying attention to *the words of the wise* (v. 17), words that are both written and preached. To these *words*, to this *knowledge*, the ear must be *bowed down* and the heart *applied* in faith, love, and careful consideration. The ear without the heart is not enough.

2. Arguments to support this exhortation. Consider:

2.1. The worth and weight of the things themselves that Solomon in this book gives us. They are not trivial (Dt 32:47), humorous proverbs. They are *excellent things*, which concern the glory of God, the holiness and happiness of our souls, the well-being of the human race, literally, "princely things," fit for kings to speak and senates to hear.

2.2. The revelation of these things and the directing of them to us in particular. The emphasis here is that "they are *made known to thee, even to thee* (v. 19), and *written to thee* (v. 20), as if the book were a letter directed to you personally. It is suited to you and to your situation." If we use these wise sayings when we speak, they will be appropriate. *They shall be fitted in thy lips* (v. 18).

2.3. The advantage intended for us by them. The *excellent things* (v. 20) God has *written to* us are not like the commands masters give their servants, which are all intended to benefit the master, but like those that teachers give their students, which are all intended to benefit the student. We cannot trust in God except while doing our duty; we are taught our duty so we may have reason to trust in God. It is desirable to know not only *the words of truth* but also *the certainty of* them (v. 21), to know that this teaching is reliable, so that our faith may be intelligent and rational and may mature to a full assurance. *If any man do his will, he shall know* for certain that the teaching comes from God (Jn 7:17). Knowledge is given us to do good with, so that others may light their candle at our lamp, and that we may in our place serve our generation according to the will of God (Ac 13:36).

Verses 22–23

After this solemn introduction, one would have expected something new and surprising; but no, here is a plain, but nevertheless necessary, warning against the inhuman practice of oppressing poor people. Notice that the sin itself is *robbing the poor* (v. 22) and making them even poorer. It is bad to rob anyone, but most absurd to rob the poor, whom we should relieve. *To oppress the afflicted* (v. 22), and so to add further affliction to them, taking unfair advantage of people because they are helpless, is not only evil and cowardly but also unnatural, and shows those who do it to be even worse than animals. Those who rob and oppress the poor do so at their peril. The oppressed will find that God will support them powerfully.

Verses 24–25

Here is a good warning against being close to people who are hot-tempered, easily provoked, irritable, and touchy, who, when they lose their temper, behave shockingly. Such people are not fit to have as friends, for they will always become angry with us, and they will expect that we should, like them, become angry with others, and that will be our sin. It is dangerous to have dealings with those who send out sparks of passion, "for if you do, you may imitate them, humor them, and so fall into bad habits."

Verses 26–27

We must not deceive people out of their money by taking on obligations we lack the means to fulfill, either by *striking hands* ourselves or by *becoming surety for others* (v. 26). If a person is unable to pay his debts, he should be pitied and helped, but one who borrows money or goods himself or becomes bound for another's debt when he knows he lacks the resources to pay is in effect picking his neighbor's pocket. Although in all cases compassion is to be the order of the day, let such a person blame himself if the law takes its course and his *bed is taken from under him* (v. 27), which could not be taken as a pledge to secure a debt (Ex 22:26–27). For if a person appeared to be so poor that he had nothing to give for security but his bed, then he ought to be relieved of the obligation to give security, and it was fitting to let him keep his bed. However, it seems the bed could be taken by the strict operation of the law to recover a debt already incurred.

Verse 28

The ancient *landmarks* or boundary stones bear witness to everyone's rights; let them not be moved away, for this will give rise to wars, conflicts, and endless disputes. Let them not be removed so as to take some of your neighbor's land as your own, for that is downright robbery and passing on the deception to future generations. Deference is to be paid, in all civil matters, to customs that have prevailed from time immemorial.

Verse 29

Truly honest and industrious people are commended here, people who are good and skilled at their work, even if in a very lowly and narrow sphere. *A man diligent* (skilled) *in his business* is a capable, expert person who knows how to do a lot of work with few resources in a short time. Although he now *stands before mean* (obscure) *men* and is employed by them, he will rise and is likely to *stand before kings*. He may well become an envoy or prime minister.

CHAPTER 23

Verses 1–3

Indulgence of our appetite for food and drink is a sin that easily entangles us (Heb 12:1), and here we are told when we are most in danger of falling into this sin: "When you have a lavish table set before you, a wide range of fine delicacies, a full spread such as you have

seldom seen." The temptation may be stronger to one who is not used to such banquets. Be afraid of becoming immoderate: "*Put a knife to thy throat* (v. 2), that is, restrain yourself, as it were, with a sword hanging over your head. But that is not enough: put the ax to the root (Mt 3:10); put to death those cravings that have such power over you (Col 3:5).

Verses 4–5

Some are liable to overeat (v. 2); others are inclined toward covetousness. We must try to live comfortably and provide for our children and families, but we must not seek things that are beyond us. Do not be like those who desire above all to be rich, who make it their main purpose (1Ti 6:9). What you have, or do, master that, and do not get enslaved to it as those do who *rise up early, sit up late*, and *eat the bread of sorrows* (Ps 127:2), all with the aim of becoming rich. The things of this world are a show, a shadow, and a sham to the soul that trusts in them. "Will you do something so absurd? What are you, a reasonable creature, doing doting on mere shadows?" Riches are very uncertain: *They make themselves* (sprout) *wings, and fly away* (v. 5). The wings they sprout and fly away on are of their own making. They have in themselves the principles of their own corruption. Riches go irresistibly and irrecoverably, as *an eagle toward heaven* (v. 5), which flies strongly and flies out of sight and out of call — it cannot be brought back; they leave people sad and troubled if they set their hearts on them.

Verses 6–8

There are those who pretend to welcome their friends but are not sincere. They speak fine words and know what they should say — *Eat and drink, saith he* (v. 7) — because it is expected that the one giving the feast should compliment the guests, but they have *an evil eye* (v. 6); they are stingy and begrudge their guests every piece of food they eat. If a person is so mean that he cannot find in his heart to make his friends welcome to enjoy what he has, he should not add to that the guilt of pretense by inviting them in the first place. "*Eat not thou the bread* (v. 6) of such a person; let him keep it for himself. Do not sponge off those who are generous, but especially don't be indebted to people who are mean and insincere."

Verse 9

It is our duty to take all suitable opportunities to speak about divine things, but some people will make jokes about everything. A wise person is advised not to *speak in the ears* of such fools. If what wise people say in their wisdom will not be heard, let the wise people be silent, and see whether the wisdom of that will be noticed.

Verses 10–11

The fatherless are taken under God's special protection. He is *their Redeemer*, their *go'el*, their kinsman-redeemer, who will take their side and stand up for them. Everyone must therefore be careful not to wrong them in anything or encroach on their rights, either by secretly moving the ancient boundary stones or by forcibly entering their fields.

Verses 12–16

Parents should persuade their children to apply themselves to the words of knowledge so that they may learn what their duty is. A loving parent finds it hard to administer correction, but for his child's good he punishes him with the rod (v. 13), gently correcting him with the *stripes* (floggings) *of the children of men* (2Sa 7:14), not those that we give animals. The correcting rod will not kill him; it will prevent him from killing himself by those evil ways that the rod will restrain him from. It is to be hoped that those who learn to *speak right things* when they are young will do *right things* when they grow up. "Children, if you are wise and good, devout and conscientious, we will think our labor in instructing you was well given. We will rejoice in the hope that you will be a credit and comfort to us if we live to be old, that you will lift high the name of Christ in your generation, that you will live comfortably in this world and happily in the next."

Verses 17–18

"*Let not thy heart envy sinners* (v. 17); do not grudge them either the liberty they have to sin or the success they have in their sin; they will have to pay dearly, and they are to be pitied rather than envied." We must *be in the fear of the Lord*, taking delight in contemplating God's glory and conforming to his will. *There will be an end of the prosperity of the wicked*; therefore *do not envy them* (Ps 73:3, 17). There will be an end to your suffering; *perfect love will shortly cast out fear* (1Jn 4:18), and *thy expectation* of the reward will be not only *not cut off* (v. 18), or disappointed, but infinitely surpassed.

Verses 19–28

1. Here is a heartfelt call: "*Hearken* (listen) *unto thy father who begat thee*, and who therefore has authority over you and affection for you, and who wants only your own good." We should *give reverence to the fathers of our flesh*, who were the instruments of our existence; much more should we obey and submit to *the Father of our spirits* (Heb 12:9), who made us and is the author of our being. And since *the mother* also, from a sense of duty to God and from love to her child, gives children good instructions, let them not *despise her*, nor her advice, *when she is old* (v. 22).

2. Here are some general commands:

2.1. *Guide thy heart in the way* (v. 19). If the heart is guided along the right way, the steps will be guided and the way of life well ordered.

2.2. *Buy the truth and sell it not* (v. 23). Truth is what the heart must be guided and directed by, for there is no goodness without truth. We must buy it no matter what it costs us; we will not repent of the bargain. Riches should be employed to obtain knowledge rather than knowledge to obtain riches. When we go to great pains to search after truth, then we buy it. "Heaven grants everything to those who work hard." We must not sell it. We are not to give it up for the pleasures, honors, riches, or anything of this world.

2.3. *Give me thy heart* (v. 26). In this exhortation, God speaks to us as to children: "Son, daughter, *give me thy heart*." *Thou shalt love the Lord thy God with all thy heart* (Dt 6:5). We must readily respond to this call, "*My father, take my heart*, such as it is, and make it such as it should be. Take possession of it, and set up your throne on it."

2.4. *Let thy eyes observe my ways* (v. 26). Our eyes must closely observe the rule of God's word, the leadership of his providence, and the good examples of his people, and then we will persevere.

3. Here are some particular warnings against the most destructive sins:

3.1. Gluttony and drunkenness. *Be not a winebibber* (v. 20). *Be not an* excessive *eater of flesh* (v. 20).

Immoderation must be avoided in food as well as in drink. Solomon draws an argument against this sin from its expensiveness. *The drunkard and the glutton* hate to be reformed, even though they are told they *shall come to poverty* (v. 21). Drunkenness is the cause of *drowsiness*; it desensitizes people and makes them inattentive to their work, and then everything goes to rack and ruin.

3.2. Prostitution. This is a sin that captivates people to their ruin: *The adulteress lies in wait as for a prey* (v. 28), as a bandit lying in wait, pretending friendship but intending to strip them of both their armor and their ornaments. It is a sin that contributes more than any other to the spreading of evil and immorality in a kingdom. One adulterous woman may be the ruin of many precious souls and may help defile a whole community. Brothels are houses where people suffer from this plague and should therefore be suppressed by those whose responsibility it is to take care of the public welfare.

Verses 29–35

Solomon here gives fair warning against the sin of drunkenness, to confirm what he said earlier (v. 20).

1. He warns everyone to keep away from temptations to it: *Look not thou upon the wine when it is red* (v. 31). In Canaan, red wine was looked on as the best wine; it is therefore called *the blood of the grape* (Dt 32:14). Do not long for what pleases the eye, but let your serious thoughts convince you that what seems delightful is really harmful.

2. Notice the harmful consequences of the sin of drunkenness: in the end *it bites* (v. 32). The drunkard is made ill by drinking too much, and he is made poor and his livelihood ruined, especially when his conscience has been awakened and he cannot reflect on it without horror and indignation at himself.

2.1. It involves people in quarrels. Many people have trouble and sorrow and cannot help it, but drunkards willfully create trouble and sorrow for themselves. The bruises people receive in defense of their country and its just rights are their honor, but *wounds without cause* (v. 29), received in the service of their sinful desires, are marks of their notoriety.

2.2. It makes people impure and arrogant (v. 33). The *eyes* grow unruly and see *strange* (loose) *women* and lust after them, and so allow adultery into the heart (Mt 5:28). The tongue also grows unruly and talks wildly; by it the *heart utters perverse things* (v. 33) against reason, religion, and ordinary politeness. What ridiculous, incoherent nonsense people talk when they are drunk!

2.3. It stupefies people and makes them foolish (v. 34). Their judgments are unclear, and they are as unsteady and rocky as someone who is asleep *upon the top of a mast*. If you put drunkards into the stocks, they are not aware of the punishment. *They have stricken me, and I was not sick; I felt it not* (v. 35). Drunkenness turns people into mere wood and stone; they are scarcely to be considered animals; they are dead while they live. *Look not upon the wine when it is red* (v. 31).

CHAPTER 24

Verses 1–2

"Never let into your mind the thought, 'Oh, I wish I could shake off the restraints of religious faith and conscience and be free to indulge my physical appetites, as I see other people doing!' No; *desire not to be with them* (v. 1), to do as they do and *cast in thy lot among* (1:14) them." Do not think with them, *for their heart studies destruction* (plots violence) to others, but it will prove destruction to them themselves. You would therefore be wise to have nothing to do with them. Nor do you have any reason to look on them with envy; rather, you should look on them with pity or just indignation at their evil practices.

Verses 3–6

With wise management, a person may increase his wealth and family by lawful and honest means, with the blessing of God on his hard work, and even if dishonest methods increase wealth a little sooner, the honesty, hard work, and blessing will last much longer. True wisdom will make people's outward affairs prosperous and successful. It will *build a house and establish it* (v. 3). People may build their houses by unrighteous practices, but they cannot establish them, for the foundation is rotten (Hab 2:9–10). Wisdom will also enrich a house and furnish it (v. 4). *By knowledge the chambers* of the soul are filled with the graces and comforts of the Spirit, those *precious and pleasant riches* (v. 4). Wisdom will strengthen a house and turn it into a castle: *Wisdom is better than weapons of war* (Ecc 9:18), whether the weapons are offensive or defensive. The spirit is strengthened by true wisdom both for spiritual work and for spiritual warfare. Wisdom will build a college or council of state. Wisdom will be useful to make an advantageous peace.

Verses 7–9

1. Wisdom is *too high* for a weak person (v. 7). It is not easy to obtain wisdom; some people may naturally have some elements of wisdom, but if they are foolish, that is, if they are lazy and will not make an effort, if they are inclined toward evil and keep bad company, it *is too high* for them; they are not likely to reach it. And because they lack it, they are unfit to serve their country: they *open not their mouth in the gate* (v. 7). They are not admitted to the assembly of the council or magistracy, or if they are, they stand there as mute statues; they say nothing, because they have nothing to say.

2. An evildoer is not only despised as a fool but also detested. On the one hand, the secret, malicious *devising* of (plotting) *evil is the thought of foolishness* (v. 9). It is bad to do evil, but it is even worse to plot it, for that contains the subtlety and poison of the old Serpent. But the verse may be taken more generally. We contract guilt not only by acts of foolishness but also by thoughts of it, even if they go no further. The first stirrings of sin in the heart are sin; they are offensive to God and must quickly be repented of, or we are ruined. On the other hand, the openly abusive *scorner*, who takes delight in being rude to people and showing contempt for them, *is an abomination to men* (v. 9).

Verse 10

In *the day of adversity* we are inclined to *faint*, to wilt and become discouraged, to stop working and to despair of ever being relieved. This is evidence that our *strength is small.* "It is a sign that you are not strong or determined, that your thoughts are not firm, that your faith—for that is the strength of a soul—is weak, if you cannot cope in times of trouble." *Be of good courage* therefore, *and God shall strengthen thy heart* (Ps 27:14).

Verses 11–12

Here a great duty is required of us: to relieve innocent people who are being oppressed. Even if the oppressed

are not people to whom we are under any particular obligation, out of a general zeal for justice we must help them. It is easy to make the excuse, *We knew it not,* or, *We forgot.* It is not easy to use such excuses to evade the judgment of God, because God *ponders the heart and keeps the soul* (v. 12); he keeps an eye on it. We should be sensitive to the lives of others and do all we can to protect them, because our lives have been precious in the sight of God, and he has graciously kept them. He will *render to every man according to his works* (v. 12), not only for committing evil works but also for neglecting to do good works.

Verse 13–14

The study of wisdom will be very pleasant. We *eat honey because it is sweet to the taste* (v. 13), and that is why we call it *good,* especially what comes first from the *honeycomb.* Canaan was said to be flowing with milk and honey, and honey was the common food of the country (Lk 24:41–42), even for children (Isa 7:15). This is how we should take in wisdom and enjoy its good instructions. Those who have experienced the power of truth and godliness are abundantly satisfied with the delights of both; they have tasted their sweetness, and all the unbelievers in the world with their reasoning, and the ungodly with all their banter, cannot make them change their mind.

Verses 15–16

Notice here the plans of evildoers against the righteous; the plot is carefully planned: they *lay wait against the dwelling of the righteous* (v. 15). They do not doubt they will *spoil his resting place* (v. 15), because his condition is lowly and distressed and he is almost ruined already. But the righteous person, whose ruin was expected, recovers. The *just man falls,* sometimes *falls seven times,* perhaps into sins of weakness through unexpected temptations, but he *rises again* in repentance (v. 16), finds mercy with God, and regains his peace. The evildoer, who expected to see the destruction of the righteous and tried to assist in it, is ruined.

Verses 17–18

If any have done us harm, or if we bear a grudge against them only because they harm our interests, then when any damage comes to them—for example, if they fall—our corrupt hearts are too inclined to conceive a secret delight and satisfaction in it. "People hope that in the destruction of their enemies or rivals they will gain revenge or win some advantage, but do not be so cruel; *rejoice not* (do not gloat) *when* your worst *enemy falls*" (v. 17). *The Lord will see it,* even though it is hidden in the heart, *and it will displease him* (v. 18), as a wise father disapproves when he sees one child gloating over the correction of another, which the gloating child should take warning from, not knowing how soon it may be his turn, because he has deserved it so often.

Verses 19–20

Even what grieves us must not *fret* us; nor must our eyes be perversely set against anyone because God is good. If evildoers prosper, we must not therefore follow their evil ways. Do not be envious of their prosperity. There is no true happiness in it. The evildoer *has his reward* (Mt 6:2); those who have their reward in this life and who will outlive it are not to be envied (Ps 17:14). Their *candle* (lamp) shines brightly, but it will presently be snuffed out (v. 20).

Verses 21–22

Religious faith and faithfulness must go together. It is our duty as human beings to honor our Creator, to worship and fear him; it is our duty as members of a community, joined together for mutual benefit, to be faithful and loyal to the government God has set over us (Ro 13:1–2). Those who are not truly religious are not truly faithful. How can people be loyal to their ruler if they are false to their God? And if faithfulness toward God and loyalty toward other people come to compete with each other, the case has already been decided: we must *obey God rather than men* (Ac 5:29). Those who have restless, factious, and turbulent spirits commonly pull down trouble on their own heads before they are aware of what is happening: *Their calamity shall rise suddenly* (v. 22).

Verses 23–26

As subjects must do their duty by being obedient to magistrates, so also magistrates must do their duty by administering justice to their subjects. They must always weigh up the merits of a cause and not be swayed by any regard, one way or the other, for the parties concerned. A good judge will recognize the truth, not recognize faces; he will not support his friends and help them when they are in the wrong, nor even omit anything that could be said or done in favor of a righteous cause when it is the cause of his enemy. He must discourage and restrain all fraud, violence, injustice, and immorality. Let magistrates and ministers, and private citizens too who are capable of doing it, *rebuke* evildoers, so that they may bring them to repentance or put them to shame, and they will take comfort from it within themselves: *To them shall be delight* (v. 25), when their consciences bear witness for them that they have been witnesses for God. They must *give a right* (honest) *answer*, that is, give their opinion and pass sentence according to the law and the true merits of the cause, and *everyone shall kiss the lips* of the judge who does so, that is, all will love and honor him with a kiss of allegiance. Those who in ordinary conversation speak relevantly and sincerely are loved and respected by everyone.

Verse 27

This is a rule of wise management of household affairs. We must put what is necessary before what would be nice to have, not spending money on things merely for show when it should really be spent on supporting the family. We must not think of building until we can afford it: "First apply thyself to *thy work without* (outside) *in the field* (v. 27); look after your farm, for that is your livelihood, and when you have gained profit from that—then, and not until then—thou mayest think of rebuilding *thy house* and making it attractive."

Verses 28–29

We are forbidden to harm our neighbor in court either as *a witness* or as a plaintiff or prosecutor. "Never bear testimony against any man *without cause* (v. 28); never give testimony unless what you say is something you know to be precisely true and you have a clear call to testify it. Never bear false testimony against anyone. And if there is occasion to bring an action or information against your neighbor, let it not be done from a spirit of revenge." Even a righteous cause becomes unrighteous when it is pursued with malice.

Verses 30–34

Here is the view Solomon took of *the field and vineyard of the slothful* (v. 30). He looked at a *field* and a

vineyard unlike all the others: although the soil was good, there was nothing growing in it except *thorns and nettles* (v. 31), and if there had been any fruit, it would all have been eaten up by the animals, for there was no fence. He paused a little *and considered it, looked* again *upon it, and received instruction* (v. 32). He did not break out into any emotional outburst to criticize the owner, but he tried to benefit from the observation. Plutarch relates a saying of Cato the Elder: "Wise people profit more from fools than fools do from wise people, for wise people will avoid the faults of fools, but fools will not imitate the virtues of wise people." See how outrageous laziness is, and how harmful to the family, and also to spiritual matters. Our souls are our fields and vineyards, which each one of us is to take good care of, to cultivate, and to keep. They are capable of being improved by good cultivation. These fields and vineyards are often in a very bad condition; not only is no fruit produced, but they are all overgrown with *thorns* and *nettles*: scratching, stinging, excessive desires and passions, pride, covetousness, ungodliness, and malice; those are the thorns and nettles, the wild grapes, that the unsanctified heart produces; no protection is kept against the enemy, with the *stone wall broken down* (v. 31). Where it is like this, it is because of the sinner's own laziness and foolishness.

CHAPTER 25

Verse 1

This verse is the title of this further collection of Solomon's proverbs. The publishers were Hezekiah's servants, who probably acted as his servants in that, among other good works he did *in the law and in the commandments* (2Ch 31:21), he appointed them to do this good service for the church. They copied out these proverbs from the records of Solomon's reign and published them as an appendix to the former edition of this book. It may be an act of good service to the church to publish other people's works that have lain hidden in obscurity.

Verses 2–3

Here is an example of the honor of God: *It is his glory to conceal a matter* (v. 2). There are unfathomable depths to his judgments (Ro 11:33). We see what he does, but we do not know why he acts as he does. It is God's glory that he need not *search into a matter* (v. 2), because he knows it without searching; but it is the honor of kings to search out matters that are brought before them, to take pains in examining offenders and not to give judgment hastily.

Verses 4–5

The vigorous attempts of a ruler to suppress evil and reform the lives of his people are the most effective way to support his government. The duty of magistrates is to use their power to bring terror on evil works and evildoers, not only to banish those who are corrupt but also to frighten them in such a way that they cannot spread the defilement of evil among their subjects. This is called *taking away the dross from the silver* (v. 4), which is done by fire. The reformation of the court will promote the reformation of the kingdom (Ps 101:3, 8).

Verses 6–7

Religious faith is so far from destroying good manners that it teaches us to give honor to those to whom it belongs. It also teaches us humility and self-denial, which is a better lesson than that of good manners. This is the real way to advancement, as our Savior shows in a parable that seems to be borrowed from this (Lk 14:8–10). It is better, and better for our satisfaction and reputation, to be advanced above our pretensions and expectations than to be pushed down below them.

Verses 8–10

"Do not be hasty about bringing an action; do not bring it before you yourself have considered the matter and consulted your friends about it. Do not bring an action before you have tried to settle matters amicably (v. 9): *Debate thy cause with thy neighbour* privately, and perhaps you will understand each other better and see that there is no occasion to go to court." "Reveal not the secret of another" is how some read it. "Do not, in revenge, to shame your enemy, disclose what should be kept private and what has nothing to do with the case." Be cautious in going to court; otherwise the case will be in danger of going against you. It will result in your disgrace if you are described as contentious.

Verses 11–12

Instruction, advice, or encouragement, given at the apposite time and suitably expressed, suited to the situation of the person spoken to and befitting the character of the person speaking—is *like golden* balls resembling *apples*, brought to the table in a silver basket, or a silver box of filigree work, through which the golden apples might be seen. It was then no doubt a well-known table ornament. A word of correction given with discretion by *a wise reprover*, and well received by an *obedient ear*, is an *earring of gold* and an *ornament of fine gold* (v. 12), very graceful and good for both the rebuker and the rebuked.

Verse 13

A servant should be *faithful to him that sends him*, and see to it that he does not, by mistake or intentionally, betray his trust. This will be the satisfaction of the master; it will *refresh his soul* as much as the *cold of snow*—which in hot countries is preserved in icehouses year-round nowadays—refreshed workers at harvest, who *bore the burden and heat of the day* (Mt 20:12).

Verse 14

A person may be said to boast about a false gift if he pretends to have received what he never had or to have given what he never gave. He blows his own trumpet about all his great achievements and good services, but it is all false; he is not what he pretends to be. He is like a morning cloud that disappears and disappoints those who expected rain from it to water the parched ground (Jude 12); he is like *clouds without water*.

Verse 15

Two things are here commended for dealing with others:

- Patience, to respond to the strong feelings of another without losing our temper, and to wait for the right opportunity to suggest our point of view and give people time to consider it. This is how even *a prince* may be *persuaded*.
- Gentleness, to speak without expressing strong feelings or reacting to provocation: *A soft tongue breaks the bone*; it calms the roughest spirits and overcomes the surliest people, like lightning, which, it is said,

sometimes breaks the bone, but does not pierce the flesh.

Verse 16

Hast thou found honey? It is not forbidden fruit to you, as it was to Jonathan (1Sa 14:24–28); you may eat it with thanksgiving to God. *Eat as much as is sufficient*, and no more. We must treat all pleasures as we treat honey, restraining our appetite. Physical pleasures lose their sweetness by being excessively indulged in; those who eat too many sweet things like honey find that they turn sour in the stomach, and then they become nauseous.

Verse 17

It is polite to visit our neighbors sometimes. It is wise, as well as polite, to avoid being troublesome to our friends by visiting them too often or staying too long, to avoid just turning up at mealtimes or busying ourselves in their family life. "After the third day, fish and company become distasteful." Familiarity breeds contempt. How much better a friend is God than any other friend; the more often we come to him, the more welcome we are.

Verse 18

A false testimony is very dangerous; it *is a maul*—a club to knock someone's brains out with, or a flail, which there is no protection against; it is a *sword* to wound close at hand and a *sharp arrow* to wound at a distance. We therefore need to pray, *Deliver my soul, O Lord! from lying lips* (Ps 120:2).

Verse 19

Confidence in an unfaithful man, in someone we thought was trustworthy but who turns out to be otherwise, proves not only useless but also painful and troublesome, like *a broken tooth, or a foot out of joint*.

Verse 20

The absurdity here criticized is *singing songs to a heavy heart*. We should encourage those who are very sad by showing them sympathy, comforting them, and mourning with them. We take a wrong course with them, however, if we think we will relieve them by being too cheerful with them, trying to make them laugh. *Taking away a garment* from someone in *cold weather* makes him feel the cold even more, and pouring *vinegar upon nitre* (soda) ferments it. It is similarly incongruous to sing pleasant songs to someone with a troubled heart. Some read it in the opposite sense: "As he that puts on a garment in cold weather" warms the body, or as *vinegar upon nitre* (soda) dissolves it, so the person who *sings songs* of comfort to a person in sorrow refreshes him and dispels his sorrows.

Verses 21–22

However much the teachers of the law and Pharisees had corrupted the law, the commandment of loving our brothers and sisters—and also that of loving our enemies—was not only a new, but also an old commandment. It was an Old Testament commandment, although our Savior has added new force to it with his own great example of loving us when we were still his enemies (Ro 5:10). We will soften our enemies just as refiners melt metal in a crucible, not only by putting it over the fire but also by heaping coals of fire on it. The way to turn an enemy into a friend is to be friendly to them.

Verse 23

Slander would not be so readily spoken as it is if it were not readily listened to; good manners would silence the slanderer if he realized that his stories displeased his company. If we cannot rebuke in any other way, we may still do so by our looks. Who knows but it may silence and drive away *a backbiting tongue*? Many people abuse those they are speaking about only in the hope of gaining favor with those they are speaking to.

Verse 24

This is the same as what was said in 21:9. Those who are unequally yoked (2Co 6:14) are to be pitied, especially those yoked to a person who is brawling and contentious, whether husband or wife, for it is equally true of both.

Verse 25

We are sometimes impatient to hear news from people who live in distant countries; our souls thirst for it. How acceptable good news will be when it does come: it will be as refreshing as cold water is to someone who is thirsty. Heaven is a faraway country; how refreshing it is to hear good news from there, both in the eternal Gospel, which means "good news," and in the witness of the Spirit with our spirits that we are God's children (Ro 8:16).

Verse 26

For the righteous to fall into sin in the sight of evildoers *troubles the fountains* by grieving some and *corrupts the springs* by defiling others and making them defiant, so that they are emboldened to do likewise. For the righteous to be oppressed and trampled on by the violence or subtlety of evildoers is a troubling of the wells of justice and a corruption of the very springs of government (28:12, 28; 29:2). For the righteous to be cowardly, to give way to evildoers, reflects badly on religion and so is like a *troubled fountain* and a *corrupt spring*.

Verse 27

We must be graciously dead to the pleasures of the senses. It is true of all human delights that one can have too much of them and that they will never fully satisfy, and they are dangerous to those who allow themselves to use them too liberally. We must also be dead to the praise of other people. *For men to search their own glory*, to seek applause, is not their glory but their shame. Everyone will laugh at them for it. Some give another sense of this verse: "To eat much honey is not good," but to look into glorious things is to be greatly commended. It is true glory; we cannot develop that too much.

Verse 28

A wise and upright person is one who has *rule over his own spirit*. An evil person, one who has no rule over his own spirit, is *like a city that is broken down and without walls*. He lies exposed to all the temptations of Satan and becomes an easy target.

CHAPTER 26

Verse 1

Evildoers, who have neither good sense nor grace, are sometimes preferred by rulers and praised and applauded by the people. It is absurd and inappropriate: it is as out of place *as snow in summer* and as harmful *as rain in harvest*, which hinders the laborers and spoils the crops when they are ready to be gathered in.

Verse 2

A person who is cursed without good cause, whether by furious imprecations or solemn denunciations, will be harmed by the curse no more than by a bird flying overhead, no more than David by Goliath's curses (1Sa 17:43).

Verse 3

Evildoers are compared to *the horse* and *the ass*. They are so rough, and are to be controlled only by force or fear. This is how far sin has sunk human beings, far below their true dignity. *An* unbroken *horse* needs *a whip* to correct it, and an *ass a bridle* to direct and restrain it when it wants to turn aside. In the same way, evildoers, those who want to set themselves free from the guidance and restraint of religion and reason, should be whipped and bridled; they should be severely rebuked and be restrained from offending anymore.

Verses 4–5

The style of Scripture seems to contradict itself but really does not. Wise people need to be instructed about how to deal with fools, and they never need wisdom more than in dealing with such people, to know when to keep silent and when to speak, for there may be a time for each. In some situations, a wise person will not pit his wit against a fool's so far as to *answer him according to his folly* (v. 4). "If the fool is boasting about himself, do not answer him by boasting about yourself. If he is ranting and raving, do not talk back to him in anger. If he tells one big lie, don't tell another to match it. If he mocks you, don't respond in similar terms, *lest thou be like him*" (v. 4). But in other situations, a wise person will use his wisdom to convict a fool, when he thinks that by taking notice of what the fool says he may be able to do good. "If you have reason to think that your silence will be taken as evidence of weakness, in such a case *answer him*, and let it be an answer that is directed at the fool's character. Play him at his own game, and that will be a pointed answer. If the fool offers anything that looks like an argument, then reply, *lest he be wise in his own conceit* (or else the fool will be wise in his own eyes) (v. 5) and boast that he has beaten you."

Verses 6–9

Solomon here shows that fools are fit for nothing; they are either stupid, and never think at all, or evil, and never think as they ought. They are not fit to be entrusted with any business, not fit to go on an errand (v. 6): *He that* even *sendeth a message by the hand of a fool*, of a careless, heedless person, will find the message misunderstood, and so many blunders made that he might as well have *cut off his legs*, that is, never have sent the messenger in the first place. He *will drink damage*; he will suffer very much for having employed such a person. People will tend to judge the master by his messenger. *To give honour to a fool* (v. 8) is like putting a sword into the hand of one who is mad. We have no idea what trouble he may wreak with it, even to those who put it into his hands. *A parable in the mouth of fools* (v. 7) stops being a parable and becomes a mere joke. Just as *the legs of the lame are not equal* (v. 7), and so they walk awkwardly, so it is inconsistent for a fool to pretend to speak wise maxims and give advice. His good words raise him up, but then his bad life pulls him down, and so his *legs are not equal*. He will only cause trouble to himself and others, as drunkards do with thorns, or any other sharp object they pick up, with which they injure themselves and those around them because they do not know how to deal with it.

Verse 10

Our translation gives this verse different readings in the text and in the margin, and so it expresses either:

1. The justice of a good God. *The great God that formed all things* in the beginning and still directs them according to his infinite Wisdom, repays everyone according to his work (Ps 62:12; Pr 24:12; Ro 2:6). He *rewards the fool*, who sinned through ignorance, *with few stripes* (Lk 12:47–48), and he *rewards the transgressor*, who sinned arrogantly, *with many stripes.* Or:

2. The iniquity of a bad ruler, as the margin reads: "A great man grieves all, and he hires the fool; he hires also the transgressors." When an evildoer gets power into his hands, by himself and by the fools whom he employs, he grieves everyone under him and is troublesome to them.

Verse 11

How detestable sin is. When sinners' consciences have been convinced, or they suffer from their sin, they are sick of it. They seem then to detest it and be willing to part with it. But sinners who have been only convinced, not converted, return to their sin, forgetting how sick it made them.

Verse 12

Self-conceit is a spiritual disease. Many people, *wise in their own conceit* (eyes), have little sense, but are proud of it. They think so much of their own abilities that they become opinionated, dogmatic, and judgmental. *There is more hope of a fool*, one who knows and acknowledges he is such, *than of* such a person.

Verse 13

The slothful man dreads *the way, the streets*, the place where work is to be done and a journey is to be made. He dreams of and pretends to dread *a lion in the way.* When urged to get down to hard work, either in his worldly affairs or in his religious faith, this is his excuse. *There is a lion in the way*, some insuperable difficulty or danger that he cannot hope to grapple with. It is foolish to frighten ourselves from real duties by imaginary difficulties (Ecc 11:4).

Verse 14

Having seen the lazy person afraid of his work, we see him here loving his ease. He lies on his bed on one side until he becomes weary of that, and then he turns to the other side—still on his bed, when it is late in the day and work should have been finished. He is like a door moving on its hinges: it changes its position but not its location. Notice the character of the sluggard: he does not want to get out of bed but seems to be attached to it, *as the door* that turns *upon the hinges.* He does not want to go forward with his business; he stirs a little, but he is just playing at it; he remains where he is.

Verse 15

The sluggard has now, with a lot of fuss and bother, gotten out of bed, but he might as well have stayed there. He *hides his hand in his bosom* for fear of catching cold; the next best thing to his warm bed is his warm body. Or he pretends he is lame, as some do who make a business out of begging; something troubles his hands; he wants it thought that his hands are blistered because of hard work the day before. He himself loses by it, for he is starving himself: *It grieves him to bring his hand to his mouth*, that is, he cannot find it in his heart to eat. It is a fine hyperbole, emphasizing his sin, that he cannot bear to make the slightest effort. Those who are lazy in their religious faith will not make any effort to feed their own souls with the word of God or the bread of life, or to bring in the promised blessings by prayer.

Verse 16

The sluggard thinks he is *wiser than seven men*, than seven wise people, for they are such as *can render a reason.* One who exerts himself in matters of religious faith can give a good reason for it; he knows he is working for a good Master and that *his labour shall not be in vain* (1Co 15:58). But *the sluggard* thinks himself *wiser than seven* such people (v. 16). It is *the sluggard*, above all people, who is so self-conceited. His good opinion of himself is the cause of his laziness; he will not lift a finger to obtain wisdom because he thinks he is wise enough already. His laziness is the cause of his high opinion of himself. If he would only sit up, think, and examine himself, he would have other thoughts of himself.

Verse 17

What is condemned here is *meddling with strife that belongs not to us.* If we can be instrumental in making peace between those who are at odds, we must do so, but to busy ourselves in other people's matters and take sides in other people's quarrels is to court trouble. It is like taking a snarling dog *by the ears.* It will snap at you and bite you.

Verses 18–19

Those who have no scruples about *deceiving their neighbours* (v. 19) are *as madmen that cast firebrands, arrows, and death* (v. 18). They pride themselves as scheming people, but really they are *as madmen.* There is no greater madness in the world than intentional sin. The excuse that people commonly make for the trouble they cause is that they did not mean it; they were only joking: *Am I not in sport?* (v. 19). But playing with fire and joking with cutting tools will prove dangerous. Those who sin in jest must repent in earnest, or their sin will be their destruction. Truth is too valuable to be sold as a joke, and so is the reputation of our neighbor.

Verses 20–22

Quarrels are like fires; they heat the spirits, burn up everything that is good, and set families and communities on fire. We must not listen to *talebearers* (gossips) (v. 20), for they feed the fire of contention with fuel. In fact, they spread it with combustible matter; the stories they carry are fireballs. Those who suggest that people are corrupt, who reveal secrets and misrepresent words or actions, are to be banished, and then quarrels will end as surely as the fire will go out when it has no fuel. Whisperers and backbiters are agitators who should not be allowed in a community. They wound love and kindness, and they fatally wound friendship and Christian fellowship. We must not associate with perverse, hot-tempered people. These *are contentious* people, who *kindle strife* (v. 21). The less we have to do with them the better, for it will be very difficult to avoid quarreling with people who are quarrelsome.

Verse 23

This may refer to either:

1. *A wicked heart* showing itself in *burning lips*, angry words, burning with evil. Evil words and ill feelings go

together as well as *a potsherd* (piece of earthenware) and the *dross of silver*, which, now that the pot has been broken and the dross separated from the silver, are fit to be thrown out with the garbage. Or:

2. *A wicked heart* disguising itself with *burning lips*, burning with professions of love and friendship. This is *like a potsherd covered with* the scum or *dross of silver*, which a weak person may be deceived into thinking valuable, but a wise person soon becomes aware of the deception.

Verses 24–26

It is here said to be common that people's professions of friendship lack sincerity and that such professions are used to serve the most cruel intentions (v. 24): *He that hates* his neighbor and is planning to cause him trouble *dissembles with his lips*, talks kindly with them, as Cain did with Abel; such a person *lays up deceit within him* (v. 24). That is, he keeps in mind the trouble he wants to cause to his neighbor. Remember to distrust when a person *speaks fair*; do not be too eager to *believe him* unless you know him well, for it is possible there may be *seven abominations in his heart* (v. 25). Though the fraud may be carried on plausibly for a time, it will be brought to light (v. 26). He *whose hatred is covered by deceit will* be discovered sooner or later. Love, it is said, is the best armor, but the worst cloak, and it will help hypocrites no more than the disguise Ahab put on and died in (1Ki 22:29, 37).

Verse 27

Notice here what effort people take to cause trouble to others: they conceal their petty scheming by professions of friendship. This is *digging a pit*, it is *rolling a stone*, hard work, but people will not stop at that to satisfy their anger and revenge. Their cruel actions will return on their own heads; they will themselves *fall into the pit they digged*, and the stone they rolled *will return upon them* (Ps 7:15–16; 9:15–16).

Verse 28

There are two kinds of lies, both of which are equally detestable:

- A slandering lie: *A lying tongue hates those that are afflicted by it*; it afflicts them by slander and insults because it hates them. The trouble of this is obvious; it afflicts, it hates, and it openly acknowledges itself, and everybody sees it.
- A flattering lie secretly works ruin. It is hardly suspected, and people betray themselves by believing the compliments that are given them. A wise person will therefore be more afraid of a flatterer who kisses and then kills than of a slanderer who openly declares war.

CHAPTER 27

Verse 1

Boast not thyself, not even about *tomorrow*, much less about many days or years to come. This does stop us from preparing for tomorrow, but it warns us against presuming on tomorrow. We must not put off the great work of conversion, the one thing that is needed (Lk 10:42), until tomorrow, as if we were sure of it, *but* do it *today, while it is called today* (Heb 3:13), when we hear God's voice. *We know not what a day may bring forth*, what event may be in the growing womb of time. God has wisely kept us in the dark about future events so that he may train us to continually depend on himself and always be ready for every event (Ac 1:7).

Verse 2

Let our own works be such that they will bring commendation to us, even *in the gates* (31:31) (Php 4:8). But when we have done good, we must not commend ourselves, for that is evidence of our pride. There may be a just occasion for us to vindicate ourselves, but it is not right for us to praise or congratulate ourselves.

Verses 3–4

The wrath of a fool, who when provoked does not care what he says or does, is more troublesome than a heavy stone or a weighty load of sand. Those who cannot control their temper sink under its burden. The wrath of a fool lies heavily also on those he is angry with. We would therefore be wise not to provoke a fool, but if he has lost his temper, we would be wise to get out of his way. Deep-rooted hatred is much worse. *Wrath is cruel* and does many terrible things, but secret enmity toward another person, envy of his prosperity, and a desire for revenge for some insult are a much greater problem. One may avoid a sudden fit of anger, as David escaped Saul's spear, but when anger gradually gets worse, as Saul's did, and becomes a well-established envy, there is no *standing before it* (v. 4).

Verses 5–6

It is good for us to be corrected and told our faults by our friends. *Faithful are the reproofs of a friend*, even though they are painful as *wounds* for the present (v. 6; Heb 12:11). Doctors are concerned to cure the illnesses of patients, not to satisfy their desire for appreciation. It is dangerous to be treated kindly and flattered by *an enemy*, whose *kisses are deceitful* (v. 6). Joab's kiss (2Sa 20:9) and Judas's (Mt 26:49) were deceitful. Some read it: "May the Lord deliver us from an enemy's kisses, from lying lips, and from a deceitful tongue."

Verse 7

Solomon here, as often in this book, shows that the poor have in some respects an advantage over the rich, for they have greater enjoyment. Hunger is the best sauce. Plain food, with a hearty appetite, has a tangible pleasantness. Those who eat and drink lavishly every day become ill when they eat delicacies. To those who eat no more than their necessary food, it *is sweet* (v. 7), even though it is such as *the full soul* would call *bitter*; they eat it with pleasure, digest it, and are refreshed by it. They are more thankful: *the hungry will* bless God for bread and water, while those who are *full* think the greatest delicacies hardly worth giving thanks for.

Verse 8

There are many people who do not know when they are well off. They love to wander, are glad to have any excuse to go far away, and do not want to stay long in any one place. Those who abandon the post assigned to them are like *a bird that wanders from her nest*. They are always wavering, like birds that wander and hop from branch to branch and come to rest nowhere. When a bird wanders from its nest, its eggs and young ones are neglected. Those who love to be away from home neglect their work at home.

Verses 9–10

Here is a command to be faithful and loyal to our old friends. It is good to have a close friend, with whom we can be ourselves. It is also good to have a special respect for those who have been friends of our family: *"Thy own friend, especially if he has been thy father's friend, forsake not* (v. 10). He is a long-standing friend; he knows your life well; therefore let him advise you." It is a duty we owe to our parents, when they have died, to love their friends. Solomon's son ruined himself by abandoning the advice of his father's friends (1Ki 12; 14:21–31). There is a great deal of *sweetness* in talking with a close friend. It is like *ointment and perfume*, which exhilarate our spirits. It *rejoices the heart* (v. 9); our anxieties are relieved when we share our burdens with our friends. *The sweetness of* friendship lies not in hearty merriment but in *hearty counsel*, faithful, honest advice, sincerely given and without flattery, literally, "by counsel of the soul." We are here advised not to go into *a brother's house* (v. 10), not to expect relief from relatives simply because they are relatives—but rather to turn to our neighbors, who are close by, and be ready to help them in times of crisis. It is wise to please them by being neighborly.

Verse 11

Children may be a comfort to their parents and *make their hearts glad*, even when *the evil days come* (Ecc 12:1), and so repay them for their care (23:15). They may be a credit to them: *"That I may answer him that reproaches me* for having been too strict and harsh in bringing up my children." Those who have been blessed with a religious education should behave themselves so as to silence those who say, "Young saint, old devil," and to prove the opposite, "Young saint, old angel."

Verse 12

Evil may be foreseen. Where there is temptation, it is easy to foresee that if we throw ourselves into it, it will lead to sin. Then the evil of punishment will follow. Usually, God warns before he wounds, and the *prudent man, foreseeing the evil*, forecasts accordingly, *and hides himself, but the simple* is either so stupid that he does not foresee it or so stubborn and lazy that he is not careful to avoid it.

Verse 13

Here we see those to whom poverty will soon come: those who have such little consideration as to put up security for anyone who asks them and those who have relationships with wayward women. Such people will borrow money as far as their credit will stretch, and no doubt they will cheat their creditors in the end; in fact, they have been cheating them all along.

Verse 14

We should give everyone their due praise, applaud those who excel in knowledge, goodness, and usefulness, and acknowledge the kindnesses we have received with thankfulness. But if we do this *with a loud voice, rising early in the morning*, always harping on it, whoever we are with, even to our friend's face, or if we extravagantly praise the merits of our friend, then this is excessive. It is even more foolish to be fond of receiving extravagant praise. Modest praise invites those who are present to add to the commendations, but immoderate praise tempts them rather to do the opposite, to criticize the person they hear commended too much. Praising someone too much

makes them the object of envy, and the greatest danger of all is that it is a temptation to pride (2Co 12:6).

Verses 15–16

Here, as before, Solomon expresses grief for the man who has a perverse, hot-tempered wife. It is a grievance that cannot be avoided, for it is like *a continual dropping in a very rainy day* (v. 15). The contentions of a neighbor may be like a sharp shower, troublesome for a time, but while it lasts, you may take shelter; but *the contentions of a wife* are like a constant, soaking rain, for which there is no remedy but patience. See also 19:13. A wise man would hide it if he could, but he cannot, any more than he can hide the noise of the wind when it blows or the smell of strong perfume. Those who are perverse and quarrelsome will declare their own shame, even when their friends, in kindness to them, want to cover it up.

Verse 17

Wise and profitable discussion sharpens people's understanding, and even those who know much may still learn more by discussing matters with others. The graces of good people are sharpened by talking things over with those who are good, and evildoers' sinful desires and passions are sharpened by talking with other evildoers, as iron is sharpened by its like, especially by the file. People who once were rough, dull, and inactive are filed and made smooth, bright, and fit for business by conversation.

Verse 18

Even if work is laborious and contemptible, those who are faithful in it will find something to be gained from it. Let not a poor gardener, who *keeps the fig tree*, be discouraged. Even though the fig tree needs constant care and attention to help it grow to maturity and keep it in good order, so that it produces figs in the appropriate season, all his hard work will pay off: he *shall eat the fruit* of it (1Co 9:7). A poor servant, if he is conscientious in *waiting on his master*, if, literally, "he keeps his master," if he does all he can so that his master's possessions are not wasted, such a servant *shall be honoured*; he will be advanced and rewarded. God is a Master who has committed himself to honor those who serve him faithfully (Jn 12:26).

Verse 19

Just as the water is a mirror in which we may see our faces as a reflection, so are mirrors by which the *heart of a man* is revealed to *a man*, that is, to himself. Let us examine our own conscience, our thoughts, intentions, and attitudes. Let us see our *natural face in the glass* of the divine law (Jas 1:23), and then we may discern what kind of people we are and know our true character, which is useful for each one of us to know. As there is a likeness between the human face and its reflection in the water, so also between the heart of one person and the heart of another, for God has made human hearts similar.

Verse 20

Two things are insatiable and closely related—death and sin. People work for things that sate them but do not satisfy them. Those whose eyes are always toward the Lord (Ps 25:15) are satisfied in him and will be so forever.

Verse 21

Silver and gold are tested by putting them into the crucible and furnace; so are people tested by praising them.

If a person becomes proud and scornful from the praise he receives, if he takes glory for himself that he should pass on to God, that will show that he is foolish and worthless and that nothing in him is truly praiseworthy. If, on the contrary, a person is made more thankful to God by the praise he receives, if he is more respectful toward his friends and more diligent to do good to others, this will show that he is wise and good (2Co 6:8).

Verse 22

Earlier Solomon said (22:15), *The foolishness* that *is bound in the heart of a child may be driven out by the rod of correction*, for at that age the mind can be molded, because the evil habits have not taken root. Here he shows that if it is not done then, it will be next to impossible to do it later. Some are so bad that rough and harsh methods must be used with them, since gentle means have been tried and have had no effect; they must be *brayed* (ground) *in a mortar*. God will use this method with them by his judgments; the magistrates must use this method with them by the rigors of the law. Force must be used with those who will not be ruled by reason, love, and their own interests.

Verses 23–27

We have here:

1. A command given us to be conscientious in our callings. It is directed to farmers and shepherds, but it is to be extended to all other lawful callings. We should not lead idle lives. We should understand our business and not interfere with things we do not understand. We should use our own eyes to inspect the *state of our flocks* (v. 23); it is the master's eye that makes them prosper.

2. Reasons given to reinforce this command:

2.1. The uncertainty of worldly wealth. *Riches are not for ever* (v. 24). "*Look well to thy flocks and herds* (v. 23), your wealth in the country and the livestock there, for these are your staple commodities, which will last forever, whereas riches in trade will not; the *crown* itself may not be so guaranteed to your family as your flocks and herds."

2.2. The goodness and generosity of the God of nature. *The hay appears* (v. 25). In taking care of the *flocks and herds*, "there need be no great work, no plowing or sowing; food for them is the spontaneous product of the land; you have nothing to do but put them into the fields in the summer, *when the grass shows itself*, and *gather the herbs* (grass) *of the mountains* for them for the winter. God has done his part; if you do not do your part too, you are ungrateful to him, and unjustly refuse to serve his providence."

2.3. The benefit of good management in a family: "Keep your sheep, and your sheep will help to maintain you; you will have food for your children and servants, *goats' milk enough* (v. 27); and 'Enough is as good as a feast.' You will also have clothing: the *lambs' wool shall be for thy clothing* (v. 26). You will have money to pay the rent; the goats you will have to sell will be *the price of thy field*" (v. 26); in fact, as some understand it, "You will become a buyer," and so "you will buy land to leave to your children." Plain food and plain clothing, if they are adequate, are all we should aim at. "Consider yourself well looked after if you are clothed with homespun cloth from the fleece of your own lambs, and fed with goats' milk; be satisfied to serve yourself the same food that is the *food of thy household and the maintenance of thy maidens* (v. 27). Do not desire delicacies that are 'far fetched and dear bought.'"

CHAPTER 28

Verse 1

Guilt in the consciences of evildoers makes them a terror to themselves, so that they are ready *to flee when none pursues*, like a person who absconds to avoid paying a debt, who thinks everyone he comes across is a bailiff. Sin makes people cowards. *The righteous are bold as a lion*, as a young lion. When they are in great danger, they trust in a God of almighty power. *Therefore will not we fear though the earth be removed* (Ps 46:2).

Verse 2

National sins bring national disorder. *For* (Because of) *the transgression of a land*, and its general defection from God and religious faith to idolatry, ungodliness, or immorality, *many are the princes thereof*. It has many rulers, many claiming sovereignty at the same time, causing the people to break up into many parties and factions, biting and devouring one another (Gal 5:15); or it has many successive rulers in a short time, who are soon destroyed. The government sometimes suffers from the sins of the people. Wisdom will prevent or put right these grievances: *By a man*, that is, by a people, *of understanding*, who come to their right mind (Mk 5:15), things are kept in good order. We cannot imagine how much good one wise person may do for a nation at a critical time.

Verse 3

Those who know from experience the miseries of poverty should be compassionate toward those who suffer similarly, but they are inexcusably cruel if they wrong them. Notice how arrogant people usually are when they get into power after having been poor and needy. If a ruler promotes a poor person, the latter forgets he was ever poor, and no one will be so oppressive to the poor as he is, and no one will crush others so cruelly. He *is like a sweeping rain*, which washes away the grain on the ground and lays flat and beats out what has grown, so that it *leaves no food*.

Verse 4

Those who *praise the wicked* make it clear that they themselves *forsake the law* and disobey it, for forsaking the law is what brings condemnation on evildoers. Evildoers will speak well of one another, and so strengthen one another's hands in their evil ways, hoping thereby to silence the clamors of their own consciences and serve the interests of the Devil's kingdom. Those who are careful to follow the law of God themselves will, where they are, vigorously oppose sin.

Verse 5

Sinful desires are so pervasive because of the darkness of people's understanding, and the darkness of their understanding comes from the power of their sinful desires. *Men understand not judgment*; they are *evil*. People's *seeking the Lord* is a good sign that they understand much, and it is a good way for them to increase in understanding all things necessary for them. If a person *does the Lord's will*, he will *know his doctrine* (Jn 7:17).

Verse 6

It is a paradox to a blind world that one who is honest, godly, and poor is better than one who is evil, ungodly, and rich; the former has a better character, is in a better condition, has more comfort in himself, is a greater blessing to the world, and is worthy of much more honor and respect. It is certain not only that his situation will be better at death but also that it is better in this life.

Verse 7

Religious faith is true wisdom, and it makes people wise in every aspect of their life. Evil brings shame not only on the sinner himself but also on everyone related to him.

Verse 8

What is gained wrongly, though it may greatly increase, will not last long. A person may perhaps increase in wealth in a short time by charging exorbitant interest and by fraud, but it will not last long. He gathers his wealth for himself, but another person's wealth will be raised up from its ruins. Sometimes God in his providence so orders things that what has been gained unjustly is used charitably by another.

Verse 9

God speaks to us by his law, and he expects us to listen to him and obey him; we speak to him by prayer, and we wait for favorable answers to it.

Verse 10

The seducers, who attempt to draw good people into sin and trouble, will not be successful; they will *fall themselves into their own pit*, and having been not only sinners but also tempters, they will receive the greater condemnation (Mt 23:14–15). The sincere will not only be kept from evil ways that evildoers try to lure them into; they will also have the assurance and grace of God's Spirit.

Verse 11

Those who are rich tend to think they are wise, because whatever else they are ignorant of, they know how to get and save, and so they expect that all they say should be regarded as authoritative and a law. *A poor man* who takes pains to obtain wisdom and who, unlike a rich person, has no other way to gain a reputation, *searches him out* (sees through him) and makes it clear that he is not the scholar or politician he is thought to be.

Verse 12

For the people of God to live in comfort and safety is the honor of the nation in which they live. A *great glory* dwells in the land when *the righteous do rejoice*, when they have their liberty, can freely exercise their religious faith, and are not persecuted. The promotion of evildoers is the eclipsing of the beauty of a nation: *When the wicked rise* and make progress, they advance against all that is sacred, and then *a man is hidden*, a good person is driven into obscurity.

Verse 13

Here we see the foolishness of indulging in sin, excusing it, denying or extenuating it, diminishing it, pretending it is not there, or putting the blame for it on others: *He that covers his sins shall not prosper.* David acknowledges himself to have been in a constant state of turmoil while he *covered his sins* (v. 13; Ps 32:3–4). As long as patients are not willing to admit they are ill, they cannot hope to be healed. *He that confesses* his guilt to God and is careful not to return to sin will *find mercy* with God. His conscience will be relieved, and his destruction prevented. See 1Jn 1:9; Jer 3:12–13.

Verse 14

Most people think that those who never fear are the ones who are happy; but there is a fear that, far from containing torment, has the greatest joy. Happy is the one who always keeps before him a holy awe and reverence of God, who is always afraid of incurring his displeasure, who keeps his conscience sensitive and fears any appearance of evil. *He that hardens his heart*, however, who mocks at such fear (Job 39:22) and defies God and his judgment, *shall fall into mischief*; his arrogance will lead to his destruction.

Verse 15

It is written, *Thou shalt not speak evil of the ruler of thy people* (Ac 23:5), but if the ruler is evil and oppresses the people, this Scripture calls him *a roaring lion and a ranging* (charging) *bear*. He is violent, cruel, and bloodthirsty; he is to be put among the wild animals.

Verse 16

A ruler who loves corruption will neither do justly nor love mercy (Mic 6:8), and the people under him will be bought and sold. *He that hates covetousness shall prolong* his government and peace (Isa 9:7); he will be happy in the affections of the people and the blessing of his God.

Verse 17

This agrees with that old law, *Whoso sheddeth man's blood, by man shall his blood be shed* (Ge 9:6). The person who has committed murder, even though he flees for his life, will be continually haunted with terrors, will himself *flee to the pit*, betray himself, and torment himself, like Cain. Those who acquit the murderer or do anything to help him get off free share in the guilt of the bloodshed.

Verse 18

Those who are honest are always safe. One who acts with sincerity, speaks as he thinks, and does everything rightly, to the glory of God and for the good of his brothers and sisters, *shall be saved* in the future life. He will also be secure now. Integrity and uprightness will give him a holy security in the worst times. He may be injured, but he cannot be harmed. Those who are false and dishonest are never safe.

Verse 19

One who *tills his land*, who looks after his business affairs, whatever they are, *shall have plenty of bread*, what he needs for himself and his family and also the resources he needs to be kind to the poor; he will *eat the labour of his hands* (Ps 128:2). Those who are lazy and careless and keep company with worthless people are following a miserable way of life, though they may think they are indulging in an easy and pleasant life.

Verse 20

Here we are shown the true way to be happy, and that is to be holy and honest. The person who is *faithful* to God and other people will be blessed by the Lord. Usefulness will be the reward of faithfulness, and it is a good reward. We are warned against a false way to happiness, and that is to suddenly increase one's wealth without regard for right or wrong. One who does so will not be considered innocent by his neighbors but will be an object of their hatred and their hateful words. Solomon does not say that such a person *cannot be innocent* but that he probably will not prove so: *He that hasteth with his feet sinneth*— misses the way, stumbles, or falls (19:2).

Verse 21

It is a fundamental error in administering justice to show partiality by considering the people involved in a case rather than the merits of the case. The result may be to favor one person because he is a gentleman, my compatriot, my old friend, or one who belongs to my group or is of my persuasion, and to be hard on the other party because he is a stranger or a poor man, has been my rival, or has voted against me. Those who show partiality will be contemptible. Once people have broken through the bonds of justice and defiled their consciences, they will ultimately be so corrupt that *for a piece of bread* they will give judgment against their consciences, though at first it must have taken some great bribe to bias them.

Verse 22

Solomon shows the sin and foolishness of those who want to *be rich*, to get rich quick. They *have an evil eye*, that is, they are stingy and always resentful of those who have more than they. *Poverty shall come upon* them.

Verse 23

Flatterers may for a time please those who on second thought will detest and despise them. Rebukers at first may displease those who later, when the anger has died down and the bitter medicine begins its good work, will love and respect them. One who cries out to their doctor for hurting them when the doctor is probing a wound will still pay the doctor well, and be grateful, when they are healed.

Verse 24

As Christ shows the evil of children who think they have no duty to maintain their parents (Mt 15:5), so Solomon here shows the evil of those who think it is not a sin to rob their parents, whether by force, by wheedling them, by threatening them, or by running into debt and leaving them to pay the bills. The one who does it is *the companion of a destroyer*, a partner to one who destroys; he is no better than a highway robber.

Verse 25

Those who are arrogant and quarrelsome make themselves poor and continually uneasy, for they are here contrasted to those who will prosper. Those who constantly depend on God and his grace make themselves prosper and are always at peace: *He who puts his trust in the Lord*, the one who, instead of struggling for himself, commits his cause to God, *shall be made fat*, that is, prosperous.

Verse 26

A *fool trusteth to his own heart*, in his own wisdom, his own strength, his own merit and righteousness, and the high opinion he has of himself. A wise person *walketh wisely*; he does not trust in his own heart but is humble and diffident. He lives his life in the strength of the Lord his God. He *shall be delivered* and kept safe.

Verse 27

He that gives to the poor will himself never be poorer for doing so; he *shall not lack. He that hides his eyes*, so that he may not look at the misery of the poor—for then his eyes might affect his heart and force him to help them—*shall have many a curse*, both from God and from other people.

Verse 28

This is to the same effect as v. 12. When power is put into the hands of *the wicked, men hide themselves*; wise people retire into seclusion and decline public business, not wanting to work under evildoers; rich people get out of the way for fear of being squeezed out of what they have, and good people leave because they despair of doing good and fear mistreatment. When evildoers are disgraced and power is taken from them, then *the righteous increase*, for *when the* evildoers *perish*, good people will be put in their place.

CHAPTER 29

Verse 1

The obstinacy of many evildoers is to be greatly mourned. They are *often reproved by* parents and friends, by judges or ministers, but they *harden their necks*, they remain stiff-necked. Perhaps they rush off and will not even listen to the correction. Those who continue in their sin in spite of warnings *shall be destroyed*; if the rod of discipline does not fulfill its purpose, then the ax (Mt 3:10) must be expected. Literally, they *shall be destroyed* "and no healing."

Verse 2

This is what was said before (28:12, 28). *The people* will have cause to *rejoice* or *mourn* according to whether their rulers are *righteous* or *wicked*. If *the righteous* are in *authority*, sin will be punished and restrained, *but if the wicked* gain power, religious faith and religious people will be persecuted, and so the ways of government will be corrupted. *The people will* also actually *rejoice* or *mourn* according to whether their rulers are *righteous* or *wicked*.

Verse 3

A virtuous young man *loves wisdom*; he is a *philosopher*, "a lover of wisdom," for the religious faith that produces true virtue is the best philosophy; such a person avoids bad company, especially the company of immoral women. An evil young man hates *wisdom*; he *keeps company with* immoral women, who will ruin him both spiritually and physically.

Verse 4

A ruler should *establish the land*, give it security, maintain its laws, settle the minds of his subjects, and secure their liberties and land from hostilities forever. A ruler must do this *by judgment*, that is, justly, by the stable administration of justice, without showing partiality. "A man of oblations," as the margin reads, *overthrows the land*; a man who is either sacrilegious or superstitious, who in exchange for a bribe will ignore those who are most guilty and in expectation of a bribe will persecute the innocent—such a ruler will ruin a country.

Verse 5

People may be said to *flatter their neighbours* when they applaud good in them that really either does not exist or is not as the flatterers describe it. These *spread a net for their* neighbors' *feet*. Flattery harms those who are flattered; it puffs them up with pride and so turns out to be a net that catches them in sin. Flatterers also set a trap for their own feet, as some understand the verse. Those who flatter others in expectation that they will return the compliment and flatter them only make themselves look ridiculous and abhorrent, even to those on the receiving end of the flattery.

Verse 6

The danger in the path of sin lies not only in the punishment at the end of it but in the *snares* along the way. One sin serves as a temptation to another, and there are troubles that, like *a snare*, come suddenly on evildoers in their disobedience. The trap that is *in the transgression of evil men* spoils all their happiness, *but righteous* people are kept from those snares or are rescued from them; they walk at liberty (Ps 119:45), and therefore they *sing and rejoice.*

Verse 7

A *righteous* judge *considers the cause of the poor.* It is everyone's duty to consider the poor (Ps 41:1), but to consider *the cause of the poor* is the duty of those who administer justice. A sense of justice must make both judge and defense attorney as careful and diligent in looking after the legal cases of the poor as if they hoped to gain the greatest advantage by that work. A *wicked* person, on the other hand, *regards to know not* the case of a poor person, has no such concern for it, for nothing is to be gained by it; he does not care which way it goes, regardless of right or wrong. See Job 29:16.

Verse 8

When *scornful men* (mockers) are employed in the business of the state, they do things in a rush because they scorn deliberation. They scorn "being restricted," as they see it, by laws and constitutions. They scorn being bound by their word. In this way they *bring a city into a snare* by their evil leadership and behavior, or (as the margin reads it) they "set a city on fire"; they sow the seeds of dissension (6:14, 19) among the citizens and throw them into confusion. *Wise men* promote religious faith, which is true wisdom, and so *turn away the wrath* of God; and by wise guidance they reconcile warring groups.

Verse 9

If a wise man contend with a wise man, he may hope to be understood and, as far as he has reason and justice on his side, to be successful and settle a dispute amicably, but if he *contend with a foolish man, there is no rest*; he will see no end of it. Whether the foolish man receives what is said to him angrily or scornfully, whether he rants and raves at it or mocks it, there will be *no rest.* The wisest man must expect to be either scolded or ridiculed if he *contends with a fool.* Whether the wise man himself *rages or laughs* (scoffs), whether he takes the serious or lighthearted way of dealing with the fool, no good is done.

Verse 10

Bad people hate their best friends: *The bloodthirsty,* all the offspring of the old Serpent, who *was a murderer from the beginning* (Jn 8:44), *hate the upright.* Bloodthirsty people especially *hate upright* judges, who try to restrain and reform them. *The just,* on the other hand, whom the bloodthirsty hate, *seek their soul,* pray for their conversion, and would gladly do anything for their salvation. Christ taught us this. *Father, forgive them* (Lk 23:34).

Verse 11

A person is *a fool* if he *utters all his mind,* if, however a conversation starts, he quickly loses his temper, if when provoked he will say anything that is in his mind, no matter who may be affected by it. *A wise man will* not *utter all his mind* at once, but will take time to have second thoughts or will keep back the present thought for later,

for a more suitable time. He will not make one continuous, formal speech, but will punctuate what he says with pauses, so that he may listen to any objections there may be and respond to them.

Verse 12

Lies will be told to those who will listen to them, and those who listen to them are as bad as those who tell them. Those who do so will have *all wicked servants* (officials): the officials will appear evil, for they will have lies told about them; and they will be evil, for they will tell lies to their rulers.

Verse 13

This shows how wisely God in his greatness serves the intentions of providence by people with very different temperaments. Some are *poor,* honest, and hardworking; others are rich, lazy, and *deceitful.* They *meet together* in the business of this world, and *the Lord enlightens both their eyes.* He gives his grace to some of both kinds of people. He gives sight to the poor by giving them patience, and he gives sight to the oppressors by giving them repentance, as for example to Zacchaeus. We are ready to look on *the poor and the deceitful* as blemishes of providence, but God makes even them display the beauty of providence.

Verse 14

The rich will look to themselves, but the ruler must *defend the poor* and needy (Ps 82:3) and plead for them (31:9). Those judges who do their duty *shall be established for ever.*

Verse 15

Parents must not only tell their children what is right and wrong but also correct them if need be. If a *reproof* will serve without *the rod,* well and good, but *the rod* must never be used without a reasoned and serious *reproof*; and then it will *give wisdom. A child* who is not restrained or rebuked, but is *left to himself,* as Adonijah was (1Ki 1:6), may do well if he chooses well, but if he follows the wrong way, he will prove a disgrace to his family and *bring his mother to shame.*

Verse 16

The more sinners there are, the more sin there is. In the old world, when *men began to multiply* (Ge 6:1), they began to corrupt themselves and one another. The more sin there is, the closer comes the time when sinners are ruined. Let not *the righteous* have their faith and hope shocked by the increase of sin and sinners. Let them not say that *God has forsaken the earth,* but wait patiently; the sinners' downfall will come; they will fall into disgrace and destruction.

Verse 17

It is a pleasure for parents, a pleasure no one knows except those who are blessed by it, to see the happy fruit of the good upbringing they have given their children, and to have a prospect of their doing good for earth and heaven. Children must be trained, not allowed to do what they want and to go without rebuke when they do wrong.

Verse 18

1. People who lack a settled ministry are miserable. *Where there is no vision,* no prophet to explain the law, no priest or Levite to teach the necessary knowledge of

the Lord, no means of grace, where the word of the Lord is rare and there is *no open vision* (1Sa 3:1)—where it is so, *the people perish*; the word translated *perish* has many meanings.

1.1. "The people are made naked," stripped of their ornaments and so exposed to shame, stripped of their armor and so exposed to danger. How bare does a place look without Bibles and ministers, and what an easy target it is to the enemy of souls!

1.2. "The people rebel," not only against God but also against their ruler. Good preaching makes people good subjects, but if they lack revelation, they are uncontrolled and unruly.

1.3. "The people are idle," or "they play," as schoolchildren tend to do when their teacher leaves the room.

1.4. "They *are scattered as sheep having no shepherd*, because they lack leaders to call them and keep them together" (Mk 6:34).

1.5. *They perish*; they are *destroyed for lack of knowledge* (Hos 4:6).

2. People who have a settled, successful ministry are happy.

Verse 19

An unprofitable, lazy, evil servant (Mt 25:26, 30) does not serve from conscience or love, but purely from fear. No reasonable words will influence him; he *will not be corrected* and reformed by fair means or even by foul *words*. No rational words will be gained from him. He is determined and morose, and *though he understands* the questions you ask him, he *will not* give you an *answer*.

Verse 20

Seest thou a man that is hasty in his words, who has a light and halfhearted understanding, who gallops through a book, taking no time to digest it? *There is more hope* for making a wise student out of someone who is dull-witted and slow in his studies than out of someone who has such a volatile mind and cannot settle down seriously to something. *Seest thou a man that is* eager to speak about every subject that comes up, as if he were an authority on everything? *There is more hope* for a modest *fool*, who is aware of his foolishness, than for someone who is so conceited.

Verse 21

It is unacceptable in a servant to behave insolently because he has been pampered. The humble prodigal thinks he is unworthy *to be called a son* and is content to be a servant (Lk 15:19); the pampered slave thinks he is too good to be called *a servant*, and wants to be *a son at the length* (in the end), to be on the same level as his master, and perhaps claim the inheritance.

Verse 22

An angry, hot-tempered, furious disposition makes people provoke one another. It makes people provoke God. Undue anger is a sin that leads to many other sins.

Verse 23

Those who think they will gain respect by lifting themselves up, talking big, appearing fine, and applauding themselves will expose themselves to contempt, lose their reputation, and provoke God to bring them down and lay them *low* by humbling providences. Those who *humble themselves shall be exalted* (Mt 23:12) and established in their dignity.

Verse 24

Those who are drawn away by the temptation of sinners incur guilt: a person does so if he becomes a *partner with* (accomplice of) those who rob and defraud. Accomplices are as bad as the thieves themselves; by joining them in committing the sin, they cannot escape joining them in concealing it, even though it may involve the most terrible perjury, curses, or oaths. They even *hate their own souls*, for they deliberately do what will inevitably destroy them.

Verse 25

We are warned not to dread the power of human beings. Slavish fear *brings a snare*, that is, it exposes people to many insults, or rather to many temptations. Abraham, *for fear of man*, denied his wife (Ge 12:10–20), and Peter denied his Master (Mt 26:69–75), and many people have denied their God and their faith. Whoever puts his trust in the Lord will be set high above human power and fear of that power.

Verse 26

To advance and enrich themselves, people *seek the ruler's favour*. Solomon was himself a *ruler*, and he knew how often people turned to him, some on one errand, others on another, but all to seek his *favour*. Haman had *the ruler's favour*, but it did him no good. Look up to God, seek the favor of the Ruler of rulers, for *every man's judgment cometh from the Lord*. Then it does not matter whether we please the ruler or not; it is as God wants.

Verse 27

This expresses not only the inherent opposition between good and evil but also the old enmity that has always been between the seed of the woman and the seed of the Serpent (Ge 3:15). All who are sanctified have a deep-rooted hatred toward evil and evildoers. They have goodwill to the souls of everyone, but they hate the ways and practices of those who are ungodly. *An unjust* man makes himself repugnant *to the just*, and it is one aspect of his present shame and punishment that good people cannot endure him. All who are unsanctified have a similar deep-rooted hatred toward godliness and godly people.

CHAPTER 30

This and the next chapter are an annex to Solomon's proverbs, but each chapter, in its first verse, calls itself a prophecy (oracle), by which it appears that their authors were divinely inspired. This chapter was written by one who bears the name of Agur the son of Jakeh. We have: 1. His confession of faith (vv. 1–6). 2. His prayer (vv. 7–9). 3. A warning against wronging servants (v. 10); four evil generations (vv. 11–14). 4. Four insatiable things (vv. 15–16), to which is added a reasonable warning to undutiful children (v. 17). 5. Four unsearchable things (vv. 18–20); four intolerable things (vv. 21–23). 6. Four things that are small and wise (vv. 24–28). 7. Four stately things (vv. 29–33).

Verses 1–6

Agur was "a collector," as the name means, a collator, one who collected the wise sayings and observations of others (v. 3): "I have not *learned wisdom* myself, but have been a scribe or copyist to others who are wise and learned." *Ithiel and Ucal* are mentioned as the names of Agur's pupils. Probably they wrote down what he dictated, as Baruch wrote what Jeremiah said. Or the words may refer to the subject of Agur's sayings. *Ithiel* means "God with me," the application of *Immanuel*, "God with us." *Ucal* may mean "the Mighty One," for it is One who is mighty who helps us. The prophet here aims at three things:

1. To abase or humble himself. Before he confesses his faith, he confesses his own foolishness and the weakness and deficiency of reason, which make it so necessary that we be guided and directed by faith. When Agur was turned to by others as wiser than most, he acknowledged himself more foolish than anyone. Whatever high opinion others may have of us, we should have humble thoughts of ourselves. He speaks of himself as lacking a revelation to guide him in the ways of truth and wisdom. The natural man, the natural powers, do not perceive, in fact, they *receive not, the things of the Spirit of God* (1Co 2:14).

2. To advance Jesus Christ, and the Father in him (v. 4): *Who hath ascended up into heaven?* Some understand this to refer to God and his works, which are both incomparable and unsearchable. Others refer it to Christ, to Ithiel and Ucal, the Son of God, for it is the Son's name as well as the Father's that is here sought after, and a challenge is given to anyone to rival him. What is the *name* of *his Son* (v. 4), by whom he does all these things? The Old Testament saints expected the Messiah to be the *Son of the Blessed* (Mk 14:61), and he is spoken of here as a person who is distinct from the Father, but whose name is still secret.

3. To assure us of the truth of the word of God and to commend it to us (vv. 5–6). Agur's students expect to be taught by him in the things of God. "Alas!" he says. "I cannot undertake to teach you; go to the word of God. *Every word of God is pure*; it does not contain the slightest falsehood or flaw." God in his word, God in his promises, is *a shield*, an effective protection, to all those who *put their trust in him* (v. 5). His word is sufficient, and so we must not add to it (v. 6). We must be content with what God has thought right to reveal to us of his mind, and not want to be *wise above what is written* (1Co 4:6).

Verses 7–9

After Agur's confession and creed comes his litany, in which we may notice:

1. The introduction to his prayer: *Two things have I required* (v. 7)—that is, asked—of you, O God! Before we pray, it is good to consider what we need, and what the things are which we need to ask God for.

2. The prayer itself. The *two things* he requires are sufficient grace and the food he needs.

2.1. Grace that is sufficient for his soul: *Remove from me vanity* (falsehood) *and lies* (v. 8). Some understand this as a prayer for the forgiveness of sin, for when God pardons sin, he takes it away.

2.2. The food that is necessary for his body. "Feed me with the bread of my allowance (v. 8, margin), such food as you think fit to give me." Our Savior seems to refer to this when he teaches us to pray, *Give us this day our daily bread* (Mt 6:11). He prays against the two extremes of abundance and lack: *Give me neither poverty nor riches* (v. 8). He intends to express the value that wise and good people have for a condition of life that is moderate, and, while submitting to the will of God, he desires that that might be his condition, neither great honor nor great contempt. He gives a godly reason for his prayer (v. 9): "*Lest I be full* and sin, or *poor* and sin." Sin is what a good person is afraid of in every condition and event. Prosperity makes people proud and forgetful of God, as if they did not

need him. A good person also dreads the temptations of a poor condition: *Lest I be poor and steal* (v. 9). Poverty is a strong temptation to dishonesty; the reason Agur fears that he would steal is that in so doing he would dishonor God.

Verses 10–14

Here is:

1. A warning not to abuse other people's servants any more than our own, nor to cause trouble between them and their masters. "Hurt not a servant with thy tongue" is the reading of the margin, for it shows a corrupt disposition to strike anybody secretly with the lash of the tongue, especially a servant, who is no match for us.

2. An account of some evil generations that are justly detestable to all who are good.

2.1. Those who are abusive to their parents. *There is a generation* of such (vv. 11–14); young men of such evil character commonly form a gang and incite one another against their parents, because they cannot endure discipline.

2.2. Those who are conceited and *are not cleansed from their filthiness* (v. 12), the filthiness of their hearts, which they claim to be their best part.

2.3. Those who are haughty and arrogant to those around them (v. 13). There is a generation of such people, on whom the One who *resists the proud will* (Jas 4:6) pour contempt.

2.4. Those who are cruel to the poor and cruel to all who lie at their mercy (v. 14); their teeth are as iron and steel, *swords and knives*, instruments of cruelty, with which they *devour the poor* with the greatest possible pleasure, and as greedily as hungry people cut up their food and devour it.

Verses 15–17

Agur has spoken of those people who devour the poor (v. 14); he now speaks about their insatiableness in doing this. They are prompted to it by covetousness and cruelty, *two daughters* of the *horseleech*, its genuine offspring, which continually cry out, "*Give, give* (v. 15), give more blood, give more money," for the bloodthirsty are continually bloodthirsty; being drunk with blood, they add thirst to their drunkenness, and continue to seek blood.

1. He specifies four other things that are insatiable:

1.1. The grave, into which many people fall and still more will fall. It swallows them all up and returns no one.

1.2. The *barren womb*, which is impatient with the affliction of barrenness and cries out, as Rachel did, *Give me children* (Ge 30:1).

1.3. The *parched ground* (Isa 35:7) in times of drought, especially in those hot countries, which always soaks in the rain that falls abundantly on it and soon wants more.

1.4. The *fire*, which when it has consumed a lot of fuel, still devours all the combustible matter thrown onto it. So insatiable are the corrupt desires of sinners, and so little satisfaction have they even when they are gratified.

2. He adds a terrible threat to disobedient children (v. 17). Those who dishonor their parents will be hanged in chains, as it were, for birds of prey to peck out their eyes, those eyes with which they looked so scornfully on their good parents. The dead bodies of evildoers were not to hang all night, as before nightfall the ravens would have pecked out their eyes.

Verses 18–23

Here is:

1. An account of four things that are *too wonderful* to be fully known:

1.1. The first three are natural things and are only intended as comparisons to illustrate the last. We cannot fathom:

- *An eagle in the air* (v. 19). Which way it has flown cannot be discovered, nor can we explain the amazing speed of its flight.
- *A serpent upon a rock* (v. 19). We may find the path of a snake in the sand by tracking it, but not that of a snake on hard rock.
- *A ship in the midst of the sea* (v. 19) leaves no traces behind it. The kingdom of nature is full of wonders *past finding out* (Job 9:10).

1.2. The fourth is a mystery of sin, more inexplicable than any of these; it belongs to the depths of Satan. On the one hand, there is the cursed way an evil adulterer uses to defile a young woman and persuade her to yield to his evil, detestable lusts. On the other, there is the cursed way an evil, adulterous woman uses to hide her evil; so secret are her intrigues that it is as impossible to track her down as it is to track an eagle in the air. She eats the forbidden fruit and then wipes her mouth, so that she may not betray herself, and says with a defiant arrogance, "I have done nothing wrong." She denies the fault to her own conscience. This is how many destroy their souls, by calling evil good (Isa 5:20), defying their convictions, and justifying themselves.

2. An explanation of four intolerable things, that is, four kinds of people who are very troublesome:

2.1. A servant who is promoted. Of all people, he is most disrespectful and arrogant.

2.2. A fool—a silly, rude, boisterous, cruel person—who has become rich and is enjoying the pleasures of the table. He will disturb all the company with his extravagant talk.

2.3. A disagreeable, perverse woman when she gets a husband, one who, having made herself unloved by her pride and sourness, so that you would not have thought anyone would ever love her, finally marries, and then that honorable state makes her more intolerably defiant and spiteful than ever. A gracious woman, when married, will be even more obliging.

2.4. A woman servant who has persuaded her mistress to leave her what she has. She will be as intolerably proud and hateful as the perverse wife, and will think herself wronged if anything is left to anyone else. Let those therefore whom Providence has advanced from humble beginnings to positions of honor carefully watch against pride and arrogance.

Verses 24–28

1. Having mentioned four things that seem great but are really contemptible, Agur here mentions four things that are small but wonderful, great in miniature. They teach us:

1.1. Not to wonder at physical bulk, beauty, or strength, but to judge people by their wisdom and behavior, their diligence and application to their work.

1.2. To wonder at the wisdom and power of the Creator in the smallest and lowliest creatures, in an ant as much as in an elephant.

1.3. To blame ourselves when we do not act as much in our own true interests as the lowliest creatures do in theirs.

1.4. Not to despise the weak things of the world (1Co 1:27); there are those that are *little upon the earth*, but *are exceedingly wise* (v. 24). The margin reads, "They are wise, made wise," by the special instinct of nature. All

who are wise to salvation (2Ti 3:15) are made wise by the grace of God.

2. Those he mentions are:

2.1. The *ants*, which are tiny and very weak but nevertheless work very hard to gather proper food in summer, which is the right time. This is such a great act of wisdom that we may learn from them to be wise for the future (6:6).

2.2. The *conies*, the hyraxes or rock badgers, weak creatures and very timid, but still so wise as to *make their houses in the rocks* (v. 26), where they are well protected. A sense of our own need and weakness should drive us to the One who is *a rock higher than we* (Ps 61:1) for shelter and support.

2.3. The *locusts* also are small and *have no king*, as the bees have, but *they go forth all of them by bands*, they advance together in ranks (v. 27), like an army arrayed for battle (Joel 2:25). *They go forth all of them* "gathered together" (margin); a sense of weakness should make us keep together, so that we may strengthen one another.

2.4. The *spider*. Spiders are very clever at weaving their webs with a fineness and precision that no skill can claim to come near: they *take hold with their hands* (v. 28) and spin a fine thread from their own bodies with a great skill, and they are not only in the cottages of the poor but also in *kings' palaces* (v. 28).

Verses 29–33

Here is:

1. A list of four things that are majestic and stately in their bearing:

1.1. *A lion*, the king of beasts, because it is *strongest among beasts* (v. 30). The lion neither *turns away* (v. 30) nor changes its pace for fear of being pursued.

1.2. *A greyhound*, whose body is fit for running, or (as the margin reads) "a horse."

1.3. *A he-goat*, whose stately bearing appears when it goes in front and leads a flock. It is the beauty of a Christian's bearing to be in the vanguard in a good work and to lead others along the right path.

1.4. *A king*, who when he appears in his majesty is looked on with reverence and awe, and *there is no rising up against* him (v. 31). And if *there is no rising up* against an earthly ruler, *woe to him* then *that strives with his Maker* (Isa 45:9). It is intended that we should learn courage and bravery from the *lion* and *not turn away for any* difficulty we may encounter. From the greyhound we may learn speed, from the he-goat the care of our family and those in our responsibility, and from a king to have our children in sincere submission, and from them all to *go well*, so that we may not only be safe but also move with stately bearing (v. 29).

2. A warning to us to keep our temper at all times, no matter how we are provoked. We must be ashamed of ourselves whenever we are justly accused of a fault; we must not insist on our own innocence. If we have *lifted up* (exalted) *ourselves* (v. 32) in perverse opposition, we have *done foolishly*. If we have only *thought evil* (v. 32), if we are aware in ourselves that we have cherished evil intentions in our minds, even then we must *lay our hand upon our mouth* (v. 32), that is, humble ourselves for what we have done wrong. We must keep the evil thought we have conceived in our minds from breaking out in evil words. It is bad to think wrong thoughts, but it is much worse to speak them out, for that implies a consent to the evil thought. We must not stir up the passions of others. Some are so provocative in their words and behavior that they even *force wrath* (stir up anger) and thereby *bring*

forth strife, and where there is strife, *there is confusion and every evil work* (Jas 3:16). Just as the forceful stirring of cream draws the goodness out of the milk, and the hard *wringing* (twisting) *of the nose* draws blood from it, so also this *forcing of wrath* (v. 33) wastes both the body and the spirits of a person and robs them of all the good that is in them. The spirit is gradually heated with strong passions; one angry word leads to another, and so it goes on until it ends in an irreconcilable feud.

CHAPTER 31

Some, equating King Lemuel with King Solomon, think this chapter was added to the rest of the proverbs because it was written by the same author; others think it was added only because it deals with the same kind of subject, even though it was written by another author named Lemuel. Whichever is true, it is a prophecy, an oracle, given by inspiration of God, who directed Lemuel to write it and his mother to dictate to him the substance of it. Here is: 1. An exhortation to Lemuel, a young ruler, to beware of the sins he would be tempted to commit and to do the duties of the position he was called to (vv. 1–9). 2. The description of a noble woman, a wife and the female head of a family. Lemuel's mother drew it up, either as a set of instructions to her daughters—as the previous verses were directed to her son—or as directions to her son for choosing a wife (vv. 10–31).

Verses 1–9

Some commentators think Lemuel is Solomon; the name means one that is "for God" or "devoted to God"; *Lemuel* may have been an affectionate name by which his mother called him. One would rather tend to think it is Solomon who tells us here what *his mother taught him* (v. 1), because he tells us in 4:4 what his father taught him. Some think, however, that Lemuel was a ruler in some neighboring country, whose mother was a daughter of Israel. It is the duty of mothers as well as fathers to teach their children about good and evil so that they may do the one and avoid the other. When children are young and tender, they are most under the mother's eye, and she then has the opportunity of molding their minds well.

1. She pleads with the young ruler, speaking as one who is thinking about what advice to give him. "You are descended from me; you are *the son of my womb*, and so what I say comes from the authority and affection of a parent. You are a piece of me. Be wise and good, and then I will have been well repaid. You are *the son of my vows*, the son I prayed to God to give me and promised to give back to God." Our children who by baptism have been dedicated to God, and for whom and in whose name we covenanted with God, may well be called *the children of our vows*.

2. She warns him against the two destructive sins of immorality and drunkenness. *Give not thy strength unto women*, to adulterous women. He must not be weak and indulgent. Sexual immorality lessens the honor of kings and makes them inferior. Are those who themselves are slaves to their own lusts fit to govern others? If they want to keep their people from immorality, they themselves must be models of purity. The king must also avoid *drinking wine* or *strong drink* to excess; *it is not for kings* to allow themselves that liberty (v. 4). It is beneath the dignity of kings; it dishonors their crown by confusing the head that wears it. All Christians are *made to our God kings and priests* (Rev 5:10). *It is not for* Christians to

drink to excess; it is inconsistent with the life of those who are heirs of the kingdom and spiritual priests (Lev 10:9). It is saddening to read the complaint made of the priests and prophets in Isa 28:7, that *they have erred through wine, and through strong drink they are out of the way* and stumble when making decisions.

3. She advises him to do good with his wealth. "You have wine and strong drink at your disposal; instead of doing yourself harm with it, do good to others with it; give it to those who need it. We must deny ourselves physical gratifications so that we may have enough to spare to relieve the anguish of others. Wine can be used medicinally and is therefore to be used in times when people are in need, not when they are immoral. An example is Timothy, who was advised to *drink a little wine, only for his stomach's sake and his often infirmities* (1Ti 5:23). The king must do good with his power and knowledge, and must administer justice with care, courage, and compassion (vv. 8–9). He must *judge righteously* and pass sentence fairly, without fear of other people: *Open thy mouth*, speak up; rulers and judges are to speak freely when passing sentence. He must especially look on himself as obliged to support oppressed innocence, especially those who are *dumb* and do not know how to speak up for themselves, whether through fear or being confused by the prosecutor or overawed by the court.

Verses 10–31

This description of the *virtuous woman*, the wife of noble character (v. 10), is intended to show what kind of wives women should be and what kind of wives men should choose. It consists of twenty-two verses, each beginning with a letter of the Hebrew alphabet in order, which makes some people think it was a poem by itself, written by someone else; that it may have been commonly repeated; and that it was to promote this custom that it was made alphabetical, for ease of memorization. We have its summary in the New Testament in 1Ti 2:9–10; 1Pe 3:1–6, where the duties set down for wives correspond to this description of a noble wife. Here is:

1. A general search for a wife of such noble character (v. 10). The one who is sought is a *virtuous woman*—"a woman of strength" is the sense; she is the weaker partner (1Pe 3:7), but she is made strong by wisdom, grace, and the fear of God: it is the same word that is used in describing good judges (Ex 18:21): *A virtuous woman* is a woman of spirit, who has command of her own spirit (16:32) and knows how to manage those of other people. *A virtuous woman*, a wife of noble character (v. 10), is a woman who has determination, who, having embraced good principles, holds them firmly and steadily. *Who can find* (v. 10) her? Good women are very scarce. But the man who wants to marry should make sure he is not biased by superficial beauty or good humor, wealth or background, dressing well or dancing well, for all these may be present in a woman who is not noble. The rarer good wives are, the more they should be valued.

2. A particular description of her and her excellent qualifications.

2.1. She works very hard to commend herself to her husband's respect and affection. She conducts herself in such a way that he can put his full confidence in her. She trusts her to remain faithful to him. He trusts her to act with wisdom and good sense in every matter. He trusts her to be faithful to all his interests. When he goes out to attend to public matters, he trusts her to deal with all the arrangements at home. She contributes so much to his happiness *that he shall have no need of spoil*, he lacks nothing of value (v. 11); he does not need to go around complaining or scraping together a living, as some men have to do whose wives are proud and wasteful at home. He is so happy with her that he does not envy those who have more of this world's wealth; he does not need it: he has enough, because he has such a wife! She shows her love for him not merely by a simple fondness but also by doing those thoughtful things that make their relationship enjoyable and deepen it, speaking good words to him, not bad ones, even when he is out of sorts, trying to provide what is right for him both in health and in sickness. This is her concern *all the days of her life*: not only when they were first married or now and then, when she is in a good mood, but always. If she survives him, she continues to do him good by caring for their children and possessions and his good name. She adds to his reputation in the world (v. 23): *Her husband is known in the gates* (respected at the city gate); he is known to have a good wife. By his cheerful face and pleasant mood it is clear that he has a delightful wife at home, who takes care of him.

2.2. She is one who is careful to do her duty where she is and who takes pleasure in it. She hates to sit still and do nothing: *She eats not the bread of idleness* (v. 27). She is careful to fill up time, so that no minutes are lost. When daylight is over, then because her business lies indoors and her work is worth the candlelight, she uses that to extend the day, and *her candle goes not out by night* (v. 18). *She rises* early, *while it is yet night* (v. 15), to give her servants their breakfast, so that they may be ready to go about their work cheerfully. She is not one of those people who sit up playing cards or dancing till midnight, or till morning, and then lie in bed until noon. She applies herself to the business that is right for her. She does not occupy herself with the work of a student, political leader, or farmer, but with the work of a woman. *She seeks wool and flax* at the place where she may select the best of each at the cheapest price. She has a stock of both, and with this she not only sets the poor to work, which is a very kind act, but also works herself, *works willingly, with her hands. She lays her* own *hands to the spindle*, or spinning wheel, *and her hands hold the distaff* (v. 19), and she does not consider it a restriction on her liberty. The spindle and the distaff are here mentioned as her honor, while the ornaments of the daughters of Zion are reckoned as their disgrace (Isa 3:18–23). She does not employ herself only in sitting work, or fine finger work—there are kinds of work that are scarcely one step away from doing nothing—but, if need be, she pursues her work with all the strength she has, which she will use as one who knows it is the way to gain more.

2.3. She is the kind of person who turns what she does to good advantage. She knows she can make things herself better and more cheaply than she can buy them. She brings in provisions of all things that are necessary and convenient for her family (v. 14). She buys land and enlarges the family's estate (v. 16): *She considers a field, and buys it.* She considers what benefits it will bring to the family. Though she has it very much in mind, she will not buy it till she has thought about it first: whether it is worth her money, whether the land actually corresponds to the description given of it, and whether she has the money at her disposal to pay for it. *She* also *plants a vineyard*, but it is *with the fruit of her hands*; she plants it using money she has earned by her work and saved up, not borrowed money. She provides well for her house and has good clothing for herself and her family (v. 22): *She*

makes herself coverings of tapestry to hang in her rooms, and she herself has made them. *Her* own *clothing* is rich and fine: it is *silk and purple.* She has rich clothes and wears them well. The senator's robes that her husband wears have been spun by her, and they look better and wear better than any that have been bought. She also gets good warm clothing for her children. She does not need to be afraid of the cold of the severest winter, for she and her family are well supplied with clothes. *All her household are clothed in scarlet* (v. 21), strong cloth suitable for winter, but also good-looking. She makes more than she and her household need, and so when she has stocked her family sufficiently, *she sells fine linen and girdles* (sashes) *to the merchants* (v. 24), who carry them to Tyre, the market of the nations, or some other trading city. She stores up for later times: *She shall rejoice in time to come* (v. 25), having provided a good supply for her family.

2.4. She takes care of her family and all its concerns, *gives meat* (food) *to her household* (v. 15). *She looks well to the ways of her household* (v. 27).

2.5. She is kind *to the poor* (v. 20). She is as intent on giving to others as she is on getting for herself. *She* also *reaches forth her hands to the needy* who are far away.

2.6. She is wise: she is not talkative, critical, or perverse. When she does speak, her words show good sense and are very much to the point: *In her tongue is the law of kindness* (v. 26). The law of love, faithfulness, and kindness is written on her heart, but it shows in her words. She is full of godly conversation, which shows how full her heart is of another world even when her hands are very busy in this world.

2.7. What completes and crowns her character is that *she fears the Lord* (v. 30). With all those good qualities she does not lack the *one thing needful* (Lk 10:42). The fear of God reigning in a heart is the beauty of the soul; it commends those who have it to the favor of God and is extremely valuable in his sight; it will last forever and defy death itself, which consumes the beauty of the body but consummates the beauty of the soul.

3. The happiness of this noble wife.

3.1. She has the comfort and satisfaction of her goodness within herself (v. 25). She has a firm and positive spirit that will endure many crosses and disappointments, and this is her clothing, for defense as well as decency. She treats everyone honorably *and shall rejoice in time to come*; she will remember with comfort when she grows old that she was not idle or useless in her younger days. In fact, *she shall rejoice* with *fulness of joy and pleasures for evermore* (Ps 11:16).

3.2. She is a great blessing to her relatives (v. 28). Her children grow up in her home, and they call her blessed. Her husband is so happy with her that he takes every opportunity to speak well of her.

3.3. She gains a good reputation with all her neighbors. A woman who fears the Lord will receive praise from God (Ro 2:29). She will be highly praised (v. 29): *Many have done virtuously*, but she surpasses them all. If what people do deserves commendation, then they should be praised. If her children are dutiful and respectful toward her, they then give her the fruit of her hands; she reaps the benefits of all the care she has taken of them. Her own works will praise her; if her relatives and neighbors are silent, her good works will nevertheless declare her praise. And so we come to the end of this mirror chapter for women, which shows them how they should dress and behave, and if they live in this way, then when Jesus Christ returns, their adornment will be shown to have been to his praise, honor, and glory (1Pe 3:3; 1:7).

Twenty chapters of the book of Proverbs (chapters 10 to 29), consisting mostly of entire sentences in each verse, could not be easily classified under proper headings so that their contents might be collated. I have therefore put the contents of all these chapters together here, which may be of some use to those who want to see all that is said on any one heading in these chapters.

1. The comfort or grief that parents have in their children, according to whether they are wise or foolish, godly or ungodly (10:1; 15:20; 17:21, 25; 19:13, 26; 23:15–16, 24–25; 27:11; 29:3).
2. The world's insufficiency, and religion's sufficiency, to make us happy (10:2–3; 11:4) and the preference therefore to be given to the benefits of goodness above those of this world (15:16–17; 16:8, 16–17; 17:1; 19:1; 28:6, 11).
3. Laziness and diligence (10:4, 26; 12:11, 24, 27; 13:4, 23; 15:19; 16:26; 18:9; 19:15, 24; 20:4, 13; 21:5, 25–26; 22:13, 29; 24:30–34; 26:13–16; 27:18, 23, 27; 28:19), especially making the most of or neglecting opportunities (6:6; 10:5).
4. The happiness of the righteous and the misery of the wicked (10:6, 9, 16, 24–25, 27–30; 11:3, 5–8, 18–21, 31; 12:2–3, 7, 12–13, 21, 26, 28; 13:6, 9, 14–15, 21–22, 25; 14:11, 14, 19, 32; 15:6, 8–9, 24, 26, 29; 20:7; 21:12, 15–16, 18, 21; 22:12; 28:10, 18; 29:6).
5. Honor and dishonor (10:7; 12:8–9; 18:3; 26:1; 27:21); boasting (25:14, 27; 27:2).
6. The wisdom of obedience and the foolishness of disobedience (10:8, 17; 12:1, 15; 13:1, 13, 18; 15:5, 10, 12, 31–32; 19:16; 28:4, 7, 9).
7. Causing trouble and being useful (10:10, 23; 11:9–11, 23, 27; 12:5–6, 12, 18, 20; 13:2; 14:22; 16:29–30; 17:11; 21:10; 24:8; 26:23, 27).
8. The praise of wise and good words, and the hurt and shame of an ungoverned tongue (10:11–14, 20–21, 31–32; 11:30; 14:3; 15:2, 4, 7, 23, 28; 16:20–21, 23–24; 17:7; 18:4, 7, 20–21; 20:15; 21:23; 23:9; 24:26; 25:11).
9. Love and hatred, peacefulness and strife (10:12; 15:17; 17:1, 9, 14, 19; 18:6, 17–19; 20:3; 25:8; 26:17, 21; 29:9).
10. The rich and the poor (10:5, 22; 11:28; 13:7–8; 14:20, 24; 18:11, 23; 19:1, 4, 7, 22; 22:2, 7; 28:6, 11; 29:13).
11. Lying, fraud, and pretense, and truth and sincerity (10:18; 12:17, 19, 22; 13:5; 17:4; 20:14, 17; 26:18–19, 24–26, 28).
12. Slander (10:18; 16:27; 25:23).
13. Talkativeness and silence (10:19; 11:12; 12:23; 13:3; 17:27–28; 29:11, 20).
14. Justice and injustice (11:1; 13:16; 16:8, 11; 17:15, 26; 18:5; 20:10, 23; 22:28; 23:10–11; 29:24).
15. Pride and humility (11:2; 13:10; 15:25, 33; 16:5, 18–19; 18:12; 21:4; 25:6–7; 28:25; 29:23).
16. Despising and respecting others (11:12; 14:21).
17. Gossiping (11:13; 16:28; 18:8; 20:19; 26:20, 22).
18. Rashness and deliberation (11:14; 15:22; 18:13; 19:2; 20:5, 18; 21:29; 22:3; 25:8–10).
19. Putting up security (11:15; 17:18; 20:16; 22:26–27; 27:13).
20. Good and bad women or wives (11:16, 22; 12:4; 14:1; 18:22; 19:13–14; 21:9, 19; 25:24; 27:15–16).
21. Mercifulness and unmercifulness (11:17; 12:10; 14:21; 19:17; 21:13).

22. Love toward the poor, and unkindness (11:24–26; 14:31; 17:5; 22:9, 16, 22–23; 28:27; 29:7).
23. Covetousness and contentment (11:29; 15:16–17, 27; 23:4–5).
24. Anger, and humility and patience (12:16; 14:17, 29; 15:1, 18; 16:32; 17:12, 26; 19:11, 19; 22:24–25; 25:15, 28; 26:21; 29:22).
25. Low spirits and joy (12:25; 14:10, 13; 15:13, 15; 17:22; 18:14; 25:20, 25).
26. Hope and expectation (13:12, 19).
27. Prudence and foolishness (13:16; 14:8, 18, 33; 15:14, 21; 16:21–22; 17:24; 18:2, 15; 24:3–7, 27; 26:6–11; 28:5).
28. Treachery and trustworthiness (13:17; 25:13, 19).
29. Good and bad company (13:20; 14:7; 28:7; 29:3).
30. The education of children (13:24; 14:14; 19:18; 20:11; 22:6, 15; 23:12; 29:15, 17).
31. The fear of the Lord (14:2, 26–27; 15:16, 33; 16:6; 19:23; 22:4; 23:17–18).
32. True and false witness bearing (14:5, 25; 19:5, 9, 28; 21:28; 24:28; 25:18).
33. Mockers (14:6, 9; 21:24; 22:10; 24:9; 29:9).
34. Credulity and caution (14:15–16; 27:12).
35. Kings and their subjects (14:28, 34–35; 16:10, 12–15; 19:6, 12; 20:2, 8, 26, 28; 22:11; 24:23–25; 25:2–5; 28:2–3, 15–16; 29:4, 12, 14, 26).
36. Envy, especially the envy of sinners (14:30; 23:17–18; 24:1–2, 19–20; 27:4).
37. God's omniscience and his universal providence (15:3, 11; 16:1, 4, 9, 33; 17:3; 19:21; 20:12, 24; 21:1, 30–31; 29:26).
38. A good and ill name (15:30; 22:1).
39. People's good opinion of themselves (14:12; 16:2, 25; 20:6; 21:2; 26:12; 28:26).
40. Devotion toward God and dependence on him (16:3; 18:10; 23:26; 27:1; 28:25; 29:25).
41. The happiness of God's favor (16:7; 29:26).
42. Incentives to obtain wisdom (16:16; 18:1; 19:8, 20; 22:17–21; 23:15–16, 22–25; 24:13–14; 27:11).
43. Cautions against temptations (16:17; 29:27).
44. Old age and youth (16:31; 17:6; 20:29).
45. Servants (17:2; 19:10; 29:19, 21).
46. Bribery (17:8, 23; 18:16; 21:14; 28:21).
47. Reproof and correction (17:10; 19:25, 29; 20:30; 21:11; 25:12; 26:3; 27:5–6, 22; 28:23; 29:1).
48. Ingratitude (17:13).
49. Friendship (17:17; 18:24; 27:9–10, 14, 17).
50. Self-indulgence (21:17; 23:1–3, 6–8, 19–21; 27:7).
51. Drunkenness (20:1; 23:21, 29–35).
52. The universal corruption of nature (20:9).
53. Flattery (20:19; 26:28; 28:23; 29:5).
54. Undutiful children (20:20; 28:24).
55. The brevity of ill-gotten gains (20:21; 21:6–7; 22:8; 28:8).
56. Revenge (20:22; 24:17–18, 29).
57. Sacrilege (20:25).
58. Conscience (20:27; 27:19).
59. The preference of moral duties before ceremonial (15:8; 21:3, 27).
60. Extravagance and wastefulness (21:20).
61. The triumphs of wisdom and godliness (21:22; 24:15–16).
62. Perversity and tractableness (22:5).
63. Sexual immorality (22:14; 23:27–28).
64. Faltering in suffering (24:10).
65. Helping the distressed (24:11–12).
66. Loyalty to the government (24:21–22).

67. Forgiving your enemies (25:21–22).
68. Causeless curses (26:2).
69. Answering fools (26:4–5).
70. Unsettledness and unsatisfiedness (27:8, 20).
71. Cowardliness and courage (28:1).
72. The people's interest in the character of their rulers (11:10–11; 28:12, 18; 29:2, 16).

73. The benefit of repentance and holy fear (28:13–14).
74. The punishment of murder (28:17).
75. Eagerness to get rich quick (28:20, 22).
76. The enmity of evildoers against the godly (29:10, 27).
77. The necessity of the means of grace (29:18).

A PRACTICAL AND DEVOTIONAL EXPOSITION OF THE BOOK OF
Ecclesiastes

The account we have of Solomon's turning away from God at the end of his reign (1Ki 11:1) is the tragic part of his story; he may have spoken his Proverbs in the prime of his time, while he kept his integrity, but delivered Ecclesiastes when he had grown old—for he speaks feelingly about the burdens and decays of age (ch. 12)—and was, by the grace of God, restored from his backsliding. In Proverbs he dictated his observations; here he wrote his own experiences. This is how days speak (Job 32:7); this is the wisdom that many years have taught.

1. Ecclesiastes is a sermon in print; the text is (1:2), *Vanity of vanities, all is vanity*, utterly meaningless, everything is meaningless; that is the teaching too; it is proved in detail by many arguments, and objections are answered, and at the end we have its application, by way of an exhortation to *remember our Creator* (12:1), to *fear him*, and to *keep his commandments* (12:13). There are indeed many things in this book that are dark and difficult to understand, and some things that people *wrest* (distort) *to their own destruction* (2Pe 3:16) for lack of distinguishing between Solomon's arguments and the objections of unbelievers, but there is enough that is easy and clear to convince us of the meaninglessness of the world and its complete insufficiency to make us happy, of the evil of sin and its certain tendency to make us miserable, and of the wisdom of being religious and the solid comforts and assurance that are to be gained by doing our duty both to God and to our fellow human beings.

2. It is a penitential sermon; it is a sermon of confession, in which the preacher sadly mourns his own foolishness in promising himself satisfaction from the things of this world and even from the forbidden self-indulgent pleasures, which he now finds bitterer than death. His fall is proof of the weakness of human nature: *Let not the wise man glory in his wisdom* (Jer 9:23), since Solomon himself, the wisest person who ever lived, was such an outrageous fool; nor *let the rich man glory in his riches* (Jer 9:23), since Solomon's wealth was such a great trap to him and did him much more harm than Job's poverty did him. His restoration proves the power of God's grace: it was strong enough to bring back to God a person who had gone so far from him.

3. It is a practical and profitable sermon. Having been brought to repentance, Solomon resolves, like his father, to *teach transgressors God's way* (Ps 51:13). The fundamental error that people make is the same as that of our first parents: hoping to be like God by taking what seems *good for food, pleasant to the eyes, and desirable to make one wise* (Ge 3:5–6). The thrust of this book is to show that this is a great mistake, that our happiness consists not in being gods to ourselves in order to have what we want and do what we want, but in having our Maker as our only God. In this book, Solomon assures us that *to fear God and to keep his commandments is the whole duty of man* (12:13). He shows the meaninglessness of those things in which people commonly look for happiness, such as mere human learning and wisdom, self-indulgent pleasures, honor and power, wealth and great possessions. He also prescribes remedies. Although we cannot heal these things of their meaninglessness, we may prevent the trouble they give us by not holding onto them, but instead having low expectations of them and accepting the will of God, and especially by remembering God in the days of our youth (12:3) and continuing to live in his fear and service throughout our lives.

CHAPTER 1

In this chapter we have: 1. The title of the book (v. 1). 2. The general doctrine of the meaninglessness of creation established (v. 2) and explained (v. 3). 3. The proof of this doctrine, taken: 3.1. From the brevity of human life (v. 4).

3.2. From the changeable nature of all creatures and the perpetual ebb and flow of the sun, wind, and water (vv. 5–7). 3.3. From the wearisome toil of human beings (v. 8). 3.4. From the constant return of the same things, which shows the limit of all perfection (Ps 119:96)

916

(vv. 9–10). 3.5. From the oblivion to which all things are condemned (v. 11). 4. The first example of this doctrine: the meaninglessness of human knowledge. Solomon performed an experiment on human knowledge (vv. 12–13, 16–17) and rendered the judgment that it is all meaningless (v. 14). There is no satisfaction in it (v. 18). If human knowledge is a meaningless chasing after the wind, all other things in this world, being much less than this in dignity and worth, must be so too.

Verses 1–3

Here is:

1. An account of the author of this book. It was Solomon, for no other son of David was king of Jerusalem, but he conceals his name *Solomon*, "peaceable," because he has brought trouble on himself and his kingdom by his sin; he has broken his peace with God and so is not worthy to be called by that name anymore. Call me not *Solomon*, call me *Mara* (Ru 1:20), for *behold, for peace I had great bitterness* (Isa 38:17). But he calls himself:

1.1. *The preacher*, which shows his present role. He is *qoheleth*, which comes from a word that means "to gather." Or perhaps the word *soul* must be added, and so *qoheleth* is:

1.1.1. A *penitent soul*, or a *gathered* one, one who had gone astray like a lost sheep but was now taken back from wandering. The spirit that had been dissipated after a thousand meaningless acts was now collected and made to center on God. It is only the penitent soul that God will accept, the heart that is broken, not the head that is bowed low like a bulrush only for a day. And it is only the gathered soul that comes back from the byways of sin.

1.1.2. A *preaching soul*, or a *gathering* one. Being himself *gathered* and reconciled to the church, he tried to gather to the assembly others who had gone astray as he had. God by his Spirit made him a preacher, as a sign of his being reconciled to him; a commission is a tacit pardon. Christ sufficiently testifies his forgiving of Peter by committing his lambs and sheep to his trust.

1.2. *The son of David* (v. 1). He looked on it as greatly aggravating his sin that he had such a father. On the other hand, his being the son of David also encouraged him to repent and hope for mercy, for David had fallen into sin but had repented and found mercy; here he followed David's example and found mercy as David did.

1.3. *King of Jerusalem* (v. 1). God had done much for him by raising him to the throne, but he had repaid God so badly. He thought it not beneath him, as a king, to be a preacher, and the people would respect him more as a preacher because he was a king.

2. The general intention and theme of this book, which is to make us truly religious, to lower our respect for and expectation of the things of this world. In order to do this, he shows:

2.1. That they are *all vanity*, meaningless (v. 2). It is *all vanity* (v. 2) not only when it is abused, when it is corrupted by sin, but even when it is used. It is expressed here emphatically; not only *All is vain* (meaningless) but also, in the abstract, *All is vanity* (meaninglessness), as if meaninglessness were an attribute of the things of this world, part of their nature. They are not only vanity but even *vanity of vanities* (v. 2), vanity in the highest degree. Many speak contemptuously about the world because they are hermits and do not know it, or beggars and do not have it, but Solomon knew it. He had described the depths of nature (1Ki 4:33), and he had the wealth of this world, perhaps more than anyone else had ever had. He spoke in God's name and was divinely inspired to speak

as he did, and he spoke deliberately; what he spoke he set down as a fundamental principle on which he based the necessity of being religious. One main thing he intended to show was that the eternal throne and kingdom that God had promised to David must be of another world, for all things in this world are meaningless and therefore do not have enough in them to fulfill the scope of that promise.

2.2. That they cannot make us happy. *What profit has a man of all the pains he takes*, what does a person gain from all his labor? (v. 3). The business of this world is labor; the word refers to both care and toil. It is work that makes people tired. *What profit has a man of all that labour?* (v. 3). Solomon says in Pr 14:23, *In all labour there is profit*, but here he denies there is any profit. As to our present condition in the world, it is true that it is from our labor that we obtain what we call *profit*; we *eat the labour of our hands* (Ps 128:2). But here he determines that it has no real lasting benefits. In short, the wealth and pleasures of this world, even if we have much of them, are not sufficient to make us happy. As goods increase, worries about them increase, and *those are increased that eat of them* (5:11), and a little thing will make bitter all the strength and encouragement we derive from them, and then *what profit has a man* (v. 3) from all his labor? If this is true of our present condition, then how much more truly may we say for the soul and our future life, *What profit has a man of all his labour?* (v. 3). All that people gain will not supply the needs of the soul or satisfy its desires, nor atone for the sin of the soul or heal its diseases.

Verses 4–8

To prove the meaninglessness of all things under the sun Solomon here shows:

1. That the time of our enjoyment of these things is very short. We live in this world for only one generation, which is continually passing away to make way for another, and we are passing away with it. While the stream of people continually flows, how little can one drop of that stream enjoy the pleasant banks between which it glides! We may give God the glory for the constant succession of generations, but as to our own happiness, let us not expect it within such narrow limits, but in eternal rest and peace.

2. That when we leave this world, we leave the earth behind us, which *abides for ever* (v. 4). It is good for the human race in general that the earth endures to the end of time, when it and all the works in it will be burned up, but what is that to individual people, when they move to the world of spirits?

3. That human beings remain on the earth for only a little while. The sun sets every night, but it rises again every morning, as bright and fresh as ever. *But man lies down and rises not* (Job 14:7, 12).

4. That all things in this world are movable and changeable, never resting; the only thing we can be certain of is uncertainty. And can we expect rest in a world where all things are so *full of labour* (wearisome) (v. 8), on a sea that is always ebbing and flowing, and its waves continually running and rolling?

5. That the human mind is as restless in its pursuits as the sun, wind, and rivers; it is never satisfied or contented. The more it has of the world, the more it wants; and it would be no sooner filled with the streams of outward prosperity than the sea is with *all the rivers that run into it* (v. 7); it is still as it was, *a troubled sea that cannot rest* (Isa 57:20).

6. That *all things continue as they were from the beginning of the creation* (2Pe 3:4). The earth is where it was;

the sun, winds, and rivers follow the same course. We must therefore look beyond the sun for satisfaction and for a new world. Our senses are unsatisfied, and the objects of them unsatisfying. Curiosity is still inquisitive because it is still unsatisfied, and the more it is indulged, the fussier and more perverse it becomes, crying, *Give, give* (Pr 30:15).

Verses 9–11

There are two things in which we tend to take much pleasure and satisfaction and on the basis of which we evaluate ourselves. Solomon shows us we are mistaken in both.

1. The novelty of our discoveries. How good it is to think that no one has ever made such advances in knowledge and such discoveries as we have, that no one has ever so increased their wealth. We boast about our contemporary fashions, our innovative thinking, our new methods, and the latest expressions that jostle out the old and take their place. But this is all a mistake. What is there in the kingdom of nature about which we may say, *This is new?* The powers of nature and series of natural causes are still the same as ever. People's hearts and their corruption are still the same; their desires, pursuits, and complaints are still the same. When Tatian, the Syrian Christian teacher, showed the Greeks how all the arts that they prided themselves on owed their origin to the nations they considered barbaric, he reasoned with them: "Shame on you, do not call those things inventions which are mere imitations." What reason have we to think that the world should be any kinder to us than it has been to the people who have gone before us, since it contains nothing new, and our predecessors have made as much of it as they could? If we want to be entertained by new things, we must come to know the things of God; we must get a new nature; then *old things pass away, and all things become new* (2Co 5:17). The Gospel puts *a new song into our mouths* (Ps 40:3).

2. The memorableness of our achievements. Many people think they have found enough satisfaction in foreseeing that their names will be remembered forever, that future generations will celebrate their noble actions. How many *former things* (v. 11) and people have there been, who looked very great and significant in their day, but of whom now *there is no remembrance* (v. 11)? Here and there one remarkable person emerges or an action occurs that happens to be recorded by a kind historian, but at the same time there are others, no less remarkable, who are neglected.

Verses 12–18

What seems most likely to bring happiness to reasonable beings is knowledge and learning; if this is meaningless, then everything else must also be so. Now as to this:

1. Solomon tells us how he had devoted himself to study and conducted an experiment to see if true satisfaction could be found in knowledge and learning. He conducted it under such conditions that if true satisfaction could be found in this way, he would have found it. He had his royal seat *in Jerusalem*, which then deserved, more than Athens ever did, to be called "the eye of the world." Solomon's great wealth and honor enabled him to make his court the center of learning and the meeting place of learned people. He made it his business to get to know *all the things that are done under the sun* (v. 14), everything that is done either by divine Providence or by human skill and wisdom. Although he was a ruler, he made himself a slave to learning; he was not discouraged by its intricate difficulties, nor did he give up halfway through his studies. He did all this not simply to satisfy his own thirst

for learning, but to qualify himself to serve God and his generation (Ac 13:36) and to see how far the deepening of knowledge would go toward giving his mind calmness and rest. He *saw all the works that were done under the sun* (v. 14), on the one hand the works of nature in the higher and lower worlds, and on the other hand works of art, of human ingenuity and imagination either in a personal or social capacity. He had as much satisfaction in the success of his explorations as anyone ever had. Solomon must be acknowledged as a competent judge of this matter, for not only was his head full of grand ideas, but also his *heart had great experience of wisdom and knowledge* (v. 16), of the power and benefits of knowledge as well as the enjoyment of it. He digested what he came to know, and he knew how to use it. Solomon was so diligent in seeking to better himself in knowledge that he gained instruction from both the wisdom of the prudent and the madness of the foolish, by *the field of the slothful* (Pr 24:30) as well as of *the diligent*.

2. He tells us what were the results of this experiment, to confirm what he had said, that *all is vanity* (meaningless) (v. 1).

2.1. He found that his search for knowledge was very tiring to both his body and his mind (v. 13). As food for the body must be obtained and eaten *in the sweat of our face* (Ge 3:19), so also must that for the soul.

2.2. He found that the more he saw of *the works done under the sun*, the more he saw of their futility; in fact, the sight often brought him *vexation of spirit* (v. 14): "*I have seen all the works* of a world full of business; I have noticed what people are doing; *and behold*, whatever people think of their own works, I see that *all is vanity and vexation of spirit*, all of them are meaningless, a chasing after the wind." The more we see of this world, the more we see that makes us uneasy and the more we look on it, like the Greek philosopher Heraclitus, with weeping eyes. Solomon realized especially that the knowledge of *wisdom and folly* was *vexation of spirit* (v. 17). It troubled him to see many who had wisdom and did not use it, and many who were foolish and did not fight against their foolishness.

2.3. He found that when he had obtained some knowledge, he could neither gain that satisfaction for himself that he had expected to gain nor do the good to others with it that he had expected to do (v. 15). Human minds and ways are twisted and perverse. Solomon thought that by using both his wisdom and his power he might be able to thoroughly reform his kingdom, but he was disappointed in this. All the philosophy and politics in the world will not restore corrupt human nature. Learning will not change people's natural attitudes or cure them of their disease of sin. *That which is wanting* (lacking) in our knowledge is so much that it *cannot be numbered* (v. 15). The more we know, the more we know our ignorance. In the end, therefore, he concluded that great scholars only make themselves great mourners; *for in much wisdom is much grief* (v. 18). Those *that increase knowledge* have so much the quicker and sharper awareness of the adversities of this world. Yet let us not for that reason be turned away from pursuing any useful knowledge, but patiently break through its sorrows; on the other hand, let us despair of finding true happiness in this knowledge, and expect it only in knowing God and carefully fulfilling our duty toward him.

CHAPTER 2

Having declared everything meaningless, Solomon goes on to show why he has become tired of this world, and how little reason people have to be fond of it. 1. He shows there is no true happiness and satisfaction to be gained in the delights of self-indulgence (vv. 1–11). 2. He reconsiders wisdom and concedes that it is excellent and useful, but he sees that it cannot make people happy (vv. 12–16). 3. He asks how far wealth will go toward making people happy, and he concludes from his own experience that to those who set their hearts on it, it is vanity and vexation of spirit, it is meaningless and a chasing after the wind (vv. 17–23), and that if there is any good in it, it is only to those who do not cling to it (vv. 24–26).

Verses 1–11

In his pursuit of human happiness, Solomon moves out of his study, where he has sought to find it in vain, into the park and his garden; he exchanges the company of the philosophers and serious senators for the company of the witty and high-spirited people of his generation, to see if he can find true satisfaction and happiness among them. Here he takes a great step downward, from the noble pleasures of the intellect to unrefined physical pleasures.

1. He decided to test mirth and wit: *"Enjoy pleasure* (v. 1) and have your fill of it; throw all cares to the wind, go on—make up your mind to be merry!" But many who are poor, who lack the fine things Solomon had, are very merry; beggars in a barn are proverbially so. Mirth comes short of the substantial delights that we find in the use of the mind, yet it is to be preferred to indulging in fleshly delights. Some distinguish human beings from animals not only by their rationality but also by their ability to laugh. "Try, therefore," says Solomon, "to laugh and be rich, to laugh and be merry." The conclusion of this experiment: *I said of laughter, It is mad*—or, "You are mad"—*and of mirth, What doeth it?* Innocent mirth, well balanced, appropriate, and in moderation, is good; it oils the wheels of life and work and helps soften the toil of life, but when it is excessive and immoderate, it is foolish and fruitless. It merely dulls the pain of our present life.

2. Finding himself not happy in what pleased his frivolous imaginings, he decided next to see what would please his sense of taste (v. 3). *I sought in my heart to give myself unto wine*, that is, to good food and drink. Solomon applied himself to it critically, and only to perform an experiment. He sought *to lay hold on* (embrace) *folly* (v. 3), to see the utmost that it could do toward making people happy. He decided that foolishness would not take hold of him, that it would not control him. He took care at the same time to *acquaint* himself *with wisdom*, to manage himself wisely in his self indulgence so that he would not be harmed or disqualified from being a competent judge of pleasure. Solomon proposed this to himself, but he found it *vanity* (meaningless). *Wine is a mocker* (Pr 20:1), and it will be impossible for anyone to say that they will give themselves to it so far but no farther. What he aimed at was not to indulge his appetite, but to find the way to human happiness. Notice the description he gives of human happiness—it is *that good for the sons of men which they should do under the heaven all their days* (v. 3). *Good Master, what good thing shall I do?* (Mt 19:16). Our happiness consists not in being lazy but in doing right, in being usefully employed. But that anyone would give themselves to wine in the hope of finding that to be the best way to live in this world is an absurdity that Solomon here, on reflection, condemns.

3. Realizing quickly that it was foolish of him to give himself to wine, he next tried the most costly entertainments and amusements.

3.1. He undertook a great deal of building work, both in the city and in the country, and having gone to such vast expense at the beginning of his reign to build a house for God, he could be excused if later he pleased himself by building for himself. In building, he had the pleasure of employing poor people and of doing good for future generations. We read of Solomon's buildings in 1Ki 9:15–19, and they were all *great works*. Notice his mistake: he sought the *good* works he should do (v. 3), and he applied what he learned in that inquiry by applying himself to *great* works. *Good* works indeed are truly great, but many works reputed to be great are far from good.

3.2. He loved gardening, which to some is as enthralling as building. He *planted himself vineyards* (v. 4); he *made himself* fine *gardens and orchards* (v. 5). He had not only forests of timber trees but also *trees of all kinds of fruit*, which he himself had planted.

3.3. He spent a great deal of money on reservoirs, ponds, and canals, not for entertainment or diversion but for use, *to water the wood that brings forth trees* (v. 6); he not only planted but also watered, and then left it to God to give the increase (1Co 3:6).

3.4. When he proposed to do *great works*, he had to employ many people, and so he acquired *servants and maidens*, and from those he *had servants born in his house* (v. 7).

3.5. He *had large possessions of great and small cattle* (v. 7), herds and flocks, as his father had before him (1Ch 27:29, 31).

3.6. He became very rich and was not made poor at all by his building and gardening.

3.7. He had all sorts of music, both vocal and instrumental. These are called *the delights of the sons of men* (v. 8).

3.8. He enjoyed, more than anyone ever did, a combination of pleasures of both the mind and body at the same time. In the midst of these entertainments *his wisdom remained with him* (v. 9). But his judgment and conscience did not restrain his pleasures, nor did they prevent him from extracting the very essence from his self-indulgence (v. 10). He had as much pleasure in his work and life as anyone ever had: *My heart rejoiced in all my labour* (v. 10). The fact that he enjoyed success from his business sweetened it, and it sweetened his enjoyments that success was the product of his business, so that, in general, he was as happy as the world could make him.

3.9. We have the conclusion he came to from all this (v. 11). When Solomon reviewed *all his works that his hands had wrought* with the greatest cost and care, *and the labour that he had laboured to do* to make himself at ease and happy, nothing fulfilled his expectations; *behold, all was vanity and vexation of spirit*, everything was meaningless, a chasing after the wind. *There was no profit under the sun* in this present world, no profit from either the employments or the enjoyments of this world.

Verses 12–16

Having tried to see what satisfaction could be gained from learning and then from self-indulgence, Solomon here compares one with the other and passes judgment on them.

1. He sets himself to consider both wisdom and foolishness again (see 1:17) to see if, on second thoughts, he could gain more satisfaction. Let us accept Solomon's judgment of the things of this world and not think of repeating the experiment, for we can never have such advantages as he had to make the experiment with or conduct it with equal application of mind.

2. He far prefers wisdom to foolishness. "I soon *saw*," he says, "*that there is an excellency in wisdom more than in folly* (v. 13), as much as there is in light more than darkness." Although the pleasures of wisdom are not enough to make people happy, they are vastly better than the pleasures of wine. Wisdom enlightens the soul with surprising discoveries and the guidance necessary for it to direct itself rightly, but self-indulgence clouds the mind and is like darkness to it. *The wise man's eyes are in his head* (v. 14), where they should be, ready to see both the dangers to be avoided and the advantages to be made the most of. *Fools*, however, *walk in darkness* and are always either at a loss or about to fall.

3. But he maintains that, with respect to lasting happiness and satisfaction, the wisdom of this world gives very little advantage. The same sickness, the same sword, devours wise and foolish people. Solomon applied this mortifying observation to himself (v. 15). Why should I take so much effort to obtain wisdom when, as for this life, it will do me so little good? *Then I said in my heart that this also is vanity.* Wise and foolish people are all forgotten (v. 16): *There is no remembrance of the wise more than of the fool.* The righteous are promised that they *shall be had in everlasting remembrance* (Ps 112:6), that *their memory shall be blessed* (Pr 10:7), and that they will soon *shine as the stars* (Da 12:3), but no such promises are made about the wisdom of this world, that that will make people's names last forever, for it is only those names that are *written in heaven* that will last forever (Lk 10:20). There is a great difference between the death of a godly person and that of an evildoer, but not between the death of a wise person and that of a foolish person.

Verses 17–26

After a life of contemplation and pleasure, Solomon turned to activity, but found no more satisfaction in it than in any other way; he found it still to be *all vanity and vexation of spirit* (v. 17):

1. The work he tried was work *under the sun*, in this present world (vv. 17–20), with the things of this world; it was the work and business of a king. It is *labour under the sun* that Solomon here speaks about with so little satisfaction, labor in this present world (v. 20), labor for the *meat* (food) *that perishes* (Jn 6:27; Isa 55:2). It was the better kind of work, *labour in wisdom, and knowledge, and equity* (v. 21). It was work that involved his mind and related to the government of his kingdom. It was work in which he *showed himself wise* (v. 19), which many people have in mind more than anything else in their pursuit of worldly business.

2. He soon became tired of it. He *hated all his labour* (v. 18). After he had built all his fine houses and gardens, he soon began to look down on them with contempt. This does not express a gracious hatred of these things, which is our duty, to love them less than God and religious faith (Lk 14:26); nor is it a sinful hatred of them, which would be foolish to have—to become tired of the place God has assigned us and its responsibilities; rather, it is a natural hatred of them, arising from an excess and a sense of disappointment in them. Have we all not dug deeply into this earth searching for some rich mine of satisfaction, only to find not the slightest sign of it; have we not always been frustrated in the search, and will we not finally despair of ever finding it? He *hated life itself* (v. 17), because it is subject to so much toil, trouble, and disappointment.

3. Two things made him weary:

3.1. His work was such a toil to himself: the *work that he had wrought under the sun* (in this present world) *was*

grievous unto him (made him sad) (v. 17). A person who works is described as being uneasy both in his *going out* and in his *coming in*; he does not rest (v. 23). He is deprived of his pleasure by day; he is disturbed in his rest *by night*. Notice how foolish those are who make themselves drudges to the world and do not make God their rest; day and night they can only be uneasy. The result is that generally *all is vanity*, meaningless (v. 17).

3.2. The gains of his business must all be left to others. To a gracious soul this is not troublesome in any way; why should we not rather be pleased that when we have gone, those who come after us will get along better because of our wisdom and hard work? He does not know whether the person he leaves his wealth to will turn out to be *a wise man or a fool* (v. 19), a wise person who will make more out if it or a fool who will bring it to nothing. It is probable that Solomon wrote this from the heart, because he was afraid of how Rehoboam would turn out.

4. The best use, therefore, that can be made of the wealth of this world is to use it cheerfully and do good with it. He concludes the chapter with this (vv. 24–26). Notice:

4.1. What is the good that is commended to us here, what is the greatest pleasure and advantage we can expect or draw from the business of this world, what is the most we can do to rescue it from its *vanity* (meaninglessness) and *vexation*, its chasing after the wind.

4.1.1. We must do our duty with our wealth: we must be more concerned to use our possessions well, for the purposes for which we were entrusted with them, than to increase them.

4.1.2. We must take comfort from them. If we use them to support the body so that the body can keep up with the soul in its service to God, then we have turned them to good account. He does not suggest we give up our work and take our ease to *eat and drink*. We must *enjoy good in our labour* (v. 24); we must use these things; we must not excuse ourselves from them, but be conscientious and cheerful in undertaking our worldly business.

4.1.3. We must *acknowledge God* in our wealth. We must see that the *good things* themselves are *from the hand of God* (v. 24), from his bountiful providence, and that a heart to enjoy them is the gift of God's grace.

4.2. Why we should keep this good before our eyes and look to God for it.

4.2.1. Solomon himself, with all his wealth, could aim at no more and desire no better (v. 25). He could not, however, obtain this good by his own wisdom, without the special grace of God, and so he tells us to expect it from the hand of God and pray to him for it.

4.2.2. Riches are a blessing or a curse according to whether people have or do not have a heart to use them well. God makes riches a reward to one who is good, if with them he also gives *wisdom, and knowledge, and joy* (v. 26), to enjoy them cheerfully and share them generously with others. He makes them a punishment to an evildoer, for the evildoer does not have a heart to take comfort from them; they only tantalize the evildoer and tyrannize them. *Godliness, with contentment, is great gain* (1Ti 6:6). Ungodliness is commonly punished with discontent and an insatiable greed, which are sins that are their own punishment.

CHAPTER 3

Having shown the meaninglessness of studies, pleasures, and work and having made it clear that happiness is not to be found in the schools of the learned, in the gardens of Epicurus, or in the marketplace, Solomon concludes that we should cheerfully content ourselves with and make use of what God has given us. He proves this by showing: 1. The changeability of all human affairs (vv. 1–10). 2. The unchangeability of God's purposes (vv. 11–15). 3. The futility of worldly honor and power (v. 16). To restrain proud oppressors and show them their futility, he reminds them that they will be called to account in the other world for their oppression (v. 17) and that their condition in this world is no better than that of the animals (vv. 18–21). He therefore concludes that we would be wise to use what power we have for our own well-being and not to oppress others with it (v. 22).

Verses 1–10

We live in a world of change. The events of time and the conditions of human life are very diverse, and we are continually passing to and fro between different events and between different conditions. In the *wheel of nature* (Jas 3:6: *course* [literally, *wheel*] *of nature*) sometimes one spoke is uppermost, and then soon the opposite is; there is a constant ebb and flow, a waxing and waning from one extreme to the other. When we are successful, we should be at peace, but not self-confident — not self-confident, because we live in a world of change, and yet at peace; and, as Solomon already advised us (2:24), we ought *to enjoy the good of our labour*, humbly depending on God, neither exalted with hopes nor downcast with fears, but prepared with a calmness of mind.

1. A general proposition is laid down: *To everything there is a season* (v. 1). Those things that seem most opposite to one another will, as the wheel of life rotates, each have their turn and come into play. The day will give way to the night, and the night will give way to the day. Is it summer? It will soon be winter. Is it winter? Wait a little while, and it will be summer. Every purpose has its time.

2. Some of these changes are purely the act of God; others depend more on human will. Everything *under heaven* (v. 1) is therefore changeable, but in heaven there is an unchangeable state. There is:

2.1. *A time to be born and a time to die* (v. 2). But just as there *is a time to be born and a time to die*, so also there will be a time to rise again.

2.2. *A time* for people *to plant*, a time of year, a time of their lives, but when *that which was planted has* grown fruitless and useless, it *is time to pluck it up* (uproot it) (v. 2).

2.3. *A time to kill*, when the judgments of God are out and about in a land and devastate everything, but when he comes in mercy, then *is a time to heal* (v. 3) what *he has torn* (Hos 6:1–2), to comfort a people after he has *afflicted them* (Ps 90:15).

2.4. *A time to break* (tear) *down* (v. 3) a family, a kingdom, or wealth when it has become ripe for destruction, but God will find *a time*, if people return and repent, to rebuild what he has broken down.

2.5. *A time* when God's providence calls people *to weep and mourn* (v. 4). But on the other hand, a time comes when God calls people to be cheerful, *a time to laugh and dance* (v. 4), and he expects us then to *serve him with joyfulness and gladness of heart* (Dt 28:47).

2.6. *A time to cast away* (scatter) *stones*, by breaking down fortifications, when God gives peace in a country's borders, but there is also *a time to gather stones together*, to build up strongholds (v. 5).

2.7. *A time to embrace* a friend when we find that friend faithful, but *a time to refrain from embracing* (v. 5)

when we find they are unfair or unfaithful. It is commonly applied to marital embraces and explained by 1Co 7:3–5; Joel 2:16.

2.8. *A time to get* money, promotion, good bargains, when opportunities smile, a time when wise people will, literally, "search." When they are setting out in the world and have a growing family, when they are in their prime, then it is time for them to be busy and "make hay while the sun shines." There will come *a time to lose* (v. 6), when what has been gained will soon be scattered.

2.9. *A time to keep*, when we may use what we have gained, but there may come *a time to cast away* (v. 6), when our love for God may make us throw away what we have, because we will deny Christ and wrong our consciences if we hang on to it (Mt 10:37–38).

2.10. *A time to rend* garments, as on the occasion of some great sorrow, *and a time to sew* them again (v. 7), as a sign that the sorrow has past.

2.11. *A time* when it is our duty *to keep silence* (v. 7), when it is an *evil time* (Am 5:13) or when we are in danger of speaking wrongly (Ps 39:2), but there is also *a time to speak* (v. 7) for the glory of God, when silence would betray a righteous cause.

2.12. *A time to love*, to be friendly, to be expansive and cheerful, but there may come *a time to hate* (v. 8), when we will see cause to break off the relationship with some whom we have been fond of, and to be reserved.

2.13. *A time of war*, when God draws the sword for judgment, when people draw the sword for justice, but we may hope for *a time of peace* (v. 8), when the sword of the Lord will be put back in its sheath and he will *make wars to cease* (Ps 46:9). War will not last forever, nor can any peace on this side of eternal peace be called a lasting peace.

3. If our present state is subject to such changes, *What profit has he that works?* We must look on ourselves as serving, as it were, a probationary period in this life. There is indeed no profit *in that wherein we labour*; the thing itself, when we have it, will do us little good, but if we make right use of the guidance received from Providence through it, there will be profit in that (v. 10): *I have seen the travail which God has given to the sons of men*, which he sends not to create happiness in them but *to exercise* them, so that they may absorb the various graces that come with living through various events, have their dependence on God tested by every change, and be trained and taught. Every change brings some new work for us, which we should be more concerned about than about the event itself.

Verses 11–15

Solomon shows God's hand in all those changes.

1. We must make the best of *that which is*; we must believe it to be best for the present, and we must come to terms with it: *He has made every thing beautiful in his time* (v. 11). Cold is as good in winter as heat is in summer. The night, in its turn, is a black beauty, just as the day, in its turn, is a bright one. There is a wonderful harmony in God's providence and all its ways, so that when its events are considered in their relationships and trends, together with their seasons, it appears very beautiful, to the glory of God and the encouragement of those who trust in him. Although we do not see the complete beauty of providence now, we will still see it — and it will be a glorious sight — when the mystery of God is accomplished (Dt 32:4; Eze 1:18).

2. We must wait patiently for the full revelation of what seems complex and perplexing to us, acknowledging that we *cannot find out* (fathom) *the work that God makes*

from the beginning to the end (v. 11), and so we must judge nothing before the time (1Co 4:5). While the picture is still being drawn, and the house is still being built, we do not see the beauty of either, but when the artist has put the finishing touch to them, then all will appear very good. We see only the middle of God's works, not their beginning—if we saw that, we would see how wonderfully the plan was established in God's purposes—nor their end, which crowns the action—if we saw that, we would see the final outcome to be glorious; we must wait until the curtain is torn (Mt 27:51; 2Co 3:14). Those words, *He has set the world in their hearts* (v. 11), are variously understood.

2.1. Some understand them to be a reason why we may know more of God's works than we do. If people would only give themselves to exactly observing things, they might in most of them perceive a wonderful order and design.

2.2. Others understand them to be a reason why we do not know as much of God's works as we might: "We have the world so much in our hearts, we are so taken up with the thoughts and cares of worldly things, that we have neither the time nor the spirit to see God's hand in them."

3. *There is no* certain, lasting *good in* these things (vv. 12–13). All the *good* there is *in them is to do good* with them, to our families, our neighbors, the poor, the public, and its civil and religious interests. Why else do we exist? What else do we have our being, our abilities, our wealth for, but to be in some way useful to our generation (Ac 13:36)? Notice that our business is *in this life* (6:12), where we are serving, as it were, a state of probationary trial for another life. Every person's life is their opportunity to do what will prepare them for eternity. Let us give ourselves peace, *rejoicing and enjoying the good of our labour* (v. 13), as *it is the gift of God* (v. 13), and so enjoying God in it and giving him thanks.

4. We must be satisfied with the ways of God's providence, as to both our personal and public concerns. Let us say, "May it be as God wills," for however bad it may be for our comfort, intentions, and interests, God's will remains wise. His purposes need not be changed. If we could see it all together at one time, we would see that everything is so perfect that *nothing can be put to it*—for it contains no deficiencies—*nor anything taken from it* (v. 14), for there is nothing in it that is unnecessary or that can be spared.

5. We must work hard to fulfill all that God aims at in his providence. Whatever changes we may see or feel in this world, we must acknowledge the unbreakable faithfulness of God's rule. The revolutions of the sun and moon follow the same way as they have from the beginning; so it is with the events of providence (v. 15): *That which has been is now.* The world, as it has been, is and will be constantly changing, for *God requires that which is past*, that is, he repeats what he has formerly done. No change has happened to us *but such as is common to men* (1Co 10:13).

Verses 16–22

Solomon continues to show that everything in this world, without godliness and the fear of God, is meaningless. In these verses he shows that power and life itself are nothing without the fear of God.

1. Here is the futility of powerful human beings on the throne, people in the place of justice, where, if judges are ruled by the laws of religion, they are God's vice-regents. But without the fear of God it *is meaningless*, for if you set that aside:

1.1. Judges will not judge rightly. Solomon perceived that there was *wickedness in the place of judgment. Man being in honour, and not understanding* what he should do, *becomes like the beasts that perish* (Ps 49:12), like wild animals. It would have been better for the people to have no judges than to have such corrupt ones. It would have been better for the judges to have no authority than to use it so wrongly.

1.2. The judges will themselves be judged for not judging rightly. *I said in my heart* that this unrighteous judgment is not conclusive, for there will be a review of the judgment; *God shall judge* between *the righteous and the wicked*; he will judge for the righteous and plead their cause. It is to the indescribable comfort of the oppressed that their cause will be heard again. Let them therefore wait for it with patience, for there is another *Judge* that *stands before the door* (Jas 5:9). *There is a time* to rehear causes, redress grievances, and reverse unjust decrees, even though we may not see it here (Job 24:1).

2. Here is the futility of mortal human beings. Solomon now comes to speak more generally *concerning the estate of the sons of men* (v. 18) in this world and shows that their reason, without religious faith and the fear of God, advances them only little above the animals. Notice:

2.1. What he aims at in this description of the human state.

2.1.1. That God may be honored, justified, and glorified: "that they might clear God," as the margin of v. 18 reads. If people have a troubled life in this world, they must not blame God. Let them not say that he made this world to be a prison for people and made life to be a penance. God made human beings a *little lower than the angels* (Ps 8:5); if they are lowly and miserable, it is their own fault.

2.1.2. That people may be humbled, reviled, and mortified. It is not easy to convince proud people that *they are but men* (Ps 9:20), and it is much more difficult to convince evildoers *that they are beasts* (v. 18), because they are devoid of religious faith.

2.2. How he verifies this account. A worldly, ungodly, earthly-minded person *has no preeminence above the beast, for all* that they set their heart on *is vanity* (v. 19). *That which befalls the sons of men* is no different from what *befalls beasts*; death brings about much the same change in an animal as it does in a human being. As for their bodies, the change is completely the same, except the different respects that are paid to them by the survivors. Solomon here observes that *all go unto one place*; the dead bodies of human beings and animals all decompose in the same way; *all turn to dust again* (v. 20) in their decay. As for their spirits, there is a vast difference, but it is not visible (v. 21). It is certain that *the spirit of* human beings at death *goes upwards* to the Father of spirits (Heb 12:9), who made it; it does not die with the body but *is redeemed from the power of the grave* (Ps 49:15). The soul of a human being is like a candle taken out of a dark lantern, which leaves the lantern useless, but itself shines more brightly. Those who live only according to their senses, as all ungodly people do, who *walk in the sight of their eyes*, have no *preeminence above the beasts* (v. 19). It is not strange that those who think they will die like animals live like animals; the noble faculties of reason are lost on such people. A conclusion is drawn from this (v. 22): *There is nothing better*, as to this world, *than that a man should rejoice in his own works.* This means, first, that we keep a clear conscience and never allow *iniquity* in the place of righteousness (v. 16). It means, second, that we live a cheerful life. If God has prospered the work of our hands, let us rejoice in it; let us not make it a burden to ourselves and leave others to enjoy it, for it is *our portion* (lot) (v. 22).

CHAPTER 4

Solomon shows: 1. The temptation that the oppressed feel to be discontented and impatient (vv. 1–3). 2. The temptation that those who love their comforts have to take their ease (vv. 4–6). 3. The foolishness of hoarding an abundance of worldly wealth (vv. 7–8). 4. A remedy against that foolishness, which is to be made aware of the benefits of companionship and mutual assistance (vv. 9–12). 5. The unpredictability even of royal status, not only because of the foolishness of the ruler himself (vv. 13–14) but also because of the fickleness of the people (vv. 15–16).

Verses 1–3

Solomon had deep understanding (1Ki 4:29), and it appeared in this way, among other things: he had a very great concern for those who were oppressed and afflicted. He earlier took the oppressors to task (3:16–17); now he takes notice of those who have been oppressed, and he does this as a preacher. He shows:

1. The troubles of their condition (v. 1), which grieved him. Servants and laborers were oppressed by their masters, debtors by cruel creditors and creditors by fraudulent debtors, tenants by harsh landlords and orphans by treacherous guardians, and, worst of all, subjects by despotic rulers and unjust judges. He *beheld the tears of such as were oppressed* (v. 1) and unable to help themselves: *On the side of their oppressors there was power* (v. 1); when they had done wrong, they had power to stand by it and succeed in it, so that the poor were kept down with a strong hand and had no way to obtain redress.

2. The temptations of their condition. Being so harshly abused, they were tempted to envy those who were dead and in their graves and to wish they had never been born (vv. 2–3). Solomon was ready to agree with them: "*I praised the dead that are already dead* before they have properly begun to live. I concluded that it is better with them than with *the living that are yet alive* (v. 2), merely alive, dragging along the long, heavy chain of life and wearing out its tedious minutes." Better never to have been born than be born to *see the evil work that is done under the sun*, in this present world (v. 3), and not only to be unable to put matters right but also to be punished for doing right. However adverse the condition of good people may be while they are in this world, they cannot have good reason to wish they had never been born, since they are glorifying the Lord even in the fires of their suffering.

Verses 4–6

1. If a person is sharp, skilled, and successful in his work, he will be envied by his neighbours (v. 4), and the more so because of the reputation he has gained by his honesty. Cain envied Abel, Esau Jacob, and Saul David, all for their right works. This is sheer devilry. Those who excel in goodness will always be offensive to those who exceed in evil, yet this should not discourage us from doing right, but drive us to expect praise for it, not from other people but from God.

2. If people are stupid and stumbling in their work, they wrong themselves (v. 5): *The fool* who goes about his work as if *his hands* were wrapped up and *folded together*, who does everything awkwardly, *the sluggard* who loves his ease and *folds his hands together* to keep them warm, *eats his own flesh*, is a cannibal, bringing himself into such a poor condition that he has nothing to eat but his own flesh. The following words (v. 6), *Better is a handful with quietness than both the hands full with travail and vexation of spirit*, may be taken either:

2.1. As the sluggard's excuse for his idleness, as if a little with idleness were better than abundance with honest labor. Or:

2.2. As Solomon's advice to keep to the intermediate position between *travail* and laziness, and I prefer this view. Let us work hard and honestly and take hold of the handful God gives us so that we may not lack what is necessary, but let us not grasp to have both hands full, which will only be for us a chasing after the wind. Moderate pains and moderate gains will be best.

Verses 7–12

Solomon focuses on another example of the futility of this world, that frequently the more people have of it the more they want, and they are so intent on this that they have no enjoyment of what they have.

1. Selfishness is the cause of this evil (vv. 7–8): *There is one alone*, who pays attention to and cares for no one but himself; *there is not a second*, nor does he want one: he thinks one mouth is enough in a house. He is a slave to his work. Although *he has neither child nor brother*, no one to look after except himself, no marriage partner—for fear of the expense of a family!—*yet is there no end of his labour.* He never thinks he has enough: *His eye is not satisfied with riches* (v. 8). He has enough for his back, for his stomach, for his calling, for his family, for living decently in the world, but in his own eyes he does not have enough. Yet he denies himself the comfort of what he has: he *bereaves* (deprives) *his soul of good* (v. 8). And he has no excuse for doing this: *He has neither child nor brother* (v. 8); there is no one dear to him and no one poor who is near him. It is wise for those who are toiling for this world to consider whom they are toiling for, whether it is really worthwhile. If people do not consider this, it is *vanity, and a sore travail*, meaningless—a miserable business (v. 8); they shame and trouble themselves in vain.

2. Companionship is the cure for this evil. People are so corrupt because they are only concerned for themselves. Solomon shows, by different ways, that *it is not good for man to be alone* (Ge 2:18); his intention is to commend to us both marriage and friendship.

2.1. Solomon lays down as a truth that *two are better than one* (v. 9), happier jointly than either could be separately. *They have a good reward of their labour* (v. 9). One who serves only himself has only himself to pay his wages. But one who is kind to others has *a good reward*; the pleasure and benefits of holy love will be a great reward for all the *work and labour of love* (Heb 6:10).

2.2. He proves it by citing examples of the benefits of friendship and good conversation. It is good for two to travel together, *for if* one happens to *fall*, the other will be ready *to help him up* (v. 10). If a person falls *into sin*, his friend will help *restore him with the spirit of meekness* (Gal 6:1). Good and gracious feelings are stirred by good company, and Christians warm one another by *provoking one another to love and to good works* (Heb 10:24). If an enemy finds a person alone, he is likely to *prevail against him* (v. 12); but if the one who is attacked has a companion, he may do well enough: *two shall withstand him* (v. 12). As was said of the ancient Britons when the Romans invaded them, "When they fight in detached parties, they sacrifice the general cause." We may help one another in our spiritual warfare as well as in our spiritual work; next to the encouragement of fellowship with God comes that of the fellowship with God's people. Solomon concludes with this proverb: *A threefold cord is not easily broken* (v. 12), any more than a bundle of arrows, though a single thread or a single arrow is easily broken. He compares two together to *a threefold cord,* for where two are closely joined in holy love and fellowship, Christ will come to them by his Spirit and make the third, as he joined the two disciples going to Emmaus, and then there is *a threefold cord* that can never *be broken.*

Verses 13–16

1. A king's situation is not happy unless he has wisdom (vv. 13–14). The one who is truly *wise* and godly, even if *poor* in the world and very young, *is better than an old king* if he is *foolish,* if he will not accept any warning or advice from others. Foolishness and stubbornness often go together, and those who most need warning bear it worst, but neither age nor titles will ensure that people are respected if they do not have true wisdom and goodness to commend them, whereas wisdom and goodness will gain honor for people even if they suffer from the disadvantages of youth and poverty.

2. A king is not likely to continue if he does not have a strong influence on the affections of the people. The king must also have a successor, *a second, a child that shall stand up in his stead,* his own son or perhaps that *poor and wise child* spoken of in v. 13. People are never satisfied for long: *There is no end,* no rest, *of all the people* (v. 16); they continually want changes, though they do not really know what they want. As it has been, so it is likely to continue: *Those that come after* (v. 16) will have the same disposition and *shall not* long *rejoice in him* (v. 16) whom they seemed to be very fond of at first. Today, *Hosanna,* but tomorrow, *Crucify.* It must bring great grief to rulers to see themselves shown such disrespect by those they have sought to oblige and have depended on; there is no faithfulness or steadfastness in people. *This is vanity and vexation of spirit,* a meaningless and a chasing after the wind (v. 16).

CHAPTER 5

In this chapter Solomon writes about: 1. The worship of God, seeing that as a remedy against all the futility he has already observed in wisdom, learning, pleasure, honor, power, and business. If our religious faith is meaningless, how great is that meaninglessness (Mt 6:23)! Let us therefore watch out for meaninglessness as we listen to the word, offer sacrifices (v. 1), pray (vv. 2–3), make vows (vv. 4–6), and think of pretending to have divine dreams (vv. 7–8). 2. The wealth of this world and the meaninglessness and trouble that are part of it. The fruits of the earth are necessary to support life (v. 9), but silver and gold and riches are unsatisfying (v. 10). They are unprofitable (v. 11); they are disturbing (v. 12); they often prove harmful and destructive (v. 13); they are perishing (v. 14); they must be left behind when we die (vv. 15–16). If we do not have a heart to use them, they cause a great deal of uneasiness (v. 17). We can learn from this chapter how to manage the business of religious faith and the business of this world—the two things that take up most of our time—so that we may turn both to good account.

Verses 1–3

Solomon's purpose in driving us away from the world by showing us its futility is to drive us to God and to our duty.

1. He sends us to *the house of God* (v. 1), to the place of public worship. Let our disappointment in the creation make us turn our eyes to the Creator. In the word and prayer there is balm for every wound.

2. He tells us here how to behave well in the house of God. Religious exercises are not futile, but if we mismanage them, they become futile to us.

2.1. We must deal with ourselves with all possible seriousness and care: "*Keep thy foot,* guard your steps (v. 1), do not withdraw your foot from the house of God (as in Pr 25:17), but *look well to thy goings, ponder the path of thy feet* (Pr 4:26), so that you may not take a false step. Turn to the worship of God with solemn contemplation and take time to compose yourself, not going about it in a rushed way, which is called *hasting with the feet* (Pr 19:2). Keep your thoughts from wandering; keep your thoughts from running after wrong objects." Some think *keep thy foot* alludes to the responsibility given to Moses and Joshua to *put off their shoes* (Ex 3:5; Jos 5:15).

2.2. We must make sure that the sacrifice we bring is not *the sacrifice of fools* (v. 1), that we do not trust in the signs and ceremonies, the outward aspect of worship, without considering its sense, meaning, and purpose, for that is the *sacrifice of fools.* People may be doing evil even when they do not know it, when they do not consider it. Evil minds can only choose sin, even in their acts of devotion.

2.3. We must be *ready to hear* (v. 1) and must conscientiously listen to the word of God read and preached. The word for *hearing* often means *obeying,* and that is *better than sacrifice* (1Sa 15:22; Isa 1:15–16). "Let the word of the Lord come," a good person once said, "and if I had 600 necks, I would bow them all to the authority of it."

2.4. We must be very cautious in all our approaches to God (v. 2): "*Be not rash with thy mouth* in making prayers, promises, or vows; *let not thy heart be hasty to utter anything before God.*" If we come without a purpose, we will leave without any benefit. What we *utter before God* must come from *the heart,* and so we must never let our tongue run ahead of our thoughts in our devotions. Thoughts are words to God. It is not enough that what we say comes from the heart; it must come from a composed heart, not from a sudden emotional outburst.

2.5. We must be sparing in our words, that is, reverent and deliberate. *God is in heaven* (v. 2), where he is *far exalted above all our blessing and praise* (Ne 9:5). *We are on earth* (v. 2), the footstool of his throne (Isa 66:1; Mt 5:35), unworthy to have any fellowship with him. We must therefore be serious, humble, and reverent in speaking to him.

Verses 4–8

We are encouraged to do four things in these verses:

1. To be conscientious in paying our vows.

1.1. A vow is a personal commitment (Nu 30:2). When, while suffering some affliction (Ps 66:14) or pursuing some mercy (1Sa 1:11), you have made a vow *unto God,* know that *thou hast opened thy mouth unto the Lord and thou canst not go back* (Jdg 11:36); and so fulfill what you have promised; *pay* (fulfill) *that which thou hast vowed* (v. 4); *pay* it fully and *keep not back any part of the price* (Ac 5:2). Have we vowed to *give our own selves unto the Lord?* Let us then be as good as our word. *Defer not to pay* (fulfill) *it* (v. 4).

1.2. Two reasons are given here why we should fulfill our vows quickly and cheerfully. First, because otherwise we show disrespect to God; we are playing around with him, as if intending to trick him, and *God has no pleasure in fools* (v. 4). Second, because otherwise we wrong ourselves; we incur the penalty for not fulfilling it; it would have been a great deal better *not to have vowed* in the first place. Not to have *vowed* would have been but an omission, but to *vow and not pay* (fulfill) (v. 4) incurs the guilt of treachery and perjury; it is *lying to God* (Ac 5:4).

2. To be cautious in making our vows. We must make sure we never vow anything that is sinful or may cause sin, for such a vow is improperly made and must be broken. *Suffer not thy mouth*, by such a vow, *to cause thy flesh to sin*, as Herod's rash promise caused him to cut off the head of John the Baptist (Mk 6:24–28). "When you have made a vow, do not seek to avoid fulfilling it; *say not before the angel*—the temple messenger or priest, who is called the *messenger of the Lord of hosts* (Mal 2:7)—that you have had second thoughts, you have now changed your mind and want to be freed from the obligation of your vow; no, stick to it, and do not look for some loophole to get out of it." If we treacherously revoke our vows and the words of our mouths, God will justly defeat our plans.

3. To maintain the fear of God (v. 7). Many people in former times claimed to know the mind of God by *dreams*; they almost made God's people forget his name because of their attention to those *dreams* (Jer 23:25–26); and many now are confused by their strange or frightening dreams, as if they forecast some disaster. Those who take notice of dreams will find many of them, but they all contain *divers vanities* (are meaningless) (v. 7). So never take any notice of them; instead of repeating them, do not emphasize them at all. Do not draw any disturbing conclusions from them, but *fear thou God* (v. 7).

4. Every good person, everyone with a sense of justice and a concern for other people, is angry to see *the oppression of the poor* and the *violent perverting of judgment and justice in a province* (v. 8), oppression in the name of the law and supported by power. The kingdom in general may have a good government, but it may so happen that a particular province is under the authority of an evildoer. When things look so sad, we may satisfy ourselves with the thought that although oppressors are *high*, God is *higher than the highest* (v. 8) creature. He is higher than the highest ruler. God is the *Most High over all the earth* (Ps 83:18), and his *glory is above the heavens* (Ps 8:1). Although oppressors feel secure, God *regards* them, keeps an eye on them, and he will deal with them for all their violent perversion of justice.

Verses 9–17

Solomon shows there is as much futility in great riches, and the *lust of the eye* on them, as there is in the sinful cravings of those who have them and in their boasting about what they have and do (1Jn 2:16), and people can make themselves no happier by hoarding wealth than by spending it.

1. He grants that the crops of the earth are valuable to support and give contentment in human life (v. 9). There is an increase to be gained from the earth, and it is *for all*; *everyone* needs it; it is appointed for all, and there is enough for all. It is not only for all people but also for all the lower creatures (Ps 104:14). *The king himself is served of the field* (v. 9), and he would not be served—would in fact be completely starved—without its products. This puts a great honor on the calling of farmers, who are very important in supporting human life.

2. He maintains that the riches that are more than these, those that are to be saved rather than used, are *vain things* and will not give people peace or happiness.

2.1. The more wealth people have, the more they want (v. 10). Natural desires come to rest when what is desired is obtained, but corrupt desires are insatiable. There are physical desires that silver itself will not satisfy; if a person is hungry, ingots of silver will no more satisfy their hunger than clods of clay will. Much less will worldly abundance satisfy spiritual desires.

2.2. The more people have, the more uses they find for it, and so they are no better off: *When goods increase, they are increased that eat them* (v. 11). The more food, the more mouths. Is wealth increasing? And does not the family at the same time grow more numerous and the children grow up to need more? The more people have, the better houses they have to keep. And then *what good is there to the owners* (v. 11) themselves except the pleasure of *beholding it with their eyes* (v. 11)? The owners of a thing see it as their own even though those around them enjoy as much of the real benefit of it as they do. Only the owners, however, have the satisfaction of doing good to others with it, which indeed is a satisfaction to one who believes what Christ said, that *it is more blessed to give than to receive* (Ac 20:35).

2.3. The more people have, the more anxiety they have about it, which perplexes them and disturbs their rest (v. 12). Refreshing sleep is as much the support and strength of this life as food is. Those who sleep best are commonly those who work hard and have only what they work for: the sleep of the laborers is *sweet*. Those who have everything else often fail to have a good night's sleep.

2.4. The more people have, the more danger they are in both of making trouble and of having it (v. 13): *There is an evil, a sore evil, riches kept for the owners thereof*—who have diligently hoarded them and kept them safe—to *their hurt*; they would have been better without them. They also *do hurt with their riches*, which not only enable them to satisfy their own sinful desires but also give them an opportunity to oppress others and treat them harshly. And they often sustain *hurt* from others because of *their riches*. They would not be envied or robbed if they were not rich. Those riches that have been stored up so painstakingly *perish by evil travail* (become lost by some misfortune), by the very effort and care that their owners have taken to protect and increase them. Many have lost all they had by trying to seize all they could.

2.6. However much people have when they die, they must leave it all behind them (vv. 15–16): *As he came forth of his mother's womb naked, so shall he return*. With respect to the body, we must leave this world as we came into it; the dust will return to the earth as it was. But our case is sad if the soul returns as it came, unsanctified. This is *a sore evil* (v. 16)—at least, it is so in the thought of one whose heart is glued to this world; to him it is a *sore evil* that he *shall take nothing of his labour which he may carry away in his hand* (v. 15); his riches will not go with him into another world or do him any good there. If we work hard in our religious faith, we may take the grace and comfort we have gained from that hard work in our hearts, and we will be the better for it to eternity; that is food that endures (Jn 6:27). People will see that they have *laboured for the wind* (v. 16) when at death they find that the profit of their labor has all gone, gone like the wind, they do not know where to.

2.7. Those who have a great deal, if they set their hearts on it, have not only uncomfortable deaths but also uncomfortable lives (v. 17). The covetous worldly person considered here, who is so bent on increasing his wealth, *all his days eats in darkness and much sorrow, and it is his sickness and wrath*; he not only has no pleasure in his wealth, nor any enjoyment of it himself—for he is *eating the bread of sorrow* (Ps 127:2)—but also is troubled when he sees others eat it.

Verses 18–20

Solomon looks at the futility of stored riches and concludes that the best course of action to follow is to use well what we have, to serve God with it, do good with it, and take comfort from it for ourselves and our families; he urged this before (2:24; 3:22).

1. What is commended to us here is not to indulge our fleshly appetites, but to use soberly and moderately what Providence has allotted to us. Life is God's gift, and he has appointed us *the number of the days* of our life (Job 14:5); let us therefore spend those days in *serving the Lord our God with joyfulness and gladness of heart* (Dt 28:47). We must not do the business of our calling as mere drudgery and become enslaved to it, but must *rejoice in our labour* (v. 19); we must not grasp at more business than we can take on without becoming confused or disturbed, but take pleasure in our calling.

2. To commend this to us, it is urged, first, that *it is good and comely* (proper) (v. 18). Those who cheerfully use what God has given them honor the One who has given it, fulfill the intention of the gift, act rationally and generously, do good in the world, and use what they have for good, and this is both to their credit and to their encouragement; *it is good and comely*; there is a sense of both duty and propriety about it. Second, a heart to do this is a gift of God's grace that crowns all the gifts of his providence. Finally, to use well what we have is the way to relieve ourselves in the many toils and troubles that come to us on earth (v. 20): *He shall not much remember the days of his life*, the days of his sorrow and hard work, his days spent weeping. He will either forget them or remember them as "water under the bridge"; he will not take his adversities to heart, nor will he cherish bitter thoughts about them for long, *because God answers him in the joy of his heart* (v. 20); God balances out all the grievances of his toil with joy, and he rewards him for it by giving him to *eat the labour of his hands* (Ps 128:2).

CHAPTER 6

In this chapter: 1. The royal preacher goes on to show the futility of worldly wealth. Riches in the hands of a person who is wise and generous are good for something, but in the hands of a corrupt and covetous miser they are good for nothing. 1.1. Solomon takes an account of the possessions and enjoyments that such a person may have. He has wealth (v. 2), he has children to inherit it (v. 3), and he lives long (vv. 3, 6). 1.2. He describes this person's foolishness in not taking comfort from it; he has no power to eat it, allows strangers to devour it, and at the end receives no burial (vv. 2–3). 1.3. He prefers the condition of a stillborn child to the condition of such a person (v. 3). The stillborn child's unhappiness is only negative (vv. 4–5), but that of the covetous worldly person is positive (v. 3). 1.4. Solomon shows the futility of riches as things that belong to the body and afford no satisfaction to the mind (vv. 7–8), and he shows the futility of those unlimited desires with which covetous people trouble themselves (v. 9), which, if they are fully gratified, leave a person still as he is: a mere human being (v. 10). 2. Solomon concludes this speech about the meaninglessness of created things (Ro 1:25) with the clear general conclusion that it is foolish to think about

making ourselves happy from the things of this world (vv. 11–12). Our satisfaction must be in another life, not in this one.

Verses 1–6

Solomon now shows the evil of having but not using. This *is an evil which* Solomon himself saw *under the sun* (v. 1). As a king, he took notice of this evil as an injustice, as harmful to the public, who are damaged not only by people's wastefulness on the one hand but also by their stinginess on the other. As it is with blood in the physical body, so it is with the wealth of the wider community: if instead of circulating, it stagnates, it will cause harm. As a preacher, Solomon observed the evils that were being done so that he might correct them and warn people against them. Notice:

1. The great reasons the miser has to serve God. *Riches* and *wealth* commonly gain people *honour. Riches, wealth, and honour* (v. 2) are God's gifts, the gifts of his providence, but they are given to many people who do not make good use of them. The miser *wants* (lacks) *nothing for his soul of all that he desires* (v. 2). Nor does he *want*—desire—grace for his soul, the better portion (Lk 10:42); all he desires is enough to satisfy his physical appetites, and he does that. It is supposed that he has numerous offspring, that he *begets a hundred children* (v. 3), which are the support and strength of his house and in whom he has the prospect of having his name built up. To complete his happiness, it is supposed, he *lives many years* (v. 3), *a thousand years twice told* (v. 6).

2. The little heart he has to use what God gives him for the ends and purposes for which it was given. This is his fault. He cannot find it in his heart to make good use of what he himself has. He has food set before him, but he does not have the *power to eat thereof* (v. 2). His corrupt, miserly attitude will not allow him to spend any of his money, not even on himself. Because he lacks the will to serve God with it, God denies him the power to serve himself with it. God so arranges matters that *a stranger eats it* (v. 2). This may be well called *vanity and an evil disease* (v. 2). Our worst diseases are those that arise from the corruption of our own hearts. He deprives himself of the good he might have gained from his worldly possessions. *His soul is not filled with good* (v. 3). He *has no burial* (v. 3), not one that suits his rank; he does not receive a decent burial, but is given *the burial of an ass* (Jer 22:19).

3. The preference that the preacher gives to *an untimely birth*: a stillborn child, who is carried from the womb to the grave, *is better than he* (v. 3). An untimely birth (v. 3) is very sad for many reasons (vv. 4–5): The child *comes in with vanity* (without meaning), and *he departs in darkness*; little or no notice is taken of him. Being stillborn, he has no *name*, or if he does, it will soon be forgotten and buried in oblivion; it will *be covered with darkness*, as the body is with the earth. In fact (v. 5), *he has not seen the sun*; from the darkness of the womb he is rushed immediately to the darkness of the grave, and, what is worse than not being known to anyone, he has not *known any thing*.

Verses 7–10

The preacher here further shows the futility and foolishness of storing up worldly wealth and expecting happiness from it.

1. However much we toil in the world and however much we get out of it, we have for ourselves no more than will just keep us going (v. 7). A little will be enough to sustain us comfortably, and a great deal can do no more.

2. Those who have a great deal are still craving for more; even if a person toils very much *for his mouth, yet the appetite is not filled* (v. 7). The desires of the soul find nothing in the wealth of the world to give them any satisfaction. Literally, "The soul is not filled."

3. A fool may have as much worldly wealth and may enjoy as much pleasure in it as one who is wise, and perhaps not be so aware of its trouble: *What has the wise more than the fool?* (v. 8). A fool can fare as well, can dress as well, and can cut as dashing a figure in any public appearance as someone who is wise. The result is that if there were not pleasures and honor special to the intellect, which *the wise man has more than the fool* (v. 8), the two would be on the same level as regards the things of this world.

4. Even someone who is poor, who has business and is sensible and diligent in managing it, may get as comfortably through this world as the one who has very large wealth. *What hath the poor, that knoweth to walk before the living,* who knows how to act decently and do his duty? Why, he is better loved and more respected among his neighbors and has more influence than many rich people who proudly clutch at things.

5. The enjoyment of what we have must be acknowledged as more reasonable than a greedy grasping for more (v. 9): *Better is the sight of the eyes,* making the best of what is present, *than the wandering of the desire.* People who are always content even if they have very little are much happier than people who are always craving for more even if they have much. Yet we cannot say, *Better is the sight of the eyes than the* fixing *of the desire* on God, the resting of the soul in him.

6. Whatever we gain in this world, we are still only human, and even the greatest possessions cannot lift us above the common adversities of life. That busy animal that makes such a noise in the world *is named already.* The One who made him gave him his name, *and it is known that it is man* (v. 10), and it is a humbling name (Ge 5:2). He *called their name Adam*; and all theirs have the same character, "red earth." It is good for rich and great people to know and consider that they are *but men* (Ps 9:20).

Verses 11–12

There be many things (words) *that increase vanity* (meaninglessness) (v. 11); even what seems to increase wealth and pleasure only increases the meaninglessness of human life and the futility of its pursuits. We do not know what to wish for, because what we promise ourselves most satisfaction from often proves most vexatious to us. Thoughtful people earnestly desire to do everything for the best, and they would if they knew how, but the corruption of our hearts is shown in our tendency to desire as good for us what is really harmful. Furthermore, since everything is meaningless, *Who can tell a man what shall be after him under the sun?* (v. 12). He can no more please himself with the hopes of *what shall be after him,* to his children and family, than with the enjoyment of what is with him, since he cannot predict himself, nor can anyone else predict to him, *what shall be after him.*

CHAPTER 7

Solomon has given many proofs of the futility of this world. In this chapter: 1. He commends to us some good ways to put right these grievances so that we may make the best of the bad: 1.1. The care of our reputation (v. 1). 1.2. Seriousness (vv. 2–6). 1.3. Calmness of spirit (vv. 7–10). 1.4. Prudence in managing all our affairs (*vv. 11–12*). *1.5. Submission to the will of God in all events* (*vv. 13–15*). *1.6. Conscientious avoidance of all dangerous extremes* (*vv. 16–18*). *1.7. Humility and tenderness toward those who have wronged us* (*vv. 19–22*). *In short, we must be composed and maintain our self-control. 2. He mourns his own iniquity, having many wives, by which he was drawn away from God and his duty* (*vv. 23–29*).

Verses 1–6

In these verses Solomon sets down some great truths that seem absurd.

1. The honor of goodness is really more valuable and desirable than all the wealth and pleasure in this world (v. 1): "A good name is better than fine ointment." *Good ointment* here stands for all the gains of the earth, among the products of which oil was reckoned as one of the most valuable; it stands for all physical delights, and it is called *the oil of gladness* (Ps 45:7); in fact, it stands for the highest titles of honor, for kings are anointed. *A good name* is better *than* all *riches* (Pr 22:1). Christ paid Mary for her ointment with *a good name* (v. 1), a name that would live on (Mt 26:13).

2. If we have lived so as to deserve *a good name, the day of our death* (v. 1), which will put an end to all our cares, toil, and sorrows and move us to a place of rest, joy, and eternal assurance, *is better than the day of our birth* (v. 1).

3. It will do us more good to go to a funeral than to go to a festival (v. 2). We may possibly glorify God, do good, and be blessed with good in the house of feasting, but considering how we tend to be proud, shallow, overconfident, and self-indulgent, *it is better* for us *to go to the house of mourning* (v. 2), not to see the pomp of the funeral but to share in its sorrow. In *the house of mourning* (v. 2) we find information: *That is the end* (destiny) *of all men* (v. 2). We also receive a warning: *The living will lay it to his heart* (v. 2). Nothing is more easy and natural than for the deaths of others to remind us of our own death. Some people perhaps *will lay that to heart* and be led to *consider their latter end* (Dt 32:29) even though they would not take a good sermon to heart. *The house of mourning* (v. 4) is the school for wise people, where they have learned many good lessons. A fool, whose *heart is in the house of mirth* (v. 4), has their heart set on being glad and jolly. If they go to *the house of mourning* at any time, they are restrained; their heart at the same time *is in the house of mirth.*

4. The proverb says, "An ounce of mirth is worth a pound of sorrow," but the preacher teaches us the opposite lesson: *Sorrow is better than laughter. By the sadness* that appears in *the countenance, the heart is* often *made better,* because a sad face is good for the heart (v. 3).

5. It is much better for us to have our corrupt state humbled by the *rebuke of the wise* than to have it gratified by *the song of fools* (v. 5). And how absurd it is for people to be so fond of such short-lived pleasure as *the laughter of a fool* (v. 6), which may be compared to the burning *of thorns under a pot* (v. 6), which makes a great noise and a great blaze for a short time, but quickly scatters its ashes and contributes hardly anything to creating heat, for that requires a constant fire! *The laughter of a fool* is noisy and flashy and is not true joy. *This is also vanity* (meaningless) (v. 6).

Verses 7–10

Solomon has often complained before about *oppressions* (extortion) (v. 7) that he has seen, which were a great discouragement to goodness and godliness.

1. He grants that the temptation is strong (v. 7): *Surely it is often too true that oppression makes a wise man mad.* If wise people are oppressed greatly and for a long time, they tend to speak and act unlike themselves, to break out into immoderate complaints against God and other people. The end of v. 7 may be understood, "It destroys the heart of a gift"; even the generous heart is destroyed by being oppressed. We should therefore make great allowances to those who have been abused; we do not know what we would do if we were in their shoes.

2. The character of oppressors is very bad, as some understand v. 7. If one who had the reputation *of a wise man* becomes an *oppressor*, he becomes *mad*; and *the gifts* that he takes only *destroy his heart* and completely extinguish any remnants of goodness in him, and he is to be pitied rather than envied. He should be left alone, and he will destroy himself in a little while. Yet the outcome will be good: *Better is the end of a thing than the beginning thereof* (v. 8). *Better was the end of* Moses' treaty with Pharaoh, that proud oppressor, when Israel was victorious, *than the beginning* of it, when there were a great number of bricks to be made and everything looked so discouraging.

3. If we do not want to be driven mad by oppression, we must be clothed with humility (1Pe 5:5), *for the proud in spirit* (v. 8) are those who become outraged when they are beset with difficulties. We must also put on patience (Col 3:12), submitting to the will of God in the affliction and waiting patiently for God to have his way in his time. We must govern ourselves with wisdom and grace (v. 9): *Be not hasty in thy spirit to be angry*; those who cannot stand delays tend to get angry if they are not immediately satisfied. And, "Don't be angry for long," for although anger may enter the heart of a wise person and pass through it as someone on a journey, it *rests* only *in the bosom of fools* (v. 9). We must make the best of the present situation (v. 10): "Don't take it for granted *that the former days were better than these*; don't ask *what is the cause* that they were so, for it is not wise to ask such questions. You are so much a stranger to former times, and such an incompetent judge even of the present, that you cannot expect to receive a satisfactory answer to the question. It is foolish to praise the goodness of former times, since doing so detracts from the mercy of God to us in our own times—as if God had been unjust and unkind to us in giving us our present times, compared with the golden ages, "the good old days" that went before us. Such a thought arises from nothing but anxiety, discontent, and a tendency to pick quarrels with God himself. We are not to think there is any universal decay in nature or general degeneracy in morals. God has always been good, and people have always been bad, and if the times are now worse than they have been in some respects, perhaps they are better in other respects.

Verses 11–22

Here are:

1. Commendations of wisdom. Wisdom is necessary to manage and make the most of our worldly possessions: *Wisdom is good with an inheritance* (v. 11), that is, an inheritance is good for little without wisdom. Wisdom is not only good for the poor but also good for the rich, good *with* riches, to keep a person from getting hurt by them and to enable him to do good with them. *Wisdom is good* (v. 11) in itself, and it makes a person useful, but if he also has wealth, that will enable him to be even more useful and to use his wealth to be of greater service to his genera-

tion (Ac 13:36) than he could have been without it. Wisdom contributes to our security and is a shelter to us from the storms of trouble and its scorching heat; it is, literally, "a shadow," *as the shadow of a great rock in a weary land* (Isa 32:2). *Wisdom is a defence, and money* (that is, "as money") *is a defence* (v. 12). As rich people make their wealth, so wise people make their wisdom, *a strong city* (Pr 10:15; 18:11). Wisdom is joy and true happiness to a person. This is *the excellency* (advantage) *of knowledge* (v. 12), divine knowledge—this is how it surpasses not only money but also human wisdom, *the wisdom of this world* (1Co 3:19): it *gives life to those that have it* (v. 12). *The fear of the Lord, that is wisdom* (Job 28:28), and that is life; it prolongs life. Wisdom will strengthen people and be their support and power (v. 19): *Wisdom strengthens the wise*, strengthens their spirits and makes them bold and resolute by keeping them always on sure ground.

2. Some of the principles of wisdom.

2.1. *Consider the work of God.* To silence our complaints concerning adverse circumstances, let us consider the hand of God in them and not open our mouths against his actions. Consider that every work of God is wise, just, and good, that there is a wonderful harmony in his works, and that all will ultimately be seen to have been for the best. *Who can make that straight which he has made crooked?* Who can change the nature of things from what has been determined by the God of nature?

2.2. We must reconcile ourselves to the various ways of Providence that concern us and do the work and duty of the day on its day (v. 14). Day and night, summer and winter, are set *the one over against the other* (v. 14), so that we may rejoice in prosperity *as though we rejoiced not* and may weep in adversity *as though we wept not* (1Co 7:30), and it is *to the end that man may find nothing after him* (v. 14), that he may live in dependence on Providence and be ready for whatever happens. Our religious faith, in general, must be the same in every condition, but our practice of it will vary with our outward circumstances. *In a day of prosperity* we must *be joyful* (v. 14), be doing good and gaining good things, maintaining a holy cheerfulness, *and serving the Lord with gladness of heart in the abundance of all things* (Dt 28:47). *In a day of adversity consider* (v. 14); we cannot fulfill God's purpose in afflicting us unless we consider why he contends with us.

2.3. We must not be offended by the greatest prosperity of evildoers or by the saddest adversities that may come to the godly in this life (v. 15). Wisdom will teach us how to interpret those dark chapters of Providence so as to reconcile them with the wisdom, holiness, goodness, and faithfulness of God. *All things have I seen in the days of my vanity*; although Solomon was so wise, he still called the days of his life *the days of his vanity* (this meaningless life of his), for compared with the days of eternity, the best days on earth are as meaningless as this. The adversities of the righteous are preparing them for their future blessedness, and the days of evildoers are prolonged to prepare them for destruction. There is a judgment to come, which will put right this apparent irregularity, and we must wait with patience until that time.

2.4. Wisdom will be useful both to warn saints on their path and to restrain sinners on their path. *A just man may perish in his righteousness* (v. 15), but let him not, by his own imprudence and rash zeal, pull trouble down on his own head and then reflect on Providence as having dealt harshly with him. "*Be not righteous overmuch* (do not be overrighteous)" (v. 16). Self-denial and mortification of the flesh are good (Ro 8:13; Col 3:5), but if we harm our health by them and make ourselves unfit to serve God, we are *righteous overmuch.* Do not be too dogmatic and proud of your own abilities. Do not set yourself up as a critic, to find fault with everything that is said and done. As to sinners, it is true *there is a wicked man that prolongs his life in his wickedness* (v. 15), but let no one say that therefore they may safely be as evil as they want to be; no, *be not overmuch wicked* (v. 17); "do not be so foolish as to lay yourself open to the law; *why shouldst thou die before thy time?*" (v. 17).

2.5. Wisdom will guide us to steer a middle course and avoid two extremes, keeping us always on the path of duty, which we will find to be clear and safe (v. 18): "*It is good that thou shouldst take hold of this*, this wisdom, this care, not to fall into traps. *Yea, also from this withdraw not thy hand.* Take a firm hold of the bridle by which your headstrong emotions must be held, as one holds *the horse and mule that have no understanding* (Ps 32:9), and having taken hold of it, keep your grip. Be conscientious but also cautious, and work at getting the right balance."

2.6. Wisdom will teach us how to behave in reference to others. Wisdom teaches us not to expect that the people we deal with will be faultless; we ourselves are not so; no one is so. This *wisdom strengthens the wise* and arms them against provocation (v. 19), and so they are not disturbed by it. Those they have dealings with are not incarnate angels, but sinful sons and daughters of Adam. Even the best people are so, insomuch that *there is not a just man upon earth, that doeth good and sinneth not* (v. 20). Wisdom teaches us not to be too quick either to take offense or to resent offense, but to turn a blind eye to many of the wrongs that are done to us and act as if we have not seen them (v. 21): "*Take no heed to all words that are spoken*; *set not thy heart to them.* Don't be too concerned or inquisitive to know what people are saying about you. Approve yourself to God and your own conscience, and then don't take any notice of what people say about you. If you take notice of every word that is spoken, perhaps *thou wilt hear thy own servant curse thee* (v. 21) when they think you are not listening." It is easier to pass by twenty such offenses than to avenge one. Wisdom reminds us of our own faults (v. 22): "Don't become angry at those who speak badly about you, *for oftentimes*, if you withdraw into yourself, into your own little world, then your own conscience will tell you *that thou thyself hast cursed others*, spoken badly about them, and you will be paid back in your own coin." If we are truly angry with ourselves, as we should be, for criticizing and bad-mouthing others, we will be less angry with others for bad-mouthing and criticizing us

Verses 23–29

Up to this point, Solomon has been proving the futility of the world and its complete insufficiency to make people happy; he now comes to show the evil of sin and its sure tendency to make people miserable. Here, as before, he proves this from his own experience, and it was a costly experience. He is here, more than anywhere in the whole book, putting on the clothing of a penitent.

1. He recognizes and mourns the weaknesses of his wisdom. Having discovered the futility and poverty of the world, he found that there were many other things he could not prove by wisdom.

1.1. His searches were thorough. God had given him the ability to increase in knowledge more than anyone else. He decided that if it was possible to be successful, he would be successful: *I said, I will be wise* (v. 23). He decided to spare no effort (v. 25): "*I applied my heart. I*

set *myself to know, to search, and to seek out wisdom*, to become accomplished in every branch of useful learning—science, philosophy, and theology."

1.2. But his success was not fitting or satisfying: "*I said, I will be wise, but it was far from me* (v. 23); I could not grasp it. After all, the more I know, the more I see that there is to be known, and the more aware I am of my own ignorance. *That which is far off, and exceedingly deep, who can find it out?*" (v. 24). He is referring to God himself, his purposes and his works; when he searched into these, he immediately found himself puzzled and at a loss. Bless God that there is nothing we have to do that is not clear and easy (Pr 8:9); *the word is nigh us* (Dt 30:14; Ro 10:8); but there is a great deal that we would like to know that is *far off.*

2. He recognizes and mourns the examples of his foolishness in which he had excelled; in folly he has excelled, while in wisdom he has come short. Here is:

2.1. His question concerning the evil of sin. He *applied his heart to know the wickedness of folly, even of foolishness and madness* (v. 25). Sin has many disguises, because it is unwilling to show itself in its true colors, and it is very hard to strip it of these and see its real nature. It is necessary for our repentance of sin that we come to know the evil of sin, just as knowing the nature, causes, and seriousness of a disease is necessary in order to heal it. Solomon, who in the days of his foolishness had set himself to dream up schemes of having fun and was clever at finding out how to satisfy the desires of the flesh, is equally diligent, now that God has opened his eyes, to find out about the terrible nature of sin and so to give an edge to his repentance. Clever sinners should be clever penitents. Solomon emphasizes most the *wickedness of folly* (v. 25), by which perhaps he is referring to his own sin, the sin of sexual immorality, for that was commonly called *folly in Israel* (Ge 34:7; Dt 22:21; Jdg 20:6; 2Sa 13:12). When he indulged in it, he made light of it; but now he wants to see its *wickedness.* As there is evil in foolishness, so there is foolishness in evil; it is sheer stupidity and madness.

2.2. The result of this investigation.

2.2.1. He now discovered the evil of that great sin that he himself had been guilty of, the *loving of many strange* (foreign) *women* (1Ki 11:1). He found the remembrance of the sin very painful. *I find it more bitter than death* (v. 26). The heart of the adulterous woman is *snares and nets* (v. 26). Unwary souls are enticed into them by the bait of pleasure. The hands of the adulterous woman are *as bands* (chains), *with which, pretending to engage in* fond embraces, she holds the men fast whom she has seized. *He that pleases God shall escape from her* (v. 26): God may show a man great favor by preserving him either from being tempted to commit this sin or from being overcome by the temptation.

2.2.2. He now discovered more than ever the general corruption of human nature. He tried to find out the number of his actual sins (v. 27). He wanted to find them out as a penitent, so that he might confess them in detail. He soon found himself at a loss and realized his sins could not be counted (v. 28): *Which yet my soul seeks*; I am still counting, but I cannot count them all. I am still making new discoveries of the evil there is in my own heart (Jer 17:9–10). He illustrates this by comparing the corruption of his own heart and life with the corruption of the world, where he can scarcely find one upright man among a thousand. He found (v. 20) that he had sinned even in doing good. The source of all the foolishness and madness in the world is in human beings' turning away from God and their corruption from their original uprightness (v. 20). Human beings, as they were originally made by God, were, as we may put it, small portraits of their Maker, who is *good and upright.* Human beings were marred, and in effect ruined, by their own foolishness and badness: *They have sought out many inventions* (schemes) (v. 29)—*they,* our first parents, or the whole human race, all in general and each one in particular. Instead of being in favor of God's institutions, people wanted to follow their own desires and schemes.

CHAPTER 8

In this chapter, Solomon commends wisdom to us as the most powerful antidote to temptations and troubles. Here are: 1. The benefits and commendation of wisdom (v. 1). 2. Some particular examples of wisdom: 2.1. We must duly submit to the government God has set over us (vv. 2–5). 2.2. We must prepare for sudden evils, especially sudden death (vv. 6–8). 2.3. We must strengthen ourselves against the temptation into which an oppressive government leads us (vv. 9–10). The impunity of oppressors makes them more daring (v. 11), but in the end things will go well for the righteous and badly for evildoers (vv. 12–14). 2.4. We must cheerfully use the gifts of God's providence (v. 15). 2.5. We must accept the will of God with complete contentment (vv. 16–17).

Verses 1–5

Here is:

1. An encomium of *wisdom* (v. 1), that is, true godliness, guided in all its exercises by good sense and discretion. The wise person is a good person; he knows God and glorifies him. *Who is as the wise man?* (v. 1). Heavenly wisdom will make a person incomparable. No one who lacks grace, however highly educated, noble, or rich, can be compared with one who has true grace and is therefore accepted by God. This wisdom also makes him useful among his neighbors: *Who* but the *wise man knows the interpretation of a thing,* the explanation of things (v. 1), that is, who understands the times and events (1Ch 12:32)? *Wisdom makes his faces to shine* (v. 1), as Moses' did when he came down from the mountain; it honors him and puts a glow on his whole life. *The boldness* (hardness, severity, or strength) *of his face shall be changed* by wisdom and made kind and agreeable. Even those whose natural temper is rough and morose are strangely changed by *wisdom.* It emboldens a person against his enemies. *The boldness of his face shall be* (v. 1) doubled by wisdom; it will add to his courage when he not only has an honest cause to plead but also knows by his wisdom how to manage it.

2. A specific example of wisdom: submission to authority. Notice:

2.1. How the duty of subjects is described.

2.1.1. We must observe the laws. In all those things in which the civil power is responsible, whether legislative or judicial, we should submit to its order. *I counsel thee;* "I command you," not only as a ruler but also as a preacher; "I commend it to you as a wise thing to do; I say—whatever may be said by those who want change—*keep the king's commandment*" (v. 2). Literally, "Observe the mouth of a king." Some understand the following clause as restricting this obedience: *Keep the king's commandment* in such a way that you have *a regard to the oath of God* (v. 2), that is, so as to keep a good conscience and not break your obligations to God, which take precedence over, and are higher than, your obligations to the king.

2.1.2. We must not be eager to find fault with the public administration (v. 3): *"Be not hasty to go out of his* (the king's) *sight* when he is displeased with you (10:4) or when you are displeased with him; don't suddenly lose your temper or abandon the kingdom."

2.1.3. We must not persist in a fault when it is shown us: *"Stand not in an evil thing* (v. 3); humble yourself in any offense you have given to your ruler, and do not justify yourself, for that will make the offense even worse."

2.1.4. We must wisely adjust to our opportunities to right wrongs, both those we think have been done to us and those done against the public: *A wise man's heart discerns both time and judgment* (will know the proper time and procedure) (v. 5).

2.2. What arguments are used to encourage them to do their duty. There are three. First, *for conscience sake* (Ro 13:5). "*Keep the king's commandments* (v. 2), for he has sworn to rule you in the fear of God, and you have sworn, in that fear, to be faithful to him." It is called *the oath of God* (v. 2) because he bears witness to it and will avenge disobedience to it. Second, *for wrath's sake,* because of the sword that the ruler bears (Ro 13:4). Third, for the sake of our own comfort: *Whoso keeps the commandment* and lives a quiet and peaceful life (1Ti 2:2) *shall feel no evil thing* (v. 5).

Verses 6–8

Solomon here shows that:

1. Even the wisest people may still be caught by an unforeseen tragedy, and that we would therefore be wise to expect and prepare for sudden changes. A person himself *knows not that which shall be;* and *who can tell him when* or how *it shall be?* (v. 7). The stars cannot predict what will happen, nor can divination. In his wisdom, God has hidden from us the knowledge of future events, so that we may be always ready for changes. *Because to every purpose there is* (v. 6) only one way, one proper procedure, one proper opportunity, *therefore the misery of man is great upon him* (v. 6). People are miserable because they are not sufficiently wise and attentive.

2. Whatever other evils may be avoided, we all have to die (v. 8). When the soul is required (Lk 12:20), it must be given up. *There is no man that has power over* his own *spirit, to retain it,* when it is summoned to return to God who gave it (12:7). Death is an enemy that we must all fight with sooner or later: *There is no discharge in that war* (v. 8). Human evil, by which people often avoid or defy the justice of the ruler, cannot protect them from death, nor can the most stubborn sinners harden their hearts against those terrors.

Verses 9–13

In these verses Solomon encourages us concerning the trouble caused by tyrannical and oppressive rulers.

1. He had observed that many times *one man rules over another to his hurt,* that is:

1.1. To the harm of those who are ruled, as many understand it. It is sad for a people when those who should protect their religious faith and rights aim to destroy both.

1.2. To the harm of the rulers, which is how we understand it: *to their own hurt.* The harm people do to others will ultimately return to harm them.

2. He had observed them successfully abusing their power (v. 10): *I saw* those *wicked* rulers *come and go from the place of the holy,* go and return in pomp from the court of law—which is called "the place of the Holy One" because *the judgment is the Lord's* (Dt 1:17). These tyrants

continued all their days in *office*; they were never brought to account for their maladministration, but died in honor and were buried magnificently. *And they were forgotten in the city where they had so done* (v. 10); their evil practices were not remembered against them when they had died.

3. He had observed that their prosperity hardened them in their evil (v. 11). It is true of all sinners in general, and especially of evil rulers, that *because sentence against their evil works is not executed speedily*, they think it will never be carried out, and therefore they defy the law and *their hearts are full in them to do evil*; they dare to make even more trouble; they are arrogant in their iniquity. Sentence is passed against evil works and evildoers by the righteous Judge of heaven and earth; he judges the evil works of rulers and famous people as well as of lesser people. The execution of this sentence is often delayed, and the sinner continues to be not only unpunished but also prosperous and successful. Sinners are deceiving themselves, for although the *sentence* is *not executed speedily* (v. 11), it will ultimately be carried out more severely.

4. Even if an evil ruler does something unjust *a hundred times*, we should not be discouraged. "*It shall be well with those that fear God*—I say with all those, and only those, *who fear before him*" (v. 12). When God's people are at the mercy of proud oppressors, they fear God more than they fear them. And therefore, "*surely I know*—I know it by the promise of God and the experience of all the saints—*that*, however things go with others, *it shall go well with them*" (v. 12). A good person's days contain substance; they live to good purpose. An evildoer's days are all *as a shadow*, empty and worthless. These days *shall not be prolonged* (Isa 13:22) to what they promised themselves. Although they may be *prolonged* (v. 12) beyond what others expected, the evildoer's day to fall will come. They will fall short of eternal life, and then their long life on earth will be worth little.

Verses 14–17

Wise and good people have always been perplexed by the difficulty of reconciling the prosperity of evildoers and the troubles of the righteous on the one hand with the holiness and goodness of the God who rules the world on the other. Solomon here gives us his thoughts on this:

1. He does not want us to be surprised at it, as though it were something strange, for he himself saw it in his days (v. 14). He saw *just men to whom it happened according to the work of the wicked*, righteous people who suffered very hard things despite their righteousness. He saw *wicked men to whom it happened according to the work of the righteous*, evildoers who prospered as remarkably as if they had been rewarded for some good deed. We, too, see just people troubled and perplexed in their own minds and evildoers living relaxed, fearless, and self-confident lives.

2. He wants us not to accuse God of sin but to accuse the world of meaninglessness. No fault is to be found with God, but as to the world, *This is vanity upon the earth*, and again, *This is also vanity*, that is, it is certain evidence that the things of this world are not the best things and that they were never intended to bring us happiness, for if they were, God would not have allocated so much of this world's wealth to his worst enemies and so much of its troubles to his best friends. There must, therefore, be another life after this one, and the joys and griefs in that life must be real and substantial.

3. He does not want us to be anxious about it, but to cheerfully enjoy what God has given us in the world and make the best of it, even though things may be going much better with others who we think are very unworthy (v. 15): *Then I commended mirth*, or "joy," a holy security and peace of mind arising from a confidence in God, his power, and his promises, *because a man has no better thing under the sun than to eat and drink*, that is, to soberly and thankfully use the things of this life, *and to be merry*, or rather, "cheerful," whatever happens, *for that shall abide with him of his labour.* Our present life is a life *under the sun*, but we look for *the life of the world to come* (Jn 6:51), which will begin and continue when *the sun shall be turned into darkness* (Joel 2:31) and shine no longer.

4. He does not want us to undertake to give reasons for what God does, for *his way is in the sea and his path in the great waters* (Ps 77:19), beyond finding out (vv. 16–17; Job 9:10; Ro 11:33). Both Solomon himself and many others had very closely studied the point; they had searched deeply into the reasons for the prosperity of evildoers and the suffering of the righteous. It was all labor in vain (v. 17). When we look on *all the works of God* and his providence, comparing one part with another, we *cannot find* that there is any certain pattern by which *the work that is done under the sun* is undertaken. God's ways are far beyond ours, nor is he restricted to his own former ways; *his judgments are a great deep* (Ps 36:6).

CHAPTER 9

Solomon further proves the futility of this world, and he gives us four observations. He observed: 1. That usually, as regards outward things, good and bad people fare much the same (vv. 1–3). 2. That death brings all our work and enjoyment in this world to a definite end (vv. 4–6). From this he concludes that we would be wise to enjoy the comforts of life and take care of the work of life while life lasts (vv. 7–10). 3. That great adversities often surprise people (vv. 11–12). 4. That wisdom often makes people very useful, but people of great merit are shown disrespect (vv. 13–18). What is there then in this world that should make us fond of it?

Verses 1–3

It has been observed concerning those who have claimed to search for the philosophers' stone that although they could never find what they were looking for, during the search they have nevertheless hit on many other useful discoveries and experiments. So with Solomon here. When, at the close of the previous chapter, he *applied his heart to know the work of God* (8:16), he despaired of comprehending it; yet he found something else that greatly rewarded him in his search, and *He considered all this in his heart* (v. 1), weighing it up deliberately so that he might *declare* it for the good of others. The great difficulty that Solomon met with in studying Providence was the little difference between good and bad people in the distribution of comforts and adversities. This has bewildered the minds of many wise people. What Solomon says about this may prevent it from becoming a stumbling block to us.

1. Before he describes the power of this temptation, he establishes a great and unquestionable truth. Job, before he speaks about this matter, establishes the doctrine of God's omniscience (Job 24:1), Jeremiah the doctrine of his righteousness (Jer 12:1), another prophet that of his holiness (Hab 1:13), the psalmist that of his goodness and special favor to his own people (Ps 73:1); and this last doctrine is what Solomon here decides to abide by: that although good and evil seem to be randomly dispensed, God still

has a particular care and concern for his own people: *The righteous and the wise, and their works, are in the hand of God* (v. 1); they are all under his special protection and guidance. All their affairs are directed by him for their good, to be rewarded in the other world, though maybe not in this one. Whatever happens, all God's saints are in his hand (Dt 33:3; Ps 31:15; Jn 10:29).

2. He establishes it as a rule that the love and hatred of God are not to be measured and judged by people's outward condition. *No man knows either love or hatred* by those things that they can sense. We may know love and hatred by what is in us; if we love God with all our heart, we may know that he loves us, just as we may know that we are under his wrath if we are controlled by the ungodly mind. Love and hatred will be known by what will happen hereafter in our eternal state.

3. Having established these principles, he acknowledges that *all things come alike to all*, all share a common destiny (v. 2). Some consider this and all that follows to v. 13 to be the perverse reasoning of unbelievers against the doctrine of God's providence, but I prefer to consider it a concession Solomon could make now that he had established those truths that are enough to guard against any wrong use that may be made of what he states. Notice here (v. 2):

3.1. The great difference between the characters of the righteous and evildoers.

3.1.1. The righteous are *clean*, have *clean hands and pure hearts* (Ps 24:4); evildoers are *unclean*, under the control of impure desires. God will certainly make a distinction *between the clean and the unclean* (v. 2) in the next world, though he does not seem to do so in this one.

3.1.2. The righteous *sacrifice* both in inward and outward worship: the wicked *sacrifice not*, that is, they neglect God's worship and begrudge giving up anything for his honor.

3.1.3. The righteous do good in the world.

3.1.4. Evildoers swear; they have no respect for the name of God; but the righteous person *fears an oath* (v. 2), taking it only with great reverence.

3.2. The little difference between the conditions of the righteous and evildoers in this world: *There is one event to* (v. 3) both; the same destiny overtakes all. Is David rich? So is Nabal. Is Ahab killed in a battle? So is Josiah. There is a vast difference between the nature of an event as it relates to one person and the nature of the same event as it relates to another; its effects are vastly different for the two. The same Providence is to the one *a savour of life unto life* and to the other *of death unto death* (2Co 2:16), although outwardly it looks the same.

4. He acknowledges this to be a difficulty to those who are wise and good: "*This is an evil*, something very perplexing, *among all things that are done under the sun*, in this present world" (v. 3). It hardens unbelievers and strengthens the hands of evildoers. When they see that *there is one event to the righteous and the wicked*, that all share a common destiny (v. 2), they corruptly reason from this that it is all the same to God whether they are righteous or evil.

5. To further clear up this great difficulty, he concludes with the doctrine of the misery of evildoers. However they may prosper, *madness is in their heart while they live, and after that they go to the dead* (v. 3).

Verses 4–10

Solomon had been anxious when he had *praised the dead more than the living* (4:2), but here he seems to be in a different mood when he considers the advantages of life from the point of view of preparing for a better life.

1. He shows the advantages that the living have over the dead (vv. 4–6). If a person's condition is bad for any reason, *there is hope* it will get better. If *the heart be full of evil, and madness be in it* (v. 3), there is still life while *there is hope* (v. 4) that by the grace of God a blessed change may be brought about. *The living know they shall die*; it is something still to come, and so provision should be made for it. But *the dead know not any thing* (v. 5). *They have no more a reward* (v. 5) for their toil in the world, but all they must be left to others. They have a reward for their holy actions, but not for their worldly ones. The things of this world will not be a reward for the soul. The world can only be an annuity for life, not *a portion* (reward) *for ever* (v. 6). There is an end to our affections, friendships, and enmities: *Their love, and their hatred, and their envy have now perished* (v. 6).

2. He reasons from this that we would be wise to make the best use of life while it lasts.

2.1. Let us enjoy the comforts of life while we live. Having himself become caught up in the abuse of self-indulgent pleasures, Solomon warns others of the danger, not by totally prohibiting those pleasures but by advocating the moderate use of them. "Let your spirit be at peace and pleasant; then let there be *joy* and *a merry heart* within." We must enjoy ourselves, enjoy our friends, and enjoy our God; we are to be careful to keep a clear conscience in this. We must serve God with gladness (Dt 28:47; Ps 100:2) by using what he gives us and be generous in sharing it with others, not allowing ourselves to be oppressed by excessive anxiety about the world. "Make use of the comforts and enjoyments God has given you. Show your cheerfulness (v. 8). *Let thy garments be always white*. Be neat, wear clean linen, and don't be slovenly. Get along well with your relatives: *Live joyfully with the wife whom thou lovest* (v. 9). Do not keep enjoyment to yourself, not caring about what happens to those around you, but let them share with you, and make their lives comfortable too. Keep to your wife, to one woman, and do not have more than one. *Live joyfully with her* (v. 9), and be happiest when you are with her. Take delight in your family, your vine and your olive plants" (Ps 128:3). Those people whose works God has accepted have reason to be cheerful and should be so. God loves to have his servants sing at their work. "Live joyfully. Let a gracious peace of mind be a powerful antidote to the meaninglessness of the world. *That is thy portion in the* things of *this life*, this is your lot in life (v. 9). In God, and another life, you will have a better lot."

2.2. Let us give ourselves to the work of life while life lasts, using its enjoyments in such a way as to equip ourselves for work: "*Eat with joy* and *a merry heart* (v. 7) so that your soul may take more effort and so that the joy of the Lord may be its strength (Ne 8:10) and oil to its wheels" (v. 10). This is the world of service; the world to come is the world of reward. This is the world of preparation for eternity. Harvest days are busy times; and we must "make hay while the sun shines." Serving God and working out our salvation must be done with *all that is within us* (Ps 103:1), and all that is little enough.

Verses 11–12

The preacher has encouraged us (v. 10) to do what we have to do *with all our might*, but here he reminds us that when we have done everything (Lk 17:10; Eph 6:13), we must leave the outcome with God.

1. We are often disappointed that we have not received the good we had great hopes of (v. 11). Events, both in public and in private matters, do not always correspond with the most rational prospects and probabilities. One would have thought that the most nimble creature would, when running, win the prize, but *the race is not* always *to the swift* (v. 11); some accident happens to slow them down, or they are too self-confident and allow those who are slower to overtake them. One would have thought that in fighting, the most numerous and powerful army would always be the conqueror, and that in a fight, the powerful champion would win, but *the battle is not* always *to the strong* (v. 11). An army of Philistines was once defeated by Jonathan and his servant; the goodness of the cause has often triumphed over the most formidable power. One would have thought that wise people would always be wealthy and have great land, but it does not always turn out so. Even *bread is not* always *to the wise*, much less *riches* always *to men of understanding* (v. 11). One would have thought that those who understand people, those who have brilliant management skills, would always be promoted, but many clever people have spent their days in obscurity. All these disappointments to us seem accidental, and we call them *chance*, but really God's activities are according to his purposes, here called *time*, in the language of this book (3:1; Ps 31:15). *Time and chance happen to them all* (v. 11).

2. We are often surprised by evils (v. 12): *Man knows not his time*, the time when tragedy will come. It is *not for us to know the times* (Ac 1:7), when or how we will die. God in wisdom has kept us in the dark so that we may be always prepared. We may meet with trouble in the very thing from which we promise ourselves satisfaction, just as fish and birds are drawn into a trap and net by the bait. People often find their bane to be in what they sought their bliss in. Let us always be ready for changes, so that although they may come suddenly, they may not make us terrified.

Verses 13–18

Solomon still commends wisdom to us as necessary to preserve our peace. This wisdom that makes people serve their country out of pure goodwill, when they themselves gain no benefit from it, is the wisdom that Solomon says *seemed great unto him* (v. 13).

1. Solomon gives an example here, probably a real case, *of a poor man* who used his wisdom to fulfill some great service in a time of public distress and danger (v. 14): *There was a little city* with only a few people in it, who were ready to give up their city as if it were already lost. *A great king* came against this little city with a strong army and besieged it. Did victory and success attend the *strong?* No; among the few people who lived in this little city there was one *poor wise man* (v. 15), one who was not promoted to any high-earning or powerful job. We should notice two things about this man. First, being wise, he served the city even though he was poor. In their distress they went to him (Jdg 11:7) and begged his advice and assistance, and *he by his wisdom delivered the city* (v. 15), either by the wise instructions he gave to the besieged, directing them to some unthought-of strategy for their own protection, or by making a wise treaty with the besiegers, as the woman at Abel did (2Sa 20:16). Second, being poor, he was disrespected by the city. *No man remembered that same poor man* (v. 15); no reward was given to him, no honors put on him; he lived in as much poverty and obscurity as before.

2. From this example he draws some useful conclusions.

2.1. He observes that *Wisdom is better than strength* (v. 16) and *better than weapons of war*, whether offensive or defensive (v. 18). He observes that *The words of wise men are heard in quiet*; what they speak, being rational and to the point, spoken calmly and with deliberation, will gain respect. They will have more sway with people than the domineering shouts of the one who *rules among fools*, who chose him to be their ruler because of all his noisy blustering. A few concise arguments are worth a great many big words. He observes that wise and good people, nevertheless, must often be content with the satisfaction of having done good when they cannot receive the praise they should. Wisdom enables a man to serve his neighbors, but if he is poor, his wisdom is despised and his *words are not heard* (v. 16). Many people have been buried alive in poverty and obscurity who, if they had only received the right encouragement, might have been a great blessing to the world; many a pearl is lost in its shell. But a day is coming when wisdom and goodness will be honored and the *righteous shall shine forth* (Mt 13:43).

2.2. From what he has observed of the great good that one wise and good man may do, he infers what a great deal of trouble one evildoer may do. A sinful condition is wasteful to the sinner. How many good gifts both of nature and of Providence does one sinner destroy. One sinner who makes it his business to defile others may defeat and frustrate the intentions of a great many good laws.

CHAPTER 10

This chapter seems to be, like Solomon's proverbs, a collection of wise sayings; the preacher set in order many proverbs (12:9) to be included in his preaching. The general scope is to commend wisdom to us. 1. He commends wisdom to private citizens, who are in humble positions in life. We would be wise: 1.1. To preserve our reputation by managing our affairs skillfully (vv. 1–3). 1.2. To submit to our superiors if we have offended them at any time (v. 4). 1.3. To live quiet and peaceful lives (2Ti 2:2), having nothing to do those who are factious and rebellious (vv. 8–11). 1.4. To control our tongues (vv. 12–15). 1.5. To be conscientious in our work and provide for our families (vv. 18–19). 1.6. Not to speak evil of our rulers (v. 20). 2. He commends wisdom to rulers; let them not think that because their subjects must be submissive under them, they may do what they please. Let them be careful whom they promote to positions of trust and authority (vv. 5–7); let them be generous and not childish, moderate and not self-indulgent (vv. 16–17).

Verses 1–3

In these verses Solomon shows:

1. That *a little folly* (v. 1) is a great blemish to *him that is in reputation for wisdom and honour* (v. 1), and is as harmful to his good name as *dead flies* are to a sweet perfume. True wisdom will give a person a good reputation, which is like a box of precious ointment (7:1). The reputation that is gained by a great deal of wisdom may be easily lost by a *little folly* (v. 1), because envy focuses on eminence and makes the worst of the mistakes of those who are praised for wisdom.

2. That *a wise man's heart is at his right hand*, so that he goes about his business with skill. But a *fool's heart is at his left hand*; it always has to be looked for when he

has anything to do that is important, and so he goes about his work awkwardly.

3. How fools often tend to declare their own foolishness and expose themselves. One who is either silly or evil *says to every one he meets that he is a fool* (v. 3), that is, he reveals his foolishness as plainly as if he had said he was foolish.

Verses 4–11

The purpose of these verses is to keep subjects loyal and dutiful to the government.

1. Let not subjects pursue a quarrel with their ruler with any private, personal disgust (v. 4): "*If the spirit of the ruler rise up against thee*, if he is displeased with you, *leave not thy place*, don't forget your duty as a subject, don't rebel from your allegiance, don't suddenly lose your temper and leave your post in his service."

2. Let not subjects start a quarrel with their ruler. Solomon grants that *there is an evil often seen under the sun* (v. 5), an evil that only the king can cure, for *it is an error which proceeds from the ruler* (v. 5). It is a mistake that rulers are too often guilty of, one that they make when they consider their personal feelings more than public interests: they do not promote people according to their merit, but *set folly in great dignity* (v. 6). It is wrong for evildoers to be advanced and worthy people to be kept tucked away out of sight. This is illustrated in v. 7: "*I have seen servants upon horses*, people not so much of humble background, but with corrupt, servile, and mercenary attitudes."

2.1. Let neither ruler nor people violently attempt changes. Let not rulers encroach on the rights and liberties of their subjects; let subjects not rebel against their rulers, for:

2.1.1. *He that digs a pit* for another is highly likely to *fall into it* (v. 8). If rulers become tyrants or subjects become rebels, we know from history what is likely to be their fate.

2.1.2. *Whoso breaks a hedge*, an old hedge, which has been a landmark for a long time, let him expect that *a serpent*, or snake, the kind that lives in old hedges, will *bite him* (v. 8).

2.1.3. *Whoso removes stones*, to pull down a wall or building, is merely piling them onto himself; he will be *hurt therewith* (v. 9). Those who go around trying to disturb a well-modeled, well-settled government will quickly realize that it is easier to find fault than to put things back together.

2.1.4. *He that cleaves* (splits) *the wood* (v. 9), especially if, as in the following verse, he has unsharpened tools (v. 10), *shall be endangered thereby* (v. 9); the chips, or his own axhead, will fly in his face. If we meet with knotty pieces of timber, people of perverse and uncontrolled spirits, and we think we can overpower them by force and violence, the attempt may turn out unpleasantly and we may be damaged in return.

2.2. It would be better if both ruler and people acted toward each other wisely, humbly, and in a good frame of mind: *Wisdom is profitable to direct* (v. 10) the ruler how to skillfully administer a people who are inclined to be restless, so that he will neither embolden and encourage them to rebellion by neglecting them nor provoke them to rebellion by undue rigor and severity. Wisdom is also profitable for directing subjects how to act toward a ruler who is inclined to be hard on them, so that they will not alienate his affections but win him over by humble appeals and peaceful methods. Let wisdom guide us to use gentle methods and hold back from using forceful ones. Wisdom

will teach us to sharpen the tools we use rather than, by leaving them blunt, make it necessary to exert much *more strength* (v. 10). We must sharpen before we cut, that is, consider and think over what is right to say and do in every difficult situation. Time spent sharpening our tools is never wasted. Wisdom will teach us to charm a snake we are to fight with, rather than think it can be gotten rid of by hissing louder than it does (v. 11): *The serpent will bite* if it is not charmed by singing and music, and *a babbler is no better.* The expression rendered *babbler* means literally, "He that is lord of the tongue"; such a lord, a ruler who may say whatever he wants, is as dangerous to deal with as an uncharmed snake. To those who may say anything it is wise to say nothing provocative.

Verses 12–15

Solomon shows us here how troublesome foolishness is.

1. Fools talk a great deal of nonsense, and they show their foolishness by the arrogance of their words. In contrast, *the words of a wise man's mouth are gracious*; they do good to everyone around him. But *the lips of a fool* not only expose him to disgrace but *will also swallow up himself* (v. 12) and destroy him. A fool's talk arises from his own weakness and evil: *The beginning of the words of his mouth is foolishness* (v. 13); the foolishness bound up in his heart (Pr 22:15) is the corrupt spring from which all these polluted streams flow. *The end of his talk is madness* (v. 13). *A fool also is full of words*, especially a passionate fool, who never knows when to stop. He must have the last word, even though it is the same as the first. Many people who are devoid of sense are *full of words*; as the proverb puts it, "Empty vessels make the most sound." The fool is *full of words*, for even if he has only the most trite or ordinary thing to say, one *cannot tell what shall be*, what he will say next, because he so loves to hear himself talk that he will keep on repeating it, and *what shall be after him who can tell him?* (v. 14).

2. Fools toil a great deal without achieving anything (v. 15). *The labour of the foolish*, to achieve their plans, *wearies every one of them*. All their labor is for the world, the body, and food that perishes (Jn 6:27). The foolish never bring anything substantial to pass, *because they know not how to go to the city* (v. 15), that is, because they do not have the capacity to understand the clearest thing, such as the route to town, which one would think it impossible to miss.

Verses 16–20

Solomon here notices:

1. That the happiness of a country depends on the character of its rulers. The people cannot be happy when their rulers are childish and self-indulgent (v. 16): "*Woe unto thee, O land!* when *thy king is a child*, not so much in age as in understanding." When the ruler is as weak and foolish as a child, fickle, anxious, and unpredictable, things are going badly for the people. Nor is it much better for a people when their rulers *eat in the morning* (v. 16), that is, make a god of their stomach (Php 3:19) and make themselves slaves to their appetites. If the rulers and privy councilors are wise, the country may do better, but if they are devoted to pleasure before undertaking public business, making themselves unfit for it by eating and drinking *in a morning* (v. 16), if judges want only to enjoy life, if they do not eat to live, but live to eat—what good can a nation expect? The people must be happy when their rulers are generous and active, sober and temperate, and people who work well (v. 17). Wisdom, goodness, the

fear of God, generosity, and a readiness to do good to all people all make the royal blood noble. When lesser judges are more concerned to discharge their trusts than to satisfy their own appetites, when they *eat in due season*, at the proper time (v. 17), that is, when they have done their business, the country is blessed. Magistrates should *eat for strength* (v. 17), so that their bodies may be made fit to serve their souls in serving God and their country. It goes well with a people when their rulers are examples of moderation, when those who have most to spend on themselves also know how to deny themselves.

2. What bad consequences laziness brings to both private and public affairs (v. 18): *By much slothfulness and idleness of the hands*, neglect of business and the love of ease and pleasure, *the building decays* (the rafters sag), *drops through* at first, and gradually the house begins to spring leaks. If the king is *a child* and will take no care, if the *princes eat in the morning* (v. 16) and make no effort in their work, the affairs of the nation will suffer loss. All its foundations will be out of joint through the laziness and self-seeking of those who should be the *repairers of its breaches and the restorers of paths to dwell in* (Isa 58:12).

3. How industrious people generally are, both rulers and people, in order to gain money, because that serves every purpose (v. 19). Solomon seems to prefer money to happiness. On the one hand, *A feast is made for laughter*, not the laughter of the fool, which is madness, but that of wise people, by which they make themselves fit for business and serious study. *But money*, on the other hand, is the measure of all things. With money, but not with the *wine* that *makes merry*, we can supply all our needs and even make a feast. Money by itself is not the answer; it will neither feed nor clothe people. And it brings no spiritual benefits; it will not obtain pardon for sin, the favor of God, or peace of conscience. But used in trade and commerce, it fulfills all the needs of this present life.

4. How careful subjects need to be that they do not harbor any disloyal purposes in their thoughts or get involved in any group to plot the overthrow of the government. "*Curse not the king, no, not in thy thought*, do not wish harm to the government in your thoughts. *Curse not the rich*, the rulers and governors, *in thy* bedchamber (v. 20), in a little group of people dissatisfied with the government; do not associate with such people; *come not into their secret* (council) (Ge 49:6); do not join them in plotting against it. Although the plan may be carried out with the greatest secrecy, *a bird of the air shall carry the voice* (v. 20) to the king, who has more spies than you are aware of, *and that which has wings shall tell the matter* (v. 20), to your confusion and ruin."

CHAPTER 11

Here is: 1. An urgent exhortation to do works of kindness to the poor (vv. 1–6). 2. A serious warning to prepare for death and judgment (vv. 7–10).

Verses 1–6

Solomon here urges rich people to be very generous to the poor.

1. The duty itself is commended to us (v. 1). *Cast thy bread upon the waters*, "thy bread-corn upon the low places," as some understand it, alluding to farmers, who *go forth, bearing precious seed* (Ps 126:6), holding back grain from their family for the seed, knowing that without that they can have no harvest the following year. In the

same way, generous people sow some of their grain to produce the next year's crop: they take away from themselves some of their provisions to supply the poor, so that they may be found to have *sowed beside all waters* (Isa 32:20), because as they sow, so will they reap (Gal 6:7). Give your bread freely to the poor, even though it may seem thrown away and lost when you do this, like what is *cast upon the waters* (v. 1). Send it on a voyage; risk it, as merchants do in trading across the ocean. Trust it *upon the waters*; it will not sink. "*Give a portion to seven and also to eight* (v. 2), that is, be generous in your giving." Give not a pittance but *a portion*, a meal. Give to many, *to seven, and also to eight* (v. 2); if you meet with seven people who need your kindness, give to them all, and then, if you come across an eighth, give to that person, too, and if you meet eight more, then give to them all too. God is rich in mercy to all (Eph 2:4; Ro 10:12), to us, even though we are unworthy; he *gives liberally, and upbraids not*, does not rebuke our requests because he has already given us so many gifts (Jas 1:5).

2. Reasons are urged on us. "Although you *cast it upon the waters* (v. 1) and it seems lost, yet *thou shalt find it after many days* (v. 1), as farmers find their seed again in a plentiful harvest. The return may be slow, but it is nevertheless sure and will be so much the more plentiful because you have waited longer for it." Wheat, the most valuable grain, lies longest in the ground. Our opportunity for doing good is uncertain: "*Thou knowest not what evil may be upon the earth* (v. 2) that may deprive you of your wealth and make you unable to do good." Many people use this as an argument against giving to the poor: they do not know what hard times may come on them when they themselves may be in need; but we should see a reason to be charitable in the assurance that when *evil days* (days of trouble) *come* (12:1), we will have the comfort of having done good while we could.

3. The excuses of the uncharitable.

3.1. Some people will say that what they have is their own and will ask, "Why should we *cast* it thus *upon the waters*?" (v. 1). "Look up," says Solomon, "and consider how soon you would be starved in a barren ground *if the clouds* over your head were to plead this, that they have their waters for themselves. Are the heavens so generous to the poor earth that is beneath them, and will you begrudge giving some of your wealth to your poor brother, who is *bone of thy bone*?" (Ge 2:23; 2Sa 5:1; etc.).

3.2. Some will say that their sphere of usefulness is humble and narrow; they cannot do the good they see others doing, who are in more prominent positions, and so they will sit still and do nothing. "No," he says, "*in the place where the tree falls*, or happens to be, *there it shall be* (v. 3), for the benefit of those to whom it belongs." Everyone must work to be a blessing to the place, wherever it is, where God in his providence has put them; wherever we are we may find good work to do if only we have the heart to do it.

3.3. Some will object that they have met with many discouragements in their giving. They have been criticized for it as being proud and pharisaical; they will be despised if they do not give as others do; they have taxes to pay, and they do not know what use will be made of their charity. He answers these, and a hundred such objections, in a few words (v. 4): *He that observes the wind shall not sow*, which stands for doing good; *and he that regards the clouds shall not reap*, which stands for obtaining good. If we stand around magnifying every little difficulty, raising objections and imagining hardships where there are none, we will never do anything with our work. If farmers were to refuse to sow, or stop sowing, for the sake of every fleeting cloud and give up reaping for the sake of every gust of wind, they would not have much to show for it at the end of the year.

3.4. Some people will say, "We do not see how what we give in charity would ever be made up to us." To this he responds, *"Thou knowest not the work of God* (v. 5), nor is it right you should. You may be sure he will fulfill his promise even though he does not tell you how." Solomon shows our ignorance of the work of God in two instances:

3.4.1. We *know not what is the way of the Spirit* (v. 5), "of the wind," according to some; we *know not whence it comes, or whither it goes* (Jn 3:8), or when it will change direction, but the sailors are ready, waiting for it to turn in their favor. This is how we must do our duty, in expectation of the time appointed for the blessing. Or it may be understood as referring to the human soul; we know that God made us and gave us these souls, but we do not know how they entered into these bodies or how they give our bodies life and operate on them; the soul is a mystery to itself, and it is no wonder that *the work of God is* (v. 5) so to us.

3.4.2. We do not know *how the bones are fashioned in the womb of her that is with child* (v. 5). We cannot describe either how the body is formed or how the soul is inspired; we know both are *the work of God* (v. 5), and we accept his work. Let the One who has done the greater thing for us be happily depended on to do the lesser.

3.5. Some people say, "We have been charitable but have yet to see any return for it. Many days have gone by, and we have not *found it again*." To this Solomon answers (v. 6), "Still go on, continue to do good. *In the morning sow thy seed, and in the evening do not withhold thy hand. In the morning* of youth do good; give out of the little you have; *in the evening of* old age do not give in to the common temptation of old people to be tightfisted. Even then, *withhold not thy hand,* but do good to the last, *for thou knowest not* which work of charity *shall prosper,* both as to others and as to yourself, *this or that,* but have reason to hope that *both shall be alike good."*

Verses 7–10

Having spoken many excellent commands teaching us how to live well, the preacher comes now to teach us how to die well.

1. He turns to the elderly. *Truly the light is sweet;* the light *of the sun is* so; it is *a pleasant thing for the eyes to behold* it. It is pleasant to see the light; the pagans were so charmed by its pleasure that they worshiped the sun. It is pleasant to use it to see other things. It cannot be denied that life is sweet. It is sweet to everyone. Nature says it is sweet; nor can death be desired for its own sake, but only if it comes as an end to present evils or is a passage to future good. *If a man lives many years, yet let him remember that the days of darkness* (v. 8) are coming. Here is:

1.1. An enjoyable summer's day suggested—it is supposed that life may continue long, perhaps many years, that by the goodness of God those years may be comfortable, and that people may *rejoice in them all* (v. 8). However, some people rejoice in their many years more than others. If a prosperous state and a cheerful spirit come together, they may indeed do much toward enabling a person to *rejoice in them all,* but even the most cheerful spirit is sometimes dampened. Happy sinners have their sad qualms, and cheerful saints have their gracious sorrows; and so it is simply a supposition, not a real case, that a man should *live many years and rejoice in them all.* But:

1.2. A winter's night suggested as to be expected after this summer's day: *Yet let* this hearty old person *remember*

the days of darkness, for they shall be many (v. 8). They are many, but they are not infinite. As the longest day will have its night, so also the longest night will have its morning. *The days of darkness* will come with much less terror if we have thought of them beforehand.

2. He turns to the young people to wake them up to think about death (vv. 9–10). We have here:

2.1. An ironic concession to the worthless pleasures of youth: *Rejoice, O young man! in thy youth* (v. 9). Solomon is speaking ironically to a young man to expose his foolishness and the absurdity of a self-indulgent, evil way of life.

2.2. A powerful restraint given to these worthless pleasures: *Know thou that for all these things God shall bring thee into judgment* (v. 9).

2.3. A word of warning and exhortation concluded from all this (v. 10). Let young people look to themselves and handle well both their souls and their bodies. Let them take care that their minds are not lifted up with pride or disturbed with anger or any sinful passion: *Remove sorrow,* or anger, *from thy heart;* the word refers to any disorder or disturbance of the mind, for example, anxiety. Young people tend to be impatient about any restraint or control, about anything that humbles them: their proud hearts rise against everything that contradicts them. Let them keep far away from everything that on reflection will cause sorrow or anxiety. Let them take care that their bodies are not defiled by overindulgence, immorality, or any sinful desires: *Put away evil from the flesh* (v. 10), and so do not use parts of your body as instruments of unrighteousness (Ro 6:13).

3. The preacher urges the great theme of his sermon, the futility of all present things and their uncertainty and insufficiency.

3.1. He reminds old people of this (v. 8): *All that comes is vanity* (meaningless), even though *a man live many years and rejoice in them all.*

3.2. He reminds young people of this: *Childhood and youth are vanity* (meaningless) (v. 10). The pleasures and advantages of childhood and youth are fleeting and pass away quickly; these flowers wither, and these blossoms fall (Isa 40:7–8; 1Pe 1:24); let them therefore grow into good fruit, which will continue and produce good results.

CHAPTER 12

The wise and penitent preacher here brings his sermon to a conclusion. He closes it with what is likely to make the best impressions and have a powerful and lasting effect on his listeners. Here is: 1. An exhortation to young people to begin early in life to have religious faith and not put it off to old age (vv. 1–7). 2. A repetition of the great truth he has undertaken to prove in this sermon, the futility of the world (v. 8). 3. A confirmation and commendation of what he has written in this and his other books, as worthy to be duly weighed and considered (vv. 9–12). 4. The whole matter summed up and concluded with a command to everyone to be truly religious (vv. 13–14).

Verses 1–7

Here is:

1. A call to young people to think about God and take care of their duty to him when they are young: *Remember now thy Creator in the days of thy youth* (v. 1). "You who are young flatter yourselves with expectations of great things from the world, but it yields no solid satisfaction to a soul. So *remember your Creator* (v. 1). If you do this,

you will guard against the troubles that arise from the futility of the creation." It is the royal physician's antidote to the particular diseases of youth, the self-indulgence that childhood and youth are subject to. To prevent and cure this, *remember thy Creator* (v. 1). God is our Creator; he *made us and not we ourselves* (Ps 100:3), and he is therefore our rightful Lord. We must give him the honor and duty that we owe him as our Creator. *Remember thy Creators* (v. 1); the word is plural, as it is in Job 35:10. For God said, *Let us make man* (Ge 1:26)—*us*: Father, Son, and Holy Spirit. "Begin at the beginning of your days to remember the One from whom you had your being. Call him to mind through all the days of your youth; never forget him. In this way guard against the temptations of youth, and make the most of its advantages."

2. A reason to support this command: *while the evil days come not, and the years of which thou shalt say, I have no pleasure in them* (v. 1).

2.1. Do it quickly: before sickness and death come, and before old age comes, *years of which we shall say, We have no pleasure in them* (v. 1), when our *strength* will be *labour and sorrow* (Ps 90:10), when there will be *no pleasure* (v. 1) except in reflecting on a good life on earth and expecting a better life in heaven.

2.2. He enlarges on these two arguments in the following verses, but reverses the order, speaking first of old age and then of death. He shows:

2.2.1. It is the greatest absurdity and ingratitude to give the cream of our days to the Devil and reserve the husks, refuse, and dregs for God. If the difficulties of age are such as are described here, we will need something to support and comfort us then, and nothing will be more effective than having the testimony of our consciences that we began early to remember our Creator. How can we expect God to help us when we are old if we will not serve him when we are young?

2.2.1.1. The weaknesses of old age are here elegantly described in figurative expressions. In old age:

2.2.1.1.*1*. The sun and the light of it, the moon and the stars and the light that they take from the sun, will be darkened* (v. 2). They look dim to old people because of their failing eyesight; their intellectual powers and faculties, which are as lights in the soul, are weakened. Their understanding and memory fail them.

2.2.1.1.*2*. The clouds return after the rain* (v. 2); sometimes, no sooner has one cloud blown over than another succeeds it; so it is with old people: when they have gotten free from one pain or ailment, another one immediately comes on them.

2.2.1.1.*3*. The keepers of the house tremble* (v. 3). The head, which is like the watchtower, shakes, and the arms and hands, which are used to protect the body, also shake and become weak.

2.2.1.1.*4*. The strong men shall bow themselves* (v. 3); the legs cannot be used for walking as they once were, but are soon tired out.

2.2.1.1.*5*. The *grinders cease because they are few* (v. 3); the teeth stop playing their part *because they are few.*

2.2.1.1.*6*. Those that look out of the windows are darkened* (v. 3). Moses was a rare instance of a person who, when 120 years old, had good eyesight.

2.2.1.1.*7*. The doors are shut in the streets* (v. 4). Old people stay indoors and do not want to go out for amusement.

2.2.1.1.*8*. Old people *rise up at the voice of the bird* (v. 4). They do not sleep soundly as young people do; a little thing—even the chirping of a bird—disturbs them.

2.2.1.1.*9*. With them, *all the daughters of music* are *brought low* (v. 4). Old people become deaf and unable to distinguish sounds and voices.

2.2.1.1.*10*. They are *afraid of that which is high* (v. 5), afraid to go to the top of any high place, either because they are out of breath and cannot reach it or because they become dizzy. They dare not go there.

2.2.1.1.*11*. The almond tree flourishes* (v. 5). The old man's hair has grown white, so that his head looks like an almond tree in blossom.

2.2.1.1.*12*. The grasshopper is a burden, and desire fails* (v. 5). Old people can bear nothing; the lightest thing sits heavily on them, both on their bodies and on their minds. A little thing sinks and breaks them.

2.2.1.2. Solomon probably wrote this when he himself was old and could speak feelingly about the infirmities of old age, which perhaps grew faster on him because of his indulgence in physical pleasures. All this makes a good reason why we should *remember our Creator in the days of our youth* (v. 1), so that he may remember us when *evil days come* (v. 1) and so that his comforts may delight our souls when our enjoyment of ordinary things has to a large extent petered out.

2.2.2. How great a change death will make to us.

2.2.2.1. Death will fix us in an unchangeable state: *Man* will then *go to his long* (eternal) *home* (v. 5). He has gone to his rest, to the place where he is to remain. He has gone "*to his house of eternity.*" It should make us willing to die to know that at death we will *go home*, and why should we not long to go to our Father's house (Jn 14:2)?

2.2.2.2. Death will bring sorrow to our friends, who love us. When *man goes to his long* (eternal) *home, the mourners go about the streets* (v. 5), both the real mourners and the mourners who have been paid to weep for the dead; there are mourners who express their own grief and those who mourn to arouse mourning in others.

2.2.2.3. Death will dissolve this frame of nature, take down this earthly tent we live in, which is elegantly described in v. 6. Then will *the silver cord*, by which soul and body were wonderfully fastened together, *be loosed*, that sacred knot will be untied, and *the golden bowl*, which held the waters of life for us, will *be broken. The pitcher* with which we used to fetch water to constantly support life and to repair its deterioration will *be broken*, even *at the fountain*, so that it can carry no more; and *the wheel*—all those organs that serve to collect and distribute nourishment—will be *broken* and made unable to carry out its functions anymore. The body will become like a watch with a broken spring: because the movement of all its wheels has stopped, they all stand still.

2.2.2.4. Death will bring us back to our first principles (v. 7). Human beings are strange creatures, a ray of heaven united to a clod of earth. At death these are separated, and each goes to the place from which it came. The body, that clod of clay, *returns to* its own *earth*. The soul, that beam of light, *returns to* that *God* who, when he *made man of the dust of the ground, breathed into him the breath of life*, to make him *a living soul* (Ge 2:7). The soul does not die with the body; it is *redeemed from the power of the grave* (Ps 49:15); it can survive without it and will live in a state of separation from it, as a candle burns, and burns more brightly, when it is taken out of a dark lantern.

Verses 8–12

Solomon is here drawing toward a close. He repeats his text (v. 8). He commends to our serious consideration what he has written on this subject by divine direction and inspiration.

1. They are the words of one who was a convert, a penitent who could speak from his own real and costly experience of the futility of the world and the foolishness of expecting great things from it. He was *qoheleth* (v. 8), "one gathered" in from his wanderings (see commentary at 1:1). *Vanity of vanities* (meaningless, meaningless), *saith the* penitent (v. 8).

2. They are the words of one who was wise, endowed with an extraordinary degree of wisdom, famous for it among his neighbors, who all sought him *to hear his wisdom* (1Ki 10:24), and therefore competent to judge this matter.

3. He was one who made it his business to do good and to use wisdom rightly.

4. He took a great deal of pains and care to do good, planning to *teach the people knowledge* (v. 9). He chose the most profitable way of preaching, using proverbs or short sentences.

5. He expressed what he had to say in terms that he thought would be most pleasing: *He sought to find out acceptable words, just the right words*, the *mots justes*, delightful words (v. 10), so that his good content was not spoiled by bad style.

6. *That which was written was upright* and sincere, *words of truth* (v. 10). Most want nice, pleasant words that flatter and make them feel good, rather than the best words, to show them the right way (Isa 30:10), but to those who understand themselves and their own interests, *words of truth* will always be *acceptable words*.

7. What he and other holy people wrote (2Pe 1:21) will be very useful to us, especially by its explanation (v. 11). The words are *as nails* to those who waver and are inconsistent, to establish them in doing what is good. They are *as goads* (v. 11) to those who are lethargic and draw back and as *nails* to those who are unsteady and draw aside, so that any good in us may be *as a nail fastened in a sure place* (Isa 22:25) (Ezr 9:8). Sacred meetings for religious worship are an ancient divine institution, intended for the honor of God and the edification of his church. There must be leaders in these assemblies, and those leaders are Christ's ministers. Their business is to fasten the *words of the wise* (v. 11), to really nail them down, and for this reason the word of God is also described as *a hammer* (Jer 23:29).

8. What is written, and thereby commended to us, is of divine origin. Although it comes to us through various

hands—many *wise* people and many leaders of assemblies—it is still *given by one* and the same *shepherd* (v. 11), the *shepherd of Israel, that leads Joseph like a flock* (Ps 80:1).

9. If only we will make use of them, the sacred inspired writings are sufficient to guide us along the path to true happiness. "*And further*, nothing now remains but to tell you that *of making many books there is no end*." Even if people write very many books on the way to live, if they write until they have tired themselves out with much study, they cannot give better instructions than the ones we already have in the word of God.

Verses 13–14

The great quest that Solomon has pursued in this book has been, *What is that good which the sons of men should do* (2:3)? What is the right way to be truly happy, the sure way to fulfill our great end? He has found it by the help of the revelation that God made to the human race in ancient times (Job 28:28), that sincere godliness is the only way to true happiness: *Let us hear the conclusion of the whole matter* (v. 13):

1. The summary of religious faith. Setting aside all matters where there are differences of opinion, to be religious is to *fear God and keep his commandments* (v. 13).

1.1. The basis of religious faith is the fear of God reigning in the heart, a reverence of his majesty, a respect for and submission to his authority, and a dread of his wrath.

1.2. The rule of religious faith is the law of God revealed in the Scriptures. Our fear toward God must be taught by his commandments (Isa 29:13), and we must keep those and carefully observe them.

2. The immense importance of it: *This is the whole of man*, the whole duty of every human being (v. 13; *duty* is not in the original but is supplied); it is all our business and all our blessedness; our whole duty is summed up in this, and our whole comfort is bound up in this.

3. A powerful incentive to this (v. 14). We will see how immensely important it is to us that we have religious faith if we consider the account each one of us must soon give of himself or herself to God: *God shall bring every work into judgment* (v. 14). The great thing to be then judged concerning *every work* is whether it is good or evil, and so we should be greatly concerned now to be very careful about how we walk with God, so that we may *give up our account with joy* (Heb 13:17).

A PRACTICAL AND DEVOTIONAL EXPOSITION
OF THE
Song of Solomon

In our belief in both the divine origin and the spiritual explanation of this book we are confirmed by the consistent testimony of both the church of the Jews and the Christian church.

1. This Song of Solomon's is very different from the songs of his father David; here is no mention of the name of God; it is never quoted in the New Testament; we do not find in it either any expressions of natural religion or godly devotion, on the one hand, or any of the marks of direct revelation, on the other. It seems as hard as any part of Scripture to be made a fragrance of life to life (2Co 2:16). In fact, to those who come to read it with ungodly minds and corrupt desires, it is in danger of being made a smell of death. The Jewish teachers therefore advised their young people not to read it until they were thirty years old, so that they would not abuse what is purest and most sacred and thereby kindle the flames of lust with the fires of heaven. But:

2. On the other hand, with the help of the many faithful guides available to understand this book, it appears to be a bright and powerful ray of heavenly light, wonderfully suited to arouse godly devotion in holy souls and improve their friendship and fellowship with God. It is an allegory, the letter of which kills those who look no further, but the spirit of which gives life (2Co 3:6; Jn 6:63). It is a parable, which makes divine things more difficult to those who do not love them but clearer and more pleasant to those who do (Mt 13:14, 16). Experienced Christians find here something equivalent to their experiences, and it is intelligible to them. It is a nuptial song expressing the love between a bridegroom and his bride, and in it the mutual affection that passes between God and a remnant of the human race is set out and illustrated. It is a pastoral song; the bride and bridegroom are brought in as a male and female shepherd.

2.1. This song could easily be taken in a spiritual sense by the Jewish church, for whose use it was first composed. God betrothed the people of Israel to himself; he entered into covenant with them, and it was a marriage covenant. He had given abundant proofs of his love to them and required of them that they love him with all their heart and soul. Idolatry was often spoken of as spiritual adultery, and this song was written to prevent it.

2.2. It may be more easily taken in a spiritual sense by the Christian church, because the condescension and communications of divine love appear richer and freer under the Gospel than they did under the Law, and the fellowship between heaven and earth more intimate. God sometimes spoke of himself as the husband of the Jewish church (Isa 62:5; Hos 2:16, 19) and rejoiced in it as his bride (Isa 62:4–5). But more frequently Christ is represented as the bridegroom of his church (Mt 25:1; Ro 7:4; 2Co 11:2; Eph 5:32), and the church as the bride, as the Lamb's wife (Rev 19:7; 21:2, 9). The best key to this book is Ps 45, which we find applied to Christ in the New Testament (Heb 1:8–9). It requires some effort to discover the probable meaning of the Holy Spirit in the various parts of this book. As many of David's songs are at the level of the capacity of the lowliest people, and there are shallows in them in which a lamb may wade, so this song of Solomon's will exercise the capacities of the most learned, and it has depths in which an elephant may swim.

CHAPTER 1

In this chapter, after the title of the book (v. 1), we have Christ and his church, Christ and a believer, expressing their respect for each other. 1. The bride, the church, speaks to the bridegroom (vv. 2–4), to the daughters of Jerusalem (vv. 5–6), and then again to the bridegroom (v. 7). 2. Christ, the bridegroom, speaks in answer to the complaints and requests of his bride (vv. 8–11) 3. The church expresses the great value she has for Christ and the delights she takes in fellowship with him (vv. 12–14). *4. Christ commends the church's beauty (v. 15). 5. The church returns the commendation (vv. 16–17).*

Verse 1

This book is *a song* to stir our devotion. It is evangelical, and Gospel times should be times of joy, for Gospel

939

grace puts *a new song* into our mouths (Ps 98:1). The author is Solomon. It is not the song of fools (Ecc 7:5), as many of the songs of love are, but the song of the wisest person. No one can give better proof of their wisdom than to celebrate the love of God to the human race. Solomon's songs numbered 1,005 (1Ki 4:32); those that were on other subjects are lost, but this one about angelic love remains. Like his father, Solomon was devoted to poetry, and in whatever realm a person's talents lie, they should try to honor God and build up the church with it. It is not certain when Solomon wrote this sacred song. Some think that he wrote it after he was restored by the grace of God from his backsliding. It is more probable that he wrote it at the beginning of his reign, when he kept close fellowship with God. It is suitably placed here after Ecclesiastes, for in reading that book we have been thoroughly convinced of the futility of the creation and its insufficiency to satisfy us and make us happy. We will then be encouraged to seek happiness in the love of Christ and that transcendent pleasure which is to be found only in fellowship with God through him.

Verses 2–6

In this dramatic poem, the bride is here introduced addressing herself first to the bridegroom and then to the daughters of Jerusalem.

1. To the bridegroom, not giving him any name or title, but beginning abruptly: *Let him kiss me* (v. 2). The bride desires two things:

1.1. The bridegroom's friendship (v. 2): "*Let him kiss me with the kisses of his mouth*, that is, may he be reconciled to me, and may I know that he is so; may I have the signs of his favor." Here we see how the Old Testament church wanted Christ's revelation of himself in the flesh. "May he no longer send for me, but may he himself come. May he no longer speak by angels and prophets, but may I receive the word from his own mouth (Heb 1:1–2:5), those *gracious words* (Lk 4:22) that will be to me as the *kisses of his mouth* (v. 2), sure signs of reconciliation, as Esau's kissing of Jacob was." All our Gospel grace is summed up in his kissing us, as the father of the prodigal son kissed him when he returned in repentance (Lk 15:20). It is a kiss of peace. The bride gives several reasons for this desire.

1.1.1. Because of the great respect she has for his love: *Thy love is better* (more delightful) *than wine* (v. 2). Gracious souls take more pleasure in loving Christ and being loved by him, in the fruits and gifts of his love, than anyone has ever taken in the finest physical delights.

1.1.2. Because of the fragrance of his love and its fruits (v. 3): "*Because of the savour of thy good ointment, because of the fragrance of your perfumes*—because your grace and encouragement are pleasant to all those who rightly understand both them and themselves—because of this *savour, thy name is as ointment* (perfume) *poured forth*. Your very name is precious to all your people; it is a fine perfume that gladdens the heart" (Pr 27:9).

1.1.3. Because of the great devotion that all holy souls have for him: *Therefore do the virgins love thee* (v. 3). It is Christ's *love shed abroad in our hearts* (Ro 5:5) that draws them out in love to him. All who are pure from the defilement of sin are the virgins who love Jesus Christ and *follow him whithersoever he goes* (Rev 14:4). Christ is the favorite of all the *pure in heart* (Mt 5:8).

1.2. The bridegroom's fellowship (v. 4). Notice:

1.2.1. Her request for divine grace: *Draw me* (v. 4). "Draw me to yourself, draw me closer, draw me home to you." Christ has told us that no one may come to him unless the Father draws them (Jn 6:44).

1.2.2. Her promise to make the most of that grace: *Draw me*, and then *we will run after thee* (v. 4). The flowing forth of the soul after Christ and its ready submission to him are the effects of his grace; we could not run after him unless he drew us (2Co 3:5; Php 4:13). When Christ pours out his Spirit on the church in general, which is his bride, all its members receive enlivening and quickening influences.

1.2.3. The immediate answer that was given to this prayer: *The King has* drawn me; he has *brought me into his chambers*. It is not so much an answer drawn by faith from the word of Christ's grace as an answer drawn by experience from the activity of his grace. Those who are drawn to Christ are brought not only into his courts, into his palaces (Ps 45:15), but also into his inner room where he receives his personal friends.

1.2.4. The wonderful delight that the bride takes in being *brought into the chamber* (v. 4): "We have what we want. Our desires are crowned with indescribable delights; all our sorrows have vanished, and *we will be glad and rejoice* (v. 4). All our joy will center on God: *We will rejoice* not in the perfume or the palace but *in thee*. It is only God who is our *exceeding joy* (Ps 43:4). We have no joy except joy in Christ."

1.2.5. The fellowship that a gracious soul has with all God's people in this fellowship with Christ. In the chambers to which we are brought we meet not only him but also one another. Whatever differences of thought or devotion there may be among Christians in other matters, they are all agreed on this: Jesus Christ is precious to them.

2. *To the daughters of Jerusalem* (vv. 5–6). The believer speaks to those who are in the church but not of it, or to weak Christians, babes in Christ, who are willing to be taught the things of God. She observed these bystanders looking disdainfully at her because of her blackness, the blackness of both her sins and her sufferings, on account of which they think she has little reason to expect the kisses she wishes for (v. 2) or to expect they will join with her in her joys (v. 4). She acknowledges she is *black*. Guilt blackens; the heresies, scandals, and offenses that take place in the church make her *black*, and the best saints have their failings. Sorrow blackens; that seems to be referred to especially. The church is often mean, poor, and contemptible, her beauty sullied by weeping.

2.1. She asserts that she is attractive nevertheless (v. 5): *I am black, but comely* (lovely). She is black *as the tents of Kedar*, in which the shepherds lived, which were very rough and never whitened, weather-beaten and discolored by long use; but she is attractive *as the curtains of Solomon*. The church is sometimes *black* with persecution but attractive in patience, faithfulness, and encouragement. True believers are *black* in themselves but lovely in Christ, with the attractiveness he puts on them, *black* outwardly, for the *world knows them not*, but *all glorious within* (Ps 45:13).

2.2. She gives an account of how she came to be so black. The blackness was not natural but contracted, and was because of the harsh treatment she had received: *Look not upon me* so scornfully *because I am black* (v. 6). *I am black* because of my sufferings: *The sun has looked upon me* (v. 6). She was fair and lovely; whiteness was her proper color. But she obtained this blackness by the *burden and heat of the day* (Mt 20:12), which she was forced to bear. But what was the matter? She fell under the displeasure of those of her own house: *My mother's children were angry with me* (v. 6). She was *in perils by false brethren* (2Co 11:26). The Samaritans, who claimed to be related to the Jews, were troubled at anything that led to the prosperity of Jerusalem (Ne 2:10). They dealt very harshly with her: *They made me the keeper of the vineyards* (v. 6), that is:

2.2.1. "They persuaded me to sin and drew me into false worship, into serving their gods, which was like dressing the vineyards *of Sodom*" (Dt 32:32). These are the grievances that good people complain most about in times of persecution, that their consciences are worried.

2.2.2. "They brought me into trouble, imposed on me what was laborious and disgraceful." Keeping the vineyards was the work of the lowliest people. Her mother's children made her the drudge of the family. And yet "my sufferings are such as I have deserved, for I have not kept my own vineyard."

Verses 7–11

Here is:

1. The humble request that the bride presents to her beloved, that the church and every believer presents to Christ, for a freer and more intimate fellowship with him. She turns from the *daughters of Jerusalem* (v. 5) and looks to heaven for help and relief (v. 7). Notice:

1.1. The title she gives to Christ: *O thou whom my soul loveth.*

1.2. The opinion she has of him as the good shepherd of the sheep; she does not doubt that he *feeds his flock* and *makes them rest at noon* (v. 7). Jesus Christ graciously provides both food and rest for his sheep. Is it now a midday of outer troubles and inner conflicts with God's people? Christ has rest for them.

1.3. Her request to him that she might be admitted into his company: *Tell me where thou feedest* (v. 7). "Tell me where to find you, where I may talk with you, *where thou feedest* and tendest thy flock, so that I may enjoy some of your company there."

1.4. The plea she uses to support this request: "*For why should I be as one that turns aside by* (or "after") *the flocks of thy companions* (v. 7)—those who pretend to be your companions but are really your competitors and rivals?" Turning away from Christ to follow other lovers is what gracious souls dread. Good Christians will be afraid of giving any reason to those around them to question their faith in Christ and their love for him.

2. The gracious response that the bridegroom gives to this request (v. 8). See how ready God is to answer prayer. Notice how affectionately he speaks to her: *O thou fairest among women!* In the eyes of the Lord Jesus, believing souls are more beautiful than any other. Notice how mildly he restrains her for her ignorance: *If thou know not* (v. 8). "What! Do you not know where to find me and my flock?" Compare this with Christ's answer to a similar comment of Philip's (Jn 14:9): *Have I been so long time with you, and yet hast thou not known me, Philip?* Notice, too, with what tenderness he tells her where she can find him. "Follow the track, ask for the good old way (Jer 6:16), observe *the footsteps of the flock,* and *go forth by* them" (v. 8). Sit under the direction of good ministers: "*Feed* thyself *and thy kids beside the tents of the shepherds* (v. 8). Bring those you are responsible for with you; they will all be welcome. *The shepherds* will be helpers; therefore remain by their tents." Those who want to have deeper friendship and fellowship with Christ must abide by holy worship and must join his people. Those who have responsibility for families must bring them with them to

religious meetings; let their *kids,* their children, their servants, have the benefit of *the shepherds' tents* (v. 8).

3. The glowing praise that the bridegroom gives to his bride.

3.1. He calls her his *love* (v. 9); it is a term of endearment that is often used in this book: "My friend, my companion, my intimate one."

3.2. He compares her to a set of strong and stately *horses in Pharaoh's chariots.* Egypt was famous for the best horses. The church had complained about her own weakness and the danger of being attacked by her enemies: "Do not be afraid," Christ says, "*I have made thee like a company of horses* (v. 9); I have put strength into you, so that you will laugh at fear (Job 39:22). *I have compared thee to my company of horses* that triumphed over *Pharaoh's chariots* (v. 9), the holy angels, *horses of fire*" (Hab 3:15).

3.3. He wonders at her beauty and the jewelry she wears (v. 10): *Thy cheeks are comely* (beautiful) *with rows of jewels* (earrings), the adornments of your head, curls of hair or knots of ribbons; *thy neck also with chains* (strings of jewels), such as are worn by women of the highest rank, *chains of gold.* The decrees of Christ are the ornaments of the church. The graces, gifts, and assurance of the Spirit adorn every believing soul and make it beautiful.

4. His gracious purpose to add to her ornaments, for where God has given true grace, he will give even more grace. She will be made even more beautiful (v. 11): *We will make thee borders of gold,* inlaid or enameled *with studs of silver.* The same God who is the author will also be the perfecter of the good work; it cannot fail (Heb 12:2; Php 1:6).

Verses 12–17

Endearments are exchanged between Christ and his bride.

1. Believers take great delight in fellowship with Christ. Notice:

1.1. The humble reverence believers have for Christ as their Sovereign (v. 12). He has fellowship with them and joy in them; he *sits at his table* (v. 12) to make them welcome. In any religious duty, especially in the ordinance of the Lord's Supper, where the King is pleased to *sit* with us *at his* own *table,* when good Christians have their graces exercised, when they have their hearts broken in repentance, healed by faith, and inflamed with holy love, then the *spikenard sends forth the smell thereof,* then the perfume spread its fragrance (v. 12).

1.2. The strong devotion they have for Christ as their *beloved,* their *well-beloved* (v. 13). Christ is not only *beloved* by all believing souls, but is their *well beloved,* their best beloved, their only beloved. Christ is considered *a bundle* (sachet) *of myrrh* (v. 13) and *a cluster of camphire* (henna blossoms) (v. 14), everything that is pleasant and delightful. The teaching of his Gospel and the assurance of his Spirit are very refreshing to them. They rest in his love. The word translated *camphire* is *koper,* the same word that also means "atonement" or "propitiation." Christ is *a cluster of* merit and righteousness to all believers; *he is the propitiation for their sins* (1Jn 4:10). He shall lie *all night between my breasts* (v. 13), near my heart. Christ has his beloved disciples reclining next to him; why then should not they lay their beloved Savior close to them?

2. Jesus Christ has a great love for his church and every true believer; they are pleasant to his eyes (v. 15): *Behold, thou art fair, my love;* and again, *Behold, thou art fair.* He says this to show that there is a real beauty in holiness, that

all who are sanctified are made beautiful by that; they are truly beautiful. One example of the beauty of the bride is mentioned here, that she *has doves' eyes* (4:1). In Christ's sight, those who are beautiful do not have the piercing eye of the eagle, but the pure eye of the *dove*, not an eye like that of the hawk, which, when it soars upwards, still has its eye on the prey below, but a humble, modest eye, the kind of eye that is a sign of a godly, simple sincerity and a dove-like innocence enlightened and guided by the Holy Spirit.

3. The church expresses how greatly she values Christ and responds with respect (v. 16): *Behold, thou art fair.* "Lord," says the church, "do you call me *fair*? I am fair in no other way than that I have your image stamped on me. You are *pleasant* to all who are yours." Having expressed her respect for her husband's person, she, as a loving bride, praises the accommodations into which he has welcomed her: his *bed*, his *house*, his *rafters* (beams or galleries) (v. 16), which may appropriately be applied to those services of worship in which believers have fellowship with Jesus Christ and receive the signs of his love and respond in godly devotion to him. She calls these *ours*; Christ and believers having a joint interest in them. They are his institutions and their privileges; Christ and believers meet in them. All is *ours* if we are Christ's. Do the color of the bed and the furnishings belonging to it help set it off? *Our bed is green* (v. 16), a color that in pastoral poetry is preferred to any other because it is the color of the fields and groves. *The beams of our house are cedar* (v. 17), which probably refers to the temple Solomon had just built for fellowship between God and Israel, which was of *cedar*, a strong wood, sweet, durable, a wood that would never rot and was therefore a type of the firmness and continuation of the church. The galleries for walking are made of *fir* or *cypress*, wood that was pleasing both to the sight and to the smell, suggesting the delight that God's people take in walking with Christ. Everything in the covenant of grace is firm, fine, and fragrant.

CHAPTER 2

In this chapter: 1. Christ speaks about both himself and his church (vv. 1–2). 2. The church speaks: 2.1. Remembering the delight and joy she has had in fellowship with Christ (vv. 5–4). 2.2. Enjoying the present signs of his favor (vv. 5–7). 2.3. Triumphing in his approaches toward her (vv. 8–9). 2.4. Repeating the gracious calls he has given her to accompany him walking—invited by the pleasures of the returning spring (10–13)—out from her obscurity (v. 14), and the command he has given to the servants to destroy what would be harmful to his vineyard (v. 15). 2.5. Rejoicing in her interests in him (v. 16). 2.6. Longing for his arrival (v. 17). Those whose hearts are filled with love for Christ and the hope of heaven know best what these things mean.

Verses 1–2

Notice here:

1. He who is the Son of the Highest calls and acknowledges himself *the rose of Sharon, and the lily of the valleys* (v. 1), to express his presence with his people in this world, his accessibility to them, and the beauty and sweetness that they find in him. *The rose* is the chief flower as regards beauty and fragrance, and our Savior prefers the clothing of *the lily* to that of *Solomon in all his glory* (Lk 12:27). Christ is *the rose of Sharon* (v. 1), where the best roses grew, "the rose of the field," as some call it, showing that the Gospel salvation is open to all. Christ is not a rose

locked up in a garden. He is *a lily* for whiteness, *a lily of the valleys* (v. 1) for sweetness. He is a *lily of the valleys* (v. 1), or "low places," in his humiliation. Humble souls see most beauty in him. To those who are in the *valleys* he is *a lily.*

2. His church is *as a lily*; he himself is *the lily* (v. 1). The beauty of believers consists in their likeness to Jesus Christ. They are like lilies, for those in whose hearts his *love is shed abroad* are made like Christ (Ro 5:5). The church of Christ far surpasses all other communities as much as a bed of roses surpasses a thorn bush. She is *as a lily* surrounded by *thorns.* Evildoers, *the daughters* of this world, who have no love for Christ, are as *thorns*, worthless, useless, and harmful. God's people are *as lilies among* them, scratched and torn by them, shaded and obscured by them; they are precious to Christ but are exposed to hardships and troubles.

Verses 3–7

Here:

1. The bride commends her beloved and prefers him to all others: *As the apple tree among the trees of the wood* (v. 3), useful, yielding pleasant and profitable fruit, while the other trees are not very useful, not even the cedars until they are cut down, *so is my beloved among the sons* (v. 3).

2. She remembers the deep joy and encouragement she gained in fellowship with him: she *sat down* by him *with great delight* (v. 3), as shepherds sometimes rest. She found two benefits in sitting down so near the Lord Jesus:

2.1. Refreshing shade: *I sat down under his shadow* (v. 3). Christ is to believers *as the shadow* of a great tree. Those who *are weary and heavily laden* may find *rest* in Christ (Mt 11:28). We must *sit down under this shadow with delight* (v. 3). We must put our entire confidence in the protection he offers.

2.2. Pleasing, nourishing food. This tree drops its fruits to those people who *sit down under its shadow* (v. 3). They will find them *sweet unto their taste* (v. 3). Promises are sweet to a believer. Pardon is sweet, and peace of conscience is sweet; the assurance of God's love, joy in the Holy Spirit, the hope of eternal life, and the present pledges and foretastes of it are all sweet to those who have their spiritual senses awakened and exercised.

3. She acknowledges herself to be obliged to Jesus Christ for all the benefit and encouragement she had in fellowship with him (v. 4): "*I sat down under* the apple tree (v. 3), but he admitted me into more intimate fellowship with him. He brought me to the house* of wine" (v. 4). One of the rabbis understands *the banqueting house* (v. 4) to refer to the Tent of Meeting. Surely we may apply it to Christian meetings, where the Gospel is preached and Gospel ordinances are administered, particularly the Lord's Supper, that *banquet of wine.* We would never have come *into the banqueting house*, never have come to know spiritual pleasures, if Christ had not first brought us. *His banner over me was love* (v. 4); he brought me in with a banner displayed over my head. The Gospel is compared to *an ensign* or banner (Isa 11:12), and what is presented in this banner is *love.* This is the reception in *the banqueting house!*

4. She professes her strong devotion and most passionate love for Jesus Christ (v. 5): *I am sick of love*, faint, overcome, overpowered, by it. She cries out: "Oh *stay me with flagons* (raisins, ointments, or flowers), anything that is reviving; *comfort me with apples* (v. 5), with the fruits

of the *apple tree* of Christ (v. 3), with the merit and mediation of Christ and the sense of his love for my soul."

5. She experiences the power and tenderness of divine grace, relieving her in her present fainting (v. 6). Although he seemed to have withdrawn, he was still even then an ever-present help (Ps 46:1). *"His left hand is under my head* (v. 6) to support it, in fact, as a pillow to sustain it. For, in the meantime, *his right hand embraces me* (v. 6) and so gives me an unquestionable assurance of his love." Believers owe all their strength and comfort to the supporting left hand and embracing right hand of the Lord Jesus.

6. Finding her beloved so near to her, she is very concerned that her fellowship with him not be interrupted (v. 7): *I charge you, O you daughters of Jerusalem.* She charges them *by the roes* (gazelles) *and the hinds of the field* (v. 7), that is, by everything that is pleasant in their eyes and precious to them, like *the loving hind and the pleasant roe* (deer) (Pr 5:19). Those who experience the sweetness of fellowship with Christ must desire that these blessed prospects and this deep sense of assurance continue.

Verses 8–13

The church here pleases herself with the thoughts of further delight in Christ.

1. She rejoices in his approach (v. 8). She hears him speak: "It is *the voice of my beloved* calling to me to tell me he is coming." She sees him come. This may very well be applied to the prospect that the Old Testament saints had of Christ's coming in the flesh. *Abraham saw his day* at a distance *and was glad* (Jn 8:56). Those who waited for the consolation of Israel (Lk 2:25) with an eye of faith saw him come and triumphed in the sight. He comes joyfully, leaping and skipping *like a roe* and like *a young hart* (v. 9), as one who is pleased and who has his delights with the people. He comes overcoming all the difficulties that lie in his way; he comes "leaping over the mountains, skipping over the hills," making nothing of discouragements. The curse of the Law, the death of the cross, must all be undergone; the powers of darkness must be grappled with. But in the strong presence of his love, these great mountains become plains. Whatever opposition is given at any time to the rescue of God's church, Christ will break through it. He comes quickly, *like a roe* (gazelle) or *a young hart* (young stag) (v. 9); they thought they had waited long, but in reality he came quickly.

2. She pleases herself with the glimpses she has of him: "He *stands behind our wall* (v. 9); I know he is there, for sometimes *he looks forth at the window* (v. 9) and shows *himself through the lattice*" (v. 9). Such was the state of the Old Testament church while it waited for the coming of the Messiah. They had him near them; they had him with them, even though they could not see him clearly. They saw him looking through the windows of the ceremonial institutions and smiling through those lattices; in their sacrifices and purifications Christ revealed himself to them. He gave them intimations and pledges of his grace. Christ is near us in the sacraments, but it is *behind the wall* of external signs, through *those lattices* he reveals himself to us, but we will soon *see him as he is* (1Jn 3:2).

3. She repeats the gracious invitation he had given her to come walking with him (vv. 10–13).

3.1. He called her his love and his beautiful one. Christ will acknowledge as his those who take him as their beloved; never was any love lost that was shown to Christ.

3.2. He called her to *rise and come away* (v. 10 and again v. 13).

3.3. He gave as a reason the return of spring and the pleasantness of the weather.

3.3.1. The season is elegantly described. The dark, cold, and barren *winter is past* (v. 11); winter does not last forever. And the spring would not be so pleasant as it is if it did not come after winter, which is a contrast to its beauty (Ecc 7:14). *The rain is over and gone* (v. 11); the cold, stormy winter rain is now over, and *the dew is as the dew of herbs* (the morning) (Isa 26:19). *The flowers appear on the earth* (v. 12). All winter flowers are dead and buried in their roots, and there is no sign of them, but in the spring they revive and show themselves in a wonderful variety of flourishing green. *The time of the singing of birds has come* (v. 12). The little birds, which all winter lie hidden and withdrawn and scarcely live, forget all the adversities of winter when spring returns. They sing out praises of their Creator to the best of their ability. No doubt the One who understands the birds that cry out in need (Ps 147:9) takes notice of those that *sing for joy* (Ps 104:12). *The voice of the turtle* (cooing of doves) *is heard in our land* (v. 12); the dove is one of the seasonal birds mentioned in Jer 8:7, which observe their particular time to come and sing and so shame us who do not understand the times (1Ch 12:32; Mt 16:3) or sing at the time for singing. *The fig tree puts forth her green figs* (v. 13), by which *we know that summer is nigh* (Mt 24:32).

3.3.2. This description of the returning spring as a reason for coming away with Christ is applicable:

3.3.2.1. To the introducing of the Gospel in place of the Old Testament dispensation, during which it had been winter for the church. Christ's Gospel warms what was cold and makes fruitful what was earlier dead and barren. When it comes to an area, it gives beauty and glory to that place (2Co 3:7–8). Springtime is a pleasant time, and so is Gospel time.

3.3.2.2. To the rescuing of the church from the power of persecuting enemies after a winter of suffering and restraint. When the storms of trouble are over and gone, when the *voice of the turtle* (cooing of doves) (v. 12), the joyful sound of the Gospel of Christ, is heard again, and when public worship is enjoyed with freedom, then *arise and come away* (v. 13); sing in the ways of the Lord. When the churches had rest, they were strengthened (Ac 9:31).

3.3.2.3. To the conversion of sinners from a state of nature to a state of grace, which is like the return of spring, a universal change, a new creation (Gal 6:15); it is being born again (Jn 3:3). The soul that was hard, cold, frozen, and unprofitable, like the earth in winter, becomes fruitful, like the earth in spring, and gradually, like it, brings its fruits to maturity. This blessed change comes about only because of the approaches and influences of the sun of righteousness (Mal 4:2).

3.3.2.4. To the encouragement of God's people after a state of despondency. A child of God under doubts and fears is like the earth in winter. But encouragement will return; the birds will sing again, and the flowers will appear again. "Arise, therefore, poor drooping soul, and *come away.*"

3.3.2.5. To the resurrection of the body at the last day. The bones that have lain in the grave, as the roots of plants in the ground during the winter, will at the resurrection *flourish as a herb* (Isa 26:19; 66:14). That will be an eternal farewell to winter and a joyful entrance to an eternal spring.

Verses 14–17

Here is:

1. The invitation that Christ gives to the church and to every believing soul to come into fellowship with him (v. 14).

1.1. David had called the church God's *turtledove* (Ps 74:19), and she is called that here: a dove in her beauty, innocence, and inoffensiveness. A gracious spirit is a dove-like spirit, loving, quiet, and pure, and faithful to Christ, as the dove is to her mate. The Spirit descended *like a dove* (Mt 3:16) on Christ, and so he does on all Christians, making them of a *meek and quiet spirit* (1Pe 3:4).

1.2. This dove is *in the clefts of the rock and in the secret places of the stairs*, in the hiding places on the mountainside (v. 14). Christ is the rock to whom she flies for shelter and in whom she finds safety, like a dove in the hole of a rock when attacked by the birds of prey (Jer 48:28). She withdraws into the hiding places on the mountainside, where she may be alone and may better be able to commune with her own heart (Ps 4:4). Christ often withdrew to a mountain *himself alone*, to pray (Mt 14:23).

1.3. Christ calls her out of her withdrawal: come, *let me see thy countenance, let me hear thy voice* (v. 14).

1.4. For her encouragement, he tells her: "*Sweet is thy voice* (v. 14); your praying voice is music to God's ears."

2. The command that Christ gives to his servants to suppress what is a terror to his church (v. 15): *Take* (catch for) *us the foxes, the little foxes* that creep in unawares, for even though they are little, they *spoil the vines*, especially now when our vines have *tender grapes* that must be preserved because otherwise the crop will fail. Believers are like vines; their fruits are as *tender grapes* at first, which need time to reach maturity. This command to *take* (catch) *the foxes* is:

2.1. A command to believers to put to death their own sinful desires and passions, which are as *foxes, little foxes*, that destroy their graces, crush good beginnings, and prevent their reaching maturity. Seize the *little foxes*, the first risings of sin, those sins that seem little, for they often turn out to be very dangerous.

2.2. A command to everyone to oppose and prevent the spreading of such opinions and practices as may lead to the corrupting of judgments, defiling of consciences, confusing of minds, and discouragement of goodness. Persecutors are foxes (Lk 13:32); false prophets are foxes (Eze 13:4). Those who sow weeds of heresy or schism and hinder the progress of the Gospel are the *foxes, the little foxes*, which must be tamed, or else restrained from causing trouble.

3. The profession that the church makes of her relationship with Christ, and the satisfaction she takes in her interest in him and fellowship with him (v. 16). He had called her to *rise* and *come away* with him. Now this is her response to that call.

3.1. She comforts herself with the thoughts of her relationship with her beloved: "*My beloved is mine*"; this shows ownership. Believers share in Christ; they are taken not only into covenant but also into fellowship with him. All he has promised in the Gospel, all he has prepared in heaven, all is yours (1Co 3:21–22). All true believers have given themselves to Christ (2Co 8:5). If we are his, he is wholly and his only, his forever, we may take encouragement from his being ours.

3.2. She comforts herself with the thoughts of the assurance of his grace to his people: *He feeds among the lilies* (v. 16). He *feeds* among believers, that is, he takes pleasure in them and their meetings.

4. The church's hope and expectation of Christ's coming.

4.1. She does not doubt that the *day will break* and the *shadows will flee away* (v. 17). The Gospel day will dawn, and the shadows of the ceremonial law will fly away. This was the comfort of the Old Testament church. Or it may refer to the second coming of Christ and the eternal happiness of God's people.

4.2. She begs the presence of her beloved, in the meantime, to support and comfort her: "*Turn, my beloved* (v. 17), come to me, *be with me always to the end of the age* (Mt 28:20). Come even over *the mountains* that get in the way, with some gracious signs of your light and love."

CHAPTER 3

In this chapter: 1. The church gives an account of a severe trial with which she was troubled because her beloved seemed to have left her (vv. 1–5). 2. The daughters of Jerusalem marvel at the honors of the church (v. 6). 3. The church wonders at Jesus Christ in the person of Solomon, his bed (carriage) and the bodyguards around it (vv. 7–8), and his chariot (vv. 9–11).

Verses 1–5

It was hard for the Old Testament church to find Christ in the ceremonial law. The consolation of Israel was sought for a long time before it came (Lk 2:25). At length Simeon had in his arms the one *whom his soul loved*. This passage can be applied to individual believers; they often walk in darkness, but those who seek Christ to the end will ultimately find him. Notice:

1. How the bride sought him in vain *upon her bed* (v. 1). She lacked the fellowship she used to have with him, as David did when he *thirsted for God, for the living God* (Ps 42:2). She sought him, but she did not see the signs of his presence that she was used to, but she still sought them nevertheless. She failed in her attempt.

2. How she sought him in vain out in the city (v. 2). She had gone through the duties of private devotion, even in the *night watches* (Ps 63:3), but still she had no assurance of his presence. Yet she is not driven away by disappointment. She resolves, "*I will rise now* (v. 2), I will not lie here if I cannot find my beloved here. *I will rise now* without delay and seek him immediately, for otherwise he may withdraw further from me." Those who seek Christ must not be shaken by difficulties. "*I will rise, and go about the city* (v. 2), the Holy City, in the streets and the broad ways"—for she knew he would not be found in any blind alleyway. We must seek in the city, in Jerusalem, that is, in the Gospel church, of which Jerusalem was a type; we must seek him there in holy worship. She had a good purpose in mind when she said, *I will arise now* (v. 2), but actually carrying out that good work was most important. And so she arose and *sought him*. And yet she *found him not* (v. 2). This complaint is repeated with emphasis: *I sought him, but I found him not!* (v. 2).

3. How she asked the watchmen about him (v. 3). At night the watchmen *go about the city* to preserve its peace and safety. The watchmen met her as she was walking about, and she asked them if they could give her any news about her beloved. Gracious souls press through crowds of other delights in their pursuit of Christ. *Saw you him whom my soul loveth?* We must search the Scriptures, be devoted in prayer, keep close to his ordinances, and do all with this on our heart: *Saw you him whom my soul loveth?* (v. 3). Only those who have themselves seen Christ are likely to direct others to a sight of him.

4. How she eventually found him (v. 4). She *passed from* the watchmen as soon as she realized they could give her no news of her beloved. But soon after she left the watchmen, she found the one she was looking for. Those who continue to seek Christ will eventually find him, perhaps when they were almost ready to despair of ever finding him. See Ps 42:7–8; 77:9–10; Isa 54:7–8.

5. How close she kept to him when she had found him. She is now as much afraid of losing him as she earlier was concerned to find him. Those who hold on to Christ firmly in the arms of faith and love will *not let him go* (v. 4); he will remain with them.

6. How much she wanted others to come to know him: "*I brought him to my mother's house* (v. 4) so that all my relatives, all who are dear to me, might enjoy the benefits of fellowship with him." Wherever we find Christ, we must take him home with us to our houses, especially to our hearts. The church is our mother (Gal 4:26), and we should be concerned for her interests, so that she may have Christ present with her.

7. How concerned she was that he not be disturbed (v. 5); she repeats the command she gave before (2:7) to the *daughters of Jerusalem* not to *stir up or awake her love.* Let all *clamour and bitterness be put* far *from you,* for that *grieves the Holy Spirit of God* (Eph 4:30–31). Some consider this to be Christ's command not to disturb his church or trouble the minds of the disciples.

Verse 6

These are the words of the *daughters of Jerusalem,* to whom the command was given (v. 5). Earlier they looked warily at the bride because she was black (1:6), but now they admire her and speak of her with great respect: *Who is this?* How beautiful she looks! Who would have expected such a person to *come out of the wilderness* (v. 3)?

1. This can be applied to the situation of the Jewish church when, after forty years' wandering in the desert, they left it to take possession of the Promised Land. Balaam said, when he stood in wonder at them: *From the top of the rocks I see him. How goodly are thy tents, O Jacob!* (Nu 23:9; 24:5).

2. It is also applied to the restoration of a gracious soul from feeling abandoned and discouraged. She rises up *out of the wilderness* (v. 6), the dry and barren land, *like pillars of smoke* (v. 6), like a cloud of incense rising up from the altar. This suggests a fire of godly devotion in the soul. Christ's return to the soul gives life to its devotion, and its fellowship with God is most refreshing when it rises up *out of a wilderness* (v. 6). She is *perfumed with myrrh and frankincense* (v. 6). She is filled with the graces of God's Spirit, which are like sweet spices, or like the holy incense. She is now not only acceptable to God but also pleasing in the eyes of others, who ask in wonder, *Who is this?* What a memorial of mercy is this! The grace and encouragement with which she is *perfumed* are called the *powders of the merchant* (v. 6), for they have been bought at a high price by our Lord Jesus, the blessed merchant, who took a long voyage and purchased them for us with nothing less than his own blood,.

Verses 7–11

The *daughters of Jerusalem* (v. 5) stand admiring the bride and commending her, but she transfers all the glory to Christ and directs them to look from her to him. He is called *Solomon* three times here, but it is Christ who is referred to, One who is greater than Solomon (Mt 12:42), and of whom Solomon was an eminent type in his wisdom and, especially, in his building the temple. She admires him for three things:

1. The security of his *bed* (v. 7): *Behold his bed,* even *Solomon's,* very rich and fine, for such were *the curtains of Solomon* (1:5).

1.1. Even though Christ had *not where to lay his head* (Mt 8:20), his bed is better than Solomon's. The church is his bed, for he has said of it, *This is my rest for ever; here will I dwell* (Ps 132:14). The hearts of believers are his bed, for he lies all night by them (Eph 3:17).

1.2. It is *Solomon's bed* (v. 7), and his name means "peace." What she admires about his bed is the guard that surrounds it. Those who rest in Christ live not only in peace—many do so who are still in great danger—but also in security. This bed had *threescore valiant men about it* (v. 7) as yeomen of the guard, well armed: *They all hold swords* (v. 8) and know how to hold them; they are *expert in war.* They take up positions of defense, *every man* with *his sword upon his thigh* and his hand on his sword, ready to draw it at the call to battle, and they are so positioned *because of fear in the night,* that is, because of the danger feared.

1.3. Or, *because of the fear* (v. 8) of danger and the apprehension of it that the bride may feel, these guards are set to assure her, so that she may be *quiet from the fear of evil* (Pr 1:33), which believers themselves are subject to when they are under a cloud as regards their spiritual state.

1.4. Christ himself was under the special protection of his Father; he had legions of angels at his command (Mt 26:53). The church is well guarded; more are with her than are against her (2Ki 6:16). The whole nature of God is committed to the security of believers. His peace protects those in whom it rules (Php 4:7). Our danger is from *the rulers of the darkness of this world* (Eph 6:12), but we are secure in the *armour of light* (Ro 13:12).

2. The stateliness of his chariot (vv. 9–10). Solomon himself planned and made this chariot; the materials were very rich, *silver* and *gold* and *cedar* and *purple.* Some understand this *chariot*—the word is not used anywhere else in Scripture—to refer to the human nature of Christ, in which the divine nature rode as in an open chariot. It was divine workmanship (Eph 2:10)—*A body hast thou prepared me* (Heb 10:5)—the structure was very fine, but its base was love, pure love for the human race. Others think it refers to the eternal Gospel, in which, as in an open chariot, Christ shows himself. *The pillars* are of *silver,* for the words of the Lord are *as silver tried* (Ps 12:6). It is hung with *purple,* a royal color; all its decorative features are dyed in the precious blood of Christ. But what completes its glory is *love*; *it is paved with love* (v. 10); its interior is lovingly inlaid, *love* of *the daughters of Jerusalem* (v. 10), a holy *love.* Silver is better than cedar, and gold is better than silver, but love is better than gold, better than everything, and it is put last, for nothing can be better than it. The Gospel is all *love.*

3. The splendor of his royal person when he appears in his greatest pomp (v. 11). Notice here:

3.1. The call that is given to the *daughters of Zion: Go forth, and behold* him. Christ reveals himself in his Gospel. Let each one of us add to the number of those who honor him. Look with delight at Christ in his glory. Look at him with the settled eye of faith.

3.2. The instruction given them to take notice of his *crown,* either the crown of gold, adorned with jewels, that he wore on his coronation day, or the garland or crown of flowers and greenery tied with ribbons that his mother made for him, to adorn the sacred marriage ceremony. Applying this to Christ, it speaks of both the honor and the dishonor shown him. It shows the honor given him by his Father: *Go forth* and see King Jesus *with the crown wherewith his* Father *crowned him* (v. 11) when he declared him his *beloved Son, in whom* he was *well pleased* (Mt 3:17), when he *set him as King upon his holy hill of Zion* (Ps 2:6). It speaks of the dishonor shown him by his persecutors. Some apply this to the *crown of thorns* with which *his mother*, the Jewish church, *crowned him* on the day of his death, which was the day of his wedding to his church, when he *loved it, and gave himself for it* (Eph 5:25). It seems to refer especially to the honor shown him by his church, as his mother, and by all true believers. When believers accept him as theirs and join themselves to him in an eternal covenant, it is his coronation day in their souls. Before their conversion they were crowning themselves, but then they begin to crown Christ, and they continue to do so from that day on. It is *the day of his espousals* (wedding) (v. 11), in which he pledges them to be married to him forever in unfailing love and mercy. It is *the day of the gladness of his heart* (v. 11); he is pleased with the honor that his people do him.

CHAPTER 4

In this chapter: 1. Jesus Christ, having himself promised to marry his church (3:11), highly commends her beauty (vv. 1–5 and again v. 7). 2. He withdraws from the mountains of terror to those of delight (vv. 6, 8) and invites her to come to him; he professes his love to her (vv. 9–14). 3. She ascribes all she has that is valuable in her to him (vv. 15–16).

Verses 1–7

Here is:

1. A detailed account of the beauties of the church and of gracious souls on whom the image of God is renewed (Col 3:10), consisting *in the beauty of holiness* (1Ch 16:29; Ps 29:2; 96:9). Those who honor Christ he will honor (1Sa 2:30).

1.1. He does not flatter her, but encourages her in her present unhappiness. She was pledged to be married to him, and that made her beautiful.

1.2. As to the description here given of the beauty of the church, the images are certainly bright, the shades strong, and the comparisons bold. Seven details are specified, a perfect number, for the church is enriched with many graces by *the seven spirits* that *are before the throne* (Rev 1:4; 1Co 1:5, 7).

1.2.1. Her *eyes*. A good eye contributes much to beauty: *Thou hast doves' eyes* (v. 1), clear and pure and often looking up to heaven. Wisdom and knowledge are the eyes of the new self; they must be clear but not proud, *not exercised in things too high for us* (Ps 131:1). When our aims and intentions are sincere and honest, then we have *doves' eyes*. The *doves' eyes* are *within the locks* (v. 1), which are like a shade on them. They cannot fully see. As long as we live in this world, we *know but in part* (1Co 13:12).

1.2.2. Her *hair*; it is compared to *a flock of goats* (v. 1), which looked white and, on the top of mountains, looked like a fine head of hair. Some understand *hair* to refer to the outer behavior of a believer, which should be attractive and decent, corresponding to holiness in the heart.

1.2.3. Her *teeth* (v. 2). Ministers are the church's teeth; like nurses, they chew the food for the babes of Christ.

These are here compared to *a flock of sheep* (v. 2). Christ called his disciples and ministers *a little flock* (Lk 12:32). It is the praise of teeth to be *even*, to be white, and to be kept clean, *like sheep from the washing* (v. 2).

1.2.4. Her *lips*; these are compared to *a thread of scarlet* (v. 3). Red lips are beautiful and a sign of health, as the paleness of the lips is a sign of faintness and weakness. When we praise God with *our lips, and with the mouth make confession* of him *to salvation* (Ro 10:10), then they are as *a thread of scarlet*. All our good works and good words must be *washed in the blood of Christ*, dyed like the *scarlet thread*, and then they are acceptable to God.

1.2.5. Her *temples*, or cheeks, which are here compared to *a piece of a pomegranate* (v. 3), a fruit that, when cut in two, has rich veins or specks in it, like a blush on the face. Humility and modesty, blushing at remembering a sin and a sense of our unworthiness of the honor put on us, will make us very beautiful in the eyes of Christ.

1.2.6. Her *neck*; this is here compared to *the tower of David* (v. 4). This is generally applied to the grace of faith, by which we are united to Christ, as the body is *united* to the head by the neck; this *is like the tower of David*, providing us with weapons of war, especially *bucklers* and *shields*, as the soldiers were supplied with them from that tower, *for faith is our shield* (Eph 6:16). Those who have this armor never lack *a buckler* (shield), for God will surround them *with his favour as with a shield* (Ps 5:12).

1.2.7. Her *breasts*; these *are like two young roes* (fawns) *that are twins* (v. 5). The church's breasts are comforting (Isa 66:11). Some apply these to the two Testaments; others to the two sacraments, the seals of the covenant of grace; others to ministers, who are to be spiritual nurses to the children of God and to give them the *sincere milk of the word, that they may grow thereby* (1Pe 2:2), and who, to that end, are themselves to *feed among the lilies* where Christ feeds (2:16).

2. The bridegroom's resolution then to withdraw *to the mountain of myrrh* (v. 6) and to live there. This *mountain of myrrh* is supposed to represent Mount Moriah, on which the temple was built, where incense was daily burned to the honor of God. Christ will dwell there *till the day break and the shadows flee away* (v. 6). His parting promise to his disciples, as the representatives of the church, corresponds to this: *Lo, I am with you always, even to the end of the world* (Mt 28:20). Where the ordinances of God are duly administered, Christ will be there. The holy hill, some notice, is called here both *a mountain of myrrh*, which is bitter, and *a hill of frankincense* (v. 6), which is sweet, for there we have occasion both to mourn and to rejoice; repentance is bittersweet. But in heaven it will be all frankincense, all sweetness, and no myrrh, no bitterness.

3. His repeated commendation of the beauty of his spouse (v. 7): *Thou art all fair, my love*. He declares the details, as he did those of the Creation, *all very good*. "*Thou are all fair, my love* (v. 7). There is nothing wrong in you. You have all beauty in you; you are *sanctified wholly* (1Th 5:23) in every part; *all things have become new* (2Co 5:17); there is not only a new face and a new name but also a new self and a new nature (Eph 4:24; Col 3:10).

Verses 8–14

These are still the words of Christ to his church, expressing his affection for her. Notice:

1. The endearing names and titles by which he calls her to express his love to her, assure her of it, and allure and excite her love to him. Twice here he calls her *My spouse* (bride) (vv. 8, 11) and three times *My sister, my*

spouse (bride) (vv. 9–10, 12). His wedding day was mentioned in 3:11, and after that she is called his *spouse*, but not before. There is a marriage covenant between Christ and his church, between Christ and every true believer. Christ calls his church his *spouse* (bride). Because no one human relationship is sufficient to display Christ's love for his church, and in order to show that all this must be understood spiritually, he acknowledges her in two relationships: *My sister, my spouse* (vv. 9–10). His calling her *sister* is based on his taking our nature on himself in his incarnation.

2. The gracious call he gives her to accompany him as a faithful bride.

2.1. All who by faith have come to Christ must come with Christ, in holy obedience to him and compliance with him. Being united with him, we must also walk with him. This is his command to us daily: *"Come with me, my spouse* (v. 8); come with me to God as a Father; come with me onward, toward heaven; *come with me from Lebanon, from the top of Amana, from the lions' dens"* (v. 8). These mountains are to be considered:

2.1.1. As apparently delightful places. Lebanon is called *that goodly* (fine) *mountain* (Dt 3:25). We read of the pleasant *dew of Hermon* (Ps 133:3) and the *joy of Hermon* (Ps 89:12). This is Christ's call to his bride to come away from the world, not clinging to worldly delights. Even if they are sitting on top of the world, on *the top of Amana* (v. 8), they must still *come away* and live above the tops of the highest hills on earth, so that they may have *their conversation in heaven* (Php 3:20). *From the tops of Shenir and Hermon* (v. 8), which were on the other side of the Jordan, as from Pisgah, they could see the land of Canaan. We must look out from this world and forward to the better country (Heb 11:16).

2.1.2. As really dangerous places. These hills indeed look pleasant enough, but they actually contain *lions' dens*; they are *mountains of the leopards* (v. 8), mountains of wild animals, even though they seem *glorious and excellent* (Ps 76:4). On the tops of these mountains there are many dangerous temptations. *"Come with me from* the temples of idolaters and the company of evildoers; *come out from among them, and be you separate* (2Co 6:17). *Come from* under the control of your own sinful desires, which are as *lions* and *leopards"* (v. 8).

2.2. It may be taken as a promise: you will *come with me from Lebanon, from the lions' dens* (v. 8), that is: "Many will be brought home to me from every point on the compass to be living members of the church, from Lebanon in the north, Amana in the west, Hermon in the east, Senir in the south, from every direction, to *sit down with Abraham, Isaac and Jacob*" (Mt 8:11). See Isa 49:11–12.

3. The great delight Christ takes in his church and in all believers. He delights in them:

3.1. As in a delightful bride. No expressions of love can be more passionate than these here in which Christ reveals his love for his church, but that great proof of his love, his dying for it, goes far beyond them all. A bride so dearly bought and paid for must indeed be dearly loved. Notice:

3.1.1. How devoted he is to his bride: *Thou hast ravished my heart* (v. 9), you have captivated or stolen my heart. The word is used only here in all of Scripture; new words are coined to express the inexpressibleness of Christ's amazing love for his church.

3.1.2. What it is that so moves him with delight.

3.1.2.1. The respect she has for him: *Thou hast ravished my heart with one of thy eyes* (v. 9), those *doves' eyes*, clear and pure, that were commended in v. 1.

3.1.2.2. The ornaments she has from him, that is, the obedience she gives him—for that is the *chain of her neck* (v. 9)—and the graces that enrich her soul. Having shaken off the *bands of our neck*, by which we were tied to this world (Isa 52:2), we are bound with the *cords of love* (Hos 11:4) as with *chains of gold* (1:10) to Jesus Christ, and our necks are brought under his sweet and easy yoke.

3.1.2.3. The devotion she has for him: *How fair is thy love!* (v. 10), how beautiful it is! How good it is for believers to love Christ in this way. Nothing commends us to Christ as this does.

3.1.2.4. The perfume, the fragrance with which she is scented, that is to say, the gifts and graces of the Spirit, her good works, which *are an odour of a sweet smell* (a fragrant offering), *a sacrifice acceptable, wellpleasing to God* (Php 4:18). Love and obedience to God are more pleasing to Christ than sacrifices or incense. *The smell* (fragrance) *of her garments* (v. 11) too, the visible, public profession she makes of religious faith and of her relationship with Christ, is like *the smell of Lebanon* (v. 11).

3.1.2.5. Her words, words of devotion and words spoken to other people (v. 11): *Thy lips O my spouse! drop as the honeycomb*, drop sweetness freely and plentifully. If what God speaks to us is *sweeter* to us *than the honey and the honeycomb* (Ps 19:10), what we say to him in prayer and praise will also be pleasing to him. The word of God contains sweet and wholesome nourishment, milk for babies and honey for those who have grown up.

3.2. As in a pleasant garden. The church is appropriately compared to *a garden* that, as was usual, has *a fountain in it* (vv. 12–14). Notice:

3.2.1. The special nature of this garden. It is *a garden enclosed* (locked up), a paradise separate from ordinary ground. It is reserved for God; he has *set it apart for himself* (Ps 4:3); Israel belongs to God. It is enclosed to be concealed; God's people are his hidden ones (Ps 83:3). Christ walks in his garden unseen. It is enclosed for safety; a hedge surrounds it for protection, which all the powers of darkness cannot find or make a hole in. It has a spring and a fountain in it, but it is *a spring shut up* and *a fountain sealed* (v. 12), so that it may not be muddied or defiled by those who want to harm it. The souls of believers are as *gardens enclosed*; grace in them is as *a spring shut up* (v. 12) there in *the hidden man of the heart* (1Pe 3:4), where the water that Christ gives is *a well of living water* (Jn 4:14; 7:38). The Old Testament church was *a garden enclosed* by the partition wall of the ceremonial law (Eph 2:14). The Bible was then a *spring shut up* and *a fountain sealed*; it was confined to one nation. Now, however, the wall of separation has been removed, and the Gospel is preached to every nation: *in Jesus Christ there is neither Greek nor Jew* (Col 3:11).

3.2.2. The crops of this garden. *Thy plants*, or plantations, *are an orchard of pomegranates with pleasant fruits* (v. 13). Here are *fruits, pleasant fruits, all trees of frankincense*, and *all the chief spices* (v. 14). Here is a wide range of fruits, each the best of its kind. Their finest spices were much more valuable than the finest flowers we have. Saints in the church, and graces in the saints, are very appropriately compared to these *fruits and spices*, for *the trees of righteousness* are the *planting of the Lord* (Isa 61:3). Saints are the blessings of this earth. They are permanent, and they will have been preserved to good purpose when flowers have withered and are good for nothing. Grace, matured to glory, will last forever.

Verses 15–16

These seem to be the words of the bride, the church, in answer to the commendations that Christ, the bridegroom, has given of her as a pleasant and fruitful garden.

1. She acknowledges her dependence on Christ himself to make this garden fruitful. She looks to him (v. 15) as the *fountain of gardens*. She gives him all the glory of her fruitfulness, as being nothing without him. The church expresses praise to Christ and says to him, *All my springs are in thee*; you are *the well of living waters* (Jer 2:13). Those who are gardens to Christ must acknowledge him as being a fountain to them, from whose fullness they receive (Jn 1:16) and because of whom their souls are like *a watered garden* (Jer 31:12).

2. She implores the Holy Spirit to shed his influence and make this garden fragrant (v. 16): *Awake, O north wind! and come, thou south.* This is a prayer for the church in general, that there may be a plentiful outpouring of the Spirit. This prayer was answered in the outpouring of the Spirit on *the day of Pentecost*, ushered in by *a mighty wind* (Ac 2:1–2); at that time the apostles, who previously had been restricted, flowed out and were *a sweet savour to God* (2Co 2:15). Sanctified souls are like gardens of the Lord, enclosed for him. Graces in the soul are like spices in these gardens. The Holy Spirit, in his activity on the soul, is like the *north and the south wind* (v. 16). There is the north wind of conviction and the south wind of encouragement. The flowing out of the spices of grace depends on the strong wind of the Spirit.

3. She invites Christ to the best reception the garden offers: *"Let my beloved* then *come into his garden and eat his pleasant fruits* (v. 16); let him have the honor of all the crops of the garden, and let me have the encouragement of his acceptance of them."* Believers can take little delight in their garden unless Christ, the beloved of their souls, comes to them; nor will they enjoy any of its fruits unless those fruits lead in some way or other to the glory of Christ.

CHAPTER 5

In this chapter we have: 1. Christ's gracious acceptance of the invitation that his church had given him (v. 1). 2. The account the bride gives of her own foolishness in showing disrespect for her beloved, and the distress she was in because of his withdrawal (vv. 2–8). 3. The inquiry of the daughters of Jerusalem concerning the qualities of her beloved (v. 9) and her detailed response to that question (vv. 10–16). To you who believe he is thus precious (1Pe 2:7).

Verse 1

These words are Christ's answer to the church's prayer at the end of the previous chapter, *Let my beloved come into his garden* (4:16); he has come here. She called him *her beloved* because she loved him; in response he called her his *sister and spouse*. Those who make Christ their best beloved will be acknowledged by him in the closest and most precious relationships. She invited him to *come into his garden* (v. 1), and he says, *I have come* (v. 1). Those who throw open the door of their souls to Jesus Christ will find him ready to come in to them (Rev 3:20), and he will meet his people and bless them everywhere he records his name (Ex 20:24). She wanted him to *eat* only *the fruits* (4:16) of the garden, but he brought along with him something more, *honey* and *wine* and *milk*, which provide substantial nourishment and which were the products of Canaan, Emmanuel's land (Isa 8:8). The great work of human redemption and the riches of the covenant of grace are a feast for the Lord Jesus (Jn 4:34), and they should also be for us.

Verses 2–8

In this song of love and joy we have here a sad scene; the bride is speaking here not *to* her beloved but *about* him, and she tells a sad story about her own foolishness and wrong behavior. Notice:

1. Lethargy had seized her (v. 2). *She slept*, that is, her godly devotion cooled down, and she neglected her duty and became negligent in it. True Christians do not always keep the same level of vitality in their religious faith. But grace remained, nevertheless: "*My heart wakes* (v. 2); my own conscience rebukes me for it and continues to try to rouse me from my sluggishness. I am asleep, but it is not a dead sleep; I am fighting against it; I cannot be at peace in this condition." We should take notice of our own spiritual sleep and illnesses, and we should reflect on them with sorrow and shame that we have fallen asleep when Christ has been close to us in his garden.

2. The call Christ gave to her when she was suffering in this way: *It is the voice of my beloved* (v. 2); she knew it was his voice, which was a sign that her heart was awake. Like the child Samuel, she heard him when he first called (1Sa 3:4–5), but she did not, like him, mistake the person; she knew it to be the voice of Christ. He knocks to awaken us to come and let him in. He knocks by his word and Spirit; he knocks in our suffering and in our own consciences. Those whom he loves he will not leave in their negligence; he will find some way or other to wake them up, to rebuke and correct them. Notice how moving the call is: *Open to me, my sister, my love* (v. 2). He who may demand entrance pleads for it; he who could easily knock down the door knocks on it. He gives her all the most endearing titles possible: *My sister, my love, my dove, my undefiled* (v. 2); he calls her by no bad names. *His lovingkindness he will not utterly take away* (Ps 89:33). *Open to me* (v. 2). Can we deny access to such a friend and guest? He begs to be admitted as a poor traveler who needs lodging: "*My head is wet with the dew* (v. 2). Consider what hardships I have gone through to deserve you, which surely should evoke from you such a small kindness as this." When Christ was crowned with thorns, then was his head *wet with the dew*. Is this how we requite his love?

3. The excuse she made to put off her obedience to this call (v. 3): *I have put off my coat. How shall I put it on again?* She is half asleep; she knows the voice of her beloved but cannot find it in her heart to open to him. She is undressed; she has *washed her feet* (v. 3) and does not want to wash them again. Frivolous excuses are the language of a controlling laziness in matters of religious faith; Christ calls to us to open up our lives to him, but we pretend we do not have the inclination, or the strength, or the time. Those who cannot find it in their hearts to withstand the cold or get out of a warm bed for Christ show great contempt for him.

4. The powerful influences of divine grace, by which she was made willing to rise and open to her beloved. When he could not persuade her, he *put in his hand by the hole of the door* to unbolt it, as one who was weary of waiting (v. 4). This suggests a work of the Spirit on her soul. The conversion of Lydia is described by the *opening of her heart* (Ac 16:14).

5. Her ultimate submission to these methods of divine grace: *My bowels were moved for him* (v. 4). She was moved with compassion for her beloved, because his *head*

was wet with dew (v. 2). Did Christ redeem us in his pity? Let us then in pity receive him, and for his sake let us receive those who are his when they are in distress at any time. He made her ashamed of her previous slowness and laziness (v. 5): *I rose up, to open to my beloved.* It was her own act, and yet he brought it about in her. And now her *hands dropped with myrrh upon the handles of the lock* (v. 5). Either:

5.1. She found the myrrh there when she applied her hand to the lock to push it back; he who *put in his hand by the hole of the door* (v. 4) left the fragrant substance there as evidence he had been there. When Christ has done a powerful work on a soul, he leaves a blessed sweetness in it. Or:

5.2. She brought it there. When she came to open the door to him, she made preparations to anoint his head and thereby refresh and comfort him. She was in such a hurry to meet him that she would not stay to make the usual preparations, but dipped her hand in her box of ointment so that she might quickly anoint his head. Those who open the doors of their hearts to Christ, those *everlasting doors* (Ps 24:7), must meet him with an active and genuine expression of faith and other graces and must anoint him with these.

6. Her sad disappointment when she did open up to her beloved. *I opened to my beloved*, as I intended, but alas! *My beloved had withdrawn himself, and was gone* (v. 6). Literally, "My beloved was gone, was gone."

6.1. She did not open to him at his first knock, and now she came too late. Christ wants to be sought while he may be found (Isa 55:6); if we let the opportunity pass, we may miss our means of access. Christ justly rebukes our delays and suspends his provision of assurance to those who are careless.

6.2. She still calls him her *beloved*, having decided, however cloudy and dark the day is, that she will not abandon her relationship with him. She now remembers the words he said to her when he called her: "*My soul failed when he spoke* (v. 6); his words melted me when he said, *My head is wet with dew* (v. 2), but I lay still and made excuses and did not open up to him." She goes to search for him: *I sought him; I called him* (v. 6). *I could not find him; he gave me no answer* (v. 6). This shows us that there are those who have a true love for Christ but who do not receive immediate answers to their prayers for his favor, and yet he responds to them with something equivalent if he makes them bold in their souls to continue to seek him (Ps 138:3). The apostle Paul was not successful in his prayer for the *thorn in the flesh* to be removed (2Co 12:7), but was answered by the Lord's response: "My grace is sufficient for you" (2Co 12:9). She is treated badly by the watchmen: *They found me; they smote me; they wounded me* (v. 7). They think she was an immoral woman, and so they beat and wound her. Miserable saints are thought to be sinners and are criticized as such. When she is rendered unfit to pursue her inquiry herself, she charges those around her to help her (v. 8): "*I charge you, O you daughters of Jerusalem!* all my friends and acquaintances, *if you find my beloved*, speak a good word for me; tell him that *I am sick of love.*" It is better to be faint with love for Christ than at ease in love for the world.

Verses 9–16

Here:

1. The daughters of Jerusalem answer the charge she has given them (v. 9). Notice the respectful title they give to the bride: *O thou fairest among* (most beautiful of) *women!* The church is the most noble community in the

whole world, and the beauty of the sanctuary is an all-surpassing beauty. Holiness is the beautiful harmony of the soul. Even those who know little of Christ, such as these daughters of Jerusalem, must see beauty in those who bear his image. Their question about her beloved: "*What is thy beloved more than another beloved?* How is your beloved better than others?" (v. 9). Some take this as a scornful question, blaming her for making such a fuss about him. Worldly hearts see nothing excellent or extraordinary in the Lord Jesus, in his person or his work, in his teaching or his kindness. Others take it as a serious question and suppose that those who asked it intended to comfort the bride, who they knew would be encouraged if she only spoke for a while about her beloved. They wondered what had moved the bride to ask them to make promises about her beloved with so much concern and concluded there must be something more in him than in any other. There begins to be hope for people when they begin to ask about Christ. Sometimes the extraordinary zeal of one person in seeking Christ may be a means of stirring many people to action (2Co 9:2).

2. The account the bride gives of her beloved in answer to this question. She assures them, in general, that he is a person of incomparable excellencies and unparalleled worthiness (v. 10); everything in him is lovely: *My beloved is white and ruddy.* This points not to any extraordinary beauty of the body he would have when he became incarnate, but to his divine glory in the eyes of those who are enlightened to discern spiritual things. We may behold in him the *beauty of the Lord* (Ps 27:4); he was the *holy child Jesus* (Ac 4:27); that was his beauty. His love to us makes him lovely. He is *white* in the spotless innocence of his life, *ruddy* in the bloody sufferings he went through at his death, *white* in his glory, as God, *ruddy* in his assuming human nature, *Adam*, "red earth." He has that beauty in him that is not to be found in any other person: he is *the chief among ten thousand* (v. 10). She gives particular details of his achievements; she does not hide his power or beautiful appearance. Here she gives ten examples of his goodness. Their general intention is to show that he is qualified for his undertaking in every way and has everything in him that should commend him to our respect, love, and confidence. Christ's appearance to John (Rev 1:13) may be compared with the description that the bride gives of Christ here, the scope of both being to describe him as transcendently glorious.

2.1. *His head is as the most fine gold* (v. 11). *The head of Christ is God* (1Co 11:3). Christ's head speaks of his sovereign authority over all and his vital influence on his church and all its members.

2.2. *His locks are bushy* (his hair is wavy) *and black* (v. 11), *black as a raven* (v. 11), whose blackness is his beauty. They are *black and bushy*, showing that he is always young and there is in him nothing that becomes old.

2.3. *His eyes are as the eyes of doves* (v. 12), fair and clear, pure and kind.

2.4. *His cheeks are as a bed of spices and as sweet flowers* (v. 13), or towers of sweetness yielding perfume. The least revelations Christ makes of himself to the soul are reviving and refreshing, fragrant above the richest flowers or perfumes.

2.5. *His lips are like lilies* (v. 13), sweet and pleasant. Such are *the words of his lips* to all who are sanctified: *grace is poured into his lips* (Ps 45:2). Those who heard him *wondered at the gracious words which proceeded out of his mouth* (Lk 4:22).

2.6. *His hands are as gold rings set with the beryl* (chrysolite), a noted precious stone (v. 14). Famous people had their hands adorned with gold rings on their fingers, set with precious stones, but in her eyes, *his hands* themselves were *as gold rings*; all the accomplishments of his power, the works of his hands, all the actions of his providence and grace are precious, like gold, like *the precious onyx and the sapphire* (Job 28:16). All are suitable for the purpose for which they were designed, and all are beautiful, *as rings set with beryl*.

2.7. "His bowels are as bright ivory" (v. 14)—it is the same word that was used for *bowels* in v. 4. It refers to his tender compassion and affection for his bride. His love is like *bright ivory*, finely polished and richly *overlaid with sapphires* (v. 14). The love itself is strong and firm, bright and sparkling.

2.8. *His legs are as pillars of marble* (v. 15). This speaks of his stability and firmness. He is able to bear all the weight of the government that is on his shoulders (Isa 9:6).

2.9. *His countenance* (his appearance) *is as Lebanon* (v. 15), that stately hill; his expression is beautiful and delightful, *excellent as the cedars* (v. 15).

2.10. *His mouth is most sweet*; it is, literally, "sweetnesses" (v. 16). The words of his mouth are all sweet to a believer. The tokens of his love have a transcendent sweetness about them and are most delightful to those who have their spiritual senses exercised. *To you that believe he is precious* (1Pe 2:7).

3. She concludes with a full assurance both of faith and of hope and so gets her trouble under control. Here is a full assurance of faith about the complete beauty of the Lord Jesus: *He is altogether lovely* (v. 16). Here is a full assurance of hope concerning her own interest in him: "*This is my beloved, and this is my friend* (v. 16), and so it is not surprising that I long for him. He is mine, *my Lord and my God* (Jn 20:28), mine according to the terms of the Gospel covenant, mine in every relationship, given to me, to be all to me all that my poor soul needs." This is here spoken of with an air of triumph: "This is the One whom I have chosen, and to whom I have given myself. No one but Christ; no one but Christ. This is the One on whom my heart is set, for he is my best beloved. This is the One in whom I am trusting and from whom I expect all good, for *this is my friend*" (v. 16).

CHAPTER 6

In this chapter: 1. The daughters of Jerusalem, moved with the description the church has given of Christ, ask after him (v. 1). 2. The church tells them where they may meet him (vv. 2–3). 2. Christ is now found by those who sought him (Jer 29:13–14), and he intensely praises the beauty of his bride (vv. 4–7), preferring her to all others (vv. 8–9), commending her to the love and respect of all her neighbors (v. 10), and expressing the great delight he takes in her (vv. 10–13).

Verses 1–3

Here is:

1. The question the daughters of Jerusalem ask about Christ (v. 1). They still continue to have elevated thoughts about the church, and they call her, as before, the *fairest among women*. And now they raise their thoughts higher about Christ: *Whither* (where) *has thy beloved gone, that we may seek him with thee?* This would be an unacceptable compliment if the song were not to be understood spiritually, for love is jealous of rivals, but those who truly love Christ want others to love him too. The bride has

expressed her own love for him, and that flame in her heart scattered sparks into theirs. Just as an outbreak of sinful desires defiles many people, so the godly zeal of some may stir many people to action (2Co 9:2).

2. The answer that the bride gives to this question (vv. 2–3).

2.1. Now she knows very well where he is (v. 2): "*My beloved* is not to be found in the streets of the city and in the crowd and noise there; he *has gone down to his garden* (v. 2), a place of retirement." The more we withdraw from the hustle and bustle of this world, the more likely we are to come to know Christ, who took his disciples into a garden to witness there the agonies of his love. Christ's church is an enclosed garden (4:12), *his garden*, which he has planted. Those who want to find Christ may expect to meet with him in *his garden*, the church; they must wait on him in the ordinances he has instituted, the word, the sacraments, and prayer, in which he will be with us *always, even to the end of the world* (Mt 28:20). When Christ comes down to his church, he comes to feed his flock, which he does not feed in the open fields, as other shepherds do, but in his garden. He comes to feed his friends and receive them, *for the Lord takes pleasure in those that fear him* (Ps 147:11). He has many gardens, many individual churches of different sizes and shapes, but as long as they are his, he reveals himself to them all and is pleased with them. He picks the lilies one by one and gathers them to himself. There will be a general harvest of them at the great day.

2.2. She is very confident of her own relationship with him (v. 3): *I am my beloved's, and my beloved is mine*. She has acted unkindly toward her beloved, and he has justly withdrawn himself from her. There is now therefore need for her to take fresh hold of the covenant, which continues firmly between Christ and believers despite their failings and his frowns (Ps 89:30–35). "I have been careless and negligent in my duty, but *I am my beloved's* (v. 3). He has justly hidden his face from me, and *yet my beloved is mine*." When we do not have a full assurance of Christ's love, we must still live according to a faithful loyalty to him. "Even though I do not sense the encouragement and assurance I used to, I will still cling to this: *Christ is mine and I am his*."

Verses 4–10

We must presume now that Christ has graciously returned to his bride, having forgiven and forgotten all her unkindness, for he speaks very tenderly and respectfully to her.

1. He declares her truly pleasant (v. 4): *Thou art beautiful, O my love! as Tirzah*, a town in the tribe of Manasseh, whose name signifies "pleasant" or "acceptable." *Thou art comely* (lovely) *as Jerusalem*, a city compact together (Ps 122:3), a city Solomon had built and made beautiful. It was the Holy City, and that was its greatest beauty; and the church is appropriately compared to it. The Gospel church is *the Jerusalem that is above* (Gal 4:26), *the heavenly Jerusalem* (Heb 12:22); God has *his sanctuary* in it and is present there in a special way; and so it is as lovely as Jerusalem, and because it is so, it is *terrible* (majestic) *as an army with banners* (v. 4).

2. He acknowledges himself to be in love with her (v. 5), although for a short time he has hidden his face from her. Some read v. 5, "Turn your eyes toward me"—that is, "turn the eyes of faith and love toward me," — "for they have lifted me up"; "look to me and be encouraged." When we are calling to God to turn the eye of his favor

toward us, he is calling to us to turn the eyes of our obedience toward him.

3. He repeats, almost word for word, part of the description he gave earlier of her beauty (4:1–3), *her hair*, *her teeth*, her *temples* (vv. 5–7), to show that he still keeps the same respect for her that he had before.

4. He sees all the beauties and perfections of others meeting and centering on her (vv. 8–9): "*There are, it may be, threescore queens*, who, like Esther, have by their beauty reached the royal state and dignity, *and fourscore concubines, virgins without number*, but *my dove, my undefiled* (perfect one), *is but one* (unique), a holy one." She surpasses them all. Go throughout the world and view communities that consider themselves wise and happy: kingdoms, courts, senates, councils. None of them will compare to the church of Christ. There are individual people who are well known for what they have achieved, the beauties of their language and actions, but the beauty of holiness is beyond every other beauty. "Although there are many individual churches, some of greater honor, others of less, some of longer standing and others of shorter, and many individual believers, each with different gifts and achievements, nevertheless, they all make up one universal church, are all parts of that whole, and that *is my dove, my undefiled*" (v. 9). Christ is the center of the church's unity.

5. He shows how much she is respected, not only by him but also by all who know her. As Solomon himself is said to have been *tender and an only one in the sight of his mother* (Pr 4:3), so is she *the only one of her mother* (v. 9), as precious as if she had been an only child, *the choice one of her that bore her* (v. 9). In Christ's account, all the kingdoms of the world, and all their glory, are nothing compared with the church. She is admired by all who know her, not only *the daughters*, her juniors, but even *the queens and the concubines*, who might have reason to be jealous of her as a rival. *They* all *blessed her, praised her* (v. 9), and spoke well of her. Those who have any correct sense of things must be convinced in their consciences (whatever they say) that godly people are excellent people; many will speak well of them, and more give them their goodwill. Jesus Christ is pleased with those who honor people who fear the Lord, and he is displeased with those who *offend any of his little ones* (Mt 18:6).

6. He refers to the praise given of her and makes it his own (v. 10): *Who is she that looks forth as the morning?* This may be applied both to the church in the world and to grace in the heart. Christians are, or should be, the lights of the world (Mt 5:14). The patriarchal church appeared as the dawn (v. 10) when the promise of the Messiah was first made known and *the dayspring from on high visited* (Lk 1:78) this dark world. The Jewish church was as *fair as the moon* (v. 10); the ceremonial law was an imperfect light; it shone by reflection, did not make day, nor had *the sun of righteousness yet risen* (Mal 4:2). But the Christian church *is clear as the sun* (v. 10), exhibiting a great *light to those that sat in darkness* (Mt 4:16). The beauty of the church and of believers is as awesome *as an army with banners* (v. 10). In this world, the church is *as an army*, like the camp of Israel in the desert. It is on war footing; it is in the midst of enemies and is engaged in constant conflict with them. Believers are soldiers in this army. It has its *banners*; the Gospel of Christ is an ensign (Isa 11:12). It is marshaled and kept in order and under discipline. It is *terrible* to its enemies. When the church preserves her purity, she protects her honor and victory. When she is *fair as the moon* and *clear as the sun* (v. 10), she is truly great and formidable.

Verses 11–13

Christ has now returned to his bride, the rift has been completely healed, and here he gives an account of the separation and of the reconciliation.

1. When he had withdrawn from his church as his bride, even then he still looked on it as his garden, which he took care of (v. 11): "*I went down into the garden of nuts* (the grove of nut trees) *to see the fruits of the valley*, with concern, to see them as my own." When he was out of sight, he was no further away than in the garden, hidden among the trees, observing *how the vine flourished* so that he might do what was necessary for it to flourish further. He went to see whether *the pomegranates budded*. Christ observes the beginnings of the good work of grace in the soul and the early blossoming of devotion and godly inclinations there, and is pleased with them, as we are with blossoms in spring.

2. Yet he could not be content himself with this for long. He suddenly felt a powerful inclination to return to his church, being moved by her expressions of sadness after him (v. 12): "*Or ever I was aware* (before I realized it), *my soul made me like the chariots of Amminadib*; I could not keep away any longer; and I immediately decided to flee to my love." And now the bride realizes that he *heard the voice of her supplications* (Ps 28:6; 31:22) and became *like the chariots of Amminadib* (v. 12), which were noted for their beauty and swiftness. Christ's people should be a willing people. If they continue to seek Christ and long for him even when he seems to withdraw from them, he will return to them in due time.

3. He, having returned to her, kindly encouraged her return to him, despite the discouragements she labored under. Let her take encouragement from the return of her beloved (v. 13). Here the church is called the *Shulamite*, referring to *Salem*, the place of her birth and residence, as the woman of *Shunem* is called the *Shunammite*. Heaven is the Salem from which God's people are born (*Salem* is a shortened form of *Jerusalem* [Ps 76:2] and is related to the Hebrew word for "peace" [Ed.]) and where they have their citizenship (Php 3:20). She is invited to return. As rebelling sinners need to be called to again and again— *Turn you, turn you, why will you die?* (Eze 33:11)—so troubled saints need to be called to again and again: "*Turn you, turn you, why will you faint? Why art thou cast down, O my soul?*" (Ps 42:5, 11; 43:5). Having returned, she is asked to show her face, "*that we may look upon thee* (v. 13). Do not go about anymore with your face covered up like a mourner." Christ is pleased with the humble and cheerful confidence of his people and wants them to look pleasant. A short description is given of what is to be seen in her. The question is asked, *What will you see in the Shulamite?* (v. 13). And the answer comes, *As it were the company of two armies* (v. 13).

3.1. Some think she gives this description of herself. "Alas!" she says. "*What will you see in the Shulamite?* Nothing worth looking at, nothing but *as it were, the company of two armies* actually engaged, where, nothing is to be seen except blood and slaughter." The watchmen have wounded her, and she bears in her face the marks of those wounds, looking as if she has been fighting. She said earlier (1:6), *Look not upon me because I am black*, and here she says, "Look not on me because I am bloodstained."

3.2. Others think her beloved gives this account of her. "I will tell you what you will *see in the Shulamite* (v. 13); you will see as noble a sight as that of two armies, or two divisions of the same army, arrayed in rank and file, not only *as an army with banners* (v. 10), but also as *two armies*, with a majesty double what was described earlier (v. 10). She is like *Mahanaim*, like the two hosts that Jacob saw (Ge 32:1–2), an army of saints and an army of angels ministering to them; the church militant, the church triumphant."

CHAPTER 7

In this chapter: 1. Christ, the royal bridegroom, continues to describe the beauties of his bride, the church, and to express his love to her (vv. 1–9). 2. The bride, the church, expresses her great delight in him and her desire for fellowship with him (vv. 10–13).

Verses 1–9

The title that Jesus Christ here gives to the church is a new one: *O prince's daughter!* (v. 1); this corresponds to Ps 45:13, where she is called *the king's daughter*. She is called this because of her new birth; she is born from above (Jn 3:3, 7, where "born again" may also be translated "born from above"), born of God (Jn 1:13), and his workmanship (Eph 2:10), bearing the image of the King of kings and guided by his Spirit. She is the daughter of a prince by marriage. Christ, by promising her in marriage to himself, has made her *a prince's daughter* (v. 1), although he found her lowly and shameful. We have here:

1. A full description of the beauty of the bride, which seems to be given by Christ himself and to be intended to express his love for her, as before (4:1; 6:5–6). The comparisons are different from before, to show that the beauty of holiness is such that nothing in nature can reach it. The earlier commendation of the bride (ch. 4) was on the wedding day (3:11); this commendation is on her return from a byway (6:13). This surpasses that one, to show the faithfulness of Christ's love to his people; *he loves them to the end* (Jn 13:1). The bride has described the beauty of her beloved in ten ways (5:11–16); and now he describes her in as many. The beauties of the church are reckoned from foot to head.

1.1. Her *feet* are praised here; the feet of Christ's ministers are beautiful in the eyes of the church (Isa 52:7), and her feet are said to be beautiful in the eyes of Christ. *How beautiful are thy feet with shoes!* (v. 1). When believers are set free from the captivity of sin (Ac 12:8), they have *their feet shod with the preparation of the Gospel of peace* (Eph 6:15), and they walk steadily according to the rule of the Gospel, and then their *feet are beautiful with shoes* (v. 1). They tread firmly.

1.2. *The joints of the thighs* (graceful legs) *are* said to be *like jewels* (v. 1), jewels skillfully worked by an artist (v. 1). This is explained by Eph 4:16; Col 2:19, where the mystical body of Christ is said to be held together by *joints and bands* (ligaments and sinews), like the hips and knees, both of which are *the joints of the thighs* and serve the natural body in its strength and movement. The church is beautiful in Christ's eyes when these joints move firmly and easily by holy love and unity.

1.3. The *navel* is here compared to a rounded cup or goblet (v. 2). The fear of the Lord is said to be *health to the navel*. See Pr 3:8.

1.4. The *belly* (waist) *is like a heap of wheat* (v. 2) in the storeroom, which perhaps was sometimes adorned with flowers. The *wheat* is useful, the *lilies* are beautiful; the church has everything its members might want for either the use or the adornment of that body. All the body is nourished from the *belly*; the image shows the spiritual prosperity of a believer and the healthy constitution of the soul.

1.5. The *breasts are like two young roes that are twins* (v. 3). We had this comparison before (4:5).

1.6. The *neck*, which before was compared to *the tower of David* (4:4), is here compared to *a tower of ivory*, so white and precious; such is the faith of the saints, by which they are joined to Christ their head.

1.7. The *eyes are* compared to *the fishpools in Heshbon*, or the artificial fishponds, *by a gate*, either of Jerusalem or of Heshbon, which is called *Bath-rabbim* (v. 4), which means "the daughter of many," perhaps because it was a great thoroughfare. The understanding, the intentions of a believer, are as clean and clear as these pools.

1.8. The *nose* is like *the tower of Lebanon* (v. 4); the forehead or face is set *like a flint* (Isa 50:7), as undaunted as that tower was impregnable. This shows the holy boldness and courage of the church, or, according to others, a spiritual wisdom to discern different things, as animals inexplicably distinguish things by smell. This tower *looks towards Damascus* (v. 4), the main city of Syria, showing the boldness of the church in facing its enemies.

1.9. The *head* is *like Carmel*, a very high hill near the sea (v. 5). The head of a believer is *lifted up above his enemies* (Ps 27:6), above the storms of the lower region, as the top of Carmel was, pointing heavenward.

1.10. *The hair of the head* is said to be *like purple* (v. 5). This represents the pleasantness of a believer in the eyes of Christ, even including *the hair*, or, as some understand it, the pins with which *the hair* is dressed.

2. The church that has been made beautiful and adorned in this way, and truly lovely if she is so in his eyes. His love makes this beauty truly valuable.

2.1. He delighted to look on his church. *The king is held in the galleries* (v. 5) and cannot leave them. And if Christ has such delight *in the galleries* of fellowship with his people, much more reason have they to delight in them.

2.2. He marveled at the beauty of his church (v. 6): *How fair and how pleasant art thou, O love!* "How fair you are made!" is the sense, "not born fair, but made so by the beauty that I have put on you."

2.3. He determined to maintain fellowship with his church. He compares her *stature to* that of *a palm tree* (v. 7); she appears so straight and strong. The *palm tree* has been observed to flourish most when it is laden with fruit, as has the church: the more it has been burdened by suffering, the more it has multiplied, and its branches are emblems of victory. Christ says, "*I will go up to the palm tree* to enjoy its shade (v. 8), and *I will take hold of its boughs* and observe their beauty." He compares her *breasts*—her devotion toward him—*to clusters of grapes*, a most pleasant fruit (v. 7), and he repeats it (v. 8): "they *shall be*—that is, they will be to me—*as clusters of the vine*, which *make glad the heart*" (Ps 104:15). "Now that I come *up to the palm tree*, your graces will be stimulated and exercised." *The smell of* their nostrils (of their breath) is *like the smell of apples* (v. 8), or oranges, which is pleasing and reviving. *The roof of her mouth is like the best wine* (v. 9); her spiritual taste and enjoyment of the words she speaks to God and other people, which come from *the roof of the mouth*, are pleasing to God. *The prayer of the upright is his delight* (Pr 15:8). It is like wine that is full of flavor. It *goes down sweetly* (v. 9). Nothing *goes down so sweetly* with a gracious soul as the wine of God's deep assurance. The presence of Christ by his Spirit with his people will be reviving and refreshing to them, like the strong wine that makes *the lips even of those that are asleep*—those who are ready to faint away in a fever — *to speak* (v. 9). Unconverted sinners are asleep; saints are often sleepy and listless; but the word and Spirit of Christ will put life and energy into the soul, and *out of the abundance of the heart* that is filled in this way *the mouth will speak* (Mt 12:34).

Verses 10–13

These are the words of the bride, the church, the believing soul.

1. She triumphs here in her relationship with Christ. She says with holy delight (v. 10), "*I am my beloved's*, not my own, but completely devoted to him and acknowledged by him." Glorying in the fact that she is his and desiring to serve him, she encourages herself with the knowledge that his *desire is toward her* (v. 10). Christ's desire was strongly toward his chosen remnant when he came from heaven to earth to seek and save them (Lk 19:10). It is a comfort to believers that, whoever shows them any disrespect, Christ still loves them. Such desire will again bring him from heaven to earth to receive them to himself.

2. She humbly and fervently desires fellowship with him (vv. 11–12): "*Come, my beloved*, let us walk together so that I may receive advice, instruction, and encouragement from you and may freely tell you my needs and sorrows, without interruption." Similarly, Christ walked with the two disciples who were going to the village called Emmaus, and he talked with them till he made their *hearts burn within them* (Lk 24:32). She wants to go out into the fields and villages to have such fellowship with him. Those who want to talk with Christ must leave the world; they must avoid everything that would distract their minds and hinder the conversation. They should be wholly taken up with Christ. *Let us get up early to the vineyards* (v. 12). This shows she is concerned to make the most of opportunities of talking with her beloved. She will be content to take up her lodging in the villages. His presence will make them fine and pleasant. A gracious soul can come to terms with the poorest accommodations as long as it may have fellowship with God in them.

3. She desires to come to know better the state of her own soul, the present disposition of its affairs (v. 12): *Let us see if the vine flourish*. Our own souls are our vineyards. We are made keepers of these vineyards, and so we should be concerned to look into them often, to examine the state of our own souls to see whether the *vine flourishes*, whether we are fruitful in the fruits of righteousness. Let us especially ask whether *the tender grapes appear* and whether *the pomegranates bud forth* (v. 12), what good attitudes there are in us that are still only young and tender, so that they may be protected and nurtured with special care and may produce mature fruit. And if we want to get to know ourselves more, we must beg him to search and test us (Ps 139:23), to help us in the search and reveal us to ourselves.

4. She promises her beloved the best reception she can give him, for he will come in to us and will eat with us (Rev 3:20).

4.1. She promises him her best devotion.

4.2. She promises him her best provisions (v. 13). "We will find pleasant scents there, for *the mandrakes give a smell*. We will also find what is good for food, as well as delightful to the eye (Ge 3:6): *At our gates are all manner of pleasant fruits*" (v. 13). The fruits and exercises of grace are pleasant to the Lord Jesus. These must be carefully devoted to his service and honor; they must always be available, as what is stored up at our gates. There is a wide variety of these pleasant fruits, and our souls should

be well stocked with them; we must have grace for every occasion. Those who truly love Christ will think all they have, even their most *pleasant fruits* (v. 13), and what they have treasured up most carefully, to be too little to be given to him.

CHAPTER 8

The affection between Christ and his bride is as strong as ever in this final chapter of the song. 1. The bride continues her bold request for more intimate fellowship with him (vv. 1–3). 2. She charges the daughters of Jerusalem not to interrupt her fellowship with her beloved (v. 4), and they wonder at her dependence on him (v. 5). 3. She begs her beloved to confirm by his grace that blessed union with him to which she was admitted (vv. 6–7). 4. She makes intercession for others also, that they might be cared for (vv. 8–9) 5. She recognizes that she is his tenant for a vineyard she holds for him at Baal Hamon (vv. 11–12). 6. The song concludes with an exchange of parting requests. Christ charges his bride to let him hear from her often (v. 13), and she begs him to come back to her quickly (v. 14).

Verses 1–4

Here:

1. The bride wants constant intimacy and freedom with the Lord Jesus Christ. She was obliged to refrain from intimacy and keep some distance away. She therefore wishes she may be taken as his sister, since he has called her so (5:1), and that she may have the same pure and innocent familiarity with him that a sister has with a brother. It is the wish of all believers to enjoy more intimate fellowship with Christ so that they might *receive the Spirit of sanctification* (2Th 2:13) and so that Christ might be as their brother, that is, so that they may be as his brothers and sisters, which they are when by grace they participate in the divine nature (2Pe 1:4).

2. She promises herself that she would then have the satisfaction of making a more open profession of her relationship with him than she can make at present: "*When I should find thee without* (outside), anywhere, even in front of other people, *I would kiss thee* (v. 1), as a sister does her own brother." Since Christ's incarnation, the church can acknowledge him better than she could before, when she would have been laughed at for being so much in love with One who had not yet been born. Christ has become as our brother (Mt 12:50; Heb 2:11); wherever we find him, let us be ready to acknowledge our relationship with him and our love for him.

3. She promises to make the most of the opportunity she would then have to cultivate her friendship with him (v. 2): "*I would lead thee*, as my brother; I would bring *thee into my mother's house*, into the church, into the sacred meetings (3:4), and *there thou wouldst instruct me*." It is Christ's presence in and with his church that makes the word and ordinances instructive to her children, who all want to be taught by God.

4. She promises him that she will make him welcome with the best she has; she will *cause him to drink of her spiced wine and the juice of her pomegranate* (v. 2). The exercise of grace and the fulfillment of our duty are very acceptable to the Lord Jesus, as ways that we express gratitude for his favors.

5. She does not doubt that she will experience his tender care of her, that she will be supported by his power — *His left hand shall be under my head* — and that she will be

comforted by his love—his *right hand shall embrace me.* While we cling to Christ, his *right hand sustains us* (Ps 63:8). *Underneath are the everlasting arms* (Dt 33:27).

6. She charges those around her to do nothing to interrupt the pleasant fellowship she is enjoying with her beloved (v. 4). The church, the mother of us all (Gal 4:26), charges all her children never to do anything to provoke Christ to withdraw.

Verses 5–7

Here:

1. The bride is very much admired by those around her (v. 5). This verse is included as a parenthesis, but in it Gospel grace lies as clearly, and as much on the surface, as anywhere in this mystical song: *Who is this that comes up from the wilderness, leaning upon her beloved?* (v. 5). They are the words of the daughters of Jerusalem, to whom she just now spoke (v. 4); they see her and bless her. The Jewish church came up from the desert supported by God's power and favor (Dt 32:10–11). The Christian church was raised up from lowly desolation by dependence on divine grace (Gal 4:27). Individual believers are wonderful, and divine grace is to be wondered at in them, when by the power of that grace they are brought *up from the wilderness, leaning* (v. 5) with holy confidence *upon* Jesus Christ, *their beloved.* This speaks of the beauty of a soul and also the wonders of divine grace.

2. She speaks to her beloved.

2.1. She reminds him of the experience that she and others have had of encouragement in turning to him.

2.1.1. On her own part: "*I raised thee up under the apple tree* (v. 5), that is, I have many times wrestled with you in prayer and been successful. When I was alone in my devotion, solitary in the orchard, under *the apple tree,* meditating and praying, then *I raised thee up* (I roused you) (v. 5), to help me and strengthen me," as the disciples woke up Christ in the storm, saying, *Master, carest thou not that we perish?* (Mk 4:38).

2.1.2. Others have had similar experience of strength in Christ. There *thy mother brought thee forth* (v. 5), the universal church, or believing souls, in whom Christ was formed (Gal 4:15). Those who had *travailed* in convictions ultimately *brought forth* in encouragement, and the *pain was forgotten* for joy of the Savior's birth (Jn 16:21–22).

2.2. She begs him that her union with him might be confirmed, and her fellowship with him continued and made even more intimate (v. 6): *Set me as a seal upon thy heart, as a seal upon thy arm.* "May I have a place in your heart, the privilege of knowing your love. Be my high priest; may my name be written on your breastpiece, close to your heart. May your power be active for me as evidence of your love for me; may I be not only *a seal upon thy heart* but also *a seal upon thy arm* (v. 6); may I always be carried in your arms and be sure of it."

2.3. To support this request, she pleads the power of love.

2.3.1. Love is a vigorous passion. It is *strong as death* (v. 6). Christ's love for us was *strong as death;* it broke through death itself. *He loved us, and gave himself for us* (Eph 5:2). The love of true believers for Christ is *strong as death,* for it makes them dead to everything else. *Jealousy is cruel as the grave* (v. 6), which swallows up and devours all; those who truly love Christ are jealous of everything that would draw them away from him. *The coals thereof* burn with incredible power and irresistible force, as the *coals of fire that have a most vehement flame,* "a flame of

the Lord," as some understand it. Holy love is a fire that gives birth to an intense heat in the soul and burns up its dross and chaff.

2.3.2. Love is a valiant and victorious passion. Holy love is so; the reigning love of God in the soul is constant and firm and will not be drawn away from him by *life or death* (Ro 8:38). Death, and all its terrors, will not frighten a believer away from loving Christ; although *many waters* will quench fire, they *cannot quench this love;* not even will *floods drown it* (v. 7). No waters could quench Christ's love for us, nor will any rivers wash it away; he waded through the greatest difficulties, even seas of blood. Love ruled as king over the waters; let nothing lessen our love for him. Life, and all its comforts, will not entice a believer away from loving Christ. Love will enable us to repel and triumph over temptations from the smiles of the world as much as over those from its frowns.

Verses 8–12

Having sufficiently confirmed that their love for each other is *strong as death* (v. 6) and unbreakable, Christ and his bride are here talking together about their lives. When husband and wife have laid their hearts together, they also put their heads together.

1. They are discussing their sister, their little sister, and what to do with her.

1.1. The bride presents the situation with compassionate concern (v. 8): *We have a little sister, and she has no breasts*—she has not yet grown to puberty—*what shall we do for* this *little sister of ours in the day that she shall be spoken for?*

1.1.1. This may be understood as spoken by the Jewish church concerning the Gentile world. God had promised the church of the Jews in marriage to himself, and she was richly endowed, but what will become of the poor Gentiles? Their condition according to the godly Jews is very wretched; they are *sisters,* but they are *little,* because they are not honored by the knowledge of God; they *have no breasts,* no divine revelation, no Scriptures, no ministers, no encouragement, being *strangers to the covenants of promise* (Eph 2:12). *What shall we do for* them (v. 8)? We can only pity them and pray for them. But now the tables are turned; the Gentiles are promised in marriage to Christ and should return the kindness by having an equal concern for the bringing in of the Jews again, our elder sister, who once had breasts but now has none.

1.1.2. It may also be applied to any others who belong to the election of grace but have not yet been called. They are remotely related to Christ and his church and are sisters to them both, *other sheep that are not of this fold* (Jn 10:16; Ac 18:10). Those who through grace are brought to Christ themselves should seek what they may do to help others come to him, to carry out the great purpose of his Gospel, which is to bring souls to Christ, to convert sinners to the One whom they have left.

1.2. Christ soon determines what to do in this case, and his bride agrees with him (v. 9): "*If she be a wall,* if the good work has been begun (Php 1:6) with the Gentiles, with the souls that are to be called in, if the *little sister, when she shall be spoken for* (v. 8) by the Gospel, will only receive the word and build on Christ the foundation (1Co 3:11), *we will build upon her a palace of silver* (v. 9). We will carry on the good work that has begun until the wall becomes a palace, the wall of stone a palace of silver." Once this *little sister* is united with the Lord, she will *grow into a holy temple, a habitation* (a dwelling) *of God through the Spirit* (Eph 2:21–22). *If she be a door*

(v. 9), then when this palace is finished, *we will enclose her with boards of cedar* (v. 9). Although the beginnings of grace are small, they will greatly increase in the end. The church is concerned for those who have not yet been called. Christ says, "Leave it to me to do all that is necessary for them. Trust me to do this."

1.3. The bride takes this opportunity to acknowledge with thankfulness his kindness toward her (v. 10). She is very willing to trust him with her *little sister*, for she herself has had great experience of his grace, and on her part, she owes everything to him: *I am a wall, and my breasts like towers. Then was I in his eyes as one that found favour* (v. 10). With what joy and triumph we should speak of God's grace toward us, and with what assurance we should look back on the special times and seasons when *we were in his eyes as those that find favour* (v. 10); those days are never to be forgotten.

2. They are discussing *a vineyard* they have in the country, the church of Christ on earth considered in the form of *a vineyard* (vv. 11–12): *Solomon had a vineyard at Baal-hamon*. His vineyard was a type of the church of Christ. Our Savior has given us a key to these verses in the parable of the vineyard rented out to ungrateful farmers (Mt 21:33–41). The bargain was that each one of the tenants had so much of the vineyard assigned to him as would contain 1,000 vines, and each was to pay the annual rent of *a thousand pieces of silver* (v. 11), for we read (Isa 7:23) that in a fruitful soil there were *a thousand vines at a thousand silverlings* (worth a thousand silver shekels).

2.1. Christ's church is his vineyard, a pleasant place; he delights to walk in it and is pleased with its fruits.

2.2. He has entrusted each of us with his vineyard, as *keepers of* it. The privileges of the church are the good that he has committed to us, to be kept as a sacred trust. The service of the church is to be our business.

2.3. He expects rent from those who are employed in his vineyard and entrusted with it. *He comes, seeking fruit* (Lk 13:7) and requires all those who enjoy privileges under the Gospel to fulfill its duties.

2.4. Although Christ has *let out his vineyard to keepers* (v. 11), it is still his, and he always has his eye on it for good. Some take these as Christ's words (v. 12): *My vineyard, which is mine, is before me*; and they notice how he lives on his property: it is *my vineyard, which is mine*; his church is so precious to him; it is *his own in the world* (Jn 13:1), and so he will always protect it.

2.5. But the church, which enjoys the privileges of the vineyard, must have the privileges always in mind. The keeping of the vineyard requires constant care and conscientiousness. And so these are actually the words of the spouse: *My vineyard, which is mine, is before me* (v. 12). She has mourned her own fault and foolishness in not keeping her *own vineyard* (1:6), but now she decides to mend her ways. Our hearts are our vineyards, and we must *keep* them *with all diligence* (Pr 4:23).

2.6. Our great concern must be to pay our rent for what we have of Christ's vineyard. *Thou, O Solomon! must have a thousand* shekels (v. 12), and you will have. The main profits belong to Christ; all our fruits must be dedicated to him.

2.7. If we are careful to give Christ the praise for our church privileges, we may then allow ourselves their encouragement and benefit. If the owner of the vineyard receives his due, its keepers will be well paid for their effort and pains; they will have 200 shekels, a sum that no doubt was looked on as a good profit.

Verses 13–14

Christ and his bride are here apart for a while; she must stay below *in the gardens* (v. 13) on earth, where she has work to do for him; he must move to *the mountains of spices* (the spice-laden mountains) (v. 14) in heaven, where he has business to attend to for her, as *an advocate with the Father* (1Jn 2:1).

1. He desires to hear often from her. "*Thou that*, for the present, *dwellest in the gardens*, tending and keeping them until you move from the garden below to the paradise *above—thou*, O believer! *that dwellest in the gardens* of sacred worship, *in the gardens* of church fellowship— *the companions* are so happy to hear *thy voice; cause me to hear it* too." *The communion of saints is* an article of our covenant as well as an article of our creed; we are *to exhort one another daily* (Heb 3:13). *Hearken to the voice* (v. 13) of the church, as far as it agrees with the voice of Christ. In the midst of our fellowship with one another we must not neglect our fellowship with Christ; he speaks of this here: "*The companions hearken to thy voice*; it is a pleasure to them; *cause me to hear it* (v. 13). Pour out your heart to me." We *cause him to hear* (v. 13) our prayers when we not only pray but wrestle and strive in prayer.

2. She wants him to return quickly to her (v. 14): "*Make haste, my beloved*, to come again and receive me to yourself; *be thou like a roe, or a young hart, upon the mountains of spices*." *Even so, come, Lord Jesus, come quickly* (Rev 20:22). True believers are also moving quickly toward what they are looking for, the coming of that *day of the Lord*. The bride, after an endearing discussion with her beloved, finds that it must end, and so she concludes with this affectionate request for the perfecting of this happiness in the future state forever. It is good to conclude our devotions with a joyful expectation of the glory to be revealed and holy, humble longings for it. We should not part except with the prospect of meeting again. It is good to conclude every Sabbath with thoughts of the eternal Sabbath, which will have no night at its end, nor any weekday to follow it. It is good to conclude every sacrament with thoughts of the eternal feast, when we will all sit down with Christ at his table in his kingdom. And it is good to end every religious meeting in the hope of *the general assembly of the church of the firstborn* (Heb 12:23), when there will be no more time and days.

A PRACTICAL AND DEVOTIONAL EXPOSITION OF THE BOOK OF THE PROPHET

Isaiah

A prophet is one who enjoys great intimacy with heaven and great privileges there and so has commanding authority on earth. Prophecy was most usually communicated by dreams, voices, or visions, first to prophets and then by them to the people (Nu 12:6). Before the sacred canon of the Old Testament began to be written, there were prophets who served the church in place of Bibles. Our Savior seems to count Abel among the prophets (Mt 23:31, 35). Enoch was a prophet; Noah was a preacher of righteousness (2Pe 2:5). God said about Abraham, *he is a prophet* (Ge 20:7). Jacob foretold things to come (Ge 49:1). Moses was incomparably the most famous of all the Old Testament prophets, for the Lord spoke to him *face to face* (Dt 34:10).

But after the death of Moses, for some time the Spirit of the Lord appeared and acted in the church of Israel more as a military spirit than as a spirit of prophecy; in the time of the judges, he inspired people more to act than to speak. We find the Spirit of the Lord coming on Othniel, Gideon, Samson, and others to serve their country with their swords, not their pens. In all the book of Judges there is not one mention of a prophet [Ed. note: Matthew Henry seems to have overlooked the unnamed prophet of Jdg 6:8], except that Deborah is called *a prophetess* (Jdg 4:4). Then the word of the Lord was rare; there were not many visions (1Sa 3:1).

But prophecy revived in Samuel, and in him a famous period of the church began, a time of great light in a constant and uninterrupted succession of prophets, until some time after the Exile, when the canon of the Old Testament was completed. Then prophecy ceased for nearly 400 years. We read about prophets raised up for special public services, among whom the most famous were Elijah and Elisha in the kingdom of Israel. There was nothing of their own writing except one letter of Elijah (2Ch 21:12).

Toward the end of the kingdoms of Judah and Israel, however, it pleased God to direct his servants the prophets to write some of their sermons. The dates of many of their prophecies are uncertain, but the earliest of them may have been in the days of Uzziah (Azariah) king of Judah (2Ch 26) and Jeroboam II (2Ki 14:23–29), his contemporary, king of Israel, about 200 years before the Exile, not long after Joash had killed Zechariah the son of Jehoiada (2Ch 24:20–21). Even if they begin to murder the prophets, they will not be able to murder their prophecies; these will remain as witnesses against them. Hosea may have been the first of the prophets to write down his prophecy, and Joel, Amos, and Obadiah may have circulated their prophecies about the same time. Isaiah began a little later, but his prophecy is placed first because it is the longest and speaks most about the One to whom all the prophets bore witness (Ro 3:21–22). Indeed it contains so much of Christ that Isaiah is justly called "the evangelical prophet" and, by some of the old commentators, "the fifth Evangelist." Here we read:

1. About the prophet himself. He was, if we may believe the tradition of the Jews, of the royal family; it is said his father was the brother of King Uzziah. He was certainly often at court, especially in Hezekiah's time. The Spirit of God sometimes served his own purpose by the particular genius of the prophet, for prophets were not megaphones, through which the Spirit spoke, but speaking human beings, by whom the Spirit spoke, making use of their natural powers, both their light and their fire, and advancing them beyond themselves.

2. About his prophecy. It is transcendently useful, serving to bring about conviction of sin, direction in duty, and comfort in trouble. Two great distresses of the church are referred to here: Sennacherib's invasion, which happened in Isaiah's own time, and the exile in Babylon, which happened long after. In the encouragement laid up for these times of need we find much of the grace of the Gospel (Heb 4:16). There are not as many quotations in the Gospels from any other prophecy of the Old Testament, perhaps not from all the other prophecies, as from this one, nor such explicit testimonies concerning Christ, for example, that of his being born of a virgin (7:14) and of his sufferings (ch. 53). The beginning of this book contains

many rebukes for sin and threats of judgment; its end is full of good and comforting words. The Spirit of Christ formerly used this method in the prophets, and he does so still; he first convinces and then comforts, for those who want to be blessed by comfort must first submit to conviction.

CHAPTER 1

The first verse of this chapter is intended as a title for the whole book. The sermon in this chapter contains: 1. A great accusation in God's name against the Jewish church and nation for their ingratitude (vv. 2–3), for their incorrigibleness (v. 5), for the universal corruption of the people (vv. 4, 6, 21–22), and for the perversion of justice by their rulers (v. 23). 2. A sad complaint about the judgments of God that they had brought on themselves by their sins and by which they were brought to almost complete destruction (vv. 7–9). 3. A just rejection of this shadow of religion that they kept up among them despite their general apostasy (vv. 10–15). 4. A serious call to repentance and reformation, setting before them life and death (Dt 30:15, 19) (vv. 16–20). 5. A threat of destruction to those who would not be reformed (vv. 28–31). 6. A promise of a happy reformation ultimately, and a return to their original purity and prosperity (vv. 25–27).

Verse 1

Here is:

1. The name of the prophet, *Isaiah*, which in the New Testament is read as *Esaias* (Isaiah). His name means "the salvation of the Lord"—a proper name, especially for this prophet, who prophesies so much about Jesus the Savior and the great salvation he brought. He is said to be *the son of Amoz* (v. 1), the brother, or son, of Amaziah king of Judah, though this tradition is as uncertain as that rule the Jews give that, where a prophet's father is named, the father also was himself a prophet.

2. The nature of the prophecy. It is a vision. The prophets were called *seers*, and so their prophecies are appropriately called *visions*. It was what Isaiah saw with the eyes of his mind, and he foresaw as clearly by divine revelation as if he had seen it with his physical eyes.

3. The subject of the prophecy. There are some chapters in this book about Babylon, Egypt, Tyre, and other neighboring nations, but it takes its title from what is its main substance and is therefore said to be *concerning Judah and Jerusalem* (v. 1). Isaiah brings to them especially:

3.1. Instruction, for they were entrusted with the very words of God (Ro 3:2; 9:4).

3.2. Rebuke and threats, for if sin is found in Judah, or in Salem (Ps 76:2), they will be judged for it sooner than any other people.

3.3. Comfort and encouragement in evil times, for the children of Zion will be joyful in their king (Ps 149:2).

4. The date of the prophecy. Isaiah prophesied *in the days of Uzziah, Jotham, Ahaz,* and *Hezekiah* (v. 1). By this it appears:

4.1. That he prophesied for a long time, especially if, as the Jews say, he was finally put to death by Manasseh, being sawn in two, to which some think the writer to the Hebrews refers (Heb 11:37). From the year that King Uzziah died (6:1) to Hezekiah's sickness and recovery was about forty-seven years; how much he prophesied before and after this is not certain.

4.2. That he passed through wide-ranging times. Jotham was a good king, and Hezekiah a better one, and no doubt both of them took advice from this prophet, but

between them, and when Isaiah was in the prime of his life, the reign of Ahaz was very ungodly and evil.

Verses 2–9

1. Although the prophet speaks in God's name, he still despairs to gain the hearing of his people, and so he addresses himself to the heavens and the earth (v. 2): *Hear, O heavens! and give ear, O earth!* Inanimate creatures, which observe the law and fulfill the purpose of their creation, are more likely to listen than this stupid and senseless people. Let the lights of heaven shame their darkness, the fruitfulness of the earth shame their barrenness, and the strictness of each to its time shame their irregularity. Moses begins in this way in Dt 32:1.

2. He accuses them of sheer ingratitude. Let heaven and earth listen and wonder at:

2.1. God's gracious dealings with such a perverse and offensive people: "I have nourished and brought them up as children; they have been well fed and well taught" (Dt 32:6).

2.2. Their ill-natured behavior toward him, who was so kind to them: *"They have rebelled against me."*

3. He attributes their rebellion to their ignorance and inconsideration (v. 3): *The ox knows, but Israel does not.* Notice:

3.1. The intelligence of the ox and the donkey, creatures of the stupidest kind. The ox, however, has such a sense of duty as to know its owner and to serve them. The donkey has such a sense of interest as to know where its master feeds it and to stay there. Human beings are shamed in knowledge by these silly animals and are not only sent to school with them (Pr 6:6–7) but put in a class below them (Jer 8:7).

3.2. The foolishness and stupidity of Israel. God is their owner. He made us and has provided well for us, but many who are called the people of God ask, *"What is the Almighty, that we should serve him?"* (Job 21:15). They do not know or understand. They know, but their knowledge does them no good because they do not consider and understand what they know; they do not apply it to their situation or put their minds to it. A lack of consideration of what we do know is as great an enemy to us in religious faith as ignorance of what we should know. People rebel from God and rebel against him.

4. He mourns the corruption of their church and kingdom. The disease of sin was epidemic, and all kinds of people had become infected by it: *Ah sinful nation!* (v. 4).

4.1. Their evil was universal. They were a sinful nation; most of the people were evil and ungodly. Their evil lay on them as *a talent of lead* (Zec 5:7–8). They came from bad families and were a *seed of evildoers* (v. 4). Treachery ran in their blood. They were a race and family of rebels. They were not only corrupt children but also *children that were corrupters* (v. 4), who spread evil and infected others with it. *They have provoked the Holy One of Israel unto anger* (v. 4) willfully and deliberately; they knew what would anger him, and they did it.

4.2. He illustrates it by a comparison taken from a sick and diseased body that has an infectious skin disease all over it or, like Job's, is covered by painful sores (vv. 5–6). The disease has caught hold of the vital organs and so threatens to be fatal. They have become corrupt in their judgment: the disease has reached the head. It has spread over the whole body and so has become extremely deadly. There is *no soundness* (v. 6), no good motives, no religious faith—for that is a sign of a sound and healthy soul—nothing but *wounds and bruises* (v. 6), guilt and corruption. No attempts have been made toward reformation, or, if they have been, they have proved ineffective: the wounds *have not been closed, nor bound up, nor mollified with ointment* (v. 6). While sin remains unrepented of, the wounds are not dealt with or closed up, and nothing is done toward healing them.

5. He sadly mourns the judgments of God that they have brought on themselves. Their kingdom has been almost devastated (v. 7). "Look and see how things are; *your country is desolate*; and as for the fruits of your land, which should be food for your families, *strangers devour them* (v. 7) *before your eyes*. You cannot prevent it; you starve while your enemies are sating themselves." Jerusalem, which is like the Daughter of Zion—the temple built on Zion was a mother to Jerusalem—is now lost, deserted, and exposed *as a cottage* (shelter) *in a vineyard* (v. 8), which, when the vine harvest has finished, nobody lives in. Everyone is afraid of coming near it as if it were *a besieged city* (v. 8). This sermon was probably preached in the reign of Ahaz, when Judah was being invaded by the kings of Syria and Israel, the Edomites and the Philistines, who killed many people and took many away into exile (2Ch 28:5, 17–18). National ungodliness and immorality bring national desolation. But they did not mend their ways, and so God threatened to act differently with them (v. 5). By way of righteous judgment, God sometimes stops correcting those who have hardened themselves against him, because he intends to destroy them for their hardness.

6. He comforts himself with the consideration of a remnant that will be a testament to divine grace and mercy despite the general corruption and devastation (v. 9). *The Lord of hosts left unto them a very small remnant* (v. 9), who were kept pure from the general apostasy and kept safe and alive from the general disaster. This is quoted by the apostle Paul (Ro 9:29) and applied to those few of the Jewish nation who embraced Christianity in his time. This remnant is often very small. Numbers are no mark of the true church. Christ's flock is little (Lk 12:32). It is good for a people who have been saved from complete destruction to look back and see how close they came to it, to see how much they owed to a few good people who stood in the gap (Eze 22:30), and to see that that was because of a good God who left them these good people.

Verses 10–15

Here:

1. God calls out to them to listen to his word, but in vain (v. 10). The title he gives them is very strange: *You rulers of Sodom* and *people of Gomorrah*. This suggests that God would have been righteous if he had dealt with them like Sodom and Gomorrah (v. 9). The rulers are boldly attacked here by the prophet as rulers of Sodom, for he does not know how to give them a flattering title. The tradition of the Jews is that long afterward he was put to death for this. His demand of them is very reasonable: "*Hear the word of the Lord* and *give ear to the law of our God* (v. 10); listen to what God has to say to you, and let his word be a law to you."

2. He justly refuses to listen to their prayers and accept their services, their sacrifices and burnt offerings, the fat and blood of the sacrifices (v. 11), their attendance at his courts (v. 12), their offerings, their incense, and their sacred assemblies (v. 13), their New Moon festivals and their appointed feasts (v. 14), their most devout prayers (v. 15). These are all rejected, because their hands are full of blood.

2.1. There are many who are strangers, even enemies, to the power of religious faith, but who seem very zealous for its external forms and shadows (2Ti 3:5; Col 2:17). This sinful nation brought many sacrifices to the altar of the God of Israel, both fellowship offerings, which they themselves shared in, and burnt offerings, which were wholly consumed to the honor of God; and their sacrifices were the best of their kind. They prayed often, offered many prayers, thinking they would be heard for their many words (Mt 6:7), but their hearts were empty of true devotion. They came to *appear* before God (v. 12), "to be seen" before him, as the margin reads. Their hands were full of blood: they were guilty of committing murder, pillage, and oppression in the name of law and justice. In God's sight, malice is murder committed in the heart; someone who hates their brother in their heart has, in effect, their hands full of blood.

2.2. When sinners come under the judgments of God, they will more easily be brought to flee to their devotions than to abandon their sins and reform their lives.

2.3. The most ostentatious and costly devotions of evildoers, without a thorough reformation of the heart and life, are so far from being acceptable to God that they are really detestable to him. A great variety of expressions is given here to show that *to obey is better than sacrifice* (1Sa 15:22), that, in fact, sacrifice without obedience is nothing but an insult and offense to God. Their sacrifices are here described as useless and unimportant: *To what purpose is the multitude of your sacrifices?* (v. 11). They are meaningless offerings (v. 13). Their attention to God's institutions is all futile and does not serve any good purpose: *Who has required these things at your hands?* (v. 12). They pray, but God will not listen, for although they offer many prayers, none of them come from an upright heart. "They are *your* sacrifices; they are not mine. I am full of them, I am sated with them." Their coming into his courts he calls *treading them*, or trampling on them. Even though their incense is very fragrant, it is detestable to him, for it is burned in hypocrisy and with evil intentions. He cannot bear their sacred assemblies; he cannot consider them with any patience. God is never weary of listening to the prayers of the upright, but he soon becomes weary of the costly sacrifices of evildoers. Sin is hateful to God, so hateful that it makes even people's prayers and their religious services hateful to him. Pretended godliness is double iniquity

Verses 16–20

Notice:

1. A call to repentance and reformation: "If you want to have your sacrifices accepted and your prayers answered, you must begin your work at the right end. Be converted to my law, but otherwise do not expect to be accepted in your devotion." As justice and charity will never atone for godlessness and ungodliness, so prayers and sacrifices will never atone for fraud and oppression.

1.1. They must *cease to do evil*, must do no more wrong, shed no more innocent blood. This is the meaning of washing themselves and *making themselves clean* (v. 16). We must not only put away the evil of our actions by abstaining from gross acts of sin but also crush and put to death the roots and habits of sin that are in our hearts.

1.2. They must *learn to do well* (v. 17). This was necessary to complete their repentance. We must do good, the good that the Lord our God requires. We must learn to do well, make an effort to gain the knowledge of our duty. He urges them particularly to do the duties of the second table of the Ten Commandments: "*Seek judgment* (justice) (v. 17); ask what is right, so that you may do it. *Relieve the oppressed* (v. 17). Avenge those who suffer wrong, and the fatherless and the widows, who, because they are weak and helpless, are trampled on by proud people and are abused by them. Speak up for those who do not know how to speak for themselves and who do not have the resources to repay you for your kindness."

2. A demonstration, in the court of right reason, of the justice of God's proceedings with them: "*Come now, and let us reason together* (v. 18). While your hands are full of blood, I will have nothing to do with you, even though you bring me many sacrifices. If you wash and make yourselves clean, however, you are welcome to draw near to me. Come on, let us talk the matter over." Religious faith has reason on its side; there is every reason in the world why we should do as God wants us to do. The case needs only to be stated, and it will settle itself.

2.1. They could not reasonably expect any more than that if they repented and reformed, they would be restored to God's favor despite their former offenses. Here no penance is imposed, nor is the yoke made heavier. He does not say, "If you are perfectly obedient," but, "If you are *willingly* so," for if there is a willing mind, it is accepted. All their sins would be pardoned and would not be mentioned against them. Although our sins have been as scarlet and crimson, as deep dye, although we have often been dipped into sin by our frequent backsliding, and though we have lain soaking a long time in it, as the cloth does in the scarlet dye, pardoning mercy will thoroughly cleanse the stain. If we make ourselves clean by repentance and reformation (v. 16), God will make us white by complete forgiveness. "Only be willing and obedient, and *you shall eat the good of the land* (v. 19), the Land of Promise." If sin is pardoned, assurance is real.

2.2. They could not reasonably expect anything else than that if they obstinately continued in their disobedience, the sentence of the law would be carried out on them (v. 20).

Verses 21–31

Here:

1. The wretched corruption of Judah and Jerusalem is sadly mourned. The royal city used to be a faithful city, faithful to God and the interests of his kingdom, faithful to the nation and its public interests. *It was full of judgment* (justice) (v. 21); justice was properly administered: *Righteousness lodged in it* (v. 21). But that beautiful, lovely bride has now become a prostitute; righteousness no longer lives in Jerusalem; even murderers live undisturbed there. The rulers themselves are so cruel and oppressive that they have become no better than murderers. The corruption of Jerusalem is illustrated by metaphors (v. 22): *Thy silver has become dross.* The degenerate condition of the magistrates is as great a disgrace and wrong to the kingdom as would be the debasing of their money and the turning of their silver into dross. *Thy wine is mixed with water* (v. 22), and so has become flat and sour. Dross may shine like silver, and wine mixed with water may keep the color of wine, but both are worthless. In this way, they kept up a show and pretense of goodness and justice, but with no true sense of either. The prophet also gives examples of their corruption. "Your rulers, who should keep others loyal to God and obeying his law, are themselves rebellious and defy God and his law. Those who should

restrain thieves are themselves companions of thieves. They throw in their lot with the thieves they protect in their ill-gotten gains. Their only aim is to make as much money as possible, to gain the greatest advantage over them, rightly or wrongly. They should protect those who are wronged, but *they judge not the fatherless* (v. 23); they are not concerned to protect orphans, *nor does the cause of the widow come unto them* (v. 23), because the poor widow can offer no bribe with which to make headway in her cause."

2. A decision is taken up to put right these grievances (v. 24): *Therefore saith the Lord, the Lord of hosts, the Mighty One of Israel—who* has power to fulfill what he says—*Ah! I will ease me of* (get relief from) *my adversaries.* God will find a time and a way to relieve himself of this burden. If God's professing people do not conform to his image as the Holy One of Israel (v. 4), they will feel the weight of his hand as the Mighty One of Israel. God will relieve himself of this grievance in two ways:

2.1. By reforming his church and replacing corrupt judges with good ones. Although the church contains a great deal of dross, it will still not be completely rejected, but will be refined (v. 25): "*I will purely purge away thy dross.* Evil will be suppressed and oppressors deprived of their power to cause trouble." The reformation of a people is God's own work: "*I will turn my hand upon thee* (v. 25); I will do for the revival of religious faith what I did in the beginning in planting it." He does it by blessing them with good judges and ministers of state (v. 26): "*I will restore thy judges as at the first*, to enact laws against evildoers, *and thy counsellors*, to deal with public affairs, *as at the beginning*." He does it by planting in people's minds motives of justice and ruling their lives by those motives (v. 27). People may do much by external restraints, but God does it effectively by the influences of *his Spirit*. All the redeemed of the Lord (Ps 107:2; Isa 51:11) will be converts, and their conversion is their redemption: "*Her converts*, or 'they that return of her' (v. 27, margin), will be redeemed with righteousness." The reviving of a people's goodness is the restoring of their honor: *Afterwards thou shalt be called the city of righteousness* (v. 26).

2.2. By cutting off those who hate to be reformed. They will be destroyed, not merely disciplined. The openly ungodly, who have completely rejected all religion, and the hypocrites, who live evil lives under the cloak of religious profession, will be destroyed together. *And those that forsake the Lord*, to whom they formerly united themselves, *shall be consumed* (will perish) (v. 28), as water in a pipe soon stops when its supply is cut off. Their idols will not be able to help them, *the oaks which they have desired, and the gardens which they have chosen* (v. 29), that is, the images which they have worshiped in their groves and under the green trees (1Ki 14:23), for which they abandoned the true God, and which they have worshiped privately in their own garden. This was the practice of sinners, but they will be ashamed of it, not with a show of repentance, but of despair (v. 29). They will be ashamed of their idols, for the idols themselves *shall go into captivity* (46:1–2). They will not be able to help themselves (v. 31): "*Even the strong man shall be as tow* (will become tinder), not only soon broken and pulled to pieces but also easily catching fire, and 'his work' (v. 31, margin) will be as a spark to his own tinder."

3. Now all this can be applied to:

3.1. The sacred work of reformation that was brought about in Hezekiah's time after the detestable corruption of the reign of Ahaz.

3.2. Their return from exile in Babylon.

3.3. The Gospel kingdom and the outpouring of the Spirit, by which the New Testament church would be made a New Jerusalem, a city of righteousness (v. 26).

3.4. The second coming of Christ, when he will thoroughly clear his threshing floor (Mt 3:12).

CHAPTER 2

With this chapter there begins a new sermon, which is continued in the following two chapters. The subject is Judah and Jerusalem (v. 1). In this chapter the prophet speaks about: 1. The glory of the Christians, Jerusalem, the Gospel church in the final days, about the admission of many people into it (vv. 2–3) and the great peace it would introduce to the world (v. 4), from which he infers the duty of the house of Jacob (v. 5). 2. The shame of the Jews, Jerusalem as it then was and as it would be after its rejection of the Gospel and its being rejected by God. 2.1. Their sin was their shame (vv. 6–9). 2.2. By his judgments, God would humble them and put them to shame (vv. 10–17). 2.3. They themselves would be ashamed of their confidence in their idols and in human strength (vv. 18–22).

Verses 1–5

The particular title of this sermon (v. 1) is the same as the general title of the book (1:1), except what is called there the *vision* is here called *the word which Isaiah saw*. This sermon begins with the prophecy relating to the last days, the days of the Messiah, when his kingdom would be set up in the world, at the end of the Mosaic dispensation. In the last days of the earthly Jerusalem, just before its destruction, this heavenly Jerusalem would be set up (Heb 12:22; Gal 4:26). Gospel times are the last days, for:

- They were waited for a long time by the Old Testament saints but came ultimately.
- We are not to look for any dispensation of divine grace except what we have in the Gospel (Gal 1:8–9).
- We are to look forward to the second coming of Jesus Christ at the end of time (1Jn 2:18).

The prophet here foretells:

1. The planting of the Christian faith in the world. Christianity will then be *the mountain of the Lord's house* (v. 2). The Gospel church will then be the meeting place of all the spiritual descendants of Abraham (Gal 3:29). It is promised here:

1.1. That Christianity will be openly preached and professed; it will be "prepared" (v. 2, margin) on the top of the everlasting mountains, in the view and hearing of all. What the apostles did was not *done in a corner* (Ac 26:26). It was the lighting of a beacon and the setting up of a standard.

1.2. That it will be firmly fixed and rooted; it will be established on the top of the eternal mountains, built on *a rock*, so that the *gates of hell shall not prevail against it* (Mt 16:18)—unless they could uproot the mountains.

1.3. That it will not only overcome all opposition but also rise above all rivals; it will be *exalted above the hills* (v. 2). This *wisdom of God in a mystery* (1Co 2:7) will surpass all the wisdom of this world, all its philosophy and all its politics.

2. The bringing of the Gentiles into the Christian church.

2.1. The nations will be allowed into it, even the uncircumcised, who were forbidden to come into the courts of the temple at Jerusalem.

2.2. *All nations shall flow into it* (v. 2); having free access, many will embrace the Christian faith.

3. The mutual help and encouragement that this stream of converts will give to one another. "*Come, and let us go up to the mountain of the Lord*; although the way is uphill and against the heart, it is *the mountain of the Lord*, who will help the willingness of our souls toward him." The Gospel church is here called not only *the mountain of the Lord* but also *the house of the God of Jacob* (v. 3), for in it God's covenant with Jacob and his praying descendants is maintained and has its fulfillment. It is worthwhile to make the effort to go up to his holy mountain to be taught his ways, and those who are willing to make that effort will never find that their labor is in vain (1Co 15:58). "If he will *teach us his ways*, we will *walk in his paths* (v. 3); if he will let us know our duty, we will by his grace carefully do it."

4. The means by which this will be brought about: *Out of Zion shall go forth the law* (v. 3), the New Testament law, the law of Christ, as formerly the Law of Moses from Mount Sinai, *the word of the Lord from Jerusalem* (v. 3). The Gospel is a law, a law of faith; it is the *word of the Lord*. And in the temple on Mount Zion the disciples preached the Gospel (Ac 5:20). It was by this Gospel, which began in Jerusalem, that the Gospel church was established as chief among the mountains (v. 2).

5. The setting up of the kingdom of the Redeemer in the world: *He shall judge among the nations*. By the activity of his Spirit on human consciences he will judge people. He will test people and restrain them; his kingdom is spiritual *and not of this world* (Jn 18:36).

6. The great peace that will be the effect of the success of the Gospel in the world (v. 4): *They shall beat their swords into ploughshares* (v. 4). *Nation shall then not lift up sword against nation*, as they do now, *neither shall they learn war any more* (v. 4), for they will have no more need to do so. The purpose and intention of the Gospel is to make peace and bring all hostility to an end. The Gospel contains the most powerful obligations and incentives for peace. The Gospel of Christ, as far as it is effective, makes people inclined to be peaceful. It softens the human spirit and makes it sweet. When the love of Christ is poured out into the heart (Ro 5:5), it causes people to love one another. The first Christians were well known for their mutual love; even their enemies noticed it. Here is a practical conclusion drawn from all this (v. 5): *O house of Jacob! come you, and let us walk in the light of the Lord.* By the *house of Jacob* is meant either Israel according to the flesh, or spiritual Israel, all who are brought to the God of Jacob. Will God teach us his ways? Will he show us his glory in the face of Christ (2Co 4:6)? Let us walk with assurance in the light of this peace. Will there be no more war? Let us then go on our way rejoicing (Ac 8:39).

Verses 6–9

Here is:

1. Israel's condemnation. This is set out in two words, the first and the last of this paragraph, but they are two terrible words:

1.1. Their case is very sad (v. 6): *Therefore thou hast forsaken thy people.* The people whom God has forsaken are miserable. This was the deplorable case of the Jewish church after they had rejected Christ. *Your house is left unto you desolate* (Mt 23:38).

1.2. Their case is wholly desperate (v. 9): *Therefore forgive them not.* This prophetic prayer amounts to a threat that they will not be forgiven. This does not refer to any particular persons—many of them repented and were forgiven—but to the main group of people that made up that nation.

2. Israel's deserving of this condemnation and the reasons on which it is based. In general, it is sin that provokes God to abandon his people. The particular sins that the prophet specifies are those that were greatly in evidence among them at that time. A partial and temporary rejection of them came with the exile in Babylon, which was a type of their final destruction by the Romans and which the sins mentioned here brought on them. Their sins were of the kind that directly contradicted all God's kind and gracious purposes for them.

2.1. God set them apart for himself as his own people, dignified above all other people (Nu 23:9), but they were *replenished from the east;* they *naturalized* foreigners but did not *convert* them; they encouraged them to settle among them, and they mixed with them (Hos 7:8). Their country was populated by Arameans and Babylonians, Moabites and Ammonites, and when they admitted the people, they admitted also their fashions and customs and thus *pleased themselves in the children of strangers* (v. 6). In this way they dishonored their crown and their covenant.

2.2. God gave them his word, the Scriptures and the prophets, but they slighted these and became soothsayers like the Philistines, introducing divination and listening to those who used the stars, the clouds, the flight of birds, and the entrails of animals. The Philistines were noted diviners (1Sa 6:2).

2.3. God assured them that he would be their wealth and strength, but they distrusted his power and promise and set their hope on gold. They provided themselves with horses and chariots (1Ki 1:5), depending on them for their security (v. 7). It is not having silver and gold, horses and chariots, that is an offense to God, but desiring them insatiably.

2.4. God himself was their God, and he instituted ordinances of worship for them, but they slighted both him and his institutions (v. 8). Their land was full of idols; every city had its god (Jer 11:13). Those who love idols will always want more of them. They were so foolish that they *worshiped the work of their own hands* (v. 8). God had enriched them with silver and gold, but they had used that silver and gold to make idols.

2.5. God had put honor on them, but they had been corrupt (v. 9): *The mean man boweth down to his idol,* a thing below the lowest person that has any spark of reason left. Nor is it only the illiterate who do this; even *the great man* (v. 9) forgets his grandeur and humbles himself to worship idols. He deifies people who are no better than himself, and he consecrates stones that are much baser than he.

Verses 10–22

The prophet here goes on to show what desolation will be brought on their land when God abandons them. This may refer particularly to their destruction first by the Babylonians and later by the Romans. God will find a way:

1. To startle and wake up sinners who defy him and his judgments (v. 10): "*Enter into the rock;* God will attack you with such terrible judgments that you will be forced to *enter into the rock, and hide yourself in the dust, for fear of the Lord.* You will lose all your courage and tremble at the shaking of a leaf" (Lev 26:36). V. 19 is to the same effect: *They shall go into the holes of the rocks, and into the caves of the earth,* the darkest, deepest places. It was particularly like this in the destruction of Jerusalem by the Romans (Lk 23:30) and in the destruction of the persecuting powers (Rev 6:16). And the sinners will do all this *for fear of the Lord, and of the glory of his majesty*

(v. 19). Those who will not fear God and flee to him will be forced to fear him and flee from him to a refuge of lies (28:15). It will be futile to think of finding refuge in the caves of the earth when the earth itself is shaken. There will be no shelter then except in God and in things above (Col 3:2).

2. To humble and abase proud sinners (v. 11): *The lofty looks of man shall be humbled.* It is repeated (v. 17), *The loftiness of man shall be bowed down.* The arrogance of human beings will be humbled either by the grace of God convincing them of the evil of their pride and clothing them with humility (1Pe 5:5) or by the providence of God depriving them of all those things they were proud of and humbling them. This will be done because the *Lord alone will be exalted* (v. 11 and again v. 17). It will be done by humbling judgments that will mortify people and bring them low (v. 12): *The day of the Lord of hosts,* the day of his wrath and judgment, *shall be upon every one that is proud.* This day of the Lord is here said to be on *all the cedars of Lebanon, that are high and lifted up* (v. 13), which were the straightest and loftiest; on the oaks of Bashan, which were the strongest and sturdiest; on the natural elevations, *the high mountains and the hills that are lifted up* (v. 14), which rose up above the valleys and seemed to push back the skies; and on the artificial strongholds, *every high tower and every fenced wall* (v. 15). We may understand these:

2.1. As standing for the proud people themselves, who in their own minds are like the cedars and the oaks, firmly rooted and unable to be stirred by any storm, looking on everyone around them as shrubs. The highest hills are most exposed to lightning. These boastful people, who are like lofty towers in which noisy bells are hung, these fenced walls, which fortify themselves with their native hardiness and entrench themselves in their strongholds, will be brought down.

2.2. As showing the things they are proud of and about which they boast. He will *take from them all their armour wherein they trusted* (Lk 11:22). They were proud of their trade abroad, but the day of the Lord will be *upon all the ships of Tarshish* (v. 16); they will founder at sea or be shipwrecked in harbor. The day of the Lord will be *upon all pleasant pictures* (v. 16), the fine paintings they brought home in their ships from other countries.

3. To make idolaters ashamed of their idols and of the respect they have given them (v. 18): *The idols he shall utterly abolish.* When the Lord alone is exalted (v. 17), he will show contempt not only to arrogant people but also, and much more, to all false gods. Their friends will abandon them; their enemies will destroy them. They cannot even protect themselves, let alone protect their worshipers. Their worshipers will abandon them either from a conviction of their worthlessness and falsehood or from a sad experience of their inability to help them (v. 20). When people are themselves frightened by the judgments of God to flee into the caves in the rocks, they will throw their idols, which they have made their gods and hoped to make their friends in times of need, to the rodents and the bats. God can make people sick of those idols they have been most fond of. Greedy people make silver and gold their idols; they make money their god, but the time may come when they may feel it as much their burden as they made it their confidence. There was a time when the sailors threw the cargo, and even the *wheat, into the sea* (Jnh 1:5; Ac 27:38). The darkest holes, where the rodents and the bats live, are the most appropriate places for idols, because they have eyes but do not see (Ps 115:5; 135:16). It is possible that sin may be both detested and left but not

truly repented of out of love for God, only from a cringing fear of his wrath.

4. To make those who have trusted in human strength ashamed of their confidence (v. 22): "*Cease from man,* stop trusting in human beings. Consider how weak human beings are: their *breath is in their nostrils,* puffed out every moment, soon gone forever. *Put not your trust in man.* Do not fear him. Let him not be your hope, but look up to the power of God, to which all human powers are subject and subordinate. Let your *hope be in the Lord your God*" (Ps 146:5).

CHAPTER 3

In this chapter the prophet continues to foretell the devastations that are coming on Judah and Jerusalem because of their sins, both the devastation by the Babylonians and that by the Romans, which completed their destruction. God threatens: 1. To deprive them of all the supports of both their life and their government (vv. 1–3). 2. To leave them to fall into confusion and disorder (vv. 4–5, 12). 3. To deny them the blessing of judges (vv. 6–8). 4. To strip the daughters of Zion of their ornaments (vv. 17–24). 5. To devastate everything by the sword of war (vv. 25–26). The sins that provoked God were: 5.1. Their defiance of God (v. 8). 5.2. Their arrogance (v. 9). 5.3. The abuse of power in oppression and tyranny (vv. 12–15). 5.4. The pride of the daughters of Zion (v. 16). In the middle of the chapter the prophet is directed to assure good people that things will go well with them (v. 10) and assure evildoers that trouble will still come on them, however much God might remember mercy in judgment (Hab 3:2) (v. 11).

Verses 1–8

God is now about to destroy all the confidence they have placed in the creation, so that they will meet with nothing but disappointments in all their expectations (v. 1): *The stay and the staff* (supply and support) *will be taken away.* Their church and kingdom have now grown old and are decaying, and they are like old people (Zec 8:4) leaning on a cane: God now threatens to take away their support. Jerome refers this to the observable decay of the Jewish nation after they had crucified our Savior (Ro 11:9–10). I prefer to take it as a warning to all nations not to offend God.

1. Bread is the staff of life, but God can take away all supplies of bread and all supplies of water (v. 1). He does so justly when what was given as a provision for life is used to satisfy sinful desires. He can take away bread and water by withholding rain (Dt 28:23–24). He can withhold his blessing so that the bread is not nourishing nor the water refreshing. Christ is the bread of life and the water of life; if he is our support, we will find that this is a good part and will not be taken away (Jn 6:27, 35; 4:14; Lk 10:42).

2. Their army—their generals and commanders—will be taken away. *The mighty man, and the man of* war (v. 2), and even the subordinate officer, *the captain of fifty* (v. 3), will be removed. Let not the strong therefore glory in their strength (Jer 9:23), nor any people trust too much in their warriors.

3. Their ministers of state, the learned people, their politicians, their clergy, will also be taken away: *the judges; the prophets; the prudent,* who help the judges—literally, "diviners," or soothsayers, who used unlawful arts; and *the ancients,* elders in age and in office. When the whole supply breaks down, *the cunning artificer* (skilled worker)

(v. 3) will also be taken away. The last is *the eloquent orator* (v. 3), who is skilled at speaking and in some cases may do good service. Moses cannot speak well, but Aaron can. God will take all these away.

4. It is the business of the sovereign to hold firmly the pillars of the land (Ps 75:3). But it is threatened here that this support will fail them. When the warriors and the wise are removed, mere *children shall be their princes:* *children* in age (v. 4), who must still be under tutors and governors, and children in understanding and disposition, childish people, no more fit to rule than a child in a cradle. These will rule over them, with all the foolishness, familiarity, and fickleness of a child.

5. The unity of the subjects among themselves, their good order and good understanding, will break down. It is threatened here that God will send an evil spirit among them too (Jdg 9:23), which will make them unneighborly toward one another (v. 5): *The people shall be oppressed every one by his neighbour,* and because their leaders are children, they will not restrain the oppressors or relieve the oppressed. Something is seriously wrong with a people when the rising generation is disobedient and uncontrollable.

6. The condition of the government will be so desperate that no one with any sense or substance will want to have anything to do with it.

6.1. The government will begin to beg (v. 6). It is assumed that there is no way of putting right all these grievances and bringing things to order again except by good judges, and that those judges must be invested with power by common consent and use that power for the good of the community. The case is described as deplorable, and things as having come to a sad condition, for since children are their leaders, everyone will think they are qualified to recommend someone as a judge. *A man shall take hold* (v. 6) by violence of someone to make them a leader; *a man* will urge it on *his brother.* It will be looked on as sufficient reason to promote a man as leader that he has better clothing than his neighbors. It would have made some sense to say, "You have wisdom, integrity, and experience; you be our leader." But it was absurd to say, *Thou hast clothing; be thou our ruler* (v. 6).

6.2. Those who are pressed into office in this way will cry out in protest, because they still know they cannot bear the responsibilities of the office (v. 7): *He shall swear*—will lift up the hand, the ancient ceremony used in taking an oath—*I will not be a healer; make not me a ruler. Leaders must be healers, and good leaders will be;* they must work hard at uniting their subjects, not widening the differences among them. But why will he not be a leader? Because *in my house is neither bread nor clothing* (v. 7). It was a sign that the case of the nation was very bad when no one was willing to accept a place in governing it. God brought things to this sad condition not for lack of goodwill to his country. *Jerusalem is ruined,* and *Judah is fallen,* and they have only themselves to blame that they are in such a condition. They have brought destruction onto their own heads, for *their tongue and their doings are against the Lord* (v. 8). They broke the law of God in word and action. They offended him to his face, as if the more they knew of his glory, the greater pride they took in insulting it.

Verses 9–15

God continues his dispute with his people. Notice:

1. The reason for his dispute. It is because of sin that God has contended with them; if they bother to look, they will see that they have only themselves to blame for the

situation they are in: *Woe unto their souls! For they have rewarded evil unto themselves.* It may be read, "Alas for their souls!" as an expression of mourning, for they have brought disaster on themselves (v. 9). They are accused of rejecting the shame that should have restrained them and becoming arrogant. This hardens people against repenting as much as anything. Those who are beyond shame are "beyond redemption," as we say, and then beyond hope (v. 12): "*Those who lead thee* (the rulers, priests, and prophets) mislead thee; they *cause thee to err.*" Their judges, who should support and protect the oppressed, are themselves the greatest oppressors (vv. 14 – 15). The people's elders and rulers *have eaten up the vineyard* (v. 14). They have "burned" (which is the literal meaning of the word) God's vineyard, which they were appointed to tend and look after. God reasons with these great people (v. 15): "*What mean you, that you beat my people into pieces?* What do you mean by crushing my people? Do you think that was why power was given you?" *You grind the faces of the poor* (v. 15); you put them in as much pain and terror as if they were ground in a mill.

2. How this dispute is handled. God himself is the prosecutor (v. 13): *The Lord stands up to plead,* and he *stands to judge the people,* to speak up for those who are oppressed; and he will *enter into judgment with the princes* (v. 14). The greatest people cannot exempt themselves from the scrutiny and sentence of God's judgment. The accusation is proved: "Look at the oppressors, and the *show of their countenance witnesses against them* (v. 9); look at the oppressed, and you see how their faces are battered and abused" (v. 15). To punish those who have abused their power, God sets over them those who do not have the sense to use their power well: *Children are their oppressors, and women rule over them* (v. 12), men who have as weak judgments and strong passions as women and children. And God makes a distinction between individual persons (vv. 10 – 11); if they had been righteous, things would have gone well with them, but if trouble is falling on them, it is because they are evil and will remain so. When the whole *stay of bread is taken away* (v. 1), in the *day of famine the righteous shall be satisfied* (Ps 37:19); they *shall eat the fruit of their doings* (v. 10)—they will have the testimony of their consciences that they kept themselves pure from sin, and so the common disaster is not the same for them as it is for others. There is anguish for evildoers, and disaster will come on them.

Verses 16 – 26

The prophet's work was to show all kinds of people what they had contributed to the national guilt and what share they must expect in the coming national judgments. Here he rebukes and warns the daughters of Zion. Notice:

1. The sin the daughters of Zion are accused of (v. 16). They stand here accused of two things—pride and immorality. They have revealed their hearts by the way they walked and behaved. They are haughty, for they *walk with stretched forth necks* (v. 16), so they may seem tall. Their eyes are immoral; "deceiving" is the sense. They affect a formal way of walking, *mincing,* tripping along with quick short steps. They make a *tinkling with their feet* (v. 16), having, as some think, little bells or other ornaments on their shoes. These were the daughters of Zion, who should have behaved with the modesty and seriousness that is appropriate for women who profess godliness.

2. The punishments threatened for this sin, and they correspond to the sin as the image corresponds to a face in a mirror (vv. 17 – 18).

2.1. They *walked with stretched forth necks* (v. 16), but God will *smite with a scab the crown of their head* (bring sores on the heads) (v. 17), which will make them ashamed to show their heads, because they have been obliged to cut off their hair.

2.2. They did not care what money they spent on a great variety of fine clothes, but God will reduce them to such poverty and distress that they will not have enough clothes to cover their nakedness.

2.3. They were extremely proud of their ornaments, but God will strip them of those ornaments when their houses are plundered, their treasures ransacked, and they themselves taken into exile. It is not significant to ask what precise kind of ornaments these were. Fashions change, as do the names of fashionable items. Many of these things, we may presume, were ridiculous and, if they had not been in fashion, would have been laughed out of court. Those things that were decent and beneficial, such as *the linen, the hoods, and the veils* (shawls), did not need to be provided in such abundance and variety.

2.4. They were very fussy about their clothes, but God would make their bodies a disgrace and burden to them (v. 24): *Instead of sweet smell*—those tablets, or boxes, of perfume, "houses of breath," as they are called in v. 20, margin—*there shall be stink* (a stench), garments that have become filthy because they have been worn for such a long time. *Instead of a* rich, embroidered *girdle* (sash) used to keep the clothes in place, there will be *a rent:* old, rotten clothes torn into rags or rope. *Instead of well-set hair,* there will be *baldness,* the hair being plucked out or shaven, as was usual in times of great suffering (15:2; Jer 16:6) or great slavery (Eze 29:18). *Instead of a stomacher,* or sash, there will *be a girding of sackcloth,* as a sign of deep humiliation, *and burning* (branding) *instead of beauty.* When those who have a good complexion are taken into exile, they will be tanned and sunburned; the best complexions are the ones soonest harmed by the weather. Let us learn from all this not to wear or use what is showy and costly.

2.5. They intended to use these ornaments to charm the gentlemen and win their affections (Pr 7:16 – 17), but no one will be charmed by them (v. 25): *Thy men shall fall by the sword, and thy mighty in the war.* And when Zion's guards are destroyed, it is not surprising that Zion's gates *lament and mourn* (v. 26). The city itself, being desolate, will *sit upon the ground* (v. 26) like a destitute widow.

CHAPTER 4

In this chapter we have: 1. A threat that men will be few and scarce (v. 1). 2. A promise of the restoration of Jerusalem's peace and purity, righteousness and security, in the days of the Messiah (vv. 2 – 6). And so, mercy is remembered in wrath (Hab 3:2).

Verse 1

Here we have the effect of that great killing of men. Providence has so wisely ordered things that on average there is nearly an equal number of males and females born into the world, but through devastations caused by war, there would be scarcely one man in seven left alive to Judah. As there are deaths accompanying childbirth, which are specific to the woman, so there are deaths that are specific to men, those by the sword, which perhaps kills more than childbirth does. It was foretold that there would be *seven women to one man* (v. 1). Because of the scarcity of men, whereas men usually court women, the women would now seize the men. Seven would now, by consent, become the wives of one man, and whereas by the Law the husband was obliged to provide food and clothes for his wife (Ex 21:10), these women would bind themselves to supply these things on their own. They would *eat bread of their own earning, and wear apparel of their own working* (v. 1), and the man they courted would not have to pay; they would desire only to be called his wives, to *take away the reproach* (v. 1) of a single life. They would be willing to be wives on any terms, their only concern being to get husbands. Perhaps—though this would be sad—this means that they would not be humbled by God's punishments (3:18), that they would forget modesty and think the shame of evil nothing compared with the shame of virginity.

Verses 2–6

In light of the previous threats everything looks sad. But here the sun breaks out from behind the clouds. We have very many great and precious promises in these verses, giving assurance of comfort. These certainly point to the kingdom of the Messiah and the great redemption to be brought about by him; God's people would see types of this kingdom and redemption in the restoration of Judah and Jerusalem by the reforming reign of Hezekiah after Ahaz and in the return from exile in Babylon. The passage may have some reference to both these events, but it chiefly refers to Christ.

1. God will raise up a righteous Branch (Jer 23:5), which will produce fruits of righteousness (Php 1:11) (v. 2): *In that day*, when Jerusalem is destroyed and the Jewish nation dispersed, the kingdom of the Messiah will be set up.

1.1. Christ himself will be exalted. He is the *branch of the Lord* (v. 2); it is one of his prophetic names, *my servant the branch* (Zec 3:8; 6:12), *a rod out of the stem of Jesse and a branch out of his roots* (11:1). The ancient Aramaic paraphrase reads, "The Christ, or Messiah, of the Lord." He himself will be advanced to the glory that he had with the Father before the world began (Jn 17:5).

1.2. His Gospel will be embraced. The success of the Gospel is the fruit of the Branch of the Lord; all the grace and encouragement of the Gospel come from Christ. But it is called *the fruit of the earth* (v. 2) because it sprang up in this world. We may understand this to refer to both the people and the things that are the products of the Gospel. If the Branch of the Lord is beautiful and glorious in our eyes, even the fruit of the earth will be dignified and glorious, because then we may take it as the fruit of the promise (Ps 37:16; 1Ti 4:8).

2. God will reserve for himself a holy seed (6:13) (v. 3). When most people will be cut off as withered branches because of their own unbelief, some will be left.

2.1. This is a remnant of those who are *written* (recorded) *among the living* (v. 3). Those who are kept alive in times of killing were recorded for life in the book of divine Providence, *written in the Lamb's book of life* (Rev 13:8). All who were *written among the living* will be found to be among the living, every one, for Christ will lose none of all who were given to him (Jn 17:12).

2.2. It is a remnant *under the dominion of grace*, for everyone who is *written among the living* will be called *holy* and so will be accepted by God.

3. God will reform his church and put right whatever is wrong in it (v. 4). The time when the remnant will be *called holy* will be the time *when the Lord shall have washed away their filth*, washed it from among them by destroying evildoers, washed it from within them by cleansing what is evil. Although Jerusalem is the Holy

City, it needs reformation. *The daughters of Zion* may refer to the country towns and villages, to which Jerusalem was related as the mother city and which needed reformation. The filth will be washed away, for evil, especially bloodshed, is filthiness. *The Lord shall do it.* Reformation is a work of God. But how? Sinners are destroyed by the judgment of his providence, but it is by the Spirit of his grace that they are reformed and converted. The Spirit acts here, enlightening the mind, convicting the conscience, guiding, separating the precious and the worthless, quickening and invigorating the affections, making people zealous to do a good work.

4. God will protect his church and all who belong to it (vv. 5–6). Those who are sanctified are well fortified.

4.1. Their dwelling places will be defended (v. 5). Their houses where they live and rest, where they worship God with their families, will be protected. God takes particular care of the dwelling places of his people, the humblest cottage as well as the grandest palace. Their meetings or tents of meeting for religious worship as well, all the congregations of Christians, even though only two or three meet together in Christ's name (Mt 18:20), will be taken under the special protection of heaven. This writ of protection is drawn up using a metaphor that refers to the security of the camp of Israel when it marched through the desert. God will give the Christian church evidence of his care for them that is just as real as the evidence he then gave to Israel. Although miracles have ceased, God is still the same to the New Testament church as he was to Israel in former times. Another metaphor is also used, referring to the outside cover of skins of rams and sea cows that was on the curtains of the tabernacle, as if every dwelling place and every assembly were as precious to God as that tabernacle was: *Upon all the glory shall be a defence* (canopy) (v. 5) to protect it from wind and weather. Gospel truths and ordinances, the Scriptures and the ministry, are the church's glory, and there is a canopy on all this glory. If God himself is the glory in its midst, he will himself be an impenetrable and impregnable wall of fire around it. Grace in the soul is its glory, and those who have it are *kept by the power of God* as in a stronghold (1Pe 1:5).

4.2. Their tabernacle will be a canopy to them (v. 6). Divine power and goodness will be a tabernacle to all God's people. God himself will be their hiding place (Ps 32:7); they will be at home in him (Ps 91:9). God is a refuge to his people at all times and in all weathers.

CHAPTER 5

In this chapter the prophet, in God's name, shows the people of God their disobedience and the judgments that are to be brought on them for their sins: 1. By a parable of an unfruitful vineyard, describing the favors God has given, their disappointing of his expectations of them, and the destruction they deserve (vv. 1–7). 2. By a listing of the sins among them, with a threat of the punishments that will correspond to the sins: 2.1. Covetousness and greed, which will be punished by famine (vv. 8–10). 2.2. Rioting, reveling, and drunkenness (vv. 11–12, 22–23), which will be punished by exile (vv. 13–17). 2.3. Arrogance and defiance of the justice of God (vv. 18–19). 2.4. Confusing the distinction between good and evil and so undermining the principles of religion (v. 20). 2.5. Self-conceit (v. 21). 2.6. Perverting the course of justice, for which great and general devastation is threatened (vv. 24–25), which will be carried out by a foreign invasion (vv. 26–30), referring perhaps to the havoc made not long afterward by Sennacherib's army.

Verses 1–7

To wake sinners up to repent, God sometimes speaks in plain terms and sometimes in parables, sometimes in prose and sometimes in song, as here. God the Father dictates it to the honor of Christ, his beloved Son, whom he has made Lord of the vineyard (Mt 21:33–46). The prophet sings it to the honor of Christ. The Old Testament prophets were friends of the bridegroom. Christ is God's beloved Son and our beloved Savior. This parable was put into a song so it might be all the more moving and all the more easily learned, remembered, and passed on to future generations. It is an explanation of the Song of Moses (Dt 32:1–47), showing that what he then foretold was now fulfilled. Here we have:

1. The great things that God had done for the Jewish church and nation. The soil they were planted in was *a very fruitful hill* (a fertile hillside) (v. 1), "the horn of the son of oil," as the margin reads. There was plenty, and there were delicacies: they ate rich portions and drank the sweet wine. Notice further what God did for this vineyard:

1.1. He fenced it. If they had not thrown away their hedge, no inroads would have been made on them (Ps 125:2; 121:4).

1.2. He cleared it of stones. He offered his grace to take away the stony heart.

1.3. He planted it with the best, the choicest, vines; he set up pure religion among them.

1.4. He built a tower in its midst for defense. The temple was this tower.

1.5. He also set up a winepress there, his altar, to which the sacrifices, as the fruits of the vineyard, were to be brought.

2. The disappointment of his just expectations: *He looked that it should bring forth grapes* (v. 2). From those who enjoy vineyard privileges God expects vineyard fruit. Good purposes and good beginnings are good, but not enough: there must also be fruit, a good heart and a good life; there must be fruit of the *vineyard*, thoughts and affections and words and actions that are pleasing to the Spirit. His expectations are frustrated: *It brought forth wild grapes* (v. 2). Wild grapes are the fruit of the corrupt nature, hypocritical religious activities that look like grapes.

3. An appeal to the people themselves as to whether God must not be justified and they condemned (vv. 3–4). *O inhabitants of Jerusalem, and men of Judah! judge, I pray you, betwixt* (between) *me and my vineyard.* Here is a challenge to show any situation in which God has not done enough for them: *What could have been done more to my vineyard, that I have not done in it?* (v. 4). They had everything they needed. "Why, what reason can you give that when I looked for grapes, the vine should produce wild grapes?"

4. Their condemnation read and sentence passed on them (vv. 5–6). "*And now,* since nothing can be offered to excuse the crime or to stop the judgment, *I will tell you what I am determined to do to my vineyard. I will* be troubled with it no more. In short, it will stop being a vineyard and will be turned into a desert: the church of the Jews will be excluded: *I will take away the hedge thereof* (v. 5), and then it will become bare." God will remove all their defenses, and they will become an easy target for their enemies. They will no longer look like a vineyard, no longer have the form and shape of a church and community, but will be leveled and devastated. Those who would not produce good fruit will bear none. The curse of barrenness is the punishment of the sin of barrenness (Mk 11:14). This had its partial fulfillment in the

destruction of Jerusalem by the Babylonians and its complete fulfillment in the final rejection of the Jews, and it has its frequent fulfillment in the departure of God's Spirit from those who have long resisted him.

5. The explanation of this parable, or a key to it (v. 7). The vineyard is *the house of Israel*, the body of the people, joined into one church and community, and the vines are the people of Judah. He has dealt graciously with them, and he expected from them an appropriate return. We are told what is meant by the grapes that were expected and the wild grapes that were produced: *He looked for judgment and righteousness*, that the people would be honest and the judges would administer justice strictly. This might reasonably be expected. But the reality was the complete opposite. Instead of justice there was the cruelty of the oppressors, and instead of righteousness came the cries of the oppressed.

Verses 8–17

Eagerness for the things of the world and indulgence of the flesh are the two sins against which the prophet here declares woes in God's name. These were sins that were then prevalent among the people of Judah, some of the wild grapes they produced (v. 4).

1. Here is a woe to those who set their hearts on the wealth of the world (v. 8), who *join house to house and lay field to field, till there be no place*, no room for anyone to live by them. If they could succeed, they would monopolize all possessions and advancement. They are immoderate in their desires to make themselves rich. They are careless of others. They do not care what hardships they place on those they have power over or what evil ways they use to store money for themselves. The punishment of this sin is that neither the houses nor the fields will be reckoned to their advantage (vv. 9–10). The houses they are so fond of will be deprived of tenants and stand empty for a long time: *Many houses shall be desolate* (v. 9), and the people living in them will be destroyed by the sword, famine, or plague or be taken into exile. We have a saying that fools build houses for wise people to live in, but sometimes it turns out that they are built for no one to live in. The fields they are so fond of will be unfruitful (v. 10): *Ten acres of vineyard shall yield* only such grapes as will make but *one bath* of wine, about six gallons (about twenty-two liters), *and the seed of a homer*, probably six bushels of sowing seed, will yield only an ephah, the tenth part of a homer, that is, about three-fifths of a bushel (about twenty-two liters), so that they will not have more than a tenth of their seed back.

2. Here is a woe to those who are too fond of the pleasures of this world (vv. 11–12). Sensuality ruins people as much as worldliness and oppression.

2.1. The sinners against whom this woe is declared are those who are given to drink. They sit drinking all day *and continue till night, till wine inflame them* (v. 11) and inflames their sinful desires. They are those who never give their minds to anything serious: *They regard not the work of the Lord* (v. 12); they take no notice of his power, wisdom, and goodness in those they abuse, nor do they take notice of the goodness of his providence in giving them the good things they use to fuel their sinful desires.

2.2. It is foretold here that they will be dislodged; the land will spew out these drunkards (Lev 18:28; 20:22) (v. 13): *My people have gone into captivity, because they have no knowledge.* How can they have any knowledge when their excessive drinking makes them fools? They will become poor and come to lack what they have wasted and excessively abused: even *their honorable men* (those of high rank) *are famished*, are subject to famine and killed by it, and *their multitude are dried up with thirst* (v. 13). Multitudes will be destroyed by famine and sword (v. 14): *Therefore hell has enlarged herself.* Tophet, the common burial place, will prove too small; there will be so many bodies to bury that they will be forced to enlarge it (30:33) [Ed. note: the Hebrew translated *hell* is *sheol*, "the grave"]. They will be humbled, and all their honor laid in the dust (Ps 7:5).

2.3. As a result of these judgments, first, God will be glorified (v. 16); he will be exalted in the righteousness of these judgments. Second, good people will be helped and relieved (v. 17): *Then shall the lambs feed after their manner* (will graze as in their own pasture); the meek of the earth, who followed the Lamb, who were persecuted and frightened by those proud oppressors, will feed quietly, and no one will make them afraid (17:2; Eze 34:28; etc.). Finally, the country will be devastated and become an easy target to its neighbors: *The waste places of the fat ones* (the ruins of the rich) (v. 17), the possessions of those rich people who lived in ease, will be eaten by others who are not related to them in any way. The church of the Jews, those rich ones, was laid waste, and their privileges were transferred to the Gentiles, all who were lambs of Christ's flock.

Verses 18–30

Here:

1. Sins that will bring judgments on the people are described. Although it may relate primarily to the people of Judah, it is intended as a warning to all peoples in all ages. Those who are said to be in a desperate condition are those:

1.1. Who are violent in their sinful pursuits (v. 18), who *draw iniquity with cords of vanity*, who draw sins along with *cords of vanity* (deceit), who make as much effort to sin as cattle do to haul a load. They think they are as sure of the fulfillment of their evil plans as if they were pulling it toward them with strong cart ropes, but those ropes will turn out to be *cords of vanity*, which will break when stress is put on them. Those who sin through weakness are drawn away by sin; those who sin arrogantly draw sin to them, in spite of the oppositions of providence and the restraining voice of conscience. Some by *sin* pull God's judgments onto their own heads, as it were, with cart ropes.

1.2. Who defy the justice of God and challenge the Almighty to do his worst (v. 19): *They say, Let him make speed, and hasten his work.* They ridicule the prophets and mock them. They will not believe the revelation of God's wrath from heaven (Ro 1:18) unless they see it carried out. If God were to appear against them, as he has threatened, they would still think themselves able to resist him successfully. "We have heard his word, but it is all mere words; let God hurry up and do what he says he will, but we will take care of ourselves well enough."

1.3. Who confound the distinctions between moral good and evil, *who call evil good and good evil* (v. 20). Such people do a great deal of wrong toward God, religious faith, and conscience, and to their own souls and the souls of others. They call drunkenness "good fellowship" and covetousness "good management," and on the other hand, they call seriousness "spitefulness" and falsely say all kinds of evil concerning godliness (Mt 5:11).

1.4. Who, though they are guilty of such gross mistakes, still have a high opinion of their own judgments (v. 21): they are *wise in their own eyes*; they think they can outwit infinite Wisdom and go against Providence itself.

1.5. Who glory that they are able to take a great deal of strong drink without being overcome by it (v. 22), *who are mighty to drink wine* and use their strength in serving their sinful desires. Drunkards ungratefully abuse their physical strength, which God has given them for good purposes, and what they do gradually, but inevitably, weaken it.

1.6. Who, as judges, pervert the course of justice: they *justify the wicked for reward*, they acquit the guilty for a bribe (v. 23), finding some pretense or other to clear them from their guilt and protect them from punishment; and they condemn the innocent, *taking away their righteousness from* (deny justice to) *them* (v. 23).

2. The judgments that these sins will bring on them are described. The righteous God will take vengeance (vv. 24–30). Notice:

2.1. How complete this destruction will be. God has compared this people to a vine that, it was hoped, would be fruitful (v. 7), but the grace of God was received in vain, and the root became rotten. Because it then dried up from below, its blossom would blow away as dust. Sin weakens the strength, the roots, of a people, so that they are easily uprooted; it defaces the beauty, the blossom, of a people, and takes away the hope of fruit. Sinners make themselves like stubble and chaff: *As the fire devours the stubble* (v. 24), chaff is consumed, and no one offers any pity or help.

2.2. How just the destruction will be. God does not reject people for every act of disobedience of his law and word, but when his word is despised and his law is rejected, what can they expect but that God will completely abandon them?

2.3. Where this destruction will come from (v. 25): the Almighty. The justice of God appoints it, for that is *the anger of the Lord* that is *kindled against his people*, his necessary vindication: *He has stretched forth his hand against them* (v. 25). That hand that had been stretched out many times for them against their enemies is now stretched out against them.

2.4. The results and continuation of this destruction. When God comes in wrath against a people, the mountains shake; fear seizes even their great people. What sight can be more terrible than human carcasses thrown "as dung" (v. 25, margin) *in the midst of the streets*? This suggests that many people will be killed, that not only soldiers but also those who live in the cities will be coldbloodedly killed, and the survivors will have neither hands nor hearts to bury them.

2.5. The instruments: this destruction will be done by a foreign enemy who will devastate everything. Those who do not know God are made use of to fulfill his purposes.

2.5.1. He can send far away for help. If God sets up his banner, he can incline people's hearts to enlist themselves under it, even though they perhaps do not know why.

2.5.2. He can make them come into his service with great speed: *Behold, they shall come with speed swiftly* (v. 26).

2.5.3. He can continue them in service with great eagerness and fury. This is described in elegant and exalted expressions in vv. 27–30. Although their journey is long, yet *none among them shall be weary* (v. 27). Although the way is rough, yet none of them will *stumble.* Although they are forced to keep constant watch, yet *none shall slumber nor sleep* (v. 27). They will not desire any rest or relaxation; they will neither take off their clothes nor *loose the girdle of their loins* (v. 27), but will always have their belts on and swords by their sides. Not *a latchet of their shoes shall be broken* that they must stop to mend

(Jos 9:13). Their arms and ammunition will all be ready for action and in good condition, *their arrows sharp, and all their bows bent* (v. 28), none unstrung. Their horses and chariots will all be ready for service, their horses so strong that *their hoofs shall be like flint* (v. 28). The wheels of their chariots will not be broken or battered, but *swift like a whirlwind* (v. 28). All the soldiers will be bold and daring (v. 29): *Their roaring shall be like a lion*, which encourages itself with its roaring and terrifies all those around. *They shall roar like the roaring of the sea* (v. 30) in a storm. There will not be the slightest prospect of help or relief. If the light is darkened in the heavens, how great that darkness must be (Mt 6:23)! If God hides his face, it is not surprising that the heavens hide theirs and appear gloomy (Job 34:29).

CHAPTER 6

Up to this time, Isaiah, having only an implicit and unspoken commission, and perhaps having seen little success in his ministry, began to think of giving it up, and so God saw fit to renew his commission in such a way as would encourage his zeal, even though he seemed to labor in vain (Ps 127:1–2; 1Co 15:58). In this chapter we have: 1. An awesome vision that Isaiah saw of the glory of God (vv. 1–4), the dread it put into him (v. 5), and the relief given him from that terror by an assurance of the forgiveness of his sins (vv. 6–7). 2. An awesome commission that Isaiah received to go as a prophet in God's name (v. 8) and, by his preaching, to harden the impenitent in sin (vv. 9–12), but with a reservation of mercy for a remnant (v. 13). These things were shown and said to him as to an evangelical prophet.

Verses 1–4

The vision that Isaiah saw when he was, as is said of Samuel, *established to be a prophet of the Lord* (1Sa 3:20) was intended to confirm his faith. Similarly, God appeared at first as a God of glory to Abraham (Ac 7:2) and to Moses (Ex 3:2). Ezekiel's prophecies and those of the apostle John also begin with visions of divine glory. Those who are to teach others the knowledge of God should themselves know him well.

The vision was *in the year that king Uzziah died* (v. 1), who had reigned as well as any of the kings of Judah, and for more than fifty years. About the time that he died, Isaiah saw this vision of God on a throne. Israel's king dies, but Israel's God still lives. King Uzziah (Azariah) died a *leper* (2Ch 26:21) in a house, but the King of kings still sits on his throne.

1. See God on his throne, and that throne *high and lifted up* (v. 1), not only above other thrones, as it surpasses them, but also over other thrones, as it rules them. Isaiah does not use *Jehovah* here—the essence of God, whom no one has seen or can see—but *Adonai*—the word for God in his authority and power. He saw the Lord Jesus Christ; as this vision is explained in Jn 12:41, Isaiah now saw Christ's glory. See the authority of the eternal Monarch: he sits *upon a throne* (v. 1)—a throne of glory, before which we must worship, a throne of government, to which we must submit, and a throne of grace, to which we may come boldly (Heb 4:16).

2. See his temple, his church on earth, filled with the revelation of his glory. His *train*, the skirts of his robes, *filled the temple* (v. 1), the whole world, for it is all God's temple. Or rather *the temple* is indeed the church, which is filled, enriched, and made beautiful with the signs of God's special presence.

3. See the bright and blessed attendants on his throne (v. 2): *Above the throne the seraphim stood*, the holy angels, who are called *seraphim*, "burning ones," for he *makes his ministers a flaming fire* (Ps 104:4). They burn because of their love for God, zeal for his glory, and zeal against sin. It is the glory of the angels that they are seraphim, that they have heat in proportion to their light; they have an abundance not only of divine knowledge but also of holy love. *Each of them* had *six wings* (v. 2), but they were not spread out above, as those that Ezekiel saw (Eze 1:11). Instead, four were covering; the two upper wings were used to cover their faces, and the two lowest wings to cover their feet. This speaks of their great humility and reverence. They cover not only their feet but even their faces. Two were used for flying; when angels are sent on God's errands, they fly swiftly (Da 9:21). This teaches us to do the work of God with cheerfulness and speed.

4. Listen to the song of praise that the angels sing to the honor of the One who sits on the throne (Rev 4:9–10) (v. 3). With intense zeal they *cried* aloud, and with unanimity they *cried* "one to another" without the slightest jarring to break their harmony. The song was the same as that sung by the four living creatures (Rev 4:8). The church above is the same in its praises; there is no change of times or notes there. Here God is praised with one of his most glorious titles: he is *the Lord of hosts* (v. 3), of all powers; and he is praised for one of his most glorious qualities, his holiness. Power without purity to guide it would terrorize the human race. God's power was spoken of twice (Ps 62:11), but his holiness three times: *Holy, holy, holy* (v. 3). The repetition may refer to the three persons of the Godhead, Holy Father, Holy Son, and Holy Spirit, for it follows (v. 8), *Who will go for us?* Or perhaps it refers to *that which was, and is, and is to come. The earth is full of his glory* (v. 3), of the glory of his power and purity, for he is holy in all his works (Ps 145:17).

5. Notice the signs of terror with which the temple was filled at this vision of divine glory (v. 4). The house was *shaken*; even *the posts of the door*, which were firmly fixed, *moved at the voice of him that cried*, at the voice of God, who called to judgment (Ps 50:4). The house was darkened; it was *filled with smoke*, which was as a *cloud spread* on the *face of his throne* (Job 26:9). In the temple above, everything will be seen clearly. God lives in light there, but here he *makes darkness his pavilion* (2Ch 6:1; Ps 18:11).

Verses 5–8

We have here:

1. The prophet's dismay at seeing this vision of the glory of God (v. 5): *Then said I, Woe is me!* One would think he would have said, "I am happy, nothing will trouble me now," but, on the contrary, he cries out, "*Woe is me! for I am undone* (v. 5)." Notice:

1.1. What it was that the prophet reflected on concerning himself that terrified him: "I am ruined, because I am a man of unclean lips." Some think he was referring especially to some rash word he had spoken, or to his sinful silence in not rebuking sin with boldness. But it may be taken more generally: "I am a sinner; more particularly, I have offended in word." We all have reason to mourn this before the Lord:

1.1.1. That we ourselves are of unclean lips; our lips are not consecrated to God. We are unworthy to take God's name onto our lips. The impurity of our lips should sadden our spirits, for by our words we will be justified or condemned (Mt 12:37).

1.1.2. That we too live among those who are of unclean lips. The disease is hereditary and epidemic, which, so far from lessening our guilt, should rather increase our sorrow, considering that we have not done what we should have done to cleanse the defilement of other people's lips; we have rather learned their ways and spoken their language, as Joseph learned the courtier's oath in Egypt (Ge 42:16).

1.2. What caused these sad reflections: *My eyes have seen the King, the Lord of hosts* (v. 5). We are ruined if there is not a Mediator between us and this holy God (1Sa 6:20). Isaiah was humbled in this way to prepare him for the honor he was now to be called to as a prophet.

2. The silencing of the prophet's fears by the encouraging words with which the angel answered him (vv. 6–7). One of the seraphim immediately flew to him to purify him. Those who are struck down with the visions of God's glory will soon be raised up again with the coming of his grace. Here one of the seraphim was dismissed for a time from the throne of God's glory to be a messenger of his grace to a good man, and he came flying to him. To our Lord Jesus himself, in his agony, there *appeared an angel from heaven, strengthening him* (Lk 22:43). The seraph *brought a live coal from the altar* (v. 6) and touched his lips with it to cleanse them. The Holy Spirit works as fire (Mt 3:11). The seraph put life into the prophet, for the way to cleanse the lips from the uncleanness of sin is to fire the soul with the love of God. "*Lo, this has touched thy lips*, to assure thee that *thy iniquity is taken away and thy sin purged* (v. 7). The guilt of your sin is taken away by pardoning mercy, the guilt of the sins of your tongue, and your sin has been atoned for. Your corrupt disposition to sin has been removed by renewing grace, and so nothing can prevent you from being accepted by God as a worshiper or from being used by God to give his message to people."

3. The renewing of the prophet's mission (v. 8). Here is an interaction between God and Isaiah. How can we expect God to speak through us if we have never heard him speaking to us? God is here deliberating with himself: *Whom shall I send? And who will go for us?* This is how he wants to teach us that the sending out of ministers is a work to be done only with mature deliberation. It puts an honor on the ministry that when God wants to send a prophet to speak in his name, he appears in all the glory of the upper world. Notice that God was waited on by holy angels, but he still asked, *Whom shall I send?* (v. 8), for he wanted to send them *a prophet from among their brethren* (Dt 18:18) (Heb 2:17). God reveals his mind using people like ourselves, who themselves have an interest in the messages they bring. Those who are workers together with God (2Co 6:1) are sinners and sufferers together with us. Who is equal to such a task (2Co 2:16)? Such a degree of courage, such concern for human souls, and such an insight into the mysteries of the kingdom of heaven are seldom encountered. No one is allowed to go for God except those who are sent by him (Ro 10:15). It is Christ's work to put people into the ministry (1Ti 1:12). The office seemed to need someone to fill it, and everyone declined it, but Isaiah offered himself: "I will go and leave the success to God. *Here am I; send me*." Notice what he says shows readiness: "Here am I, a volunteer, not someone forced into service." "Here am I." "*Here I am* (v. 8), ready to encounter the greatest difficulties. *I have set my face as a flint*" (50:7).

Verses 9–13

God takes Isaiah at his word and here sends him on a strange mission—to foretell the ruin of his people and even to prepare them for that destruction. And this was to

be a type of the state of the Jewish church in the days of the Messiah, when they would stubbornly reject the Gospel and would therefore be rejected by God. These verses are quoted in part, or referred to, six times in the New Testament. Isaiah is here given to understand four things:

1. That most of the people to whom he is sent will turn a deaf ear to his preaching and deliberately close their eyes to all the revelations of the mind and will of God that he has to make to them (v. 9).

2. That insofar as they will not be made better by his ministry, they will be made worse by it. Those who are deliberately blind will be judicially blinded (v. 10): "They will not understand or perceive you, and so you will be instrumental in *making their heart fat*, calloused and insensitive, so *making their ears* even more *heavy* (dull) and *shutting their eyes* more tightly, so that ultimately their restoration and repentance will be completely impossible." Even the word of God often proves a means of hardening sinners.

3. That the result of all this will be their *utter ruin* (vv. 11–12). The prophet asks, "*Lord, how long?*"—an abrupt question—"Will it always be like this? Must I and other prophets always work in vain among them, and will things never get better?" In response to this, he is told that it will lead to the final destruction of the Jewish church and nation. "Their cities will be uninhabited, and the land will be uncultivated; there will be 'desolate with desolation'" (v. 11, margin). Spiritual judgments often bring physical judgments on people and places. This was in part fulfilled in the destruction of Jerusalem by the Babylonians, but because the foregoing predictions are so expressly applied in the New Testament to the Jews in our Savior's time, this no doubt points to the final destruction of that people by the Romans.

4. That nevertheless a remnant will be reserved to be a memorial to mercy (v. 13). *But in it shall be a tenth*, a certain number, but a very small number in comparison with the great number who will perish in their unbelief. Concerning this tithe, this saved remnant, we are told:

4.1. That they will return (v. 13; 10:21); they will return from sin to God and their duty; they will return from exile to their own land.

4.2. That they will be eaten, that is, will be accepted by God as the tithe was, which was food in God's house (Mal 3:10).

4.3. That they will be like a tree in winter, which has life even though it has no leaves: *As a teil tree* (terebinth) *and as an oak, whose substance is in them even when they cast their leaves* (v. 13), so this remnant, even though they may be stripped of their outward prosperity, will still recover, as trees do in the spring, and flourish again.

4.4. That this special remnant will be the support of the public interests. *The holy seed* (v. 13) in the soul is the substance of human beings; the principle of grace reigning in the heart will keep life there; those who are *born of God* have *his seed remaining in them* (1Jn 3:9). As the trees that grow on either side of the raised way, or terrace walk, that leads from the king's palace to the temple (1Ki 10:5) support the causeway by retaining the earth, which would otherwise crumble away, so the small residue of religious, serious, praying people support the state and help keep things together and save them from decay.

CHAPTER 7

This chapter is a sermon for a particular occasion, in which the prophet sings of both mercy and judgment (Ps 101:1) to those who do not understand either. Here is:

1. *The consternation of Ahaz because of an attempt by the allied forces of Aram and Israel against Jerusalem (vv. 1–2). 2. The assurance that God, by the prophet, sent him for his encouragement, that the attempt would be defeated and Jerusalem would be preserved (vv. 3–9). 3. The confirmation of this by a sign that God gave to Ahaz (vv. 10–16). 4. A threat of the great destruction God would bring on Ahaz and his kingdom by the Assyrians, despite their escape from this present storm, because they continued to do evil (vv. 17–25).*

Verses 1–9

The prophet Isaiah had his commission renewed in the year that King Uzziah (Azariah) died (6:1). Jotham his son reigned, and reigned well, for sixteen years. All that time, no doubt, Isaiah prophesied as he was commanded, but we do not have in this book any of his prophecies dated from the reign of Jotham; this one, put first, came in the days of Ahaz, the son of Jotham. Here is:

1. A formidable plot against Jerusalem by Rezin king of Aram and Pekah king of Israel. These two had attacked Judah separately (2Ki 15:37), but now, in the second or third year of the reign of Ahaz, they entered into an alliance against Judah. Because Ahaz began his reign with idolatry even though he found the sword over his head, *God delivered him into the hand of the king of Syria* (Aram) *and of the king of Israel* (2Ch 28:5). Flushed with this victory, they went up toward Jerusalem to besiege it.

2. The great distress that Ahaz and his court were in when they received news of this plot. The house of David was told that Aram and Ephraim had signed an alliance against Judah (v. 2). When news came that the two armies of Aram and Israel had taken the field, *the heart of Ahaz was moved with fear*, and then it is not surprising that *the heart of his people was so, as the trees of the wood are moved with the wind* (v. 2). What caused this fright was the sense of guilt and the weakness of their faith. They had made God their enemy and did not know how to make him their friend.

3. The orders given to Isaiah to encourage Ahaz in his distress because he was a son of David and king of Judah. God was kind to him for the sake of his father, who must not be forgotten, and of his people, who must not be abandoned. Notice:

3.1. God appointed the prophet to meet Ahaz even though Ahaz did not send for the prophet to speak with him and did not ask the prophet to inquire of the Lord for him (v. 3): *Go to meet Ahaz.*

3.2. He ordered Isaiah to take his little son with him, because he carried a sermon in his name, *Shear-jashub,* "a remnant will return." This son was so called to encourage those of God's people who were taken captive, assuring them that they would return.

3.3. He told him where he would find Ahaz: *at the end of the conduit* (aqueduct) *of the upper pool* (v. 3), where he was working out how to protect the waterways for the city (22:9–11; 2Ch 32:3–4) or giving some necessary directions to fortify the city.

3.4. He put words in his mouth; otherwise the prophet would not have known how to bring a message of good to such a bad man. Such a person ought to be afraid (33:14), but God intended the message as a support for the faithful Israelites.

3.4.1. The prophet must rebuke their fears (v. 4): "*Take heed, and be quiet* (keep calm). Be brave and be encouraged, be courageous."

3.4.2. He must teach them to despise their enemies, not in pride or false security but in faith and dependence on God. Ahaz's fear called them two powerful political rulers, for either of whom he was an unequal match. "No," the prophet said, "they are *two tails of smoking firebrands* (two stubs of smoldering firewood) (v. 4); they are angry and fierce, like fireballs, and they make one another worse by being allies, as sticks of firewood burn together more intensely, but they are only stubs of firewood, *tails* (stubs) of smoldering firewood, partly burned out already; their force has been exhausted; you may put your foot on them and tread them out."

3.4.3. He must assure them that the present intention of these great allies—as they thought themselves—against Jerusalem would certainly be defeated and come to nothing (vv. 5–7). Judah had done them no wrong; they had no reason to quarrel with Ahaz; but without any reason, they said, *Let us go up against Judah, and vex it* (tear it apart) (v. 6). They counted on dividing the kingdom into two parts, one for the king of Israel, the other for the king of Aram; the latter had agreed on one viceroy—a *king* to be *set in the midst of it, even the son of Tabeal* (v. 6), some obscure person, it is uncertain whether an Aramean or an Israelite. They were so sure of being successful that they divided the plunder even before they had won. God himself gave them his word that the attack would not succeed (v. 7): *Thus saith the Lord God, It shall not stand, neither shall it come to pass.*

3.4.4. He must give them a prospect of the ultimate destruction of these enemies. Neither of them would enlarge his dominions or push his conquests any farther: *The head of Syria* (Aram) *is Damascus, and the head of Damascus is Rezin*; he glories in this, and let him be content with it (v. 8). *The head of Ephraim has long been Samaria, and the head in Samaria is* now Pekah *the son of Remaliah* (v. 9). These two will both be made to know what is their own; their boundaries are fixed, and they will not pass them (Job 14:5); they will not control the cities of Judah, much less attack Jerusalem. Ephraim, which perhaps was the more malicious and zealous enemy of the two, would soon be completely uprooted, and, far from seizing other people's lands, they would not be able to hold their own. It was most foolish for those who were themselves marked out for destruction and so near it to be destroying their neighbors. Isaiah must urge Judah to have faith in promises (v. 9): "*If you will not believe* what is said to you, *surely you shall not be established.* The things told you are encouraging, but they will not be so to you unless you are willing to take God at his word."

Verses 10–16

Here:

1. God, by the prophet, makes a gracious offer to Ahaz to confirm the foregoing predictions by such a sign or miracle as Ahaz will choose (vv. 10–11): *Ask thee a sign of the Lord thy God.* He knows what we are like (Ps 103:14) and that because we live in a physical world, we tend to want proof that we can see, and he has favored us with such proof in the sacramental signs and seals. This shows us how gracious God is even to the evil and unthankful; Ahaz is asked to choose his sign, as Gideon asked about the fleece (Jdg 6:37).

2. Ahaz rudely refuses this gracious offer (v. 12): *I will not ask.* The true reason why he would not ask for a sign was that, depending for help on the Assyrians, their forces, and their gods, he did not want to be so indebted to the God of Israel. But he claims a godly reason: *I will not tempt the Lord.*

3. The prophet rebukes him and his court for their contempt of prophecy (v. 13): "*Is it a small thing for you to*

weary men (is it not enough for you to try the patience of human beings) by your oppression, and *will you weary* (will you try the patience of) *my God also* with the disrespect you show him? In showing disrespect to the prophets, you think you are showing disrespect only to people like yourselves; you are forgetting you are also showing disrespect to God himself, whose messengers they are."

4. The prophet, in God's name, gives them a sign. *"The Lord himself shall give you a sign* (v. 14):

4.1. "A sign in general of his goodwill to Israel and to the house of David. From your nation, your family, the Messiah is to be born, and you cannot be destroyed while that blessing is in you (65:8). This Messiah will be introduced:

4.1.1. "In a glorious way. You have been told that he will be born among you; I am now further telling you he will be born of a virgin, which will show both the divine power and the divine purity with which he will be brought into the world." This, although it was to be fulfilled more than 500 years later, was a most encouraging sign to the house of David and an assurance that God would not reject them.

4.1.2. "On a glorious mission, clothed in his glorious name: they *shall call his name Immanuel* (v. 14), 'God with us,' God in our nature, God at peace with us, in covenant with us." This was fulfilled in their calling him *Jesus*, "Savior" (Mt 1:21–25), for if he had not been *Immanuel*, "God with us," he could not have been *Jesus*, "Savior." "The promised seed will be *Immanuel*, 'God with us'; let that word comfort you (8:10), that *God is with us* and (v. 8) that your land is Immanuel's land. Let not *the heart of the house of David* be shaken (v. 2), and let not Judah fear the setting up of the son of Tabeel (v. 6), for nothing can cut off the inheritance of the Son of David who will be Immanuel." The strongest encouragements in times of trouble are those that are taken from Christ, our relationship with him, our interests in him, and our expectations of him and from him. It is further foretold about this child (v. 15) that he will be truly human and will be nursed and brought up like other children: *Butter* (curds) *and honey shall he eat.*

4.2. Here is another sign in particular of the quick destruction of these rulers who are now a terror to Judah (v. 16). "Before *this* child"—for so it should read: "this child whom I have now in my arms"; Isaiah is referring not to Immanuel but to Shear-Jashub, his own son (v. 3)—*"shall know how to refuse the evil and choose the good* (v. 16), before this child is three or four years older, *the land that thou abhorrest* (v. 16), these allied forces of Israelites and Arameans, *shall be forsaken of both their kings* (v. 16), both Pekah and Rezin." This was completely fulfilled, for within two or three years after this, Hoshea conspired against Pekah and killed him (2Ki 15:30), and before that, the king of Assyria captured Damascus and put Rezin to death (2Ki 16:9). In fact, this prediction was fulfilled in a present event, one that happened immediately. *Shear-jashub* means "the remnant will return," and the name no doubt points to the wonderful return of those 200,000 captives whom Pekah and Rezin had taken away, who were brought back by the Spirit of the Lord Almighty (Zec 4:6). Read the story in 2Ch 28:8–15. Because the prophetic naming of this child had its fulfillment, no doubt this other prophecy would also be fulfilled. Aram and Israel would both be deprived of their kings.

Verses 17–25

After encouraging promises are made to Ahaz as a branch of the house of David, terrible threats come against him as a corrupt branch of that house. His sin will be *chastened with the rod* (2Sa 7:14).

1. The judgment threatened is great (v. 17); it is to be brought on the ruler himself, the people, the royal family, *upon* all *thy father's house.*

2. The enemy to be used as the instrument of this judgment is the king of Assyria. Ahaz has put great confidence in that ruler for help against the allied powers of Israel and Aram (2Ki 16:7–8). Now God threatens that that king of Assyria, whom Ahaz has made his support instead of God, will become a scourge to him. From now on the kings of Assyria will be for a long time painful thorns to Judah. Notice:

2.1. The summons given to the invaders (v. 18): *The Lord will hiss* (whistle) *for the fly and the bee.* See 5:26. Enemies that seem as contemptible as a fly or a bee, and are as easily crushed, will, when God wishes, do his work as effectively as lions, as young lions (5:29).

2.2. Possession taken by them (v. 19). It seems the country is in no condition to offer resistance. The invaders have no difficulty forcing their way; all of them *come and rest in the desolate valleys*, the steep ravines that the inhabitants have abandoned on the first call to battle. They will come and rest in the low ground like swarms of flies and bees, will make themselves invulnerable by taking shelter in the crevices of the rocks, as bees often do, and will show themselves formidable by appearing openly on all the thornbushes; so generally will the land be overcome by them.

2.3. Great devastation made, and the country generally abandoned and depopulated (v. 20): *The Lord will shave the hair of the head, and beard, and feet;* he will sweep everything away. God will make what Ahaz hired for his own service into an instrument of Ahaz's destruction. Many people are beaten with the arm of flesh (2Ch 32:8; Jer 17:5) that they trusted in rather than the power of the Lord.

2.4. The results of this general abandonment and depopulation. The flocks of cattle will be all destroyed, so that a man will with much difficulty save for his own use a young cow and two sheep—a poor stock (v. 21). The few cattle that are left will have so much ground to feed on that they will give abundance of milk, such as will produce enough *butter* (curds) (v. 22). There will also be such a lack of people that the milk of one cow and two sheep will be enough for a whole family, which used to keep servants and consume a great deal. The country will be so depopulated that there will be enough curds and honey for the few left in it. Good land, which used to be profitably let out to tenants, will all be overrun by briers and thorns (v. 23). The farming tools will become instruments of war (v. 24), bows and arrows, with which the remnant will hunt for wild animals in the thickets or defend themselves from robbers. There will be many briers and thorns where they should not be, but none where they should be (v. 25). *The hills that shall be digged with the mattock* (hoe), for special use, which the cattle used to be kept away from for fear of briers and thorns, will now be thrown open, the *hedges broken down for the boar out of the wood to waste* that land (Ps 80:12–13).

CHAPTER 8

This chapter and the four following it (to the end of chapter 12) are all one continuous speech, the theme of which is to show the great destruction that will soon be brought on the kingdom of Israel, but rich encouragement is given to those who fear God in those dark times.

In this chapter we have: 1. A prophecy of the destruction of the allied kingdoms of Aram and Israel by the king of Assyria (vv. 1–4). 2. A prophecy of the devastation of the land of Israel and Judah by that proud, victorious ruler (vv. 5–8). 3. Great encouragement given to the people of God in the midst of those adversities. They are assured: 3.1. That the enemies will not gain the upper hand over them (vv. 9–10). 3.2. That if they maintain the fear of God and subdue their fear of people, they will find God their refuge (vv. 11–14), and while others fall into despair, they will be enabled to wait for God to bring better times (vv. 15–18). 4. A necessary warning to everyone not to consult mediums and spiritists (vv. 19–22).

Verses 1–8

In these verses we have a prophecy of the successes of the king of Assyria against Damascus, Samaria, and Judah: that the first two would be devastated by him and the last very frightened. We have here:

1. Orders given to the prophet to write down this prophecy so that it might be read by all people, so that when events came to pass, they might know that God had sent him, for that was one purpose of prophecy (Jn 14:29). He must *take a great roll* (a large scroll) (v. 1) and write on it all that he had foretold about the king of Assyria's invasion of the country. He must *write it with a man's pen* (v. 1), in the usual way. The prophet is directed to call his book *Maher-shalal-hash-baz*, "Quick to the plunder, swift to the spoil," suggesting that the Assyrian army would come on them with great speed and take great plunder.

2. The concern of the prophet to see this record well attested (v. 2): *I took unto me faithful witnesses to record*; he wrote the prophecy in their presence so that they might be ready to testify under oath that the prophet had so long before foretold the invasion that the Assyrians made on that country. He names his witnesses. One was Uriah the priest; he is mentioned in the story of Ahaz (2Ki 16:10–11).

3. The naming of his child after the title of his book. Because his wife was the wife of a prophet, she is called *the prophetess*; she *conceived and bore a son*, another son who must carry a sermon in his name, just as the previous one had (7:3), but with this difference: the name of the other one spoke mercy, *Shear-jashub*, "The remnant will return," but because that mercy was slighted, this name speaks of judgment, *Maher-shalal-hash-baz*, "Quick to the plunder, swift to the spoil," or "He has gone quickly to the plunder." Every time the child was called by his name, or any part of it, it would serve as a reminder of the coming judgments.

4. The prophecy itself, which explains this spiritual name.

4.1. That Aram and Israel, who were now in alliance against Judah, would in a short time become an easy target to the king of Assyria (v. 4): *"Before the child*, now newly born and named, will have *knowledge to cry, My father, and, My mother"*—that is, "in about a year or two"—*"the riches of Damascus, and the spoil of Samaria*, those cities that are now so self-confident, *shall be taken away before the king of Assyria*, who will plunder both city and country as trophies of his victory."

4.2. That because there were many in Judah who were secretly allied to the interests of Aram and Israel and were dissatisfied with the house of David, God would rebuke them also by means of the king of Assyria. Notice:

4.2.1. What was the sin of the discontented party in Judah (v. 6): *This people*, whom the prophet here speaks

to, *refuse the waters of Shiloah that go softly*, despise their own country and love to criticize it because, in the world, it does not look as great and make as much noise as some other kings and kingdoms do. They refuse the encouragement that God's prophets offer them from the word of God, but *they rejoice in Rezin and Remaliah's son*, who are the enemies of their country and are now actually invading it. Many a country harbors such snakes within its ranks, who eat its bread but are loyal to its enemies and are ready to "jump ship" if it seems to falter.

4.2.2. The same king of Assyria who will devastate Ephraim and Aram will be a scourge and terror to those of their party in Judah (vv. 7–8). Because they *refuse the waters of Shiloah* (v. 6), *the Lord brings upon them the waters of the river, strong and many*, the Euphrates River. Assyria will pay no respect to the land of Judah, because it has no river to boast of that can compare with that. "Well," God says, "if you are such admirers of the Euphrates, you will have more than enough of it; the king of Assyria, whose country lies on that river, will come with his great army. God will bring that army on you." Let us be pleased with the waters of Shiloah, which flow gently, for rapid streams are dangerous. It is threatened that the Assyrian army will break in on them like a flood coming down menacingly, with all its mighty power. *He shall reach even to the neck* (v. 8), that is, he will advance so far as to lay siege to Jerusalem. In the greatest floods of trouble God can and will keep his people's heads above water. Though the outspread wings of the Assyrian, that bird of prey, though the right and left wing of its army, will fill the breadth of the land of Judah, it is still *thy land, O Immanuel!* (v. 8). It was to be Christ's land, for that was where he was to be born.

Verses 9–15

The prophet here returns to speak of the present distress that Ahaz and his court and kingdom are in because of the threatening alliance of the ten tribes and the Arameans against them.

1. He triumphs over the invading enemies and, in effect, bids them do their worst (vv. 9–10): *"O you people, you of far countries*, listen to what the prophet says to you in God's name. We do not doubt that you will now do your utmost against Judah and Jerusalem. You *associate yourselves* in alliance. You *gird yourselves* (prepare for battle), and again you *gird yourselves*, you *take counsel together. You speak the word*, you determine what to do and are confident that the matter will be fulfilled without even speaking a word. But all your efforts will be useless. You *shall be broken in pieces*. Not only will your attempts be destroyed, but also your attempts will be your destruction; you will be shattered by those plans you have worked out against Jerusalem. *For God is with us*, he is on our side, to take our side and fight for us, and *if God be for us, who can be against us?"* (Ro 8:31).

2. He strengthens and encourages the people of God with the same encouragements that he himself has received (2Co 1:4).

2.1. The prophet tells us how he himself was taught by God not to give way to such fear and dismay (v. 11): *"The Lord spoke to me with a strong hand not to walk in* (follow) *the way of this people*, not to say as they say and not to do as they do, not to approve of making peace on any terms or of calling on the help of the Assyrians." God taught the prophet not to follow that path. There is a tendency in even the best people to be frightened at threatening clouds, especially when fears are epidemic.

2.2. Now what is it that he says to God's people?

2.2.1. He warns them against a sinful fear (v. 12). It seems this was how the people were at this time, and fear is contagious. Those whose hearts fail them make the hearts of others fail like theirs (Dt 20:8), and so, "*Say you not, A confederacy, to all those to whom this people shall say, A confederacy* (v. 12). Do not join with those who, through unbelief and distrust in God and their cause, want to make an alliance with the Assyrians. Do not, when any little thing is wrong, cry out, 'There is a plot!' When they talk, there is dismal news: '*Syria is joined with Ephraim*; what will happen to us?' But do not fear their fear."

2.2.2. He advises them to have a gracious religious fear: *But sanctify the Lord of hosts himself* (v. 13). A believing fear of God is a special means of preventing the disturbing fear of people; see 1Pe 3:14–15, where this is quoted and applied to suffering Christians.

2.2.3. He assures them of a holy security and peace of mind if they do so (v. 14): "*He shall be for a sanctuary*; make him your fear, and you will find him your hope, help, defense, and mighty deliverer. He will be your sanctuary, to which you may flee for safety and where you need not fear any evil."

3. He threatens the destruction of the ungodly and unbelieving, both in Judah and in Israel. They have no share in the foregoing encouragement. The prophet foresees that the greatest part of both of the houses of Israel will not *sanctify the Lord of hosts* (v. 13). What is a fragrance of life to others will be the smell of death to them (2Co 2:16), "so that *many among them shall stumble and fall*" (v. 15).

Verses 16–22

In these verses we have:

1. The overwhelming privilege that the people of God enjoy in having the words of God, the sacred writings, entrusted to them. So that they may sanctify the Lord Almighty, let them make him their fear (v. 13) and find him their sanctuary, and *bind up the testimony* (v. 16).

1.1. This revelation is a *testimony* and *a law*; God has declared it, and he has prescribed it. As a testimony it tells us what we are to believe; as a law it tells us how we are to live; and we should submit to both its truths and its commands.

1.2. This testimony and this law are bound up and sealed, for we are not to add to them or take anything away from them (Dt 4:2; 12:32).

1.3. They are placed as a sacred deposit into the hands of the disciples of *the children of the prophets and the covenant* (Ac 3:25). This is the good that is committed to them (2Ti 1:13–14).

2. The good use we should make of this privilege. We are taught this:

2.1. By the prophet's own practice and resolutions (vv. 17–18). He embraced the law and the testimony and drew encouragement from them in the midst of the many discouragements he faced. Notice:

2.1.1. The discouragements he faced. He specifies two. First, there was the disapproval of God toward his people, whose interests lay very close to his heart: "He *hides his face from the house of Jacob* (v. 17), seems to be neglecting them and putting them under the signs of his displeasure." Second, there was the contempt and shame of other people, not only on himself but also on his disciples, among whom the law and the testimony were sealed: "*I and the children whom the Lord has given me are for signs and wonders* (v. 18); we are looked at as being outlandish." Christ looks on believers as his children, whom the Father gave him (Jn 17:6), and both he and they are

as signs and wonders, spoken against (Lk 2:34), spoken against everywhere (Ac 28:22).

2.1.2. The encouragement he took concerning these discouragements. He saw the hand of God in everything that was discouraging to him, and he kept his eye on God. He therefore decided to serve the Lord and look for him, to worship as usual even while God hid his face, and to humbly wait for his response in mercy.

2.2. By the advice that he gives to his disciples, to whom were committed the living words of God (Ro 3:2).

2.2.1. He thinks that in the day of their distress they will be tempted to consult *those that had familiar spirits* (v. 19). This is what Saul did when he was in difficulties: he turned to the witch of Endor (1Sa 28:7, 15), and Ahaziah to the god of Ekron (2Ki 1:2). These conjurers *peeped and muttered* (v. 19). The words here may refer either to the muffling of their heads or to the muffling of their voices, their manner of speaking. They did not speak with boldness and clarity, but as those who want to entertain people rather than instruct them. There were explicit laws against this evil (Lev 19:31; 20:27), but it was still found in Israel and is found even in Christian nations. Dread the use of spells and charms; dread sorcerers who claim to tell fortunes and cure diseases.

2.2.2. He provides them with an answer to this temptation. "If anyone goes about trying to entrap you, reply to them in this way: *Should not a people seek to their God? What! for the living to the dead?* Why consult the dead on behalf of the living (v. 19)? Tell them that a people should seek their God. Jehovah is our God, and so we should seek him, consult him, not those who are mediums and spiritists (Mic 4:5). Should not a people who are under guilt and in trouble seek their God for pardon and peace? Should not a people in doubt, in need, and in danger seek their God for direction, supply, and protection?" What can be more absurd than to expect that our friends who are dead can do for us—when we make gods of them and pray to them—what our living friends cannot do? Mediums and spiritists, such as the witch of Endor, consulted the dead, and so declared their own foolishness.

2.2.3. He tells them to consider the words of God. If the prophets who live among them do not speak directly to every situation, they still have the written word, and they must turn to that. Those who know how to make good use of their Bibles will never be drawn to consult mediums and spiritists. Make God's statutes your counselors (Ps 119:24), and you will be counseled rightly. Notice:

2.2.3.1. What use we must make of the law and the testimony. We must *speak according to that word* (v. 20), that is, we must make it our standard (1Ti 6:3).

2.2.3.2. Why we must make this use of it: because those who do not agree with the word of God are showing that *there is no light* (v. 20), no "light of dawn," *in them*. Those who reject divine revelation do not even have human understanding; nor is the authority of reason rightly admitted by those who will not admit the authoritative words of God. Some read it as a threat: "If they do not speak according to this word, there will be no light to them; they will be driven to darkness and despair," as described here (vv. 21–22). What light did Saul have when he consulted the witch (1Sa 28:18, 20)?

2.2.4. He reads the condemnation of those who seek mediums and spiritists and do not consider God's law and testimony; they may expect horror and misery (vv. 21 22). They will *pass through* the land, unsettled. They will be *hardly bestead* (distressed) (v. 21), uncertain where to go for the necessary supports of life. Those who used to be fully satisfied will be hungry. Those who turn away from God leave the way of goodness. These people, *when they shall be hungry, shall fret themselves* (will become enraged) (v. 21) and be very provocative to everyone around them. They will forget all the rules of duty and decency and will treasonably *curse their king* (v. 21) and blasphemously curse *their God* (v. 21). When they have broken the ties of their loyalty, it is hardly surprising if the ties of their faith do not hold them for long: they move on to cursing their God, curse him and die (Job 2:9). They will look upward, but heaven will frown on them and look gloomy, and how can it be otherwise when they curse their God? They will look to the earth, but what encouragement can that give to those with whom God is at war?

CHAPTER 9

In this chapter the prophet says to the righteous, It will be well with thee, but Woe to the wicked, it will be ill with him (3:10–11). 1. Gracious promises are given to those who are faithful to the law and the testimony. While those who consult spiritists will be driven into darkness and dimness (8:19–22), the faithful will see a great light, relief in the midst of their distresses. This light is a type of Gospel grace (vv. 1–3) as it appears in the doctrine of the Messiah, in his victories (vv. 4–5), and in his rule as Immanuel (vv. 6–7). 2. Terrible threats are uttered against the people of Israel, who have rebelled (vv. 8–10): that their neighbors will attack them (vv. 11–12), that because of their impenitence and godlessness, all their enhancements and supports will be cut off (vv. 13–17), and that by the wrath of God against them and their wrath against one another, they will be brought to complete ruin (vv. 18–21).

Verses 1–7

The first words of this chapter clearly refer to the close of the previous chapter, where everything looked sad and black: *Behold, trouble, and darkness, and dimness* (8:22); yet *to the upright there shall arise light in the darkness* (Ps 112:4). And the dimness *shall not be such dimness* (gloom) (v. 1) as there has sometimes been. In the worst of times God's people have a *but* to balance out their troubles; they are persecuted but not abandoned (2Co 4:9), sorrowful but always rejoicing (2Co 6:10). And it is a matter of comfort to us, when things are at their darkest, that he who *forms the light and creates the darkness* (45:7) has appointed limits to both and set one against the other (Ge 1:4; Ecc 7:14).

1. Three things are promised here, and they all point ultimately to the grace of the Gospel, with which the saints will encourage themselves on every cloudy and dark day:

1.1. A glorious light, which will gradually dispel the gloom, so that it will not be as it has sometimes been, *not such as was in her vexation* (distress) (v. 1), *when at first he lightly afflicted the land of Zebulun and Naphtali*—which was remote and most exposed to the inroads of the neighboring enemies—*and* when *afterwards he more grievously afflicted the land by the way of the sea and beyond Jordan* (v. 1). If a light adversity does not humble and reform us, we must expect to be afflicted more severely. Israel has been *without the true God and a teaching priest, and in those times there was no peace* (2Ch 15:3, 5). But the fearful gloom threatened in 8:22 will not succeed to such a degree, for (v. 2) *the people that walked in darkness have seen a great light.* At this time when the prophet lived, there were many prophets in Judah and Israel, whose prophecies were a great light both for

direction and for encouragement to the people of God, prophets who were faithful to the law and the testimony. This was to have its complete fulfillment when our Lord Jesus appeared as a prophet and began to preach the Gospel in the land of Zebulun and Naphtali, and in Galilee of the Gentiles (v. 1).

1.2. A glorious increase and a universal joy arising from that increase (v. 3) *"Thou, O God, hast multiplied* (enlarged) *the nation.* It has been decreased by one severe judgment after another; now you have begun to multiply it again." But it follows, *"Thou hast not increased the joy* (v. 3)—the worldly joy and enjoyment. But despite that, *they joy before thee* (v. 3); there is a great deal of deep spiritual joy among them, joy in the presence of God." This applies very much to the times of Gospel light, spoken of in v. 2. "And to him," as the Masoretes read it, "you have magnified the joy, to everyone who receives the light." The following words favor this reading: *"They joy before thee*; they come before you in holy worship with great joy; their happiness is not like that of Israel under their vines and fig trees (1Ki 4:25; 2Ki 18:31; etc.)—you have not increased that joy; their happiness is in the favor of God and in the signs of his grace." It is holy joy: *They joy before thee* (v. 3); they rejoice in spirit, as Christ did before God (Lk 10:21). It is a great joy; it is *according to the joy in harvest* (v. 3), when those who sowed in tears and have long waited patiently for the precious fruits of the earth reap in joy (Ps 126:5), and as in war soldiers rejoice when, after a dangerous battle, *they divide the spoil* (v. 3). The Gospel brings plenty and victory.

1.3. A glorious liberty and release (vv. 4–5): "They will rejoice in your presence, and with good reason, too, *for thou hast broken the yoke of his burden*, for he (the righteous person) will no longer be a slave, and you have broken *the staff of his shoulder and the rod of his oppressor*," as the Midianites' yoke was broken from the neck of Israel by the agency of Gideon. *Do unto them as to the Midianites.* What temporal rescue this refers to is not clear; probably it was the preventing of Sennacherib from controlling Jerusalem, which was done, *as in the day of Midian* (v. 4), by the direct hand of God, silently and without noise. But doubtless it also looks further, to that great light that would come to those who sat in darkness; it would bring *deliverance to the captives* (Lk 4:18). The purpose of the Gospel is to break the yoke of sin and Satan, to take away the burden of guilt and corruption, so that we may be brought into the glorious liberty of the children of God (Ro 8:21). Christ broke the yoke of the ceremonial law (Ac 15:10; Gal 5:1) and rescued us *out of the hand of our enemies* so that we might *serve him without fear* (Lk 1:74–75). This is done by the Spirit working like fire (Mt 3:11), not as the battle of the warrior is fought, with confused noise. No; the weapons of our warfare are not worldly (2Co 10:4).

2. But who and where is the One who will undertake and accomplish these great things for the church? The prophet tells us (vv. 6–7) they will be done by the Messiah, *Immanuel* (7:14), and he speaks about it, in prophetic style, as something already done: the *child is born* (v. 6), because the church before his incarnation reaped great benefits. As he was the Lamb that was slain *from the foundation of the world* (Rev 13:8), so also he was the child born from that time. All the great things that God did for the Old Testament church were done by him as the eternal Word and for his sake because he is the Mediator. The Jewish nation, especially the house of David, was preserved many times from imminent destruction only because that blessing was in it (65:8). The Aramaic

paraphrase understands this to refer to the man who will endure forever, namely Christ.

2.1. See him in his humiliation. The same One who is *the mighty God is a child born* (v. 6); this was how he humbled and emptied himself (Php 2:7), to exalt and fill us. He is born into our world. *The Word was made flesh, and dwelt among us* (Jn 1:14). God loved the world so much that he gave him (Jn 3:16). He is born *to us*, he is given to us.

2.2. See him in his exaltation. This child, this Son of God, this Son of Man, is invested with the highest honor and power, so that we must be happy if he is our friend.

2.2.1. See the dignity he is advanced to. His name is above every name. He will be called *Wonderful, Counsellor, mighty God, everlasting Father, Prince of Peace.* His people will know him and worship him by these names. He is *wonderful, counsellor.* Justly is he called *wonderful* (v. 6), for he is both God and a human being. He is the *counsellor,* for he knew intimately the counsels, or purposes (Ac 2:23), of God from eternity, and he gives counsel to people. He is the wisdom of the Father and is made by God to be wisdom to us (1Co 1:24, 30). He is *the mighty God* (v. 6), "God, the mighty One." As he has wisdom, so also he has strength. He is able to save completely (Heb 7:25). He is *the everlasting Father* (v. 6), or "the Father of eternity"; he is God, one with the Father (Jn 17:11), who is from everlasting to everlasting (Ps 90:2). He is the author of eternal life and happiness to his people, and is therefore the Father of a blessed eternity to them. He is *the prince of peace* (v. 6). As a King, he preserves, commands, and creates peace in his kingdom. He is our peace (Eph 2:14).

2.2.2. See the power he is advanced to. His throne is above every throne (v. 6): *The government shall be upon his shoulder*—only his. He will not only wear its emblems on his shoulder—the *key of the house of David* (22:22)—but also bear its burden. Glorious things are here spoken of Christ's government (Ps 87:3) (v. 7). It will be multiplied; the radiance will increase, and it will shine more and more brightly in the world (Pr 4:18). It will be a peaceful government, according to his character as the Prince of Peace. He will rule by love, and as his government increases, so will the peace increase. It will be administered with wisdom and justice: *He shall order it, and settle it, with justice and judgment* (v. 7). It will be an eternal kingdom: *There shall be no end of the increase of his government.* God himself has undertaken to bring all this about: *"The Lord of hosts,* who has all power in his hand and all creatures at his command, *shall perform this"* (v. 7).

Verses 8–21

Here are terrible threats directed primarily against Israel, the kingdom of the ten tribes, here called *Ephraim and Samaria.* This prophecy foretells the ruin of Israel, which took place within a few years, but it also looks further and announces the condemnation of all the nations that ignore God and refuse to have Christ reign over them (Lk 19:14, 27). Notice:

1. The introduction to this prophecy (v. 8): *The Lord sent a word into Jacob,* sent it by his servants the prophets. He warns before he wounds. But they were not concerned to turn away his wrath, and so it fell on them as a storm of rain and hail from on high, which they could not avoid.

2. The sins that the people of Israel are accused of, which provoked God to bring these judgments on them.

2.1. Their arrogant defiance of the justice of God, their thinking themselves a match for him: "They say,

in the pride and stoutness of their heart (v. 9), 'Let God do his worst. If he ruins our houses, we will repair them and make them stronger. If the houses that were built of bricks are demolished in the war, we will rebuild them with dressed stone. If the enemy cuts down the fig trees, we will plant cedars.'"

2.2. Their incorrigibleness under all the rebukes of Providence up to that time (v. 13): *The people turn not* (have not returned) *unto him that smiteth* (struck) *them, neither do they seek the Lord of hosts;* either they are atheists and have no religious faith, or they are idolaters and seek those gods that are the creations of their own imagination and the works of their own hands.

2.3. Their general corruption in life and their great ungodliness. Those who should have reformed them helped defile them (v. 16): "*The leaders of this people* mislead them and *cause them to err.*" Things are seriously wrong with a people when their doctors are their worst disease. "*Those that bless this people*" — or "call them blessed," as the margin reads — "who flatter them and soothe them in their evil ways and cry out *Peace, peace, to them* (Jer 6:14; 8:11), lead them astray." We have reason to fear those who speak well of us when we do wrong; see Pr 24:24; 29:5. Evil was universal, and all were defiled by it (v. 17): *Every one is a hypocrite and an evil doer.* Everyone was ungodly toward God and an evildoer toward their fellow human beings. These two commonly go together: those who have no fear of God do not care what people think.

3. The judgments threatened against them for their evil.

3.1. In general, they had exposed themselves to the wrath of God. It would devour as fire (v. 18): *Wickedness shall burn as the fire.* When the fire consumes the briers and thorns, it will *mount up like the lifting up of smoke* (v. 18), so that the whole land will be darkened; they will be in trouble and see no way out (v. 19): *The people shall be as the fuel of the fire.*

3.2. God would strengthen the neighboring powers against them (vv. 11–12). At this time Israel was in league with Aram against Judah. But the Assyrians were the enemies of the Arameans, and when they had conquered the Arameans, they would invade Israel. And it would be God who would set the enemies of Israel in such an alliance — though the enemies themselves did not consider each other allies. Those who share with each other in sin, as Aram and Israel did in invading Judah, must expect also to share in the punishment of sin. The Arameans themselves, whom Israel was now in league with, would be a scourge to them, attacking them in front while the Philistines attacked their side or rear. They would be surrounded by enemies, who would *devour them with open mouth* (v. 12). The Philistines were not now looked on as formidable enemies, and the Arameans were looked on as firm friends, but these would devour Israel.

3.3. God would take from their midst those they trusted in (vv. 14–15). *The Lord will cut off head and tail, branch and rush,* which is explained in the next verse.

3.3.1. Their judges, who were honorable by birth and office, were *the head* and the *branch*, but because they led the people astray, they would be cut off

3.3.2. Their false prophets were *the tail* and the *rush*, the most contemptible of all. An evil minister is the worst kind of person. The best things become the worst when they are corrupted.

3.4. The devastation would be as general as the corruption had been, and no one would escape it (v. 17): *The Lord shall have no joy in their young men,* who were in the flower of their youth, nor will he say, *Deal gently with the young men for my sake* (2Sa 18:5). He *shall not have mercy on their fatherless and widows* (v. 17), even though he especially is the patron and protector of such. They had corrupted their ways like all the others.

3.5. Everyone would help forward the common destruction: *No man shall spare his brother* (v. 19). Civil wars soon devastate a kingdom. There were such wars in Israel in these quarrels. People *snatched on the right hand, and yet were hungry* still, and ate the *flesh of their own arms*, preyed on themselves because they were so hungry (v. 20). This speaks of famine and scarcity. These quarrels would be not only among particular individuals and private families but also among the tribes (v. 21): *Manasseh shall devour Ephraim, and Ephraim Manasseh.* Those who could unite against Judah could not unite with one another. Mutual hatred among the tribes of God's Israel is a sin that prepares them for destruction and is a sad symptom of destruction coming quickly.

3.6. Although they would be followed with all these judgments, God would not abandon his dispute with them. It is the refrain of this song (vv. 12, 17, 21): *For all this his anger is not turned away, but his hand is stretched out still.* They do not repent and reform. His anger therefore continues to burn against them, and *his hand is stretched out still. The people turn not to him that smites them* (v. 13), and so he continues to strike them.

CHAPTER 10

In this chapter, the prophet deals with: 1. The proud oppressors of his people at home, who abused their power (vv. 1–4). 2. A threatening invader of his people from abroad, Sennacherib king of Assyria. Concerning him, observe: 2.1. The commission given him to invade Judah (vv. 5–6). 2.2. His pride and arrogance in carrying out that commission (vv. 7–11, 13–14). 2.3. A rebuke given to his pride and a threat that he would fall and come to ruin when he had served the purposes for which God had raised him up (vv. 12, 15–19). 2.4. A promise of grace to the people of God to enable them to endure this affliction (vv. 20–23). 2.5. Great encouragement to them not to fear this threatening storm, but to hope that it would all end with the destruction of this formidable enemy (vv. 24–34).

Verses 1–4

It is not certain whether those against whom the prophet announced this woe were the rulers and judges of Israel or of Judah, or both. Here is:

1. The indictment drawn up against these oppressors (vv. 1–2). They are accused of:

1.1. Making unjust laws and edicts: they *decree unrighteous decrees.* Woe to the higher powers that make these decrees! And woe to the lower officers who draw them up and record them—those who *write the grievousness.*

1.2. Perverting the course of justice by executing the laws that were made.

1.3. Enriching themselves by oppressing those who were at their mercy. They *rob the fatherless* (v. 2) of the little that is left to them, because they have no friends to speak up for them.

2. A challenge given them. Let them, with all their pride and power, defy the judgments of God (v. 3): "*What will you do? To whom will you flee?* You can trample on the widows and fatherless, but *what will you do when God riseth up?*" (Job 31:14). "*Where will you leave your glory* (v. 3), to find it again when the storm is over?" The

wealth they have gained is their glory, and they have no safe place in which to deposit it.

3. Sentence passed on them, by which they are condemned. Some are condemned to imprisonment and exile—*they shall bow down under* (or among) *the prisoners*—others to death. Those who have trampled on the widows and fatherless will themselves be trodden down (v. 4). "It will come to this," God says, "*without me,* that is, because you have abandoned me and driven me away from you."

Verses 5–19

The destruction of the kingdom of Israel by Shalmaneser king of Assyria was foretold in the previous chapter, and it was fulfilled in the sixth year of Hezekiah (2Ki 18:10). It was complete and final; head and tail were both destroyed (9:14). Now the correction of the kingdom of Judah by Sennacherib king of Assyria is foretold in this chapter, and this prediction was fulfilled in the fourteenth year of Hezekiah (2Ki 18:13, 17). It ended in the confusion of the Assyrians and the great encouragement of Hezekiah and his people in their return to God.

1. God, in his sovereignty, appointed the king of Assyria to be his servant and used him as a tool (vv. 5–6): "*O Assyrian!* Know this, that you are *the rod of my anger,* and I will send you to be a scourge to *the people of my wrath.*" The Jews, though they appeared good, were *a hypocritical nation,* who professed religion, and at this time particularly professed reformation, but were not truly religious, not truly reformed. Some read it, "a profane (ungodly) nation." Hezekiah had to a large extent healed them of their idolatry, and now they became ungodly; hypocrisy is ungodliness. Because they were a godless, hypocritical nation, they were the people of God's wrath. Notice what a change sin made: those who had been God's chosen and holy people had now become the *people of his wrath* (Am 3:2). The Assyrian, even though he appeared very great, was only *the rod of God's anger* (v. 5), an instrument God used to rebuke his people. *The staff* (club) *in their* (the Assyrians') *hand,* with which they struck his people, *was his indignation* (v. 5); it was his wrath that put the club into their hand. Sometimes God makes an idolatrous nation, which does not serve him at all, to be a scourge to a godless nation that does not serve him in sincerity and truth. The Assyrian is called the *rod of God's anger* (v. 5) because he was employed by him. *I will send him; I will give him a charge* (v. 6). The Assyrian was *to take the spoil and to take the prey,* to seize loot and snatch plunder (v. 6), not to shed any blood. He was to plunder the country, ransack the houses, drive away the cattle, deprive the people of all their wealth and ornaments, and *tread them down like the mire of the streets* (v. 6). But why must the Assyrian triumph like this against them? Not so they may be destroyed, but so they may be reformed.

2. The king of Assyria, in his pride, claimed to be absolute and acting for his own honor. *God ordained him for judgment,* to be an instrument of bringing his people to repentance, *howbeit he means not so* (but this is not what he intends), *nor does his heart think so* (nor is this what he has in mind) (v. 7).

2.1. He does not think that he is either God's servant or Israel's friend. God intends to correct his people, heal them of their hypocrisy, and bring them closer to himself, but was that Sennacherib's intention?

2.2. He intends nothing but *to destroy and to cut off nations not a few* (v. 7) and to take control of them. He wants to satisfy his own greed and to set himself up as a universal monarch.

2.3. The prophet here describes him as boasting and intimidating, and his general's letter to Hezekiah, written in his name, seems to show that boasting and arrogance have entered into his spirit. His pride and arrogance are described here partly to portray him as ridiculous and partly to assure the people of God that he will be brought down.

2.3.1. He boasts about the great things he has done to other nations. He has made their kings his courtiers (v. 8): "*My princes are altogether* (my commanders are all) *kings.* Those who are now my commanders are those who have been kings." Or those who are absolute rulers in their own dominions hold their crowns under him and pay him homage. He himself has taken control of their cities. He names several that were all conquered by him (v. 9). *Calno* yielded as quickly as *Carchemish* did, *Hamath* could not hold out any more than *Arpad*, and *Samaria* has become his, as has *Damascus.* He *found out the kingdoms of the idols* and found ways to make them his own (v. 10). Sennacherib vainly imagines that every conquest of a kingdom was the conquest of a god. He has enlarged his own territories and *removed the bounds of the people* (v. 13), enclosing many large territories within the limits of his own kingdom. *I have robbed their treasures* (v. 13). Great conquerors are often no better than great robbers. "*I have put down the inhabitants as a valiant man* (v. 13). Those who were proud I have humbled."

2.3.2. He boasts about the way in which he has dealt with them. He boasts he has done all this by his own skill and power (v. 13): "*By the strength of my hand,* for I am strong, *and by my wisdom, for I am prudent* (have understanding)." He has done all this with no difficulty and has made it but a diversion, as if he had been taking eggs from birds' nests (v. 14): *My hand has found as a nest the riches of the people.* "*As one gathers the eggs that are left* in the nest by a bird, so easily *have I gathered all the earth.*" Like Alexander, he thinks he has conquered the world.

2.3.3. He threatens what he will do to Jerusalem, which he is now about to lay siege to (vv. 10–11). He blasphemously calls the God of Israel an *idol,* setting him on the same level as the false gods of other nations, as if none were the true God except Mithras, the sun, which he worships. He might have known that the worshipers of the God of Israel were expressly forbidden to make any idols, and that if any did, they did it secretly, and so their idols could not be so rich and ostentatious as those of other nations. If he is referring to the ark and the atonement cover, he speaks like himself, very foolishly. Those who make external show and splendor a mark of the true church follow the same rule. Because he has conquered Samaria, he concludes that Jerusalem will fall. But it does not follow, for Jerusalem has been faithful to its God, whereas Samaria has abandoned him.

3. God, in his justice, rebukes his pride and reads his condemnation.

3.1. He shows the futility of Sennacherib's bold, arrogant boasts (v. 15): *Shall the axe boast itself against him that hews therewith? Or shall the saw magnify itself against him that shaketh it?* "Oh look at how much dust I'm making!" said the fly on the cartwheel in the fable. "What destruction am I making among the trees!" says the ax. The ax may be said to *boast itself against him that hews with it* in two ways.

3.1.1. By way of resistance and opposition. Sennacherib blasphemed God, threatening to deal with him as he had with the gods of the nations; now this was as if the ax would go completely against the person who was cutting with it. The tool fighting against the worker is no less

absurd than the clay striving against the potter (45:9). Just as it cannot be justified for people to fight against God with the knowledge, wealth, and power he gives them, so also it cannot be tolerated.

3.1.2. By way of competition. Will the ax take for itself the praise for the work it has done? This is how absurd it was for Sennacherib to say, *By the strength of my hand I have done it, and by my wisdom* (v. 13). It was as if the rod, when it was wielded, boasted that it guided the hand that wielded it, whereas "when the staff is lifted up, is it not still wood?"

3.2. He foretells his fall and ruin.

3.2.1. When God has done his work through him, he will do his work on him (v. 12). With reference to Sennacherib's invasion, God intends to do good to Zion and Jerusalem by this providence. When God brings his people into trouble, it is to remind them of their sin and to awaken them to a sense of duty, teaching them to pray and to love and help one another. When these things have, to some extent, been achieved by the suffering, it will be removed in mercy (Lev 26:41–42). The rod will *accomplish that for which God sends it* (Isa 55:11). When God has carried out this work of grace for his people, he will carry out a work of wrath on their invaders: *I will punish the fruit of the stout heart of the king of Assyria* (punish the king of Assyria for the willful pride of his heart) (v. 12).

3.2.2. This attempt on Zion and Jerusalem will certainly be thwarted and come to nothing (vv. 16, 19). God himself will do it, as *the Lord of hosts* and as *the light of Israel.* We are sure he can do it, for he is the Lord Almighty, Lord of all the powers of heaven and earth. We have reason to hope he will do it, for he is *the light of Israel, and his Holy One* (v. 17). This destruction will be like a wasting disease sent on the body: *The Lord shall send leanness among his fat ones* (v. 16). Sennacherib's numerous army, which is like a body covered with fatness, will be reduced, waste away, and become like a skeleton. *Under his glory he will kindle a burning, as the burning of a fire* (v. 16), which will destroy his army as suddenly as a raging fire reduces a stately home to ashes. *The light of Israel shall be for a fire* to the Assyrians, as the same pillar of cloud was a light to the Israelites and a terror to the Egyptians at the Red Sea. *It shall burn and devour its thorns and briers* (v. 17), burn his officers and soldiers like thorns and briers. "Even *the glory of his forest* (v. 18), the best troops in his army, which he valued as people do their timber trees (the glory of their forest) or their fruit trees (the glory of their Carmel) [Ed. note: compare 2Ki 19:23; *Carmel* means "fruitful field"], will be put as briers and thorns into the fire." The prophet tells us the army will be reduced to a very small number: *The rest of the trees of his forest shall be few* (v. 19). Those few who remain will be completely discouraged: *They shall be as when a standard-bearer fainteth* (v. 18).

Verses 20–23

The prophet has said (v. 12) that by Sennacherib's invasion of the land, *the Lord will perform his whole work upon Mount Zion and upon Jerusalem.* That work will be of two parts:

1. The conversion of some people, in whom this providence will produce the peaceful fruit of righteousness, even though for the present it is not joyful, but painful (Heb 12:11); these are only *a remnant* (v. 22), *the remnant of Israel* (v. 20), *the remnant of Jacob* (v. 21). This remnant of Israel is said to be *such as have escaped of the house of Jacob* (v. 20), survivors who escaped the corruptions of the house of Jacob and kept their integrity in

times of general apostasy. "They *shall no more again stay* (rely) *upon him that smote* (struck) *them* (v. 20); they will never depend on the Assyrians for help against their other enemies, finding that the Assyrians are themselves their worst enemies." *"The remnant shall return"*—which was shown by the name of the prophet's son, *Shear-jashub* (7:3)—*"even the remnant of Jacob"* (v. 21). They will return, after the lifting of the siege of Jerusalem, not only to the quiet possession of their houses and lands but also to God and their duty. They will repent, pray, seek his face, and reform their lives." This promise of the conversion and salvation of a remnant of Israel (vv. 22–23) is applied by the apostle Paul (Ro 9:27–28) to the remnant of the Jews that received the Gospel when it was first preached.

2. The complete destruction of others: *The Lord God of hosts shall make a consumption* (v. 23). This meant the destruction of the possessions and families of many of the Jews by the Assyrian army. It is *determined* that there will be such a destruction; literally, it will be "cut out"; it is particularly appointed how far it will extend and how long it will continue. God will justly bring this destruction on an offensive people, but he will wisely and graciously set limits to it.

Verses 24–34

In his preaching, the prophet distinguishes between the precious and the worthless. In speaking of Sennacherib's invasion, he spoke terror to the godless, who were the *people of God's wrath* (v. 6). But here he speaks comfort to the sincere, who are the people of God's love. We have here:

1. An encouragement to God's people not to be frightened at this threatening disaster. *Let the sinners in Zion be afraid* (33:14), but *O my people, that dwellest in Zion, be not afraid of the Assyrian* (v. 24).

2. Considerations to silence their fears. The Assyrian will do nothing against them except what God has appointed and decreed. The storm will soon blow over (v. 25): *Yet a very little while*—"a little, little while" is the meaning—*and the indignation shall cease, even my anger*, which is *the staff in their hand* (v. 5). The enemy that threatens them will be judged. He *lifted up his staff* against Zion, but God *shall stir up a scourge for him*, lash him with a whip (v. 26); he is a terror to God's people, but God will be a terror to him. To encourage God's people, the prophet quotes precedents. The destruction of the Assyrian will be *according to the slaughter of Midian*, which was brought about by an invisible power; and just as *at the rock of Oreb* (v. 26) one of the leaders of Midian was killed after the battle (1Sa 15:32), so will Sennacherib be killed after the defeat of his forces. And *as his rod was upon the sea* (v. 26), the Red Sea, first to divide it for Israel to escape and then to close it to destroy their pursuers, so will his rod now be *lifted up, after the manner of Egypt* (v. 26), to rescue Jerusalem and destroy the Assyrian. They will be completely rescued from the power of the Assyrian and from the fear of it (v. 27). The yoke will not only be taken away; it *shall be destroyed because of the anointing* (v. 27), for the sakes of those who shared in the anointing.

- For the sake of Hezekiah, the anointed of the Lord, an active reformer, precious to God.
- For the sake of David. This is why God would defend Jerusalem from Sennacherib (37:35).
- For the sake of his people Israel, the good people among them.
- For the sake of the Messiah, the Anointed One of God.

3. A description of how terrible the enemy was and the terror with which many were struck by them. Notice:

3.1. How formidable the Assyrians were. Here is a particular description of the march of Sennacherib, what swift advances he made: *He has come to Aiath* (v. 28). *At Michmash he has laid up his carriages* (stored up supplies) (v. 28), as if he had no further need for his heavy artillery, so easily was every place subdued; or the store cities of Judah, which had been fortified, had now become his storehouses. He had taken some remarkable pass: *They have gone over the passage* (v. 29).

3.2. How cowardly the people of Judah were, the corrupt seed of that lion's cub (Ge 49:9). They fled on the first alarm. And *poor Anathoth*, a priests' town, which should have been an example of courage, shrieked more loudly than any other (v. 30). Those who *gathered themselves together* did not do so to fight, but to flee together (v. 31). This shows how fast the news of the enemy's progress flew through the kingdom: *He has come to Aiath*, says one; no, says another, *He has passed to Migron* (v. 28).

3.3. How powerless Sennacherib's attempt on Jerusalem will be: *He shall remain at Nob*, from which he may see Mount Zion, and there *he shall shake his hand* against it (v. 32). He will threaten it, and that will be all.

3.4. How fatal it will prove to him. When he *shakes his hand at Jerusalem* (v. 32), *the Lord shall lop the bough with terror and cut down the thickets of the forest* (vv. 33–34). The high and stately trees will be cut down, that is, the proud will be humbled. *The thickets of the forest he shall cut down* (v. 34). When the Assyrian soldiers were armed, their spears upright, they looked like a forest, like Lebanon, but when in one night they all became corpses (2Ki 19:35), Lebanon was suddenly cut down *by a mighty one* (v. 34), by the destroying angel, and if this is the departure of that proud invader, let not God's people be afraid of him.

CHAPTER 11

It is a very good transition in prophecy to pass from the prediction of the temporal rescue of the church to that of the great salvation that in the fullness of time would be brought about by Jesus Christ, of which the other rescues were types. On the occasion of the prophecy of the rescue of Jerusalem from Sennacherib there comes a prophecy about Messiah the Ruler. 1. His rise from the house of David (v. 1). 2. His qualifications for his great undertaking (vv. 2–3). 3. The justice of his government (vv. 3–5). 4. The peacefulness of his kingdom (vv. 6–9). 5. The admission of the Gentiles to it (v. 10), and with them the remnant of the Jews, who would be united with them in the Messiah's kingdom (vv. 11–16). And God would soon give them a type of all this, some shadowy representation, in the excellent government of Hezekiah, the great peace the nation would enjoy under him after Sennacherib's plans were overturned, and the return of many of the ten tribes from their dispersion to their own people in the land of Judah.

Verses 1–9

The prophet spoke earlier about a child who would be born, on whose shoulders the government would rest (9:6). He said (10:27) that *the yoke would be destroyed because of the anointing*; now here he tells us on whom that anointing would rest.

1. The Messiah would, in due time, rise up out of the house of David as that *branch* of the Lord that the prophet

had said (4:2) would be glorious. This branch would come up from *Jesse*. He would be the son of David, with whom the royal covenant was made. David is often called *the son of Jesse*, and Christ is also called this. He is called *a rod* (shoot) and *a branch*; both words refer to a small, tender product, "a twig" and "a sprig," such as is easily broken off. The enemies of God's church have just been compared to stately boughs (10:33), and Christ is compared to a tender shoot (53:2), yet he will be victorious over them. He is said to come from Jesse rather than David, because Jesse lived and died in lowliness and obscurity; his family was insignificant (1Sa 18:18). The Messiah will come up from the *stem*, or stump, of Jesse. The house of David was reduced and brought very low at the time of Christ's birth, as seen in the obscurity and poverty of Joseph and Mary. The Aramaic paraphrase reads: "There shall come forth a King from the sons of Jesse, and the Messiah" — or "Christ" — "shall be anointed out of his sons' sons."

2. He would be qualified in every way for that great work to which he was intended. This tender branch would be so watered by the dew of heaven (Da 4:15, 23, 25) as to become a strong rod for a scepter to rule (v. 2). *The Spirit of the Lord shall rest upon him*. He will have the Spirit not in a limited way, but without limit (Jn 4:34), the fullness of the Godhead dwelling in him (Col 1:19; 2:9). He began his preaching with this: *The Spirit of the Lord is upon me* (Lk 4:18). He will have *the spirit of wisdom and understanding, of counsel and knowledge* (v. 2). He will know how to administer the affairs of his spiritual kingdom so as to fulfill its two great intentions, the glory of God and the well-being of people. He was well-known for the courage he showed by teaching the way of God in truth and not being swayed by what people thought or said (Mt 22:16).

3. He would be precise and exact in the administration of his government and the exercise of the power committed to him (v. 3): the Spirit with whom he will be clothed *shall make him of quick understanding in the fear of the Lord*. Jesus Christ had the Spirit without limit (Jn 4:34), so that he might completely understand his undertaking.

4. He would be just and righteous in all the acts of his government: *He shall not judge after the sight of his eyes*, showing partiality (Job 34:19), nor *reprove after the hearing of his ears* (v. 3), by what others said about a person, as human beings often do. Nor does he judge people by the fine words they speak, *calling him, Lord, Lord* (Mt 7:21); rather, he will judge by the hidden spirit of the heart (1Pe 3:4) and the inner motives and principles that direct people's lives, of which he is an infallible witness. He will make righteous judgments (v. 5): *Righteousness shall be the girdle of his loins* (will be his belt). It will constantly surround him and will be his honor; he will be prepared for every action, will put on his sword for war in righteousness. *With righteousness shall he judge the poor*; he will judge in favor and defense of those who have right on their side, even though they are poor in the world, and because they are poor in spirit (Mt 5:3). Christ is the poor man's King (Ps 72:2, 4). He will *rebuke with equity for the meek of the earth* (v. 4), or of the land. Some read it, "He shall reprove or correct the meek of the earth with equity." If his own people, the meek of the land, do wrong, he will *visit their transgression with the rod. But he shall smite* (strike) *the earth*, earthly mortals who oppress (Ps 10:18), *with the rod of his mouth* (v. 4), the word of his mouth, speaking terror and ruin to them. *With the breath of his lips* (v. 4), by the activity of his Spirit, according to his word, *he shall slay* (kill) *the wicked*.

5. There would be great peace and tranquility under his government (9:6). Peace means two things:

5.1. Unity or concord, suggested in these figurative promises. Even *the wolf shall dwell* peacefully *with the lamb* (v. 6); people with the most fierce and furious temperaments will have their temper so wonderfully changed by the grace of Christ that they will live in love even with the weakest people and those whom they previously attacked. Christ, who is our peace (Eph 2:14), came to remove all enmity and to establish lasting friendships among his followers, especially between Jews and Gentiles. *The leopard shall* not only not tear the goat, but *lie down with her*: even *their young ones shall lie down together* (v. 6) and be brought up to live in blessed harmony. *The lion* will stop being greedy and *shall eat straw like the ox* (v. 7), as some think all the wild animals did before the Fall. *The asp* (cobra) and *the cockatrice* (viper) will stop being poisonous, so that parents will let their children *play* with them. A generation of vipers (Mt 3:7) will become a seed of saints. This is fulfilled in the wonderful effect of the Gospel on the minds of those who sincerely accept it; it changes the nature, so that those who used to trample on the meek of the earth become not only meek like them but also affectionate toward them. Some hope it will be further fulfilled in the last days, when *swords shall be beaten into ploughshares* (2:4; Mic 4:3).

5.2. Safety or security. Christ, the great Shepherd, will take such care of his flock that not only will they not destroy one another, but no enemy from outside will be allowed to harm them in any way. God's people will be rescued not only from evil but also from the fear of it.

5.3. The effect of this peace will be people who are amenable and willing to receive instruction: *A little child shall lead those* (v. 6) who formerly defied being controlled even by the strongest person. The cause of this peace will be the knowledge of God. The deeper the knowledge of God is, the greater the disposition to peace. *The earth shall be full of the knowledge of the Lord* (v. 9), which will extinguish human rage and anger. There is much more of the knowledge of God to be gained by the Gospel of Christ than could be gained by the Law of Moses.

Verses 10–16

Here is a further prophecy of the enlargement and advancement of the kingdom of the Messiah, under the type and figure of Judah at the end of Hezekiah's reign, after the defeat of Sennacherib.

1. This prediction was partially fulfilled when the great things God did for Hezekiah and his people proved to be like a banner, inviting the neighboring nations to them to *inquire of the wonders done in the land* (2Ch 32:31); it was on such a mission that the king of Babylon's envoys came. The Gentiles, the nations, rallied to and sought them, and Jerusalem was then glorious (v. 10). At that time many of the Israelites of the ten tribes, who were forced by the king of Assyria to flee for shelter to all the countries around, were encouraged to return to their own country and put themselves under the protection of the king of Judah. This is said to be a *second time* to reclaim them (v. 11), an example of the power of God like their first rescue from Egypt. The *outcasts* (exiles) *of Israel* would be brought home, and those of Judah too. The old enmity between Ephraim and Judah would be forgotten, and they would join against the Philistines and their other common enemies (vv. 13–14). When God's time has come for the rescue of his people, mountains of opposition will become clear before him. Let us not despair,

therefore, when the interests of the church seem to be very low; God can soon turn gloomy days into glorious ones.

2. It had a further reference to the days of the Messiah and the admission of the Gentiles to his kingdom, for to these things the apostle Paul applies v. 10, of which the following verses are a continuation. *There shall be a root of Jesse; and he that shall rise to reign over the Gentiles, in him shall the Gentiles trust* (Ro 15:12). That verse is a key to Isaiah's prophecy, which speaks about Christ as the root of Jesse, or *a branch out of his roots* (v. 1), *a root out of a dry ground* (53:2).

2.1. *He shall stand*, or be set up, *for an ensign of* (as a banner for) *the people* (v. 10). When he was crucified, he was *lifted up from the earth*, so that, as an ensign or banner, he might *draw* the eyes and the hearts of *all men unto him* (Jn 12:32). He is set up as a banner in the preaching of the eternal Gospel, in which the ministers, as standard-bearers, display the banner of his love (SS 2:4).

2.2. *To him shall the Gentiles seek* (v. 10). We read of Greeks that did so: *We would see Jesus* (Jn 12:21).

2.3. *His rest shall be glorious* (v. 10). Some understand this to refer to the death of Christ—the triumphs of the cross made even that glorious—others to his ascension, when he sat down to rest at the right hand of God (Heb 1:3). Or it may refer to the Gospel church.

2.4. Both Jews and Gentiles will be gathered to him (v. 11), a remnant of both, a small remnant in comparison, reclaimed with great difficulty. There will be a remnant of the Jews gathered in: *The outcasts* (exiles) *of Israel and the dispersed* (scattered people) *of Judah* (v. 12), many of whom, when they were brought to Christ, were *Jews of the dispersion*.

2.5. There will be a happy settlement between Judah and Ephraim, and both will be safe from their enemies and rule over them (vv. 13–14). The combination of Judah and Israel at that time was a type of the uniting of Jews and Gentiles, for when Judah and Ephraim are at peace with one another, *they shall fly upon* (swoop down on) *the shoulders of the Philistines* (v. 14) as an eagle strikes at its prey and will extend their conquests eastward over the Edomites, Moabites, and Ammonites; and similarly, some of all nations will become obedient to the Christian faith.

2.6. Everything that might hinder the progress and success of the Gospel will be taken out of the way; when Jews and Gentiles are to be brought together into the Gospel church, all obstructions will be removed (vv. 15–16), difficulties that seemed insuperable will be strangely overcome, and *the blind shall be led by a way that they knew not*. See 42:15–16; 43:19–20. Converts will be brought in chariots and in wagons (66:20).

CHAPTER 12

The salvation promised in the previous chapter was compared to that of Israel in the day that he came up out of the land of Egypt (11:16). As Moses and the children of Israel then sang a song of praise to the glory of God (Ex 15:1–21), so will the people of God do on that day when the root of Jesse will stand as a banner for the people (11:10) and will be the desire and joy of all nations (Hag 2:7). On that day: 1. Every believer will sing a song of praise (vv. 1–3). Thou shalt say, Lord, I will praise thee (v. 1). 2. Many will join together in praising God for the common benefit arising from this salvation (vv. 4–6).

Verses 1–3

This is the first part of the hymn of praise prepared for the use of the church, of the Jewish church when God

rescued them and of the Christian church when the kingdom of the Messiah was to be set up in the world. When the scattered church is united as one body, it will, as one, praise God in this way:

1. The promise is sure, and its blessings, when given, will provide the church with abundant matter for thanksgiving.

2. *Thou shalt say*, that is, "you should say so." *In that day*, when many are brought home to Jesus Christ and flock to him as doves to their windows (60:8), *thou shalt say, O Lord! I will praise thee*.

2.1. Believers are taught here to give thanks to God for the turning away of his displeasure and the return of his favor. (v. 1): *O Lord! I will praise thee, though thou wast angry with me*. Even God's frowns must not put us out of tune for praising him. By Jesus Christ, the root of Jesse (11:10), God's anger against the human race was turned away, for *he is our peace* (Eph 2:14). God strengthens those whom he is reconciled to. God sometimes brings his people into a desert so that there he may speak tenderly to them (Hos 2:14).

2.2. They are taught to triumph in God (v. 2): "*Behold*, and wonder; *God is my salvation*; not only my Savior, by whom I am saved, but also my salvation, in whom I am safe." We have work to do and temptations to resist, and we may depend on him to make us able to accomplish both. We have many troubles to experience, and we may depend on him to encourage us and strengthen us in all our troubles, for he *giveth songs in the night* (Job 35:10). Notice the title given to God here: *Jah, Jehovah* (v. 2). *Jah* is the contraction of *Jehovah*, and both refer to his eternity and unchangeableness, which are a great comfort and encouragement to those who depend on him as their strength and their song.

2.3. They are taught to draw comfort to themselves from the love of God (v. 3): "Therefore, because the Lord Jehovah is your strength and song and will be your salvation, *out of the wells of salvation* in God, who is the fountain of all good to his people, *you shall draw water with joy*. God's promises, which are revealed, confirmed, and given to us in his ordinances, are wells of salvation."

Verses 4–6

This is the second part of this evangelical song; in the first, believers stir up themselves to praise God, and here they invite and encourage one another to do so. Notice:

1. Who are called on to praise God here—*The inhabitants of Zion* and Jerusalem, whom God had protected from Sennacherib's force (v. 6). They should be most eager and zealous to praise him. *Thou inhabitress of Zion*; the word is feminine. Let the weaker sex be strong in the Lord, and then out of their mouths his praise will be made complete (Mt 21:16).

2. How they must praise the Lord.

2.1. By prayer: *Call upon his name* (v. 4). Seeking further mercy is graciously accepted as a thankful acknowledgment of the mercies already received.

2.2. By preaching and writing. We must not only speak to God but also speak to others about him: "proclaim his name." *Declare his doings* (what he has done) *among the people* (v. 4), among the nations, so that they may be brought into fellowship with Israel and the God of Israel. When the apostles preached the Gospel to all nations, beginning at Jerusalem, then this Scripture was fulfilled: "*Cry out and shout* (v. 6); welcome the Gospel to yourselves and declare it to others with hurrahs and loud congratulations, as those who shout for victory (Ex 32:18) or for the coronation of a king" (Nu 23:21). *Great* is the Holy One (v. 6), for he is glorious in holiness (Ex 15:11); he is great because he is holy. It is the happiness of Israel that the God who is in covenant with them, and among them, is infinitely great.

CHAPTER 13

Up to this time the prophecies in this book related only to Judah and Israel, especially Jerusalem, but now the prophet begins to read the condemnation of several neighboring states and kingdoms, for the One who is King of saints is also King of nations. But the nations to whom these prophecies relate were all those the people of God were in some way or other connected with. The threats we find here against Babylon, Moab, Damascus, Egypt, Tyre, and so on were intended to encourage and strengthen those in Israel who feared God but were terrified and oppressed by those powerful neighbors and to alarm those among them who were evil. This chapter and most of the next contain what God had to say to Babylon and Babylon's king, who would in the course of time become a greater enemy to them than any other enemy had been, for which God would judge them ultimately. In this chapter we have: 1. A general meeting of the forces to be employed against Babylon (vv. 1–5). 2. The bloody work that those forces would do in Babylon (vv. 6–18). 3. The complete ruin and desolation of Babylon (vv. 19–22).

Verses 1–5

The general title of this book was *The vision of Isaiah the son of Amoz* (1:1), but the particular title of this sermon is *the burden of* (NIV: oracle concerning) *Babylon* (v. 1). It is a burden, a lesson they were to learn, as some understand it, but they would be reluctant to learn it, and so it would be a load that would lie heavily on them. It is the burden of Babylon or Babel, which at this time was dependent on the Assyrian monarchy, the capital of which was Nineveh, but soon afterward rebelled and became a monarchy by itself, a very powerful one, under Nebuchadnezzar. This prophet afterward foretold the exile of the Jews in Babylon (39:6). In these verses a summons is given to those powerful nations whom God would use as instruments for the destruction of Babylon. He names them (v. 17) *the Medes*, and it was they, in conjunction with the Persians and under the command of Darius and Cyrus, who were the ruin of the Babylonian monarchy.

1. Babylon is called *the gates of the nobles* here (v. 2), because of the many houses of nobles that were in it. But *the whole land* is doomed to destruction (v. 5), for although the nobles were the leaders in persecuting, the whole land agreed with them in it.

2. The people brought together to devastate Babylon are called here God's *sanctified ones* (v. 3), set apart for this service by the purpose and providence of God. This suggests that it was God's intention, though not theirs, that the war be a holy war; they wanted the enlargement of their own empire, but God had in mind the release of his people. Cyrus, the person mainly concerned, was justly called *a sanctified one* (v. 3), for he was God's anointed one (45:1) and a type of the One who was to come, They are called God's *mighty ones* (v. 3), because they received their power from God and were now to use it for him. It is said of Cyrus that in this expedition *God held his right hand* (45:1). Although Cyrus did not know God, God still used him as his servant—*I have surnamed thee my servant, though thou hast not known me* (45:4). They are very numerous, *a multitude, a great people, kingdoms*

of nations (v. 4), not inexperienced and cruel, but regular troops. *They come from a far country, from the end of heaven* (v. 5). The vast country of Assyria lay between Babylon and Persia.

3. The summons given them is effective. *A banner is lifted up upon the high mountain* (v. 2). It is the *Lord of hosts that musters the host of the battle* (v. 4).

Verses 6–18

We have here a description of the terrible destruction that will be brought about in Babylon by the Medes and Persians. Those who are now self-confident are told *to howl* (wail) and mourn, for:

1. *The day of the Lord is at hand* (v. 6), a minor day of judgment, when God will act as a just avenger of his own and his people's injured cause. *The day of the Lord cometh* (v. 9). God will deal severely with them for the harshness they exercised toward God's people.

2. Their hearts will fail them, and they will have neither courage nor comfort left (vv. 7–8). Those who on the day of peace were *proud, haughty,* and *terrible* (v. 11) will, when trouble comes, be discouraged and at their wits' end: *All hands shall be faint* (will go limp) (v. 7) and unable to hold a weapon, *and every man's heart shall melt* (v. 7); *they shall be amazed* (aghast) *at one another* (v. 8). In frightening themselves, they will frighten one another. *Their faces shall be as flames* (v. 8), pale as flames, through fear, or red as flames blushing at their cowardice.

3. All hope will fail them (v. 10): *The stars of heaven shall not give their light*, but will be clouded, and *the sun shall be darkened in his going forth*, a sure sign of bad weather.

4. God will punish them *for their iniquity*, especially the sin of pride (v. 11). That pride must now have its fall: *The haughtiness of the terrible* must now be *laid low* (v. 11), particularly the pride of Nebuchadnezzar and his son Belshazzar, who in their pride had trampled on the people of God.

5. There will be such a great slaughter that it will produce a scarcity of men (v. 12): *I will make a man more precious than fine gold.* Populous countries are soon depopulated by war.

6. Such confusion in their affairs will be like the *shaking of the heavens* with thunder and the *removing of the earth* by earthquakes. Everything will go to rack and ruin *in the day of the wrath of the Lord of hosts* (v. 13). Babylon, which used to be like a roaring lion and a raging bear (Pr 28:15), will become *as a chased roe* (hunted gazelle) *and as a sheep that no man takes up* (a sheep without a shepherd) (v. 14). The army, consisting of troops of several nations, will be so discouraged and dispersed that they will *turn every man to his own people* (v. 14).

7. There will be a scene of awful bloodshed, as is usual where the sword devours. The conqueror gives no mercy, but puts everyone to the sword. Those of other nations who come to help them will be destroyed with them. Since the most sacred laws of nature, and of humanity itself, are silenced by the fury of war, the conquerors will most cruelly *dash the children to pieces, and ravish the wives* (v. 16).

8. The enemy will be unstoppable. These Medes, together with the Persians, will accept no bribes (v. 17). The Medes *shall not regard silver.* They will show no pity (v. 18), not to the *young men* who are in the prime, not to the age of innocence—*they have no pity on the fruit of the womb, nor spare little children* (v. 18).

Verses 19–22

The great havoc and destruction that would, it was foretold, be made by the Medes and Persians in Babylon here end in its final destruction.

1. Babylon was a noble city. It was *the glory of kingdoms and the beauty of the Chaldees' excellency* (the glory of the Babylonians' pride) (v. 19); it was that *head of gold* (Da 2:37–38); it was called *the lady* (queen) *of kingdoms* (47:5), *the praise of the whole earth* (Jer 51:41); the word translate *roe* in v. 14 also means "pleasant," and so it was "like a pleasant roe," but it will be *as a chased roe* (hunted gazelle) (v. 14).

2. It is prophesied that it will be completely destroyed, like Sodom and Gomorrah. Babylon was taken when Belshazzar was partying, and although Cyrus and Darius did not demolish it, it gradually went to ruin. It is foretold here (v. 20) *that it shall never be inhabited*; during the reign of the Roman emperor Hadrian (AD 117–138) nothing remained but the wall. And whereas it was prophesied concerning Nineveh that when it would be deserted and left desolate, flocks would still lie down in its midst (Zep 2:13–14), it is here said concerning Babylon that *the Arabians*, who were *shepherds, shall not make their folds there* (v. 20); the country will be so barren that there will be no grazing for sheep. It will be occupied by *wild beasts*, which like to be by themselves. The houses of Babylon *shall be full of doleful creatures, owls and satyrs* (v. 21), which will themselves be frightened into them, and by those beasts all others will be frightened out of those houses. Benjamin Bar-Jona, in his *Itinerary*, speaking of Babel, has these words: "This is that Babel which was thirty miles in breadth; it is now laid waste. There are ruins of a palace of Nebuchadnezzar, but people dare not enter in for fear of snakes and scorpions, which possess the place." It is said that this destruction will come soon (v. 22): *Her time is near to come.* This prophecy of the destruction of Babylon was intended to support and strengthen the people of God when they were prisoners there and were greatly oppressed; the fulfillment of the prophecy came nearly 200 years after it was delivered.

CHAPTER 14

In this chapter: 1. The burden of Babylon is made heavier. 1.1. Israel's cause is pleaded in this quarrel with Babylon (vv. 1–3). 1.2. The king of Babylon will be brought down (vv. 4–20). 1.3. All the Babylonians will be cut off (vv. 21–23). 2. A confirmation of the prophecy of the destruction of Babylon, which was far away, is given in the prophecy of the destruction of the Assyrian army who invaded the land, which happened not long afterward (vv. 24–27). 3. The success of Hezekiah against the Philistines is foretold, along with the advantages that his people would gain from that (vv. 28–32).

Verses 1–3

Babylon must be ruined, because God has mercy in store for his people. The wrongs done to his people must be revenged on their persecutors. The yoke that Babylon has long placed on their necks must be broken, and they must be set free. Notice:

1. The basis of these favors to Jacob and Israel—God's commitment to be kind to them and his choice of them (v. 1): "*The Lord will have mercy on Jacob*, the seed of Jacob who are now exiles in Babylon, and *will yet choose them*, though he has seemed for a time to refuse and reject them."

2. The particular favors he intends for them: the *Lord will set them in their own land* (v. 1), out of which they were driven, the Holy Land, the Land of Promise. *Strangers* (foreigners) *shall be joined with them* (v. 1), saying, *We will go with you, for we have heard that God is with you* (Zec 8:23). These converts will be very helpful to them in their return home: *The people* among whom they live *shall take them*, take care of them, and *bring them to their place* (v. 2). The converts will be friends and servants, willing to do them all the good they can. In the return of the exiles from Babylon, all who were around them, according to Cyrus's proclamation, contributed to their move (Ezr 1:4, 6), not, like the Egyptians, because they were sick of them, but because they loved them. Many will choose to go with them; Israel *shall possess them in the land of the Lord for servants and handmaids* (v. 2). The advantages of that land made it paradise for those servants who had been strangers to the covenants of promise (Eph 2:12), for there was *one law to the stranger and to those that were born in the land* (Ex 12:49). Those who will not be reconciled will be subdued and humbled by them: *They shall take those captives whose captives they were* (take captive those whose captives they have been) *and shall rule over their oppressors* (v. 2), righteously but not vengefully. Israel will see a happy end to all their grievances (v. 3): *The Lord shall give thee rest from thy sorrow and thy fear, and from thy hard bondage.* God himself undertakes to work a blessed change.

Verses 4–23

The kings of Babylon, successively, were oppressors of God's people. The Babylonian monarchy was likely to be an absolute, universal, and perpetual one, and, in these claims, rivaled the Almighty; it was therefore very justly brought down, and the last monarch, Belshazzar, *was slain* (killed) *on that night* that Babylon was taken (Da 5:30). Notice:

1. The fall of the king of Babylon, and a most curious composition is prepared here to attach lasting marks of infamy to his memory. It gives us an account of the life and death of this mighty monarch, how he *went down slain to the pit* even though he had been *the terror of the mighty in the land of the living* (Eze 32:27). Here we have:

1.1. The vast extent of wealth and power that this monarch and monarchy reached. Babylon was *a golden city* (v. 4). The king of Babylon, having so much wealth, used it to help him *rule the nations* (v. 6), gave them the law and took pleasure in *weakening the nations* (v. 12), so that they might not be able to act against him. He brought upon vast armies onto the field that he *made the earth to tremble, and shook kingdoms* (v. 16); all his neighbors were afraid of him and were forced to submit to him.

1.2. The wretched abuse of all this wealth and power, in two ways:

1.2.1. Great oppression and cruelty. He is known by the name *oppressor* (v. 4); he has *the sceptre of the rulers* (v. 5), but it is *the staff of the wicked* (v. 5). *He smote the people* (he struck down peoples), not in justice, to correct and reform them, but *in wrath* (v. 6), *with a continual stroke.* He ruled them *in anger*; he who had directed everyone and everything around him could not control himself. He *made the world as a wilderness* (v. 17). He was harsh toward his prisoners (v. 17). He *opened not the house of his prisoners*; he would not let his captives go home; he kept them in close confinement and never allowed any to return to their own land. This refers especially to the Jewish people. He was also oppressive to his own subjects (v. 20): *Thou hast destroyed thy land, and slain* (killed) *thy people.*

1.2.2. Great pride and arrogance. Notice is taken here of his *pomp*, the extravagance of his retinue (v. 11). But it was his attitude that prepared him for destruction (vv. 13–14): *Thou hast said in thy heart*, like Lucifer (v. 12), *I will ascend into heaven.* The king of Babylon here promises himself he will surpass all his neighbors, that he will in fact be as far above those around him as heaven is above the earth. Belshazzar, in his last drunken cavorting, seems to have had a particular spite against God's Mount Zion when he called for the goblets of the temple at Jerusalem in order to desecrate them; see Da 5:2. He had the same attitude when he said, *I will sit upon the mount of the congregation* (assembly) *in the sides of the north* (v. 13), where Mount Zion is said to be situated (Ps 48:2). Perhaps Belshazzar was planning an expedition to Jerusalem at the time when God destroyed him. He wanted to rival the God of Israel, about whom he had heard that he had his residence *above the heights of the clouds* (v. 14). "*I will ascend* there," he says, "and be as great as he; I will be like the One whom they call *the Most High*" (v. 14). Some of the first founders of the Assyrian monarchy were deified, and stars took their names from them. "But," he says, "*I will exalt my throne above them*" (v. 13) all."

1.3. The complete ruin that would be brought on him. It is foretold:

1.3.1. That his wealth and power would be broken. He had long been an oppressor, but he would stop being so (v. 4). God would bring to an end those who would not stop sinning. *The Lord*, the righteous God, *has broken the staff of that wicked prince* (v. 5).

1.3.2. That he himself would be seized: *He is persecuted* (v. 6); violent hands are laid on him. It is the common fate of tyrants to be deserted by their flatterers. Tiberius and Nero saw themselves abandoned in this way.

1.3.3. That he would be killed and therefore be *weak as the dead* and *like unto them* (v. 10). *His pomp is brought down to the grave* (v. 11), that is, it perishes with him. This powerful ruler, who used to lie on a luxurious bed, would now have the *worms* (maggots) *spread under him and the worms covering him* (v. 11), which, although he thought he was a god, proved he came from the same mold as other humans.

1.3.4. That he would not have the honor of a burial, much less of a decent one. *The kings of the nations lie in glory* (v. 18), *every one in his own house* (v. 18), that is, in his own burial place. But this king of Babylon is *cast* (thrown) *out* and has no grave (v. 19); his dead body is thrown, like that of an animal, into the ditch, *like an abominable branch* of some harmful, poisonous plant, which no one will touch, or like the clothes of evildoers who are put to death, who, by the hand of justice, are *thrust through with a sword* (v. 19), on whose dead bodies heaps of stones are raised. The king of Babylon's dead body would be *trodden under feet* (v. 19) by the horses and soldiers and crushed to pieces. And so he *shall not be joined with his ancestors in burial* (v. 20).

1.4. The many who would triumph in his fall.

1.4.1. Now that he is gone, *the whole earth is at rest and is quiet*, for he was the great disturber of the peace. Now they all *break forth into singing*; the pine trees and cedars of Lebanon now feel safe; there is no danger now of their being cut down to provide him with timber. The neighboring princes, who are compared to pine trees and cedars (Zec 11:2), may now rest and no longer be afraid of being dispossessed of their rights.

1.4.2. The dead will welcome him, especially those whom he cruelly hastened there (vv. 9–10): *Hell from beneath is moved for thee, to meet thee at thy coming*, many people in the grave are very excited about meeting you when you go down there. *The chief ones* (leaders) *of the earth*, who when you go down there. were kept in awe by him, will mockingly rise from their thrones and ask him if he will be pleased to sit down on them, as he used to do on their thrones on earth. "*Hast thou also become weak as we?* (v. 10). Who would have thought it? You who ranked yourself among the immortal gods, have you come to take your fate among us poor mortals? *How hast thou fallen from heaven, O Lucifer! son of the morning!* (vv. 11–12). Has such a star become a lump of clay? Did anyone ever fall from such a height of honor and power into such an abyss of shame and misery?" *Those that see him shall narrowly look upon him, and consider him* (vv. 15–16). "Never was death so great a change to anyone as it is to him. Is it possible that a man who a few hours before looked so great should now look so ghastly, contemptible, and neglected? *Is this the man that made the earth to tremble and shook kingdoms?* (v. 16). Who would have thought he would ever come to this?" (Ps 82:7).

1.5. A conclusion drawn from all this (v. 20): *The seed of evildoers shall never be renowned.* The rulers of the Babylonian monarchy were evildoers, and so they had this infamy passed on as an inheritance to them. The way of sin does not have a good name.

2. The complete ruin of the royal family is foretold here, together with that of the royal city.

2.1. The royal family is to be completely destroyed. The Medes and Persians, who are to be used in this work of destruction, are ordered, when they have killed Belshazzar, to *prepare slaughter for his children* (v. 21). Nebuchadnezzar killed Zedekiah's sons (Jer 52:10), and because of that sin, his offspring are paid back in the same way, so that they *may not rise up to possess the land* (v. 21) and cause as much trouble in their day as their ancestors did in theirs. The providence of God provides for the well-being of nations more than we are aware of by destroying some who, if they had lived, would have caused trouble.

2.2. The royal city is to be demolished and deserted (v. 23). It will be occupied by solitary, timid birds, particularly *the bittern* (owl), joined by the cormorant (desert owl) and the great owl (24:11).

Verses 24–32

It was almost 200 years from this prediction of Babylon's fall to its fulfillment. The people to whom Isaiah prophesied might ask, "What has this to do with us? How will we be any better for it?" He answers these questions by the prediction of the destruction of both the Assyrians and the Philistines. These would be a pledge of their future rescue. Here is:

1. Assurance is given of the destruction of the Assyrians (v. 25): *I will break the Assyrian in my land.* Sennacherib brought a formidable army into the land of Judah, but there God crushed it. He undertook to do it himself. "*I will break the Assyrian* (v. 25); leave me alone to do it" (Ex 32:10). The crushing of the power of the Assyrian would be the removing of the yoke from the neck of God's people. *His burden shall depart from off their shoulders* (v. 25), the burden of quartering that vast army and paying tribute. This prophecy is here confirmed by an oath (v. 24): *The Lord of hosts hath sworn.* What is said here about this particular intention is true of all God's purposes. The breaking of the Assyrian power is made an example of

what God would do with all the nations engaged against him and his church (v. 26), not only *upon* the Assyrian Empire, which was then reckoned to be all the world, as afterward the Roman Empire was (Lk 2:1)—for many nations that depended on it fell with Assyria. It is still true and always will be: *Cursed is he that curses God's Israel* (Nu 24:9). God will be an enemy to his people's enemies (Ex 23:22). All the powers on earth are defied to change God's purposes (v. 27): "*The Lord of hosts has purposed* to break the Assyrian's yoke, *and who has power to turn it back* (v. 27) or to stop the course of his judgments?"

2. Assurance is also given of the destruction of the Philistines and their power. This came in *the year that king Ahaz died*, which was the first year of Hezekiah's reign (v. 28).

2.1. The Philistines are rebuked for triumphing in the death of king Uzziah (Azariah). He had been like a snake to them (v. 29), had brought them very low (2Ch 26:6). He *warred against the Philistines, broke down their walls, and built cities among them.* But when Uzziah abdicated, it was told with joy in Gath and *published in the streets of Ashkelon* (2Sa 1:20). They retaliated against Ahaz and captured and occupied many towns of Judah (2Ch 28:18), but *out of the root* of Uzziah *would come a cockatrice* (viper), a more formidable enemy than Uzziah, namely Hezekiah, the fruit of whose government would be to them *a fiery flying serpent* (v. 29), for he would fall on them with incredible speed and fury. *He smote* (defeated) *the Philistines even to Gaza* (2Ki 18:8).

2.2. The destruction of the Philistines by famine and war is prophesied. "When the people of God, whom the Philistines have devastated, distressed, and impoverished, enjoy plenty again," and when *the firstborn of their poor shall feed*—when their poorest have the food they need—then, as for the Philistines, God will destroy *their root with famine.* When the *needy* of God's people *shall lie down in safety* (v. 30), delighting in the songs of peace, then every gate and city of the Philistines will wail and howl (v. 31), and there will be a total dissolution of their state, for from Judea, which lay north of the Philistines, *there shall come a smoke*—a vast army raising great dust, smoke indicating that a consuming fire is near—*and none* of all that army *shall be alone in his appointed times*; there will be none who straggle or are missing when they are to be involved.

3. The good use that would be made of all these events to encourage the people of God (v. 32): *What shall one then answer the messengers of the nations?*

3.1. This implies that the great things God does for his people are noticed by their neighbors. Envoys will be sent to ask about them. We should always be ready to give an answer, *with meekness and fear*, to everyone who asks us to give the reason for the hope we have in the providence of God (1Pe 3:15).

3.2. The answer that is to be given to the messengers: God is and will be a faithful friend to his church and people. Tell the messengers that the *Lord has founded* (established) *Zion* (v. 32). God, by all the revolutions of states and kingdoms, is establishing Zion; he is aiming at the advancement of his church's interests. The envoys of the nations, when they sent to ask about Hezekiah's successes against the Philistines, expected to learn of politics and military skill, but they were told that these successes were not because of anything like that, but because of the care God took of his church. *The poor of his people shall trust in it* (will find refuge) (v. 20), his poor people who have just been brought very low. The *poor receive the Gospel* (Mt 11:5). They will trust in this, this great truth,

that the Lord has established Zion; they will build their hopes on this, not on human strength. However matters may go with individual groups, because the church has God himself as its founder and Christ the rock as its foundation (1Co 3:11; 10:4), it must surely stand firm. They will not fear what other people may do to them.

CHAPTER 15

This chapter and the one that follows are the oracle about Moab—a prophecy of a great devastation that would come on that country, which bordered on this land of Israel and had often been troublesome to it and had wronged it. This trouble would come on Moab even though the Moabites were descended from Lot, Abraham's relative and companion, and even though the Israelites, by the appointment of God, had spared them when they could both easily and justly have destroyed them with their neighbors. In this chapter we have: 1. Great lament made by the Moabites, and by the prophet himself for them (vv. 1–5). 2. The great disasters that caused that lament and justified it (vv. 6–9).

Verses 1–5

The country of Moab was small in extent, but very fruitful. It bordered on the allotted territory of Reuben on the other side of Jordan and on the Dead Sea. Naomi went to stay there when there was a famine in Canaan (Ru 1:1–2). This is the country that, it is foretold here, would be devastated and severely troubled, though not completely ruined; for its ruin is prophesied elsewhere (Jer 48) and was brought about by Nebuchadnezzar. Isaiah's prophecy was to be fulfilled *within three years* (16:14), and so it was, either by the army of Shalmaneser, about the time of the capturing of Samaria, in the fourth year of Hezekiah, or by the army of Sennacherib, which, ten years later, invaded Judah. The prophet communicated this prophecy to his own people to show them that there is a Providence that directs the world and all its nations and that the worshipers of false gods were accountable to the God of Israel. The fulfillment of this prophecy soon (*within three years*) could be taken as a confirmation of the prophet's mission and of the truth of all his other prophecies. About Moab it is foretold:

1. That their main cities will be unexpectedly attacked and conquered in a night by the enemy (v. 1): there will be great grief, *because in the night Ar of Moab is laid waste, and Kir of Moab*, the two main cities of that kingdom. *In the night that they were taken*, or sacked, *Moab was cut off* (v. 2). The seizing of them laid the whole country open and made its wealth an easy target. As the country feeds the cities, so the cities protect the country, and neither can say to the other, *I have no need of thee* (1Co 12:21).

2. That the Moabites will turn to their idols for help (v. 2): *He* (that is, the king of Moab) *has gone up to Bajith* (or rather to the house or temple of Chemosh), *and Dibon*, the inhabitants of Dibon, *have gone up to the high places*, where they worshiped their idols, to make their complaints there.

3. That there will be universal grief throughout the country. It is described here very movingly. Moab will be a vale of tears (Ps 84:6)—a little version of this world (v. 2). The Moabites will mourn the loss of Nebo and Medeba, two significant cities, which, it is likely, were plundered and burned. They will tear their hair out in grief so much that *on all their heads shall be baldness, and they shall cut off their beards*, according to the custom of mourning in those times and places. *In the streets*

they shall gird themselves with sackcloth (v. 3). They will go up to *the tops of their houses*—which had flat roofs—and there they will *weep abundantly*, will *howl* and wail, crying out to their gods. "They shall come down with weeping" (v. 3, margin); they will come down from their housetops weeping as much as they did when they went up.

4. That the courage of their armed soldiers will fail them. Although they are experienced soldiers, they still *shall cry out* and shriek for fear, and each one of them will have *his life become grievous to him* (his heart become faint) (v. 4).

5. That the outcry at these disasters will spread grief to every surrounding part (v. 5). The prophet's spirit was greatly moved by the prediction of this: "*My heart shall cry out for Moab*; even though they are enemies of Israel, they are still our fellow creatures." God's ministers should have a tender, sensitive spirit; they should be like their master, who wept over Jerusalem even when he gave her up to ruin (Lk 19:41–44), and like their God, *who desires not the death of sinners* (2Pe 3:9). All the neighboring cities will echo the lamentations of Moab. *The fugitives*, who are doing the best they can to keep safe, will take the cry *to Zoar* (v. 5), the city to which their ancestor Lot fled for shelter from Sodom's flames and which was spared for his sake. They will make as great a noise with their cry *as a heifer of three years old* does when she goes *lowing* for her calf (1Sa 6:12). They will go up the hill of *Luhith*, as David continued up the Mount of Olives, with many weary steps, weeping as he went (2Sa 15:30), and they will go in *way of Horonaim* (v. 5), the way that leads to the two Beth Horons, Upper and Lower, which we read about in Jos 16:3, 5.

Verses 6–9

"By this time *the cry has gone round about* all *the borders of Moab*" (v. 8). It has reached *Eglaim*, a town at one end of the country, and *Beer-elim*, a settlement far in the other direction.

1. *The waters of Nimrim are desolate* (dried up) (v. 6), that is, the country has been plundered and made poor. Famine is usually the sad effect of war. Look at the houses; they are stripped bare too (v. 7): the wealth they acquired with a great deal of hard work, and *that which they laid up* with a great deal of care, *shall they carry away to the brook of the willows*. Either the owners will take it there to hide it or the enemies will pack it up and send it home, by water perhaps, to their own country.

2. *The waters of Dimon are turned into blood* (v. 9), that is, the inhabitants of the country are killed in great numbers. *Dimon* means "bloody"; the place will correspond to its name. The verse means literally, "I will bring additions upon Dimon," additional plagues; "I have even more judgment in reserve for them." *For all this, God's anger is not turned away* (9:12). Some escape, others are overlooked and are as a remnant of the land, but on both God *will bring lions*, wild animals.

CHAPTER 16

This chapter continues and concludes the oracle about Moab. In it: 1. The prophet gives good advice to the Moabites, to reform, especially to be kind to God's people, to prevent the judgments previously threatened (vv. 1–5). 2. Fearing they will not accept this advice, he goes on to foretell the devastation of their country that will come within three years (vv. 6–14).

Verses 1–5

God has made it clear that he does not delight in the destruction of sinners (2Pe 3:9) by telling them what they may do to prevent the ruin; so he does here to Moab.

1. He advises them to be just to the house of David, paying the tribute they once agreed to pay (v. 1): *Send you the lamb to the ruler of the land.* David made the Moabites bring him tribute (2Sa 8:2). Afterward they paid their tribute to the kings of Israel (2Ki 3:4) and paid it in lambs. Now the prophet requires them to pay it to Hezekiah. Let it be levied from all parts of the country, *from Sela*, a frontier city of Moab on the one side, *to the wilderness*, a boundary of the kingdom on the other side: and let it be sent *to the mount of the daughter of Zion* (v. 1), the City of David. Some think it is spoken ironically: "Now you would be glad to make the God of Israel your friend, but it is too late." I prefer to consider it good advice seriously given, like that of Daniel to Nebuchadnezzar when he was reading him his doom (Da 4:27). It may be applied to the great Gospel duty of submission to Christ, as the ruler of the land and our ruler. When you come to God, the great ruler, come in the name of the Lamb, the Lamb of God. *The daughters of Moab*—the country villages or the women of your country—will flutter about the *fords of Arnon* (v. 2), attempting to use that to escape to some other land, *like a wandering bird thrown out of the nest* (v. 2) half fledged.

2. He advises them to be kind to the descendants of Israel (v. 3): *Take counsel*, reverse all the unrighteous decrees you have made, by which you have put hardships on the people of God.

2.1. The prophet foresees a storm coming on the people of God, who, by his merciful providence, escaped the fury of the Assyrian army but were put into a critical position and had to fend for themselves. The danger and trouble they were in were like the scorching heat at high noon.

2.2. He speaks of a shelter that they will find in the land of Moab when their own land is made too difficult for them. This is the justice Moab must grant (v. 12); they must deal kindly with the people of God. If they want to continue to live in the same dwellings, let them now open their doors to the dispersed members of God's church, becoming like a cool shade to those who have to *bear the burden and heat of the day* (Mt 20:12). "*Betray not him that wandereth* (v. 3), and do not hand him over," as the Edomites did (Ob 13–14), "but *hide the outcasts* (fugitives)" (v. 3). "In fact, not only hide them for a time but, if need be, let them be naturalized: *Let my outcasts dwell with thee, Moab* (v. 4); find somewhere they can stay, and *be thou a covert to them.*" They are *outcasts*, but they are *my outcasts* (v. 4). The Lord knows those who are his wherever he finds them (2Ti 2:19), even where no one else knows them. He himself will be their dwelling place if they have no other (Ps 90:1), and they will be at home in him.

2.3. He assures them of the mercy God has in store for his people. They will not need the Moabites' kindness for long or be troublesome to them: *For the extortioner* (oppressor) *is almost at an end already, and the spoiler* (destroyer) *ceases* (v. 4). Before long his people will be in a position to return the Moabites' kindness (v. 5): "Although the throne of the ten tribes has been overturned, yet *the throne of David shall be established in mercy*, and let your throne be established by the same methods, if you please. Make Hezekiah your friend; he *shall sit upon the throne in truth* (v. 5). Then he will sit *judging*, and he will then protect those who have been a shelter to the people of God." Notice in Hezekiah the character of a good magistrate. He will *seek judgment* (justice) (v. 5); that is, he will seek opportunities to do right to those who have been wronged. He will *hasten* (speed the cause of) *righteousness* (v. 5); he will not delay to do justice. Let the Moabites learn from this example and then assure themselves that their state will be established.

Verses 6–14

Here we have:

1. The sins Moab is accused of (v. 6). The prophet seems to rebuke himself for giving good advice to the Moabites. He wanted to heal them, but they did not want to be healed. Perhaps there are more precious souls ruined by pride than by any other sin. The Moabites were notorious for this: "*We have heard* in both ears *of the pride of Moab* (v. 6). They think they are too wise to be advised, and so they will not learn from the example of Hezekiah to act justly and love mercy (Mic 6:8). We have heard of *his* (Moab's) *wrath* too—for those who are very proud are often very angry—particularly his wrath against the people of God, whom he would rather persecute than protect. It is with *his lies* that he satisfies his pride and his passion; *but his lies shall not be so* (lies are empty) (v. 6); he will not complete the proud and angry projects as he hoped he would."

2. The sorrows with which Moab is threatened (v. 7): *Therefore shall Moab howl* (wail) *for Moab.* Notice:

2.1. The causes of this sorrow. On the one hand, their towns will be destroyed. *For the foundations of Kir-hareseth shall you mourn* (v. 7). That great and strong town, which has held out against a mighty force (2Ki 3:25), will now be leveled to the ground. On the other hand, their country will be devastated. Moab was famous for its fields and vineyards, but those will all be laid waste by the invading army (vv. 8, 10). It was planted with choice vines, noble vines, with *principal plants*, which reached *even to Jazer* (v. 8) and wound themselves along the framework on which they were spread, even *through the wilderness* of Moab. There were vineyards there, *stretched out*, even to *the sea*, the Dead Sea. They had shouted many times *for their summer fruits, and for their harvest* (v. 9). They had had *joy and gladness* (v. 10) in their fields and vineyards, *singing* and *shouting at the treading of their grapes*. Nothing is said about their praising God for their abundance or giving him the glory for it. They made it a food and fuel of their sinful desires, and so they will be stripped of everything. "The fields will wither. The soldiers"—called here *the lords of the heathen* (the rulers of the nations) (v. 8)—"will break down all the plants, *principal plants* (v. 8), the choicest vines that could be obtained. The joy of harvest has ended; there is no more singing; the ruin of their country has spoiled their happiness." Destroy the vines and the fig trees, and you make all the gladness of a worldly heart come to an end (Hos 2:11–12). But a gracious soul can rejoice in the Lord as the God of its salvation even when the fig tree does not blossom and there is no fruit on the vine (Hab 3:17–18).

2.2. The agreement of the prophet with them in this sorrow: "*I will with weeping bewail Jazer, and the vine of Sibmah* (v. 9), and look with a compassionate concern on the devastation of such a pleasant country. I *will water thee with my tears, O Heshbon!* (v. 9), and mix them with your tears"; in fact, it appears to be an inner grief: *My bowels* (heart) *shall sound like a harp for Moab* (v. 11). The afflictions of the world, as well as those of the church, should also be our afflictions. See also 15:5.

3. At the end of the chapter:

3.1. The inability of the gods of Moab to help them (v. 12). "Moab will be soon *weary of the high place.* He will spend his spirits and strength in vain in praying to his idols; they cannot help him, and he will be convinced that they cannot." But when he is weary of his high places, he will not go, as he should, to God's sanctuary, but to *his* sanctuary, to the temple of Chemosh, the principal idol of Moab (as it is generally understood); and he will pray there to as little purpose.

3.2. The ability of the God of Israel, the only true God, to fulfill what he has spoken against them. The thing itself was been determined long before (v. 13): *This is the word*, this is the thing, *that the Lord has spoken concerning Moab, since the time* that he began to be so proud, arrogant, and abusive to God's people. The country was long ago destined for destruction. It was now made known when it would be done. *The Lord has spoken* that it will be *within three years* (v. 14). God makes known his mind gradually; the light of divine revelation shone more and more (Pr 4:18), as does the light of divine grace in the heart. *The glory of Moab shall be contemned* (despised) (v. 14), that is, it will be contemptible, when all those things they have gloried in will come to nothing. It was the glory of Moab that their country was very populous and their forces courageous, but the little remnant that is left will be *very small and feeble* (v. 14). This will happen *within three years, as the years of a hireling* (a servant bound by contract) (v. 14), that is, at the end of three years exactly, for a servant who is hired for a fixed term keeps a record of it to the day. Reasonable warning is given, and with it the opportunity to repent; if they had made the most of their warning, as Nineveh did, we have reason to think the judgments threatened would have been prevented.

CHAPTER 17

Syria *(Aram) and Ephraim were allied against Judah (7:1–2), and because they worked so closely together, although this chapter is entitled the burden of Damascus (v. 1)—which was the capital city of Aram—it also describes the condemnation of Israel. 1. The destruction of the strong cities of both Aram and Israel is foretold here (vv. 1–5 and again vv. 9–11). 2. In the midst of judgment, mercy is remembered to Israel (Hab 3:2), and a gracious promise is made that a remnant will be preserved from the disasters and that they will benefit from them (vv. 6–8). 3. The overthrow of the Assyrian army before Jerusalem is pointed to (vv. 12–14). In order of time, this chapter should be placed after chapter 9, for the destruction of Damascus, foretold here, happened in the reign of Ahaz (2Ki 16:9).*

Verses 1–5

We have here the oracle about Damascus; the Aramaic paraphrase reads, "The burden of the cup of the curse to drink to Damascus in," and because the ten tribes were allied with Damascus, they must expect to be coupled with it in this cup that makes people reel (51:17).

1. Damascus itself, the capital city of Aram, must be destroyed. The houses will probably be burned down; at least, its walls, gates, and fortifications will be demolished, and its inhabitants taken away as captives, so that it is *taken away from being a city* and is reduced to *a ruinous heap* (v. 1).

2. The country towns are abandoned by their inhabitants. *The cities of Aroer* (a province of Aram so called) *are forsaken* (v. 2); the places that should be lived in are for

flocks to lie down in (v. 2). Stately houses are converted into houses for sheep to sleep in.

3. The strongholds of Israel, the kingdom of the ten tribes, will be brought to ruin: *The fortress shall cease from Ephraim* (v. 3). The Arameans were the ringleaders in the alliance against Judah, and so they are punished first and most severely, and now that Israel is weakened, *The remnant of Syria* (Aram) *shall be as the glory of the children of Israel* (v. 3); those few Arameans who remain will be in as low and contemptible a condition as the children of Israel are. The glory of Jacob is weakened like that of a person with a wasting disease (v. 4). *The glory of Jacob* was their numbers, but this glory *shall be made thin* when many are cut off and few are left. Israel died of a lingering disease; the kingdom of the ten tribes wasted gradually. It was all gathered and taken away by the Assyrian army. The victorious army, like the careful reapers in the Valley of Rephaim, where the grain was extraordinary, would not, if they could help it, leave a head of grain behind.

Verses 6–8

Mercy is reserved here, as an aside in the middle of judgment, for a remnant that would escape the general destruction of the kingdom of the ten tribes. The meek of the earth were still hidden in the day of the Lord's anger (Ps 76:8–9); they had escaped with their lives and so were able to withdraw to the land of Judah.

1. They will be only a small remnant, who will be marked out to be saved (v. 6): *Gleaning grapes shall be left in it.* Most of the people were taken into exile. Those who are left will be only like the poor remains of an olive tree when it has been carefully shaken; perhaps there will be *two or three berries* (olives) *in the top of the uppermost bough* (on the topmost branches) (v. 6), out of reach of those who shook it, but that is all.

2. They will be a sanctified remnant (vv. 7–8). They will be those who have repented of their sins and reformed their lives and were therefore snatched as burning sticks out of the fire (Am 4:11; Zec 3:2). They will look to their Creator; they will acknowledge his hand in every aspect of their lives, in mercy and in suffering, and will submit to his hand. They will look away from their idols, the creations of their own imagination. They will no longer worship them and expect help from them. He who looks to his Maker must not *look to the altars, the work of his hands* (v. 8), must not keep the least respect for *that which his fingers have made* (v. 8), but break it to pieces.

Verses 9–11

Here the prophet returns to foretell the desolation that will be made in Israel by the army of the Assyrians.

1. The cities will be deserted. Even the strong cities, which should protect the country, will not be able to protect themselves: they *shall be as a forsaken bough and an uppermost branch* (v. 9) of an old tree, which has gone rotten, bare, dry, and dead. As the Canaanites fled before Israel, so Israel will now flee from the Assyrians.

2. The country will be devastated (vv. 10–11). "It is *because thou hast forgotten the God of thy salvation* (v. 10) and all his great rescues and *hast not been mindful of the rock of thy strength* (v. 10). If he had not been your strength on many occasions, you would have been broken long ago." They took great care to improve their land and make it even more pleasant. It was like a garden and a vineyard, filled with plants, the best it could produce. And yet, not content with these plants, they sent to all the neighboring countries for *strange slips*, imported vines.

This seems to be included to show in general their great diligence in cultivating their ground. They made sure their plants would grow and flourish. But *the harvest shall be a heap*, all confused, *in the day of grief and of desperate sorrow* (v. 10). The harvest had sometimes been a day of sadness, if the crop was thin, but in that case there was hope that the next year's harvest would be better. But this will be a time of desperate sorrow, for they will see not only this year's crops taken away, but the very character of the ground changed and their conquerors lords of it.

Verses 12–14

These verses read the condemnation of those who rob the people of God. If the Assyrians and Israelites invade and plunder Judah, if the Assyrian army takes God's people captive and devastates their country, let them know that ruin will come to them. The Assyrian army was made up of diverse nations: it was *the multitude of many people* (v. 12), and in the force of their numbers they placed their hopes of victory. They were noisy, like the roaring of the seas, to frighten God's people from resisting them. In their speeches and letters, Sennacherib and the field commander made a great noise in an attempt to strike terror on Hezekiah and his people; the nations that followed them *made a rushing like the rushing of many waters* (v. 12). They thought they would win simply because of the loud noise they made, but he *shall rebuke them* (v. 13), that is, God will, *and* then *they shall flee afar off* (v. 13). Sennacherib, the field commander, and the remains of their forces will be chased by their own terror, *as the chaff of the mountains*, which stands helpless *before the wind, and like a rolling thing before the whirlwind* (v. 13), like "thistledown" (v. 13, margin). God will make *them like a rolling thing*, and *make them afraid with his storm* (Ps 83:13, 15). This will be done suddenly (v. 14): *At eveningtide* they are very troublesome and are threatening trouble for the people of God, but *before the morning they are not.* When they sleep, they are put into a deep sleep (Ps 76:5–6). It was at night that the angel drove out the Assyrian army.

CHAPTER 18

Whatever country it is that is referred to here by the land shadowing with wings *(v. 1), God has a quarrel with it because of his people. 1. They threaten God's people (vv. 1–2). 2. All the neighbors are called to notice what the outcome will be (v. 3). 3. Although God seems for a time unconcerned at the distress of his people, he will eventually appear against their enemies and destroy them (vv. 4–6).*

Verses 1–7

Interpreters are very much at a loss as to the exact location of this land that lies *beyond* the rivers of *Ethiopia* (Cush). Some consider it to be Egypt. However, a strong objection to this is that the next chapter is distinguished by the title *the burden of Egypt* (19:1). Others take it to be *Ethiopia* (Cush), of which Tirhakah was king. He thought he would protect the Jews, as it were, under *the shadow of his wings* (v. 1) by giving a powerful diversion to the king of Assyria when he was attacking Jerusalem (2Ki 19:9). But though he used his envoys to defy the king of Assyria, God will use another way to protect Jerusalem. Because of a hint in Dr. Lightfoot's *Harmony of the Old Testament*, however, I incline to understand this chapter as a prophecy against Assyria and therefore as a continuation of the last three verses of the previous chapter. That prophecy was against the army of the Assyrians that attacked Judah; this one is against the land of Assyria itself, which lay beyond the Euphrates and Tigris rivers. Here is:

1. The attempt made by this land, wherever it precisely is, on *a nation scattered and peeled* (NIV: smooth-skinned) (v. 2). Whether this refers to Cush waging war with the Assyrians, or the Assyrians with Judah, it teaches us that a people that has been *terrible from their beginning*, feared far and wide, and has become influential, may still become stripped and scattered, and may even be divided by its own rivers, rivers that ought to enrich both the farmers and the merchants. "It is a nation that has been terrible, and it is now a stripped and scattered nation and easy prey for us."

2. The alarm sounded to the surrounding nations, by which they are summoned to notice what God is about to do. *He lifts up an ensign upon the mountains, and blows a trumpet* (v. 3), by which he declares war against the enemies of his church and calls in all her friends. He is about to do some great work, as the *Lord of hosts* (v. 7).

3. The assurance God gives to his prophet, to be given through him to his people, that although he might seem to sit by as an unconcerned spectator for a time, he will still certainly appear to strengthen his people and confound his and their enemies (v. 4): *So the Lord said unto me.*

3.1. He will take care of his people and shelter them. He will regard his *dwelling place* (v. 4); Zion is his rest forever (Ps 132:14), and he will "look after it," as some understand it. He will be like *a clear heat* "after rain" (v. 5, margin), like dew and *a cloud in the heat of harvest* (v. 4), which are very welcome, the dew to the ground and the cloud to the laborers. Great people have their winter houses and their summerhouses (Am 3:15), but those who are at home with God have both in him.

3.2. He will judge his and their enemies (vv. 5–6). When the Assyrian army promises itself a plentiful harvest in capturing Jerusalem, God will destroy that army as easily as a gardener cuts off the sprigs of the vine with pruning knives or *takes away and cuts down the branches* (v. 5). This seems to point to the dead bodies of the soldiers scattered like the branches of a wild vine (2Ki 19:35), cut to pieces. *And they shall be left to the fowls* (birds of prey) *of the earth* (v. 6) to seize and kill.

4. The tribute of praise that will be brought to God through all this (v. 7): *In that time*, when this will be fulfilled, *shall the present be brought unto the Lord of hosts*. Those who were *a people scattered and peeled, meted out, and trodden down* (v. 2) will be brought as a gift to the Lord, and although they seem useless and worthless, they will be acceptable to the One who judges people by the sincerity of their faith and love, not by the show and prosperity of their outward condition. It is prophesied that *Ethiopia* (Cush) *shall soon stretch out her hands unto God* (Ps 68:31). Others understand it to refer to the plunder of Sennacherib's army, out of which presents were brought to *the Lord of hosts* (Nu 31:50).

CHAPTER 19

As Assyria was a breaking rod to Judah, with which Judah was struck, so Egypt was a broken reed, with which it was deceived (2Ki 18:21), and so God had a quarrel with both of them. Here we have the oracle about Egypt: 1. That it would be brought low and would be as contemptible among the nations as it was now significant (vv. 1–17). 2. That ultimately God's holy faith would be brought to Egypt, in part by the Jews who would flee there for refuge, but more fully by the preachers of the

Gospel of Christ, through whose ministry churches would be planted in Egypt in the days of the Messiah (vv. 18–25).

Verses 1–17

Although the land of Egypt had formerly been a land of slavery for the people of God, the unbelieving Jews trusted in Egypt for help (30:2), and in disobedience to God's explicit command (Jer 43:7), they fled there when things were brought to a crisis in their own country. The field commander rebuked Hezekiah for this (36:6). While they kept up an alliance with Egypt, they did not stand in awe of the judgments of God: they depended on Egypt to protect them. To prevent all this trouble, Egypt must be humbled.

1. The gods of Egypt will be seen to be completely unable to help them (v. 1). "*The Lord rides upon a cloud, a swift cloud, and shall come into Egypt.* As a judge goes in procession to try and condemn evildoers, so God will come to Egypt with his judgment." In all of this oracle about Egypt there is no mention of any foreign enemy invading them, but God himself will come against them and raise up the cause of their destruction from among themselves. When he comes, *the idols of Egypt shall be moved* (v. 1). Because the idols of Egypt—Isis, Osiris, and Apis—were unable to help their worshipers, they will be disowned and rejected by them. When they are at their wits' end, the Egyptians *shall seek to* (consult) *the idols* and consult *the charmers and wizards* (v. 3), but it will all be in vain.

2. The militia of Egypt, who are famous for their bravery, will be disheartened. Their heroes, who used to be celebrated for their courage, will be ridiculed as cowards: *The heart of Egypt shall melt in the midst of it*, like wax in front of a fire (v. 1); *the spirit of Egypt shall fail* (v. 3). They *shall be like women* (v. 16); they will be weak, frightened, and confused by the slightest alarm.

3. The Egyptians will be embroiled in quarrels among themselves. There will be no need to bring a foreign force on them to destroy them; they will destroy one another (v. 2): *I will set the Egyptians against the Egyptians; they shall fight every one against his brother and neighbour, city against city, and kingdom against kingdom*. Egypt was then divided into twelve provinces, or dynasties, but Psammetichus, the governor of one of them, set them in conflict with one another and so eventually made himself master of them all. A kingdom divided against itself would soon be devastated (Mt 12:25).

4. Their plans will be turned to foolishness. When God destroys the nation, he will *destroy the counsel thereof* (v. 3). They will make fools of one another, each betraying their own foolishness, and divine Providence making fools of them all (v. 11). The nobles of Egypt boasted much about their ancient wisdom, producing fabled records of their succession for more than 10,000 years. This attitude was prevalent among them about this time, as can be seen from Herodotus; their common boast was that Egypt was thousands of years older than any other nation. "But *where are thy wise men?* (v. 12). Let them use all their so-called skill to *know what the Lord of hosts has purposed upon Egypt* (v. 12) and protect themselves accordingly. In fact, so far are they from doing this that they themselves are, in effect, working toward the ruin of Egypt and quickening it (v. 13). *The princes of Noph* (leaders of Memphis) not only are deceived themselves but also *have seduced Egypt*." Things are sad for a people when those who undertake to look after their safety are helping toward their destruction, as here (v. 14): *They have caused Egypt to err in every work thereof.*

5. The rod of government will be turned into the snake of tyranny and oppression (Ex 4:3) (v. 4): "*The Egyptians will I give over into the hand of a cruel lord*, not a foreigner, but one who will rule over them by hereditary right; and yet he will rule them fiercely and harshly."

6. Egypt was famous for its Nile River, which was its wealth and strength, and it is threatened that *the waters shall fail from the sea* and the river will be *wasted and dried up* (v. 5). The fruitfulness of the country depended wholly on the overflowing of the river. If that dried up, their fruitful land would soon become barren and their harvests would come to an end: *Every thing sown by the brooks will wither*, of course, *will be driven away, and be no more* (v. 7). If plants by the very mouth of *the brooks* wither, then much more so the grain, which lies farther away. But this is not all; the drying up of their rivers:

6.1. Will be the destruction of their fortifications, for rivers are *brooks of defence* (v. 6). But these *shall be emptied and dried up* (v. 6), not by an enemy, like Sennacherib, who with the *sole of his foot dried up mighty rivers* (37:25), but by the providence of God, which sometimes *turns watersprings into dry ground* (Ps 107:33).

6.2. Will *kill the fish* (Ps 105:29), and so will ruin those who make it their business to catch fish, whether by angling or by nets (v. 8); they will *lament* and *languish*, for their trade will have come to an end. There were those who *made sluices and ponds for fish* (v. 10), but *they shall be broken in the purposes thereof*; their business will fail for lack of water to fill their ponds. The loss of these advantages by the river is their own doing (v. 6): *They shall turn the rivers far away*. Their kings and leaders will drain water from the main river to their own houses, preferring their private convenience to the public good. Herodotus tells us that Pharaoh Neco, planning to cut a means of access by water from the Nile to the Red Sea, employed a vast number of workers to make a channel for that purpose, damaged the river, lost 120,000 people, and still left the work unfinished.

7. Egypt was famous for the manufacture of linen, but that trade will be ruined. Solomon's merchants traded with Egypt for linen yarn (1Ki 10:28). Their country produced the best flax and the best hands to work it, but *those that work in fine flax shall be confounded* (will despair) (v. 9). The trade of Egypt must fall, for (v. 15) *there shall not be any work for Egypt*, and where there is nothing to be done there is nothing to be gained. There will be *no work which either head or tail, branch or rush, may do*; nothing for highborn or lowborn, weak people or strong people, to do.

8. A general fear will seize the Egyptians; they *shall be afraid and fear* (v. 16), which will be both evidence of general decay and a means and premonition of ruin (v. 17). When they hear of the devastation made in Judah by the army of Sennacherib, they will conclude that it will be their turn next to be plundered by that victorious army. They will *fear* (v. 16) *because of the shaking of the* (the uplifted) *hand of the Lord of hosts* and (v. 17) *because of the counsel* (plans) *of the Lord of hosts*. From the uplifting of his hand they will conclude *he has determined* against Egypt as well as Judah. For if judgment begins with the family of God (1Pe 4:17), where will it end?

Verses 18–25

The sun breaks out here, out of the threatening clouds of the prophecy, and it is the sun of righteousness (Mal 4:2). God still has mercy in store for Egypt, and he will show it by bringing true religious faith among them, calling them to the worship of the one true God. The preaching, so it

is thought, of Mark the Evangelist led to the founding of Christian churches in Egypt. Many prophecies of this book point to the days of the Messiah, and why not this one too? It is not unusual to speak of Gospel graces and ordinances in the language of Old Testament institutions. And in these prophecies, the words *in that day* perhaps do not always refer to what goes immediately before, but have a special significance pointing to that day when the rising sun from heaven would visit this dark world (Lk 1:78; Mal 4:2). But it is not improbable that this prophecy was partly fulfilled when those Jews who fled their own country to shelter in Egypt upon Sennacherib's invasion of their land took their religious faith with them. Josephus tells us that Onias, the son of Onias the high priest and living as an outlaw at Alexandria, obtained permission from Ptolemy Philometor and Cleopatra his queen to build in Bubastis a temple to the God of Israel like that in Jerusalem, and that Onias claimed to have authority to do this from this prophecy in Isaiah, which foretells that there will be an *altar to the Lord in the land of Egypt* (v. 19). The conversion of Egypt is described:

1. They will *speak the language of Canaan*, the holy language, the language of Scripture; they will not only understand it but also use it (v. 18). *Five cities in Egypt* (v. 18) will speak this language; many Jews will come to live in Egypt, and they will soon populate five cities, one of which will be Heliopolis, where the sun was worshiped, the most notorious of all Egyptian cities for idolatry. Even there a wonderful reformation will come.

2. They will swear to the Lord Almighty, not only swear by him but also take a solemn oath to devote themselves to his honor and commit themselves to his service.

3. They will set up the public worship of God in their land (v. 19): *There shall be an altar to the Lord* in the *midst of the land of Egypt*, an altar on which *they shall do sacrifice and oblation* (grain offerings) (v. 21); this must be understood spiritually, for according to the Law of Moses there was to be no altar for sacrifice except that at Jerusalem (Dt 12:5, 11, etc.; 1Ki 8:29; 9:3; 14:21, 23). In Christ Jesus all distinction between nations is swept away, and a spiritual altar, a Gospel church, in Egypt, is as acceptable to God as one in Israel.

4. There will be an expression of religious faith in the nation. Not only in the heart of the country, but even in its *borders, there shall be a pillar* (v. 19) inscribed, *To Jehovah*, to his honor. Even in the land of Egypt he will have some faithful worshipers, who made his name their strong tower (Pr 18:10).

5. Being in distress, they will seek God, and he will be found by them (1Ch 28:9; Jer 29:13–14), and this *shall be a sign and a witness for the Lord of hosts* then he is a *prayer-hearing God* to *all flesh* that *come to him* (v. 20).

6. They will be saved by the great Redeemer. Repenting Egyptians will find the same favor with God that repenting Ninevites did (Jnh 3:5, 8, 10). All these rescues that were carried out for them prefigured, like those for Israel, salvation through the Gospel.

7. The knowledge of God will be effective among them (v. 21). Perhaps this partly refers to the translation of the Old Testament from Hebrew into Greek in the Septuagint (a Greek version of the Old Testament), which was carried out at Alexandria in Egypt. By the help of this — the Greeks having introduced their language into that country — *the Lord was known to Egypt* (v. 21). It is promised that *the Egyptians shall know* (acknowledge) *the Lord* (v. 21).

8. They will come into the fellowship of saints. Because they are committed to the Lord, they will be added to the church.

8.1. Enmities will be removed. There had been mortal feuds between Egypt and Assyria, but now *there shall be a highway between Egypt and Assyria* (v. 23); they will trade with each other, and everything that passes between them will be friendly. *The Egyptians shall serve with the Assyrians* (v. 23). Those who have fellowship with the same God and meet at the same throne of grace (Heb 4:16) should serve each other, put an end to all quarreling and animosity, and unite hearts in holy love.

8.2. The Gentile nations will not only unite with each other in the Gospel community under Christ the Great Shepherd but also all be united with the Jews. When Egypt and Assyria become partners in serving God, *Israel* will *make a third with* them (v. 24); they will become a *threefold cord, not easily broken* (Ecc 4:12). Because they are united in this way, they will be a *blessing in the midst of the land, whom the Lord of hosts shall bless* (vv. 24–25). They will all be blessed by the Lord. Although Egypt was formerly a land of slavery for the people of God, and Assyria their unjust invader, all this will now be forgiven and forgotten, and they will be as welcome to God as is Israel. They are all alike his people, whom he takes under his protection.

CHAPTER 20

This chapter is a prediction of the carrying away of many Egyptians and Ethiopians (Cushites) into exile by the king of Assyria. Here is: 1. The sign by which this was foretold, which was the prophet's going barefoot and almost naked for some time, like a poor prisoner (vv. 1–2). 2. The explanation of that sign, applying it to Egypt and Ethiopia (Cush) (vv. 3–5). 3. The good use that the people of God will make of this, which is never to trust in human strength, because that will fail them (v. 6).

Verses 1–6

As King of the nations, God here brings a severe disaster on Egypt and Cush, but as King of saints, he brings good to his people from it. Notice:

1. The date of this prophecy. It was in the year that Ashdod, a strong city of the Philistines, was besieged and captured by an army of the Assyrians. It is uncertain what year of Hezekiah's reign that was. The king of Assyria at that time is called *Sargon*. *Tartan*, the supreme commander in this expedition, was one of Sennacherib's officers, sent by him to defy Hezekiah, together with his field commander (2Ki 18:17).

2. The causing of Isaiah to be a sign by his unusual clothing. By the sackcloth he had worn, he had been a sign to his own people of the miserable times that had come and were coming on them. Perhaps sackcloth was the clothing common to prophets, by which he showed himself dead to the world. Elijah wore clothes made of hair (2Ki 1:8), as did John the Baptist (Mt 3:4), but Isaiah has orders to *loose his sackcloth from his loins* (v. 2), to exchange it not for better clothing, but for none at all; and he must *put off his shoes* (v. 2) and go barefoot. This was a great hardship for the prophet and would expose him to contempt and ridicule, but God told him to do it so that he might prove his obedience to God and so put to shame his people who disobeyed him. When doing our duty, we can trust God with both our reputation and our safety.

3. The explanation of this sign (vv. 3–4). It was intended to show that the Egyptians and the Cushites would be taken captive by the king of Assyria and stripped, as Isaiah was. God calls him his *servant Isaiah* (v. 3) because in this matter he has shown himself to be God's willing, obedient servant, and for this very thing God glories in him. Isaiah is said to have *walked naked and barefoot three years* (v. 3), that is, whenever he appeared as a prophet during that time. The Assyrian army will make three successive campaigns to plunder the Egyptians and Cushites and take them captive; they must go around stripped, scarcely having rags to cover up their nakedness. The prophecy is particularly declared to be *to the shame of Egypt* (v. 4), because the Egyptians were a proud people.

4. The use and application of this sign (vv. 5–6). Those countries that were in danger of being overrun by the Assyrians expected Tirhakah, king of Cush, to put an end to the progress of Assyria's victorious army and be a barrier that protected Tirhakah's neighbors, and they thought that Egypt, a kingdom so famous for skill and competence, would oblige Assyria to raise the siege of Ashdod and withdraw. But instead, by attempting to oppose the king of Assyria the Egyptians only made their country an easy target for him. Then all the nations around Egypt and Cush became more afraid than ever of the increasing power of the king of Assyria, in the path of whom Egypt and Cush proved to be like briers and thorns set to stop a consuming fire (10:17; 27:4). The Jews in particular would be convinced of their foolishness in resting on such splintered reeds (2Ki 18:21) (v. 6): *The inhabitants of this isle*—the land of Judah, situated on the sea though not surrounded by it—everyone in Judah, will now have their eyes opened and will say, "*Behold, such is our expectation* (v. 6). We have fled to the Egyptians and Cushites and have hoped they would rescue us from the king of Assyria, but now that they have been broken, how will we escape, since we are not able to bring such armies onto the field as they did?"

CHAPTER 21

In this chapter we have a prophecy of sad times that were coming, and heavy burdens: 1. On Babylon, here called the desert of the sea (v. 1), that it would be destroyed by the Medes and Persians (vv. 1–10). 2. On Dumah, or Idumea (vv. 11–12). 3. On Arabia, or Kedar (vv. 13–17).

Verses 1–10

We had one oracle about Babylon before (13:1–22); here we have another prediction of its downfall. Babylon sometimes claimed to be Israel's friend (39:1), and God wanted to warn them not to trust in that friendship; sometimes Babylon really was their enemy, and God wanted to warn them not to be afraid of that enmity. Babylon is marked out for ruin, and all who believe God's prophets can see it tottering. Babylon is here called the *desert* or "plain" *of the sea*, for it was a flat country, full of lakes, and was abundantly watered by the many streams of the Euphrates River. It had just begun to be famous, Nineveh having surpassed it while the monarchy was in Assyrian hands, but it became the finest kingdom, and before Nebuchadnezzar's time, God had by this prophet plainly foretold its fall again and again, so that his people might not be terrified at its rise nor despair of relief when they were its prisoners (Job 5:3; Ps 37:35, 36). Here is:

1. The powerful invasion that the Medes and Persians will make on Babylon (vv. 1–2): they will come *from the desert, from a terrible land.* The northern parts of Media and Persia were waste and mountainous, formidable to strangers. *Elam* (that is, Persia) is summoned to go up

against Babylon and, together with the forces of Media, to besiege it. These forces come *as whirlwinds from the south* (v. 1). As is usual in such cases, some traitors will go over to them: *The treacherous dealers will deal treacherously* (v. 2). Historians tell us of Gadatas and Gobryas, two leading officials of the king of Babylon, who went over to Cyrus and, knowing well all the roads of the city, led a party directly to the palace, where Belshazzar was killed. And so with the help of the *treacherous dealers, the spoilers* (looters) *spoiled* (v. 2). The Persians will give the Babylonians a taste of their own medicine; those who used fraud, unrighteous wars, and deceitful treaties to attack their neighbors will meet their match.

2. The different impressions this will make on those concerned. To the poor captives it will be welcome news, for they have been told long before that Babylon's destroyer will rescue them, and so, when they hear that Elam and Media are coming to besiege Babylon, *all their sighing will be made to cease* (v. 2). To the proud oppressors, on the other hand, it will be a dire vision (v. 2), especially to the king of Babylon, and it seems he is the one who is mentioned here mourning his inevitable fate (vv. 3–4): *Therefore are my loins filled with pain; pangs have taken hold upon me*, which was literally fulfilled in Belshazzar, for that very night in which his city was taken and he was killed, when he saw a hand writing mysterious characters on the wall, *his countenance was changed and his thoughts troubled him, so that the joints of his loins were loosed and his knees smote one against another* (Da 5:6). He was killed on the very night when he was at the height of his revelry, with his cups and concubines around him and a thousand lords reveling with him.

3. Babylon's position when surprised by the enemy: festive, bold self-confidence (v. 5): "Prepare the tables with all kinds of delicacies. Set the guards; let them watch in the watchtower while we have a good time, and if any alarm is raised, the officers will get up and oil the shields and be ready to give the enemy a warm reception."

4. The alarm that will be given to Babylon upon its being overpowered by Cyrus and Darius. The Lord showed the prophet the watchman posted in his watchtower, so that, according to the duty of a watchman, he might *declare what he sees* (v. 6). This watchman discovered a chariot with teams of horses, in which the commander in chief rode. He saw riders on donkeys, much in use among the Persians, and riders on camels, much in use among the Medes, so that these two chariots stand for the two nations combined against Babylon. *He cried, A lion* (v. 8); the meaning of this word coming from a watchman's mouth was no doubt something everybody knew. *Or he cried as a lion*, very boldly and loudly, because the occasion was urgent. "*I stand, my lord, continually upon the watchtower* (v. 8) until now. Up to this time everything has seemed safe and quiet." He shouts again (v. 9): *Here comes a chariot of men with a couple of horsemen*.

5. A definite account eventually given of the overthrow of Babylon. The one in the chariot *answered and said*—when he heard the watchman speak—*Babylon has fallen, has fallen* (v. 9). Or perhaps God said it in answer to the prophet's inquiry as to how these matters would turn out: *All the graven images of her gods he has broken unto the ground* (v. 9).

6. Notice given to the people of God, who were then captives in Babylon, that this prophecy of the downfall of Babylon was particularly intended to encourage them (v. 10).

6.1. The title the prophet gives them in God's name: *O my threshing, and the corn of my floor*, my people, crushed

on the threshing floor. The prophet calls them *his* because they are his compatriots, but he speaks it as from God. The church is God's floor. True believers are the grain of God's floor. Hypocrites are as mere chaff and straw (Ps 1:4). The grain of God's floor must expect to be threshed by suffering and persecution. Even then God acknowledges it as his own threshing; it still belongs to him.

6.2. The assurance he gives them to build their hope on: *That which I have heard of the Lord of hosts, the God of Israel, have I declared unto you* (v. 10).

Verses 11–12

This prophecy concerning Dumah is very short and difficult to understand. Some think that Dumah was a part of Arabia and that the inhabitants were descended from Dumah, the sixth son of Ishmael. Others understand Dumah to refer to Idumea, the country of the Edomites, because Mount Seir is mentioned here. Some of Israel's neighbors are certainly intended, and their distress is foretold not only to warn them to prepare for it but also to warn Israel not to depend on them, but only on God. We have here:

1. A question put by an Edomite to the watchman. Someone *called out of Seir* (v. 11), as the man of Macedonia whom Paul saw in a vision wanted him to come over and help them (Ac 16:9). The question is serious: *What of the night?* (v. 11). It is good to ask the right person, the *watchman*. The Edomite repeats the question as one who is serious. God's prophets and ministers are appointed to be watchmen. They are as watchmen in the city in times of peace, to see that everything is safe, to knock at every door by making personal inquiries—"Is it locked? Is the fire protected?" They are as watchmen in the camp in time of war (Eze 33:7). They are to take notice of the enemy and sound the warning. It is our duty to ask again and again, *What of the night?* (v. 11). "Watchman, what is the time? After a long dark night, is there any hope of dawn?" "What from the night?" according to some; "What vision has the prophet had tonight? We are ready to receive it." Or: "What is going on tonight? What is the weather like? What news is there?"

2. The watchman's answer to this question. The watchman was neither asleep nor silent. Even though it was a man of Mount Seir who called him, he answered, "The morning comes. First comes a morning of light, peace, and opportunity; you will enjoy one more day of comfort. But afterward will come a night of trouble and disaster." Make the most of the present morning in preparation for the night that follows it. "*Inquire, return, come* (v. 12). Be inquisitive, be penitent and obedient."

Verses 13–17

Arabia was a large country eastward and southward of Canaan. The Dedanites (v. 13) were descended from Dedan, Abraham's son by Keturah; the inhabitants of Tema and Kedar were descended from Ishmael (Ge 25:3, 13, 15). The Arabians lived in tents, kept cattle, and were a hardy people used to labor. The Jews depended on them as a wall between them and the more belligerent eastern nations, and so, to alarm the Jews, the prophet reveals *the burden* (oracle) *of Arabia* (v. 13).

1. A destroying army will be brought on these peoples with a sword, with *a drawn sword*, with *a bow bent* and ready, and with all the *grievousness of war* (v. 15). It is probable that the king of Assyria captured Arabia and made easy prey of it.

2. The poor country people will be forced to flee for shelter, so that *the travelling companies of Dedanim*

(caravans of Dedanites) will have to *lodge in the forest in Arabia* (v. 13).

3. They will lack refreshment in their flight from the invading army: "*O you inhabitants of the land of Tema!*" (who probably were the closest neighbors to the caravans of Dedanites) "bring water"—so the margin reads it—"to him that is thirsty, and prevent with your bread (bring food for) those that flee (v. 14), for they are objects of your compassion; they flee from the sword" (v. 15). Let us learn from this to look with compassion on those who are in distress and to relieve them cheerfully. It is here remembered to the commendation of the land of Tema that they relieved even those who were falling.

4. All the glory of Kedar will disappear and fail. Their numerous herds and flocks will all be driven away by the enemy. Their archers, instead of foiling the enemy, will fall themselves. *The residue of their number* (surviving archers) *shall be diminished* (v. 17); their able-bodied archers will become very few, for they will be most exposed and will fall first by the enemies' sword.

5. All this will be done in a short time: "*Within one year according to the years of a hireling* (v. 16)—within one year precisely reckoned—will this judgment come on Kedar." This fixing of the time might have been very useful to the Arabians, to awaken them to repentance, so that, like the people of Nineveh, they might prevent the judgment when they were told it was just at the door (Jnh 3:8–10).

6. It is all confirmed by the truth of God (v. 16): "*Thus hath the Lord said to me.*" And again (v. 17): *The Lord God of Israel hath spoken it.*

CHAPTER 22

This chapter is the burden of the valley of vision, *Jerusalem (v. 1); now let Jerusalem hear its own doom. This chapter concerns: 1. The city of Jerusalem itself and its neighborhood. Here is: 1.1. A prophecy of the severe distress they would soon experience from Sennacherib's invasion and siege (vv. 1–7). 1.2. A rebuke given them for their misconduct in two things: not looking to God in using the means to preserve their lives (vv. 8–11) and not humbling themselves under his mighty hand (vv. 12–14). 2. The court of Hezekiah and the officers of that court. 2.1. The ousting of Shebna, an evildoer, and the expelling of him from the treasury (vv. 15–19, 25). 2.2. The promotion of Eliakim, who would serve his country better (vv. 20–24).*

Verses 1–7

The title of this prophecy is *the burden of the valley of vision,* an oracle concerning the Valley of Vision (v. 1), that is, concerning Judah and Jerusalem. Jerusalem is called a valley, for the mountains were around it, and the land of Judah abounded with valleys. It is called a *valley of vision* (v. 1) because it was there that God was known (Ps 76:1) and there that the prophets came to know his mind by visions. Because Babylon was a stranger to God, it was called *the desert of the sea* (21:1) even though it was rich and great, but because Jerusalem was trusted with his oracles (Ro 3:2), it was a *valley of vision* (v. 1). The *burden of the valley of vision* (v. 1) would only frighten it, not completely ruin it, for the prophecy does not refer to the destruction of Jerusalem by Nebuchadnezzar, but to the attempt made on it by Sennacherib. Here is foretold:

1. The fear that the city would be in on the approach of Sennacherib's army. It used to be a city of great trade, populous and noisy, a joyous city of revelry. "But what

troubles you now? The shops are all empty, and *thou hast wholly gone up to the housetops* (v. 1) to protect yourself from the enemy." But why is Jerusalem in such a state of shock? *Her slain men are not slain with the sword* (v. 2), but by famine, according to some. Or else by fear: they are so discouraged that they seem as effectively stabbed by fear as if they had been run through with a sword.

2. The ignominious flight of the rulers of Judah, who fled from all parts of the country to Jerusalem (v. 3) and were *found* in Jerusalem, having left their respective cities to be the victims of the Assyrian army, which, because it met with no opposition when it *came up against all the defenced cities of Judah,* easily *took them* (36:1). These rulers *were bound,* literally, "from the bow"; they not only left their cities like cowards but trembled when they came to Jerusalem, so that they could not even draw a bow.

3. The great grief that this would cause to all serious people, the prophet taking it to heart himself (vv. 4–5). He is not willing to publicly show his sorrow, and so he tells those around him to look away from him. He will weep secretly. But what is the cause of his grief? A poor prophet had little to lose, and he had become used to hardship, but it was for *the spoiling of the daughter of his people,* the destruction of his people (v. 4). "Our enemies trample on us, and our friends do not know how to be kind to us. The enemies use battering rams to break down the walls, and in vain we are *crying out to the mountains* to ward off the enemy or to fall on us and cover us (Hos 10:8; Lk 23:30), or in vain we appeal to the mountains to hear our dispute (Mic 6:1) and judge between us and our neighbors."

4. The great strength of the enemy, who would besiege their city (vv. 6–7). Elam, that is, the Persians, comes with quivers full of arrows and with chariots. Kir, that is, the Medes, prepares for battle, to besiege Jerusalem. Then the rich valleys around Jerusalem, which used to be clothed with flocks, will be full of chariots of war, and *the horsemen shall set themselves in array* (be posted) at the city gates (v. 7) to prevent all provisions from going in.

Verses 8–14

What is meant by *the covering of Judah* (v. 8), which at the beginning of this paragraph is said to be *discovered,* is not agreed on. The fenced cities of Judah were a covering, or defense, to the country, but because these were taken by the army of the Assyrians, they stopped being a shelter. The weakness of Judah now appeared, so the defense of Judah was stripped away. Its storehouses were now opened up for public use. Dr. Lightfoot gives this another sense, that by this distress into which Judah would be brought, God would reveal their hypocrisy (2Ch 32:31). Now they revealed both their ungodly confidence (v. 9) and their ungodly self-confidence (v. 13).

They were in great fright, and in their fright they showed:

1. Great contempt for God's goodness and his power to help them. They made use of all the means they could think of to preserve their own lives, but in doing this they did not acknowledge God. Notice:

1.1. How careful they were to make the most of all their advantages. When Sennacherib had made himself master of all the cities of Judah with defenses, the people in Jerusalem decided to take up a defensive position, and not to tamely surrender. They inspected the storehouses to see if they were well supplied with arms: *They looked to the armour of the house of the forest,* which Solomon built in Jerusalem as an armory (1Ki 10:17). They viewed the fortifications, the *breaches of the city of David* (v. 9);

they walked around the walls and observed where they were broken for lack of repairs. There were many such breaches. Public distresses should wake us up to *repair our breaches* and put right what is wrong. They made sure of water for the city: *You gathered together the water of the lower pool* (v. 9). They *numbered the houses of Jerusalem* (v. 10), so that every house might send in its quota of men for the public service or contribute money, so much per house. Because private property should give way to public security, those houses that were in their way when the wall was to be strengthened were torn down. They made a *ditch* (reservoir) between the outer and inner walls to increase the security of the city, and they devised a way of drawing the water of the Old Pool to the ditch, so that they might have plenty of water themselves and might deprive the besiegers of it, so that the Assyrian army *would* not *come and find much water* (2Ch 32:4).

1.2. How negligent they were toward God in all these preparations: *But you have not looked unto the Maker thereof* (v. 11), that is, the Maker of Jerusalem, the city you are so concerned to defend, the Maker of all the advantages that nature has provided it for its defense. It is God who made his Jerusalem, who formed it long ago in his purposes. They are accused here of failing to look to God. They strengthened Jerusalem because it was a rich city and their own houses were in it, not because it was the Holy City and God's house was in it. They did not depend on him for a blessing on their work, but thought their own powers would be enough. It is said about Hezekiah himself that *he trusted in God* (2Ki 18:5), and especially on this occasion (2Ch 32:8), but there were those around him, it seems, who were great political leaders and warriors and yet had little religious faith.

2. Great contempt for God's wrath and justice (vv. 12–14). Notice here:

2.1. What was God's intention in bringing this disaster on them: to humble them, to bring them to repentance. In that day of trouble, the Lord called them *to weeping and mourning* (v. 12), to all the expressions of sorrow, even to *baldness* (tearing out their hair) *and girding with* (putting on) *sackcloth* (v. 12). All this was for the purpose of mourning their sins, backing up their prayers, and preparing to reform their lives. God called them to this by his prophets' explaining his providences.

2.2. How much they went against God's intentions (v. 13). They were as self-confident and cheerful as if there were no enemy, or as if they were in no danger. When they had taken precautions to secure themselves, they then defied danger and decided to indulge in revelry: *Let us eat and drink, for tomorrow we shall die* (v. 13). This was the language of the ungodly scoffers who *mocked the messengers of the Lord and misused his prophets* (2Ch 36:16). They made fun of death. They also made fun of the doctrine of a future state on the other side of death. A practical disbelief in another life after this one lies at the root of the ungodly self-confidence and senseless worldliness that are the sin, shame, and ruin of so many people. God showed his anger toward it to the prophet, *revealed it in his ears* to be declared by him from the roofs: *Surely this iniquity shall not be purged from you till you die* (v. 14). Those who are hostile toward God will find that he will be hostile toward them; he will show his displeasure toward those who are stubbornly perverse.

Verses 15–25

We have here a prophecy about the ousting of Shebna, a great officer at court, and the promotion of Eliakim to the position of honor and trust vacated by Shebna. By the accomplishment of what was foretold about these individuals God wanted to confirm his word in the mouth of Isaiah about other and greater events. It is probable that this prophecy was communicated at the same time as the one in the former part of the chapter and that it began to be fulfilled before Sennacherib's invasion, for now Shebna was in charge of the palace (v. 15), but later Eliakim was (36:3), and Shebna was demoted to secretary. Here is:

1. The prophecy of Shebna's disgrace. He is called *this treasurer* (steward) (v. 15), being entrusted with the management of the revenue, and he is also said to be *over the house* (in charge of the palace) (v. 15). The Jews say, "He maintained traitorous dealings with the king of Assyria and was in league with him to hand over the city to him." In this message to Shebna we have:

1.1. A rebuke of his pride, vanity, and self-confidence (v. 16): "*What hast thou here* (what are you doing here), *and whom hast thou here?* What a mighty noise you make! Are you not lowly and obscure, one who does not know where he comes from? What is the meaning of all this, that you have built yourself a fine house, *hast graved thyself a habitation* (resting place)?" (v. 16). It seemed engraved in a rock because it was founded so firmly and was so impregnable. "In fact, *thou hast hewed thee out a sepulchre*" (v. 16), as if he wanted his pomp to survive his funeral.

1.2. A prophecy of his fall and of the defiling of his glory. *I will drive thee from thy station* (v. 19). High positions are slippery, and those who are proud of their position are justly deprived of their honor. V. 25 refers to this. "The peg that is *now fastened in the sure place*—that is, Shebna, who thinks himself immovably fixed in his office—*shall be removed, and cut down, and fall.*" After a while he would not only be driven out from his position but be driven out from his country: *The Lord will carry thee away with the captivity of a mighty man* (vv. 17–18). Some think the Assyrians seized him and took him away; perhaps Hezekiah, discovering his treachery, banished him. The Dutch jurist and theologian Hugo Grotius thinks he was struck down by a skin disease, which was commonly supposed to have come directly from God's displeasure, particularly to punish the proud. Because of this disease, he was *tossed like a ball* (v. 18) out of Jerusalem. Shebna thinks his place too restricted for him; God will therefore send him *into a large country* (v. 18), where he will have space to wander but will never find his way back again. *There the chariots* (v. 18) that have been the chariots of his glory will serve only to rebuke him for his former grandeur, *to the shame of his lord's house* (v. 18), the court of Ahaz, who promoted him.

2. The prophecy of Eliakim's advancement (v. 20). He is God's servant. He has shown himself to be faithful in other employments, and so God will call him to this high position (Mt 25:23). It is here foretold:

2.1. That Eliakim would be put into Shebna's place of lord chamberlain of the household, lord treasurer, and prime minister of state. The prophet must tell Shebna this (v. 21). "He will have *thy robe*, the badge of honor, and *thy girdle*, the badge of power, for he will have *thy government*." *I will clothe him*; and then it follows, *I will strengthen him* (v. 21). Those who are called to positions of trust and power should seek God for grace to enable them to fulfill the responsibilities of those positions. Eliakim's promotion is further described as the laying of the *key of the house of David upon his shoulders* (v. 22). He had access to *the house of the precious things, the silver, and the gold, and the spices*, and to the *house of the* armour and the *treasures* (39:2), and he made use of the stores for the public service as he thought fit.

2.2. That he would be firmly established in that office. He would have it for life (v. 23): "*I will fasten him as a nail in a sure place*, not to be removed or brought down." He would be a blessing to his country (v. 21): *He shall be a father to the inhabitants of Jerusalem and to the house of Judah.* He would take care not only of the affairs of the king's household but also of all the public interests in Jerusalem and Judah. Things are fortunate for a people when the court, city, and country have no separate interests, when the courtiers are true patriots, when the people the court blesses are also blessed by the country. He will be a blessing to his family (vv. 23–24): *He shall be for a glorious throne to his father's house.* Eliakim is *a nail in a sure place* (v. 23), and all his family are said to depend on him, as in a house the vessels that have handles on them are hung up on nails and pegs. The comparison also shows that he will take care of them all generously, bearing the weight of that responsibility: *All the vessels*, not only *the flagons* (jars) but also *the cups, the vessels of small quantity* (v. 24), the lowliest in his family, will be provided for by him. Our Lord Jesus, having the key of the house of David, is as *a nail in a sure place* (v. 23), and all *the glory of his father's house hangs* on him (v. 24). That soul cannot perish, nor that enterprise fall to the ground, which is hung on Christ by faith, even if it is very heavy.

CHAPTER 23

This chapter is about Tyre, an old, wealthy city situated on the sea and famous for trade and commerce. The allotted territory of the tribe of Asher bordered it. See Jos 19:29, where it is called the strong city Tyre. We rarely find it a dangerous enemy to Israel, but sometimes their faithful ally, as in the reigns of David and Solomon, for trading cities keep their great status not by the conquest of their neighbours but by commerce with them. In this chapter is foretold: 1. The lamentable desolation of Tyre by Nebuchadnezzar and the Babylonian army, about the time they destroyed Jerusalem (vv. 1–14). 2. The restoration of Tyre after seventy years and the return of the Tyrians from captivity to their trade (vv. 15–18).

Verses 1–14

Because Tyre was a seaport, this prophecy of its overthrow fitly begins and ends with, *Howl, you ships of Tarshish* (v. 1 and again v. 14), for all its business, wealth, and honor depended on its shipping. If its shipping was ruined, the ships that traded with it would all be ruined. Notice:

1. Tyre flourishing. *The merchants of Zidon*, who traded at sea, had at first *replenished* (enriched) *her* (v. 2). Sidon was an older city, situated about twenty-five miles (about forty kilometers) north of Tyre on the same coast, and Tyre was originally only its colony, but the daughter had outgrown the mother. Egypt had helped very much to raise her (v. 3). Shihor was a branch of the Nile River: by that river and the sea into which it ran, the Egyptians traded with Tyre. Tyre became rich and great by sheer hard work, though it had no other plows than those that plow the waters. It was a *joyous city*, noted for revelry (v. 7). This made its citizens very reluctant to consider any warnings God gave them by his servants. The city's *antiquity* was *of ancient days* (v. 7), and that helped increase its self-confidence. It was *a crowning city* (v. 8), one that produced kings. *Her merchants are princes* (v. 8), and *her traffickers* (traders), whatever country they go to, *are the honourable of the earth* (v. 8), respected by all.

2. Tyre falling. It does not seem that this city brought trouble onto itself by provoking its neighbors, but rather by tempting them with its wealth, but if it was this that led Nebuchadnezzar to attack Tyre, he was disappointed, for after it had withstood a siege of thirteen years, the inhabitants got away by sea, with their families and goods, and left Nebuchadnezzar nothing but the bare city.

2.1. Notice how the destruction of Tyre is foretold:

2.1.1. The haven will be plundered, or at least neglected. There will be no convenient harbor to receive the ships of Tarshish; all will be *laid waste.* The ships that used to come from Tarshish and Kittim (Cyprus) will receive the sad news: there is no more business there.

2.1.2. The inhabitants will be so overwhelmed by grief that they will not be able to express it.

2.1.3. The neighbors will be stunned, embarrassed, and in anguish at them: *Zidon is ashamed* (v. 4), for the rolling waves of the sea will bring this news from Tyre to Sidon, and there *the strength of the sea*, a high spring tide, will declare it: "*I travail not, nor bring forth children* (v. 4) now. I do not bring shiploads of young people to Tyre, to be brought up there to be involved in trade and business," which was the thing that had made Tyre so rich and well populated. It is true that Egypt had a much larger and more significant kingdom, but Tyre had so many good trading relationships that all the surrounding nations would be in as much anguish at news of the ruin of that one city as they not long after would be at the news of the ruin of all Egypt (v. 5).

2.1.4. The merchants will move their effects to other places and abandon Tyre. "*You* who have long been *inhabitants of this isle*, it is time to wail now, for you must pass over to Tarshish. The most advantageous course you can take is to make your way as best you can to Tarshish, to the sea." Those who could not make their escape must expect nothing other than to be taken captive (v. 7): *Her own feet shall carry her afar off to sojourn*; they will be hurried away on foot into captivity. Many of those who attempt to escape will fall into the hands of the enemy. Tyre will *pass through her land as a river* (v. 10), running down into the abyss of misery; *there is no more strength* (v. 10); her citizens fall as easy prey to the enemy. And just as Tyre has no more strength, so her sister Zidon has no more comfort (v. 12): "*Thou shalt no more rejoice, O oppressed virgin, daughter of Zidon*, who are now ready to be overpowered by the victorious Babylonians!"

2.2. But from where does all this trouble come? God will be its author; it is a *destruction from the Almighty* (13:6). It will be asked (v. 8), "*Who has taken this counsel against Tyre?*" God has intended it, the One who is infinitely wise and just. God did not bring those disasters on Tyre to show arbitrary power, but to punish the Tyrians for their pride. Many other sins, no doubt, reigned among them, but the sin of pride was the particular basis for God's dispute with Tyre. God tells the world what he meant. He intended to convince people of the futility and uncertainty of all earthly glory, to show them how withering it is, even when it seems substantial. Do people consider learning and wealth, pomp and power, their glory? Look at the ruins of Tyre, and see all this glory defiled, humbled, and buried in the dust. *He stretched out his hand over the sea.* The Babylonians will be the instruments of doing it (v. 13): *Behold the land of the Chaldeans*; how easily they and their land were destroyed by the Assyrians. Although their own hands *founded it*, though they themselves *set up the towers* of Babylon and *raised up its palaces*, the Assyrians still brought it to ruin, and so will Tyre later be destroyed by Nebuchadnezzar. If we took more notice of the falling of others, we would not be so confident as we often are of our own standing (1Co 10:12).

Verses 15–18

Here is:

1. The time fixed for the continuation of the desolation of Tyre, which was not to be a *perpetual desolation* (Jer 25:9, 12): *Tyre shall be forgotten seventy years* (v. 15). It was destroyed by Nebuchadnezzar about the time that Jerusalem was, and it lay in ruins just as long. He trampled on the pride of Tyre, and here he served God's purpose, but did it with greater pride, for which God humbled him soon afterward.

2. A prophecy of the restoration of Tyre to its former glory: *After the end of seventy years, according to the years of one king* (v. 15), or one dynasty, that of Nebuchadnezzar. And we may presume that Cyrus at the same time when he released the Jews and encouraged them to rebuild Jerusalem, also released the Tyrians and encouraged them to rebuild Tyre. It is foretold:

2.1. That God's providence will again smile on this ruined city (v. 17): *The Lord will visit Tyre* in mercy, for he will not contend forever (57:16).

2.2. That she will use her best endeavors to recover her trade. She will sing like a prostitute who has for some time been under correction for her immorality and has been set free; she will use her old skills of temptation. When the Tyrians have returned from their captivity, they will seek to force trade, obtain the best goods, and be pleasant to all their customers, just as a prostitute who has been forgotten, when she comes to be spoken of again, commends herself to men by singing and playing, *takes a harp, goes about the city* (v. 16), serenading. Tyre will gradually come to be the marketplace of nations; she will *return to her hire*, to her trade, *and shall commit fornication*—that is, she will ply her trade, for the prophet continues the comparison of a prostitute—*with all the kingdoms of the world* (v. 17) that she had formerly traded with in her prosperity. The love of worldly wealth is spiritual unfaithfulness, and so greedy people are called *adulterers and adulteresses* (Jas 4:4).

2.3. That, having recovered her trade again, Tyre will make better use of it than before (v. 18): *Her merchandise, and her hire, shall be holiness to the Lord*. The trade and earnings of Tyre, and all the profits from its trade, will be devoted to God and employed in his service. It will not be hoarded, but be spent in acts of godliness and kindness. What they can spare from the maintenance of themselves and their families *shall be for those that dwell before the Lord* (v. 18), for the priests, the Lord's ministers, so that they and their families may *eat sufficiently* (v. 18) and may have *durable clothing* (v. 18), strong and lasting. This supposes that religious faith would be set up in New Tyre, that its citizens would come to the knowledge of the true God and into fellowship with the Israel of God. We find people of Tyre then living in the land of Judah (Ne 13:16). Tyre and Sidon were better disposed to religious faith in Christ's time than the cities of Israel were, for if Christ had gone among them, *they would have repented* (Mt 11:21). And we meet with Christians at Tyre (Ac 21:3–4). Both the merchandise of the traders and the hire of the laborers will be devoted to God. It must be the same with us. Both our *merchandise* (the work we follow) and our *hire* (the profit from our work) must *be holiness to the Lord*; the phrase alludes to the motto engraved on the gold plate on the high priest's turban (Ex 39:30) and to the separation of the tithe under the Law (Lev 27:30). We must first give ourselves to be holiness to the Lord before what we do,

or have, or get can be so. When we are generous in relieving the poor, supporting the ministry, and encouraging the Gospel—then our profit and our earnings are holiness to the Lord, if we sincerely look to his glory in them.

CHAPTER 24

Here begins a new sermon, which continues to the end of chapter 27. And in it the prophet tells the righteous in many precious promises that it will be well with them and says of the wicked, in many terrible threats, "Woe to the wicked, disaster is upon them" (3:10–11), and these illustrate each other. This chapter is mostly taken up with threats. It is not the oracle about any particular city or kingdom, as those before were, but the oracle of the Lord's devastation of the whole earth. Some think that it is a prophecy about the great havoc that Sennacherib and his Assyrian army would make in Isaiah's own time. Others think it points to similar devastations that, about 100 years later, Nebuchadnezzar and his armies would make in the same countries. The promises that are mixed with the threats are intended to encourage the people of God in those terrible times. The prophet intends here to describe the calamitous state of the human race in general. Prophecies were written and preserved for our learning (Ro 15:4) and therefore should not be looked on as coming about by private interpretation (2Pe 1:20). In this chapter we have: 1. A threat of devastating judgments for sin (vv. 1–12), to which is added an assurance that in the midst of them good people would be comforted (vv. 13–15). 2. A further threat of similar devastation (vv. 16–22), to which is added an assurance that in the midst of everything God would be glorified.

Verses 1–12

It is a very dark and sad scene that this prophecy presents.

1. The earth is stripped; it is *made empty and waste* (v. 1), as if it were reduced to its original chaos, *tohu* and *bohu*, confusion and emptiness (Ge 1:2), formless and empty. *Earth* sometimes refers to the land, and the same word, *eres*, is translated *earth* in v. 1 and *land* in v. 3: *The land will be utterly emptied and utterly spoiled*. But it could be translated *the earth* in v. 3 as well as in v. 1. Many countries are empty of all solid comforts and satisfaction; a small thing devastates them. We often see abundant wealth completely devoured and destroyed by one judgment or another. Sin has turned the earth *upside down*; the earth has become a totally different place for human beings from what it was when God originally made it to be his dwelling place. Sin has also *scattered its inhabitants*. The rebellion at Babel brought about a dispersion. V. 4 is to the same effect: *The earth mourns, and fades away*; it disappoints those who placed their happiness in it. *The whole world languishes and fades away*. It is like a flower, which withers in the hands of those who are too pleased with it (40:7–8). And just as the earth itself becomes old, so those who live in it are desolate; people have weak bodies and are often alone and confined by suffering (v. 6). *The inhabitants of the earth are burned*, or consumed, some by one disease, others by another, and there are only a *few men left*.

2. It is God who brings all these disasters on the earth. *The Lord* who made the earth fruitful and beautiful, to provide for and strengthen human beings, now *makes it empty and waste* (v. 1), for its Creator is and will be its Judge. It is *the Lord* who *has spoken this word*, and he will do the work (v. 3).

3. People of all ranks and conditions will share in these disasters (v. 2): *It will be as with the people, so with the priest.* The honor of magistrates and ministers will not protect them. The priests have been as evil as the people, and if their position did not restrain them from sin, how can they expect that it will protect them from judgment? As with the servant, so with his master; as with the maid, so with her mistress. Those who have money in hand will fare no better than those who are poor.

4. It is sin that brings these disasters on earth. The earth is made empty and fades away because it is defiled by its inhabitants (v. 5), and so it is made desolate by the judgments of God. They have disobeyed the laws of their creation and rejected their commitment to the God of nature. They *have changed the ordinances* (violated the statutes) (v. 5) of revealed religion, "neglected the ordinances," as some read it, and not been careful to observe them. They have ignored the laws by committing sin and have ignored the statutes by omitting to do their duty. Here they have broken the everlasting covenant, which is a perpetual commitment and will be an eternal blessing to those who keep it.

5. These judgments will humble people's pride (v. 4): *The haughty people of the earth do languish,* for they have lost the reason that supported their pride. Their merriment is spoiled. This is explained in detail (vv. 7–9): *All the merryhearted do sigh.* This is what worldly, godless merriment is like; it is only *as the crackling of thorns under a pot* (Ecc 7:6). Worldly joy is noisy, but its noise will soon come to an end, and it will end in mourning. Two things excite and express worthless merriment:

5.1. Drinking: *The new wine mourns* (dries up) (v. 7); it has turned sour for lack of being drunk. *The vine languishes* (withers) (v. 7); it gives little hope of a good harvest, and so the merrymakers groan (v. 7), for if you *destroy their vines and their fig trees, you make all their mirth to cease* (Hos 2:11–12).

5.2. Music: *The mirth of tabrets ceases, and the joy of the harp* (v. 8), which used to be heard at their festivals (5:12). In short, *All joy is darkened* (turns to gloom) (v. 11); there is not a happy face to be seen, and no one has even the energy to force a smile.

6. The cities will suffer from this devastation (v. 10): *The city of confusion is broken down*; it lies exposed to invading powers. *Every house is shut up* (v. 10), perhaps because of the plague, so that there are *few men left* (v. 6). *In the city,* in Jerusalem itself, there will be left nothing but *desolation*; grass will grow in the streets, and *the gate is smitten with destruction* (battered to pieces) (v. 12); all who used to pass to and fro through the gate will be crushed.

Verses 13–15

Here is mercy remembered in the midst of wrath (Hab 3:2). In Judah and Jerusalem, and the neighboring countries, when they are overrun by the enemy, Sennacherib or Nebuchadnezzar, there will be a remnant preserved from the general destruction. Notice:

1. The small number of this remnant (v. 13). When all goes to ruin, *there shall be as the shaking of an olive tree, and the gleaning grapes,* here and there one or two who will escape the general disaster. These few are dispersed like the gleanings of the olive tree, and they are hidden under the leaves. The Lord knows those who are his (2Ti 2:19); the world does not.

2. The great devotion of this remnant, which is the greater for their having so narrowly escaped this great destruction (v. 14): *They shall lift up their voice; they shall sing.* Those who rejoice in the Lord can rejoice even in trouble (Php 4:4, 6). They will sing not only for the mercy but also *for the majesty of the Lord* (v. 14). Their dispersion will help spread the knowledge of God, and they will make even remote shores ring with his praises (11:9).

3. Their holy zeal to motivate and inspire others to the same devotion (v. 15), both those who are *in the fires* (v. 15), in the furnace of affliction, the fires by which the *inhabitants of the earth are burned* (v. 6), and those who are *in the isles of the sea* (v. 15), to where they are banished or forced to flee for shelter. They have gone *through fire and water* (Ps 66:12), but in both let them glorify the Lord.

Verses 16–23

These verses, like those before, speak clearly of:

1. Comfort to saints. They may be driven by general disasters to *the uttermost parts of the earth* (Ps 2:8), or perhaps they are forced there for their religious beliefs, but there they are singing, not sighing. And this is their song: *even glory to the righteous* (v. 16). The word is singular and may refer to *the righteous God.* Or the meaning may be, "These songs contribute to the glory of the righteous people who sing them."

2. Terror to sinners. The prophet returns to mourn the wretchedness he sees breaking out on the earth: "*But I said, My leanness! My leanness! Woe unto me!* I'm getting weaker and weaker; how terrible it is for me! The very thought of it worries me and makes me waste away and become weaker" (v. 16). He foresees:

2.1. The prevalence of sin, that sin will be great (v. 16): *The treacherous dealers have dealt treacherously,* the treacherous betray. People are false to one another; there is universal dishonesty. Truth, that sacred bond of society, has departed, and there is nothing but treachery in people's dealings with one another. Everyone is also unfaithful to their God; all have dealt very treacherously with him, departing from their loyalty to him.

2.2. The prevalence of wrath and judgment for that sin.

2.2.1. The inhabitants of the earth will be pursued from place to place by one trouble or another (vv. 17–18): *Fear, and the pit, and the snare* (terror of the pit and the snare) await them wherever they are. It is a common example of the disastrous state of human life that when we seek to avoid one trouble, we fall into a worse one.

2.2.2. The earth itself will be shaken to pieces. It will be literally so ultimately, when all *the works therein shall be burnt up* (2Pe 3:10), and it is often figuratively so before that time. This is expressed in vv. 19–20: *The earth is utterly broken down; it is clean dissolved* (split open); *it is moved exceedingly,* thoroughly shaken from its place. Those who lay up their treasure in worldly things (Mt 6:19–20) put their confidence in things that will soon be *utterly broken down and dissolved. The earth shall reel to and fro like a drunkard* (vv. 19–20). Worldly people live in it as in a castle, an impregnable tower, but it sways like a hut in the wind (v. 20), so easily and suddenly and with so little loss to the great landlord. It *shall fall, and not rise again* (v. 20), but there will be a new heavens and a new earth (Rev 21:1), in which nothing but righteousness will live (Rev 21:27). But what is it that shakes the earth in this way and sinks it? It is the guilt of its rebellion that will fall heavily on it. Sin is a burden to the whole creation (Ro 8:22). Sin is the destruction of states, kingdoms, and families.

2.2.3. God will have a particular dispute with the kings and leaders of the earth (v. 21): *He will punish the host* (powers) *of the high ones.* The powerful, who think they are out of the reach of any danger, will have all their pride and cruelty brought against them by God; it will return on their own heads. Let those who are trampled on by the powerful ones on earth encourage themselves with this, that although they cannot resist them, there is still a God who will call them to account. It is foretold in particular (v. 22) that they will be herded together as prisoners, as convicted and condemned prisoners are herded together in a dungeon, and there they will be kept in close confinement. Let not free people glory in their freedom, any more than strong people in their strength (Jer 9:23), for they do not know what restraints they are reserved for. But after many days *they will be visited*, either in wrath or in mercy. They will ultimately be *visited* in wrath, that is, punished, for they are being reserved for the day of execution, for the judgment on the great day (Jude 6). Or they will be *visited* in mercy; they will be released from imprisonment and will again gain, if not their dignity, then their liberty. Nebuchadnezzar took many kings and princes as his prisoners, and he kept them in the dungeon in Babylon, and among them was Jehoiachin king of Judah. However, a long time after, when Nebuchadnezzar had died, his son visited them with kindness, particularly to Jehoiachin, whom he gave a seat of honor higher than those of other kings who were with him (Jer 52:32).

2.3. Glory to God in all this (v. 23). When the proud enemies of God's church are humbled, it will be clear beyond contradiction that the Lord reigns. When the kings of the earth are punished for their tyranny, then it will be proved to all the world that God is King of kings, that he reigns as *Lord of hosts*, Lord of all their hosts; that he reigns in Mount Zion and in Jerusalem, in his church; and that he reigns before *his ancients* (elders). God's elders, the old disciples, the experienced Christians, who have often gone into the sanctuary of God in Zion and Jerusalem when they have been perplexed, will see more than others of God's rule and sovereignty (Ps 73:17; 2Ki 19:14–34). Then it will be clear that he reigns gloriously, in such brightness and splendor that the moon will be *confounded* (abashed) and the sun ashamed, as the smaller lights are eclipsed and extinguished by the greater ones. The glory of the Creator infinitely surpasses the glory of the brightest creation.

CHAPTER 25

We have here: 1. Thankful praises that the prophet offers to God for what he has done (vv. 1–5). 2. Precious promises of what God will do further for his church, especially in the grace of the Gospel (vv. 6–8). 3. The church's triumph in God over her enemies (vv. 9–12). This chapter looks as agreeably on the church as the previous chapter looked terribly on the world.

Verses 1–5

Here:

1. The prophet determines to praise God himself (v. 1): "*O Lord! thou art my God*, a God in covenant with me." When God is punishing *the kings of the earth upon the earth* (24:21), a poor prophet can go to him and say with humble boldness, *O Lord! thou art my God*, and so *I will exalt thee, I will praise thy name* (v. 1).

2. He pleases himself with the thought that others will also be brought to praise God (v. 3). "Therefore, because of the desolations you have brought on the earth and the just vengeance you have taken, the strong people will glorify you together, and cities of ruthless nations will fear you." This may be understood as referring to:

2.1 Those who have been the enemies of God's kingdom: they will either be converted and glorify God by joining with his people in his service or, at least, be convinced, acknowledging that they have been conquered. Or:

2.2. Those who will be now made strong and terrible for God and by him, even though earlier they were weak. God will so visibly support those who fear and glorify him that all will stand in awe of them.

3. He mentions what should be the subject of this praise. We must exalt God and praise him, for:

3.1. He has done marvelous things, according to the purpose of his own will (v. 1). These *wonderful things*, which are new and surprising to us, are according to his *counsels of old*.

3.2. He has in particular humbled the pride and broken the power of the mighty ones of the earth (v. 2): "*Thou hast made of a city a heap of rubbish*. You have brought to ruins many fortified towns, which thought they were well guarded both by nature and by human skill. Many a town so richly built that it might be called *a palace* (stronghold), and visited so often by people from all parts of the world that it might be called a *palace of strangers*—you have made such a city into a heap of rubble; it has been razed to the ground and will never again be rebuilt." Cities that once flourished have decayed and are now scarcely known—except by urns or coins that have been excavated. How many of the cities of Israel have long since become heaps and ruins!

3.3. He has relieved his needy people (v. 4): *Thou has been a strength to the poor, a strength to the needy*. He strengthens the weak who are humble and who trust in him. In fact, he not only makes them strong but is himself their strength. He is a refuge from the storm of rain or hail, and a shadow from the scorching heat of the sun in summer. When *the blast of the terrible ones is as a storm against the wall*, God will come to ensure the safety of his people; the blast makes a great noise but cannot knock down the wall. The enemies of God's poor are ruthless. Their rage is like a blast of wind, loud, blustering, and furious, but, like the wind, it is under divine restraint, for God *holds the winds in his fist* (Pr 30:4). A storm beating against a ship tosses it about, but one that beats against a wall never moves it (Ps 76:10; 138:7).

3.4. He does and will shelter those who trust in him from the arrogance of their proud oppressors (v. 5): "You will, or you do, *bring down the noise of strangers* (silence the uproar of foreigners); you will abate and still it, as *the heat in a dry place* is moderated *by the shadow of a cloud* intervening." The oppressors of God's people are called *strangers*, for they forget that those they oppress are of the same blood as they. They are called *terrible* (ruthless) *ones*; they would rather be feared than loved. The branches, even the top branches, of the ruthless ones will be broken off. If the laborers in God's vineyard are called to *bear the burden and heat of the day* (Mt 20:12), God will refresh them, as with the shadow of a cloud.

Verses 6–8

If we suppose (as many do) that this refers to the great joy there would be in Zion and Jerusalem when the army of the Assyrians was routed by an angel (2Ki 19:35), or when the Jews were released from captivity in Babylon (2Ch 36:22–23), we still cannot avoid making it look further, to the grace of the Gospel and the glory that is the crown and consummation of that grace. We have here a prophecy of the salvation and the grace brought to us by Jesus Christ, into which *the prophets inquired and searched diligently* (1Pe 1:10), a prophecy:

1. That the grace of the Gospel would be a royal feast for all people, not like that of Xerxes, intended only to show the splendor of the one who gave the feast (Est 1:4), for this is intended to please the guests.

1.1. God himself is the One who gives the feast.

1.2. The guests invited are *all people*, Gentiles as well as Jews. *Go preach the Gospel to every creature* (Mk 16:15).

1.3. The place is *Mount Zion*: the preachers must begin at Jerusalem (Lk 24:47). The Gospel church is the Jerusalem that is above. It is *a feast of fat things* (rich food) *and full of marrow* (the best of meats) (v. 6); the comforts of the Gospel are very nourishing to all those who feast on them. It is a feast *of wines on the lees* (v. 6), the strongest-bodied wines, which have been kept a long time and then are well refined.

2. That the world would be freed from that darkness of ignorance and failure in the mists of which it had been so long lost and buried (v. 7): *He will destroy in this mountain the face of the covering* (the shroud or covering of the face). Their faces are covered like those of condemned or dead people. There is *a veil spread over* (a sheet that covers) *all nations* (v. 7), for they all sit in darkness (Mt 4:16; Isa 9:2; 42:7). The Jews themselves, among whom *God was known*, had a *veil upon their hearts* (2Co 3:15). But the Lord will destroy this veil by the light of his Gospel shining in the world, and the power of his Spirit will open people's eyes to receive it.

3. That death would be conquered, its power broken: *He will swallow up death in victory* (v. 8).

3.1. Christ himself, in his resurrection, will triumph over death. The grave seemed to swallow him up, but really he swallowed it up.

3.2. The happiness of the saints will be out of the reach of death.

3.3. Believers may triumph over death as a conquered enemy: *O death! where is thy sting?* (1Co 15:55). It is the last enemy (1Co 15:26).

4. That grief will be banished and there will be endless joy: *The Lord God will wipe away tears from off all faces* (v. 8). In the covenant of grace there will be something provided that is enough to balance out all the sorrows of this present time (Ro 8:18). And in heaven God will *wipe away all tears* (Rev 7:17; 21:4). Then *there shall be no more sorrow*, because *there shall be no more death*. The hope of this should now wipe away all excessive tears, all the weeping that hinders sowing.

5. That all the disgrace poured on religious faith will be forever rolled away (Jos 5:9): *The rebuke* (disgrace) *of his people* (v. 8), the slander and misrepresentations by which their character has been blackened, *shall be taken away*.

Verses 9–12

Here is:

1. The welcome that the church will give to these blessings (v. 9): *It shall be said in that day*, with humble exultation, *Lo, this is our God; we have waited for him!* With such a triumphant song as this will glorified saints *enter into the joy of their Lord* (Mt 25:21). His coming is an encouragement to hope for the perfection of this salvation: *We have waited for him, and he will save us* (v. 9); he will carry on what he has begun, for *as for God*, our God, *his work is perfect* (Dt 32:4; Ps 18:30).

2. A prospect of further blessings. *In this mountain will the hand of the Lord rest* (v. 10). The church and people of God will have continual proofs of God's presence with them. The power of their enemies will be broken. *Moab* here stands for all the enemies of God's people; they *shall*

all *be trodden down* or trampled—for in those days they thrashed out the grain by trampling on it—and will be thrown out on the rubbish heap like straw (v. 10), because it is good for nothing else. Because God has *caused his hand to rest upon this mountain*, he will *spread forth his hands, in the midst* of his people, *like one that swims* (v. 11), which suggests he will strongly use and exert his power for them. He will be continually active on their behalf, for this is how swimmers progress. *He shall bring down the pride* (v. 11) of their enemies—and Moab was notoriously guilty of pride (16:6)—by one humbling judgment after another. He will bring down *the spoils of their hands* (v. 11); he will take from them what they have gained by plunder and robbery. He will ruin all their fortifications (v. 12); there is no fortress that is impregnable to almighty God. This destruction of Moab is a type of Christ's victory over death (described in v. 8), his disarming the powers and authorities by the cross (Col 2:15).

CHAPTER 26

This chapter is a song of holy joy and praise, in which the great things God has committed himself to do for his people are celebrated. It was to be sung when that prophecy would be fulfilled, for we must meet God in our thanksgiving when he comes to us with his mercies. The people of God are taught here: 1. To triumph in the holy security that the church in general and every member of it has under the divine protection (vv. 1–4). 2. To triumph over all opposing powers (vv. 5–6). 3. To walk with God and wait for him in the darkest times (vv. 7–9). 4. To mourn the stupidity of those who do not consider the providence of God (vv. 10–11). 5. To encourage themselves with the hope that God will continue to do them good (vv. 13–14), and to engage themselves to continue in his service (v. 13). 6. To recollect the kind providences of God toward them (vv. 15–18). 7. To rejoice in hope of a glorious rescue (Ro 5:2), which will be as a resurrection to them (v. 19), and to rest in expectation of it (vv. 20–21).

Verses 1–4

A song of praise is fittingly added to the prophecies of Gospel grace. *In that day this song shall be sung* (v. 1). It will be sung in the *land of Judah* (v. 1), which prefigured the Gospel church, for the Gospel covenant is said to be made *with the house of Judah* (Heb 8:8).

1. The church of God is strongly fortified against evildoers (v. 1): *We have a strong city.* It is a city incorporated by the charter of the eternal covenant, made ready for the reception of all who are set free by that charter. It is a strong city, as Jerusalem was, as long as it was a city firmly built (Ps 122:3), with God himself as a wall of fire around it. The church is a strong city, for it has *walls and bulwarks* appointed by God, for he has, in his promise, set salvation as its defense.

2. The people of Jerusalem, if they are such as they should be, are its strength (Zec 12:5). The gates are here ordered to be opened, so *that the righteous nation, which keeps the truth, may enter in* (v. 2). They were banished and driven out by the sin of former times, but now they are free to enter again.

3. All who belong to it are safe and at peace and have a security and calmness of mind in the assurance of God's favor. *Thou wilt keep him in peace*, in *perfect peace*, inner peace, outer peace, peace with God, peace of conscience, peace in all events. Those who trust in God must have their minds firmly set on him. God will keep in perpetual

peace those who do so, and that peace will keep them (Ps 112:7). Trust in him forever, at all times, when you have nothing else to trust in. Whatever we trust in the world for is restricted to the limits of time. But what we trust in God for will last as long as we will last. For in the *Lord Jehovah—Jah, Jehovah*, in him who was, is, and is to come (Rev 1:4)—there is, literally, a "Rock of ages" (v. 4), a firm and lasting foundation for faith to build on, and the house built on that rock will stand secure in a storm (Mt 7:24–25).

Verses 5–11

The prophet encourages us to trust in the Lord, for:

1. He will make the souls who are humble and trust in him victorious over their proud enemies (vv. 5–6). Even the lofty city Babylon itself, or Nineveh, he lays low (25:12). He does not say, "Great armies will tread them down," but, "When God wants it to be done, even the feet of the poor will do it" (Mal 4:3). See also Ps 147:6; Ro 16:20.

2. He takes notice of the path his people take and has delight in it (v. 7): *The way of the just is* level; they walk with God in consistent obedience. *Thou, most upright, dost weigh* (or make smooth) *the path of the just* (v. 7), by removing those things that would be stumbling blocks. God *weighs* it; he considers it and will give them grace that is sufficient to help them through all difficulties (2Co 12:9; Heb 4:16).

3. It is our duty to wait for God in the darkest and most discouraging times (vv. 8–9). This has always been the practice of God's people: *"In the way of thy judgments we* have still *waited for thee*; when you have corrected us, we have looked to no one else than you to relieve us." Our troubles must never turn us away from God; rather, *the desire of our soul must* still *be to his name and to the remembrance of him* (v. 8). Our great concern must be for God's name: *"Father, glorify thy name* (Jn 12:28), and we are satisfied." The thoughts we remember God with must be our great support and pleasure. Our desires toward God must be inner, fervent, and sincere (Ps 42:1).

4. It is God's intention in his judgments to bring *men to seek him*: *When thy judgments are upon the earth* (v. 9), devastating everything, we have reason to expect that not only God's people, but even *the inhabitants of the world, will learn righteousness* (v. 9). They have their mistakes put right and their lives reformed.

5. Those who will not be persuaded by the methods God takes to reform them are truly evil, and it is necessary for God to deal with them severely by his judgments. Sinners walk contrary to God (v. 10). *Favour is shown* to them. They receive many mercies from God, and the intention of this is that they may be won over to love and serve God, but all is in vain: *they will not learn righteousness* (v. 10). They live *in a land of uprightness* (v. 10), in a land of *evenness*, where there are not so many stumbling blocks as in other places, in a land of *correction*, where evil and godlessness are punished, but there they *will deal unjustly* (v. 10) and continue perversely in their evil ways. Those who act corruptly deal unjustly both with God and with other people, as well as with their own souls, and, having refused to be reclaimed by the justice of the nation, they may expect to receive the judgments of God on them. They *will not behold the majesty of the Lord* (v. 10). Even when we receive the mercy of the Lord, we must still behold the *majesty of the Lord and his goodness* (v. 10; Hos 3:5). *They will not see* (v. 11), and there are none so blind as those who will not see, who ascribe a divine rebuke to chance or common fate. *They will not see, but*

they shall see (v. 11), will be made to see, whether they want to or not, that God is angry with them. Unbelievers, mockers, and the self-confident will soon feel that *it is a fearful thing to fall into the hands of the living God* (Heb 10:31). *They shall see* that they have done God's people a great deal of wrong, and so *they shall be ashamed* of their enmity and harsh treatment of those who deserved to be treated better. Their condemnation, therefore, is that since they showed disrespect toward the happiness of God's friends, *the fire of his enemies shall devour them*.

Verses 12–19

In these verses, the prophet looks back and then looks forward:

1. His reviews and reflections are mixed. When he looks back on the state of the church, he finds:

1.1. That God in many instances has done great things for them (v. 12): *Thou hast wrought all our works in us*, or for us. Whatever good work is done by us, it is because of a good work accomplished by the grace of God in us. In particular (v. 15): *"Thou hast increased the nation, O Lord*, so that a little one has become a thousand—in Egypt they multiplied greatly, and later in Canaan, so much that they filled the land—and in this *thou art glorified*," as faithful to his covenant with Abraham (Ge 17:7).

1.2. That still he has them under his rebukes.

1.2.1. The neighboring nations have sometimes tyrannized them (v. 13): *"O Lord our God*, you who have the sole right to rule over us, whose subjects and servants we are, we complain to you that *other lords besides thee have had dominion over us*." When they had been careless in serving God, God allowed their enemies to rule over them, so that they might know the difference between his service *and the service of the kingdoms of the countries* (2Ch 12:8). It may be understood as a confession of sin, their serving other gods, by which other lords—for they called their idols *baals*, "lords"—ruled over them, besides God. But now they promise that it will be so no longer: "From this time on *by thee only will we make mention of thy name* (v. 13); we will worship only you, and only in the way that you have instituted and appointed." The same may be our penitent reflection: *Other lords, besides God, have had dominion over us* (v. 13); every sinful desire has been our lord, and we have wronged both God and ourselves.

1.2.2. They have sometimes been taken prisoner by their enemies (v. 15): "The nation that at first you increased you have now diminished and *removed to all the ends of the earth, driven out to the utmost parts of heaven*," as is threatened in Dt 28:64; 30:4.

1.2.3. The prophet remembers that when they have been oppressed and taken captive, they have cried out to God, which showed that they neither had completely abandoned him nor had been completely abandoned by him, and that there were merciful intentions in the judgments they were under (v. 16): *Lord, in trouble have they visited thee*. Adversity brings us to God, encourages us to do our duty, and shows us our dependence on him. Adversity brings us to secret prayer, in which we may be more free and detailed in what we say to him than we can be in public. The prophet complains that their struggles for their liberty have been painful and perilous, but that they have not been successful (vv. 17–18). "We have been like a woman in labor, who cries out in labor pain; we have endured a great deal of anxiety and toil in trying to help ourselves, and our troubles have been increased in those attempts." Whenever they came to *present themselves before the Lord* with their complaints and requests, they were in agony like that of a woman in labor. "*We have been with child* (v. 18); we have had great expectation of a happy salvation. But alas! *We have as it were brought forth wind* (v. 18); it has proved a miscarriage; our expectations have been frustrated. All our efforts have proved abortive: *We have not wrought any deliverance* (salvation) *in the earth* (v. 18), for ourselves or for our friends, *neither have the inhabitants of the world fallen* (v. 18) before us: they are still as high and arrogant as ever."

2. His prospects and hopes are very pleasant. In general, "*Thou wilt ordain peace for us*" (v. 12). Whatever trouble may be appointed to the people of God for a time, peace will ultimately be established for them, for the *end of those men is peace* (Ps 37:37). "You have heard the desire of the humble, and so we will give glory for it only to you and will depend only on your grace to enable us to do so." *They are dead*, those *other lords* who *have had dominion over us* (v. 13); their power is broken. He has *made all their memory to perish* (v. 14). Although the church does not rejoice in the birth of the male child for whom she suffered much in labor (Jn 16:21; Rev 12:5), *but has as it were brought forth wind* (v. 18), the disappointment will be balanced out. *Thy dead men shall live* (v. 19). A spirit of life from God will enter into the slaughtered witnesses (Rev 11:11). The *dry bones shall live* and become an *exceedingly great army* (Eze 37:10). *Together with my dead body shall they arise* (v. 19). When God's time comes, Jerusalem, the city of God, now lying like a dead body, will arise; the church will be rebuilt and flourish again. And so let the poor, desolate, sad inhabitants, who live as in dust, *awake and sing*. The dew of God's favor will be to the city as the evening dew is to the grass that has been parched by the heat of the sun throughout the day; his dew will revive and refresh them. As the plants that have lain buried in the earth come out and blossom when watered by the spring dews, so will they flourish again. Dr. Lightfoot applies it to the spiritual resurrection, by the power of Christ, of those who were dead in sin. "The Gentiles will live; with my body will they arise; that is, they will be called in after Christ's resurrection. They will rise with him and sit with him in heavenly places (Eph 2:5–6); in fact, they will arise with my body; they will become the mystical body of Christ and will rise as part of him."

Verses 20–21

These two verses are thought not to belong to the song that takes up the rest of the chapter, but to begin a new subject, and to be an introduction to the following chapter rather than the conclusion of this one.

1. God invites the people (v. 20): "*Come, my people, come to me, come with me; let the storm that disperses others bring you closer together. Come, and enter into thy chambers*; do not stay outside, or you will be caught in the storm." We must by faith find a way into these rooms and hide there; we must put ourselves under divine protection with peace of mind. "Come, as Noah did into the ark, for he *shut the doors about him*" (v. 20) (Ge 7:16). When dangers are threatening, it is good to withdraw and remain hidden, as Elijah did by the Kerith Ravine (1Ki 17:3). "*Enter into thy chamber* (v. 20), to examine yourself, meditate, pray, and humble yourself before God."

2. He assures them that the trouble will be over in a very short time: "*Hide thyself for a moment* (v. 20), the smallest possible instant of time. When it is over, it will seem like nothing to you." When the church father Athanasius (ca. 293–373) was banished from Alexandria by a decree of the Roman emperor Julian (331–363), and his friends greatly mourned it, he told them to be cheerful. "It is a little cloud that will soon blow over."

3. He assures them that their enemies will be judged for all the trouble they have caused them by the sword (v. 21). The Lord comes out of his place to punish the people of the earth for *their iniquity*. God *comes out of his place to punish* (v. 21). Some observe that God's place is the mercy seat; he delights to be there. When he punishes, he leaves that place, for he has no pleasure in the death of sinners (Eze 18:23; 33:11). The criminals will be convicted: *The earth shall disclose her blood* (v. 21); the innocent blood of the saints and martyrs that has been shed will now be brought to light (Ge 4:10–11; Job 20:27).

CHAPTER 27

In this chapter the prophet goes on to show what great things God would do for his church and people in the rescue of Jerusalem from Sennacherib and the destruction of the Assyrian army, but it is expressed generally, in order to encourage the church in later times. 1. Proud oppressors would be judged (v. 1); 2. Care would be taken of the church, as of God's vineyard (vv. 2–3). 3. God would drop his displeasure with the people when they returned to him (vv. 4–5). 4. He would greatly multiply and increase them (v. 6). 5. As to their adversities, their nature would be changed (v. 7), and they would be lessened and moderated (v. 8) and sanctified (v. 9). 6. Although the church might be ravaged and deserted for a time (vv. 10–11), it would still be restored, and the scattered members would be gathered together (vv. 12–13).

Verses 1–6

The prophet is here singing about judgment and mercy (Ps 101:1):

1. Judgment on the enemies of God's church (v. 1). When the Lord *comes out of his place, to punish the inhabitants of the earth* (26:21), he will be sure to punish *leviathan*, the *dragon that is in the sea* (v. 1), every proud, oppressing tyrant that is the terror of the mighty (Eze 32:27) and, like Leviathan, is so *fierce that none dares stir him up* (Job 41:10, 24–25). So Sennacherib was in his day, Nebuchadnezzar in his, and Antiochus in his; so Pharaoh had been formerly, and is called *leviathan* and *the dragon* (51:9; Ps 74:13–14; Eze 29:3). The New Testament church has had its leviathans; we read of an enormous red dragon ready to devour it (Rev 12:3). Those evil, persecuting powers are here compared to the Leviathan for bulk and strength and to dragons for their rage and fury. They are also compared to *piercing serpents*, penetrating in their objectives, and to *crooked serpents* (v. 1), subtle and insinuating, but perverse and troublesome. If great rulers oppose the people of God, they are as dragons and serpents in God's sight, plagues on the human race. They are too big for people to deal with and call to account, and so God in his greatness will take the matter into his own hands. He has *a sore* (fierce), *and great, and strong sword* (v. 1), when the limit of their sins has been reached (Ge 15:16; Mt 23:32) and their *day has come to fall*. In *that day* (v. 2) he will punish, on his day, which is coming (Ps 37:13). This may be applied to the spiritual victories gained by our Lord Jesus over the powers of darkness. He not only disarmed the prince of this world (Col 2:15; Jn 12:31) but, with his strong sword, the power of his death, and the preaching of his Gospel, even now *destroys him that had the power of death, that is, the devil* (Heb 2:14), that great Leviathan, that old Serpent, the Dragon (Rev 20:2–3).

2. Mercy to the church.

2.1. She is God's vineyard and is under his special care (vv. 2–3). She is, in God's eye, *a vineyard of red wine*. The world is like a worthless desert, but the church is enclosed like a vineyard, from which precious fruits are gathered, with which the church's members honor God and people. It is a vineyard of *red wine*, producing the best and finest grapes, suggesting the reformation of the church, that it now produces good fruit for God, whereas before it produced bad grapes (5:4). *I the Lord do keep it* (v. 3). He has undertaken to be the keeper of Israel (Ps 121:4–5). Those who produce fruit for God are under his protection. God's vineyard in this world is very much exposed to harm; there are many who want to harm it (Ps 80:13). God, however, will allow no real harm to be done to it, no harm except what he will bring good out of. God will guard it not only in the night of danger and persecution but also in days of peace and prosperity, the temptations of which are no less dangerous. This vineyard will be well protected. *I will water it every moment* (v. 3), but it will not be watered too much. The still and silent dews of God's grace and blessing will fall on it continually. God waters his vineyard by the ministry of the word through his servants the prophets. Paul plants, and Apollos waters, but God makes it grow (1Co 3:6).

2.2. Though sometimes he contends with his people, he will be reconciled to them when they submit to him (vv. 4–5). *Fury is not in him* toward his vineyard. It is true that if he finds in it briers and thorns instead of vines, he will trample on them and burn them, but otherwise, "If I am angry with my people, let them humble themselves, pray, and seek my face, and so *take hold of my strength*; let them come to me for refuge (v. 5) with a sincere desire to make peace with me, and I will be reconciled to them, and all will be well." Here is a quarrel imagined between God and human beings. It is an old quarrel, one that began when sin first entered the world. Here also is a gracious invitation given to us to settle this quarrel. Pardoning mercy is called the power of our Lord; let them take hold of that. Christ is the *arm of the Lord* (53:1). Christ *crucified is the power of God* (1Co 1:24); let them take hold of him by a living faith. God is willing to be reconciled to us if we are only willing to be reconciled to him.

2.3. The church of God in the world will be a growing body (v. 6). "In times to come," as some read it, "in later times," when these calamities are past, or in the days of the Gospel, *he shall cause Jacob to take root*, deeper root than ever. Many will be brought into the church; there will be many converts, some from all the nations around, and the converts will be fruitful in the fruits of righteousness (Php 1:11). The preaching of the Gospel *brought forth fruit in all the world* (Col 1:6), fruit that will last (Jn 15:16).

Verses 7–13

Here is the prophet again singing about mercy and judgment to the church (Ps 101:1), and mercy mixed with that judgment.

1. Here is judgment threatened even to Jacob and Israel. *They shall blossom and bud* (v. 6), but:

1.1. Some will be *smitten* (struck) and *slain* (killed) (v. 7). Judgment will begin with the people of God (1Pe 4:17).

1.2. Jerusalem, their *defenced city, shall be desolate* (vv. 10–11). "After God has tried a range of methods to reform them, which have proved ineffective on many of them, he will ravage their country for a time," which was fulfilled when Jerusalem was destroyed by the

Babylonians; then that *habitation* was abandoned for a long time.

1.2.1. Jerusalem had been a well-fortified city, not so much by human skill or by nature as by God's grace and protection, but when God was provoked to withdraw, she was left as in the desert. "Cattle will graze in the pleasant gardens of Jerusalem; they will lie down there, and there will be none to drive them away, and they will eat the tender branches of the fruit trees," which perhaps further shows that the people would become an easy target for their enemies.

1.2.2. "*When the boughs thereof are withered* (v. 11) as they grow on the tree, blighted by winds and frosts and not pruned, *they shall be broken off* for fuel, and *the women* and children will *come and set them on fire* (v. 11). There will be total destruction, for the trees themselves will be destroyed." And this is a figure of the deplorable state of the vineyard (v. 2). Our Savior seems to refer to this when he says about the branches of the vine that *abide not in him* that they are *cast forth and withered, and men gather them, and cast them into the fire, and they are burned* (Jn 15:6).

1.2.3. The comparison is explained: *It is a people of no understanding* (v. 11), who do not enjoy or savor divine things, like a withered branch without sap, and this lies at the root of all sins. Evildoers have no understanding of the most important concerns. *He that formed them* (v. 11) into a people to declare his praise, seeing that they do not fulfill the purpose of their formation, but hate to be reformed, will reject them and *show them no favour* (v. 11). If the One who made us by his power does not make us happy in his favor, it would have been better if we had never been made.

2. Here is great mercy mixed with this judgment, for there are good people mixed with those who are corrupt and degenerate, those on whom God will have mercy.

2.1. Although they will be struck and killed, they will not be to the same extent, and in the way, that their enemies will be struck and killed (v. 7). God's people and God's enemies are here described struggling with each other. In this contest there are those who are killed on both sides. God makes use of evildoers not only to strike his people but also to kill them, for they are his sword (Ps 17:13). But when the cup that makes people stagger comes to be put into the hand of these evildoers (51:17), it will be much worse with them than it ever was with God's people in their greatest troubles. The seed of the woman has only his heel bruised, but the serpent has its head crushed and broken. There really is a vast difference between the suffering and deaths of good people and the suffering and deaths of evildoers.

2.2. The adversity will be mitigated, moderated, and exercised in proportion to their strength, not in proportion to what they deserve (v. 8). This is how God orders the troubles of his people, not *suffering* (permitting) *them to be tempted above what they are able* (1Co 10:13). He considers what we can bear when he begins to correct, and when it is the *day of his east wind* (v. 8), not only blustering and noisy but also blighting and harmful, then, nevertheless, he restrains his fierce wind; he checks it and sets bounds to it. When he is winnowing his grain, it is with a gentle gale, which will blow away only the chaff, not the good grain.

2.3. Although God will afflict them, he will make their afflictions work for the good of their souls (Ro 8:28); he will correct them as parents correct their children (Pr 3:11–12), to drive out the foolishness that is in their hearts (Pr 22:15) (v. 9): *By this therefore shall the iniquity of Jacob be purged* (will Jacob's guilt be atoned for). Because the suffering is moderated and the fierce wind is restrained, we may conclude that he intends it as a way of reforming them, not destroying them. The particular sin that the adversity was intended to heal was the sin of idolatry. But by the exile in Babylon they were not only weaned from this sin but also set against it. *Ephraim shall say, What have I to do any more with idols?* (Hos 14:8). Jacob has his sin taken away *when he makes all the stones of the altar* (v. 9)—of his idolatrous altar, the stones of which were precious and sacred to him—*as chalkstones that are beaten asunder* (crushed to pieces) (v. 9). He not only has contempt for them and values them no more than chalk stones but, in holy revenge, crushes them to pieces as easily as a person breaks up chalk stones. *The groves and the images* (Asherah poles or incense altars) *shall not* stand before this penitent (v. 9), but will be thrown down too, never to be set up again. This was according to the law for the demolishing and destroying of every trace of idolatry (Dt 7:5), and since the exile in Babylon, no people in the world have such a deep-rooted aversion to idols and idolatry as the Jews.

2.4. Although Jerusalem will be desolate and forsaken for a time, there will still come a day when its scattered friends will return to it from all the countries to which they had been dispersed (vv. 12–13). Where will these scattered Israelites be gathered from? *The Lord shall beat them off* (v. 12) as fruit from the tree or thresh them as kernels from the heads of grain. He will separate them from those among whom they live, *from the channel of the river* Euphrates, northeast, *unto* Nile, *the stream* (Wadi) *of Egypt* (v. 12), which lay southwest; he will find those who are driven into the land of Assyria and are prisoners there in the land of their enemies, and he will find those who are exiled in the land of Egypt (v. 13), where many of those who were not taken into exile in Babylon went, against God's explicit command (Jer 43:6–7), living there as outcasts; God has mercy in store for them all. Though they are outcasts, they are not rejected. *"You shall be gathered one by one* (v. 12), silently and, as it were, in secret, dropping in, first one, and then another." *The great trumpet shall be blown, and* then *they shall come* (v. 13). Cyrus's proclamation of liberty to the captives (2Ch 36:22–23; Ezr 1:1–4) is this great trumpet, which woke up the Jews who were asleep in their bondage. They will be gathered up: *To worship the Lord in the holy mount at Jerusalem* (v. 13). When the captives rallied and returned to their own land, the main thing they applied themselves to was the worship of God. The holy temple was in ruins, but they had the holy mount, *the place of the altar* (Ge 13:4). Freedom to worship God is the most valuable and desirable liberty.

CHAPTER 28

In this chapter: 1. The Ephraimites are rebuked and threatened for their pride and self-indulgence (vv. 1–8). Yet in the midst of this there is a gracious promise of God's favor to the remnant of his people (vv. 5–6). 2. They are likewise rebuked and threatened for their dullness, stupidity, and unwillingness to learn from the instructions the prophets gave them in God's name (vv. 9–13). 3. The rulers of Jerusalem are rebuked and threatened for their arrogant contempt and defiance of God's judgments, and after a gracious promise of Christ and his grace, it is impressed upon them that they will certainly be deceived by the futile hope with which they flatter themselves, the hope that they will escape the

judgments of God (vv. 14–22). 4. All this is confirmed by a comparison taken from the ways in which farmers use their ground and grain, according to which the prophet's listeners must expect God will deal with his people, whom he has just called his threshing and the corn of his floor (21:10) (vv. 23–29). All this is written down as a warning to us (1Co 10:11) and is profitable to correct us (2Ti 3:16).

Verses 1–8

Here:

1. The prophet warns the ten tribes of the judgments coming for their sins, judgments that were carried out when the king of Assyria devastated their country and took the people into exile. Ephraim took his name from *fruitfulness* (Ge 41:52), and the land belonging to the tribe descended from him had a great many *fat* (fertile) *valleys* (vv. 1, 4); and Samaria, situated on a hill, was *on the head of the fat* (fertile) *valleys* (v. 1). Their country was the glory of Canaan, and their valleys were covered over with grain and vines. Notice:

1.1. How they misused their plenty. The goodness with which God crowned their years was to them a *crown* (wreath) *of pride* (v. 1). Pride was a sin that prevailed among them, and so the prophet boldly declared a *woe to the crown of pride* (v. 1). They abandoned themselves to self-indulgence. Ephraim was notorious for drunkenness, and Samaria, the head of the fertile valleys, was full of those who were *overcome with wine* (v. 1), were "broken" with it (margin), laid low by it. Drunkards make fools of themselves. Sin overcomes them and *brings them into bondage* (2Pe 2:19). Their constitution is broken by it, and their health is ruined. They are brought to ruin by it. Their peace with God is broken. And all this is to satisfy their corrupt, sinful desires. Woe to these *drunkards of Ephraim!* (v. 1). There is a particular woe to the drunkards of Ephraim, for they belong to God's professing people. Some think the *crown of pride* (v. 1) belongs to the drunkards and that the expression here refers to the garlands that were placed as a crown on those who obtained the victory in their corrupt drinking matches, those who drank more than the rest of their company.

1.2. The justice of God in taking away their plenty, which they had misused. Their *glorious beauty*, the plenty they were proud of, *is a fading flower* (v. 1). God can easily *take away their corn in the season thereof* (Hos 2:9) and recover those goods of his that they prepared for Baal. God has an official who is ready to seize the property for him, *a mighty and strong one* (v. 2), namely the king of Assyria, who *shall cast down to the earth with the hand* all that they are proud of (v. 2). Then *the crown of pride* and *the drunkards of Ephraim shall be trodden under foot* (v. 3). In their foolishness, drunkards tend to talk proudly, but in so doing they make themselves ridiculous. The beauty of their valleys will wither by itself and has in itself the principles of its own corruption. *The hasty fruit* (v. 4), as soon as it is discovered, is plucked and eaten. In the same way, the wealth of this world, besides being subject to decay by itself, is subject to being swallowed up by others as greedily as the first ripe fruit.

2. He next turns to the kingdom of Judah, whom he calls the *residue* (remnant) *of his people* (v. 5), for they were only two tribes, while the other kingdom was ten.

2.1. He promises them God's favors; they will be taken under his guidance and protection when the beauty of Ephraim will be exposed to be trampled on and eaten up (vv. 5–6). *In that day*, when the Assyrian army is ravaging Israel, God will be all that the remnant of his people need and can desire; he will be so not only to the kingdom of Judah but also to those of Israel who have kept their integrity. When the Assyrian is in Israel as *a tempest of hail*, noisy and battering, as *a destroying storm* (v. 2), and as *a flood of mighty waters overflowing* the country (v. 2), then *in that day will the Lord of hosts* (v. 5) act by special favor and set apart his people, those who have distinguished themselves by a firm loyalty to him. He will be to them *for a crown of glory and for a diadem of beauty* (beautiful wreath) (v. 5). He will support them in such a way as to make it clear that they have his image renewed on them, and that will be to them a beautiful wreath. He will give them all the wisdom and grace they need. He will himself be *a spirit of judgment* (justice) *to those that sit in judgment* (v. 6); the councilors will be guided by wisdom and good sense, and the judges will rule by justice and fairness. He will give them all the courage they need to carry them through difficulties. He will be *for strength to those that turn the battle to the gate* (v. 6), to the gates of the cities they besiege, or to their own gates, when they go out against the enemies who besiege them. Where God gives these, he is a crown of glory to that people. This may well be supposed to refer to Christ, and this is how the Aramaic understands it: "In that day shall the Messiah be a crown of glory."

2.2. He complains about the many corrupt ones (v. 7): *But they also*, many of those of Judah, *have erred through wine*. There are drunkards in Jerusalem as well as in Ephraim. Ephraim's sins are found in Judah, but not Ephraim's destruction. *They have erred through wine* (v. 7). Their drinking to excess is itself a practical error; they ruin their judgment, and they think they will preserve their health by drinking to excess and that it will help their digestion (1Ti 5:23), but they spoil their constitution and hasten diseases and death. Their understanding is clouded by it, and their conscience defiled by it, and so they have corrupt ideas and form their minds in favor of their sinful desires. Three things are heightening their sin:

2.2.1. That the guilty are those who should have set a better example: *The priest and the prophet are swallowed up of wine* (v. 7); their office is drowned and lost by it. The priests, as those bringing the sacrifices, were obliged by a specific law to be temperate (Lev 10:9). The prophets were a kind of Nazarite (as is seen by Am 2:11) and were obligated to keep as far away as possible from the sins they rebuked in others, but many of them were trapped in this sin.

2.2.2. That its consequences were very harmful, and not only by the adverse influence of their example: when the prophet was drunk, he *erred in vision* (v. 7). The priest *stumbled in judgment and forgot the law* (Pr 31:5); he reeled and staggered as much in the thoughts of his mind as in the movements of his body.

2.2.3. That the disease was epidemic: *All tables are full of vomit* (v. 8). It is bad-mannered enough to make those who look at it sick, for the tables where they eat their food are filthily stained.

Verses 9–13

The prophet here complains about the wretched stupidity of this people, that they were unteachable:

1. Their prophets and ministers intended to *teach knowledge*, the knowledge of God and his will, and *to make them understand doctrine* (v. 9). This is God's way of dealing with people, to enlighten the mind first with the knowledge of his truth, and so to gain their devotion and bring their wills into submission to his laws.

2. They used every possible means to do them good, teaching them as little children who are beginning to learn, who are taken from the breast to the book (v. 9), for among the Jews it was usual for mothers to nurse their children until they were three years old and almost ready for school. It is good to teach children as soon as they are capable of receiving the message—the good knowledge of the Lord—and to instruct them even when they have just been weaned from their mothers' milk. They had been taught, as children are taught to read, by *precept upon precept*, and taught to write *by line upon line, a little here* and *a little there* (v. 10): a little of one thing and a little of another, so that the instruction might have a pleasant variety; a little at one time and a little at another, so that their memories might not be overtaxed; a little from one prophet and a little from another, so that everyone might be pleased with listening to those they liked and admired. We need to constantly receive God's detailed commands and instructions in our lives, with one instruction enforcing another. The precepts of justice must be built on those of godliness, and the precepts of love and kindness to others must be built on those of justice. The same commands and instructions should often be repeated. Teachers should adjust their teaching style to what their learners can take in, giving them what they need most, and a little at a time (Dt 6:6–7). The ministers and prophets persuaded them to learn (v. 12). God, through his prophets, said to them, "*This* way that we are directing you in *is the rest wherewith you may cause the weary to rest; and this will be the refreshing* of your own souls and will bring your country rest from the wars with which it has been long troubled."

3. They were as unwilling to learn as young children (v. 9). They *would not hear* (v. 12) what would be rest to them. They kept up the old custom of being present at the prophet's preaching and hearing it beating on them, but it beat nothing into them.

4. God would judge them severely for this. He would deprive them of the privilege of clear preaching and speak to them *with stammering lips and another tongue* (v. 11). Those who will not listen to the encouraging voice of God's word will be made to hear the dreadful voice of his rod. By their ungodly contempt of God and his word they were only moving more quickly toward their own ruin and preparing themselves for it; they were left to their contempt so *that they might go and fall backward* (v. 13), proceeding from one sin to another until they were completely *broken* (injured), *snared, and taken* (captured), and ruined (v. 13).

Verses 14–22

Having rebuked those who made fun of the word of God, the prophet here went on to rebuke those who made fun of the judgments of God. He spoke to *the scornful men who ruled in Jerusalem*, the magistrates of the city (v. 14).

1. These scoffers challenged God Almighty to do his worst (v. 15): *You have said* (boasted), *We have made a covenant with death and the grave*. They thought they were as sure of their lives—even when judgments were present—as if they had made a bargain with death not to take them away by forceful means, but rather by old age. If we are at peace with God, we have in effect made a covenant with death that, whenever it comes, it will be no terror to us nor do us any real harm (1Co 3:22–23). To think of making death our friend, however, while we live in sin and make God our enemy, is the greatest possible absurdity. It was silly of these scoffers to think, "*When the overflowing scourge shall pass through* our country and

others fall under it, yet *it shall not come to us*" (v. 15). But what was the basis of their confidence? *We have made lies our refuge* (v. 15). Now, these lies may have been the things that the prophet told them would deceive them, but that they themselves looked on as a substantial protection. On the other hand, they may have been the things that would be lies and falsehood to the enemy, who was the scourge of God. The rulers of Jerusalem thought they would protect themselves by deceiving the enemy with their strategies of war or with their pretended submission in treaties of peace. They thought they were better politicians than those in the country towns; they would compliment the king of Assyria with a promise to surrender their city or to pay him tribute, intending all along to shake off his yoke as soon as the danger was over. Those who pursue their intentions by trickery and fraud may perhaps accomplish them, but they cannot expect any encouragement from them.

2. God, by the prophet, shows them the foolishness of their self-confidence.

2.1. He tells them on what basis they can be secure. He does not disturb their false confidence until he has first shown them a firm basis on which they can rest (v. 16): *Behold, I lay in Zion for a foundation a stone.* The foundation is made up of:

2.1.1. The promises of God in general: his covenant with Abraham is a foundation of stone, firm and lasting, for faith to build on; it is *a tried stone* (v. 16), for all the saints have rested on it, and it has never failed them.

2.1.2. The promise of Christ in particular, for this is expressly applied to him in the New Testament (1Pe 2:6–8). He is that stone that has become *the head of the corner.* Jesus Christ is a foundation laid by God. He is a tested stone, a cornerstone or capstone, in whom the sides of the building are united, the *head stone of the corner* (Ps 118:22). And *he that believes* these promises and rests on them *shall not make haste* (NIV: be dismayed) (v. 16). No; he will have a fixed heart and will quietly await the outcome (Ps 112:7), saying, *Welcome the will of God.*

2.2. He tells them that the grounds they are now building on cannot be safe (v. 17): *Judgment will I lay to the line, and righteousness to the plummet.* This refers to:

2.2.1. The building up of his church. Having laid the foundation (v. 16), he will raise the structure, as builders do, with the aid of a plumb line (Zec 4:10). Righteousness will be the plumb line and justice the measuring line. The church, being founded on Christ, will be formed and reformed by Scripture. Or:

2.2.2. The punishing of the church's enemies, against whom God will act by an exact rule. And when God comes to execute judgment:

2.2.2.1. These scoffers will be made ashamed of the vain hopes with which they had deluded themselves. Those who make lies their refuge are building on sand, and when the storm comes, the building will fall (Mt 7:26–27) and will bury the builder in its ruins. They thought that when the overwhelming scourge was going to sweep through the land, it would not come near them, but the prophet tells them (v. 19) that they will be the first who will fall by it: "*From the time it goes forth it shall take you*, as if it came on purpose to seize you. *Morning by morning shall it pass over* (v. 19); you will never be safe; there will be a plague stalking in the darkness and destruction devastating at noon" (Ps 91:6). The very report of it at a distance will be a terror to you. Bad news is a terror to scorners. The person whose heart is fixed, *trusting in God, is not afraid of* bad news (Ps 112:7), but scorners, when the overwhelming scourge comes,

will be abandoned by all comforts and everything they have trusted in (v. 20). *The bed is shorter than that a man can stretch himself upon it* (v. 20), so that he is forced to restrict himself. What they thought would shelter them turns out to be inadequate: *The covering is narrower than that a man can wrap himself in.*

2.2.2.2. God will be glorified in the fulfillment of his counsels. When God comes to contend with these scoffers, *He will do his work and bring to pass his act* (v. 21) as the righteous Judge of the earth. He will do it now against his people as formerly he did it against their enemies; he will now *rise up against Jerusalem as*, in David's time, against the Philistines *in Mount Perazim* (v. 21) (2Sa 5:20) and as, in Joshua's time, against the Canaanites *in the valley of Gibeon* (v. 21). If those who profess to be members of God's church make themselves by their pride and scoffing like Philistines and Canaanites, they must expect to be dealt with as such. This will be *his strange work, his strange act* (v. 21). It is work that he is not used to carrying out against his own people. It is a truly strange work if he *turns to be their enemy and fights against them* (63:10). Here is the application of all this (v. 22): "*Therefore be you not mockers* (stop mocking); do not dare ridicule either the rebukes of God's word or his judgments. *Be you not mockers, lest your bands be made strong* (or your chains will become heavier) (v. 22), both the chains by which you are bound under the power of sin and the chains by which you are bound over to the judgments of God." Let not these mockers make light of divine threats, for the prophet assures them that the Lord God Almighty has *determined a consumption* (destruction) *upon the whole earth* (v. 22), and can they expect to escape?

Verses 23–29

This parable, which—like many of our Savior's parables—is borrowed from the work of farmers, is introduced with a solemn preface: *He that has ears to hear, let him hear* (Mt 11:15), (v. 23).

1. The parable here is clear enough, that the farmer applies himself to the work of his calling with diligence and wisdom and that he observes a method and order in his work:

1.1. In his plowing and sowing: *Does the ploughman plough all day to sow?* (v. 24). Yes; he *ploughs in hope and sows in hope* (1Co 9:10). *Does he open and break the clods?* (v. 24). Yes, so that the land may be fit to receive the seed. And *when he has thus made plain the face thereof* (v. 25), does he not sow seed suitable to the soil? The farmer knows what grain is suitable for clay ground and what for sandy ground, and he sows accordingly, each in its place: *wheat in the principal place* (v. 25), for it was a staple commodity of Canaan (Eze 27:17), *and barley in the appointed place* (v. 25).

1.2. In his threshing (vv. 27–28). He fits the threshing method to the seed that is to be threshed. Because the *fitches* (caraway) *and the cummin* are easily removed from their husk or ear, they are threshed with only *a staff and a rod*, but the seeds of *the bread corn* (grain) require more force, and so to beat the germ out of them, the farmer must *bruise* (ground) them with *a threshing instrument*, a sledge strengthened with iron, which was drawn backward and forward over them. But *he will not be ever threshing it*, nor any longer than is necessary to loosen the grain from the chaff. *He will not break it*, or crush it *with the wheel of his cart, nor bruise it* to pieces with his horses (v. 28); the grinding of it is reserved for another operation. Notice what effort is to be taken not only for earning our necessary food but also for preparing it, and yet when all is said and done, it is food that spoils. Will we then begrudge laboring much more for the food that endures to eternal life (Jn 6:27)? *Bread corn is bruised* (v. 28). Christ was too; *it pleased the Lord to bruise him* (53:10), so that he might be the bread of life to us.

2. The interpretation of the parable is not so clear. Most interpreters consider it a further response to those who defy the judgments of God: "As farmers will not always plow, but will eventually sow their seed, so God will not always be making threats, but will eventually bring on sinners the judgments they have deserved—but in wisdom, so that they may be reformed and brought to repentance." But we may give this parable greater application:

2.1. It is God who *instructs the husbandman to discretion*, as *his God* (v. 26). Farmers need good sense with which to organize their affairs. Advances in agriculture serve a more useful purpose to the whole human race than developments in most other human skills. The skill of farmers comes from God. This takes some of the edge off the weight of the sentence passed on humans for sin: when God, in executing his sentence, sent them to till the ground, he taught them how to do it to their greatest benefit. It is God who gives people the ability to do this work, an inclination to do it, and a delight in it, and farmers must seek God for direction, for they, above other people, have an immediate dependence on divine Providence. As to the second kind of threshing, that of grain, it is said, *This also comes forth from the Lord of hosts* (v. 29). And if it is from him that people do things wisely, we must acknowledge him to be *wise* (wonderful) *in counsel and excellent in working* (magnificent in wisdom) (v. 29).

2.2. God's church is his field (1Co 3:9). If Christ is the true vine, his Father is the gardener (Jn 15:1), and he is continually cultivating the vine by his word and ordinances. Does not God by his ministers break up the fallow ground? God sows his word by the hand of his ministers (Mt 13:19). Whatever the soil of the heart is like, there is some seed or other in the word that is proper for it (Mt 13:3–20). And in this way the rod of God, like the word of God, is wisely used. Adversities are God's threshing instruments, designed to loosen us from the world, to separate us from the worthless chaff in us, but he will proportion them to our strength. If the rod and the staff will fulfill their purposes, he will not need to use his cartwheel and his horses.

CHAPTER 29

The woe to Ariel in this chapter is the same as the burden *of the valley of vision (22:1), and it may well point to the same event—the besieging of Jerusalem by the Assyrian army, which was cut off there by an angel (2Ki 19:35), but it may also apply to the destruction of Jerusalem by the Babylonians and its later destruction by the Romans. Here is: 1. The event itself foretold, that Jerusalem would be greatly distressed (vv. 1–4, 6), but that its enemies would be defeated (vv. 5, 7–8). 2. A rebuke to three kinds of sinners: those who paid no attention to warnings (vv. 9–12), those who were merely formal and hypocritical in their religious rituals (vv. 13–14), and those politicians who profanely despised God's providence (vv. 15–16). 3. Precious promises of grace and mercy to a remnant whom God would sanctify (vv. 17–24).*

Verses 1–8

It is agreed that what is here called *Ariel* is Jerusalem, for that was the city where David lived; the part of it that was called *Zion* was the City of David in a particular way, because it was the part in which both the temple and the

palace were situated. But why Jerusalem is called *Ariel* is uncertain. Cities, as well as people, have surnames and nicknames. *Ariel* may mean "the lion of God" or "the strong lion": as the lion is king among animals, so was Jerusalem among the cities. While Jerusalem was a righteous city, it was bold as a lion. Some consider *Ariel* to mean "the altar of burnt offerings" or "the altar hearth," which devoured the beasts offered in sacrifice as the lion does its prey. I prefer to take it as a woe to *Jerusalem, Jerusalem*; it is repeated here, as it is in Mt 23:37, so that it might be more rousing. Here:

1. The distress of Jerusalem is foretold. Although Jerusalem is a strong city, nevertheless, if sin is found there, it will be terrible for it.

1.1. Let Jerusalem know that the external performance of religious services will not exempt them from the judgments of God (v. 1): "*Add year to year*; continue in your cycle of annual festivals, let all your males appear there three times a year before the Lord, and none come empty-handed, and let them never miss any of these festivals: *let them kill the sacrifices* (v. 1) as they used to do, but as long as their lives are not reformed and their hearts not humbled, let them not think that their actions will pacify an offended God and turn away his wrath."

1.2. Let Jerusalem know that it will be *visited of the Lord of hosts* (v. 6); the city's sins will be punished with alarms like *thunder and earthquakes, storms and tempests, and devouring fire* (v. 6).

1.2.1. Jerusalem will be besieged. He does not say, "I will destroy Ariel," but, *I will distress Ariel* (v. 2), and the reason the city will be brought into a state of distress is so that, being stirred to repent, it may not be brought to destruction. *I will encamp against thee round about* (all around) (v. 3). Although it is the enemy's army that will encamp against it, God says that he will do it. When people are fighting against us, we must, in them, see God contending with us.

1.2.2. Jerusalem will be in sorrow to see the country devastated. "*There shall be heaviness and sorrow* (v. 2), they will repent, reform, and return to God, and then the city will be to me like Ariel, that is, Jerusalem will be like itself, will become to me a Jerusalem again, a holy city" (1:26).

1.2.3. Jerusalem will be humbled and mortified (v. 4): "*Thou shalt be brought down* from the height of arrogance and *speak out of the ground, out of the dust, as one that has a familiar spirit* (with a voice like a ghost), *whispering out of the dust*" (v. 4). They will be faint and feeble, like those who are sick, their speech low and mumbled, since they will be afraid that their enemies might overhear them.

2. The destruction of Jerusalem's enemies is foretold (vv. 5, 7): *Thou shalt be brought down* (v. 4), *to speak out of the dust*; you will be reduced so low. "But"—so it may be rendered—"*the multitude of thy strangers and thy terrible ones*, the numerous armies of the enemy, *shall* themselves *be like small dust*, unable to speak at all, even so much as to whisper; they will be like *chaff that passes away* (v. 5). You will be brought low, but they will be completely dispersed and killed (27:7). *Yea, it shall be in an instant, suddenly* (v. 5): the enemy will be surprised at the destruction, and you at the salvation." The army of the Assyrians was killed on the spot by an angel, in an instant, suddenly (2Ki 19:35). *The multitude of the nations that fight against Zion shall be as a hungry man who dreams that he eats* (v. 8) but still is hungry. Whereas they hoped to attack Jerusalem and enrich themselves with plunder, their hopes will prove vain. Both they themselves and

all their pomp, power, and prosperity will vanish like a dream.

Verses 9–16

Here:

1. The prophet stands stunned at the stupidity of most of the Jewish nation. They had Levites, who taught *the good knowledge of the Lord*. They had prophets, who brought them messages directly from God. *Surely this great nation, which has all the advantages of divine revelation, will be a wise and understanding people* (Dt 4:6). But, unfortunately, it was completely different (v. 9). The prophet turns to speak to the sober thoughtful part of them. "The rest sport themselves with their own deceit; they riot and revel, but you *cry out*, mourn their foolishness, cry out to God in prayer for them." But what are we to wonder at?

1.1. We may well wonder that most of the people were so foolish and ignorant, as if they were intoxicated (v. 9). They were drunk with the love of pleasure, with their prejudices against religion, and with the corrupt motivations they had taken in. Like drunkards, they were not aware of the divine rebukes they were under. *They have beaten me, and I felt it not*, says the drunkard (Pr 23:35). There is such a thing as spiritual drunkenness.

1.2. It is even stranger that God himself would *pour out upon them a spirit of deep sleep and close their eyes* (v. 10) by righteous judgment, to punish them for their *loving darkness rather than light* (Jn 3:19), their loving sleep. They said, *Yet a little sleep, a little slumber* (Pr 6:10), and so he gave them up to strong delusions (2Th 2:11) and said, *Sleep on now* (Mt 26:45). This is applied to the unbelieving Jews who rejected the Gospel of Christ and were justly hardened in their unfaithfulness until great wrath came on them. *God has given them the spirit of slumber* (Ro 11:8).

1.3. It is very sad that this should be the case with those who were their prophets, rulers, and seers, that those who should have been their guides were themselves blindfolded. This was fulfilled when, in the latter days of the Jewish church, the chief priests, the teachers of the law, and the elders of the people were those who greatly opposed Christ and his Gospel (Mk 8:31; 14:43) and brought themselves under a judicial confounding.

1.4. The sad effect of this was that all the means of conviction, knowledge, and grace that they enjoyed were ineffective and did not fulfill their purpose (vv. 11–12). Every vision, particularly the vision that this prophet had seen and made known, had become unintelligible. They had it among themselves, but they were never any the wiser because of it, any more than someone—even someone who is a good scholar—is after receiving a book that is sealed up. Such a person sees it is a book, and that is all. So they knew that what Isaiah said was a vision and prophecy, but its meaning was hidden from them. "The same vision that to you is *a savour of death unto death* is and will be to others *a savour of life unto life*" (2Co 2:16). Knowledge is easy to those who understand.

2. In God's name, the prophet threatens those who are merely formal and hypocritical in their devotion (vv. 13–14).

2.1. Their sin is making a pretense of their religious activities (v. 13). The One who knows the heart cannot be deceived by show and pretense. If the heart is full of his love and fear, the mouth will speak out of that abundance (Mt 12:34). But there are many whose religion is only lip service. It is only from the teeth outward. They do not apply their minds to the service. They do not make the word of God the rule of their worship, or his will their reason: *Their fear towards me is taught by the precept of men* (v. 13). The tradition of the elders was of more value than the laws that God commanded Moses. Our Savior applies this to the Jews in his time, who were merely formal in their devotions (Mt 15:2–9).

2.2. It is a spiritual judgment with which God threatens to punish them for their spiritual evil (v. 14): *I will proceed to do a marvellous work.* They removed all sincerity from their hearts. Now God will remove all wisdom from their heads. *The wisdom of their wise men shall perish* (v. 14). They played the hypocrite, thinking they could deceive God, and now they are left to themselves to play the fool, to be easily deceived by everyone around them. This is a terrifying work—that wise people should suddenly lose their wisdom and be given up to strong delusions (2Th 2:11).

3. He shows the foolishness of those who thought they could act independently of God and keep secrets from him. Their plans are described (v. 15): they *seek deep to hide their counsel from the Lord*, so that he may not know either what they are doing or what they are thinking. The absurdity of their plans is demonstrated (v. 16): *Surely your turning of things upside down*, your inverting the order of things and thinking you can make God's providence serve your plans, turning things upside down and beginning at the wrong end, *shall be esteemed as the potter's clay* (v. 16). God will turn and manage you, and all your purposes, with as much ease as the potter fashions clay.

Verses 17–24

God tells them here that he will turn things upside down in his own way. They do not believe in providence: "Wait a while," God says, "and you will be convinced that there is a God who rules the world." The wonderful change foretold here may refer primarily to the happy settlement of Judah and Jerusalem after the defeat of Sennacherib's attempt to overthrow Jerusalem. But it may look further, to the rejection of the Jews at the first planting of the Gospel.

1. In general, a great change is foretold (v. 17). *Lebanon*, which was a forest, *shall be turned into a fruitful field*, and Carmel—for that is the word here used to mean "fruitful field"—will become a forest. It was a sign of the defeat of Sennacherib that the ground would be more than usually fertile (37:30): *You shall eat this year such as grows of itself;* food for people will be—as food for animals is—the spontaneous product of the soil. Then Lebanon became so fertile that what used to be reckoned as a fertile field in comparison with it was now looked on as a mere forest. When a great harvest of souls was gathered in to Christ from among the Gentiles, the desert became a fertile field (54:1).

2. In particular:

2.1. Those who were ignorant will become intelligent (v. 18). Those who did not understand this prophecy when it was spoken will understand it when it is fulfilled. They will acknowledge not only the hand of God in the actual fulfillment but also the voice of God in its prediction: *The deaf shall then hear the words of the book.* The poor Gentiles will then have divine revelation brought among them, and those who sat in darkness will see a great light (9:2; Mt 4:16), for the Gospel was sent to them to *open their eyes* (Ac 26:18).

2.2. Those who were in error will become orthodox (v. 24): *Those that erred* (who were wayward) *in spirit* will come to a right understanding of things; the Spirit of truth will lead them into all truth (Jn 16:13). Those who grumbled about the truths of God as hard sayings will learn the true meaning and will be better reconciled to them. Those who misunderstood the providence of God and grumbled at it will see the outcome of things and be aware of what God was intending in everything (Hos 14:9).

2.3. Those who were sad will become cheerful and pleasant (v. 19): *The meek also shall increase their joy in the Lord*. This suggests that even in their distress they have kept up their joy in the Lord, but now they will increase it. The grace of humility will lead very much to a growing holy joy. Sennacherib, that *terrible* (ruthless) *one*, and his great army will be *brought to nought* (v. 20). The power of Satan, that terrible Evil One, will be broken by the supremacy of Christ's Gospel (Heb 2:14–15).

2.4. The persecutors will be quieted. To complete the rest of God's people, the mockers at home will be consumed and cut down by Hezekiah's reformation. They have persecuted God's people and prophets, probably especially the prophet Isaiah. And this can also be applied to the chief priests and Pharisees who persecuted Christ and his apostles and were cut down for that sin. They lay in wait for an opportunity to strike them. By their spies they *watched for iniquity* (had an eye for evil) (v. 20), to see if they could discover anything that was said or done that could be called evil. On the basis of a wrong or misplaced word, they *made a man* out to be guilty (v. 21), even if he was very wise and good and if they must have known it was well meant (v. 21). Those who *reprove in the gates* (v. 21), *who* were bound as prophets, judges, and magistrates to show people their disobedience—the persecutors hated these rebukers and tried to trap them, just as the Pharisees, who hated our Savior, sent their envoys to watch him so that they might *entangle* (trap) *him in his talk* (Mt 22:15). *They turned aside the just for a thing of nought*, deprived the innocent of justice with false testimony (v. 21). They ran people down and misrepresented them using every trick in the book, as they did with our Savior.

2.5. Jacob, who was made to blush by the rebukes of his enemies, will now be relieved by the rolling away of those reproaches (Jos 5:9): *Thus saith the Lord who redeemed Abraham* out of his troubles and will redeem all who are by faith his genuine seed out of theirs. He who began his care of his church in the redemption of Abraham will appear for the house of Jacob, and they will not be ashamed, nor will *their* faces now grow pale; they will take courage.

2.6. Jacob, who thought his family would be extinct, will see his children, very many believers, and he *shall not be ashamed* (v. 22), but will contend with his enemy in the gate (Ps 127:5). It is some encouragement to parents to think that their children are God's creatures, the work of the hands of his providence. But it will be much more of an encouragement to them to see their children as his new creatures, the work of the hands of his grace.

CHAPTER 30

This chapter seems to relate to the approaching danger of Sennacherib's invasion. Here is: 1. A just rebuke to those who were in a rush to obtain help from Egypt (vv. 1–7). 2. A terrible threat against those who showed disrespect for the good advice that God gave them by his prophets (vv. 8–17). 3. A gracious promise to those who trusted in God, that they would see happy days, times of joy and reformation, outwardly good things and increasing joys

and triumphs (vv. 18–26); and many of these promises may be applied to Gospel grace. 4. A prophecy of the total rout of the Assyrian army, which would be an introduction to those happy times (vv. 27–33).

Verses 1–7

It was often the fault and foolishness of the Jewish people, when they were insulted by their neighbors on one side, that they sought help from their neighbors on the other side instead of looking to God and putting their confidence in him. Against the Israelites they sought help from the Arameans (2Ch 16:2–3). Against the Arameans they looked to the Assyrians (2Ki 16:7). Against the Assyrians they here looked to the Egyptians (2Ki 18:21).

1. Their sin is described. They would not consult God. "They *take counsel* among themselves and with one another, but they do not ask advice—much less will they take advice—from me. They *cover with a covering* (v. 1), *but not of my Spirit* (v. 1). And so it will prove too weak an alliance and a refuge of lies" (28:17). They *strengthened themselves in the strength of Pharaoh* (v. 2). *The shadow of Egypt* (v. 2), which was only shade, was the covering with which they wrapped themselves.

2. The evil of this sin was that it showed them to be *rebellious children* and that they *added sin to sin*. They claimed to be God's children, but because they did not trust in him, they were justly stigmatized as *rebellious*. They added sin to sin when they took so much effort to make sure the Egyptians were their allies: *They walk to go down to Egypt* (v. 2), travel up and down to find an advantageous road there, but they *have not asked at my mouth* (v. 2), never considered whether God would approve of it. They went to vast expense to do it (v. 6). They loaded *the beasts of the south*, animals of the Negev—horses taken from Egypt, which lay south of Judea—with their riches, thinking, as is common with people when they are frightened, that they were safer anywhere than where they were there. Or they sent their riches there as bribes to Pharaoh's courtiers. God would have helped them freely, but if they wanted to have help from the Egyptians, they must pay dearly for it. They took their effects to Egypt "through a land"—so it may read—*of trouble and anguish*, that barren, howling desert that lay between Canaan and Egypt (Dt 32:10), *whence come the lion and fiery serpent* (Dt 8:15).

3. We read of its consequences. The Egyptians would receive their officials and be willing to deal with them (v. 4): *His princes were at Zoan*, and Pharaoh encouraged them to depend on the help he would send them. But the Egyptians would not fulfill their expectations: they *could not profit them* (v. 5). God says, *They shall not profit them* (v. 6). The forces the Egyptians were to provide them with could not be raised in time, or the Egyptians would secretly be disposed toward the Assyrians. *The Egyptians shall help in vain, and to no purpose* (v. 7). "*The strength of Pharaoh*, which was your pride, *shall be your shame*, and you will rebuke yourselves for your foolishness in trusting it. And the *shadow of Egypt*, that *land shadowing with wings* (18:1), which was your confidence, will be your confusion." The officials of Israel, who were so eager to make an alliance, *shall all be ashamed of a people that could not be a help or profit to them, but only a shame and reproach* (disgrace) (v. 5). Those who put their confidence in any created thing will find that sooner or later it becomes a disgrace to them. The Creator is a Rock of ages (26:4); created things are mere splintered reeds. We cannot expect too little from human beings nor too much from God. "*Therefore have I cried concerning this* matter. *Their strength is to sit still*, in humble dependence on

God, and not to wander about to seek help from this or that other creature."

Verses 8–17

Here:

1. The introduction is terrible. The prophet must write it (v. 8), *write it in a table* (on a tablet), *in a book* (on a scroll), to be preserved for future generations as a constant testimony against this evil generation. Let it be written to shame the people of the present age. Their children may profit by it, even though they will not. People will be tempted to think God was too harsh on them unless they know how bad they were and what reasonable means God used with them before he brought matters to this critical point. It is intended to warn those in the most distant places and ages.

2. The characterization given of the ungodly and evil Jews is that they are *a rebellious people* (v. 9). They rebelled against their own convictions and covenants: "They are *lying children* (v. 9), they will not stand by what they say." They also rebelled against divine authority: "They are *children that will not hear the law of the Lord* (v. 9) or take any notice of it."

3. The charge drawn up against them is very great, and the sentence passed on them is dreadful.

3.1. They forbade the prophets to speak to them in God's name.

3.1.1. Their sin is described. They *said to the seers*, in effect, *See not*. The prophets told them their faults and warned them of their danger because of their sin, and they could not bear that. The prophets must speak to them *smooth* (pleasant) *things*. No matter how right and true a word was, if it was not pleasant, they would not hear it. Those who want to be deceived deserve to be. The prophets stopped them in their sinful pursuits, standing in their way like the angel in Balaam's way (Nu 22:22–33), with the sword of God's wrath drawn in their hand. When they continued perversely following the way of their hearts, they said to the prophets, *Get you out of the way, turn aside out of the paths* (v. 11). The prophets were continually telling them about the Holy One of Israel and how severely he will judge sinners, and they could not bear to listen to this. If the prophets are to speak to them, they will make it part of the bargain that they will not call God *the Holy One of Israel* (v. 11), for God's holiness is that aspect of his nature that evildoers dread most of all.

3.1.2. The condemnation passed on them for this is in vv. 12–13. *Thus saith the Holy One of Israel.* We must tell people that God is the *Holy One of Israel.* The basis of the judgment is, *Because they despise this word* (v. 12), either, in general, every word that the prophets say to them, or this word in particular, which declares God to be *the Holy One of Israel* (v. 12). They *trust in oppression and perverseness* (deceit) (v. 12), in the wealth they have gained by fraud and violence, or in the sinful ways they have used for their own security. They depend on these, and so it is just that they should fall. Judgment is passed on them: "*This iniquity shall be to you as a breach ready to fall*, this sin will become for you like a high wall, cracked and bulging (v. 13). This confidence of yours will be like a house built on the sand (Mt 7:26–27). Your contempt of that word of God, the word that you could have built on, will make everything else you trust in like a bulging wall, which, if any weight is placed on it, often sinks under its own weight." *The breaking shall come suddenly, at an instant* (v. 13). "You and all your confidence will be not only as weak as the potter's clay (29:16) but *broken to pieces as the potter's vessel.* Once it has been

broken so as to be unfit for use, let it all be dashed and crushed to pieces, so that not even one shred will remain that is big enough to take a coal or scoop up water—two things that we need daily and that poor people commonly carry in a piece of a broken pitcher.

3.2. They showed disrespect for the gracious directions God gave them; they wanted to follow their own ways (vv. 15–17). Notice here:

3.2.1. The way God gave them for salvation and strength. The God who knew them and desired their welfare gave them this prescription, and it is commended to us all. If we want to be saved from the evil of every calamity, it must be *in returning and rest* (v. 15), in repenting toward God and resting in him as our peace. Let us turn from our evil ways and settle in the way of God and duty: that is the way to be saved. "Turn away from this plan of going down to Egypt. *In returning*—in the thorough reformation of your hearts and lives—*and in rest*—in a complete submission of your souls to God—*you shall be saved*" (v. 15). If we want to be strengthened to do what is required of us, it must be *in quietness and in confidence* (v. 15). We must trust in God with a holy confidence that he can do what he will and that he will do what is best for his people. And this will be our strength.

3.2.2. The contempt they showed toward this prescription; they would not take God's advice even though it was for their own good. Those who will not take God as their doctor will justly die of their disease. They would not even go so far as try the method God prescribed: "*But you said, No* (v. 16), we will not calm ourselves, for *we will flee upon horses* and *we will ride upon the swift*; we will hurry here and there to draw in foreign help." When Sennacherib captured all the fortified towns of Judah, those rebellious children would not be persuaded to patiently expect God's supporting them, as he did wonderfully in the end.

3.2.3. The sentence passed on them for this. Their sin will be their punishment: "*You will flee* (are determined to flee) (v. 16), and so *you shall flee* (v. 17); you will go as fast as you can, and so will those who pursue you." Dogs tend to run barking after those who run away quickly. The conquerors protected those who sat still but pursued those who made their escape. It is foretold (v. 17) that they would be easily cut down; one of the enemy would defeat a thousand of them, and the threat of five would make an army flee. Only here and there would one escape alone in a solitary place and be left *as a beacon* (flagstaff) *upon the top of a mountain* (v. 17), as a warning to others.

Verses 18–26

Some understand the closing words of the previous paragraph—*You shall be left as a beacon* (flagstaff) *upon a mountain* (v. 17)—as a promise that a remnant of them would be reserved as memorials of mercy, so that here the prophet continues the thought by telling the people of good times to come. On the other hand, the first words in this paragraph may be read as introducing a contrasting idea, "Despite this, yet" *will the Lord wait that he may be gracious* (v. 18).

1. God will be gracious to them and have mercy on them. "He *will wait to be gracious* (v. 18); he will wait until you repent and seek his face, and then he will be ready to meet you with mercy. He will stir himself up to rescue you, he will be exalted and will be *raised up out of his holy habitation* (dwelling) (Zec 2:13), *and thus he will be exalted* (v. 18), that is, he will glorify his name. *He will be gracious to thee at the voice of thy cry* (v. 19), the cry of your need, when your needs are most urgent—the

cry of your prayer, when it is most fervent. *When he shall hear it*, you will not need to pray any more; at the first word *he will answer thee* (v. 19), saying, *Here I am*." Those who were disturbed in their possessions will again enjoy them quietly. When the danger is over, *the people shall dwell in Zion, at Jerusalem* (v. 19), as they used to do; they will live securely, free from the fear of evil. Those who live in Zion, the Holy City, will find enough there to wipe away the tears from their eyes. This is based on two great truths:

- That *the Lord is a God of judgment* (justice) (v. 18); he is both wise and just in all the ways of providence, true to his word and kind toward his people.
- That therefore all those who *wait for him* are blessed (v. 18), all who not only wait on him with their prayers but also wait for him with their hopes.

2. They will not again know the lack of the means of grace (vv. 20–21).

2.1. It is supposed that they might be brought into troubles and difficulties after they have been rescued. It was promised (v. 19) that they would *weep no more* and that God would be *gracious to them*, but here it is taken for granted that God may give them the *bread of adversity and the water of affliction*.

2.2. It is promised that their eyes will *see their teachers* (v. 20), that is, that they will have faithful teachers among them and will have hearts to respect them and not offend them as they had, and then they will be able to more easily come to terms with the bread of trouble and the water of suffering. It was a common saying among the old Puritans, "Brown bread and the Gospel are good fare [food]." It seems that the teachers of Judah had been moved into hiding. But God will find a time to call the teachers out of hiding again, and to return them to their sacred meetings.

2.3. It is also promised that they will have the benefit not only of the public ministry but also of private warnings and advice (v. 21): "*Thy ears shall hear a word behind thee*, calling after you as someone calls out to travelers when they are going along the wrong road." This word will come "from *behind thee* (v. 21), from someone whom you cannot see, but who sees you. Your eyes see your teachers, but this teacher is out of sight; it is your own conscience, which will now by the grace of God be awakened to fulfill its role." The word will be, *This is the way, walk you in it* (v. 21). This word will come *when you turn to the right hand or to the left* (v. 21). There are errors on the right hand and the left hand, extremes on each side of virtue; the tempter is busy persuading us to turn aside. It is beneficial, then, if, by the particular advice of a faithful minister or friend, or the restraints of conscience and the strivings of God's Spirit (Ge 6:3), we are put right and prevented from going wrong. "Not only will it be spoken, but also your ears will listen to it; whereas God has formerly *spoken once, yea, twice*, and you have *not perceived it* (Job 33:14), now you will listen attentively to these secret whispers and hear them with an obedient ear."

3. They will be healed of their idolatry, will give up their idols and never be reconciled to them again (v. 22). They will break off from their favorite sin. Notice how mad about their idols they had been in the day of their apostasy. They had *graven images of silver* and *molten images of gold* (v. 22), and although gold needs no painting, they had coverings and ornaments on these; they spared no cost in honoring their idols. Notice, too, how mad they now were *at* their idols, what a righteous anger

they conceived against them on the day of their repentance. They not only degraded their images but also defaced them, throwing away, in godly fury, the gold and silver they were made of. Probably this was fulfilled in many people, who, by the rescue of Jerusalem from Sennacherib's army, were convinced of the foolishness of their idolatry and abandoned it. It was fulfilled in the Jewish nation at their return from exile in Babylon, for they detested idols ever after, and it is fulfilled daily in the conversion of souls, by the power of divine grace, from spiritual idolatry to the fear and love of God.

4. God will then give them plenty of all good things. When he gives them their teachers and they give him their hearts, *then all other things shall be added to them* (Mt 6:33). And when the people are brought to praise God, *then shall the earth yield her increase, and with it God, even our own God, shall bless us* (Ps 67:5–6). So it follows: "When you have abandoned your idols, *then shall God give the rain of your seed*" (v. 23). God will give you rain to water the seed you sow in the ground. *Thou shalt sow the ground* (v. 23), which is your part, and then *God will give the rain of thy seed* (v. 23), which is his part. This is also true of spiritual fruit. The increase of the earth will be "fat and fat," very rich and very good, *fat and plenteous*, good and enough of it. *The cattle shall feed in large pastures* (broad meadows) (v. 23), and the oxen and donkeys *shall eat clean provender* (fodder and mash) (v. 24). The grain will not be given them in the chaff to make it go further; rather, they will have good clean grain *winnowed with the fan* (v. 24). Even the tops of the mountains will be so well watered by the rain that there will be *rivers and streams* running down to the valleys (v. 25). This will happen *in the day of the great slaughter* made by the angel in the camp of the Assyrians, *when the towers* they have set up to siege of Jerusalem *shall fall*.

5. The effect of all this will be comfort and joy to the people of God (v. 26). Light will increase; that is, knowledge will increase—when the prophecies are fulfilled, they will be fully understood. *The light of the moon shall become as* bright and as strong as *that of the sun, and that of the sun* will increase proportionately and be *as the light of seven days, when the Lord binds up the breach of his people* (v. 26), heals the wounds that have been given them by this invasion and makes up all their losses. The light that the Gospel brought into the world to those who sat in darkness (9:2; 42:7; Mt 4:16) as far surpassed the Old Testament light as that of the sun does that of the moon.

Verses 27–33

This terrible prediction of the ruin of the Assyrian army is part of the promise to the Israel of God that God would deter the Assyrians from doing something similar again. Here is:

1. God Almighty introduced in all the power and all the terror of his wrath (v. 27). *The name of Jehovah*, which the Assyrians disdain, *behold, it comes from far*. A messenger comes in the name of the Lord, a messenger of wrath, *burning with* the Lord's *anger*. God's *lips are full of indignation* at the blasphemy of the field commander, who compared the God of Israel with the gods of the nations (2Ki 18:32–35); God's *tongue is as a devouring fire* (v. 27). He does not stifle his anger, but *shall cause his glorious voice to be heard* (v. 30). He will display *the indignation of his anger* as *the flame of a devouring fire*, with a *scattering* of the Assyrian troops, or, as it may also be read, "with lightning," and with *tempest and hailstones*.

2. The execution carried out by this anger of the Lord. God will *show the lighting down of his arm* (v. 30). Those people who *would not see the lifting up of his arm* (26:11) will feel it coming down and find to their cost that its burden is heavy (v. 27). Five things are for the execution here:

2.1. Here is *an overflowing stream* that *shall reach to the midst of the neck* (v. 28). The Assyrian army has been to Judah *as an overflowing stream, reaching even to the neck* (8:7–8), and now the breath of God's wrath will be so to it.

2.2. Here is *a sieve of vanity* (destruction), with which God will sift those nations that make up the Assyrian army (v. 28). He will sift them so as to shake them against one another, put them into a state of great fear, and shake them all away ultimately, for it is a sieve of destruction.

2.3. Here is *a bridle* (bit) (v. 28) to restrain them from doing trouble and to force them to serve God's purposes against their own will (10:7).

2.4. Here is a *rod* and a *staff*, the voice of the Lord, giving orders with which the Assyrian will be *beaten down* (v. 31). There is no escaping it. In every place where an Assyrian is found, the Lord will *lay it upon him* and cause it to rest (v. 32).

2.5. Here is *Tophet ordained* and *prepared* for them (v. 33). The valley of the son of Hinnom, adjoining Jerusalem, was called *Topheth*. It is thought that many of the Assyrian regiments were camped in that valley and were killed there by the destroying angel.

3. The Assyrian's fall is Jerusalem's triumph (v. 29): "*You shall have a song as in the night*, a psalm of praise such as is sung by those who *by night stand in the house of the Lord* (Ps 134:1), and you shall sing to the glory of him who *gives songs in the night*" (Job 35:10).

CHAPTER 31

This chapter is a summary of the previous chapter. Here is: 1. A woe to those who, when the Assyrian army invaded them, trusted in the Egyptians, and not God, for help (vv. 1–3). 2. Assurance given of the care God would take of Jerusalem in that time of danger (vv. 4–5). 3. A call to repentance and reformation (vv. 6–7). 4. A prediction of the fall of the Assyrian army (vv. 8–9).

Verses 1–5

Notice:

1. The sin rebuked here (v. 1). They *go down to Egypt for help* (v. 1) in every urgent need, as if the worshipers of false gods were more likely to have success on earth than the servants of the living and true God. The Egyptians had many chariots and horses and horsemen, and if the people of Judah could obtain forces from there and avail themselves of them, they would think themselves more able to deal with the king of Assyria. In this way they showed disrespect toward the God of Israel: *They look not to the Holy One of Israel* (v. 1).

2. The absurdity of this sin.

2.1. They neglect the One whom, if they will not hope in him, they still have reason to fear. They do not seek the Lord, *yet he also is wise* (v. 2). Would not infinite Wisdom, engaged on their side, be more useful to them than all the plans of Egypt? They want to go down to Egypt, a long journey, although they would receive better help by looking up to heaven. But if they will not seek God's wisdom, he *will arise against the house of the evildoers* (v. 2), this little group who go down to Egypt.

2.2. They trust in those who are unable to help them and will soon be seen to be so (v. 3). Let them know that

the Egyptians, on whom they depend so much, *are men* (mortals) *and not God*. Everyone knows this, that the Egyptians are not God and their horses are not spirit, but those who look to them for help do not consider it, or else they would not put such confidence in them.

2.3. The Egyptians will be judged soon, as is seen in the *burden of Egypt* (ch. 19), and then those who fled to them for shelter and help will fall with them.

2.4. They have taken God's work out of his hands. They pretended to take a great deal of care to preserve Jerusalem by forming an alliance with Egypt. The prophet here tells them that Jerusalem will be preserved without help from Egypt and that those who stay in Jerusalem will be safe while those who flee to Egypt will be ruined. God will fight against Jerusalem's enemies with the boldness of a *lion over his prey* (v. 4). When the lion comes out to seize his prey, a *multitude of shepherds come out against him*. These shepherds dare not come near the lion; all they can do is to make *a noise* and think they will frighten him with that. But does he take any notice of it? No; he *will not be afraid of their voice* (shouts). Thus *will the Lord of hosts come down to fight for Mount Zion*; he will as easily and irresistibly destroy the Assyrian army as a lion tears a lamb to pieces. Whoever fights against God is merely a band of poor, simple shepherds shouting at a lion. God will support Jerusalem's friends with the tenderness of a bird over its young (v. 5). *As birds flying* (v. 5) to their nests as quickly as possible when they see them attacked, hovering over their young ones to protect them, drive away the attackers, so *will the Lord of hosts defend Jerusalem* with such compassion and affection (v. 5). *Defending, he will deliver it* (v. 5). *Passing over he will preserve it* (v. 5); the word for *passing over* is used in this sense only here and in Ex 12:12–13, 27, where it refers to the destroying angel's "passing over" the houses of the Israelites when he killed all the firstborn of the Egyptians. The Assyrian army is to be routed by a destroying angel who will "pass over" Jerusalem. They will be killed by the plague, but none of the besieged will be infected. In this way he will again "pass over" the houses of his people and protect them.

Verses 6–9

1. Jerusalem will be reformed, and so the city will be rescued from its enemies within the walls (vv. 6–7). Here is a gracious call to repentance, the Lord's voice crying out in the city and the voice of the prophets interpreting the judgment: "*Turn you* from your evil ways, *unto God*, return to your faithfulness to him from whom you, *O children of Israel*, have so strongly rebelled." He reminds them of their birth and parentage. They have been backsliding children, but they are still children; therefore let them return, and their backsliding will be healed. Here also is a gracious promise (v. 7): *In that day every man shall cast away his idols*, in obedience to Hezekiah's orders, though until the people were alarmed by the Assyrian invasion, many refused to do this. It is a good shock that frightens us out of our sins. It will be a general reformation: everyone will reject their own idols. And it will be a reformation motivated by godliness, not expediency. They will throw away their idols because they have caused them to sin.

2. Jerusalem's besiegers will be routed. When the people have thrown away their idols, *then shall the Assyrian fall* (vv. 8–9). The army of the Assyrians will die on the spot by the sword of the Lord in the hand of the angel. The king of Assyria will flee from that invisible sword to one of his own strongholds. *His princes* (commanders)

who accompany him *shall be afraid of the ensign* (will panic at the sight of the battle standard) (v. 9), of every banner they see, suspecting it is a group of Jews pursuing them. But who will do this? It is *the Lord, whose fire is in Zion, and his furnace in Jerusalem* (v. 9). God keeps home there, as people do where their fire and oven are. Let the Assyrians not think they can turn him out of his own house. He is himself *a wall of fire round about Jerusalem*, so that whoever attacks that city does so at their peril (Zec 2:5; Rev 11:5).

CHAPTER 32

Here is: 1. A prophecy of the good work of reformation with which Hezekiah would begin his reign (vv. 1–8). 2. A prophecy of the great disturbance there would be in the kingdom in the middle of his reign because of the Assyrian invasion (vv. 9–14). 3. A promise of better times afterward (vv. 15–20), a promise that may be thought to look as far forward as the days of the Messiah.

Verses 1–8

We have here the description of a flourishing kingdom. It may be taken as a direction to both magistrates and subjects or as a commendation of Hezekiah. It is both promised and prescribed:

1. That magistrates shall do their duty in their situation, and the powers that be shall fulfill the great purpose for which they were ordained (vv. 1–2). The rulers must have a king, a monarch over them as supreme authority, in whom they can unite, and the king must have rulers under him as officers, by whom he can act (1Pe 2:13–14). They shall use their power according to the law, and not against it. They shall reign in righteousness with wisdom and fairness. Christ himself reigns according to a rule. In this way they shall be a great blessing to the people (v. 2): *A man, that king who reigns in righteousness, shall be as a hiding place.* When rulers are as they should be, people are as they want to be. This good magistrate shelters subjects from the storms of wrong and violence; he *defends the poor and fatherless* (Ps 82:3). He is *as rivers of water in a dry place* (v. 2), cooling the earth and making it fruitful, and *as the shadow of a great rock* (v. 2), under which poor travelers may shelter from the scorching heat. Christ Jesus is all this and much more to all the willing, faithful subjects of his kingdom. In him we find rivers of water for those who hunger and thirst for righteousness (Mt 5:6), all the refreshment that a needy soul can desire, and the shadow of a great rock to shelter travelers. Christ is like the rock, our shelter and our hiding place; he received the battering of the wind and storm for us.

2. That subjects shall do their duty in their situation.

2.1. They shall be willing to be taught and shall lay aside their prejudices against their rulers and teachers and submit to the light and power of truth (v. 3). When this good work of reformation is set in motion and people fulfill their parts in it, *the eyes of those that see*, of the prophets, the seers, *shall not be dim* (will not be closed); God will bless them with visions, to be communicated by them to the people. Then *the ears of those that hear the word preached shall hearken.*

2.2. There shall be a wonderful change brought about in them (v. 4). *The heart of those that were hasty and rash* will now be healed of their hastiness and *shall understand knowledge*, for the Spirit of God will open their understanding. Christ carried out this sanctifying work in his disciples after his resurrection (Lk 24:45). *The tongue of the stammerers*, who used to stumble whenever they

spoke about the things of God, *shall now be ready to speak plainly* (v. 4), as those who understand, those who believe, and therefore speak (Ps 116:10; 2Co 4:13).

2.3. The differences between good and evil shall be no more confused by those who see darkness for light and light for darkness (5:20) (v. 5): *The vile shall no more be called liberal*, no longer will the fool be called noble.

2.3.1. Evildoers shall no longer be promoted by the rulers. *Vile* (contemptible) people, when they are advanced, are called *liberal* and *bountiful benefactors* (Lk 22:25), but when the world becomes wiser, people will be promoted according to their merit.

2.3.2. Evildoers shall no longer be held in esteem among the people. In short, things are going well with a people when individuals are valued by their virtue, usefulness, and generosity to others and not by their wealth or titles of honor. To enforce this rule, here is a description both of the foolish person and of the noble.

2.3.2.1. Fools and scoundrels will cause trouble, and all the more so if they have power in their hands; their honors will make them worse (vv. 6–7). These corrupt and evil people are always plotting something unjust. There does not appear in them the slightest spark of generosity. The more intrigue and machination there is in a sin, the more there is of Satan in it. They *speak villany* (foolishness) (v. 6). When they lose their temper, you can see what they are really like by the bad language they use to those around them. They *utter error against* (spread error concerning) *the Lord* (v. 6), and here they practice *hypocrisy* (ungodliness). Nothing can be more arrogantly done against God than to use his name to support evil. Instead of supplying the needs of the poor, they make them even poorer; they *make empty the souls of the hungry* (v. 6), either taking away the food the poor have or denying the supply they have to give to the poor. And they *cause the drink of the thirsty to fail* (v. 6); they cut off the relief the thirsty used to have, even though they need it as much as ever. These scoundrels and fools have always had others around them who are ready to serve their corrupt purposes: *All their servants are wicked* (Pr 29:12).

2.3.2.2. One who is truly noble, who deserves the honor of being called so, makes it his business to do good to everybody according to their sphere (v. 8). He *devises liberal things* (makes noble plans). Charity must be guided by wisdom, so that charity may not be misplaced. *By liberal things he shall stand* (v. 8). The providence of God will reward him with a settled prosperity and an established reputation. The grace of God will give him peace within him.

Verses 9–20

In these verses we have God rising up to judge the contemptible people but returning in mercy to the noble to reward them for their generosity.

1. When there was such a great corruption of conduct, bad times might well be expected. The alarm is sounded to the *women that are at ease* (v. 9) and the *careless daughters*, whose husbands and fathers, to feed these women's pride and self-indulgence, are tempted to starve the poor. "*Rise up, and hear* with reverence and attention."

1.1. God is about to bring devastating and desolating judgments on the land in which they have *lived in pleasure and been wanton* (self-indulgent) (Jas 5:5). This seems to refer primarily to the devastation made by Sennacherib's army when he seized all the fortified towns of Judah, but if so, then the words *many days and years* (v. 10) must be translated, as the margin reads, "days above a year"; that is, in little more than a year this havoc will be made: it was that long from the time that that army first entered the land of Judah to the time of its overthrow. *You shall be troubled, you careless women* (v. 10). The prophet here tells them that the country from which they have their income and luxuries will soon be devastated: *"The vintage* (grape harvest) *shall fail*, and then what will you do for wine to make merry? *The gathering* (harvest) *of fruit shall not come*, for there will be none to be gathered in (v. 10). You will lack *the teats*, the good milk from the cows, and you will lack *the pleasant fields* (v. 12) and their crops." The cities of Judah, too, where they live in complacency, will be devastated (vv. 13–14): *Briers and thorns*, the fruits of sin and the curse, *shall come up*, not only *upon the land of my people* but also on *all the houses of joy in the joyous cities* (v. 13). Then the grand homes *shall be for dens* (be a wasteland) *for ever* (v. 14), houses that have been like forts and towers because of their strength and splendor.

1.2. In the foresight of this, let them *tremble* and *be troubled, strip themselves, and gird sackcloth upon their loins* (v. 11). This suggests not only that God's judgments will strip them but also that the best way to prevent the trouble would be to repent and humble themselves before God in true remorse and godly sorrow. The best preparation for the trouble would be to deny themselves and not to cling to worldly pleasures.

2. As long as there was still a remnant who kept their integrity, they had reason to hope for good times to come ultimately. They saw such times at the end of the reign of Hezekiah, but the prophecy may well be thought to look further, to the days of the Messiah, who is *King of righteousness* and *King of peace* (Heb 6:20–7:2). Notice:

2.1. How those wonderful times will be introduced: by the *pouring out of the Spirit from on high* (v. 15), which speaks not only of the goodwill of God toward us but also of the good work of God in us. God's *giving his Holy Spirit to those that ask him* is in effect his giving them all good things, as can be seen by comparing Lk 11:13 with Mt 7:11. This is the great thing that God's people encourage themselves with the hope of, that *the Spirit shall be poured out upon them* (v. 15). When God intends to give favors to his church, he also pours out his Spirit to qualify those whom he wants to use as instruments of his favor. The kingdom of the Messiah was both brought in and set up by the pouring out of the Spirit (Ac 2:1–13), and so it will be to the end.

2.2. What a wonderfully happy change will then be made. What was *a wilderness*, dry and barren, *shall become a fruitful field* (v. 15; compare 29:17). *Then shall the earth yield her increase* (harvest) (Ps 67:6). It is promised that in the days of the Messiah the *fruit of the earth shall shake like Lebanon* (Ps 72:16). Some apply this to the admission of the Gentiles into the Gospel church, which made the desert a fruitful field. Three things go into making these times happy.

2.2.1. Justice and righteousness (v. 16). When the Spirit is poured out on a land, *then judgment* (justice) *shall dwell in the wilderness* and turn it into a fruitful field, and *righteousness shall remain in the fruitful field* and make it even more fruitful. Ministers will explain the law, and magistrates will implement it, so judiciously and faithfully that evildoers will be made good and the good made even better. Among all kinds of people—the poor, low, and unlearned, who are neglected as the desert, and the rich, great, and learned, who are valued as the fruitful field—there will be right thoughts of things.

2.2.2. Peace and quietness (vv. 17–18). This peace is of two kinds:

2.2.2.1. Inner peace (v. 17). This follows from the indwelling of righteousness (v. 16). It is itself peace, and its effect is *quietness and assurance* (confidence) *for ever* (v. 17), that is, a holy serenity and security of mind. The quiet and peaceful lives are those that are spent *in all godliness and honesty* (1Ti 2:2). *The work* (fruit) *of righteousness shall be peace* (v. 17). In doing our duty, we will find true pleasure. Although the work of righteousness may be tiring and exposes us to contempt, it is peace. *The effect of righteousness shall be quietness and assurance* (v. 17) to the endless ages of eternity.

2.2.2.2. Outer peace (v. 18). When the terror of Sennacherib's invasion was over, the people were more aware than ever of the mercy of a quiet dwelling place, not disturbed by the fear of war. Let every family keep itself quiet from conflict or disharmony within the home and put itself under God's protection. Jerusalem will be a peaceful dwelling place; compare 33:20. Even *when it shall hail* and there is a violent battering storm *coming down on the forest* (v. 19) that is bare and wind-swept, even then Jerusalem will be *a quiet resting place, for the city shall be low* (leveled) *in a low place* (v. 19), under the wind, not exposed to the rage of the storm, but sheltered by the *mountains that are round about Jerusalem* (Ps 125:2).

2.2.3. Plenty and abundance. There will be good crops gathered in everywhere, and every year. God will give the harvest (1Co 3:6–7), but the farmers must also work hard and sow by every stream (v. 20), and if they do this, the grain will grow so thickly that they will get their cattle, both oxen and donkeys, to eat the tops of it and control its growth. Some think it points to the ministry of the apostles, who, like farmers, went out to sow their seed (Mt 13:3) by every stream. When God sends these happy times, blessed are those who make the most of them by doing good with what they have, who sow by every stream.

CHAPTER 33

This chapter relates to the same events as the previous chapter, the distress of Judah and Jerusalem caused by Sennacherib's invasion and their rescue by the destruction of the Assyrian army. Notice: 1. The great distress that Judah and Jerusalem would then experience (vv. 7–9). 2. The particular fear that the sinners in Zion would then be in (vv. 13–14). 3. The prayers of good people to God in this distress (v. 2). 4. The holy security that they would enjoy in the midst of this trouble (vv. 15–16). 5. The destruction of the army of the Assyrians (vv. 1–3). 6. The enriching of the Jews with the plunder of the Assyrian camp (vv. 4, 23–24). 7. The happy settlement of Jerusalem and the Jewish state. Religious faith will be uppermost (v. 6), and their civil state will flourish (vv. 17–22).

Verses 1–12

Here we have:

1. The proud and false Assyrian, for all his deceit and violence, laid under a woe (v. 1). He had destroyed the people of God, acted treacherously, and broken his treaty of peace with them. The Assyrian destroyed those who had never done him any wrong and whom he had no pretense to quarrel with, and he had dealt treacherously with those who had always dealt faithfully with him. He who destroyed the towns of Judah will have his own army destroyed by an angel. The Babylonians will deal treacherously with the Assyrians and rebel from them. Two of Sennacherib's own sons will deal treacherously

with him and cruelly murder him at his devotions. When he has done his worst, gone as far as God allows him to go, then the cup that makes people stagger will be put into his hand (51:17).

2. The praying people of God, who seek fervently at the throne of grace for mercy for the land now in its distress (v. 2): "*O Lord! be gracious to us.*" They prayed:

2.1. For those who were employed in military services for them: "*Be thou their arm* (strength) *every morning* (v. 2). Hezekiah, the rulers under him, and all the warriors need continual supplies of strength and courage from you. Every morning, when they go out and perhaps have new work to do and new difficulties to encounter, let them be invigorated, and *as the day, so let the strength be*" (Dt 33:25).

2.2. For the body of the people: "*Be thou our salvation also in the time of trouble* (v. 2), the salvation of us who sit still and do not venture out onto the battlefield." They depend on God not only as their Savior, to rescue them, but also as their salvation itself.

3. The Assyrian army ruined, and their camp made a rich but easy prey to Judah and Jerusalem. No sooner is the prayer offered (v. 2) than it is answered (v. 3); it is more than answered. They prayed that God would save them from their enemies, but he did more than that: he gave them victory over their enemies. The strength of the Assyrian camp was broken when the destroying angel killed so many thousands of them (v. 3): *At the noise of the tumult,* the rest of *the people fled.* The plunder of the Assyrian camp was seized, by way of reprisal, for all the devastation of the fortified towns of Judah (v. 4): *Your spoil shall be gathered* by the inhabitants of Jerusalem, *like the gathering of the caterpillar* (harvest of young locusts) and *as the running to and fro* (swarming) *of locusts,* that is, the destroyers will as easily and as quickly make themselves masters of the riches of the Assyrians as a swarm of locusts denudes a field or tree.

4. God and his Israel glorified. The plunder of the enemy has been gathered, and in this *the Lord is exalted* (v. 5). His people will receive the blessing of it. When God rises up to scatter the nations allied against Jerusalem (v. 3), *he has filled Zion with judgment* (justice) *and righteousness* (v. 5), a sense of justice. It will again be called *The city of righteousness* (1:26). Hezekiah and his people are encouraged (v. 6) with an assurance that God will stand by them in their distress. *Wisdom and knowledge shall be the stability* (sure foundation) *of thy times, and strength of salvation* (v. 6). Here is a desirable end, and that is *the stability of our times,* that things are not disturbed at home, and the *strength of salvation,* rescue from enemies away from home. Here is also a godly expression for Hezekiah and his people to use as a rule in how they conduct themselves: *The fear of the Lord is his treasure* (v. 6). True religion is the true treasure of any ruler or people; it designates them as rich.

5. The great distress that came upon Jerusalem described. It is foretold here:

5.1. That the enemy will be very arrogant, and there will be no dealing with him, either by treaties of peace—*for he has broken the covenant* (v. 8), as if it were beneath him to be a servant to his word—or by preparations of war, for *he has despised the cities* (v. 8). He laughs at their requests for mercy. He meets with so little resistance that he despises them, and he does not regret it in any way when he kills everyone. He neither fears God nor has any respect for people (Lk 18:2, 4).

5.2. That therefore he will not be brought to any terms of reconciliation. *The ambassadors* sent by Hezekiah to negotiate peace will find him unmanageable and *shall weep bitterly* (v. 7) in distress like children, despairing to find a way of pacifying him.

5.3. That the country will be devastated for a time by his army. No one will dare travel on the roads; this will mean that trade and commerce ceases: *The highways lie waste* (v. 8). *The wayfaring man ceases.* No one will have any profit from the land (v. 9). The desolation will be universal. That part of the country which belonged to the ten tribes was already laid waste: "*Lebanon* famous for cedars, *Sharon* for roses, *Bashan* for cattle, *Carmel* for grain, all very fruitful, have now become like deserts, *are ashamed* to be called by their old names, because they are so unlike what they once were. They *shake off their fruits* (v. 9) before their time into the hands of those who have come to destroy."

6. God appearing, at length, against this proud invader (v. 10). It seemed he was merely looking on as an unconcerned bystander, but he will demonstrate not only that there is a God who judges but also that he is God over all. When all other helpers fail, then it is God's time to help. He will bring down the Assyrian. "O Assyrians! *You shall conceive chaff, and bring forth stubble* (and give birth to straw) (v. 11), which is worthless except as fuel for the fire, which it cannot escape, since *your* own *breath as fire shall devour you* (v. 11). The threats and slaughter you breathe out against the people of God (Ac 9:1) will devour you." God will make their own breath fan the fire that will consume them. It is then no wonder that the people are *as the burnings of lime* (v. 12) in a lime kiln, and *as thorns cut up* (v. 12), which are withered, and so are soon burned up. Such was the destruction of the Assyrian army.

Verses 13–24

What has God done? In what deeds of his must we acknowledge his power?

1. He has struck terror on the sinners in Zion (v. 14): *Fearfulness has surprised the hypocrites* (godless). There are sinners who enjoy Zion's privileges and services, but whose hearts are not right in the sight of God. Now those sinners in Zion, although always subject to secret fears and terrors, were struck with an extraordinary fear from the convictions of their own consciences. When they saw the Assyrian army besieging Jerusalem, ready to set fire to it, they could not escape to Egypt, and, distrusting the promises God had made through his prophets, they were at their wits' end, crying out, "*Who among us shall dwell with devouring fire?* (v. 14). Let's abandon the city and fend for ourselves somewhere else." Or the question may mean that they saw the Assyrian army destroyed, for the destruction of that is the fire spoken of immediately before (vv. 11–12). When sinners in Zion saw what terrible results the wrath of God had, they were very fearful, being aware that they had offended this God by secretly worshiping other gods.

2. He has graciously provided for the security of his people who trust in him: *Hear this, and acknowledge his power* in causing those who *walk righteously* and *speak uprightly* to *dwell on high* (vv. 15–16). We have here:

2.1. The character of this good person even in times of general iniquity. He walks righteously. He acts according to rules of justice, renders to all their due, to God what is his due, as well as to other people what they are due. He speaks uprightly, "what is right"; he speaks with honest intention. He thinks it is corrupt and dishonest to enrich himself by putting hardships on his neighbor. If he has a bribe thrust into his hands at any time, to pervert the course of justice, he *shakes his hands from holding it*

(v. 15), taking it as an affront to have been offered it. He *stops his ears from hearing* (v. 15) anything that tends toward murder, or any suggestions that may lead to revenge (Job 31:31). He *shuts his eyes from seeing evil* (v. 15). He has such a detestation of sin that he cannot bear to see others commit it. Those who want to preserve the purity of their souls must close their ears to temptations and turn away their eyes from looking at worthless things.

2.2. The good person's comfort, which he can keep even in times of general disaster (v. 16). He will be safe; he will have fellowship with the God who is a consuming fire (Dt 4:24; Heb 12:29), who will instead be a rejoicing light to him (Pr 13:9; 15:30). And as to present troubles, *he shall dwell on high*; he will not be really harmed by them. *The floods of great waters shall not come nigh him* (Ps 32:6). Or, if they do attack him, *his place of defence shall be the munitions of rocks* (mountain fortresses) (v. 16), fortified by nature as well as by human beings. God, the Rock of ages (26:4), will be his high tower (2Sa 22:3; Ps 18:2; 144:2). He will lack nothing he needs: *Bread shall be given him* (v. 16), even when the siege is at its most difficult, and *his waters shall be sure* (v. 16). Those who fear the Lord will not lack anything good for them (Ps 34:10).

3. He will protect Jerusalem and rescue it out of the hands of the invaders.

3.1. Hezekiah will remove his sackcloth and will appear publicly in his beauty, in his royal robes (v. 17), to the great joy of all his loving subjects. Those who walk uprightly will also have the eye of faith to see the King of kings in his beauty, the beauty of holiness, and that beauty will be on them (Ps 15:2; 84:11).

3.2. Because the siege is raised, they will now be free to go out without danger of falling into the hands of their enemy: *They shall behold the land that is very far off* (v. 17); they will visit the farthest corners of the nation. Similarly, believers look at the heavenly Canaan, the land that is very far away, and encourage themselves with the prospect of it in evil times.

3.3. The remembrance of the fear they were in will add to the pleasure of their rescue (v. 18): *"Thy heart shall meditate terror* with pleasure when it is over. You will think you can still hear the alarm in your ears. 'To arms! Everyone to their positions! *Where is the scribe?'"* (v. 18)—the chief officer or secretary of war—"'Let him come to draw up the muster roll. *Where is the receiver?'"* (v. 18)—the one who took the revenue and was paymaster of the army—"'Let him see what is in the bank, to pay the defense costs. *Where is he that counted* (the officer in charge of) *the towers?* (v. 18). Let him bring in the account of them, so that care may be taken to put a competent number of soldiers in each.'"

3.4. They will no longer be terrified by the sight of the Assyrians, who were an arrogant people and spoke a strange language, so that the Jews could understand neither their requests nor their complaints, and therefore pretended to be deaf to them. Nor could they themselves be understood: "They are *of a deeper speech than thou canst perceive* (v. 19), which will make them more formidable (v. 19). But your eyes will no longer see them as arrogant; their faces will be changed when they all become corpses."

3.5. They will no longer fear for the safety of Jerusalem (v. 20). *"Look upon Zion, the city of our solemnities,* the city where our sacred festivals are kept, where we used to meet to worship God in religious gatherings." The good people suffered most because they were very concerned about Zion, as they worried that the conquerors would burn their temple. Two things are promised here to Jerusalem:

3.5.1. A well-founded security. It will be *a quiet habitation* (v. 20) for the people of God; they will not be disturbed, as they have been, by the fear of war or persecution (29:20). *"Thou shalt see the good of Jerusalem, and peace upon Israel;* you will live to see it and share in it."

3.5.2. An unmoved stability. Jerusalem, *the city of our solemnities* (festivals), is indeed only *a tabernacle* in comparison with the New Jerusalem. The present revelations of divine glory and grace are nothing in comparison with those that are reserved for the future state. Yet Jerusalem is such a tabernacle as *shall not be taken down* (will not be moved) (v. 20). After this trouble is over, it will enjoy a long-established peace. Its sacred privileges, which are the stakes and ropes of the tabernacle, will not be moved. God's church on earth is a tabernacle, which, though it may move from one place to another, will not be taken down while the world stands, for in every age Christ will have those who serve him. The promises of the covenant are its stakes, and the ordinances and institutions of the Gospel are its ropes, which will never be broken.

3.6. God himself will be their protector and Savior (vv. 21–22). This is the main basis of their confidence. God will be the Savior of Jerusalem and its glorious Lord:

3.6.1. As a guard against the enemies of Judah in other countries. He will be *a place of broad rivers and streams* (v. 21). Jerusalem had no significant river running by it, so it lacked one of the best natural fortifications, as well as one of the greatest advantages for trade and commerce. However, the presence and power of God are sufficient at any time to make up to us the deficiencies of the creation. If there are broad rivers and streams around Jerusalem, these are rivers and streams *in which shall go no galley with oars* (v. 21).

3.6.2. As a guide to their lives at home: *"For the Lord is our Judge* (v. 22), whose judgment we accept. *He is our lawgiver;* and to him every thought is brought into obedience (2Co 10:5). *He is our King,* to whom we pay homage, and therefore *he will save us."*

3.7. The enemies will be broken like a ship at sea, which cannot ride out the storm, which, because its tackle is torn and its masts split and it has nothing with which to repair them, is given up as a wreck (v. 23). They thought they were sure to capture Jerusalem, but when they were just entering the port, as it were, and thought all was theirs, they *could not spread their sail* (v. 23).

3.8. The wealth of their camp will become rich plunder for the Jews: *Then is the prey of a great spoil* (an abundance of spoils) *divided* (v. 23). They *left their tents as they were* (2Ki 7:10). All the treasure fell into the hands of the besieged, and even the *lame took the prey* (carried off plunder) (v. 23). In this way God brought good out of evil, not only rescuing Jerusalem but also enriching it.

3.9. Both illness and sin will be taken away. *The inhabitant shall not say, I am sick* (v. 24). As *the lame shall take the prey* (v. 23), so will the sick. There will be such universal joy that even those who are ill will forget their illness and join in the joy; the rescue of their city will be their cure. Or those who are ill will endure their illness without complaining as long as they see things going well with Jerusalem. *The people that dwell therein shall be forgiven their iniquity* (v. 24). Sin is the illness of the soul. When God pardons the sin, he heals the illness.

CHAPTER 34

In this chapter we have the fatal condemnation of all the nations who are the enemies of God's church and people. This prophecy was probably fulfilled in the great devastation made by the Assyrian army among those nations that were neighbors of Israel and had in some way wronged them, or, more likely, it was fulfilled in the devastation by Nebuchadnezzar's army on those nations some time after. That powerful conqueror took pride in bloodshed and in devastating countries, and here, completely beyond his intention, he was fulfilling what God threatened against his and his people's enemies. Here is: 1. A demand for universal attention (v. 1). 2. A terrible scene of bloodshed and confusion (vv. 2–7). 3. The reason given for these judgments (v. 8). 4. The continuation of this desolation (vv. 9–15). 5. The solemn confirmation of all this (vv. 16–17).

Verses 1–8

Here we have a prophecy, as elsewhere we have a history, of the wars of the Lord (Nu 21:14), which we are sure are both righteous and effective. He does good to this world, as it is his creation, but as it is in the influence of Satan, who is called *the god of this world* (2Co 4:4), he fights against it.

1. War is declared (v. 1). All nations must hear and pay attention, because they are all concerned in it. God is angry with them; his indignation is on all nations.

2. The declaration is made known, setting out:

2.1. Whom he makes war against (v. 2): *The indignation of the Lord is upon all nations*; they are all in league against God and religious faith, all in league with the Devil. As they have all had the benefit of his patience, so now they must all expect to feel his anger. *His fury is especially upon all their armies* (v. 2). With their armies the nations have caused trouble to the people of God, and with them they hope to resist the justice and power of God, and so God's fury will come on them first.

2.2. Whom he makes war for, and what are the reasons for the war (v. 8): *It is the day of the Lord's vengeance.* Just as there is a day of the Lord's patience, so also there will be a day of his vengeance, for although he is patient for a long time, he will not always be so. It is *the year of recompences for the controversy of Zion* (the year of retribution to uphold Zion's cause) (v. 8). Zion is the Holy City, a type of the church of God in the world. Zion has a just quarrel with its neighbors for the wrongs they have done to them. Zion has left it to God to plead their cause, and he will do so when the time comes.

3. The operations of war are settled on with infallible assurance.

3.1. The sword of the Lord is *bathed in heaven* (has drunk its fill in the heavens) (v. 5). This may allude to some custom they had of bathing their swords in liquor to harden them or brighten them (Eze 21:9–11). God's sword is *bathed in heaven*, in his counsel and decrees, in his justice and power.

3.2. *It shall come down upon Idumea* (Edom), *the people of God's curse* (v. 5), the people who are under his curse. God's sword of war is always a sword of justice.

3.3. In accordance with the sentence, a terrible slaughter will be made among them (v. 6). When the day of God's wronged mercy and patience has past, the sword of his justice gives no mercy. By their own sin people have lost the honor of human nature and made themselves like perishable animals; they are therefore killed as animals, and nothing more is made of killing an army of people

than of butchering a flock of lambs or goats and feeding on *the fat of the kidneys of rams*. In fact, the sword of the Lord will judge not only the lambs and goats, the poor common soldiers, but (v. 7) *the unicorns* (wild oxen) too, which *shall* be made to *come down with them, and* also *the bullocks* (bull calves) *with the bulls*, that is, *the great men, and the mighty men, and the chief captains* (Rev 6:15)—the sword of the Lord will attack them as easily as the lambs and the goats. The greatest people are nothing before the wrath of the great God. Even *the mountains*, which are hard and rocky, *shall be melted* (soaked) *with their blood* (v. 3). These expressions are hyperbole and are used because they sound terrible to us.

3.4. This great slaughter will be a great sacrifice to the justice of God (v. 6). Sacrifices were intended for the honor of God, to make it clear that he hates sin and demands atonement for it and that nothing but blood will make atonement (Nu 35:33; Heb 9:22). And in the same way, the whole earth would have been soaked with the blood of sinners if Jesus Christ, the great atoning sacrifice, had not shed his blood for us.

3.5. These who have been killed will be detestable to the human race (v. 3). The effect will be universal confusion and desolation, as if the whole frame of nature were dissolved and melted down (v. 4). *The heavens* themselves *shall be rolled together as a scroll* of parchment that is set aside when we have finished with it, or that is shriveled up by the heat of the fire. The stars will fall like autumn leaves. All the beauty, joy, and comfort of the conquered nation will be lost and done away with; the judiciary and government will also be abolished.

Verses 9–17

This prophecy describes the sad changes that are often made by divine Providence in countries, cities, palaces, and families. Places that have flourished go into decline. We do not know where to find the exact locations where many of the great towns that are celebrated in history once stood. The prophecy also describes the judgments that are the just punishment that God will inflict when the year of retribution to uphold Zion's cause has come (v. 8). Those who aim to destroy the church can never do that; they will infallibly destroy themselves.

1. The country will become like the lake of Sodom (vv. 9–10). *The streams thereof*, which watered the land and refreshed those who lived there, *shall* now *be turned into pitch*, will be congealed. *The dust thereof shall be turned into brimstone* (burning sulfur) (v. 9); sin has made their land so combustible that it will catch fire at the first spark of God's wrath. It will burn continually and *shall not be quenched night nor day* (v. 10). The torment of those in hell, or who have a hell within them in their own consciences, is continuous and without interruption. As long as there are offensive sinners on earth, *from one generation to another* (v. 10), it will be found, however light people make of it, that it is *a fearful thing to fall into the hands of the living God* (Heb 10:31).

2. The cities will become like old, decayed houses, deserted by people and occupied by wild animals or ominous birds. God will mark their citadels out for ruin and destruction. *He shall stretch out upon Bozrah the line of confusion* (the measuring line of chaos) *with the stones* (or plumb lines) *of emptiness* (desolation) (v. 11). The chaos and desolation that will spread over the face of the whole country will be like that of the whole earth when it was *tohu* and *bohu* (the very words used here), *without form and void* (Ge 1:2). Sin will soon turn a paradise into a chaos and spoil the beauty of the whole creation. When

there is chaos, there will soon be desolation. Their great people will all be cut off, and none of them will dare to appear (v. 12): they will call the *nobles of the kingdom* to take care of the arduous affairs that lie before them, but no one will be available.

3. Even the citadels will become as deserts (v. 13); *thorns shall come up, in her palaces* (citadels), *nettles and brambles in the fortresses thereof.*

4. These mighty buildings will become the residence and meeting place of fearful animals and birds. This desolation is dealt with at some length (v. 11). *The cormorant* (desert owl) *shall possess it,* which likes to be solitary (Ps 102:6); and *the bittern,* which makes a hideous screeching noise, *the great owl,* a melancholy bird, and *the raven,* a bird of prey, invited by the dead carcasses, will live there, all the unclean birds, not useful for human beings (v. 13). What was once a court for princes will now be for owls or ostriches (v. 14). *The wild beasts of the desert* will meet with the wild animals of the island, the wet, marshy country. *The satyr* [Ed. note: desert demon; NIV: wild goats, connected with demons in Hebrew thought] *shall cry to his fellow* (v. 14) to go with him to this desert place. There will *the screech owl rest* (v. 14). *The great owl shall there make her nest* (v. 15) *and lay and hatch. The vultures,* which feast on carcasses, *shall be gathered there, every one with his mate* (v. 15). What a dismal change sin makes; it makes a fruitful land barren, a busy city into a desert.

5. Here is an assurance given of the fulfillment of this prediction (vv. 16–17): *Seek you out of the book of the Lord and read.* What God's word has appointed, his Spirit will bring about, for no word of God will fall empty to the ground (1Sa 3:19). There is an exact order and proportion observed: *He has cast the lot* (v. 17) for these birds and animals, so that each one will know its place: *They shall not break their ranks, neither shall one thrust another* (Joel 2:7–8). Ancient Jerusalem recovered from its ruins, and later it gave way to the Gospel Jerusalem, and that, in turn, may be brought low, but will be rebuilt and will continue until it gives way to the heavenly Jerusalem.

CHAPTER 35

Just as after a prediction of God's judgments on the world (ch. 24) comes a promise of great mercy for his church (ch. 25), so here after a dark scene of confusion we have a bright and pleasant one, which, though it foretells the flourishing state of Hezekiah's kingdom at the end of his reign, still also surely looks as far beyond that as the prophecy in the previous chapter looks beyond the destruction of the Edomites. Both were types of the kingdom of Christ and the kingdom of heaven. The Gospel church will be set up and flourish. 1. The Gentiles will be brought into it (vv. 1–2, 7). 2. Those who wished it well but were weak and fearful will be encouraged (vv. 3–4). 3. Miracles will be performed both on the souls and on the bodies of human beings (vv. 5–6). 4. The Gospel church will be led on the way of holiness (vv. 8–9). 5. It will ultimately be brought to endless joy (v. 10). We find, therefore, more of Christ and heaven in this chapter than one would have expected in the Old Testament.

Verses 1–4

In these verses we have:

1. A desert turned into a good land. When the land of Judah was freed from the Assyrian army, the country that had been made a desert began to recover and blossom like the crocus. When the Gentile nations, which had long

been like a desert, producing no fruit for God, received the Gospel, joy came to them (Ps 67:3–4; 96:11–12). When Christ was preached in Samaria, there was *great joy in that city* (Ac 8:8). Converting grace causes the soul that was *a wilderness to rejoice with joy and singing* and to *blossom abundantly* (v. 2). Whatever is valuable in any institution is brought into the Gospel. All the beauty of the Jewish church was admitted into the Christian church, as can be seen in the letter to the Hebrews. Whatever was desirable in the Mosaic era is translated into the ways of the Gospel.

2. The glory of God shining out: *They shall see the glory of the Lord* (v. 2). God will reveal himself more than ever in his grace and love to the human race. This is what will make the desert blossom. The more we see by faith of the glory of the Lord, the more joyful and the more fruitful will we be.

3. The weak and fainthearted encouraged (vv. 3–4). God's prophets and ministers are charged, because of their office, to *strengthen the weak hands,* to encourage those who have difficulty recovering from the fears they have been put into by the Assyrian army; they must encourage them with an assurance that God will now return in mercy to them. This is the purpose of the Gospel:

3.1. To strengthen those who are weak and to confirm them. Among true Christians there are many who have weak hands and feeble knees, who are still only babes in Christ (1Co 3:1), but it is our duty (Lk 22:32) not only to bear with the weak but also to do what we can to confirm them (Ro 15:1; 1Th 5:14). It is our duty also to strengthen ourselves (Heb 12:12), making the most of the strength God has given us.

3.2. To encourage those who are afraid and discouraged: "*Say to those that are of a fearful heart* (v. 4), who are, literally, 'hasty,' who want to turn and flee at the first sign of danger, who say, in their haste, 'We are cut off and ruined' (Ps 31:22)," there is enough in the Gospel to silence these fears. He who says to us, *Be strong,* has provided help for us through One who is mighty.

4. Assurance given of the approach of a Savior: "*Your God will come with vengeance* (v. 4). God will support you against your enemies; he will come with retribution both for their wrongs and for your losses." Those whose *hearts tremble for the ark of God* (1Sa 4:13) and who are concerned for his church in the world may silence their fears with the assurance that God will take the work into his own hands.

Verses 5–10

"*Then,* when your God comes, Christ himself, look for great things."

1. Wonders will be performed in the kingdoms of both nature and grace.

1.1. Wonders will be performed on human bodies (vv. 5–6): *The eyes of the blind shall be opened;* this was often done by our Lord Jesus when he was here on earth (Mt 9:27; 12:22; 20:30; Jn 9:6). By his power the ears of the deaf also were unstopped, with one word, *Ephphatha,* "Be opened" (Mk 7:34). Many who were lame had the use of their limbs restored (Ac 3:8). The mute were enabled to speak (Mt 9:32–33). Christ performed these miracles to prove that he was sent by God (Jn 3:2); in fact, working them in his own name, he proved that he was God, the same One who originally made the human mouth, the hearing ear, and the seeing eye (Pr 20:12).

1.2. Wonders, greater wonders, will be performed on human souls. By the word and Spirit of Christ those who were spiritually blind were enlightened (Ac 26:18), those who were deaf to the calls of God were made to hear them readily, such as Lydia, whose heart *the Lord opened, so that she attended* (responded) (Ac 16:14). Those who were mute and did not know how to speak about God or to God will have their understandings opened to know him and their lips opened to declare his praise (Ps 51:15).

2. The Spirit will be poured out from heaven. There will be *waters and streams in the wilderness* (v. 6), where one would least expect it. This was fulfilled when the *Holy Ghost fell upon the Gentiles* who *heard the word* (Ac 10:44). These waters are said to *break out* (gush forth), a surprise to the Gentiles, which brought them, as it were, into a new world. The blessed effect of this will be that the *parched ground shall become a pool* (v. 7). In *the thirsty land*, where there was no water or ordinances (Ps 63:1), there will be *springs of water* (v. 7), a Gospel ministry, *the river that makes glad the city of our God* (Ps 46:4). In *the habitation of dragons* (haunt of jackals) (v. 7), animals that chose to live in the parched, scorched ground (34:9, 13), these waters will flow, and they will dispossess the jackals, so that *where each lay, shall be grass with reeds and rushes* (v. 7). This is how it was when Christian churches were planted and flourished greatly in the cities of the Gentiles, which for many ages had been haunts of jackals, or rather demons. When they were converted to Christianity, then the haunts of jackals became fruitful fields (32:15).

3. The way of religious faith and godliness is here called *the way of holiness* (v. 8). "When our God comes to save us, he will outline the way to us by his Gospel, as it has never been described before." It will be an appointed way, *a highway*. It is the King's highway, the highway of the King of kings, in which, though we may be intercepted, we cannot be stopped. The *way of holiness* is the way of God's commandments; it is the *good old way* (Jer 6:16). *The unclean shall not pass over it* (v. 8), either to defile it or to disturb those who walk along it. *It shall be for those* whom the Lord has *set apart for himself* (Ps 4:3); it will be reserved for them: *The redeemed shall walk there* (v. 9), out of reach of attack from this evil world. *The wayfaring men*, who choose to travel in it, *though fools* (v. 8), who are weak in other things, will have such clear directions from the word and Spirit of God that they *shall not err therein* (v. 8). They are sure to reach the destination of their journey. Those who walk along the narrow way, even though some may fall into one path and others into another, not all equally right, will nevertheless all meet finally at the same point. The Spirit of truth will lead them into all the truth they need (Jn 16:13). The way to heaven is a clear way and easy to reach. It will also be a safe way: *No lion shall be there, nor any ravenous beast* (v. 9), none *to hurt or destroy* (11:9; 65:25). Those who keep close to this way keep out of reach of Satan, the roaring lion (1Pe 5:8). Those who walk in the way of holiness may proceed with peace of mind, knowing that nothing can do them any real harm. Those who walk in the *way of holiness* must separate themselves from the unclean and *save themselves from an untoward generation* (Ac 2:40). Let them walk *with the redeemed* who *shall walk there* (v. 9).

4. The end of this way will be everlasting joy (v. 10). Here is good news for the citizens of Zion: *The ransomed of the Lord shall return and come to Zion* (v. 10). God will open up to them a door of escape from their captivity. They will join the Gospel church, that *Mount Zion*, that *city of the living God* (Heb 12:22). Those who by faith are made citizens of the Gospel Zion may *go on their way rejoicing* (Ac 8:39). They rejoice in Christ Jesus, and

those who mourn are blessed, for they will be comforted (Mt 5:4). When God's people returned out of Babylon to Zion, they came *weeping* (Jer 50:4), but they will come to heaven singing a new song, which no one can learn (Rev 14:3). Their joy will be visible, and no longer secret, as it is here in this world. It will be made known, to the glory of God. Our joyful hopes and prospects of eternal life should swallow up all the sorrows and joys of this present time.

CHAPTER 36

In this and the three following chapters, the prophet Isaiah is a historian. Many of the prophecies of the previous chapters had their fulfillment in Sennacherib's invading Judah and besieging Jerusalem and in the miraculous defeat he met with there, and so the story is inserted here to confirm the prophecy. The key of prophecy is to be found in history, and here, so that we might enter more easily and readily, the key is, as it were, hung near the door. The exact fulfilling of this prophecy could serve to confirm the faith of God's people in the other prophecies, whose fulfillment was farther away. Whether this story was taken from the book of the Kings and added here, or whether it was first written by Isaiah here and taken into the book of Kings, is not significant. But the story is the same almost word for word in 2Ki 18–19 and here, and a shorter version of it appears in 2Ch 32. In this chapter we have: 1. The attack the king of Assyria made on Judah (v. 1). 2. The meeting he wanted to have with Hezekiah (vv. 2–3). 3. The field commander's (Rabshakeh's) blasphemous speech, with which he intended to frighten Hezekiah into submission (vv. 4–10). 4. His appeal to the people, to persuade them to desert Hezekiah and thereby force him to surrender (vv. 11–20). 5. The report of this made to Hezekiah by his officials (vv. 21–22).

Verses 1–10

People may be doing their duty but may meet with trouble and distress. We must not wonder if, when we are doing well, God sends afflictions to encourage us to do even better, to do our best and to press forward toward perfection. The enemies of God's people try to conquer them by frightening them, especially by frightening them away from their confidence in God. This is the ploy of *Rabshakeh* (the field commander) here, who uses noise and ridicule to belittle Hezekiah as being completely unable to cope with the field commander's master. We should therefore be concerned to keep up our spirits by maintaining our hope in God, so that we may stand our ground against the enemies of our souls (Eph 6:12–13). Those who abandon God's service forfeit his protection. It is easy and very common for those who persecute the church and the people of God to claim to have received a commission from him for doing so. The field commander could say, *Have I now come up without the Lord?* (v. 10), when really he had come up *against* the Lord (37:28).

Verses 11–22

We may learn these lessons from these verses:

1. While rulers and counselors have public matters under debate, it is not fair to appeal to the people. It is therefore an unfair practice to anger subjects against their rulers by evil insinuations.

2. The more reasonably proud mockers are spoken to, the more evil they respond with. Nothing could have been spoken more mildly and respectfully than what Hezekiah's officials said to the field commander: *Speak,*

we pray thee (v. 11). But this made him even more spiteful and imperious.

3. When Satan wants to tempt people away from trusting in God, he does so by insinuating that in submitting to Satan they can be in a better condition. When the world and the flesh say to us, "*Make an agreement* with us *and come out to us* (v. 16), submit to our power and come over to our side, and *you shall eat every one of his own vine*" (v. 16), they are only deceiving us, promising us freedom when they want to lead us into the most evil captivity and slavery. Therefore, *when they speak fair, believe them not* (Jer 12:6).

4. Nothing can be more absurd in itself, nor a greater insult to the true and living God, than to compare him with the gods of the nations. They are nothing; he is the great *I AM*. They are the figments of human imagination and the works of human hands; he is the Creator of all things.

5. Arrogant sinners are ready to think that because they have been too strong for their fellow creatures, they are therefore a match for their Creator. They have subdued this and the other nation, and so the Lord himself will not rescue Jerusalem from their hands. But although the potsherds may strive with the potsherds of the earth, let them not strive with the potter (45:9).

6. It is sometimes wise not to *answer a fool according to his folly* (Pr 26:5). Hezekiah's command was, "*Answer him not* (v. 21); leave it to God to silence his mouth, for you cannot." Yet although they *answered him not a word* (v. 21), they tore their clothes in zeal for the glory of God's name and anger at the contempt shown it.

CHAPTER 37

In this chapter the story about Sennacherib, which we had before in 2 Kings, continues. In the previous chapter we saw him conquering and threatening to conquer (compare Rev 6:2). In this chapter we see him falling, and eventually fallen, in answer to prayer and in fulfillment of many of the prophecies we have read in the previous chapters. We have: 1. Hezekiah's godly reception of the ungodly speech of Rabshakeh *(the field commander) (v. 1). 2. The gracious message he sent to Isaiah to request his prayers (vv. 2–5). 3. The encouraging answer Isaiah sent him from God, assuring him that God would plead his cause against the king of Assyria (vv. 6–7). 4. An abusive letter that the king of Assyria sent to Hezekiah, to the same effect as the field commander's speech (vv. 8–13). 5. Hezekiah's humble prayer to God when he received this letter (vv. 14–20). 6. The answer God sent him by Isaiah, promising him that his affairs would soon take a turn for the better (vv. 21–35). 7. The immediate fulfillment of this prophecy in the ruin of Sennacherib's army (v. 36) and his murder (vv. 37–38).*

Verses 1–7

The best way to frustrate the evil intentions of our enemies against us is to be driven by them to God and our duty. *Rabshakeh* (the field commander) intended to frighten Hezekiah away from the Lord, but it turns out that he frightens him toward the Lord. As in the fable, the wind, instead of forcing the traveler's coat off his body, makes him wrap it more closely around him. The more the field commander heaped insults on God, the more Hezekiah sought to honor him. Hezekiah sent messengers to Isaiah to request his prayers, remembering how much Isaiah's prophecies had looked toward the events of the present day. He depended on the prophecies, but

he wanted their fulfillment to be in answer to prayer. *This is a day of trouble* (v. 3), and so let it be a day of prayer. Now the *children are brought to the birth*, but *there is not strength to bring forth* (v. 3); now let prayer come. When pains are strongest, let prayers be most vital. Prayer is the midwife of mercy, who helps to give birth to it. *It may be the Lord thy God will hear; who knows but he will return and repent?* (Jnh 3:9). The field commander has blasphemed against God, and so let Hezekiah not be afraid of him (v. 6). Judgment will certainly be given against him. Sinners' fears are only the introductions to their falls. Sennacherib will *hear the rumour* (v. 7; 2Ki 19:7) of the slaughter of his army, which will force him to withdraw to his own land, and he will be killed there.

Verses 8–20

In his promise, God may confirm us in enduring reproach silently. God answered Hezekiah, yet it seems Hezekiah did not send any answer to the field commander, but quietly left the matter with God. *So Rabshakeh* (the field commander) *returned* to the king his master for fresh instructions (v. 8). Sennacherib, without provocation given to him or warning given by him, went to wage war against Judah, and now with as little ceremony the king of Ethiopia goes to wage war against him (v. 9). Those who are quarrelsome may expect to be quarreled with. It is bad to talk proudly and profanely, but it is even worse to write in that way, for this shows more deliberation and intention, and what is written spreads further, lasts longer, and causes more trouble. Great successes often harden sinners' hearts and make them more daring. The kings of Assyria do not doubt they will destroy God's land; because the idolatrous kings of Hamath and Arpad became an easy target to them, the religious, reforming king of Judah must be so too. Hezekiah took Sennacherib's letter and spread it out before the Lord, not intending to make any complaints against Sennacherib except those based on what he himself had written. Let the matter speak for itself; here it is in black and white: *Open thy eyes, O Lord, and see* (v. 17). He encouraged himself with the knowledge that the God of Israel is the *Lord of hosts* (v. 16), that he is God *alone*. He is *God of all the kingdoms of the earth* (v. 16), for he made heaven and earth, and so he can do anything. When we are afraid of people who are very destructive, we may come with humble boldness and appeal to God as the great Savior.

Verses 21–38

1. Those who receive messages of terror from people with patience and send messages of faith to God by prayer may expect messages of grace and peace from God for their comfort. Isaiah sent a long answer to Hezekiah's prayer in God's name: "*Whereas thou hast prayed to me* (v. 21), know, for your encouragement, that your prayer is heard."

2. Those who exalt themselves against God and his people are really making themselves contemptible: "*The virgin, the daughter of Zion, has despised* (v. 22) Sennacherib. She knows that while she preserves her integrity, she is sure of divine protection."

3. Those who mistreat the people of God are insulting God himself. *Whom hast thou reproached* (insulted)? It is *the Holy One of Israel* (v. 23). And it made the indignity Sennacherib showed to God worse that he set his servants to do the same: "*By thy servants*, the worthless ones, *thou hast reproached* (heaped insults on) *the Lord*" (v. 24).

4. Those who boast about their own achievements reflect badly on God and his providence: "*Thou hast said,*

'*I have digged, and drunk water*' (v. 25), and you will not acknowledge that *I have done it*' (vv. 24–26). The most active people are no more than God makes them: "*What I have formed of ancient times*, in an eternal counsel, *now have I brought to pass, that thou shouldst be to lay waste defenced cities* (v. 26); it is therefore intolerable arrogance to speak as if it were your own doing."

5. All the hatred of the church's enemies is known and restrained by the church's God. Sennacherib was active and quick, here, there, and everywhere, but God knew when he went out and when he came back (v. 28). And although he was very stubborn and unruly, God could and would *turn him back by the way which he came* (v. 29). *Hitherto he shall come and no further* (Job 38:11). God had signed Sennacherib's commission against Judah (10:6); here he supersedes it. Jerusalem will be defended (v. 35); the besiegers will not come into it but will be defeated before they begin the siege (v. 33). But this is not all; God will come in mercy to his people. Their land will be extraordinarily fruitful, so that their losses will be abundantly made up for. And let them not think that the desolations of their country would excuse them from observing the sabbath year; though they did not now have their usual store of produce for that year, they must religiously observe it and depend on God to provide for them. There is no standing before the judgments of God when he commissions them. One angel will, in one night, put to death a vast army on the spot when God commissions him so to do (v. 36). The greatest people cannot stand before them: *The great king, the king of Assyria* (v. 33), looks very little when he is forced to return with terror and fear, thinking that the angel that has destroyed his army might also destroy him. He is made to look even smaller when his own sons, who should have guarded him, sacrifice him to his idol, whose protection he sought (vv. 37–38). The One who has rescued his people continues to do so and will do so in the future.

CHAPTER 38

This chapter continues the history of Hezekiah. 1. His illness and the sentence of death he received within himself (2Co 1:9) (v. 1). 2. His prayer in his illness (vv. 2–3). 3. The favorable answer that God gave to that prayer, and a sign to confirm his faith, that the sun would go back ten steps (vv. 4–8). We read this before (2Ki 20:1–11). But: 4. Here is Hezekiah's thanksgiving for his recovery, which we have not had before (vv. 9–20). To this is added the means used (vv. 21–22). This is a chapter that will encourage those who are confined by sickness.

Verses 1–8

We may here notice the following good lessons:

1. Neither human greatness nor human goodness will exempt people from the being arrested by illness and death. Hezekiah, a power on earth and a favorite of heaven, is struck down with a disease, which, without a miracle, will certainly prove fatal, and this comes in the middle of his life and usefulness. This sickness seizes him in the middle of his triumphs over the ruined army of the Assyrians.

2. We should be concerned to prepare when we see death approaching: "*Set thy house in order*, especially your heart" (v. 1). Our being ready for death will never make it come sooner, but it will come more easily, and those who are ready to die are most ready to live.

3. Is anyone suffering an illness? *Let him pray* (Jas 5:13). Prayer is a lotion for every sore, personal or public.

Suffering brings us to our Bibles and to our knees. When Hezekiah was in good health, he *went up to the house of the Lord* (2Ch 29:20) to pray. When he was sick in bed, he *turned his face towards the wall* (v. 2), probably toward the temple.

4. The testimony of our consciences that by the grace of God we have walked closely and humbly with God (Mic 6:8) will be a great comfort to us when we come to look death in the face. And though we may not depend on it as our righteousness, as what will justify us before God, we may still humbly plead it as evidence of our privilege of sharing the righteousness of the Mediator. Hezekiah does not demand a reward from God for his good services, but modestly begs that God would remember how he has approved himself to God (2Ti 2:15) wholeheartedly and with a pure eye: *I have walked before thee in truth*, faithfully and in sincerity, *and with a perfect heart*, wholeheartedly (v. 3), for that is a key quality of life under the Gospel.

5. God has a gracious ear open to the prayers of his afflicted people. The same prophet who was sent to Hezekiah with a warning to prepare for death is sent to him with a promise that he will not only recover but also be restored to a confirmed state of health and live fifteen years more. When we pray in our sickness, even though God does not send us such an answer as he sent to Hezekiah here, nevertheless, if by his Spirit he tells us to be cheerful and assures us that our sins are forgiven, that his grace will be sufficient for us (2Co 12:9), and that, whether we live or die, we will be his (Php 1:21), we have no reason to say that we pray in vain. God answers us if he *strengthens us with strength in our souls*, even if not with physical strength (Ps 138:3).

6. Good people cannot take much comfort in their own health and prosperity unless they also see the welfare and prosperity of the church of God. God, knowing what was close to Hezekiah's heart, promised him not only that he would live but also that he would *see the good of Jerusalem all the days of his life* (Ps 128:5). Jerusalem, now rescued, will still be defended from the Assyrians.

7. God is *willing to show to the heirs of promise the immutability of his counsel* (Heb 6:17) so that their faith may have an unshaken faith in it. God had given Hezekiah repeated assurances of his favor, but as if all that were thought too little, a sign is given him. The sign is the going back of the shadow on the *sundial* (stairway) *of Ahaz*. The sun is a faithful measurer of time, and the One who set that clock going can set it back when it is his will, for the Father of all lights (Jas 1:17) is also the One who directs them.

Verses 9–22

We have here Hezekiah's song of thanksgiving, which he wrote under divine direction after his recovery. He might have taken some of the psalms of his father David, but this occasion was extraordinary, and because his heart was full of godly devotion, he wanted to offer up his own psalm of thanksgiving in his own words. It is good to write a memorial of our affliction, noting the attitude of our hearts in the suffering, to keep a record of the thoughts we had when we were ill, and to write a thanksgiving to God. This is an excellent piece of writing that Hezekiah left here upon his recovery, but we find (2Ch 32:25) that *he rendered not again according to the benefit done to him*. The impressions, one would think, would never have worn off, but it seems they did. Thanksgiving is good, but "thanksliving" is better. Now in this writing he records:

1. The deplorable condition he was in when his disease prevailed, and his despair of recovery (vv. 10–13).

1.1. As he remembers his thoughts:

1.1.1. He blames himself for his despondency, for giving himself up as done for. We should not make the worst of our case or think that every sick person must soon die. The One who brings low can raise up.

1.1.2. He reminds himself of the fear he had of approaching death, so that he may always know and consider his own weakness and mortality.

1.1.3. He exalts the power of God in restoring him when his case was desperate. David sometimes, similarly, when he was rescued from trouble, looked back and thought about the black and sad conclusions he had made about his own situation when he was in trouble, and what he had then *said in his haste* (Ps 31:22; 77:7–9).

1.2. Let us see what Hezekiah's thoughts of himself were.

1.2.1. He reckoned that he was being cut off in the prime of life. He was now about thirty-nine years of age, with a fair prospect of many happy years. He concluded that this illness that had now suddenly seized him would be the *cutting off of his days*, that he would now be *deprived of the residue* (robbed of the rest) *of his years* (v. 10). If he died, he would be robbed not only of the comforts of life but also of all the opportunities he had to serve God and his generation (Ac 13:36).

1.2.1.1. To the same effect is v. 12, *"My age has departed* and gone and has been taken from me as a shepherd's tent, out of which I have been forcibly removed by its being suddenly pulled down." Our present residence is a little like that of a shepherd in a tent, a poor, cold, lowly lodging that will easily be taken down. But its removal is only to another world, where the coarse, black, weatherbeaten tents of Kedar that are taken down are to be set up again in the New Jerusalem, *comely* (lovely) *as the curtains of Solomon* (SS 1:5).

1.2.1.2. He adds another comparison: *I have cut off, like a weaver, my life*, like a weaver I have rolled up my life (v. 12). Not that he cut off the thread of life by any act of his own, but because he was told he must die, he was forced to cut off all his plans; his *purposes were broken off*, even the *thoughts of his heart*, as Job's were (Job 17:11). Our days are compared to the weaver's shuttle (Job 7:6), passing backward and forward very swiftly, every throw leaving a thread behind it, and when they are finished, the thread is cut off, and the piece taken out of the loom and shown to our Master, to be judged as to whether it has been well woven or not, so that we may *receive according to the things done in the body* (2Co 5:10). But just as when weavers have cut off their threads and have completed their work, so also when good people's lives are cut off, their cares are also cut off, and they rest from their labors. "But did I say, *I have cut off my life?* (v. 12). No; my times are not in my own hand; they are in God's hand (Ps 31:15), and it is he who 'will cut me off from the thrum [warp-threads left unwoven]'"—as the margin reads—"he has appointed what will be the length of the piece, and when it comes to that length, he will cut it off."

1.2.2. He reckoned that he would go to the gates of the grave, the gates of which are always open, for it is always crying, *Give, give* (Pr 30:15).

1.2.3. He reckoned that he was deprived of worshiping God and doing good in the world (v. 11): *"I said, I shall not see the Lord*, as he reveals himself in his temple, *even the Lord* here *in the land of the living.* And *I shall see man no more"* (v. 11). He would see his subjects no more, whom he now protected and helped; he would no longer see his friends.

1.2.4. He reckoned that the agonies of death would be very sharp and severe: *"He will cut me off with pining sickness* (v. 12), which will quickly waste me and wear me out." He concluded that God, whose servants all diseases are, would by them, *as a lion, break all his bones* with grinding pain (v. 13). He thought that the following morning would be the last he could expect to live in such pain and misery. *From day even to night wilt thou make an end of me* (v. 13). When we are sick, we tend to calculate our time in this way, but after all, we are still uncertain. We should be more concerned about how to reach the next world safely than about how long we are likely to live in this world.

2. The complaints he made in this condition (v. 14): *"Like a crane, or swallow* (swift or thrush), *so did I chatter*; I made a noise like those birds make when they are frightened." What a change illness makes in a short time. Some think he is referring to his praying in his suffering; it was so interrupted with groanings that could not be uttered (Ro 8:26) that it was more like the chattering of a swift or a thrush. He had such humble thoughts about his own prayers, yet they were acceptable to God. He *mourned like a dove* (v. 14), sadly, but also silently and patiently. He had found that God was ready to answer his prayers at other times, but now his *eyes failed*, and so he prayed, *"I am oppressed* (troubled) and about to sink; *Lord, undertake for me* (come to help me). Come between me and the gates of the grave, to which I am being rushed." When we receive the sentence of death within ourselves (2Co 1:9), we are ruined if divine grace does not help carry us through the valley of the shadow of death (Ps 23:4), to the heavenly kingdom on the other side of it (2Ti 4:18; 1Co 1:8)—if Christ does not do everything we need and cannot do for ourselves.

3. The grateful acknowledgment he makes of God's goodness to him in his recovery. *"What shall I say? He has spoken unto me*; he has sent his prophet to tell me that I will recover and live fifteen years more, *and he himself has done it* (v. 15). It is as sure to be done as if it were already done, for no word of his will fall empty to the ground" (1Sa 3:19). Because God has spoken it, Hezekiah is sure of it (v. 16): *Thou wilt restore me, and make me to live.* And because he has this hope:

3.1. He promises himself always to retain the impressions of his affliction (v. 15): *I will go softly all my years in the bitterness of my soul*, as one who is sad for his complaints in his suffering. When God has rescued me, I will walk cheerfully with him, as having tasted that he is gracious (Ps 34:8; Heb 6:5).

3.2. He will encourage himself and others with the experiences he has had of the goodness of God (v. 16): *"By these things* that you have done for me, *they live*; by the same power and goodness that have restored me, all people have their souls held in life (Ps 66:9). *In all these things is the life of my spirit* (v. 16); that life is maintained by what God has done to preserve my natural life."

3.3. He magnifies the mercy of his recovery, for several reasons.

3.3.1. He was brought back from a grave crisis (v. 17): *Behold, for peace I had great bitterness.* Upon the defeat of Sennacherib, he was suddenly seized by sickness, which made him bitter, and it seemed to be the bitterness of death *itself—bitterness, bitterness*, nothing but gall and wormwood (La 3:19). This was his condition when God sent him relief.

3.3.2. It came from the love of God, from love for his soul. *He delivered me because he delighted in me* (Ps 18:19), and the word here stands for a very affectionate love: "Thou hast loved my soul from the pit of corruption [destruction]" (v. 17) is the rendering in the original. This can be applied to our redemption by Christ: *In his love and in his pity he redeemed us* (63:9). And the preservation of our bodies is doubly encouraging when it is done out of love for our souls—when God repairs the house because he wants to show his kindness toward those who live in it.

3.3.3. It was the effect of the forgiveness of sin: "*For thou hast cast all my sins behind thy back* and so hast *delivered my soul from the pit of corruption* (v. 17) out of love for it." When we face our sins in true repentance, as David did when his sin was always before him (Ps 51:3), God puts them behind his back.

3.3.4. It was the extension of his opportunity to glorify God in this world. If this sickness had been his death, it would have put an end to that course of service for the glory of God and the good of the church that he was now pursuing (v. 18). Having recovered from it, he resolved not only to proceed in praising and serving God but also to abound in that work (v. 19): *The living, the living, he shall praise thee.* Not only should we praise him all the days of our life, but *the father to the children should make known thy truth* (v. 19), so that the ages to come may give God the glory of his truth by trusting in it. Hezekiah, no doubt, did this himself, but his son Manasseh did not walk in his footsteps. Parents may give their children many good things, good instructions, good examples, good books, but they cannot give them grace.

4. In the last two verses of this chapter we observe two lessons:

4.1. That God's promises are intended not to take the place of, but to encourage, human action. Hezekiah is sure to recover, but he must *take a lump* (poultice) *of figs and lay it on the boil* (v. 21). We must not put doctors or medicine in the place of God, but we must use them in submission to God and his providence; help yourself and God will help you.

4.2. That the chief end we should aim at in desiring life and health is that we may exalt God, do good, and grow in knowledge and grace (2Pe 3:18). When Hezekiah meant, *What is the sign that I shall recover?* he asked, "*What is the sign that I shall go up to the house of the Lord,* to honor God there?" (v. 22).

CHAPTER 39

The story of this chapter, like that of the previous three, is one that we have had before (2Ki 20:12–19). It is repeated here not only as a very memorable passage but also because it ends with a prophecy of the exile in Babylon, and just as the former part of the prophecy of this book frequently referred to Sennacherib's invasion, so the latter part of this book speaks much of the Jews' exile in Babylon and their restoration. We have here: 1. The pride and foolishness of Hezekiah in showing his treasures to the king of Babylon's envoys who were sent to congratulate him on his recovery (vv. 1–2). 2. Isaiah's examination of him concerning it, and his confession (vv. 3–4). 3. The sentence passed on him for it, that all his treasures would in the course of time be carried off to Babylon (vv. 5–7). 4. Hezekiah's penitent and patient submission to this sentence (v. 8).

Verses 1–4

We may learn these lessons from these verses:

1. Humanity and common civility teach us to rejoice with our friends and neighbors when they rejoice

(Ro 12:15), particularly when they recover from sickness. When the king of Babylon heard that Hezekiah had recovered, he sent a message to congratulate him.

2. It is good for us to honor those whom our God honors. The sun was the god of the Babylonians, and when they understood that it was with respect to Hezekiah that the sun had gone back ten steps on a certain day, they thought themselves obliged to give Hezekiah all the honor they could.

3. Those who do not value good people for their goodness may still be led to show them great respect by other inducements and for the sake of their worldly interests. The king of Babylon paid homage to Hezekiah not because he was godly but because he was prosperous, as the Philistines wanted to make a treaty with Isaac (Ge 26:28). The king of Babylon was an enemy of the king of Assyria, and so he was warm toward Hezekiah, because the Assyrians were so weakened by the power of Hezekiah's God.

4. It is hard to keep one's spirit humble in the midst of great advancements. Hezekiah was a wise and good man, but when one miracle after another was performed in his favor, he found it hard to stop his heart from becoming trapped by pride.

5. It is a great weakness for good people to esteem themselves much on the basis of public recognition shown them by the people of this age (Lk 20:34–36). What a poor thing it was for Hezekiah, whom God had honored so much, to be so excessively proud of the recognition shown him by an ungodly ruler, as if that added anything to him!

6. We must expect to be called to account for the actions of our pride. As far as we have reason to suspect that the sly and subtle sin of pride has wormed its way into our hearts, let us be ashamed of it, as Hezekiah was here.

Verses 5–8

Let us notice from these verses:

1. If God loves us, he will humble us. A mortifying message is sent to Hezekiah to humble the pride in his heart and convict him of its foolishness.

2. It is just of God to take away from us what is the subject of our pride. When Hezekiah boasts about his treasures, he is told that he is like foolish travelers who show their money and gold to a person who turns out to be a thief and so is tempted to rob them.

3. If we could only consider the future, we would be ashamed of our thoughts about things in the present. If Hezekiah had known that the successors of this king of Babylon would later ruin his family and kingdom, he would not have complimented his envoys as he did, and when the prophet told him that it would be so, we may well imagine how he was annoyed with himself for what he had done.

4. Those who are fond of a friendship or alliance with irreligious people will have enough of it and will have cause to repent of it. Hezekiah thought he was very happy in the friendship of Babylon, although it was the mother of prostitutes and idolatry (Rev 17:5), but Babylon, who now curried favor with Jerusalem, in the course of time conquered it and took it captive.

5. Those who truly repent of their sins will take it well to be rebuked for them and will be willing to be told about their faults. The word of the Lord that Hezekiah here reckoned to be good was the word that made him aware of what he had done wrong.

6. True penitents will quietly submit not only to the correction of the word but also to the correction of

Providence for their sins. When Hezekiah was told about the punishment of his iniquity, he said, *Good is the word of the Lord* (v. 8).

CHAPTER 40

The latter part of the prophecy of this book begins with this chapter, which is not only separated from the first part by the intervening historical chapters but also distinguished from it by its scope and style. This is all one continuous speech, and the prophet is not named even once. The first part of the prophecy consisted of many oracles and woes; this consists of many blessings. The distress that the people of God were in because of the Assyrians is spoken of here as something past (52:4), and the exile in Babylon and their rescue from that, which were much greater events, are here foretold in detail. Before God sent his people into exile, he gave them precious promises to support them in their trouble, and we may well imagine how much it must have helped dry their tears by the rivers of Babylon (Ps 137:1). But it looks even further, and to greater things: Christ and Gospel grace. As if it were intended to be a prophetic summary of the New Testament, it begins with the beginning of the Gospels, the voice of one crying in the wilderness (v. 3), and concludes with the conclusion of the book of Revelation, The new heavens and the new earth (66:22). While the prophet is speaking about redemption of the Jews, he has a more glorious salvation in his thoughts.

In this chapter: 1. Orders are given to preach and declare the good news of redemption (vv. 1–2). 2. This good news is introduced by a voice in the desert, which gives assurance that all obstructions will be removed (vv. 3–5) and that the word of God will be established and fulfilled (vv. 6–8). 3. A joyful prospect of this redemption is given to the people of God (vv. 9–11). 4. The sovereignty and power of God are exalted (vv. 12–17). 5. Idols are therefore triumphed over, and idolaters rebuked for their foolishness (vv. 18–26). 6. A rebuke is given to the people of God for their fears (vv. 27–31).

Verses 1–2

Here the commission and instructions are given to declare comfort to God's people. They are given not only to this prophet but to all the Lord's prophets, to all Christ's ministers. Let them be sure that despite all this, God still had mercy in store for them. It was especially a direction to the prophets who would live in the time of the Exile, when Jerusalem was in ruins; they must encourage the captives to hope. Gospel ministers, who are employed by the blessed Spirit as comforters and as helpers of the joy of Christians, are here reminded of the work they are called to.

1. Comforting words are directed to God's people in general (v. 1). The prophets have instructions from their God to comfort the people of God. There is a people in the world who are God's people. It is the will of God that his people be a comforted people, even in the worst of times. Words of conviction, such as we had in the former part of this book, must be followed by words of comfort, such as we have here, for the One who has torn us will heal us also (Hos 6:1).

2. Comforting words are directed to Jerusalem in particular: "*Speak*," literally, "*to the heart of Jerusalem*" (v. 2). Do not whisper it, but *cry unto her*: show saints their comforts as well as sinners their disobedience; make her hear it. *Her warfare is accomplished* (v. 2), the time

of her hard service has been completed; the campaign has now come to an end." Human life is hard service (Job 7:1); the Christian life much more so. But the struggle will not last forever; the hard service will soon be completed, and then the good soldiers will not only enter into rest but also be sure of their pay. "The cause of her trouble is removed, and when that is taken away, the effect will cease. Tell her that *her iniquity is pardoned* (v. 2); God is reconciled to her." Nothing can be spoken more comforting than this: *Son, be of good cheer; thy sins are forgiven thee* (Mt 9:2). When sin is forgiven, troubles are removed in love. "*She has received of the Lord double for* the cure of *all her sins* (v. 2), more than sufficient to come between her and her idols," the worship of which was the great sin. God intended to restore them by their exile in Babylon. It gave birth in them to a deep-rooted hatred toward idolatry and was a doubly strong medicine to cleanse that iniquity. True penitents have indeed, in Christ and his sufferings, *received of the Lord's hand double for all their sins* (v. 2), because the atonement Christ made by his death was of such infinite value that it was more than double the punishment of sin, *for God spared not his own Son* (Ro 8:32).

Verses 3–8

Because the time to favor Zion has come (Ps 102:13), the people of God must be prepared, by repentance and faith, for the favors intended for them. We have here *the voice of one crying in the wilderness* (v. 3), which may be applied to those prophets with the captives who, when they saw the day of their restoration dawning, fervently called on them to prepare for it. But it must be applied to John the Baptist, for although God was the speaker, John was *the voice of one crying in the wilderness* to *prepare the way of the Lord* (Mt 3:3), to incline human hearts to receive the Gospel of Christ. The way of the Lord is prepared:

1. By repentance for sin; this was what John the Baptist preached to all Judea and Jerusalem (Mt 3:2, 5), thereby *making ready a people prepared for the Lord* (Lk 1:17). God is coming on the way with mercy, and we must prepare for him (vv. 3–5). If we apply this to the Exile, it may be taken as a promise that whatever difficulties may lie in the people's way will be removed when they return. This voice in the wilderness sets pioneers to work to level the roads. It is the same duty that we are called to, in preparation for Christ's coming into our souls. We must cultivate the spiritual attitude that will make us ready to receive Christ and his Gospel: "*Prepare you the way of the Lord* (v. 3), and let all that might obstruct his entrance be suppressed. Make room for Christ: *Make straight a highway for him*" (v. 3). Those who are prevented from receiving comfort in Christ by their despondency are the valleys that must be raised up. Those who are prevented from receiving comfort in Christ by proud thoughts are the mountains and hills that must be made low. Those who have harbored prejudices against the word and ways of God, who are insensitive and unresponsive toward him, are the rough areas that must be leveled. When this is done, *the glory of the Lord shall be revealed* (v. 5). When the captives are prepared to be restored, Cyrus will proclaim it. When John the Baptist has for some time preached repentance, and so made ready a people prepared for the Lord (Lk 1:17), then the Messiah himself will be revealed in his glory, performing miracles and by his grace binding up and healing with comfort those whom John had wounded with convictions (Hos 6:1). This revelation of divine glory will be *a light to lighten the*

Gentiles (Lk 2:32). *All flesh shall see it together* (v. 5), not only the Jews, as the return from exile was taken notice of by the neighboring nations (Ps 126:2).

2. By confidence in the word of the Lord, and not in any part of the creation. Because *the mouth of the Lord has spoken it* (v. 5), the voice has this to cry out as well: *The word of our God shall stand for ever* (v. 8). By the fulfillment of the prophecies and promises of salvation in John the Baptist, and their being completely carried out in due time, it is shown that the word of the Lord is dependable. When human power appears to act against God's salvation, it is not to be feared, for it will be as grass before the word of the Lord: it will wither and be trodden underfoot. The gloating Babylonians are merely like grass. When human power appears to restore them, it is not to be trusted, for it is like mere grass. When God is about to work salvation for his people, he will take them away from depending on mere created things, and from looking for salvation from hills and mountains (Ps 127:1). The word of our God—that glory of the Lord that is now to be revealed, the Gospel—and that grace that is brought to us with the word and worked in us by the word, will stand forever. To prepare the way of the Lord, we must be convinced that all people are like grass, weak and withering. We ourselves are like that and so cannot save ourselves. All the beauty of the creation is simply as the *flower of grass* (Jas 1:10–11; 1Pe 1:24); the promise of God will provide us with a happiness that will run parallel to the life of our souls, which must live forever.

Verses 9–11

It was promised (v. 5) *that the glory of the Lord shall be revealed*. We are told here:

1. How it will be revealed (v. 9). Notice will be given of it to the remnant who are left in Zion and Jerusalem, the poor of the land, who were left as vinedressers and farmers (2Ki 25:12); it will be told them that their brothers and sisters will return to them. This will be told also to the captives who belong to Zion and Jerusalem. Zion is said to *dwell with the daughter of Babylon* (Zec 2:7), and there she receives notice of Cyrus's gracious declaration (2Ch 36:22–23; Ezr 1:1–4). It will also be declared *by* Zion and Jerusalem, by those who remain there, or who have already returned. Let them make it known as loudly as they can, let them *lift up their voice with strength* (with a shout) (v. 9). Let them say to the towns of Judah and all who live in the country, *Behold your God* (v. 9). *This is our God, we have waited for him* (25:9). This may refer to the invitation from the people in Jerusalem to those who had settled in the towns of Judah to come and join them in their sacrifices, an invitation issued soon after the return from exile, as soon as an altar had been set up in Jerusalem (Ezr 3:2–4). But this was to have its complete fulfillment in the apostles' public and fearless preaching of the Gospel to all nations, beginning at Jerusalem (Lk 24:47; Ac 1:4, 8).

2. What it is that will be revealed. "Your God will come. *He will come with strong hand*, a power that is too strong to be obstructed, even though it may be opposed. He will reward everyone according to their works, as a righteous Judge: *His reward is with him. His work is before him* (v. 10), that is, he knows perfectly well what he has to do and how to do it. *He himself knows what he will do* (Jn 6:6). God is the *Shepherd of Israel* (Ps 80:1); Christ is the Good Shepherd (Jn 10:11). *He shall feed his flock like a shepherd* (v. 11). His word is food for his flock to feed on; his services of worship are fields for them to feed in; his ministers are undershepherds. He takes

particular care of those who need his care most: the lambs that are weak, unaccustomed to hardship, and unable to help themselves, and *those that are with young* (v. 11), pregnant and, if injured, in danger of miscarrying. He particularly takes care to see that a succession does not fail and is not cut off. The Good Shepherd has a tender care for children, for young converts, for weak believers and those who are of a sorrowful spirit. These are the lambs of his flock. He will gather them back when they wander off, he will gather them up when they fall, he will gather them together when they are dispersed, and he will gather them home to himself eventually; and he will do all this with his own powerful hand, out of which no one will be able to snatch them (Jn 10:28). He will gently lead them.

Verses 12–17

These verses describe the greatness and glory of the Lord Jehovah, the God of Israel, and were written to encourage his people who were captives in Babylon to hope and to depend on him to be restored. They were also written to fill those who receive the good news of redemption by Christ with a holy awe and reverence of God.

1. His power is unlimited (v. 12).

1.1. He has a vast reach. If we look at the celestial globe, God in his greatness *metes the heavens with a span*; he has marked off the heavens with the breadth of his hand. All the waters in the world he can *measure in the hollow of his hand* (v. 12), and he *comprehends* (holds) *the dust of the earth in a measure* (basket) (v. 12), or with his three fingers; it is no more to him than a small handful or what we take up between our thumb and two fingers.

1.2. He has vast power and can as easily move mountains as a worker heaps goods onto scales; he balances them with his hand as exactly as if he were weighing them out on a pair of scales.

2. His wisdom is unsearchable (Ro 11:33) (vv. 13–14). As no one can do what God has done, so no one can suggest anything to him that he has not thought of. When the Lord made the world (Job 26:13), there was no one who gave him any advice. Nor does he need any counselor to guide him in governing the world.

3. The nations of the world are nothing in comparison with him (vv. 15, 17). If we take all the great and powerful nations, the most pompous kings, the most populous kingdoms, if we take the islands in their huge numbers, the islands of the Gentiles, even then, *before him* they are *as a drop of the bucket* compared with the vast ocean, or like *the small dust of the balance* (v. 15)—which is so insignificant that it is not even counted on the scales—in comparison with all the dust of the earth. He takes them up *as a very little thing* (fine dust) (v. 15). *They are counted by him*, and are to be counted by us, as *less than nothing, and vanity* (worthless) (v. 17). He can bring them all to nothing as easily as he originally brought them out of nothing. They are all *vanity*; the word used here is the same used for the chaos in Ge 1:2. It exalts God's love to the world that although it is of such small account with him, nevertheless, to redeem it he *gave his only begotten Son* (Jn 3:16).

4. The services of the church can make no addition to him. *Lebanon is not sufficient to burn* (v. 16): not its wood as fuel for the altar, nor its animals for sacrifices. He is exalted *far above all blessing and praise* (Ne 9:5), all burnt offerings and sacrifices.

Verses 18–26

The prophet here rebukes those who make idols and then say that they are like God and pay homage to them.

He also rebukes those who put creatures in the place of God, who fear them more than God or love them more than God. Twice the challenge is made here, *To whom will you liken God?* (v. 18 and again v. 25). *To whom will you liken me?* This shows the absurdity of making visible idols of the One who is invisible, imagining the idol to be enlivened by the deity. It also shows the foolishness of making creatures equal to God in our affections. Proud people make themselves equal with God; covetous people make their money equal to God; and whatever we esteem or love, fear or hope in, more than God, we are making that part of creation equal to God, which is the greatest possible insult to him. Now, to show the absurdity of this:

1. The prophet describes idols as worthy of the greatest contempt (vv. 19–20): "Look at the better kinds of idols, made of some worthless metal, fashioned into whatever shape the founder pleases and overlaid with gold plate so that it may pass for a golden image. It is a creation, for the metalworker has made it; *therefore it is not God* (Hos 8:6). It is a fraud, for it is gold on the outside but lead or copper underneath, and in this it represents the deities themselves, which are not what they seem. *He that is so impoverished* (v. 20) that he has scarcely enough to offer as a sacrifice to his god when he has made it will nevertheless not be without an enshrined deity of his own. If he cannot make one out of bronze or stone, he will have a wooden one rather than none at all, and so he *chooses a tree that will not soon rot* (v. 20) and has his idol made of that. The better sort have silver chains to fasten theirs in place, and even if it is only a wooden idol, care is taken that it *shall not be moved*" (v. 20). See how these idolaters shame their own reason by dreaming that gods of their own making — nehushtans, pieces of bronze or logs of wood — will be able to do them any kindness! Notice how these idolaters shame us, who worship on the only living and true God. They spared no expense on their idols; we, on the other hand, may sometimes begrudge as "a waste of money" what is spent on serving our God.

2. He describes God as infinitely great and worthy of the greatest reverence. To prove the greatness of God he appeals:

2.1. To what his people have *heard of him by the hearing of the ear* (Job 42:5) (v. 21): "*Have you not known* by the very light of nature? *Has it not been told you from the beginning*, or, 'by your fathers' and teachers, according to the constant tradition received from your ancestors and predecessors, even from the beginning? *Have you not understood* it as always acknowledged *from the foundation of the earth* (v. 21) that God is a great God and a great King above all gods?" (Ps 95:3). The invisible things of God are *clearly seen from the creation of the world* (Ro 1:20). "You only have to ask your father and your elders" (Dt 32:7). *Ask those that go by the way* (Job 21:29), ask the first person you come across. God has the command of all creatures. The heaven and the earth themselves are under his management: *He sits upon* (above) *the circle*, or globe, *of the earth* (v. 22). He is still stretching out the heavens, and he will do so until the day comes when they will be rolled up like a scroll (34:4; Rev 6:14). He spreads them out as easily as we draw a curtain, opening these curtains in the morning and drawing them together again at night. And the heaven is to this earth *as a tent to dwell in* (v. 22); it is a canopy drawn over our heads. The many people who live on this earth are in his sight like grasshoppers are in ours, as little and as easily crushed. If the spies thought themselves like grasshoppers in the presence of the descendants of Anak (Nu 13:33), what

are we in the presence of God in his greatness? Grasshoppers live a short time, and live carelessly, not like ants (Pr 6:6; 30:25); so do most people. Those who act against God will certainly be humbled by his mighty hand (vv. 23–24). *They shall not be planted; they shall not be sown* (v. 24); and those are the two ways of propagating plants, either by seed or cutting. And if they are so planted or sown, yet *their stock shall not take root in the earth* (v. 24); they will not continue long in power.

2.2. To what *their eyes have seen of him* (v. 26): "*Lift up your eyes on high*; do not always pore over this earth, but sometimes look up: look at the glorious lights of heaven, consider the One who created them." What we see of the creation should lead us to the Creator. When the idolaters looked at the starry host of heaven, they looked no farther but worshiped them (Dt 4:19; Job 31:26). The Creator *brings out their host by number* (v. 26), as a general draws out the squadrons and battalions of his army; *he calls them all by names* (v. 26) (Ps 147:4), and *by the greatness of his might, not one of them fails* (v. 26); every one does the work to which it has been appointed.

Verses 27–31

Here:

1. The prophet rebukes the people of God, captives in Babylon, for their unbelief and distrust of God (v. 27): "*Why sayest thou, O Jacob*, to yourself and those around you, *My way is hidden from the Lord?*"

1.1. The titles he here gave them were enough to shame them out of their distrust: O Jacob! O Israel! They bore these names because they were God's professing people, a people in covenant with him.

1.2. The way of rebuking them is by reasoning with them: "Why?" Many of our foolish fears would disappear if we closely investigated their causes.

1.3. They spoke about God as if he had rejected them.

1.4. The wrong statement they uttered was an expression of despair about their present condition. They were ready to conclude:

1.4.1. That God would not notice them: "*My way is hidden from the Lord* (v. 27). There are such difficulties in our case that even divine wisdom and power will be perplexed about them."

1.4.2. That God could not help them: "*My judgment is passed over from my God* (v. 27); my case is beyond help, so far beyond it that God himself cannot put things right."

2. He reminds them of the things that would be sufficient to silence all such fears and distrust. To convict idolaters (v. 21), he appeals to what they have known. Jacob and Israel were a knowing people (Dt 4:6), and their knowledge came by hearing (Ro 10:17). Among other things, they had heard that *God had spoken once, twice* (Job 33:14); in fact, they had *heard it* many times, *that power belongs unto God* (Ps 62:11):

2.1. He is himself an almighty God. He must be so, for he is *the everlasting God* (v. 28), and so with him there is no decay. He is without beginning or end, and so there are no changes with him (Mal 3:6). He is also *the Creator of the ends of the earth* (v. 28) and is therefore the rightful ruler of all. He is as able to save his church as he was able in the beginning to make the world. *There is no searching out of his understanding* (v. 28), to defeat its intentions. No one can say, "God's wisdom can go so far, but no farther" (Job 38:11). *He faints not, nor is weary* (v. 28). He upholds the whole creation, governs all the creatures, and has power to relieve his church when it is brought to a low point.

2.2. He gives strength to his people and helps them to help themselves. The One who is the strong God is the strength of Israel.

2.2.1. He can help the weak (v. 29).

2.2.2. He will help the willing; he will help those who, in humble dependence on him, help themselves, and he will do well for those who do their best (vv. 30–31). *The youth* and *the young men* are strong but tend to think themselves stronger than they are. And they *shall faint and be weary*; they *shall utterly fail* (v. 30) in their conflict and under their burdens; they will soon be made to see how foolish it is to trust in themselves. *But those that wait on the Lord* (v. 31), who by faith rely on him and commit themselves to his guidance, will find that God will not fail them. They will have grace that is sufficient for them (2Co 12:9): they *shall renew their strength* (v. 31). God will be their *arm every morning* (33:2). They will use this grace for the best purposes. They will soar upward toward God. Devotions are the eagles' wings on which gracious souls mount up (Ps 25:1). They will press forward toward heaven. They will walk and run in the way of God's commandments (Ps 119:32, 35), cheerfully and with liveliness.

CHAPTER 41

This chapter is intended both to convict idolaters and to comfort all God's faithful worshipers. And however much it might be primarily intended to convict the Babylonians and comfort the Israelites, no doubt it was also intended both to warn and encourage us: 1. God through the prophet shows the foolishness of those who worship idols (vv. 1–9). 2. He encourages his faithful ones to trust in him (vv. 10–20). 3. He challenges the idols (vv. 21–29). The chapter may be summed up in those words of Elijah, If the Lord be God, follow him, but if Baal, then follow him (1Ki 18:21).

Verses 1–9

God's care for his people Israel in raising up Cyrus to rescue them is a proof of his sovereignty above all idols and of his power to protect his people.

1. God, in general, challenges to the worshipers of idols (v. 1). He renews the challenge (v. 21): *Produce your cause* (present your case). The court is set, and summonses have been sent to the islands. Silence, as is usual, is declared while the case is being heard: "*Keep silence before me* (v. 1), and judge nothing before the time" (1Co 4:5). The defenders of idolatry are called on to say what they can in their defense: "*Let them renew their strength* (v. 1) in opposition to God, *Let them come near* (v. 1) to vindicate and honor their idols. Let them speak freely: *Let us come near together to judgment*, let us meet together at the place of judgment" (v. 1).

2. He particularly challenges the idols to do for their worshipers what he has done and will do for his worshipers.

2.1. What is to be proved is:

2.1.1. That *the Lord is God* alone, *the first and with the last* (v. 4), that he is infinite, eternal, and unchangeable, that he has ruled the world from the beginning and will continue to do so to the end of time.

2.1.2. That *Israel is his servant* (v. 8), whom he protects and uses and in whom he is and will be glorified.

2.2. To prove this he shows:

2.2.1. That it was he who called Abraham, the father of this despised nation, out of an idolatrous country. Abraham is *the righteous man whom God raised up from*

the east (v. 2). The Aramaic paraphrase expressly understands it to refer to him: "Who brought Abraham publicly from the east?" To maintain the honor of the people of Israel, it was right to point to this great ancestor of theirs, and in v. 8 God calls Israel the *seed of Abraham my friend*. Also, to show contempt for Babylonian idolatry, it was right to show how Abraham was called from serving other gods (Jos 24:2–3). Further, to encourage the captives in Babylon to hope that God would find a way for them to return to their own land, it was right to remind them how he brought their father Abraham out of the same country into this land to give it to him as an inheritance (Ge 15:7). He was *a righteous man*, who *believed God, and it was counted to him for righteousness*, and so he became the father of all those who by faith in Christ are made the *righteousness of God through him* (Ro 4:3, 11; 2Co 5:21). God *raised him up from the east* (v. 2), from Ur first and afterward from Haran, which lay northeast of Canaan. He raised him up out of iniquity and made him godly, raised him out of obscurity and made him famous. He *called him to his foot* (v. 2), to follow him with implicit faith, for he *went out not knowing whither he went*, but knowing whom he followed (Heb 11:8). We must all either come to his feet or be made his footstool (Ps 110:1; Mt 22:44; etc.). *He gave nations before him* (v. 2), the nations of Canaan, and the Hittites acknowledged him as a mighty ruler (Ge 23:6). He *made him rule over* those *kings* (v. 2) whom he conquered in order to rescue his relative Lot (Ge 14:1–24). And when God *gave them as dust to his sword, and as driven stubble to his bow* (v. 2), he then *pursued them, and passed safely* (v. 3), or in peace, under divine protection.

2.2.2. That it is he who will before long raise up Cyrus from the east. It is spoken of as something past, as if it had already been done. "God will raise him up in righteousness," according to one reading of 45:13; he *will call him to his foot* (service), use him as he pleases, and make him victorious over the nations that oppose his coming to the throne. He will be a type of Christ, who is righteousness itself, whom God will, in the fullness of time, raise up and make victorious over the powers of darkness.

3. He exposes the foolishness of idolaters, who obstinately persist in their idolatry (v. 5): *The isles of the Gentiles saw this*—not only what God did for Abraham himself but also what he did for his descendants—how he brought them out of Egypt and made them *rule over kings*, and *they feared* (Ex 15:14–16). They were afraid, *drew near, and came* (v. 5), but instead of helping to reason one another out of their foolish idolatry, they helped confirm one another in it (vv. 6–7). They said to one another, "*Be of good courage* (v. 6); let us unanimously agree to keep up the reputation of our gods." One worker encourages another to join an alliance to maintain the noble craft of making gods. They not only turned to their old gods for protection but also made *new ones* (Dt 32:17). *So the carpenter*, having done his part to the woodwork, *encouraged the goldsmith* to do his part in gilding or overlaying it, and when it came into the goldsmith's hands, *he that smooths with the hammer* (v. 7), who polishes it, or beats it thin, quickened *him that smote* (struck) *the anvil*, told him it was *ready for the soldering*, which perhaps was the last operation on it, and then it was *fastened with nails* (v. 7)—and before long, there you have a god.

4. He encourages his own people to trust in him (vv. 8–9): *But thou, Israel, art my servant*. "Idolaters put themselves under the protection of these powerless gods. *Those that make them are like unto them, and so is every one that trusts in them* (Ps 115:3; 135:18), but

you, O Israel, are the servant of a better Master." They are God's servants. He has *chosen* them to be his own special people. They are the descendants of Abraham his friend (v. 8). It was the honor of Abraham that he was *called the friend of God* (Jas 2:23). The people of Israel were loved for the sake of Abraham. God had not yet rejected them, though they had often provoked him, and so he would not now abandon them.

Verses 10–20

The purpose of these verses is to silence the fears and encourage the faith of the servants of God in their distress. Perhaps it is intended, in the first place, to support God's Israel in exile, but all who faithfully serve God *through patience and comfort of this scripture may have hope* (Ro 15:4). Here is a word of caution, counsel, and comfort that is repeated so often, *Fear thou not* (v. 10) and again (vv. 13 and 14), *Fear not*. It is against the wishes of God for his people to be a fearful people.

1. They may depend on his presence with them as their God: *I will hold thy right hand* (v. 13), "go hand in hand with you," according to some: he will be our guide. When we are weak, he will hold us up; he will encourage us and *so hold us by the right hand* (Ps 73:23). He will silence fears: *saying unto thee, Fear not* (v. 13). He has said it again and again in his word, but he will go further; he will by his Spirit say it to their hearts.

2. Though their enemies are now very formidable, the day is coming when God will judge them. There are those who rage against God's people, who *strive with* (oppose) *them* (v. 11), who war against them (v. 12), who hate them. But let God's people await God's time. Those enemies will be convinced of the foolishness of opposing God's people; *They shall be ashamed and confounded* (disgraced) (v. 11), which could bring them to repentance, but will rather fill them with rage. They will be ruined and undone (v. 11): *They shall be as nothing* before the justice and power of God. This is repeated (v. 12).

3. God's people themselves will become a terror to those who are now a terror to them, and victory will turn to their side (vv. 14–16). Jacob and Israel are subdued and brought very low. It is the *worm Jacob*, so little, weak, and defenseless, trampled on by everybody, forced to crawl into the earth for safety. Yet we must not wonder at this, since Jacob's King, Jesus Christ, calls himself *a worm and no man* (Ps 22:6). God's people are sometimes as worms, but not vipers, the seed of the Serpent (Ge 3:15), as their enemies are (Mt 3:7; 12:34; etc.). God regards Jacob's lowly estate and says, "*Fear not, thou worm Jacob*; do not be afraid that you will be crushed; and *you men of Israel*" (v. 14)—for which the alternative readings include "little Israel," "you few men," and "you dead men"—"do not give yourselves up as ruined." *By whom shall Jacob arise, for he is small?* (Am 7:2). We are told here: *I will help thee, saith the Lord* (v. 14), and it is the honor of God to help the weak. The Lord will help them by enabling them to help themselves and making Jacob become *a threshing instrument* (v. 15). Notice that he is only an instrument, a mere tool in God's hand. But if God makes him a threshing instrument, he will make him fit for use, *new* and *sharp* and *having teeth*, or sharp spikes, and then by divine direction and strength, *thou shalt thresh the mountains* (v. 15), the highest, strongest, and most stubborn of your enemies. He pursues the metaphor (v. 16). Having threshed them, *thou shalt winnow them, and the wind shall scatter them*. This had a partial fulfillment in the victories of the Jews in the times of the Maccabees, but it seems intended to declare the

final condemnation of all the implacable enemies of the church of God in the triumphs of the cross of Christ over the powers of darkness, and *he that overcomes shall have power over the nations* (Rev 2:26).

4. They will have great comfort in God, and God will have great honor from them: *Thou shalt rejoice in the Lord* (v. 16). "You will also *glory in the Holy One of Israel* (v. 16), in what he has done for you."

5. If occasion arises, God will again do for them as he did for Israel on their journey from Egypt to Canaan (vv. 17–19). When the captives, either in Babylon or in their return from there, lack water or shelter, God will take care of them. Their return from Babylon was a type of our redemption by Christ, and so the contents of these promises:

5.1. Were provided by the Gospel of Christ. That glorious revelation of his love has given full assurance that God has provided sufficient comforts to supply all their needs and to answer all their prayers.

5.2. Are applied by the grace and Spirit of Christ to all believers, so that they may have encouragement on their way and complete happiness at the end of their lives. It is supposed here that as the people of God pass through this world, they are often in difficulties: *The poor and needy seek water, and there is none* (v. 17); *the poor in spirit hunger and thirst after righteousness* (Mt 5:3, 6). The human soul seeks satisfaction somewhere, but soon despairs of finding it in the world. It is promised here that the grievances of these poor and needy will be satisfactorily dealt with. "*I the Lord will hear them* (v. 17), will answer them. I will be with them as I have always been in their distress." While we are in the wilderness of this world, this promise is to us what the pillar of cloud and fire was to Israel, an assurance of God's gracious presence. They will have fresh water, as Israel had, even where one would least expect it (v. 18): *I will open rivers in high places*, rivers of grace and delight, *rivers of living water*, a phrase Jesus used in speaking of the Spirit (Jn 7:38–39). The preaching of the Gospel to the world turned that desert into a pool of water. "*I will plant in the wilderness the cedar* (v. 19), so that they will pass through with as much peace and joy as people do when walking in their orchard. These trees will be to them what the pillar of cloud was to Israel, a shelter from the heat." Christ and his grace are like this to believers. When God sets up his church in the Gentile desert, there will be as great a change in human character as if thorns and briers were turned into cedars. Believers will see and acknowledge the hand of God in this (v. 20). God will do it so *that they may see* (v. 20) that this wonderful change is beyond the ordinary course of nature and therefore comes from a higher power.

Verses 21–29

The Lord, through the prophet, repeats here the challenge to idolaters: "*Produce your cause* (present your case) (v. 21) and *bring forth the strongest reasons* you have to prove that your idols are gods and worthy of worship."

1. The idols are challenged here to bring proof of their knowledge and power. Understanding and active power are human accomplishments. Whoever pretends to be a god must have these qualities perfectly.

1.1. "They are so ignorant that they can tell us nothing we did not know before. We challenge them to inform us:

1.1.1. "What has happened in the past: *Let them show the former things* (v. 22). What did they ever do that was worth taking notice of?

1.1.2. "What will happen, to declare to us *things to come*" (v. 22 and again v. 23). No creature can foretell things to come with any certainty, except by divine revelation.

1.2. "They are so powerless that they can do nothing that we cannot do ourselves." What these idols are accused of is that *they are of nothing* (v. 24). Some read it: "*The work they do is of nought*, and so is all the fuss being made about them. Therefore *he that chooses you and gives you your deity is an abomination* to God." Servants are at liberty to choose their master, but people are not at liberty to choose their God.

2. God produces here proofs that he is the true God and that there is no other god besides him.

2.1. He has irresistible power. He will soon make this clear by raising up Cyrus, a type of Christ (v. 25): *He will raise him up from the north* and *from the rising of the sun*. On his father's side Cyrus was a Mede, and on his mother's a Persian, and his army consisted of Medes, whose country lay north of Babylon, and Persians, whose country lay east of it. God will raise him up to great power, and he will come against Babylon to serve his own purposes. But:

2.1.1. "He shall proclaim God's name," as it may be understood. So he did when, in his declaration to release the Jews, he acknowledged that the Lord God of Israel was *God*.

2.1.2. All opposition will fall before him: *He shall come upon the princes* (rulers) (v. 25) of Babylon and trample on them as potters tread out clay. Christ, as a human being, was raised up from the north, for Nazareth lay in the northern parts of Canaan; as the Angel of the covenant, he ascends from the east (Rev 7:2). He maintained the honor of heaven—*he will call upon my name*—and came on the Prince of Darkness as one walks on mortar, and he trod him down.

2.2. He has infallible foresight. Now the false gods not only could not do it but also could not foresee it.

2.2.1. He challenges them to produce any of their alleged gods or diviners (v. 26): "*Who has declared from the beginning* anything like this salvation I have planned for my people?"

2.2.2. He claims for himself the sole honor of doing it and foretelling it (v. 27): "I am he that *will give to Jerusalem one that brings good tidings*" (v. 27). This may be applied to the work of redemption, in which the Lord has given to us the good news of reconciliation.

3. Judgment is given here on this trial.

3.1. None of all the idols had foretold this work of wonder. Other nations besides the Jews were released from captivity in Babylon by Cyrus, but none of them received any information about it beforehand by any of their gods or prophets. None of all the gods of the nations have shown their worshipers the way of salvation, which God will show by the Messiah.

3.2. None of those who pleaded for them could produce any example of their knowledge or power that contained any kind of proof that they were gods. Judgment must therefore be given against the defendant on the grounds of their failure to answer because they are mute.

3.3. Sentence is therefore given according to the charge shown against them (v. 24).

CHAPTER 42

The prophet seems here to launch out still further into the prophecy of the Messiah and his kingdom under the type of Cyrus. Here is: 1. A prophecy of the Messiah's
coming with humility, but also with power (vv. 1–4). 2. His commission revealed, which he received from the Father (vv. 5–9). 3. The joy with which the good news would be received (vv. 10–12). 4. The success of the Gospel, to overthrow the Devil's kingdom (vv. 13–17). 5. The rejection of the Jews for their unbelief (vv. 18–25).

Verses 1–4

We are sure that these verses are to be understood as referring to Christ, for the evangelist tells us explicitly that this prophecy was fulfilled in him (Mt 12:17–21). Here is:

1. The Father's confidence in him. God acknowledges him:

1.1. As One who fulfills his work: he is *my servant*. Although he was a Son, yet, as a Mediator, he *took upon him the form of a servant* (Php 2:7).

1.2. As chosen by him: he is *my elect*. Infinite Wisdom made the choice and then affirmed it.

1.3. As One he puts confidence in: "He is my servant on whom I lean," as some read it.

1.4. As One he takes care of: he is *my servant whom I uphold* (v. 1). The Father stood by him and strengthened him. His delight was in him from eternity.

2. His qualifications for his office: *I have put my Spirit upon him* (v. 1) to enable him to go through with his undertaking (61:1).

3. The work to which he was appointed; it was to *bring forth judgment to the Gentiles* (bring justice to the nations) (v. 1), that is, to set up a religious faith in the world to which the Gentiles would become bound and the blessings of which they would enjoy.

4. The mildness and tenderness with which he will pursue this undertaking (vv. 2–3). He will carry it out without noise. He will have no trumpet sounded before him, nor will any noisy retinue follow him. He will not resist the opposition he meets with, but will patiently *endure the contradiction of sinners against himself* (Heb 12:3). His kingdom is spiritual, and so its weapons are not weapons of the world (2Co 10:4), nor is its appearance self-important. He will be patient with evildoers; when he has begun to crush them, so that they are as bruised reeds, he will give them opportunity to repent. Although they are offensive, like smoking flax (65:5), he will still bear with them, as he did with Jerusalem. He will not despise those who are as weak as a reed, oppressed by doubts and fears, *as a bruised reed*, who are like *smoking flax* (v. 3), like the wick of a newly lit candle, which is about to go out. More is implied than is expressed. *He will not break the bruised reed* (v. 3) but will strengthen it, so it may become as a cedar in the courts of our God (Ps 92:12–13). *He will not quench the smoking flax* but will fan it into flame.

5. The courage and faithfulness with which he will persevere (v. 4) until he is able to say, *It is finished* (Jn 19:30). And he will enable his apostles and ministers not to fail or be discouraged until they also have finished their testimony (Rev 11:7). He *sets judgment* (establishes justice) *in the earth* (v. 4). He sets up his government in the world, a church for himself on earth. He reforms the world by the power of his Gospel and grace.

Verses 5–12

Here is:

1. The covenant God made with and the commission he gave to the Messiah (vv. 5–7).

1.1. The royal titles by which God in his greatness here makes himself known reveal his glory (v. 5). He is the fountain of all being and so the fountain of all power. In the upper world, *he created the heavens and stretched them out* (40:22). In the lower world, *he spread forth the earth* (v. 5) and made it a dwelling place, *and that which comes out of it* (v. 5) is produced by his power. And *He gives breath to the people upon it* (v. 5); he gives *spirit*, the powers and faculties of a rational soul. Now this introduces God's covenant with the Messiah and the commission given him, to show that the work of redemption was to restore human beings to the faithfulness they owe God as their Maker.

1.2. The assurances he gives to the Messiah of his presence with him speak much encouragement to him (v. 6). The Messiah was called by God. He was no intruder (Heb 5:4). When an angel was sent from heaven to strengthen him in his agony, the Father himself was with him, and this promise was fulfilled (Lk 22:43).

1.3. The great intentions of this commission express encouragement and strength to people. In giving us Christ, God has in him freely given us all the blessings of the new covenant (Ro 8:32; 1Co 2:12). In his Gospel, Christ brings with him two glorious blessings to the Gentile world: light and liberty. He is given *for a light to the Gentiles* (v. 6). By his Spirit in the word he presents the object; by his Spirit in the heart he prepared the organ with which to perceive the object. He is sent to proclaim liberty to the captives (61:1; Lk 4:18), as Cyrus did, *to bring out the prisoners* (v. 7), not only to open the prison doors and allow them to go out, which was all that Cyrus could do, but also to bring them out, to enable them to make use of their liberty. Christ does this by his grace.

2. The confirmation of this gift. Consider:

2.1. The authority of the One who makes the promise (v. 8): *I am the Lord, Jehovah, that is my name.* If he is the Lord who gives existence and birth to all things, he will give existence and birth to this promise.

2.2. The fulfillments of the promises he had formerly made concerning his church, which are proofs of the love he has for his people (v. 9): "*Behold, the former things have come to pass, and* now *new things do I declare* (v. 9). Now I will make new promises; now I will give you new favors. You have had an abundance of Old Testament blessings; now I declare New Testament blessings, not a fruitful country and rule over your neighbors, but *spiritual blessings in heavenly things* (Eph 1:3). *Before they spring forth* in the preaching of the Gospel, *I tell you of them* (v. 9), under the type of the former things."

3. The song of joy and praise that will then be sung to the glory of God (v. 10): *Sing unto the Lord a new song,* a New Testament song. The giving of Christ for *a light to the Gentiles* (v. 6) was something new. The praises of God's grace will be sung with joy and thankfulness:

3.1. By those who live *in the end of the earth* (v. 10), in countries that are farthest away from Jerusalem.

3.2. By sailors and merchants and all who *go down to the sea* (v. 10). The Jews traded little at sea; if, therefore, God's praises are to be sung by those who go down to the sea, it must be by the Gentiles.

3.3. By *the islands and the inhabitants thereof* (v. 10 and again v. 12).

3.4. *By the wilderness and the cities thereof, and the villages of Kedar* (v. 11). These lay east of Jerusalem, as the islands lay west.

3.5. *By the inhabitants of the rock* and those who live on *the tops of the mountains* (v. 11). *The inhabitants of the rock* may refer to the inhabitants of that part of Arabia that is called *Petraea*, "the rocky."

Verses 13–17

These verses may be the song itself that is to be sung by the Gentile world or a prophecy of what God will do to prepare for the singing of that song.

1. He will appear in his power and glory more than he ever has before. He did so in the preaching of his Gospel and in the wonderful success it had in the *pulling down of Satan's stronghold* (2Co 10:4) (vv. 13–14). *He will have long held his peace,* but now *he shall go forth* to attack the Devil's kingdom and give it a fatal blow. In the going out of the Gospel, Christ went out conquering and to conquer (Rev 6:2). The ministry of the apostles is called their *warfare* (2Co 10:4), and they were the soldiers of Jesus Christ. *He shall stir up jealousy* (his zeal) (v. 13); he will be more zealous than ever for his own name and against idolatry. *He shall cry* in the preaching of his word, *cry like a travailing woman* (a woman in childbirth) (v. 14), for the ministers of Christ preached passionately and were in the pains of childbirth until they saw Christ formed in the souls of the people (Gal 4:19). He will conquer by the power of his Spirit. As a type and figure of this, to make way for the redemption of the Jews from Babylon, God will break the power of their oppressors and *will at once destroy and devour* (v. 14) the Babylonian monarchy. In bringing about this destruction of Babylon by the Persian army under Cyrus, *he will make waste mountains and hills,* level the country, and *dry up all their herbs* (vegetation) (v. 15). The army will drain the fens and low grounds to make way for the march of their army. And similarly, when the Gospel is preached, it will have free course.

2. He will show his favor and grace. He will show the way to those who ask the way to Zion (Jer 50:5), and he will lead them in it (v. 16). God will *lead by a way that they knew not* (v. 16); he will show them the way to life and happiness in Jesus Christ, who is the Way (Jn 14:6). We see, for example, in the conversion of Paul, that he was struck blind first, and then God revealed his Son in him and made the scales fall from his eyes. God will *make darkness light before them* (v. 16). Insuperable difficulties lie in the way of their obedience, but God will make *crooked things straight* (rough places smooth) (v. 16); their way will be level. As a type of this, he will lead the Jews on a prepared road to their own land again.

3. He will confound those who are devoted to idols (v. 17). When the Babylonians see how the Jews, who despise their idols, are acknowledged and rescued by the God they worship, they will be ashamed that they ever said to these images, *You are our gods* (v. 17). In times of reformation, when sin and iniquity become unfashionable, we hope that those who would not otherwise be reclaimed will be when they realize the shame of idolatry.

Verses 18–25

Having encouraged the believing Jews, the prophet turns here to those among them who are unbelieving. In them there was a type of the Jews who rejected Christ and were rejected by him. Notice:

1. The call that is given to this people (v. 18): "*Hear, you deaf,* and listen to the joyful sound (Ps 89:15), *and look, you blind, that you may see* the joyful light." This call to the deaf to hear and to the blind to see is like the command given to the man who had the withered hand to stretch it out (Mt 12:10); even though he could not do this because it was withered, yet, if he had not attempted to do it, he would not have been healed.

2. How they are characterized (vv. 19–20): *Who is blind, but my servant, or deaf as my messenger?* The Jewish people professed to be God's servants, and their priests

and elders his messengers (Mal 2:7), but they were deaf and blind. He complains about their foolishness—they are blind—and about their stubbornness—they are deaf. They were even worse than the Gentiles themselves. Blindness and deafness in spiritual matters are worse in those who profess to be God's servants and messengers than in others. The prophet goes on (v. 20) to describe the blindness and stubbornness of the Jewish nation, just as our Savior describes it in his time (Mt 13:14–15).

3. The care God will take of the honor of his own name despite their blindness and deafness. The Scripture was fulfilled in the rejecting of the Jews as well as in the calling in of the Gentiles. *He will magnify* (make great) *the law*—divine revelation in every part—*and will make it honourable* (v. 21). The law is truly honorable and glorious, and if people will not make it great by their obedience to it, God will exalt it by punishing them for their disobedience.

4. The calamities God will bring on the Jewish nation for their deliberate blindness and deafness (v. 22). They are *robbed and spoiled* (plundered and looted). Those who were impenitent and unreformed in Babylon were sentenced to perpetual captivity. It was because of their sins that they were plundered of all their possessions. Some of them were *snared in holes* (trapped in pits), and others *hidden in prison houses* (v. 22). They lie there, and they are likely to remain lying there. This had its complete fulfillment in the final destruction of the Jewish nation by the Romans.

5. The counsel given them to help them, for although their case is sad, it is not desperate.

5.1. Most of them are deaf; they will not listen to the voice of God's word. He will therefore use his rod of discipline and see *who among them will give ear to that* (v. 23). If one method is not effective, another one may be. We may all of us, if we want to, hear the voice of God. In listening to the word we must listen for the hereafter; we must especially listen for eternity.

5.2. The counsel itself is that they must acknowledge the hand of God in suffering and, whoever were the instruments, look to him as the Prime Mover (v. 24): "*Who gave Jacob and Israel*, that people who used to have such a privileged position in heaven and such rule on earth? Who made them loot for the plunderers, as they are now to the Babylonians and to the Romans? *Did not the Lord?*" They must also acknowledge that they had caused God to abandon them and had brought all these calamities on themselves. It is he *against whom we have sinned* (v. 24); the prophet includes himself among the sinners (Da 9:7–8). Notice the trouble sin causes; it provokes God to be angry with a people and so kindles a universal fire, setting everything ablaze.

CHAPTER 43

The contents of this chapter are much the same as those of the previous one: 1. Precious promises made to God's people in their suffering that he would be with them to support them in it and that he would rescue them from it (vv. 1–7). 2. A challenge to idols to compete with the omniscience and omnipotence of God (vv. 8–13). 3. Encouragement given to the people of God to hope for their rescue from Babylon (vv. 14–21). 4. A method taken to prepare the people by reminding them of their sins, so that they might repent and seek mercy (vv. 22–28).

Verses 1–7

This chapter has a clear connection with the end of the previous chapter. It was said there that Jacob and Israel would not walk in God's ways, and now one would have thought it would have followed that God would abandon them, but no! The next words are, *But now, fear not, O Jacob! O Israel! I have redeemed thee, and thou art mine* (v. 1). Although many of them would not change from their hardened ways, God would still continue his love for his people, and the main part of that nation would still be reserved for mercy (1Ki 19:18; Ro 11:4). Now the sun suddenly breaks out from behind a thick and dark cloud and shines with a pleasant surprise. The expressions of God's goodwill to his people here convey much encouragement to all the spiritual descendants of upright Jacob and praying Israel. Here we have:

1. The reasons for God's care and concern for his people. Although Jacob and Israel are sinful and miserable, they will still be looked after, for:

1.1. They are God's *workmanship, created by him unto good works* (Eph 2:10). He has created them, not only given them existence but also formed them into a people, constituted their government, and incorporated them by the charter of his covenant.

1.2. They are the people he has bought: he has redeemed them. Out of the land of Egypt he first redeemed them, and out of many other forms of slavery, *in his love and in his pity* (63:9); much more will he take care of those who have been redeemed by the blood of his Son.

1.3. They are his own special people: he has called them out by name.

1.4. He is their God in a covenant relationship with them (v. 3). Those who have God for them need not fear who or what can be against them (Ro 8:31).

2. Former examples of this care.

2.1. God has paid a high price for them: *I gave Egypt for thy ransom* (v. 3). The Ethiopians (Cushites) invaded them in Asa's time, but they would be destroyed rather than Israel be disturbed. What are Cush and Seba, all their lives and all their treasures, compared with the blood of Christ?

2.2. He has prized them accordingly, and they are very dear to him (v. 4).

3. Further examples God would still show them of his care and kindness.

3.1. He would be present with them in their greatest difficulties and dangers (v. 2).

3.2. He would still, when the occasion arose, make all the interests of the nations give way to the interests of his own children.

3.3. Those of them who were scattered and dispersed in other nations would all be gathered and share in the blessings of the community (vv. 5–7). Some of the descendants of Israel were dispersed to all countries, but those whose hearts God had moved to go to Jerusalem would be drawn from all parts (Ezr 1:4). But who are the descendants of Israel that will be so carefully gathered? He tells us (v. 7) that they are those whom God has marked out for mercy. They are called by his name. They are created for his glory. God is with the church, and so let his church not fear; no one who belongs to the church will be lost.

Verses 8–13

God here challenges the worshipers of idols to prove that their false gods are divine.

1. Their gods have *eyes and see not, ears and hear not*, and those who make them and trust in them are like them (Ps 115:8). Idolaters have human shape, abilities, and faculties, but they are, in effect, devoid of reason and common sense, or they would never worship gods of their own making.

2. God's witnesses are summoned to appear and give evidence for him (v. 10): "*You, O Israelites*, all you who are *called by my name, you are all my witnesses, and so is my servant whom I have chosen.*" It was Christ himself who was described in this way (42:1): *My servant and my elect.*

2.1. All the prophets who testified to Christ, and Christ himself, the great Prophet, are here appealed to as God's witnesses. God's people are witnesses for him and can declare, according to their own experience, the power of his grace. But it is particularly the Messiah who is given as a witness for God to the people, having been in the closest possible relationship with his Father from eternity.

2.2. Let us see what the point is that these witnesses are called to prove (v. 12): "*You are my witnesses, saith the Lord, that I am God.* I am a Being who is self-existent and self-sufficient. I am the One whom you are to fear, worship, and trust in. In fact (v. 13), *before the day was,* from ancient days, before the first day of time, before light was created, and so from eternity, *I am he.*" The idols were gods, or rather, they were fictitious gods, created by human beings. *By nature they were no gods* (Gal 4:8). But God has existed from eternity, before there were either idols or idolaters — let us not forget that truth is more ancient than error — and he will exist to eternity. "*I, even I, am the Lord,* the great Jehovah, who is, was, and is to come (Rev 1:4), and *besides me there is no Saviour*" (v. 11)." God has infinite and infallible knowledge, as is clear from the predictions of his word (v. 12): *I have declared and I have shown* what has been fulfilled without fail. He has infinite and irresistible power. He pleads not only, "I have *shown,*" but also, "I have *saved*" (v. 13). The gods of the nations cannot even inspire a historian, much less a prophet. They are challenged to take issue with this: *Let them bring forth their witnesses* (v. 9) to prove their perfect knowledge and power.

Verses 14–21

1. God here takes to himself titles that are very encouraging to his people. He is *the Lord their Redeemer* (v. 14), the *Holy One of Israel* (v. 14), and again (v. 15), *their Holy One,* and he will therefore fulfill every word he has spoken to them. He is *the Creator of Israel,* the One who made them to be a people out of nothing, and he is their *King.*

2. He assures them he will break the power of their oppressors (14:17). God will take care to send a ruler to Babylon who will bring down all their nobles and all their people too, even the Babylonians, *whose cry is in the ships,* or whose cry is to the ships, as their refuge when the city is taken, so that they may escape by the river.

3. He reminds them of the great things he did for their ancestors when he brought them out of Egypt (vv. 16–17). "He who did this can make a way for you in the sea when you return from Babylon."

4. He promises to do even greater things for them than he has done in the past. They will see them repeated; in fact, they will see them surpassed (v. 18): "Do not remember the former things so as to undervalue what is going on at present, as if the former days were better than these times (Ecc 7:10). Behold, the Lord will do something new." The best explanation of this is in Jer 16:14–15; 23:7–8. Although former mercies must not be forgotten, fresh mercies must be especially made the most of.

5. He promises not only to rescue them from Babylon but also to lead them safely and comfortably to their own land (vv. 19–20): *I will make a way in the wilderness and rivers in the desert.* The same power that *made a way in*

the sea (v. 16) can also make *a way in the wilderness.* And the One who made dry land in the waters can also produce water in the driest land, in such abundance as to give *drink* not only *to his people, his chosen,* but also to the wild animals (v. 20), *the dragons* (jackals) and *the owls,* which are therefore said to honor God for it. This looks forward not only to God's care of the Jewish church between their return from Babylon and the coming of Christ but also to the grace of the Gospel, especially as it is revealed to the Gentile world. The Gentile sinners, who had been as the wild animals, running wild, fierce as the jackals, stupid as the owls, will be brought to honor God for his grace.

6. He traces all these promised blessings back to their great origin (v. 21): *This people have I formed for myself,* and so I do all this for them, so that they may *show forth my praise.* The new heaven, the new earth, the new humanity (Eph 2:15; 4:24; Col 3:10), are God's handiwork; they are fashioned according to his will. Just as he formed us, so he also feeds us, keeps us, and leads us.

Verses 22–28

This accusation is included here to clear God's justice in taking them into exile. They neglected God and rejected him, and so he justly rejected them and *gave them to the curse* (v. 28), and they must be brought to confess this before they are prepared to be rescued. Notice:

1. The sins that they are accused of here.

1.1. Omissions of the good that God had commanded. Notice how it begins with a *but* (v. 22); compare v. 21, where God tells them what favors he has given them and what his just expectations of them are. But they had made a very poor response to him for his favors. They had rejected prayer: *Thou hast not called upon me, O Jacob!* (v. 22). Jacob was a man famous for prayer (Hos 12:4). To boast about the name of Jacob but live without prayer is to mock God and deceive ourselves. They had become weary of their religion. They begrudged the expense of their devotion. They wanted a religious faith on the cheap, and they wanted to be excused from those acts of devotion that were costly. They had *not brought* even their *small cattle* (v. 23), the sheep or lambs and kids, which God required for *burnt offerings* (v. 23); much less did they bring their greater cattle. *Sweet cane,* or fragrant calamus, was used for the holy oil, incense, and perfume, but they were not willing to bear the cost of that (v. 24). Their sacrifices were, in effect, as good as no sacrifices at all (v. 23): *Neither hast thou honoured me with thy sacrifices.* Sacrificing, as God had appointed it, was not burdensome; it was not a service they had any reason to complain about: "*I have not caused thee to serve with an offering* (v. 23); I have not made it a drudgery to you. I have *not wearied thee with incense*" (v. 23). They had many festivals and good days, but only one day in the whole year on which they were to humble their souls, on the Day of Atonement (Lev 16:29, 31). Although in comparison with Christ's easy yoke the ordinances of the ceremonial law are spoken of as heavy (Ac 15:10), in comparison with the service that idolaters gave to their false gods, they were light. God did not require them to sacrifice their children, as Molech did.

1.2. Commissions of the evil that God had forbidden: *Thou hast made me to serve* (burdened me) *with thy sins* (v. 24). When we make God's gifts the fuel for our sinful desires, then we are burdening God with our sins. God had not burdened them with their sacrifices, but they had burdened him with their sins. The master had not tired out the servants with his commands, but they had tired him out with their disobedience.

2. What emphasized their sin (v. 27):

2.1. That they were children of disobedience (Eph 5:6; Col 3:6), for their *first father*—that is, their ancestors—*had sinned.*

2.2. That they had learned disobedience too, for *their teachers had transgressed against God* (v. 27). Those he had sent to teach them were guilty of gross, scandalous sins, and the people, no doubt, would learn from them to follow those sins.

3. What were the signs of God's displeasure toward them for their sins (v. 23). *I have profaned the princes of the sanctuary* (have disgraced the dignitaries of your temple) (v. 28), that is, the priests and Levites who presided with great dignity in the temple services. They disgraced themselves and made themselves corrupt by their heinous sins, and then God dishonored them and made them despised and humiliated by their calamities (Mal 2:9). Similarly, the honor of their state was ruined: "*I have given Jacob to the curse* (I will consign Jacob to destruction) (v. 28), that is, to be cursed, hated, and mistreated by all their neighbors, *and Israel to reproach* (v. 28), to be scorned, ridiculed, and gloated over by their enemies."

4. What were the riches of God's mercy toward them nevertheless (v. 25): *I, even I, am he who* despite all this *blotteth out thy transgressions.*

4.1. This gracious declaration of God's readiness to forgive sin is strangely included. The accusation ran very high: *Thou hast wearied me with thy iniquities* (v. 24). Now one would have thought it would follow: "*I, even I, am he* who will destroy you and will burden myself no longer with being concerned for you." No; *I, even I, am he that will forgive thee*—as if God in his greatness wants to teach us that forgiving wrongs is the best way to keep ourselves from being wearied with them. We may apply this to the forgiving of the sins of every individual believing penitent. Notice how the pardon is expressed: he *will blot them out,* as a cloud is blotted out by the rays of the sun (44:22), as a debt is blotted out so as not to appear against the debtor—the account line is crossed out as if the debt were paid, because it is pardoned on the basis of the payment that has been pledged. He *will not remember* (v. 25) the sin: not only will he remit the punishment, but the sin will not lessen his love in the future. When God forgives, he forgets. It is not for the sake of anything in us, but for his own sake, for his mercies' sake, and especially for his Son's sake.

4.2. The words (v. 26) *Put me in remembrance* may be understood either:

4.2.1. As a rebuke to a proud Pharisee, who expects to find favor for his merits and not to be indebted to free grace (Lk 18:11–12): "If you have anything to offer for the sake of which you should be pardoned, remind me of it." Or:

4.2.2. As a direction and encouragement to a penitent tax collector (Lk 18:13). Let us remind God of the promises he has made to those who repent, and of the atonement his Son has made for them. This is the only way, and it is a sure way, to peace. *Only acknowledge thy transgression* (Jer 3:13).

CHAPTER 44

God, through the prophet, continues in this chapter: 1. To encourage his people with the assurance of great blessings he has in store for them at their return from exile. These blessings were types of much greater blessings in the days of the Messiah (vv. 1–8). 2. To expose the foolishness of idol makers and idol worshipers (vv. 9–20).

3. To confirm the assurance he has given his people of those great blessings and to raise their joyful expectations (vv. 21–28).

Verses 1–8

Two great truths are explained in these verses:

1. That the people of God are a happy people, especially because of the covenant between them and God. Three things complete their happiness:

1.1. The covenant relationship in which they stand with God (vv. 1–2). Israel is called *Jeshurun* here, "the upright one," for only those, like Nathanael, in whom there is nothing false are true Israelites (Jn 1:47). Jacob and Israel were described as very offensive to God and provoking to his wrath, but mercy steps in with a *yet*: "*Yet now hear, O Jacob my servant!* (v. 1), you and I will be friends again despite all this." "I will do such and such for them," says God (Heb 8:12), *for I will be merciful to their unrighteousness.* The relationship in which his people now stand with him is very encouraging. They are his *servants.* They are his *chosen* ones, and he will maintain his choice. He takes those whom he has chosen under his special protection. They are his creatures. He *made them,* and so he will help them overcome their difficulties in their service.

1.2. The covenant blessings he has kept for them and theirs (vv. 3–4):

1.2.1. Those who are aware of their spiritual needs and of the insufficiency of any part of the creation to satisfy them will find deep satisfaction in God: *I will pour water upon him that is thirsty* (v. 3).

1.2.2. Those who are as barren as dry ground will be watered by the grace of God.

1.2.3. The water God will pour out is *his Spirit* (Jn 7:39). This is the great New Testament promise, that having sent his servant Christ and upheld him, God will also send his Spirit to uphold us. God will give the spirit of adoption (Ro 8:15) to all who share in the privileges of adoption (Gal 4:5; Eph 1:5). Through these covenant blessings there will be a great increase of the church. It will be spread to distant places (v. 4).

1.3. The assent they cheerfully give to their side of the covenant (v. 5). Many people of other nationalities joined themselves to the Jews when they returned from their captivity, invited by that glorious appearance of God for them (Zec 8:23; Est 8:17). No doubt this verse looks further, too, to the conversion of the Gentiles. These converts are *one and another,* very many people of different ranks and nations, and all are welcome to God (Col 3:11). Everyone will say for themselves, "*I am the Lord's* (v. 5); whether I live or die, I will belong to him." They will *call themselves by the name of Jacob* (v. 5). They will love all God's people and be willing to share their lot with them in every scene of life. They will do this very solemnly. Some of them will *subscribe* (write) *with their hand unto the Lord* (v. 5), as, when confirming an agreement, we write our signature on it and make a formal act and deed. The more explicit we are in covenanting with God, the better (Ex 24:7; Jos 24:26–27; Ne 9:38).

2. That just as the Israel of God is a happy people, so the God of Israel is a great God, and he alone is God. This speaks deep satisfaction to all who trust in him (vv. 6–8). The God we trust in is a God of undeniable sovereignty and irresistible power. He is *the Lord,* Jehovah, self-existent and self-sufficient. He is *the Lord of hosts,* Lord of all the powers of heaven and earth, of angels and human beings. He is *the King of Israel and his Redeemer* (v. 6), and those who take God as their King

will have him as their Redeemer. He is God from eternity, before the world was, and will be so to eternity. If there were not a God to create things, nothing would ever have existed, and if there were not a God to uphold everything, all would soon come to nothing again. He alone is God (v. 6): *Besides me there is no God.* There is no God besides Jehovah. He is all-sufficient, and so there need be no other god. His people need not put their hope in any other god. Those on whom the sun shines need neither moon nor stars nor the light of their own fire. His people also need not fear any other god. None besides God can foretell future things, which God now by his prophet gives notice of to the world, more than 200 years before they come to pass (v. 7).

Verses 9–20

This speech is intended:

- To strengthen the people of Israel against the strong temptation to worship idols when they were in exile in Babylon because it was the custom of the country and because they wanted to please those who were then their lords and masters.
- To heal them of their tendency to idolatry, which was the sin that most easily entangled them (Heb 12:1), the sin they were sent into Babylon to be reformed away from. As the rod of God's correction is used to enforce the word, so the word of God is useful to explain the rod of correction.
- To provide them with something to say to their Babylonians taskmasters. When their taskmasters gloated over them, when they asked, *Where is your God?* the Jews could in response ask them, *What are your gods?*

To convict the idolaters, we have:

1. A challenge given them to clear themselves from the allegation of the most shameful foolishness (vv. 9–11). They set their minds to conceive idols and their hands to make them, and they call them *their delectable things* (the things they treasure). We tell them that they are only deceiving themselves and one another. *Their delectable things shall not profit* (the things they treasure are worthless to) (v. 9) them; they can neither supply them with good nor protect them from evil. The *graven images* are *profitable for nothing* at all (v. 10). Their worshipers *are their own witnesses* (v. 9); they witness against themselves — if only they could allow their own consciences to deal faithfully with them — that they are blind and ignorant in doing this. *Who has formed a god?* (v. 10). Who but someone who is mad or out of their mind would think of making a god? If they make something and treat it as a god, whom do they suppose their own maker to be? *The workmen* that formed this god are only human beings (v. 11). They are weak and helpless and so cannot possibly make a being that will be all-powerful.

2. A particular account of the whole process of making a god.

2.1. The people employed in this task are skilled workers of the lowliest sort, the same that you would employ in making ordinary tools like a cart or a plow. You must have *a smith*, a blacksmith, who *with the tongs works in the coals* (v. 12), and it is hard work. He cannot allow himself time to eat or drink, for *he drinks no water, and so is faint* (v. 12). The plates with which the smith is to cover the idol, or whatever ironwork is to be done around it, he fashions with hammers, and he works precisely, according to the model given him. Then comes the carpenter, and he takes as much care and effort over the timberwork (v. 13). He brings his box of tools with him, for he needs them

all. He stretches out his ruler against the piece of wood, marking off with a line the point at which it must be cut off. He fits it, or polishes it, with planes, the greater first and then the lesser, and he uses compasses to mark its size and shape; it is then just as he wants.

2.2. The form in which it is made is that of a human being, a poor, weak mortal, but it is the noblest form that he knows. He makes the idol according to the beauty of the human form, which is appealing and attractive to human beings but altogether inappropriate to represent the beauty of the Lord. God put great honor on human beings when, in regard to their souls, he made them in the image of God. Human beings, however, show great dishonor to God when they make him, in respect of physical parts, in the image of human beings. All the beauty of the physical human form, when claimed to be given to the One who is infinite Spirit, is a deformity to and a diminishing of him. And when the attractive piece is finished, it must remain in the shrine or temple prepared for it.

2.3. The material of which it is mostly made is a sorry substance to make a god from; it is *the stock of a tree* (a block of wood) (v. 19).

2.3.1. The tree itself was taken from the forest, where it grew among other trees and was no better or more valuable than its neighbors. It was a cedar, or perhaps a cypress or an oak (v. 14). Perhaps he had his eye on it some time before to use it in this way, and *he strengthened it for himself*, somehow made it stronger and made it grow better than other trees. Or, it may be, he prefers to take an ash, which grows more quickly, which he himself had planted for this use and which has been nurtured by rain from heaven. What disrespect he is showing the God of heaven by setting up as a rival what was nourished by his rain, the rain that falls on the just and unjust (Mt 5:45).

2.3.2. The branches of this tree were good for nothing except fuel; they were put to that use, and so were the pieces that were cut off (vv. 15–16). We can see that that tree has no innate goodness for its own protection, for it is as capable of being burned as any other tree, and we can see that he who chose it put no greater value on it than on any other tree, for he has no qualms about throwing part of it onto the fire as ordinary rubbish; he asks no question for conscience's sake. It serves as a fire to keep him warm: *He will take thereof and warm himself* (v. 15), and he finds comfort from it. *Aha! I am warm; I have seen the fire*, and certainly the part of the tree that served as fuel, the use for which God and nature intended it, does him much greater kindness and gives him more satisfaction than will the part he uses to make a god. It serves as a fire to cook things on: he *roasteth roast* (his meat) *and is satisfied* that he has not done wrong to use it in this way. It serves as an oven: *He kindles it and bakes bread* with its heat, and no one accuses him of doing wrong.

2.3.3. Yet after all this, the block of wood that remains will serve to make a god out of, though it might as well have been used to make a bench. When the foolish idolater has served the lowest purposes with part of his tree, and the rest has had time to season, *he makes it a graven image* (an idol), *and falls down thereto* (bows down to it) (v. 15), that is, *the residue thereof* (from the rest) he *makes a god, even his graven image* (v. 17). He *falls down to it, and worships it*; *he prays to it*, depending on it and having great expectations of it; *he saith, Deliver me, for thou art my god.*

3. Here is judgment given on this whole matter (vv. 18–20). Human beings have become worse than the beasts that perish (Ps 49:12, 20), for the beasts act according to the dictates of sense, but human beings do

not act according to the dictates of reason (v. 18). People who act rationally in other matters act most absurdly here. They are rebels against the great principle of stopping to think (v. 19). *None considers in his heart*, no one stops to think, nor has so much diligence as to reason with himself: "I have burned part of this tree in the fire, for baking and roasting, and now shall I use what is left to make a detestable thing? Shall I be such a fool as to fall down to the block of wood—something that is simply lifeless and helpless?" These idolaters deceive themselves (v. 20): *They feed on ashes*; they will be as disappointed as would a person who expected to be nourished by feeding on ashes. The apostasy of sinners from God is owing entirely to themselves and to the evil heart of unbelief that is within them. None of them can be persuaded to suspect themselves and say, *Is there not a lie in my right hand?* Is not this thing in my right hand a lie? and so to think of saving their soul. Being suspicious of ourselves is the first step toward rescuing ourselves.

Verses 21–28

In these verses we have:

1. The duty that Jacob and Israel, now in exile, were called to, so that they might be qualified for restoration. Our first concern must be to gain good from our afflictions, and then we may hope to leave them. The duty is expressed in two words: *Remember* and *return*.

- "*Remember these, O Jacob!* (v. 21). Remember the foolishness of idolatry and that *thou art my servant* (v. 21), and so you must not serve other masters."
- *Return unto me* (v. 22).

2. The favors of which Jacob and Israel, now in exile, were assured; and what God here promises to give them when they remember and return to him is in a spiritual sense promised to all who similarly return to God. When we begin to remember God, he will begin to remember us. It is he who remembers us first. Notice:

2.1. The basis on which God's favorable intentions to his people rest.

2.1.1. They are his servants, and so he has a just quarrel with those who detain them. *Let my people go, that they may serve me* (Ex 7:16).

2.1.2. He formed them into a people (v. 24). From the early beginnings of their growth into a nation they were under his particular care.

2.1.3. He has redeemed them in the past. He is still the same God. *The Lord has redeemed Jacob* (v. 23); he is about to do it and has determined to do it because he is the Lord their Redeemer (v. 24).

2.1.4. He has *glorified himself in them* (v. 23) and so will continue to do so (Jn 12:28).

2.1.5. He has pardoned their sins, which were the only obstruction to their being rescued (v. 22). He will break the yoke of exile *because he has blotted out, as a thick cloud, their transgressions*. Our offenses and our sins, like a cloud, come between heaven and earth. When God pardons sin, he sweeps away this thick cloud, so that relations with heaven are restored.

2.2. The universal joy that will accompany the rescue of God's people (v. 23): *Sing, O you heavens!* The whole creation will have cause to rejoice at the redemption of God's people. The creation is assured that although it now groans, being burdened, it will ultimately be rescued from bondage to decay (Ro 8:21–22). The greatest establishment of the world is the kingdom of God in it (Ps 96:11–13; 98:7–9). The angels will rejoice in it. The heavens will sing, for the Lord has done it. And there is

joy in heaven when God and people are reconciled (Lk 15:7). Even the inhabitants of the Gentile world will join in these praises, because they share in these joys.

2.3. The encouragement we have to hope that although great difficulties lie in the way of the church's restoration, yet, when the time comes, they will all be easily overcome, for "*thus saith Israel's Redeemer, I am the Lord that maketh all things* (v. 24). I am the One who made them at first and is still making them," for providence is a continuing creation.

2.4. The confusion that this will give the so-called oracles of Babylon by conclusively refuting the claims of their religion (v. 25). By rescuing his people from Babylon, God will *frustrate the tokens of the liars*, foil the signs of all the false prophets, who said the Babylonian monarchy would last for many years in the future. He will baffle not only their false prophets but also their celebrated politicians: he overthrows the learning of the wise (v. 25). Those who come to know Christ see all their previous knowledge to be foolishness in comparison with knowing him, and his enemies will find all their advice turned into foolishness (2Sa 15:31; 17:14) and see themselves *taken in their own craftiness* (1Co 3:19).

2.5. The confirmation this would give to the true authority of God, which the Jews had distrusted and their enemies despised: *God confirms the word of his servant* (v. 26) and *performs the counsel* (predictions) *of the messengers* whom he has sent to his people many times.

2.6. The particular favors God intended for his people, who were now in exile (vv. 26–28).

2.6.1. It is supposed here that Jerusalem and the towns of Judah will for a time lie in ruins, depopulated and uninhabited, but it is promised that they will be rebuilt and repopulated. God has said to Jerusalem, *Thou shalt be inhabited* (v. 26), for while the world stands, God will have a church in it. The towns of Judah will be rebuilt. The Assyrian army under Sennacherib only took them, and then, on the defeat of that army, the towns returned undamaged to the rightful owners, but the Babylonian army demolished them and, by taking away their inhabitants, left them to decay. But these desolations will not last forever. God will *raise up the* wastes and *decayed places thereof* (v. 26).

2.6.2. It is supposed here that the temple too will be destroyed and that it will lie for a time razed to its foundations, but it is promised that its foundations will again be laid, and then no doubt they will be built on. Just as the desolation of the sanctuary was the most mournful part of the destruction to all the godly Jews, so its restoration and reestablishment will be the most joyful part of their restoration.

2.6.3. It is supposed here that very great difficulties will lie in the path of this restoration, but it is promised that by divine power they will all be removed (v. 27): *God saith to the deep, Be dry*. He did this when he brought Israel out of Egypt, and he will do so again when he brings them out of Babylon. "*Who art thou, O great deep?* Are you slowing down their passage and thinking you can block it? You will be dry." When Cyrus took Babylon by draining the Euphrates River into many channels and so making it passable for his army, this was fulfilled. *God saith of Cyrus, He is my shepherd* (v. 28). Israel is God's people and the sheep of his pasture (Ps 100:3). These sheep are now in the midst of wolves; they have been impounded for trespassing. Now Cyrus will be his shepherd, employed by him to release these sheep. It was more commendable for Cyrus to be God's shepherd than to be emperor of Persia. God makes what use he pleases of people; in those very things in which they are serving themselves, not looking beyond that, God is serving his own purposes through them.

CHAPTER 45

In the previous chapter Cyrus was named as God's shepherd; he was to be a type of the great Redeemer. We have here: 1. The great things God would do for Cyrus so that he might release God's people (vv. 1–4). 2. The proof God would give of his eternal power (vv. 5–7). 3. A prayer for the hastening of this restoration (v. 8). 4. A restraint to the unfaithful Jews (vv. 9–10). 5. Encouragement given to the faithful Jews, who trusted in God and continued to be bold in prayer (vv. 11–15). 6. A challenge given to the worshipers of idols and their condemnation read out, and satisfaction given to the worshipers of the true God and their comfort secured (vv. 16–25).

Verses 1–4

Cyrus was a Mede, descended, according to some, from Astyages, king of Media. The pagan writers are not agreed in their accounts of his origin. Some tell us that in his infancy he was an outcast, left exposed, and was saved from perishing by a herdsman's wife. However, it is agreed that Croesus king of Lydia attacked his country, and that Cyrus repelled the attack, pursuing the advantages he had gained against Croesus with such vigor that in a short time he took Sardis and controlled the rich kingdom of Lydia and its many provinces. This made him very great, for Croesus was proverbially rich, but it was nearly ten years later that, together with his uncle Darius and with the forces of Persia, he made this famous attack on Babylon. Babylon had now grown rich and strong. Some say the walls were so thick that six chariots could drive abreast on them. Cyrus had a great ambition to control this place, and at last he accomplished it. Here, years before it took place, we are told:

1. What great things God will do for him to put it into his power to release his people. In order to do this Cyrus will become a mighty conqueror and a wealthy monarch, and nations will pay him tribute and help him with both soldiers and money. Cyrus is here called God's *anointed*, because he was intended for this great service by God, and he was to be a type of the Messiah. God commits himself to take hold of Cyrus's right hand, as Elisha put his hands on the king's hands when he was to shoot his arrow against Aram (2Ki 13:16). Being under such direction:

1.1. He will extend his conquests very far and will make light of all opposition. Well-populated kingdoms will give in to him. God *will subdue nations before him* (v. 1). The battle is God's, and so the victory is his. Powerful rulers will fall before him: *I will loose the loins of kings* (v. 1), and this was literally fulfilled in Belshazzar, for when he was terrified by the writing on the wall, *the joints of his loins were loosed* (Da 5:6). Great cities will surrender to him. God will incline the keepers of the city to *open before him the two-leaved gates* (v. 1), from a full conviction that it is futile to oppose him. The longest and most dangerous marches will be made easy for him, and the path ready for him: *I will go before thee* to clear the way and lead you on it, and then the *crooked places* will be made *straight* (v. 2), or, as some read it, the mountains will be leveled and made even. No opposition will stand before him. The One who gives him his commission *will break in pieces the gates of brass* (break down the gates of bronze) that are shut against him, *and cut asunder* (through) *the bars of iron* (v. 2) with which they

are fastened. This was fulfilled literally if what Herodotus reports is true, that the city of Babylon had 100 bronze gates, with posts and hooks of the same metal.

1.2. He will fill his coffers (v. 3): *I will give thee the treasures of darkness*, treasures of gold and silver that have been buried underground by the inhabitants. Cyrus acknowledged God's goodness to him and, in consideration of that, released the captives. *God has given me all the kingdoms of the earth* (Ezr 1:2) and so has made *me build him a house at Jerusalem*.

2. What God intended in doing all this for Cyrus.

2.1. *"That thou mayest know* by all this *that I the Lord am the God of Israel*, for I have *called thee by thy name* (v. 3) long before you were born."

2.2. It was that the Israel of God might be released (v. 4). Though he did not know God, God indicated he was his shepherd. He called him by his name, *Cyrus*, and called him his *anointed*. And why did God do all this for Cyrus? Not for Cyrus's own sake; it is questioned whether he was a good man or not. Although when Xenophon wanted to describe the heroic virtues of an excellent ruler, he used Cyrus's name, other historians describe him as haughty, cruel, and bloodthirsty. The reason God advanced him was *for Jacob his servant's sake* (v. 4). Cyrus was a type of Christ, victorious over principalities and powers (Eph 1:21; Col 2:10) and entrusted with unsearchable riches (Eph 3:8) for the use and benefit of God's servants. *When he ascended on high, he led captivity captive* (Eph 4:8), took captive those who had taken others captive, and *opened the prison to those that were bound* (61:1).

Verses 5–10

God here asserts his exclusive sovereignty, revealed to the world in all the great things he did for and through Cyrus. Notice:

1. This teaching is set down here in two things:

1.1. That there is no God besides him. This is a fundamental truth that, if it were firmly believed, would remove idolatry from the world. Notice the awesome, commanding air of majesty and authority with which God in his greatness here declares it to the world: *I am the Lord, I the Lord, Jehovah*, and *there is none else, there is no God besides me* (v. 5), no other self-existent, self-sufficient, infinite, and eternal. *I am the Lord, and there is none else.* This is said to Cyrus here not only to heal him of the sin of his ancestors, which was the worshiping of idols, but also to prevent his falling into the sin of some of those before him who had achieved victory and universal monarchy, the sin of setting themselves up as gods and being idolized. Let Cyrus remember that he remains only human and that there is no God but one.

1.2. That he is Lord of all, and nothing is done without him (v. 7): *I form the light, and I create darkness. I make peace*—which stands here for all good—and *I create evil*, not the evil of sin—God is not the author of that—but the evil of punishment. Light and darkness are opposites. In the revolution of every day, each takes its turn. The same cause of both is he who is the Prime Mover, the ultimate cause of everything. He who formed the natural light (Ge 1:3) still forms the light of providence. He who originally made peace among the disharmonious principles of nature makes peace in human lives. He who allowed the natural darkness, which was mere deprivation, creates providential darkness.

2. How this teaching is here proved and declared.

2.1. It is proved by what God did for Cyrus: *There is no God besides me*, for (v. 5) *I girded* (strengthened) *thee, though thou hast not known me*. It can be seen from this that the God of Israel makes whatever use he pleases even of those who do not know him and who worship other gods.

2.2. It is declared to all the world by the word of God, by his providence, and by the testimony of the suffering Jews in Babylon. The wonderful restoration of the Israel of God declared to all the world that *there is none like unto the God of Jeshurun, that rides on the heavens for their help* (Dt 33:26).

3. How this teaching is here made the most of and applied. It is used:

3.1. To encourage those who quietly waited for the redemption of Israel (v. 8): *Drop down, you heavens, from above.* Some take this as the saints' prayer to be rescued. I prefer to take it as God's command for it, for he is said to *command deliverances* (Ps 44:4). All the creatures will play their part in carrying out this great work. We must not expect salvation without righteousness, for they spring up together, and together the Lord has created them. Christ died to save us from our sins, not in our sins, and he has become our redemption by becoming our righteousness and sanctification (1Co 1:30). This great restoration is from heaven, and if our hearts are open to receive it, the fruit will be the fruits of righteousness (Php 1:11) and his great salvation (Heb 2:3).

3.2. To rebuke those of the church's enemies who opposed this salvation, or those of its friends who despaired of it (v. 9): *Woe unto him that strives with his Maker!* Woe to the insulting Babylonians who defy God and will not let his people go (Ex 5:1; 7:16; etc.)! Let not the oppressed, in dejection, quarrel with God about the prolonging of their exile, "*Shall the clay say to him that forms it, 'What makest thou?* (v. 9). Why are you making me this shape and not that one?'" Will we challenge God's wisdom or question his power, we who are ourselves so fearfully and wonderfully made (Ps 139:14)? Will we say of the One whose hands made us and in whose hands we are, *He has no hands* (v. 9)? This is as unnatural as children finding fault with their parents, saying to their father, *What begettest thou?* or to their mother, "*What hast thou brought forth?* (v. 10). Why was I not born an angel, exempt from the weaknesses of human nature and the adversities of human life?"

Verses 11–19

The people in exile reconciled themselves to the will of God and were content to wait to be delivered in his time, and they are assured they will not wait in vain.

1. They are invited to ask about the outcome of their troubles (v. 11). "*Ask of me things to come*; turn to the prophets and see what they say. Ask the watchmen, *What of the night?* Ask them, *How long?*" We may not fight against our Maker by making emotional complaints, but we may wrestle with him in faithful and fervent prayer. Notice the power of prayer and its effectiveness with God: *Thou shalt cry, and he shall say, Here I am* (58:9); *what would you that I should do unto you?* (Mk 10:51).

2. They are encouraged to depend on the power of God when they are brought to a very low position and are completely unable to help themselves (v. 12). Their *help stands in the name of the Lord, who made heaven and earth* (Ps 121:2).

3. They are particularly told what God will do for them. This will lead them to expect a more glorious Redeemer, of whom Cyrus was a type.

3.1. Liberty will be proclaimed to them (v. 13). Cyrus is the man who will proclaim it: *I have raised him up in righteousness*, that is, according to my promises; and *I will direct all his ways* (v. 13). Cyrus must do two things for God:

3.1.1. Jerusalem is God's city, now in ruins, and he must rebuild it.

3.1.2. Israel is God's people, but they are now exiles, and he must release them, not demanding any ransom. Christ is anointed to do for poor, captive souls what Cyrus was to do for the captive Jews, to declare the *opening of the prison to those that were bound* (61:1), bound in a worse slavery than that in Babylon.

3.2. Provision will be made for them. They went out poor and unable to bear the expenses of their reestablishment, and so it is promised that the products of Egypt and other nations will *come over to them and be theirs* (v. 14). They did not go out empty-handed from Babylon any more than they did from Egypt. Those who are redeemed by Christ will be also enriched. Those whose spirits God stirs up (Ezr 1:5) to go to the heavenly Zion may depend on him to bear their expenses. The world is theirs as far as it is good for them.

3.3. Converts will be brought over to them: *Men of stature shall come after thee in chains; they shall fall down to thee, saying, Surely God is in thee* (v. 14). This was partially fulfilled when many of the people of the land became Jews (Est 8:17), *saying, We will go with you, for we have heard that God is with you* (Zec 8:23). But this was to have its complete fulfillment in the Gospel church, when the Gentiles would become obedient by word and deed to the faith of Christ (Ro 15:18).

4. They are taught to trust God more than they can see him. The prophet puts this word into their mouths (v. 15): *Verily, thou art a God that hidest thyself.* He hid himself when he was bringing them out of the trouble. The salvation of the church is carried out mysteriously, by the Spirit of the Lord Almighty working on human spirits (Zec 4:6), by weak and unlikely instruments, small and incidental events, but this is our encouragement: although God hides himself, we are sure he is *the God of Israel, the Saviour* (v. 15). See also Job 35:14.

5. They are instructed to triumph over idolaters and all the worshipers of other gods (v. 16).

6. They are assured that those who trust in God will never be ashamed of their confidence in him (v. 17). They will be saved in him, for his name will be their strong tower (Pr 18:10). Beyond this physical restoration they must think of the salvation by the Messiah that is the salvation of the soul, a restoration to eternal bliss. "You will not only be rescued from the *everlasting shame and contempt* that will be the reward of idolaters (Da 12:2); you will also have eternal honor and glory." Those who are ashamed as penitents for their own sin will not be put to shame as believers in God's promises and power.

7. They are exhorted to remain forever faithful to God and never to abandon him. That the Lord we serve and trust is God alone is shown by the two great lights (Ge 1:16), that of nature and that of revelation.

7.1. It is shown by the light of nature, for he made the world, and so he may justly demand its worship (v. 18): "*Thus saith the Lord, that created the heavens and formed the earth, I am the Lord*, the sovereign Lord of all, *and there is none else.*" When he had made it, he established it, *founded it on the seas* (Ps 24:2), *hung it on nothing* (Job 26:7), as at first he made it out of nothing. He fitted it for the service of humans, to whom he wanted to give it. He made nothing in vain, but intended everything for some purpose. If anyone proves to have been made in vain, it is their own fault.

7.2. It is shown by the light of revelation. As the works of God abundantly prove that only he is God, so does his word, through the revelation he has made of himself and of his mind and will in it. All that God has said is plain: *I have not spoken in secret, in a dark place of the earth.* The pagan gods communicated their words out of dens and caves, in a low and hollow voice, and in ambiguous expressions; the mediums and spiritists whispered and muttered (8:19). But God communicated his Law from the top of Mount Sinai, distinctly, audibly, and intelligibly. The vision is written and made clear, so that a messenger can read it and run to announce it (Hab 2:2). If it is obscure to anyone, they have only themselves to blame. Christ pleaded in his own defense what God says here, *In secret have I said nothing* (Jn 18:20). God has in his word invited people to seek him, and so he never denied their faithful prayers. If he did not think it right to give them the particular thing they prayed for, he still gave them such grace, strength, and encouragement in their souls as were the equivalent. What we say about winter is also true of prayer: "It never goes rotten in the skies."

Verses 20–25

What is said here is intended:

1. To convince idolaters, to show them their foolishness in worshiping gods that cannot help them and neglecting a God who can. Let all *that have escaped of the nations* (v. 20), not only the Jewish people but also those of other nations who were released by Cyrus, hear what is to be said against worshiping idols: *They set up the wood of their graven image* (idols of wood) (v. 20). Although they cover the idols with gold and ornaments and make gods of them, those idols are still only wood. They *pray to a god that cannot save.* "Summon them all; tell them that the great cause will again be tried between God and Baal. *There is no other God besides me*" (v. 21). No one besides him is qualified to rule. No one besides him is able to help. Just as he is a righteous god, so also he is *the Saviour* (v. 21).

2. To strengthen and encourage God's faithful worshipers, whoever they are (v. 22). God says to all his people, though they seem to have become lost and forgotten in their dispersion, "Let them simply *look to me* by faith and prayer, look beyond circumstances, look to me, and they will *be saved.*" When Christ is lifted up from the earth, as the bronze snake was on the pole (Nu 21:6–9), he will draw the eyes of all people to him (Jn 3:14–15; 12:32). *I have sworn by myself*—and God can swear by no one greater (Heb 6:13)—*the word has gone out of my mouth,* that the One who made everything is Lord of all and that since all beings are derived from him, they should all be devoted to him. He has assured us that the kingdoms of the world will become his kingdom (Rev 11:15). This is applied to the rule of our Lord Jesus (Ro 14:10–11): *Unto him shall men of distant countries come,* to implore his favor. *All that are incensed against him* (v. 24) *shall be ashamed* (v. 24); some will be brought to penitential shame for it, others to a ruin with no way out. In the Lord the exiled Jews had both righteousness—that is, grace both to sanctify their afflictions and to qualify them to be rescued—and strength for their support and for their departure from exile. In the Lord Jesus we have righteousness to commend us to the goodwill of God toward us, and we have strength to begin and continue the good work of God in us (Php 1:6). In the Lord, the people of the Jews will be justified before all people, and they will openly *glory* (exult) in their God. All true Christians, who depend on Christ for strength and righteousness, will be justified in him and will exult in that.

CHAPTER 46

God, by the prophet, prepares Israel for restoration by giving them a detestation for idols and a faithful confidence in God. 1. Let them not be afraid of the idols of Babylon (vv. 1–2), but let them trust that the God who has often rescued them will do so now (vv. 3–4). 2. Let them not think they can make idols of their own (vv. 5–7); they are to look to God in his word, not to an idol; let them depend on God's promises and power to fulfill all the predictions of his word (vv. 9–11). And let them know that human unbelief will not nullify the word of God (vv. 12–13).

Verses 1–4

We are told here:

1. The false gods will certainly fail their worshipers (vv. 1–2). Bel and Nebo were two famous idols of Babylon. As Bel was a deified prince, so, according to some, Nebo was a deified prophet, for this is what *Nebo* may mean. Bel and Nebo may well have been their Jupiter and their Mercury or Apollo. God here tells them what will become of these idols. When Cyrus defeats Babylon, out go the idols. Bel and Nebo, which are set up high, will *stoop and bow down* (v. 2) at the feet of the soldiers who plunder their temples. And because there is a great deal of gold and silver on them, Cyrus's army will take them away with the rest of the plunder. The mules will be laden with these and their other idols, to be sent among other baggage—for it seems the conquerors considered them so rather than as treasure—into Persia. *They stoop, they bow down together.* They are all alike, tottering, and their day has come to fall.

2. The true God will never fail his worshipers. He formed them to be a people and gave them their nature. Every good person is what God makes them. You have been *borne by me from the belly* and *carried from the womb* (v. 3). And as God began to do them good early, so he had constantly continued to do them good: he had carried them from the time they were born up to this day. We, too, have been carried in the arms of his power and in his love and pity. Our spiritual life is sustained by his grace as necessarily and constantly as our natural life is by his providence. "You have been *borne by me from the belly* (v. 3), nursed when you were children; and *even to your old age I am he* (v. 4), when, because of your infirmities, you will need as much help as in your infancy." Israel was now growing old. And they had moved quickly into their old age and its problems because of their sins. But God is still their God and will continue to carry them in the same everlasting arms that were laid under them in Moses' time (Dt 33:27). "I will now carry them on eagles' wings out of Babylon, as in their infancy I carried them out of Egypt." This promise to aged Israel may be applied to every aged Israelite. "*Even to your old age* (v. 4), when you grow unfit for business, when you are surrounded by weaknesses, and perhaps your relatives become weary of you, yet *I am he,* I am the One who is the same One by whom you have been upheld since you were conceived and who has carried you since your birth. You change, but I remain the same. I *will carry you* (v. 4); I will uphold you and take you home at the end of your life."

Verses 5–13

The restoration of Israel by the destruction of Babylon is again promised, to convict idolaters and oppressors.

1. To convict those who make and worship idols, especially those of Israel who do so:

1.1. He challenges them to make an image that would be thought to resemble him (v. 5): *To whom will you liken me?* It is absurd to think of representing an infinite and eternal Spirit by the figure of any creation. No one has ever seen any form of him, nor can they see his face and live (Ex 33:20).

1.2. He exposes the foolishness of those who make idols and then pray to them (vv. 6–7). *They lavish gold out of the bag,* even though they make their families feel the pinch and lessen their wealth by it. *They weigh silver in the balance* (scales), either to use it as material for their idol or to pay the workers' wages. They are very concerned about their idols (v. 7): *They bear him upon their own shoulders;* they *carry him, and set him in his place,* more like a corpse than a living God. They set him on a pedestal, *and he stands.* They make an effort to fix him in position, and *from his place he shall not remove,* although they know he can neither move his hand nor budge at all to do them any kindness. When the goldsmith has made what they please to call a god, *they fall down, yea, they worship it* (v. 6). Now will anyone who has some knowledge of the true and living God make a fool of themselves in this way?

1.3. He puts the matter to their own reason; let that be the judge (v. 8): "*Remember this,* that idols are senseless and helpless, *and show yourselves men,* not animals, adults and not babies. Act with reason, and scorn the thought of belittling your own judgment as you do when you worship idols."

1.4. He again produces undeniable proofs that he is God (v. 9): "*I am God, and there is none like me. Remember the former things of old* (v. 9), what the God of Israel did for his people in their beginnings. Remember those things, and you will acknowledge that *I am God and there is none else*" (v. 9). He alone is God, for it is only he who *declares the end from the beginning* (v. 10). Many prophecies in Scripture that were communicated long ago have not yet been fulfilled, but the fulfillment of some in the meantime is a pledge of the fulfillment of the rest in due time. The fulfillment of this particular prophecy, which relates to the elevation of Cyrus and his being used to restore God's people from exile, is mentioned to confirm this truth. According to his plan, God *calls a ravenous bird from the east,* a bird of prey, *Cyrus,* who, some say, had a nose like the beak of a hawk or eagle. Some think this description alludes to that; others think it alludes to the eagle that was his banner, as it was afterward that of the Romans, to which there is thought to be a reference in Mt 24:28. Cyrus came from the east at God's command: "*I have spoken it* by my servants the prophets, and what I have spoken is what *I have purposed*" (v. 11). For although God has many things in his plans that are not in his prophecies, he has nothing in his prophecies except what is in his plans.

2. To convict those who oppose God's plans, assurance is given that those plans will be fulfilled very soon (vv. 12–13).

2.1. This is addressed to the *stouthearted,* that is, either:

2.1.1. The proud and stubborn Babylonians, who *are far from righteousness* (v. 12), who say they will never let the oppressed go free in spite of their requests or God's predictions. Or:

2.1.2. The unhumbled Jews, who have long been in the furnace of affliction but are not melted. They are like their ancestors, the unbelieving, complaining Israelites in the desert, who could not enter the Land of Promise because of their unbelief: they keep good things from themselves,

and even push them further away. This may be applied to the Jewish nation when they rejected the Gospel of Christ; even though they *followed after the law of righteousness,* they *attained not to righteousness, because they sought it not by faith* (Ro 9:31–32).

2.2. Now God says that, whatever they think, the one in presumption, the other in despair:

- Salvation will certainly be accomplished for God's people. If people will not do them justice, God will. He *will place salvation in Zion* (v. 13), that is, he will make Jerusalem a place of security and defense to all those who will plant themselves there.
- It will be accomplished very soon.

CHAPTER 47

Infinite Wisdom could have ordered things so that Israel might have been released and Babylon unharmed, but if the Babylonians are going to harden their hearts and not let the people go, they have only themselves to blame that their ruin prepares the way for Israel's release. That ruin is here foretold to encourage Israel's faith and hope concerning their restoration and so that that ruin might be a type of the downfall of that great enemy of the New Testament church that, in the book of Revelation, goes under the name of Babylon. *In this chapter we have: 1. The ruin threatened, that Babylon would be brought down to the dust (vv. 1–5). 2. The sins that caused God to bring this ruin on them: 2.1. Their cruelty to the people of God (v. 6). 2.2. Their pride and false, worldly security (vv. 7–9). 2.3. Their contempt of God (v. 10). 2.4. Their use of and dependence on sorcery and astrology (vv. 11–15).*

Verses 1–6

In these verses God through the prophet sends to Babylon a message like that of Jonah to Nineveh: "The time is near when Babylon will be destroyed" (Jnh 3:4). Fair warning is given to Babylon, so that she may repent and prevent the ruin and thereby extend her tranquility. Notice:

1. God's dispute with Babylon. She has made God her enemy; let her know that the righteous Judge, to whom vengeance belongs (Dt 32:35; Ps 94:1; Heb 10:30), has said (v. 3), *I will take vengeance.* He says, *I will not meet thee as a man* (v. 3), not with human power, which can easily be resisted, but with the power of God, which cannot be resisted. Not with human justice, which may be bribed, but with the justice of God, which cannot be avoided.

2. The particular reason for this dispute. God will plead his people's cause against Babylon. It is acknowledged (v. 6) that God had given his people into the hands of the Babylonians. He had used them to correct his children; he had used them to *pollute* (desecrate) *his inheritance.* But the Babylonians took matters too far, and when they had his people in their hands, they trampled over them with an evil and harsh spirit *and showed them no mercy* (v. 6). They *laid the yoke on very heavily* (v. 6), adding even further suffering to those who were already suffering; they laid it even *on the ancient* (v. 6), the aged, those advanced in years, who were past their working age and who would surely sink under a yoke; the word may also refer to those who were elders by office, judges and magistrates.

3. The terror of this dispute. Babylon has reason to tremble when she is told who it is that has this quarrel with her (v. 4). "He is *the Lord of hosts,* the Lord Almighty

(v. 4), who has all creatures at his command and so has *all power both in heaven and in earth* (Mt 28:18). He is the *Holy One of Israel* (v. 4), a God in covenant with us." These names may be appropriately applied to Christ, our great Redeemer. He is both Lord Almighty and the Holy One of Israel.

4. The consequences of it for Babylon. She is as beautiful as a virgin and is courted by all around her; she has been called *tender and delicate* (v. 1) and *the lady* (queen) *of kingdoms* (v. 5), but now the situation has changed. Her honor is gone, and she must say farewell to all her dignity. Her power is gone, and she must say farewell to all her dominion. *There is no throne*, none for you, *O daughter of the Chaldeans* (Babylonians)! (v. 1). Those who abuse their honor or power cause God to deprive them of it and to make them *come down and sit in the dust* (v. 1). Her peace and pleasure are gone: "She will *no more be called tender and delicate* (v. 1), but will be made to work hard and feel both need and pain." Her liberty is gone, and she is brought into a state of extreme slavery. Even the leaders of Babylon must now receive the same law from the conquerors that they used to give to the conquered: "*Take the millstones and grind meal* (v. 2), get down to work, to hard labor, which will make thee sweat so that thou must throw off all thy headdresses and *uncover thy locks* (take off your veil)" (v. 2). At the whims of their masters, they are forced to wade through the streams, to *make bare the leg* and *uncover the thigh*, so that they may *pass over the rivers* (v. 2), which is a great humiliation. All her glory and all her boasting are gone. Instead of glory, she has disgrace (v. 3): *Thy nakedness shall be uncovered, and thy shame shall be seen*, according to the way the Babylonians corruptly and cruelly treated their prisoners. Instead of boasting, she *sits silently, and gets into darkness* (v. 5), ashamed to show her face, for she *shall no more be called the lady* (queen) *of kingdoms*.

Verses 7–15

Babylon, now condemned to ruin, is here justly rebuked for her pride in her prosperity, and particularly in the forecasts and advice of her astrologers.

1. The Babylonians are here rebuked for their pride and haughtiness; this attitude was reflected in the language of both the government and the body of the people: *Thou sayest in thy heart, I am, and none else besides me* (vv. 8, 10). It is the same word that God has often said about himself, *I am, and none else besides me*, showing his self-existence, his infinite and incomparable qualities, and his sole supremacy.

2. They are rebuked for their self-indulgence and love of an easy, comfortable lifestyle (v. 8): "*Thou that art given to* (who love) *pleasures* and *dwellest carelessly* (you lounge in your security) and takest nothing to heart." Great wealth and plenty are great temptations to delighting in worldliness, and where there is a surfeit of bread, there is commonly much idleness.

3. They are rebuked for their worldly, worthless self-confidence. Notice:

3.1. The cause of their self-confidence. They thought themselves safe. They lulled themselves into a false sense of security because of their ease and pleasure and dreamed about nothing else except that *tomorrow should be as this day, and much more abundant* (56:12). They did not *remember the latter end of it* (v. 7)—what might happen in the future, that their prosperity would end, that it is a fading flower and will wither (40:7–8)—and the outcome of their sin, which would be bitterness. "She did not remember her latter end" is how some read it.

3.2. The basis of their self-confidence. They trusted in their evil and their wisdom (v. 10). Their power and wealth, which they had gained by fraud and oppression, were what they put their confidence in. They did not doubt that they would be too harsh on all their enemies, because they dared to lie, kill, and commit perjury; in fact, they would do anything as long as it was in their own interests. Their politics and cunning, which they called their *wisdom*, were what they trusted in. But their *wisdom and knowledge perverted* (misled) *them* (v. 10).

3.3. The expressions of their self-confidence. This proud and haughty monarch said three things in her security:

3.3.1. "*I shall be a lady for ever*" (v. 7). This is what the New Testament Babylon says: *I sit as a queen, and shall see no sorrow* (Rev 18:7).

3.3.2. "*I will not sit as a widow*, in loneliness and sorrow; I will never lose the power and wealth I am so devoted to; the monarchy will never lack a monarch to support and protect it and be a husband to the state; *nor will I know the loss of children*" (v. 8).

3.3.3. "*No one sees me* when I do wrong, and so there will be none to call me to account" (v. 10).

3.4. The punishment of their self-confidence. It will be their ruin: "*These two things will come on thee*—the very two things that you defied—loss of children and widowhood (v. 9). Both your princes and your people will be cut off, so that you will no longer be a government or nation." Their punishment will be sudden and unexpected. "*Evil* (disaster) *will come on thee* (v. 11), and you will have neither the time nor means to prepare for it, *for thou shalt not know whence it rises*, and so you will not know where to stand on your guard." Babylon claims to have great wisdom and knowledge (v. 10), but with all her knowledge she cannot foresee the ruin threatened, nor with all her wisdom prevent it. Fair warning of this catastrophe was certainly given them by Isaiah and other prophets of the Lord, but they paid no attention to that notice and would not believe it.

4. They are rebuked for their divination, their sorcerous magic and astrology. This is one of their provocative sins (v. 9). "These evils will come on you to punish you *for the multitude of thy sorceries, and the great abundance of thy enchantments* (your powerful magic spells)." Witchcraft is a sin that gives to the Devil the honor that is due only to God, making God's enemy our guide. In Babylon it had the protection of the government. They are rebuked here for the great effort they have taken with their sorceries: thou hast *laboured in them from thy youth* (v. 12). They have their *astrologers*, or those who look up at the heavens, claiming to foretell future events by them; they view the heavens and forget the One who made them. They have their *stargazers*, who read the doom of states and kingdoms by looking at the movements of the stars and their relative positions. They are rebuked for the complete inability and insufficiency of all these pretenders in times of distress. "*Let them stand up* and see whether their power can save you." This confusing of the diviners was literally fulfilled on the night that Babylon was taken and Belshazzar was killed, when all his astrologers, soothsayers, and wise men were completely baffled by the handwriting on the wall that pronounced the fatal sentence (Da 5:8). They are rebuked concerning the fall of the wise men themselves in the general ruin (v. 14). *They shall be as stubble* before the consuming fire. The Persians will destroy the wise men of Babylon to make room for their own wise men; that *fire shall burn* the Babylonian wise men, and *they shall not deliver themselves from the power*

of the flame. The astrologers who worked in magic were in effect their merchants; fortune-telling was one of the best trades in Babylon. But when some were devoured, others fled their country, *everyone to his quarter* (v. 15), and there was no one to save Babylon.

CHAPTER 48

In the previous chapter we read how God judged the Babylonians. In this chapter, God comes to show the house of Jacob their sins, but also the mercy he has in store for them, so that by their repentance and reformation they may be prepared for that mercy. 1. He accuses them of hypocrisy in doing what is good and of stubbornness in doing what is evil, especially in their idolatry (vv. 1–8). 2. He assures them that their restoration will come about purely for the sake of God's name (vv. 9–11). 3. He encourages them to depend only on God's power and promise for this restoration (vv. 12–15). 4. He shows them that just as it was by their own sin that they brought themselves into exile, so it will be only by the grace of God that they will obtain their release (vv. 16–19); he declares their release, but with a proviso that evildoers will not benefit from it (vv. 20–22).

Verses 1–8

We may notice here:

1. The hypocritical profession that many of the Jews made of religion and their relationship with God. Notice:

1.1. How high their profession of religion was raised and what a good face they put on a bad heart.

1.1.1. They were the *house of Jacob* (v. 1); they had a place and a name in the visible church. *Jacob have I loved* (Ro 9:13).

1.1.2. They were *called by the name of Israel* (v. 1), an honorable name. *Israel* means "a prince with God" (Ge 32:28) [Ed. note: it is now known to mean "he struggles with God"], and they prided themselves on coming from that royal race.

1.1.3. *They came forth out of the waters of Judah* (v. 1) and were of the royal tribe, the tribe that was faithful to God when the rest rebelled.

1.1.4. They *swore by* (took oaths in) *the name of the Lord* (v. 1), so acknowledging him to be the true God.

1.1.5. They *made mention of the God of Israel* (v. 1) in their prayers and praises.

1.1.6. They *called themselves* citizens *of the holy city* (v. 2).

1.1.7. They *stayed themselves* (relied) *upon the God of Israel* (v. 2), boasting about his promises and his covenant with them; they *leaned on the Lord* (Mic 3:11).

1.2. How low their profession of religion sank, despite all this. All their religion was in vain; their hearts were not true or right in these professions.

2. The means God used to keep them close to him and prevent them from turning aside to idolatry. The many excellent laws he gave them would not be enough to restrain them from sin, and so God added remarkable prophecies to those, and also remarkable providences, which were all intended to convince them that it was their duty to remain faithful to him.

2.1. He favored them with remarkable prophecies (v. 3): *I have declared the former things from the beginning.* Nothing substantial happened to their nation from its origin that had not been prophesied about beforehand—their slavery in Egypt, their rescue from there, the situation of their tribes in Canaan, and so on. God had declared to them from the beginning the very disasters they were now

groaning under in Babylon (Lev 26:31; Dt 28:36; 29:28). He also declared to them their return to God and to their own land again (Dt 30:4; Lev 26:44–45).

2.2. He dignified them with remarkable providences (v. 6): *I have shown thee the new things from this time.* He also showed them new things through the prophets of their own day; indeed, he *created* them. They were *hidden things*, which the people could not otherwise know, such as the prophecy about Cyrus and the exact time of their release from Babylon. These things God *created now* (v. 7). "Consider," God says, "that however much it is talked about now, it was told you by the prophets when it was the furthest thing from your thoughts, when you had no reason to expect it (vv. 7–8), when the thing seemed completely impossible." God had shown them hidden things and done for them great things "Now," he says (v. 6), "*thou hast heard; see all this.* You have heard the prophecies; look at their fulfillment. Will you not acknowledge that your God has been good to you? Declare this to his honor and your own shame."

3. The reasons why God would use this method with them.

3.1. Because he wished to preempt their boasting about themselves and their idols. "I spoke of it," God says, "*lest thou shouldst say, My idol has done it or has commanded it to be done*" (v. 5). Those who were not so ungodly that they would ascribe the thing itself to an idol were still so proud that they would claim that they foresaw it by their own wisdom.

3.2. Because he wanted to leave them inexcusable (Ro 2:1). God took an effort with them because he knew they were obstinate (v. 4). "I knew that you were hard" is the sense. "The sinews of your neck were iron (v. 4), unwilling to submit to the yoke of God's commandments, inflexible to God's will, not submissive to his providence. Your forehead is bronze (v. 4); you are arrogant and have no scruples, but will force your way forward, following your own heart." God sent his prophets to them, but they did not listen; they did not want to know. "You were *called a transgressor from the womb* (a rebel from birth), and the name was not wrong" (v. 8). They were prone to idolatry, grumblers as soon as they began their journey to Canaan. Therefore *I knew that thou wouldst deal very treacherously* (v. 8).

Verses 9–15

The release of God's people from exile in Babylon was so improbable that God's people needed to be encouraged about it. Two things were discouraging: their own unworthiness that God would do it for them and the many difficulties in the thing itself; now both of these discouragements were taken away, for here was:

1. A reason why God would do it for them, even though they were unworthy (vv. 9–11).

1.1. It was true that they had been very offensive. Their exile was the punishment of their sin. "But," God says, "*I will defer my anger*" (v. 9), "delay, stifle, and suppress it." And why will God halt his hand in this way? *For my name's sake* (v. 9); because this people were called by his name, and if they were wiped out, the enemies would blaspheme his name. *It is for my praise* (v. 9), because it would lead to the honor of his mercy.

1.2. It was true that they were corrupt and disposed to evil, but God would make them fit for the mercy he intended to give them: "*I have refined thee* (v. 10), so that you might be made an object of honor" (Ro 9:21; 2Ti 2:21). And this explains his bringing them into the trouble and leaving them in it so long as he did. It was not to destroy them, but to do them good. He therefore takes them as they are, refined only in part, not thoroughly. *"I have chosen thee in the furnace of affliction* (v. 10) and then destined you for great things." It has been in the furnace of affliction that many have been brought home to God as chosen vessels (Ac 9:15) and had a good work of grace begun in them (Php 1:6). God will do it not because he owes them such a favor, but so that they may not be defamed by the arrogant triumphs of the nations, who, in triumphing over Israel, thought they triumphed over the God of Israel. Moses pleaded this often with God: Lord, *what will the Egyptians say?* (Ex 32:12; Nu 14:13–14).

2. A proof that God could do it for them, although they were unable to help themselves and the thing seemed altogether impracticable. They are *called according to his purpose* (Ro 8:28), called by him out of Egypt (Hos 11:1) and now out of Babylon. He will also rescue them by his own power. They need not fear then, for:

2.1. He alone is God, and he is the eternal God (v. 12): *"I am he* who can do what I will and will do what is best. *I am the first; I also am the last."* What room then is left to doubt their restoration, since the One who undertakes it has purposes that are well set out, for he is the first, and that are well carried out, for he is the last?

2.2. He is the God who made the world, and the One who did that can do anything (v. 13). "If the palm of my right hand," as the margin reads, has gone so far as to stretch out the heavens, what will he do with his outstretched arm? He also has command of all the powers of the heavens and the earth. *They stand up together* (v. 13), helping one another in the service of their Maker. If God, therefore, wishes to restore his people, he cannot be at a loss for instruments to bring about that restoration.

2.3. He has already foretold it, and no doubt he has almighty power to bring it about. *"All you* of the house of Jacob, *assemble yourselves, and hear* this for your comfort: *Which among them,* among the nations' gods or their wise men, *has declared these things,* or could declare them?" (v. 14). None can see more than he can, and so we may be sure that none can outdo him. Cyrus is the man who must do it. *The Lord has loved him* (v. 14); he has done him the honor of making him an instrument in redeeming his people. In this, he was a type of the great Redeemer, God's beloved Son, *in whom he was well pleased* (Mt 3:17). *I have called him* (v. 15) and will therefore support him. *"I have brought him from* (v. 15) a far country, brought him step by step beyond his own intentions." Cyrus will *do God's pleasure on* (carry out God's purpose against) *Babylon* (v. 14). *His arm*—Cyrus's army, and in it God's arm—*shall* come and *be upon the Chaldeans* (Babylonians) to defeat them (v. 14), for if God calls him, he will certainly *make his way prosperous* (give him success in his mission) (v. 15).

Verses 16–22

Jacob and Israel are called to listen to God speaking through the prophet. Those who draw near to God may depend on this, that his secret will be with them (Ps 25:14).

1. God refers them to what he said to them and did for them formerly. He had always spoken clearly to them *from the beginning,* through Moses and all the prophets: *I have not spoken in secret* (v. 16); he did not communicate his words obscurely and ambiguously, but in such a way that they could be understood (Hab 2:2). *"From the time* that they were first formed into *a people there am I"* (v. 16)—he sent them prophets, raised up judges for

them, and frequently fought for them—"and therefore there I will continue to do these things."

2. The prophet himself asserts his own commission: *Now the Lord God has by his Spirit sent me* (v. 16). Those whom God sends are sent by the Spirit.

3. God by the prophet sends them a gracious message. The introduction to this message is both fearful and encouraging (v. 17): *Thus saith Jehovah,* the eternal God, *thy Redeemer,* for he is *the Holy One,* who cannot deceive. The same words that introduce the Law, giving authority to that, introduce the promise and give it validity: *I am the Lord thy God* (Ex 20:2; Dt 5:6).

3.1. Here is the good work that God undertakes to fulfill in them. The One who is their Redeemer will be their instructor: *"I am thy God that teaches thee to profit* (v. 17), that is, who teaches you the things that concern your peace" (Lk 19:42). Those whom God redeems he teaches; those whom he intends to rescue from their afflictions he first teaches to learn from their afflictions. *He leads them* to the way and *in the way by which they should go* (v. 17). He not only enlightens their eyes (Ezr 9:8; Ps 19:8) but also directs their steps. By his grace he leads them along the path of duty; by his providence he leads them on the path of restoration.

3.2. Here is the goodwill that God declares he has for them (vv. 18–19).

3.2.1. Just as when he gave them his Law he fervently wished they might be obedient (Dt 5:29; 32:29), so, when he had punished them for disobedience to his Law, he wished they had been obedient: *O that thou hadst hearkened to my commandments!* (v. 18). This confirms what God said and swore elsewhere, that he has *no pleasure in the death of sinners* (Eze 33:11).

3.2.2. He assures them that if they had been obedient, that not only would have prevented them from being sent into exile but also would have advanced their prosperity and made it last forever. *"Thy peace would have been as a river* (v. 18); you would have enjoyed a series of mercies, one continually following another, like the waters of a river, which always last." Their honor and the justice of their cause would in all cases have defeated the opposition by their own strength, *as the waves of the sea* (v. 18). Their righteousness would have been such that nothing would have withstood them, whereas now that they had been disobedient, the flow of their prosperity was interrupted and their righteousness was overpowered. The rising generation would have been numerous and prosperous, whereas they were now very few, as it appears from the small number of the returning exiles (Ezr 2:64). The honor of Israel would still have been unstained and untouched: *His name should not have been cut off,* as now it is in the land of Israel, which is either desolate or inhabited by foreigners; nor would Israel's name have *been destroyed from before God* (v. 19). *This* should engage us—we might almost say, *enrage* us—against sin: it has not only deprived us of the good things we have enjoyed but also prevented the good things God had in store for us. Nothing but the prior and exclusive privilege of mercy would have saved them.

3.3. Here is assurance given of the great work that God intended for them, namely their liberation from exile. God declared, long before Cyrus did, that whoever wanted to could return to their own land (v. 20). "Send news of it by word of mouth *to the ends of the earth"* (v. 20). It prefigured the declaration of the Gospel to all the world. Let them all know that those whom God acknowledges as his are those he has dearly bought and paid for: *The Lord has redeemed his servant Jacob* (v. 20). The bonds God had loosed tied them more firmly to him. The One who redeemed us has an unquestionable right to us. We are not our own; we belong to him (1Co 6:19–20). He will take care of those whom he intends to bring home to himself, so that they do not lack the necessary expenses for their journey. *Through the deserts*, they *thirsted not* (v. 21), for the water out of the rock followed them in all their moves (1Co 10:4). He can draw in necessary supplies for his people in ways they think least likely. This refers to what he did for them when he brought them out of Egypt, when all this was literally true. But it would now in effect be done again when they returned from Babylon. God does his work as effectively by marvelous providences as by miracles. This may be applied to those treasures of grace laid up for us in Jesus Christ, from which all good flows to us as the water did to Israel from the rock, for that rock is Christ (1Co 10:4). But (v. 22) although God's thoughts were thoughts of peace (Jer 29:11), yet to those who are *wicked* and hate to be reformed *there is no peace*, no peace with God or their own consciences. What have those to do with peace who are enemies to God (2Ki 9:18–19, 22)?

CHAPTER 49

Glorious things were spoken (Ps 87:3) in the previous chapters about the restoration of the Jews from exile in Babylon, but the prophecy had a further intention. That intention was to have its complete fulfillment in a redemption that would as far surpass these expressions as the restoration from exile seemed to come short of them, namely the redemption of the world by Jesus Christ. In this chapter we have: 1. The appointing of Christ, using Isaiah as the type, to his office as Mediator (vv. 1–3). 2. The assurance given him of the success of his undertaking among the Gentiles (vv. 4–8). 3. The redemption that would be brought about by him (vv. 9–12). 4. The encouragement this would give to the afflicted church (vv. 13–17). 5. The addition of many people to the church and the setting up of a church among the Gentiles (vv. 18–23). 6. A confirmation of the prophecy of the Jews' release from Babylon, which was to be the type of all these blessings (vv. 24–26). If this chapter is rightly understood, we will see ourselves to be more involved in the prophecies relating to the Jews' deliverance from Babylon than we thought we were.

Verses 1–6

Here:

1. An audience is called together. The previous chapter was directed to the house of Jacob and the people of Israel (vv. 1, 12), but this chapter is directed to the islands—that is, the Gentiles, for they are called *the isles of the Gentiles* (Ge 10:5)—and to *the people from far*, those who were *strangers to the commonwealth of Israel* (Eph 2:12) and were far away. Let these listen (v. 1). The news of a Redeemer is sent to the Gentiles, and they listened to the Gospel when the Jews were deaf to it.

2. The great author of the redemption gives proof of his authority from heaven.

2.1. God has appointed him: "*The Lord has called me from the womb* to this office and *made mention of my name* (v. 1), named me to be the Savior." By an angel he called him *Jesus—a Saviour*, who *should save his people from their sins* (Mt 1:21). This was said about some of the prophets, who were types of him (Jer 1:5). Paul was set apart for apostleship from his mother's womb (Gal 1:15).

2.2. God has fitted him for service. He *made his mouth like a sharp sword* and *made him* like *a polished shaft*

(v. 2), or a bright arrow, so that, by his word, he might fight God's battles against the powers of darkness (Col 1:13), conquer Satan, and bring back God's rebellious subjects to their allegiance: that word is the *two-edged sword* (Heb 4:12).

2.3. God has advanced him to the service for which he has reserved him: *He has hidden me in the shadow of his hand* (v. 2), which shows:

2.3.1. Concealment. The Gospel of Christ, and the calling in of the Gentiles by it, were hidden for a long time in the shadow of the ceremonial law and the Old Testament types.

2.3.2. Protection. The house of David was under the special care of divine Providence because that blessing was in it (65:8). Christ in his infancy was sheltered from the rage of Herod.

2.4. God has acknowledged him and had said to him, *Thou art my servant* (v. 3), you are Israel, in effect, *the prince with God* (Ge 32:28). Some read the words in two clauses: *Thou art my servant*—as Christ is (42:1)—and "it is Israel in whom I will be glorified by thee"; it is the spiritual Israel, the chosen ones, in the salvation of whom God will be glorified by Jesus Christ.

3. He is assured of the success of his undertaking:

3.1. He raises the objection of the discouragement he met with when he first set out (v. 4): "Then I said, with a sad heart, *I have laboured in vain*; those who were careless and were strangers to God remain so: *I have called, and they have refused*; I have *stretched out my hands to a gainsaying* (obstinate) *people*" (Ro 10:21). This was Isaiah's complaint. The same cause for complaint was given to Jeremiah, tempting him to decide he would labor no longer (Jer 20:9). It is the complaint of many faithful ministers, who have not wasted their time, but worked hard, who have not spared their strength but spent it, and themselves with it, and who have found that nevertheless, with regard to many of their hearers, it is all in vain; people will not repent and believe. But here it seems to point to the stubbornness of the Jews, among whom Christ went in person preaching the Gospel of the kingdom. He worked and spent his strength, but the leaders and the main part of the nation rejected him and his teaching. Let not ministers think it strange when they are shown disrespect, since their Master himself was.

3.2. He strengthens himself in this discouragement by realizing that it is God's cause in which he is engaged: "*Yet surely my judgment is with the Lord*, who is the Judge of all, *and my work with my God* (v. 4), whose servant I am." His encouragement may be the encouragement of all faithful ministers when they see little success from all their hard work. They are with God and for God; they are on his side and are workers together with him (2Co 6:1). "*He knows the way that I take* (Job 23:10); *my judgment is with the Lord* (v. 4), to determine whether I have not saved my soul and left the blood of those who perish to fall on their own heads." Although the labor is in vain for those who are labored with, it will not be in vain to the laborers themselves if they are faithful (1Co 15:58): the Lord will justify them and support them, even though other people condemn them. The work is with the Lord, to give them success according to his plan and in his own way and time.

3.3. He receives from God a further answer. God is fashioning and preparing those whom he wants to employ as his servants. He is doing this work when perhaps neither they nor others are aware of it. Christ was to be *his servant, to bring Jacob again to him* (v. 5), who had treacherously left him. The offspring of Jacob according to the flesh must therefore be dealt with first, and ways must be used to bring them back. Christ, and the word of salvation through him, are sent first *to the lost sheep of the house of Israel* (Mt 10:6). But what if Jacob will not be brought back to God? What if Israel will not be gathered? In that case:

3.3.1. Christ will be glorious in the eyes of the Lord. Although few of the Jewish nation were converted by Christ's preaching and miracles, and many showed him shame, God still made him glorious. At his baptism and in his transfiguration God spoke to him from heaven, he sent angels to minister to him (Mt 4:11), and he made even his shameful death glorious, and his resurrection much more so. In his sufferings God was his strength, so that although he met with every possible discouragement, he did not fail and was not discouraged (42:4). An angel was sent from heaven to *strengthen him* (Lk 22:43). Although faithful ministers may not see the fruit of their labors, they will still be accepted by God, and in that they will be truly glorious.

3.3.2. The Gospel will be glorious in the eyes of the world. It will still be received by the nations (v. 6). The Messiah seemed as if he had been primarily intended to *bring Jacob back* (v. 5). But that is a comparatively small matter; a larger realm of usefulness is intended for him: "And therefore *I will give thee for a light to the Gentiles, that thou mayest be my salvation to the end of the earth*" (v. 6). It is from this that Simeon learned to call Christ *a light to lighten the Gentiles* (Lk 2:32), and the apostle Paul's explanation serves as a key to the context (Ac 13:47). He says, "We turn to the Gentiles, to preach the Gospel to them, *because so has the Lord commanded us, saying, I have set thee to be a light to the Gentiles.*" In this the Redeemer was truly glorious; the setting up of his kingdom in the Gentile world was more his honor than if he had raised up all the tribes of Jacob. This promise has been partially fulfilled already and will have its complete fulfillment when the fullness of the Gentiles will be brought in (Ro 11:25).

Verses 7–12

In these verses we have:

1. The humiliation and exaltation of the Messiah (v. 7). He was One *whom man despised* (v. 7). He is *despised and rejected of men* (53:3). People whom he came to save and to honor despised him and showed him contempt. They made him not only contemptible but also repugnant. He was *one whom the nation abhorred* (v. 7); they cried out, *Crucify him, crucify him* (Lk 23:21). He was *a servant of rulers* (v. 7), trampled on, abused, scourged, and crucified as a slave. Yet Herod the king stood in awe of him, saying, *It is John the Baptist* (Mk 6:14); nobles, rulers, and centurions came and knelt before him. It is for the honor of his kingdom on earth when its leaders support him and praise him. This will be the fulfillment of God's promise, and he will give him the nations as his inheritance (Ps 2:8).

2. The blessings he has in store for all those to whom he is made salvation. God will acknowledge and stand by him in his work (v. 8). Violent attacks will be made on the Lord Jesus by the powers of darkness, when their time comes, to drive him away from his work of redemption, but God has promised to keep him safe and will preserve his kingdom, although he is fought against on every side. And when he has accomplished his work, God will authorize him to give to his church the benefits of it.

2.1. Christ will be the guarantee of the covenant of peace between God and humanity: I will *give thee for a covenant of the people* (v. 8). It was in him that God was

reconciling the world to himself (2Co 5:19); the One who *spared not his own Son* (Ro 8:32) will deny us nothing. He is given as a covenant, as he is the blessed *daysman* (arbitrator) *who has laid his hand upon us both* (Job 9:33).

2.2. He will repair the decays of the church and build it on a rock (Mt 16:18). He will *cause the desolate heritages to be inherited* (reassign its desolate inheritances) (v. 8), as the towns of Judah were again inherited after the return from exile, and so the church, which in the last and degenerate ages of the Jewish nation had been like a ravaged country, was again replenished by the fruits of the preaching of the Gospel.

2.3. He will free human souls from the slavery of guilt and corruption and bring them into the glorious liberty of God's children (Ro 8:21). He will *say to the prisoners* who were bound under the power of Satan, *Go forth* (come out) (v. 9). Pardoning mercy is a release from the curse of the law, and renewing grace is a release from the power of sin. Both come from Christ. It is Christ who says, *Go forth*; it is the Son who makes us free, and then we are truly free (Jn 8:36). He said *to those that are in darkness, Show yourselves* (v. 9); "not only *see* but also *be seen*, to the glory of God and your own encouragement."

2.4. He will provide for those he sets free to travel comfortably to their place of contented settlement (vv. 9–11). These verses refer to the provision made for the Jews' return, but they may also be applied to the guidance of divine grace that all who belong to God's spiritual Israel know. The world leads its followers by broken cisterns (Jer 2:13) or streams that fail in summer (Job 6:15–17), but God leads his own people by springs of water. And those whom God guides will find a ready road (v. 11): *I will make all my mountains a way* (into roads).

2.5. He will bring them all together from all parts, so that they may return as one and encourage one another. They were dispersed as their enemies pleased, to prevent them from combining their forces. But when God's time comes to bring them home together, one spirit will encourage them all (v. 12). A group will come from far away, some from the north, some from the west, some from the land of Sinim, a country belonging to one of the chief cities of Egypt, called Sin, of which we read in Eze 30:15–16.

Verses 13–17

The return of the people of God and the eternal redemption to be brought about by Christ, of which that return was a type, would be great occasions of joy and great evidence of the compassion God has for the church.

1. Nothing can provide us with better reasons for songs of praise and thanksgiving (v. 13). Let there be joy in heaven; let the earth and the mountains *be joyful* and *break forth into singing* (v. 13) (Ro 8:19, 21), for *God has comforted his people* (v. 13) who were sorrowful.

2. Nothing can provide us with more convincing arguments to prove the most tender concern God has for his church.

2.1. The troubles of the church have given some people occasion to question God's care for it (v. 14). *Zion*, in distress, *said, The Lord has forsaken me* and looks after me no more. Unbelievers say in their presumption, *God has forsaken the earth* (Eze 8:12). Weak, despondent believers are ready to say that God has abandoned his church. But we have no more reason to question his promise and grace than we have to question his providence and justice.

2.2. The triumphs of the church after her troubles will put the matter beyond question. We are told what God will do for Zion (v. 17). Her friends, who had deserted her, will return to her: *Thy children shall make haste.* Converts to the faith of Christ are the children of the church; they will join themselves to the church with great readiness. "Thy builders shall make haste," as some read it, "those who will build up your houses and walls, especially your temple." Her enemies, who had made threats, will be forced to withdraw from her. By Christ is the prince of this world, the great destroyer, driven out (Jn 12:31), and his attempts completely thwarted. Zion's suggestions were altogether without basis. God had not forsaken her or forgotten her, and he never will. "You think I have forgotten you. *Can a woman forget her sucking child?*" (v. 15). A woman must be concerned for her own child, for the child is a part of herself, one who has just come from her. Yet it is possible that she may forget. "But," God says, "*I will not forget thee*" (v. 15). He has a constant care for his church and people (v. 16): *I have engraven thee upon the palms of my hands.* This alludes to the custom of those who tie a string on their hands or fingers to remind them of something they might forget, or to the wearing of a signet ring in memory of a dear friend. God's setting his people in this way as a seal on his arm stands for his setting them as a seal on his heart and for his always thinking about them and their interests (SS 8:6). He adds, "*Thy walls shall be continually before me* (v. 16); although your ruined walls are not pleasant to look at, they will be in my compassionate thoughts. The plan and model of your walls, which are to be rebuilt, is before me, and they will certainly be built according to it."

Verses 18–23

Two things are promised here, which were to be partially fulfilled in the reviving of the Jewish church after its return, but more completely in the planting of the Christian church by the preaching of the Gospel of Christ:

1. The church will be replenished with the great numbers that are added to it. It was promised (v. 17) that *her children would make haste*:

1.1. Many people will flock to the church from every part. *Look round, and see how they gather themselves to thee* (v. 18), by locally joining the Jewish church. They come to Jerusalem, for that was then the center of their unity, but under the Gospel, that center is the mystical body of Christ, to which believers are spiritually joined in faith and love.

1.2. Those who are added to the church will not be a burden and blemish to her, but her strength and adornment. *As I live, saith the Lord, thou shalt surely clothe thyself with them all* (v. 18). When those who are added to the church are serious, holy, and exemplary in their way of life, they adorn it.

1.3. The country that was waste, desolate, and *without inhabitant* (5:9; 6:11) will again be populated; in fact, it will be overpopulated (v. 19): "*Thy waste and thy desolate places,* which have lain so for so long, *and the land of thy destruction,* your land that was destroyed with you, will now be so full of people that there will not be enough room for them all." In this way, the *kingdom of God among men,* which had been impoverished and almost depopulated, was again populated and enriched by the setting up of the Christian church.

1.4. The new converts will remarkably increase and multiply. After Jerusalem has lost the abundance of her children by sword, famine, and captivity, she will have a new family growing up, children that she *shall have after she has lost the other* (v. 20), like Seth, who was *appointed another seed* (child) *instead of Abel* (Ge 4:25). God will repair his church's losses and keep safe for himself

offspring to serve him in it. The children will complain for lack of room. "Our numbers are increasing so fast that *the place is too strait* (small) *for us,*" as the company of the prophets complained (2Ki 6:1). But, small though the place is, still more will want to come in; even when the *poor and the maimed, the halt and the blind,* are brought in, *yet still there is room,* room enough for those who are already in and still room for more (Lk 14:21–22). The mother will stand amazed at the increase of her family (v. 21). She will say, *Who has begotten* (borne) *me these?* and, *Who has brought up these?* They come to her with all the affection of children, but she never bore any pain for them, but has them already brought up by her side. The church is not perpetually visible; there are times when it is made desolate and few. Yet on the other hand, its desolations will not last forever. God will raise up children to Abraham out of stones (Mt 3:9). Sometimes this is done in a very surprising way, as when a nation is born suddenly (66:8).

1.5. This will be done with the help of the Gentiles (v. 22). The Jews were rejected, among whom it was expected that the church would be built up. The Gentiles will be called in. God *will lift up his hand to them* (v. 22) to invite or beckon them, having in vain held it out all day to the Jews (65:2). And he *will set up his standard* (banner) *to them,* the preaching of the eternal Gospel, and *they shall bring thy sons in their arms* (v. 22). When the sons of Zion who are found among them return to their own country, the Gentiles will help them. God can raise up friends for returning Israelites even among Gentiles. "Do you ask, *Who has begotten and brought up these?* Know that they were born and brought up among the Gentiles, but they are now brought into your family."

2. The church will have an effective influence in the nations (vv. 22–23). *Kings shall be thy nursing* (foster) *fathers* (v. 23), to carry your children in their arms, like Moses (Nu 11:12); and *their queens shall be thy nursing mothers* (v. 23). This promise was partially fulfilled to the Jews after their return from exile. Several of the kings of Persia supported and encouraged them, like Cyrus, Darius, and Artaxerxes; Esther the queen was a nursing mother to the Jews who remained in their exile, putting her life in her hands to snatch the child out of the flames. After a long captivity, the Christian church was fortunate in some such kings and queens as Constantine and his mother Helena, and afterward Theodosius and others, who nursed the church with every possible care and tenderness. The church in this world is in its infancy, and it is in the power of rulers and magistrates to do it great service. Others who resist the church's interests will be forced to yield: *They shall bow down to thee and lick the dust* (v. 23). The promise to the church of Philadelphia seems to be taken from this (Rev 3:9): *I will make those of the synagogue of Satan to come and worship before thy feet.*

Verses 24–26

Here is:

1. An objection against the promise of the Jews' release, suggesting that it was not to be expected, for they were plunder in the hands of the warriors (v. 24), and so it was unlikely they would be rescued by force. They were lawful captives; because they had broken the law of God, they were justly handed over to be exiled, and by the law of nations, being taken in war, they were justly kept in captivity until they were ransomed or exchanged. Now this is spoken either by the enemies, as justifying them in their refusal to let them go, or by their friends,

either by way of distrust or thankfulness. "Who would have thought that the plunder would ever be *taken from the mighty* (v. 24)? But it is done." This may be applied to our redemption by Christ.

2. This objection answered by an explicit promise (v. 25): "*Even the captives of the mighty*, though they are mighty, will be taken away, *and the prey* (plunder) *of the terrible* (fierce), though they are fierce, will be retrieved; they cannot with all their arrogance defy the rescue and the purposes of God for it." Here is a further promise that God that will bring judgments on the oppressors and so bring salvation for the oppressed: "*I will contend with him that contends with thee* (v. 25), and this is how *I will save thy children*" (v. 25). The captives will be rescued by *leading captivity captive* (Ps 68:18), that is, sending into captivity those who had held God's people captive (Rev 13:10). "*I will feed those that oppress thee with their own flesh*, and *they shall be drunken with their own blood* (v. 26). The proud Babylonians will become easy prey to one another. Their ruin, which was begun by a foreign invasion, will be completed by internal divisions. They will *bite and devour one another*, until they are *consumed one of another*" (Gal 5:15). Notice how cruel people sometimes are to themselves and to one another. They not only thirst for blood but also drink it with as much pleasure as if it were sweet wine.

3. The effect of Babylon's ruin: *All flesh* (the whole human race) *shall know that I the Lord am thy Saviour* (v. 26). God will make it clear to all the world that although Israel seems lost, they have a Redeemer.

CHAPTER 50

In this chapter: 1. Those people to whom God sends a message of adversity are justly accused of bringing all their troubles on themselves, because it has been made clear that God was able and ready to help them if they had been ready to be rescued (vv. 1–3). 2. The One whom God sends produces his commission (v. 4), declares his own readiness to submit to all the suffering he has been called to in fulfilling that commission (vv. 5–6), and assures himself that God, who sent him, will support him against all opposition (vv. 7–9). 3. The message that is sent is life and death (Dt 30:15, 19), comfort to discouraged saints and terror to presumptuous sinners (vv. 10–11). Now all this seems to have a double reference: on the one hand, to the unbelieving Jews in Babylon and the prophet Isaiah, and, on the other, to the unbelieving Jews in our Savior's time, whose own fault it was that they were rejected, because Christ had preached a great deal to them and suffered a great deal from them. The prophet concludes with an exhortation to trust in God, not in ourselves.

Verses 1–3

Those who have professed to be the people of God and yet seem to be dealt with severely tend to complain about God. But in response to their murmurings, we have:

1. A challenge given them to prove that the quarrel began on God's side (v. 1). He had been a husband to them, and husbands were then allowed power to put away their wives for any small thing they found displeasing (Dt 24:1; Mt 19:7). But they could not say that God had dealt with them like that. It was true that they were now separated from him and had remained many days without ephod, altar, or sacrifice, but whose fault was that? He had been a father to them, and fathers then had the power to sell their children as slaves to their

creditors to pay debts. Now it was true that the Jews were sold to the Babylonians then, and afterward to the Romans, but did God sell them for payment of his debts? No; he was not indebted to any of those to whom they were sold.

2. A charge, showing that they themselves were the authors of their own ruin: "*Behold, for* (because of) *your iniquities*, for the pleasure you took in them and for the gratification of your own corrupt sinful desires, *you have sold yourselves; for your iniquities you are sold* (v. 1). You sold yourselves to do evil, and so God justly sold you into the hands of your enemies" (2Ch 12:5, 8). The Jews were sent into Babylon because of their idolatry, and they were finally rejected for crucifying the Lord of glory (1Co 2:8); these were the sins for which they were sold and put away.

3. The confirmation of this challenge and this charge. God came and offered them his favor, he offered them his helping hand, either to prevent their trouble or to rescue them from it, but they scorned him and his grace. "Are you blaming me?" God says. "Tell me, then, why, *when I came, was there no man to* meet me? Why, *when I called, was there none to answer me?*" (v. 2). God came to them through his servants the prophets, but *was there* no one who paid any attention to the warnings the prophets gave them. Because they *mocked the messengers of the Lord, God brought upon them the king of the Chaldeans* (Babylonians) (2Ch 36:16–17). Last of all *he sent unto them his Son* (Mt 21:37). He *came to his own*, but *his own received him not* (Jn 1:11); they did not know, because they did not want to know, the things that concerned their peace. It was this disobedience that meant they were put away and their house was left desolate (Mt 21:41; 23:37–38; Lk 19:41–42). It is clear that it was not because of a lack of power in God, for he is almighty and could have restored them from such a great death; nor was it because of a lack of power in Christ, for he is *able to save to the uttermost* (Heb 7:25). *Can this man save us?* For *himself he cannot save* (Mt 27:41). "But," God says, "*is my hand shortened at all* (v. 2), or is it weakened?" Can any limits be put on almighty God? Is he who is the great Redeemer unable to redeem? The expression our Savior sometimes used concerning the power of faith, that it will *remove mountains and plant sycamores in the sea* (Mt 21:21), is not unlike this; if their faith could do that, no doubt their faith would save them.

Verses 4–9

Having proved himself able to save, our Lord Jesus here shows himself to be as willing as he is able. We think the prophet Isaiah is also saying something about himself in these verses, encouraging himself to continue in his work as a prophet despite hardships, not doubting that God will strengthen him. Like David, he speaks about himself as a type of Christ. We see him as:

1. An acceptable preacher. Isaiah, as a prophet, was qualified for the work to which he was called, but Christ was anointed with the Spirit more than anyone else. To make believers perfect (2Ti 3:17), he has:

1.1. *The tongue of the learned* (an instructed tongue), to know how to give instruction, *how to speak a word in season to him that is weary* (v. 4). God gave to Christ an instructed tongue, to encourage and sustain those who are weary and burdened under the weight of sin (Mt 11:28). Notice what is the best learning of a minister, to know how to comfort troubled consciences and to speak properly and clearly to the various needs of poor souls. An ability to do this is God's gift.

1.2. The ear of the learned, to receive instruction. Prophets have as much need of this as of an instructed tongue, for they must hear the word from God's mouth attentively so that they may speak it exactly (Eze 3:17). No one must undertake to be a teacher who has not first been a learner. Christ's apostles were first disciples [Ed. note: the word translated "disciple" in the New Testament literally means "learner"]. Those who want to listen to learn must be awake, for we are naturally drowsy and hear incompletely and do not take any notice. We need to be awakened *morning by morning* (v. 4). The morning, when our spirits are liveliest, is a good time for fellowship with God. The people came *early in the morning* to hear Christ in the temple (Lk 21:38), for it seems he gave instruction in the morning.

2. A patient sufferer (vv. 5–6). Those who are commissioned to speak encouragement to the weary have hard work to do and harsh treatment to experience. *My ear hast thou opened; then said I, Lo, I come* (Ps 40:6–7). *I was not rebellious, neither turned away back* (v. 5). Although he foresaw difficulty and discouragement, although he was to serve constantly as a servant, although he was to humble himself very much, yet he did not break away or fail and was not discouraged (42:4). In this submission he submitted to being scourged: *I gave my back to the smiters* (to those who beat me) (v. 6). He also submitted to being knocked about: *I gave my cheeks to those that* not only beat them but also *plucked off the hair* of the beard (v. 6), which was more painful and shameful. And he submitted to being spit on: *I hid not my face from shame and spitting* (v. 6). Christ underwent all this for us, and voluntarily, to convince us of his willingness to save us.

3. A courageous champion (vv. 7–9). The Redeemer is as famous for his boldness as for his humility and patience, and although he yields, he is more than a conqueror (Ro 8:31). Notice:

3.1. The dependence he has on God. What was the prophet Isaiah's support was the support of Christ himself (v. 7): *The Lord God will help me,* and again in v. 9. Having laid help on his Son for us (Ps 89:19), he gave help to him, and his hand was all along *with the man of his right hand* (Ps 80:17). *He is near that justifieth me* (v. 8). Isaiah, no doubt, was scorned and slandered, as other prophets were, but he despised the reproach (Heb 12:2), knowing that God would roll it away (Jos 5:9) and make his righteousness shine like the dawn, perhaps in this world (Ps 37:6), or at the latest at the great day, when there will be a resurrection of names as well as bodies, and the righteous will shine as the morning sun (Mt 13:43).

3.2. The confidence he then has of the success in his undertaking: "If God will help me, if he will justify me, stand by me, and support me, then *I shall not be confounded* (disgraced) (v. 7): *I know that I will not be ashamed.*"

3.3. The defiance he shows to all opponents and opposition: "God will help me, and *therefore have I set my face like a flint* (v. 7). The prophet was bold in rebuking sin, in warning sinners (Eze 3:8–9), and in asserting the truth of his predictions. Christ continued in his work as Mediator with a steadfast faithfulness and undaunted resolution: "*Who will contend with me,* either in law or by the sword? *Let us stand together* (v. 8) as combatants, or as the plaintiff and defendant." Many offered to dispute with Christ, but he silenced them all. The prophet speaks this out in the name of all faithful ministers; those who keep close to the pure word of God in communicating their message need not fear contradiction. *Great is the truth and it will prevail* (1 Esd 4:49). Christ speaks this out in the name of all

believers; he speaks it as their champion. *Who is he that shall condemn me?* Perhaps the prophet was condemned to die; we are sure Christ was, but both could say, *Who is he that shall condemn?* For there is no condemnation for those whom God justifies (Ro 8:1). The righteous cause of Christ and his prophets will survive all opponents. The *moth shall eat them up* (v. 9) silently and imperceptibly; a little thing will be enough to destroy them.

Verses 10–11

Having now an instructed tongue, the prophet uses it here. His word is the summary of the Gospel. *He that believes shall be saved,* even though for a while he walks in darkness, but *he that believes not* (Mk 16:16), though for a while he walks in the light of his own fire, will still *lie down in sorrow* (v. 11).

1. Comfort is spoken here to discouraged saints, and they are encouraged to trust in God's grace (v. 10). Children of God are those who fear the Lord with a childlike fear, who stand in awe of his majesty and are afraid of incurring his displeasure. They are those who obey the voice of God's servant and are willing to be ruled by the Lord Jesus in the great work of human redemption. Those who truly fear God will obey the voice of Christ. It is nothing new for the children and heirs of light (Jn 12:36; Eph 5:8) sometimes to walk in darkness, and for a time not to have any glimpse or gleam of light. Let the one who is in the dark in this way *trust in the name of the Lord* (v. 10), in the goodness of his nature, his wisdom, power, and goodness. *The name of the Lord is a strong tower* (Pr 18:10). If they walk before God, which someone may do even though they walk in the dark, they will find God all-sufficient for them. Let them keep hold of their covenant relationship with God and call God *their God,* as Christ on the cross, *My God, My God* (Mt 27:46).

2. Presumptuous sinners are warned not to trust in themselves (v. 11). They *kindle a fire* and *walk in the light of that fire.* They depend on their own righteousness, burning their incense with that fire—as did Nadab and Abihu (Lev 10:1)—and not with the fire from heaven. They *compass themselves about with sparks of their own kindling* (provide themselves with flaming torches) (v. 11). As they trust in their own righteousness, and not in the righteousness of Christ, so they place their happiness in their worldly possessions and enjoyment, not in the favor of God. Creature comforts are like flaming torches, short-lived and soon gone. These sinners are ironically told to *walk in the light of their own fire* (v. 11). Those who make the world their comfort and make their own righteousness their confidence will meet with bitterness in the end (2Sa 2:26). A godly person's way may be miserable, but their end will be peace (Ps 37:37) and everlasting light (Isa 60:19–20). An evildoer's way may be pleasant, but their end will be darkness.

CHAPTER 51

This chapter is intended to comfort and encourage those who fear God and keep his commands (Ecc 12:13) even when they walk in darkness and have no light. Whenever the church of God is in distress, her friends and well-wishers may encourage themselves and one another with these words: 1. That God, who originally raised his church out of nothing, will take care that it will not perish (vv. 1–3). 2. That the righteousness and salvation he intends for his church are very near and can be depended on (vv. 4–6). 3. That the persecutors of the church are weak (vv. 7–8). 4. That the same power that did wonders for the church in the past is now engaged and employed to protect and save her (vv. 9–11). 5. That God himself, the Maker of the world, has undertaken both to rescue his people from their distress and to encourage them in it, and he has sent his prophet to assure them of this (vv. 12–16). 6. That, deplorable though the condition of the church now is (vv. 17–20), her persecutors and oppressors will soon be reduced to the same terrible circumstances, and even worse (vv. 21–23).

The first three paragraphs of this chapter begin with Hearken unto me (vv. 1, 4, 7), and it is God's people who are all along called to listen, for even when comforts are spoken to them, sometimes they hearken not, through anguish of spirit (Ex 6:9); therefore they are called again and again to listen (vv. 1, 4, 7). The two other paragraphs of this chapter begin with Awake, awake; in the former (v. 9) God's people call on him to awake and help them, and in the latter (v. 17) God calls on them to awake and help themselves.

Verses 1–3

Notice:

1. How the people of God to whom this word of encouragement is sent and who are called on to listen to it are described here (v. 1). They are those who follow after righteousness, those who mean business with God, who are pressing on with him, to have his favor restored to them and the image of God renewed in them (Col 3:10).

2. How they are directed to look back to their origin, to the smallness of their beginnings: "Look unto the rock whence you were hewn (from which you were cut)" (v. 1)—the idolatrous family in Ur of the Chaldeans, out of which Abraham was taken, the generation of slaves that the leaders and fathers of their tribes were in Egypt. "Look to the hole of the pit (quarry) out of which you were digged, as clay, when God formed you into a people." How hard was that rock out of which we were cut, disinclined to receive impressions, and how miserable the quarry out of which we were dug! Consideration of this should fill us with low thoughts of ourselves and high thoughts of God's grace. "Look unto Abraham your father, the father of all the faithful, of all who follow after the righteousness of faith as he did (Ro 4:11), and unto Sarah that bore you and whose daughters you all are as long as you continue to do good (1Pe 3:6). Think how Abraham was called alone, but was still blessed and multiplied, and let that encourage you to depend on the promise of God. Look to Abraham, and see what he gained by trusting in the promise of God; imitate Abraham and follow God with implicit faith."

3. How they are assured here that their present sowing of tears will ultimately end in a harvest of joy (Ps 126:5) (v. 3). God will find a time and way to comfort Zion. It is the greatest comfort to the church to be made useful to the glory of God, to be as his garden, in which he delights. He will make them cheerful and so give them hearts to rejoice. With the fruits of righteousness (Php 1:11), joy and gladness shall be found therein (v. 3), for the more holiness people have and the more good they do, the more gladness they have.

Verses 4–8

Both these declarations end with an assurance of the eternal nature of God's righteousness and his salvation.

1. This encouragement belongs to "my people, and my nation (v. 4), those whom I have set apart for myself, who acknowledge me and are acknowledged by me." They are able to form a right judgment about truth and falsehood,

good and evil. Just as they have good minds, so also they have good hearts, for they have the law of God in them, written and ruling there. God acknowledges as his people those in whose hearts his law is (v. 7). Even those who know righteousness, who have the law of God in their hearts, may still be in great distress and sorrow, loaded down by others' scorn and contempt, but their God will strengthen and encourage them.

2. The encouragement that belongs to God's people is that:

2.1. The Gospel of Christ will be preached and declared to the world: A law shall proceed from me (v. 4), a Gospel law, the law of Christ, the law of faith (2:3). This law is that law of liberty (Jas 1:25) by which the world will be ruled and judged. It will take firm and deep root in the world. And it will rest, not only for the benefit of the Jews but also as a light of the people (v. 4) of other nations.

2.2. This law will open up a ready way to people, so that they may be justified and saved (v. 5). There is no salvation without righteousness, and wherever there is the righteousness of God (Ro 3:21; 2Co 5:21), there will also be his salvation.

2.3. This righteousness and salvation will appear very soon: My righteousness is near (v. 5). It is near in time and place (Ro 10:8).

2.4. This Gospel righteousness and salvation will not be confined to the Jewish nation but will be extended to the Gentiles: My arms shall judge the people (v. 5). Those who will not yield to the justice of God's mouth will be crushed by the justice of his hand. Some will be judged by the Gospel, because for judgment Christ came into this world (Jn 9:39); but others, and those of the isles, shall wait upon him and welcome his Gospel, its commands as well as its comforts. It was an encouragement to God's people, to his nation, that very many people would be added to them. It is added, And on my arm shall they trust (v. 5), the arm of the Lord that is revealed in Christ (53:1).

2.5. This righteousness and salvation shall be for ever. Just as it will spread through all the nations of the earth, so also it will last through all the ages of the world. The visible heavens above will vanish like smoke (v. 6); they will be rolled up like a scroll (34:4; Rev 6:14). The earth will wax (become) old like a garment (v. 6). But when heaven and earth pass away, when all flesh and its glory withers as the grass, the word of the Lord endures for ever (1Pe 1:25). Those whose happiness is bound up in Christ's righteousness and salvation will have the comfort of it when time and days have come to an end.

3. If God's righteousness and salvation are near to them, then let them not fear the reproach of men (v. 7), the taunts of mere mortals, or be afraid of their revilings or spiteful mocking, those who ask you to sing the songs of Zion (Ps 137:3), or who ask you scornfully, Where is now your God? Those who cannot bear a harsh word for Christ cannot bear much for him. Let us not fear people who make fun of us. They will be quickly silenced (v. 8): The moth shall eat them up like a garment (50:9). The worm shall eat them like wool, or woolen cloth. The falsehood of all their taunts and scorn will be detected, and truth will triumph. Clouds may darken the sun, but they cannot obstruct its progress through the sky.

Verses 9–16

In these verses we have:

1. A prayer that God would, in his providence, appear and come to rescue his people. Awake, awake! Put on strength, O arm of the Lord! (v. 9). The arm of the Lord is Christ, or perhaps it stands for God himself (Ps 44:23).

Awake! Why sleepest thou? The arm of the Lord is said to awake when the power of God is stretched out for action. God does not need to be reminded or animated by us, but he allows us to ask him humbly and earnestly to show his power so as to bring himself praise. The church sees her situation as bad, her enemies to be many and powerful, her friends few and feeble, and so she depends purely on the strength of God's arm to help her.

2. The pleas to back up this prayer.

2.1. They plead precedents: the experiences of their ancestors, the great things God has done for them. "Let the powerful arm of the Lord be shown to act on our behalf. It did wonders against the Egyptians; it *cut Rahab* to pieces (v. 9) with one terrible plague after another, *and* it *wounded* Pharaoh, *the dragon* (Ps 74:13). It did wonders for Israel. *It dried up the sea* to open up *a way* through the sea *for the ransomed to pass over*" (v. 10). Past experiences are good pleas in prayer. *Thou hast; wilt thou not?* (Ps 85:1–6).

2.2. They plead promises (v. 11): *And the redeemed of the Lord shall return*, that is, as it may be read by supplying what is implied, "Thou hast said, they shall return," referring to 35:10. When sinners are brought out of the slavery of sin into the glorious liberty of God's children (Ro 8:21), they can come singing, like birds released from their cage. When the souls of believers are saved from the prison of the body, they come with singing to the heavenly Zion. Will not the One who intends in the end to bring us such joy bring about such rescues for us as we need in the meantime?

3. The answer immediately given to this prayer: *I, even I, am he that comforteth you* (v. 12). They prayed for the activity of his power; he answers them with the comfort of his grace, which may well be accepted as its equivalent. If God does not answer immediately *with the saving strength of his right hand*, we must be thankful if he answers us, as an angel himself was answered (Zec 1:13), *with good words and comfortable words*. Notice how God decides to comfort his people: he takes the work into his own hands: *I, even I*, will do it.

3.1. He comforts the fearful by rebuking them: *Why art thou cast down, and why disquieted?* (Ps 42:5, 11; 43:5) (vv. 12–13). Notice:

3.1.1. The absurdity of those fears. It is a dishonor to us to give way to them: *Who art thou, that thou shouldst be afraid* (v. 12)? It is absurd to have such dread of mere mortals. What! *Afraid of a man that shall die*, die certainly and soon, afraid *of the son of man* (of human beings), *who shall be made as grass* (v. 12), who will wither and be trodden underfoot or eaten up? This teaches us that we should look on every person as mortal. Those we admire, love, and trust in are mortal: they will die. We must consider how foolish it is for the servants of the living God to be afraid of mere mortals, who are here today and gone tomorrow. It is absurd to *fear continually every day* (v. 13). Now and then a danger may be near and threatening, and it may be wise to fear it, but to be always tossed about, anxious about danger at every turn, and to tremble at the shaking of every leaf (Lev 26:36) is to make ourselves all our lifetime *subject to bondage* (Heb 2:15). It is absurd to fear without good reason: "You are *afraid of the fury of the oppressor* (v. 13). It is gone in an instant, and the danger is over before you are aware." *Pharaoh king of Egypt is but a noise* (Jer 46:17), and the king of Babylon is no more. What has become of all the furious oppressors of God's Israel, who intimidated and threatened them and were a terror to them? They have passed away; see, they died, and so will these.

3.1.2. The ungodliness of those fears: "Thou art *afraid of a man that shall die and forgettest the Lord thy Maker*, who is also the Maker of all the world." This shows us that our excessive fear of other people is a tacit forgetfulness of God. When we are disturbed by fear of other people, we forget that there is a God above them and that the greatest people have no power except what is given them from above (Jn 19:11). We forget the experiences we have had of his care for us, and we forget his timely intervention to help us on many occasions, when we thought the oppressor was about to destroy; we forget our Jehovah-jirehs, "the Lord will provide" (Ge 22:14), monuments of mercy on the mountain of the Lord.

3.2. He comforts those who are in chains (vv. 14–15). Notice here what they do for themselves: *The captive exile hastens that he may be loosed* (v. 14) and may return to his own country, from which he has been banished; his concern is *that he may not die in the pit*—not die a prisoner—and that his *bread should not fail*. Some understand this as the captive's fault. He is distrustfully impatient with delays, cannot wait for God's time, and thinks he will undoubtedly die in the dungeon if he is not released immediately. Others take it to be to the captive's praise, that when the doors are thrown open, he does not linger. And then it follows, *But I am the Lord thy God* (v. 15), which shows what God will do for the captives, that is, what they cannot do for themselves. He will find a way to still the threatening storm and bring them safely to the harbor. *The Lord of hosts is his name*, his name forever, the name by which his people have long known him.

3.3. He comforts all his people who depend on what the prophets say to them in the name of the Lord and build their hopes on it. When the rescues that the prophets speak about either do not come so soon as they expected them or do not reach all their expectations, they begin to think themselves unfortunate, but as for this, they are encouraged (v. 16) by what God says to his messenger: *I have put my words in thy mouth, that* by them *I may plant the heavens* (v. 16). God undertook to comfort his people (v. 12), but he continues to do so by his prophets, by his Gospel, and so that he may do it through them, he here tells us:

3.3.1. That his word in them is true. He acknowledges that what they have said is what he directed and told them to say: "*I have put my words in thy mouth*, and so those who receive you and them receive me" (Mk 9:37). God's Spirit not only revealed to the prophets the things they spoke of but also dictated to them the words they were to speak (2Pe 1:21; 1Co 2:13).

3.3.2. That his word is secure: I have *covered thee in the shadow of my hand*. He said this before (49:2), expressing special protection of not only the prophets but also their prophecies, not only of Christ but also of Christianity and the Gospel of Christ.

3.3.3. That when this word comes to be fulfilled, the fulfillment will be very great. "*I have put my words in thy mouth* not so that by their fulfillment I may plant a nation or found a city, but so *that I may plant the heavens and lay the foundations of the earth* (v. 16), so that I may do for my people what will be a new creation." This must look as far forward as to the great work done by the Gospel of Christ and the setting up of his holy faith in the world. Just as it was by Christ that God made the world in the beginning (Heb 1:2) and later formed the Old Testament church (Zec 6:12), so by him, and the words put into his mouth, he will set up a new world; he will again plant the heavens and found the earth. Because sin has put the whole creation into disorder, Christ's taking away the sin of the world (Jn 1:29) put all into order again.

Verses 17–23

Having awoken to comfort his people, God here calls on them to awake, not so much out of the sleep of sin—though that is also necessary for their being ready to be rescued—as out of the stupor of despair. When the inhabitants of Jerusalem were in exile, they were so overwhelmed by the sense of their troubles that they had no heart or spirit to consider anything that led to their comfort or relief.

1. It is acknowledged that Jerusalem has long been in the depths of misery.

1.1. She has been under the signs of God's displeasure. He has put into her hand *the cup of his fury* (v. 17), that is, her share of his displeasure and wrath. She had provoked him to anger most bitterly and was made to taste the bitter fruits of his wrath. The cup of God's wrath is, and will be, a *cup of trembling*, the goblet that makes people stagger, to all those who have it put into their hands. It is said (Ps 75:8) concerning *the dregs of the cup*, the loathsome sediments at the bottom, that *all the wicked of the earth shall wring them out, and drink them*. Wherever there has been a cup of unfaithfulness—as there had been in Jerusalem's hand when she was idolatrous—sooner or later there will be a cup of wrath, *a cup of trembling*.

1.2. Those who should have helped her in her distress failed her (v. 18). She staggers and is very unsteady. She does not know what she is saying or doing, much less what she ought to say or do, and in this unhappy condition, *of all the sons that she has brought forth* and brought up, that she has borne and educated, *there is none to guide her*, no one to take her by the hand to help her out of her trouble or speak comfort to her in it.

1.2.1. Her trouble was very great. *These two things have come unto thee* (v. 19) to complete your ruin and destruction: *the famine and the sword*, by which the citizens perished. Or perhaps these two things that had come on Jerusalem were the same as the two things that were later to come on Babylon (47:9), *loss of children and widowhood*—a pitiful case, and yet, "when you have brought it on yourself by your own sin and foolishness, *who shall be sorry for thee?*"

1.2.2. Those who should have been her comforters were their own tormentors (v. 20): *They have fainted*, being completely discouraged and driven to despair; they have no patience in which to keep possession of their own souls and enjoy themselves, nor any confidence in God's promise. They throw themselves on the ground, in anguish at their troubles, and there *they lie at the head of all the streets*. They lie there like *a wild bull* (NIV: an antelope caught) *in a net*, ranting and raging, struggling and pulling to help themselves but entangling themselves all the more and making their condition even worse by their own fury and discontent. Those who are of a perverse spirit (19:14) never ask why he is contending with them, and so nothing appears in them except anger with God.

2. It is promised that Jerusalem's troubles will finally come to an end and be transferred to her persecutors (v. 21–22): "*Nevertheless hear this, thou afflicted. Thus saith thy Lord, the Lord, and thy God—the Lord*, who is able to help you—your God, in covenant with you and who has undertaken to make you happy. He is the God *who pleads the cause of his people* (v. 22), who takes what is done against them as being done against himself." It is his own cause; he has embraced it, and so he will plead it. "*I will take out of thy hand the cup of trembling*, the goblet

that makes you stagger (v. 22), that bitter cup; it will pass from you" (Mt 26:39). In fact, it is promised, "*Thou shalt no more drink it again.*" Their persecutors and oppressors will be made to drink from the same bitter cup from which the oppressed have drunk so deeply (v. 23). Here the New Testament Babylon follows in the steps of that old oppressor, tyrannizing the human conscience, laying down the law, making God's people suffer great strain and compelling them to make sinful agreements. But Babylon's case will be as bad as Jerusalem's. Daniel's persecutors will be thrown into Daniel's den (Da 6:24).

CHAPTER 52

Most of this chapter is on the same subject as the previous chapter, the restoration of the Jews from Babylon, but the last three verses are on the same subject as the next chapter, the person of the Redeemer, his humiliation, and his exaltation. Notice: 1. The encouragement given to the Jews in exile to hope that God would save them in his own way and time (vv. 1–6). 2. The great joy for both ministers and people on that occasion (vv. 7–10). 3. The call given to those who remained in exile to leave when liberty was proclaimed (vv. 11–12). 4. A short description given of the Messiah, which is enlarged on in the next chapter (vv. 13–15).

Verses 1–6

Here:

1. God's people are stirred to act vigorously for their own deliverance (vv. 1–2). Let them wake up from their despondency and encourage themselves and one another. Let them wake up from their distrust, look above them, look around them, look into the promises, and look into the providences of God that were working for them. Let them raise their expectations of great things from God. Let them wake up from their dullness. God here gives them an assurance:

1.1. That they will be reformed by their captivity: *There shall no more come into thee the uncircumcised and the unclean* (the uncircumcised and defiled will not enter you again) (v. 1); the idolatrous customs of such people will no longer be introduced, or at least not harbored. Similarly, the Gospel Jerusalem is purified by the blood of Christ and the grace of God and is truly made a holy city (Rev 21:27).

1.2. That they will be restored from captivity, that they will not be invaded anymore: "There shall no more come against thee," as it may read, *the uncircumcised and the unclean*. If they keep close to God and keep faith with him, God will keep the enemy away, but if they corrupt themselves again, Antiochus will defile their temple and the Romans will destroy it. However, they will have peace for some time. Let them prepare for joy: "*Put on thy beautiful garments* (garments of splendor) (v. 1), no longer appearing in mourning. Put on a new face, one that smiles, now that a new and pleasant scene is beginning to open up before you." Let them prepare for liberty: "*Shake thyself from the dust* (v. 2) into which your proud oppressors have trodden you (51:23), or into which you have in your sorrow rolled yourself." "Arise and set up," as it may be read. "O Jerusalem! Get clear of all the marks of slavery: *Loose thyself from the bands of* (chains on) *thy neck* (v. 2); assert your own liberty." The Gospel declares liberty to those who have been bound by fears and makes it their duty to take hold of their liberty. Let those who have been weary under the heavy burden of sin find relief in Christ and set themselves free from those chains, for *if the Son shall make them free, they shall be free indeed* (Jn 8:36).

2. God stirs himself to restore his people. He considers several things:

2.1. The Babylonians who oppressed them never acknowledged God any more than Sennacherib did (10:6–7). *"You have sold yourselves for nought;* you gained nothing by it, nor did I" (v. 3). The Babylonians gave him no thanks for them, but rather despised and blasphemed his name on that account. "And therefore they, having so long had you for nothing, will at last restore you for nothing: *You shall be redeemed without price"* (v. 3), as was promised (45:13).

2.2. They have often been in similar trouble before, and it would be a pity for them now to be left in the hands of these oppressors (v. 4): *"My people went down into Egypt* to settle there in a friendly way, but the Egyptians enslaved them and ruled them harshly." And then they were rescued. Why may we not think God will save his people now? At other times *the Assyrian oppressed the* people of God *without cause*, as when the ten tribes were taken captive by the king of Assyria; soon afterward Sennacherib, another Assyrian, made himself master of all the fortified towns of Judah. The Babylonians could be called Assyrians, their monarchy being a branch of the Assyrians, and they now oppressed them without cause.

2.3. God's glory is suffering by the wrongs done to his people (v. 5): *What have I here*, what do I gain by it, *that my people are taken away for nought?* The captives are so discouraged that they cannot praise him. *Those that rule over them make them to howl*, as the Egyptians previously made them cry out (Ex 2:23). Nevertheless, God has heard them and come to rescue them, as he rescued them out of Egypt (Ex 3:7–8). The natives have blasphemed, boasting that they are too powerful for God because they are too powerful for his people, and they have defied him as unable to save his people. "Now," God says, "I will go down to save them, for their oppressors will neither praise God themselves nor allow them to do it."

2.4. His glory will be shown by their restoration (v. 6): *"Therefore*, because my name is constantly blasphemed, I will arise, and *my people shall know my name*, my name Jehovah."

Verses 7–12

The taking of the Jews from Babylon and the application of v. 7 to the preaching of the Gospel by the apostle Paul (Ro 10:15) clearly show that that rescue was a type and figure of the redemption of humanity by Jesus Christ.

1. It is spoken of here as a great blessing, which should be welcomed with joy.

1.1. Those who bring the news of their release will be very acceptable (v. 7) as they come over the mountains around Jerusalem. The verse is meant to refer to some of the Jews, who either immediately went themselves to Jerusalem or sent their own messengers there, to tell the few who remained there that their brothers and sisters would soon be with them. The message was delivered in this way because it was to be declared as proof that Zion's God reigns, and indeed that was what the messengers said to Zion: *Thy God reigns* (v. 7). This must be applied to the preaching of the Gospel, which is a proclamation of peace and salvation; it is truly Gospel, good news of victory over our spiritual enemies and freedom from spiritual bondage. The good news is that the Lord Jesus reigns. Christ himself brought this news first (Lk 4:18; Heb 2:3), and v. 7 speaks about him: *How beautiful are his feet!*

his feet that were nailed to the cross, how beautiful on Mount Calvary.

1.2. Zion's watchmen will rejoice (v. 8). The watchmen (62:6) are those whom God has set on the walls of Jerusalem to mention his name and to continue in urgent prayer to him till he again *makes Jerusalem a praise in the earth* (62:7). They stand on their watchtower waiting for an answer to their prayers (Hab 2:1). When the good news comes, they are the first to receive it. They will *lift up the voice, with the voice together shall they sing* (v. 8), to invite others to join with them in their praises. They will see an exact agreement between the prophecy and the event, the promise and the fulfillment; they will see how these words and events look to one another *eye to eye*, and they will be satisfied that the same God spoke the one and did the other. Applying this also, like v. 8, to Gospel times, it is a promise of the outpouring of the Spirit on Gospel ministers, as a spirit of wisdom and revelation (Eph 1:17), to lead them into all truth (Jn 16:13), so that they will *see eye to eye*, or face to face, and be unanimous in this great matter of salvation. Zion's ruins will then rejoice because they will be surprisingly comforted (v. 9): *Break forth into joy, sing together, you waste places* (ruins) *of Jerusalem.* The redemption of Jerusalem is the joy of all God's people (Lk 2:38). God will have the glory of it (v. 10). He *has made bare his holy arm*—shown and displayed his power—*in the eyes of all the nations.*

2. When liberty is proclaimed, let the people of God hasten out of Babylon as fast as they reasonably can: *Depart, depart* (v. 11), *go out from the midst of her;* be gone. Babylon is no place for Israelites (Ezr 1:5). And it is a call to all those who are still in the slavery of sin and Satan to make use of the freedom that Christ has proclaimed to them. Let them make sure they do not take with them any of the defilements of Babylon: *Touch no unclean thing* (v. 11). Let them depend on the presence of God with them and his protection in their move (v. 12): *You shall not go out with haste.* They are to go with diligent haste, but not with an insecure, distrustful haste, as if they were afraid of being pursued. Cyrus will discharge them honorably, and they will return honorably; they will not have to steal away, *for the Lord will go before them* (v. 12). God will both lead their vanguard and bring up their rear.

Verses 13–15

This prophecy, which begins here and continues to the end of the next chapter, points as clearly as possible to Jesus Christ. The ancient Jews understood it to refer to the Messiah, although some modern Jews want it to refer to Jeremiah. But Philip has put it beyond dispute that of *him speaks the prophet this*, of him and of no other man (Ac 8:34–35).

1. God acknowledges Christ to be commissioned for his undertaking. He is appointed to it. "He is *my servant*, whom I employ and will therefore uphold." In his undertaking, Christ does his Father's will, seeks his Father's honor, and serves the interests of his Father's kingdom. He *shall deal prudently, for the spirit of wisdom and understanding* will rest on him (11:2).

2. He gives a short description of both his humiliation and his exaltation. *Many were astonished* (appalled) *at him* (v. 14) because of his sorrows; *His visage was marred more than any man's* when he was buffeted, struck on the cheek, and crowned with thorns, and did not hide his face from shame and spitting (50:6). He was a *man of sorrows* (53:3). Never was there sorrow like his sorrow (La 1:12). But notice how highly God exalted him because he

humbled himself (Php 2:9). Three words are used for this (v. 13): *He will be exalted and extolled and be very high.* God will exalt him, people will extol him, and with both he will be lifted up higher than the highest, higher than the heavens. Many nations will be the better for him, for he will sprinkle them; the blood of sprinkling will be applied to their consciences to purify them (Heb 12:24), for in his death was *a fountain opened* (Zec 13:1). He will do it by baptism. This promise had its fulfillment when Christ sent his apostles to disciple all nations by baptizing or sprinkling them. *Kings will shut their mouths at him* (v. 15), that is, they will not open their mouths against him, as they have done. They will receive his words and laws with great humility and reverence. They will see what has not been told them; the Gospel brings to light things that will awaken the reverence of kings and kingdoms. They will consider and understand the glory of God shining in the face of Christ (2Co 4:6), which before they have not been told about—*they have not heard* (v. 15). Christ disappointed the expectations of those, like the worldly Jews, who looked for a Messiah according to their own thoughts, but far surpassed the expectations of those who looked for such a Messiah as was promised.

CHAPTER 53

The two great things that the Spirit of Christ in the Old Testament prophets predicted were the sufferings of Christ and the glories that would follow (1Pe 1:11). But nowhere in the whole Old Testament are these two so clearly and fully prophesied as here in this chapter. This chapter is so full of the unsearchable riches of Christ (Eph 3:8) that it may be called the Gospel of the evangelist Isaiah rather than the prophecy of the prophet Isaiah. 1. The shame of Christ's sufferings—the lowliness of his appearance, the greatness of his grief, and the prejudice that many people had against his teaching (vv. 1–3). 2. The rolling away of this shame and reproach (Jos 5:9) and the stamping of immortal honor on his suffering by four considerations: that he did his Father's will (vv. 4, 6, 10); that he made atonement for the sin of the human race (vv. 4–6, 8, 11–12), for it was not for any sin of his own that he suffered (v. 9); that he bore his sufferings with an invincible patience (v. 7); and that he would prosper in his undertaking, and his sufferings would end in his immortal honor (vv. 10–12).

Verses 1–3

At the end of the previous chapter, the prophet foresaw and foretold the sympathetic reception that the Gospel of Christ would find among the Gentiles. Now here he foretells, with wonder, the unbelief of the Jews, despite the previous announcements they had of the coming of the Messiah. Notice:

1. The contempt they showed for the Gospel of Christ (v. 1). It is also applied to the little success that the apostles' preaching met with among Jews or Gentiles (Ro 10:16). Few believed the prophets who spoke about Christ. When he himself came, none of the rulers or any of the Pharisees followed him, and only one or two of the ordinary people here and there did. When the apostles announced this message throughout the world, some in every place believed, but comparatively few. Even to this day, out of the many who profess to believe this message, there are only a few who warmly embrace it and submit to its power (2Ti 3:5). They do not discern the divine power that accompanies the word, that activity of the Spirit that makes the word effective. They do not believe the

Gospel because, by rebelling against the light they had (Job 24:13), they forfeited the grace of God.

2. The contempt they showed for the person of Christ because of the lowliness of his appearance (vv. 2–3). Notice here:

2.1. The lowly condition he submitted to, how he humbled and emptied himself. The entry he made into the world and his character while in it did not in any way correspond to the ideas that the Jews had formed of the Messiah.

2.1.1. It was expected that his background would be very great and noble. He was to be the Son of David, but he sprang up out of this royal and illustrious family when it was reduced to a very low level, and Joseph was only a poor carpenter. This is what is meant here by his being *a root out of a dry ground* (v. 2), that he was born of a lowly and despised family, in the north, in Galilee, of a family out of which, like a dry and desert ground, nothing green, nothing great, was expected, in a country with such a bad reputation that it was thought that nothing good could come out of it (Jn 1:46).

2.1.2. It was expected that he would make a public entry and come in pomp and with honor, but instead of that, he grew up before God, not before people. *He grew up as a tender plant* (v. 2), silently and imperceptibly, as the grain grows up, *we know not how* (Mk 4:27).

2.1.3. It was expected that he would have some unusual beauty in his face and person, which would charm the eyes, attract the heart, and raise the expectations of everyone who saw him. But there was nothing of the kind about this man; not that he was deformed or misshapen, but *he had no form nor comeliness* (no beauty or majesty) (v. 2), none of the extraordinary features that one might have expected to meet in an incarnate deity. When Moses was born, he was *exceeding fair*, to such a degree that it was looked on as a sign of good things to come (Ac 7:20; Heb 11:23). When David was anointed, he was *of a beautiful countenance, and goodly to look to* (1Sa 16:12). But our Lord Jesus appeared in the world having nothing of tangible glory. His Gospel is preached *not with the enticing words of man's wisdom* (1Co 2:4), but with all plainness.

2.1.4. It was expected that he would live a pleasant life, which would have attracted every kind of person to him, but on the contrary, he was *a man of sorrows and acquainted with grief* (v. 3). His condition was sorrowful for many reasons. He had an unsettled life, had nowhere to lay his head (Mt 8:20), lived on the gifts of other people, was opposed and threatened, and *endured the contradiction* (opposition) *of sinners against himself* (Heb 12:3). His spirit was tender, and he allowed himself to express his sorrow. He was intimately acquainted with grief, for he knew the griefs of others and sympathized with them.

2.2. The low opinion that people had of him for this reason. There was in him the beauty of holiness (Ps 29:2; 96:9) and the beauty of goodness, enough to render him *the desire of all nations* (Hag 2:7), but most of the people among whom he lived saw nothing of this beauty, for it was spiritually discerned. He was rejected as a bad man. *We hid as it were our faces from him* (v. 3). It may be read, "He hid as it were his face from us," concealing the glory of his majesty and drawing a veil over it, and so *he was despised and we esteemed him not* (v. 3), because we could not see through that veil.

Verses 4–9

In these verses we have:

1. A further description of the sufferings of Christ. More is said here of the condition to which he humbled

himself, to which he became obedient to the death of the cross (Php 2:8).

1.1. He had griefs and sorrows. He bore them and did not blame his lot in life; he neither shrank from them nor sank under them, but persevered to the end, until he said, *It is finished* (Jn 19:30).

1.2. He had blows and bruises; he was *stricken, smitten, and afflicted* (v. 4). All along he was struck with the harsh words of other people, when people contradicted him, described him as being the worst character, and said all kinds of evil against him (Mt 5:11). Finally, he was struck with blows, blow after blow, from the hands of those who despised him.

1.3. He was scourged, not under the merciful restriction of the Jewish law, which allowed not more than forty lashes to be given to the worst offender, but according to the custom of the Romans. Pilate intended it as an equivalent for his crucifixion, but it turned out to introduce it. He was wounded in his hands, feet, and side.

1.4. He was wronged and abused (v. 7): *He was oppressed*, but our Lord Jesus kept possession of himself.

1.5. He was *taken from prison and judgment* (v. 8). He was judged as an evildoer; he was apprehended, taken into custody, and imprisoned; he was judged: accused, tried, and condemned.

1.6. He was *cut off by* an untimely death *from the land of the living* (v. 8). He made his grave *with the wicked*—for he was crucified between two thieves, as if he had been the worst of the three—but also *with the rich* (v. 9), for he was buried in a grave that belonged to Joseph, a prominent member of the Sanhedrin (Mk 15:43)

2. An account of the meaning of his sufferings. It is natural to be stunned and ask, "How did all these things come about? What evil had he done?" His enemies *esteemed him stricken, smitten of God, and afflicted* (v. 4). Because they hated and persecuted him, they thought that God hated him and persecuted him too. It was true that he was *smitten of God* (v. 4), or, as some read it, "he was God's smitten and afflicted," the Son of God, although struck down and afflicted; but not in the sense in which *they* meant it.

2.1. He never did anything in the least to deserve this harsh treatment. Whereas he was accused of corrupting the nation and sowing sedition, these charges were completely false; he had *done no violence* (v. 9), but went about doing good. And while he was called *that deceiver* (Mt 26:63), *there was no deceit in his mouth* (v. 9) (1Pe 2:22). He never offended either in word or in deed. The judge that condemned him acknowledged he could find no fault in him (Lk 23:4, 14), and the centurion who executed him professed that he was surely a righteous man (Lk 23:47).

2.2. Although he was *oppressed and afflicted*, yet he *opened not his mouth* (v. 7), not even to plead his own innocence, but instead freely offered himself to suffer and die for us. This takes away the scandal of the cross, that he voluntarily submitted to it for great and holy purposes. By his wisdom he could have evaded the sentence, and by his power he could have resisted the execution, but *thus it was written, and thus it behoved him* (it was necessary for him) *to suffer* (Lk 24:46). *This commandment he received from his Father* (Jn 10:18), and so he was led *as a lamb to the slaughter* (v. 7). *As a sheep is dumb before the shearers*—in fact, before the butchers—so he *opened not his mouth* (v. 7), which shows his cheerful submission to his Father's will. By this will we are sanctified: his making his own soul, his own life, an offering for our sin (v. 10).

2.3. It was for our good and in our place that Jesus Christ suffered. This is asserted here clearly and fully.

2.3.1. It is certain that we are all guilty before God. All of us have sinned and have come short of the glory of God (Ro 3:23) (v. 6): *All we like sheep have gone astray.* Every individual not only is stained with original corruption but also stands accused of many actual transgressions. We have gone astray like sheep, which tend to wander and are disinclined to find the way home again. That is our true character; we are prone to backslide from God and are completely unable to return to him by ourselves. Each one of us *turns aside to his own way*, and so we set up our own will in competition with God and his will, and this willfulness is the evil of sin.

2.3.2. Our sins are our sorrows and our griefs (v. 4), or, as it may be read, "our sicknesses and our wounds."

2.3.3. Our Lord Jesus was appointed and undertook to make atonement for our sins. For *the Lord has laid on him the iniquity of us all* (v. 6). The laying of our sins on Christ implies the taking of them away from us; we will not fall under the curse of the law if we submit to the grace of the Gospel. They were laid on Christ when he was *made sin*, that is, a sin offering, *for us* (2Co 5:21). This was how he put himself in a position to give peace to those who are weary and come to him under the burden of sin (Mt 11:28). See Ps 40:6–12. No one but God had power to lay our sins on Christ, both because the sin was committed against God and because Christ was his own Son, who himself had no sin. It was *the iniquity of us all* (v. 6) that was laid on Christ; for in Christ there is enough goodness for the salvation of all, and a serious offer made of that salvation to all, which excludes none who do not exclude themselves. God laid on him our iniquity, but did he consent to it? Yes, he did; for some think that the true reading of the next words (v. 7) is, "It was exacted, and he answered."

2.3.4. Having undertaken to pay our debt, he experienced its penalty. *He bore our griefs and carried our sorrows* (v. 4). Christ bore our sins and so *bore our griefs*; he took them away from us so that we would never be under pressure beyond our ability to endure (2Co 1:8). *He was wounded for our transgressions.* Our sins were the thorns in his head, the nails in his hands and feet, the spear in his side. *He was bruised*, or crushed, *for our iniquities*; they were the cause of his death. V. 8 is to the same effect: for *the transgression of my people was he smitten; the stroke* was *on him* that should have been on us.

2.3.5. The result of this is our peace and healing (v. 5). *The chastisement of our* (the punishment that brought us) *peace was upon him. He is our peace* (Eph. 2:14). Christ suffered pain so that we might have peace, knowing that through him our sins are forgiven. This is also how we have healing, *for by his stripes* (wounds) *we are healed* (v. 5). Sin is not only a crime for which we were condemned to die but also a disease that leads directly to the death of our souls and for which Christ provided the cure. By his wounds he bought for us the Spirit and grace of God to put to death our corruption, which is the disease of our souls, and to put our souls into a good state of health, so that they may be fit to serve God. The control of sin is broken in us and we are strengthened against what feeds the disease.

2.3.6. The result of this to Christ was his resurrection, for, being *delivered for our offences*, he was *raised again for our justification* (Ro 4:25). He rose *to die no more; death had no more dominion over him* (Ro 6:9). He that *was dead is alive* and *lives for evermore* (Rev 1:18).

Verses 10–12

In v. 9 the prophet testified of the sufferings of Christ; here, after mentioning the sufferings, he foretells at length the glory that will follow. Notice:

1. The service and suffering of Christ's humiliation. Come and see how he loved us; see what he did for us:

1.1. He submitted to the disapproval of heaven (v. 10): *Yet it pleased the Lord to bruise him, to put him to grief.* People considered him stricken by God for some very great sin of his own (v. 4). It was true that he was stricken down by God, but it was because of our sin.

1.2. He substituted himself for sinners as a sacrifice. He *made his soul an offering for sin* (v. 10); he himself explains this (Mt 20:28), that *he came to give his life a ransom for many.* We could not put him in our place, but he put himself in our place.

1.3. He subjected himself to what to us is the wages of sin (Ro 6:23) (v. 12): *He has poured out his soul unto death,* poured out his life as water (Ps 22:14), so little account did he make of it when laying it down as the appointed means of our redemption and salvation.

1.4. He allowed himself to be ranked with sinners, but he also offered himself to be an intercessor for sinners (v. 12). He was *numbered with transgressors* (v. 12), not only condemned as an evildoer but also executed in company with two notorious criminals, and between them, as if he had been the worst of the three. In his whole life he was numbered among the transgressors, for he was called and considered one who broke the Sabbath (Mk 2:24; 3:2–4; Lk 13:14), a drunkard, and a friend of tax collectors and sinners (Mt 11:19). In his sufferings he *made intercession for the transgressors* (v. 12), for those who reviled and crucified him, for he prayed, *Father, forgive them* (Lk 23:34), showing not only that he forgave them but also that he was now doing something on which their forgiveness and the forgiveness of all other sinners was to be based. That prayer was the language of his blood, crying out, yet not for vengeance, but for mercy (Ge 4:10; Heb 12:24).

2. The grace and glories of his exaltation. The Father promises to glorify him with the glories of the Mediator:

2.1. He will have the glories of an everlasting Father (9:6). The Redeemer will have offspring who serve him and lift up his name (Ps 22:30). True believers are the offspring of Christ; the Father gave them to him to be so (Jn 17:6). He will live to see his offspring, and because he lives, they also will live, for he is their life. He himself will continue to take care of the affairs of this family: *He shall prolong his days* (v. 10). Christ will not commit the care of his family to anyone else. *Of the increase of his government and peace there shall be no end* (9:7), for he lives forever. His great undertaking will fulfill its expectations: *The pleasure of the Lord shall prosper in his hand* (v. 10). God's purposes will succeed, and not one jot or tittle of them will fail (Mt 5:18). He will himself have abundant satisfaction in it (v. 11): *He shall see of the travail of his soul, and shall be satisfied.* This may be understood to mean that he will see it beforehand; with the prospect of his sufferings he will have a prospect of the fruit of them. He will see the fruit when it is fulfilled in the life and salvation of poor sinners. Christ does and will see the blessed fruit of the travail of his soul in the founding and building up of his church and the eternal salvation of all who were given him.

2.2. He will have the glory of bringing in an eternal righteousness. We can learn from this:

2.2.1. The great privilege that flows to us from the death of Christ is justification from sin, our being acquitted from the guilt that alone can ruin us, to be accepted into God's favor, which alone can make us happy.

2.2.2. Christ, who purchased our justification for us, applies it to us by his intercession made for us, his Gospel preached to us, and his Spirit witnessing in us (Ro 8:16).

2.2.3. It is by faith that we are justified, by our submission to Christ and the covenant of grace; this is how we are saved.

2.2.4. Faith is the knowledge of Christ, and without knowledge there can be no true faith.

2.2.5. That knowledge of Christ, and that faith in him, by which we are justified, refers to him both as a servant to God and as a surety for us. It is according to God's will that he does it. He is righteous, and we have all received from his righteousness (Jn 1:16). We must know him and believe in him as One who bore our sins, who saved us from sinking under the burden by taking it on himself.

2.3. He will have the glory of obtaining an unquestionable victory and universal dominion (v. 12). "I will set him among the great ones, highly exalt him, and give him a name above every name" (Php 2:9). Christ reaches his glory by conquest. He has defeated powers and authorities (Col 2:15), sin and Satan, death and hell, the world and the flesh; these are the strong ones he has disarmed and taken the spoils from. The spoils that he has divided consist of the vast multitudes of willing, faithful, and loyal subjects who will be brought to him; this is how some read it: "I will give many to him, and he shall obtain many for a spoil." God will *give him the heathen* (the nations) *for his inheritance and the uttermost parts of the earth for his possession* (Ps 2:8). The spoils that God divided to Christ are divided and distributed by Christ among his followers, for when he *led captivity captive* (Ps 68:18), he *received gifts for men,* so that he might give gifts to them.

CHAPTER 54

The death of Christ is the life of the church and of all who truly belong to it, and so it is appropriate that after foretelling the sufferings of Christ, the prophet foretells the flourishing of the church, which is a part of his glory, and foretells his exaltation, which was the reward of his humiliation. He was promised that he would see his offspring, and this chapter is an explanation of that promise. This chapter does of course have a primary reference to the welfare and prosperity of the Jewish church after their return from Babylon, which was a type of the glorious liberty of the children of God (Ro 8:21), the liberty that we are brought into through Christ. It cannot be denied, however, that this chapter also has a further reference to the Gospel church, into which the Gentiles were to be admitted. And since the opening words of the chapter were understood by the apostle Paul to refer to the New Testament Jerusalem (Gal 4:26–27), they may serve as a key to the whole chapter and what follows.

It is promised here concerning the Christian church: 1. That although its beginnings were small, it would be greatly enlarged by the accession of many Gentiles (vv. 1–5). 2. That although sometimes God might seem to withdraw from her, he would return in mercy (vv. 6–10). 3. That although for a while she was oppressed and sad, she would finally be advanced to greater honor (vv. 11–12). 4. That knowledge, righteousness, and peace would flourish and prevail (vv. 13–14). 5. That all attempts against the church would be thwarted (vv. 15–17).

Verses 1–5

If we apply these verses to the state of the Jews after their return from exile, it is a prophecy of the increase of their nation after they were settled in their own land. Jerusalem had been in the condition of a wife who had never given birth or a desolate, solitary widow, but now it was promised that the city and the country would be repopulated, that the ruins of Jerusalem would be repaired, and that the land that had for many years been wrongfully held by the Babylonian Gentiles would now return to its rightful owners. God would again be their husband, and the shame of their captivity and the small number to which they were then reduced would be forgotten. But we must also apply these verses to the church of God in general, to the kingdom of God on earth, God's city in the world. Notice:

1. The low state of religion in the world long before Christianity came in. It was like a *barren* woman, one *that did not bear* (v. 1), or a desolate one, who had lost her husband and children; the church was very small and produced little fruit. The Gentiles had less religion among them than the Jews, and the children of God, like the children of a broken, reduced family, were *scattered abroad* (Jn 11:52).

2. Its recovery from this low condition by the preaching of the Gospel and the planting of the Christian church.

2.1. Many were converted to turn from idols to the living God. Those who were born again, who shared in the new and divine nature through the word, were the church's children. There were more found in the Gentile church when that was established than were ever found in the Jewish church. The increase of the church is the joy of all its friends, and it strengthens their hands. Even in heaven, among the angels of God, there is uncommon joy over one sinner who repents (Lk 15:7), and then much more for a nation that does so.

2.2. The boundaries of the church were extended much further than ever before (vv. 2–3).

2.2.1. It is here imagined that the present state of the church is like a tabernacle; it lives in tents, like the heirs of promise in former times (Heb 11:9). The enduring city is reserved for the next world (Heb 13:14). A tent is soon taken down and moved, and when God pleases, it is easily set up elsewhere.

2.2.2. Although it is a tabernacle state, it is sometimes remarkably a growing state; it does not matter if it is in a tent. This is how it was in the first preaching of the Gospel; it was the work of the apostles to disciple all nations. In this way, they would lengthen the cords of this tabernacle, so that more could come in, which would make it necessary to strengthen the stakes so that they could bear the weight of the enlarged curtains. The more numerous the church grows, the more careful she must be to strengthen herself against errors and corruption and support her seven pillars (Pr 9:1).

2.2.3. It was a proof of divine power that the church *grew and prevailed mightily* everywhere (Ac 19:20). The Gospel spread to every part of the world; there were eastern and western churches.

2.3. This honored and encouraged the church (v. 4): *Fear not, for thou shalt not,* as before, *be ashamed* of your confined borders and the small number of your children.

2.4. This was owing to the relationship in which God stood to his church as her husband (v. 5): *Thy Maker is thy husband.* Jesus Christ is the church's Maker, by whom she is formed into a people, and her Redeemer, by whom she is brought out of exile, the slavery of sin, which is the worst form of slavery. This is the One who married her; he is *the Lord of hosts* (v. 5), the Holy One of Israel, the same One who presided in the affairs of the Old Testament church and was the Mediator of the covenant made with it.

Verses 6–10

The help and relief that God sent to his captives in Babylon are foretold here as a type of all God's comforts treasured up for all believers in the covenant of grace.

1. Look back to former troubles and God's favors to his people (vv. 6–8).

1.1. How sad the church's condition had been. She had been like a woman who had been deserted even though she was a *wife of youth* (v. 6), or who had been rejected and was very discontented. Even those who are married to God may still seem to be forsaken. The comparison is explained (vv. 7–8). When God keeps his people in trouble for a long time, he seems to desert them; this is how their enemies interpret it (Ps 71:11). It was in wrath that he abandoned them and hid his face from them (57:17), but it was only *in a little wrath* in comparison with what they deserved and what others justly suffer. It was but *for a moment, a small moment* (v. 7). As he is slow to anger (Ne 9:17), so also he is swift to show mercy.

1.2. How sweet the return of mercy would be to them when God came and encouraged them. God's gathering his people arises from his mercy, not any merit of theirs, and it is with *great mercies* (v. 7), *with everlasting kindness* (v. 8).

2. Look ahead to future dangers, and see God's favor to be constant and his kindness everlasting, for it is formed into a covenant *of peace* (v. 10).

2.1. This covenant is like the *waters of Noah* (v. 9), that is, like the promise that was made about the Flood that there would never again be a similar flood (v. 9); see Ge 8:21–22; 9:11. And God has kept his word, even though the world has been very offensive. The covenant of grace is just as unbreakable: *I have sworn that I would not be wroth with thee,* as I have been, *and rebuke thee,* as I have done (v. 9).

2.2. It is firmer than the strongest parts of the visible creation (v. 10): the mountains will depart, and the hills will be removed (Hab 3:6). Mountains have sometimes been shaken by earthquakes and been destroyed, but the promises of God have never been broken by the shock of any event. When our friends fail us, our God does not, and does his kindness depart? No! Do the kings of the earth and the rulers set themselves against the Lord (Ps 2:2)? They will depart and be removed. God's kindness will never depart from his people, for those whom he loves he loves to the end. The covenant is immovable and unbreakable, because it is built not on our merit but on God's mercy, which is from everlasting to everlasting (Ps 103:17).

Verses 11–17

Very precious promises (2Pe 1:4) are made here that God will not only continue his love toward his people in their troubles but also raise them to greater prosperity than any they have enjoyed up to now. In the previous chapter we read about the humiliation and exaltation of Christ; here we have the humiliation and exaltation of the church, for if we suffer with him, we will also reign with him (2Ti 2:12). Notice:

1. The distressed state of the church (v. 11): "O *thou afflicted,* poor, and needy city, who *art tossed with tempests,* like a ship lashed by storms and about to be swallowed up by the waves, not comforted by any prospect of rescue." This was the condition of the Jews in Babylon, and later, for a time, under Antiochus. It is often the condition of Christian churches and of believers. Like the disciples in the storm, they are ready to perish, and where is their faith (Mk 4:38–40)?

2. The glorious state the church is advanced to by the promise of God. Let the people of God, when they are afflicted and tossed, understand God to be speaking comfort to them by these words. In all their afflictions, he is

afflicted (63:9), and he encourages her with the assurance of the great things he will do for her.

2.1. God promises what will be her beauty and honor.

2.1.1. This is promised by comparing the church with a city, for the church is the city of the living God, the heavenly Jerusalem. Whereas Jerusalem now lies in ruins, a heap of rubbish, it will be beautiful and appear more splendid than ever. Its stones will be laid not only firmly but also finely. Its foundations will be decorated with *sapphires*, for the church's foundation, that is, Christ (1Co 3:11), and the foundation of the apostles and prophets (Eph 2:20) are more precious than anything else. The windows of this house, city, or temple will be made of *agates* (rubies), the gates of *carbuncles* (sparkling jewels), and all the *borders* — the walls that enclose the courts — of precious stones (v. 12). God has graciously undertaken to build his church; the glory of the New Testament church will far exceed the glory of the Jewish church in those gifts and graces of the Spirit which are infinitely valuable.

2.1.2. Those things that will be the beauty and honor of the church are knowledge, holiness, and love, the very image of God, in which human beings were created, renewed, and restored. These are the sapphires and sparkling jewels, the precious stones with which the Gospel temple will be made beautiful, *built upon the foundation* (1Co 3:12). The church is all glorious (Ps 45:13):

2.1.2.1. When it is full of the knowledge of God (11:9): *All thy children shall be taught of the Lord* (v. 13). They will be taught by those whom God will appoint and whose labors will be under his direction and blessing. It is a promise of the Spirit of enlightenment. Our Savior quotes the verse with application to Gospel grace (Jn 6:45).

2.1.2.2. When its members live in love and unity among themselves: *Great shall be the peace of thy children* (v. 13). *All* who are taught by God are taught to *love one another* (1Th 4:9).

2.1.2.3. When holiness reigns, for that above anything is the beauty of the church (v. 14): *In righteousness shalt thou be established*. The restoration of a right way of living, the restoration of purity, the proper administration of public justice, and the triumph of honesty and fair dealing are the strength and stability of any church or state.

2.2. Whereas she is now in danger, God promises her protection and security.

2.2.1. He promises that though on the day of her distress there were conflicts on the outside and fears within, now he will protect her from both (2Co 7:5). There will be no fears within (v. 14): *"Thou shalt be far from oppression*, not only from evil but also from the fear of evil." Nor will there be conflicts outside. Although attempts will be made on them, none of them will succeed (v. 15). It is acknowledged, *"They shall surely gather together against thee*; you must expect it." As long as there is a devil in hell, and a persecutor out of it, God's people must expect frequent alarms, but God will not acknowledge them as his. Their attempt will end in their own ruin: *"Whosoever shall gather together against thee*, they *shall fall for thy sake* (v. 15), or they will fall before you."

2.2.2. So that we may with the greatest assurance depend on God for the security of his church, we have here:

2.2.2.1. God's power over the church's enemies asserted (v. 16). The smith who makes weapons is created by God, and God gave him his skill to work in iron and bronze (Ex 31:3–4) and make proper instruments for warlike purposes. *The smith blows the coals in the fire* (v. 16) to make his iron malleable, so that it may harden into steel

and so that *he may bring forth an instrument proper for the work of those that seek to destroy*. The iron age is the age of war. But *God has created the smith*, and so he can tie his hands, so that the plans of the enemy will fail. The church's enemies must have soldiers, and it is *God that created the waster to destroy* (v. 16). The military esteem themselves for their splendid titles, but God calls them *wasters made to destroy* (destroyers to wreak havoc), for destroying and wreaking havoc are their business. They think their own cleverness, labor, and experience made them soldiers, but it was God who created them; he will also serve his own purposes and intentions through them.

2.2.2.2. The promise of God concerning the church's security laid down as *the heritage of the servants of the Lord* (v. 17). *"No weapon that is formed against thee shall prosper* (v. 17). It will not prove strong enough to harm the people of God; it will recoil in the face of the one who uses it against you." When the weapons of war do not succeed, there are tongues that will rise up in judgment. They are those who misrepresent them, who falsely accuse them to try to make them repugnant to the people and undesirable to the government. The enemies of the Jews did this to make the kings of Persia angry with them (Ezr 4:12; Est 3:8). "But you will silence these insulting, threatening tongues by doing good (1Pe 2:15), by doing what will give you a clear conscience even in the sight of your adversaries and show that you are not what you are represented as being." *This is the heritage of the servants of the Lord* (v. 17). God's servants are his sons. God's promises are their *heritage for ever* (Ps 119:111).

CHAPTER 55

In this chapter we have much about the covenant of grace made with us in Christ. The sure mercies of David, which are promised here (v. 3), are applied by the apostle Paul to the benefits that flow to us from the resurrection of Christ (Ac 13:34). Here is: 1. A free and gracious invitation to all to come and benefit from Gospel grace (v. 1). 2. Vital arguments to reinforce this invitation (vv. 2–4). 3. A promise of the success of this invitation among the Gentiles (v. 5). 4. An urgent call to repentance and reformation (vv. 6–9). 5. The confirming of all this by reference to the certain effectiveness of the word of God (vv. 10–11). And a particular example of the fulfillment of this promise appears in the return of the Jews from exile, which was a sign of the fulfillment of all the other promises.

Verses 1–5

Here:

1. We are all invited to come and take the provision that the grace of God has made for poor souls in the new covenant. Notice:

1.1. Who is invited: *Ho, every one* (v. 1), not only the Jews but also the Gentiles, the poor and the maimed, the lame and the blind, whoever can be lifted up out of the roads and country lanes (Lk 14:21, 23). Ministers are to make a general offer of life, and in Gospel times the invitation would be sent to the Gentiles. The Gospel covenant excludes none who do not exclude themselves.

1.2. What is the qualification required — they must thirst. Those who are satisfied with the world and its enjoyments — those who depend on the merit of their own works as righteousness — such people do not thirst. They have no sense of need; they are not in pain or are not uneasy about the state of their souls. But those who thirst are invited to come to the waters, as those who are weary and burdened are invited to Christ for rest (Mt 11:28). Where God gives grace, he first gives a thirst for it; and where he has given a thirst for it, he will give it (Ps 81:10).

1.3. To where they are invited: *Come you to the waters* (v. 1). Come to Christ, for he is the fountain that has been opened; he is the rock that has been stricken (Ex 17:6–7; Nu 20:11; Isa 53:4; 1Co 10:4). Come to holy services of worship, to those streams that make glad the city of our God (Ps 46:4). To those who believe in Christ the things signified will be like wine and milk, fully refreshing. Come to the healing waters; come to the living waters. Our Savior referred to it: *If any man thirst, let him come to me and drink* (Jn 7:37).

1.4. What they are invited to do.

• "*Come and buy* (v. 1). Come and buy, do not stand hesitating about the terms, nor deliberating whether you will agree to them.
• "*Come and eat*; make it still more your own, as what we eat is more our own than what we only buy."

1.5. What is the provision they are invited to: "*Come and buy wine and milk* (v. 1), which will not only quench the thirst"—ordinary water would do that—"but also nourish the body and revive the spirits." Christ far surpasses our expectations. We come to the waters and would be glad to have them, but we find there wine and milk, which were the staple commodities of the tribe of Judah. We must give up the water we find in mere puddles—which is like poison in comparison—so that we may obtain this wine and milk.

1.6. The free supply of this provision: *Buy it without money and without price* (v. 1). Our buying without money shows:

1.6.1. That the gifts offered us are invaluable and such that no price can be set on them.

1.6.2. That the One who offers them does not need us or any response we can make him.

1.6.3. That the things offered have already been bought and paid for. Christ purchased them, not with money but with *his own blood* (1Pe 1:19).

1.6.4. That we will be welcome to receive the benefits of the promise, and we must acknowledge this so that if Christ and heaven are ours, we may see ourselves as indebted to free grace forever.

2. We are urgently pressed to accept this invitation.

2.1. What we are urged to do is to listen to God and his proposals: "*Hearken diligently unto me* (v. 2). Not only give me a hearing but also apply it to yourselves (v. 3): *Incline your ear* as you incline it to what you find yourselves pleased with; come to me on my terms."

2.2. The arguments used to persuade us are taken:

2.2.1. From the unspeakable wrong we do to ourselves if we refuse this invitation: "*Wherefore do you spend money for that which is not bread* (v. 2), when with me you may have wine and milk without money? *Wherefore do you spend your labour* and toil *for that which will* not be so much as dry bread to you, for it *satisfies not?*" (v. 2). The things of this world are not bread, not proper food for a soul; *They satisfy not* (v. 2). The children of this world spend their money and labor for these very uncertain and unsatisfying things.

2.2.2. From the kindness we do to ourselves if we accept this invitation and submit to it. First, we gain joy and satisfaction in the present. "If you listen to Christ, you *eat that which is good* (v. 2), that which is both wholesome and pleasant, good in itself and also good for you."

God's good word and promise, a good conscience, and the encouragement of God's good Spirit are a continual feast (Pr 15:15) to those who listen obediently to Christ. Second, we gain for ourselves lasting happiness: *Hear, and your soul shall live* (v. 3). Third, the great God graciously keeps all this for us: "Come to me, *and I will make an everlasting covenant with you* and so show you *the sure mercies of David*" (v. 3). The benefits of this covenant are the blessings of David, such blessings as God promised to David (Ps 89:28–29), which are called *the mercies of David his servant* and are appealed to by Solomon (2Ch 6:42). By David here we are to understand the Messiah. Covenant blessings are all *his* mercies; they are purchased by him and are given to us from his hands. He is the Mediator and trustee of the covenant. They are guaranteed blessings, for the promises are all "Yes" and "Amen" in Christ (2Co 1:19–20).

3. Jesus Christ is promised to fulfill all the other promises that we are here invited to accept (v. 4). He is the David whose guaranteed blessings are all the blessings and benefits of the covenant. There was nothing in us to deserve such favor, but Christ is the gift of God. We do not know how to find the way to the waters where we will be supplied, but Christ is given to be *a leader*. We do not know what to do, but he is given as *a commander* to show us what to do and enable us to do it. Christ is a commander by his commands and a leader by his example; our task is to obey him and follow him.

4. Now that the Master of the feast has been established, next comes the supplying with guests. The Gentiles will be called to this feast. "*Thou shalt call a nation that thou knowest not* (v. 5), that is, one that was not formerly called and acknowledged as your nation." They will come at the call: *Nations that knew not thee shall run unto thee* (v. 5). There will be a meeting of believing Gentiles with Christ, who, being lifted up from the earth, will draw all people to him (Jn 12:32). The Gentiles will flock to Christ in this way because he is the Son of God. God will bring them to Christ because God is the Holy One of Israel, who is true to his promises and has promised to glorify Christ by giving him the nations as his inheritance (Ps 2:8).

Verses 6–13

Here is a further account of the covenant of grace that is made with us in Jesus Christ. This gracious revelation of God's goodwill is not to be confined either to Jews or to Gentiles, to the Old Testament or to the New, much less to the captives in Babylon. The commands and promises are here given to all, to *every one that thirsts after happiness* (v. 1).

1. Here is a gracious offer made of pardon, peace, and all happiness to poor sinners, on the terms of the Gospel (vv. 6–7).

1.1. Let them pray, and their prayers will be heard and answered (v. 6): "*Seek the Lord while he may be found.* Call on him now while he is near and within reach. Pray to him to be reconciled and, being reconciled, pray to him for everything else you need." His patience is now waiting on us (2Pe 3:9), his word is calling us, and his Spirit is striving with us (Ge 6:3). Let us now make the most of our advantages and opportunities, for now is the accepted time (2Co 6:2; Isa 49:8).

1.2. Let them repent and reform, and their sins will be pardoned (v. 7). Here is a call to the unconverted, to *the wicked and the unrighteous*—to evildoers, who continue to live in known gross sins, and to the unrighteous, who live in the neglect of plain duties: the message of this salvation is sent to them, and every possible assurance is given that penitent sinners will find God a pardoning God. There are two things involved in repentance:

1.2.1. It is to turn away from sin; it is to abandon it. There must be a change of mind; the unrighteous must *forsake their thoughts* (v. 7). If repentance is true, it strikes at the root of our lives and washes the heart from evil. We must change our judgments about people and things, remove the corrupt thoughts, and give up the vain pretense under which an unsanctified heart shelters itself.

1.2.2. To repent is to *return to the Lord* (v. 7), against whom we have rebelled. It is to turn to the Lord as the fountain of life. If we do so, God *will have mercy* (v. 7). Misery is the object of mercy. With God there is tender mercy (Ps 119:156; 145:9). *He will abundantly pardon* (v. 7). Literally, "He will multiply to pardon," as we have multiplied in offending.

2. Here are encouragements given us to accept this offer and to dare to rest our souls on it.

2.1. If we look up to heaven, we find God's purposes there high and transcendent, his thoughts and ways infinitely above ours (vv. 8–9). Evildoers are urged to abandon their evil ways and thoughts (v. 7) and to bring their ways and thoughts to comply with his, "for," he says, "my thoughts and ways are not as yours. Yours deal only with things below, but mine are above, *as the heaven is high above the earth* (v. 9), and if you want to show yourselves to be true penitents, your thoughts must be so too, and your heart must be set on things above" (Col 3:2). Sinners may fear that God will not be reconciled to them because they have not been willing to be reconciled to him when they have so wickedly and so frequently offended him. "But," God says, "my thoughts in this matter are not as yours; they are as far above them as heaven is above the earth." We think God is inclined to take offense and is slow to forgive—that if he forgives once, he will not forgive a second time. Peter thought it a lot to *forgive seven times* (Mt 18:21), but God meets returning sinners with pardoning mercy. We forgive and cannot forget, but when God forgives sin, he remembers it no more (Jer 31:34; Heb 8:12; 10:17).

2.2. If we look down to this earth, we find God's word there powerful and effective (vv. 10–11). He says to the snow, "Be on the earth." He appoints when it will come, how much, and how long it will lie there; he says so *to the small rain and the great rain of his strength* (Job 37:6). It does not return with the matter unfinished, without having fulfilled its purpose, but waters the earth. And the watering of the earth is in order for it to be fruitful. This is how he makes it *bring forth and bud* (v. 10), and so it gives not only *bread to the eater* (v. 10), present maintenance to the owner and his family, but also *seed to the sower* (v. 10), so that they may have food for another year. The farmer must be a sower as well as an eater, or else they will soon see the end of what they have. "*So shall my word be*, as powerful in the mouth of prophets as it is in the hand of providence; *it shall not return unto me void* (v. 11), *but it shall accomplish that which I please, and it shall prosper* (v. 11) in the thing for which I sent it." These promises of mercy and grace will have as real an effect on the souls of believers for their sanctification and encouragement as the rain ever had on the earth to make it fruitful. Christ's coming into the world, like the dew from heaven (Hos 14:5), will not be in vain.

2.3. If we take a special view of the church, we will find what great things God has done and will do for it (vv. 12–13): *You shall go out with joy, and be led forth with peace.* This refers:

2.3.1. To the restoration and return of the Jews from Babylon. They will leave captivity and be led out toward their own land again. They will go out *with joy* and *peace.* They will have the goodwill and good wishes of all the countries they pass through. *The hills* and their inhabitants *shall break forth into singing* (v. 12). When they come into their own land, it will be ready to welcome them.

2.3.2. To something more, without doubt. This will *be for an everlasting sign* (v. 13), that is:

2.3.2.1. The redemption of the Jews from Babylon will be a confirmation of those promises that concern Gospel times.

2.3.2.2. That redemption will be a representation of the blessings promised and a figure of them. Gospel grace will set free those who were in slavery to sin and Satan. They *shall go out and be led forth* (v. 12). *Jacob shall rejoice, and Israel shall be glad* (Ps 14:7). It will make a great change in people's characters. Those who were as thorns and briers, good for nothing but the fire, will become pleasant and useful like the fir tree and the myrtle tree. The raising of pleasant trees in the place of briers and thorns is a sign of the removal of the curse of the law and the introduction of Gospel blessings. The covenant of grace is eternal, for its present blessings are signs of eternal blessings.

CHAPTER 56

We have here: 1. A solemn command given to us all to be careful to do our duty (vv. 1–2). 2. Great encouragement given to foreigners who were willing to come under the terms of the covenant (vv. 3–8). 3. An accusation drawn up against the watchmen of Israel, who were careless in discharging their duty (vv. 9–12). This seems to be the beginning of a new sermon, a sermon of rebuke continued in the following chapters.

Verses 1–2

When God is coming toward us in mercy, we must go to meet him by doing our duty.

1. God tells us here what are his intentions of mercy to us (v. 1): *My salvation is near to come* (close at hand)—the great salvation brought by Jesus Christ, of which the salvation of the Jews from Sennacherib or from Babylon was a type.

1.1. The Gospel salvation is the salvation of the Lord.

1.2. God's righteousness is revealed in that salvation, which the apostle Paul makes the basis of his glorying in it. The law revealed the righteousness of God by which all sinners stand condemned, but the Gospel reveals the righteousness of God by which all believers stand acquitted.

1.3. The Old Testament saints saw this salvation coming long before it came, and they received notice from the prophets that it was approaching.

2. He tells us the duties he expects us to do. Do not say, "We see the salvation close at hand, and so we may live as we wish, for there is no danger now of missing it or falling short of it"; that is turning the grace of God into reckless immorality. But on the contrary, when salvation is near, redouble your guard against sin. What is required here to qualify and prepare us for the approaching salvation is:

2.1. That we be honest and just in all our dealings: *Keep you judgment and do justice* (v. 1). God is true to us; let us therefore be so to one another.

2.2. That we religiously observe the Sabbath day (v. 2). We are not just if we rob God of his time. Sabbath consecration here stands for all the duties of the first table of the Ten Commandments, the fruits of our love to God, just as justice stands for all those of the second table, the fruits of our love to our neighbor. When, in exile, the Israelites could not observe the other institutions of the law, they could still set themselves apart from the nations by making a difference between God's day and other days.

2.3. That we have nothing to do with sin: *Blessed is the man* that *keeps his hand from doing evil* (v. 2), from doing any wrong to his neighbor, in body, goods, or good name—or, more generally, from doing anything that is displeasing to God and harmful to his own soul. The best evidence of our having kept the Sabbath well will be a carefulness in maintaining a good conscience the whole week. It will be seen that we have been on the mountain with God if our faces shine in our holy walk among other people (Ex 34:29).

Verses 3–8

The prophet is here, in God's name, encouraging those who were committing themselves to God and yet labored under great discouragements.

1. They were discouraged for one of two reasons:

1.1. Some were discouraged because they were not descendants of Abraham. They had *joined themselves to the Lord* (v. 3), but they questioned whether God would accept them, because they were of *the sons of the stranger* (v. 3). They were Gentiles, foreigners to the covenants of promise (Eph 2:12), and therefore feared that they did not share in the matter. They said, *"The Lord has utterly separated me from his people* (v. 3) and will not acknowledge me as one of them, nor will he admit me to their privileges."

1.2. Others were discouraged because they were not fathers in Israel. The eunuch said, *Behold, I am a dry tree* (v. 3). He was thought to be useless because he had no children, nor was ever likely to have any. This was more painful because eunuchs were not admitted to be priests (Lev 21:20), nor to *enter into the congregation* (Dt 23:1). But God did not want the eunuchs to think that they would be excluded from the Gospel church and from being spiritual priests. As the taking down of the dividing wall of hostility (Eph 2:14), as contained in ordinances, admitted the Gentiles, so also it allowed access to those who had been kept out by ceremonial defilement.

2. Suitable encouragements are given:

2.1. To those who have no children of their own, though they have the honor to be the children of the church and the covenant themselves. Notice:

2.1.1. What a good character they have. They *keep God's sabbaths* (v. 2) as he appointed them to be kept. They *choose those things that please God* (v. 4). They *take hold of his covenant.* The covenant of grace is offered to us in the Gospel; to take hold of it is to accept the offer deliberately and sincerely, to take God to be our God and to give ourselves to be his people. We take hold of it as offenders took hold of the horns of the altar to which they fled for refuge (1Ki 1:50).

2.1.2. The comfort they may have if they fulfill these characteristics, even though they are not built up into families (v. 5): *Unto them will I give a better place* (NIV: memorial) *and name.* There is a place and a name that we have from sons and daughters, but a better place and a better name are possessed by those who are in covenant with God, and it is enough to balance out the lack of the former. A place and a name stand for rest and reputation. Although they do not have children to be the music of their house, they still *shall* have a place and a name. God will give it to them by promise; he will himself be both their place and their name. He will give it to them

in his house and within his walls; there they will have a place. Our relationship with God, our enjoyment of our privileges in Christ, and our hope of eternal life are things that give us a blessed place and a blessed name in God's house. It will be *an everlasting name that shall never be cut off* (v. 5).

2.2. To those who are themselves the children of foreigners.

2.2.1. It is promised here that they will now be welcome to the church (vv. 6–7). When the people of God's Israel come out of Babylon, let them bring their neighbors along with them, and God will find room enough for them all in his house.

2.2.1.1. Let them know that the sons and daughters of foreigners will have a place and a name in God's house provided that they abandon other gods, that they commit themselves to him as subjects to their ruler and soldiers to their general, by an oath of loyalty and obedience, and that they commit themselves to him as friends to his honor, *to love the name of the Lord* (v. 6). Serving him and loving him go together, and obedience is most acceptable to him when it flows from a motive of love, for then *his commandments are not grievous* (burdensome) (1Jn 5:3).

2.2.1.2. Three things are promised to them when they come to God:

- Assistance: *"I will bring them to my holy mountain,* not only make them welcome when they come but also dispose them to come; I will show them the way and lead them in it."
- Acceptance: *"Their burnt offerings and their sacrifices shall be accepted on my altar* (v. 7); those offerings will not be less acceptable because they are theirs, even though they are sons and daughters of a foreigner."
- Assurance: They will not only be accepted but will themselves have the pleasure of it: *I will make them joyful in my house of prayer* (v. 7). Many a sorrowful spirit has been given joyful assurance in the house of prayer.

2.2.2. It is promised here that many Gentiles will come to the church: *My house shall be called a house of prayer for all people* (v. 7). It is promised about this house:

2.2.2.1. That it will not be a house of sacrifice, but a house of prayer.

2.2.2.2. That it will be a house of prayer not only for the people of the Jews but for all people. This was fulfilled when Peter was made not only to realize himself, but also to tell the world, that *in every nation he that fears God and works righteousness is accepted of him* (Ac 10:35). It has been declared again and again that *the stranger that comes nigh shall be put to death* (Nu 1:51), but Gentiles will now be looked on no longer as foreigners and strangers (Eph 2:19). And it is shown here (v. 8) that when the Gentiles are called in, they become one body with the Jews, so that, as Christ says (Jn 10:16), there may be *one fold and one Shepherd.* There are still more and more to be brought in: the church is a growing body. We may still hope there will be more, until the church as the body of Christ is completed. *Other sheep I have* (Jn 10:16).

Verses 9–12

Here the prophet makes a sudden change of style and moves from words of encouragement to words of rebuke in the following three chapters. Some commentators see a new sermon beginning here. He has assured the people that in due time God will restore them from exile. Now here he shows what their sins and offenses are.

1. Devastating judgments are summoned here (v. 9). The sheep of God's pasture (Ps 100:3) are now to be made the sheep of his slaughter, to fall as victims to his justice, and so *the beasts of the field and the forest* are called to come and devour. If this refers primarily to the attack on them by the Babylonians and their devouring them, it may also look further, to the destruction of Jerusalem and the Jewish nation by the Romans. The Roman armies came on them as forest animals to devour them, and they completely *took away their place and nation* (Jn 11:48).

2. The reason for these judgments is given here. The shepherds, who should have been the watchmen of the flock, were treacherous and did not faithfully discharge the trust rested in them, and so the sheep became an easy target for the wild animals. Now this may refer to the false prophets in the times of Isaiah, Jeremiah, and Ezekiel and to the priests who ruled by following what the false prophets said. Or it may refer to the evil rulers, the sons of Josiah, who *did evil in the sight of the Lord* (2Ki 23:37), and evil magistrates under them, who betrayed their trust, so attracting more of the fierce anger of the Lord instead of doing anything to turn it away. Or it may refer to those who were the nation's watchmen in our Savior's time, the chief priests and the scribes, who should have announced to the people the approach of the Messiah but instead opposed him. *Woe unto thee, O land!* (Ecc 10:16) when your guides are like such people.

2.1. They were ignorant of their work and unfit to teach, being so badly taught themselves: *His watchmen are blind* (v. 10) and unfit to be watchmen. Christ describes the Pharisees as *blind leaders of the blind* (Mt 15:14). The wild animals come to devour, and the watchmen are blind and are not aware of them. *They are all ignorant* (v. 10), *shepherds that cannot understand* (v. 11), who do not know what is to be done about the sheep.

2.2. Just as they were blind watchmen, who could not discern danger, so they were also *dumb dogs* (v. 10), which could not give any warning of it. They barked at God's prophets, bit them, and attacked the sheep, but did not oppose the wolf or thief.

2.3. They were lazy and loved their ease, *loving to slumber* (v. 10).

2.4. They were covetous, *greedy dogs that could never have enough* (v. 11). They kept on asking about what more they could get and never mentioned what they could do. Each one of them looked to their *own way*, being concerned only with their personal interests and having no regard at all for the public welfare. Everyone wanted to further their own opinion and advance their own party, while the ordinary concerns of the public were wretchedly neglected and set aside.

2.5. They were never so much in their element as when they were in their drunken revels (v. 12): *Come, they say, I will fetch wine—and we will fill ourselves,* or be drunk, *with strong drink.* They had the people sit and drink with them, and so those whom they should have rebuked were instead confirmed in their evil ways. How could the people think being drunk was harmful when the watchmen themselves joined them and led them to it!

2.6. They were very self-confident that their prosperity and ease would continue; they said, *"Tomorrow shall be as this day and much more abundant* (v. 12); we will have as much to spend on our sinful desire tomorrow as we have had today."

CHAPTER 57

The prophet makes his observations about: 1. The deaths of good people (vv. 1–2). 2. The flagrant idolatry and spiritual unfaithfulness that the Jews were guilty of and the judgments they were bringing on themselves (vv. 3–12). 3. The gracious return of God to his people to end their exile and reestablish their prosperity (vv. 13–21).

Verses 1–2

The prophet has condemned the watchmen for their ignorance and foolishness; here he shows the general stupidity and mindlessness of the people. Notice:

1. The providence of God in taking good people out of this world. *The righteous,* as to this world, *perish.* Godliness exempts no one from death. Righteousness rescues us from the sting of death (1Co 15:55–56) but not from its attack. Those who could be least spared are often taken away; the fruitful trees are cut down by death, and the barren ones are left to burden the ground (Lk 13:7).

2. The thoughtless world disregarding these providences: *No man lays it to heart, none considers it* (v. 1). There are very few who mourn it as a public loss, very few who take notice of it as a public warning. When children are small, they mourn the death of their parents least, because they do not know what a loss it is to them.

3. The benefit to the righteous in their being taken away. They *are taken away from the evil to come* (v. 1). When the Flood is coming, they are called into the ark. This is done in wrath to the world; those who stood in the gap to turn away the judgments of God are taken away (Eze 22:30). It is a sign that God intends war when he calls home his ambassadors. When the righteous man dies, he *enters into peace* and *rests in his bed* (v. 2). Those who practice uprightness and persevere in it to the end will find that things go well with them when they die. Their souls then enter into peace.

Verses 3–12

Here is a great accusation, but also a just one, against that evil generation out of which God's righteous ones were taken because the world was not worthy of them (Heb 11:38). Notice:

1. The name and title by which they stand indicted (v. 3). They are called to account as *sons of the sorceress,* or of a witch, *the seed of an adulterer and a whore.* Sin is sorcery and spiritual adultery, for it is departing from God and dealing with the Devil. They were *children of disobedience* (Eph 2:2; 5:6). "Come," the prophet says, "draw near, and I will read out your condemnation; you are *children of transgression* and *a seed of falsehood"* (v. 4).

2. The particular crimes they are accused of:

2.1. Scoffing at God and his word. They are a generation of mockers (v. 4): "*Against whom do you* mock? You think it is only against the poor prophets, whom you trample on, but really it is against God himself, whose message they communicate." They made wry faces at the prophets and stuck out their tongues at them, against all the laws of good upbringing. They did not even treat God's prophets with common civility.

2.2. Idolatry. This was the sin that the people of the Jews were most notoriously guilty of before the exile, but that affliction healed them of it. In Isaiah's time they were full of it, as can be seen from the detestable idolatry of Ahaz, which some think is particularly referred to here, and of Manasseh.

2.2.1. They were obsessively fond of their idols; they inflamed themselves with them by their violent passions in worshiping them (1Ki 18:26, 28). They worshiped their idols *under every green* (oak) *tree* (v. 5), in the open air and in the shade; the beauty of the oak trees made them even more fond of the idols that they worshiped there.

2.2.2. They were unnaturally cruel in their worship of idols. They killed their children and offered them in sacrifice to their idols in the valleys and *under the cliffs of the rock* (v. 5), in dark and solitary places, most appropriate for such works of darkness.

2.2.3. They were insatiable in their idolatry.

2.2.3.1. They had gods in the valleys, which they worshiped by the waterside (v. 6): *Among the smooth stones of the valley*, or brook, *is thy portion*. If they saw a smooth carved stone, they were ready to worship it. And having taken these idols as their allotted portion, they spared no expense in honoring them: "*To them hast thou poured a drink offering and offered a meat* (grain) *offering* (v. 6), as if they had given you your food and drink." Have we taken the true God as our portion? Let us then serve him with our food and drink, not by depriving ourselves of the use of them but by eating and drinking to his glory. Here, in parentheses, comes an expression of God's just anger at their evil: *Should I receive comfort in these*, in such a people as this? (v. 6). Can those who serve Baal with God's gifts expect that God will take any pleasure in them or their devotions? "Should I have compassion on these?" is how some understand this; "Should I repent concerning these?" according to others.

2.2.3.2. They also had gods of the hills (v. 7): "*Upon a lofty and high mountain hast thou set thy bed*, your idol, your idol's temple and altar, the bed of your immorality, where you commit spiritual adultery. *Thither wentest thou up* readily enough, even though it was uphill, *to offer sacrifice*" (v. 7).

2.2.3.3. As if these were not enough, they had household gods too, as the Romans had their *lares* and *penates. Behind the doors and the posts* (v. 8), where the law of God should be written, they set up reminders of their idols to show others how attentive they were to them and to remind their children of them. They were hardened in their evil ways. They went about as publicly, and in as great crowds, to the idol temples as they had ever gone to God's house. They were like an arrogant prostitute: they were *discovering* (uncovering) *themselves to another than God* (v. 8). They *enlarged their bed*, that is, their idol temples, and, as the margin reads the following words, "thou hewedst it for thyself larger than theirs," larger than the idol temples of those from whom they copied it (2Ki 16:10). "*Thou has made a covenant with them* (v. 8), with the idols, with the idol worshipers, to live and die together. *Thou lovedst their bed* (v. 8), that is, the temple of an idol, wherever you saw it."

2.3. Their trusting in foreign help and contracting an alliance with the Gentile powers (v. 9): *Thou wentest to the king*, which some understand to refer to Molech, whose name means "a king." Or it may refer to the king of Assyria, whom Ahaz paid court to, or the king of Babylon, whose ambassadors Hezekiah was kind to, so that they might strengthen themselves by an alliance with them. They went *with ointments and perfumes* (v. 9), either to make their own faces look beautiful and so make themselves worthy of the friendship of the greatest king or to present these things to those whose favor they desired. They discredited themselves and put the honor of their crown and nation in the dust: *Thou didst debase thyself* (descended) *even unto hell* (the grave) (v. 9). They devalued themselves by submitting to the neighboring nations

and depending on them when they had a God to go to who is all-sufficient and who was in covenant with them.

3. What made their sin even worse.

3.1. They had been tired with disappointments in their evil ways, but they would not be convinced how foolish they were (v. 10): "*Thou art wearied in the greatness of thy way*; you have undertaken a mighty task, to find true satisfaction and happiness in what is a worthless lie." "Thou art wearied in the multitude [or multiplicity] of thy ways" is how some read it; those who forsake the only right way wander endlessly up and down a thousand byways and lose themselves in the many schemes they have thought up.

3.2. Although they were convinced that the way they were following was sinful, yet, because they had found worldly pleasure and profit by it, they could not persuade themselves to be sorry about it: "*Thou hast found the life* (margin, "living") *of thy hand*, you found renewal of your strength" (v. 10); *you are not grieved* (you did not faint), any more than Ephraim when he said (Hos 12:8), "*I have become rich; I have found out substance.*" Prosperity in sin is a great barrier to conversion from sin.

3.3. They had dealt contemptibly with God through their sin, for they pretended that the reason why they left God was that he was too terrible a majesty for them; they must have gods that they could be more familiar with. "But," God says, "*of whom hast thou been afraid or feared, that thou hast lied?* (v. 11). What did I ever do to frighten you away from me?" Although they pretended reverence for God, it is certain that they had no true reverence for him: "*Thou hast not remembered me* (v. 11), neither what I have said nor what I have done; you have *not laid them to thy heart* (v. 11), as you would have done if you had truly feared me." They were hardened in their sin by the patience of God.

4. God's determination to call them to account (v. 12): "*I will declare thy righteousness*, which you are boasting about, and let the world see, and you too, to your confusion, that it is all sham. I will declare your works; they will not benefit you or give you any advantage."

Verses 13–16

Here:

1. God shows how inadequate idols and creatures are to help those who worship them (v. 13): "*When thou criest out in distress*, calling for help, *let thy companies* (collection of idols) *deliver thee*, your idol gods, the troops of the allied forces that you have depended on so much; let them rescue you; expect no help except what they can give." *The wind shall carry them all away* (v. 13); they have made themselves as chaff, and so the wind will naturally blow them away (Ps 1:4).

2. He shows that there is a sufficiency, an all-sufficiency, in him: "*He that puts his trust in me* (v. 13), and only in me, will be happy, both for soul and for body, for this world and the other." Those who trust in God's providence are following the best way to secure their secular interests. They *shall possess the land* (v. 13), as much of it as is good for them. Those who trust in God's grace are following the best way to secure their sacred interests. They *shall inherit my holy mountain* (v. 13). They will enjoy the privileges of the church on earth and ultimately be brought to the joys of heaven. No wind will take them away from that. More particularly, the captives who trust in God will be released (v. 14): *They shall say*—that is, the messengers of his word and all the ministers of his providence in that great event will say—*Cast you up*

(build up), *cast you up, prepare the way*. When God's time comes for them to be rescued, the way of bringing it about is made plain and obstacles will be removed. This refers to the provision that the Gospel and its grace have made for our prepared passage through this world to a better world. The way of religious faith is now built up; it is a highway; ministers' business is to guide people along it. The contrite, who trust in God, will be *revived* (v. 15). God's glory appears here very bright:

2.1. In his greatness and majesty: he is *the high and lofty One that inhabits eternity* (v. 15). *He is the high and lofty One* (v. 15), and there is no creature like him, nor can any be compared with him. The language also suggests his sovereignty over everything and his incontrovertible right to decree law and justice to all. He is both immortal and unchangeable. There is an infinite righteousness in his nature. His name is *holy*, and all who want to come to know him must know him as a holy God. "*I dwell in the high and holy place* (v. 15), and I want all the world to know it." Whoever has any dealings with God must come to him as their Father in heaven (Mt 6:9), for that is where he lives. Although he is so high, he still concerns himself with the lowly; the One who rides on the clouds with his name JAH stoops to concern himself with poor *widows* and the *fatherless* (Ps 68:4–5).

2.2. In his grace and mercy. He has tender compassion on the humble and contrite. If they are his people, he will not overlook them even if they are poor and despised and trampled all over by other people; but what he is really referring to here is their attitude. He will have tender compassion on those who, when they suffer, come to terms with their adversity and reflect on their condition; God will live with such people. He will come to them graciously and will deal with them through his word and Spirit, as we do with those in our own family. The One who lives in the highest heavens also lives in the lowliest hearts, and the One who lives in eternity also lives in sincere hearts. He delights in these. He will revive their hearts and spirits; he will speak to them and work in them through the word and Spirit of his grace. Those whom he accuses will, if they trust in him, be relieved and received into his favor (v. 16). He will *revive the heart of the contrite ones*, for he will not accuse forever. It is not promised that he will never be angry with his people — for their sins are displeasing to him — or that he will never accuse them — for they must expect the rod of correction — but he *will not contend* (accuse) *for ever* (v. 16). As he does not become angry quickly, so he is not angry for long. "If I should accuse forever, *the spirit would fail before me, even the souls which I have made*" (v. 16). Although the Lord is interested in the body, he is chiefly concerned for the souls of his people; he is concerned to see that the spirit does not fail, nor its graces and comforts.

Verses 17–21

The main group of the people of Israel, in this account of God's dealings with them, are spoken of as one particular person (vv. 17–18), but they are divided into two kinds and dealt with differently — some who are children of peace, to whom peace is spoken (v. 19), and others who are not, who have nothing to do with peace (vv. 20–21). Notice:

1. The just rebukes that came on the people because of their sin: *For the iniquity of his covetousness I was wroth, and smote him*, I was enraged by his sinful greed; I punished him (v. 17). Greed was a prevalent sin. Those who did not worship idols were still carried away by this spiritual idolatry, for greed is such; it is making a god out of money (Col 3:5). Yet, greedy though they were, they were extravagant in serving their idols (v. 6). It is hard to say whether their extravagance in that or their greed in everything else was more offensive. Greed is a sin that is very displeasing to the God of heaven. He punished them, rebuked them for it through his prophets, corrected them through his providence, and punished them in those very things they were so devoted to and were greedy for. God hid himself from them when they were under these rebukes. When we are under God's discipline, we may bear it better if God reveals himself to us, but if he hides himself from us, sends us no prophets, speaks to us no word of assurance, we are truly miserable.

2. Their stubbornness and persistence under such punishment: *He went on frowardly in the way of his heart*, he kept on in his evil willful ways (v. 17). Notice also how insufficient suffering is to reform people unless God's grace works with them.

3. God's wonderful return in mercy to them.

3.1. The greater part of them went on stubbornly wanting their own way, but there were some among them who mourned the obstinacy of the others, and God determined not to accuse them forever. Such are the riches of divine mercy and grace, and God is so averse to judgment, that it follows, *I have seen his ways and will heal him* (v. 18). Where sin has increased, grace has increased all the more (Ro 5:20). God would first give him grace, and then, and not until then, give him peace: "I have seen their way, that they will never turn to me by themselves, and so I will turn them."

3.1.1. God would heal them of their corrupt and evil disposition. There is no spiritual disease so hardened that almighty grace cannot conquer it.

3.1.2. God would *lead him also* (v. 18). They carried on willfully, like Saul of Tarsus, still breathing out murderous threats (Ac 9:1), but God would lead them to a better state of mind and a better path. And then:

3.1.3. He would restore those comforts that they had forfeited and for the return of which he had prepared them. A wonderful reformation was brought about on the captives in Babylon, and then a wonderful redemption was brought for them.

3.2. Now, just as some of the people who went into exile were good figs and others bad, and their captivity was, accordingly, for their good or for *their hurt* (Jer 24:8–9), so, when they came out of exile, some of them were still good and others bad, and their restoration affected them accordingly.

3.2.1. To those among them who were good, their return from exile was peace, a type of the peace that would be preached by Jesus Christ (v. 19): *I create the fruit of the lips, peace*. Creation is out of nothing, and this is surely out of worse than nothing, when God creates reasons for praise for those who continue willfully in the ways of their heart. In order for this to happen, peace will be declared: *Peace, peace to him that is afar off* as well as *to him that is near* (v. 19). Peace of conscience, a holy security and serenity of mind, after the many reproaches of conscience and the turbulence of spirit they had been under in their captivity. When he speaks peace to us, we must respond by speaking praises to him. This peace is itself created by God. It is the fruit of preaching lips and praying lips; it is the fruit of Christ's lips, sweetness from the honeycomb (SS 4:11): *He came and preached peace to you* (Eph 2:17), who were far away, you Gentiles as well as the Jews, who were near — to later ages, who were far away in time, as well as those of the present age.

3.2.2. To those among them who were bad, though they could return with the others, their return was no peace (v. 20). Wherever evildoers are, in Babylon or in Jerusalem, they carry with them the source of their own uneasiness. The evildoers would not be healed by the grace of God and so will not be healed by his comforts. They are always like the sea in a storm, for they carry with them:

3.2.2.1. Unmortified corruption. They are not healed, and their uncontrolled sinful desires and passions make them like the tossing sea.

3.2.2.2. Unpacified conscience. They are under a fearful apprehension of guilt and wrath, like Cain, who always lived in the land of shaking (Nod, "wandering" [Ge 4:16]) [Ed. note: the root word can mean "shake"]. What this prophet had said before (48:22) and repeats here (v. 21) is still a certain truth: *There is no peace to the wicked*, no reconciliation to God as long as they continue in their sins.

CHAPTER 58

In this chapter the prophet has his commission renewed to rebuke the sinners in Zion (v. 1). It is intended as a warning to all godless hypocrites and is not to be confined to those of any particular age. Some think it refers primarily to those who lived at the time Isaiah prophesied; see 33:14; 29:13. Others think it refers to the captives in Babylon, the evildoers among them. They thought they would protect themselves with their external duties, particularly their fasting, which they maintained in Babylon and for some time after their return to their own land (Zec 7:3). Others think it is principally intended for the godless hypocrisy of the Jews, especially the Pharisees before and in our Savior's time: they boasted about their fasting, but Christ—like the prophet here—showed them their rebellion (Mt 23). Notice: 1. The plausible profession of religion that they made (v. 2). 2. The boasts they made of that profession and the blame they placed on God for taking no notice (v. 3). 3. The sins they are accused of, which spoiled the acceptableness of their fasting (vv. 4–5). 4. Instructions given them how to keep fasts in the right way (vv. 6–7). 5. Precious promises made to those who do keep fasts in such a way (vv. 8–12). 6. Similarly precious promises made to those who sanctify the Sabbath rightly (vv. 13–14).

Verses 1–2

When our Lord Jesus promised to send the Counselor, he added, *When he shall come, he shall convince* (Jn 16:7–8; KJV: *he will reprove*), for conviction must prepare the way for comfort. God earlier appointed this prophet to comfort his people (40:1); here he appoints him to convict them and show them their sins.

1. He must tell them how bad they really are (v. 1).

1.1. He must deal faithfully and plainly with them. "Though they are called *the people of God* and *the house of Jacob*, do not flatter them. Instead, show them their rebellion, both their sins that they do not know about and their sins that they do not acknowledge as sins. Although they are reformed in some things, they are still as bad as ever in others."

1.2. He must *cry aloud and not spare* (v. 1), not hold back; even if they hate him for it and he gets himself a bad name, he must not hold back.

2. He must acknowledge how good they seem to be, nevertheless (v. 2): *Yet they seek me daily.* They plead that they can see no rebellion, for, after all, they

are conscientious and regular in attending worship services—and what more could God want of them? Now:

2.1. He acknowledges this fact to be true. As far as godless hypocrites do what is good, they will not be denied commendation for it. It is acknowledged that they have a form of godliness (2Ti 3:5).

2.1.1. They go to church and observe their hours of prayer: *They seek me daily* (v. 2).

2.1.2. They love to hear good preaching: *They delight to know my ways* (v. 2); they are like Herod, who heard John gladly (Mk 6:20).

2.1.3. They seem to take pleasure in the exercises of religion: *They delight in approaching to God* (v. 2), not for the sake of the One whom they approach, but for the sake of some pleasant circumstances, perhaps the company, or the festival itself.

2.1.4. They ask all the right questions about their duty and seem to want to know the answers: *They ask of me the ordinances* (commands) *of justice* (v. 2), the rules of godliness for worshiping God and the rules of justice for dealing with people, both of which are *ordinances of justice*.

2.1.5. They appear to the eyes of the world as if they were carefully doing their duty: *They are as a nation that did righteousness and forsook not the ordinances of their God* (v. 2); others took them as such, and they themselves claimed to be such. People may go a long way toward heaven but still come short of it; they may go to hell with a good reputation. But:

2.2. He suggests this is so far from being a cover for their sin that it really makes it worse.

Verses 3–7

Here we have:

1. These hypocrites' displeasure with God (v. 3): *Wherefore* (why) *have we fasted, say they, and thou seest not?* They were like Cain, who was angry with God and greatly insulted that his offering was not accepted (Ge 4:5). They exalted what they themselves had done: "*We have fasted and afflicted our souls* (humbled ourselves) (v. 3); we have not only sought God every day (v. 2) but also kept certain times for more serious devotion." Some think this refers to the yearly fast—the Day of Atonement—others to occasional fasts. The Pharisee said, *I fast twice in the week* (Lk 18:12). They thought God should take great notice of what they had done, that he was indebted to them for their service. They accused God of injustice and showing partiality; they seemed determined to reject their religion and justified themselves in doing so by saying that they had found no *profit in praying* to God (Job 21:14–15; Mal 3:14).

2. The true reason why God did not accept their fasting or answer the prayers they made on their fast days: that they did not fast rightly. It was true that they fasted, but they did not, like the Ninevites, turn away from their evil ways (Jnh 3:5–9); *in the day of their fast* (v. 3) they went on to *find pleasure* (v. 3), that is, to do whatever seemed right in their own eyes and pleased them (Jdg 17:6; 21:25), making their own inclinations fit their interpretation of the law.

2.1. They were still as greedy and unmerciful as they had been: "*You exact all your labours* (v. 3) from your servants; you exploit your workers and will neither release them according to the law nor ease the rigor of their servitude." "You exact all your dues, your debts," is how some read it; "you are as harsh and severe as you ever were in demanding that the poor pay what they owe you, extorting it from them, even though it is at the end of the yearly fast that the release is declared."

2.2. They were argumentative and spiteful (v. 4): *Behold, you fast for strife and debate*. When they proclaimed a fast to pray to be saved from God's judgments, they claimed to search for those sins that caused God to threaten them with his judgments, and under that pretense perhaps particular individuals were falsely accused, such as Naboth in the day of Jezebel's fast (1Ki 21:12). And so, instead of considering their own lives, which is the proper task of a day of fasting, they condemned one another. They fasted and quarreled, following the letter rather than the spirit of the law (2Co 3:6) on fast days. Nor was it only quarrels with the tongue that were stirred up in the times of fasting; they also attacked one another *with the fist of wickedness*. Now while they continued in sin in this way, in those very sins that were directly contrary to the intentions of a day of fasting, God would not allow them to continue such ceremonies: "*You shall not fast* at all if you fast *as you do this day, causing your voice to be heard on high* (v. 4). *Bring me no more* of these empty, noisy, *vain oblations* (meaningless offerings)" (1:13).

3. Plain instructions given about the true nature of a religious fast.

3.1. In general, a fast is intended:

3.1.1. To honor and please God.

3.1.2. To humble and abase ourselves. A fast is *a day to afflict* (humble) *the soul* (v. 5); if it does not express a genuine sorrow for sin and does not promote a real putting to death of sin, it is not a true fast.

3.2. It concerns us therefore to ask, on a day of fasting, what it is that will be acceptable to God and what will humble our corrupt nature.

3.2.1. We are told here, negatively, what is not the fast that God has chosen:

3.2.1.1. It is not enough to look modest, to put on a sad and serious face, to bow the head like a reed that is withered and broken, as the hypocrites did, who were *of a sad countenance, and disfigured their faces, that they might appear unto men to fast* (Mt 6:16). Hanging his head in shame was right for the tax collector, whose heart was truly humbled and broken because of sin, and who therefore, as a sign of that, *would not so much as lift up his eyes to heaven* (Lk 18:13), but when it was only imitated, as here, it was justly ridiculed. It is merely *hanging down the head like a bulrush* (v. 5).

3.2.1.2. It is not enough to do penance and be slightly sorry, to humble the body a little, while the body of sin itself remains untouched (Ro 6:6). *Wilt thou call this a fast?* (v. 5). No; it is merely the shadow and shell of a true fast.

3.2.2. We are told here, positively, what the fast is that God has chosen. It is not "humbling the soul for a day" that will be enough, as some read v. 5; no, it must be the attitude of our whole lives. It is required here:

3.2.2.1. That we be just toward those with whom we have dealt harshly (v. 6): *To loose the bands of wickedness*, the chains that we have corruptly tied and by which others are bound. "Let the prisoner who has no debts to pay be discharged, let the troublesome lawsuit be quashed, let the servant who has been forcibly detained beyond time of his service be released, and so *break every yoke* (v. 6). Not only let go those who have been wrongfully kept under the yoke, but break the yoke of slavery itself."

3.2.2.2. That we be kind to those who are needy (v. 7). We are to contribute to the rescue and ransom of those who are oppressed by others, to the release of captives, and to the payment of the debts of the poor. This, then, is the fast that God has chosen.

3.2.2.2.1. To provide food for those who lack it. It is *to break thy bread to the hungry* (v. 7). Notice that it must be *thy* bread, what is honestly gained, the bread you yourself need, your own food. We must deny ourselves something so that we may have something to give those who are in need of it (Eph 4:28). "This is the true fast: to share your food with the hungry, not only to give them what is already broken meat but also to break bread deliberately for them, to give them whole loaves, not merely a few crumbs or a few slices of bread you can spare."

3.2.2.2.2. To provide shelter for those who lack it: it is *to take care of the poor that are cast out* (v. 7). "If they suffer unjustly, have no qualms about sheltering them; not only find quarters for them and pay for their lodging elsewhere but—what is a greater act of kindness—bring them to your own house, make them your own guests. Do not forget to welcome strangers, for although you may not, as some have done, entertain angels (Heb 13:2), you may entertain Christ himself (Mt 25:40), who will reward it in the resurrection of the just (Lk 14:14). *I was a stranger, and you took me in*" (Mt 25:35).

3.2.2.2.3. To provide clothing for those who lack it: "*When thou seest the naked, that thou cover him* (v. 7), *hide not thyself from thy own flesh* (do not turn away from your own flesh and blood)" (v. 7). Some understand this to refer to a person's own family and relatives: "If those of your own house and family fall on hard times, you are *worse than an infidel* (an unbeliever) if you do not *provide* for them" (1Ti 5:8). Others understand it more generally; all who share in human nature are to be looked on as our own flesh and blood, for have we not all one Father (Mal 2:10)?

Verses 8–12

Here are precious promises (2Pe 1:4) for those who keep the fast God has chosen; let them feast freely and cheerfully on those promises. Here is:

1. A further account of the duty to be done (vv. 9–10):

1.1. We must abstain from all acts of violence and fraud. "Those must be *taken away from the midst of thee*" (v. 9), "from thy person, out of thy heart," according to some; "you must not only refrain from practicing wrong but also put to death in you every inclination toward it." Or "from the midst of thy people." Those in authority must do all they can to prevent oppression in everyone within their jurisdiction. They must not only *break the yoke* (v. 6) but also take away the yoke; similarly, they must not threaten their slaves (Eph 6:9) and not point the finger (v. 9) at those who are poor and miserable, so exposing them to contempt. They must not *speak vanity* (v. 9), that is, flattery or deceitful words; let all their conversation be governed by sincerity.

1.2. We must give ourselves fully to all acts of kindness and generosity. We must give freely and cheerfully and from a motive of kindness and love. We must *draw out our soul to the hungry* (v. 10), not only draw out money but also do this from the heart, with a tender affection for those we see in misery. Let the heart go along with the gift, for God loves a cheerful giver (2Co 9:7), and so does someone who is poor. When our Lord Jesus healed and fed the crowds, he did so with compassion on them (Mt 14:14; 15:32). We must give plentifully and generously, so as not to tease, but to *satisfy, the afflicted soul* (v. 10).

2. A full account of the blessings and benefits that accompany the fulfillment of these duties.

2.1. God will surprise them with the return of mercy after great suffering, which will be as welcome as the light of the morning after a long and dark night (v. 8): *Then will thy light break forth as the morning*, and (v. 10) *thy light will rise in obscurity* (darkness). God will make those who are cheerful in doing good cheerful in enjoying good and finding satisfaction, and this is a special gift of God (Ecc 2:24). Those who have helped others out of trouble will themselves obtain help from God when it is their turn.

2.2. God will honor them. Good works will be rewarded with a good reputation; this is included in the light that rises up out of darkness.

2.3. They will always be secure under divine protection: "*Thy righteousness will go before thee* as thy vanguard (v. 8), to protect you from enemies who charge against you in the front, and the glory of the Lord will be your rear guard, the gathering forces, to bring up those of your number who are weary and are lagging behind and to protect you from the enemies, who, like Amalek, attack your rear." Good people are kept safe on every side. Their defense is their righteousness, and the glory of the Lord, which is, as some think, Christ, is the One who is our rear guard, on whom alone we can depend for safety when our sins pursue us and are ready to take hold of us.

2.4. God will always be near them to listen to their prayers (v. 9). "Then you will call out on your days of fasting, which should be days of prayer, and the Lord will answer: he will give you the things you call out to him for. You will cry out when you are in any distress or sudden fear, and he will say, 'Here I am.'" Whenever they pray, God says, "Here I am listening; I am in your midst." He is near to them in everything (Dt 4:7).

2.5. God will guide them in every difficult situation (v. 11). *The Lord shall guide thee continually*. While we live in the wilderness of this world, we need continual guidance from heaven.

2.6. God will give them abundant satisfaction in their own minds. God gives good people not only wisdom and knowledge but also joy; they are satisfied with the testimony of their conscience and the assurances of God's favor. "These will satisfy your soul; they will put gladness into your heart even in the drought of suffering; these will strengthen your frame—will give you a pleasure that will support you as bones support the body. You will be like a well-watered garden, fruitful in graces, and like a spring of water, whose waters do not fail in times of drought or frost." Just as a spring of water is continually sending out its streams but always remains full, so also kind people are full of good as they give themselves fully to doing good and are never the poorer for all their generosity.

2.7. They and their families will be blessings to the wider community. "Those who come from you in the future, your descendants, will be of service to their generation (Ac 13:36), as you are to yours." They will build up the ancient ruins, which had long lain desolate. This was fulfilled when the captives, after their return from exile, repaired the towns of Judah, as well as many of the cities in Israel. They will continue and finish the good work that had been begun long before. *They shall raise up* to the top that building whose *foundation* was laid long ago, that building whose construction has been in progress for *many generations* (v. 12). This was fulfilled when the building of the temple was revived after it had stood still for many years (Ezr 5:2). They will have the blessing and praise of everyone around them: "*Thou shalt be called the repairer of the breach* (the Repairer of Broken Walls) (v. 12). You will be *the restorer of paths*, safe and quiet roads not only to travel on but also to *dwell in*, so safe and quiet that people will have no difficulty in building their houses by the roadside." The conclusion is that if they

keep such fasts as God has chosen, he will settle them again in their former peace and prosperity, and no one will be able to make them afraid (17:2; Eze 34:28; etc.).

Verses 13–14

Great emphasis was always laid on the due observance of the Sabbath, and it was especially required of the Jews when they were in exile in Babylon, because by keeping that day in honor of the Creator they set themselves apart from the worshipers of the gods that have not made the heavens and the earth. See 56:1–2. Notice:

1. How the Sabbath is to be sanctified (v. 13); this law of the Sabbath is still binding on us on our Lord's Day.

1.1. Nothing must be done that dishonors the Sabbath day. We must keep our feet from breaking the Sabbath, from trampling over it; we must keep our feet from doing as we please on that holy day, that is, from living without restraint and taking liberties to do what we please on Sabbath days, without any control of our conscience. On Sabbath days we must not walk in our own ways—that is, we are not to do our jobs—nor find our own pleasure—that is, not pursue sport and recreation—in fact, we must not speak our own idle words, for we must make religious faith the work of that day. We must speak about divine things as we sit at home or walk along the road (Dt 6:7; 11:19). In everything we say and do we must make a distinction between this day and other days.

1.2. We must call it a delight, not a task or a burden. We must not only count it a delight but also call it so. We must call it so to God by giving thanks for it. We must call it so to others to invite them to come and share in its delights, and we must call it so to ourselves so that we may not harbor the slightest thought of wishing the Sabbath to be over so that we may go and sell our grain.

2. The reward of Sabbath: sanctification (v. 14).

2.1. We will have comfort from it; the work will be its own wages. *If we call the sabbath a delight, then shall we delight ourselves in the Lord* (v. 13); he will reveal himself more and more to us. If we go about our Sabbath duty cheerfully, we will go from it with satisfaction.

2.2. We will have the honor of it: *I will cause thee to ride upon the high places of the earth* (on the heights of the land) (v. 14), which shows not only a great security but also great dignity; God will honor those who honor him (1Sa 2:30) and his Sabbath. If God by his grace enables us to live above the world and to manage it in such a way that we are not hindered by it, then he makes us *ride on the high places of the earth*.

2.3. We will gain from it: I will *feed thee with the heritage of Jacob thy father* (v. 14), that is, with all the blessings of the covenant and all the precious crops of Canaan—which was a type of heaven—for these were the inheritance of Jacob.

CHAPTER 59

In this chapter we see sin appearing very sinful (Ro 7:13) and grace appearing exceedingly gracious, and just as what is here said about the sinner's sin (vv. 7–8) is applied to the general corruption of the human race (Ro 3:15), so what is here said about a Redeemer (v. 20) is applied to Christ (Ro 11:26). These people are accused of stopping the flow of God's favors to them (vv. 1–8). 2. They are told what the judgments are that they have brought on their own heads (vv. 9–11) and also what the sins are that caused God to send those judgments (vv. 12–15). 3. It is promised here that despite this, God will rescue them (vv. 16–19), and he will keep mercy in store for them and pass it on as an inheritance to them (vv. 20–21).

Verses 1–8

The prophet here puts right the mistake of those who have been quarreling with God because they have not received the rescues that they have fasted and prayed for (58:3).

1. The fault does not lie with God. He is still as able to help as ever: *His hand is not shortened* (v. 1); his power is not lessened. God can still reach as far as ever and with as strong an arm as ever. His hand has not become weak, nor is it too short. *Has the Lord's hand waxed short* (become too short)? said God to Moses (Nu 11:23). No, it has not, and he will not let it be thought that it has. None of the following can shorten or restrict the power of God: time, the power of enemies, or the weakness of his instruments. He is still as ready and willing to help in answer to prayer as he ever was: *His ear is not heavy, that it cannot hear* (v. 1). More is implied than is expressed; not only is his ear not dull, but also he is quick to hear. *Even before they call, he answers* (65:24). If your prayers are not answered, it is not because God is weary of hearing prayer, but because we are weary of praying, not because his ear is dull when we speak to him, but because our ears are dull when he speaks to us.

2. They stood in their own light and put a bar over their own door. *Your iniquities have kept good things from you* (Jer 5:25).

2.1. Notice what trouble sin causes. It prevents God's mercy; it is a dividing wall between us and God (Eph 2:14). Sin *hides his face from us,* which shows his great displeasure (Dt 31:17). The consequences of sin show that it is totally harmful, separating us from God and so separating us not only *from all good* but *to all evil* (Dt 29:21).

2.2. The prophet shows how many and great their iniquities are, according to the command given (58:1) *to show God's people their transgressions.*

2.2.1. He must begin with their thoughts, for that is where all sin begins: *Their thoughts are thoughts of iniquity* (v. 7). *They conceive mischief* (trouble) and then give birth to evil (v. 4). Although their sins may be born in pain, when they run against the oppositions of providences and the restraints of their own consciences, yet, when they have achieved their evil purposes, they look on their sins with as much pride as if there were *a man child born into the world* (Jn 16:21). This reminds us of Jas 1:15: *when lust has conceived, it bringeth forth sin.* This is called *hatching the cockatrice's egg* (the eggs of vipers) *and weaving the spider's web* (v. 5). The spider's web is weak and insignificant, something that a brush sweeps away in a moment: such are the thoughts that worldly people occupy, building castles in the air. They hatch the eggs of the adder, which are poisonous and produce venomous creatures; such are the thoughts of evildoers who delight in causing trouble. *He that eats of their eggs* — that is, has any dealings with them — *dies* — that is, is in danger of having some trouble or other done to him — *and that which is crushed,* or which begins to be hatched, *breaks out into a viper* (v. 5), which you interfere with at your peril.

2.2.2. Their mouth speaks out of this abundance of evil in the heart (Mt 12:34), and yet it does not always speak out; rather, to achieve their troublesome purpose more effectively, they cover up the evil *with much fair* (persuasive) *speech* (Pr 7:21) (v. 3): *Your lips have spoken lies,*

and again (v. 4), *They speak lies,* pretending to be kind where they really intend trouble. *Your tongue has muttered perverseness* (v. 3). Backbiters are called *whisperers.*

2.2.3. Their actions are all of a piece with their thoughts and words. They are guilty of shedding innocent blood: *Your hands are defiled with blood* (v. 3); blood is defiling: it leaves an indelible stain of guilt on the conscience, which nothing but the blood of Christ can cleanse. *Their feet run to this evil; they make haste to shed innocent blood.* With other iniquities are their *fingers defiled* (v. 3); they make everything theirs that they can lay their hands on. *They trust in vanity* (rely on empty arguments) (v. 4); they depend on their skill in deceiving people to make themselves rich, and in deceiving others they will only deceive themselves. *The act of violence is in their hands* (v. 6), according to the arts of violence in their heads and the thoughts of violence in their hearts.

2.2.4. No methods are taken to put right these grievances and reform these abuses (v. 4): *None calls for justice.* When justice is not carried out, blame is to be put not only on the magistrates but also on the people. Private individuals should contribute to the public good by showing up secret evil. Truth is opposed, and no one *pleads for it;* there is no one who has the courage to confront a prosperous fraud. *The way of peace* (v. 8) is as little regarded as the way of truth; they *know it not,* that is, they never seek the things that make for peace (Ro 14:19). *There is no judgment in their goings* (no justice in their paths) (v. 8); they have no sense of justice in the way they live.

2.2.5. In all this, they act very foolishly and against their own interests. Those who practice iniquity rely on empty arguments (v. 4). *Their webs,* which they weave so skillfully and diligently, *shall not become garments, neither shall they cover themselves,* either for shelter or for adornment, *with their works* (v. 6). There is nothing to be gained by sin, and that will be clear when profit and loss are compared. Those ways of iniquity are *crooked* (v. 8) and will therefore perplex them and never bring them to their journey's end.

Verses 9–15

In this paragraph, as in the last, it is shown that sin causes great trouble. In this paragraph it seems to be spoken by the people to God, as an acknowledgment of their humble submission to the justice of God's proceedings.

1. They acknowledge that God has opposed them (vv. 9–11).

1.1. They are in distress, oppressed by their enemies, and God has not supported them to plead their just but wronged cause: *"Judgment is far from us, neither does justice overtake us"* (v. 9). Although, as to our persecutors, we are sure that we have right on our side and that they are the wrongdoers, we have not acted justly toward one another, and so God allows our enemies to deal unjustly with us."

1.2. Their expectations have been sadly disappointed: *We wait for light* as those who wait for the morning (Ps 130:6), *but behold obscurity* (all is darkness); *we look for judgment* (justice), *but there is none* (v. 11). We look for salvation because we think God has promised it and because we have prayed for it with fasting, but *we* continue to *walk in darkness* (v. 9).

1.3. They are at their end of their tether (v. 10): *We grope for the wall like the blind.* Those who love darkness rather than light will receive their condemnation accordingly.

1.4. They have sunk into despair: *We are in desolate places as dead men* (v. 10). The state of the Jews in

Babylon is represented by *dead and dry bones* (Eze 37:4, 12), and the explanation of the comparison (Eze 37:11) explains this text: *Our hope is lost; we are cut off.* The anguish of some is loud and noisy: *We roar like bears* (v. 11); the sorrow of others is silent and preys more on their spirits: *We mourn sore* (mournfully) *like doves*, like doves in the valleys.

2. They acknowledge that they have provoked God (vv. 12–15).

2.1. They confess they have sinned. "We are witnesses against ourselves: *As for our iniquities, we know them* (v. 12), even though we may have foolishly tried to cover them up."

2.2. They confess the evil of sin; it is *transgressing and lying* (rebellion and treachery) *against the Lord* (v. 13). The sins of God's people are worse than the sins of other people, because in rebelling, they *lie against the Lord.* They misrepresent him, treacherously breaking covenant with him, which is *lying against him.*

2.3. They confess there has been a general decay of moral integrity, and those who were false to their God were also unfaithful to one another. They have *spoken oppression*, though it is rebelling against truth. They have *conceived and uttered words of falsehood* (lies) (v. 13). Many lies are spoken in haste because they are not thought about, but these are conceived and spoken deliberately and on purpose. They are lies, but they are said to be spoken *from the heart* (v. 13), because they still agree with the hatred and evil of the heart and are its natural language; it is *a double heart* (Ps 12:2).

2.4. They confess that what might have been done to reform the land and put right what was wrong was not done (v. 14). "*Judgment* (justice), which should run its course like a river, like a mighty stream (Am 5:24), *is turned away backward*; it is driven back to go in the opposite direction. The administration of justice has become a cover-up for the greatest injustice. *Justice stands afar off* (v. 14), far away even from our courts of justice. *Truth is fallen* (has stumbled) *in the street* (v. 14), *yea, truth fails* (is nowhere to be found) (v. 15) even in ordinary conversation, so that one does not know whom to believe or whom to trust."

2.5. They confessed that there is a prevalent enmity toward those who are good: *He that does evil goes unpunished*, but *he that departs from evil makes himself a prey* (v. 15). To these enemies of good, to refuse to do as they do is offensive enough to be a crime, and they treat as enemies those who will not share with them in their evil ways. "He that departs from evil is accounted mad," the margin reads.

2.6. They confess that all this must be displeasing to the God of heaven. Though done in secret and covered up by falsehood and pretense, it still could not be hidden from his all-seeing eye. Yet even though the sin displeased him, he would soon have been reconciled to the sinners if they had returned from their evil ways.

Verses 16–21

Sin increased in the earlier part of the chapter; in these verses grace increased all the more (Ro 5:20). Notice:

1. Why God worked salvation despite their offenses. It was purely for his own name's sake.

1.1. He took notice of their weakness and evil: *He saw that there was no man* (v. 16) who would do anything to support religion and goodness among them. Most people were evil, and those who were not so were weak. *There was no intercessor* (v. 16), no one to intercede with God (v. 14), no one to speak a good word for those who were

attacked because they kept their integrity (v. 15). They complained that God did not support them (58:3), but God, with much more reason, complained that they did nothing for themselves.

1.2. He engaged his own strength and righteousness to work for them. They will be saved. The work of reformation—which is the first and main aspect of their salvation—will be brought about by the immediate influence of divine grace on the human conscience. When God stirred up the spirit of Cyrus (2Ch 36:22; Ezr 1:1) and brought his people out of Babylon, *not by might, nor by power, but by the Spirit of the Lord of hosts* (Zec 4:6), then his own arm, which is never shortened, brought about salvation. Divine justice, which they have offended by their sins, appears for them through grace. Although they cannot expect any favor as if it were due to them, he will, in righteousness, punish the enemies of his people; see Dt 9:5: *Not for thy righteousness, but for the wickedness of these nations* they are driven out. In our redemption by Christ, since we had no righteousness of our own to support us, he brought in a righteousness by the merits and mediation of his own Son—which is called *the righteousness which is of God by faith* (Php 3:9). God *put on righteousness as a breastplate* (v. 17), protecting his own honor as a breastplate protects the vital organs, and put *a helmet of salvation upon his head* (v. 17). When righteousness is his coat of arms, salvation is his crest. In allusion to this, among the pieces of a Christian's armor we find *the breastplate of righteousness*, and as a helmet *the hope of salvation* (Eph 6:14–17; 1Th 5:8), and it is called *the armour of God*, because he wore it first and so fitted it for us. Because they have no spirit or zeal to do anything for themselves, God will *put on the garments of vengeance for clothing, and clothe himself with zeal as a cloak* (v. 17); he will cause both his justice toward his enemies and his jealousy for his glory to appear clearly.

2. What the salvation is that will be brought about by the righteousness of God himself.

2.1. There will be a present physical restoration worked for the Jews in Babylon, or those elsewhere in distress and captivity. This is promised (vv. 18–19) as a type of something more. It is promised here:

2.1.1. That God will judge his enemies and repay them according to the deeds they have done. He will deal with the enemies of his people abroad and with the enemies of justice and truth at home, for they are God's enemies, too. He will deal with both as they have deserved, literally, "according to former retributions," as he has repaid his enemies in the past, *fury to his adversaries, recompense* (retribution) *to his enemies* (v. 18). His fury will not exceed the rules of justice. Even *to the islands*, which lie farthest away, if they have appeared against him, he will act in retribution, for *his hand shall find out all his enemies* (Ps 21:8), and his arrows will reach them.

2.1.2. That whatever attempts the enemies of God's people may later make to disturb their peace will be brought to nothing: *When the enemy shall come in like a flood* (v. 19), then *the Spirit of the Lord shall lift up a standard against him* (v. 19), and, as the margin reads, "put him to flight."

2.1.3. That all this will lead to the glory of God and the advancement of religious faith in the world (v. 19). This had its complete fulfillment in Gospel times, when many came *from the east and west* to fill up the places of *the children of the kingdom* who were *cast out*, when eastern and western churches were set up (Mt 8:11).

2.2. There will be a more glorious salvation brought about by the Messiah in the fullness of time (Gal 4:4;

Eph 1:10). We have here the two great promises about that salvation:

2.2.1. That the Son of God will come to us as our Redeemer (v. 20). The coming of Christ as the Redeemer is the summary of all the promises both of the Old and New Testaments, and this was the redemption in Jerusalem that the believing Jews looked for (Lk 2:38). Christ is our *go'el*, our closest relative, who redeems both the person and the possessions of the poor debtor (Ge 38:8; Dt 25:5–6; Ru 2:20; etc.). Notice:

2.2.1.1. The place where this Redeemer will appear: he *shall come to Zion* (v. 20), for there, on that holy hill, the Lord will set him up as his King (Ps 2:6). Zion was a type of the Gospel church.

2.2.1.2. The people who will receive comfort from the Redeemer's coming, knowing that their redemption draws near. He will come *to those that turn from ungodliness in Jacob* (v. 20), but only to those who turn away from their sins, who repent and reform.

2.2.2. That the Spirit of God will come to us as our sanctifier (v. 21). But the promise is made to a single person: my *Spirit that is upon thee* (v. 21); this promise is directed either:

2.2.2.1. To Christ as the head of the church, who received so that he might give (Ps 68:18; Eph 4:8). Or:

2.2.2.2. To the church, and so it is a promise of the lasting continuation of the church in the world until the end of time, parallel to those promises that the throne and offspring of Christ will endure forever (Ps 22:30; 89:29, 36). *Instead of the fathers shall be the children* (Ps 45:16). It will be kept up—henceforth and for ever (v. 21), even *unto the end of the world* (62:11). The Spirit that was on Christ will always continue in the hearts of the faithful; there will be some in every age on whom he will work and in whom he will live, and so the Counselor will remain with the church for ever (Jn 14:16). There will be some in every age who, *believing with the heart* to righteousness, will *with the tongue make confession unto salvation* (Ro 10:10). The church is built on these foundations, standing firmly and forever, with Christ himself as the chief cornerstone (Eph 2:20).

CHAPTER 60

This whole chapter is a part of God's covenant with his church. The long continuation of the church, even to the farthest ages of time, was promised in 59:21, and here the large extent of the church is promised, even to the farthest regions of the earth. It is promised here: 1. That the church will be enlightened (vv. 1–2). 2. That it will be enlarged (vv. 3–8). 3. That the new converts will be greatly useful to the church (vv. 9–13). 4. That the church will be held in great honor (vv. 14–16). 5. That it will enjoy deep peace and tranquility (vv. 17–18). 6. That because all its members are righteous, its glory and joy will be eternal (vv. 19–22). This has some reference to the peaceful and prosperous condition that the Jews were in after their return to their own land, but it looks further and was to have its complete fulfillment in the kingdom of the Messiah, the enlargement of that kingdom by the bringing in of the Gentiles into it, and the spiritual blessings in heavenly things by Christ Jesus with which it would be enriched (Eph 1:3).

Verses 1–8

It is promised here that the Gospel temple will be radiant and very large.

1. It will be radiant: *Thy light has come* (v. 1). When the Jews returned from exile, they had *light and gladness,*

and joy and honour (Est 8:16); they then *knew the Lord* and *rejoiced in his great goodness*. Notice:

1.1. What this light is and where it springs from: *The Lord shall arise upon thee* (v. 2); *the glory of the Lord* (v. 1) *shall be seen upon thee*. When God appears to us, then *the glory of the Lord rises upon us* (v. 1) like the morning light. When he appears for us, then his glory is seen on us. When Christ arose as the Sun of Righteousness (Mal 4:2), and in him *the dayspring from on high visited us* (Lk 1:78), then *the glory of the Lord was* seen on us, the glory *as of the first-begotten of the Father* (Jn 1:14).

1.2. What a contrast there will be to this light: *Darkness shall cover the earth* (v. 2); but although it is thick darkness, which will spread over the people, the church will have light at the same time (Ex 10:23).

1.3. What is the duty that the rising of this light calls for: "*Arise, shine*; not only receive this light and," as the margin reads, "'be enlightened' by it, but also reflect this light; *arise and shine* with rays borrowed from it."

2. It will be very large. When the Jews were resettled in their own land after the exile, many of the people of the land joined themselves to them, but we must look further, to the bringing of the Gentiles into the Gospel church, not their flocking to one particular place. There is no place now that is the center of the church's unity; the promise concerns their flocking to Christ and coming by faith, hope, and holy love into that family that is named from him (Eph 3:15). *You have come unto Mount Zion, to the city of the living God, the heavenly Jerusalem* (Heb 12:22); this verse serves as a key to this prophecy. See also Eph 2:19. Notice:

2.1. What will invite such multitudes to join the church: "They will *come to thy light and to the brightness of thy rising*" (v. 3). This light, which reveals so much of God and his goodwill to human beings, and by which life and immortality are brought to light (2Ti 1:10), will invite all serious, well-disposed people to come and join the church. The purity and love of the first Christians, their heavenly-mindedness, and their patience in suffering were the brightness of the church's rising, which drew many people to it.

2.2. What multitudes will come to the church. Great numbers *shall come, Gentiles* (v. 3) (or nations) *of those that are saved. Nations* will be discipled (Mt 28:19). They come from all parts (v. 4): "*Lift up thine eyes round about, and see* them coming, *devout men out of every nation under heaven* (Ac 2:5). Sons and daughters will come most dutifully, as your sons and daughters, deciding to join your family." Those people who want to enjoy the honors and privileges of Christ's family must submit to its discipline.

2.3. What they will bring with them and what benefits will come to the church by their joining it. The merchants will write *holiness to the Lord* on their profit and their earnings (23:18). "*The abundance of the sea* (v. 5) (the fish, the pearls), or what is imported by sea, *shall all be converted to thee* (v. 5) and to thy use." The wealth of the rich merchants will be spent on works of godliness and charity. Those who are powerful in the nations will use their power in the service of the church: "*The forces of the Gentiles shall come unto thee* (v. 5) to guard your coasts and fight your battles." *The camels that bring* gold and incense, those of Midian and Sheba, will bring the richest goods of their country, not to trade with, but to honor God with. This was partly fulfilled when the wise men of the east came to Christ and presented to him treasures of gold, frankincense, and myrrh (Mt 2:11). Great numbers of sacrifices will be brought to God's altar, and although they are brought by Gentiles, they will be accepted (v. 7). Kedar was famous for its flocks, and probably the fattest rams were those of Nebaioth; these will be accepted on God's altar. This was fulfilled when by the decree of Darius the governors beyond the rivers were ordered to provide the temple at Jerusalem *with bullocks, rams, and lambs, for the burnt offering of the God of heaven* (Ezr 6:9).

2.4. How God will be honored by the increase of the church. When they bring their gold and incense, it will be to *show forth the praises of the Lord* (vv. 6–7). The church is the house of God's glory, where he reveals his glory to his people and receives that praise by which they honor him. And it is for the glory of this house that the Gentiles will bring their offerings to it.

2.5. How the church will herself be affected by this ·increase of her numbers (v. 5). "*Thou shalt see* and *flow together*," or "flow to and fro." There will be a mixture of fear with this joy: "*Thy heart shall fear* (v. 5), doubting whether it is lawful to *go in to the uncircumcised* and *eat with them*" (Ac 11:3). Peter was so impressed with this fear that he needed a vision and voice from heaven to help him overcome it (Ac 10:28). "When this fear is conquered, your heart will be so released that you will have room in it for all the Gentile converts." These converts flocking to the church will be greatly wondered at (v. 8): *Who are these that fly as a cloud?* The conversion of souls is like the flying of a cloud: in great numbers, but also with great unanimity, like clouds flying on the wings of the wind. They will *fly as doves to their windows* (v. 8), many together. They will fly on the wings of the harmless dove, which flies low, showing innocence and humility. They fly to Christ, to the church, as doves instinctively fly to their own windows, to their own home.

Verses 9–14

The promises made to the church are repeated to encourage the Jews after their return from exile, but the promises also look further, to the enlargement and advancement of the Gospel church.

1. God will be very gracious and favorable toward the church. "All will now seek your favor, *for in my wrath I smote* (struck) *thee*, while you were in exile, but now *in my favour have I had mercy on thee*, and so I have all this mercy in store for you" (v. 10).

2. Many people will be brought into the church, even from countries far away (v. 9): *Surely the isles shall wait for* (look to) *me*; they will welcome the Gospel. *The ships of Tarshish* (v. 9), transport ships, will carry the ministers of the church to distant parts to preach the Gospel. They live so far away that they cannot bring their flocks, and so they will *bring their silver and gold with them*.

3. Those who come into the church will be welcome. "*Therefore thy gates shall be open continually* (v. 11), not only because you have no reason to fear your enemies but also because you have reason to expect your friends." It is usual for us to leave our doors open, or to have someone available to open them, all night if we are awaiting the late arrival of a child or a guest. The gates of mercy are always open, night and day, or will soon be opened to those who knock (Mt 7:7).

4. All who are around the church will be useful to it in some way or other (v. 10): "Even *the sons of strangers*, who do not know you and who were not kindly disposed to you, *shall build up thy wall, and their kings shall*, in that and other things, *minister unto thee*" (v. 10). This was fulfilled when the king of Persia and the governors

of the provinces under his orders helped Nehemiah with the rebuilding of the walls of Jerusalem. Even those who do not belong to the church may protect it. However, *the nation and kingdom that will not serve thee shall perish* (v. 12).

5. There will be much beauty added to the services of divine worship (v. 13): *The glory of Lebanon*, the strong and stately cedars that grow there, will come to you, as they did to Solomon when he built the temple (2Ch 2:16), and with them will come other kinds of wood, to be used for the carved paneling. The temple, the place of God's sanctuary, will be not only rebuilt but also made beautiful. Similarly, it was adorned with beautiful stones and gifts (Lk 21:5), to which this promise may refer, but Christ spoke about them so lightly that we must suppose it to have its complete fulfillment in the splendors of holiness.

6. The church will appear truly great and honorable (v. 14). After the Jews returned from exile, they gradually became more considerable. This prophecy is further fulfilled when those who have been the enemies of the church are persuaded by the grace of God to see the error of their ways: "The sons of those who afflicted you—if not they themselves, then their children—will bow down before you; they will beg your pardon for their foolishness and seek your favor to be allowed into your family" (1Sa 2:36). The poor, oppressed ones of the church will have the opportunity of doing good to those who have done evil to them and of saving those who have afflicted and despised them. It is a pleasure to good people, and they count it as an honor, to show mercy to those with whom they have found no mercy.

Verses 15–22

The happy and glorious state of the church is further foretold here, referring ultimately to the Christian church under the type of that glimmer of eternal peace that the Jews sometimes enjoyed after their return from exile. This is here spoken of:

1. As compared with what it had been before.

1.1. She had been despised, but now she would be honored (vv. 15–16). Jerusalem had been forsaken and hated, but now it would be *the joy* of good people for *many generations* (v. 15). Yet considering how short Jerusalem's glory was and how short it came of the vast range of this promise, we must look for the complete fulfillment of the promise in the eternal glories of the Gospel church and the glorious privileges and advantages of the Christian faith. Two things will be her glory and joy:

1.1.1. She will find herself supported by her neighbors. The nations, and their kings, that are brought to embrace Christianity will give themselves for the good of the church. "*Thou shalt suck the milk of the Gentiles*, not suck their blood—that is not the spirit of the Gospel—you *shalt suck the breast of kings*, who will be to you as nursing fathers" (49:23).

1.1.2. She will find herself supported by her God: "*Thou shalt know that I the Lord am thy Saviour and thy Redeemer* (v. 16). You will know it from experience." They know before that the Lord was their God; they now know him as their Savior, their Redeemer.

1.2. She had been poor, but now she would be made rich (v. 17). Those who were raised up from the dust would have gold in their purses instead of bronze, and silver vessels in their houses instead of iron. So would the spiritual glory of the New Testament church exceed the external show and splendor of the Jewish era. When we had baptism in place of circumcision, the Lord's Supper in place of the Passover, and a Gospel ministry in place of a Levitical priesthood, we had gold instead of bronze. Sin turned gold into bronze when Rehoboam made bronze shields to replace the golden ones he had pawned, but when God's favor returns, it will turn bronze again into gold.

1.3. She had been oppressed by her own rulers (59:14), but now all such grievances would be put right (v. 17): "*I will make thy officers peace. They will be peace*, that is, they will sincerely seek your welfare, and you will enjoy good through them."

1.4. She had been insulted by her neighbors, invaded, and plundered, but now she would be so no longer (v. 18): "*Violence shall no more be heard in thy land.* Everyone will peacefully enjoy their lives. There will be no *wasting* (ruin) *nor destruction*; instead, *thy walls shall be called salvation, and thy gates shall be praise.*"

2. As compared with what it would be. At the end of this chapter we are directed to look even further, as far forward as to the glory and happiness of heaven, under the type of the flourishing state of the church on earth. As the prophets sometimes pass imperceptibly from the blessings of the Jewish church to the spiritual blessings of the Christian church, which are eternal, so sometimes they move from the church militant to the church triumphant, where all the promised peace, joy, and honor will be complete and perfect.

2.1. God will be all in all in the happiness promised here (1Co 15:28) (v. 19): *The sun and the moon shall be no more thy light.* "Idolaters worshiped the sun and moon, which some have thought the most ancient and plausible idolatry, but these *shall be no more thy light*, will no more be idolized, for the Lord will be a constant light to you in the nights of adversity as well as in the days of prosperity."

2.2. The happiness promised here will never change (v. 20): "*Thy sun shall no more go down*; there will be eternal sunshine with you. Your sun will not be like the sun you have now, which is sometimes eclipsed, is often clouded over, and will certainly set and leave you in the dark and cold; rather, *God himself* will be a sun; he is the *Father of all lights*, with whom there is *no variableness* or *shadow of turning*" (Jas 1:17). The comforts and joys of heaven will include both glories provided for the soul, which will be like the light of the sun, and glories prepared for the glorified body, which will be like the light of the moon, and none of these will ever even begin to cease. *And the days of thy mourning shall be ended* (v. 21).

2.3. Those who are entitled to this happiness will never lose possession of it (v. 21). And those who will fill the New Jerusalem will be *all the righteous* (v. 21) together. And because they are *all righteous*, they will *inherit the land for ever* (v. 21), for nothing but sin can turn them out of it.

2.4. The glory of the church will lead to the honor of the church's God: "They will be seen to be the *branch of my planting* (the shoot I have planted), *the work of my hands* (v. 21), and I will acknowledge them as such."

2.5. They will appear even more glorious, and God will be more glorified in them, if we compare their present state with their past state (v. 22): *A little one shall become a thousand, and a small one a strong nation.* The captives who returned from Babylon multiplied remarkably and became a strong nation. The Christian church was very small at first—it once numbered only 120 (Ac 1:15)—but it became a thousand. When the saints reach heaven and look back at the smallness of their beginnings, they will wonder how they got there. The fulfillment of the promise here may seem to be delayed, but

just as the Lord will do it, so he will *hasten it*; he will do it at the time appointed by his wisdom, not at the time dictated by our foolishness. And this is really hastening it, for although it seems to be delayed, it is not delayed if it comes at God's time.

CHAPTER 61

In this chapter: 1. We find the grace of Christ under the type of Isaiah's subject, which was the rescue of the Jews from Babylon, which he foretold (vv. 1–3). 2. We also find the glories of the church of Christ, its spiritual glories, described under the type of the Jews' prosperity after their return. It is promised that the ruins of the church will be restored (v. 4); that those from outside will be made useful to the church (v. 5); that the church will be a royal priesthood (1Pe 2:9), maintained by the riches of the Gentiles (v. 6); that she will have honor and joy instead of shame and sorrow (v. 7); that her affairs will prosper (v. 8); that future generations will enjoy these blessings (v. 9); that righteousness and salvation will be the eternal reasons for the church's rejoicing and thanksgiving (vv. 10–11).

Verses 1–3

The One who is the best expositor of Scripture has given us the best explanation of these verses, namely our Lord Jesus Christ himself, who read this out in the synagogue at Nazareth—perhaps it was the lesson for the day—and applied it completely to himself, saying, *This day is this scripture fulfilled in your ears* (Lk 4:17–18, 21). As Isaiah was directed to proclaim freedom to the Jews in Babylon, so Christ, God's messenger, was directed to make known a more joyful jubilee to a lost world. We are told:

1. How he was fitted and qualified for this work: *The Spirit of the Lord God is upon me* (v. 1). The prophets had the Spirit of God moving them at times, both instructing them what to say and stirring them to say it. Christ had the Spirit always resting on him without limit (Jn 3:34). When he began his prophetic office, the Spirit, as a dove, *descended upon him* (Mt 3:16). This Spirit he communicated to those whom he sent to declare the same good news, saying to them, when he gave them their commission, *Receive you the Holy Ghost* (Jn 20:22).

2. How he was appointed and ordained to this work: *The Spirit of God is upon me, because the Lord God has anointed me* (v. 1). This is why the Redeemer was called the *Messiah*, the *Christ*, "the Anointed One," because he was *anointed with the oil of gladness above his fellows* (Ps 45:7). And *he has sent me* (v. 1).

3. What the work was to which he was appointed and ordained.

3.1. He was to be a preacher who was to carry out the office of a prophet. He must preach "good news"—the meaning of the word *gospel*—*to the meek* (v. 1), to the penitent, humble, and poor in spirit; the news of a Redeemer would be truly good news to them.

3.2. He was to be a healer. He was sent to *bind up the brokenhearted* (v. 1). Those whose hearts are broken because of sin, who are truly humbled under the sense of guilt and fear of wrath, are provided in the Gospel of Christ with what will give them peace and silence their fears.

3.3. He was to be a deliverer. He was sent as a prophet to preach, as a priest to heal, and as a king to issue declarations:

3.3.1. Declarations of peace to his friends: he will *proclaim liberty to the captives* (v. 1)—as Cyrus did to the Jews in exile (2Ch 36:22–23; Ezr 1:1–2)—and the *opening of the prison to those that were bound* (v. 1). Whereas, because of the guilt of sin, we are under obligation to the justice of God, sold for sin, Christ lets us know that he has made atonement for that debt so that divine justice has been satisfied. If we plead that and give ourselves and all we have to him, we may by faith apply for pardon. There is, and will be, *no condemnation to us* (Ro 8:1). And whereas, by the power of sin in us, we are under the power of Satan, Christ lets us know that he has conquered Satan and provided for us sufficient grace to enable us to shake off the yoke of sin and to loose ourselves from *those bands of our neck* (52:2). *The Son* is ready by his Spirit to *make us free* (Jn 8:36). This is the Gospel proclamation, and it is like the blowing of the jubilee trumpet, which declared the great year of release (Lev 25:9, 40), in allusion to which the time announced by the prophet is here called *the acceptable year of the Lord* (v. 2). Or it is called the *year of the Lord* (v. 2) because it makes known his free grace, and it is called an *acceptable year* because it brings good news to us and thus brings what must be very acceptable to those who know the needs of their own souls and what they are capable of receiving.

3.3.2. Declarations of war against his enemies. Christ declares *the day of vengeance of our God* (v. 2):

• On sin and Satan, death and hell, and all the powers of darkness, to be destroyed in order to rescue us. Christ triumphed over these in his cross.
• On those people who resist his great offer of life.

3.4. He was to be a comforter, and so he is, as preacher, healer, and deliverer; he is sent to *comfort all who mourn* (v. 2), and those who mourn seek him, not the world, for comfort. As *blessings out of Zion* are spiritual blessings, so *mourners in Zion* are holy mourners, those who carry their sorrows to the throne of grace (Heb 4:16). It is for such people as these that Christ by his Gospel has appointed those comforts which will not only support them in their sorrows but also turn their sorrows into songs of praise, and he will give these comforts to them by his Spirit (v. 3). He will give them:

3.4.1. *Beauty for ashes* (v. 3). Here is an elegant play on words in the original: he will give them pe'er, "beauty," for *epher*, "ashes"; he will turn their sorrow into joy as quickly and as easily as you transpose a letter, for he simply has to speak and it is done.

3.4.2. *The oil of joy* (v. 3), which *makes the face to shine* (Ps 104:15), instead of *mourning*, which *disfigures the countenance* and makes it unattractive.

3.4.3. *The garments of praise* (v. 3), such beautiful garments as were worn on days of thanksgiving, instead of the *spirit of heaviness* (v. 3), "despair or dullness"; they will have open joy instead of secret mourning.

3.5. He was to be a planter, for the church is God's field (1Co 3:9). All that Christ does for us is in order to make us God's people, useful to him in some way as living trees, *planted in the house of the Lord* and *flourishing in the courts of our God* (Ps 92:13), so that others may take God's favor shining on his people and his grace shining in them as a reason to praise him, so that he may be forever *glorified in his saints* (2Th 1:10).

Verses 4–9

Promises are made here to the Jews who have now returned from exile, and these promises are to be extended to the Gospel church, which through grace is rescued from spiritual slavery.

1. It is promised that their houses will be rebuilt (v. 4), that their cities will be raised up from the ruins. The setting up of Christianity in the world repaired the decay of natural religion and restored the godliness and honesty that had been stripped away for many generations to the shame of the human race. An unsanctified soul is like a city that is broken down, but by the power of Christ's Gospel and grace it is fitted to be a dwelling place of God through the Spirit.

2. Those who were recently servants, working for their oppressors, will now have servants to do their work. *Strangers and the sons of the alien* will *keep their sheep, till their ground,* and *dress their gardens,* and *strangers shall feed your flocks* (v. 5).

3. They will be released and honorably employed (v. 6): "While strangers are *keeping your flocks,* you will be keeping *charge of the sanctuary* (Nu 3:28, 38); instead of being slaves to your taskmasters, *you shall be named the priests of the Lord,* which is a high and holy calling." God sets to work those whom he sets free; he *delivers them out of the hands of their enemies* so they may *serve him* (Lk 1:74–75; Ps 116:16). But his service is perfect freedom. And the Gospel church is *a royal priesthood* (1Pe 2:9).

4. The wealth and honors of the Gentile converts will lead to the benefit and good reputation of the church (v. 6). Those who were formerly strangers will become *fellow-citizens with the saints* (Eph 2:19).

4.1. They will *eat the riches of the Gentiles* (v. 6), which will be honorably presented to them as *gifts brought to the altar.*

4.2. They will *boast themselves in their glory* (v. 6). Whatever was the honor of the Gentile converts before their conversion will turn to the reputation of the church that they have joined. Whatever is their glory after their conversion—their holy zeal, their patient endurance, and that blessed change that divine grace has made in them—will be very much for the glory of God.

5. They will have great joy (v. 7). The Jews were privileged in this way after their return; they were in a new world and now knew how to value their liberty. And those whom Christ has brought into the glorious liberty of being God's children (Ro 8:21) rejoice much more, especially when the privileges of their adoption are completed in the resurrection of the body.

5.1. *They shall rejoice in their portion* (v. 7). Although their houses as well as their temple are inferior, they still will be pleased with them and thankful for them, because they are *in their land* (v. 7), their own land, the Holy Land, Immanuel's land (8:8), and so they will rejoice.

5.2. *Everlasting joy shall be unto them* (v. 7), which will last much longer than the exile lasted. But we must look for the fulfillment of this promise in the spiritual joy that believers have in God and the eternal joy they hope for in heaven.

5.3. This will compensate them double for all the shame and trouble they suffered in their exile: "*For your shame you shall have double* honor, and *in your land you shall possess double* (v. 7) wealth, the blessing of God on it. You will be acknowledged not only as *God's sons* but even as his *firstborn* (Ex 4:22), and so you will be entitled to a double portion." As the miseries of their captivity were so great that in them they are said to have received *double for all their sins* (40:2), so the joys of their return will be so great that in them they will receive *double for all their shame* (v. 7). The former may be applied to the fullness of Christ's atonement, in which God received *double for all our sins* (40:2); the latter to the fullness of heaven's joys, in which we will receive more than *double for all services* and sufferings. Job's case illustrates this: when God *turned again his captivity* (Ps 126:4), he gave him *twice as much as he had before* (Job 42:10).

6. God will be in covenant with them (v. 8): *I will direct their work in truth.* By his providence, God will direct their affairs for the best. As a reason both for this and for the previous promise, the first part of the verse includes the words *I the Lord love judgment* (justice). He loves justice to be done among people, both between magistrates and subjects and among neighbors, and so he hates all injustice. If people do not act justly, he loves to act justly himself by making amends for those who suffer wrong and by punishing those who do wrong. Ritual ceremonies will never atone for the sin of breaking moral commands, nor will it justify anyone's robbery to say, "It was for burnt offerings," or to say *Corban*, "It is a gift" (Mk 7:11).

7. God will pass on a blessing as an inheritance to future generations (v. 9): *Their seed*—the children of those people who are now the blessed by the Lord, or the church's offspring—will *be accounted to the Lord for a generation* (Ps 22:30).

7.1. They will be known among the Gentiles, will distinguish themselves, especially by that mutual love by which everyone will know them to be Christ's disciples (Jn 13:35). God will honor them by making them the blessings of their age and instruments of his glory.

7.2. God will be glorified for this, for all who see them will see so much of the grace of God in them that they will acknowledge them to be the offspring that the Lord has blessed and continues to bless.

Verses 10–11

We are taught here to rejoice with holy joy, to God's honor:

1. In the beginning of this good work, the clothing of the church *with righteousness and salvation* (v. 10). This is why *I will greatly rejoice in the Lord.* The first Gospel song begins like this: *My soul doth magnify the Lord, and my spirit hath rejoiced in God my Saviour* (Lk 1:46–47). The salvation God worked for the Jews and his reformation that appeared among them made them look as glorious as if they were wearing stately robes. Christ has clothed his church with eternal salvation by clothing it with the righteousness of both justification and sanctification. Notice how these two are put together; those people, and only those people, who are wearing the robe of righteousness now will be clothed with the garments of salvation in the hereafter. Such is the beauty of God's grace in those who are wearing the robe of righteousness.

2. In the progress and continuation of this good work (v. 11). It is not like a day of triumph, which is glorious for the present but is soon over. The church rejoices to think that these invaluable blessings will both spring up in future ages and spread to distant regions. They will spring up for ages to come like the fruits of the earth that are produced every year. *As the garden* that is enclosed *causes the things that are sown in it to spring forth* (v. 11) in their season, so constantly *will the Lord God cause righteousness and praise to spring forth* (v. 11) because of the covenant of grace. Although it may sometimes be winter with the church, when those blessings seem to wither and do not appear, their roots are still well established, and spring will come, when they will again flourish. They will spread far, *springing forth before all the nations* (v. 11).

CHAPTER 62

The work of prophets was both to preach and to pray. 1. The prophet is determined to apply himself constantly to *this business (v. 1). 2. God appoints him and his other prophets to continue to encourage his people while their rescue is being delayed (vv. 6–7). 3. There is a repetition and confirmation of the promises about the great things God will do for the Jews after their return from exile and for the Christian church when it is set up in the world. 3.1. The church will be made honorable in the eyes of the world (v. 2). 3.2. It will be seen to be very dear to God, precious and honorable in his sight (vv. 3–5). 3.3. It will enjoy great plenty (vv. 8–9). 3.4. It will be released from exile and become a significant nation again, particularly favored by heaven (vv. 10–12).*

Verses 1–5

The prophet here tells us:

1. What he will do for the church. Just as a prophet is a seer, so also he is a spokesman. He *will not hold his peace* (keep silent); he *will not rest.* Notice:

1.1. What the prophet's decision is: *He will not hold his peace* (v. 1). He will continue to preach with urgency. He will also continue to be bold in prayer (Ro 12:12).

1.2. What is the motivation of this decision: *for Zion's sake, and for Jerusalem's* (v. 1), not for the sake of any private interest of his own, but for the church's sake, because he has an affection and concern for Zion, which lies close to his heart. It is God's Zion and his Jerusalem, and it is precious to the prophet because it is precious to God.

1.3. He decides to continue this boldness until the promises of the church's righteousness and salvation, given in the previous chapter, are fulfilled. His prophecies will continue to speak about these things, and a remnant in every age will continue to pray for them. Then the church's *righteousness* and *salvation will go forth as brightness* and *as a lamp that burns* (v. 1), a light not only to the eyes but also to the feet, and to *the paths* of those who before *sat in darkness and in the shadow of death* (Ps 107:10).

2. What God will do for the church.

2.1. The church will be greatly wondered at. When the righteousness that is her salvation, her praise, and her glory is displayed, the Gentiles will see it. "Even kings will see and be in love with *the glory of thy righteousness*" (v. 2).

2.2. She will be truly wonderful. God is the fountain of honor, and the church's honor comes from him: "*Thou shalt be called by a new name* (v. 2), and those around you will have new thoughts about you." God will give her two names:

2.2.1. He will call her his crown (v. 3): *Thou shalt be a crown of glory in the hand of the Lord*, not on his head—as adding any real honor or power to him, as crowns do to those who are crowned with them—but in his hand, as a glory and beauty to him. "You will be *a crown of glory* and *a royal diadem* through the good hand of your God on you" (Ne 8:18).

2.2.2. He will call her his bride (vv. 4–5). This is an even greater honor, considering what a dejected condition she has been in. During the exile she was called *forsaken*, and her land was called *desolate*, like a woman shamefully divorced or left miserable. Such was the state of religion in the world before the preaching of the Gospel. But now, instead of those two shameful names, she will be called by two honorable names. She will be called *Hephzibah*, which means "my delight is in her," a proper name for a wife. By his grace God has created in his church what makes her his delight, because she has been refined, reformed, and brought home to him. She will also be called *Beulah*, which means "married." Whereas previously she had been desolate, *she shall be married.* Her sons will heartily embrace their native land: *Thy sons shall marry thee* (v. 5), that is, they will live with you and take delight in you. When they were in Babylon, they seemed to have embraced that land, for they were told to seek its peace (Jer 29:5–7). But now they will again marry their own land, *as a young man marries a virgin* (v. 5). *Her God, too, will* take pleasure in his church: *As the bridegroom rejoices over the bride, so shall thy God rejoice over thee* (v. 5).

Verses 6–9

Two things are promised to Jerusalem here:

1. A plentiful supply of the means of grace, that is, good preaching and good praying (vv. 6–7). Provision is made:

1.1. That ministers may do their duty as watchmen. God will set *watchmen on their walls who shall never hold their peace* (v. 6). They must take every opportunity to warn sinners, in season and out of season (2Ti 4:2); they must never betray the cause of Christ by a treacherous or cowardly silence. They must never keep silent at the throne of grace; they must *pray, and not faint* (Lk 18:1; Isa 40:31).

1.2. That people may do their duty. Let them not think it enough that their watchmen are praying for them; let them also pray for themselves. God's professing people must be a praying people; they must be public-spirited in prayer.

2. Plenty of all other good things (v. 8). Their grain had been food for their enemies. Here was a double adversity: they themselves lacked what was necessary to support life, while their enemies were strengthened by it. God is said to give their grain to their enemies because he ordered it to be given to them as the just punishment of his people's abuse of plenty. The wine that they had labored for was drunk by foreigners to satisfy their sinful desires. But notice the great fullness and satisfaction they would now be restored to (v. 9): *Those that have gathered it shall eat it, and praise the Lord.* We must gather carefully and diligently what God gives; we must eat it freely and cheerfully. We must also serve him with our abundance, use it in works of godliness and charity, eat it and *drink it in the courts of his holiness* (sanctuary) (v. 9), where the altar, the priest, and the poor must all receive their share. *The Lord has sworn by his right hand, and by the arm of his strength* (v. 8), that he will do this for his people. It is a great encouragement to those who build their hopes on God's promise to be sure that *what he has promised he is able to perform* (Ro 4:21).

Verses 10–12

This, like many similar passages before, refers both to the restoration of the Jews from Babylon and, under that type, to the great redemption brought by Jesus Christ and the declaring of Gospel grace and freedom through him.

1. A way will be made for this salvation (v. 10). The gates of Babylon will be thrown open, and the way from Babylon to the land of Israel will be prepared; causeways will be made and built up through wet and muddy places, and the stones removed from rough and rocky places. John the Baptist was sent to *prepare the way of the Lord* (Mt 3:3).

2. Notice will be given of this salvation (vv. 11–12). It will be declared to the prisoners that they are set free. Let it be said to Zion, to comfort and encourage her, *Behold, thy salvation comes* (v. 11), that is, your Savior, who brings salvation, is coming. When he comes, he will bring with

him a *work* of reformation and humiliation and a *reward* of comfort and peace. It follows that they will be called *The holy people* and the *redeemed of the Lord* (v. 12). *The work before him* (v. 11), which will be done in them and on them, will cause them to be called a holy people, healed of their tendency to worship idols and consecrated only to God; and the *reward with him* (v. 11), their salvation, will cause them to be called the *redeemed of the Lord* (v. 12). Jerusalem will then be called *Sought out* (Sought After), *a city not forsaken* (v. 12). She will be sought and visited as much as ever. When Jerusalem is called *a holy city,* then it is called "Sought After," for holiness draws respect. But this declaration to the ends of the earth must refer to the Gospel of Christ. It is declared directly to the church, but it is echoed to every nation: *Behold, thy salvation cometh* (v. 11). Christ is not only the Savior but also salvation itself. Christians will be called *saints* (1Co 1:2), *the holy people* (v. 12), for they are chosen and called *to salvation through sanctification* (2Th 2:13). They will also be called *the redeemed of the Lord* (v. 12).

CHAPTER 63

In this chapter we have: 1. God coming toward his people by way of mercy and restoration, and this is to be connected to the end of the previous chapter, where it was said to Zion, Behold, thy salvation comes *(62:11), for here it is shown how it comes (vv. 1–6). 2. God's people meeting him with their devotions, and this part of the chapter is carried on to the end of the next. In this chapter we have: 2.1. A thankful acknowledgment of the great favors God has bestowed on them (v. 7). 2.2. The exalting of these favors upon consideration of God's relationship with them (v. 8), his compassionate concern for them (v. 9), their unworthiness (v. 10), and former mercies (vv. 11–14). 2.3. A very humble prayer to God to support them in their present distress, pleading God's mercy (v. 15), their relationship with him (v. 16), their desire for him (v. 17), and the arrogance of their enemies (vv. 18–19).*

Verses 1–6

A glorious victory is gained by the providence of God over the enemies of Israel. The victory is obtained over the Edomites, who triumphed in the destruction of Jerusalem by the Babylonians (Ps 137:7) and cut off the Jews who, making their way as far as they could from the enemy, escaped to the Edomites (Ob 12–13); the Edomites were therefore judged when Babylon was. But this victory over Edom is given as an example of the similar victories gained over other nations that had been Israel's enemies. This is a victory won not only by the providence of God over earthly enemies but also by the grace of God in Christ over our spiritual enemies. We find the garments dipped in blood adorning the One whose name is called *The Word of God* (Rev 19:13). In this description of the victory we have:

1. A wondering question put to the conqueror (vv. 1–2) by the church, or by the prophet in the name of the church. He sees a mighty hero returning in triumph from a bloody battle and is bold enough to ask him two questions:

1.1. Who is he? The prophet notices him coming from the country of Edom in such clothes as were glorious for a soldier, smeared with blood and dirt. He notices that he does not come either frightened or tired out, but *travels in the greatness of his strength* (v. 1). The question *Who is this?* (v. 1) is perhaps like Joshua's (Jos 5:13): *Art thou for us or for our adversaries?*

1.2. "*Wherefore art thou red in thy apparel* (why are your garments red)*?* (v. 2). What hard service have you been engaged in, that you carry with you these marks of toil and danger?" Is it possible that One who has such majesty should be employed in the servile work of *treading the winepress*? (v. 3).

2. A wonderful answer given by him.

2.1. He says who he is: *I that speak in righteousness, mighty to save* (v. 1). He is the Savior. He speaks *in righteousness* (v. 1), and so he will fulfill every word he has spoken: he is *mighty to save* (v. 1), able to bring about the promised redemption.

2.2. He tells how he came to appear in this color (v. 3): *I have trodden the winepress alone.*

2.2.1. He gains the victory purely by his own strength (v. 3). Certainly he needed no assistance; yet his people did not even offer it. Though it was for them that salvation was to be accomplished, they were weak and helpless, despondent and lethargic. They had no heart to do anything (v. 5): "*I looked, and there was none to help, none to uphold,* no one who had the courage to join Cyrus against their oppressors; *therefore my arm brought* about *the salvation; not by* created *might or power,* but *by the Spirit of the Lord of hosts* (Zec 4:6), my own powerful arm." God can help when every other helper fails; that is his time to help. But this may be most fully applied to Christ's victories over our spiritual enemies, which he gained in a single battle. He trod the winepress alone and triumphed over powers and authorities *in himself* (Col 2:15). When he fought against the powers of darkness, *all his disciples forsook him and fled* (Mt 26:56).

2.2.2. He undertakes the war purely out of his own zeal. God brought salvation for the oppressed Jews purely because he was angry with the oppressing Babylonians, angry at their idolatry, their pride and cruelty, and the wrongs they did to his people. Our Lord Jesus brought our redemption out of a holy zeal for the honor of his Father and the happiness of the human race and out of a righteous anger at the outrageous attacks Satan had made on both. He had zeal against his and his people's enemies: *The day of vengeance is in my heart* (v. 4). He had zeal for his people and for all whom he intended to make sharers in the intended salvation: "The year of my redeemed has come, the year appointed for their redemption." Notice with what pleasure he speaks about his people; they are his redeemed ones; they are his own people, who are precious to him. Although their redemption has not yet been worked out, he still calls them his redeemed, because the work will as surely be done as if it were done already.

2.2.3. He will gain complete victory over them all. Much has already been done, for he now appears wearing red garments. In the destruction of the anti-Christian powers we meet with much bloodshed (Rev 14:20; 19:13), which, nevertheless, according to the language of prophecy, may be understood spiritually, and no doubt so may this here.

Verses 7–14

At the end of this chapter and in the next, the prophet, even before God comes, is recognizing thankfully his dealings with his church all along. The prophet is like a watchman on the walls, fervently praying to God for his compassion toward the church in her present deplorable state.

1. Here is a general acknowledgment of God's goodness to them all along (v. 7). He mentions the *kindness of God* (v. 7), his unfailing love—the springs of divine mercy are so plentiful that he speaks of it in the plural—his *loving-kindnesses.* He also mentions his *praises,* that is, the thankful acknowledgments of his unfailing love. He speaks about the goodness that is from God, *all that the Lord has bestowed* (v. 7) on us concerning life and godliness, in our personal and family lives. We must bless God for the blessings enjoyed by others as well as for those enjoyed by ourselves. He also speaks of the goodness that is in God. God does good because he is good; what he gives us must be traced back to the origin: it is *according to his mercies*—not according to what we deserve—and *according to the multitude of his loving-kindnesses* (v. 7).

2. Here are the steps of God's mercy to Israel ever since it was formed into a nation:

2.1. His expectation that they would live good lives (v. 8). When he brought them out of Egypt and took them into covenant, he said, "*Surely they are my people, children that will not lie,*" who will not make a pretense with God in their covenant dealings.

2.2. The favor he showed them with these expectations in mind (v. 8): *So he was their Saviour* (v. 8) out of the slavery of Egypt, and he had been their Savior many times since. Notice:

2.2.1. The motive that moved him to bring about salvation for them was *his love and his pity* (v. 9). This is strangely expressed here: *In all their affliction he was afflicted* (in all their distress he too was distressed) (v. 9). This was the extent to which he sympathized with them, that he took wrongs done to them as done to himself. Their cries move him (Ex 3:7), as if he had their pain. *Saul, Saul, why persecutest thou me?* (Ac 9:4). God is so far from *afflicting willingly* (La 3:33) that if they humble themselves, he is *afflicted in their affliction,* as tender parents are afflicted by the severe medical treatments their sick children need. There is another reading of these words in the original: "In all their affliction there was no affliction"; although they were in great affliction, it was changed by the grace of God for their good, and it was balanced out with mercy. They were so wonderfully supported, and it ended so well, that it was in effect no affliction. The troubles of the saints are not afflictions, but medicines. Saints are enabled to call them *light,* to say that they last *but for a moment* (2Co 4:17), and, looking to heaven as all in all, to make light of them.

2.2.2. The person employed in their salvation—*the angel of his presence* (v. 9) (or face). The highest angel in heaven, even the angel of his presence, is not thought too great to be sent on this mission. Similarly, the little ones' angels are said to be those that *always behold the face of our Father* (Mt 18:10). But this should rather be understood as referring to Jesus Christ, the eternal Word, that angel of whom God spoke to Moses (Ex 23:20–21), whose *voice Israel was to obey.* He is the Angel of the covenant, God's messenger to the world (Mal 3:1). He is the *angel of God's face,* for he is *the express image of his person* (Heb 1:3), and the glory of God shines in the face of Christ (2Co 4:6). The One who would work out the eternal salvation worked out the temporal salvations that were types of it.

2.2.3. The progress and perseverance of this favor. He not only redeemed them from slavery but also *bore them* (lifted them up) *and carried them all the days of old* (v. 9). When they were at war with the nations, he stood by them, and although they were perverse, he bore with them (Ac 13:18).

2.3. Their deceit and the trouble they brought on themselves (v. 10): *But they rebelled.* They rebelled against their loyalty to God and took up arms against him: *They* rebelled, and vexed (grieved) his Holy Spirit (v. 10) with their unbelief and murmuring. The ungrateful rebellion of God's children against him greatly grieves his Holy Spirit. Then he justly withdrew his protection. He who had been so much their friend was turned to be their enemy and fought against them (v. 10), by one judgment after another, both in the desert and when they settled in Canaan. Sin makes God an enemy even to those for whom he has been a good friend and angers the One who was all love and pity. Sinners willfully lose him as a friend. This refers especially to those adversities that had been brought on them by their exile in Babylon for their idolatry and other sins.

2.4. A particular reflection on what God did for them when he first formed them into a people: Then he remembered the days of old (v. 11).

2.4.1. This may be understood as referring either to the people or God himself.

2.4.1.1. We may understand it as referring to the people. Israel then, spoken of as one person, remembered the days of old (v. 11) and reasoned: "Where are all the wonders that our fathers told us of (Jdg 6:13)? Where is he that brought them up out (v. 11) of Egypt? Is he not as able to bring us up out of Babylon? Where is the Lord God of Elijah? Where is the Lord God of our fathers?" (2Ki 2:14). Their ancestors had been an offensive people but had found him to be a pardoning God, and why may not they find him so if they also turn back to him? They use it as a plea with God in prayer to release them from captivity, like that in 51:9–10.

2.4.1.2. We may understand it as referring to God; he reminded himself of former days, of his covenant with Abraham (Lev 26:42). "Why should I not support them now as I did their ancestors, who were as undeserving, as ill deserving, as they are?" He might have said, "I have rescued them already, but they have again brought trouble on themselves (Pr 19:19); therefore I will deliver them no more" (Jdg 10:13). But mercy turns the argument the other way: "I have rescued them formerly, and so I will do so now."

2.4.2. Whichever way we take it, whether the people plead it with God or God pleads it with himself, these verses recall what God did through Moses for his people, especially in bringing them through the Red Sea: God led them by the right hand of Moses (v. 12) and the miracle-working rod in his hand. It was not Moses who led them any more than it was Moses who fed them (Jn 6:32), but God through Moses. God was the owner of the flock, but Moses was a shepherd under him, and by his being trained to keep the flock of his father Jethro, he was made used to hard work and patience and so was equipped for this pastoral care. Here he was a type of Christ the Good Shepherd, who lays down his life for the sheep (Jn 10:15). God put his holy Spirit within Moses (v. 11); the Spirit of God was among them, and not only his providence but also his grace worked for them. He carried them safely through the Red Sea: He divided the water before them (v. 12), so that it gave them not only passage but also protection, a wall on both sides. He led them through the deep as a horse in the wilderness, or in the plain (v. 13). If God makes a way for us, he will make it plain and level. He brought them safely to a place of rest: As a beast goes down into the valley, carefully and gradually, so the Spirit of the Lord caused him to rest (v. 14). They had resting places provided for them many times on their journey through the desert. And ultimately they were made to rest in Canaan, and the Spirit of the Lord gave them that rest according to the promise. God did it by his glorious arm; "the arm of his power" is the sense.

Verses 15–19

This prayer, continued to the end of the next chapter, is a warm, bold, pleading prayer. It is composed for use during the time of the exile. The Jews had prayers as well as promises prepared for them for times of such need. Some good interpreters think this prayer looks further and that it expresses the complaints of the Jews under their last rejection from God and destruction by the Romans. Notice:

1. The requests they offered to God: Look down from heaven, and behold. Look down from the habitation (lofty throne) of thy holiness and of thy glory (v. 15). God's holiness is his glory. Heaven is his dwelling place, the lofty throne of his glory (v. 17): "Return; change your way toward us, return in mercy, and let us have your gracious presence with us." God's people fear nothing more than they fear his departure from them, and they want nothing more than they want his return to them.

2. The complaints they made to God.

2.1. That they were given up to themselves, and God's grace did not restore them (v. 17). It is a strange complaint: Why hast thou made us to err from thy ways? And thou hast hardened our heart from thy fear (v. 17). Some consider this the language of those who were ungodly; when the prophets rebuked them for the error of their ways, they had the brazen arrogance to accuse God of their sin, making him its author. But I prefer to take it as the language of those who mourned the unbelief and impenitence of their people, not accusing God of being the author of their evil, but complaining about it to him. They acknowledged that they had erred from God's ways, that their hearts had been hardened from his fear (v. 17), and that this was the cause of all their wandering from his ways, or from his fear (v. 17). This may mean "from the true worship of God." They complained about this as their great misery and burden, that because of their sins, God had allowed them to err from his ways (v. 17) and had justly withheld his grace, so that their hearts were hardened from his fear (v. 17). When they ask, Why hast thou done this? it is not accusing him of wrong, but mourning it as a harsh judgment. God had caused them to err and hardened their hearts (v. 10) by a judicial sentence. Their troubles had separated many of them from God and prejudiced them against his service. Their afflictions were their temptations, and those temptations were invincible to many of them.

2.2. That they were given up to their enemies (v. 18): Our adversaries have trodden down thy sanctuary. They complained not so much about the adversaries trampling down their houses and cities as about their trampling down God's sanctuary, because in doing so they insulted God directly and robbed his people of the encouragement they valued most.

3. Their pleas for mercy and their rescue.

3.1. They pleaded the tender compassion God used to show to his people (v. 15). The most effective arguments in prayer are those that are taken from God himself. It could not be that divine zeal, which is infinitely wise and just, had cooled off, that divine strength, which is infinite, had become weaker. Had God, who so often remembered to be gracious, now forgotten to be so? Has he in anger shut up his tender mercies? (Ps 77:9). It can never be.

3.2. They pleaded God's relationship with them as their Father (v. 16). "Your tenderness and compassion are not restrained, for they are the tenderness and compassion of a father." However things may be, we know God is good, for he is our Father. When the father is dead, his sons come to honour and he knows it not (Job 14:21). Our natural fathers may call themselves *ever loving*, but they are not *ever living*; it is only God who is the immortal Father, who always knows us and is never far away from us. "*Thou, O Lord! art our Father still*—and so *our Redeemer from everlasting is thy name* (v. 16), the name by which we will know and acknowledge you. We are so degenerate and corrupt that Abraham and Israel would not acknowledge us as their children, but we flee to you as our Father. Abraham drove out his son Ishmael (Ge 21:14); Jacob disinherited his son Reuben (Ge 49:3–4) and cursed Simeon and Levi (Ge 49:5–7), but our heavenly Father, in pardoning sin, is *God, and not man*" (Hos 11:9).

3.3. They pleaded that he was their Lord: "We are your servants; whatever service we can do for you, you are entitled to, and so we should not serve foreign kings and foreign gods: *Return for thy servants' sake*" (v. 16). We are the *tribes of thy inheritance* (v. 17), not only your servants but also your tenants. Will you allow your own servants and tenants to be humiliated in this way?

3.4. They pleaded that they had only briefly enjoyed the Land of Promise and the privileges of the sanctuary (v. 18): *The people of thy holiness have possessed it but a little while*. From Abraham to David was only fourteen generations, and from David to the exile only fourteen more (Mt 1:17), and that was only a short time in comparison with what might have been expected from the promise of the *land of Canaan for an everlasting possession* (Ge 17:8).

3.5. They pleaded that those who had their land were those who were foreigners to God: "*Thou never didst bear rule over them* (v. 19), nor did they ever obey you at all. Will God allow those who do not stand in any relationship with him to trample on those who do?"

CHAPTER 64

This chapter continues that passionate, pleading prayer: 1. They pray that God would support them in some remarkable way against his and their enemies (vv. 1–2). 2. They plead what God has done and always been ready to do for his people in the past (vv. 3–5). 3. They confess that they deserve the judgments that are now suffering (vv. 6–7). 4. They appeal to the mercy of God as a Father and submit to his sovereignty (v. 8). 5. They fervently pray for their sin to be pardoned and for God's anger to be turned away (vv. 9–12).

Verses 1–5

Here:

1. The request is that God would appear wonderfully for them now (vv. 1–2). When God rescues his people in some extraordinary way, he is said to *shine forth* (Ps 80:1), to show himself strong; and so here they pray that he would *rend* (open up) *the heavens and come down* (v. 1). This may be applied to the second coming of Christ, when *the Lord himself shall descend from heaven with a shout* (1Th 4:16). They want "*the mountains to flow down* (tremble) *at thy presence* (v. 1), that the fire of your wrath may even dissolve the rockiest mountains and melt them as metal is melted in a furnace and thereby made liquid"; this is how *the melting fire burns* (v. 2). Let there be a great upheaval, to bring about a glorious revolution in favor of the church: *As the fire causes the waters to boil* (v. 2). They want this to lead to the glory and honor of God, to *make his name known* (v. 2) not only to his friends but also to his adversaries, so that they may know it and *tremble at his presence* (v. 2). If his presence is not

a stronghold for us into which we may run and find safety (Pr 18:10), it will prove a stronghold against us, beyond the reach of which we cannot run and be safe.

2. The plea is that God has appeared wonderfully for his people in the past.

2.1. They plead what he did for his people Israel when he brought them out of Egypt (v. 3). He then *did terrible things* in the plagues of Egypt, *which they looked not for* (did not expect). Then he came down on Mount Sinai in such terror as made that mountain and those adjacent to it *flow down at his presence* and *skip like rams* (Ps 114:4). Some think this refers to the defeat of Sennacherib's powerful army, which was as surprising an example of divine power as the melting of rocks and mountains would be.

2.2. They plead the provision he has made for the security and happiness of his people.

2.2.1. This provision is rich (v. 4). We cannot conceive, we have neither heard nor seen, what God has *prepared for those that wait for him*. It is all the goodness that God has *laid up for those that fear him, and wrought for those that trust in him* (Ps 31:19). Much of it was hidden in former ages; the people of those ages did not know it because the *unsearchable riches of Christ* (Eph 3:8) were *hidden in God*, were *hidden from the wise and prudent* (Mt 11:25). These were revealed, however, in later times by the Gospel; this is how the apostle Paul applies this (1Co 2:9), for it follows, *But God has revealed them unto us by his Spirit* (1Co 2:10). What people had not heard *since the beginning of the world* (v. 4) they would hear before it came to an end. This provision cannot be fully comprehended by human understanding; it is spiritual and will far surpass our expectations. Even the present peace of believers, and much more their future happiness, surpasses all expression (Php 4:7). We must conclude from God's works of his wonderful grace, as well as from the works of his wonderful power, from the kind things he does as well as from the great things he does, that there is *no god like him* (1Ki 8:23).

2.2.2. It is ready (v. 5): "*Thou meetest him that rejoices and works righteousness*; you meet him with the good that you have prepared for him (v. 4), and you do not forget *those that remember thee in thy ways*" (v. 5). What fellowship there is between a gracious God and a gracious soul. In order to have this fellowship with him, we must do our duty cheerfully; we must *rejoice and work righteousness* (v. 5); we must delight in God and sing while we work. And then we may expect that he will *meet us*. This suggests the friendship, fellowship, and familiarity that God allows to his people. He will *anticipate them with the blessings of his goodness* (Ps 21:3), *will rejoice to do good* (Jer 32:41) to those that *rejoice in working righteousness*, and he will wait to be gracious to those who *wait for him* (30:18; NIV: longs to be gracious). He meets his penitent people with forgiveness, as the father of the prodigal met his returning son (Lk 15:20). He meets his praying people with favorable answers while they are still speaking (65:24).

2.3. They plead the unchangeableness of God's favor and the stability of his promise: "*Behold, thou hast* many times *been wroth* (angry) *with us because we have sinned* (v. 5), and we have been suffering under the signs of your wrath. *But in those* ways of yours, the ways of mercy in which we have *remembered thee, in those is continuance*" (v. 5), or "in those thou art ever"—his mercy endures forever. We hope to be saved by the continuation of the covenant, for it is an eternal covenant for our salvation.

Verses 6–12

Here are the Lamentations of Isaiah. Like those of Jeremiah, they concern the destruction of Jerusalem by the Babylonians and the sin of Israel that brought on that destruction:

1. The people of God confess and mourn their sins in their suffering. Now that they are being rebuked by God because of their sin, they have nothing to trust in except the sheer mercy of God.

1.1. There is a general corruption in the way they live (v. 6): *We are all as an unclean thing*, or as an unclean *person*, as one covered by an infectious skin disease, who is to be excluded from the camp. *Even all our righteousnesses are as filthy rags* (v. 6). "The best people are like this; we are all corrupt and defiled. The best of our actions are like this. There is not only a general defilement in the way we live, but also a general defect in our devotion."

1.2. There is a general coldness of devotion among them (v. 7). Prayer is particularly neglected: *"There is none that calls on thy name* (v. 7), no one who looks to you for grace to reform us or looks for mercy to help us and take away the judgments that our sins have brought on us." If here and there one person calls on God's name, it is with a great deal of indifference; they have a "take-it-or-leave-it" attitude: *There is none that stirs up himself to take hold of God.* To pray is to *take hold of God* (v. 7), by faith to take hold of the promises God has made of his goodwill to us. It is to take hold of God as we take hold of someone we are wrestling with. But when we take hold of God, we are like a boatman using a hook to take hold of the quay, as if he were pulling the shore to him; in reality it pulls him to the shore. Similarly, we pray not in order to bring God to us, but to bring ourselves to him. Those who want to take hold of God in prayer must stir themselves to do it. We must use all that is within us to fulfill this duty (Ps 103:1)—and all that would be little enough. Our thoughts are to be fixed and our devotion glowing.

2. They acknowledge their suffering to be the fruit and product of their own sins and God's anger. *"We are all as an unclean thing, and so we do all fade away as a leaf* (v. 6). We not only wither and lose our beauty but also fall and drop off"—this is the sense—"like leaves in autumn. Our profession of religion withers away, and we become dry and sapless. Then *our iniquities like the wind have taken us away* (v. 6) and rushed us into captivity, as the winds in autumn blow away the faded and withered leaves" (Ps 1:3–4).

3. They claim to have a relationship with God as their God, and they humbly plead it with him (v. 8): *"But now, O Lord! thou art our Father.* Although we are foolish and careless, poor, despised by our enemies, you are still our Father. We therefore turn back to you in repentance." God is their Father: he gave them existence, formed them into a people, and shaped them as he pleased: "We are the clay and you are our potter, and so we will hope that you who made us will make us new, form us into new people, even though we have unmade and deformed ourselves. *We are all as an unclean thing* (v. 6), but we are all the work of your hands, and so *forsake us not*" (Ps 138:8). *We are thy people* (v. 9), and should not a people seek their God (8:19)? We are yours; save us (Ps 119:94).

4. They are bold with God in asking him to turn away his anger and pardon their sins (v. 9). They pray that God would be reconciled to them, and then they will not mind whether the suffering continues or is taken away: "Do not be angry beyond measure, but let your anger be lessened by the mercy and compassion of a father."

5. They bring their sad case to the court of heaven.

5.1. Their own houses are in ruins (v. 10). The cities and towns of Judah are destroyed by the Babylonians, and their inhabitants have been taken away: *Thy holy cities are a wilderness.* The cities of Judah are called *holy cities*, for the people were a kingdom of priests to God (Ex 19:6), and so here they mourn the fact that those cities are in ruins. Even *"Zion is a wilderness* (v. 10); the City of David itself lies in ruins; *Jerusalem*, which was *beautiful*, has become the scorn and scandal of the whole earth. That noble city has become a heap of rubbish."

5.2. God's house is in ruins (v. 11). They mourn this most of all, that *the temple was burnt with fire.* It was *their holy and beautiful house* (v. 11); in their sight, its holiness was its greatest beauty, and so its desecration was the saddest part of its desolation. It was the place *where their fathers praised God* (v. 11) with their sacrifices and songs; how sad that it should lie in ashes when for so many years it had been the glory of their nation! *All their pleasant things are laid waste* (v. 11), all those things they used in serving God, not only the furnishings of the temple, the altars and table, but the Sabbaths, and all religious feasts, which they used to joyfully keep.

6. They conclude by humbly arguing with God about their present desolation (v. 12): *"Wilt thou refrain thyself for these things?* Will you hold yourself back?" When we are mistreated, we are quiet about it, because vengeance is not ours (Dt 32:35; Ro 12:19). When God's honor is wronged, it may justly be expected that he will speak to vindicate it. His people do not give orders as to what he will say, but their prayer is as here: *"Keep not thou silence, O God!* (Ps 83:1). Speak up to convict your enemies, speak to comfort and help your people, for *wilt thou afflict us for ever?"* (v. 12). God has said that he *will not contend for ever* (57:16), and so his people may depend on him that their sufferings will neither be greater than they can bear nor last to eternity, but be *light* and *for a moment* (2Co 4:17).

CHAPTER 65

We are coming to the end of this evangelical prophecy, the last two chapters of which tell us to look as far forward as the new heavens and the new earth, the new world that the Gospel era would usher in. And why should it seem absurd that the prophet here should speak about what all the prophets testified about (1Pe 1:10–11)? The rejection of the Jews and the calling of the Gentiles are often mentioned in the New Testament as what was foreseen and foretold by the prophets (Ac 10:43; 13:40; Ro 16:26). In this chapter we have: 1. The looking forward to the certain Gospel call of the Gentiles (v. 1). 2. The rejection of the Jews for their stubbornness and unbelief (vv. 2–7). 3. The saving of a remnant by bringing them into the Gospel church (vv. 8–10). 4. The judgments of God that would pursue the rejected Jews (vv. 11–16). 5. The blessings reserved for the Christian church (vv. 17–25). But these things are prophesied about here under the type of the difference God would make between some Jews and others after their exile, between those who feared God and those who did not.

Verses 1–7

The apostle Paul has told us which event is pointed to here, namely, the calling of the Gentiles and the rejection of the Jews by the preaching of the Gospel (Ro 10:20–21). And he observes that here *Esaias* (Isaiah) *is very bold* (Ro 10:20) in foretelling it to the Jews, who would take it as a great insult to their nation.

1. It is foretold here that the Gentiles, who had been far away, would be drawn near (Eph 2:13) (v. 1). Paul

reads it in this way: *I was found of those that sought me not; I was made manifest to those that asked not for me* (Ro 10:20).

1.1. Those who had long been without God in the world (Eph 2:12) will now be set to seek him; those who had not said, *Where is God my maker?* will now begin to ask after him. With what delight the great God speaks here of his being sought. There is great joy in heaven over sinners who repent (Lk 15:7).

1.2. God will anticipate their prayers with his blessings: *I am found of those that sought me not* (v. 1). This delightful communication between God and the Gentile world began on his side. Though after conversion God is found by those who seek him (Pr 8:17), in conversion he is found by those who are not seeking him: *therefore we love him because he first loved us* (1Jn 4:19).

1.3. God gave the advantages of divine revelation to those who had never professed any religious faith: *I said, Behold me, behold me* (here am I), to those who *were not called by my name* (v. 1), as the Jews for many ages had been. Christ said, *Behold me, behold me* with the eye of faith; *look unto me, and be you saved* (45:22).

2. It is foretold here that the Jews, who had long been a people close to God, would be rejected and set far away (v. 2). The apostle Paul applies this to the Jews of his time: *But to Israel he saith, All day long I have stretched forth my hands unto a disobedient and gainsaying* (obstinate) *people* (Ro 10:21). Notice:

2.1. How the Jews were courted by divine grace. God himself, by his prophets, his Son, and his apostles, stretched out his hands to them. God spread out his hands to them, as one reasoning and pleading with them. When Christ was crucified, his hands were spread out and stretched out, as if he were preparing to receive returning sinners. He waited to be gracious (30:18); he did not become tired of waiting. Even those who came at the eleventh hour of the day were not rejected.

2.2. They refused the invitation; they were invited to the wedding feast but would not come (Mt 22:2–5). They rejected God's purposes for their own lives. Here we have:

2.2.1. The bad character of this people. The world will see that it was not for nothing that they were rejected by God.

2.2.1.1. Their character in general was such as one would not expect of the favorites of heaven. They were very willful. They did right or wrong just as they pleased. God had told them his thoughts, what his mind and will were, but they wanted to follow their own thoughts and do what they thought best. This was God's complaint about them all along—they grieved him and his Holy Spirit, as if they wanted to see how they could make him their enemy.

2.2.1.2. The prophet speaks more particularly of their sins and the sins of their ancestors as the basis of God's rejecting them (v. 7).

2.2.1.2.1. The most offensive sin of their ancestors was idolatry. This was the sin that took them into exile, and although the exile pretty well cured them of it, still, when the final ruin of that nation came, that was again brought into account against them. Perhaps there were many, long after the exile, who, although they did not worship other gods, were still guilty of the violations mentioned in these verses, for they married foreign wives (Ezr 9:1–2; Ne 13:23–24). They abandoned God's temple and sacrificed in gardens or groves, doing it their own way, for they did not like God's institutions. They abandoned God's altar and burned incense on bricks, on altars they themselves

had made rather than on the golden altar God appointed them. They consulted the dead, and in order to do that they *remained among the graves, and lodged in the monuments* (spent their nights keeping secret vigil). They disobeyed the laws of God about their food and disregarded the distinction between clean and unclean before it was taken away by the Gospel. They ate the flesh of pigs. *And the broth*, or pieces, of other forbidden meats, called here *abominable things*, was in their vessels and was used as food. The forbidden meat is called detestable, and those who share in it are said to make themselves detestable (Lev 11:42–43). Perhaps this here stands figuratively for all forbidden pleasures. But those who were so proud as to venture on the borders of sin were in danger of falling into its depths.

2.2.1.2.2. The most offensive sin of the Jews in our Savior's time was their pride and hypocrisy, that sin of the scribes and Pharisees against which Christ declared so many woes (Mt 23) (v. 5). They said, *"Stand by thyself*, keep to your own companions; do not come near me, or you may defile me; *touch me not, for I am holier than thou."* *"These are a smoke in my nose,"* said God, *"the kind of smoke that does not come from a quick fire, which soon glows and becomes pleasant, but from a fire of wet wood, which *burns all the day* (v. 5) and is nothing but smoke."

2.2.2. The dispute God had with them about this. The proof against them is clear: *Behold, it is written before me* (v. 6). The *iniquity of their fathers* (v. 7) will come against them. However, their own sin deserved whatever judgments God brought on them, and much worse, and they acknowledged this (Ezr 9:13). *Your iniquities and the iniquities of your fathers* (v. 7) together, the one making the other worse, will be *measured into their bosom.*

Verses 8–10

This is explained by the apostle Paul in Ro 11:1–5. Having considered the rejection of the Jews, he asks, *Hath God then cast away his people?* and he answers, no, for *at this time there is a remnant according to the election of grace.* This prophecy refers to that special remnant. Some of the Jews will be brought to embrace the Christian faith; they will be added to the church and so be saved (Ac 2:47). Our Savior told us that *for the sake of these elect* the days of the destruction of the Jews would be shortened, and an end would be put to the desolation.

1. This is illustrated here by a comparison (v. 8). When a vine is so withered that there seems to be no sap or life in it, and the dresser of the vineyard wants to cut it down, yet, if even a little juice of the grape can be found, even if only in one cluster, someone steps in and says, *Destroy it not, for a blessing is in it;* there is life in the root. Sometimes God spares whole cities and nations for the sake of a few (Ge 18:23–33).

2. Those who will make up this saved remnant are those who:

2.1. Serve God. It is *for my servants' sake* (v. 8), and it is *my servants* who *shall dwell there* (v. 9). God's faithful servants *serve their generation* (Ac 13:36).

2.2. Seek God, who make it the aim of their lives to call on him.

3. Here is an account of the mercy God has in store for them. The remnant will resettle happily in their own land as *a seed out of Jacob* (v. 9). These are types of the remnant of Jacob that will be incorporated into the Gospel church by faith. They will inherit *my mountains*, the holy mountains on which Jerusalem and the temple were built. They will have a green pasture for their flocks (v. 10).

Sharon, to the west, *and the valley of Achor*, to the east, will again be filled with cattle. They will regain possession of the whole land. Gospel ordinances are the fields and valleys where the sheep of Christ *shall go in and out and find pasture* (Jn 10:9) and where they are *made to lie down* (Ps 23:2), like Israel's herds, in *the valley of Achor* (Hos 2:15).

Verses 11–16

Here are the different states of the godly and evildoers, of the Jews who believed and those who persisted in unbelief.

1. The terrible condemnation of those who persisted in idolatry after they were delivered from Babylon and of those who persisted in their unfaithfulness after the preaching of the Gospel of Christ. Notice:

1.1. The condemnation that is threatened here: "*I will number* (destine) *you to the sword* as sheep for the slaughter, and there will be no escaping; *you shall all bow down to it*" (v. 12).

1.2. The sins that make them fall to the sword.

1.2.1. Idolatry was their old, habitual sin (v. 11): "*You are those* who, instead of serving me as my people, *forsake the Lord* and reject him to go after other gods. You *forget my holy mountain* to burn incense on the mountains of your idols (v. 7). You have forsaken the only living and true God." They *prepared a table for that troop of* deities that the nations worshiped and *poured out drink offerings to that* (v. 11), an endless number of them, for those who thought one God too few never thought scores and hundreds were enough.

1.2.2. Unfaithfulness was the sin of the Jews in later times (v. 12): *When I called, you did not answer*, which refers to the same situation as v. 2, and that is applied to those who rejected the Gospel (Ro 10:21). Our Lord Jesus Christ himself called—he *stood and cried* (Jn 7:37)—but they refused to answer. It is not strange that those who will not be persuaded to choose what is good persist in choosing what is evil.

2. The emphasizing of this condemnation. It appears even worse when one considers the happy state of those who were brought to repentance and faith. The blessedness of those who serve God and the terrible condition of those who rebel against him are here contrasted with one another so that their sharp differences may be seen (vv. 13–16). It will add to the grief of those who perish to see the happiness of God's servants, and especially to think that they might have shared in their happiness if it had not been their own fault. The difference of their states lies in two things.

2.1. In their comfort and joy. God's servants will lack nothing that is good for them (Ps 34:10), but those who set their hearts on the world will be hungry and thirsty. They will always be empty, always craving, for it is not bread (55:2). They have too much of the things of this world, but those things do not give them a lasting satisfaction. God's servants *shall rejoice* (v. 13) and *sing for joy* in their hearts (v. 14). Heaven will be a world of eternal joy to all who now sow in tears (Ps 126:5). Those who abandon the Lord, on the other hand, are excluding themselves from all true joy, for *they shall be ashamed of* (v. 13) their empty confidence in their own righteousness and in the hopes they had built on that.

2.2. In their honor and reputation (vv. 15–16). *The memory of the just is*, and will be, *blessed, but the name of the wicked shall rot* (Pr 10:7). The name of the idolaters will be *for a curse to God's chosen* (v. 15), that is, as a warning to them. The name of God's chosen ones will become a blessing: *He shall call his servants by another name* (v. 15). The children of the covenant will be called *Christians*; and to them, under that name, will all the promises and privileges of the new covenant be guaranteed. This other name will not be confined to one nation; instead, with it people will *bless themselves in the earth* (v. 16), throughout the world. God wants servants out of all nations. They will bless themselves *in the God of truth* (v. 16). They will honor God both in their prayers and in their solemn oaths. This is a part of the homage we owe to God; we must bless ourselves in him, that is, recognize that we have enough to make us happy and can want nothing more if we have him as our God. Worldly people bless themselves in the great quantity they have of this world's goods (Ps 49:18; Lk 12:19), but God's servants bless themselves in him, as a God who is all-sufficient for them. They will honor him as the *God of truth*; "the God of the Amen" is the meaning; some understand this to refer to Christ, in whom all the promises are *yea and amen* (2Co 1:20). They will honor him as the author of this blessed change, as the one who has made them forget their former troubles because their memory has been swallowed up in their present comforts.

Verses 17–25

If these promises were partially fulfilled when the Jews, after their return from exile, were settled peacefully in their own land and brought as it were into a new world, they still were to have their complete fulfillment in the Gospel church. We are to look for this new heaven and new earth in the graces and comforts that believers have in and from Christ. It is in the Gospel that *old things have passed away and all things have become new*, and it is by the Gospel that those who are in Christ are *new creatures* (2Co 5:17). It was a happy and powerful change that was described in v. 16, that *the former troubles were forgotten*, but here it rises far higher: even the *former world* will be *forgotten* and *shall no more come into mind* (v. 17). When God is reconciled to us, which gives us a new heaven, the creatures are also reconciled to us, which gives us a new earth.

1. There will be new joys. All the church's friends and all who belong to her will rejoice (v. 18): You will *be glad and rejoice for ever in that which I create. I create Jerusalem a rejoicing and her people a joy*. The church will not only rejoice but also be rejoiced in. The prosperity of the church will be a matter of rejoicing in God himself, who delights in the prosperity of his servants (v. 19): *I will rejoice in Jerusalem's* joy and will *joy in my people*, for *in all their affliction he was afflicted* (63:9). There will be no dispelling of this joy: *The voice of weeping shall be no more heard in her* (v. 19). The former occasions for sadness will not return. But in heaven this joy will have its complete fulfillment; there *all tears shall be wiped away* (Rev 7:17).

2. There will be new life (v. 20). Untimely deaths by the sword or sickness will no more be known as they have been. Through Christ, believers will be satisfied with life even if they live for only a short time on earth. Even the child will be reckoned to die a hundred years old, for they will rise again at full age: they will rise to eternal life. And as for old people, it is promised that they will fill their days with the fruits of righteousness (Php 1:11), which they will continue to display in old age (Ps 92:14). An old person who is wise, good, and useful may truly be said to have filled their days. Old people who have their hearts set on the things of this world have never filled their days. Unbelievers will be unsatisfied and unhappy in life even if

they live very long lives. Although sinners may live to be a hundred years old, they will still be cursed, and their long life is simply a reprieve. The important thing, therefore, is not whether our lives on earth are long or short, but whether we live the lives of saints or the lives of sinners.

3. There will be a new enjoyment of the comforts of life. Whereas before these were very uncertain and precarious, now it will be otherwise. They will build houses and live in them; they will plant vineyards and eat the fruit of them (vv. 21–22). Strangers or foreigners will not break in on them to drive them out, as sometimes they have: *My elect will wear out*, or *long enjoy, the work of their hands* (v. 22). It is honestly gained, and it will wear well; it is *the work of their hands*, which they themselves have labored for, and not the bread of idleness (Pr 31:27) or the bread of deceit (Pr 20:17). If we live to enjoy the work of our hands for a long time, it is the gift of God's providence, for that is promised here: *As the days of a tree are the days of my people*; as *the days of an oak* (6:13), whose substance is in it even though it drops its leaves (6:13). Even though it is stripped every winter, it lasts many years, like the days "of the tree of life," as the Septuagint (the Greek version of the Old Testament) reads.

4. There will be a new generation rising up in their place to inherit and enjoy these blessings (v. 23): *They shall not labor in vain*, for they will not be the only ones to enjoy the work of their hands; they will leave it with confidence to those who will come after them. God will make their children who rise up a comfort to them; they will have the joy of seeing them walk in the truth (2Jn 4; 3Jn 4). He will make later times an encouragement to their children.

5. There will be a good relationship between them and their God (v. 24): *Even before they call, I will answer*. Even before their prayers are spoken, God will answer them with the blessings of his goodness. The father of the prodigal son met him on his return (Lk 15:20). God's readiness to listen to prayer appears much more in the grace of the Gospel than it ever did under the Law.

6. There will be good relationships between them and their neighbors (v. 25): *The wolf and the lamb will feed together*. Even though God's people are as sheep in the midst of wolves (Mt 10:16), they will be unharmed, for God will not so much break the power of their enemies as he did in the past, but rather turn their hearts; he will change their characters by his grace. When Paul, who had been a persecutor of the disciples—and who, coming from the tribe of Benjamin, was a ravenous wolf (Ge 49:27)—joined them and became one of them, then *the wolf and the lamb fed together* (v. 25). People will be changed: *The lion* will no more be a beast of prey but *shall eat straw like the bullock* (v. 25), will *know his owner* and *his master's crib* (1:3) as *the ox* does. When those who lived off the plunder they gained by ravaging and who wanted to make themselves rich without regard to right or wrong are brought by the grace of God to live by honest labor—when those who once stole no longer steal, but work with their hands and do what is good (Eph 4:28)—then this is fulfilled, that *the lion shall eat straw like the bullock* (v. 25). Satan will be chained, the dragon bound, *for dust shall be the serpent's meat again* (v. 25). That great enemy has had his fill and entertained himself with the precious blood of saints, who by his instigation have been persecuted, and with the precious souls of sinners, who by his instigation have ruined themselves eternally. But now he will be confined to dust, according to the sentence, *On thy belly shalt thou go, and dust shalt thou eat* (Ge 3:14). Christ will reign as Zion's king until

all the enemies of his kingdom are made his footstool (Ps 110:1).

CHAPTER 66

The first verse of this chapter is applied by Stephen to the dismantling of the temple by the planting of the Christian church (Ac 7:49–50), which may serve as a key to the whole chapter. We have here: 1. The contempt God has for ceremonial services compared with moral duties (vv. 1–4). 2. The salvation God will in due time bring about for his people, taking them out of the hands of their oppressors (v. 5). He speaks words of terror to the persecutors (v. 6) and of comfort to the persecuted, and he speaks a complete and quick restoration (vv. 7–9), a joyful settlement (vv. 10–11), and the accession of the Gentiles to them (vv. 12–14). 3. The terrible vengeance that God will bring on the enemies of his church and people (vv. 15–18). 4. The happy establishment of the church on a large and certain foundation (vv. 19–24). We may well expect this evangelical prophet, at the close of his prophecy, to look as far forward as to the last days, to the final day, to the days of eternity.

Verses 1–4

Here:

1. The temple is slighted in comparison with a gracious soul (vv. 1–2). The prophets and Christ foretold the ruin of the temple, that God would leave it and that it would then soon become desolate. After it was destroyed by the Babylonians, it soon recovered and the ceremonial services were revived, but the Romans destroyed it forever, and the ceremonial law was abolished with it. God did not need the temple, for heaven is the throne of his glory and rule. The earth is his footstool, on which he stands, sovereign over all its affairs according to his will. If God has such a bright throne, such a large footstool, *where then is the house they can build* to God as the home of his glory, or *where is the place of his rest* (v. 1)? What satisfaction can the eternal Mind take in a house made by human hands? If he needed a house to live in, he would have made one for himself when he made the world. So he had no need of a temple made by human hands. Nor would he take as much notice of the temple as he does of a humble, penitent, gracious heart. He has a heaven and earth that he has made and a temple that humans have made, but he overlooks them all so that he may look with favor on the person who is poor in spirit (Mt 5:3), humble and sincere, self-abasing and self-denying, whose heart is truly contrite for sin, penitent for it, and in anguish for it to be pardoned. Such a heart is a living temple for God; he lives there, and it is the place of his rest. It is like heaven and earth, his throne and his footstool.

2. Sacrifices are slighted when they come from ungracious hands. *The sacrifice of the wicked* is not only unacceptable but also *an abomination to the Lord* (Pr 15:8); this is shown in detail here (vv. 3–4). Notice:

2.1. How detestable their sacrifices were to God. When the worldly Jews returned from exile, they became very lax in serving God; they brought the *torn, and the lame, and the sick* for *sacrifice* (Mal 1:8, 13). This made their services detestable to God. *He that kills an ox* for his own table is welcome to do it, but when a person kills it for God's altar now, it is *as if he slew a man* (v. 3). Those who do that are in effect setting aside Christ's sacrifice. *He that sacrifices a lamb*, if it is imperfect and not the best he has, is insulting God instead of pleasing him; it is *as if he cut off* (were breaking) *a dog's neck* (v. 3), and the dog was a creature that in the eyes of the law was so worthless that, whereas a donkey could be redeemed, the price of a dog was never to be brought into the treasury (Dt 23:18). *He that offers an oblation* (sacrifice) (v. 3), a grain offering or drink offering, is like one who expects to make atonement with *swine's blood* (v. 3), and the swine was a creature that must not be eaten nor touched, the *broth of which* was detestable (65:4), and much more so its blood. *He that burns incense to God* (v. 3), thereby showing contempt for the incense of Christ's intercession, is like one who *blesses an idol* (v. 3).

2.2. What their evil was that made their sacrifices so detestable. *They had chosen their own ways*, the ways of their own evil hearts, and *their souls delighted in their abominations* (v. 3). They were corrupt and immoral, choosing the way of sin rather than the way of God's commands. This made their sacrifices offensive to God (1:11–15). They turned a deaf ear to all the warnings of divine justice and all the offers of divine grace. They *chose their own ways*, and so, God says, *I also will choose their delusions* (harsh treatment for them) (v. 4). "They have made their choice, and now I will make mine; they have taken whatever course they pleased with me, and I will take whatever course I please with them." They will be deceived by that empty self-confidence with which they have deceived themselves. God will make their sin their punishment; they will be rushed headlong toward destruction by their own foolish choices.

Verses 5–14

Having declared God's judgments against a hypocritical nation, who laughed at God's word, the prophet turns here to speak to those who *tremble at his word* (v. 5), to comfort and encourage them; they will not be involved in the judgments that are coming on their unfaithful nation. The word of God has comforts in store for those who are truly humble for sin, who are prepared to receive those comforts. There were those (v. 4) who, when *God spoke, would not hear*, but if the heart *trembles at the word* (v. 5), the ears will be open to it.

1. God will plead their just but wronged cause against their persecutors (v. 5): *Your brethren that hated you said, Let the Lord be glorified. But he shall appear to your joy.* This should be thought to refer to the apostles. They were Jews by birth, but even in the cities of the Gentiles the Jews they met were their most bitter and implacable enemies and *stirred up the Gentiles* against them (Ac 14:2). Their own people, who should have loved them and encouraged them for their work's sake, hated them and rejected them from their synagogues. And when they did it, they said, *Let the Lord be glorified* (v. 5); they pretended to be conscientious and zealous for the honor of God and the church in doing this, and they did it with all the formalities of devotion. Our Savior explains this, and in so doing he seems to refer to this passage (Jn 16:2). *They shall put you out of their synagogues*, and *whosoever kills you will think that he does God service.* Yet they were encouraged under these persecutions: "Let your faith and patience last a little while longer. Your enemies hate and oppress you, your brothers and sisters hate and reject you, but your Father in heaven still loves you, and he will support you when no one else will or dares to." This was fulfilled when, on the signals given of Jerusalem's approaching ruin, the *Jews' hearts failed them for fear*, but the disciples of Christ, whom they had hated and persecuted, *lifted up their heads with joy, knowing that their redemption drew nigh* (Lk 21:26, 28).

2. God's support for them will make a great noise in the world (v. 6): there will be *a voice of noise from the city, from the temple*. Some think this refers to the joyful and triumphant voice of the church's friends; others think it refers to the mourning voice of her enemies, fleeing in vain to the temple for shelter. These voices are simply an echo of the *voice of the Lord*, who is now rendering *a recompence to his enemies* (v. 6). A confused noise was in the city and temple when Jerusalem, after a long siege, was finally captured by the Romans. Some think this prophecy was fulfilled in the extravagances that existed before that destruction of Jerusalem, related by Josephus in his *History of the Wars of the Jews* (book 7, chapter 31), where he writes that the temple doors flew open suddenly by themselves, and the priests heard a noise of movement in the Most Holy Place, and immediately a voice, saying, "Let us depart hence." And some time after, one Jesus Bar-Annas went up and down the city at the Feast of Tabernacles, continually crying out, "A voice from the east, a voice from the west, a voice from the four winds, a voice against Jerusalem and the temple, a voice against all this people."

3. God will establish a church for himself in the world (v. 7): *Before she travailed, she brought forth.*

3.1. This is to be applied as a type to the restoration of the Jews from exile in Babylon, which was brought about very easily and silently, without any pain or struggle. The child of the deliverance is rejoiced in, but the mother never went into labor for it (compare Jn 16:21); *before her pain came, she was delivered* (v. 7). This is altogether without precedent, unless we recall the story that the Egyptian midwives told about the Hebrew women (Ex 1:19), that *they were lively and were delivered ere* (before) *the midwives came in unto them*. But *shall the earth be made to bring forth her fruits in one day* (v. 8)? No; it is the work of some weeks in the spring to *renew the face of the earth* (Ps 104:30). *Shall a land be brought forth in one day* (v. 8), or *shall a nation be born at once* (v. 8)? As a Latin saying puts it, "God does nothing abruptly." Yet in this case, *as soon as Zion travailed, she brought forth* (v. 8). Cyrus's declaration was no sooner issued than the captives were ready to make their way as best they could back to their own land (Ezr 1:4–5). And the reason is given in v. 9, that *it is the Lord's doing* (Ps 118:23). If he brings to the moment of birth the preparing of his people to be restored, he will *cause to bring forth* the fulfillment of the restoration. When everything is ready, will he not then give strength to give birth? Will God, who causes the human race and every species of living creatures to multiply and *replenish the earth* (Ge 1:28), nevertheless *restrain Zion*? Will he not make her fruitful by giving a blessed offspring to populate the church?

3.2. But this was a type of the setting up of the Christian church in the world and the populating of that family with children to be named from Jesus Christ (Eph 3:14–15). When the Spirit was poured out, very many people were converted in a short time and with little effort. The success of the Gospel was amazing. The same day as the Spirit was poured out, 3,000 souls were added to the church (Ac 2:41), *so mightily grew the word of God and prevailed* (Ac 19:20).

4. Their present sorrows will soon be turned to great joy (vv. 10–11). The church's friends are those who *love her and mourn* with her and *for her* (v. 10). Those who have a sincere devotion to the church have a warm sympathy for her. Such people are encouraged: *Rejoice with her* (v. 10), and again *I say, Rejoice* (Php 4:4). Jerusalem will have reason to rejoice; the days of her mourning will come to an end (60:20). "You who mourned for her in her sorrows must surely have the same motivation to rejoice

with her in her joys." We must *suck and be satisfied with the breasts of her consolations* (v. 11). The word of God, the covenant of grace—especially the promises of that covenant—the worship of God, and all the opportunities of waiting on him and talking with him are *the breasts of her consolations*, which the church calls and counts as her comforting breasts. We must take pleasure in our relationship with God and fellowship with him. Whatever is the glory of the church must be *our glory and joy*, particularly her purity, unity, and increase.

5. He who gives them this call to rejoice will also give them reason and hearts to do so (vv. 12–14). *I will extend peace to her*—that is, all good to her—*like a river* that runs in a constant stream. The Gospel brings with it, wherever it is received in power, such peace as this, which will continue *like a river*, supplying souls with all good and making them fruitful, as a river does the lands it passes through. *The glory of the Gentiles* will come to them *like a flowing stream* (v. 12). God will be glorified in everything, and that should be a greater reason for our joy than anything else (v. 14): *The hand of the Lord shall be known towards his servants*, and at the same time he will make known *his indignation towards his enemies* (v. 14). God's mercy and justice will both be revealed. God will not only give them reason to rejoice but also speak comfort to *their hearts*. Their country will be their tender nurse: you will be *carried on her sides*, in her arms, as small children are, and will be *dandled upon her knees* (v. 12). The great Shepherd *gathers the lambs in his arms and carries them in his bosom* (40:11), and so must the undershepherds do, so that children may not be discouraged. God will himself be their powerful comforter: *As one whom his mother comforts* when he is ill or sad, *so will I comfort you* (v. 13), not only with the arguments of the mind that a wise father uses but also with the tender devotion and compassion of a loving mother. They will feel the blessed effects of this assurance in their own souls (v. 14). This was fulfilled in the wonderful joy Christ's disciples had in the success of their ministry. Christ tells them (Jn 16:22), *Your heart shall rejoice, and your joy no man taketh from you. Then your bones*, which were dried and withered, will regain their youthful strength and vigor and *shall flourish like a herb* (v. 14).

Verses 15–24

These verses have a dark side toward the enemies of God's kingdom but a bright side toward his faithful and loyal subjects. They probably refer to the Jews in exile in Babylon, of whom some hated to be reformed and would therefore be ruined by the adversity (Jer 24:9). Others were sent them for their good and would in due time come through it. But no doubt the prophecy looks farther, to the judgment for which Christ came once (Jn 9:39) and will come again (2Ti 4:1).

1. Christ will appear to the confusion of all those who resist him. Sometimes he will appear in temporal judgment. The Jews who persisted in being unfaithful were destroyed *by fire* and *by his sword* (v. 16). The *Lord* then *pleaded with all flesh* (all people) (v. 16). Because those who resist God are killed by his sword, they are called *his slain*. Idolaters will especially be opposed on the day of wrath (v. 17). Perhaps some of those who returned from Babylon had their *idols in their gardens* and there *purified themselves* when they went about their idolatrous ritual, *one after another*, or, as our translation reads it, *behind one tree in the midst*, behind *ahad* or *ehad*, "one"; there was some idol in whose honor they ate the flesh of pigs *and other abominations*, such as *the mouse*, rats, or some

other similar animal. But the prophecy may also refer to all those judgments that God will bring on sinners in general, who are devoted to the world and the flesh: they shall meet their end and *be consumed together* (v. 17). God knows both what people do and with what intentions they do it.

2. He will appear to give comfort and joy to all who are faithful to him in setting up the kingdom of grace, the firstfruits of the kingdom of glory. The time will come that he will *gather all nations and tongues to himself* so that they may *come and see* God's *glory* as it shines in the face of Jesus Christ (2Co 4:6) (v. 18). This was fulfilled when all nations were to be discipled and the gift of tongues was given to Christ's disciples to help them do this. Up to that time the church had been confined to one nation and God was worshiped in only one tongue. It is promised:

2.1. Some of the Jewish nation will, by the grace of God, be set apart from the rest and marked out for salvation: "I will not only *set up a gathering ensign*, or banner, among them (11:12), but also set on some of them a 'differencing sign'"—the literal meaning of the word here translated *sign* (v. 19). Although they are a corrupt and degenerate nation, God will still set apart a remnant of them who will be devoted to him, and a mark will be set on them, showing with what certainty God will own and acknowledge them (Eze 9:4). Christ's sheep are marked.

2.2. Those who are themselves set apart in this way will be commissioned to be *sent to the nations* (v. 19) to take the Gospel to them and preach it to every creature (Mk 16:15). They will be sent to *the nations*, several of which are named here, *Tarshish, Pul, Lud*, and others. It is uncertain which countries are meant. *Tarshish* may mean in general "the sea," but some consider it to be Tarsus in Cilicia. *Pul* is the name of one of the kings of Assyria; perhaps some part of that country also bore that name. *Lud* is thought to be Lydia, a warlike nation famous for its archers (Jer 46:9). *Tubal*, some think, is Italy or Spain, and *Javan* Greece, the Ionians. And the *isles afar off* probably refers to the *isles of the Gentiles*, populated by the descendants of Japheth (Ge 10:5). God was known only in Judah (Ps 76:1; Am 3:2), and other countries sat in darkness (Ps 107:10; Isa 42:7); they did not hear the joyful sound (Ps 89:15) or see the joyful light. It is a pity that any human being should ever be so far away from their Maker as not to hear his name and see his glory. Those who are sent to the nations will go on God's mission, to *declare his glory among the Gentiles* (v. 19). The Jews who will be dispersed among the nations will declare the glory of God's providence concerning their nation. Some out of the nations will *take hold of the skirt* (hem of the robe) *of him that is a Jew*, asking him to notice them, "for *we will go with you, having heard that God is with you*" (Zec 8:23).

2.3. Many converts will be made (v. 20). *They shall bring all your brethren*—for converts should be acknowledged and embraced as brothers and sisters—*as an offering unto the Lord*. Some will come *upon horses* because they came from far away. Some will come in *chariots*, and the elderly, the infirm, and small children will be brought *in litters* or covered wagons, and the younger people *on mules and swift beasts* (camels) (v. 20). They will spare no trouble or expense to get to Jerusalem. They will come not as they used to come, to be offerers, but to be themselves *an offering unto the Lord* (v. 20). This must be understood spiritually, as referring to their being presented to God as *living sacrifices* (Ro 12:1). They will be brought *as the children of Israel bring an offering in a clean vessel* (v. 20), taking great care that they are holy, purified from sin, and consecrated to God. It is said of the converted Gentiles (Ac 15:9) that *their hearts were purified by faith.* The writer to the Hebrews says about all true Christians that they *have come to Mount Zion, and the heavenly Jerusalem* (Heb 12:22), which explains this passage and shows that the meaning of all this procession is only that they will be brought into the church by the grace of God as carefully, safely, and comfortably as if they were carried in chariots and wagons.

2.4. A Gospel ministry will be set up in the church (v. 21): *I will take of them* — the Gentile converts — *for priests and for Levites,* to minister holy things. Up to that time the priests and Levites were all taken from among the Jews and were all of one tribe, but in Gospel times God will take some from the converted Gentiles to minister to him. They are to teach the people, to be the stewards of the mysteries of God (1Co 4:1) as the priests and Levites were under the Law, and to be pastors and teachers, or overseers (*bishops*), who *give themselves to the word and prayer*; and God will give them deacons to *serve tables* and, as the Levites did, to take care of the *outward business of the house of God* (Php 1:1; Ac 6:2–4; Ne 11:16). The apostles were all Jews, and so were the seventy disciples (Lk 10:1). The great apostle of the Gentiles was himself *a Hebrew of the Hebrews* (Php 3:5), but when churches were planted among the Gentiles, they had ministers who came from *themselves, elders in every church* (Ac 14:23; Tit 1:5). God says, *I will take of them,* some of them. It is God's work originally to choose ministers by qualifying them and disposing them to serve him, and it is his work also to make ministers by commissioning them.

2.5. The church and ministry is so well established that it will be maintained from one generation to another (v. 22). The kingdom of the Messiah will *be a new* world (65:17). *Old things have passed away;* see *all things have become new* (2Co 5:17). The old, exclusive covenant is set aside, and a new covenant, a covenant of grace, is established (Heb 8:13). New commandments are given concerning both heaven and earth, and new promises are made about both, and both together make a New Testament. The change that comes about will be an abiding change; the new world will always be new. The Gospel era is to continue to the end of time. It will be maintained in an offspring that will serve Christ: *Your seed,* and in them *your name, shall remain* (v. 22); as one generation passes away, another will come. Even though the gates

of hell fight against the church, they will not *prevail* (Mt 16:18), nor will they *wear out the saints of the Most High* (Da 7:25).

2.6. The public worship of God in religious assemblies will be attended to by all who are brought *as an offering to the Lord* (v. 23). This is described in expressions suited to the Old Testament era, to show that although the ceremonial law will be abolished and the temple service will come to an end, God will still be as regularly worshiped as ever. Up to that time only Jews went up to appear before God, and they had to attend only three times a year, and only males; but now all flesh, Gentiles as well as Jews, women as well as men, will *come and worship before God* (v. 23), in his presence, though it will be in assemblies throughout the world rather than in his temple at Jerusalem; and these assemblies will be to them as the Tent of Meeting was to the Jews. In them God will record his name, and even when only two or three meet together, he will be among them and bless them (Mt 18:20). There is no need for only one definite place, as the temple was in former years. Christ is our temple, in whom all believers meet by faith. But it is right that there should be a definite appointed time so that established services may be frequently observed, as a sign of the spiritual fellowship that all Christians have with one another in faith, hope, and holy love. Where the Lord's Day is consecrated weekly, the Lord's Supper celebrated monthly, and both duly attended, the Christian New Moon festivals and Sabbaths are observed there.

2.7. Their thankful sense of God's special favor toward them will be increased by considering the destruction of those who persist in their ungodliness (v. 24). Evildoers are people who have *transgressed* (rebelled) *against God* (v. 24); they have not only broken his laws but also broken the covenant with him. The phrase may refer especially to the unfaithful Jews who rejected the Gospel of Christ. Their misery is represented by the spectacle of a battlefield covered with the *carcases* of the slain. They are therefore *abhorring to all flesh* (loathsome to the whole human race) (v. 24); nobody wants to come near them. Now this is fulfilled in the destruction of Jerusalem and the Jewish nation by the Romans. It may refer also to the spiritual judgment that came on the unfaithful Jews, which the apostle Paul considers and shows us (Ro 11:8). It will brighten the joys and glories of the blessed ones to see that they were themselves like burning sticks plucked out of that fire (Am 4:11).

A PRACTICAL AND DEVOTIONAL EXPOSITION OF THE BOOK OF THE PROPHET

Jeremiah

Concerning this prophet Jeremiah we may notice:

1. That he began young, and so he could say from his own experience that it is good for people to bear the yoke while they are young, the yoke of both service and affliction (La 3:27): Jerome observes that Isaiah, who had more years behind him, had his tongue touched with a coal of fire to atone for his sin (Isa 6:7), but when God touched Jeremiah's mouth, nothing was said about atoning for his sin (1:9), because he was still young.

2. That he continued for a long time as a prophet: according to some, fifty years, and according to others, more than forty. He began in the thirteenth year of Josiah, that good king, but he continued through all the evil reigns that followed.

3. That he was a prophet who rebuked; he was sent in God's name to tell Jacob about their sins and to warn them of the judgments of God. Commentators observe that his style is plainer and rougher, and less polite, than that of Isaiah and some other prophets. Plain dealing is best when we are dealing with sinners to bring them to repentance.

4. That he was a weeping prophet, as he is commonly called, not only because he wrote Lamentations but also because he was throughout a mournful spectator of the sins of his people.

5. That he was a prophet who suffered. He was persecuted by his own people more than any other prophet, as we will read in this book. He lived and preached just before the Jews' destruction by the Babylonians, when their character seems to have been the same as it was just before their destruction by the Romans, when they *killed the Lord Jesus and persecuted* his *disciples, did not please God, and were contrary to all men, for wrath had come upon them to the uttermost* (1Th 2:15–16). The last account we have of him is that the remaining Jews forced him to go down with them into Egypt, whereas the current tradition among both Jews and Christians is that he suffered martyrdom. Hottinger, from Elmakin, an Arab historian, relates that Jeremiah continued to prophesy in Egypt against the Egyptians and other nations and was stoned to death, and that long afterward, when Alexander entered Egypt, he took the bones of Jeremiah from the place where they had been buried in obscurity, carried them to Alexandria, and buried them there.

The prophecies that we have in the first nineteen chapters of this book seem to be the headings of the sermons he preached by way of general correction for sin; the prophecies after that are more detailed, mixed with the history of his day, but not placed in due time order. With the threats are many gracious promises of mercy to those who repent, promises of the restoration of the Jews from exile, some of which refer clearly to the kingdom of the Messiah. The Apocrypha contains a letter said to be written by Jeremiah to the exiles in Babylon, warning them against the worship of idols by exposing the worthlessness of idols and the foolishness of idolaters. That supposed letter of Jeremiah is chapter 6 of Baruch. But it is not thought to be authentic; nor does it have, in my opinion, anything like the life and spirit of Jeremiah's writings. It is also related concerning Jeremiah (2 Macc 2:5–7) that when Jerusalem was destroyed by the Babylonians, he, by direction from God, took the ark and the altar of incense and, carrying them to Mount Nebo, placed them in a cave and sealed up the entrance. Some followed him and thought that they had noted the location, but when they looked for it, they could not find it. He blamed them for seeking it, telling them that the place would remain unknown until the time that God would gather his people together again.

CHAPTER 1

We have here: 1. The general title of this book, with the time of Jeremiah's public ministry (vv. 1–3). 2. The call of Jeremiah to the office of prophet, his modest objections to it answered, and a full commission given him (vv. 4–10). 3. The visions of an almond branch and a boiling pot, signifying the approaching ruin of Judah and Jerusalem by the Babylonians (vv. 11–16). 4. Encouragement given to the prophet to continue undaunted in his work (vv. 17–19).

Verses 1–3

Here are the genealogy of this prophet and the timing of this prophecy.

1. We are told what family he came from. He was *the son of Hilkiah* (v. 1), one *of the priests that were in Anathoth* (v. 1). The name Jeremiah means one "raised up by the Lord." He was *of the priests* (v. 1), and because he was a priest, he was authorized and appointed to teach the people, but God added to that appointment the extraordinary commission of a prophet. Ezekiel also was a priest. This was how God supported the honor of the priesthood at that time when, by their sins and God's judgments on them, it was sadly eclipsed. Jeremiah was one of the priests in Anathoth, a village of priests, which lay about three miles (about five kilometers) from Jerusalem. Abiathar had his country house there (1Ki 2:26).

2. We have the general date of his prophecies.

2.1. He began to prophesy in the thirteenth year of Josiah's reign (v. 2). In the twelfth year of his reign Josiah began a work of reformation, and he earnestly applied himself to cleanse Judah and Jerusalem of the *high places, and the groves, and the images* (2Ch 34:3). At just the right time this young prophet was raised up to help the young king in that good work. Now one would have expected that when these two joined forces, such a ruler and such a prophet, as in a similar case (Ezr 5:1–2), and since both were young, such a complete reformation would be brought about that it would prevent the ruin of the church and state, but it turned out quite differently. In the eighteenth year of Josiah there were still very many remnants of idolatry that were not cleansed, for what can the best rulers and prophets do to prevent the ruin of a people who hate to be reformed (Lev 26:23)? And so Jeremiah continued to prophesy judgments that were coming on them. Josiah and Jeremiah would have healed them, but they did not want to be healed.

2.2. He continued to prophesy through the reigns of Jehoiakim and Zedekiah, each of whom reigned eleven years. He prophesied *to the carrying away of Jerusalem captive* (until Jerusalem went into exile) (v. 3). He continued to prophesy after that (40:1), but this figure is used because from the thirteenth year of Josiah to the exile was just forty years. In this prophet God endured his people's ill manners for forty years, and he finally swore in his wrath that they would not continue in his rest (Heb 3:7–11; Ps 95:7–11).

Verses 4–10

Here is:

1. Jeremiah's early call to the office of a prophet (vv. 4–5): *The word of the Lord came to him*, and God told him:

1.1. That he had *ordained him a prophet to the nations* (v. 5), the nation of the Jews in the first place, but also to the neighboring nations, to whom he was to *send yokes* (27:2–3) and whom he must make *drink of the cup* of the Lord's anger (25:17). In his writings, he is still a prophet to the nations, including our own, to tell them what national judgments may be expected for national sins.

1.2. That he had appointed him a prophet in his eternal purposes. This commission was given him according to God's purposes for him even before he was born: "*I knew thee, and I sanctified thee*" (v. 5), that is, "I determined that you would be a prophet and set you apart for that office." What God has intended people for, he will call them to. As a Latin saying puts it: "Original endowment, not education, makes a prophet."

2. Jeremiah's modestly declining this honorable work (v. 6). "*Ah, Lord God! behold, I cannot speak* to great people and to many people, as prophets have to do; I cannot speak fluently or with any authority, *for I am a child*, and my youth will be despised" (1Ti 4:12). It is good for us, when we have any service to do for God, to be afraid that we may make a mess of it and that the work may suffer through our weakness.

3. The assurance God graciously gave him that he would stand by him and support him in his work.

3.1. Let him not object that he is only a child; he will be a prophet nevertheless (v. 7). "You have God's command, and let not your being young prevent you from obeying it. Go to all *to whom I shall send thee and speak whatsoever I command thee.*" God was angry with Moses for even his modest excuses (Ex 4:14). Samuel communicated a message from God to Eli when he was a small child. God can, when he pleases, make children become prophets; he can *ordain strength out of the mouth of babes and sucklings* (Ps 8:2).

3.2. Let him not object that he will encounter much opposition; God will protect him (v. 8): "*Be not afraid of their faces*, though they look big and therefore think they can defy you. You speak in the name of the King of kings and by his authority, and you may confront them with that." Those who have messages to communicate from God must not be *afraid of the face of man* (Eze 3:9).

3.3. Let him not object that he cannot speak as he should. God will enable him to speak:

3.3.1. As one who knows God (v. 9). Now that he had a vision of God's glory, the Lord gave him the gift of speaking; he *put forth his hand, touched his mouth*, and with that touch *opened his lips*, so that his mouth would declare God's praise (Ps 51:15). God not only put knowledge into his head but also put *words into his mouth*, for there are *words which the Holy Ghost teaches* (1Co 2:13).

3.3.2. As one who had authority from God (Mt 7:29) (v. 10). *See, I have this day set thee over the nations and over the kingdoms.* This sounds very great, but Jeremiah is still a poor priest; he is not set over the kingdoms as a leader to rule them by the sword, but as a prophet he is set over the nations to let loose the power of the word of God. Jeremiah is *set over the nations* (v. 10) not to demand tribute from them, but to *root out, and pull down*, and also *to build and plant* (v. 10). He must attempt to reform the nations, to *root out and destroy* (v. 10) idolatry and other evils among them, corrupt habits and customs that were firmly established, to *throw down* the kingdom of sin, so that religious faith and goodness may be *planted* and *built* among them. He must set before them *life and death, good and evil* (Dt 30:19, 18:9–10). He must assure those who persist in their evil ways that they will be *rooted out and destroyed* (v. 10), and he must assure those who repent that they will be *built and planted* (v. 10).

Verses 11–19

Here:

1. God gives Jeremiah, in a vision, a view of the most important mission he is to go on, which is to foretell the destruction of Judah and Jerusalem by the Babylonians for their sins, especially their idolatry.

1.1. He suggests to him that the people are quickly preparing themselves for ruin and that ruin is coming quickly toward them. He asks him, "*Jeremiah, what seest thou?* Look around and notice." Jeremiah replies, "*I see a rod* (branch), standing for suffering and rebuke, a rod of correction hanging over us, and it is a *rod of an almond tree* (v. 11), which is one of the earliest trees in spring—it buds and blossoms quickly, when other trees are scarcely out at all." This is why in Hebrew it is called the "hasty tree." God explained it in the next words (v. 12): *Thou hast well seen.* God commended him that he was so observant as to be aware, even though it was the first vision he had ever seen, that the branch was from an almond tree. "You have seen a 'hasty tree,' for I will hasten to carry out what I have spoken" (v. 12). Jeremiah will prophesy what he himself will live to see fulfilled.

1.2. He hints to him where the intended ruin will come from. Jeremiah is asked a second time, *What seest thou?* and he sees *a seething* (boiling) *pot* on the fire (v. 13), representing Jerusalem and Judah in great agitation, like boiling water because of the attack of the Babylonian army, evaporating and growing less and less before the people's eyes. Now the face of the furnace over which this pot boiled was *toward the north* (v. 13), for it was from there that the fire and the fuel were to come that must make the pot boil in this way. And this is how the vision is explained (v. 14): *Out of the north an evil shall break forth.* It had long been intended by the justice of God and long deserved by the sin of the people, and the enemies had intended it, but up to that time God's patience had restrained it; now, however, all restraints would be taken away, and the *evil would break forth* (v. 14). Look for this storm to arise *out of the north, whence fair weather usually comes* (Job 37:22). Sometimes the fiercest storms come from where we have expected fair weather from. This is further explained in v. 15: *I will call all the families of the kingdoms of the north, saith the Lord.* All the northern crowns would unite under Nebuchadnezzar and join him in this expedition. God's summons would be obeyed; those whom he called would come. The commanders of the troops of different nations would take up their positions in besieging Jerusalem and other towns of Judah.

1.3. He tells him clearly what the cause of all these judgments was; it was the *sin of Jerusalem* and of the *cities of Judah* (v. 16): "I will pass sentence upon them," as it may be read, "because of *all their wickedness.*" They *have forsaken God* and have *burnt incense to other gods,* new gods, foreign gods, and all false gods. Jeremiah was young, and perhaps he did not know what detestable idolatry his people were guilty of, but God told him so that he himself might be satisfied with the justice of the sentence that he was to pass on them in God's name.

2. God encourages Jeremiah. A great trust is committed to him. He is sent as a chief herald, for God gives warning of his judgments beforehand so that sinners may be awakened to meet him with repentance and thereby *turn away his wrath.* Jeremiah has a responsibility given him with this trust (v. 17). He must be quick: *Arise,* and lose no time. He must be busy: *Arise, and speak unto them* in season and out of season (2Ti 4:2). He must be bold: *Be not dismayed at their faces*—as he was told before (v. 8).

2.1. He must be faithful in two things:

2.1.1. He must speak all that he is given responsibility for: *Speak all that I command thee* (v. 17). He must keep back nothing for fear of offending someone; he must *declare the whole counsel of God* (Ac 20:27).

2.1.2. He must not whisper it in a corner (Ac 26:26) to a few particular friends, but appear *against the kings of Judah* (v. 18), if they are evil kings. He must not spare *the priests thereof* (v. 18), even though he himself is a priest and is concerned to maintain the dignity of his order. He must declare judgment against the *people of the land* (v. 18), even though they are his own people, insofar as they are against the Lord.

2.2. He is given two reasons why he should do this:

2.2.1. Because he has reason to fear the wrath of God if he is false: "*Be not dismayed at their faces* (v. 17), so as to abandon your office or shrink from its duties, *lest I confound and dismay thee before them*"; the fear of God is the best antidote to the fear of people. It is better to have all the people in the world as our enemies than to have God as our enemy.

2.2.2. Because he has no reason to fear human wrath if he is faithful (v. 18). This mere youth of a prophet is made like a fortified city by the power of God, strengthened with *iron pillars* and surrounded by *brasen* (bronze) *walls*; he sallies out on the enemy issuing rebukes and threats and *keeps them in awe.* They attack him on every side; the kings and rulers thrash him with their power, and the priests thunder against him with their censures, and *the people of the land* (v. 18) shoot their arrows at him, that is, slanderous and bitter words, but he keeps his ground and will still restrain them (v. 19): *They shall fight against thee, but they shall not prevail to destroy thee, for I am with thee to deliver thee.*

CHAPTER 2

This chapter was probably Jeremiah's first sermon after his ordination, and it is a most lively and passionate sermon. He can no longer say, I cannot speak, for I am *only* a child *(1:6), for because God has touched his mouth and put his words into it, no one can speak better. The aim of the chapter is to show God's people their disobedience by way of rebuke and conviction, so that they might be brought to repent. The sin that they are most especially accused of is idolatry. They are told: 1. That this was showing ingratitude to God (vv. 1–8). 2. That it was without precedent that a nation should change their god (vv. 9–13). 3. That in doing so they had ruined themselves (vv. 14–19). 4. That they had broken their covenant and degenerated from their good beginnings (vv. 20–21). 5. That their evil was too bad to be excused (vv. 22–23, 35). 6. That they persisted willfully and obstinately in it (vv. 24–25, 33, 36). 7. That they put themselves to shame by their idolatry and would soon be made ashamed of it when they discovered their idols could not help them (vv. 26–29, 37). 8. That they had not been convinced and reformed by the rebukes of Providence (v. 30). 9. That they had shown great contempt for God (vv. 31–32). 10. That they had mixed most unnatural murder with their idolatry, shedding the blood of poor innocents (v. 34).*

Verses 1–8

Here is:

1. A command given to Jeremiah to take a message from God to the people of Jerusalem. Let ministers carefully compare with the word of God whatever they have to communicate, and let them see that they agree with that word, so that they may be able to say not only, *The Lord sent me,* but also, "He sent me to *speak this.*" Jeremiah must go from Anathoth, where he lived in pleasant retreat, studying the Law, and appear at Jerusalem, that noisy city, and *cry in their ears:* "Cry aloud, so that everyone may hear. Get close to them, and *cry in the ears* (v. 2) of those who have stopped up their ears" (Zec 7:11; Ac 7:57).

2. The message he was commanded to deliver. He must rebuke them for their terrible ingratitude in abandoning the God who had formerly been so kind to them.

2.1. God reminds them here of the favors he gave them when they were first formed into a people (v. 2):

"*I remember thee, the kindness of thy youth and the love of thy espousals*" — or, "*I remember* 'for thy sake,' and cannot forget, *the kindness of thy youth* (devotion) *and the love of thy espousals* (how as a bride you loved me), and I want you to remember it and make the most of remembering it for your good."

2.1.1. This may be understood as referring to their devotion for God; it was not such that they had any reason to boast about it, but God is pleased to mention it, for although it was only a weak love and devotion they showed him, he took it kindly. When *they believed the Lord and his servant Moses* (Ex 14:31), when they *sang God's praise at the Red Sea*, when at the foot of Mount Sinai they promised, *All that the Lord shall say unto us we will do and will be obedient* (Ex 24:7), then they showed the *kindness of their youth and the love of their espousals* (v. 2). When they seemed so eager for God, he said, *Surely they are my people* and will be faithful to me; surely they are *children that will not lie* (Isa 63:8). The devotion of their youth (v. 2) was seen in two things:

2.1.1.1. They followed the direction of the pillar of cloud and fire in the desert and for forty years *went after God in the wilderness*, trusting him to provide for them even though it was *a land that was not sown* (v. 2). God took this kindly. In the same way, although Christ often rebuked his disciples, when he parted from them he still commended them for continuing with him (Lk 22:28).

2.1.1.2. They set up the tabernacle among them. Israel *was then holiness to the Lord* (v. 3). This was how they *began in the Spirit*, and God reminds them of this, so that they may be ashamed of ending *in the flesh* (Gal 3:3).

2.1.2. Or it may be understood as referring to God's kindness to them; he speaks in detail about that later. *When Israel was a child, then I loved him* (Hos 11:1).

2.1.2.1. God took them to himself. They were the *first fruits of his increase* (harvest) (v. 3), the first constituted church he had in the world, but the full harvest was to be gathered in from among the Gentiles.

2.1.2.2. Having taken them in marriage, he embraced their cause and became an *enemy to their enemies* (Ex 23:22). Whoever wronged the people of God did so at their peril. He especially had a dispute with those who attempted to defile them and draw them away from being *holiness to the Lord* (v. 3), as can be seen in his *quarrel with the Midianites about the matter of Peor* (Nu 25:17–18).

2.1.2.3. He *brought them out of Egypt* with a mighty hand and with great and awesome deeds (Dt 4:34), and yet with a kind hand and great tenderness he led them through a barren, howling wilderness (Dt 32:10) (v. 6). They walked through that dark valley for forty years, but *God was with them*, and even there God *prepared a table for them* (Ps 23:4–5); he gave them bread from the clouds (Ex 16:4) and drink from the rocks (Ex 17:6; Nu 20:7–11). All God's spiritual Israel must acknowledge their obligation to him for safely leading them through the wilderness of this world, which is no less dangerous to the soul than that physical wilderness was to the body.

2.1.2.4. He finally settled them in Canaan (v. 7): *I brought you into a plentiful country*. They *ate the fruit thereof* and the *goodness thereof*. "I brought you into a fertile land," literally, "a land of Carmel"; Carmel was a place of extraordinary fruitfulness, and Canaan was like one great fruitful field (Dt 8:7).

2.1.2.5. God gave them the means of knowledge, grace, and fellowship with him; this is implied in v. 8.

2.2. He rebukes them for their ingratitude (v. 4).

2.2.1. He challenges them to produce any example of his being unjust and unkind to them. He puts the question fairly to them to see if they can come up with a reason for deserting him (v. 5): "*What iniquity have your fathers*, or you either, *found in me*? Have you found God to be a hard taskmaster? You who have forsaken the worship of God, can you say that his service was boring and tedious? The disappointments you have met with were because of yourselves, not God. The yoke of his commandments is easy (Mt 11:30), and in the *keeping of them there is great reward*" (Ps 19:11). Although he afflicts us, he does us no wrong; all the sin is with us.

2.2.2. He charges them with being unjust and unkind to him nevertheless. "*They have gone from me*; in fact, they have gone *far from me*" (v. 5). *They have walked after vanity* (v. 5), that is, worthless idols. With their idolatry they had introduced all kinds of evil. When they entered the land that God gave them, they defiled it (v. 7) by defiling themselves. It was God's land, a holy land, Immanuel's land (Isa 8:8), but they *made it an abomination* (v. 7). Having abandoned God, they had no thoughts of returning to him. Neither the people nor the priests asked after him, nor did they express any desire to regain his favor. The *people* did not say, *Where is the Lord?* (v. 6). The *priests* did not say, *Where is the Lord?* (v. 8). Those who should have taught the people the knowledge of God were not concerned to gain the knowledge of him themselves. The scribes, who *handled the law* (v. 8), did not know God or his will. The pastors, who should have kept the flock from rebelling against him, were themselves ringleaders in their rebellion: *They have transgressed against me* (v. 8). They claimed to prophesy by Baal, and they were supported by the evil kings in confronting the Lord's prophets.

Verses 9–13

The prophet shows their unparalleled fickleness and foolishness (v. 9): *I will yet plead with you*. Before God punishes sinners, he pleads with them to bring them to repentance. Here he pleads with those who persist in that *vain conversation* (empty way of life) *received by tradition from their fathers* (1Pe 1:18), and he pleads *with their children's children* (v. 9), that is, with all who in every age follow in their footsteps.

1. He showed that they were acting contrary to the customs of all nations. Their neighbors were more firm and faithful to their false gods than they were to the true God. Let them survey the present state of the coasts of Kittim, Greece, and the European islands, the countries that were more civilized and learned, and of Kedar. They would not find one example of a nation that had *changed their gods* (v. 11). Those nations had such respect for their gods that although they were gods of wood and stone, they would not change them for gods of silver and gold, and not even for the living and true God. We praise them not (1Co 11:22), and yet it may well be urged, to the disgrace of Israel, that they, who were the only people that had no reason to change their God, were nevertheless the only people that had changed him. The zeal and faithfulness of idolaters should shame Christians out of their coldness and unfaithfulness.

2. He showed that they were acting against the principles of common sense, changing for the worse, making a bad bargain for themselves.

2.1. They abandoned a God who made them truly glorious, for his glory had often appeared on their tabernacle.

2.2. They accepted gods that could do them no good, gods that *do not profit* (v. 11) their worshipers. Heaven itself is here called on to stand appalled at the sin and foolishness of those who have turned away from God (vv. 12–13): *Be astonished* (appalled), *O you heavens!*

at this. The meaning is that the behavior of this people toward God was:

2.2.1. Such as may well be wondered at—that human beings, who pretend to be rational, should ever do something so absurd.

2.2.2. Such as we should have a holy indignation at as being ungodly and a great insult to our Maker.

2.2.3. Such as we may tremble to think about the consequences of. "*My people*, whom I have taught, *have committed two great evils* (v. 13), ingratitude and foolishness; they have acted contrary to both their duty and their interests."

2.2.3.1. They have insulted their God by turning their backs on him. "*They have forsaken me, the fountain of living waters* (v. 13), in whom they have an abundant and constant supply." God is their *fountain of life* (Ps 36:9). In him there is all-sufficient grace and strength; all our springs are in him (Ps 87:7). He has been to us a *fountain of living waters,* overflowing, flowing constantly. To abandon him is, in effect, to deny this. He has been to us a generous giver, a *fountain of living waters* (v. 13), overflowing in the gifts of his favor; to abandon him is to withhold that tribute of love and praise which his kindness calls for.

2.2.3.2. They have also deceived themselves. They abandoned *their own mercies* for worthless idols (Jnh 2:8). They took a great deal of effort to *hew* (dig) *themselves out cisterns,* but these proved to be *broken cisterns* that could *hold no water* (v. 13). When they came to quench their thirst there, they found nothing but mud and mire and the filthy sediments of a stagnant pool. The idols were as such to their worshipers. If we make an idol of any creature—wealth, pleasure, or honor—if we make it our joy and love—we will find it a broken cistern. Although we may take a great deal of effort to dig it out and fill it, at best it will hold only a little water, and that water will be dead and flat. It is a broken cistern, which cracks in hot weather, so that the water is lost when we need it most (Job 6:15). Let us therefore remain faithful only to the Lord, for he has *the words of eternal life* (Jn 6:68).

Verses 14–19

The foolishness of abandoning God had already cost them dearly, for this was the reason for all the disasters their country was suffering:

1. Their neighbors who were their professed enemies defeated them.

1.1. They were made slaves and lost their liberty (v. 14): *Is Israel a servant?* No; *Israel is my son, my firstborn* (Ex 4:22). They are children; they are heirs (Ro 8:17), the descendants of Abraham. They were intended to rule, not to be slaves. *Why then is he spoiled* (plundered) of his liberty? Why is he treated as a servant, as a slave by birth (v. 14)? Why does he *make himself a slave* to his sinful desire and idols, to what is worthless (v. 11)? What is this, that such a birthright should be sold for a mess of pottage (Ge 25:29–34), such a crown dishonored and placed in the dust? The rulers made slaves of their subjects, and masters made slaves of their servants (34:11), and so they made their country lowly and wretched, a country that God had made happy and honorable. The neighboring rulers and powers broke in on them, making some of them slaves even in their own country and perhaps selling others as slaves to foreign countries. For *their iniquities they sold themselves* (Isa 50:1). We may apply this spiritually. Is the human soul *a servant*? Is it a slave by birth? No; it is not. Why then is it plundered? It is because it has sold its own liberty and made itself a slave to sinful desires and passions.

1.2. They were made poor and had lost their wealth. God brought them into a fertile land (v. 7), but all their neighbors attacked it (v. 15): *Young lions roar aloud over him and yell* (growled). Sometimes one powerful enemy, and sometimes another, and sometimes many together, attacked them and triumphed over them. They carried off the fruits of their land, made it *waste,* and *burned their cities.*

1.3. They were mistreated, insulted, and struck by everybody (v. 16): "Even *the children of Noph and Tahapanes,* contemptible people, not well known for military courage or strength, *have broken the crown of thy head.*" We read how terrible the condition of Judah had just been in the reign of Manasseh (2Ch 33:11)

1.4. All this was because of their sin (v. 17): *Hast thou not procured this unto thyself* (have you not brought this on yourselves)? By their sinful alliances with the nations and their conformity to their idolatrous customs, they had made themselves contemptible. "You have forsaken your God at the time that he was leading you by the way," as it may read.

2. Their neighbors who claimed to be friends did not help them, and this was also because of their sin.

2.1. It was futile for them to look to Egypt and Assyria for help (v. 18): "*What hast thou to do in the way of Egypt?* You want to *drink the waters of Sihor*" (v. 18), that is, the Nile. "You are relying on the fair promises they make you. At other times you want to go *in the way of Assyria* (v. 18), going there quickly to get reinforcements. You think you can satisfy yourself with the *waters of the river Euphrates;* what *hast thou to do* there? What will you gain by turning to them? They will *help in vain* (Isa 30:7), and what you thought would be a river to you will turn out to be just a broken cistern" (v. 13).

2.2. This also was because of their sin. "*Thy own wickedness shall correct thee* (v. 19), and then it is impossible for them to save you; *know and see that it is an evil thing that thou hast forsaken God,* for this is what makes your enemies your enemies, and your friends are friends in vain." Sin is *forsaking the Lord* as our God; it is the soul's separation from him. The cause of sin is that *his fear is not in us* (v. 19). Sin is an evil that contains no good. It is *bitter.* The wages of sin is death (Ro 6:23), and death is bitter. Just as it is in itself evil and bitter, so also it has a direct tendency to make us miserable: "*Thy own wickedness shall correct thee, and thy backslidings shall reprove thee* (v. 19). The punishment will so inevitably follow the sin that the sin will itself be said to punish you. Your own evil will convince you and silence your mouth forever, and you will be forced to acknowledge that *the Lord is righteous.*"

Verses 20–28

In these verses the prophet continues with his charges against this backsliding people. Notice:

1. The sin itself: idolatry.

1.1. They frequented the places of idol worship (v. 20): "*Upon every high hill and under every green tree,* in the high places and the groves, *thou wanderest,* unsettled and unsatisfied, but it is all *playing the harlot* (lying down as a prostitute)," which is spiritual immorality and was commonly accompanied by physical immorality.

1.2. They made idols for themselves and gave them honor as gods (vv. 26–27). Not only the common people did this; even the kings and rulers, the priests and prophets, were themselves so stupid as to *say to a stock* (piece of wood), "*Thou art my father*—that is, you are my god, the author of my being, to whom I owe duty and on whom I depend"—and *to a stone*, to an idol made of stone, *"Thou hast* given me birth; therefore protect me." What greater insult could people show God, our true Father and the One who has made us? When these idols were first made the objects of worship, then it was supposed that they were given life by some heavenly power or spirit, but gradually that thought became lost, and so the idolaters become futile in their thinking (Ro 1:21); the very idol was supposed to be their father and was worshiped accordingly!

1.3. They multiplied these false gods endlessly (v. 28): *According to the number of thy cities are thy gods, O Judah!* They could not agree on the same god. One town wanted one god, and another, another god.

2. The proof of this. They claimed they could acquit themselves from this guilt; they *washed themselves with nitre* (soda) and *took much soap* (v. 22). They pretended they worshiped these not as gods but as demons, or that it was not divine honor that they gave them, but polite respect. This was how they tried to evade the convictions of God's word. They said, *I am not polluted* (defiled), *I have not gone after Baalim* (v. 23). Because it was done in secret and they worked hard to hide it (Eze 8:12), they thought it could never be proved that they were guilty. But they were convicted nonetheless. *"How canst thou* deny the facts and *say, I have not gone after Baalim?"* (v. 23). "It is ingrained so deeply and stained before me," as some read it. "Although you try to wash it out, as murderers try to get the stain of the blood of the person they have killed out of their clothes, you can never get it out." *See thy way in the valley* (v. 23)—they had worshiped idols not only on the high hills but also in the valleys (Isa 57:5–6), in the valley opposite Beth Peor, according to some (Dt 34:6; Nu 25:3); but if a particular valley is meant, surely it is the *valley of the son of Hinnom* (2Ch 28:3), for that was the place where they sacrificed their children to Molech and which therefore witnessed against them more than any other.

3. The things that made this sin that they were accused of even worse.

3.1. God had done great things for them, but they had rebelled from him and against him (v. 20): *Of old time I have broken thy yoke* (tore off) *thy bonds.* The bonds that God had loosed from them should have bound them forever to him.

3.2. They had begun promisingly but had not fulfilled their promise: *Thou saidst, I will not transgress* (v. 20).

3.3. They had wretchedly degenerated from what they had been when God originally formed them into a people: *I had planted thee a noble vine* (v. 21). *Israel served the Lord* and kept close to him *all the days of Joshua, and the elders that outlived Joshua* (Jos 24:31). The very next generation *knew not the Lord, nor the works which he had done* (Jdg 2:10), and so they became worse and worse (2Ti 3:13) until they turned into *the degenerate plants of a strange* (a corrupt wild) *vine* (v. 21).

3.4. They were violent and eager in pursuing their idolatry, and they would not be restrained either by the word of God or by his providence. They are compared to *a swift dromedary traversing her ways*, a female camel hunting for a male (v. 23), and, to the same effect, *a wild ass used to the wilderness* (v. 24), not tamed by the experience of laboring for human beings and therefore very rebellious, *snuffing* (sniffing) *up the wind at her pleasure* (in her craving) (v. 24), and on such an *occasion who can turn her away?* (v. 24). Who can hinder her from what she is lusting after? *Those that seek her* then *will not weary themselves for her* (v. 24), but will wait until she is heavily pregnant, and then *they shall find her* (v. 24), and she cannot

outrun them. Excited lust is wild, and those who will not be turned away from it are to be reckoned as wild animals. Let them not be looked on as rational creatures. Idolatry is strangely intoxicating. *Ephraim is joined to idols; let him alone* (Hos 4:17). Yet the time will come when the fiercest will be tamed. When distress and anguish come on them, their ears will be open to discipline.

3.5. They continued obstinately in their sin, and just as they could not be restrained, so they would not be reformed (Lev 26:23) (v. 25). He would certainly take them into a miserable exile, and on their way, they would be forced to travel barefoot and would be denied reasonable water, so their throats would dry up with thirst. Those who turn after foreign gods and their ways of worship will justly be made prisoners to a foreign king in a foreign land. They said to those who tried to persuade them to repent and reform, *"There is no hope*; it's no use, don't expect us to throw away our idols, for *we have loved strangers* (foreign gods), *and after them we will go"* (v. 25). But just as we must not despair of the mercy of God, but believe that if we repent and seek that mercy, then we will find his mercy sufficient to forgive our sins—even though they are terrible—so neither must we despair of the grace of God, but believe that it is able to subdue our corruption, although that may be strong, if we pray for and use that grace. We must never say, *There is no hope* (v. 25), as long as we are on this side of hell.

3.6. They had shamed themselves by pushing away from the One who would have helped them (vv. 26–28). *As the thief is ashamed* when found and brought to punishment, *so are the house of Israel ashamed*, not with a penitent shame for the sin they have been guilty of but with a penal shame for the disappointment they met with in that sin. In their prosperity they turned their backs on God. In a time of trouble, however, they will find no satisfaction except in turning to him; then *they will say, Arise, and save us* (v. 27). To bring them to this point of being ashamed, in case they might be brought to repentance, they are sent *to the gods whom they have chosen* and served (Jdg 10:14). They cried out to God, *Arise, and save us* (v. 27), but God says about the idols, *"Let them arise and save thee* (v. 28), for you have no reason to expect that I will."

Verses 29–37

1. The prophet declares that the truth of the charge is clear beyond contradiction (v. 29): *"Wherefore will you plead with me?* You know you have all transgressed (v. 29), one person as well as another; why then do you *quarrel with me* for accusing you?"

2. He emphasizes it with a consideration of their incorrigibleness and ingratitude. They had been under divine rebukes of many kinds. God's intention was to bring them to repentance, but it was *in vain*. Their consciences were not awakened, nor were their hearts softened. *They received no instruction* by the *correction*, were not made any better by it. They *did not receive* the correction, and so they were *smitten* (punished) *in vain* (v. 30). They had not been persuaded by the word of God that he had sent them through the mouth of his servants the prophets; they had killed the messengers for the sake of the message: *Your own sword has devoured your prophets like a destroying* (ravenous) *lion* (vv. 30–31). *"O generation!"*—he does not speak to them as harshly as he might (Mt 3:7; 17:17), but gently: "O you people of this generation!"—*"see the word of the Lord*; do not only hear it." As we are told to listen to *the rod* (Mic 6:9)—for that has its voice—so also we are told to *see the word*, for that has its visions and views. It is written as with a ray of the sun, so that a

messenger can read it as he runs with it (Hab 2:2): *Have I been a wilderness to Israel, a land of darkness* (v. 31)? The service of God had been neither an unpleasant nor an unprofitable service to any of them. God had sometimes led his people *through a wilderness* and *a land of darkness* (v. 31), but at such times he was to them all that they needed; he fed them with manna and led them by a pillar of fire, so that they were in a fruitful field (Isa 32:15) and a land of light. Yet they had become intolerably arrogant. They say, *We are lords; we will come no more unto thee* (v. 31). It is absurd for us who are beggars to say, *We are lords*, that is, "We are rich, and so we will no longer come to God."

3. He puts the blame for all their evil on their forgetting God (v. 32): *They have forgotten me*; they had avoided all those things that would remind them of God. They had neglected him *days without number* (v. 32), from time immemorial. How many days of our lives have passed without our having properly remembered God? Who can count those empty days? They did not have such a regard for him as young women have for their fine clothes: *Can a maid forget her ornaments or a bride her attire?* (v. 32). No; they are always thinking and speaking about them.

4. He shows them what a bad influence their sins had had on others (v. 33): *Why trimmest thou thy way to seek love?* How skilled you are at pursuing love! Here is an allusion to immoral women who commend themselves by their amorous looks, flirting, and bright clothes, like Jezebel, who *painted her face and tired her head* (2Ki 9:30). This was how they had sought the favor of their neighbors to join in sinful alliances with them and *taught the wicked ones their ways* (v. 33) of mixing God's institutions with their idolatrous customs. Those who by their fellowship with the unfruitful works of darkness (Eph 5:11) make evildoers more evil than they would be otherwise will have a great deal to answer for.

5. He accuses them of the guilt of murder (v. 34): *Also in thy skirts is found the blood of the souls*, the lifeblood of the poor innocents. The reference is to the children who were offered in sacrifice to Molech, or it may be taken more generally for all the *innocent blood* that Manasseh shed and with which he had *filled Jerusalem* (2Ki 21:16). This blood was found *not by secret search* (v. 34), not, literally, by "digging," but *upon all these*; it was above ground and in full view of the people. This suggests that the guilt was openly made known and shameless.

6. He overrules their plea of "Not guilty." *I will plead with thee* (v. 35) and convince thee of thy mistake. They think that God's anger toward them is without reason and that by pleading innocence they have proved it to be so. They therefore conclude that God will immediately drop his action and *his anger shall be turned from them* (Hos 14:4). This is very offensive, and God will convince them that his anger is just, and he will never drop his dispute until they, instead of justifying themselves, judge and condemn themselves.

7. He rebukes them for the shameful disappointments they met with in what they put their confidence in, even as they made God their enemy (vv. 36–37). It was an act of spiritual idolatry that they trusted in human strength and that their hearts *departed from the Lord. Why gaddest thou about* (why do you go about) *so much to change thy way?* (v. 36). Those who set their hope in God and continually depend on him need not go about changing their ways, for their souls may return to him and find him to be their rest. They first trusted in Assyria (2Ki 16:7–9), and when that turned out to be a broken reed, they depended on Egypt, but that proved no better (2Ki 18:21). "*Thou*

shalt be ashamed of Egypt (v. 36), which you are now trusting in, as formerly *thou wast of Assyria*"—*who distressed them and strengthened them not* (2Ch 28:20). "Your ambassadors or envoys will return from Egypt disappointed and with the matter unaccomplished, mourning the desperate condition of their people." Or, "Thou shalt go forth hence," that is, into exile in a foreign land, *with thy hands upon thy head* (v. 37). "And Egypt, which you are relying on, will not be able to prevent it nor rescue you from captivity." *As there is no counsel* (plan) *or wisdom* (Pr 21:30) that can succeed against the Lord, so there is none that can succeed without him.

CHAPTER 3

In this chapter gracious invitations are given to the people to return and repent, despite the great number of their offenses, which are specified here to show that as sin increased, grace increased all the more (Ro 5:20). Here: 1. It is shown how bad they have been, but also how ready God is to receive them into his favor when they repent (vv. 1–5). 2. The impenitence of Judah is emphasized (vv. 6–11). 3. Great encouragements are given to these backsliders to turn back to God and repent, and promises are made of the great mercy God has in store for them (vv. 12–19). 4. The charge against them for their turning away from God is renewed, and the invitation is repeated, to which are added the words that they must use in returning to God (vv. 20–25).

Verses 1–5

These verses open a door of hope; God wounds so that he may heal (Job 5:18; Hos 6:1). Notice:

1. How corruptly this people had abandoned God and prostituted themselves from him. To have admitted one foreign God among them would have been bad enough, but they were insatiable in their lust for false worship: *Thou hast played the harlot with many lovers* (v. 1). They had sought opportunities for their idolatry and had set about seeking new gods: *In the high places* (barren heights) *hast thou sat for them* (v. 2), like *the Arabian in the wilderness* (v. 2)—"the Arabian huckster," according to some, who seeks customers, or "the Arabian thief," according to others, who watches for people to rob. They defiled not only themselves but also *their land with their whoredoms* (prostitution) *and with their wickedness* (v. 2), for it became a national sin. And yet (v. 3) "*thou hadst a whore's forehead*, a brazen look of a prostitute." *Thou refusedst to be ashamed* (v. 3). Blushing is the color of virtue, or at least a remnant of it, but those who have gone beyond shame are beyond all hope.

2. How gently God had corrected them for their sins. He only *withheld the showers from them* (v. 3), and that for only one part of the year.

3. How justly God might have refused ever to receive them again; this would have been going by the known rule of divorces (v. 1). *They say* (Dt 24:4) that if a woman is once divorced and is joined to *another man*, her first husband will never take her again to be his wife: such playing fast and loose with the marriage bond would be a terrible desecration of that commitment and would *greatly pollute* (defile) *that land* (v. 1).

4. How graciously he invites them to turn back to him. "Though you have been bad, *yet return again to me*" (v. 1). God has not limited himself to the laws he made for us, nor does he have any perverse human resentment. He will be kinder to Israel than ever any wronged husband was to an adulterous wife. He kindly tells them what to

say to him (v. 4): "*Wilt thou not from this time cry unto me?* Now that you have been made to see your sins (v. 2) and to suffer for them (v. 3), will you not now abandon them and return to me, saying, *I will go and return to my first husband, for then it was better with me than now?*" (Hos 2:7). He expects them to claim a relationship with God as theirs: *Wilt thou not cry unto me, My father, thou art the guide of my youth?* (v. 4). They will surely come toward him as a father to beg his forgiveness for their irresponsible behavior toward him. Or they will come to him as *the guide of their youth* (v. 4), that is, as their husband (Mal 2:14) or friend. "Although you have gone after many lovers, surely you will finally remember your marriage promises and return to the *husband of thy youth*" (Joel 1:8). Youth needs a guide. When we return to God, we must remember with thankfulness that he *was the guide of our youth* (v. 4) to strengthen and encourage us. When we return to God, we must make a covenant with him that he will be our guide from that time on in doing our duty.

Verses 6–11

The date of this sermon was *in the days of Josiah* (v. 6), who set in motion a blessed work of reformation, in which he was sincere but the people were insincere. The two kingdoms of Israel and Judah are compared, the *ten tribes* who had rebelled from the throne of David and the temple of Jerusalem and the *two tribes* who remained faithful to both.

1. Here is a short account of Israel, the ten tribes. She is called faithless Israel because that kingdom was first founded in turning away from divine institutions, both in church and in state. They had *played the harlot* (committed adultery) *upon every high mountain and under every green tree* (v. 6), that is, they had worshiped other gods in their high places and groves. God by his prophets had invited and encouraged them to repent and reform (v. 7): "*After she had done all these things,* for which she might justly have been abandoned, yet *I said* to her, '*Turn thou unto me* and I will receive you.'" God still sent his prophets among them to call them to *return to him* and worship only him, not insisting so much on their return to the house of David but urging their return to the house of Aaron. We do not read that Elijah, that great reformer, ever called them to return to the house of David. But despite God's calls to repentance, they had persisted in their idolatry: *But she returned not,* and God *saw it* (vv. 7–8). He had therefore given them into the hands of their enemies (v. 8): "When I saw that I had to send her away for all the adultery she had committed, I gave her a certificate of divorce." He scattered all their synagogues and the schools of the prophets and excluded them from making any further claim on the covenant made with their ancestors.

2. Here is the case of Judah, the kingdom of the two tribes. She is called *treacherous* (unfaithful) *sister Judah* (v. 8), a sister because they descended from the same stock, Abraham and Jacob, but just as Israel had the character of a *backslider,* so Judah is called *treacherous,* because although she professed to keep close to God when Israel had been faithless—she had remained faithful to the kings and priests who were appointed by God—yet she proved treacherous. Israel's captivity was intended to warn Judah, but it did not have the intended effect. Judah thought she was safe because she had Levites as her priests and sons of David as her kings. She *defiled the land* and made it detestable to God, for she *committed adultery with stones and stocks* (wood) (v. 9), with the most corrupt idols. In the reigns of Manasseh and

Amon, all the country was corrupted. God tested them to see whether they would be good in a good reign, but their evil disposition remained the same: *They returned not to me with their whole heart, but feignedly* (only in pretense) (v. 10). Josiah went further in destroying idolatry than the best of his predecessors had done, and he *turned to the Lord with all his heart and with all his soul* (2Ki 23:25). The people were forced into an outward compliance with him (2Ch 34:32; 35:17), but they were insincere in it; their *hearts were not right with God* (Ps 78:37). This was why God said at that time, *I will remove Judah out of my sight, as I removed Israel* (2Ki 23:27). I know of no religion except one that is sincere.

3. The lives of these sister kingdoms are compared, and of the two, Judah was the worse (v. 11). This comparative justification will give Israel little advantage; what good will it do us to be able to say, *We are not so bad as others,* when we are still not really good in ourselves? Judah was in two respects worse than Israel:

3.1. More was expected from Judah than from Israel; Judah disgraced a more sacred profession and falsified a more solemn promise than Israel did.

3.2. Judah could have taken warning from the ruin of Israel, but would not.

Verses 12–19

There is a great deal of the Gospel in these verses. The prophet is told to *proclaim these words toward the north* (v. 12), for they are a call to faithless Israel, the ten tribes who were taken captive into Assyria, which lay north of Jerusalem. He must look that way to rebuke the people of Judah for their stubbornness in refusing to answer the calls given them. Faithless *Israel will* sooner accept mercy, and therefore receive its benefit, than unfaithful Judah (v. 11). And perhaps the declaring of these words toward the north looks as far forward as the *preaching of repentance and remission of sins unto all nations, beginning at Jerusalem* (Lk 24:47).

1. Here is an invitation given to faithless Israel, and in them to the faithless Gentiles, to *return unto God,* the God from whom they have rebelled (v. 12): *Return, thou backsliding Israel.* And again (v. 14): "*Turn, O backsliding children!* Come back to the good way, from which you have turned aside." They are encouraged to return. "You have incurred God's displeasure, but return to me, and *I will not cause my anger to fall upon you*" (v. 12). They are told how to return (v. 13): "*Only acknowledge thy iniquity,* confess your faults and so be ashamed of yourself and give glory to God" (Jos 7:19). It will only aggravate the condemnation of sinners that the terms of forgiveness and peace were brought so low and yet they would not reach up for them. *If the prophet had told thee to do some great thing, wouldst thou not have done it? How much more when he says, Only acknowledge thy iniquity?* (2Ki 5:13). We must acknowledge our actual sins: "*That thou hast transgressed against the Lord thy God* (v. 13); you have insulted and offended him." We must acknowledge the great number of our rebellions: "That *thou hast scattered thy ways to the strangers,* that you have run here and there in pursuit of your idols, *under every green tree* (v. 13). You have not obeyed my voice. Acknowledge that, and let that humble you more than anything else."

2. Here these faithless children are given precious promises that they will be greatly blessed if they turn back to him, promises that were partially fulfilled in the return of the Jews from exile; but the prophecy is to have its complete fulfillment in the Gospel church and the gathering together of *the children of God that were scattered abroad*

(Jn 11:52): "Return, for although you have backslidden, you are still children; although an unfaithful wife, you are still a wife, for *I am married to you* (v. 14) and will not disown that relationship." This is how God remembers his covenant with their ancestors (Lev 26:42).

2.1. He promises to gather them together from all places to which they are dispersed and scattered (Jn 11:52), *I will take you, one of a city, and two of a family,* or clan; *and I will bring you to Zion* (v. 14). Of the many who have backslidden from God, there are only a few who return to him, *one of a city and two of a country.* Of those few, not even one will be lost even though they are dispersed (Jn 17:12; 18:9). Although there is only *one in a city* (v. 14), God will find that one. God's chosen ones, scattered throughout the world, will be brought to *the Gospel church,* that Mount Zion, the heavenly Jerusalem, that holy hill on which Christ reigns.

2.2. He promises to set over them those who will be a blessing to them in every way (v. 15): *I will give you pastors after my heart.*

2.2.1. When a church is gathered, it must be led. *"I will bring them to Zion* (v. 14) to be disciplined, to live not like wild animals but like sheep under the direction of a shepherd." *I will give them pastors* (shepherds) (v. 15), that is, both magistrates and ministers.

2.2.2. Things are going well with a people when their pastors are *after God's own heart* (v. 15), pastors who make his will their rule in all their ministry and who rule for him and, as they are able, rule like him.

2.2.3. Those who are pastors after God's own heart are the ones who feed the flock (Jn 21:15–18); they do not seek to *fleece the flocks* but to *feed them with wisdom and understanding* (v. 15). Those who are not only pastors but also teachers must feed them with the word of God, which is able to make us wise for salvation (2Ti 3:15).

2.3. He promises there will be no more need for the *ark of the covenant* (v. 16), which has been the sign of God's presence with them. That will be set aside (v. 16): *When you shall be multiplied and increased in the land,* when the kingdom of the Messiah is set up, then *they shall say no more, The ark of the covenant of the Lord* (v. 16), because they will set up a pure and spiritual way of worship, in which all the external ordinances of the ceremonial law will be set aside, for Christ, the truth of all those types, as shown to us in the word and sacraments of the New Testament, will take the place of all those ordinances. In the Gospel temple Christ himself *is the ark;* he is the mercy seat, and it is the spiritual presence of God in his ordinances that we are now to expect. Many expressions are used here concerning the setting aside of the ark: that it will not *come to mind,* that they *shall not remember it,* that they will *not visit it* (it will not be missed) (v. 16), that none of these things will be *any more done,* for the *true worshippers shall worship the Father in spirit and in truth* (Jn 4:24).

2.4. He promises that the Gospel church, here called *Jerusalem,* will become renowned (v. 17). Two things will make it famous:

2.4.1. God's special residence and rule in it. It will be called *the throne of the Lord,* of his glory, of *his government* (Isa 9:7), of *his grace* (Heb 4:16).

2.4.2. The accession of the Gentiles to it. *All the nations shall* become subjects to the *throne of the Lord* (v. 17) that is set up there.

2.5. He promises there will be a wonderful reformation worked in the church: *They shall not walk any more after the imagination of their evil hearts* (v. 17). They will not live as they want but live according to God's

rules, according to the will of God. Notice what leads to *sin—the imagination of our own evil hearts;* sin *is walking after* that imagination, being ruled by our futile thinking and corrupt motives. Notice what converting grace does: it takes us away from following our own desires and brings us to be directed by religious faith and right reason.

2.6. He promises that Judah and Israel will be happily united in one body (v. 18). They were so in their return from exile and their resettlement in Canaan. This happy union of Israel and Judah in Canaan was a type of the uniting of Jews and Gentiles in the Gospel church, when, because all enmities had been removed, they would become one *sheepfold under one shepherd* (Jn 10:16).

3. Difficulties lie in the way of all this mercy.

3.1. God asks, *How shall I do this for you?* It is not as if God showed his favor with reluctance, but we are utterly unworthy of his favors; there is nothing in us that deserves them. How should we who are so lowly and weak, so worthless and unworthy, and so offensive ever be *put among the* (treated as his) *children* (v. 19)? To those whom God treats as the children he will *give the pleasant land* (v. 19), the land of Canaan. It was a type of heaven, where there are *pleasures for evermore* (Ps 16:11). Who could expect a place in that *pleasant land* when they have so often *despised it* (Ps 106:24) and so are unfit for it?

3.2. He himself responds in answer to this question: *But I said, Thou shalt call me, My Father* (v. 19). God himself answers all the objections. So that he may treat returning penitents as his children, he will give them the *Spirit of adoption,* teaching them *to cry, Abba, Father* (Ro 8:15; Gal 4:6). "*Thou shalt call me, My Father* (v. 19); you will return to me and submit to me as children to their father, and that will commend you to my favor." He will *put his fear in their hearts* (32:40), so that they may never *turn from him* but may persevere to the end (Mt 10:22; 24:13).

Verses 20–25

Here is:

1. The charge against Israel for their unfaithful abandonment (v. 20). They were joined to God by the marriage covenant, but they broke that covenant; they *dealt treacherously* with God.

2. Their confession of the truth of this charge (v. 21). When God rebuked them for their apostasy, there were some whose *voice was heard upon the high places weeping and praying,* humbling themselves before the God of their ancestors, acknowledging that *they had perverted their way and forgotten the Lord their God* (v. 21). Sin is the turning aside to corrupt ways. Forgetting the Lord our God is at the root of all sin. If people would remember God, they would not disobey him.

3. The invitation God gives them to turn back to him (v. 22): *Return, you backsliding children.* He calls them *children* out of tenderness and compassion for them; they are perverse as children but still *his* sons and daughters, whom, though he corrects them, he will not disinherit. God is patient toward such children, as parents must be too. When they are convicted of their sin (v. 21), they are being *invited* to *return,* as Christ invites those to him who are *weary* and *heavy laden* (Mt 11:28). The promise to those who turn back to him is, *I will heal your backslidings* (v. 22). God *will heal our backslidings* by his pardoning mercy, his quieting peace, and his renewing grace.

4. The ready agreement they give to this invitation. This is an echo of God's call; as a voice is returned from broken-down walls, so this comes from broken hearts. God says, *Return;* they answer, *Behold, we come.* It is an immediate response.

4.1. They come devoting themselves to God as their God: "*Thou art the Lord our God*" (v. 22). It is only because of our sin and foolishness that we have gone away from you."

4.2. They come claiming help from God: "*In vain is salvation hoped for from the hills and from the multitude of the mountains*" (v. 23). They worshiped their idols on hills and mountains (v. 6), but now they will have nothing more to do with them. Therefore:

4.3. They come depending on God alone as their God: *In the Lord our God is the salvation of Israel* (v. 23). It may be applied very much to the great salvation from sin, which Jesus Christ brought us; that is the *salvation of the Lord* (La 3:26), his *great salvation* (Heb 2:3).

4.4. They come justifying God in their troubles and judging themselves for their sins (vv. 24–25). They attribute all the adversities they have suffered to their idols: *Shame* (shameful idols) *has devoured the labour of our fathers*. True penitents have learned to call sin *shame*. They have also learned to call it death and ruin. "It has *devoured* all those good things that our ancestors *laboured for* and left to us. We have found *from our youth* that our idolatry has destroyed our prosperity." When they speak of the labor of their ancestors, which their idols have devoured, they mention particularly *their flocks and their herds, their sons and their daughters* (v. 24). They are ashamed of their sin and foolishness (v. 25): "*We lie down in our shame*, being unable to stand up in it. *Our confusion* (disgrace) *covers us*, that is, the shame both from the penalty we have suffered and from our penitence." Sin is "in our blood": "*We and our fathers have sinned.* We have sinned *from our youth*; we have continued to sin. We have sinned *even unto this day*, although we are often called on to repent and abandon our sins. *We have not obeyed the voice of the Lord our God* commanding us, when we have sinned, to repent." All this seems to be the language of the penitents *of the house of Israel* (v. 20), of the ten tribes, either of those who were in exile or of those who remained in their own land. And the prophet comments on their repentance to cause the people of Judah to imitate their holiness.

CHAPTER 4

It might seem that the first two verses of this chapter would have been better added to the previous chapter, for they are directed to Israel, the ten tribes, encouraging them to hold firmly to their resolution (vv. 1–2). The rest of the chapter concerns Judah and Jerusalem. 1. They are called to repent and reform (vv. 3–4). 2. They are warned of the advance of Nebuchadnezzar and his forces against them (vv. 5–18). 3. To affect them all the more, the prophet himself bitterly mourns and sympathizes with his people concerning the disasters that this desolation will bring on them (vv. 19–31).

Verses 1–2

When God called to faithless Israel to turn back to him (3:22), they immediately answered, *Lord, we return*. God here takes notice of their response:

1. "Do you say, *I will return*? Then you must *return unto me* (v. 1); make a thorough work of it. Return to the instituted worship of the God of Israel. You must completely abandon all sin and not hang onto any of the remains of idolatry: *Put away thy abominations* (detestable idols) *out of my sight*" (v. 1). Their idolatry was not only obvious to the eye of God but also offensive to it; it was an offense to the pure eyes of God's glory. They must

not return to sin; this is how some understand *Thou shalt not remove*, reading it, "Thou shalt not [or: you must not] wander." They must give God the glory due to his name (Ps 29:2; 96:8) (v. 2): "*Thou shalt swear, The Lord liveth.* His existence will be the most sacred fact for you.

2. He encourages them to remember their resolutions, for if they keep them:

2.1. They will be blessed themselves. "*If thou wilt return to me*, then"—as it may be read—"you shall return, that is, you will be brought back out of exile into your own land, as was promised in former times" (Dt 4:29; 30:2).

2.2. They will be a blessing to others (Ge 12:2), for their turning back to God will be a means of turning others to him who never knew him. See Isa 65:16. They will bless themselves *in the God of truth*, not in false gods; *in him shall they glory* (v. 2); they will make him their glory.

Verses 3–4

The prophet here turned his speech, in God's name, to the people in the place where he lived. We have heard what words he declared *toward the north* (3:12), for the comfort of those who were now in exile. Let us now see what he said to the *men of Judah and Jerusalem* (v. 3), who were now living in prosperity, to convict and awaken them. In these two verses he exhorts them to repent and reform in order to prevent the devastating judgments that are about to break in on them. Notice:

1. The duties required of them.

1.1. They must act toward their hearts as they did toward land that they expected to gain any good from; they must plow it (v. 3): "*Break up your fallow ground.* Plow your land, *sow not among thorns*, so that you do not labor in vain, as you have long been doing. Put yourselves into the right attitude to receive mercy from God and put away everything that keeps him from you, and then you may expect to receive mercy and to prosper in your endeavors to help yourselves." An unconvinced, unhumbled heart is like fallow ground, uncultivated and unoccupied. It is ground that can be made better, but it is unfenced, unfruitful, and overgrown with thorns and weeds, which are the natural products of the sinful heart. Unless it is renewed with grace, rain and sunshine are lost on it (Heb 6:7–8). We should be concerned to get this fallow ground plowed. We must look deeply into our own hearts and uproot those impurities that, like thorns, choke our endeavors.

1.2. They must do to their souls what was done to their bodies when they were taken into covenant with God (v. 4): "*Circumcise yourselves to the Lord, and take away the foreskins of your heart.* Put to death the flesh and its sinful desires (Ro 13:14; Gal 5:24). Do not boast about physical circumcision, for that is simply a sign and has no meaning without the thing signified. It is a sign of dedication. Do in sincerity what was done in profession by your circumcision; devote and consecrate yourselves to the Lord."

2. The danger threatened. "Repent and reform, *lest my fury come forth* (or my wrath will break out and burn) *like fire*" (v. 4). What is to be feared by us more than anything else is the wrath of God. It is the *evil of our doings* (actions) (v. 4) that kindles the fire of God's wrath against us. The consideration of the imminent danger should wake us to *sanctify ourselves to God's glory* and to see to it that we are *sanctified by his grace*.

Verses 5–18

God's usual method is to warn before he wounds. In these verses God gives notice to the Jews of the general devastation that will soon be brought on them by a foreign invasion. This must be declared in all the cities and towns of Judah and the streets of Jerusalem, so that everyone may hear and be either brought to repentance or left without excuse (Ro 2:1).

1. The war is declared, and notice is given of the advance of the enemy. It is made known now, some years before, by the prophet (vv. 5–6). The *trumpet* must be *blown*, the *standard* (signal) must be raised, and a summons must be issued to the people to *gather together* and draw *toward Zion*, either to guard it or because they expect to be guarded by it. The militia must be raised, and all the forces mustered. Those who are fit for service must go into the fortified cities to guard them. Those who are weak must *withdraw* and *not stay*.

2. A message comes with information of the approach of the king of Babylon and his army. The enemy is compared here:

2.1. To *a lion* that *comes up from his* (its) *thicket* when it is hungry, to seek its prey (v. 7). The helpless animals are terrified and so become an easy target for it. Nebuchadnezzar is this roaring, tearing lion, *the destroyer of the nations*, now *on his way* toward the land of Judah. The *destroyer of the Gentiles* will be the *destroyer of the Jews* too when by their idolatry they have made themselves like the Gentiles. He has *gone forth from his place*, from Babylon, against *this land*; the cities will be *laid waste, without inhabitants*: they will be "overgrown with grass as a field," as some read it.

2.2. To a *drying*, blasting *wind* (v. 11), which blights the fruits of the earth and withers them, a wind such as comes *out of the north* and *drives away rain* (Pr 25:23), a *black*, freezing wind. Wherever they go, it will surround them. It is *a wind of the high places* (barren heights) *in the wilderness* (v. 11), or of the plain, a wind that beats down on the tops of the hills or carries everything in front of it on the plain. It will come in its full force *toward the daughters of my people* (v. 11), who have been brought up so tenderly. This fierce wind will come against them *not to fan, nor cleanse* (v. 11) them; it will be *a full wind* (v. 12). *This* will come *to me*, or rather "for me"; it will come at God's command and will fulfill the purpose for which he sends it (Isa 55:11).

2.3. To clouds and a whirlwind for speed (v. 13). The Babylonian army will *come up as clouds* driven by the wind. The horses are *swifter than eagles* (v. 13) when they attack their prey.

2.4. To watchers and the guards of a field (vv. 15–17). *The voice declares from Dan*, the northernmost city of Canaan. They received the news and passed it on to Jerusalem. Now, what is the news? *"Make ye mention to the nations*, the cities of the ten tribes, so that they may take care of their own safety; but to Jerusalem *publish* it, declare it, for that is the game being shot at. Let them know that *watchers have come from a far country* (v. 16), that is, a besieging army, soldiers, who will watch for every opportunity to cause trouble. They are coming at full speed, and they *give out their voice against the cities of Judah* (v. 16). Just as *keepers* (guards) *of a field* (v. 17) surround it to keep everyone out of it, so they will surround the cities of Judah until they surrender. They are *against her round about, compassing her in on every side*." See Lk 19:43.

3. The terrible cause of this judgment is stated.

3.1. They sinned against God; it is all their own fault: *She has been rebellious against me, saith the Lord* (v. 17). The Babylonians are breaking in on them, and it is sin that has opened up the gap where they will enter: *Thy way and*

thy doings have procured (your own conduct and actions have brought) *these things unto thee* (v. 18). Sin is the cause of all our troubles.

3.2. God is angry with them for their sin. It is the *fierce anger of the Lord* (v. 8) that will make the army of the Babylonians so fierce.

3.3. In his just anger he has condemned them to this punishment: *Now also will I give sentence against them* (v. 12).

4. The terrible effects of this judgment are described. The people who want to fight will despair and will not have the heart to resist the enemy in the least (v. 8): *"For this gird yourself with* (put on) *sackcloth, lament and howl* (wail)." Instead of putting on the sword and preparing for battle, they will put on sackcloth. While the enemy is still far away, they will give themselves up and cry out, *Woe unto us! For we are spoiled* (ruined) (v. 13). Judah and Jerusalem had been famous for brave soldiers, but notice the effects of sin: by depriving people of their confidence toward God, it deprives them of their courage toward others. *At that day the heart of the king shall perish*, both his wisdom and his courage. His rulers and privy councillors will be as much in despair as he. The work of priests was to encourage the people; they were to say, *Fear not, and let not your hearts faint* (Dt 20:2–3). But now *the priests* themselves *shall be astonished* (horrified) (v. 9) and will have no heart to encourage the people. Our Savior foretold that at the last destruction of Jerusalem *men's hearts* would *fail them for fear* (Lk 21:26).

5. The prophet complains about the people's being deceived (v. 10). It is expressed strangely: *Ah! Lord God, surely thou hast greatly deceived this people, saying, You shall have peace.* We are sure that God deceives no one. But:

5.1. The people deceived themselves with the promises that God had made; they relied on the promises even though they were not concerned to fulfill the conditions on which the promises depended. They therefore deceived themselves and then corruptly complained that God had deceived them.

5.2. The false prophets deceived them with the promises of peace that they made to them in God's name (23:17; 27:9).

5.3. God had allowed the false prophets to deceive and allowed the people to be deceived by them, giving both up to *strong delusions* to punish them *for not receiving the truth in the love of it* (2Th 2:10–11).

5.4. It may be read as a question: *"Hast thou indeed thus deceived this people?* (v. 10). It is clear that they are greatly deceived, for they expect *peace*, whereas the *sword reaches unto the soul"* (v. 10). Now, was it God who deceived them? No; he has often warned them of judgments, but their own prophets deceive them and cry out peace to those to whom the God of heaven does not speak peace. It is pitiful to see people flattered to their own destruction, promising themselves peace when war is at their door.

6. The prophet attempts to free them from their deception.

6.1. He shows them their wound. They can discern their punishment in their sin (v. 18): *"This is thy wickedness, because it is bitter.* It produces bitter sorrow that *reaches unto the heart*; the sword *reaches to the soul"* (v. 10).

6.2. He shows them the cure (v. 14). *"O Jerusalem! wash thy heart from wickedness, that thou mayest be saved."* By *Jerusalem* he means each one of the inhabitants of Jerusalem, for everyone has his own heart, and it is personal reformation that must help the public one.

Everyone must turn away from *his own evil way* (35:15) and cleanse *his own evil heart* (v. 14). Reformation is absolutely necessary for salvation. No reformation saves except one that reaches the heart. There will be no effective reformation of the way of life without a reformation of the mind. In the second part of the verse he reasons with them: *How long shall thy vain thoughts lodge within thee* (will you harbor wicked thoughts)? (v. 14). *Thoughts of iniquity* (Isa 59:7) or evil are the corrupt thoughts that are the offspring of the evil *heart*, from which all other sins are produced (Mt 15:19). Some understand the *vain thoughts* here to be the frivolous excuses the people used to brush aside the rebukes and calls of the word, supporting themselves in their own evil ways.

Verses 19–31

The prophet is in anguish here and cries out like someone in intense pain. The expressions are passionate enough to melt a heart of stone. *My bowels! My bowels! I am pained at my very heart* (v. 19). A good man, in such a bad world as this is, must be a *man of sorrows* (Isa 53:3). *My heart makes a noise in* (my heart pounds within) *me* (v. 19), through the turmoil of my spirits, and *I cannot hold my peace* (v. 19). It is not for himself or any suffering in his family that he is grieving as he is, but purely because of the public: it is his people's situation that he takes so much to heart.

1. They are very sinful and do not want to be reformed (v. 22). These are the words of God himself. God calls them his people even though they are foolish. They have rejected him, but he has not rejected them (Ro 11:1). They are *foolish*, for *they have not known me* (v. 22). They are *wise* (skilled) *to do evil*, to plan trouble against those who live quietly in the land; they are skilled enough at working out how they can satisfy their sinful desires and then cover them up and disguise them. But *to do good they have no knowledge* (v. 22); they will not apply their minds to it.

2. They are very miserable and cannot be helped.

2.1. He cries out, *Because thou hast heard, O my soul! the sound of the trumpet*, and *seen the standard*, both giving the battle cry (vv. 19, 21). He does not say, "Thou hast heard, O my ear!" but, *O my soul!* because it is by the spirit of prophecy that he sees it. His *soul* heard it from the words of God, as if he had heard it with his physical ears. Although he foretold this disaster, he was far from *desiring the woeful day* (17:16). He tried to wake them up to a holy fear so that they might prevent judgment by a true and prompt repentance.

2.2. Let us see the destruction foretold here:

2.2.1. It is swift and *sudden*: *Destruction upon destruction is cried* (v. 20), *breach upon breach* (Job 16:14), one sad disaster on the heels of another. The death of Josiah opened the floodgates; three months after that, his son and successor Jehoahaz was deposed by the king of Egypt. Within two or three years, Nebuchadnezzar besieged Jerusalem and took it, and from that time on he was continually attacking the land of Judah, until he completed the ruin in the destruction of Jerusalem: but *suddenly were their tents spoiled, and their curtains* (shelter) *in a moment* (v. 20). Though the cities held out for some time, the country was laid waste at the beginning, the shepherds and everyone who lived in tents were plundered immediately. When the Babylonian army first came into the land, therefore, we find the Recabites, who lived in tents, withdrawing to Jerusalem (Jer 35:11).

2.2.2. This war continued long, for the people were stubborn and refused to submit to the king of Babylon; they took every opportunity to rebel against him. This is

complained about (v. 21): *How long shall I see the* battle *standard?* Will the sword continue to devour forever (2Sa 2:26)?

2.2.3. *The whole land is spoiled*, destroyed or plundered (v. 20). This was how it was in the beginning, when the country was laid waste, and ultimately the whole land was reduced to chaos.

2.2.3.1. The earth was *without form, and void* (v. 23), as it was at the creation. It was *tohu* and *bohu*—the same words are used in the creation account (Ge 1:2)—as far as the land of Judea was concerned.

2.2.3.2. The *heavens* too were *without light*. This refers to the *darkness* that was *upon the face of the deep* (Ge 1:2). Not only did the earth fail them; heaven frowned on them. They had darkness with their trouble, for they could not see through their troubles. The smoke of their houses and cities that were burned by the enemy darkened the sun, so that *the heavens had no light* (v. 23). Or it may be taken figuratively: *The earth* (that is, the common people) was made poor and confused, and the *heavens* (that is, the leaders and rulers) *had no light* (v. 23), no wisdom in themselves, nor were they any comfort to the people or a guide to them.

2.2.3.3. *The mountains trembled, and the hills moved lightly* (swayed) (v. 24). The *everlasting mountains* seemed to be *scattered* (Hab 3:6). The mountains on which they had worshiped their idols trembled, as if they were aware of the people's guilt. The hills moved to and fro, relieved of the burden *of a sinful nation* (Isa 1:4).

2.2.3.4. Not only the earth but also the air was depopulated and left uninhabited (v. 25): *I beheld the cities, and, lo, there was no man* to be seen. Even *the birds of the heavens*, which used to fly about and *sing among the branches* (Ps 104:12), were no more seen or heard. The *land of Judah* had now become like the *lake of Sodom*; see Dt 29:23.

2.2.3.5. Both the ground and the houses were devastated (v. 26): *Lo, the fruitful place was a wilderness*. The *cities*, too, and their gates and walls were *broken down* and leveled. Those who look no farther than secondary causes will attribute it to the plans and rage of the invaders, but the prophet, who looks beyond that to the primary cause, says that it is *at the presence of the Lord* (v. 26).

2.2.3.6. The meaning of all this was that the nation would be completely ruined, both the country and the town. *The whole land shall be desolate*; arable land and pastureland would all be laid waste (v. 27). And *the whole city shall flee for fear of the horsemen and bowmen*. Rather than lie exposed to their rage, the inhabitants would *go into the thickets*. They would *climb up upon the rocks*, for *every city shall be forsaken* (v. 29). This is a gloomy picture of the approaching desolation, but in the midst of all these threats came one encouraging word (v. 27): *Yet will not I make a full end*, for God would reserve a remnant. Jerusalem would be rebuilt, and the land would be inhabited again. This was included to encourage those who *trembled at God's word* (Isa 66:5).

2.2.4. Their case was helpless. God would not help them; he told them this plainly (v. 28). They would not repent and turn back from their sins (2:25), and so God would not relent and turn back from his judgments. Nor could they help themselves (vv. 30–31). They flattered themselves with the hopes that they would still find some means. But the prophet told them that when the judgment approached, they would be completely at a loss: *When thou art spoiled, what wilt thou do?* They would be despised by their allies whom they depended on. He compared Jerusalem to a prostitute abandoned by all the immoral men who used to seek her. She did what she could to make herself look good among the nations, to look like a valuable ally. She complimented them through her ambassadors. She *clothed herself with crimson*, as if she were rich, and *decked herself with ornaments* (jewels) *of gold*, as if her treasuries were still full. She *rent her face with painting* (v. 30), putting the best possible colors on her present distresses. But although this painting makes the face look beautiful for the present, it really "rends" it, for paint spoils the skin, cracks it, and makes it rough. "And in the end, *in vain shalt thou make thyself fair* (v. 30); all your neighbors are aware to what a lowly condition you have been brought. The Babylonians will strip you of your scarlet and jewels." This seems to be an allusion to the story of Jezebel, who thought that by making herself look fair and fine she would defy her fate, but in vain (2Ki 9:30, 33). They will find their troubles to be like the pain of a woman in labor, which she cannot escape: *I have heard the voices of the daughter of Zion* (v. 31), her groans echoing to the triumphant shouts of the Babylonian army. Since her neighbors refused to pity her, Zion *bewailed herself*, gasping for breath, and she *spread her hands* (v. 31), reaching them out to receive help.

CHAPTER 5

Rebukes for sin and threats of judgment come together in this chapter. Judgments are threatened so that the rebukes for sin might be more effective in bringing the people to repentance. 1. The sins they are accused of are injustice (v. 1), hypocrisy in religion (v. 2), their hardness against God (v. 3), corruption and defilement among both poor and rich (vv. 4–5), idolatry and adultery (vv. 7–8), unfaithfulness to God (v. 11), defiance of him (vv. 12–13), and at the root of all this, lack of the fear of God (vv. 20–24). At the end of the chapter they are charged with violence and oppression (vv. 26–28), which defile the nation (vv. 30–31). 2. The judgments threatened are terrible (vv. 9, 29). A foreign enemy will be brought against them (vv. 15–17), take them into captivity (v. 19), and keep everything good from them (v. 25). But: 3. Here is an intimation given twice that God will not completely destroy them (vv. 10, 18). This was the theme and purpose of Jeremiah's preaching at the end of Josiah's reign and the beginning of Jehoiakim's.

Verses 1–9

Here is:

1. A challenge to produce one truly honest person in Jerusalem (v. 1). Jerusalem had become like the old world, in which *all flesh had corrupted their way* (Ge 6:12). "Look in *the streets*; look in *the broad places* (squares), where they keep their markets; *see if you can find a man*, 'a magistrate' (according to some), *that executes judgment* (v. 1), who administers justice impartially." *Truth has fallen in the street* (Isa 59:14). If there were only ten righteous people in Sodom (Ge 18:32), if only one out of a thousand (Ecc 7:28), or ten thousand, in Jerusalem, the city would be spared. "What do you make of those people in Jerusalem who continue to profess religion? Are they not people for whose sakes Jerusalem may be spared?" No; they are insincere in their profession (v. 2): *They say, the Lord liveth*, and will swear only by his name, but they *swear falsely*.

2. A complaint that the prophet makes to God of the willfulness of these people. God appealed to their eyes (v. 1), but here the prophet appeals to God's eyes (v. 3): "*Are not thy eyes upon the truth?* Do you not see every

person's true character? *They have made their faces harder than a rock. Thou hast consumed them*, crushed them severely, *but they have refused to receive correction*. They refused to receive instruction and learn from the correction."

3. The testing of both rich and poor, and the bad characterization given of both.

3.1. The poor were ignorant. He found many who *refused to return* (v. 3), for whom he was willing to make an excuse (v. 4): "*Surely these are poor, they are foolish*. They never had the advantage of a good education, and they do not have the resources to help themselves now by teaching themselves." Prevalent ignorance is the sad cause of great ungodliness and sin. There are not only God's poor but also the Devil's, who, despite their poverty, could *know the way of the Lord* (v. 5) so as to walk in it (Isa 30:21) and do their duty without being "walking encyclopedias" of religious facts, but remain stubbornly ignorant.

3.2. The rich were arrogant and proud (v. 5): "*I will get me to the great men* (leaders) and see if I can find them more open to the word and providence of God. But although *they know the way of the Lord and the judgment of their God*, they also are too stiff to submit to his rule: *These have altogether broken the yoke and burst the bonds*. They think they are too important to be corrected even by the sovereign Lord himself. The poor are weak, and the rich are stubborn, and so neither do their duty."

4. Some particular sins mentioned, the ones they were notoriously guilty of. *Their transgressions* indeed *were many*, and they added to their number and became more arrogant in them (v. 6). But two sins especially were to be looked on as unpardonable: spiritual and physical adultery. Their spiritual adultery gave to idols the honor that is due only to God: *They have sworn by them that are not gods* (v. 7). "They have sworn to them," as it may be read; they have joined them and made a covenant with them. Because they had abandoned God and served idols, he gave them up to their corrupt affections, and so they committed physical adultery as well. Those who dishonored him were left to dishonor themselves and their own families. They *committed adultery* without any sense of shame or fear of punishment, for they *assembled themselves by troops in the harlots'* (thronged to prostitutes') *houses* (v. 7) and were not embarrassed in the slightest to be seen by other people. Their lust was so arrogant that they became animals (v. 8); like well-fed horses, they *neighed every one after his neighbour's wife* (v. 8).

5. God's wrath against them for the universal defilement of their land. A foreign enemy will break in, and their country will be as if it were overrun and completely controlled by *a lion of the forest*, or by *a wolf of the evening* (v. 6), one that comes out at night, when it is hungry, and is very fierce and ravenous, or by *a leopard*, which is very swift and cruel. The enemy will *watch over their cities* to put the inhabitants into this sad dilemma: if they stay, they are starved; if they move, they are killed. *Every one that goeth out thence shall be torn in pieces* (v. 6). All this bloody work is caused by the *multitude of their transgressions* (v. 6). It is sin that makes the slaughter. "*Shall I not visit* (punish) *for these things?* Can you think that a God who is infinitely pure will turn a blind eye to such detestable immorality?" *Shall not my soul be avenged on such a nation as this?* (v. 9). It is not that those who have been guilty of these sins have not found mercy with God—Manasseh himself did (2Ch 33:1–13)—but it would not be for the glory of God to let a nation pass without some clear signs of his displeasure, because nations, as such, are punishable only in this life.

Verses 10–19

We may notice in these verses, as before:

1. The sin of this people, which condemns them to destruction (v. 10). *The house of Israel and the house of Judah*, though in conflict with one another, have agreed to *deal very treacherously* (completely unfaithfully) *against God*. They abandoned their worship of him and were hypocritical. They defied the judgments of God and the threats that have come from him by the mouth of his prophets (vv. 12–13). Many people are ruined by being made to believe that God will not be strict. *Neither shall we see sword nor famine* (v. 12). The prophets gave them fair warning, but they laughed it all off: "They are only talking like that because that's their job. It is not the word of the Lord, but only the language of their sad imaginations." They threatened the prophets: *"They shall become wind*, and *thus shall it be done unto them"* (v. 13). Do they try to frighten us by all this talk of famine? Let them be *fed with the bread of affliction* (1Ki 22:27). Are they telling us about the sword? Let them themselves perish by the sword!" (2:30).

2. The punishment of this people for their sin.

2.1. The threats they laughed at will be carried out (v. 14). God turns to the prophet Jeremiah, who has been among the prophets who have been ridiculed: *Behold, I will make my words in thy mouth fire, and the people wood* (v. 14). By their sin, sinners make themselves fuel.

2.2. The enemy they thought was not dangerous to them will be brought upon them. God gives the enemy their commission (v. 10): *"Go you up upon her walls*, climb them, trample on them, tread them down. With God's commission, walls of stone will become walls of mud. You may *take away her battlements* and leave the enclosed, fortified towns exposed, for her battlements *are not the Lord's*, and so he will not protect and strengthen them." The terrible work these invaders will make is described (v. 15): *Lo, I will bring a nation upon you, O house of Israel!* This nation of the Babylonians is here said to be a distant nation; it is *brought upon them from afar* (v. 15), and so it will stay long, so that the soldiers may pay themselves well for such a long march. It is a *mighty nation*, an *ancient nation*, which prides itself on how old it is and will therefore soon become proud and imperious. It is *a nation whose language thou knowest not* (v. 15); they spoke Aramaic. The difference in language will make it more difficult for them to discuss terms of peace. "They will not store up, but *eat up thy harvest* in the field *and thy bread* in the house, *which thy sons and thy daughters should eat. They shall eat up thy flocks and herds*, out of which you have taken sacrifices for your idols; they will not leave you the fruit of *thy vines and fig trees* (v. 17). They *shall impoverish thy fenced cities*, those cities *wherein thou trustedst* (v. 17) as a protection for the country."

3. A suggestion of the tender compassion God still has for them. The enemy is commissioned to destroy and devastate but must *not make a full end* (not destroy them completely) (v. 10). "Even *in those days*, dismal though they are, *I will not make a full end with you*," and if God will not, then neither will the enemy.

4. The justification of God in these proceedings. Just as he will be seen to be gracious in not destroying them completely, so he will also be seen to be righteous in coming near it. The people *will say, Wherefore* (why) *doth the Lord our God do all this unto us? —* as if there did not appear to be enough reason to act against such a sinful nation. The prophet is instructed what answer to give them. He must tell them that God is doing this against them because of what they have done against him, and so they may read their sin in their punishment. Have they forgotten how often they *served strange* (foreign) *gods in their own land* (v. 19)? Is it not just of God, therefore, to make them *serve strangers* in a foreign land?

Verses 20–24

Having rebuked them, the prophet is here sent to them on another mission, which he must declare in Judah; its purpose is to persuade them to fear God.

1. He complains about the shameful stupor in which this people lies: they are *a foolish people and without understanding* (v. 21); they do not discern the mind of God even though it is plainly declared to them by his prophets and by his providence (v. 21): *They have eyes, but they see not, ears, but they hear not*. They have intellectual faculties, but they do not use them as they should. Their wills are stubborn and they cannot submit to the rules of divine Law (v. 23): *This people has a revolting* (obstinate) *and a rebellious heart*. It is the corrupt bias of the will that makes the understanding foolish and senseless. The character of this people is the true character of all people until the grace of God has brought about a change. We are *foolish, slow of understanding*, and have stubborn and rebellious hearts, not only rebelling from him by a deep-rooted aversion to what is good, but also rebellious toward him by a strong inclination to do what is evil.

2. He ascribes this to the lack of the fear of God. When he observes them to be senseless, he asks, *"Fear you not me, saith the Lord, and will you not tremble at my presence?"* (v. 22). When he observes that they have turned aside and gone away, he adds, as the cause of their apostasy (v. 24), *Neither say they in their hearts, Let us now fear the Lord our God*. Bad thoughts come into their mind because they will not admit and receive good thoughts.

3. He suggests some of those things that are suitable for giving us a holy fear of God.

3.1. We must fear the Lord and his greatness (v. 22). The prophet gives one example of God's greatness: he keeps the sea within limits. Although the tides flow with great power twice a day and would drown the world if they continued to flow, although in a storm the waves dash against the shore with incredible force, they still return, and no harm is done. *This is the Lord's doing*, and if it were not what usually happens, it would be *marvellous in our eyes* (Ps 118:23). A wall of sand will be as effective as a wall of bronze to restrain the flowing waves, to teach us that *a soft answer turns away wrath*, calms a foaming rage, when *grievous words* (Pr 15:1), like hard rocks, only exasperate. This boundary is placed *by a perpetual decree* (v. 22), or "by an ordinance of antiquity," and this reading sends us back to the creation of the world, when God separated the sea and the dry land (Ge 1:9–10) (which is admirably described in Ps 104:6–26 and Job 38:8–41). It is *a perpetual decree* (v. 22); it has had its effect to this day and will continue until day and night come to an end. This is a good reason why we should fear God, for we see that he is a God of universal sovereignty.

3.2. We must fear the Lord and his goodness (Hos 3:5). We must *fear the Lord our God*, that is, we must worship him, because he is continually doing us good. He gives us both *the former and the latter rain* (spring and autumn rains), the former a little after sowing, the latter a little before harvest, and this is how *he reserves to us the appointed weeks of harvest* (v. 24). God is therefore to be acknowledged in the mercy of harvest for his power, goodness, and faithfulness, for they all come from him.

This is a good reason why we should fear him: we should want to keep ourselves in his love because we have a necessary dependence on him.

Verses 25–31

Here:

1. The prophet shows them what trouble their sins have caused them: "It is *your sin* that *has withholden good from you* (v. 25) when God was ready to give it to you." It is what makes the heavens like bronze and the earth like iron (Dt 28:23).

2. He shows them how great their sins are. When they abandoned the worship of the true God, even moral integrity was lost among them: *Among my people are found wicked men* (v. 26), and they are so much the worse for being found among God's people.

2.1. They are spiteful and nasty, delighting to cause trouble. They have been *found* (that is, caught) in the very act of committing evil. Just as hunters or fowlers set traps for their game, so they *lie in wait to catch men* (v. 26). They make a sport of it. They plan ways of causing trouble to good people, whom they hate for their goodness; they especially seek to harm those who faithfully correct them (Isa 29:21) or those whose possessions they covet: it was for this reason that Jezebel trapped Naboth to gain his vineyard.

2.2. They are false and unfaithful (v. 27): *As a cage is full of birds*, and of food to fatten them up for the table, so are *their houses full of deceit*, of wealth obtained fraudulently. Whoever deals with them will be cheated by them if they can be. Their evil deeds know no limits (v. 28). Those who act deceitfully in the name of the law and justice perhaps cause more trouble than evildoers who are openly forceful and violent. The people even prosper in these evil ways, and so their hearts become hardened in them. *They have become great* and powerful in the world; they have become rich (v. 27), and they thrive on it. They are sleek and smooth: *They shine* (v. 28); they look fair and bright; everybody admires them. And they "pass by matters of evil," as some read the following words. They *are not in trouble as other men* (Ps 73:5), much less as we might expect bad people to be.

2.3. When they become powerful, they do not do good with it: *They judge not the cause, the cause of the fatherless and the right of the needy* (v. 28). And *yet they prosper* still; *God layeth not folly to them*, God charges no one with wrongdoing (Job 24:12). Certainly, then, the things of this world are not the best things, for often the worst people have the most of them; yet we are not to think that God approves of their practices. No; although *sentence against* their *evil works be not executed speedily* (Ecc 8:11), it will still be executed.

2.4. There is a general corruption (vv. 30–31): *A wonderful* (shocking) *and horrible thing is committed in the land*. The corruption of such people, who are privileged and advanced, is shocking, horrible, to be detested. The leaders mislead the people: *The prophets prophesy falsely* (v. 31). Religious faith is never more dangerously attacked than under the cloak of divine revelation. And the priests make use of these prophets, for they *bear rule by their means* (v. 31); they support themselves in their grandeur and wealth, laziness and self-indulgent luxury, by the help of the false prophets. The people, for their part, are very happy to be misled: "They are *my people*," God says, "and should have borne witness against the evil of their priests and prophets, but they *love to have it so*" (v. 31). They love to be led by a loose rein, and they are fond of those rulers who will not restrain their sinful desires.

3. He shows them how fatal the consequences of this will be. *Shall not I visit for* (punish) *these things?* Sometimes mercy triumphs over judgment (Jas 2:13). Here, however, judgment triumphs over mercy: *Shall I not visit* (punish)? (v. 29). We are sure that infinite Wisdom knows how to reconcile matters between the two. *Shall not my soul be avenged?* (v. 29). Yes, without doubt, if the sinners do not repent. *What will you do in the end thereof?* (v. 31). Those who walk in wrong ways would do well to consider that such ways lead to greater sin and complete destruction.

CHAPTER 6

In this chapter, as before, we have: 1. A prophecy of the invading of the land of Judah and the besieging of Jerusalem by the Babylonian army (vv. 1–6), the plunder they would take of the country (v. 9), and the terror at that time (vv. 22–26). 2. An account of those sins of Judah and Jerusalem that caused God to bring this devastating judgment: their oppression (v. 7), their contempt of the word of God (vv. 10–12), their worldliness (v. 13), the unfaithfulness of their prophets (v. 14), their arrogance in sin (v. 15), and their stubbornness in correction (vv. 18–19), which made their sacrifices unacceptable to him (v. 20) and for which he gave them up to ruin (v. 21), first testing them (v. 27) and then rejecting them as incapable of being reformed (vv. 28–30). 3. Good advice given them in the midst of all this, but in vain (vv. 8, 16–17).

Verses 1–8

Here is:

1. Judgment threatened against Judah and Jerusalem. The city sees no clouds gathering; everything looks calm and peaceful. The prophet tells them, however, that they will soon be invaded by a foreign power *from the north*, which will devastate everything. It is foretold:

1.1. That the alarm and signal will be loud and terrible: this is described in v. 1. The children of Benjamin, in whose territory part of Jerusalem lies, are here called to flee for their lives to the country, for the city, to which it was first thought advisable for them to flee (4:5–6), will soon be made too difficult for them. They are told to raise the signal throughout the country and to do what they can for their own safety: *Blow the trumpet in Tekoa*—a town that lay some eleven miles (about seventeen kilometers) south of Jerusalem, although some scholars think it was twelve miles (about nineteen kilometers) north of Jerusalem. *Set up a sign of fire* (that is, light the beacons) *in Beth-haccerem* (v. 1)—the "house of the vineyard," which lay on a hill between Jerusalem and Tekoa. This may be taken ironically: "Do your best to preserve your lives; it will all be in vain. When you have done your best, there will still be a great destruction, for it is futile to oppose God's judgments."

1.2. That the attempt on them will be formidable. *The daughter of Zion*, on whom the attack is made, is compared *to a comely* (beautiful) *and delicate woman* (v. 2). Because she is not used to hardship, she will be less able either to resist the enemy or to bear the destruction. The generals and their armies are compared to *shepherds* and *their flocks* (v. 3); they will come in such numbers, with the soldiers following their leaders as sheep follow their shepherds. Just as shepherds easily make themselves masters of an open field, which is common land, owned by no one—they *pitch their tents* (v. 3) in it, and their flocks quickly eat it bare—so will the Babylonian army easily break in on the land of Judah, forcefully making for themselves free quarters where they want to and devouring everything in a short time. God will commission them to make this destruction. It is he who says (v. 4), *Prepare you war against her*, for he is the Lord of Hosts, and he has said (v. 6), *Hew* (cut) *you down trees, and cast a mount* (build siege ramps) *against Jerusalem*. God has said, "*This is the city to be visited* (v. 6) by divine justice, and this is the time of her punishment." The Babylonians will decide to be very swift: *Arise, let us go up at noon* (v. 4), although it is the hottest time of the day; in fact (v. 5), *Arise, let us go up by night*, even though it is dark. "*Let us go up*, and let us destroy her palaces and control their wealth."

2. The cause of this judgment given: it is their evil; they have brought it on themselves. They will be oppressed because they have been the oppressors; they have dealt harshly with one another, each in their own way, as they have had power and advantage, and now the enemy will come and deal harshly with them all. Sin has become natural to them (v. 7): she *casts* (pours) *out wickedness*, in hatred and trouble, *as a fountain casts* (pours) *out her waters*, plentifully and constantly. The cry of this wickedness has come before God as that of Sodom did (Ge 18:20): *Before me continually are grief and wounds* (v. 7)—the complaints of those who find themselves unjustly wounded in bodies or spirits, in possessions or reputation. The One who is the common Parent of the human race sees and feels, and sooner or later will take revenge on, the troubles and wrongs that people do to one another.

3. How to prevent this judgment (v. 8). "*Be thou instructed, O Jerusalem!* Receive the instruction given you both by the Law of God and by his prophets; come to your senses finally and be wise about your own lives, *Lest my soul depart*, or turn away, *from thee.*" This suggests what tender affection and concern God had for them; his very soul had been joined to them, and nothing but sin could separate it. The God of mercy is reluctant to depart even from an offensive people, and he is serious in wanting them to truly repent and reform to prevent things coming to such a critical point.

Verses 9–17

The subjects of this paragraph are the same as those of the last, for we need to have God's commands repeated to us often and in detail.

1. The ruin of Judah and Jerusalem is threatened here. We heard earlier of the speed with which the Babylonian army will go (vv. 4–5); now here we have the havoc they will wreak. The enemy will be insatiable in thirsting for treasure. *They shall thoroughly glean the remnant of Israel as a vine* (v. 9), just like those who, gathering grapes, are determined to leave none behind and therefore again pass their hands over the branches to put more in. Perhaps the people were *given to covetousness* (v. 13) and had not observed the law of God that forbade them to *glean all their grapes* (Lev 19:10), and now they themselves will be *thoroughly gleaned* (v. 9). The children will perish in the disaster that the ancestors' sins have caused. The execution will reach *the assembly of young men*, their happy times together; they will be *cut off together* (v. 11). *Even the husband with the wife shall be taken, and the old with the full of days* (v. 11), whose deaths can contribute no more to their safety than their lives could contribute to their service. *Their houses shall then be turned to others* (v. 12).

1.1. The prophet justifies himself in preaching so terribly (v. 11): *I am full of the fury of the Lord.* He takes no pleasure in making the threat, but he cannot contain himself; he is *weary with holding in* (v. 11), but he is so *full of power by the Spirit of the Lord of hosts* (Mic 3:8) that he must speak.

1.2. He condemns the false prophets (vv. 13–14): *The priest and the prophet* have *dealt falsely*; they have not told the people their faults and the danger they were in. They should have been their doctors, but they killed their patients by giving them everything they wanted, flattering them with assurances that they were in no danger (v. 14): they have *healed the hurt of the daughter of my people slightly*. They merely soothed people in their sins, and gave them sleeping pills to give them some relief, while the disease was attacking their vital organs. They said, "*Peace, peace*—everything will be fine." They cried out that all was well, even though *there was no peace* (v. 14), because they continued in their arrogant ungodliness. Those who flatter us sinfully are to be considered our false friends—that is, our worst and most dangerous enemies.

2. The sin of Judah and Jerusalem, which caused God to bring this ruin, is declared.

2.1. They cannot bear to be told about their danger. God tells the prophet to warn them of the judgment to come (v. 9), "but," he says (v. 10), "*to whom shall I speak and give warning? I cannot speak that they may hear*, for *their ear is uncircumcised*. The *word of the Lord is unto them a reproach* (is offensive to them); the rebukes and threats that are considered offensive will certainly be turned into woes."

2.2. They are devoted to the things of this world and carried away by the love of it (v. 13): "*From the least of them even to the greatest, every one is given to covetousness*, greedy for dishonest gain." This has made them oppressive and violent (vv. 6–7). This has hardened their hearts against the word of God and his prophets.

2.3. They have even gone beyond the point of being ashamed. Their hearts were so hardened that *they were not at all ashamed, neither could they blush* (v. 15); their faces were so insensitive to God. They decided to defy God himself. Those who will not submit in penitential shame will not escape complete destruction: *Therefore they shall fall among* those *that fall* (v. 15); they will be made to tremble, because they would not blush. Those who sin and cannot be ashamed of it are in desperate situation now, and things will be worse with them soon. At first, they hardened themselves and would not be ashamed; later they were so hardened that they could not be. As Seneca wrote: "They have lost the only good which once was mixed with much bad, that is, shame for having done wrong."

3. They are reminded of the good advice that has often been given them in vain. They have had a great deal said to them:

3.1. By way of advice concerning their duty (v. 16). God has been used to saying to them, *Stand in the ways and see.* He wanted them to do as travelers who want to go along the way that will bring them to their destination: they ask which is the right way. Oh that people were so *wise for their souls* (Pr 9:12)! "*Ask for the old paths* (v. 16), *inquire of the former age* (Job 8:8), *ask thy father, thy elders* (Dt 32:7), and you will find that the way of godliness has always been the way God has acknowledged and blessed and in which people have prospered. Ask for the *old paths*, the time-honored paths that the patriarchs traveled, Abraham, Isaac, and Jacob; and if you hope to inherit the promises made to them, follow in their footsteps. *Ask for the old paths: Where is the good way?*"

(v. 16). But there is an *old way which wicked men have trodden* (Job 22:15). When we ask for the old paths, it is only to find the *good way*. This shows us that the way of religious faith and godliness is a good old way, the way that all the saints in all ages have walked on. "When you have found the good way, *walk therein* and persevere in it." Some believe this advice was to be given them with reference to the struggles between the true and false prophets: "*Stand in the way*" (v. 16), God says, "and inquire which of these two agrees with the written word and the usual methods of God's providence, which directs you to the good way, and follow it. *Walk in the good old way*, and you will enjoy God and yourselves, and the way will lead you to true rest. You will find an abundant reward at the end of your journey." *But they said, "We will not walk therein* (v. 16); we will still not deny ourselves and our inclinations in order to *walk in it."*

3.2. By way of warning concerning their danger. Because they refused to be ruled by fair reasoning, God used lesser judgments to threaten greater, and he sent his prophets to frighten them with the thought of the danger they were in (v. 17): *Also I set watchmen over you.* This was the chorus of the prophets' song; *Hearken to the sound of the trumpet* (v. 17). In his providence, God sounds the trumpet (Zec 9:14); the watchmen hear it (4:19), and they call on others to listen to it too. *But* the people *said, "We will not hearken* (v. 17); we will not take any notice; the prophets may as well save themselves and us the trouble."

Verses 18–30

Here:

1. God appeals to the whole world to recognize how justly he is dealing with Judah and Jerusalem (vv. 18–19): "*Hear, you nations, and know* especially, *O congregation* of the powerful leaders of the nations. Judah and Jerusalem all wonder that *I* should *bring evil upon this people* (v. 19), who are in covenant with me. *Wherefore has the Lord done thus to this land?* they ask (Dt 29:24). Know then that the evil brought on them is *the fruit of their thought* (v. 19). They thought that by making an alliance with foreigners they would strengthen themselves, and by that they weakened and exposed themselves. That is the just punishment of their disobedience and rebellion. It is because they *have not hearkened to my words nor to my law* (v. 19), but rejected it all. Therefore you cannot say that anything wrong is being done to them."

2. God rejects their plea, by which they insisted that their services were adequate to atone for their sins. Unfortunately, this plea is empty (v. 20): "*To what purpose come there to me incense and sweet cane, to be burned as perfume on the golden altar? What do I care about your burnt offerings and your sacrifices?"* Sacrifice and incense were appointed to point them to a Mediator and help their faith in him. Where this good use was made of them, they were acceptable; God respected them and those who offered them. But when they were offered with the thought that with them the people purchased a license to continue sinning, then, far from being pleasing to God, these offerings greatly provoked him.

3. He foretells the devastation. God intends to destroy them because they hate to be reformed (Lev 26:23) (v. 21): *I will lay stumbling blocks before this people*, occasions for falling not into sin but into trouble. God will slow down all the means they use to provide for their own safety. The friends of the enemy will be obstacles to them, and *the fathers and the sons* of the people of Judah *together* (parents and children) *shall fall upon them*—upon those

obstacles (v. 21); neither the parents with their wisdom nor the children with their strength will escape the enemy. He will make the Babylonians his instruments. Babylon, far to the north, and some of the countries that are subject to the king of Babylon, must be used in this service (vv. 22–23). They are *a great nation*, a warlike people. *They lay hold on bow and spear* and know how to use them. *They ride upon horses* and therefore move all the more swiftly and press even harder in battle. They *are cruel and have no mercy*; their voice *roars like the sea.* They are *set in array* (in battle formation) *against thee, O daughter of Zion!*

4. He describes the fear that Judah and Jerusalem will be in when this formidable enemy approaches (vv. 24–26). "When *we have but heard the fame* (reports) *thereof, our hands wax feeble* (hang limp) (v. 24), and we have no heart to offer any resistance. *Anguish has taken hold of us,* and we are like *a woman in travail"* (v. 24). A sense of guilt discourages people on the approach of trouble. They confine themselves to their houses; they would rather die tamely than fight or flee to help themselves. They say one to another (v. 25), "*Go not forth into the field, nor walk by the way.* Your life will be in danger if you do, for the *sword of the enemy* and the fear of it are *on every side.*" The prophet calls on them to sadly mourn (v. 26): "*O daughter of my people,* listen to your God calling you to mourning. Do not only put on sackcloth for a day; do not only put ashes on your head, but *wallow thyself* (roll) *in ashes,* as parents *mourn for an only son.*"

5. He appoints the prophet as a judge over this people who are now standing on trial: *I have set thee for a tower,* or as a guard on a tower, *among my people, that thou mayest know and try their way* (v. 27). God appeals to the prophet himself in this way, to his own observation, so that the prophet may be fully satisfied in the justice of God's actions against the people. God set him up as a tower, but also made him *a fortress, a strong tower* (Ps 61:3; Pr 18:10), giving him courage to bear the brunt of their displeasure. He will find:

5.1. That they are miserably defiled (v. 28): *They are all grievous revolters* (rebellers)—literally, "rebellers of rebellers," the worst of rebellers. They *walk with slanders,* slandering one another. They are *brass* (bronze) *and iron,* base metals. They were like silver and gold, but they have become corrupt. As *they are all revolters* (rebellers), *so they are all corrupters,* also keen to defile others.

5.2. That they will never be reclaimed and reformed; it is futile to think of reforming them, for various ways have been tried, all to no effect (vv. 29–30). He compares them to ore that is thought to contain some good metal and is therefore put into the furnace by the refiner, but turns out to be all worthless dross. God has used ways to refine this people by his prophets and his providences, but it was all in vain. By a series of adversities, they have been constantly refined, but it was all useless. *The bellows* have been kept so near the fire to blow on it that they *are burnt* with its heat (v. 29). The *lead*—which was then used to refine silver, as quicksilver once was too—*is consumed of the fire* and has not done its work (v. 29). *The founder melts* (the refining goes on) *in vain*; the work is lost, *for the wicked are not plucked away* (not purged out) (v. 29); no care is taken to drive out of fellowship those who, being corrupt, are in danger of defiling others. Doom is pronounced on them (v. 30): *Reprobate silver shall they be called*, useless and worthless; they glitter as if they had some silver in them, but there is nothing of real goodness to be found among them, and *the Lord has rejected them* (v. 30). God has *no pleasure in the death* (Eze 18:32) and destruction of sinners. He did not reject them until he had used every proper means to reform them; nor did he abandon them as dross until it was clear that they were *reprobate silver* (v. 30).

CHAPTER 7

Having rebuked the people in God's name for their sins, the prophet continues trying to humble and awaken them: 1. He shows them the invalidity of the plea that they have the temple of God among them and constantly attend its services (vv. 1–11). 2. He reminds them of the desolation of Shiloh and foretells that the destruction of Jerusalem will be similar (vv. 12–16). 3. God describes to the prophet their detestable idolatry (vv. 17–20). 4. God sets before the people that maxim that to obey is better than sacrifice *(1Sa 15:22), telling them he will not accept the sacrifices of those who persist in disobedience (vv. 21–28). 5. God threatens to devastate the land for their idolatry and ungodliness (vv. 29–34).*

Verses 1–15

These verses begin another sermon, which is continued in the two following chapters, to reason with them to repent. Notice:

1. The orders given to the prophet. This was *a word that came to him from the Lord* (v. 1). We are told:

1.1. Where it must be preached — *in the gate of the Lord's house* (v. 2), through which they entered into the outer court. It would show disrespect to the priests, exposing the prophets to their fury, but the prophet must not fear human beings.

1.2. To whom it must be preached — to the men of *Judah, that enter in at these gates to worship the Lord* (v. 2); probably it was at one of the three festivals, when all the males were to appear, making sure not to *appear empty* (Ex 34:20).

2. The contents of the sermon itself. It is spoken in the name of *the Lord of hosts, the God of Israel* (v. 3), who commands the world and who also covenants with his people. The prophet tells them here:

2.1. What the true words of God are. In short, if they repent and return to God, he will restore their peace, set right their grievances, and return to them by mercy (v. 3): *Amend your ways and your doings* (actions). God shows them where and how they must reform, and he promises to accept them: "*I will cause you to dwell* quietly and peaceably *in this place* (v. 3), and an end will be put to what threatens your expulsion." They must *thoroughly amend* (v. 5); it must be a universal, constant, persevering reformation, not wavering but constant. They must be honest and just in all their dealings. Those who have power must *thoroughly execute judgment between a man and his neighbour* (v. 5), without partiality. They must not *oppress the stranger, the fatherless, or the widow* (v. 6), nor protect those who do oppress. They must *not shed innocent blood*, defiling with it both *this place* (v. 6) and the land in which they live. They must keep closely to the worship of the only true God: *Neither walk after other gods* (v. 6); do not follow them. "Set about such a work of reformation as quickly as possible, *and I will cause you to dwell in this place*, this temple. It will continue to be the refuge, the place where you may meet with God and one another, and you will never be turned out either from God's house or from your own." They will enjoy it by covenant: not by providence, but by promise. They will not be disturbed *for ever and ever*; nothing except sin could cause them to be thrown out. An eternal inheritance

in the heavenly Canaan is kept safe for all who lead godly and blameless lives.

2.2. What are the deceptive words of their own hearts, which they must not trust. He warns them: "*Trust not in lying words.* You are told in what way you may be safe and happy. Do not flatter yourselves by thinking that you may be so in any other way (v. 4). Yet *behold*, it is clear that *you* do *trust in lying words*, despite what has been said to you; you trust in *words that cannot profit* (v. 8). Now these deceptive words are, "*The temple of the Lord, the temple of the Lord, the temple of the Lord are these* (v. 4). Here he resides, here he is worshiped, and here we meet three times a year to show our loyalty to the One who is our King in his palace." They think this is security enough to keep God and his favors from leaving them. When the prophets tell them how sinful they are, they still appeal to the temple. It is the song of the day; it is on their lips all the time. The privileges of *a form of godliness* (2Ti 3:5) are often the pride and confidence of those who are strangers and enemies to its power, and it is common for those who are farthest from God to boast about how close they are to the church (Zep 3:11). To convince them what little good this plea will do them:

2.2.1. God shows them its gross absurdity. If they knew anything about either the *temple of the Lord* or the *Lord of the temple* (v. 4), they would have to recognize that to plead that in order to excuse their sin was most unreasonable. God is a holy God, but this plea suggested he supported sin (vv. 9–10). "When you have done the worst you can against God, will you barefacedly *stand before him in this house which is called by his name*, stand before him as servants seeking his favor? It is as if you said, *We are delivered* (safe) *to do all these abominations*" (v. 10). Some read it in this way: "You present yourselves before God with your sacrifices and sin offerings and then say, *We are delivered* (v. 10), we have been acquitted from our guilt. But all this is done to blind the world, so that you may more easily *do all these abominations* (v. 10). *Has this house, which is called by my name* and is a sign of God's kingdom, set up in opposition to the kingdom of sin and Satan — has *this become a den of robbers in your eyes* (v. 11)? Do you think it was built to be a refuge to evildoers?" Though the horns of the altar were a sanctuary to those who killed someone unintentionally, they were not a sanctuary to deliberate murderers (Ex 21:14; 1Ki 2:29). *Behold, I have seen it, saith the Lord* (v. 11); I have seen through the counterfeit godliness to the real sin.

2.2.2. He shows them that this plea was judged inadequate long before in the case of Shiloh.

2.2.2.1. It is certain that Shiloh was ruined, even though it had God's sanctuary in it, when by its evil it desecrated that sanctuary (v. 12): *Go you now to my place which was in Shiloh.* God *set his name* there *at the first*; the tabernacle was set up there (Jos 18:1). But those who ministered in the service of the tabernacle corrupted both themselves and others there, and from them arose the *wickedness of his people Israel* (v. 12). And what came of it? Was it protected because it had the tabernacle in it? No; God *forsook* it (Ps 78:60); he sent his ark into captivity and cut off the house of Eli, who presided there. *Remember Lot's wife* (Lk 17:32); remember Shiloh and the seven churches of Asia; and know that the ark and lampstand may be moved (Rev 2:5; Mt 21:43).

2.2.2.2. Shiloh's fate would be Jerusalem's doom unless a speedy and sincere repentance prevented it. Jerusalem was now as sinful as Shiloh ever was. "*You have done all these works*; you cannot deny it" (v. 13). God spoke, but they *heard not*, they were not in the slightest concerned;

he *called them*, but they *answered not*; they would not respond to his call. And so Jerusalem would soon be as miserable as Shiloh ever was: *Therefore I will do unto this house as I did to Shiloh*, destroy it and devastate it (v. 14). "This house," God says, "*is called by my name* (v. 14), and so you may think I should protect it. The people of Shiloh, however, flattered themselves in this way and were only deceiving themselves." He quotes another precedent (v. 15), the ruin of the kingdom of the ten tribes; they too were the descendants of Abraham, but their idolatry drove them out and destroyed them.

Verses 16–20

The temple and its service would not be sufficient to prevent the threatened judgment. But there was still the prophet's intercession for them; his prayers would do them more good than their own pleas. Yet now even that support was taken away from them. The case of those who have lost their share in the prayers of God's ministers and people is truly sad.

1. God here forbids the prophet to pray for them (v. 16): "The decree has been made known: *pray not thou for this people*, that is, do not pray for the threatened judgment to be prevented; they have *sinned unto death*, and so pray not for their life but for the life of their souls" (1Jn 5:16). God's prophets are people who pray; Jeremiah foretold the destruction of Judah and Jerusalem, and yet he prayed for them to be preserved. Even when we threaten sinners with condemnation, we must pray for their salvation, that they may *turn and live* (Eze 18:32). Jeremiah was persecuted and reproached by his people, but he still prayed for them. God's praying prophets have great privileges in heaven. Those who will not consider the preaching of good ministers cannot expect to receive any benefit from their prayers. If you will not listen to us when we speak from God to you, God will not hear us when we speak to him for you.

2. He gives him a reason for this prohibition.

2.1. They have decided to persist in their rebellion against God (v. 17): *Seest thou not what they do* openly and publicly, without either shame or fear, *in the cities of Judah and in the streets of Jerusalem?* This suggests that the sin was clear and that the sinners committed their evil even in the prophet's presence. He saw what they did, but they still did it, which was an insult to the One whose officer he was. Their idolatrous respects were paid to the *queen of heaven* (v. 18), the moon, that is, either an idol of the moon or the moon itself, or both. They probably worshiped it under the name of *Ashtaroth* (44:17, 19). They worshiped the creation instead of the One who made it (Ro 1:25), the gifts instead of the Creator. Along with *the queen of heaven* they worshiped *other gods* (v. 18), for those who abandon the true God wander endlessly after false ones. They offered *cakes* as grain offerings to these gods of their own making and *poured out drink offerings* to them (v. 18). *The children* were sent to *gather wood; the fathers kindled the fire* to heat the oven; *the women kneaded the dough* (v. 18) with their own hands. Let us be taught even by this bad example how to serve God rightly.

2.1.1. Let us *honour him with our substance* (Pr 3:9), as those who have all we need from him, and eat and drink to the glory of the One from whom we receive our food and drink.

2.1.2. Let us not decline the hardest services by which God may be honored, for no one will *kindle a fire on God's altar for nought* (Mal 1:10).

2.1.3. Let our children be employed in doing something toward keeping up religious exercises. Notice the

direct tendency of this idolatry: "It is *that they may provoke me to anger* (v. 18); they cannot intend anything else in it. Is it because I am easily provoked? It is their own doing; and they alone will bear it" (Pr 9:12). But (v. 19) *is it against God that they provoke him to wrath?* It is spite against God, but it is powerless spite; it cannot hurt him, but it will hurt them.

2.2. God has decided to proceed in his judgments against them, and he will not be turned way by the prophet's prayers (v. 20): "*Thus saith the Lord God; Behold, my anger and my fury shall be poured out upon this place.* It will reach both human beings and animals, like the plagues of Egypt, and will destroy the *trees of the field and the fruit of the ground* (v. 20), which they have *prepared for Baal* and from which they have made *cakes for the queen of heaven*" (v. 18). There is no extinguishing this fire: *It shall burn and shall not be quenched* (v. 20); prayers and tears will then be useless.

Verses 21–28

Having shown the people that the temple will not protect them as long as they defile it with their evil, God shows them here that their sacrifices will not atone for them as long as they continue to be disobedient. He speaks about their ceremonial services (v. 21): "*Put your burnt offerings to your sacrifices.* Add one kind of sacrifice to another; turn your *burnt offerings* into *peace offerings*, so that you may *eat flesh*, but do not expect any other benefit from them." "Keep your sacrifices to yourselves" is how some understand it; "let them be served at your own table, for they are not acceptable at God's altars."

1. He shows them that obedience is the only thing he requires of them (vv. 22–23). He appeals to the original contract by which they were first formed into a people when they were brought out of Egypt. God did not make them *a kingdom of priests* (Ex 19:6) for himself so that he might be regaled with their sacrifices, as were the devils that the pagans worshiped (Dt 32:38). No; *I spoke not to your fathers concerning burnt offerings or sacrifices* (v. 22), not *at first*. The commands of the moral law were given before the ceremonial institutions, and those came later, as trials of their obedience. The Levitical law begins in this way: *If any one of you will bring an offering*, they must do such and such (Lev 1:2; 2:1), as if it were intended to regulate sacrifices rather than to require them. The condition of their being God's own people was this (Ex 19:5): *If you will obey my voice indeed.* "Be careful both to undertake the duties of natural religion and to observe from a motive of obedience those institutions I have explicitly laid down, and then *I will be your God, and you shall be my people* (v. 23). Let your way of life be consistent: *Walk* within the guidelines I have set and *in all the ways that I have commanded you*, and then *it shall be well with you*" (v. 23). The demand here is very reasonable, that we should be guided by infinite Wisdom, that the One who made us should command us, and that the One who gives us our existence should give us his law.

2. He shows them that disobedience is the only thing for which he has a quarrel with them.

2.1. They set up their own wills in competition with the will of God (v. 24): *They hearkened not* to God and to his law; they *inclined not their ear* to listen to it, much less their hearts to submit to it. *Their own counsels* were their guide. *The imagination* (stubborn inclinations) *of their evil heart*, its appetites and passions, would be a law to them.

2.2. They *went backward* (v. 24) when they talked about choosing a new leader and returning to Egypt;

already then they did not want to go forward under God's leadership. They started off well, saying, *All that the Lord shall say unto us we will do* (Ex 19:8), but they drew back into the ways of sin and became worse than ever.

2.3. When God sent them prophets, they continued to be disobedient. God had his servants among them in every age to tell them of their faults; he *rose up early to send them* (v. 24, as before, v. 13), but they were as deaf to the prophets as they were to the law (v. 26). Their practice and character remained the same. They were worse, and not better, *than their fathers* (v. 26). Jeremiah could himself bear witness against them: "*Thou shalt speak all these words to them. They will not hearken to thee* (v. 27), nor listen to you. Either they will give you no answer at all or they will not give you an obedient answer; they will not come when you call them." The prophet must therefore go and tell them to their faces that they were disobedient and ripe for destruction (v. 28): "*Say unto them, This is a nation that obeys not the voice of the Lord their God.* They are notorious for being stubborn; they sacrifice to the Lord, but they refuse to be ruled by him. They will not receive either the instruction of his word or the correction of his rod; they will not be restored or reformed by either. They are false both to God and other people."

Verses 29–34

We have here:

1. A loud call to weeping and mourning (v. 29). Jerusalem, which had been a joyful city, must now *take up a lamentation on high places*, where the people had worshiped their idols. As a sign of both sorrow and slavery, Jerusalem must now *cut off her hair and cast* (throw) *it away*. The word refers particularly to the hair of the Nazarites, which was the sign of their dedication to God (Nu 6:5–7). Jerusalem had been a city that was a Nazarite to God, but she must now *cut off her hair*, be degraded, and be separated from God, as previously she had been set apart for him. It is time for those who have lost their holiness to set aside their joy.

2. Just reasons given for this great lament:

2.1. The sin of Jerusalem appears here as terrible (v. 30): "*The children of Judah have done evil in my sight*; they have defied me to my face." Here are two things they were accused of. First, they were arrogant toward God and defied him: *They have set their abominations in the house that is called by my name*, in the very courts of the temple, *to pollute* (defile) *it* (v. 30), as if they would reconcile heaven and hell, God and Baal. Second (v. 31), they had particularly *built the high places of Tophet*, where the image of Molech was set up, *in the valley of the son of Hinnom*, adjoining Jerusalem; and there *they burnt their sons and their daughters in the fire*, burned them alive, to honor or appease their idols, which were devils and not gods. When they exchanged the glory of God for the image of an animal (Ro 1:23), surely it was by way of a righteous judgment that God gave them over to affections so corrupt as to make them even worse than animals. God says about this that it was *what he commanded them not*. It never *came into his heart* to have children offered to him, but the people had abandoned his service to serve gods that showed themselves to be true enemies of humanity.

2.2. The destruction of Jerusalem will be extremely miserable in general (v. 29): *The Lord hath rejected and forsaken the generation of his wrath*. Sin makes those who have been the generation of God's love become the generation of his wrath. God will reject those who have by their impenitence made themselves *vessels of wrath fitted*

to destruction (Ro 9:22). *Verily, I say to you, I know you not* (Mt 25:12).

2.2.1. Death will triumph over them (vv. 32–33). *Tophet shall be called the valley of slaughter* (v. 32), for many people will be killed there, falling into the hands of the besiegers when they try to escape. This valley of Tophet was a place where they sacrificed some of their children to Molech and dedicated others to him, and it was there that they would fall as victims to divine justice. Tophet was once the burial place, or burning place, of the dead bodies of the besiegers, the Assyrian army under Sennacherib (Isa 30:33), and God will now turn it into a burial place for the besieged. So great will that slaughter be that even the spacious valley of Tophet will not be big enough to contain all those who are killed, and ultimately there will not be enough people who are left alive to bury the dead, so that *the carcases of the people shall be meat* (food) for the birds of prey and wild animals (v. 33), which will feed on them like carrion.

2.2.2. Joy will depart from them (v. 34): *Then will I cause to cease the voice of mirth*. It is threatened here that there will be nothing to rejoice in. There will be none of the joy of weddings; there will be no mirth, because there will be no marriages. Nor will there be any joy of harvest, *for the land shall be desolate*, uncultivated and left fallow. Both *the cities of Judah and the streets of Jerusalem* will look sad.

CHAPTER 8

In this chapter the prophet proceeds to justify the destruction that God is bringing on this people. 1. He describes the judgments as so terrible that death will be desired (vv. 1–3). 2. He emphasizes the wretched foolishness and willfulness of this people as the cause of this ruin (vv. 4–12). 3. He describes the great confusion and fear that the whole land will be in (vv. 13–17). 4. The prophet is himself deeply affected (vv. 18–22).

Verses 1–3

These verses give a further description of the terrible destruction that the Babylonian army will make of the land.

1. Death will not now be, as it always used to be, the resting place of the dead. The ashes of the dead, even of *kings* and *princes*, will be disturbed, and their *bones scattered at the grave's mouth* (Ps 141:7). It was threatened at the end of the previous chapter that those who were killed would not be buried, but here we find that the graves of those who were buried will be cruelly opened by the enemy, who out of greed, hoping to find treasure in the graves, *shall bring out the bones of the kings of Judah and the princes* (v. 1). The status of their graves will not be able to protect them. The bones of the priests and prophets will also be dug up and thrown about. The cruel nations were sometimes guilty of these absurd and inhuman triumphs over those they had conquered. After the bones have been dug out of the graves, they will be exposed on the surface of the earth in contempt. *They shall be spread before the sun* and before *the moon and stars*, even *all the host of heaven*, whom God's people have made idols of (v. 2). Their dead bodies will be thrown and left to rot before these lights of heaven, whose favor they have sought.

2. Death will now be what it never used to be, the choice of the living, though not because there appears anything delightful in it; everything in this world will become so distressing, and everything will look so black, that *death shall be chosen rather than life* (v. 3). This will

be done not in a confident hope of happiness in the other life but in utter despair of any peace in this life. The survivors will be so few that the nation will then be reduced to a *family*. These few will *remain* alive, just barely, in the many *places whither* (to which) *they were driven* by the judgments of God. Some were prisoners in the country of their enemies, others beggars in their neighbor's country, and yet others fugitives and vagabonds in their own country.

Verses 4–12

The prophet is instructed here to set before this people the foolishness of their impenitence. They are described as a senseless people who have refused to be made wise by all the methods that infinite Wisdom has taken to bring them to themselves.

1. They would not listen to the dictates of reason. They would not act in spiritual matters with the same common wisdom with which they acted in other matters. *Come, and let us reason together, saith the Lord* (Isa 1:18). *Shall men fall and not arise?* (v. 4). If people happen to fall to the ground, fall into the dirt, will they not get up again as fast as they can? Will *a man turn aside* out of the right way? The most careful travelers may lose their way, but then, as soon as they are aware of it, *will they not return?* This is how people act in other things. *Why then has this people of Jerusalem slidden back by a perpetual backsliding?* (v. 5). Why do they not quickly get up and repent when they have fallen into sin? Why do they not correct their errors and reform their ways when they see they have missed their way? Sin is *a backsliding*, going back from the right way, going not merely onto a byway but onto a path in the opposite direction, away from the way that leads to life and back to the one that leads to destruction. Sinners not only wander endlessly; they are also moving continually toward ruin. The tempter both brings people to sin and keeps them in it, and they contribute to their own captivity: *They hold fast* (cling to) *deceit* (v. 5). The excuses they make for their sins are deceitful, but they refuse to be freed from their error, and so *they refuse to return* (v. 5).

2. They would not listen to the dictates of conscience, which is our reason reflecting on our inner selves and our own actions (v. 6). The prophet listened to see what effect his preaching had on them; God himself listened, as One who does not desire the death of sinners (Eze 18:23, 32), who would have been glad to hear anything that promised repentance. These expectations were disappointed (v. 6): "*They spoke not aright*; they did not speak as I thought they would." God did not find any repenting of their national evil, which might have helped to drain the cup of public guilt that was filling up. They did not even take the first step toward repentance; they did not say, *What have I done?* They continued in their sins with determination: *Every one turned to his course, as the horse rushes into the battle*, scorning to be restrained.

3. They would not listen to the dictates of providence nor understand the voice of God in them (v. 7). They had not realized the true meaning of either mercy or suffering. They did not know how to make the most of the grace that God gave them when he sent them his prophets or how to act in the light of the rebukes when *his voice cried in the city* (Mic 6:9). It emphasized their foolishness that there is so much wisdom in the lower creatures. *The stork in the heaven knows her appointed times*, as do other seasonal birds, *the turtle, the crane, and the swallow* (dove, swift, and thrush) (v. 7). These have a natural instinct to change their quarters, as the air alters; they come when

spring comes and go when winter approaches, probably to warmer climates.

4. They would not listen to the dictates of the written word.

4.1. They said, *We are wise*, but *how* could they say so (v. 8)? They thought they were wise because *the law of the Lord was with them*, the Book of the Law and its interpreters (Dt 4:6). But their claims were without foundation. They might as well have been without the Law, considering how little use they made of it. *The pen of the scribes*, of those who first wrote the Law and of those who now wrote explanations of it, *was in vain* (v. 8).

4.2. But it might be said that there were some wise people among them. To this it was answered (v. 9): *The wise men are ashamed* that they have not made better use of their wisdom and lived up to it more properly. *They are dismayed and taken*; all their wisdom has not been enough to keep them from those ways that led to their destruction. They talked about their wisdom, but *Lo, they had rejected the word of the Lord* (v. 9). Those who claimed to be wise and said, "*We are wise, and the law of the Lord is with us*" (v. 8), were the priests and the false prophets, and the prophet here deals plainly with them.

4.2.1. He threatens the judgments of God against them. Their families and land will be ruined (v. 10): *Their wives shall be given to others* when they are taken prisoner, *and their fields* will be taken away from them by the victorious enemy and will be given *to those that shall inherit them*. And despite all their claims to be wise and holy, *they shall fall among those that fall* (v. 12). *In the time of their visitation* (v. 12), when the evil in their land comes to be examined, it will be found that they have caused it more than anyone else.

4.2.2. He gives a reason for these judgments (vv. 10–12). They are greedy to have the wealth of this world. The *priests teach for hire*, and the *prophets divine for money* (Mic 3:11). *Every one deals falsely* (v. 10), looks one way and rows their boat the other way. There is no such thing as sincerity among them. They flatter people in their sins and pretend to be the ones who care for the health of the state, but they do not know how to apply proper remedies; they *heal them slightly*, killing patients by giving merely superficial relief, silencing their fears with a soothing, "*Peace, peace* (v. 11), everything is fine, carry on as you have been doing and all will be well; you are not in any danger." *They cannot blush* (v. 12). They have no sense whatsoever of virtue or honor.

Verses 13–22

In these verses we have:

1. God threatening the destruction of a sinful people. He has long been patient with them, but their offenses provoke him more and more. They will be stripped of all their comforts (v. 13): *There shall be no grapes on the vine*, nothing left for them with which to *make glad their hearts*. It is explained in the last clause: *The things that I have given them shall pass away from them* (v. 13). Abused mercies are forfeited, and then God is just to take them away. *I will send serpents among you*, the Babylonian army, fiery snakes, and they *shall not be charmed* with music (v. 17). These are snakes of a different kind; they are as *the deaf adder, that stops her ear, and will not hear the voice of the charmer* (Ps 58:4–5).

2. The people sinking into despair under the pressure of these disasters. Those who were devoid of fear will be devoid of all hope when fear breaks in on them. They will have neither the heart nor the mind to try to oppose it or withstand it (v. 14): "*Why do we sit still here?* Let's

assemble and go as a group *into the defenced cities."* Although in the end they can expect nothing other than to be wiped out there, that will not happen so quickly there as in the country, and so they will say, *"Let us go, and be silent there.* Let us not try to do anything, not even make a complaint, for what good would it do?" It is a sullen silence. Notice what will make them sink:

2.1. They will be aware that God is angry with them: *"The Lord our God has put us to silence,* has struck us with dismay and *given us water of gall* (poisoned water) *to drink* (v. 14). *Thou hast made us to drink the wine of astonishment* (wine that makes us stagger) (Ps 60:3). Why oppose our fate when God himself fights against us?" They will seem to quarrel with God as if he had dealt harshly with them by not allowing them to speak up for themselves. Yet this will show that they have finally begun to see the hand of God extended in their adversities and disasters and to acknowledge that they have provoked him.

2.2. They will be aware that the enemy is likely to be too strong for them (v. 16). *The snorting of the horses was heard from Dan;* news of the strength of the enemy cavalry will soon be carried throughout, and everybody will *tremble at the sound of the neighing of his steeds.* *"They have come,* and they cannot be opposed; they *have devoured the land and all that is in the city."*

2.3. They will be disappointed in their expectations of being rescued. *"We looked for peace, but no good came,* no good news from abroad. We looked *for a time of health* and prosperity for our nation, but *behold, trouble,* the noise of war." Their false prophets have cried *Peace, peace* to them (v. 11), but the rescue will not come even when they have long expected it (v. 20): *The harvest is past, the summer is ended;* that is, a great deal of time has past. Harvest and summer are times of the year. The meaning, therefore, is, "One year passes after another, one campaign after another, but our lives are as bad as ever. No relief is coming. *We are not saved."* The time for action will then be over, summer and harvest gone, and a cold and sad winter coming. God often keeps his people expecting his salvation for a long time for his wise and holy purposes. And yet they are standing in their own light and putting a bar over their own door; they are not saved because they are not yet ready for salvation.

2.4. They will be deceived in the things that they thought would have kept their peace for them (v. 19): *The daughter of my people* cries aloud, *because of those that dwell in a far country,* because of the foreign enemy that comes from a far country to possess ours: *Is not the Lord in Zion? Is not her king in her?* These are the two things that they have all along depended on:

- That they had among them the temple of God and the signs of his special presence with them.
- That they had the throne of the house of David. *Is not Zion's king in her?* (v. 19). And will not Zion's God protect Zion's king and his kingdom? Their outcry dishonors God, and so he responds immediately: *Why have they provoked me to anger with their graven images?* (v. 19).

3. More of the lamentations of Jeremiah. He was an eyewitness to the devastation of his country (v. 18): *"My heart is faint in me. When I would comfort myself against my sorrow,* every attempt to lighten my grief only makes it worse." Sometimes sorrow is such that the more it is repressed, the more it hits back. This may be the situation of very good people, as it was of the prophet here, whose soul refused to be comforted. He tells us (v. 21): "It is *for the hurt of the daughter of my people* that *I am* thus *hurt;* it is for their sin and for the misery they have brought on themselves by it. This is why *I am black,* why I mourn and go about in black as mourners do; and this is why *astonishment* (horror) *has taken hold on me* (v. 21), so that I do not know which way to turn." A gracious spirit will be a public spirit, a tender spirit, and a mourning spirit. Jeremiah had prophesied the destruction of Jerusalem, and although the truth of his prophecy was questioned, he still did not rejoice in the proof of its truth, putting the welfare of his country before his own reputation. Notice how few his hopes were (v. 22): *"Is there no balm in Gilead*—no medicine that is right for a sick and dying kingdom? *Is there no physician there*—no skillful and faithful hand to give the medicine?" This verse may be understood as putting all the blame for the incurableness of their disease on the people themselves. The question must be answered affirmatively: *"Is there no balm in Gilead*—*no physician there?* Yes, certainly there is; God is able to help and heal them." Gilead was a place in their own land, not far away. They had among themselves God's Law and his prophets, with the help of whom they could have been brought to repentance and their destruction could have been prevented. They had rulers and priests, whose business was to reform the nation and put right their grievances. *Why then was not* their health restored? Certainly it was not for lack of balm or a doctor but because they would not accept the application and submit to the treatment. Doctor and medicine were both available, but the patient was willful and did not want to be restrained by the rules.

CHAPTER 9

In this chapter the prophet continues to faithfully rebuke the people for their sin and to threaten God's judgments for it, but also to bitterly lament both. 1. He expresses his great grief for the miseries of Judah and Jerusalem, and his detestation of their sins (vv. 1–11). 2. He justifies God in the destruction brought on them (vv. 9–16). 3. He calls on others to mourn the deplorable case (vv. 17–22). 4. He shows them the foolishness and futility of trusting in their own strength or wisdom, or in anything except God (vv. 23–26).

Verses 1–11

The prophet is commissioned to foretell destruction and to point out sin. What he said about both came from the heart, and one would have thought it would reach the heart.

1. He abandons himself to sorrow when he thinks about the disastrous condition of his people.

1.1. He mourns the bloodshed and the lives lost (v. 1): *"O that my head were waters* (a spring of water), *that my eyes* might be *fountains of tears,* always sending out floods of tears because there is always fresh cause for them!" The Hebrew word here translated "eye," *'ayin,* can also by extension mean "fountain," as if in this land of sorrows our eyes were intended for weeping as well as seeing. When we find our hearts to be such fountains of sin, it is right that our eyes should be fountains of tears. But Jeremiah's grief here is on behalf of the nation: he will *weep day and night for the slain of the daughter of his people,* for many of his compatriots who were killed by the sword. When we hear about the great numbers of people killed in battles, we should be very much affected; they have the same human nature as we do, whatever nation they come from. So many precious lives are lost, and they are as dear to them as ours are to us.

1.2. He mourns the devastation of the country. "Not only for the towns and cities but also *for the mountains will I take up a weeping and wailing"*—the fruitful hills that were plentiful in Judea—and for *the habitations of the wilderness* (desert pastures) (v. 10), or rather the pastures of the plain, which used to be *clothed with flocks or covered with corn* (Ps 65:13). Now *they are burnt up* by the Babylonian army. Everything looks so sad, for they *hear not the voice of the cattle.* The havoc that war produces on a country must be mournful for all tender spirits, for it is a tragedy that destroys the stage it is acted on.

2. He abandons himself to solitude. While all his neighbors are fleeing to the fortified cities (4:5–6), he is planning to withdraw to some desert, detesting his people's sin (v. 2): *"O that I had in the wilderness a lodging place of wayfaring men,* such as they have in the deserts of Arabia for travelers, *that I might leave my people and go from them!"* We must not *go out of the world* (1Co 5:10), bad as it is, before our time; if Jeremiah could not do good to many people, he might still be able to benefit some of them. Yet it made him weary of his life to see them dishonoring God and destroying themselves. Though he was in the courts of God's house, Jeremiah wished he were in a desert. To justify his willingness to leave them, he showed:

2.1. What he himself had observed among them. He would not think of leaving them because they were in distress, but because they were evil. They were filthy: *They are all adulterers,* that is, most of them were (5:8). This sin makes people despicable. They were also false. Those who had been unfaithful to their God were also unfaithful to one another. If you were to go to church, court, or market, you would find a crowd of unfaithful people. They enjoyed deliberate cheating, for (v. 3) *they bent their tongues, like their bow, for lies,* with skill. Their tongue turned as naturally to lies as a bow turns to the string. *But they are not valiant for the truth upon the earth* (v. 3). They could do good service if they used skill and determination as masters in the cause of truth, but they refused to do so. Those who want to be faithful to the truth must be *valiant* and not fear opposition. We must someday answer not only for our enmity in opposing truth but also for our cowardice in not defending it properly. They would cheat their own brothers and sisters—*every brother will utterly supplant* (is a deceiver) (v. 4). Jacob had his name from the word meaning "supplanting"; it is the word used here. If you were to keep company with them, you would find there was nothing sincere or honest among them. No one thought they should be either grateful or sincere. *Every neighbour will walk with slander* (v. 4); they did not care what bad things they said about one another, even false things. They followed the way of slander; they *walk with it.* They have taught their tongue to speak lies; they weary *themselves to commit iniquity* (v. 5). They were wearied *with* their sinful pursuits but not weary *of* them. They grew worse and worse (2Ti 3:13) (v. 3): *They proceed from evil to evil,* from one degree of sin to another. No one reaches the depths of vice immediately. They began by equivocating, then finally came to downright lying.

2.2. What God had told him about their corrupt ways and what he had decreed against them.

2.2.1. God had noticed their sin. He could tell the prophet—and he told him with compassion for him—what kind of people they were (v. 6): *"Thy habitation is in the midst of deceit,* you live surrounded by deception; everyone around you is addicted to it; therefore be on your guard." This charge is explained more fully in v. 8. Earlier their tongue was *a bow bent* (v. 3), plotting

and preparing trouble; here it is *an arrow shot out.* It is "a slaying arrow," as some readings have it; their tongue had been an instrument of death to many people. They *speak peaceably to their neighbours,* against whom they are at the same time *lying in wait* (v. 8), as Joab kissed Abner when he was about to kill him. When fair words are not accompanied by good intentions, they are contemptible, but when they are intended as a cloak to cover up evil intentions, they are detestable. Sinners could be taught the good knowledge of the Lord, but they would not learn, and where there is no knowledge of God, what good can be expected (Hos 4:1)?

2.2.2. God had marked them out for destruction (vv. 7, 9, 11). Those who refuse to acknowledge God as their lawgiver will be made to know him as their judge. Some would be refined (v. 7): "Because they are so corrupt, *behold, I will melt them and try* (refine and test) *them* to see whether the furnace of affliction will purify them of their dross and whether, when they are refined, they can be cast anew in a better mold." They would not be *rejected as reprobate silver* until *the founder had melted in vain* (6:29–30). He spoke as One who could not find it in his heart to give them up to destruction until he had first used every possible means to bring them to repentance. The rest would be ruined (v. 9): *Shall I not visit* (punish) them) *for these things?* Fraud and falsehood are sins that God hates and that he will judge. The sentence had been passed; the decree had been declared (v. 11): "*I will make Jerusalem heaps* of rubbish; it will be fit for nothing but to be *a den of dragons* (haunt of jackals), and *the cities of Judah* will be *a desolation."*

Verses 12–22

The prophet intends two things in these verses concerning the approaching destruction of Judah and Jerusalem:

- To convince people of the justice of God, that by their sin they have brought it on themselves.
- To move people by the greatness of the desolation so that its terrible prospect might wake them up to repentance and reformation.

1. He calls for the thinking people to show others that God's proceedings are just, even though his ways seem harsh (v. 12): "*Who,* where, *is the wise man,* or the prophet, *to whom the mouth of the Lord hath spoken?* You boast about your wisdom and the prophets you have among you; show me one, and such a person will soon understand that there is a just basis for God to bring these charges against this people." Do these wise people ask, *"For what does the land perish* (v. 12)? It used to be a land that God cared for, but it is now a land that he has abandoned. *Wherefore has the Lord done thus unto this land?"* God here gives a full answer. He produces from the record:

1.1. The indictment presented against them, upon which they have been found guilty (vv. 13–14).

1.1.1. They have rebelled from their allegiance to their rightful Sovereign. The reason God has *forsaken their land* is that they have *forsaken his law* and have not *obeyed his voice* or *walked in* his ways.

1.1.2. They have entered into the service of usurpers; they have not only withdrawn from their obedience to their ruler but also taken up arms against him. They have set up their own will, the will of their sinful mind and nature, in contradiction to the will of God: *They have walked after the imagination* (stubbornness) *of their own hearts* (v. 14). They want to do as they please, whatever God and their conscience say to the contrary. *They have walked after Baalim:* the word is plural; they had many

Baals, Baal of Peor and Baal Berith, the Baal of this place and the Baal of that place, for they had *lords many* (1Co 8:5; *Baal* means "lord" [Ed.]), which *their fathers taught them* to worship, but which had again and again been forbidden them by the God of their ancestors. This was why *the land perished* (v. 12).

1.2. The sentence on the convicted rebels that must now be carried out: *The Lord of hosts, the God of Israel, hath said it* (vv. 15–16), and who can reverse his decision? Their comforts at home will be poisoned and made bitter to them: *I will feed this people with wormwood*—or rather with wolfsbane, some herb that is both nauseous and harmful—*and I will give them water of gall*, or hemlock juice or some other poisonous herb, *to drink*. Everything around them will become a terror to them. God will *curse their blessings* (Mal 2:2). Their dispersion to distant places will be their destruction (v. 16): *I will scatter them among the heathen* (nations). They will lose themselves where they lost their virtue, among the nations. They have violated the truth that is the bond of society and commerce, and so they are justly crumbled to dust and *scattered among the heathen* (nations). Now we see why the land perishes; all this devastation is what their deeds deserved.

2. He calls for the mourning women to mourn these sad adversities that have come or are coming on them, so that the nation may prepare for them: *The Lord of hosts himself says, Call for the mourning women, that they may come* (v. 17).

2.1. Here is work for the counterfeit mourners: *Send for the cunning* (skillful) *women*, who are used at funerals to make up for the lack of true mourners. Let these *take up a wailing* for us (v. 18). Or, rather, the verse shows the extreme futility of the people, who have not taken the judgments to heart. God sent his mourning prophets to them to call them to mourning, but his word in their mouths had no effect on their faith. Rather, therefore, than let them go laughing to their destruction, he will call the mourning women to come and work on them.

2.2. Here is work for the real mourners.

2.2.1. There is the lament itself. The present scene is very tragic (v. 19): *A voice of wailing is heard out of Zion.* Some think this is the song of the mourning women, but it is rather its echo, returned by those whose affections were moved by their wailing. In Zion, the voice of joy and praise used to be heard, as long as the people kept close to God. But sin has altered the tune; it is now the *voice of lamentation*. "*We are confounded* because *we have forsaken the land*—forced to do so by the enemy—not because we have forsaken the Lord, being drawn aside *of our own lust and enticed* (Jas 1:17); we are confounded *because our dwellings have cast us out* (because our houses are in ruins), not because our God has cast us off." This is how unhumbled hearts mourn their adversity but not their sin, which is its cause.

2.2.2. There is more still to come that will be a subject for lament (Eze 19:14). Those whose land has *spewed them out*—and justly so, because they followed in the steps of their predecessors, the Canaanites, who were driven out before them (Lev 18:24–28)—complain that they are driven into the city, but after a while those people in the city, along with these who are fleeing to the city, will be forced to flee from there too: "*Yet hear the word of the Lord* (v. 20); let *the women* hear it, for the men will not listen to it patiently. The prophets will be glad to preach to a congregation of women who *tremble at God's word* (Isa 66:5). Let the women *teach their daughters wailing. Let every one teach her neighbour lamentation*"; this suggests

that the trouble will spread far; it will go from house to house. The judgment threatened here is made to look terrible. Many people will be killed (v. 21). Death will ride triumphantly, and there will be no escaping its attack. Nor does it attack only the homes of the lowly; it has also *entered into our palaces*. And those who are killed will be left unburied (v. 22).

Verses 23–26

The prophet has been trying to instill in the people a holy fear of God and his justice, but they continue to turn to some sad means or other to excuse themselves in their obstinacy. He therefore sets himself here to drive them away from these refuges of lies (Isa 28:15, 17).

1. When they were told how inevitable the judgment would be, they pleaded the defense of their wisdom and power, which, with their wealth and treasure, they thought made their city impregnable. In answer to this he shows them how foolish it is to trust in these supports as long as they do not have a God in covenant with them (vv. 23–24). He shows here:

1.1. What we may not depend on in times of distress: *Let not the wise man glory in his wisdom* (v. 23), as if with that help he could find some way to evade the enemy. "But if human wisdom is inadequate, people may surely succeed and conquer by their power and courage." No; *Let not the strong man glory in his strength*, for the battle is not always to the strong (Ecc 9:11). David the youth proves too strong for Goliath the giant (1Sa 17). All human force is nothing without God; in fact, it is worse than nothing against him. But may not the *rich man's wealth* be *his strong city* (Pr 10:15; 18:11)? Is not money the answer to all things (Ecc 10:19)? No; *Let not the rich man glory in his riches*, for they may expose him and make him a better target. Let the people not boast about their *wise men, and mighty men, and rich men* among them, as if they could successfully resist the Babylonians because they have wise men to offer military advice, mighty warriors to fight their battles, and rich people to pay the costs of war.

1.2. What we may depend on in times of distress. Our only comfort in trouble will be that we have done our duty. Those people who *refused to know God* (v. 6) will boast in vain about their wisdom and wealth, but those who *know God* intelligently, who *understand* rightly *that he is the Lord*, may *glory in this*: it will be the lasting source of their joy in days of evil. Our only confidence in trouble will be that, having by his grace done our duty to some extent, we will find God to be all-sufficient for us. We may *glory in this*: that wherever we are, we know a God who *exercises loving-kindness, and judgment* (justice), *and righteousness in the earth* (v. 24), who is just to all his creatures and kind to all his children and will protect them and provide for them. They may cheerfully trust in the God they faithfully conform to, even in times of greatest difficulty. But the prophet suggests that most of the people were not concerned about this.

2. When they were told how offensive their sins were to God, they pleaded in vain the covenant of circumcision. They were undoubtedly the people of God: they had the mark of being his children in their flesh. The prophet answered this: God would punish all evildoers, without distinguishing between the circumcised and uncircumcised (vv. 25–26). The people of Judah had lived in the same way as the uncircumcised nations, and so they had forfeited the benefit of that distinction. The Judge of all the earth is impartial (Ge 18:25), and no one will fare any better in his court of law because of any external

advantages. The condemnation of impenitent sinners who are baptized will be as certain as that of impenitent sinners who are not baptized. It is supposed that those *in the utmost corners, that dwell in the wilderness,* were the people of Kedar and those of the kingdoms of Hazor, as can be seen by comparing 49:28–32. Some think they are called those *in the utmost corners* because they lived, as it were, in a corner of the world; others think they are so called because they had "the hair of their head polled (cut short) into corners" (v. 26, margin). Be that as it may, they were uncircumcised in the flesh, and the Jews are ranked with them, for *all the house of Israel are uncircumcised in the heart* (v. 26); they have the sign, but not the thing the sign stands for (4:4).

CHAPTER 10

The prophecy of this chapter has a double reference: 1. To those who were taken into the land of the Babylonians, a country notorious for its idolatry and superstition. They are warned not to follow the way of the nations (vv. 1–2), for their astrology and idolatry are both foolish (vv. 3–5), and the worshipers of idols are senseless (vv. 8–9). This will be clear when they are judged (vv. 14–15). Similarly, the people are encouraged to remain faithful to the God of Israel, for there is none like him (vv. 6–7). He is the true God, he rules over the world (vv. 10–13), and his people are happy in him (v. 16). 2. To those who still remained in their own land. They are warned against false security (vv. 17–18); a foreign enemy will be brought on them by God for their sin (vv. 20–22). The prophet laments this disaster (v. 19) and prays that it will be mitigated (vv. 23–25).

Verses 1–16

The prophet Jeremiah here arms the people against the idolatrous customs of the nations, so that, being convinced and reclaimed by the word of God, they may prevent the rod of discipline from falling on them; and this is *written for our learning* (Ro 15:4). Notice:

1. A solemn command given to the people of God not to conform to the ways of the nations. Let Israel hear this word from the God of Israel: "*Learn not the way of the heathen* (nations) (v. 2); do not approve of it, do not be indifferent to it. Do not let any of their customs creep in among you or insidiously become part of your religion." Worshiping the heavenly bodies—the sun, moon, and stars—was part of the ways of the nations; they gave divine honor to them, and they expected divine favor from them. Now God does not want his people to be *dismayed* (terrified) *at the signs of heaven,* either to revere the stars as deities or to frighten themselves with any forecasts based on them. Let them fear the God of heaven, and then they need not be terrified at signs in the sky, for the *stars in their courses* (Jdg 5:20) do not fight against those who are at peace with God.

2. Good reasons given to support this command.

2.1. The way of the nations is absurd and is condemned by the dictates of right reason (v. 3). The statutes of the nations are themselves futile. The Babylonians pride themselves on their wisdom, in which they think they excel all their neighbors, but the prophet here shows that they are senseless, along with all others who worship idols and expect help from them.

2.1.1. Consider what the idol is that is worshiped.

2.1.1.1. It was a *tree cut out of the forest* originally. It was prepared by *the hands of the workman* (v. 3), squared, sawn, and worked into shape; see Isa 44:12. But at the end of the day, it was merely a piece of wood, better to be used as a gatepost than anything else. But to hide the wood, *they deck it with silver and gold* (v. 4). *They fasten it* to its place *with nails and hammers,* so that it will not fall down or be stolen (v. 4). The idol is made upright; the skilled workers did their part: it *is upright as the palm tree* (v. 5). It looks impressive and stands as if it were going to speak to you, but it *cannot speak;* it cannot take one step toward helping you. If it has to be moved for any reason, it must be lifted up in a procession, for it *cannot go.*

2.1.1.2. The warning here is appropriate: "Do not be afraid of incurring their displeasure, for *they can do no evil.* Do not be afraid of losing their favor, for *neither is it in them to do good*" (v. 5). Idols of gold and silver are as unworthy to be worshiped as wooden gods. "*The stock is a doctrine of vanities* (v. 8). The stock of wood that is the idol teaches lies about God. It is 'an instruction of vanities'; it is wood."

2.1.1.3. A great deal of skill is used, and a great deal of effort taken, to make it. It is not mere ordinary workers who are employed with these idols, such as the workers who were concerned with wooden gods (v. 3). These are skilled workers; it *is the work of the workman*; the engravers must do their work when it has passed through *the hands of the founder* (goldsmith) (v. 9). And so that these gods might be revered as kings, *blue and purple are their clothing,* the color of royal robes (v. 9); but they are no better for all that. For what are the idols when they are made, when the workers have made the best they can out of them? *They are falsehood* (v. 14), deceit and fraud. They are not what they pretend to be. They are worshiped as gods that give breath and life and sense, whereas in reality they are themselves lifeless and senseless, and *there is no breath in them* (v. 14). There is, literally, "no spirit in them"; there is no spark of life in them. They do not even have the *spirit of a beast that goes downward* (Ecc 3:21). *They are vanity* (worthless), *and the work of errors* (the object of mockery) (v. 15). They are the figments of a deluded imagination.

2.1.2. The idolaters who worship these idols (v. 8) *are altogether brutish* (senseless) *and foolish.* Although in the works of creation they cannot help seeing the *eternal power and godhead* of the Creator, they still have become *vain in their imaginations, not liking to retain God in their knowledge* (See Ro 1:20–21, 28).

2.2. The God of Israel is the one and only living and true God; to set up any rival to compete with him is the greatest affront that can be given. For:

2.2.1. He is incomparable. The prophet turns from speaking with the greatest disdain about the idols of the nations to speak with the deepest and most fearful reverence of the God of Israel (vv. 6–7). What is the glory of a human being who devised a useful skill or founded a flourishing kingdom—and this was a sufficient basis among the nations to entitle someone to the status of a god—compared with the glory of the One who is the Creator of the world and who *forms the spirit of man within him* (Zec 12:1)? What is the glory of the greatest ruler or power compared with the glory of the One whose *kingdom rules over all* (Ps 103:19)? The prophet acknowledges (v. 6), "*O Lord! thou art great,* infinite and immense, and *thy name is great in might.*" Not only should the house of Israel worship the great Jehovah as the *God of Israel,* the *King of saints* (Rev 15:3–4); all the families of the earth should worship him as *King of nations*; for *to him it appertains,* that is, the worship of all is due him.

2.2.2. His reality and truthfulness are as clear as the idol's emptiness (v. 10). Idols are the work of human hands, but *the Lord is the true God*, the God of truth; he is God in truth. He is *the living God*. He is life itself, has life in himself, and is the fountain of life to all creatures. The gods of the nations are dead things, but ours is the living and immortal God. He is *an everlasting king*, "a King of eternity." Even if the nations joined together, they would still be completely unable to resist or even *to abide his indignation* (endure his wrath).

2.2.3. He is the God of nature, the fountain of all being, and all the powers of nature are at his command (vv. 12–13).

2.2.3.1. If we look back, we find that the whole world owed its origin to him as its First Cause. It was a common saying even among the Greeks—"The one who sets himself up to be another god should first make another world." God made us and all things. *The earth contains* valuable treasures in its depths, and the crops on its surface are even more valuable. He has *made* it and them *by his power*; and it is by no less than an infinite power that it *hangs upon nothing* (Job 26:7). The *world*, the inhabited part of the earth, is wonderfully fitted for human use and service, and *he hath established it so by his wisdom. The heavens* are wonderfully *stretched out by his discretion*, and the movements of the heavenly bodies are directed for the benefit of this lower world. These movements *declare his glory* (Ps 19:1), and they oblige us declare it, and not to give to the heavens the glory that is due only to the One who made them.

2.2.3.2. If we look up, we see his providence to be a continued creation (v. 13): *When he uttereth his voice, there is a multitude of waters in the heavens*, which are poured out on the earth: *He causes the vapours to ascend from the ends of the earth*. The whole earth pays the tribute of *vapors* (clouds), because the whole earth receives the blessing of rain. And so the moisture in the universe, like money in a kingdom and blood in the body, is continually circulating for the good of the whole. There is no kind of weather except what gives us proof and an example of the wisdom and power of the great Creator.

2.2.4. This God is Israel's God in covenant. Let the house of Israel therefore remain faithful to him and not abandon him to go after idols, for (v. 16) *the portion of Jacob is not like them*; their rock is not as our rock (Dt 32:31), nor ours like their molehills. If we have satisfaction in God as our portion (Ps 16:5; 73:26), he will have a gracious delight in us as his people, whom he acknowledges to be *the rod of his inheritance* (v. 16), with whom he lives and by whom he is served and honored. It is the indescribable comfort of all the Lord's people that the One who is their God is *the former of all things* (v. 16).

2.3. Having compared the gods of the nations to the God of Israel, the prophet reads out the condemnation of all those pretenders, and he directs the Jews, in God's name, to read it out to the worshipers of idols (v. 11). *Thus shall you say unto them: The gods which have not made the heavens and the earth shall perish*. The first Christians would say, when urged to worship such a god, "Let him make a world and he will be my god." When God comes to judge idolaters, he will make them tired of their idols and glad to be rid of them. They will *cast them to the moles and to the bats* (Isa 2:20).

Verses 17–25

In these verses:

1. The prophet threatens, in God's name, the approaching ruin of Judah and Jerusalem (vv. 17–18). The Jews who remained in their own land, after some were taken into exile, were very self-confident. They thought themselves *inhabitants of a fortress* (v. 17). Their country was their stronghold; they thought it was impregnable. But here they must prepare to go after their brothers and sisters and pack up their belongings in expectation: "*Gather up thy wares out of the land* (v. 17); sort out your affairs, and make your baggage as compact as you can. Let what you have not be scattered, for the Babylonians will soon attack you again, to execute the sentence God has passed on you (v. 18): *Behold, I will sling out the inhabitants of the land at this once*; they have up to this time dropped out only a few at a time, but they will be hurled out as a stone out of a sling. They will be thrown out violently and soon driven to a place far off." He adds, *And I will distress them, that they may find it so*. Wherever they go, they will be continually perplexed and in difficulties, so that they may feel what they would not believe. They were told that their sin would be their ruin, but now *they shall find it so*.

2. He describes the people sadly mourning their disastrous situation (v. 19): *Woe is me for my hurt* (because of my injury)*!* Some consider this to be the prophet's own lamentation, not for himself but for the devastation that has come to his country. But it may also be taken as the language of the people considered as a body and therefore speaking as one person. The prophet puts into their mouths the words they *will* say; whether they want to say them or not, they will have cause to say them. In his vision Jeremiah sees that:

2.1. They mourn that the affliction is great and difficult to bear. "*Woe is me for my hurt* (because of my injury), not because of what I fear but because of what I feel." It is *a wound* that is *grievous*.

2.2. There is no remedy but patience. "Why complain? *This is a grief, and I must bear it* as well as I can." But this expresses a patience that is compelled, not a patience that is well motivated. To say, "This is something that is harming me, *and I must bear it* because I cannot help it," shows a lack of the good thoughts about God that we should always have, even in suffering, saying not only that God can and will do what he pleases but also, *Let him do what he pleases* (1Sa 3:18).

2.3. The country is ravaged (v. 20): *My tabernacle is spoiled* (my tent is destroyed). Although Jerusalem was a strong city, it now proves weak: their government has collapsed, and their state has fallen to pieces. Their church is ruined, and all its supports fail. It is a general destruction of church and state, city and country, and there is no one to repair this destruction. "*My children have gone forth of me*; some have fled, others have been killed, and others have been taken into exile, so that *they are not*, for *there is none to stretch forth my tent any more*, none of my children to do me any service."

2.4. The rulers take no proper measures to reestablish their ruined state (v. 21): *The pastors* (shepherds) *have become brutish* (senseless). When the shepherds' tents were destroyed (v. 20), it was the shepherds' business to look after them, but they are foolish shepherds. The kings and rulers are not at all bothered with the public welfare. The priests, the pastors of God's tabernacle, do a great deal toward destroying religion but nothing toward restoring it. They neither acknowledge justice from his hand nor expect deliverance from it. *Therefore they shall not prosper* (v. 21); none of their attempts to keep and protect the public safety will succeed. Those who do not by faith and prayer take God along with them in all their ways cannot expect to prosper.

2.5. The report of the enemy's approach is terrible (v. 22): *The noise of the bruit has come* (the report is coming), which at first was only whispered here and there, as without confirmation. It now proves true: *A great commotion* arises *out of the north country*, a commotion that threatens to make all *the cities of Judah desolate and a den of dragons* (a haunt of jackals), for they must all expect to be sacrificed to the greed and fury of the Babylonian army.

3. He turns to God and addresses himself to him, finding it ineffective to speak to the people.

3.1. The prophet here acknowledges the sovereignty of divine Providence. Our lives are not at our own disposal but under divine direction; the outcome is often governed by God so as to be completely the opposite of our expectations. Some think that the prophet is comforting himself here with the thought that the way of the Babylonian army is not directed by the Babylonians themselves; they can do no more than what God allows them to do. He can set limits to these proud waves, saying, *Hitherto they shall come, and no further* (Job 38:11).

3.2. He prays to be saved from divine wrath, that it might not fall on God's Israel (v. 24). He speaks not only for himself but also on behalf of his people. "*O Lord, correct me, but with judgment*, no more than is necessary to drive out the foolishness that is bound up in our hearts (Pr 22:15). Let it *not* be *in thy anger*, but from your love, and let it be made to work for good. Let it not *bring us to nothing*, but to bring us home to yourself. Let it not be according to what our sins deserve (Ezr 9:13), but according to the purposes of your grace." As long as we know that God corrects those he loves and are aware in ourselves that we need correction and deserve it, we cannot pray in faith that we may never be corrected.

3.3. He calls down divine wrath on the persecutors of Israel (v. 25): *Pour out thy fury upon the heathen* (nations) *that know thee not.* This prayer does not come from a spirit of malice or revenge. It is an appeal to his justice. It is as if the prophet had said, "Lord, we are an offensive people, but are there not other nations that are more so? We are your children and may expect a fatherly correction, but they are your enemies, and your anger should be directed against them, not us." The nations are strangers to God and are content to remain so. They *know him not*; they do not acknowledge him and do not want to know him. They live without prayer and have nothing of religious faith among them; they *call not on God's name.* They are persecutors of the people of God. *They have eaten up Jacob* with as much greediness as those who eat when they are very hungry. They have *devoured him, and consumed him, and made his habitation desolate*, that is, they have destroyed his homeland, in which he lives, or the temple of God, which is his dwelling place among them.

CHAPTER 11

1. God by the prophet reminds the people of the covenant he made with their ancestors (vv. 1–7). 2. He accuses them of having obstinately refused to obey him (vv. 8–10). 3. He threatens to punish them with complete destruction because of their disobedience (vv. 11, 13). He tells them that their idols will not save them (v. 12) and that their prophets will not pray for them (v. 14). He justifies his actions with the consideration that they have brought all this trouble on themselves (vv. 15–17). 4. Here is an account of a conspiracy against Jeremiah by his fellow citizens, the people of Anathoth: God's revelation of it to him (vv. 18–19), his prayer against them (v. 20), and a prediction of God's judgments on them for it (vv. 21–23).

Verses 1–10

The prophet draws up an indictment against the Jews for their willful disobedience to the commands of their rightful Sovereign.

1. God has commanded him to *speak it to the men of Judah* (vv. 1–2). In the original it is plural: not "Speak thou this" but "Speak ye this." What he said to Jeremiah was the same as he ordered all his servants the prophets to say. None of them said anything different from what Moses had said in the Law; and so it is in that that they must instruct the people: "*Hear the words of this covenant*; be judged by them." Jeremiah must now declare this in the towns *of Judah and the streets of Jerusalem* (v. 6), so that everybody may listen; it concerns everyone. "By comparing yourselves with the covenant, you will soon be aware of the terms on which you now stand with God."

2. He begins with the charter on which their state was founded and by which they have kept their privileges. They have forgotten its basic tenets and are living as if they thought that they could do as they pleased and still have what God had promised. Or they are living as if they thought that keeping the ceremonial observances was all that God required of them. He therefore shows them that God insists on *obedience*, which is *better than sacrifice* (1Sa 15:22). He says, *Obey my voice* (v. 4 and again v. 7). "Acknowledge God as your Master. *Do my commandments, according to all which I command you.* Be careful to do the moral duties especially; do not limit yourselves to those that are merely ritual. Listen to the words of the covenant and do them."

2.1. This was the original contract, made between God and them when he first formed them into a people. It was what he *commanded their fathers* when he first *brought them forth out of the land of Egypt* (vv. 4, 7). He redeemed them out of the service of the Egyptians, which was sheer slavery, so that he might take them into his own service, which is complete freedom (Lk 1:74–75).

2.2. This was made the condition of the relationship between them and God: "*So shall you be my people, and I will be your God* (v. 4); *I will* acknowledge you as mine, and you may call on me as yours."

2.3. It was on these terms that the land of Canaan was given them as their possession: *Obey my voice, that I may perform the oath sworn to your fathers, to give them a land flowing with milk and honey* (v. 5).

2.4. This obedience was not only made a condition of the blessing but also required under penalty of a curse. *Cursed be the man*, even if it is only one person, *that obeys not the words of this covenant*, and much more so when it is most of the nation that rebels.

2.5. In case this covenant should be forgotten, God had from time to time called to them to remember it by his servants the prophets.

2.6. This covenant was agreed to (v. 5): *Then answered I, and said, So be it, O Lord!* These may be the words of the prophet, expressing his own agreement to the covenant for himself and his desire to enjoy its benefits or expressing his good will that his people might enjoy its benefits; or perhaps the verse expresses his people's agreement to the covenant: "*Then answered I*, in the name of the people, *So be it.*"

3. He accuses them of breaking the covenant, with such a breach as amounted to a forfeiture of their charter (v. 8). God had said many times, "*Obey my voice*, do as you are told to do, and all will be well," *yet they obeyed not.* They walked every one in the imagination (stubbornness) *of their evil heart.* Everyone did as their imagination

led them, rightly or wrongly, lawfully or unlawfully, both in their devotions and in their lives more generally; see 7:24. What then could they expect but to fall under the curse of the covenant? What made their defection from God even worse was that it was general; it was *by consent* (vv. 9–10). Jeremiah himself saw that many people lived in open disobedience to God, but the Lord told him that the matter was worse than he thought: *A conspiracy is found among them.* There was a conspiracy against God and religious faith, a dangerous plot being hatched to overthrow God's government and introduce false gods. They wanted to overthrow divine revelation and persuade people not to listen to the words of God. Human reason would be their god, an inner light their god, an infallible judge their god, saints and angels their gods, or the god of this or that other nation would be theirs. This was how, using several different disguises, they were allied *against the Lord and against his anointed* (Ps 2:2). *The inhabitants of Jerusalem* were conspiring with *the men of Judah* (v. 9). Those of this generation seemed to have joined in the conspiracy with those of the previous generation in order to carry on the war against religious faith from age to age. Judah and Israel, the kingdom of the ten tribes and that of the two, which were often at odds with one another, were joined together *in a conspiracy* to *break the covenant* God had made with *their fathers*, even with the heads of all the twelve tribes. The house of Israel began the rebellion, but the house of Judah soon joined the conspiracy.

Verses 11–17

This paragraph contains much of God's wrath: *Therefore I will bring evil* (a disaster) *upon them* (v. 11), the disaster of punishment for the evil of sin.

1. They cannot help themselves. It is *evil which they shall not be able to escape,* or "go forth out of," by any means whatever.

2. Their God will not help them: *Though they shall cry unto me, I will not hearken to them.* For he has clearly told us that those who *turn away their ears from hearing the law,* as they did—for they *inclined not their ear* (v. 8)—will find that even their prayers will be detestable to him.

3. Their idols will not help them (v. 12). They will *go, and cry to the gods to whom they* now *offer incense; they shall not save them at all.* It is only God who is a friend in times of need, *a present,* powerful *help in time of trouble* (Ps 46:1). If the idols could have done any real kindness for their worshipers, they would have done it for this people, who had as many of them as the number of their towns (v. 13), who had idols in Jerusalem—in fact, idols *according to the number of their streets.*

4. Jeremiah's prayers will not help them (v. 14). God will give no encouragement to the prophets to pray for them, not for the body of the people. Yet he will put it into their hearts to pray for the remnant among them, for their eternal salvation, though not for their rescue from the physical judgments.

5. The profession they make of religion will do them no good (v. 15). Once they had a place *in God's house;* they shared at God's altar; they ate of the meat of their fellowship offerings, here called the *holy flesh* (consecrated meat). What harm could come to those who were God's beloved, who were under the protection of his house? They gloried in this privilege. Even when they *did evil, they* still *rejoiced* and gloried in this. Their confidence, however, will deceive them; they themselves have forfeited the privileges. They have *wrought lewdness with many* (v. 15);

they have worshiped many idols, and so God's temple *will yield them no protection.* Nor will God's altar yield them any satisfaction: "*The holy flesh* (consecrated meat) *has passed from thee,* that is, an end will soon be put to your sacrifices, when the temple will be destroyed, and where will the consecrated meat be then, that meat that you are so proud of?" A holy heart will be a comfort to us when the consecrated meat has passed from us; an inner source of grace will make up for the lack of the outer means of grace. But we are unfortunate if the departure of the consecrated meat is accompanied by the departure of the Holy Spirit.

6. God's former favors to them will do them no good (vv. 16–17). God had *called Israel's name a green olive tree* and had made them so. He had *planted* them (v. 17), had formed them into a people, with all the advantages they could have to make them a fruitful and flourishing people: their Law and land were so good. He had planted them as a green olive, a good olive, but they had turned into a *wild olive* (Ro 11:17). Both *the house of Israel* and the *house of Judah* had *done evil,* had *provoked God to anger in burning incense unto Baal,* setting up other mediators besides the promised Messiah. Now that the One who planted this green olive tree and expected fruit from it had found it barren and wild, he *had kindled fire upon it* to burn it as it stood, for, being without fruit, it was *twice dead, plucked up by the roots* (Jude 12), *cut down and cast into the fire* (22:7). Its *branches,* its high and lofty boughs, would be *broken down;* both rulers and priests would be cut off. And so it turned out that the evil done against God was really done *against their own souls.*

Verses 18–23

The prophet Jeremiah has much in his writings about himself; the times he lived in were very worrying. Here we have the beginning of his sorrows, which arose from the people of his own city, Anathoth, a priest's town. Notice:

1. Their plot against him (v. 19). They *devised devices against him,* put their heads together to work out how they might take his life. They said about Jeremiah, *Let us destroy the tree with the fruit thereof*—a proverbial expression, meaning, "Let us completely destroy him, root and branch." Or rather, "both the prophet and the prophecy; let us kill the one and defeat the other. Let us destroy his good name and so spoil the reputation of his predictions." The persecutors of God's prophets *hunt for* no less than *the precious life* (Pr 6:26). They thought they would put an end to his days, but he survived most of his enemies; they thought they would blight his memory, but it lives on to this day and will as long as time endures.

2. The information that God gave him of this conspiracy. He knew nothing about it himself, because they had concealed it so skillfully. He came to Anathoth fearing no harm, *like a lamb or an ox,* which thinks it is being driven as usual to the field *when it is brought to the slaughter* (v. 19). There was just a short step between Jeremiah and death (1Sa 20:3), but then *the Lord gave him knowledge of it,* by dream or vision or an impression on his spirit, so that he might save himself, as the king of Israel did on the information Elisha gave him (2Ki 6:10). Jeremiah came to *know it.* God *showed him their doings* (v. 18). Notice what care God takes of his prophets: he *suffers* (allows) *no man to do them wrong* (1Ch 16:21); all the rage of their enemies cannot succeed in taking them away until they have finished bearing their testimony.

3. His appeal to God about this (v. 20). When people treat us unjustly, we have a God we can turn to who will plead the cause of wronged innocence and support those who have been wronged. God's justice is a terror to evildoers, but it is an encouragement to the godly. He knew the integrity that was in Jeremiah's heart and knew the evil in the hearts of his enemies, even though it was skillfully covered up. Now Jeremiah prayed for judgment against them: "*Let me see thy vengeance on them*; act in justice between me and them in such a way as is your will." Some think there was something of human frailty in this prayer; at least Christ has taught us another lesson, both by command and by pattern, which is to pray for our persecutors (Mt 5:44). Jeremiah turned his case completely to the judgment of God: "*Unto thee have I revealed my cause*, neither desiring nor expecting to interest any other person in it." When we are wronged, we have a God we can commit our cause to, deciding to accept his definitive sentence and agree with what he does, not giving orders to him as to what he should do.

4. Judgment given against his persecutors, *the men of Anathoth.* It was useless for him to appeal to the courts at Jerusalem; the priests there would stand by the priests at Anathoth. But God himself would take notice of his situation, and we are sure that his judgment is based on truth (Ro 2:2). Their crime was that they sought to take the prophet's life; they forbade him to prophesy on penalty of death, and this was in effect seeking to take his life, because it was an attempt to defeat the purpose of his life and to rob him of the comforts of fulfilling that purpose. The provocation he gave them was his prophesying *in the name of the Lord* and not prophesying the smooth things that they always required. It is as bad for God's faithful ministers to have their mouth stopped as to have their breath stopped. It used to be said that a prophet could not perish except at Jerusalem, for there the great council sat, but the people of Anathoth were so bitter toward Jeremiah that they would undertake to kill him themselves. For this, God says, *I will punish them.* The sentence passed on them for this crime was that *the sword* would devour their *young men,* even though they were young priests, and *famine* would destroy the *sons and daughters* (vv. 22–23). They sought to take Jeremiah's life, and so they would die. They wanted to destroy him *root and branch,* so that *his name* might be *no more remembered* (v. 19), and so *there shall be no remnant of them* (v. 23).

CHAPTER 12

We have here: 1. The success of evildoers in their evil practices (vv. 1–2) and the prophet's appeal to God about his own integrity (v. 3), with a prayer that God would bring the evil to an end (vv. 3–4). 2. God's rebuke to the prophet for his uneasiness at his present troubles (vv. 5–6). 3. A sad lament at the present deplorable state of the Israel of God (vv. 7–13). 4. An intimation of mercy to God's people in a declaration of wrath against their neighbors, foretelling that those enemies would be uprooted but also promising that if they finally joined the people of God, they would come and share in their privileges (vv. 14–17).

Verses 1–6

The prophet does not doubt that it would be useful to others to know what passed between God and his soul, and so:

1. He tells us what freedom he humbly had to reason with God about his justice (v. 1). He intended to *plead* with God; he did not want to find fault with his ways but to ask about their meaning. We may not *strive with our Maker* (Isa 45:9), but we may reason with him. When we are most in the dark about the meaning of God's ways with us, we must still decide to keep right thoughts about God, being confident that he never did and never will do the slightest wrong to any of his creatures. When we find it hard to understand particular providences, we must turn back to general truths as our basic principles and accept them. However dark providence may be, *the Lord is righteous*; see also Ps 73:1.

2. He tells us what it was in the ways of divine Providence that he stumbled at. The intentions and plans of evildoers seem to be successful: *The way of the wicked prospers*; they fulfill their evil purposes. Hypocrites are chiefly the ones referred to here, as appears in v. 2—those who pretend to have faith but depart from their good beginnings, deal faithlessly, and *yet are happy.* Concerning the particular evildoers he has observed, the prophet shows (v. 2) that God has been indulgent to them: "They have been planted in a good land, a land flowing with milk and honey, and *thou hast planted them*; in fact, you drove out the nations to plant them" (Ps 44:2; 80:8). *They have taken root*; their prosperity seems to be confirmed and settled. God has favored them in this way even though they dealt faithlessly with him: *Thou art near in their mouth and far from their reins* (v. 2), you are always on their lips but far from their hearts. Though they do not care to think about God or have any sincere affection for him, they can still easily persuade themselves to speak about him with an air of seriousness. Godliness from the teeth outward is not difficult. Although they always have the name of God ready in their mouth and have words and expressions that seem devout, they cannot maintain the fear of God in their hearts.

3. He tells us what strength he had in appealing to God concerning his own integrity (v. 3): *But thou, O Lord! knowest me.* God knew he was not a deceiver and false prophet. Those who abused him in this way did not know him (1Co 2:8). We are as our hearts are, and our hearts are good or bad according to what they are, or are not, toward God.

4. He prayed that God would turn against these evildoers and not allow them to prosper always, though they had prospered long: "Let some judgment come to *pull them out* of this rich pasture *as sheep for the slaughter,* to make it clear that their long prosperity was only like the feeding of lambs to *prepare them for the day of slaughter*" (Hos 4:16). God had allowed them to prosper so that in their pride and self-indulgence they might reach the limit of their sins (Ge 15:16; Mt 23:32) and so be ready for destruction. Since, therefore, they had caused so much trouble to others, the prophet thought, they themselves should fall into trouble; the longer they continued on the land, the more harm they did, like the plagues of their generation (v. 4): "*How long shall the land mourn for the wickedness of those that dwell therein?* Lord, will those who destroy all around them prosper?" *The herbs* (grass) *of every field wither*—the grass is burned up, the animals perish. This was the effect of a long drought that happened at the end of Josiah's reign and the beginning of Jehoiakim's (3:3; 8:13; 9:10, 12; ch. 14). Now why was it that this *fruitful land* was *turned into barrenness* other than *for the wickedness of those that dwelt therein* (Ps 107:34)? The prophet therefore prayed that these evildoers might

die for their own sin (2Ch 25:4) and that the whole nation might not suffer for it. *They said, He shall not see our last end* (what will happen to us) (v. 4). That is, either, "God himself will not see this; he does not know what way we take or what it will end in," or, "Jeremiah *shall not see our last end.*" They looked on him as a false prophet.

5. He provides us with the answer God gave to his complaints (vv. 5–6). Ministers have lessons to learn as well as lessons to teach, and they themselves must hear God's voice and preach it to themselves. Jeremiah complained much about the evil of the people of Anathoth and their prosperity in their evil. Now this seems to be an answer to that complaint.

5.1. It was allowed that he had cause to complain (v. 6): "*Thy brethren,* the priests of Anathoth, of *the house of thy father, even they have dealt treacherously with thee* and, under the guise of friendship, have caused you all the trouble they could. They *have called a multitude after thee,* raised the mob to attack you, to whom they tried to make you contemptible. They are truly those you cannot believe, *though they speak fair words to thee.* They seem to be your friends, but they are really your enemies."

5.2. But he was told that he had taken the unkindness of his compatriots too much to heart. *They had wearied* him because it was *in a land of peace wherein he trusted* (v. 5). It had been very painful for him to be hated in this way and abused by his own relatives. It had disturbed him in his mind and discouraged him in his work, so that he had become tired of prophesying and begun to think of giving it all up. He did not see that this was only the beginning of his sorrow and that he had more difficult trials ahead of him, and that whereas he should, by patiently bearing this trouble, prepare himself for greater ones, by his uneasiness he was only unfitting himself for what lay ahead of him: "*If thou hast run with the footmen and they have wearied thee* and exhausted your breath, *then how wilt thou contend with horses?*" If the wrongs done to him by the people of Anathoth had made such an impression on him, what would he do when the rulers and chief priests at Jerusalem set on him with their power (20:2; 32:2)? If he had so quickly become tired *in a land of peace,* where there was little danger, *what would he do in the swellings* (floodings) *of Jordan,* when that river overflowed all its banks and frightened even lions out of their thickets (49:19)? How will we preserve our integrity and peace when we come to *the swellings* (floodings) *of Jordan*? We must acquit ourselves well in our present, smaller trials; we must keep up our spirits and keep hold of the promises, with our eye on the prize, running so that we may obtain it (1Co 9:24).

Verses 7–13

The people of the Jews are here marked out for destruction.

1. God is seen here as abandoning his people. It is a terrible word that he says here (v. 7): *I have forsaken my house*—the temple, his palace; they have desecrated it and so forced him out of it: "*I have left my heritage* (abandoned my inheritance) and will look after it no more." If they had behaved properly, he would have made the best of them, for they were *the beloved of his soul,* but they have provoked him to *give them into the hand of their enemies.* They have become corrupt and have become like *beasts of prey,* which no one loves and everyone avoids (v. 8). *My heritage is unto me as a lion in the forest.* They *cry out against God* in the threats they breathe out (Ac 9:1) against his prophets who speak to them in his name.

They blaspheme his name, oppose his authority, and defy his justice, and so they *cry out against him as a lion in the forest.* Those who were the *sheep of God's pasture* (Ps 100:3) have become cruel and ravenous and as wild and uncontrollable as lions in the forest. That is why *he has hated them,* for what delight could the God of love take in people who had become as roaring lions and raging beasts, a source of fury to everyone around them? They have become like *birds of prey,* unworthy to have a place in God's house, where neither wild animals nor birds of prey are allowed to be offered in sacrifice (v. 9): *My heritage is unto me* "as a bird with talons," as some understand it, and as the margin reads; they by their unnatural fighting have turned their country into a cockpit. Or his heritage is to him *as a speckled bird,* sprinkled or sprayed with the blood of its prey. The *birds round about are against her.* Some take *speckled* to mean pied or motley, because the people mixed superstitious customs of the nations with divine institutions in the worship of God. They wanted a "pick-and-mix" religion.

2. The enemies are seen attacking and destroying them. Some think this is why they are compared to a speckled bird, because birds usually make a fuss about a bird of an odd or unusual color. God's people are, among the children of this world, like *men wondered at* (Zec 3:8), like a *speckled bird* (v. 9), but this people have in their own foolishness made themselves so. Let *all the birds round be against her* (v. 9), for God has abandoned her. The complete destruction of the land by the Babylonian army is spoken of here as something already done, because it is so near. God speaks of it as something he has no pleasure in, any more than in the death of other sinners (Eze 18:32; 33:11).

2.1. Notice with what tender affection he speaks of this land, despite its sinfulness, remembering his covenant: it is *my vineyard, my portion, my pleasant portion* (my field, my pleasant field) (v. 10). This shows us that God has kindness and concern for his church even though there is much that is wrong in it.

2.2. Notice with what tender compassion he speaks about the desolation of this land: *Many pastors* (shepherds)—the Babylonian generals who controlled the country and devoured it with their armies as easily as the Arabian shepherds with their flocks eat up the fruits of the common ground—*have destroyed my vineyard* (v. 10). What was a pleasant land they have turned into *a desolate wilderness* (v. 10). It is made so by the sword of war (v. 12): *The spoilers* (destroyers), the Babylonian soldiers, *have come through the plain upon all high places.* They have taken control of all the strongholds. *The sword devours from one end of the land to the other;* the army of the invaders disperse to every corner, so that *no flesh shall have peace.*

2.3. Notice from where all this misery comes. It is *the sword of the Lord* that *devours* (v. 12). While God's people keep close to him, the sword of their protectors and deliverers is the sword of the Lord, as can be seen in the case of Gideon (Jdg 7:18, 20). When they have abandoned him, however, the sword of their destroyers becomes the *sword of the Lord,* as can be seen in the case of the Babylonians. It is *because of the fierce anger of the Lord* (v. 13). It is their sin that has made God their enemy (v. 11): the land *mourns unto me;* the country that lies desolate pours out, as it were, its complaint, but the inhabitants are so senseless and foolish that *none of them lays it to heart.* They do not mourn their sinfulness to God, even as the very ground shames them (v. 13): "*They have sown wheat, that* is, they have taken effort to secure their own protection, but it is all in vain. *They shall reap thorns*, that is, what will prove troublesome to them. *They shall be ashamed of your revenues* (harvest), ashamed that they have depended so much on their preparations for war." Money is the lifeblood of war; they thought they had enough of that, but they will be embarrassed, for their silver and gold will not gain them anything in the day of the Lord's anger.

Verses 14–17

Here is a message to all those who have wronged God's people one way or another. Notice:

1. What the quarrel is that God has with them. They are *his evil neighbours* (v. 14), evil neighbors to his church, and what they have done against it he took as done against himself. These evil neighbors are the Moabites, Ammonites, Arameans (*Syrians*), Edomites, and Egyptians, who have been evil neighbors to Israel by helping to defile them and draw them away from God and who are now helping to make them desolate, joining the Babylonians against them. Notice what God accuses them of: they have *touched*, or "meddled with," *the inheritance which I have caused my people Israel to inherit.* They sacrilegiously turned to their own use what was given to God's own people. The One who said, *Touch not my anointed* (1Ch 16:22), also said, *Touch not their inheritance.*

2. What course he will take with them. He will break the power they have gained over his people: *I will pluck out* (uproot) *the house of Judah from among them* (v. 14). God's people have been taken captive by them or, fleeing to them for shelter, have been made prisoners. But now, by his Spirit, he will compel them to come out and compel their taskmasters to let them go, just as he plucked Israel out of Egypt. And he will bring on Israel's enemies the same disasters they have been instrumental in bringing on his people; as he plucked Israel from among their enemies, he will *pluck* those enemies *out of their land.* Judgment began with the house of God (1Pe 4:17), but it did not end there.

3. What mercy God has in store for those among them who will join him and become his people (vv. 15–16). They have drawn God's people to join them in serving idols. If they will now be drawn by a returning people to join them in serving the true and living God, they will be received on the same level as the Israel of God. This was partially fulfilled when, after the return from exile, many of the people who had been evil neighbors of Israel became Jews (Ezr 6:21), and it was to have its complete fulfillment in the conversion of the Gentiles to the faith of Christ. *After that I have plucked them out*, in justice for their sins, *I will return and have compassion on them.*

3.1. God will show favor to them always, provided *that they will diligently learn the ways of my people* (v. 16). There are good ways that are especially *the ways of God's people.* The ways of holiness and heavenly-mindedness, love and peace, the ways of prayer and Sabbath sanctification and conscientious attendance to services of worship—these and similar ways are *the ways of God's people.* These enemies of God's people must learn to say, *The Lord liveth*—they must learn to acknowledge him, to adore him, and to follow his judgment—just *as they taught my people to swear by Baal.* We must not despair of the lives of the worst people, not even of those who have been instrumental in corrupting and defiling others. Even they may still be brought to repentance, and if they are, they will find mercy. The conversion of the deceived may turn out to be a happy occasion of the conversion of even the deceivers. In this way, those who fall together into the ditch (Mt 15:14) are sometimes taken together up out of it.

3.2. When they return to God and God to them, he will *bring them again every man to his heritage* (inheritance) (v. 15). They will become entitled to the spiritual privileges of God's Israel: *then shall they be built in the midst of my people* (v. 16). They will have a name and a place in the house of the Lord—where there was a court for the Gentiles—and they will also be built among them.

4. What will become of those who are still settled in their own evil ways even though many around them have turned to the Lord: *If they will not obey*, if any continue to resist me, *I will utterly pluck up* (uproot) *and destroy that nation*, that family, that particular person, *saith the Lord* (v. 17).

CHAPTER 13

Here the prophet continues to try to wake up this stubborn people to repent: 1. He is to tell them by the sign of a ruined linen belt that their pride will be ruined (vv. 1–11). 2. He is to tell them by the sign of wineskins filled with wine that their purposes will be thwarted (vv. 12–14). 3. He is to call them to repent and humble themselves in consideration of this (vv. 15–21). 4. He is to convince them that it is because of their stubbornness that the judgments of God last so long (vv. 22–27).

Verses 1–11

Here is:

1. A sign, the spoiling of a *linen girdle* (belt), which the prophet had worn for some time, by hiding it in a crevice in the rocks near the *Euphrates* River [Ed. note: Hebrew *Perath*, perhaps the same as Parah (Jos 18:23), three miles northeast of Anathoth]. He was to wear a linen belt for some time (vv. 1–2). Some think he wore it under his clothes, because it is said to have *cleaved to his loins* (be bound round his waist) (v. 11). More likely it would be worn on his clothes; it may have been a fine sash, such as officers wear. He must *not put it in* (not let it touch) *water*, so that it would be less likely to rot. The prophet, like John the Baptist, was not one of those people who wear soft clothing (Mt 11:7–8; Mk 1:6), and so it would have been strange to see him with a linen belt. After he had worn this linen belt for some time, he must go and *hide it in a hole of a rock* (v. 4) by the water's side, where it would become wet when the water was high and become dry again when the water fell, and so would soon rot. Many days later, he would find it spoiled and ruined, completely good for nothing (v. 7). It seems hard to imagine that the prophet would be sent on two such long journeys to the Euphrates. For this reason most tend to think that the journey, at least, was only in a vision, and that the explanation of this sign was likewise given only to the prophet himself (v. 8), not to the people.

2. The thing referred to by the sign (vv. 9–11):

2.1. The people of Israel had been to God like this belt in two respects:

2.1.1. He had taken them into covenant and fellowship with himself: *As the girdle cleaves* very closely *to the loins of a man* and surrounds him, *so have I caused to cleave to me the houses of Israel and Judah*, for as a belt is bound around the waist, so I bound the whole house of Israel and the whole house of Judah to me. He *caused them to cleave* to him by the law he gave them, the prophets he sent them, and the favors he showed them.

2.1.2. When he took them to be *to him for a people*, it was so that they might be to him *for a name, and for a praise, and for a glory* (v. 11), as a belt adorns a person, especially as the *curious* (skillfully woven) *girdle of the ephod* adorned the high priest *for glory and for beauty* (Ex 28:2, 8).

2.2. By their idolatry and other sins they had loosed themselves from him, buried themselves in the earth—and foreign earth too—and allied themselves to the nations, and were so corrupted that they were *good for nothing*. They would not be faithful to God, but *walked after other gods, to serve them, and to worship them* (v. 10). They were devoted to the gods of the nations that were toward the Euphrates, and so they were completely ruined in their service of their own God and were like this spoiled, rotten belt.

2.3. God would by his judgments separate them from him, send them into exile, and deface their beauty, so that they would be like a fine belt that has become ruined, a worthless people. Similarly, God would *mar the pride of Judah and the great pride of Jerusalem*. He speaks of *the pride of Judah*—the country people were proud of their good land—but of *the great pride of Jerusalem*; the temple was there, and the royal palace, and so those citizens were prouder. Pride will lead to a fall, for God opposes the proud (Jas 4:6; 1Pe 5:5). Even the temple, when it became Jerusalem's pride, was destroyed and turned to ashes.

Verses 12–21

Here is:

1. A judgment threatened against this people (v. 12): *Thus saith the Lord God of Israel, every bottle* (wineskin) *shall be filled with wine*, that is, those people who have by their sins made themselves *vessels of wrath fitted to destruction* (Ro 9:22) will be filled with the wrath of God as a wineskin is filled with wine. They will be as brittle as *bottles*; and like old wineskins into which new wine is put, they will burst and be broken to pieces (Mt 9:17). Or they will have their heads as full of wine as wineskins are, for this is how it is explained in v. 13: *They shall be filled with drunkenness*; compare Isa 51:17. They are not aware of the prophet's meaning; they ridicule him for it (v. 12): "*Do we not certainly know* that *every bottle* (wineskin) *shall be filled with wine?*" Perhaps they were so sensitive toward the prophet because they thought this was a reflection on them for their drunkenness, and it was probably partly intended in this way. They *loved flagons of wine* (Hos 3:1). "Well," the prophet says, "you will have your *bottles full of wine*, but not such wine as you want." What he meant was this:

1.1. That they would be as dizzy as people who are drunk. Someone who is drunk is rightly compared to a wineskin full of wine, for "when the wine is in, the wit it out," and along with it all wisdom and all that is good for anything. Now God threatens (v. 13) that they will all be *filled with drunkenness*; they will be fully confused in their minds; they will falter and stagger. They will expose themselves to the contempt of everyone around them. The priests and false prophets are as self-indulgent as the people and will therefore justly be deprived of their sense, and *all the inhabitants* both *of the land* and *of Jerusalem* will be as far gone as they. Those whom God will destroy he brings to no good.

1.2. That, being drunk, they will cause trouble to themselves and one another (v. 14): *I will dash* (smash) *a man against his brother*. Their destruction will be helped along not only by their drunken foolishness but also by their drunken frays. When this decree against them has been declared, God says, *I will not pity, nor spare, nor have mercy, but destroy them*, for they *will not pity, nor spare,*

nor have mercy, but destroy one another; see also Hab 2:15–16.

2. Good advice given, which, if followed, will prevent this devastation. It is, in short, to *humble themselves under the mighty hand of God* (1Pe 5:6). This is what God has to say to them: *Be not proud* (v. 15). This was one of the sins God accused them of earlier (v. 9). "*Be not proud*; when God speaks to you through his prophets, do not think yourselves too good to be taught. Do not be scornful."

2.1. They must seek to honor God. "*Give glory to the Lord your God* (v. 16), not your idols. Give him glory by confessing your sins and accepting the punishment of your sins (Jos 7:19). Give him glory by sincerely repenting and reforming your ways." We will begin to live to some good purpose only when we repent. "Do this quickly, *before he cause darkness* (v. 16), before he brings his judgments on you, which you will see no way of escaping from." Their attempts to escape will speed up their destruction: *Their feet shall stumble* when they are moving as quickly as they can over *the dark mountains* (v. 16). This shows us that those who think they can run ahead of the judgments of God will find their road impassable. Their hopes of a better state of things will be disappointed: *While you look for light*, for comfort and relief, he will *turn it into the shadow of death* and make it *gross darkness* (deep gloom) (v. 16), like that of Egypt when Pharaoh continued to harden his heart, which was a darkness that could be felt (Ex 10:21).

2.2. They must humble themselves. The prerogative of the king and queen will not exempt them from this (v. 18): "*Say to the king and queen* that, great as they are, they must *humble themselves* in true repentance, thereby giving glory to God and setting a good example to their subjects." Otherwise, "When you are led away as captives, where will your crown and all the emblems of royalty be then?"

3. This advice backed up by some arguments. If they continue to be proud and not humbled:

3.1. It will be the prophet's indescribable grief (v. 17): "*If you will not hear it*, will not submit to the word, but continue to be hardened and willful, not only my eye but also *my soul shall weep in secret places*." It will grieve him to see their sins unrepented of: "*My soul shall weep for your pride*, your haughtiness, stubbornness, and arrogant confidence." The sins of others should be a matter of sadness to us. We must mourn for what we cannot put right, and mourn all the more for it because we cannot put it right.

3.2. It will be their own inevitable ruin (vv. 19–21). *The cities of the south shall be shut up*. Some understand this to refer to the cities of Egypt, which lay south of Judah; the places there that they expect help from will fail them, and they will find no access to them. *Judah shall be carried away captive*. This is what happened in the last captivity under Zedekiah, because they did not repent. The enemy who is now at hand will do this (v. 20): "*Lift up your eyes. Behold those that come from the north*, from the land of the Babylonians; notice how fast they are advancing and how fierce they appear." The prophet addresses this to the king, or rather, because the pronouns are feminine, to the city or state. "What will you do now with the people who are committed to your charge and whom you should protect? *Where is the flock that was given thee, thy beautiful flock?* How can they escape these ravenous wolves?" Leaders of families who neglect their children and allow them to perish for lack of a good education, and ministers who neglect their people, should think they hear God asking them this question: "*Where is* the flock that was given thee to feed, that beauteous flock (v. 20)? What will thou say when he shall punish thee for, or visit upon thee, the former days (v. 21)? You cannot say anything, except that God is just in all that is brought upon thee (Ne 9:33). How will you endure the trouble that is close at hand? Shall not sorrows take thee as a woman in travail? And your sorrows will be all the more painful in that there is no child to be born" (Jn 16:21).

Verses 22–27

Here is:

1. Ruin threatened as before. The Jews will go into exile and fall under all the miseries of poverty and slavery. They will be stripped of their clothes, their skirts discovered (uncovered) for lack of upper garments to cover them, and their heels made bare for lack of shoes (v. 22). This is how armies used to keep prisoners of war when they took them into captivity: naked and barefoot (Isa 20:4). Taken off into a strange country, they will be scattered as the stubble (chaff) that is blown away by the wind of the wilderness. They will be stripped of all their ornaments and exposed to shame like prostitutes.

2. An inquiry made by the people into the cause of this ruin (v. 22). Thou wilt say in thy heart, Wherefore came these things upon (why have this things happened to) me? They cannot see that they have done anything that might justly provoke God to be so angry with them.

3. An answer to this inquiry (v. 22). God will be justified when he speaks (Ps 51:4) and will make us justify him, and he will set out the sin of sinners before them. The evil that has come upon them is all their own fault.

3.1. It is because of the greatness of their sins (v. 22). God does not take advantage of them for small faults; the sins he now punishes them for are heinous—he punishes them for "the multitude of thy iniquity," as it may read, sins of every kind and often repeated. Some think we are in greater danger from the great number of our smaller sins than from the detestable nature of our greater sins.

3.2. It is because of their obstinacy in their sins (v. 23): "Can the Ethiopian change his skin, which is by nature black, or the leopard his spots, which are woven into its skin?" It is morally impossible to reclaim and reform these people. They were taught to do evil; they have served their apprenticeship to it. Their prophets have despaired of ever bringing them to do good. Those who have long been accustomed to sin have shaken off restraints of fear and shame; their consciences are seared. The habits of sin are confirmed. Sin is blackness of the soul and its deformity. But almighty grace is available that is able to change the Ethiopian's skin, and that grace will not be lacking to those who sense their need of it and seek it from the heart.

3.3. It is because of their faithless departures from the God of truth (v. 25): "This is thy lot, to be driven away; this is the portion of thy measures from me, the punishment assigned and appointed to you. It is because thou hast forgotten me, the favors I have shown you; you have no remembrance of these." Forgetfulness of God lies at the root of all sin, as the remembrance of our Creator early in life (Ecc 12:1) marks the happy and hopeful beginnings of a holy life.

3.4. It is because of their idolatry. Idolatry is of all sins most offensive to the jealous God (Ex 20:5). They are exposed to a shameful adversity (v. 26) because they have been guilty of shameful sin but remain shameless in it (v. 27): "I have seen thy adulteries, your excessive fancying of foreign gods, even the lewdness of thy whoredoms (your shameless prostitution), your eager worshiping of

idols on the hills in the fields, on the high places. This is why a woe is declared against you, O Jerusalem!"

4. An affectionate pleading with them about the whole matter. While there is life there is still hope, and so he continues to reason with them to bring them to repentance (v. 27). Wilt thou not be made clean? It shows the wonderful grace of God that he wants sinners to repent and be converted and thinks it a long time until they are brought to repent, but it shows the incredible foolishness of sinners that they put off over and over what is so absolutely necessary. They do not say that they will never be cleansed, just not yet.

CHAPTER 14

This chapter was written on the occasion of a great drought. This judgment began at the end of Josiah's reign but continued to the beginning of Jehoiakim's. It was mentioned several times before, but in this chapter it is dealt with more fully. Here is: 1. A sad description of this disaster (vv. 1–6). 2. A prayer to God to end it (vv. 7–9). 3. A severe threat that God would continue to accuse them, because they continued in their sin (vv. 10–12). 4. The prophet's excusing the people by putting the blame on their false prophets (vv. 13–16). 5. Directions given to the prophet that instead of interceding for them, he should mourn for them (vv. 17–22).

Verses 1–9

The first verse is the title of the whole chapter: it does indeed all concern the dearth (drought), but much of it consists of the prophet's prayers about it. These are not inappropriately said to be the word of the Lord which came to him about it, for every acceptable prayer is what God puts into our hearts. Our word that comes to him is nothing except what is first his word that comes from him. In these verses we have:

1. The language of nature mourning the disaster. When the heavens were as bronze and distilled no dew, the earth was as iron and produced no fruit (Dt 28:23); the grief and confusion were widespread.

1.1. The people of the land were all weeping. Judah mourns (v. 2) not for the sin but for the withholding of rain. The gates thereof, all who go in and out by their city gates, languish, look pale and grow feeble for lack of the necessary support of life and for fear of further judgment. The gates now look dismal; the inhabitants are leaving through them to look for bread in other countries. Even those who sit at the gates languish; they are black unto the ground, they go about in black like mourners and sit on the ground like beggars. They fall to the ground through weakness. The cry of Jerusalem has gone up, that is, the cry of its citizens—for the city is served by the field (Ecc 5:9)—or the cry of people from every part of the country who met at Jerusalem to pray for rain. But we fear it was the cry of their trouble rather than the cry of their prayer.

1.2. The leaders of the land suffered from this judgment (v. 3): The nobles sent their little ones to the water. Or perhaps the phrase means their meaner ones, their servants; they sent these to look for water, but none could be found. They returned with their vessels empty; the springs had all dried up, since there was no rain to feed them, and then they—their masters—were ashamed and confounded. The farmers suffered most immediately (v. 4): The ploughmen were ashamed (dismayed), for the ground was so parched and hard that it would not admit the plow. They were ashamed to be lazy. Notice what a direct dependence farmers have on divine Providence, for they cannot plow or sow in hope (1Co 9:10) unless God *waters their furrows* (Ps 65:10). The case of even wild animals was pitiable (vv. 5–6). Judah and Jerusalem had sinned, but what had the does and the wild donkeys done? Does are particularly tender to their young, but these does, contrary to their instincts, left their young to look for grass elsewhere, even when their young most needed them, and if they could find none, they *abandoned* them, because they could not suckle them. It did not grieve the doe so much that she did not have enough grass for herself as that she had none for her young, which will shame those who spend on their sinful desires what they should keep for their families. One would be sorry even for the wild donkeys, for the *barren land* was now too hot for them, so hot that they went to the *highest places* they could reach, where the air was coolest, and *snuffed up the wind like dragons* (panted like jackals), creatures that are continually panting for breath. *Their eyes failed*, and so did their strength, *because there was no grass*.

2. The language of grace mourning the sin and complaining to God about the disaster. The people are not eager to pray, but the prophet here prays for them and so stirs them to pray for themselves (vv. 7–9). In this prayer:

2.1. Sin is humbly confessed. If we quarrel with God that he is dealing with us unjustly or unkindly in afflicting us, our sins bear witness that we do him wrong, "*for our backslidings are many* and too detestable to be excused, for they are against you."

2.2. Mercy is fervently sought: "*Though our iniquities testify against us, yet do thou it.*" As is right for penitents and beggars, they leave the matter with God: "Do with us as you think fit (Jdg 10:15). We have nothing to plead in ourselves but everything in you." There is another petition in this prayer (v. 9): "*Leave us not*; do not withdraw your favor and presence."

2.3. Their relationship with God and their expectations from him are pleaded (vv. 8–9). They look on him as the One who they have reason to think should rescue them. In him mercy has often triumphed over judgment (Jas 2:13). God has encouraged his people to hope in him; in calling himself so often the *God of Israel*, the *rock of Israel*, and the *Holy One of Israel*, he has made himself the *hope of Israel*. They plead, "*Thou art in the midst of us*; we have the special signs of your presence with us, your temple, your ark, and your oracles, and *we are called by thy name*, the *Israel* of God. We therefore hope you will not leave us; *we are thine, save us*" (Ps 119:94). It grieves them to think that he does not appear to rescue them: "*What will the Egyptians say?*" (Ex 32:12). They will say, 'Israel's hope and Savior does not look after them; he has become *as a stranger in the land*, who shows no concern for all its interests; his temple, which he called *his rest for ever* (Ps 132:14), is no more so; he is in it *as a wayfaring man* (traveler), *that turns aside to tarry* (stay) *but for a night* in an inn.' The enemies once said, 'Because the Lord *was not able to bring* his people to Canaan, he let them *perish in the wilderness*' (Nu 14:16), and so they will now say, 'Either his wisdom or his power fails; either he is *as a man astonished* (taken by surprise)—who, though he has human reason, is completely at his wits' end—or as a *mighty man*, human and therefore limited in power.' Either of these would be an intolerable insult to God's perfections, and so why has the God who we are sure *is in the midst of us* become *as a stranger*? Why does almighty God seem powerless to save?"

Verses 10–16

The dispute in this chapter between God and his prophet seems to be like that about the barren fig tree between the owner and the one who took care of the vineyard (Lk 13:7). The justice of the owner condemns it to be cut down; the mercy of the one who looks after it intercedes to gain a reprieve.

1. God overrules the prophet's plea on the people's behalf. *Thus saith the Lord* concerning *this people* (v. 10). He does not say, "concerning *my people*," because they have broken the covenant with him. It is true that they were *called by his name*, but they have sinned and caused God to withdraw from them. God here tells Jeremiah:

1.1. That they are not qualified to receive a pardon. The prophet has acknowledged *their backslidings were many* (v. 7); and although they were, there was still hope for them if they returned. But *this people* show not the slightest inclination to return; *they have loved to wander* (v. 10). They have chosen to be unfaithful, which should have been their shame. It is not through necessity that they wander; they love to wander. Their wanderings mean they lose God's favor, but it is their love of wandering that completely cuts them off from it. They have been warned what their wandering would lead to, but they have not taken the warning and *refrained* (restrained) *their feet*. This is what God is now judging them for. When he denies them rain from heaven, he is *remembering their iniquity* and *visiting* (punishing) *their sin*. This is why their *fruitful land* is thus *turned into barrenness* (Ps 107:34).

1.2. That they have no reason to expect that the God they have rejected will accept them, even though they use fasting and prayer and burnt offerings and sacrifice: *The Lord doth not accept them* (v. 10). The sense is that he takes no pleasure in them. "*When they fast* (v. 12), which is a proper expression of repentance and *reformation*, and *when they offer a burnt offering and an oblation* (grain offerings), which is intended to be an expression of faith in a Mediator, although their prayers are supported by these actions, which used to be acceptable, nevertheless, because those prayers do not proceed from humble, penitent, and renewed hearts, but from hearts that still *love to wander, I will not hear their cry*. Nor *will I accept them*: not their persons or what they do." They have lost all the benefits of the prophet's prayers for them because they have not considered his preaching. This is the meaning of that repeated prohibition given to the prophet: *Pray not thou for this people for their good* (v. 11; also 7:16; 11:14). This did not forbid him from expressing his goodwill to them, but it forbade them from expecting any good effects from it as long as they *turned away their ear from hearing the law* (Pr 28:9). It therefore follows, *I will consume them* (v. 12).

2. The prophet offers another plea as an excuse for the people's obstinacy. The prophets, who claim to have received a commission from heaven, deceive them and flatter them with assurances of peace (v. 13). He speaks of it with mourning: "*Ah! Lord God*, there are those who in your name tell them they *shall not see the sword nor famine*. They say it as coming from you: '*I will* keep you in this place and give you assured peace.' I tell them the contrary, but I am one against many. Therefore, Lord, pity and spare them, for *their leaders cause them to err*." This excuse would have carried some weight if they had not been warned before about false prophets.

3. God not only overrules this plea but also condemns both the blind leaders and the blind followers to fall together into the ditch (Mt 15:14). He disowns the

flattery (v. 14): *They prophesy lies in my name.* They have not received a commission from God to prophesy at all: *I neither sent them, nor commanded them, nor spoke unto them.* Those who accept their own thoughts in opposition to God's word—God indeed speaks the truth, but they think otherwise—walk in the *deceit of their heart,* and it will be their ruin. He passes sentence on the flatterers (v. 15): let them know that they will have no peace themselves. They have undertaken to guarantee the people that *sword and famine* will *not be in the land,* but they themselves will be destroyed by the sword and famine. The *people to whom they prophesy lies,* and who willingly allow themselves to be so deceived, *shall die by sword and famine* (v. 16). Their bodies will be *cast* (thrown) *out,* even *in the streets of Jerusalem.* They will lie unburied there. This is how God will *pour their wickedness upon them,* that is, the punishment of their evil acts.

Verses 17–22

The present deplorable state of Judah and Jerusalem is here made the subject of the prophet's mourning (vv. 17–18) and of his prayer for them (v. 19), and the latter as well as the former came by divine direction. The words (v. 17) *Thus shalt thou say unto them* refer to the intercession as well as to the mourning, and so it amounts to a recalling of the directions given to the prophet not to pray for them (v. 11).

1. The prophet stands weeping over the ruins of his country. Jeremiah must say not only to himself but also to them, *Let my eyes run down with tears* (v. 17). This is how he must show them that he foresees *the sword* coming, and another kind of famine, one that will be in the city through the difficulty of the siege. The prophet speaks as if he already saw the miseries that will come with the attack that the Babylonians make on them: *The virgin daughter of my people is broken with a great breach* (has suffered a grievous wound), *with a very grievous* (crushing) *blow,* more painful than any she has sustained up to this time, for (v. 18) *in the field* many people lie dead who were *slain by the sword,* and in the city many people lie dying for lack of food. "*The prophets and the priests,* the false prophets who flattered them with their lies and the evil priests who persecuted the true prophets, are expelled and *go about* either as captives or as restless wanderers, wherever they can find shelter *in a land that they know not.*" Some understand this as referring to the true prophets Ezekiel and Daniel, who were taken to Babylon with the others. The prophet's eyes must run *with tears day and night* in considering this, so that the people may be convinced not only that this terrible day will certainly come but also that he would gladly have brought them messages of peace if he only had warrant from heaven to do it.

2. He stands up to make intercession for them. There are still some who will join with him in his devotions and set the seal of their *Amen* to them.

2.1. He humbly pleads with God about their situation (v. 19). Their expectations from their God have failed them; they thought he had declared Judah to be his, but now, it seems, he has *utterly rejected* it. They thought Zion was beloved, but now *his soul* even *loathes Zion,* loathes even the services carried out there. All their other expectations have failed them as well: *They have been smitten* (afflicted), their wounds are many, but there is *no healing* for them. They *looked for peace,* because after a storm usually comes a calm. They looked for a *healing time* but could not even gain so much as a breathing space. "*Behold, trouble* at the door, by which we hoped

peace would come in. But will you not finally in wrath also remember mercy?" (Hab 3:2).

2.2. He makes a penitent confession of sin, one that they all should have spoken, although only a few did (v. 20): "*We acknowledge our wickedness,* the great evil of our land, *and the iniquity of our fathers,* which we have imitated. *We know, we acknowledge,* that *we have sinned against thee,* and so you are just in everything that has come on us, but because we confess our sins, we hope to find you faithful and just to forgive our sins" (1Jn 1:9).

2.3. He prays to be saved from God's displeasure, and by faith he appeals to his promise (v. 21). His request is, "*Do not abhor* (despise) *us*; though you make us suffer, *do not abhor us*; even if your hand is turned *against* us, let not your heart be so, nor let your mind be alienated from us." They acknowledge that God could justly despise them, but they pray: "*Do not abhor us, for thy name's sake,* your name, by which we are called and which we call on." The honor of his sanctuary is pleaded: "Lord, do not despise us, for that will *disgrace the throne of thy glory.* We deserve to have disgrace put on us, but let not the desolation of the temple cause the nations to despise the One who used to be worshiped there." We may be sure that God will not *disgrace the throne of his glory* on earth (v. 21). They are humbly bold to remind him of this: *Remember thy covenant with us, and break not* that covenant.

2.4. He professes a dependence on God for the mercy of rain (v. 22). They will never turn to the idols of the nations. *Are there any among the vanities of the Gentiles* (worthless idols of the nations) *that can cause rain?* In a time of great drought in Israel in the days of Ahab, even though all Israel presented their prayers to Baal, Baal could not help them; it was only the God who *answered by fire* who could answer *by water* too (1Ki 18). *Can the heavens give showers?* Not without orders from the God of heaven, for he is the One with the key to the clouds, who *opens the bottles of heaven* (Job 38:37) and *waters the earth from his chambers* (Ps 104:13). All their expectation is therefore from him (Ps 62:5): "*Art not thou he, O Lord our God!* from whom we may expect help and to whom we must turn? Are you not the One who *causest rain* and *givest showers?* For *thou hast made all these things*; you gave them existence, and so you decree them and have them all at your command. We will *ask of the Lord rain* (Zec 10:1). We will trust him to give it to us in due time."

CHAPTER 15

1. Despite the prophet's prayers, God here confirms the sentence against the people (vv. 1–9). 2. The prophet himself, despite the assurance he has in his fellowship with God, still finds himself spiritually out of sorts. 2.1. He complains to God about his continual struggle with his persecutors (v. 10). 2.2. God assures him that he will be taken under special protection, even though there is a general devastation coming on the land (vv. 11–14). 2.3. He appeals to God about his sincerity in fulfilling his prophetic office (vv. 15–18). 2.4. Fresh security is given him to assure him that, on condition that he remains faithful, God will continue to care for him and show his favor toward him (vv. 19–21).

Verses 1–9

There are scarcely anywhere more moving expressions of divine wrath against an offensive people than in these verses. The prophet had prayed fervently for the people and found some who would join him, but no reprieve was gained, nor the slightest reduction in the judgment. Notice:

1. What the sin was on which this severe sentence was based. The sentence lies on them:

1.1. Because of Manasseh, for what he did in Jerusalem (v. 4). We are told in 2Ki 24:3–4 what that was and that it was why Jerusalem was destroyed. It was because of his idolatry and *the innocent blood which he shed, which the Lord would not pardon*.

1.2. In consideration of their present impenitence. Their sin is described (v. 6): "*Thou hast forsaken me*, my service and your responsibility to me; *thou hast gone backward* and become the opposite of what you should have been." The impenitence is described (v. 7): *They return not from their ways*, the ways of their own hearts, back to the ways of God's commandments. There is mercy for those who have turned aside if they return, but what favor can be expected by those who persist in turning away from God?

2. What the sentence is. It is ruin.

2.1. God himself abandons them: *My mind cannot be toward them* (v. 1). It is not in a fit of anger, but with a just and holy indignation, that he says, "*Cast them out of my sight*, and let *them go forth*, for I will not be troubled with them anymore."

2.2. He will not allow any intercession to be made for them (v. 1): "*Though Moses and Samuel stood before me* to reconcile me to them by prayer or sacrifice, I still could not admit them into my favor."

2.3. He condemns them all to one destructive judgment or another. When God rejects them from his presence, *whither shall they go forth?* (v. 2). *Such as are for death to death*, or *for the sword to the sword*. It is the kind of choice David was given, a choice that put him into great distress (2Sa 24:14). *Captivity* is mentioned last, some think, because it is the harshest judgment, being both a complication and a continuation of miseries. The judgment by *the sword* is repeated (v. 3) and is made the first of another set of four destroyers. As those who escape *the sword* will be destroyed by plague, famine, or captivity, so those who fall by the sword will be cut off by divine vengeance. There will be *dogs to tear* in the city and *fowls of the air* and *wild beasts* in the field to devour. And if anyone thinks they can outrun justice, *they shall be removed into all kingdoms of the earth* (v. 4), like Cain, who became a restless wanderer on earth (Ge 4:12).

2.4. They will fall without being helped.

2.4.1. God, even their own God (Ps 67:6), will fight against them: *I will stretch out my hand against thee*; it will be a deliberate stroke, which will wound deeply. *I am weary with repenting*, I can no longer show compassion (v. 6); by their faithless professions of repentance, they have strained even infinite patience to the limit. Now he will grant no more reprieves.

2.4.2. Their own country will expel them; it will be ready to *spew them out*, for this was threatened (Lev 18:28). *I will fan them with a fan* (I will winnow them with a winnowing fork) *in the gates of the land*, in their own gates, or "into the gates of the earth," into the cities of all the nations around them (v. 7).

2.4.3. Their own children will be cut off from them: *I will bereave them of children*; they will have little hope that the next generation will restore their affairs, for *I will destroy my people*.

2.4.3.1. The destroyer will be brought on them (v. 8). Nebuchadnezzar is here called *a spoiler* (destroyer) *at noonday*, not a thief in the night afraid of being discovered, but one who without fear breaks through (Mt 6:19) and destroys. "I have brought against the mother a young man, a spoiler," as some read it, for when Nebuchadnezzar first invaded Judah, he was but *a young man*, in the first year of his reign. Our translation reads it, *I have brought upon them*, even *against the mother of the young men, a spoiler*, that is, against Jerusalem, a mother city, which had a very large family of young men. God *caused him to fall upon it*, that is, on the plunder delivered to him, *suddenly*, and then *terrors* came *upon the city*. "I will cause to fall suddenly upon her [Jerusalem] a watcher and terrors," for the word is used for a watcher (messenger) (Da 4:13, 23), and the Babylonian soldiers were called watchers (4:16).

2.4.3.2. The destruction made by this destroyer will be a terrible slaughter. Wives will be deprived of their husbands: *Their widows are increased above the sand of the seas* (v. 8). God says, *They are increased to me*. Although the husbands will be destroyed by the sword of his justice, their poor widows will be gathered to the arms of his mercy; among the titles of his honor is *the God of the widows*. Parents will be deprived of their children. When the children are killed, the mother will *give up the ghost*, for her life was bound up with theirs: *Her sun has gone down while it was yet day* (v. 9). Some understand the languishing mother to refer to Jerusalem mourning the death of her inhabitants as passionately as a poor mother wails for her dead children.

2.5. They will fall without being pitied (v. 5): "*For who shall have pity on thee, O Jerusalem?* When your God has *cast thee out of his sight* (2Ki 17:20), neither your enemies nor your friends will have any compassion on you. *O Israel! thou hast destroyed thyself*" (Hos 13:9).

Verses 10–14

Jeremiah has now returned from his public work and withdrawn to his private room (Mt 6:6); we have an account in these verses of what took place between him and his God there.

1. The complaint that the prophet made to God about the many discouragements he faced in his work (v. 10).

1.1. He met with a great deal of contradiction and opposition. He was *a man of strife and contention*. Both city and country fought against and quarreled with him, doing all they could to oppose him. He was a peaceful man, and yet he was *a man of strife*, not a man striving but a man who was striven with; he was for peace, but when he spoke, they were for war (Ps 120:7). The real cause of their quarrels with him was his faithfulness to God and to their souls. He showed them their sins that were leading to their destruction and showed them how they could prevent that ruin, but they were angry with him. The Gospel of peace (Ro 10:15; Isa 52:7) brings division (Mt 10:34–35; Lk 12:49, 51). Now this made Jeremiah very uneasy. He cried out, *Woe is me, my mother, that thou hast borne me* (v. 10); he was angry that she had *borne him a man of strife*. This appears to be a sign of weakness, but we rather hope that it was intended to be no more than a passionate lament for his situation. Even those who are most peaceful are often made to be people of strife. But if we cannot live as peacefully with our neighbors as we would like, we must not be so disturbed as to lose calmness in our own minds and make ourselves anxious.

1.2. He met with a great deal of scorn and insults. They branded him as factious, as one who sowed the seeds of discord (Pr 6:14, 19) and incited them to rebellion. They should have blessed him and blessed God for him, but they cursed God's messenger and did all they could to make his life horrible. But one would tend to suspect that surely Jeremiah had given them some cause to be offended as they were; but no: *I have neither lent money nor borrowed* money. It is implied here that those who deal much in the business of this world are often involved in strife and contention. It showed Jeremiah's wisdom that because he was called to be a prophet, he *entangled not himself in the affairs of this life* (2Ti 2:4), so that he might not give the least suspicion that he aimed at secular advantages in his work. He did not lend any money, for he was no usurer; he borrowed no money, for he was no merchant. We find in 16:2 that he had neither wife nor children to keep. But he was still exposed to a general hatred because of the sin of those times.

2. The answer God gave to this complaint.

2.1. God assured him that he would weather the storm and finally be at peace (v. 11). "If I do not take care of you, may I never be considered faithful; *verily it shall go well with thy remnant*, with the remainder of your life," as the word may mean; "the remainder of your days will be more comfortable to you than those up to this time have been." "Thy end shall be good" is the Aramaic reading. It seems that Jeremiah was not only vexed by the way his people treated him but also uneasy at the apprehension of sharing in the public judgments he foresaw would come: "If my friends are so abusive to me, what will my enemies do?" But God quieted his mind with this promise: "*Verily I will cause the enemy to entreat* (plead with) *thee well in the time of evil*, when everything around you is devastated." This promise was fulfilled when Nebuchadnezzar, having taken the city, charged the commander of the imperial guard to be kind to Jeremiah and let him have everything he asked for (39:11–12). When the following words, *Shall iron break the northern iron, and the steel* (bronze)? (v. 12), are compared with the promise of God made to Jeremiah (1:18), that he would make him an *iron pillar* and *brazen* (bronze) *walls*, they seem intended to encourage him. The people were continually clashing with him and were rough and hard as iron, but because Jeremiah was armed with power and courage from heaven, he was like northern iron, which is naturally stronger, and like steel, which is hardened by human skill, and so they would not prevail against him; compare this with Eze 2:6; 3:8–9.

2.2. God assured him that his enemies and persecutors would be lost in the storm (vv. 13–14). God turned here from speaking to the prophet to addressing the people. To them v. 12 may also be applied: *Shall iron break the northern iron, and the steel?* Will their courage and strength, will the boldest and most vigorous of their efforts, be able to resist either the purpose of God or the army of the Babylonians, which are as inflexible and invincible as the northern iron and steel? Let them therefore listen to their condemnation: *Thy substance* (wealth) *and thy treasure will I give to the spoil* (as plunder), and that *without price* (without charge). The prophet was poor; he had nothing to lose, neither wealth nor treasure, and so the enemy would treat him well. But the people who had great financial wealth or great lands would be killed for what they had. Every part of the country, even those that were most remote, had contributed to the national guilt, and all would now be brought to account. "*I will make thee to pass with thy enemies*, who will lead you in triumph *into a land that thou knowest not*, and one you can therefore expect to find no comfort in."

Verses 15–21

Here, as before, we have:

1. The prophet's humble address to God, "*O Lord! thou knowest*; you understand my sincerity, which people have decided they will not acknowledge; you know my distress, which people scorn to notice."

1.1. The prophet prays (v. 15):

1.1.1. That God would consider his case and be mindful of him: "*O Lord! remember me*; think about me for good."

1.1.2. That God would communicate strength and comfort to him: *Visit me.*

1.1.3. That God would support him: *Revenge me of my persecutors*, or rather, "Vindicate me. Vindicate me from them: release me; vindicate me against them: avenge me; vindicate me in their eyes: justify me. Render judgment against them, and let that judgment be carried out so far as is needed to vindicate me and to make them acknowledge that they have wronged me." Good people will not want God to avenge them further than this. Let something be done to convince the world that Jeremiah is a righteous man and that the God whom he serves is righteous.

1.1.4. That God would still spare him: "*Take me not away* by a sudden stroke, but *in thy longsuffering* lengthen my days." Although he had complained passionately about his birth (v. 10), he still did not want his death to come quickly, for life is sweet to nature, and the life of a useful person is sweet to grace.

1.2. He offers several pleas in support of his prayers:

1.2.1. That God's honor is at stake in this situation: *Know*, and make it known, *that for thy sake I have suffered rebuke* (v. 15). If it is for doing good that we suffer, and for righteousness' sake that people say all kinds of evil things against us (Mt 5:11), we may hope that God will vindicate our honor with his own. V. 16 is to the same effect: *I am called by* (I bear) *thy name, O Lord of hosts!*

1.2.2. That he has experienced the word of God in his own soul; his task is to preach that to others, and so he has been given the graces of the Spirit, as well as his gifts, to qualify him for God's favor. Jeremiah can say (v. 16): "*Thy words were found*, found *by me*, found *for me. I* not only tasted them but also *did eat them*, received them completely. They were welcome to me, as food is to someone who is hungry." The prophet was told to *eat the roll* in Eze 2:8 and Rev 10:9. *I did eat it*—that is, as it follows, it *was to me the joy and rejoicing my heart*; nothing could be more agreeable. We may understand this to refer to:

1.2.2.1. The message itself that he was to communicate. Although he was to foretell the ruin of his country, which was dear to him, and whose ruin he would share deeply in, all natural affections were swallowed up in zeal for God's glory. Because these messages of wrath were divine messages, they gave him assurance. He also rejoiced, at first, in the hope that the people would accept the warning and so avert the judgment. Or:

1.2.2.2. The commission he received to communicate this message. Although the work he was called to was not accompanied by any worldly advantages, but, on the contrary, exposed him to contempt and persecution, it was his *meat and drink to do the will of him that sent him* (Jn 4:34). Or:

1.2.2.3. The promise God gave him that he would help and acknowledge him in his work (v. 18).

1.2.3. He pleads that he has applied himself to the duty of his office with seriousness and self-denial, even though recently he has received only a little satisfaction from it

(v. 17). He has *sat alone*, spent a great deal of time in his room, *because the hand* of the Lord has been strong on him to help him continue his work (Eze 3:14). "*For thou hast filled me with indignation* (v. 17), with such messages of wrath against this people as have always given me so much to think about." It is his complaint that he has had only a little pleasure in his work. It originally gave joy to his heart but recently it has made him depressed, so that he has no heart to *sit in the meeting of those that make merry* (30:19; 31:4). He has *sat alone*, grieving over the people's obstinacy and the little success of his labor among them.

1.2.4. He throws himself on God's pity and promise by pleading very passionately (v. 18), "*Why is my pain perpetual*, and nothing done to relieve it? Will the God who has promised me a sense of his presence *be to me as a liar*? Will the God on whom I depend be to me *as waters that fail*? No; I know you will not be." God is not a human being that he should lie (Nu 23:19). The fountain of life will never be to his people as *waters that fail*.

2. God's gracious answer to this address (vv. 19–21). Notice:

2.1. What God required of him here. God would acknowledge him, but:

2.1.1. He must regain his temper and become reconciled to his work. He must *return*; he must shake off these distrustful and discontented thoughts and emotions, not giving way to them.

2.1.2. He must decide to be faithful in his work. Although there was no cause at all to accuse Jeremiah of unfaithfulness, and God knew his heart was sincere, God still saw fit to give him this caution. You must *take forth the precious* (worthy) *from the vile* (worthless) (v. 19). The righteous are the precious even if they are very humble and poor; evildoers are worthless even if they are very rich and great. In our congregations these are mixed, wheat and chaff in the same room; we cannot distinguish them by name, but we must by character, and must give to each a portion, comfort to precious saints and terror to worthless sinners: *Let them return to thee, but return not thou to them*, that is, he must do all he can in his preaching to bring people back to the mind of God. As for those who had run away from God, "*Let them return to thee*. Let them have second thoughts, accept my terms, but do not *return to them*, do not compliment them or think you can make matters easier for them than the word of God has made it."

2.2. What God promised here. If Jeremiah proved himself well:

2.2.1. God would calm his mind and his present spiritual turmoil: *If thou return, I will bring thee again, will restore thy soul* (Ps 23:3).

2.2.2. God would use him in his service as a prophet: "*Thou shalt stand before me* to receive instructions from me, as servants do from their masters, and *thou shalt be as my mouth* to communicate my messages to the people, as an ambassador is the mouthpiece of a ruler who sends them."

2.2.3. He would have the strength and courage to face the many difficulties in his work, and his spirit would not fail as it now had (v. 20): "*I will make thee unto this people as a fenced brazen* (bronze) *wall*, which the storm batters and beats violently against but cannot shake. *Return not thou to them* by any sinful alliances, and then trust with holy determination that your God will protect you by his grace. Do not be cowardly, and God will make you bold." He had complained that he was made *a man*

of strife (v. 10). "Expect to be so," God says. "They *will fight against thee; but they shall not prevail against thee*" (v. 20).

2.2.4. He would have God to rescue him: *I am with thee to save thee* (v. 20). Those who have God with them have a Savior with them who has enough wisdom and strength to deal with the most formidable enemy (v. 21). Many things appear very frightening but do not prove at all harmful to good people.

CHAPTER 16

In this chapter: 1. The greatness of the disaster that is coming on the Jewish nation is illustrated by prohibitions given to the prophet: he must not set up a house of his own (vv. 1–4), not go into the house where there is a funeral meal (vv. 5–7), and not go into the house of feasting (vv. 8–9). 2. God is justified in acting so severely against them because of their great sin (vv. 10–13). 3. An indication is given of mercy in reserve (vv. 14–15). 4. Some hope is given that the punishment of the sin will lead to the reformation of the sinners (vv. 16–21).

Verses 1–9

The prophet is to be a sign to the people here. They would not consider what he *said*; so let there be a test to see whether they will consider what he *does*. He must conduct himself as befits one who expects to see his country in ruins very soon. He foretold this, but he is to show that he himself is fully convinced of its truth. He is forbidden marriage, mourning for the dead, and joy.

1. Jeremiah must not marry or think of having a family (v. 2). The Jews prided themselves on their early marriages and numerous children, but Jeremiah must live a celibate life. By this it is made clear that such a discipline was advisable only in times of disaster and times of *present distress* (1Co 7:26); the undertaking of it was part of the disaster itself. When we see such times approaching, it is wise for everyone, and especially prophets, to keep themselves from being encumbered with what will bring more care, fear, and grief, the closer it is to them. The reason given is that the *fathers* and *mothers, the sons and the daughters, shall die of grievous deaths* (die of deadly diseases) (vv. 3–4). Those with wives and children will have such a burden on them that they cannot escape death. The death of every child, and its circumstances, will be a new death to the parent. It would be better to have no children than to give birth to them and have them brought up *for the murderer* (Hos 9:13–14), better to have none than to see them live and die in misery. Mourning the dead and burying them are denied (v. 4): *They shall not be lamented*, but will be carried away, as if all the world were weary of them. In fact, they *shall not be buried*, but left exposed. *They shall be as dung upon the face of the earth*, not only contemptible but also detestable. Since they will be *consumed*, some *by the sword* and some *by famine, their carcases shall be meat for the fowls of heaven and the beasts of the earth.*

2. Jeremiah must not go to the house of mourning, to any house where there is a funeral meal upon the death of any of his neighbors or relatives (v. 5). It was usual to express one's condolences to those whose relatives had died, to *bemoan them* (weep with them), *cut themselves*, and *make themselves bald* (v. 6), which were expressions of mourning, though forbidden by the Law (Dt 14:1). Sometimes, in an outburst of grief, they *tore themselves for them* (v. 7). They used to mourn *to comfort them for*

the dead, as the Jews did with Martha and Mary, and they showed their sympathy by *giving them a cup of consolation to drink* (v. 7), providing drinks for them to keep them going in their grief. Those who were grieving would then know that although they had lost *their father or their mother* (v. 7), they still had friends who were concerned for them. It is good to *go to the house of mourning* (Ecc 7:2). The prophet Jeremiah did such kind acts habitually. But now God tells him not to mourn the death of his friends. His sorrow for the coming destruction of his country in general must swallow his sorrow for individual deaths. People will be involved so much in death that they will have no time, opportunity, or heart for the ceremonies that used to accompany death. All will be mourners then, and no one will be comforters; everyone will find it enough to bear their own burden, for (v. 5), God says, "*I have taken away my peace from this people*, brought to an end their prosperity, deprived them of health, wealth, quiet, friends, and everything with which they might comfort themselves and one another." Whatever peace we enjoy, it is God's peace. It is his gift, and *if he give quietness, who then can make trouble?* But if we do not use his peace well, he can and will take it away (Job 34:29). Then we can say farewell to all that is good, for it will all be gone when God takes away from us his unfailing love and his mercy.

3. Jeremiah must not go to the house of mirth (Ecc 7:4) any more than to the house of mourning (v. 8). God was coming against them in his judgment, and it was time for them to *humble themselves* (Jas 4:10). Ministers should be examples of self-denial. His friends wondered that he would not meet them as he used to in the house of feasting. But he told them it was to show them that all their feasting would soon come to an end (v. 9): "*I will cause to cease the voice of mirth.* You will have nothing to feast on, nothing to rejoice in. Instead, you will be surrounded by adversities that will spoil and dampen your joy." God can find ways of restraining the happiest people. "This will be done *in this place*, in Jerusalem, which used to be the *joyous city* (Isa 22:2; 23:7; 32:13) and thought her joys were all secure. It will be done *in your eyes*, in your sight, to be upsetting to you, who now look so proud and so joyful." They had stopped the voice of praise by their sins and idolatry, and so God had justly stopped *the voice of mirth and gladness* among them. They no longer listened to the voice of God's prophets, and so no longer would *the voice of the bridegroom and of the bride*, the songs that used to grace the wedding feast, be heard among them. See also 7:34.

Verses 10–13

Here:

1. An inquiry is made into the reasons why God will bring those judgments (v. 10): "*What is our iniquity? Or what is our sin?* What crime have we ever been guilty of that is proportionate to such a sentence?" Instead of humbling and condemning themselves, they try to justify themselves and suggest that God has wronged them in decreeing this disaster on them.

2. A clear and full answer is given to this inquiry. Do they ask the prophet why God is so angry with them? The righteous God is never *angry without cause*, without good cause, and so he must tell them particularly what it is, so that they may be humbled, or at least so that God may be justified.

2.1. God is punishing them because of the sins of their ancestors (v. 11): *Your fathers have forsaken me, and have not kept my law.* They shook off divine institutions and *walked after other gods*, whose worship was brighter and

showier. Because they liked variety and indulging in the latest thing, they *served them and worshipped them.* This was the sin that God had said, in the second commandment, he would *visit upon their children*, who would follow such idolatrous customs.

2.2. God is also judging them for their own sins (v. 12): "You have made your ancestors' sins your own and have become liable to receive the punishment that was deferred in their days, for *you have done worse than your fathers.*"

2.2.1. If they had made good use of their ancestors' reprieve and been led by the patience of God to repentance, the judgment would have been prevented and the reprieve turned to a national pardon. But they have been more arrogant and obstinate in sinning than their ancestors were. They have allowed their own passions to be expressed noisily, so that they might drown out the voice of their consciences.

2.2.2. It is not surprising, then, that God has made this decision (v. 13): "*I will cast* (throw) *out of this land*, this land of light, this valley of vision (Isa 22:1, 5), into a far country, *a land that you know not, neither you nor your fathers.*" Two things will make their situation there very miserable, and both of them relate to the soul. First: "It is the happiness of the soul to be employed in serving God, but *there shall you serve other gods day and night* (v. 13), perhaps compelled to do so by your cruel taskmasters, and when you are forced to worship idols, you will be as sick of such worship as you were fond of it when it was forbidden you by your godly kings." Second: "It is the happiness of the soul to have some signs of the unfailing love of God, but you will go to a foreign land, *where I will not show you favour.*"

Verses 14–21

There is both mercy and judgment in these verses, and some seem to look as far forward as the times of the Gospel.

1. God will certainly carry out his judgment on them for their idolatry. The decree has been declared.

1.1. God sees all their sins (v. 17), even though they commit them in great secrecy and cover them up very skillfully: *My eyes are upon all their ways.*

1.2. God is highly displeased, especially at their idolatry (v. 18). As his omniscience convicts them, so his justice condemns them: "*I will recompense their iniquity and their sin double*, not double what it deserves, but double what they expect." The sin for which God has a dispute with them is that they have *defiled God's land* with their idolatry. Idols are *carcases of detestable things*. God hates them, and so should we.

1.3. He will raise up instruments of his wrath that will *cast* (throw) *them out of their land*, according to the sentence passed (v. 16): *I will send for many fishers and many hunters*—the Babylonian army, which will have ways of trapping them, by trickery, like fishermen, and by force, like hunters. These fishermen and hunters will discover them wherever they have hidden themselves, in *hills, mountains*, or *holes of the rocks*.

1.4. Their exile in Babylon will be more painful than their slavery in Egypt, their taskmasters more cruel, and their lives more bitter. This is implied in the promise (vv. 14–15) that their restoration from Babylon will be more welcome to them than their rescue from Egypt. Their slavery in Egypt came on them gradually; their exile in Babylon came on them suddenly and with all the fearful circumstances of terror. In Egypt they had a

Goshen of their own (Ge 45:10; 46:34), but they had no place like that in Babylon. In Egypt they were treated as servants who were useful, but in Babylon as captives who had been hateful.

1.5. They will be warned; these judgments have a voice, and they speak instruction to the people. When God corrects them, he teaches them. God uses this rod of discipline to plead with them (v. 20): *"Shall a man make gods to himself* (do people make their own gods)?" These judgments also speak honor to God, for he will be known by the judgments he executes (Ps 9:16). "For *this once,* and no more, *I will cause them to know my hand,* how far it can reach and how deeply it can wound."

2. But he has mercy in store for them. It was said, with a note of severity (v. 13), that God would banish them to a strange land, but words of comfort immediately follow.

2.1. *The days will come,* days of joy, when the same hand that dispersed them will gather them again (vv. 14–15). They will be driven out, but not rejected totally. *I will bring them again into their own land* and settle them there. And the following words (v. 16) may be understood as a promise; God will send for fishermen and hunters, the Medes and Persians, who will find them in the countries where they are scattered and send them back to their own land.

2.2. Their restoration from Babylon will be more memorable than their rescue from Egypt. The fresh mercy will be so surprising and welcome that it will even abolish the memory of the earlier one. The rescue of Israel out of Egypt was done *by might and power,* but their rescue from Babylon was done *by the Spirit of the Lord of hosts* (Zec 4:6). In this later rescue there was more forgiveness than in that one, for their exile in Babylon contained more punishment of sin than their slavery in Egypt.

2.3. Their restoration from exile will be accompanied by a blessed reformation, and they will return healed of their tendency to idolatry. They have defiled their own land with their *detestable things* (v. 18). But when they have suffered for so doing, they will come and humble themselves before God (vv. 19–21).

2.3.1. They will be brought to acknowledge that only their God is the true God. Like Jeremiah, they will call him *"my strength* to support and comfort me, *my fortress* to protect and shelter me, *and my refuge* to whom I may flee *in the day of affliction."*

2.3.2. They will be quickened to return to him by the conversion of the Gentiles: *"The Gentiles shall come to thee from the ends of the earth* (v. 19), and so shall we not come?" The prophet comforts himself with the hope of this: *"O Lord! my strength and my fortress,* I am now at peace, since you have given me a view of many people who will *come to thee from the ends of the earth,* of both Jewish and Gentile converts."

2.3.3. They will acknowledge the foolish ways of their ancestors, as will befit them, since they will be suffering for their ancestors' sins: *"Surely our fathers have inherited lies, vanity, and things wherein there is no profit* (worthless idols that did them no good). We are now aware that they were deceived in their idolatrous worship; it did not deliver what it promised, and so what have we to do with it anymore?"

2.3.4. They will reason themselves out of their idolatry, and the reformation that arises from a rational conviction of the great absurdity of sin is likely to be long-lasting.

2.3.5. They will here give honor to God because he has made his name known to them by making his power known to them (v. 21). Nothing less than the mighty power

of divine grace, known in our own experience, can make us rightly know the name of God as it is revealed to us.

2.4. Their restoration from exile will be a type and figure of the great salvation to be brought about by the Messiah, who will *gather together in one the children of God that were scattered abroad* (Jn 11:52).

CHAPTER 17

1. God convicts the Jews of the sin of idolatry and condemns them to captivity for it (vv. 1–4). 2. He shows them the foolishness of all their worldly confidence (vv. 5–11). 3. The prophet makes his appeal to God on the occasion of the hatred of his enemies toward him, committing himself to God's protection and begging God to support him (vv. 12–18). 4. Through the prophet, God warns the people to keep the Sabbath day holy, assuring them that if they do, their tranquility will be extended (vv. 19–27).

Verses 1–4

The people have asked (16:10), *What is our iniquity, and what is our sin?*

1. The accusation is fully proved to the captives, both its fact and the blame for it. They cannot plead *Not guilty,* for their sins are recorded in their own conscience. Their sins are obvious to the world (vv. 1–2). They are *written* before God in the most legible and indelible characters (Dt 32:34). They are engraved there with *a pen of iron and with the point of a diamond* (with an iron tool and a flint point). What is written will not be worn out with time; the sin of sinners is never forgotten until it is forgiven. *It is graven upon the table of their heart* (v. 1). What is *graven on the heart* cannot be erased. In fact, we need not appeal to the tablets of the heart; we need go no further to prove the charge than *the horns of their altars,* on which the blood of their idolatrous sacrifices is sprinkled. Their neighbors will bear witness against them, and their own children will *remember the altars and the groves* (Asherah poles) to which their parents took them when they were little (v. 2). Their hearts are still biased as strongly as ever toward their idols, and they have not been persuaded either by the word of God or by his discipline to reduce their affection for them. It is written *upon the horns of their altars,* for they have given up their names to their idols and have committed themselves, as with cords.

2. Because the accusation has been proved, the judgment and the sentence are confirmed (vv. 3–4). Their treasures will be given into the hands of foreigners. Jerusalem is God's *mountain in the field;* it was built on a hill in the middle of a plain. But God will give *all the treasures* of that wealthy city *to the spoil* (as plunder). *"My mountain"*—as the whole land was (Ps 78:54; Dt 11:11)—"you have turned into *your high places for sin.* You have worshiped your idols on *the high hills* (v. 2), and now they will be *given for a spoil in all your borders."* They will be forced to give up their inheritance and will be taken captive to a foreign land (v. 4). Sin brings about a loss of our comforts and deprives us of enjoying what God has given us. It is intimated that when they repent, they will regain possession. But for the present, *you have kindled a fire in my anger* (v. 4), which burns so strongly that it seems as if it would burn *for ever.*

Verses 5–11

The prophet's sermons were not all prophetic; some of them were practical. Let us learn:

1. About the disappointment and trouble that will certainly come to those who depend on created things for success and help in times of trouble (vv. 5–6): *Cursed*—that is, miserable—*is the man* who does so, for he is depending on a splintered reed (2Ki 18:21). The sin that is condemned here is *making flesh the arm* we depend on (v. 5; 2Ch 32:8), the power we work with and on which we rely for protection. God is his people's *arm* (strength) (Isa 33:2). Notice the great offense there is in this sin: it is the *departure of the evil heart of unbelief from the living God* (Heb 3:12). Those who trust in human beings perhaps draw near to God with their mouth, but really *their heart departs from him* (v. 5; Isa 29:13). Clinging to the cistern is leaving the fountain (2:13) and is therefore taken as an insult by the One who is our only fountain. One who puts his confidence in his fellow human beings not only offends God but also deceives himself, for (v. 6) he *shall be like the heath in the desert,* a sad bush or shrub, the crop of barren ground, useless, worthless, and without nourishment. His strength will fail him, and he will wither, be dejected, and be trampled underfoot by everyone around him. *When good comes,* he *shall not see* it and share in it; when times get better, he will not get better with them, but will *inhabit the parched places in the wilderness.* When others enjoy a harvest, he will have none. Those who trust in their own righteousness (Lk 18:9) and think they can do well enough without the grace of Christ *make flesh their arm* (strength), and then their souls cannot prosper; they can neither produce the fruits of services that are acceptable to God (Mt 3:8; Ro 12:1) nor reap the fruits of saving blessings from him; they *dwell in a dry land* (Ps 68:6).

2. About the abundant satisfaction of those who put their confidence in God, who live by faith and rest in him and his love in the most difficult times (vv. 7–8). The duty required of us is to *make the Lord our hope* (v. 7), his favor the good we hope for, and his power the strength we hope in. The one who puts his confidence in God will be *as a tree planted by the waters* (v. 8), a good tree, which has had great care taken that it be set in the best soil. He will be like a tree that *spreads out its roots,* firmly established, spreading them out *by the rivers,* from which it draws deep nourishment. Those who put their hope in God are at peace and enjoy continual security and calmness of mind. A tree that is planted and watered in this way will *not see when heat comes*; it will not sustain any damage from the most scorching heats of summer. It is so well moistened by its roots that it will be sufficiently strong in times of drought. Those who make God their hope will flourish like a tree that is *always green,* whose leaf does not wither (Ps 1:3); they will be cheerful in themselves and beautiful in the eyes of others. They will be established with inner peace and satisfaction: they *shall not be careful* (will have no worries) *in a year of drought,* when there is a lack of rain, for just as the tree has *seed in itself* (Ge 1:11), so it has *its moisture* (Lk 8:6). We need not be worried about a cistern breaking as long as we have the fountain (2:13). Those who trust in God, who by faith in him derive strength and grace from him, *shall not cease from yielding fruit.*

3. About the sinfulness of the human heart and the divine scrutiny it is always under (vv. 9–10). It is foolish to trust in mere mortals, for they are not only frail but also false and deceitful. We think we trust in God when really we are not doing so, as becomes clear when we observe that our hopes and fears rise or fall according to whether our circumstances are good or bad. There is evil in our hearts that we ourselves are not aware of and do not suspect is there. *The heart,* the human conscience, in the corrupt and fallen state, *is deceitful above all things* (v. 9). It calls evil good and good evil (Isa 5:20), giving false descriptions to things. When people say in their hearts that there is no God (Ps 14:1) or that he does not see (Ps 94:7), in these and a thousand similar suggestions the heart is deceitful. The situation is truly bad if the conscience, which should put right the errors of the other faculties, is itself a source of falsehood and a ringleader in the delusion. We cannot know our own hearts or what they will do in times of temptation—Hezekiah did not (2Ki 18:13–16; 20:12–18), and Peter did not (Mt 26:33–35, 69–75). Much less can we know the hearts of others or depend on them. Whatever evil there is in the heart, God sees it (v. 10): *I the Lord search the heart.* The judgment God makes of the heart is made *to give to every man according to his ways and according to the fruit of his doings.*

4. About the curse that comes on wealth that is gained unjustly (v. 11): *He that gets riches and not by right,* even though he may put his hope in them, will never enjoy them. He who has gained *treasures* by deceit and lies may congratulate himself on his success and say, *I am rich,* but the wealth will be taken from away him, or he will be parted from his riches. Those who obtain grace, on the other hand, will be wise *in the latter end*; they will have the strength and encouragement of that grace in death and to eternity (Pr 19:20). Those who place their happiness in the wealth of the world will regret its folly when it is too late. They are like *the partridge that sits on eggs and hatches them not*; they are broken (as Job 39:15) or stolen (as Isa 10:14), or they become rotten. Rich people take a great deal of effort to gather their wealth, and then they sit brooding on it, but they never have any true and deep comfort or satisfaction in it.

Verses 12–18

The prophet withdraws for private meditation, to be *alone with God.*

1. He acknowledges the great favor of God to his people in establishing a revealed religion among them and honoring them with divine institutions (v. 12): *A glorious high throne from the beginning is the place of our sanctuary.* The temple at Jerusalem, where God revealed his special presence, where the people showed their faithfulness to their Sovereign, and to which they fled for refuge in distress, was the *place of their sanctuary.* It was a throne of holiness, God's throne. Jerusalem is called the *city of the great King* (Ps 48:2), not only Israel's King but also the King of the whole earth, so that it might justly be considered the royal city of the world. It was *from the beginning* (2Ch 2:9). Jeremiah here mentions this either as a plea with God for mercy to their land or to emphasize the sin of his people in abandoning God even though his throne was among them.

2. He acknowledges the righteousness of God in abandoning to ruin those who have rebelled from their allegiance to him (v. 13). He speaks to God as one who agrees that his judgment is just: "*O Lord! the hope of* those in Israel who remain faithful to you, *all that forsake thee shall be ashamed.*" "Let them be ashamed" is how some read it, and on that reading it is a request for his grace, to make them penitently ashamed. "*Those that depart from me,* from the word of God that I have preached, are in effect abandoning God," as those who return to God are said to turn to the prophet (15:19). "*Those that depart from thee,*" as some read it, "will be *written in the earth*

(dust). They will soon be blotted out, as what is written in the dust. They have *forsaken the Lord, the fountain of living waters*—that is, spring waters—for broken cisterns" (2:13).

3. He prays to God for healing and saving mercy for himself (v. 14): Lord, *heal me* and *save me.* He was wounded in spirit for many reasons. He was continually exposed to the hatred of unreasonable people. To back up this request he pleads, *Heal thou me, and then I shall be healed.* If God upholds us, we will live; if he protects us, we will be safe. "Thou shalt be my praise" is how some read it; "heal me and save me, and you will receive the glory for it."

4. He complains about the unfaithfulness and arrogant ungodliness of the people to whom he has preached. He has faithfully communicated God's message to them, and what answer does he have to give to the One who sent him? *Behold, they say unto me, Where is the word of the Lord? Let it come now* (v. 15; Isa 5:19). They ridicule the prophet. They deny the truth of what he says: "If that is the *word of the Lord* that you are speaking to us, *where is it?* Why has it not been fulfilled?" They defy the terror of what he says. "Let God Almighty do his worst; let all he has said come to pass; we will be fine; the lion is not as fierce as it is painted!" (Am 5:18).

5. He appeals to God concerning the faithful fulfillment of the duty to which he was called (v. 16). He has continued to be faithful in his work, but his office as a prophet, instead of protecting him, has exposed him to contempt and injury. "But," he says, *"I have not hastened from being a pastor after thee; I have not run away from being your shepherd. I have not left my work."* Jeremiah was a true pastor, or shepherd, to the people of God, feeding them on the good word of God, and although he faced as much difficulty and discouragement as anyone ever has, he still did not run away, as Jonah did (Jnh 1), or want to be excused from going on any more of God's missions. He maintained his love for the people. Even though they were very abusive toward him, he remained compassionate toward them: *I have not desired the woeful day* (the day of despair). The day of the fulfillment of his prophecies would truly be a desperate day for Jerusalem, and so he wished it would never come. God does not, and so ministers must not, desire the death of sinners, but instead they should desire that sinners turn back to God and live (Eze 18:32; 33:11). He kept closely to his instructions. Although he could have sought the favor of the people if he had not been so sharp in his rebukes, he would continue to communicate his messages faithfully.

6. He humbly begs God to acknowledge him, protect him, and enable him to continue in the work to which he has so clearly called him. He wants two things here:

6.1. That he might have comfort in serving the God who sent him (v. 17): *Be not thou a terror to me.* He pleads, "Thou art my hope, and then nothing else is my fear. My dependence is on you, and so *be not a terror to me."*

6.2. That he might have the courage to deal with the people to whom he was sent (v. 18). The people persecuted him when they should have received and encouraged him. "Lord," he says, *"let them be confounded*—may they be ashamed of their obstinacy, or may the judgments threatened be finally carried out on them—*but let not me be confounded,* do not let me be terrified by their threats so that I betray my trust." As to his persecutors, he prays, *Bring upon them the day of evil,* in the hope that its coming on them might prevent it from coming on the whole country.

Verses 19–27

These verses are a sermon concerning keeping the Sabbath holy. This message about keeping the Sabbath was probably sent in the days of Josiah, to further that work of reformation that he had set in motion. It must be declared first at the court gate, the gate *by which the kings of Judah come in and go out* (v. 19). Let them be told their duty first, for if Sabbaths are not kept holy, *the rulers of Judah are to be contended with* (rebuked), for they are certainly failing in their duty. Jeremiah must also preach it *in all the gates of Jerusalem.* It is a matter of great and general concern, and so let them all take notice of it. Notice:

1. How the Sabbath is to be kept holy, what the law about it is (vv. 21–22). They must rest from their worldly work on the Sabbath day. They must *bear no burden* (carry a load) into the city or out of it. Farmers' loads of grain must not be carried in, manure must not be carried out, nor traders' loads, nor merchandise. A loaded horse, cart, or wagon must not be seen on the Sabbath in the streets or on the roads; those carrying loads must not work on that day, nor must servants be allowed to take in provisions or fuel. It is a day of rest, and so must not be made a day of labor, except in cases of necessity. *"Hallow you the sabbath* (v. 22), that is, consecrate it to the honor of God; keep it holy and spend it in serving and worshiping him." Worldly business must be set aside, so that we may devote ourselves to the work that requires and deserves the whole person. *"Take heed to yourselves* (v. 21), for your lives are in danger if you rob God of the part of your time that he has reserved for himself." Let not the soul be burdened by the cares of this world on the Sabbath. "This is no new imposition, but is what *I commanded your fathers"* (v. 22).

2. How the Sabbath has been desecrated (v. 23): "Your ancestors were required to keep the Sabbath holy, *but they obeyed not*; they *hardened their necks* against this as well as other commands given them." Where Sabbaths are neglected, all religion decays significantly.

3. What blessings God has in store for them if they will be careful to keep the Sabbath holy. The court will flourish. *Kings* in succession, with the other *princes* (officials) who *sit upon the thrones of* judgment, will ride in great pomp *through the gates of Jerusalem* (v. 25). The city will flourish. Jerusalem, *the holy city, shall remain for ever*; "it will be forever inhabited"; it will not be destroyed and depopulated, as is threatened. The country will flourish (v. 26): *The cities of Judah and the land of Benjamin* will be filled with vast numbers of inhabitants; they will have much and live in peace. The church will flourish: *Meat offerings* (grain offerings), *and incense, and sacrifices of praise* (thank offerings) will be brought *to the house of the Lord.* A people truly flourish when religious faith flourishes among them. And this is the effect of Sabbath sanctification; when that branch of religious faith is kept up, other instances of it are also kept up, but when that is lost, devotion is lost either in superstition or in worldliness. The streams of all religious faith run either deep or shallow according to whether the banks of the Sabbath are maintained or neglected.

4. What judgments they must expect to come on them if they persist in desecrating the Sabbath (v. 27): *"If you will not hearken* (listen) *to me in* this matter, to keep the gates shut on Sabbath days, so that there is no unnecessary *entering in or* going out on that day—if you will break through the guidelines of divine law and treat that day the same as any other day—know that God will *kindle a fire in the gates* of your city." Gates will justly be set on fire

when they have not been used, as they should have been, to shut sin out, keep people in, and keep them attending to their duty.

CHAPTER 18

In this chapter we have: 1. God's ways in dealing with nations and kingdoms (vv. 1–6). If he threatens their ruin, then when they repent, he will return in mercy to them, and when he is coming toward them in mercy, nothing but their sin will stop the advance of his favors (vv. 7–10). 2. A particular demonstration of the foolishness of the people of Judah and Jerusalem in abandoning their God to follow idols (vv. 11–17). 3. The prophet's complaint to God about the corrupt ingratitude and hatred of his enemies, and his prayers against them (vv. 18–23).

Verses 1–10

The prophet is here sent to *the potter's house* (v. 2), not to preach a sermon but to prepare a sermon, or rather to receive it already prepared. "*Go to the potter's house* and notice how he works, and there *I will cause thee*, by silent whispers, *to hear my words.* There I will give you a message to be communicated to the people." The prophet went down to the potter's house (v. 3) and took note of how he worked at the wheel. When a lump of clay he wanted to form into one shape proved too stiff or had a stone in it or came to be *marred in his hand* (v. 4), he immediately formed it into another shape, just *as seems good to the potter.* Ministers will use well their dealings with the business affairs of this life if they take from them examples that help them speak more clearly and familiarly to people about the things of God and explain what the Scriptures mean. While Jeremiah looks carefully at the potter's work, God puts into his mind two great truths that he must preach to *the house of Israel*:

1. That God has both an undeniable authority and an irresistible ability to form kingdoms and nations as he pleases to serve his own purposes: *Cannot I do with you as this potter? saith the Lord* (v. 6). Yes, he can; God has a clearer entitlement to rule over us than the potter has over the clay, for the potter only gives it its form, whereas we have both matter and form from God. This suggests that God has an incontestable sovereignty over us, and it would be as absurd for us to dispute this as for the clay to answer back and quarrel with the potter. It is very easy for God to make what use he pleases of us. One turn of the hand, one turn of the wheel, completely changes the shape of the clay, makes it a pot, unmakes it, and makes it again. In the same way, our times are in God's hand (Ps 31:15). It is spoken here of nations. This is explained by Job (Job 12:23; Ps 107:33; and compare Job 34:29). If the potter's pot is spoiled for one use, it will serve another; those who refuse to be memorials of mercy will become memorials of justice. God formed us out of the clay (Job 33:6); we are still like clay in his hands (Isa 64:8).

2. That in exercising this authority and ability, he acts according to settled rules of justice and goodness. He shows his favor in his sovereignty, but he never punishes arbitrarily. When God is coming against us by way of judgment, we may be sure that it is for our sins. National repentance will stop the progress of his judgment (vv. 7–8). *If God speaks concerning a nation to pluck up* (uproot) its fences that protect it and so exposes the fruit trees that enrich it, and if he removes its fortifications so that the enemy may freely enter—if *that nation* repents of

their sins and reforms their lives, and everyone turns from their evil ways back to God, then God will return in mercy to them (Jnh 3:8–10). It is undoubtedly true that a sincere conversion from the evil of sin will effectively prevent a disastrous punishment, and God can as easily raise up a penitent people from their ruins as the potter can make a fresh jar of clay when it is *marred in his hand* (v. 4). When God is coming toward us in mercy, if there is any delay in the progress of that mercy, it is nothing but sin that causes it (vv. 9–10). Sin is the great troublemaker between God and a people; it makes them lose the right to benefit from his promises and spoils the effectiveness of their prayers. It defeats his kind intentions for them (Hos 7:1).

Verses 11–17

Here is the application to the Jews of the general truths set down in the previous part of the chapter.

1. "*Go, and tell* them," God says, "*Behold, I frame evil* (am preparing a disaster) *against you and devise a device* (a plan) *against you.* Providence in all its operations is clearly working toward destroying you."

2. He invites them by repentance and reformation to meet him and so prevent his further action against them: "*Return you now every one from his evil ways*, so that God may turn from the disaster he had planned to do to you, and then that Providence, which seemed to be formed like a pot on the wheel against you, will immediately be thrown into a new shape, and the outcome will be in your favor."

3. He foresees their stubbornness and their perverse refusal (v. 12): "*They said, There is no hope.* We despair of ever being restored, for we have decided that *we will walk after our own devices.* It is useless for the prophets to say anything further to us. *We will do every one the imagination* (stubbornness) *of his own evil heart* and will not come under the restraints of God's law." They call it liberty to live without restraint, but the reality is that those who are slaves to their own sinful desires are held captive by the worst form of slavery.

4. He rebukes them for the absurd foolishness of their stubbornness and for their hating to be reformed (Lev 26:23) (v. 13): *Ask you among the heathen* (nations)—those without the benefit of divine revelation, with no oracles or prophets—*Who hath heard such a thing?* When the Ninevites were warned in this way, they turned from their evil ways (Jnh 3:6–10). But *the virgin of Israel* defies the call to repent, whatever conscience and Providence say to the contrary, and so *has done a horrible thing.* She should have kept herself pure for God, who had promised her in marriage to himself, but she has separated herself from him and refuses to return to him. Willful impenitence is the most terrible form of suicide, and that is horrible.

5. He shows their foolishness in two things:

5.1. In the nature of the sin itself: they abandoned God for idols (vv. 14–15): "*Will a thirsty traveler leave the snow* that, having melted, runs down from the mountains *of Lebanon*, passes over *the rock of the field*, and *flows* in clear, clean, crystal streams? Will thirsty travelers pass these by and think they will drink better from some mere dirty puddle water? *Or shall the cold flowing waters that come from any other place be forsaken* in the heat of summer?" When people who are dried up with heat and drought come across cool, refreshing streams, they use them. The margin reads, "*Will a man* who is traveling along the road 'leave my fields,' which are plain and level, 'for a rock,' which is rough and hard, or 'for the snow of Lebanon,' which, lying in great drifts, makes the road impassable? *Or shall the running waters be forsaken for the strange cold waters?* But *my people have forgotten me* (v. 15); they have abandoned *a fountain of living waters for broken cisterns* (2:13). *They have burnt incense to* idols (v. 15) that are not what they pretend to be and cannot do what is expected from them." They left *the ancient paths* (v. 15), which had been appointed by God's Law, had been walked in by all the saints, and were therefore the safe and right way to their destination. But when they were advised to keep to the good old way, they positively refused to (6:16). They chose byways; they walked *in a way not cast* (built) *up*, not on the King's highway. Such was the way of idolatry.

5.2. In its troublesome consequences. The direct result was *to make their land desolate* and so make themselves miserable. *Every one that passes by* their land will remark on it, *be astonished* (appalled), *and wag* (shake) *his head*, some wondering, others commiserating, others triumphing at the desolation of a country that was once *the glory of all lands* (Eze 20:6). And it is threatened that when, in the process of their destruction, *their land* has been made *desolate* (v. 17), *I will scatter them as with a* violent *east wind*. What completes their misery is that *I will show them the back, and not the face, in the day of their calamity*. Disasters may be borne relatively easily if God looks toward us and smiles on us, but if he turns *his back* on us, if he shows he is displeased, if he leaves us to ourselves, we are ruined.

Verses 18–23

Here the prophet mentions his own life, for our instruction. Notice:

1. The common methods persecutors use. We read about Jeremiah's enemies (v. 18) that:

1.1. They put their heads together to consider what they could do against him, both to take revenge on him for what he had said and to silence him in the future: *They said, Come and let us devise devices* (plans) *against Jeremiah*, not only against his person but also against the word he communicated to them.

1.2. Here, they pretended to have a mighty zeal for the church, which, they suggested, was in danger if Jeremiah was allowed to preach as he did: *"Come,"* they said, "let us silence and crush him, *for the law shall not perish from the priest. The law of truth is in their mouths* (Mal 2:6), and we will seek it there; the administration of ordinances according to the Law is in their hands, and neither the one nor the other will be taken away from them." They insinuated two things:

1.2.1. That Jeremiah could not himself be a true prophet, but was a pretender, because he was not commissioned by the priests, nor did he agree with the other prophets.

1.2.2. That the theme of his prophecies could not have come from God, because it sometimes reflected badly on the prophets and priests. He had accused them of being the ringleaders of all the trouble (5:31) and deceiving the people (14:14). He had foretold that their *heart would perish* and *be astonished* (horrified) (4:9), that *the wise men would be dismayed* (8:9–10), and that the priests and prophets would be drunk (13:13).

1.3. They agreed to do all they could to ruin his reputation: *Come, let us smite* (attack) *him with the tongue* (v. 18).

1.4. To set others an example, they decided that they themselves would pay no attention to anything he said. *Let us not give heed to any of his words* (v. 18)—for, right

or wrong, they would look on them as *his words*, not the words of God.

1.5. So that they might effectively silence him, they decided to kill him (v. 23): *All their counsel against me is to slay me*. They *hunt for the precious life* (Pr 6:26).

2. The common relief of the persecuted. We may see this in what Jeremiah does. He immediately turns to his God in prayer.

2.1. He refers himself and his cause to God's awareness (v. 19). They would not pay any attention to a word he said, they would not accept his complaints, and they did not take any notice of his criticism; "but, *Lord*," he says, "*do thou give heed to me*. Listen to the voice of those who accuse me, how noisy and wild they are, how false and malicious their words are, and may they *be judged out of their own mouth* (Lk 19:22); *cause their own tongues to fall upon them*" (Ps 64:8).

2.2. He complains about their great ingratitude to him. (v. 20): *"Shall evil be recompensed for good*, and will it go unpunished? Will you not repay me good for bearing this evil?" (2Sa 16:12). *They have dug a pit for my soul* (v. 20); they aimed to take away his life in a dishonest, cowardly, and secret way: *they dug pits for* him, against which there was no protection (Ps 119:85). But notice how great the good was that he did for them: *Remember that I stood before thee to speak good for them*; he has been an intercessor with God for them. But it was not strange that those who had forgotten their God did not know who their best friends really were. It was very painful to him, as it was to David. *For my love they are my adversaries* (Ps 35:13; 109:4). Sinners deal with the great Intercessor just as deceitfully, crucifying him afresh and speaking against him on earth while his blood speaks for them in heaven (Heb 12:24). It was an encouragement to the prophet that when they behaved so spitefully against him, he had the testimony of his conscience that he had done his duty to them.

2.3. He invokes the judgments of God on them, not with a vengeful attitude but in indignation against their wickedness (vv. 21–23). He prays:

2.3.1. That their families may be starved for lack of bread.

2.3.2. That they may be destroyed *by the sword* of war.

2.3.3. That the terrors and desolation of war may come on them suddenly and by surprise, so that their punishment may correspond to their sin (v. 22).

2.3.4. That they may be dealt with as their sin deserves, because it is without excuse.

2.3.5. That God's wrath against them may destroy them: *Let them be overthrown before thee* (v. 23). This is not written for us to imitate. Jeremiah was a prophet, and he could pray by the compulsion of the spirit of prophecy, foreseeing the certain ruin coming on his persecutors, but we are not to pray such prayers. Our Master has taught us, by his command and example, to *bless those that curse us and pray for those that despitefully use us* (Mt 5:44).

CHAPTER 19

The theme of this chapter is the same sad subject as that of the last several—the approaching ruin of Judah and Jerusalem for their sins. 1. Jeremiah must set out their sins before them (vv. 4–5). 2. He must describe the particular judgments that were now quickly coming on them (vv. 6–9). 3. He must do this in the Valley of Ben Hinnom with great solemnity (vv. 2–3). 4. He must summon a company of the elders to witness this (v. 1). 5. He must confirm this with a sign, which was the breaking of a clay jar, meaning that they would be dashed to pieces like a potter's jar (Ps 2:9) (vv. 10–13). 6. When he had done this in the Valley of Ben Hinnom, he confirmed it in the court of the temple (vv. 14–15).

Verses 1–9

The prophet was here sent with a message he had often communicated.

1. He must take some of the elders of the people and some of the priests, leaders in both church and state, to be an audience and witnesses to what he said—the *ancients of the people and the ancients of the priests*. Although most of the elders were discontented with him, there were probably a few who looked on him as a prophet of the Lord and would pay this respect to the heavenly vision.

2. He must *go to the valley of the son of Hinnom* and deliver this message there, for *the word of the Lord* is not limited to any one place. As good a sermon may be preached in the Valley of Ben Hinnom as in the gates of the temple. Christ preached on a mountain and from a boat. This sermon must be preached in *the valley of the son of Hinnom*:

2.1. Because it was there that they had been guilty of the most evil form of their idolatry, the sacrificing of their children to Molech (32:35), and the sight of the place could serve to remind them of this.

2.2. Because it was there that they would feel the most severe adversity. Because it was the common sewer of the city, let them notice how miserable this magnificent city would look when it would be all like the Valley of Ben Hinnom. God told him, "*Proclaim there the words that I shall tell thee* when you come there." God's messages were frequently not revealed to the prophets before they were to deliver them.

3. He must give general notice of a widespread ruin that would now soon come on Judah and Jerusalem (v. 3). "*Hear you the word of the Lord,* even though it is a terrible word." Both rulers and ruled must listen to it. The *kings of Judah,* the king and his sons, the king and his privy councillors, must listen to the word of the King of kings, for, high as they were, he was above them. The *inhabitants of Jerusalem* must also listen to what God had to say to them. Both rulers and people had contributed to the national guilt and must agree to repent nationally, or they would both share in the national destruction. "*He will bring evil upon this place*—on Judah and Jerusalem—that will be so surprising and so dreadful that *whosoever hears* it, *his ears shall tingle.*" The ruin of Eli's house is described in this way (1Sa 3:11), as is that of Jerusalem (2Ki 21:12).

4. He must clearly tell them what their sins were (vv. 4–5). They were accused of turning away from God—*They have forsaken me*—and of abusing the privileges of the visible church, with which they had been honored—they *have estranged this place* (they have made this a place of foreign gods). He accused them of being devoted to and adoring false *gods,* those that *neither they nor their fathers had known.* They took them as their gods without really thinking about it; in fact, because they liked change and new things, they liked those gods more than the true God, and new fashions in religion pleased their fancies as much as new fashions in other things. They also stood accused of deliberate, premeditated murder: *They have filled this place with the blood of innocents.* And as if idolatry and murder committed separately were not bad enough, they had consolidated them into one complex crime, that of burning their children in the fire to Baal (v. 5).

5. He must try to move them with the greatness of the devastation that was coming on them. He must tell them that this *valley of the son of Hinnom* would gain a new name, *the valley of slaughter* (v. 6), for (v. 7) many people would *fall* there *by the sword,* either when they ventured out to kill the besiegers and were repelled or when they tried to escape and were seized. As for those who remained in the city and would not surrender to the besiegers, they would die for lack of food, but only after they had eaten *the flesh of their sons and daughters* and closest *friends* because of the *straitness* (difficulty) *wherewith their enemies would straiten* (distress) *them* (v. 9). Lastly, the whole *city* would be *desolate.* The place that holiness had made *the joy of the whole earth* (Ps 48:2) would be made the shame of the whole earth by sin.

6. He must assure them that all their attempts to prevent and avoid this ruin would be fruitless and futile so long as they continued not to repent and reform (v. 7): *I will make void* (ruin) *the counsel of Judah and Jerusalem,* the advice of the rulers and leaders *in this place.* There is no fleeing from God's justice except by fleeing to his mercy.

Verses 10–15

The message communicated in the previous verses is here backed up:

1. By a visible sign. The prophet is to take along with him an *earthen bottle* (a clay jar) (v. 1), and when he has communicated his message, he is to *break the bottle* in pieces (v. 10). He compared his people in the previous chapter to the potter's clay, which is spoiled as easily as it is formed. But some people might say, "We are past all that; we have been made and hardened long ago." "And although you may be," Jeremiah says, "the finished potter's jar is as soon broken in anyone's hand as the form of the jar in soft clay is spoiled in the potter's hand. But the case of the finished jar is much worse, for as long as the jar is soft clay, even if it is spoiled, it may be molded again, but if it is broken after it is hardened, it can never be put back together again." Symbols and sacramental signs have been used in teaching since ancient times.

1.1. As the bottle is easily and irrecoverably smashed, so will *Judah and Jerusalem* be smashed by the Babylonian army (v. 11). They have depended very much on the firmness of their constitution and on their determined courage, which they think makes them as hard as a bronze jar, but the prophet shows that that has only hardened them like an earthen jar, which, though hard, is brittle and breaks more quickly than what is not so hard. It is God himself, who made them, who has decided to undo them: *I will break this people and this city,* smash them to pieces like *a potter's vessel.* This was the fate of the nations (Ps 2:9; Rev 2:27), but it is now Jerusalem's fate (Isa 30:14). *A potter's vessel,* once broken, *cannot be made whole again,* cannot be repaired. The destruction of Jerusalem will be complete; no one will be able to repair it except the One who has broken it, and if they return to him, then even though he has torn, he will heal (Hos 6:1).

1.2. This is to be done in Topheth, in the Valley of Ben Hinnom, to show two things:

1.2.1. That Topheth will be the container for those who are killed: *They shall bury in Tophet till there be no place to bury* even one more there.

1.2.2. That the whole city will be like Topheth (v. 12): *I will make this city as Tophet.* As they have filled the valley with the dead bodies they sacrificed to their idols, so God will fill the whole city with those who will die as sacrifices to the justice of God. After Josiah desecrated Topheth (2Ki 23:10) because it had been abused by idolatry, whatever it was before, from then on it was looked on as a detestable place. Dead carcasses and other filth of the city were carried there, and a fire was continually kept there to burn it, and so it came to be looked on as such a disgusting place that in the language of our Savior's time, in allusion to this valley, hell was called *Gehenna, the valley of Hinnom* (Mt 5:22, 29, 30; 10:28; etc.). Even *the houses of Jerusalem and* those *of the kings of Judah shall be defiled as the place of Tophet* (v. 13), because of the idolatry committed there. The flat roofs of their houses were sometimes used by devout people as convenient places for prayer (Ac 10:9), but they were used by idolaters as high places, on which they sacrificed to foreign gods, especially to *the host of heaven*, the sun, moon, and stars. We read elsewhere about those who *worshipped the host of heaven upon the housetops* (Zep 1:5). This sin on the housetops brought a curse onto the house.

2. By a solemn recognition and confirmation *in the court of the Lord's house* of what he has said in the valley (vv. 14–15). The prophet returns from Topheth to the temple, which stood on the hill over the valley, and confirms there what he said earlier.

2.1. The fulfillment of the prophecies is the judgment threatened. The people flatter themselves with the belief that the threat has been made simply to frighten them, but the prophet tells them that they are deceiving themselves. *For thus saith the Lord of hosts*, who is able to fulfill his words, *I will bring upon this city, and upon all her towns, all the evil that I have pronounced against it.* God will act as terribly against sin and sinners as the Scriptures say.

2.2. The contempt of the prophecies is here the sin they are accused of. It is *because they have hardened their necks* and would *not hear my words.*

CHAPTER 20

If such plain dealing did not convince and humble the people, it would provoke and exasperate them. We find here: 1. Jeremiah persecuted by Pashhur for preaching that sermon (vv. 1–2). 2. Pashhur threatened for doing so, and the word that Jeremiah had preached confirmed (vv. 3–6). 3. Jeremiah complaining to God about this persecution (vv. 7–10). But he encourages himself in God, appealing to him and not doubting that he will yet praise him (Ps 42:5, 11; 43:5) (vv. 11–13), but perversely cursing the day of his birth (vv. 14–18), from which it is clear that he was a human being just like us (Jas 5:17).

Verses 1–6

Here is:

1. Pashhur's unjust displeasure against Jeremiah and the fruits of that displeasure (vv. 1–2). Pashhur was a priest and therefore should have protected Jeremiah, who was also a priest, and all the more so because Jeremiah was a prophet of the Lord, whose interests the priests should consider. But this priest was also a persecutor. He was *the son of Immer*; that is, he was of the sixteenth division of priests, of which Immer was father when these divisions were first settled by David (1Ch 24:14). This Pashhur is therefore distinguished from another of the same name mentioned in 21:1, who was of the fifth division. This Pashhur was chief officer in the temple; perhaps he was only so temporarily, while the division he was head of awaited its turn. This was Jeremiah's great enemy.

We cannot suppose that Pashhur was one of those who went with Jeremiah to the valley of Topheth to hear him prophesy. However, when he came into the courts of the Lord's house (v. 1), *He heard that Jeremiah prophesied these things*, and he could not bear that Jeremiah should dare preach in the courts of the Lord's house, where he was chief officer, without his permission. Because Pashhur was angry with Jeremiah:

1.1. He *smote* him (v. 2), beat him with his hand or staff of authority. Perhaps it was a blow that was intended only to disgrace him. Such a method was illegal; the high priest, and the rest of the priests, should have been consulted, and Jeremiah's credentials examined. But these rules were set aside as mere formalities; rightly or wrongly, Jeremiah must be dealt with severely.

1.2. He *put him in the stocks.* Jeremiah stayed there all night, and in public too, *in the high gate of Benjamin, which was in*, or by, *the house of the Lord* (v. 2), probably a gate that passed between the city and the temple. Pashhur intended by this to rebuke him, to expose him to contempt so that no one would pay him any attention if he did prophesy.

2. God's just displeasure against Pashhur. *On the morrow Pashur* set Jeremiah free, *brought him out of the stocks* (v. 3). And now Jeremiah had a message from God for him. When he released Jeremiah from the stocks, God put a word into the prophet's mouth, which would awaken Pashhur's conscience, if he had any.

2.1. Did he aim to establish himself by silencing one who told him his faults and would probably lessen his reputation with the people? He will not win here, for:

2.1.1. Even if the prophet remained silent, Pashhur's own conscience would make him always uneasy. To confirm this he will be given a new name, Magor-Missabib, which means "terror on every side." It seems to be a proverbial expression, describing someone in despair, in terror on every side. *The wicked flee when no man pursues* (Pr 28:1) and are in *great fear where no fear is* (Ps 53:5). This will be Pashhur's situation (v. 4): "*Behold, I will make thee a terror to thyself*, and your own imagination will constantly make you uneasy." Those who will not listen when told their faults by God's prophets will be made to hear about them from their own conscience, which will bring rebukes within them. But the terror will not remain confined within them: "*I will make thee a terror to all thy friends*; you will express yourself with so much horror that all your friends will choose to stand aloof from your torment."

2.1.2. His friends will all fail him. God will allow him to live miserably, like Cain, in the "land of shaking" (Ge 4:16) [Ed. note: *Nod* can mean "shaking"], in such a continual state of fear that wherever he goes the question will be asked, "Why is this man in such a state of continual terror?" It will be answered, "It is God's hand on him for putting Jeremiah in the stocks." His friends, who should encourage him, will *fall by the sword of the enemy, and his eyes shall behold it* (v. 4).

2.1.3. He will find that divine vengeance is awaiting him (v. 6); he and his family will *go into captivity*, even *to Babylon*; he will die as a captive and be buried in his chains, he *and all his friends*. This is the fate of Pashhur.

2.2. Did he aim to keep the people at peace, to prevent the destruction Jeremiah prophesied and, by lowering his reputation, make his words fall empty to the ground (1Sa 3:19)? It appears from v. 6 that he set himself up as a prophet and told the people they would have peace. He *prophesied lies to them*, and because Jeremiah's prophecy contradicted his, he set himself against him. But can he win this point? No; Jeremiah stands by what he has said against Judah and Jerusalem:

2.2.1. The country will be ruined (v. 4): *I will give all Judah into the hand of the king of Babylon.* It has long been God's own land, but he will now transfer his ownership of it to Nebuchadnezzar; he will control the country and dispose of the inhabitants as he pleases, and no one will escape him.

2.2.2. The city will be ruined too (v. 5). The king of Babylon will take all that is valuable in it off to Babylon. He will seize their military stores, here called *the strength of the city,* and turn them against them. He will take away all their products, wares, and merchandise, here called *their labours.* He will plunder their fine houses, taking away their furniture, here called their *precious things.* He will rifle the treasury and take away the jewels of the crown and *all the treasures of the kings of Judah.*

Verses 7–13

Jeremiah is here, through the weakness of the flesh, strangely in turmoil within himself. On the occasion of the great wrong that Pashhur did Jeremiah, it seems there was a struggle within him between grace and corruption. Here is:

1. A sad representation of the wrong that was done him. He complains:

1.1. That he is ridiculed and laughed at; they make fun of everything he says and does. *I am in derision; I am mocked* (vv. 7–8). What was it that so exposed him to contempt and scorn? It was nothing but his faithful and zealous discharge of the duty of his office (v. 8). They can find no reason why they should laugh at him except his preaching; it was *the word of the Lord* that *was made a reproach.* They laugh at him for two things:

1.1.1. The manner of his preaching: *Since he spoke, he cried out.* He had always been a lively and passionate preacher, and since he had begun to speak in God's name, he had always spoken as someone who was serious; he *cried aloud.* Lively preachers are the scorn of careless, unbelieving hearers.

1.1.2. The matter of his preaching: he *cried violence and spoil* (destruction). He rebuked them for violence and destruction toward one another, and he prophesied that violence and destruction would be brought on them as punishment. For the former they ridicule him as too precise, and for the latter as too willing to believe whatever came into his mind. This is bad enough, but he complains even more.

1.2. That he is conspired against, and his ruin is plotted; he is not only ridiculed as weak but also reproached and misrepresented as bad and dangerous to the government (v. 10). But there are those who act with greater subtlety.

1.2.1. They whisper bad things about him behind his back. *I heard,* second hand, *the defaming of many, fear on every side* — "of many Magor-Missabibs," as some read it—*defaming by many such people as Pashhur. They* represent Jeremiah as a man who instills fear and jealousy into the minds of the people and so makes them uneasy with the government and disposes them to rebel. Notice how Jeremiah's enemies contrive matters: *Report, say they, and we will report it.* "Let some very bad thing be said about him to render him loathsome to the government, and even though it is false, we will support it, spread it, and add to it."

1.2.2. They flatter him to his face in the hope they can find something from him on which they can base an accusation, as the spies did who came to Christ (Lk 11:53–54; 20:20). "If we approach him kindly, we will

somehow persuade him to speak words of treason. Then *we shall prevail against him* and *take our revenge on him* for telling us our faults and threatening us with the judgments of God."

2. An account of the temptation he has suffered.

2.1. He is tempted to quarrel with God for making him a prophet. He begins with this (v. 7): *O Lord! thou hast deceived me, and I was deceived.* This is the language of Jeremiah's foolish corruption. He knows how the prophets before him have been persecuted (Mt 5:12), and he has no reason to expect any better treatment. In fact, God explicitly told him that all the *princes, priests, and people of the land would fight against him* (1:18–19). Christ told his disciples what opposition they would meet with, *that they might not be offended* (Jn 16:1–2). But the words may very well be read thus: "You have persuaded me, and I was persuaded." This reading accords best with what follows. Jeremiah was very reluctant to undertake the prophetic office; he pleaded that he was too young and unfit to serve God in this way, but God overruled his pleas and told him that *he must go* (1:6–7). "Now, Lord," he says, "since you have given me this position, why do you not stand by me in it? Had I thrust myself on it, I might justly have been laughed at, but why am I so when you thrust me into it?"

2.2. He is tempted to quit his work, partly because he himself has met with so much hardship in it and partly because those to whom he was sent, instead of being built up and made better, have been made angry and worse (v. 9).

3. An account of his faithful devotion to his work and his cheerful dependence on his God nevertheless.

3.1. He found the grace of God to be powerful enough in him to keep him to his business: "*I said,* in my haste (Ps 31:22; 116:11), *I will speak no more in his name*; what I have in my heart to communicate I will stifle and suppress. But I soon found it was *in my heart as a burning fire shut up in my bones* (v. 9), which glowed inwardly and must be expressed. It was impossible to smother it. While *I kept silence from good, my heart was hot within me*; it was *pain and grief to me,* and I must speak so that I might be refreshed" (Ps 39:2–3; Job 32:20). Jeremiah soon became weary with refusing to preach, and he could not contain himself. Nothing gives faithful ministers so much pain as being silenced; nothing gives them so much terror as silencing themselves. Their convictions will soon triumph, for *woe is unto me if I preach not the Gospel,* whatever it costs me (1Co 9:16).

3.2. He was assured of God's presence with him, which would be sufficient to frustrate all the attempts of his enemies (v. 11): "They say, *We shall prevail against him.* But I am sure *they shall not prevail, they shall not prosper. I* can defy them, for *the Lord is with me* to support me against them (Ro 8:31). He is with me to support me under these burdens. He is with me to make the word I preach fulfill his purposes. He is with me to strike terror on them and so overcome them." The most formidable enemies who act against us appear contemptible when we see the Lord for us as a *mighty, terrible one* (v. 11; Ne 4:14). Jeremiah is now speaking with good assurance: If *the Lord be with me, my persecutors shall stumble,* so that when they pursue me, they will not overtake me (Ps 27:2), and then *they shall be greatly ashamed* of their powerless hatred and futile attempts to mock me.

3.3. He appealed to God against them as a righteous Judge and prayed for justice for his cause (v. 12). The One who examines the righteous also examines the unrighteous, for he *sees the reins* (probes the mind) *and the heart* and can therefore pass infallible judgment on their words and actions. *Unto thee have I opened my cause.* Not that God did not perfectly know his cause, and all its merits, but we must spread out the cause we commit to God before him (2Ki 19:14). He knows it, but he wants to know it from us. He allows us to be detailed in laying it before him, not to move him, but to move ourselves.

3.4. He greatly rejoiced in and praised God, in full confidence that God would support him (v. 13). He stirred himself and others with great delight and joy to give God glory: *Sing unto the Lord, praise you the Lord.* Here a great change had apparently come over him since he began this speech; the clouds had blown over; his complaints had all been silenced and had become thanksgiving. It was the living exercise of faith that made this happy change, which turned his sighs into songs and his trembling into triumph. "He rescued me formerly when I was in distress, and now recently from the hands of Pashhur, and he will continue to rescue me (2Co 1:10). He will rescue my soul from the sin that I am in danger of falling into when I am persecuted in this way."

Verses 14–18

What do these verses mean? Does there *proceed out of the same mouth blessing and cursing* (Jas 3:10)? Could the one who said so cheerfully, *Sing unto the Lord, praise you the Lord* (v. 13), also say so passionately, *Cursed be the day wherein I was born* (v. 14)? It seems to be an account of the turmoil he had been in while he was in the stocks, out of which by faith and hope he had recovered, rather than a fresh temptation. When grace has won the victory, it is good to remember the struggles, so that we may be ashamed of ourselves and our own foolishness and may wonder at the goodness of God in not taking us at our word. Notice:

1. The prophet's language in this temptation.

1.1. He directed a curse on his birthday (v. 14), as Job did in a fit of temper (Job 3:1). He wished he had never been born. Judas in hell has reason to wish this (Mt 26:24), but no person on earth has, because they do not know whether they may still become an object of mercy (Ro 9:23); and much less does any good person have reason to wish this.

1.2. He wished harm to the messenger who brought his father news of his birth (v. 15). He was fierce in the curses he declared (v. 16): "*Let him be as the cities* of Sodom and Gomorrah"—for these are the cities he means—"*which the Lord utterly overthrew, and repented not. Let him hear the cry* of the invading, besieging enemy *in the morning,* as soon as he stirs, and by noon let him hear their *shouting* for victory. And so let that messenger live in constant terror."

1.3. He was angry that he was not *slain from the womb,* that his first breath was not his last, and that he was not strangled as soon as he was born (v. 17).

1.4. He thought his present adversities sufficient to justify this emotional outburst (v. 18): "*Wherefore* (why) *came I forth out of the womb*—in which I was hidden and was not hated, in which I lay safely and knew no evil—to see all this *labour and sorrow,* to have my *days consumed with shame,* to be continually abused, to have my life wasted and worn away by trouble?"

2. What use we may make of this. It is not recorded for us to imitate, but we may still learn good lessons from it. Notice:

• The futility of human life and the trouble that is part of it.

• The foolishness and absurdity of sinful passion, how unreasonably it talks when it is allowed to wander. What nonsense it is to curse a day—to curse a messenger for the sake of his message! When the heart is angry, let the tongue be restrained (Ps 39:1–2).

CHAPTER 21

The prophecies of this book are not placed in the same order in which they were preached, for there are chapters after this one that concern Jehoahaz, Jehoiakim, and Jehoiachin, who all reigned before Zedekiah, in whose reign the prophecy of this chapter is dated. Here is: 1. The message Zedekiah sent to the prophet to ask him to inquire of the Lord for them (vv. 1–2). 2. The answer Jeremiah, in God's name, sent to that message, in which: 2.1. He foretold the certain and inevitable ruin of the city (vv. 3–7). 2.2. He advised the people to go over to the king of Babylon (vv. 8–10). 2.3. He advised the king and his family to repent and reform (vv. 11–14).

Verses 1–7

Here is:

1. A very humble message that king Zedekiah sent to Jeremiah the prophet when he was in distress. He humbled himself so far as to request the prophet's help but not so far as to take his advice or to be guided by him. Notice:

1.1. The distress King Zedekiah was now in: *Nebuchadrezzar made war upon him* (v. 2); he had invaded the land and besieged the city.

1.2. The messengers he sent—*Pashur and Zephaniah.* It would have been better if he had sought a personal meeting with the prophet, which he could have had if he had been willing to humble himself that far. When these priests were commanded by the king, they must carry a respectful message to the prophet, which was both a mortification to them and an honor to Jeremiah.

1.3. The message itself: *Inquire, I pray thee, of the Lord for us* (v. 2). Now that the Babylonian army had penetrated their borders, they were convinced that Jeremiah was a true prophet, although they were reluctant to acknowledge it. Finally convinced, they wanted him to stand as their friend with God: "*Inquire of the Lord for us;* ask him what course of action we should take in our present difficulty, for the measures we have taken up to this time have all failed." Those who will not be directed by God's grace on how to get clear of their sins may still be glad to hear the directions of his providence on how to get clear of their troubles. "Entreat the Lord for us," it may be read; "be an intercessor with God for us. *It may be the Lord will deal with us* now *according to the wondrous works he wrought for our fathers,* that the enemy may raise the siege and *go up from us.*" All their concern is to get rid of their trouble; they do not care about making their peace with God and being reconciled to him: "That our enemy may *go up from us,*" not, "That our God may return to us." This is similar to Pharaoh's approach (Ex 10:17). All their hope is that God may do what he has done before: he performed wonders before when he saved Jerusalem from the siege of Sennacherib in response to Isaiah's prayer (2Ch 32:20–21), and who can tell whether he may destroy these besiegers in response to Jeremiah's prayer? But they do not consider how different the character of Zedekiah and his people is from that of Hezekiah and his people: Hezekiah's days were days of general reformation and piety; these are days of general corruption and apostasy.

2. A very startling, cutting reply that God, through the prophet, sent to that message. God knew their hearts better than Jeremiah, and he sent them an answer that scarcely contained one word of comfort. Jeremiah sent it to them in the name of *the Lord God of Israel* (v. 3), to show them that although God allowed himself to be called the *God of Israel*, had done great things for Israel formerly, and still had great things in store for Israel, this would not do any good to the present generation, who were Israelites only in name. It is foretold:

2.1. That God will make all their attempts to maintain their own security fruitless and ineffective (v. 4).

2.2. That the besiegers will soon come to control Jerusalem, with all of its wealth and strength: *I will assemble in the midst of this city* those who are now surrounding it.

2.3. That God himself will be their enemy, and then who can befriend them? Not even Jeremiah himself (v. 5). Those who rebel against God may justly expect him to make war on them.

2.4. That those who, for their own safety, decline to go out against the besiegers, and so avoid their sword, will still not escape the sword of God's justice (v. 6): "I will strike down those who live in the city, both people and animals; *they shall die of a great pestilence.*"

2.5. That the king himself, and all the people who escape the *sword, famine,* and *pestilence,* will fall *into the hands* of the Babylonians (v. 7): they *shall not spare them* or *have pity* on them.

Verses 8–14

From the polite message the king sent to Jeremiah it appeared that both he and the people had begun to have respect for him, but the reply God makes him give is enough to crush that little respect and make them even more angry with him. They found offensive not only the predictions in the previous verses but also the prescriptions in these:

1. He advised the people to surrender to the Babylonians; this was the only option left to save their lives (vv. 8–10). This advice was displeasing to those who had been flattered by their false prophets into a desperate determination to hold out to the last, trusting in the power of their walls and their military courage or expecting foreign aid to lift the siege. The prophet assured them, *"The city shall be given into the hand of the king of Babylon,* and he will not only plunder it but also *burn it with fire,* for God himself has *set his face against this city for evil and not for good* (v. 10). Therefore, if you want to make the best of a bad situation, you must beg mercy from the Babylonians and surrender as prisoners of war." It was the best course of action they could follow now that God was against them. Both the Law and the Prophets had often set out before them life and death in another sense—life if they obeyed the voice of God, death if they persisted in disobedience (Dt 30:19). The prophet used the same expression here, but in a different sense. *Behold, I set before you the way of life and the way of death,* he said, but this time it was not, like those earlier declarations, a fair proposal, but a sad dilemma, advising them to choose the lesser of two evils. *"He that abides in the city* will certainly die either by *the sword* outside the walls or by *famine* or *pestilence* inside them. But he who can leave his vain hopes, go out, and fall *to the Chaldeans, his life shall be given him for a prey* (v. 9); he will save his life as plunder that is taken away from those who are powerful." They thought they would plunder the Babylonian camp, as their ancestors had plundered that of the Assyrians (Isa 33:23),

but if, by surrendering unconditionally, they could only save their lives, that would be all the plunder they could promise themselves.

2. He advised the king and rulers to reform. In the reply there was a particular word for *the house of the king,* to give them good counsel (vv. 11–12): *"Execute judgment in the morning;* administer justice carefully and diligently. Do it quickly, and do not delay in administering justice on appeals made to you. You want to be rescued from the hands of those who distress you, and you expect God to do you justice there; see to it then that you do justice to those who turn to you, and *deliver them out of the hand of their oppressors, lest my fury go out like fire,* with the result that you who think you will escape best actually fare worst, *because of the evil of your doings"* (v. 12). It was the *evil of their doings* that kindled the fire of God's wrath. This was how plainly he dealt even with the *house of the king,* for those who want to benefit from a prophet's prayers must also gratefully accept a prophet's rebukes. The rulers must begin and set a good example, and then the people would be encouraged to reform. The rulers must use their powers to punish wrong, and then the people would be obliged to reform. The prophet reminded them that they were *the house of David,* who administered justice to his people, and so they should follow in his footsteps.

3. He showed them the futility of all their hopes so long as they continued to lead unreformed lives (vv. 13–14). Jerusalem was an *inhabitant of the valley,* guarded by mountains on all sides, which were their natural fortifications, making it difficult for an army to approach them. It was *a rock of the plain* (a rocky plateau), which made it difficult for an enemy to undermine them. They trusted in these advantages more than in the power and promises of God. They thought their city impregnable, and so they defied the judgments, saying, *"Who shall come down against us?"* God soon showed the futility of their challenge, *Who shall come down against us?* when he said, *Behold, I am against thee* (v. 13). He came out against them as a judge who could not be resisted, for he said (v. 14), *I will punish you* by the due course of law, *according to the fruit of your doings.*

CHAPTER 22

Here are sermons that Jeremiah preached at court in some preceding reigns; they are recorded here so that it might be seen that his listeners had received fair warning. Here is: 1. A message sent to the royal family, it would seem, in the reign of Jehoiakim, relating partly to Jehoahaz, who was taken captive into Egypt, and partly to Jehoiakim, who succeeded him and is now on the throne (vv. 1–9). Jehoahaz, here called Shallum, is mourned (vv. 10–12). Jehoiakim is rebuked and threatened (vv. 13–19). 2. Another message sent to them in the reign of Jehoiachin (Jeconiah), the son of Jehoiakim. He is charged with an obstinate refusal to listen, and it is foretold that in him Solomon's house will fail (vv. 20–30).

Verses 1–9

Here we have:

1. Orders given to Jeremiah to go and preach before the king (v. 2): *Hear the word of the Lord, O king of Judah!* The *king of Judah* is here spoken to as *sitting upon the throne of David,* who was a man after God's own heart (1Sa 13:14); the king now reigning holds his dignity and power by the covenant made with David. Let him

therefore conform to David's example, so that he may enjoy the benefit of the promises made to David. The king's *servants* (officials) are spoken to with him.

2. Instructions given him what to preach.

2.1. He must tell them what the Lord their God requires of them (Mic 6:8) (v. 3). They must be careful to:

- Do all the good they can with the power they have. They must administer justice in defense of those who have been wronged.
- Do no harm with it. They must *do no wrong to the stranger* (foreigner), *fatherless, and widow*, for God especially looks after and supports such people (Ex 22:21–22).

2.2. He must assure them that by faithfully fulfilling their duty, they will advance their prosperity (v. 4). There will then be an uninterrupted succession *upon the throne of David*, enjoying tranquility and living in dignity. The most effective way for the government to preserve its status is to fulfill its responsibilities.

2.3. Similarly, he must assure them that if they persist in the sins, they will be the ruin of their family (v. 5). Sin has often been the ruin of royal palaces, even if very strong and grand. Sin will be the ruin of the houses of rulers as well as of lowly people.

2.4. He must show how fatal their evil will be to their kingdom as well as to themselves, especially to Jerusalem, the royal city (vv. 6–9). Judah and Jerusalem have been valuable in God's eyes: *Thou art Gilead unto me, and the head of Lebanon* (v. 7). They have been given a place that is as rich and pleasant as Gilead; Zion is a stronghold and as stately as Lebanon: they trust in this as their security. But the country that is now as fruitful as Gilead will be made *a wilderness*. The cities that are now as strong as Lebanon will be cities *not inhabited*. There will be those who will do it effectively (v. 7): "*I will prepare destroyers against thee*"; literally, "I will sanctify them." And who can oppose the destroyers that God himself has prepared? There will be those who will be ready to justify God in what he has done (vv. 8–9); people of *many nations*, when they *pass by* the ruins of *this city* in their travels, will ask, "*Wherefore* (why) *hath the Lord done thus unto this city?*" "Ask the next person you meet, and they will tell you it was because they changed their gods" (2:11). God never rejects anyone until they first reject him.

Verses 10–19

1. Here is the doom of Shallum, who doubtless was the same as Jehoahaz, for he was the son of Josiah king of Judah who reigned *in the stead of Josiah his father* (v. 11), which Jehoahaz did by the act of the people, who made him king even though he was not the eldest son (2Ki 23:30; 2Ch 36:1). Perhaps the people preferred him to his elder brother because they thought him a more active and young man, and fitter to rule, but God soon showed them the foolishness of their injustice, for within three months the king of Egypt attacked him, deposed him, and took him away as a prisoner into Egypt, as God had threatened (Dt 28:68). It does not appear that any of the people were taken into captivity with him. We have the story in 2Ki 23:34; 2Ch 36:4. Notice:

1.1. The people were directed to mourn him rather than his father Josiah: "*Weep not for the dead*; do not weep anymore for Josiah." Jeremiah had himself been a true mourner for him (2Ch 35:25), but now he wanted them to turn their tears to another channel. They must weep greatly for Jehoahaz, who had gone into Egypt. Josiah went to the grave in peace and honor; "*Weep not for him,*

but for his unhappy son, who is likely to live and die in disgrace and misery as a wretched captive." Dying saints may justly be envied, while living sinners are justly to be pitied.

1.2. He would never return from captivity, as he and his people expected, but would die there. They were unwilling to believe this, and so it was repeated here again and again. This came about because he abandoned the good example of his father and usurped the right of his elder brother.

2. The doom of Jehoiakim, who succeeded him. He ruled no better, and in the end fared no better. We have here:

2.1. His sins rebuked. Jehoiakim was not accused of idolatry here, but the crimes for which he was rebuked here were:

2.1.1. Pride, love of pomp, and splendor, as if a king's only responsibility were to look great and as if to do good were the least of his concerns. He had to build for himself a grand palace, a *wide house*, and *large chambers* (v. 14). He must have *windows cut out* in the latest style. The rooms must be *ceiled* (paneled) *with cedar*, the finest wood, painted with *vermilion*, or as some read it, *indigo*. Those who are enlarging their houses, therefore, and making them more lavish, need to look to their own motives in doing it and carefully watch against boasting. He reigned his first three years by the permission of the king of Egypt, and all the rest by the permission of the king of Babylon, but he who was no better than a viceregent sought to rival the greatest monarchs.

2.1.2. Worldly security and confidence in his wealth. He thought he must reign without any disturbance or interruption because he had *closed himself in cedar*, because he had more and more cedar (v. 15).

2.1.3. Sacrilege, according to some—robbing the house of God to make his own house beautiful. He *cut him out* "my" *windows* (v. 14, margin), which some understand as if he had taken windows out of the temple to put into his own palace and then *painted them with vermilion*, so that his theft would not be discovered.

2.1.4. Extortion, oppression, violence, and injustice. He *built his house by unrighteousness* (v. 13), with money unjustly gained and materials not honestly come by. God notices the wrong done by the greatest people to their poor servants and laborers, and he will repay in justice those who will not in justice pay those they employ. What was at the root of everything was greed, that love of *money which is the root of all evil* (1Ti 6:10). *Thy eyes and thy heart are not but for covetousness* (v. 17), that and nothing else. In greed, the heart walks after the eyes: it is therefore called *the lust of the eye* (1Jn 2:16; Job 31:7).

2.1.5. What made all his sins worse was that he was the son of a good father, who had set him a good example, if only he would have followed it (vv. 15–16). Jeremiah told him that his father's practice directed him to do his duty: Josiah *did judgment and justice*. He not only did not abuse his power to support wrong but also used it to maintain what was right and just. He *judged the cause of the poor and needy* (v. 16). Josiah's prosperity, on the other hand, encouraged Jehoiakim to do his duty. God accepted Josiah: "*Was not this to know me, saith the Lord* (is that not what it means to know me)?" And Josiah had encouragement from this acceptance: *Did he not eat and drink* soberly and cheerfully, so as to make himself fit for his work, *for strength and not for drunkenness?* (Ecc 10:17). God blessed him with abundance, and he enjoyed it himself and was very hospitable and charitable. It was Jehoiakim's pride that he had built a fine house, but

Josiah's true praise was that he kept a good house. It is better to live with Josiah in an old-fashioned house and do good than to live with Jehoiakim in a stately house and leave debts unpaid.

2.2. Jehoiakim's doom faithfully read out (vv. 18–19). We may suppose that Jeremiah's own life was in danger here when he foretold the shameful death of Jehoiakim, but *thus said the Lord concerning* him, and so he declared it. Jehoiakim would die unmourned; he would make himself so repugnant by his oppression and cruelty that no one would do him the honor of shedding one tear for him. His relatives would not *lament him* (v. 18), *His* subjects would not lament him—as they used to do at the graves of their rulers. Jehoiakim would be *buried with the burial of an ass* (v. 19), that is, he would have no burial at all; his dead body would be thrown into a ditch or onto a rubbish heap. It would be *drawn*, or dragged away, ignominiously and *cast forth beyond the gates of Jerusalem*. Josephus says that Nebuchadnezzar put him to death at Jerusalem and left his body exposed somewhere far away from the *gates of Jerusalem*.

Verses 20–30

This prophecy seems to have been intended for the inglorious reign of Jehoiachin (*Jeconiah*), the son of Jehoiakim, who reigned only three months and was then taken into exile in Babylon, where he lived for many years (52:31).

1. The destruction of the kingdom was now coming on quickly (vv. 20–23). Jerusalem and Judah are here spoken to as a single person: "*I spoke unto thee in thy prosperity*, spoke rebukes, warnings, words of advice through my servants the prophets, *but thou saidst, I will not hear*." It is common for those who lead self-indulgent, self-confident lives to live in contempt of the word of God. *This has been thy manner from thy youth.* "When thou seest *all thy lovers destroyed* (allies crushed), when you find that your idols are unable to help you and your foreign alliances are failing you, you will cry out, *Help, help, or we are lost*; thou wilt *lift up thy voice* with fearful shrieks on *Lebanon* and *Bashan*. You will *cry from the passages*, from the roads. You will cry out to everyone around you. Your cries will be in vain, however, for (v. 22) *the wind shall eat up all thy pastors*, who should provide for your safety. They will be driven away, withered as buds and blossoms are by a bleak or freezing wind. *Thy lovers* (allies), whom you have affection for, will *go into captivity* and will not even be able to save themselves. When no relief from any of your allies comes, *then shalt thou be ashamed and confounded* (disgraced) *for all thy wickedness*" (v. 22). The Jewish state is here called *an inhabitant of Lebanon* because that famous forest was within its border (v. 23), and all its country was as well guarded as Lebanon's natural fortresses. However, the people were so proud that they were said to *make their nest in the cedars*, out of the reach of all danger, from where they looked down with contempt on everyone around them. "But, *how gracious wilt thou be* (how you will groan) *when pangs come upon thee!* Then you will humble yourself before God and promise to mend your ways." Some give this another sense: "What good will all your pomp do you? No more than *a woman in travail*, full of pain and fears, can take comfort in her fashion accessories when she is in that condition."

2. The king is disgraced; his name was *Jeconiah* (Jehoiachin), but he is here again and again contemptuously called *Coniah*. Two examples of dishonor will be laid on him:

2.1. He will be taken away *into captivity* and will spend and end his days in exile. God will abandon him (v. 24). "*Though he were the signet upon my right hand, I would pluck him thence.*" The godly kings of Judah were as precious as signet rings on God's right hand, so near and dear to him. He gloried in them. But this king will be captured by the king of Babylon. Those who have removed themselves from God's protection do not know what trouble they are exposed to (v. 25). The Babylonians hated Jehoiachin; they *sought his life*. These were the kind of people he feared. He and his family will be taken to Babylon, where they will spend many long years in a miserable *captivity*; *he and his mother* (v. 26), *he and his seed* (children) (v. 28), that is, he and all the royal family, will all be expelled to another country, *a country where they were not born, a land which they know not*, in which they have no friends from whom they can expect any kindness. *To the land whereunto they desire to return, thither shall they not return* (v. 27). Jehoahaz was taken to Egypt, the land of the south, and Jehoiachin to Babylon, the land of the north, and they would never meet again, nor breathe their native air. There is something very emphatic in this part of the threat (v. 26): *In the country where you were not born, there shall you die.* This fate will render him contemptible in the eyes of all his neighbors. They will be ready to say (v. 28), "*Is this Coniah* (Jehoiachin) *a despised broken idol?*" There was a time when he was dignified, in fact, when he was almost deified. The people who had seen his father recently deposed were ready to worship Jehoiachin when they saw him on the throne, but now *he is a despised broken idol*.

2.2. He will leave no descendants to inherit his honor. Let all the world notice these judgments of God on a nation and a family that once were precious to him, and let them reason from this that God is impartial in administering justice. Now what is here to be taken notice of is that Jeconiah *is written* (recorded as) *childless* (v. 30), that is, as it follows, *No man of his seed shall prosper, sitting upon the throne of David*. Some think that he had children born in Babylon (v. 28) and that they died before him. We read in the genealogy in 1Ch 3:17 of seven sons of *Jeconiah Assir* (that is, Jehoiachin the captive) of whom *Salathiel* (Shealtiel) is the first. Some think they were only his sons by adoption, and that when it is said (Mt 1:12), *Jeconiah begat Salathiel*, no more is meant than that he bequeathed to him the claims he had to the government, because *Salathiel* is called the *son of Neri* of the *house of Nathan* (Lk 3:27, 31). Whether he had children by birth or by adoption, none of his descendants ruled as kings of Judah.

CHAPTER 23

The prophet, in God's name, is speaking out his rebukes: 1. Among the careless rulers, or shepherds of the people (vv. 1–2), but promising to take care of the flock (vv. 3–8). 2. Among the evil prophets and priests, for deceiving the people with their claimed inspirations, for which they must expect to be punished (vv. 9–32). 3. Among the worldly people who ridicule God's prophets (vv. 33–40).

Verses 1–8

1. Here is a word of terror to the negligent shepherds. *Woe be to the pastors*—to the *shepherds*, both in church and in state—who should be pastors who lead, feed, protect, and take care of God's people. They do not own the sheep. God calls his people *the sheep of my pasture* here,

"those whom I have provided good pasture for." How terrible it will be for those who are commanded to feed God's people and claim to do it but instead *scatter the flock* (v. 1) by their violence and oppression. In not looking after the sheep, *the pastors* have in effect been driving them away. The wild animals have scattered them, and the shepherds, who should have kept them together, are to blame.

2. Here is a word of comfort to the neglected sheep. Although the undershepherds take no care of them, the Chief Shepherd will look after them (1Pe 5:4). God will fulfill his promise, even though those he employs do not fulfill their duty.

2.1. The dispersed Jews will eventually return to their own land and settle there happily under a good government (vv. 3–4). Although there is only a remnant of God's flock left, he will gather that remnant from wherever they are and bring them back out of all countries *whither he had driven them* (v. 3). *They shall be brought* to their former homes, as sheep are to their folds, and there *they shall be fruitful and increase* in numbers. Formerly they were continually disturbed, but now *they shall fear no more, nor be dismayed* (v. 4). Such pastors as Zerubbabel and Nehemiah, though they did not live in the pomp that Jehoiakim and Jehoiachin lived in, were as great blessings to the people as the others were scourges to them.

2.2. Messiah the Prince, that great and good Shepherd of the sheep (Heb 13:20), will in the last days be raised up to bless his church and to be *the glory of his people Israel* (vv. 5–6; Lk 2:32). The house of David seemed to have been ruined by that threat against Jehoiachin (22:30), but here is a promise that effectively secures the honor of the covenant made with David, for by this promise, the house will be raised up from its ruins to shine more brightly than ever. We do not have as many prophecies of Christ in this book as we had in that of the prophet Isaiah, but here we have an outstanding one. The first words show that it would be a long time before this promise would be fulfilled: *The days come* (v. 5), but they are not yet. *I shall see him, but not now* (Nu 24:17).

2.2.1. Christ is spoken of here as a *Branch from David*: his appearance lowly, his beginnings small, like those of a bud, and his rise apparently out of the earth, but growing to be loaded with fruits. He will be a branch from David's family, arising when it seemed to be *a root in a dry ground* (Isa 53:2), buried and not likely to revive. In him the *horn of David* buds (Ps 132:17–18). He is *a righteous branch* (v. 5), for he is righteous himself, and through him many—in fact all who are his—are made righteous. As an advocate, he is *Jesus Christ the righteous* (1Jn 2:1).

2.2.2. He is spoken of here as his church's King. He will set up a kingdom in the world that will be victorious over all opposition. In the chariot of the eternal Gospel he will go out *conquering and to conquer* (Rev 6:2). Christ, by his Gospel, will break the usurped power of Satan, establish a perfect rule of holy living, and, as far as that rule is effective, make all the world righteous. The result of this will be a holy security and peace of mind in all his faithful, loyal subjects. *In his days*, under his rule, *Judah shall be saved and Israel shall dwell safely* (v. 6). See Lk 1:74–75; Ro 8:31. In the days of Christ's government in the soul, when he rules there, the soul *dwells at ease* (Ps 25:13).

2.2.3. He is spoken of as *the Lord our righteousness* (v. 6). As God, he is *Jehovah*, the inexpressible name of God, referring to his eternity and self-existence. He is always with his people and is always working on their behalf. As Mediator, he is *our righteousness*. By making atonement for human sin to satisfy the justice of God, he has brought in an eternal righteousness, and in the covenant of grace he has transferred that righteousness to us in such a way that upon our consent to that covenant, it becomes ours. He is a sovereign, all-sufficient, and eternal righteousness. All our righteousness has its being from him, and it exists because of him. *This is the name whereby he shall be called*; he will not only be our righteousness but also be known to be so. That which God allows as a plea on the basis of which we are justified before him, acquitted from guilt, and accepted into his favor is *our righteousness*; and we have no plea except "Christ has died—indeed, has risen again"; and we have taken him as our *Lord*.

2.3. This great salvation, which will come to the Jews in the last days, after their return from Babylon, will far surpass the rescue of Israel out of Egypt (vv. 7–8): *They shall no more say, The Lord liveth that brought up Israel out of Egypt; But, The Lord liveth that brought them up out of the north*. After they came out of Babylon, Messiah the Prince set up the Gospel temple, the greatest glory of that nation that was so wonderfully brought out of Babylon.

Verses 9–32

Here is a long lesson for false prophets. The prophet complained to God earlier about those false prophets (14:13), and he often foretold that they would be involved in the common destruction, but here they have woes of their own.

1. He expresses what trouble it is to him to see people who claim to have received a divine commission and inspiration ruining both themselves and the people among whom they live by their falsehood and treachery (v. 9): *My heart within me is broken; I am like a drunken man*. Jeremiah was a man who took things very much to heart, and what was in any way threatening to his country made a deep impression on his spirit. He is in trouble here:

1.1. *Because of the prophets* (v. 9) and their sin, the false doctrine they preach and the evil lives they lead, claiming to have received instruction from God.

1.2. "*Because of the Lord* and his judgments, which by means of the false prophets' sin are brought on us like a flood." He trembles to think of the ruin and desolation that are coming *from the face of the Lord* (Ps 34:16; 1Pe 3:12) *and from the face of the word of his holiness* (v. 9).

2. He mourns the great and detestable evil of the land and the present signs of God's displeasure the false prophets are facing because of it (v. 10): *The land is full of adulterers*; it is full of both spiritual and physical prostitution. Their land mourns now under the judgment of famine; the *pleasant places*, the pastures, are dried up for lack of rain, but still we can see no signs of repentance. They have a great deal of determination, but it is channeled in the wrong way. They are *zealously affected*, but not *in a good thing*, even though they see God opposing them.

3. He blames the prophets and priests, especially the prophets, for all this. They are *both profane* (godless) (v. 11); the priests defile the ordinances of God they pretend to administer; the prophets defile the word of God they claim to communicate. They both "play the hypocrite," as some read it; they use a sacred profession as a cover for their corrupt intentions: *in my house have I found their wickedness*. In the temple, where the priests minister and the prophets prophesy, is where they are guilty of both idolatry and immorality. They are accused of two things:

3.1. That they teach people to sin by their examples. He compares them to the prophets of Samaria, the leading city of the kingdom of the ten tribes, which was long since devastated. The prophets of Samaria were so foolish as to *prophesy in Baal*, in Baal's name; and so *they caused my people Israel to err*, to abandon the service of the true God and to worship Baal (v. 13). Now the prophets of Jerusalem do not do this; they prophesy in the name of the true God and pride themselves on that, that they are not like the prophets of Samaria, who prophesied by Baal. But they defile the nation as much by their immorality as the others did by their idolatries. They make use of the name of the holy God but at the same time also wallow in all kinds of impurity. They use the name of the God of truth but *walk in lies* (v. 14). In this way they encourage sinners, for everyone will say, "Surely we can do as the prophets do! You can't expect us to be better than our teachers!" This is why Judah and Jerusalem have become *as Sodom and Gomorrah*: God looks on them as fit for nothing but to be destroyed.

3.2. That they encourage people to sin according to their false prophecies. They have made themselves believe there is no harm or danger in sin, and so they practice it accordingly. It is then not surprising that they have made others believe this too (v. 16): *They speak a vision of their own heart*; it is *not out of the mouth of the Lord*. They tell sinners that things will go well with them even though they persist in their sins (v. 17). Those who are devoted to their own pleasures show contempt for their God. These prophets flatter the people: they should have been still saying, "There is no peace to those who go on in their evil ways," but they still said, *You shall have peace; no evil shall come upon you* (v. 17), and, what is worst of all, they tell them, *God has said so*.

4. God denies all that these false prophets have said to soothe people in their sins (v. 21): *I have not sent these prophets*; they were never sent by God. But they were very *forward—they ran*; they were very *bold—they prophesied* without any of that *difficulty* with which the true prophets sometimes struggled. They said to sinners, *You shall have peace*. But (v. 18): "*Who hath stood in the counsel of the Lord?* You communicate this message with a great deal of assurance, but have you consulted God about it? You have not *perceived and heard his word*; you have not compared this with Scripture; if you had taken notice of the constant tenor of that, you would never have spoken such a message." The fact that they did not *stand in God's counsel* or *hear his word* is proved later (v. 22). *If they had stood in my counsel*, as they claim:

4.1. They would have made the Scriptures their standard: *They would have caused my people to hear my words*.

4.2. They would have made the conversion of souls their business and would have aimed at that in all their preaching.

4.3. They would have had some seal on their ministry. *If they had stood in my counsel*, and the words they had preached had been *my words*, then they would *have turned them from their evil way*.

5. God threatens to punish these prophets for their evil. They promised the people *peace*, and to show them that that was foolish, God tells them that they will have no peace themselves. Evil is coming on them, and they are not aware of it. Because the prophets and priests are godless, *their ways shall be unto them as slippery ways in the darkness* (v. 12). They claim to show others the way, but they themselves will remain in the dark or in a mist. They claim to give assurances to others, but they themselves

will find no firm footing. They claim to put the people at ease with their flatteries, but they will themselves be uneasy: *They shall be driven*; trying to make their escape, *they shall fall in the way*. They claim to prevent the disaster that threatens others, but God will *bring evil upon them, even the year of their visitation* (v. 12). *The year of visitation* is the year of calamitous punishment. It is further threatened (v. 15), *I will feed them with wormwood*, which is not only nauseous but also toxic, and *make them drink waters of gall*, or, as some read it, "hemlock juice"; see also 9:15.

6. The people are warned here not to believe these false prophets (v. 16): "Take notice of what God says and *hearken not to the words of these prophets*, for you will find that God's word will stand, and not theirs. They tell you, *No evil shall come upon you*, but listen to what God says (v. 19): *Behold, a whirlwind of the Lord has gone forth in fury*. They tell you, 'Everything will be peace and calm,' but God tells you, 'A storm is coming, *a whirlwind of the Lord*; no one can stand in the presence of it.'" This sentence is irreversible (v. 20): *The anger of the Lord shall not return*. God will not change his mind or allow his anger to be turned away *till he has executed* the sentence and *performed the thoughts of his heart*. They will not consider this now, but *in the latter days you shall consider it perfectly*, consider it "clearly," "with understanding," or "with consideration."

7. Several things are offered here for these false prophets to consider so that they might be brought to realize their error.

7.1. Let them consider that although they may deceive people, God is too wise to be deceived.

7.1.1. God asserts his omnipresence and his omniscience in general (vv. 23–24). Though God's throne is in the heavens, he is still a God here in this lower world, which seems *afar off* from him, as well as in the upper world, which seems to be *at hand* (v. 23). The eye of God is the same on earth as it is in heaven. The power of God is the same on earth among those who live here as it is in heaven among its armies. With us nearness and distance make a great difference both in what we see and in what we do, but it is not so with God; to him darkness and light, nearby and far away, are both alike (Ps 139:7–12). People's characters and purposes cannot possibly be concealed from God's all-seeing eye (v. 24): "*Can any hide himself in the secret places?* Can anyone hide their plans and intentions in the secret places of the heart, so that I will not see them?" He is present everywhere; he not only rules heaven and earth but also *fills heaven and earth* by his essential presence (Ps 139:7–8). No place can either include him or exclude him.

7.1.2. He applies this to these prophets, who are skilled at disguising themselves (vv. 25–26). God will show them that he knows all the shame they have given to the world in the name of divine revelation. God has uncovered the deception, and he cries out, "*How long?* Is it in the hearts of those prophets to be always prophesying lies and prophesying the deceits of their own hearts?"

7.2. Let them consider that their palming off false revelations on people and claiming their own ideas are divinely inspired is the ready way to bring all religious faith into contempt and turn people into atheists and unbelievers. *Thus saith the Lord, they think to cause my people to forget my name by their dreams* (v. 27). The great thing Satan aims at is to make people forget God and his name, God and everything by which he has made himself known. Sometimes he does it by setting up false gods—by causing people to love Baal, and then they soon forget the name of God—sometimes by misrepresenting the true God.

7.3. Let them consider what a vast difference there is between their prophecies and those that are spoken by the true prophets of the Lord (v. 28): *The prophet that has a dream, let him tell it as a dream.* "Let him emphasize it no more than people do their dreams, nor expect it to be held in higher regard than a dream. But let the true prophet, who *has my word, speak my word faithfully,* speak it 'as a truth,'" as some read it; "let him keep closely to his instructions, and you will soon notice a vast difference between the dreams of the false prophets and the divine dictates the true prophets speak. Those who have their spiritual senses exercised will be able to discern the difference, for *what is the chaff to the wheat?*" (v. 28). Human imagination is light and worthless, as the chaff *which the wind drives away* (Ps 1:4). But the word of God contains substance; it is of value, it is food for the soul, the bread of life (Jn 6:35, 48). "*Is not my word like a fire? saith the Lord* (v. 29). Is their word so? Has it the power and effectiveness of the word of God?" Fire has different effects, according to the substance on which it works. It hardens clay but softens wax; it consumes the dross but purifies gold. The word of God is similar: to some *a savour of life unto life, to others of death unto death* (2Co 2:16). Similarly, his word is compared to *a hammer breaking the rock in pieces* (v. 29). The unhumbled human heart is like a rock; if it will not be melted by the word of God as a fire, it will be broken to pieces by it as an object is broken to pieces by a hammer.

7.4. Let them consider that as long as they continue in these ways, God is against them. They are told this three times (vv. 30–32). *They steal my word every one from his neighbour* (v. 30). Those who are strangers to the spirit of the true prophets imitate their words, picking up some of their good expressions and passing them on to the people as if they were their own, but they do this awkwardly; the plagiarized parts do not fit. Others understand this to refer to the word of God as it was received by some of the people; the false prophets steal it from their hearts, as the Evil One in the parable is said to steal the good seed of the word (Mt 13:19). By their insinuations they diminish the authority, and so weaken the power, of the word of God on the minds of those people who seem to be under its conviction. God is against them (v. 31), because they *use their tongues* however they please in their messages to the people, and then say God is the author of their messages: "He said it." Some read it, "They smooth their tongues"; they are very polite and flattering to the people and say nothing except what seems pleasant and acceptable. "I *am against them* (v. 32), for they cheat and *prophesy false dreams,* claiming their own thoughts to have been divinely inspired." It is true that it is the people's fault that they err, that they take things on trust, but it is much more the prophets' fault that they cause God's people to *err by their lies and by their lightness* (reckless boasting). God denies that they have any commission from him: I *sent them not, nor commanded them*; they are not God's messengers, and *therefore they shall not profit this people at all.*

Verses 33–40

The ungodliness of the people, along with that of the priests and prophets, is rebuked here in a particular example; it may seem insignificant, but ungodliness in ordinary conversation and the corrupting of the language of a nation are a stark sign of the prevalence of evil in it.

1. The sin they are accused of here is ridiculing God's prophets and the language they used. They asked, *What is the burden of* (the message from) *the Lord?* (vv. 33–34). This was the word that gave great offense to God; whenever they spoke of *the word of the Lord,* they called it, in scorn and derision, *the burden of the Lord.* This was a word that the prophets used often, and they used it seriously to show how heavy the weight of the word of God was on their spirits. Now the godless scoffers took this word and made a joke of it. Making fun of God's messengers was a way of not allowing his message to be heard and obeyed. Some think that when the *word of the Lord* is called *a burden* it refers to some rebuke or threat; if so, then this use of the expression *the burden of the Lord* in mocking tones reflected badly on God as always being harsh on them and always frightening them; in that case, the scoffers were speaking of the word of God as something that was continually uneasy to them. Those who were guilty of this sin were some of the false prophets, some of the priests, and some of the people, the people having learned from the godless priests and prophets to take liberties with the things of God.

2. When they are rebuked for this godless way of speaking, they are told how to express themselves properly. We find the word *burden* used to refer to a word from God long after this (Zec 9:1; Mal 1:1; Na 1:1; Hab 1:1), but here God wants to have the prophet keep to the rule he was given earlier (15:19): *Let them return unto thee, but return not thou unto them.* "Do not stop using this word, but let others stop abusing it. You—priests, prophets, and people—*shall not mention the burden of the Lord any more* in this godless and careless way" (v. 36). How then must they express themselves? He tells them (v. 37): "*Thus shalt thou say to the prophet* when you are inquiring of him: *What hath the Lord answered thee? And what hath the Lord spoken?*" And they must speak in this way when they inquire of *their neighbours* as well (v. 35).

3. They will still say, *The burden of the Lord,* even though God has told them not to (v. 38). Those who distort the words of God in this way and who misinterpret them will be severely judged; mocking God's messengers is a great offense to him. *Every man's word shall be his own burden*; that is, the guilt of this sin will fall heavily on him. God will make sure they have enough of their joke, so that they will have no heart to mention *the burden of the Lord* anymore; it will be too serious to make fun of. Do they ask, *What is the burden of the Lord?* Let the prophet ask them, *What burden* are you referring to? Is it this: *I will even forsake you* (v. 33)? This is the message that will be laid on them (vv. 39–40): *Behold, I, even I, will utterly forget you, and I will forsake you.* God's word will be exalted and honored when those who mock it be reviled and made contemptible.

CHAPTER 24

At the end of the previous chapter we had a general prediction of the complete destruction of Jerusalem, which made the prophet himself sad. In this chapter, God encourages him by showing him that although the destruction seems to be universal, all the people will not be equally involved in it, since God knows how to distinguish the worthy and the worthless. Some have already gone into exile with Jehoiachin, but God tells him that it will turn out for their good. Others remain hardened in their sins, but God tells him those will go into exile. To inform the prophet of this, here is: 1. A vision of two baskets of figs, one very good and the other very poor (vv. 1–3). 2. The explanation of this vision, applying the good figs to those who have already been sent into exile for their good (vv. 4–7), and the bad figs to those who will later be sent into exile for their harm (vv. 8–10).

Verses 1–10

This short chapter helps us to put an encouraging interpretation on many long ones, by showing us that the same providence that is a savour of death unto death to some may by the grace of God be made a savour of life unto life (2Co 2:16) to others, and that even when God's people share with others in a disaster, it is intended for their good; it is a correcting rod in the hand of a tender Father (Pr 13:24). Notice:

1. The date of this sermon. It was a little after the captivity of Jehoiachin (Jeconiah) (v. 1). Jehoiachin was himself a despised broken vessel, but some very valuable persons were taken with him, Ezekiel for one (Eze 1:12). Many of the princes (officials) of Judah went into captivity. Of the rest of the people, only the carpenters and the smiths (artisans and other skilled workers) were forced away, because the Babylonians needed workers of those trades: they had many astrologers and stargazers, but too few artisans and other skilled workers. Many good people were taken away in that captivity, which the prophet took to heart, while there were others who triumphed in this loss and gloated over those to whose lot it fell to go into exile.

2. The vision by which this distinction of the captives was presented to the prophet's mind. He saw two baskets of figs, set before the temple, ready to be offered as firstfruits to the honor of God. The figs in one basket were extraordinarily good, while those in the other basket were extremely bad. Human beings are all like the fruits of the fig tree, capable of being made useful to God and other people (Jdg 9:11). Some, however, are like good figs, than which nothing is more pleasant, while others are like damaged, rotten figs, than which nothing is more sickly. The good figs were like those that ripen early, which are most welcome (Mic 7:1) and most prized. The bad figs were the kind that could not be eaten, they were so evil. They were neither pleasant nor good to eat. If God does not receive honor, or even any service, from human beings, they are like bad figs that cannot be eaten, which will not fulfill any good purpose. Of the people presented to the Lord at the door of his tabernacle, some were sincere, and they were very good; others play-acted with God, and they were very bad.

3. The explanation and application of this vision. God intended it to raise the dejected spirits of those who had gone into exile by assuring them of their happy return, and to humble and awaken the proud spirits of those who continued to live in Jerusalem by assuring them of a miserable captivity.

3.1. Here is the lesson of the good figs (v. 5), the ones that ripened early. These represented the godly captives, those who seemed to be the ones that were ripe for ruin first, for they went into exile first; they would turn out to be the ones who were ripe for mercy first, and their captivity would help ripen them. They were pleasing to God and would be carefully preserved. Notice here:

3.1.1. Those who were already taken into exile were the good figs. When God's judgments have been declared, those who are the first ones to be seized by them are not always the worst. In fact, early suffering sometimes proves to be best. The sooner the child is corrected, the better effect the correction is likely to have. Those who went

into exile first were like the son whom the father loves and therefore chastens betimes (Pr 13:24), chastens while there is hope. But those who stayed behind were like a child long left to himself (Pr 29:15), who, when later corrected, is stubborn and has been made worse (La 3:27).

3.1.2. God considered their exile as his action (v. 5): I have sent them out of this place into the land of the Chaldeans (Babylonians). It is God who puts his gold into the furnace, and he does so to test it (Isa 1:25; Job 23:10). His hand is especially seen in the suffering of good people. The judge orders the evildoer into the hands of the executioner, but the father corrects the child with his own hand.

3.1.3. Even this exile was intended by God for their benefit, and his intentions are never frustrated: I have sent them for their good. It seemed to hurt them in every way, not only because it destroyed their possessions and liberty but also because it depressed their spirits, discouraged their faith, deprived them of the benefit of God's messages and services of worship, and exposed them to temptations. Nevertheless, it was intended for their good, and eventually it turned out so. Their suffering convicted them of sin, humbled them under the hand of God, weaned them from the things of the world, taught them to pray, and turned them away from their sin.

3.1.4. God promised them that he would acknowledge them in their exile. The scornful relatives they left behind would barely acknowledge them, but God said, I will acknowledge them.

3.1.5. God assured them of his protection in their trouble. Being sent into exile for their good, they would not be lost there; it would be for them as it is with gold that the refiner puts into the furnace. He had his eye on his gold while it was there, and it was a watchful eye, to see that the gold sustained no damage: "I will set my eyes upon them for good." He would take his gold out of the furnace again as soon as the intended work had been completed: I will bring them again to this land (v. 6). They were sent away to improve their lives under severe discipline. They would be brought back to their Father's house. He would fashion his gold when he had refined it. He would make it an object of honor (Ro 9:21) fit for his use. The result would be that when God had brought them back from their trial, he would build them and make them a dwelling place for himself; he would plant them and make them a vincyard for himself. Their exile was to knock off the harsh edges of the rough stones and make them fit for his building, to prune the young trees and make them fit for him to plant.

3.1.6. He wanted to prepare them for these temporal mercies that he intended for them by giving them spiritual blessings (v. 7). They would learn more of God by his providences in Babylon than they had learned by all his messages and institutions in Jerusalem. It is promised here, I will give them not so much a head to know me as a heart to know me. They shall return to me with their whole heart (v. 7). God was committing himself to see to it that they would turn back to him, and if he turns us, we will be turned (31:18). In this way, they would again be taken into covenant with God: They shall be my people, and I will be their God. If those who have backslidden from God turn back to him sincerely, they are admitted as freely as anyone to all the privileges and encouragements of the eternal covenant.

3.2. Here is the lesson of the bad figs (v. 8). Zedekiah and his princes (officials) and supporters yet remain in the land, proud and self-confident (Eze 11:3). Many had fled into Egypt for shelter and safety, and so they boasted that although they had gone against the command of God, they had still acted wisely for themselves. Now, in both cases, it was threatened here against those who looked with contempt on those who had gone into exile:

3.2.1. That whereas those who had already been taken into exile were settled in one country, where they had the comfort of one another's company, the bad figs would be dispersed *and removed into all the kingdoms of the earth* (v. 9).

3.2.2. That whereas those already in exile were taken as captives for their good, the bad figs would be taken into all countries *for their hurt*. Their adversities would harden them; they would not bring them closer to God, but set them farther away from him.

3.2.3. That whereas those already in exile would have the honor of being acknowledged by God in their troubles, the bad figs would have the shame of being abandoned by the whole human race: *In all places whither I shall drive them they shall be a reproach and a proverb* (v. 9).

3.2.4. That whereas those already in exile would *return to their own land* (v. 6), the bad figs would be *consumed* (destroyed) *from that land* (v. 10), never to see it again.

3.2.5. That whereas those already in exile were reserved for better times, the bad figs were reserved for worse; wherever they were removed to, *the sword, and famine, and pestilence* would be sent after them. It is probable that this is a type of the later destruction of the Jews by the Romans, in which those who believed were taken care of but those who continued stubbornly in their unbelief were driven into all countries as objects of ridicule and cursing.

CHAPTER 25

The prophecy of this chapter is dated some time before the immediately previous chapters. It is dated in the first year of Nebuchadnezzar, that remarkable year when the sword of the Lord began to be drawn. Here is: 1. A review of the prophecies that had been given to Judah and Jerusalem for many previous years, by Jeremiah himself and other prophets, and an account of the little attention given them (vv. 1–7). 2. An explicit threat of the destruction of Judah and Jerusalem by the king of Babylon for their continuing in sin (vv. 8–11); to this threat is attached a promise of their restoration from exile in Babylon after seventy years (vv. 12–14). 3. A prediction of the devastation of several other nations by Nebuchadnezzar; the devastation is represented by a "cup of God's wrath" put into their hands (vv. 15–28), by a sword sent among them (vv. 29–33), and by the desolation brought about among the shepherds, flocks, and pastures (vv. 34–38).

Verses 1–7

This is a message from God concerning all the people of Judah (v. 1), which Jeremiah spoke to all the people of Judah (v. 2), probably when they had all come up to Jerusalem to worship at one of the sacred festivals.

This prophecy is dated in the fourth year of Jehoiakim and the first of Nebuchadnezzar. It was now that this military ruler began to set himself up to control the world. It was now that God, through his prophet, gave notice that Nebuchadnezzar was his servant. Nebuchadnezzar would not have moved so far toward universal monarchy (universal tyranny) except that God had his own purposes to fulfill through him. In this message notice the great efforts that were taken with the people to bring them to repentance, which were reminded of here, as justifying God in his action against them.

1. Jeremiah, for his part, had been a constant preacher among them for twenty-three years. *These* twenty-*three years have I come seeking fruit on this fig tree* (Lk 13:7). All this while, God had constantly sent messages to them, whenever they needed them: "From that time *to this very day the word of the Lord has come into me*, for you to use." In this way God's Spirit was contending with them, as he did with the old world (Ge 6:3). Jeremiah had been faithful and conscientious in communicating those messages. *I have spoken to you, rising early and speaking* (v. 3). He had declared to them the *whole counsel of God* (Ac 20:27).

2. Besides him, God had sent them other prophets on the same mission (v. 4). Many others from among God's *servants the prophets* preached awakening sermons, which were never published.

3. All these prophets told them about their faults, *their evil way* and their evil practices. Those who flattered them as if there were nothing wrong were not sent by God. The true prophets all rebuked them for their idolatry, their *going after other gods, to serve them and to worship them*, gods that were *the work of their own hands* (v. 6). The true prophets all called on them to repent of their sins and reform their lives. This was the chorus of every song they sang; personal reformation must be insisted on as necessary for national restoration: *every one* must *turn from his* own *evil way* (v. 5). The street will not be clean unless everyone sweeps the path in front of their own front door. And these prophets assured them that if they did reform, the mercies they enjoyed would continue to them: "*You shall dwell in the land*, live in peace in this good land, which the Lord has given you and your fathers. Nothing but sin will turn you out of it, and that will not do so if you turn from it."

4. But all this had no effect. They were not persuaded to follow the only right method to turn away the wrath of God. Jeremiah was a very lively and warm preacher, but *they hearkened* (listened) *not* to him (v. 3). The other prophets dealt faithfully with them, but they neither *hearkened to them* nor *inclined their ear* (v. 4).

Verses 8–14

Here is the sentence based on the foregoing accusation: "*Because you have not heard my words*, I must take another course of action with you" (v. 8). Sinners must either be parted from their sin or perish in it.

1. The ruin of the land of Judah by the king of Babylon's armies is decreed here (v. 9). God sent to Judah *his servants the prophets*, but they paid no attention to them, and so God will send for *his servant the king of Babylon*; the messengers of God's wrath will be sent against those who refuse to receive the messengers of his mercy.

1.1. Although Nebuchadnezzar was a stranger to the true God, in the attack he made on this country he was *God's servant*, an instrument in God's hand to correct his people. He was really serving God's intentions when he thought he was only serving his own ends. The most powerful and absolute monarchs are God's servants. Nebuchadnezzar, who is an instrument of God's wrath, is as truly his servant as Cyrus (Isa 44:28–5:1), who is an instrument of his mercy.

1.2. The complete destruction of this and all the neighboring lands is described here (vv. 9–11). This devastation will ruin their reputation among their neighbors; it will *make them an astonishment and a hissing*, an object of horror and scorn. *I will take from them the voice of mirth* (v. 10); they will have neither cause to be glad nor the heart for it. *The sound of the millstones shall not be heard,* for when the enemy has seized their stores, the sound of the grinding must fade (Ecc 12:4). All their business will be brought to an end; *the light of a candle* will not be seen, for there will be no work to be done that is worth the candlelight.

1.3. And, finally, they will be deprived of their liberty: *Those nations shall serve the king of Babylon seventy years* (v. 11). The fixing of the time during which the exile would last would be very useful not only to confirm the prophecy but also to encourage the people of God in their adversity and to help their faith and prayer. *Known unto God are all his works from the beginning of the world* (Acts 15:18), which shows that when he has thought fit, some of his works have been made known to his servants the prophets and through them to his church.

2. The ultimate ruin of Babylon is foretold here (vv. 12–14), as it was long before by Isaiah. The destroyers must themselves be destroyed. This will happen when *seventy years are accomplished* (v. 12). It is uncertain when these *seventy years* commence; some date them from the exile in the fourth year of Jehoiakim and the first of Nebuchadnezzar, others from the exile of Jehoiachin eight years later. When the set time to favor Zion has come (Ps 102:13), the king of Babylon must be punished, and all his tyranny judged. Then that nation will be punished *for their iniquity.* That land must then be *a perpetual desolation,* such as they had made other lands. When this destruction comes to Babylon at the hands of the Medes and Persians, reference will be made to what God has said: *I will bring upon that land all my words* (v. 13). The same Jeremiah who prophesied the destruction of other nations by the Babylonians also foretold the destruction of the Babylonians themselves: *I will recompense* (repay) *them according to their deeds,* by which they disobeyed the Law of God, even when they were made to serve his purposes. They themselves will be enslaved by *many nations and great kings,* allied with Cyrus king of Persia. Cyrus and his allies will make themselves masters of the Babylonians' country and make them the footstool by which they will seek to mount the throne of universal monarchy.

Verses 15–29

The universal desolation that is now coming is represented here by using the metaphor of a cup being passed round. The cup in the vision is to be a sword in the fulfillment of the vision, as explained in v. 16.

1. Concerning the circumstances of this judgment, notice:

1.1. From where this destroying sword would come: *from the hand of God* (v. 15). Evildoers are used as his sword (Ps 17:13). It is *the wine cup of his fury.* It was the righteous anger of God that sent this judgment. The signs of this anger are compared to some intoxicating drink that the nations would be forced to drink, as, in times past, condemned evildoers were sometimes executed by being compelled to drink poison. Evildoers are said to *drink the wrath of the Almighty* (Job 21:20; Rev 14:10).

1.2. By whose hand it would be sent to them: by the hand of Jeremiah as the judge *set over the nations* (1:10) to pass sentence on them, and by the hand of Nebuchadnezzar as the executioner. Jeremiah must *take the cup at God's hand* and compel the nations to *drink it.*

1.3. On whom it would be sent: on all the nations within Israel's communication. Jeremiah took the cup and *made all the nations to drink of it,* that is, he prophesied concerning each of the nations mentioned here that they would share in this great devastation.

1.3.1. *Jerusalem and the cities of Judah* are put first (v. 18), for *judgment begins at the house of God* (1Pe 4:17), at the sanctuary (Eze 9:6). And this part of the prophecy had already begun to be fulfilled; this is shown by that parenthesis *as it is this day* (v. 18), for in the fourth year of Jehoiakim, things had gotten into a very bad condition.

1.3.2. *Pharaoh king of Egypt* comes next, because the Jews trusted in that broken reed (2Ki 18:21) (v. 19); their survivors fled to Egypt, and Jeremiah particularly foretold the destruction of that country (43:10–11). All the other nations that bordered on Canaan must drink a toast to Jerusalem from this bitter cup. So must the *mingled people* (vv. 20, 24), who were either the Arabians or pirates from various nations who lived by pillaging; and so must the *kings of the land of Uz,* which was joined to the country of the Edomites. The Philistines had been troublesome to Israel, but now their towns would become the plunder. Edom, Moab, Ammon, Tyre, and Sidon are places well known to border on Israel; the *isles beyond,* or beside, *the sea,* are thought to be those parts of Phoenicia and Syria that lay on the coast of the Mediterranean Sea. Dedan and the other countries mentioned (vv. 23–24) seem to have been on the borders of Idumea and the Arabian Desert. The people of Elam were the Persians with whom the Medes were joined. The *kings of the north* (v. 26), which was nearer to Babylon, would be seized by the victorious sword of Nebuchadnezzar.

1.3.3. He would impel his victories with such incredible fury that *all the kingdoms of the world* (v. 26) would be sacrificed to his ambition. In the same way, Alexander is said to have conquered *the world,* and the Roman Empire is called *the world* (Lk 2:1). Or perhaps the phrase may be taken as reading the fate of *all the kingdoms* of the earth; at one time or other, they will all feel the terrible effects of war. The world has been and will be a great arena as long as the desires within human beings wage war against each other (Jas 4:1). *The king of Sheshach shall drink after them,* that is, the king of Babylon himself, who had given his neighbors all this trouble, would finally have it return on his own head. It is clear from 51:41 that *Sheshach* means Babylon. Babylon's ruin was foretold earlier as well (vv. 12–13).

1.4. What would be its effects. The devastation in all these kingdoms is represented by the consequences of excessive drinking: *They shall drink, and be moved, and be mad* (v. 16). *They shall be drunken, and spew, and fall and rise no more* (v. 27). People who are drunk often *fall and rise no more*; it is a sin that is its own punishment. When God sends the sword on a nation with authority to devastate it, that nation soon becomes like someone who is drunk, filled with confusion. The advisers become *mad*; they are at their wits' end. They are sick at heart with continual troubles, *falling* down in front of the enemy and unable to do anything to help themselves.

1.5. Its undoubted certainty, with the reason given (vv. 28–29). They would *refuse to take the cup* at Jeremiah's *hand.* They would not believe the prediction of such a despised person as Jeremiah. But he must tell them that it was *the word of the Lord of hosts,* and it was futile for them to struggle against Omnipotence: *You shall certainly drink* (v. 28). And he must give them this reason: the time of punishment has come, the day of reckoning, and Jerusalem has been called to account already: *I begin to bring evil on the city that is called by my name,* and *should you be utterly unpunished* (v. 29)? If Jerusalem was to be punished for learning idolatry from the nations, would not the nations be punished, from whom they learned it? *I will call for a sword upon all the inhabitants of the earth*, for they have helped to defile the inhabitants of Jerusalem.

2. Concerning this whole matter, we may notice that there is a God who judges the earth, to whom all the nations of the earth are responsible and whose judgment they must accept. Those who have been troublesome to the people of God will ultimately be judged for that. The year of the redeemer will come, the year of retribution. The message of the Lord will at last be seen in his judgments. Isaiah had prophesied long ago against most of these nations (Isa chapters 13 to 23), and now all his prophecies would be fulfilled. Nebuchadnezzar was so proud of his power that he had no sense of right. These are the men who turn the world upside down and yet expect to be admired and adored. Alexander thought himself a great ruler when others thought him no better than a great pirate. The greatest pomp and power in this world will not continue forever. Kings themselves must yield and become captives to Nebuchadnezzar's great power.

Verses 30–38

Here is a further description of the terrible devastation the king of Babylon would cause with his armies in all the countries around Jerusalem. They will soon become aware that Nebuchadnezzar is waging war on them, but the prophet is instructed to tell them that it is God himself who is waging war on them.

1. War is declared (v. 30): *The Lord shall roar from on high.* He *shall mightily roar upon his habitation* on earth from his home above. He roars *as a lion that has forsaken its covert* (lair) (v. 38) and is going out seeking something to devour.

2. The proclamation is published (v. 31): *The Lord has a controversy with the nations.* His quarrel with them is because of their evil, that is, their contempt for his authority and for his kindness to them. *He will give those that are wicked to the sword.* They have provoked God to anger, and so it is from him that all this destruction comes.

3. The alarm is sounded and taken (v. 31): *A noise will come even to the ends of the earth.* The alarm will not be sounded by the trumpet or drum, but by *a great whirlwind*, a storm that will be *raised up from the coasts*, the remote ends *of the earth* (v. 32). The Babylonian army will be like a hurricane that is raised in the north but is carried from there with speed, bearing down on everything in its path. Now the shepherds, that is, the kings and rulers, will *howl and cry*, and so will the leaders of the earth, the *principal*, or best, *of the flock*. They used to be the ones who were most courageous, but now their hearts will fail them; *they shall wallow themselves in the ashes* (v. 34). There will be *a voice of the cry of the shepherds*, and *a howling of the principal of the flock shall be heard* (v. 36). Perhaps, to continue this metaphor of a roaring lion, the verse alludes to the great fright that shepherds are in when they hear a roaring lion coming toward their flocks and neither they nor the leaders *of their flock* can find *any way to flee* for their own safety (v. 35) or *escape* the predator.

4. The progress of this war is described (v. 32): *Behold, evil shall go forth from nation to nation.* Every nation will have its share and take warning by the disasters of another to repent and reform. When our neighbor's house is on fire, it is time to be concerned for our own. When one nation is in the arena of war, every neighboring nation should hear, fear (Dt 31:12, 13), and make its peace with God.

5. The dreadful consequences of this war are foretold: *The days of slaughter and dispersions are accomplished*, that is, they have fully come (v. 34). Many people will fall by the sword of the merciless Babylonians, so that *the slain of the Lord* will be found everywhere. Those who are killed because of sin are the *slain of the Lord*. They will have no friends left to bury them, and the enemies will not have enough humanity in them to do them even this small favor. The effect of this war will be the *desolation of the whole land* in which it takes place (v. 38), one land after another. But here are two further expressions that make the case piteous. First, *You shall fall like a pleasant vessel* (v. 34). The most desirable people among them, who were looked on as fine, honorable objects, will fall by the sword. "You will fall as fine, delicate Venetian glass or as a fragile China dish, which is quickly shattered to pieces." Second, even the *peaceable habitations* (peaceful meadows) will be cut down (v. 37). Those who used to be quiet, not harming any of their neighbors, those who lived in peace and never provoked anyone—even those who will not escape. This is one of the terrible effects of war. We bless God, however, that there is *a peaceable habitation* (dwelling) above for all the children of peace, which is beyond reach of fire and sword.

CHAPTER 26

Just as in the Acts of the Apostles the accounts of the apostles' preaching and those of their suffering are interwoven, so it is in the account we have of the prophet Jeremiah. We have here: 1. How faithfully he preached (vv. 1–6). 2. How spitefully he was persecuted for doing so by the priests and the prophets (vv. 7–11). 3. How bravely he stood by his teaching in the face of his persecutors (vv. 12–15). 4. How wonderfully he was protected and rescued by the wisdom of the officials and elders (vv. 16–19). Though Uriah, another prophet, was put to death by Jehoiakim at about the same time (vv. 20–23), Jeremiah met with people who protected him (v. 24).

Verses 1–6

Here is the sermon Jeremiah preached that caused such offense that he was in danger of losing his life for it. It is left on record as an appeal to the judgment of impartial people throughout the ages.

1. God told him where to preach this sermon, and when, and to what audience (v. 2). God gave him orders to preach *in the court of the Lord's house* (v. 2), which was within the special jurisdiction of his sworn enemies, the priests. He must preach this message at the time of one of the most sacred festivals, when people had come from all the *cities of Judah* to *worship in the Lord's house.* These worshipers probably had great respect for their priests and would support them against Jeremiah. But none of these things must make him afraid. He must preach this sermon, which, if it were not convincing, would be offensive. God told him particularly *not to diminish* (omit) *a word*, but to speak *all the words* that he had commanded him.

2. God told him what to preach. He must assure them that if they would *repent of their sins* and turn from them, then even though judgments were near, a stop would be put to them, and God would go no further in his accusations against them (v. 3). This was the main purpose God intended in sending him to them. God *waits to be gracious* (Isa 30:18); he waits until we are duly qualified, until we are fit, and in the meantime he tries a variety of methods to make us so. Jeremiah must, on the other hand, assure them that if they continued obstinately not to pay any attention to all God's calls, it would certainly end in

the ruin of their city and temple (vv. 4–6). What God required of them was that they should *walk in all his law which he set before them* (v. 4), the Law of Moses and its ceremonies and commandments, and that they should *hearken* (listen) *to the words of his servants the prophets* (v. 5). The Law was what God himself had given them. The prophets were his own servants, sent by him to them. Up to that time the people had been deaf both to the Law and to the prophets: *You have not hearkened* (v. 5). All he expected now was that they would finally listen to and take note of what he said and make his word their rule of life. If they refused to listen, this city, and the temple in it, would suffer the same fate as their predecessors, Shiloh and the tabernacle there, for similarly refusing to listen. This was not the first time he had given them warning to this effect; see also 7:12–14.

Verses 7–15

Instead of awakening their convictions, the sermon only made their corruption even worse.

1. Jeremiah was charged with preaching such a sermon as if it were a crime, and he was detained for it as a criminal. The *priests* and *false prophets* and *people heard him speak these words* (v. 7). The leaders based their indictment on this: "He said, '*This house shall be like Shiloh*'" (v. 9). Notice how unfairly they represented his words. He had said, in God's name, *If you will not hearken to me, then will I make this house like Shiloh* (vv. 5–6), but they conveniently left out God's hand in the desolation as well as their own hand in it in not listening to the voice of God. They accused him of *blaspheming this holy place*, the crime that both our Lord Jesus (Mt 26:61) and Stephen (Ac 6:13–14) were accused of: "He said, '*This house shall be like Shiloh.*'" When the accusation was based on such weak foundations, it is no wonder that the sentence was unjust: *Thou shalt surely die* (v. 8). What he had said agreed with what God had said earlier (1Ki 9:6–8), "*If you shall at all turn from following after me, then this house shall be* abandoned," but he was condemned to die for saying it. This outcry of the priests and prophets raised the mob, and *all the people were gathered together against Jeremiah* in a general uproar (v. 9), ready to tear him to pieces.

2. He was arraigned and indicted for it. The *princes* (officials) *of Judah* were his judges (v. 10). When those who filled *the thrones of judgment* (Ps 122:5), the elders of Israel, heard this uproar in the temple, they *came up from the king's house*, where they usually sat, *to the house of the Lord* to ask what was going on. They *sat down in the entry of the new gate of the Lord's house* and held court. The *priests and prophets* were Jeremiah's prosecutors and accusers and were violently against him. They appealed to *the princes* and *to all the people* whether *this man* was not *worthy to die* (v. 11). When Jeremiah prophesied in the house of the king about the fall of the royal family (22:1), the court, though very corrupt, bore it patiently, and we do not find that they persecuted him for it. When he came into the *house of the Lord*, however, and touched the tenure of the priests and contradicted the lies and flatteries of the false prophets, then he was judged *worthy to die*.

3. Jeremiah made his defense in front of the officials and the people. He did not deny the words. He would stand by what he had said, even if it cost him his life; he had prophesied against *this house* and *this city* (v. 12), but he asserted that he did this by good authority, not maliciously nor rebelliously; "*The Lord sent me* to prophesy in this way." This was how he began his defense (v. 12) and also

how he concluded it (v. 15): *Of a truth the Lord hath sent me unto you to speak all these words.* As long as ministers keep closely to the instructions they have received from heaven, they need not fear the opposition they may meet with from hell or earth. Jeremiah was under divine protection, and any insult to the ambassador would be taken as against the Prince who sent him. It was said not by way of fatal sentence, but by way of fair warning (v. 14): "*As for me*, what becomes of me is not important; *behold, I am in your hand*. I have no power to oppose you, nor is it so much my concern to save my own life. *Do with me as seems meet* (good and right) *unto you.*" But as for them, he told them that their lives would be in danger if they put him to death (v. 15): *You shall surely bring innocent blood upon yourselves.*

Verses 16–24

Here is:

1. The acquitting of Jeremiah. He had indeed spoken the words made in the accusation, but they were not considered likely to cause rebellion or treason, and the court found him not guilty. The priests and prophets continued to demand judgment against him, but the officials and all the people stated clearly that *this man is not worthy to die* (v. 16), for, as they said, *he hath spoken to us* not by himself, but *in the name of the Lord our God*. Were they willing to acknowledge that he did indeed speak to them *in the name of the Lord* and that that Lord was their God? If so, then why did they not reform their ways and actions?

2. A precedent quoted to justify them in acquitting Jeremiah. Some of the *elders of the land*, or the more intelligent people, stood up and reminded the priests and prophets of a former case. The case referred to is that of Micah.

2.1. Was it thought strange that Jeremiah prophesied against this city and the temple? Micah did so before him, even in the reign of Hezekiah, that reign of reformation (v. 18). Micah had spoken as publicly as Jeremiah had now spoken, and to the same effect: "*Zion shall be ploughed like a field*; the buildings will all be destroyed, so that nothing will stop it from being plowed; *Jerusalem shall become heaps of* ruins, and *the mountain of the house*, on which the temple is built, will be *as the high places of the forest*, overrun with briers and thorns" (Mic 3:12). From this it is clear that a man may be, as Micah was, a true prophet of the Lord and yet prophesy the destruction of Zion and Jerusalem.

2.2. Was it thought right by the officials to justify Jeremiah in what he had done? It was what Hezekiah did before them in a similar case. Did Hezekiah and the people of Judah put Micah to death? On the contrary, they accepted the warning he gave them. Hezekiah set an excellent example for his successors, because he *feared the Lord* (v. 19). Micah's preaching drove him to his knees; he *besought the Lord* to turn away the threatened judgment and be reconciled to them, and he found it was not in vain, for *the Lord repented* (relented) *him of the evil* and returned in mercy to them. He sent an angel, who defeated the army of the Assyrians that threatened to plow Zion like a field (2Ki 19:35).

3. An example of another prophet who was put to death by Jehoiakim for prophesying as Jeremiah had (v. 20). Some believe this was urged by the prosecutors as a case that favored the prosecution, a modern case, in which speaking such words as Jeremiah had spoken was judged treason. Others think that the elders, who were advocates for Jeremiah, alleged this to show that by killing a prophet

they might bring a terrible disaster on themselves, for it would be adding sin to sin. Jehoiakim, the present king, had already killed one prophet; let them not reach the limit by killing another (Ge 15:16; Mt 23:32). But some good interpreters believe the voice in this narrative is that of the historian who wrote the book, Jeremiah himself, or Baruch. Notice:

3.1. Uriah's prophecy was *against this city and this land according to all the words of Jeremiah* (v. 20). The prophets of the Lord agreed in their testimony, and one would have thought that the word would have been taken notice of from the mouth of so many witnesses (Dt 19:15; Mt 18:16).

3.2. His being pursued for it (v. 21). Jehoiakim and his courtiers were angry with Uriah and *sought to put him to death*.

3.3. His running away: *When he heard* that the king sought to take his life, *he was afraid, and fled, and went into Egypt* (v. 21). This was certainly an effect of the weakness of his faith, and accordingly, things turned out badly. He distrusted God and his power to protect and support him. It was especially unbecoming to flee *into Egypt*. There are many who have much grace but little courage, who are very honest but also very timid.

3.4. His execution nevertheless. Jehoiakim's hatred, one might think, would possibly have been content with Uriah's banishment, but his revenge was so ruthless that he sent soldiers to Egypt, and they brought Uriah back by force. They *brought him to Jehoiakim*, and Jehoiakim *slew* (killed) *him with the sword* (v. 23). He loaded the dead body with infamy, throwing it into *the graves of the common people* as if Uriah had not been a prophet of the Lord. This was how Jehoiakim hoped both to ruin Uriah's reputation with the people, so that his predictions might not be listened to, and to deter others from prophesying similarly; but his attempts were futile. Herod thought he had won a victory when he had cut off John the Baptist's head, but he found himself deceived when, soon afterward, he heard about Jesus Christ and said in a fright, *This is John the Baptist* (Mt 14:2).

4. Jeremiah's rescue. Although Uriah had just been put to death, God still wonderfully preserved Jeremiah, even though he did not run away, but stood his ground. He who had an extraordinary mission could expect extraordinary protection. God raised up a friend for Jeremiah; he took him by the hand in a friendly way and helped him. It was *Ahikam the son of Shaphan*, one of the ministers of state in Josiah's time; we read about him in 2Ki 22:12. He had great influence among the officials, and he used it on behalf of Jeremiah.

CHAPTER 27

Jeremiah the prophet, unable to persuade the people to submit to God's commands and so prevent the destruction of their country, here persuades them to submit to God's providence by yielding to the king of Babylon and becoming his tributaries, which is the wisest course they can now take, because it will prevent their country from being devastated by fire and sword. 1. He gives this advice, in God's name, to the kings of the neighboring nations, assuring them that there is no way out for them except to serve the king of Babylon, but that there will be relief, for his power will last only seventy years (vv. 1–11). 2. He gives this advice to Zedekiah king of Judah especially (vv. 12–15), and to the priests and people, assuring them that the king of Babylon will still proceed against them until things come to a crisis,

and patient submission will be the only way to reduce the impact of the disaster (vv. 16–22).

Verses 1–11

There is some difficulty in dating this prophecy. Dr. Lightfoot solves it in this way: at the beginning of Jehoiakim's reign Jeremiah was to make these bonds and yokes and put them on his own neck as a sign of Judah's submission to the king of Babylon, which began at that time. However, he was to send these objects to the neighboring kings later, in the reign of Zedekiah; it is by way of prediction, then, that mention is made of Zedekiah's succession to Jehoiakim and of the ambassadors sent to him.

1. Jeremiah was to prepare a sign of the general submission of all these countries to the king of Babylon (v. 2): *"Make thee bonds and yokes,"* yokes with straps to fasten them, so that the animal may not slip its neck from the yoke." The prophet must put his own neck into these, for everyone would ask, "What do Jeremiah's yokes mean?" We find him with one on in 28:10. Here he was showing that he advised them to do nothing except what he had decided to do himself.

2. He was to send this, with a sermon attached to it, to all the neighboring rulers; those that lay closest to the land of Canaan are mentioned (v. 3). It seems there was a treaty of alliance in existence between the king of Judah and all those other kings. Jerusalem was the appointed place for the treaty. That was where they all sent their envoys, and it was agreed they would bind themselves in a league that was both offensive and defensive, in opposition to the threatening greatness of the king of Babylon. They had great confidence in the strength they gained by uniting in this way, but when the envoys were returning to their respective masters with the confirmation of this treaty, Jeremiah gave each of them a yoke to carry back to his master, to show them that they must become a servant of the king of Babylon. In the sermon:

2.1. God asserts his own indisputable right to dispose of kingdoms as he pleases (v. 5). He is the creator of all things; he *made the earth* at first and established it, and it remains; it is still the same, even though *one generation passes away and another comes* (Ecc 1:4). He still continues his work of creation, producing *man and beast upon the ground* by his *great power* and *outstretched arm*. As he has graciously *given the earth to the children of men* in general (Ps 115:16), so also he gives to each their share of it, to some more and to some less.

2.2. He declares a gift of all these countries to Nebuchadnezzar. "This is to certify to all whom it may concern that I have *given all these lands*, with all their wealth, into *the hands of the king of Babylon*; even the animals of the field, whether tame or wild, *have I given to him* (v. 6), parks and pastures; they are all his own." Nebuchadnezzar is a proud and evil person, an idolater, but God in his providence gives him this large dominion, these vast possessions. This shows us that the things of this world are not the best things, for God often gives the largest share of them to evildoers, who are rebels against him. Power is not based on grace. Nebuchadnezzar is a bad man, but God still calls him his servant, because he will use him as an instrument of his providence to correct the nations.

2.3. He assures them that they will all be unavoidably brought under the power of the king of Babylon for a time (v. 7): *All nations*, all these nations and many others, will serve *him, and his son, and his son's son*. His son was Evil-Merodach, and his son's son Belshazzar, in whom his kingdom ended. It was then that the time of reckoning came, and *many nations and great kings*, incorporated into the empire of the Medes and Persians, *served themselves of him* (subjugated him), as was foretold earlier (25:14).

2.4. He threatens those who stand out against the king of Babylon and will not submit to him (v. 8): the nation that will not *put their neck under his yoke I will punish with sword and famine*, with one judgment after another, until it is *consumed by his hand.*

2.5. He shows them the futility of all the hopes they feed themselves with, that they will preserve their liberty (vv. 9–10). These nations, like Israel, had their prophets, who claimed to foretell future events by the stars, dreams, or mediums, to please their patrons, and who assured them that they *would not serve the king of Babylon.* In this way, they wanted to encourage their people to resist vigorously. But Jeremiah tells them that it will turn out to be their destruction. Later we will read particular prophecies against these nations that bordered on Israel (48:1–49:39; Eze 25:1–17).

2.6. He puts them in a position to prevent their destruction by a quiet and easy submission (v. 11). The nations that will be content to *serve the king of Babylon* and pay him tribute for seventy years—*those will I let remain still in their own land. Serve the king of Babylon, and you shall till the land* and *dwell therein.* Some among them will condemn this as evidence of a weak spirit, but the prophet here commends it as a sign of a humble spirit, which yields to necessity and, by a quiet submission to the hardest turns of providence, makes the best of a bad situation. Many might have prevented destroying providences by humbling themselves under humbling providences. It is better to take up a lighter cross along our way than to pull a heavier one down onto our heads.

Verses 12–22

What was said to all the nations is here applied with particular tenderness to the Jews, for whom Jeremiah was concerned. The situation at present was as follows: Judah and Jerusalem had fought with the king of Babylon and were always beaten; many of their valuable people and goods had already been taken to Babylon, especially some of the *vessels of the Lord's house* (v. 16). Now what would be the outcome of this struggle? There were those at Jerusalem who claimed to be prophets and told them to hold out and regain all they had lost. Now Jeremiah was sent to tell them to yield, for otherwise, instead of recovering what they had lost, they would lose everything that remained.

1. Jeremiah humbly addresses the king of Judah to persuade him to surrender to the king of Babylon. The king's act will represent the people's, and so Jeremiah speaks to him as to them all (v. 12): *Bring your necks under the yoke of the king of Babylon and live.* Are they wise to submit to the heavy iron yoke of a cruel tyrant so that they may secure the lives of their bodies? Is it not much wiser to submit to the sweet and easy yoke of our rightful Lord and Master Jesus Christ, that we may secure the lives of our souls (Mt 11:29–30)? Humble your spirits to repentance and faith, and that is the way to lift your spirits to heaven and glory.

2. He addresses himself similarly to the priests and the people (v. 16), to persuade them to *serve the king of Babylon* so that they might *live* and might prevent the devastation of the city (v. 17): "*Wherefore* (why) *should it be laid waste*, as certainly it will be if you resist?"

3. In both these addresses he warns them against believing the false prophets who have rocked them to sleep in their security: "*Hearken* (listen) *not to the words of the prophets* (v. 14), *your prophets* (v. 16). They are not God's

prophets; he never sent them; they are yours, for they say what you want them to say, and they aim at nothing but to please you." Their prophets said two things:

3.1. That the power that the king of Babylon had gained over them would now soon be broken. They said (v. 14), "*You shall not serve the king of Babylon*; you need not submit voluntarily, for you will not be compelled to submit." They prophesied this *in the name of the Lord* (v. 15), as if God had sent them, but it was a lie: *I have not sent them, saith the Lord.*

3.2. They prophesied that the articles of the temple, which the king of Babylon had already taken away, would now soon be brought back (v. 16), knowing how acceptable it would be to the priests, since they loved the *gold of the temple* more than the *temple that sanctified the gold* (Mt 23:17). These vessels were taken away when Jehoiachin was taken captive to Babylon (v. 20). We have the sad story in 2Ki 24:13, 15; 2Ch 36:10. The temple was their pride, and the stripping of that was too clear a sign of what the true prophet told them, that their *God had departed from them* (Jdg 16:20; 1Sa 28:15). Their false prophets therefore had no other way to give them peace than to tell them that the king of Babylon would be forced to restore them in a little while. Now here Jeremiah tells them to think of preserving by their prayers the articles that remained rather than of bringing back by their prophecies those that had gone (v. 18): *If they be prophets*, as they claim to be, and if *the word of the Lord be with them*—if they have any relationship with heaven—let them stand *between the living and the dead*, between what is carried away and what remains, so that *the plague may be stayed* (Nu 16:48). *Let them make intercession with the Lord of hosts*, so that the articles that remain do not go with the rest. Instead of prophesying, let them pray. He assures them that the bronze articles will go the same way as the golden ones (vv. 19–20). Nebuchadnezzar will be sure to come again and take all he can find, not only in *the house of the Lord* but also in the *king's house*. But Jeremiah concludes with a gracious promise that the time will come when they will all be returned: *Until the day that I visit them in mercy*, and *then I will bring* those articles *up again, and restore them to this place* (v. 22). Surely these things were under the protection of a special providence; otherwise they would have been melted down; but there was to be a second temple, for which they were to be reserved. We read particularly of their return in Ezr 1:8. Although the return of the church's prosperity may not come in our time, we must not therefore despair of it, for it will come in God's time.

CHAPTER 28

In the previous chapter Jeremiah had charged with lies those prophets who foretold the speedy breaking of the yoke of the king of Babylon and the return of the articles of the sanctuary; now we have his contest with a particular prophet. 1. Hananiah, who claimed to be a prophet, foretold the reduction of Nebuchadnezzar's power and the return of both the people and the articles that had been taken away (vv. 1–4), and as a sign of this, he broke the yoke from Jeremiah's neck (vv. 10–11). 2. Jeremiah wished Hananiah's words could prove true, but he appealed to actual events, not doubting that events would prove Hananiah wrong (vv. 5–9). 3. The doom of both the deceived and the deceiver is read here. The people would have their yoke of wood turned into a yoke of iron (vv. 12–14), and the prophet would soon be destroyed by death (vv. 15–17).

Verses 1–9

This struggle between a true prophet and a false one is said to have happened *in the beginning of the reign of Zedekiah*, but *in the fourth year* (v. 1), for the first four years of his reign might well be called *the beginning*, because it was then that he reigned under the power of the king of Babylon and as one who paid tribute to him. During the rest of his reign, however, which might well be called its latter part as distinct from the former part, he reigned in rebellion against the king of Babylon. In this fourth year of his reign he went in person to Babylon (as we find in 51:59). This probably gave the people some hope that he would be able end the war, and the false prophets, Hananiah particularly, encouraged them in this hope. We have here:

1. The prediction that Hananiah solemnly delivered; he delivered it *in the house of the Lord*, in the name of the Lord, and *in the presence of the priests and of all the people*. In speaking this prophecy, he faced Jeremiah, addressing it to him (v. 1) and intending to contradict him, as much as to say, "Jeremiah, you are a liar." His prediction was that the king of Babylon's power over Judah and Jerusalem would soon be broken, that *within two full years* (v. 3) the articles of the temple would be brought back and Jeremiah and all the exiles taken away with him would return, whereas Jeremiah had foretold that the yoke of the king of Babylon would be bound more tightly and that the articles and exiles would not return for seventy years (vv. 2–4). On reading this false prophecy and comparing it with the messages God sent by the true prophets, we may observe the vast difference between them. Here is nothing of the spirit and life, the sublime expression, that appear in the messages of God's prophets. But what is especially lacking here is a note of godliness; Hananiah spoke about the return of the people's prosperity, but he spoke not even a word of good advice to repent, to return to God, to pray and seek his face. He promised them physical blessings in God's name, but made no mention of those spiritual blessings God always promised (24:7): *I will give them a heart to know me.*

2. Jeremiah's reply to this false prophecy.

2.1. He heartily wishes it could prove true, since he has great affection for his country, and a true desire that their ruin might be prevented. He says, *Amen; the Lord do so; the Lord perform thy words* (vv. 5–6). This was not the first time Jeremiah had prayed for his people even though he had prophesied against them, as Christ prayed, *Father, if it be possible, let this cup pass from me* (Mt 26:39), when he nevertheless knew it must not pass from him. Although God himself has determined the death of sinners, he does not desire it (Eze 18:23; 33:11), but wants *all men to be saved* (1Ti 2:4).

2.2. He appeals to the actual outcome of events to prove it false (vv. 7–9). The false prophets maligned Jeremiah, as Ahab did Micaiah, because he never *prophesied good concerning them, but evil* (1Ki 22:8). Prophets in former times had prophesied against *many countries and great kingdoms* (v. 8). They had been bold in communicating the messages God sent them, and they were far from fearing other people or seeking to please them, as Hananiah did. They had no difficulty, any more than Jeremiah does, in threatening war, famine, and plague, and what they said was regarded as coming from God. Why then should Jeremiah be criticized as *a pestilent fellow and a sower of sedition* (Ac 24:5), since he preaches nothing different from what God's prophets have always preached before him? But the prophet that *prophesies of peace* (v. 9) and prosperity—especially, as Hananiah does, absolutely and

unconditionally, without adding the necessary condition that the people must not by willful sin obstruct their own lives and stop the flow of God's favors—will be proved a true prophet only by the fulfillment of his prediction. If it comes to pass, then it will be known that *the Lord has sent him*, but if not, he will be seen to be a cheat and an impostor.

Verses 10–17

We have here an example of:

1. The arrogance of the false prophet. To complete the insult he intended for Jeremiah, *he took from off his neck the yoke* (v. 12) that he carried as a memorial of what he had prophesied about the enslaving of the nations to Nebuchadnezzar, and he broke it, so that he might give a sign of the fulfillment of his prophecy, as Jeremiah had given of his, and might seem to have defeated the intention of Jeremiah's prophecy. The lying spirit in the mouth of this false prophet (1Ki 22:23–23) imitates the language of the Spirit of truth: *Thus saith the Lord, So will I break the yoke of the king of Babylon*, not only from the neck of this nation but *from the neck of all nations, within two full years* (v. 11).

2. The patience of the true prophet. Jeremiah quietly *went his way*; not that he had nothing to say in reply, but he was willing to wait until God provided him with a direct answer, which as yet he had not received. He expected God to send a special message to Hananiah. *I, as a deaf man, heard not, for thou wilt hear*, and *thou shalt answer, Lord, for me* (Ps 38:13, 15).

3. The justice of God in judging between Jeremiah and his adversary. Jeremiah went his way, as a man *in whose mouth there was no rebuke* (Ps 38:14), but God soon put a word into his mouth. Let not Jeremiah himself distrust the truth of what he had spoken in God's name because it met with such contradiction. If what we have spoken is the truth of God, we must not withdraw it because people contradict it, for *great is the truth and will prevail* (1 Esd 4:41). Hananiah had broken the *yokes of wood*, but Jeremiah must make for them *yokes of iron*, which cannot be broken (v. 13), for God said, "*I have put a yoke of iron upon the neck of all these nations*, which will lie on them more heavily and bind them more tightly (v. 14), *that they may serve the king of Babylon*." What was said before is repeated: *I have given him the beasts of the field also*—as if there were something significant in that. By their evil, people had made themselves *like the beasts that perish* (Ps 49:12, 20), and so they deserved to be ruled as wild animals are, and Nebuchadnezzar ruled with such a power, for *whom he would he slew, and whom he would he kept alive* (Da 5:19). Hananiah was sentenced to death for contradicting it, and when Jeremiah had received commission from God, he boldly told him so to his face. The crimes for which Hananiah stood convicted were deceiving the people and insulting God: *Thou makest this people to trust in a lie* (v. 15); *thou hast taught rebellion against the Lord* (v. 16). The judgment given against him was, "*I will cast thee off from the face of the earth* (v. 16). *This year thou shalt die*, die as a rebel against the Lord." This sentence was executed (v. 17). Hananiah died the same year, within two months.

CHAPTER 29

The contest between Jeremiah and the false prophets was carried out before by preaching, and here by writing. Here is: 1. A letter Jeremiah wrote to the exiles in Babylon against the prophets they had there (vv. 1–3), in which: 1.1. He tries to reconcile them to their captivity (vv. 4–7). 1.2. He warns them not to believe their false prophets, who feed them with hopes of a quick release (vv. 8–9). 1.3. He assures them that God will restore them in mercy to their own land again at the end of seventy years (vv. 10–14). 1.4. He foretells the destruction of those who have not so far gone into exile (vv. 15–19). 1.5. He prophesies the destruction of two of their false prophets in Babylon, who soothe them in their sins and set them bad examples (vv. 20–23). 2. A letter that Shemaiah, a false prophet in Babylon, wrote to the priests at Jerusalem to stir them to persecute Jeremiah (vv. 24–29), and here is a pronouncement of God's wrath against him for writing such a letter (vv. 30–32).

Verses 1–7

1. Jeremiah wrote to the exiles in Babylon in the name of the Lord. Jehoiachin had surrendered himself as a prisoner, with the queen his mother, the court officials of his household — called here the *eunuchs* — and many of *the princes* (leaders) *of Judah and Jerusalem. The carpenters and smiths* (artisans and other skilled workers) had been given over as well, so that those who remained might not have any proper means to strengthen their city. By this submission it was hoped that Nebuchadnezzar would be pacified, but the imperious conqueror wanted further concessions. Not content with this, when these had *departed from Jerusalem*, he came again and took many more of *the elders, the priests, the prophets, and the people* (v. 1). The situation of these exiles was very sad, especially because they looked as if they were greater sinners than all those who lived in Jerusalem. Jeremiah therefore wrote them a letter to encourage them. This letter of Jeremiah's was sent to the exiles in Babylon by the hands of the ambassadors King Zedekiah sent to Nebuchadnezzar, whom he sent probably to pay him his tribute and renew his submission to him. Jeremiah chose to use such messengers to send this message by because it was a message from God.

2. A copy of the full letter follows here and continues to v. 24.

2.1. He assures them that he is writing in the name of the *Lord of hosts, the God of Israel* (v. 4); Jeremiah is merely the scribe or copyist. It will be encouraging to them in their exile to hear that God is *the Lord of hosts*, able to help and restore them. He is the *God of Israel*, in covenant with his people. This will be a warning to stand on their guard against all temptations to succumb to the idolatry of Babylon. God's writing this letter to them can encourage them, as it is evidence that he has not rejected them; he has not disinherited them, even though he has been displeased with them and is correcting them.

2.2. God, by him, acknowledges the hand he had in their exile: *I have caused you to be carried away* (v. 4). If God caused them to be taken as exiles, they can be sure that he neither did them any wrong nor meant them any harm.

2.3. He tells them to think of nothing except settling there, and so let them decide to make the best of the situation (vv. 5–6): *Build yourselves houses and dwell in them*, and so on. They must not feed themselves with the hope of a speedy return from captivity. Let them therefore come to terms with it as best they can. Let them *build*, *plant*, and *marry*, and deal with their children there as if they were in their own homeland. If they live in the fear of God, what can stop them from living comfortably in Babylon? They cannot but *weep* sometimes *when they remember Zion* (Ps 137:1). But let not weeping stop them from sowing in all conditions of life. We would be

wise to make the best of our existing situation and not to throw away the comfort of what we may have because we do not have all we want. We have a natural affection for our native country, but if Providence moves us to another country, we must decide to live at peace there. If the *earth is the Lord's* (Ps 24:1), then wherever children of God go, they do not go away from their Father's land. They must not disturb themselves with fears of intolerable hardships in their exile.

2.4. He tells them to seek the good of the country where they are in exile (v. 7), to pray for it, to try to promote it. This forbids them to attempt to do anything against the public peace as long as they are subjects of the king of Babylon. They must live *quiet and peaceable lives* under him, *in all godliness and honesty* (1Ti 2:2), not plotting to shake off the chains that hold them, but patiently leaving it to God to bring about their restoration at the right time. *For in the peace thereof you shall have peace* (v. 7). Similarly, the first Christians, according to the spirit of their holy religious faith, prayed for the governing powers, even though they were persecuting powers. Every passenger is concerned with the safety of the ship.

Verses 8–14

To make the people settled and at peace in their captivity:

1. God takes them away from building on the false foundation their false prophets have laid (vv. 8–9). The false prophets tell them their captivity will be short and that they must therefore not think of putting down roots in Babylon. "Now here *they deceive you*," God says; "they *prophesy a lie to you*, even though they prophesy *in my name*. But *let them not deceive you*; do not allow yourselves to be deluded by them." *Hearken not* (do not listen) *to your dreams, which you cause to be dreamed* (v. 8). He is referring either to the dreams, or false thoughts, that the people please themselves with or to the dreams the prophets dream and base their prophecies on. The people *cause them to be dreamed*, for they encourage the prophets to deceive them, asking them to prophesy nothing but *smooth things* (Isa 30:10). Whether dreamed by the people or by the prophets, they are dreams that the people themselves have asked for.

2. He gives them a good foundation to base their hopes on. God promises them here that although they will not return quickly, they will return finally, *after seventy years be accomplished* (v. 10). He will put an end to *their captivity*. Even though they are dispersed, some in one country and some in another, he *will gather them from all the places whither they are driven* (v. 14) and join them together again in one body. They will be brought back to their own land, *to the place whence* they were *carried captive* (v. 14).

2.1. This will be the fulfillment of God's promise to them (v. 10): *I will perform my good word toward you*. Their return from exile will be made very encouraging by the assurance that it is the fulfillment of God's good word to them, the product of a gracious promise.

2.2. This will be according to God's purposes for them (v. 11): *I know the thoughts that I think toward you*. His thoughts are all working toward the *expected end*, which he will show in due time. Let them be patient until the fruit is ripe, and then they will have it. He will give them, literally, "an end and expectation," a future and a hope. When things are at the worst, they will begin to get better; he will allow them to see *the end* — a comforting termination — of their trouble and the glorious perfection of their restoration. The One who in the beginning completed the *heavens and the earth* and all the *hosts* of both will complete all the blessings of both to his people. God does nothing by halves. He will also allow them to see their future *expectation*, the *end* that they desire. He will give them not the expectations of their fears or the expectations of their imaginations, but the expectations of their faith.

2.3. This will be in answer to their prayers (vv. 12–15). *Then shall you call upon me*, and *you shall go and pray unto me*. When restoration is coming, we must go out in prayer to meet it. *I will hearken unto you*, and *I will be found of you*. God has said it, and we may depend on it: *Seek and you shall find* (Isa 55:1). A general rule is laid down for us (v. 13): *You shall find me when you shall search for me with all your heart.*

Verses 15–23

Jeremiah here turns to those who show disrespect for the advice and encouragement he has ministered and who depend on the false prophets. When this letter comes from Jeremiah, they will be ready to say, "Why should he be so interfering? Why take it upon himself to advise us? *The Lord has raised us up prophets in Babylon* (v. 15). We are satisfied with those prophets and can depend on them. We don't need to listen to any prophets in Jerusalem." These prophets of their own tell them that no more will be taken into exile, but that those who are in exile will soon return. In answer to this:

1. The prophet foretells here the complete destruction of those who remain in Jerusalem: "As for the *king* and *people* who *dwell in the city*, who, you think, will be ready to welcome you back when you return, you are deceived. They will be followed by one judgment after another, *sword, famine,* and *pestilence* (plague), which will destroy many people, and the poor and miserable remnant will be *removed into all kingdoms of the earth*" (vv. 16, 18). And so God *will make them*, or rather deal with them, *like vile figs*. This refers to the vision and the prophecy we had in ch. 24. The reason given is the same: *Because they have not hearkened to my words. I called, but they refused* (v. 19).

2. He foretells the judgment of God on the false prophets in Babylon. He calls on all the people in exile, who boast about them as prophets whom God has raised up (v. 20): "Stand still, and listen to the fate of the prophets you are so fond of." The two prophets named here are *Ahab* and *Zedekiah* (v. 21). Notice:

2.1. The crimes they are accused of—impiety and immorality: they *prophesy lies in God's name* (v. 21), and again, they have *spoken lying words in my name* (v. 23). Saying the God of truth was the author of their lies was worst of all. It is seen here why they flattered others in their sins—because they could not rebuke them without condemning themselves.

2.2. The judgments threatened against them: *The king of Babylon shall slay them before your eyes*; in fact, he will put them to a miserable death, *roast* (burn) *them in the fire* (v. 22). We may suppose that it was not because of their ungodliness and immorality that Nebuchadnezzar punished them so severely, but for rebellion, for some attempts of their tumultuous spirits to destroy the public peace and stir the people to rebel. Their names will be a curse among the exiles in Babylon (v. 22). When people want to invoke the greatest punishment on one they hate, they will think they cannot bring on them a heavier curse, in fewer words, than to say, *The Lord make thee like Zedekiah and like Ahab.*

Verses 24–32

The false prophets were angry at the contents of Jeremiah's letter. One of them, Shemaiah, showed his hatred toward the prophet:

1. This troublemaking fellow is called *Shemaiah the Nehelamite*, the "dreamer," as the margin of v. 24 reads, because he claimed to have received all his prophecies from God in a dream. He had gotten a copy of Jeremiah's letter to the exiles, or information was given to him about it, and it irritated him greatly. He will answer it—yes he will. But how? He does not write to Jeremiah to justify his own mission; he writes to the priests and instigates the persecution of Jeremiah through them. He writes in his own name, as if he must dictate his plans to the whole human race. It is a circular letter that he sends, to the priests at Jerusalem and the rest of the people, but it is chiefly directed to Zephaniah, who was either the immediate son of Maaseiah or a member of the twenty-fourth division of the priests, of which Maaseiah was the father and leader. He was not the high priest, but deputy high priest, or in some significant position of command in the temple, as Pashur was (20:1).

1.1. Shemaiah reminds Zephaniah and the other priests of the duty of their position (v. 26): *The Lord hath made thee priest instead of Jehoiada the priest.* Some think he is referring to the famous Jehoiada, that great reformer in the days of Joash. On the other hand, it may have been some other Jehoiada, Zephaniah's immediate predecessor in this office, who perhaps was taken to Babylon among the priests (v. 1). Zephaniah is promoted sooner than expected to this place of trust and power, and Shemaiah wants him to think that Providence has advanced him so that he may persecute God's prophets, that he has come to this position in government for such a time as this (Est 4:14). These priests' work, says Shemaiah, is to examine *every man that is mad and makes himself a prophet* (any crazy person who acts like a prophet) (v. 26). God's faithful prophets are described as prophets of their own making, usurpers of the office, lay intruders, crazy people, motivated by some demon, people who are mad and frenzied.

1.2. He informs the priests of the letter Jeremiah wrote to the exiles (v. 28). Why should this be objected to? The false prophets said that the exile would never come (14:13). Jeremiah said it would come, and the outcome has already proved him to be right.

1.3. He demands judgment against Jeremiah, assuming that he is *mad* and *makes himself a prophet*. He expects that the priests will order him to be put *in prison* and *in the stocks* (v. 26), and he hopes that if Jeremiah loses credibility in Jerusalem, the exiles in Babylon will not be influenced by him. He takes it on himself to rebuke Zephaniah for his neglect (v. 27): *Why hast thou not rebuked and restrained Jeremiah of Anathoth?* God has confirmed his word in the mouth of Jeremiah, and it has *taken hold of* the people (Zec 1:6), but because he does not prophesy to them the pleasing things they want, they have decided to look on him as not duly called to the office of a prophet. They have now been sent into a miserable exile for *mocking the messengers of the Lord* and *misusing his prophets*. Adversity will not cure people of their sins unless the grace of God works alongside it; without grace, adversity will rather make worse the corruption it is intended to put to death (Pr 27:22). *Though thou shouldst bray a fool in a mortar, yet will not his foolishness depart from him.*

2. *Zephaniah read this letter in the ears of Jeremiah.* He has respect for Jeremiah—for we find him employed

in messages to him as *a prophet* (21:1; 37:3)—and so protects him. He tells Jeremiah the contents of the letter, so that he may see what enemies he has even among the exiles.

3. Sentence is passed on Shemaiah for writing this letter. God sends him an answer. It is ordered to be sent *to those of the captivity*, who encouraged and supported him as if he had been a prophet raised up by God (vv. 31–32). Shemaiah has made fools of them. He promised them peace in God's name, but God did not send him; he forged a commission, made the people *trust in a lie*, and by preaching false comfort to them deprived them of true comfort. He has made traitors of them; he has *taught rebellion against the Lord*, as Hananiah did (28:16). At his end *he shall also be* (prove to be) *a fool*—as it is expressed in 17:11—his name and family will be buried in oblivion: *He shall not have a man to dwell among this people* (v. 32). Neither he nor any who come from him will *behold the good that I will do for my people*.

CHAPTER 30

The sermon in this and the next chapter is very different from those before. Most of what he has said up to this time has been by way of reproof, but these two chapters are wholly taken up with precious promises of a return from exile, which was a type of the glorious things reserved for the church in the days of the Messiah. The prophet is told to write it down, because it is intended to strengthen and encourage future generations (vv. 1–3). It is promised here: 1. That they will later have a joyful restoration: 1.1. Though they are now in great terror (vv. 4–7). 1.2. Though their oppressors are strong (vv. 8–10). 1.3. Though they are not restored (v. 11). 1.4. Though all means of their restoration seem to fail and be cut off (vv. 12–14). 1.5. Though God himself sent them into exile (vv. 15–16). 1.6. Though everyone looks on their case as desperate (v. 17). 2. That after their joyful restoration they will be happily settled, and their city will be rebuilt (v. 18), their numbers increased (vv. 19–20), their government established (v. 21), God's covenant with them renewed (v. 22), and their enemies destroyed (vv. 23–24).

Verses 1–9

Here:

1. Jeremiah is told to *write* what God has spoken to him in the hope that those people who have not benefited by what he said when they heard it the first time might take more notice of it when they have greater opportunity to read it and consider it. He must collect the promises and put them together, and God will now add to them many similar words. He must write them for future generations, who will see them fulfilled. He must write them not *in a letter* but *in a book* (v. 2), to be preserved in the archives. This prophecy must be written so that it may be read, and so that it may be seen how exactly the fulfillment corresponds to the prediction. It is suggested they will be *beloved for their fathers' sake* (Ro 11:28), for God will bring them again to Canaan, because it was *the land that he gave to their fathers*, which *they shall possess* (v. 3).

2. Jeremiah is told what to write. The very words are such as the Holy Spirit teaches (1Co 2:13) (v. 4).

2.1. He must write a description of the consternation that the people are now in and are likely to be in every time the Babylonians attack (v. 5): *We have heard a voice of trembling*—shrieks of terror echoing to the noise of

danger. The false prophets told them they would have *peace*, but "there is fear and not peace," as the margin of v. 5 reads. Even the warriors will be overwhelmed by the calamities of their nation. They will look like *women in labour*, whose pains come on them with extreme intensity and who know they cannot escape them (v. 6). *Alas! For that day is great*, a day of judgment—the final Day of Judgment is called the *great day*, the *great and terrible day of the Lord* (Joel 2:31; Jude 6)—great, such that *there has been none like it*. The last destruction of Jerusalem is spoken of by our Savior as unparalleled (Mt 24:21). *It is even the time of Jacob's trouble* (v. 7), a sad time, when God's professing people will be in greater distress than any other people. The whole time of the exile was a time of Jacob's trouble.

2.2. He must write God's assurances that these adversities will come to a favorable end.

2.2.1. Jacob's troubles will cease: *He shall be saved out of them* (v. 7).

2.2.2. Jacob's troublers will be made unable to cause him any further trouble (v. 8): "*I will break his yoke from off thy neck*, that yoke that has lain so heavy for so long and has angered you so much. *I will burst thy bonds* and restore you to liberty and peace; they will no more enrich themselves either by your possessions or by your labors."

2.2.3. What crowns and completes the mercy is that their freedom to exercise their religious faith will be restored (v. 9). When the time comes that they are *saved out of their trouble*, God will prepare and qualify them for it by giving them *a heart to serve him* and the opportunity to serve him. We are *delivered out of the hands of our enemies* so that we may *serve God* (Lk 1:74–75). They will serve their own God, and they will be neither inclined nor compelled, as they were in exile, to serve other gods. They will serve *David their king*, such rulers as God will from time to time set over them, from the line of David (e.g., Zerubbabel). But this has a further meaning. The Aramaic paraphrase reads, "They shall obey [or listen to] the Messiah [the Christ], the Son of David, their king." The Jewish interpreters apply it to him. The era that began at their return from exile brought them to the Messiah. He is called *David their King* because he was the *Son of David* (Mt 22:42) and he answered to the name (Mt 20:31–32). In the New Testament God is often said to have *raised up* Jesus as a King (Ac 3:26; 13:23, 33). Those who serve the Lord as their God must give themselves to Jesus Christ to be ruled by him. All people must *honour the Son as they honour the Father* (Jn 5:23), and they must come into the service and worship of God by the Son as Mediator. Those to whom he gives rest must take his yoke on them (Mt 11:28–29).

Verses 10–17

The deplorable case of the Jews in exile is set out, but many precious promises are given them.

1. God himself acted against them: he *scattered* them (v. 11); he did *all these things unto them* (v. 15). This was intended by him as a fatherly correction and nothing more (v. 11): "*I will correct thee in measure*, I will discipline you with justice, no more than you deserve, in fact, no more than you can bear." God hates sin most in those who are closest to him. God here corrects his people *for the multitude of their iniquity* and *because their sins were increased* (vv. 14–15). Yet what God intended as a fatherly correction the Jews and others interpreted as an act of hostility; they looked on him as having *wounded them with the wound of an enemy* and *with the chastisement of a*

cruel one (v. 14). It is true, it did seem as if God had dealt severely with them, as if he had fought against them (Isa 63:10). Job complains that God has become cruel to him and *multiplied his wounds* (Job 9:17).

2. Their friends abandoned them. If we are criticized, we expect our friends to appear to vindicate us. If we are sick, distressed, or wounded, we expect our friends to sympathize with us and, if need be, help us in healing. Here, however, there is no one to do that, "no one to bind up your wounds. *All thy lovers* (allies) *have forgotten thee.*" When God is against a people, who will be for them? Their case seemed desperate and beyond relief (v. 12): *Thy bruise is incurable, thy wound grievous* (beyond healing), and (v. 15) *thy sorrow is incurable.* Their sorrow could not be alleviated; they seemed to be hardened in it. In this deplorable condition they were looked on with disdain (v. 17): *They called thee an outcast,* abandoned to ruin; they said, *This is Zion, whom no man seeks after.* Now everything was in ruins. When foreigners looked at the people who formerly lived in Zion but were now in exile, they called them outcasts. These were the ones who belonged to Zion, but *no man sought after* them or asked about them.

3. In spite of all this, God will work restoration and salvation for them at the appropriate time.

3.1. Although he seems far away from them, he still assures them of his presence with them: *I will save thee* (v. 10). *I am with thee, to save thee* (v. 11).

3.2. Although they are remote from their own land, *afar off in the land of their captivity,* salvation will still find them; it will take them and their *seed* from there (v. 10).

3.3. Although they are now full of fears, the time will come when they *shall be in rest and quiet,* at peace and secure, *and none shall make them afraid* (v. 10).

3.4. Although the nations to which they are dispersed will be brought to ruin, they will be preserved (v. 11): *Though I make a full end of* (completely destroy) *the nations whither I have scattered thee, yet I will not make a full end of thee.* God's church may sometimes be brought very low, but he *will not make a full end of it* (5:10, 18).

3.5. Although God may correct them, and justly so, he will still return in mercy to them, and even their sin will not prevent their restoration when God's time comes.

3.6. Although their adversaries are powerful, God will break their power (v. 16): *All that devour thee shall be devoured.* "They *shall every one of them,* without exception, *go into captivity,* and the day will come when *those that* now *spoil thee shall be a spoil.*"

3.7. Although the wound seems incurable, God will heal it (v. 17): *I will restore health unto thee.*

4. They are warned against excessive fear and grief, for there is enough in these precious promises to silence both. *Fear thou not, O my servant Jacob! Neither be dismayed.* They must not grieve as those who have no hope (1Th 4:13) (v. 15). "*Why criest thou for thy affliction?* It is *for thy sin* (vv. 14–15), and so, instead of complaining, you should repent."

Verses 18–24

Here are further signs of the favor God has reserved for them after the days of their adversities are over.

1. The city and temple will be rebuilt (v. 18). *Jacob's tents* and *his dwelling places* felt the effects of *the captivity,* for they lay in ruins when the inhabitants were taken captive, but those homes will be repaired, and in this way God will *have mercy upon their dwelling places,* which have been memorials to his justice. Then *the city* of Jerusalem *shall be built upon her own heap,* her own hill, even though it is now no better than a heap of ruins. The One

who can *make of a city a heap* (Isa 25:2) can *make of a heap a city* again when he pleases. *The palace* (the temple, God's palace) *shall remain after the manner thereof;* it will be built following the old model.

2. The sacred festivals will again be celebrated (v. 19): *Out of* the city and the temple and all the dwelling places of Jacob *shall proceed thanksgiving and the voice of those that make merry* (rejoice).

3. The people will be multiplied or increased: *They shall not be few, they shall not be small* (v. 19), but will be significant among the nations, for *I will multiply them* and *I will glorify them.* It is for the honor of the church to have many added to it who will be saved (Ac 2:47). There will be a constant succession of faithful magistrates in the congregation of the elders and a constant succession of faithful worshipers in the congregation of the saints.

4. They will be blessed with a good government (v. 21): *Their nobles* and judges *shall be of themselves,* of their own nation, and the people will no longer be ruled by foreigners and enemies. *Their governor shall proceed from the midst of them,* will be one who has shared with them in the adversities of their exile. This alludes to Christ, our *governor, David our King* (v. 9); he is one like us, *in all things made like unto his brethren* (Heb 2:17). *And I will cause him to draw near;* this may be understood to refer either:

4.1. To the people, Jacob and Israel: "*I will cause* them *to draw near* (v. 21) to me in the temple service, as before, to come into covenant with me as *my people*" (v. 22). Or:

4.2. To the governor, for it is a single person that is spoken of: *Their governor shall* be duly called to his office, and he will *draw near* to God to discuss matters with him on every occasion. But it also looks further, to Christ as Mediator. The proper work and office of Christ, as Mediator, is *to draw near and approach unto* God for us, and in our name and place, as the high priest of our profession (Heb 3:1). God the Father did *cause* Jesus Christ to *draw near and approach* him as Mediator in this way. He anointed him for this purpose and declared he was pleased with him (Mt 3:17). And Christ's own voluntary undertaking, in compliance with his Father's will and in compassion to fallen humanity, committed him.

5. They will be taken again into covenant with God, according to the covenant made with their ancestors (v. 22): *You shall be my people,* and it is God's good work in us that makes us *to him a people, a people for his name* (Ac 15:14).

6. Their enemies will be judged and humbled (v. 20): *I will punish all* those *that oppress them,* so that it will be clear to everyone that it is dangerous to *touch God's anointed* (Ps 105:15). We had these two verses before (23:19–20); there they were a pronouncement of God's wrath against the ungodly hypocrites in Israel; here they are against the evil oppressors of Israel. The wrath of God against evildoers is here represented as being irresistible, like a storm. Storms usually last for a short time, but this will be *a continuing whirlwind.* It will fulfill the reasons for which it is sent (Isa 55:11): *The anger of the Lord shall not return till he have done it* (v. 24). The purposes of his wrath, as well as the purposes of his love, will all be fulfilled; he will *perform the intents of his heart.*

CHAPTER 31

Here are good and encouraging words to strengthen the exiles, assuring them that God will in due time make them a great and joyful nation again, especially by sending them the Messiah, in whose kingdom and grace many of these promises will have their complete fulfillment. 1. They will be restored to peace and joy (vv. 1–14). 2. The sorrow for the loss of their children will come to an end (vv. 15–17). 3. They will repent of their sins, and God will graciously accept them (vv. 18–20). 4. They will be increased, both their children and their cattle (vv. 21–30). 5. God will renew his covenant with them and enrich it with spiritual blessings (Eph 1:3, 7) (vv. 31–34). 6. These blessings will be kept safe for their own families after them (vv. 35–37). 7. As a pledge of this, the city of Jerusalem will be rebuilt (vv. 38–40).

Verses 1–9

God assures his people:

1. That he will again take them into a covenant relationship with himself. His own people will be acknowledged by him as the children of his love: "*I will be the God*—that is, I will show myself to be the God—*of all the families of Israel* (v. 1), not only of the two tribes but of all the tribes; not only of their state in general but also of their individual families and their interests." These will all enjoy a special relationship with God. If we and our households serve the Lord (Jos 24:15), we and our households will be protected and blessed by him (Pr 3:33).

2. That he will do for them, in bringing them out of Babylon, what he did for their ancestors when he rescued them from Egypt.

2.1. He reminds them of what he did for their ancestors when he brought them out of Egypt (v. 2). They were then, as are these whom Jeremiah now addresses, *a people left of* (who survived) *the sword*, that sword of Pharaoh that he used to kill all the male children as soon as they were born (Ex 1:16). They were then *in the wilderness*, where they seemed to be lost and forgotten, as these are now in a foreign land, but they found grace in God's sight and were acknowledged and greatly honored by him, and he was at this time going *to cause them to rest* in Canaan. God is still the same.

2.2. They remind him of what he did for their ancestors, indicating that they now do not see such signs and are ready to ask, as Gideon did, "*Where are all the wonders that our fathers told us of?* (Jdg 6:13). The years of long ago were glorious years, but now things are different; what good will it do us that he *appeared of old* to us when now he is *a God that hides himself* from us (Isa 45:15)?"

2.3. To this he answers with an assurance of the constancy of his love: *Yea, I have loved thee,* not only with an ancient love but also *with an everlasting love* (v. 3), a love that will never fail, however much the assurance of it may be suspended for a time. Nothing can separate them from that love (Ro 8:35–39). Those whom God loves with this love he will draw into covenant and fellowship with himself by the influence of his Spirit on their souls.

3. That he will again form them into a people and joyfully establish them in their own land (vv. 4–5). They will take up their harps, which will have long been hanging on the willow trees (Ps 137:2); they will tune them and will themselves be in tune to use them. Is the joy of the city maintained by the products of the country? Yes, it is, and so it is promised (v. 5), *Thou shalt yet plant vines upon the mountains of Samaria.* Before the fall of the kingdom of Israel, Samaria was its leading city, in opposition to that of Judah, but they will now be united (Eze 37:22). There will be such perfect peace and security that people will apply themselves wholly to improving their land: *The planters shall plant,* not fearing that the soldiers will come to eat the fruits of what they had planted or to

uproot it, and they themselves *shall eat them* freely, as *common things*, not forbidden fruits.

4. That they will have the freedom and opportunity to worship God in his own appointed religious services (v. 6): *There shall be a day,* and it will be a glorious day, when *the watchmen upon Mount Ephraim,* who stand on guard there to warn of the approach of the enemy, finding that all is very quiet and that there is no appearance of danger, will ask when they can be discharged from their post so that *they* may *go up to Zion* to praise God for the public peace. But what is most significant here is *that the watchmen of Ephraim* will be eager to encourage the worship of God at Jerusalem, whereas formerly *the watchman of Ephraim,* that is, the prophet, *was hatred against the house of his God* (Hos 9:8) and, instead of inviting people to Zion, set traps for those who went there (Hos 5:1).

5. That God will have the glory for this wonderful change, and the church will have both the honor and the comfort of it (v. 7): *Sing with gladness for Jacob,* that is, let all her friends and well-wishers be glad with her (Dt 32:43). *Rejoice, you Gentiles, with his people* (Ro 15:10). *Publish you, praise you* (v. 7). In declaring this news, praise the God of Israel, praise the Israel of God, speak honorably about both.

6. That they will joyfully return from the land of their captivity, so that they can be happily settled in their own land (vv. 8–9).

6.1. Although they are scattered to places far away, they will still be brought together *from the north country, and from the coasts of the earth.*

6.2. Although many of them are very unfit for travel, that will not be a hindrance to them: *The blind and the lame* will come; there will be such goodwill about making their journey, and they will be in such good heart to do it, that they will not make their blindness and lameness an excuse for staying where they are. Their companions will be ready to help them; they will be *eyes to the blind and legs to the lame,* as good Christians should be to one another in their travels heavenward (Job 29:15). But above all, their God will help them, and let no one plead that they are blind if they have God as their guide, or plead that they are lame if they have God as their strength. *The women with child* are heavy, and it is not right that they should undertake such a journey, much less those *that travail with child;* but when the reason to travel is to return to Zion, neither the one nor the other will find it difficult. When God calls, we must not plead any inability to come, for the One who calls us will help us and strengthen us.

6.3. Although their return will be a matter of joy to them, they will bring prayers and tears, which will be both their stores and their artillery (v. 9): *They shall come with weeping and with supplications.* When they are restored from exile, they will weep with greater bitterness and sensitivity because of their sin than they ever did when they were groaning under it. Prayers help wipe away tears. "With favors will I lead them" is the reading of the margin.

6.4. Although they are on a dangerous journey, they will still be safe in the company of a divine escort. Is the country they pass through dry and thirsty? *I will cause them to walk by the rivers of waters,* not the waters of a flood that fail in summer (Job 6:15). Is it a desert without road or track? *I will cause them to walk in a straight way* (v. 9), which they will not miss. Is the country rough and rocky? Yes, it is, but *they shall not stumble.* Wherever God gives his people a clear call, he will either find or prepare the way for them. A reason is given why God will take all this care of his people: *For I am a Father to Israel* and will therefore maintain them (Ps 103:13). *Ephraim is my firstborn*; even *Ephraim*, who, having gone astray from God, is *no more worthy to be called a son* (Lk 15:19), will be acknowledged as *a firstborn*, especially precious, and heir of a double portion of the Father's blessings. The same reason that was given for their release from Egypt is given for their release from Babylon; they are freeborn and so must not be enslaved; they are born to God and so must not be servants (Ex 4:22 – 23): *Israel is my son, even my firstborn; let my son go, that he may serve me.*

Verses 10 – 17

The theme of this paragraph, like that of the last one, is the purposes of God's love for his people. This is *a word of the Lord* that the *nations* must *hear* (v. 10), for it is a prophecy of a work of the Lord. It will be news that will spread throughout the world. It is foretold:

1. That those who are dispersed will be brought together from being scattered: *He that scattereth Israel will gather him* (v. 10), and when he has gathered him into one body, one fold, he *will keep him, as a shepherd does his flock*, from being scattered again.

2. That those who are sold and who belong to others will be redeemed and brought back (v. 11). Although the enemy that has gained possession of him is *stronger than he*, yet *the Lord*, who is stronger than all, *has redeemed and ransomed him*, not by price but by power.

3. That with their liberty they will have an abundance and joy, and God will be honored (vv. 12 – 13). When they have returned to their own land, *they shall come and sing in the high place of Zion*. They will sing to the praise and glory of God on the top of that holy mountain. We read that they did so when the foundation of the temple was laid there (Ezr 3:11). They *shall flow together to the goodness of the Lord*; that is, they will flock in great numbers and with great joyfulness, as flowing streams of water, *to the goodness of the Lord*, to the temple where he causes his goodness to pass in front of his people (Ex 33:19). They will come together in sacred meetings to *praise him for his goodness* and to pray for its continuation. They will come to bless him for his goodness in giving them *wheat, and wine, and oil, and the young of the flock and of the herd* (v. 12). Once again they will have unchallenged ownership of these good things, and so they will honor God with the firstfruits of them and bring offerings to his altar from them. Our souls are like gardens when they are watered with the dews of God's Spirit and grace. There follows a precious promise that *they shall not sorrow any more at all*, it is only in the New Jerusalem *that all tears shall be wiped away* (Rev 21:4). However, the returning exiles did not have the causes for sorrow that they had previously. *Young men and old shall rejoice together*, therefore (v. 13).

4. That both the ministers and those they minister to will have great satisfaction in what God gives them (v. 14): *I will satiate* (satisfy) *the soul of the priests with fatness* (abundance); there will be such an abundance of sacrifices brought to the altar that those who *live upon the altar* will live comfortably; they and their families will be satisfied with abundance. *My people shall be satisfied with my goodness.* This may be applied to the spiritual blessings that the redeemed of the Lord (Isa 51:11) enjoy in Jesus Christ, which are infinitely more valuable than grain, wine, or oil (Ps 4:7).

5. That especially those who have been sad at the loss of their children who were taken into exile will have that sorrow turned to joy on the return of their children (vv. 15 – 17). Here we have:

5.1. The sad mourning of the mothers for the loss of their children (v. 15): *In Ramah was there a voice heard*, when the general captivity took place, nothing but *lamentation, and bitter weeping*, more there than in other places, because there Nebuzaradan had a general meeting of his captives, as appears in 40:1, where we find him sending Jeremiah back from Ramah. *Rachel* is here said to *weep for her children*. The grave of Rachel was between Ramah and Bethlehem. Benjamin, one of the two tribes, and Ephraim, leader of the ten tribes, were both descendants of Rachel. She had only two sons, the elder of whom his father grieved for and *refused to be comforted* (Ge 37:35); the other she herself called *Ben-oni* (Ge 35:18), "the son of my sorrow." Now, similarly, the inhabitants of Ramah *grieved for their sons and their daughters* who were taken away (1Sa 30:6). The tender parents even *refused to be comforted for their children, because they were not*, were not with them, but in the hands of their enemies; they were likely never to see them again. This is applied by the evangelists to the great mourning at Bethlehem for the murder of the infants by Herod (Mt 2:17 – 18), and this Scripture is said to be fulfilled then.

5.2. Prompt encouragement administered to them in reference to this (vv. 16 – 17). Although we mourn, we must not murmur. In order to repress excessive grief, we must consider that *there is hope in our end* (v. 17), hope that the trouble will not last forever and that there will be a happy end: the end will be peace (Ps 37:37). Although one generation falls in the desert, the next will enter Canaan. *Thy* suffering *work shall be rewarded.* God makes his people *glad according to the days wherein he has afflicted them* (Ps 90:15), and so there is a balance between joys and sorrows, as there is between reward and work. There is hope for children taken away by death that they will *return to their own border*, to the happy lot assigned them in the resurrection, their inheritance in the heavenly Canaan, that land of his sanctuary.

Verses 18 – 26

We have here:

1. Ephraim's repentance and return to God. *Ephraim shall say, What have I to do any more with idols?* Ephraim, the people, will be as one in their repentance. Ephraim is here seen as weeping for sin, perhaps because Ephraim, the person from whom that tribe had its name, had a sensitive spirit, *mourned for his children many days* (1Ch 7:21 – 22), and sorrow for sin is compared to that *for an only son* (6:26; Am 8:10). We see the penitent:

1.1. Moaning about his present miseries. True penitents do moan in this way.

1.2. Accusing himself, in the first place, of impatience when he was being corrected: *"Thou hast chastised me;* I have suffered under the rod of your correction, and I needed it, I deserved it. I was justly disciplined *as a bullock* (unruly calf), which would never have felt the goad if it had not first rebelled against the yoke." This is the sin he finds himself guilty of now, but in v. 19 he reflects on his sins in the days of his youth. Now he remembers *the reproach* (disgrace) *of his youth.*

1.3. Being angry with himself, having a righteous anger at himself for his sin and foolishness: he *smote upon his thigh*, as the tax collector beat his breast (Lk 18:13). He was stunned at his own stupidity and perverseness: he *was ashamed, yea even confounded.*

1.4. Commending himself to the mercy and grace of God. He finds he cannot by any power of his own keep himself close to God, much less bring himself back to God when he has rebelled, and so he prays, *Turn thou me, and I shall be turned.* See 17:14: *Heal me and I shall be healed.*

1.5. Rejoicing in the experience he had of the wonderful effect of divine grace: *Surely after that I was turned, I repented.* All the godly workings of our heart toward God are the consequence of the working of his grace in us. When sinners come to a right knowledge, they will come to follow a right way. Ephraim was disciplined, and that did not produce the desired effect; it went no further: *I was chastised,* and that was all. But when the instructions of God's Spirit accompanied the corrections of his providence, then the work was completed.

2. God's compassion on Ephraim and the kind reception Ephraim finds with God (v. 20).

2.1. God acknowledges him as a child, even though he has been an undutiful child and a wasteful son: *Is Ephraim my dear son? Is he a pleasant child?* Or, as it is sometimes presented, *Is not Ephraim my dear son?* "Is he not a pleasant child?" Yes, now that he repents and returns.

2.2. He relents toward him and speaks about him with much tender compassion: *I do earnestly remember him still*; my thoughts toward him are thoughts of peace (29:11). When God afflicts his people, he still does not forget them; when he drives them out of their land, he does not reject them from his sight or put them out of mind. It was God's compassion that reduced Ephraim's punishment—*My heart is turned within me* (Hos 11:8–9)—and now the same compassion accepts Ephraim's repentance. He decides to do him good: *I will surely have mercy upon him, saith the Lord*

3. Gracious encouragement given to the people of God in Babylon to prepare for their return to their own land. Let them not tremble and lose their spirits; let them not trifle and lose time. Instead, let them have a firm determination and great diligence to address themselves to their journey (vv. 21–22).

3.1. They must think about nothing except coming back to their own country: *"Turn again, O virgin of Israel!*—a virgin to be given in marriage to your God. *Turn again to these thy cities* (v. 21); although they are laid waste and in ruins, they are *thy cities* that your God gave you, and so *turn again* to them."

3.2. They must return the same way that they came, so that the memory of the sorrows that accompanied them, or that their ancestors told them about, might make them even more thankful for being restored. Those who departed to become slaves of sin must return to the duties they have neglected; they must *do their first works* (Rev 2:5).

3.3. They must commit themselves and all that is within them in this matter (Ps 103:1): *Set thy heart toward the highway*; the way from Babylon to Zion, from the slavery of sin into the glorious liberty of God's children (Ro 8:21), is a highway, but no one is likely to walk on it unless they *set their hearts toward it.*

3.4. They must provide themselves with everything necessary for the journey: *Set thee up way marks, and make thee high heaps,* or guideposts; send in front of you those who will set up road signs and guideposts wherever there is any danger of missing the road. Let those who go first and who know the way best set up such directions for those who are to follow.

3.5. They must prepare themselves for their journey: *How long will thou go about, O backsliding daughter?* (v. 22). Let their minds not wander or be uncertain. Let them not be distracted by anxieties or fears. Let them throw themselves on God, and then let their minds be fixed on him.

3.6. They are encouraged to do this by an assurance God gives them that he will *create a new thing in the earth, a woman shall compass a man.* The church of God, which is as weak as a woman, not well disposed for military action (Isa 54:6), will besiege and prevail against a powerful man. The church is compared to a woman (Rev 12:1). And whereas we later find *armies compassing* (surrounding) *the camp of the saints* (Rev 20:9), now the camp of the saints will surround them. Many good interpreters understand this *new thing* to be the incarnation of Christ, which had sometimes been given to them as a sign (Isa 7:14; 9:6). *A woman,* the virgin Mary, enclosed in her womb *the Mighty One,* for this is the meaning of *geber,* the word used for *man* at the end of v. 22. God is called *Gibbor, the Mighty God* (32:18), as is Christ in Isa 9:6, *El-Gibbor,* the *mighty God.*

4. A prospect given them of being happily settled in their own land again. All their neighbors will say good things about them and offer good prayers for them (v. 23): *As yet,* or rather *yet again*—even though Judah and Jerusalem have long been scorned—*this speech shall be used,* as it was formerly, *concerning the land of Judah and the cities thereof: The Lord bless you, O habitation of justice* (righteous dwelling) *and mountain of holiness!* This suggests that they will return much reformed and that this reformation will be so clear that everyone around them will take notice of it. The *cities,* which used to be the homes of plunderers, will be righteous dwellings; the *mountain of Israel,* and especially Mount Zion, will be *a mountain of holiness.* There will be a plentiful supply of all good things among them (vv. 24–25): *There shall dwell in Judah itself* both farmers and shepherds, the two ancient and honorable employments of Cain and Abel (Ge 4:2), though it has been desolate for a long time. "I have *satiated the weary and sorrowful soul*"; those who have been sad in exile for a long time will now enjoy great plenty. This can be applied to the spiritual blessings God has in store for all true penitents.

5. The prophet telling us what delight the discovery of this brought (v. 26). "*Upon this I awaked,* overcome with joy, which burst the chains of sleep. I then reflected on my dream, and it was such as had made *my sleep sweet* (pleasant) *to me*; I was refreshed, as people are when they have slept soundly."

Verses 27–34

It is further promised here:

1. The people of God will become both numerous and prosperous. Israel and Judah will be filled both with people and with cattle (v. 27). This will be a type of the wonderful increase of the Gospel church. God will build them and plant them (v. 28). He *will watch over them* to do them good (24:6). Everything will for a long time have been set so much against them that it will seem as if God has *watched over them to pluck up and to throw down.* Now, however, everything will happily strengthen and advance their interests.

2. They will be judged no more for the sins of their *fathers* (parents) (vv. 29–30). Our Savior tells the evil Jews in his days that they will suffer for their fathers' sins because they have persisted in them (Mt 23:35–36). But it is promised here that God will proceed no further for their ancestors' sins, but will remember his covenant with their ancestors and do them good according to that covenant: *They shall no more* complain, as they have, that the *fathers have eaten sour grapes, and the children's teeth are set on edge*; rather, *every one shall die for his own*

iniquity. God will judge individual people who offend against him.

3. God will renew his covenant with them, so that they will have all these blessings not only by providence but also by promise. But this covenant also looks forward to Gospel times, the latter days that *shall come*, for the writer to the Hebrews understands it as referring to Gospel grace in Heb 8:8–12, where this whole passage is quoted as a summary of the covenant of grace made with believers in Jesus Christ. Notice:

3.1. This covenant is made with *the house of Israel and Judah*, with the Gospel church, *the Israel of God* on which *peace shall be* (Gal 6:16), with the spiritual offspring of faithful Abraham and praying Jacob. Judah and Israel were two separate kingdoms for a time, but after their return they were united in the joint favors God gave them, as were Jews and Gentiles in the Gospel church and covenant.

3.2. It is a *new covenant* and *not according to the covenant made with them when they came out of Egypt*. The services of worship and promises are more spiritual and heavenly under this new covenant, and the revelation much clearer. God made that earlier covenant with them when he *took them by the hand*, as if they had been blind, lame, or weak, *to lead them out of the land of Egypt*, and that *covenant they broke* (v. 32). It was God who made that covenant, but it was the people who broke it, for our salvation comes from God, but our sin and ruin are brought about by ourselves.

3.3. The particular articles of his covenant all contain spiritual blessings; not, "I will give them the land of Canaan and numerous descendants," but, "I will give them pardon, peace, and grace, good minds and good hearts." He promises:

3.3.1. That he will dispose them to do their duty; *I will put my law in their inward part and write it in their heart* (v. 33).

3.3.2. That he will take them into relationship with himself: "*I will be their God*, a God who is all-sufficient to them, and *they shall be my people* (v. 33), a loyal, obedient people to me."

3.3.3. That there will be an abundance of the knowledge of God among all kinds of people. Those who rightly know God's name will seek him, serve him, and put their trust in him (v. 34): *All shall know me*; all will be welcome to know God and will have the means of that knowledge; *his ways shall be known upon earth* (Ps 67:2), whereas, in many previous times, *in Judah only was God known* (Ps 76:1; Am 3:2). The priests preached only now and then, and in the temple, and to a few people in comparison, but now all will or may know God by joining Christian meetings, where, throughout every part of the church, the good knowledge of God will be taught. In short, the things of God will be brought by the Gospel of Christ to a clearer light than ever (2Ti 1:10), and the people of God will be brought by the grace of Christ to a clearer sight of those things than they ever had before (Eph 1:17–18). Sin will be pardoned. This is made the reason for everything else: *For I will forgive their iniquity, will forgive* and forget: *I will remember their sin no more* (v. 34).

Verses 35–40

Glorious things have been spoken (Ps 87:3) in vv. 1–34 about the Gospel church. But can we depend on these promises? Yes; we have them confirmed here. The great thing guaranteed to us is that as long as the world stands, God will have a church in it, which, though it may sometimes be brought very low, will still be raised

up again, and its interests reestablished; it is *built upon a rock, and the gates of hell shall not prevail against it* (Mt 16:18).

1. The building of the world, and the firmness and lastingness of this building, are evidence of the power and faithfulness of God, who has undertaken to establish his church. *He that built all things* at first *is God* (Heb 3:4). The faithfulness of the kingdom of nature can encourage us to depend on his promises that the glories of the kingdom of grace will continue. Let us notice:

1.1. The glories of the kingdom of nature, and let us reason from them how fortunate are those who have this God, the God of nature, as their God for ever and ever. *He gives the sun for a light by day* (v. 35). Not only did he make it originally to be so, but he still continues to make it so, for its light and heat and all its influences continually depend on its great Creator. He gives *the ordinances of the moon and stars for a light by night*; their movements are called *ordinances* (decrees) because they are regular and under his rule. See Job 38:31–33. Notice the government of the sea and the restraint imposed on its proud waves: *The Lord of hosts divides the sea*, or, as some read it, "settles the sea when its waves roar." Notice the vastness of the heavens and their immeasurable extent; the *heavens above cannot be measured* (v. 37), but God fills them. Notice the mystery of even that part of the creation in which we live. Notice the immovable firmness of all these (v. 36): *These ordinances* (decrees) *cannot depart from before God, for all are his servants* (Ps 119:90–91). The sky is often clouded over, and the sun and moon often in shadows; the earth may quake, and the sea may toss and turn; but they all keep their place: they may move, but they are not removed.

1.2. The security of the kingdom of grace, which may be reasoned from that: *the seed of Israel shall not cease from being a nation* (1Pe 2:9). When Israel according to the flesh is no longer a nation, the *children of the promise are counted for the seed* (Ro 9:8), and God *will not cast off all the seed of Israel*, even though they have acted very wickedly (v. 37). The God who has undertaken to keep the church is a God of almighty power, who *upholds all things by his* almighty *word* (Heb 1:3). *Our help stands in the name of the One who made heaven and earth* (Ps 124:8), and so he can do anything. God would not take all this care of the world without taking some glory from it. And how will he do so except by providing himself with a people in it, a church, a people who *shall be to him for a name and a praise* (13:11)? If the order of the creation continues firmly because it was originally well established, and if it is not changed because it does not need to be, the method of grace will continue unchanged for the same reason, as it was well established in the beginning. He who has promised to preserve a church for himself has proved he is faithful to the word that he has spoken about the stability of the world.

2. The rebuilding of Jerusalem, now in ruins, will be a pledge of these great things that God will do for the Gospel church, the *heavenly Jerusalem* (vv. 38–40). *The days will come*, though they may not come for a long time, when Jerusalem will be completely rebuilt, as large as ever. The wall that Nehemiah built and that, to fulfill the prophecy more precisely, began near the *tower of Hananeel*, mentioned here (Ne 3:1), enclosed as much ground as is referred to here, though we cannot determine for certain the places called here *the gate of the corner, the hill Gareb*. When this wall is built, it will be consecrated to God and his service (v. 38), and even the pasturelands and adjacent fields *shall be holy unto the Lord*. The whole

city will be, as it were, one temple, one Holy Place, as the New Jerusalem is, which has no temple, because it is all temple (Rev 21:22). It will continue for a very long time: the time of the new city from the return to its later destruction was as long as that of the old from David to the exile. This promise was to have its complete fulfillment, however, in the Gospel church, which, as it is the spiritual Israel, will not be rejected by God. It is the Holy City, and therefore all human power *shall not pluck it up, nor throw it down*.

CHAPTER 32

In this chapter we have: 1. Jeremiah imprisoned for foretelling the destruction of Jerusalem and the exile of King Zedekiah (vv. 1–5). 2. Jeremiah buying land by divine appointment as an assurance that in due time a happy ending would come to his present troubles (vv. 6–15). 3. The prayer he offered to God on that occasion (vv. 16–25). 4. A message God entrusted him to communicate to the people. 4.1. He must foretell the complete destruction of Judah and Jerusalem for their sins (vv. 26–35). But: 4.2. At the same time he must assure them that although the destruction was total, it would not be final (vv. 36–44).

Verses 1–15

The devastation of Judah and Jerusalem by the Babylonians came gradually on them, and because they did not respond in repentance at God's judgments, he proceeded until all was ravaged, which was in the eleventh year of Zedekiah. What is recorded here took place in the tenth. The king of Babylon's army had now besieged Jerusalem and was continuing the siege vigorously.

1. Jeremiah prophesies that both the city and the court will fall into the hands of the king of Babylon. He tells them that God, whose city it is, will give it into their hands and put it beyond his protection (v. 3). He also prophesies that though Zedekiah will attempt to escape, he will be overtaken and handed over as a prisoner into the hands of Nebuchadnezzar. Zedekiah will hear the king of Babylon pronounce his fate, and he will see with what fury and anger he will look on him—*His eyes shall behold his eyes* (v. 4). Zedekiah will be taken away to Babylon and continue his life as a miserable captive there *until God visit him*, that is, until God puts an end to his life by a natural death, as Nebuchadnezzar long before put an end to his natural life by putting out his eyes.

2. For prophesying this, he is imprisoned, not in the common jail, but in the *king of Judah's house* (v. 2), and not closely confined there either, but sheltered from the abuse of the mob. It is, however, a prison, and Zedekiah puts him in prison for prophesying as he did (vv. 2–3). He is so far from *humbling himself before Jeremiah* (2Ch 36:12) that he *hardens himself* against him. Although he formerly acknowledged him to be a prophet so far as to want him to *inquire of the Lord for them* (21:2), he now rebukes him for prophesying (v. 3) and confines him, perhaps to restrain him from prophesying anymore.

3. Being confined, he buys from a near relative of his a piece of ground in Anathoth (vv. 6–7).

3.1. One would not have expected that he would buy a *piece of land* when he himself knew that the whole land was to be devastated and fall into the hands of the Babylonians. But it was the will of God that he buy it, and so he submitted, even though it seemed that the money was being thrown away. His near relative came to offer it to him; it was not something he himself sought. Moreover,

the *right of redemption* belonged to him (v. 8), and if he refused, he would not fulfill the role of the nearest relative. It was land that lay within the pastureland of a priests' city, and if he refused it, there was danger that in such times of disorder it might be sold to one of the other tribes, which was against the law. It would also be a kindness to his relative, who probably was at this time in great need of money.

3.2. Two things may be observed about this purchase:

3.2.1. How fairly the bargain was made. When Jeremiah knew by Hanamel's coming to him, as God had foretold he would, that *it was the word of the Lord*, that it was God's will that he make this purchase, he had no more difficulties with it, but *bought the field* (v. 9). He was very honest and exact in paying. He *weighed him the money*; he did not urge him to take his word for it that the amount was correct. It was *seventeen shekels of silver*. We will not be surprised at the low price if we consider how scarce money was at this time and how little land was counted on. He was very wise in preserving the written statement. It was signed *before witnesses*. One copy was *sealed up*, and the other was *open* (v. 11). The deeds of purchase were put in the hands of Baruch before witnesses, and he was ordered to put them in an *earthen vessel*—so that they might *continue many days*, for the use of Jeremiah's heirs.

3.2.2. What the intention was of having this bargain made. It was to show that although Jerusalem was now besieged, and the whole country was likely to be devastated, the time would still come when *houses, and fields, and vineyards would be again possessed in this land* (v. 15). Just as God appointed Jeremiah to confirm his predictions of the approaching destruction of Jerusalem in his own life by living as an unmarried person, so he now appointed him to confirm his predictions of the future restoration of Jerusalem by his own action in buying this field. The Roman historian Lucius Florus relates it as a great example of the bravery of the Roman citizens that at the time of the second Punic War, when Hannibal besieged Rome and was very near controlling it, a field on which part of his army lay, being offered for sale at that time, was immediately bought, in the firm belief that the Roman bravery would lift the siege (book 2, chapter 6). And have not we much more reason to risk our all on the word of God?

Verses 16–25

We have here Jeremiah's prayer to God on the occasion of the revelations God made to him about his purposes for this nation, to uproot it and, in time, rebuild it, which puzzled the prophet. Although he spoke his messages faithfully, yet on reflecting on them, he was greatly at a loss as to how to reconcile them. In his perplexity, he poured out his soul to God in prayer. Jeremiah is confined, in distress, and in the dark about the meaning of God's providences, and then he prays.

1. He adores God and gives him the glory due to his name (Ps 29:2; 96:8) as the Creator (vv. 17–19). When we are perplexed about the particular ways of providence at any time, it is good for us to satisfy ourselves with the general teachings of God's wisdom, power, and goodness. Let us consider, as Jeremiah does here:

1.1. That God is the fountain of all being, power, life, movement, and perfection: he *made the heaven and the earth with his outstretched arm* (v. 17).

1.2. That with him nothing is impossible (Mt 17:20; Lk 1:37): *Nothing is too hard for thee*.

1.3. That he is a God of boundless mercy: "You not only are kind but also *show loving-kindness*, and not to a few, to one here and there, but *to thousands* (v. 18), thousands of people, thousands of generations" (Ex 20:6).

1.4. That he is a God of impartial and firm justice.

1.5. That he is a God of universal dominion and command: he is *the great* God, for he is *the mighty God*. He is *the Lord of hosts*, of all powers; that *is his name*.

1.6. That he plans everything for the best: he is *great in counsel* (v. 19). So deep are the intentions of his wisdom.

2. He acknowledges the universal awareness God has of all the actions of the people (v. 19): *Thy eyes are open upon all the sons of men* everywhere, looking at the evil and the good, noticing all *their ways*, not as an unconcerned spectator but as an observant judge, for people will find that God acts toward them as they act toward him.

3. He recounts the great things God did for his people Israel formerly.

3.1. He brought them out of Egypt, that land of slavery, with *signs and wonders* (v. 21). *Israel* was reminded of it every year by the ordinance of the Passover. All the neighboring nations spoke about it, as what led very much to the glory of the God of Israel and *made him a name* (gave him renown) *as at this day*.

3.2. He brought them into Canaan, that *land flowing with milk and honey.* He *swore to their fathers to give it them*, and he gave it to the children (v. 22), *and they came in and possessed it* (v. 23). It is good for us often to reflect on the great things God did for his church in former times, especially when it was first set up in that great miracle.

4. He mourns the rebellion they have been guilty of against God and the judgments that have brought on them for such rebellion. He gives here a sad account of the ungrateful conduct of that people toward God. God has done everything he promised to do, but they have *done nothing of all that he commanded them to do* (v. 23).

4.1. Jeremiah compares the present state of Jerusalem with God's predictions, and he finds that what God *has spoken* has *come to pass*. God gave them fair warning of it before, and if they had taken notice of this, Jerusalem's ruin would have been prevented.

4.2. He commits the present state of Jerusalem to God's compassion (v. 24): *Behold the mounts* — or siege ramps that they were to use to batter down the city — *"Behold, thou seest it.* Is this the city that you have chosen to put your name within? And will it be abandoned in this way?" He neither complains about God for what he has done nor gives orders to God as to what he should do, but wants only for God to consider their case. Whatever trouble we are in, we may comfort ourselves with the knowledge that God sees it and sees how to put it right.

5. He seems to want to be let further in on the meaning of the order God has now given him to buy his relative's field (v. 25): "*Though the city is given into the hands of the Chaldeans* (Babylonians), and no one is likely to enjoy what he has, *thou hast said unto me, Buy thou the field.*" As soon as he understood that it was the mind of God, he did it, but when he had done it, he wanted to better understand why God had ordered him to do it. Although we are committed to follow God with implicit obedience, we should still try to make sure it is a more and more intelligent obedience. We must never dispute God's statutes and judgments, but we may and must ask, *What mean these statutes and judgments?* (Dt 6:20).

Verses 26–44

Here is God's answer to Jeremiah's prayer to quiet his mind. It is a full revelation of the purposes of God's wrath against the present generation and the purposes of

his grace concerning the future generations. Jeremiah did not know how to *sing both of mercy and of judgment* (Ps 101:1), but here God teaches him to sing to him about both. When Jeremiah was ordered to buy the field in Anathoth, he hoped that God was about to order the Babylonians to lift the siege. "No," God says, "the execution of the sentence will go on; Jerusalem will be devastated." But in case Jeremiah thinks his being ordered to buy this field is a sign that all the mercy God has in store for his people after their return is only that they will possess their own land again, God informs him that that is merely a type of those spiritual blessings that will then be abundantly given to them. Those blessings will be indescribably more valuable than fields and vineyards. In this *word of the Lord* to Jeremiah, we have, first, as terrible threats as perhaps any in the Old Testament, and then as precious promises.

1. The ruin of Judah and Jerusalem is declared here.

1.1. God here asserts his own sovereignty and power (v. 27): *Behold, I am Jehovah*, the self-existent, self-sufficient God in covenant with his people. *I am that I am* (Ex 4:13); *I am the God of all flesh*, that is, of the whole human race.

1.2. He keeps to what he has often said about the destruction of Jerusalem by the king of Babylon (v. 28): *I will give this city into his hand, and he shall take it. The Chaldeans* (Babylonians) *shall come and set fire to it*, will burn it and all the *houses in it*, not excluding God's house and the king's.

1.3. He gives the reason for this severe action against the city. It is sin that ruins it.

1.3.1. They were bold and arrogant in sinning. They *offered incense to Baal*; and they did not hide away in corners to do this, as those who were ashamed, but did it on the *tops of their houses* (v. 29).

1.3.2. They did it *to provoke me to anger* (v. 29). *They have only provoked me to anger with the works of their hands* (v. 30). Again (v. 32), *All the evil which they have done was to provoke me to anger.* They decided to test his jealousy and provoke him in his sight. "Jerusalem has been *to me a provocation of my anger and fury*" (v. 31).

1.3.3. They began early and continued all along to provoke God: "They have *done evil before me from their youth*, ever since they first became a people (v. 30), as can be seen from their grumbling and rebellion in the desert." And as for Jerusalem, even though it is the *holy city*, it has been *a provocation from the day that they built it, even to this day* (v. 31).

1.3.4. All contributed to the common guilt, and so they were justly involved in the common ruin. Not only the *children of Israel*, who had rebelled from the temple, but also *the children of Judah*, who were still faithful to it.

1.3.5. God had again and again called them to repentance, but they rudely turned their backs on the One who "*taught them a better way of life, rising up early in teaching them*, working hard to adapt the teaching to what they could take in; it was all in vain."

1.3.6. Their idolatry showed their ungodly contempt for God, for (v. 34) *they set their abominations* — their abominable idols — *in the house which is called by my name, to defile it*.

1.3.7. They were guilty of the most unnatural cruelty to their own children, for they *sacrificed them to Moloch* (v. 35). They *caused Judah to sin* (v. 35). The whole country was infected with the contagious idolatry and sins of Jerusalem.

2. The restoration of Judah and Jerusalem is promised here (v. 36). In judgment, God will remember mercy

(Hab 3:2), and a set time will come to favor Zion (Ps 102:13). Notice:

2.1. The despair to which this people was now finally brought. When the threatened judgment was a long way away, they had no fear; when it attacked them, they had no hope. They said about the city (v. 36), *It shall be delivered into the hand of the king of Babylon*, by *the sword, famine, and pestilence* (plague). They said about the country, with troubled hearts (v. 43), *It is desolate, without man or beast*; there is no help coming; we cannot see a way out. *It is given into the hand of the Chaldeans* (Babylonians).

2.2. The hope that God gives them of mercy. Although their carcasses must fall in exile, their children will again see this good land and the goodness of God in it.

2.2.1. They will be brought back from their exile and will come and settle again in this land (v. 37). He will have dispersed them and *driven them into all countries*. Those who flee will disperse themselves; those who fall into enemy hands will be dispersed by them out of a desire to prevent them from conspiring together. God's hand will be in both. But then God will *gather them out of all the countries whither they were driven*, as he promised in the Law (Dt 30:3–4). When they have reformed and have returned to God, neither their own consciences nor their enemies will make them fear. He promises (v. 41): *I will plant them in this land assuredly*; also they will here enjoy a holy security and rest, and they will put down roots here, will be *planted in stability*.

2.2.2. God will renew his covenant with them—a covenant of grace—the blessings of which are spiritual. It is called an *everlasting covenant* (v. 40) not only because God will be faithful to it forever but also because its effects will be eternal. There is no doubt that these promises look further than physical Israel and are assured for all believers. True Christians may apply these promises to themselves and plead them with God.

2.2.2.1. God will acknowledge them as his and declare himself to be theirs (v. 38): *They shall be my people*. He will make them his by working in them all the character and disposition of his people. "And to make them truly, completely, and eternally happy, *I will be their God*."

2.2.2.2. God will give them a heart to fear him (v. 39). What he requires of those whom he takes into covenant with him as his people is that they revere his majesty, fear his wrath, stand in awe of his authority, pay homage to him, and give him the glory due to his name (Ps 29:2; 96:8). It is repeated (v. 40): "*I will put my fear in their hearts*, that is, I will inspire in them gracious motives and attitudes, which will influence and direct their whole way of living." Teachers may put good things into our minds, but it is only God who can put them into our hearts, only he who can work in us *both to will and to do* (Php 2:13).

2.2.2.3. He will *give them one heart and one way*. Each of them will be at one with himself or herself, and all of them will be one with one another.

2.2.2.4. He will effectively provide for their perseverance in grace and the continuation of the covenant between himself and them. God will never leave them or abandon them: *I will not turn away from them, to do them good* (v. 40). Earthly rulers are fickle, but God's *mercy endures for ever* (33:11). God may seem to turn away from this people (Isa 54:8), but even then he does not turn away from doing them good and intending them good. We have no reason to distrust God's faithfulness, but we do have reason to distrust our own, and so it is promised here that God will *give them a heart to fear him for ever* (v. 39).

2.2.2.5. He will pass on an inheritance of blessing to their descendants; he will give them grace to fear him, *for*

the good of them and of their children after them. Just as their disloyalty to God has harmed their children, so their loyalty and faithfulness to God will be to the advantage of their children. We cannot do better for the good of our descendants than by setting up the fear and worship of God in our families.

2.2.2.6. He will take delight in their descendants and will do everything to advance them (v. 41): *I will rejoice over them to do them good*. When he punishes them, he does so reluctantly. *How shall I give thee up, Ephraim?* (Hos 11:8). But when he restores them, he rejoices in doing them good. He is himself a cheerful giver, and so he loves cheerful servants (2Co 9:7). All things will be seen at last to have worked for the good of the church (Ro 8:28), so that it will be said that the One who rules the world is completely taken up with the care of his church.

2.2.2.7. These promises will as surely be performed as the previous threats were: *As I have brought all this great evil upon them*, according to the threats and for the glory of divine justice, *so I will bring upon them all this good*, according to the promise and for the glory of divine mercy.

2.2.2.8. As a pledge of all this, houses and lands will again be sold for a good price in Judah and Jerusalem (vv. 43–44): *Fields shall be bought in this land*; people will want to have lands here rather than anywhere else. In *the places about Jerusalem, in the cities of Judah* and of Israel, in all parts of the country, *men shall buy fields, and subscribe evidences* (deeds will be signed). Trade will revive; farming will come back. Laws will again take their due course, for people will sign and seal legal deeds. This is mentioned to reconcile Jeremiah to his new purchase. Although he has bought a piece of land and cannot go to see it, this is the pledge of many purchases, and those purchases themselves will be faint resemblances of the purchased possessions in the heavenly Canaan that are reserved for all those who have God's fear in their hearts.

CHAPTER 33

The scope of this chapter is much the same as that of the previous chapter—to confirm the promise of the restoration of the Jews, despite the present desolation of their country and the dispersion of their people. And these promises refer, in type, as far forward as the Gospel church. It is promised here: 1. That the city will be rebuilt and reestablished (vv. 1–6). 2. That the captives, having their sins pardoned, will be restored (vv. 7–8). 3. That this will lead to the glory of God (v. 9). 4. That the country will have both joy and plenty (vv. 10–14) 5. That the way will be made for the coming of the Messiah (vv. 15–16). 6. That the house of David, the house of Levi, and the house of Israel will again flourish, and all three in the kingdom of Christ; a Gospel ministry and the Gospel church will continue as long as the world stands (vv. 17–26).

Verses 1–9

1. The date of this encouraging prophecy was after the prophecy in the previous chapter, when things were still becoming worse and worse; it was the second time. God *speaketh once, yea, twice* (Job 33:14) for the encouragement of his people. We are not only so disobedient that we need *precept upon precept* (Isa 28:10) to make us do our duty, but also so distrustful that we need promise on promise to bring us comfort, strength, and encouragement. This word, like the earlier one, *came to Jeremiah* when *he was in prison* (v. 1).

2. Concerning the prophecy itself, notice:

2.1. Who it is who secures this comfort for them (v. 2): it is *the Lord, the maker thereof, the Lord that framed it.* He is the maker and former of heaven and earth. He is the maker and former of Jerusalem, of Zion; he built them originally, and so he can rebuild them. He built them for his own praise, and so he *will* do so. He is the maker and former of this promise; he has laid the plans for Jerusalem's restoration, and the One who has made the promise will fulfill it, for Jehovah *is his name*; he is a God who gives life to his promises by fulfilling them, and when he does this, he is known by that name (Ex 6:3), known to be a perfect God. When the heavens and the earth were finished, then, and not until then, the Creator was called *Jehovah* (Ge 2:4).

2.2. How this comfort must be gained by prayer (v. 3): *Call upon me, and I will answer thee.* Christ himself must *ask, and it shall be given him* (Ps 2:8). *I will show thee great and mighty things, hidden things, which,* though partially revealed, *thou knewest not.* Promises are given not to replace prayer but to encourage it. See Eze 36:37.

2.3. The condition of Jerusalem made it necessary that such comforts be provided (vv. 4–5): *The houses of this city,* not excluding those *of the kings of Judah, are thrown down by the mounts,* or siege ramps, *and by the sword,* or axes or hammers. The strongest, stateliest houses were leveled to the ground. Those who *came to fight with the Chaldeans* (Babylonians) did more harm than good, provoked the enemy to be more cruel and violent in their attacks, so that the houses in Jerusalem were filled *with the dead bodies of men.* God says that they were those he had *slain* (put to death) *in his anger,* for the enemies' sword was his sword. But it seems the people who were killed had distinguished themselves by their evil, and they were the very ones *for whose wickedness* God now *hid himself from this city.*

2.4. The blessings that God has in store for Judah and Jerusalem, which will put right all their grievances.

2.4.1. God will provide healing, even though the disease is thought to be fatal and incurable (8:22). *"The whole head is sick, and the whole heart faint* (Isa 1:5), but *I will bring it health and cure* (v. 6); I will prevent death, remove the sickness, and set everything right again" (30:17). The sin of Jerusalem is its sickness (Isa 1:6); its reformation will therefore be its recovery. *I will reveal unto them the abundance of peace and truth. Peace* stands here for all good; peace and *truth* are peace and true religious faith, peace and the true worship of God, in opposition to the many falsehoods and deceptions by which they were led away from God. We may also apply it more generally. Peace and truth are the great subject matter of divine revelation. These promises here lead us to the Gospel of Christ, and God has revealed to us *peace and truth* in that — *truth* to guide us, peace to put us at rest. *Grace and truth,* and an abundance of both, *come by Jesus Christ* (Jn 1:17). Peace and truth are the life of the soul, and Christ *came that we might have* that *life, and might have it more abundantly* (Jn 10:10). Christ rules by the power of truth (Jn 18:37), and by it he gives *abundance of peace* (Ps 72:7; 85:10). The divine revelation of peace and truth brings health and healing to all those who receive it by faith.

2.4.2. Are they scattered and enslaved, and is their nation in ruins? *"I will cause their captivity to return* (v. 7), bringing back both Israel and Judah."

2.4.3. Is sin the main cause of all their troubles? That will be pardoned and subdued, and so the root of the judgment will be killed off (v. 8). Just as those who were

ceremonially unclean, and were therefore excluded from the tabernacle, regained free access to it when they were sprinkled with the *water of purification,* so people will have free access to their own land and its privileges when God has *cleansed them from their iniquities.*

2.4.4. Have both their sins and their sufferings turned to the dishonor of God? Their reformation and restoration will lead as much to his praise (v. 9). The neighboring nations will look on the growing greatness of the Jewish nation as formidable, and they will be afraid of making them their enemies. When the church is *fair as the moon* and *clear as the sun,* she is *terrible as an army with banners* (SS 6:10).

Verses 10–16

Here is a further prediction of the happy and fortunate state of Judah and Jerusalem after their glorious return from exile, leading gloriously and finally to the kingdom of the Messiah.

1. It is promised that the people who have long been sad will again be filled with joy. Everyone concluded that the country would lie desolate for ever, that *no beasts* would be found in the land of Judah and no inhabitant *in the streets of Jerusalem* (v. 10), but although weeping may last for a time, joy will return. There will be ordinary joy there, *the voice of the bridegroom and the voice of the bride* (v. 11); marriages will again be celebrated, as formerly, with songs. There will be religious joy there; temple songs will be revived, *the Lord's songs,* which the people could not *sing in a strange land* (Ps 137:4). They will praise him both as *the Lord of hosts* and as the God who *is good* and whose *mercy endures for ever.* This was an old song, but because it was sung on this fresh occasion, it will become a new song. We find this literally fulfilled at their return from Babylon (Ezr 3:11). All the sacrifices were intended for the praise of God, but this seems to refer to the spiritual sacrifices of humble adoration and joyful thanksgiving, *the calves of our lips* (Hos 14:2), which *shall please the Lord better than an ox or bullock* (Ps 69:31).

2. It is promised that the country, which will have long been depopulated, will again be populated and filled with people. *In all the cities of Judah and Benjamin there shall be a habitation of* (pastures for) *shepherds* (vv. 12–13). After their return, the country will not be a dwelling place for beggars, who have nothing, but for shepherds and farmers. The offspring of Jacob, in the beginning, gloried in their being shepherds (Ge 47:3), and so they will now be shepherds again. They will give themselves wholly to that innocent employment, *causing their flocks to lie down* (v. 12) and to *pass under the hands of him that telleth* (counts) *them* (v. 13), flocks to be counted, so that they may know if any are missing. Now because it seemed incredible that a people who were reduced as they now were would ever recover such peace and plenty, here is added a general confirmation of these promises (v. 14): *I will perform that good thing which I have promised.*

3. To crown all these blessings that God has in store for them, here is a promise of the Messiah and of the eternal righteousness he will bring in (vv. 15–16). Probably this is *that good thing* (v. 14), that great good thing, that in the last days, days that were still to come, God would *perform,* as he had promised to Judah and Israel, which their return from exile and their resettlement in their own land made way for. *From the captivity to Christ* is a significant period (Mt 1:17). We had this promise of the Messiah before (23:5–6), and there it came as a confirmation of the promise of the shepherds whom God would set over

them, which would make one think that the promise here about the shepherds and their flocks, which introduces the promise about the Messiah, is to be understood figuratively. Christ is here prophesied:

3.1. As a rightful king. He is *a branch of righteousness*, not a usurper, for he *grows up unto David* (v. 15).

3.2. As a righteous king, righteous in enacting laws, waging wars, and administering justice, righteous in upholding those who suffer wrong and punishing those who commit wrong: *He shall execute judgment and righteousness in the land.*

3.3. As a king who will protect his subjects from all wrong. By him *Judah shall be saved* from wrath and the curse, and because they are saved, *Jerusalem shall dwell safely*, quiet from the fear of evil and enjoying peace of mind in dependence on this Prince of their Peace (Isa 9:6).

3.4. As a king who will be praised by his subjects: "This is the name by which they shall call him," as the Aramaic, the Syriac, and the Vulgate read; "they will triumph in and celebrate his name, and they will call on him using this name." The city is called *The Lord our righteousness*, because they glory in Jehovah as their righteousness. What was before said to be the name of Christ (23:6) is here made the name of Jerusalem, the city of the Messiah, the church of Christ. He is the One who imparts righteousness to her, for he is *made of God to us righteousness* (1Co 1:30), and by bearing that name, she professes to have her whole righteousness not from herself but from him.

Verses 17–26

Three of God's covenants, that of royalty with David and his descendants, that of the priesthood with Aaron and his descendants, and that with Abraham and his descendants, seemed all to have been broken and lost as long as the exile lasted, but it is here promised that their true meaning will be abundantly revealed in the New Testament blessings, of which the blessings given to the Jews after their return from exile were types.

1. The covenant of royalty will have its complete fulfillment in the kingdom of Christ, the Son of David (v. 17). The throne of Israel was overthrown in the captivity; there was not *a man to sit on the throne of Israel*. After their return, the house of David became significant again, but it is in the Messiah that this promise will be fulfilled that *David shall never want* (lack) *a man to sit on the throne of Israel*. For as long as the man Christ Jesus (1Ti 2:5) sits at the right hand of the throne of God, the glorified head over all things (Eph 1:22)—as long as he is *King upon the holy hill of Zion* (Ps 2:6)—David does not lack a successor, nor is the covenant with him broken. *The Lord God shall give him the throne of his father David, and he shall reign over the house of Jacob for ever* (Lk 1:32–33). To confirm this, it is promised:

1.1. That the covenant with David will be as firm as the laws of nature. There is a covenant of nature that is here called *a covenant of the day and the night* (vv. 20, 25), because one of its articles is that there will be *day and night in their season*. God divided light and darkness and established the ruling of each. This meant that the sun would *rule by day*, and *the moon and stars by night* (Ge 1:4–5, 16). The *morning and* the *evening* each have their regular *outgoings* (Ps 65:8); the *dayspring knows its place* (Job 28:12), *knows its time*, and keeps both, as do *the shadows of the evening*, and as long as the world stands, this course will not be changed and this covenant will not be broken. This is how firm the covenant of redemption

will be with the Redeemer—God's servant, but David our King (v. 21). Christ will have a church on earth to the end of the world, until time comes to an end. Christ's *kingdom is an everlasting kingdom* (Ps 145:13), and when *the end cometh*, and not until then, it *shall be delivered up to God*, even *the Father* (1Co 15:24). But its condition in this world will be mixed, prosperity and adversity succeeding each other, as do day and night. Though the sun will set tonight, it will rise again tomorrow morning, whether we live to see it or not, and so we may be sure that although the kingdom of the Redeemer in the world may be clouded over by corruption and persecution for a time, it will still shine out at the appointed time.

1.2. That *the seed of David*, that is, the spiritual descendants of the Messiah, born to him by the power of his Gospel and his Spirit working with it, will be as numerous *as the host of heaven*. Christ's descendants are not, as David's were, his successors, but his subjects; the day is coming, however, when they also will reign with him (2Ti 2:12) (v. 22).

2. The covenant of priesthood will be kept safe, and its promises will also have their complete fulfillment. During the captivity there was no altar or temple service for the priests to attend, but this too will be revived. Immediately after they came back to Jerusalem, priests and Levites were ready to *offer burnt offerings* and to *do sacrifice continually* (Ezr 3:2–3), as is promised here (v. 18). But that priesthood soon became corrupt; *the covenant of Levi was profaned*—as can be seen from Mal 2:8—and in the destruction of Jerusalem by the Romans it came to a final end. The priesthood of Christ supersedes that of Aaron and is the reality of that shadow. As long as that great *high priest of our profession* (Heb 3:1) is always appearing *in the presence of God for us* (Heb 9:24), it may truly be said that *the Levites do not want a man before God to offer continually* (Heb 7:3, 17). He is a priest forever (Ps 110:4; Heb 5:6). As long as there are faithful ministers to take the lead in religious assemblies and to offer the spiritual sacrifices of prayer and praise, *the priests, the Levites*, do not lack successors; indeed, such ministers *have obtained a more excellent ministry*. The apostle Paul puts those who preach the Gospel in the place of those who served at the altar (1Co 9:13–14). All true believers are *a holy priesthood, a royal priesthood* (1Pe 2:5, 9), who are *made to our God kings and priests* (Rev 1:6); they *offer up spiritual sacrifices, acceptable to God*, offering themselves first of all, as *living sacrifices* (Ro 12:1). This promise must be understood to refer to these Levites (v. 22), as saying that they will be as numerous *as the sand of the sea*, for all God's spiritual Israel are spiritual priests (Rev 5:9–10; 7:9, 15).

3. The covenant that set aside Abraham's descendants as God's people will similarly be kept safe, and the promises of that covenant will have their complete fulfillment in the Gospel Israel. This covenant was looked on as broken during the captivity (v. 24): *Considerest thou not what this people have spoken? This people* may refer either to the enemies of Israel or to the unfaithful Israelites themselves. The latter have broken covenant with God, as if he had not dealt faithfully with them. "*Thus have they despised my people*, that is, despised the privilege of being my people as if it were a worthless privilege." The covenant stands despite all this, as firmly as the covenant with day and night. God will sooner allow day and night to come to an end than he *will cast away the seed of Jacob*. This cannot refer to the physical descendants of Jacob, for they are rejected; it must refer to the Christian church, on which all these promises were to be settled, as the apostle Paul

says in Ro 11:1. Christianity will continue in the kingdom and rule of Christ, and the submission of Christians to him, until day and night come to an end. *I will cause their captivity to return.* Having brought them back, *I will have mercy on them.* To whom this promise refers appears in Gal 6:16, where all that *walk according to the gospel rule* are made to be the *Israel of God,* on whom *peace and mercy* will rest.

CHAPTER 34

Here are two messages that God sent by Jeremiah: 1. One to foretell the fate of Zedekiah king of Judah, that he would fall into the hands of the king of Babylon as a captive but would die in peace in exile (vv. 1–7). 2. Another to read out the fate of both ruler and people for their unfaithful dealings with God, in returning to slavery the servants whom they had released according to the law (vv. 8–11). They had walked recklessly with God, and so God would bring the Babylonian army again when they began to hope that they had gotten clear of them (vv. 12–22).

Verses 1–7

This prophecy concerning Zedekiah was given to Jeremiah, and by him to the parties concerned, before he was confined in prison. Notice:

1. When this message was sent to Zedekiah: *when the king of Babylon,* with all his forces, *fought against Jerusalem and the cities thereof* (v. 1), intending to destroy them. The cities that now remained, that still held out, are named (v. 7): *Lachish and Azekah.* This suggests that matters had now come to a head, but Zedekiah obstinately resisted.

2. The message that was sent to him. He is told what he has often been told before, that the city will be taken by the Babylonians *and burnt with fire* (v. 2) and that he will be made a prisoner, brought before Nebuchadnezzar, and taken captive to Babylon (v. 3). Ezekiel, however, prophesied that he *would not see Babylon,* and he did not, for his eyes were put out (Eze 12:13). He will die a captive, but *not by the sword;* he *shall die in peace* (v. 5). We are willing to hope that he repented of what evil he had *done in the sight of the Lord* in his captivity and that, God being reconciled to him, he could truly be said to *die in peace.* Someone may die in prison but still *die in peace.* Perhaps it was a change brought about in him by *his* afflictions that caused his death to be looked on as such a great loss. It is better to live and die penitent in a prison than to live and die impenitent in a palace. *They will lament thee, saying, Ah lord!* This was an honor that his brother Jehoiakim did not have (22:18).

3. Jeremiah's faithfulness in speaking out this message. Although he knew it might prove dangerous to himself, as indeed it did—for he was imprisoned for it—he still *spoke all these words to Zedekiah* (v. 6).

Verses 8–22

We have here another prophecy on a particular occasion.

1. When Jerusalem was closely besieged by the Babylonian army, the leaders and people agreed on a reformation concerning their servants.

1.1. The Law of God required very explicitly that those of their own nation must not be held in slavery for more than seven years; after serving the length of one apprenticeship, they must have their liberty, even if they had sold themselves to pay their debts, or even if they were *sold by the judges* for the punishment of their

crimes. Those of other nations taken in war or bought with money could be enslaved forever, but their fellow Jews must serve only seven years. God calls this the covenant he made with them when he *brought them out of the land of Egypt* (vv. 13–14). This was the first of the judicial laws God gave them (Ex 21:2). God had brought them out of slavery in Egypt, and he wanted them to express their thankfulness for that favor by releasing those to whom their houses were *houses of bondage,* as Egypt had been to their ancestors. God's compassion toward us should make us compassionate toward our brothers and sisters; we must release as we are released.

1.2. They and their ancestors had broken this law. Their worldly profit was more important to them than God's covenant. When the servants had lived seven years with their masters, they understood their responsibilities better than they had when they had first come to them, and so their masters did not want to part with them. *Your fathers hearkened not to me* in this matter (v. 14). They thought they could do it because their ancestors did it. God was now bringing them into slavery because of this sin, and their ancestors', and justly so.

1.3. When they were besieged by the Babylonian army and then were told of their fault in this matter, they immediately reformed, releasing all their servants who were entitled to their freedom, as Pharaoh, when the plague was on him, agreed to *let the people go* (Ex 13:17). The prophets warned them about their sin. They heard from the prophets that they must let their Hebrew servants go *free* (v. 10). The *king,* the *princes* (leaders), and *all the people* agreed to *let go their servants.* The people had to follow to avoid a sense of shame. They bound themselves by a solemn oath and covenant that they would do this, and in this covenant they committed themselves to God and one another. This covenant was made in a holy place, *made before me, in the house which is called by my name* (v. 15), in the presence of God. It was confirmed by a significant sign; they *cut a calf in two, and passed between the parts thereof* (vv. 18–19), signifying this fearful imprecation: "May we be similarly torn apart if we do not fulfill what we now promise." They conformed themselves here to the command of God and *let their servants go,* even though the city was besieged and they could hardly spare them. In this they did *right in God's sight* (v. 15).

2. When there was some hope that the siege was to be lifted and that the danger was over, they undid the good they had done and forced the servants they had released to go back into their service. The *king of Babylon's army* had now *gone up from them* (v. 21). Pharaoh was bringing an army of Egyptians to stop the progress of the king of Babylon's victories, and the Babylonians lifted the siege for a time (37:5). This was a great shame for the servants, but it especially showed disrespect to God; in doing this they *polluted* (profaned) *his name* (v. 16).

3. They are severely threatened for dealing so treacherously with God. *Be not deceived; God is not mocked* (Gal 6:7). Those who think they can deceive God by a partial, temporary reformation will greatly deceive their own souls. Since the people of Jerusalem have not given freedom to their servants to go where they please, God will give freedom to all his judgments to take their course (v. 17): *You have not proclaimed liberty to your servants.* "*Therefore I will proclaim a liberty for you; I will* discharge you from my service and put you beyond my protection, which those who withdraw from their loyalty to me forfeit the right to. You will have the freedom to choose which of these judgments you will be cut off by: *sword, famine, or pestilence* (plague)." Since they have brought

their servants back into confinement in their houses, God will *make them to be removed into all the kingdoms of the earth* (v. 17), where they will live in slavery. "I will make the men who have transgressed my covenant like the calf that they cut in two; I will tear them apart as they tore it apart." They have all dealt treacherously with God, and so they will all be involved in the common destruction. Since the retreat of the Babylonian army from them emboldened them to return to their sin, against their covenant, God will bring that army on them again: "They have now *gone up from you*, and your terror is over for now, but I *will command them* to return to where they were; they will *return to this city, and take it and burn it*" (v. 22). If we repent of the good we had intended, God will repent of the good he had intended. *With the froward* (crooked) *thou wilt show thyself froward* (shrewd) (Ps 18:26).

CHAPTER 35

A wide range of methods is tried to awaken the Jews to a sense of their sin and to bring them to repentance. The scope of many of the prophet's sermons was to frighten them out of their disobedience by setting before them what that would lead to if they persisted in it. The scope of the sermon in this chapter is to shame them out of their disobedience if they had any sense of honor left in them. 1. He sets before them the obedience of the family of the Recabites to the commands left them by Jonadab, their ancestor (vv. 1–11). 2. He uses this to emphasize the disobedience of the Jews to God and their contempt for his commands (vv. 12–15). 3. He foretells the judgments of God on the Jews for their ungodly disobedience (vv. 16–17). 4. He assures the Recabites of the blessing of God on them for their godly obedience (vv. 18–19).

Verses 1–11

What is contained in this chapter was said and done *in the days of Jehoiakim* (v. 1), toward the end of his reign, for it was after the king of Babylon *came up into the land* with his army (v. 11), which seems to refer to the invasion mentioned in 2Ki 24:2, on occasion of Jehoiakim's rebellion against Nebuchadnezzar. Jeremiah sets out before the rebellious people the example of the Recabites, a family that set themselves apart. They were originally Kenites, as emerges from 1Ch 2:55: *These are the Kenites that came out of Hemath, the father of the house of Rechab.* The Kenites, at least those of them who settled in the land of Israel, were the descendants of Reuel, Moses' father-in-law (Jdg 1:16). One family of these Kenites had their name from Recab. His son, or a descendant from him, was Jonadab, a man famous in his time for his wisdom and godliness. He flourished in the days of Jehu, king of Israel, nearly 300 years before this (2Ki 10:15–16). We are told here:

1. The rules of living that Jonadab told his children and his descendants to religiously observe. They were probably what he himself had observed throughout his life.

1.1. They were commanded to obey two remarkable decrees:

1.1.1. He forbade them to *drink wine*, according to the law of the Nazarites. We tend to abuse wine and get hurt by it so much that it is a commendable act of self-denial either not to use it at all or to use it only very sparingly and medicinally, as Timothy did (1Ti 5:23).

1.1.2. He appointed them to *dwell in tents*, not to build houses, buy land, or rent or occupy either (v. 7). This was an example of strictness and self-denial. Tents were lowly dwellings, and this would teach them to be humble; they

were cold, and this would teach them to be hardy and not to indulge the body; they were portable dwellings, and this would teach them not to think of settling or putting down roots anywhere in this world. They must live in tents *all their days*. They must get used to enduring hardship (2Ti 2:3).

1.2. Why did Jonadab prescribe such rules of living to his descendants? It was to show his wisdom and the real concern he had for their welfare. He did not, however, bind them by an oath or vow; he only advised them to conform to this discipline insofar as they found that it built them up. His ancestors had devoted themselves to a pastoral life (Ex 2:16), and he wanted his descendants to keep to it. Moses had given them the hope that they would be naturalized (Nu 10:32), but they were still *strangers* (nomads) *in the land* (v. 7). They received no inheritance from it, and so they must live by their employment and get used to living the hard life; humility and contentment in obscurity are often the wisest and safest way to live. Jonadab saw the general corruption of the lives of those around him; the drunkards of Ephraim were many (Isa 28:1, 3), and he was afraid his children might be corrupted by them. He therefore obliged them to live by themselves in a secluded state in the country, and, so that they might not fall into any unlawful pleasures, he obliged them to deny themselves the use of even lawful delights. Jonadab could foresee the destruction of a people who were so corrupt, and he wanted his family to be prepared, so that, if they could not have peace *in the peace thereof* (29:7), yet even in the midst of the troubles, *they might have peace.* Let them not cling to what they had, and then they could be stripped of it less painfully. They must learn to live by rule and discipline. It is good for us all to do so, and to teach our children to do so.

2. How strictly his descendants observed these rules (vv. 8–10). They had all *obeyed the voice of Jonadab their father* in their respective generations; they had *done according to all that he commanded them.* They *drank no wine*, even though they lived in a country where there was plenty of it. They built no houses and cultivated no ground, but lived on what their cattle produced. Now, as to one of the particulars of Jonadab's command, they dispensed with it in a case of necessity (v. 11): *When the king of Babylon came into the land* with his army, even though they had lived in tents up to that time, they now left their tents and came and lived in houses in Jerusalem. The rules of a strict discipline must not be made too strict, but should allow exemption when cases of necessity call for it. These Recabites would have been tempting God, not trusting him, if they had not used proper means to ensure their own safety despite the law and tradition of their family. Jeremiah took them into the temple (v. 2), into a *prophet's chamber* (a side room), because he had a message from God. There he not only asked the Recabites whether they would drink any wine but also set *pots full of wine before them*, making the temptation as strong as possible, and said, *"Drink you wine*, you will have it freely. You have broken one of the rules of your order by coming to live at Jerusalem; why may you not break this rule too? When in the city, why not do as they do there?" But they refused absolutely. They all agreed in their refusal. "No, *we will drink no* wine, for it is against the law with us." The prophet saw they were determined to stand by their decision.

Verses 12–19

The trial of the Recabites' faithfulness was intended as a sign; here we have its application.

1. The Recabites' observance of their father's command to them is used to emphasize the disobedience of the Jews to God. Let them see it and be ashamed. The prophet asks them in God's name, "*Will you not* finally *receive instruction?* (v. 13). Will nothing succeed in revealing your sin and duty? You see how obedient the Recabites are to their father's commandment (v. 14), but *you have not inclined your ear to me*" (v. 15). The Recabites were obedient to one who was a human being like themselves, but the Jews were disobedient to an infinite and eternal God, who had absolute authority over them, as the Father of their spirits (Heb 12:9). The Recabites were never reminded of their obligations to their father, but God often sent his prophets to his people (v. 14). God had given his people *a good land*, and he promised them that if they were obedient, they would continue to live in it, so that they were bound both by gratitude and by interest to be obedient, but they would not *listen*.

2. Judgments are threatened, as often before, against Judah and Jerusalem. The Recabites will rise up in judgment against them, for they *performed the commandment of their father*, continuing to obey it (v. 16), but *this* rebellious and contradictory *people* have not *hearkened unto me*. "*I will bring upon them* by the Babylonian army, *all the evil pronounced against them* both in the Law and in the Prophets, for *I have spoken to them, I have called to them*—spoken by my word, called out by my providence—but they have not *heard* nor *answered*" (v. 17).

3. Mercy is promised here to the family of the Recabites for their steady loyalty to the laws of their house. Although it was only to shame Israel that their faithfulness was tested, yet because they were unshaken, it was *found unto praise, and honour, and glory* (1Pe 1:7) (vv. 18–19). The family would *never want* (lack) *a man* to inherit what they had, even though they had no inheritance to leave. Although they were neither priests nor Levites, nor appear to have had any position in the temple service, they would still stand before God to minister to him in a faithful, regular devotion.

CHAPTER 36

Here is another way that is tried to affect this careless and perverse people, but in vain. A scroll is provided, containing an abstract of all the sermons Jeremiah had preached to them. We have here: 1. The writing of this scroll by Baruch, as Jeremiah dictated it (vv. 1–4). 2. The public reading of the scroll by Baruch, to all the people on a day of fasting (vv. 5–10), then a private reading by Baruch, to the officials (vv. 11–19), and lastly a reading by Jehudi to the king (vv. 20–21). 3. The burning of the scroll by the king, with orders to prosecute Jeremiah and Baruch (vv. 22–26). 4. The writing of another scroll, with large additions, particularly concerning Jehoiakim's fate for burning the previous scroll (vv. 27–32).

Verses 1–8

In the beginning of Ezekiel's prophecy we meet with *a roll* written *in vision* (Eze 2:9–10; 3:1). Here, at the end of Jeremiah's prophecy, we meet with *a roll* written *in fact*, to reveal the things contained in it to the people. We have here:

1. The command God gave to Jeremiah to write a summary of all the sermons he had given ever since he first began to be a preacher, in the thirteenth year of Josiah, *to this day*, which was in the fourth year of Jehoiakim

(vv. 2–3). What they had heard once must be gone over again, so that what was forgotten could be called to mind again and what made no impression on them when they heard it the first time might make an impression on them when they heard it a second time. Notice the reason given here for the writing of this scroll (v. 3): *It may be that the house of Judah will hear.* Notice what it is hoped they will listen to: *All that evil which I purpose to do unto them.* Notice what it is hoped will be the effect of listening: *They will hear, that they may return every man from his evil* way. The conversion of sinners is what ministers should aim at in preaching, and people hear the word in vain if that point is not gained. *That I may forgive their iniquity.* This clearly shows God's justice. It is inconsistent that he should forgive the sin unless sinners repent of it. It also clearly expresses his mercy, showing that he is very ready to forgive sin and only waits until the sinner is ready to receive forgiveness; he uses various ways to bring us to repentance so *that he may forgive.*

2. The instructions Jeremiah gave to Baruch, his scribe, according to the command he had received from God (v. 4). God told Jeremiah to write, but it seems he did not have the *pen of a ready writer* (Ps 45:1). He could not write as fast or as well as Baruch, and so he used him as his secretary. The apostle Paul wrote only a few of his letters with his own hand (Gal 6:11; Ro 16:22). God distributes his gifts to different people; some are good at speaking, others at writing, and neither one can say to the other, "We have *no need of you*" (1Co 12:21). The Spirit of God dictated to Jeremiah, and he to Baruch. If we may credit the apocryphal book that bears Baruch's name, he was later himself a prophet to the captives in Babylon. Baruch wrote in *a roll of a book*, on pieces of parchment or vellum, which were joined together, making one long scroll, which was perhaps rolled on a staff.

3. The orders Jeremiah gave to Baruch to read out to the people what he had written. Jeremiah, it seems, was *shut up* (restricted) and *could not go to the house of the Lord* himself (v. 5). Although he was not a confined prisoner—for then there would have been no need to send officers to seize him (v. 26)—he was still forbidden by the king to appear in the temple. Similarly, the apostle Paul wrote letters to the churches that he could not visit in person. When God ordered the reading of the scroll, he said, *It may be they will hear and return from their evil ways* (v. 3); when Jeremiah orders it, he says, *It may be they will pray* and will *return from their evil way.* Prayer to God for grace to turn us is necessary for us to turn. According to these orders, Baruch did read *out of the book the words of the Lord*, whenever there was a *holy convocation* (v. 8).

Verses 9–19

It seems that before the very sacred reading of the book all at once that is spoken of here, Baruch had frequently read out of it to all who would listen to him, for the directions about reading from the book were given in the *fourth year of Jehoiakim*, whereas this reading was done in *the fifth year* (v. 9). Some think, however, that the writing of the book took so much time that it was another year before it was completed.

1. The government appointed a public fast to be religiously observed (v. 9), because of either the distress caused them by the Babylonian army or the lack of rain (14:1): *They proclaimed a fast to the people.* Great acts of godliness and devotion may be found even among those who, though they keep up these *forms of godliness,* are foreigners and enemies to *the power* of it (2Ti 3:5).

But what good will such hypocritical service do? Fasting without reforming and turning away from sin will never turn away the judgments of God (Jnh 3:10).

2. Baruch repeated Jeremiah's sermons publicly in the temple of the Lord on the day of fasting. He stood in a room that belonged to Gemariah and spoke from a window or balcony to the people who were in the courtyard (v. 10).

3. An account of this was brought to the officials who were now together in the secretary's office, here called *the scribe's chamber* (secretary's room) (v. 12). It seems that although the officials had called the people to meet in the temple of God to fast, pray, and listen to the word, they did not see fit to be present there themselves. Micaiah told the officials about what Baruch had read, for his father, Gemariah, supported Baruch so far as to lend him his room.

4. Baruch was sent for and ordered to sit down among them and read it all over again to them (vv. 14–15), which he did readily.

5. The officials were very moved by the word that was read to them (v. 16). And *when they had heard all, they were afraid*, all of them, *one* as well as *another*, like Felix, who trembled at Paul's reasoning (Ac 24:25). The rebukes were just, and the predictions were now set to be fulfilled, so that they were in a state of great fear. We are not told what impression this reading of the scroll made on the people (v. 10), but the officials were made afraid by it and, as some read it, "looked at one another," not knowing what to say. They agreed to *tell the king of all these words* (v. 16), and if he thought fit to believe them, they would. At the same time, they knew the king's mind so much that they advised Baruch and Jeremiah to hide themselves (v. 19) and to do all they could for their own safety, expecting that the king, instead of being convinced, would become angry.

6. They asked Baruch the trifling question, *How didst thou write all these words?* (v. 17), as if they suspected there was something extraordinary in it, but Baruch gave them a direct answer, that Jeremiah dictated to him and he wrote the words down (v. 18).

Verses 20–32

Here we follow the path of the scroll from the officials to the king:

1. On notice given him concerning it, he sent for it and ordered it to be read to him (vv. 20–21). He did not want Baruch to read it himself, though he could read it more intelligently and with more authority and affection than anyone else; rather, Jehudi, one of his pages in waiting, who was sent to fetch it, was told to read it. Those who so despise the word of God will soon make it clear, as this king did, that they hate it as well, that they have not only low, but also bad, thoughts about it.

2. He did not have the patience to listen to it read through as the officials had, but, when he had heard *three or four leaves* read, angrily *cut it with his penknife* and threw it piece by piece *into the fire*, so that he might be sure to see it *all consumed* (vv. 22–23). This was a most arrogant act of disrespect to the God of heaven, whose message this was. In this way:

2.1. He showed his impatience with rebuke.

2.2. He showed his anger toward Baruch and Jeremiah; he was in such a rage that he would have cut them in pieces and burned them if he had had them within his reach.

2.3. He expressed his obstinate determination never to submit to the intentions of the warnings given him.

2.4. He foolishly hoped to defeat the threats declared against him.

2.5. He thought he had effectively made sure that the things contained in this scroll would spread no further.

3. Neither the king himself nor any of his officials were at all affected by the word: *They were not afraid* (v. 24), not even those officials who *trembled at the word* when they heard it the first time (v. 16). They showed some concern until they saw how lightly the king took it, and then they shook off all that concern.

4. Three of the officials had so much sense and grace left as to intervene to prevent the scroll from being burned, but in vain (v. 25).

5. Jehoiakim, having in effect burned God's warrant by which he was arrested, now — by way of revenge — signed a warrant to arrest Jeremiah and Baruch, God's ministers, *but the Lord hid them* (v. 26).

6. Jeremiah had orders and instructions to write on another scroll the same words that were written on the scroll Jehoiakim had burned (vv. 27–28). Enemies may succeed in burning the Bible, but they cannot do away with the word of God or defeat its fulfillment. Although the tablets of the Law had now been broken, they were renewed (Ex 32:19; 34:1), and so out of the ashes of the scroll that had been burned arose another Phoenix. *The word of the Lord endures for ever* (1Pe 1:25).

7. The king of Judah, although a king, was severely judged by the King of kings for this indignity done to the written word. Jehoiakim was angry because it was *written therein, saying*, surely *the king of Babylon shall come and destroy this land* (v. 29). God and his prophets had *become his enemies because they told him the truth*, told him about the coming devastation; yet at the same time they had put him in a position to prevent it. The wrath of God would come on him and his family, in the first place, by the hand of Nebuchadnezzar. He would die, and in a few weeks his son would be taken off the throne and exchange his royal robes for prison garments, so that *he would have none to sit upon the throne of David. His dead body* would lie unburied, or *he would be buried with the burial of an ass* (22:19), that is, thrown into the ditch. Even *his seed and his servants* would suffer because of their relationship with him (v. 31), for they would be punished, not for his sin, but so much the sooner for their own. All the evil declared against Judah and Jerusalem in that scroll would be brought on them.

8. When the scroll was written afresh, *there were added* to the former *many like words* (v. 32), many more threats, for since they would yet *walk contrary to God* (Lev 26:21, 23, etc.), he would *heat the furnace seven times hotter* (Da 3:19).

CHAPTER 37

This chapter brings us close to the destruction of Jerusalem by the Babylonians, for its story comes at the end of Zedekiah's reign. We have in it: 1. A general idea of the bad character of that reign (vv. 1–2). 2. The message that Zedekiah, nevertheless, sent to Jeremiah to request his prayers (v. 3). 3. The false hopes that the Babylonians would give up the siege of Jerusalem (v. 5). 4. The assurance God gave them by Jeremiah, who was now free (v. 4), that the Babylonian army would renew the siege and capture the city (vv. 6–10). 5. The imprisonment of Jeremiah under the pretense that he was a deserter (vv. 11–15). 6. The kindness Zedekiah showed him when he was a prisoner (vv. 16–21).

Verses 1–10

We have here:

1. Jeremiah's preaching insulted (vv. 1–2). Zedekiah succeeded *Coniah*, or Jehoiachin, and although he saw in his predecessor the fatal consequences of condemning the word of God, he himself still did not heed the warning. *Neither he nor his* officials *nor the people of the land hearkened unto the words of the Lord* (v. 2), even though they had already begun to be fulfilled.

2. Jeremiah's prayers requested. Zedekiah sent messengers to him, saying, *Pray now unto the Lord our God for us* (v. 3). He did so before (21:1–2), and one of the messengers who were used then, Zephaniah, serves in that role here as well. Zedekiah is to be commended for this, and it shows there was some good in him, some sense of his need of God's favor. When we are in distress, we should desire the prayers of our ministers and Christian friends, for then we are honoring prayer and showing respect for our brothers and sisters. Kings themselves should look on their praying people as the strength of the nation (Zec 12:5, 10). And yet this only helps condemn Zedekiah out of his own mouth. If he really did look on Jeremiah as a prophet, whose prayers could be effective, why did he not *hearken to the words of the Lord* (v. 2) that the Lord spoke by Jeremiah? How can we expect God to listen to others speaking to him for us if we will not listen to them speaking to us from him and for him? When Zedekiah sent Jehucal to the prophet to pray for him, it would have been better if he had sent for the prophet to pray *with* him.

3. Jerusalem flattered by the retreat of the Babylonian army from it. Jeremiah was now at liberty (v. 4). Jerusalem also, for the present, was at liberty (v. 5). Although Zedekiah was paying tribute to the king of Babylon, he had entered into a private alliance with Pharaoh king of Egypt (Eze 17:15). In accordance with this alliance, when the king of Babylon came to rebuke him for his treachery, the king of Egypt sent forces to relieve Jerusalem when it was besieged. The Babylonians lifted the siege. They did this probably not out of fear of the Egyptians, but in wisdom, in order to fight them far away, before any of the Jewish forces could join them. The Jews encouraged themselves with this to hope that Jerusalem had been rescued for good.

4. Jerusalem threatened with the return of the Babylonian army. Zedekiah sent Jehucal to Jeremiah to ask him to pray that the Babylonian army might not return, but Jeremiah sends him word that the decree has been issued and that it is foolish of them to expect peace. *Thus saith the Lord, Deceive not yourselves* (v. 9). Satan himself, though he is the great deceiver, could not deceive us unless we deceived ourselves. Jeremiah uses no dark metaphors, but tells them clearly:

4.1. That the Egyptians will retreat to *their own land*.

4.2. That the Babylonians will return and renew the siege: *They shall not depart* for good and all (v. 9); *they shall come again* (v. 8); they will *fight against the city.*

4.3. That Jerusalem will certainly be handed over to the Babylonians: *They shall take it, and burn it with fire* (v. 8). "In fact, *though you had smitten* (defeated) their army, so that many were killed and all the rest wounded, those *wounded men should rise up and burn this city*" (v. 10).

Verses 11–21

We have here a further account concerning Jeremiah, who relates more information about himself than any other prophet.

1. When Jeremiah had opportunity, he tried to withdraw from Jerusalem into the country (vv. 11–12): *When the Chaldeans* (Babylonians) had *broken up from Jerusalem* because *of Pharaoh's army*, Jeremiah decided *to go into the* country and, as the margin of v. 12 reads, "to slip away from Jerusalem in the midst of the people," who, in that interval in the siege, went out into the country to look after their livelihood. He tried to steal away in the crowd, for although he was well known, he was content to be lost in the crowd and buried alive in a cottage. Jeremiah found he could do no good in Jerusalem; he had worked in vain among them, and so he was determined to leave them.

2. In this attempt, he was seized as a deserter and committed to prison (vv. 13–15): *He was in the gate of Benjamin* when *a captain of the ward* (guard), who probably was in charge of that gate, recognized him and *took him* into custody. He was the grandson of Hananiah, who according to the Jews was Hananiah the false prophet, who opposed Jeremiah (28:10), and they add that this young captain bore a grudge against Jeremiah for that reason. What the guard accused him of was, *Thou fallest away to the Chaldeans* (you are deserting to the Babylonians)—an unlikely story, because the Babylonians had now gone; Jeremiah therefore denied the charge with good reason, and with the confidence and the mildness of an innocent man: "*It is false; I fall not away to the Chaldeans*; I am going about my own lawful business." Jeremiah's declaration of his integrity, even though he was a prophet and was ready to give his word as a priest, was not listened to, and he was brought before the privy council. On the basis of the evil insinuation of the captain of the guard and without examining Jeremiah, they lost their temper with him: they *were wroth*. They beat him and then *put him in prison*, in the worst prison they had, the one *in the house of Jonathan the scribe*. Jeremiah was thrust into this prison, *into the dungeon*, which was dark, cold, damp, and dirty. He had to stay in the vaulted cells or *cabins*. *There Jeremiah remained many days* (v. 16).

3. Zedekiah finally sent for him, finally showed him some favor, although this probably did not happen until the Babylonian army had returned and had set a fresh siege on the city. When their futile hopes had all vanished, then they were more confused and fearful than ever. "Oh then," Zedekiah says, "send quickly for the prophet; let me talk with him."

3.1. The king sent for him to give him a private audience as an ambassador from God. He *asked him secretly* (privately) *in his house*, being ashamed to be seen in his company, "*Is there any word from the Lord?* (v. 17). Any word of comfort? Can you give us any hope that the Babylonians will again withdraw?" Jeremiah's life and comfort are in Zedekiah's hands, and he now has a request that he will ask Jeremiah to grant as a favor, and yet, having this opportunity, Jeremiah tells him clearly that though *there is a word from the Lord*, it is no word of encouragement for him or his people: *Thou shalt be delivered into the hand of the king of Babylon* (v. 17). If Jeremiah had consulted with *flesh and blood* (Mt 16:17), he would have given the king an agreeable answer, and although he would not have told him a lie, he might still have thought twice before telling him the worst at this time. But Jeremiah was one who had *obtained mercy of the Lord to be faithful* (1Co 7:25) and would not, to obtain human mercy, be unfaithful either to God or to his ruler. He therefore tells him the truth, the whole truth. Jeremiah uses this occasion to rebuke him and his people for their trust in the false prophets, who told them that *the king of Babylon* would *not come* at all or who, when he had withdrawn, told them he would *not* come again *against* them (v. 19). *"Where are now your prophets*, who told you you would have peace?"

3.2. Jeremiah made the most of this opportunity to present his private petition as a poor prisoner (vv. 18, 20). He humbly pleaded with the king: *"What have I offended against thee, or thy servants, or this people*, what law have I broken, *that you have put me in prison?"* Having thus pleaded, he begged fervently and emotionally (v. 20), *Cause me not to return* to that terrible jail, *to the house of Jonathan the scribe, lest I die there. Hear me, I pray thee, O my Lord the king! Let my supplication, I pray thee, be accepted before thee.* Here is not one word of complaint about the officials who unjustly committed him to prison, but modest supplication to the king. A lion in God's cause must be a lamb in his own.

3.2.1. The king granted him his request, took care that he would not die in the dungeon, and ordered that he have the liberty of the *court of the prison* (courtyard of the guard), where he could breathe the fresh air.

3.2.2. He ordered for him his *daily bread out of the public store, till all the bread was spent* (v. 21). Zedekiah should have released him, but he did not have the courage to do that; it was good that he did as he did. God can make even confinement turn to advantage, and the courtyard of a prison become as green pastures.

CHAPTER 38

Here Jeremiah is greatly humbled under the disapproval of the officials, but also highly honored by the favor of the king. They abused him as a criminal; the king used him as his privy councillor. 1. Because of his faithfulness, Jeremiah is put into the cistern by the officials (vv. 1–6). 2. At the intercession of Ebed-Melech, a Cushite, by special order from the king, he is lifted up out of the cistern and confined to the courtyard of the guard (vv. 7–13). 3. He has a private conference with the king on present affairs (vv. 14–23). 4. Care is taken to keep that conference private (vv. 24–28).

Verses 1–13

Here:

1. Jeremiah persists in his direct preaching (v. 3): *This city shall be given into the hand of the king of Babylon*; even though it holds out for a long time, it will finally be captured. He would have not repeated this unwelcome message so often except that he considered it the only way he could put them in the position of saving themselves, even if they could not save the city (v. 2). Let them *go forth to the Chaldeans* (go over to the Babylonians) and throw themselves on their mercy before things come to a crisis, and then they *shall live*; the Babylonians will give them mercy, and they will escape *the famine and pestilence* (plague), which will be the death of very many people in the city.

2. The officials persist in their hatred toward Jeremiah. He has been faithful to his country and to the trust put in him as a prophet, and although he eats the king's bread at this time, that has not stopped his mouth. But his persecutors complain that he is abusing his freedom by walking about the courtyard of the guard, for although he cannot go to the temple to preach, he still says the same things in private conversation to those who come to visit him, and so (v. 4) they describe him to the king as someone who is dangerous, disloyal toward the government he lives under: *He seeks not the welfare of this people, but the hurt.* No one has done more for the good of Jerusalem than he has.

Yet they describe his preaching *as weakening the hands* of the soldiers and discouraging them (v. 4). It is common for evildoers to look on God's faithful ministers as their enemies, only because ministers show them what enemies they are to themselves as long as they remain impenitent.

3. With the king's permission, Jeremiah is then put into a *dungeon* (cistern), to kill him there. Although Zedekiah feels a conviction that Jeremiah is a prophet sent by God, he does not have the courage to acknowledge it: *He is in your hand* (v. 5). Those who, though secretly kind and well disposed toward good people, dare not acknowledge it in times of need will have a great deal to answer for. The officials, having received this general authority from the king, immediately put poor *Jeremiah into the dungeon* (cistern) *of Malchiah, that was in the court of the prison* (v. 6). It must have been a deep cistern, for they *let him down* into it *with cords*; it must have been dirty, for *there was no water* in it, *but mire*, and he *sunk in the mire*, "up to his neck," according to Josephus. Those who put him there no doubt intended him to die of hunger and cold, and so die an obscure death, fearing that if they put him to death openly, the people might become angry with them. Many of God's faithful witnesses have been privately put away in prisons and starved to death in this way, and their blood will be brought to account on the Day of Judgment. What Jeremiah did in his distress, he tells us himself in La 3:55, 57: *I called upon thy name, O Lord! out of the low dungeon, and thou drewest near, saying, Fear not.*

4. A petition is brought to the king by Ebed-Melech, one of the officials of the royal palace, on behalf of the poor sufferer. Ebed-Melech was an *Ethiopian, a stranger to the commonwealth of Israel* (Eph 2:12), but he had in himself more humanity, and more theology too, than Israelites had. Christ found more faith among Gentiles than among Jews (Mt 8:5–10). Ebed-Melech lived in an evil court and in a corrupt and degenerate time, but he had a great sense of both justice and godliness. God has his remnant in every place. There were *saints* even *in Caesar's household* (Php 4:22). The king was now *sitting in the gate of Benjamin* to receive appeals and requests. Ebed-Melech went immediately there, for the case could not be delayed. He boldly asserted that Jeremiah had had a great deal of wrong done him, and he was not afraid to tell the king this. He did not mince his words; he told the king faithfully—let the king take it as he wishes—*These men have done ill in all that they have done to Jeremiah* (v. 9). God can raise up friends for his people in distress where they are little thought of.

5. Orders are immediately given for Jeremiah to be released, and Ebed-Melech makes sure the orders are carried out. The king has had his heart suddenly and wonderfully changed, and he now wants Jeremiah to be released in defiance of the officials, for he orders no fewer than thirty men to be employed in lifting him up out of the cistern, in case the officials should raise a party to oppose it (v. 10). Ebed-Melech has been successful, and he soon brings Jeremiah the good news. Special notice is taken of his great tenderness in providing soft old rags for Jeremiah to put under his armpits to keep the cords with which he was lifted up from hurting him, his armpits probably being made sore by the cords with which he was let down. Nor does Ebed-Melech throw the rags or worn-out clothes down to him, in case they should get lost in the mud; rather, they are let down carefully (vv. 11–12). Jeremiah is brought up out of the cistern, and is now where he was, *in the court of the prison* (v. 13).

Verses 14–28

The king is in close conference with Jeremiah, though (v. 5) he earlier handed him over to his enemies. Notice:

1. The honor that Zedekiah showed the prophet. When he was newly brought up out of the cistern, he sent for him to meet with him privately. He met him in *the third entry*—or, as the margin reads, "the principal entry"—that *was in*, or led toward, *the house of the Lord* (v. 14). Perhaps he intended to show respect for *the house of God*, now that he wanted to hear *the word of God*. Zedekiah wanted to ask *Jeremiah a thing*; it would be better translated "a word." "I am here asking you for *a word of prediction*, advice, and encouragement, *a word from the Lord* (37:17). Whatever word you have, *hide it not from me*; let me know the worst." He hoped to receive a more pleasant answer, as if God, who is *in one mind* (Job 23:13), were altogether like men (Ps 50:21), a human being, who could not make up his mind.

2. The agreement that Jeremiah insisted on before he would give the king his advice (v. 15). "And if I do," Jeremiah says, "*wilt thou not put me to death?* I am afraid thou wilt," as some take it; "what else can I expect when you are led blindfold by the officials?" It was not that Jeremiah was reluctant to seal his preaching with his blood, but in doing our duty we should use all lawful means to preserve our own lives; even the apostles of Christ did so. He was willing to give the king wholesome advice, and he did not rebuke him for his unkindness in allowing him to be put in the cistern. "*Wilt thou not hearken unto me?* (v. 15). Surely you will; I hope to find you open to receiving advice and, now *in this thy day, willing to know the things that belong to thy peace*" (Lk 19:42). Some read it as spoken in despair: "If I give you advice, you will not listen to me. I have reason to fear you will not, and then I might as well keep my advice to myself." Zedekiah did not reply; he would not promise to listen to his advice. As for the prophet's safety, he promised him, on the word of a king, *I will neither put thee to death nor deliver thee into the hands of those that will* (v. 16). Zedekiah's oath on this occasion was solemn: "*As the Lord liveth, who made us this soul* (v. 16), who gave me my life and you yours, I dare not take away your life unjustly, knowing then I would forfeit my own to the One who is the Lord of life."

3. The good advice Jeremiah gave him, with good reason why he should accept it, not out of any prudence or political shrewdness of his own, but in the *name of the Lord, the God of hosts* and *God of Israel*. Jeremiah advised him not as a statesman but as a prophet, and he said that he should surrender himself and his city *to the king of Babylon's princes*: "*Go forth to them* and make the best terms you can with them" (v. 17). This was the advice he had given to the people (v. 2 and before 21:9), to submit to divine judgments. To persuade the king to take this advice, he set before him good and evil, life and death (Dt 30:15). If the king would yield, he would save his children from the sword and Jerusalem from the flames. If he would simply acknowledge God's justice, he would experience his mercy: *The city shall not be burnt*, and *thou shalt live and thy house*. But if he obstinately resisted, it would lead to the ruin of both his house and Jerusalem (v. 18). This is the situation of sinners before God; if they humbly submit to his grace and government, they will live.

4. The objection that Zedekiah made against the prophet's advice (v. 19). If he had had due regard to God's authority, wisdom, and goodness, then as soon as he understood what the mind of God was, he would have immediately accepted. Instead, however, he suggested in response some wise opinions of his own. All he suggested was, "*I am afraid*. I am not afraid of the Babylonians; their officials are honorable. But I am afraid of the Jews who have already gone over to the Babylonians; when they see *me* follow them, me, who had so much opposed their going, they will laugh at me and say, *Hast thou also become weak as water?*" (Isa 14:10). Yet even if it had been really the greatest personal trouble possible, he still should have ventured to obey God and preserve his family and city.

5. The urgent boldness with which Jeremiah followed up the advice he had given the king. He assured him that if he would submit to the will of God, the thing he feared would not come on him (v. 20): "*They shall not deliver thee up*, but treat you as is right. *Obey, I beseech thee, the voice of the Lord*, because it is his voice, and so it *shall be well unto thee*." But he told him what would be the consequences if he did not obey. He himself would *fall into the hands of the Chaldeans* (Babylonians). "*Thou shalt not escape*, as you hope to do" (v. 23). He himself would be responsible for the destruction of Jerusalem: "*Thou shalt cause this city to be burnt with fire*, which by a small submission and self-denial you could have prevented." He would certainly be justly disgraced if he resisted—and by women, too (v. 22), who would make fun of him when all his wives and children were attacked by the conquerors (v. 23).

6. The care that Zedekiah took to keep this meeting private (v. 24): *Let no man know of these words*. He raised no objections against Jeremiah's advice, but he would not follow it. Zedekiah was concerned to keep matters private not so much for Jeremiah's safety as for his own reputation. Jeremiah was instructed what to say to the officials if they examined him about it. He must tell them that he had been pleading with the king not to send him back to *the house of Jonathan the scribe* (vv. 25–26), and he did tell them so (v. 27), and no doubt it was true.

CHAPTER 39

The prophet Jeremiah, having foretold in detail the handing over of Jerusalem into the hands of the king of Babylon, gives a particular account of that sad event. We have that sad story in this chapter, which serves to confirm the word of God's messengers. 1. Jerusalem, after eighteen months' siege, was taken by the Babylonian army (vv. 1–3). 2. King Zedekiah, attempting to escape, was captured and made a miserable prisoner of the king of Babylon (vv. 4–7). 3. Jerusalem was burned to the ground, and the people were taken away captive, except the poor (vv. 8–10). 4. The Babylonians were very kind to Jeremiah and took special care of him (vv. 11–14). 5. Ebed-Melech, too, for his kindness, received protection from God himself on this day of devastation (vv. 15–18).

Verses 1–10

Jeremiah abode patiently in the court of the prison until the day that Jerusalem was taken (38:28). He did not disturb the officials any further with his prophesying, nor did they him disturb with their persecution.

1. The city was finally captured by attack; Nebuchadnezzar's army laid siege to it in the *ninth* year of Zedekiah, *in the tenth month* (v. 1). Nebuchadnezzar left his generals to continue the siege, and they renewed it with redoubled vigor. Finally, *in the eleventh year, in the fourth month*,

they entered the city, because the soldiers were now so weak from famine that they could not offer any resistance (v. 2). Sin had caused God to withdraw his protection, and then, like Samson when his hair was cut (Jdg 16:17–21), it was weak as other cities.

2. The officials of the king of Babylon took possession of the *middle gate* (v. 3). Some think this was the *second gate* (Zep 1:10), in the middle wall that divided one part of the city from the other. Here they cautiously came to a halt and dared not go forward—among people who perhaps would sell their lives as dearly as they could—until they had given directions that the whole city be searched, so that they might not be surprised by any ambush. And they sat in the *middle gate*. There, where *Eliakim* and *Hilkiah*, who bore the name of the God of Israel, used to sit, now sat *Nergal-sharezer*, *Samgar-nebo*, and so on, who bore the names of the pagan gods. *Sarsechim* was the name of the *Rab-saris*, that is, the captain of the guard (commander of the imperial guard), and *Nergal-sharezer* was the *Rab-mag*, the camp-master or quartermaster. What Jeremiah had prophesied was now fulfilled (1:15), that the families of the kingdoms of the north would come and set up their thrones in the entrance of the gates of Jerusalem.

3. Zedekiah thought it was time to fend for himself, and, burdened by guilt and fear, he *went out of the city* under protection of *the night* (v. 4). He was discovered, pursued, and overtaken *in the plains of Jericho* (v. 5). From there he was brought as prisoner to Riblah, where the king of Babylon pronounced sentence. *The king of Babylon slew his sons before his eyes* (v. 6). Zedekiah himself was now only thirty-two years old, and witnessing the deaths of these children must have been like dying so many deaths himself, especially when he considered that his own obstinacy was their cause. *They shall bring forth thy wives and children to the Chaldeans* (38:23). Nebuchadnezzar also *slew all the nobles of Judah* (v. 6). He ordered *Zedekiah to have his eyes put out* (v. 7), so condemning forever to darkness the one who had shut his eyes to the clear light of God's word. He *bound him* "with two brazen chains or fetters," as the margin says, to take him away to Babylon to spend the rest of his days in misery there.

4. Some time afterward the city was burned, temple and palace and everything, and its walls broken down (v. 8).

5. The people who were left were all *carried away captives to Babylon* (v. 9). They must be driven hundreds of miles, like wild animals, before the conquerors, who were now their cruel taskmasters. They must lie at their mercy in a foreign land. A few, *the poor of the people*, never offered any resistance, and they were left to stay at home. *The captain of the guard gave them vineyards and fields at the same time*, such as they had never controlled before (v. 10). The rich had been proud oppressors, and now they were justly punished for their injustice; the poor had been patient sufferers, and now they were graciously rewarded for their patience.

Verses 11–18

Here we must sing about mercy, just as in the first part of the chapter we sang about judgment (Ps 101:1); we must sing to God about both. We may notice here:

1. A gracious providence concerning Jeremiah. Nebuchadnezzar had given orders that care should be taken of him and that he should be treated well in every respect (vv. 11–12). Nebuzaradan and the rest of the king of Babylon's officials discharged him from prison and did everything to put him at his ease (vv. 13–14). This was:

1.1. A very generous act of Nebuchadnezzar, who took notice of this poor prophet. No doubt he had received

information that Jeremiah had foretold the king of Babylon's successes against Judah. It was honorable of the king to give this command even before the city was taken, and it was honorable of the commanders to observe it even in the heat of the battle, and it is recorded for us to imitate.

1.2. An act of disgrace to Zedekiah and the officials of Israel. They had put Jeremiah in prison, and the king of Babylon and his officials took him out.

1.3. The fulfillment of God's promise to Jeremiah that he would reward him for his services. *I will cause the enemy to treat thee well in the day of evil* (15:11). Jeremiah had been faithful to the trust put in him as a prophet, and now God showed himself faithful to him and to the promise he had made him. What was used as an instrument to punish the persecutors was used as an instrument to relieve the persecuted, and Jeremiah never thought any worse of his rescue for its coming through the hand of the king of Babylon; rather, he saw the hand of God in it all the more clearly.

2. A gracious message to Ebed-Melech to assure him of a reward for his kindness to Jeremiah. He relieved *a prophet in the name of a prophet, and so he received a prophet's reward* (Mt 10:41). Jeremiah told him that God would certainly bring on Jerusalem the ruin that had long been threatened, and for his further satisfaction in having been so kind to Jeremiah he would see him abundantly proved to be a true prophet (v. 16). He would be rescued from sharing in the common disaster: *I will deliver thee; I will surely deliver thee* (v. 18). He had been instrumental in rescuing God's prophet from the cistern, and now God promised to rescue him, *because thou hast put thy trust in me, saith the Lord*. Ebed-Melech trusted in God that he would acknowledge him and stand by him, and then he was not afraid of any mere mortal. Those who trust God, as this good man did, in doing their duty, will find that their hope will not make them ashamed (Ro 5:5) in times of greatest danger.

CHAPTER 40

In this and the four following chapters, notice the story of those few Jews who were left in the land after their brothers and sisters were carried away. It is a very sad story, for they soon appeared to be as stubborn in their sin as ever, not humbled or reformed. Here: 1. A more detailed account is given of Jeremiah's discharge and his settlement with Gedaliah (vv. 1–6). 2. The Jews who remain scattered in the neighboring countries turn in great numbers to Gedaliah, who was made their governor under the king of Babylon, and for a while they are in a good position under him (vv. 7–12). 3. A treacherous plot is hatched against Gedaliah by Ishmael (vv. 13–16).

Verses 1–6

In these verses we have Jeremiah staying with Gedaliah on the advice of Nebuzaradan. Jeremiah was honorably taken from the courtyard of the guard by the king of Babylon's officials (39:13–14), but later, when he was found among the people in the city, when orders were given to the subordinate officers to bind in chains everyone they found there in order to take them as captives to Babylon, he, by the ignorance and mistake of these officers, was bound among the rest and rushed away. But when the captives were brought in chains to Ramah, Jeremiah was soon set apart from the rest and discharged.

1. The commander of the guard solemnly acknowledges him to be a true prophet (vv. 2–3): "*The Lord thy*

God has by you *pronounced this evil upon this place.* They received fair warning, but they refused to accept the warning, and *now the Lord hath brought it*, and as he said it by your mouth, so by my hand *he hath done what he said.*" He tells everyone who is now in chains in front of him, *It is because you have sinned against the Lord that this thing has come upon you* (v. 3). The officials of Israel would never be brought to acknowledge this, but this pagan official plainly sees it.

2. He gives the prophet leave to do as he pleases. He *looses him from his chains* a second time (v. 4) and invites him to come to Babylon as a friend and companion. "I will set my eye upon you" is the sense of the next clause; "I will show you respect and see that you are well provided for." If Jeremiah does not want to go to Babylon, he can live where he pleases in his own country.

3. He advises him to go to Gedaliah and settle with him. This Gedaliah, *made governor of the* land under *the king of Babylon*, was an honest Jew who probably went over to the Babylonians and showed he was so honorable that this great trust was put into his hands (v. 5). *While* Jeremiah has *not yet gone back*, but stands considering what he should do, Nebuzaradan suggests he *go to Gedaliah*. Nor does he give him only his liberty and approval of any measures he may take to provide for himself; he also provides for his support: he *gave him victuals* (provisions) *and a present*, either in clothes or in money, *and so let him go*. Jeremiah accepts his kindness, takes his advice, goes to Gedaliah at Mizpah, *and dwells with him* (v. 6). It does not turn out at all for his benefit. However, we may commend his heartfelt devotion for the land of Israel, that he would not abandon it, but chose rather to live with the poor in the Holy Land than with officials in an unholy one.

Verses 7–16

We have in these verses:

1. A bright sky opening up on the remaining Jews who were left in their own land, and a prospect given them of peace and quietness after the many years of trouble and terror. Providence seemed to raise and encourage such an expectation, and it would be as life from the dead to that miserable people.

1.1. Gedaliah, one of their own, was made *governor in the land* by *the king of Babylon* (v. 7). He was *the son of Ahikam, the son of Shaphan*, one of the officials. His father (26:24) took Jeremiah's side against the people. Gedaliah seems to have been a man of great wisdom and mild temper, under whose government the few people who were left could have been very happy.

1.2. All those who were now dispersed Jews came and put themselves under his government and protection. The leaders who had escaped the Babylonians came and quietly submitted to Gedaliah. Several are named here (v. 8). *They came* with *their men*, their servants, and their soldiers. The king of Babylon had such a high opinion of Gedaliah that he was not anxious about the increase in their numbers; rather, he was pleased with it. The poor who had escaped by fleeing into the neighboring countries of Moab, Ammon, and Edom were motivated by the love they had for their own land to return as soon as they heard that Gedaliah was in authority there (vv. 11–12). In wrath God remembered mercy (Hab 3:2); he still admitted some of the Jews back into their land for a further test of their obedience.

1.3. The model of this new government was drawn up and settled by an original contract (v. 9). "Come," Gedaliah said, "*fear not to serve the Chaldeans.*" Although the divine

law had forbidden them to make alliances with the nations, the divine sentence had made them submit to the king of Babylon. "It is therefore no disgrace to anyone to submit to him. Do not be afraid of consequences. If only you will live at peace, you will live; do not disrupt the government, and it will not disturb you. *Serve the king of Babylon, and it shall be well with you.*" Gedaliah—probably by instruction from the king of Babylon—undertook to act for them on all occasions (v. 10): "*As for me, behold, I will dwell at Mizpah, to serve the Chaldeans*, to represent you before the Babylonians in the name of the whole body if need be, to receive orders and pay them their tribute when they *come to us.*" Gedaliah gave them the assurance of an oath that he would protect them, but being charitable, he did not require an oath from them that they would be faithful to him; otherwise the trouble that followed could have been prevented. On the condition that they acknowledge that their land belonged to the Babylonians, they would freely enjoy the land and all the profits they gained from it (v. 10): "*Gather you wine and summer fruits* and take them for your own use; *put them in your vessels* (storage jars) to be stored for the winter, as do those who live in a land of peace and hope to *eat the labour of their hands.*" And so they *gathered wine and summer fruits very much*, because their grain harvest was over some time before Jerusalem was captured. Gedaliah left them to enjoy the advantages of the public abundance, and it appears that he demanded no tribute from them, for he did not seek his own profit, but the profit of many (1Co 10:33).

2. A dark cloud gathering over this infant state and threatening a dreadful storm. *Baalis the king of the Ammonites* hated Gedaliah and was planning to kill him, either out of malice toward the Jews or in personal anger against Gedaliah (v. 14). Some think Baalis was the queen mother of the king of the Ammonites, or queen dowager. One would have thought this little remnant might have been safe when the great king of Babylon protected it, but it was ruined by the plots of this petty prince or princess. Fortunate are those who have the King of kings on their side, for the greatest earthly king cannot with all his power keep us safe from treachery. Baalis employed *Ishmael, the son of Nethaniah*, as the instrument of his hatred, instigated him to murder Gedaliah, and, so that he might have a good opportunity, directed him to enlist among Gedaliah's subjects and promise to be loyal to him. Ishmael came from a royal family, and so he would be easily tempted to envy one who was set up as a governor in Judah but was not of David's line. Johanan, a brisk and active man, having gotten wind of this plot, told Gedaliah about it: "*Dost thou certainly know?* Surely you do" (v. 14). He gave Gedaliah private information about it (v. 15). He offered his service to prevent it: *I will slay* him. *Wherefore* (why) *should he slay thee?* Gedaliah, however, being a sincere man himself, would not at all believe the information given him. He said, *Thou speakest falsely of Ishmael.* Many have been ruined by being overconfident in the faithfulness of the people around them.

CHAPTER 41

A very tragic story is related in this chapter, a story showing that evil pursues sinners. The black cloud that gathered in the previous chapter breaks out in a terrible storm. Those few Jews who escaped the exile were proud to think that they were still in their own land, and they were self-confident under Gedaliah's protectorship. 1. Gedaliah was cruelly killed by Ishmael (vv. 1–2). 2.

All the Jews who were with him were also killed (v. 3), and a cistern was filled with their dead bodies (v. 9). 3. Eighty godly men, who were going toward Jerusalem, were drawn in by Ishmael and also murdered (vv. 4–7). Only ten of them escaped (v. 8). 4. Those who escaped the sword were taken prisoner by Ishmael and taken away to Ammonite country (v. 10). 5. By the leadership and courage of Johanan, the prisoners were recovered, and he now became their commander in chief (vv. 11–16). 6. His plan is to take them into Egypt (vv. 17–18).

Verses 1–10

Such evil, cruel, bloody work is undertaken here by men who by their birth should have been honorable and who by their religion should have been just, and all this was done to people of their own nation and their own religion, who were their brothers in affliction; and it was done for no offense and in cold blood.

1. Ishmael and his party treacherously killed Gedaliah himself in the first place. The king of Babylon had made him a great man and *governor of the land,* and God had made him a good man and a great blessing to his country, and he was used to bring, as it were, life from the dead; but neither his commission nor his goodness could protect him. Ishmael was of *the seed royal* (v. 1) and so was jealous of Gedaliah's increasing greatness. He had *ten men* with him who, like him, were *princes* (officers) *of the king,* and they were guided by the same corrupt resentments. These had put themselves under Gedaliah's protection (40:8), and now they came to him again, *and they did eat bread together in Mizpah.* Gedaliah welcomed them generously. They pretended to be friends and gave him no warning to stand on his guard. But those who *ate bread* with him *lifted up the heel* (Ps 41:9; Jn 13:18) against him. They watched for an opportunity when they were alone with him, and they assassinated him (v. 2).

2. They also killed all, both Jews and Babylonians, who were employed under Gedaliah. The vinedressers and the farmers were busy in the fields and knew nothing about this bloody massacre; it was so craftily concealed.

3. Some good, honest men who were going to mourn the desolations of Jerusalem were murdered with the others. They came (v. 5) *from Shechem, Samaria,* and *Shiloh,* places that had been famous but were now subdued. They were going to *the house of the Lord,* the temple at Jerusalem, to pay their respects to its ashes. They took *offerings and incense in their hand,* so that they might not be without something to offer. They showed their goodwill, even though the altar was gone. These went with *their clothes rent* and *their heads shaven.* As they approached, they were decoyed into a fatal snare by Ishmael's hatred. He hated these pilgrims for the sake of the mission they were on. Ishmael went out to meet them with crocodile tears, pretending to mourn the desolations of Jerusalem as much as they did and watching to see how they were disposed toward Gedaliah and his government. He encouraged them to come and found they had a respect for Gedaliah, which confirmed him in his resolution to murder them. *He said, Come to Gedaliah,* pretending he wanted them to come and live with him, when really he intended that they come and die with him (v. 6). When Ishmael had them *in the midst of the* town, he fell on them and *slew them* (v. 7). He took the dead bodies of these men and the others he had killed, and he threw them into a great *pit* (cistern) (v. 7), the same cistern that Asa king of Judah had dug long before when he built or fortified Mizpah (1Ki 15:22) *for fear of Baasha king of Israel* (v. 9), to be a frontier garrison against Baasha. Among these last who were doomed

to be killed were ten who obtained a pardon by working on the greed of those who had them at their mercy (v. 8). They *said to Ishmael, Slay us not, for we have treasures in the field,* country treasures, large stocks from the land, *wheat and barley, and oil and honey.* This bait proved effective; Ishmael saved them—not because he loved mercy, but because he loved money.

4. He took the people away as prisoners. *The king's daughters* and the poor people in the country, the vinedressers and farmers, who were committed to the responsibility Gedaliah gave them, were all taken away as prisoners toward the country of *the Ammonites* (v. 10). These prisoners thought, *Surely the bitterness of death,* and of captivity, *is past* (1Sa 15:32), but some died by the sword and others were taken into exile. Many ships are wrecked in the harbor (1Ki 22:48). We can never be sure of peace this side of heaven.

Verses 11–18

It would have been good if Johanan, when he told Gedaliah about Ishmael's plot of treason, had stayed with Gedaliah, for Johanan and his army officers and their forces could have been a bodyguard for Gedaliah, but it seems they were out on some expedition when they could have done their best service. Those who are inclined to wander are often unavailable when they are most needed. However, they finally heard about all the crimes Ishmael had committed (v. 11).

1. We sincerely wish Johanan could have taken revenge on the murderers, but he was successful only in rescuing the captives. He gathered what forces he could *and went to fight with Ishmael* (v. 12). He pursued him and overtook him by the great *pool of Gibeon,* which we read about in 2Sa 2:13. And when he appeared with such force, Ishmael's heart failed him, and he dared not stand his ground. The poor captives *were glad when they saw Johanan* and *the captains that were with him,* seeing them as their rescuers (v. 13), and they found a way to turn around and come over to them (v. 14). Ishmael did not try to detain them; he left his spoils to save his life and *escaped with eight men* (v. 15). It seems that two of his ten men, who were his brigands or assassins (spoken of in v. 1), deserted him. He made his way to the Ammonites, and we hear no more about him.

2. We sincerely wish that Johanan, when he had rescued the captives, had sat down quietly with them and ruled them peaceably, as Gedaliah did. Instead he wanted to lead them into Egypt. This resolution was very rash; nothing was enough for him except to *go to enter into Egypt* (v. 17), and in order to do that, he had them encamp for a time *in the habitation of Chimham, by Bethlehem,* David's city. Johanan made his headquarters here, steering his course toward Egypt, either from a personal affection for that country or an ancient national confidence in the Egyptians (Nu 14:3; 2Ki 18:21). Some of the *mighty men of war,* it seems, had escaped; he took them with him as well as *the women and children whom he had recovered from Ishmael.*

CHAPTER 42

Because Johanan and the officers were set on going to Egypt, advised to do so either by their affections or by their politics, they had a great desire that God would direct them to do so too—like Balaam, who, when he was determined to go and curse Israel, asked God's permission. Here is: 1. The arrangement that was made between Jeremiah and them about consulting God in this matter (vv. 1–6). 2. The message that God sent them, in which: 2.1. They were commanded to remain in the land of Judah and assured that if they did so, things would go well with them (vv. 7–12). 2.2. They were forbidden to go to Egypt and told that if they did, it would be their ruin (vv. 13–18). 2.3. They were accused of making a fatal mistake in asking what God's will was and disobeying God when they were told what his will was; and accordingly, sentence is passed on them (vv. 19–22).

Verses 1–6

Jeremiah the prophet escaped Ishmael's sword, and it was not the first time the Lord hid him. Now, finally, when he is needed, Jeremiah is sought out, and *all the captains,* including Johanan himself, *with all the people from the least to the greatest,* pay him a visit. They *came near* (v. 1). Up to this time they have kept their distance from the prophet and been reluctant to consult him.

1. They want him to pray and ask direction from God about what they should do at this present critical point (vv. 2–3). They express themselves with great respect for the prophet. Although he is poor and lowly, they still turn to him with humility as petitioners seeking his help: *Let, we beseech thee, our supplication be accepted before thee* (v. 2). They compliment him in the hope of persuading him to say what they want him to say. "*Pray for us,* because we do not know how to pray for ourselves. *Pray to the Lord thy God,* for we are unworthy to call him ours, nor do we have any reason to expect any favor from him." They speak of themselves as objects of compassion: "*We are but a remnant, but a few of many*; such a remnant will be easily swallowed up. *Thy eyes* see what distress we are in; if you can do anything, do help us (Mk 9:22). *Let the Lord thy God* think about the ruin we face and *show us the way wherein we may walk,* so that we may expect to have his presence with us, *and the thing that we may do,* the course of action we may take for our own safety" (v. 3).

2. Jeremiah faithfully promises he will pray for guidance for them and that, whatever message God sends them through him, he will communicate it to them just as he received it (1Co 11:23; 15:3). Although they have shown him disrespect, yet, like Samuel when he was dishonored, he will not *sin against the Lord in ceasing to pray for* them (1Sa 12:23). He will *declare to them the whole counsel of God* (Ac 20:27), so that they may show that they have been faithful to their trust.

3. They promise that they will be directed by the will of God as soon as they know what it is (vv. 5–6). They now call God *their* God, for Jeremiah has encouraged them to do this (v. 4): *I will pray to the Lord your God.* They promise to *obey his voice* because they sent the prophet to him to consult him. They will do what God appoints them to do, *whether it be good* (favorable) *or whether it be evil* (unfavorable): "Although it may seem unfavorable to us, we still believe that if God commands something, it is certainly good, and we must not dispute it, but do it. Whatever God commands, whether it is easy or difficult, if it is our duty, we will do it."

Verses 7–22

We have here the answer Jeremiah was sent to speak to those who asked him to seek direction from God.

1. It did not come till *ten days after* (v. 7). They were kept this long in suspense, perhaps, to punish them for their hypocrisy or to show that Jeremiah did not speak from himself, but had to wait for instructions. *The vision is for an appointed time, and at the end it shall speak* (Hab 2:3).

2. When it did come, he spoke it publicly, both to the *captains* (officers) and to all the *people,* fully and faithfully, just as he received it. What he had to advise, however, was what *the Lord the God of Israel said,* to whom they had sent him.

2.1. It is the will of God that they should stay where they are, and his promise is that if they do so, it will be *well with them* (v. 10). Their brothers and sisters were forced out of it into exile; let them therefore count it a mercy that they may stay in their land and count it a duty that they must stay there. God expresses a very tender concern for them in their disastrous condition: *It repenteth me of the evil* (I am grieved over the disaster) *that I have done unto you.* It was not that God changed his mind, but he was very ready to change his ways and to return in mercy to them. He answers the argument they have against remaining in the land. *They fear the king of Babylon* (41:18), that he might come and avenge the death of Gedaliah on them, though they were not in any way an accessory to it. "*Be not afraid of the king of Babylon,* for that fear will become a trap. Do not fear, for *I am with you,* and if God is for you to save you, who can be against you to harm you?" (Ro 8:31). He assures them that if they will remain in this land, they will not only be safe from the king of Babylon but also be made happy by the King of kings: "*I will build you and plant you* (42:10); you will put down your roots again and become the new foundation of another state, a kingdom that rises up out of the ashes of the previous one." God will show them mercy in that the king of Babylon not only will not destroy them but also will *have mercy upon them* and help them settle down again. God has made our duty what is really our privilege, and our obedience will be its own reward.

2.2. They must by no means think of going to Egypt, of all places — not to the land from which God rescued their ancestors and with which he has so often warned them not to make an alliance (Dt 17:16; Isa 30:2–3; 31:1). "You begin to say, *We will not dwell in this land* (v. 13), not even if God himself undertakes to protect us. We will *go into the land of Egypt,* and *there will we dwell,* whether God gives us permission and goes along with us or not" (v. 14). It is supposed that their hearts are set on it: "*If you wholly set your faces* (are determined) *to enter into Egypt,* then you must accept what follows." Now the reason for their resolution is that "*in Egypt we shall see no war, nor have hunger of bread,* as we have had for a long time in this land" (v. 14). The sentence passed on them for this sin, if they will persist in it, is declared in God's name (v. 15): "*Hear the word of the Lord, you remnant of Judah,* who think that because you are a remnant you must of course be spared" (v. 2). Do the sword and famine frighten them? Those very judgments will follow them into Egypt and overcome them there (vv. 16–17): "*You* think that just because war and famine have raged for a long time in this land, they are its inheritance. The reality, however, is that if you trust in God, he can turn even this land into a land of peace for you." Those people who go to Egypt against God's will to escape *the sword and famine* will *die in Egypt by sword and famine.* Does the devastation of Jerusalem frighten them? Do they want to get as far as they can from it? They will meet with the second part of that in Egypt too (v. 18). When God's professing people associate closely with unbelievers and seek their favor, they lose their honor and disgrace themselves.

2.3. God knows their hypocrisy in their inquiries of him, and that when they asked what he wanted them to do, they were determined to go their own way. The prophet solemnly declares he has faithfully spoken God's message (v. 19). The conclusion of the whole matter (Ecc 12:13) is, *"Go not down into Egypt.* You are disobeying the command of God if you go. I have plainly *admonished you*; you cannot now plead ignorance of God's mind." He accuses them of deception in the petition they made to him for divine direction (v. 20). *"You dissembled* (erred) *in your hearts*; you professed one thing but meant another, promising what you never meant to fulfill." "You have used deceit against your souls," as the margin reads. *Know certainly that you shall die by the sword* (v. 22). God's threats may be reviled, but cannot be canceled, by human unbelief.

CHAPTER 43

Jeremiah had faithfully spoken out his message from God. In this chapter we read about: 1. The people's contempt for this message; they denied it to be the word of God (vv. 1–3). Into Egypt they went, taking Jeremiah himself along with them (vv. 4–7). 2. God's pursuit of them with another message, foretelling the king of Babylon's pursuit of them to Egypt (vv. 8–13).

Verses 1–7

What God said to the builders of Babel may be truly said about this people: *Now nothing will be restrained from them which they have imagined to do* (Ge 11:6). Their desire is to go to Egypt, and to Egypt they will go, whatever God himself says. Jeremiah made them listen to everything he had to say. It was what the Lord their God had sent him to say to them, and it all must be said to them. Now let us see their response:

1. They deny it to be a message from God: *Johanan, and all the proud men, said to Jeremiah, Thou speakest falsely* (v. 2).

1.1. The cause of their disobedience was pride. Those who accused Jeremiah of lying were *proud* and arrogant men. They could not bear to have their ideas contradicted or their plans restrained—no, not even by God's wisdom and will. Either they were not convinced that what had been said had come from God or, though convinced of it, they would not acknowledge it.

1.2. The pretext for their disobedience was that *"the Lord hath not sent thee* on this mission to us." Had they not consulted Jeremiah as a prophet? Had he not waited to receive instructions from God on what to say to them? And had not God proved him a true prophet? They had some good thoughts about Jeremiah himself, but, they suggested (v. 3), *Baruch sets thee on* (is inciting you) *against us.* If Jeremiah and he had been so well disposed to the Babylonians, they would have gone away with Nebuzaradan to Babylon and not have stayed to share their lot with this despised and ungrateful remnant. If Baruch, on the other hand, had been so ill disposed toward his compatriots, could they think Jeremiah would be so influenced by him as to use God's name as an authority to support such an evil purpose?

2. They determine to go to Egypt nevertheless. They decide not to *dwell in the land of Judah*, as God ordered them to (v. 4), but to go as one to Egypt. Those who came *from all the nations whither they had been driven, to dwell in the land of Judah*, out of a sincere affection for that land, will not be left to choose freely, but are forced to go with Johanan's party to Egypt (v. 5), *men, women, and children* (v. 6). These proud and arrogant men compel even Jeremiah the prophet and Baruch his scribe to go along with them to Egypt. They *came to Tahpanhes*, a

famous city in Egypt named in honor of one of its queens (1Ki 11:19). Pharaoh's house was there (v. 9). If they had had the spirit of Israelites, they would have chosen to live in the desert of Judah rather than in the grandest, most well-populated cities of Egypt.

Verses 8–13

Here, as also in the next chapter, Jeremiah is prophesying in Egypt. Jeremiah was now in Tahpanhes, among idolatrous Egyptians and treacherous Israelites, but there he received *the word of the Lord*; it *came to him* (v. 8). God can find his people, when he comes by his grace, wherever they are. The spirit of prophecy was not restricted to the land of Israel. When Jeremiah was taken to Egypt by force, God did not withdraw his usual favor from him. He passed on to the people what he received from the Lord (1Co 11:23; 15:3). Jeremiah was appointed and entrusted to speak these two messages when he was in Egypt, one in this chapter, relating to Egypt and foretelling its destruction, and the other in the next chapter, about the Jews in Egypt. God had told them that if they went into Egypt, the sword would follow them; here he told them also that the sword of Nebuchadnezzar would follow them.

1. This is foretold by a sign. Jeremiah must take *great stones* and *lay them in the clay of the* furnace, or *brickkiln*, which is *at the entry to*—that is, "in the open way to" or "beside the way that leads to"—*Pharaoh's house* (v. 9). Egypt was famous for its brick kilns, but the foundation of Egypt's desolation was now put in those brickkilns, in *that clay*. Jeremiah must do this *in the sight of the men of Judah* to whom he was sent, so that because he did not prevent them from going to Egypt, he might bring them to repent of their having gone.

2. It is foretold:

2.1. That the present king of Babylon, Nebuchadnezzar, would come in person against the land of Egypt and would *set his throne* in the very place where *these stones* were laid (v. 10). This detail was foretold especially so that when it was fulfilled, the Jews could be confirmed in their belief in the certainty of God's foreknowledge, in which even the smallest events are established. God called Nebuchadnezzar his servant because he carried out God's will in this matter.

2.2. That he would destroy many Egyptians and have them all at his mercy (v. 11): *He shall smite* (attack) *the land of Egypt*; he would kill whomever he wanted to. And those whom he wanted to save he would save and take into *captivity*.

2.3. That the king of Babylon would destroy the idols of Egypt, the temples and the idols of their gods (v. 12): *He shall burn the houses of the gods of Egypt. Beth-shemesh*, or "the house of the sun," was so named from a temple built there to the sun. He would *break in pieces* the statues (v. 13). The king of Babylon himself was a great idolater and had his temples and idols in honor of the sun, but he was employed to destroy the idols of Egypt.

2.4. That he would make himself master of the land. *He shall array himself with the rich spoils of the land of Egypt.* He would array himself with them as ornaments and as armor, and though it would be heavy booty, he would slip it on with as much ease *as a shepherd slips on his garment* when he goes to turn out his sheep in a morning. He would make no more of the spoils of the land of Egypt than of a shepherd's coat. He would *go forth in peace*, unharmed; the land of Egypt would be so powerfully subdued. This destruction of Egypt by the king of Babylon is foretold in Eze 29:19; 30:10.

CHAPTER 44

Here: 1. Jeremiah preaches a rousing sermon to the Jews in Egypt to rebuke them for their idolatry (vv. 1–14). 2. The people respond to this warning with contempt and express their determination to persist in their idolatry despite what God and Jeremiah said (vv. 15–19). 3. Sentence is passed on them: they will all—except a very small number—be destroyed and perish in Egypt, and, as a sign of this, the king of Egypt will soon fall into the hands of the king of Babylon and be unable to protect them any longer (vv. 20–30).

Verses 1–14

The Jews in Egypt had now dispersed to various parts of the country, into *Migdol, Noph*, and other places, and Jeremiah was sent on a mission from God to them (v. 15).

1. God reminds them of the devastation of Judah and Jerusalem, which the fugitives in the cities of Egypt seem to have forgotten (v. 2): *"You have seen* what a deplorable condition Judah and Jerusalem have been reduced to; now will you consider where such devastation came from? It came from the wrath of God; it was his anger that made Jerusalem and *the cities of Judah waste and desolate"* (v. 6).

2. God reminds them of the sins that brought this devastation on Judah and Jerusalem. It was because of *their wickedness* (v. 3), giving to false deities the honor that they should have given only to the true God. They abandoned the God who was known among them: *"Neither they nor you nor your fathers* could give any rational reason why worship of *the God of Israel* was exchanged for worshiping such impostors."

3. God reminds them of the frequent and fair warnings he gave them by his word not to serve other gods (v. 4). *The prophets* were sent with a great deal of care to call out to them, saying, *Oh! do not this abominable thing that I hate.* We should warn one another of the dangers of sin: "Oh! *do not* do it. If you love God, do not commit sin, for it is offensive to him. If you love your own selves, avoid sin, for it will destroy you." If God hates it, you too should hate it. But *"they hearkened not* (did not listen), *nor inclined their ear* (v. 5). This was intended as a warning for you, who have not only heard the judgments of God's mouth, as they did, but also seen the judgments of his hand."

4. He rebukes them for their continued idolatry (v. 8): *You burn incense to other gods in the land of Egypt.* Those who went against God's will to Egypt became more wedded than ever to their idolatry. When we push ourselves into places of temptation, God is just to leave us on our own to do as we wish. They caused a great deal of harm to themselves and their families: *"You commit this great evil against your souls"* (v. 7). "It is the sure way to *cut yourselves off* from every encouragement and hope (v. 8), to destroy your name and honor. The result will be that by your sin and your misery, you will become an object of cursing and a reproach among all the nations." They filled up the container of sins that their ancestors had been filling (Mt 23:32), and they even added more to it (v. 9): "*Have you forgotten the wickedness* of those who have gone before you?" "Have you forgotten the punishments of your fathers?" is how some read it. He reminds them of the sins and punishments *of the kings of Judah, the wickedness of their wives*, who had persuaded them to lapse into idolatry. In the original it reads, "and of his wives," which, according to Dr. Lightfoot, tacitly reflects

on Solomon's wives, particularly his Egyptian wives. *"Have you forgotten your own wickedness and the wickedness of your wives*, when you lived prosperous lives in Jerusalem, and what ruin it brought on you?"

5. He threatens their complete destruction for persisting in their idolatry now that they were in Egypt. They will perish in Egypt. Those who think they can not only affront God Almighty but also confront him will find themselves shamed to silence. They will not be ravaged by natural deaths, as Israel was in the desert, but by harsh judgments. No one, except a very few who will narrowly escape, will ever *return to the land of Judah* (v. 14). Those who are perverse and discontented will be uneasy and want to move no matter where they are. When the Israelites were in the land of Judah, they wanted to go to Egypt (42:22), but when they were in Egypt, they wanted to *return to the land of Judah*; they "lifted up their soul" to it (v. 14, margin), which shows a fervent desire.

Verses 15–19

We have here the people's stubborn refusal to submit to the power of the word of God through the mouth of Jeremiah.

1. The people who defied God and his judgments were those who knew either themselves or their wives to be guilty of the idolatry Jeremiah had rebuked them of (v. 15). The women had been more guilty of idolatry and superstition than the men. This was not because the men were closer to the true God, but because they were generally unbelievers, who wanted no God and no religious faith at all, and so could easily allow their wives to follow a false religion. It was consciousness of their guilt that made them impatient with being rebuked: *They knew that their wives had burnt incense to other gods* and that they had supported them in it, *and the women that stood by* knew that they had joined them in idolatrous customs. When Jeremiah spoke, his message touched them at a sensitive spot.

2. The reply these people gave to Jeremiah, and through him to God himself, was in effect, *Depart from us; we desire not the knowledge of thy ways* (Job 21:14).

2.1. They declared they were determined not to do as God commanded them, but only what they themselves wanted to do. They wanted to worship the moon, here called *the queen of heaven*. Some understand this to refer to the sun, which was worshiped a great deal in Egypt (43:13) and had been at Jerusalem (2Ki 23:11). Others understand it to refer to all the starry host, that is, all the heavenly bodies. These arrogant sinners did not now go about making excuses for refusing to obey, nor did they suggest that Jeremiah spoke from himself and not from God, as they had before (43:2). "Nevertheless," they told him roundly, *"We will not hearken* (listen) *unto thee*; we will do what is forbidden and run the risk of incurring any threats." Those who live in disobedience to God commonly become worse and worse (2Ti 3:13), and their hearts are increasingly hardened by the *deceitfulness of sin* (Heb 3:13). These Jews expressed the thoughts of many people. It is what young people want *in the days of their youth*; they want to do everything they have a mind to (Ecc 11:9).

2.2. They gave a variety of reasons to support their determination.

2.2.1. They pleaded many of the things that Roman Catholics plead as the marks of a true church. They pleaded antiquity: "we are determined *to burn incense to the queen of heaven*, for *our fathers* did so" (v. 17). They pleaded authority. Those who had power practiced it themselves and passed it on to others: "*Our kings and our princes*, whom God set over us and who were descended from David, did these things." They pleaded unity. "We are all of one mind. We who are *a great multitude* (v. 15), we did it." They pleaded universality: It was done *in the cities of Judah*. They pleaded visibility: it was not done only in dark and shady groves, but also *in the streets*, openly. They pleaded that it was the practice of the first church: it had been done in *Jerusalem*. They pleaded prosperity: "*Then had we plenty of* bread *and* of all good things; we *were well and saw no evil.*" But even if we suppose all these reasons to be true, this does not excuse them from idolatry. The law of God remains what we must be judged by, not human practice.

2.2.2. They suggested that the judgments they had been under were brought on them for *leaving off to burn incense to the queen of heaven* (v. 18). This also happened when Christianity first began, when God rebuked the nations with public adversities for opposing Christians and persecuting them. These calamities were misinterpreted, and it was suggested they were punishments for ignoring and tolerating Christians; people therefore cried out, "Throw the Christians to the lions."

2.2.3. They pleaded that although the women were most active in their idolatry, they still did it with the approval of their husbands; the women were busy *making cakes* for grain offerings *to the queen of heaven* and preparing *and pouring out the drink offerings* (v. 19). "But *did we* do it *without our husbands?* No, the men took the lead; they taught us." Some understand this question as spoken by the husbands (v. 15), who pleaded that they did not do it *without their men*, that is, without their elders and rulers; but because the making of the *cakes* and pouring out of *the drink offerings* are explicitly spoken of as being the work of women (7:18), it seems rather to be understood as the women's plea.

Verses 20–30

Prophets may be oppressed, but God cannot be; in fact, here the prophet refused to be.

1. Jeremiah has something to say to them from himself. They said that these miseries came on them because they had now *left off burning incense to the queen of heaven*. "No," Jeremiah says, "it was because you had done it before, not because you stopped doing it now." The incense that they and their ancestors had burned to other gods did indeed go unpunished for a long time, for God was patient, and while he was patient with them things went perhaps, as they said, *well with them, and* they *saw no evil*. However, finally they became so offensive *that the Lord could no longer bear* their evil actions (v. 22), and then some of them reformed their ways slightly. But because their old corrupt inclinations were still the same, God remembered against them the idolatry of *their fathers, their kings, and their princes, in the streets of Jerusalem*, which they gloried in (v. 21). They were held responsible for all the *abominations which they had committed*, and that is why *their land is a desolation and a curse, as at this day* (v. 22). It was because of their former disobedience that all *this evil happened to them, as at this day* (v. 23).

2. Jeremiah has something to say to them, especially *to the women*, from *the Lord of hosts, the God of Israel*. They have given their answer; now let them listen to God's reply (v. 24).

2.1. Since they are fully determined to persist in their idolatry, he will continue to punish them. God repeats what he said (v. 25): "*You and your wives* are agreed

in your stubbornness; *you have spoken with your mouths and fulfilled with your hands*. You have said, *We will surely perform our vows that we have vowed, to burn incense to the queen of heaven*," as if even though it was a sin, simply vowing to do it was sufficient to justify them in doing it. The reality, however, is that no one can by vowing make something lawful to themselves, much less their duty, when the act they vow to commit has already been declared by God to be sinful.

2.1.1. He has sworn that what little remains of religious faith there are among them will be lost (v. 26). Although they have joined with the Egyptians in their idolatry, they still continue to invoke the name of Jehovah, particularly in their solemn oaths. They say, *Jehovah liveth*, he is the *living God*: this is what they acknowledge him to be. Even though they worship dead idols, they swear, *The Lord liveth* (5:2). But God declares that his *name shall no more be* so *named* by *any man of Judah in all the land of Egypt*. Those whom God has so far left to themselves that they have completely forgotten their religious faith are very miserable.

2.1.2. He has sworn that what little remnant of people there is will all be destroyed (v. 27): *I will watch over them for evil*. Those whom God finds to be impenitent sinners he will act toward as an unyielding Judge. They say that they will recover when they return to worship *the queen of heaven*; God says they will ruin themselves.

2.2. He tells them that few of them will *escape the sword* and *return into the land of Judah, a small number* (v. 28) in comparison with the great numbers who will return from the land of the Babylonians.

2.3. He gives them a sign that all these threats will be fulfilled in Egypt. *Pharaoh-hophra*, the present *king of Egypt*, will be delivered *into the hands of his enemies that seek his life* (v. 30)—"the hands of his own rebellious subjects" under Amasis, who usurped his throne, according to some; *the hand of Nebuchadnezzar king of Babylon*, who invaded his kingdom, according to others; the former is related by Herodotus, the latter by Josephus. The Jews expected more from Pharaoh than from Zedekiah king of Judah; he was a more powerful ruler. "But," God says, "*I will give him into the hand of his enemies*, as I gave Zedekiah."

CHAPTER 45

The prophecy in this chapter concerns only Baruch. It comes after the story of the destruction of Jerusalem and the dispersion of the Jews, but it was spoken long before, in the fourth year of Jehoiakim. We find here: 1. How Baruch was terrified when he fell into trouble for writing and reading Jeremiah's scroll (vv. 1–3). 2. How his fears were restrained and silenced with a promise of special preservation (vv. 4–5).

Verses 1–5

Baruch was employed in writing Jeremiah's prophecies and reading them, and he was threatened for doing so by the king. He escaped under divine protection. This chapter should have been added to that story, but because it refers to a private individual, it is put here toward the end of the book. Notice:

1. The dismay poor Baruch felt when he was sought by the king's messengers, and the notice that God took of him. He was a young man, willing to serve God and his prophet. But when he found that it exposed him to contempt, he cried out, "I am in despair; I will fall into the pursuers' hands, be imprisoned, put to death, or banished:

The Lord has added grief to my sorrow (v. 3). After the grief of writing and reading the prophecies of my country's destruction, I now have the sorrow of being treated as a criminal for so doing. It is a burden that is too heavy for me. I *fainted in my sighing, and I find no rest.*" Young disciples in religious faith tend to be discouraged by the small difficulties they face when they begin to serve God. They merely *run with the footmen*, and it *wearies them* (12:5); they *faint* at the very dawn of *the day of adversity*, and it shows that *their strength is small* (Pr 24:10) and their faith is weak. Baruch should have been glad that he was counted worthy to suffer for such a good cause (Ac 5:41) and with such good company, but instead he reflected badly on his God, as if God were dealing harshly with him.

2. Jeremiah was troubled to see him so agitated and did not know what to say to him. He was reluctant to scold him, but he thought he deserved it; he was willing to encourage him, but he did not know how to go about it. God told him, however, what he must *say to him* (v. 4). We are too fond of the good things of this present age, and that makes us impatient when difficulties come. God showed Baruch that he was foolishly to blame in desiring an abundance of the wealth and honor of this world. The ship was sinking; ruin was coming on the Jewish nation: "*That which I have built*, to be a house for myself, *I am breaking down, and that which I have planted*, to be a vineyard for myself, *I am plucking up, even this whole land* (v. 4), the Jewish church and state; dost thou now *seek great things for thyself* (v. 5)? Do you expect to be rich, honorable, and important? Can you expect to receive great things when everyone has been brought low?"

3. God gave him hope that although he would not be great, he would still be secure: "*I will bring evil upon all flesh*, all nations, *but thy life will I give to thee for a prey*, I will let you escape with your life, *in all places whither thou goest.* You must be rushed about from one place to another and be in danger, but you will escape with your life, though often only barely. You will have your life, but it will be like *a prey*, booty, a prize of war, gained with much difficulty and danger; you will be saved as by fire" (1Co 3:15).

CHAPTER 46

Judgment began with the house of God (1Pe 4:17), but it did not end there. In this and the following chapters we have prophecies of the devastation of the neighboring nations, brought on them mostly by the king of Babylon, until Babylon itself finally came to be judged. The prophecy against Egypt is put first: 1. A prophecy of the defeat of Pharaoh Neco's army by the Babylonian forces at Carchemish (vv. 1–12). 2. A prophecy of the attack Nebuchadnezzar would mount on the land of Egypt, which was fulfilled some years after the destruction of Jerusalem (vv. 13–26). 3. A word of encouragement to the Israel of God in the midst of those disasters (vv. 27–28).

Verses 1–12

The first verse is the title of the part of this book that relates to the neighboring nations. It is *the word of the Lord which came to Jeremiah against the Gentiles* (nations). In the Old Testament we have *the word of the Lord* against *the Gentiles*; in the New Testament we have *the word of the Lord* for *the Gentiles*, for those who were *afar off are made nigh* (Eph 2:13).

Jeremiah begins with Egypt, because they have long been Israel's oppressors and more recently their deceivers. In these verses he foretells the overthrow of *the army of Pharaoh-necho* by Nebuchadnezzar *in the fourth year of Jehoiakim* (v. 2). This defeat (as we find in 2Ki 24:7) made Neco pay dearly for his expedition against the king of Assyria four years before, in which he killed Josiah (2Ki 23:29). This event is prophesied here in noble expressions of triumph over Egypt's defeat, which Jeremiah would speak of with pleasure, because the death of Josiah was now avenged on Pharaoh Neco.

1. The Egyptians are rebuked for the great preparations they made for this expedition, in which the prophet challenges them to do their utmost: "Come then, *order the buckler*, prepare your shields; let the weapons of war be gotten ready" (v. 3). Egypt was famous for *horses*—let them be *harnessed*, and let the cavalry be mounted: *Get up, you horsemen, and stand forth* (v. 4). He compares this expedition to the rising of their Nile River (vv. 7–8): *Egypt* now *rises up like a flood*, threatening to overflow over all the neighboring lands. It is a formidable army. The prophet calls them (v. 9): *Come up* (charge), *you horses; rage* (drive furiously), *you chariots.* He challenges them to bring all their allied troops together: *the Ethiopians*, who descended from the same stock as the Egyptians (Ge 10:6) and were their neighbors and allies, and *the Libyans and Lydians*, both in Africa, to the west of Egypt, from whom the Egyptians drew their auxiliary forces. It will all be futile; they will be shamefully defeated, for God will fight against them (Pr 21:30–31).

2. They are rebuked for the great expectations they have of this expedition. They know their own thoughts, and God knows them, *but they know not the thoughts of the Lord, for he gathers them as sheaves into the floor* (Mic 4:11–12). Egypt says (v. 8), "*I will go up; I will cover the earth*, and no one *shall hinder me; I will destroy the city*, whatever city stands in my way. Like Pharaoh in former times, *I will pursue, I will overtake*" (Ex 15:9). But God says that it will be his day: *This is the day of the Lord God of hosts* (v. 10), on which he will be exalted in defeating the Egyptians.

3. They are rebuked for their cowardice (vv. 5–6): "*Wherefore* (Why) *have I seen them*, despite all these great and vast preparations, *dismayed* (terrified) *and turned back*, with no spirit left in them, when the Babylonian army faces them?" Even *their mighty ones*, whom one would have expected to stand their ground, withdraw and flee together in confusion. They have neither the time nor the courage to *look back; fear is round about* them (v. 5). They cannot make their escape. *They shall stumble* in their flight *and fall toward the north*, toward enemy country, for they were so confused that instead of going homeward, they went onward.

4. They are rebuked for their inability ever to recover from this blow (vv. 11–12). The maiden, *the daughter of Egypt*, who lived in a state of great show, is severely wounded by this defeat. Let her now look for *balm in Gilead*; let her use all the medicines her wise men can prescribe to repair the loss sustained by this defeat. It will all be futile, however; "no cure shall be to them"; they will never be able to bring such a powerful army onto the battlefield again. "*The nations* who sounded out your glory and strength *have* now *heard of thy shame*, how shamefully you were defeated and how you have been weakened by it." *Thy cry hath filled* the surrounding country: they were in such confusion.

Verses 13–28

In these verses we have:

1. Confusion and terror spoken to Egypt. The fulfillment of the prediction in the first part of the chapter prevented the Egyptians from trying to attack any other nation, but they still remained strong at home, and none of their neighbors dared attack them. The theme of the prophecy here is to show *how the king of Babylon would soon come and smite* (attack) *the land of Egypt* (v. 13). This was fulfilled by the same hand as fulfilled the earlier prophecy, Nebuchadnezzar's, but many years later.

1.1. The alarm of war is sounded in Egypt (v. 14). The enemy is approaching, *the sword is devouring round about* in the neighboring countries, and it is time for the Egyptians to prepare to face the enemy. This must be declared in every part of Egypt, especially in Migdol, Memphis (*Noph*), and Tahpanhes, because in these places the Jewish refugees had settled, in contempt of God's command (43:4, 7; 44:1). Let them find out what a poor shelter Egypt is likely to prove to be for them.

1.2. The retreat of the forces of other nations that the Egyptians had in their pay is prophesied here. It is spoken of in the past tense, as if it had already taken place. When the prophecy was fulfilled, some were positioned at the borders to guard them, where they were beaten off by the invaders and put to flight. The *valiant men* (warriors) were then *swept away* (v. 15) as with *a sweeping rain*—it is the same word that is used in Pr 28:3. None of them could stand their ground, *because the Lord drove them* from their positions; he drove them away by enabling the Babylonians to subdue them. If it was God's will, they would be caused to *fall upon one another, every man's sword against his fellow. Her hired men*, the mercenaries that Egypt had in its service, were truly *in the midst of her like fatted bullocks* (fattened calves) (v. 21), strong, ablebodied warriors, ready to be strong against the enemy, but *they were turned back*; and, instead of fighting, they *fled away together*. They all went homeward toward their own country (v. 16): *They said, "Arise, and let us go again to our own people*, safe *from the oppressing sword* of the Babylonians, which is defeating everything and everyone in its path." In times of crisis, little confidence is to be put in mercenaries, who fight purely for pay. They spoke out vehemently against Pharaoh, whose bad management was the probable cause of their defeat. When he positioned them on the borders of his country, he probably told them he would come himself with a bold army to support them, but he failed them. It is hardly surprising that they deserted, crying out, *Pharaoh king of Egypt is but a* (is only a loud) *noise. He has passed the time appointed* (v. 17); he did not keep his word.

1.3. The formidable power of the Babylonian army is described as defeating all in its path. *The King* of kings, *whose name is the Lord of hosts*, has said it: *As I live, saith* this *King, as Tabor* is higher than *the mountains and Carmel* overlooks *the sea, so shall* the king of Babylon overcome all the forces of Egypt (v. 18). He and his *army shall come against* Egypt *with axes, as hewers of wood* (v. 22), and the Egyptians will be no more able to resist them than a tree can resist a woodcutter who comes with an ax to *cut it down*.

1.4. The devastation of Egypt is prophesied, the desolation of that rich country. *Egypt is* now *like a very fair heifer*, or calf (v. 20), fat and shining, not used to the discipline of submission, and inclined to stray like a wellfed heifer. Some consider this an allusion to Apis, the bull or calf that the Egyptians worshiped, from whom

the children of Israel learned to worship the golden calf. Egypt is as beautiful as a goddess, *but destruction comes*; "cutting up comes," as some read it; "a gadfly is coming," according to others. *It comes out of the north*; the Babylonian soldiers will come from there to kill and cut up this *fair heifer. The daughters of Egypt shall be confounded* (v. 24); they will be put to shame. *Their voice shall go like a serpent*, that is, it will be very low and submissive. They will not dare make loud complaints about the cruelty of the conquerors, but will express their grief in silent murmurs. They will not now answer roughly, but, with *the poor, use entreaties* and beg for their lives. They will be taken away as prisoners into enemy country (v. 19): "*O thou daughter! dwelling securely and finely in Egypt, furnish thyself* (pack your belongings) *to go into captivity.* Instead of rich clothes, which will only tempt the enemy to strip you, wear plain and warm clothes; get used to hardship, so that you may bear it better." The Egyptians must prepare to flee, for their cities will be evacuated. Memphis (*Noph*) particularly *shall be desolate, without an inhabitant. The multitude of No shall be punished*: it is called *populous No* (Na 3:8). *Though hand join in hand* (Pr 11:21; 16:5), they will not escape; nor can anyone think they can disappear with the crowd. Pharaoh will be defeated, and so will *all those that trust in him* (v. 25), especially the Jews who came to stay in his country, trusting in him rather than God. All these will be *delivered into the hands of the northern nations* (v. 24).

1.5. An indication is given that in due time Egypt will recover (v. 26): *Afterward it shall be inhabited.*

2. Encouragement and peace spoken to the Israel of God (vv. 27–28). This may refer to the exiles in Babylon, whom God had mercy in store for, or, more generally, to all the people of God, to encourage them in the most difficult times, when the judgments of God are coming on the nations. Let evildoers on earth tremble, *but fear not thou, O my servant Jacob! And be not dismayed, O Israel!* And again: *Fear thou not, O Jacob!* God does not want his people to be a fearful people. God's people will be found and gathered together even though they are far away. Evildoers are *like the troubled sea when it cannot rest* (Isa 57:20); they *flee when none pursues* (Lev 26:17, 36, 37). But because Jacob is at home in God, he *shall be at rest and at ease, and none shall make him afraid* (v. 27), for *what time he is afraid*, he has a *God to trust to* (Ps 56:3). Nations come to an end, but the Gospel church, God's spiritual Israel, still continues, and will continue until the end of time.

CHAPTER 47

This chapter concerns the destruction of the Philistines, as the previous chapter concerned that of the Egyptians, and both come from the same hand, that of Nebuchadnezzar. It is short but terrible, and it includes Tyre and Sidon, which will share with the Philistines in the destruction. It is foretold: 1. That forces will come from the north (vv. 1–5). 2. That the war will continue for a long time, and the Philistines' attempts to end it will be futile (vv. 6–7).

Verses 1–7

Just as the Egyptians had often proved false friends to the Israel of God, so the Philistines had always been sworn enemies, and they had been all the more dangerous because they were such close neighbors. They were humbled in David's time, but it seems they had become significant again and remained so until Nebuchadnezzar destroyed them with their neighbors, which is the event foretold here. The date of this prophecy was *before Pharaoh attacked Gaza.* It is uncertain when this attack on Gaza from the king of Egypt happened, but this word of the Lord came to Jeremiah against the Philistines when they were in no danger from any enemy, and Jeremiah still foretold their ruin. It is foretold here:

1. That a foreign enemy will attack them: *Waters rise up out of the north* (v. 2). Now a terrible storm comes from that cold climate. The Babylonian army will flood the land like a deluge.

2. That they will all be in a state of fear about it. The people will have no heart to fight: *All the inhabitants of the land shall howl,* so that nothing but mourning will be heard everywhere. Before it comes to the slaughter, the very *stamping of the horses* and *rattling of the chariots* will strike them with such terror that parents will seem devoid of natural affection, *for they shall not look back to their children* (v. 3) to provide for their safety.

3. That the country of the Philistines will be plundered and devastated. Tyre and Sidon were strong and wealthy cities, and they used to help the Philistines in difficulties, but now they themselves will be involved in the common destruction, and God will cut off from them every *helper that remains* (v. 4). Who the *remnant of the country of Caphtor* was is uncertain, but the Caphtorites were closely related to the Philistines (Ge 10:14), and probably when their own country was destroyed, those who remained settled with their relatives the Philistines. Some individual places are named here, *Gaza and Ashkelon* (v. 5). *Baldness has come upon them;* the invaders have stripped them of all their ornaments, and they are *cut off.* The prophet asks them first with his usual tenderness (v. 5), *How long will you cut yourselves,* as people do in extreme sorrow and anguish? But he turns from the effect to the cause: *They cut themselves,* for the sword of the Lord cuts them. *O thou sword of the Lord! how long will it be ere* (before) *thou be quiet?* (v. 6). He begs it to *put up itself into the scabbard.* This shows the prophet's fervent desire to see an end to the war, looking with compassion even on the Philistines, but he silences himself against his own complaint (v. 7): *How can it be quiet, seeing the Lord hath given it a charge* against such and such places? When the sword is drawn, we cannot expect it to be sheathed until it has fulfilled its commission. Just as the word of God will achieve the purpose for which he sends it (Isa 55:11), so will his rod and sword.

CHAPTER 48

Moab comes next to judgment. We have also had prophecies about Moab in Isa 15–16 and Am 2:1. Isaiah's predictions concerning Moab were fulfilled when the Assyrians, under Shalmaneser, invaded and brought distress on Moab. But this is a prophecy of the devastation of Moab by the Babylonians, which was fulfilled under Nebuzaradan, about five years after he had destroyed Jerusalem. Here is: 1. The destruction foretold: that it would be great and general, extending to every part of the country (vv. 1–6, 8 and again vv. 20–25, 28, 34); that destroyers would come on them and force some to flee (v. 9), taking many others into exile (vv. 12, 46); that the enemy would come soon (v. 16) and swiftly and surprise them (vv. 40–41); that he would be thorough (v. 10) and devastate the country (vv. 14–15); that none would escape (vv. 42, 45); that this would force them to

abandon their idols (vv. 13, 35) and would put an end to all their joy (vv. 33–34); that their neighbors would mourn them (vv. 17–19), as the prophet himself did (vv. 31–32, 36). 2. The cause of this destruction given: their pride and worldly self-confidence (vv. 7, 11, 14, 29) and their contempt of God and his people (vv. 26–27, 30). 3. A promise of the restoration of Moab (v. 47).

Verses 1–13

We may notice in these verses:

1. The author of Moab's destruction is *the Lord of hosts* and *the God of Israel* (v. 1), who will plead the cause of his Israel against a people who have always been troublesome to them. He will punish them now for the wrongs done to Israel in former times.

2. The instruments of Moab's destruction: *Spoilers shall come* (v. 8), will come with a sword that will *pursue them* (v. 12). "*I will send unto him wanderers,* those who come from far away, as if they had missed their way, but they will *cause him to wander.*" These destroyers *have devised evil against Heshbon* (plotted its downfall), one of the main cities of Moab, and they aim at ruining the kingdom: *Come, and let us cut it off from being a nation* (v. 2). In God's name, the prophet commits them to undertake the work thoroughly, not lazily, applying to this work the general rule given to all who are employed in any service for God (v. 10): *Cursed be he that does the work of the Lord deceitfully* (in a lax way).

3. The effects of this destruction. The cities will be devastated; they will be *spoiled* (v. 1) and cut down (v. 2); they will be *desolate, without any to dwell therein* (v. 9). The *country* also will be devastated, the *valley shall perish,* and the *plain shall be destroyed* (v. 8). The grain and the flocks, which used to cover the plains and make the valleys glad (Ps 65:13), will all be destroyed, eaten up, trodden on, or taken away. The *priests and princes shall go together into captivity* (v. 7). Chemosh, the god they worship, will share with them in the general destruction; his temples will be laid in ashes, and his idol taken away with the rest of the plunder. The consequences will be shame and confusion: *Kiriathaim is confounded,* and Misgah is too. "There will be no more boasting in Moab about Heshbon," as v. 2 might be read. Nor will they boast anymore about their gods (v. 13); they *shall be ashamed of Chemosh as Israel was ashamed of Bethel,* of the golden calf they had at Bethel, for it was not able to save them from the Assyrians; nor will Chemosh be able to save the Moabites from the Babylonians. If you go up to the hills or down to the valleys, you meet with *continual weeping* ("weeping with weeping"); everyone is in tears; you meet no one with dry eyes. They will cry to one another, "Away, away! *Flee, save your lives* (v. 6); run away, even though you escape as naked as the *heath,* bush, or dry shrub, *in the wilderness.* Take shelter, even if it is in a barren wilderness. The danger will come on you suddenly and swiftly. Therefore *give wings unto Moab*" (v. 9).

4. The sins for which God will now judge Moab. First, they have been self-confident and have trusted in their own wealth and strength, *in their works* and *in their treasures* (v. 7). They trusted *in the abundance of their riches* and strengthened themselves in their wickedness (Ps 52:7). Second, they have not made the most of the days of their peace and prosperity (v. 11). They have long been undisturbed: *Moab has been at ease from his youth.* It was an ancient kingdom before Israel existed, and it has enjoyed great tranquility, even though it is a small country. It has not been unsettled, nor *gone into captivity,* but it is an evil, idolatrous nation and one of the allies

against *God's hidden ones* (Ps 83:3, 6). It has been corrupt and unreformed during all this time that it has been undisturbed: Moab *has settled on his lees* (been left on his dregs); he has put his confidence in his prosperity. *His taste remained in him, and his scent is not changed*; he is still the same, as bad as ever.

Verses 14–47

The destruction is further prophesied here in moving language, intended not only to awaken them to prevent the trouble through national repentance, or to prepare for it through a personal repentance, but also to move us with the dreadful state of human life and with the power of God's anger toward an offensive people.

1. The destruction threatened here is surprising and sudden. They thought they were *strong for war* and able to deal with the most powerful enemy (v. 14), and yet their downfall is near, and they are not able to keep it away. As an eagle swoops on its prey, the enemy *shall spread the wings* of his army *over Moab*, so that no one can escape. *The strongholds* of Moab will be taken *by surprise* (v. 41), so that all their strength will do them no good. It requires extraordinary courage not to be *afraid of sudden fear*.

2. It will devastate Moab completely: *Moab is spoiled* (v. 15), totally destroyed, is *confounded and broken down* (disgraced and shattered) (v. 20). The kingdom will be deprived of its honor and authority: *The horn of Moab is cut off*, the horn of its strength and power, both offensive and defensive; *his arm is broken*, so that he can neither attack nor defend (v. 25). The youth of the kingdom will go down to the battle promising they will return victorious, but God tells them that they will go *down to the slaughter*. Those who are enemies to God's people will soon be made no people.

3. It will be a lamentable destruction and will turn joy to a heavy spirit.

3.1. The prophet himself mourns the passing of Moab. His very *heart shall mourn for* them (v. 31); he will *weep for the vine of Sibmah* (v. 32); his heart *shall sound like pipes for Moab* (v. 36). The ruin of sinners gives God no pleasure (Eze 18:23, 32; 33:11), and so it should also be painful to us. These passages, and many others in this chapter, are much the same as Isaiah's in his prophecies against Moab (Isa chapters 15 and 16), for although there was a long time between that prophecy and this one, they were still both dictated by one and the same Spirit.

3.2. Moabites themselves will lament. Those who sat in *glory*, surrounded by wealth and merriment, will *sit in thirst*, in a dry land, where there is no water or comfort (Ps 63:1) (v. 18). The Moabites in the distant corners of the country will ask everyone *that escapes, What is done?* (v. 19). And when they are told that everything is gone, they will *howl and cry* in anguish of spirit (v. 20). They will *leave the cities* and live among the rocks (v. 28), where they may feel as sad as they like. There will be no more singing birds, but only mourning birds, *like the dove* (v. 28), *the doves of the valley* (Eze 7:16). What Moab used to rejoice in was its pleasant fruits and the abundance of rich wines. Their sole joy was in physical delights. If those are taken away, if their gardens and vineyards are destroyed, you make *all their mirth to cease* (Hos 2:11–12). *Take joy and gladness from the plentiful field*, and you take it away *from the land of Moab* (v. 33). Those who make physical delights their chief joy subject themselves to the tyranny of the greatest grief, since these are things they may be easily deprived of in a brief time, whereas those who rejoice in God may do so even when

the fig tree does not blossom and there is no fruit in the vine (Hab 3:17). All the Moabites' neighbors are called to mourn with them and sympathize with them because of their destruction (v. 17): *All you that are about him bemoan him.* Let no one become proud and put their confidence in their strength or beauty, for neither will protect them from the judgments of God.

4. It will be a shameful destruction and one that will expose them to contempt: *Moab is made drunk* (v. 26).

5. It will be the destruction of what is dear to them, not only of their summer fruits and their grapes but also of their wealth (v. 36): *The riches that he has gotten have perished.* Riches, like dust, slip through our fingers even when we hold them fast. But this is not the worst of their judgment; even those whose religion was false were fond of it more than anything else, and so what was really a promise was to them a threat (v. 35), that God *will cause to cease him that offers in the high places*. The high places will be destroyed, and the fields of offerings will be devastated, and the priests themselves, *who burn incense to their gods*, will be killed or taken into exile (v. 7).

6. It is a just destruction, one that they have deserved and brought on themselves by sin.

6.1. The sin that they themselves have been most notoriously guilty of is pride. It is mentioned six times (v. 29). *We have* all *heard of the pride of Moab.* They were accused of this earlier by Isaiah (Isa 16:6), but here it is expressed in more detail than there. Two examples are given here of the pride of Moab:

6.1.1. He has behaved very arrogantly toward God. He must be humbled by shame (v. 26), for *he* has *magnified himself against the Lord.* The Moabites preferred Chemosh to Jehovah and thought they were a match for the God of Israel.

6.1.2. He has behaved very scornfully toward Israel in their recent troubles. This is why Moab will fall into the same trouble and become an object of ridicule, for Israel has been an object of ridicule to him (vv. 26–27). The Moabites persistently declared their joy, gloating over every Israelite they met with in distress and laughing at them.

6.2. Besides this, they have been guilty of hatred toward God's people and of treachery in their dealings with them (v. 30). They made a joke of the devastation of Judah and Jerusalem. "But," God says, "*I know his wrath*; I know this ridicule comes from the old enmity he has toward the worshipers of the true God. But the nation whose fall he triumphs in will recover."

7. It is a complicated destruction, involving one instance of judgment after another. What was said about sinners in general (Isa 24:17–18), that those who *flee from the fear shall fall into the pit* and those who come *up out of the pit shall be taken in the snare*, is here particularly foretold concerning the sinners of Moab (v. 44). The figurative expressions used in v. 44 are explained in v. 45 as referring to *those that will flee* out of the villages for fear of the enemy's forces; they will put themselves *under the shadow of Heshbon*, and they will stand there thinking they are safe, as armies sometimes withdraw under the cannon of a fortified city, but here they will be disappointed, for when *they flee out of the pit, they shall fall into the snare.* They think Heshbon will shelter them, but it will devour them, as Moses foretold long before (Nu 21:28).

8. The chapter concludes with a short promise of the Moabites' return out of *captivity in the latter days.* God, who brings them into captivity, *will bring again* their *captivity* (v. 47). This is how tenderly God deals with

Moabites, and if he does so, then how much more tenderly will he deal with his own people! Even with Moabites he *will not contend for ever, nor be always wroth* (Isa 57:16). This prophecy concerning Moab is long, but it ends here on an encouraging note: *Thus far is the judgment of Moab* (v. 47).

CHAPTER 49

The cup of trembling (Isa 51:17) is still passed on, and the nations must all drink of it (25:15). This chapter puts it into the hands of: 1. The Ammonites (vv. 1–6). 2. The Edomites (vv. 7–22). 3. The Arameans (vv. 23–27). 4. The people of Kedar and the kingdoms of Hazor (vv. 28–33). 5. The Elamites (vv. 34–39).

Verses 1–6

The Ammonites were closest to the Moabites according to both family ties and location.

1. Judgment is given here in God's name against the Ammonites because they encroached illegally on the rightful possessions of the tribe of Gad, which lay next to them (v. 1). They are called on to show their entitlement to those territories, which, when the Gileadites were taken away by the king of Assyria (2Ki 15:29; 1Ch 5:26), were left almost depopulated and an easy target to the next invader. "Are there no Gadites left, to whom the right of inheritance belongs? Or if there are not, are there no Israelites, is there no one left from Judah, which is more closely related to them than you are?" *Why then does their king*, as if he were entitled to the forfeited estates, or why does *Milcom* (Molech), their idol, as if he had the right to dispose of it to his worshipers, *inherit Gad, and* why do *his people dwell in the cities* that fell by lot to that tribe of God's people? The Ammonites *magnified themselves against* God's *border* and boasted it was their own (Zep 2:8). People will find themselves mistaken if they think everything they can lay their hands on is their own. Just as there is justice owing to owners, so also there is justice owing to their heirs, and it is a great sin to defraud heirs out of what is rightfully theirs, even if they either are not aware of their rights or do not know how to defend them.

2. Judgment is given here against them for this aggression. God *will cause an alarm of war to be heard*, even *in Rabbah*, their very strong capital city (v. 1). Their cities will be devastated. Their country, which they are so proud of, will be devastated (v. 4). They are accused of backsliding, for they are the descendants of righteous Lot (Ge 19:36–38; 2Pe 2:7). Some understand the word translated *backsliding* to mean "perverse and disobedient." Having abandoned their *God, they glory in their valleys*. They have forcefully taken these away from Israel. They boast about the power of their valleys, which are so surrounded by mountains that they are inaccessible; they boast in their crops. They flatter themselves that they will never be disturbed in enjoying them: *Tomorrow shall be as this day* (Isa 56:12); they therefore defy God and his judgments. *Their king and his princes* (officials), and Molech, their god, *and his priests, shall go into captivity* (v. 3), *and every man shall be driven out right forth* (headlong), fleeing as best he can (v. 5). And to complete their misery, *none shall gather up him that wanders*; none will open their doors to him. Then the country of the Ammonites will fall into the hands of the remaining Israelites (v. 2).

3. But there is a prospect of mercy later (v. 6), as there had been earlier for Moab.

Verses 7–22

The Edomites are next to hear their fate from God through the mouth of Jeremiah: they too were enemies of God's Israel. Many of the expressions used in this prophecy *concerning Edom* (v. 7) are borrowed from the prophecy of Obadiah, which is also *concerning Edom* (Ob 1), because all the prophets are inspired by one and the same Spirit.

1. The country of Edom will be completely devastated; *the calamity of Esau* will be *brought upon him*, the disaster he has deserved because of his former sins (v. 8). The time is near when God *will visit him* and call him to account, and then the Edomites will *flee* from the sword, *turn back* from the battle, and *dwell deep* in caves, hiding there. All they have will be taken away by the conqueror; those who destroy them will never be satisfied (vv. 9–10). They will make *Esau* quite *bare*, strip the Edomites of everything they have. *His brethren* the Moabites *and his neighbours* the Philistines, whom he might have expected to receive help from, or at least shelter, will be destroyed as well. The Aramaic translation treats these words as those of God to his people, setting them apart from the Edomites in this disaster, and it reads, "But you, O house of Israel! you shall not leave your orphans; I will secure them, and I will let your widows rest on my word." "Whatever happens to the widows and orphans of the Edomites, I will take care of yours." The Edomites have been significant, but God will make *them small among the heathen*, and those who despised God's people will themselves be *despised among men* (v. 15; Ob 2). *Edom shall be* such a *desolation* that no one will care to come near its ruins; *no man shall abide there* (v. 18).

2. The instruments of this destruction will be very determined and formidable. God has determined that Edom will be ravaged, and then the one who is to be employed in devastating it will come swiftly and strongly. Nebuchadnezzar is the one about whom it is foretold he *shall come up like a lion*, with fierceness and rage, like a lion made angry by *the swelling of Jordan* overflowing its banks, which forces it out of hiding by the waterside to higher ground (v. 19). In fact, a fierce lion is not needed to do it: *Even the least of the flock shall draw them out* (v. 20); the lowliest servant in Nebuchadnezzar's retinue will *draw them out* to kill them; he will force them to surrender. Nebuchadnezzar will come not only like a lion, the king of the animals, but also like an eagle, the king of the birds (v. 22): *He shall fly as the eagle* on its prey, so swiftly and strongly, and immediately *the hearts of the mighty men* will fail them, for they will realize it is futile to struggle against such an enemy.

3. The Edomites' confidence will fail them in the day of their distress.

3.1. They trust in their wisdom, but that will do them no good. This is the first thing focused on in this prophecy against Edom (v. 7). That nation used to be famous for its wisdom, and their political leaders were thought to excel in politics, but now they will follow such wrong courses of action, and be so thwarted in all their intentions, that people will ask, with wonder, "What is the matter with the Edomites?" *Is wisdom no more in Teman?* It is like this when God intends to destroy a people, for he confuses those he is going to destroy. See Job 12:20. *Has their wisdom vanished?* Or, as others render these words: "Is it tired?" "Is it worn out?" "Has it become useless?"

3.2. They trust in their strength, but that will not do them any good (v. 16). They have terrorized all their neighbors. Because no neighboring nation dares to meddle with them, they think no nation in the whole world dares to. Their country is mountainous, having many passes, which they think would resist any invader (Ob 3–4, 8).

4. Their destruction will be inevitable.

4.1. God has determined it (vv. 12–13), he has *sworn it*, that they will *drink the cup of trembling* (Isa 51:17) that is put into the hands of all their neighbors.

4.2. All the world will take notice of it (v. 21): *The earth is moved*, and all the nations are caused to be concerned *at the noise of their fall. The noise of the outcry is heard to the Red Sea*, which flows on the coasts of Edom. It will even be heard among the ships that lie in the Red Sea to take cargo (1Ki 9:26).

Verses 23–27

The kingdom of Aram, north of Canaan, had often been troublesome to God's Israel. Damascus was the capital of that kingdom. Hamath and Arpad, two other significant cities, are named (v. 23), and *the palaces of Ben-hadad*, which he built, are especially marked out for ruin (v. 27); see also Am 1:4. The judgment of Damascus begins with fright and discouragement. They *hear evil tidings* (bad news), that the king of Babylon is coming against them with all his forces, and *they are confounded* (dismayed) (v. 23); their courage has melted away, and they are terrified; *they are fainthearted*. They are like *the troubled sea, that cannot be quiet* (Isa 57:20), or like men *in a storm* at sea (Ps 107:26); or the sorrow that begins in the city will go to the coast. *Damascus* now *waxes* (becomes) *feeble* (v. 24) and acknowledges that it is as useless to think about opposing its fate as for *a woman in* labor to do anything about her labor pains, which she cannot escape. It was a *city of praise* (v. 25), not praise to God but to itself, a city very much admired by all strangers who visited it. It was *a city of joy*. But now it is all overwhelmed with fear and grief. The judgment ends with terrible destruction and fire. The inhabitants are killed (v. 26): the *young men*, who should defend the city, *shall fall* by the sword *in her streets, and all the men of war shall be cut off*. The city will be burned to ashes (v. 27): the *fire is kindled by* the besiegers *in the wall*, but it will devour everything, especially *the palaces of Ben-hadad*, where so much trouble has been plotted against God's Israel.

Verses 28–33

These verses foretell the devastation that Nebuchadnezzar and his forces would cause among the people of Kedar (who were descended from Kedar the son of Ishmael and lived southeast of Judah) and of Hazor. The people of Hazor were perhaps originally Canaanites, from the kingdom of Hazor, to the north of Canaan, which had Jabin as its king, but because they were driven from there, they had settled in the deserts of Arabia (Jos 11; Jdg 4). Notice about these people:

1. They lived in *tents* and had *curtains*, not walls (v. 29), no fortified cities; they had *neither gates nor bars* (v. 31). They were shepherds and had no treasure, no money or wealth except flocks and camels. They had no soldiers among them, for they *dwelt alone* (v. 31) and so were not afraid of invaders. Although they had no trade or treasures, it is here said that they were a *wealthy nation* (v. 31). Those who have enough to supply their needs and know when they have enough are truly rich. We need not go after the treasures of kings and provinces or the cash of merchants to look for wealthy people; they may be found among shepherds *that dwell in tents*.

2. The intention of the king of Babylon against them and the attack he launched on them: *He has taken counsel*

(plotted) *against you* (v. 30). He has decided that it will never be said that he—who has conquered so many strong cities—leaves unconquered those *that dwell in tents*. It was strange that that eagle should stoop to snatch these flies. These people had lived inoffensively among their neighbors. Yet God said (v. 28): *Arise, go up to Kedar, and spoil* (destroy) *the men of the east*. God orders it to correct an unthankful people.

3. The dismay this put them into and the devastation caused among them: *They shall cry unto them*; those on the borders will raise the alarm to every part of the country, which will be put into the greatest confusion. They will cry out, *"Fear is on every side*—we are surrounded by the enemy"; none of them will have the heart to offer any resistance. The enemy need not strike a single blow; they will shout them out of their tents (v. 29). There are *fears on every side* when there are enemies on every side. The Babylonians will *take to themselves their curtains and vessels*; even though these things are only plain and coarse, the Babylonians will take them for spite; they will plunder for the sake of plundering. *They shall carry away their tents and their flocks* (v. 29). *Their camels* will also be plunder to those who came for nothing else (v. 32). It is not said that any of the people will be killed, for they do not attempt to offer any resistance, and their tents and flocks are accepted as a ransom for their lives; but they will be removed and dispersed. Their country will lie uninhabited; it does not have either cities or lands that welcome strangers. No one will care to succeed them as residents, and so *Hazor shall be a desolation for ever* (v. 33).

Verses 34–39

This prophecy is dated to the beginning of Zedekiah's reign. The Elamites were the Persians, descended from Elam the son of Shem (Ge 10:22); yet some think it was only the part of Persia lying nearest to the Jews that was called *Elymais* and was next to Media-Elam, and it was this Media-Elam, they say, that had acted against God's Israel and *borne* (took up) *the quiver* in a mission against them (Isa 22:6). They must, therefore, be judged with the others. It is foretold here, in general, that God *will bring evil upon them, even* his *fierce anger*.

1. Their forces will be disabled. The Elamites were famous archers, but, *Behold, I will break the bow of Elam* (v. 35), will ruin their artillery, and then *the chief* (mainstay) *of their might* is gone. God often arranges it so that what we most trust in fails us first, and what was the mainstay of our strength proves to help us the least.

2. Their people will be dispersed. Enemies will come against them from every part, and they will all take some of them away as captives to their respective countries (v. 36). *The four winds* will be brought on them; the storm will come sometimes from one direction and sometimes from another.

3. Their officials will be destroyed, and the government completely changed (v. 38): *I will set my throne in Elam*. The throne of Nebuchadnezzar will be set there, or the throne of Cyrus, who began his conquests with Elymais. Or it may refer to the throne on which God sits in judgment. The king of Elam was famous in former times (Ge 14:1). Kedorlaomer was king of Elam, and he was powerful in his day; his successors were probably significant too. But the king of Elam is no more to God than any another person.

4. But the destruction of Elam will not last forever (v. 39): *In the latter days I will bring again the captivity of Elam*. When Cyrus had destroyed Babylon and brought

the empire into the hands of the Persians, the Elamites no doubt returned in triumph and resettled in their own country. But this promise was to have its complete fulfillment in the days of the Messiah, when we find Elamites among those who, when the Holy Spirit was given on the Day of Pentecost, heard spoken *in their own tongues the wonderful works of God* (Ac 2:9, 11), and that is the most desirable return from captivity.

CHAPTER 50

In this chapter and the one that follows we have the judgment of Babylon, which comes as the last of Jeremiah's prophecies against the Gentiles because it was the last to be fulfilled. Babylon was used as the rod in God's hand to correct all the other nations, and now finally that rod will be thrown onto the fire. The destruction of Babylon by Cyrus was foretold by Isaiah and now again by Jeremiah, when it had reached the greatness of its power, for although at this time he saw that kingdom flourishing like a green bay tree (Ps 37:35), at the same time he also foresaw it withered and cut down. And just as Isaiah's prophecies about the destruction of Babylon and the restoration of Israel seem intended to be types of the Gospel triumphs of all believers over the powers of darkness and the great salvation brought by our Lord Jesus Christ, so Jeremiah's prophecies of the same events seem intended to point to the apocalyptic triumphs of the Gospel church over the New Testament Babylon. Because the kingdom of Babylon was much larger and stronger than any of the other kingdoms prophesied against here, its fall was the more significant, and what was often foretold in general before (25:12; 27:7) is described here in more detail, and with a great deal of prophetic heat as well as light. Babylon was destroyed to make way for the return from exile of God's people. Here is: 1. The ruin of Babylon (vv. 1–3, 9–16, 21–32, 35–46). 2. The redemption of God's people (vv. 4–8 and again vv. 17–20, 33–34).

Verses 1–8

1. Here is a word spoken against Babylon. The king of Babylon had been very kind to Jeremiah, but Jeremiah must foretell the ruin of that kingdom, for God's prophets must not be ruled by favor or affection. Whoever our friends are, if they are God's enemies, we dare not speak words of peace to them.

1.1. The destruction of Babylon is spoken of here as something already done (v. 2).

1.2. It is spoken of as something done thoroughly. The very idols of Babylon, which the people want to protect as carefully as possible, will be destroyed. Bel and Marduk (*Merodach*), their two chief gods, will be *confounded* (put to shame), and their idols *broken to pieces*. The country will be devastated (v. 3) out *of the north*, from Media, which lies north of Babylon, and from Assyria, through which Cyrus will attack Babylon; from there will come the nation that will make *her land desolate*.

2. Here is a word spoken for the people of God to encourage them, both *the children of Israel* and those *of Judah* (v. 4):

2.1. It is promised that they will return to their God first and then to their own land. The promise of their conversion and reformation makes way for all the other promises (vv. 4–5). They will *lament after the Lord*, as the whole house of Israel did in Samuel's time (1Sa 7:2); they will *go weeping*. These tears flow from godly sorrow (2Co 7:10). They are tears of repentance for sin, tears

of joy at the goodness of God, at the dawn of the day of their restoration from exile. The dawning of that day *leads them to repentance* now that their adversities have not been effective to drive them to it. They will *inquire after the Lord*; they will not sink under their sorrows, but go *weeping to seek the Lord their God*. They will *seek the Lord as their God* and will now have nothing more to do with idols. They will think of returning to their own country; they will think of it not only as a mercy but also as a duty (v. 5): *They shall ask the way to Zion with their faces thitherward*. The journey is long, and they do not know the road, but they will *ask the way*. This describes the return of poor souls to God. In all true converts there is both a sincere desire to reach the destination and a constant concern to keep on the way that leads to it. They will renew their covenant to walk with God more closely in the future: *Come, and let us join ourselves to the Lord in a perpetual covenant*.

2.2. Their present case is mourned as very sad and as having long been so: "*My people have been lost sheep* (v. 6). They have *gone from mountain to hill* and been unable to find pasture. *They have forgotten their resting place* in their own country and cannot find their way to it.*" They were *led astray by their own shepherds*, their own rulers and priests. Those shepherds turned them away from their duty, so provoking God to turn them out of their own land. It was as if they were wandering sheep; *all that found them have devoured them* and attacked them. Their enemies laughed at them, telling them that the attack was what their own prophets had many times told them they deserved. God's people had put contempt on the temple and on the tradition of their ancestors, and so they deserved to suffer these hardships.

2.3. They are called on to move away quickly, as soon as the door of liberty is open to them (v. 8): "*Remove* (flee), not only away from the borders, but *out of the midst of Babylon*. Move quickly to Zion, and *be as the he-goats before* (goats that lead) *the flocks*; do your best to see which one of you will be first, which will take the lead in such a good work."

Verses 9–20

Here God through his prophet continues his dispute with Babylon. Notice:

1. The commission given to the instruments that are to be used to destroy Babylon. The army that is to undertake this work is called *an assembly* (alliance) *of great nations* (v. 9), the Medes and Persians. God will *raise them up* to do it and equip them for this service. He *will cause them to come up*, to *put themselves in array* (take up their positions) *against Babylon* (v. 14). God will tell them to *shoot at her and spare no arrows* (v. 14). When God gives commands, he also gives success. They are told not only to *shoot at her* (v. 14) but also to *shout against her* (v. 15) with triumphant roars, as those who are already sure of victory.

2. The devastation and destruction that will be brought on Babylon. This is set out using a wide range of expressions.

2.1. The wealth of Babylon will be a rich and easy target for the conquerors (v. 10).

2.2. The country of Babylon will be depopulated and lie uninhabited (v. 13).

2.3. Their ancestors will be ashamed of the cowardice they show by fleeing at the start (v. 12), or, *Your mother*, Babylon itself, the mother city, *shall be confounded* (greatly ashamed) when she sees herself deserted.

2.4. The great admirers of Babylon will see it made contemptible: *it shall be* the very tail of the nations, *a wilderness, a dry land, a desert* (v. 12).

2.5. The great city, its head, will be completely ruined. It is the vengeance of the Lord, which nothing can resist either in law or in battle.

2.6. There will not be left in Babylon so much as *the poor of the land for vine-dressers and husbandmen* (52:16; 2Ki 25:12) (v. 16). Harvest will come, but there will be no reapers; seedtime will come, but there will be no one to sow the seed.

3. The cause of this destruction. It comes from God's displeasure; he has been provoked to anger; it is *because of the wrath of the Lord* that Babylon *shall be wholly desolate* (v. 13). His wrath is righteous, for (v. 14) *she hath sinned against the Lord*, and so *spare no arrows*. What they did against Jerusalem they did with pleasure (v. 11): *You were glad, you rejoiced*. When Titus Vespasianus destroyed Jerusalem, he wept over it, but these Babylonians gloated over it. They used the plunder of Jerusalem to feed their own luxury. Those who have swallowed riches in this way must vomit them up again. That is why the Babylonians have *given their hand* (v. 15). They aimed at nothing less than the complete destruction of God's Israel: *Israel is a scattered sheep*, as was said before (v. 6), a sheep that is not only barked at and attacked by dogs but also roared at and *driven away* by lions (v. 17). One king of Assyria took the ten tribes away and devoured them; another invaded Judah and impoverished it, tearing the fleece and flesh of this poor sheep. Now, at last, this Nebuchadnezzar has fallen on him and *broken his bones*, and so the king of Babylon must be punished as the king of Assyria was (v. 18).

4. The mercy promised to the Israel of God. They will be released from bondage and *brought again to their own habitation* as sheep that have been scattered return to their own fold (v. 19). He will restore their prosperity; they will not only live in their own land again but live there comfortably; they will *feed upon Carmel and Bashan*, the richest and most fruitful parts of the country. They will *inquire the way to Zion* (v. 5), where God is to be served and worshiped. This will be what they chiefly aim at when they return, but God will bring them to Carmel and Bashan, where they will abundantly feed themselves. God will pardon their iniquity; this is the foundation of everything else (v. 20): *In these days the iniquity* (guilt) *of Israel will be sought for, and there shall be none*. Not only will the punishments of their sin be taken away, but the offense that it gave to God will be forgotten, and he will be reconciled to them. This shows how fully God forgives sin; he *remembers it no more* (31:34). This may also include a thorough reformation of their hearts and lives, as well as a full forgiveness of sins. God reserves those whose sins he pardons for something very great, for those *whom he justifies, them he* glorifies (Ro 8:30).

Verses 21–32

Here:

1. The forces have been gathered and are commissioned to destroy Babylon. The forces of Cyrus are called to go up against Babylon (v. 21), to *come against her from the utmost border*. Let all come together, for there will be enough work and pay for them all (v. 26). *The archers* particularly must be *called together against Babylon* (v. 29). This is how *the Lord hath opened his armoury*, "his arsenal or treasury," *and hath brought forth the weapons of his indignation* (v. 25). Media and Persia are now God's arsenal; he takes from there the weapons of his wrath, Cyrus and his officers and armies.

2. They are instructed what to do. They must *open her storehouses* (v. 26), rifle its treasures, *cast her up as heaps*. Their officials and leaders will fall by the sword, not as warriors on the battlefield but as animals (v. 27).

3. Assurances are given them of success. If they do what God commands, they will fulfill what he threatens. Cyrus will without doubt win, for he is fighting under God.

4. Reasons are given for this harsh treatment of Babylon.

4.1. Babylon has been very troublesome and harmful to all its neighbors; it has been *the hammer of the whole earth* (v. 23). The One who is the God of nations will sooner or later assert the wronged rights of nations against those who unjustly and violently invade them.

4.2. Babylon has defied God himself: *Thou hast striven against* (opposed) *the Lord* (v. 24), as in law or battle; therefore *thou art* now *found, and caught*, as in a trap.

4.3. Babylon ruined Jerusalem, the Holy City, and the holy house there (v. 28). The burning of the temple and the taking away of its vessels were part of the accusation against Babylon on which greater emphasis was put than on its being *the hammer of the whole earth*, for Zion was *the joy* and glory *of the whole earth* (Ps 48:2).

4.4. Babylon has been proud and arrogant and so must fall. They will fall not so much because others push them down as because they themselves stumble, for they hold their heads so high that they never look down at their feet.

Verses 33–46

We have in these verses:

1. Israel's sufferings and their rescue from those sufferings. *Israel and Judah were oppressed together* (v. 33). It seems that when the kingdoms of Assyria and Babylonia united, those who remained of the exiles of the ten tribes came and mixed with those of the two tribes, so that they were *oppressed together*. This is their encouragement in their distress: although they are weak, *their Redeemer* (their Avenger) *is strong* (v. 34). *The Lord of hosts is his name*, and he will answer to his name, and he will be to them all that they depend on him to be. *He shall thoroughly plead their cause, that he may give rest to the land*, to his people's land, rest from all their enemies around them (Dt 32:25; Jos 23:1; 2Sa 7:1). This may be applied to all believers who complain about the power of sin and corruption and about their own weakness. Let them know that *their Redeemer is strong*; he is able to keep what they commit to him (2Ti 1:12). Sin will not be their master; he will *make them free*, and they will be *free indeed* (Jn 8:36); he will give them *rest*, that *rest which remains for the people of God* (Heb 4:9).

2. Babylon's sin and their punishment for that sin.

2.1. The sins they are accused of are idolatry and persecution.

2.1.1. They oppressed the people of God; they *held them fast* and would not let *them go*. They *opened not the house of his prisoners* (Isa 14:17).

2.1.2. They wronged and robbed God himself, giving to others the glory that is due only to him, for (v. 38) *it is the land of graven images, and*, literally, "with the terrors they will go mad"; the word here used for idols properly signifies "terrors"—*Emim*, the name given to giants, who were formidable (Dt 2:10–11). The Babylonians made the images of their gods look frightening, to strike terror on fools and children. And Babylon was *the mother of harlots* (Rev 17:5), the source of idolatry.

2.2. The judgments of God on them for these sins are such as will ruin them.

2.2.1. All that should be their defense and support will be destroyed by the sword. The Babylonians have long been God's sword, which he has used to judge the sinful nations around them, but now, because they are as bad as any of those other nations, or worse, *a sword* is brought on them (v. 35). It is a sword of war, and in God's hand it is also a sword of justice. It will fall on *upon their princes* and *their wise men* and on their philosophers, their political leaders, and their privy councillors; their learning and wisdom will neither protect them nor do the public any good. It will fall on their soothsayers and astrologers, here called *the liars* (v. 36), for they deceive people with their false prophecies of peace and prosperity. The sword on these deceivers will make them lose their minds, so that they will talk like fools. The Babylonians' *mighty men shall be dismayed* and will no longer be *mighty men. The sword shall be upon their horses and chariots*; the invaders will seize their horses and chariots. The troops of other nations who are in their service will be discouraged: *The mingled people* (foreigners) *shall become as* weak and timid as *women. The sword* will be *upon her treasures*, which support war, *and* those treasures *will be robbed* and used by the enemy against them.

2.2.2. The country will be devastated (v. 38): *The waters shall be dried up*, the water that keeps the city. Cyrus drew the Euphrates River into so many channels that it became passable for his army, so that they easily reached the walls of Babylon, which that river was thought to have made inaccessible. "Similarly, the water that made the country fruitful will *be dried up*" (v. 39). This was foretold about Babylon in Isa 13:19–21.

2.2.3. The king and kingdom will be put into the greatest confusion and fear by the enemies' invasion (vv. 41–43). Those who have dealt cruelly, who have shown no mercy, may expect to be dealt with cruelly and to find no mercy themselves.

2.2.4. They will be as much hurt as frightened, for the invader will *come up like a lion* to tear down and destroy (v. 44) and will make them and their *habitation* (pasture) *desolate* (v. 45), and the devastation will be so shocking that all the nations around will be terrified by it (v. 46). We had these three verses before in the prophecy of the destruction of Edom (49:19–21), which was fulfilled *by* the Babylonians, and they are repeated here in the prophecy of the destruction of Babylon, which was to be fulfilled *on* the Babylonians.

CHAPTER 51

In this chapter the prophet continues with the prediction of Babylon's downfall, to which other prophets also bore witness. Here is: 1. The detailed record of Babylon's fate and of many circumstances that made her fall worse, with great encouragements to the Israel of God, who suffered such hard things from her (vv. 1–58). 2. The representation and confirmation of this by the throwing of a copy of this prophecy into the Euphrates River (vv. 59–64).

Verses 1–58

We have here:

1. An acknowledgment of the great show and power that Babylon had had and how God in his providence had used it (v. 7): *Babylon hath been a golden cup*, a rich and glorious empire, *a golden city* (Isa 14:4), *a head of gold* (Da 2:38), *a golden cup in the Lord's hand*. He had made

the earth *drunk with this cup*; some were drunk with her pleasures, others drunk with her terrors and destroyed by her. In both senses, the New Testament Babylon is said to have made the kings of the earth drunk (Rev 17:2; 18:3). Babylon had also been God's *battle axe* (war club); it was so at the time when Jeremiah prophesied (v. 20). The forces of Babylon were God's *weapons of war*, tools in his hand, with which he broke in pieces *nations and kingdoms* (v. 20). With those tools he broke *horses* and *chariots*, which are very much the strength of kingdoms (v. 21); *man and woman, young and old*, with which kingdoms are filled (v. 22); and *the shepherd and his flock, the husbandman and his oxen*, with which kingdoms are maintained and supplied (v. 23). The Babylonians had made such havoc when God used them as instruments of his wrath to rebuke the nations, but now Babylon itself must fall.

2. An accusation drawn up against her by the Israel of God.

2.1. She is complained about because of her persistent evil (v. 9). The people of God who were captives among the Babylonians tried (10:11) to convince them of the foolishness of their idolatry, but the Babylonians could not accept it. Some understand this, however, as spoken by the forces the Babylonians had hired to help them, declaring that they had done their best to save Babylon from destruction, but that it was all futile, and so they might as well go home to their respective countries, "for *her judgment reaches unto heaven*, and it is futile to withstand it or think it can be averted."

2.2. She is complained about because of her persistent hatred toward Israel. Other nations have been treated harshly by the Babylonians, but only Israel complains to God about it and appeals to him with confidence (vv. 34–35). *Zion and Jerusalem shall say*, "May the violence done to me and my children, who are *my* own *flesh* and part of myself, and may all the blood of my people, which they have shed like water, *be upon* them; may the guilt of it fall on them, and may they be judged for it."

3. Judgment declared on this appeal by the righteous Judge of heaven and earth, on behalf of Israel against Babylon. He answers (v. 36), "*I will plead* (defend) *thy cause.* Leave matters with me; I will in due time defend it effectively *and take vengeance for thee*, and every drop of Jerusalem's blood will be accounted for with interest." God deals better with Israel than they deserve, and despite their sins and his harshness, *Israel is not forsaken.* God is still their God, and he will act for them as the Lord Almighty, a God of power. *The Lord God of recompenses* (retribution), the *God to whom vengeance belongs* (Dt 32:35; Ps 94:1), *will surely requite* (v. 56), will pay them back; he *will render unto Babylon all the evil they have done in Zion* (v. 24). Cyrus will deal with the Babylonians in the same way they dealt with the Jews. Zion's children will triumph (v. 10): *The Lord has brought forth our righteousness*; he has supported us against those who dealt unjustly with us, and he has remedied the injuries done to us. Let therefore be spoken of to his praise: *Come and let us declare in Zion the work of the Lord our God*, so that others may be invited to join us in praising him.

4. A declaration of the sovereignty of God, who embraces Zion's cause and undertakes to judge this proud and powerful enemy (v. 14). He will fill Babylon with vast numbers of the enemy's forces, *will fill it with men as with caterpillars* (a swarm of locusts), who will overpower it. But who is the One who can break such a powerful kingdom as Babylon? The prophet describes him from the account he gave earlier (10:12–16). It is repeated here

to show that those who would not be convinced by God's word that he is *God over all* will be convinced by his judgments.

4.1. He is the God who made the world (v. 15).

4.2. He commands every creature he has made (v. 16); his providence is a continuing creation.

4.3. The idols that oppose the fulfillment of his word are false, and their worshipers are senseless (vv. 17–18). But there is no comparison between the God of Israel and these gods of the nations (v. 19): *The portion of Jacob is not like them*; the God who speaks this and will do it is the One who forms all things; he is *the Lord of all hosts*, and there is a close relationship between him and his people, for he is *their portion*, and they are his.

5. A description of the instruments that are to be employed in this service. God has *raised up the spirit of the kings of the Medes* (v. 11), Darius and Cyrus, who come against Babylon by divine instinct, for *God's device* (purpose) *is against Babylon to destroy it*. Those whom God uses to judge Babylon are compared to *a destroying wind* (v. 1), which either by its coldness withers the fruits of the earth or by its fierceness blows down everything in its path. This wind is *brought out of God's treasuries* (storehouses) (v. 16), *raised up against those that dwell in the midst of the Chaldeans*, those from other nations who have joined them. These enemies are compared to *fanners* (winnowers) (v. 2), who will *drive them away as chaff* is driven away (Ps 1:4). The Babylonians themselves winnowed God's people (15:7), and now they will be winnowed.

6. A full commission given these instruments to devastate everything. Let them *bend their bow* against the archers of the Babylonians (v. 3). Let all necessary preparations be made. They are called to do this (vv. 27–28). Let *a standard be set up*, under which the soldiers will enlist; *let a trumpet be blown* to call the soldiers together to it. Let the nations, out of which Cyrus's army is to be raised, prepare their recruits. Let the kingdoms of *Ararat, Minni, and Ashkenaz*, of Armenia, both the higher and the lower, and of Ascania, around Phrygia and Bithynia, send their quota of soldiers for his service; let them devastate the country as locusts do (Joel 1:4).

7. The weakness of the Babylonians, and their inability to make headway against this threatening force. They are called on to prepare for action, but the call comes ironically (v. 11): *Make bright* (sharpen) *the arrows*, which have grown rusty through disuse; *gather* (take up) *the shields*, which in a long time of peace and security have been scattered and thrown out (v. 12); *set up the standard upon the walls of Babylon*. But they will not have the courage to respond to the call (v. 29). *The mighty men of Babylon have forborne to fight* (have stopped fighting) (v. 30). Because God will take away their strength and courage, they will *remain in their holds* (strongholds), so that the enemy will *burn her dwelling places* and *break her bars* without any resistance. The same thing happens in vv. 56–58. When the destroyer attacks Babylon, her strong people will be immediately captured; *every one of their bows shall be broken*. Their human wisdom will fail them. Their rulers, officials, and commanders will sit in council as drunkards, intoxicated by stupidity or despair. The *walls of their city* will fail them (v. 58). When the enemy has found ways to ford the Euphrates, which is thought impassable, surely, they think, the walls will be impregnable. They are the *broad* (thick) *walls of Babylon*. Some say that there was a threefold wall around the inner city and something similar around the outer city, but these

will be *utterly broken*, and *the high gates and towers shall be burnt*.

8. The destruction that will be brought about in Babylon by these invaders.

8.1. It is a certain destruction; divine power is engaged against Babylon, a power that cannot be resisted (v. 8), although when Jeremiah prophesied this, and for many years after, it was at the height of its power and greatness.

8.2. It is a righteous destruction. Babylon has made herself ready for it, and so it cannot fail to happen, for (v. 25) *Babylon* has been a *destroying mountain, destroying all the earth*, as the stones that fall from high mountains devastate the ground around them, but now it will itself be *rolled down from its rocks*. Again (v. 33): "*Babylon is like a threshing floor*, in which the people of God have long been threshed, but now the time has come that she herself will be threshed."

8.3. It is an unavoidable destruction. Babylon seems to be well fortified against it: *She dwells upon many waters* (v. 13); the march of an enemy is made difficult by rivers; *Babylon is abundant in treasures*. And yet "*thy end has come*, and neither your waters nor your wealth will protect you."

8.4. It is a gradual destruction, which they could have foreseen and been warned of (v. 46): "*A rumour will come one year* that Cyrus is making great preparations for war, *and after that, in another year, shall come a rumour* that his eyes are set on Babylon"; when he was a long way off they could have sent a messenger to negotiate conditions of peace (Lk 14:31–32), but they were too proud, and their hearts were hardened to their destruction.

8.5. But when it comes, it will be a surprising destruction: *Babylon has suddenly fallen* (v. 8). The king of Babylon was himself so far away from the place where the attack was made that it took a long time for him to receive information that the city had been taken; those positioned near the place sent one messenger after another (v. 31). They were to tell him that the enemy had seized the river crossings (v. 32) and that, having passed over the river, they had set fire to the reeds on the riverside to instill fear in the city's population, so that all the warriors surrendered. The messengers came with this news, which was immediately confirmed by the enemy's being in the palace, killing the king himself (Da 5:30). That ungodly feast they were celebrating at the very time when the city was captured seems to be referred to here (vv 38–39): *They will roar together like lions*, as people do when reveling, when the wine has affected them. They have passed their cup around; now *the cup of the Lord's right hand shall be turned unto them* (Hab 2:15–16); let them be as merry as they could with that bitter cup, for on that night, in the middle of all their merriment, *Belshazzar was slain* (Da 5:30).

8.6. It is to be a universal destruction. The strength of the enemy is here compared to an inundation of waters (v. 42): *The sea has come up upon Babylon*—and there is no protection against the sea once it has broken through its limits—so that the city is *covered with the multitude of its waves*, overcome by a numerous army; *her cities* then become *a desolation*, an uninhabited and uncultivated desert (v. 43).

8.7. It is a destruction that will reach the gods and idols of Babylon. "As a sign that *the whole land shall be confounded*, that all *her slain shall fall*, and that throughout all the country *the wounded shall groan, I will do judgment upon her graven images*" (v. 47 and again v. 52).

Although the invaders are themselves idolaters, they will destroy the idols and temples of the gods of Babylon. Bel was the chief idol that the Babylonians worshiped, and so that is marked out for destruction by name (v. 44): *I will punish Bel*, that idol to which so many sacrifices have been offered. His altars will be abandoned; no one will pay them any more attention, and so the idol will fail them.

8.8. It will be a final destruction. *Babylon* will become a heap of ruins (v. 37), and the ruins will not be put to any use. *They shall not take of thee a stone for a corner, nor a stone for foundations* (v. 26).

9. A call to God's people to leave Babylon. When the ruin is approaching, they will be wise to leave the city (v. 6): "*Flee out of the midst of Babylon*, so that you may not be cut off in her sins." They would be wise to *get out of the midst of Babylon*, for otherwise, though they may not be involved in her ruins, they may yet be involved in her fears (vv. 45–46). Those who do not have enough grace to keep their temper in temptation should be wise enough to keep out of the way of temptation. They are told this (vv. 50–51): "*You Israelites, who have escaped the sword of the Chaldeans* (Babylonians) your oppressors and of the Persians their destroyers, *go away, stand not still*, go quickly back to your own country, for this is not the place where you are to rest; Canaan is."

9.1. He reminds them of the incentives they have to return: "*Remember the Lord afar off*: his presence with you now, his presence with your ancestors."

9.2. The returning captives (v. 51), being reminded of Jerusalem, cry out, "*We are confounded* (disgraced); we cannot bear the thought of it. *Shame covers our faces* at the mere mention of it, for *we have heard of the reproach of the sanctuary*, which has been desecrated and ruined by foreigners; how can we think of it with any delight?" Jeremiah answers (v. 52) that the God of Israel will now triumph over the gods of Babylon, so that their reproach will be rolled away forever (Jos 5:9).

10. The various emotional responses aroused by Babylon's fall.

10.1. Some will mourn the destruction of Babylon. There *is the sound of a cry* from Babylon (v. 54) lamenting this great destruction (v. 55). They will say in their lamentations (v. 41), "*How is Sheshach taken* (Sheshach being a cryptogram for Babylon), and how we are mistaken concerning her! How that city is surprised that was the boast, the glory, of the whole earth!"

10.2. But some will rejoice at Babylon's fall, not because it is the misery of their fellow creatures, but because it reveals the righteous judgment of God and opens up the way for the release of God's exiles (v. 48).

Verses 59–64

1. A copy is made of this prophecy, by Jeremiah himself, it seems, for Baruch his scribe is not mentioned (v. 60): *Jeremiah wrote in a book all these words that are here written against Babylon.*

2. It is sent to Babylon, to the exiles there, by the hand of Seraiah, who goes there as an attendant on King Zedekiah *in the fourth year of his reign* (v. 59). He *went with Zedekiah*, or, as the margin reads, "on the behalf of Zedekiah," *into Babylon*. The characterization given of him is that *Seraiah was a quiet prince*, a peaceful official. He was in a position of honor, but not passionate and headstrong, leading his own little group. He had a calm temperament and worked at the things that made for peace (Ro 14:19). Jeremiah could safely entrust such a man with

his mission. The real honor of great persons lies in being quiet persons.

3. Seraiah is asked to read it to his compatriots who have already gone into exile: "*When thou shalt come to Babylon, and shalt see* (v. 61) what a magnificent place it is, how large a city, how rich and well fortified it is, and when you are therefore tempted to think, 'Surely, it will stand forever,' *then thou shalt read all these words* to yourself and your friends, to encourage them in captivity: let them look with the eye of faith to see the end of these threatening powers."

4. He is directed to make a solemn declaration of God's authority and the certainty of what he has read (v. 62). Although Seraiah sees Babylon flourishing, after he has read this prophecy he must foresee Babylon falling. When we see what this world is really like, how glittering its outward appearance is and how flattering its proposals, let us read in the Book of the Lord that it is passing away, and we will learn to look on it with a holy contempt.

5. He must then tie a stone to the book and throw it into the Euphrates River as a confirming sign of the things contained in it. He is to say, "*Thus shall Babylon sink, and not rise*" (vv. 53, 64). In the sign it was the stone that sank the book, but in the thing referred to it was the book that sank the stone; it was the divine sentence passed on Babylon in this prophecy that sank that city, which seemed *as firm as a stone*. The last words of the chapter seal the vision and prophecy of this book: *Thus far are the words of Jeremiah*. This prophecy was dated in the *fourth year* of Zedekiah (v. 59), long before he finished his testimony, but it was the last of all his prophecies against the nations to be fulfilled (46:1). The remaining chapter in the book of Jeremiah is purely historical and, some think, was added by a different writer.

CHAPTER 52

History is the best expositor of prophecy, and so, to understand better the prophecies of the destruction of Jerusalem and the kingdom of Judah, we are here given an account of that sad event. It is much the same as the history in 2Ki 24–25, but the subject matter is repeated here to give light to the book of the Lamentations. We have here: 1. The bad reign of Zedekiah (vv. 1–3). 2. The besieging and capture of Jerusalem by the Babylonians (vv. 4–7). 3. The severe treatment that Zedekiah and the officials faced (vv. 8–11). 4. The destruction of the temple and the city (vv. 12–14). 5. The captivity of the people (vv. 15–16) and the numbers of those who were taken into exile (vv. 28–30). 6. The taking away of plunder from the temple (vv. 17–23). 7. The slaughter of the priests and other great men (vv. 24–27). 8. The better days that King Jehoiachin lived to see at the end of his life, after the death of Nebuchadnezzar (vv. 31–34).

Verses 1–11

This narrative begins in the beginning of the reign of Zedekiah, although there were two captivities before, one in the fourth year of Jehoiakim and the other in the first of Jehoiachin. We have here:

1. God's just displeasure against Judah and Jerusalem for their sin (v. 3). He determined to *cast them out from his presence*. He expelled them from the good land that had such signs of his presence in his providential goodness, and he expelled them from that holy city and temple that had such signs of his presence in covenant grace and love.

2. Zedekiah's bad conduct and management, for which God punished him. Zedekiah had reached maturity by the time he came to the throne; he *was twenty-one years old* (v. 1). He was not the worst of the kings—we never read about his idolatry—but he *did evil in the eyes of the Lord* (v. 2), for he did not do the good he should have done. But the evil deed of his that especially hastened this destruction was his *rebelling against the king of Babylon*, which was both his sin and his foolishness and brought ruin on his people. God was greatly displeased with him for his treacherous dealings with the king of Babylon.

3. The Babylonians gaining Jerusalem after eighteen months' siege. It was in the tenth month that they laid siege to it and in the fourth month that they took control of it, and to remember these two steps toward their ruin, the Jews kept *a fast in the fourth month and a fast in the tenth* while they were in exile (Zec 8:19); the fast in the *fifth month* was in memory of the burning of the temple, and the one in the *seventh* in memory of the murder of Gedaliah. For a year and a half the city was besieged. Supplies of food were cut off. In spite of constant attacks, the garrison refused to surrender, but soon there was the *famine in the city* (v. 6), *no bread for the people of the land*. The soldiers lacked strength to stand guard. It is then not surprising that *the city was broken up* (v. 7). Walls, in such a position, will not hold out long without guards, any more than guards without walls; nor will both together do people any good without God and his protection (Ps 127:1).

4. The king and his army getting out of the city *by night* (v. 7), but the king was overtaken by pursuers *in the plains of Jericho*, his guards were dispersed, and all his army was *scattered from him* (v. 8).

5. The sentence imposed on Zedekiah by the king of Babylon. He treated him as a rebel and *gave judgment* (pronounced sentence) *upon him* (v. 9). *His sons were slain* (killed) *before his eyes*, as well as all *the princes* (officials) *of Judah* (v. 10); then *his eyes were put out*, and he was *bound in chains* and carried in triumph to Babylon. He was condemned to imprisonment forever, to live out the remainder of his life—we cannot say *his days*, for he never saw daylight again—in darkness and misery. Jeremiah had often told him where it would all lead, but he refused to accept the warning when he could have prevented the threatened punishment.

Verses 12–23

Here is an account of the terrible havoc made by the Babylonian army under the command of Nebuzaradan, the *captain of the guard*, a month after the city was captured.

1. He burned the temple to ashes, having first plundered it of everything valuable: he *burnt the house of the Lord* (v. 13), that holy and beautiful house, where the *fathers* of the Jews had *praised him* (Isa 64:11).

2. He burned down the royal palace, probably what Solomon built after he had built the temple, which ever since had been called *the king's house*.

3. He burned *all the houses of Jerusalem*.

4. He *broke down all the walls of Jerusalem* to take revenge on them for standing in the way of his army so long. This was how the fortified city was made a ruin (Isa 25:2).

5. He *carried away many into captivity* (v. 15); he took away *certain of the poor of the people*, that is, of the people in the city, for *the poor of the land* (the poor of the country) he left for *vine-dressers and husbandmen* (v. 16). He also carried off *the residue of the people that remained*

in the city, those who had escaped the sword and famine, and the deserters.

6. The articles that were still in the temple were looted. Every article of great value had been taken away before, *the vessels of silver and gold*, but some of that kind remained (v. 19). Yet most of the temple plunder that was taken now was of bronze, which, being less valuable, was taken away last. When the walls of the city were demolished, the pillars of the temple were pulled down, too, and both happened as a sign that God, who was the strength and mainstay of both their civil and ecclesiastical government, had departed from them. No walls can protect those, nor can pillars sustain those, from whom God withdraws. These pillars of the temple were decorative. They were called *Jachin*, "He will establish," and *Boaz*, "In him is strength" (1Ki 7:21), so that the breaking of these showed that God would no longer establish his house or be its strength. These pillars are described here (vv. 21–23; 1Ki 7:15). All the articles that belonged to the bronze altar were taken away, for the sin of Jerusalem, like that of Eli's house, was not to be atoned for by sacrifice or offering (1Sa 3:14). It is said (v. 20), *The brass of all these vessels was without weight* (more than could be weighed); so it was when they were made (1Ki 7:47): *the weight of the brass was not then found out* (determined) (2Ch 4:18). Those who took the pillars as plunder did not weigh them before taking them, as purchasers do.

Verses 24–30

Here is a very sad account:

1. Of the slaughter of some great men in cold blood at Riblah. As they are reckoned in 2Ki 25:18–19, there were seventy-two—according to the number of the elders of Israel (Nu 11:24–25). The account here agrees with that, except there it is said that there were five of *those that were near the king* (royal advisers), whereas here there were seven (v. 25). Dr. Lightfoot thinks that the captain of the guard took away seven of those near the king, but two of them were Jeremiah and Ebed-Melech, both of whom were discharged, so that only five of them were put to death. *Seraiah the chief priest* is put first. Seraiah the prince was *a quiet prince* (51:59), but perhaps Seraiah the priest was turbulent and had made himself repugnant to the king of Babylon. The leaders of this people had caused them to go astray, and now they were objects of divine justice.

2. Of the exile of the rest. *Judah was carried away captive out of his own land* (v. 27). Here is an account:

2.1. Of two exiles, one in the seventh year of Nebuchadnezzar's reign (v. 28)—the same one as is said to have been in his eighth year in 2Ki 24:12—another in his eighteenth year (v. 29), the same one as is said in v. 12 to be in his nineteenth year. But the numbers here are small in comparison with those we find expressed in the other account (2Ki 24:14, 16) concerning the first of these two exiles; there it is said that 18,000 were taken captive, whereas here they are said to be 3,023. Concerning the other exile mentioned here, similarly, when all who remained in the city were taken away (v. 15), one would think there would have been more than 832 people. Dr. Lightfoot therefore conjectures that since these numbers immediately follow the story of the killing of the great men at Riblah, all who are here said to have been taken away were *put to death* as rebels.

2.2. Of a third captivity, not mentioned before, which was in the twenty-third year of Nebuchadnezzar's reign, four years after the destruction of Jerusalem (v. 30): then *Nebuzaradan* came and *carried away* 745 Jews; it is probable that this was done in revenge for the murder of Gedaliah, which was another rebellion against the king of Babylon, and that those who were now taken were put to death; yet this is not certain. If this is the sum total of the captives, and not only of those who were put to death—*all the persons were* 4,600 (v. 30)—then in this figure we see how strangely they were reduced from what they had once been, but the Lord made them fruitful in the land of their suffering, and the more they were oppressed, the more they multiplied (Ex 1:12).

Verses 31–34

We have also read this story about the release of King Jehoiachin before, in 2Ki 25:27–30, except that there it is said to have been done on *the twenty-seventh day of the twelfth month*, whereas here it is said to have been done *on the twenty-fifth*. Probably the orders for his release were given on the twenty-fifth day, but he was not presented to the king until the twenty-seventh. Nebuchadnezzar had kept this unhappy king in prison for a long time, and his son, though well disposed toward the prisoner, could not

gain any favor for him. However, when the old man had died, his son supported Jehoiachin and made him a favorite. Jehoiachin fell from a throne into a prison, but here he is advanced again to a seat of honor (v. 32), though not to a throne of power. As, earlier, the robes were changed into prison clothes, so now they are converted back into robes. Although the night of suffering may last a very long time, we must still not despair: dawn will finally come. Jehoiachin was a prisoner for thirty-seven years, held in confinement and in contempt since he was eighteen years old. Let those people whose sufferings have been extended encourage themselves with this example; the vision at the end will speak words of assurance, and so wait for it (Hab 2:3). God can make his people find favor in the eyes of their oppressors, and he can turn their hearts to pity them. *He made them to be pitied of all those that carried them captives* (Ps 106:46). It is not in vain to hope and to quietly *wait for the salvation of the Lord* (La 3:6). And now, comparing the prophecy and the history of this book, we may learn that it is nothing for churches and people that are highly honored to become corrupt, that sin leads to the ruin of those who harbor it, and that if it is not repented of and abandoned, it will certainly end in ruin.

A PRACTICAL AND DEVOTIONAL EXPOSITION OF THE BOOK OF

Lamentations

Let us consider:

1. The title of this book; in the Hebrew it has none, but is called, as the books of Moses are, by the first word, which in this case is *'ekah*, "How"; yet the Jewish commentators call it, as the Greeks do, and we from them, *qinot*, "Lamentations." As we have sacred songs of joy, so we have sacred elegies or songs of mourning.

2. The writer of this book; it is Jeremiah the poet, and this book therefore is appropriately attached to his book of prophecy and is like an appendix to it. There we had the predictions of the destructions of Judah and Jerusalem, and then the account of them, to show how the predictions were fulfilled. Here we have the expressions of his sorrow when they actually took place. When he saw these disasters from a distance, he wished that his head *were waters and his eyes fountains of tears* (Jer 9:1), and when they came, then, far from being disloyal toward his country, he wept. Although his country had been unkind to him, and although its ruin was proof that he was a true prophet, he still sadly mourned it.

3. The occasion of these lamentations; it was the destruction of Judah and Jerusalem by the Babylonian army and the dissolution of the Jewish state, both civil and ecclesiastical. Some consider these to be the lamentations that Jeremiah wrote on the occasion of the death of Josiah (2Ch 35:25). But they seem to be written in the sight, rather than in the foresight, of the disasters that followed Josiah's death, and there is nothing about Josiah in the lamentations, as there surely would have been if his death had been their occasion. No; it is Jerusalem's funeral that this is an elegy on.

4. Its composition, which is not only poetic but also alphabetical, in every chapter except chapter 5. The verses of chapters 1, 2, and 4 begin with successive letters of the Hebrew alphabet, the first verse with *aleph*, the second with *beth*, and so on; chapter 3 is a triple alphabet, the first three verses beginning with *aleph*, the next three with *beth*, and so on. This method of composition was a help to the memory and yielded a form then considered elegant. In chapters 2, 3, and 4 the letter *pe* is put before *ayin*, though this is the reverse of their order in the Hebrew alphabet. Dr. Lightfoot offers the conjecture that the letter *ayin*, which also signified the number 70, would, by being displaced, remind them of the seventy years at the end of which God would restore their fortunes.

5. Its use to the godly Jews in their sufferings, providing them with spiritual language to express their natural grief and helping them preserve the memories of Zion when they were in Babylon. They are taught here to mourn for sin and mourn to God.

CHAPTER 1

We have here the first alphabet of this lamentation, twenty-two stanzas, in which the miseries of Jerusalem are mourned and her present deplorable condition is emphasized by being compared with her former, prosperous state. Sin is acknowledged as the cause of all these miseries, and God is appealed to for justice against their enemies and for compassion toward them. Here is: 1. A complaint made to God about the disasters they suffered (vv. 1–11). 2. The same complaint made to their friends (vv. 12–17). 3. An appeal to God and his righteousness concerning their situation (vv. 18–22), in which he is humbly sought.

Verses 1–11

Such pitiful lamentations are found here that one would think that those who are inclined in any way to *weep with those that weep* (Ro 12:15) would scarcely be able to stop themselves from crying at reading these verses.

1. The miseries of Jerusalem are complained about, miseries:

1.1. In their civil state.

1.1.1. A city that was well populated is now deserted (v. 1). She was full of her own people, who *replenished* her (Ge 1:28), and full of the people of other nations that turned to her, with whom she had profitable trade, but now her own people are taken into exile, and she *sits solitary* (deserted). The *chief places of the city* are not now a *place of concourse* (meeting), as they used to be. *How has she become as a widow!* (v. 1). Her king, who was like a husband to her, is gone; her God has departed from her, giving her a certificate of divorce (Jer 3:8); she has been emptied of her children and is as lonely and sad as a widow.

1.1.2. A city that once ruled others is now subject to others (v. 1). She was *great among the nations*, greatly loved by some and greatly feared by others. Some gave her presents, and others paid her taxes. She therefore really was a *princess among the provinces*. But now she not only has lost her friends and *sits solitary*; she has lost her freedom and sits *tributary* (has become a slave); she was a slave first to Egypt and then to Babylon. Sin brings a people not only into solitude but also into slavery.

1.1.3. A city that used to be full of merriment has now become full of grief (v. 2). Jerusalem used to be a joyful city, to which tribes went to express their joy in the presence of the Lord: she was *the joy of the whole earth* (Ps 48:2); but now *she weeps sorely* (bitterly). She weeps *in the night*, in silence and solitude; *in the night*, when others rest, her thoughts are set on her troubles. Her head is *as waters, and her eyes fountains of tears*, so that she *weeps day and night* (Jer 9:1); *her tears are* continually *on her cheeks*.

1.1.4. Those who were separated from the pagan nations now *dwell among the heathen* (v. 3); those who were a special people are now a mixed people: *Judah has gone into captivity*, out of her own land into the land of her enemies, among those who are foreigners to God and the covenants of promise (Eph 2:12), with whom *she finds no rest*. "*Her children have gone into captivity before the enemy* (v. 5); those who were to have been the next generation have been taken off, so that the land is likely to remain desolate for lack of heirs." Those who live among their own people, a free people and in their own land, would be more thankful for mercies if only they would consider the miseries of those forced to go to foreign countries.

1.1.5. Those who used to conquer others have now been conquered: *All her persecutors overtook her between the straits* (v. 3), so that her people unavoidably *fell into the hand of the enemy*, for there was no way of escape (v. 7). Everywhere *her adversaries were the chief and her enemies prosper* (v. 5).

1.1.6. Those who were once a dignified people, whom God honored and to whom their neighbors paid respect, are now brought into contempt (v. 8): *All that honoured her* before *despise her*. Her people have degraded themselves by their sins: *The enemies magnify themselves against them* (v. 9). *Sin is the reproach of any people* (Pr 14:34).

1.1.7. Those who lived in a fruitful land are ready to perish for lack of necessary food (v. 11): *All her people sigh* in despondency and despair. There was *no bread for the people of the land* (Jer 52:6), and in exile they had to work hard to get bread (5:6). *They have given their pleasant things* (treasures) *for meat to relieve the soul*, or, as the margin reads, "to make the soul come again," when they were about to faint.

1.2. In their ecclesiastical state.

1.2.1. Their religious festivals are no longer observed (v. 4): *The ways of Zion do mourn. The solemn feasts* were neglected and desecrated (Isa 1:11–12), and so an end is now justly put to them. And just as *the ways of Zion mourn, so the gates of Zion*, in which the faithful worshippers used to meet, *are desolate*.

1.2.2. *Her priests sigh* at the desolation of the temple (v. 4). Their songs are turned into sighs. In the day of Zion's prosperity, *among them were the damsels playing with timbrels* (Ps 68:25), and notice is taken of their lack now. *Her virgins are afflicted*, and so *she is in bitterness*; that is, all the inhabitants of Zion *are sorrowful for the solemn assembly*, and to them *the reproach of it is a burden* (Zep 3:18).

1.2.3. Their religious places were desecrated (v. 10): *The heathen* (pagan nations) *entered into her sanctuary*, into the temple itself, into which no Israelite was permitted to enter, even very reverently and devoutly, except the priests. The pagan nations now crowd rudely in, not to worship, but to plunder.

1.2.4. All the rich things with which the temple was adorned, and which were used in the worship of God, have fallen into the hands of the enemy (v. 10): *The adversary has spread out his hand upon all her pleasant things* (treasures). What these treasures are may be seen from Isa 64:11, where the following words are added to the complaint of the burning of the temple: *All our pleasant things are laid waste*, the ark and the altar and all the other signs of God's presence with them. Treasured above others, they were now broken in pieces and taken away. From *the daughter of Zion all her beauty has departed* (v. 6). *The beauty of holiness* was the *beauty of the daughter of Zion* (1Ch 16:29); when the temple, that holy and beautiful house, was destroyed, her beauty was gone.

1.2.5. Their religious days are made fun of (v. 7): *The adversaries saw her, and did mock at her sabbaths*. They laugh at the Jews for observing one day in seven as a day of rest. Juvenal, a pagan poet, ridiculed the Jews of his day for losing a seventh part of their time: "They keep their sabbaths to their cost, / For thus one day in sev'n is lost," whereas the reality is that if Sabbaths are sanctified as they should be, they will become more useful than all the other days of the week. Whereas the Jews in exile profess that they keep the Sabbath out of obedience to their God, their adversaries ask them, "What benefit have you gained by keeping the decrees of your God, who now abandons you in your distress?"

1.2.6. Her state at present is just the reverse of what it used to be (v. 7). *Now, in the days of affliction and misery*, when everything is black and dismal, *she remembers all her pleasant things that she had in the days of old*. God often teaches us the worth of mercies by removing them.

2. The sins of Jerusalem are the reasons for all these disasters. It is *the Lord who has afflicted her* (v. 5), and he has done it as a righteous Judge, for *she has sinned*. Are her troubles many? Yes, but her sins are even more. See Jer 30:14. They are heinous (v. 8): *Jerusalem has grievously sinned*; she has "sinned sin" is how the original reads, sinned willfully and deliberately. Jerusalem, who makes such a profession and enjoys such privileges, *sinned grievously* (v. 8), and so (v. 9) she *came down wonderfully* (her fall was astounding). The people of Judah have been oppressive and are therefore justly oppressed (v. 3): *Judah has gone into captivity*, and it is *because of affliction and great servitude*, because the rich among them afflicted the poor, especially, as the Aramaic paraphrases it, because they oppressed their Hebrew servants, which they are accused of in Jer 34:11. *All that honoured her despise her* (v. 8), for *her filthiness is in her skirts*; she has rolled them in the sinful mire.

3. Jerusalem's friends are here complained about as false and unkind: they *have all dealt treacherously with* (have betrayed) *her* (v. 2), so that, in effect, *they have*

become her enemies. Her princes are like harts (v. 6), who, at the first signs of fear, rush away. They *are like harts* famished because they can find no *pasture*, and so *are gone without strength* (in weakness) *before the pursuer*. Her neighbors are unneighborly. There is no one *to help her* (v. 7). *She has no comforter*, no one to sympathize or alleviate her grief (vv. 7, 9).

4. Jerusalem's God is here sought, and all is turned to his compassionate consideration (v. 9): "*O Lord! Behold my affliction*," and (v. 11), "*See, O Lord! And consider.*" The only way to get peace when we have burdens is to give them to God first, and leave him to do with us as seems good to him (1Sa 3:18).

Verses 12–22

In these verses the prophet, in the name of the mourning church, especially acknowledges the hand of God in this disaster and the righteousness of his hand.

1. The church in distress exalts her adversity. She appeals to all spectators: *See if there be any sorrow like unto my sorrow* (v. 12). This might perhaps be truly said about Jerusalem's sorrows, but we tend to be oversensitive and apply it too readily to ourselves when we are in trouble. If our troubles were to be seen in perspective together with the common store of the burdens of other people, and then they were all equally shared out, each of us would say, "Please give me back my own share."

2. The church looks beyond the instruments here to the author of her troubles: "It is *the Lord* who *has afflicted me*, and he has *afflicted me* because he is angry with me. It is *in the day of his fierce anger*" (v. 12). She is like someone suffering from a fever: "*He has sent fire into my bones*" (v. 13). She is like someone caught in a net: the more she struggles to get out of it, the more she is caught up in it. She is like someone in a desert, whose way is solitary: "*He has turned me back*, so that I cannot go on, *has made me desolate*, so that I have nothing to support me with, but am *faint all the day.*" She is like someone in a yoke, not yoked for service, but for penance (v. 14): *The yoke of my transgressions is bound by his hand.* The yoke of Christ's commands is an *easy yoke* (Mt 11:30), but the yoke and burden of our own sins is heavy. When conscience, his deputy, binds us to his judgment, then *the yoke is bound* and *wreathed* (woven together) *by the hand* of his justice, and nothing except the hand of his forgiving mercy will loose it. It is he who has *trodden under foot all her mighty men* (v. 15). She is like someone in a winepress, and it is God who has *trodden the virgin, the daughter of Judah.* She is in the hand of her enemies, and it is the Lord who has handed her over to them (v. 14). The One who has many times *commanded deliverances for Jacob* (Ps 44:4) now commands an invasion against Jacob, because Jacob has disobeyed the commands of his law.

3. The church justly demands a share in the compassion of those who see her misery (v. 12): "*Is it nothing to you, all you that pass by*? Can you look on me without concern? Is it nothing to you that your neighbor's house is on fire?"

4. The church justifies her own grief (v. 16): "*For these things I weep*; I weep in the night (v. 2), when no one can see; *my eye, my eye runs down with water.*" Zion spreads forth her hands (v. 17), which is here an expression of despair rather than desire. Her God has withdrawn from her. It is hardly surprising that the souls of the saints are weak when God, who is the only comforter who can relieve them, keeps far away. Her children are taken away from her and are unable to help her. They cannot help themselves, and how could they help her? Both the young women and young men, who were her joy and hope, *have gone into captivity* (v. 18). Her friends have failed her, some refusing to help her and others unable to. She *spreads forth her hands*, begging for relief, but *there is none to comfort her* (v. 17). Her idols were her lovers, but they *deceived* her. Egypt and Assyria were her trusted friends, but they deceived her. The *priests* and the *elders*, who should have taken the lead, died of hunger (v. 19) or went begging for bread to keep them alive. *Abroad* (outside) *the sword bereaved* and killed all that came in its path, and *at home* (inside) all provisions were cut off by the besiegers, so that *there was as death* (v. 20), that is, famine. The enemies, who were the instruments to bring this disaster, were cruel, and so were those who were bystanders, the Edomites and Ammonites, who were hostile toward Israel: they *heard of my trouble and were glad that thou hadst done it* (v. 21). It pleased them to find that God and his Israel had fallen out.

5. The church justifies God, acknowledging that her sins have deserved these rebukes. The burden that lies so heavily and binds so firmly is the *yoke of her transgressions* (v. 14). It is with our own rod that we are beaten. She acknowledges the fairness of God's actions by acknowledging the sins of her own: *I have rebelled against his commandments* (v. 18), and again (v. 20), *I have grievously rebelled*. We cannot speak badly enough of sin, and we must always speak the worst about our own sin; we must call it *rebellion, grievous rebellion*. Sorrow for sin must be great and must have an effect on the soul.

6. The church appeals to both the mercy and the justice of God in her present situation. *Behold, O Lord! For I am in distress*. She appeals to the justice of God concerning the wrongs her enemies did her (vv. 21–22): "*Thou wilt bring the day that thou hast called*, the day that is set in the purposes of God and declared in the prophecies, when my enemies *shall be like unto me*, when the *cup of trembling* (Isa 51:17), now put into my hands, will be put into theirs." It may be read as a prayer, "May the appointed day come," and so it continues, "*Let their wickedness come before thee*; may that day come quickly when you will deal with them for their sins as you have dealt with me for mine." This prayer amounts to a protest against all thoughts of a coalition with them. Our prayers must agree with God's word, and although we are bound in charity to forgive our enemies and pray for them, we may still in faith pray for the fulfillment of what God has spoken against his and his church's enemies.

CHAPTER 2

The second alphabetical elegy is set to the same mournful tune as the first, and its substance is much the same; it begins with 'ekah, as the first did: "How sad is our case! Woe to us!" Here is: 1. The anger of Zion's God as the cause of her adversities (vv. 1–9). 2. The sorrow of Zion's children as the effect of her adversities (vv. 10–19). 3. The matter referred to God's compassionate consideration (vv. 20–22). The hand that wounded must also make whole (Job 5:18; Hos 6:1).

Verses 1–9

A very sad description is given here of the state of God's church, of Jacob and Israel, of Zion and Jerusalem, but the emphasis in these verses seems to be placed throughout on the hand of God. The grief is that God appears angry with them. He is the One who is rebuking them and corrects them *in his hot displeasure* (Ps 6:1; 38:1).

1. There was a time when God's delight was in his church and he supported her as a friend. But now he is angry with her and appears against her as an enemy. To those who know how to value God's favor, nothing appears more fearful than his anger; corrections in love are relatively easily endured, but rebukes in love wound deeply. It is God's wrath that *burns against Jacob like a flaming fire* (v. 3), but it was their sin that kindled this fire. God is such a tender Father toward his children that we may be sure he is never angry with them except when they give him cause to be angry. Now he has become an enemy toward them; at least he is *as an enemy* (v. 5). He has *bent his bow like an enemy* (v. 4). He stands *with his right hand* stretched out against them and with a drawn sword in it, *as an adversary*. God is not really his people's enemy, not even when he is angry with them and corrects them in anger. But sometimes God is *as an enemy* toward them, when all his providences concerning them seem outwardly to lead toward their ruin. But we bless God that Christ is *our peace* (Eph 2:14), our peacemaker, who has dealt with and taken away the enmity.

2. There was a time when God's church appeared very bright, significant among the nations, but now *the Lord has covered the daughter of Zion with a cloud* (v. 1), a dark cloud, through which she cannot see his face. It is *a thick cloud*, a black cloud, not like the one that led them through the wilderness or the one by which God took possession of the temple and filled it with his glory; no, the side of the cloud that is now turned toward them is the side that was turned toward the Egyptians in the Red Sea. He *turned back their right hand* (v. 3), so that they were unable to ward off the blows they received. What can their right hand do against the enemy when God draws it back and withers it, as he did Jeroboam's (1Ki 13:4)?

3. There was a time when Jerusalem and the towns and cities of Judah were strong and well fortified. But now the Lord has in anger *swallowed them up* (vv. 2, 5). They are ruined so totally that they seem to have been *swallowed up*. He has *swallowed up all her palaces* (v. 5), even though those were very grand, strong, rich, and well guarded. He has destroyed not only their dwelling places but also their *strongholds*. This is how he *increased in the daughter of Judah mourning and lamentation*; they saw all their defenses leave them. This is insisted on again in vv. 7–9. He has *given up into the hand of the enemy the walls of her palaces*. The walls of the palaces cannot give adequate protection unless God himself is a wall of fire around them. Whatever desolations God makes in his church, they are all according to his purposes. But when he was about to do it, he *stretched out a line*, a measuring line, to do it according to his exact measure. The destruction will go up to a certain point and no farther.

4. There was a time when their government flourished and the balance of power was on their side, but now it is completely different: *He has polluted* (brought down) *the kingdom and the princes thereof* (v. 2). They first defiled themselves with their idolatry, and then God dealt with them as with things that have been defiled. It is not surprising that the king and the priest, whose characters have always been greatly respected, are despised by everybody when God has, *in the indignation of his anger, despised the king and the priest* (v. 6). The crown has fallen from their heads, for *her king and her princes are among the Gentiles*, among them as prisoners (v. 9), and treated as the basest persons, without any thought given to their position. God is just to dishonor by his judgments those who have dishonored themselves by their sin.

5. There was a time when the ordinances of the worship of God were administered in purity, when the people had those signs of God's presence with them, but now that part of the *beauty of Israel* which was truly their greatest glory is gone.

5.1. The ark was God's footstool (so called in 1Ch 28:2; Ps 99:5; 132:7), under the atonement cover, between the cherubim; of all the symbols of God's presence, this was the most sacred; it was there that the *Shechinah*, the visible presence of the divine glory, rested. But now he has *not remembered his footstool* (v. 1). The ark itself was allowed, it seems, to fall into the hands of the Babylonians. The signs of his presence have little value when his presence is gone! God and his kingdom can stand without that footstool.

5.2. Those who ministered holy things used to be *pleasant to the eye in the tabernacle of the daughter of Zion* (v. 4); they were *purer than snow, whiter than milk* (4:7). But now these have been killed, and their *blood is mingled with their sacrifices* (Lk 13:1).

5.3. The temple was God's tabernacle—as the tabernacle, while that existed, was called *his temple* (Ps 27:4)—and *he has violently taken this away* (v. 6); he has uprooted its stakes and cut the cords. It will no longer be a tabernacle, much less his. When people desecrate God's tabernacle, God is just to take it away from them. He has now *abhorred his sanctuary* (v. 7); it has been defiled with sin, the only thing he hates, and for the sake of that he even rejects his sanctuary, which he had previously delighted in and called *his rest for ever* (Ps 132:14). Some understand the *places of the assembly* (v. 6) to refer not only to the temple but also to the synagogues and the schools of the prophets, which the enemy *burnt up* (Ps 74:8).

5.4. The sacred festivals and the Sabbaths used to be carefully remembered, but now the Lord has *caused those to be forgotten*, even in Zion itself. Now that Zion is in ruins, no distinction is made between Sabbaths and other days; every day is a day of mourning, so that all the *solemn feasts are forgotten* (v. 6).

5.5. The altar that once sanctified their gifts (Mt 23:19) is now rejected, for God will no longer accept their gifts or be honored by their sacrifices (v. 7). The altar was *the table of the Lord* (Mal 1:7), but God will no longer keep his house among them; he will neither feast them nor feast with them. They were once blessed with prophets and teachers of the law, but now *the law is no more* (v. 9); it is no longer read by the people, no longer explained by the scribes. The tables of the Law have gone with the ark; the Book of the Law has been taken away from them. *Her prophets also find no vision from the Lord*. They persecuted God's prophets and despised the visions they had from the Lord, and so God is just to say they will have no more prophets or visions.

Verses 10–22

Justly is this book called *Lamentations*, expressions of grief, like the contents of Ezekiel's scroll (Eze 2:10).

1. Vivid images of lamentation are here presented.

1.1. The judges and magistrates, who used to appear in robes of state, have been stripped of them and are wearing clothes of mourning (v. 10); the elders no longer sit in the seats of judgment, *the thrones of the house of David* (Ps 122:5), but *sit upon the ground*. They *keep silence*, overwhelmed with grief, not knowing what to say. They have *cast dust upon their heads and girded themselves with sackcloth.*

1.2. *The virgins of Jerusalem hang down their heads to the ground*; those who were always merry now know sorrow.

1.3. The prophet himself is an example to the mourners (v. 11). His *eyes do fail with tears*; he has wept until he can weep no more; he wept himself blind. Jeremiah himself has received better treatment than his neighbors, and better than he had received earlier from his own compatriots; their destruction was his restoration. Nevertheless, his personal interests are swallowed up in his concern for the public, and he mourns the *destruction of the daughter of his people*, as if he himself had suffered the greatest in that terrible disaster.

2. Calls to lamentation are given here (v. 18): *The heart of the people cries unto the Lord.* Some fear it was a cry of bitter complaint, but many of them sincerely cry out to God for mercy in their distress, and the prophet tells them to continue to do so: *O wall of the daughter of Zion!* This opening phrase means either "you who stand on the wall, you *watchmen on the walls*" (Isa 62:6), or "because of the breaking down of the wall"—which was not done until about a month after the city was captured. With this latter reading, the sentence would mean, "Because of the breaking down of *the wall of the daughter of Zion*, let her continually lament." This was something Nehemiah lamented long afterward (Ne 1:3–4). "*Let tears run down like a river day and night*, weep without stopping, give yourself no rest from weeping, *let not the apple of thy eye cease.*" The calamities will continue, and the causes of grief will recur, and they will be given fresh occasion every day and night to mourn their sad condition. They will gradually tend to grow insensitive, and so they will continually need to be called to humble their souls, until their proud and hard hearts are thoroughly humbled and softened.

3. Causes for lamentation are given here:

3.1. Many people perish by famine. God corrected them with a scarcity of provisions due to a lack of rain some time before (Jer 14:1), and now God uses the greater severity of the siege to bring upon them the most extreme form of the same judgment. The children die of hunger in their mothers' arms (v. 11). This is mentioned again in v. 19: *They faint for hunger in the top of every street.* There are also little children who are killed and eaten by their mothers (v. 20). Something similar was done in the siege of Samaria (2Ki 6:29).

3.2. Many people fall by the sword, which destroys one as well as the other (2Sa 11:25), especially when it is in the hand of such cruel enemies as the Babylonians. They spare no age, not even those who, by reason of their young or old age, are exempt from taking up the sword, for even they *perish by the sword.* They spare neither sex: *My virgins and my young men have fallen by the sword.* This was the *Lord's doing* (Ps 118:23). But to say what follows, *Thou hast killed, and not pitied*, is very harsh toward God, for his soul is *grieved for the misery of Israel* (Jdg 10:16).

3.3. Before Jerusalem fell, their false prophets deceived them (v. 14). This was something Jeremiah mourned long before and observed with great concern (Jer 14:13): *Ah! Lord God, the prophets say unto them, You shall not see the sword*; and he includes it among his lamentations here. Their visions came from their own imagination, and it is most likely that they themselves knew that the visions they claimed to have received were false. The people set them up and told them what to say, so that they were *prophets after their hearts* (Eze 13:2). Prophets

should tell people their faults and show them their sins, so that they may come to repentance and prevent their ruin, but these prophets knew that that would lose them the people's affections and contributions. Therefore *they have not discovered* (exposed) *thy iniquity* (v. 14), even though that might have been the means of warding off their captivity by taking away their sins.

3.4. Their neighbors now laugh at them (v. 15): *All that pass by thee clap their hands at thee. Is this the city*, they say, *that men called the perfection of beauty?* (Ps 50:2). How has such perfection become deformed! Where is all its beauty now?

3.5. Their enemies gloat over them (v. 16). Those who wish harm to Jerusalem now *open their mouths*; in fact, they open them wide. They *hiss* (scoff) *and gnash their teeth* in scorn and indignation: "*We have swallowed her up*, we have done it, and it is our gain; it all belongs to us now. *Certainly this is the day that we have looked for* a long time; *we have found it; we have seen it. Aha! So would we have it* (Ps 35:25)."

3.6. Their God has gone against them in all this (v. 17): *The Lord has done that which he had devised* (planned). What God plans against his people is intended for them, and that will be seen to be so in the outcome of events. When he gave them his Law through Moses, he told them what judgments he would certainly inflict on them if they disobeyed that law, and now that they have been guilty of disobeying this law, he has carried out its sentence according to Lev 26:16; Dt 28:15.

4. Comforts to heal these lamentations are here sought for and prescribed.

4.1. They are sought for (v. 13). The prophet seeks some suitable, acceptable words to say to her in this situation: *Wherewith shall I comfort thee, O virgin! daughter of Zion?* We try to comfort our friends by telling them that their case is not special, that there are many people who have greater troubles than theirs; but this cannot be applied in Jerusalem's case: "*What thing shall I liken to thee*, or *what shall I equal to thee, that I may comfort thee?* What city or country is there whose case is parallel to yours? Unfortunately, there is not one, no one has sorrow like yours, because there is none whose honor was like yours." Or we may tell our suffering friends that their case is not desperate and that it may easily be put right, but that will not be accepted here either, considering human probabilities, for "*thy breach* (wound) *is great, like the sea* (v. 13), like a breach that the sea sometimes makes on the land, which gradually becomes wider and wider and cannot be repaired. You are wounded, and *who shall heal thee?*" No wisdom or human power can make good such a broken, shattered state. It is futile, therefore, to administer any of these common medicines.

4.2. The cure prescribed is that they should turn to God, committing their situation to him by penitent prayer and being constant and urgent in such prayer (v. 19): "*Arise* out of the dust and your despondency; *cry out in the night.* When others are asleep, you are to be on your knees, boldly seeking God for mercy; *in the beginning of the watches*, of each of the four watches of the night, *pour out thy heart like water before the Lord.* Be free and full in prayer, be sincere and serious in prayer, open your hearts and minds, spread out your case before the Lord. *Lift up thy hands toward him* in holy desire and expectation; beg for *the life of thy young children.* What have these poor lambs done (2Sa 24:17)? Take with you these words (v. 20): '*Behold, O Lord! and consider to whom thou hast done this.* Are they not your own people, the descendants of Abraham your friend and of Jacob your chosen one? Lord, have compassion on them!'"

CHAPTER 3

The theme of this chapter is the same as that of the two previous chapters, but its composition is different; those were in long verse, this is in short, another kind of meter; those were in single alphabets, this is in a treble one. We have here: 1. A sad complaint of God's displeasure and its fruits (vv. 1–20). 2. Words of encouragement to God's people (vv. 21–36). 3. Duty prescribed in this afflicted state (vv. 37–41). 4. The complaint renewed (vv. 42–54). 5. Encouragement taken to hope in God (vv. 55–66). Some think all this was spoken by the prophet himself when he was imprisoned and persecuted, but to me it seems rather to have been spoken in the person of the church, now in exile and desolate; and the prophet was in fact especially interested in the desolation of the church. But the complaints here are more general than those in the previous chapter, and they are intended more for use in the private room than in the sacred assembly. Some think Jeremiah makes these complaints not only as an intercessor for Israel but also as a type of Christ.

Verses 1–20

The title of Ps 102 might appropriately be used as an introduction to this chapter: the *prayer of the afflicted, when he is overwhelmed and pours out his complaint before the Lord.* The prophet complains:

1. That God is angry. This gives both birth and bitterness to the affliction (v. 1): *I am the man that has seen affliction,* and has felt it strongly, *by the rod of his wrath.* God is sometimes angry with his own people, yet this anger is not a sword to cut off his people, but only a rod to correct them. It is to them *the rod of his wrath,* which, though painful at the time, is advantageous in the end (Heb 12:11). We must expect to *see affliction* through this rod, and if we are made to experience extraordinary affliction, we must not quarrel, for we are sure that the anger is just and that the affliction is mixed with mercy.

2. That he is in the dark. Darkness stands for trouble and bewilderment; this is the case of the one who complains (v. 2), "*He has led me* by an inexplicable chain of events *into darkness and not into light,* the darkness I feared, not the light I hoped for." And (v. 6), "*He has set me in dark places,* dark as the grave, *like those that are dead of old,* who are completely forgotten."

3. That God appears against him as an enemy: "*Surely against me is he turned* (v. 3), as far as I can discern, for his hand *is turned against me all the day. I am chastened every morning*" (Ps 73:14). When God's hand is turned against us, we are tempted to think that his heart is turned against us too. "*He was unto me as a bear lying in wait,* surprising me with his judgments, *and as a lion in secret places,* so that whichever way I turned, I could never feel safe (v. 10). *He has bent his bow* (v. 12). *He has set me as a mark for his sorrow,* and *the arrows of his quiver enter into my reins* (heart), give me an inner wound (v. 13)."

4. That the Jewish state may be fitly compared to a man who has become wrinkled with old age (v. 4): "*My flesh and my skin has he made old*; they are wasted and withered away, and *he has broken my bones* (v. 15). *He has filled me with bitterness,* a bitter sense of these adversities. *He has mingled gravel* with my bread, so that *my teeth are broken with it* (v. 16). *He has covered me with*

ashes*," as mourners used to be, or, as some read it, "he has fed me with ashes."

5. That he is unable to discern any way of escape (v. 5): "*He has built against me,* as forts and siege works are set up around a besieged city. Where there once was an open way, it is now completely closed: *He has compassed* (walled) *me* in on every side *with gall and travail*; I am troubled, anxious, and worn out; I am seeking a way out but cannot find one (v. 7). *He has hedged me about, that I cannot get out.* I am chained, and as notorious evildoers are doubly fettered, so he *has made my chain heavy. He has* also (v. 9) *enclosed* (barred) *my ways with hewn* (with blocks of) *stone,* with a stone wall, which cannot be broken through, so that *my paths are made crooked.* I want to go this way or that way but am continually turned back." And again (v. 11), "*He has turned aside my ways,* ruined my proposals. He has *pulled me in pieces* and *made me desolate*; he has deprived me of all comfort in my own soul."

6. That God turns a deaf ear to his prayers (v. 8): "*When I cry and shout,* as one who is serious with God and wants to make him listen, he still *shuts out my prayer.*" Sometimes God seems to be angry even against *the prayers of his people* (Ps 80:4), and their case is truly miserable when they are denied not only an answer but even the assurance of acceptance.

7. That his neighbors laugh at his troubles (v. 14): *I was a derision* (laughing-stock) *to all my people,* to all the evildoers among them, who made fun of the public judgments and made others do so too, especially the prophet Jeremiah's griefs.

8. That he is ready to despair of rescue: "You have not only taken peace away from me but also *removed my soul far off from peace* (v. 17). *I forget prosperity*; it is so long since I had it that I have lost any idea of what it is like. I have become so used to sorrow and harsh treatment that I no longer know what joy and liberty mean. *My strength and my hope have perished from the Lord* (v. 18). I can no longer rest in God as my support; even my God seems relentless."

9. That grief returns whenever he remembers his troubles, and his reflections are as sad as his prospects (vv. 19–20). "My affliction and my transgression," as some read it, "my trouble and my sin that brought it on me; this is *the wormwood and the gall* in *the affliction and the misery.*" It is sin that makes the cup of affliction bitter. The exiles in Babylon had all the miseries of the siege continually in their mind, and they *wept when they remembered Zion*; in fact, they could *never forget Jerusalem* (Ps 137:1, 5).

Verses 21–36

Here the clouds begin to disperse, and the sky to clear up. Here the tune changes, and the mourners in Zion begin to appear more optimistic. If it were not for hope, the heart would break. To save the heart from being completely broken, something that gives grounds for *hope* is *called to mind* (v. 21). "I cause to return to my heart" is the reading of the margin. What we have had in our hearts is sometimes as if it were forgotten until God by his grace makes it return to our hearts. "*I recall it to mind; therefore have I hope* and am saved from complete despair." Let us see what he calls to mind.

1. Bad as things are, it is because of the mercy of God that they are not even worse. We are *afflicted by the rod*

of his wrath, but *it is of the Lord's mercies that we are not consumed* (v. 22).

1.1. The streams of mercy are acknowledged: *We are not consumed* (v. 22). The church of God is like Moses' burning bush, burning but *not consumed* (Ex 3:2). It is *persecuted* by people *but not forsaken* by God, and so although it is *cast down*, it is *not destroyed* (2Co 4:9); it is corrected but *not consumed*, refined in the furnace as silver is, but *not consumed* as dross.

1.2. These streams flow from the fountain: *It is of the Lord's mercies* (v. 22). God is an inexhaustible *fountain of mercy, the Father of mercies* (2Co 1:3). If we had been dealt with *according to our sins*, we would have been consumed long ago, but we have been dealt with *according to God's mercies*.

2. Even in the depths of their suffering, they still experience the tenderness of God's pity and the truth of his promises. They have several times complained that God has not shown compassion (2:17, 21), but here they correct themselves and acknowledge:

2.1. That *God's compassions fail not* (v. 22); they really do not fail, not even when he seems in his anger to have *shut up his tender mercies*. These rivers of mercy flow fully and constantly and never run dry. *They are new every morning* (v. 23). Every morning we have fresh instances of God's compassion toward us; *every morning does he bring his judgment to light* (Zep 3:5). When our strength fails, God's compassion does not.

2.2. That *great is his faithfulness*. Although Jerusalem is in ruins, *the truth of the Lord endures for ever* (Ps 117:2).

3. God is and always will be the all-sufficient happiness of his people, and they depend on him to be this (v. 24): *The Lord is my portion, saith my soul*; that is:

3.1. "When I have lost everything I have in the world, my liberty, livelihood, and almost life itself, I still have not lost my relationship with God.

3.2. "While I have a relationship with God, I have enough; I have what is sufficient to balance out all my troubles and make up for all my losses.

3.3. "This is what I depend on: *Therefore will I hope in him*. I will trust in him, wait for him, when every other support failed me."

4. Those who deal with God will find it is not futile to trust in him. While we *wait for him* by faith, we must *seek him* by prayer. Our seeking will help maintain our waiting. *It is good*—it is our duty and will be to our overwhelming comfort and satisfaction—*to hope and quietly to wait for the salvation of the Lord*, to hope that his time will come. We must wait until he does come, remaining calm and silent, not quarreling with God, but accepting his divine arrangements. *Father, thy will be done* (Mt 26:39).

5. Afflictions are really good for us, and if we bear them rightly, they will benefit us. It is not only good to wait for the salvation; it is also good to suffer in the meantime (v. 27): *It is good for a man that he bear the yoke in his youth*. Many of the young men were taken into captivity. He tells them that it is good for them to *bear the yoke* of that captivity, and they will find it so if they will seek to fulfill God's purposes in placing that heavy yoke on them. This can be applied to the yoke of God's commands, but here it seems to refer to the yoke of affliction. Many have found it beneficial to bear this in their youth; it has made them humble when otherwise they would have become proud and unruly, and *as a bullock unaccustomed to the yoke* (Jer 31:18). But when are we *bearing the yoke*

in such a way that it is really *good for us to bear it in our youth*?

5.1. When we are quiet under our afflictions, when we *sit alone and keep silence*, so that we may talk with God and *commune with our own hearts* (Ps 4:4), silencing all thoughts of discontent or distrust.

5.2. When we are humble and patient under our affliction. The person who *puts his mouth in the dust* benefits from the yoke—the one who not only *lays his hand upon his mouth* (Job 40:4), as a sign of submission to the will of God, but also *puts it in the dust* (v. 29), as a sign of sorrow at remembering the sin. Those who are truly humbled because of their sin will be glad to obtain a good hope, through grace, even if they *put their mouth* (bury their faces) *in the dust* because of it.

5.3. When we are meek toward those who are the instruments of our trouble, having a forgiving spirit (v. 30). Our Lord Jesus has left us an example of this, for he *gave his back to the smiter* (Isa 50:6). Those who can bear contempt and disgrace, not *rendering railing for railing* (1Pe 3:9) and bitterness for bitterness, will find that *it is good to bear the yoke*, that it will turn to their spiritual advantage.

6. God will graciously return to his people with encouragements *according to the time that he has afflicted them* (vv. 31–32). We may support ourselves with this:

6.1. That when we are cast down, we are not cast away; when parents correct their children, they are not disinheriting them.

6.2. That although we may seem to have been cast away for a time, we are not in reality cast away.

6.3. That whatever we are suffering, his hand is in it, and so we may be assured it is *for a season* (1Pe 1:6).

6.4. That God has compassion and encouragement in store even for those whom he himself has grieved. He has torn, and he will bind up our wounds (Hos 6:1).

6.5. That when God comes to us to deal graciously with us, it will not be according to what we deserve, but according to his mercies.

7. When God does bring grief, it is for his wise and holy purposes, and he does not take delight in our calamities (v. 33). He does not do it *willingly*, not, literally, "from the heart."

7.1. He afflicts us only when we give him cause to do so. If he shows us kindness, it is because *so it seems good* to him (Mt 11:26), but if he designates bitter things for us, it is because we both deserve them and need them.

7.2. He does not delight either in the death of sinners (Eze 18:23; 33:11) or in the disquiet of saints, but punishes with reluctance. He does not delight in the misery of any of his creatures; he is so far from it that in all their suffering he suffers too (Isa 63:9), and his soul is grieved for the misery of Israel (Jdg 10:16).

7.3. He maintains his kindness for his people even when he brings affliction on them. If he does not *willingly grieve the children of men*, then much less so his own children. They may by faith see love in his heart even when they see frowns on his face and the rod of correction in his hand.

8. Although he uses people as his hand, or rather as instruments in his hand, to correct his people, he is far from pleased with the injustice and the wrong those instruments do to his people (vv. 34–36). In two ways the people of God are oppressed by their enemies, and the prophet here assures us that God does not approve of either of them:

8.1. If people wrong them by using force, God does not approve of that. He does not himself *crush under his feet the prisoners of the earth* (v. 34), but hears their cry; nor does he approve when human beings crush their prisoners. It is cruel to trample on those who are down.

8.2. If people commit wrongs while pretending to administer justice, if they *turn aside the right of a man* (v. 35), so that he cannot find out what his rights are or cannot reach them, if they *subvert a man in his cause* (deprive a person of justice) (v. 36), bringing in a wrong verdict or giving a false judgment, let them know that God sees them. It is *before the face of the Most High* (v. 35). God does not approve of them. More is implied than is expressed. The perversion of the course of justice and the depriving of justice are a great insult to God, and he will still sooner or later severely judge those who act in this way.

Verses 37–41

1. We must not quarrel with God because of any suffering he places upon us at any time (v. 39): *Wherefore does a living man complain?* From the teaching of God's sovereign and universal providence Jeremiah infers, *Wherefore does a living man complain?* The sufferers in captivity must submit to the will of God in all their suffering. Will *a living man complain, a man for the punishment of his sins?* We are sinners, and what we complain about is the just *punishment of our sins*; it is far less than our sins have deserved. Then let us not complain; instead of repining, we must repent, and as a sign that God is reconciled to us, we must try to reconcile ourselves to his holy will.

2. We must set ourselves to fulfill God's intention in bringing troubles on us, which is to remind us of our sin and bring us back home to himself (v. 40). *Let us search and try our ways.* Let conscience be used to examine and test. *Let us try our ways*, so that by them we may *try* ourselves, for we are to judge our state not by our weak wishes, but by our steps, not by one individual step, but by our ways, the ends we are aiming at and the rules we follow, considering whether the tenor of our lives is agreeable to those ends and rules. When we are suffering, it is a good time to *consider our ways* (Hag 1:5), so that what is wrong may be repented of and put right for the future, and so that we may fulfill the intention of the suffering. In times of public disaster, we tend to reflect on other people's ways and blame them, but our business is to *search and try our own ways*. "Let us *turn again to the Lord*. We have been with him, and things have never gone well with us since we abandoned him; let us therefore now return to him." Our hearts must accompany our prayers. We must *lift up our hearts with our hands*, as we must pour out our souls with our words. Praying is lifting up the soul to God (Ps 25:1) as to *our Father in heaven*, and the soul that hopes to be with God in heaven forever will continue to learn the way there and press on toward it in frequent acts of devotion.

Verses 42–54

The prophet has acknowledged that living people should not complain, but here the clouds return after the rain (Ecc 12:2).

1. They confess the righteousness of God in afflicting them (v. 42): *We have transgressed and have rebelled.* If we call sin disobedience and rebellion, then we are giving it the right names.

2. They complain about the suffering they are experiencing, not without some reflections upon God.

2.1. They complain about the signs of his displeasure (v. 42): *Thou hast not pardoned. Thou hast not pitied* (v. 43). They complain that there is a wall that divides them and God: "*Thou hast covered us* up as human beings who have been buried are covered up and forgotten." It prevents their prayers from reaching God (v. 44): "*Thou hast covered thyself with a cloud* so thick *that our prayers* seem as if they have become lost in it."

2.2. They complain about the contempt of their neighbors (v. 45): "*Thou hast made us as the off-scouring.*" If they had not made themselves contemptible, their enemies could not have made them so.

2.3. They complain about the destruction that their enemies carry out on them (v. 47): the *destruction of the daughter of my people* (v. 48), *of all the daughters of my city* (v. 51). Their enemies have chased them until they completely defeated them (v. 53): *They have cut off my life in the dungeon* (pit). They are, so to speak, thrown into the pit or grave, and *a stone cast upon them*, such as used to be *rolled to the door of the sepulchers* (Mt 27:60). They look upon the Jewish nation as dead and buried. Their destruction is compared to the sinking of living human beings into the water.

2.4. They complain about their own excessive grief and fear (vv. 48–49). It is added (v. 51), "*My eye affects my heart.* The more I look at the desolation of the city and country, the sadder I am."

2.5. In the midst of these sad complaints here is one word of comfort (v. 50). We continue weeping *till the Lord look down and behold from heaven*. Bad as the case is, one favorable look from heaven will set everything right. While they continue to weep, they also continue to wait; nothing will wipe tears from their eyes *till he look down*.

Verses 55–66

There has been a struggle within the prophet between sense and faith, fear and hope, but faith has the last word and becomes conqueror. The prophet and his friends have found God good in three things:

1. He has *heard their prayers* (v. 56), although they have been ready to fear that the cloud of wrath is such that their *prayers cannot pass through* (v. 44). When they were *in the low dungeon* (deep pit), as *free among the dead* (Ps 88:5), they *called upon God's name* (v. 55). "Thou didst not hide thy ear at my breathing, at my cry" (v. 56). Notice how he calls prayer *his breathing*, for in prayer we breathe toward God; we breathe after him. Prayer is the breath of the new self, sucking in the air of mercy in petitions and returning it in praise; it is both a sign of and the way to maintain the spiritual life.

2. He has silenced their fears (v. 57): "*Thou drewest near in the day that I called upon thee.*" When we draw near to God in our duty, we may by faith see him drawing near to us in his mercy. *Thou saidst, Fear not.*

3. He has already begun to appear for them (v. 58): *O Lord! Thou hast pleaded the causes of my soul*, that is, as it follows, *thou hast redeemed my life.* He encourages himself by appealing to God's justice and omniscience. "*O Lord! Thou hast seen my wrong*, that I have done no wrong at all, but am now suffering a great deal. *Thou hast seen all their imaginations* (plots) *against me* (v. 60). They amuse themselves and one another with my misery, as the Philistines made fun of Samson (Jdg 16:23–25). May they be dealt with as they have dealt with us; may your hand be against them as their hand has been against us."

CHAPTER 4

This chapter is another single alphabet of lamentations for the destruction of Jerusalem, like those in the first two chapters. 1. The prophet here mourns the indignities done to those to whom respect was once shown (vv. 1–2). 2. He mourns the effects of the famine (vv. 3–10). 3. He mourns the sacking of Jerusalem (vv. 11–12). 4. He acknowledges that the sins of their leaders were the cause of all these calamities (vv. 13–16). 5. He gives up everything as doomed (vv. 17–20). 6. He foretells the destruction of the Edomites who triumphed at Jerusalem's fall (v. 21). 7. He foretells the eventual restoration of the fortunes of Zion (v. 22).

Verses 1–12

The elegy in this chapter begins with a lamentation of the sad change in Jerusalem. The city that was once like *the most fine gold* (v. 1) has lost its radiance; it has become dross.

1. The temple, which was the glory of Jerusalem and its protection, was devastated. And some understand the gold (v. 1) to be the *gold of the temple*, the fine gold with which the whole interior was overlaid (1Ki 6:22). When the temple was burned, its gold was sullied. *The stones of the sanctuary* were brought down by the fire and thrown about at the head of every street; they lay mixed among the general ruins.

2. The princes and priests, who were in a special way the *sons of Zion*, were abused (v. 2). Israel was richer in them than in treasures of gold and silver. But now they were broken as pots of clay. They had become poor, had been taken into exile and rendered lowly and contemptible.

3. Little children were starved for lack of bread and water (vv. 3–4).

4. People of rank were reduced to poverty (v. 5). Those who were well born and well brought up were stripped by the war; they were *desolate in the streets*. They did not have a bed to lie on. As sometimes the *needy* are *raised out of the dunghill* (Ps 113:7), so there are instances of the *wealthy* being brought *to the dunghill*.

5. People who were well known for honor, perhaps for sanctity, shared with others in the general disaster (vv. 7–8). *Her Nazarites*, like her gold (v. 1), were changed. These *Nazarites*, because of their modest diet, especially the delight they had in devoting themselves to God, which made their faces shine like *Moses'* (Ex 34:29), were *purer than snow* and *whiter than milk* (v. 7). Drinking no wine or strong drink meant they had a healthy complexion and more cheerful looks. But now *their visage was marred* (appearance was disfigured), as is said about Christ (Isa 52:14); it was *blacker than a coal* (soot); they looked miserable, partly through hunger and partly through grief and perplexity. *They were not known in the streets* (v. 8); those who had respected them now took no notice of them.

6. Jerusalem died a slow, lingering death, because the famine contributed more to her destruction than any other judgment. Jerusalem died gradually, died so as to feel she was dying. The sin of Jerusalem was worse than that of Sodom; it is not surprising, then, that its punishment was too. Sodom never had the means of grace that Jerusalem had. *The hands of the pitiful women had* killed and then *sodden* (boiled) *their own children.* The case was sad enough when they did not have enough resources to feed their children and prepare food for them (v. 4), but it was much worse when they could find it in their hearts to eat their own children. The destruction of Jerusalem was complete (v. 11), and it was an incredibly terrifying destruction (v. 12). It came as a surprise to the kings of the earth and to *all the inhabitants of the world* who knew Jerusalem. They knew that it was the *city of the great King* (Ps 48:2), and so they thought it was so much under God's protection that it would be futile for any of its enemies to attack it.

Verses 13–20

We have here:

1. The sins for which God brought this destruction on them and which served to justify him in this punishment (vv. 13–14). He punished them, in particular, *for the sins of her prophets* and the *iniquities of her priests*, and the particular sin they are accused of is persecution; the false prophets and corrupt priests united to *shed the blood of the just in the midst of her.* They shed not only the blood of their innocent children, whom they sacrificed to Molech, but also the blood of the righteous people among them, whom they sacrificed to the crueler idol of enmity to the truth and true religious faith. There is nothing that will make prophets and priests hated so much as a spirit of persecution.

2. The testimony of their neighbors to convict them of sin and show the justice of God's dealings against them. These neighbors rebuked them for pretending to live in purity while they really lived in sin. *They cried to them, Depart you; it is unclean.* They all cried out "Shame" to them and could easily foresee that God would not allow such an offensive people to live for long in such a good land. They foresaw that the land would vomit them out, as it had done their predecessors (Lev 18:28), and when they saw the dispersed of *Jacob fleeing and wandering,* they told them that this would be their fate. They said that now *the anger of the Lord had divided them* (v. 16). They said, when they saw them expelled, *God will no more regard them* (v. 16), and how then could they help themselves? Here the neighboring nations were mistaken. God had not rejected them, even for all this.

3. Their despair under their calamities. "*As for us,* we look upon our situation as especially helpless. *Our end is near* (v. 18), the end of both our church and our state." The refuges they fled to let them down. They looked for help from this and that powerful ally, but it was all pointless; they looked for what never came (v. 17). They *watched in watching for a nation* that frustrated their expectations. The persecutors overcame them (v. 18): *They hunt our steps,* so *that we cannot go in our streets.* When the Babylonians besieged the city, they raised their fortified siege works so high above the walls that they could shoot at people as they went along the streets. They *hunted them* with the arrows from place to place. Their *persecutors were swifter than the eagles of heaven* (v. 19).

Verses 21–22

David's psalms of lamentation commonly conclude with some word of comfort, which is like life from the dead (Ro 11:15) and light shining out of darkness, and the lamentation in this chapter does so. It is foretold here, to encourage God's people:

1. That an end will be put to Zion's troubles (v. 22). The troubles of God's people will last only until they have completed the work for which they were sent.

2. That an end will be put to Edom's triumphs. It is spoken ironically (v. 21): "*Rejoice and be glad, O daughter of Edom! The cup* that makes people stagger (Isa 51:17, 22), which it is now Jerusalem's turn to drink deeply

from, *shall pass through unto thee.*" The destruction of the Edomites was foretold by this prophet (Jer 49:7). "*The cup* that *shall pass unto thee* will intoxicate you. *Thou shalt be drunken* and at thy wits' end. You will stagger and stumble, and then, like Noah when he was drunk, *thou shalt make thyself naked* (v. 21) and expose thyself to contempt" (Ge 9:21).

CHAPTER 5

Although this chapter has the same number of verses as chapters 1, 2, and 4, it is not arranged alphabetically. We have here: 1. A description of the present disastrous state of God's people in exile (vv. 1–16). 2. A declaration of their concern for God's sanctuary (vv. 17–18). 3. A humble request to God for him to respond in mercy (vv. 19–22). Some ancient versions call this chapter "The Prayer of Jeremiah."

Verses 1–16

The people of God, overwhelmed with grief, express their sorrows at the throne of grace (Heb 4:16). "*Remember what is* past," they pray. "*Consider and behold* what is present, and *let not all the trouble* we are in *seem little to thee*, and not worth taking notice of" (Ne 9:32). The one word in which all their grievances are summed up is *reproach* (disgrace): *Consider, and behold our reproach*. Just as their suffering is a disgrace to them, so also it reflects badly on the name and honor of the God who has acknowledged them as his people.

1. They acknowledge the disgrace of sin, *the reproach* (disgrace) *of their youth*, of the early days of their nation. It is a penitent confession of the sins of their ancestors, which they themselves have persisted in, for which they now justly suffer.

2. They describe the reproach they bear, in several details, which contribute greatly to their disgrace.

2.1. They have been robbed of the good land that God gave them (v. 2). "It is turned over to foreigners. They are living in the houses we built, and this is our disgrace."

2.2. Their state and nation are like widows and orphans (v. 3): "*We are fatherless,* that is, helpless. Our king, who is the father of the country, is cut off; in fact, God our Father seems to have abandoned us. *Our mothers,* our cities, *are* now *as widows,* exposed to wrong and injury, and this is our disgrace."

2.3. They are hard pressed for necessities. Water used to be free, but now (v. 4), *We have drunk our water for money.* Formerly they had fuel that they could simply take, but now, "*Our wood is sold to us,* and we have to pay a high price for every bundle of twigs." But what can they do for bread? Some of them have sold their freedom for it (v. 6): "*We have given the hand to the Egyptians and to the Assyrians,* have made the best deal we could, so that we might *be satisfied with bread. We got our bread with the peril of our lives.*" During the siege, they stole out of the city to obtain some supplies, and were then in danger of being killed by the sword, *the sword of the wilderness* (v. 9), as it is called.

2.4. They are brought into slavery, and this as much as anything is their reproach (v. 5): *Our necks are under the* painful yoke *of persecution.* The poor exiles in Babylon *labour and have no rest,* either at night or on the Sabbath.

They refused to be ruled by their God and by his servants the prophets, whose rule was gentle and gracious, and so they are justly ruled harshly by their enemies and their servants.

2.5. Those who used to be feasted are now famished (v. 10): *Our skin was black like an oven,* dried and parched too, *because of the terrible famine;* the "storms of famine" is the sense.

2.6. All kinds of people are abused and dishonored. The *women* are *ravished,* even *the women in Zion,* that holy mountain (v. 11).

2.7. An end has been put to all their happiness (v. 14): *The young men,* who used to be happy, have ceased *from their music.* This has happened with most of the people (v. 15): *The joy of their heart ceased; our dance is turned into mourning.* This may refer to the joy of their sacred festivals, and their dancing in them (Jdg 21:21), which was not only modest but also sacred.

2.8. An end has been put to all their glory. The public administration of justice was their glory, but that is gone (v. 14). The royal honor was their glory, but that also has gone: *The crown has fallen from our head* (v. 16); not only has the *king* himself fallen into disgrace, but also *the crown.* He has no successor. Earthly crowns fade and fall, but we bless God that there is *a crown of glory that fades not away* (1Pe 5:4), which never fails, *a kingdom that cannot be moved* (Heb 12:28).

Verses 17–22

Here:

1. The people of God express the deep concern they have for the ruins of the temple, which is greater than their concern for any of their other disasters (vv. 17–18). "The people have desecrated the *mountain of Zion* with their sins, and God has justly made it *desolate; the foxes* (jackals) *walk upon it* as freely and commonly as they do in the woods."

2. They comfort themselves with the doctrine of God's eternity (v. 19): but *thou, O Lord! remainest for ever.* What shakes the world does not disturb the One who made it; whatever changes may happen on earth, there is no change in the eternal Mind. God is still the same and *remains for ever* infinitely wise and holy, just and good.

3. They humbly plead with God about the frowns of heaven they sense (v. 20): "*Wherefore dost thou forget us for ever,* as if we were completely driven out of your thoughts? You are the same, and although the throne of your sanctuary has been demolished, will you not be the same toward us?" Although we may not quarrel with God, we may still plead with him (Jer 12:1).

4. They fervently pray to God for mercy and grace: "Lord, do not reject *us for ever,* but *turn thou us unto thee; renew our days*" (v. 21). Although these words do not come last, the Jewish authorities, not wanting the book to conclude with the sad words of v. 22, repeat this prayer at the end, making these the last words both in writing and reading this chapter. This corresponds to that repeated prayer (Ps 80:3, 7, 19), "*Turn us again, and then cause thy face to shine. Turn us* from our idols back to yourself, by a sincere repentance and reformation, *and* then *we shall be turned.*" If God by his grace renews our hearts, he will by his favor *renew our days.*

A Practical and Devotional Exposition of the Book of the Prophet

Ezekiel

༺ ⁓ ༻

The writings of the prophets, which speak about the *things that should be hereafter*, seem to utter the same call that John had (Rev 4:1): *Come up hither*. However, the prophecy of this book is as if the voice said, *Come up higher*; as we go forward in time—for Ezekiel prophesied in the exile, as Jeremiah prophesied just before it—so we soar upward in even more sublime revelations of God's glory. These waters of the sanctuary still become deeper; they are so far from being fordable that in some places they are scarcely fathomable. Deep though they are, however, out of them flow streams that *make glad the city of our God* (Ps 46:4).

1. The writer was Ezekiel; his name means "the strength of God" or the one "strengthened by God." He prepared his mind for service, and God put strength into him. *I have made thy face strong against their faces* (3:8). If we are to believe the tradition of the Jews, he was put to death by the exiles in Babylon for his boldness in rebuking them; it is stated that his brains were dashed out. An Arab historian says he was put to death and was buried in the sepulcher of Shem the son of Noah.

2. The scene is set in Babylon, when it was a land of slavery for the *Israel of God*; the prophecies of this book were written there when both the prophet himself and the people to whom he prophesied were exiles there. Ezekiel prophesied at the beginning of the exile, Daniel at its end. It was an indication of God's goodwill and his gracious intentions in their suffering that he raised up prophets both to convince them when they were unhumbled at the beginning of their troubles, which was Ezekiel's responsibility, and to comfort them when they were dejected and discouraged at the end of their troubles.

3. Concerning its subject and theme:

3.1. There is much that is mysterious, dark, and hard to understand (2Pe 3:16), especially at the beginning and the end. The Jews therefore forbade the reading of it to their young men until they were thirty years old, so that the difficulties they met might not make them prejudiced against the Scriptures. However, if we read these difficult parts with humility and reverence, examining them diligently, then even though we may not untie all the knots, any more than we can solve all the phenomena in the book of nature, we may still learn from them, as we can from the book of nature, and gather a great deal to confirm our faith and encourage our hope in God.

3.2. Although the visions here are so intricate that an elephant may swim in them, the sermons are mostly so plain that a lamb may wade in them. Their chief intention was to *show God's people their transgressions* (Isa 58:1), so that they might in their exile repent and not repine. Just as it was very useful to the oppressed exiles themselves to have a prophet with them, so it was a testimony for their religion against their oppressors who ridiculed it and them.

3.3. Although the rebukes and threats here are sharp and bold, toward the close of the book very encouraging assurances are given of the great mercy God has in store for them, and there you find some reference to Gospel times, something that was to have its fulfillment in the kingdom of the Messiah. By opening the *terrors of the Lord*, Ezekiel prepares the way for Christ. We have the visions that were the prophet's credentials in chs. 1–3 and the rebukes and threats in chs. 4–24., Between these threats and the comforts at the end of the book we have messages sent to the nations that bordered the land of Israel, whose destruction is foretold in chs. 25–35 to make way for the restoration of God's Israel and the reestablishment of their city and temple, which are foretold in chs. 36–48.

CHAPTER 1

In this chapter we have: 1. The circumstances of the prophecy now to be given, the time when it was given (v. 1), the place where (v. 2), and the person by whom
(v. 3). 2. The introduction to it by a vision of the glory of God: 2.1. In the higher world, where his throne is surrounded by angels, here called living creatures (vv. 4–14). 2.2. In his providences for the lower

world, represented by the wheels and their movements (vv. 15–25). 2.3. In the face of Jesus Christ sitting on the throne (vv. 26–28). The more we are familiar with, and the more intimately we deal with, the glory of God in these three aspects, the more powerful influence divine revelation will have on us.

Verses 1–3

The circumstances of the vision that Ezekiel saw, and in which he received his commission, are set down here in detail to show that the narrative is authentic. It may be useful to keep an account of when and where God has revealed himself to our souls in a special way. Here we have:

1. The time when Ezekiel had this vision: it was *in the thirtieth year* (v. 1). Some believe this was the thirtieth year of the prophet's age; because he was a priest, he could enter into the complete responsibilities of the priestly office at that age. Others consider it the thirtieth year from the beginning of the reign of Nabopolassar, the father of Nebuchadnezzar. The Aramaic paraphrase, however, establishes it in another era by saying that this was the thirtieth year after "Hilkiah the priest found the Book of the Law in the house of the sanctuary, at midnight, after the setting of the moon, in the days of Josiah the king." It was in the *fourth month,* corresponding to our June, and on the *fifth day of the month,* that Ezekiel had this vision (v. 2). It was probably on the Sabbath, because we read that *at the end of seven days* (3:16), the next Sabbath, the word of the Lord came to him again.

2. The sad circumstances he was in when God honored him. He was *among the captives, by the river of Chebar, and it was in the fifth year of king Jehoiachin's captivity.*

2.1. Some of the people of God were *captives in the land of the Chaldeans.* Most of the Jewish nation remained in their own land, but these were the firstfruits of the exile, and they were some of the best (Jer 24:5). The word of instruction and the rod of correction working together may be very useful to us, the word to explain the rod and the rod to enforce the word; together they give wisdom. In their exile, these Jews did not have the ordinary helps to encourage their souls, and so God raised up for them these extraordinary ones, for if God's children are hindered in their education in one way, they will have it made up in another way. The Jews who remained in their own land had Jeremiah with them, and those who had gone into exile had Ezekiel with them, for wherever the children of God are scattered abroad, he will find teachers for them.

2.2. The prophet himself was among the exiles by *the river Chebar.* Interpreters are not agreed what river this Kebar was. The best people, those who are most precious to God, often share in the public and national judgments that are inflicted for sin. Those who contributed nothing to the guilt still have to suffer. The exiles would be best instructed by one who was an exile among them and knew their sorrows in his own experience. Wherever we are, we may maintain our fellowship with God. When Paul was a prisoner, the Gospel had free rein. When John was banished to the Isle of Patmos, Christ visited him there.

3. The revelation that God made of himself to the prophet. He tells us here what he saw, heard, and felt.

3.1. He *saw visions of God* (v. 1). No one can *see God and live* (Ex 33:20), but many people have seen visions of God, displays of his glory that have instructed them. Ezekiel was employed in turning the hearts of the people to the Lord their God (Lk 1:16), and so he himself must

see the visions of God. Those whose business is to bring others to know and love him should themselves know God well for themselves and be very much moved by their knowledge of him. So that he might see the *visions of God, the heavens were opened;* the darkness and distance that hindered his visions were overcome.

3.2. He heard the voice of God (v. 3): *The word of the Lord came expressly* to him, and what he saw was intended to prepare him for what he was to hear. "The essential Word," as we may read it, *the Word who is, who is what he is* (Ex 3:14), *came to Ezekiel,* to send him on his mission.

3.3. He felt the power of God opening his eyes to see the visions, opening his ear to hear the voice, and opening his heart to receive both.

Verses 4–14

1. The scope and intention of these visions is:

1.1. To possess the prophet's mind with high and honorable thoughts of the God by whom he was commissioned. It was *the likeness of the glory of the Lord* that he saw (v. 28). Such a great God as this must be served *with reverence and godly fear* (Heb 12:28).

1.2. To strike terror both on the sinners who remained in Zion and on those who had already come to Babylon, who, feeling secure in their exile, defied the threats of Jerusalem's ruin. That this vision refers to the destruction of Jerusalem seems clear from 43:3.

1.3. To speak comfort to those who feared God and humbled themselves under his mighty hand. "Let them know that although they are exiles in Babylon, they still have God close to them. Although they do not have *the place of the sanctuary,* they still have the God of the sanctuary." Dr. Lightfoot observes, "Now that the church is to be planted for a long time in another country, the Lord shows a glory first in their midst (Zec 2:5), as he did when the church was first formed in the desert." The first part of the vision represents God as attended and served by an innumerable company of angels, who are all his ministers, *doing his commandments* and *hearkening to the voice of his word* (Ps 103:20).

2. The introduction to this vision of the angels is magnificent and stirring (v. 4). The prophet, seeing the heavens opening, *looked* up. To clear the way, *behold, a whirlwind* (windstorm) *came out of the north,* which would drive away the mists. God can use a windstorm to clear the sky and air, and he can produce that peace of mind that is necessary for our fellowship with heaven. This whirlwind came to Ezekiel, as one came to Elijah (1Ki 19:11), to *prepare the way of the Lord* (Isa 40:3).

3. Then the vision itself is described. *A great cloud* was the vehicle of this vision (v. 4), for God's canopy in which he rests, his chariot in which he rides, is *darkness and thick clouds* (Ps 18:11; 104:3).

3.1. The cloud was accompanied by *a fire,* as on Mount Sinai. There God resided in *a thick cloud,* but *the sight of his glory was like devouring fire* (Ex 24:16–17), and his first appearance to Moses was in *a flame of fire in the bush* (Ex 3:2), for *our God is a consuming fire* (Heb 12:29).

3.2. The fire was surrounded by glory: *A brightness was about it* (v. 4). Although we cannot see into the fire—we cannot probe the limits of almighty God—we can still see the brightness around it. Moses was allowed to see God's back, but not his face (Ex 33:23). Nothing is easier than to determine that God is, but nothing is more difficult than to describe what he is.

3.3. Out of this fire there shone *the colour of amber* (v. 4). The first thing he noticed before he viewed the details was that the vision was *of the colour of amber,* or "the eye of amber," that is, it looked as amber does to the eye, with a bright, glowing, fiery color. The *living creatures* that he saw coming *out of the midst of the fire* were *seraphim,* "burners."

3.4. What came out of the fire, of a glowing amber color, was *not* the *living creatures* themselves — angels are spirits and cannot be seen — but *the likeness* of them, such as God saw fit to show the prophet. *The likeness of these living creatures came out of the midst of the fire* (v. 5). The prophet himself explains this vision (10:20): *I knew that the living creatures were the cherubim.* We have here an account of:

3.4.1. Their nature. They were living creatures, the creatures of God, the work of his hands. The sun, according to some, is a flame of *fire enfolding itself,* but it is not a living creature.

3.4.2. Their number. They were four; this was how many they were here, even though they were innumerable. The prophet's seeing four of these living creatures was intended to suggest that they were sent toward the four winds of heaven (Mt 24:31). Zechariah saw them as four chariots going out from east, west, north, and south (Zec 6:1). God has messengers to send in every direction.

3.4.3. Their qualifications. These are set out figuratively and by using comparisons, as is proper in visions. These living creatures are described here:

3.4.3.1. By their general appearance: *They had the likeness of a man* (v. 5); they were reasoning, intelligent beings, who had that *spirit of a man* which is the *candle of the Lord* (Pr 20:27). The angels of God appeared in *the likeness of man* because in *the fulness of time* the Son of God would not only appear in that likeness but also assume that nature.

3.4.3.2. By their faces: *Every one had four faces* (v. 6), looking in four different ways. They *all four had the face of a man* (v. 5), but besides that, they had *the face of a lion, an ox,* and *an eagle,* each domineering in its kind, *the lion* among *wild* animals, *the ox* among *tame* ones, and *the eagle* among birds (v. 10). The scattered perfections of the living creatures on earth meet in the angels of heaven. They have *the understanding of a man,* and such as far exceeds it; they also resemble people in tenderness and humanity. But *a lion* excels human beings in strength and boldness; the angels, therefore, who resemble them in this, put on the *face of a lion. An ox* surpasses human beings in conscientiousness and patience in the work to be done. The angels, therefore, employed in serving God and the church, put on *the face of an ox. An eagle* surpasses human beings in speed and piercing sight, and in soaring high. The angels, therefore, who seek things above and see far into divine mysteries, put on *the face of a flying eagle.*

3.4.3.3. By their wings: *Every one had four wings* (v. 6). Faith and hope are the soul's wings, on which it soars upward; godly devotions are the wings on which it is carried forward. Their wings were joined (v. 9 and again v. 11) as a sign of their complete and perfect unity and unanimity. Two of their wings were used in covering their bodies, the spiritual bodies they assumed.

3.4.3.4. By their feet. Their feet were *straight feet* (v. 7); they stood straight, firm, and steady. "Their feet were winged," according to the Septuagint (a Greek version of the Old Testament); they went so swiftly that it was as if they flew (v. 8).

3.4.3.5. By their hands (v. 8). They had not only wings for movement but also hands for action. They were *the hands of a man,* which are wonderfully made and fitted for service, guided by reason and understanding. Calves' feet denote the swiftness of their movement.

3.4.4. Their movements. The living creatures were moving; angels are active beings.

3.4.4.1. Whatever service they went about, *they went every one straight forward* (vv. 9, 12). If *our eye is single,* our *whole body will be full of light* (Mt 6:22). The singleness of the eye is the sincerity of the heart. *They went straight forward,* each to their own work; they did not thwart one another.

3.4.4.2. *They turned not when they went* (vv. 9, 12). They were not distracted; just as they did not turn back, so they did not turn aside.

3.4.4.3. *They went whither the Spirit was to go* (v. 12). Wherever *the Spirit* of God wanted them to *go,* that was where *they went.*

3.5. The prophet saw these living creatures (v. 13) by their own light, for *their appearance was like burning coals of fire.* He saw them also by the light of *lamps* that *went up and down among* them, whose light *was* very bright. The angels of light are in the light, but we see them and their works only by candlelight, by the dim light *of lamps* that go *up and down among* them; when *the day breaks, and the shadows flee away* (SS 2:17; 4:6), we will see them clearly.

Verses 15–25

The prophet is very exact in making and recording his observations about this vision. We have here:

1. The vision of the *wheels* (vv. 15–21). The glory of God appears not only in the splendor of the higher world but also in the steadiness of his government here in this lower world. As *he beheld the living creatures* and was contemplating the glory, this other vision came into view.

1.1. The ways of providence are compared to *wheels,* the wheels of a chariot. Although the *wheels* do not move by themselves, as *the living creatures* do, they are still made movable.

1.2. The wheel is said to have been *by the living creatures* (v. 15).

1.2.1. There was such a close connection between *the living creatures* and the *wheels* that they moved and rested together. *When the living creatures went, the wheels went by them;* when God has work to do by the ministry of angels, secondary causes are all found, or made ready, to fit in with it. *If the living creatures were lifted up from the earth,* were elevated to any service above the ordinary course of nature, the wheels moved together with them, and *were lifted up over against them* (vv. 19–21).

1.2.2. This shows us that all lower creatures are, move, and act as the Creator directs and influences them by the ministry of angels. The reason is that *the spirit of the living creatures was in the wheels;* the same wisdom, power, and holiness of God, who guides and directs the angels, order all the movement of the creatures in this lower world. God is the soul of the world, and he gives life to the whole, both the world above and that below, so that they move together in perfect harmony, as the upper and lower parts of the natural body do, so that *whithersoever the Spirit is to go* — whatever God wills and plans to be done — *thither their spirit is to go.*

1.3. The wheel is said to have four *faces,* looking in four different directions (v. 15), showing that the providence of

God exerts itself east, west, north, and south, and extends to its remotest corners. At first Ezekiel saw it as *one wheel* (v. 15), one sphere, although afterward he saw it was four, but *they* four *had one likeness* (v. 16). Various events fulfill the same intention.

1.4. *Their appearance and their work* are said to have been *like the colour of a beryl* (sparkled like chrysolite) (v. 16), literally, "like the appearance of Tarshish"; that is, of the sea. The nature of things in this world is like that of the sea, in a continual state of flux but with a constant coherence. The sea ebbs and flows, as does providence in all its ways. The sea looks blue, as the air does, because of the shortness of our sight, and we can see only a little of either. We cannot find out what God does *from the beginning to the end* (Ecc 3:11). We see but *parts of his ways* (Job 26:14), and everything beyond that looks blue. It is *far above out of our sight* (Ps 10:5).

1.5. *Their appearance and their work* are also said to have been *as it were a wheel in the middle of a wheel* (v. 16). We cannot pretend to give a mathematical description of it. The disposals of Providence seem to us intricate, perplexing, and inexplicable, but they will finally be seen to have been all wisely ordered.

1.6. The movement of these wheels was steady and constant: *They turned not*, or did not return, *when they went* (v. 17), because they never went wrong. God takes his work in front of him, and he wants to move it forward, and it is moving on even when it seems to us to be going backward. *They went* as the Spirit directed them, and so they *returned not*. We would not need to return as we need to, to undo by repentance what we have done wrong and do it over again, if only we were *led by the Spirit* and followed his direction. "The Spirit of life," as some read it, "was in the wheels," and the Spirit carried them on with ease and evenness.

1.7. The *rings*, or rims, *of the wheels* were *full of eyes round about*, plainly showing that the movements of providence are all directed by infinite Wisdom. The outcome of events is not determined by blind fortune, but by the *eyes of the Lord*, which *run to and fro through the earth* (2Ch 16:9) and *are in every place, beholding the evil and the good* (Pr 15:3).

2. The notice he took of *the firmament* above, *over the heads of the living creatures*. What is done on earth is done under heaven, under its inspection and influence. Ezekiel saw that *the firmament was as the colour of the terrible crystal* (v. 22); its vastness and brightness struck him with fearful reverence. God is high, *above the firmament*; the angels are *under the firmament*, which shows their submission to God's rule. Ezekiel heard the *noise of the angels' wings* (v. 24), which beat the air to awaken the attention of the prophet to what God was about to say to him from above the expanse (v. 25). He heard a *voice from the firmament*, from the One who sits on the throne (v. 25). When the angels had used their wings to rouse a careless world, they stood still and *let down their wings*, so that there might be a profound silence and God's voice might be better heard (Rev 8:1). The voice of Providence is intended to open human ears to the voice of the word.

Verses 26–28

The other parts of this vision were merely an introduction to this. In them, God had made himself known as Lord of angels and the supreme ruler of all the affairs of this lower world. But now that a divine revelation is to be given to a prophet, we must look higher than the living creatures or the wheels and must expect that revelation to come from the eternal Word. When Ezekiel heard a voice from above the expanse, he looked up, as John did, to *see the voice that spoke with him*, and he *saw one like unto the Son of man* (Rev 1:12–13).

1. This glory of Christ that the prophet saw *was above the firmament* that was *over the heads* of the living creatures (v. 26). This honor and rule of the Redeemer before his incarnation exalt his condescension in his incarnation.

2. The first thing Ezekiel noticed was *a throne*, for divine revelation comes backed by a royal authority. We must look with the eye of faith to God and Christ as on a throne. The first thing that John saw in his visions was *a throne set in heaven* (Rev 4:2). It is a throne of glory, a throne of grace, a throne of triumph, a throne of government, and a throne of judgment.

3. On the throne he saw *the appearance of a man* (v. 26). It is good news to human beings that the throne above the expanse is filled with One who is not ashamed to appear, even there, in the likeness of man.

4. He saw him as a prince and judge on this throne, in more than human glory (v. 27), for God lives in light (1Ti 6:16) and *covers himself with light as with a garment* (Ps 104:2). From his waist, both upward and downward, there was the *appearance of fire*. The fire above his waist was *round about within the amber*; it was inward and involved. That below the waist was outward. Some consider the former to represent Christ's divine nature, hidden within the *colour of amber*; it is what no one has ever seen or can see (1Ti 6:16). They think the latter is his human nature, the glory of which is visible, the glory as of *the only begotten of the Father, full of grace and truth* (Jn 1:14).

5. The throne was surrounded by a rainbow (v. 28). It is so surrounded in John's vision as well (Rev 4:3). Just as it is a display of majesty, so it is also a sign of mercy, for it confirms the gracious promise God has made. Now that the fire of God's wrath was breaking out against Jerusalem, he would *look upon the bow and remember the covenant*, as he promised to do in such a case (Ge 9:16; Lev 26:42).

6. Lastly, we have the conclusion of this vision. *This was the appearance of the likeness of the glory of the Lord* (v. 28). Here, as all along, the prophet is careful to guard against all obviously physical thoughts of God. He does not say, "This was the Lord," for he is invisible, but, *This was the glory of the Lord*, in which he revealed himself as a glorious being; yet it was not *the glory of the Lord*, but *the likeness of that glory*, some faint resemblance of it. Nor was it any adequate likeness of that glory, but only *the appearance of that likeness*, a shadow of it, and not the very *image of the thing* (Heb 10:1). *When I saw it, I fell upon my face*. He was overcome by it. He fell on his face as a sign of that holy awe and reverence with which his mind was possessed and filled. Yet all he saw was only to prepare him for what he was to hear, for *faith comes by hearing* (Ro 10:17). God delights to teach those who are humble.

CHAPTER 2

What our Lord Jesus said to the apostle Paul (Ac 26:16) may appropriately be applied to the prophet Ezekiel: "Rise and get to your feet, for I have appeared to you to make you a minister." Here we have Ezekiel's ordination to his office: 1. He is commissioned to go as a prophet to the house of Israel, now in exile in Babylon (vv. 1–5).

2. He is warned not to be afraid of them (v. 6). 3. He is instructed what to say to them, which is represented by the vision of a scroll (vv. 7–10).

Verses 1–5

God calls him *Son of man* (vv. 1, 3), "Son of Adam, Son of the earth." We may take it:

- As a humbling title. So that Ezekiel will not become conceited because of the surpassingly great revelations he received (2Co 12:7), he is reminded that he is still *a son of man*. Or:
- As an honorable title, for it is one of the titles of the Messiah in the Old Testament (Da 7:13): *I saw one like the Son of man come with the clouds of heaven.*

1. Ezekiel is led to stand up so that he may receive his commission (vv. 1–2). He is raised up:
1.1. By divine command: *Son of man, stand upon thy feet.* His lying prostrate was a position of greater reverence, but his standing up will be a position of greater readiness.
1.2. By divine power accompanying that command (v. 2). God makes him *stand up*, but because he does not have the strength of his own to get to his feet or the courage to face the vision, *the Spirit enters into him* and *sets him upon his feet.* The *Spirit sets him upon his feet*, makes him willing to do as he is told, and then he *hears him that speaks* to him.
2. Ezekiel is sent with a message to the children of Israel (v. 3): *I send thee to the children of Israel.* They have now been sent into exile for mistreating God's messengers, but even there God sends this prophet among them. Notice:
2.1. The rebellion of the people to whom this ambassador is sent. They are called *children of Israel*; they keep the name of their godly ancestors, but they have become corrupt and degenerate; they have become *goim*, "nations," the word commonly used for the Gentiles. They have been a rebellious generation all along and have persisted in rebellion: *They and their fathers have transgressed against me* (v. 3). They are now hardened, *impudent children* (v. 4), brazen and self-willed.
2.2. The rule of the ruler by whom this ambassador is sent. He has authority to command the one whom he sends: "*I do send thee unto them,* and so *thou shalt say* this to them" (v. 4). He also has authority to use the one he sends to command those to whom he sends him: *Thou shalt say unto them, Thus saith the Lord God.* All he says to them must be spoken in God's name, enforced by his authority, and communicated as from him. The writings of the prophets are the word of God and are therefore to be taken notice of. When people's hearts are made to burn under the word (Lk 24:32), and their wills to submit to it, then they know and bear witness in themselves that it is not the *word of men, but of God* (Jn 1:13). If they turn a deaf ear to his word, they will still be made to know that the One whom they slighted was truly a prophet (v. 5), by the condemnation of their own consciences and the just judgments of God on them for refusing him.

Verses 6–10

Having received his commission, the prophet receives here a charge. It is required of him:
1. That he be bold. *Son of man, be not afraid of them* (v. 6). Those to whom God sends him are like *briers and thorns* (v. 6), troubling, whichever way he turns. Evildoers are like briers and thorns, which hinder God's farming.

They are *scorpions*, venomous and malignant. The sting of a scorpion is a thousand times more harmful than the scratch of a brier. Ezekiel has been caught up in a vision, talking with angels, but when he comes down from this mountain, he finds he *dwells with scorpions.* They will threaten and intimidate him to discourage him from being a prophet, or at least from threatening them with the judgments of God.
2. That he be faithful (v. 7) to Christ, who sent him, and to the souls of those to whom he is sent. "It is true that they are *most rebellious*, but *speak my words* to them, whether they are pleasing or unpleasing to them."
3. That he observe:
3.1. The instructions that are given him in the book that is *spread before him* (v. 10). The scroll is *written within and without*, on the inside and on the outside. One side contains their sins; the other side contains the judgments of God coming on them for those sins. Ezekiel is being sent on an unhappy mission; the matter contained in the book is *lamentations, and mourning, and woe.* What could be more lamentable, more mournful, and more woeful than seeing a holy, happy people sunk into such sin and misery?
3.2. The explicit charge given to him as to both how he must receive his message and how he must speak it. He is to listen to it carefully: *Son of man, hear what I say unto thee* (v. 8). If ministers ignore sin and humor sinners for fear of displeasing them, in so doing they share in their guilt: "Do not only *hear what I say unto thee*, but also *open thy mouth, and eat that which I give thee* (v. 8). Eat it willingly and with an appetite." He who brought it to the prophet *spread it before him*, so that he fully understood its contents and then received it and made it his own.

CHAPTER 3

Here is the further preparation of the prophet for the work to which God called him. 1. His eating the scroll that was presented to him (vv. 1–3). 2. Further instructions and encouragements (vv. 4–11). 3. The mighty impulse he was under, with which he was carried to those who were to hear him (vv. 12–15). 4. His role and work as a prophet, described through the metaphor of a watchman (vv. 16–21). 5. The restraining and restoring of the prophet's liberty of speech (vv. 22–27).

Verses 1–15

Some translators attach these verses, appropriately, to the previous chapter, considering them a continuation of the same vision. Here the prophet is taught:
1. How he must receive divine revelation himself (v. 1). "*Son of man, eat this roll*, impress it on your mind; let your soul be nourished and strengthened by it. Be full of it, as you are of the food you have eaten." Whatever we find to be the word of God, whatever is brought to us by the One who is the Word of God, we must receive without argument. If the One who *opens the roll* and, by his Spirit, unrolls it out before us did not also *open our understanding* and, by his Spirit, give us the knowledge of it and *cause us to eat* it, we would always be strangers to it. Although *the roll was filled with lamentations, and mourning, and woe*, it was still to the prophet *as honey for sweetness.*
2. He must communicate to others the divine revelation he himself has received (v. 1): *Eat this roll, and* then *go, speak to the house of Israel.* He is not sent to the Babylonians to rebuke them for their sins, but *to the house*

of Israel to rebuke them for theirs, for parents correct their own children first if they do wrong, not the children of strangers.

2.1. Here are the instructions that were given to the prophet.

2.1.1. He must tell them all that God said to him, and only that. *Thou shalt speak with my words unto them* (v. 4), or "in my words."

2.1.2. He must remember that those to whom he is sent to speak are *the house of Israel,* God's house and his own. They are those he knows intimately, being not only their compatriot but also their *companion in tribulation* (Rev 1:9).

2.1.3. He must remember what God has already told him about the character of those to whom he is sent, so that if he faces discouragement and disappointment, he may not be offended. They *are impudent* (obstinate) *and hard-hearted* (v. 7); no convictions of sin will make them ashamed, and no declarations will make them tremble. They are obstinate toward God himself: "They *will not hearken* (listen) *unto thee,* and that is hardly surprising, *for they will not hearken unto me.*" They are prejudiced against the law of God, and that is why they turn a deaf ear to his prophets, whose business it is to enforce his law.

2.1.4. He must decide to put on courage. God will enable him to make the best of the situation: "*I have made thy face strong against their faces* (v. 8), endowed you with all firmness and boldness." The more stubborn evildoers are in opposing religious faith, the more openly and resolutely God's people should defend it. When evil is being shamelessly displayed, let not goodness be silent. Ezekiel is therefore commanded to be courageous and to continue in his work, taking no notice of the criticism or the threats of his enemies. Let not angry faces, which drive away a backbiting tongue (Pr 25:23), restrain in any way a tongue that rebukes.

2.1.5. He must continue to preach to them urgently, whatever the outcome (v. 11). He must *tell them* not only what the Lord said but also that the Lord said it: *Thus saith the Lord God; tell them so, whether they will hear or whether they will forbear* (v. 11). Not that we should be unconcerned as to whether our ministry is successful or not, but whether it is or not, we must continue with our work and leave the outcome to God.

2.2. Having been told how full instructions are given to the prophet, we are told:

2.2.1. With what satisfaction his mission is applauded by the holy angels. He *hears a voice of a great rushing* (a loud rumbling sound) (v. 12), as if the angels thronged and crowded to see the inauguration of a prophet. He *hears the noise of their wings that touch,* and *the noise of the wheels* of providence moving *over against* the angels and together with them. But all this sound ends in the voice of praise. He hears them saying, *Blessed be the glory of the Lord from his place* (v. 12).

2.2.2. With what reluctance in his own spirit, but with what a mighty power of *the Spirit of God,* the prophet is led to carry out his office. The Spirit leads him with a strong hand. God tells him to go, but he does not stir until *the Spirit takes him up* (v. 14), *lifts him up, and takes him away* to his work. Ezekiel would willingly have kept all he heard and saw to himself, but he is taken and led on by the prophetic impulse, so that he cannot *but speak the things which he has heard and seen,* as the apostles did (Ac 4:20). He follows with a sad heart: *The Spirit took me away,* he says, *and then I went,* but it was *in bitterness, in*

the heat (anger) *of my spirit* (v. 14). He has perhaps seen what a hard task Jeremiah had at Jerusalem, what harsh treatment he had encountered, and all to no purpose. "*I went,* not *disobedient to the heavenly vision* or shrinking from the work, like Jonah, but *I went in bitterness,* not at all pleased with it." He goes *in the heat* (anger) *of his spirit,* because of the discouragements he foresees, *but the hand of the Lord is strong upon* him, to equip him and encourage him in the difficulties he will meet. When he finds it to be so, he is reconciled to his work and applies himself to it: *Then he came to those of the captivity* (v. 15) *and sat where they sat,* and he remained *among them seven days* to hear what they said and observe what they did, all that time waiting for *the word of the Lord* to come to him. He was *there astonished,* stunned and overwhelmed by grief at the sins and misery of his people and overcome by the vision he had seen.

Verses 16–21

These further instructions were given to the prophet by God *at the end of seven days,* that is, on the seventh day after the vision he had. It is probable that both that day and this day were Sabbaths. Ezekiel met them near the river where they were accustomed to meet for prayer, and *the word of the Lord* then and there *came to* him (v. 16). He who had been musing and meditating on the things of God all week was ready to speak to the people in God's name on the Sabbath, and to hear God speak to him. He was plainly, and by a metaphor, told what his duty was, which he was to communicate to the people. Notice:

1. The *office* to which the prophet was called: *Son of man, I have made thee a watchman to the house of Israel* (v. 17). He was *a watchman,* appointed to be *a watchman* in the city, *a watchman* over the flock, and *a watchman* in the camp, in an invaded country or besieged town, to watch for the movements of the enemy and raise the alarm when they approached. This implied that *the house of Israel* was in a military state and was exposed to enemies who were subtle. Watchmen are in danger of death from the enemy, who will win if they kill the guard, but they dare not abandon their posts on pain of death from their general. The church's watchmen are in such a dilemma; people will curse them if they are faithful, and God will curse them if they are false.

2. The work of a watchman is to take notice and to give notice.

2.1. The prophet, as a watchman, must take notice of what God said concerning this people. He must not, as other watchmen, look around to spy out danger and gain intelligence, but look up to God, and he need not look any further: *Hear the word at my mouth* (v. 17).

2.2. He must give notice of what he heard not in his own name, or as from himself, but in God's name and from him.

2.2.1. Some of those he had to do with were evildoers (vv. 18–19). God has said, and does say, to all evildoers that if they continue in their trespasses, they will *surely die. Their iniquity* will undoubtedly be their ruin. If a *wicked man turn from his wickedness* and *from his wicked way, he shall live* (33:19), and the threatened ruin will be prevented. In order for such people to turn, they have to be warned of the danger they are in. It is the duty of ministers both to warn sinners of the danger of sin and to assure them of the benefits of repentance. Those who are faithful will have their reward even if they are not successful.

2.2.2. Some of those he had to deal with were *righteous,* and he must warn them not to *turn away from their righteousness* (vv. 20–21). One good way to keep us from falling is to keep up a holy fear of falling (Heb 4:1). When people *turn from their righteousness*, they soon learn to commit iniquity. When they grow careless and slack in the duties of God's worship, they become easy prey to the tempter. The righteousness that people give up will do them no good, because it is not continued. We must not only not flatter evildoers; we must also not flatter even the righteous, as if they were perfectly secure anywhere on this side of heaven. Nothing is more beautiful than a *wise reprover upon an obedient ear* (Pr 25:12); the one *shall live because he is warned*, and the other *has delivered his soul*.

Verses 22–27

After all this revelation that God had made of himself to the prophet, and the full instructions he had given him, his work, at first, seems not in proportion to his call.

1. Here he has withdrawn for further learning. From Ezekiel's unwillingness to go, it would seem as if he were not convinced of God's ability to support him, and so, to encourage him in the face of the difficulties he foresees, God favors him with another vision of his glory. God calls him out *to the plain* (v. 22) to *talk with him*. See the condescension of God in speaking in such an ordinary way with a human being, a poor exile, in fact, with a sinner, who goes *in bitterness of spirit* (v. 14) and is at this time dissatisfied with his work. It is very encouraging to be alone with God, withdrawn from the world to speak with him, and a good person will say that they are never less alone than when they are alone in such a way. Ezekiel *went forth into the plain* more willingly than he went *among those of the captivity* (v. 15). He *went out into the plain*, and there saw the same vision that he had seen *by the river of Chebar*. God calls him out to *talk with him*, but he does more than that: he shows him his *glory* (v. 23) (Ex 33:19). We are not to expect such visions now, but we must acknowledge that we have a favor done for us if by faith we so *behold the glory of the Lord* as to be *changed into the same image, by the Spirit of the Lord* (2Co 3:18).

2. Here he is restrained from further teaching for the moment. One would have expected God to send him directly into the noisy streets now (Pr 1:21) and to make him and his message acceptable, so that he would have a wider door of opportunity opened to him. However, what is said here to him is the opposite of all this. Instead of sending him to a public assembly, he orders him to confine himself to his own lodgings: *Go, shut thyself within thy house* (v. 24). He was not willing to appear in public, and when he did, the people did not pay him any attention, and as a just rebuke both to him and them, to him for his shyness and to them for their coldness, God forbids him to appear in public. He must *shut himself within his house* so that he can receive further revelations of the mind of God. *The elders of Judah* visited him and *sat before him in his house* (8:1) to be witnesses of his ecstasies, but it was not till 11:25 that he *spoke to those of the captivity all the things that the Lord had shown him*. Instead of obtaining for him the respect and affection of those to whom he sent him, God tells him that *they shall put bands upon him* and bind him (v. 25) in order to further punish him as one who is disturbing the peace. Even though they themselves were sent into exile in Babylon for persecuting the prophets, they continue to persecute them there. They will bind him, claiming he is out of his mind. Instead of opening his lips so that his mouth might declare God's praise (Ps

51:15), God silences him, so that he is silent for a considerable time. The one who can speak best is forbidden to speak at all. The reason given is that *those* to whom he is sent *are a rebellious house* and not worthy to have him as a *reprover*. But *when* God *speaks with* him, and intends to speak by him, he *will open* his *mouth* (v. 27). Instead of giving him an assurance that he will succeed when he speaks to the people at any time, God leaves the matter in doubt here, and Ezekiel must not become confused or disturbed about it, but let things be as they are.

CHAPTER 4

The exiles in Babylon still had Jerusalem on their hearts; the godly looked toward it with the eye of faith, and the presumptuous looked toward it with the eye of pride, flattering themselves with the thought that they would soon return. Those who remained corresponded with the captives and supported them with the hope that everything would still be well as long as Jerusalem was standing strong. God gave the prophet a very clear and moving vision of the besieging of Jerusalem by the Babylonian army and the disasters that would accompany that siege. Two things were represented in the vision: 1. The fortifications that would be raised against the city (vv. 1–8). 2. The famine that would rage within the city (vv. 9–17).

Verses 1–8

The prophet is ordered here to describe *the siege of Jerusalem* using signs, and this amounts to a prediction.

1. He is ordered to engrave a drawing of Jerusalem on *a tile* (clay tablet) (v. 1). It was Jerusalem's honor that God had *graven her upon the palms of his hands* (Isa 49:16), and the names of the tribes were engraved in precious stones on the breastplate of the high priest, but now that *the faithful city has become a harlot*, a worthless, brittle tablet of clay is thought good enough to *portray it upon*.

2. He is ordered to build small siege works against this model of the city, resembling the ramps raised by the besiegers (v. 2). Between the city and the besieger he is to set up an *iron pan*, as an *iron wall* (v. 3). This represents the inflexible determination of both sides; the Babylonians will resolve never to leave until they have conquered, and the Jews will resolve never to surrender.

3. He is ordered to lie on his side in front of it, to surround it, as it were, representing the Babylonian army lying in front of it to block it off. He is to lie on his left side for 390 *days* (v. 5); the siege of Jerusalem is reckoned to have lasted eighteen months (Jer 52:4–6), but if we deduct from that a five-month interval, when the besiegers withdrew on the approach of Pharaoh's army (Jer 37:5–8), the number of the days of the close siege will be 390. But the number also has another meaning. The 390 days signify 390 years, and when the prophet lies so many days on his side, he bears the guilt of the iniquity that *the house of Israel*, the ten tribes, have borne for 390 years, reckoning from their first apostasy under Jeroboam to the destruction of Jerusalem, which completed the ruin of those few remaining who had joined Judah. He is then to lie forty days *upon his right side*, bearing for that long *the iniquity of the house of Judah*, the kingdom of the two tribes, because the limit-reaching sins of that people were those they were guilty of during the last forty years before their exile. Judah, who had Josiah and Jeremiah, reaches the limit of its sins in less time than Israel does. The prophet lies every day at a certain time of the day.

When he receives visits he is found lying 390 *days on his left side* and *forty days on his right side* in front of his model of Jerusalem, which all can understand to refer to the besieging of that city.

4. He is ordered to pursue the siege vigorously (v. 7): *Thou shalt set thy face toward the siege of Jerusalem*, as one who is wholly set on it. This is how the Babylonians will be. Nebuchadnezzar's anger at Zedekiah's treachery in breaking his alliance with him made him pursue the siege furiously so as to rebuke that faithless ruler and people. The Babylonians will exert themselves to the limit in all the operations of the siege, which the prophet is to represent by the *uncovering of his arm*, the "stretching out" of his arm, as it were, to deal blows. He is said to *make bare his arm* (Isa 52:10). In short, the Babylonians will be earnest and resolute both in taking up the business of the siege and in carrying it out.

4.1. This is intended to be *a sign to the house of Israel* (v. 3), both to those in Babylon and to those who remain in their own land. The prophet is *dumb* and *cannot speak* (3:26), but God *leaves not himself without witness* (Ac 14:17), but orders him to make signs, to *make known his mind*—the mind of God—to the people, who through their senselessness and dullness must be taught as children are, by pictures. Or the prophet uses signs for the same reason that Christ used parables, so that *hearing they may hear and not understand*, and *seeing they may see and not perceive* (Mt 13:14–15).

4.2. This is how the prophet *prophesies against Jerusalem* (v. 7); and there were those who were more moved by it because it was represented in this way, for visual images make deeper impressions on the mind than words do, and this is why sacraments are instituted to represent divine things. The power of imagination, if used rightly and kept under the direction and correction of reason and faith, may be very useful to kindle heartfelt devotion. Imagination is like fire, *a good servant but a bad master*.

4.3. This whole transaction seems childish and tiresome, but our comfort must at times be sacrificed to our duty, and we must never call God's service hard. It must have gone against the grain to appear as he did against Jerusalem, the city of God, but he is a prophet. He must follow his instructions, not his feelings, and must plainly preach the ruin of a sinful place, even though its welfare is what he passionately desires. All this that the prophet sets before his people about the destruction of Jerusalem is intended to bring them to repentance. But notice that it is a day of punishment per year of sin: *I have appointed thee each day for a year.* The siege is a disaster of 390 days.

Verses 9–17

The best explanation of this part of Ezekiel's prediction of Jerusalem's desolation is Jeremiah's lamentation of it (La 4:3–4; 5:10).

1. The prophet here, to move the people with the prophecy, must confine himself for 390 days to rough food and short rations of poor quality, for the people would lack both food and fuel.

1.1. His food was to be of the worst kind, made of only a little wheat and barley, and the rest of beans, lentils, millet, and spelt, such as we feed horses or hogs with. This was mixed, like the grain in the bag of a beggar, who receives a bowl full of one kind of corn at one house and of another kind at another house (v. 9).

1.2. It was to be the least that someone could be kept alive with. The prophet must eat only twenty *shekels'*

weight of food each day (v. 10), that is, about eight ounces (about 0.2 kilogram), and he must drink only the *sixth part of a hin of water*, that is, two-thirds of a quart (about 0.6 liter) (v. 11). The prophet in Babylon had enough food and to spare, but so that he might confirm his prediction and be a sign to the children of Israel, God made him live this sparingly. Nature is content with a little, grace with less, but sinful desires with nothing. It is good to restrict ourselves by choice, so that we may better bear it if ever we have to restrict ourselves by necessity.

1.3. He must *bake it with man's dung* (v. 12), using that as fuel to heat his oven. He must implement this nauseous cookery publicly, *in their sight*, so that they might be all the more moved by the approaching disaster. In the extremity of the famine they would not only have nothing on hand that was a delicacy but also nothing that was clean. The prophet humbly requested to be excused from the circumstance of this sign, the baking of his food with human excrement (v. 14); it seemed to be ceremonial defilement, for there was a law that human excrement should *be covered with earth*, so that God might *see no unclean thing in their camp* (Dt 23:13–14). Does the prophet have to go and gather something so offensive, and then use it to prepare his food in the sight of the people? "*Ah! Lord God*," he says, "*behold, my soul has not been polluted* (v. 14), and I am afraid that this would defile it." The defilement of the soul by sin is what good people dread, but sometimes tender consciences fear it without cause, having scruples concerning lawful things, as the prophet did here, not yet having learned that it is not what *goes into the mouth that defiles the man* (Mt 15:11). Now, because Ezekiel made known this scruple with a clear, tender conscience, God excused him in this matter. God allowed Ezekiel to use *cow's dung* instead of *man's dung* (v. 15).

2. This sign signified:

2.1. That those who remained in Jerusalem would be brought to extreme misery for lack of essential food. All supplies would be cut off from Jerusalem by the besiegers, including food (v. 16). Many of them would die of famine; they would die so as to *feel themselves die*. And it was sin that brought all this misery on them: "They shall consume away in their iniquity," as it may read. God is righteous to deprive us of enjoyments that we have made the food and fuel of our sinful desires.

2.2. That those who were taken into exile would be forced to *eat their defiled bread among the Gentiles* (v. 13), to eat food prepared by Gentile hands in a way other than that prescribed by the law of the Jewish church, food that they were always taught to call *defiled*. Or they would be forced to eat putrid food, such as their oppressors would allow them in slavery, and such as they formerly would have scorned to touch.

CHAPTER 5

Here is a further, and no less terrible, declaration of the judgments of God that were coming on the Jewish nation. 1. This destruction of Judah and Jerusalem is here represented by a sign: the cutting, burning, and scattering of hair (vv. 1–4). 2. That sign is explained and applied to Jerusalem. 2.1. Jerusalem is charged with sin as the cause of this desolation—the sin of contempt for God's Law (vv. 5–7) and that of defiling his sanctuary (v. 11). 2.2. Wrath is threatened (vv. 8–10), a variety of miseries (vv. 12, 16–17), which will be their shame and destruction (vv. 13–15).

Verses 1–4

We have here the sign by which the complete destruction of Jerusalem is set out, and here, as before, the prophet was himself the sign, so that the people might see how much he was moved by the situation of Jerusalem and how it lay close to his heart.

1. He must *shave off the hair of his head and beard* (v. 1), an act that symbolized God's completely rejecting that people as a worthless generation, one that could well be spared. Jerusalem had been the head, but having become corrupt, it had become like the *hair*, and hair, when it grows thick and long, is a burden. Ezekiel must not only cut off the hair that was superfluous; he must *cut it all off*, showing the end that God would make of Jerusalem.

2. He must *weigh the hair* and *divide it into three parts* (v. 1). Some believe the shaving of the hair shows their loss of liberty and honor: it was looked on as a sign of disgrace, as in the disgrace Hanun showed toward David's ambassadors (2Sa 10:4). It also shows the loss of their joy, for they shaved their heads on occasions of great mourning.

3. He must dispose of the hair so that it might all be destroyed (v. 2).

3.1. One *third part* must *be burnt in the midst of the city*, showing that many people would die from famine and the plague, and perhaps in the burning down of the city, *when the days of the siege were fulfilled*.

3.2. Another third was to be *cut in pieces with a knife*, representing the many people who, during the siege, were killed by the sword.

3.3. Another third was to be *scattered in the wind*, showing the carrying away of some to the land of the conqueror and the escape of others to the neighboring countries for shelter.

4. He must preserve a small quantity of the last third to be *scattered in the wind*, and he must *bind them in his skirts* (tuck them in the folds of his garment) (v. 3). This perhaps symbolized the small handful of people who were left under the government of Gedaliah, who, it was hoped, would keep possession of the land when most of the people were taken into exile. God would have done well for them in this way if they had done well for themselves.

Verses 5–17

The explanation of the foregoing metaphor: *This is Jerusalem*. The prophet's head, which was to be shaved, symbolized Jerusalem, which by the judgments of God was now to be stripped of its ornaments, emptied of its inhabitants, and made *naked and bare* (16:39), to be *shaved with a razor that is hired* (Isa 7:20). The head of one who was a priest, prophet, and holy person was fittest to represent Jerusalem, the Holy City. We have here:

1. The privileges Jerusalem was honored with (v. 5): *I have set it in the midst of the nations and countries that are round about her.* Jerusalem was situated in the center of kingdoms that were populated, civilized, and famous for learning, arts, and sciences. It was *set in the midst of them* as surpassing them all, set in the middle of them as a lamp on a lampstand to spread the light of divine revelation to all the dark corners of the neighboring nations to the ends of the earth. Jerusalem was to be as the heart is in the body, to give divine life to this dead world (1Ki 4:34). If they had preserved this reputation, what a blessing would Jerusalem have been to all the surrounding nations! But because it failed to be so, the fulfillment of

this intention was reserved for its latter days, *when out of Zion went forth the* Gospel *law, and the word of the Lord* Jesus *from Jerusalem* (Isa 2:3).

2. The offenses Jerusalem was guilty of. An accusation is here drawn up and proved beyond contradiction. She had *not walked in God's statutes* or *kept his judgments* (v. 7); in fact, the inhabitants of Jerusalem had *refused his judgments and his statutes* (v. 6). The people had not only broken God's laws but also perverted and abused them in such a way that they had made them the excuse and cover for their evil. They introduced the detestable traditions of the nations in place of God's institutions. *She has changed my judgments*, by idolatry and false worship, *more than the nations* (v. 6), and she has *multiplied* idols and altars, gods and temples, *more than the nations that are round about*. Israel's God is one, his name is one, and his altar is one. They multiplied their gods. They corrupted revealed religion more than the Gentiles had corrupted natural religion. Jerusalem desecrated the holy things, which she had been both entrusted and honored with (v. 11).

3. The punishments that Jerusalem would fall under:

3.1. God would take this work of punishing Jerusalem into his own hands. "You think it is only the Babylonian army that is against you, but they are God's hand, or rather the staff in his hand; it is *I, even I*, who *am against thee*, to speak against you through prophets, to act against you through providence." Those who will not take notice of the judgments of God's mouth will not escape the judgments of his hand.

3.2. These punishments would come from his displeasure. They would not be a correction in love for most of the people, but *in furious rebukes* (v. 15), unusual expressions to come from a God who said, *Fury is not in me* (Isa 27:4), and who has declared himself *gracious and merciful* and *slow to anger* (Ps 103:8). But their purpose was to show the awfulness of sin. Just as when God is dishonored by human sins, he is said to be *grieved* (Ps 95:10), so when he is honored by their destruction, he is said to *be comforted*.

3.3. Punishments would be public and open: *I will execute* these *judgments in the sight of the nations* (v. 8). Public sins call for public reproofs; likewise, if reproofs are not effective, public sins call for public judgment. The nations would fear the God of Israel when they saw how severely he punished sin even in those who were closest to him: *It shall be an instruction to the nations* (v. 15). Jerusalem should have taught her neighbors the fear of God by her godliness and goodness, but because she did not do that, God would teach it to them by her ruin.

3.4. These punishments would be such as had no precedent (v. 9): "*I will do in thee that which I have not done* in you before, though you have long deserved it." This is a rhetorical expression of the most severe judgments, like the description of Solomon that tells us that there was *none like him, before or after him* (1Ki 3:12). The strongest bonds of natural affection would be broken, which would be a just punishment for their willful breaking of the commitments of duty to God (v. 10): *The fathers shall eat the sons, and the sons shall eat the fathers*, because of the famine, or they would be compelled to do it by their barbaric conquerors. Some would be taken away by the plague (v. 12); the *pestilence shall pass through thee* (v. 17). Others *shall be consumed with famine*. Others *shall fall by the sword round about* Jerusalem; others would be devoured by *evil beasts*, which would attack those who fled for shelter to the deserts and mountains. And the last third, who would escape, would be *scattered into* all parts of the world, *into all the winds*, as it is expressed in vv. 10, 12.

3.5. These punishments would turn out to destroy them gradually. They would be *diminished* (v. 11), *bereaved* (v. 17), emptied of all that was their joy and confidence. We may well deduce that this prediction looks further, to the final destruction of that great city by the Romans.

3.6. All this is confirmed by divine authority and trustworthiness: *And they shall know that I the Lord have spoken it* (v. 13). There were those who thought it was only the prophet who spoke this in a state of delirium, but God's word would prove it is true.

CHAPTER 6

We have here: 1. A threat of the destruction of Israel because of their idolatry, and of the destruction of their idols with them (vv. 1–7). 2. A promise of the gracious return of a remnant of them to God by true repentance and reformation (vv. 8–10). 3. Directions given to the prophet to mourn the sin and the adversities of Israel (vv. 11–14).

Verses 1–7

Here:

1. The prophecy was directed to *the mountains of Israel* (vv. 1–2); the prophet must *set his face toward* them. If he could see so far as the land of Israel, *the mountains* would be the first part seen. He must look toward them steadfastly, as a judge looks at a prisoner when passing sentence. Although *the mountains of Israel* are very strong, he must *set his face against* them, as one who has punishment to declare that would shake their foundations. *The mountains of Israel* had been *holy mountains*, but now that the people had defiled them with their high places, God set his face against them and called on them to *hear the word of the Lord* (v. 3), and so must the prophet. But from *the mountains the word of the Lord* would echo *to the hills, to the rivers, and to the valleys*, for *the Lord God* speaks to them also.

2. What was threatened was the complete destruction of the idols and the idolaters. God himself said, *Behold, I, even I, will bring a sword upon you* (v. 3); the sword of the Babylonians would come at God's command. The *high places*, which were on the mountaintops (v. 3), would be leveled *and made desolate* (v. 6). The *altars*, on which they offered sacrifices to foreign gods, would *be broken* to pieces and *laid waste*; the *images* and *idols* would be defaced, *be broken and cease* (vv. 4, 6). *As all their high places would be laid waste*, so would all *their dwelling places* too, even *all their cities* (v. 6). It was added as a remarkable circumstance that they would fall *before their idols* (v. 4), that their *dead carcases* would be *laid*, and their *bones scattered, about their altars* (v. 5). In this way, the idols were rebuked for their inability to help their worshipers, and idolaters were rebuked for their foolishness in trusting them.

Verses 8–10

Up to this time, judgment has triumphed, but in these verses mercy triumphs over judgment (Jas 2:13). The ruin seems to be total, but *yet will I leave a remnant*, a small remnant; it is God who leaves them.

1. It is a preserved remnant, saved from the destruction (v. 8). None of those who are to *fall by the sword about* Jerusalem *shall escape*, for they trust in Jerusalem's walls for security. But some of them *shall escape the sword*

among the nations, where, because they are deprived of all other support, they depend only on God. They will be the seed of another generation, out of which Jerusalem will flourish again.

2. It is a penitent remnant (v. 9): *Those who escape of you shall remember me.* Where God intends to give grace to repent, he allows opportunity to repent. Yet many who have the opportunity lack the grace; many who *escape the sword* do not abandon their sin. Notice here:

2.1. The occasion of their repentance, which will be a mixture of judgment and mercy. They will be *carried captives*, but also they will *escape the sword* in their exile. True repentance will be accepted by God even though we are brought to it by our troubles; in fact, sanctified suffering often proves the means of conversion.

2.2. The root and driving force of their repentance: *They shall remember me among the nations* (v. 9). The prodigal son did not think about his father's house until he was about to die of hunger far away (Lk 15:14–18). Their remembering God will be the first step they take in returning to him. They *departed from* God, from his word, which they should have made their rule; they departed from his work, which they should have made their business. *Their hearts departed from* him; *their eyes* also went *after their idols*. The terrible aspect of this sin is that it is spiritual unfaithfulness; it is a *whorish heart* that *departs from* God. They will remember how this has grieved him and how he was angry with it. On the day of their repentance what will humble them more than anything will be not so much that their peace was broken, and their country broken, but *that God was broken* by their sin.

2.3. The evidence of their repentance: *They shall loathe themselves for the evils which they have committed in all their abominations* (all their detestable practices) (v. 9). True penitents see sin as detestable, as that *abominable thing which the Lord hates* and which makes sinners, and even their service, repugnant to him (Jer 44:4; Isa 1:11). It defiles the sinner's own conscience and makes them, unless they are beyond feeling, detestable to themselves.

2.4. The glory that will be given to God because of their repentance (v. 10): "*They shall know that I am the Lord*, finding that what I have said is fulfilled, caused to work for good, and caused to fulfill a good intention."

Verses 11–14

The same threats we had before are repeated, with an instruction to the prophet to lament them.

1. He must use gestures in preaching to express the sense he has of the sins and the adversities of the house of Israel (v. 11): *Smite* (strike) *with thy hand and stamp with thy foot.* The prophet must mourn two things in this way:

1.1. National sins. *Alas! for all the evil abominations* (detestable practices) *of the house of Israel* (v. 11). The sins of sinners are the sorrows of God's faithful servants.

1.2. National judgments. It is our responsibility to be moved not only by our own sins and sufferings but also by the sins and sufferings of others, and to look with compassion on the misery that evildoers bring on themselves, as Christ *beheld Jerusalem and wept over it* (Lk 19:41).

2. He must inculcate in them what he said before about the destruction that was coming on them.

2.1. They will be overcome and ruined by a range of judgments that will find them out and follow them wherever they are (v. 12).

2.2. They will read their sin in their punishment (vv. 5–7). Where they had prostrated themselves in honor of their idols, God will lay them dead, to their own shame and the shame of their idols.

2.3. The country will all be laid waste (v. 14), as was earlier said of *the cities* (v. 6): *I will make the land desolate.*

CHAPTER 7

The prophet must tell the people: 1. That the ruin of the land of Israel will be a complete destruction and make a miserable end of them (vv. 1–6). 2. That it is just at the door (vv. 7–10). 3. That it is unavoidable (vv. 10–15). 4. That their strength and wealth will be no protection against it (vv. 16–19). 5. That the temple will itself be ruined (vv. 20–22). 6. That the destruction will be national, because the sin that brought it on was national (vv. 23–27).

Verses 1–15

The prophet announces here, *An end! An end! It has come, it has come* (v. 2). *He that hath ears to hear, let him hear* (Mt 11:15).

1. The end that all the previous judgments have been moving toward, as a means of bringing it about, was a long time in coming, but *it has now come.* This perhaps looks further, to the last destruction of that nation by the Romans. And even further than that: *The end of all things is at hand,* and Jerusalem's last end was a type of *the end of the world* (Mt 24:3).

2. *An evil, an only evil, behold, has come* (v. 5). Sin is *an evil, an only evil, an evil* that contains no good; it is the worst of evils. But this is spoken of the evil of disaster. It is a disaster that is unheard of and without precedent or parallel, a disaster that stands alone; you cannot produce another such example of disaster. Evildoers have to drink *the dregs of that cup* which is full of *mixtures of mercy* to the righteous (Ps 75:8).

3. *The time has come,* the set time; *there is a time* (Ecc 3:1), a proper time for all God's purposes. Although threatened judgments may be long delayed, they will not be dropped. Although God's patience may postpone the judgments, nothing but sincere repentance and reformation will set them aside.

4. The whole body of the nation has become a *vessel of wrath, fitted for destruction* (Ro 9:22). Those who made light of mercy when it was offered them will *have judgment without mercy* (Jas 2:13).

5. All this is the just punishment for their sins, and it is what they have brought on themselves by their own foolishness. Two sins are particularly specified as causing God to bring these judgments on them—pride and oppression.

• God will humble them by his judgments, for they have exalted themselves. *The rod* of affliction *has blossomed,* but it was *pride* that *budded* (v. 10).
• Their enemies will deal harshly with them, for they have dealt harshly with one another (v. 11).

6. There is no escape from these judgments. People will be safe nowhere, for *he that is in the field shall die by the sword*—every field will become a battlefield for them—*and he that is in the city,* even though it is a holy city, will not find that it gives *protection,* but that *famine and pestilence devour him.* Sin has abounded in both city and country. Those who fall will not be mourned (v. 11): *There shall be no wailing for them,* for there will be no one left to wail for them. *None ever hardened his heart against God and prospered* (Job 9:4). Those who strengthen themselves in their evil will be found not only to weaken themselves but also to ruin themselves (Ps 52:7). *The multitude* can neither resist the torrent of these judgments nor make any headway against them (v. 14): *They have blown the trumpet* to call their soldiers. All is in vain, however: "*Let not the buyer rejoice* that he is increasing his estate and has become a purchaser; nor let *the seller mourn* that he is reducing his estate and has become bankrupt" (v. 12). Notice the futility of the things of this world and how worthless they are in times of trouble. It is added (v. 13), "*The seller shall not return*—at the Year of Jubilee, according to the Law (Lev 25:10, 13–17)—*to that which is sold,* even if he escapes the sword and lives until that year comes, for no inheritance will be enjoyed here until the seventy years have passed, and then people will return to their possessions and reclaim them" (2Ch 36:21; Jer 25:11).

Verses 16–22

Some of them *shall escape* (v. 16), but will they fare any better? Each good person dies once, whereas those who lead wretched lives die a thousand deaths, escaping only like Cain, to be restless wanderers; they are afraid of being killed by everyone they come across (Ge 4:13–14); so will these be.

1. They will have no comfort or satisfaction in their own minds, for wherever they go, they will take with them their guilty consciences, which will make them a burden to themselves. They will always be solitary, alone *upon the mountains,* ashamed of the lowly circumstances to which they have been reduced. They will always be sad. Those who once thought themselves as bold as lions will now become like the *doves of the valleys* (v. 16). This is how timid and discouraged they will be, ready to *flee when none pursues* and to tremble at the mere shaking of a leaf (Lev 26:17, 36). Sooner or later sin will produce one form of sorrow or another, and those who will not repent of their sin may justly be left to pine away in it. They will be deprived of all their strength in body and mind (v. 17). They will be deprived of all their hopes (v. 18).

2. They will gain no benefits from their wealth and riches (v. 19). They think their wealth will be *their strong city* (Pr 10:15; 18:11), that they will be able to use it to bribe enemies and buy friends, that it will be the price of their lives. But it will bring no relief to them now in their day of adversity, for *gold and silver* cannot protect them from the judgments of God. Their *gold and silver* cannot satisfy their hunger or even suffice to make up one good meal for them. We could survive better without mines of gold than without fields of corn. Much less can these things satisfy their souls or give them any inner comfort. Their *gold and silver shall be thrown into the streets* (v. 19), because it would be an encumbrance to them and slow down their flight, or because it would expose them to danger and be a temptation to the enemy to cut their throats for their money.

3. God's temple will do them no good (vv. 20–22). God did them a great honor by setting up his sanctuary among them, but here is the great dishonor they have done to God in defiling his sanctuary: they *made the images of their* false gods. They set these up in God's temple, and no greater disrespect could have been shown him. And so they will be deprived of the temple, and it will bring no help to them. Let the soldiers do as they want; let them *enter into the secret place,* into the Most Holy Place. Its defense has departed.

Verses 23–27

Here is:

1. The prisoner brought into court: "Prepare a chain," in which to drag the criminal to the bar. The chain signified the siege of Jerusalem, the slavery of those taken into exile, or that they were all bound by the righteous judgment of God.

2. The accusation drawn up against the prisoner: *The land is full of bloody crimes* (v. 23); literally, it is full of "the judgments of blood"; it is full of such crimes as were to be punished with death under the Law, "the judgment of the blood." Idolatry, blasphemy, witchcraft, homosexual practices, and others were *bloody crimes*.

3. Judgment given on this accusation. God will judge them not only for the desecrating of his sanctuary but also for perverting the course of justice between one human being and another. Since they have walked in the way of the nations and behaved worse than they did, God will *bring the worst of the heathen* (nations) *upon them* (v. 24) to destroy them. Since they have filled their house with goods they gained unjustly and have used their power to oppress the weak, God will give their houses to be possessed by foreigners and *make the pomp* (pride) *of the strong to cease.* Since they have set up the images of other gods in the temple, God will remove from there the signs of the presence of their own God. Since they have followed one sin with another, God will pursue them with one judgment after another, *mischief upon mischief* and *rumour upon rumour* to frighten them, like the waves in a storm. While in the troubles, they will not have the direction that they expect (v. 26). *They shall seek a vision of the prophet* to be assured of a happy outcome. They will want a vision, not to rebuke them for sin or to warn them of danger, but to promise them rescue. But they refused to listen to what God had to say to them by way of conviction, and so he has nothing to say to them by way of encouragement. *Counsel shall perish from the ancients*; the elders of the people, who should advise them what to do at this difficult point, will be at their wits' end. None of the powerful people will *find their hands* (Ps 76:5).

CHAPTER 8

Having given the prophet a clear vision of the people's misery that is coming on them very shortly, God gives him here a clear insight into the people's evil. Here God, in a vision, brings him to Jerusalem to show him the sins that are committed there (vv. 1–4). There he sees: 1. The idol of jealousy set up at the gate of the altar (vv. 5–6). 2. The elders of Israel worshiping all kinds of idols in a secret room (vv. 7–12). 3. The women weeping for Tammuz (vv. 13–14). 4. The men worshiping the sun (vv. 15–16). God then appeals to him as to whether such an offensive people should have any pity shown them (vv. 17–18).

Verses 1–6

Ezekiel was now in Babylon, but the messages of wrath he had spoken that are recorded in the previous chapters related to Jerusalem. Here he had a vision of what was happening at Jerusalem, and this vision continues to the end of chapter 11. Notice:

1. The date of this vision. The first vision he had was in *the fifth year of the captivity, in the fourth month* and on *the fifth day of the month* (1:1–2). This was only fourteen months later. Perhaps it was after he had lain 390 days on his left side to bear the iniquity of Israel, and before he

began the forty days on his right side to bear the iniquity of Judah, for he was now sitting in his house, not lying.

2. The prophet was himself *sitting in his house* (v. 1), perhaps deep in contemplation. *The elders of Judah*, who were now in exile with him, *sat before him*. Some think it was on some special occasion that they were with him, to inquire of the Lord, and so they *sat down* at his feet to *hear his word*. Now that the elders of Judah were in exile, they paid more respect to God's prophets, and to his word in their mouth. A minister's house should be a church for all their neighbors. Paul preached in his own rented house at Rome, and God acknowledged him there, and *no man forbade him* (Ac 28:30–31).

3. The divine influence that the prophet was now under: *The hand of the Lord fell there upon me.*

4. The vision that the prophet saw (v. 2). He *beheld a likeness*, all *brightness* above and all *fire* below, fire and flame. This agrees with the description we had in 1:27 of the vision he had earlier.

5. The prophet's vision of Jerusalem. He was *lifted up between heaven and earth* (v. 3), and then, perhaps in a transport of delight, he had the following visions; and we may suppose that he *could not tell whether* he was *in the body or out of the body*, any more than Paul could in a similar case (2Co 12:2), and much less we. Those who by divine grace have been raised up above the earth and its things are best prepared for fellowship with God and the sharing of divine light. He was taken in the vision to Jerusalem, to God's sanctuary there.

6. The revelations made to him.

6.1. He saw the glory of God (v. 4), the same appearance that he had seen before (ch. 1). Ezekiel had this repeated vision of the glory of God both to support and to honor the following revelations. But it seems to have a further intention here; it was to emphasize the sin of Israel in exchanging a God of so much glory for false, scandalous gods. The more glorious we see God to be, the more repugnant we will see sin to be, especially the sin of idolatry.

6.2. There he saw the reproach and shame of *Israel—the image of jealousy*, set *northward, at the gate of the altar* (vv. 3, 5). This was probably an idol of Baal or of the carved Asherah pole, both of which Manasseh made and set in the temple (2Ki 21:7; 2Ch 33:3), and which Josiah removed. It seems that Josiah's successors put it back there, as they probably also did the *chariots of the sun* that he found *at the entering in of the house of the Lord* (2Ki 23:11), said here to be *in the entry*. Whatever idol it was, the prophet tells us that it was *the image of jealousy*, to convince our consciences that it was most offensive to God and *provoked him to jealousy* (Ps 78:58). And now God appealed to him as to whether this was not sufficient basis for God to reject this people. By their idolatry they had, in effect, like the Gadarenes, asked him *to depart out of their coasts* (Mt 8:34), and so he would depart. He would no more honor and protect his sanctuary, but would give it up to shame. *But turn thyself yet again* (v. 6). Where there is one abomination, it will be found that there are many more. Sins do not go alone.

Verses 7–12

Here we have a further revelation of the detestable practices committed at Jerusalem within the confines of the temple. Notice:

1. How this revelation is made. God, in a vision, brings Ezekiel to the *door* (entrance) *of the court*, the outer court, along the sides of which are the priests' lodgings. But,

behold, a hole in the wall (v. 7), a spy hole. This *hole in the wall* is made wider by Ezekiel, and *behold a door* (v. 8). He goes in by this doorway into the treasury, or some of the apartments of the priests, and sees *the wicked abominations that they do there* (v. 9).

2. What the revelation is. He sees a room with idolatrous pictures all around (v. 10). This was a kind of collection of all the idols together. Although the letter of the second commandment forbids any graven images, painted ones are as bad and as dangerous. He sees this chamber filled with idolatrous worshipers (v. 11): there are *seventy men of the elders of Israel* offering incense to these painted idols. Each one of them has a censer in his hand. They all want to be their own priests. They think themselves out of God's sight: *They say, The Lord seeth us not* (v. 12).

Verses 13–18

Here we have:

1. More detestable practices revealed to the prophet. First, there are *women weeping for Tammuz* (v. 14). Some think it was for Adonis, an idol among the Greeks, that they shed these tears; others think it was for Osiris, an idol of the Egyptians. It is said that the idol was caused to weep and that the worshipers then wept with it. They mourned the death of this Tammuz and immediately rejoiced at its returning to life. These mourning women *sat at the door of the gate of the Lord's house*, and they shed their idolatrous tears there, and some think that along with the spiritual adultery of their idolatry, they prostrated themselves as prostitutes. There were also *men worshiping the sun* (v. 16). This was practiced *in the inner court of the Lord's house at the door of the temple of the Lord, between the porch* (portico) *and the altar*. They turned *their backs toward the temple of the Lord* and turned *their faces toward the east, and worshiped the sun*, the rising sun.

2. The inference drawn from these discoveries (v. 17): *"Hast thou seen this, O son of man*, and could you have ever thought you would see such things being done in the temple of the Lord?" He appeals to the prophet himself. "Is it excusable in those who have God's oracles and ordinances (Ro 3:2; 9:4) *that they commit the abominations which they commit here*? Do not those who sin in this way deserve to suffer? They *return to provoke me*—they repeat the offense; they do it, and do it again *and lo, they put the branch to their nose"* — a proverbial expression that perhaps shows their *scoffing* at God. "They put the branch to their wrath," or "to his wrath," as the Masoretes read it, that is, they are still bringing more fuel to the fire of divine wrath, which they have already kindled. *"Though they cry in my ears with a loud voice, yet will I not hear them*, for their sins continue to cry out more loudly for vengeance than their prayers cry out for mercy."

CHAPTER 9

Here is: 1. Preparation made of instruments that were to be employed to destroy the city (vv. 1–2). 2. The removal of the Shechinah, the visible presence of the divine glory, from the cherubim to the threshold of the temple (v. 3). 3. Orders given to mark a remnant to be preserved from the common destruction (vv. 3–4). 4. The warrant signed and the execution begun (vv. 5–7). 5. The prophet's intercession for the sentence to be reduced (vv. 8–10).

6. The report made by the one who was to mark the godly remnant that he had completed the matter (v. 11).

Verses 1–4

In these verses we have:

1. The call given to Jerusalem's destroyers. God's angels had received a charge now to lay that city waste, which they had long had responsibility to protect and watch over. They were close by, as destroying angels, as ministers of wrath, for *every man has his destroying weapon in his hand*, like the angel that kept the way of the tree of life with a flaming sword (Ge 3:24).

2. Their appearance, on this summons, recorded. Immediately *six men came* (v. 2), one for each of the principal gates of Jerusalem. The nations of which the king of Babylon's army was composed, which some reckon to be six, and the commanders of his army—of whom *six* are named as the main ones (Jer 39:3)—may be *the slaughter* (deadly) *weapons* that are said to be in the hands of the angels. They came *from the way of the higher gate, which lies toward the north* (v. 2), either because the Babylonians came from the north (Jer 1:14) or because the image of jealousy was set *up at the door of the inner gate that looks toward the north* (8:3, 5).

3. The notice taken of one among the destroying angels. It seems he was not one of the six, but *among them*, to see that mercy was mixed with judgment (v. 2). This *man was clothed with linen*, as priests were, and he had *a writer's inkhorn* (kit) hanging at *his side*, as attorneys once did; he had this tool for his task just as the other six had their *destroying weapons* for their task. Here the honors of the pen exceeded those of the sword: those who bore the sword were angels, but the One who used the *writer's inkhorn* (kit) was the Lord of angels, for it is generally agreed that he represented Christ as Mediator, saving those who were his from the flaming sword of divine justice. As high priest, he wears fine *linen* (Rev 19:8). As a prophet he wears the *writer's inkhorn* (kit). The Book of Life is the Lamb's book (Rev 21:27). The great things of the Law and Gospel that God has written down for us are written down by him, and the Bible is *the revelation of Jesus Christ* (Rev 1:1). Among the destroyers and the destructions around, there is a Mediator, a great high priest (Heb 4:14).

4. The removal of the appearance of the divine glory from over the cherubim. Some think it refers to the display of God's glory that the prophet now saw over the cherubim in a vision. Ezekiel immediately observed that *the glory of the God of Israel had gone up from the cherub* (v. 3), and what good is a vision of angels if God has gone?

5. The charge given *to the man clothed in linen* to protect the godly remnant from the general desolation. We do not read that this Savior was summoned and sent for, as the destroyers were, for he is always ready, *appearing in the presence of God for* us (Heb 9:24). This remnant that was to be saved were those who *sighed and cried*, sighed in themselves, as people in distress, crying out to God in prayer. These godly few had witnessed against the detestable practices of others in the city and had done what they could to suppress them. Orders were given to find all those who had such a godly public spirit: *"Go through the midst of the city* seeking them (v. 4); find them *and set a mark upon their foreheads."* A work of grace in the soul is to God *a mark upon the forehead*, which he will acknowledge as his mark, and by which *he knows those that are his* (2Ti 2:19). God will set a mark on his mourners; he will note their sighs and bottle their tears (Ps 56:8).

Verses 5–11

In these verses we have:

1. A command given to the destroyers to carry out their commission.

1.1. They were ordered to destroy all. This was fulfilled in the death of many people by famine and the plague, and especially by the sword of the Babylonians, as far as the military execution went. Sometimes even such a work of bloodshed has been God's work. But then see how evil sin is, which provokes the God of infinite mercy to go to such severe measures. *Let not your eye spare, neither have you pity* (v. 5). Those who live in sin and hate to be reformed will die in sin. They might easily have prevented the ruin, but refused to do anything that would have prevented it.

1.2. They were warned not to cause the slightest harm to those who were marked out for salvation: "*Come not near any man upon whom is the mark*; do not even threaten or frighten any of them." God had promised that *it would go well with his remnant* and they *would be well treated* (Jer 15:11), and we have reason to think that none of the mourning, praying remnant were killed by the sword of the Babylonians. In the last destruction of Jerusalem by the Romans, the Christians were all secured in a city called Pella, and none of them perished.

1.3. They were instructed to *begin at the sanctuary* (v. 9). They must begin there because that was where the evil that caused God to send these judgments began. God's temple is a sanctuary, a refuge and protection for penitent sinners, but not for anyone who *goes on still in his trespasses* (Ps 68:21).

1.4. They were appointed to *go forth into the city* (vv. 6–7). Though *judgement begins at the house of God* (1Pe 4:17), it will not end there.

2. Execution carried out. They observed their orders. *They began at the* elders, *the ancient men that were before the house,* either those seventy elders who worshiped idols at their shrines (8:12) or those twenty-five who *worshiped the sun between the porch and the altar.* Then they proceeded to the ordinary people.

3. The prophet's intercession for the judgment to be lessened (v. 8): *While they were slaying them, and I was left, I fell upon my face.* He speaks as one who narrowly escaped the destruction, attributing it to God's goodness, not to his own deserving. We must look on that and recognize that we too are spared only because of God's mercy, so that we may do good where we are, especially by our prayers.

4. God's denial of the prophet's request for the judgment (vv. 9–10). God was as willing to show mercy as the prophet could desire; he always is so. But here the situation would not allow it; it was such that mercy could not be granted without wronging justice. The sinners justified themselves in their sin with the same faithless, ungodly principle with which they flattered themselves in their idolatry (8:12): "*The Lord has forsaken the earth* and left it to us to do what we want; he will not interfere in its affairs, and whatever wrong we do, he *sees not.*" Now how can those who so defy God's justice expect to benefit by his mercy?

5. A report brought back concerning the order of protection that was issued to keep safe those who mourned in Zion (v. 11): *The man clothed with linen reported the matter*; he gave an account of what he had done. He had found all who mourned in secret for the sins of the land and who cried out against them, and he had marked them all on the forehead. Lord, *I have done as thou hast commanded me.*

CHAPTER 10

Again the prophet sees the vision of the glory of God as he saw it by the Kebar River: 1. The scattering of the coals of fire on the city, taken from between the cherubim (vv. 1–7). 2. The removal of the glory of God from the temple (vv. 8–22).

Verses 1–7

To inspire us with a holy awe and fear of God and to fill us with reverence of him, we may notice in this part of the prophet's vision:

1. The glorious appearance of divine majesty. Something of the invisible world is made visible here, faint representations of its radiance and beauty, shadows, but such as are not to be compared with the truth and substance any more than a picture is compared with real life. He is *in the firmament above the head* (above the expanse over the heads) *of the cherubim* (v. 1) here. It is *the firmament of his power* and his viewpoint, for it is from there that *he beholds* all *the children of men* (Ps 33:13; 11:4; 14:2). He is on the throne here. God's glory and rule infinitely transcend all the brightest ideas our minds can either form or receive. The appearance of his glory is veiled with a cloud, but out of that cloud comes a dazzling radiance; in *the house* and *inner court* there was *a cloud* and darkness, which filled them, but the outer court *was full of the brightness of the Lord's glory* (vv. 3–4). In the same way, in Hab 3:4, *he had rays coming out of his hand, and yet there was the hiding of his power.* Nothing is clearer than that God is, nothing darker than *what* he is. *God covers himself with light* (Ps 104:2), but he *makes darkness his pavilion* (Ps 18:11).

2. The terrible directing of his wrath. Further orders are to be given to destroy Jerusalem. Here we have a command to burn the city to ashes by *scattering coals of fire* on it, which in the vision were taken *from between the cherubim* (v. 2). *The glory of the Lord* was lifted *up from the cherub* and stood *on the threshold of the house,* to imitate the courts of judgment, which the Israelites kept in the gates of their cities. The One who sat on the throne called *to the man clothed in linen* to go *in between the wheels, and fill his hand with coals of fire from between the cherubim, and scatter them over the city* (v. 2). This shows the burning of the city and temple by the Babylonians. The fire on God's altar, where atonement was made, had been insulted. When the prophet first saw this vision, he observed that there were *burning coals of fire* and *lamps* that *went up and down among the living creatures* (1:13); it was from there that this fire was taken (v. 7). The *spirit of burning* (Isa 4:4), *the refiner's fire* (Mal 3:2), by which Christ purifies his church, is of divine origin.

Verses 8–22

Here is a further account of the vision of God's glory that Ezekiel saw, which is intended to introduce the departure of the glory from them.

1. Ezekiel saw the glory of God shining in the sanctuary, as he had seen it *by the river of Chebar.* Ezekiel saw here the operations of divine Providence in the government of the lower world. The agency of the angels in directing the affairs of this world is represented by the close communication between the *living creatures* and the *wheels,* the wheels being guided by them in all their movements, as the chariot is by the one who drives it. But the fact that the same Spirit is in both the *living creatures* and the *wheels* (v. 17; 1:21) shows the infinite wisdom that serves its own purposes by the service of angels and all the events of this

lower world. The prophet noticed that this was *the same vision* as the one he saw by the Kebar River (vv. 15, 22). This world is subject to change. Its course of affairs is represented by *wheels* (v. 9). Their appearance was as if there were a *wheel in the midst of a wheel* (a wheel intersecting a wheel) (v. 10), which suggests the references of providences to each other, their dependence on each other, and their tendency to serve one common purpose even though their movements are intricate and seemingly contrary. There is a wonderful harmony and uniformity in the various events of Providence (v. 13): *although the wheels moved several ways, it was cried to them, O wheel!* They were all as one, being guided by one Spirit to one purpose. The movements of Providence are steady and regular, and whatever the Lord pleases he does. *The wheels turned not as they went* (v. 11), and the *living creatures went every one straight forward* (v. 22). The Spirit of God directs all the creatures, both higher and lower, so as to make them serve God's purpose. Events are not determined by the *wheel of fortune*, which is blind, but by the *wheels of Providence*, which are full of eyes.

2. Ezekiel saw the glory of God moving out of the sanctuary, the place where God's honor had long dwelt, and this sight was sad. Earlier it was said that the *glory of the Lord stood over the threshold* (v. 4). But now it *departed from off the threshold* and *stood over the cherubim*, those that Ezekiel now saw in a vision (v. 18). And immediately *the cherubim lifted up their wings* (v. 19) and *mounted up from the earth*, and *when they went out*, the wheels of this chariot were not drawn *beside them*, but went by instinct, by which it appeared that *the Spirit of the living creatures was in the wheels* (v. 17; 1:21). In the courts of the temple the people of Israel had dishonored their God, and now the *cherubim, and the glory of God above them, stood at the door of the east gate of the Lord's house* (v. 19). But with many stops and pauses God departs, as if reluctant to go, as if to see whether there is anyone who will intercede with him to return. God moves gradually from an offensive people, and when he is ready to depart in displeasure, he would return to them in mercy if only they were a repenting, praying people.

CHAPTER 11

This chapter concludes the vision that Ezekiel saw. Here we have: 1. A message of wrath against those who continue at Jerusalem (vv. 1–13). 2. A message of comfort to those who were taken into exile to Babylon and are very despondent there. And just as the former are assured that God has judgments in store for them, so the latter are assured that God has mercy in store for them despite their present distress (vv. 14–21). And so the glory of God moves further away (vv. 22–23). The vision disappears (v. 24), and Ezekiel faithfully gives his hearers an account of it (v. 25).

Verses 1–13

We have here:

1. The self-confidence of the leaders of Jerusalem. The prophet was brought, in a vision, to the gate of the temple where these leaders sat in council. *The Spirit lifted me up, and brought me to the east gate of the Lord's house, and behold twenty-five men were there* (v. 1). They were charged not with corruption in worship, but with maladministration in government; two of them are named, *Pelatiah* and *Jaazaniah* son of Azzur. Some tell us that Jerusalem was divided into twenty-four wards and that

these were the aldermen of those wards with their mayor or president. "*These are the men that devise mischief* (plot evil) under pretense of public safety. They harden people in their sins and take away their fear of the judgments of God that are threatened by the prophets. They *give wicked counsel in this city*, advising the inhabitants to silence the prophets, to rebel against the king of Babylon, and to be determined to hold until all else fails." They were accused for words spoken at their council meeting (v. 3). They spoke to this effect: "*It is not near*—the destruction of our city, so often threatened by the prophets." Where Satan cannot persuade people to look on the judgment to come as something doubtful and uncertain, he still wins his victory by persuading them to look on it as something far off. If the destruction is not near, they conclude, "*Let us build houses; let us count on things continuing as they are, for this city is the cauldron, and we are the flesh*" (v. 3). This seems to be a proverb, signifying, "We are as safe in this city as meat that is being boiled in a pot; the walls of the city will be to us as *walls of brass* (Jer 1:18; 15:20) and will not be damaged by the besiegers any more than the *cauldron* is by the *fire under it*." Perhaps it has reference to *the flesh of the peace offerings* (fellowship offerings), which it was a great offense for the priests to take out of the *cauldron* while the meat was being boiled (as we find in 1Sa 2:13–14), and if this is the reference, then it suggests they felt more self-confident because Jerusalem was the Holy City, and they thought themselves a holy people in it, not to be meddled with.

2. The method taken to wake them up out of their self-confidence. To help them to understand, the word of God was sent to them to give them warning (v. 4): *Therefore prophesy against them* and try to get them to see the truth. *Prophesy, O son of man!* on these dead and dry bones (37:4). *The Spirit of the Lord fell upon him*, to make him full of power and courage, and *said unto him, Speak* (v. 5). Let them know that God notices (v. 5): "*I know the things that come into your minds every one of them*, what secret reasons you have for these decisions, putting such a good appearance on something you know to be bad." God knows not only the things that come out of our mouths but also the things that come into our minds, not only all we say but also all we think. "In this way, you, with all your stubbornness, have *filled the streets of Jerusalem with the slain* (dead)" (v. 6). These slain, these people who have been killed, were the only flesh that would be left in this pot (v. 7). They had provoked God to abandon the city and thought they would do well enough by their own wisdom and strength when he was gone, but God wanted them to know that there is no peace for those who have left their God. Let them know that all this was the due punishment for their sin, and *the revelation of the righteous judgment of God* (Ro 2:5) against them: *You shall know that I am the Lord* (vv. 10, 12).

3. The awakening providence that immediately followed this awakening word (v. 13). *It came to pass, when I prophesied, that Pelatiah the son of Benaiah died*. It seems this was done in a vision now, but it was an assurance that when this prophecy was made known it would be fulfilled in fact. The death of Pelatiah was a pledge of the complete fulfillment of this prophecy. Though the sudden death of Pelatiah was a confirmation of Ezekiel's prophecy, he was still deeply concerned about it, taking it to heart as if he had been his relative or friend: *He fell on his face and cried with a loud voice, "Ah! Lord God, wilt thou make a full end of the remnant of Israel?* Will the remnant who have escaped the sword die in the same way, by the direct hand of heaven?"

Verses 14–21

The prophet Ezekiel, having received instructions to try to wake up those who were *at ease in Zion*, was in these verses given words of encouragement for those who mourned in Babylon when they *remembered Zion* (Ps 137:1). Notice:

1. How the godly exiles were trampled on and gloated over by those who stayed in Jerusalem (v. 15). God said to the prophet, "They are *thy brethren*; they are your fellow exiles. They are the whole house of Israel." God considered them so because it was only they who had kept their integrity. They were not only of the same family and nation as Ezekiel, but of the same spirit. Those who were at ease scorned their compatriots who were humbled. They cut them off from being members of their church. Because the exiles had, in submission to the will of God, surrendered themselves to the king of Babylon, their leaders excommunicated them, saying, "Go far away from the Lord; we will have nothing to do with you. *Unto us is this land given in possession*; you have lost your estates by surrendering to the king of Babylon, and we have become entitled to own them."

2. The gracious promises that God made to them. Those who hated them and rejected them said, *Let the Lord be glorified*. However, he *shall appear to their joy* (appear and bring them joy) (Isa 66:5). God acknowledged that his hand had gone out against the exiles (v. 16): "It is true that I have sent them far away among the nations and scattered them among the countries; they look as if they were an abandoned people. But I have mercy in store for them." He would make up to them the lack of the temple (v. 16): *I will be to them as a little sanctuary in the countries where they shall come*. Those at Jerusalem have the temple but are without God; those who are in Babylon have God, though without the temple. God would in due time put an end to their adversities; he would bring them out of exile and resettle them or their children in their own land (v. 17). "*You* will have the entitlement as the patriarchs had, and *they* (v. 18)—those who come after you—will have the possession." Their exile would effectively heal them of their idolatry. God would plant good motivations within them; he would make the tree good (v. 19). This is a Gospel promise, and it is fulfilled to all those whom God intends to go to the heavenly Canaan. All who are sanctified have *a new spirit*. They act from new motivation, walk by new rules, and aim at new purposes. A new name or a new face will not be enough without a new spirit. This is God's work, his gift by promise. Their practices would be consistent with those principles: *That they may walk in my statutes* in every aspect of their lives and keep my ordinances in every act of religious worship (v. 20). *But as for those* who have no grace, what have they *to do with peace* (2Ki 9:17, 19)? Their *heart walks after the heart of their detestable things* (v. 21). They have a *heart after the heart of their idols*.

Verses 22–25

Here is:

1. The departure of God's presence from the city and temple. When the message was committed to the prophet, when he was fully informed of it, *then the cherubim lifted up their wings and the wheels beside them* (v. 22) as before (10:19). The glory of the Lord moved *to the mountain which is on the east side of the city* (v. 23). On this mountain the people had set up their idols, to confront God in his temple (1Ki 11:7). There was a full view of the city from that mountain; it

was to there that God moved, to fulfill what he had said in Dt 32:20, *I will hide my face from them, I will see what their end shall be*. It was from this mountain that Christ *beheld the city and wept over it* (Lk 19:41), foreseeing its destruction by the Romans. *The glory of the Lord* moved there to be, as it were, still within call, ready to return if, *in this their day*, they would *understand the things that belonged to their peace* (Lk 19:42).

2. The departure of this vision from the prophet: it *went up from him* (v. 24); he saw it rise upward until it went out of sight, confirming to his faith that it was a heavenly vision. The same spirit that had carried him in a trance or ecstasy to Jerusalem brought him back to Babylonia, for that was his place of service. He spoke his message very honestly: he *spoke all that* God *had shown* him, and only that. It is better to be in Babylon under the favor of God than in Jerusalem under his wrath and curse.

CHAPTER 12

Although the vision of God's glory has gone up from the prophet, God's word continues to come to him. 1. By removing his belongings and leaving his lodgings, the prophet must be a sign to symbolize Zedekiah's flight from Jerusalem in the greatest confusion when the Babylonians take the city (vv. 1–16). 2. By eating his food with trembling, the prophet must be a sign to symbolize the famine in the city during the siege (vv. 17–20). 3. A message is sent from God to the people to assure them that all these predictions will be soon fulfilled (vv. 21–28).

Verses 1–16

Since the vision of the glory of God had gone up from him, Ezekiel perhaps reflected with so much pleasure on it that he often wished it would come down to him again, but we do not find that he ever saw it again. However, *the word of the Lord comes to* him. We may keep up our fellowship with God without raptures and ecstasy. In these verses the prophet is instructed:

1. By what signs and actions to express the approaching captivity of Zedekiah king of Judah. That is what is to be foretold, and it is foretold to those who are already in exile, because as long as Zedekiah is on the throne, they flatter themselves with the hope that he will rescue them soon. It is therefore necessary to convince them that Zedekiah, instead of being the one who will rescue them, will very soon suffer with them. To prepare them, the prophet must first give them a sign; he must reveal to their eyes first, and then to their ears. And here we have:

1.1. The reason why he must use this method (v. 2): it is that they are a senseless, dull, and unthinking people. He must speak to them in signs, as one teaches deaf people.

1.2. The method he uses to awaken and move them; he must provide himself with all necessaries *for removing* (moving) (v. 3), provide clothes and money for a journey. He must *remove from one place to another*, as one who is unsettled and forced to move on. He must do this *by day, in the sight of the people*; he must bring out all his household belongings to be packed up and sent away (v. 4). Because all the doors and gates are either locked up or guarded, he must *dig through the wall* and transfer his goods in secret through the gap he makes (v. 5). He must take his goods away himself on his own shoulders, *in the twilight*, so that he may not be discovered. He must himself steal away *at evening in their sight*, with fear and trembling, and must go *as those that go forth into captivity* (v. 4); he must *cover* his *face* (v. 6) as a sign of great sorrow and must leave as a poor, broken person who leaves their country. In this way, Ezekiel must himself be a sign to them; God says (v. 3), "*It may be they will consider*, and that they will lose their worthless confidence, *though they be a rebellious house.*"

1.3. Ezekiel's ready obedience to the orders God has given him (v. 7): *I did so as I was commanded.*

2. How he is to explain those signs and actions.

2.1. It is presumed that the people will ask the meaning of this sign, or at least they should (v. 9): *Hath not the house of Israel said unto thee, What doest thou?* This is why the prophet must do a strange, unfamiliar thing, so that they may ask what it means.

2.2. The prophet is to tell them its meaning. In general (v. 10), this oracle concerns the prince in Jerusalem. They know who that is, and though they are now in exile, they glory in the knowledge that they still have a prince of their own in Jerusalem and that *the house of Israel* is still intact there. "But tell them," God says, "that in what you have done they may read the doom of their friends at Jerusalem. Say, 'I am your sign'" (v. 11).

2.2.1. The people will be led away into exile (v. 11): *As I have done, so shall it be done unto them*; they will be forced from their own houses, never to return to them.

2.2.2. The prince will make a futile attempt to escape, for he also will go into exile. Ezekiel here foretells it to those who promise themselves relief through him.

2.2.2.1. The prince himself will take away his own goods (v. 12). God can turn a prince into a porter. The one who used to have regalia carried before him will now himself carry his goods on his back and steal away out of the city at dusk. Because all the roads to the palace are carefully watched by the enemy, *they* (the king and those with him) *shall dig through the wall to carry out* (their possessions) *thereby*.

2.2.2.2. He will attempt to escape in disguise, wearing a mask, which will cover his face, so that he will not see the ground with his eyes.

2.2.2.3. He will be taken prisoner into exile in Babylon (v. 13). Jeremiah said that King Zedekiah would see the king of Babylon and that he would go to Babylon; Ezekiel says that he will be brought to Babylon, but he will not see it, even though he will die there. One said that he would see the king of Babylon, while the other said that he would not see Babylon, but both proved true: he did see the king of Babylon at Riblah, where he passed sentence on him for his rebellion, but it was there that Nebuchadnezzar had Zedekiah's eyes put out, so that he did not see Babylon when he was taken there. The captives could have had little joy in seeing him when he could not see them.

2.2.2.4. All his guards will be dispersed (v. 14): *I will scatter all that are about him to help him*, so that he will be left helpless; *I will scatter them among the nations* and disperse them in the countries (v. 15). But some of Zedekiah's scattered troops will escape (v. 16), *that they may declare all their abominations* (acknowledge all their detestable practices) *among the heathen whither they come*. They will then acknowledge the justice of God and make confession of their sins. This will show that they were spared in mercy.

Verses 17–20

Here again the prophet is made a sign to them of the devastation that is to come on Judah and Jerusalem.

1. He must himself eat and drink in anxiety and despair, especially when in company (vv. 17–18), in order to express the disastrous condition of those who will be in Jerusalem during the siege.

2. He must tell them that *the inhabitants of Jerusalem*, too, will eat and drink with anxiety and despair (vv. 19–20), either because they are afraid that supplies will not last or because they are continually expecting terror from the enemy. The decay of goodness in a nation brings about a decay of everything else, and when neighbors devour one another, God is just to bring enemies on them to devour them all.

Verses 21–28

Various methods have been used to wake up this self-confident and careless people so that they might be stirred by repentance and reformation. The prophecies of their destruction were confirmed by visions and illustrated by signs, but we are told here how they evade the conviction by telling themselves and one another that although the threatened judgments will come eventually, they will not come for a long time.

1. They have a saying that has become proverbial in the land of Israel (v. 22): "*The days are prolonged* (the days go by); because the destruction has not come, it will never come. We are never going to trust a prophet again, for we have been more frightened than hurt in the past." And another saying is, "*The vision is for a* great while *to come*; it refers to events far away, so that we need not trouble ourselves about them" (v. 27). The patience of God that should have led them to repentance hardened them in sin.

2. They are assured that they are deceiving themselves: *Tell them, therefore, The days are at hand* (v. 23), and again, *There shall none of my words be prolonged any more* (v. 28). God will certainly silence the lying proverbs and prophecies that support their worthless hopes. *There shall be no more any vain* (false) *vision* (v. 24). God will certainly, and very soon, fulfill every word he has spoken. Note with what majesty he says it (v. 25): *I am the Lord! I am Jehovah!* Those who *see the visions of the Almighty* do not see false visions; God *confirms the word of his servants* (Isa 44:26) by fulfilling it. *The days are at hand* when you will see *the effect of every vision* (v. 23).

CHAPTER 13

God's faithful prophets were nowhere so sharp toward any kind of sinners as they were toward false prophets, not because the false prophets were their most spiteful enemies, but because they showed the greatest disrespect to God and caused the greatest trouble to his people. The prophet shows here the sin and punishment: 1. Of the false prophets (vv. 1–16). 2. Of the false women prophets (vv. 17–23). The two have agreed to encourage the people in their sins and flatter them with the hope that they will still have peace. However, these prophets will be proved to be liars, their prophecies sham, and the expectations of the people illusory.

Verses 1–9

Some of the false prophets were at Jerusalem (Jer 23:14): *I have seen in the prophets at Jerusalem a horrible thing*; and some of them were among the exiles in Babylon, for Jeremiah writes to them (Jer 29:8), *Let not your diviners, that be in the midst of you, deceive you.* Ezekiel must prophesy against them in the hope that the people might be warned not to listen to them. He had explicit orders to *prophesy against the prophets of Israel*

(v. 2); this was what they called themselves, as if no one but them were worthy of being called Israel's prophets, though they were really Israel's deceivers. Ezekiel is instructed:

1. To reveal their sin to them. They are called here *foolish prophets* (v. 3). The accusations:

1.1. They claimed to have received a commission from God, but he never sent them. They pushed themselves forward into the prophetic office without authority from *the Lord God* of the holy prophets, which was foolish, for how could they expect God to recognize them in a work that he had never called them to? They were "prophets out of their own hearts," as the margin of v. 2 reads, those who prophesied out of their own imagination (v. 6). They condemned divine revelation, lessened its trustworthiness, and weakened its credibility. When these pretenders were found to be deceivers, unbelievers would deduce from this that all prophets were like that.

1.2. They claimed to have received instructions from God, but he never made himself and his mind known to them: *they followed their own spirit* (v. 3); they spoke as a message from God what was simply the product of either their own personal invention or their own crazy and passionate imaginations. For *they had seen nothing*; they had not really seen any heavenly vision. *You have spoken vanity* (false words) *and seen lies* (lying visions); what they saw and what they said was all the same, a mere sham. Again (v. 9), they *see vanity and divine lies*, they saw false visions and uttered lying divinations; they claimed to have had visions, as the true prophets had, but their so-called visions were either creations of their own imaginations—and that was *seeing vanity*—or stories made up out of their own mere human knowledge, and they knew they had no vision, and so they *saw lies and divined lies*.

1.3. They did not try to prevent the judgments of God from breaking in on the kingdom. They were like *the foxes in the deserts* (jackals among ruins), seeming to be in a great hurry, but only to get away and fend for themselves, not to do any good. They should have made intercession to turn away the wrath of God, but they were not praying prophets. They should have made it their business to bring people to repentance and reformation by preaching and by giving advice, for in this way they could have *made up* (repaired) *the hedge*. However, they were taken up with how to flatter and please the people, not how to see that they benefited.

2. To declare the judgments of God against them for these sins, for their claiming to be prophets will not exempt them from these judgments. They are sentenced to be excluded from all the privileges of citizenship of Israel (Eph 2:12), for they are judged to have lost the right to them all (v. 9). *They shall not be in the secret* (confidence) *of my people*; their foolishness will be so clear that they will never be consulted, nor their advice asked; nor will they be in the assembly of God's people for religious worship. They will die in captivity; they will die childless.

Verses 10–16

Notice:

1. How the people have been deceived by the false prophets. Those flatterers have seduced them, saying, *Peace, and there was no peace* (v. 10). They told the idolaters and other sinners that there was no harm or danger in the way they lived. This was how they *seduced God's people*. Now this is compared to the building of a flimsy wall, or, according to our Savior's metaphor (Mt 7:26), the *building of a house upon the sand*, which seems to

be a shelter and protection for a while but will fall when a storm comes. One false prophet built the wall, setting up the idea that God was not displeased with Jerusalem, but that the city would be victorious over the powers that now threatened it. This idea was very pleasing, and the person who started it made himself very acceptable by it, which invited others to say the same. They made the matter look even more plausible and promising; they *daubed* (covered) *the wall* that the first person had built, but it was with *untempered mortar* (NIV: whitewash) (v. 10). And what happens to a wall built in this way? When it is subject to pressure or stress, it will bulge, fall, and gradually collapse.

2. How they will soon be made to see the truth by the judgment of God, which, we are sure, is based on truth (Ro 2:2). The attack that the Babylonian army will make on Judah and the siege that they will lay to Jerusalem will be like *an overflowing shower* (torrential rain). The fury of Nebuchadnezzar and his leaders, who were deeply angry at Zedekiah's treachery, made the invasion formidable, but that was nothing in comparison with God's fury. This storm will overturn the wall: *it shall fall*, and the wind will *rend it* (tear it apart) (v. 11); the *hailstones shall consume it* (v. 13). *I will break it down* (v. 14) and *bring it to the ground*, so that the *foundation thereof shall be discovered* (laid bare) and it will be seen how false and rotten it was, to the prophetic shame of the builders. Human anger cannot shake what God has built, but God's anger will overthrow what people have built in opposition to him. The builders of the wall and those who covered it with *untempered mortar* will themselves be buried in its ruins: *It shall fall, and you shall* be *consumed in the midst thereof* (v. 14). Both the deceivers and the deceived, when they perish together, will justly be ridiculed (v. 12): *"When the wall has fallen, shall it not be said unto you* by those who believed the true prophets and feared the word of the Lord, 'Now where is the daubing wherewith you have daubed the wall?* What has become of all the fair promises with which you flattered and all the assurances you gave that the troubles of the nation would soon come to an end?' They will say to you (v. 15), '*The wall is no more, neither he that daubed it;* your hopes have vanished, and so have the people who supported them, *the prophets of Israel*'" (v. 16).

Verses 17–23

As God has promised that when he pours out his Spirit on his people, both *their sons and their daughters shall prophesy* (Joel 2:28), so when the Devil acts as a spirit of lies and falsehood, he is so in the mouth of not only false male prophets but also false female prophets: *Son of man, set thy face against the daughters of thy people* (v. 17). The women claim to have a spirit of prophecy, and they sing the same song as the men. They *prophesy out of their own heart* (imagination), too; they say the first thing that comes into their minds. The prophet must *set his face against them*.

1. The sin of these false women prophets is described.

1.1. They told deliberate lies to those who consulted them and came to them to be given advice and to be told their fortune: "You cause trouble by lying to my people, who listen to your lies" (v. 19).

1.2. They dishonored the name of God: "*You pollute* (profane) *my name among my people* (v. 19), using that to support your lies." They did this for gain, and poor gain at that: mere *handfuls of barley and pieces of bread*. They would sell you a false prophecy that would please you for a beggar's portion—and that was more than it was worth.

1.3. They kept people in awe and terrified them with their claims: *You hunt the souls of my people* (v. 18), *hunt them to make them flee* (v. 20). They claimed that they would *save the souls alive that came to them* (v. 18). In this way they deceived unstable souls who had a concern for salvation.

1.4. They discouraged those who were honest and good and encouraged those who were evil and corrupt: "You have promised sinners life in their sinful ways; you have told them that they will have peace even though they continue in those ways, which has strengthened their hands and hardened their hearts."

1.5. They imitated the true prophets by giving signs to illustrate their false predictions—as Hananiah did (Jer 28:10)—signs consistent with being women. They sewed little *pillows to all armholes* (NIV: magic charms on the people's wrists) to show that the people could rest and not be shaken by any trouble. And they made *kerchiefs*, veils of various lengths for their heads, for people of every age, young and old (v. 18). These veils were badges of liberty or triumph, showing they would be rescued from the Babylonians. Some think these practices were superstitious rituals that they used with those to whom they gave their divinations, preparing them by putting enchanted pillows under their arms and handkerchiefs on their heads.

2. God declares himself against the ways they use to delude and deceive (v. 20). They will be defeated in their attempts (v. 23). God's people will be saved from their hands. *The pillows* (magic charms) *shall be torn from their arms*, and the *kerchiefs* (veils) *from their heads* (vv. 20–21). The falsehoods will be exposed, their fraud shown up for what it truly is, and the people of God will no longer be in their hands, to be hunted as they have been.

CHAPTER 14

1. The elders of Israel come to hear the word by inquiring of the prophet, but because they are not properly qualified, they meet with rebuke instead of acceptance (vv. 1–5) and are called on to repent of their sins and reform their lives (vv. 6–11). 2. It is supposed that Noah, Daniel, and Job might pray for this people, but their prayers would not be answered (vv. 12–21). But at the close, it is promised that a remnant will escape (vv. 22–23).

Verses 1–11

Here is:

1. The address that some of the elders of Israel made to the prophet to seek guidance from the Lord through him. They *came and sat before him* (v. 1). From his harsh response, one would suspect they intended to trap the prophet.

2. The account of their real character that God gives the prophet privately concerning them (v. 3); they are idolaters and are consulting Ezekiel only as they would any authority of a false god, to satisfy their curiosity, and so God says: *Should I be inquired of at all by them?* They *have set up their idols in their heart.* This may be understood to refer to spiritual idolatry; those whose affections are placed on the wealth of the world (Col 3:2) and physical pleasures, who worship their money, *whose god is their belly* (Php 3:19)—they *set up their idols in their heart.* Also, *they put the stumbling-block of their iniquity before*

their own *faces* (vv. 3, 7), stumbling on it even though they see it in front of them. The expression shows that they are determined to continue in sin, whatever the consequences. *I have loved strangers, and after them I will go* (Jer 2:25): that is the language of their hearts. Can those who continue to act against God and his ways expect a favorable answer from him?

3. The answer that God orders Ezekiel to give them (v. 4). Let them know that it is a rule for *every man of the house of Israel* that if he continues to be devoted to his idols and comes to inquire of God, God will answer him according to his real sin, not according to his pretended godliness. *I the Lord*, who *speak and it is done, I will answer him that cometh, according to the multitude of his idols.* He will give them up *to their own hearts' lust,* leaving them to themselves to be as bad as they want to be until they *have filled up the measure of their iniquity* (Ge 15:16; Mt 23:32). If God finds them, if he binds them over to his judgment, it is all by *their own hearts. O Israel, you have destroyed yourself* (Hos 13:9)!

4. The extent of this response that God gives him: it is for all *the house of Israel* (vv. 7–8); and yet it concerns not only everyone of the house of Israel, as before (v. 4), but also *the stranger that sojourns in Israel* (v. 7); even converts will not be supported if they are not sincere. Hypocrites *separate themselves from* God by their fellowship with idols; they cut themselves off from their relationship with God. The hypocrite will receive his answer not from the words of the prophet, but by the judgments of God. *And I will set my face against that man.* God will make an example of him, for *thus shall it be done to the man that separates himself from* God but pretends to *inquire concerning him.* The hypocrite thought he could pass himself off as belonging to God's people, but God *will cut him off from the midst of his people* (v. 8).

5. The doom of those people who claim to prophesy when they support those who claim to be godly (vv. 9–10). Even though Ezekiel will not give an encouraging response to these hypocritical inquirers, they still hope to meet with some other prophets who will. If they do, as perhaps they may, let them know that God allows those lying prophets to deceive them as punishment. But notice the fearful doom of the lying prophet himself: *I will stretch out my hand upon him and will destroy him* (v. 9).

6. The advice that is given them to prevent this terrible doom (v. 6): "*Therefore repent, and turn yourselves from your idols.* Turn away from them as you do from detestable practices you are sick of, and then you will be welcome to seek the Lord."

7. The good outcome of all this: the false prophets and the false saints will perish together, so that when some are made examples of, most of the people will be reformed, and so *that the house of Israel may go no more astray from me* (v. 11).

Verses 12–23

The theme of these verses is to show that:

1. National sins bring national judgments. *When the land sins against me,* when evil reaches epidemic proportions, when gross ungodliness and immorality is widespread, *then I will stretch forth my hand upon it* to punish it (v. 12).

2. God has a range of judgments with which he punishes sinful nations. Four harsh judgments are specified here:

2.1. *Famine* (v. 13). The denying and withholding of common mercies is itself judgment enough. He *cuts off man and beast* by cutting off the supplies that nature makes in the annual products of the earth.

2.2. Harmful wild animals. God can cause these *to pass through the land* (v. 15), *so that no man may pass through because of the beasts.* When people rebel from their allegiance to God, God is just to make lesser creatures rise up in arms against people (Lev 26:22).

2.3. War. God often rebukes sinful nations by bringing a sword on them. He says, *Sword, go through the land* (v. 17).

2.4. *Pestilence* (plague) (v. 19), a dreadful disease, which has sometimes depopulated cities.

3. When God's professing people rebel against him, they may justly expect to receive many judgments on them.

4. There commonly are some very good people even in those places that are ripened for ruin by sin. Even in a land that has *trespassed grievously*, there may be *three* such *men* as *Noah, Daniel, and Job.* Daniel was already famous, and yet he was taken away into captivity (Da 1:6). Some of the better kinds of people in Jerusalem might perhaps think that if Daniel—whose fame in the king of Babylon's court they had heard much about—had only remained in Jerusalem, it would have been spared for his sake. "No," God says, "even if you had him, one who was as markedly good in bad times and places as Noah was in the old world and Job in the land of Uz, a reprieve would still not be obtained."

5. God often spares evil places for the sake of a few godly people in them. This is implied here as the expectation of Jerusalem's friends: "Surely God will stop his challenge, for are there not some among us who by their prayers are emptying the container of national guilt, as others are filling it by their sins? And rather than *destroy the righteous with the wicked* (Ge 18:23), God will preserve *the wicked with the righteous.*"

6. Such men as Noah, Daniel, and Job will be successful, if any people can be, to turn away the wrath of God from a sinful people. Noah kept his integrity, and for his sake, his family, even though one of them was wicked (Ham), was saved in the ark. Job was effective in praying for his children and friends, and God restored his fortunes when he prayed. Daniel, one of their own fellow Jews and a *companion in tribulation*, is a person of great humility, urgent and faithful in prayer, enjoying the same good privileges in heaven as Noah or Job. Why may not God raise up as great and good people now as he did in former times, and do as much for them?

7. When the sin of a people has reached its height and the decree has been issued to destroy them, the godliness and prayers of the best people will not be effective enough to bring the dispute to an end. *Though these three men were in* Jerusalem at this time, they would *deliver neither son nor daughter* (v. 20).

8. Though godly, praying men may not be successful in saving others, *they* still *shall deliver their own souls by their righteousness*, so that although they may suffer in the general disaster, it is not to them what it is to evildoers; it is sanctified and does them good. If their bodies are not saved, their souls still are.

9. Even when God makes the greatest devastation by his judgments, he keeps some people as memorials to his mercy (vv. 22–23). In Jerusalem itself, though that is marked out for complete destruction, *there* still *shall be left a remnant*, who will be taken into exile, both *sons and daughters*, the seed of a new generation. The young ones *shall be brought forth* by the victorious enemy, and

behold, they shall come forth to you who are in exile, and they will come more willingly to Babylon because so many of their friends have gone there before them. When they come, *you shall see their ways and their doings*; you will hear them make a free confession of sins and a humble profession of repentance with promises of reformation. You will also see examples of reformation in their lives; you will see what good their suffering has done for them. *They shall comfort you when you see their ways* (v. 23). "*You shall be comforted concerning all the evil that I have brought upon Jerusalem* when you understand better. *You shall know that I have not done without cause*, not without just provocation, but also not without gracious intentions, *all that I have done in it.*"

CHAPTER 15

Again and again, Ezekiel has foretold the complete ruin of Jerusalem in God's name, but it seems he finds it hard to reconcile himself to it. Here, in this short chapter, God shows him that it is as necessary for Jerusalem to be destroyed as for dead and withered branches of a vine to be cut off and thrown onto the fire. The comparison is pleasant (vv. 1–5), but the explanation of the comparison is terrible (vv. 6–8).

Verses 1–8

The prophet, we may suppose, was thinking how glorious a city Jerusalem was and that it was therefore a pity that it should be destroyed. God responds to these thoughts by comparing Jerusalem to a vine. It is true that if a vine is fruitful, it is a most valuable plant. Jerusalem was *planted a choice and noble vine, wholly a right seed* (Jer 2:21), and if it had produced fruit that befitted it as a holy city, it would have been the glory of both God and Israel. But if a vine is not fruitful, it is as worthless as thorns and briers. *What is the vine more than any tree if the branch of it be as the trees of the forest?* That is, what good is it if it bears no fruit, as forest trees seldom do, being intended to produce timber, not fruit? Now there are some fruit trees that, if they do not bear fruit, are nevertheless very useful, as their wood may be put to good use, but the vine is not of this kind: if it does not fulfill its purpose as a fruit tree, it is worth nothing as a timber tree. Notice:

1. How this comparison is expressed. The wild vine, or the *empty* (spreading) *vine*, which Israel is compared to in Hos 10:1, is good for nothing. Its *wood* is not *taken to do any work*; one cannot even make *a pin* (peg) *of it to hang a vessel* (things) *upon* (v. 3). Among herbaceous plants, the roots of some, the seeds or fruits of others, the leaves of others, and the stalks of some are most useful to us. In the same way, among woody plants, some are strong and unfruitful, such as oaks and cedars; others are weak but very fruitful, such as the vine. The unfruitful tree is not *meet* (useful) *for any work*, and so *it is cast into the fire* (v. 4). When it is good for nothing else, it is useful this way.

2. How this comparison is applied to Jerusalem. That holy city has become unprofitable and good for nothing. It was once like *the vine tree among the trees of the* vineyard, producing many fruits of righteousness to the glory of God. When the pure worship of God was kept, a joyful grape harvest was gathered from it, and while it continued to yield this fruit, God protected it; it was his *pleasant plant* (Isa 5:7); he *watered it every moment* and *kept it night and day* (Isa 27:3). Now, however, it has become *the degenerate plant of a strange vine* (Jer 2:21),

a vine tree among the trees of the forest, which, being wild, *brings forth wild grapes* (Isa 5:4), not only useless but also sickly and harmful (Dt 32:32): *their grapes are grapes of gall, and their clusters are bitter.* It is explained in v. 8, which reads literally, "They have trespassed a trespass"; they have treacherously gone astray from God. When the Jewish nation, once famous for being a holy people, became evil, they were then *good for nothing*; they also lost all their usefulness and became the most corrupt and contemptible people under the sun, *trodden under foot of the Gentiles* (Lk 21:24) (v. 6). Those who are not fruitful to the glory of God's grace will be fuel to the fire of his wrath. *The inhabitants of Jerusalem* were like a vine branch, rotten and difficult, and so (v. 7), *I will set my face against them*, as they set their faces against God, to defeat all his purposes. *I will make the land quite desolate*, and so, when they *go out from one fire, another fire shall devour them* (v. 7). They will go from misery in their own country to misery in Babylon.

CHAPTER 16

God shows the prophet, and orders him to show the people, that he is punishing them only as their sins deserve. In the previous chapter he compared Jerusalem to an unfruitful vine; in this chapter he compares it to an adulteress, who, according to justice, should be abandoned. Here the following is put before us: 1. The unimpressive and deplorable beginnings of that church and nation (vv. 3–5). 2. The many honors and favors God has shown them (vv. 6–14). 3. Their ungrateful abandonment of God for the services of idols (vv. 15–34). 4. A threat of judgments that God will bring on them for this sin (vv. 35–43). 5. A comparison with Sodom and Samaria (vv. 44–59). 6. A promise of mercy that God will show to a penitent remnant (vv. 60–63).

Verses 1–5

Ezekiel was now among the exiles in Babylon, but as Jeremiah at Jerusalem wrote for the benefit of the exiles (Jer 29:1–21), so Ezekiel wrote for the people of Jerusalem. Jeremiah wrote to the exiles to encourage them; Ezekiel was directed to write to the people living in Jerusalem to convict and humble them.

1. This is his commission (v. 2): "*Cause Jerusalem to know her abominations*, her detestable practices; confront her with them." We can learn from this that we need to know our sins so that we may confess them.

2. So that Jerusalem may be confronted by her detestable practices, she must be reminded of the great things God has done for her. In these verses she is made to know from what poor beginnings God raised her and how unworthy she is of his favor. Jerusalem here stands for the Jewish church and nation, which is compared to an outcast child, of humble birth and abandoned.

2.1. The ancestry of the Jewish nation was lowly: "*Thy birth is of the land of Canaan* (v. 3); from the very beginning you had the spirit and disposition of a Canaanite." The patriarchs lived in Canaan, and they were there merely *strangers and sojourners*, not having any ground they could call their own except a burial place. Abraham and Sarah were indeed their *father and mother*, but they were merely lodgers with the Amorites and Hittites, who, having the power, seemed to be parents to the seed of Abraham (Ge 23:4, 8), as can be seen from the patriarchs' dependence on their neighbors the Canaanites and their fear of them (Ge 13:7; 34:30). When the patriarchs first came to

Canaan, they *went from one nation to another* (Ps 105:13), as tenants go from one farm to another. Their fathers had *served other gods in Ur of the Chaldees* (Jos 24:2); even in Jacob's family there were *strange gods* (Ge 35:2).

2.2. When the children of Israel began to become a people, they were thrown out of the country intended for them; a famine drove them from there (Ge 42–47). Egypt was *the open field* (v. 5) into which they were thrown; there they were ruled harshly and their lives were made very hard. The nation of Israel was doomed to destruction, like a newborn infant, not clothed, *not swaddled*, because not *pitied* (vv. 4–5). This infant is said to have been *cast out, to the loathing of her person. The Israelites were an abomination to the Egyptians*, as we find in Ge 43:32; 46:34. Moses told them (Dt 9:24), *You have been rebellious against the Lord from the day that I knew you.* They were not *supplied* (NIV: made clean) or *washed* or *swaddled*; they were not at all manageable or put into good shape. God took them to be his people not because he saw anything in them that was inviting or promising, but rather because *so it seemed good in his sight* (Mt 11:26).

Verses 6–14

Here is an account of the great things God did for the Jewish nation in gradually raising them up to be significant.

1. God saved them from the ruin they were on the brink of in Egypt (v. 6). Those to whom God commands life will surely live. God looked on the human race intending *life, and that more abundantly* (Jn 10:10). God says to the soul, through converting grace, *Live.*

2. He looked on them with kindness and a tender affection. He *set his love upon them* (Dt 7:7); there was nothing lovely in them, but *I looked upon thee*, and, *behold, thy time was the time of love* (v. 8). It was *the kindness and love of God our Saviour* (Tit 3:4) that sent Christ to redeem us, who sends the Spirit to sanctify us, who brought us out of a state of nature into a state of grace.

3. He took them under his protection. "*I spread my skirt over thee* (v. 8) to shelter you." God took them into his care as an *eagle bears her young ones upon her wings* (Dt 32:11–12). When God sent Moses to Egypt to rescue them, then he *spread his skirt over them.*

4. He cleared them from the discredited character that their slavery in Egypt had given them (v. 9). All the disgrace of their slavery was rolled away (Jos 5:9) when they were brought, *with a high hand and a stretched-out arm* (Dt 5:15; Ex 14:8), *into the glorious liberty of the children of God* (Ro 8:21).

5. He multiplied them and built them up into a people. This is mentioned (v. 7) before his *spreading his skirt over them*, because *their numbers increased exceedingly* while they were still slaves in Egypt.

6. He admitted them into covenant with himself. This was done at Mount Sinai: "When the covenant between God and Israel was sealed and ratified, then *thou becamest mine.*" God called them his people, and himself the God of Israel.

7. He adorned them beautifully. This young woman cannot forget her ornaments (Jer 2:32), and she is gratified with having many of them (vv. 10–13). We need not try to apply each one in detail. Her wardrobe was well furnished with rich clothes. It may be taken figuratively to refer to all the blessings of heaven that adorned both their church and their state. In a short time they received or became *excellent ornaments* (beautiful jewels) (v. 7). The laws and ordinances that God gave them were to them like

ornaments of grace to the head and chains about the neck (Pr 1:9). God's sanctuary, which he set up among them, was *a beautiful crown upon their head* (v. 12); it was the *beauty of holiness* (1Ch 16:29; Ps 29:2; 96:9).

8. He fed them with many delicacies. In Canaan they ate bread to the full, the finest of the wheat (Dt 32:13–14).

9. He gave them a great reputation among their neighbors and made them significant: *Thou didst prosper into a kingdom* (v. 13), and *thy renown went forth among the heathen* (your fame spread among the nations) *for thy beauty* (v. 14). Solomon's wisdom and Solomon's temple were very much the fame of that nation, and if we put all the privileges of the Jewish church and kingdom together, we must acknowledge that it was the most accomplished beauty of all the nations on earth. We may apply this spiritually. Sanctified souls are truly beautiful; they are so in God's sight, and they themselves may take comfort from it.

Verses 15–34

Here is an account of the great evil of the people of Israel, despite the great favors God had shown them. Their evil is represented here by the immoral and scandalous conduct of that beautiful young woman who was rescued from ruin. Their idolatry was the greatly offensive sin they were guilty of; it began at the end of Solomon's time and continued from then until the exile, and although it was now and then restrained by the reforming kings, it was never totally suppressed. This is portrayed here by comparing it to sexual immorality and adultery, because it is the violation of the marriage covenant with God, the corrupting and defiling of the mind, the enslaving of the spiritual part of human beings, and the defiling of the conscience. Notice:

1. The causes of this sin.

1.1. They became proud (v. 15): "*Thou trustedst to thy beauty*, expecting that that would make you prominent, and *playedst the harlot* (became a prostitute)." Solomon allowed idolatry to satisfy his wives and their relatives.

1.2. They forgot their humble beginnings (v. 22).

1.3. They were weak in understanding and will (v. 30). The strength of the desires of human beings shows the weakness of their hearts.

2. The details.

2.1. They worshiped all the idols that came their way, all that they were ever invited to worship; they were at the beck and call of all their neighbors (v. 15).

2.2. They adorned their idol temples, groves, and high places with the fine, rich clothing that God had given them (vv. 16, 18).

2.3. They used the jewels God had given them to make idols for worship (v. 17): *The jewels of my gold and my silver which I had given thee.* It is God who gives us our gold and silver. It remains his, and so we should serve and honor him with it, and we are accountable to him for how we use it. Every coin has God's image on it as well as Caesar's (Mt 22:20–21).

2.4. They served their idols with the good things God gave them (v. 18): "*Thou hast set my oil and my incense before them*, on their altars. You entertained their hungry priests with *my meat* (food), *and fine flour, and oil*, and the honey that Canaan flowed with, and *wherewith I fed thee* (v. 19). You made an offering of it to them for *a sweet savour*. The One who knows all things knows it."

2.5. They had sacrificed their children to their idols. *Thou hast taken thy sons and thy daughters* (vv. 20–21),

and you have not only made them pass through the fire, as a sign of their being dedicated to Molech, but also *sacrificed them to be devoured* (v. 20). It was an irreparable wrong to God himself: they are *my children* (v. 21), the *sons and daughters which thou hast borne unto me* (v. 20). He is the *Father of spirits* (Heb 12:9), and rational souls are his in a special way, and so the unjust taking away of human life is an act of outrageous disrespect to the *God of life*. How absurd was this, that the children who were born to God should be *sacrificed to devils*! The children of parents who are members of the visible church are to be looked on as born to God, as his children, and as such, they are to be loved by us, prayed for by us, brought up for him by us, and, if he calls for them, cheerfully parted with, for *may he not do what he will with his own?*

2.6. They built temples to honor their idols. "*After all thy wickedness* of this kind committed in private, you have finally reached such heights of arrogance as to declare it openly; now you cannot even blush" (vv. 23–25). *Thou hast built there an eminent place* (mound), "a brothel-house," as the margin reads, and such were their idol temples. *Thou hast made thy beauty to be abhorred.* When the Jewish nation left their own God and became devoted to the gods of the nations around them, they made themselves contemptible in the eyes of even their pagan neighbors.

3. What made this sin even worse.

3.1. They were fond of the idols of the nations that had oppressed and persecuted them, such as the Egyptians and the Assyrians.

3.2. They had suffered the rebukes of Providence, but they persisted (v. 27): "*I have stretched out my hand over thee* to threaten and frighten you." God did this before he *laid his hand upon them* to destroy them. That is his method, to try initially to bring people to repentance by lesser judgments.

3.3. They were insatiable in their spiritual unfaithfulness: *thou couldst not be satisfied* (vv. 28–29).

3.4. They went to great expense on their idolatry, spending a great deal of wealth in idols and altars and hiring priests to attend them from other countries. This is greatly insisted on (vv. 31–34).

4. What Jerusalem's response will be to being challenged about their sin. In all this, has not Jerusalem now been confronted with her detestable practices? Here we see with stunned horror how human nature is when God leaves people to themselves, even though they have the greatest advantages encouraging them to be good and become better.

Verses 35–43

This notorious adulteress was found guilty, and sentence is now passed on her. It is introduced with solemnity (v. 35). An apostate church is a prostitute. Jerusalem is like that if she becomes an idolater. *How has the faithful city become a harlot!* (Isa 1:21).

1. The crime is stated and the accusation summed up (vv. 36, 43):

1.1. Disobedience to the first two commandments of the first table of the Ten Commandments by idolatry, her *whoredoms* (promiscuity) *with her lovers*, that is, with all the idols of her detestable practices.

1.2. Disobedience to the first two commandments of the second table of the Ten Commandments by murdering their own innocent infants: *The blood of thy children which thou didst give unto them.* Their sins are made worse by a consideration of their corrupt ingratitude: "*Thou hast* not remembered the days of thy youth and the kindness that was shown to you then, when otherwise you would have perished" (v. 43). "Thou hast fretted (enraged) me in all these things, not only angered me but also grieved me."

2. The sentence is passed in general: I will judge thee as women that break wedlock (commit adultery) and shed blood are judged (v. 38), and those two crimes were punished by an ignominious death. This criminal must be exposed to public shame (v. 37). The calamities of Jerusalem will be the grief of her friends and the joy of her enemies. Those whom they have allowed to rob them of their goodness will see them stripped. They shall stone thee with stones and thrust thee through with their swords (v. 40). When the walls of Jerusalem were battered down with stones shot against them, and the inhabitants of Jerusalem were killed by the sword, then this sentence was executed literally. They shall throw down thy eminent place (tear down your mounds), and (v. 41) they shall burn thy houses, as the homes of bad women are destroyed. It was the complaint in the best reigns of the kings of Judah that the high places were not taken away. Now, however, the Babylonian army will break them down. The exile in Babylon made the people of Israel stop forever from being unfaithful; it effectually healed them of their inclination toward idolatry. Then (v. 42) "my jealousy shall depart (my jealous anger will turn away from you), and I will be calm and no longer angry."

Verses 44–59

God through the prophet now shows Jerusalem:

1. That she is as bad as her mother, that is, as the cursed Canaanites who possessed this land before her. As is the mother, so is her daughter (v. 44). The character of the mother was that she loathed her husband and her children and had all the marks of an adulteress, and that is what the daughter is like. When God brought Israel into Canaan, he particularly warned them not to follow the detestable practices of the men of that land, who went before them, and their disobedience of this commandment was the reason the land had spewed them out (Lev 18:27–28). They had learned their ways and followed in their footsteps. It might truly be said that their mother was a Hittite and their father an Amorite (v. 45), for they were more like them than like Abraham and Sarah.

2. That she was worse than her sisters Sodom and Samaria, who were also adulteresses and were also weary of the gods of their ancestors, and always wanting to introduce new gods and follow the new fashions in religion. Notice:

2.1. Who Jerusalem's sisters were (v. 45). Samaria is called the elder sister, or rather the "greater," because it was much larger and was more closely allied to Israel. This city of Samaria and its villages had recently been destroyed for their spiritual unfaithfulness. Sodom, with adjacent towns and villages, was her less sister, less than Jerusalem, less than Samaria, and these were destroyed long ago for their physical sexual immorality (Jude 7).

2.2. Jerusalem's sins were like her sisters', particularly Sodom's (v. 49): This was the iniquity of Sodom: pride, fulness of bread, and abundance of idleness. Their going after strange flesh (Jude 7), which was Sodom's most notorious form of evil, is not mentioned. The sins mentioned were those that opened the door to these more terrible crimes that they committed to satisfy their unnatural lusts. Pride was the first of these initiating sins. It was also the first sin that turned angels into devils, and the garden of the Lord (Ge 13:10; Isa 51:3) into a hell upon earth.

Gluttony was the second initiating sin, here called fulness of bread (v. 49). Idleness was the third, abundance of idleness, a fear of hard work and a love of ease. Idleness may allow much sin to enter. Stagnant waters collect dirt, and the sitting duck is the fowler's target. Nor did Sodom strengthen the hands of the poor and needy (v. 49); this probably implies that she weakened their hands and broke their arms (Job 22:9).

2.3. The sins of Jerusalem exceeded those of Sodom and Samaria. The evil of that holy city, which was so precious to God, was more offensive to him than the evil of Sodom and Samaria, which did not have Jerusalem's privileges and means of grace. Samaria has not committed half thy sins (v. 51), has not worshiped half as many idols or killed half so many prophets. By this they justified Sodom and Samaria (v. 51). They pretended in their pride to judge them, and in former days, when they maintained their integrity, they judged them (v. 52). But now it would appear to mitigate the sins of those sister cities that, bad though they were, Jerusalem was worse, and for this Jerusalem should be greatly ashamed: "You who have judged thy sisters and cried out shame on them, now bear thy own shame, for thy sins which thou hast committed are more abominable than theirs" (v. 52). There is nothing in sin that we have more reason to be ashamed of than that by our sin we have encouraged others to commit sin. Jerusalem had looked down on her neighbors disdainfully: Thy sister Sodom was not mentioned by thee in the day of thy pride (v. 56). If the Jews had only talked more frequently and seriously to one another and to their children concerning the wrath of God revealed from heaven against Sodom's ungodliness and unrighteousness (Ro 1:18), it might have prevented them following in their steps.

2.4. What devastation God had brought and was bringing on Jerusalem for these evil acts, in which they exceeded Sodom and Samaria.

2.4.1. She had already long ago been disgraced among her neighbors and fallen into contempt among them (v. 57).

2.4.2. She was now in captivity, or moving quickly toward captivity, not only for her unfaithfulness (v. 58) but also for her treachery and covenant breaking (v. 59). Those who will not remain loyal to God as their God have no reason to expect that he will continue to acknowledge them as his people.

2.4.3. The exile of the evil Jews, and their destruction, would be as irrevocable as that of Sodom and Samaria. Most interpreters take vv. 53, 55 in this sense, as a threat. Sodom and Samaria were never brought back, nor ever returned to their former estate, and so Jerusalem should not expect it, that is, those who now remained there, whom God would deliver to be removed into all the kingdoms of the earth for their hurt (Jer 24:9–10).

Verses 60–63

At the close of the chapter, after a most shameful conviction of sin and most fearful judgments, mercy is remembered for those who will come later. As God swore in his wrath that those who came out of Egypt would not enter Canaan (Ps 95:11) and yet said to them, "Your little ones will," so also here. Some think that what is said about the return of Sodom and Samaria (vv. 53, 55), and of Jerusalem with them, is a promise. It may be understood in this way, if by Sodom we understand the Moabites and Ammonites, the descendants of Lot, who once lived in Sodom (Jer 48:47; 49:6). But these closing verses are, without doubt, a precious promise, which was partly fulfilled at the return of the penitent and reformed Jews from Babylon, but was to have its complete fulfillment in Gospel times in that *repentance and* that *remission of sins preached to all nations, beginning at Jerusalem* (Lk 24:47). Notice:

1. From where this mercy would come: from God himself, from his remembering his covenant with them (v. 60): "*Nevertheless, I will remember my covenant with you*, the covenant that I made with you in the days of your youth, and will revive it. Although you have broken the covenant (v. 59), I will remember it, and it will flourish again."

2. How they would be prepared and qualified for this mercy (v. 61): "*Thou shalt remember thy ways*, your evil ways. God will remind you of them and set them out before you so that you may be ashamed of them."

3. The mercy that God had in reserve for them.

3.1. He would take them into covenant with himself (v. 60): *I will establish to thee an everlasting covenant*, and again (v. 62), "*I will establish*, reestablish, and establish more firmly than ever, my covenant with you."

3.2. He would bring the Gentiles into church fellowship with them (v. 61): "*Thou shalt receive thy sisters*, the Gentile nations that are around you, elder and younger, nations ancient and modern, and I will give them to you as daughters. They will be nursed and educated by the Gospel, which will go out of Zion and Jerusalem (Isa 2:3; Mic 4:2). The result will be that all the neighbors will call Jerusalem mother. They will be your daughters, but not by your covenant, not as converts to the Jewish faith, but as converts with you to the Christian faith." Or *not by thy covenant* may mean "not on the basis of such terms as you will think fit to impose on them as conquered nations, whom you may command at will. They will be your daughters by my covenant, the covenant of grace made with you and them. I will be a Father to both Jews and Gentiles, and so they will become sisters of one another."

4. What the fruit and effects of this would be.

4.1. God would be glorified (v. 62): "*Thou shalt know that* I am the Lord. It will be known that the God of Israel is a God of power, faithful to his covenant. You will know it to your comfort."

4.2. They would be more humbled on account of their sin (v. 63): "*That thou mayest be* the more confounded at the *remembrance of all that thou hast done* amiss, that you may never open your mouth again to contradict God, but may forever be submissive *because of thy shame.*"

CHAPTER 17

God is dealing with the king of Judah for his treachery in breaking the covenant with the king of Babylon. Zedekiah is scheming with the king of Egypt in a treacherous plan he has formulated to shake off the yoke of the king of Babylon and withdraw the loyalty he swore to him. For this, God, through the prophet: 1. Threatens the ruin of Zedekiah and his kingdom, issuing the threat by a parable of two eagles and a vine (vv. 1–10) and by the explanation of that parable (vv. 11–21), but at the close: 2. Promises later to raise up the royal family of Judah again, the house of David, in the Messiah and his kingdom (vv. 22–24).

Verses 1–21

The prophet is appointed to *put forth a riddle* to the house of Israel (v. 2), but not to puzzle them; he is to tell them its meaning immediately. Yet he must express this message in a riddle, or parable, so that they may remember it better and tell it to others. Ministers should try various methods to do good; they should both bring what is familiar into their preaching and bring their preaching into their ordinary speech. Having told the riddle, Ezekiel must also explain it to *the rebellious house* (v. 12).

1. Nebuchadnezzar had some time before taken away Jehoiachin (*Jeconiah*), when he was only eighteen years old and had reigned in Jerusalem a mere *three months*, him and his leaders, and had brought them as captives to Babylon (2Ki 24:12). This is represented in the parable by an eagle's breaking off the top branch of *a cedar*, the tenderest branch, and carrying it into *a land of traffic* (merchants), a city of traders (vv. 3–4), which is explained in v. 12. The *king of Babylon* took the *king of Jerusalem*, who could no more resist him than a young twig of a tree can oppose the strongest bird of prey, which easily snaps it off and uses it perhaps in making *her nest*. In this parable, Nebuchadnezzar is the king of birds, *a great eagle*, which lives off plunder. His dominion extends far and wide, like the great and long wings of an eagle; the people are numerous, for the eagle is *full of feathers*; the court is splendid, for it has *divers* (varied) *colours*, which look like plumage. Jerusalem is Lebanon, a forest of houses. The royal family is *the cedar*; Jehoiachin is the *top branch*, the *top of the young twigs.* Babylon is the land of merchants and city of traders where this tender branch is *set*, or planted (v. 4).

2. When Nebuchadnezzar took Jehoiachin to Babylon, he made Jehoiachin's uncle Zedekiah king in his place (vv. 5–6). His name was *Mattaniah*, "the gift of the Lord," which Nebuchadnezzar changed to *Zedekiah*, "the justice of the Lord," to remind him to be as just as the God he called his. This was *one of the seed of the land*, a native, not one of Nebuchadnezzar's Babylonian rulers; he was *planted in a fruitful field*, for Jerusalem was like that then. The king of Babylon *placed it by great waters*, like *a willow tree*, which grows quickly and grows best in moist ground but is never expected to be a stately tree. He *set it with* care; he wisely provided for it to grow, but not too big. *He took of the king's seed*, as it is explained in v. 13, and *made a covenant with him* that he would have the kingdom, enjoying royal power, provided he held it as his servant. He *took an oath of him*, made him swear allegiance by his own God, the God of Israel, that he would be his faithful subject (2Ch 36:13). He also *took away the mighty of the land*, the leading warriors, as hostages for the fulfillment of the covenant, and so that the king would be less tempted to break the alliance. We are told what he intended to do (v. 14): *That the kingdom might be base* (brought low), neither a rival with its powerful neighbors nor a terror to its feeble ones, that *it might not lift up itself* to rival the kingdom of Babylon. But he still intended that by *the keeping of this covenant it might stand* and remain a kingdom. How sad a change sin made to the royal family of Judah. There was a time when all the nations around were subjects to it.

3. As long as Zedekiah continued to be faithful to the king of Babylon, he acted very well, and if only he had reformed his kingdom and returned to God and his duty, he might soon have recovered his former position (v. 6). This plant grew, and even though it was *set as a willow tree* and insignificant, it became *a spreading vine of low stature*, a blessing to his own country, and his fruits *made glad their hearts* (Ps 104:15). It is better to be a low spreading vine than a useless lofty cedar. Nebuchadnezzar was pleased, for *the branches turned toward him* and rested on him as

a vine rests on a wall, and he had his share of the fruits of this vine; *the roots thereof*, too, were *under him* and at his disposal. The Jews had reason to be pleased, for they sat under their own vine (1Ki 4:25; 2Ki 18:31), which *brought forth branches, and shot forth sprigs*. Notice how gradually the judgments of God came on this offensive people, giving them opportunity to repent. Before making them no kingdom, he brought their kingdom low to see if that would humble them.

4. Zedekiah did not know when he was well off; he became impatient with being subject to the king of Babylon and entered into a private treaty with the king of Egypt. If he had acted faithfully, he might have been *a goodly vine*. But there was *another great eagle* that he had affection for and put confidence in, and that was the *king of Egypt* (v. 7). Those two great powers, the kings of Babylon and Egypt, were merely two great eagles, *birds of prey*. This great eagle of Egypt is said to have *great wings* but not to be *long-winged* like the king of Babylon, because the kingdom of Egypt was not as vast as that of Babylon. It is said to have *many feathers*, much wealth and many soldiers, but they really were no more than so *many feathers*. Zedekiah, promising himself liberty, made himself subject to the king of Egypt. *This vine* secretly and underhandedly *bent her roots toward* the king of Egypt, and after a while she openly sent *forth her branches toward him*, showing him how much she wanted an alliance with him, so *that he might water it by the furrows of her plantation*, whereas it was *planted by great waters* (v. 5) and did not need any help from him. This is explained in v. 15: Zedekiah *rebelled against the king of Babylon in sending his ambassadors into Egypt* so that they would *give him horses and much people*, enabling him to challenge the king of Babylon.

5. God here threatens Zedekiah with the complete destruction of him and his kingdom for his treacherous rebellion from the king of Babylon. This is represented in the parable (vv. 9, 19) by the *plucking up of this vine by the roots, the cutting off of the fruit*, and *the withering of the leaves*. The plan will be thwarted; it will *utterly wither*. Will he *break the covenant, and be delivered* (v. 15) from that vengeance which is the just punishment of his treachery? No.

5.1. His doom is ratified by the oath of God (v. 16): *As I live, saith the Lord God, he shall die* for it.

5.2. It is justified by the detestable nature of his crime. He has been very ungrateful to his benefactor, who *made him king* when he could so easily have made him a prisoner. He had been very deceitful; he *despised the oath* and broke it (vv. 15–16, 18–19). The oath by which he had bound himself to the king of Babylon was a solemn oath. An emphasis is laid on this (v. 18): *when, lo, he had given his hand* in pledge to the king of Babylon, as his friend, the joining of hands being a sign of the joining of hearts. God says (v. 19), "It is *my oath* that he has despised and *my covenant that he has broken*." The oath of allegiance to a ruler is especially called *the oath of God* (Ecc 8:2). Now Zedekiah's breaking this oath is the sin that God *will recompense upon his own head* (v. 19), the *trespass which he has trespassed against God*. Though Nebuchadnezzar is a worshiper of false gods, the true God will avenge this quarrel in which one of his worshipers breaks his covenant with Nebuchadnezzar, for truth is an obligation that is due to every person. Having *despised the oath* and *broken the covenant*, Zedekiah *shall not escape*.

5.3. The punishment is made to fit the sin. He has rebelled against the king of Babylon, and the king of

Babylon will be his powerful conqueror (v. 16). God himself will now join the king of Babylon against him: *I will spread my net upon* (for) *him* (v. 20). He has relied on the king of Egypt, and the king of Egypt will be ineffective in helping him: *Pharaoh with his mighty army shall not make for* (will be of no help to) *him in the war* (v. 17). On the approach of the Egyptian army, the Babylonians withdrew from the siege of Jerusalem; on the retreat of Egypt, the Babylonians returned to it and took it. It is true that Zedekiah had *bands* (troops), but although those troops were probably the best soldiers his kingdom could afford, they would become fugitives; they would fall by the sword of the enemy (v. 21). This was fulfilled when the city was broken up and the whole army fled (Jer 52:7).

Verses 22–24

Human unbelief will not cancel out the promise of God. He will find another *seed of David* in which the promise will be fulfilled.

1. The house of David will again be exalted, and another phoenix will rise up out of its ashes. The metaphor of a tree, used earlier in the threat, is here presented in the promise (vv. 22–23). This promise was partially fulfilled when Zerubbabel, a branch of the house of David, was raised up to lead the Jews in their return from exile, rebuild the city and temple, and reestablish their church and state, but it was to have its complete fulfillment in the kingdom of the Messiah (Lk 1:32).

1.1. God himself undertakes to restore the house of David. Nebuchadnezzar attempted to reestablish the house of David in dependence on him (v. 5), but his plantation withered and was uprooted. "Well," God says, "the next will be planted by myself: *I will also take of the highest branch of the high cedar and I will set it.*"

1.2. The house of David is revived in *a tender one cropped from the top of his young twigs*. Zerubbabel was this one; what was hopeful in him was the *day of small things* (Zec 4:10), but before him *great mountains* were *made plain* (Zec 4:7). Our Lord Jesus was *the highest branch of the high cedar*, the furthest of all from *the root* but the closest of all to heaven, for his kingdom was not of this world (Jn 18:36). He was *taken from the top of the young twigs, a tender plant and a root out of a dry ground* (Isa 53:2), but *a branch of righteousness* (Jer 33:15), *the planting of the Lord* (Isa 61:3).

1.3. This branch is planted *in a high mountain* (v. 22), in the *mountain of the height of Israel* (v. 23). God brought Zerubbabel there in triumph; it was there that he raised up Jesus to gather the *lost sheep of the house of Israel* (Mt 15:24) that were *scattered upon the mountains* (1Ki 22:17); he set him as *his king* on *his holy hill of Zion* (Ps 2:6) and sent out the Gospel from *Mount Zion, the word of the Lord from Jerusalem* (Mic 4:2). There the Christian church was first planted. The churches of Judea were the earliest churches.

1.4. It spreads far and wide from there. Although the Jewish state began very low in Zerubbabel's time and was like a tender branch, which could easily be uprooted, it put down firm roots and spread out, and after some time people of other nations, *fowl of every wing* (birds of every kind), put themselves under its protection. When the Gentiles flocked into the church, then birds of every kind came and *dwelt under the shadow of this goodly cedar*. See Da 4:21.

2. God himself will be glorified in this (v. 24). Never was greater proof given of the truth that all things are governed by an infinitely wise and mighty Providence than what was given by the exaltation of Christ and the

establishment of his kingdom on earth. *All the trees of the field shall know* (v. 24):

2.1. That the tree that God wants *brought down* and *dried up* will be.

2.2. That the trees that God wants to exalt and cause to flourish will be exalted and will flourish, even though they are lowly and dry. The house of Nebuchadnezzar, which now seems so important, will be destroyed; the house of David, now so humble, will again become famous; and the Jewish nation, now insignificant, will become significant. The kingdom of Satan, which has had such a great influence for so long, will be broken, and the kingdom of Christ, which was looked on with contempt, will be established.

CHAPTER 18

This chapter appears to concern us all, for, without any particular reference to Judah and Jerusalem, it establishes the rule of judgment according to which God will deal with individuals. Here is: 1. The corrupt proverb used by the worldly Jews, which gave rise to the message sent them here (vv. 1–3). 2. The reply given to this proverb, in which God asserts his sovereignty and justice (v. 4). Woe to the wicked! Disaster is upon them (Isa 3:11) (vv. 4, 20). But tell the righteous it will be well with them (Isa 3:10) (vv. 5–9). In particular, he assures us: 2.1. That it will go badly with an evildoer even if he had a good father (vv. 10–13). 2.2. That it will go well with a good person even if he had a wicked father (vv. 14–18). God is righteous in this (vv. 19–20). 2.3. It will go well with penitents even if they began badly (vv. 21–23, 27–28), but it will go badly with apostates even if they began well (vv. 24, 26). The purpose of all this is: 2.4.1. To justify God and show the justice of all his ways (vv. 25, 29). 2.4.2. To engage and encourage us to repent of our sins and turn to God (vv. 30–32).

Verses 1–9

Sometimes evil proverbs produce good prophecies. Here is:

1. An evil proverb commonly used by the Jews in their exile. This proverb accuses God of injustice: "You use this proverb *concerning the land of Israel*, now that it is devastated by the judgments of God: *The fathers have eaten sour grapes, and the children's teeth are set on edge* (v. 2). We are being punished for the sins of our ancestors, which is as absurd as if children had their teeth set on edge by their parents' eating sour grapes, whereas if people eat or drink anything wrong, it is only they themselves who suffer by it." It must be acknowledged that God had often said that he would *visit the iniquity of the fathers upon the children* (Ex 20:5), especially the sin of idolatry, so showing the evil of sin. He had often declared through his prophets that in bringing the present ruin on Judah and Jerusalem he had considered the sins of Manasseh and other preceding kings. But dealing with them now for the sins of previous ages was only like making a man, *when he is old, possess the iniquities of his youth* (Job 13:26), and God is not unrighteous in doing so (Ro 9:14). Yet the Jews intended their proverb as a charge that God was unjust to deal with them as he did. It is true that those who are guilty of deliberate sin *eat sour grapes*; sins will set the sinner's teeth on edge. When conscience has been wakened, it will spoil the enjoyment. But those who quoted the proverb suggested that it was unreasonable that the children should suffer for their parents' foolishness, feeling pain for what they never tasted the pleasure of.

2. A just reply to this proverb: "Your own consciences will tell you that you yourselves have eaten the same sour grapes that your parents ate before you; otherwise your teeth would not have been set on edge." God does not punish the children for the parents' sins unless they follow in their parents' footsteps and *fill up the measure of their iniquity* (Mt 23:32). It is only in physical disasters that children fare worse for their parents' evil, and God can make those disasters work for good to those who are punished by them (Ro 8:28). But as regards spiritual and eternal misery—and that is the death spoken about here—the children will in no way suffer for their parents' sins. In his reply:

2.1. He asserts his own absolute sovereignty: *Behold, all souls are mine* (v. 4). The One who is the Maker of *all things* is the *Father of spirits* (Heb 12:9) in a special way, for his image is stamped on the human soul; it was so in their creation; it is so in their renewal. He *forms the spirit of man within him* (Zec 12:1). God bears goodwill to both parent and child, and he will put no hardship on either. He has such a kindness for all souls that no one dies except by their own fault.

2.2. Yet he waives his sovereignty, instead establishing a just and unexceptionable rule of judgment. Sinners who persist in sin will certainly die. *The soul that sins shall die* (v. 4). As sin is the act of the *soul*, so the punishment of sin is the *tribulation and the anguish of the soul* (Ro 2:9). Righteous people who persevere in righteousness, on the other hand, will certainly live. *If a man be just, do judgment and justice* (v. 5), *he shall surely live, saith the Lord God* (v. 9). He is careful to keep himself clean from the defilements of sin:

2.2.1. Sins against the second commandment. In the matters of God's worship, he has not even *eaten upon the mountains*, that is, not had any fellowship with idolaters by *eating things sacrificed to idols* (1Co 10:20).

2.2.2. Sins against the seventh commandment. He always keeps the physical appetites subject to reason and goodness.

2.2.3. Sins against the eighth commandment. The one who has not *oppressed any* by fraud or *spoiled any by violence* (committed robbery) (v. 7) is a just man. He will not take advantage of his neighbor's needs, but is willing to share a loss as well as profit. This is how he acts toward his neighbors; he is just and true. But to complete his character he must also be so toward God (v. 9). This is the just man, and *he shall surely live*, or, literally, *living he shall live*.

Verses 10–20

Through the prophet, God has laid down the general rule of judgment, and in these verses he proceeds to show that a person's parentage will not change the situation.

1. He applies the case both ways. It often happens that godly parents have evil children and evil parents have godly children. Now he shows here:

1.1. A wicked man will perish in his iniquity even if he is the son of a godly father. It is supposed here that he gives himself to all those sins and crimes that his good father dreaded.

1.2. A righteous man will be happy even if he is the son of a wicked father. Although the parents ate sour grapes, if the children do not meddle with them, they will never fare the worse for that. The graceless father alone will die in his iniquity, but his gracious child will live.

2. He appeals to the Jews as to whether they are not wronging God with their proverb. "The situation is clear,

and *yet you say, Does not the son bear the iniquity of the father?* No, he does not; he will not if he will himself *do that which is lawful and right*" (v. 19). But this people who bear the iniquity of their parents have not done what is lawful and right, and so they justly suffer for their own sin and have no reason to complain that God's actions against them have been unjust, though they do have reason to complain that the bad example their parents left them was very unkind. *Our fathers have sinned and are not, and we have borne their iniquity* (La 5:7). It is true that there is a curse passed on by inheritance to evil families, but it is just as true that the inheritance may be cut off by repentance and reformation. Let the impenitent and unreformed therefore blame themselves if they fall under God's judgment. The established rule of judgment is therefore repeated (v. 20): *The soul that sins shall die*, and not another soul for it. The guidance God has given to earthly judges (Dt 24:16) will be pursued by God himself: *The son shall not die*, not die eternally, *for the iniquity of the father*, unless he follows in his father's steps, nor the father *for the iniquity of the son*, if he tries to do his duty to prevent it. In *the day of the revelation of the righteous judgment of God* (Ro 2:5), which is now clouded and eclipsed, *the righteousness of the righteous shall* appear before all the world to be *upon him*, to his eternal comfort and honor, on him as a robe and crown. In the same way, *the wickedness of the wicked* will be *upon him*, to his eternal shame, on him as a chain and burden, as a mountain of lead to make him sink to the bottomless pit.

Verses 21–29

Here is another rule of judgment by which the justice of God's government is demonstrated. Here he shows that he will reward or punish according to the change made in the person himself. While we are in this world, we are serving, as it were, a probationary period; the time of trial lasts as long as our lives. See here:

1. The case fairly stated, much as it was before (3:18), and here it is established twice (vv. 21–24 and again vv. 26–28), because it is a matter of life and death:

1.1. A fair invitation is given to the wicked to turn from their wickedness. Assurance is given that *if the wicked will turn*, he will *surely live* (vv. 21, 27). The first step toward conversion is consideration (v. 28): *Because he considers and turns*. This consideration must produce an aversion to sin. He must turn from *all* his sins without keeping anything back at all. This must be accompanied by turning to God and our duty. One who turns from sin to God in this way will *save his soul alive* (v. 27). A repenting, returning sinner is aware that his obedience for the future can never make up for his former disobedience, but he also knows that God's nature and delight is to have mercy and to forgive (v. 23).

1.2. A fair warning is given to righteous people not to turn from their righteousness (vv. 24–26).

2. An appeal to the consciences of members of the house of Israel, even though they are very corrupt, concerning God's justice in every way he acts. The charge they drew up against God is blasphemous (vv. 25, 29), but God's reasonings with them are very gracious, for God wants even these blasphemers to be convinced and saved rather than condemned.

Verses 30–32

Look, a miracle of mercy; the day of grace and divine patience is still extended, and so, although God will ultimately judge *every one according to his ways* (v. 30), he still waits to be gracious (Isa 30:18), and he closes with a call to repentance and a promise that people will be pardoned if they do repent.

CHAPTER 19

The theme of this chapter is much the same as that of chapter 17, to prophesy and mourn the ruin of the house of David (v. 1). The prophet does so using comparisons. 1. The kingdom of Judah and house of David are compared here to a lioness, and the rulers to lions, which were fierce and ravenous but were hunted down and taken in nets (vv. 2–9). 2. That kingdom and that house are compared here to a vine, and these rulers to branches, which had been strong and flourishing but were now broken and burned (vv. 10–14).

Verses 1–9

Here are:

1. Orders given to the prophet to mourn the downfall of the royal family. The kings of Judah are called here *princes of Israel*, for their glory was diminished.

2. Instructions given him what to say. The prophet must compare the kingdom of Judah to *a lioness* (v. 2). The royal family was like a mother to the kingdom, a *lioness*, fierce, cruel, and ravenous. She *nourished her whelps* (cubs) *among young lions*, taught the young princes the way of tyrants. If they had remained faithful to God's law and promise, God would have preserved for them the power and majesty of a lion, which is strong and formidable to its enemies at a distance, and he does so in Christ, the *Lion of the tribe of Judah* (Rev 5:5). But these *lions' whelps* acted in this manner toward their own subjects; they were cruel and oppressive toward them. Jehoahaz, one of the cubs, *became a young lion* (v. 3); he was made king and thought he was anointed so that he could do as he pleased. He did not prosper long in his tyranny: *The nations heard of him* (v. 4); *he was taken*, like a wild animal, *in their pit* and *brought in chains to the land of Egypt*. Jehoiakim, instead of taking notice of the warning of his brother's fate, followed in his brother's steps: *He went up and down among the lions* (v. 6). And he soon learned to *catch the prey*, and he *devoured men* (v. 6); he seized his subjects' estates and devoured all that stood in his way. He learned the art of discovering the treasures that they had hoarded: he *knew their desolate places* (strongholds) (v. 7). By his *oppression he laid waste their cities*. It only quickened his own destruction (v. 8). God brought Aramean, Moabite, Ammonite, and Babylonian raiders against Jehoiakim (2Ki 24:2), and he was *taken in their pit*. *Nebuchadnezzar bound him in fetters to carry him to Babylon* (2Ch 36:6). An end came to his tyranny: he was *buried with the burial of an ass* (Jer 22:19).

Verses 10–14

Jerusalem, the mother city, is described here using another comparison; she is a vine, and the princes are her branches. We had this comparison before (ch. 15).

1. Jerusalem is like *a vine*; so is the Jewish nation: it is *like a vine in thy blood* (v. 10). Places of great evil may prosper for a while, and a vine planted in blood may be full of branches, for blood in the soil contributes very much to the flourishing and fruitfulness of vines. Jerusalem was full of able magistrates, who were *strong rods*, branches of uncommon strength, or poles to support this vine, for this is what magistrates are like. The boughs had grown to such maturity that they were fit to make white staves for

the sceptres of those that bore rule (v. 11). When the royal family of Judah was numerous and the courts of justice were filled with people of good sense and integrity, then *Jerusalem's stature was exalted among thick branches.* "In thy quietness," as some read the phrase we translate *in thy blood* (v. 10), "you were such a vine." When Zedekiah was quiet and at peace under the king of Babylon's yoke, his kingdom flourished.

2. This vine is now destroyed. When Nebuchadnezzar, provoked by Zedekiah's treachery, *plucked up* the vine *in fury* (v. 12), ruined the city, and cut off all the branches of the royal family, *the vine was planted in the wilderness* (v. 13). Babylon was like a desert to those who were taken there as captives. The land of Judah was like a desert to Jerusalem. The *strong rods* (v. 12), the men of the house of David who should have been fit to govern, had been instruments of oppression, and now they were destroyed with him. Tyranny allows anarchy to come in, and when the rod of government becomes the serpent of oppression (Ex 7:8–10), God is just to say, "There will be no strong rod to be a scepter to rule, but let people become as *the fishes of the sea* (Hab 1:14), where the greater devour the less."

CHAPTER 20

1. The prophet is consulted by some of the elders of Israel (v. 1). 2. He is instructed by his God what answer to give them. 2.1. He must show God's displeasure against them (vv. 2–4). 2.2. He must show them what just cause God has for that displeasure by relating to them the history of God's good dealings with their ancestors in Egypt (vv. 5–9), in the desert (vv. 10–26), and in Canaan (vv. 27–32). 2.3. He must declare the judgments of God against them (vv. 33–36). 2.4. He must tell them what mercy God has in store for them (vv. 37–44). 2.5. Here is another word dropped toward (v. 46) Jerusalem, which is explained in the next chapter (vv. 45–49).

Verses 1–4

Certain of the elders of Israel came to inquire of the Lord (v. 1). Their inquiry was whether, now that they were captives in Babylon, where they had no temple or synagogue for the worship of God, it was not lawful for them to join in worship with *the families of these countries,* who *served wood and stone* (v. 32). They must be made to know that God was justly angry with them (v. 4): "*Wilt thou judge them, son of man, wilt thou judge them? See, I have set thee over the nation* (Jer 1:10); will you not declare to them the judgment of the Lord? Cause them therefore *to know the abominations of their fathers.*"

Verses 5–9

We have here:

1. The gracious purposes of God's law concerning Israel in Egypt, where they were slaves to Pharaoh.

1.1. He chose Israel to be his own special people—though their condition was bad and their character worse—so that he might have the honor of restoring both.

1.2. He *made himself known to them* by his name *Jehovah,* a new name (Ex 6:3), when because of their slavery they had almost lost the knowledge of that name by which he was known to their ancestors, *God Almighty.*

1.3. He made himself their God in covenant: "*I lifted up my hand unto them* (v. 5), saying and confirming with an oath, '*I am the Lord your God.*'"

1.4. He promised to bring them out of Egypt, and he fulfilled what he promised.

1.5. He assured them that he would give them possession of the land of Canaan. He brought them out of Egypt so *that he might bring them into a land that he had spied out for them* (v. 6), a second garden of Eden.

2. The reasonable commands he gave them: "*Cast you away every man* his images that he uses for worship, which should be detestable to him. *Defile not yourselves with the idols of Egypt.*"

3. Their unreasonable disobedience to these commands, for which God might justly have cut them off as soon as they were formed into a people (v. 8). It was strange that all the plagues of Egypt were not successful in healing them of their affection for the *idols of Egypt* (v. 7). He could justly have said, "Let them die with the Egyptians."

4. The wonderful rescue that God brought them, nevertheless. Although they forfeited the favor even as it was being given, mercy triumphed over judgment (Jas 2:13), and God did what he intended purely *for his own name's sake* (v. 9). When nothing in us gives him a reason for his favors, he himself provides one.

Verses 10–26

The history of the struggle between the sins of Israel, by which they tried to ruin themselves, and the mercies of God, by which he tried to save them and make them happy, continues here. The story of Israel in the desert is referred to in the New Testament (1Co 10 and Heb 3), as well as often in the Old, to warn us as Christians. Notice:

1. The great things God did for them, which he reminds them of, not to show that he begrudged them his favor, but to show how ungrateful they had been. It was a great favor that God *brought them forth out of Egypt* (v. 10), even though, as it follows, he *brought them into the wilderness* and not immediately into Canaan. It is better to be free in a desert than slaves in a land of plenty. But when they met with difficulties in the desert, some wished they were in Egypt again. It was also a great favor to them that God gave them the Law on Mount Sinai (v. 11). In fact, he not only *gave them his statutes* (decrees) but also *showed them his judgments,* not only enacted laws for them but also showed them that those laws were reasonable and just. And he revived the ancient institution of the Sabbath, which was lost and forgotten while they were slaves in Egypt. Sabbaths are signs; the Sabbath is a sign that people have a sense of religious faith. If Sabbaths are appropriately sanctified, they are the means of our sanctification.

2. Their disobedient, undutiful behavior toward God, for which he could justly have rejected them from the covenant (v. 13): *They rebelled in the wilderness.* There, where they received so much mercy from God and were on their way to Canaan, they often broke out in open rebellion against the God who led them and fed them.

3. God's determination to destroy their generation in the desert. What lay at the root of their disobedience to God and their neglect of his institutions was a secret devotion to the gods of Egypt: *Their heart went after their idols.*

4. When he looked on them, he had compassion on them and did not *make an end of them,* but reprieved them until a new generation was brought up.

5. The rebellion of the next generation from God, by which they also made themselves liable to the wrath of God (v. 21): *The children rebelled against me* too. They

polluted (defiled) *God's sabbaths*, as their parents had. It is said of the children (v. 24) that *their eyes went after their fathers'* (parents) *idols*. If they must have gods, they wanted to have those they could see.

6. The judgments of God on them for their rebellion. God *gave them statutes and judgments* that *were not good*, and *by which they would not live* (v. 25). This may help us understand the different ways by which God punished them while they were in the desert—the plague that broke in on them, the snake, and so on—which are called *judgments* because they were inflicted by the justice of God, and *statutes* because he commanded devastation, just as sometimes he had commanded rescues. Spiritual judgments are to be feared most. He made their sin become their punishment, and he gave them up to a *reprobate mind*, as he did the Gentile idolaters (Ro 1:24, 26). God sometimes makes sin its own punishment. Nothing more is needed to make people miserable than to give them up to their own sinful appetites and passions.

Verses 27–32

The prophet keeps on describing their rebellion.

1. They had persisted in rebelling even after they had settled in the land of Canaan (v. 27). They were often very close to being destroyed in the desert, but they eventually came to Canaan. Even God's Israel reach heaven via the gates of hell, just as hypocrites reach hell via the gates of heaven. The transgressions of God's Israel are so many, and their corruptions so strong, that it is a miracle of mercy they are ultimately happy. But once there, they broke his commands against idolatry again, and they obstinately persisted in doing so despite all the warnings they were given (v. 29).

2. They are persisting still. The prophet must *say to* the present *house of Israel*, some of whose elders are now sitting before him, *"Are you polluted after the manner of your fathers*, will you defile yourselves the way your ancestors did?" These elders seem to have been planning an alliance with the pagan nations. The prophet is ordered here to tell those who want to settle the differences between God and Baal that they will have no comfort or benefit from either. There is nothing to be gained by sinful compliances, and the worldly plans of hypocrites will do them no good.

Verses 33–44

The intention that is afoot among the elders is that the people of Israel should conform to the people among whom they live, but God has told them that the plan will not take effect (v. 32). In these verses, he shows how it will be frustrated.

1. Babylon will not protect them or any of the nations, for God will drive them out of his protection, and then which prince or place can serve as a sanctuary for them? They will be brought *into the wilderness of the people* (v. 35), either to Babylon, which is called *a wilderness* (19:13), or to some other place that, though full of people, will be a place where God will *plead with them face to face*, as he *pleaded with their fathers in the wilderness of Egypt* (v. 36), a place where he will avenge disobedience to his law with as much terror as he gave it with in the desert of Sinai.

2. Israel will be no more able to protect them than Babylon could. There will come a day of distinguishing, when God will separate the precious and the worthless (Jer 15:19); he will *cause them*, as the shepherd causes every tenth sheep, to *pass under the rod* (Lev 27:32), so

that he may mark those that are God's, and *he will bring them into the bond of the covenant* (v. 37). Or the phrase may refer to those among them who repent and reform; he will cause them to pass under the rod of affliction, and then he will bring them again *into the bond of the covenant*. The judgments of God will find them out, and their claiming to belong to Israel will not protect them. It is promised that those who preserve their integrity, who refuse to serve idols in other lands, will return to their prosperity and serve the true God in their own land: *All of them in the land shall serve me.* He will give them true repentance for their sins (v. 43). He will give them the knowledge of himself: *They shall know* by experience that *he is the Lord*, kind to his people and faithful to his covenant with them.

Verses 45–49

Here is a prophecy of wrath against Judah and Jerusalem, which would more fitly have begun the next chapter than concluded this one. When the people complained that this was a parable that they did not understand, the beginning of the next chapter explained it. In this parable:

1. A forest is prophesied against, *the forest of the south field*, Judah and Jerusalem. These lay south of Babylon, and so he was told to *set his face toward the south* (v. 46), to show that God had set his face against them. But although it was a message of wrath, he must speak it with tenderness. He must *drop his word toward the south*; his teaching must *distil as the rain* (Dt 32:2), so that people's hearts could be softened by it. Judah and Jerusalem are called *forests* because they had been empty of fruit, for fruit trees do not grow in a forest. Those people who should have been like the garden of the Lord had become like a forest, overgrown with *briers and thorns*.

2. A fire kindled in his forest is what is prophesied (v. 47). *I will kindle a fire in thee* (v. 47). The One who himself was once a protecting fire around Jerusalem is now a consuming fire (Dt 4:24) in it. *All faces*, that is, all that covers the face of the earth, *from the south* of Canaan to the north, from Beersheba to Dan (1Ch 21; 2Ch 30:5), will be *burnt therein*. The people, on the occasion of this speech, said, *Does he not speak parables?*

CHAPTER 21

Here is: 1. An explanation of the prophecy at the end of the previous chapter about the fire in the forest (vv. 1–5), with directions to the prophet to show himself deeply moved by it (vv. 6–7). 2. A further prediction of the sword that was coming on the land (vv. 8–17). 3. A prospect given of the king of Babylon's approach to Jerusalem (vv. 18–24). 4. Sentence passed on Zedekiah king of Judah (vv. 25–27). 5. The destruction of the Ammonites by the sword foretold (vv. 28–32).

Verses 1–7

The prophet faithfully communicated the message in the terms in which he received it, but when he complained that the people found fault with him for speaking parables, the word of the Lord came to him again and gave him a key to that figurative speech.

1. The prophet is instructed here against whom he is to direct the arrow of this prophecy. He must *drop his word toward the holy places* (v. 2), toward Canaan, the Holy Land, Jerusalem, the Holy City, and the temple, the holy house.

2. The meaning of the fire that was to consume the forest of the south was that it represented the sword of war that would ravage the land (v. 3). Did the fire devour *every green tree* and *every dry tree*? The sword, similarly, will *cut off the righteous and the wicked*. The righteous were *cut off from the land of Israel* when they were sent as exiles to Babylon. Already at the beginning of Israel's troubles, such excellent people as Daniel and his fellows and Ezekiel were cut off from it and taken to Babylon. But far be it from us to think that *the righteous are as the wicked* (Ge 18:25). God's graces and comforts make a great difference. *The good figs* are sent into Babylon *for their good* (Jer 24:5–6).

3. By expressing his own grief and concern for these coming disasters, the prophet must try to move the people to similar feelings. He must *sigh* as if his heart were about to burst, *sigh with bitterness*.

Verses 8–17

Here is another prophecy of the sword. The sword was unsheathed in the previous verses; here it is fitted to carry out its work, which the prophet is commanded to mourn. Here we see:

1. How the sword is described. It is *sharpened*. It is *furbished* (polished), so that *it may glitter* (may flash like lightning), to the terror of those against whom it is drawn. This sword is *that rod of iron* that despises every tree and will cut it down (Ps 2:9). Or, this sword is *the rod of my son*, a correcting rod, to discipline the disobedience of God's people (2Sa 7:14), not to destroy them from being a people (Ps 83:4; Jer 48:42). "It is a sword to others, a rod to my son."

2. How the sword is put here into the hand of the executioners. *It is given into the hand*, not of the fencer to be played with, but *of the slayer* to carry out execution.

3. Against whom it is sent (v. 12): *It shall be upon my people*; they will fall by this sword. *The sword* of the nations will be drawn against God's own people. But if the sword is drawn against God's people at any time, do they not have enough courage to protect themselves against everything that is frightful? They have, as long as they behave as befits his people, but these people have not done so, and so *terrors, by reason of the sword*, will be on those who call themselves *my people*. This sword is directed especially *against the great men* (v. 14), for they have been the people's greatest sinners. The *point of this sword* is directed against *all their gates* (v. 15), against all those things that they thought would keep it out. This sword is sent with a general warrant (v. 16): "*Go thee, one way or other*, whichever way you will; turn *to the right hand or to the left*, and you will find there people who are repugnant, for no one is free from guilt."

4. The nature of this sword, and the limitations of it as to the people of God (v. 13). It is designed for correction; what is a sword to others is a rod to them. This is a word of encouragement that comes in the middle of these terrible messages. Fears are silenced with an assurance that the sword will not forget the mission on which it is sent: *It is a trial* (v. 13), and it is *no more than a trial*. It is a matter of encouragement to the people of God, when his judgments are about, that *when they are tried, they shall come forth as gold* (Job 23:10), and the proving of their faith will make it even better.

5. That the prophet and the people must show themselves moved by these threatened judgments. The prophet must not work hard to seek fine words, but must warn them of the coming war: *A sword! A sword!* (v. 9). "Let the sword be doubled* the *third time* in your preaching" (v. 14). He must also *cry and howl* (v. 12), wailing and mourning the coming devastation. Again (v. 14), "*Prophesy, and smite thy hands together*; strike *thy hands* together in mourning."

Verses 18–27

In the previous verses, the prophet had shown them the coming sword; he shows them here that they should not flatter themselves with the hope that the sword will be diverted.

1. He must show the Babylonian army coming against Jerusalem. The prophet must *appoint him two ways*, that is, he must draw out two roads on paper (v. 19); he must bring the king of Babylon's army to the fork where the roads part, for they will make a stand there. One road leads to Rabbah, the capital of the Ammonites, and the other to Jerusalem. Nebuchadnezzar is determined to destroy both, but he has not decided which to attack first. Many of the inhabitants of Judah have now taken shelter in Jerusalem, and so it is called *Judah in Jerusalem the defensed* (Judah and fortified Jerusalem). The prophet must describe this dilemma (v. 21), for *the king of Babylon stood*—that is, he will stand—*at the head of the two ways*. In this scenario that the Lord presents to the prophet, it seems the king of Babylon did not know what was in his own best interests or could not make up his own mind. To come to a resolution he *used divination*. He *made his arrows bright*, to be drawn as lots. Perhaps *Jerusalem* was written on one arrow and *Rabbah* on the other, and whichever was drawn out first he decided to attack first. Or he heard the observations that the diviners made on the entrails of the sacrifices: *he looked in the liver* (v. 21). Because Jerusalem was the set mark, the campaign was opened.

2. He must show the people and the prince that they bring this destruction on themselves by their own sin.

2.1. The people do so (vv. 23–24). They disregard the warnings given them of the coming judgment. Ezekiel's prophecy is to them a *false divination* (false omen).

2.2. The prince likewise brings his ruin on himself. Zedekiah was evil, as he promoted sin among his people; he sinned and made Israel sin (1Ki 14:16; 16:2; 21:22; etc.). He has forfeited his crown, and he will no longer wear it. His ungodliness has meant he has desecrated his crown, and it will be thrown to the ground (v. 26): *Remove the diadem* (crown). Crowns and diadems may be lost; it is only in the other world that there is a crown of glory that never fades away (1Pe 5:4). Attempts to reestablish the government will come to nothing. This monarchy will never be restored until it is established forever in the hands of the Messiah (v. 27).

Verses 28–32

The prediction of the destruction of the Ammonites was carried out by Nebuchadnezzar about five years after the destruction of Jerusalem.

1. The sin of the Ammonites is shown here (v. 28). The reproach they put on the Israel of God, triumphing in their suffering, was inhuman. They thought they were better than Israel because they were spared when Israel was destroyed, and this made them so proud that they even *trod on the necks of the Israelites that were slain*.

2. The total destruction of the Ammonites is threatened. God is angry at the indignity and wrongs done to his people, considering them done to him (v. 31). "*I will judge thee where thou wast created*, where you were first

formed into a people and have been settled ever since, where you seemed to have put down roots; *the land of thy nativity* (ancestry) will be the land of your destruction."

CHAPTER 22

Here are three separate messages that God entrusts the prophet with to speak about Judah and Jerusalem to show them their sins and the judgments that are coming. 1. Here is a list of their sins (vv. 1–16). 2. They are condemned as dross to the fire (vv. 17–22). 3. All are found guilty (vv. 23–31).

Verses 1–16

The prophet is authorized to *judge the bloody city,* the city of bloodshed (v. 2). Jerusalem is given this name because the land is full of bloodshed and the city is full of violence (7:23), which defiled her in her own blood.

1. He is to find Jerusalem guilty of many detestable crimes. Let us consider the sins Jerusalem is accused of:

1.1. Murder: *The city sheds blood,* even *in the midst of it,* where the magistrates would, if anywhere, be watchful.

1.2. Idolatry: *She makes idols against herself to destroy herself* (v. 3). And again (v. 4), *Thou hast defiled thyself.* Idolaters deceive themselves to their own destruction, and they defile themselves, making themselves repugnant to God.

1.3. Disobedience to parents (v. 7): *In thee have* the children *set light by their father and mother,* treated them with contempt, mocked them.

1.4. Oppression and extortion. To enrich themselves they wronged the poor (v. 7): *They dealt by oppression* and *deceit with the stranger,* taking advantage of the stranger's needy condition and of their ignorance of the laws, and they have *greedily gained of* their *neighbours* by *violence* and *wrong* (v. 12).

1.5. Desecration of the Sabbath and other holy things. *Thou hast despised my holy things* (v. 8), holy authority, holy ordinances.

1.6. Sexual immorality and all kinds of sins against the seventh commandment. Jerusalem had been famous for its purity, but now *in the midst of thee they commit lewdness* (v. 9).

1.7. Neglect of God lay at the root of all this evil (v. 12): *"Thou hast forgotten me;* otherwise you would not have acted in this way."

2. He is to pass sentence on Jerusalem for these crimes. Let her know that she has filled up the measure of her iniquity (Ge 15:16; Mt 23:32) and that her sins call for speedy vengeance. She has caused *her time to come* (v. 3), *her days to draw near* for punishment (v. 4). God has justly exposed her to the contempt and scorn of all her neighbors (v. 4). Since she has walked in the ways of the nations and learned their works, she will have enough of them (v. 15): "*I will* not only send you *among the heathen,* out of your own land; *I will scatter thee* among them and *disperse thee in the countries.*"

Verses 17–22

1. The wretched corruption of the house of Israel is described. In David's and Solomon's times, it had been *a head of gold;* when the kingdoms were divided, it was like the *arms of silver* (Da 2:32). It has degenerated into a base metal: *They are all brass* (copper), *and tin, and iron, and lead,* which some commentators think represent different kinds of sinners among them. *The house of Israel*

has become dross to me. This is what she is like in God's sight. They were silver, but now they are *even the dross of silver;* the word stands for all the dirt, rubbish, and worthless stuff that becomes separated from silver in its washing, melting, and refining.

2. The terrible destruction of this corruption of the house of Israel is foretold. They are all gathered together in Jerusalem; people have fled there from every part of the country as to a city of refuge. Now God tells them that their flocking to Jerusalem will be like the gathering of various kinds of metal into the furnace or crucible to be melted down and have the dross separated from them.

Verses 23–31

Here is:

1. A general idea given of the land of Israel, how well it deserves the judgments coming to destroy it and how much it needs these judgments to refine it. Let the prophet tell her plainly, "*Thou art the land that is not cleansed,* not refined as metal is, and so you again need to be put into the furnace."

2. A change that they have all helped to fill up the measure of the nation's guilt (Ge 15:16; Mt 23:32), but no one has done anything toward emptying it.

2.1. They have each one *corrupted his way* (Ge 6:12).

2.1.1. The *prophets,* who claim to declare the mind of God to them, are not only *deceivers* but also *devourers* (v. 25). They have devoured souls by flattering sinners into having a false peace.

2.1.2. The priests, who are teachers by office, have disobeyed the law of God, which they should have observed and taught others to observe (v. 26). They have not *put a difference between the holy and profane, the clean and the unclean,* according to the directions of the Law. They *have hid their eyes from God's Sabbaths,* looking the other way, whereas they should have supervised the behavior of the people on Sabbaths.

2.1.3. The officials have been as bold transgressors of the law as anyone (v. 27): *They are like wolves ravening* (tearing) *the prey,* for this is what power without justice and goodness to direct it looks like. The *prophets have daubed them with untempered mortar* (whitewash) (v. 28), told them in God's name that there is no harm in what they do. Daubing prophets are the great supporters of devouring rulers.

2.1.4. The people with any power in their hands learned from their officials how to abuse it (v. 29).

2.2. There is no one who appears as an intercessor for them (v. 30): *I sought for a man among them that should stand in the gap, but I found none.* Sin makes a gap in the protection that surrounds a people, and through that gap good things run out of them and evil things pour in on them. There is a way of standing in the gap, by repentance, prayer, and reformation. Moses stood in the gap when he made intercession for Israel to *turn away the wrath of God* (Ps 106:23).

CHAPTER 23

This chapter is a history of the apostasy of God's people from him, using the metaphor of prostitution. The kingdoms of Israel and Judah, the ten tribes and the two, with their capital cities, Samaria and Jerusalem, are considered individually: 1. The apostasy of Israel and Samaria from God (vv. 1–8) and their ruin (vv. 9–10). 2. The apostasy of Judah and Jerusalem from God (vv. 11–21) and the similar sentence passed on them (vv. 22–35). 3.

The joint evil of them both (vv. 36–44) and the joint ruin of both (vv. 45–49).

Verses 1–10

The sinners who are to be exposed here are *two women,* two kingdoms, sister kingdoms, Israel and Judah, *daughters of one mother,* having been for a long time but *one people.* Notice:

1. Their character when they were one (v. 3): *They committed whoredoms* (prostitution) *in Egypt,* for they were guilty of idolatry there, as we read before (20:8).

2. Their names when they became two (v. 4). The kingdom of Israel is called the *elder sister,* because she was the first to make the break—the "greater sister" is the sense, for ten tribes belonged to that kingdom and only two to the other. In this parable, Samaria and the kingdom of Israel have the name of *Aholah* (Oholah), meaning "her own tabernacle," because the places of worship that that kingdom had were of their own choosing and the worship itself was their own invention. Jerusalem and the kingdom of Judah bear the name of *Aholibah* (Oholibah), meaning "my tabernacle is in her," because their temple was the place where God himself had *chosen* to *put his name* (1Ki 11:36).

3. The unfaithful departure of the kingdom of Israel from God (v. 5). Although the ten tribes had abandoned the house of David, God still acknowledged them as *his;* as long as they worshiped only the God of Israel, even though by idols, he did not completely reject them. But Aholah was unfaithful, bringing in the worship of Baal (1Ki 16:31) in competition with Jehovah (1Ki 18:21); as a corrupt adulteress *dotes on her lovers,* so she doted on her neighbors, particularly the Assyrians. She wondered at their idols and worshiped them.

4. The destruction of the kingdom of Israel for their apostasy from God (vv. 9–10): *I have delivered her into the hand of her lovers.* God first justly gave her up to her sinful desires and then gave her up *to her lovers.* We have the story in detail in 2Ki 17:6–23.

Verses 11–21

In the time of the prophet Hosea, he noticed that the two tribes kept their integrity to a great extent when the ten tribes had committed apostasy (Hos 11:12). Although, by some unfortunate marriages between the house of David and the house of Ahab, the worship of Baal had been brought into the kingdom of Judah, it had been removed by the reforming kings. But this did not last long. In the reign of Manasseh, soon after the kingdom of Judah had seen the destruction of the kingdom of Israel, they became more corrupt than Israel had been in their excessive love of idols (v. 11).

1. Jerusalem, who had been *a faithful city, became a harlot* (Isa 1:21). She, like Israel (v. 7), *doted upon* (lusted after) *the Assyrians* (v. 12); she joined in alliance with them and joined in their worship. This was how the Jews grew to like everything foreign and began to despise their own nation. Even their nation's religion seemed lowly and homely. She longed to see the Babylonian commanders whose portraits she saw on walls (vv. 15–16), and she joined in alliance with that kingdom, even sending for models of their idols, altars, and temples and using them in their worship. And when she had had enough of the Babylonians, she sought the favor of the *Egyptians* (v. 20), seeking an alliance with them, and wanted to join them in their idolatry. This was how she carried her prostitution still further: she repeated her former unfaithfulness and

encouraged herself by calling *to remembrance the days of her youth* (v. 21). Those who, instead of reflecting on their former sins with sorrow and shame, reflect on them with pleasure and pride, defy all calls to repentance. They called it *God's remembrance,* provoking him to remember it against them.

2. God justly gave a certificate of divorce to this now unfaithful city (Jer 3:8). Sin separates God's mind from the sinner, and justly so, for it is the separation of the sinner's mind from God.

Verses 22–35

Jerusalem stands accused by the name of Oholibah, a false traitor to her sovereign Lord, the God of heaven. She does not have his fear always before her eyes (Ps 36:1), but is motivated by Satan and has rebelled from her loyalty to God.

1. Her old allies must be her executioners (v. 12): "*I will raise up thy lovers against thee,* the Babylonians, whom formerly you admired and with whom you have treacherously broken the covenant."

2. The execution to be carried out on her is very terrible. Her enemies will come against her *on every side* (v. 22). They will come with military force (v. 24), a vast army that is well equipped. They will have justice on their side: *I will set judgment before them* (v. 24). Because it is a war of revenge, *they shall deal with thee hatefully* (v. 29). She will be stripped of the *clothes* and the *fair jewels* (fine jewelry) with which she tried to commend herself to her lovers (v. 26). Both city and country will be made poor, and her children will go into exile. She will be stigmatized and deformed: "They will *take away thy nose and thy ears,* marking you as a harlot and rendering you repugnant forever" (v. 25). Some want these words to be understood figuratively, and they think the nose refers to the royal position, and the ears to the position of the priesthood.

3. Because she has followed in the steps of Samaria's sins, she must expect nothing other than Samaria's fate (v. 31).

4. In all this, God will be justified, they will be reformed, and so the outcome will be God's glory and their good. They have been very bad, and that justifies God in all that is brought on them (v. 30): *I will do these things unto thee because thou hast gone a whoring after the heathen* (lusted after the nations) and (v. 35) *because thou hast forgotten me and cast* (thrust) *me behind thy back.* Forgetfulness of God is at the root of all our treacherous departures from him. This fire, though consuming many people, will be refining to a remnant (v. 27). Before the exile, no nation, all things considered, was more recklessly bent on idols and idolatry than they were; after the exile no nation was more passionately set against idols and idolatry.

Verses 36–49

After the ten tribes were taken into exile, that kingdom's remains were gradually incorporated into the kingdom of Judah, and many of them gained a settlement in Jerusalem, so that the *two sisters* had in effect become *one* again. Therefore, "You will now be employed, in God's name, to *judge them* (20:4) jointly. The matter is worse rather than better since the union."

1. Let them be led to see the sins they are guilty of: *Declare unto them* openly and boldly *their abominations* (v. 36). They have been guilty of gross idolatry, here called *adultery* (v. 37); they have broken their marriage

covenant with God. They have committed the most barbaric murders by sacrificing their children to Molech. They have desecrated the sacred things with which God honored them and set them apart. They *defiled the sanctuary* on *the same day* that they *profaned the sabbath.* They have courted foreign alliances. This, too, is represented by the sin of adultery, for it was a departure from God, *in* whom alone they should put their trust. Great preparation was made for the reception of these foreign ministers, for their public arrival and public audience, and this preparation is compared to the pains that an adulteress takes to make herself look beautiful. The *men of the common sort* were there to increase the crowd, and *with them were brought Sabeans from the wilderness.* The margin reads "drunkards from the wilderness," who would drink toasts to the prosperity of this grand alliance. But an alliance between the nation of the Jews and a pagan nation can never be to the advantage of either. They are like chalk and cheese and cannot mix; God will never bless such an alliance.

2. Let them be made to foresee the judgments that are coming on them for these sins (v. 45). The *righteous men, they shall judge them.* Some understand *the righteous men* to refer to the prophets, whose responsibility it was, in God's name, to judge them and pass sentence on them. Because this judgment is given by the righteous, the righteous God will award execution (vv. 46–47), the same as before (v. 23). The destruction of God's city, like the death of God's saints, will do for the saints what ordinances and providences before could not do, so that Jerusalem will rise up out of its ashes as a new lump (1Co 5:7), as gold comes out of the furnace purified from its dross.

CHAPTER 24

There are two sermons in this chapter, preached on a particular occasion, and they are both from Mount Sinai, the mount of terror (Ex 19:16; 20:18), both from Mount Ebal, the mount of curses (Dt 27:12–26; Jos 8:33–34); both speak of the approaching fate of Jerusalem. Their occasion was the king of Babylon's laying siege to Jerusalem. 1. The sign of meat boiling in a cooking pot over the fire showed the miseries that Jerusalem would suffer during the siege (vv. 1–14). 2. The sign of Ezekiel's not mourning the death of his wife showed that the calamities coming on Jerusalem would be too great to be lamented; they were so great that the people would sink under them into silent despair (vv. 15–27).

Verses 1–14

We have here:

1. The notice God gives to Ezekiel in Babylon of Nebuchadnezzar's laying siege to Jerusalem (v. 2): "Son of man, take note, the king of Babylon, who is now with his army—and you do not know where he is—is setting himself against Jerusalem today." He tells the prophet so that the prophet can tell the people, so that when it proves to be precisely true, it will confirm the prophet's mission.

2. The notice he orders him to take of it. He must enter it in his book; he is to write down that *in the ninth year* of Jehoiachin's captivity, in the tenth month, on the tenth day of the month, the king of Babylon laid siege to Jerusalem, and the date here agrees with the date recorded in 2Ki 25:1.

3. The notice he orders him to give to the people. A rebellious house will soon be a ruinous house.

3.1. He must show them this by a sign, that of a *boiling* (cooking) *pot.* This corresponds with Jeremiah's vision many years before: *I see a seething pot,* said Jeremiah, *with the face toward the north* (Jer 1:13); and according to the explanation of this vision (Jer 1:15), the image stands for the besieging of Jerusalem by the *northern* nations, to confront the worthless confidence of the leaders of Jerusalem, who have said (11:3), *This city is the caldron, and we are the flesh,* meaning, "We are as safe here as if we were surrounded by walls of bronze." "Well," God says, "it will be so; you will be boiled in Jerusalem as the *flesh in the caldron.*" Those who have fled from all parts of the country to Jerusalem for safety will be sadly disappointed, but there will be no escape: they will have to stay there, as the meat has to remain in a cooking pot.

3.2. He must give them a comment on this sign. It is to be interpreted as a *woe to the bloody city* (to the city of bloodshed) (v. 6). During the siege, Jerusalem is like a pot boiling over the fire. Care is taken to keep a good fire under the pot, and the strength of the fire represents the closeness of the siege. Commission is given to the Babylonians (v. 10) to *heap on wood and kindle the fire.* Here no measuring line is used (2Sa 8:2), no casting of lots for mercy; all go to destruction. God would not follow these severe methods with Jerusalem except that he has been provoked to do so (vv. 7–8). Jerusalem is to be made an example of to the world and is therefore made a spectacle to the world. Because she is incurably evil, she is abandoned to ruin with no way of escape. Methods to reform her have been tried in vain (v. 13). It is therefore decided that no more such methods will be used: *Thou shalt not be purged from thy filthiness any more.* The fire will be no longer a refining fire, but a consuming fire.

Verses 15–27

These verses conclude Ezekiel's prophecies of the destruction of Jerusalem, for after this, although he prophesied much about other nations, he said nothing more about Jerusalem until he heard of its destruction, almost three years later (33:21). Notice here:

1. The sign by which this was portrayed to them.

1.1. He must lose a good wife, who would suddenly be taken away from him by death. God gave him notice of it beforehand (v. 16). A beloved wife is the *desire of the eyes.* When the desire of our eyes is suddenly taken away, we must see and acknowledge the hand of God in it: *I take away the desire of thy eyes.*

1.2. He must deny himself the satisfaction of mourning for his wife, which would have been both an honor to her and a relief to the oppression of his own spirit. Ezekiel was not allowed to do this, even though he would perhaps be badly thought of by the people around him if he did it not. Nor may he eat *the bread of men,* the customary food of mourners, or expect his neighbors and friends to send him provisions, as they usually did in such situations, presuming that the mourners had no heart to provide for themselves. If it was sent, he must not eat it. It must surely have gone greatly against the grain of his humanity not to lament the death of one he loved so dearly, but this was God's command, and *I did in the morning as I was commanded* (v. 18). He appeared in public without any signs of mourning. For Ezekiel to make himself a sign to the people, he must exercise extraordinary self-denial.

2. The application of this sign. The people asked about its meaning (v. 19): *Wilt thou not tell us what these things are to us that thou doest so?* They knew that the death of

his wife was a great adversity to him and that he would not appear so unconcerned about it except for some good reason.

2.1. Let them know that as Ezekiel's wife was taken away from him in one blow, so God would take from them all that was dearest to them (v. 21). If a faithful servant of God was tested by such suffering, how would such a generation of rebels against God go unpunished? God would *take away that which their soul pitied* (the object of their affection), that is, the thing of which they would say, "What a pity it is that it should be cut off and destroyed!" And what was that? First, it was their public pride, the temple: "I *will profane* (desecrate) *my sanctuary* by giving it into the enemy's hand to be plundered and burned." Second, it was their family pleasure, what they looked on with delight: "*Your sons and your daughters*, who are more precious to you because they are only a few left of many (Jer 42:2), the rest having perished by famine and plague, will *fall by the sword* of the Babylonians." This was the punishment of sin.

2.2. Let them know that just as Ezekiel did not weep in his suffering, so neither would they weep in theirs. He must say, *You shall do as I have done* (v. 22). *You shall not mourn nor weep* (v. 23). Their grief would be so great that they would be overwhelmed. Their calamities would come on them so fast that by a habit of sorrowing they would be *hardened in their sorrows* (Job 6:10), stunned by them. There would be none of that sense of sorrow which would help bring them to repentance, but only that which would drive them to despair: "*You shall pine away for your iniquities* (v. 23) with hardened consciences and reprobate minds, and *you shall mourn* not to God in prayer and confession of sin, but *one toward another,*" complaining about God.

3. An appeal to actual events to confirm all this (v. 24): "*When this comes,* as it is foretold, when Jerusalem, which is now besieged, is completely destroyed, which now you cannot believe will ever happen, *then you shall know that I am the Lord God,* who has given you fair warning. Then you will remember that Ezekiel was a sign to you." The prophet would be given notice of this not by revelation, but in an ordinary way (v. 26): "*He that escapes in that day* will, by special direction of Providence, *come to thee* to bring you news of it," which we find happened (v. 21). From this time to that, Ezekiel would be silent insofar as he prophesied no more against the land of Israel, but against the neighboring nations, as we will find in the following chapters; when he received that notice, however, he would have orders given him to *speak again to the children of his people* (33:2, 22). When God was speaking so loudly by the rod, there was less need for him to speak by the word.

CHAPTER 25

Ezekiel had finished his testimony relating to the destruction of Jerusalem, and as regards that, he was ordered to say nothing more, but to await the outcome of events. He must not remain silent, however; there were several nations bordering the land of Israel that he must prophesy against, as Isaiah and Jeremiah had done before. In this chapter we have his prophecy: 1. Against Ammon (vv. 1–7). 2. Against Moab (vv. 8–11). 3. Against Edom (vv. 11–14). 4. Against Philistia (vv. 15–17). What each of them was accused of was their cruel and arrogant behavior toward God's Israel.

Verses 1–7

1. The prophet is ordered to address the Ammonites in the name of *the Lord Jehovah* the *God of Israel,* who is also the God of the whole earth. He is told to *set his face against the Ammonites* (v. 2), for he is God's representative, and so he must demonstrate that God has *set his face against them,* for *the face of the Lord is against those that do evil* (Ps 34:16). He must show that although he has prophesied so long *against Israel,* he is for Israel, and, though he has borne witness against their corruption, he glories in God's covenant with them.

2. He is told what to say to them. Ezekiel is now an exile in Babylon and knows little about the nations around Israel, but God tells him what they are doing and what he is about to do with them.

2.1. He must rebuke the Ammonites for their arrogant and cruel triumphs over the people of Israel in their adversities (v. 3). The Ammonites, of all people, should not have been glad at Jerusalem's ruin, but should rather have trembled, because they themselves had such a narrow escape (21:20). And they had reason to think that the king of Babylon would attack them next. And it is wrong to be glad at the calamities of anyone.

2.2. He must threaten the Ammonites with complete destruction for their arrogance. He has predicted the destruction of the Ammonites before (21:28). If they had repented, that sentence would have been revoked, but it is now confirmed: *I will deliver thee to the men of the east* (v. 4). First came the Babylonians and their army from the northeast, under the command of Nebuchadnezzar, and they destroyed the country of the Ammonites about five years after the destruction of Jerusalem, and when the Babylonians had devastated the country, then the Arabians, who were properly the *children of the east* (Jdg 6:3, 33; 1Ki 4:30), came and took possession of it for themselves. They even used the royal city for their cattle (v. 5): *I will make Rabbah,* that splendid city, *a stable for camels.* This is how God will preserve his own honor, and he will make it clear that he is the God of Israel even though he allows them for a time to be in exile in Babylon. This is how he will bring those who were strangers to him to come to know him.

Verses 8–17

Three more of Israel's ill-natured neighbors are condemned to destruction here for contributing to and triumphing in Jerusalem's downfall.

1. The Moabites. Seir, the seat of the Edomites, is joined with them (v. 8). Notice:

1.1. The sin of the Moabites. They said, *Behold, the house of Judah is like unto all the heathen* (nations). They were pleased to see them abandon their God to worship idols. Let the Moabites know that although there are those of the house of Judah who have made themselves like the nations, there is still a remnant who retain their integrity; the religious faith of the house of Judah will recover. They also triumphed at the calamities of Israel, saying, "*The house of Judah is like all the heathen.* Their God can no more rescue them from this *overflowing scourge* of these parts of the world than the gods of the nations can." Those who judge only by outward appearances are ready to conclude that the people of God have lost all their privileges when they have lost their worldly prosperity.

1.2. The punishment of Moab for this sin. Their country will be overthrown in the same way as that of the Ammonites, who were guilty of the same sin (vv. 9–10).

The frontier towns, which were Moab's strength, will be demolished by the Babylonian forces, and thus *opened*. When *the men of the east* come to take possession of the country of the Ammonites, they will also seize the country of the Moabites. The Arabians, who are shepherds and live quietly in tents, will by an overruling providence be given possession of the land of the Moabites, who are soldiers and who live turbulent lives. The Babylonians will gain it by war, and the Arabians will enjoy it in peace.

2. The Edomites, the descendants of Esau. Between them and Jacob there had been an ancient hostility (v. 12). They not only rejoiced over the ruin of Judah and Jerusalem, as the Moabites and Ammonites had done, but also took advantage of the present distressed state to which the Jews were reduced to cause them some real trouble. They probably made inroads at their frontiers and plundered their country. Amaziah had rebuked them severely (2Ki 14:7), and for this they *took vengeance*; now they wanted to settle all the old scores. God will take them to task for it (v. 13): *I will stretch out my hand upon Edom.* Their country will be desolate *from Teman* in the south, and *they shall fall by the sword unto Dedan*, which lay north. They suffered much through the Babylonians, which seems to be referred to in Jer 49:8. We find that *Judas fought against the children of Esau in Idumea, gave them a great overthrow, abated their courage, and took their spoils* (1 Macc 5:3), and Josephus says (*Antiquities* bk. 13, ch. 17) that Hircanus made the Edomites pay tribute to Israel.

3. The Philistines. Their sin is much the same as that of the Edomites. They have *dealt by revenge* with the people of Israel and have *taken vengeance with a despiteful heart* (with malice in their hearts) to *destroy them* because of the ancient grudge they bore toward Israel (v. 15). Their punishment, similarly, is much the same (v. 16). Their country was devastated by the Babylonian army not long after the destruction of Jerusalem, which is foretold in Jer 47.

CHAPTER 26

The city of Tyre is the next to come to court. Because this was a place of such immense trade, it was known throughout the world, and so there are three chapters, this and the two that follow, devoted to prophesying the destruction of Tyre. We have the burden *(oracle) of Tyre in Isa 23; the city is merely mentioned in Jeremiah (Jer 25:22; 27:3; 47:4); but Ezekiel is ordered to speak in detail about that subject. In this chapter we have: 1. The sin Tyre is accused of, which is gloating over the destruction of Jerusalem (vv. 1–2). 2. The destruction of Tyre itself foretold: 2.1. The extreme nature of this destruction (vv. 4–6, 12–14). 2.2. The instruments of this destruction (v. 3), including the king of Babylon with his immense victorious army (vv. 7–11). 2.3. The surprise of the neighboring nations (vv. 15–21).*

Verses 1–14

This prophecy is dated in the eleventh year, which was the year that Jerusalem was captured, and *in the first day of the month*, but it is not said what month. Notice:

1. The pleasure with which the Tyrians looked on the ruins of Jerusalem (v. 2): "*Aha! She is broken*, broken to pieces, she who was *the gates of the people*. All the wealth, power, and privileges that Jerusalem had will go to Tyre, and so *now* that *she is laid waste, I shall be replenished*." The Tyrians were businesspeople and so were not of a persecuting spirit; all they wanted was to add to their possessions and increase their trade, and they looked on

Jerusalem not as an enemy, but as a rival. Tyre promised herself that the downfall of Jerusalem would give her an advantage with respect to trade and commerce, that now she would have Jerusalem's customers, and so the prosperity of Tyre would rise up out of the ruins of Jerusalem. God is just to frustrate the plans of those who want to raise themselves up on the ruins of others.

2. The displeasure of God against them for it. Tyre was a pleasant and wealthy city and might have continued to be if she had sympathized with Jerusalem in her adversities. But instead she was pleased at her neighbor's downfall; so then God says, *Behold, I am against thee, O Tyrus! Many nations shall come against thee* (v. 3), an army made up of many nations, or one nation that will be as strong as many. The person is named who will bring this army on *them—Nebuchadnezzar king of Babylon, a king of kings*, who has many kings paying tribute to him, besides those who are his captives (Da 2:37–38). He will come with a vast army, *horses and chariots*. He will set up siege works, build a ramp (v. 8), and batter the walls with battering rams. His troops will raise dust that will cover the city (v. 10). The city held out in a long siege, but it finally fell. Not only the soldiers who bear weapons but also the ordinary citizens will be *put to the sword*, because the king of Babylon is very angry with them for holding out so long. The wealth of the city will all become plunder for the conqueror (v. 12). All the *pleasant houses* will be *destroyed* (v. 12). When Jerusalem was destroyed, it was *ploughed like a field* (Mic 3:12). But the destruction of Tyre will be carried further; its very soil will be scraped away, and it will be made *like the top of a rock* (vv. 4, 14) that has no earth to cover it. It will only be a place *for the spreading of nets* (vv. 5, 14); fishermen will use it to dry their nets on.

Verses 15–21

Notice:

1. How significant and great Tyre has been, how unlikely it was ever to come to this. She was *inhabited of seafaring men* (v. 17), inhabited by those who traded at sea, by those who came there from everywhere by sea, and she was *strong in the sea*, fortified by a *wall of water* that made her impregnable. Everybody stood in awe of the Tyrians and was afraid of displeasing them.

2. How insignificant, how small, Tyre is made (vv. 19–20). This *renowned city* will be made *a desolate city*, a city overflowed by a flood of waters, which will *cover* it; it will be a city on which the *deep is brought up*. The Tyrians will be lost among the nations, so that people will look in vain for Tyre in Tyre: *Thou shalt be sought for, and never found again* (v. 21).

3. What distress the inhabitants of Tyre will be in (v. 15): *There is a great slaughter made in the midst of thee.*

4. What fear all the neighbors will be in at the downfall of Tyre. The *islands* will *shake at the sound of thy fall* (v. 15). The *princes of the sea* (coast) will be affected, those who rule those islands. The rich merchants, who live like princes (Isa 23:8), and the captains of ships, who command like princes, will mourn the fall of Tyre. When Jerusalem, the Holy City, was destroyed, there were no such laments for it; it was *nothing* to *those that passed by* (La 1:12). But when Tyre, the trading city, fell, it was universally bemoaned.

5. The irreparable ruin of Tyre is emphasized by the prospect of the restoration of Israel. Tyre will sink *when I shall set glory in the land of the living* (v. 20). The Holy

Land is the *land of the living*, for none but holy souls are properly living souls.

CHAPTER 27

In this chapter we have: 1. A detailed account of the dignity, wealth, and splendor Tyre had while it was strong (vv. 1–25). 2. A prediction of its downfall and ruin (vv. 26–36). And this is intended to enable us to see the worthlessness and uncertainty of worldly riches, honors, and pleasures.

Verses 1–25

Here:

1. The prophet is told to take up a lament for Tyre (v. 2). It was still at the height of its prosperity, with not the slightest symptom of its decay apparent, but the prophet must lament it, because its prosperity is its snare, which will make its downfall more terrible.

2. He is told what to say, and to say it in the name of *the Lord Jehovah*.

2.1. He must rebuke Tyre for her pride: *O Tyrus! thou hast said, I am of perfect beauty* (v. 3), literally, of "universal beauty," well built and well provided with money and trade.

2.2. He must rebuke Tyre for her prosperity, which was the subject of her pride.

2.2.1. The city of Tyre was well situated, standing at the east end of the Mediterranean, convenient for trade by land into all the eastern parts, so that she became *a merchant of the people for many isles* (v. 3). Being situated between Greece and Asia, she became the meeting place of merchants from all parts of the world: *Thy borders are in the heart of the seas* (v. 4).

2.2.2. It was skillfully built, according to the style of that time. *Thy builders have perfected thy beauty* (v. 4); they had refined the art of architecture.

2.2.3. It had its haven *replenished* (enriched) with many *gallant* (mighty) *ships* (Isa 23:2; 33:21). The Tyrians made their *sails of fine linen* obtained from Egypt, and that *embroidered* too (v. 7). The word means "a banner" as well as "a sail." They hung rooms on board ship with *blue and purple*, the richest cloths and the richest colors they could get. Tyre was itself famous for purple, which is therefore called the *Tyrian dye*.

2.2.4. These mighty ships were well staffed. The pilots and captains of the ships were of their own city (v. 8): *Thy wise men, O Tyrus! that were in thee, were thy pilots. The inhabitants of Arvad and Zidon were thy mariners.* Veteran craftsmen from Gebal in Syria came as shipwrights, as *calkers*, to seal up the seams of the ships when the ships came home after long voyages for repairs.

2.2.5. Their city was guarded by a significant military force (vv. 10–11). Even though the land of Israel lay adjacent to them and supplied them with timber, we do not find that it supplied them with people—that would have infringed the liberty and position of the Jewish nation (2Ch 2:17–18).

2.2.6. They had an immense trade and good connections with all parts of the then known world. The identity of many of the places listed here is uncertain, but we will observe what is practical concerning them.

2.2.6.1. Ezekiel knew little, from his own knowledge, about the trade of Tyre. He was a priest, taken captive far from Tyre, and he had been in captivity eleven years. However, he speaks about the particular merchandise of Tyre in as much detail as if he had been in charge of its custom house. It is God who *saith this* (v. 3).

2.2.6.2. God looks at individual people, taking notice of what they do when they are employed in their worldly business, which is a good reason why we should *keep a conscience void of offense* (Ac 24:16) in every aspect of our lives.

2.2.6.3. The wisdom and goodness of God as the common Father of the human race is seen in making one country have much of one commodity and another of another, all commodities being more or less useful. One land does not supply all varieties of products. Providence distributes its gifts differently, some to each and all to none, so that there may be mutual dealings among those whom God has *made of one blood*, even though they are made *to dwell on all the face of the earth* (Ac 17:26). Let every nation, therefore, thank God for the products of its country; although its products may not be so rich as those of others, there is still some use for them in the public service of the world.

2.2.6.4. Notice what a blessing trade and merchandise are to humanity, especially when followed in the fear of God and with respect not only to private advantage but also to common benefits. *The earth is full of God's riches* (Ps 104:24).

2.2.6.5. Notice how many things are mentioned that serve only to please human desires, that are made valuable only by human taste and custom; and yet God allows us to use them, trade in them, and part with those things that we can spare that have intrinsic worth far beyond them

2.2.6.6. It is significant that Judah and the *land of Israel* were merchants in Tyre. They traded mostly *in wheat*, a substantial commodity. Tyre was maintained by grain obtained from the land of Israel.

2.2.6.7. Tyre gained plenty by buying and selling, importing commodities from one place and exporting them; yet manufacturing trades were not neglected. The *wares of their own making*, and *a multitude of such wares*, are here spoken about (vv. 16, 18). A nation is wise to encourage industry, for it contributes much to the wealth and honor of a nation to send abroad *wares of their own making*.

2.2.6.8. All this made Tyre very great and very proud: *The ships of Tarshish did sing of thee in thy market* (v. 25).

Verses 26–36

The destruction of Tyre was sudden. Her *sun went down at noon* (Am 8:9). All her wealth and grandeur, pomp and power, only emphasized her ruin. She was like a great, richly laden ship that is sunk by the rashness of those steering it: *Thy rowers have* themselves *brought thee into great* and dangerous *waters* (v. 26); the rulers of the city involved them in a war with the Babylonians that led to the ruin of their state. By their arrogance they provoked Nebuchadnezzar to attack them and, obstinately resisting to the end, enraged him so much that he was determined to destroy their state; *like an east wind*, he *broke them in the midst of the seas* (v. 26). All her wealth will be buried with her, *her riches, her fairs* (wares), *and her merchandise* (v. 27); all will *fall with her into the midst of the seas in the day of her ruin*. The *pilots*, her princes and officers (v. 27), when they see how wretchedly they have mismanaged affairs and how they have contributed to their own ruin, will *cry out* so loud that they make even the *suburbs* (shorelands) *shake* (v. 28). Tyre will be rebuked for her former prosperity (vv. 32–33); she who was Tyre the *renowned* will now be called *Tyrus the destroyed* in the *midst of the sea.* Some will be *sorely afraid* (appalled) and *troubled* (v. 35). Others will *hiss at her* (v. 36) and ridicule her pride and bad management, and think her ruin just.

CHAPTER 28

We have here: 1. A prediction of the downfall and ruin of the king of Tyre, who, in the destruction of that city, is particularly set up as a target for God's arrows (vv. 1–10). 2. A lament for the king of Tyre, even though he falls through his own sin (vv. 11–19). 3. A prophecy of the destruction of Sidon, which was near Tyre (vv. 20–23). 4. A promise of the restoration of the Israel of God, even though they were gloated over by their neighbors on the day of their adversity (vv. 24–26).

Verses 1–10

The ruler of Tyre is singled out from the rest. Here is a *message to him from God,* which the prophet must send him.

1. He must tell the king about his pride. His *heart was lifted up* (v. 2). Out of the pride of his heart he said, *I am a god.* He thought that the city of Tyre depended as much on him as the world depended on the God who made it, "*I am the strong God*"—for the root of the word for *God* here means "strength"—"and so will not be contradicted, because I cannot be controlled. *I sit in the seat of God; I* sit as safely as God, as securely *in the heart of the seas,* and as far beyond the reach of danger, as the One who sits in the *height of heaven.*" He would now be told, "*Thou art a man, and not God* (v. 2), a dependent creature, a dying creature; you are *flesh, and not spirit*" (Isa 31:3). Although the king of Tyre had such a powerful influence, and though he was flattered by his courtiers and made a god of by his poets, he was *but a man;* he knew it; he feared it. What he was proud of was his wisdom and his wealth. When the king of Tyre dreamed he was a god, he said, I am *wiser than Daniel. There is no secret that they can hide from thee.* He who was *wiser than Daniel* was prouder than Lucifer (Isa 14:12). His wisdom led him to pursue wealth. Just as some of the kings of Judah loved the soil (2Ch 26:10), so the king of Tyre loved trade, and by it *he got riches, increased his riches, and filled his treasures with gold and silver* (vv. 4–5). He attributed the increase of his wealth to himself and not to the providence of God, forgetting the One who *gave him power to get wealth* (Dt 8:17–18). He thought that he was wise because he was rich, whereas a fool can have possessions (Ecc 2:19).

2. Since *pride goes before destruction, and a haughty spirit before a fall* (Pr 16:18), he must tell the king about that destruction, that fall. "Because you have claimed to be a god (v. 6), you shall not be a man for much longer" (v. 7). *I will bring strangers* (foreigners) *upon thee*—the Babylonians. They are people of a *strange language.* They are the *terrible of the nations;* it was an army made up of many nations, formidable both for strength and for fury. "*They shall draw their swords against the beauty of thy wisdom* (v. 7), against all those things that you gloried in as your beauty and as the products of your wisdom." The king of Tyre glories in his palace, treasury, city, navy, and army as his pride and joy; the victorious enemy will defile, deface, and deform these. He will be so reviled in his death that he can despair of being made a god after his death. The sentence of death passed on the king of Tyre here is confirmed by divine authority: *I have spoken it, saith the Lord God* (v. 10). "When the conqueror sets his

sword to your body and you see no way of escape, *wilt thou then say, I am God?* (v. 9). The fear of it will force you to acknowledge that you are not a god, but a weak, fearful, trembling, dying human being."

Verses 11–19

After the ruin of the king of Tyre is prophesied, he is mourned.

1. This is commonly understood to refer to the ruler who then reigned over Tyre, who was addressed in v. 2. His name was *Ethbaal,* or *Ithobalus,* as the Greek historian Diodorus Siculus calls the one who was king of Tyre when Nebuchadnezzar destroyed it. He was an accomplished man, but his sin was his ruin.

2. Some think that *the king of Tyre* refers to the whole royal family. He is spoken of here as having lived in great splendor (vv. 12–15). He was thought to be as wise as human reason could make him and as happy as the wealth of this world and the enjoyment of it could make him. He seemed to be as wise as Adam in innocence (v. 13): "*Thou hast been in Eden, even in the garden of God;* you have lived, as it were, in paradise all your days, having power over everything around you, as Adam had." His rooms were decorated with jewels, so that *he walked in the midst of* jewels, and then it seemed to him as if he were as glorious as God, surrounded by many angels, who are compared to a *flame of fire* (Heb 1:7). *Gold* is mentioned last, as far less valuable than these other precious stones, and he was accustomed to speaking about it accordingly. Another thing that made him think his palace was a paradise was the fine music he had, the *tabrets and pipes,* hand instruments and wind instruments. He appeared in as much splendor as the high priest had when he was clothed with his garments in glory and beauty (v. 15): "*Thou wast perfect in thy ways;* you were successful in all your affairs, and everything went well with you *from the day thou wast created till iniquity was found in thee,* and that spoiled everything." And once iniquity was *found in him,* it increased; he grew worse and worse (v. 18). The king had so much to do with his trading, and was so wholly intent on making as much wealth as possible from that, that he neglected to act justly, to give redress to those who suffered wrong and to protect them from violence (v. 16): "*Thy heart was lifted up because of thy beauty* (v. 17); you were in love with yourself." He disgraced the crown he wore, and so forfeited it, and he would be destroyed *from the midst of the stones of fire,* the precious stones with which his palace was decorated.

Verses 20–26

God's glory is his great purpose. He will be glorified:

1. In the destruction of Sidon, a city near Tyre, one that was more ancient but not as significant; it depended on Tyre, and stood and fell with it. The Sidonians were more devoted to idolatry than the Tyrians, who, because they were businesspeople, were less prone to bigotry and superstition. The Sidonians were noted for the worship of Ashtoreth. Jezebel was a daughter of the king of Sidon, who introduced the worship of Baal to Israel (1Ki 16:31), and so God had been greatly dishonored by the Sidonians. The punishments that will be inflicted on Sidon are war and the plague (v. 23). Nor is it only Tyre and Sidon on which God will inflict punishment, but also all those who have despised his people Israel and gloated over their adversities, for this is now God's dispute with the nations that are *round about them* (v. 26).

2. In the restoration of his people to their former prosperity. He has been dishonored by the sins of his people,

and their sufferings have also given cause to the enemy to blaspheme (Isa 52:5), but God will now both heal them of their sins and relieve them of their troubles, and so he *will be sanctified in them in the sight of the heathen* (v. 25). They will enjoy great peace there. When those who have been troublesome to them are taken away, they will live in quietness; there will no more be *a pricking brier nor a grieving thorn* (v. 24). They will enjoy a contented settlement, for they will *build houses* and *plant vineyards*, and there will be no one to disturb them or make them afraid (Isa 17:2; Eze 34:28; etc.) (v. 26). But the complete fulfillment of this promise is reserved for the heavenly Canaan, where everything offensive will be removed and all griefs and fears banished forever.

CHAPTER 29

Here begin four chapters about Egypt and its king. Egypt was once a land of slavery for God's people; recently they had depended too much on it, and so, whether the prediction reached Egypt or not, it would still be useful to Israel, to take them away from their confidence in their alliance. In this chapter we have: 1. The destruction of Pharaoh foretold, because of his deceitful dealings with Israel (vv. 1–7). 2. The desolation of the land of Egypt foretold (vv. 8–12). 3. A promise of the restoration of Egypt, in part, after forty years (vv. 13–16). 4. A promise that Nebuchadnezzar would be given possession of the land of Egypt (vv. 17–20). 5. A promise of mercy to Israel (v. 21).

Verses 1–7

Here is:

1. The date of this prophecy against Egypt. It was in the *tenth year of the captivity* (v. 1). The first prophecy against Egypt was just at the time when the king of Egypt was coming to relieve Jerusalem and lift the siege (Jer 37:5) but did not fulfill the expectations of the Jews.

2. The scope of this prophecy. It is directed against *Pharaoh king of Egypt and against all Egypt* (v. 2). It begins with the ruler because it began to be fulfilled in the rebellions of the people against the ruler not long after this time.

3. The prophecy itself. Pharaoh Hophra, as the Pharaoh reigning at the time was called, is represented here by *a great dragon* (great monster), or crocodile, which *lies in the midst of his rivers* to *play therein* (Ps 104:26) (v. 3). The Nile River was famous for crocodiles. Notice here:

3.1. The pride and self-confidence of Pharaoh. He boasts that he is an absolute ruler, a sole ruler, who has neither partner nor competitor in the government. Pharaoh's reason for his claims is absurd: "My *river is my own*, for *I have made it for myself.*" Here he usurps two of the divine prerogatives, to be the author and to be the purpose of his own existence and happiness. Self is the great idol that all the world worships, in defiance of God and his sovereignty.

3.2. How God will humble this proud man. He is a great monster in the waters, and God will deal with him accordingly (vv. 4–5).

3.2.1. He will draw him out of his rivers, for he has *a hook and a cord* for this *leviathan* (Job 41:1): "*I will bring thee up out of the midst of thy rivers*, will drive you out of all those things in which you take such delight and in which you trust." Herodotus said about this Pharaoh that he had reigned in great prosperity for twenty-five years and was so elevated with his successes that he said that

God himself could not cast him out of his kingdom; but he will soon be convinced of his mistake.

3.2.2. *All his fish* will be drawn out with him, his servants, his soldiers, and all who depend on him. These will *stick to his scales* (v. 4), adhere to their king, being determined to live and die with him. But king and army, the monster and all the fish that stick to his scales, will perish together, as fish thrown up on dry ground (v. 5). This is thought to have had its fulfillment soon afterward, when this Pharaoh, in defense of Aricius king of Libya, who had been expelled from his kingdom by the Cyrenians, mustered a great army and went out against the Cyrenians to reestablish his friend. However, he was defeated in battle, which offended his subjects so much that they rose up in rebellion against him. In this way he was *thrown into the wilderness, he and all the fish of the river* with him.

3.3. The basis on which God challenges the Egyptians; it is that they have cheated his people. They failed them (vv. 6–7). When any stress was laid on them, they either could not or would not do for them what was expected of them. The king of Egypt had probably encouraged Zedekiah to break his alliance with the king of Babylon and promised that he would stand by him if he did; but he failed to support Zedekiah in this way. God had told them long before that the Egyptians were broken reeds (Isa 30:6; see also Isa 36:6), and now they found it so.

Verses 8–16

These verses explain the foregoing prophecy, which was figurative and looked to something further. Here is a prophecy:

1. Of the ruin of Egypt. This threat is precise, and the sin is their pride (v. 9). God is against the king and against the people, *against thee and against thy rivers*. Waters stand for *people and multitudes* (Rev 17:15). Many will die by war, the sword of civil war. The country will be depopulated. The *land of Egypt shall be utterly waste*, "wastes of waste," as the margin reads, *and desolate* (v. 10); *neither men nor beasts shall pass through it, nor shall it be inhabited* (v. 11); it will be *desolate in the midst of the countries that are so* (v. 12). This was the effect of the war that the king of Babylon waged on them. The people will be dispersed and scattered among the nations (v. 12), so that those who thought the balance of power was in their hands will now become contemptible.

2. Of the restoration of Egypt after a while (v. 13). Egypt will *lie desolate forty years* (v. 12), and then *I will bring again the captivity of Egypt* (bring them back) (v. 14). The forty years ended about the first year of Cyrus's reign, when the seventy years' exile of Judah ended, or soon afterward. God will gather the Egyptians and make them to *return to the land of their habitation* (ancestry) (v. 14). Yet they will not be as significant as they have been. Egypt will be *a kingdom* again, but it will be the *basest* (lowliest) *of the kingdoms* (v. 15). It will be humbled in this way for two reasons:

- So that it may not lord it over its neighbors, but know what it is to be lowly and despised.
- So that it may not deceive the people of God (v. 16): Egypt shall no longer be the source of confidence for the people of Israel; they will no more trust it.

Verses 17–21

The date of this prophecy is in the twenty-seventh year of Ezekiel's captivity, sixteen years after the prophecy in the earlier part of the chapter. After the destruction of

Jerusalem, Nebuchadnezzar spent two or three campaigns in the conquest of the Ammonites and Moabites. He then spent thirteen years in the siege of Tyre. During all that time, the Egyptians were embroiled in war with the Cyrenians, which made them much weaker and poorer. At the end of the siege of Tyre, God delivers this prophecy to Ezekiel to show him that the complete destruction of Egypt, which he foretold fifteen or sixteen years before, will now be completely fulfilled by Nebuchadnezzar. The prophecy that begins here is continued, it seems, to 30:20. It is the last prophecy we have of this prophet, but it is put here so that all the prophecies against Egypt might appear together. Notice:

1. The success God would give to Nebuchadnezzar against Egypt (vv. 19–20). It was cheap and easy plunder. Jeremiah foretold that Nebuchadnezzar would *array himself with the land of Egypt as a shepherd puts on his coat* (Jer 43:12), which intimates what a rich and easy plunder it would be.

2. This success was a reward for the hard service with which he had made his army serve against Tyre (vv. 18, 20).

2.1. The taking of Tyre cost Nebuchadnezzar much blood and treasure. In this siege, *every head was made bald* (rubbed bare), *and every shoulder peeled* (made raw) (v. 18), with carrying heavy loads and laboring hard in the water when they had a strong tide to contend with.

2.2. In this service God acknowledges that they *wrought for him* (v. 20). He set them at work to humble a proud city and its king, even though *they* who were employed in it *meant not so, neither did their heart think so* (Isa 10:7).

2.3. For this service he had *no wages*. He went to vast expense to capture Tyre, and he promised himself good plunder, but the Tyrians sent their best effects away by ship and threw the rest into the sea, so that the Babylonians had nothing but bare walls.

2.4. He will have the plunder of Egypt to reward him for his service against Tyre.

3. The mercy God had in store for the house of Israel. When the tide is at its highest point, it will turn, as it will when it is at its lowest. Nebuchadnezzar was at the height of his glory when he had conquered Egypt, but within a year of that he went mad (Da 4:28–37). When he was at the highest point, Israel was at its lowest, but *in that day the horn of the house of Israel shall bud forth*, on that day I will make a horn grow for the house of Israel (v. 21). Their restoration will begin with some small revival in the honor that will be done:

3.1. To their rulers; they are the *horns of the house of Israel*, the seat of their glory and power. These began to grow when Daniel and his fellows were greatly advanced in Babylon (Da 2:49). Within a year after the conquest of Egypt they were promoted, and soon afterward three of them were made famous by the honor God gave them by bringing them alive out of the burning fiery furnace (Da 3:20–26). This promise had its further fulfillment in the release of Jehoiachin king of Judah (Jer 52:31–32).

3.2. To their prophets: and *I will give thee the opening of the mouth*. Though none of Ezekiel's prophecies after this are recorded, we have reason to think he continued to prophesy, and with more liberty, when Daniel and his fellows were in power, ready to protect him.

CHAPTER 30

Here is: 1. A continuation of the prophecy against Egypt that was spoken just before the devastation of that once flourishing kingdom was completed by Nebuchadnezzar. In this prophecy the destruction of all Egypt's allies is foretold (vv. 1–19). 2. A repetition of a former prophecy against Egypt, spoken just before its devastation was begun by the bad conduct of its own people, which gradually weakened them and prepared the way for the king of Babylon (vv. 20–26).

Verses 1–19

The prophecy of the destruction of Egypt is very detailed.

1. It will be a lamentable destruction, one that will cause great sorrow (vv. 2–3). "You have your day now, when you are successful in all your undertakings and trample on everyone around you, but God will soon have his day. It will be *a cloudy day*, dark and dismal, and on it a storm will be seen threatening. *It shall be the time of the heathen*, a time of reckoning with the nations for all their pagan practices."

2. It will be the destruction of Egypt and of all the countries allied to her.

2.1. Egypt herself will fall (v. 4).

2.2. Her neighbors will fall with her. When those who are killed fall so thickly in Egypt, *great pain shall be in Ethiopia*, both the part in Africa and that in Asia. There were those of other countries who for some reason or another lived in Egypt, as did also *the men of the land that is in league* (v. 5), some of the remnants of the people of Israel and Judah, the *children of the covenant*, as they are called (Ac 3:25). These people stayed in Egypt against God's command, and these will *fall with them*.

3. All who claim to support the sinking interests of Egypt will fall with her (v. 6). Even *the multitude of Egypt shall be made to cease* (v. 10). That well-peopled country will be depopulated. Is the Nile River her support, and are its various streams a defense to her? *I will make the rivers dry* (v. 12). Are her idols a support to her? They will be destroyed. Is her royal family her support? *There shall be no more a prince in the land of Egypt*; the royal family will be uprooted. Is her courage her support? *I will put a fear in the land of Egypt*. Is the rising generation her support? Alas! *The young men shall fall by the sword* (v. 17), and *the daughters shall go into captivity* (v. 18), and so she will be robbed of all her hopes.

4. God will inflict these devastating judgments on Egypt (v. 8).

5. The king of Babylon and his army will be used as instruments of this destruction (v. 10). Those who undertook to protect Israel from the king of Babylon will not be able to protect themselves.

6. No place in the land of Egypt will be exempt from the rage of the Babylonian army, not the strongest or the most remote: *The sword shall go through the land.* Various places are named here: *Pathros* (Upper Egypt), *Zoan, and No* (Thebes) (v. 14); *Sin* (Pelusium) *and Noph* (Memphis) (vv. 15–16); *Aven and Phi-beseth* (Heliopolis and Bubastis) (v. 17); and *Tahpanhes* (v. 18). These will be devastated. The *pomp of their strength shall cease*, and *a cloud shall cover them*. The Ethiopians (Cush) who are far away from them, as well as those who are mixed in with them, will share in their pain and terror as well. The close of this prediction leaves:

• The land of Egypt humbled: *Thus will I execute judgments* (inflict punishment) *on Egypt* (v. 19).
• The God of Israel glorified: *They shall know that I am the Lord* (v. 19).

Verses 20–26

This short prophecy of the weakening of the power of Egypt was delivered about the time that the army of the Egyptians, which attempted to lift the siege of Jerusalem, was frustrated and returned without accomplishing its purpose.

1. It is foretold here that the king of Egypt will grow weaker and weaker.

1.1. This has partly been done already (v. 21): *I have broken the arm of Pharaoh.* One arm of that kingdom might well be considered broken when the king of Babylon routed the forces of Pharaoh Neco at Carchemish (Jer 46:2) and occupied *all that pertained to Egypt from the river of Egypt to Euphrates* (2Ki 24:7). Before Egypt's heart and neck were broken, its arm was.

1.2. This is to be done again. Now (v. 22), *I am against Pharaoh and will break both his arms.* The king of Egypt will be discouraged when he finds he is in danger from the king of Babylon's forces: *he shall groan before him with the groaning of a deadly wounded man* (v. 24). The people of Egypt will be dispersed (vv. 23, 26): *I will scatter them among the nations.*

2. It is foretold here that the king of Babylon will grow stronger and stronger (vv. 24–25).

CHAPTER 31

The prophecy of this chapter, like that of the two chapters before, is against Egypt and is designed to humble Pharaoh. Pharaoh stands accused for his pride and arrogance and for the wrongs he has done to God's people. He, however, thinks that he is too high to be accountable to any authority and too strong to be conquered. The prophet is therefore told to report to him the case of the king of Assyria, whose capital city was Nineveh. 1. He must show him how great a monarch the king of Assyria was, what a vast empire he had (vv. 3–9). 2. He must then show him how similar he is to the king of Assyria in pride (v. 10). 3. He must next read him the history of the downfall and ruin of the king of Assyria (vv. 11–17). 4. He must leave the king of Egypt to apply all this to himself, to see his own face in the mirror of the king of Assyria's sin and to foresee his own fall (v. 18).

Verses 1–9

This prophecy is dated the month before Jerusalem was taken; the one at the end of the previous chapter was dated about four months before. When God's people were in the depths of their distress, it would be some comfort to them to be told from heaven that the cup of God's wrath was being passed round, that it would soon be taken out of the hands of God's people and put into the hands of those who hated them (Isa 51:22–23).

1. The prophet is told to send Pharaoh to search for a case parallel to his own (v. 2). The falls of others, both into sin and into ruin, are intended to warn us not to be self-confident or *high minded*, nor to think we stand beyond any danger.

2. He is told to show him an example of one to whom he is similar in greatness (v. 3), and that is the king of Assyria. Sennacherib was one of the mighty rulers of that monarchy, but it sank soon after him, and the monarchy of Nebuchadnezzar was built on its ruins. The king of Assyria is compared here to a beautiful cedar (v. 3).

2.1. The Assyrian monarch was a tall cedar, of *high stature, his top among the thick boughs.* He surpassed all the rulers around him; they were all shrubs to him (v. 5):

His height was exalted above all the trees of the field; he towered over them all (v. 8).

2.2. He was also a spreading cedar, which shows that his territories were large; he extended his conquests far and his influences much further. His large dominions were well managed. His government was admirable in the eyes of all. In all the surrounding nations there was no ruler who was so much admired and courted as the king of Assyria.

2.3. He was useful for his shadow (v. 6). The *fowls* and the *beasts* took refuge under him, that is, *Under his shadow dwelt all great nations;* they all fled to him for safety and were willing to swear allegiance to him if he would undertake to protect them. But the greatest security that any created thing, even the king of Assyria himself, can give is only like the shadow of a tree, which is but scanty protection. God will take us *under the shadow of his wings,* where we will be warmer and safer than under the shadow of the strongest and stateliest cedar (Ps 17:8; 91:4).

2.4. He seemed to be established in his greatness and power. This cedar was not like the *heath in the desert, made to inhabit the parched places* (Jer 17:6); it was not a *root in a dry ground* (Isa 53:2). He had much wealth to support his power and grandeur (v. 4): *The waters made him great.* He had vast treasures, which were like *the deep that set him up on high, as rivers running round about his plants.* These enabled him to strengthen and protect his interests everywhere, for he *sent out his little rivers to all the trees of the field,* to water them; *their country was nourished by the king's country* (Ac 12:20), and they would be useful and faithful to him.

Verses 10–18

The king of Egypt resembles the king of Assyria in grandeur, power, and prosperity.

1. He also resembles him in his pride (v. 10). The same temptations of a prosperous state by which some are overcome are fatal to many others too. *"Thou, O king of Egypt! hast lifted up thyself in height,* hast been proud of thy wealth and power (29:3). And in just the same way, when the king of Assyria *shot up his top among the thick boughs,* he grew arrogant and imperious, defied God, and trampled on his people."* Notice, in his messages to Hezekiah (Isa 36:4–10; 2Ki 19:10–13), how proudly he spoke of his achievements!

2. He will therefore resemble him in his fall:

2.1. Here is the fall of the king of Assyria. Cyaxares, king of the Medes, together with Nebuchadnezzar king of Babylon, destroyed Nineveh, and with it the Assyrian Empire. Three things are affirmed about the Assyrian king:

2.1.1. It was God himself who ordered his ruin: *I have delivered him into the hand* of the executioner; *I have driven him out* (v. 11).

2.1.2. It was his own sin that led to his ruin: *I have driven him out for his wickedness.*

2.1.3. It was *a mighty one of the heathen* (ruler of the nations) who was the instrument of his ruin. In this history of the fall of the Assyrian king there is still the metaphor of the cedar. He grew very tall and extended his boughs very far, but his day to fall came. This beautiful cedar was dropped: *The terrible* (most ruthless) *of the nations have cut him off* (v. 12). They first lopped off his branches, cities or countries that were broken off from the Assyrian monarchy. He was deserted: *All the people of the earth* who had fled to him for shelter went *down from his shadow and left him. Upon his ruin shall all the fowls of the heaven remain;* they trod on the broken branches of this cedar. *All the trees of Eden* that had fallen before him, *all that drank water of* the rain of heaven, like the stump of the tree that is left in the *south* (Da 4:23), *shall be comforted in the nether parts of the earth* (v. 16); they were consoled when they saw this proud cedar brought as low as themselves. But the trees of Lebanon, those that were still standing, *mourned for him*, because they must have read their own destiny in his fall. The cutting down of this cedar represents the slaughter of this mighty monarch and all his supporters. God wanted to instill fear into surrounding nations (v. 16): *I made the nations to shake at the sound of his fall.* He also wanted to warn their kings (v. 14). It would have been well for Nebuchadnezzar, who was himself active in bringing down the Assyrian, if he had taken notice of the warning.

2.2. Here is a prophecy of the fall of the king of Egypt in a similar manner (v. 18).

CHAPTER 32

The destruction of Pharaoh and Egypt is expanded on. 1. Perhaps it looks as far back as the book of Genesis (Ge 15:14). 2. Perhaps it looks as far forward as the book of the Revelation, where we find that the great enemy of the Gospel church is figuratively called Egypt (Rev 11:8). If so, there is some analogy between this prophecy of the ruin of Egypt and the prophecy of the destruction of the anti-Christian generation. We have two distinct prophecies in this chapter relating to Egypt, both in the same month. They are both laments, to show how much the prophet himself would lament it out of a generous motive of love for the human race. The destruction is represented here using two similes: the killing of some devouring creature (vv. 1–16), and the funeral of a great commander (vv. 17–32).

Verses 1–16

Here:

1. The prophet is told to *take up a lamentation for Pharaoh king of Egypt* (v. 2).

2. He is told to show reasons for that lament.

2.1. Pharaoh has been a troubler of the nations, even his own nation. He is *like a young lion of the nations* (v. 2), threatening like a lion when it roars. He is like *a whale in the seas*, troublesome, like the *leviathan*, which *makes the deep to boil like a pot* (Job 41:31). When Pharaoh engaged in an unnecessary war with the Cyrenians, he *came forth with his rivers*, with his armies, *troubling the waters* and disturbing both his own kingdom and the neighboring nations.

2.2. He who has troubled other people must expect to be troubled himself, for the Lord is righteous (Jos 7:25).

2.2.1. This is set out by a simile. Is Pharaoh like *a great whale*? God has a net strong enough to hold him (v. 3): *I will spread my net over thee*, even the army of the Babylonians, *a company of many people. The flesh of* this great monster will be *laid upon the mountains* (v. 5), and the *valleys* will *be filled with his height.* So many of Pharaoh's soldiers will be killed that the dead bodies will be scattered on the hills and piled up in the valleys.

2.2.2. It is set out by a prophecy of the deep impression that the destruction of Egypt will make on the neighboring nations. When Pharaoh, who has been like a blazing, burning torch, is *put out* and *extinguished*, it will make everything around him look black (v. 7). The *hearts of* many people will be *vexed* (troubled) to see the word of the God of Israel fulfilled in the destruction of Egypt, and that all the *gods of Egypt* were not able to relieve it. It will fill them with wonder (v. 10): they will be *amazed* (appalled) *at thee*, will wonder to see such *great riches* and power *come to nothing* (Rev 18:17). It will fill them with fear. When others are ruined by sin, we have reason to shudder with terror, knowing ourselves guilty and liable to receive his punishment. It is the *sword of the king of Babylon* that will *come upon thee* (v. 11), the *swords of the mighty*, even the *terrible of the nations, all of them* (v. 12). The hordes of Egypt will be destroyed. The pride of Egypt will be spoiled. The cattle of Egypt, which used to feed by the rivers, will be destroyed (v. 13), either slaughtered by the sword or taken away as plunder. The *waters of Egypt*, which used to flow briskly, will now grow slow and heavy and will *run like oil* (v. 14), a figurative expression signifying that there will be such universal sadness and heaviness on the whole nation that even the rivers will flow softly and silently like mourners. The whole country of Egypt will be stripped of its wealth (v. 15), and *then shall they know that I am the Lord.*

Verses 17–32

This prophecy completes the oracle of Egypt.

1. Here we attend the funeral of that once flourishing kingdom.

1.1. This dead kingdom is brought to the grave. The prophet is told to foretell their destruction (v. 18). But he must foretell it as one with an affectionate concern for them; he must *wail for the multitude of Egypt*, even when he consigns them to the pit. When Egypt is put to death, let her have an honorable funeral; let her be buried *with the daughters of the famous nations.*

1.2. This corpse of a kingdom is welcomed to the grave, and Pharaoh is freely admitted to the assembly of the dead, but not without some pomp and ceremony. There lies the Assyrian Empire and all the rulers and leaders of that monarchy (v. 22). There lies the kingdom of Persia, which perhaps had been wasted and brought down within human memory at that time: *There is Elam and all her multitude*, the king of Elam and his numerous armies (vv. 24–25). There lies the Scythian power: Meshech and Tubal, those cruel northern nations, had recently launched an attack on the Medes, living among them and insisting on having the provision of free board and lodging for the troops for some years. Finally, however, Cyaxares, king of the Medes, made the invaders leave his country (v. 26). These Scythians are not buried with marks of honor, for *their iniquities shall be upon their sons.* There lies the kingdom of Edom, which flourished for a long time but was completely laid waste before the destruction of Egypt, as was foretold (25:13). Among the graves of the nations is Edom (v. 29). There lie the princes of the north and all the Sidonians. These were as familiar with maritime affairs as the Egyptians, who depended much on that part of their strength, but they have gone down with those who have been killed with the sword (v. 30). All this is applied to Pharaoh and the Egyptians, who have no reason to flatter themselves with hopes of peace when they see how the wisest, wealthiest, and strongest of their neighbors have been devastated (v. 28).

2. The view that this prophecy gives us of ruined states may show us something of this present world and the empire of death in it. People are ingenious at finding ways to destroy one another. It is not only a great pit but a great cockpit.

CHAPTER 33

The prophet now returns to his people. 1. He must let them know that he is a watchman and has received a commission concerning them (vv. 1–9). We have had the substance of this before (3:17). 2. He must let them know on what terms they stand with God, that they are on trial (vv. 10–20). 3. A particular message is sent to those who remain in the land of Israel (vv. 21–29). 4. A rebuke is given to those who personally listen to Ezekiel's ministry but are not sincere in their professions of devotion (vv. 30–33).

Verses 1–9

Now that Jerusalem has been captured, the prophet is appointed again to direct his speech to the Jews, and here his commission is renewed. We have here:

1. The position of a watchman established, the trust rested in him, and the commission given him (vv. 2, 6).

1.1. It is supposed that a public danger is what gives rise to the appointing of a watchman. When a country fears a foreign invasion, then, so that they may not be surprised, but may have early notice of it, so that they can give the invader a hostile reception, they *set a man of their coast* to be *their watchman* (v. 2). This will be some suitable person who lives on the borders of their country. One person may be of public service to a whole country.

1.2. It is supposed that public trust is lodged in the watchman and that he is accountable to the public for fulfilling his duties. If he fulfills his part, if he acts as "an early-warning system," he has fulfilled his trust and has not only saved himself but also earned his wages. If the people take no notice of the warning, it is their own fault. The blame is not to be laid on the watchman. If the watchman does not do his duty, and *blows not the trumpet* to *warn the people*, so that some are surprised and destroyed *in their iniquity* (v. 6), he will be found guilty because he did not *give warning*. However, if the watchman does his part and the people do theirs, all is well.

2. The application of this to the prophet (vv. 7, 9).

2.1. He is *a watchman to the house of Israel*. He has occasionally given warning to the surrounding nations, but his responsibility is to be a watchman to the house of Israel. They did not *set him for a watchman*, but God acted for them; he appointed a watchman for them.

2.2. His responsibility as a watchman is to give warning to sinners of their danger because of their sin. This is the word he must *hear from God's mouth* and *speak to them*. God has said, *The wicked man shall surely die* (v. 8). Unless he repents, he will be cut off from God. The wrath of God is revealed from heaven (Ro 1:18) not only against evil nations but also against evildoers. It is the will of God that the evildoer should be warned about this: *Warn them from me* (v. 7). This suggests there is a possibility of preventing the punishment; otherwise it would be foolish to give warning of it; God wants it to be prevented. It is the work of ministers to say to the evildoer, *It shall be ill with thee* (Isa 3:11). He must say this not in passion, to anger sinners, but in compassion, to *warn the wicked from his way*, warn him to *turn from it*, so that he may live.

2.3. If souls perish through the watchman's neglect of his duty, he brings guilt on himself.

2.4. If he does his duty, he may take comfort from it even if he is not successful (v. 9).

Verses 10–20

Notice here:

1. The complaints of the people against God's way of dealing with them. God had *set life before them* (Dt 30:15, 19), but they pleaded that he had set it beyond their reach. The prophet had said, *You shall pine away for your iniquities* (24:23), and they used this to rebuke him, as if it had been spoken to drive them to despair, whereas in reality it was spoken conditionally, to bring them to repentance. They said, *The way of the Lord is not equal* (just) (vv. 17, 20), suggesting that God showed favoritism in his ways and that he was more severe against sin and sinners than was reasonable.

2. A satisfactory answer given to both these complaints.

2.1. When they spoke of *pining away in their iniquity*, God quickly sent the prophet to them to tell them that there was still *hope in Israel*. God takes no delight in the ruin of sinners, nor does he desire it. They questioned whether they would *live*, even if they repented and reformed; "Yes," God says, "as sure *as I live*, true penitents will live also, for *their life is hid with Christ in God* (Col 3:3)." It is certain that if sinners die unrepentant, it is because of what they are in themselves; they die because they want to die.

2.2. If those who make the most credible profession of faith turn away from God, they will certainly perish forever in their apostasy from God, and if the most notorious sinners repent, they will certainly be happy forever in their return to God. These rules of judgment are so clearly just that they need no other confirmation than to be repeated. If those who have made a great profession of religious faith abandon their profession, the profession they made will do them no good (vv. 12–13, 18). Those who lead a consistently godly life will live. Surely such people must be happy. The righteous, who have very good hopes for themselves, are still in danger of sinning by trusting in their righteousness. Or they trust in the strength of their own righteousness, and so, presuming on their own sufficiency, they are led to commit sin. If those who have lived an evil life repent and reform, their sins will be forgiven and they will be justified and saved. In this way, even the threats of the word are to some, by the grace of God, the fragrance of life, while the promises of the word become to others, by their own corruption, the smell of death (2Co 2:16). There is many an evildoer who is hastening to destruction who is persuaded by the grace of God to return and repent. He *turns from his sin* (v. 14), and, as evidence of his repentance, he gives back what he took in pledge for a loan (v. 15) and returns what he has stolen and taken unjustly from the rich. Not only does he *cease to do evil*; he also *learns to do well* (Isa 1:16–17). In this good way, he perseveres *without committing iniquity*; though not free from weakness, he is not under the controlling power of any sin. He *shall surely live; he shall not die* (v. 15). And again (v. 16), *he shall surely live*. Again (v. 19), *he has done that which is lawful and right*, and *he shall live thereby*. Now that there is a settled separation between him and sin, there will be no longer a separation between him and God. *None of the sins that he has committed shall be mentioned unto him* (v. 16), either to hinder his pardon or as any lessening of the glory that has been prepared for him. The conclusion of the whole matter (Ecc 12:13) is v. 20: "*O you house of Israel*, even though you are all involved now in the common disaster, a distinction between people will be made in the spiritual and eternal state, and *I will judge you every one after his ways*."

Verses 21–29

Here we have:

1. The news brought to Ezekiel of the burning down of Jerusalem by the Babylonians. The city was burned in the eleventh year of the exile, in the fifth month (Jer 52:12–13). News was brought to the prophet a year and almost five months later by one who was an eyewitness to the destruction (v. 21). This was the first time he had an account of it from a refugee, one who escaped.

2. The divine influences he was under to prepare him for this bad news (v. 22): *The hand of the Lord was upon me before he came, and had opened my mouth* to speak to the house of Israel. He prophesied now with greater freedom and boldness. Now *the hand of the Lord came upon him*, renewed his commission, gave him fresh instructions, and *opened his mouth*, giving him power to speak to the people *as he ought to speak* (Eph 6:20).

3. The particular message he was entrusted with, about the Jews who still remained in the *land of Israel, inhabiting the wastes* of that land (v. 24). A few who had escaped the sword and exile still continued to live there and began to think about settling down there again. Here we have:

3.1. An account of the pride of these remaining Jews who lived in the ruins of the land of Israel. Although the providence of God concerning them had been very humbling and was still very threatening, they still were unbearably haughty: *They said, "The land is given us for inheritance* (v. 24). Because our partners have gone, it now all belongs to us; we have it all to ourselves." They thought they could conclude that they were as entitled by God to have this land as Abraham was: "If God *gave this land* to him, who was only one worshiper of him, as a reward of his service, then surely much more will be given it to us, who are many worshipers of him, as the reward of our service."

3.2. A restraint to this pride. Since God's providences neither humbled them nor terrified them, he sends them a message sufficient to do both. To humble them, he tells them of the evil they still persist in, which makes them completely unworthy to possess this land. "You have no scruples about eating forbidden fruit, forbidden food: *You eat with the blood* (v. 25). Idolatry is still the sin that most easily entangles you (Heb 12:1). You are as fierce, cruel, and barbaric as ever: *You shed* innocent *blood*. You trust in your own strength: *You stand upon your sword* (v. 26). You think you will triumph over everything within sight by sheer force of arms. You are guilty of all manner of detestable practices. Especially, *you defile every one his neighbour's wife* (v. 26), *and shall you possess the land?*" To terrify them, the prophet tells them of the further judgments God has in store for them. Those people who live in the cities, here called the *wastes*, will *fall by the sword*, either by the sword of the Babylonians or by one another's swords. Those who are in the open field will be *devoured by* wild *beasts*. Those who are *in the forts* (strongholds) *and in the caves*, who think they are safe in artificial or natural strongholds, will *die of the pestilence* (v. 27).

Verses 30–33

Those who are now in exile in Babylon are rebuked; they are under divine rebukes but have not been reformed by them. They have made some show of religious faith and devotion, but their hearts are not right with God. What they are accused of here is *mocking the messengers of the Lord* (2Ch 36:16). They mocked the prophet Ezekiel in two ways:

1. By invidious, ill-natured reflections on him, privately among themselves. The prophet does not realize it, but God comes and tells him, *The children of thy people are still talking against thee* (v. 30). Those who can make the preaching and hearing of the word of God a matter of fun and ridicule have reached a great level of ungodliness, even if they do it in private conversation.

2. By deceiving him in their attendance on his ministry. Hypocrites mock God and mock his prophets. Notice here:

2.1. The plausible profession that these people make. They are like those (Mt 15:8) who *draw nigh to God with their mouths and honour him with their lips, but their hearts are far from him.* They are diligent and constant in being present at the means of grace: *They come unto thee as the people come* (v. 31). In Babylon they have no temple or synagogue, but they go to the prophet's house (8:1). Now these hypocrites come, *according to the coming of the people*, as properly and as early as any of the prophet's hearers. They behave themselves very decently and reverently in the public assembly. They listen very attentively to the word that is preached. They pretend to show great kindness and respect for the prophet. Although behind his back they do not have a good word to say for him, *they show much love* to him and his teaching to his face. They take great delight in the word. Ezekiel is to them like one *that has a pleasant voice* and can sing well *or* can *play well on an instrument*. People may have their own desires satisfied by the word but not have their consciences touched or their hearts changed; the itching ear is gratified (2Ti 4:3), but the corrupt nature is not sanctified.

2.2. The hypocrisy of these claims and professions. While they *show much love*, it is only *with the mouth*, from the teeth outward; *their heart goes after their covetousness* (v. 31). They are as much attached to the world as ever. They *hear thy words*, but it is a mere hearing, for they *do them not*, do not put them into practice (v. 31).

2.3. What it will lead to: *Shall their unbelief* and carelessness *make the word of God of no effect?* (Ro 3:3–4; Mk 7:13). No. God will confirm the prophet's word, even though they make light of it (v. 33). When it actually takes place, *they shall know* to their cost that *a prophet has been among them*, even though they made nothing more of him than to say that he was one who *had a pleasant voice*.

CHAPTER 34

In this chapter the shepherds of Israel, their rulers both in church and in state, are called to account. Here is: 1. A great accusation brought against them for their negligence and unfaithfulness in managing public affairs (vv. 1–6 and again v. 8). 2. Their discharge from their trust (vv. 7–10). 3. A gracious promise that God would take care of his flock, even though they did not (vv. 11–16). 4. Another accusation, this one against those of the flock who were strong, for the wrongs they did to those who were weak (vv. 17–22). 5. Another promise, that God would in the fullness of time send the Messiah to be the great and good Shepherd of the sheep (Heb 13:20; Jn 10:14), who would set everything right with the flock (vv. 23–31).

Verses 1–6

The prophecy of this chapter is not dated, nor any of those that follow it, until ch. 40.

1. The prophet is ordered to *prophesy against the shepherds of Israel* (v. 2)—the rulers and judges, the priests

and Levites, especially the kings, for there were two now in exile in Babylon, who, as well as the people, must have their sins shown them, so that they might repent. *Woe to the shepherds of Israel!* Although they are shepherds of Israel, the prophet still must not spare them.

2. They are charged with two things:

2.1. That they are concerned only with advancing themselves, enriching themselves, and making themselves great. *Should not the shepherds feed the flocks?* (v. 2). They betray their trust if they do not. But *these* shepherds *feed themselves*, working at every possible means of satisfying and indulging their own appetites. They make sure they obtain the fleece and *clothe themselves with the wool.*

2.2. That they are not concerned about the benefit and welfare of those who are committed to their responsibility: *You feed not the flock* (v. 3). The rulers and judges show no concern for those who suffer wrong by putting things right for them. They do not look after the poor. The priests show no concern for the ignorant; they do not instruct them. The ministers of state are unconcerned about, and unwilling to restrain, the growing tensions within the kingdom. They are not concerned enough to fulfill their duty to those of the flock who have been driven away by enemies and forced to seek shelter wherever they could, or who *wander* by choice on *the mountains and hills* (v. 5). The reason these sheep are *scattered* is that *there is no shepherd* (v. 5). Christ complains that his flock are *as sheep having no shepherd* (Mt 9:36), although the scribes and Pharisees *sat in Moses' seat* (Mt 23:2).

Verses 7–16

Notice here:

1. How very displeased God is with the shepherds. Their crimes are repeated (v. 8). God's flock were plundered by the deceivers who drew them to idolatry and by the destroyers who took them into exile, and these shepherds were not concerned to prevent either the one or the other. God is *against them*, and they will realize it. They will be made responsible for the way in which they have discharged their trust: "*I will require my flock at their hands* (v. 10) and hold them accountable for letting so many of them become missing." *They shall cease from feeding the flock* (v. 10), that is, from pretending to feed it. *Neither shall the shepherds feed themselves any more.*

2. How very concerned God is for the flock, for *with him the fatherless finds mercy* (Hos 14:3). The precious promises made here were to have their fulfillment in the return of the Jews from exile and their reestablishment in their own land. Let the shepherds *hear this word of the Lord* and know that they have no share in the matter (Ac 8:21).

2.1. God will gather together his sheep that were scattered, and he will bring back to the fold those who had wandered from it. "*I will both search my sheep and find them out* (v. 11), as *a shepherd* does (v. 12), and bring them back as a shepherd brings back on his shoulders the sheep that have gone astray, *from all the places where they have been scattered in the cloudy and dark day.*" God will both incline their hearts to come by his grace and open a door for them by his providence, and remove every difficulty that lies in the way. *I will seek that which was lost and bring again that which was driven away* (v. 16). This was done when so many thousand Jews returned triumphantly from Babylon under the leadership of Zerubbabel, Ezra, and others.

2.2. God will bring the returning captives safely to their own land (v. 13) and *feed them upon the mountains*

of Israel, and that is *a good pasture, a fat pasture* (v. 14). *Their fold* (grazing land) will be there, and it is good. There God will *cause them to lie down* (v. 15), which shows that, their wanderings over, they will have rest and a continuing home.

2.3. He will help those who are hurt, *binding up that which was broken, strengthening that which was sick* (v. 16), and comforting those that *mourn in Zion* and with Zion.

Verses 17–31

The prophet now has a message to communicate to the flock. God has told him to speak tenderly to them and assure them of the mercy he has in store for them. But here he is told to differentiate between the worthy and the worthless (Jer 15:19) and then give them a promise of the Messiah. Here is:

1. Conviction declared to those of the flock who are sleek and strong, the *rams and the he goats* (v. 17), those who, though they do not have the power of shepherds and rulers, yet, because they are rich and wealthy, make use of the opportunity that their wealth gives them to be harsh toward their poor neighbors. *The rams* and the *he goats* not only keep all the good pasture to themselves but also will not let the poor of the flock have any enjoyment of the little that is left for them; they *tread down the residue of the pastures and foul the residue* (muddy the rest) *of the waters* (vv. 18–19). They not only rob the poor to make them poorer but also trouble the sick and weak of the flock (v. 21).

2. Comfort promised to those of the flock who are poor and feeble and who wait for the consolation of Israel (Lk 2:25) (v. 22): "*I will save my flock*, and they will no more be attacked by the wild animals, by their own shepherds, or by the rams and goats among themselves." On this occasion, as is usual in the prophets, there comes a prediction of the coming of the Messiah and the setting up of his kingdom. Notice what is foretold:

2.1. About the Messiah himself. He will have his commission from God: I will *set him up* (v. 23); *I will raise him up* (v. 29). He will be the great *Shepherd* of the sheep (Heb 13:20), who will do for his flock what no one else could do. He is the *one Shepherd*, under whom Jews and Gentiles will be *one fold* (Jn 10:16). He is *God's servant* to reestablish his kingdom. He is David, one after God's own heart (1Sa 13:14), set as his king on the holy hill of Zion (Ps 2:6), made the capstone (Ps 118:22), with whom the royal covenant is made (2Sa 7:5–16), and to whom God will *give the throne of his father David* (Lk 1:32). He is the *plant of renown*, because he is a *righteous branch* (Jer 23:5), *beautiful* and *glorious* (Isa 4:2). Some understand this to refer to the church, the *planting of the Lord* (Isa 61:3).

2.2. About the great charter by which the kingdom of the Messiah will be founded (v. 25): *I will make with them a covenant of peace.* The covenant of grace is a covenant of peace. The thrust of this covenant is, "*I the Lord will be their God*, a God who is all-sufficient for them (v. 24)." Those, and only those, who have the Lord Jesus as *their prince* have the Lord Jehovah as *their God.*

2.3. About the privileges of those who are the faithful subjects of this kingdom of the Messiah. These privileges are set out here figuratively, as the blessings of the flock. But we have a key to it in v. 31. Those who belong to this flock, even though they are spoken of as sheep, are really people.

2.3.1. They will enjoy a holy security under divine protection. Christ, our good Shepherd, has rid the land of evil animals (v. 25), having defeated all our spiritual enemies. Sin and Satan, death and hell, are conquered. And now the Messiah's subjects will live in safety, not only in good grazing land but also in the fields, in the desert, in the woods. Through Christ, God rescues his people not only from the things they have reason to fear but also from their fear even of death itself.

2.3.2. They will enjoy a spiritual plenty of all good things. They will no longer be consumed with hunger in the land (v. 29). Showers of blessings will come on them (vv. 26–27). The heavens will yield their dews (Zec 8:12); the trees of the field will also yield their fruit. All who are near Zion will live better for it; the nearer the church, the nearer its God. The effect of this plenty is, *I will make them a blessing* (v. 26); they will be blessings to everyone around them. Those who are the blessed of the Lord must seek to make themselves blessings to the world. Those who are good should do good; those who have received the gift, the grace, should serve one another with it (1Pe 4:10).

CHAPTER 35

This chapter enlarges on the promise concerning the destruction of the enemies of the church; the next chapter on the promise concerning the filling of the church with blessings. Mount Seir (that is, Edom) is the enemy prophesied against in this chapter, but it is appropriately used here, as in the prophecy of Obadiah, to represent all the enemies of the church. We have here: 1. The sin of the Edomites are accused of, which is their hatred toward Israel (vv. 10–13). 2. The ruin threatened: God will be against them (v. 2), and then their country will be ruined (v. 4), made completely desolate (vv. 6–9), and left like that when other nations that have been devastated will recover (vv. 14–15).

Verses 1–9

Mount Seir was associated with Moab in one of the threats we had before (25:8), but here it has woes of its own. The prophet must let the Edomites know:

1. Why God is against them (v. 5). God embraces his people's cause and takes what is done against them as done against himself. It is on their account, therefore, that God now accuses the Edomites:

1.1. Because of the enmity they have against the people of God. "You have had *a perpetual hatred* (ancient hostility) toward them, toward the very name of an Israelite." The Edomites have maintained a *hereditary* hatred against Israel, the same that Esau bore to Jacob. The descendants of Esau would never be reconciled to the descendants of Jacob. It is strange how deeply rooted national hatred sometimes is, and how long it lasts.

1.2. Because of the wrongs they have done to the people of God. They have not attacked them as fair and open enemies, but have lain in wait for them, to *cut off* those of them who escaped (Ob 14).

2. What the effect and outcome of God's challenge against them will be. If God stretches out his hand against the country of Edom, he *will make it most desolate* (v. 3). *Thou hast not hated blood* (v. 6) implies, "You have delighted in it and thirsted after it." Some read it, "Unless thou hatest blood (that is, unless you repent and put away this disposition to shed blood), *blood shall pursue thee.*" Those who help forward the desolation of Israel may expect to be made desolate themselves. And what completes the judgment is that Edom will be made *perpetual desolations*, desolate for ever (v. 9).

Verses 10–15

Here is:

1. A further account of the sin of the Edomites, their bad behavior toward the people of God. Elsewhere we find the church complaining about them for siding with the Babylonians and encouraging them to act against Jerusalem, saying, *Rase it, rase it* (Ps 137:7), inflaming a rage that needed no encouragement. Here they are further charged with gloating over Jerusalem's ruin and the desolation of the country. They pleased themselves with the hope that when the people of Israel were destroyed, they would be allowed to possess their country. Those who desire the death of others because they hope to gain by it, or who are pleased with their failures because they expect to inherit their possessions, have the spirit of Edomites. But in this case of the Edomites' coveting and seeking the land of Israel, there was a particular insult to God. They expected possession when the land became vacant, because Israel was driven out, *whereas the Lord was* still *there* (v. 10). It was Immanuel's land (Isa 8:8); he was to be born in it.

2. The notice God took of the cruel arrogance of the Edomites, and the doom passed on them for it: *I have heard all thy blasphemies* (contemptible words) (v. 12). And again (v. 13), *You have multiplied your words against me* (spoken against me without restraint), and *I have heard them.* God has heard the Edomites' contemptible words; let them therefore hear their doom (vv. 14–15). It was a national sin, and so they will be punished by a national desolation. The punishment will correspond to the sin: "*As thou didst rejoice in the desolation of the house of Israel,* God will give you an excess of desolation; since you are so fond of it, *thou shalt be desolate*; *I will make thee so.*" Some read v. 14 so as to complete the correspondence between the sin and the punishment: "The whole earth will rejoice when I make you desolate, as you rejoiced when Israel was made desolate."

CHAPTER 36

This chapter contains two distinct prophecies: 1. One concerning the physical state of the Jews, in which their present deplorable condition is described, but it is promised that their grievances will be dealt with and that in due time they will resettle in their own land, surrounded by peace and plenty (vv. 1–15). 2. Another concerning their spiritual state, in which they are reminded of their former sins (vv. 16–20), but it is promised: 2.1. That God will glorify himself by showing mercy to them (vv. 21–24). 2.2. That he will sanctify them by giving them his grace and making them fit for his service, in answer to their prayers (vv. 25–38).

Verses 1–15

Now that God is returning in mercy, the prophet must speak good and encouraging words (v. 1 and again v. 4). *You mountains of Israel, hear the word of the Lord,* and what he says to them he says *to the hills, to the rivers, to the valleys, to the desolate wastes* in the country, and to the cities *that are forsaken* (v. 4 and again v. 6). The people are gone; nothing remains to be spoken to except for the places, the mountains and valleys; the Babylonians could not take these away with them. To show the mercy God has in reserve for the people, the prophet is to speak of him as having a dormant kindness for the place. We have here:

1. The compassionate notice God takes of the present deplorable condition of the land of Israel. It has become both *a prey and a derision to the heathen* (plundered and ridiculed by the nations) *that are round about* (v. 4).

1.1. They are all enriched with its spoils. No one thought it any crime to strip an Israelite. It is commonly cried out, when someone is down, "Down with him!"

1.2. It has been ridiculed by them. *The enemy said, "Aha! Even the ancient high places are ours in possession* (v. 2)." God takes notice of it here to emphasize the present calamity of Israel: *You are taken up in the lips of talkers and are an infamy of the people* (v. 3).

2. The expressions of God's just displeasure against those who have gloated over the devastation of the land of Israel, especially Edom.

2.1. They carved out large possessions for themselves from God's land, for that is what it was: "*They have appointed my land into their possession* (v. 5), and so not only invaded their neighbor's property but also infringed God's rights." Those who did not have an opportunity to plunder God's people scorned them, which meant that they were *the shame of the heathen* (v. 6).

2.2. God has decided to judge them for it, and this *in the fire of his jealousy* (burning zeal), both for his own honor and for the honor of his people (v. 5). In their malice, these enemies spoke against God's people, and so God will speak *in his jealousy and in his fury* (v. 6). *Surely the heathen that are about you, they shall bear their shame* (will also suffer scorn).

3. The promises of God's favor to his Israel and assurances given of great mercy in store for them. The prophet must say to the *mountains of Israel*, now *desolate and despised*, that God is *for them* and will *turn to them* (v. 9). Their rightful owners will return to possess them: *My people Israel are at hand to come* (v. 8). Though dispersed in many countries, they will *come again to their own border* (Jer 31:17). The time is at hand for them to return. The mountains of Israel are now desolate, but God will *cause men to walk upon them* again, *even his people Israel*, not as travelers, but as inhabitants. Canaan here was a type of the heavenly Canaan, to which all God's children are heirs. When the land had *enjoyed her sabbaths* for so many years, she would be all the more fruitful. *You shall be tilled and sown* (v. 9) and will *yield your fruit to my people Israel* (v. 8). The people of Israel will have a comfortable settlement in their own land: the *cities shall be inhabited; the wastes shall be builded* (v. 10). And *I will settle you after your old estates* (v. 11). *I will do better unto you* now *than at your beginnings*. God will bring back to the land *all the house of Israel, even all of it*—notice the emphasis placed on that (v. 10)—all *whose spirits God stirred up* to return (Ex 35:21; Ezr 1:1–3; Hag 1:14). God's kingdom in the world is a growing kingdom, and his church, though for a time it may decrease in numbers, will recover and be replenished. The reproach long ago given to the land of Israel by the faithless spies, and recently revived, that *it is a land that eats up the inhabitants* of it (Nu 13:32) by famine, sickness, and the sword, will be completely rolled away (Jos 5:9). *Thou shalt no more bereave them of men* (never again deprive them of their children) (v. 12), will no longer devour people (v. 14). When the nation is made to flourish in peace (v. 15), then its people *hear no more the shame of the heathen* (v. 15), especially when it is reformed. When sin is taken away, then they *hear no more the reproach of the people*.

Verses 16–24

We read here:

1. How God's name had suffered both from the sins and from the miseries of Israel.

1.1. God's glory had been dishonored by the sin of Israel when they were in their own land (v. 17). It was a good land, a land that had the eye of God watching over it. *But they defiled it by their own way.* What was unclean could not be used. By abusing the gifts of God's goodness, we lose the right to use them, and because the mind and conscience are defiled with guilt, no comfort is given to us, *nothing is pure* to us (Tit 1:15). They *shed blood and worshiped idols* (v. 18) and with those sins *defiled the land*. This was why God *poured out his fury* on them, *scattered them among the heathen*. God was righteous in this, for *he judged them according to their way and according to their doings* (v. 19).

1.2. When they *entered into the land of the heathen* (went among the nations), God gained no glory from them there; on the contrary, his holy name was profaned (v. 20). The enemies of God used that as an opportunity to pour scorn on God, as a God who was unable to protect his own worshipers and give the gifts he had promised.

2. How God would restore his honor by bringing a great reformation on them and then bringing a great salvation for them. "*I will gather you out of all countries and bring you into your own land* (v. 24). *Not for your sake*, for you are most unworthy, but *for my holy name's sake* (v. 22), so that *I may sanctify my great name*" (v. 23).

Verses 25–38

The people of God had cause to be discouraged in their hopes of a restoration by the sense not only of their unworthiness but also of their unfitness. That objection is resolved in these verses with the promise that God, by his grace, would prepare them for the mercy and then give it. And this was partly fulfilled in that wonderful effect which the exile in Babylon had on the Jews there, that it effectively cured them of their inclination to idolatry.

1. God promises here that he will perform a good work in them (vv. 25–27).

1.1. He will cleanse them from the defilement of sin (v. 25): *I will sprinkle clean water upon you*, which represents both the blood of Christ, sprinkled on the conscience to purify it and take away the sense of guilt, and the grace of the Spirit, sprinkled on the whole soul to purify it from all corrupt inclinations, as Naaman was cleansed from his leprosy by dipping himself in the Jordan (2Ki 5:14). *I will save you from all your uncleannesses* (v. 29).

1.2. He will give them *a new heart* (v. 26), an inner disposition vastly different from what it was before.

1.3. To replace their *heart of stone* (v. 26), a heart that is insensitive and disinclined to receive divine influences and respond with heartfelt devotion, he will give *a heart of flesh*, a soft, tender, responsive heart, one that has spiritual senses exercised, submitting in everything to the will of God.

1.4. Because, in addition to our inclination to sin, we also complain about our inability to do our duty, God *will cause them to walk in his statutes* (v. 27), and thoroughly supply them with the wisdom, the will, and the active powers they need for every good work.

2. God promises here that he will take them into covenant with himself. We have here the essence of the covenant of grace (v. 28).

3. When they are prepared for mercy, they will return to their possessions and be resettled in them (v. 28): *You*

shall dwell in the land that I gave to your fathers. This will follow on the blessed reformation God will work among them (v. 33): "*In the day that I shall have cleansed you from all your iniquities*, and so will have made you fit for the inheritance, *I will cause you to dwell in the cities and so give you possession of the inheritance.*" And this is indeed God's way of showing mercy: first to separate people from their sins and then to restore them to their comforts. Then they will enjoy a plentiful supply of all good things. *I will call for the corn and will increase it* (v. 29). The land that has long *lain desolate in the sight of all that passed by*, all who looked at it, some with contempt and some with compassion, will again *be tilled* (v. 34). God will command such a blessing (Ps 133:3) on the *hand of the diligent* (Pr 10:4) that all who pass by will wonder and take notice of it (v. 35). Crowds are a lovely sight in God's temple.

4. He shows what will be the good effects of this blessed change. It will bring them to frank repentance for their sins (v. 31): *Then shall you remember your own evil ways and shall loathe yourselves.* It will have a beneficial effect on their neighbors, too, for it will bring them to a clearer knowledge of God (v. 36).

5. He proposes these things to them not as the reward of their merits, but as the response to their prayers. They must acknowledge that the mercies they receive from God are not only not merited but also a thousand times forfeited. They must be so far from boasting about their good works that they must be ashamed of their evil ways, and that is the best preparation for mercy. When God is coming toward his people in his mercy, he requires them to *seek him*. They must pray for it, for God is sought through prayer.

CHAPTER 37

The promises of restoration that we have here toward the end of the book are to encourage a humble faith. God had assured them that he would gather all the house of Israel to return them to their own land. There were two things, however, that made this very unlikely: 1. That they were so dispersed among their enemies and so discouraged in their own minds. For these reasons, they are here, in a vision, compared to a valley full of the dry bones of the dead, which would be brought together and raised to life. We have a vision of this (vv. 1–10) and its explanation, with its application to the present situation (vv. 11–14). 2. That they were so divided among themselves, since too much of the ancient enmity between Judah and Ephraim remained even in exile. But a sign of two sticks made into one in the hand of the prophet is made to show the happy reunion there would be between the two nations of Israel and Judah on their return (vv. 15–22). This is a type of the uniting of Jews and Gentiles, Jews and Samaritans, in Christ and his church. And so the prophet moves into a prediction of the kingdom of Christ (vv. 23–28).

Verses 1–14

Here is:

1. The vision of resurrection from death to life.

1.1. It is without doubt a most vivid representation of a threefold resurrection:

1.1.1. The resurrection of souls from the death of sin to the life of righteousness, to a holy, heavenly, spiritual, and divine life, by the power of divine grace accompanying the word of Christ (Jn 5:24–25).

1.1.2. The resurrection of the Gospel church from a state of suffering and persecution to liberty and peace.

1.1.3. The resurrection of the body at the great day, especially the bodies of believers, which will rise to eternal life.

1.2. Let us consider the details of this vision:

1.2.1. The wretched condition of these dead bones. The prophet was, in a vision, taken and set *in the midst of a valley*, probably the plain spoken of in 3:22, and there God then *talked with him*, and it was *full of bones*, of dead human bones, scattered on the face of the ground, as if some battle had been fought there, blood had been shed, and those killed had been left unburied. Nothing was left but the bones, separate from one another and scattered. *Lo, they were very dry* (v. 2), having long been exposed to the sun and wind. The Jews in Babylon were like those dead, dry bones, unlikely ever to come together again, less likely to become a body, and least of all a living body. He was made to acknowledge that their case was deplorable and could not be helped by any power less than that of God himself (v. 3): "*Son of man, can these bones live?* Can your knowledge of nature reach so far as to put life into dry bones, or your knowledge of politics to restore a captive nation?" "Lord, you know whether they can and whether they will; if you do not put life into them, they certainly cannot live."

1.2.2. The means used to bring these scattered bones together, to enable these dead and dry bones to live. Ezekiel was ordered to *prophesy upon these bones* (v. 4 and again v. 9), to *prophesy to the wind*. So he *prophesied as he was commanded* (vv. 7, 10). He must preach, and he did so, and the dead bones came alive by a power that accompanied the word of God that he preached. He must pray, and he did so, and the dead bones came alive in answer to prayer, for *a spirit of life* entered into them. Notice the power of the word and prayer, and the need for both, to raise dead souls. God's ministers must *prophesy upon the dry bones*. But we call in vain and they remain dead: they are still very dry. We must therefore plead with God in prayer for the working of the Spirit with the word: *Come, O breath*, and breathe on them! God's grace can save souls without our preaching, but our preaching cannot save them without God's grace, and that grace must be sought by prayer.

1.2.3. The wonderful effect of these means. Those who do as they are commanded in the face of the greatest discouragements need not doubt they will be successful. Ezekiel looked down and prophesied on the bones in the valley, and they became human bodies.

1.2.3.1. What he had to *say to them* was that God would infallibly raise them to life (vv. 5–6).

1.2.3.2. What was immediately done for them was that they were molded once again into shape. Even dead and dry bones begin to move when they are called to hear the word of the Lord. This was fulfilled when, on Cyrus's declaration of liberty, those whose spirits God had stirred (Ezr 1:5) began to think of using that liberty and getting ready to go.

1.2.3.2.1. But this was not all: *The bones came together, bone to his bone*, under divine direction, and although as human beings we have many bones, of all the bones of those many people who had been killed not one was missing. Not one missed its place; each knew and found its fellow bone. The scattered bones came together, and the displaced bones were knit together. This is what it was like at the return of the Jews; those who were scattered to different parts of the province of Babylon came to their respective families.

1.2.3.2.2. Gradually, *sinews* (tendons) and *flesh* came on these bones, and the *skin covered them* (v. 8). This was fulfilled when the exiles gathered their belongings around them and the *men of their place helped them* with *silver* and *gold* and whatever they needed for their move (Ezr 1:4). But still there was *no breath in them*; they lacked the spirit and courage for such a difficult and hazardous enterprise as returning to their own land. Ezekiel then looked up and prophesied to the *wind*, or *breath*, or *spirit*, and said, *Come, O breath, and breathe upon these slain!* (v. 9). In answer to this request, *the breath* immediately came *into them* (v. 10). The spirit of life is from God; the One who at first breathed into human beings the breath of life in creation will also do so at the resurrection. The discouraged exiles were animated with determination to break through all the discouragements that lay in the path of their return. And then they *stood upon their feet, an exceedingly great army*, not only living human beings, but also effective, equipped for service, and formidable.

2. The application of this vision to the present disastrous condition of the Jews in exile: *These bones are the whole house of Israel* (v. 11), both the ten tribes and the two. Notice:

2.1. The depth of despair to which they are now reduced. When troubles continue for a long time, with all hope frustrated, nothing but an active, living faith in the power, promises, and providence of God will keep the spirit from completely fading away and dying.

2.2. "*Therefore*, because things have come to such a critical point, *prophesy to them* and tell them that now is God's time to appear for them. *Jehovah-jireh* (Ge 22:14): 'on the mount of the Lord it shall be seen'" (vv. 12–14).

Verses 15–28

Precious promises are made here concerning the favorable state of the Jews after their return to their own land, but they also have a further reference to the kingdom of the Messiah and the glories of Gospel times. It is promised here:

1. That Ephraim and Judah will be happily united. Ever since the desertion of the ten tribes from the house of David under Jeroboam, there has been continual feud and animosity between the two kingdoms of Israel and Judah, even in exile. Now there will be a coalition between them. This is illustrated here by a sign. The prophet is to take *two sticks*, and he is to write on one, *For Judah* (including Benjamin, those of the *children of Israel* that were *his companions*), and on the other, *For Joseph*, including the rest of the tribes (v. 16). These two sticks must be brought together in such a way as to fall into *one in his hand* (v. 17). The meaning is that Judah and Israel will become *one in the hand of God* (v. 19).

1.1. They will be one nation (v. 22). They will set aside their separate interests and so will have no divided desires. They have been two sticks crossing and thwarting each other, beating and bruising each other, but now they will become one, supporting and strengthening each other.

1.2. They will be one in *God's hand* (v. 19); they will be united by his power. They will be one in his hand, for his glory will be the center of their unity and his grace the cement that joins them.

1.3. They will be one in their return from exile (v. 21). Their having suffered jointly will contribute to this blessed act of coming together. If you put many pieces of metal together into a furnace, when they have melted, they will all fuse together. God's loving them all was a good reason why they should love each other.

1.4. They will all be the subjects of one king, and so they will become one. After the Jews returned, they were under one government, and were not divided as formerly. But this certainly looks further, to the kingdom of Christ; he is that one King in submission to whom all God's spiritual Israel will cheerfully unite.

2. That the Jews will be cured of their tendency to idolatry by their exile (v. 23). God will use two ways to cure them of their idolatry: bringing them out of the temptation to commit it and changing their attitude: "*I will cleanse them*" (v. 23).

3. That they will be the people of God and the subjects and sheep of Christ their King and Shepherd. These promises are repeated here (vv. 23–24) to encourage the faith of Israel. *David, my servant, shall be king over them.* Christ is this David, Israel's King of old.

4. That they will live comfortably (vv. 25–26). They will live in the land of Israel. They will have it by covenant; they will be restored to their previous entitlement because of the gift made to *Jacob*, God's *servant*. They will come to it by a claim founded on their ancestors' long-held previous possession. It was the inheritance of their ancestors, and so it will be theirs. They are *beloved for their fathers' sakes* (Ro 11:28). *They shall dwell therein* all their time and leave it as an inheritance *to their children and their children's children for ever*. And they will live under a good government.

5. That God will live among them: *I will set my sanctuary in the midst of them for evermore; my tabernacle also shall be with them* (vv. 26–27). They will have the opportunity of having fellowship with God, which will bring encouragement and strength to their lives. They will enjoy the means of grace. They will be made wiser and better people through the word of God in his tabernacle, and all their children will be taught by the Lord. In this way, their covenant relationship with God will be made the most of and its commitments strengthened.

6. That both God and Israel will have the honor of this among the nations (v. 26). "The very nations will be made to understand that *the Lord sanctifies* Israel, because his sanctuary is, and will be, among them."

CHAPTER 38

This chapter and the one that follows it concern Gog and Magog, a powerful enemy of the people of Israel. They would launch an attack on Israel, but their army and their plans would be defeated. This prophecy was most probably fulfilled after the return of the people of Israel, in the struggles they had with the kings of Syria (Aram), especially Antiochus Epiphanes, or in some other way. Through the prophet, God had assured his people of happy times after their return to their own land, but he told them here, as Christ told his disciples, that they would have trouble in the world, but they should take heart, for they would be victorious ultimately (Jn 16:33). But the Old Testament prophecies had their fulfillment in the Jewish church as the New Testament prophecies will have theirs, when the time comes, in the Christian church. We have here: 1. The attempt that Gog and Magog would make to attack the land of Israel: the vast army they would bring onto the battlefield, their immense preparations (vv. 4–7), their plans and purposes in it (vv. 8–13), and God's hand in it (vv. 4, 17). 2. The great terror that this would strike on the land of Israel (vv. 15–16, 18–20). 3. The divine protection that Israel would be under (vv. 2–4 and again v. 14). 4. The defeat that would be given to those enemies by the direct hand of God (vv. 21–23).

Verses 1–13

The commentators have their work cut out to identify Gog and Magog. Some think they are to be identified as distant nations in Scythia, Tartary, and Russia. Others think they are to be identified nearer the land of Israel, in Syria (*Aram*) and Asia Minor. Gog seems to be the king and Magog the kingdom. Ezekiel is appointed to prophesy against Gog and tell him that *God is against him* (vv. 2–3). Let us notice:

1. The confusion that God intends to put this enemy in. It is remarkable that this is put first in the prophecy; before it is foretold that God will *bring him forth* against Israel, it is foretold that God *will put hooks into his jaws* and *turn him back* (v. 4).

2. The undertaking that he intends to engage this enemy in, in order to bring about his defeat.

2.1. The nations that will be allied against Israel are many, great, and powerful (vv. 5–6), *Persia, Ethiopia* (Cush), and so on. Antiochus had an army made up of all the nations named here.

2.2. They are well supplied with *arms* and with *horses and horsemen* (v. 4), well equipped *with all sorts of armour, bucklers and* (large and small) *shields* for defense, *and all handling* (brandishing) *swords* for offense. "*Be thou prepared, and do thou prepare*" (v. 7). This call to prepare seems to be ironical—"do *thy worst,* but I *will turn thee back*"—like that in Isa 8:9.

2.3. Their intention is set against *the mountains of Israel* (v. 8), against *the land that is brought back from the sword*. It was not long ago that it was harassed by the sword of war, and it has scarcely recovered any strength since it was brought down by war. It is a people who *dwell safely, all of them, in unwalled villages*, feeling secure and *having neither bars nor gates* (v. 11). They do not intend to cause trouble for their neighbors, for they fear no trouble from them.

2.4. What the enemy has in mind in devising this project is to enrich himself and make himself master, not of the country, but of its wealth. It came into Antiochus's mind what an extraordinary people these religious Jews were, and how their worship condemned the idolatry of their neighbors, and so, out of hostility toward their religion, he would harass them. It came into his mind how wealthy they were, that they had *gotten cattle and goods in the midst of the land* (v. 12). And so he came to this decision (vv. 11–12): "*I will go up to the land of unwalled villages*; yes, I will. It will cost me nothing to taken possession of them." These were the thoughts that came into the mind of this evil ruler, and God knew them.

2.5. According to this scheme that he devised, he pours all his forces into the land of Israel and finds those who are prepared to come to help him with the same plans (v. 9).

Verses 14–23

This second part of the chapter repeats the first part.

1. It is again foretold that this malicious enemy will make a formidable attack on the land of Israel (v. 15). The words (v. 14) *When my people Israel dwell safely, shalt thou not know it?* may be taken in two ways:

1.1. As showing his motivation. "You will have information that the people of Israel are a rich and easy target, and you will soon decide to attack them."

1.2. As showing his disappointment in this attempt. "You will soon find that there is *no enchantment* (sorcery) *against Jacob* (Nu 23:23), that *no weapon formed against them shall prosper* (Isa 54:17); you will know to your cost and shame that although they have no walls, bars, or gates,

they have God himself, a *wall of fire, round about them,* and that the One who *touches them touches the apple of his eye* (Zec 2:8); whoever interferes with them interferes to their own detriment." The enemy said, *Let us take the spoil and take the prey*, but they *knew not the thoughts of the Lord* (Mic 4:11–12), who had said, *I will bring thee against my land*. This is strange news, that God will not only allow his enemies to attack his own children but even bring them himself. Yet we will be reconciled even to this if we understand that the reason is "so *that the heathen* (nations) *may know me* to be the only living and true God *when I shall be sanctified in thee*, O Gog! that is, when I am sanctified in your defeat and destruction *before their eyes,* so that all the nations may see and say, *There is none like unto the God of Jeshurun, that rides on the heavens for the help of his people* (Dt 33:26)."

2. Reference is made here to the predictions of the former prophets (v. 17): "*Art thou he of whom I have spoken in old time*, about whom Moses spoke in his prophecy of the latter days (Dt 32:43), and about whom David spoke in Ps 9:15 and often elsewhere in the Psalms?" This is Leviathan, about whom Isaiah spoke (Isa 27:1); this is the meeting of the nations about which Joel spoke (Joel 3:1).

3. It is foretold here that the army of this furious, formidable enemy will be completely destroyed in his attempt to attack Israel. Many commentators think this was fulfilled in the many defeats given by the Maccabees to the forces of Antiochus. *When he comes up* in pride and anger *against the land of Israel*, then *God's fury shall come up in his face,* which is an allusion to something that happens to human beings: our color rises in our faces when we are shown some disrespect (v. 18). The enemy's forces will be put into the greatest possible confusion and panic (v. 19): *There shall be a great shaking of* them *in the land of Israel* (v. 20), which will affect the *fishes* and *fowls* (birds), the *beasts* and *creeping things*, and much more *the men that are upon the face of the earth*. He will be defeated and completely ruined; both earth and heaven will be armed against him. From the earth (v. 22), *I will plead against him with pestilence and blood*. The weapons of heaven will also be drawn out against them: *I will rain upon him an overflowing rain* (v. 22). He comes like a storm on Israel (v. 9), but God will come like a storm on him.

CHAPTER 39

This chapter concludes the prophecy against Gog and Magog, in whose destruction God crowns his favor to his people Israel. Here is: 1. An explicit prediction of the complete destruction of Gog and Magog (vv. 1–7). 2. The vastness of that destruction: the burning of their weapons (vv. 8–10), the burying of those who were killed (vv. 11–16), and the feasting of the birds on the dead bodies of those who were not buried (vv. 17–22). 3. A declaration of God's gracious purposes concerning his people Israel (vv. 23–29).

Verses 1–7

This prophecy begins as the previous one (38:3–4): *I am against thee, and I will turn thee back.*

1. The enemy's soldiers will be disarmed and so be unable to continue their enterprise.

2. He and the greatest part of his army will be killed on the battlefield (v. 4). *Thou shalt fall upon the open field* (v. 5). Even on the mountains, he will not find a pass that he will be able to keep to, and on the open field he will not find a road for his escape. Never was an army so

totally routed as this. And to add to the enemies' notoriety and disgrace, their bodies will be a feast for the birds of prey (v. 4).

3. His country also will be made desolate: *I will send a fire on Magog* (v. 6) and *among those that dwell carelessly*, or confidently, *in the isles*, that is, the coastlands or nations of the Gentiles. When his people Israel see this, they will come to know more of God's name, his power and his goodness, his care of them and his faithfulness to them. This is God's way of dealing with people: first to enlighten their understanding, and by that means to influence the whole person. He first makes us know his holy name, and so keeps us from defiling it and commits us to honor it. The nations who never knew it or would not acknowledge it will *know that I am the Lord, the Holy One in Israel* (v. 7).

Verses 8–22

Although this prophecy was to be fulfilled in the latter days, it is spoken of here as if it were already fulfilled, because it is certain (v. 8). To represent the routing of the army of Gog as very great, two things are mentioned here as its consequences. It was God himself who gave the defeat; we do not find that the people of Israel drew a sword or struck a stroke. But:

1. Israel will *burn their* enemies' *weapons*, their *bows and arrows*, which *fell out of their hands* (v. 3), everything that is combustible. They will not need to *take wood out of the field or forests* for *seven years* without ceasing (v. 10); such vast quantities of weapons will be left on the open field where the enemy fell.

2. They will bury their dead. Those who have been killed will be so dispersed on the mountains of Israel that it would take a very long time for their survivors to find them all, and so it will be left to the house of Israel to bury them. A place will be appointed for their burial, *the valley of the passengers* (travelers), *on the east of the sea* (v. 11), either the Salt Sea or the Sea of Tiberias. It will be called *The valley of Hamon-gog*, that is, "of the hordes of Gog." Acts of humanity add much to the honor of God's Israel. Burying the dead is a good work, even if the corpses are those of foreigners and enemies to the citizens of Israel (Eph 2:12).

Verses 23–29

This refers not only to the predictions about Gog and Magog but also to all the prophecies of this book about the exile of the people of Israel and about their restoration and return from exile.

1. God will let the nations know the meaning of his people's troubles. Upon their reformation and return to him, he will restore their fortunes, bring them back to their own land, and bring about great salvation for them. Then it will be made clear even to the nations that there is no basis whatsoever for their thought that Israel went into exile because God could not protect them. It will be clear that it happened because by their sin Israel had forfeited his favor and thrown themselves out of his protection (vv. 23–24). That was the true reason why God *hid his face from them* and *gave them into the hand of their enemies*. The glory of God will appear clearly when the world is made to know:

1.1. That God punishes sin even in his own people, because he hates it most in those who are nearest and dearest to him (Am 3:2).

1.2. That when God hands his people over to become plunder, it is to correct them and reform them, not to satisfy their enemies (Isa 10:7; 42:24).

1.3. That no sooner do God's people humble themselves under the rod than he returns in mercy to them.

2. God will let his own people know what favor he has in store for them (vv. 25–26).

2.1. Now God *will have mercy upon the whole house of Israel* because they repent of their sins. God has justly brought them into a land of trouble, where everyone makes them afraid, because they trespassed against him in a land of peace, where no one made them afraid. When they humble themselves under humbling providences, God will bring them back from captivity.

2.2. As God was dishonored by the disgrace they were under during their exile, so he will be sanctified when they are reformed and made into a holy people again, and he will be glorified when they are restored and made into a happy, glorious people again. Then they will enjoy the benefits of it (v. 28): *They shall know that I am the Lord their God.* The providences of God have the grace of God accompanying them to teach his people to look to God as their God.

CHAPTER 40

The waters of the sanctuary that this prophet saw later in this vision (47:1–5) are a proper representation of this prophecy. Now the waters have risen and have become a river that cannot be crossed. Here is one continuous vision, beginning at this chapter and continuing to the end of the book, which is justly looked on as one of the most difficult parts of Scripture. Many commentators, both ancient and modern, have acknowledged that they are at a loss to understand it. But though it is hard to understand, we must humbly search it, reaching as far as we can into it and drawing as much as we can out of it. When we despair of solving every difficulty, we must bless God that our salvation does not depend on it, but that the things that are necessary for our salvation and godly living are clear enough.

Here the prophet sees a vision of a glorious temple (in this chapter and chs. 41–42); sees God taking possession of it (ch. 43); hears orders concerning the priests who are to minister in this temple (ch. 44); sees the division of the land, what portion must be allotted for the sanctuary, what for the city, and what for the prince (ch. 45); and receives further instructions for himself and the people (ch. 46). After the vision of the holy waters, we have the borders of the Holy Land, the portions assigned to the tribes, and the dimensions and gates of the Holy City (chs. 47–48).

Some suggest that this represents the situation during the flourishing state of the Jewish church, how glorious Solomon's temple was in its best days, so that the exiles might see what they had lost by their sin. But that seems improbable. I take its general scope to be: 1. To assure the captives that they would not only return to their own land and settle there but also be encouraged to build another temple. God would acknowledge that temple, he would meet them and bless them there, the ordinances of worship would be revived, and the sacred priesthood would serve there. 2. To direct them to look further than all this, to expect the coming of the Messiah, who had been prophesied about before under the name of David. Because the dimensions of these visionary buildings are so large, it is clearly shown, as Dr. Lightfoot observes, that these things must be understood spiritually, not literally. However, the Gospel temple, erected by Christ and his apostles, was so closely connected with the second physical temple, and was erected so carefully just at the time when the other fell into decay, that it was appropriate enough for them both to be referred to in the same vision. The spiritual worship of Gospel times is foreshadowed under the type and figure of a temple and altar, priests and sacrifices, and finally perfected in the kingdom of glory, in which perhaps these visions will have their complete fulfillment. Some think this will happen in some happy and glorious state of the Gospel church this side of heaven, in the last days.

In this chapter we have: 1. A general account of this vision of the temple and city (vv. 1–4). 2. A detailed account of it, including a description of the outside wall (v. 5); the east gate (vv. 6–19); and the north gate (vv. 20–23); the south gate (vv. 24–31); the rooms, porticos, and so on, belonging to these gates; the inner court, both toward the east and toward the south (vv. 32–38); the tables (vv. 39–43); the rooms for the singers and the priests (vv. 44–47); and the portico of the temple (vv. 48–49).

Verses 1–4

Here:

1. The date of this vision is given. It was in the twenty-fifth year of Ezekiel's captivity (v. 1), which some calculate to be the thirty-third year of the first exile, said here to be the fourteenth year after the city was smitten (fell). "Then the hand of the Lord was upon me and brought me thither to Jerusalem, now that it was in ruins, desolate and deserted," a pitiful sight for the prophet.

2. The prophet was brought, in the visions of God, to the land of Israel (v. 2). He was taken there to have a pleasing prospect of it in its glory. He was set upon a very high mountain, as Moses was set on the top of Pisgah (Dt 34:1), to view this land, which was now for a second time a land of promise. From the top of this mountain he saw that this city was a temple as large as a city. It was a city for people to live in; it was a temple for God to live in, for in the church on earth God lives with people, and in the church in heaven people live with God.

3. The particular revelations of this city were made to him by a man whose appearance was like the appearance of brass (bronze) (v. 3), Jesus Christ. It is through Christ that we both know and have access to the benefits and privileges of God's house. His appearing like bronze suggests both his brightness and his strength.

4. The dimensions of this city or temple were taken with a line of flax (linen cord) and a measuring reed (measuring rod) (v. 3).

5. Directions are given here to the prophet to receive this revelation from the Lord and communicate it purely and entirely to the church (v. 4).

Verses 5–26

The measuring rod that was in the hand of the surveyor was mentioned before (v. 3). Here we are told (v. 5) what its exact length was. It was six cubits long, not the standard cubit, but the cubit of the sanctuary, and that was a handbreadth (that is, about three inches or eight centimeters) longer than the standard cubit; the standard cubit was eighteen inches, this was twenty-one; see 43:13. Some critics contend that the length of this measuring-reed was only six standard cubits plus one handbreadth added to the whole. The former seems more probable. Here is an account:

1. Of the outer wall surrounding the house, which shows the separation between the church and the world.

2. Of the different gates with the rooms attached to them.

2.1. He begins with the east gate, because that was the usual way of coming into the lower end of the temple, the Most Holy Place being at the west end. Notice, in the description of this gate, that:

2.1.1. He went up to it by stairs (v. 6), for when we go to worship God we must ascend; this is the upward call (Rev 4:1).

2.1.2. The rooms adjoining the gates were only little chambers (alcoves), about ten feet (about three meters) square (v. 7). These were for those who attended the service of the temple to stay in.

2.1.3. The chambers were each foursquare, so they were all of one measure, so that there might be equality among the attendants.

2.1.4. There were very many rooms, for there are many mansions in our Father's house (Jn 14:2), in his house above and in that on earth. Some believe these rooms represent the particular congregations of believers, which are parts of the great temple, the universal church.

2.1.5. It is said (v. 14), He made also the posts (projecting walls). The One who measured them was the same One who made them, for Christ is the builder of his church and so is most able to tell us about it.

2.1.6. There are projecting walls of sixty cubits, which, some think, was literally fulfilled when Cyrus, in his decree for rebuilding the temple at Jerusalem, ordered that their height should be sixty cubits, that is, thirty yards (about thirty meters) (Ezr 6:3).

2.1.7. There were windows (parapet openings) for the alcoves and windows for the projecting walls and arches, that is, the portico or cloisters below (v. 16), to represent the light from heaven with which the church is illuminated. There were lights for the alcoves, even the smallest. Even the smallest and least significant parts of the church will have light given them. However, they are narrow windows, like those in the temple (1Ki 6:4). The revelations made to the church on earth are narrow compared with what will be in the future state.

2.1.8. Different courts are spoken about here; an outermost one, then an outer court, followed by an inner, and the innermost, into which only the priests entered. These courts had porticos around them to shelter those who were in them from wind and weather.

2.1.9. The faces of the projecting walls were decorated with palm trees (v. 16) to show that the righteous shall flourish like the palm tree in the courts of God's house (Ps 92:12). The more the righteous are burdened with suffering, the more strongly they grow, as it is said about palm trees.

2.1.10. Notice is taken of the pavement of the court (vv. 17–18). The word suggests that the pavement was made of porphyry, an Egyptian rock of the color of burning coals, for the brightest glories of this world should be put under our feet when we draw near to God.

2.2. The gates that faced north (v. 20) and south (v. 24) were much the same as that which faced east, after the measure of the first gate (v. 21). This temple had not only a gate facing east, to allow in the children of the east, who were famous for their wealth and wisdom, but also a gate facing north and another facing south, to admit people from the poorer and less civilized nations. The New Jerusalem has twelve gates, three toward each corner of the world (Rev 21:13), for many will come from all parts to sit down there (Mt 8:11).

Verses 27–38

Here is a description of the inner court. The survey of the inner court begins with the south side (v. 27), proceeds to the east (v. 32), and then to the north (v. 35). These gates to the inner court exactly matched those to the outer court. The work of grace is substantially the same in mature Christians as it is in young beginners. The ascent into the outer court at each gate was by *seven steps*, but the ascent into the inner court at each gate was by *eight steps*. This is explicitly mentioned (vv. 31, 34, 37) to show that the closer we approach God, the more we should rise above the things of this world. The people who worshiped in the outer court must rise seven steps above other people, but the priests who served in the inner court must exceed them by at least one step more than the number by which they exceeded those who remained outside.

Verses 39–49

In these verses we have a description:
1. Of the tables that were in the porch of the gates of the inner court. Here eight tables were provided on which to *slay* (kill) *the sacrifices* (v. 41). They are included to show the many spiritual sacrifices that would be brought to God's house in Gospel times. Here were the meat tables for the altar (v. 43). They also washed the burnt offerings there (v. 38), to show that before we draw near to God's altar we must wash our hands and our hearts, those spiritual sacrifices.
2. Of the use of the rooms.
2.1. Some rooms were for the *singers* (v. 44). The singing of psalms would continue as a Gospel ordinance. Christians should sing.
2.2. Other rooms were for *the priests*, both those who kept *the charge of the house*, to cleanse it and keep it in good repair (v. 45), and those who *kept the charge of the altar* (v. 46).
3. Of the inner court, the court of the priests, which was a hundred cubits square (v. 47). The altar that *was before the house* (in front of the temple) was placed in the middle of this court. Christ is both our altar and our sacrifice, to whom we must look with faith whenever we approach God.
4. Of the *porch* (portico) (vv. 48–49) of the house, to teach us not to rush hastily and thoughtlessly into the presence of God, but seriously, passing first through the outer court, then the inner, then the portico, before we enter the temple.

CHAPTER 41

In this chapter we come to the temple itself, the description of which creates many difficulties for commentators. It is sufficient for us to notice: 1. The dimensions: its jambs (v. 1), the entrance (v. 2), the wall and the side rooms (vv. 5–6), the foundations and wall of the rooms, their entrances (vv. 8–11), and the temple itself (v. 13). 2. The dimensions of the Most Holy Place (vv. 3–4). 3. An account of another building facing the temple court-yard (vv. 12–15). 4. The way in which the temple was built (vv. 7, 16–17). 5. The ornaments (vv. 18–20). 6. The altar of incense and the table (v. 22). 7. The doors of the outer sanctuary and the Most Holy Place (vv. 21, 23–26). There is so much difference in the terms of architecture between one age and another, one place and another, that it should not be a stumbling block that there is so much that is difficult to understand. To an ordinary Jewish carpenter or mason at that time, we

may presume, all this was understood easily enough in its literal sense.

Verses 1–11

1. Having studied the courts, the prophet was finally *brought to the temple* (v. 1). If we conscientiously listen to the instructions given us in the clearer parts of religious faith, and benefit from them, we will be led into a deeper knowledge of the mysteries of the kingdom of heaven. Those who are willing to dwell in God's courts will finally be brought into his temple.
2. When our Lord Jesus spoke about destroying *this temple*, which his hearers understood to refer to this second temple of Jerusalem, he was speaking about the temple of his body (Jn 2:19, 21). Ezekiel's vision concerned both, including Christ's mystical body, the church, called the *house of God* (1Ti 3:15), and all the members of that body, *living temples* (1Pe 2:5), in which the Spirit lives (1Co 3:16).
3. The jambs of this temple, the doorposts, were far apart, so the door was wide. Comparing life under the law with life under grace, we may say, Wide is the gate that leads into the church (compare Mt 7:13), since the ceremonial law, that wall of hostility that restricted the gate so much (Eph 2:14), has been taken down.
4. The Most Holy Place was an exact square (v. 4). The New Jerusalem is exactly square (Rev 21:16), showing its stability.
5. The upper floors were larger than the lower ones (v. 7). Care was taken, however, that the timber might have a firm hold—although God builds high, he builds firmly. The higher we build ourselves up in our most holy faith, the more our hearts, those living temples, should be enlarged.

Verses 12–26

Here is:
1. A description of a building that was facing the temple courtyard *at the end toward the west* (v. 12). This stood in a court by itself. Perhaps in this vision it represented setting up a church among the Gentiles that was not inferior to the Jewish temple, but of a completely different nature.
2. A description of the ornaments of the temple and the other building. The walls on the inside from top to bottom were decorated with *cherubim and palm trees*, placed alternately. Each cherub is said to have two *faces*, the *face of a man* and the *face of a young lion* (v. 19). These seem to represent the angels, who have more than the wisdom of a human being and the courage of a lion, and the palms of victory are in front of them.
3. A description of the doorframes of both the outer temple and the Most Holy Place; they were *squared* (rectangular) (v. 21). In the tabernacle and in Solomon's temple, the entrance to the Most Holy Place was narrower than that of the temple, but here it was as wide, for in Gospel times the way into the holiest of all is made more *manifest* (disclosed) than it was under the Old Testament (Heb 9:8). These doors are described (vv. 23–24).
4. A description of the altar of incense, said to be an *altar of wood* (v. 22). Without being overlaid with gold, it would not bear the fire with which the incense was to be burned—unless it shows that the incense to be offered in the Gospel temple will be purely spiritual, and that the fire is spiritual. This altar is therefore called a table. The great sacrifice has now been offered; what we have to do is to feast on the sacrifice at the Lord's Table.

CHAPTER 42

This chapter concludes the description and measurement of this mystical temple: 1. A description of the rooms around the courts (vv. 1–13) and the uses for which they were intended (vv. 13–14). 2. A survey of the whole temple area and its courts (vv. 15–20).

Verses 1–14

The prophet has taken a very precise view of the temple and is now brought again into the outer court. Here is:

1. A description of rooms, which seems to us to be intricate. We will only notice, in general:

1.1. That around the temple, which was the place of public worship, were private rooms. We must not only worship in the courts of God's house but must, both before and after attending there, go into our own rooms, to read and meditate and *pray to our Father in secret* (Mt 6:6).

1.2. That these rooms were many; there were *three stories* of them (vv. 5–6). There were enough for all such devout people as Anna the prophet, who *departed not from the temple night or day* (Lk 2:37).

1.3. That although these rooms were private, they were still near the temple. Our religious activities in our own rooms must prepare us for exercises of devotion in public.

1.4. That in front of these rooms were *walks* (inner passageway) *of ten cubits broad* (v. 4), in which those who lodged in these rooms could meet, talk together, and share their experiences. Human beings are social beings, and Christians are made to have fellowship.

2. The appointed use of these rooms (vv. 13–14).

2.1. They were *for the priests* who approach the Lord. They are called *holy chambers* because they were for those who ministered in holy things to use during their time of service.

2.2. There the priests were to deposit *the most holy things*, the part of the offerings that belonged to them.

2.3. There the priests were to place the vestments that God had appointed for them to wear when they served at the altar. We read of priests being provided with garments after their return from exile (Ne 7:70, 72). When they had ended their service at the altar, they must set aside those garments and *put on other garments*. They must wear what other people wore when they *approached to those things which were for the people* (v. 14), that is, to teach them the law and to answer their questions.

Verses 15–20

We now see how far the holy ground on which we tread extends.

1. Each way it reached 500 measuring rods (vv. 16–19), each rod more than three and a half yards, so that it reached in every direction about a mile. The outlying areas of this mystical temple were so large to show the great extent of the church in Gospel times. Room must be made in God's courts for the numerous Gentiles (Isa 49:18; 60:4–5).

2. The dimensions were so large to *make a separation*, by putting a distance *between the sanctuary* and *the profane place* (to separate the holy and the common). A distinction is to be made between common and holy things (Jer 15:19), between God's name and other names, between his day and other days, his book and other books.

CHAPTER 43

Having given us a view of the mystical temple, the Gospel church, as he received it from the Lord, the prophet now describes the worship that will be carried out in it, under the type of the Old Testament services. Here is: 1. Possession taken of this temple by the glory of God filling it (vv. 1–6). 2. A promise given of God's presence remaining with his people on condition of their return to the instituted way of worship and their abandoning idolatry (vv. 7–12). 3. A description of the altar of burnt offerings (vv. 13–17). 4. Directions given for the consecration of that altar (vv. 18–27). Ezekiel seems to stand between God and Israel here, as Moses the servant of the Lord did when the sanctuary was first set up.

Verses 1–6

Having patiently surveyed the temple of God, the greatest glory of this earth, Ezekiel is honored with seeing the glories of the upper world; *Come up hither* (Rev 4:1). He has seen the temple, spacious and splendid, but until the glory of God comes into it, it is only like the dead bodies he saw in his vision in ch. 37, which had *no breath* until the Spirit of life entered them. Here therefore he sees the house filled with God's glory.

1. He has a vision of *the glory of God* (v. 2), *the glory of the God of Israel*, who is in covenant with Israel. The idols of the nations have no glory except what they owe to the goldsmith or the painter. This glory *came from the way of the east*. Christ's *star was seen in the east* (Mt 2:9). He is the morning star (Rev 22:16), the sun of righteousness (Mal 4:2). Ezekiel noticed two things in this appearance of the glory of God:

1.1. The power of his word, which he heard: *His voice was like a noise of many* rushing *waters* (v. 2). Christ's Gospel, in the glory of which he shines, was to be declared aloud, to be sounded so that it could be heard from far away.

1.2. The brightness of his appearance, which he saw: *The earth shone with his glory*, for God is light, and none can bear the radiance of his light; none *has seen* nor *can see it* (1Ti 6:16). The glory of God that shines in the church shines on the world.

2. He has a vision of the entrance of this glory into the temple. When he saw this glory, he *fell upon his face* (v. 3) in humble and reverent adoration. But the Spirit *took him up* (v. 5) when the *glory of the Lord* had *come into the house* (v. 4), so that he might see how the temple was filled with it. This was to have its fulfillment in the glory of the divine grace that shines so brightly in the Gospel church and fills it. Here there is no mention of a cloud filling the temple as formerly, for we now *with open face behold the glory of the Lord* (2Co 3:18), in the face of Christ, and not, as formerly, through clouds of types.

3. He receives instructions more directly from the glory of the Lord, as Moses did when God had taken possession of the tabernacle (Lev 1:1): *I heard him speaking to me out of the house* (v. 6).

Verses 7–12

God is here, in effect, renewing his covenant with his people Israel by retaking possession of the house.

1. Through the prophet, God reminds them of their former offenses. This is spoken to make way for the encouragement that will follow. They formerly *defiled God's holy name* (v. 7). *They and their kings* brought contempt on the religion they professed by setting up altars to their idols even in the courts of the temple, than which nothing could

be a more shameless insult to the divine Majesty. They set up a separation *wall between him and them*, which stopped the flow of his favors to them. It often proves too true, "The nearer the church, the further from God."

2. He calls on them to repent (v. 9): "*Now let them put away their whoredom* (prostitution); and now that God is returning in mercy toward them and setting up his sanctuary again among them, let them throw away their idols, those detestable *carcases of their kings*." This is timely advice now that the prophet has the model or pattern of the temple to set before them.

2.1. If *they see that pattern* (plan), they will surely be ashamed of their sins (v. 10). The goodness of God toward us should lead us to repentance. Let them consider the plan themselves and see how much it surpasses the previous plan, and let them work out from that the great things God has in store for them.

2.2. If *they be ashamed* of their sins, they will surely see more of the plan (v. 11). "*Show them the form of the house*; show them its laws and regulations." Along with the privileges of God's house, we must also come to know its responsibilities. *Show them* these regulations so that they may *keep them* and *do them*.

3. He promises that they will be as they should be, and then he will be to them as they want him to be (v. 7). Then *I will dwell in the midst of them for ever* (v. 7 and again v. 9).

4. The general law of God's house is established (v. 12). Whereas formerly only the chancel, or sanctuary, was *most holy*, now, in Gospel times, the whole *mountain of the house* will be so. The whole church will have the privilege of the *holy of holies*, that is, of close access to God. All believers have now, under the Gospel, *boldness to enter into the holiest* (Heb 10:19). Whereas the high priest entered by virtue of the blood of bulls and goats, we enter by virtue of the blood of Jesus, and wherever we are, through him we have *access to the Father* (Eph 2:18).

Verses 13–27

This relates to the altar in this mystical temple, and that is mystical too, for Christ is our altar. After their return from exile, the Jews had an altar long before they had a temple (Ezr 3:3). But this was an altar in the temple. Here we have:

1. The measurements of the altar (v. 13). It was about six yards (about six meters) square at the top and about seven yards (about seven meters) square at the bottom; it was four yards and a half (about four meters) high; it had a lower ledge, called here *a settle*, a yard (about one meter) from the ground, on which some of the priests stood to minister, and another one two yards (about two meters) above that, on which other priests stood. What was to be burned on the altar was handed up by the offerers to those on the lower ledge, and handed by them to those on the higher, and they laid it on the altar.

2. The regulations of the altar. Directions are given:

2.1. About its dedication. *Seven days* were to be spent in this, and sacrifices were to be offered every day (v. 25). Neither what we are as people nor what we do can be acceptable to God unless sin is taken away, and that cannot be taken away except by the blood of Christ, which sanctifies both the altar and the gift on the altar (compare Mt 23:18–19). The dedication of the altar is called here its *cleansing* and *purging* (vv. 20, 26). All the sacrifices must be seasoned with salt (v. 24; see also Lev 2:13). *Grace* is the *salt* with which all our religious activities must be seasoned (Col 4:6).

2.2. About the constant use that would be made of the temple when it was dedicated (v. 27). It was *sanctified*, so that it might *sanctify the gift* offered on it (Mt 23:18–19). Notice:

2.2.1. Who were to serve at the altar: the *priests of the seed of Zadok* (v. 19). His name means "righteous," for those who are priests to God are the righteous *seed*, or descendants, through Christ *the Lord our righteousness* (Mal 4:2).

2.2.2. How they would prepare for this service (v. 26). Before we minister to the Lord in holy things, we must consecrate ourselves.

CHAPTER 44

Here: 1. Access to the outer gate of the sanctuary facing east is restricted to the prince (vv. 1–3). 2. A rebuke is sent to the house of Israel for their former desecration of God's sanctuary (vv. 4–9). 3. Those Levites who had formerly been guilty of idolatry are demoted, and the priesthood is established in the family of Zadok, who had kept their integrity (vv. 10–16). 4. Various laws and regulations are given concerning the priests (vv. 17–31).

Verses 1–3

The prophet is brought a third time to the east gate and finds it shut, which indicates that the rest of the gates were open at all times to the worshipers. But the account given of this gate's being shut puts honor:

1. On the God of Israel. It was for his honor that the gate of the inner court, through which his glory entered when he took possession of the house, was kept shut forever after (v. 2).

2. On the prince of Israel (v. 3).

2.1. He will *sit in this gate* to *eat his* share of the peace offerings *before the Lord*.

2.2. He will *enter by the way of the porch* (portico) *of that gate*, by some little door or opening. Some understand *prince* here to refer to the high priest, and they believe that only he was allowed to enter by this gateway, for he was God's representative. Christ is the high priest of our profession (Heb 3:1), who himself entered into the Holy Place and *opened the kingdom of heaven to all believers*.

Verses 4–9

The prophet must look again at what he saw before and must be told again what he heard before. Here, as before, he sees the house *filled with the glory of the Lord*, which strikes awe on him: *I fell upon my face* (v. 4).

1. God commands the prophet to take notice of all he sees and all that is said to him (v. 5).

1.1. "Look with your eyes at what is shown you, especially the entrance of the temple and all the exits of the sanctuary.

1.2. "Hear with your ears all that I say to you about the laws and *ordinances* of the temple, so that you may instruct the people."

2. He sends him on a mission to the people, *to the rebellious, even to the house of Israel* (v. 6).

2.1. He must show the house of Jacob their sins (Isa 58:1). They have admitted to the privileges of the sanctuary those people who are not entitled to them. If these foreigners had been devout, then even though they were not circumcised, the crime would not have been so great, but they were *uncircumcised in heart* too, strangers indeed to God and all goodness. The people have employed in the service of the sanctuary those who were not fit for it. *"You have set keepers of my charge in my sanctuary for yourselves* (v. 8), those you liked or favored: *thus you have not kept the charge of my holy things."*

2.2. He must tell them their duty (v. 9): "No foreigner may enter my sanctuary until they have first submitted to its laws."

Verses 10–16

The Master of the house is about to set up house again here, and so he takes account of his servants the priests and sees who are fit to be kept.

1. Those who have been treacherous are demoted. Those Levites or priests who were formerly taken down the stream of the apostasy of Israel (v. 10), who complied with the idolatrous kings of Israel or Judah, who *ministered to them before their idols* (v. 12), are put lower, justly put under the mark of God's displeasure. They are sentenced to be deprived of part of their office and are demoted from the position of priests to the condition of ordinary Levites. But there is a mixture of mercy in this sentence; God mitigates it (vv. 11, 14). They will still help to *slay the sacrifice*, which the Levites were permitted to do, and which in this temple was done not at the altar, but *at the tables* (40:39). They will be porters *at the gates of the house.*

2. Those who have been faithful are honored and established (vv. 15–16). "But the sons of Zadok, who kept their integrity during a time of general apostasy, who did not go astray when others did, will come near to me and my table."

Verses 17–31

God's priests must be "regular," not "lay," and so here rules are laid down for them.

1. About their clothes; they must wear *linen garments* when they *go in to minister*, and nothing that is *woollen*, because it would *cause sweat* (vv. 17–18). When they have completed their service, they must change their clothes, storing their linen garments in the rooms appointed for that purpose (v. 19, as before in 42:14).

2. About their hair; they must avoid both extremes in that (v. 20). They must not shave their heads, in imitation of the Gentile priests; nor, on the other hand, must they allow their hair to grow long, so that they might be thought to be Nazarites when really they were not. No; instead they must be serious and modest, trimming their hair to keep it short.

3. About their diet; they must be sure to drink no wine when they minister, so that they may not drink excessively and forget the law (v. 21).

4. About their marriages (v. 22). Here, considering the reputation of their office, they must not marry a woman who has been divorced and is therefore at least under the suspicion of immodesty, nor a widow, unless she is a priest's widow, used to the life of a priest's family.

5. About their preaching and church government. It is part of their responsibility to teach the people, and here they must show themselves both skillful and faithful (v. 23). It is part of their responsibility to judge appeals made to them (Dt 17:8–9), and in disputes they must serve as judges (v. 24). They must have the integrity and honesty to stand up for what is right, and when they have passed a right judgment, must have the courage to stand by it. Another part of their work, as church governors, is to keep God's Sabbaths holy, to see that God's people also sanctify that day and do nothing to defile it.

6. About their mourning for dead relatives; the rule here agrees with the Law of Moses (Lev 21:1, 11). A priest must not come near any dead body—for he must be purified *from dead works* (Heb 9:14)—except that of one of his closest relatives, (v. 25).

7. About their livelihood; they must live from the altar at which they serve (v. 28). Some land is allowed them (48:10), but their principal subsistence will be through their office. Notice:

7.1. What the priests are to receive from the people for their maintenance and encouragement. They must have the flesh of many of the offerings. They must also have every dedicated thing in Israel, which is in many cases to be turned into money, which is then given to the priest. This is explained in v. 30. They are to have *the first of the dough* when it is going to the oven, as well as the first of their fruits when they are going to the barn. Because the priests are so well provided for, it would be inexcusable of them if they should *eat that which is torn or which died of itself* (v. 31).

7.2. What the people can expect from the priest as their reward. Those who are kind to a prophet or priest will have a prophet's or a priest's reward (Mt 10:41) (v. 30). It was part of the priest's work to *bless the people in the name of the Lord*, not only their congregations but also their families.

CHAPTER 45

In this chapter the prophet is further shown, in a vision: 1. The division of the Holy Land, so much for the temple and the priests who attended its service (vv. 1–4), so much for the Levites (v. 5), so much for the city (v. 6), so much for the prince, and the remainder for the people (vv. 7–8). 2. The statutes of justice that were given both to prince and to people (vv. 9–12). 3. The special gifts they were to offer (vv. 13–17), especially at the beginning of the year (vv. 18–20), the Passover, and the Feast of Tabernacles (vv. 21–25).

Verses 1–8

Directions are given here for the dividing of the land after the people's return to it:

1. Here is the portion of land assigned to *the sanctuary*, in the middle of which the temple was to be built (v. 1), *an oblation* (a sacred district) *to the Lord*, for what is given to maintain the worship of God and advance religious faith is accepted by God as given to him. This *holy portion of the land* was to be measured, and its borders fixed. The priests and Levites who were to come near to minister were to have their homes in this *portion of the land* that was around the sanctuary.

2. Next to the lands of the sacred district the lands of the city were assigned. In them the Holy City was to be built, and the citizens were to be maintained with the income and profits from them (v. 6).

3. The next allotment after the church lands and the city lands was of the crown lands (vv. 7–8). They are said to lie *on the one side and on the other side* of the church lands and city lands, to show that the prince with his wealth and power was to protect both. *My princes shall no more oppress my people* (v. 8), for God will make the *officers peace* and the *exactors righteousness* (Isa 60:17). Nehemiah was one who did not do as the *former governors* (Ne 5:15, 18).

4. The rest of the lands were to be distributed to the people *according to their tribes.*

Verses 9–12

Some general rules of justice are set down for both prince and people. Let it be enacted:

1. That *princes do not oppress their subjects*, but appropriately and faithfully administer justice among them (v. 9). Let them *take away their exactions*, relieve their subjects of those taxes that lie heavily on them, and let them *execute judgment and justice* according to law.

2. That one neighbor is not to cheat another in trade (v. 10): *You shall have just balances*. God's Israel should be honest, just, and accurate in all their dealings, prompt and exact in rendering to everyone what is their due, because otherwise they spoil the acceptableness of their profession with God and the reputation of it in the eyes of other people.

Verses 13–25

Having set down the rules of righteousness toward other people, the prophet comes next to give some directions for their religious faith toward God.

1. It is required that they offer *an oblation* (special gift) to the Lord (v. 13): *All the people of the land* must give a special gift (v. 16). They have offered a sacred district out of their real estates (v. 1), *a holy portion of their land*; now they are told to offer a special gift out of their goods and belongings.

2. The proportion of this special gift is determined here, which was not done by the Law of Moses.

2.1. Out of their corn they were to offer a sixtieth part (v. 13).

2.2. Out of their oil they were to offer a hundredth (v. 14).

2.3. Out of their flocks they were to give only *one lamb* out of 200 (v. 15); however, it must be *out of the fat pastures of Israel*. They must offer to God the fattest and best they had for *burnt offerings* and *peace offerings*. These sacrifices were to *make reconciliation* for them. Christ is our sacrifice of atonement, by whom reconciliation is made.

3. This special gift must be given *for the prince in Israel* (v. 16). Some read it "to" the prince and understand it to refer to Christ, to whom we must offer our sacrifices of praise to be presented to the Father (Heb 13:15). Or, they will give it "with" the prince (v. 17). The people were to bring their special gifts to him, and he was to bring them to the sanctuary, and to make up himself what fell short.

4. Some specific ceremonies are appointed here:

4.1. At the beginning of the year was the annual ceremony of cleansing the sanctuary.

4.1.1. *On the first day of the first month* they were to offer a sacrifice for the *cleansing of the sanctuary* (v. 18) and to seek grace to better fulfill the service of the sanctuary the following year. By this sacrifice atonement was intended to be made for the sins of all the servants who served that house, the sins of priests, Levites, and people—the sins that were found in all their services. They were appointed here to *cleanse the sanctuary* on the first day of the month because on the fourteenth day of the month they were to eat the Passover, an ordinance that, of all Old Testament institutions, contained the most of Christ and Gospel grace.

4.1.2. This sacrifice was to be repeated on *the seventh day of the first month* (v. 20). It was then intended to make atonement *for every one that erred and for him that was simple*, anyone who sinned through ignorance, mistake, or inadvertence.

4.2. The Passover was to be religiously observed at the appointed time (v. 21). Christ is *our passover*, who

is *sacrificed for us* (1Co 5:7). We celebrate the memorial of that sacrifice in the Lord's Supper, which is our Passover feast.

4.3. The Feast of Tabernacles is spoken of next (v. 25), and there is no mention of the feast of Pentecost, which came between that of the Passover and that of Tabernacles. Notice the deficiency of the legal sacrifices for sin; they were often repeated, not only every year but also every feast, every day of the feast. Notice the necessity of our frequently repeating the same religious exercises. Although the sacrifice of atonement is offered *once for all* (Heb 10:10), the sacrifices of acknowledgment, that of a broken and thankful heart (Ps 51:17), those spiritual sacrifices that are acceptable to God through Christ Jesus, must be offered every day.

CHAPTER 46

In this chapter we have: 1. Some further rules given to both the priests and the people, relating to their worship (vv. 1–15). 2. A law concerning the prince's disposal of his inheritance (vv. 16–18). 3. A description of the places provided for the cooking of the sacrifices and the baking of the grain offerings (vv. 19–24).

Verses 1–15

We do not find in the history of the the Jewish church after the exile that they governed themselves by these regulations, but only by the Law of Moses, looking on these regulations as belonging to the next age, as mystical, not literal.

1. The place of worship was established, and rules were given to prince and people.

1.1. The east gate, kept shut at other times, was to be opened on the Sabbath days, on the New Moons (v. 1), and whenever the prince offered a freewill offering (v. 12). Some think he went in with the priests and Levites into the *inner court*, and these interpreters suggest that judges and ministers should go hand in hand in promoting the service of God. However, it seems rather that he went *by the way of the porch of the gate*, stood *at the post of the gate*, and *worshiped at the threshold of the gate* (v. 2), where he had a full view of the priests' actions at the altar, and that the people stood behind him at *the door of that gate* (v. 3).

1.2. As to the north gate and south gate, by which they entered into the *court of the people, whoever* came in at the *north gate* must go out at the *south gate*, and whoever came in at the *south gate* must go out at the *north gate* (v. 9). Some think this was to prevent pushing and shoving.

1.3. *The people must worship at the door of the east gate*, where the prince did, both *on the sabbath and on the new moons* (v. 3).

2. The ordinances of worship were fixed.

2.1. Every morning they must offer *a lamb for a burnt offering* (v. 13).

2.2. On the Sabbath days, whereas by the Law of Moses two lambs were to be offered (Nu 28:9), six lambs must be offered.

2.3. On the New Moons, at the beginning of their months, there was the additional offering of a young bull (v. 6).

2.4. All the sacrifices were to be *without blemish*, as Christ, the great sacrifice, was (1Pe 1:19), and as Christians, who present themselves to God as living sacrifices, should be—*blameless, and harmless, and without rebuke* (Php 2:15).

2.5. All the sacrifices were to have their *meat offerings* (grain offerings) attached to them, to show that we should honor him with the fruit of our ground as well as with the fruit of our cattle (Dt 28:4). The grain offerings here are much larger in proportion than they were by the Law of Moses, which shows that under the Gospel, because the great atoning sacrifice has been offered, these sacrifices that do not involve bloodshed will be offered more generously.

Verses 16–18

Here is a law to limit the power of the prince in disposing of crown lands.

1. If he has a *son* who has deserved well, he may, as a reward for his son's services, settle some parts of his lands on him (v. 16).

2. But if he has a servant who is a favorite, he may not settle lands on him (v. 17). He may give him lands to be held until the Year of Jubilee, but then they must revert to the family (v. 17).

3. Any possessions he gives his children must be from his own (v. 18): he *shall not take of the people's inheritance*. It is in the interests of princes to rule in the hearts of their subjects. It is better to gain their loyalty by protecting their rights than to gain their possessions by invading them.

Verses 19–24

Here are the places for cooking the flesh of the offerings (v. 20). Some were at the entrance to the inner court (v. 19), and others in all four corners of the outer court (vv. 21–23). In those places they were to *boil the trespass offering* (cook the guilt offering) *and the sin offering* (v. 20), those parts that were allotted to the priests. There, too, they were to *bake the meat* (grain) *offering*.

CHAPTER 47

We have here: 1. The vision of the holy waters: their rise, extent, depth, and healing power, and the fish in them; and an account of the trees growing on their banks (vv. 1–12). 2. An appointment of the borders of the land of Canaan, which was to be divided by lot to the tribes of Israel and the foreigners who stayed among them (vv. 13–23).

Verses 1–12

This part of Ezekiel's vision must have a mystical and spiritual meaning. It may be explained by the prophecy in Zec 14:8, which speaks of *living waters* that will *go out* from Jerusalem, *half of them toward the former sea and half of them toward the hinder sea*. There is a clear reference to this in St. John's vision of *a pure river of water of life* (Rev 22:1). That vision seems to represent the glory and joy that are grace perfected. This one seems to represent the grace and joy that are glory begun. Most interpreters agree that these waters represent the Gospel of Christ and the gifts and power of the Holy Spirit; the Gospel went out from Jerusalem and spread to the surrounding countries, and because of the gifts and power of the Holy Spirit that accompanied it, it spread far and produced blessed effects. Notice:

1. The source of these waters (v. 1). Waters flowed out from the threshold of the house eastward, and from under the right side of the house, that is, the south side of the *altar*. Again (v. 2), *There ran out waters on the right side*, showing that *from Zion will go out the law,*

and the word of the Lord from Jerusalem (Isa 2:3). It was there that the Spirit was poured out on the apostles and endowed them with the gift of tongues to enable them to take these waters to all nations. They were to stand and preach the words of this life in the temple (Ac 5:20). They must preach the Gospel to all nations but must begin at Jerusalem (Lk 24:47). Christ is the temple (Jn 2:19–21); he is the gate (Jn 10:7, 9); those living waters flow from his pierced side (Jn 19:34). It is by believing in him that we receive from him *rivers of living water*, and *this spoke he of the Spirit* (Jn 7:38–39). The origin of these waters was not above ground, but from under the threshold, for the fountain of a believer's life is a mystery; it is hidden with Christ in God (Col 3:3).

2. The progress and increase of these waters: they *went forth eastward* (v. 3), *toward the east* country (v. 8). The prophet and his guide followed the stream as it ran down from the holy mountains, and when they had followed it about a thousand cubits (about 1,500 feet, or about 450 meters), they went across to discover its depth, and it came up to the ankles (v. 3). Then they walked along on the bank of the river on the other side, a thousand cubits more, and then, to discover its depth, they waded through it a second time, and it reached their knees (v. 4). They walked along by it a thousand cubits more, and then crossed it a third time, and it then came up to their middle—the waters were to the waist. They then walked a thousand cubits further and attempted to cross it a fourth time, but found it impracticable: *The waters had risen*, so that there were *waters to swim in, a river that could not be passed over* (v. 5). This shows us:

2.1. The waters of the sanctuary are running waters, like those of a river, not still waters, like those of a pond. Grace in the soul is continually pressing onward; *onward still*, until it reaches perfection.

2.2. They are increasing waters. Just as this river runs constantly, so also the further it goes, the fuller it grows. The Gospel church was very small in its beginnings, like a tiny rippling brook, but it gradually came *to the ankles, to the knees*: many were added to it daily (Ac 2:47). The gifts of the Spirit increase by being exercised, and grace is growing, like the light of the morning, which *shines more and more to the perfect day* (Pr 4:18).

2.3. It is good for us to follow these waters. Notice the progress of the Gospel in the world; consider the process of the work of grace in the heart; observe the motions of the blessed Holy Spirit, as Ezekiel did here. If we search into the things of God, we will find some very clear and easy to understand, like the waters that came up to the ankles; others more difficult, like the water to the knees; and some quite beyond our reach, impenetratable to us; and yet, despairing to find their bottom, we must, with the apostle Paul, sit down at their edge and adore their *depth* (Ro 11:3).

3. The extent of this river: *It issues* (flows) *toward the east country* but *goes down into the desert*, and so *goes into the sea*, either into the Dead Sea (v. 8), which lay southeast, or the Sea of Tiberias, which lay northeast, or the Great Sea, which lay west. This was fulfilled when the Gospel was preached throughout all the regions of Judea and Samaria (Ac 8:1); and afterward the surrounding nations, and even the islands, were enlightened.

4. The healing power of this river. When the waters are *brought forth into the sea*, the sulfurous lake of Sodom, even those *waters shall be healed* (v. 8), will become fresh and healthy. This intimates the blessed change that the Gospel would make, as great a change as the turning of

the Dead Sea into a fountain of gardens. The Gospel was like the salt that Elisha threw into the waters of Jericho, with which he *healed them* (2Ki 2:20–21). When Christ came into the world to be its physician, he sent his Gospel as the great medicine. Wherever these rivers come, they *make things to live* (v. 9); they are *the water of life* (Rev 22:1, 17). Christ came so *that we might have life* (Jn 10:10), and that is why he sends his Gospel. The grace of God makes dead sinners alive and living saints active; everything is made fruitful and flourishing by it. However, its effect is according to how it is received and according to how the mind is prepared and disposed to receive it.

5. The great plenty that will be in this river. Every living, moving thing will be found here, will *live here* (v. 9).

6. The trees that are on the banks of this river—*many trees on the one side and on the other* (vv. 7, 12); they are *trees for meat* (food), and the *fruit* of them *shall not be consumed*, for it will produce fresh fruit *every month*. The *leaf* will be *for medicine*, and it *shall not fade*. This part of the vision corresponds to St. John's vision (Rev 22:2), in which it is said that the *tree of life* grew on either side of the river and *yielded her fruit every month*, and that *the leaves* were *for the healing of the nations*. The actual leaves of these trees *are for medicine*, "for bruises and sores" (v. 12, margin). Good Christians do good to those around them; they *strengthen the weak* (Isa 35:3) and bind up the brokenhearted (Isa 61:1). Their cheerfulness *does good like a medicine* (Pr 17:22). Their *leaf shall not fade*, having not only life in their root but also sap in all their branches. Each one of them will produce fruit monthly, which shows an abundant disposition to bearing fruit—they will never become weary of well-doing. And they will be so extraordinarily fruitful *because their waters issue out of the sanctuary*; their fruitfulness is to be ascribed to the continual supply of divine grace.

Verses 13–22

The land of Canaan is guaranteed to them here as an inheritance (v. 14): *I lifted up my hand to give it unto your fathers.* God has not forgotten his oath that he swore to their ancestors. *I lifted up my hand to give it,* and so it will without fail *fall to you for an inheritance* (v. 14). The boundaries are fixed. It is God who appoints the boundaries of our lands. The land is ordered here to be distributed among the tribes of Israel, with two portions for Joseph to make up the number of twelve, since Levi was removed to attend the sanctuary and had his lot adjoining that (vv. 13, 21): *You shall inherit it, one as well as another* (v. 14). The foreigners who stay among them, *who shall beget children* and be built up into families, and so help to populate their country, *shall have inheritance among the tribes, just as if they had been native-born Israelites* (vv. 22–23). This certainly looks forward to Gospel times, when the wall between Jew and Gentile was taken down (Eph 2:14) and both were put on the same level before God, both made one in Christ, in whom *there is no difference* (Ro 10:12).

CHAPTER 48

Particular directions are given here for the distribution of the land. We have: 1. The portions of the twelve tribes, seven to the north of the sanctuary (vv. 1–7) and five to the south (vv. 23–29). 2. The allotment of land for the sanctuary and the priests (vv. 8–11), for the Levites (vv. 12–14), for the city (vv. 15–20), and for the prince (vv. 21–22). 3. A plan of the city and its gates, and the

new name given to it (vv. 30–35), which concludes the vision and prophecy of this book.

Verses 1–30

A short way is taken to divide the land among the twelve tribes. In this distribution of the land we may notice that:

1. It differs very much from the division in Joshua's time. It is to be understood not so much literally as spiritually, though its mystery is very much hidden from us. *Behold, all things have become new* (2Co 5:17) in Gospel times. The Israel of God has a new way of doing things.

2. The tribe of Dan, which was provided for last in the first division of Canaan (Jos 19:40), is provided for first here (v. 1). In dispensing his grace, God does not follow the same method as he does in his providence.

3. All the ten tribes that were taken away by the king of Assyria, as well as the two tribes that were taken to Babylon long afterward, have their allotment in this visionary land. We believe this distribution has its intended fulfillment in the establishment and enlargement of the Gospel church and in the sure and sweet enjoyment of the privileges of the new covenant, in which there is enough for all and enough for each.

4. Every tribe in this visionary distribution has its particular allotment assigned it by divine appointment. We must not only acknowledge, but also accept, the hand of God appointing us our lot, and be pleased with it, believing it is most appropriate for us: *He shall choose our inheritance for us* (Ps 47:4).

5. The tribes lie next to one another. By *the border* of one tribe is *the portion* of another. This prefigures the fellowship of churches and saints governed by the Gospel; thus, although they are many, they are still one, and should stay together in holy love and mutual help.

6. The lot of Reuben, which before lay far beyond Jordan, now lies next to Judah, just one tribe away from the sanctuary, for the scandal Reuben lay under, for which he was told he should not excel (Ge 49:4), began by this time to wear off.

7. The sanctuary is *in the midst* of them. Seven tribes are to the north of it, and the portions for the Levites, the prince, and the city, with that of the other five tribes, are to the south of it. It therefore is, as it should be, *in the heart of the kingdom.*

8. The priests are where the sanctuary is: *For them, even for the priests, shall this holy oblation* (special portion) *be* (v. 10).

9. The priests who showed themselves faithful to God in times of testing are the ones who have the priests' share of these lands (v. 11): *It shall be for the sons of Zadok,* who, it seems, distinguished themselves at some critical point, not *going astray* when the *children of Israel,* and the other *Levites, went astray.*

10. The land that is set aside for the ministers of the sanctuary must by no means be passed to other hands. They cannot *sell it or exchange it* (v. 14). It is sacrilege to convert to other uses what is dedicated to God.

11. The land allotted for the city and its *suburbs* (pasturelands) is called *profane* (v. 15), or common. In comparison with the sanctuary, it is a common place.

12. The city is made to be exactly square, with the pasturelands extending equally on every side, as the Levites' cities did in the first division of the land (vv. 16–17); and since this was never literally fulfilled in any city, it must be understood spiritually, as referring to the beauty and stability of the Gospel church, that *city of the living God* (Heb 12:22).

13. Whereas previously the inhabitants of Jerusalem were principally of Judah and Benjamin, in whose tribe the city lay, now *those that serve the city* and hold office in it *shall serve it out of all the tribes of Israel* (v. 19).

14. Those who applied themselves to public business in the city as well as in the sanctuary must have an honorable, comfortable maintenance; lands are appointed, *the increase* (produce) of which *shall be food unto those that serve the city* (v. 18).

15. The prince has a lot assigned to himself, suited to the dignity of his high position (v. 21).

16. As Judah has his lot next the sanctuary on one side, so Benjamin has his lot closest to it on the other side, an honor that was reserved for those who were faithful to the house of David and the temple at Jerusalem when the other ten tribes turned away from both.

Verses 31–35

Here is a further account of the city that would be built for those who would come to worship in the adjoining sanctuary. It is nowhere called Jerusalem, nor is the land called Canaan, for *old things are done away; behold, all things have become new* (2Co 5:17). Notice concerning this city:

1. The measurements of its exits and of the land around it (v. 35); the form of measurement used here is uncertain, however. These things are to be understood spiritually.

2. The number of its gates. It had twelve gates in all, three on each side, inscribed with the names of the twelve tribes. In John's vision, the New Jerusalem has *twelve gates*, three on each side, and on them are written *the names of the twelve tribes of the children of Israel* (Rev 21:12–13). There is free access by faith into the church of Christ for all who come out of every tribe, from every quarter. Christ has *opened the kingdom of heaven for all believers*.

3. The name given of this city will not be, as previously, *Jerusalem*, "the vision of peace," but what is the origin of that, *Jehovah Shammah*, "The Lord is there" (v. 35). This suggested that:

3.1. The exiles, after their return, would have clear signs of God's presence with them and his residence among them.

3.2. The Gospel church, too, would have the presence of God in it; though it would not have that presence in the *Shechinah*, as in ages past, it would have it in a form that was no less certain, that of his Spirit. *Lo, I am with you always even unto the end of the world* (Mt 28:20). It may be truly said of every soul that has a living spring of grace in it, *The Lord is there*.

3.3. The glory and happiness of heaven would consist chiefly in the knowledge that *the Lord is there*.

A PRACTICAL AND DEVOTIONAL EXPOSITION OF
THE BOOK OF THE PROPHET
Daniel

The book of Ezekiel left Jerusalem all in ruins, but with a joyful prospect of being glorious again. Appropriately, the book of Daniel follows. Ezekiel told us what was seen, and what was foreseen, by him in the earlier years of the exile; Daniel tells us what was seen, and foreseen, in the later years of the exile. It was also an encouragement to the exiles that they first had one prophet and then another, to show them that God had not completely rejected them. Let us ask:

1. About this prophet. His Hebrew name was *Daniel*, which means "the judgment of God"; his Babylonian name was *Belteshazzar*. He was of the tribe of Judah and of the royal family, eminent for wisdom and godliness. Ezekiel, his senior, spoke about him as an authority when he rebuked the king of Tyre for his pride: *Thou art wiser than Daniel* (Eze 28:3). Noah, Daniel, and Job were counted as three men who had the greatest influence in heaven (Eze 14:14). Some of the Jewish rabbis rank his book among those that they call the Writings, not among the prophecies. One reason is that he did not live such a mortified life as Jeremiah and other prophets, but lived like a prince and became prime minister of state; yet we find him persecuted as other prophets (ch. 6) and humbling himself as other prophets did, declining to *eat pleasant bread* (10:3), and exhausted and ill when he was under the power of the Spirit of prophecy (8:27). Another reason they suggest is that he had his visions and wrote his book in a pagan country rather than in the land of Israel; but if that were a good reason for expunging a person from the roll of the prophets, Ezekiel, too, would be expunged. But the true reason why the rabbis reject Daniel is that he speaks so clearly of the time of the Messiah's coming that they do not want to listen to it. Yet Josephus calls him one of the greatest of the prophets. He lived a long, active life in the courts and councils of some of the greatest monarchs: Nebuchadnezzar, Cyrus, and Darius. The Spirit, like the wind, blows where it pleases (Jn 3:8), and if those who have much to do in the world plead that as an excuse for the unimportance of their dealings with God, Daniel will condemn them.

2. About this book. Its first six chapters are historical and are clear and easy; the last six are prophetic and contain many things that are hard to understand (2Pe 3:16), which would be more intelligible if we had a more complete history of the Jewish nation from Daniel's time to the coming of the Messiah. The first chapter and the first three verses of chapter 2 are in Hebrew; from there to chapter 8 is in Aramaic, and from there to the end is in Hebrew. Mr. Broughton observes that since the Babylonians were kind to Daniel, giving him cups of cold water when he asked, rather than the king's wine, God would not have them lose their reward (Mt 10:42), but gave their language honor in his writings. According to his reckoning, Daniel continues the holy story from the first surprise attack on Jerusalem by the Babylonian Babel, when he himself was taken captive, until its last destruction by Rome, the mystical Babel (9:27). The stories of Susanna and of Bel and the Dragon are apocryphal, have been found only in Greek, and have never been acknowledged by the Jewish church. There are some histories and prophecies of this book that are dated to the end of the Babylonian monarchy, and others that are dated to the beginning of the Persian monarchy. But both Nebuchadnezzar's dream, which Daniel interpreted, and Daniel's own visions point to the Greek and Roman monarchies, and especially to the Jews' troubles under Antiochus Epiphanes.

CHAPTER 1

Here is an account of the beginning of Daniel's life. Daniel began with the study of human learning, and afterward came divine visions. We have here: 1. Jehoiakim's first captivity (vv. 1–2), in which Daniel, with others of the royal family, was taken to Babylon.

2. The choice of Daniel and some other young men to be educated in the Babylonian way in order to equip them to serve the government (vv. 3–7). 3. Their devout refusal to eat the king's food and their decision to live on vegetables and water, which the chief of the king's court officials allowed them to do, finding that it suited them very well (vv. 8–16). 4. Their wonderful advancement above all their fellow students in wisdom and knowledge (vv. 17–21).

Verses 1–7

Here we have an account of:

1. The first attack that Nebuchadnezzar king of Babylon made on Judah and Jerusalem, in the first year of his reign, which was the third year of the reign of Jehoiakim (vv. 1–2). He *besieged Jerusalem*, conquered it, seized the city, took whomever and whatever he pleased, and then left Jehoiakim to reign as his tributary.

2. The way he made the most of this success. He did not destroy the city or kingdom, but made what was just the first threat of trouble by Babylon. It was declared against Hezekiah, for showing his treasures to the king of Babylon's ambassadors (Isa 39:6–7), that the treasures and the children would be taken away. And so:

2.1. Many of the holy articles were taken away by the king of Babylon and brought to the *house of his god* (v. 2), to whom he gave praise for his success with blind devotion. Notice here the righteousness of God: his people had brought idols of other gods into his temple, and now he allowed the articles of the temple to be taken away to the treasure houses of those other gods. It was only *part* (some) *of them* that went now; some were left, to see if the Jews would follow the right course of action to prevent the rest of them from being taken away. See Jer 27:18.

2.2. The children and young men, especially those of noble or royal extraction, handsome and promising, were taken away. They were taken away as security for the faithfulness of their parents in their own land and as a "seed to serve him" (compare Ps 22:30). He took them away to train them up for employment and promotion. Notice the directions that the king of Babylon gave for choosing these youths (v. 4). His officials must not choose those who had any physical defect, but those who were good-looking and handsome, *skilful in all wisdom* (showing aptitude for every kind of learning), *cunning*, well-informed, sharp, and quick to understand. He chose those who were young, because they would be submissive and likely to forget their own people and become Babylonians. They must be those who would be able to *stand in the king's palace* and preside in his affairs. Notice also the care that he took with their education. They were to be taught *the learning and tongue of the Chaldeans* (the language and literature of the Babylonians). They must be taught in such learning as might qualify them to serve their generation (Ac 13:36). They had *daily provision of the king's meat, and of the wine which he drank* (v. 5). This showed his generosity and humanity. A generous maintenance should go alongside a liberal education.

3. A particular account of Daniel and his fellows. They were of the *children of Judah* (v. 6), the royal tribe, and probably of the house of David. The *prince of the eunuchs* (chief official) changed the names of Daniel and his fellows as a sign of their being naturalized and made Babylonians. Their Hebrew names, which they received at their circumcision, had something of God, or Jah, in them: *Daniel*, "God is my Judge"; *Hananiah*, "the grace of the Lord"; *Mishael*, "he that is the strong God"; *Azariah*, "the Lord is a help." To make them forget the God of their fathers, the guide of their youth (Pr 2:17), the Babylonians gave them names that smacked of Babylonian idolatry. *Belteshazzar* means "the keeper of the hidden treasures of Bel"; *Shadrach*, "the inspiration of the sun," which

the Babylonians worshiped; *Meshach*, "of the goddess Shach," under which name Venus was worshiped; *Abednego*, "the servant of the shining fire," which they also worshiped.

Verses 8–16

We notice here, very much to our satisfaction:

1. That Daniel was a favorite with the chief official (v. 9), as Joseph was with the keeper of the prison.

2. That Daniel still held firm to his religious faith. They had changed his name, but they could not change his nature. Whatever name they wished to call him, he still retained the spirit of a true Israelite. He was resolved that *he would not defile himself with the portion of the king's meat*, and so he refused it, along with *the wine which he drank* (v. 8). *His* fellows reached the same decision (v. 12). They all did this from a principle of conscience. It was not in itself unlawful for them to *eat of the king's meat* or to *drink of his wine*. But:

2.1. They had scruples about eating food that might be sinful to eat. Sometimes there might be set before them food that was forbidden by their law, such as pork, or perhaps they were afraid it had been offered in sacrifice to an idol or blessed in the name of an idol. The Jews were set apart from other nations very much by their food (Lev 11:45–46). If God's command was against it, they must be faithful to that.

2.2. They took jealous care of themselves, for though it was not sinful in itself, it might cause them to sin. Besides, Jerusalem was in great trouble, and they themselves were in exile. They had no heart *to drink wine in bowls*; so much were they *grieved for the affliction of Joseph* (Am 6:6).

3. That God wonderfully acknowledged him in this. When Daniel asked to be excused from eating the king's food or drinking the wine, the chief official objected that if Daniel and his fellows were not in as good condition as their companions, he, the chief official, would be in danger of losing his head (v. 10). Daniel expressed the wish that the matter be put to the test. He asked the subordinate officer, *Melzar*: "*Prove* (test) *us for ten days* (v. 12); let us have nothing but *pulse to eat*, nothing but vegetables and fruits, parched peas or lentils, and nothing but *water to drink*, and see how we can live on that" (v. 13). The test was then made. Daniel and his fellows lived for ten days on vegetables and water. *At the end of the ten days* they were found *fairer and fatter in flesh* than *all those who did eat the portion of the king's meat* (v. 15). This was in part a natural effect of their temperance, but it must also be ascribed to the special blessing of God, which will make a little go a long way.

4. That the steward did not force them to eat against their consciences, but, as they wished, *gave them pulse and water* (v. 16). This self-denial prepared them for their eminent service. They kept their minds clear and unclouded. Those who had gotten used to hardship in this way and had lived a life of self-denial could more easily venture into the fiery furnace and the lions' den.

Verses 17–21

Concerning Daniel and his fellows we have here:

1. The great learning that God gave them (v. 17), which:

1.1. Made up for what they lost. Because of the sins of their ancestors, they had been deprived of honors and pleasures, but to make amends for that, when God gave them learning, he gave them better honors and pleasures.

1.2. Rewarded them for their integrity. They were faithful to their religious faith, even in the minutest details, and now God rewarded them: to Daniel he gave a double portion; he had *understanding in visions and dreams* (v. 17) by a divine wisdom that God gave him.

2. Their great acceptance with the king. After *three years* spent on their education they were presented to the king (v. 18). The king examined them and *communed* (talked) *with them* himself (v. 19). He examined them *in all matters of wisdom and understanding* and found that they had *more understanding than the ancients* (Ps 119:99–100). He freely acknowledged that when the test had been completed, he found those poor young exiled Jews wiser and *better than all the magicians that were in all his realm* (v. 20). These four young students were *ten times* better than all the old practitioners. After this judgment had been given, they *stood before the king* (v. 19).

CHAPTER 2

This chapter is the story of a prophecy that was given through a dream and its interpretation. The prophecy concerned the four monarchies and Israel's relation to them; it also concerned the kingdom of the Messiah, which would be set up in the world on their ruins. We have here: 1. The great perplexity that Nebuchadnezzar felt through a dream, and his command to the magicians to tell him what it was (vv. 1–11). 2. Orders given to destroy all the wise men of Babylon, including Daniel and his friends (vv. 12–15). 3. The revelation of this mystery to Daniel in answer to prayer, and the thanksgiving he offered to God (vv. 16–23). 4. His admission to the king and his revelation to him of both his dream and its interpretation (vv. 24–45). 5. The great honor that Nebuchadnezzar put on Daniel as a reward for this service, and the promotion of his companions with him (vv. 46–49).

Verses 1–13

It is difficult to date this story; it is said to be in the second year of the reign of Nebuchadnezzar (v. 1). Daniel was taken to Babylon in his first year and, it seems, was educated by tutors for three years before he was presented to the king (1:5). How then could this happen in *the second year*? Perhaps Daniel advanced so quickly in his studies that he was given a job after only one year. Some understand it to be the second year after Nebuchadnezzar began to reign alone, but the fifth or sixth year since he began to reign in partnership with his father. Some read it, *And in the second year*—the second year after Daniel and his friends stood before the king—*in the kingdom of Nebuchadnezzar*, or *in the reign of Nebuchadnezzar*, this happened. It appears in Ezekiel that Daniel was soon famous both for wisdom and for effectiveness in prayer. He came to be famous for both early in Nebuchadnezzar's reign. Here we may notice:

1. The perplexity that Nebuchadnezzar felt because of a dream that he had forgotten (v. 1). There was something in the impression it made on him that was evidence of its divine origin and its prophetic significance. Nebuchadnezzar was a troubler of God's Israel, but here God troubled him (Jos 7:25; 1Ch 2:7). All the *treasures* and *delights* (Ecc 2:8–11) that this mighty monarch had could not gain for him a little rest when, because of his troubled mind, his *sleep broke from him*.

2. The test he gave to his magicians and enchanters. They were immediately sent for to *show the king his*

dreams (v. 2). His dream had slipped out of his mind, and he could not possibly recollect it. The magicians were probably proud of being sent for into the king's room. He told them that he had *dreamed a dream* (v. 3). They asked him to tell them his dream and assured him they would interpret it (v. 4). But the king insisted that they must tell him the dream. He also said that if they could not do this, they would all be put to death as deceivers (v. 5); they themselves would be *cut to pieces*, and *their houses made a dunghill* (turned into piles of rubble). If they could do it, they would be rewarded (v. 6). The magicians insisted that the king must tell them the dream, and then, if they did not tell him its interpretation, it would be their fault (v. 7). But arbitrary power is deaf to reason. The king lost his temper, spoke to them harshly, and accused them of trying to insult him: *You have prepared lying and corrupt words to speak before me* (v. 9). He told them that they were playing with him to gain time (v. 8), *till the time* (situation) *be changed* (v. 9), either until the king's desire to know his dream had passed or until they had reason to hope he had so completely forgotten his dream that they could tell him whatever they wanted. Therefore, they must tell him the dream without delay. They pleaded in vain:

2.1. That there was *no man on earth* who could reclaim the king's dream (v. 10). They acknowledged that the gods could indeed *declare unto man what is his thought* (Am 4:13). But those who can do this are gods (v. 11), and it is only they who can do it. Notice here an example of the ignorance of these magicians, that they speak about many gods, whereas there is, and can be, only one infinite God, yet notice their knowledge that there is a God who is a Spirit and who knows perfectly the spirits of human beings and all their thoughts.

2.2. That there was no king on earth who would expect or require such a thing (v. 10).

3. The condemnation passed on all the magicians of Babylon. There was but *one decree* (penalty) *for them all* (v. 9): each one of them must be put to death (v. 13), including *Daniel and his fellows* (friends), even though they knew nothing about the matter. Nebuchadnezzar was seen here to be a tyrant in his true colors, speaking death when he could not speak sense.

Verses 14–23

When the king sent for his wise men to have them tell him his dream (v. 2), Daniel was not summoned to appear. How unfortunate is the situation of those who live under an arbitrary government, such as this of Nebuchadnezzar! Daniel was famous both for wisdom and for prayer; as a prince he had power with God and people; through prayer he had power with God, through wisdom he had power with people, and in both he overcame (Ge 32:28). In these verses we have a remarkable instance of both.

1. Daniel had the wisdom to deal with people. When *Arioch the captain of the guard*, who was appointed to put to death all the wise men of Babylon, seized Daniel, Daniel *answered with counsel* (tact) *and wisdom* (v. 14); he did not lose his temper, but mildly asked (v. 15): *Why is the decree so hasty?* Daniel offered to give the king all the satisfaction he wanted, if he could just have a little time (v. 16).

2. Daniel knew how to talk to God in prayer, how to present both requests and thanksgiving. Notice:

2.1. His humble request for mercy, that God would reveal to him what the king's dream was, along with its interpretation. He *went to his house* to be alone with his

God, for from him alone, the *Father of lights* (Jas 1:17), he expected to receive this great gift.

2.1.1. He also engaged his companions to pray for it (vv. 17–18). The apostle Paul often asked his friends to pray for him. This is how we must show that we value our friends and their prayers.

2.1.2. He was specific in this prayer but also looked to and depended on the general mercy of God: he requested that his friends *would desire* (plead for) *the mercies of the God of heaven concerning this secret* (mystery) (v. 18). Whatever we are concerned about must be the subject of our prayer; we must desire the mercy of God about all things that cause us trouble and fear. God allows us to be humbly free with him. We may still in faith pray to him who has all hearts in his hand and who in his providence does wonders, that he would reveal what is out of our sight and grant us what is out of our reach.

2.1.3. The mercy that Daniel and his friends prayed for was given. The mystery was revealed to Daniel in a night vision (v. 19). Some think that when he was asleep, he dreamed the same dream that Nebuchadnezzar had dreamed.

2.2. His grateful thanksgiving for this mercy (v. 19). In the same way that he had prayed with full assurance that God would do this for him, he also gave thanks with full assurance that God had done it: *Blessed be the name of God for ever and ever* (v. 22). There is in God what is to be blessed and praised forever; it is unchangeably and eternally in him. His companions were present with Daniel when the revelation was made, or as soon as he knew it he told them, so that those who had joined him in their prayers might join him in their praises; his linking them with him shows his humility. In the same way, the apostle Paul sometimes links Silas, Timothy, or some other minister with himself in the introductions to many of his letters.

Verses 24–30

We have here the introduction to Daniel's declaration of the dream and its interpretation.

1. He immediately requested the reversing of the sentence against the wise men of Babylon (v. 24). He went as fast as he could to Arioch: *Destroy not* (do not execute) *the wise men of Babylon.*

2. With great assurance, he offered to go to the king and tell him his dream and its interpretation (vv. 24–25).

3. He contrived as much as possible to give honor to God on this occasion. The king acknowledged that it was a bold undertaking (v. 26). *Art thou able to make known unto me the dream?* The less likely it appeared to the king that Daniel could do this, the more God was glorified in enabling him to do it. Daniel drew the king's favor away from his soothsayers (v. 27): "They cannot explain this mystery to the king. Therefore let not the king be angry with them for not doing what they cannot do, but rather let him reject them because they cannot do it. Although they cannot reveal the secret, let not the king despair of having it revealed, for there is a God in heaven who makes known secrets" (v. 28).

4. He confirmed the king in his opinion that the dream was very valuable. It was a divine revelation, a ray of light darted into his mind from the higher world, relating to the great affairs of this lower world. In it, God made known to the king what would happen *in the latter days*, in days to come (v. 28). Some think that the thoughts about what would take place in the future that are said to have come into the king's mind on his bed were his own thoughts when he was awake. They think that just before he fell asleep,

he was musing about what would be the outcome of his increasing greatness, what his kingdom would be like in the future, and so the dream was an answer to those thoughts.

5. He solemnly professed that he could not claim to have deserved from God the favor of this revelation (v. 30): "*But as for me,* this secret has not been found out by me, but has been revealed to me. It has been revealed to me not because of any *wisdom that I have* that qualifies me to receive such a revelation." The secret was made known to him for the sake of his people, his brothers and sisters and companions in misfortune. God revealed this thing to Daniel so that he could make it known to the king. Prophets receive so that they may give, so that the revelations made to them may be communicated to the people who are concerned in them.

Verses 31–45

Daniel fully satisfied Nebuchadnezzar about his dream and its interpretation here. Now the king was abundantly repaid, and because he received this prophet, though not in the name of a prophet, he received a prophet's reward (Mt 10:41). Here is:

1. The dream itself (vv. 31, 45). Nebuchadnezzar was a worshiper of *images* (statues), and now a large statue was set before him in a dream. This was the statue of an erect man: *It stood before him,* like a living human being, and because those monarchies represented by it were wondered at by their friends, the *brightness of* this image *was excellent* (dazzling). Moreover, because they were formidable to their enemies, the *form* of this image is said to have been *terrible* (awesome); both the features of the face and the positions of the body made it so. However, what was most remarkable was the different metals of which it was composed—the *head of gold* (the richest and most durable metal), the *breast* (chest) *and arms of silver* (the next most valuable), the *belly and sides* (or *thighs*) *of brass* (bronze), the *legs of iron* (baser metals), and lastly the feet, which were *part of iron and part of clay.* Notice what the things of this world are like: the further we go with them, the less valuable they appear. Some comment that in Daniel's visions the monarchies were represented by four animals (ch. 7), and in his wisdom he saw it from below, earthly and a tyrannical power, which had more in it of the beast than of human beings. However, to Nebuchadnezzar, a pagan prince, these kingdoms were represented by a showy, proud human statue, for he was an admirer of the *kingdoms of this world and the glory of them* (Mt 4:8). But what became of this statue? In the next part of the dream we see it broken to pieces, reduced to powder and brought to nothing (v. 34). He saw a stone cut out of the quarry by an unseen power, and this stone fell on the *feet of the image,* which were *of iron and clay,* and *broke them to pieces.* Then the statue must fall, and the gold, silver, bronze, and iron were all broken to pieces, smashed so small that they became like the *chaff of the summer threshing floors* (v. 35), but the stone *cut out of the mountain* became itself a *great mountain, and filled the earth.*

2. The interpretation of this dream.

2.1. This statue represented the kingdoms of the earth that would successively rule among the nations and influence the affairs of the Jewish church. The four monarchies were not represented by four distinct statues, but by one statue, because they were all of one and the same spirit, and all more or less against the church. It was the same power, only placed within four different nations.

2.1.1. The *head of gold* represented the Babylonian monarchy, which was now in existence (vv. 37–38):

"You are the *highest of kings* on earth at this time. It is *the God of heaven* who has *given thee a kingdom, power, and strength, and glory*, a kingdom that exercises great authority and stands firmly." The extent of his dominion is set out (v. 38): *wheresoever the children of men dwelt* in all the nations of that part of the world, he was *ruler over them all*. He was therefore "*the head of gold*; you and your son and your grandson, for seventy years." Compare this with Jer 25:9, 11, and Jer 27:5 – 7. There were other powerful kingdoms in the world at this time, such as that of the Scythians, but it was the kingdom of Babylon that reigned over the Jews. It is called *a head* for its wisdom and absolute power, a head of *gold* for its wealth (Isa 14:4). Some believe this monarchy began with Nimrod, and so they include in it all the Assyrian kings. However, it had not been a monarchy of such vast extent for as long as that, and therefore others believe only Nebuchadnezzar, Evil-Merodach, and Belshazzar belong to this *head of gold*.

2.1.2. The *breast* (chest) *and arms of silver* signified the monarchy of the Medes and Persians (Medo-Persia). *There shall arise another kingdom inferior to thee* (v. 39), not so rich, powerful, or victorious. This kingdom was founded by Darius the Mede and Cyrus the Persian in alliance and was therefore represented by two arms. Cyrus was himself a Persian through his father, a Mede through his mother.

2.1.3. The *belly and thighs of brass* (bronze) represented the monarchy of the Greeks, founded by Alexander, who conquered Darius, the last of the Persian emperors. This is the *third kingdom, of bronze*, inferior in wealth and extent to the Persian monarchy, but in Alexander himself it would by the power of the sword *bear rule over all the earth* (v. 39), for Alexander boasted that he had conquered the world.

2.1.4. The *legs and feet of iron* represented the Roman monarchy. It was in the time of that monarchy, when it was at its height, that the kingdom of Christ was set up in the world by the preaching of the eternal Gospel. The Roman kingdom was strong as iron (v. 40) and *broke in pieces* the Greek Empire and afterward destroyed the nation of the Jews. Toward the end of the Roman monarchy it became weak and branched into ten kingdoms, which were like the toes of these feet. Some of these were as weak as clay, others as strong as iron (v. 42). *They shall not cleave one to another* (will not remain united) (v. 43). This empire divided the government for a long time between the senate and the people, the nobles and the common people, but they did not coalesce. There were civil wars between Marius and Sulla, Caesar and Pompey, whose parties were like iron and clay.

2.2. The stone *cut out without hands* (vv. 34, 45) represented the kingdom of Jesus Christ, for it would be neither raised nor supported by human power or wisdom.

2.2.1. The Gospel church is a kingdom *not of this world* (Jn 18:36), but set up in it; it is the kingdom of God on earth.

2.2.2. The *God of heaven* was to set up this kingdom, to give authority to Christ, to set him as *King upon his holy hill of Zion* (Ps 2:6). It is often called the *kingdom of heaven* in the New Testament, for its origin is from above and its focus is upward.

2.2.3. It was to be set up *in the days of these kings*, the kings of the fourth monarchy, of which particular notice is taken in Lk 2:1. When these kings were fighting against one another, God would do his own work and fulfill his own purposes.

2.2.4. It is a kingdom in which there will be no decay, and it will not allow any succession or revolution. Just as Christ is a monarch who has no successor—for he

himself will reign forever—so his kingdom is a monarchy that will have no revolution. The kingdom of God was indeed taken from the Jews and given to the Gentiles (Mt 21:43), but it was still Christianity that ruled, the kingdom of the Messiah.

2.2.5. It is a kingdom that will be victorious. It will *break in pieces and consume all those kingdoms*, as the *stone cut out of the mountain without hands* broke in pieces the statue (vv. 44 – 45). In the kingdoms that submit to the kingdom of Christ, tyranny, idolatry, and everything that causes their shame will, as far as the Gospel of Christ gains ground, be broken. Our Savior seems to refer to this when he says, *On whomsoever* this stone *shall fall, it will grind him to powder* (Mt 21:44).

2.2.6. It will be an eternal kingdom. *The Lord shall reign for ever*, not only to the end of time but also when there will be no more time and days and *God shall be all in all* to eternity (1Co 15:28).

3. A solemn assertion with which Daniel closed after he had interpreted the dream in this way, in which he affirmed:

- The divine origin of this dream: *The great God* has *made known to the king what shall come to pass hereafter* (v. 45), which the gods of the magicians could not do.
- The undoubted certainty of the things foretold by this dream. We may depend on whatever God has made known.

Verses 46 – 49

Instead of resenting Daniel's words as an insult, the king received them as an authoritative message, and we are told here what impressions this message made on him.

1. He was ready to look on Daniel as a little god. He concluded that Daniel certainly had divine qualities in him, worthy of his adoration, and so he *fell upon his face and worshiped Daniel* (v. 46). This was how God exalted divine revelation *and made it honourable*. That Daniel said something to him that turned his eyes and thoughts another way is suggested by what follows: *The king answered Daniel* (v. 47).

2. He readily acknowledged the God of Daniel to be the great God. If Daniel would not allow himself to be worshiped, the king would *worship God*, by confessing, *Of a truth your God is a God of gods* (v. 47), over all gods in authority and power.

3. He promoted Daniel, *making him a great man* (placed him in a high position) (v. 48). The king *gave him many great gifts*. He made him *ruler over the whole province of Babylon*; he also made him chancellor of the university, *chief of the governors over all the wise men of Babylon*.

4. He promoted his companions for his sake, and on his request (v. 49), Daniel himself *sat in the gate of the king* and obtained positions in the government for Shadrach, Meshach, and Abednego. Because these devout Jews were advanced to such a high position in Babylon, they had a great opportunity to serve their brothers and sisters in exile.

CHAPTER 3

Here we have those same three men under the king's displeasure as much as they were in his favor before, but more highly honored by their God than they were honored by their prince, by the grace with which he enabled them to suffer rather than to sin. It is a memorable story and a great encouragement to the faithfulness of his people in difficult times. The writer to the Hebrews mentions, among the believing heroes, those who by faith quenched the violence of fire (Heb 11:34). We have here: 1. Nebuchadnezzar's setting up a golden image and requiring all his subjects to fall down and worship it; and we see the general submission of his people to that command (vv. 1–7). 2. Information given against the Jewish young men for refusing to worship this golden image (vv. 8–12). 3. Their constant persistence in refusing to do so, despite his threats (vv. 13–18). 4. The throwing of them into the fiery furnace for refusing (vv. 19–23). 5. Their miraculous preservation by the power of God and their invitation by the king to come out of the fire, since he was now convinced by this miracle that he had done wrong by throwing them in (vv. 24–27). 6. The honor that the king then gave to God and the favor he showed those faithful men (vv. 28–30).

Verses 1–7

1. A *golden image was set up* to be worshiped. Babylon was full of idols. Those who have forsaken the one and only living God and begin to set up many gods will find the gods they set up so unsatisfying that they will multiply them without limit. It was *an image of gold*. It was *threescore cubits high and six cubits broad*, as if monstrously would make up for lifelessness. Perhaps he set it up as an image of himself and intended to be worshiped through it. The good impressions made on him earlier by the dream were quickly and completely lost. Then, he had acknowledged that the God of Israel is *God of gods* and a *Lord of kings* (2:47); now, in defiance of the explicit law of that God, he set up an image to be worshiped. The dream that had then made him worship the true God now made him set himself up as a bold competitor with God.

2. The officials were called to attend the dedication of this image (vv. 2–3). Many took long journeys on a foolish mission, but just as idols are senseless, so are their worshipers.

3. A declaration was made commanding that when the signal was given, all people present must fall down and worship the image.

4. The assembly agreed to this command (v. 7). It had been declared that whoever would not *worship this golden image* would be immediately thrown *into the midst of a burning fiery furnace* already prepared for that purpose (v. 6).

Verses 8–18

It was strange that Shadrach, Meshach, and Abednego were present at this assembly when, as is likely, they knew why it had been called; surely it was because they wanted to obey the king's orders as far as they could and wanted to be ready to bear public testimony against this gross idolatry.

1. Information is brought to the king against these three by *certain Chaldeans* (astrologers) (v. 8). Perhaps *Chaldeans* here refers specifically to some of those *magicians or astrologers* who were called Chaldeans (2:2). Perhaps they were astrologers who envied the young Jews their promotion, *and who can stand before envy* (Pr 27:4)? They appeal to the king:

1.1. To remind him of the law he just made, that all people, without exception as regards nation or language, should *fall down and worship this golden image* (vv. 10–11).

1.2. To inform him that these three men, Shadrach, Meshach, and Abednego, had not conformed to this decree (v. 12). To anger the king even more against them:

1.2.1. They remind him of the position to which the criminals have been advanced. It is therefore an insufferable act of arrogance for them to disobey the king's command. The high position they are in will make their refusal even more scandalous.

1.2.2. They suggest that it has been done to show defiant contempt of him and his authority.

2. These three devout Jews are brought before the king and examined on this information. Nebuchadnezzar becomes very angry and *in his rage and fury commands* them to be seized (v. 13).

3. The king asks them whether it is true that they have not worshiped the golden image when others did so (v. 14). Maybe on second thought they will change their minds. The king is willing to let them be tested again; if they *will worship the golden image*, then all well and good; their former omission will be pardoned. Yet he is determined that if they persist in their refusal, they will immediately be *cast into the fiery furnace* (v. 15). *Turn or burn*, he says, and because he knows they support themselves in their refusal with a confidence in their God, he defies him: *"And who is that God that shall deliver you out of my hands? Let him, if he can."*

4. They answer that they will remain faithful to their decision and determination not to worship the golden image (vv. 16–18). We call these the *three children* (they were indeed *young men*), but we should rather call them three champions, the first three of the Worthies of God's kingdom [Ed. note: there is a traditional list of classical, Jewish, and Christian heroes called the Nine Worthies]. They did not go out of their way to seek martyrdom, but when they were duly called to the fiery trial, they acquitted themselves bravely. This showed:

4.1. Their contempt of death and their noble disregard of the dilemma: *O Nebuchadnezzar, we are not careful to answer* (we do not need to defend ourselves before) *thee in this matter* (v. 16). They do not sullenly deny him an answer, but tell him that they are not concerned about it. They need no time to deliberate concerning their answer, for they do not hesitate as to whether they should obey or not. It is a matter of life and death; but when the sin and duty in the case are determined by the letter of the second commandment, and no opportunity is left to question what is right, then the life and death that are in the case are not to be considered. The three friends are not working out some evasive answer when a direct answer is expected from them.

4.2. Their confidence in God and their dependence on him (v. 17). They trust in the living God, and they choose to remain committed to that faith rather than to sin, even if it means suffering. "If we must be thrown into the fiery furnace unless we serve your gods, then know that although we do not worship *thy gods*, we are not unbelievers; there is a God whom we call ours. We serve this God. We are convinced that this God is *able to deliver us from the burning fiery furnace*. But if he does not rescue us from the fiery furnace, he *will deliver us out of thy hand*." Nebuchadnezzar can only torment and kill the body (Mt 10:28), and after that, there is nothing more he can do. God will rescue us either from death or in death.

4.3. Their determination to be faithful to their principles, whatever the consequences might be (v. 18). They are not being required to disown their God or renounce his worship. It is only one single act that is required of them, which can be done in a minute, and they can declare their sorrow for it afterward. They could be excused if they went with the stream when it was so strong. Had not all the ten tribes for many years worshiped gods of gold at Dan and Bethel? If they obeyed the king's decree, they would save their lives and so be able to be of great service to their brothers and sisters. But there is enough in that one word of God with which to answer and silence these and many more such worldly reasons: *Thou shalt not bow down thyself to any images, nor worship them* (Ex 20:5). They must suffer rather than sin and must not do evil so that good may come. Truly, their being saved from this sinful obedience was as great a miracle as their being saved from the fiery furnace.

Verses 19–27

In these verses we have:

1. The throwing of these three faithful servants of God into the fiery furnace. Instead of being convinced by what they said, Nebuchadnezzar was exasperated (v. 19). It made him *full of fury*, and the *form of his visage* (his attitude) *was changed* toward these men. In his temper, Nebuchadnezzar exchanged the awesome majesty of a prince for the fearful rage of a *wild bull in a net* (Isa 51:20). Instead of reducing their punishment, he ordered that it be heightened, that his servants should *heat the furnace seven times more than it was wont* (usually) *to be heated* for other evildoers (v. 19). He ordered them to be bound in their clothes and thrown into the middle of the burning fiery furnace, which was done (vv. 20–21). God's providence ordered it to heighten the miracle, in that their clothes were not even singed. The men who bound them and threw them into the furnace were themselves consumed or suffocated by the flames (v. 22). However, these men were only the instruments of cruelty; the one who told them to do it had the greater sin. Nebuchadnezzar himself was reserved for a later reckoning.

2. The rescue of these three faithful servants of God from the furnace.

2.1. Nebuchadnezzar found them walking in the fire. *He was astonished, and rose up in haste* (v. 24). In his amazement he called his advisers: *Did we not cast three men bound into the fire?* "True, O king," they said. "But now," the king said, "I have been looking into the furnace, and *I see four men, loose, walking in the midst of the fire*" (v. 25). They were released from their bonds. The fire that did not even singe their clothes burned the cords with which they were bound, and set them free. They *walked in the midst of the fire*. The furnace was large, so that they had room to walk about; they were unhurt, so that they were able to walk; their minds were at peace, so that they felt like taking a walk, as in a paradise or garden of pleasure. There was a fourth person seen with them in the fire, whose form, in Nebuchadnezzar's judgment, was *like the Son of God* (v. 25); he appeared as a divine person, a messenger from heaven, not as a servant, but as a son. In the apocryphal narrative of this story it is said, *The angel of the Lord came down into the furnace* (S of III Ch 1:26), and Nebuchadnezzar says in v. 28, God *sent his angel and delivered them*. It was also an angel that shut the lions' mouths when Daniel was in the den (6:22). However, some think it was the eternal Son of God. Those who suffer for Christ have his gracious presence with them in their sufferings, even in the fiery furnace, even in the valley of the shadow of death, and so they need *fear no evil* even there (Ps 23:4).

2.2. Nebuchadnezzar called them out of the furnace (v. 26): he *came near to the mouth of the burning fiery furnace* and told them to come out and come to him. He was convinced by their miraculous preservation that he had done evil by throwing them into the furnace. The fourth, whose form was like the Son of God, withdrew, but the other three came out of the fire, as *brands out of the burning* (Am 4:11). They had not sustained the least damage in the fire (v. 27). Not even a hair on their head had been singed. Their clothes did not change color or smell of fire, and much less were their bodies scorched or blistered; no, *the fire had no power on them*. The Babylonians worshiped fire, as a sort of image of the sun, so that, in restraining the fire now, God showed contempt not only for their king but also for their god.

Verses 28–30

Let us now see what effect this had on Nebuchadnezzar.

1. He gave glory to the God of Israel as a God who is able and ready to protect his worshipers: *Blessed be the God of Shadrach, Meshach, and Abednego* (v. 28). God can draw out confessions of his blessedness even from those who have been ready to curse him to his face.

1.1. He gave him the glory for his power: *There is no other God that can deliver after this sort* (v. 29). If God can work acts of rescue that no other god can, then it is right that he may demand such obedience as no other god may.

1.2. He gave him the glory for being ready to do it (v. 28): *He has sent his angel and delivered his servants.* Bel could not save his worshipers from being burned at the mouth of the furnace, but the God of Israel saved his worshipers from being burned when they were thrown into the middle of the furnace because they refused to *worship any other god*.

2. He applauded the faithfulness of these three men in their religion and described it to their honor (v. 28). They surrendered their own bodies to be thrown into the fiery furnace rather than forsake their God. They *changed the king's word* (defied the king's command); they went against it and so made him repent. They depended on their God, trusting that he would either bring them out of the fiery furnace on earth or lead them through the fiery furnace forward to their place in heaven. In this confidence, they were without concern for their own lives.

3. He issued a royal decree strictly forbidding anyone to speak evil of the God of Israel (v. 29). The miracle now brought about by the power of this God in defense of his worshipers, and done publicly in the sight of the thousands of Babylon, was a sufficient justification for this decree. It is a great mercy to the church when its enemies, even though their hearts have not yet turned, still have their mouths silenced and their tongues tied.

4. He not only reversed the condemnation of these three men but also restored them to their positions in the government—"made them prosper" is the sense.

CHAPTER 4

The story recorded here concerning Nebuchadnezzar is given us in his own words. Here is: 1. The introduction to his narrative, in which he acknowledges God's rule over him (vv. 1–3). 2. The narrative itself, in which he relates: 2.1. His dream (vv. 4–18). 2.2. The interpretation of his dream by Daniel, who showed him his own downfall, advising him to repent and reform (vv. 19–27). 2.3. The fulfillment of it in his becoming mad for seven years and then recovering his sanity (vv. 28–36). 2.4.

The concluding of the narrative with a humble acknowledgment and adoration of God as Lord of all (v. 37).

Verses 1–3

Here is:

1. The form that was usual in proclamations issued by the king (v. 1). The royal style is short and unaffected: *Nebuchadnezzar the king.* The declaration is directed *to all people, nations, and languages that dwell in all the earth* (v. 1). He uses the usual form in saluting those to whom he writes: *Peace be multiplied unto you,* may you prosper greatly (v. 1).

2. The substance. He writes this:

2.1. So that others may know the providences of God as they have related to him: *I thought it good to show the signs and wonders that the high God* (v. 2)—note what he calls the true God—*has wrought toward me.* He thinks it a debt he owes to God and the world, now that he has recovered from his confusion, to tell how justly God humbled him and how graciously he eventually restored him. We should give glory to God not only by praising him for his mercies but also by confessing our sins and accepting the punishment for our sins (Jos 7:19–20).

2.2. So that he may show how much he himself is convinced by them (v. 3). He wonders at God's actions. Nebuchadnezzar was now old, having reigned more than forty years, and had seen much of the world and changes, but not until now was he brought to wonder at God's signs and wonders. Now, *How great, how mighty,* are they! He deduces God's rule from these. *His kingdom is an everlasting kingdom,* not like Nebuchadnezzar's own kingdom, which he saw, in a dream, moving quickly toward an end. Other reigns are confined to one generation, and other dynasties to a few generations, but God's *dominion is from generation to generation* (v. 3).

Verses 4–18

Before Nebuchadnezzar relates the judgments of God brought on him because of his pride, he gives an account of the fair warning he had of them before they came. Here we have:

1. The time when this alarm was given to him (v. 4), when he was *at rest in his house, and flourishing* (contented and prosperous) *in his palace.* He had recently conquered Egypt, thereby completing his victories and ending his wars, about the thirty-fourth or thirty-fifth year of his reign (Eze 29:17). Then he had this dream, which was fulfilled about a year later. His madness continued for seven years, and on his recovery from it he wrote this declaration, then lived about two years longer and died in his forty-fifth year.

2. The impression it made on him: *I saw a dream which made me afraid* (v. 5). His *thoughts upon his bed* made him uneasy, and the *visions of his head,* what he saw in his own imagination, *troubled him.*

3. His consulting the magicians and astrologers in vain. This time he had not forgotten the dream, as he had before (ch. 2). He wanted to know its interpretation (v. 6). Orders were immediately given to summon *all the wise men of Babylon* to see if any could interpret the king's dream. His expectations of them were disappointed: he *told them the dream* (v. 7), but they *could not tell him the interpretation of it,* though they had boasted with great assurance (vv. 4, 7). Then was fulfilled what Isaiah foretold in Isa 47:12–13, that when the ruin of Babylon was drawing near, her *enchantments* and *sorceries,* her *astrologers* and *stargazers,* would not be able help her.

4. His humble request that Daniel explain his dream to him: *At the last Daniel came in* (v. 8). Many make God's word their last refuge, never turning to it until they have been driven away from all other forms of help. The king complimented Daniel very highly. He applauded his rare gifts: Daniel had *the spirit of the holy gods,* as the king told him to his face (v. 9). Here was a strange contradiction in Nebuchadnezzar, but one that is common in those who side with their corruptions against their convictions. He was an idolater, and his speech gave him away. He spoke about many gods. Some also think that when he spoke of *the spirit of the holy gods,* he was thinking that there were some evil, malignant gods and some who were good, kind gods, and that Daniel was being inspired by the spirit of the latter. He also applauded Daniel as *master of the magicians* (v. 9)—not as *a servant of God* (6:20; 9:11). How weak his convictions were, and how easily he dropped them. He had once called the God of Israel a *God of gods* (2:47). Now he set him on the same level as the rest of those whom he called the *holy gods.* Nebuchadnezzar did not proceed with acknowledgments of the sovereignty of the true God, but soon *went backwards,* though he professed to have a high opinion of Daniel, whom he knew to be a servant of the true God.

5. The account he gave him of his dream:

5.1. He saw an impressive flourishing tree *planted in the midst of the earth* (v. 10), appropriately representing him as the one who reigned in Babylon, the middle of the then known world. His position was represented by the height of this tree, which was *exceedingly great* (enormous); it *reached unto heaven.* He was higher than those around him and aimed to have divine honors given him. This tree had everything in it that was pleasant to the eye and good for food (Ge 2:9; 3:6) (v. 12): *The leaves thereof were fair,* showing the pomp and splendor of Nebuchadnezzar's court. This tree was:

- For protection; its boughs gave shelter. Rulers should protect their subjects *from the heat* and *from the storm.*
- For provision. The Assyrian was compared to *a cedar* (Eze 31:6), which gives only shade, but this tree had much fruit—in it was *meat* (food) *for all,* and *all flesh* (every creature) *was fed of it.* This mighty monarch, it seems from this, not only was great but also did good.

5.2. He heard the doom of this tree read out. The sentence was passed on the tree by an angel, whom he saw *come down from heaven* and heard declare this sentence aloud. This angel is called here *a watcher* or *watchman.* This angel was "a messenger or ambassador," as some read it, and *a holy one.*

5.2.1. Orders were given for the tree to be cut down (v. 14).

5.2.2. Care was taken that the root would be preserved (v. 15): "*Leave the stump of it in the earth,* exposed to all kinds of weather. Let it be bound with *a band of iron and brass* (bronze) to keep it firm." God remembers mercy in judgment (Hab 3:2), and he may still have good things in store for those whose condition seems most forlorn. There is *hope of a tree, if it be cut down, that it will sprout again, that through the scent of water it will bud* (Job 14:7–9).

5.2.3. The meaning of this was explained to Nebuchadnezzar by the angel himself (v. 16). Whoever is the person represented by this tree is sentenced to be deposed from the dignity of a human being, to be deprived of reason and to live like a wild animal until *seven times pass over him. Let a beast's heart be given unto him.* This is surely the saddest and harshest of all physical judgments. Those proud tyrants who *set their heart as the heart of God* (Eze 28:2) may justly be deprived of the use of a human mind and be given the mind of an animal.

5.2.4. Its truth was confirmed (v. 17). The angels of heaven had agreed to it. It was by *the decree of the watchers* (messengers). Such was Nebuchadnezzar's doom; it was by the *decree of the watchers*. The saints on earth requested it, as well as the angels in heaven: *The demand is by the word of the holy ones.* God's suffering people, who had groaned for a long time under the heavy yoke of Nebuchadnezzar's tyranny, made their demands, and God answered in this way.

5.2.5. Its intention was declared: orders were given for this tree to be cut down, *to the intent that the living may know that the Most High rules* (v. 17).

And so Nebuchadnezzar fully and faithfully told his dream, what he saw and what he heard, and then demanded its interpretation from Daniel (v. 18).

Verses 19–27

Here is the interpretation of Nebuchadnezzar's dream, and once it was declared that he was the tree in the dream, once it was said, *Thou art the man* (2Sa 12:7), little more needed to be said, in one sense, to explain the dream. The thing was so clear that when Daniel heard the dream, he was *astonished for one hour* (v. 19). He was stunned, greatly perplexed, and struck with terror at such a great judgment coming on such a great prince. He was also struck with confusion when he found himself the one who must bring to the king *these heavy tidings.*

1. The king noticed that he looked greatly perplexed and, thinking he was reluctant to speak out for fear of offending him, encouraged him to deal clearly with him: *let not the dream, nor the interpretation thereof, trouble thee.* He said this either:

1.1. As one who sincerely desired to know the truth. Or:

1.2. As one who despised the truth and defied it. Daniel was concerned for him, and so he wished, *"The dream be to those that hate thee* (v. 19). May the bad things it warns about fall on the heads of your enemies, not on your own." Although Nebuchadnezzar was an oppressor of the people of God, he still was, at that time, Daniel's prince.

2. The interpretation itself was only a repetition of the dream, with application to the king. "As for *the tree* that you saw *flourishing* (vv. 20–21), *it is thou, O king!"* (v. 22). He showed the king his present prosperous state in the mirror of his own dream (2:37–38). "As for the doom passed on the tree (v. 23), it is *the decree of the Most High, which comes upon my lord the king*" (v. 24). He must be deposed from his throne, *driven from men,* and, being deprived of his reason and having the mind of an animal given him, he would live *with the beasts of the field.* He would *eat grass as oxen,* and, like them, lie *exposed in every weather, until seven times (seven years) pass over him,* and then he would know that the *Most High rules.* When he was brought to realize and acknowledge this, he would be restored to his position (v. 26). God is called *the heavens* here, and the influence that the visible heavens have on this earth is intended to be a faint representation of the rule that the God of heaven has over this lower world; we are said to *sin against heaven* (Lk 15:18).

3. The end of the interpretation is the devout advice that Daniel, as a prophet, gave the king (v. 27). Notice:

3.1. How humbly he gave his advice, and with what tenderness and respect: *"O king! Let my counsel be acceptable unto thee."*

3.2. He did not advise him to go and consult a doctor to prevent his mental illness, but to break away from his sin. He had wronged his own subjects and dealt unfairly with his allies. He had been cruel to the poor.

3.3. The motive with which he backed up this advice: *If it may be a lengthening of thy tranquillity* (then your prosperity will continue).

Verses 28–33

Nebuchadnezzar's dream was fulfilled, and Daniel's application of it to him justified and confirmed. We have here:

1. God's patience with him: *All this came upon him,* but not till *twelve months after* (v. 29). There was such a long *lengthening of his tranquillity,* though it does not seem that he *broke off his sins* or showed any *mercy to the poor* captives. God gave him opportunity to repent; he *let him alone this year also* (Lk 13:8), this *one* year more.

2. His pride, haughtiness, and abuse of that patience. He walked *in the palace of the kingdom of Babylon* in all his pomp and pride. He thought everything in Babylon looked great, *"and this great Babylon I have built."* Babylon was built many years before he was born, but he boasted that he had built it, as Augustus Caesar boasted about Rome, "I found it as brick, but I left it as marble." He boasted that he had built it *for the house of the kingdom* (v. 30), the capital city of his empire.

3. His punishment. There came from heaven the powerful word by which he was immediately deprived:

3.1. Of his honor as a king: *The kingdom has departed from thee* (v. 31).

3.2. Of his honor as a human being. He lost his reason, and that meant he lost his authority: *They shall drive thee from men* (v. 32). And it was fulfilled: he was *driven from men the same hour* (v. 33). Suddenly he fell stark raving mad. His understanding and memory went, and all his reasoning faculties failed. He went about naked and on all fours, like an animal, running wild into the fields and woods. He was made to *eat grass as oxen.* Nebuchadnezzar wanted to be more than a human being, and so God justly made him less than one; the one who set himself up as a rival to his Maker was put on the same level as the animals. See also Job 40:11–13.

Verses 34–37

We have here Nebuchadnezzar's restoration from his insanity and his return to his right mind *at the end of the days,* that is, at the end of the seven years. *At the end of the days,* he said, *I lifted up my eyes unto heaven* (v. 34), no longer looking down toward the earth as an animal, but beginning to look up as a human being. But there was more in it than this; he looked up as someone who was penitent, as a humble petitioner for mercy.

1. He had the use of his mind restored to him to such an extent that he used it to glorify God, humbling himself before him. People never rightly use their reason until they begin to be religious, nor do they live a fully human life until they live to the glory of God. The king's foolishness was the means by which he became wise. To be brought to himself, he must first be *beside himself* (Mk 3:21; Ac 26:24; 2Co 5:13). His flatterers often complimented Nebuchadnezzar with, *O king! Live for ever.* But he was now convinced:

1.1. That no king lives forever, but that it is only the God of Israel who lives forever.

1.2. That God's kingdom is like God, *everlasting*, and his *dominion from generation to generation* (v. 34); there is no succession, no change, in his kingdom.

1.3. That *all nations* before him are *as nothing* (v. 35).

1.4. That his power is irresistible, for he *does according to his will*.

1.5. That everything that God does is done well: his *works are truth*, for they all correspond to his word. *His ways are judgment* (v. 37), both wise and righteous, consistent with the rules of wisdom and justice.

1.6. That he has power to humble the proudest enemies. *Those that walk in pride he is able to abase.*

2. He had his mind restored to him to such an extent that he could use it to know his true self again (v. 36). He was now reestablished in his kingdom as firmly as if there had been no interruption. Afflictions will last no longer than the time necessary for them to complete the work for which they were sent. When Nebuchadnezzar was restored to his kingdom, he praised, extolled, and honored the King of heaven (v. 37).

It was not long after this that Nebuchadnezzar's life and reign ended. The Greek historian Abydenus, quoted by Eusebius, bishop of Caesarea (*Praeparatio Evangelica* 1.9), reports that on his deathbed Nebuchadnezzar foretold the taking of Babylon by Cyrus. Whether he continued in the same good state of mind that he seems to have been in here we are not told. If our charity may reach so far as to hope he did, we must wonder at free grace, by which he lost his senses for a while so that he might save his soul forever.

CHAPTER 5

Belshazzar now reigned in Babylon; some reckon he had reigned seventeen years, others only three. About two years before this, Cyrus king of Persia, a monarch who was increasing in power, came against Babylon with a great army; Belshazzar met him, fought him, and was defeated by him in a pitched battle. He and his scattered forces withdrew into the city, where Cyrus besieged them. They were secure because the Euphrates River was their defense and they had twenty years' provisions in the city, but Cyrus captured it in the second year of the siege. We have here: 1. The riotous, idolatrous, and sacrilegious feast that Belshazzar gave (vv. 1–4). 2. The alarm given him by the writing on the wall, which none of his wise men could read (vv. 5–9). 3. The interpretation of the mystical characters by Daniel, who dealt plainly with Belshazzar, showing him his doom written there (vv. 10–29). 4. The immediate fulfillment of the interpretation in the killing of the king and the seizing of the kingdom (vv. 30–31).

Verses 1–9

Here we see Belshazzar the king very merry, but then suddenly very gloomy. He affronted God, and God frightened him.

1. He affronted God. He *made a great feast*, or *banquet of wine* (v. 1); probably it was some anniversary. Historians say that Cyrus, who was now besieging Babylon, knew about this feast and, presuming that the inhabitants would then be off their guard, overcome by sleep and wine, took that opportunity to attack the city and so controlled it. Belshazzar invited *a thousand of his lords* (nobles) *to come and drink with him*. In this lavish feast:

1.1. He defied God's judgments. His city was now besieged; his life and kingdom were at risk. He should

therefore have proclaimed a fast, but because he was determined to walk against God's ways, he declared a feast.

1.2. He insulted the temple of God (v. 2). *While he tasted the wine, he commanded to bring the vessels* (goblets) of the temple, to drink from them.

1.3. He insulted God himself and defied his deity, for *they drank wine, and praised the gods of gold and silver* (v. 4).

2. God frightened him, striking terror on him. Belshazzar and his nobles were in the middle of their reveling. However, the hour had now come for the fulfillment of what had been said long before about the king of Babylon (Isa 21:2–4). *The night of my pleasures has he turned into fear to me* (Isa 21:4).

2.1. The fingers of a human hand appeared in front of the king's face, writing on the plaster of the wall (v. 5). There was no destroying angel with a sword drawn, only a pen in the hand, writing on the wall near the lampstand, where they could all see it by the light of their own candle. The king saw *the part of the hand that wrote* but not the person whose hand it was. What we see of God, the part of the hand that writes in the book of the Scriptures, may be enough to give us fearful thoughts about the things of God that we cannot see. If this is the finger of God, what is his arm laid bare like (Isa 52:10)?

2.2. The king was immediately seized with panic (v. 6): *His countenance was changed*—the color in his face drained away and he turned pale; *the joints of his loins were loosed*; and his knees knocked together. Why was he in such a panic? His thoughts troubled him; his own guilty conscience told him he had no reason to expect good news from heaven. God can soon make the heart of the boldest sinner tremble, and there need be nothing more than to let loose that person's own thoughts on them.

2.3. The wise men of Babylon were called for, to see what sense they could make of this writing on the wall (v. 7). Whoever wants to may read the mind of God in the Scriptures. The king promised that whoever gave him a satisfactory account of this writing would be given the highest honors.

2.4. The king was disappointed; none of them could understand the writing, much less interpret it (v. 8), which increased the king's confusion (v. 9).

Verses 10–29

Here is:

1. The information given by the queen mother to the king about Daniel, how fit he was to be consulted in this difficult situation. It is thought that this queen was the widow of Evil-Merodach and was the famous Nitocris whom Herodotus mentions as a woman of extraordinary wisdom. News being brought to her apartment, she came herself to the banquet hall to recommend to the king a doctor for his illness. She could not read the writing herself, but she directed him to one who could; let *Daniel be called* for now, who should have been called for originally. He *is a man in whom is the spirit of the holy gods* (v. 11), who has something in him more than human. She spoke honorably of him as a man who had *light, and understanding, and wisdom*. It was clear he was divinely inspired. He had *knowledge* and *understanding* beyond all the other wise men for *interpreting dreams*. He had a wonderfully good heart: *An excellent spirit was found in him*. "*The king thy father*," that is, your grandfather, "*made him master of the magicians* (v. 11)." He *named him Belteshazzar*, according to the name of his god,

thinking to honor him. *Let Daniel be called, and he will show the interpretation* (v. 12).

2. The introduction of Daniel to the king (v. 13). The king asked with an air of pride (v. 13), *Art thou that Daniel who art of the children of the captivity?* Yet he acknowledged that all the wise men of Babylon were baffled; they could not read this writing or give its interpretation (v. 16). He promised Daniel the same rewards that he had promised them if he would do it (v. 16).

3. The interpretation Daniel gave of these mysterious characters, which, far from relieving the king of his fears, increased them. Daniel was now old and Belshazzar was young, and this is why Daniel seems to have taken greater liberty in dealing with him plainly and forcefully than he had done on similar occasions with Nebuchadnezzar.

3.1. Daniel undertook to read and interpret the writing that put them into this panic (v. 17). He rejected the offer of rewards, for he was not one of those who prophesy for money. *Let thy gifts be to thyself,* you may keep your gifts for yourself, for they will not be yours for long, and *give thy rewards to another* (v. 17). Let us do our duty in the world, reading God's writing and making known its interpretation.

3.2. Daniel recounted to the king God's dealings with his father Nebuchadnezzar (vv. 18, 21). He described the great honor and power to which divine Providence had advanced Nebuchadnezzar (vv. 18–19). His ability was so strong that it was irresistible. His authority was so absolute that it was uncontrollable. *Whom he would he slew, and whom he would he saved alive* (v. 19), even if both were equally innocent or equally guilty. *Whom he would he set up, and whom he would he put down.* Daniel set before Belshazzar the sins Nebuchadnezzar had been guilty of, which had provoked God against him. The description given of Nebuchadnezzar's power suggests his abuse of power. He behaved arrogantly toward the God above him and grew proud and haughty (v. 20). Daniel reminded Belshazzar of the judgments of God that were brought on Nebuchadnezzar for his pride and obstinacy, how he was deprived of his sanity and so was deposed from his royal throne (v. 20) and driven away from people to live with the wild donkeys (v. 21).

3.3. In God's name, Daniel presented the articles of impeachment against Belshazzar. Before he read him out his doom from the writing on the wall, he showed him his crime. Belshazzar had taken no notice of the judgments of God on his father (v. 22): *Thou his son, O Belshazzar! hast not humbled thy heart, though thou knewest all this.* He had insulted God more arrogantly than Nebuchadnezzar himself had done, as can be seen from the revels of that very night. "*Thou hast lifted up thyself against the Lord of heaven* (v. 23). You have desecrated the goblets of his house, made the articles of his sanctuary instruments of your sin, and praised the gods of silver and gold, which cannot see, hear, or know anything, as if they were to be preferred to the God who sees, hears, and knows everything." The king had not fulfilled the purpose of his creation and maintenance: *The God in whose hand thy breath is, and whose are all thy ways, hast thou not glorified* (v. 23). This is a general charge, which stands against us all. Notice our dependence on God as our Creator, preserver, benefactor, owner, and ruler; not only did our breath come from his hand in the beginning, but also our breath is still in his hands. He is the One who holds our souls in life (Ps 66:9), and if he takes away our breath, we die. We should glorify him, devote ourselves to his honor, and employ ourselves in his service. *We have*

all sinned, and have come short of the glory of God (Ro 3:23). This is the indictment directed against Belshazzar.

3.4. Daniel then proceeded to read the sentence, as he found it *written upon the wall* (v. 5): "Then," said Daniel, "when you reached such depths of ungodliness as to trample on the most sacred things, when you were in the middle of your sacrilegious, idolatrous feast, then was *the part of the hand,* the writing fingers, sent *from him,* from God; he *sent them,* and *this writing,* as you now see, *was written*" (v. 24). Now the writing was, *Mene, Mene, Tekel, Upharsin* (v. 25). The meaning is, *he has numbered, he has weighed, and they divide.*

3.4.1. *Mene* is repeated, for the thing is certain—*Mene, mene*; that means, both in Hebrew and in Aramaic, "he has *numbered and finished,*" which Daniel explained (v. 26): "*God has numbered thy kingdom.* Here is an end of your kingdom."

3.4.2. *Tekel* signifies in Aramaic, "You are weighed," and in Hebrew, "You are too light." God did not declare judgment against him until he had first pondered his actions and considered the merits of his case.

3.4.3. *Upharsin* (v. 28): "*Thy kingdom is divided;* it is torn away from you, and it is *given to the Medes and Persians* as plunder to be divided among them." Belshazzar was so far convicted by his own conscience of the reasonableness of all Daniel said that he gave Daniel the reward he promised him: he put on him the *scarlet gown* and the *gold chain* and made him the *third ruler in the kingdom* (v. 29).

Verses 30–31

Here is:

1. The death of the king. Pagan writers speak of Cyrus's taking Babylon by surprise, with the help of two deserters who showed him the best way into the city.

2. The transferring of the kingdom to other hands. From the head of gold we now descend to the chest and arms of silver. *Darius the Mede took the kingdom* in partnership with, and with the agreement of, Cyrus, who had conquered it (v. 31).

CHAPTER 6

Daniel does not give us a continuous history, but selects particular passages of the story that serve to confirm our faith in God. By faith Daniel stopped the mouths of lions (Heb 11:33) and so obtained a good report (Heb 11:39). The three children were thrown into the fiery furnace for not committing a known sin, but Daniel was thrown into the lion's den for not omitting a known duty. We have: 1. Daniel's advancement in the court of Darius (vv. 1–3). 2. The envy and hatred of his enemies against him (vv. 4–5). 3. The decree they obtained against prayer for thirty days (vv. 6–9). 4. Daniel's faithfulness and commitment in prayer despite that decree (v. 10). 5. Information given against him because of it, and his being thrown into the lions' den (vv. 11–17). 6. His miraculous preservation and rescue (vv. 18–23). 7. The throwing of his accusers into the den and their destruction there (v. 24). 8. The decree that Darius made on this occasion in honor of the God of Daniel, and the prosperity of Daniel afterward (vv. 25–28).

Verses 1–5

We are told concerning Daniel:

1. What a *great man* he was. When Darius came to the crown of Babylon by conquest, he set up new governmental

arrangements and made Daniel chief minister of state. Darius *set over the kingdom* 120 *princes* (satraps) (v. 1), and he appointed them their districts. Over these princes there was a triumvirate, *three presidents* (administrators), who were to administer and state the public accounts, so *that the king should have no damage* (v. 2), so that he would not sustain loss in his revenue. Daniel was the chief of these three, *preferred above the presidents and princes* (v. 3). Daniel had been a great man in the kingdom that had been conquered, and for that reason one would think he would have been imprisoned or banished. He was a native of a foreign kingdom, and a ruined one, and might have been despised as a foreigner and captive. But Darius soon became aware that Daniel had something extraordinary in him. Therefore, when he found that Daniel excelled in wisdom and goodness, he made him his right-hand leader; he had probably heard of his being divinely inspired. Although Daniel was now very old, he was still as able as ever to undertake business, and he won respect from everyone by being like an oak, not by being like a willow, by being faithful in virtue, not by yielding to corruption.

2. What a good man he was. *An excellent* (extraordinary) *spirit was in him* (v. 3). There was *no error or fault to be found in him* (v. 4).

3. What ill will was shown to him because of his greatness and his goodness. The administrators and satraps envied him because he was promoted above them. Notice:

3.1. The cause of envy, which is everything that is good. The better a person is, the worse they are thought of by their rivals.

3.2. The effect of envy, which is everything that is bad. Those who envied Daniel sought nothing less than his ruin. They set spies to watch him; they *sought to find occasion against him* (v. 4). They eventually reached the conclusion that they could find no basis for any charges against him except *concerning the law of his God* (v. 5). It seems that Daniel maintained his profession of religious faith, and there was no law that required him to follow the king's religion or rendered him unable to bear office in the state unless he did. He was at the king's service in his official duties, but he was free to pursue his own religious faith. It was in this matter, therefore, that his enemies hoped to trap him.

Verses 6–10

Daniel's enemies devised a new law that they hoped would trap him, and such was his faithfulness to his God that they were successful. Here is:

1. Darius's ungodly *law*; it was Darius's because he gave his royal assent to it, but strictly speaking it was not his: the administrators and satraps framed the decree. They intimated to the king that it had carried unanimously: "*All the presidents* (administrators) are of this mind," but we are sure that Daniel, the chief of the three, did not give his agreement to it. These evildoers claimed to give honor to the king, and they urged him to pass a law—to make it a royal statute—that *whosoever shall ask a petition of any god or man for thirty days, save of the king, shall be cast into the den of lions* (v. 7). Now:

1.1. It contained nothing that had the least appearance of good. All people must be made to believe that the king was so ready to respond to all petitioners that no one in any distress needed to turn either to God or to other people for help, but only to the king. For thirty days, therefore, he would be ready to listen to everyone who had any petition to present to him. It is a king's honor to help his subjects,

but if a king undertakes to usurp God's place in helping his people, it is his disgrace.

1.2. It contained a great deal that was obviously evil. It is bad enough to forbid people from making requests of their fellows. Must a beggar not ask alms, or one neighbor not ask a kindness from another? If children lacked bread, must they not ask for it from their parents, or be cast into the den of lions if they do? However, it was an arrogant insult to all religion to forbid asking a petition *of any god*. To prohibit prayer for thirty days is to rob God of all the tribute he receives from people and to rob people of all the comfort they may obtain in God. Does not everyone's heart tell them to call on God when they are in need or distress, and must this be considered treason? If they had suggested only prohibiting the Jews from praying to their God, Daniel would have been as effectually trapped, but they knew the king would not pass such a law, and so they made it general.

2. Daniel's devout disobedience of this law (v. 10). He did not withdraw into the country, but stood his ground, knowing that he now had a good opportunity of honoring God in front of the people.

2.1. Daniel *prayed in his house*, sometimes himself alone and sometimes with his family, and he made it his solemn business. Every house not only may be, but also should be, a house of prayer; where we live, God must have his altar, on which we must offer spiritual sacrifices (1Pe 2:5). In every prayer Daniel gave thanks. When he prayed and gave thanks, he *kneeled upon his knees*. Kneeling is a posture for begging, and we come to God as beggars, beggars for our lives. Daniel *opened the windows of his chamber*, so that the sight of the visible heavens would move his heart with awe. He *opened them toward Jerusalem*, the Holy City, even though it now lay in ruins, to show his affection even for its stones and dust (Ps 102:14). He did this *three times a day*. It is good to have our set hours of prayer, not to compel us, but to remind us, and if we think our bodies require refreshment through food three times a day, can we think that we can receive spiritual nourishment less frequently? All who knew him knew it to be his practice, and he was not ashamed of it.

2.2. Daniel's faithfulness to this practice even when it was made a capital offense by the law. When he knew that *the writing was signed*, he continued to do *as he did aforetime* (v. 10). Many people, indeed, many good people, would have thought it wise to omit this duty for these thirty days when they could not do it without putting their lives in danger. Daniel, however, who had so many eyes on him, must act with courage, and we must make sure that we are not found guilty of being cowards in the cause of God under the pretense of discretion.

Verses 11–17

Proof was given that Daniel was praying to his God despite the recent decree to the contrary (v. 11): *These men assembled*; "they came tumultuously together" is the sense. They came together to visit Daniel at the time that they knew to be his usual hour of devotion, perhaps claiming they were coming to see him on some business matter, and they *found him on his knees praying* and *making supplication before his God* (asking his God for help). They lost no time in turning to the king (v. 12) and proceeded to accuse Daniel (v. 13). They described him in terms designed to exasperate the king and make him even more angry with him than he would be simply because Daniel had broken the law: "He is *of the children of the captivity of Judah*, an exile in a contemptible condition, who can call nothing his own except what he has by the king's favor, but *he regards not* (pays no attention to) *thee, O king, nor the decree that thou hast signed.*" They did not say, "He is making his petition to his God," in case Darius should take notice of that to Daniel's honor, but only, *He makes his petition,* which was what was forbidden by the law. The king now perceived that, whatever they claimed, it was not out of honor to him, but out of spite for Daniel (v. 14). Now the king *set his heart to deliver Daniel;* both by argument and by authority he worked hard *till the going down of the sun* to *deliver him,* that is, to persuade his accusers not to insist on the prosecution. The prosecutors demanded justice (v. 15). We are not told what Daniel said; the king himself was his advocate. But the prosecutors insisted that the law must take its course. The Persians exalted the wisdom of their king by supposing that whatever law he solemnly confirmed had been so well made that there could be no need to change it. The king himself, with the greatest reluctance, and against his conscience, signed the warrant for Daniel's execution. Daniel, that honored, thoughtful man, whose face shone with majesty and sweetness, was *thrown into the den of lions* to be devoured by them (v. 16), purely for worshiping his God. To make sure the sentence was carried out, the stone *laid upon the mouth of the den was sealed* (v. 17). Darius encouraged Daniel to trust in God: *Thy God whom thou servest continually, he will deliver thee* (v. 16). He cleared Daniel from guilt, acknowledging his only crime to be continually serving his God. He left it to God to free him: *He will deliver thee.*

Verses 18–24

Here is:

1. The sad night that the king spent on Daniel's account. He could not forgive himself for throwing him into the danger. He *passed the night fasting* (v. 18). He forbade music or any other form of entertainment.

2. The early inquiry he made about Daniel the next morning (vv. 19–20). He *went in haste to the den of lions.* When he came to the den, he cried, *with a lamentable* (anguished) *voice, O Daniel! servant of the living God,* has *thy God whom thou servest* made it clear that he is *able to deliver thee from the lions?*

3. Daniel alive, safe and well, and unhurt in the lions' den (vv. 21–22). He knew the king's voice: *O king! live for ever.* He did not reproach him, but had heartily forgiven him. The account Daniel gave the king was triumphant.

3.1. God had preserved his life by a miracle. "He is *my God,* whom I acknowledge, and who acknowledges me, for *he has sent his angel.*" The same angel that was seen in *the form of the Son of God* with the three children in the fiery furnace had come to Daniel and had *shut the lions' mouths.* Notice the care God takes of his faithful worshipers. He in effect *stops the lions' mouths* so that they cannot hurt them.

3.2. God had pleaded his cause. Daniel was portrayed to the king as disloyal to him and his government. We do not find that he said anything to vindicate himself; rather, he left it to God to establish his integrity, and God did so powerfully by performing a miracle to preserve his life.

4. The discharge of Daniel from his confinement. His prosecutors had to acknowledge that the law had been satisfied, even though they were not. No cause could be shown why Daniel should not be brought out of the lions' den.

5. The committing of his prosecutors to the same prison (v. 24). Darius was brought to life by this miracle

done for Daniel, and he now began to take courage and act like himself. Daniel's accusers had the same punishment inflicted on them that they had inflicted on him, now that his innocence had been proved.

Verses 25–28

Darius seeks here to make amends for the dishonor he showed both to God and to Daniel.

1. He gives honor to God by a decree published to all nations, by which they are required to fear and reverence the true God. He sends this decree *to all people, nations, and languages, that dwell in all the earth* (v. 25). The decree is that *men tremble and fear before the God of Daniel.* This goes further than Nebuchadnezzar's decree, for that only restrained people from *speaking amiss* of this God, but here they are required to *fear before him.* Yet although this decree goes far, it does not go far enough; if Darius had lived up to his new convictions, he would have commanded all people not only to have fear and reverence for this God but also to love him and trust in him, to abandon their worship of idols and worship only him. There is good reason why all people should fear this God, for:

- His being is transcendent.
- His government is indisputable.
- Both his being and his government are unchangeable.
- He has ability that is sufficient to support such authority (v. 27). He rescues his faithful servants from trouble and saves them out of trouble.
- He has given fresh proof of all this by *delivering* his servant *Daniel from the power of the lions.*

2. He gives honor to Daniel (v. 28): *So this Daniel prospered.*

CHAPTER 7

The six first chapters of this book were historical; we now enter with fear and trembling into the six later ones, which are prophetic, and in which there are many things that are dark and difficult to understand (2Pe 3:16), which we dare not positively determine. But they also contain many things that are clear and profitable. We have: 1. Daniel's vision of the four beasts (vv. 1–8). 2. His vision of God's throne of government and judgment (vv. 9–14). 3. The interpretation of these visions (vv. 15–28). Whether the visions look as far forward as the end of time or whether they were to have more immediate fulfillment is difficult to say, and the best commentators are not agreed on these matters.

Verses 1–8

The date of this chapter places it before chapter 5, which was in the last year of Belshazzar, and chapter 6, which was in the first of Darius. Belshazzar's name here, in the original, is spelled *Bel-eshe-zar,* "Bel is on fire by the enemy." Bel the god of the Babylonians had prospered but was now to be consumed. We have here Daniel's vision of the four monarchies who oppressed the Jews. Notice:

1. The circumstances of this vision (v. 1): he *had visions of his head* (visions passed through his mind) *upon his bed* when he was asleep. This was how God sometimes revealed his mind to people, when deep sleep fell on them (Job 33:15). When Daniel was awake, he *wrote the dream.* He *told the sum of the matters* (the substance of his dream) to his brothers, giving it to them in

writing so that it could be preserved for their children, who would see these things fulfilled. The Jews misunderstood Jeremiah and Ezekiel, flattering themselves with the expectation that after their return they would enjoy uninterrupted tranquility. Through this prophet, however, God let them know that they would have trouble.

2. The vision itself:

2.1. He noticed the *four winds* that *strove upon* (churned up) *the great sea* (v. 2). They made great efforts to see which could blow the strongest and, ultimately, blow by itself. This represents the contests among rulers for empire. The four winds strove for mastery. That is what the kings of the nations are contending for in their wars, which are as noisy and violent as the battle of the winds.

2.2. He saw four great beasts come up from the sea, from the troubled waters. The monarchs and monarchies are represented by beasts. These beasts were separate from one another (v. 3), to show the different nature of the nations.

2.2.1. The first beast was like a lion (v. 4). This was the Babylonian monarchy, which was fierce and strong and made its kings absolute. This lion had eagle's wings, showing the speed with which Nebuchadnezzar conquered kingdoms. However, Daniel soon saw the wings plucked. Different countries that had paid them tribute rebelled, so that this winged lion was forced to *stand upon the feet as a man, and a* human heart was given to it. It had lost the heart of a lion, which it had been famous for (the English king Richard I was called *Coeur de Lion*, Lion Heart), becoming feeble, dreading everything and daring nothing.

2.2.2. The second beast was like a bear (v. 5). This was the Persian monarchy, less strong and generous but no less ravenous. This bear raised itself up on one side against the lion and soon conquered it. "It raised up one dominion," as some read it. Persia and Media now set up a joint government. This bear had three ribs in its mouth between the teeth, the remains of those nations it had devoured; stuck in its teeth were still some ribs, nations that it could not conquer. It was then told, "Arise, devour much flesh; devour what will be easier prey." The rulers would press on with their conquests and let nothing stand in their way.

2.2.3. The third beast was *like a leopard* (v. 6). This was the Greek monarchy, founded by *Alexander the Great*, active, crafty, and cruel, like a *leopard*. He had *four wings of a fowl*, for although Nebuchadnezzar settled his conquests speedily, Alexander did so even more swiftly. Within six years he gained the whole empire of Persia and a great part of Asia, as well as Syria, Egypt, India, and other nations. This beast had *four heads*; on Alexander's death his conquests were divided among his four chief commanders: Seleucus Nicator had Asia the Great; Perdiccas, and after him Antigonus, had Asia Minor; Cassander had Macedonia; Ptolemy had Egypt.

2.2.4. The *fourth* beast was more fierce and formidable than any of the others (v. 7). The commentators are not agreed on the identity of this anonymous beast; some believe it to be the Roman Empire, which comprised ten kingdoms: Italy, France, Spain, Germany, Britain, Sarmatia, Pannonia, Asia, Greece, and Egypt. They consider the little horn that rose by the fall of three of the other horns (v. 8) to be the Turkish Empire, which arose in the place of Asia, Greece, and Egypt. Others consider this fourth beast to be the kingdom of Syria, the family of the Seleucids, which was very cruel to the Jewish people, as we find in

Josephus and the history of the Maccabees. Their armies were the *great iron teeth* with which they *devoured and broke in pieces* the people of God and *trampled upon the residue* of them. The *ten horns* are then thought to be ten kings that reigned successively in Syria, and therefore the *little horn* is Antiochus Epiphanes, the last of the ten, who undermined three of the kings and gained the government. He was a man of great ingenuity and so is said to have eyes *like the eyes of a man*.

Verses 9–14

Whether we understand the fourth beast to represent the Syrian Empire or the Roman, it is clear that these verses were intended to encourage the people of God in the persecution they were likely to sustain. Three things are revealed here that are encouraging:

1. That there is a judgment to come, and God is the Judge. People have their day now. *I beheld till the thrones were cast down* (v. 9), not only the thrones of these beasts but also *all rule, authority, and power* that are set up to defy the kingdom of God on earth (1Co 15:24): such are the thrones of the kingdoms of the world in comparison with God's kingdom. "I beheld till thrones were set up," as it may well read — Christ's throne and the throne of his Father. It is the *judgment* that is *set* here (v. 10). This is intended to proclaim God's wise and righteous government of the world by his providence. Perhaps it points to the destruction brought about on Syria or Rome for their tyrannizing the people of God. It seems principally designed to describe the Last Judgment. Many of the New Testament predictions of the judgment to come have a clear allusion to this vision, especially St. John's vision of that judgment (Rev 20:11–12). The Judge is the Ancient of Days himself, God the Father. He is called the *Ancient of days* (v. 9) because he is God from eternity to eternity. The glory of the Judge is set out in his garment, which is white as snow, showing his splendor and purity, and the hair of his head is as pure wool, white and venerable. The throne is *like the fiery flame* (v. 9), fearful to evildoers. Its *wheels* are *as burning fire*, to devour the adversaries. This is enlarged on in v. 10. His attendants are numerous. The *Shechinah* is always attended by angels; it is so here: *Thousand thousands minister to him*, and *ten thousand times ten thousand stand before him* (v. 10). *The judgment is set* (the court is seated) publicly, and *the books are opened*.

2. That the cruel enemies of the church of God will be humbled in due time (vv. 11–12). This is represented here:

2.1. In the destruction of the fourth beast. God's quarrel with this beast is *because of the voice of the great words which the horn spoke*, defying heaven. The Syrian Empire, after Antiochus, was destroyed. He himself died of a miserable disease, his family was uprooted, and the kingdom was wasted by the Parthians and Armenians and eventually made a province of the Roman Empire by Pompey. The Roman Empire itself, if we take that to be represented by the fourth beast, after it began to persecute Christianity, declined and wasted and was destroyed.

2.2. In the weakening of the other three beasts (v. 12): they have *their dominion taken away* and so are rendered unable to cause trouble to the people of God, but *a prolonging in life is given them for a time and a season*. The power of the previous kingdoms is broken, but their people still remain in a weak and lowly condition. This is how God deals with his church's enemies; sometimes he crushes the persecution but reprieves the persecutors, so that they may have opportunity to repent.

3. That the kingdom of the Messiah will be set up in the world in spite of all the opposition of the powers of darkness. Daniel sees this in a vision and comforts his friends.

3.1. The Messiah is called here the Son of Man—*one like unto the Son of man* (v. 13), for he was *made in the likeness of sinful flesh* (Ro 8:3) and was *found in fashion as a man* (Php 2:8). *I saw one like unto the Son of man.* Our Savior seems clearly to refer to this vision when he says that the *Father* has *given him authority to execute judgment* because he is *the Son of man* (Jn 5:27).

3.2. He is said to *come with the clouds of heaven* (v. 13). Some think this refers to his incarnation. I think rather that it refers to his ascension (Ac 1:9). It is worthwhile asking where the cloud carried him when it received him out of the sight of his disciples, and we are told here that he ascended to *his Father and our Father*, to *his God and our God* (Jn 20:17). He was *brought near* as our high priest, who enters within the veil for us, and as our forerunner (Heb 6:19–20). He is represented as having a mighty influence on this earth (v. 14). When he went to be glorified with his Father, he had *a power given him over all flesh* (Jn 17:2, 5). Daniel and his friends are encouraged with the prospect of this, that not only will the dominion of the church's enemies be taken away (v. 12), but also the church's head will have *dominion given him*; to him *every knee shall bow* and *every tongue confess* (Php 2:9–10). *His dominion* will not *pass away*. The church will continue militant to the end of time, and it will be triumphant to the endless ages of eternity.

Verses 15–28

Here we have:

1. The deep impressions that these visions made on the prophet (v. 15): *I Daniel was grieved* (troubled) *in my spirit, in the midst of my body.* The word here used for *body* means "a sheath," for the body is a sheath to the soul. The *visions of my head troubled me*; he was deeply troubled by his thoughts (v. 28). The way in which these things were revealed to him completely overwhelmed him.

2. His fervent desire to understand the meaning (v. 16).

3. The key that was given him.

3.1. *The great beasts* are great *kings* and their kingdoms, *which shall arise out of the earth*, as those beasts did *out of the sea* (v. 17).

3.2. Daniel understands the first three beasts, but he wants to know more about the fourth beast. He especially wants to know the identity of the *little horn* that *had eyes* and *a mouth that spoke very great things* (v. 20). It was this horn that *made war with the saints, and prevailed against them* (v. 21). It is time to ask, "What does this mean? What is this horn that will defeat the saints?" His interpreter answers (vv. 23–25) that this *fourth beast is a fourth kingdom*, which *shall devour the whole earth*, or, as it may read, "the whole land." The *ten horns are ten kings*, and the *little horn* is another king who will subdue three kings and be very abusive to God and his people. He will act.

3.2.1. In a very ungodly way toward God, defying him (v. 25).

3.2.2. In a very arrogant way toward the people of God. He will *wear out* (oppress) *the saints of the Most High*. He will *think to change times* (set times) *and laws*, to abolish all the ordinances and institutions of religious faith. In these bold attempts he will prosper and be successful for

a time; God's people will be given into his hand *until time, times, and half a time* (that is, for three and a half years). However, at the end of that time the *judgment shall sit and take away his dominion* (v. 26), by which the angel here explains the beast's being *slain* (killed) *and his body destroyed* (v. 11). And, as Mr. Joseph Mede reads v. 12, "as to the rest of the beast," the ten horns, especially the little "ruffling" horn, they had their dominion taken away. Now the question is, "Who is this enemy?" Interpreters are not agreed on this. Some see the fourth kingdom as that of the Seleucids and the little horn as Antiochus, and they show the fulfillment of all this in the history of the Maccabees. Others, however, consider the fourth kingdom to be that of the Romans; of those who hold this view, Calvin considers the *little horn* to be Julius Caesar and the succeeding emperors, and Mr. Joseph Mede considers it to be the antichrist, that is, the papal kingdom. Others consider the *little horn* to be the Turkish Empire; this is the opinion of Luther, Vatablus, and others. Since prophecies sometimes have many fulfillments, I am willing to allow that they are both right. This prophecy refers primarily, I would say, to the Syrian Empire and was intended to encourage the Jews who suffered under Antiochus. However, it also has a further reference, foretelling the persecuting power of Rome against the Christian religion. St. John in his visions, which point primarily at Rome, has reference to these visions of Daniel.

3.3. He has a joyful prospect given him of God's kingdom on earth and its final victory over all opposition. This is brought in abruptly (vv. 18, 22), before it is interpreted in its place in the vision (vv. 26–27). And this also refers to:

3.3.1. The prosperous days of the Jewish church after it had weathered the storm under Antiochus.

3.3.2. The setting up of the kingdom of the Messiah in the world by the preaching of his Gospel.

3.3.3. The second coming of Jesus Christ. *The Ancient of days shall come* (v. 22). God will judge the world through his Son, to whom he has *committed all judgment* (Jn 5:22). *The judgment* (court) *shall sit* (v. 26). God *judges in the earth*, both in wisdom and in justice. The *dominion* of the enemy will be *taken away* (v. 26). All Christ's enemies will be made his footstool (Ps 110:1). *Judgment is given to the saints of the Most High.* The apostles are entrusted with the preaching of a Gospel by which the *world shall be judged*. What is most insisted on is that *the saints of the Most High shall take the kingdom, and possess the kingdom for ever* (v. 18); again (v. 22), *The time came that the saints possessed the kingdom*; and again (v. 27), *The kingdom and dominion, and the greatness of the kingdom under the whole heavens, will be given to the people of the saints of the Most High*. This shows the spiritual dominion of the saints over their own sinful desires and corruptions, their victories over Satan and his temptations, and the triumphs of the martyrs over death and its terrors. It also promises that the Gospel kingdom will be set up, a kingdom of light, holiness, and love. The saints will possess the kingdom forever, in fact, *for ever and ever*, and the reason is that the One whose saints they are is the *Most High* and *his kingdom is an everlasting kingdom* (v. 27). *Because I live, you shall live also* (Jn 14:19). His kingdom is theirs.

At the close, Daniel tells us what impressions this vision made on him; it overwhelmed his spirit so much that his *countenance* was *changed* (his face turned pale) (v. 28), but he *kept the matter in his heart* (v. 28)—not to keep it from the church, but to keep it for the church.

CHAPTER 8

This chapter is written not in Aramaic, for the benefit of the Babylonians, as the six previous chapters were, but in Hebrew, for the benefit of the Jews, as are the remaining chapters to the end of this book. We have: 1. The vision of the ram, the goat, and the little horn that would fight and triumph over the people of God for a limited time (vv. 1–14). 2. The interpretation of this vision by an angel, showing that the ram signified the Persian Empire, the goat the Greek, and the little horn a king of the Greek monarchy, Antiochus Epiphanes, who would be set against the Jews (vv. 15–27). The Jewish church had all along been blessed with prophets, men divinely inspired to explain God's mind to them, but soon after Ezra's time, divine inspiration ceased, and there were no more prophets until the Gospel day dawned. Therefore, the events of that time were foretold here by Daniel, and his words are left on record.

Verses 1–14

Here is:

1. The date of this vision (v. 1). It was *in the third year of the reign of Belshazzar*, his last year, as reckoned by many, so that according to chronological order, this chapter should come before the fifth. So that Daniel would not be surprised at the destruction of Babylon, which was now at hand, God gave him a foresight of the destruction of other kingdoms later. This vision reminds him of a former vision that *appeared to him at the first*, and it is an explanation and confirmation of that earlier vision and points to many of the same events.

2. The scene of this vision. The place where it happened was in *Shushan the palace* (the citadel of Susa) (v. 2), situated in the province of Elam, the part of Persia next to Babylon. Daniel was not there in person, for he was now in Babylon, an exile. However, he was there in vision, as Ezekiel was often brought in the spirit to the land of Israel when an exile in Babylon. The soul may be at liberty when the body is in captivity, for when we are bound, the Spirit of the Lord is not bound (2Ti 2:9).

3. The vision itself.

3.1. He saw a *ram with two horns* (v. 3). This was the second monarchy, of which the kingdoms of Media and Persia were the two horns. The horns were *very high* (long), but the one that grew up later was the longer. The kingdom of Persia, which rose up last, in Cyrus, became more eminent than that of the Medes.

3.2. He saw this *ram pushing* (charging) all around him with his horns (v. 4), *westward* (toward Babylon, Syria, Greece, and Asia Minor), *northward* (toward the Lydians, Armenians, and Scythians), and *southward* (toward Arabia, Ethiopia, and Egypt), for the Persian Empire attacked all these nations in an attempt to extend its dominion. In the end the ram became so powerful that *no beasts might stand before him*. The kings of Persia did according to their will and *became great*.

3.3. He was considering the *ram*, and *behold, a he-goat came* (v. 5). This was Alexander the Great, the son of Philip king of Macedonia. He *came from the west*, from Greece. He, in effect, conquered the world. He moved so lightly that he *touched not the ground*, that is, he met with little or no opposition. This male *goat*, or buck, had *a notable* (prominent) *horn between his eyes*. He had strength, and he knew his own strength. Alexander pushed his conquests on so fast and with so much fury that none had the courage to stand against him. This *goat* came to the *ram that had two horns* (v. 6). Alexander with

his victorious army — consisting of no more than 30,000 foot soldiers and 5,000 horses — attacked the kingdom of Persia. He overtook Darius Codomannus, then emperor of Persia, being *moved with choler* (furiously) *against him* (v. 7). Alexander was too strong for him whenever he engaged him, and he *smote* (struck) *him, cast* (knocked) *him down to the ground*, and *stamped upon him*; some think these three expressions refer to the three famous victories that Alexander gained over Darius, at Granicus, Issus, and Arbela, which meant he was finally, totally routed, having, in the last battle, lost 600,000 men. Alexander then became absolute master of all the Persian Empire, having *broken his two horns*, the kingdoms of Media and Persia.

3.4. He saw the goat made significant, but the *great horn*, which had carried out all this, *was broken* off (v. 8). Alexander was twenty years old when he began his wars. When he was twenty-six, he conquered Darius and controlled the whole Persian Empire, but when he was thirty-two *years of age*, in his full strength, he was *broken*. He died of excessive drinking or, as some suspect, by poison, and left no child to survive him (Ecc 4:8).

3.5. He saw this kingdom divided into four parts, and in the place of one great horn there came *up four notable* (prominent) *ones*, Alexander's four commanders. These *four notable horns* were toward the *four winds of heaven* (v. 8), the kingdoms of Syria and Egypt, Asia and Greece.

3.6. He saw a *little horn* that became a great persecutor of the church and people of God. All agree that this was Antiochus Epiphanes. He is called here (as before, in 7:8) a *little horn*, because his origin was contemptible: others were ahead of him in line of succession, and he had been a hostage and prisoner at Rome. But he escaped and gained the kingdom. He seized Egypt and invaded Persia and Armenia. But what is noted here is the trouble he caused to the Jewish people.

3.6.1. He set himself against *the pleasant land*, the Beautiful Land, the land of Israel. Mount Zion was *beautiful for situation*, the *joy of the whole earth* (Ps 48:2). We should consider a place beautiful if it is a holy place, a place where God lives and where we may have fellowship with him.

3.6.2. He fought against the *host of heaven* (v. 10), that is, the people of God, the church militant here on earth.

3.6.3. He *cast* (threw) *down some of the* host to the ground and trampled on them. Some of those most eminent in church and state, burning and shining lights in their generation (Jn 5:35), were either forced by him to submit to his idolatry or put to death, as good old Eleazar and the seven brothers were, whom he put to death with cruel tortures because they would not eat pork (2 Macc 7:1).

3.6.4. He *magnified himself even to the prince of the host* (v. 11). He set himself against the high priest, Onias, or against God himself.

3.6.5. He *took away the daily sacrifice* (v. 11). Antiochus forbade the morning and evening lamb, which God appointed to be offered on his altar.

3.6.6. He *cast down the place of his sanctuary* (v. 11). He did not burn the temple, but made it the temple of Jupiter Olympius and set up his idol in it. He also *cast* (threw) *down the truth to the ground*, trampled on the Book of the Law, burned it. God would not have allowed it if his people had not provoked him to do so. It was *by reason of transgression*, the transgression of Israel, that Antiochus was used to give them all this trouble. The great transgression of the Jews after the exile was contempt and desecration of holy things, sniffing contemptuously at the service of God, *bringing the torn and the lame for sacrifice*, as if the *table of the Lord* were *a contemptible thing* (Mal 1:7–8) and that was why God sent Antiochus to *take away the daily sacrifice* and *cast down the place of his sanctuary*.

3.7. He heard the time of this disaster limited, *how long it should last*, so that when they no longer had any *prophets to tell them how long*, they would have this prophecy to give them a prospect of rescue. One *saint* asked another, "*How long shall be the vision concerning the daily sacrifice?* How long will the prohibition of this sacrifice continue?*" (v. 14). The angels are here called *saints*, for they are *holy ones* (4:13); some consider the angel to whom the question was addressed to be the *eternal Word*, the *Son of God*. The answer was given to Daniel rather than to the angel who asked, because the question was asked for his sake: *He said unto me*. Christ, the angel who was asked, assured Daniel that the trouble would end; it would continue 2,300 *days and no longer*, so many "evenings and mornings." We should understand them as 2,300 "natural days," which make six years, three months, and about eighteen days; it was just so many days that are reckoned from the defection of the people—brought about by Menelaus the high priest in the 142nd year of the kingdom of the Seleucids, the sixth month of that year, and the sixth day of the month (as Josephus dates it)—to the cleansing of the sanctuary and the reestablishment of religious practices among them, which was in the 148th year, the ninth month, and the twenty-fifth *day of the month* (1 Macc 4:52).

Verses 15–27

Here we have:

1. Daniel's fervent desire to have this vision explained to him (v. 15): *I sought the meaning*.

2. One *in the appearance of a man*—who some think was Christ himself—ordering Gabriel to *make Daniel understand this vision* (v. 16).

3. The fear Daniel was in when his instructor approached (v. 17): *When he came near, I was afraid.* Prostrate on the ground, he *fell into a deep sleep* (v. 18).

4. The relief the angel gave to Daniel. He *touched him* and *set him upright*, on his feet (v. 18). He promised to explain the visions to him: "*Understand, O son of man!* (v. 17). You will understand, if you will only apply your mind to understand." He assured him that he would be allowed to know *what would be in the last end of the indignation* (what would happen later in the time of wrath) (v. 19). Let those who live to see these disastrous times take courage from knowing that an end of them would come; *the indignation shall cease* (Isa 10:25); it *shall be overpast* (Isa 26:20). Good would be brought out of it. The angel told him (v. 17), "*At the time of the end shall be the vision*; when the final end of God's wrath comes, when the course of this providence has been completed, then the vision will be made clear and intelligible by the event."

5. The explanation he gave him of the vision.

5.1. About the two monarchies of Persia and Greece (vv. 20–22). The *ram* represented the succession of the kings of Media and Persia; *the goat* signified the kings of Greece; the *great horn* was Alexander; *the four horns* that rose up in his place were the four kingdoms we read about before (v. 8). Josephus relates that when Alexander had captured Tyre and was marching toward Jerusalem, Jaddas, then high priest, fearing his rage, turned to God in prayer and was warned in a dream that when Alexander approached, he must open the gates of the city, and that

he and the rest of the priests must go out to meet him in their garments, and all the rest of the people must go out in white. When Alexander saw this company at a distance, he went alone to the high priest and, having prostrated himself, first saluted the priest, and then, when asked by one of his own commanders why he had done so, said that while he was still in Macedon, pondering the conquest of Asia, there appeared to him a man wearing such clothes, who invited him into Asia and assured him of success in conquering it. The priests led him to the temple, where he offered sacrifices to the God of Israel as they instructed him, and they showed him this book of the prophet Daniel, where it was foretold that a Greek would destroy the Persians. This encouraged him on the mission against Darius. He then took the Jews and their religion under his protection, promising to be kind to those of their religion in Babylon and Media, to where he was now marching (Josephus, book 11).

5.2. About Antiochus and his oppression of the Jews. The angel said that this would happen in the *latter time of the* kingdom of the Greeks, when the *transgressors are come to the full* (when rebels have become completely wicked) (v. 23). Notice:

5.2.1. His character. He would be a king of fierce countenance (stern-faced), not fearing God or having respect for human beings (Lk 18:2), *understanding dark sentences*, or a master of intrigue, well versed in the hidden, dishonest things.

5.2.2. His success and the end he would come to. He would make havoc of the nations: *His power shall be mighty*, bearing down on all in its path (v. 24), with the help of his allies, Eumenes and Attalus, partly by the treachery and evil of many of the Jews. Now:

5.2.2.1. He *destroyed wonderfully* (astoundingly) indeed, for he destroyed the *mighty people*. The princes of Egypt would not be able to withstand him with all their forces. He would also destroy the *holy people*, or the *people of the holy ones*; their sacred character would not deter him. He would gain this success by his deception, cunning, and shrewdness (v. 25), by deceit and diabolical subtlety. He would *cause craft* (deceit) *to prosper*; he would be successful through the art of persuading, using soft, flattering words. He would trick them into subjection to him; as others destroyed by war, *by peace* (when they feel secure) *he would destroy many*, claiming treaties, leagues, and alliances. Sometimes when a truly brave nation has gained in a righteous war, a truly evil nation has regained in a treacherous peace. *He would magnify himself in his heart*, so that he would *stand up against the Prince of princes*, that is, against God himself. He would desecrate his temple and altar and persecute his worshipers.

5.2.2.2. And yet his destroying would come to an end: *He shall be broken without hand.* He would not be killed in war, nor would he be assassinated; instead, he would fall into the hands of the living God and die (Heb 10:31). When Antiochus heard that the Jews had thrown the idol of Jupiter Olympus out of the temple, where he had put it, he became so angry that he vowed he would make Jerusalem *a common burial place*, but no sooner had he spoken these proud words than he was struck with an incurable plague, and he remained in this misery for a long time. At first he persisted in intimidating the Jews, but finally, despairing of ever recovering, he acknowledged that he had wronged the Jews in many ways and had desecrated the temple at Jerusalem. Then he wrote courteous letters vowing that if he recovered he would allow them to freely exercise their religion. When he realized his disease was killing him, he said, "It is right to submit to God, for mortals not to set themselves in competition with God." So he died in a strange land, on the mountains of Pacata, near Babylon.

6. The conclusion of this vision, and the charge is given to Daniel to keep it to himself for the present: *Shut thou* (seal) *up the vision* (v. 26), *for it shall be for many days*; seal it, for it concerns the distant future. Let it be kept for generations, who would live at about the time of its fulfillment, for it would be most useful to them.

CHAPTER 9

We have here: 1. Daniel's prayer for the restoration of the Jews in exile (vv. 1–19). 2. An immediate answer to his prayer, in which: 2.1. He is assured of the quick release of the Jews from captivity (vv. 20–23). 2.2. He is informed about the redemption of the world by Jesus Christ (vv. 24–27). It is the clearest prophecy of the Messiah in the whole Old Testament.

Verses 1–3

Daniel here is employed in better business than any the king had for him, speaking to God and listening to him, and not only for himself but also for the church.

1. Daniel had this fellowship with God (v. 1) *in the first year of Darius the Mede*, who had just become king of the Babylonians, Babylon being conquered by him and his nephew, or grandson, Cyrus. In this year, the seventy years of the Jews' exile came to an end.

2. What brought about his address to God in prayer (v. 2): he *understood by books* (understood from the Scriptures) that seventy years was the time that had been fixed for the continuation of *the desolations of Jerusalem* (v. 2). The *book* by which he understood this was the book of Jeremiah, in which he found it expressly foretold (Jer 29:10), *After seventy years be accomplished in Babylon I will visit you, and perform my good word toward you.* It was also said (Jer 25:11), *This whole land shall be seventy years a desolation*; the word is *chorba*, the same that Daniel uses for the *desolations of Jerusalem* (v. 2), which shows that Daniel had Jeremiah's prophecy before him when he wrote this.

3. How serious and solemn his address to God was. Now *Daniel sought by prayer and supplications*, in the hope that the people would be prepared by the grace of God for the restoration that God was about to work out for them. This prayer, *I set my face unto* (turned to) *the Lord God to seek him* (v. 3), denotes the fixedness of his thoughts and the firmness of his faith in the duty. Probably, as a sign of his turning toward God, he turned toward Jerusalem. As a sign of his deep humility before God for both his own sins and the sins of his people, when he prayed, he *fasted* and put on *sackcloth* and *ashes*.

Verses 4–19

We have here Daniel's prayer to God as his God and the confession that was part of that prayer: *I prayed, and made my confession* (v. 4). In every prayer we must confess not only our sins but also our faith in God. We have here:

1. His humble, reverent address, in which he gave glory to God:

1.1. As a God to be feared: "*O Lord! the great and dreadful God* (v. 4), you who are able to deal with the greatest and most terrible of the church's enemies."

1.2. As a God to be trusted: *Keeping the covenant and mercy to those that love him* and who, to prove their love to him, *keep his commandments* (v. 4). He will be

even better than his word, for he *keeps mercy to them*, something more than was in the covenant. It was right for Daniel to consider God's mercy now that he was to lay before him the miseries of his people, and it was right to think about God's covenant now that he was to seek the fulfillment of a promise.

2. A penitent confession of sin (vv. 5–6). When we seek national mercies, we should humble ourselves for the sins of our nation. Two things emphasized their sins:

2.1. That they had disobeyed the laws God had given them through Moses.

2.2. That they had shown disrespect toward the reasonable warnings God had given them through the prophets (v. 6): "*We have not hearkened* (listened) *to thy servants the prophets*, who have reminded us of your laws."

3. A self-abasing acknowledgment of the righteousness of God in all the judgments brought on them. Daniel acknowledged that it was sin that brought on them all these troubles. Israel was *dispersed* through *all the countries* around, and therefore weakened, impoverished, and exposed. It was *because of their trespass that they have trespassed* (v. 7). They associated closely with the nations, with the result that they were defiled by them, and now God closely associated them with the nations so that they might be stripped by them. Daniel notes the fulfillment of the Scriptures in what was brought on them. *The curse is poured upon us, and the oath*, that is, the curse that was confirmed by an oath in the Law of Moses (Dt 27:15–26) (v. 11). God was only inflicting the penalty of the law. "It is not one of the common adversities of life that we are complaining about, but something that has in it special marks of divine displeasure, for *under the whole heaven has not been done as has been done upon Jerusalem*" (v. 12). Jeremiah mourned in the name of the church, *Was ever sorrow like unto my sorrow?* (La 1:2), to which we must add another, similar question, "Was ever sin like my sin?" Daniel put shame on the whole nation, from the highest person to the lowest. If Israel had continued to be a holy people, they would have been *high above all nations in praise, and name, and honour* (Dt 26:19), but now that they had *sinned and done wickedly*, shame and disgrace belonged to them, to *the men of Judah and the inhabitants of Jerusalem*, to *all Israel*, both to the two tribes *that are near*, by the rivers of Babylon, and to the ten tribes *that are afar off*, in the land of Assyria. Daniel blamed the continuation of the judgment on their incorrigibleness while they had been under it (vv. 13–14). "We have not sought the favor of the Lord our God" is the sense; "we have not been careful to make our peace with God and become reconciled to him." If people were brought to *understand God's truth* in the right way and to submit to its power and authority, they would turn from the errors of their ways. The first step toward this is to *make our prayer before the Lord our God*, so that the suffering may be consecrated before it is taken away.

4. A confident appeal to the mercy of God.

4.1. God had always been ready to pardon sin (v. 9). He is "a God of pardons" (Ne 9:17, margin); he *multiplies to pardon* (Isa 55:7).

4.2. Daniel looked back to encourage his faith (v. 15): "*Thou hast* formerly *brought thy people out of Egypt with a mighty hand*, and will you not now restore them with the same mighty hand from Babylon? And has not God said that their restoration from Babylon will surpass even that from Egypt?" (Jer 16:14–15).

5. An emotional complaint of the scorn that God's people lay under and the ruins that God's sanctuary lay

in. Their neighbors laughed at them in scorn and gloated over their disgrace. This shows us that God's Holy Place was desolate. Jerusalem, the Holy City, was an object of scorn (v. 16), the holy house was desolate (v. 17), and its altars and all the buildings lay in ashes.

6. A bold request to God to restore the captive Jews: *O Lord! I beseech thee* (v. 16). *Now therefore, O our God! hear the prayer of thy servant and his supplication* (v. 17). Now what are his petitions? What are his requests?

6.1. That God would turn away his wrath from them; that is what all the saints dread and pray against more than anything: *O let thy anger be turned away from thy Jerusalem, thy holy mountain!* (v. 16). He did not pray for the restoring of their fortunes—let the Lord do with them as seems good in his eyes (Jdg 10:5)—but he prayed first for the *turning away of God's wrath.* Take away the cause, and the effect will end.

6.2. That he would turn his face toward them (v. 17): *Cause thy face to shine upon thy sanctuary that is desolate.* The shining of God's face on the desolation of the sanctuary leads directly toward its repair, and it must be rebuilt on that foundation. If its friends want to begin their work at the right end, therefore, they must first pray fervently to God for his mercy.

7. Several pleas and arguments to support these petitions. God allows us not only to pray but also to plead, not to move him—he himself knows what he will do—but to move ourselves and encourage our faith.

7.1. They disdain to depend on any righteousness of their own; they do not pretend to deserve anything from God's hand except wrath and the curse (v. 18). Moses had told Israel that whatever God did for them was *not for their righteousness* (Dt 9:4–5).

7.2. They take their encouragement in prayer only from God, knowing they are seeking grace and mercy from him.

7.2.1. "Do it *for thy own sake* (v. 19), to accomplish your own purpose, to fulfill your own promise.

7.2.2. "Do it for the Lord's sake." Christ is *the Lord;* he is Lord of all. It is for his sake that God causes his face to shine on sinners when they repent and turn to him, because of the atonement he has made.

7.2.3. "Do it *according to all thy righteousness* (v. 16), that is, plead for us against our persecutors and oppressors *according to thy righteousness.*

7.2.4. "Do it *for thy great mercies* (v. 18), to show that you are a merciful God.

7.2.5. "Do it for the sake of the relationship we stand in with you. The sanctuary that is desolate is your sanctuary (v. 17). Jerusalem is your city and your holy mountain (v. 16); it is the city that is called by your name (v. 18). The people who have become an object of scorn are *thy people*; they are *called by thy name* (v. 19). *They are thine, save them*" (Ps 119:94).

Verses 20–27

Here is the answer that was immediately sent to Daniel's prayer, which contains the most glorious prediction of Christ and Gospel grace in the whole Old Testament. Notice:

1. The time when this answer was given.

1.1. It was while Daniel was at prayer. He called attention to this and strongly emphasized it: *While I was speaking in prayer* (v. 21), before he got up from his knees, and while there was even more he intended to say. He was confessing sin and mourning *my sin and the sin of my people Israel.* Now God fulfilled what he had spoken through Isaiah: *While they are yet speaking, I will*

hear (Isa 65:24). Daniel was very fervent in prayer (vv. 18–19), and *while he was speaking,* the angel came to him with a gracious answer. We cannot now expect God to send us answers to our prayers through angels, but if we pray fervently for what God has promised, we may by faith take the promise as an immediate answer to the prayer, for *he is faithful that has promised* (Heb 10:23). He had a revelation made to him of a far greater and more glorious redemption that God would work for his church in the last days.

1.2. It was *about the time of the evening oblation* (v. 21). The altar was in ruins, and there was no sacrifice offered on it, but the devout Jews in exile remembered daily the time when it should have been offered, and they hoped that their prayer would be *set forth before God as incense* and that the *lifting up of their hands,* and their hearts with their hands, would be acceptable in his sight *as the evening sacrifice* (Ps 141:2). The evening sacrifice was a type of the great sacrifice that Christ was to offer in the evening of the world, and it was because of that sacrifice that Daniel's prayer was accepted when he prayed *for the Lord's sake.*

2. The messenger by whom this answer was sent. It was not given him in a dream or by a voice from heaven, but by an angel appearing in human form who was deliberately sent to give this answer to Daniel. If Michael the archangel is, as many suppose, Jesus Christ, Gabriel is the only created angel who is named in Scripture. He was the one *whom I had seen in the vision at the beginning,* and Daniel learned his name when he heard him called by it at that time (8:16). When this angel said to *Zacharias, I am Gabriel* (Lk 1:19), he intended to remind him of this announcement to Daniel. Notice the instructions received from the Father of lights (Jas 1:17), to whom Daniel prayed (v. 23): *At the beginning of thy supplications* the word, *the commandment, came forth* (was given) from God. Perhaps it was *at the beginning of Daniel's supplications* that *Cyrus's word, or commandment, went forth to restore and to build Jerusalem* (v. 25). "The thing was done *this very day*; the declaration of liberty to the Jews was signed this morning, just as you were praying for it." He *touched him* (v. 21) to nudge him to break off his prayer and listen. He *talked with him* (v. 22), familiarly, so that *his terror might not make him afraid* (Job 33:7). *I have come to show thee* (v. 23). He had explained to him about the troubles of the church under Antiochus, and about the end of those troubles (8:19), but now he had greater things to explain to him. "In fact, *I have now come forth to give thee skill* (insight) *and understanding* (v. 22), not only to tell you these things but also to *make thee understand* them." He assured him that he was a favorite of heaven. I *have come to show thee, for thou art greatly beloved.* Those to whom, and in whom, God *reveals his Son* may consider themselves greatly beloved by him.

3. The message itself. It was recorded with great precision, but in it there are things that are dark and hard to understand (2Pe 3:16). Daniel, who understood from the prophet Jeremiah the expiration of the seventy years of exile, was now employed to make known to the church another more glorious release, at the end, not of seventy years, but of seventy weeks of years.

3.1. The times decreed here are somewhat hard to understand. In general, it is seventy weeks, that is, seventy times seven years, which makes 490 years. The great affairs that were still to come about concerning the people of Israel and the city of Jerusalem would lie within the range of these years. The land had enjoyed its Sabbaths, in a sad sense, for seventy years (Lev 26:34), but now the people of the Lord would enjoy their Sabbaths seven times seventy years, and in them seventy sabbatical years, which makes ten jubilees.

3.1.1. Difficulties arise concerning the time when these seventy weeks begin. They are dated here from the *going forth* of the commandment to restore and to build Jerusalem (v. 25). I am inclined to understand this to refer to the edict of Cyrus mentioned in Ezr 1:1. It also looks as though the seventy weeks should begin immediately on the expiration of the seventy years, except that by this reckoning the Persian monarchy, from the capture of Babylon by Cyrus to Alexander's conquest of Darius, lasted only 130 years, whereas, by the particular account given of the reigns of the Persian emperors, it is calculated that it continued for 230 years. This is the reckoning of Thucydides, Xenophon, and others. Mr. Poole, in his Latin *Synopsis*, has a vast and elaborate collection of what has been said for and against the different beginnings of these weeks. Concerning their end, too, interpreters are not agreed. Some believe they ended at the death of Christ. Others think, however, that because it is said that in the middle of the week—that is, the last of the seventy weeks—he will cause the sacrifice and the offering to cease, the 490 years ended three and a half years after the death of Christ. The division of the period into seven weeks and sixty-two weeks and one week is as hard to explain as anything else. In the first seven weeks, or forty-nine years, the temple and city were built, and in the last single week Christ preached his Gospel, by which the foundations were laid for the Gospel city and temple.

3.1.2. However, whatever uncertainty we may labor under concerning the exact establishing of these times, there is enough that is certain to cover the two great objectives of determining them.

3.1.2.1. It was useful to raise and support the expectations of believers. By the light of this prophecy they were guided to approximately what time to expect the Messiah.

3.1.2.2. It is useful to refute and silence the expectations of unbelievers, who will not acknowledge that Jesus is *the One who should come*, but still *look for another* (Mt 11:3). Whichever commandment to build Jerusalem we choose as a date from which to begin, it is certain that these 490 years expired more than 1,500 years ago [Ed. note: this commentary was published in 1712]. We are confirmed in our belief that the Messiah has come and that our Jesus is the One by observing that he came just at the time that had been predetermined.

3.2. The events foretold here are easier to understand. Notice what is foretold:

3.2.1. About the return of the Jews now quickly to their own land and their resettlement there. Let the devout Jews be encouraged by the assurance that a *commandment* will *go forth to restore and to build Jerusalem* (v. 25). God will carry on his own work; he will build up his Jerusalem and make it beautiful and strong, *even in troublous times*.

3.2.2. About the Messiah. The worldly Jews looked for a Messiah who could rescue them from the Roman yoke and give them physical power and wealth, whereas they were told here that the Messiah would come on another mission, purely spiritual.

3.2.2.1. Christ came to take away sin. Sin had brought a division between God and human beings; it had separated people from God and provoked God against human beings. It was this that brought misery on the human race. Christ undertakes to destroy the works of the devil (1Jn 3:8). Gabriel does not say to "finish your transgressions and your sins," but *to finish transgression and sin* in general (v. 24),

for he is the atoning sacrifice for the sins of the whole world (1Jn 2:2). He came to *finish transgression* (v. 24), to "restrain" it, according to some, to break its power and establish a kingdom of holiness and love in the hearts of human beings. He came to *make an end of sin*, to abolish it, to "seal up sins" (v. 24, margin), so that they may not break out against us. And he came to *make reconciliation for iniquity*, as by a sacrifice, to make peace and bring God and human beings together. He is not only the peacemaker but the peace (Eph 2:14). He himself is the atonement.

3.2.2.2. He came to *bring in an everlasting righteousness* (v. 24). God could justly have put an end to sin by putting an end to sinners, but Christ found another way, putting an end to sin in such a way as to save sinners, by providing a righteousness for them. The merit of his sacrifice is our righteousness. By faith we apply this to ourselves and plead it with God, and our faith is credited to us as righteousness (Ro 4:3, 5).

3.2.2.3. He came to seal up the vision and prophecy, all the prophetic visions of the Old Testament that had referred to the Messiah. He sealed them up, that is, he accomplished them.

3.2.2.4. He came to *anoint the most holy*, that is, himself, the Holy One. He is called the *Messiah* (vv. 25–26), Christ, which means "the Anointed One" (Jn 1:41), because he received the anointing both for himself and for all who are his.

3.2.2.5. In order to do all this, the Messiah must be *cut off*, must die a violent death, and so be *cut off from the land of the living*, as was foretold (Isa 53:8). For this reason, when Paul preaches the death of Christ, he says that he preaches nothing except what the prophet said would happen (Ac 26:22–23). And *thus it behoved Christ* (was necessary for the Christ) *to suffer* (Lk 24:46). He must be cut off, but not for himself. It was to atone for our sins, to purchase life for us. He must cause the sacrifice and offering to cease. By offering himself as a sacrifice once for all, he will put an end to all the Levitical sacrifices.

3.2.3. About the final destruction of Jerusalem and of the Jewish church and nation, which follows immediately from the cutting off of the Messiah, because it was the just punishment of those who put him to death. He died to take away the ceremonial law, to abolish that law of commandments. However, the Jews would not be persuaded to abandon it: they stoned Stephen for saying that Jesus would change the customs that Moses handed down to them (Ac 6:14). It is foretold here that *the people of the prince that shall come* (v. 26) will be the instruments of this destruction, that is, the Roman armies, belonging to a monarchy still to come. The *city* and *sanctuary*, in particular, will be *destroyed* and completely devastated. Titus the Roman general wanted to save the temple, but his soldiers were so angry with the Jews that he could not restrain them from burning it to the ground. The *sacrifice and oblation* (offering) will be *made to cease*. There will be *an overspreading of abominations* (v. 27), which refers to the armies of the Romans. These are the words to which Christ refers in Mt 24:15 when he says, *When you shall see the abomination of desolation, spoken of by Daniel, stand in the holy place, then let those who shall be in Judea flee*, which is explained in Lk 21:20.

CHAPTER 10

This chapter and the two following chapters make up one complete vision and prophecy that is communicated to Daniel for the use of the church, not by signs and figures,

*as before (chs. 7–8), but by clear words. Daniel prayed
daily, but he saw a vision only now and then. In this
chapter we have things that introduce the prophecy, in
the eleventh chapter individual predictions, and in the
twelfth its conclusion. This chapter shows us: 1. Daniel's
solemn fasting and abasement before he had this vision
(vv. 1–3). 2. A glorious appearance of the Son of God to
him (vv. 4–9). 3. The encouragement given him to expect
that future events that would be useful both to others and
to him would be revealed to him, and to expect that he
would be enabled to understand the meaning of this revelation (vv. 10–21).*

Verses 1–9

This vision is dated in the *third year of Cyrus,* that is,
in the third year of his reign after the conquest of Babylon,
the third year since Daniel came to know him. Here is:

1. A general idea of this prophecy (v. 1): *The thing was
true, but the time appointed was long,* to the end of the
reign of Antiochus, which was 300 years. This prophecy
looks as far forward as the end of the world and the resurrection of the dead, for the events foretold here are types
of those things; Daniel might well say, therefore, *The time
appointed was long.*

2. An account of Daniel's humbling of himself before
he had this vision. He *was mourning full three weeks* (v. 2)
for his own sins and the sins of his people and for their
sorrows. Some think that the reason for his mourning
was the laziness of many of the Jews, who, though free to
return to their own land, still remained in the land of exile.
Others think that it was because he heard of the obstruction caused to the building of the temple by the enemies of
the Jews, who *hired counsellors against them, to frustrate
their purpose, all the days of Cyrus* (Ezr 4:4–5). *Daniel
ate no flesh, drank no wine, nor anointed himself* for those
three weeks (v. 3).

3. A description of that glorious person whom Daniel saw in vision, who, it is generally agreed, could be
none other than Christ himself, the eternal Word. He
was by the side of the *Hiddekel* (Tigris) River (v. 4),
probably walking in contemplation, as Isaac walked in
the field, to meditate (Ge 24:63). There he *looked up*
and saw even *the man Christ Jesus* (1Ti 2:5) (vv. 5–6).
His attendants *saw not the vision.* Similarly, Paul's
companions were aware of the *light* but *saw no man*
(Ac 9:7; 22:9). Although Daniel's attendants did not see
the vision, *a great quaking fell upon them, so that they
fled to hide themselves* (v. 7), probably among the willows that grew by the riverside. Only Daniel saw it, but
he could not bear the sight of it. It overwhelmed his
spirit, so that *there remained no strength in him* (v. 8).
Although Daniel was so discouraged with the vision of
Christ, however, he still *heard the voice of his words*
and knew what he said. When the vision of Christ terrified Daniel, the voice of his words composed him and
laid him to sleep in a holy security and peace of mind:
"*When I heard the voice of his words, I fell into a slum
ber,* a sweet slumber, *on my face,* with *my face toward
the ground*" (v. 9).

Verses 10–21

Daniel was gradually brought back to himself.

1. The hand that *touched him* set him at first *upon his
knees and the palms of his hands* (v. 10). Afterward he
was helped up, but he *stood trembling* (v. 11) for fear
that he might fall again. Before God *gives strength and
power unto his people,* he makes them aware of their own

weakness. Daniel finally recovered not only the use of his
feet but also the use of his tongue, and when he *opened
his mouth* (v. 16), what he had to say was to excuse his
having been silent so long. *My sorrows are turned upon
me,* I am overcome with anguish. And again (v. 17), half-
dead with fright: "As for me, *straightway there remained
no strength in me* to receive these manifestations of divine
glory and these revelations of the divine will; in fact, *there
is no breath left in me.*"

2. The angel who was used by Christ to talk with
Daniel gave him all the encouragement and strength he
needed. Christ himself encouraged John when he, in a
similar case, fell at his feet as though dead (Rev 1:17), but
here he did it through the angel.

2.1. He offered him his hand to help him up (v. 10), for
otherwise he would still have lain prostrate on the ground;
he touched his lips (v. 16), for otherwise he would still
have been mute. He touched him again (v. 18) and put
strength into him. One touch from heaven brings us to our
knees, sets us up on our feet, opens our lips, and strengthens us, for it is God who works on us, and works in us,
both to will and to do what is good (Php 2:13).

2.2. He assured him of the favor God had for him: you
are *a man greatly beloved* (v. 11), and again (v. 19), *O man
greatly beloved!* Those people whom God loves are truly
greatly beloved, and it is enough comfort to know it.

2.3. He silenced his fears and encouraged his hopes with
good words and encouraging words (Zec 1:13). *Fear not,
Daniel* (v. 12), and again (v. 19), *O man greatly beloved!
fear not; peace be to thee; be strong, yea, be strong.* Now
that Daniel had experienced the power of God's strengthening word and grace, he was ready for anything.

2.4. He assured him that his fasting and prayers had
come up as a memorial offering before God (Ac 10:4):
Fear not, Daniel (v. 12). From the first day that we begin
to look toward God by way of duty, he is ready to meet us
by way of mercy.

2.5. Why did this angel come to Daniel? He told him
(v. 14): *I have come to make thee understand what will
befall thy people in the latter days.* What the angel was
entrusted to communicate to Daniel, and what Daniel was
encouraged to expect from him, were not speculations,
even though he was an angel, but what he had received
from the Lord (1Co 11:23). It was the revelation of Jesus
Christ that the angel gave to the apostle John to be communicated to the churches (Rev 1:1). So here (v. 21): *I
will show thee what is written in the scriptures of truth*
(Book of Truth). The decree of God is something written;
it is Scripture that remains and cannot be altered.

2.6. He gave him a general account of the adversaries
of the church's cause.

2.6.1. The *kings of the earth* are and will be its adversaries (Ps 2:2). The angel told Daniel that the prince of
the Persian kingdom resisted him twenty-one days, just
the three weeks that Daniel had been fasting and praying. This new king of Persia, by hindering the temple,
had hindered the good news that he would otherwise have
brought him. "When *I have gone forth* from the kings of
Persia, when their monarchy is brought down for their
unkindness to the Jews, then *the prince of Grecia shall
come*" (v. 20). Although the Greek monarchy was favorable to the Jews at first, as the Persian was, it would yet
become a problem to them.

2.6.2. The God of heaven is, and will be, its protector.
Here is:

2.6.2.1. The angel Gabriel. He had resolved that when
he had dealt with this errand to Daniel, he would *return*

to fight with the prince of Persia and would finally bring down that proud monarchy (v. 20).

2.6.2.2. Michael our prince, the great protector of the church, *the first of the chief princes* (v. 13). Some understand this name to refer to a created angel. Others think that *Michael the archangel* is none other than Christ himself (v. 5). He *came to help me* (v. 13), and there is *none but he that holds with me in these things* (v. 21). Christ is the church's prince; angels are not (Heb 2:5).

CHAPTER 11

The angel Gabriel fulfills the promise he made to Daniel that is recorded in the previous chapter, that he would show him what should befall his people in the latter days *(10:14), according to what was* written in the scriptures of truth *(10:21). Here is a prediction: 1. Of the setting up of the Greek monarchy on the ruins of the Persian one (vv. 1–4). 2. Of the activities of the two kingdoms of Egypt and Syria with reference to each other (vv. 5–20). 3. Of the rise of Antiochus Epiphanes and of his actions and successes (vv. 21–29). 4. Of the great trouble he would do to the Jewish nation and religion, and of his contempt of all religion (vv. 30–39). 5. Of his final fall and ruin (vv. 40–45).*

Verses 1–4

Here:

1. The angel Gabriel tells Daniel the good deed he has done for the Jewish nation (v. 1): "*In the first year of Darius the Mede*, who destroyed Babylon and released the Jews from exile, *I stood to confirm and strengthen him*." This is how the angel, at the request of *the watcher* (4:23), destroyed the golden head (2:32, 38); this is how the ax was laid to the root of the tree (Mt 3:10). God's care of his church in the past encourages us to depend on him in further difficulties in the present and future.

2. He foretells the reign of four Persian kings (v. 2).

2.1. *Three kings in Persia* will appear besides Darius, in whose reign this prophecy is dated (9:1). Mr. Broughton understands these three to be Cyrus; Artaxasta or Artax- erxes, called by the Greeks *Cambyses*; and Ahasuerus, who married Esther and was called *Darius son of Hystaspes*. The Persians attributed these qualities to them: Cyrus was a father, Cambyses a master, and Darius a hoarder (Herodotus).

2.2. There will be a fourth, *far richer than them all*, that is, Xerxes, whose wealth the Greek authors take note of. By *his strength* (his vast, powerful army, consisting of at least 800,000 soldiers) and *his riches he shall stir up all* against *the realm of Greece*. Xerxes' expedition against Greece ended in shameful defeat. About thirty years after the first return from exile, Darius, a young king, revived the building of the temple, acknowledging the hand of God against his predecessors for hindering that work (Ezr 6:7).

3. He foretells Alexander's conquests and the partition of his kingdom (v. 3). The one who is a *mighty king* will *stand up* against the kings of Persia and will *rule with great dominion* and despotic power, for he will *do according to his will*. But his *kingdom* will soon be *broken* up and *divided* into four parts, *but not to his posterity* (v. 4). His *kingdom shall be plucked up* (uprooted) for others outside those of his own family. Philip Arrhidaeus, his brother, was made king in Macedonia; Olympias, Alexander's mother, killed Arrhidaeus and poisoned his two sons, Hercules and Alexander. In this way, his family was uprooted by its own hands.

Verses 5–20

Here are foretold:

1. The rise and power of two great kingdoms from the remains of Alexander's conquests (v. 5).

1.1. Egypt was made significant by Ptolemy Lagus, one of Alexander's commanders. He is called the king of the *south*, that is, Egypt (vv. 8, 42–43). The countries that at first belonged to Ptolemy are Egypt, Phoenicia, Arabia, Libya, and Ethiopia.

1.2. The kingdom of Syria was set up by Seleucus Nicator, or "Seleucus the Conqueror"; he was one of Alexander's officers and was the most powerful of all Alexander's successors. Both of these rulers *were strong* (v. 5) against Judah: Ptolemy invaded Judea, and took Jerusalem *on a sabbath*, pretending a friendly visit; Seleucus also disturbed Judea.

2. The futile attempt to unite these two kingdoms like the iron and clay in Nebuchadnezzar's image (v. 6): "*At the end of certain years*, about seventy after Alexander's death, the Lagidae and the Seleucids will unite, but not sincerely. Ptolemy Philadelphus, king of Egypt, will marry his daughter Berenice to Antiochus Theos, king of Syria," who already had a wife named Laodice. "Berenice will come to the *king of the north* to make an alliance, but *she shall not retain the power of the arm*; neither she nor her descendants will establish themselves in the kingdom of the north. *She shall be given up* (handed over), *and so* will *those that brought her*." Antiochus divorced Berenice and returned to his former wife, Laodice, who poisoned him, had Berenice and her son murdered, and set up as king her own son by Antiochus, Seleucus Callinicus.

3. A war between the two kingdoms (vv. 7–8). A branch from the same root as Berenice *shall stand up in his estate*, that is, he will take the place of Ptolemy Philadelphus. Ptolemy Euergetes, Philadelphus's son, will come against Seleucus Callinicus, king of Syria, to avenge his sister's quarrel. He will be victorious, carry away rich spoil into Egypt, and *continue more years than the king of the north*. However, he will be forced to *come into his kingdom* and *return into his own land* (v. 9) to keep the peace there, and so he will no longer be able to carry on the war abroad.

4. The long reign of *Antiochus the Great*, king of Syria. Seleucus Callinicus, that king of the north who was defeated (v. 7) and died miserably, left two sons, Seleucus and Antiochus. These are the sons of the *king of the north* who will be *stirred up and shall assemble a multitude of great forces* to recover what their father lost (v. 10). But Seleucus, the elder, was poisoned, and reigned for only two years; his brother, Antiochus, succeeded him, reigned thirty-seven years, and was called *the Great*.

4.1. The *king of the south* will at first have great success in this war. Ptolemy Philopator, moved with indignation at the indignities done by *Antiochus the Great*, will *come forth and fight with him*, bringing a vast army. The *other multitude*, the army of Antiochus, will *be given into his hand*. After Ptolemy Philopator gained this victory, *his heart was lifted up*, and he went into the temple at Jerusalem and entered the Most Holy Place.

4.2. The *king of the north, Antiochus the Great*, will *return* with a *greater army* than *the former*, and "at the end of times" (that is, years) he will *come with a mighty army and great riches* against the *king of the south*, that is, Ptolemy Epiphanes, who succeeded Ptolemy Philopator, his father. In this expedition Antiochus had powerful allies (v. 14), including Philip V of Macedon. Antiochus defeated the king of Egypt, destroying most of his army, and then the Jews joined him and helped him besiege Ptolemy's garrisons. Then *the robbers of thy people shall exalt themselves to establish the vision* (v. 14), but *they shall fall and* come to nothing. Following that, the *king of the north* (v. 15), this same Antiochus, will pursue his intentions against the king of the south another way.

4.2.1. He will surprise his stronghold; all that the king of Egypt has gained in Syria and Samaria, and *the arms of the south* (v. 15), will not be able to resist Antiochus.

4.2.2. He will take control of the land of Judea (v. 16): *He that comes against him* (that is, the king of the north, who comes against the king of the south) will defeat all in his path; *by his hand* Israel, *the glorious land* (the Beautiful Land), was devastated and consumed. The land of Judea lay between these two powerful kingdoms of Egypt and Syria, so that in all the struggles between them it was sure to suffer.

4.2.3. He will still press on his war against the king of Egypt. He will *set his face to enter with the strength of his whole kingdom*, taking advantage of the infancy of Ptolemy Epiphanes (v. 17).

4.2.4. He will go to war against the Romans (v. 18): he will *turn his face to the isles* (coastlands) (v. 18), Greece and Italy. He took many of the islands around the Hellespont, but a *prince*—or "state," according to some—will *turn* the insolence back *upon him*. This was fulfilled when the two Scipios were sent with an army against Antiochus and totally defeated him. This will put an end to his insolence.

4.2.5. He will fall. When he was defeated by the Romans and forced to abandon all he had in Europe to them, he *turned to his own land* and, to raise money to pay his tribute, plundered a temple of Jupiter, which so angered his own subjects against him that they killed him; so he *fell* and *was no more found* (v. 19).

4.2.6. A successor arose in his place (v. 20), *a raiser of taxes*, "a sender forth of the extortioner." Seleucus IV Philopator, the elder son of Antiochus the Great, was a great oppressor of his subjects and exacted a great deal of money from them. He also attempted to rob the temple at Jerusalem. However, *within a few days he shall be destroyed, neither in anger nor in battle*; he was poisoned by Heliodorus, his own prime minister.

5. What we may learn from all this:

- That God in his providence sets up one and pulls down another, as he pleases. Some have called leaders "the footballs of fortune"; rather, they are the tools of providence.
- This world is full of *wars and fightings*, which come from the sinful desires of human beings (1Pe 2:11).

Verses 21–45

All this is a prophecy of the reign of Antiochus Epiphanes, the *little horn* (8:9), a sworn enemy of the Jewish faith and a bitter persecutor. Some things in this prediction concerning Antiochus are alluded to in the New Testament predictions of the Antichrist, especially vv. 36–37.

1. His character: he called himself Epiphanes, "the illustrious." The pagan writers describe him as an "odd-humored" man, boisterous, foolish, and immoral. He would sometimes steal out of the court into the city and join any notorious company in disguise. Some took him to be foolish; others thought him mad. He is called a *vile* (contemptible) *person* here (v. 21), for he had been a hostage at Rome so that his father would remain faithful after the Romans had subdued him.

2. His accession to the crown. He used a trick to get Demetrius, the heir of his elder brother, Seleucus IV Philopator, to be sent as a hostage to Rome in exchange for him, and because Seleucus was killed by Heliodorus (v. 20), his own prime minister, Antiochus took the kingdom. The states of Syria did not *give it* to *him* (v. 21); he *came in peaceably*, pretending to reign for, Demetrius, who was then a hostage at Rome. However, *by flatteries* (through intrigue) *he obtained the kingdom*, crushing Heliodorus and all others who opposed him, even to *the prince of the covenant*, his nephew, the rightful heir, with whom he pretended to make a covenant that he would resign whenever he returned (v. 22). Nevertheless, *after the league made with him he shall work deceitfully* (v. 23), as one whose avowed maxim is that princes should not be bound by their word any longer than is in their interests. Following this, he will *become strong with a small people*, who at first remain faithful to him, and *he shall enter peaceably upon the fattest places* (richest provinces) of the kingdom of Syria (v. 24). He will *scatter* among the people the *prey, and the spoil, and riches* to worm himself into their affections. At the same time, however, he will *forecast his devices against the strongholds* (plot the overthrow of fortresses) in order to control them. When he has gained control of the garrisons, he will not distribute his plunder anymore, but rule by force.

3. His war with Egypt, which was his second expedition there (vv. 25, 27). Antiochus will *stir up his power and courage* against Ptolemy Philometor king of Egypt. Ptolemy *shall* then *be stirred up to battle* against him. Antiochus's army will *overthrow* the Egyptian army. The king of Egypt will be betrayed by his own counselors. After the battle, a treaty of peace will be set in place, and these two kings will meet, but neither of them will be sincere in it. It is no wonder that *it shall not prosper*. The peace will not last.

4. Another expedition of his against Egypt. From the previous expedition he *returned with great riches* (v. 28), and so he took the first opportunity to invade Egypt again, two years later (v. 29), but this attempt did not succeed, for (v. 30) *the ships of Chittim* (the western coastlands) *shall come against him*, that is, the navy of the Romans, or ambassadors from the Roman senate, who came in ships. Because Ptolemy Philometor king of Egypt was now in a strict alliance with the Romans, he requested their help against Antiochus, who had besieged him and his mother, Cleopatra, in the city of Alexandria. The Roman senate then sent an embassy to Antiochus to command him to raise the siege, and, fearing the Roman power, he was forced to give orders for the raising of the siege and the retreat of his army from Egypt. This is how Livy and others relate the story.

5. Antiochus's rage and cruel practices against the Jews. On his return from his expedition into Egypt (v. 28), he *did exploits* against the Jews; he plundered the city and temple. However, the most terrible storm came on his return from Egypt, two years later (v. 30). He then took Judea on his way home, and since he could not gain victory in Egypt because of the intervention of the Romans, he wreaked revenge on the Jews.

5.1. He had a deep-rooted hatred toward the Jews' religion: *His heart* was *against the holy covenant* (v. 28), and *he had indignation against the holy covenant* (v. 30). He hated the Law of Moses and the worship of the true God and was angered by the privileges of the Jewish nation and the promises made to them.

5.2. He pursued his malicious intentions against the Jews with the help of some apostate Jews. He kept up *intelligence with those that forsook the holy covenant* (v. 30). We read much in the book of the Maccabees of the trouble caused to the Jews by these treacherous men of their own nation, Jason and Menelaus, and their group. *"Such as do wickedly against the covenant* he will *corrupt with flatteries,* to use them as decoys to draw in others" (v. 32).

5.3. He desecrated the temple. *Arms shall stand on his part* (armed forces will rise up) (v. 31), not only his own army but also deserters from the Jewish religion, and they will *pollute the sanctuary of strength.* We have the story of this in 1 Macc 1:21; *Antiochus went into the most holy temple, Menelaus, that traitor to the laws and to his own country, being his guide* (2 Macc 5:15). Antiochus also *took away the daily sacrifice* (v. 31). Then he *set up the abomination of desolation upon the altar* (1 Macc 1:54), an *idol altar* on top of the altar of burnt offering (1 Macc 1:59), and called the temple the temple of *Jupiter Olympius* (2 Macc 6:2).

5.4. He persecuted those who maintained their integrity. Although there are many who *forsake the covenant,* there is also a people who do *know their God,* and *they shall be strong and do exploits* (v. 32). Good old Eleazar, one of the *principal scribes,* when he had a piece of pork thrust into his mouth, bravely spit it out again, even though he knew he would be tormented to death for doing so (2 Macc 6:19). The mother and her seven sons were put to death for being faithful to their religion (2 Macc 7). This might well be called *doing exploits,* for to choose suffering rather than sin is a firm act. Right knowledge of God is the strength of the soul, and in the strength of that, gracious souls do great deeds. Concerning this people who knew their God, we are told here:

5.4.1. *They shall instruct many* (v. 33). They will explain to others what they have learned about the difference between truth and falsehood, good and evil. Some understand this as referring to a society that had just been set up to spread divine knowledge, called Assideans (Hasidim), or pietists (as the name means).

5.4.2. *They shall fall* by the cruelty of Antiochus, will be put to death through his rage. Their sufferings *for righteousness' sake* will test and cleanse the Jewish nation.

5.4.3. When they shall fall, they will *not be utterly cast down* (Ps 37:24), but *shall be holpen* (helped) *with a little help* (v. 34). It is also foretold that *many shall cleave to them with flatteries* (v. 34). When they see the Maccabees prosper, some Jews will join them; they will only pretend friendship, either with the intention of *betraying them* or in the hope of *rising with them.* However, the *fiery trial* (1Pe 4:12) (v. 35) will separate the *precious and the vile* (Jer 15:19). Although these troubles may continue for a long time, they will have *an end.*

5.5. He grew arrogant and ungodly and, becoming puffed up by his conquests, defied heaven and trampled on everything that was sacred (v. 36). And so it is foretold here that he will irreverently dishonor the God of Israel, called here *the God of gods* (v. 36). He will, in defiance of God, *do according to his* own *will* against God's people and his holy religion. This was fulfilled when Antiochus forbade sacrifices to be offered in God's temple and ordered the *Sabbaths* to be *profaned* and *the sanctuary* and the *holy people to be polluted, to the end that they might forget the law and change all the ordinances,* and this on pain of death (1 Macc 1:45–49). Antiochus showed no respect for any god, but exalted himself above them all (v. 37). And so he "got away with everything" until the wrath was completed (v. 36). Antiochus will not show any

respect for the gods of his ancestors; he made laws to abolish the religion of his country and to introduce the idols of the Greeks. He will set up an unknown god, a new god (v. 38). *In his estate,* in the place of the gods of his ancestors, he will honor the *god of forces* (NIV: of fortresses), a supposed god of power, a god whom his ancestors did not know or worship. This seems to refer to Jupiter Olympius, which was never introduced among the Syrians until Antiochus introduced it. He will do this *in the most strong holds,* in the strongest fortresses (v. 39), that is, in the temple of Jerusalem, which is called *the sanctuary of strength* (the temple fortress) (v. 31); there he will set up the idol of this *strange god.* Some understand the *Mahuzzim,* or *god of forces,* that Antiochus will worship to be "money," the love of which is the root of all evil (1Ti 6:10).

6. Still another expedition of his into Egypt. It seems Ptolemy, that *king of the south,* will engage him in battle (v. 40), making an attempt on some of his territories, and then Antiochus, the king of the north, will come against him like a whirlwind, with incredible speed and fury, with chariots, cavalry, and many ships, a great force. He will invade many countries and sweep through them like a flood. In this speedy march, many countries will be defeated by him, and he will enter the glorious land (the Beautiful Land), the land of Israel. Some will escape his fury, particularly Edom and Moab and the leaders of Ammon (v. 41). However, the land of Egypt will not escape. *He shall have power over the treasures of gold and silver, and all the precious things of Egypt* (v. 43).

7. The prediction, as before (8:25), that he will fall and come to ruin when he is at the height of his honor; news from the east and the north will *trouble him* (v. 44). This made Antiochus drop the enterprises he had in hand and go against the Persians and Parthians. Now comes the last effort of his rage against the Jews. When he finds himself perplexed and frustrated in his affairs, *he will go forth with great fury to destroy and utterly to make away many* (v. 44), but he will give orders that Jerusalem be destroyed after he is gone, and he will set up his royal pavilion near Jerusalem as a sign that although he could not be present himself, he still gave full power to his commanders to wage war against the Jews with the most intense rigor. When ungodliness becomes very arrogant, we may see its ruin near. *He shall come to his end, and none will help him* (v. 45). This is the same as was foretold in 8:25: *he will be broken without hand.*

CHAPTER 12

After the prediction of the troubles of the Jews under Antiochus, prefiguring the troubles of the Christian church under the anti-Christian power, we have here: 1. Encouragement to God's people in those times of trouble (vv. 1–4). 2. A conversation between Christ and an angel concerning the extent of these events (vv. 5–7). 3. Daniel's question for his own assurance (v. 8), and the answer he received to that question (vv. 9–13).

Verses 1–4

1. Jesus Christ will appear as his church's patron and protector: *At that time,* when the persecution is at its most intense, *Michael shall stand up, the great prince* (v. 1). Christ is that *great prince. At that time* Michael will arise to work out our eternal salvation; the Son of God will become incarnate, will be *manifested to destroy the works of the devil* (1Jn 3:8). Christ *stood for the children of our people* when he was made sin and a curse for them; he

stood in their place as a sacrifice, bearing the curse for them in order to bear it away from them.

2. When Christ appears, he will repay tribulation to those who trouble his people. There will *be a time of trouble*, threatening to all. This is applicable:

2.1. To the destruction of Jerusalem, which Christ calls such *a great tribulation as was not since the beginning of the world to this time* (Mt 24:21). Or:

2.2. To the judgment of the great day, which will be such *a day of trouble* as never has been to all those whom Michael our prince stands against.

3. He will work salvation for his people: "*At that time thy people shall be delivered* from the trouble and ruin designed for them by Antiochus."

4. There will be a resurrection of those who *sleep in the dust* (v. 2).

4.1. When God rescues his people from persecution, it is a kind of resurrection; the Jews' release from Babylon was represented in this way in a vision (Eze 37), and so was the rescue of the Jews from Antiochus; they were as *life from the dead* (Ro 11:15).

4.2. When, on the appearing of Michael our prince, his Gospel is preached, many of those who *sleep in the dust*, both Jews and Gentiles, will be awakened by it to take on a profession of their religious faith. But:

4.3. It must refer to the general resurrection on the last day: *The multitude of those that sleep in the dust shall awake* (v. 2).

5. There will be a glorious reward given to those who were *wise* (v. 3) and who *instructed many* (11:33) in times of trouble and distress. It was foretold earlier (11:33) that they would perform an important service but would *fall by the sword and by flame*. Now, if there were not another life after this, they would be *of all men most miserable* (1Co 15:19), and so we are assured here that they will be rewarded *in the resurrection of the just* (v. 3). Those who turn *men to righteousness*, who *turn sinners from the errors of their ways* and help to *save their souls from death* (Jas 5:20), will share in the glory of those they have helped to heaven, which will be a great addition to their own glory.

6. This prophecy of those times, though closed up and sealed now, would be very useful to those who would live then (v. 4). Daniel must now *shut up the words and seal the book*, because the *time would be long* before these things would be fulfilled. He must keep it safely, as a treasure of great value stored for the ages to come. Those things of God that are now dark and obscure will in the future be made clearer and easier to understand. "Truth is the daughter of time." Scripture prophecies will be explained by their fulfillment.

Verses 5–13

Daniel had been caused to foresee the amazing changes in states and kingdoms as far as the Israel of God was concerned in them; in them he foresaw troubled times for the church. Two questions are asked and answered here: *When will the end be?* and, *What will the end be?*

1. The question *When will the end be?* was asked by an angel (vv. 5–6). We may notice:

1.1. Who it was who asked the question. Daniel had had a conversation with the angel Gabriel, and now he looked, *and, behold, there stood other two* (v. 5), two angels he had not seen before, *one on the bank of the river on one side and the other on the other side*. Christ stood *on the waters of the river* (v. 6), *between the banks of Ulai*. Daniel had not seen them before, but now, when they began to speak, he looked up and saw them.

1.2. To whom the question was put, to the man clothed in linen, about whom we read before (10:5), to Christ our great high priest (Heb 4:14), who was on the waters of the river.

1.3. What the question was: *How long shall it be to the end of these wonders?* (v. 6). The angel asked as one concerned, *How long shall it be?* What is the time for the *end of these wonders*, these astonishing, suffering, testing times, which are to come on the people of God?

1.4. What answer was given. Here:

1.4.1. The angel who asked the question was given a general account of the duration of these troubles (v. 7). They would continue *for a time, times, and a half*, that is, a year, two years, and half a year, as was intimated before (7:25). Some understand it indefinitely, as a certain time representing an uncertain one; it would be *for a time* (a considerable time), for *times* (a longer time), but only *half a time*; when it was over it would seem not half so much as had been feared. However, it should rather be taken as a certain time; we meet it in Revelation, where it is sometimes called three and a half days, standing for three and a half years, sometimes forty-two months, sometimes 1,260 days. This Mighty One that Daniel saw stood with *both feet* on the water and swore with *both hands* lifted up. God's time to help and relieve his people is when their affairs are brought to the ultimate crisis; *in the mount of the Lord it shall be seen* that Isaac is saved just when he is about to be sacrificed (Ge 22:14). Now the event fulfilled the prediction; Josephus says that Antiochus surprised Jerusalem "and held it three years and six months" and was then "cast out of the country" by the Maccabees. Christ's public ministry continued *three years and a half*, during which time he endured the opposition of sinners and lived in poverty and disgrace, but when at his death his enemies triumphed over him, he obtained the most glorious victory and said, *It is finished* (Jn 19:30).

1.4.2. In what was said to Daniel in vv. 11–12, some more details were added concerning the duration of those troubles. The time of the trouble was to be dated from the *taking away of the daily sacrifice* by Antiochus and the *setting up* of the image of Jupiter on the altar, which was the *abomination of desolation*. The Jews' trouble would last 1,290 days, *three years* and *seven months*, or, as some calculate it, *three years, six months*, and *fifteen days*, and then, probably, the daily sacrifice was restored and the abomination that causes desolation was taken away. It appears that the beginning of the trouble came in the 145th year of the Seleucids, and its end in the 148th year. We may learn from this that:

- A time is fixed for the end of the church's troubles and the bringing about of their rescue.
- This time must be waited for with faith and patience.
- When it comes, it will abundantly reward us for our long expectation.

2. The question *What shall the end be?* was asked by Daniel. Notice:

2.1. Why Daniel asked this question; it was because although he *heard what was said* to the angel, he still did not *understand* it (v. 8).

2.2. What the question was: *O my Lord! What shall be the end of these things?* (v. 8). He directed his inquiry not to the angel who talked to him, but directly to Christ. When we take a view of the affairs of this world, and of the church of God in it, we see things moving as if they would end in the complete destruction of God's kingdom on earth. When we see evil and ungodliness, the decay of religious faith, the sufferings of the righteous, and the triumphs of the ungodly, we may well ask, *O my Lord! what will be the end of these things?*

2.3. What answer was given to this question.

2.3.1. Daniel must content himself with the revelations that had been made to him: "*Go thy way, Daniel* (v. 9). *Go thy way, and record what thou hast seen* (Rev 1:2) and heard, for the benefit of future generations, and do not desire to see and hear more at present."

2.3.2. He must not expect that what had been said to him would be fully understood until it was fulfilled.

2.3.3. He must depend on nothing other than the assurance that as long as the world stands, it will always contain a mixture of good and bad (v. 10).

2.3.3.1. There is no remedy; evildoers *will do wickedly.* Bad people will do bad things, and *a corrupt tree will never bring forth good fruit* (Mt 7:18). Corrupt practices are the natural products of corrupt principles and dispositions. As we were told before, the *wicked will do wickedly.* They *will not understand*; they close their eyes to the light; and there are none so blind as those who will not see. Deliberate sin is the effect of deliberate ignorance; they *will not understand* because *they are wicked*; they *hate the light* and do not come to the light *because their deeds are evil* (Jn 3:19).

2.3.3.2. Yet, bad though the world is, God will keep for himself a remnant of good people in it. There will be many to whom the providences and ordinances of God will be *a savour of life unto life* (2Co 2:16). *Many shall be purified, and made white, and tried* (v. 10) by their troubles (compare 11:35). The word of God will do them good. When the *wicked understand not,* but stumble at his word, the *wise shall understand* (v. 10). Those who are ruled by divine law and love will be illuminated with divine light. For those who *do his will* will *know the truth* (Jn 7:17).

2.3.4. He must encourage himself with the pleasing prospect of his own happiness in death, in judgment, and to eternity (v. 13). Time and days will have an end; not only will our time and days end very soon, but also all times and days will finally come to an end. In a short while, time will be no more; all its changes will be accounted for and finished. It was an encouragement to Daniel, and it is an encouragement to all the saints, that, whatever may be their allotted portion in the days of time, they will have a happy allotted inheritance at *the end of the days* (v. 13). A confident hope and prospect of a blessed allotted inheritance in the heavenly Canaan at the end of our days will provide us with real comfort in our dying moments.

A Practical and Devotional Exposition of the Book of the Prophet

Hosea

1. We now have in front of us the twelve Minor Prophets, which were sometimes grouped together as one book. These books are called the Minor Prophets not because they have less authority than the writings of the greater prophets, but only because they are shorter than the others. These prophets preached as much as the others but did not write so much. These twelve, Josephus says, were put into one volume by "the men of the great synagogue" in Ezra's time. These are the fragments of prophecy, carefully collated by divine Providence and the care of the church. Nine of these prophets prophesied before the exile, and the last three after the return of the Jews to their own land. There is some difference of opinion as to the order of these books. We place them as the ancient Hebrew did, and all agree to put Hosea first; the Septuagint, on the other hand (a Greek version of the Old Testament), places the first six in this order: Hosea, Amos, Micah, Joel, Obadiah, and Jonah. But it does not matter.

2. We have in front of us the prophecy of Hosea, who was the first of all the writing prophets. The ancients say he came from Beth Shemesh, in the tribe of Issachar (Jos 19:22). He continued to be a prophet for a very long time. Jerome observes that Hosea prophesied the destruction of the kingdom of the ten tribes, then lived to see and mourn it himself. The scope of his prophecy is to reveal sin and to declare the judgments of God against a people who refused to be reformed (Lev 26:23). The style is concise, and in some places it seems like the book of Proverbs, without connection from one verse to the next, and should be called Hosea's *sayings* rather than Hosea's *sermons*.

CHAPTER 1

In the first three chapters, the mind of God is revealed to this prophet, and by him to the people, by signs and types, but afterward only by messages. In this chapter we have: 1. The title (v. 1). 2. Some detailed instructions Hosea was ordered to give to the people of God. 2.1. He must convince them of their sin in being unfaithful to God (vv. 2–3). 2.2. By the names of his sons he must foretell the ruin coming on Israel for their sin (vv. 4–6, 8–9). 2.3. He must speak words of encouragement to the kingdom of Judah, who still retained the pure worship of God (v. 7). 2.4. He must let them know what great mercy God had in store for Israel and Judah in the latter days (vv. 10–11).

Verse 1

Here we have:

1. The prophet's name: *Hosea,* or *Hoshea,* the same as Joshua's original name; it means "a savior." His surname was *Ben-Beeri,* or *the son of Beeri. Beeri* means "a well," which may remind us of living waters (Jer 2:13; 17:13) from which prophets must continually draw.

2. His authority and commission: *The word of the Lord came to him.* What he said and wrote was by divine inspiration. This book was therefore accepted among the canonical books of the Old Testament, which is confirmed by what is quoted from it in the New Testament (Mt 2:15; 9:13; 12:7; Ro 9:25–26; 1Pe 2:10).

3. A detailed account of the times in which he prophesied—*in the days of Uzziah, Jotham, Ahaz, and Hezekiah, kings of Judah, and in the days of Jeroboam the son of Joash, king of Israel.* Now by this account given of the reigns in which Hosea prophesied it appears that he prophesied a long time, that he began when he was young and continued until he was very old. But the longer they enjoyed him, the less they respected him; first they despised his youth (1Ti 4:12), and then later his age. Some of these kings were good, and encouraged him; others were bad, and frowned on him and discouraged him, but he remained the same. He began to prophesy in Israel at a time when their kingdom was prospering, as in the reign of Jeroboam II (2Ki 14:25). Yet at that very time, Hosea boldly told them about their sins and foretold their destruction.

Verses 2–7

These words, *The beginning of the word of the Lord by Hosea,* may refer either:

- To that glorious group of prophets that was raised up. About this time the following lived and prophesied: Joel, Amos, Micah, Jonah, Obadiah, and Isaiah, although Hosea was the first of them who foretold the destruction of Israel. Or, rather:
- To Hosea's own prophecies. This was the first message God sent him with to this people, to tell them that they were *an evil and an adulterous generation* (Mt 12:39).

He might have wanted to be excused until he had gained some authority and the benefit of their affection. No; he must *begin* with this, so that they would know what to expect from a prophet of the Lord.

1. The prophet must show them *their sin*, as it were, in a mirror. The prophet is ordered to *take unto him a wife of whoredoms* (an adulterous wife) *and children of whoredoms* (unfaithfulness) (v. 2). And he does so (v. 3). He marries a prostitute, a woman of ill repute, *Gomer the daughter of Diblaim*, one who has lived scandalously while single. To marry such a woman was not wise and was therefore forbidden to the priests, and it would be a burden to the prophet, but not a sin. Most commentators think that it was done *in vision*, or that it is nothing more than a parable. He must take an adulterous wife and have children by her that, though born in wedlock, everyone would suspect to be children of unfaithfulness. "Now, Hosea," God says, "this people is to me such a dishonor, and such a grief and trouble, as a *wife of whoredoms* and *children of whoredoms* would be to you. *For the land has committed great whoredoms* (the vilest adultery)." The adultery they are accused of here is, especially, their idolatry. *Idolatry is great whoredom*, worse than any other; it is departing from *the Lord. The land has committed whoredom*; the whole land is defiled with it. Is it not offensive to the *holy God* to have such a people called by his name and given a place in his house? It was as if he had married Gomer the daughter of Diblaim, a noted prostitute. The land of Israel was like Gomer the daughter of Diblaim. *Gomer* means "corruption," and *Diblaim* means "two cakes," or "two lumps of figs"; this shows that Israel was close to ruin and that their self-indulgence was the cause of that. It shows that sin is the daughter of plenty and destruction is the daughter of the abuse of plenty.

2. The prophet must, as it were, through a magnifying glass, show them their ruin, and he does this in the names given to the children born of this adulteress.

2.1. He foretells the downfall of the royal family in the name he is appointed to give to his first child, who is a son: *Call his name Jezreel* (v. 4). *Jezreel* means "the seed of God," but it also means the "scattered of God." *Call them not Israel*, which means "dominion," but *Jezreel*, which means "dispersion," for those who have departed from the Lord will wander endlessly. Jezreel was the name of one of the royal seats of the kings of Israel, and it is with allusion to that city that this child is called *Jezreel, for yet a little while, and I will revenge the blood of Jezreel upon the house of Jehu*, the blood that Jehu shed when he destroyed the house of Ahab as well as all the worshipers of Baal. God approved of what he did (2Ki 10:30). Yet God will here avenge that *blood upon the house of Jehu*, when the time has expired during which it was promised that his family would reign. It was the execution of a righteous sentence passed on the house of Ahab, and, as such, it was rewarded, but Jehu did not do it for the right reasons. He did it with hatred against the sinners, but not with any hatred toward the sin, for he maintained the worship of the golden calves (2Ki 10:31). Therefore, when God came to judge them, the first article in the account is for the blood of the house of Ahab, here called the *blood of Jezreel*. Some understand those words to say, "I will visit," or "appoint," *the blood of Jezreel upon the house of Jehu*; and the words refer, say these interpreters, not to the revenging of that bloodshed, but to the repeating of that bloodshed: "I will punish the house of Jehu as I punished the house of Ahab." After the death of Zechariah, the last of the house of Jehu, the kingdom

of the ten tribes decayed. In order to bring about its ruin, it is threatened: *I will break the bow of Israel in the valley of Jezreel* (v. 5). The *breaking of the bow* shows a sinking, ruined power.

2.2. He foretells God's abandoning the whole nation in the name he gives to the second child. Call this daughter *Lo-ruhamah*, "not loved" (Ro 9:25) or *not having obtained mercy* (1Pe 2:10). This indicates that God has shown them great mercy, but they have abused his favors and thereby forfeited them. Though God may be patient for a long time with a people who hate to be reformed, he will not always be so.

3. He must show them what mercy God has in store for the house of Judah at the same time that he is opposing the house of Israel (v. 7): *But I will have mercy upon the house of Judah*. When the Assyrian armies had destroyed Samaria and taken away the ten tribes into exile, they proceeded to besiege Jerusalem, but God had mercy on the house of Judah, saving them by the vast slaughter that an angel made in one night in the *camp* of the Assyrians; they were then *saved by the Lord their God*, not by sword or bow. This may refer also to the salvation of Judah from idolatry, which qualified and prepared them for their other salvations. Just at the time that the kingdom of Israel was *utterly taken away*, under Hoshea, the kingdom of Judah was gloriously reformed, under Hezekiah, and in Babylon God saved them from their idolatry first, and then from their exile. Some understand this promise to look forward to the great salvation that, in the fullness of time, was to be brought about *by the Lord our God*, Jesus Christ.

Verses 8–11

We have a prediction here:

1. Of the rejection of Israel for a time, which is represented by the name of another child that Hosea has by his adulterous wife (vv. 8–9). *When she had weaned* her daughter, *she conceived and bore a son*. Some think that her bearing another son refers to that people's persistence in their evil; sinful desires still *conceived* and *brought forth sin* (Jas 1:15). The name given him is *Lo-ammi*, "Not my people." When they were told that God would *no more have mercy on them*, they did not pay any attention to it, but buoyed themselves up with the thought that they were God's people, whom he must have mercy on. He therefore snatches away that stick from under them, disowning all relationship with them: *You are not my people, and I will not be your God*. This was fulfilled in Israel when they were *utterly taken away* into the *land of Assyria*. They were no longer *God's people*; no prophets were sent to them, and no promises made to them as were made to the two tribes in their exile.

2. Of the subduing and restoration of Israel in the fullness of time. Here, as before, mercy is remembered in the midst of wrath (Hab 3:2); just as the rejection will not be total, so it will not be final (vv. 10–11).

2.1. Some think that these promises were fulfilled in the return of the Jews from exile in Babylon, when many of the ten tribes joined Judah, came out of the countries into which they had dispersed to their own land, appointed Zerubbabel their leader, and formed one people. When they are in their own land, God will acknowledge them as his children through his prophets.

2.2. Others think that these promises will not have their fulfillment completely until the general conversion of the Jews in the final days.

2.3. This promise was certainly fulfilled in the setting up of the kingdom of Christ and the bringing in of both Jews and Gentiles (Ro 9:25–26; 1Pe 2:10).

2.3.1. This Israel will greatly multiply. Although Israel in the flesh has diminished, the spiritual Israel will be innumerable. In the multitudes who by the preaching of the Gospel have been brought to Christ, in the first ages of Christianity and ever since, this promise is fulfilled (Rev 7:4, 9; Gal 4:27).

2.3.2. God will renew his covenant with the Gospel Israel, and he will make it a church by as full a charter as the one by which the Old Testament church was incorporated. Both the *abandoned Gentiles* in their respective places and the *rejected Jews* in theirs will be blessed. There, where the ancestors were rejected for their unbelief, the children, when they believe, will be taken in. The privilege is enlarged; now it is not only *You are my people*, as formerly, but also *"You are the sons of the living God,"* whether by birth you were Jews or Gentiles." They were as children, "under age"; now, under the Gospel, they have grown up to greater understanding and greater freedom (Gal 4:1-2). The sonship of believers will be acknowledged. *You are the sons of the living God* (v. 10). Their honor will be even greater when they are honored with the signs of God's favor in that very place where they had long lain under the signs of his displeasure.

2.3.3. Those who have been in conflict will be happily brought together (v. 11): *Then shall the children of Judah and the children of Israel be gathered together.* This reuniting of Judah and Israel is mentioned only as an example, or one instance, of the fortunate effect of the establishment of Christ's kingdom in the world. The first disciples were partly Jews and partly Galileans. When the Samaritans believed, even though there was much greater enmity between them and the Jews, in Christ there was perfect unanimity (Ac 8:14). Through the death of Christ, the dividing wall of the ceremonial law was taken down. See Eph 2:14-16.

2.3.4. Jesus Christ will be the center of unity to all God's spiritual Israel. To believe in Christ is to appoint him as our head, that is, to agree to God's appointment and willingly commit ourselves to his guidance and government, with all true Christians who make him their head; though we are many, therefore, we are one in him and so become one with each other.

2.3.5. Having appointed Christ as their head, *they shall come up out of the land*; they will come, some of all sorts, from all parts. It shows not a movement through space—for they are said to be in the same place (v. 10)—but a change of mind, a spiritual ascent to Christ. When all this is fulfilled, *great shall be the day of Jezreel* (v. 11). Israel is called *Jezreel* here, the "seed of God." This seed is now sown in the earth and buried, but its day will be great when the harvest comes.

CHAPTER 2

1. God, through the prophet, reveals to them the sin of their idolatry, their spiritual adultery (vv. 1-2, 5, 8). 2. He threatens to take away from them all the good things with which they have served their idols (vv. 3-4, 6-7, 9-13). 3. But he promises that in the end he will return to them in mercy (v. 14), restore them to their former plenty (v. 15), heal them of their inclination to idolatry (vv. 16-17), renew his covenant with them (vv. 18-20), and bless them with all good things (vv. 21-23).

Verses 1-5

Some believe the first words of this chapter belong at the end of the previous chapter. When they have appointed Christ their head, then let them say to one another with triumph and exultation, *"Ammi* (my people) and *Ruhamah* (my loved one)"; and let the prophets call them these names again, for they will no longer lie under the shame and doom of *Lo-ammi* and *Lo-ruhamah*; they will now be *my people* again and will *obtain mercy.*

1. The *mother* (v. 2) seems to be the same as the *brethren* and *sisters* (v. 1), the church of the ten tribes; and in a special manner *mother* seems to refer to the heads and leaders, who were like the mother by whom the others were brought up and nursed. But who are the children who must *plead with their mother* in this way? Either:

1.1. The godly who were among them, who witnessed against the sins of the times: let those who had not bowed the knee to Baal (1Ki 19:18) reason with those who had. Or:

1.2. The sufferers among them, who shared in the disasters of the times: let them not complain about God or lay the blame on him, as if he had dealt harshly with them, and not like a tender father. No, let them *plead with their mother* and lay the fault on her, where it should be laid; compare Isa 50:1.

2. They must remind her of the relationship in which she had stood with God, the kindness he had had for her. Let them tell their *brothers* and *sisters* that they had been *Ammi* and *Ruhamah*, God's people and objects of his mercy.

3. They must accuse her of breaking the marriage covenant between her and God. Tell her (v. 2) that *she is not my wife, neither am I her husband*, that by her spiritual unfaithfulness she has forfeited her relationship with God. They must bring this charge home to her: *Their mother has played the harlot* (v. 5); "their congregation has run after idols," which they were encouraged to do by their false prophets.

4. They must rebuke her for being ungrateful toward God, her benefactor, by attributing to her idols the glory of the gifts he had given her (v. 5). *She said*, "Whatever is offered to the contrary, *I will go after my lovers*," or "after those that cause me to love them." The Aramaic understands this to refer to the nations whose alliance Israel courted, who supplied them with what they needed. "I will go after my lovers, because they give me *my bread and my water*, which are necessary to sustain the body, *my wool and my flax*, which are necessary to clothe the body, and pleasant things, *my oil* and *my drink*"—literally, "my liquors," "my wine and strong drink." The idolaters made Ceres the goddess of their grain and Bacchus the god of their wine, and then they foolishly imagined they received their grain and wine from them, forgetting the Lord their God, who gave them both that good land and *power to get wealth* out of it (Dt 8:18).

5. They must rebuke her for her horrible ingratitude and persuade her to repent and reform. God will disown her if she persists in her adultery (v. 2). Let her be convinced that it is possible for her to reform. True penitents will abandon both their open sins and their secret sins (Ps 19:12-13); they will both avoid the outward opportunities for sin and put to death the inner disposition to it.

6. They must explain about the complete and certain destruction that will be the consequence of her sin if she does not repent and reform (v. 3). She will be starved and will be deprived of her honors, her comforts, and the essential supports of life. She will be famished, will be made *as a wilderness* and *a dry land* and be *slain with thirst* (let her die of thirst) (v. 3). Some understand it in this way: *"I will make her as* she was in the *wilderness,"*

setting her as she was *in the desert land*, where she was sometimes about to perish *for thirst. I will* set her *as in the day that she was born*, for it was in the vast, howling wilderness that Israel was first formed into a people (Dt 32:10).

Verses 6 – 13

God goes on to threaten what he will do with this treacherous, idolatrous people, and he warns so he may not wound.

1. They will be confused and thwarted in their purposes and disappointed in their expectations. This is threatened in vv. 6 – 7. However, to the threat is attached a promise that this will be a means to convince them of their foolishness and bring them back to do their duty.

1.1. God will raise up difficulties and troubles: *I will hedge up thy way with thorns.* She said, "*I will go after my lovers; I will* pursue my alliances with foreign powers and depend on them." But God says, "She will be frustrated in these plans and not be able to proceed in them." She will be like a traveler who finds no way at all to go forward. And then *she shall follow after her lovers, but shall not overtake them*; she will try to secure influence with the Assyrians and Egyptians and to have them as her protectors, but she will not be successful. This is the sort of mercy Balaam met when the angel stood in his way to prevent him from going forward to *curse Israel* (Nu 22:22). Crosses and obstacles on an evil path are great blessings. They are God's hedges to restrain us from wandering and to make the sinful path difficult.

1.2. These difficulties that God raises up in their way will raise in their minds thoughts of turning back. Two things will be drawn out of this degenerate, apostate people here:

1.2.1. A just acknowledgement of the foolishness of their apostasy.

1.2.2. A good desire to come back again to their duty: *I will go and return to my first husband* (v. 7); and she knows so much of his goodness and readiness to forgive that she speaks without doubt of his receiving her.

2. The necessary supports and comforts of life will be taken away from them, because they have dishonored God with them (vv. 8 – 9). Notice:

2.1. How graciously their abundance was given them. God not only gave them grain but also *multiplied* (lavished on them) *their silver and gold*, which they could use to trade with other nations. He gave them *wool and flax*, too, to *cover their nakedness* (Eze 16:10).

2.2. How corruptly their plenty was abused by them.

2.2.1. They robbed God of the honor of his gifts: *She did not know that I gave her corn and wine* (v. 8); she did not remember it.

2.2.2. They served and honored his enemies with them: *They prepared them for Baal* (v. 8); they decorated their idols with *gold and silver* (Jer 10:4) and decorated themselves to worship their idols (v. 13).

2.3. How justly their plenty will be taken away from them: "*Therefore will I return; I will* alter my dealings with them, will take another course: I *will take away my corn* (v. 9) and other good things that I gave her." Those who abuse the mercies that God gives them and so dishonor him cannot expect to keep enjoying them for long.

3. They will lose *all their honour* and be exposed to contempt (v. 10): "*I will discover her lewdness*, will bring to light her secret evil, to her shame. Moreover, this will happen *in the sight of her lovers*, in the sight of the neighboring nations with whom she sought an alliance and on whom she depended; they will not think her worthy of

their friendship any longer." Those who will not hand themselves over to God's mercy cannot be rescued from the hand of his justice.

4. They will lose all their pleasure and will be left in a sad condition (v. 11): *I will cause her mirth to cease.*

4.1. God will take away the occasions of their sacred *mirth — their feast days, their new moons, their sabbaths, and all their solemn feasts* (v. 11). God instituted these to be observed in a religious manner, and they were to be observed with rejoicing (Dt 16:14). They still maintained the observance of these, not at God's temple at Jerusalem, for they had long since forsaken that, but probably at Dan and Bethel, where the calves were (1Ki 12:28 – 29). In this way, when they had lost the power of godliness, nevertheless, to satisfy their worldly minds, they kept up its form (2Ti 3:5), and this was how their New Moons and their Sabbaths became an iniquity that God *could not away* (bear) *with* (Isa 1:13).

4.2. God will take away their provisions for these ceremonies (v. 12): *I will destroy her vines and her fig trees.* He will wither them, or he will bring on Israel a foreign enemy who will devastate the country, so that their vineyards will become *a forest* (thicket); the enclosures will be torn down, so that the *beasts of the field* (wild animals) will eat their grapes and their figs. This will destroy their merriment: God will *cause all her mirth to cease*. "*I will destroy her vines and her fig trees*, take away her worldly pleasures, and then she will think herself truly ruined." This will be the punishment for their idolatry (v. 13): "*I will visit upon* (punish) *her the days of Baalim*." The *days of Baalim* were the solemn festival days that they kept in honor of their idols. These were the days on which she *burnt incense* to idols and *decked herself with her earrings and her jewels*, so that the honor she did to Baal might be thought greater.

Verses 14 – 23

The state of Israel, restrained by divine grace, looks bright and pleasant here, and it is surprising that the promises follow the threats so closely. When it was said, *She forgot me*, one would have thought it would follow, "Therefore I will abandon her; I will never look after her again." No; *Therefore I will allure her.* God's thoughts and ways of mercy are infinitely above ours (Isa 57:17 – 18). Because she will not be restrained by the declarations of wrath, God will see whether she will be persuaded by the offers of mercy. Some think it may be translated, "Afterward *I will allure her*," or, "Nevertheless, *I will allure her.*" It all comes to the same thing: the clear intention is to exalt free grace to those on whom God will have mercy, purely for mercy's sake.

1. Although now Israel is ready to despair, they will be revived with encouragement and hope (vv. 14 – 15). This is expressed here with an allusion to God's dealings with that people when he brought them out of Egypt and through the desert to Canaan, *in the day that they were born* (v. 3). They will be newly formed by the same kind of miracles of love and mercy as they were originally formed by. Notice:

1.1. The gracious methods God will use with them.

1.1.1. He will *bring them into the wilderness*, as he did when he brought them out of Egypt. The land of their exile will be to them now, as that desert was then, the *furnace of affliction*, in which God will *choose them*. When God rescued Israel from Egypt, he led them into the desert, to *humble them and prove them, that he might do them good* (Dt 8:2 – 3, 15 – 16), and he will do so again. Those people whom God has mercy in store for he first *brings into a wilderness*—into solitude and seclusion, so that they may speak with him more freely, being away from the noise of this world, and sometimes into outward distress and trouble, so opening up the ear to receive discipline (Job 36:10).

1.1.2. He will then *allure them and speak comfortably to them, will persuade them* and *speak to their hearts*, that is, he will by his word and Spirit both incline and encourage their hearts to return to him. "By the hand of my servants the prophets I will speak comfort to her heart," reads the Aramaic. This refers to the offer of divine grace in the Gospel, by which we are drawn to abandon our sins and turn to God. By the promise of rest in Christ we are invited to take his yoke on us (Mt 11:29–30), and the work of conversion may be advanced by comforts as well as by convictions.

1.1.3. *He will give them their vineyards thence* (v. 15). From that place where he has afflicted them and brought them to see their foolishness, and from that time on, he will *do them good*. He will *destroy their vines* (v. 12), but then he will give them whole *vineyards*, and so they will be repaid. They will have not only the grain that they need but also vineyards for delight. These represent the privileges and encouragements of the Gospel that are prepared for those who *come up out of the wilderness leaning upon* Christ as *their beloved* (SS 8:5). He will give them *the valley of Achor for a door of hope* (v. 15). *The valley of Achor* was the one in which Achan was stoned; it means "the valley of trouble," because he troubled Israel, and God troubled him there (Jos 7:24–26). So when God returns to his people in mercy, and they turn back to him in duty, it will be to them as happy a sign as anything. If they put away the devoted things from among them (Jos 7:13), if by putting sin to death they stone the Achan that has troubled their camp, their subduing that enemy within themselves is a pledge for them of victory over all the kings of Canaan.

1.2. The great rejoicing with which they will receive God's gracious response toward them: *She shall sing there as in the days of her youth* (v. 15). This clearly refers to that triumphant and prophetic song that Moses and the children of Israel sang at *the Red Sea* (Ex 15:1). When they are restored from exile, they will repeat that song, and it will be a new song to them.

2. Although they have been very devoted to the worship of Baal, they will then abandon all appearances of idolatry and remain faithful only to God (vv. 16–17). The very *names of Baalim* will be *taken out of their mouths*. The apostle Paul states that we should feel hatred toward all sexual immorality or impurity in the same way: *Let them not be once named among you* (Eph 5:3). God's grace in the heart will change the language by causing a beloved sin to be loathed. The very word *Baal* will be set aside, even in its innocent meaning. God says, *Thou shalt call me Ishi, and call me no more Baali* (v. 16); both mean *my husband*, and both had been used about God. *Thy Maker is thy husband* (Isa 54:5)—in Hebrew, "your *Baal*," "your patron and protector"; but *Ishi* is an expression of love, sweetness, and familiarity.

3. Although they have been in continual troubles, as if the whole creation had been at war with them, they will then enjoy perfect peace and tranquility, as if they were in an alliance or friendship with the whole creation (v. 18). The lower creatures will do them no harm, as they did when the wild animals devoured their vineyards (v. 12). God can make *the beasts of the field honour* him and contribute to his people's comfort, as he has promised (Isa 43:20). And it is our part of the covenant not to abuse

them. However, this is not all. People are in greater danger from one another than from wild animals, and so it is further promised that God will *make wars to cease* (Ps 46:9); he will disarm the enemy: *I will break the bow, and sword, and battle.* He will do it for those whose *ways please him*, for he *makes even their enemies to be at peace with them* (Pr 16:7). This corresponds with the promise that in Gospel times *swords shall be beaten into ploughshares* (Isa 2:4).

4. Although God has given them a certificate of divorce for their adultery, yet, when they repent, he will take them back into marriage covenant (vv. 19–20). *I will betroth thee unto me*, and a second and third time, *I will betroth thee* (vv. 19–20). *All* who are sincerely devoted to God are betrothed to him; God will love them, protect them, and provide for them. The covenant itself will be unbreakable: "God will not break it on his part, and you will not on yours, and the blessings of it will be eternal." "And," God says, "I will renew the covenant *in righteousness*." But will it not reflect badly on his wisdom to take back into covenant a people who have acted so treacherously? "No," God says; "I will do it *in judgment* (justice). I will do it in *loving-kindness and in mercies*." God will act tenderly and graciously in making the covenant with them. It will be a covenant of grace, made with compassionate consideration of their weaknesses. *Thou shalt know the Lord* (v. 20). This is a promise not only that God will reveal himself to them more fully than ever, but also that he will give them *a heart to know him*; they will know him in another way. They will all be *taught of God* to know him.

5. Although the heavens have been like bronze to them, and the earth like iron (Dt 28:23), now the heavens will yield their dew (Dt 33:28; Zec 8:12), and the earth its fruits (vv. 21–22). This promise of *corn and wine* is to be taken also in a spiritual sense; what is promised here using the metaphor of temporal blessings is an outpouring of those blessings and graces that concern the soul, the dew of heaven as well as the richness of the earth, and so heaven is put first, as in the blessing of Jacob (Ge 27:28). "But," the heavens say, "we have no rain to give unless the One who has the key of the clouds unlocks them, unless he opens these containers, and so, *if the Lord do not help you* (2Ki 6:26), we cannot." God will graciously take notice of their addresses to him. Then *I will hear the heavens* (v. 21); "I will answer them," as it may be read, and then they will *hear and answer the earth* and pour down seasonable rain on it. Notice here the coherence of secondary causes with one another, as links in a chain, and the necessary dependence they all have on God, the Primary Cause.

6. Whereas they will have been divided and scattered throughout the world, God will turn this curse into a blessing: "I will not only water the earth for her but also *sow her unto me in the earth*" (v. 23). Her dispersion will not be like that of the chaff on the floor, which *the wind drives away* (Ps 1:4), but like that of the seed in the field, in order to grow more; wherever they are scattered, they will *take root downward and bear fruit upward* (2Ki 19:30). *The good seed are the children of the kingdom. I will* sow her to me." When Christianity gained a footing in all parts of the world, then this promise was fulfilled.

7. Whereas they will have been *Lo-ammi*, "not a people," and *Lo-ruhamah*, "not finding mercy" with God, then they will be restored to his favor (v. 23). God had mercy on those who *had not obtained mercy* (v. 23). His mercy must not be despaired of anywhere on this side of hell. He says to them, "*Thou art my people* (v. 23), whom

I will acknowledge and bless," and they will say, "*Thou art my God*, whom I will serve and worship, and to whose honor I will be forever devoted."

CHAPTER 3

God continues to inculcate the same matter into this careless people through the prophet, and, as before, he does it by a sign, that of the dealings of a husband with an adulterous wife. We have here: 1. The bad character of the people of Israel (v. 1). 2. The lowly condition to which they would be reduced by their exile (vv. 2–4). 3. The blessed reformation that would be brought on them in the last days (v. 5).

Verses 1–5

Some think that this chapter refers to Judah, the two tribes, just as the adulterous woman the prophet married in 1:3 represented the *ten tribes*. However, the *children of Israel* were the ten tribes, and so it is more probable that this parable is to be understood as about them.

1. In this parable we may notice:

1.1. God's goodness and Israel's badness serving to contrast each other (v. 1). Israel is as a woman *beloved of her friend* (v. 1), and *yet an adulteress*; such is the situation between God and Israel. If they were restrained from submitting to idols, they still looked at them amorously, with *eyes full of* that spiritual *adultery* (2Pe 2:14). They also loved *flagons of wine*; they joined the idolaters because they lived in high spirits and drank well. Idolatry and immorality often go together. Yet their badness had not put an end to God's goodness. "Such is my *love to the children of Israel*; it is love to the loveless, to the unlovely, to those who have forfeited it a thousand times."

1.2. The way found to bring a God who is so good and a people who are so bad together. Notice here:

1.2.1. The way God humbles them (v. 2): *I bought her to me for fifteen pieces of silver, and a homer and a half homer of barley*, that is, "I courted her to encourage her to return to her first husband," as he said he would in 2:14. The present that the prophet brings to her to buy her favor is very small, and it reduces her to short rations and makes her look very lowly in order to punish her for her pride; yet she must be content to live on it for a long time, until her husband thinks fit to restore her to her original possessions. God gave Egypt as Israel's ransom once (Isa 43:3), but now that they have been unfaithful to him, he will give only fifteen pieces of silver for them because they have lost so much value through their sin.

1.2.2. The new terms on which God is willing to return (v. 3). They must be a people to him, and he will be a God to them. They must themselves be ashamed of their apostasy from him: *Thou shalt abide for me many days* in *solitude* and silence, as a widow who is *desolate* and sad. They must *lay aside their ornaments* and wait with patience and submission to know what God will do with them. It is not enough to be ashamed of ourselves for the sins we have committed and to justify God in correcting us for them; we must also be determined, in the power of God's grace, not to offend anymore. In the land of their exile they will be attracted to worship the idols of the country; that will be a long time of testing for them, which will last many days: "But if you keep your ground and hold firmly to your integrity, if, when *all this comes upon thee*, thou dost not *stretch out thy hand to a strange god*, you will be qualified for God's favor to return."

2. In the last two verses we have the interpretation of the parable and its application to Israel. *They shall abide many days without a king, and without a prince* (v. 4); a nation in this condition may well be called *a widow. They shall* live *without a sacrifice* and *without an image*—or "a statue," "pillar," or "sacred stones" (the word is used for the pillars Jacob set up [Ge 28:18; 31:45; 35:20])—and *without an ephod and teraphim*. The meaning is that in their exile they will not look like a nation, nor will they look like a church. They will have *no ephod* nor *teraphim*, no legal priesthood. This was the case of the Jews in exile, and even today the scattered Jews, though they have their synagogues, have no temple service. They will eventually be received again as a wife (v. 5): *Afterward*, in the course of time, when they have gone through this discipline, *they shall return*. The Aramaic reads, "They will seek the service of the Lord their God and obey Messiah, the Son of David their king." Compare this with Jer 30:9; Eze 34:23; 37:25. *They shall fear the Lord and his goodness* (blessings) (v. 5). Some understand his *goodness* to refer to the temple, toward which they will look in worshiping God. The Jews say there were three things that Israel rejected in the days of Rehoboam—the *kingdom of heaven*, the *family of David*, and the *house of the sanctuary*. However, God's *goodness* here should instead be understood as the attribute of God that he showed as his glory (Ex 33:18–29) and by which he made known his name (Ex 34:5–7). It is not only the Lord and his greatness that we are to fear, but also the Lord and his goodness, not only his majesty but also his mercy.

CHAPTER 4

Prophets were sent to tell people their faults and warn them of the judgments of God, and that is how this prophet is employed in this and the following chapters. As attorney for the King of kings, he states the charges brought against the people of Israel. 1. He tells them God's charges against them: a general prevalence of evil and ungodliness (vv. 1–2), ignorance and neglect of God (vv. 6–7), the worldly-mindedness of the priests (v. 8), drunkenness and immorality (v. 11), divination and witchcraft (v. 12), sacrifices on the high places (v. 13), prostitution (vv. 14, 18), and bribery among magistrates (v. 18). 2. He tells them what the results will be. God will punish them for these things (v. 9). The whole land will be devastated (v. 3), all kinds of people destroyed (v. 5), their honor lost (v. 7), their creature comforts made unsatisfying (v. 10), and they themselves made ashamed (v. 19). And the most severe judgment of all will be that they are left alone in their sins (v. 17); they will not rebuke one another (v. 4), and God will not punish them (v. 14); in fact, he will allow them to prosper (v. 16). 3. He warns Judah not to follow in the steps of Israel (v. 15).

Verses 1–5

Here:

1. The court is set and attention demanded: *Hear the word of the Lord, you children of Israel* (v. 1). They are ready enough to listen when God speaks words of encouragement to them, but are they willing to listen when he brings charges against them?

2. The accusations are read, by which the whole nation stands charged with crimes by which God is greatly offended.

2.1. They are charged with national omissions of the most important duties. The people seem to have no sense at all of honesty. Much less do they have any sense of mercy or of being under any obligation to have compassion on and help the poor. What good can be expected where there is no knowledge of God?

2.2. They are accused of national commissions of repugnant sins against both the first and second table of the Ten Commandments. *Swearing, lying, killing, stealing,* and *committing adultery,* which are sins against the third, ninth, sixth, eighth, and seventh commandments, respectively, are to be found in every corner of the land (v. 2). They *break out,* that is, they break all bounds of reason and conscience and the divine law. When they break out in this way, *blood touches blood* (bloodshed follows bloodshed); murders are committed in every part of the country. It was about this time that there was so much bloodshed in trying to seize the crown.

3. Sentence is passed on this guilty land (v. 3). It will be completely devastated. The valleys are said to *mourn* when they are made desolate by war and famine. The destruction of the fruits of the earth will be so great that there will not be enough for even the *fowls of the air* to pick.

4. A court order is issued (v. 4): *Yet let no man strive nor reprove another* suggests that as long as there is any hope we should rebuke sinners for their sins. However, sometimes they are so hardened in their sin that it will be to little effect either to deal with them or to deal with God for them. *Thy people are as those that strive with the priests.* Those who rebel against the rebuke of their ministers, which is an ordinance of God for their reformation, have lost the benefit of mutual rebuke too. Perhaps this may refer to the recent evil of Joash, king of Judah, and his people, who stoned Zechariah (2Ch 24:21). *"Therefore, because you will accept no rebuke, thou shalt stumble and fall in the day,* and *the prophet,* the false prophet who flattered you, will *fall with thee in the night.* The darkness of night will not help cover you from trouble, nor will the light of day help you to flee from it." Do the children think that when they are in danger of stumbling, their mother will help them? It will be futile to expect it, for *I will destroy thy mother,* Samaria, the mother city, which is like a mother to every part. It will all be *made silent.*

Verses 6–11

1. The people *strive with the priests;* they are therefore justly *destroyed for lack of knowledge* (v. 6). Those who rebel against the light (Job 24:13) can expect nothing other than to perish in the dark. Or it is a charge against the priests, who should have been continually *teaching the people knowledge* (Ecc 12:9), but do not.

2. Both priests and people have rejected knowledge, and God will therefore justly *reject them.* The reason why the people did not learn and the priests did not teach was not that they did not have the light, but hated it (Jn 3:20).

3. They *have forgotten the law of God* (v. 6) and do not want to pass on the memory of it to future generations, and so God will *forget* them and *their children,* the people's children. Or it may refer to the priests' children; they will not succeed them in the office of priests (1Sa 2:36).

4. They have dishonored God (v. 7). It was their honor that they had increased in number, wealth, power, and status. The beginnings of their nation were small, but they *greatly increased.* But *as they were increased, so they sinned* against God. Their wealth, honor, and power only made them more daring in sin. Therefore, says God, *will I change their glory into shame.*

5. The priests feed on the sin of God's people, and so *they shall eat and not have enough* (v. 10). They have abused the maintenance that was given to the priests

(v. 8). They have *set their hearts* on the people's *iniquities;* they have *lifted up their soul* to them (Ps 24:4), that is, they are glad when people commit sins, because then they have to atone for the sins with an offering, of which the priests have their share. God will therefore deny them his blessing on their maintenance: *They shall eat and not have enough* (v. 10). Although they enjoy great plenty through the abundance of offerings, they will have no satisfaction from it.

6. The more they have increased, the more they have sinned (v. 7), and so although *they commit whoredom* (engage in prostitution), although they use the most corrupt methods to multiply their people, yet *they shall not increase.*

7. The people and the priests have hardened one another in sin, and so they will justly share in the punishment: *There shall be, like people, like priest* (v. 9).

8. They have indulged in sensory delights to keep their hearts lifted up, but they will find that these delights *take away their hearts* (v. 11): *Whoredom* (prostitution), *wine, and new wine take away the heart.*

Verses 12–19

In these verses we have, as before:

1. The sins the people of Israel are charged with:

1.1. Spiritual prostitution, or idolatry. They have in them *a spirit of whoredoms,* a strong inclination to that. Israel has *played the harlot* (committed adultery) (v. 15); their behavior in worshiping their idols has been like that of a prostitute, reckless and arrogant. *Israel slideth back as a backsliding heifer* (v. 16), like an "untamed" heifer (according to some), or like a "stubborn" heifer (according to others), one that is turned loose and runs wildly about the field or, if put under the yoke, which seems to be alluded to here, will draw back instead of going forward, will struggle to remove its neck from the yoke and its feet from the furrow. The people of Israel are so unruly, ungovernable, and intractable. *My people ask counsel at their stocks,* their wooden gods. They *say to a stock, Thou art my father* (Jer 2:27). This probably refers to corrupt methods of divination, such as consulting a *piece of wood* or *a staff,* as when Nebuchadnezzar divined *by his arrows* (Eze 21:21). They offer sacrifices to them as gods (v. 13) to atone and pacify them, and they *burn incense* to them to please and satisfy them. They choose places *upon the tops of the mountains* and *upon the hills,* foolishly imagining that being high off the ground will give them some advantage in approaching heaven; or they choose places *under oaks and poplars and elms* (terebinth), *because the shadow thereof is* pleasant to them and they think that a dense shade will give the heart some proper awe for devotion.

1.2. Physical prostitution: *They have committed whoredom* (prostitution) *continually* (v. 18). They have made a business out of prostitution. Their false gods have drawn them to it; for the devil whom they worship, though a spirit, is an evil spirit. To punish them for that sin, God gave up their wives and daughters to similar unnatural relations.

1.3. The perversion of justice (v. 18). *Their rulers do love, Give ye,* that is, they use shameful ways such as bribes, and they have them continually in their mouths. Justice, properly administered, is refreshing, as a drink is to someone who is thirsty, but when the course of justice is perverted, and rulers take rewards either to acquit the guilty or to condemn the innocent, the *drink is sour.*

2. The signs of God's wrath against them for their sins:

2.1. Their wives and daughters will not be punished for the wrong and disgrace they have done to their families: *I will not punish your daughters* (v. 14), and because they are not punished for their sin, they will continue in it. This shows us that the exemption of one sinner is sometimes made the punishment of another.

2.2. They themselves will be successful for a while, but their prosperity will help destroy them: *The Lord will feed them as a lamb in a large place* (meadow) (v. 16), but it will only be to prepare them for slaughter, as is a lamb that is fed in this way. Other people, however, understand them to feed as *a lamb on the common*, a truly large place, but one with short grass, and where they will be exposed. The Shepherd of Israel will turn them both out of his pastures and out of his protection.

2.3. No means will be used to bring them to repentance (v. 17): "*Ephraim is joined to idols*, is in love with them and is devoted to them, and so *let him alone*"—as in v. 4: "*Let no man reprove* him." The father does not correct the rebellious son anymore when he has decided to disinherit him. Those who are not disturbed in their sin will be destroyed for their sin.

2.4. They will be swept away by a swift and shameful destruction (v. 19).

3. The warning given to Judah not to sin in the same way Israel did. *Though thou, Israel, play the harlot* (commit adultery), *yet let not Judah offend* (let not Judah become guilty).

3.1. This was a necessary warning. The people of Israel were close neighbors to the people of Judah; Israel was more numerous, and at this time it was prosperous, and so there was danger that the people of Judah might learn their ways and that their souls might become entrapped.

3.2. It was a reasonable warning: Judah had greater means of knowledge than Israel; Judah had the temple and priesthood, and a king of the house of David; it was from Judah that Shiloh was to come (Ge 49:10). Therefore *let not Judah offend*, for more was expected from them than from Israel, and God would take it more unkindly from them. If Israel committed adultery, let not Judah do so too, for then God would have no professing people in the world. *Come not you unto Gilgal*, where *all their wickedness is* (9:15; 12:11); they *multiplied transgression* there (Am 4:4). For the same reason Judah must *not go up to Bethel*, called here the "house of wickedness," for that is the meaning of *Beth Aven*, not the "house of God," as *Bethel* means.

CHAPTER 5

Here: 1. Israel and Judah are called to listen to the charge (vv. 1, 8). 2. They are accused of many sins, which are here emphasized: persecution (vv. 1–2), spiritual prostitution (vv. 3–4), pride (v. 5), apostasy from God (v. 7), and the oppression of the leaders and the weakness of the people in submitting to it (vv. 10–11). 3. They are threatened with God's displeasure for their sins (v. 3), and he reveals his wrath against them for it (v. 9). 3.1. They will stumble in their sin (v. 5). 3.2. God will abandon them (v. 6). 3.3. Their heritage will be devoured (v. 7). 3.4. God will rebuke them (vv. 9–10). 3.5. They will be oppressed (v. 11). 3.6. God will be like a moth to them in secret judgments (v. 12) and like a lion in public judgments (v. 14). 4. They are blamed for the wrong course they followed in their suffering (v. 13). 5. It is suggested that they will eventually take a right course (v. 15).

Verses 1–7

Here:

1. All orders and kinds of people are officially summoned to appear and answer (v. 1): "*Hear you this, O*

priests! Listen, *you house of Israel*, the common people, and *give ear, O house of the king!*" Let them all take notice, for they have all contributed to the national guilt and will share in the national judgments.

2. A witness is produced against them, one instead of a thousand (Job 9:3; 33:23); it is God's omniscience (v. 3): *I know Ephraim, and Israel is not hidden from me*. They have not known the Lord (v. 4), but the Lord has known them.

3. They are accused of very bad things.

3.1. They have been diligent at drawing people either into sin or into trouble: "You have been *a snare on Mizpah, and a net spread upon Tabor*" (v. 1).

3.2. They have been both crafty and cruel in pursuing their intentions (v. 2): the rebels are *profound to make* (are deep in) *slaughter*.

3.3. They have *committed whoredom* (turned to prostitution), have defiled their own bodies with sinful desires and defiled their own souls with the worship of idols (v. 3).

3.4. They have no inclination whatsoever to come to know God and enjoy fellowship with him. Because the spirit of prostitution has caused them to go astray from him, it keeps them wandering endlessly (v. 4).

3.4.1. They *have not known the Lord*, nor do they want to know him.

3.4.2. Therefore *they will not frame their doings* (direct their actions) *to turn to their God*. It is true that we cannot turn to God through our own power, without his special grace, but we may make proper use of our own faculties and the general help of his Spirit to *frame our doings* to turn to him.

3.4.3. They are guilty of notorious arrogance and insolence in sin (v. 5): *The pride of Israel doth testify to his face*; it witnesses against him that he is a rebel against God and his government in the joviality and gaudiness of their worship, as a prostitute is known by her clothes (Pr 7:10).

3.4.4. They have abandoned God to turn to idols (v. 7): *They have dealt treacherously against the Lord*, like a wife who lives in adultery with another man. And so *they have begotten strange* (illegitimate) *children*; they have brought up their children in idolatry (v. 7). People deal treacherously with God when they not only turn from following him themselves but also train their children to follow in their evil ways.

4. Very sad things are appointed to be their doom (v. 1): "*Judgment is toward you*. God is coming out to oppose you, to show his displeasure against you for your sins." They will *fall in their iniquity*. This follows from their pride testifying to their face (v. 5). *Therefore shall Israel and Ephraim fall in their iniquity*. They will fall short of God's favor when they profess to seek it (v. 6): *They shall go with their flocks and with their herds to seek the Lord*, but in vain; *they shall not find him*. This seems to be spoken mainly about Judah. They went as usual to the sacred festivals *with their flocks and herds* to *seek the Lord*, but their hearts were not *entire* (wholehearted) *for him*. Those who go only *with their flocks and their herds* to seek the Lord, and not with their hearts and souls, cannot expect to find him, for his favor is not to be bought with *thousands of rams* (Mic 6:7). They and their *portions* (fields) will all be swallowed up. They have *dealt treacherously against the Lord*, but *now* shall *a month devour them with their portions* (v. 7). Perhaps *portions* means their idols, whom they chose as their inheritance instead of God. A *month* will *devour* them. The judgments of God sometimes make

quick work of a sinful people. A month devours more, and more heritage, than many years can repair.

Verses 8–15

Here:

1. A loud alarm is sounded, giving notice of coming judgments (v. 8): *Blow you the cornet* (trumpet) *in Gibeah* and *in Ramah*, two cities in the confines of the two kingdoms of Judah and Israel, Gibeah a frontier town of the kingdom of Judah, Ramah of Israel, so that the warning is sent to both kingdoms here. "*Cry aloud at Beth Aven*, or Bethel." The prophet spoke before about the judgments as being certain; he speaks of them here as being near. The blowing of this trumpet is explained in v. 9: *Among the tribes of Israel have I made known that which shall surely be*; the phrase signifies what is certain or true.

2. The basis of God's challenge is given. He challenges *the princes of Judah* because they have been bold leaders in sin (v. 10). They have encroached even on God's rights, have trampled on the distinction between good and evil. Some commentators have noticed that the leaders of Judah ruled more absolutely, and assumed a more arbitrary power, than the leaders of Israel did; now, for this reason, God challenges them: *I will pour out my wrath upon them like water*. He challenges the *people of Ephraim* because they have been contemptible followers in *sin* (v. 11): *He willingly walked after the commandment*, that is, the commandment of Jeroboam and the succeeding kings of Israel, who obliged all their subjects by law to worship the calves at Dan and Bethel and never to go up to Jerusalem to worship. It is for this that *Ephraim is oppressed and broken in judgment*, has his civil rights and liberties broken. Nothing gives greater advantage to a mastiff-like tyranny, one that is fierce and violent, than a spaniel-like submission, one that is fawning and flattering.

3. The prophet shows the different ways God would use both with Judah and with Ephraim.

3.1. He would begin with lesser judgments, which would sometimes work silently and insensibly (v. 12): *I will be*—that is, "my providences will be"—*unto Ephraim as a moth*; or, as it might better be read, "my providences are unto Ephraim as a moth," for it is the kind of *sickness* that Ephraim sees already now (v. 13). The judgments of God on a sinful people are sometimes *as a moth* to them, and *as rottenness*, or like a worm. His judgments work silently, so that even the sinners will not be aware of it. They will think they are safe and thriving, but they will find they are wasting and decaying. His judgments come slowly and with long delays and intervals, so that he may give them *space to repent* (Rev 2:21).

3.2. When it appeared that those had not been effective in doing their work, he would come on them with greater judgments (v. 14): *I will be unto Ephraim as a lion, and to the house of Judah as a young lion*. If lesser judgments do not do their work, it may be expected that God will send greater ones. "*I, even I*, will take the work into my own hands"; there is a more direct work of God in some judgments than in others. *I will tear, and go away*. He will go away not fearing them and not helping them.

4. We see the different effects of those different ways. When God opposed them with lesser judgments, they looked to created things for relief, but they sought in vain (v. 13). Then they turned to the Assyrian for help; they courted King Jareb, who, some think, was one of the names of Tiglath-Pileser, king of Assyria, to whom both Israel (2Ki 15:19) and Judah (2Ki 18:14) turned for relief in their distress, hoping by an alliance with him to reestablish their declining interests. In times of trouble, worldly hearts see their sickness but do not see the sin that is its cause. Instead of going immediately to the Creator, who could help them, they look to created things, who cannot help them at all. The kings of Assyria, whom Judah and Israel looked to, caused them trouble and did not help them (2Ch 28:16). They had sent *king Jareb a present* (10:6) and, having so engaged him to represent them, they did not doubt his loyalty to them, but he deceived them. When God brought greater judgments on them, they would then eventually be forced to turn to him (v. 15). First, he would leave them: *I will go and return to my place*, to heaven, or to the mercy seat, the throne of grace. When God punishes sinners, he comes out of his dwelling (Isa 26:21), but when he intends to show them favor, he returns to his dwelling, where he waits to be gracious (Isa 30:18). He would eventually work on them and bring them home to himself, through their misery, no longer withdrawing from them. Two things are aspects of their return:

4.1. Their penitent confession of sin: *Till they acknowledge their offence* (v. 15), "till they be guilty" (margin), that is, until they are aware of their guilt and humble themselves before God for it. When people begin to complain more about their sins than about their suffering, there begins to be some hope for them.

4.2. Their humble petition for the favor of God: till they *seek my face* (v. 15). If they seek him in this way, though it might be called seeking him late, nevertheless, it is not too late.

CHAPTER 6

The closing words of the previous chapter gave us some hope that God and his Israel might still be happily reconciled, despite their sins and his wrath. Now this chapter takes that matter further. Some did repent and reform. Notice: 1. Their decision to return to God, and the encouragement they gave themselves in their return (vv. 1–3). 2. The instability of many of them in their promises of repentance, and the course that God therefore took with them (vv. 4–5). 3. The covenant God made with them and his expectations of them (v. 6); their disobedience to that covenant (vv. 7–11).

Verses 1–3

These verses may be taken either as the words of the prophet to the people, calling them to repentance, or as the words of the people to one another. Notice:

1. What it is that they commit themselves to do (v. 1): "Let us look no longer to Assyria or send to King Jareb for help; let us *return to the Lord*, turn to worshiping him and putting our hope firmly in him."

2. What inducements and encouragements they take hold of to stir one another up.

2.1. The experience they have had of his displeasure: "Let us return to him, for *he has torn, he has smitten* (he has torn us to pieces and has injured us). We have been torn to pieces, and he was the One who did that. He did it because we rebelled from him, and so we cannot expect him to be reconciled to us until we turn back to him."

2.2. The expectation they have of his favor: "He who has torn us to pieces *will heal us*; he who has injured us will *bind us up*," as a skillful surgeon uses tender hands to bind up a broken bone or a bleeding wound. This is an acknowledgment of both God's power and his mercy on our behalf; he both can and will heal us. Indeed, he has torn *so that* he may heal. Some commentators think this points especially to the return of the Jews from Babylon. The favor they expect is described in several aspects.

2.2.1. They promise themselves that their restoration from their troubles will be to them like *life from the dead* (Ro 11:15) (v. 2): *"After two days he will revive us*—in a short time, in a day or two—*and the third day,* when it is expected that the dead body would be buried *out of our sight,* then he will *raise us up* and *we shall live in his sight;* we will see his face with comfort, and it will revive us. Although he *forsake* for *a small moment* (Isa 54:7), he *will gather* with *everlasting kindness."* This seems also to have a further reference to the resurrection of Jesus Christ, and the time may be a figure of Christ's rising on the *third day,* for all the prophets testified of *the sufferings of Christ and the glory that should follow* (1Pe 1:11). Although Hosea's listeners may not have been aware of this mystery in these words, the fact that they are now fulfilled to the letter in the resurrection of Christ is a confirmation that *this is he that should come,* and we are to *look for no other* (Mt 11:3). It is appropriate that a prophecy of Christ's resurrection should be expressed by saying, "He will raise *us* up, and *we* will live," for Christ rose as the firstfruits, and we are revived with him; we live through him.

2.2.2. They will then make the most of the knowledge of God (v. 3): *Then shall we know, if we follow on to know the Lord* (v. 3). When God returns in mercy to his people, he will give them more knowledge of himself; the earth will be *full of that knowledge* (Isa 11:9). It may be taken as the fruit of Christ's resurrection and of the life we live through him that we will have not only greater means of knowledge but also grace to apply that knowledge. Our knowledge will be perfected and yet also eternally increasing.

2.2.3. They will then receive many divine consolations: *His going forth is prepared as the morning,* that is, the response of his favor is thus prepared, the favor that he withdrew from us when he *returned to his place. He shall come to us,* and be as welcome to us, *as the rain, as the latter and former rain unto the earth,* which refreshes it and makes it fruitful. This also looks further than their restoration from captivity; it had its complete fulfillment in Christ and the grace of the Gospel. *His going forth was prepared as the morning* (v. 3), for he came in the fullness of time, was prepared by *John the Baptist,* and he was himself the *bright and morning star* (Rev 22:16) *He shall come down as the rain upon the mown grass* (Ps 72:6). The grace of God in Christ is both the *latter and the former rain,* for by it the good work of our bearing fruit is both begun and carried on.

Verses 4–11

Judah and Ephraim are both charged here with two evil things:

1. That they are unsteady, *unstable as water* (vv. 4–5). *O Ephraim! what shall I do unto thee? O Judah! what shall I do unto thee?* Not that God is at a loss, but he speaks like a human being to show how absurd and unreasonable they are. God wants to do them good, but they are not qualified to receive his goodness: *"What shall I do unto thee?* What else can I do but reject you, when I cannot in honor save you?" Notice here:

1.1. Their conduct toward God: their goodness, or kindness, is like the morning cloud. The good that sometimes appears in them soon vanishes like the morning mist and the early dew. Will he accept their goodness? No, he cannot, for it disperses; goodness will never be

either pleasing to God or profitable to us when it is like the morning mist or early dew. When people make promises but do not fulfill them, when they waver unsteadily and unevenly, then their *goodness is as the morning cloud and the early dew.*

1.2. What action God has taken with them: "Because they were like that, *I have hewn them* (cut them in pieces) *by the prophets,* as timber or stone is cut for use; *I have slain them by the words of my mouth."* When the prophets dealt faithfully with them, they were ready to say that the prophets killed them. They wavered in their religious faith (v. 4), and so God cut them down. The hearts of sinners are not only as hard as stone but also as rough as stone, which needs a great deal of work to shape it properly, or like knotty timber, which is not squared without a great deal of difficulty. There are those people whom ministers must rebuke sharply; every word should cut, and although the rebuked may fly in the face of the rebuker and count them as an enemy because they tell the truth, the rebuker still continues with their work. God fulfilled what was foretold: *"I have slain them* by my judgments, according to the words of my mouth." The word of God will be the death of either the sin or the sinner. His prophets have taken great effort over them, but these means have not had the desired effect. They cannot accuse God of being severe with them if he brings on them the threatened miseries. The prophet acknowledges, *Thy judgments are as the light that goes forth* (v. 5), clearly just and righteous.

2. That they are not faithful to God's covenant with them (vv. 6–7). Notice:

2.1. The covenant that God made with them (v. 6): "*I desired mercy and not sacrifice* and insisted on the knowledge of God more than* on *burnt offerings." Mercy* here is the same word that in v. 4 is rendered *goodness*—*hesed,* "devotion, sanctity." It stands for all practical religion; it is the same as *charity* in the New Testament, the powerful love of God and our neighbor. This is fully explained in Jer 7:22–23. Perhaps this is mentioned here to show a difference between the God whom they abandoned and the gods whom they went over to. The *power of godliness* is the main thing God looks for and requires, and without it the *form of godliness* is useless (2Ti 3:5).

2.2. How little attention they have given to this covenant. There were *good things committed* to them to keep, the jewels of mercy and devotion and the knowledge of God in the cabinet of sacrifices and burnt offerings, but they betrayed their trust, keeping the cabinet but pawning off the jewels to satisfy their corrupt sinful desires. This is why God is just in challenging them (v. 7). "They, like Adam, have transgressed the covenant," as it might read, for *Adam* means "man"; just as he disobeyed the covenant of innocence, so they disobeyed the covenant of grace. Dealing unfaithfully with God is called here *dealing treacherously against him,* for it is both an insult and in opposition to him.

2.2.1. Look on the other side of the Jordan, to the country most exposed to neighboring nations, and where, therefore, the people need to keep themselves under divine protection, and there you will find the boldest provocations of divine Majesty (v. 8). Gilead, which lies in the allotted territory of Gad and the half tribe of Manasseh, is *a city of the workers of iniquity.* Perhaps the name refers to Ramoth Gilead, which was one of the three cities of refuge on the other side of the Jordan, and a Levites' city. Its inhabitants, though from the sacred tribe, are *workers of iniquity.* For a bribe, they will protect those who are guilty of deliberate murder. Those whose business is to minister in holy things are as bad as the worst (v. 9). The *companies of priests* are cruel and bloodthirsty. They are cunning. "They murder in the way to Shechem"—according to the margin, which interprets it as a proper name—they murder those going to Jerusalem to worship—for Shechem lay in that direction. Or, as some interpret "in the way to Shechem," they murder as their father Levi, with Simeon his brother, murdered the Shechemites (Ge 34:1–31), by fraud and deceit.

2.2.2. *There is the whoredom of Ephraim*, both physical and spiritual prostitution, too plain to be denied. Look into Judah, and you find them sharing in Israel's fate: "*Also, O Judah! he has set a harvest for thee* (v. 11); you who have *ploughed iniquity* and *sown wickedness* will *reap the same* (Job 4:8)."

CHAPTER 7

We have here: 1. A general charge drawn up against Israel for those grave crimes and misdemeanors by which they have obstructed the flow of God's favors to them (vv. 1–2). 2. A particular accusation: 2.1. Against the court—the king, princes, and judges (vv. 3–7). 2.2. Against the country. Ephraim is accused of conforming to the nations (v. 8), foolishness under the judgments of God (vv. 9–11), ingratitude to God for his mercies (v. 13), insincerity under his judgments (v. 14), contempt of God (v. 15), and hypocrisy in pretending to return to him (v. 16). They are also threatened with severe correction, which will humble them (v. 12), and, if that is not effective, then with complete destruction (v. 13), especially of their leaders (v. 16).

Verses 1–7

Notice:

1. A general idea of the present state of Israel (vv. 1–2).

1.1. God graciously intended to do them good: *I would have healed Israel.* He would have reformed them, would have cleansed the corruptions that were among them. He would have rescued them from their troubles and restored their peace and prosperity to them. Their own foolishness set them back again.

1.2. They stood in their own light and placed a bar across their own door. When God *would have healed them,* the wickedness that had been covered up was *found out.* When attempts were made to reform them, their corruption grew even more outrageous. Their professions of repentance were hypocritical.

1.3. A practical disbelief in God's omniscience and government lay at the root of all their evil (v. 2): "*They consider not in their hearts,* they never say to their own hearts, never realize, *that I remember all their wickedness.*" This is the sinner's unbelief; it is as good as saying there is *no God* (Ps 14:1) as to say that he is either ignorant or forgetful. However, the time will come when those who deceive themselves in this way will be made to see things in the right way: *Now their own doings have beset them about* (engulfed them).

1.4. God had begun his judgments: *The thief comes in, and the troop of robbers spoils without* (v. 1). Some take this to be an example of their evil, that they stole things from and attacked one another. It seems rather to be a punishment of their sin; they had been infiltrated by secret thieves among them and by *troops of robbers,* foreign invaders, who openly and forcefully *spoiled abroad.*

2. A particular account of the sins of the court, of the king and princes.

2.1. They were pleased with the evil of their subjects (v. 3): *They make the king and princes glad with their wickedness.*

2.2. Drunkenness and reveling were very much in evidence at court (v. 5). The *day of our king* was a festive day for them, and they *made him sick with bottles of wine.* When he was so drunk, he *stretched out his hand with scorners* (joined hands with the mockers). The one who was entrusted with the government of a kingdom then lost the government of himself (Pr 16:32).

2.3. Adultery and immorality were very prevalent among the courtiers. This is spoken of in vv. 4, 6–7, and the accusation against drunkenness is included among these charges, for wine is oil to the fire of lust (Pr 23:33). *Adulterers* (v. 4) are here compared again and again to an oven heated by the baker: *They have made ready their heart like an oven* (v. 6); *they are all hot as an oven* (v. 7). An immoral heart is like a heated oven. The baker kindles a fire in his oven and puts sufficient fuel in it. In the morning he finds his oven well heated and ready for his purpose. Similarly, these evildoers, when they have hatched some plan to satisfy their covetous or immoral lusts, have their hearts so fully set to commit evil (Ecc 8:11) that, although they may stifle them for a while, the fire continues to glow inside, and as soon as there is an opportunity, their purposes break out into actions, just as a fire bursts into flame when it receives a blast of air.

2.4. They resisted the proper methods of reformation: *They have devoured their judges* (v. 7), those few good judges and rulers among them who would have put out these heated fires. *All their kings* have *fallen* one after another, and their families with them, which must have put the kingdom into confusion. There are hearts that burn; they are as *hot as an oven* with rage and malice against one another, and this causes the *devouring of their judges* and the *falling of* their *kings.* In the middle of all this disorder, *there is none among them that calls unto God.*

Verses 8–16

The *iniquity of Ephraim is discovered* (exposed), as well as *the sin of Samaria* (v. 1), of people as well as leaders.

1. They did not separate themselves from the nations, as God had separated them: *Ephraim, he has mingled himself among the people,* has associated closely with them, become like them, and lost his distinctive character among them. They went up and down among the nations, begging help from one of them against another. Nor were they completely devoted to God: *Ephraim is a cake not turned* (like a flat cake not turned over), and therefore burned on one side with uncooked dough on the other side, but good for nothing on either side.

2. They were strangely insensitive to the judgments of God. They were slowly drawing toward the ruin of their state partly by the encroachments of foreigners: *Strangers* (foreigners) *have devoured* (sapped) *his strength* (v. 9). Some destroyed them in open wars—as in 2Ki 13:7, when the king of Aram made them *like the dust by threshing*—others pretended to make treaties of peace, in which they made Ephraim pay dearly for what did them no good (2Ki 16:9). They were defeated partly by their own maladministration: *Yea, gray hairs are here and there upon him,* that is, the sad symptoms of a decaying and declining state, which is growing *old* and *ready to vanish away* (Heb 8:13).

3. They went on in their corrupt ways (v. 10): *The pride* (arrogance) *of Israel* still *testifies to his face* (against him), as it had done before (5:5); their hearts remain

unhumbled. They *do not return to the Lord their God*; although they suffer for going astray, they do not think of turning to God.

4. They followed wrong methods in their distress (vv. 11–12): *Ephraim is like a silly dove without heart.* To be harmless as a dove is commendable, but to be as foolish as a dove is shameful.

4.1. The silliness of this dove was that:

4.1.1. She did not mourn the loss of her young that were taken away from her; she intended to make her nest again in the same place. Ephraim had their people taken away by the enemy but continued to have dealings with those who dealt cruelly with them.

4.1.2. She was easily enticed into the net, having *no heart*, no understanding, to discern the danger she was in. Ephraim was drawn into alliances with neighboring nations who brought about their ruin.

4.1.3. When she was frightened, she did not have the courage to stay where she was safe, under the careful protection of her owner, but hovered, seeking shelter first in one place, then in another, so exposing herself more. And so the people in distress did not fly *like the doves to their windows* (Isa 60:8), where they might have been kept safe from the birds of prey, but threw themselves out of God's protection. They *called to Egypt*, then *Assyria*, to seek the help that they would, by repentance and prayer, have found in their God.

4.2. Notice what happens to this *silly dove* (v. 12): They are ensnared: "*I will spread my net upon them*, bring them into difficulties, so that they may see their foolishness and think of returning to God." They soar upward, proud of their foreign alliances, but *I will bring them down. I will chastise them as their congregation has heard*; they have been told many times that *vain is the help of man* (Ps 60:11; 108:12), that *in the son of man there is no help* (Ps 146:3). They have heard from both the Law and the prophets, and *as they have heard*, now *they shall see* (Job 42:5; Ps 48:8), they will feel.

5. They rebelled against God despite the methods he took to retain them (vv. 13–15). God, as a gracious sovereign toward a people who are precious to him, had *redeemed them* (v. 13) from Egypt and rescued them out of many difficulties since then. He had *bound and strengthened their arms* (v. 15). When their power was weak, like a broken arm, God set it again. He had given Israel victories over the Arameans (2Ki 13:16–17), had restored their boundaries (2Ki 14:25–26), and had strengthened them for battle. He had taken them into covenant, but they ran away from him as if he had been their dangerous enemy. He had given them his laws, which were all holy, just, and good, by which he intended to keep them on the right path, but they *transgressed against him*. They rejected his messages sent to them through his prophets. In their hypocritical professions of religious faith and promises of a reformed life, they lied to the Lord. He had good intentions for them, but they *imagined mischief* (plot evil) *against* him (v. 15). Sin is evil and troublesome; it is troublesome against God; it is treason. They will be punished for this (v. 13): *Woe to them! for they have fled from me.*

6. Their shows of devotion were just that—mere shows (v. 14).

6.1. They pretended to be devout, but this devotion was insincere (v. 14). When they were suffering personal troubles and called on God, they were insincere. They may have used good words, but they did not *cry with their heart*, and so God did not consider it true crying out to him. Moses is said to have *cried unto God* when

he did not speak a word, when only his heart was praying with faith (Ex 14:15). These people made a great noise but did not *cry to God*, because their hearts were not *right with him*. God was so far from approving their prayer and accepting it that he called it *howling*. Some think this suggests the noisiness of their prayers, that they were like the prayers they used to cry out to Baal. They did not pray for the grace of God, that God would forgive their sins, but only that he would not take away from them *their corn and wine*. Worldly hearts seek only temporal mercies and dread nothing except temporal judgments.

6.2. They pretended to reform their lives, but that was insincere too (v. 16). *They return*, that is, they acted as if they were going to return. God, however, said (Jer 4:1), *If thou wilt return, O Israel! return to me*; not only *turn toward me*, but also *return to me*. Their pretense made them like *a deceitful bow* (Ps 78:25), which is thought to be fit for use and is therefore bent and drawn, but breaks when pressure is put on it; either the bow or the string breaks. The sin of the leaders of Israel was *the rage of their tongue*, quarreling with God and with everyone around them. The leaders would *fall by the sword* of either their enemies or their own people, and *this* would *be their derision* (v. 16).

CHAPTER 8

This chapter, like the one before, divides itself into the sins and punishments of Israel. Here: 1. The sin of Israel is set out in many general expressions (vv. 1, 3, 12, 14) and in many individual examples: setting up kings without God (v. 4), setting up idols against God (vv. 4–6, 11), seeking alliances with neighboring nations (vv. 8–10), and still maintaining a profession of religious faith and of a relationship with God (vv. 2, 13–14). 2. The punishment of Israel is set out as corresponding to the sin. God would bring an enemy on them (vv. 1, 3). All their plans would prove worthless (v. 7). Their confidence in their idols and their foreign alliances would disappoint them (vv. 6, 8, 10). Their strength at home would fail them (v. 14).

Verses 1–7

The prophet must sound the alarm, for an enemy is coming to seize their land. Here we see:

1. A general accusation drawn up. The people have *transgressed my covenant* (v. 1). They have not only behaved foolishly but also dealt deceitfully. They have *trespassed against my law* (v. 1). They have *cast off the thing that is good* (v. 3), the service and worship of God, which is, in effect, rejecting God.

2. General threats of wrath and ruin for their sin: *The enemy shall come as an eagle against the house of the Lord* (v. 1) and *shall pursue him* (v. 3). If by *the house of the Lord* we understand the temple at Jerusalem, then we must presume the eagle to refer either to Sennacherib or to Nebuchadnezzar, who burned down the temple. However, if we consider these verses to point to the destruction of the kingdom of the ten tribes by the king of Assyria, we must reckon *the house of the Lord* to refer to the main group of the people to whom, as Israelites, *pertained the adoption, the glory, and the covenants* (Ro 9:4). Those who break their covenant of friendship with God make themselves a cheap and easy target.

3. The people's hypocritical claim of a relationship with God (v. 2). In their distress, *Israel shall cry unto me* and claim to have the kind of knowledge of God's ways

that in their prosperity they *desired not*, but *despised*. What good will it do a person to be able to say, *My God, I know thee* (v. 2), when that person cannot say, "My God, I love you"?

4. The prophet's pleading (v. 5): *How long will it be ere they attain to innocency* (before they reach purity)*?* Absolute innocence is not meant here, but how long would it be before they became innocent of and free from the sin of idolatry? In trouble they cried out, "*How long will* it be before God turns to us in mercy?" But they did not hear him ask, "*How long* will it be before they turn back to God in duty?"

5. Some particular sins:

5.1. In their civil affairs, they *set up kings without God* (v. 4). This was what they did when they rejected Samuel and chose Saul (1Sa 8:5, 7). This was what they did when they set up Jeroboam (1Ki 12:20–24). This was how they acted now at about the time when Hosea prophesied, when it seems to have become fashionable to *set up kings* and then depose them again (2Ki 15:8–26).

5.2. In their religious matters they did much worse, for they *set up calves against God*. They called them *gods—Behold thy gods, O Israel!* (1Ki 12:28)—but God called them *idols*; the word means "griefs or troubles," because they are offensive to God and will ruin those who worship them. To show the people their foolishness, God told them:

5.2.1. Where their gods came from. If one traced them to their origin, they would be found to be creations of the people's own imaginations and the work of their hands (v. 6). The calf they worshiped is called here *the calf of Samaria*, probably because when Samaria became the capital of the kingdom in Ahab's time, a calf was set up there so that it would be near the court. It was dreamed up by them, some think, not taken from the Egyptians, for although the Egyptians worshiped Apis in the form of a living cow, they never worshiped *a golden calf*. The gold and silver from which it was made was collected from the people of Israel: it is a poor god indeed whose creation depends on assessing taxes. *The workmen made it; therefore it is not God* (v. 6). A god that is made is no God at all.

5.2.2. What their gods would come to. If they were not true gods, they would not last.

5.2.3. What their gods would bring them to. *They have made for themselves idols, so that they may be cut off* (destroyed) (v. 4) from God, from their own land, and from the land of the living. Those who allow themselves to be deceived *into* idolatry will certainly find themselves deceived *in* it. The people's disappointment in their idols is illustrated (v. 7) by a metaphor.

5.2.3.1. They gained no good for themselves by worshiping idols: *They have sown the wind* (v. 7). They had gone to a great deal of trouble and expense to make and worship their idols, as a farmer does to sow corn, in expectation of reaping advantage from it. They did it to be as successful as the neighboring nations, who worshiped idols. But it was like *sowing the wind*, which can produce no harvest.

5.2.3.2. They brought ruin on themselves by it. They would *reap the whirlwind*, "a great whirlwind." They not only did not have their false gods to support them; they also set the true God against them. The service of idols is unprofitable, and the works of darkness are unfruitful (Eph 5:11); *The end of those things is death* (Ro 6:21).

Verses 8–14

It was the honor and happiness of Israel that they had only one God, but they did not know how well off they were.

1. They multiplied their alliances (v. 9): *They had hired lovers.* They went to great expense to buy the friendship of the nations around them. Without doubt, those who have no lovers except what they hire have behaved badly among their neighbors. Notice here:

1.1. The contempt that Israel was under among the nations (v. 8): *Israel was swallowed up*; they had been devoured by foreigners, and their land eaten up (v. 7), and, having become poor, they had lost their reputation, like a trader who has become bankrupt.

1.2. The favor that Israel sought from the nations nevertheless (v. 9): they had *gone to Assyria* to help them, and here they were like *a wild ass alone by himself*, headstrong and unruly.

1.3. The adversities they were likely to face in their alliances with the neighboring nations (v. 10): *Though they had hired among the nations*, what they provided for their own safety would only make them easier prey to their enemies. The king of Assyria, whose friendship they sought (Isa 10:8), laid *burdens* on Israel and levied taxes on them (2Ki 15:19–20), and for these *they* would *sorrow* (waste away) *a little.* "They have begun to be diminished," as some read it, *by the burden of the king of princes.*

2. They had many altars and temples. Notice:

2.1. How they denied *the power of godliness* (2Ti 3:5) (v. 12): *I have written to him the great things of my law.* The things of God's law are the great things of God. They declare the greatness of the Lawmaker, things that are important to us; they are our life (Dt 32:46–47), and our eternal welfare depends on our observance of them and obedience to them. It is a great privilege to have the things of God's written law. They are written by God himself, for Moses and the prophets were his secretaries, and holy prophets wrote as they were carried along by the Holy Spirit (2Pe 1:21). Furthermore, if those who had the *great things of God's law* written for them were happy, how much happier are we who have the much greater things of his Gospel written for us! However, the great things of the law were *counted as a strange* (foreign) *thing*, as unintelligible and unreasonable: *We desire not the knowledge of thy ways* (Job 21:14).

2.2. How they kept up the form of godliness (2Ti 3:5), nevertheless, and to what little effect.

2.2.1. They had many altars (v. 11): *Ephraim made many altars to sin.* The altars would lead them into further sin, because their many altars dedicated to the God of Israel would introduce altars dedicated to other gods.

2.2.2. They had many sacrifices (v. 13). Their altars were smoking altars: they *sacrificed flesh for the sacrifices of God's offerings*, as if they hoped that by their observation of their own ceremonial law they could excuse themselves from the obligation of all God's moral commands. *The Lord accepts them not.* How could he, when they sacrificed only meat, not the spiritual sacrifice of a penitent, faithful heart? A petition to be allowed to commit sin amounts to an invoking of the curse for sin, and this is how it will be answered, *according to the multitude of the idols* (Eze 14:4). *Israel has forgotten his Maker and builds temples* (v. 14). Some understand *temples* here to refer to "palaces": Israel was so self-confident that they defied God's judgments with a pride like that of Nebuchadnezzar (Da 4:30). Judah, similarly, was accused of *multiplying fenced cities* (fortifying many towns) and trusting in them for security when God was judging his people.

CHAPTER 9

In this chapter: 1. God threatens to deprive this corrupt seed of Israel of all their worldly enjoyments (vv. 1–5). 2. He condemns them to ruin for their own sins and the sins of their prophets (vv. 6–8). 3. He rebukes them for the evil of their ancestors, whose steps they have followed in (vv. 9–10). 4. He threatens them with the uprooting of their descendants (vv. 11–17).

Verses 1–6

1. The people of Israel are accused of spiritual adultery: *O Israel! thou hast gone a whoring from* (been unfaithful to) *thy God* (v. 1). When they set up idols and worshiped them, they were unfaithful to God and honored the pretenders with the affection, adoration, and confidence that were due only to God. *They loved a reward upon every corn floor* (v. 1), the offerings and firstfruits they gave their idols at every threshing floor. Or they loved to receive rewards from their idols, and they reckoned the fruits of the earth to be such rewards.

2. They are forbidden to rejoice: *"Rejoice not, O Israel! for joy.* What right do you have to either *peace* or joy while your acts of unfaithfulness and sorcery are so many?"* (2Ki 9:19–22). Some think that at this time they had particular reasons for joy, probably the making of a treaty with some powerful ally.

3. They are threatened with judgments for their spiritual unfaithfulness.

3.1. Their land will not yield its usual harvest. Canaan, that *fruitful land*, will be *turned into barrenness for the wickedness of those that dwell therein* (Ps 107:34) (v. 2). *The floor and the winepress shall not feed them*, much less feast them.

3.2. Their land will not only stop feeding them but also stop being their dwelling place; it will spew them out, as it did the Canaanites before them (Lev 18:28) (v. 3). It was a sad and harsh judgment to be driven out of such a land; it was like the expelling of our first parents from the Garden of Eden. Those who refuse to submit to the Lord's laws cannot expect to live in the Lord's land.

3.3. They will have no rest or contentment in any other land. Some will *return into Egypt*, the old land of slavery; they will flee there from Assyria (8:13). Others will be taken captive to Assyria and be forced to *eat unclean things* there, things unfit for Jews to eat because they are prohibited by their law.

3.4. In the land of their enemies they will have no opportunity either to give honor to God or to obtain favor with him by offering any acceptable sacrifice to him. They will have no sacrifices to offer, nor any altar. They will not so much as *offer drink offerings* to the Lord, much less any other sacrifices. Instead of sacrifices of joy, they will *eat the bread of mourners* (v. 4). Their *bread for their soul*, the bread they need to support their lives, *shall not come into the house of the Lord*. The return of the days of their sacred festivals will therefore be uncomfortable for them (v. 5).

3.5. They will perish in the land of their dispersion (v. 6): *For, lo, they have gone* out of the Lord's land, *gone because of destruction*, gone to Egypt because of the destruction of their own country by the Assyrians, flattering themselves that they will return when the storm has passed. However, they will find that there are *graves in Egypt*, as their murmuring ancestors said (Ex 14:11).

3.6. Their land, which they leave behind and to which they will hope to return, will become desolate: as for *their tabernacles* (tents), where they formerly lived and kept their stores, *the pleasant places for their silver*, they will be laid in ruins, be overgrown with *nettles*.

Verses 7–10

To awaken them even more, it is threatened here:

1. That the destruction spoken of will come quickly. It is at the door (v. 7): *The days of visitation* (punishment) *have come, the days of recompence* (reckoning) *have come*, and the time of the divine patience has expired.

2. That by the speedy arrival of this destruction they will be made ashamed of their attitudes toward their prophets.

2.1. They will then know that the false prophets, who flattered them in their sins and rocked them to sleep in their self-confidence—as Ahab's prophets did (1Ki 22:24)—were *fools* and *madmen*.

2.2. They will then recognize the *true prophets*, God's faithful ambassadors to them. Mocking the messengers of the Lord was the sin they were punished for.

3. That by its speedy arrival the evil of the false prophets will be revealed, to their shame (v. 8): "*The watchman of Ephraim* pretends to have been *with my God* and introduces his lies with, *Thus saith the Lord*, but he is *a snare of a fowler in all his ways.*" When the best things are corrupted, they become the worst.

4. That God will judge them for the sins of their ancestors (vv. 9–10). The people of Ephraim now are as bad as their ancestors: *They have deeply corrupted themselves*; they are far gone in the *depths of Satan* (Isa 31:6). Evil and immorality are as brazen and arrogant now as in the *days of Gibeah* (Jdg 19), and so what can be expected but such vengeance as was then taken on Gibeah? God uses this occasion to rebuke them for the corruption of their ancestors (v. 10). God first formed them into a people: *I found Israel like grapes in the wilderness* (v. 10). He took as much delight in them as poor travelers would in grapes they found in a desert. God set them apart for himself as his own special people, but they went to Baal of Peor, joining the Moabites in sacrificing to that corrupt, false god (Nu 25:2–3), and they *separated themselves unto that shame*, that shameful idol. This was the way of their ancestors; God had done the good, but they had acted ungratefully toward him; and in the same way the present generation have *deeply corrupted themselves*.

Verses 11–17

We have here:

1. The sin of Ephraim. Their worship is corrupt (v. 15): *All their wickedness is in Gilgal*, a place that was infamous for idolatry, as is clear from 4:15; 12:11; Am 4:4; 5:5. That place had been famous in other ages for solemn transactions between God and Israel (Jos 5:2, 10; 1Sa 10:8; 11:15). Grotius thinks there is a mystical sense here. *Golgotha* in Syriac (Aramaic) refers to the same place as *Gilgal* in Hebrew, and so he thinks this may have reference to the putting of Christ to death at Golgotha, which was the greatest sin of the Jewish nation, and about which it could truly be said, "*All their wickedness* was summed up in that."

2. The displeasure of God against Ephraim. He *departs from them* (v. 12). He hates them. *In Gilgal*, where *all their wickedness is, there I hated them* (v. 15). Where their sinful, detestable practices are committed is the place where God detests sinners. *For the wickedness of their doings, I will drive them out of my house.* They will be *castaways* (v. 17).

3. The fruit of this displeasure, which comes in the cutting off and abandoning of their descendants. The name

Ephraim is derived from *fruitfulness* (Ge 41:51). Moses' blessing foretold the *ten thousands of Ephraim* (Dt 33:17). This was his glory (v. 11). Ephraim is as strong and rich as Tyre ever was, and as proud and self-confident. Yet *their glory shall fly away like a bird* (v. 11); their children will be taken away, and the hopes of their families cut off. *Ephraim is smitten; their root is dried up; they shall bear no fruit* (v. 16). They will perish by themselves, by the immediate hand of God (v. 11): they will *fly away from the birth, and from the womb, and from the conception*. They will also perish at the hands of their enemies. They will die violent deaths (v. 12). Again (v. 13), *Ephraim shall bring forth his children to the murderer*. The mothers will labor in pain to give birth to their children, and yet a cruel enemy will come and put all to the sword. The Aramaic paraphrase suggests, and many of the rabbis think, that the *murderers* to whom the children were brought out were those who sacrificed their children to Molech. Those few who escape will be dispersed (v. 17): they will be *wanderers among the nations*. Notice the prophet's prayer about this (v. 14): *Give them, O Lord! What wilt thou give?* Rather let them have no children than have the children made miserable. Christ said, *Blessed is the womb that never bore and the paps that never gave suck* (Lk 23:29). "Give, therefore, *a miscarrying womb and dry breasts*; for it is better to fall into the hands of the Lord, whose mercies are great, than into human hands" (2Sa 24:14).

CHAPTER 10

Here: 1. The people of Israel are accused of gross corruption in the worship of God (vv. 1–2, 5–6, 8). 2. They are accused of corruption in the administration of the civil government (vv. 3–4, 7). 3. They are accused of imitating the sins of their ancestors and of being self-confident in their own sins (vv. 9–11). 4. They are fervently invited to repent and reform (vv. 12–15).

Verses 1–8

Notice:

1. National sins bring national judgments.

1.1. They were not fruitful, that is, they did not produce fruits of righteousness (Php 1:11). Here all their evil acts began (v. 1): *Israel is an empty vine*. Of all trees, a vine is the least useful if it does not bear fruit. It is then good for nothing (Eze 15:3, 5).

1.2. They had many altars and sacred stones, and the more generous God's providence was to them, the more extravagant they were in serving their idols.

1.3. Their hearts were *divided* (v. 2). They were in conflict about their idols and in conflict about their kings, and there was no such thing as friendship among them. They *halted between God and Baal* (1Ki 18:21), so their *hearts were divided*.

1.4. They were not concerned about what they said and what they did in the most solemn manner (v. 4). They *swore falsely in making a covenant*; subjects broke their oaths of allegiance, and kings broke their coronation oaths; they broke their treaties with the nations. God is greatly offended by corruption, not only in his own worship but also in the administration of justice between people.

2. They will have no joy from their kings or their government. *Now they shall say, "We have no king*, that is, we are as if we had none, none to preserve the public peace and none to fight our battles, and these things have justly come on us." Those who keep themselves in the fear

and favor of God may say, "What can the greatest person do against us?" But those who reject his protection must say, with despair, "What can the greatest person do for us?" Their civil government will be not only weakened but completely destroyed (v. 7): *As for Samaria*, the royal city, *her king is cut off as the foam from the water*. The foam makes a great show on the surface of the water, but it is only a heap of bubbles. The kings of Israel were like this after their rebellion from the house of David, mere scum; their government had no foundation. He *shall break down their altars*. God will do it by means of the hands of the Assyrians, and the Assyrians will do it on God's orders: *He shall spoil their images* (destroy their sacred stones) (v. 2). If the grace of God is not effective in destroying the love of sin in us, God in his providence will destroy the food and fuel of sin around us. *The thorn and the thistle* will *come up on their altars*, that is, the altars will lie in ruins. In this way, idolaters are brought in trembling when God arises to *shake terribly the earth* (Isa 2:21). Here (v. 8), *They shall say to the mountains, Cover us, and to the hills, Fall on us*.

Verses 9–15

Here:

1. Israel is reminded of the sins of their ancestors. They were told in 9:9 that they had *corrupted themselves, as in the days of Gibeah*, and here again they are told (v. 9), "*O Israel! thou hast sinned from the days of Gibeah*. The evil that was committed in that age is revived in this one, and reenacted. It has been continued in a constant series and succession through all the intervening ages. The case was bad then, for *there they stood* (remained), and *the battle in Gibeah against the* children of sin did not reach them until the third encounter, and then did not overwhelm them all, for 600 escaped (Jdg 20). However, your sin is worse than theirs."

2. They have received warning of the judgments of God that were coming on them (v. 10). God has pitied and spared them up to now. Because God does not desire the death and ruin of sinners (Eze 18:23, 32), he does desire their correction. "Because they did not receive correction from me through my prophets, who rebuked them in my name, I will correct them by the hands of the people who will be *gathered against them, when they will bind themselves in their two furrows*," that is, within a double entrenchment. Or, "when I will bind them for their two transgressions," as the margin reads, meaning their physical and spiritual adultery. Or, "when I will bind them to their two furrows," that is, bring them into the slavery of the Assyrians, as oxen with a plow, which are bound to the two furrows up and down the field. In this way, those who would not be God's free people will be their enemies' slaves.

3. Ephraim is like a heifer that has been taught to tread out the corn and enjoys that work, because, not muzzled, she has the freedom to eat at will. "But," God says, "I have a yoke to put on her fair neck. *I will make Ephraim to ride*, that is, I will cause them to be ridden by the Assyrians and other conquerors, who will rule them harshly, as people do the animals they ride on (Ps 66:12). Judah will be made to plow, and Jacob to break up the ground," that is, they will be treated harshly, but not so harshly as Ephraim. Dr. Pocock gives another sense to these words; he believes they offer a reason why Ephraim should return to obedience to God's law: God used such gentle methods with this people to bring them into obedience to his law. He had managed them as farmers manage cattle that they

are training for service. Because Ephraim, a docile heifer, was fit to be employed, God took hold of her fair neck to get her used to the hand, harnessed her, or put the yoke of his commandments on her, giving his people Israel a law, so that they would not be tempted by the customs of the nations to go astray. He has used all fair and likely means with them to keep them obeying; he set Judah to plow and Jacob to break up the ground. Yet they would not maintain that obedience, but started to go astray.

4. They are invited and encouraged to turn back to God by prayer, repentance, and reformation (vv. 12–13). They are God's field (1Co 3:9), and the duties are taken from the language of farming. Let them break up the fallow ground; let them cleanse their hearts from all corrupt and sinful attitudes and desires, which are like weeds and thorns, and let them have a broken and contrite spirit (Ps 51:17). Let them prepare to receive the divine commands, like the ground that is plowed is broken up to receive the seed so that it may take root. See Jer 4:3. Let them sow righteousness for themselves; let them return to the practice of good works, and let them sow to the Spirit, as the apostle Paul writes (Gal 6:7–8). Let them seek the Lord; let them look up to him for his grace and beg him to bless the seed that has been sown. It is the right time to do it. If we sow righteousness for ourselves—if we are careful and conscientious in doing our duty, depending on his grace—he will shower down his grace on us; he will *rain righteousness*, the very thing that those who are to sow righteousness need most. We have *ploughed wickedness and reaped iniquity*, and our past is enough to show that we have done so (v. 13). "You have taken a great deal of effort to serve sin. Will you begrudge bearing the burden and heat of the day in God's service? You have done much to condemn your souls; will you not undo that work and do something to save them? You trusted in your own way of life, in your great numbers; you have put your confidence in created things, your own power and knowledge, and your hopes have deceived you. Now come and seek the Lord, and your hope in him will not deceive you."

5. They are threatened with complete destruction, for both their worldly practices and their worldly confidence (vv. 14–15). *A tumult* (the roar of battle) *shall arise among thy people*, either from insurrections at home or from invasions from abroad, and the *fortresses* they trust in will be seized and rifled, as *Shalman spoiled* (devastated) *Beth-arbel in the day of battle* (v. 14). This refers to some event that had just taken place. Shalman is probably the same as Shalmaneser, king of Assyria, who had lately carried out a military execution against some town or castle—*Beth-arbel is the house of Arbel*—to terrify other garrisons into speedy surrender. God tells them that this is how Samaria will be devastated. The inhabitants will be put to the *sword*, as it was at *Beth-arbel. In a morning shall the king of Israel utterly be cut off* (v. 15). Hoshea was the last king of Israel; in him the whole kingdom was *cut off*; the verse may refer to him or to some of his predecessors who were cut off through treachery. It will be done *in a morning*, as suddenly as a day dawns. What is the source of this bloodshed? He tells us in v. 15: *So shall Bethel do unto you*. Bethel was the place where one of the golden calves was (1Ki 12:28–29); Gilgal, where *all their wickedness* is said to have been, was close by; their *great wickedness* was there—literally, "the evil of their evil"—the sum and essence of their sin. He does not say, "So will the *king of Assyria* do to you," but, "So will *Bethel* do to you." Whatever trouble happens to us, it is sin that does it.

CHAPTER 11

We have here: 1. The great goodness of God toward his people Israel (vv. 1, 3–4). 2. Their ungrateful behavior toward him (vv. 2–4, 7, 12). 3. Threats of wrath against them for their unfaithfulness (vv. 5–6). 4. Mercy remembered in the midst of wrath (Hab 3:2) (vv. 8–9). 5. Promises of what God would still do for them (vv. 10–11). 6. An honorable description of Judah (v. 12).

Verses 1–7

Here we find:

1. God being very gracious to Israel.

1.1. He showed kindness to them when they were young (v. 1): *When Israel was a child, then I loved him*; when they first began to increase to a nation in Egypt, God then *set his love upon them*, and he *chose them because he loved them* (Dt 7:7–8). When they were as helpless as children, foolish as children, when they were outcasts and vulnerable children, then God *loved them*. Those who have grown up—in fact, those who have grown old—should often reflect on the goodness of God toward them in their childhood.

1.2. He rescued them from the land of slavery: *I called my son out of Egypt*, because he was a beloved son. These words are said to have been fulfilled in Christ when, on the death of Herod, he and his parents were *called out of Egypt* (Mt 2:15). The calling of Christ out of Egypt prefigured the calling of all who are his, through him, out of spiritual slavery.

1.3. He gave them a good education and took care of them. *I taught Ephraim also to go*, as a child is taught to walk with the guidance of leading strings. *He taught them to go* the way of his commandments by the institutions of the ceremonial law, which were like tutors (Gal 4:2).

1.4. When anything was wrong with them, he was their doctor: *I healed them*.

1.5. He brought them into his service mildly and gently (v. 4): *I drew them with cords of a man, with bands of love.* He draws *with the cords of a man*, with such cords as are used by human beings—by those who are humane. He draws *with bands of love*, or "cart ropes" of love. This word stands for stronger cords than the word translated *cords*.

1.6. He relieved them of burdens: *I was to them as those that take off the yoke on their jaws* (v. 4); this alludes to the concern of good farmers, who are compassionate to their animals and will not tire them with constant hard labor.

1.7. He supplied them with the food they needed. In Egypt they led a hard life, but when God brought them out, he *laid meat* (food) *unto them*, as farmers feed their cattle when they have unyoked them. God rained manna around their camp (Ex 16:11–35), bread from heaven (Ps 105:40), angels' food (Ps 78:24–25).

2. Israel being ungrateful to God.

2.1. They were deaf and disobedient to his voice.

2.2. They were fond of idols and worshiped them. Idolatry was the sin that from the beginning, and throughout, had entangled them most (Heb 12:1).

2.3. They did not show any concern for God and his favors toward them: *They knew not that I healed them* (v. 3). Ignorance lies at the root of ingratitude (2:8).

2.4. They were strongly inclined to apostasy. This is the most severe aspect of this accusation (v. 7): *My people are bent to backsliding from me.* They were *bent to backslide*; they were ready to sin. It also suggests that they were determined in sin; their hearts were *fully set in them to do evil* (Ecc 8:11).

2.5. They were strangely averse to repentance and reformation. *They refused to return* (v. 5). God's prophets and ministers called on them to turn back to the God from whom they had rebelled, to the Most High God, from whom they had sunk into wretched corruption, but the call was in vain.

3. God being very angry with Israel, and justly so. He had brought them out of Egypt to take them as his own people, but they would not be faithful to him (v. 5): "*Israel shall not return into the land of Egypt*, even though that was a land of terrible slavery, but will go into even harder service, for *the Assyrian shall be his king*, who will treat them worse than Pharaoh did." God, who gave them Canaan, would bring his judgments on them there (v. 6): *The sword* would come on them, the sword of a foreign enemy triumphing over them. They continued to rebel against God, and so God continued his judgments on them.

Verses 8–12

In these verses we have:

1. God's wonderful unwillingness to destroy Israel (vv. 8–9): *How shall I give thee up?* Notice here:

1.1. God's discussion within himself about Israel's situation, a discussion between justice and mercy, in which victory clearly inclines toward mercy (Jas 2:13). Not that there are such struggles in God as there are in us, but that God used these human expressions to show the severity that the sin of Israel deserved and the divine grace that would spare them nevertheless. *How shall I give thee up?* Notice here:

1.1.1. The proposals that justice makes for Israel. Let Ephraim be given up as an incorrigible son. Let Israel be handed over to the enemy as a lamb is to the lion to be torn to pieces; let them be made like Admah and Zeboim, the two cities that were destroyed with Sodom and Gomorrah. Ephraim and Israel deserve to be abandoned in this way, and God will do them no wrong if he deals with them like this.

1.1.2. The opposition that mercy makes to these proposals: *How shall I do it?* It is as a tender father reasons with himself, "How can I reject my perverse son? He is still my son. I cannot do it. They have been a people who are precious to me; there are still some good people among them; they may still repent and reform, and so how can I do it?" God speaks as if he were conscious of a strange struggle within himself, involving his compassion toward Israel: *My repentings are kindled together* (all my compassion is aroused).

1.2. His gracious decision in this discussion. After a long struggle, mercy triumphs over judgment (Jas 2:13); mercy is victorious (v. 9). It is decreed that the reprieve will be extended even longer, and *I will not* now *execute the fierceness of my anger.* They will be corrected but not consumed.

1.3. The reason for this determination: *For I am God and not man, the Holy One of Israel* (v. 9). He is Lord of his anger, whereas the anger of a human being often dominates them. It is a great encouragement to our hope in God's mercies to remember that he is *God, and not man.*

2. His wonderful eagerness to do good for Israel, which is clear from his promise that he will qualify them to receive the good he intends for them (vv. 10–11): *They shall walk after the Lord.* It is spoken about the ten tribes, and it had its partial fulfillment when some of them

returned with a group from the two tribes in Ezra's time. It had its more complete fulfillment, however, in God's spiritual Israel, the Gospel church, brought together by the Gospel of Christ. Notice:

2.1. How they were to be called and brought together: *The Lord shall roar like a lion.* The voice of the Gospel was heard from far away, like the *roaring of a lion*, and it was a *mighty voice.* See Joel 3:16.

2.2. What impression this call would make on them, the kind of impression the roaring of a lion makes on all the animals of the forest: *When he shall roar, then the children shall tremble.* When those whose hearts the Gospel reached trembled and cried out, *What shall we do?* (Ac 2:37), when they were to work out their salvation and worship God with fear and trembling (Php 2:12), then this promise was fulfilled. *The children shall tremble from the west* (v. 10). This seems to refer to the calling of the Gentiles who lay westward of Canaan, for the Gospel spread especially that way. The apostle Paul speaks *of mighty signs and wonders* that were brought by the preaching of the Gospel from *Jerusalem round about to Illyricum* (Ro 15:19). It was at such a time as this that the children trembled from the west. Whereas the people of Israel were dispersed in Egypt and Assyria, it was promised that they would be effectively summoned from there (v. 11): *They shall tremble*; they would come with all speed, *as a bird* on the wing, *out of Egypt*, and *as a dove out of the land of Assyria.*

2.3. What effect these impressions would have on them. Being *moved with fear* (Heb 11:7), *they shall walk after the Lord* (v. 10). Those who lay farthest away from each other would meet in Christ and be joined in the church. Our holy trembling at the word of Christ will draw us to him, not drive us away from him. When he *roars like a lion*, the slaves tremble and flee from him, but the children tremble and flee to him.

2.4. What reception they would meet with when they returned (v. 11): *I will place them in their houses*—all those who come at the Gospel call will have a place and a name in the Gospel church. They will live in God and be at home in him as a person is in their own home. They will have mansions, for there are many in *our Father's house* (Jn 14:2).

3. A sad complaint about the unfaithfulness of Ephraim and Israel, which may be an indication that it is not the people of Israel to whom the foregoing promises belong, but rather the spiritual Israel, for as for this Ephraim, this Israel, they *compass* (surround) *God about with lies and deceit.*

4. A pleasant commendation of the integrity of the two tribes, to emphasize the unfaithfulness of the ten tribes and show why God had mercy in store for Judah that he did not have for Israel (1:6–7). *Judah rules with God*, that is, he serves God, and the service of God is dignity and dominion. They *walk in the way of good men* (Pr 2:20), and those who do so *rule with God* (v. 12); they enjoy great privileges in heaven.

CHAPTER 12

We have here: 1. A great accusation drawn up against both Israel and Judah for their sins (vv. 1–2), especially the sin of fraud and injustice, which Ephraim is accused of (v. 7) and justifies himself in (v. 8), and the sin of idolatry (v. 11), which causes God to bring charges against them (v. 14). 2. An emphasis on the sins they are accused of, taken from the honor God had shown to their father

Jacob (vv. 3–5), their advancement from humble, lowly beginnings to nationhood (vv. 12–13), and the provision he had given them of spiritual help through the prophets he sent them (v. 10). 3. A call to the unconverted to turn to God (v. 6). 4. An intimation of mercy that God has in store for them (v. 9).

Verses 1–6

In these verses:

1. Ephraim is convicted of foolishness for trusting in Egypt and Assyria when he was in difficulties (v. 1): *Ephraim feeds on wind.* The people of Ephraim think they can obtain the Assyrians' support by a solemn alliance: *They make a covenant with the Assyrians,* but they will find that that powerful prince will honor his word not a moment longer than he pleases. They think they will gain the Egyptians as their allies by making a rich present: *Oil is carried into Egypt.* However, when the Egyptians received the bribe, they dropped the cause.

2. *The Lord has also a controversy with Judah,* for though a while ago Judah *ruled with God* and was *faithful with the saints* (11:12), he is now beginning to become corrupt.

3. Both Ephraim and Judah are reminded of their father Jacob so that they will be encouraged to turn back to God. God called this people Jacob (v. 2), threatening to punish them, but (11:8) *how shall I give them up?* How can that dear name be forgotten? From what took place between God and Jacob we may learn that *Jehovah, the Lord God of hosts, is the God of Israel* (2Sa 7:26); he was the God of Jacob, and this is *his memorial* (his name of renown) throughout all generations of descendants of Jacob (v. 5). Here are two memorials by which he is set apart from all others and is to be acknowledged by us. The first shows that his existence is of himself. He is Jehovah, the *I AM,* the One who *was, and is, and is to come* (Rev 4:8), infinite, eternal, and unchangeable. Jehovah is *his memorial,* his special name. The second shows his dominion over all: he is the *God of hosts;* he has all the powers of heaven and earth at his command. God's names, titles, and attributes are his memorials; there is no need for idols to be such. *"Therefore turn thou to thy God.* The One who was the God of Jacob is the God of Israel, is *thy God.* You have rebelled from him; therefore, turn back to him in repentance and faith, turn to him as yours, to love him, obey him, and depend on him. *Keep mercy and judgment* (maintain love and justice), *mercy* in helping and relieving the poor and distressed, *judgment* in giving everyone their due; be kind to all."

Verses 7–14

These verses contain:

1. Rebukes for sin. Ephraim is accused of turning away from his God by idolatry and breaking the laws of justice.

1.1. He is accused of injustice, of violating the commands of the second table of the Ten Commandments (vv. 7–8). Notice here:

1.1.1. The sin he is accused of: *He is a merchant.* The margin reads it as a proper name: "He is Canaan," or a Canaanite, unworthy to be given the name of Jacob and Israel. See Am 9:7. However, *Canaan* sometimes means *a merchant,* and so most likely it does here, where Ephraim is accused of deceit in commerce. Although God had given his people a land flowing with milk and honey (Ex 3:8, 17; etc.), he still did not forbid them from making themselves rich by trading. Moreover, if they had traded fairly, it would have brought no shame on them

at all. Ephraim, however, is the same type of merchant as the Canaanites are, who cheat everyone they possibly can. Ephraim deceives and so oppresses with a great deal of skill and cunning: *The balances of deceit are in his hand* (v. 7).

1.1.2. How he justifies himself in this sin (v. 8). He stands accused of common deception, yet he does not deny the charge, but insists on justifying himself. Suppose it were true that he used dishonest scales; nevertheless:

1.1.2.1. He has gained good possessions. Let the prophet say what he wants to about his deceit; Ephraim still cannot be convinced there is any harm in it: *"Yet I have become rich, I have found me out substance* (I have become wealthy) (v. 8)." Worldly hearts are often confirmed in their evil ways by their worldly prosperity and success. It is a great mistake, however. Every word in what Ephraim says here declares his foolishness. It is foolish to:

1.1.2.1.1. Call the riches of this world *substance,* for they are insubstantial (Pr 23:5).

1.1.2.1.2. Think that what we have is for ourselves. *I have found me out substance*—as if we had it for our own use, whereas we are only entrusted with it as stewards.

1.1.2.1.3. Think that becoming rich sinfully makes us innocent or will keep us safe. See also Isa 47:10; Pr 1:32.

1.1.2.2. He pleads that he has kept up a good reputation. Worldly hearts tend to build up a good opinion of themselves on the basis of the good reputation they have among their neighbors. He excuses himself for the fraud, and so no one condemns it: *"They shall find no iniquity in me that were* (would be) *sin,* nothing very bad, nothing except what is very excusable." It is a fashionable sin; it is the same thing that everybody is doing. No one will think the worse of them for what they have done. God, however, does not see as human beings see (1Sa 16:7); he does not judge as human beings judge.

1.2. He is also accused of idolatry, which is against the commands of the first table—idolatry, that sin that is especially worthless, the making and worshiping of idols, which are worthless (v. 11): *Surely they are vanity.* They do not bring profit, but only deceive. The prophet mentions two places that are notorious for idolatry:

1.2.1. Gilead, on the other side of the Jordan, which was branded as scandalous before (6:8): *Is there iniquity in Gilead?* It is something to be wondered at; it is a thing to be sadly lamented.

1.2.2. Gilgal, too, where they *sacrifice bullocks* (v. 11) and *their altars* are as thick *as heaps* of manure *in the furrows of the field* that is to be sown (8:11).

2. Threats of wrath for sin. Some take v. 9 to be a threat: *I will make thee to dwell in tabernacles as in the days of the appointed time,* as the Israelites did when they lived in tents and wandered for forty years; that was the *time appointed* in *the wilderness.* Ephraim thinks that there is no sin in him that deserves to be called sin (v. 8), but God tells him that there is sin in him, and it will be found to be sin if he does not repent and reform. *Ephraim provoked him to anger most bitterly* (v. 14). God will take away his forfeited life: *He shall leave his blood upon him* (will leave upon him the guilt of his bloodshed) (v. 14), that is, he will not hold him guiltless (1Ki 2:9). *His blood shall be upon his own head* (2Sa 1:16). *His reproach shall his Lord return upon him* (the Lord will repay him for his contempt) (v. 14).

3. Memories of former mercy, which come to convict those who are corruptly ungrateful. Let them remember that:

3.1. God raised them from lowliness. When Ephraim became rich, he forgot what God made his people acknowledge every year: *A Syrian ready to perish was my father* (Dt 26:5). But God reminds him of it here (v. 12). Let them remember not only the honors of their father Jacob (v. 3) but also what a lowly servant he was to Laban. *Jacob fled into Syria* from a malicious brother, and there he served a covetous uncle *for a wife*, and *for a wife he kept sheep*, because he had no estate. He was a quiet man, staying among the tents (Ge 25:27), and kept sheep, and so *balances of deceit* (v. 7) were unbecoming to his descendants. God wonderfully preserved him, and this exalts the goodness of God both to him and to them and also leaves them with the stain of corrupt ingratitude to the God who was their founder and benefactor.

3.2. God rescued them from misery and raised them up out of poverty and slavery (v. 13). God *brought Israel out of Egypt by a prophet*, Moses, who, though he is called *king in Jeshurun* (Dt 33:5), still acted for Israel *as a prophet*, by direction from God and by the power of his word. This shows how ungrateful this people were in rejecting their prophets. They should have loved and valued his prophets and have tried to fulfill God's purpose in sending them, for the sake of the prophet through whom God had brought them out of Egypt.

3.3. God took care of their education as they grew up. We have this instance of God's goodness in v. 10. As he rescued them through a prophet, so it was also *by prophets* that he still continued to speak to them.

4. Intimations of further mercy in the midst of sin and wrath (Hab 3:2), as some understand v. 9: *"I that am the Lord thy God from the land of Egypt*, who took you then and there to be my people and have shown myself to be your God ever since by a constant series of merciful providences, still have kindness for you, though you are bad, and I *will make thee to dwell in tabernacles*, not as in the desert, but *as in the days of the solemn feast*," the Feast of Tabernacles, which was celebrated with great joy (Lev 23:40).

CHAPTER 13

Here: 1. The people of Israel are rebuked and threatened for their idolatry (vv. 1–4). 2. They are rebuked and threatened for their recklessness, pride, self-indulgence, and other abuses of their wealth and prosperity (vv. 5–8). 3. The ruin coming on them is foretold (vv. 12–13, 15–16). 4. Those among them who still maintain respect for their God are encouraged to hope that he will come to help them (vv. 9–11, 14).

Verses 1–4

Idolatry was the sin that most easily entangled the Jewish nation (Heb 12:1) until after the exile; the ten tribes were guilty of it initially, but especially after the days of Ahab. Notice:

1. The provision that God made to prevent their falling into idolatry. We have this in v. 4. He made himself known to them as *the Lord their God*. He told them this from heaven at Mount Sinai. He continued to prove this to them by his prophets and his providences. He gave them a law forbidding them to worship any other: *Thou shalt know no God but me*. He gave them a good reason for this law: *There is no saviour besides me* (v. 4).

2. The honor that Ephraim had as long as he kept clear of idolatry (v. 1): as long as *Ephraim spoke trembling*, or "with trembling," so long *he exalted himself in Israel*.

Those that humble themselves, especially those who humble themselves before God, *shall be exalted* (Mt 23:12).

3. The lamentable growth of idolatry among them (v. 2): *Now they sin more and more*. They make themselves *molten images* (idols). They make them of *their silver*. They make them *according to their own understanding*, according to their own imagination. Or "according to their own likeness," in human form. Though the work of their hands, the idols are loved by their souls, for they say about them, *Let the men that sacrifice kiss the calves* (v. 2).

4. Threats of wrath for their idolatry. Because they are so fond of kissing their calves, God will convict them of their foolishness and make them feel the conviction keenly (v. 3). God tells them that they will be disappointed and *driven away in their wickedness* (Pr 14:32). They will be like the *morning cloud*, the *early dew*. Both *pass away*, and the day proves as dry and hot as ever; their prosperity will be transient, and they themselves will be like the *chaff*, light and worthless, and like the *smoke*, harmful and offensive (see Isa 65:5); and they will be driven away *as the smoke out of the chimneys*.

Verses 5–8

Notice here:

1. The abundant provision God had made for Israel (v. 5): *"I did know thee in the wilderness*, made provision for you even in *a land of great drought*, when no relief was to be found in ordinary ways." The God who knew them and fed them there was "a friend indeed."

2. Their unworthy, ungrateful abuse of God's favor toward them. God not only took care of them in the desert but also gave them possession of Canaan: *according to their pasture, so were they filled* (v. 6). When they came into Canaan, they fed themselves *to the full* and were satisfied. Their situation would have been more promising if they had been more moderate in using their plenty. *They were filled, and their heart was exalted* (they became proud). Their self-indulgence made them proud, arrogant, and self-confident. The best comment on this is that of Moses: *But Jeshurun waxed* (became) *fat and kicked* (Dt 32:13–15). They began to think they had no further need of God: *Their heart was exalted; therefore have they forgotten me* (v. 6). We should acknowledge that we live on God when we live on common providence, even though we do not live on miracles, as Israel did in the desert.

3. God's just displeasure against them for their corrupt ingratitude (vv. 7–8). *I will be unto them as a lion* and *as a leopard*. Some read it—and the original will bear this sense—"I will be as a leopard in the way of Assyria." The judgments of God will surprise them just when they are going to the Assyrians to seek protection and help from them. He will *rend the caul of their heart* (attack them and rip them open) (v. 8). The lion is seen to aim at the heart of the animal it is attacking, and God will *devour them like a lion*. The judgments of God against impenitent sinners will be terrible. They will tear open their hearts and fill the soul with confusion.

Verses 9–16

The first of these verses is the summary, or contents, of all the rest (v. 9). All the blame of Israel's ruin is laid on themselves: *"O Israel! thou hast destroyed thyself*," or, "It has destroyed thee, O Israel!" All the glory of Israel's help, on the other hand, is ascribed to God: *But in me is thy help*. "Your case is bad, but it is not desperate. *Thou hast destroyed thyself*, but come to me and I will help you." Now, in the remaining verses, we may see:

1. How the people of Israel have destroyed themselves. It is said (v. 16) that they *rebelled against God*.

1.1. They store up wrath for themselves for the day of wrath (Ro 2:5), and so they destroy themselves. Their former sins contributed to their present destruction, for they were *laid up in store with God* (Dt 32:34–35; Job 14:17). The sin of sinners is not forgotten until it is forgiven.

1.2. They are their own ruin because they will not do what they should toward their own salvation (v. 13). They will be thrown into pangs and agonies, very sharp and severe and yet, like the pains of a woman in labor, hopeful and promising, tending toward their deliverance, and though God punishes them by these, he intends them for their good, as correction. They are corrected so that they may not be destroyed. But they do not repent and so cannot expect the joy of deliverance (v. 13). Those who delay their conversion are in danger of miscarrying in it. Here is a sad description of the desolation they are condemned to (vv. 15–16). It is assumed that *Ephraim is fruitful among his children*; but sin turns this fruitful tribe into barrenness. The instrument is an *east wind*, representing a foreign enemy that will invade it. It is called the *wind of the Lord*. Is Ephraim a rich tribe? The foreign enemy will make it poor and exhaust its sources of wealth. Is it a populous and numerous tribe? The enemy will depopulate it and make its people few: *Samaria shall become desolate*, without inhabitants.

2. How God will help this self-destroying people, how he will be their only help (v. 10): *"I will be thy King,* to rule and save you."* Although they have rebelled against him, he will still be their king. Our situation would be truly sad if God were not better to us than we are to ourselves.

2.1. God will be their king when they have no other king. *Where is the king that may save thee in all thy cities? Where are thy judges,* who by administering public justice should preserve the public peace? Their demand, *Give me a king and princes,* refers:

2.1.1. To the foolish, evil desire that the whole nation had for a kingly government. They rejected Samuel, and in him *the Lord* (1Sa 8:7), when they said, *Give us a king* like the nations, whereas the *Lord was their King* (1Sa 12:12).

2.1.2. To the desire that the ten tribes had for a kingly government different from that of the house of David, because they thought that was too harsh on them and hoped they would better themselves by making Jeroboam king. Providence gave them first Saul and later Jeroboam. Were they any better for them? Saul was *given in anger*—given in *thunder* (1Sa 12:18–19)—and soon after was *taken away in wrath* on Mount Gilboa (1Sa 31:1). The kingly government of the ten tribes was given in anger also, because of their hostility toward the house of David, and God was now about to take that away in wrath through the power of the king of Assyria.

2.2. God will do for them what no other king could do if they had one (v. 14): *I will ransom them from the power of the grave*. Their rescue will come about by ransom, and we know who it was who paid their ransom and what the ransom was, for it was the Son of Man who *gave his life a ransom for many* (Mt 20:28). Christ has abolished death; he has broken its power and changed its nature and so enabled us to triumph over it. Thanks be to God, therefore, who gives us the victory (1Co 15:57)!

CHAPTER 14

This chapter is a lesson for penitents, and there were some of those in Israel. Here are: 1. Directions for repenting (vv. 1–3). 2. Encouragements to repent, based on God's readiness to receive sinners who turn back to him (vv. 4, 8) and the benefits he has for them (vv. 5–7). 3. A solemn commendation of these things (v. 9).

Verses 1–3

Here we have:

1. A kind invitation given to sinners to repent (v. 1). It is directed to Israel, God's professing people. They are called to *return*. Conversion must be preached even to those who are within the confines of the church, not just to those outside. *"Thou hast fallen by thy iniquity,"* "hast stumbled," as some read it. Their idols were their *stumbling blocks* (Zep 1:3), their downfall. Sin is a downfall, and it is necessary for those who have fallen in sin to get up again in repentance. *"Return to the Lord thy God;* return to him as *the Lord* whom you have dependence on, as *thy God."* Return *even to the Lord;* come home to the Lord. The ancient Jews had a saying based on this: "Repentance is a great thing, for it brings people back to the throne of glory."

2. Instructions as to how to repent.

2.1. They must come to themselves and consider what to say to God when they come to him (Lk 15:17): *Take with you words* (v. 2). They are required to bring not sacrifices and offerings, but penitential prayers, the fruit of their lips, yet not only of the lips but also of the heart. The heart must dictate to the tongue.

2.2. They must come to themselves and consider what to do. They must not only take with them words but must turn back to the Lord: inwardly in their hearts and outwardly in their lives.

3. Words teaching them what to say, which God is willing to put into their mouths for their assistance and encouragement. They are:

3.1. Words of petition. We are here told to ask for two things:

3.1.1. To be acquitted from guilt. When we turn back to the Lord, we must say to him, "Lord, *take away all iniquity* (forgive all our sins) (v. 2). Lift it as a burden or as the stumbling block that we have often fallen over. Take it all away by a free and full forgiveness, for we cannot strike it away by ourselves."

3.1.2. To be accepted as righteous in God's sight: *"Receive us graciously* (v. 2). Let us enjoy your favor and love. Receive our prayer graciously; be pleased with the good that we have been enabled to do through your grace." "Take good" is the sense; "take it to give to us"; the margin reads, "Give good." This follows from the petition for taking away sin, for until sin is taken away, we have no reason to expect any good from God. "Give good, the good that will make us good and keep us from turning to sin again."

3.2. Words of promise. These are also put in their mouths, not to move God, but to move themselves. They are to promise and vow two things:

3.2.1. Thanksgiving. "Forgive our sins and accept us, and *will we render the calves of our lips.*" "The fruit of our lips" is the reading of the Septuagint (a Greek version of the Old Testament), and the word for "fruit" is one that was used for burnt offerings, and so it agrees with the Hebrew. The writer to the Hebrews quotes this phrase (Heb 13:15) and considers the *fruit of our lips* to mean the *sacrifice of praise to God, giving thanks to his name.*

3.2.2. Amendment of life. They are taught to promise not only verbal acknowledgments but also a real reformation of life. They will not trust in their alliances abroad: *Asshur* (Assyria) *shall not save us* (v. 3). "We will not seek the help of the Assyrians when we are in distress, as we did before (5:13; 7:11; 8:9); we will sneer at being indebted to the Assyrians for help. *We will not ride on horses,* that is, we will not court Egypt," for that was where they acquired their horses (Dt 17:16; Isa 30:16; 31:1, 3). We must promise that we will not set our hearts on the gains of this world or pride ourselves on our external religious acts, for that is, in effect, to *say to the work of our hands, You are our gods.*

3.3. Words of pleading put into their mouths: for *in thee the fatherless find mercy* (compassion) (v. 3). People who are truly aware of their helplessness and are willing to acknowledge it may expect to find help in God. They plead God's unfailing love to those who are in that condition: *With thee the fatherless* not only may find, but *do find,* and will find, *mercy.*

Verses 4–7

Here is a favorable answer to the prayers of returning Israel. They seek God's face, and they will not *seek in vain* (Isa 45:19).

1. Do they dread God's displeasure and pray to be saved from it, and do they turn back to him for that reason? He assures them that when they submit, *his anger is turned away from them.* This is given as the basis for all the other favors promised here.

2. Do they pray for the *taking away of iniquity* (forgiveness of their sins)? He assures them that he will cure them of their backsliding, as he promised (Jer 3:22). He will heal the guilt of their backsliding by forgiving mercy and heal their tendency to backslide by renewing grace.

3. Do they pray that God will receive them graciously? In answer to that, it is promised, *I will love them freely* (v. 4).

4. Do they pray that God will "give good," that he will make them good? In answer to that, it is promised, *I will be as the dew unto Israel* (v. 5). This guarantees spiritual blessings in heavenly things (Eph 1:3), and it follows from the curing of their backsliding, for forgiving mercy is always accompanied with renewing grace. Because the bad is made good by the grace of God, they will be made better by the same grace, for grace, wherever it is true, is growing. They will grow like the lily. The growth of the lily is very fast. Its roots seem lost in the ground all winter, but when they are refreshed by the spring dews, the flower starts to grow quickly. This is how the grace of God makes the most of young converts, sometimes very quickly. They will grow downward and be firmer. The lily indeed grows fast and grows fine, but it soon fades and is easily uprooted. It is therefore promised to Israel here that along with the flower of the lily they will have the root of the cedar: they will *cast forth* (send down) *their roots as Lebanon,* like the trees of Lebanon, which, having taken deep root, cannot be uprooted (Am 9:15). Spiritual growth mostly consists in growth in the roots, which is out of sight. The more we depend on Christ and draw sap and power from him, the more deeply motivated our religious faith is and the more dedicated and resolved we are in it—the more we *cast forth our roots* (v. 6): *His branches shall spread* on all sides. Ephraim will grow like the vine, whose branches extend furthest of any woody plant (v. 7). They will be graceful and acceptable both to God and to other people. They are compared here to trees that are delightful:

4.1. To the sight: *His beauty shall be as the olive tree,* which is always green (Jer 11:16). Services of worship are the beauty of the church. Holiness is the beauty of a soul.

4.2. To the smell: *His smell* (fragrance) will be *as Lebanon* (v. 6), and *his scent* as *the wine of Lebanon* (v. 7). The church is compared to a garden of spices. Grace is the perfume of the soul (Ecc 7:1). The "memorial thereof" will be like the wine of Lebanon (v. 7, margin); their surviving honors when they are gone will be like the wine of Lebanon, which has a delicate flavor. The church is compared here to the vine and the olive, which produce useful fruits, to the honor of God and human beings.

Verses 8–9

Let us now hear the conclusion of the whole matter (Ecc 12:13):

1. About Ephraim (v. 8).

1.1. His repentance and reformation: *Ephraim shall say, What have I to do any more with idols?* Some read it as God reasoning and arguing with him here as to why he should renounce idolatry: "O Ephraim! What more have I to do with idols? What agreement can there be between me and idols?" As our translation reads it, however, God promises to bring Ephraim to this conclusion and keep him to it: *Ephraim shall say,* "What have I to do anymore with idols?" He has promised not to *say any more to the works of his hands, You are my gods* (v. 3). Ephraim has been *joined to his idols* (4:17); but God will produce such a change in him that he will loathe them as much as he loved them.

1.2. The gracious notice God takes of it: *I have heard him, and observed him.* "I have heard and will look on him," as some read it. God *observed* Ephraim to see whether he would produce fruits in keeping with his profession of repentance (Mt 3:8).

1.3. The mercy of God that is intended for him. Before, Israel was compared with a tree, but now God compares himself to one. He will be to his people like the branches of a tree: "*I am like a green fir tree* and will be so to you." He will be either a sun and a shield (Ps 84:11) or a shade and a shield (Ps 121:5), according to what they need. He will also be like the root of a tree: *From me is thy fruit found* (v. 8): from him we receive grace and strength to enable us to do our duty. Whatever fruits of righteousness (Php 1:11) we produce, all the praise for them is due to God.

2. About everyone who reads the words of the prophecy of this book (v. 9): *Who is wise? He shall understand these things.* Those who are wise in doing their duty, who are discerning in matters of practical religious faith, are most likely to know and understand the truths and providences of God that are a mystery to others (Jn 7:17). To those who are good, the right ways of God are and will be the fragrance of life (2Co 2:16): *The just shall walk in them.* But to those who are evil, the right ways of God will be the smell of death (2Co 2:16): *The transgressors shall fall* not only in their own wrong ways but even *in the right ways of the Lord.* The influence of what is received depends on the qualities of the receiver. The same sun softens wax and hardens clay. Of all sinners, however, those who have the most dangerous falls are those who fall *in the ways of God.*

A Practical and Devotional Exposition of the Book of the Prophet

Joel

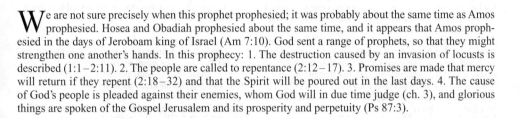

We are not sure precisely when this prophet prophesied; it was probably about the same time as Amos prophesied. Hosea and Obadiah prophesied about the same time, and it appears that Amos prophesied in the days of Jeroboam king of Israel (Am 7:10). God sent a range of prophets, so that they might strengthen one another's hands. In this prophecy: 1. The destruction caused by an invasion of locusts is described (1:1–2:11). 2. The people are called to repentance (2:12–17). 3. Promises are made that mercy will return if they repent (2:18–32) and that the Spirit will be poured out in the last days. 4. The cause of God's people is pleaded against their enemies, whom God will in due time judge (ch. 3), and glorious things are spoken of the Gospel Jerusalem and its prosperity and perpetuity (Ps 87:3).

CHAPTER 1

This chapter is the description of a terrible invasion of the country of Judah by locusts. Some think that the prophet was speaking about it as something to come and that he was giving a warning in advance, since the prophets usually warned of coming judgments. Others think that it was now happening and that he wanted to stir the people by it and wake them up to repent. 1. It is spoken of as a judgment (vv. 1–7). 2. All kinds of people sharing in the calamity are called on to mourn it (vv. 8–13). 3. They are directed to look to God in their mourning and to humble themselves before him (vv. 14–20).

Verses 1–7

Joel spoke about the harsh judgment that was now coming, or was to come, on Judah, for their sins. Notice:

1. The judgment was unparalleled in previous ages or in the memory of anyone living (v. 2). Those who surpass their predecessors in sin may expect to fall under greater judgments than any of their predecessors knew. It was also such as would not be forgotten in future ages (v. 3): "*Tell you your children of it* so that they may take warning and learn obedience by the things you have suffered. Let *your children tell their children, and their children another generation* also; let them tell it to *teach their children* to stand in awe of God and his judgments and tremble before him."

2. The judgment is an invasion of the country of Judea by a great army.

2.1. Many interpreters both ancient and modern understand it to refer to armies of men, the forces of the Assyrians, who, under Sennacherib, *took all the defended cities of Judah* and wreaked havoc on the country. Some suggest that the four kinds of creatures named here (v. 4) represent the four monarchies that, each in turn, oppressed the Jewish people, one destroying what had escaped the fury of the other.

2.2. However, it seems much more likely that the images should be understood to refer literally to armies of insects

coming on the land and eating up its fruits. The plague of locusts in Egypt lasted only a few days (Ex 10:1–20); this plague seems to have continued for four years successively, as some think, because four kinds of insects are mentioned here (v. 4); but others think they came all in one year. Although a devastation by these insects is primarily intended here, it is expressed in language that may be applied to the destruction of the country by a foreign enemy. If this nation of locusts does not subdue them, then another nation will come to ruin them. These creatures are *locusts* and *caterpillars, palmerworms* and *cankerworms* (v. 4). They were all small insects, but when they came in vast swarms, they were formidable and consumed everything in their path. The weaker the instrument that God employs, the greater his power is exalted. They are called here *a nation* (v. 6) because they act as if with a common purpose, for although *the locusts have no king, yet go they forth all of them by bands* (Pr 30:27). They are said to have *teeth of a lion* because they complete such a great and terrible work. Locusts become like lions when they come armed with a divine commission. They destroy not only the grass and grain but also the trees (v. 7): the *vine is laid waste*. Vermin eat the leaves that would shelter the fruit while it is ripening. They even eat the bark of the fig tree and so kill it. Therefore the *fig tree does not blossom*, nor is there *fruit in the vine* (2:22).

3. A call to the drunkards to mourn this judgment (v. 5): *Awake and weep, all you drinkers of wine.* It would touch them at a tender spot; the *new wine* they loved so much would be *cut off from their mouth.* The more people base their happiness on satisfying physical desires, the more critical physical afflictions are on them. The people who drank water did not need to worry when the vine was destroyed; they could live just as well without it as they had been living.

Verses 8–13

They are called to mourn (v. 8) as a virgin mourns the death of her lover to whom she was betrothed, or as a

1299

young woman recently married, from whom the *husband of her youth*, or the husband to whom she was married when she was young, is suddenly taken away by death.

1. Let the farmers and vine growers mourn (v. 11). They will see the fruit of their labor being devoured before their eyes, and they will not be able to save any of it. *The field is laid waste* (v. 10): all that was produced is ruined. *The land mourns*: the ground is dried up and looks sorrowful. The people are justly brought to mourn their loss and lack of the *wheat and barley*. The trees are destroyed, not only the *vine and the fig tree* (as before v. 7) but also the *pomegranate, palm tree*, and *apple tree*, all the *trees of the field*, as well as those of the orchard, trees for timber as well as fruit trees. See how necessary it is that we depend continually on God and his providence, for our own hands are insufficient for us.

2. Let the priests, the Lord's ministers, mourn, for they share deeply in the disaster: *Gird yourselves* with sackcloth (v. 13). The ministers of the altar must *lament and howl*, for the *meat offering* (grain offering) and *drink offering* are *cut off from the house of the Lord* (v. 9). "He is your God in a special way, and so it is expected that you should be more concerned than others about what hinders the service of his sanctuary." As far as any public trouble obstructs the course of religion, it is to be sadly mourned for that reason more than any other, especially by the priests, the Lord's ministers.

Verses 14–20

Many tears were shed at the destruction of the crops of the earth by the locusts; now those tears must be channeled in the right way, to repentance and humiliation before God.

1. The priests are ordered to appoint a general fast, and a proclamation is issued calling on all to observe it. When we are suffering public judgments, there should be public humiliation.

1.1. A day is to be set aside for this purpose, "a day of restraint" (v. 14, margin), a day on which people must be restrained from their ordinary business.

1.2. It must be *a fast*, a religious abstaining from food and drink, from anything more than is absolutely necessary. When we take part in such a fast, we acknowledge that we are unworthy of necessary food, that we have forfeited the right to it. We punish ourselves and deny our physical appetite.

1.3. There must be a sacred assembly. Everyone has contributed to the national guilt, all share in the national disaster, and so they must all join in professions of repentance.

1.4. They must come together in the temple, *the house of the Lord* their *God*, because that is the house of prayer, and it is there that they can hope to meet with God, because it is the place he *chose to put his name there* (1Ki 11:36).

1.5. They must *sanctify* this fast, must observe it with sincere devotion.

2. Some considerations are suggested to motivate them to declare this fast and observe it strictly.

2.1. God is beginning his challenge toward them. It is time to *cry unto the Lord*, for *the day of the Lord is at hand* (v. 15). "The day of his judgment is very near, *at hand*; it *will not slumber* (2Pe 2:3), and so you should not." It will be very terrible. There is no fleeing from him except by fleeing to him.

2.2. They see themselves already suffering under the signs of his displeasure. It is time to fast and pray, for their distress is very great (v. 16). They should look into their own houses to see that there is no plenty there, and they

should look into God's house and see the effects of the judgment there; joy and gladness have been *cut off from the house of God* (v. 16).

2.3. The prophet returns to describe the disaster in terrible detail. Grain and cattle are the farmers' staple commodities; here they are deprived of both.

2.3.1. The locusts have devoured the grain (v. 17). *The seed is rotten under the clods* (seeds are shriveled), either through too much rain or lack of rain, or perhaps some insects underground ate it all up.

2.3.2. The cattle perish too for lack of grass (v. 18): *How do the beasts groan!* Even *the flocks of sheep*, which live on very short grass, *are made desolate* and are suffering.

3. The prophet stirs them to cry out to God in imitation of the examples of others.

3.1. His own example (v. 19): *O Lord! to thee will I cry.* The motivation that makes him cry out to God is not so much any personal suffering as the national disaster: the *fire has devoured the pastures of the wilderness* (v. 19), which seems to refer to some parching and scorching heat of the sun, which consumed them all.

3.2. The example of the lower creatures: "*The beasts of the field* not only *groan* but also *cry unto thee* (v. 20)." The complaints of the wild animals here are due to a lack of water and grass.

CHAPTER 2

We have here: 1. A further description of the terrible destruction that would be made on the land of Judah by the locusts (vv. 1–11). 2. A call to the people to turn back to God to repent, fast, pray, and seek him for mercy, with directions for how to do this rightly (vv. 12–17). 3. A promise that on their repentance God would remove the judgment and restore to them an abundance of good things (vv. 18–27). 4. A prediction of the establishment of the kingdom of the Messiah in the world by the outpouring of the Spirit in the last days (vv. 28–32). The beginning of this chapter is terrible with the signs of God's wrath, but its end is encouraging with assurances of his favor. The result is that although it is only the last paragraph of this chapter that points directly to Gospel times, the whole of it may be considered as a type and figure, representing the curses of the law coming on people for their sins and the comforts of the Gospel flowing from their repentance.

Verses 1–11

God accuses his own professing people of their sins and carries out on them the judgment written in the Law (Dt 28:42): *The fruit of thy land shall the locust consume.* Here:

1. War is declared (v. 1): *Blow the trumpet in Zion* to sound the alarm to Judah and Jerusalem that judgment is coming, so that they can *prepare to meet their God* (Am 4:12) by their prayers and tears. It was the priests' work to blow the trumpet (Nu 10:8), both as an appeal to God in times of distress and as a summons to the people to come together to seek his face. It is the work of ministers to express warnings from the word of God concerning the fatal effects of sin.

2. A general idea is given of the day of battle that *is nigh at hand* (v. 1). It is the *day of the Lord*, the day of his judgment, *a day of darkness and gloominess* (v. 2), literally so, for the swarms of locusts are so large and dense that they will darken the sky (Ex 10:15). The darkness of this day will come as suddenly *as the morning spreading upon the mountains*, and as irresistibly.

3. The army is drawn up in array (v. 2): they are a *great people, and a strong*. The army is here described as daring: they *are as horses* (v. 4); and, like war horses and like *horsemen*, galloping along with martial fire and fury, *so they shall run* (v. 4). Some of the old commentators noticed that the head of a locust is very like the head of a horse in shape. They are loud and noisy — *like the noise of chariots* driven furiously over rough ground *on the tops of the mountains* (v. 5). The noise is like the crackling *noise of a flame* that *devours the stubble*. When God's judgments are about, they make a great noise. These soldiers are also very regular, keeping ranks *as a strong people set in battle array* (v. 5). *They shall not break their ranks, nor one thrust another* (not swerve from their course and not jostle each other) (vv. 7–8).

4. A terrible execution is carried out by this formidable army in both the country and the city (v. 3). If you look at the fields they have eaten up, they are *as a desolate wilderness*, and in the city they will *climb the wall* (v. 7), *run upon the houses*, and *enter in at the windows like a thief* (v. 9).

5. Strong impressions are made on the people by this invasion. These enemies are invulnerable and therefore irresistible (v. 8). "One person is in anguish for their field, another for their vineyard, *and all faces gather blackness* (every face turns pale)." When God frowns on people, the lights of heaven will give them little joy.

6. The commander in chief of this formidable army is God himself (v. 11). This makes the *great day* of the Lord *very terrible*.

Verses 12–17

God brings us into difficulties so that he may bring us to repentance and so bring us back to himself. Here is a gracious invitation:

1. To personal repentance, exercised in the soul. Everyone must amend their own life and mourn for their own sin, and then we would all be amended and all be found among God's mourners. Notice:

1.1. What it is to repent, for it is the same thing that the Lord our God still requires of us (Mic 6:8).

1.1.1. We must be truly humbled for our sins, be sorry we have offended God by our sin, and be ashamed we have wronged ourselves by our sin. There must be outward expressions of sorrow and shame, *fasting, weeping*, and *mourning* (v. 12). But the outward expressions of sorrow must spring from within. And so it follows, *Rend* (tear) *your heart, and not your garments* (v. 13). Rending the heart is what God looks for and requires; it is the *broken and contrite heart* that he *will not despise* (Ps 51:17).

1.1.2. We must be thoroughly converted to our God, coming back home to him when we separate ourselves from sin: *Turn you even to me, saith the Lord* (v. 12), and again (v. 13), *Turn unto the Lord your God*.

1.2. What arguments are used here to persuade this people to turn back to the Lord in this way *with all their hearts*. We are sure that he is a good God. We must *turn to the Lord our God* not only because he has been just and righteous in punishing us for our sins but also because he is *gracious and merciful* (v. 13) in receiving us when we repent. *He repents him of the evil*; not that human beings change his mind, but when the sinner's mind is changed, God's way toward him is changed; the sentence is reversed, and the curse of the law is taken away and he relents from sending disaster. There is no question at all that if we truly repent of our sins, God will forgive them and be reconciled to us, but whether he will remove this or that form of suffering that we are under may be questioned. The possibility of it, however, should encourage us to repent.

2. To a public and national repentance, a national act by which the people could give glory to God and show the neighboring nations what it was that qualified them for God's gracious response in mercy to them. The congregation must be called together (vv. 15–16). The trumpet was blown earlier (v. 1) to sound an *alarm of war*, but now it must be blown to announce a peace treaty. What was said in 1:14 is repeated here: "*Call a solemn assembly; gather the people; sanctify the congregation*; appoint a set time for sacred preparation beforehand and get them into the right frame of mind to prepare themselves. Let not the greatest people be excused, but *assemble the elders*, the judges and magistrates. Let not the lowliest be passed over, but *gather the children, and those that suck the breasts* (v. 16)." Private joys must give way to public sorrows, both those for affliction and those for sin. The priests, *the Lord's ministers*, must lead the assembly, being God's mouthpiece to the people and theirs to God. They must officiate *between the porch* (the temple porch) *and the altar*. The people must see them weeping and wrestling with God there, like their ancestor Jacob (Ge 32:24–28), and be helped to have the same devout godliness. Their request must be, *Spare thy people, O Lord!* (v. 17). "Let the nations not make them a proverb, or 'a byword,'" as some read it; "let it never be said, 'As poor and beggarly as an Israelite.'"

Verses 18–27

They prayed that God would *spare them*, and notice here with what *good words and comfortable words* (Zec 1:13) he answered them, for God's promises are real answers to the prayers of faith. Notice:

1. From where the promised mercy will arise (v. 18): God will *be jealous for his land* and *pity his people*. He will restore their forfeited comforts to them.

2. What his mercy will be, in several examples:

2.1. The destroying army will be dispersed and defeated (v. 20): "*I will remove far off from you the northern army*, that army of locusts that invaded you from the north. Nothing will remain of these swarms of insects except their stench." Many interpreters understand this northern army to refer to that of Sennacherib, which was dispersed when by it God had *accomplished his whole work upon Mount Zion and upon Jerusalem* (Isa 10:12).

2.2. The destroyed land will be watered and made fruitful. It is promised (v. 22) that *the pastures of the wilderness*, the open pastures that the locusts left as bare as the desert, will again *spring*, and the *trees shall again bear their fruit*, especially the *fig tree and the vine*. It will be so, for "*the Lord has given* and will give you the *former rain and the latter rain* (v. 23)," and will give them moderately and in due season, the *latter rain in the first month*, when it is needed and expected.

2.3. All their losses will be made up for (v. 25): "*I will restore to you the years that the locust has eaten*; you will be comforted according to the time that you have suffered (Ps 90:15) and will have years of plenty to compensate for the years of famine."

2.4. They will have a plentiful supply of all good things. If you look into their storehouses, you will find *the floors full of wheat, and the fats* (vats) *overflowing with wine and oil* (v. 24), whereas in the day of their distress the *wine and oil languished* and *the barns were broken down* (1:10, 17). Some expositors understand these promises figuratively, as pointing to Gospel grace. When God sends us his promises for us to enjoy, his grace to be their basis and his Spirit to be their author, he has sent us, according to his promise here (v. 19), *corn, and wine, and oil*, or what is indescribably better.

3. What use will be made of this response of God's mercy.

3.1. God will receive the glory, for they will *rejoice in the Lord their God* (v. 23). They will not praise their idols or call their grain and wine the *rewards that their lovers have given them* (Hos 2:12).

3.2. They will have the comfort and spiritual benefit of them. Their reputation will be regained (v. 19): "*I will no more make you a reproach among the heathen* (I will never again make you an object of scorn to the nations), who triumphed over your disasters and gloated over you (vv. 26–27)." Their joys will be revived (v. 23). They will *rejoice in the Lord their God*, not so much in the good things themselves that have been given them as in the good hand that gives them. The *joy of harvest* and the joy of a festival must both end in God, whose love we should taste in all the gifts of his goodness, so that we may make him our chief joy, just as he is our chief good and the fountain of all good to us (Jer 2:13). Their faith in God will be confirmed and increased. This is promised here (v. 27): *You shall know that I am in the midst of Israel, the Holy One in the midst of thee* (Hos 11:9), *and that I am the Lord your God, and none else*. We should seek to come to know God more in all providences, those involving mercy and those involving suffering.

Verses 28–32

The promises of grain, wine, and oil would be acceptable to a devastated country, but we must not rest in those things. These verses refer to better things (Heb 11:40; 12:24), both the kingdom of grace and the kingdom of glory. Notice:

1. How the kingdom of grace will be introduced by a plentiful outpouring of the Spirit (vv. 28–29). The apostle Peter has given us an assurance that when the Spirit was poured out on the apostles, on the Day of Pentecost (Ac 2:1), that was the very thing *which was spoken of here by the prophet Joel* (vv. 16–17). We often read in the Old Testament of the Spirit of the Lord coming in droplets, as it were, on the judges and prophets whom God raised up for extraordinary service, but now the Spirit will be poured out plentifully in a full stream, as was promised (Isa 44:3). The time fixed for this is *afterward*; after the fulfillment of the foregoing promises, this will be fulfilled. The Spirit will be *poured out upon all flesh*, not only on Jews, as up to that time, but also on Gentiles, for in Christ there is no distinction between Jew and Greek (Ro 10:11–12). The Jews understand the phrase to refer to all flesh in the land of Israel, and Peter himself did not fully understand it as speaking of the Gentiles until he saw it fulfilled in the descent of the Holy Spirit on Cornelius and his friends, who were Gentiles (Ac 10:44–45), which was simply a continuation of the same gift that was given on the Day of Pentecost. "*Your old men*, who are past their prime and whose spirits are beginning to decay, and *your young men*, who have now only a little experience of divine things, will still *dream dreams* and *see visions*. God will reveal himself by dreams and visions to both young and old. *They shall prophesy*; they will receive new revelations of divine things, not only for their own private use but also for the benefit of the church. They will interpret Scripture and speak about things distant and future. By these extraordinary gifts the Christian church was first founded and set up, the Scriptures written, and the ministry settled.

2. How the kingdom of glory will be introduced by the change of nature (vv. 30–31). The outpouring of the Spirit will give great assurance to the righteous, but let the unrighteous hear this and tremble. There is a great and terrible Day of the Lord coming. This is to have its complete fulfillment at the end of time. It was fulfilled in part in the death of Christ, which is called the *judgment of this world* (Jn 12:31), when the earth quaked and the sun was darkened; and it was fulfilled more fully in the destruction of Jerusalem, which was a figure of the general judgment. The judgments of God on a sinful world and the frequent destruction of evil kingdoms by fire and sword are signs of the judgment of the world on the last day.

3. How the security and happiness of all true believers will be assured in both the first and the second coming of Jesus Christ (v. 32). This speaks of individual people, for the New Testament is more concerned with them, and less with kingdoms and nations, than the Old. Notice that there is:

3.1. A salvation that is worked out. Although the Day of the Lord *will* be great and terrible, *in Mount Zion and in Jerusalem there shall be deliverance* from its terror. Christ is himself not only the *Saviour* but also *the salvation*; he is so *to the ends of the earth* (Ac 13:47). This deliverance, which is stored up for us in the covenant of grace, fulfills the promises made to the ancestors. See Lk 1:72.

3.2. A remnant who share in this salvation and are saved. The pledges of that salvation are *in* the souls and spirits of *that remnant. Christ in you, the hope of glory* (Col 1:27). Those who will be saved on the great day are:

3.2.1. Those who sincerely call on God: *Whosoever shall call upon the name of the Lord*, whether Jew or Gentile (Ro 10:13), *shall be delivered*. This calling on God presumes knowledge of him, faith in him, desire toward him, dependence on him, and a careful obedience to him, for without that, crying out *Lord, Lord* (Lk 13:25), will not do us any good.

3.2.2. Those who are effectively called by God. The deliverance is certain to *the remnant whom the Lord shall call*.

CHAPTER 3

At the end of the previous chapter we read a gracious promise of deliverance in Mount Zion and Jerusalem; this chapter is a comment on that promise, showing what that deliverance will be like, how it will be carried out by the destruction of the church's enemies, and how it will be completed in the eternal rest and joy of the church. This was fulfilled in part in the deliverance of Jerusalem from the attempt that Sennacherib made on it in Hezekiah's time (2Ki 19:35–37), and later in the return of the Jews from exile in Babylon, and in other deliverances brought about for the Jewish church between that and Christ's coming. It has a further reference, however, to the great redemption brought for us by Jesus Christ and to the destruction of our spiritual enemies and all their agents. Here is a prediction: 1. Of God's judging the enemies of his people (vv. 1–8). 2. Of God's judging all nations when the limit of their sins has been reached (Ge 15:16; Mt 23:32) (vv. 9–17). 3. Of the provision God has made to refresh his people (vv. 18–21). Those promises were written to teach us, so that we, through endurance and the encouragement of the Scriptures, can have hope (Ro 15:4).

Verses 1–8

The *year of the redeemed* (Isa 63:4) and the *year of recompences for the controversy of Zion* (a year of retribution, to uphold Zion's cause) (Isa 34:8) will come. Here we have a prophecy of what will be done whenever it comes, because it comes often, and at the end of time it will come once and for all.

1. It will be the *year of the redeemed*, for God will *bring again the captivity* (restore the fortunes) *of Judah and Jerusalem* (v. 1). Although the slavery of God's people may be painful and long, it will not be eternal. The slavery in Egypt ended eventually. *Let my son go, that he may serve me* (Ex 4:23). The exile in Babylon will also end well. The Lord Jesus will provide for the effective redemption of enslaved souls from the control of sin and Satan and will proclaim that *acceptable year*, and the *opening of the prison to those that were bound* (Isa 61:1–2; Lk 4:18–19).

2. It will be the year of retribution, to uphold Zion's cause. God will *lead captivity captive* (Ps 68:18); he will take captive those who took his people captive (Rev 3:10). Notice:

2.1. Who will be judged—*all nations* (v. 2). This shows that:

2.1.1. All nations have exposed themselves to the judgment of God for doing wrong to his people.

2.1.2. Whichever nation wronged God's nation, they would not go unpunished, for those who disturb the Israel of God will be made to realize that they are disturbing the apple of his eye (Zec 2:8). The neighboring nations, however, will be particularly judged—*Tyre, and Sidon, and all the coasts of Palestine*, or the Philistines, who have been troublesome neighbors to the Israel of God (v. 4).

2.2. The sitting of this court of law for judgment. All these nations will be *gathered* (v. 2). They will be *brought down into the valley of Jehoshaphat*, which lay near Jerusalem, and there *God will plead* (enter into judgment) *with them*. It was in this valley of Jehoshaphat, as Dr. Lightfoot suggests, that Sennacherib's army, or part of it, lay when it was destroyed by an angel (2Ki 19:35–37).

2.3. The plaintiff being called, on whose behalf this prosecution is set in motion; it is *for my people, for my heritage Israel*. It is their cause that God will now jealously argue.

2.4. The charge leveled against the nations. They have insulted God many times through their idolatry, but the basis of the charge God has against them is the disrespect they have shown his people and the vessels of his sanctuary. They have been abusive to the people of Israel, *scattering them among the nations* (v. 2). They have *parted their land, cast lots for my people*, and *sold them* (v. 3). When they took them prisoners, they did *not increase their wealth by their price* (Ps 44:12), but sold them for pleasure rather than profit. They *gave a boy* taken in war for the *hire of a harlot*, and *a girl* for as many bottles of wine as would be enough for them in one drinking bout—*a goodly price* (Zec 11:13) for a son and daughter of Israel to be a slave and a drudge in a tavern or a brothel. What is gained by one sin is commonly spent on another. When the Tyrians and Philistines seized any of the children of Judah and Jerusalem, they sold them to the Greeks, so that they *might remove them far from their* own *border* (v. 6). The nations have unjustly seized *God's silver and gold* (v. 5), which some understand to refer to the wealth of Israel. However, it seems more likely to refer to the *vessels* and *treasures of the temple*, which God here calls his *goodly pleasant things* (his finest treasures). They *carried* these *into their temples* as trophies of their victory over God's Israel, thinking that in so doing they triumphed over Israel's God—and even that their idols triumphed over him. This was why the ark was put in Dagon's temple (1Sa 5:2). Can they claim that either God or his people have done them any wrong, for which they may justify themselves in causing them this trouble?

2.5. The sentence passed on them. Those who oppose God will find they are unable to defend themselves against him. He will repay them *suddenly*. They will not fulfill their purpose in the trouble they intended to bring against God's people. They wanted to *remove them so far from their border* that they would never return to it (v. 6). "But," God says, "*I will raise them out of the place whither you have sold them*, and they will not, as you intended, be buried alive there." The sellers will be paid back in their own coin. They will be justly *sold to the Sabeans*, to *a people far off*. Some think this was fulfilled in the victories gained by the Maccabees over the enemies of the Jews; others think it looks as far forward as the last day.

Verses 9–17

The notice of God's judging the nations may refer to the destruction of Sennacherib, Nebuchadnezzar, Antiochus, and especially the Antichrist, and all the proud enemies of the Christian church. Some of the best interpreters both ancient and modern, however, think that the purpose of these verses is to set out the day of the Last Judgment. We have here:

1. A challenge given to all the enemies of God's kingdom (vv. 9–11). It seems to be spoken ironically here: "*Proclaim you this among the Gentiles*; let all the forces of the nations be summoned to join in alliance against God and his people, if they dare." This is how a God of almighty power defies all the opposing powers of darkness. The nations *come up to the valley of Jehoshaphat* to receive their condemnation (v. 12). *Jehoshaphat* means "the judgment of the Lord." Let them come to the place of God's judgment—which perhaps is the chief reason for the use of this name. The challenge (v. 9) is turned into a summons (v. 12).

2. A charge given to the ministers of God's justice to appear and act against these enemies of his kingdom on earth: *cause thy mighty ones to come down, O Lord!* (v. 11). Some think the words (vv. 9–10) *Prepare war, wake up the mighty men* are not a challenge to the enemies' forces, but a charge to God's forces. However, in v. 13 it is clear that the charge is given to God's forces: *Put you in the sickle, for the harvest is ripe*; that is, *their wickedness is great*, they are ready for destruction.

3. The great gathering that will appear on that solemn day (v. 14): *Multitudes, multitudes in the valley of decision*, the same valley that was called the *valley of Jehoshaphat* before. The Day of Judgment will be the *day of decision*. This will take place in "the valley of the distribution of judgment" (Aramaic), when *every man shall receive according to the things done in the body* (2Co 5:10). It will be in "the valley of threshing" (v. 14, margin), continuing the metaphor of the *harvest* (v. 13). The proud enemies of God's people will then be made as the *dust of the summer threshing floors* (Da 2:35).

4. The amazing change that will then be brought about in the kingdom of nature (v. 15): *The sun and moon shall be darkened*, as before (2:31). Their glory and brightness will be eclipsed by the far greater brightness of that glory in which the Judge will then appear.

5. The different impressions that that day will make.

5.1. It will be a terrible day for evildoers. *The Lord will then speak from Zion and Jerusalem* (v. 16), from the throne of his glory. To evildoers, his speaking will be as terrible as the roaring of a lion—this is the sense of the word.

5.2. It will be a joyful day for the righteous. Their longings will be satisfied: *The Lord will be the hope of his people* (v. 16). He will be the refuge of his people, their home. Their happiness will be confirmed. Their holiness will be completed (v. 17): *Then shall Jerusalem be holy*, the *holy city* indeed. The Gospel church is a holy community, even in its militant state, but will never itself be holiness until it comes to be triumphant. Nothing will enter the New Jerusalem that defiles or produces sin (Rev 21:27). *So shall you know that I am the Lord your God* (v. 17). It is experiential knowledge. They will find him their *hope and strength* (v. 16) in the most difficult times, and so they will *know that he is the Lord their God*.

Verses 18–21

The promises are partially fulfilled in the kingdom of grace, but they will have their complete fulfillment in the kingdom of glory.

1. It is promised that the enemies of the church will be overcome and brought down (v. 19). Egypt, that old enemy of Israel, and Edom, which had an inveterate enmity toward Israel, *shall be a desolation*, not to be inhabited anymore. The reason why God challenges these kingdoms is that they have done *violence against the children of Judah*; see Eze 25:3, 8, 12, 15; 26:2.

2. It is promised that the church will be very happy in its spiritual privileges, even during its militant state, but much more so when it becomes triumphant. Three things are promised:

2.1. Purity. This is mentioned last here, as a reason for the others (v. 21), but we may consider it first, as the basis of the others: *I will cleanse their blood that I have not cleansed.* What could not be cleansed by the sacrifices and purifications of the ceremonial law will be cleansed by the blood of Christ. Although the refining and reforming of the church is a work that carries on slowly, and there is still something that *is not cleansed*, a day is coming when everything that is wrong will be put right.

2.2. Plenty (v. 18). It shows the abundance of vineyards and of cattle in the fields. In order to make the land produce abundant grain, the *rivers of Judah shall flow with water*, so that the country will be like the Garden of Eden (Ps 65:9). This seems to be meant spiritually, however; the graces and comforts of the new covenant are compared to *wine and milk* (Isa 55:1), and the Spirit to *rivers of living water* (Jn 7:38). Moreover, these gifts abound much more in the New Testament than they did in the Old. The fountain of this plenty is in the *house of God*; from there the streams flow out, as those *waters of the sanctuary* flow from *under the threshold of the house* in Ezekiel's vision (Eze 47:1). Christ himself is the fountain; his merit and grace cleanse and refresh us. This fountain is said to water *the valley of Shittim* (valley of acacias), which lay on the other side of the Jordan, a barren valley, which shows that Gospel grace, flowing from Christ, will reach far, even to the Gentile world.

2.3. Perpetuity. This crowns all the others (v. 20): *Judah shall dwell for ever*, and Jerusalem will continue *from generation to generation*. The church of Christ will continue in the world to the end of time.

A Practical and Devotional Exposition of the Book of the Prophet

Amos

A mos was a country farmer. *Amos* means "a burden bearer," and from his name derives a tradition of the Jews that he spoke with a stammer; we may rather say that his speech was weighty and his word was the *burden of the Lord* (Jer 23:33). He was, as most think, from Judah but prophesied chiefly against Israel, and at Bethel (7:13). Some think his style is more direct and rustic than that of some of the other prophets. It appears from his contest with Amaziah the priest of Bethel that he met with opposition but was faithful and bold in rebuking sin and urging the people to repent and reform their lives. He begins with threats against the neighboring nations who are Israel's enemies (ch. 1–2). He then calls Israel to account and judges them for their idolatry and their incorrigibleness under God's judgments (chs. 3–4). He calls them to repentance (ch. 5) and foretells the desolations coming on them despite their self-confidence (ch. 6); he predicts some individual judgments (ch. 7), especially on Amaziah; and after other rebukes and threats (chs. 8–9), he concludes with a promise of the establishment of the Messiah's kingdom and the happiness of God's spiritual Israel.

CHAPTER 1

We have here: 1. The general title of this prophecy (v. 1), with its general theme (v. 2). 2. God's particular declarations against Aram (vv. 3–5), Philistia (vv. 6–8), Tyre (vv. 9–12), and Ammon (vv. 13–15) for their cruelty to his people. This explains God's entering into judgment with the nations (Joel 3:2).

Verses 1–2

Here is:

1. The general character of this prophecy. It consists of *the words which the prophet saw* (v. 1). The prophet saw these words, that is, they were revealed to him in a *vision*, as John is said to see *the voice* that spoke to him (Rev 1:12).

2. The person through whom this prophecy was sent—*Amos, who was among the herdmen of Tekoa* and was one of them. Some think he was a rich dealer in cattle. Others think he was a poor keeper of cattle, for we find (7:14–15) that he was also *a gatherer of wild figs*, which suggests that he could only just earn his living. When God wanted to send a prophet to rebuke and warn his people, he used a shepherd.

3. The people concerned in the prophecy of this book; they are the *ten tribes*, who are now rapidly ripening for ruin. God has raised up for them prophets from among themselves (2:11), but they have paid them no attention. God therefore sends them one from Tekoa, in the land of Judah.

4. The time when these prophecies were delivered, which was in the days of *Uzziah king of Judah*, when the affairs of that kingdom went very well, and of *Jeroboam II king of Israel*, when the affairs of that kingdom went fairly well. However, they must both be told about the sins and the judgments that were coming on them, so that they would not be led by the present gleam of prosperity to flatter themselves into thinking they were secure. It was *two years before the earthquake*, the earthquake that is said to have occurred *in the days of Uzziah* (Zec 14:5).

5. The introduction to these prophecies, containing their general theme (v. 2): *The Lord will roar from Zion.* His threats through his prophets will be as terrible as the roaring of a lion is to the shepherds and their flocks. See Hosea (Hos 11:10) and Joel (Joel 3:16).

Verses 3–15

What the Lord says here may be explained by what he says in Jer 12:14 concerning his *evil neighbors.* Damascus was a close neighbor to Israel on the north, Tyre and Gaza on the west, Edom to the south, Ammon and Moab on the east; all had been evil neighbors.

1. Let us see what is repeated concerning each of these nations. Although those nations will not worship him as their God, they will still be made to realize that they are responsible to him as their Judge.

1.1. The indictment drawn up against them all is the same in the following ways.

1.1.1. They are charged in general with *three transgressions, and with four,* that is, with many sins—as we say "one or two" to mean "a few" and say "three or four" to mean "many." Or it may be read "with three [that is, a variety of] sins, and a fourth" especially, which is specified concerning each of them, though the other three are not.

1.1.2. That the particular sin, which is the fourth, is the sin of persecution.

1.2. The judgment given against them all is the same in the following ways:

1.2.1. That because their sin has plumbed to such depths, *God will not turn away the punishment thereof.* Justice will take its course.

1.2.2. That God *will kindle a fire* among them; this is said concerning all these *evil neighbours* (vv. 4, 7, 10, 12, 14). God will *send a fire* into their cities.

2. Let us see what is distinctive:

2.1. About Damascus, the capital of Syria, a kingdom that was often troublesome to Israel.

2.1.1. The particular sin of Damascus: *They threshed Gilead with threshing instruments of iron* (v. 3), which may be understood literally, as referring to their torturing the inhabitants of Gilead whom they received into their hands, as David put the Ammonites under *saws and harrows* (2Sa 12:31). Or it may be taken figuratively: *He destroyed them, and made them like the dust by threshing* (2Ki 13:7).

2.1.2. The particular punishment of Damascus is that:

2.1.2.1. Fire will be directed not on the chief city but on *the house of Hazael*, which he built, and *it shall devour the palaces* (fortresses) *of Ben-hadad*.

2.1.2.2. The enemy will force his way into the city (v. 5): *I will break the bar of Damascus*. This may be understood figuratively: the strength and security of that great city will prove insufficient and fail.

2.1.2.3. The people will be destroyed with the sword: *I will cut off the inhabitant from the plain of Aven*, the valley of idolatry.

2.1.2.4. The main part of the nation will be taken away. The *people shall go into captivity unto Kir*, which was in the country of the Medes. We find this fulfilled about fifty years later (2Ki 16:9).

2.2. About Gaza, a city of the Philistines.

2.2.1. The particular sin of the Philistines was *carrying away captive the whole captivity*, either of Israel or Judah, which some think refers to the inroads made on Jehoram (2Ch 21:17); it may, however, refer to the Philistines' seizing those who fled to them for shelter when Sennacherib invaded Judah and then *selling them to the Grecians* (Joel 3:4–6) or the Edomites.

2.2.2. The particular punishment of the Philistines is that fire will devour the palaces (consume the fortresses) of Gaza, and that the *inhabitants* of the other cities of the Philistines—Ashdod (or Azotus), Ashkelon, and Ekron—will all be *cut off*.

2.3. About Tyre, that famous city that was itself a kingdom (v. 9).

2.3.1. The particular sin of Tyre is *delivering up the whole captivity to Edom*, that is, selling to the Edomites those whole communities of Israel who fled to them for shelter.

2.3.2. In the punishment of Tyre *the palaces thereof* will be *devoured* (her fortresses will be consumed), which was done when Nebuchadnezzar took it after thirteen years' siege.

2.4. About Edom, the descendants of Esau.

2.4.1. Their particular sin was that they tirelessly, mercilessly pursued the people of God and caused them trouble at every opportunity (v. 11). He did *pursue his brother with the sword*, not only in former times (Nu 20:18) but also ever since. Whenever any other enemy had made Judah or Israel flee, then the Edomites attacked the rear, killing those who were already half dead and *casting off all pity*.

2.4.2. In their punishment, *a fire* will be *sent to devour their palaces* (consume their fortresses).

2.5. About the Ammonites (vv. 13–15). Notice:

2.5.1. The fire of their anger turned against the people of God. They *ripped up the women with child of Gilead*. It was done with a diabolical intention to destroy the race of Israel by killing not only all who were born but also all

who were to be born. It was so *that they might enlarge their border* (v. 13), so that they could take the land of Gilead for themselves. We find that the Ammonites *inherited Gad* (that is, Gilead) under the pretense that Israel had no heirs (Jer 49:1).

2.5.2. How violently the fire of God's anger burned against them. *Shall not his soul be avenged?* (Jer 5:9). The fire will be set alight *with shouting in the day of battle* (v. 14), that is, war will set the fire alight. It is especially threatened that *their king and his princes* (officials) *shall go together into captivity*; they were taken away by the king of Babylon. *Milcom* (1Ki 11:5) *shall go into captivity*; some understand this to refer to the god of the Ammonites, whom they called *Moloch*, "a king."

CHAPTER 2

1. God, through the prophet, proceeds against Moab as he did against other nations (vv. 1–3). 2. He shows what he has against Judah (vv. 4–5). 3. He eventually begins his charges against Israel, to which all that has gone before is merely an introduction. Notice: 3.1. The sins they are accused of: injustice, oppression, and sexual immorality (vv. 6–8). 3.2. The emphasizing of those sins: the temporal and spiritual mercies God gave them, to which they have responded with such ingratitude to him (vv. 9–12). 3.3. God's complaint against them because of their sins (v. 13) and his threats to destroy them (vv. 14–16).

Verses 1–8

Here is:

1. The judgment of Moab.

1.1. Moab's fourth sin was cruelty. The cruelty described here was not inflicted on the people of God: the king of Moab *burnt the bones of the king of Edom into lime* (v. 1). There was a war between the Edomites and the Moabites in which the king of Moab offered his own son as a burnt offering to appease his god (2Ki 3:26–27). Afterward he, or his successors, when in a position of advantage over the *king of Edom*, seized him alive and burned him to ashes, killed him and burned his body, or dug up the bones and *burnt them to lime*.

1.2. Moab's condemnation for this sin is death. *Moab shall die*. The Moabites will be destroyed with the sword. The king, judges, and leaders will be destroyed together.

2. The judgment of Judah, which is also a close neighbor of Israel and has made itself like the nations and mixed with them, and is therefore accused in the same form: *For three transgressions of Judah, and for four, I will not turn away the punishment thereof.* The sentence is the same as that against the other nations (v. 5): "*I will send a fire upon Judah*, and it will *devour the palaces* (consume the fortresses) *of Jerusalem*, even though it is the Holy City and God has formerly been *known in its palaces for a refuge*" (Ps 48:3). The sin that Judah is accused of here, however, is different from all the rest. The other nations were judged for wrongs done to human beings, but Judah is judged for dishonor shown to God (v. 4). *They have despised the law of the Lord*, and here they despised the wisdom, justice, and goodness, as well as the authority and sovereignty, of the Lawmaker. They honored his rivals, their idols or false gods, here called *their lies*, which *caused them to err*.

3. *The words* that *Amos saw concerning Israel* (1:1). He begins with them as with the others: *For three transgressions of Israel, and for four, I will not turn away the punishment thereof* (v. 6). Their sins are:

3.1. Perverting the course of justice. They think nothing of selling a righteous person for a piece of silver; the bribe always tips the scales. Those who will wrong their consciences for anything will eventually come to sell justice *for a pair of* old *shoes*.

3.2. Oppressing the poor. *They pant after the dust of the earth on the head of the poor* (v. 7). They attack those who have dust on their heads in sorrow. When poor orphans are mourning their parents, these oppressors seize them to obtain their possessions.

3.3. Detestable immorality, even incest.

3.4. Enjoying themselves immoderately and pretending to honor their God with what they have gained by oppression and extortion (v. 8). They *lay themselves down* at ease on *clothes laid to pledge*, which they should have restored the same night according to the Law (Dt 24:12–13). They *drink the wine of the condemned*, of those they have fined, spending on their physical pleasures what they have gained from their injustice. They think they can make up for this by *drinking this wine in the house of their God*, in the temples where they worship their calves.

Verses 9–16

Here:

1. God reminds his people Israel of the great things he has done for them (vv. 9–10). "Israel, remember (Lk 16:25) that God brought you out of *Egypt*, where you would otherwise have died in slavery. He *led thee forty years* through a desert and fed you in a *wilderness*." He made space for them in Canaan: *I destroyed the Amorite before them*. The Amorites were of great stature—*whose height was like the height of the cedars* (v. 9)—and the people of Israel were like shrubs compared with them. The Amorites were *strong as the oaks*. But *I destroyed his fruit from above and his roots from beneath* (v. 9), so that these enemies of Israel were no longer a nation. Here we see how highly God valued Israel. How ungrateful then were those who showed him so much contempt!

2. He rebukes them because of the spiritual privileges they enjoyed as a holy nation (v. 11). They had prophets who were divinely inspired and commissioned to make known the mind of God to them. It was an honor that they had children of their own who were to be God's messengers to them. They also had Nazarites who were good examples of godliness. God raised these up to be his witnesses against the ungodliness of that corrupt age.

3. He charges them with abusing the means of grace they enjoyed (v. 12). They did what they could to defile good people: *You gave the Nazarites wine to drink*, contrary to their vow. They did what they could to silence good ministers, to shut up their mouths: *You commanded the prophets, saying, Prophesy not*, and threatened to harm them if they did prophesy (7:12).

4. He complains about the wrong they have done him by their sins (v. 13): "*I am pressed under you*, I am crushed by you (Isa 1:24; Hos 11:8–9). I am loaded down and burdened by you. *I am pressed under you* and the burden of your sins *as a cart is pressed that is full of sheaves*, loaded down with grain in the middle of the *joy of harvest* till it will not hold one more kernel."

5. He threatens them with inevitable destruction. As some understand v. 13, "Behold, I will press [crush] your place, as a cart full of sheaves presses [crushes]"; they will be loaded with judgments until they sink. How can we expect anything else than for God to load us with his judgments if, when he loads us down daily with his benefits, we, despite that, load him with our sins? When the Assyrian army comes to devastate the country by sword

and captivity, no one will escape. *He that is swift of foot shall not deliver himself* (the fleet-footed soldier will not get away) (v. 15). Or do they say, *We will flee upon horses*, and *we will ride upon the swift*? Nevertheless, they will be overtaken. It will also be futile to think of fighting it out. *The strong shall not strengthen his force* (will not muster their strength). *The mighty* will not be able to *deliver himself*. Just as physical strength will fail, so will the weapons of war. *Neither shall he stand that handles the bow* (the archer will not stand his ground) (v. 15). *He that is courageous among the mighty* (even the bravest warriors), who used to look danger in the face, will *flee away naked in that day* (v. 16).

CHAPTER 3

A stupid, careless people are called on to take notice: 1. Of the judgments of God against them and the warnings he gives them, to be woken up from their self-confidence (vv. 1–8). 2. Of the sins among them that have caused God to threaten and punish them as he has done, so that unless they repent and reform, they can expect nothing else than for God to continue his accusations (vv. 9–15).

Verses 1–8

The *children of Israel* would not pay any attention to the words of advice that God spoke to them, and now they will be made to listen to the words of rebuke. Let them know that:

1. The gracious notice God has taken of them and the favors he has shown them will not exempt them from the punishment due for their sins. Israel is *a family* whom *God brought up out of the land of Egypt* (v. 1), and it was no more than a family when it went there. It was from Egypt that God rescued that family. It is a family that God has especially acknowledged: *In Judah is God known* (Ps 76:1), and so Judah is known by God. God has made a covenant with them and talked with them. *Therefore I will punish you for all your iniquities* (v. 2). If the favors of God do not restrain us from sin, they will not exempt us from punishment. It is necessary for God to vindicate his own honor by making it clear that he hates sin and that he hates it most in those who are closest to him.

2. They cannot expect any encouraging fellowship with God unless they first make their peace with him (v. 3): *Can two walk together except they be agreed?* Where there is no friendship, there can be no fellowship.

3. The warnings God has given them of the coming judgments were not without cause (v. 4): "*Will a lion roar in the forest when he has no prey* in view? No; he roars at his prey. Nor would God so express warnings to you if he were not really about to afflict you with judgments." The threats of the word and the providence of God are not imaginary terrors to frighten children and fools, but are the certain results of human sin and the certain signs of the coming judgments of God.

4. Their own evil was the cause of these judgments (v. 5). It is their own sin that has entangled them, for *can a bird fall in a snare upon the earth where no gin is* (snare has been set) *for him?* Nothing but their own repentance can disentangle them.

5. All their troubles came from the hand of God's providence (v. 6).

6. Their prophets, who warn them of coming judgments, communicate nothing to them except what they have *received from the Lord* (1Co 11:23) (v. 7): *Surely the Lord Jehovah will do nothing*, none of that disaster spoken

of in the city (v. 6), *but he reveals it* (without revealing it) *to his servants the prophets* (v. 7). The *secret* of God is in a special way with the prophets (Ps 25:14), to whom the Spirit of prophecy (Rev 19:10) is a Spirit of revelation. The prophets must make known to the people what God has made known to them (v. 8): *The Lord God has spoken; who can but prophesy?* They receive a command from God to communicate the message he has entrusted them with, and they would be false to their trust if they did not do so.

7. They should tremble before God as they would at the sounding of a trumpet. Some read v. 6, "Shall a trumpet be blown in the city, and the people not be afraid or run together?" However, when God notifies them of their danger through his prophets, it makes no impression.

Verses 9–15

The Israelites are again convicted and condemned.

1. Notice is given of it to their neighbors. The prophet is ordered to *publish it in the palaces* (proclaim it to the fortresses) *of Ashdod*, one of the chief cities of the Philistines; the summons must go even to *the palaces* (fortresses) *in the land of Egypt* (v. 9). God's accusations against sinners do not fear scrutiny; even Philistines and Egyptians will be led to see that *the ways of the Lord are equal* (just) but that *our ways are unequal* (unjust) (Eze 18:25).

1.1. Let them observe the behavior of the inhabitants of Samaria, seeing how unruly they are and hearing how loud the voice of their sin is, as Sodom's was. In their streets, you will see *great tumults in the midst thereof* (v. 9); reason and justice are shouted down by the fury of an outrageous mob. *The oppressed* are *in the midst thereof* (v. 9), thrown down and crushed by their oppressors. In the courts of justice, those who lead *know not to do right* (v. 10); they act as if they had no concept at all of justice. Their treasures and stores are filled with *violence and robbery* (v. 10), with what was unjustly gained and is unjustly kept.

1.2. Let them see how severe the condemnation is (vv. 11–12). The country of Samaria will be invaded and ruined. The Assyrian forces will surround it and overrun it. Samaria *stored up robbery in their palaces* (fortresses) (v. 10), and so their *palaces shall be spoiled* (fortresses will be plundered). The people of Samaria will not escape (v. 12). They will fall into the hands of the enemy as a lamb falls into the mouth of a lion; they will be devoured and eaten up, and very few people will escape, and those who do will be from the lowliest and least important, like *two legs* (leg bones or shanks) of a lamb, or *a piece of an ear* that the lion drops or that *the shepherd* takes away from him when he has eaten the body. In this way, perhaps, one here and there may escape from Samaria and Damascus, but those will do so with the greatest danger, by hiding themselves in the *corner of a bed* or under the bed, which shows that their spirits will be completely discouraged and broken.

2. Notice is given to them themselves (v. 13). Let this be *testified* and *heard in the house of Jacob*, for it is spoken *by the Lord God, the God of hosts*.

2.1. It will be terrible for *their altars*, for God *will visit* (destroy) them. He will consider all their superstition and idolatry. *The horns of the altar shall be cut off* and *fall to the ground* (v. 14), and with them the altar itself will be broken to pieces. Some consider *the horns of the altar* (v. 14) to represent all those things they flee to for refuge. All those things will be destroyed, with the result that the people will have nothing to take hold of.

2.2. It will be terrible for their houses, for God will tear them down too. He will investigate the sins they have been guilty of in their houses, the fruits of robbery they have stored up and the self-indulgence in which they live: *and I will smite the winter house with the summer house* (v. 15). *The houses of ivory shall perish*, be burned down or pulled down, *and the great houses shall have an end*; their extravagance will be included in the total of their sins and foolishness.

CHAPTER 4

1. The oppressors in Israel are threatened because of their oppression of the poor (vv. 1–3). 2. The idolaters in Israel are given over to their own hearts' sinful desires (vv. 4–5). 3. All the sins of Israel are shown to be made worse by their refusal to turn back to God and reform their ways (vv. 6–11). 4. They are still invited to humble themselves before God (vv. 12–13).

Verses 1–5

Oppressors will be humbled, and idolaters will be hardened.

1. Proud oppressors will be humbled for their oppression, for *he that does wrong shall receive according to the wrong that he has done* (2Co 5:10). Notice:

1.1. How their sin is described (v. 1). They are compared to the *kine* (cows) *of Bashan*, a very strong breed of cattle, especially if they were fed on *the mountain of Samaria*. Amos has been a shepherd, and he speaks in the dialect of his calling, comparing the rich people, who live in careless self-indulgence, to the cows of Bashan, which are reckless and unruly, breaking through the hedges and trespassing on neighboring land. Nor is that all they do; they also push and gore smaller cattle. Those who have their summerhouses on the mountains of Samaria are as troublesome and hurtful to those around them as the cows on the mountains of Bashan. They oppress the poor and *crush* them to squeeze something out of them. They are also allied to others who do so. They *say to their masters*—to the masters of the poor, who take away from them what they have, whereas they should relieve them—"*Bring, and let us drink*; if we feast with you on the gains of your oppression, then we will protect you, stand by you in it, and reject the appeals of the poor against you."

1.2. How their punishment is described (vv. 2–3). God *will take them away with hooks, and their posterity* (the last of you) *with fishhooks*; he will send the Assyrian army on them, who will not only capture the main part of the nation in their net but also fish for individual people, taking them prisoner as with fishhooks, drawing them out of their own land as fish are drawn up out of the water. Some will attempt to escape: *You shall go out at the breaches* made in the wall of the city, *every cow at that which is before her* (v. 3), to fend for themselves, and then the unruly cows of Bashan will themselves be crushed, just as they themselves crushed the poor and needy. Others will think they can take shelter: "You shall throw yourselves," as some read it, or "throw them"—that is your children—*into the palace*, where the enemy will find them ready to be seized.

1.3. How their sentence to this punishment is confirmed: *The Lord God has sworn it by his holiness* (v. 2). He swears by *his holiness*, the aspect of his nature that is so much his glory.

2. Obstinate idolaters will be hardened in their idolatry (vv. 4–5): *Come to Bethel, and transgress*. It is spoken

ironically: "Do so; let your actions take their course; *multiply* your *transgressions* by multiplying your sacrifices, *for this liketh you* — this is what you love to do — but what will you do in the end?" Here we see:

2.1. How determined they were to serve their idols. They *brought their sacrifices, tithes*, and *free-will offerings*, hoping to be accepted by God, but it was all detestable to him.

2.2. How they mimicked God's institutions. They had their *daily sacrifice* at the altar of Bethel, just as God had at his altar; their worship had its *thank offerings*, just as the worship of God had, except that they allowed *leaven* in them. Holy bread was not good enough for them unless it tasted pleasant.

2.3. How pleased they were with these services: "*This liketh you, O you children of Israel!* (v. 5). This is what you love!"

2.4. How they were rebuked for it. "Your foolish hearts will be made more and more darkened and foolish (Ro 1:21), and you will be completely *given up* to these *strong delusions, to believe a lie*" (2Th 2:11). This is what Christ said to the Jews: *Fill you up the measure of your fathers* (Mt 23:32).

Verses 6 – 13

Here:

1. God has shown them his displeasure by several signs to lead them to repentance, but it has not had that effect.

1.1. It is repeated five times in these verses, as the chorus of the charge, "*Yet have you not returned unto me, saith the Lord*" (vv. 6, 8, 9, 10, 11); there is no sign of amendment." This shows that God's intention in all his rebukes was to influence them to turn back to him. If they had turned back to their God, they would have been accepted. It is no *pleasure to the Almighty that he should afflict* (Eze 18:32).

1.2. He recalls the lesser judgments with which he has tried to bring them to repentance.

1.2.1. There has sometimes been a scarcity of provisions (v. 6): "*I have given you cleanness of teeth in all your cities*, for you had no food to chew on." Or, "*I have given you emptiness of teeth*, empty stomachs, no food to fill your mouths with." Some think this refers to the *seven years' famine* in Elisha's time, which we read of in 2Ki 8:1.

1.2.2. Sometimes they have lacked rain: *I have withholden the rain from you* (v. 7). The rain was withheld *when there were yet three months to the harvest.*

1.2.3. Sometimes the crops of their ground have been eaten up by locusts or blighted by mildew (v. 9). They took no notice of the warning, however: *Yet have you not returned unto me.*

1.2.4. Sometimes the plague has raged among them, and the sword of war has killed many people (v. 10). It was *a pestilence after the manner of Egypt*, "in the way of Egypt" (v. 10, margin); when they were either making their escape to Egypt or going there to seek aid, the plague took hold of them on the way. The dead carcasses of those who were killed by either sword or plague were so many: the *stench of their camps came up into their nostrils*. This was not effective, however, in making them religious. In these judgments, some were remarkably destroyed and made memorials to justice, while others were remarkably spared and made memorials to mercy. (v. 11): *I have overthrown some of you, as God overthrew Sodom and Gomorrah*. Others had a narrow escape: "Many of you *were* as a *firebrand plucked out of the burning* (like a burning stick snatched from the fire), like Lot out of

Sodom, but you hate sin none the more for it, nor do you love God any more for the rescue he has brought you."

2. God calls on his people, now on this their *day*, to understand the things that concern their peace before they are hidden from their eyes (Lk 19:42) (vv. 12 – 13). He threatens them with harsher judgments than any they have suffered so far. Nothing but reformation will prevent the destruction of a sinful people. *I will punish you yet seven times more, if you will* not *be reformed* (Lev 26:23 – 24). "Decide, therefore, to meet him as a humble petitioner, to meet him as *thy God*, in covenant with you, to submit and stop resisting." Since we cannot run away from God, we must be concerned to prepare to meet him, and so he gives us advance warning, so that we may prepare. He sets out his greatness and power as a reason why we should prepare to meet him (v. 13). The One who formed the *great mountains* can *make them plain* (Isa 40:4) when they stand in the way of his people's salvation. He *declares unto man what is his thought* (v. 13). Through his servants the prophets he reveals the thoughts of his justice against impenitent sinners and the good thoughts he thinks (Jer 29:11) toward those who repent. He knows the thought that is in the human heart; he *understands it afar off* (Ps 139:2). He *treads upon the high places of the earth* (v. 13); he tramples on proud people and on the idols that are worshiped on the highest places. *Jehovah the God of hosts is his name* (v. 13), for he has his being in himself (Ex 3:13 – 14). He is the fountain of all being, and all the forces of heaven and earth are at his command. Let us therefore humble ourselves before this God.

CHAPTER 5

The prophet tells them here: 1. What preparations they must make: they must seek the Lord, *and not idols (vv. 4 – 8); they must seek good and love it (vv. 14 – 15). 2. Why they must make this preparation to meet their God: 2.1. Because of their present wretched condition (vv. 1 – 3). 2.2. Because it was their sin that brought them into such a condition (vv. 7, 10 – 12). 2.3. Because it will be their happiness to seek God, and he is ready to be found by them (vv. 8 – 9, 14). 2.4. Because he will proceed to completely destroy them if they do not seek him (vv. 5 – 6, 13, 16 – 17). 2.5. Because all they trust in will fail them if they do not make him their friend: their contempt of God's judgments will not protect them (vv. 18 – 20); their external religious services will not be effective (vv. 21 – 24); their having long possessed church privileges will not protect them (vv. 25 – 27). There is therefore no way open to them to save themselves except the way of repentance and reformation.*

Verses 1 – 3

This chapter begins with *Hear this word* (v. 1). It is the *word which I take* up — not only I the prophet but also I the God who sent him. It is *the word that the Lord has spoken* (3:1). Here is a terrible description of the present state of the kingdom of Israel and a prediction of its destruction. *The virgin of Israel has fallen* (v. 2), *she has fallen* into contempt and is universally disrespected. *She shall no more rise*; she will never regain her former position. *She is forsaken upon* (deserted in) *her land* (v. 2). Not only those she was allied with abroad failed her; friends at home deserted her also. She would not have been taken captive into a strange land if she had not first been *forsaken upon her own land*. The people from among them who should have helped them up were diminished (v. 3). The city that had a militia 1,000 strong will find only 100

AMOS 5

left after the battle, and, in proportion, the city that sent out 100 will find that only *ten* come back.

Verses 4–15

Here is a message from God to the house of Israel:

1. They are told their faults.

1.1. God tells them, in general (v. 12), "*I know your manifold transgressions, and your mighty sins*, and you will be made to know them too." What a vast number of worthless thoughts reside within us! What a vast number of idle, evil words have been spoken by us! In what a vast number of instances have we indulged our corrupt appetites and passions! Moreover, how many times have we neglected to do our duty?

1.2. He specifies some of these great sins.

1.2.1. They corrupted the worship of God and turned to idols; this is implied in v. 5. They had *sought to Bethel*, where one of the golden calves was (1Ki 12:28–29); they had frequented Gilgal, a place where they chose to set up idols. Beersheba, famous in the days of the patriarchs, was now another meeting place of idols.

1.2.2. They perverted the course of justice among themselves (v. 7): "*You turn judgment to wormwood*, that is, you make your administrations of justice bitter and displeasing to God and people."

1.2.3. They were very oppressive to the poor; they trampled on those whom they could gain nothing from (v. 11). The judges aimed only at making themselves rich, and so they *took from* the poor *burdens of wheat* by extortion. The poor had no other way to save themselves than by presenting to them horseloads of the grain that they and their families needed to live on. These judges took from the poor "debts of wheat," as some read it. They are again charged with this sin of oppression (v. 12): *They afflict the just* by turning the law against those who are innocent and *quiet in the land*. Those who *departed from evil* were liable to be attacked by them. They accepted a bribe from the rich to support and protect them in oppressing the poor. In this way, they *turned aside the poor in the gate*, in the courts of justice, *from their right*, from the justice due them (v. 12).

1.2.4. Furthermore, they were the malicious persecutors of God's faithful ministers and people (v. 10). They could not bear to be rebuked by the reading and explaining of the Law and by the messages the prophets communicated to them in the name of the Lord. *They hate him that rebukes in the gate*. Though things were generally very bad, there were some among them who *spoke uprightly* and condemned them: that was why *they abhorred them*. They were such hardened enemies of honesty that they could not endure the sight of someone who was honest. Prophets cannot keep silent; the compulsion they sense will not allow them to act out of prudence; they must *cry aloud, and not spare* (shout aloud and not hold back) (Isa 58:1). *The prudent*, who were *wise as serpents* (Mt 10:16), were so cautious as to say nothing, because they did not know how what they said might be misrepresented. Those who are cautious will say to a bold rebuker, as Erasmus said to Luther, "Away to your cell, and cry out, 'Have mercy on me, O Lord!'" *Evil times* will not bear plain dealing, that is, *evil men will not*.

2. They are told about what judgments they are liable to because of their sins. The places of their idolatry are in danger of being ruined (v. 5). *Gilgal*, the headquarters of idolatry, *shall go into captivity, and Bethel* with its golden calf *shall come to nought*. Most of the kingdom is in danger of being destroyed with them (v. 6). "There is a danger that if you do not seek God, he will *break out like a fire in*

the house of Joseph and devour it. And there shall be none to quench it in Bethel (v. 6)." God tells them that when the fire of his judgments sets fire to them, all the gods they served at Bethel will not be able to quench it. What they have gained by extortion will be taken away from them (v. 11): "*You have built houses of hewn stone*, which you thought would endure for a long time, *but you shall not dwell in them*, for your enemies will burn them down and take you into exile. *You have planted pleasant* (lush) *vineyards*, but you will never *drink wine of them*."

3. They are told their duty and are given great encouragement to set about doing it. The duties prescribed here are godliness and integrity, seriousness in their relationship with God and justice in their dealings with people.

3.1. They are encouraged to be sincere and devout in their relationship with God (v. 4). God is not sought truly unless he is sought exclusively: "*Seek you the Lord, and seek not Bethel* (v. 5), for you *forsake your own mercies* if you observe those worthless idols (Jnh 2:8). *Seek the Lord* (vv. 6, 8); inquire after him; seek to know his mind as your rule." Seeking God will be *our life* (Dt 32:47). This is what he tells them (v. 4): *Seek you me, and you shall live*. So also the prophet tells them (v. 6): *Seek the Lord, and you shall live*. "You will be rescued from the judgments you are threatened with, your nation will live, it will recover from its present doldrums, your souls will live (Jer 38:17, 20), and you will be sanctified, strengthened, encouraged, and made blessed forever. *You shall live*." The God whom we are to *seek* (vv. 8–9) is a God of almighty power. Various examples are given here of God's power as Creator. Compare 4:13.

3.1.1. The stars are the work of his hands. The *stars of your god* (v. 26) are God's creatures and servants. He *makes the seven stars* (Pleiades) *and Orion*, two constellations that Amos had particularly noted as a shepherd while he kept his cattle by night. God made them, and he either *binds* or *looses* their *sweet influences* (beauty). See Job 9:9; 38:31.

3.1.2. The constant succession of day and night is under his direction. He is the One who *turns* the night *into the morning* by the rising of the sun, and who by the setting of the sun *makes the day dark with night*. The same power that can turn suffering and sorrow into prosperity and joy for humble penitents can as easily turn the success of arrogant sinners to darkness.

3.1.3. The rain rises and falls as he appoints. He *calls for the waters of the sea*; out of them vapor is drawn up by the heat of the sun and forms clouds, which are *poured out upon the face of the earth* to make it fruitful. It is God who has *made these things; Jehovah is his name*. As a God of almighty power, he *gives strength and power unto his people* who seek him, and if they *wait upon him* for it (Isa 40:31), he *renews strength* to those who had lost it (v. 9). He *strengthens the spoiled against the strong*. This is an encouragement to the people to *seek the Lord*, that if they do so, they will find him able to restore their fortunes.

3.2. They are encouraged to be upright and just in their dealings with people (vv. 14–15): *Seek good, and not evil. Hate the evil, and love the good, and establish judgment in the gate* (courts); reestablish it there, from where it has been expelled (v. 7). If the right course of action is followed, grievances may be compensated for and abuses set right: justice may still triumph where injustice currently tyrannizes. To this end, good must be loved and sought, and evil must be hated. We must love good motives as a foundation: love to do good, loving good people, and whatever good we do, we must do it from a motivation of love, and with delight. "He will be with you *as you have spoken*, that is, as you have 'gloried'; you will have in reality what you only boasted about as if you had it." Or, "as you have prayed when 'you sought the Lord.' Live up to your prayers, and you will receive what you pray for." This is the likeliest way to make the nation happy: "If you seek and love what is good, you may contribute to the saving of the land from ruin."

Verses 16–20

Here is:

1. A terrible threat of coming destruction (vv. 16–17). The threat is introduced with more than ordinary solemnity, to strike awe on them. It is not only the word of the prophet but also the word of the *Lord Jehovah*, the *God of hosts, Adonai*, "the Lord," who has absolute sovereignty. He is the One who can and will fulfill his words. The land of Israel will be put into a state of mourning. If you look at the cities, you will find that *wailing shall be in all streets*. If you look at the country, *they shall say in all the highways, Alas! Alas!* Farmers will be called away from their plow by the disasters coming on their country. Even in all the vineyards, where there used to be nothing but happiness and pleasure, there will be a general wailing when a foreign force invades the country. "*I will pass through thee* as the destroying angel passed through the land of Egypt."

2. A rebuke to those who make light of these threats (v. 18). "Woe to you who *desire the day of the Lord*, who really wish for times of war and confusion," as some do who have restless spirits and long for changes. Or it is spoken to those who, in their mourning for the disasters, wish they could die. Or, rather, it is spoken to those who speak jokingly of the day of the Lord. "Let him do his worst, *let him make speed* and *hasten his work*" (Isa 5:19). In response to this, the prophet shows how foolish people are when they arrogantly wish for God's judgments: "*To what end is it for you* (why do you long) for the day of the Lord to come? You will find that it is not something to be made fun of. *The day of the Lord is darkness, and not light* (v. 18)." Moreover, when God makes a day dark, all the world cannot make it light. The prophet also shows how foolish people are when they long for *the day of the Lord* in the hope of improving themselves or, at least, of knowing the worst. But the prophet tells them that they do not know what they are asking (Mt 20:22) (v. 19). It is *as if a man did flee from a lion and a bear met him*, or as if a man *went into the house for security*, to escape all external dangers, and *leaned his hand on the wall* to rest, and there *a serpent bit him*.

Verses 21–27

These verses show how little God valued their shows of devotion as long as they continued in their sins. Notice:

1. How displeasing their hypocritical service was to God. They had their *feast-days* at Bethel, in imitation of those at Jerusalem. They had their *solemn assemblies* for religious worship. They offered to God *burnt offerings*, to the honor of God, together with the *meat offerings* (grain offerings). They offered the *peace offerings* (fellowship offerings) to implore God's favor, and they offered the *fat* (choice) *beasts* they had (vv. 21–22). Similarly, in imitation of the temple music, they had the *noise of their songs* and the *melody of their viols* (harps) (v. 23). They hoped to use such services to obtain permission to continue in their sin. He *hated*, he *despised* their *feast days*. Nothing is more hateful or more despicable than hypocrisy. God would not stand *their solemn assemblies*, for there was

nothing in them that was pleasing to him; in fact, there was a great deal that was offensive. He would not accept them. This shows that:

1.1. Sacrifice itself is of little significance with God in comparison with moral duties; to love God and our neighbor is *better than all burnt offering and sacrifice* (Hos 6:6; Mk 12:33).

1.2. The sacrifice of evildoers is really detestable to him (Pr 15:8). Pretended godliness is a double sin.

2. What it was that he required, what it was that would make their sacrifices acceptable and without which no sacrifice would be acceptable (v. 24): *Let judgment run down as waters* among you, *and righteousness as a mighty stream*, that is, "Let there be a general reformation in your way of life; let religion (God's *judgment*) and *righteousness* have their due influence on you. Let your land be watered with it, and let it overcome all evil and profaneness. Let it run as wide as overflowing waters but as strong as a never-failing stream. Let justice be properly administered: let its flow not be stopped by partiality or bribery. Let it be as pure as running water, not muddied by corruption. Let it run *like a mighty stream*."

3. What little emphasis God had placed on the law of sacrifices in comparison with the moral commands (v. 25): "*Did you offer unto me sacrifices in the wilderness forty years?* No; you did not." For part of that time sacrifice was neglected. After the second year, the Passover was not celebrated until they reached Canaan yet he never considered their omission as a fault of the people, but continued to be kind to them: it was because of their murmuring and unbelief that God was displeased with them. Although ritual sacrifices may be dispensed with, spiritual sacrifices will not; even justice and honesty will not make up for the lack of prayer and praise, a broken heart and the love of God.

4. What little reason they had to expect that their sacrifices would be acceptable to God, when they and their ancestors had all along devoted themselves to the worship of other gods. This is how some understand v. 25: "*Did you offer to me sacrifices*, that is, only to me? No, and therefore not acceptably at all to me. *But you have borne the tabernacle of your Moloch* (v. 26), the little shrines to your king that you carried. You have had the images of your *Moloch*, 'your king'"—probably representing *the sun*, the king of the heavenly bodies—"and *Chiun*, or *Remphan* (Rephan)"—as Stephen calls it (Ac 7:43), following the Septuagint (a Greek version of the Old Testament); *Chiun* and *Remphan* probably represented Saturn. The worship of the sun, moon, and stars was the most ancient and most plausible form of idolatry. They *made to themselves* the *star of their God*, some star whose name they gave to their god.

5. What punishment God would inflict on them for their persistent idolatry (v. 27): *I will cause you to go into captivity beyond Damascus*. Their place of exile under the Assyrians was far beyond that under the Arameans. Or the exile of Israel under Shalmaneser was far beyond that of Damascus under Tiglath-Pileser, much more severe, as was foretold (1:5).

CHAPTER 6

In this chapter we have: 1. A sinful people disregarding God's threats and making them appear trivial (vv. 1–3), trusting in their power (v. 13) and devoted to their pleasures (vv. 4–6). 2. A serious prophet seeking to take seriously God's threats and to make them appear terrible (v. 7), by showing these people that God is abandoning them and theirs to death (vv. 8–11) and bringing desolation on them (vv. 12–14).

Verses 1–7

The first words of the chapter give the contents of these verses: *Woe to those that are at ease!* Here is:

1. A description of their pride, false security, and self-indulgence, for which God would judge them.

1.1. They were vainly conceited about their own position, thinking that that would protect them from the threatened judgments.

1.1.1. Those who lived in Zion thought that their residence there was enough honor and protection; God's sanctuary would protect them from his judgments.

1.1.2. Those who lived *in the mountain of Samaria* trusted in it, because it was the center of a powerful kingdom and the headquarters of its religion.

1.1.3. Both of these kingdoms prided themselves on their relationship with Israel, that prince with God (Ge 32:28), a relationship that they looked on as making them the *chief of the nations*. The *house of Israel* came to them, that is, was divided into the kingdoms whose mother cities were Zion and Samaria. Those who were *at ease* in their complacency were the princes and rulers. Great nations and great people tend to esteem themselves too highly. However, to restrain their pride, the prophet told them to take notice of the cities that had been as famous in their time as Zion or Samaria but were nevertheless destroyed (v. 2). "Go to Calneh"—an ancient city built by Nimrod (Ge 10:10)—"it now lies in ruins. The same has happened to *Hamath the great*, one of the chief cities of Aram. Gath, too, was devastated by Hazael (2Ki 12:17). Now *were they better than these kingdoms* of Judah and Israel? Yes, and *their border greater than your border*, so they had more reason than you to be confident of their safety, but see what has become of them, and dare you be so smug and complacent?"

1.2. They persisted in their evil ways because they presumed they would never be called to account for them (v. 3). You *put it far away*. You therefore *cause the seat of violence to draw near*.

1.3. They indulged in all kinds of physical pleasures and delights (vv. 4–6). What they are accused of here is not in itself sinful—these things could be used soberly and in moderation—but they based all their happiness on gratifying their physical appetites. They were extravagant and lazy. They "abounded in superfluities," as the margin of v. 4 reads, when many of their poor brothers and sisters lacked necessities. They had to have the finest of everything—and plenty, too! They ate *the lambs out of the flock* and the *calves out of the midst of the stall*. Some people show their ingenuity only in their self-indulgence; they devote all their ingenious faculties to that. Or it shows their godlessness in their revelry; they imitated the temple music and made fun of it, perhaps because it was old-fashioned and they took pride in mocking it. They drank excessively and put on the strongest perfumes to increase their love for their own bodies.

1.4. They showed no concern at all for the interests of God's church and of the nation: *They are not grieved for the affliction of Joseph*; the church of God, including both the kingdoms of Judah and Israel, which are called *Joseph* (Ps 80:1), was in distress and was invaded. As to their own kingdom, great breaches were made in its peace and welfare. They were so confused that they were unaware of them. It was all the same to them whether the nation sank or swam, as long as they could live in pleasure. Some think that in calling the afflicted church *Joseph*, the

prophet alluded to the story of Pharaoh's cupbearer, who *remembered not Joseph, but forgot him* (Ge 40:21, 23). They *drank wine in bowls* but *were not grieved for the affliction of Joseph*.

2. The sentence passed on them (v. 7): *Therefore now shall they go captive* (into exile) *with the first that go captive* (into exile). Those who lived in luxury will lose even their liberty. Those who *stretched themselves* will be forced to reduce their lavish circumstances.

Verses 8–14

Here we see God loading them down with punishments. Notice:

1. How strongly this burden is bound on them. It is bound on them by *the Lord the God of hosts*.

2. How heavily this burden lies.

2.1. God will detest and abandon them, and that implies enough misery. Their temple, altar, and priesthood have been the pride of Jacob, but now that these are defiled by sin, God detests them. Moreover, if God detests them, he will *deliver up the city with all that is therein* to the hands of the enemy, who will devastate it and plunder all its wealth.

2.2. There will be a great and general mortality among them (v. 9). But what makes this judgment even more painful is that their hearts seem hardened under it.

2.3. Their houses will be destroyed (v. 11). God *will smite the great house with breaches* (smash the great house to pieces), *and the little house with clefts* (into bits).

3. How justly they are burdened. If we understand the matter rightly, we will say, *The Lord is righteous* (La 1:18). God has sent them his prophets to *break up their fallow ground*, but the prophets found them as hard as rock. Though they are the house of Israel, he will *raise up against them a nation* that they have hoped in many times, namely the Assyrians, and this nation will *afflict them* all the way from the *entering in of Hamath*, in the north, to *the river of the wilderness*, the river of Egypt, Sihor or Nile, in the south.

CHAPTER 7

In this chapter: 1. God is contending with Israel. The people are threatened with lesser judgments but are reprieved at the prayer of Amos (vv. 1–6); God's patience is worn out by their stubbornness, and they are sentenced (vv. 7–9). 2. Israel is contending with God by opposing his prophet. Amaziah brings malicious information against Amos (vv. 10–11) and does what he can to rid the country of him (vv. 12–13). Amos justifies himself in what he does as a prophet (vv. 14–15) and declares the judgments of God against Amaziah his prosecutor (vv. 16–17).

Verses 1–9

God is patient with an offensive people for a long time, but he will not be patient with them always.

1. Here are two examples of God's sparing mercy.

1.1. God came against this sinful nation here, first by one judgment and then by another.

1.1.1. He began with the judgment of famine. The prophet saw this in a vision. He saw God *forming grasshoppers*, or locusts (v. 1), as instruments of his wrath. The wisdom and power of God appears as much in the structure of an ant as in that of an elephant. These locusts were sent *in the beginning of the shooting up of the latter growth, after the king's mowings* (after the king's share had been harvested and just as the second crop was coming up) (v. 1). The judgment was lessened by the mercy that preceded it. God could have sent these insects to devour the grass at the beginning of the first crop, in the spring, when the grass was most necessary, but God allowed that to grow and allowed the people to gather it in. The locusts were commissioned to devour only the *latter growth*, the later grass, which is less valuable than the first mowing. Remembering the blessings of the first growth should make us submissive to the will of God when we meet with disappointments in later stages. Some understand this figuratively, as referring to a devastating and destroying army brought on them.

1.1.2. He proceeded to the judgment of fire (v. 4): *The Lord God called to contend* (was calling for judgment) *by fire*. A fire was kindled among them, which may perhaps have been a great drought—the heat of the sun, which scorched the earth and burned up the roots of the grass that the locusts had eaten the tops of—or to a raging fever, which was like a fire in their bones, or to lightning, fire from heaven, which burned down their houses, as it burned down Sodom and Gomorrah (4:11). Or it was the burning down of their cities, either by accident or by the hand of the enemy. The towns were ravaged in this way, as the country was ravaged by the locusts. This fire *devoured the great deep* (v. 4), as the fire that fell from heaven on Elijah's altar licked up the water in the trench (1Ki 18:38).

1.2. The prophet sought by prayer to turn away his wrath (v. 2). It was the business of prophets to pray for those to whom they prophesied, and so they did not *desire the woeful day* (Jer 17:16). Notice:

1.2.1. The prophet's prayer: "*O Lord God! Forgive, I beseech thee*, and take away the sin" (v. 2). He saw that sin was at the root of the trouble and that the pardon of sin must lie at the root of the deliverance. *Cease, I beseech thee*, and take away the judgment; *cause thy anger toward us to cease*. Take away the cause, and the effect will stop.

1.2.2. The prophet's plea to support this prayer: *By whom shall Jacob arise, for he is small?* (v. 2). This is repeated (v. 5). It was Jacob whom he was interceding for, the professing people of God, called by his name. *Jacob is small*, weakened and brought low by former judgments, and if these come, he will be brought to nothing. The people were unable to help themselves or one another. Sin would soon reduce their numbers and weaken the courageous. *By whom shall he arise?* He had no friend to help him, no one to lift him up, unless the hand of God did it.

1.2.3. God graciously dropping his accusations in answer to the prophet's prayer (v. 3): *The Lord repented* (relented) *for this*. He did not change his mind; he changed his way, took another course in mercy. He said, *It shall not be*. And again (v. 6), *This also shall not be*. This was not the first time that Israel's life was begged for and thereby saved. What a blessing praying people, praying prophets, are to a land. Amos seeks a reprieve and gains it because God inclines to give it. It is the glory of God that he *multiplies to pardon* (the literal sense of *will abundantly pardon* in Isa 55:7), that he spares and forgives more than seventy times seven (Mt 18:22).

2. Here is the final rejection of those who had often been reprieved but never brought back to their duty. This is represented to the prophet by a vision (vv. 7–8).

2.1. The vision is of *a plumb line*, a line with a plummet at its end, such as stonemasons and bricklayers use to build a wall by, so that their work may be straight and true. Israel was a wall that God had set up as a bulwark to his sanctuary. This wall was *made by a plumb line*, exact and firm. It had long stood as firm as a bronze wall (Jer 1:18; 15:20). But God now *stood upon it with a plumb line in his hand* to measure it. This was how God would bring the people of Israel to a time of testing to show where they went wrong. He would set *a plumb line in the midst of them* to mark off how far their wall must be pulled down.

2.2. The prediction is of complete destruction (v. 9).

2.2.1. The body of the people will be destroyed. They are called here *the house of Isaac* (v. 16), in allusion, some think, to the meaning of Isaac's name ("laughter"). They would become a joke among all their neighbors. They thought their castles were safe and their temples sacred, but these would be *laid waste* to punish them for their idolatry and their worldly self-confidence.

2.2.2. The royal family would sink first. Jeroboam II was now king of the ten tribes; his family was destroyed in his son Zechariah (2Ki 15:10).

Verses 10–17

Amos is persecuted.

1. Malicious information was brought to the king against the prophet Amos (vv. 10–11). The informer was *Amaziah the priest of Bethel*, the chief of the priests who ministered to the golden calf there, "the president of Bethel," as some read it. He complained against Amos because Amos prophesied against his altars, which would soon be deserted if Amos's preaching was believed. Priests have been the bitterest persecutors. Notice:

1.1. The crime Amos was charged with was treason: "*Amos has conspired against thee* to depose and murder you; he is aiming at succeeding you. *The land is not able to bear his words*." It was slyly insinuated that the country was angry with Amos. It is nothing new for the accusers of our brothers and sisters to misrepresent them as enemies of the king and kingdom, when in reality they are the best friends of both.

1.2. The words in the indictment to support this charge (v. 11): *Amos says*—and they had witnesses ready to prove it—*Jeroboam shall die by the sword, and Israel shall be led away captive*. Amaziah did not tell the king how Amos had interceded for Israel, turning away first one judgment and then another. He did not tell him that Amos had often assured them that if they would repent, the ruin would be prevented. It does not appear that Jeroboam took any notice of this information; perhaps he revered a prophet and stood more in awe of divine authority than Amaziah his priest did.

2. We are told the method Amaziah used to persuade Amos to leave the country (vv. 12–13). He wormed himself into his acquaintance to try to persuade him to go and prophesy in the *land of Judah*, not at Bethel. He suggested to him:

2.1. That Bethel was not a proper place for him to exercise his ministry, for it was *the king's chapel*, or *sanctuary*. It was also *the king's court*, or *the house of the kingdom*, where the royal family resided and where the thrones of judgment were set (Ps 122:5), and so *prophesy not any more* here. And why not? Because:

- Amos was too direct, plain, and blunt a preacher for the court and the king's chapel.
- The worship that was in the king's chapel would continually trouble Amos.
- It was not appropriate that the king and his house should be shown such disrespect in their own court and chapel by rebukes and threats in the name of the Lord.

• Amos could not expect to be encouraged there at all, but, on the contrary, to be ridiculed and threatened. He should not think he would persuade anyone to turn away from the idolatry that was supported by the authority and example of the king. To preach his doctrine there was only, as we put it, "like banging his head against a brick wall."

2.2. That the land of Judah was the best place for him. "*Flee thee away* there as fast as possible, and *there eat bread*, and *prophesy there* (v. 12). You will be safe and welcome there." Notice:

• How willing evildoers are to get clear of those who will rebuke them.
• How inclined worldly people are to measure others by themselves. Amaziah, as a priest, aimed at nothing but the profits of his position, and he thought Amos, as a prophet, had the same attitude.

3. Amos replied to Amaziah's suggestions. He did not *consult with flesh and blood* (Gal 1:16), nor did he desire to make himself rich, but to *make full proof of his ministry*; he desired not to escape injuries but to keep a good conscience, and so he determined to remain at his post, and, in answer to Amaziah:

3.1. He justified himself in his faithfulness to his work and his place (vv. 14–15). He had received a divine commission. "*I was no prophet, nor prophet's son*, neither born nor brought up to this office, as Samuel and Jeremiah were, but *was a herdsman*, a keeper of cattle, and *a gatherer of sycamore fruit*." He was an ordinary man from the country, brought up and employed in country work and used to country living. God made him a prophet, and a prophet to them, appointed him his work and his position. He therefore would not be silenced, for:

3.1.1. He could produce a divine commission for what he did. People will find they are in danger if they oppose anyone who comes in God's name. Contempt shown to an ambassador is contempt shown to the ruler who sends the ambassador.

3.1.2. The lowly character he had before he received the commission strengthened his authority.

3.1.2.1. He had no thoughts whatever of ever being a prophet, and so his prophesying was due to a divine motivation.

3.1.2.2. He was not instructed in the art of prophesying, and so he must have received his abilities for it directly from God, which was an undeniable proof that he had his mission from him. Similarly, the apostles were originally unlearned and ignorant, but they showed that they owed their knowledge to their having *been with Jesus* (Ac 4:13).

3.1.2.3. He had an honest calling by which he could comfortably maintain himself and his family, and so he did not need to prophesy for bread, as Amaziah suggested (v. 12). If God, who sent him, had not strengthened him, he could not have *set his face as a flint* (Isa 50:7). A shepherd from Tekoa puts to shame a priest from Bethel when he receives authority from God to act for him.

3.2. In the name of the Lord and by authority from him, he condemned Amaziah for opposing him (vv. 16–17).

3.2.1. For his opposition to Amos, God would bring ruin on him and his family. He would have no comfort in his relatives: *Thy wife shall be a harlot. Thy sons and thy daughters shall fall by the sword* of war. He would be stripped of all his possessions. He himself would perish in a foreign country, in a *polluted land*, an unclean, pagan country.

3.2.2. Amos was accused for saying, *Israel shall be led away captive* (v. 11), but he stood by it and repeated it. The *burden of the word of the Lord* (Mal 1:1) cannot be shaken off. Silencing the mouths of God's ministers will not stop the progress of God's word, for it will not return to him empty (Isa 55:11).

CHAPTER 8

Sinful times are accompanied by sadness here. 1. The vision of a basket of summer (ripe) fruit stands for the speedy coming of the threatened ruin (vv. 1–3). 2. Oppressors are called to account for abusing the poor (vv. 4–10). 3. A famine of the word of God is made the punishment of a people who turn to other gods (vv. 11–14).

Verses 1–3

1. The approach of the threatened ruin is represented *by a basket of summer* (ripe) *fruit* that Amos saw in a vision. He saw *a basket of summer fruit* gathered and ready to be eaten, which signified:

1.1. That they were ripe for destruction; the people were ready to be eaten up.

1.2. That the year of God's patience was coming toward an end; it was autumn with them.

1.3. Fruits that will not keep until winter, but must be used up immediately, and are therefore a fitting symbol for this people, who had nothing consistent in them.

2. The intention and meaning of this vision is nothing more than this: *the end has come upon my people Israel.* What was said in 7:8 is repeated here as God's determined resolution: *I will not again pass by them any more* (I will spare them no longer).

3. The consequence of this will be total desolation (v. 3). Here in a sinful world, in a sinful nation:

3.1. Sorrow reigns so much that *the songs of the temple shall be howlings* (will turn to wailing). When God's judgments are about, they will turn joy to heaviness, and they will turn the temple songs, which used to sound so pleasant, into loud wailing.

3.2. Death reigns. There will be *many* dead bodies *in every place* (Ps 110:6), put to death by the sword or plague. The survivors will not even have the bell tolled for the dead, but will *cast them forth* (be flung) *with silence.*

Verses 4–10

God is opposing proud oppressors here and showing them:

1. The terrible nature of the sin they are guilty of. They have the character of the unjust judge who neither *feared God nor regarded man* (Lk 18:2).

1.1. If you look at them in their devotions, you will say, "They have no reverence for God." They keep up a show of godliness (2Ti 3:5); they observe the *sabbath* and the *new moon*, but they soon become fed up with them. They say, *When will the sabbath be gone, that we may sell corn?* They are tired of the restraints of the Sabbaths and the New Moon festivals and wish them over. They are fond of market days; they long to be *selling corn* and *setting forth wheat* (v. 5). Those who love market days better than Sabbaths, who would rather be selling grain than worshiping God, are strangers to him and are their own enemies.

1.2. If you look at how they live, you will see that they have no respect for people. They neither *do justly* nor *love mercy* (Mic 6:8). When they *sell their corn*, they deceive the buyer. They measure out the grain using their own measures, but they *make the ephah small*. When they receive money from the buyer, they weigh it on their own scales, using their own weights, and they *make the shekel great*, so that the payment is found too light and they must have more money added to it. They do not have in their hearts the fear or the love of the God, who has clearly said that *false weights and balances are an abomination to him* (Pr 20:23). Another example of their deceitful trading is that they *sell the refuse of* (the sweepings with) *the wheat*, taking advantage of their neighbor's ignorance or necessity and making them take it at the same price at which they sell the *finest of the wheat* (Ps 81:16; 147:14). They are cruel and unmerciful to the poor: they *swallow up the needy* and *make the poor of the land to fail* (v. 4). However, the one who *reproaches the poor despises his Maker*, in whose hands *rich and poor meet together* (Pr 22:2). They trample on the poor by driving hard bargains with them, and they humiliate them in order to have their labor for next to nothing. This is how *they buy the poor for silver* (v. 6); they bring them and their *children into bondage* (Ne 5:2–5). Moreover, so many poor people have been reduced to this crisis that the price of a slave is very low. You can buy a poor man to be your slave *for a pair of shoes*. Property was the first basic principle to be invaded, and then liberty; oppressors first make people beggars and then make them their slaves.

2. The punishment that will be inflicted on them for this sin. God will remember their sin against them. He swears, *Surely I will never forget any of their works. I will never forget them* is as much as to say, "I will never forgive them." He will bring ruin and destruction on them. There will be universal fear and terror (v. 8). When God comes out against them, the waters of trouble and disaster will *rise up wholly as a flood*, which swells when it is dammed up and soon overflows its banks. The whole land *shall be cast out* (stirred up) *and drowned*, put under water, as the land of Egypt is every year by the overflowing of the Nile River. It will come on them when they least expect it (v. 9): "*I will cause the sun to go down at noon*, when it is in its full strength and brightness. The *earth* will be *darkened in the clear day*, when everything looks pleasant and promising." This will change their tune and spoil all their happiness (v. 10): *I will turn your feasts into mourning*, as he will turn the *songs of the temple into howlings* (v. 3). The state of impenitent sinners becomes worse and worse, and the last state of all will be the worst of all.

Verses 11–14

In these verses are threatened:

1. A spiritual famine coming on the whole land, *a famine of the word of God*, the failing of authoritative messages and the scarcity of good preaching. *The days will come* when another kind of darkness will come on that land of light. When Amos prophesied, and for a considerable time afterward, Israel had many prophets, abundant opportunities of *hearing the word of God*. God threatens that in the future he will deprive them of this privilege. They will have plenty of bread and water, but their teachers will be removed. Having the word of God made their nation great and high, for *to them were committed the oracles of God* (Ro 3:2), but when these were taken away from them, their beauty was stained and their honor placed in the dust (Ps 7:5). This was a sign of God's most intense displeasure against them. We should say at any time—and we *will* say in times of trouble—that a famine of the word of God is the most severe famine, the most serious form of judgment (v. 12): *They shall wander*

(stagger) *from sea to sea*, from the Sea of Tiberias (Jn 6:1; 21:1) to the Great Sea, to see if God will send them prophets. *In the day* of this famine *the fair virgins and the young men shall faint for thirst* (v. 13). Some commentators think *virgins* and *young men* refer to the Jewish churches and the masters of their synagogues. Other commentators think *fair virgins* and *choice young men* refer to those who trust in their own merit and think they have no need of Christ; they will *faint for thirst*, whereas those who *hunger and thirst after the righteousness* (Mt 5:6) of Christ will be filled.

2. The particular destruction of those who were ringleaders in idolatry (v. 14). They *swear by the sin of Samaria*, that is, by the god of Samaria, the idol that was worshiped at Bethel, not far from Samaria. They say, *Thy God, O Dan! liveth*; that was the other golden calf, a mute, dead idol, but treated as if it had been the living God. They say, *The manner*, or power or way, *of Beersheba liveth*; they swear by the religion of Beersheba. Those who give to idols the honor due only to God *shall fall*, and the gods cannot stand as their friends, and so they will *never rise again*.

CHAPTER 9

Here: 1. Judgment is threatened, which the sinners will not escape (vv. 1–4), which an almighty power will inflict (vv. 5–6), and which the people of Israel have deserved (vv. 7–8); and yet it will not be the total destruction of their nation (v. 8), for a remnant of good people will escape (v. 9). Evildoers, however, will perish (v. 10). 2. Mercy is promised, to be given in the last days (vv. 11–15), as is clear from its application to the days of the Messiah (Ac 15:16).

Verses 1–10

Here we have the justice of God passing sentence on this offensive people, and notice:

1. With what solemnity the sentence is passed. The prophet sees in a vision *the Lord standing upon* (by) *the altar* (v. 1), the altar of burnt offerings. He has moved from the *mercy seat* between the *cherubim*. He stands by the altar to prohibit sacrifice. Now the order given is, *Smite the lintel of the door* of the temple with such a blow *that the posts may shake*, and *cut them*, wound them *in the head, all of them*; break down the door of God's house, as a sign that he is going out from it, abandoning it. "Strike the king, who is like the pillar of the door, so that the rulers, who are like *the posts*, may *shake*; *cut them in the head*, cut them down, *all of them, and I will slay the last of them*."

2. The effective care taken that no one will escape the execution of this sentence. God's judgments will overtake the swiftest of those who think they can outrun them (v. 2).

2.1. Hell itself, though it has its name in English from its being "covered over" or "hidden," cannot hide them (v. 2): "Although *they dig into hell*, into the center of the earth, even *thence shall my hand take them*." The grave is a place for the righteous to hide from the hatred of the world (Job 3:17), but it will not be a place for evildoers to hide from the justice of God.

2.2. Heaven, though it may derive its name from being "heaved," or lifted up, will not put them out of reach of God's judgments (v. 2): *thence* (from there) *will I bring them down*.

2.3. *The top of Carmel* (v. 3) will not protect them: "*Though they hide themselves there*, where they imagine no one will go looking for them, *I will search and take them out thence* (from there)."

2.4. The *bottom of the sea* will not be able to conceal them. *Thence will I command the serpent, and he shall bite them,* the *crooked serpent, even the dragon that is in the sea* (Isa 27:1).

2.5. Distant countries will not become their friends, nor will lesser judgments excuse them from greater (v. 4).

3. God Almighty passes this sentence on them, and he himself will carry it out. Threats are more or less formidable according to the power of the person who is making them. We laugh at impotent wrath, but the wrath of God is not powerless; it is almighty wrath. He will *make the land melt* and tremble and make *all that dwell therein mourn,* and he can do it with the greatest ease, for:

3.1. It is *the Lord God of hosts* who undertakes to do it. The situation of those who have the Lord of Hosts against them is miserable indeed, for they have *hosts,* God's armies, the whole creation, at war with them.

3.2. He is the Creator and ruler of the higher world: *It is he that builds his stories* (lofty palace) *in the heavens* (v. 6) — the heavenly bodies, or orbs — one above the other like so many stories in a high and stately palace.

3.3. He has the command of this lower world too, *earth* and *sea.* Do they think they can fight on land? He *has founded his troop in the earth,* his troops of guards, to protect his subjects and punish his enemies. All the creatures on earth make one "bundle" (as the margin of v. 6 reads), one bundle of arrows, out of which he takes what he wants to shoot against the persecutors (Ps 7:13). Do they think they can fight at sea? He commands the waters of the sea too; even its waves, the most tumultuous, rebellious waters, obey him.

4. How justly God passes this sentence on the people of Israel. He does not destroy them by an act of sovereignty, but by an act of righteousness. Because this is a sinful kingdom:

4.1. Notice how God makes light (v. 7) of the relationship in which he stands to it: *Are you not as children of the Ethiopians unto me, O children of Israel?* A sad change! Those who were trained in the knowledge and fear of God — who showed great potential — reject their profession and become as bad as the worst people. This foreshadows the rejection of the unfaithful Jews in the days of the Messiah; because they did not embrace the doctrine of Christ, the kingdom of God was taken away from them. They were dischurched and rejected from the covenant.

4.2. Notice how he makes light of the favors he has given them. They think he will not reject them and put them on the same level as other nations, because he has done for them what he has not done for other nations. "No," he says, "the favors shown to you are not so distinctive as you think they are: *Have not I brought up Israel out of the land of Egypt?* I have also brought the *Philistines from Caphtor* (Crete or Cappadocia). In the same way, the *Syrians* (Arameans) were brought up from Kir, where they had been taken away to (2Ki 16:9). If God's Israel lose their distinctive holiness, they lose their distinctive privileges.

5. How graciously God will separate the worthy and the worthless (Jer 15:19) on the day of retribution. Although the evil Israelites will be like the evil Ethiopians, and their being called Israelites will give them no advantage, the devout Israelites will not be like the *wicked ones. I will* distinguish, as befits a righteous judge. The house of Israel will be *sifted as corn is sifted* (v. 9), but they will remain in the hands of God, as the sieve is in

the hands of the one who is sifting: *I will sift the house of Israel among all nations.* None of the righteous ones among them, who are like the solid grain, will perish; *not the least grain shall fall on the earth,* so as to be lost and forgotten. Not the smallest "pebble," literally, for the good grain is as heavy as a stone in comparison with what we call *light corn.*

Verses 11–15

The prophet here bears testimony to the One to whom all the prophets bear witness (Ac 10:43). The prophet speaks of *that day* in which God will do great things for his church by setting up the kingdom of the Messiah. The promise here may refer to the planting of the Christian church (Ac 15:15–17). It is promised that:

1. In the Messiah the kingdom of David will be restored (v. 11). The church militant, in its present state, living as in shepherds' tents to eat and soldiers' tents to fight, is the *tabernacle of David.* In Amos's time the royal family had become very poor and its power had been reduced, because many of that race had become corrupt, and it lost its imperial position in the exile. This is how the church of the Jews was; in its later days, its glory had departed (1Sa 4:21–22). It was like a tent brought to ruin. But these tents were raised and rebuilt by Jesus Christ. In him, God's covenant with David had its fulfillment, and the glory of that house revived. The spiritual glory of the family of Christ far exceeded the temporal glory of the family of David. In Christ also God's covenant with Israel was fulfilled, and in the Gospel church the tabernacle of God was set up among human beings again. This is quoted in the first council at Jerusalem as referring to the calling in of the Gentiles and God's *taking out of them a people for his name* (Ac 15:14).

2. That kingdom will be enlarged (v. 12) so that the house of David may possess the *remnant of Edom, and of all the heathen* (nations), that is, so that Christ may have them given him as his *inheritance.* Christ died to *gather together in one the children of God that were scattered abroad* (Jn 11:52), who are said here to be those that were *called by his name.*

3. In the kingdom of the Messiah there will be great plenty (v. 13): *The ploughman shall overtake the reaper,* that is, there will be such a plentiful harvest every year that it will last all summer, even until autumn, when it is time to begin to plow again. The hills that were dry and barren will be moistened and will melt with the richness or mellowness of the soil. This must be understood to refer to the spiritual blessings with which all those who are sincerely added to Christ and his church (Ac 2:47) are blessed. They will have the bread of life to *strengthen their hearts* (Ps 104:15) and the wine of divine encouragement and strength to *make them glad — meat indeed* and *drink indeed* (Jn 6:55) — all the benefits that come to the human soul from the word and Spirit of God. When great multitudes were converted and when the preachers of the Gospel were *always caused to triumph in* (2Co 2:14) the success of their preaching, then the *ploughman overtook the reaper.*

4. The kingdom of the Messiah will be well populated; there will be mouths to enjoy this food (Ecc 5:11) (v. 14). Those who take effort with their religious faith, as people do with their vineyards and gardens, will obtain both pleasure and profit from it. The *bringing again* of the *captivity* of God's Israel, which is promised here, may refer to the canceling of the ceremonial law and the giving to them of the liberty with which Christ came to set his church free (Gal 5:1).

5. The kingdom of the Messiah will take such deep root in the world as never to be uprooted from it (v. 15): *I will plant them upon their land.* The church may become corrupt, but it will not completely abandon God; it may be persecuted, but it will not be completely abandoned by God. Two things will ensure that the church will last forever:

- God's gifts to it: it is *the land which I have given them.*
- Its privileges in him: he is *the Lord thy God*, who has said it and will fulfill it, who will *reign for ever* (Rev 11:15) *unto all generations* (Ps 119:90). Moreover, because he lives forever, the church will live forever too.

A Practical and Devotional Exposition of the Book of the Prophet

Obadiah

This is the shortest book in the Old Testament, but it is not to be overlooked, for this coin has Caesar's image and title on it (Mt 20:22); it is stamped with a divine authority. It is entitled *The vision of Obadiah.* Who this Obadiah was is not revealed. Some of the old commentators thought he was the same Obadiah who was in charge of Ahab's palace (1Ki 18:3), and if so, the one who hid and fed the prophets truly had a prophet's reward (Mt 10:41) when he himself was made a prophet. However, there is no basis for that conjecture. This Obadiah probably lived later; some think he was a contemporary of Hosea, Joel, and Amos; others think he lived about the time of the destruction of Jerusalem, when the children of Edom triumphed so cruelly in that destruction. Whichever is true, what he wrote was what he saw; it is his *vision*. It is a foolish thought of some Jews that because he prophesied only about Edom, he himself was an Edomite by birth, but a convert to the Jewish religion. Other prophets prophesied against Edom, and some of them seem to have borrowed from him in their prophecies against Edom (Jer 49:7; Eze 25:12).

This book is wholly about Edom, a nation adjoining Israel, but an enemy of Jacob's offspring, inheriting the enmity of their father Esau toward Jacob. We have here, after the introduction (v. 1): 1. Threats against Edom: that their pride would be humbled (vv. 2–4), their wealth would be plundered (vv. 5–7), their wisdom would be brought to nothing (vv. 8–9), and their spiteful behavior toward God's Israel would be avenged (vv. 10–16). 2. Gracious promises to Israel: that they would be restored and reformed and would be victorious over the Edomites (vv. 17–20) and that the kingdom of the Messiah would be set up by the bringing in of the great salvation (v. 21).

CHAPTER 1

Verses 1–9

Edom is the nation against which this prophecy is directed, and some think it stands for all the enemies of Israel. Although Edom was destroyed in the times of the Maccabees, as it had been before by Jehoshaphat, its destruction still seems to have been a type, like the rejection of the Edomites' father, Esau (Ro 9:13), and to have had further reference to the destruction of the enemies of the Gospel church. Some have noted well that it must have been a great trial to the people of Israel to see themselves, the children of beloved Jacob, in trouble, and the Edomites, the descendants of hated Esau, gloating over them in their troubles. God therefore gives them a prospect of the destruction of Edom and of a happy outcome of their own correction. Here is:

1. A declaration of war against Edom (v. 1): "*We have heard a rumour*, or rather a message, *from the Lord*, almighty God. He has given the word of command that all who trouble his people will certainly bring trouble on themselves. We have heard that God is preparing his throne for judgment (Ps 9:7). *An ambassador is sent among the heathen* (nations)," a herald or envoy, to alarm the nations: "*Arise ye*, stir yourselves and one another, *and let us rise up against* Edom *in battle*." The allied forces under Nebuchadnezzar prepare to swoop on that country: *Gather yourselves together, and come against her*, as it is in the parallel reference (Jer 49:14).

2. A prediction of the success of that war. Edom will certainly be subdued. Are they depending on:

2.1. How grand they look among the nations, their influence on them? That will dwindle (v. 2): "*Behold, I have made thee small among the heathen* (nations), so that none of your neighbors will seek an alliance with you; *thou art greatly despised* among them, as a nation that has been unfaithful." Consequently, *the pride of thy heart has deceived thee* (v. 3).

2.2. The fortifications of their country? Those too will deceive them. They *dwelt in the clefts of the rock* (v. 3) like an eagle in its nest, and their home was on the heights, fortified against their enemies, and they thought they were so high as to be out of the reach of danger. Edom says in the pride of his heart: *Who shall bring me down to the ground?* He speaks with confidence in his own strength and with contempt of God's judgments. Worldly self-confidence is a sin that easily entangles people (Heb 12:1) in their pride, power, and prosperity. If people dare challenge almighty God, that challenge will be taken up: *Who shall bring me down?* says Edom. "*I will,*" God replies. "*Though thou exalt thyself as the eagle* that soars high to the heights, in fact, *though thou set thy nest among the stars*, it is only in your own imagination, and *thence will I bring thee down.*" We had this in Jer 49:15–16.

2.3. Their wealth and treasures, their resources for war? Their money will expose them rather than protect them; it will become plunder for the enemy, and they will become prey because of it (vv. 5–6). "How you have fallen, and how great your fall is!" "How art thou stupefied!" as the Aramaic reads. The prophet shows that the coming judgment will be their total destruction, not an "ordinary" disaster. It is indeed ordinary for those who have wealth to have it stolen, to lose a little from their plenty. *Thieves come to them* and steal no more than they think they can take away, and when there is plenty, small amounts that are stolen are scarcely missed. But it will not be so with Edom; his wealth will be completely taken away; nothing will escape the hands of the destroying army (v. 6). *How are his hidden things*, his hidden treasures, plundered, rifled, and *sought up* (pillaged).

2.4. Their alliances with neighboring states and powers? They too will fail them (v. 7): "The *men of thy confederacy*, all your allies, the Ammonites and Moabites and other allies who were at *peace with thee, did eat thy bread*; they were entertained by you and lived off you. They *brought thee even to the border* of your land, were respectful to your envoys and took them on their way home, but then they *deceived thee*; they flew back and retreated in your hour of need. They *prevailed against* (overpowered) *thee*; they proved too powerful for you in the treaty imposed on you, bringing you into danger and leaving you there as an easy prey to the enemy. They have *laid a wound under thee*; that is, they have laid under you as a support what will turn out to wound you, not only as thorns but as swords." If God puts under us the arms of his power and love, these will be firm (Dt 33:27); the God of our covenant will never deceive us. But if we trust in our allies and what they will give us, it may turn out to be a trap and *dishonour*. Just censure is spoken here to Edom for trusting in those who played tricks on him: "*There is no understanding in him*, for otherwise he would never have put such confidence in them, putting himself in their power to betray."

2.5. The wisdom of their counselors? That too will fail them (v. 8). Edom has been famous for its great political leaders, but now the *counsellors* have become *fools*. *Shall I not in that day destroy the wise men out of Edom?* This was just punishment of their foolishness in trusting in an arm of flesh (2Ch 32:8): *There is no understanding in them* (v. 7); they do not have the sense to trust in the living God. It was also the forerunner of their destruction. A nation is certainly marked out for ruin when God hides the things that will bring it peace from the eyes of those who are entrusted with its decisions (Lk 19:42).

2.6. The strength and courage of their soldiers? They are able-bodied warriors with spirit and courage, but now (v. 9), *Thy mighty men, O Teman! shall be dismayed*; their courage will fail them, *to the end that every one of the mount of Esau may be cut off by slaughter*, and no one will escape.

Verses 10–16

Many things were wrong in Edom; they were a sinful people and *a people laden with iniquity* (Isa 1:4). However, that one single crime that they are accused of as bringing this destruction on them is the wrong they did to the people of God. "It is *for thy violence against thy brother Jacob* (v. 10), that ancient grudge that you have borne against the people of Israel, that all this *shame shall cover thee* and *thou shalt be cut off for ever*. It is violence *against thy brother*, to whom you should be a

go'el, 'a kinsman-redeemer' (Dt 25:5–10), for whom it is your duty to put things right if others wrong him. Thou *slanderest* and *abusest thy own mother's son*" (Ps 50:20). The violence is made much worse if it is done against one of God's people; "it is your brother Jacob, who is in covenant with God and precious to him. You hate the one whom God has loved." Here we are told about:

1. The violence that Edom did against his brother Jacob. What they are accused of is their cruel behavior toward Judah and Jerusalem when they were in distress and ready to be destroyed, probably by the Babylonians. It is charged against the Edomites that *in the day of Jerusalem they said, Rase it* (tear it down) (Ps 137:7); see also Eze 25:12. "You *should not have looked*, you *should not have entered*, but you did so (vv. 12–14)." Let us see:

1.1. The situation of Judah and Jerusalem when the Edomites gloated over them. With the Edomites it was a day of prosperity; with the Israelites it was a day of calamity, for judgment commonly *begins at the house of God* (1Pe 4:17). Children are corrected when foreigners are left alone. It was *the day of their destruction* (v. 12), when *foreigners entered into the gates of Jerusalem*, when the great officers of the king of Babylon's army sat in the gates as the judges of the land. It was a day when the *strangers carried away captive his forces* (v. 11). The Edomites, their neighbors and brothers, should have pitied them and helped them.

1.2. The conduct of the Edomites for which they are condemned. They looked unconcerned and with pleasure on the suffering of God's people (vv. 12–13). Those who are idle spectators of the troubles and afflictions of their neighbors when they could be actively helping them have a great deal to answer for. They *rejoiced over the children of Judah in the day of their destruction* (v. 12). They went even further, for they *entered into the gate* of God's people and *laid hands on their substance* (seized their wealth) (v. 13). Although they did not help to conquer them, they helped plunder them. They not only robbed their brothers and sisters but even murdered them (v. 14). When the victorious sword of the Babylonians was working bloodshed among the Jews, many escaped, but the Edomites cruelly intercepted them; they *stood in the cross way*. They cruelly killed some; they handed others over to the pursuers. In all this they joined with the open enemies and persecutors of Israel: *Even thou wast as one of them*.

2. The shame that will cover them for their violent acts. When they come to be in the same disastrous condition that Israel is now in, they will be ashamed (v. 15): *The day of the Lord is near upon all the heathen* (nations), when God will show his retribution toward people who trouble his church. *As you have drunk upon my holy mountain* (v. 16)—that is, as God's professing people have drunk deeply of the cup of suffering—*so shall all the heathen* (nations) *drink* of the same bitter cup. They may expect their case to be worse on the day of distress than that of Israel on their day. The afflictions of God's people lasted only for a moment, but their enemies will *drink continually the wine of God's wrath* (Rev 14:10). The dregs of the cup are reserved for the *wicked of the earth* (Ps 75:8); they will *drink and swallow down*, or "sup up," as the margin of v. 16 reads, will drink it to the bottom.

Verses 17–21

This prophecy, like those of Joel and Amos, concludes with precious promises of the salvation of the church. Although they might have been partially fulfilled in the return of the Jews from Babylon, they would doubtless have their complete fulfillment in that great salvation brought by Jesus Christ.

1. There will be salvation on Mount Zion: *Upon Mount Zion shall be deliverance* (v. 17). A remnant of Israel *upon the holy mountain* will be saved (v. 16).

2. Where there is salvation, there will be sanctification: *And there shall be holiness* to prepare and qualify the children of Zion for this deliverance, for wherever God intends glory he gives grace.

3. This salvation and sanctification will spread and triumph: the *house of Jacob,* this *Mount Zion,* with the deliverance and the holiness produced there, will *possess their possessions;* that is, the Gospel church will be set up among the nations and fill the earth. The apostles of Christ will gain possession of the hearts of human beings, and when they possess their hearts, they will *possess their possessions,* for those who have given themselves to the Lord give up all they have to him. It is foretold here:

3.1. How this possession will be gained (v. 18): *The house of Jacob shall be a fire, and the house of Joseph a flame,* for their God is a consuming fire (Heb 12:29). *The house of Esau will be as stubble.* The Gospel, preached in the house of Jacob and Joseph, will be like a fire and a flame to melt hard hearts, to burn up the dross, so that they may be purified with the *spirit of judgment and* the *spirit of burning* (Isa 4:4). The word of God in the mouth of his ministers is said to be like fire, and the people like wood to be consumed by it (Jer 5:14). Those who are not refined as gold by the fire of the Gospel will be consumed as dross by it.

3.2. How far this possession will extend (vv. 19–20). The *captivity of this host of Israel*—the company of Israelite exiles, still called the *children of the captiv-*ity—will regain their own land and gain ground from their neighbors adjoining them. Some will become converts and join the Jews, who, by possessing them in holy fellowship, will possess their land. The kingdom of Israel will join with that of Judah in both civil and sacred interests, and the two kingdoms, as friends and brothers and sisters, will mutually possess and delight in one another. Together they will *possess the Canaanites,* even as far as Zarephath, which *belongeth to Zidon,* and Jerusalem will possess the *cities of the south,* even as far as Sepharad. This is how the Jews enlarged their borders on all sides. The promise here, however, no doubt has a spiritual meaning, and had its fulfillment in the setting up of the Christian church in the world, the Gospel Israel, and will have its gradual fulfillment in the church's enlargement, until the mystical body is completed.

4. The kingdom of the Redeemer will be set up, bringing encouragement to his loyal subjects and shame to his enemies (v. 21): *The kingdom shall be the Lord's,* the Lord Christ's. The mountain of Zion will be saved. On it *saviours* will *come,* the preachers of the Gospel, who are called *saviours* because their business is to save themselves and those who hear their message. In this they are *workers together with Christ* (2Co 6:1). The mountain of Esau will be judged, and those who come as saviors on Mount Zion will *judge the mountain of Esau,* for the word of the Gospel in the mouth of these preachers convinces and condemns the people of Edom. In the course of God's providence his Scripture is fulfilled; when God raises up friends for the church in her distress, then *saviours come on Mount Zion* to save it. When the enemies of the church are brought down, then the *mount of Esau is judged.* This will be done in every age in such a way as God thinks best.

A Practical and Devotional Exposition of the Book of the Prophet

Jonah

Although this book of Jonah is located among the prophetic books, it is a history rather than a prophecy; it contains one line of prediction, *Yet forty days, and Nineveh shall be overthrown* (3:4), the rest of the book being a narrative of the introduction to and the effects of that prediction. Probably Jonah himself wrote this book, recording his own faults, like other inspired writers, which is evidence that their purpose in these writings was God's glory, not their own. We read about this same Jonah in 2Ki 14:25, where we find that he was from Gath Hepher in Galilee, a town that belonged to the tribe of Zebulun, in a distant corner of the land of Israel. He was a messenger of mercy to Israel in the reign of Jeroboam II, for the *restoring of the coast* (boundaries) *of Israel* is said to have been *according to the word of the Lord which he spoke by the hand of his servant Jonah the prophet* (2Ki 14:25). The story contains remarkable instances of both human weakness and God's mercy: of human weakness in Jonah and of God's mercy in both his forgiving of repentant sinners, as in Nineveh, and his bearing with discontented saints, such as Jonah.

CHAPTER 1

We have here: 1. A command given to Jonah to preach at Nineveh (vv. 1–2). 2. Jonah's disobedience to that command (v. 3). 3. The pursuit and stopping of him for that disobedience by a storm (vv. 4–6). 4. The discovery that he and his disobedience were the cause of the storm (vv. 7–10). 5. The throwing of him into the sea to calm the storm (vv. 11–16). 6. The miraculous preservation of his life inside the fish (v. 17), which reserved him for further service.

Verses 1–3

Notice:

1. The honor God showed to Jonah by commissioning him to go and prophesy against Nineveh. *Jonah* may mean "a dove," a proper name for all God's prophets, all his people, who should be *harmless as doves* (Mt 10:16) and should *mourn as doves* for the sins and calamities of the land. His father's name was *Amittai*, "my truth," because God's prophets should be sons of truth. It was to him that *the word of the Lord* (v. 1) came; to him were now given the orders, *Arise, go to Nineveh, that great city* (v. 2). Nineveh was the center of the Assyrian monarchy (Ge 10:11), *a great city*, great in its number of inhabitants and great in power and dominion. It was the city that for some time *ruled over the kings of the earth*. Great cities, however, as well as great people, are under God's rule. Nineveh was also a pagan city; its inhabitants did not know or worship the true God. And it was evil: *Their wickedness has come up before me* (v. 2); they sinned defiantly. Jonah must *cry against it*. He must bear witness against their great evil, and he must warn them of the destruction coming on them because of it. *Cry aloud, spare not* (Isa 58:1). He must not whisper his message, but make it known in the streets of Nineveh; *he that hath*

ears to hear, let him hear (Mt 11:15) what God has to say against that evil city through his prophet. Jonah must *go to Nineveh* and cry out there against its evil. Other prophets were ordered to *send* messages to the neighboring nations, but Jonah must go and take the message himself.

2. The dishonor Jonah showed to God by refusing to go (v. 3): *But Jonah*, instead of rising to go to Nineveh, *rose up to flee to Tarshish*, to *the sea*, not bound for any port, but simply wanting to get away *from the presence of the Lord*. He *consulted with flesh and blood* (Gal 1:16) and declined the message, because he was jealous for the rights of his country and unwilling for any other nation to share in the honor of divine revelation. He himself acknowledged (4:2) that the reason for his dislike was that he foresaw that the Ninevites would repent and that God would forgive them and take them into his favor, which would bring disgrace on the people of Israel, who had so long been God's own special people. He went to Joppa, a famous port in the land of Israel, looking for a ship that was sailing for Tarshish, and he found one there. Providence seemed to give him an opportunity to escape. The ready way is not always the right one. He found the ship and set sail for Tarshish. So he *paid the fare thereof*. He went *with them*, the sailors, the passengers, the merchants, whoever they were who were going to Tarshish. Jonah forgot his position as well as his duty; he went along with them.

Verses 4–10

1. God sent a pursuer after Jonah, *a mighty tempest* (a violent storm) *in the sea* (v. 4). The effect of this wind was like that of *a mighty tempest*, because when the winds get up, the waves rise. The storm raged so much that the *ship was likely to be broken* (threatened to break up). This wind was sent after Jonah to draw him back to God and his duty, and it is a great mercy to be recalled homeward

when we are going astray, even though it may be through a violent storm.

2. The ship's crew were alarmed by this violent storm, but only Jonah was unconcerned (v. 5). The sailors were *afraid*; although their work led them to such dangers and they were used to making light of them, now the oldest and bravest of them began to tremble, fearful that there was something extraordinary in this storm because it arose so suddenly and raged so strongly. They *cried every man unto his god*. Many will not be brought to prayer until they are frightened into it: if you want to learn to pray, go to sea. Having called on their gods to help them, they did what they could to help themselves. They *cast forth the wares* (threw the cargo) *that were in the ship into the sea, to lighten it of them*, as Paul's sailors did in a similar situation (Ac 27:18–19, 38). But where is Jonah all this time? One would have expected him to be busier than anyone else, but we find him down in *the hold, between the sides of the ship* (below deck), and he is lying there *fast asleep*; neither the noise outside nor the sense of guilt within him woke him up.

3. The captain of the ship called Jonah up to his prayers (v. 6). The *shipmaster came to him* and told him he should be ashamed of himself and get up, both to *pray for life* and to *prepare for death*. *What meanest thou, O sleeper?* We commend the captain. We pity Jonah, who needed this rebuke; as a prophet of the Lord, if he had been in the right place, he might have been rebuking the king of Nineveh, but, being outside his duty, he was open to the rebukes of an insignificant captain. We must wonder at God's goodness, however, in sending him this timely rebuke, for it was the first step toward his recovery, as the crowing of the cock was to Peter (Mt 26:74–75). "*Arise, call upon thy God*; each one if us is here crying out to his god. Why do you not get up and cry out to yours?" *If so be that God will think upon us, that we perish not* (v. 6). It seems that the many gods they called on were considered by them only as mediators between them and the supreme God, for the captain spoke about only one God from whom he expected relief.

4. Jonah was found to be the cause of the storm.

4.1. The sailors noticed so much that was uncommon and distinctive in the storm that they concluded that it was a messenger of divine justice sent to arrest someone onboard the ship who was guilty of some great crime (Ac 28:4); it must be for his sake they suffered.

4.2. They decided to cast lots to see which of them was the criminal who had caused this storm: *Let us cast lots, that we may know for whose cause this evil is upon us* (v. 7). They suspected one another and were determined to find out who it was. These sailors wanted to know the person who was the burden in their ship, so that that one man might *die for the people* (Jn 11:50) and so that the whole ship *might not be lost*. In order to find this out, they cast lots, by which they appealed to the judgment of God.

4.3. The *lot fell upon Jonah*, who could have saved them this trouble if only he had told them what his own conscience told him: *Thou art the man* (2Sa 12:7). We may suppose there were those in the ship who were greater sinners than Jonah, but he was the man the storm was pursuing. The storm was sent after Jonah because God had a work for him to do, and it was sent to draw him back to it.

4.4. Jonah was brought to be examined by the captain and the sailors. He was a stranger; none of them had anything to accuse him of, and so they must extract a confession from him and judge him *out of his own mouth* (Lk 19:22). They did not attack him outrageously, but calmly inquired into his case. Compassion is due to offenders when they are discovered and convicted. They inquired of him about two things:

4.4.1. Whether he would acknowledge that he was the person for whose sake the storm was sent: "*Tell us for whose cause this evil* (calamity) *is upon us* (v. 8); are you responsible for it? What is the offense for which you are being pursued in this way?"

4.4.2. His calling and his country. *What is thy occupation? Whence comest thou?*

4.5. Jonah revealed everything. He told them he was *a Hebrew* (v. 9), and so he was more ashamed to acknowledge he was a criminal, for the sins of Hebrews, who made such a profession of religion, were all the more sinful because of that. He also gave an account of his religious faith, for that was his calling: "*I fear the Lord Jehovah*; that is the God I worship, *the God of heaven*, the sovereign Lord of all, who has *made the sea and the dry land* and has command of both." He acknowledged that he had *fled from the presence of the Lord*, that he was running away from his duty, and that the storm had been sent to draw him back.

4.6. The sailors *were exceedingly afraid* (v. 10), and justly so, for they perceived that God was angry with the one who feared and worshiped him because the man had run away from his work just once. "If a prophet of the Lord is so severely punished for one offense, what will become of us who have been guilty of so many great, detestable, heinous offenses?" They said to him, "*Why hast thou done this?* Why have you involved us in this pursuit?"

Verses 11–17

Something more still had to be done, because *the sea wrought and was tempestuous* (v. 11 and again v. 13); it was getting rougher and rougher.

1. They asked Jonah himself what he thought they should do with him (v. 11). He appeared to be guilty, but he also appeared to be penitent. They would not *cast him into the sea* if he could think of any other way by which to *save the ship*.

2. Jonah read his own doom (v. 12): *Take me up, and cast me forth into the sea*. This is the language of true penitents, who fervently want no one but themselves to fare worse because of their sins and foolishness. How ready Jonah was to take all the guilt on himself and look on all the trouble as theirs. "If it is I who have raised the storm, it is not throwing the cargo into the sea that will make it calm again; no, you must throw me in." When conscience is awakened, and a storm raised, nothing will turn it calm except parting with the sin that caused the disturbance.

3. The poor sailors did what they could to avoid throwing Jonah into the sea, but it was in vain (v. 13): *They rowed hard to bring the ship to the land*, so that if they had to part with Jonah, they could set him safely on the shore, *but they could not*.

4. When they threw Jonah into the sea, they first prayed to God that his blood would not lie on them (v. 14). They prayed to the *God of Israel*, now being convinced by the providences of God toward Jonah and the information he had given them that God is the only God. "Lord," they said, "*let us not perish for this man's life*."

5. Having prayed to be saved from the guilt, they carried out the act (v. 15): *They took up Jonah* and threw *him into the sea*. When sin is the Jonah that raises the storm, it must be thrown in this way into the sea; we must drown what otherwise will *drown us*.

6. The throwing of Jonah into the sea immediately brought an end to the storm. If we turn away from our sins, God will soon turn from his anger.

7. The sailors were even more confirmed in their belief that Jonah's God was the only true God (v. 16). As evidence, they *offered sacrifice* to him when they came ashore on the land of Israel, and for the present they made vows that they would continue to do so to express their thankfulness for being saved.

8. Jonah's life was saved by a miracle. In the middle of judgment, God *remembered mercy* (Hab 3:2). Although Jonah was fleeing from the presence of the Lord and seemed to have fallen into his avenging hands, God still had a work for him to do and had therefore *prepared a great fish to swallow up Jonah* (v. 17), *a whale* (a huge fish), as our Savior calls it (Mt 12:40), one of the largest kinds of whales, which have wider throats than others; in the belly of such a creature there has been found the dead body of a man in armor. It was because of the Lord's mercies that Jonah was not now consumed (La 3:22). Through this preservation, Jonah was intended to become a memorial to divine mercy, a successful preacher to Nineveh, and an eminent type of Christ, who was buried and rose again according to the Scriptures (1Co 15:4); for just as Jonah was in the whale's belly three days and three nights, so was the Son of Man in the heart of the earth three days and three nights (Mt 12:40). Was Jonah's grave a strange or a new one? So was Christ's, one in which no one had been laid before. Was Jonah there the best part of three days and three nights? So was Christ, but both were there in order to rise again and take the teaching of repentance to the Gentile world.

CHAPTER 2

God brings his people through fire and water (Ps 66:12), and we see that through God's power, Jonah the prophet is still alive. In this chapter, God hears from him, for we find him praying; in the next chapter, Nineveh hears from him, for we find him preaching. In his prayer we have:
1. The great distress and danger he was in (vv. 2–3, 5–6). 2. The despair he was almost reduced to (v. 4). 3. The encouragement he took to himself (vv. 4, 7). 4. The assurance he had of God's favor toward him (vv. 6–7). 5. The warning and instruction he gave to others (v. 9). 6. The praise and glory given to God for everything (v. 9). In the last verse we have Jonah's rescue, and he comes safe and sound onto dry land again.

Verses 1–9

God and his servant Jonah had separated in anger, and the quarrel began on Jonah's side; he fled from his country in order to run away from his work. The reconciliation began on God's side. At the end of the previous chapter we found God returning to Jonah by way of mercy, *delivering him from going down to the pit,* having *found a ransom* (Job 33:24); in this chapter we find Jonah returning to God by way of duty. Notice:

1. When he prayed—when he was in trouble: *Then Jonah prayed* (v. 1). When he was under the sense of sin and the signs of God's displeasure with it, *then* he prayed. And when there was a sign of hope that he would be delivered, having been preserved alive by miracle, *then* he prayed.

2. Where he prayed—in *the fish's belly.* No place is the wrong place to pray. Wherever God puts us, we may find a way open toward heaven. All who have Christ dwelling in their hearts through faith (Eph 3:17) take their altars, which *sanctify the gifts* (Mt 23:19), along with them

wherever they go and are thus *living temples* (2Co 6:16). People may shut us out from fellowship with one another, but not from fellowship with God. Jonah was now at the bottom of the sea, but *out of the depths he cried to God.*

3. To whom he prayed—*to the Lord his God.* He had been fleeing from God, but now he saw how foolish that was and returned to him.

4. What his prayer was. He reflects on the activity of his heart toward God when he was in distress, on the conflict that was within him between faith and sense, between hope and fear.

4.1. He reflects on the fervency of his prayer and God's readiness to listen to and answer it (v. 2). He says, *I cried, by reason of my affliction, unto the Lord. Out of the belly of hell* (depths of the grave) *cried I.* His cry was not in vain: *God heard him, heard the voice of his distress.*

4.2. He reflects on the miserable condition he was in when he was in the belly of the grave. He was thrown very low (v. 3): *Thou hadst cast me into the deep.* The mariners hurled him there, but he saw the hand of God doing it. Notice how terribly he was engulfed: *The floods compassed me about* (the currents swirled about him). The channels and springs of the waters of the sea engulfed him; it was high water with him. *All thy billows and thy waves passed* (waves and breakers swept) *over me.* These words are clearly quoted by Jonah from Ps 42:7, where in the original David's complaint is the same, word for word. If ever any person's case was special, surely Jonah's was, but, to his great satisfaction, he found that even the man after God's own heart (1Sa 13:14) made the same complaint about God's *waves and billows going over him.* Our path of trouble is not an untrodden path. V. 5 is to the same effect: *The waters compassed me about even to the soul.* This is also borrowed from David's complaint: the *waters have come in unto my soul* (Ps 69:1). How firmly he was held (v. 6): He *went down to the bottom* (roots) *of the mountains;* the *earth with her bars was about him;* it was likely to be wrapped around him forever.

4.3. He reflects on the black and desperate conclusion he was then about to make concerning himself and recalls the relief he obtained from that conclusion (vv. 4, 7). He began to sink into despair. When the *waters compassed him about even to the soul,* it was no wonder that *his soul fainted within him.* What hope could he have of being saved from a trouble that his *own ways and doings* had brought on him? He said, *I am cast out of* (I have been banished from) *thy sight.* Sometimes the condition of God's people may be such in this world that they may think they are excluded from God's presence, so as to see him no more. However, this is only the thought of unbelief, for God has not *cast away his people whom he has chosen* (Isa 41:9). Jonah recovered from sinking into despair, with some comfortable prospects of rescue. Faith corrected and controlled the thoughts of fear and distrust. Here was a fierce struggle between sense and faith, but faith had the last word and came off conqueror. Jonah's faith said, *Yet I will look again towards thy holy temple* (v. 7). When Hezekiah wanted to be assured of his recovery, he asked, *What is the sign that I shall go up to the house of the Lord?* (Isa 38:22), as if that were the only thing for the sake of which he wished for health. In the same way, Jonah here hoped he would *look again towards the temple* (v. 7). Notice how modestly Jonah expressed himself; he was conscious in himself of his own guilt and unworthiness, and he dared not speak of living in God's house, but he hoped he might be admitted to look toward it. Or these words may be taken as Jonah's vow when he was in distress, and he spoke (v. 9) of paying what he vowed. His sin for which God pursued him was *fleeing from the presence of the Lord*. He would never again look toward Tarshish, but he would look toward the temple again, and would *go from strength to strength till he appeared before God there* (Ps 84:7). When our souls faint, we must remember God, and when we think of him, we should call on his name.

4.4. He reflects on the favor God showed him when he sought and trusted him in this distress. God graciously accepted his prayer: *My prayer*, being sent to him, *came in unto him*, even *into his holy temple* (v. 7); it was heard in the highest heaven, even though it was prayed in the lowest depths. And God wonderfully rescued him (v. 6): *Yet hast thou brought up my life from corruption, O Lord my God!* Some think he said this when he was vomited onto the dry ground. *The earth with her bars was about me for ever*, but *thou hast brought up my life from the pit*, from "the bars of the pit" (v. 6). Or we may suppose it to have been spoken while he was still inside the fish, and if so, then it expresses his faith: "You have kept me alive in the pit, and so you can and will *bring up my life from the pit*"—or *from corruption*, as our translation reads it; and he spoke of his rescue with as much assurance as if it were already done: *Thou hast brought up my life*. If the Lord is our God, he will be to us the *resurrection and the life* (Jn 11:25), he will redeem our lives from destruction (Ps 103:4), from the power of the grave (Ps 49:15).

4.5. He gives warning to others to keep close to God (v. 8): *Those that observe lying vanities forsake their own mercy*, that is, those who worship other gods, as the pagan sailors did, expecting relief and comfort from them, *forsake their own mercy*. They turn their backs on their own happiness. Or, those who follow their own desires, as Jonah himself did when he *fled from the presence of the Lord* to go to Tarshish, *forsake their own mercy*, the mercy that they could find if only they kept close to God and their duty.

4.6. He recalls how he solemnly committed his soul with a vow that if God would rescue him, the God of his mercies would be the God of his praises (v. 9). Jonah promised that besides offering a sacrifice of thanksgiving, he *would mention the loving-kindness of the Lord* for the Lord's glory and the encouragement of others. He will now honor him by a prompt performance of the vows. Probably his vow was that if God rescued him, he would readily go wherever God wished to send him, even if it was Nineveh. He concludes with an acknowledgment of God as the Savior of his people: *Salvation is of the Lord*; it *belongs to the Lord* (Ps 3:8). Jonah's experience will encourage others in all ages to trust in God as the God of their salvation.

Verse 10

Jonah's release from his imprisonment and his rescue from death may be considered as an example of God's mercy to a poor penitent who prays to him in his distress. When God had him at his mercy, he showed him mercy; he did not *contend for ever* (Isa 57:16). It seems a type and figure of Christ's resurrection. He died and was buried to calm the storm that our sin had raised, and he lay in the grave, as Jonah did, three days and three nights, a prisoner for our debt, but on the third day he came out to preach repentance and forgiveness of sins through his messengers, even to the Gentiles.

CHAPTER 3

We have here: 1. Jonah's mission renewed, and the command given him a second time to go and preach at Nineveh (vv. 1–1–2). 2. Jonah's message to Nineveh

faithfully communicated (vv. 3–4). 3. The repentance, humiliation, and reformation of the Ninevites (vv. 5–9). 4. God's gracious revoking of the sentence passed on them (v. 10).

Verses 1–4

We have further evidence here of the reconciliation between God and Jonah, and we see that it was a thorough reconciliation, even though the disagreement between them had been great.

1. Jonah's commission was renewed and readily obeyed. God was completely reconciled to Jonah, and the fresh commission given him was evidence of the pardon of his former disobedience. *The word of the Lord came unto Jonah the second time* (v. 1). After he had been thrown into the sea and thrown out of it again, God came and asked him, "Jonah, will you now go to Nineveh?" Jonah would be trusted. God could justly have said, as we would concerning someone who had dealt treacherously with us, that although he would not proceed to apply the law rigorously against him, nevertheless, he would never again put his trust in him. But see! The word of the Lord came to him again, to show that when God forgives, he forgets, and those whom he forgives he receives into his family and restores to their former estate. God's making use of us is the best evidence of his being at peace with us. Jonah was reconciled to God; he was not now *disobedient to the heavenly vision* (Ac 26:19). He neither tried to avoid hearing the command nor declined to obey it. Now, without murmuring and disputing, *Jonah arose, and went unto Nineveh, according to the word of the Lord* (v. 3). He went directly to Nineveh, even though it was a long way away and was probably a place he had never been to before. He went there *according to the word of the Lord*.

2. Let us see the command or commission given him and what he did to carry it out.

2.1. The command given him was to go in the name of the God of heaven and declare war on Nineveh (v. 2): "*Arise, go up to Nineveh, that great city*," that capital, and *preach unto it*, preach "against it" (the Aramaic reading). Jonah was sent to Nineveh, which was at this time the chief city of the Gentile world, as a sign of God's gracious intentions to make the light of divine revelation shine in those dark regions. God knew that if Sodom and Gomorrah, Tyre and Sidon, had had the means of grace, they would have repented (Mt 11:21, 23). He knew that if Nineveh now had the means of grace, they would repent, and he gave them those means. He sent Jonah. "Go and preach," God says, "*the preaching* (message) *that I bid thee*. Tell the people of Nineveh that their evil has come up to God and God's vengeance is coming down on them." This was the message Jonah had been reluctant to communicate earlier and had fled by taking off for Tarshish. When Jonah was brought to face up to it a second time, however, God did not change the message to indulge him at all or make it more palatable. No; Jonah must now preach the same message that he had been ordered to preach before but had refused to preach. It was an encouragement to him that God would go with him, that the Spirit of prophecy would rest on him when he was in Nineveh to give him further instructions. Jonah must go with implicit faith. When admirals are sent abroad, they are sometimes forbidden to open their commission until they have sailed a fair distance at sea; this was how Jonah must go to Nineveh, and when he reached there, he would be told what to say.

2.2. He faithfully and boldly undertook his mission. When he reached Nineveh, he found it was an *exceedingly great city of three days' journey* (v. 3), literally, "a city great to God," *exceedingly great*. The greatness of Nineveh consisted chiefly in its extent; it was much larger than Babylon, such a city as no one built ever again, according to Diodorus Siculus. When Jonah came there, he lost no time, but opened his commission immediately, according to his instructions, and *cried, and said, Yet forty days, and Nineveh shall be overthrown*; he may have said more, but this was the substance of his message. He meant, and they understood him as meaning, that it would be overthrown not by war but by some immediate stroke, either by an earthquake or by fire and burning sulfur, as Sodom was. God would wait that long to see if, when this alarm was given, they would humble themselves, put right their actions, and so prevent the threatened ruin. But he would wait no longer. Forty days is a long time for a righteous God to delay his judgments, but it is only a short time for an unrighteous people to repent and reform. The fixing of the day in this way, with all possible certainty, would help persuade them that it was a message from God.

Verses 5–10

Here is:

1. A wonder of divine grace in the repentance and reformation that Nineveh undertook on being warned of their approaching destruction. Nineveh *will rise up in judgment against the men of* the *Gospel generation, and condemn them; for the Ninevites repented at the preaching of Jonas, but behold, a greater than Jonas is here* (Mt 12:41). In fact, it did condemn the impenitence and stubbornness of Israel at that time. God sent many prophets to Israel, well known as *mighty in word and deed* (Ac 7:22), but he sent only one to Nineveh, and he was a foreigner, who looked insignificant, and his *bodily presence weak* (2Co 10:10) after such a long journey. Nineveh repented, however, but Israel did not. Jonah preached only one sermon, and we do not find that he gave them any sign or wonder, but they were persuaded, while Israel continued to be stubborn. Jonah only threatened wrath and ruin; we do not find that he gave them any encouragement to hope that they would find mercy if they did repent, and yet they repented. Israel, however, persisted in impenitence even though the prophets that were sent to them drew them *with cords of a man, and with bands of love* (Hos 11:4). Let us see how Nineveh repented:

1.1. The people of Nineveh *believed God*; they believed the word that Jonah spoke to them in the name of God. They believed that there was only *one living and true God*, that they were accountable to him, that they had sinned against him, and that this notice sent to them of the approaching ruin came from him. They also believed that he is a merciful God and that there might be some hope of his turning away his threatened wrath if they turned away from the sins for which it was threatened.

1.2. They brought word to the king of Nineveh, who is thought by some to have been Sardanapalus. Jonah was not sent to the royal court to make his proclamation, but to the streets of Nineveh; however, an account was brought to the king. It was not brought as information against Jonah for disturbing the public peace, but as a message from heaven brought by those who were concerned for the public welfare.

1.3. The king set them a good example of humiliation (v. 6). When he heard the *word of God* that was sent to him, he *rose from his throne* in sorrow and shame for the sin by which he and his people had offended. He set aside his royal robe and other signs of his imperial position, as an acknowledgment that, not having used his power as he

should have to restrain violence and wrong and maintain justice, he had forfeited the signs of that power to the justice of God. Even the king himself did not think it beneath him to put on the clothes of a penitent, for he *covered himself with sackcloth, and sat in ashes* (v. 6).

1.4. The people followed the example of the king, or rather, it seems, they led the way. They *put on sackcloth, from the greatest of them even to the least of them* (v. 5). Though physical exercise alone is not useful (1Ti 4:8), and a person's *spreading sackcloth and ashes under him*, if that is all, is not significant—it is the heart that God looks at (1Sa 16:7; Isa 58:5)—yet when God *calls to mourning and girding with sackcloth* (Isa 22:12), we must use outer expressions of inner sorrow to *glorify God with our bodies* (1Co 6:20), at least by setting aside the finery we put on them.

1.5. A general fast was observed throughout that great city (vv. 7–9). Let us observe:

1.5.1. What was required by the fast. First, it was to be strictly observed. On the day appointed, *let neither man nor beast taste anything*, not even *drink water*. Let them make themselves physically uncomfortable to show how uncomfortable they were in their minds because of their sorrow for sin and their fear of divine wrath. Second, they must add prayer and supplication to God to their fasting and mourning, for the fasting was intended to equip the body to serve the soul in prayer. In prayer, we must cry out urgently, with firm thoughts, faith, and a fervency of godly devotion. Third, they must add reformation and amendment of life to their fasting and praying: *Let them turn everyone from his evil way* (v. 8), and especially *from the violence that is in their hands*. Let them restore what they had taken unjustly and make amends for the wrong they had done. It is not enough to fast for sin; we must also fast from sin.

1.5.2. From what motivation this fast was proclaimed and religiously observed (v. 3): *Who can tell if God will turn and repent?* They hoped that on their repenting and turning, God would revoke his sentence against them. Just as we pray for everything good when we pray for the favor of God, so also we pray against all evil when we pray against the wrath of God. Jonah had not told them to hope that God would turn away from his wrath; nor did they have any other prophets among them to tell them. However, they had a general notion of the goodness of God's nature and his mercy to human beings, and from this they raised some hope that he would spare them. They dared not presume, but they would not despair.

2. A wonder of divine mercy in the sparing of these Ninevites when they repented (v. 10). God saw that they turned from their evil way, and that was the thing he looked for and required. Here we read of no sacrifices being offered to God to make atonement for sin, but the *sacrifice of God is a broken spirit; a broken and contrite heart*, such as the Ninevites now had, is what he *will not despise* (Ps 51:17); it is what he will honor and look on with favor.

CHAPTER 4

In this chapter we read, with a great deal of uneasiness, about the sin of Jonah. Just as there is joy in heaven and earth at the conversion of sinners (Lk 15:7), so there is also grief for the foolishness and weakness of saints. In the first chapter we saw Jonah fleeing from the face of God, but here we have him flying in the face of God; there we had an account of his repentance and return to God, but here, though no doubt he did repent, no account is left us of his recovering. While we read with wonder at his perversity, however, we read with no less wonder at God's tenderness toward him, by which it was made clear that he had not rejected him. Here is: 1. Jonah's complaining at God's mercy to Nineveh (vv. 1–3). 2. The gentle rebuke God gave him for it (v. 4). 3. Jonah's discontent at the withering of the vine (vv. 5–9). 4. God's using the experience to convince Jonah that he should not be angry at the sparing of Nineveh (vv. 10–11).

Verses 1–4

Notice here:

1. How unjustly Jonah quarreled with God for his mercy to Nineveh. This makes us suspect that Jonah had only spoken the message of wrath against the Ninevites and had not helped them in their repentance.

1.1. Jonah begrudged them the mercy they found (v. 1): *It displeased Jonah exceedingly*, and *he was very angry*. It was very wrong that:

1.1.1. He had so little self-control as to be so displeased and angry.

1.1.2. He had so little reverence of God as to be displeased at what he did. Whatever pleases God should please us; although we cannot understand it, we must still accept it.

1.1.3. He had so little affection for people as to be angry at the conversion of the Ninevites and their acceptance into God's favor. It was a point of honor that Jonah stood on and that made him angry. He was jealous for the honor of his country. The repentance and reformation of Nineveh shamed the stubbornness of Israel, who had not repented, who *hated to be reformed* (Lev 26:23), and the favor God had shown to these Gentiles when they repented was a bad sign to the Jewish nation. Jonah was also jealous for his own honor, fearing that if Nineveh was not destroyed within forty days, he would be considered a false prophet and therefore stigmatized.

1.2. He quarreled with God about it. When his heart was stirring within him, he *spoke unadvisedly with his lips* (Ps 106:33), and here he tells us what he said (vv. 2–3): he *prayed unto the Lord*, but it is a very awkward prayer. Being discontented, he let his corruption get ahead of his graces, and when he should have been praying to benefit from the mercy of God himself, instead he complained about the benefit others gained from that mercy.

1.2.1. He now began to justify himself in fleeing *from the presence of the Lord* (1:3) when he was first ordered to go to Nineveh: "*Lord,*" he said, "*was not this my saying when I was in my own country?* Did I not foresee that if I went to preach to Nineveh, they would repent and you would forgive them?" What a strange kind of person Jonah was, dreading the success of his ministry! It is unaccountable that what all the saints had made the subject of their joy and praise should be made by Jonah a matter that reflected badly on God, as if what is the greatest glory of divine nature were an imperfection — that God is *gracious and merciful* (Ps 103:8).

1.2.2. In an emotional outburst, he now wished to die (v. 3): "*Now, O Lord! take, I beseech thee, my life from me.* If Nineveh must live, let me die rather than see your word and mine disproved, rather than see the glory of Israel pass to the Gentiles" — as if there were not enough grace in God for both Jews and Gentiles. It was absurd of him to wish to die when he had a prospect of living to such good purpose and so could hardly be spared. Our business is to prepare to die by doing the work of life, and then to turn to God to take away our life when and how he pleases.

2. How justly God rebuked Jonah for his emotional outburst (v. 4): the Lord said, "*Doest thou well to be angry? Have you any right to be angry?*" Notice how mildly God in his greatness speaks to this foolish man, to teach us to restore those who have fallen with *a spirit of meekness* (Gal 6:1), and with *soft answers* to *turn away wrath* (Pr 15:1). *Doest thou well?* We should often ask ourselves this question. When emotions run high, let them face this restraint: "Have I a right to be angry so quickly, *angry* so often, angry so long, to put myself into such a passion and speak to others in such bad language in my anger?"

Verses 5–11

Jonah persisted here in his discontent. We have here:

1. Jonah's sullen expectation of the fate of Nineveh. He withdrew, *went out of the city*, sat alone, and remained silent, because he saw the Ninevites repent and reform (v. 5). The forty days were now coming to an end, or had come to an end, and Jonah hoped that if Nineveh was not overthrown, then some judgment or other would come on it that would be enough to save his reputation. He *made himself a booth* (shelter) of the boughs of trees.

2. God's gracious provision for his shelter and refreshment when he so foolishly caused problems for himself (v. 6). Jonah was sitting in his shelter, fretting about the cold of the night and the heat of the day. God looked on him with compassion, as a tender mother looks on her perverse child. He *prepared a gourd* (vine), a plant with broad leaves, which suddenly grew up and covered his shelter. It was *a shadow over his head, to deliver him from his grief*, so that, being physically refreshed, he might be better protected from mental anxieties. A vine, one would think, was only a slender fortification at best, but Jonah *was exceedingly glad of the gourd* (v. 6). A vine in the right place may be more useful to us than a cedar. A small toy will sometimes be enough to pacify a bad-tempered child, as the vine pacified Jonah.

3. The sudden loss of this provision that God had made for his refreshment, and the return of his trouble (vv. 7–8). God *prepared a worm* to destroy the vine. The vine withered the day after it sprang up; our comforts *come forth like flowers and are soon cut down* (Job 14:2). Something little withers them; a small worm at the root destroys a large vine. Something unseen and indiscernible does it. God did not send an angel to uproot Jonah's vine, but a worm to strike it. He *prepared a wind* to make Jonah feel the lack of the gourd (v. 8). It was *a vehement* (scorching) *east wind*, which drove the heat of the rising sun violently onto Jonah's head. Poor Jonah was therefore exposed to the sun and wind.

4. The further anxiety that Jonah was caused (v. 8). "If the vine is killed off, if the vine is dead, kill me too, *let me die with the gourd* (vine)." It is just that those who love to complain should never be left without something to complain about, that their foolishness may be revealed and corrected and, if possible, healed.

5. The rebuke God gave him for this; he again reasoned with him: *Doest thou well to be angry for the gourd?* (v. 9). When afflicting providences deprive us of our relatives, possessions, and enjoyments, we must bear it patiently; we must not become angry with God, must not be angry *for the gourd*. It is a comparatively small loss, the loss of a shadow. What should especially silence our discontent is that although our vine has gone, our God has not gone.

6. Jonah's justification of his passion and discontent is strange (v. 9). He said, *I do well to be angry, even unto death*. Passion often overrules the conscience, forcing it

to give a false judgment, as Jonah did here. He had so little regard for himself as to abandon his own life, to kill himself with anxiety.

7. The turning of this passion against Jonah to convince him that he did wrong to complain at the sparing of Nineveh. God would judge him out of his own mouth. Jonah made no reply, and so we hope he returned to his right mind and recovered his right temper.

7.1. God argued (vv. 10–11): *"Thou hast had pity on the gourd*, you have (literally) 'spared' it. You said, *What a pity it is* that this vine should wither! And *should not I then spare Nineveh?* The vine you had pity on was only one, but the inhabitants of Nineveh, whom I have pity on, are numerous."* The city had a large population, as can be seen from the number of the infants—say, two years old and under—of which there were 120,000 in Nineveh. There were that many in Nineveh who were not guilty of any transgression against the Law and so had not contributed to the common guilt, but if Nineveh had been overthrown, they would all have been involved in the common calamity; "and *shall not I spare* Nineveh then, looking with compassion on them, especially?" God took notice of the great number of cattle that were in Nineveh also, which he had more reason to pity and spare than Jonah had to pity and to spare the vine, inasmuch as animal life is superior to vegetable life. Moreover:

7.2. The vine that Jonah was concerned for was not his own, nor had he made it grow, but the people in Nineveh whom God had compassion on were all the *work of his own hands*. He made them, and they were his, and so he had much more reason to have compassion on them.

7.3. The vine that Jonah had pity on had grown up suddenly, and so it was of less value; it *came up in a night*; "it was the son of a night" is the sense; but Nineveh was an ancient city, which had stood for many ages, and therefore could not be so easily given up.

7.4. The vine that Jonah had pity on *perished in a night*; it withered, and that was the end of it. However, the precious souls in Nineveh whom God had pity on are immortal. One soul is of more value than the whole world (Mt 16:26). Surely, then, one soul is more valuable than many vines. It may be that Jonah, after this, was reconciled to the sparing of Nineveh, that he became as pleased with it as he had previously been displeased. Jonah had said, *I do well to be angry* (I have a right to be angry), but he could not prove it. God said and proved, "I have a right to be merciful," and it is a great encouragement to poor sinners to hope that they will find mercy with him. Such murmurers as Jonah was here will be made to understand this teaching: however narrow their souls and motives are, and however willing they are to monopolize divine grace for themselves and those of their own persuasion, there is one *Lord over all, that is rich in mercy to all that call upon him* (Ro 10:12), and in *every nation*, in Nineveh as well as in Israel, *he that fears God and works righteousness is accepted of him* (Ac 10:35); those who repent and turn from their evil ways will find mercy with him.

A PRACTICAL AND DEVOTIONAL EXPOSITION OF THE BOOK OF THE PROPHET

Micah

There is a resemblance between Isaiah's prophecy and this one. Compare Isa 2:2–3 with Mic 4:1–2. Isaiah's prophecy is said to be concerning *Judah and Jerusalem*, but Micah's concerning *Samaria and Jerusalem*, for although this prophecy is dated only by the reigns of the kings of Judah, it still refers to the kingdom of Israel, the approaching ruin of which, in the exile of the ten tribes, Micah foretells and sadly mourns. The purpose of this book was: 1. To convince sinners of their sins in two ways: first, by accusing both Israel and Judah of idolatry, covetousness, oppression, and contempt for the word of God and accusing their rulers especially, both in church and in state, of the abuse of power; and second, by showing them the judgment of God that was coming. 2. To encourage God's people with promises of mercy and rescue, especially with an assurance of the coming of the Messiah and of the grace of the Gospel through him. Two quotations from Micah were made publicly on very solemn occasions, and both referred to great events. 2.1. One was a prediction of the destruction of Jerusalem (3:12), which we find quoted in the Old Testament by *the elders of the land* (Jer 26:17–18) to justify Jeremiah. "Micah," they said, "foretold that *Zion would be ploughed as a field*, and Hezekiah did not put him to death; why then should we punish Jeremiah for saying the same?" 2.2. Another was a prediction of the birth of Christ (5:2), which we find quoted in the New Testament by the *chief priests and scribes of the people* in answer to Herod's question as to *where Christ should be born* (Mt 2:4–6).

CHAPTER 1

We have here: 1. The title of the book (v. 1) and an introduction calling for attention (v. 2). 2. Warning given of judgments coming quickly on Israel and Judah (vv. 3–4) because of their sin (v. 5). 3. The details of the destruction (vv. 6–7). 4. The greatness of the destruction illustrated by the prophet's sorrow for it (vv. 8–9) and by the general sorrow that there would be for it in the places that must expect to share in it (vv. 10–16).

Verses 1–7

Here is:

1. A general account of this prophet and his prophecy (v. 1). The prophecy is the *word of the Lord*, a divine revelation. This word of the Lord came to the prophet clearly and powerfully; it is *the word which Micah saw*; Micah saw the vision and the particular things foretold in it as clearly as if they had already been fulfilled. The prophet is Micah of Moresheth; his name *Micah* is a contraction of *Micaiah*. His surname, the *Morasthite*, signifies that he was born, or lived, at Moresheth, which is mentioned in v. 14, or Mareshah, which is mentioned in v. 15 and Jos 15:44. The date of his prophecy is in the reigns of three kings of Judah—Jotham, Ahaz, and Hezekiah. Ahaz was one of the worst of Judah's kings, and Hezekiah one of the best. The promises and threats of this book are interwoven; even in the evil reign he preached comfort, and in the godly reign he preached conviction, for, however much times change, the word of the Lord remains the same. The prophecy is *concerning Samaria and Jerusalem*, the leading cities of the two kingdoms of Israel and Judah.

2. A solemn introduction to the following prophecy (v. 2), in which:

2.1. The people are summoned to draw near: "*Hear, you people*" ("all of them," as the margin of v. 2 reads). It is an unusual construction, but those words with which Micah begins his prophecy are the same in the original as those with which Micaiah ended his in 1Ki 22:28.

2.2. The earth is called on, with *all that therein is*, to listen to what the prophet has to say: *Hearken, O earth!* If the church and those in it will not listen, then the earth and those in it will, and they will shame the church.

2.3. God himself is appealed to for testimony against this people: "*Let the Lord God be witness against you*, a witness that you have received a fair warning but would not accept it. Let the fulfillment of the prophecy prove that it was the word of God and that no word of his will fall empty to the ground" (1Sa 3:19; Isa 55:11). He will be a witness *from his holy temple* in heaven when he comes down to execute judgment (v. 3) against those who turned a deaf ear to his words.

3. A terrible prediction of judgments that will come on Judah and Israel, which had its fulfillment soon after in Israel, and later in Judah, for it is foretold that:

3.1. God himself will appear against them (v. 3). God's way toward this people has long been a way of mercy, but now he changes his way; he *comes out of his place and will come down*.

3.2. When the Creator appears against them, it will be futile for any created thing to appear on their behalf. High places, set up for the worship of idols or for military fortifications, will all be trampled into the dust. Neither people of high rank, like the mountains, nor people of low rank, like the valleys, will protect themselves or the land from the judgments of God when they are sent with commission to devastate everything. This is applied particularly to the leading city of Israel (v. 6): *I will make Samaria*, which is now a rich and populous city, like *a heap of the field*, a heap of stones or rubble gathered together to be carried away, and *as plantings of a vineyard*, like little mounds of earth raised to plant vines in. Their *altars* have been like *heaps in the furrows of the fields* (Hos 12:11), and now their houses will be like heaps of rubble.

4. A charge of sin brought against them; that is the cause of these judgments (v. 5): *For the transgression of Jacob is all this*. All the calamities of Jacob and Israel are due to their disobedience. The question is asked, *What is the transgression of Jacob?* It is idolatry. It is the *high places*. It is the idolatry of Samaria and Jerusalem, the royal cities of those two kingdoms. These were the places that had the greatest influence on the country, by their authority and example. If the disobedience of Jacob is Samaria, *Samaria* will *become a heap*. Let the ringleaders in this sin hear and fear (Dt 31:12–13).

5. The punishment made to correspond to the sin (v. 7). The gods they worship will be destroyed: *The graven images shall be beaten to pieces* by the army of the Assyrians, *and all the idols shall be laid desolate. Samaria and her idols* were ruined by Sennacherib (Isa 10:11), and *their gods cast into the fire*, for *they were no gods* (Isa 37:19). The gifts that passed between them and their gods will be destroyed, for *all the hires thereof shall be burnt with fire*. All this wealth will become the plunder of the idolatrous nations and so be the *hire of a harlot* again, wages of an army of idolaters.

Verses 8–16

Here is the funeral of a ruined kingdom.

1. The prophet is himself chief mourner (vv. 8–9). It was usual for the prophets to express their own grief for public grievances. It was not out of any ill will that they declared the judgments of God. They dreaded it more than anything. We should mourn the punishment of sinners as well as the suffering of saints in this world; the weeping prophet did so (Jer 9:1), as did this prophet. He *makes a wailing like the dragons* (jackals), ravenous animals that meet in the night and *howl*, making terrible noises; he mourns *as the owls*, or as the screech owls, or ostriches, as some understand it. Israel's case is desperate: her *wound is incurable*. She will not help herself by repentance and reformation. There is indeed balm in Gilead and a physician there (Jer 8:22), but they will not turn to the physician. Judah is in danger as well. The cup is being passed round and is now put into Judah's hands: *The enemy has come to the gate of Jerusalem*. Soon after the destruction of Samaria, the Assyrian army, under Sennacherib, laid siege to Jerusalem; they came to the gate but could not force their way any further. However, the prophet foresaw this shock with great concern.

2. Several places are here called on to mourn, but they must not let the Philistines hear them (v. 10): *Declare it not in Gath*; this is taken from David's mourning for Saul and Jonathan (2Sa 1:20), for the uncircumcised will triumph in Israel's tears. One would not, if it could be helped, please those who amuse themselves with the sins or the sorrows of God's Israel. However, though it may be wise not to give way to noisy sorrow, it is still a duty to admit a silent sorrow when the church of God is in distress: "*Roll thyself in the dust*. In this way the house of Judah and every house in Jerusalem can become *a house*

of Aphrah, a house of dust." Places are named here that will share in this universal mourning, the names of some of which we do not find elsewhere. The meanings of these names may be intended either to indicate or to emphasize the miseries coming on the places named. Sennacherib's invasion is described in this way by the impressions of terror it would make on the various cities that fell in his path (Isa 10:28–29).

2.1. *The inhabitants of Saphir* (Shaphir) (v. 11), which means "neat and beautiful; pleasant" ("thou that dwellest fairly," as the margin of v. 11 reads), will *pass away* into captivity or be forced to flee, stripped of all their ornaments *and having their shame naked*.

2.2. *The inhabitants of Zaanan*, which may mean "the country of flocks," a populous country, where the people are as numerous as flocks of sheep, will be so taken up with their own calamities that they will *not come forth in the mourning of Bethezel*, which may mean "a near place." They will not bring relief to their neighbors in distress, for "*he shall receive of you his standing*. The enemy will find a foothold among you."

2.3. As for *the inhabitants of Maroth*—which some think stands for Ramoth, while others think it means "the rough places"—they *waited carefully* (painfully) *for good* but were disappointed, for *evil came from the Lord unto the gate of Jerusalem* when the Assyrian army besieged it (v. 12).

2.4. Lachish was a city of Judah to which Sennacherib laid siege (Isa 36:1–2). The inhabitants of that city are called to *bind the chariot to the swift beast* (harness the team to the chariot) to prepare for a speedy flight. God's quarrel with Lachish is that she is *the beginning of sin*, the sin of idolatry, *to the daughter of Zion* (v. 13); Lachish has learned it from the ten tribes, her close neighbors, and so infected the two tribes with it. Because Lachish has been found to be so much an accessory to the sin of Israel, she will certainly be judged: "*Thou shalt give presents to Moresheth-gath*"—a town of the Philistines—"to help you, but it will be in vain, for (v. 14) *the houses of Achzib*"—Aczib, a town adjoining Mareshah, or Moresheth, and mentioned with it in Jos 15:44—"*shall be a lie to the kings of Israel*." Aczib means "a lie."

2.5. Mareshah, which could not, or would not, help Israel, will herself be plundered (v. 15): "*I will bring an heir*, that is, an enemy who will take possession of your lands with as much assurance as if he were a legal heir to them. *The glory of Israel* will come to be like Adullam, a contemptible place."

2.6. The whole land of Judah seems to be called to weeping and mourning (v. 16): "*Make thee bald*, shave your heads in mourning, tear your hair; *poll thee for* (cut off your hair for) *thy delicate children*, who have been so tenderly and scrupulously brought up; *enlarge* (extend) *thy baldness as the eagle* does when it casts its feathers and is bald all over, *for they have gone into captivity from thee*. Their exile will be the more painful to them because they have not been used to hardship."

CHAPTER 2

We have here: 1. The sins that the people of Israel are accused of—covetousness and oppression, fraudulent and violent practices (vv. 1–2), dealing cruelly, even with women and children (vv. 8–9), opposition to God's prophets (vv. 6–7), and delighting in false prophets (v. 11). 2. The judgments with which they are threatened: that they will be humbled, impoverished (vv. 3–5), and banished (v. 10). 3. Gracious promises of comfort that

are reserved for the good people among them, to be ful-
filled in the Messiah (vv. 12–13).

Verses 1–5

Here is:

1. The injustice of human beings in planning evil
(vv. 1–2). It is the sin of oppression.

1.1. They desire what is not their own—that is the *root
of bitterness* (Dt 29:18; Heb 12:15), the root of all evil
(1Ti 6:10). They *covet fields and houses* (v. 2), as Ahab
did Naboth's vineyard (1Ki 21:1–4).

1.2. They devise ways of fulfilling their desires (v. 4). It
is wrong to cause trouble on a sudden impulse, but much
worse to do it with forethought and deliberation. They
plot evil *upon their beds*, when they should be asleep.

1.3. They practice the iniquity they have plotted,
because it is in the power of their hand (v. 1); they can
achieve it with the help of their wealth and the authority
and influence they have.

1.4. They are diligent, and as soon as *morning is light*,
they put it into practice.

1.5. They stop at nothing to pursue their designs;
what they *covet* they *take away*, taking people's fields by
force; they take them not only by fraud and in the name
of the law but also arrogantly and with violence. They
do not care whom they wrong. They *oppress a man and
his house*; they rob those who have families to maintain,
unconcerned that they are making them and their wives
and children go begging. They *oppress a man and his
heritage* (inheritance); they take away from people what
they have received from their ancestors, what they have in
trust to pass on to future generations.

2. The justice of God in planning punishment for this
sin (v. 3): *Therefore thus saith the Lord, Behold, against
this family do I devise an evil* (I am planning disaster),
that is, against the whole kingdom, the *house of Israel*,
especially those families in it who are cruel and oppressive. He finds them:

2.1. Very self-confident that they will escape judgment
in some way or other. He therefore tells them that it is *an
evil from which they shall not remove their neck* (from
which they cannot save themselves). They are children of
Belial, who would not endure the easy yoke of God's righteous commands, but *broke those bonds*, and God will lay
on them the heavy yoke of his righteous judgments.

2.2. Very proud, and so he tells them they will no longer walk haughtily, with *stretched forth necks and wanton
eyes, walking and mincing as they go* (Isa 3:16), for *this
time is evil*, and its events are humbling.

2.3. Very jovial, and he tells them their laughter will
be turned to mourning and their joy to heaviness (Jas 4:9)
(v. 4): "*In that day*, when God comes to punish you for
your oppression, *shall one take up a parable against you*
and *lament with a doleful lamentation*"—literally, with
"a lamentation of lamentations." Their enemies will gloat
over them and make fun of their grief, *taking up a parable*
(taunt) *against them*.

2.4. Very rich in their houses and lands, obtained by
oppression, and so he tells them that they will be stripped
of them all. They will say, "*We are utterly spoiled* (ruined);
he has changed the portion of my people (my people's
possession is divided up), so that it is now in the possession of their enemies: *How has he removed it from me!*
Turning away from us in wrath, he *has divided our fields*
and assigned them to the hands of foreigners." The margin of v. 4 reads, "Instead of restoring, he has divided our
fields." God will confirm what they say (v. 5): *Thou shalt
have none to cast a cord by lot in the congregation of the*

Lord (you will have no one in the assembly of the Lord to
divide the land by lot), no one to divide the inheritances,
because there will be no inheritances to divide. It is God's
land, a holy land, and so it will be more painful to them
to be turned out of it.

Verses 6–11

Here are two sins that the people of Israel are accused
of, and judgments for each—persecuting God's prophets
and oppressing God's poor.

1. Persecuting God's prophets, suppressing and silencing them, is a sin that provokes God, for his sending
prophets to us is a sure sign of his goodwill. Notice:

1.1. The opposition that this people gave to God's
prophets: they *said to those that prophesy, Prophesy
ye not*. They *said to the seers, See not* (Isa 30:10). "Do
not trouble us with accounts of what you have seen or
bring us any such fearful messages." They must either not
prophesy at all or prophesy only what is pleasant. Some
read it, "Prophesy not; let these prophesy." "Let us not
hear prophecy from those who tell us about our faults and
threaten us, but *let those prophesy* who will flatter us in
our sins and cry out peace to us." If a prophet will only
tell them that it is lawful for them to drink as much as they
please of their wine and strong drink, that they *shall have
peace though they go on and add drunkenness to thirst*
(Dt 29:19), this is a man after their own heart. *He shall
even be the prophet of this people*—they want a person
who will not only associate with them in their riots and
revels but also pretend to consecrate their ungodly worldliness by his prophecies.

1.2. They are pleaded with here (v. 7): "*O thou that
art named the house of Jacob*, will you silence those who
prophesy and forbid them to speak in God's name? *Is
the Lord's Spirit straitened* (restricted)*?* In silencing the
Lord's prophets, you are doing what you can to silence his
Spirit too; can you make the Spirit of God your servant?
Will you forbid him to say what does not please you? If
you silence the prophets, the Spirit of the Lord will still
find other ways to reach your consciences. Can your unbelief frustrate God's purposes?" As Jews, "You are *named
the house of Jacob*, and this is your honor, but *are these*
the actions of your ancestor Jacob?" Let them consider
how unreasonable the thing is in itself: *Do not my words
do good to those that walk uprightly?* "In this you wrong
God, who acknowledges the words of the prophets as his
words—they are *my words* (v. 7)—and who by them aims
and intends to do good to people (Ps 119:68), and will
you hinder the great benefactor from doing good?" It is
certainly for the common good of states and kingdoms
that religious faith be encouraged.

1.3. They are threatened with punishment for this sin.
They will be deprived of the benefit of a faithful ministry. Since they say, *Prophesy not*, God will take them at
their word, and *they shall not prophesy to them*. Let the
doctor no longer see the patients who do not want to be
healed, for they will not be persuaded. They will be given
up to the blind guidance of an unfaithful ministry. We may
understand v. 11 as a threat: *If a man be found walking
in the spirit of falsehood*, he *shall be the prophet of this
people*. Since they will not admit the *truth in the love of
it*, God will send them *strong delusions to believe a lie*
(2Th 2:10–11).

2. Oppressing God's poor is another sin they are
accused of (vv. 1–2). The sin is described in vv. 8–9.
Those who formerly arose against the enemies of the
nation now recently *rose up as enemies of the nation*
and, instead of defending it, destroyed it. They attacked

men, who were traveling, who *passed by securely as men averse from war*, on their lawful business. They attacked them and *pulled off the robe with the garment from them*, that is, they stripped them. They also attacked women (v. 9): *The women of my people have you cast out from their pleasant houses. They devoured widows' houses* (Mt 23:14), took possession of them. And they attacked children, whose age entitles them to tender treatment: *From their children have you taken away my glory for ever.* It was the glory of the Israelites' children that they were free, but these sinners made slaves of them, sold them to foreigners, and sent them into idolatrous countries. The sentence is passed on them for it (v. 10): *"Arise ye, and depart*; prepare to leave this land. You will neither be contented in it nor even stay in it, *because it is polluted* (defiled) by your wickedness. Not only will you be obliged to depart from this land, but *it shall also destroy you even with a sore destruction*; you will either be turned out of it or be ruined in it."

Verses 12–13

The chapter concludes, as is usual with the prophets, with promises of mercy, which were partly fulfilled when the Jews returned from Babylon and were completely fulfilled in the kingdom of the Messiah.

1. Whereas they will have been dispersed, they will be brought together again (v. 12): *"I will surely assemble, O Jacob! all of thee*, all who are *named of the house of Jacob* (v. 7) now expelled from your country (v. 10). *I will surely gather the remnant of Israel. I will put them together as the sheep of Bozrah."* Sheep are sociable creatures; these sheep will be *as the flock in the midst of their fold*, their own fold, where they are safe under the shepherd's eye and care. *They shall* also *make great noise*—as numerous flocks and herds do, with all their bleating and lowing—*by reason of the multitude of men*; the noise will not be owing to their strife and contentions, but to their great numbers. This was fulfilled when Christ through his Gospel gathered together as one *all the children of God that were scattered abroad* (Jn 11:52), uniting both Jews and Gentiles into one fold and under one Shepherd.

2. Whereas God will seem to have deserted and rejected them, then he will help them through all the difficulties in the way of their return and rescue (v. 13): *The breaker has come up before them* to break down all opposition and clear the way for them. Under his guidance *they have broken up, and have passed through the gate*, the way of escape from exile. *Their King shall pass before them* to lead the way, Jehovah—he is their king—*on the head of them* (at their head), as he led the armies of Israel through the desert. Christ is the church's King; he is Jehovah. He passes in front of them, bringing them out of the land of exile into the land of rest. Bishop Pearson applies this verse to the resurrection of Christ. *The breaker has gone up before us* out of the grave and has taken away its gates, and we go out through that opening.

CHAPTER 3

Micah is very bold in rebuking and threatening the ringleaders in sin, and he gives the reason why he is so bold (v. 8): because he has received the commission from God to say what he says; he says it by a higher spirit and power than his own. Magistracy and ministry are two great ordinances of God, but both of these were corrupted, and their intentions perverted. The prophet is very severe, and justly so, toward those who have abused them. 1. He teaches them their lesson separately,

reproving and threatening rulers (vv. 1–4) and false and flattering prophets (vv. 5–7). 2. He teaches them their lesson together, as those who have acted together to destroy the kingdom (vv. 9–12).

Verses 1–7

1. Let the rulers listen to the charges and their condemnation. The *heads* (leaders) *of Jacob* and the *princes of the house of Israel* are called on to *hear* what the prophet has to say to them (v. 1). The prophet has faithfully discharged his trust: *And I said, Hear, O princes!* He tells them:

1.1. What is expected of them. "Is it not your business to administer justice impartially, not to *know faces*—the literal meaning of the Hebrew expression for showing partiality—but to *know judgment*, the merits of every cause? Therefore stand still and listen to your own judgment."

1.2. How miserably they have disobeyed the rules of justice, even though they knew them. They *hate the good and love the evil* (v. 2). Because this is their motivation, they act accordingly; they are cruel toward those who are under their power, and whoever lies at their mercy will find that they receive none. They fleece the flock they should feed; instead of taking care of them, they take care only of themselves (Eze 34:2). They *eat the flesh of my people*. It is right that they should be clothed with wool, but that is not enough for these leaders: they *flay the skin from them* (v. 3). By imposing heavier taxes and demanding them rigorously, with fines and corporal punishment for pretended crimes, they ruin their subjects, taking away from some their lives and from others their livelihoods, and are like wild animals rather than shepherds. "They *break their bones* to come at the core of their being, and they *chop* the flesh *in pieces as for the pot."*

1.3. How they can expect God to deal with them. The rule is firm: those who have shown no mercy will receive judgment without mercy (Jas 2:13) (v. 4). *With the froward God will show himself froward* (Ps 18:26), and he often hands cruel and unmerciful people over to those who are cruel and unmerciful themselves.

2. Let the prophets listen to their charges, too, and their condemnation; they have prophesied falsely, and the rulers have governed through them. Notice:

2.1. Their sin. They have made it their business to flatter and deceive the people. "They lead them astray by crying 'Peace,' by telling them that everything will go well with them, whereas the reality is that they are following the paths of sin and are on the brink of ruin. They *cry peace*, but they *bite with their teeth*," which perhaps refers to their biting their own lips, as we tend to do when we want to suppress something. They *bite with their teeth, and cry peace*; that is, they flatter and compliment those who will feed them tasty morsels, but as for those who *put not into their mouths*, they look on them as their enemies. Whether they preach comfort or terror to people depends not on what the people are before God, but on what they are before them.

2.2. The sentence passed on them for this sin (vv. 6–7). *Night shall be upon them*, a dark, cold night of calamity, such as they, in their flattery, have led the people to hope will never come. *It shall be dark unto you; the sun shall go down over the prophets.* All comfort will depart, and all hope, too. Their minds will be full of confusion; they will be disoriented, and their own thoughts will trouble them. They kept others in the dark, and now God will bring them into the dark. They will be silenced, and all their claims to prophecy will be shamed forever. They never received any true vision; it was all a sham, and they were cheats and impostors. They will not even be able to come up with a counterfeit vision. They will be *ashamed*, be *confounded*, and *cover their lips*.

Verses 8–12

Here:

1. The prophet experienced a divine power accompanying him in his work. He could not refrain from speaking the word that God put into his mouth. The false prophets were *sensual* (following mere natural instincts), *not having the Spirit* (Jude 19), but truly, Micah says, *I am full of power by the Spirit of the Lord* (v. 8). Notice the qualifications with which this prophet was endowed: he was *full of power, and of judgment* (justice), *and of might*; he had an ardent love for God and the souls of people, a deep concern for God's glory and their salvation, and a passionate zeal against sin. He had also the courage to rebuke it and witness against it. He was a man of wisdom as well as courage; in all his preaching there was light as well as fire, a spirit of wisdom as well as zeal. Those who act honestly may act boldly, and those who are sure they have received a commission from God need not be afraid of opposition from people. He *declared to Jacob his transgression and to Israel his sin* (v. 8). Since few are humble enough to receive rebuke, those who are to speak words of rebuke need a great deal of boldness, and they must pray for a spirit of both wisdom and power.

2. The prophet exerted this power in dealing with the *heads of the house of Jacob*. He repeated the summons (v. 9), the same as we had in v. 1, to *the princes of the house of Israel*, though he means those of *Judah*, for it appears in Jer 26:18–19, where v. 12 is quoted, that this was spoken in Hezekiah's kingdom, and because the ten tribes had gone into exile, Judah was all that was now left of Jacob and Israel. He gave them their titles of *heads* and *princes*. Ministers were to be faithful to leaders, but they must not be rude or impolite to them. Notice:

2.1. The great wickedness of the *princes, priests*, and *prophets*; they were covetous, and they corrupted their offices for their love of money. The *princes abhorred all judgment* (despised justice) (v. 9); they *perverted all equity* (distorted all that is right) when it could not be turned to favor their own interests. They are accused (v. 10) of *building Zion with blood* (bloodshed). "In justifying their extortion, they pretend to build Zion; they add new streets and squares to the holy cities to grace them. It is *with blood* and *with iniquity*, however, and so it cannot succeed; nor will their good intentions for the city of God justify their acting against the law of God. *They judge for reward* (a bribe) (v. 11). The most righteous cause will not be supported without payment of a fee, and the most unrighteous cause will be pursued for a bribe." The priests' work was to teach the people, but they *taught for hire*; they were willing to be hired to teach anything that they knew would please. The prophets *divined for money*. Someone could have whatever word they wanted from them; they just had to pay them for it.

2.2. Their arrogant self-confidence: they *leaned upon the Lord*, and because by profession they were his people, they thought there was neither harm nor danger in their corrupt practices. Faith builds on the Lord, resting in him and depending on him as the soul's foundation; arrogance *leans upon the Lord* only as a crutch and uses him to serve its own purposes while the world remains the foundation that is built on. *Is not the Lord among us?* they asked. "Do we not have the signs of his presence among us, his temple, his ark, his living words?" They were *haughty because of the holy mountain* (Zep 3:11), as if their church

privileges would soften the worst practices. They thought they were secure: *No evil can come upon us*. Many are rocked to sleep in their fatal self-confidence by their church privileges, as if those would protect them in sin.

2.3. The condemnation passed on them for their sin (v. 12): *Therefore shall Zion for your sake be ploughed as a field*. This passage is quoted as a bold word spoken by Micah (Jer 26:18), which Hezekiah and his rulers took well; they repented and reformed, and so this threat was not carried out in those days. It is Zion that will be plowed as a field, the building burnt to the ground and leveled. Some notice that this was literally fulfilled in the destruction of Jerusalem by the Romans, when the ground on which the city stood was plowed up as a sign of its complete desolation. The evil of those who lead them brings ruin: "It is *for your sake* that *Zion shall be ploughed as a field*; you pretend to build Zion, but by shedding blood and by iniquity, you pull it down."

CHAPTER 4

Zion, the Jewish church, was plowed as a field (3:12), but the Christian church was built on its ruins. It is promised here that: 1. The church will be enlarged by the accession of the nations (vv. 1–2). 2. It will be protected in tranquility and peace (vv. 3–4). 3. It will be kept faithful to God (v. 5). 4. Under Christ's rule, all its grievances will be put right (vv. 6–7). 5. It will have an abundant and flourishing rule (v. 8). 6. Its troubles will be brought to a happy outcome (vv. 9–10). 7. Its enemies will be destroyed by their attempts against it (vv. 11–13).

Verses 1–7

It is a very encouraging *but* with which this chapter begins. When we sometimes see the corruption of the church, *Zion ploughed as a field*, we are ready to fear that it will one day perish. Let our faith not fail, however; out of the ashes of the church another phoenix will rise. The first words of this chapter show *the mountain of the Lord's house* being as much honored by being frequented as it had ever been disgraced by being abandoned. Although Zion is plowed as a field, God has not *cast off his people*; rather, by the fall of the Jews salvation has come to the Gentiles (Ro 11:11–12). This is the mystery that God through the prophet shows us here, and he says in the first three verses of this chapter the same thing another prophet said at the same time (Isa 2:2–4).

1. A church for God will be set up in the world in the days of the Messiah, after the defection and destruction of the Jewish church. The people of God will have a new charter; a new spiritual way of worship will be enacted. Better privileges will be granted by this new charter, and better provision made for establishing the kingdom of God on earth than had been made by the Old Testament constitution. *The mountain of the house of the Lord* will again appear as firm ground (v. 1). A church will be set up in the world, to which the Lord will be daily *adding such as shall be saved* (Ac 2:47).

2. This church will be firmly founded and well built: it *shall be established in the top of the mountains*; Christ himself will build it on a rock (Mt 16:18).

3. It will become eminent and conspicuous: it *shall be exalted above the hills*, noticed with wonder for its growing greatness from small beginnings. The glory of this present house is greater than that of the former (Hag 2:9). See also 2Co 3:7–8.

4. There will be a great addition of converts to it and a succession of converts in it. *People shall flow unto it*

continually from all parts, like a river. In Gospel times many nations will flow into the church. Ministers will be sent out to *disciple all nations* (Mt 28:19), and they will not *labour in vain* (1Co 15:58). "*He will teach us of his ways*, the ways in which he wants us to walk with him and in which we may depend on him to meet us graciously."

5. A new revelation will be declared to the world, on which the church will be founded and by which many people will be brought into it: *For the law shall go forth of Zion, and the word of the Lord from Jerusalem* (v. 2). The Gospel is called *the word of the Lord* here. It began to be spoken by the Lord Christ himself (Heb 2:3). It is also *a law*, a law of faith; we are *under the law to Christ* (1Co 9:21). This was to go *forth from Jerusalem, from Zion*. From there the Gospel must arise, to show the connection between the Old Testament and the New, that the Gospel is not set up in opposition to the Law but is an explanation and illustration of it, *a branch growing out of its roots* (Isa 11:1). It was in Jerusalem that Christ preached and performed miracles; there he died, rose again, and ascended; there the Spirit was poured out. Those who were to preach repentance and remission of sins to all nations were ordered to *begin at Jerusalem* (Lk 24:47).

6. A convincing power will accompany the Gospel of Christ in all places where it is preached (v. 3): *He shall judge among many people.*

7. An attitude of mutual peace and love will be the happy result of the setting up of the kingdom of the Messiah (Tit 3:2–3). People who before their conversion committed wrongs but would themselves bear none will after their conversion bear wrongs but themselves do none. As far as the Gospel is effective, it makes people peaceful, for such is *the wisdom from above*; it is *gentle and easy to be entreated* (Jas 3:17), and if nations were only leavened by it, there would be universal peace. The art of war, instead of being developed, which some consider to be the glory of a kingdom, will be forgotten and set aside as useless. The Gospel will make people peaceful (v. 4): *They shall sit* safely, and no one will disturb them; they will sit in security and will not disturb themselves, everyone *under his vine and fig tree*, enjoying their fruits and needing no other shelter than their leaves. *None shall make them afraid*; they will not be inclined to fear.

8. The churches will be faithful in fulfilling their responsibilities. Peace is a true blessing when it strengthens our determination to be faithful to the Lord. Notice how faithful God's people now decide to be to him: "*We will walk in the name of the Lord our God* (v. 5); we will acknowledge him in all our ways."

9. Despite the dispersions, distress, and weaknesses of the church, it will be formed and established (vv. 6–7). The state of the church became low and helpless in the latter times of the Old Testament, partly through the corruption of the Jewish nation and partly through the oppression under which they groaned. They were like a flock of sheep that were harassed, maimed, and scattered (Eze 34:16; Jer 50:6, 17). It is promised that these grievances will be put right. Christ will come himself (Mt 15:24) and send his apostles to *the lost sheep of the house of Israel* (Mt 10:6). God gathered a remnant (v. 7) from among the Jews. He also raised a strong nation from among the Gentiles. The Gospel church is such a strong nation that the gates of hell will never overcome it (Mt 16:18).

10. The *Messiah* will be the king of this kingdom to the end of time.

Verses 8–13

These verses relate to Zion and Jerusalem, called here the *tower of the flock* or the *tower of Edor* (v. 8); we read of such a place (Ge 35:21) near Bethlehem. Some believe it is the same place where the shepherds were keeping their flocks when the angels brought them news of the birth of Christ, and some think Bethlehem itself is spoken of here, as it is in 5:2. Some believe it is a tower at that gate of Jerusalem that is called the *sheep gate* (Ne 3:32) and that Christ rode in triumph through that gate into Jerusalem. However, it seems to stand for Jerusalem itself, or for Zion, the *tower of David* (SS 4:4). Now here:

1. We have a promise of the glories of the spiritual Jerusalem, the Gospel church, which is the tower of the flock, that one fold in which all the sheep of Christ are protected under one Shepherd (v. 8): "*Unto thee shall it come; even the first dominion*, a position and power equal to that of David and Solomon—that *kingdom*, which Zion was deprived of at the exile, will again *come to the daughter of Jerusalem.*" Now this was by no means fulfilled in Zerubbabel, and so it must refer to the kingdom of the *Messiah* and have had its fulfillment when God gave to our Lord Jesus *the throne of his father David* (Lk 1:32).

2. This is illustrated by a prediction of the favor God will show to the literal Jerusalem and the relief he will give it from its calamities, and this favor and relief are a type of what God will do for the Gospel Jerusalem.

2.1. Jerusalem is made to suffer by the providences of God (v. 9). "She *cries out aloud* because there is *no king in her*; she has none of that honor she used to have. Instead of ruling the nations, she is ruled by them and has become a captive. Her *counsellors* have *perished. Pangs have taken her.*" She is taken captive to Babylon. "She *goes forth out of the city* and is constrained to *dwell in the field*, exposed to all kinds of inconveniences; she *goes even to Babylon*, and there she wears out *seventy tedious* years in a miserable exile, *in pain, as a woman in travail*, waiting to be delivered (v. 10)." When she is rescued from Babylon, she is still in fear, for *now also*, when Jerusalem is being rebuilt, *many nations are gathered against her* (v. 11). They were so in Ezra's and Nehemiah's time, doing all they could to obstruct the building of the temple and the wall. They were so in the time of the Maccabees. They said, *Let her be defiled.*

2.2. Jerusalem is established peacefully by the promises of God: *Why dost thou cry out aloud?* (v. 9). Jerusalem's pain is not death throes, but labor pain, which after a while will be forgotten in the joy that a child has been born into the world (Jn 16:21–22). Let the literal Jerusalem comfort herself with the assurance that she will continue until the coming of the Messiah, for his kingdom must be set up there first, and when she is finally plowed as a field, as is threatened in 3:12, her privileges will be resigned to the spiritual Jerusalem, and the promises made to her will be fulfilled. Let Jerusalem be at peace, then, for her exile in Babylon will come to a happy end (v. 10). This was done by Cyrus, who acted as God's servant (Isa 44:28); that restoration was a type of our redemption by Jesus Christ. The intentions of Jerusalem's enemies against her later will be thwarted (vv. 12–13). Their coming together against Zion will be the occasion of their ruin. Zion will have the honor of being victorious over them (v. 13). "*Arise, and thresh, O daughter of Zion!* God will give you horns of iron to push them down and hoofs of *brass* (bronze) to tread on them when they are down, and so you will *beat in pieces many people* who have long been beating you into pieces." In this way, when God pleases, *the daughter of Babylon is made a threshing floor* and the *worm Jacob is* made *a threshing instrument*, with which God will *thresh the mountains, and make them as chaff* (Isa 41:14–15). How strangely are the tables turned since Jacob was the threshing floor and Babylon the threshing instrument (Isa 21:10)! The plunder gained by Zion's victory will be brought into the sanctuary and given to God, either in part, like that taken from Midian (Nu 31:28), or in whole, like that taken from Jericho (Jos 6:17). People variously interpret all this as pointing to the defeat of Sennacherib when he besieged Jerusalem, the destruction of Babylon, or the successes of the Maccabees, but others think it had its complete fulfillment in the spiritual victories obtained by the Gospel of Christ over the powers of darkness that fought against it. The nations thought they could destroy Christianity in its infancy, but it was victorious over them.

CHAPTER 5

We have here: 1. A prediction of the troubles and distresses of the Jewish nation (v. 1). 2. A promise of the Messiah and of his kingdom. It is a promise, specifically: 2.1. Of the birth of the Messiah (vv. 2–3). 2.2. Of his advancement (v. 4). 2.3. Of his protection of his people and his victory over his and their enemies (vv. 5–6). 2.4. Of the great increase of the church and the blessings that will come to the world through it (v. 7). 2.5. Of the destruction of the enemies of the church, both those outside and those within it (vv. 8–15).

Verses 1–6

Here, as before, we have:

1. The humiliation and distress of Zion (v. 1). For many years before the exile, the Jewish nation dwindled: *Now gather thyself in* (marshal your) *troops, O daughter of troops!* It is a summons to Zion's enemies. Or it is a challenge to Zion's friends: even if they marshal their troops, it will be futile, "for," says the prophet, in the name of the inhabitants of Jerusalem, "*He has laid siege against us,*" the king of Assyria has, the king of Babylon has, and he will go so far as *to smite the judge of Israel*—the king, the chief justice, and the other lesser judges—with *a rod upon the cheek* (v. 1), having taken them as prisoners." A complaint has been made about the judges of Israel (3:11), that they are corrupt and take bribes, and this disgrace will come justly on them because they abused their power.

2. The advancement of Zion's King. Having shown how low the house of David will be brought, Micah adds an eminent prediction of the Messiah, in whom that covenant will be established and the honors of that house revived. He does this to encourage the faith of God's people. Notice:

2.1. How the Messiah is described. He is the One who is to *be ruler in Israel, whose goings forth* (origins) *have been from of old, from everlasting* (v. 2), literally, "from the days of eternity." This description of Christ's eternal generation, or his origin as the Son of God, begotten of his Father before all worlds, shows that this prophecy must belong only to him and could never be used to describe any other being. The *going forth* is used (Dt 8:3) for a *word* that *proceeds out of the mouth*, and so it is appropriately used to refer to the eternal generation of the One who is called the *Word of God*, who was *in the beginning with God* (Jn 1:1–2). See his office as Mediator; he was to be *ruler in Israel*, king of his church; he was to *reign over the house of Jacob for ever* (Lk 1:32–33). It is a spiritual Israel that he reigns over. In the hearts of

believers he reigns through his Spirit and grace, and in their worship and fellowship he reigns through his word and ordinances.

2.2. What is foretold about him here. That:

2.2.1. Bethlehem will be the place where he will be born (v. 2). *Bethlehem* means "the house of bread," and so it would be the best place for the birth of the One who is *the bread of life* (Jn 6:48). Moreover, because it was the City of David, it was ordered by a special providence that the Messiah would be born there. It is called *Bethlehem Ephratah*, which is really two names of the same city, as appears in Ge 35:19. It was *little among the thousands of Judah*, not significant either because of the number of its inhabitants or because of their importance. Christ would give honor to the place of his birth, not derive honor from it.

2.2.2. In the fullness of time he will be born of a woman (v. 3). Although the origins of the Messiah were *from everlasting*, the *redemption in Jerusalem*, the *consolation of Israel*, must be *waited for* (Lk 2:25–38) until the time that *she who shall bring forth*—as the Virgin Mary is called, and Christ himself, similarly, is called *He that shall come*—will *bring forth*, and in the meantime *he will give them up*. Divine salvation must be waited for until the time fixed for it to be born.

2.2.3. *The remnant of his brethren shall then return to the children of Israel* (v. 3). The remnant of the Jewish nation will return to the spirit of the true children of Israel, a people in covenant with God. Some understand it to refer to all believers, Gentiles as well as Jews; they will all be incorporated into the citizenship of Israel, and, as they are all brothers and sisters of one another, so *he is not ashamed to call them brethren* (Heb 2:11).

2.2.4. He will be a glorious prince, and his subjects will be happy under his government (v. 4): *He shall stand and feed*, that is, he will both rule and teach. He will do this not as an ordinary man, but *in the strength of the Lord* (v. 4), as one clothed with divine power to undertake his work. The prophets introduced their messages with *Thus saith the Lord*, but Christ spoke not as a servant, but as a Son—*Verily, verily, I say unto you* (e.g., Mt 5:18). This was feeding *in the majesty of the name of the Lord his God* (v. 4). Christ's government will be happy for his subjects, for *they shall abide. Now shall he be great to the ends of the earth. Now* that he stands and feeds his flock, *now shall he be great*. Christ reckons it his greatness to do good.

2.2.5. He will protect the peace and welfare of his church and people against all the attacks of his and their enemies (vv. 5–6): *This man*, as king and ruler, *shall be the peace when the Assyrians shall come into our land*. This refers literally to the rescue of Hezekiah and his kingdom from the power of Sennacherib, who invaded them, but it is ultimately a promise of the security of the Gospel church and of all believers from the attacks of the powers of darkness, from Satan and all his agents, the dragon and his angels, who seek to devour the church of the firstborn (Heb 12:23) and all who belong to it (Rev 12:4). When the Assyrian comes with such a force into a land, can there be any other peace than a tame submission and an unresisted desolation? Yes; even then Christ is our peace (Eph 2:14), and as a priest, he makes atonement for sin and reconciles us to God. The One who is our peace is a king, conquering our enemies and calming anxious fears and passions; he *creates the fruit of the lips, peace* (Isa 57:19). He will find proper instruments to protect and rescue them and to defeat their enemies: *Then shall we raise against him seven shepherds and eight principal men* (v. 5), that is, a sufficient number of people, people who will have the care and tenderness of shepherds and the courage and authority of *principal men*, or commanders. *Seven* and *eight* are a certain number for an uncertain amount. Magistrates and ministers are shepherds and leaders, raised up to defend the righteous cause of religious faith against the powers of sin and Satan in the world. The opposition given to the church will be overcome, and those who oppose it will be defeated. This is represented by the devastating of Assyria and Babylon, the two nations that were the most formidable enemies of all to the Israel of God, and the destruction of them meant making Christ's enemies his footstool (Ps 110:1): *They shall waste the land of Assyria with the sword, and the land of Nimrod in the entrances thereof* (v. 6).

Verses 7–15

Glorious things are spoken here (Ps 87:3) of *the remnant of Jacob*, that remnant that was raised out of the lame one (4:7), and it seems to be that *remnant which the Lord our God shall call* (Joel 2:32), on whom the Spirit will be poured out, the remnant that will be saved (Ro 9:27).

1. They will be *as a dew* in the midst of the nations (v. 7). God's church is dispersed throughout the world; it is *in the midst of many people*, like gold in the ore, wheat in a bundle. Israel according to the flesh lived by itself, but the spiritual Israel lies scattered *in the midst of many people*, as the *salt of the earth*, or as seed sown in the ground, here a grain and there a grain (Hos 2:23). Now this remnant will be *as dew from the Lord born from above* (Jn 3:7), not of the earth, smelling like the things of the earth. They will be numerous as the drops of dew on a summer's morning. They will be pure and clear, not muddy and corrupt. They will be produced silently, as the dew distils imperceptibly; such is the way of the Spirit. They will rely on divine grace, for they are no more than what the free grace of God makes them every day. They will be great blessings to those among whom they live, as the dew and the showers are to the grass. They will be mild and gentle in their behavior, like their Master, who comes down *like rain upon the new mown grass* (Ps 72:6).

2. They will be *as a lion among the beasts of the forest*, which *treads down and tears in pieces* (v. 8). Just as they will be silent, gentle, and sharing all that is good to those who receive the truth out of love for it (2Th 2:10), so they will also be bold as a lion in witnessing against the corruption of the times and places they live in, and strong as a lion, in the strength of God, to resist and overcome their spiritual enemies.

3. They will be brought away from all the worldly things they have put their confidence in; by the providence of God they will enjoy such security that they will not need them. They have trusted in chariots and horses and multiplied them (Ps 20:7), but now God *will cut off their horses* and *destroy their chariots* (v. 10). They have depended on their fortified cities for their security, but God will make sure those are demolished (v. 11). They will have them to live in, but not as garrisons. Many of them have depended very much on the advice of their diviners and fortune-tellers, and God will cut those off. Many of them have said to the work of their hands, *You are our gods*, but now idolatry will be abolished and abandoned (v. 13). Among other memorials to idolatry, *I will pluck up thy groves* (Asherah poles) *out of the midst of thee* (v. 14). These have been planted and preserved in honor of their idols and used in the worship of them. So *will I destroy their cities*, that is, the cities dedicated to the idols.

4. Those who resist the Gospel of Christ and continue to follow their idolatry and witchcraft will fall under the wrath of God (v. 15).

CHAPTER 6

Here: 1. God prosecutes his people for their corrupt ingratitude and their wrong response to him for his favors (vv. 1–5). 2. He shows the wrong course they took when they were under conviction, the frivolous suggestions they made in answer to his charge, and the course they should have followed instead (vv. 6–8). 3. He calls on them to listen to the voice of his judgments and sets their sins out before them (v. 9), their injustice (vv. 10–15) and their idolatry (v. 16), for both of which ruin is coming on them.

Verses 1–5

Here:

1. The introductions to the message are very serious: "*Hear you now what the Lord says* (v. 1). *Arise, contend thou* (plead your case) *before the mountains*" — or "with the mountains" — and "*let the hills hear thy voice*. Plead your case with the mountains and hills of Judea, that is, with the inhabitants of those mountains and hills." Some think the reference is to those mountains on which they worshiped idols. It should be taken more generally, however, as is shown by the prophet's calling not only to the mountains but also to the *strong foundations of the earth*. He must speak as passionately as if to make even the hills hear him; "*Let the hills hear thy voice*, for this senseless, careless people will not listen to it. Let the rocks, the *foundations of the earth*, which have no ears, listen, since Israel refuses to."

2. The message itself is very moving. The prophet is to inform the whole world that God has a quarrel with his people. Notice:

2.1. Sin gives birth to a lawsuit by God against human beings.

2.2. The sins of God's own professing people are more displeasing to him than the sins of others, since they are a greater grief to his Spirit and dishonor to his name.

2.3. God will plead with those whom he has accusations against; he will plead with his people Israel so that they may be convinced and he may be justified. At the end of the previous chapter he pleaded with the nations in anger, but here he pleads with Israel in compassion and tenderness, to bring them to repentance: *Come now, and let us reason together* (Isa 1:18).

2.3.1. God challenges them here to show what he has done against them that might have given them cause to abandon him. They have rebelled against God, but had they any good reason to do so? (v. 3): *O my people! what have I done unto thee?* Here is a challenge to all who have ever been in God's service to testify against him if they have found him to be a hard Master in anything or if they have found his demands unreasonable.

2.3.2. Since they cannot show anything that he has done against them, he will show them a great deal that he has done for them. He brought them out of Egypt, the land of their slavery (v. 4). They were content with their slavery, almost in love with their chains, for the sake of the garlic and onions they had plenty of (Nu 11:5), but God *brought them up*, inspiring them with an ambition of liberty and encouraging them with a determination to boldly shake off their chains. The Egyptians held them tightly, but God *redeemed them* by force *out of the house of servants, the house of bondage* (Dt 5:6). When he brought them out of

Egypt into a howling desert (Dt 32:10), he sent *Moses, Aaron, and Miriam*, "three prophets" (according to the Aramaic paraphrase), to lead them. We must not forget the mercy of the good teachers we had when we were young. It was God who sent them before us to prepare the way. God no less glorified himself and honored his people when he brought them into the land of their rest than when he brought them out of the land of their slavery. Let them remember now what God did for them by defeating the designs of Balak and Balaam and by bringing them *from Shittim*, their final encampment before they crossed the Jordan, *unto Gilgal*, their first after crossing the Jordan. It was there, between Shittim and Gilgal, that, on the death of Moses, Joshua, a type of Christ, was raised up to give Israel possession of the Land of Promise.

Verses 6–8

Here is the proposal for the reconciliation between God and Israel. Judgment is given against Israel, and so:

1. They express their desires to be at peace with God on any terms (vv. 6–7). Each one knows the sin in their own heart, so they do not ask, *What shall this man do?* but, *What shall I do? What will the Lord be pleased with? What shall I give for my transgression?*

2. They make proposals that betray their ignorance, even while showing their zeal:

2.1. They offer much. They offer *thousands of rams* (v. 7). God required one ram as a sin offering; they offer their whole stock, as long as they may be at peace with God. They could be content to part with *their firstborn for their transgressions* if that would be accepted as atonement; they would offer the *fruit of their body for the sin of their soul* (v. 7). To those who had become futile in their thinking (Ro 1:21), this seemed a probable way of making atonement for sin, because our children are part of ourselves.

2.2. They do not offer rightly, however. It is true that some of these things were instituted by the ceremonial law, but these alone will not commend them to God. The legal sacrifices had their virtue from the reference they had to Christ, the great atoning sacrifice, but otherwise, in themselves, it was *impossible that the blood of bulls and goats should take away sin* (Heb 10:4). All the proposals of peace except those that are according to the Gospel are absurd. Some of the things the people propose to offer are evil things, such as to give our *firstborn* and the *fruit of our body* to death. Do not our children belong to God? Are they not already his, born to him? How then can they be a ransom? They neither could answer the demands of divine justice nor would serve in lieu of the sanctification of the heart and the reformation of life.

3. God tells them clearly what he demands (v. 8). We need not trouble ourselves to make suggestions; the terms have already been settled and laid down. The One whom we have offended has shown it to all human beings, not only "to you, O Israel!" but *to thee, O man!* He has shown it to Gentiles as well as Jews—to human beings, who are rational creatures, not to beasts. What is spoken to *all men everywhere* (Ac 17:30) in general must be applied by faith to us in particular, as if it were spoken *to thee, O man!* by name, and to no one else. The good that God requires of us is not the paying of a price for the forgiveness of sin, but doing the duty that is the condition of our participation in the forgiveness purchased for us.

3.1. We must *do justly*, must *render to all their due* (Ro 13:7), according to our relationship and obligation to them. We must wrong no one, but do right to all, to their bodies, goods, and reputation.

3.2. We must *love mercy*: be not only just to all we deal with but also kind to all who need us. We must not only show mercy but also *love mercy*.

3.3. We must *walk humbly with our God*. This includes all the duties of the first table of the Ten Commandments, as the two previous requirements include all the duties of the second table. Enoch's walking with God is interpreted as his *pleasing God* (Heb 11:5). We must, in our whole way of life, conform to the will of God, maintain our fellowship with God, and seek to be approved by him. We must "humble ourselves to walk with God" (as the margin of v. 8 reads); every thought within us must be humbled and be brought into obedience to God (2Co 10:5). This is what God requires, and without it the most expensive services are *vain oblations*, meaningless offerings (Isa 1:13); this is more than *all burnt offerings and sacrifices*.

Verses 9–16

Having shown the people how necessary it is that they act justly, God shows them here how clear it is that they have acted unjustly. Notice:

1. The charges that are brought against them (v. 9). God speaks to *the city*, to Jerusalem, to Samaria. When the sin of a city cries out to God (Ge 18:20–21), his voice cries out against the city (Jnh 1:2). He warns before he wounds, because he is *not willing that any should perish* (2Pe 3:9). Notice:

1.1. How the voice of God is discerned by some: *The man of wisdom will see thy name* (v. 9).

1.2. What this voice of God says to all: "*Hear you the rod, and who hath appointed it.* Listen to the rod when it is coming, hear it from far away, before you see it and sense it. Pay attention to the rod when it has come, when you feel the blow; give your attention to the cautions it speaks to you." Every rod has a voice, and it is the voice of God that is to be listened to in the rod of God. In every affliction, God *performs the thing that is appointed for us* (Job 23:14).

2. The basis for the charges, the things they are accused of.

2.1. They are accused of injustice, a sin against the second table of the Ten Commandments. After all the ways God has used to teach them to act justly, are they still dealing unjustly? It seems they are (v. 10). *Shall I*, therefore, *count them pure* (v. 11)? Those who are dishonest in their dealings will never be considered pure. God searches the houses of those citizens, and he finds there *treasures of wickedness*, which *profit nothing* (Pr 10:2); *a scant* (short) *measure*, by which they sell to the poor, cheating them; and *wicked balances and a bag of false weights*. Those who have wealth and power in their hands abuse it. They are *full of violence*, that is, they have their houses full of what is gained by violence. *The inhabitants thereof have spoken lies* (v. 12). If they are unable to use force and violence, then they use fraud and deceit.

2.2. They are accused of idolatry (v. 16): *The statutes of Omri are kept, and all the work of the house of Ahab*. Both of these kings were wicked, and the wickedness that they established by law and by example was idolatry, and this wickedness remained. People who make corrupt laws and bring in corrupt traditions are doing what perhaps may prove the ruin of unborn children.

3. The sentence God has warned (v. 9) will be brought down on them (v. 13): *Therefore also I will make thee sick, in smiting thee*. Just as they have struck the poor with the rod of their oppressions, so God will strike them, so as to make them sick of their unjust gains.

3.1. What they have will do them no good. Their food will not nourish them: *Thou shalt eat, but not be satisfied* (v. 14). People may have too much of the good things of this world but still not be satisfied (Ecc 5:10; Isa 55:2). Their country will not shelter or protect them: *"Thy casting down shall be in the midst of thee* (v. 14), that is, you will be ruined by troubles at home even though you have not been invaded by a foreign force." They will not be able to preserve what they have from a foreign force: *"Thou shalt take hold* of what is about to be taken away from you, but you will not hold it firmly; you will not retrieve it." Their wives and children, whom they have resolved not to part with, must go into exile. What they save for a time will be reserved for a future stroke: *That which thou deliverest* out of the hand of one enemy *will I give up to the sword* of another enemy (v. 14). What they have labored for they will not enjoy (v. 15): *"Thou shalt sow, but thou shalt not reap*; it will be withered, or an enemy will reap it for themselves, or you will be taken into exile and leave it to be reaped by people you do not know. *Thou shalt tread the olives*, but *thou shalt not anoint thyself with oil*, having no heart when all is being destroyed. *Thou shalt tread out the sweet wine* but *shalt not drink wine*, for many things may fall between the cup and lip."

3.2. All they have will ultimately be taken away from them (v. 13): *Thou shalt be made desolate because of thy sins*, be made *a desolation and a hissing* (I will give you over to ruin, and your people to derision) (v. 16). When a people who have been flourishing are made desolate, some witnesses are stunned and some triumph. This is how *you shall bear the reproach of my people* (scorn of the nations). Now their sins and God's judgments have made their land desolate, and their having once been the people of God only increases the scorn they receive, and their enemies will say, *These are the people of the Lord* (Eze 36:20).

CHAPTER 7

Here: 1. The prophet, in the name of the church, sadly mourns the terrible decay of religious faith in his time (vv. 1–6). 2. The prophet, for the sake of the church, gives advice as to what to do. 2.1. The people must look to God (v. 7). 2.2. They must courageously bear the arrogance of the enemy (vv. 8–10). 2.3. They must patiently bear the rebukes of their God (v. 9). 2.4. They must expect the trouble to continue long (vv. 11–13). 2.5. They must encourage themselves with the promises God made in response to the prophet's prayers (vv. 14–15). 2.6. They must foresee the downfall of their enemies (vv. 16–17). 2.7. They themselves must boast in the mercy and grace of God and his faithfulness to his covenant (vv. 18–20). And the prophecy concludes with that word of encouragement.

Verses 1–6

Some take this description of bad times as a prediction of what would happen in the reign of Manasseh. However, I prefer to think it took place in the reign of Ahaz or at the beginning of Hezekiah's time; for the best part of his life, when he had done his best to purge corruption, much remained that was wrong. The prophet laments his lot, that he happens to live in such a corrupt age, among a people who are quickly heading for a ruin that will unavoidably involve many good people. He mourns that:

1. There are so few good people to be found, even among God's people: *The good man has perished out of the earth* (has been swept out of the land) (v. 2). The good *man* is godly and merciful; the word means both. People who are devout toward God and compassionate and kind toward others, who love mercy and walk with God (6:8), are completely good. There is no such thing as a good person in the land. This is illustrated by a comparison (v. 1): They are *as when they have gathered the summer fruits*; it is as hard to find a good person as to find any of the summer fruits, the finest and best, when the harvest has past. You can find no groups of them, as you can find bunches of grapes on a healthy vine at harvest: *There is no cluster to eat*; and the best and ripest grapes are those that grow in large clusters. When we read of the devotion and charity of those who professed religious faith in former times and see the opposite in the present age, we must wish, with a sigh, "Oh, to go back to early Christianity!"

2. There are so many evildoers who cause all the harm they can: *"They all lie in wait for blood*, and they *hunt every man his brother*" (v. 2). They act as if the whole human race were at war and the use of force were the only right way to live. They are like predators toward their neighbors, for *they all lie in wait for blood* like lions for their prey."

3. The judges, who according to their office should support and protect what is right, practice and promote wrong: *That they may do evil with both hands earnestly. The prince asketh, and the judge asketh for a reward* (v. 3), for a bribe, which will help them carry on any evil plan *with both hands. So they wrap it up*; they scheme so that justice is lost like a mist, making things go whichever way they want. These leaders are described in sad terms here: *the best of them is as a brier, and the most upright is sharper than a thorn hedge* (v. 4). Moreover, when things have come to such a state, *"the day of thy watchmen comes*, that is, *the day of thy visitation*, when God will judge you for all this evil." This is called *the day of the watchmen* because their prophets, whom God set as watchmen over them, have often warned them of that day.

4. There is no trust between people; people have grown universally unfaithful (v. 5). "Those who have any sense of honor remaining in them have a firm regard for the laws of friendship; they would not harm a friend by divulging what is spoken in private conversation or revealing secrets. However, those things are made fun of now. Wise people will make the rule, 'Do not trust in a friend' (v. 5), for people will find their friends false. As for those who undertake to be *your guide* in any business that they claim to understand better than you, you cannot *put a confidence* in them, for they will mislead you if they can gain anything by it." Some understand *a guide* to refer to a husband, who is called *the guide of thy youth* (Pr 2:17; Jer 3:4), and that agrees with what follows: *"Put no confidence in* your role as *a guide. Keep the doors of thy lips from her that lieth in thy bosom*, from your own wife; be careful about what you say to her, for she may betray you."

5. Children are abusive to their parents (v. 6). It is sad when a person's betrayers and worst enemies are their children and their best friends.

Verses 7–13

Having sadly complained of the evil of the times, the prophet focuses on some considerations for encouragement. The case is bad, but it is not desperate.

1. "Although God is now displeased, he will be reconciled to us, and then all will be well (vv. 7, 9)." At such a time we must:

1.1. Turn to God in our troubles (v. 7): *Therefore I will look unto the Lord*. Everything may look bright above us when everything looks dark around us. The prophet has been complaining that there is no confidence to be put in friends and relatives, and this drives him to his God: *Therefore I will look unto the Lord.*

1.2. Submit to the will of God in our troubles: "*I will bear the indignation of the Lord* patiently, without murmuring and complaining, *because I have sinned against him.*" When we complain to God about the corruption of the times, we should be dissatisfied with the corruption in our own hearts.

1.3. Depend on God to restore us. When things are brought to such a critical state, *my God will hear me*; if the Lord is our God, he will listen to our prayers and respond to them favorably. "*When I sit in darkness*, dejected and perplexed, then *the Lord shall be a light to me*, a light to my *eyes* and my feet, a light *in a dark place.*" He will *plead my cause, and execute judgment for me* (v. 9). "*He will bring me forth to the light.* The morning of comfort will shine forth out of the long and dark night of trouble. *I shall behold his righteousness*, the fulfillment of his promises to me."

2. Although enemies triumph, they will be put to shame (vv. 8, 10). The enemies of God's people say (v. 10), *Where is the Lord thy God?* — as if their suffering showed that God had abandoned them, that they did not know where to find him with their prayers, and that he did not know how to help them with his favors. The people of God, by faith, bear up under these insults (v. 8): "*Rejoice not against* (do not gloat over) *me, O my enemy!* I am down now but will not always be so, and when my God appears for me, then *she that is my enemy shall see it and be ashamed* (v. 10)." The rescue of the church will confound her enemies.

3. Although the land continues to be desolate for a long time, it will finally be repopulated. Its salvation will not come until "after it has been desolate," as the margin of v. 13 reads. It must lie under God's rebukes for a long time, *because of those that dwell therein.* Because of all this, they must expect to suffer a great while. But when their salvation does come, it will be a complete salvation, and this seems to refer to their restoration from Babylon by Cyrus. *The decree shall be far removed* (v. 11). God's decree sending them into exile and Nebuchadnezzar's decree expressing his resolution never to release them will be set aside. Jerusalem and the cities of Judah will again be repaired: then *thy walls shall be built.* All who belong to the land of Israel, wherever they are dispersed to, far and wide, will come flocking to it again (v. 12): *He shall come even to thee.* They will come from all the distant parts, *from sea to sea and from mountain to mountain*, not turning back until they reach Zion.

Verses 14–20

Here is:

1. The prophet's prayer to God to take care of his own people (v. 14). When we see God coming toward us by way of mercy, we must go out to meet him in prayer. It is a prophetic prayer, which amounts to a promise of the good that is prayed for; what God directed his prophet to ask for he also no doubt intended to give. The people of Israel are called here the *flock of God's heritage* (inheritance) (v. 14). This flock *dwells solitarily in the wood*, or in a forest, *in the midst of Carmel* (v. 14), a high mountain. Israel was a distinctive people *that dwelt alone*, like a flock of sheep in a forest. Now they are a desolate people (v. 13);

they are in the land of their exile like sheep in a forest, in danger from the animals of the forest. The prophet prays that God would *feed them there with his rod*, that is, that he would take care of them in their exile and fulfill the part of a good shepherd to them. "Let them be ruled by your rod, not the rod of their enemies, for they are your people." He prays that God would in due time bring them back to feed in the plains of Bashan and Gilead: *Let them feed* in their own country again, *as in the days of old* (v. 14). Some apply this spiritually, considering it either the prophet's prayer to Christ or the Father's charge to Christ to take care of his church as the great Shepherd of the sheep.

2. God's promise in answer to this prayer. God answers that he *will show them marvellous things* (v. 15); he will exceed their hopes and expectations. He will do what will be a repetition of the wonders and miracles of former ages — *according to the days of thy coming out of the land of Egypt* (v. 15). He will do for them what will be a matter of astonishment to the present age: the *nations about* will take notice of it (vv. 16–17). They will be *confounded at all the might* with which the exiles — whom they thought disabled forever — will now exert themselves. They will now *lay their hands upon their mouths*, ashamed of what they have said. They will stop their ears, unwilling to hear any more of God's wonders done for that people, whom they have so despised. Those who have arrogantly confronted God himself will then be brought, in profession at least, to submit to him: *They shall lick the dust like a serpent* (v. 17), as if they were sentenced to the same curse the serpent was laid under (Ge 3:14).

3. The prophet's thankful acknowledgment of God's pardoning mercy, which lies at the root of his promise of restoration. Just as it was their sin that brought them into slavery, so it was God's pardoning of their sin that brought them out of it (Ps 85:1–2; Isa 33:24; 38:17; 60:1–2). The prophet stands amazed at this, while the surrounding nations stand amazed only at those rescues that are merely its fruits. The reasons why God pardons sin and is not angry forever are all taken from within himself; it is *because he delights in mercy* (v. 18); the salvation of sinners is what he has pleasure in, not their death and condemnation. There is *no God like unto him*; no judge forgives as God does. In this his thoughts and ways are infinitely higher than ours (Isa 55:9); in this he is *God, and not man* (Nu 23:19). His mercy *endures for ever* (e.g., 1Ch 16:34), and just as he has *shown mercy*, he will continue to do so in the future (vv. 19–20). He will renew his favors to us: *He will turn again; he will have compassion.* He will also renew *us* in order to prepare and qualify us for his favor: *He will subdue our iniquities* (v. 19). When he takes away the guilt of sin so that it may not condemn us, he will break the power of sin so that it may not control us. *Thou wilt cast all their sins into the depth of the sea* (v. 19), as when, in bringing them out of Egypt, he subdued Pharaoh and the Egyptians and hurled them into the depths of the sea. This verse suggests that when God forgives sin, he *remembers it no more* (Jer 31:34; Heb 8:12). He hurls them into the sea, not near the shore, where they may appear again at the next tide, but into *the depth of the sea*, never to rise again. *All their sins* will be cast there without exception, for when God forgives sin, he forgives all sin. With this good work, he will do all that our lives require and which he has promised (v. 20).

A PRACTICAL AND DEVOTIONAL EXPOSITION OF THE BOOK OF THE PROPHET

Nahum

The name of this prophet means "a comforter," for all the prophets were charged, *Comfort you, comfort you, my people* (Isa 40:1). This prophet, though he is wholly taken up in foretelling the destruction of Nineveh, is, even in that, a comforter to the ten tribes of Israel, who had probably recently been taken as captives to Assyria. He probably lived in the time of Hezekiah, and he probably prophesied against Nineveh after the exile of Israel by the king of Assyria, which was in the ninth year of Hezekiah's reign, and before Sennacherib's invasion of Judah, which was in Hezekiah's fourteenth year, for it is thought that the first chapter refers to that attempt and its defeat (2Ki 18–19). Huetius (French scholar [1630–1721]) thought that the other two chapters of this book were delivered by Nahum some years later, perhaps in the reign of Manasseh; the Jewish chronologies generally place him in that reign, some time before the captivity of Judah.

CHAPTER 1

In this chapter we have: 1. The inscription of the book (v. 1). 2. A magnificent display of the glory of God in a mixture of wrath and justice against evildoers and mercy and grace toward his people; and his majesty and power are revealed in both (vv. 2–8). 3. A particular application of this, as some commentators think, to the destruction of Sennacherib and the Assyrian army when they besieged Jerusalem (2Ki 19:35–36) (vv. 9–16).

Verse 1

Nineveh was the place concerned, along with the Assyrian monarchy, of which that city was the royal seat. Jonah had, in God's name, foretold the quick overthrow of this great city, but then the Ninevites repented and were spared. The Ninevites then saw clearly how much it was to their advantage to turn from their evil ways; it was the saving of their city. But soon afterward, they returned to their evil way, and it became worse than ever. Then God sent them this prophecy of their condemnation, which was now irreversible. It is *the book of the vision of Nahum the Elkoshite*. The oracle of Nineveh was something that the prophet clearly foresaw, for it was his *vision*. When he was gone, the outcome could be compared with the prophecy. All we know of the prophet himself is that he was an *Elkoshite*, of the town called *Elkes*, which Jerome says was in Galilee.

Verses 2–8

Nineveh does not know God, and therefore she is told what this God is like. This glorious description of the Sovereign of the world, like the pillar of cloud and fire, has a bright side toward Israel and a dark side toward the Egyptians.

1. He is a God of uncompromising justice; let Nineveh know this and tremble before him. Their idols are insignificant; there is nothing formidable in them. The God

of Israel, however, is to be greatly feared. He resents the dishonor shown him by those who deny his being or any of his attributes, who set up other gods as rivals to him, who destroy his laws, ridicule his word, or are abusive to his people. Let such people know that Jehovah is jealous for his own honor in matters of his worship and will not endure a rival; he is jealous for the well-being of his worshipers, *jealous for his land* (Joel 2:18), and will not have that wronged. He "has fury" is the literal sense, not as human beings have it, in whom it is an uncontrolled passion, but in a way that befits the righteous God. He is "Lord of anger"—the Hebrew phrase for *he is furious*—he has anger, but he has it at his command and under his control. Our anger often takes us over, like those who have *no rule over their own spirits* (Pr 25:28), but God is always *Lord of his anger* and *weighs a path to it* (Ps 78:50). Whoever his enemies are, he will make them feel his anger in the day of wrath (Ro 2:5). He *will not at all acquit the wicked* who sin, who stand by it and do not repent (v. 3). This revelation of the wrath of God against his enemies (Ro 1:18) is applied to Nineveh (v. 8), and all those who continue in their trespasses should apply it to themselves: *With an overrunning flood he will make an utter end of the place thereof* (v. 8). *Darkness shall pursue his enemies*; terror and trouble will follow them wherever they go. If they think about fleeing from the darkness that pursues them, they will only fall into what is in front of them.

2. He is a God of irresistible power. If we look up into the sky, we will find proofs of his power, for *he has his ways in the whirlwind and the storm* (v. 3). He spoke to Job out of the whirlwind, and even *stormy winds fulfil his word* (Ps 148:8). If we look at the great depths, we find that the sea is his, for when he pleases, *he rebukes the sea and makes it dry, drying up all the rivers* (v. 4). If we look around on this earth, we find proofs of his power when, either by the extreme heat and drought of summer or the

cold and frost of winter, *Bashan languishes, and Carmel, and the flower of Lebanon languishes* (v. 4). Earthquakes shake the mountains (v. 5) and melt the hills, leveling them with the plains. When he pleases, *the earth is burnt* (trembles) *at his presence* by the scorching heat of the sun. If God is an almighty God, we may reason from that (v. 6), *Who can stand before his indignation?* The Ninevites had once found God *slow to anger* (v. 3; Jnh 4:2), and perhaps they presumed on the mercy they had then experienced. It is futile for the boldest and strongest to think they can successfully resist the power of God's anger. God's anger is so furious that it beats down everything in its path: *The rocks are thrown down by him.* The eruption of underground fires is a faint likeness of the fury of God's anger against sinners whose hearts are as hard as rock. Sinners are like stubble in the face of the fire, the wrath of God. *Who can abide in* (endure) *the fierceness of his anger?* A person may endure some of the effects of God's displeasure in this world, but who can bear the *fierceness of his anger* when it is directed against the soul? Let us *fear before him*; let us *stand in awe, and not sin* (Ps 4:4).

3. He is a God of infinite mercy. *Let the sinners in Zion be afraid* (Isa 33:14), those who continue in their disobedience, but let not those who trust in God tremble in his presence. He *is slow to anger* (v. 3), ready to show *mercy*. When the signs of his rage against evildoers are about, he looks after his own people (v. 7): *The Lord is good* to those who are *good*, and he will be *a stronghold in the day of trouble* to them.

Verses 9–15

These verses seem to point to the destruction of the army of the Assyrians under Sennacherib, which may well be considered a part of the oracle of Nineveh, the capital city of the Assyrian Empire, and may well be considered, too, a pledge of the destruction of Nineveh itself about 100 years later. Here is:

1. The great provocation the Assyrians gave to God, the just and jealous God, for which, although he is *slow to anger*, he will take vengeance (v. 11): *There is one come out of thee, that imagines evil against the* Lord—Sennacherib, with his spokesman *Rabshakeh*, the field commander. They framed an evil letter and an evil speech, not only against Hezekiah and his people but also against God himself, implying that the Lord is on the same level as the gods of the nations and unable to protect his worshipers, urging his people to put themselves under the protection of the *great king, the king of Assyria*. The prophet says to this evil counsel (v. 9): "*What do you imagine* (What are you plotting) *against the Lord?* How foolish and evil it is for you to plot against God, as if you could outwit divine wisdom and overpower almighty God himself!"

2. The great destruction that God will bring on them for it, not immediately on the whole monarchy—the ruin of that was delayed—but:

2.1. On the army. God *will make an utter end* of it; it will be totally cut off and ruined at one blow. They have exposed themselves to divine wrath through their own actions (v. 10). They are *as thorns* that entangle one another and are *folded together*. They make one another worse. God will deal with them as farmers do with thorn bushes when they cannot separate them: they put them all into the fire together. They are *as drunken men*, intoxicated with pride and anger, and as such they will be destroyed. They will be *devoured as stubble fully dry* (v. 10), which is irresistibly and irrecoverably consumed by fire. This great army (v. 12), *though they be quiet* (have allies) *and likewise many*, thinking themselves very secure while

they are numerous, will be cut down like grass and corn when *he shall pass through*.

2.2. On the king. He *imagined evil* (plotted) *against the Lord*, and will he escape? No (v. 14): "*The Lord has given a commandment concerning thee*; the decree has been issued *that thy name be no more sown* (you will have no more descendants), that the memory of you will perish." The images he worships will be removed from their temple, which some think was fulfilled when Sennacherib was killed by his *two sons as he was worshipping in the house of Nisroch his god*. After that, probably, the temple was looked on as defiled and therefore ceased to be used, and the images were destroyed. Sennacherib's grave, some think, will be made there, in the house of his god; he will be killed there, and he will be buried there, for *he is vile*. Or the verse may refer to the shameful downfall of the Assyrian monarchy itself, on the ruins of which Babylon was raised up.

3. The great rescue that God will carry out for his own people and the city that was called by his name (Jer 25:29). The siege will be raised: "*Now will I break his yoke from off thee*, the yoke by which you are kept in slavery, and *will burst thy bonds asunder*, the bonds by which you seem bound to the Assyrian's wrath." This was a figure of the great salvation by which the Jerusalem that is above is made free (Gal 4:26). The enemy will be so weakened and discouraged that they will never make any such attempt again. The enemy will not dare attack Jerusalem again (v. 15): *The wicked shall no more pass through thee* to devastate everything, as they have done. His army will be destroyed, his spirit destroyed, and finally he himself will be destroyed. The news of this great rescue will be welcomed throughout the kingdom (v. 15). While Sennacherib was successful, every day brought bad news, but now, *behold, upon the mountains, the feet of him that bringeth good tidings* (v. 15), "the feet of the evangelist." He is seen coming from a distance on the mountains, as fast as his feet will carry him, and how pleasant it is to see once again a messenger of peace, after we have received so many of Job's messengers (Job 1:13–19)! These words are also quoted by the apostle Paul, both from Isaiah and from Nahum, and applied to the great redemption brought for us by our Lord Jesus and the declaring of it to the world by the eternal Gospel (Ro 10:15). Christ's ministers are those messengers of good news who preach *peace by Jesus Christ*. During the trouble, ordinary feasts were discontinued. While Jerusalem was *encompassed with armies*, the people could not go there to worship, but now they must return to celebrating their festivals. Now that the rescue has been carried out, they are called on to fulfill their vows.

CHAPTER 2

Nineveh, that great city (Jnh 1:2; 3:2), took no notice of the warning given her by the destruction of her armies and the downfall of her king, and she persists in being God's enemy, and so she may expect that he will continue his accusations against her. Here are foretold: 1. The approach of the enemy that will destroy Nineveh (vv. 1–5). 2. The capture of the city (v. 6). 3. The captivity of the queen, the flight of the city's inhabitants, and the seizing of all its wealth (vv. 7–10). And: 4. This is traced back to its true causes—their sinning against God and God's appearing against them (vv. 11–13). This was fulfilled when Nebuchadnezzar, in the first year of his reign, together with Cyaxares, or Ahasuerus, king of the Medes, conquered Nineveh and took control of the Assyrian monarchy.

Verses 1–10

Here is:

1. A warning of war to Nineveh. The prophet speaks of it as close at hand: "Look about you and see, *he that dashes in pieces has come up before thy face* (an attacker advances against you) (v. 1). Nebuchadnezzar is noted for tearing nations to pieces, and he will disperse you." The attempt of Nebuchadnezzar on Nineveh will be bold and daring: "He *has come up before thy face*, affirming his intention to ruin you. Therefore, stand to arms, *O Nineveh! Keep the munition* (guard the fortress), secure your towers and arsenals. *Watch the way*, set guards on all the approaches to the city. *Make thy loins strong* (brace yourselves), encourage your soldiers; stir yourself and them. *Fortify thy power mightily* (marshal all your strength)"—this is spoken ironically—"even if you do all you can, *there is no counsel or strength against the Lord* (Pr 21:30)."

2. The causes of the war (v. 2): *The Lord has turned away the excellency* (splendor) *of Jacob, as the excellency* (splendor) *of Israel*. The Assyrians have been abusive to Jacob, the two tribes, as well as Israel, the ten tribes; they *have emptied them and marred their vine-branches*. God will judge them for this, even though they did it long ago. Or it may mean God is now, through Nebuchadnezzar, about *to turn away the pride of Jacob* by the exile of the two tribes, as he did the pride of Israel by their exile. The enemy who is to do this must begin with Nineveh. God is looking at proud cities, bringing them low. Samaria is humbled, and Jerusalem is to be humbled, and will not Nineveh, that proud city, also be brought down? *Emptiers have emptied* the cities *and marred the vine-branches* in the country of Jacob and Israel.

3. A particular account given of the terrors with which the invading enemy will appear against Nineveh.

3.1. *The shields of his mighty men are made red* (v. 3), as if they were already colored with the blood they had shed.

3.2. *The valiant men are in scarlet* (v. 3): they are wearing rich clothes to show the wealth of the army.

3.3. *The chariots shall be with flaming torches in the day of his preparation* (v. 3); the wheels will strike fire on the stones. Or the Assyrians carried flaming torches with them in their open chariots when they made their approach at the night, both to be a guide to them and to set everything on fire wherever they went.

3.4. *The fir trees shall be terribly shaken* (v. 3). This refers to the leaders of Nineveh, who tower over their neighbors as stately firs do over shrubs; the very trees will be shaken by the violent pounding of that great army's feet.

3.5. The chariots of war will be very terrible (v. 4): *They shall rage in the streets*, that is, those who drive them will storm through the streets. Even *in the broad ways*, where one would think there would be enough room, they will *jostle one another*. These iron chariots will be made so bright that in the beams of the sun *shall they seem like torches* at night. Nebuchadnezzar's commanders are called his *worthies* here, his "gallants" (as the margin of v. 5 reads). "His worthies shall remember" is how some read it; they will be mindful of their duty, of the charge they have received, and be so intent on their business that they *shall stumble in their walks, for they shall make haste to the wall thereof*. The defense, or the covered way, will be prepared—something to shelter them from the darts of the besieged—and they will carry on the siege with so much vigor that the *gates of the rivers shall be opened* (v. 6). The gates of Nineveh that open on the Tigris River, on which Nineveh was built, will be forced by the enemy, and they will enter by those gates. Then the *palace shall be dissolved* (collapse), either the king's house or the house of Nisroch his god; the same word means both "a palace" and "a temple."

4. A prediction of the consequences of this.

4.1. The queen will fall into the hands of the enemy (v. 7): *Huzzab shall be led away captive*; she who was "established" or "decreed," as some read the name, thinks herself safe because she is concealed, but she will be "discovered," as the margin reads, and will be led *away captive* in disgrace. She will be *brought up in* a mock state, *and her maids* of honor *shall lead her*, because she is weak and faint. They will be *tabering upon their breasts*, beating their own breasts in grief, as if they were drumming on them.

4.2. None of the inhabitants will be able to stand their ground (v. 8): *Nineveh is of old like a pool of water*, full with people as a pool with water. It was long ago a populous city; in Jonah's time there were 120,000 little children in it (Jnh 4:11). Their commanders will cry out, "*Stand, stand* (stand firm, stop!), have a heart for it, and we will do well enough." But they will not have the least spark of courage remaining in them. They will not even look back to see who calls for them.

4.3. The wealth of the city will become plunder, and all its rich furnishings will fall into the hands of the victorious enemy (v. 9). This is how this rich city becomes *empty, and void, and waste* (pillaged, plundered, and stripped) (v. 10).

4.4. The soldiers and people will have no heart to appear to defend the city. Much pain will be *in all loins* (hearts will melt and knees give way), as is the case in extreme fear, so that they will not be able to stand. The *faces of them all shall gather blackness* (every face grows pale) also, like that of a pot that is used on the fire every day.

Verses 11–13

Here we have Nineveh's destruction:

1. Triumphed in by its neighbors, who now recall against it all the oppressions it has been guilty of in its pride and prosperity (vv. 11–12): *Where is the dwelling of the lions? Where is the feeding place of the young lions*, where they glutted themselves with prey? The rulers of Nineveh have been like lions, like wild animals. Even though no one loved them, everyone feared them, and that was all they desired. The king made it his business to use violence and extortion to enrich himself and raise his family; he *tore in pieces enough for his whelps*, and he *strangled for his lionesses*.

2. Affirmed by the righteous Judge (v. 13): *Behold, I am against thee, saith the Lord of hosts*. The oppressors in Nineveh thought they only set their neighbors against them, but they also set God against them, who is the asserter of right and the avenger of wrong. These military preparations will do them no good: *I will burn their chariots in the smoke*; he does not say *in the fire*; rather, in contempt of them, the very *smoke* of God's indignation will be enough to burn their chariots. Their children, the hopes of their families, will be cut off: *The sword shall devour the young lions*. The wealth they have heaped up by fraud and violence will not be enjoyed by them: "You will be no better off for it, but no one else will be either. *The voice of thy messengers shall no more be heard*, no more be heeded," which some think refers to the field commander.

CHAPTER 3

Here: 1. Nineveh is accused of the sins of murder (v. 1), prostitution, and sorcery (v. 4), and her evil is said to extend to all around her (v. 19). 2. Judgments are threatened against her here, blood for blood (vv. 2–3) and shame for shameful sins (vv. 5–7). 3. Instances are given of similar devastation brought on other places for similar sins (vv. 8–11). 4. The overthrow of all the things she has depended on is foretold (vv. 12–19).

Verses 1–7

Here is:

1. Nineveh accused. It is a *city of blood* (v. 1). *It is all full of lies*; truth has been banished from among its people. There is no such thing as honesty. The city is full of *robbery* and plunder. There is a *multitude of whoredoms* in it (v. 4), that is, idolatry, spiritual prostitution. She is *a mistress of witchcrafts* (sorcery), and by them she *sells families* (v. 4). What Nineveh has aimed at is a universal monarchy, to be the center of the world, compelling some and deceiving others into submitting to her. She has used her sinful charms to seduce them. This is her sorcery, with which she has inexplicably gained power.

2. Nineveh condemned to ruin on this accusation (v. 1).

2.1. Nineveh has been very cruel in terrorizing and destroying others, and so destruction and terror will be brought on her. Listen to the alarm with which Nineveh will be terrified (v. 2). It is a formidable army that is advancing against it; you can hear them from far away, *the noise* (crack) *of the whip*, the *rattling* (clatter) *of the wheels*, the *prancing* (galloping) *horses, and the jumping* (jolting) *chariots*. The very noise is frightening. Notice the slaughter with which Nineveh will be devastated (v. 3): the sword will be drawn, *the bright* (flashing) *sword lifted up and the glittering spear*, the dazzling brightness of which is terrible. Notice what havoc these weapons make when they are commissioned to kill. The destruction of Sennacherib's army, which, in the morning, were *all dead corpses* (2Ki 19:35), is perhaps looked on here as a figure of the similar destruction that would later come on Nineveh.

2.2. Nineveh has drawn other people into shameful wickedness, and so God will weigh her down with contempt (vv. 5–7): *The Lord of hosts is against her.* When it is seen that in courting her neighbors she intended to ruin her liberty and property, then her *shame will be discovered* (exposed) *to the nations.* When her proud pretensions are thwarted, then *to see the nakedness of the land do they come*, and it appears ridiculous. Then they will *cast abominable filth upon her* (they will pelt her with filth), like an adulteress held up to public shame, and *make her vile.* Those who formerly looked to her in the hope of being protected by her will then *look upon her and flee from her* for fear of being ruined with her. When Nineveh is devastated; *who will bemoan her?* Those who showed no pity in times of power can expect to find no pity in times of downfall.

Verses 8–19

To convince Nineveh that her self-confidence is futile, the prophet shows her people:

1. That Nineveh will fall unpitied and uncomforted—and she will not be able to help herself: *Art thou better than populous No?* (v. 8). The prophet quotes precedents. The city mentioned is *No* (Thebes), a great city in the land of Egypt (Jer 46:25), "No-Ammon," as some read it. Some think it was Diospolis, others Alexandria.

Just as God said to Jerusalem, *Go, see what I did to Shiloh* (Jer 7:12), so he says to Nineveh, *Go, see what I did to populous No.* Notice concerning No:

1.1. How firm her standing is (v. 8). She was fortified by both natural and artificial means, was *situate among the rivers* (situated on the Nile). The Nile watered her fields and guarded her wall. *Her rampart was the sea*, the *lake of* Mareotis. She was also supported by alliances abroad (v. 9). *Ethiopia*, Cush or Arabia, *was her strength*, either by trade or by forces supplied in military service. The whole country of Egypt contributed to this populous city; the result was that it was "infinite, and there was no end of it," as it might be translated; she set no limits on her ambition and knew no end of her wealth and strength. However, it is only God's right to be infinite. *Put and Lubim were thy helpers*, two neighboring countries of Africa, Mauritania and Libya, that is, Libya Cyrenaica [Ed. note: *Put* and *Lubim* may refer to just one country, Libya].

1.2. How fatal her downfall proved to be (v. 10): *Yet was she carried away*, and her strength failed her; even the one who seemed so strong and secure *went into captivity. Her young children* were *dashed in pieces at the top of all the streets by* the merciless conquerors. *They cast lots for her honourable men* who were made prisoners of war, to determine whom each prisoner would be given to as a slave. What a mortification this was to *populous No.* The prophet infers from this concerning Nineveh (v. 11), "You also will be intoxicated, drunk with the cup of the Lord's fury, which will be put into your hand" (Jer 25:17, 27). *Thou shalt fall and rise no more.*

2. That all those things in which they put their confidence will fail them.

2.1. Do the people of Nineveh trust in their own bravery? Their hearts will sink and fail them. *They shall be hid*, will run away in shame. They will *seek strength*, will come crawling to their neighbors to beg assistance.

2.2. Do they depend on the garrisons and strongholds they have? Those will prove walls of mere paper and will be *like the first ripe figs* (v. 12), which, if you shake the tree only a little, will *fall into the mouth of the eater* below. They may make their strongholds as strong as possible; they are challenged to do all they can to make them safe against the invader (v. 14): *Draw thee water for the siege.* Water stands here for all kinds of provision, with which Nineveh is ironically told to supply herself in expectation of a siege. "*Go into* (work the) *clay, and tread the mortar*, and *make strong the brick-kiln* (repair the brickwork); take all the effort you need to set up new fortifications; yet it will be all in vain, for (v. 15) there will be *the fire devour thee* if the stronghold is burned down, or there will *the sword cut thee off* if it is taken by storm."

2.3. Do they put their confidence in the great numbers of their inhabitants? They will only sink more quickly under the weight of their own numbers (v. 13): *Thy people in the midst of thee are women*: they will be fickle and fainthearted in times of danger and distress, adding to their fears by the power of their own imagination. Although they *make themselves many* (v. 15), like the *cankerworm* (grasshoppers) and *the locust*, which come in vast swarms, *though thou hast multiplied thy merchants above the stars of heaven*, though your market is full of wealthy traders, their hearts will fail them. Even though they are as numerous as caterpillars, the fire and sword will devour them as irresistibly as grasshoppers (v. 15). The prophet adds (v. 16), *The cankerworm spoils*, or "spreads herself," *and flies away*. Both the merchants and the enemies are compared to grasshoppers. The enemies will plunder Nineveh and carry away the spoils without opposition. Or the rich merchants, who have come from abroad to settle in Nineveh, will move somewhere else when they see the country invaded and the city likely to be besieged. They will *spread their wings* and *fly away* to where they may be safe (Pr 23:5).

2.4. Do they put their confidence in the strength of their gates? *The gates of thy land shall be set wide open unto thy enemies* (v. 13), the gates of your rivers (2:6), that is, the floodgates, or else the passes: *The fire shall devour thy bars*, and they will fly open.

2.5. Do they put confidence in their king and rulers? They will not help them (v. 17): *Thy crowned heads are as the locusts*; those who were proud and powerful as crowned heads were made feeble. "*Thy captains*, who should lead your forces, look great, but they are like the great *grasshoppers*. They may be the largest of their species, but they remain only grasshoppers, worthless and unable to help. *They encamp in the hedges, in the cold day*, the cold weather, *but when the sun arises, they flee away*, nobody knows where. This is what the mercenary soldiers do when any trouble comes: they run away to save their own lives. *The hireling flees, because he is a hireling* (Jn 10:13)." The *king of Assyria* is told that *his shepherds slumber*; they have no spirit to support the flock. The *nobles shall dwell in the dust* (v. 18), buried in silence.

2.6. Do they hope that they will still recover? They will also be disappointed in this, for when the shepherds are struck, the *sheep are scattered* (Zec 13:7); the people are dispersed *upon the mountains*, and *no man gathers them*. The judgment they are under is like an incurable wound. "Your case is desperate (v. 19), and your neighbors will *clap their hands over thee*, gloating over your downfall. *Upon whom has not thy wickedness passed continually?* You have always been causing trouble to those around you, and so they will be far from pitying you. *The troublers shall be troubled* (Jos 7:25) will be the burden of many, as it is here the *burden* (oracle) of Nineveh.

A Practical and Devotional Exposition of the Book of the Prophet

Habakkuk

It is a foolish thought of some of the Jewish rabbis that this prophet was the son whom Elisha miraculously gave to the Shunammite woman and later raised from the dead (2Ki 4:18–37), as they say also that the prophet Jonah was the son of the widow of Zarephath (1Ki 17:7–24). It is a more probable thought that he lived and prophesied in the reign of King Manasseh, when there was much evil and when destruction was being brought quickly by the Babylonians, whom this prophet mentions as the instruments of God's judgments. Manasseh was himself taken to Babylon as a pledge of what would later come. In the apocryphal story of Bel and the Dragon, Habakkuk the prophet is mentioned as being taken by an angel from the land of Judah to Babylon to feed Daniel in the lions' den; those who believe that story seek to reconcile it with our prophet's living before the exile and foretelling it. Some people have imagined that Habakkuk's feeding Daniel in the den is to be understood mystically, that Daniel then *lived by faith*, as Habakkuk had said *the just would do*; he was *fed* by that word (2:4). The prophecy of this book is a mixture of the prophet's addresses to God in the people's name and to the people in God's name, for it is the work of the prophet to take messages both ways. It is a description of the fellowship between a gracious God and a gracious soul. The whole book refers especially to the invasion of the land of Judah by the Babylonians.

CHAPTER 1

Here: 1. The prophet complains to God about the violence done by the abuse of justice among his own people and about the hardships that are thereby put on many good people (vv. 1–4). 2. Through him, God foretells the punishment of such abuse of power by the sword of war, that is, by the destruction the army of the Babylonians will cause (vv. 5–11). 3. Then the prophet is grieved that the Babylonians are so successful (vv. 12–17), so that he scarcely knows which should be more mourned, the sin or its punishment, for in both many good people suffer very greatly. It is good that there is a day of judgment and a future state ahead of us; then the present apparent disorders of providence will be set right.

Verses 1–4

The writer was *a prophet*, a man divinely inspired and commissioned, and the book itself is *the burden* (oracle) *which* he *saw*; he was as sure of its truth as if he had seen it already fulfilled with his physical eyes. The prophet sadly mourns the sin of the times: the land is *full of violence*, as the old world was (Ge 6:11). The prophet *cries out of violence* (cries out, "Violence!") (v. 2), *iniquity* (injustice) and *grievance* (wrong), *spoil* (destruction) and *violence*. It does not appear that the prophet himself has had any great wrong done him—in times of loss things went best with those who had nothing to lose—but it grieves him to see other people wronged. He complains that *the wicked doth compass about the righteous* (v. 4). One honest person, one honest cause, will have enemies surrounding them. The kingdom is broken into parties and factions that are continually biting and devouring one another (Gal 5:15). *There are* those *that raise up strife and contention* (v. 3), who stir up divisions and sow seeds of discord (Pr 6:14, 19) among brothers and sisters. If *blessed are the peacemakers* (Mt 5:9), then cursed are such peace breakers. The torrent of violence and strife runs so strongly as to defy laws and the administration of justice (v. 4). Because God does not come against them, no one else will; *therefore the law is slacked* (paralyzed); it is silent. It is, literally, "numb," *and judgment does not go forth*. Habakkuk complains about this to God but cannot obtain redress for those grievances: "*Lord*," he says, "*why dost thou show me iniquity?*" Why have you cast my lot in such a time and at such a place, when and where it is to be seen?" When God seems to ignore the wickedness of evildoers—when indeed he seems to support it by allowing them to prosper in their evil—it shocks the faith of good people. God has reasons for the reprieves of evildoers and the rebukes of good people, and so we must believe that the day will come when the cry of sin will be heard against those who commit wrong (Ge 18:20–21) and the cry of prayer will be heard for those who suffer it.

Verses 5–11

Here is an answer to the prophet's complaint. Though God will bear with them patiently for a long time, he will not always bear with this offensive people (Nu 14:27). Notice:

1. The introduction to the sentence (v. 5): *Behold, you among the heathen, and regard* (look at the nations and watch). Since they will not be brought to repentance by the patience of God, he will inflict on them:

1344

1.1. A public punishment, at which the neighboring nations will be stunned: see Dt 29:24–25. Israel will be made a spectacle to the world.

1.2. An astounding punishment, so strange that it will not be believed even by those who receive news of it from those who were eyewitnesses to it when it came (Lk 1:2): *You will not believe it, though it be told you* (v. 5). The punishment of God's professing people must be to the astonishment of everyone about them.

1.3. A speedy punishment: *"I will work a work in your days,* quickly now; this generation will not pass until the threatened judgment is fulfilled."

1.4. A punishment in which the hand of God will appear: *This is the Lord's doing.*

1.5. A punishment that will be a type of the destruction to be brought on the despisers of Christ and his Gospel. The destruction of Jerusalem by the Babylonians for their idolatry was a figure of their ruin by the Romans for rejecting Christ and his Gospel.

2. The sentence itself, which is dreadful and detailed: *Lo, I raise up the Chaldeans* (Babylonians) (v. 6). When God's professing people quarrel among themselves, growl, and devour one another (Gal 5:15), God is just to bring a common enemy on them, who will make peace by making devastation. The contending parties in Jerusalem were hardened against one another when the Romans came and *took away their place and nation* (Jn 11:48). We have here:

2.1. The people who will be raised up against Israel and be a scourge to them. They are *a bitter and hasty nation,* cruel and fierce. They show no mercy, and they spare no effort. *They are terrible and dreadful, famed* for the troops they bring onto the field; *their horses are swifter than leopards, more fierce* than the *evening wolves* (v. 8), and wolves are observed to be most ravenous toward dusk, waiting for darkness, under which *all beasts of the forest creep forth* (Ps 104:20). *"Their horsemen shall spread themselves* a great way, for they will *come from far,* from all parts of their own country." They are a law to themselves; they will not be governed by any laws of humanity, justice, or honor: *Their judgment and their dignity shall proceed of themselves* (v. 7). Their own appetites and passion rule them, not reason or conscience.

2.2. A prophecy of the terrible execution that will be carried out by this nation: *They shall march through the breadth of the land* (the earth) (v. 6). The Babylonian forces subdued all the nations in those parts, so that they seemed to have conquered the world. Or they marched through the breadth of *the land* of Israel, which was completely devastated by them. *Their faces shall sup up as the east wind*; even their faces will appear so fierce and frightful that one look will be enough to allow them to control all they want, so that they will *swallow up* all, as a desert wind nips and blasts the buds and flowers. "They will take a vast number of prisoners and send them to Babylon: *They shall gather the captivity as the sand,* in great masses (v. 9). *They shall scoff*—"he will scoff," as it is in the original, referring to Nebuchadnezzar, who, having become proud of his successes, will laugh—*at the kings* and commanders. *The princes shall be an* object *of scorn to them. He shall deride every stronghold,* for to him it will be weak, and *he shall heap dust, and take it*; a little soil thrown up in ramparts will be enough to give him all the advantage that he can want; he will make sport of capturing them. By all this he will become intolerably proud, which will be his destruction: *Then shall his mind change for* the worse (v. 11). *Bel* and *Nebo* were the gods of the Babylonians, and that people gave the glory of their successes to them. They were hardened in their idolatry, and they blasphemously argued that because they had conquered Israel, their gods were too strong for the God of Israel.

Verses 12–17

The prophet now turns to God and again speaks to him to ease his mind while he remains under the burden that he has seen. If he looks around him, he sees nothing but violence done by Israel; if he looks in front of him, he sees nothing but violence done against Israel. The prospect of the success of the Babylonians drives the prophet to his knees to plead with God about it. We have here:

1. The truths that he resolves to be faithful to, to comfort himself and his friends under the threats of the Babylonians.

1.1. God remains *the Lord our God,* and *our Holy One* (v. 12). He *is Jehovah,* the fountain of all being (Ex 3:14–15), power, and perfection. *Our rock* is not *as theirs* (Dt 32:31). "He is *my God."* He speaks in the people's name; every Israelite may say, "He is *mine.* Even though *all this has come upon us, yet have we not forgotten the name of our God* (Ps 44:17, 20). We will not harbor any harsh thoughts of him or his service because of all this."

1.2. Our God is eternal. If he is from everlasting, he will be to everlasting (Ps 90:2), and we must keep on turning back to this basic principle when things that are seen and physical are discouraging, so that we have hope and sufficient help in God, who is eternal. "Are you not *from of old,* a God in covenant with your people?" as some understand it. "Are you not the same God? You are God, *and thou changest not"* (Mal 3:6).

1.3. While the world stands, God will have a church in it. The prophet infers the perpetuity of the church from the eternity of God, for Christ has said, *"Because I live,* and so as long as I live, *you shall live also"* (Jn 14:19). *We shall not die* (v. 12).

1.4. Whatever the enemies of the church may do against her, it is according to the purposes of God and is intended and directed for his wise and holy ends (v. 12): *Thou hast ordained them; thou hast established them.* It was God who gave the Babylonians their power. He gave them their commission *to take the spoil and to take the prey* (Isa 10:6). In this, God is seen as a mighty God when it is recognized that the power of powerful people is derived from him and is under his restraint: *Hitherto shall it come, and no further* (Job 38:11). Those whom God ordains will do no more than what he has ordained. He has *ordained them for judgment* and *for correction.* God's people need correction, and they deserve it. The correction comes to drive out the foolishness in their hearts (Pr 22:15).

1.5. Although the evildoers may prosper for a while, God remains a holy God, and he does not approve of that wickedness (v. 13): *Thou art of purer eyes than to behold evil.* When the prophet observed how ruthless the Babylonians were, but how successful they were against God's Israel, he was tempted to say it was futile to serve God. However, he suppressed that thought by going back to his basic principle, that God is not the author or supporter of sin. God is *of purer eyes than to behold it* with approval. There is in God's nature an incompatibility toward those practices that are against his holy law, and although, fortunately, a way has been found for him to be reconciled to sinners, he never will and never can be reconciled to sin. Even though God sees cause to allow trouble to be done to God's people by their persecutors, he still does not approve of it.

2. The grievances he finds hard to reconcile with these truths: "Since we are sure that you are a holy God, *wherefore lookest thou* with favor *upon the Chaldeans* (Babylonians), who *deal treacherously* with your people? Why do you give them success? Why do you allow your sworn enemies to deal so cruelly with your sworn subjects, who desire to fear your name? What shall we say in response to all this?" This was a temptation for Job (Job 21:7; 24:1), David (Ps 73:2–3), and Jeremiah (Jer 12:1–2), and here Habakkuk was tempted when he observed:

2.1. That God allowed sin and was patient with the sinners.

2.2. That his patience was abused and that *because sentence* against these evil works and workers *was not executed speedily, their hearts were all the more fully set in them to do evil* (Ecc 8:11). They were false and deceitful. They hated and persecuted people because they were better than they, as Cain hated Abel because *his own works were evil and his brother's righteous* (1Jn 3:12). They thought that killing people was like catching fish. The prophet complained that because providence had delivered up the weaker to be the prey to the stronger, they were, in effect, made like *the fishes of the sea* (v. 14). They had been like this among themselves, attacking one another as bigger fish attack smaller ones (v. 3). They were *as the creeping things*, or the fish (Ge 1:26), *that have no ruler* over them. They were given over to the Babylonians as fish are given to fishermen. Those proud oppressors had no hesitation in killing God's people, any more than people hesitate when they catch fish from the water. They had various ways of destroying and plundering, as people do of catching fish. Some they *took up with the angle* (hooks) (v. 15), one by one; others *they caught* in shoals, large numbers, *in their net*, and *gathered them in their drag*, their enclosing dragnet. *Their portion was fat, and their meat plenteous* (their catch is large and luxurious, and they enjoy the choicest food). They live happily (v. 15): *Therefore they rejoiced and were glad*, because their wealth is great and their plans succeed. They wonder greatly at their own ingenuity: they *sacrificed to their own net, and burned incense to their own drag* (v. 16).

3. The hope that the prophet humbly expresses in closing, that God will not allow these destroyers of the human race to continue to prosper in this way (v. 17): "*Shall they therefore empty their net?* Will they empty their net of what they have caught, so that they may throw it back into the sea to catch even more? Must the numbers and wealth of nations be sacrificed to their net? Is not God the king of nations, and will he not assert their rights? Is he not jealous for his own honor, and will he not maintain that?" The prophet puts the matter in God's hands and leaves it with him, as the psalmist does. *Arise, O God! Plead thy own cause* (Ps 74:22).

CHAPTER 2

In this chapter the prophet looks for an answer to his complaints about the violence and victories of the Babylonians (v. 1), and the Spirit of God gives him an answer, which is: 1. That after God has served his own purposes by the Babylonians, after he has tested the faith and patience of his people, distinguishing the hypocrites and the sincere, he will humble not only that proud monarch Nebuchadnezzar but also that proud monarchy (vv. 2–8). 2. That not only they but also all other sinners like them will perish: 2.1. Those who are covetous and greedy for wealth and honors (vv. 9, 11). 2.2. Those who are oppressive and increase their possessions by ravaging

(vv. 12–14). 2.3. Those who urge drunkenness so that they may expose their neighbors to shame (vv. 15–17). 2.4. Those who worship idols (vv. 18–20).

Verses 1–4

Here:

1. The prophet humbly waits on God (v. 1): "*I will stand upon my watch*, as a guard waits on the walls of a besieged city. I will look up, around, and within *and watch to see what he will say unto me*. 'I will watch to see what he will say in me'"—as it may read—"what the Spirit of prophecy in me will dictate to me as an answer to my complaints." God not only speaks to us through his word but also speaks in us through our own consciences, whispering to us, *This is the way, walk in it* (Isa 30:21). Those who expect to hear from God must withdraw from the world and go up higher than it. They must raise their attention, fix their thoughts, study the Scriptures, consult experiences and the experienced, devote themselves to prayer, and so set themselves *upon the tower*.

1.1. When we are perplexed with doubts about the ways of Providence, when we are tempted to think it is fate, and not a wise God, that governs the world, then we must set ourselves on the tower to see if we can discover what will silence the temptation and solve the difficulties. We must go into the sanctuary of God and there seek to understand *the end* of these things (Ps 73:17).

1.2. When we have been at prayer, pouring out our complaints and requests to God, we must carefully take notice of what answers God gives through his word, his Spirit, and his providences.

2. God graciously meets with him. The prophet has complained about the success of the Babylonians. Now, to pacify him about it, God reveals to him their downfall and destruction, as Isaiah, before this, when he had prophesied the exile in Babylon, also prophesied the destruction of Babylon.

2.1. The prophet must *write the vision* (v. 2). We have reason to bless God for written visions, that God has written to us the great things of his Prophets as well as of his Law. Habakkuk must *write the vision* and *make it plain upon tables*, must write it legibly, in large characters, so that *he who runs may read*. God himself has attached his imprimatur to the prophet's words; he has said, *Make them plain*.

2.2. The people must wait for the fulfillment of the vision (v. 3): "*The vision is yet for an appointed time* to come. You will now be told that you will be restored by the breaking of the Babylonians' power and that its time has been fixed in the purposes and decrees of God, but the time is still to be deferred for a great while." God has an appointed time for his appointed work, and he will be sure to complete the work when the time comes; it is not for us to go before his appointments, but to wait for his time.

2.3. This vision will be such an exercise of faith and patience as will test and reveal people's true character (v. 4). There are some who will proudly disdain this vision. They think *their own hands sufficient for them* (Dt 33:7), and God's promise is insignificant to them. Those who are truly good and whose hearts are upright with God will value the promise and risk their all on it. They will keep close to God and their duty in the most difficult and trying times and lead assured lives in fellowship with God, depending on him with expectation.

Verses 5–14

Now that the prophet has received orders to *write the vision*, the vision itself follows. It reads the doom of

Nebuchadnezzar, some think, who was principally active in the destruction of Jerusalem, or of all such proud and oppressive powers as are hard on any people, especially God's people. Notice:

1. The charge laid down against this enemy (v. 5). The *lusts of the flesh, the lusts of the eye*, and *the pride of life* (1Jn 2:16) are snares, and we find that the one who took Israel captive is himself taken captive by each of these.

1.1. He is sensual and hedonistic, devoted to his pleasures: *He transgresses by wine* (v. 5). Drunkenness is the cause of a great deal of transgression.

1.2. He is haughty and imperious: *He is a proud man*, and his pride is a certain sign of his fall. When people are drunk, though they make themselves like animals, they still think they are as great as royalty, and they pride themselves on doing what shames them (Isa 28:1).

1.3. He is covetous and greedy for wealth, and this is the effect of his pride. The Babylonian monarchy aimed to be a universal one. He *keeps not at home*; he is not content with his own, thinks it not enough. His ambition is his eternal unease. Even if the home is a palace, it is a prison to someone who is discontented. He *enlarges his desire as hell*, or the grave, which daily receives but still cries out, *Give, give* (Pr 30:15). God is just in seeing to it that insatiable desires remain unsatisfied.

2. The sentence passed on him (v. 6): *Shall not all these take up a parable* (taunt) *against him?*

2.1. Since pride has been his sin, disgrace and dishonor will be his punishment, and he will be laughed at and despised by everyone around him.

2.2. Since he has been abusive to his neighbors, those very people whom he has abused will be the instruments of his disgrace: *All those shall take up a* taunting *proverb against him. He shall say—he* who draws up the insulting oracle will speak in this way—"Ho, he that increases what is not his! Aha!" What has become of him now? This is one way to read it, tauntingly. Here is:

2.2.1. A woe against him for increasing his own possessions by encroaching on his neighbor's rights (vv. 6–8). What he is doing *is lading himself with thick clay*. Riches are merely thick clay; what are gold and silver but white and yellow earth? People will respond by crying out to God, "How long will you allow this proud oppressor to trouble the nations?" Or they will say to one another, "Notice how long it is lasting, how long he is able to keep what he has gained so dishonestly." What he has gained by violence from others will be taken by violence from him. The Medes and Persians will plunder the Babylonians as they have plundered other nations (vv. 7–8). "There will be those who will *bite thee* and *vex thee*; those who seemed *asleep* will *rise up* and *awake* to be a plague to you. They will rise up *suddenly* when you feel most secure. According to the law of retaliation, as *thou hast spoiled many nations*, so you yourself will be *spoiled* (v. 8); *all the remnant of the people shall spoil thee.*"

2.2.2. A woe against him for coveting even more and aiming to get even higher (vv. 9–11). "Woe to him that gains an evil gain" is the reading of the margin at v. 9. There is a lawful gain that by the blessing of God may be a comfort to a house—*a good man leaves an inheritance to his children's children* (Pr 13:22)—but ill-gotten gains from fraud and injustice are a poor gain; they will bring poverty and ruin on a house. *By cutting off many people, thou hast consulted* not safety but *shame to thy house* (v. 10). It is a scandal to a family to raise possessions through sin. "*Thou hast sinned against thy own soul* and put that in danger." If the sinner pleads "Not guilty" and thinks his fraud cannot be proved against him, let him

know that *the stone shall cry out of the wall* against him, and *the beam out of the timber* in the roof *shall answer it* (v. 11).

2.2.3. A woe against him for building a town and a city by blood and extortion (v. 12). This is what Nebuchadnezzar did (Da 4:30): *Is not this great Babylon that I have built for the house of the kingdom?* It is built, however, with the blood of his own subjects, whom he has oppressed, and the blood of his neighbors, whom he has invaded. It is *established by iniquity*. The destruction of that city was the shame of the Babylonians, who had taken so much effort and gone to such vast expense to fortify it (v. 13): *Is it not of the Lord of hosts that the people* who have labored so hard to defend that city will *labour in the very fire*, will labor in vain to save it? There is no greater drudge in the world than the one who is controlled by greed. They are only poorly paid for it, for, after all, *they weary themselves for very vanity*; it is worse than meaningless and worthless; it is *vexation of spirit*, a chasing after the wind (Ecc 1:14; 2:11, 17; etc.).

Verses 15–20

The foregoing articles, on which the woes here are based, are very closely related to one another. Here are two more articles, however, of a different kind, articles that carry a *woe* to those in general to whom they belong, especially to the Babylonian monarchs, by whom the people of God were taken and held captive.

1. The promoters of drunkenness stand condemned here. Belshazzar was one of those; he was so in a remarkable way on that very night when the prophecy of this chapter was fulfilled, when he *drank wine before a thousand* of his lords (Da 5:1) and then forced them to drink his health. Perhaps this was one reason why the succeeding monarchs of Persia made it a law of their kingdom that *in drinking none should compel*, as we find in Est 1:8: they had seen in the kings of Babylon the troublesome consequences of forcing toasts and making people drunk. The woe here, however, stands firmly and fearfully against all those, whoever they are, who are guilty of this sin at any time and in any place.

1.1. The sinner accused here is a person who *makes his neighbour drunk* (v. 15). To give a drink to a neighbor with the intention of making them drunk, so that they may expose themselves, make themselves look ridiculous, or reveal their private concerns, is a detestable evil. Those who are guilty of this are rebels against God in heaven and his sacred laws. They are the agents of Satan and enemies to people on earth.

1.2. Sentence is passed on him here. There is a woe to him (v. 15) and a punishment (v. 16) that will correspond to the sin. Does he put the cup of drunkenness into the hand of his neighbor? The *cup of the Lord's right hand* will be *turned unto him*; it will finally be put into the hands of the king of Babylon, as was foretold (Jer 25:15–16, 18, 26–27). Does he take pleasure in putting his neighbor to shame? He will himself be loaded down with contempt: *Thou art filled with shame for glory*, or "with shame instead of glory" (v. 16). "Thou *also shalt drink* of the *cup of trembling* (Isa 51:17), the cup that makes you stagger, and you will expose yourself by your cowardice, which will be like the *uncovering of thy nakedness*, to your shame. For *the violence of Lebanon shall cover* (overwhelm) *thee, and the spoil of beasts* (your destruction of animals) (v. 17); you will be hunted with as much violence as any wild animals in Lebanon were."

2. The promoters of idolatry stand condemned. In his revels, Belshazzar *praised his idols*. The Babylonians are,

Jeremiah put it, *mad upon* (madly in love with) *their idols* (Jer 50:38). They have a great variety of idols, *graven images* and *molten images*. The *maker of the work* (v. 18) has performed his part admirably well, the "fashioner of his fashion" (v. 18, margin). *They lay them over with gold and silver. The maker of the work trusts therein* as his god. They pray to them: "*They say to the wood, 'Awake* for our relief,' and to the silent stone, '*Arise*, and save us.'" They consult them as oracles and expect to be directed by them. The foolishness of this is exposed. Their idols are completely devoid of both sense and reason; they are lifeless and speechless, so that the tiniest creature that has breath and movement is superior to them. It is not in their power to do their worshipers any good (v. 18): *What profits the graven image* (of what value is an idol)? Far from profiting them, it keeps them under the power of strong delusion (2Th 2:11). They say, *It shall teach*, but it is a *teacher of lies*, for it represents God as having a body, as being finite, visible, and dependent, whereas he is a Spirit, infinite, invisible, and independent. The people of God triumph in him when the idolaters shame themselves (v. 20): *Our rock is not as their rock* (Dt 32:31). Their gods are mute idols; our God is Jehovah, the living God, who is what he is (Ex 3:14), and not, like theirs, what people want to make him. They have devastated his temple at Jerusalem, but he has a temple above, which is beyond the reach of their rage and hatred but within reach of his people's faith and prayers.

CHAPTER 3

In all of chapter 3, the prophet speaks to God through the Spirit of prayer, and his prayer is in imitation of David's psalms, for it is directed to the chief singer on stringed instruments (v. 19). The prayer is left on record for the use of the church, especially for the Jews in exile while they waited to be restored. 1. He fervently begs God to help his suffering people, to come quickly to save them and in the meantime to comfort them (v. 2). 2. He recalls the experiences the church formerly had of God's glorious and gracious appearances on her behalf, when he brought Israel out of Egypt through the desert to Canaan and when he rescued them wonderfully many other times (vv. 3–15). 3. He stirs himself with a holy concern for the present troubles of the church, but he also encourages himself and others to hope that the outcome will be glorious, even though all visible means fail (vv. 16–19).

Verses 1–2

This chapter is entitled *a prayer of Habakkuk*. It is an intercession for the church. Prophets were prayerful, and sometimes they prayed even for those whom they prophesied against.

1. The prophet acknowledges receipt of God's answer to his former words and the impression it made on him (v. 2): *O Lord! I have heard thy speech*, "thy hearing," as some render it. Those who want to pray to God in the right way must carefully notice what he says to them. "I heard it *and was afraid*." It made the prophet afraid to hear how low the people of God would be brought under the Babylonians. He was afraid that their spirits would fail and that the church would be completely uprooted and, ultimately, lost.

2. He fervently prays that these *days of trouble* might be *shortened* (Mt 24:22) or moderated, or that the people of God would be supported. He thinks it a very long time to wait till the *end of the years*; perhaps he is referring to the seventy years of the exile, and so he says, "Lord, do

something on our behalf *in the midst of the years* (v. 2). Even if we are not rescued, let us not be abandoned and rejected. *Revive thy work*, your church"—the *work of God's own hand* (Isa 64:8)—"even when it *walks in the midst of trouble* (Ps 138:7–8). Revive the work of thy grace in us, by sanctifying the trouble to us and supporting us in it, even though the time has not yet come for our rescue from it. *In the midst of the years make known*; make yourself known, make known your power, your pity, your promises, your providence in ruling the world, for the safety and welfare of your church." When *in the midst of the years* of the exile God miraculously acknowledged the three children in the fiery furnace and humbled Nebuchadnezzar (Da 3), this prayer was answered.

Verses 3–15

When God's people are in distress, they help themselves by recalling their experiences, *considering the days of old*. The prophet here looks back as far as the miracles God did for them in Egypt and as he brought them through the desert. The One who brought them originally into Canaan can now bring them out of Babylon.

1. God appeared in his glory (vv. 3–4): *He came from Teman, even the Holy One from Mount Paran*. This refers to the visible manifestation of the glory of God when he gave the Law on Mount Sinai (Dt 33:2). Then *his glory covered the heavens*. The *earth also* was *full of his praise*, or of "his splendor," as some understand it. Or the earth was full of the works of God that were to be praised. Some understand the *two horns* (for the word is dual) *coming out of his hand* to refer to the *two tables of the law*. It is added: *And there was the hiding of his power*. What he did with his power was less than what he could have done; his power was more hidden than revealed.

2. God sent plagues on Egypt to humble proud Pharaoh (v. 5): *Before him went the pestilence*, which killed all the firstborn of Egypt in one night, and *burning coals went forth at his feet* when, in the plague of hail, there was fire mingled with hail—"burning diseases," as the margin at v. 5 reads. These were *at his feet*, that is, at his coming, for they are at his command; he says to them, "Go," and they go, "Come," and they come, "Do this," and they do it (Mt 8:9).

3. He divided the land of Canaan for his people Israel and expelled the nations: *He stood, and measured the earth* (v. 6), measured that land to assign it as an inheritance to Israel his people (Dt 32:8–9). *He beheld, and drove asunder the nations*, though they combined together against Israel. Then *the everlasting mountains were scattered, and the perpetual hills did bow*; the mighty princes of Canaan, who seemed as high and firmly established as the mountains, were broken to pieces. When he *drove asunder the nations of Canaan*, one could have seen the *tents of Cushan in affliction, the curtains of the land of Midian trembling*, and all the inhabitants of the neighboring countries taking fright (v. 7).

4. He divided the Red Sea (Ex 14:21–22) and Jordan (Jos 3:14–17), and he drew a river out of a rock when Israel needed it (Ex 17:6; Nu 20:8–11) (v. 8). God *rode upon his horses and chariots of salvation*, as a general at the head of his forces, powerful to save (Isa 63:1). This seems to be referred to again in v. 15. *Thou didst walk through the heap*, or mud, *of great waters* slowly, as the children and cattle walked. When they came to enter Canaan, the *overflowing of the water passed by*, that is, the Jordan, which at that time overflowed all its banks, was divided (Jos 3:15). *The deep uttered his voice* when the Red Sea and Jordan were divided; the waters roared.

They *lifted up their hands*, or sides, *on high*, for the waters *stood up on a heap* (Jos 3:16). *Thou didst cleave* (split) *the earth with rivers*; channels that seemed to split the earth were made in the desert for the waters to run in, channels that flowed out of the rock to supply the camp of Israel.

5. He stopped the movement of the sun and moon to promote Israel's victories (v. 11). *At the light*, at the direction, *of thy arrows they went*, and at *the shining of thy glittering spear*; the sun and moon acknowledged that the glittering light of his spear shone more brightly than theirs, and so whichever way that spear pointed, they directed their influences that way, as when *the stars in their courses fought against Sisera* (Jdg 5:20).

6. He completed Israel's victories over the nations of Canaan and their kings. This is insisted on as a plea with God that he would restore them to the land that they were first given possession of.

6.1. Many expressions are used here to describe the conquest of Canaan. God's *bow was made quite naked* (v. 9), taken out of the case to be employed for Israel. We should say, rather, that his sword was completely uncovered. He *marched through the land* from end to end *in indignation* (v. 12), scorning to let that evil generation of Canaanites possess such a good land any longer. He *threshed the heathen in anger*, trod them out as grain on the floor. He *wounded the heads out of the house of the wicked* (v. 13); he destroyed their rulers, cut off the heads and so *discovered the foundations of them*, even *to the neck* (stripped them from head to foot). Some apply this to Christ's victories over Satan and the powers of darkness, in which he *wounded the heads over many countries* (Ps 110:6). He *struck through with his staves the head of the villages* (v. 14). Spears will carry out the same execution as swords. When Pharaoh pursued Israel to the Red Sea, he *came out as a whirlwind*, and so did the kings of Canaan in their alliances against Israel. *Their rejoicing was as to devour the poor secretly*; they were as confident of success in their undertaking as any great person was of devouring a poor man. God confounded them, however, and their pride made their fall more shameful and God's care of his poor more eminent. He *walked* "to" *the sea with his horses*, as some understand v. 15, that is, he carried Israel's victories to the Great Sea, the Mediterranean, which was on the side of Canaan opposite that on which they had entered.

6.2. God considered three things in giving Israel victory over the Canaanites. First, he wanted to fulfill his promise to their ancestors; it was *according to the oaths of the tribes, even his word* (v. 9). He had sworn to give this land to the *tribes of Israel*. Second, he wanted to show his kindness to *his people* because of their relationship with him and his concern for them: *Thou wentest forth for the salvation of thy people* (v. 13). Third, he wanted to give a type and figure of the redemption of the world by Jesus Christ. It *is for salvation with thine anointed*, with

Joshua, who was a figure of the one whose name he bore, Jesus, our Joshua.

Verses 16–19

1. The prophet has foreseen the success of the church's enemies, and the sight has made him tremble (v. 16). Here he continues what he said in v. 2: *I have heard thy speech and was afraid*. "*When I heard* what sad times were coming, *my belly trembled* (my heart pounded); *my lips quivered at the voice*." It was no reproach to his courage. *I tremble in myself, that I might rest in the day of trouble*. The One who has joy in store for those who *sow in tears* (Ps 126:5) also has rest in store for those who tremble in his presence. *Good hope through grace* (2Th 2:16) is founded on a *holy fear*.

2. He has looked back at the church in former ages and has observed what great things God did for them, and so he falls into a rapture of holy joy, with an explicit "notwithstanding" to the calamities he sees coming.

2.1. He imagines the ruin not only of the delights of this life but also of its necessary supports (v. 17). Famine is one of the ordinary effects of war. He imagines the fruit tree to be withered and barren; *the fig tree*, which used to provide them with much of their food, *shall not blossom*. He also imagines the labour of the olive (olive crop) to *fail*, their oil, which was to them as butter is to us; *the fields shall yield no meat* (food). *The flock is cut off from the fold* (there are no sheep in the pen), *and there is no herd* (no cattle) *in the stall*.

2.2. He decides to delight and triumph in God nevertheless; when all has gone, his God has not gone (v. 18): "*Yet will I rejoice in the Lord*." Those who enjoyed God in everything when they were full can still *joy in God*, and so *enjoy all in God*, when they are emptied. They can sit down on the sad heap of the ruins and even then sing to the praise and glory of God. This is the basis of our joy in God: that he is the God of our eternal salvation, the salvation of the soul, and if he is so, we may rejoice in him in our greatest distresses, since by them our salvation cannot be hindered, but may be furthered. Joy in God is never out of season; in fact, it is especially seasonable when we meet with losses and crosses in the world, for then it may become clear that our hearts are not set on these things and that our happiness is not bound up in them. The One who is the *God of salvation* in another world will be our strength in this world, to carry us on in our journey there and help us overcome the difficulties and oppositions we face on our way. And so the prophet, who began his prayer with fear and trembling, concludes it with joy and triumph, for prayer gives relief to a gracious soul. He set his song on *Shigionoth* (v. 1), wandering tunes, "according to the variable songs," and on *Neginoth* (v. 19), *the stringed instruments*. The one who is suffering and who has prayed rightly may then be at peace, may then be happy enough to sing psalms.

A PRACTICAL AND DEVOTIONAL EXPOSITION OF THE BOOK OF THE PROPHET

Zephaniah

This prophet is placed last of all the Minor Prophets before the captivity, and not long before Jeremiah, who lived at the time of the exile. He foretells the general destruction of Judah and Jerusalem by the Babylonians and sets their sins before them. He calls them to repentance, threatens the neighboring nations with similar destructions, and gives encouraging promises of their joyful return from exile in due time.

CHAPTER 1

After the title of the book (v. 1), here is: 1. A threat of the destruction of Judah and Jerusalem by the Babylonians (vv. 2–4). 2. An accusation against them for their gross sin (vv. 5–6). He continues in the rest of the chapter to set out the judgments before them, so that they might either prevent them by repentance or prepare for them, and he continues to set out the sins that are destroying them, so that they can judge themselves and justify God in what is brought on them. 2.1. They must hold their peace because they have sinned greatly (vv. 7–9), but: 2.2. They will wail because the trouble will be great (vv. 10–18). God gave the Jews such a fair and timely warning of the coming exile.

Verses 1–6

Here is:

1. The title page of this book (v. 1); it is from heaven, and not of human origin: it is *the word of the Lord*. Zephaniah may mean "the servant of the Lord," for God *revealed his secrets to his servants the prophets* (Am 3:7). The genealogy of Zephaniah goes back four generations, and the earliest mentioned is *Hizkiah*, the same name in the original as that of Hezekiah king of Judah (2Ki 18:1). This prophet prophesied *in the days of Josiah king of Judah*, who in the twelfth year of his reign carried out a work of reformation in which he destroyed idols. It is not stated whether Zephaniah prophesied at the beginning of this reign; if he did, we may suppose his prophesying had a great influence on that reformation.

2. The summary of this book. The general proposition contained in it is that complete destruction is coming quickly on Judah and Jerusalem for their sin. He begins abruptly (v. 2): *By taking away I will make an end of all things from off the face of the land, saith the Lord*. The appointed removal will take away:

2.1. The lower creatures: *I will consume the beasts, the fowls of the heaven, and the fishes of the sea* (v. 3). The expressions are figurative, referring to universal destruction. Both those who fly very high and those who hide very close will still be attacked by their enemies and be completely swept away.

2.2. The people: "*I will consume man; I will cut off man from the land*. The land will be depopulated and left uninhabited; I will destroy not only Israel but also *man* (people). Although they will not be cut off from the Lord, they will still be *cut off from the land*." Even Judah, where God is known, and Jerusalem, where his dwelling place is (Ps 76:1–2), will find that his hand is stretched out against them if they rebel from him and rebel against him.

2.3. All evildoers and all the things they use to do evil (v. 3): "*I will consume the stumbling-blocks with the wicked*, the idols with the idolaters, the offenses with the offenders." The Babylonians will spare none of the idols of Baal or the worshipers of those idols. The *Kemarim* will be *cut off*; we read about them in the story of Josiah's reformation. *He put down the idolatrous priests* (2Ki 23:5), the *Kemarim*. The word may mean "dark men." Some think they were referred to this way because they wore black clothes; others think it was because their faces were dark from serving at the altars or at the fires in which they burned their children to Molech. They seem to have been the immediate attendants in the service of Baal. Among other idolaters, the *worshipers of the host of heaven upon the housetops* will be cut off (v. 5). It will appear as great an offense to God to give divine honor to a star as to give it to a stone or a stick. Those who also be consumed. They waver between God and Baal (1Ki 18:21), sometimes worshiping Jehovah and other times Molech, and they *swear by both*, or, as it might better be read, swear *to the Lord and to Malcham*. Those who have committed apostasy against God will be swept away with those who never gave their names to him (v. 6).

Verses 7–13

Notice is given to Judah and Jerusalem that God is coming against them. *His day*, the day of his judgment, is not far away (v. 7). People have their day now, when they do as they please, but *God's day is at hand*; it is called here his *sacrifice*, reparation to his wronged honor. Notice:

1. Those who will be punished on this day of retribution. The royal family will be punished for their pride and affectation (v. 8). They will be punished, and all like them, all who are clothed *with strange apparel* (foreign clothes). *The princes and the king's children* send abroad to foreign countries for their clothes, because they will not be satisfied unless their clothes come from far away

1350

and are expensive. Pride in clothing displeases God, and it is a symptom of the corruption of a people. *In the same day will I punish those that leap on the threshold*, a phrase that probably referred to encroaching on their neighbor's rights. They *leap on the threshold*, as if to say that the house is their own, and so they make everything in it their own, thereby *filling their masters' houses* with goods gained *by violence and deceit*. Iniquity is found among *the inhabitants of Maktesh*, probably a low part of Jerusalem, deep like a "mortar" (the meaning of the word). The *goldsmiths* and the merchants live there (Ne 3:32), and they are now *cut down*, having shut up shop and become bankrupt. *All those that bear silver are cut off* by the invaders. All the careless people, who lead lax and idle lives, are next to be judged (v. 12). God will find them out and punish them: *At that time I will search Jerusalem with candles* to find them. God will punish not only the secret idolaters but also those who are hidden in their secret, worldly godlessness. They are complacent: they *are settled on their lees*, intoxicated with their pleasures. Their ideas are godless. They can live such loose lives only by saying *in their heart, The Lord will not do good, neither will he do evil*; that is, *He will do nothing*. They deny his providential sovereignty over the world. If they were not drowned in the pleasures of their senses, they could not be so senseless.

2. What will be their punishment. He will silence them (v. 7): *Hold thy peace* (be silent) *at the presence of the Lord*. He will *sacrifice* them, for it is *the day of the Lord's sacrifice* (v. 8); he will give them over to the hands of their enemies. *In that day there shall be a noise of a cry from the fishgate*, so called because it was near the fish market. *And* there will be *a howling from the second*, which was next to that *fish gate*. The alarm will go around the walls of Jerusalem from gate to gate, and there will be *a great crashing* (a loud crash) *from the hills*, from the mountains around Jerusalem, from the acclamations of the invaders and the mourning of the invaded. The inhabitants of the city, even those in the most secure part of the city, will wail (v. 11); so loud will the grieving be. They will be stripped of all they have; it will be taken as plunder by the enemy (v. 13): *Their goods*—their household wealth and their business wealth—will *become a rich booty; their houses shall be* leveled with the ground and be *a desolation*. Those of them who have *built* new houses *shall not inherit them*; the invaders will gain and keep possession of them. They will not *drink the wine of* the *vineyards* they have planted, nor use it as relief for the friends who faint among them; instead they will be forced to part with it so that it may be used to animate their enemies who fight against them (Dt 28:30).

Verses 14–18

Here is the warning given to Judah and Jerusalem of the approaching destruction by the Babylonians. It is *the great day of the Lord* (v. 14), a kind of doomsday, as our Savior's describes the final destruction of Jerusalem by the Romans when he predicts that (Mt 24:27).

1. This *day of the Lord* is here spoken of as very near. The prophet gives the alarm like a person who wakes up a family with the cry of "Fire! Fire!" when the house next door is on fire.

2. It is spoken of as a very terrible day. The *voice of* this *day of the Lord* will make *the mighty men cry there bitterly* (v. 14). It will be a day of *trouble and distress* to the sinners; they will see no way to help or relieve themselves. It is *a day of clouds and thick darkness*; the thick clouds are heavy with storms.

3. It is spoken of as a destructive day (vv. 16–17). What fortifications, what fences, can withstand the wrath of God? "*I will bring distress upon men*, the strongest and boldest people; they will *walk like blind men*, wandering endlessly, *because they have sinned against the Lord*." Those who walk as bad people will justly be left to walk as blind people, always in doubt and danger.

4. The destruction of that day will be unavoidable and universal (v. 18). There will be no escaping it by trying to pay a ransom: *Neither their silver nor their gold shall be able to deliver them in the day of the Lord's wrath*. There will be no escaping it by trying to run away or hide, for the *whole land shall be devoured by the fire of his jealousy*, and where can there then be a hiding place?

CHAPTER 2

We have here: 1. An earnest exhortation to the nation to repent and make their peace with God (vv. 1–3). 2. The judgments of God against several of the neighboring nations who have contributed to or rejoiced in the calamity of Israel: 2.1. The Philistines (vv. 4–7). 2.2. The Moabites and Ammonites (vv. 8–11). 2.3. The Ethiopians (Cushites) and Assyrians (vv. 12–15).

Verses 1–3

The prophet's intention in giving that terrible description of approaching judgments that we had in the last chapter was not to drive the people to despair but to drive them to God and to their duty, not to frighten them out of their wits but to frighten them out of their sins. We have here:

1. The summons to come to a national assembly (v. 1): *Gather yourselves together.* The call is given to *a nation not desired*. The word means either:

1.1. "Not desiring," not having any desires toward God. "But *come together* and see if you can stir up desires in one another." Or:

1.2. *Not desirable*, having nothing in them that might commend them to God. God says, "*Gather together*, so that you may as a group humble yourselves." Some read it, "Inquire into yourselves": "Examine your consciences. Look into your hearts; search and test your ways. Collect your thoughts, so that you may find the sin that has provoked God's displeasure."

2. Arguments urged to press them to do this quickly (v. 2): "Be serious about this; do it as quickly as possible, before it is too late, *before the decree bring forth, before the day pass*."

3. Directions prescribed. They are not to gather in fear, but seriously and calmly (v. 3): *Seek you the Lord*. If the land is to be saved, it must be by the intercession of the godly few, *the meek* (humble) *of the earth*, or of the land. They must *seek the Lord*, seek his favor and grace. "Look to God for the fulfillment of his promises to you, and see to it that you abound even more in doing your duty for him."

4. Encouragements given to take these directions: *It may be, you shall be hid* (perhaps you will be sheltered) *in the day of the Lord's anger*. "*Verily it shall be well with thy remnant* (Jer 15:11). *It may be you shall be hid*; if any are hidden, then you will be." They will be hidden, as Luther says, "either in heaven or under heaven," either in the possession of heaven or under the protection of heaven.

Verses 4–7

The prophet here foretells what share the neighboring nations will have in the destruction brought by

Nebuchadnezzar. This is intended to make the Jewish people aware how great the flood of calamities will be, to make the *day of the Lord* appear more fearful so that they may perhaps be quickened to prepare for it. It is also intended to encourage them with the thought that though God has seemed to be their enemy and to fight against them, he is still so much their friend, and an enemy of their enemies, that he resents, and will avenge the dishonor shown them. In these verses we have the doom of the Philistines, who were near neighbors and old enemies of the people of Israel. They were *the inhabitants of the seacoasts* (v. 5), for their country lay on the Great Sea. The *nation of the Cherethites* (Kerethites) is joined to them here; it bordered on them (1Sa 30:14) and fell with them. The Philistines' land is called *Canaan* here because it belonged to the country that God gave to his people Israel (Jos 13:3). This land is still to be possessed, for the Philistines wrongfully kept Israel out of its possession (Jdg 3:3).

1. It is foretold here that the Philistines, the usurpers, will be dispossessed and completely destroyed. *Gaza shall be forsaken*, even though it is now a well-populated city. It was foretold by Jeremiah (Jer 47:5) that *baldness* would come on Gaza; Alexander the Great razed that city, and we find in Ac 8:26 that Gaza was a desert. *Ashkelon* will be *a desolation. Ashdod shall be driven out at noon day*, in the extremity of the scorching heat. They will be forced into exile. *Ekron*, too, which has long been taking root, will be *rooted up*. The land of the Philistines will be depopulated. The sea coast, which used to be a harbor for ships and a home for merchants, will now be deserted, and only *cottages for shepherds* and *folds for flocks* will be there (v. 6).

2. It is foretold here that the house of Judah, the rightful owners, will recover possession of it (v. 7). The remnant of those who will *return out of captivity* will *lie down* in safety (Isa 14:30) *in the houses of Ashkelon*.

Verses 8–11

The Moabites and Ammonites were both from the descendants of Lot; their countries adjoined each other.

1. They are both accused of insulting the people of God and gloating over their calamities (v. 8). They have "spoken big words," as some read it, "spoken great things" against their border (v. 8), against those of God's people who lived on the border of their country. They spoke big words against the people of the Lord as a deserted, abandoned people. "But I have heard them," God says.

2. They are both put under the same condemnation. Sentence is pronounced on them (v. 9). The Moabites and Ammonites will be like Sodom and Gomorrah, the marks of whose ruins in the Dead Sea lie next to the countries of Moab and Ammon. They will be laid waste, not to be inhabited again, or not for a long time. The country will produce nettles instead of grain, and there will be salt pits instead of fountains of water. Israel will plunder them of their goods and possess their country. And *this shall they have for their pride* (v. 10).

3. Other nations will be similarly humbled.

3.1. Pagan gods must be abolished. Their worshipers have gloried in them, but the *Lord will famish all the gods of the earth* (v. 11); he will starve them out of their strongholds.

3.2. Pagan nations must be converted. When the Gospel gains ground, it will bring people to worship the One who lives forever, *everyone from his place*. They will not need to go up to Jerusalem to worship the God of Israel, but will have access to him wherever they are.

Verses 12–15

Not only Israel's close neighbors but also those who are more remote must be judged.

1. The Ethiopians (Cushites or Arabians), who have sometimes terrorized Israel, as in Asa's time (2Ch 14:9), *shall be slain by my sword* (v. 12). Nebuchadnezzar was God's sword, the instrument with which these enemies were punished (Ps 17:14).

2. The Assyrians, with Nineveh, the capital city of their monarchy, are next to receive their fate: *He* that is God's sword *will stretch out his hand against the north and destroy Assyria.* Assyria had been the rod of God's anger against Israel (Isa 10:5), and now Babylon is the rod of God's anger against Assyria. Notice:

2.1. How flourishing Nineveh's state once was (v. 15): *This is the rejoicing city that dwelt carelessly.* Nineveh was so strong that she feared no evil.

2.2. How complete Nineveh's ruin will now be; she will be made *a desolation* (v. 13). The gloomy-sounding birds, such as *the cormorant and bittern* (desert owl and screech owl), will make their nests in the remains of the houses. The *lintels*, or capitals of the columns or pillars, the *windows* and *thresholds* (doorways), and all the fine *cedarwork* will lie exposed, and these ominous birds will perch on them, and their *voice shall sing* (v. 14). *Every one that passes by will hiss* at her and *wag his hand*—"So that's what happened to proud Nineveh!"

CHAPTER 3

Here we listen to what God says to Jerusalem: 1. Rebuke and threat for the evil that was found in her (vv. 1–7). 2. Mercy and grace, which God still keeps in reserve for them. Here are two general promises: 2.1. That God will do a glorious work of reformation among them, cleansing them from their sins and bringing them back to himself (vv. 8–13). 2.1. That he will bring about a glorious work of salvation for them when he has prepared them for it in this way (vv. 14–20). These promises were to have their complete fulfillment in Gospel times and Gospel graces.

Verses 1–7

We have here:

1. A very bad characterization given of Jerusalem in general. She shames herself; she is *filthy and polluted* (rebellious and defiled) (v. 1), "has made herself infamous," as some read it; she is the "gluttonous" city (v. 1, margin), always indulging the flesh. She wrongs her neighbors and inhabitants; she is *the oppressing city*. She is offensive to her God (v. 2). He gave her his Law, but *she obeyed not his voice*. Her confidence was placed in her alliances with the nations more than in her covenant with God. She did not draw near to her God. She stood far away and *said to the Almighty, Depart* (Job 22:17).

2. A very bad characterization of the leaders in the city. They support wickedness; those who should be her doctors are in fact her worst disease. Her *princes* (officials) are as cruel as roaring lions and are universally hated. *Her judges* are *evening wolves* (v. 3), voracious; their cruelty and covetousness are insatiable: *They gnaw not the bones till the morrow* (v. 3). They take such delight in oppression that when they have devoured a good person, they keep the bones, as it were, as a tasty morsel to be gnawed the next morning (Job 31:31). *Her prophets*, who claim to be special messengers to them from heaven, *are light and treacherous persons*, with no seriousness or firmness, persons who cannot be trusted. *Her priests* betray their trust. Their duty is to preserve the purity of the *sanctuary*,

but they themselves defile it. They corrupt the law; they distort its meaning. They twist the law to make it mean what they want and so, in effect, break it (Ps 119:26).

3. General corruption in Jerusalem.

3.1. They have the signs of God's presence, but they persist in their disobedience (v. 5). "*The just Lord* is among you as a holy God, and so your defilement is more offensive (Dt 23:14). A just God will punish both the disrespect you show him and the wrongs you do to one another." He sent his prophets to them, rising up early and sending them (Jer 7:25; 25:4; etc.): *Every morning he brings his judgment to light* (v. 5). He wakens his prophets with the rising sun to bring to light the things that lead to their peace (Lk 19:42).

3.2. God has set before their eyes memorials to his justice, intended to warn them (v. 6): *I have cut off the nations*, the seven nations of Canaan, which the land spit out because of their evil (Lev 18:28). Or the statement may refer to some of the neighboring nations devastated because of their wickedness. *Their towers were desolate*, their streets were laid waste, and their cities were destroyed and ruined; no one was to be found in them. The enemies did it, but God affirms it: *I cut them off*, he says. God intended this as a warning to Jerusalem.

3.3. He has set before them life and death, good and evil (Dt 30:15, 19). He assured them that their prosperity would continue if they would fear him and receive instruction; then *their dwelling would not be cut off* as their neighbor's was. He made them suffer the rebukes of his correcting rod, though he reprieved them from the sword. Yet they were more resolute and eager in their evil ways than ever. God rose up early to send them his prophets, but they were up before him to shut and bolt the door against them.

Verses 8–13

Things looked bad for Jerusalem in vv. 1–7; she has gotten a very bad reputation and seems to be hardened, incurable, and resistant to mercy and judgment. But see the riches of divine grace. They became worse and worse (2Ti 3:13); *therefore wait you on me, saith the Lord* (v. 8). "Since the law, it seems, will *make nothing perfect* (Heb 7:19), the bringing in of a better hope will. Let those who mourn the corruption of the church *wait on God*, until he sends his Son into the world *to save his people from their sins* (Mt 1:21) and purify for himself his own distinctive people of both Jews and Gentiles." There were, in fact, those who *waited for redemption* in Jerusalem. They looked for it for a long time until it eventually came (Lk 2:38).

1. All nations are summoned, as it were, through the Gospel of Christ preached to the whole creation (Mk 16:15), to appear together before the Lord Jesus, who is about to set up his kingdom in the world. However, since the greatest part of the human race will not obey the call, he will *pour on them his indignation* (v. 8), for those who do not believe are already condemned. Then all the earth will be consumed by the fire of his jealousy (v. 8; 1:18); both Jews and Gentiles will be judged for their hostility toward the Gospel.

2. When God intends to restore Israel, he makes way for their reformation and the revival of their goodness and godliness. God's way is first to make them holy and then to make them happy. These promises were partly fulfilled after the return of the Jews from Babylon. It is promised that:

2.1. There will be a reformation in the people's words, which have been generally corrupt but will now

be seasoned with salt and grace (Col 4:6) (v. 9): "*Then will I turn to the people a pure language*." Converting grace refines the language, not by making its expressions witty, but by making the substance wise. The Jews, after the exile, had mixed the *language of Canaan* (Isa 19:18) with that of Ashdod (Ne 13:24). Their language will be more than refined, however; it will be purified from all ungodliness, filthiness, and falsehood. "I will turn them to 'a choice language,'" as some understand it.

2.2. The worship of God, according to his will, will be more closely practiced and more unanimously agreed to. Instead of offering sacrifices and incense, they will *call upon the name of the Lord* (v. 9). Prayer is the spiritual offering with which God must be honored. They will serve God *with one consent*, with "one shoulder"—the phrase is literally "shoulder to shoulder," alluding to oxen in a yoke, which pull together. When Christians agree in the service of God, the work carries on joyfully. Purity is the way to unity; the reformation of life is the way to growth.

2.3. Those who were driven away from God will return to him and be accepted by him (v. 10). *From beyond the rivers of Ethiopia*, or from some other remote country, those who had almost forgotten God will be reminded of him, as the prodigal son was of his father's house in the far country (Lk 15:14, 17). The *daughter of his dispersed*, who is *afar off*, will be found among those whom *the Lord our God shall call* (Joel 2:32; Ac 2:39). Wherever they are, even if it is *beyond the rivers of Ethiopia*, a long way away from his house of prayer, they still are his suppliants (1Ki 8:46–52). *They shall bring my offering*. They will bring themselves as spiritual sacrifices to God (Ro 12:1).

2.4. Sin and sinners will be cleansed from among them (v. 11). *In that day shalt thou not be ashamed for all thy doings*. They will be ashamed as penitents (see Eze 16:63), but they will not be ashamed as sinners who return to their foolishness. "*I will take away out of the midst of thee* not only the ungodly but also the hypocrites, who appear beautiful outwardly and *rejoice in thy pride*, in the Holy City, the holy house." The people were *haughty because of the holy mountain* (v. 11); they were proud and scornful and defied the judgments of God. The pride that is the most offensive to God is fed by claims to holiness. God will leave a remnant of holy, humble, sincere people (v. 12): *I will leave in the midst of thee an afflicted and poor people*. This select remnant will be blessed with purity and peace (v. 13), in both words and actions: they *shall neither do iniquity nor speak lies*.

Verses 14–20

After the promises of the taking away of sin come promises of the taking away of trouble; for when the cause is removed, the effect will come to an end. The people are called on to rejoice and sing (v. 14): *Sing, O daughter of Zion! Sing for joy; shout, O Israel!* Those who love God with all their heart need all their heart to rejoice in him. *In that day it shall be said to Jerusalem*—God will say it through his prophets and his providences, their neighbors will say it, and they will say it to one another—"*Fear thou not*. Lift up your hands in prayer to God (1Ti 2:8); lift up your hands to help yourself." Let us now see what these precious promises are.

1. An end will be put to all their troubles and distresses (v. 15): "*The Lord has taken away thy judgments* (punishment); he has removed all the calamities that were the punishments of your sin; the noise of war will be silenced, the disgrace of famine done away with, and your fortunes

restored. *He has cast out thy enemy*, who has thrust himself into your land. He has 'swept out thy enemy,'" as
some read it. The way to stay clear of the harm of trouble
is to stay clear of the evil of sin, and to those who do so,
trouble has no real harm in it.

2. God will give them the signs of his presence with
them. *"The Lord is in the midst of thee, O Zion!*—of you,
O Jerusalem!—as the sun is at the center of the solar
system, to spread its light and influence to every part.
He is the *King of Israel* (v. 15) and is among you as a
king is among his people. He is the Lord your God, yours
in the covenant, among you as your God, whose you are.
He will save. He will be Jesus; he will fulfill the meaning
of his name, for he will save his people from their sins
(Mt 1:21)."

3. God will take delight in doing them good. *He will
rejoice over thee with joy.* The conversion of sinners and
the comfort of saints are the joy of angels (Lk 15:7), for
they are the joy of God himself. He will *rest in his love*,
"will be silent in his love," "be quiet over you with his
love."

4. God will comfort Zion's mourners and wipe away
their tears (v. 18): *I will gather those who are sorrowful
for the solemn assemblies, to whom the reproach of it was
a burden.* Zion is in mourning. Her calamities are many.
The city is in ruins, and the palaces are demolished; trade
has come to an end; but all these are nothing in comparison with the destruction of the temple and the altar,
to which all Israel used to come together to attend sacred
festivals three times a year. It is about those sacred assemblies that they are sorrowful. The restraining of public
assemblies for religious worship, their scattering by their
enemies, or the forsaking of them by their friends, is a
sorrowful thing for all good people. The disgrace brought
on the sacred assemblies is a burden to them.

5. God will restore the captives and bring home
those who seemed to have been banished and expelled
(vv. 19–20). *"At that time I will undo all that afflict thee*,
will break their power and thwart their purposes, so that
they will be forced to surrender the plunder they have
taken." One act of mercy and grace will serve both to
gather them from their dispersions and to lead them into
their own land. When the *people's hearts are prepared*,
the work will be done suddenly.

6. God will, in all this, gain them respect from all
around them. When God returns in mercy to his church,
it is promised here that she will regain her credibility: *"I
will get them praise and fame in every land where they
have been put to shame."* Those people who said, "This
is Zion, whom no one is looking after" (Jer 30:17), will
say, "This is Zion, whom the great God looks after." This
happened to the Jewish church when *the fear of the Jews*
fell on their neighbors (Est 8:17). This is what happened
to the Christian church when it was made to flourish in
the world, for there is something in it that may justly commend it to the esteem of all people.

A PRACTICAL AND DEVOTIONAL EXPOSITION OF THE BOOK OF THE PROPHET

Haggai

The exile in Babylon gave a very remarkable turn to the affairs of the Jewish church in both history and prophecy. Nine of the twelve minor prophets lived and preached before that exile. Haggai and Zechariah appeared eighteen years after the return, when the building of the temple was both slowed down by its enemies and neglected by its friends. *Then the prophets, Haggai the prophet and Zechariah the son of Iddo, prophesied unto the Jews that were in Jerusalem, in the name of the God of Israel, even unto them* (as we read in Ezr 5:1), to encourage them to revive that good work when it had come to a standstill for some time. Haggai began two months before Zechariah. Zechariah continued longer at the work; all Haggai's prophecies that are recorded were delivered within four months, in the second year of Darius, but we have Zechariah's prophecies dated more than two years later (Zec 7:1). The Jews ascribe to these two prophets the honor of being members of the great synagogue, which was formed after the return from exile; we think it more certain, and a much greater honor, that they prophesied about Christ. Haggai spoke about him as the *glory of the latter house* (2:9), and Zechariah as *the man, the branch* (Zec 6:12). In them, the light of that morning star (Rev 22:10) shone more brightly as they now began to see his day approaching. The Septuagint (a Greek version of the Old Testament) takes Haggai and Zechariah to be the authors of Pss 138, 146, 147, and 148.

CHAPTER 1

We have here: 1. A rebuke of the Jewish people for their tendency to delay in building the temple, and with the rebuke came an exhortation to them to resume that good work seriously (vv. 1–11). 2. The success of this sermon, as shown in the people's return and conscientious application to that work, in which the prophet encouraged them, assuring them that God was with them (vv. 12–15).

Verses 1–11

It was the complaint of the Jews in Babylon that they *saw not their signs* and that there was *no more any prophet* (Ps 74:9), and this was a just judgment for mocking the prophets. We do not read of any prophets leading or accompanying them on their return. However, the light of Old Testament prophecy will still make some glorious efforts before it expires, and Haggai is the first who appears in the role of a special messenger from heaven. This prophet was sent in the second year of the reign of Darius Hystaspes, the third of the Persian kings; the word of the Lord came to him, and it came through him to the leaders among the Jews (v. 1). The chief governor was *Zerubbabel the son of Shealtiel,* of the house of David, who was commander in chief of the Jews in their return from exile. The chief governor in the church was *Joshua the son of Josedech,* who was now *high priest.* They were great and good leaders. The prophets, who were extraordinary messengers, did not set aside the institutions of the judiciary and ministry, but tried to make both more effective. Notice:

1. The sin of the Jews at this time (v. 2). As soon as they came out of exile, they set up an altar for sacrifices, and within a year later laid the foundations of a temple (Ezr 3:10). They then seemed very eager to do this. When, however, they were served with a prohibition from the Persian court and charged not to continue, they not only yielded to the force of that order while they were actually under it, but still had no spirit to set about the work again later, when the violence of the opposition had diminished; and in fact, they allowed the work to come to a standstill. These Jews continued to be lazy until they were reminded of their duty. They suggested to one another, "*The time has not come, the time that the Lord's house should be built* (v. 2). Our losses are not yet made good. It is too great an undertaking for beginners such as we are; let's get our own houses together before we talk about building churches, and in the meantime let a bare altar be enough for us, as it was for our father Abraham" (Ge 12:7, 8; 13:18; 22:9). They did not say that they would not build a temple at all, but, "Not yet; we'll do that all in good time."

2. The judgments of God by which they were punished for this neglect (vv. 6, 9–11). So that the punishment would correspond to the sin, God by his providence kept them in debt, and the poverty that they thought they would prevent by not building the temple was brought on them by God for not building it. We need the help of God's prophets and ministers to explain not only the judgments of God's mouth but also the judgments of his hands, so that we may understand his mind and meaning in his discipline as well as in his word:

2.1. God did not send them back into exile or bring a foreign enemy on them, as they deserved, but took their correcting into his own hands, for his mercies are great (2Sa 24:14).

2.1.1. He who *gives seed to the sower* (Isa 55:10; 2Co 9:10) denied his blessing on the *seed sown*, and then it never prospered. *They sowed much* (v. 6), kept a great deal of ground under cultivation, because their land had long *lain fallow* and had *enjoyed its sabbaths* (2Ch 36:21). Having sown much, they looked for much from it, but they were disappointed: *They brought in little*, very little (v. 6); when they had made the best of it, *it came to little* (v. 9). We are told here how they came to be disappointed (v. 10): *The heaven over you is stayed from dew*; the One who has the key to the clouds in his hands shut them up and withheld the rain, and then of course *the earth was stayed from her fruit*, for if the skies are as hard as bronze, the earth is like iron (Dt 28:23). God will make us aware of our necessary and constant dependence on him through all the links in the chain of secondary causes. We will therefore never be able to say, "Now we no longer need God and his providence." See Hos 2:21. *I called for a drought upon the land*; he ordered the weather to be extremely hot, and then the fruits of the earth were burned up. The heat of the sun gives life to the plants and *renews the face of the earth* at spring (Ps 104:30). However, if it goes to an extreme, it undoes everything. This drought was *upon the mountains*, which, because they lay high, were first affected by it. The mountains were their pasturelands, which used to be *covered over with flocks*, but now there was no grass for them. It was *upon the corn, the new wine, and the oil*; all failed through the extreme hot weather. It also had a bad influence on people; the hot weather weakened some, making them weary and faint. It gave others a fever. It brought diseases on cattle too.

2.1.2. The One who gives *bread to the eater* (Isa 55:10; 2Co 9:10) denied his blessing on the bread they ate, and then that did not nourish them. When they had the grain in the barn, it was not secure: *I did blow upon it, saith the Lord of hosts* (v. 9), and that withered it. When they had it on the table, it was not what they expected: *"You eat, but you have not enough. You clothe yourselves, but there is none warm. He that earns wages* by hard labor and has it paid him in ready cash *puts it into a bag with holes*; as money falls unnoticed through the holes in such a bag, so their money wastes away imperceptibly. Everything is so scarce and expensive that they spend their money as fast as they get it."

2.2. God stopped the flow of the favors he had promised to do for them when they returned (Joel 2:24). They provoked him to oppose them in this way: *It is because of my house that is waste* (v. 9). The foundation of the temple had been laid, but the building did not continue. "Everyone *runs to his own house* to finish that, and no one bothers about the Lord's house." If God crosses us in our temporal lives and we face trouble and disappointment, we will find that this is its cause: that the work we have to do for God is left undone, and we *seek our own things more than the things of Jesus Christ* (Php 2:21).

3. The rebuke that the prophet gave them for their neglect of the temple work (v. 4): *"Is it time for you, O you! to dwell in your ceiled* (paneled) *houses*, to have them beautifully decorated, and your families settled in them?" They were not content to have the walls and roofs they needed. "It is now time," one of them says, "that my house had new wood paneling." "It is now time," another says, "for mine to be repainted." All this time, God's house *lay waste*, and nothing was done about it.

4. The good advice the prophet gave to those who despised God in this way. *"Now therefore consider your ways* (v. 5 and again v. 7). Think what you have done that has provoked God to interrupt your comforts, and think what you will do to show your repentance." He wanted them to reform their ways (v. 8): *"Go up to the mountain*, to Lebanon, *and bring wood* and other materials *and build the house* quickly." God assured them, *Build the house, and I will take pleasure in it*. That was enough encouragement for them to continue it, whatever it cost them. If those who have long postponed their return to God finally return with all their heart, they must not despair of his favor.

Verses 12–15

The foregoing sermon met with the desired success among the people, and their obedience met with due encouragement from God. Notice:

1. How the people returned to God to fulfill their duty. All those to whom that sermon was preached were persuaded to act on it. Zerubbabel, the chief governor, was a man who had been greatly useful in his day, but he did not plead his former merits in response to this rebuke for his present negligence. Joshua also, as high priest, willingly received warning and instruction. *The remnant of the people* all *obeyed the voice of the Lord their God* and submitted to his commands (v. 12). They looked on the prophet as the Lord's messenger and considered the word he spoke to be the Lord's message, and they therefore received it *not as the word of man, but as the word of almighty God* (1Th 2:13). Prophecy was new to them; they had had no special messenger from heaven for a long time, and now that they had one, they paid extraordinary regard to him. It is sometimes so; when good preaching is scarcest, it does most good, whereas the manna that comes plentifully is hated as *light bread* (Nu 21:5). Because they received this prophet so readily, God, within a month or two, raised up another for them (Zec 1:1). When they saw their own sin to be the cause of those judgments, they then feared. *The Lord stirred up* their spirits (v. 14). He encouraged them, and with those encouragements he set their hearts free (Ps 119:32). In case they should sink under the weight of fear, God stirred them up, making them cheerful and bold. They applied themselves to their work with the greatest possible energy. Everyone, according to their capacity or ability, lent a hand to further that good work. The consideration of God's covenant relationship with his people by his grace should stir our spirits to act for him and to advance the interests of his kingdom on earth. It was only on the first day of the sixth month that Haggai preached this sermon, and little more than three weeks later, they were all busy working in the house of the Lord their God (v. 15). Those who have lost time need to redeem the time.

2. How God met them by way of mercy. The same prophet who rebuked them brought them an encouraging word (v. 13): *Then spoke Haggai, the Lord's messenger, in the Lord's message, saying, I am with you, saith the Lord*. That was all he had to say, and that was enough. *I am with you*, that is, "I will forgive your neglect up to this time. *I am with you* to protect you against your enemies and give you success in your work. *I am with you* to strengthen your hands and bless their work."

CHAPTER 2

Here are three sermons preached by the prophet Haggai to encourage those who build the temple. In the first, he assures the builders that the glory of the house they are now building will, in spiritual respects, though not out-wardly, exceed that of Solomon's temple (vv. 1–9). In the second, he assures them that although their sin in delaying to build the temple has slowed down the progress of other affairs, nevertheless, now that they have set about it seriously, God will bless them and give them success (vv. 10–19). In the third, he assures Zerubbabel that, as a reward for his godly zeal and activity, he will be a favorite of heaven and one of the ancestors of Messiah the Prince (Da 9:25), whose kingdom will be set up on the ruins of all opposing powers (vv. 20–23).

Verses 1–9

Here is:

1. The date of this message (v. 1). It was sent on the twenty-first day of the seventh month, when the builders had been at work for about a month. Those who are genuine in serving God will receive fresh encouragements from him to proceed in it. If we set the wheels in motion, God will oil them.

2. The direction of this message (v. 2). *Speak to Zerubbabel, and Joshua, and the residue* (remnant) *of the people*, the same people who *obeyed the voice of the Lord* (1:12) and whose spirits God stirred up to do so (1:14); these words of encouragement are sent to them.

3. The message itself, in which notice:

3.1. The discouragements that those who were employed in this work labored under. What had dampened and alloyed their joy as they laid the foundation of the temple remained a frustration to them: they could not build a temple so large, grand, or lavish as the one Solomon built. This brought tears to the eyes of many people when the new temple's dimensions were first set out (Ezr 3:12). It was now about seventy years since Solomon's temple was destroyed, so there might still be some people alive who could remember having seen it. One person could remember the gold with which it was overlaid, another the precious stones, the porch, the pillars—where are these now? It is sometimes the fault of old people to discourage the services of the present age by praising too much the actions and achievements of the previous "golden age." *Say not thou that the former days were better than these* (Ecc 7:10), but thank God that there is any good in these times, bad though they are.

3.2. The encouragement that is given them to continue in the work, nevertheless (v. 4): "*Yet now*, even though this house is likely to be inferior to the former, *be strong, O Zerubbabel! And be strong, O Joshua!*" Let leaders do as well as they can, since they cannot do so well as they want to.

3.3. The basis of these encouragements. God himself says to them, *Fear you not* (v. 5), and he gives goods reasons for it.

3.3.1. They have God with them, his Spirit and his special presence: *Be strong, for I am with you, saith the Lord of hosts* (v. 4). The presence of God is with us, as the *Lord of hosts*, the Lord Almighty; he is enough to silence all our fears. The Jews had hosts against them, but they had the *Lord of hosts* with them. Though *he chastens them for their transgressions with the rod*, his faithfulness will not fail. It was the Spirit of God who moved their hearts to come out of Babylon (Ezr 1:5), and now to build the temple (v. 14).

3.3.2. They will have the Messiah among them soon—*him that should come* (Mt 11:3) (vv. 6–7). When the Son of Man comes, let him find faith on earth (Lk 18:8). Concerning his coming it is foretold that it will be introduced by a general disturbance (v. 6): *I will shake*

the heavens, and the earth, and the sea, and the dry land. This is applied to the establishment of Christ's kingdom in the world. God will once again act for his church as he did when he brought them out of Egypt; he shook the heavens and earth at Mount Sinai, and this will be done again when, at the birth of Christ, Herod and all *Jerusalem are troubled* (Mt 2:3) and the Messiah is *set for the fall and rising again of many*. When his kingdom was set up, it disturbed the nations. When nations are shaken, it is often so that the church may be settled and so that the things that cannot be shaken may be established.

3.3.3. The house they are now building will be filled with so much glory that its glory will surpass that of Solomon's temple. It is God's right to fill with glory; the glory that comes from him is satisfying, not worthless. Moses' tabernacle and Solomon's temple were filled with glory when God, in a cloud, took possession of them, but this house will be filled with glory of another nature. Let them not be concerned because this house will not have so much silver and gold as Solomon's temple had (v. 8). Let them be comforted with the assurance that although this temple has less gold, it will have more glory than Solomon's (v. 9): *The glory of this latter house shall be greater than of the former.* It will have in it the presence of the Messiah, the Son of God: his being presented there as *the glory of his people Israel* (Lk 2:32), his attending the temple when twelve years old, and later his preaching and working miracles there and his driving out the buyers and sellers from it. It was necessary, then, for the Messiah to come while the second temple stood, but because that has long since been destroyed, we must conclude that our Lord Jesus is the Christ, that he is *he that should come* and we are to *look for no other* (Mt 11:3). It was the *glory of this latter house* that:

3.3.3.1. Before the coming of Christ, it was always kept free from idols and idolatries. The purity of the church and its faithfulness to divine institutions are much more its glory than external pomp and splendor are.

3.3.3.2. After Christ, the Gospel was preached in it by the apostles, *all the words of this life* (Ac 5:20). In the temple, Jesus Christ was preached daily (Ac 5:42). Where Christ is, *behold, a greater than Solomon is there* (Mt 12:42); so also with the heart in which he dwells and makes a living temple: behold, it is more glorious than Solomon's temple and will be so eternally.

3.3.4. They will see an encouraging end to their present troubles and enjoy the pleasure of a happy settlement: *In this place will I give peace, saith the Lord of hosts* (v. 9). However, the Jews under the latter temple had so much trouble that we must conclude that this promise was fulfilled in the spiritual peace that Jesus Christ bequeathed to all believers (Jn 14:27). God will *give peace in this place*; he will give his Son to be the peace (Eph 2:14).

Verses 10–19

This sermon was preached two months later than that in the first part of this chapter. The people are now vigorously building the temple, and now God sends them a message that will be useful to them:

1. By way of conviction and caution. God sees that there are many among them who spoil this good work by going about it with unsanctified hearts and hands. All are warned to cleanse the hands they employ in this work. A spiritual use is to be made of the ceremonial law; it was intended not only as a divine ritual to the Jews but also as *instruction in righteousness* to all. Notice here:

1.1. What the rule of the law is. The prophet is ordered to inquire of the priests about it (v. 11); Haggai himself, though a prophet, must *ask the priests concerning the law*. It is their duty to explain the ordinances of God and give the general rules for their observance. The rules of the law, in the cases set out, are:

1.1.1. That a person who carries consecrated meat in the fold of his garment cannot transmit holiness by the touch of his clothes (v. 12).

1.1.2. A person who is ceremonially unclean by the touch of a dead body, however, does by his touch transmit that uncleanness. The law is explicit (Nu 19:22). The sum of these two rules is that defilement is more easily transmitted than sanctification.

1.2. How it is applied here (v. 14): *So is this people, and so is this nation, before me*. They think that their offering sacrifices on the altar will sanctify them and excuse their neglect in building the temple. "No," God says, "your consecrated meat and your altar will be so far from sanctifying to you your food and drink, your wine and oil, that your contempt of God's temple will bring defilement not only on your ordinary enjoyment of these good things but even on your sacrifices." If they are worldly and morally impure, then even if they work hard at building the temple and even if they offer many costly sacrifices when it is built, that will not be enough to sanctify their food and drink to them; the impurity of their hearts and lives will defile even that work of their hands and all their offerings and make them detestable to God.

2. By way of comfort and encouragement. If their hearts are right with God and they are wholehearted, God will remove the punishment of famine and restore great plenty to them. On the twenty-fourth day of the sixth month they began to prepare materials (1:15), and now on the twenty-fourth day of the ninth month they begin to *lay a stone upon a stone in the temple of the Lord* (v. 15). Let them take notice of this day:

2.1. Note how they have gone into debt before this day. Let them remember the time when there was waste and decay in all they had (v. 16). A man went to his granary, expecting to find *a heap of twenty measures* of grain, but he found it had become less and he could not explain why; when he came to measure it, *there were but ten measures*; it had dried away in being kept, or vermin had eaten it, or it had been stolen. Similarly, when he went to *the wine press*, expecting to draw *fifty vessels* (measures) of wine, he found they did not produce as they usually did, for he could get *but twenty*. *I smote you with blastings*, winds and frosts, which made all the greenery wither, *and with mildew*, which choked the grain as it was growing, *and with hail*, which battered it when it was nearly ripe. They were disappointed in this way *in all the labour of their hands* as long as they neglected to put their hands to the work of God. As long as they continued to neglect the temple work, all their affairs went backward. But:

2.2. Let them now observe their situation, and they will find that God will bless them from this day forward (vv. 18–19): "*Consider now* whether, when you begin to change your ways toward God, you do not find God

changing his ways toward you." God does not say what his blessings will be, but says only, in general, *I will bless you*; they will lack nothing to make them happy.

Verses 20–23

After Haggai's sermon to the people, there follows one to the leaders on the same day, particularly to *Zerubbabel* (v. 21): "*Speak to Zerubbabel, governor of Judah*; speak to him by himself." Zerubbabel is concerned about the community and about the neighboring nations and their governments. He is concerned about what will become of the few weak Jews and about how such a poor ruler as he is will be able to keep his ground and serve his country. "Go to him," God says, "and tell him it will be well with him and his remnant."

1. Let him expect to hear about the great commotions in the nations (vv. 21–22): *I will shake the heavens and the earth*. The world is like the sea, like a wheel, always moving, but sometimes it is especially turbulent. But, thank God, if the earth is shaken, it is to *shake the wicked out of it* (Job 38:13). In the apocalyptic visions, earthquakes are not a sign of hard times for the church. The Babylonian monarchy, which had been the throne of kingdoms, was already overthrown, and the powers that are still to come will also be overthrown; their day to fall will come. They *trust in chariots and horses* (Ps 20:7), but their *chariots* will *be overthrown*, and so will *those that ride in them*. This is the fate of all the enemies of God's church, and it seems also to be intended as a promise of Christ's victory over the powers of darkness, his overthrow of Satan's throne, that *throne of kingdoms*. All opposing *rule, principality, and power* will be destroyed, so that the *kingdom* may be *delivered up to God, even the Father* (1Co 15:24).

2. Let him be assured that he will be kept safe under divine protection in the midst of all these commotions (v. 23). Zerubbabel is eager to build a house for God, and so God makes the same promise to him as he did to David, that he will *build him a house* and establish it, even *in that day* when heaven and earth are shaken. Similarly, his successors in the government of Judah can take encouragement from this promise. However, this promise has a special reference to Christ, who was lineally descended from Zerubbabel and is the sole builder of the Gospel temple. Zerubbabel is acknowledged here as *God's servant. I have chosen thee* (v. 23) for this office. It is promised that because he is chosen, God will make him *as a signet ring*. Jehoiachin had been as the *signet on God's right hand*, but he was *plucked thence* (Jer 22:24). But Zerubbabel will be dear and precious to God, and his family will continue until the Messiah springs from it, who *is the signet on God's right hand*. Princes sign their edicts, grants, and commissions with their signet rings (Est 3:10). Our Lord Jesus is the signet ring on God's right hand, for all authority is given to him and derived from him (Mt 28:18). By him the great charter of the Gospel is signed and confirmed, and it is in him that all the promises of God are "Yes" and "Amen" (2Co 1:20).

A Practical and Devotional Exposition of the Book of the Prophet

Zechariah

This prophet was a colleague of the prophet Haggai and a worker together with him in advancing the building of the second temple (Ezr 5:1). Zechariah began to prophesy some time after Haggai. However, he continued longer, soared higher in visions and revelations, and prophesied more especially about Christ than Haggai had done. He begins with a sermon expressing the scope of his prophecy in the first five verses, but then, to the end of chapter 6, he relates the visions he saw and the instructions he received from heaven through them. In chapters 7 and 8, he takes occasion from a question put by the Jews about fasting to show them the duty of their present day and encourage them to hope for God's favor. Then there are two more sermons, both called *burdens of the word of the Lord* (one beginning at 9:1, the other at 12:1). Their scope is to rebuke sin, threaten God's judgments against the impenitent, and encourage those who feared God with an assurance of the mercy God had in store for his church, and especially of the coming of the Messiah and the setting up of his kingdom in the world.

CHAPTER 1

In this chapter, after the introduction (v. 1), we have: 1. A wake-up call to a sinful people to repent and return to God (vv. 2–6). 2. Great encouragement given to hope for mercy. This encouragement comes in the form of: 2.1. A vision of horses (vv. 7–11). 2.2. A prayer by an angel for Jerusalem and the answer to that prayer (vv. 12–17). 2.3. A vision of four carpenters (vv. 18–21).

Verses 1–6

We have here:

1. The foundation of Zechariah's ministry: *The word of the Lord came to him.* He received a divine commission to be God's mouthpiece to the people. The coming of the word was evidenced and demonstrated by the power of the Spirit, and so it was real, not imaginary. The word of the Lord came first to him *in the second year of Darius.* Before the exile, the prophets dated their writings by the reigns of the kings of Judah and Israel, but now they dated them by the reigns of the kings of Persia, to whom they were subjects. Zechariah preached his first sermon in the *eighth month* of this *second year of* Darius; Haggai preached his in the sixth month of the same year (Hag 1:1). Zechariah was *the son of Barachiah* (Berekiah), *the son of Iddo,* and he was *the prophet,* as Haggai is called *the prophet* (Hag 1:1).

2. The firstfruits of his ministry. Before he declares the promises of mercy, he issues calls to repentance, for this is how *the way of the Lord* must be *prepared* (Isa 40:3; Mt 3:1–3). The Law must first be preached, then the Gospel.

2.1. The prophet reminds them of what God had against their ancestors (v. 2): "*The Lord has been sorely displeased with your fathers.* You have seen with your eyes the fearful remains of his displeasure." The judgments of God that those who went before us were under should be taken as calls to repentance, so that we may cut off the curse and have it turned to a blessing.

2.2. He calls them in God's name to turn back and make their peace with him (v. 3). Let the rebels return to their former allegiance, and they will enjoy all the privileges of good subjects. What is most significant is that God is called the *Lord of hosts* three times here: *Thus saith the Lord of hosts. Turn you to me, saith the Lord of hosts*—this shows the authority and obligation of the command—*and I will turn to you, saith the Lord of hosts*—this shows the validity and value of the promise—so that it is no vain repetition (Mt 6:7).

2.3. He warns them not to persist in their impenitence, as their ancestors did (v. 4): *Be you not as your fathers.* We tend to be ruled very much by precedent. Some argued, "Shall we be wiser than our ancestors? They took no notice of the prophets; why then should we bother with them? They made laws against them; why should we tolerate them?" However, they are taught here how they should reason: "Our ancestors showed disrespect to the prophets, and God was very displeased with them for it; let us, therefore, consider what God says to us through his prophets." "Notice," says the prophet, "that *the former prophets cried to your fathers* as people who were in earnest, in the name of *the Lord of hosts*; and this was the substance of what they *said—Turn you now from your evil ways, and from your evil doings*—the same message that we are now preaching to you. Prompt reformation is the only way to prevent approaching ruin. And what has become of both your ancestors and the prophets who preached to them? They are all dead and gone" (v. 5). In another world both we and our prophets will live forever, and our great concern and work in this world should be to prepare for that world. "The preachers died and the hearers died, but the word of God did not die; that took effect, and not one *jot or tittle* of it fell to the ground"

(Mt 5:18). Although God's prophets could not fasten convictions on them, the threatened disasters overtook them, and they could not escape. Human unbelief cannot cancel out the threats of God's word; sooner or later they will take place if the prescribed course of action is not followed to prevent them. *"They returned, and said"* — they changed their mind and acknowledged when it was too late to prevent the ruin of their nation — *"Like as the Lord of hosts thought to do unto us according to our ways and doings, so has he dealt with us*, and we must acknowledge both his truth and his justice."

Verses 7–17

Here are visions and revelations of the Lord, for that is how God chose to speak through Zechariah in order to wake up the people's attention. Most of the following visions seem intended to comfort the Jews, recently returned from exile, and to encourage them to continue building the temple. The scope of this vision — which was an introduction to the rest — was to assure the Jews that God was taking care of them even now, when they seemed deserted and their situation seemed miserable. The vision is dated (v. 7) *the twenty-fourth day of the eleventh month*, three months after he preached the foregoing sermon (v. 1) in which he called them to repentance. Finding that it had the good effect of turning them back to God in their duty, he confirmed the assurances he had given them that God would return to them in mercy (v. 3). Notice:

1. What the prophet saw and its explanation.

1.1. He saw a grove of *myrtle trees*, a dark, shady grove, down *in a bottom* (ravine), hidden by the nearby hills. This represented the low, dark, solitary, sad condition of the Jewish church at this time.

1.2. He saw *a man* mounted on *a red horse*, standing among the shady myrtle trees. This man is no other than the *man Christ Jesus* (1Ti 2:5), the same who appeared to Joshua with *his sword drawn in his hand* as *captain of the host of the Lord* (Jos 5:13–14). Although the church was in a low condition, Christ was present among his people. He was *riding* like a speedy warrior, *riding on the heavens for the help* of his people (Dt 33:26). He rode on *a red horse*, as this same victorious prince appeared *red in his apparel* in Isa 63:1–2. Red is the color of fire, and so it showed that he was *jealous for Jerusalem* (v. 14) and angry at her enemies. Under the Law, Christ appeared on a red horse, showing that he still had ahead of him the conflict in which he was to *resist unto blood* (Heb 12:4). However, under the Gospel, he appears on *a white horse* (Rev 6:2; 19:11), showing that he has now gained the victory.

1.3. He saw a troop of horses attending the man: *Behind him there were some red horses, and* some *speckled, and* some *white*, angels attending the Lord Jesus, ready to be used by him to serve his church, some in acts of justice, others in acts of mercy, others in mixed events.

1.4. He asked the meaning of this vision. He had an angel talking to him as his instructor. Zechariah asked him (v. 9), *O my Lord! what are these?* The account given him was, *These are those whom the Lord has sent*: they are his messengers.

2. What the prophet heard and what instructions were given him.

2.1. He heard the report that the angels made (v. 11). They had been out as flying messengers, and having returned, they gave this account to the *"Angel that stood among the myrtle trees. We have walked to and fro through the earth, and, behold, all the earth sits still and is at rest.* We find the human race here very careless: *All the earth sits still, and is at rest*, while all the church is made uneasy,

tossed with tempests and not comforted (Isa 54:11)." Those who were strangers to the church were secure in their self-confidence; those who were its enemies were successful. The Babylonians and Persians lived in complacency, while the poor Jews were continually in fear.

2.2. He heard Christ's intercession with the Father for his afflicted church (v. 12). The angels related what life was like in this world, but we do not read of any prayers they made to put right the grievances. It was *the Angel among the myrtle-trees* who was the great intercessor. On the report of the angels, he immediately turned toward heaven and said, "Lord, wilt thou not have mercy on your church? *How long wilt thou not have mercy!*" The objects of compassion were Jerusalem, the Holy City, and the other cities of Judah that were now in ruins, for God had had *indignation against them* now *threescore and ten years*. The indignation lasted long, and though *now for a little space grace* had been *shown them from the Lord their God*, to *give them some reviving* (Ezr 9:8), the scars of those seventy years' exile still remained deep. The captivity was removed, as it came on, gradually. "Lord, we are still under the burden of the seventy years' wrath, *and wilt thou be angry with us for ever?"*

2.3. He heard a gracious reply given to this intercession (v. 13): *The Lord answered the angel*, this angel of the covenant, *with good words and comfortable words*, with promises of mercy and deliverance, with a promise that he would complete what he had begun.

2.4. He heard the reply that was given to the angel repeated to himself, with a commission to make it known to the children of his people to encourage and strengthen them. Now that God would *speak comfortably to Jerusalem* (Isa 40:2), Zechariah was *the voice of one crying in the wilderness, Prepare you the way of the Lord* (Mt 3:3). *The voice said, Cry.* The prophets must now cry out as loudly to show God's people their comforts as they ever did formerly to show them *their transgressions* (Isa 40:2–3, 6). Zechariah must declare the wrath God had in store for the enemies of Jerusalem (v. 14). The earth *sat still and was at rest* (v. 11), not relenting at all for all the trouble they had done to Jerusalem (v. 15). God is displeased with those who help forward the suffering even of those who suffer justly, for in such a case, true humanity is godliness. He must cry out, *"Thus saith the Lord, I have returned to Jerusalem with mercies*. I was going away in wrath, but I am now returning in love" (v. 17). *The Lord*, the Lord Almighty, was assuring them that:

2.4.1. The temple, though it met with much discouragement, would be perfected, and they would have the signs of God's presence. Jerusalem would again be *built as a city compact together* (Ps 122:3). *A line* (measuring line) would *be stretched forth upon Jerusalem* (v. 16), so that it might be rebuilt with exactness and uniformity.

2.4.2. The nation would again become well populated and rich. Not only Jerusalem but also other towns that had been subdued would *spread abroad*. The towns that would increase in this way God called his towns; they were *blessed* by him, and they would be *fruitful and multiply, and replenish the land.*

2.4.3. God had comforts in reserve for Zion and all her mourners.

2.4.4. Just as he first built them into a people when he brought them out of Egypt, so he would rebuild them now that he had brought them out of Babylon.

Verses 18–21

In this vision — the second that this prophet had — we have an illustration of God's Spirit making a stand, and even advancing, against the formidable power of the church's enemies. We have here:

1. The enemies of the church threatening to be its death: *I looked and behold four horns* (v. 18), which are explained in v. 19. They *are the horns which have scattered Judah, Israel, and Jerusalem,* that is, the Jews in both the country and the city. They had "tossed them," as some read it, as furious bulls use their horns to toss. They had scattered them, *so that no man did lift up his head* (v. 21). They were *four horns,* for the Jews were surrounded with them on every side. The people of Judah and of Jerusalem, and many of the Israelites who joined themselves to them, set about building the temple, but enemies from all sides drove them from it. Rehum, Shimshai, and the other Samaritans who opposed the building of the temple were these horns (Ezr 4:8). So were Sanballat and Tobiah and the Ammonites and Arabs, who opposed the building of the wall (Ne 4:7).

2. The friends of the church being active and effective. The prophet himself saw the four horns, but *the Lord* then *showed him four carpenters,* or craftsmen, who were empowered to cut off these horns (vv. 20–21). With our physical eyes we can see the power of the enemies of the church; however, it is with eyes of faith that we see that it is safe nevertheless. *Carpenters* or craftsmen—for the horns are thought by some to have been horns of iron—were those who had skill and ability to break the horns. Some understand these four craftsmen to be Zerubbabel and Joshua, Ezra and Nehemiah, who continued the work of God despite the opposition.

CHAPTER 2

We have here: 1. Another vision that the prophet saw for the edification of those to whom he was sent (vv. 1–2). 2. A sermon on it in the rest of the chapter: 2.1. To explain the vision, showing it to be a prediction of the repopulating of Jerusalem (vv. 3–5). 2.2. To apply this explanation by means of: 2.2.1. An exhortation to the Jews who were still in Babylon to be quick in returning to their own land (vv. 6–9). 2.2.2. Comfort to those who had returned, in reference to the many difficulties they had (vv. 10–12). 2.2.3. A warning to all not to give orders to God or limit him, but to wait patiently for him (v. 13).

Verses 1–5

This prophet was to assure the people (1:16) that *a line* (measuring line) *would be stretched forth upon Jerusalem.* Here we have that promise illustrated and confirmed.

1. He saw, in a vision, a man going to measure Jerusalem (vv. 1–2): *He lifted up his eyes again, and looked.* At the end of the previous chapter, he had seen Jerusalem's enemies defeated and broken, so now he began to hope she would not be ruined. *The man Christ Jesus* (1Ti 2:5), whom the prophet saw *with a measuring line in his hand,* is the master builder of his church (Heb 3:3), and he builds exactly, using a measuring line and spirit level. Zechariah asked him *whither he was going* with that measuring line. He readily told the prophet that he was going to *measure Jerusalem,* to take account of its dimensions each way, so that it could be worked out what was needed for building a wall around it, and so that it would be clear, by comparing its dimensions with the vast numbers who would inhabit it, what additions were necessary. When many people flock to Jerusalem (Isa 60:4), it is time for her to *enlarge the place of her tent* (Isa 54:2).

2. He was informed that this vision meant good things for Jerusalem. The *angel that talked with* the prophet went *forth,* but *another angel went out to meet him,* to ask him first to explain this vision to the prophet for his encouragement (v. 4): *Jerusalem shall be inhabited as towns without walls;* it will extend far beyond its present dimensions. It will be extended as freely as if it had no walls at all, but it will be as safe as if it had the strongest walls; such a *multitude of men*—which are the best walls of a city—*shall there be therein.* It will be secure, for God himself will be a *wall of fire round about it.* Jerusalem had no walls around it at this time; now, however, God would be a wall of fire to her. Some think this refers to fires built to frighten away wild animals, either by shepherds to protect their flocks or by travelers to protect their tents in the desert. God himself would be such a wall, a wall of fire all around them. God himself *will be the glory in the midst of it.* All this was fulfilled in part in Jerusalem, which in the course of time became a very successful city, beyond what could have been expected, considering how low it had been brought and how long it was before it recovered.

Verses 6–9

One would have thought that Cyrus's proclamation giving liberty to the exiled Jews to return to their own land would be enough to bring them all back, but it did not have that effect.

1. There were about 40,000 whose hearts God moved to go, and they went, but many stayed behind. The land of their exile was to most of them the land where they had been born; they had settled down there. They had no great affection for their own land, and they thought the difficulties insuperable. This attitude proceeded from a distrust of the power and promise of God, a love of ease and worldly wealth, and an indifference toward the religion of their country and the God of Israel himself. It was also a tacit criticism of those who did return. Here, therefore, is another proclamation by the God of Israel, commanding all his freeborn subjects, wherever they are dispersed, to return speedily to their own land. They are called on loudly (v. 6): *Ho! ho! come forth, and flee from the land of the north, saith the Lord.* This appropriately follows the promise of the rebuilding of Jerusalem. If God will build it for them, they must come and inhabit it for him and his glory, not continue skulking in Babylon. Let them consider:

2. They are now dispersed, but they should unite for the common defense (v. 6): "*I have spread you abroad as the four winds of heaven,* some into one corner of the world and some into another, and you should now think of coming together again to help one another."

3. They are now in bondage and are therefore to assert their liberty: *Deliver thyself* (escape), *O Zion!* When Christ has proclaimed that release for the captives which he has himself brought about, each of us should *deliver ourselves,* and since we are under grace, we should be determined that *sin shall not have dominion over us* (Ro 6:14). "*Deliver thyself, O Zion!* by a speedy return to your own land, and do not destroy yourself by continuing in that defiled land."

4. They have seemed to be forsaken and forgotten by God, but God will now make it clear that he embraces their cause and will plead it with jealousy (vv. 8–9). The *angel that talked with* the prophet—that is, Jesus Christ—tells him what he was commissioned to do to protect and complete their salvation. Christ, who is the *Lord of hosts, says, He*—that is, the Father—*has sent me.*

4.1. Christ is sent *after the glory.* He is sent, in the first place, to the nation and people of the Jews, *to whom* pertained the glory (Ro 9:4). However, *after the glory*, after his care of them, he is *sent to the nations, to be a light to lighten the Gentiles* (Lk 2:32); he is sent so that by the power of his Gospel he may enthrall them and bring them into obedience to himself (2Co 10:5).

4.2. He is *sent to the nations that spoiled them*, to take vengeance on them for the wrongs done to Zion. *They shall be a spoil* (plunder) *to their servants* (v. 9); they will be enslaved to those whom they had enslaved. The promise is fulfilled in Christ's victory over our spiritual enemies, his *spoiling principalities and powers and making a show of them openly* (Col 2:15).

4.3. What he will do for his church will be proof of God's affection for it: *He that touches you touches the apple of his eye* (v. 8). He takes what is done against her as being done against the very apple of his eye, the most tender part, which nature has put a double guard on. Let the people of God pray with David (Ps 17:8), *Keep me as the apple of the eye*, and let them do as Solomon directs (Pr 7:2), *keeping God's law as the apple of their eye*.

Verses 10–13

1. Here is joy declared to the church of God, to the *daughter of Zion*, who has separated herself from the *daughter of Babylon*. The Jews who have returned are in distress, their enemies in the neighborhood are malicious, and their friends who remain in Babylon are cool and decline to come and help them, but they are directed to *sing* and *rejoice* even in tribulation.

1.1. God wants to have a people among them. If their brothers and sisters in Babylon will not come to them, those of other nations will: *Many nations shall be joined to the Lord in that day* (v. 11). After the exile, the Jewish nation multiplied greatly by the accession of converts, who were naturalized and entitled to the privileges of native Israelites. It was strange that what was promised as a blessing in the prophets' times should be such a great offense to the Jews in the apostles' times.

1.2. They will have his presence among them: *Sing and rejoice, for I come*. God will come to reside with them and preside over them: *I will dwell in the midst of thee* (v. 10), and it is repeated (v. 11), because it was to be doubly fulfilled:

- In the dedication of the temple, in their regularly observing all God's institutions there. Those who have God's ordinances administered in their purity and accompanied by a divine power have God *dwelling in the midst of them*.
- In the incarnation of Christ. The One who promises to live among them is the *Lord whom the Lord of hosts has sent* (v. 11), and so he must be the *Lord Jesus*, the eternal *Word*, who was *made flesh, and dwelt among us* (Jn 1:14).

1.3. They will have all their ancient honors and privileges restored to them (v. 12). Canaan will be a holy land again. Judah will be in this holy land, no longer scattered in Babylon. Judah will be God's portion, in which he will be glorified. God will protect his people and rule them as people do their inheritance. He will *choose Jerusalem again*; it will continue to be a chosen place until it must resign that honor to the Jerusalem from above (Gal 4:26).

2. Here is silence declared to all the rest of the world (v. 13). The daughter of Zion must sing, but *all flesh* must be silent. God is about to do something unexpected and to plead his people's cause, which has long seemed neglected. Leave it to God to take his own way; neither

dictate to him what he should do nor quarrel with him about anything he does: *Be still, and know that he is God* (Ps 46:10). *Stand still, and see his salvation* (Ex 14:13).

CHAPTER 3

The vision in the previous chapter gave assurances of the reestablishing of the civil interests of the Jewish nation. Now the vision in this chapter concerns their church state and their ecclesiastical interests. Here is: 1. A vision relating to Joshua as the representative of the church in his time. The vision shows the disadvantages that he labors under and that the people labor under in him, and then shows the redress of the grievances of both. 1.1. He is accused by Satan but is acquitted by Christ (vv. 1–2). 1.2. He appears in filthy garments but has them changed (vv. 3–5). 1.3. He is assured that he will be established in his office if he behaves well (vv. 6–7). 2. A sermon relating to Christ, who is here called the Branch, by whom we would enjoy pardon and peace (vv. 8–10).

Verses 1–7

There was a Joshua who was a principal agent in the first settlement of Israel in Canaan; here is another of the same name who is very active in their second settlement there after the exile. *Jesus* is the same name, and that name means "Savior," and they were both figures of the One who was to come (Mt 11:3), our chief commander and our chief priest. The angel who talked with *Zechariah showed him Joshua the high priest*; the prophet probably saw Joshua frequently and had a close relationship with him, but he saw only how Joshua appeared before human beings. How he stands before the Lord must be shown him in a vision. He *stood before the angel of the Lord* to fulfill his *office*. He stood to consult the oracle on behalf of Israel. Guilt and corruption are our two great discouragements when we stand before God; they expose us to his justice and make us repugnant to his holiness.

1. Joshua is accused as a criminal but is justified.

1.1. Violent opposition is raised against him. *Satan stands at his right hand to resist him* (v. 1), as the prosecutor or witness. When God is about to reestablish the priesthood, Satan objects with the sins that are found among the priests. It is by our own foolishness that we give Satan an advantage against us. We must expect to meet with all the resistance that Satan's subtlety and malice can give us. Let us then resist him, and he will flee from us (Jas 4:7).

1.2. A victorious defense is made (v. 2): *The Lord* (that is, the Lord Christ) *said unto Satan, The Lord rebuke thee*. It is the joy of the saints that the Judge is their friend. Satan is restrained here by one with authority (Mt 7:29). *The Lord said*—that is, the Lord our Redeemer—*The Lord rebuke thee*, that is, the Lord the Creator. The power of God is committed to making the grace of Christ effective. Satan resists the priest, but his resistance is ineffective against Jerusalem, for *the Lord has chosen* it. He knew the worst when he chose them. *Is not this a brand plucked out of the fire?* Joshua is so, and so are the priesthood and the people, whose representative he is. Christ has something to say about them for which they are to be pitied. One cannot expect anything else than that those who only the other day were exiles in Babylon should appear lowly and contemptible. They have just been wonderfully rescued from the fire so that God could be glorified in them; will he then abandon them?

2. Joshua appears as one defiled, but is purified, for he represents the Israel of God, who are all *as an unclean*

thing (Lev 5:2). *He is clothed* in *garments* that are not only coarse but also *filthy*, such as are inconsistent with the dignity of his office and the sanctity of his work (Ex 28:2). Joshua's garments are a shame and disgrace, but *he stands* in them *before the angel of the Lord.* He has no clean linen with which to minister. This shows not only that the priesthood was poor and despised and burdened with contempt but also that there was sin clinging to the holy things. The returned Jews thought that because they were free from idolatry, they could not be charged with sin. God showed them, however, that there were many things wrong with them. There were spiritual enemies warring against them. Joshua is, however, permitted to *stand before the angel of the Lord.* Provision is made for his cleansing. Two things are done for Joshua, representing a double work of divine grace done in and for believers:

2.1. His filthy garments are taken away from him (v. 4). The meaning of this is given in what Christ says, and he says it as one having authority: *Behold, I have caused thy iniquity to pass from thee.* When God forgives our sins, he *causes our iniquity to pass from us*; he sanctifies our nature and enables us to *put off the old man* (Col 3:9), to drive away from us the filthy rags of our corrupt affections and sinful desires.

2.2. He is given fresh clothes; he has not only the shame of his filthiness removed but also the shame of his nakedness covered: *I will clothe thee with change of raiment.* Joshua has no clean linen of his own, but he will appear as lovely now as he appeared loathsome before. In this way, those whom Christ makes spiritual priests are clothed with the spotless robe of his righteousness and appear before God wearing that (Rev 7:13–15); he clothes them with the graces of his Spirit, which are ornaments to them.

3. Joshua is reinstalled and established in his office.

3.1. The crown of the priesthood is put on him (v. 5). This is done at the request of the prophet. When God intends the restoring or reviving of religious faith, he stirs his prophets and people to pray for it, and then he restores and revives in answer to their prayers. Zechariah prays that the angels will be ordered to set the *mitre* (turban) on Joshua's head, and they do it immediately, and *clothe him with* the priestly *garments.*

3.2. The covenant of the priesthood, which is called God's *covenant of peace* (Nu 25:12), is renewed with him. It is "the authority of his office," which is here declared and delivered to him before witnesses (vv. 6–7). Joshua must *walk in God's ways*; he must go before the people in the paths of God's commandments, walking carefully. He must also *keep God's charge*, seeing to it that the lesser priests perform the duties of their position. Let him be sure to fulfill his part, and God will acknowledge him. The high priest should not make any new laws for God's house or ordain any other ceremonies of worship, but must *judge God's house*, that is, he must see to it that God's laws and ordinances are observed. "*Thou shalt also keep my courts*; you will have oversight of all the courts of the temple, and you must keep them in good order for worship to be performed in them." *I will give thee places to walk among those that stand by.* Those who *walk in God's ways* may be said to *walk among the angels* themselves, for they do the will of God as the angels who are in heaven do it, and they are the angels' *fellow-servants* (Rev 19:10).

Verses 8–10

Just as the promises made to David often slide imperceptibly into promises of the Messiah, whose kingdom David's was a type of, so the promises made here to

Joshua rise as far upward, and look as far forward, as to Christ, of whose priesthood Joshua's was now a shadow. Christ is, as Joshua was, a high priest (Heb 2:17; 3:1; 4:14–15; etc.) for sinners and sufferers. See:

1. To whom this promise of Christ was directed (v. 8): "*Hear now, O Joshua!* You have heard what belongs to yourself, but behold, a greater than Joshua is at hand (Mt 12:41–42). *Hear now* concerning him, *thou* and the rest of the priests, *thy fellows* (associates), *who sit before thee* as learners, for you are *men wondered at.*" They were symbols of what was to come, as types and figures of Christ's priesthood. Or the phrase may mean "men of wonder"; they were amazed to think how much their condition had changed.

2. The promise itself, which consists of several parts, all intended to encourage Joshua and his friends in the great work of building the temple. The Messiah will come: *Behold, I will bring forth my servant the branch.* He is the Branch, as he was called in Isaiah: *The branch of the Lord* (Isa 4:2), *a branch out of the roots of Jesse* (Isa 11:1). His beginning will be small, like that of a tender branch, but in time he will become a great tree (Isa 53:2), the branch from which all our fruit must be gathered. He is *the stone laid before Joshua* (v. 9); the phrase alludes to the foundation, or chief cornerstone, of the temple, which probably was laid with great solemnity in the presence of Joshua. Christ is not only the branch, which is the beginning of a tree, but also the foundation, which is the beginning of a building. *Seven eyes shall be upon him.* The eye of his Father was on him to protect him, especially in his suffering. The eyes of all the prophets and Old Testament saints were on this one stone. The eyes of all believers are on him; they look to him and are saved. *I will engrave the graving thereof, saith the Lord of hosts* (v. 9). The builders refused this stone as rough and unsightly, but God undertakes to smooth it, polish it, and carve it, so that it will be the *head stone of the corner* (Ps 118:22; Mt 21:42). This stone is *a precious stone*, though laid as *a foundation* (Isa 28:16). Its *graving* (inscription) seems to allude to the precious stones in the breastplate of the high priest (Ex 28:21–22). By Christ sin will be taken away, both its guilt and its controlling power: *I will remove the iniquity of that land in one day.* When the high priest had the names of Israel engraved on the precious stones he was adorned with, he was said to *bear the iniquity of the holy things* (Ex 28:38). He bore the iniquity of the land, as a type of Christ, but he could not remove it. That was reserved for Christ, that blessed *Lamb of God, that takes away the sin of the world* (Jn 1:29), and he did it *in one day*, that day on which he suffered and died. Some understand the engravings with which God engraved him to stand for the wounds and stripes that were given to his blessed body, wounds that he underwent for our *transgression* and *by which we are healed* (Isa 53:5). The effect of all this will be a sweet assurance and a sweet fellowship (v. 10): *In that day you shall call every man his neighbour under the vine and fig tree.* When sin is taken away, we rest in tranquility and are quiet from the fear of evil. We sit down under Christ's shadow with delight and are sheltered by it from the scorching heat of the curse of the law.

CHAPTER 4

Here is another vision, which, as it was explained to the prophet, contained much to encourage the people of God in their present difficulties. The scope of the vision was to show that God would complete the work by his own power.

Here is: 1. The awakening of the prophet to observe the vision (v. 1). 2. The vision itself, of a lampstand with seven lights that were kept burning with oil from two olive trees that grew by it, one on either side (vv. 2–3). 3. The general encouragement to be given to the builders of the temple to continue that good work (vv. 4–10). 4. The explanation of the vision (vv. 11–14).

Verses 1–10

Here:

1. The prophet was prepared to receive the revelation: *The angel that talked with him came and waked him* (v. 1). It seems that the angel let him lose himself a little, to enable him to be fresh to receive new revelations, but then *waked him*.

2. When he was prepared in this way, the revelation was made to him. What he noticed was *a golden candlestick*. The church is a lampstand to enlighten this dark world and hold out the light of divine revelation to it. The light is God's; the church is only the lampstand. This golden lampstand had *seven lamps* branching out from it, that many bases, in each of which was a burning and shining light (Jn 5:35). The Jewish church was one. Under the Gospel, Christ is the center of unity, and not Jerusalem, or any one place. This candlestick had one *bowl* on the top, into which oil was continually dropping, and from it, by seven *pipes*, oil was distributed to the seven lights, so that without any further care they received oil as fast as they used it up. They never lacked oil or ever had too much and therefore always kept burning clear. The bowl, too, was continually supplied without any care, for (v. 3) the prophet saw *two olive trees*, one on each side of the lampstand, which naturally poured oil continually into the bowl; and two larger pipes (v. 12) dispersed the oil from the central bowl to smaller ones and so to the lights. This meant that nobody needed to attend this lampstand, and the aim of this image is to show that God can easily, and often does, fulfill his gracious purposes for his church without human work.

3. The prophet was asked the meaning of this (v. 4): *I answered and spoke to the angel*, saying, *What are these, my lord?* Zechariah saw what these *were*, but he was asking what they *signified*. The angel answered him with a question: *Knowest thou not what these be?* The prophet knew there was a golden lampstand in the tabernacle and that it was the priests' constant work to supply that with oil. When he saw such a lampstand, therefore, with lamps always burning but with no priests to attend it, he could have discerned its meaning to be that even though God had set up the priesthood again, he could continue his own work for his people without them.

4. The general intention of this vision was revealed. Its purpose was to assure the prophet that by providence and divine grace this work of building the temple would be brought to a happy conclusion even though its enemies were many and its friends few. This vision was to illustrate a word that the Lord had to say to Zerubbabel to encourage him to continue building the temple. Let him know that he is a worker together with God and that it is a work that God will acknowledge and crown.

4.1. God will carry on this work not by external force, but by internal influences on human minds. The One who says this will do it *not by* human *might or power*, but *by his own Spirit* (v. 6). It was through the *Spirit of the Lord of hosts* that the people were stirred to build the temple, and that is why they are said to be *helped by the prophets of God*, because the prophets, as the Spirit's mouthpiece, spoke to their hearts (Ezr 5:2). It was by the same Spirit

that the heart of Darius was disposed to favor that good work and that the enemies of it were frustrated so that they could not prevent it. When instruments fail, therefore, let us leave it to God to do his work himself through his own Spirit.

4.2. All the difficulties and opposition that lie in the way will be removed, even those that seem insuperable (v. 7): *Who art thou, O great mountain? Before Zerubbabel thou shalt become a plain.* The enemies of the Jews are proud and as hard as great mountains, but when God has a work to do, the mountains dwindle into molehills. Faith will remove mountains (Mt 21:21) and make them plains. Christ is our Zerubbabel; nothing is too hard for his grace to do (Ge 18:14; Jer 32:17; Mt 17:20; 19:26).

4.3. The same hand that has begun this good work will perform it (Php 1:6): *He shall bring forth the headstone* (capstone) (v. 7), and again (v. 9), *The hands of Zerubbabel have laid the foundation of this house*, and *his hands shall also finish it.* Here he is a type of Christ, who is both the *author* and the *finisher of our faith* (Heb 12:2). When the work is finished, it must be thankfully acknowledged that it was not by any power of our own, but that it was God's grace that did it—God's goodwill toward us and his good work in us and for us.

4.4. This will be a full confirmation of the foregoing prophecies about the Jews' return and resettlement. When the temple is finished, then *thou shalt know that the Lord of hosts has sent me unto you* (v. 9).

4.5. This will effectively silence those who looked with contempt on the beginning of this work (v. 10). In God's work, *the day of small things is not to be despised.* A grain of mustard seed may become a great tree (Mt 13:31–32).

4.6. Those who despaired that the work would never be finished will rejoice when they *see the plummet* (plumb line) *in the hand of Zerubbabel.*

4.7. This will exalt God's providence, which is always employed for the good of his church. Zerubbabel does his part, but he does it *with those seven, those seven eyes of the Lord* that we read of earlier (3:9). He could do nothing if the gracious providence of God did not go before him and go along with him in it. Those *seven eyes* that *run through the earth* are all *upon the stone* that Zerubbabel is laying straight with his plumb line. Moreover, people who have the plumb line in their hands must have a constant regard to divine Providence and act in dependence on its guidance.

Verses 11–14

Enough had been said to Zechariah both to encourage him and to enable him to encourage others, and that was the main intention of the vision he saw. However, he still wanted to know more about the details. Notice:

1. What his question was. He understood the meaning of the lampstand with its lights: it was Jerusalem, it was the temple, it was their salvation that was to *go forth as a lamp that burns*; but he wanted to know what these *two olive trees* were (v. 11), these *two olive-branches* (v. 12). He took notice not only that one of the olive trees grew *on the right side and the other on the left side of the candlestick*—divine grace is so near and so available to the church—but also that the *two olive branches*, from which in particular the lampstand received *the root and fatness* (nourishing sap) *of the olive*, emptied the *golden oil out of themselves through the two golden pipes* into the *golden bowl* on the head of the lampstand. Our Lord Jesus emptied himself (Php 2:7) to fill us; his precious blood is the golden oil in which we are supplied with all we need.

2. What answer is given. Now again the angel required him to acknowledge his ignorance before he answered his question (v. 13): *"Knowest thou not what these are?* If you know that the church is the lampstand, can you think that the olive trees, which supply it with oil, are anything else than the grace of God?"

2.1. If we understand the lampstand to be the visible church, especially that of the Jews at that time, for whose comfort this vision was primarily intended, these *sons of oil,* who *stand before the Lord of the whole earth,* are the two great ordinances and offices of the judiciary and ministry, which at that time were put into the hands of those two great and good leaders Zerubbabel and Joshua. Kings and priests were anointed with oil; this prince, this priest, were the anointed ones. Their wisdom, courage, and zeal were continually emptying themselves into the golden bowl to keep the lamps burning.

2.2. If we understand the lampstand to be the church of the firstborn (Heb 12:23), the church of true believers, these anointed sons may refer to Christ and the Spirit, the Redeemer and the Comforter. From Christ, the *olive tree,* through the *Spirit, the olive branch,* all the golden oil of grace is communicated to believers, which keeps their lamps burning.

CHAPTER 5

God's prophets are not only his ambassadors, to negotiate peace with the children of peace (Lk 10:6), but also heralds, to declare war against those who delight in war (Ps 68:30) and persist in their rebellion. In this chapter we have two visions, by which the wrath of God is revealed against all ungodliness and unrighteousness of men (Ro 1:18). God will do great and kind things for his people, but let sinners in Zion be afraid, for: 1. God will judge severely those individuals who are evil and ungodly, who hate to be reformed in these times of reformation. While God is showing kindness to most of the nation, they and their families will lie under the curse, which the prophet sees in a flying scroll (vv. 1–4). 2. If most of the nation become corrupt, the nation will be taken away with swift destruction, represented by a cover of lead on the mouth of a measuring basket, taking it far away on wings (vv. 5–11).

Verses 1–4

We do not find that the prophet now needed to be awakened, as he did in 4:1.

1. He looked up into the air, and *behold a flying roll* (scroll). The angel asked him *what he saw* (v. 2). The prophet gave the angel this description: *I see a flying roll;* and, as close as he could guess from what he saw, it was *twenty cubits long,* that is about ten yards (about nine meters), and *ten cubits broad,* that is about five yards (about 4.5 meters). The Scriptures of the Old Testament and the New are scrolls, in which God has *written to us the great things of his law* (Hos 8:12) and Gospel. Christ is the Master of the rolls. They are *flying* scrolls. God's word *runs very swiftly* (Ps 147:15).

2. This flying scroll was *a curse;* it contained a declaration of the righteous wrath of God against those who by swearing insulted God's majesty or by stealing invaded their neighbor's property. Notice:

2.1. The extent of this curse. This curse *went forth over the face of the whole earth,* not only over the land of Israel. The whole human race is exposed to the judgment of God. How welcome, then, would be the news of a Savior who came to *redeem us from the curse of the law* by

being himself *made a curse for us* (Gal 3:13) and, like Ezekiel, *eating this roll!* (Eze 3:1).

2.2. The criminals against whom this curse was especially leveled. The world is full of sin, as was the Jewish church at this time. However, two kinds of sinners are specified here:

2.2.1. Thieves; the curse is *for every one that steals,* especially those who convert to their own use what was devoted to God (Mal 3:8; Ne 13:10). Sacrilege is without doubt the worst kind of thieving.

2.2.2. Swearers. Sinners of the previous class offend against the second table of the Ten Commandments; these against the first. The person who swears profanely will not be held guiltless (Ex 20:7), much less the one who swears falsely (v. 4).

2.3. The enforcing of this curse: *I will bring it forth, saith the Lord of hosts* (v. 4). The One who declares the sentence will take care to see that it is executed. Who can withstand or resist the curse that a God of almighty power declares?

2.4. The effect; it is terrible: *Every one that steals shall be cut off,* not corrected but cut off. He will be cut off *as on this side*—cut off from this place, that is, from Jerusalem. God will not spare the sinners he finds among his own people, nor will the Holy City offer protection to the unholy. *It shall enter into the house of the thief and of him that swears.* God's curse cannot be kept out by bars or locks. Unless the sinner repents and reforms, there is no way to throw it out. It will *consume* that house *with the timber thereof, and the stones thereof.* Sin is the ruin of homes and families, especially the sins of injury and perjury.

Verses 5–11

The previous vision was very clear, but this one contains things that are *dark and hard to be understood* (2Pe 3:16). Some think that its scope is to foretell the final destruction of the Jewish nation and the dispersion of the Jews when, by crucifying Christ and persecuting his Gospel, they filled up the measure of their sins (Mt 23:32). The prophet was told to turn and that then he would see greater destructions (v. 5). *What is this that goeth forth?* Through either the distance or the dimness of his sight, the prophet now could not tell very well what it was (v. 6). The angel told him both what it was and what it meant.

1. He saw an *ephah,* a measuring basket with which people measured grain in those days. Moreover, *this was their resemblance,* the appearance of the Jewish nation *over all the earth,* wherever they were now dispersed. Some think that the mention of a basket, which was used in buying and selling, suggests that fraud and extortion in commerce were sins that abounded among them.

2. He saw a *woman sitting in the midst of the ephah* (measuring basket), representing the sinful church and nation of the Jews in their later, corrupt age. The One who weighs the mountains on the scales and the hills in a balance (Isa 40:12) measures nations and churches as in a measuring basket; he is so exact in his judicial dealings with them. God's people are called *the corn of his floor* (Isa 21:10). Here he put this grain into the bushel basket in order to part with it. The angel said of the woman in the measuring basket, *"This is wickedness;* it is an evil nation, for otherwise God would not have rejected it in this way; it is as evil as *wickedness* itself."

3. He saw the woman pushed back into the measuring basket and saw a *talent,* or large cover, *of lead,* pushed down over its *mouth,* by which she was confined as a prisoner in the measuring basket. This was intended to

show that the wrath of God against impenitent sinners is something they cannot escape from. It is insupportable. Guilt is like a heavy load of lead on sinners.

4. He saw the measuring basket, with the woman in it, taken away into some distant country. The instruments employed to do it were *two women* who had *wings like those of a stork*, and to make them fly more swiftly, they had the *wind in their wings*, showing the speed with which the Romans destroyed the Jewish nation. They *lifted it up between the earth and the heaven*, as unworthy of either and abandoned by both. When the prophet asked where they were carrying the prisoner (v. 10), he was told that they planned *to build it a house in the land of Shinar*. This suggests that the punishment of the Jews would be a final dispersion; they would be forced to live in distant countries. There the *ephah shall be established, and set upon her own base* (the basket will be set there in its place). Their disaster would continue from generation to generation. Their sin would continue too, and their hearts would be hardened in it.

CHAPTER 6

The two kingdoms of providence and grace are what we are all interested in, since all our temporal lives are necessarily subject to divine providence and all our spiritual and eternal concerns are in vital dependence on divine grace. These two are represented to us in this chapter—the former by a vision, the latter by a type. Here is: 1. God as King of nations, in the vision of the four chariots (vv. 1–8). 2. God as King of saints, ruling the church through the mediation of Christ in the figure of Joshua the high priest (vv. 9–15).

Verses 1–8

The prophet *turned and lifted up his eyes and looked* (v. 1). This was the seventh vision he had. Notice the sight that the prophet had of *four chariots* drawn by horses of different colors (vv. 1–5). Some understand the *four chariots* to stand for the four monarchies, and then they read (v. 5), *These are the four winds of the heavens*, and suppose that there reference is made to Da 7:2. The Babylonian monarchy, they think, is represented here by the *red horses*. The second chariot with the *black horses* is the Persian monarchy, which went out northward against the Babylonians and *quieted God's Spirit* (gave his Spirit rest) *in the north country* (v. 8), by executing his judgments on Babylon and releasing the Jews from exile. The *white*, the Greeks, went *forth after them* in the north, for they overthrew the Persians. The *grizzled* (dappled), the Romans, who conquered the Greek Empire, are said to *go forth toward the south country*, because Egypt, which lay to the south, was subdued by the Romans. The *bay horses* had been with the *grizzled* (dappled), but later went out by themselves, and, according to this reading, these were the Goths and Vandals. I am inclined, however, to understand this vision more generally, as representing the administration of the kingdom of providence in the government of this lower world. The *angels* are often called the *chariots of God* (Ps 18:10; 68:17). The various providences of God about nations and churches are represented by the different colors of horses (Rev 6:2, 4–5, 8). Notice, therefore, that:

1. The counsels and decrees of God are the spring of all events, and they are immovable, like *mountains of brass* (bronze). The *chariots* came *from between the two mountains*; for God *performs the thing that is appointed for us* (Job 23:14). We could as soon grasp the mountains in our arms as comprehend the divine purposes with our finite understanding; we could as soon move *mountains of brass* (v. 1) as change any of God's purposes.

2. God fulfills his decrees in the works of providence, which are like chariots, in which God rides like a prince. His providences move as swiftly as chariots, directed by his infinite wisdom as chariots are by their drivers.

3. The holy angels are the ministers of God's providence and are employed by him as *the armies of heaven*. They are the *chariots* or the horses that draw the chariots, very powerful. They are *chariots of fire, and horses of fire* (2Ki 2:11), to carry one prophet to heaven and guard another on earth.

4. The events of providence have different aspects, and the face of the times often changes. The *horses* harnessed to the *first chariot* were *red*, representing war and bloodshed. Those harnessed to the *second chariot* were *black*, representing the sad consequences of war. Those harnessed to the *third chariot* were *white*, representing the return of comfort, peace, and prosperity after these sad and dark times. Those harnessed to the *fourth chariot* were of a mixed color, *grizzled* and *bay*, representing interwoven events, a day of prosperity and a day of adversity set one against the other (Ecc 7:14).

5. All the instruments and all the events of providence come from God. *These are the four spirits of heaven*, the four winds, according to some, which seem to blow wherever they please (Jn 3:8), from the various directions. Or, rather, these are *the angels* who *go forth from standing before the Lord of all the earth*: they wonder at his glory in the higher world, which is their blessedness, and they serve his glory in this lower world, which is their work.

6. There is a wonderful beauty in providence, and one event serves to balance out another. *The black horses went forth* (v. 6) carrying with them very dark and sad events, but immediately *the white went forth after them* carrying joy to those who mourned. Such are God's dealings with his church and people: if the black horses go out, the white ones immediately go after them, for *as affliction abounds, consolation much more abounds* (Ro 5:20).

7. The common, general aspect of providence is mixed, but heaven is unmixed. The *grizzled* (dappled) and *bay horses* were both harnessed to the *fourth chariot* (v. 3), and though at first they went out toward the *south country*, they afterward *sought to walk to and fro through the earth* (v. 7). If we go out throughout the earth, we will find the events of providence neither all black nor all white, but dappled, gray, or mixed black and white. Such is the world we live in. Yet God is pleased with all the actions of his providence (v. 8): *These have quieted my spirit* (have given my spirit rest), these *black horses* that stand for extraordinary judgments and the *white* ones that stand for extraordinary acts of rescue, both of which *went toward the north country*. These had *quieted my spirit in the north country*, which had just been the scene of the most remarkable action with reference to the church.

Verses 9–15

God spoke not only at *sundry times* but also *in divers manners* (Heb 1:1) in the past through the prophets to his church. In the earlier part of this chapter he spoke through a vision, which only the prophet himself saw; here, in this second part, he speaks through a sign, or type, which many people saw and which was a prediction of the Messiah as the priest and king of his church. Here is:

1. The significant ceremony that God appointed, and that was the *coronation of Joshua* the high priest (vv. 10–11). There were two types of Christ named

Joshua in the Old Testament: Joshua the commander in chief, a type of Christ the captain of our salvation (Heb 2:10), and Joshua the chief priest, a type of Christ the High Priest of our profession (Heb 3:1), and both in their day were saviors and leaders in bringing their people into Canaan. Joshua was far from being ambitious for the crown, and the people were far from ambitious to have a crowned king over them, but the prophet was ordered to crown Joshua as if he had been a king. Moreover, Zerubbabel's wisdom and godliness kept this from being any insult to him.

1.1. Jews from Babylon brought an offering to the house of God; these were *some of the captivity* (some exiles), who *came from Babylon* on a visit to Jerusalem with an offering of gold and silver for the service of the house of God. Perhaps they came with this gift because they heard that the building of the temple was progressing slowly for lack of money.

1.2. The time and place were appointed for the prophet to meet them. They thought they would bring their present to the priest, but God had a prophet ready to receive them and it. This would be an encouragement to them, who, in their exile, had so often complained, *We see not our signs, there is no more any prophet* (Ps 74:9). Zechariah was to meet them in the house of Josiah, the son of Zephaniah, who probably kept the treasuries of the temple.

1.3. Crowns were to be *made* and *put upon the head of Joshua* (v. 11). It is thought that two crowns were provided, one of silver and the other of gold; the former, some think, represented his priestly position, the latter his kingly position. The sun shines like gold when he *goes forth in his strength* (Jdg 5:31), and beams of the moon, when she *walks in brightness*, we call "silver beams." Those who worshiped the sun and moon would now fall down before the golden and silver crowns of the Redeemer, before whom the sun would be ashamed and the moon confounded (Isa 24:23).

2. The significance God gave this ceremony. Everyone would be ready to ask, "What is the meaning of Joshua's being crowned in this way?" The prophet would be ready to tell them:

2.1. God would, in the fullness of time (Gal 4:4; Eph 1:10), raise up a great high priest, like Joshua. Joshua was only the figure of One who was to come (Mt 11:3), a faint shadow of him (v. 12): "*Speak unto him* in the name of the *Lord of hosts*; tell him that *the man whose name is The BRANCH* will *grow up out of his place*, out of the City of David. Although the family is a root in a dry ground (Isa 53:2), this branch will spring up out of it, as, when the sun returns in spring, the flowers spring up from the roots, in which they have lain buried out of sight and out of mind."

2.2. Just as Joshua was active in building the temple, so *the man, the branch*, would be the sole builder of the spiritual temple, the Gospel church. He *shall build the temple of the Lord*.

2.3. Christ would bear the glory. Glory is a burden [Ed. note: the Hebrew word for "glory" also means "weight"], but this burden would not be too heavy for him to bear, because he is the One who upholds all things (Heb 1:3). The cross was his glory (Gal 6:14), and he bore that, and the crown given him was *an exceeding weight of glory* (2Co 4:17), and he bears that. What he would undertake would be the true *glory of Israel*. He would "lift up the glory," as it may read; he would raise it up out of the dust.

2.4. He would have a throne and be both priest and king on his throne. A throne denotes both dignity and rule,

exalted honor with extensive power. As a priest, Christ always lives to make intercession for us (Heb 7:25), but he does so seated at his Father's right hand, as one having authority (Heb 8:1). Christ, who is ordained to offer sacrifices for us, is authorized to decree laws to us. He will not save us unless we are willing for him to rule us (Ps 110:3; Lk 19:14, 27). God has prepared for him a throne *in the heavens* (Ps 103:19), and if we want to obtain any benefit from that, we must prepare a throne in our hearts for him. This king would be a *priest upon his throne* (v. 13). With the majesty and power of a king, he would have the tenderness and simplicity of a priest.

2.5. *The counsel of peace shall be between them both*, that is, between *Jehovah* and the *man the branch*, between the Father and the Son; for the peace between God and human beings comes by the mediation of Christ. Some think the verse alludes to the former government of the Jews' state, in which the king and priest, separate officers, consulted with one another to maintain peace and prosperity in church and state, as Zerubbabel and Joshua did now.

2.6. There would be a happy partnership between Jews and Gentiles in the Gospel church, and they would both meet in Christ, the priest on his throne, who would be the center of their unity (v. 15): *Those that are far off shall come and build in the temple of the Lord*.

2.7. This would be confirmation of the truth of God's word: *You shall know that the Lord of hosts has sent me unto you*. That promise, that those who were far away would help them in *building the temple of the Lord*, was, as it were, the *giving of them a sign* (2Ch 32:24; Isa 7:14) that Zechariah, who told them about it beforehand, was sent by God. This would now be fulfilled very quickly; see Ezr 6:13–14. "*For this shall come to pass—if you will diligently obey the voice of the Lord your God* (v. 15). You will have the help of foreigners in building the temple if only you will set about it diligently yourselves."

3. The provision that was made to preserve the memory of this. *The crowns* that were used in this ceremony were not given to Joshua, but must be *kept for a memorial in the temple of the Lord* (v. 14). Either they were stored in the temple treasury or—as the Jews' tradition has it—they were hung in the windows of the temple in view of all as evidence of the promise of the Messiah.

CHAPTER 7

The prophet saw no further signs like those he had seen, but the word of the Lord continued to come to him. 1. A case of conscience is proposed to the prophet by the exiles concerning fasting (vv. 1–3). 2. The answer is given gradually and, it seems, at various times, for here are four distinct messages that all refer to this case. In this chapter: 2.1. The prophet sharply rebukes the exiles for the mismanagement of their fasts (vv. 4–7). 2.2. He encourages them to reform their lives, which would be the best way of fasting (vv. 8–14). Then, in the next chapter, having examined the wound, he binds it up and heals it, with gracious assurances of the mercy that will turn their fasts into feasts.

Verses 1–7

We have here:

1. A case presented concerning fasting. Some people were sent to ask the priests and prophets whether they should continue to observe their yearly fasts, especially the one in the fifth month, as they had done. It is uncertain whether the case was put by those who still remained in

Babylon or by those who had returned, who were called the *people of the land* (v. 5). Notice:

1.1. Who came with this inquiry. They were *Sherezer* and *Regem-Melech*, people of some rank and figure, for they came *with their men*.

1.2. They were sent, perhaps, not with *gold and silver*, as those in 6:10–11 were, but for the two great purposes that should bring us all to the house of God:

1.2.1. To intercede with God for his mercy. They were sent to *pray before the Lord* (v. 2) and *offer sacrifice*. In exile, the Jews prayed toward the temple, as can be seen from Da 6:10, but now that it was to be rebuilt, they sent their representatives to pray in it.

1.2.2. To ask God concerning his mind.

1.3. Whom they consulted. They spoke *to the priests that were in the house of the Lord and to the prophets*. The priests and the prophets were not jealous of one another, nor did they have any differences among themselves. Let not the people then make differences between them, but thank God for both.

1.4. The situation in which they wanted assurance. They asked (v. 3): *Should I weep in the fifth month, separating myself, as I have done these so many years?* They kept up the sacred stated fasts for humiliation and prayer. They mention only one, that of the fifth month, but it appears (8:19) that they observed four anniversary fasts, one in the fourth month (June 17), in remembrance of the breaking up of the wall of Jerusalem (Jer 52:6), another in the fifth month (July 4), in remembrance of the burning down of the temple (Jer 52:12–13), another in the seventh month (September 3), in remembrance of the killing of Gedaliah, and another in the tenth month (December 10), in remembrance of the beginning of the siege of Jerusalem (2Ki 25:1). Their present doubt was whether they should continue these fasts or not. The situation was put as by a single person: *Should I weep?* A religious fast must be made sacred not only by abstinence but also by a godly sorrow for sin (2Co 7:10), here expressed by weeping. "Should I still keep such *days to afflict the soul* as *I have done these so many years?*" It is said in v. 5 to have been seventy years. Something was to be said for the continuation of these fasts. The Jews were still under the signs of God's displeasure, and it is unwise for patients to break off their course of medicine while they still suffer symptoms of their illness. But there was also something to be said for stopping these fasts. God had returned in mercy to them. Now that the bridegroom had returned, why should the *children of the bridechamber fast* (Mt 9:15)? As for the fast of the fifth month, which was kept in remembrance of the burning of the temple, they should have seen that that had been superseded, because the temple was now on its way to being rebuilt.

2. An answer given to this case. Although the question looked plausible enough, those who suggested it were not conscientious about it, for they were more concerned about the ceremony than about the substance. Therefore, the first answer to their question was a very sharp rebuke of their hypocrisy.

2.1. What they did that was good was not done rightly (v. 5): *You fasted and mourned, yet did you at all fast unto me, even to me?* God appealed to their own consciences. Was it *to me, even to me?* The repetition suggests that this was emphasized as the main matter. To fast, but not fast to God, was to mock him and provoke him. If the ceremonies of our fasting, though frequent, long, and severe, do not serve to quicken prayer and change the attitude of our minds and the course of our lives for the better, God will not accept them as performed to him. The Jews had the

same view of themselves in their fasting that they had in their eating and drinking (v. 6).

2.2. The thing they should have done was left undone (v. 7): "*Should you not hear the words which the Lord has cried by the former prophets?* You must do what you have not yet done; you must repent of your sins and reform your lives. This is what we now call you to do, and it is the same as the former prophets called your ancestors to do." Zechariah reminded them of the former flourishing state of their country: Jerusalem, which was now desolate and in distress, *was* then *inhabited and in prosperity*. But then God *by the prophets cried* to them to reform their ways, for otherwise their prosperity would soon come to an end. "Now," the prophet said, "you should have taken notice of that and inferred that what they did not do is what you must do, and if you do not, all your fasting and weeping are worthless."

Verses 8–14

Here is a warning to these hypocritical inquirers, who continued in their sins when they asked with great scrupulousness whether they should continue their fasts.

1. This prophet repeated here what former prophets preached to their ancestors (vv. 9–10). The duties required are not keeping fasts and offering sacrifices, but *doing justly* and *loving mercy* (Mic 6:8). Magistrates must administer justice impartially. Neighbors must have a tender concern for one another. The weaknesses of others as well as their adversities are to be looked on with compassion. *Let none of you imagine evil against his brother in your heart.*

2. He described the stubborn disobedience of their ancestors (vv. 11–12). If they did hear what was said to them and seemed initially inclined to comply with it, then, like a bullock unused to the yoke, *they pulled away the shoulder* and would not submit to the *easy yoke and light burden* (Mt 11:30) of God's commandments. Literally, "they gave a withdrawing shoulder"; they seemed to lay their shoulder to the work, but they immediately withdrew it (Jer 34:10–11). *They made their hearts as an adamant-stone* (v. 12), as hard as diamond, the hardest stone to work, or flint. Nothing is so hard, so unmalleable, as the heart of an arrogant sinner. The reason why people are not good is that they do not want to be so; they will not consider and will not comply, and so God says, *if thou scornest, thou alone shalt bear it* (Pr 9:12).

3. He showed the fatal consequences to their ancestors: *Therefore came great wrath from the Lord of hosts.* As they had turned a deaf ear to God's word, so God turned a deaf ear to their prayers (v. 13). As they rejected their allegiance to God, so God scattered and threw them about like chaff before a whirlwind: *He scattered them among all the nations whom they knew not* (v. 14). As they disobeyed all the laws of their land, so God took away all its glories: *Their land was desolate after them, and no man passed through or returned.* It was not so much the Babylonians who did it. No; they did it themselves.

CHAPTER 8

The prophet here is ordered to change his tune, to speak words of encouragement to those who are willing and obedient. In the first of these messages (v. 1), God promises that Jerusalem will be restored and reformed (vv. 2–8), that the country will be rich, that their reputation will be restored, and that their state will be the reverse of what it has been for many previous years (vv. 9–15). He then encourages them to reform what is wrong in order to make themselves ready for these favors intended for them (vv. 16–17). He promises that their fasts will be superseded by the return of mercy (v. 19) and that they will be strengthened by the addition of foreigners to them (vv. 20–23).

Verses 1–8

The prophet wants to bring them to repentance, not drive them to despair, and so he sets out before them here the great things God has in store for them.

1. God will support Jerusalem and be avenged on Zion's enemies (v. 2). The great wrath that was against her (7:12) is now turned against her adversaries. "*I have returned to Zion* after I had seemed so long to stand far away, and I will again *dwell in the midst of Jerusalem* as before." This keeps safe for them the signs of his presence in his ordinances and in his providences.

2. There will be a wonderful reformation in Jerusalem, and religious faith will flourish there. *Jerusalem*, which has dealt treacherously both with God and with people, will become so famous for faithfulness and integrity that it *shall be called* and known as *a city of truth*, and its inhabitants will be called *children that will not lie* (Isa 63:8).

3. There will be in Jerusalem a great increase of people and all the marks of a profound tranquility. *In the streets of Jerusalem*, which once were filled with the bodies of those who had been killed, there will now live *old men* and *old women*, who have not been cut off by untimely deaths but have known the even thread of their days spun out to full length. They will go to their grave in full age, like *a shock of corn in his season*. Just as the hoary head is a crown of glory to those who wear it (Pr 16:31), so it is to the places where they live. It is a graceful thing to a city to have many old people in it; it is a sign not only of the health of the air but also of the predominance of good and the banishment of vices; it is a sign not only that the climate is temperate but also that the people are so. And one may look with as much pleasure on the generation that is arising in the place of the old (v. 5): *The streets of the city shall be full of boys and girls playing in the streets.* Their children will be healthy, strong, and cheerful. It is their enjoyable playing age; let us not grudge it to them: may it do them much good and no harm. They will not be terrified by the fear of war, but enjoy perfect security.

4. The scattered Israelites will be brought together again from all parts to which they were dispersed (v. 7): "*I will save my people from the east country, and from the west*; I will save them from being lost, or losing themselves, in Babylon or Egypt or any other country to where they were driven."

5. God will renew his covenant with them: *They shall be my people, and I will be their God* (v. 8). That is the foundation and crown of all these promises, and it includes all happiness. God will never leave nor abandon them in his mercy, as he promised them, and they will never leave nor abandon him in their duty, as they have promised him. These promises were fulfilled in the flourishing state of the Jewish church between the exile and Christ's time; they were to have a further and more complete fulfillment in the Gospel church; but the most complete fulfillment of all will be in the future state.

6. All doubts of God's people are silenced with the question (v. 6), "*If it be marvellous in the eyes of this people, should it be marvellous in my eyes?* If it seems unlikely to you that Jerusalem would ever be repaired and repopulated in this way, is it therefore impossible with God?"

Verses 9–17

Through the prophet, God gives further assurances here of the mercy he has in store for Judah and Jerusalem. These verses contain strong encouragements. We may notice:

1. To whom these encouragements belong—to those who, in obedience to the call of God through his prophets, seriously got down to the work of building the temple (v. 9). It is only those who work for God who may expect to be encouraged by him. Those who put their hands to the plow of duty will have them strengthened with the promises of mercy.

2. The discouragements they have suffered up to now. These are mentioned as a contrast to the blessings God is now about to give them. *Before these days of reformation began, there was no hire for man, nor any hire for beasts* (there were no wages for people or animals) (v. 10). The fruits of the earth were thin and poor. Merchants had no goods to export, so they did not need to hire either people or animals. There was no such thing as friendship or neighborliness among them: *I set all men every one against his neighbour* (v. 10). In this matter there was much sin, for these wars and infightings came from sinful desires.

3. What encouragement they will now have to proceed in their good work and to hope that things will go well: "You have been so harassed and afflicted, but now God will change his way toward you (v. 11). Now that you return to do your duty, the tide has turned." They will have great plenty and abundance of all good things (v. 12). The *heavens shall give their dew*, without which the earth would not yield its increase, which is a constant sign of God's generosity to us on earth and of our dependence on him. They will also regain their reputation among their neighbors (v. 13). Those blessed by the Lord are the blessing of the land and should be considered so. God himself will determine to do them good (vv. 14–15).

4. The use they are to make of these encouragements. Let them take comfort in these promises: *Fear you not* (v. 15); *let your hands be strong* (v. 9 and v. 13). Let them do the duty that those promises call for from them (vv. 16–17). "Leave it to God to fulfill for you in his own way and time what he has promised, but know that it is promised on condition that you are careful to do your duty. *These are the things then that you shall do. You* must never tell a lie, but *Speak you every man the truth to his neighbour. Execute the judgment of truth and peace in your gates.* Let the judges who sit in the gates consider both truth and peace. No one must bear hatred toward their neighbor. Great reverence must be had for oaths, with the mind set on fulfilling them. The things forbidden here are all found among the *seven things which the Lord hates* (Pr 6:16–19).

Verses 18–23

These verses contain two precious promises to encourage those Jews who were building the temple.

1. Their fasts would be converted into days of thanksgiving (v. 19). Joyful times would come to the church after troublesome times; if weeping lasted for more than a night and joy did not come the next morning (Ps 30:5), the morning would still eventually come. "Let the truths of God rule in your minds, and may the peace of God rule in your hearts."

2. A great addition would be made to the church by the conversion of many foreigners (vv. 20–23). This was fulfilled in part when, in the latter times of the Jewish church, there were many converts from countries nearby

or remote who came every year to worship at Jerusalem. This added to the grandness and wealth of that city, making it significant before our Savior's time, even though now it was only just beginning to emerge from its ruins. However, it would be fulfilled much more completely in the conversion of the Gentiles to the faith of Christ and in their joining with the faithful Jews in one body under Christ the head (Ro 16:26). The inhabitants of many cities would embrace the Gospel of Christ; *yea, many people and strong nations* (v. 22), some of *all languages* (v. 23). They would come *to pray before the Lord and to seek the Lord of hosts* (v. 21). Converts to God and members of the church are those who *seek the Lord of hosts*, who inquire for *God their Maker* and are sincerely devoted to his honor and glory. They are those who *pray before the Lord*. They would be zealous in motivating one another to do it (v. 21): *The inhabitants of one city shall go to another*, and they will say, *Let us go speedily to pray before the Lord; I will go also.* Those who are brought to know Christ themselves should do all they can to bring others; Andrew invited Peter to Christ, and Philip invited Nathanael. True grace hates monopolies. Just as iron sharpens iron, so may good people sharpen both *the countenance* and spirits of one another in doing what is good (Pr 27:17). They would join the church not for the church's sake, but for the sake of the One who lives in it (v. 23). This suggests the great respect they would have for a Jew, as one of the chosen people of God. *We will go with you, for we have heard that God is with you.*

CHAPTER 9

Here is: 1. A prophecy against the Jews' unrighteous neighbors—the Syrians, Tyrians, Philistines, and others (vv. 1–6)—with a suggestion of mercy to some of them, in their conversion (v. 7), and a promise of mercy to God's people, in their protection (v. 8). 2. A prophecy of their righteous King, the Messiah, and his coming (v. 9) and his kingdom (v. 10). 3. An account of the obligation the Jews were under to Christ for their restoration from exile (vv. 11–12). 4. A prophecy of the victories God would give the Jews over their enemies, which was a type of our great rescue by Christ (vv. 13–15). 5. A promise of the great plenty, joy, and honor that God had in store for his people (vv. 16–17).

Verses 1–8

1. The Arameans have been bad neighbors to Israel, and so the word of the Lord will be *a burden in the land of Hadrach*, that is, of *Syria* (Aram). Damascus is the center of that kingdom, and the judgments threatened here will lie on it. The reason for this oracle's resting on Damascus is that *the eyes of man, as of all the tribes of Israel*—or rather, *even of all the tribes of Israel*—are *toward the Lord*, because the people of God by faith and prayer look up to him for help and relief against their enemies. When the apostle Paul was converted at Damascus and then preached there and argued with the Jews, then the word of the Lord could be said to rest there, and then *the eyes of men*, of other people besides *the tribes of Israel*, began to be *toward the Lord*; see Ac 9:22.

2. Tyre and Sidon are next to be called to account, as in other prophecies (vv. 2–4). Tyre is flourishing, thinking she is very safe, and ready to defy God's judgments. She is also *very wise*. It is spoken ironically; she thinks she is very clever. However, there is no *wisdom* nor *counsel against the Lord* (Pr 21:30); in fact, it is his honor to confound the wise (1Co 1:27). *Tyrus did build*

herself a stronghold (v. 3), which she thought could never be brought down or overcome. By her vast trade she has *heaped up silver as the dust*, made it as common as heaps of sand, and made *fine gold* as common as *the mire of the streets*. Yet her wisdom, wealth, and strength will not be able to protect her (v. 4): *The Lord will cast her out* of that stronghold in which she has fortified herself, "will make her poor." God will *smite her power in the sea*; her being surrounded by water will not protect her; *she shall be devoured with fire*, burned down to the ground.

3. God next judges the Philistines with their great cities, which border the south of Israel. Now *Ashkelon shall see* the destruction of her friends and allies and will *fear*; *Gaza also shall see it, and be very sorrowful, and Ekron* (v. 5). What will become of their house when their neighbor's is on fire? They will themselves be destroyed and wasted. *The king shall perish from Gaza. Ashkelon shall not be inhabited.* Foreigners will take possession of their land (v. 6): *A bastard shall dwell in Ashdod.* This is how God will *cut off the pride of the Philistines.* This prophecy of the destruction of the Philistines and of Damascus and Tyre was fulfilled not long after this by Alexander the Great, who ravaged all these countries, captured the cities, and planted colonies in them. Some, on the other hand, understand v. 7 as a promise, that God will take away the sins of these *nations—their blood* and *their abominations*, their cruelty and their idolatry. He will preserve a remnant even of these nations, who will be memorials to his mercy and grace. Their birth will be no barrier to their acceptance with God; a Philistine will be as acceptable to God, on Gospel terms, as a person from Judah, and Ekron will be like the Jebusites, or people of Jerusalem.

4. In all this God intends mercy for Israel, and it is out of kindness to them that he will deal in this way with the neighboring nations. Some understand v. 7 as suggesting that God will rescue his people from their bloodthirsty enemies when they are just about to devour them and attack them. "I will *take away his blood*"—that is, the blood of Israel—"out of the mouth of the Philistines and *from between their teeth*" (Am 3:12). *He that remains*—that is, the remnant of Israel—*shall be for our God*, will be taken into his favor, will acknowledge him and be acknowledged by him, and this one who remains *shall be as a governor in Judah*. However, the sense of v. 8 is clearly that God will take his people under his special protection and weaken their neighbors so that it may not be in their power to cause them trouble in the first place: *I will encamp about my house because of the army.* When the times are dangerous, when armies are marching up and down and everyone shows their hatred toward Zion, then Providence will, as it were, redouble its defense of the church of God against marauding forces, *because of him that passes by and because of him that returns*, so that whether the enemy returns as a conqueror or as one conquered, he may do it no harm. This was fulfilled when, for some time after the struggles of the Maccabees, Judea was a free and flourishing state, or perhaps when Alexander the Great, struck with awe at Jaddus the high priest, favored the Jews and took them under his protection while he devastated the neighboring countries.

Verses 9–11

Here begins a prophecy of the Messiah and his kingdom with explicit application to Christ's riding in triumph into *Jerusalem* (Mt 21:5; Jn 12:15).

1. Notice is given of the approach of the promised Messiah as a subject of great joy for the Old Testament church: *Behold, thy king cometh unto thee.* Christ is a

king, a sovereign prince, having all power both in heaven and on earth (Mt 28:18). In the Gospel church, his spiritual kingdom is administered. "This King has been a long time in coming, but now, *behold, he cometh*; he is at the door. There are only a few more ages to elapse, and *he that shall come* (Mt 11:3) will come."

2. Here is such a description of him as makes his coming very acceptable to them.

2.1. He is a righteous ruler; *he is just.*

2.2. He is a powerful protector to all those who have faith in him and are truly faithful to him, for he *has salvation*; he has it in his power to give to all his subjects. He is a meek, humble, tender Father to all his subjects as his children; he is *lowly*; the word means "poor and afflicted"; having *emptied himself* (see commentary on Php 2:7), he was *despised and rejected of men* (Isa 53:3). He is *meek*, not proud or taking offense, but *humbling himself* from first to last. *Learn of me, for I am meek and lowly in heart* (Mt 11:29). When he made his public entry into his own city—and it was the only passage of his life that had anything magnificent in the eyes of the world—he chose to ride not on a stately horse or in a chariot, as leaders usually did, but *upon an ass* (v. 9). Nor was it a donkey ready for use, but an *ass's colt*, a small, foolish, unmanageable foal of a donkey, likely to disgrace its rider. He had no fine saddle, no trappings, no equipment, except his disciples' clothes thrown on the colt, for he *made himself of no reputation* (Php 2:7) when he visited us in great humility.

3. His kingdom is set out here to display its glory. This king has a kingdom that is not of this world (Jn 18:36); it is a spiritual kingdom, *a kingdom of heaven* (Mt 4:17). It will not be set up by worldly weapons of warfare (2Co 10:4). No; he *will cut off the chariot from Ephraim and the horses from Jerusalem* (v. 10) in kindness to his people, so that they may not cut themselves off from God by putting confidence in them that they should put only in the power of God. He will establish his kingdom by declaring peace on earth, goodwill toward all (Lk 2:14). As far as it is effective in the minds of human beings and has power over them, it will make them peaceful and remove all enmity; it will break *the battle bow* (v. 10) and *beat swords into plough shares* (Isa 2:4). The preachers of the Gospel will carry it from one country to another until the most distant corners of the world are enlightened by it.

4. The great benefit gained for the human race by the Messiah is redemption from extreme misery, of which the restoration of the Jews from exile in Babylon was a type (v. 11). "*I have sent forth thy prisoners*, sent your exiles out of Babylon, which for them was like *a pit* in which there was *no water*." Part of the covenant stated that if they sought the Lord in the land of their exile, he would be found by them (Lev 26:42, 44–45; Dt 30:4). It was *by the blood of that covenant*, which was a type of the blood of Christ, in whom all God's covenants with the human race are "Yes" and "Amen" (2Co 1:20), that they were released from captivity, and this was a mere shadow of the great salvation brought about *by thy King, O daughter of Zion!*

Verses 12–17

Having taught those who have returned from exile to attribute their restoration to the *blood of the covenant* and to the promise of the Messiah, the prophet now encourages them with the prospect of a joyful and happy settlement, but these promises have their complete fulfillment in the spiritual blessings of the Gospel that we enjoy through Jesus Christ.

1. They are invited to look to Christ and flee to him as their city of refuge (v. 12): *Turn you to the stronghold, you*

prisoners of hope. The Jews who had returned from exile into their own land were *prisoners of hope*, or "expectation," for God had given them a *little reviving in their bondage* (Ezr 9:8). Those who continued to live in Babylon still lived in the hope that at some time or other they would see their own land again. Now both of these are instructed to turn their eyes to look to the Messiah. The promise of the Messiah was the stronghold of the faithful long before his coming; they saw his day from far away and were glad (Jn 8:56; Lk 2:25, 38). This invitation to the stronghold speaks the language of the Gospel call. Sinners are prisoners, but they are prisoners of hope; Christ is a stronghold for them.

2. They are assured of God's favor toward them: "I *will render double unto thee* (v. 12), to you: every one of you prisoners of hope." As a pledge of this, God here promises that in the fullness of time (Gal 4:4; Eph 1:10) the Jews will have victory, plenty, and joy in their own land, which will be only a type of more glorious victories, riches, and joys in the kingdom of Christ.

2.1. They will triumph over their enemies. After their return, the Jews were surrounded by enemies on all sides. However, it is promised here that the Lord will save them.

2.1.1. They will be instruments in God's hand to defeat and confound their persecutors: "*I have bent Judah for me*, as my bow of steel; that *bow I have filled with Ephraim* (v. 13) as my arrows, have drawn it up fully bent, until the arrow is at the head." Let them not think, however, that they gain their successes by their own bow, for they themselves are no more than God's bow and his arrows, tools in his hands that he manages as he pleases. The following words explain this: *I have raised up* and roused *thy sons, O Zion! against thy sons, O Greece!* This was fulfilled when, against Antiochus, one of the kings of the Greek monarchy, the people who knew their God were *strong* and *did exploits* (Da 11:32).

2.1.2. God will be commander in chief in every engagement (v. 14): *The Lord shall be seen over them.* Is their army to be mustered and brought onto the field? *The Lord shall blow the trumpet* to gather the forces together and give directions. Whatever initiative the campaign is opened with, God will go out leading *with whirlwinds of the south*—which moved incredibly swiftly—"and before these whirlwinds your sons, O Greece, will be as chaff!" Is the army actually engaged in battle? God's *arrows shall go forth as lightning.* He *sent out his arrows* and *scattered them* (Ps 18:14). This alludes to what God did for Israel in former times when he brought them out of Egypt and into Canaan, and it had its fulfillment partly in the wonderful successes that the Jews had in the time of the Maccabees. It was fulfilled completely, however, in the glorious victories gained by the cross of Christ over Satan and all the powers of darkness. Do their enemies hope to swallow them up? The attempt will be turned back on them, and Israel will *devour* their enemies and *subdue* them *with sling stones. The stones of the brook* (1Sa 17:40) will serve as well as the best artillery weapons when God wishes.

2.2. They will triumph in their God. They will be encouraged and give God the glory for their successes. This is how some read v. 15. *They shall eat* (that is, they will quietly enjoy) what they have gained. In their overwhelming joy, they will offer many sacrifices to the honor of God, so that *they shall fill both the bowls and the corners of the altar* with the fat and blood of their sacrifices. They will triumph in the relationship in which they stand with him, that they are *the flock of his people* and he is their Shepherd and that they are to him *as the stones of a crown* (v. 16), very precious, of great value, and kept under a strong guard. *They shall be lifted up as an ensign upon his land*, like a royal standard displayed as a sign of triumph and joy. *For how great is his goodness, and how great is his beauty!* This is the chorus of the songs with which they will *make a noise* before the Lord (Ps 100:1). This may refer to the Messiah, to Zion's *King that cometh* (v. 9). See *that king in his beauty* (Isa 33:17), who is the *fairest of ten thousand* and *altogether lovely* (SS 5:16). Although in the eyes of the world he had no form or beauty, with the eyes of faith we see how great his beauty is. And *how great is his goodness!* How rich in mercy he is! Here is an example of his goodness to his people: *Corn shall make the young men cheerful, and new wine the maids*, that is, God will bless his people with many fruits of the earth.

CHAPTER 10

The scope of this chapter is to encourage the Jews who have returned with the hope that although they have been under divine rebukes for their negligence in rebuilding the temple and are now surrounded by enemies, God will make them prosperous at home and victorious abroad. 1. They are here told to acknowledge God's hand both in the adversities they suffer and in the comforts they desire (vv. 1–4). 2. They are encouraged to expect strength and success from him in all their struggles (vv. 5–12).

Verses 1–4

Gracious, glorious things were promised to this poor, suffering people in the previous chapter, and God shows them that he expects them to acknowledge him in all their ways (Pr 3:6) and in all his ways toward them.

1. The prophet tells them to turn to God in prayer for rain in the right season. *"Ask you of the Lord rain. Do not pray to the clouds or the stars for rain, but to the Lord."* The former rain fell at the time of sowing, in autumn; the latter rain fell in spring, between March and May, which brought the grain to maturity. If either of these rains failed, things went very badly with that land. In our prayers we must dutifully consider the ways of Providence; we must ask for mercies at their proper time and not expect God to change his usual way and method just for us. *So the Lord shall make bright clouds*—which, although without rain themselves, are still signs that rain is coming—"lightnings," as the margin of v. 1 reads, for *he maketh lightnings for the rain*.

2. He shows them the foolishness of turning to idols (v. 2): *The idols have spoken vanity*. The diviners, who were the prophets of those idols, *have seen a lie*—their visions were sheer deception—and *they have told false dreams*, which proved that they were not from God. They not only gained nothing from their false gods but also lost the favor of the true God, for *they went their way into captivity as a flock* and *were troubled* as scattered sheep are, *because there was no shepherd*. Those who wandered after foreign gods were made to wander into foreign nations.

3. He shows them the hand of God in events, both those that were against them and those that were for them (v. 3). When everything went wrong, it was God who *walked contrary to them* (Lev 26:24, 28, 41) (v. 3): *"My anger was kindled against the shepherds*, who should have fed the flock but instead neglected it and starved it. I was displeased with the evil magistrates and ministers, the idol-shepherds." The exile in Babylon was a sign of God's

anger against them; in it he *punished the goats* as well, those of the flock who were dirty and troublesome. When things began to change for the better, it was God who made them turn. "He has now *visited his flock* with favor and has made them *as his goodly horse in the battle*, managed and used them, as a person does the horse they are riding on; God has made them valuable in themselves and formidable to those around them, *as his goodly* (proud) *horse*."

4. He shows them that every created thing is to them what God makes it to be (v. 4): *Out of him came forth the corner* (cornerstone), *out of him the nail* (tent peg). *Out of him* came the combined forces of their enemies; nor could they have had such power unless it had been given them from above (Jn 19:11). Similarly, all the power that worked for them was derived from him. Out of him came *the cornerstone* of the building, the power of magistrates, which keeps the different parts of the state together. Out of him came *the nail* that fixed the state (Isa 22:23), the *nail in his holy place* (Ezr 9:8). Out of him came *the battle-bow*, the military power, and out of him *every oppressor*.

Verses 5–12

Here are precious promises made to the people of God, promises that look further than the state of the Jews and certainly have reference to the spiritual Israel of God, the Gospel church, and all true believers.

1. They will have God's favor and presence and will be acknowledged and accepted by him. This is the foundation of all the rest: *The Lord is with them* (v. 5). Again (v. 6), *I have mercy upon them*. All their honor and joy derive purely from God's mercy, and just as mercy presupposes misery, so it also excludes merit. They *shall be as though I had not cast them off*. This is how great God's favor is to returning, repenting sinners; they are admitted into such fellowship, and he gives them such freedom, that they are *as though they had never been cast off. I am the Lord their God*, according to the original contract, the covenant made with their ancestors.

2. They will be victorious over their enemies (v. 5): *They shall be as mighty men*, who are both strong in body and bold in spirit, powerful warriors. They will, as mighty warriors, *tread down their enemies in the battle because the Lord is with them*. Some would argue that they may sit still and do nothing because the Lord is with them, since he can and will do everything. No; God's gracious presence with us to help us must not replace, but must motivate, our endeavors to help ourselves. Then *the riders on horses shall be confounded*. The preachers of the Gospel of Christ went out to *war a good warfare* (1Ti 1:18); they charged bravely, because God was with them. The *riders on horses* that opposed them *were confounded*. But where do they get all this power from? It is in the Lord, and in the power of his might (Eph 6:10), that they are so (v. 6). God saves us by strengthening us, and he works out our happiness by working in us to do our duty (Php 2:13).

3. Those of them who are dispersed will be gathered together into one body (v. 6): *I will bring them again to place them*, bring them from other lands to put them in their own land. To this end (v. 8), *I will hiss for them*, or signal to them, as a shepherd uses his pipe to whistle and call together his sheep, which *know his voice* (Jn 10:4), and so *I will gather them* (Jer 32:37). *I will gather them, for I have redeemed them*. This promise has its spiritual fulfillment in the gathering in of precious souls out of a slavery that is worse than that in Egypt or Assyria and in the bringing of them into the glorious liberties of the children of God (Ro 8:21). All the Promised Land is theirs,

even Gilead and Lebanon. How will a people so dispersed be gathered together? The difficulties seem insuperable, but they will be overcome as effectively as those that lay in the way of their rescue from Egypt and their entrance into Canaan: *He shall pass through the sea with affliction* (v. 11), as he once before passed through the Red Sea. *All the deeps of the river shall dry up*, as Jordan did to make way for Israel's passage into the good land that God had given them. Does *the pride of Assyria* stand in the way of their rescue? The One who sets boundaries to the *proud waves of the sea* (Job 38:11) will restrain it. Does the scepter of Egypt oppose it? That will *depart away*. When the Gospel church was to be gathered out of all nations by the preaching of the Gospel, great opposition was raised against it by the enraged powers of earth and hell. But God's power became *mighty to the pulling down of strongholds* (2Co 10:4) and the conversion and salvation of thousands. Then the sea fled, and Jordan was *driven back at the presence of the Lord*.

4. They will greatly multiply, and the church, that new world, will be refilled (v. 8): *They shall increase as they have increased* formerly in Egypt. *In Judah* only *God* had been *known*, and his *name was great* only *in Israel* (Ps 76:1); it was only there that he revealed his *statutes* and *judgments*. However, in Gospel times, that place will be much too restricted; the church's tent must be enlarged. Then *I will sow them among the people* (v. 9). Their scattering will be like the scattering of seed in the ground, not to bury it, but to increase it. The Jews who came from all parts to worship at Jerusalem took from there the Gospel light and fire to their own countries, as those in Ac 2 and the Ethiopian eunuch did (Ac 8:26–40). Their own synagogues in the different cities of the Gentiles were the first to receive the apostles and their preaching. This is how God *sowed them among the people*, and he took care that they would *remember him* and mention his name *in far countries*. By keeping up the knowledge of God among them as he had revealed himself in the Old Testament, they would be readier to admit the knowledge of Christ as he has revealed himself in the New Testament.

5. God himself will be both their strength and their song (Ex 15:2; Ps 118:14). They will be comforted in him, and they will enjoy abundant satisfaction (v. 7). When we resolutely resist, and so overcome, our spiritual enemies, our hearts rejoice. Moreover, along with graces, joys will be spread: *Their children shall see it and be glad, and their hearts* also *shall rejoice in the Lord*. It is good to acquaint children with the delights of religious faith at an early age, making its services pleasant, so that, having learned early in life to rejoice in the Lord, they may wholeheartedly cling to him (Ac 11:23). If God strengthens us (v. 12), we must stir and must *walk up and down* in all the duties of the Christian life. For us to live must be Christ, and *whatever we do in word or deed*, we must *do all in the name of the Lord Jesus* (Col 3:17), so that we do not receive the strengthening grace of God in vain. See Ps 80:17–18.

CHAPTER 11

Here is: 1. A prediction of the destruction that will come on the Jewish nation (vv. 1–3). 2. The putting of the nation into the hands of the Messiah. 2.1. He is charged with the custody of that flock (vv. 4–6). 2.2. He undertakes it and rules it (vv. 7–8). 2.3. When he finds it corrupt, he gives it up (v. 9), breaks his shepherd's staff (vv. 10–11), resents the indignities and contempt shown to him (vv. 12–13), and then breaks his other staff (v. 14).

2.4. He turns them over to the hands of foolish shepherds, who, instead of preventing their ruin, will complete it, and both the blind leaders and the blind followers fall together into the ditch (Mt 15:14) (vv. 15–17).

Verses 1–3

In dark and figurative expressions, as is usual in the Scriptural predictions of things far off, the destruction of Jerusalem and of the Jewish church and nation is foretold here, which our Lord Jesus, when the time was near, prophesied about very clearly. We have here:

1. Preparation made for that destruction (v. 1): "*Open thy doors, O Lebanon!* You would not open them to let your king in. Now you must open them to let your ruin in." Some understand Lebanon to refer to the temple, which was built of cedars from Lebanon. It was burned down with fire by the Romans, and its gates were forced open by the rage of the soldiers. Others understand it to refer to Jerusalem, or rather the whole land of Canaan, to which Lebanon was an inlet in the north. All will be exposed to the invader, and the cedars, the powerful and famous warriors, will be devoured, which must have put fear into those of lesser rank (v. 2). If *the cedars* have *fallen*, let the *fir tree howl* (pine tree wail). How can the slender pine trees stand if stately cedars fall? Let the *oaks of Bashan*, which are exposed to every injury, *howl, for the forest of the vintage* (or the flourishing vineyard, which used to be guarded with special care) has come down, or let them howl when the *defensed forests*, such as Lebanon was, have been cut down.

2. Mourning expressed for the destruction (v. 3): *There is a voice of howling*. Those who have fallen wail in grief and shame, and those who see their own turn coming wail for fear. The leaders, especially, receive the fear with the greatest confusion. Those leaders did the work of shepherds, and as such they should have protected the flock that God had committed to their charge; it is the duty of both rulers and priests. However, they were like *young lions*, which themselves terrorized the flock. The *young lions howl*, for *the pride of Jordan is spoiled*. The pride of Jordan was the lush thickets on the banks, in which the lions rested; when the river overflowed, the lions came up from these thickets, as we read in Jer 49:19, and they came up roaring.

Verses 4–14

The prophet is made a type of Christ here, as the prophet Isaiah sometimes was, and the scope of these verses is to show that *for judgment Christ came into this world* (Jn 9:39), for judgment to the Jewish church and nation, which, about the time of his coming, were corrupted by the worldliness and hypocrisy of their rulers. Christ would have healed them, but they did not want to be healed (Jer 51:9). Notice:

1. The desperate case of the Jewish church under the tyranny of their own governors (v. 5). In Zechariah's time we find the rulers and the nobles justly rebuked for *exacting usury of their brethren* (Ne 5:7, 15). In Christ's time the Sadducees, who were deists, corrupted their judgments. The Pharisees, who were superstitious hypocrites, corrupted their morals by setting aside the commandments of God (Mt 15:16). This is how they killed the sheep of the flock, selling them. They showed great disrespect for God by giving him thanks; they said, *Blessed be the Lord, for I am rich*, as if their prospering in their evil showed that God was himself supporting their unjust practices. Christ had compassion on *the multitude because they fainted and were scattered abroad, as if they had no shepherd*

(Mt 9:36)—as in reality they had worse than none. Things are bad for a church when its pastors can look on the ignorant, the foolish, the wicked, and the weak without pity.

2. The sentence of God's wrath passed on them for their stupidity. Just as their shepherds did not pity them, so they did not grieve for themselves; God therefore said (v. 6), "*I will no more pity the inhabitants of the land.*" Those who are willing to have their consciences oppressed by those who *teach for doctrines the commandments of men* (Mt 15:9) are often punished by oppression in their civil interests, and justly so, for they forfeit their own rights if they tamely give up God's rights. He will hand them over to oppressors, *everyone into his neighbour's hand.* Everyone will be given over *into the hand of his king,* whom they chose to submit to rather than to Christ.

3. A test administered to see whether their ruin could be prevented by sending Christ among them as a shepherd (Mt 21:37). Various prophets had spoken about him as the *Shepherd of Israel* (Isa 40:11; Eze 34:23). He himself told the Pharisees that he was the *Shepherd of the sheep* (Jn 10:1–2, 11), and in saying this he apparently referred to this passage, where we have:

3.1. The responsibility he received from his Father to see what could be done with this flock: *Thus saith the Lord my God. Feed the flock of the slaughter* (v. 4). The Jews were God's flock, but they were the *flock of slaughter,* for their enemies had killed them all day long (Ps 44:22; Ro 8:36).

3.2. His acceptance of this responsibility (v. 7). Christ would care for these lost sheep; he would go about among them, *teaching* and *healing even you, O poor of the flock.* His disciples, who were his constant companions, came from the poor of the flock. *I took unto me two staves,* shepherd's staffs; other shepherds have one staff, but Christ had two, showing his care for people, care for both their bodies and their souls. David speaks about God's *rod* and his *staff* (Ps 23:4), a correcting rod and a supporting staff. One staff was called *Beauty* (Favor), representing the Temple; the other was called *Bands* (Union), representing the civil state of the nation. Christ, in his Gospel and in all he did, considered the advancement of both their civil and their sacred interests. The chief Shepherd (1Pe 5:4) *fed the flock* (v. 7), and he removed those undershepherds who were corrupt (v. 8): *Three shepherds I cut off in one month.*

4. Their enmity to Christ. He came to the sheep of his own pasture (Ps 95:7; 100:3; Jn 1:11); it might have been expected that between him and them there would be devotion; but they behaved so badly that *his soul loathed them,* "was straitened" toward them, as it may read. Whatever separation there is between God and human beings, it begins on the human side.

5. Christ's rejection of them as incurable. Here we have:

5.1. The sentence of their rejection passed (v. 9): "*Then said I, I will not feed you.* What will be attacked by the wolf, let it be attacked. Let the rest forget their own gentle nature so completely that they *eat the flesh of one another;* let these sheep fight like dogs."

5.2. A sign of it given (v. 10): *I took my staff, even Beauty, and cut it asunder* (broke it). The breaking of this staff represented the breaking of God's covenant that he had *made with all the people,* the distinctive covenant made with all the tribes of *Israel.* When Christ told them clearly that the *kingdom of God* would be *taken from them* and *given to another people,* he then broke the *staff of Beauty* (Favor) (Mt 21:43). Although Jerusalem and the Jewish nation held out forty years longer, it is from that

day that we may reckon the staff of Favor to have been broken (v. 11).

5.3. A further reason given for their rejection. It was said before, *Their souls abhorred him* (v. 8), and here we have an example of it, their buying and selling him for thirty pieces of silver. This is foretold here in somewhat obscure terms, for otherwise the clarity of the prophecy might prevent its fulfillment. The Shepherd comes to them for his wages (v. 12): "*If you think good, give me my price*; you are weary of it, and so pay me off and discharge me, and *if not, forbear.*" Compare with this what Christ said to Judas when Judas was going to sell him: "*What thou doest do quickly*; let them either accept the bargain or leave it" (Jn 13:27). They valued him at *thirty pieces of silver.* It was the ordinary price of a slave (Ex 21:32). Because the silver was in no way proportionate to his worth, it was *thrown to the potter* with contempt: "Let him take it to buy clay with." So the prophet *cast the thirty pieces of silver to the potter in the house of the Lord.* There is a particular fulfillment of this in the account of Christ's sufferings (Mt 27:9–10). *Thirty pieces of silver* was the very sum for which Christ was sold to the chief priests; the money was spent on buying *the potter's field* (Mt 27:7).

5.4. The completing of the Jews' rejection in the breaking of the other staff (v. 14). The breaking of the first staff represented the ruin of their church by breaking the covenant between God and them—that defaced their *beauty.* The breaking of this staff represented the ruin of their state by breaking the brotherhood, the family bond, between Judah and Israel. They would be crumbled into different parties and factions; this was how divided their kingdom was: it would be *brought to desolation.* Nothing ruins a people so inevitably as the breaking of *the staff of Bands* (Union), the weakening of family bonds among them.

Verses 15–17

Having shown this people being justly abandoned by the Good Shepherd (Jn 10:14), God here shows their further misery in being shamefully abused by a foolish shepherd. The prophet himself must impersonate this pretended shepherd (v. 15): *Take unto thee the instruments* or equipment *of a foolish shepherd,* such a coat, bag, and staff as a foolish shepherd would appear in, for such a shepherd will be set over them (v. 16), one who, instead of protecting them, will cause them trouble. The description given here of the foolish shepherd fits the description Christ gives of the teachers of the law and Pharisees (Mt 23:2). The people will be under the tyranny of unmerciful rulers, and they will be deceived by false Christs and false prophets, as our Savior foretold (Mt 24:5). Notice:

1. What a curse this foolish shepherd will be to the people (v. 16). He will not *visit those that are cut off* (not care for the lost), will take no care of the *young ones,* nor *heal* what was *broken,* but leave it to die of its bruises, when some small act, in time, would have saved it. He will never do anything to *support the weak* and comfort *the feebleminded* (1Th 5:14). Their shepherds will indulge themselves, *eating of the flesh of the fat* (eating the meat of the choice sheep); they will make sure they themselves have the best, *serving their own bellies* (Ro 16:18). But they will be very cruel to the flock. When they are in a rage against any of the flock, they will *tear their* very *claws in pieces* by driving them too hard.

2. What a curse this foolish shepherd will bring on himself (v. 17): *Woe to the idol* (worthless) *shepherd.* His doom is that *the sword* of God's justice will be *upon his arm* and

his right eye, so that he will completely lose the use of both. This was fulfilled when Christ said to the Pharisees, *I have come that those who see may be made blind* (Jn 9:39).

CHAPTER 12

In Gal 4:25–26, the apostle Paul distinguishes between Jerusalem which now is, and is in bondage with her children—*the Jewish church, who rejected Christ—and* Jerusalem that is from above, that is free, and is the mother of us all, *the Christian church, the spiritual Jerusalem. In the previous chapter we read the fate of the former, and in this chapter we have many precious promises (2Pe 1:4) made in the Gospel Jerusalem by the One who (v. 1) declares his power to fulfill them. It is promised: 1. That the attempts of the church's enemies against her will be to their own ruin (vv. 2–4, 6). 2. That the endeavors of the church's friends and supporters for her good will be successful (v. 5). 3. That God will strengthen the lowliest and weakest members of his church and work salvation for them (vv. 7–8). 4. That as a pledge, he will pour out on them a spirit of prayer and repentance (vv. 9–14). These promises were of use then to the devout Jews who lived in the troublesome times under Antiochus and other oppressors, and Christians in every age must continue to avail themselves of them to guide their prayers and encourage their hopes for the Gospel church.*

Verses 1–8

Here is:

1. The title of this charter of promises made to God's Israel; it is the *burden* (oracle) *of the word of the Lord,* a divine prediction. It is a heavy *burden* to all the church's enemies. However, it is *for Israel,* for their comfort and benefit.

2. The title of the One who grants this charter: he is the Creator of the world and our Creator and so has irresistible power. He *stretches out the heavens* and keeps them stretched out *like a curtain,* and he will do so until the end comes. He *lays the foundation of the earth* and keeps it fixed on its own axis, even though it is *founded on the seas* (Ps 24:1–2)—indeed, though it is *hung upon nothing* (Job 26:7). He *forms the spirit of man within him.* He *made us these souls* (Jer 38:16). He not only breathed the breath of life into the first human being (Ge 2:7); he still breathes that life into every human being.

3. The promises by which the church will be kept safe.

3.1. Whatever attacks the enemies of the church may make on her purity or peace will certainly result in their own confusion. Jerusalem is safe, and it is those who fight against it who are in danger. This is illustrated here by three comparisons:

3.1.1. *Jerusalem* will be *a cup of trembling* to all who besiege it (v. 2). In this way, Alexander the Great was struck with dismay when he met Jaddus the high priest and was therefore deterred from offering any violence to Jerusalem. When Sennacherib besieged Judah and Jerusalem, he found them to be such a cup of stupefying wine as to put all his warriors asleep (Ps 76:5–6).

3.1.2. *Jerusalem* will be *a burdensome stone* to all who attempt to remove it or take it away (v. 3). Those who want to advance the kingdom of sin in the world look at Jerusalem, the church of God, as the great obstacle to their plans, and they must get rid of it, but they cannot move it. God will keep a church in the world in spite of it; it is *built upon a rock* (Mt 16:18) and is like *Mount Zion* (Ps 125:1). This *stone, cut out of the mountain without*

hands, will break in pieces all that burden themselves with it, like that stone that *smote the image* (struck the statue) in Nebuchadnezzar's dream (Da 2:34). Our Savior seems to allude to these words when he speaks of himself as a heavy stone to those who will not have him as their foundation stone, as a stone that will *fall upon them and grind them to powder* (Mt 21:44).

3.1.3. The leaders of Judah will be like *a hearth of fire among the wood and a torch of fire in a sheaf* among their enemies, like a firepot in a woodpile, like a flaming torch among sheaves (v. 6). Those who strive against them will find that it is like the opposition of briers and thorns to a consuming fire (Isa 27:4). The fire will go through them and burn them up. The enemies thought they would be like water to this fire, but God will make them like wood—in fact, like sheaves of corn, which burn up more easily—to this fire. The persecutors of the early church found this fulfilled in it, as can be seen from the eventual confession of Julian the apostate: "Thou hast overcome me, O thou Galilean!" "If you are weary of life, persecute Christians" was once a proverb.

3.2. God will discourage the church's enemies and frustrate their plans (v. 4). The church's infantry will be too strong for the enemy's cavalry.

3.3. Jerusalem will be repopulated and replenished (v. 6). God's people will have a new Jerusalem on the same foundation, the same ground. They did this after their return from exile, but the Gospel church is a Jerusalem inhabited *in its own place;* since the Gospel is to be preached throughout the world, Jerusalem may call each place its own.

3.4. The inhabitants of Jerusalem will be enabled to defend themselves under divine protection (v. 8). God will not only be *a wall of fire* around the city but also surround individual people with his favor *as with a shield* (Ps 5:12). He does this by giving them strength and courage to help themselves. In that day the weakest inhabitants of Jerusalem *shall be as David,* as skillful and strong, as useful to Jerusalem in guarding it as David himself was in founding it. *The house of David shall be as God,* that is, *as the angel of the Lord, before them.* Zerubbabel is now the highest branch of the house of David; he will be endowed with wisdom and grace. He will go in front of the people as an angel (Ex 23:20). However, this was to have its complete fulfillment in Christ; now the house of David looked small and lowly, and its glory was eclipsed, but in Christ the house of David shone more brightly than ever.

3.5. There will be a very good understanding between the city and the country. *The governors of Judah,* the magistrates of the country, will think honorably of the citizens, *the inhabitants of Jerusalem.* Things are going well with a kingdom when its leaders know how to value its good people. God will put a special honor on Judah and so save them from the contempt of their brothers and sisters. God says (v. 4), *I will open my eyes upon the house of Judah;* in fact (v. 7), *the Lord shall save the tents of Judah first.* Those who live in tents lie most exposed, but God will rescue them before rescuing those who live in Jerusalem. Courtiers and citizens should not despise country people, those whom God *opens his eyes upon* and who are *first saved.* This promise has a further reference to the Gospel church, in which no difference will be made between high and low, rich and poor, slave and free (Gal 3:28), circumcision and uncircumcision (Gal 6:15).

Verses 9–14

The *day* spoken of here is the day of Jerusalem's defense and rescue, that glorious day, which, if it refers to the successes the Jews had against their enemies in the time of the Maccabees, certainly looks further as well, to the Gospel day, to Christ's victories over the powers of darkness and the great salvation he has brought.

1. A glorious work of God is to be carried out for his people: *I will seek to destroy all the nations that come against Jerusalem* (v. 9). Nations come against Jerusalem, but they will all be destroyed. At Christ's first coming, he *sought to destroy him that had the power of death* (Heb 2:14), and he did destroy him. At his second coming, he will complete the destruction of those nations, and *death* itself will be *swallowed up in* that *victory* (1Co 15:54).

2. A gracious work of God is to be carried out in his people. When he seeks to destroy their enemies, he *will pour upon them the Spirit of grace and supplication* (v. 10). When God intends to give great mercy to his people, the first thing he does is to set them praying. However, this promise has reference to the graces of the Spirit given to all believers (Isa 44:3): *I will pour my Spirit upon thy seed*; this was fulfilled when *Jesus was glorified* (Jn 7:39). Notice here:

2.1. On whom these blessings will be poured out:

2.1.1. *On the house of David*, on the leaders, for they are no more, and no better, than the grace of God makes them.

2.1.2. *On the inhabitants of Jerusalem*, the ordinary people. The church is Jerusalem, the heavenly Jerusalem (Gal 4:26); all true believers, who have their citizenship in heaven (Php 3:20), are inhabitants of this Jerusalem, and this promise belongs to them.

2.2. What these blessings are: *I will pour upon them the Spirit*. He *will pour his Spirit upon them*:

2.2.1. As a *Spirit of grace* (v. 10), to sanctify us and make us gracious.

2.2.2. As a *Spirit of supplications*, instructing and helping us in the privilege of prayer.

2.3. What their effects will be: *I will pour upon them the Spirit of grace*. One would have thought it would follow, "and they will rejoice," but the effect of the gift is that they will mourn, for there is a mourning that will end in rejoicing and bring a blessing as an inheritance. This mourning is a fruit of the Spirit, a sign of a work of grace in the soul. It is a mourning based on a vision of Christ: *They shall look on him whom they have pierced, and shall mourn for him*. It is foretold that Christ will be pierced, and this Scripture is quoted as having been fulfilled when Christ's side was pierced on the cross; see Jn 19:37. He is spoken of as One whom we have pierced; it is spoken primarily of the Jews, but it is true of all of us as sinners. Those who truly repent of their sin look on Christ as the One who was pierced for their sins and is pierced by them. They will mourn for sin *as one mourns for an only son*. The sorrow of parents for a child, for a firstborn, is natural; it is private and deep. Such are the sorrows of a true penitent, flowing purely from love to Christ above anyone else. It will be *like the mourning of Hadadrimmon in the valley of Megiddon*, where good King Josiah was killed, for whom there was a general mourning (v. 11). It was for this reason that they cried out, *The crown has fallen from our head. Woe unto us, for we have sinned!* (La 5:16). Christ is our King; our sins caused his death, and that is why they should be the cause of our sorrow. Not only will there be a mourning of *the land* by its representatives in a general assembly (as in Jdg 2:5, when the place was called *Bochim*, "A place of weepers"); it will also spread all through the land. *Every family apart* will mourn (v. 12), *all the families that remain* (v. 14). Four different clans are here mentioned as examples to others:

• Two of them are royal clans: the *house of David*, in Solomon, and the *house of Nathan*, another son of David (Lk 3:27–31).
• Two of them are sacred clans (v. 13): *the family of the house of Levi*, which was God's tribe, and in it especially the family of Shimei, which was a branch of the tribe of Levi (1Ch 6:17). Just as the civil leaders must mourn for the sins of the magistracy, so the priests must mourn for the *iniquity of the holy things*.

CHAPTER 13

We have here: 1. Some further promises relating to Gospel times: a promise of the forgiveness of sins (v. 1), a promise of the reformation of lives (v. 2), and, especially, a promise of the silencing of false prophets (vv. 2–6). 2. A clear prediction of the sufferings of Christ and the dispersion of his disciples (v. 7), of the destruction of the greater part of the Jewish nation not long afterward (v. 8), and of the purifying of a remnant of them (v. 9).

Verses 1–6

Behold, the Lamb of God taking away the sin of the world (Jn 1:29).

1. He takes away the guilt of sin by the blood of his cross (v. 1): *In that day*, in the Gospel day, *there shall be a fountain opened*, that is, provision will be made to cleanse from the defilement of sin all those who truly repent. *In that day*, when the Spirit of grace is poured out to set them mourning for their sins, their consciences will be purified and pacified by the *blood of Christ, which cleanses from all sin* (1Jn 1:7). This *fountain opened* is the pierced side of Jesus Christ, spoken of just before (12:10), for it was from there that *blood and water* came (Jn 19:34), both for cleansing. Sin is uncleanness; it defiles the mind and conscience and renders us repugnant to God and uneasy in ourselves, unfit for the service of God. There is enough mercy in God and enough merit in Christ to forgive the greatest sins and sinners (1Co 6:11). Under the law there were a bronze basin and a bronze Sea to wash in; those were merely furnishings, but we have a fountain, overflowing and always flowing. It is *a fountain opened*, opened not only to *the house of David* but also to *the inhabitants of Jerusalem*, to the poor and lowly as well as the rich and great.

2. He takes away the controlling power of sin by the power of his grace. Those who are washed are sanctified as well as justified. On that day:

2.1. Idolatry will be completely abolished, and the people of the Jews will be effectively healed of their inclination to idolatry (v. 2): *I will cut off the names of the idols out of the land*. This was fulfilled in the deep-rooted aversion that the Jews had to idols and idolatry after the exile, an aversion they still keep to this day. It was also fulfilled in the conversion of many people to the faith of Christ, by which they were taken away from making an idol of the ceremonial law.

2.2. False prophecy will also be brought to an end. *I will cause the prophets and the unclean spirit to pass out of the land* (v. 2). The Devil is an *unclean* spirit, and he has his prophets.

2.2.1. It is foretold here that false prophets will be brought to punishment even by their closest relatives (v. 3). Holy zeal for God and godliness will make us hate sin most in, and dread temptation most from, those whom naturally we love best.

2.2.2. False prophets will themselves be convicted of their sin (v. 4): *The prophets shall be ashamed every one of his vision*, because God has by his grace awakened their consciences and shown them their error or because the event disproves their predictions. Consequently, they will no longer *wear a rough garment*, or *garment of hair*, as the true prophets used to do, in imitation of Elijah. Let people be really as good as they seem to be, but not seem to be better than they really are. The pretender, as a true penitent, *shall say, "I am no prophet* (v. 5), as I have claimed to be. *I am a husbandman* (farmer); *I* was never taught by God to prophesy, but *taught of man to keep cattle."* We must show the truth of our repentance by returning to our duty, even though it is extremely humbling for us. When a false prophet drops his claims, everybody will be surprised, and some will ask, "Haven't you been beaten into this acknowledgment? Was it not *the rod and reproof* that made you so wise (Pr 29:15)?" He will acknowledge, "Yes, it was; these are the *wounds with which I was wounded in the house of my friends*, who bound me and brought me to my senses." Subdued by stripes, he had the good sense and frankness to acknowledge that those who had wounded him in this way to restore him were his real friends. Some good commentators think these are the words of Christ, who was wounded in his hands when they were nailed to the cross. After his resurrection, he still had the marks of these wounds. Here he is saying how he came by them; he received them as a false prophet, for the chief priests called him a deceiver (Mt 27:63), but he received them in the house of the Jews, who should have been his friends.

Verses 7–9

Here is a prophecy:

1. Of the sufferings of Christ, who was to be pierced (12:10) and was to be the fountain opened (v. 1). *Awake, O sword! against my Shepherd* (v. 7). These are the words of God the Father, giving commission to the sword of his justice to wake up against his Son when he had voluntarily *made his soul an offering for sin*, for it *pleased the Lord to bruise him* and *put him to grief*, and *he was stricken, smitten of God, and afflicted* (Isa 53:4, 10). Notice:

1.1. What he calls him. "As God, he is *my fellow*," for he thought it *no robbery to be equal with God* (Php 2:6). He and *the Father* are one (Jn 10:30). "As Mediator, he is *my Shepherd*, the Shepherd who was to lay down his life for the sheep (Jn 10:15)."

1.2. How he treats him: *Awake, O sword! against him.* If he is to be a sacrifice, he must be killed, for without the shedding of blood, the lifeblood, there is no forgiveness of sins (Heb 9:22). The command is given not to a rod to correct him, but to a sword to kill him, for God *spared not his own Son* (Ro 8:32).

2. Of the dispersion of the disciples at that point: *Smite* (strike) *the Shepherd, and the sheep shall be scattered.* Our Lord Jesus himself declared this to have been fulfilled when *all his disciples were offended because of him* in the night on which he was betrayed (Mt 26:31). They all *forsook him and fled.* They were *scattered everyone to his own, and left him alone* (Jn 16:32). Some think this refers to Christ as the *Shepherd* of the Jewish nation; he was struck; they themselves struck him. They were therefore dispersed among the nations. The words *I will turn my hand upon the little ones* may be understood either as a threat—just as Christ suffered, so will his disciples—or as a promise that God will gather Christ's scattered disciples together again and meet them in Galilee.

3. Of the rejection and ruin of the unfaithful Jews (v. 8), and this will have its fulfillment in the destruction of the corrupt and hypocritical part of the church.

4. Of the reformation of the chosen remnant, who believed, and of the Christian church in general (v. 9): *The third part shall be left.* When Jerusalem and Judea were destroyed, all the Christians in that country, having received the warning Christ gave them to *flee to the mountains* (Mt 24:16), fended for their own safety and were sheltered in a city called *Pella* on the other side of Jordan. And so we have here first the trials and then the triumphs of the Christian church. *I will bring* that *third part through the fire* of affliction *and will refine* and try them as *silver and gold are refined and tried* (v. 9). This was fulfilled in the persecutions of the early church, the *fiery trial* (1Pe 4:12). Their fellowship with God is their triumph: *They shall call on my name, and I will hear them.* They will write to God by prayer and receive from him favorable answers. Their covenant with God is their triumph: "*I will say, 'It is my people,* whom I have chosen and loved and will acknowledge,' *and they shall say, 'The Lord is my God,* all-sufficient to me.'"

CHAPTER 14

This chapter speaks of the day of the Lord that cometh *(v. 1) and repeats seven times the phrase* in that day, *a phrase that occurred often in the previous two chapters as well. What that day is that is referred to here is uncertain. Some passages here seem to look as far forward as Gospel times. The Day of the Lord brings both judgment and mercy, judgment to the church's enemies and persecutors, and mercy to his church. 1. The gates of hell are here threatening the church (vv. 1–2), but they do not overcome it (Mt 16:18). 2. The power of heaven appears for the church (vv. 3, 5). 3. The events concerning the church are represented (vv. 6–7) as turning out well in the end. 4. The spreading of knowledge is foretold, as is the establishment of the Gospel kingdom in the world (vv. 8–9), which will be the enlargement and setting up of another Jerusalem (vv. 10–11). 5. Those who fought against Jerusalem will be judged (vv. 12–15), as will those who neglect his worship there (vv. 17–19). 6. It is promised that a great number of people will turn to the church, and there will be great purity and godliness in it (vv. 16, 20–21).*

Verses 1–7

God's providences toward his church are described here as strangely changing and strangely mixed.

1. They are strangely changing. Sometimes the tide is high and is strongly against them, but now it turns.

1.1. God here appears against Jerusalem. When the *day of the Lord comes* (v. 1), Jerusalem must pass through the refining fire. The *city shall be taken by the* Romans, the houses will be ransacked, and *the women* will *be ravished. One half of the city* will then be taken *into captivity*, to be sold or enslaved.

1.2. He immediately changes his ways and appears to support Jerusalem, for although judgment begins with the house of God, it does not end there.

1.2.1. A remnant will be spared. *One half shall go into captivity*, from where they may be drawn back, *and the residue of the people shall not* be destroyed *from the city.* Many of the Jews will receive the Gospel and so will prevent their being cut off from the city of God, his church on earth.

1.2.2. Their cause will be pleaded against their enemies (v. 3): when God has used these nations as a scourge to his people, he will *go forth* and *fight against them* by his judgments. The Roman Empire never flourished after the destruction of Jerusalem as it had done before, but in many instances God fought against it.

1.2.3. Though Jerusalem and the temple are destroyed, God will still have a church in the world, into which Gentiles will be admitted and with whom the faithful Jews will be joined (vv. 4–5).

1.2.3.1. God will carefully inspect Jerusalem, even when its enemies are devastating it: *His feet shall stand in that day upon the mount of Olives* (Mk 13:3). When the refiner puts his gold into the furnace, he stands by to see that it is not damaged; so when Jerusalem, God's gold, is to be refined, he will stand by *upon the mount of Olives*; this was literally fulfilled when our Lord Jesus was often on this mountain. From there he *ascended up into heaven* (Ac 1:12). It was the last place on which his feet stood on this earth.

1.2.3.2. The wall of hostility between Jews and Gentiles will be removed (Eph 2:14). By the destruction of Jerusalem this mountain will be caused to *cleave in the midst* (split in two), and the Gentiles will be made one with the Jews by the breaking down of this *middle wall of partition* (Eph 2:14). The ceremonial law was a great mountain in the way of the Jews' conversion, but it was leveled before Christ and his Gospel.

1.2.3.3. A new and living way will be opened to the New Jerusalem (Heb 10:20). Because the mountain is divided, with one half *toward the north* and the other half *toward the south*, there will be *a very great valley*, a broad way of communication between Jerusalem and the Gentile world, through which the Gentiles will have free access to the Gospel Jerusalem, and the word of the Lord that *goes forth from Jerusalem* (Isa 2:3) will have *a free course* (2Th 3:1) into the Gentile world.

1.2.3.4. Those of the Jews who believe will come in and join the Gentiles in the Gospel church. The *valley of the mountains* (v. 5) is the Gospel church, to which there were added from the Jews daily *such as should be saved* (Ac 2:47). God *makes his mountains a way* (Isa 49:11) by making them a valley. This valley will extend to those who are now separated from God, for the Gentiles, who are far away, will be brought near the Jews (Eph 2:17), who are a *people near unto him*, and both will have mutual access to each other and joint access to God as a Father by one Spirit (Eph 2:18).

1.2.3.5. They will flee to *the valley of the mountains*, to the Gospel church, under terrible apprehensions of their danger from the curse of the Law.

1.2.4. God will appear in his glory to accomplish all this: *The Lord my God shall come, and all the saints with thee* (v. 5), which may refer to his coming to destroy Jerusalem, or to destroy the enemies of Jerusalem, or to his coming to set up his kingdom in the world, which is called the *coming of the Son of Man* (Mt 24:37), or to his last coming at the end of time. Whichever interpretation we adopt, it teaches us that the Lord will come. Some think that this may be read as a prayer: *Yet, O Lord my God! come, and bring all the saints with thee.*

2. God's providences appear here strangely mixed (vv. 6–7): *In that day* of the Lord the *light shall not be clear nor dark, not day* or *night*, but *at evening time it shall be light.* Some think this refers to all the time from then to the Messiah's coming; the Jewish church had neither perfect peace nor constant trouble, but a cloudy day. However, it may be taken more generally to describe the way God usually administers the kingdom of both providence and grace. It is so with the church of God in this world; where the Sun of righteousness has risen (Mal 4:2), it cannot be dark night, but neither will it be clear day this side of heaven. It *shall be one day which shall be known to the Lord* (v. 7). This shows beauty and harmony in such mixed events; there is one and the same intention in everything. *At evening time it shall be light*; it will be clear light, and no longer dark. We are sure of it in the next world, and we hope for it in this world—at *evening time*, when things are at their worst and the case of the church is most deplorable.

Verses 8–15

Here are:

1. Blessings promised to Jerusalem, the Gospel Jerusalem, on the day of the Messiah, and to all the earth.

1.1. Jerusalem will be a spring of living waters to the world; it was made so when the Spirit was poured out on the apostles there, and the word of the Lord spread from there to the surrounding nations (v. 8). It was the honor of Jerusalem that *thence the word of the Lord went forth* (Isa 2:3). Half of these waters will go *toward the former* (eastern) *sea* (i.e., the Dead Sea) and *half toward the hinder* (western) *sea* (i.e., the Mediterranean), as all rivers bend their course toward some sea or other, some eastward, others westward. The Gospel will spread to all parts of the world. The knowledge of God will spread every way and every day. In *summer and in winter it shall be.* Such divine power accompanies these living waters that they will not dry up, either by droughts in summer or by frosts in winter.

1.2. The kingdom of God on earth will be a universal and united kingdom (v. 9). *The Lord shall be King over all the earth. There shall be one Lord, and his name one.* All false gods will be abandoned, and all false ways of worship abolished, and just as God will be the center of their unity, so the Scripture will be the rule of their unity.

1.3. The land of Judea, and Jerusalem, its mother city, will be repaired and taken under the special protection of heaven (vv. 10–11). Some think this describes a special favor to the Jewish people, but it should rather be understood as referring figuratively to the Gospel church, of which Judah and Jerusalem was a type. The church will be like a fruitful country, abounding in all the rich products of the soil. The whole land of Judea, naturally uneven and hilly, will be *turned as a plain*; it will become a smooth, level valley, from Gibeah, its farthest border north, to Rimmon, *south of Jerusalem.* When the Gospel of Christ comes in its power, it levels the ground, so that the Lord alone may be exalted. Just as the Holy Land will be leveled, so the Holy City will be repopulated. *Jerusalem shall be lifted* up out of its low estate; it will be raised up from its ruins. The whole city will be inhabited. Its farthest limits are mentioned here, all built on, from the Benjamin Gate in the northeast to the Corner Gate in the northwest, and from the Tower of Hananeel in the south to the royal winepresses in the north. *Those that dwell in it* will live securely, and there will be "no more anathema," as some read it, no more curse.

2. Judgments threatened against the enemies of the church, who *have fought*, or fight, against Jerusalem. Those who fight against the city of God and his people will be found to be fighting against God (v. 12).

2.1. They will waste away under painful and decaying diseases.

2.2. They will be dashed in pieces against one another (v. 13): *A great tumult from the Lord shall be among them.* Those who join together against the church will justly be separated and set against one another, and the tumults they raise against God will be avenged in panic among themselves. Some think this was fulfilled in the factions and dissensions that existed among the Jews when the Romans destroyed them all.

2.3. The spoils of their camp, or the spoils of their country, will greatly enrich the people of God (v. 14): "Judah also shall eat at Jerusalem," as one learned commentator understands it; people will come from all parts to share in the plunder. The *wealth of the sinner is often laid up for the just*, and the Israel of God enriched by the spoil of the Egyptians.

2.4. Even the cattle will share in the plague with which the enemies of God's church will be cut off (v. 15).

Verses 16–21

Three things are foretold here:

1. That those who were left of the enemies of religion will be so aware of the mercy of God to them in their narrow escape that they will turn to worshiping the God of Israel and pay homage to him (v. 16). Just as some of Christ's enemies will be made his footstool (Ps 110:1), so others will be made his friends (Lk 12:4; Jn 15:13–15). They will *go up to worship* at Jerusalem, because that is the place God chose, and the temple is there as a type of Christ and his mediation. Gospel worship is represented here by the *keeping of the feast of tabernacles*, for the sake of those two great graces that were especially represented in that festival—contempt for the world and joy in God (Ne 8:17). We must go to Christ our temple with all our offerings, for only in him are our *spiritual sacrifices* acceptable to God (1Pe 2:5). They will go up *from year to year*, at the appointed times for this sacred festival. Every day of a Christian's life is a day of the *feast of tabernacles*, especially every Lord's Day.

2. That those who neglect the duties of Gospel worship will be judged for their neglect. *Upon them there shall be no rain* (v. 17). Some understand this figuratively: the rain of heavenly teaching will be withheld (Dt 32:2), along with that of heavenly grace, which should accompany that teaching. It is righteous of God to withhold the blessings of grace from those who do not attend the means of grace, to deny the *green pastures* (Ps 23:2) to those who pay no attention to *shepherd's tents* (SS 1:8). If we are barren and unfruitful toward God, then the earth is justly made so to us. What will be done to the defaulters of the land of Egypt, however, to whom the threat is no threat because they have no rain at any time? The Nile River waters their land and makes it fruitful. Yet they will, in effect, suffer the same plague. God can restrain the flooding of the river, which was equivalent to the shutting up of the clouds. It does not follow that those who can live without rain can therefore live without God. Omissions are sins, and those who *go not up to worship* at the appointed times, as they have opportunity, are guilty.

3. That those who fulfill the duties of Gospel worship will have grace to adorn their profession by the duties of Gospel conduct too.

3.1. The name and character of holiness will not be so confined as formerly. *Holiness to the Lord* has been written only on the high priest's forehead, but now it will not be limited in this way. All Christians will be *living temples* and *spiritual priests* (1Co 3:16–17; 1Pe 2:5), dedicated to the honor of God and employed in his service.

3.2. Real holiness will be more widely known than it has been. There will be a more plentiful outpouring of the Spirit of holiness and sanctification after Christ's ascension than ever before.

3.2.1. Holiness will be introduced into common things. The equipment of their horses will be consecrated to God. *Upon the bells of the horses* will be engraved *Holiness to the Lord*, or on the "bridles" of the horses (v. 20, margin) or the trappings. Travelers will have it on the bridles with which they guide their horses, to guide themselves by this rule. The furnishings of their homes also will be consecrated to God, to be employed in his service. The ordinary drinking cups they use will be *like the bowls before the altar*, which were used either to receive the blood of the sacrifices or to present the wine and oil for the *drink offerings*. The vessels that they use for their own tables will be used to the glory of God, and their meals will look like sacrifices. They will eat and drink not to themselves, but to the One who spreads their tables and fills their cups. "*Every pot in Jerusalem and in Judah shall be holiness to the Lord*, the pots and bowls in which they boil their meat, the cups out of which they drink. What they eat and drink out of these will nourish their bodies for the service of God, and they will give generously out of these to relieve the poor." Then are they *Holiness to the Lord*. When there is such real holiness, people will not be so concerned and fussy about ceremonial holiness: "*Those that sacrifice shall come and take* of these common vessels *and seethe* (cook) their sacrifices *therein*, making no distinction between them and the *bowls before the altar*." In Gospel times, the true worshipers will worship God *in spirit and in truth* (Jn 4:21). One place will be as acceptable to God as another, and one vessel will be as acceptable as another.

3.2.2. No unholiness will be introduced into their sacred things, to corrupt them: *In that day there shall be no more the Canaanite in the house of the Lord of hosts*. Some read it, "There will be no more the merchant"—for that is what *Canaanite* sometimes means—and they think it was fulfilled when Christ drove the buyers and sellers out of the temple (Mt 21:12). At the end of time, and not before, Christ will gather out of his kingdom everything that is offensive.

A PRACTICAL AND DEVOTIONAL EXPOSITION OF THE BOOK OF THE PROPHET

Malachi

God's prophets were his witnesses to his church, each in his day, for several ages, and were witnesses for him and his authority, witnesses against sin and sinners. They were affirming God's providences in his dealings with his people then and his grace concerning his church in the days of the Messiah. The Jews say that prophecy continued for forty years under the second temple, and they call this prophet the "seal of prophecy," because in him the series or succession of prophets broke off and came to an end. Let us consider: 1. The prophet himself. We have only his name, *Malachi*, and no account of his country or family background. *Malachi* means "my angel, my messenger." Prophets were messengers, God's messengers; the name of this prophet is the same word we find in the original for *my messenger* (3:1). The tradition of some of the ancients is that he came from the tribe of Zebulun and that he died young. 2. The theme of the prophecy. Haggai and Zechariah were sent to rebuke the people for delaying in building the temple; Malachi was sent to rebuke them for neglecting it when it was built and for their desecration of the temple service, for they went from the one extreme of idolatry and superstition to the opposite of ungodliness and irreligion. Now that prophecy was to come to an end, he spoke more clearly about the Messiah, as One who was close at hand. He concluded with a direction to the people of God to remember the Law of Moses while they were expecting the Gospel of Christ.

CHAPTER 1

This prophet is sent first to convict and then to comfort, first to reveal sin and rebuke it and then to promise the coming of the One who will take away sin. This is how the blessed Holy Spirit deals with our souls (Jn 16:8). He first opens up the wound and then applies the healing lotion. God had provided for Israel to stay close to himself through providence and ordinances, but it seems that they received the grace of God in vain. 1. They were ungrateful to God for his favors (vv. 1–5). 2. They were careless and negligent—especially the priests—in observing his institutions (vv. 5–14).

Verses 1–5

The prophecy of this book is entitled *The burden* (oracle) *of the word of the Lord* (v. 1), which suggests that it was weighty and important, that it would often be repeated, like the chorus of a song, and that there were those to whom it was a burden and a reproach. It would prove a true burden to them, one that would lower them to the deepest hell unless they repented. This *burden of the word of the Lord* was sent to Israel: God had sent many prophets to Israel, and now he would test them with one more. It was sent *by Malachi*; the phrase in the original is literally "by the hand of Malachi." In these verses, they are accused of ingratitude.

1. God asserts the great kindness he has had for them (v. 2): *I have loved you, saith the Lord.* The sermon begins so abruptly, so kindheartedly. In this one word God sums up all his gracious dealings with them.

2. They question his love: *Yet you say, Wherein hast thou* (how have you) *loved us?* As God traces all his favors to them back to the fountain, which was his love, so he traces all their sins against him back to the fountain, which was their contempt of his love. "Have we not been devastated, made poor, and taken captive; how then *hast thou loved us?*"

3. He demonstrates beyond contradiction that he has loved them. Some read their question, *Wherefore hast thou loved us?* as if they did acknowledge that he had loved them, but insinuate that he loved them because their father Abraham had loved him, so that it was not a love freely given, but a love given to repay a debt. To this, God replies, "*Was not Esau* as closely related to Abraham as you are? And so, if there were any right to a reward for Abraham's love, Esau had it, but *I hated Esau and loved Jacob.*" What a distinction God made between Jacob and Esau! Esau was Jacob's brother, his twin brother: "*Yet I loved Jacob and I hated Esau,* that is, I took Jacob into covenant but refused and rejected Esau." The apostle Paul quotes this (Ro 9:13). Esau was justly hated, but Jacob freely loved.

3.1. The Edomites will be made memorials to God's justice. For *Esau have I hated; I laid his mountains waste* (v. 3), the mountains of Seir, which were *his heritage.* When all that part of the world was ravaged by the Babylonian army, the country of Edom was ruined (Isa 34:6, 11). The Edomites had triumphed at Jerusalem's downfall (Ps 137:7), and so God was just to put the same *cup of trembling* (Isa 51:17) into their hands. Jacob's cities are devastated, but they are rebuilt; Edom's are devastated but never rebuilt. The sufferings of the righteous will end well; their grievances will be put right, and their sorrow turned to joy, but the sufferings of evildoers will be as Edom's ruins were (v. 4). The vain hopes of the Edomites have no promise to build on. They say, "It is true, *we are impoverished*; it is the common fate, and there is no answer, but *we will return and build the desolate places*; we are determined we will" — not even asking God permission. They build presumptuously, as Hiel built Jericho in direct contradiction to the word of God (1Ki 16:34), and things will work out accordingly. They say, *We will build*, but what says *the Lord of hosts? They shall build, but I will throw down. All* who see them will call them *the border of wickedness*, a sinful nation, incurably so, and therefore *the people against whom the Lord has indignation for ever*. Since their wickedness will never be reformed, their ruins will never be repaired.

3.2. The Israelites will be made memorials to his mercy (v. 5). *The Edomites will be stigmatized as a people hated by God, but your eyes shall see* your doubts about his love toward you silenced, for you will have cause to say, *The Lord will be magnified from* every part and border of the land of Israel." When the border of Edom remains in ruins and the border of Israel is repaired and replenished, it will be seen that God has loved Jacob. Because God's goodness is his glory (Ex 33:18–19), when he does us good, we must declare he is great, for that is exalting him.

Verses 6–14

Here the prophet calls the priests to account, even though they themselves were appointed judges and were thus charged with calling the people to account. This is what *the Lord of hosts saith to you, O priests!* (v. 6). Notice:

1. What God expected from them (v. 6): *A son honours his father*, because he is his father. Nature has written this law on the hearts of children; it did so before God wrote the law at Mount Sinai. *A servant*, though his obligation to his master is by voluntary agreement, still thinks it his duty to honor him. However, the priests, who were God's children and his servants, did not fear and honor him. They were *fathers* and *masters* to the people and expected to be called so (Jdg 18:19; Mt 22:7, 10), but they forgot their Father and Master in heaven and the duty they owed to him. Our relationship to God as our Father and Master strongly obligates us to fear and honor him. If we honor and fear our human fathers, then much more should we honor the Father and Master of our spirits (Heb 12:9).

2. What contempt the priests showed toward God. They showed contempt for God's name, which means everything by which he has made himself known — his word and ordinances; and so they caused the *sacrifices of the Lord to be abhorred*, as Eli's sons did (1Sa 2:12–17). They *profaned God's name* (v. 12). They *polluted* (defiled) it (v. 7). They not only had a low opinion of sacred things; they also corrupted them to serve the worst purposes: their own pride, covetousness, and self-indulgence. This was the general accusation against them. They pleaded *Not guilty* to this, and they challenged God to prove it against them. *You say, Wherein have we despised thy name?* (v. 6), and *wherein have we polluted thee?* (v. 7). Their defense was their offense, and their saying, *Wherein have we despised thy name?* proved they were proud, defiant, and corrupt. They could justly have been condemned on the general charge, but God showed them in detail how they had shown contempt for his name.

2.1. They despised God's name in what they said: "*You say* in your hearts, *The table of the Lord is contemptible*"

(v. 7), and again (v. 12), "*You* say, *The table of the Lord is polluted* (defiled); it is to be held in no higher regard than any other table." Either they thought this about the table in the temple, on which the consecrated bread was placed, or rather the altar of burnt offerings is called the table here. They thought this was contemptible, in comparison with their own tables and those of their leaders: *The fruit thereof, even his meat, is contemptible.*

2.2. They despised God's name in what they did, which fitted in with what they said. They thought anything would serve as a sacrifice, even if it was coarse and mean. With every sacrifice they were to bring a grain offering of *fine flour mingled with oil*, but they brought *polluted bread* (v. 7). As to the animals they offered, although the law was clear that what was offered as a sacrifice should be unblemished, they brought *the blind, and the lame* (crippled), *and the sick* (diseased) (v. 8), and again (v. 13), *the torn* (injured), *and the lame* (crippled), *and the sick* (diseased), which were ready to die by themselves. Some consider v. 8 to be a continuation of what the priests corruptly said (v. 7): *You say* to the people, *If you offer the blind for sacrifice, it is not evil; or if you offer the lame and the sick, it is not evil*. If we worship God ignorantly and without understanding, we are bringing the blind as a sacrifice; if we do it carelessly, if we are cold, dull, and lifeless in it, we bring the sick; if we depend only on physical exercise and do not make it a work of the heart (1Ti 4:8), we bring the lame, and if we allow worthless thoughts and distractions to remain within us, we bring the torn. Is it not a great insult to God and a great wrong and injury to our own souls? They would do no more of their work than what they were paid for. There was not a man among the priests who would *shut the doors*, or *kindle a fire, for nought*. Their work was sheer drudgery to them (v. 13): *You said also, Behold, what a weariness* (what a burden) *is it!* They thought the duty of their office an intolerable and troublesome burden, and they sniffed at it contemptuously as unreasonable.

3. God pleaded and reasoned with them.

3.1. Would they insult an earthly ruler in this way? "You offer to God *the lame and the sick; offer it now unto thy governor* (v. 8), either as tribute or as a present; *will he be pleased with thee?*"

3.2. Could they imagine that such sacrifices would please God? *Should I accept this at your hand, saith the Lord?* (v. 13). If God has no pleasure in the person, if the person is not in a justified state, if not sanctified, God will not accept the offering. God favored Abel first and then his sacrifice (Ge 4:4).

3.3. How could they expect their intercessions to God for the people to be effective when they so insulted God in their sacrifices?

3.4. Had God deserved such treatment from them? No; he had provided comfortably for them, giving them such encouragement in their work as ought to have made them do it cheerfully and well.

4. He called them to repentance for profaning his holy name. This is how we may understand v. 9: "*Now, I pray you, beseech God that he will be gracious to us.* Humble yourselves for your sin; call out urgently to God for forgiveness (Jnh 3:8), for all the rebukes of providence we are under *are by your means* (from your hands)."

5. He declared his determination both to protect the glory of his own name and to judge those who had dishonored it. Let them know:

5.1. That they would not triumph. God would exalt his law and honor it, even though they reviled it and made it contemptible, for *from the rising of the sun to the going* down of the same my name shall be great among the *Gentiles* (v. 11). Instead of those external ordinances, which they dishonored, a spiritual way of worship be introduced and established: *Incense shall be offered to God's name*—which represents prayer and praise (Ps 141:2; Rev 8:3)—instead of the blood and fat of bulls and goats. Instead of being worshiped and served only among the Jews, a small people in a corner of the world, he would be served and worshiped in all places, *from the rising of the sun to the going down of the same; in every place*, in every part of the world, *incense shall be offered to his name*. Nations would speak about the wonderful works of God and have them spoken to them in their own language (Ac 2:11). This is a clear prediction of that great change by which the Gentiles, who had been *strangers and foreigners*, came to be *fellow citizens with the saints and of the household of God* (Eph 2:19), and to be welcome to the throne of grace.

5.2. That they would not go unpunished (v. 14). Ungodly and careless worshipers are those who *vow and sacrifice to the Lord a corrupt thing* when they have *in their flock a male*. The priests accepted such an offering, even though God would not; they pretended to be more indulgent than he was. They were *deceivers*; they dealt falsely and fraudulently with God. Hypocrites are deceivers, and they will be proved to be self-deceivers, and so also self-destroyers. They are *cursed*; they expect a blessing, but they will receive a curse. The nations paid greater respect to their gods, even though they were idols, than the Jews did to theirs, even though he is the only true and living God.

CHAPTER 2

There are two great ordinances that divine wisdom has instituted, and the corrupt desecration of both of them is severely rebuked in this chapter. 1. The ordinance of the ministry, which is distinctive to the church, was dishonored by those who were themselves dignified with its honor. The priests dishonored the holy things of God; they are accused of this here (vv. 1–9). 2. The ordinance of marriage, which is common to the human race, was dishonored by both the priests and the people when they married foreigners (vv. 11–12), treated their wives unkindly (v. 13), divorced them (v. 16), and dealt unfaithfully (vv. 10, 14–15). What lay at the root of this and other examples of ungodliness was sheer unbelief (v. 17).

Verses 1–9

What was said in the previous chapter was directed to the priests (1:6): *Thus saith the Lord of hosts to you, O priests! that despise my name*. Yet they might think it some excuse that they offered what the people brought. But if the priests had given the people better instructions, the people would have brought better offerings, and so the blame returns to the priests: *And now, O you priests! this commandment* (warning) *is purely for you* (v. 1). Here is:

1. A repetition of the covenant God made with that sacred tribe, which was their commission for their work: The *Lord of hosts sent a commandment* to them to establish this covenant (v. 4). Let the sons of Levi, especially the sons of Aaron, know what honor God showed to their family (v. 5): *My covenant was with him of life and peace.* This is called *his covenant of life and peace* because it was intended to support religious faith, which brings life and peace to human souls. What is said here about the covenant of priesthood is true of the covenant of grace

made with all believers, as spiritual priests. It assures all believers of eternal peace and eternal life, all happiness both in this world and in the one to come. This covenant was made with the whole tribe of Levi when they were set apart from the other tribes. These great blessings of life and peace, contained in that covenant, were blessings God *gave to him*: to Levi, Aaron, and Phinehas. He entrusted them with these benefits for the use and benefit of God's Israel; they received so that they could give (v. 5). Notice:

1.1. The considerations on which this covenant was based: it was *for the fear wherewith he feared me, and was afraid before my name* (v. 5). The tribe of Levi gave clear proof of their holy fear of God when they appeared so boldly against the worshipers of the golden calf (Ex 32:26), and for their zeal in that matter God bestowed this blessing on them. Some read this not as the consideration of the gift but as its condition: *I gave them to him provided that he should fear before me.*

1.2. The trust that was placed in the priests by this covenant (v. 7). They were made *the messengers of the Lord of hosts*, messengers of that covenant of life and peace, not mediators of it, but only messengers, or ambassadors, whose task was to settle the terms of peace between God and Israel. The priests were *God's mouth* to his people. *The priests' lips should keep knowledge*, not keep it from the people, but keep it for them. Ministers must be people of knowledge; they must not only keep it but also have it ready to be communicated to others as occasions arise. The people *should seek the law at his mouth*; they should consult the priests as God's messengers.

2. A memorial of the foolishness and zeal of many of their predecessors in the priest's office, virtues that are mentioned to emphasize the sin of the current priests in turning aside from such honorable ancestors. The good priest (v. 6) knew the Scriptures very well: *The law of truth was in his mouth*, for the use of those who *asked the law at his mouth*. Truth is a law; it has a commanding power. It is by truth that Christ rules. He lived like a priest who was chosen to *walk before God* (1Sa 2:30). He walked with God in peace, *in equity. He did turn many away from iniquity*, and God crowned his endeavors with wonderful success. He helped save many souls from death, and there are many who are now in heaven blessing God that they ever knew him. As one of the rabbis observes here, "When the priest is upright, many will be upright."

3. A high accusation drawn up against the priests who violated the covenant. Many corruptions had crept into the church of the Jews at this time: mixed marriages, admitting foreigners into the house of God, and the dishonoring of the Sabbath. These were all due to the carelessness and unfaithfulness of the priests. They are accused of:

3.1. Turning away from the way: "*You have not kept my ways*, neither kept them yourselves nor fulfilled your part in keeping others in them" (v. 9).

3.2. Betraying their trust: "*You have corrupted the covenant of Levi* (v. 8). You have managed your office as if its sole purpose were to feed you and make you fat and make you look important, rather than to give glory to God and do good to human souls." Another example of their betrayal of trust was that they were *partial* (showed favoritism) *in the law* (v. 9). They showed partiality in the law they were to lay down to the people.

3.3. Causing trouble to the people, whom they should have helped save: *You have caused many to stumble at the law* (v. 8).

3.4. Refusing to listen to the rebukes of both the word and the providence of God; they *would not hear* (v. 2).

4. A record of the judgments God had brought on these priests. They had lost their assurance (v. 2): *I have already cursed your blessings.* They had no encouragement from their work, which is the assurance of doing good. They had lost their reputation (v. 9): *Therefore have I also made you contemptible and base* (despised and humiliated) *before all the people.* When they abandoned the ways of God and corrupted the covenant of Levi, they made themselves not only lowly but also contemptible in the eyes of even the common people (1Sa 3:13).

5. A sentence of wrath being passed on them (vv. 2–3). However, it was conditional: *If you will not lay it to heart,* God said—implying, "If you will, God's anger will be turned away"—*I will send a curse upon you,* so that you will neither be blessed yourselves nor be blessings to the people, but even your plenty will be a plague to you, and you will be plagues to your generation." The fruits of the earth would not comfort them: "*Behold, I will corrupt your seed*; the grain you sow will rot underground." Or it may be understood to refer to the seed of the word that they preached: *Bring no more vain oblations*; your *incense is an abomination* to me (Isa 1:13).

Verses 10–17

Corrupt practices are the genuine fruit and product of corrupt motives. In these verses we find people dealing falsely with one another, and it is because they think falsely about their God.

1. Notice how corrupt their practices were. In general, they *dealt treacherously every man against his brother* (broke faith with one another) (v. 10). It cannot be expected that those who are false to their God would be true to their friends. They are accused of two things here: taking foreign wives from the pagan nations and abusing and divorcing the wives they had from their own nation. In both matters they violated a sacred covenant.

1.1. In contempt of the covenant God made with Israel as his own distinctive people, they married foreign wives, which was expressly prohibited and provided against in that covenant (Dt 7:3). God committed to do them good on the condition that they would not associate closely with the nations; this was the covenant made with their fathers, the great charter by which that nation was incorporated. "*Have we not all one Father?* Yes, we have, for *has not one God created us?* Are we not all *his offspring* (Ac 17:28)?" Here, however, it seems to refer to the Jewish nation: *Have we not all one father,* Abraham, or Jacob? They prided themselves on this, *We have Abraham to our father* (Mt 3:9). "*Has not one God created us,* that is, formed us into a people, making us a nation by ourselves and putting life into us, to make us distinct from other nations? Therefore, should not this make us maintain the dignity of our character?" They were dedicated to God as well as set apart from the neighboring nations. *Israel was holiness to the Lord* (Jer 2:3). By marrying foreign wives, however, they desecrated this sanctuary and put its honor in the dust (Ps 7:5). *Judah has married the daughter of a strange* (foreign) *god.* The harm was not so much that she was the daughter of a foreign nation, but that she was the daughter of a foreign god. God would judge them for this (v. 12): "*The Lord will cut off the man that doeth this,* who marries the daughter of a foreign god." Such a man had, in effect, cut himself off from the holy nation. The original suggests, "God will cut him off, him and all that belongs to him." God would no longer acknowledge them as belonging to his nation, and if the priest who *offered an offering to the Lord* had married a foreign wife—as we find many of the priests did (Ezr 10:18)—he would not

escape. He would be cut off from the temple of the Lord, as others had been from the tabernacles of Jacob.

1.2. In contempt of the marriage covenant, which God instituted for the common benefit of the human race, they abused and divorced their wives from their own nation (v. 13).

1.2.1. Let us see what it is that is complained about here. They did not behave as they should have toward their wives. The wives, not daring to make their case known to any other person, complained to God, *covering the altar of the Lord with tears, with weeping, and with crying.* The good Master we serve wants his altar not to be covered with tears, but to be surrounded by joyful songs (Ps 100:2). It is a reason given why marriage partners should live in holy love and *joy—that their prayers may not be hindered* (1Pe 3:7). The men dealt treacherously with their wives (vv. 14–16). They did not fulfill their promises to them, but took in concubines to share in the affection that was due only to their wives. They *put them away,* that is, they gave them a certificate of divorce and turned them away. In all this *they covered violence with their garment*; they abused their wives and yet pretended in the sight of others to be very loving toward them.

1.2.2. Let us see the proof and emphasizing of the accusation. "*The Lord has been witness between thee and the wife of thy youth* (v. 14), has witnessed the marriage covenant between you and her, for you appealed to him about your sincerity and your faithfulness. She is *thy wife,* your own wife, your own flesh and blood, the closest relationship in the world, and to remain faithful to her means you must forsake all others. She is *the wife of thy youth,* who had your affections when they were strongest. Let not the darling of your youth be the scorn and loathing of your age. She is *thy companion*; she has shared equally with you in your cares, griefs, and joys for a long time." The wife is to be looked on not as the husband's servant, but as his companion. "She is *the wife of thy covenant,* to whom you are so firmly committed that, while she continues to be faithful, you cannot be released from her, for it was a covenant for life."

1.2.3. Let us look at the reasons why husband and wife should continue together to the end of their lives in holy love and peace, neither quarreling with each other nor separating from each other. God has joined them together (v. 15): *Did not he make one,* one Eve for one Adam, so that Adam would never *take another to her to vex her* (Lev 18:18), nor divorce her to make way for another? Intending that *Adam* would have *a help meet for him* (Ge 2:18), he made him *one wife.* If he had made more for him, he would not have had *a meet* (suitable) *help.* Why did he make only one woman for one man? It was so *that he might seek a godly seed*—"a seed of God," a seed that would bear the image of God, so that, *every man having his own wife,* and *but one,* according to the law (1Co 7:2), they might live in pure and holy love, and not like wild animals, because the children being born in holy matrimony, which is an ordinance of God, could be made a *seed to serve him.* God is very much displeased with those who go about separating *what he has joined together* (v. 16).

1.2.4. Let us see the warning deduced from all this: *Therefore take heed to your spirit, and let none deal treacherously against the wife of his youth* (v. 15), and again, *therefore take heed to your spirit, that ye deal not treacherously* (v. 16).

2. Notice how corrupt their motives were, which led to all these corrupt practices. Let us trace the streams back to the fountain (v. 17): *You have wearied the Lord with your words.* It is wearisome, even for God himself, to hear people insist on justifying their own corrupt and evil

practices. They denied him to be a holy God and even had the arrogance to say, *Every one that does evil is good in the sight of the Lord, and he delights in them.* They drew this evil deduction, without any reason, from the prosperity of sinners in their sinful ways (see 3:15). Under the pretense of making God out to be not as severe as he was commonly said to be, they said things to be as they wanted them to be, because they thought he was *altogether such a one as themselves* (Ps 50:21). They said, *"Where is the God of judgment* (justice)*?* We may do as we please; he doesn't see us, and he will not pay any attention to us."

CHAPTER 3

In this chapter we have: 1. A promise of the coming of the Messiah and of his forerunner. The Messiah's mission is described in detail (vv. 1–6). 2. A rebuke to the Jews for their corruption of God's ordinances, along with a charge to put right this matter and a promise that if they did so, God would respond in mercy to them (vv. 7–12). 3. A description of the wickedness of evildoers who speak against God (vv. 13–15) and of the righteousness of the righteous who speak for him, with precious promises made to them (vv. 16–18).

Verses 1–6

The first words of this chapter seem to be a direct response to the blasphemous, godless demand of the scoffers: *Where is the God of judgment* (justice)*?* (2:17). "He is here; he is at the door; the long-expected Messiah is about to appear, and he says, *For judgment have I come into this world* (Jn 9:39)." We have here:

1. A prophecy of the appearing of his forerunner, John the Baptist, which the prophet Isaiah had foretold (Is 40:3) as the *preparing of the way of the Lord.*

1.1. He is *God's messenger.* John the Baptist received his commission *from heaven, and not of men* (Mt 21:25). All considered John the Baptist to be a prophet (Mt 21:26), for he was God's messenger, as the prophets were, to call people to repentance and reformation.

1.2. He is Christ's forerunner. He *shall prepare the way before me* by taking them away from a confidence in their relation to Abraham *as their father*—which they thought enough without a savior—and by announcing that the Messiah is now near.

2. A prophecy of the appearing of the Messiah himself: "*The Lord, whom you seek, shall suddenly come to his temple, the God of judgment,* who you think has abandoned the earth. The Messiah has long been called *he that should come* (Mt 11:3), and he will now soon come."

2.1. He *is the Lord—Adonai,* the foundation on which the world is founded, the one *Lord over all* (Ac 10:36) who has all power committed to him (Mt 28:18) and is to *reign over the house of Jacob for ever* (Lk 1:33).

2.2. He is the *Messenger of the covenant,* or the *Angel of the covenant,* sent from heaven to negotiate a peace between God and human beings. Christ is the *Angel of this covenant,* through whose mediation it is brought about and established. That covenant that is all our *salvation began to be spoken by the Lord* (Heb 2:3). Although he is, as some understand this, "the prince of the covenant," he condescended to be its messenger.

2.3. He is the One *whom you seek, whom you delight in,* whom the devout Jews expect and desire. In looking and waiting for him, they *looked for redemption in Jerusalem and waited for the consolation of Israel* (Lk 2:25, 38). Those who seek Jesus will find delight in him. If he is our heart's desire, he will be our heart's delight.

2.4. He *shall suddenly come;* his coming draws near, and we see it not so far away as the patriarchs saw it.

2.5. He *shall come to his temple,* this temple at Jerusalem, which had just been built. It is his temple, for it is *his Father's house* (Jn 2:16).

3. An account of the great purposes of his coming (v. 2). He is the One whom they seek, but *who may abide* (endure) *the day of his coming,* even though he does not come to condemn the world, but so that the world might have life through him (Jn 3:17; 20:31)? This may refer:

3.1. To the terrors of his appearance. Even in the days of his human nature there were some displays of his glory and power that no one could stand before, namely, his transfiguration and the signs that accompanied his death.

3.2. To the troublesome times that would follow soon after. The Jewish teachers speak about the "pangs" or "griefs" of the Messiah, referring to the great suffering that would come on Israel at the time of his coming.

3.3. To the testing to which his coming would subject human beings. *He shall be like a refiner's fire,* which separates the gold and the dross by melting the ore, or *like fuller's* (launderer's) *soap,* which with much rubbing removes spots from a cloth. Christ came to reveal what people are really like, *that the thoughts of many hearts might be revealed* (Lk 2:35), to separate the precious and the unworthy (Jer 15:19), for *his fan is in his hand* (Mt 3:12). Notice the effects of the testing:

3.3.1. The Gospel will be beneficial to those who are disposed to be good; it will be the fragrance of life to them (2Co 2:16) (v. 3): *He shall sit as a refiner.* He will *purge them as gold and silver,* that is, he will sanctify them inwardly. *He will purge them* with fire, *as gold and silver are purged,* for he *baptizes with the Holy Ghost and with fire* (Mt 3:11), with the Holy Spirit working like fire. *That they may offer unto the Lord an offering in righteousness,* that is, that they may be sincerely converted to God and consecrated. He makes the tree good so that the fruit may be good (Mt 7:17–18). It then follows (v. 4), *The offering of Judah and Jerusalem shall be pleasant unto the Lord.* It will no longer be offensive, as when they brought the torn, the lame, and the sick for sacrifices (1:8, 13), but will be *acceptable.* The Messiah will, through his grace in them, make them acceptable. When he has purified and refined them, they will then offer such sacrifices as God requires and will accept. Through his intercession for them, he will make them accepted.

3.3.2. It will turn as a witness against those who are determined to continue in their evil (v. 5). This is the direct answer to their challenge, *Where is the God of judgment?* "You will know where he is, and you will know it to your terror and shame, for *I will come near to you to judgment.*" The sinners who must appear to be judged by the Gospel of Christ are the *sorcerers,* who deal in spiritual evil; the *adulterers,* who wallow in the lusts of the sinful nature; the *false swearers,* who dishonor God's name by calling him to witness to a lie; and the oppressors, who *defraud the hireling in his wages* and crush *the widow and fatherless.* What lies at the root of all this is that *They fear not me, saith the Lord of hosts. I will come near and will be a swift witness against* them.

4. The confirmation of all this (v. 6): *For I am the Lord, I change not; therefore you sons of Jacob are not consumed.* Although the sentence passed against evil works is not implemented speedily (v. 5), it will still be executed, for he is *the Lord,* he *changes not.* The people of Israel had reason to say that he was an unchangeable God, for he had been faithful to his covenant with them and their ancestors. They had been false and fickle in their behavior

toward him, and he could justly have abandoned them, but because he *remembered his covenant* (Ex 2:24; 6:5; Ps 105:8; 106:45), they were kept. We may apply this to ourselves; because we have to do with a God that *changes not, we are not consumed* (Heb 4:13; La 3:22–23).

Verses 7–12

Here is God's dispute with the people of that generation for abandoning his service and robbing him.

1. They have run away from their Master and abandoned the work he gave them to do (v. 7): *You have gone away from my ordinances and have not kept them.* Notice:

1.1. What a gracious invitation God gives them to turn back to him and repent: "*Return unto me* and to your duty, return to your allegiance, return as travelers who have missed their way, as soldiers who have deserted their colors, as a treacherous wife who has left her husband; return to me, and then *I will return unto you*, taking away the judgments you are under and preventing those you fear."

1.2. What a perverse response they give: "*But you said* with contempt—to the prophets, to one another, to your own hearts, to stifle the convictions you were under—you said, *Wherein shall we* (how are we to) *return?*" They take it as an insult to be *told of their faults* (Mt 18:15) and called on to put them right. They are so ignorant of themselves and of the strictness, extent, and spiritual nature of God's law that they think they do not need to repent. They are firmly determined to continue in their sin.

2. They have robbed their Master and embezzled his goods. Notice:

2.1. The prophet's great charge against the people. They stand accused of robbery—of sacrilege, the worst of robberies: *You have robbed me* (v. 8). *Will a man be* so daringly arrogant as to *rob God?* "Will a man do violence to God?" is how some read it. "Will a man be mean toward God or restrict him?" is how others read it.

2.2. The people's great challenge in response to that accusation. They plead *Not guilty* and challenge God to prove their guilt. They rob God and do not know what they are doing (Lk 23:34). They rob him of his honor and of what is devoted to him, what is to be employed in his service; they rob him of themselves, rob him of Sabbath time, rob him of what is given to support religious faith, and do not give him his due from their possessions; and yet they ask, *Wherein have we robbed thee?*

2.3. The plain proof of the charge. It *is in tithes and offerings.* They detained them, defrauded the priests of them, refused to pay their tithes. They did not bring the offerings that God required, or brought the torn, the lame, and the sick (1:8, 13), which were unfit for use. For this they were *cursed with a curse* (v. 9). God punished them with famine and scarcity, through unseasonable weather, or insects that ate the fruits of the earth. Because God had punished them with a scarcity of bread, they used that as an excuse for robbing him—that now, because they were so poor, they could not afford to bring their tithes and offerings.

2.4. A serious exhortation. They are urged to reform in this matter and are promised that if they do, the judgments will be removed. *Bring ye all the tithes into the storehouse.* "Bring in the full tithes to the maximum that the law requires, *that there may be meat* (food) *in God's house* for those who serve at the altar, whether there is food in your houses or not." "Let God be served first, and then *prove me herewith, saith the Lord of hosts, whether I will not open the windows of heaven.*" The expression is figurative; because every good gift comes from above

(Jas 1:17), it is from there that God will plentifully pour out on them the goodness of his providence. Very sudden plenty is expressed by *opening the windows of heaven* (2Ki 7:2). They were opened to pour down a deluge of wrath in Noah's flood (Ge 7:11). Here, however, they are opened to *pour down blessings*, so much that there will not be *room enough to receive* them. God will not only be reconciled to sinners who repent and reform; he will also be a generous benefactor to them. God has blessings that he is ready to give us, but through the weakness of our faith and the narrowness of our desires we do not have the room to receive them. Whereas fruits of their ground have been devoured by locusts and caterpillars, God will now remove that judgment (v. 11). Whereas they have fallen under the *reproach of famine*, now *all nations shall call them blessed.*

Verses 13–18

We have here:

1. The angry notice God takes of the arrogant, blasphemous talk of the sinners in Zion. Here is:

1.1. An indictment directed against them for treasonable words. *Your words have been stout* (harsh) *against me, saith the Lord.* Their words came from their vain pride, bold arrogance, and defiant contempt of God. They spoke out proudly and with contempt, scorning to be under the divine check and rule.

1.2. Their response to this indictment. *What have we spoken so much against thee*, so much that there need be all this fuss about it? They could not deny that they had spoken against God, but they made light of it.

1.3. The words themselves with which they were charged. They said:

1.3.1. That there is nothing to be gained in serving God. *It is vain* (futile) *to serve God* (v. 14), or, "He who serves God labors in vain and to no purpose; he gets only his labor in exchange for his pains, and so he is a fool for his labor. We have walked *mournfully*, or *in black*, with great solemnity and grief, *before the Lord of hosts*, have humbled our souls, but we are no better off." They wanted it thought that they had served God and had carried out his requirements, whereas it was only the external observance of the requirements that they had kept; and so they could indeed say that serving God was futile. They had *walked mournfully* (gone about like mourners) before God, whereas God had required them to serve him with gladness (Dt 28:47; Ne 8:9–11; Ps 100:2) and to walk cheerfully before him. By their own superstitions they made the service of God a chore and drudgery to themselves, and then they complained about it as hard service. They complained that they had gained nothing from their religious faith; they remained poor and suffering. Perhaps this refers to the errors of the Sadducees. They denied the future state and then said, "It is *vain to serve God*," which has indeed some truth in it, for, *if in this life only we have hope in Christ, we were of all men most miserable* (1Co 15:19).

1.3.2. They maintained that evil is the way to prosperity (v. 15). Just as the outer prosperity of sinners in their sins has weakened the hands of the godly in their godliness (Ps 73:13), so it has also strengthened the hands of evildoers in their evil acts. Wait a little while, and you will see *those that work wickedness set up* as a target for the arrows of God's vengeance, and you will see *those that tempt God delivered* to the tormentors.

2. The gracious notice God takes of the godly talk of the saints in Zion; and we see also its gracious reward. Even in this corrupt and degenerate age, there were still

some people who retained their integrity and zeal for God. Let us see:

2.1. How they distinguished themselves. They *feared the Lord* (v. 16)—the fear of the Lord is the beginning of wisdom (Ps 111:10; Pr 9:10) and the root of all religious faith; they had a reverence for the majesty of God and submitted to his authority. Every age has had a remnant who feared the Lord, even though sometimes it is a very small remnant. They *thought upon his name*, that is, they meditated on the revelations God has made of himself in his word and by his providences. They *spoke often one to another* about the God they feared. *Those that feared the Lord* kept together. They spoke kind words to one another to promote mutual love, so that that would not *wax cold* when *iniquity* was so prevalent. They spoke intelligently to one another to increase faith and holiness. At a time when sin was bold and brazen, the people of God took courage and stirred themselves, *the innocent against the hypocrite* (Job 17:8). When religious faith was misrepresented, its friends did all they could to support its reputation. When seducers were busy deceiving unwary souls with their prejudice against religious faith, those who feared God were diligent in strengthening one another's hands.

2.2. How God honored and supported them.

2.2.1. He took notice of their godly conversations and was graciously present at their meetings: *The Lord hearkened and heard it* (v. 16) and was very pleased with it. When the two disciples on the road to Emmaus were talking about Christ, he listened and heard and joined them, making a third conversation partner (Lk 24:15).

2.2.2. He kept an account of them: *A book of remembrance was written before him.* God remembers the services of his people, so that he may say, *Well done; enter thou into the joy of thy Lord* (Mt 25:21). God has a book for the sighs and tears of his mourners (Ps 56:8). Never was any good word spoken about God or for God without being registered, so that it may be rewarded.

2.2.3. He promised them a share in his glory in the future (v. 17): *They shall be mine, saith the Lord of hosts, in that day when I make up my jewels. They shall be my segullah, my peculiar treasure* (the word used in Ex 19:5), *in the day when I make* or do what I have said and intended. The saints are God's jewels; they are *a royal diadem* in his hand (Isa 62:3). There is a day coming when God *will make up his jewels.* They will be gathered out of the dirt into which they have now been thrown, from all the places to which they are now scattered.

2.2.4. He promised them a share in his grace now: *I will spare them as a man spares his own son that serves him.* The word usually signifies "to spare with compassion," *as a father pities his children* (Ps 103:13). It is our duty to serve God as his children. We must be his sons, must share the divine nature through a new birth (Jn 3:3; 1Pe 1:3). We must be his servants, too; God does not want his children to be trained up in idleness; they must serve him, from a motivation of love, with joy and delight. When Nehemiah had done much good, he still knew there is not *a just man on earth,* who *does good and sins not* (1Ki 8:46; Ecc 7:20), and so he prayed, *Lord, spare me according to the greatness of thy mercy* (Ne 13:22). God, as a Father, will show them this mercy.

2.3. How they would be set apart from the children of this world (v. 18). "You who now speak against God as making no distinction between good and bad and who say, *It is in vain to serve him* (v. 14)—you will be made to see the error of your ways." This is concerned with the clear distinction made between the Jews who were faithful and those who persisted in their unfaithfulness at the time

of the destruction of Jerusalem, and of the Jewish church and nation, by the Romans. It is to have its complete fulfillment at the second coming of Jesus Christ, however. All people are either those who serve God or those who do not serve him. In this world it is often hard to *discern between the righteous and the wicked.* There are many people who we think are serving God but who, not having their hearts right with him, will be found not to be among his servants. On the other hand, many people who did not follow us (Mk 9:38) and who we therefore thought were not serving him will be found to be his faithful servants. In Christ's court of law at the Last Judgment, it will be easy to *discern between the righteous and the wicked,* for then the character of every person will be both perfected and perfectly revealed; every person will then appear in their true colors, and their disguises will be taken off.

CHAPTER 4

Here are instructions: 1. About the state of reward and retribution before us (vv. 1–3). This is represented by a prophecy of the destruction of Jerusalem. 2. About the state of trial and preparation; the Jews are directed to keep the Law of Moses (v. 4) and to expect a further revelation of God's will through Elijah the prophet, that is, through John the Baptist, the messenger of the Messiah (vv. 5–6).

Verses 1–3

The great and terrible day of the Lord, like the pillar of cloud and fire, will have its dark side turned toward the Egyptians, who fight against God, and a bright side toward the faithful Israelites, who follow him (Ex 14:20): *The day cometh* (v. 1) refers to both the first and the second coming of Jesus Christ.

1. In both, Christ is a consuming fire to those who rebel against him. The day of his coming *shall burn as an oven* (furnace); it will be a day of wrath, of *fiery indignation.* God, who knows perfectly everyone's character, knows who are *the proud.* He also knows everyone's actions; he knows who *does wickedly,* and they will be as *stubble* to this fire. They will be consumed by it, and it is wholly because of themselves that they will be, for they make themselves stubble—that is, combustible matter—for this fire. Those who in their unbelief oppose Christ are setting themselves like *briers and thorns* in the face of *a devouring fire* (Isa 27:4–5). *The day that cometh shall burn them up,* and it will *leave them neither root nor branch.* This was fulfilled when Christ spoke words of terror and condemnation to the proud Pharisees and the other Jews who acted wickedly, when he sent on the earth that fire that burned up the chaff of the traditions of the elders and the corrupt interpretations they had put on the Law of God. It was also fulfilled when the Romans destroyed Jerusalem and wiped out the Jews as a nation. This seems to be mainly intended here; our Savior said that those would be the *days of vengeance* (Lk 21:22). The verse is certainly applicable to the Day of Judgment.

2. In both, Christ is a rejoicing light to those who serve him faithfully (v. 2). Here mercy and comfort are kept in store for all those who fear the Lord and think about his name. Here notice:

2.1. From where this mercy and comfort will flow to them: *To you that fear my name shall the Sun of righteousness arise, with healing in his wings.* The day that comes will be a fair and bright day to those who fear God; it will be as reviving as the rising sun is to the earth. Particular notice is taken of the rising of the sun on Zoar when that was mercifully set apart from the cities of the plain (Ge 19:23). When the hearts of others *fail for fear*, let those who fear the Lord *lift up their heads for joy*, for *their redemption draws nigh* (Lk 21:28). The *Sun of righteousness* certainly refers to Jesus Christ, who would keep the faithful remnant from falling with the rest at the time of the general destruction of the Jews. However, it is also to be applied:

2.1.1. To the coming of Christ in the flesh to seek and save those who were lost (Lk 19:10). Christ is the *light of the world*. He is the *light of men* (Jn 1:4); he is to the human soul what the sun is to the visible world, which without the sun would be a dark dungeon. In the same way, the human race would be darkness itself without the *light of the glory of God* shining *in the face of Christ* (2Co 4:6). He is the *Sun of righteousness*, for he is himself a righteous Savior. The word translated "righteousness" sometimes signifies "mercy" or "kindness," and it was in Christ that the *tender mercy of our God visited us* (Lk 1:78). Those who are ruled by a holy fear of God will have his *love* also *shed abroad in their hearts by the Holy Ghost* (Ro 5:5).

2.1.2. To the graces and comforts of the Holy Spirit that are brought into the human soul. The sun may be said to arise there and to bring both a delightful day and a fruitful spring along with it.

2.1.3. To Christ's second coming, which will be a glorious and welcome sunrise to all who *fear his name*.

2.2. What this mercy and comfort will bring to them: he *shall arise with healing in his wings* (v. 2). Christ came, as *the sun* comes, to bring not only light to a dark world but also health to a diseased world. The Jews have a proverb, "As the sun rises, infirmities decrease." Christ came into the world to be the great Physician — indeed, the great medicine, too: both the *balm in Gilead* and the *physician there* (Jer 8:22). When he was on earth, he went about as the sun revolves in its circuit (Ps 19:6), doing that kind of good (Ac 10:38); he *healed all manner of sicknesses and diseases among the people* (Mt 4:23). His healing physical diseases was an example of his great intention in coming into the world, which was to heal the diseases of human souls.

2.3. What a good effect it will have on them.

2.3.1. It will make them vigorous in themselves: "*You shall go forth*, as those who are healed go out and return to their work." The souls will go out of their bodies at death, and the bodies out of their graves at the resurrection, as prisoners leave their dungeons, see the light, and are set at liberty. "You will also *grow up*; being restored to health and liberty, you will increase in knowledge, grace, and spiritual strength." Those who by the grace of God are made wise and good are made wiser and better by the same grace. Their growth is compared to that of *the calves of the stall*, which is a quick, strong, and useful growth. Some read it, instead of *You shall grow up*, "You will move yourselves," or "you will leap for joy," being as playful as calves of the stall when they are let loose onto the open fields.

2.3.2. It will make them victorious over their enemies (v. 3): *You shall tread down the wicked*. When believers by faith *overcome the world* (1Jn 5:4), when they suppress their own corrupt appetites and passions, when the God of peace bruises Satan under their feet (Ro 16:20), then they *tread down the wicked*. The saints' triumphs are all because of God's victories; it is not they who do this, but God who does it for them.

Verses 4–6

This is without doubt intended as a solemn conclusion of the whole Old Testament. The Jews were not to expect any more prophecy inspired by the Spirit until the *beginning* (Mk 1:1) of the Gospel of the Messiah. Two things are required:

1. They must maintain their obedient respect for the Law of Moses (v. 4): *Remember the law of Moses my servant* and observe it, that law that *I commanded unto him in Horeb*. Notice here:

1.1. The honorable mention of *Moses*. God through Malachi calls him *Moses my servant*, for the righteous will be remembered eternally.

1.2. The honorable mention of the *law of Moses*; it was what God himself *commanded*. It is our concern to keep the law because God has commanded it and because he commanded it for us, for we are the spiritual Israel. If we expect to enjoy the benefits of the covenant with Israel (Heb 8:10), we must observe the commands given to Israel, those of them that were intended to be kept perpetually.

1.3. The summary of our duty with reference to the Law. The task of our conscience is to tell us to *remember the law*. Even when we have made considerable advances in knowledge, we must still hold on to the basic principles of practical religion and be determined to be faithful to them. Those who study the writings of the prophets and Revelation must continue to remember the Law of Moses and the four Gospels. Prophecy was now to cease in the church for some ages, and the Spirit of prophecy was not to return until the *beginning of the Gospel* (Mk 1:1); now they were told to *remember the law of Moses*. Let them live by its rules and live on its promises. As long as we have Bibles, we may maintain our fellowship with God and keep ourselves in his way.

1.4. They were to expect the coming of the Messiah, the preaching of his Gospel, and the setting up of his kingdom. Let them observe the Law of Moses, and then they could expect to enjoy the benefits of the Gospel of Christ, for *to him that has*, and uses what he has well, *more shall be given, and he shall have abundance* (Mt 13:12).

2. They must maintain a faithful expectation of the Gospel of Christ and must look for its *beginning* (Mk 1:1–3) in the appearing of Elijah the prophet (vv. 5–6). The *law and the prophets were until John* (Lk 16:16); they continued to be the only lights of the church until that morning star appeared (Rev 22:16). Notice:

2.1. Who this prophet was who would be sent; he was *Elijah* (v. 5). Some of the Jewish teachers want this to be the same Elijah who prophesied in Israel in the days of Ahab; they believe that he will come again as the forerunner of the Messiah. Others of them say he is not the same person, but another of the same spirit. However, we Christians know very well that John the Baptist was the Elijah who was to come (Mt 17:10–13), and explicitly so: *This is Elias that was to come* (Mt 11:14); this is the one about whom it is written, *Behold, I send my messenger* (3:1; Mt 11:10). Elijah was a man of great austerity, bold in rebuking sin. John the Baptist was inspired by the same spirit and power as Elijah, and, like Elijah, he preached repentance and reformation.

2.2. When he would be sent — before the appearing of the Messiah. John the Baptist gave the Jews fair warning when he told them of the *wrath to come* and gave them a way to escape it, as well as when he told them of the *fan in Christ's hand*, with which Christ would thoroughly cleanse his floor; see Mt 3:7, 10, 12.

2.3. On what mission he would be sent: *He shall turn the heart of the fathers to their children, and the heart of the children to their fathers* (v. 6), *so making ready a people prepared for him* (Lk 1:16–17). It was promised about John that he would:

2.3.1. Make a bold stand against the flood of sin and ungodliness. This is called his *coming to restore all things* (Mt 17:11).

2.3.2. Preach a doctrine that would reach people's hearts. Many people had their consciences awakened by his ministry.

2.3.3. Turn the hearts of parents "with their children" and the hearts of the children "with their parents"—as some read it—to God and to their duty.

2.3.4. Be an instrument to bind them more firmly to one another by bringing and binding them all to their God. He would prepare the way for that kingdom of heaven which would make all its faithful subjects of *one heart* and *one soul* (Ac 4:32), which would be a kingdom of love and put to death all enmities. By their impiety and impenitence, the body of the Jewish nation had exposed themselves to the curse of God. God was ready to strike them with that curse, but he wanted to test them once again. He therefore sent John the Baptist to preach repentance to them, so that their way of life might prevent their disgrace; God is so unwilling that anyone should perish (2Pe 3:9). Some notice that the last word of the Old Testament is a curse, so that we may welcome Christ, who comes with a blessing. It is with a blessing, with the finest blessing, that the New Testament ends, and let us arm ourselves with that—or, rather, may God arm us—against this curse. *The grace of our Lord Jesus Christ be with us all. Amen* (Ro 16:24).

A Practical and Devotional Exposition of the Gospel of

Matthew

W e have here:
1. The second part of the Holy Bible, called *The New Testament of our Lord and Saviour Jesus Christ*, or the *new covenant*. However, when the phrase *of Jesus Christ* is added to it, as here, making the title a reference to Christ's act, the word is most properly rendered *testament*, for he is the testator, and it comes into force *by his death* (Heb 9:16–17). All the grace contained in this book is owing to our Lord and Savior Jesus Christ, and unless we submit to him as our Lord, we cannot expect to receive any benefit from him as our Savior. This was called the *New* Testament to distinguish it from what was given by Moses. How carefully we preserve, and with what attention and delight we read, the last will and testament of a friend, who has left us a fair estate and, with it, their high expressions of love to us! How precious, then, should this testament of our blessed Savior be to us, which safeguards all his unsearchable riches for us (Eph 3:8)! It is *his* testament, for though, as is usual, it was written by others, nevertheless, he dictated it, and the night before he died, in the institution of his supper, he signed it, sealed it, and made it public in the presence of twelve witnesses. In it is declared *the whole counsel of God* concerning our salvation (Ac 20:27).

2. *The Four Gospels. Gospel* means "good news," and this history of Christ's coming *into the world to save sinners* (1Ti 1:15), is, without doubt, the best news that ever came from heaven to earth. The angel gave it this title (Lk 2:10): "*I bring you good tidings*; I bring the Gospel to you." In addition, the prophet Isaiah foretold good news (Isa 52:7; 61:1). *Gospel* is an Old English word; it means "God's spell" or "God's word." The four books that contain the record of the Redeemer are commonly called *the four Gospels*, and their inspired writers *evangelists*, or *Gospel writers*. These four Gospels were received early and constantly by the church and were read in Christian assemblies, as can be seen from the writings of Justin Martyr and Irenaeus, who lived little more than a hundred years after Christ's ascension. About the same time, Tatian compiled a harmony of these four evangelists, which he called "The Gospel made up of four." In the third and fourth centuries Gospels were forged by various sects and published, one under the name of St. Peter, another of St. Thomas, yet another of St. Philip, and so on. However, they were never acknowledged as canonical by the church.

3. *The Gospel according to St. Matthew*. The writer was a Jew by birth, a *publican* (tax collector) by calling, until Christ commanded his attendance, and then he left the tax collector's booth to follow him (9:9) and was one of those who accompanied him *all the time that the Lord Jesus went in and out, beginning from the baptism of John unto the day that he was taken up* (Ac 1:21–22). He was therefore a competent witness of what he recorded here. It was written, without doubt, in Greek, as were the other parts of the New Testament; it was not written in the language that was distinctive to the Jews, whose church and state were near an end, but in the one that was common to the world and in which the knowledge of Christ would be most effectively transmitted to the nations of the earth.

CHAPTER 1

This evangelist begins with the account of Christ's lineage and birth, the ancestors from whom he descended and how he came into the world, because it was foretold that he would be the Son of David and would be born of a virgin. We have here: 1. His genealogy from Abraham in forty-two generations, three fourteens (vv. 1–17). 2. An account of the circumstances of his birth, to show he was born of a virgin (vv. 18–25).

Verses 1–17

Notice about this genealogy of our Savior:
1. Its title. It is *the book of the generation of Jesus Christ*. The phrase can mean the account of his natural ancestors or the narrative of his birth. It is "a book of Genesis." It is a glory of the Old Testament that it begins with the book of the generation of the world, but the glory of the New Testament excels that glory by beginning with *the book of the generation of* the One who made the world.

2. Its main aim. It is not an endless or unnecessary genealogy (1Ti 1:4). It is like a lineage given as evidence, to prove a title and make a claim; the intention is to prove that our Lord Jesus is *the son of David* and *the son of Abraham*, from that nation and family out of which the Messiah was to come. Abraham and David were, in their day, the great trustees of the promise of the Messiah. Abraham was promised that Christ would descend from him (Ge 12:3; 22:18), and David was promised that he would descend from him (2Sa 7:12; Ps 7:12; 89:3; 132:11). Christ is first called *the son of David* here because it was by that title that the Christ was commonly spoken of and expected among the Jews. Those who acknowledged him to be *the Christ* called him *the son of David* (15:22; 20:31; 21:15). Therefore, the evangelist undertakes to show that he is not only *a son of David* but also that *son of David* on whose *shoulders the government was to be* (Isa 9:6); he shows that the Christ is not only *a son of Abraham* but also that *son of Abraham* who was to be *the father of many nations* (Ge 17:4–5; Ps 22:30; Isa 9:6; 53:10). In calling Christ *the son of David* and *the son of Abraham*, he shows that God is faithful to his promise and that he will fulfill every word he has spoken. He will do this:

2.1. Even though the fulfillment is delayed for a long time. Although delays of promised mercies may exercise our patience, they do not weaken God's promises.

2.2. Even though it may begin to be despaired of. This *son of David* and *son of Abraham*, who was to be the glory of his Father's house, was born when the seed of Abraham was a despised people and had recently become subject to the Roman yoke, and when the house of David was buried in obscurity, for Christ was to be *a root out of a dry ground* (Isa 53:2).

3. Its particular sequence, drawn in a direct line from Abraham onward, according to the genealogies recorded at the beginning of the books of Chronicles. We may notice some details in this genealogy:

3.1. Among the ancestors of Christ who had brothers, he generally descended from a younger brother; Abraham himself was one such, as were Jacob, Judah, David, Nathan, and Rhesa (Lk 3:27). This showed that the preeminence of Christ did not come from an unbroken succession of firstborn sons in his ancestry, but from the will of God (Jn 1:13), who *exalteth them of low degree* (Lk 1:52) and puts *more abundant honour upon that part which lacked* (1Co 12:23).

3.2. Among the sons of Jacob, besides Judah, from whom Shiloh came (Ge 49:10), notice is taken here of his brothers: *Judas and his brothers*. No mention is made of Ishmael the son of Abraham or of Esau the son of Isaac, because they were excluded from the church, whereas all the children of Jacob were taken in and so are mentioned in the genealogy.

3.3. For the same reason that the brothers of Judah are taken notice of, *Phares* (Perez) and *Zara* (Zerah), the twin sons of Judah, are also both named, though only Perez was Christ's ancestor.

3.4. Four women, and only four, are named in this genealogy. Two of them were originally foreigners to the citizenship of Israel (Eph 2:12): Rahab, a Canaanitess, and also a prostitute, and Ruth the Moabitess, for in Jesus Christ there is neither Greek nor Jew (Ro 10:12; Gal 3:28; Col 3:11). Those who are strangers and foreigners are welcome, in Christ, to the citizenship of the saints. The other two were adulteresses, Tamar and Bathsheba; this was a further mark of humiliation put on our Lord Jesus. He took on himself the likeness of sinful flesh (Ro 8:3),

and he takes even great sinners, on their repentance, into the closest relationship with himself.

3.5. Although several kings are named here, none is explicitly called a king except David (v. 6), because the covenant of royalty was made with him. The Messiah is therefore said to inherit the throne of his father David (Lk 1:32).

3.6. In the lineage of the kings of Judah, between *Joram* (Jehoram) and *Ozias* (Uzziah) (v. 8), three are left out, namely, Ahaziah, Joash, and Amaziah, and so when it is said, *Joram begat Ozias* (Jehoram became the father of Uzziah), it is meant, according to the Hebrew custom, that Uzziah was lineally descended from him.

3.7. Some notice what a mixture there was of good and bad in the succession of these kings; for instance (vv. 7–8), evil *Roboam* (Rehoboam) was the father of evil *Abia* (Abijah); evil Abijah was the father of good Asa; good Asa was the father of good *Josaphat* (Jehoshaphat); good Jehoshaphat was the father of evil *Joram* (Jehoram). Grace does not run in the blood, nor does the control of sin. God's grace is his own, and he gives or withholds it as he pleases.

3.8. The exile in Babylon is mentioned as a remarkable period in this lineage (vv. 11–12). All things considered, it was a miracle that the Jews were not lost in captivity, as other nations have been, but this suggests that the reason why the streams of that people were kept running pure through that dead sea was that from them, *concerning the flesh, Christ* was to *come* (Ro 9:5).

3.9. *Josias* (Josiah) is said to be the father of *Jechonias* (Jeconiah) and his brothers (v. 11); by *Jechonias* (Jeconiah) is meant Jehoiachin (see commentary on 2Ki 24:8–20, 2.4.4.; 1Ch 3:10–24, 2.). When *Jechonias* is said to have been recorded as childless (Jer 22:30), it is explained in this way: *no man of his seed shall prosper*. Shealtiel is said here to have been the father of *Zorobabel* (Zerubbabel), whereas Shealtiel was the father of Pedaiah, and Pedaiah was the father of Zerubbabel (1Ch 3:19), but as before—and as is often the case—the grandson is called the son.

3.10. The line comes down not to Mary the mother of our Lord, but to Joseph the husband of Mary (v. 16), for the Jews always reckoned their genealogies through males; but Mary was of the same tribe and family as Joseph, so that both by his mother and by his supposed father, he came from the house of David (see commentary on Lk 3:23).

3.11. The center in whom all these lines meet is *Jesus, who is called Christ* (v. 16). This is the One who was so fervently desired, so impatiently expected. Those who do the will of God are in a more honorable relationship with Christ than those who were related to him according to the flesh (12:50). Jesus is called the *Christ*, that is, "the Anointed One," which means the same as the Hebrew *Messiah*.

3.12. We have the general summary of all this genealogy in v. 17, where it is summed up in three fourteens, grouped in remarkable periods. In the first fourteen, we have the family of David arising and looking forward like the morning; in the second, we have it flourishing in its midday brightness; in the third, we have it declining and growing less and less, dwindling to the family of a poor carpenter, and then Christ *shines forth* out of it (Dt 33:2; Job 11:17), the *glory of his people Israel* (Lk 2:32).

Verses 18–25

The mystery of Christ's incarnation is to be adored, not meddled with. If we *know not the way of the Spirit* in the forming of ordinary people, nor *how the bones are formed in the womb of* anyone *that is with child* (Ecc 11:5), then much less do we know how the blessed Jesus was formed in the womb of the Blessed Virgin. We find here some circumstances surrounding the birth of Christ that are not in Luke, even though it is recorded there more fully. We have here:

1. Mary's being promised in marriage to Joseph. Mary, the mother of our Lord, *was espoused to Joseph*, not completely married, but promised in marriage. We read of a man who *has betrothed a wife and has not taken her* (Dt 20:7). Christ was born of a virgin, and she was a betrothed virgin (pledged to be married):

1.1. To confer respect on the marriage state and to commend it as *honourable among all* (Heb 13:4). Who was more highly favored than Mary, when she was promised in marriage (Lk 1:28)?

1.2. To save the reputation of the Blessed Virgin, which otherwise would have been exposed. It was fitting that her conception should be protected by marriage and thereby justified in the eyes of the world.

1.3. So that the Blessed Virgin would have one to be the guide of her youth (Pr 2:17), a suitable companion for her. Some think that Joseph was now a widower and that those who are called the *brethren of Christ* (13:55) were Joseph's children by a previous wife. Joseph was *a just man*; she, a *virtuous woman* (Pr 31:10). We may also learn from this example that it is good to enter into the married state with deliberation, not hastily—to introduce the marriage with a contract. It is better to take time to consider beforehand than to find time to repent afterward.

2. Her being pregnant with the promised seed; *before they came together*, she *was found with child*, which really was *of the Holy Spirit* (v. 18). We may well imagine what perplexity this might justly have caused the Blessed Virgin. She herself knew the divine origin of this conception, but how could she prove it? She would be *dealt with as a harlot* (Ge 34:31). Never was any daughter of Eve so dignified as the Virgin Mary, and yet she was in danger of falling under the imputation of one of the worst of crimes. We do not find, however, that she tormented herself about it, but rather that, being aware of her own innocence, she remained calm and at peace and committed her cause to *him that judgeth righteously* (1Pe 2:23).

3. Joseph's bewilderment and his anxiety about what to do in this situation. He was reluctant to believe something so bad of a woman whom he believed to be so good, but just as the matter was too bad to be excused, it was also too plain to be denied. Notice:

3.1. The extremity he sought to avoid. He was *not willing to make her a public example* (did not want to expose her to public disgrace) (v. 19). He could have done so (Dt 22:23–24). How different was the spirit that Joseph displayed from that of Judah, who in a similar case quickly passed the severe sentence, *Bring her forth and let her be burnt!* (Ge 38:24). How good it is to *think on things* (Php 4:8) as Joseph did here! If there were more deliberation in our criticism and judgments, there would be more mercy and moderation in them. Some people with rigorous attitudes would blame Joseph for his mercy, but it is commended here; because *he was a just man*, he was not willing to expose her. He was *a religious, good man*, and so he was inclined to be merciful, as God is, and to *forgive* as one who was *forgiven* (Eph 4:32). We should in many cases be gentle toward those who come under the suspicion of having offended. The law court of conscience that moderates the rigor of the law is called a "court of equity." Those who are found at fault were perhaps *overtaken in*

the fault and are therefore to be *restored with the spirit of meekness* (Gal 6:1).

3.2. The way he found to avoid this crisis. He was *minded to put her away privily* (had in mind to divorce her quietly), that is, to put a certificate of divorce in her hand before two witnesses and so to keep the matter quiet among themselves. The necessary criticism of those who have offended should be managed without noise. Christian love and Christian wisdom will *hide a multitude of sins* (Jas 5:20)—and great ones, too—as much as they can without having fellowship with them.

4. Joseph's release from this bewilderment by a messenger sent from heaven (vv. 20–21). *While he thought on these things* and did not know what to decide, God graciously told him what to do and gave him peace. Those who want to have direction from God must *think on things* themselves; they must consider matters. It is the thoughtful, not the unthinking, whom God will guide. When he was at a loss and had taken the matter as far as he could in his own thoughts, then God came in with his advice. God's time to come in with instruction to his people is when they are perplexed and have come to the end of themselves. The message was sent to Joseph by an *angel of the Lord*. We cannot say how far God may now, invisibly, use the service of angels to extricate his people from their difficulties, but we are sure that they are all *ministering spirits* for their good (Heb 1:14). This angel appeared to Joseph *in a dream* when he was asleep. When we are at our quietest and most composed, we are in the best attitude to receive the announcements of God's will.

4.1. Joseph was here *directed* to proceed with his intended marriage. It was necessary to remind this poor carpenter of his noble birth: "Value yourself, Joseph; you are that *son of David* through whom the line of the Messiah is to be drawn." We may say this to every true believer: "Fear not, you son of Abraham, you child of God; do not forget the dignity of your birth, your new birth." *Fear not to take Mary for thy wife.*

4.2. He was here *informed* concerning that *holy thing* with which his promised wife was now pregnant. What was conceived in her was of divine origin. He was told two things:

4.2.1. That she had conceived *by the power of the Holy Ghost*, not by natural means. The *Holy* Spirit, who produced the world, now produced the Savior of the world, *preparing him a body*, as was promised him when he said, *Lo, I come* (Heb 10:5, 7). He was the Son of God, but he shared his mother's nature in such a way that he could truly be called *the fruit of her womb* (Lk 1:42). Histories tell us of some who proudly claimed to have conceived by divine power, such as the mother of Alexander, but none ever really did so except the mother of our Lord. We do not read that the Virgin Mary herself proclaimed the honor shown her; she hid it in her heart (Lk 2:19), and so God sent an angel to declare it.

4.2.2. That she would give birth to *the Saviour of the world* (v. 21). This was indicated:

4.2.2.1. In the name that would be given to her Son: *Thou shalt call his name Jesus, a Saviour. Jesus* is the same name as *Joshua*, only with the ending changed for the sake of conforming to the Greek. Joshua is called *Jesus* in Ac 7:45; Heb 4:8, where the Septuagint, a Greek version of the Old Testament, is quoted. Christ is our Joshua, both the *Captain of our salvation* (Heb 2:10) and the *High Priest of our profession* (Heb 3:1), and, in both, our Savior—a Joshua who comes to replace Moses and does for us what *the law could not do, in that it was weak* (Ro 8:3). Joshua had been called *Hosea*, but Moses attached the first syllable of the name *Jehovah*, and so made it *Jehoshua* (Nu 13:16), to show that the Messiah, who was to bear that name, would be *Jehovah*; he is therefore *able to save to the uttermost* (Heb 7:25), *neither is there salvation in any other* (Act 4:12).

4.2.2.2. In the reason for that name: *For he shall save his people from their sins* (v. 21). Those whom Christ saves he saves *from their sins*, from the guilt of sin by the merit of his death, from the controlling power of sin by the Spirit of his grace. In saving them from sin, he saves them from his wrath and the curse and from all misery here and in the future. Those who leave their sins and give themselves to Christ as *his people* enjoy the privilege of a relationship with the Savior and the great salvation that he has brought.

5. The fulfilling of the Scripture in all this. This evangelist, writing among the Jews, more frequently observes this than any of the other three. Here the Old Testament prophecies had their fulfillment, in our Lord Jesus. Now the Scripture that was fulfilled in the birth of Christ was that promise of a sign that God gave to King Ahaz (Isa 7:14), *Behold, a virgin shall conceive*, where the prophet, encouraging the people of God to hope for the promised rescue from Sennacherib's invasion, directed them to look forward to the Messiah, who was to come from the Jewish people and the house of David.

5.1. The sign given was that the Messiah would be *born of a virgin*. "*A virgin shall conceive*, and by her he will be revealed *in the flesh*." The Hebrew word *almah*, which is used in Isa 7:14, means "a virgin" in the strictest sense, such as Mary professes herself to be (Lk 1:34): *I know not a man*. Christ would be born not of an *empress* or *queen*—for he appeared not in outward pride, show, or splendor—but of a virgin, to teach us spiritual purity.

5.2. The truth proved by this sign was that he was the Son of God and the Mediator between God and human beings, for *they shall call his name Immanuel*. *Immanuel* means "God with us." It is a mysterious name, but a very precious one, God incarnate among us and therefore God reconcilable to us, at peace with us and taking us into covenant and fellowship with himself. The Jewish people had *God with them* in types and shadows, dwelling between the cherubim (1Sa 4:4; 2Sa 6:2; etc.), but never so much as when the *Word was made flesh* (Jn 1.14)—*that* was the blessed *Shechinah*, God's presence made visible. By the light of nature, we see God as a God *above us*; by the light of the *law*, we see him as a God *against us*; but by the light of the Gospel, we see him as *Immanuel*, God *with us*, in our own nature and on our side. His great work of salvation lies in bringing God and human beings together; what he intended was to bring *God* to be *with us*, which is our great joy, and to bring *us* to *be with God*, which is our great duty.

6. Joseph's obedience to the divine command (v. 24). *Being raised from sleep* by the impression that the dream made on him, *he did as the angel of the Lord had bidden him. He took unto him his wife*. God still has ways of making known his mind in doubtful cases, by the nudges of providence, the whispers of conscience, and the advice of faithful friends. In each of these, applying the general rules of the written word, we should take direction from God.

7. The fulfillment of the divine promise (v. 25). *She brought forth her firstborn* son. The circumstances of the birth are related more fully in Lk 2:1–20. If Christ is *formed* in the soul (Gal 4:19), God himself has begun the good work that he will complete (Php 1:6); what is *conceived* in grace will no doubt be *brought forth* in glory. Although Joseph solemnized the marriage with Mary, his promised wife, he *knew her not till she had brought him*

forth (he had no union with her until she gave birth). Much has been said about the perpetual virginity of the mother of our Lord: Jerome was very angry with Helvidius for denying it. It is certain that it cannot be proved from Scripture. Dr. Whitby tends to think that when it is said, *Joseph knew her not till she had brought forth her firstborn* (v. 25), it is suggested that afterward he lived with her according to the Law (Ex 21:10). *Joseph called his name Jesus*, according to the instruction given him.

CHAPTER 2

In this chapter we have the account of our Savior's infancy: 1. The wise men's concerned inquiry about Christ (vv. 1–8). 2. Their devout attendance on him when they found where he was (vv. 9–12). 3. Christ's escape to Egypt to avoid the cruelty of Herod (vv. 13–15). 4. The barbaric murder of the infants of Bethlehem (vv. 16–18). 5. Christ's return from Egypt to the land of Israel (vv. 19–23).

Verses 1–8

It was a mark of humiliation put on the Lord Jesus that though he was the *Desire of all nations* (Hag 2:7), his coming into the world was hardly observed or taken notice of; his birth was obscure and ignored; indeed, he *came into the world*, and the *world knew him not*; indeed, he *came to his own*, and *his own received him not* (Jn 1:11). Yet, as later, so also in his birth, some rays of glory darted out from the greatest examples of his humility. The first people who took notice of Christ after his birth were the shepherds (Lk 2:15), who saw and heard glorious things about him and *made them known abroad*, to the amazement of all who heard them (Lk 2:17–18). After that, Simeon and Anna spoke about him, through the Spirit, to all who were disposed to take note of what they said (Lk 2:38). Now, one would have thought that these hints would have been taken notice of by the people of Judah and the *inhabitants of Jerusalem* and that they would embrace the long-looked-for Messiah with both arms, but it seems that he continued to live for nearly another two years at Bethlehem without any further notice being taken of him until these wise men came. Nothing will wake up those who are determined to ignore him. Notice:

1. When this inquiry was made about Christ. It was *in the days of Herod the king* (v. 1). This Herod was an Edomite, made king of Judea by Augustus and Antonius, the then chief rulers of the Roman state, a man who was known for falsehood and cruelty and yet was complimented with the title of *Herod the Great*.

2. Who and what these *wise men* were; they are here called "Magi." Some understand this in a good sense; the *Magi* among the *Persians* were their philosophers and their priests. Others think they dealt in unlawful arts; the word is used to describe Simon (Ac 8:9, 11) and Elymas (Ac 13:6), both sorcerers, and the Scripture does not use it in any other sense. Whatever kind of wise men they were before, they began to be truly *wise men* when they set themselves to ask about Christ. We are sure of the following:

2.1. They were Gentiles and did not belong to the citizenship of Israel (Eph 2:12). The Jews paid no attention to Christ, but these Gentiles sought him out. Many times those who are closest to the means are furthest from the end. See 8:11–12.

2.2. They were *scholars*. They studied knowledge and philosophy; good scholars should be good Christians, and when they *learn Christ* (Eph 4:20), then they complete their learning.

2.3. They were *men of the east*, who were noted for their *soothsaying* (Isa 2:6). Arabia is called the land of *the east* (Ge 25:6), and the *Arabians* are called *men of the east* (Jdg 6:3). The presents they brought were the products of that country.

3. What motivated them to make this search. In their country, which was in the *east*, they had seen an *extraordinary star*, such as they had not seen before. They took this to indicate the birth of an extraordinary person in the land of Judea, over which land this star was seen to hover. This was so different from anything that was common that they concluded it meant something uncommon. The birth of Christ was reported to the Jewish shepherds by *an angel*, and to the Gentile philosophers by *a star*: God spoke to both in their own language and in the way they were most familiar with. The same star they had seen in the *east* was seen long after, leading them to the house where Christ lay. It was a candle deliberately set up to guide them to Christ. The idolaters worshiped the stars as the *host of heaven* (Dt 4:19; 17:3; etc.), especially the *eastern* nations. At the birth of Christ, the stars, which had been misused, came to be put to right use, to lead people to Christ; the gods of the nations became his servants. Others attribute the inquiry of the wise men to the general expectation of that time, in those *eastern* parts, that some great ruler would appear. We may suppose a divine impression was made on their minds, enabling them to interpret this star as a sign given by heaven of the birth of Christ.

4. How they pursued their inquiry. *They came from the* east to Jerusalem, seeking this prince further. They could have said, "If such a ruler is born, we will hear about him soon in our own country, and that will be the time to pay our homage to him." But they were so impatient to know him more that they deliberately undertook a long journey to seek him. Those who truly desire to know Christ and find him will think nothing of pain or danger in seeking him.

4.1. Their question was, *Where is he that is born King of the Jews?* (v. 2). They did not ask whether such a person was born; their question was, *Where is he born?* Those who know something of Christ must want to know more of him.

4.2. They expected to find a ready answer to this question, to find all Jerusalem worshiping at the feet of this new king, but no one could give them any information. There is more gross ignorance in the world, and also in the church, than we are aware of. Many people who we think should direct us to Christ are themselves strangers to him and do not know him. These travelers pursued their inquiry: *Where is he that is born King of the Jews?* If they were asked, "Why are you asking?" their answer would be that they had *seen his star in the east.* If they were asked, "What business do you have with him? What have the men of the *east* to do with the *King of the Jews?*" they had their answer ready: *We are come to worship him* (v. 2). Those in whose hearts the morning star is risen (2Pe 1:19) and given them anything of the knowledge of Christ must make it their business to worship him.

5. How this inquiry was treated at Jerusalem. News of it eventually reached the court, and *when Herod heard it, he was troubled* (v. 3). He could not have been ignorant of the prophecies of the Old Testament about the Messiah and his kingdom, and he must have known the times Daniel's weeks had established for the Messiah's appearing, but because he himself had reigned so long and so successfully, he began to hope that those promises would fail forever and that his kingdom would be established forever in spite of them. It must have greatly disappointed

his hopes when he heard talk of this King being born. Although Herod, being an Edomite, was troubled, one would have thought that Jerusalem would be very joyful to hear that her King was coming, but it seems *all Jerusalem were troubled with* Herod, fearing the adverse consequences of the birth of this new king. The slavery of sin is foolishly preferred by many people to the glorious liberty of the children of God (Ro 8:21), only because they fear some present difficulties accompanying that necessary revolution of government in the soul. Herod and Jerusalem were troubled because of the mistaken notion that the kingdom of the Messiah would conflict and interfere with the secular powers, whereas the star that proclaimed him king clearly indicated that his kingdom was heavenly, not of this lower world.

6. What assistance they met with in this inquiry from the teachers of the law and the priests (vv. 4–6). No one can claim to tell where the King of the Jews is, but Herod asked where it was expected *he would be born.*

6.1. The people he consulted were the chief priests, who were the teachers of the law. It was generally known that Christ would be *born at Bethlehem* (Jn 7:42), but Herod wanted to have an expert opinion on this matter. He turned, therefore, to the proper people, *all the chief priests, and all the scribes,* and *demanded of them* that they tell him *where Christ should be born.* Many a good question is asked with wrong motives.

6.2. The priests and teachers of the law did not need to take long to answer this question, nor did their opinions differ; they all agreed that the Messiah must be *born in Bethlehem, the city of David,* here called *Bethlehem of Judea. Bethlehem* means "the house of bread," and so that town was the best birthplace for the One who is the true manna, *the bread which came down from heaven,* which was *given for the life of the world* (Jn 6:33). Bethlehem's honor lay not, like that of other towns, in the large number of its people, but in the magnificence of the rulers it produced. It was supreme over all the towns of Israel, therefore, in this way: that *the Lord shall count, when he writes up the people, that this man,* even *the man Christ Jesus* (1Ti 2:5), *was born there* (Ps 87:6). *Out of thee shall come a Governor,* the *King of the Jews.* Bethlehem was the *city of David,* and David the glory of Bethlehem; there, therefore, David's son and successor must be born. There was a famous well at *Bethlehem,* by the gate, that David longed to drink from (2Sa 23:15); in Christ we have not only enough bread and to spare; we may also come and take *of the water of life freely* (Rev 21:6).

7. Herod's plan for bloodshed that was brought about by this inquiry (vv. 7–8). Herod was now an old man and had reigned thirty-five years; this king was only recently born and unlikely to do anything significant for many years; but Herod was still jealous of him. Crowned heads cannot bear to think of their successors, much less of their rivals, and so nothing less than the blood of this infant king would satisfy him. Passion had gained control of his reason and conscience.

7.1. Notice how craftily he set up the project (vv. 7–8). *He privily* (secretly) *called the wise men* to discuss this matter with them. He would not openly acknowledge his fears and jealousies. Sinners are often tormented by secret fears that they keep to themselves. Herod learned from the wise men the *time when the star appeared.* He then employed them to ask further and told them to bring him an account of where the child was. All this might have looked suspicious if he had not covered it up with a show of religious fervor: *that I may come and worship him also.*

The greatest evil often conceals itself under a cloak of godliness.

7.2. Notice how strangely he was fooled and infatuated because he trusted this mission to the wise men. Bethlehem was only seven miles (about eleven kilometers) from Jerusalem; he could easily have sent spies to watch the wise men, and the spies could have reached there as quickly to destroy the child as the wise men would to worship him!

Verses 9–12

We have here the wise men's humble attendance on this newborn *King of the Jews* and the honors they gave him. From Jerusalem they went to Bethlehem, resolving to *seek till they should find*, but it is very strange that they went alone. They *came from a far country* to worship Christ, while the Jews, his relatives, would not move a step, would not even go to the next town to welcome him. We must continue to wait on Christ even if we are alone in doing so; whatever others may do, we must *serve the Lord* (Dt 10:12; 11:13; 28:47).

1. See how they found Christ by the same star that they had seen in their own country (vv. 9–10). Notice how:

1.1. Graciously God directed them. By the first appearance of the star they were given to understand where they should ask for this King, and then the star disappeared, and they were left to follow up with the usual methods for such an inquiry. Extraordinary helps are not to be expected where ordinary means are available. They then traced the matter as far as they could; they were on their journey to Bethlehem, but because that was a populous town, where would they find him when they reached there? Here they were at a loss, at their wits' end, but not at their faith's end; they believed that God would not leave them there. Nor did he, for, look, *the star which they saw in the east went before them* (v. 9). If we go as far as we can in doing our duty, God will direct and enable us to do what we by ourselves cannot do. The star had left them a long time before, but it now returned. Those who follow God in the dark will find that light is sown (Ps 97:11), is reserved, for them. This star was the sign of God's presence with them, for he is light (1Jn 1:5), and he goes in front of his people as their Guide. There is a morning star that arises in the hearts of those who seek Christ (2Pe 1:19).

1.2. Joyfully they followed God's direction: *When they saw the star, they rejoiced with exceeding great joy* (v. 10). Now they saw that they were not deceived; now they realized they had not taken this long journey in vain. They were now sure God was with them, and the signs of his presence and favor fill with unspeakable joy the souls of those who know how to value them. We cannot expect too little from people, nor too much from God. What delight, what rapture these wise men were in when they saw the star! Now they had reason to hope for a sight of *the Lord's Christ* (Rev 11:15) quickly, of *the Sun of righteousness* (Mal 4:2), for they saw the *Morning Star* (Rev 22:16). We should be glad to see anything that will show us the way to Christ. This star was sent to meet the wise men and lead them into the presence of the King. Now God fulfilled his promise of meeting those who wanted to *rejoice and work righteousness* (Isa 64:5). God sometimes favors young converts with such signs of his love as are especially encouraging to them in coping with the difficulties they face when they set out in the ways of God.

2. See how they acted when they found him (v. 11). We may well imagine what a disappointment it must have been to them to find that his palace was a mere cottage and that his own poor mother the only attendant he had! However,

these wise men were wise enough to see through this *veil*. They did not draw back, thinking their inquiry had been thwarted, but, having found the King they sought, they presented to him first themselves and then their gifts.

2.1. They presented themselves to him: *they fell down, and worshipped him* (v. 11). We do not read that they gave such honor to Herod, though he was at the height of his royal grandeur, but they gave this honor to this baby, not only as to a king but also as to a God. All who have found Christ fall down before him; they adore him and submit themselves to him. *He is thy Lord, and worship thou him* (Ps 45:11).

2.2. *They presented their gifts to him.* In the eastern nations, when subjects paid homage to their kings, they gave them presents. Along with ourselves, we must give all we have to Jesus Christ. Our gifts are not accepted, however, unless we first present ourselves to him as living sacrifices (Ro 12:1). The gifts they presented were *gold, frankincense, and myrrh*, money and things that were worth money. Providence sent this as a timely relief to Joseph and Mary in their present poor condition. These were the products of the wise men's own country; we must honor God with what he favors us with. They offered him *gold* because he was a king, paying him tribute; *frankincense* because he was God, for they honored God with the smoke of incense; and *myrrh* because he was a Man who would die, for *myrrh* was used in embalming dead bodies.

3. See how they left him when they had been with him (v. 12). Herod appointed them to *bring him word*, and, not suspecting that he wanted to use them as instruments to pursue his evil plans, they probably would have done so if they had not been commanded to do the opposite. Those who are sincere and honest easily believe that others are so too; they cannot think the world is as bad as it really is. God prevented the trouble Herod intended for the child Jesus. They were *warned not to return to Herod, nor* to Jerusalem; those who could have seen with their own eyes, yet would not, were unworthy to have reports brought them about Christ. *They departed into their own country another way* to bring the news to their compatriots, but it is strange that we never hear anything more about them.

Verses 13–15

We have here Christ's escape to Egypt to avoid the cruelty of Herod. It was only a little respect that was shown to Christ in his infancy—compared with what should have been—but even that, instead of honoring him among his people, served to expose him. Notice:

1. The command given to Joseph about it (v. 13). Joseph knew neither the danger the child was in nor how to escape it, but God, through *an angel*, told him both *in a dream*, using the same means as before to direct him (1:20). Joseph was told here what their danger was: *Herod will seek the young child to destroy him.* God knows all the cruel plans and purposes of the enemies of his church. How early was the blessed Jesus involved in trouble! Usually, even those whose more mature years are accompanied by toils and perils have a peaceful and quiet infancy, but it was not so with the blessed Jesus. His life and suffering began together. Joseph was told what to do to escape the danger: *Take the young child, and flee into Egypt.* Christ must give an example so early in his life of his own rule (10:23): *When they persecute you in one city, flee to another.* Because self-preservation is a branch of the law of nature, it is eminently a part of the law of God. *Flee!* But why *into Egypt*? Egypt was infamous for idolatry, tyranny, and enmity to the people of God. That, however, was the appointed place of refuge for the holy

child Jesus. When God pleases, he can make the worst places serve the best purposes. This may be considered:

1.1. As a test of the faith of Joseph and Mary. They might be tempted to think, "If this child is the Son of God, as we are told he is, has he no other way to protect himself from a *man, that is a worm* (Job 25:6), than by making such a lowly and inglorious retreat?" They had just been told that he would be *the glory of his people Israel* (Lk 2:32), and had the land of Israel so quickly been too difficult for him? It now became clear how well God had provided for *the young child and his mother* (v. 13) in appointing Joseph to stand in such a close relation to them. Now the gold that the wise men had brought would help them bear their expenses. God foresees his people's distresses and provides for them in advance. God indicated the continuation of his care and guidance when he said, *Be thou there until I bring thee word*, so that Joseph must expect to hear from God again and must not move without receiving fresh orders.

1.2. As an example of the humiliation of our Lord Jesus. Just as there was no room for him in the inn at Bethlehem, so there was also no quiet room for him in the land of Judea. If we and our infants are in difficulties at any time, let us remember the difficulties Christ was brought into in his infancy.

1.3. As a sign of God's displeasure toward the Jews, who took so little notice of him; he justly left those who had shown him no respect.

2. Joseph's obedience to this command (v. 14). The journey would be inconvenient and dangerous for both the young child and his mother; but Joseph *was not disobedient to the heavenly vision* (Ac 26:19); he made no objection and was not slow in obeying. As soon as he had received his orders, he immediately *arose* and went away *by night*. Those who want to make sure work of their obedience must make a quick work of it. Now Joseph went out, as his father Abraham did, with an implicit dependence on God, *not knowing whither he went* (Heb 11:8). *Joseph took the young child and his mother.* Some notice that *the young child* is put first, as the main person, and Mary is called not *the wife of Joseph*, but *the mother of the young child*, which was her greater honor. They remained in Egypt until the death of Herod. There they were far away from the temple and its services, and among idolaters. Yet although they were far from the temple of the Lord, they still had with them the Lord of the temple. Forced absence from God's ordinances and forced presence among evildoers may be the sad lot, but are not the sin, of good people.

3. The fulfillment of the Scripture in all this: *Out of Egypt have I called my son* (Hos 11:1). Of all the evangelists, Matthew takes most notice of the fulfillments of the Scriptures concerning Christ. Now this word of the prophet undoubtedly referred to the rescue of Israel from Egypt, in which God acknowledged them as his son, his firstborn (Ex 4:22), but it is applied here, by way of analogy, to Christ, the Head of the church. The Scripture has many fulfillments; God fulfills the Scriptures every day. It is nothing new for God's sons to be in Egypt, in a foreign land, in a land of slavery, but they will be taken out. They may be hidden in Egypt, but they will not be left there.

Verses 16–18

1. Here is Herod's anger at the departure of the wise men. He waited a long time for them to return. He heard, however, after making inquiries, that they had gone off another way, which made him *exceedingly wroth* (furious) (v. 16). He was then even more desperate and outraged, because he and his plans had been disappointed.

2. We also have Herod's political plotting, despite this, to remove him who was *born King of the Jews*. If he could not reach him by a particular act, he had no doubts that a general attack would strike him. It was strange that Herod could find anyone so inhuman as to be willing to undertake such a barbaric act of bloodshed, but evil hands never lack evil tools to work with. Herod was now about seventy years old, so that an infant, at this time *under two years old*, was unlikely ever to disturb him. It was purely to gratify the brute desires of his own pride and cruelty that he did this. Notice what great plans he took:

2.1. As to the time; he *slew* (killed) *all from two years old and under*. The blessed Jesus was probably then not a year old, but Herod included all infants *under two years old* to make sure he did not miss his prey.

2.2. As to the place; he killed all the male children not only *in Bethlehem* but also *in all the coasts* (vicinity) *thereof*, in all the villages of that town. This was being *overmuch wicked* (Ecc 7:17). An unbridled wrath armed with unlawful power often makes people do the most terrible and unreasonable acts of cruelty. We are not to infer from the suffering of these children that they *were sinners above all that were in Israel* (Lk 13:2). However, we must look on this murder of the infants from a different angle; it was their martyrdom. They shed their blood for the One who later shed his blood for them. These were the infantry of *the noble army of martyrs*.

3. Here we have the fulfillment of Scripture (vv. 17–18): *then was fulfilled* that prophecy, *A voice was heard in Ramah* (Jer 31:15). That prediction was fulfilled in Jeremiah's time, but now the prophecy was again fulfilled in the great sorrow at the death of these infants. The Scripture was fulfilled:

3.1. In the place of this mourning. Its noise was heard from Bethlehem to Ramah, for Herod's cruelty extended itself to *all the coasts of Bethlehem*, even into the allotted territory of Benjamin, among the children of Rachel. Rachel's sepulcher was near Bethlehem (Ge 35:16, 19; 1Sa 10:2). These mothers were like Rachel; they lived near Rachel's grave, and many of them were descended from Rachel, and so their lamentations were excellently represented by *Rachel's weeping*.

3.2. In the extent of this mourning. It was *lamentation, weeping, and great mourning*, yet all little enough to express how they were affected by this devastating calamity. There was a great outcry in Egypt when the firstborn were killed (Ex 12:30), and so there was here when the youngest was killed, for we naturally have a particular tenderness for our youngest child. This sorrow was so great that they *would not be comforted*. We bless God that there is no cause of grief in this world, not even what is supplied by sin itself, that will justify us in refusing to *be comforted*! They *would not be comforted, because they were not*, that is, *they were not* in the land of the living, *were not* as they were, in their mothers' arms. If it were true *they were not*, there might be some excuse for sorrowing as though we had no hope (1Th 4:13), but we know they are not lost, but gone before. If we forget that *they are*, we lose the best reason for our encouragement. If we look further into this prophecy, we will find that *the bitter weeping* in Ramah introduced the greatest joy, for it follows, *Thy work shall be rewarded, and there is hope in thy end* (Jer 31:16). The worse things are, the sooner they will get better.

Verses 19–23

We have here Christ's return from Egypt to the *land of Israel*. Egypt may serve as a place to stay in or take shelter in temporarily, but not to remain in. Christ was *sent to the lost sheep of the house of Israel* (Mt 15:24), and so he must return to them. Notice:

1. What it was that made way for his return — the death of Herod, which happened not long after the murder of the infants. Divine vengeance made such quick work! Of all sins, the guilt of shedding innocent blood fills up the measure the soonest (23:32). Herod was so passionate and impatient that he tormented himself and intimidated all who attended him. Notice what kind of people have been the enemies and persecutors of Christ and his followers! Few have opposed Christianity except those who have first deprived themselves of humanity.

2. The orders given from heaven concerning their return, and Joseph's obedience to those orders (vv. 19–21). God had sent Joseph into Egypt, and he stayed there until the same One who brought him there ordered him away from there. In all our moves, it is good to see our way clear, to see God going before us; we should not move either one way or the other without orders from him. No place is outside God's gracious visits. Angels came to Joseph in Egypt, to Ezekiel in Babylon, and to John in Patmos.

2.1. The angel informed him of the death of Herod and his accomplices: *They are dead, which sought the young Child's life.* They were dead, but the young Child lived. Persecuted saints sometimes live long enough to tread on the graves of their persecutors. This is how the church's King weathered the storm, and the church has weathered many storms since.

2.2. He told him what to do. He must *go and return to the land of Israel*, and he did so without delay. God's people follow his directions wherever he leads them, wherever he puts them.

3. The further directions he received from God, as to which way to steer and where to settle in the land of Israel (vv. 22–23). God could have given him these instructions with the earlier ones, but God reveals his mind to his people gradually, to keep them waiting on him and expecting to hear further from him. Joseph probably received these orders *in a dream*, through the ministry of an angel, like those before. Now the direction given this holy, royal family was that:

3.1. They must not settle in Judea (v. 22). Joseph might think that because Jesus was *born in Bethlehem*, he must also be brought up there, but he was wisely *afraid for the young Child*, because *he heard that Archelaus reigned* in place of Herod, but only over Judea. Notice what a succession of enemies fight against Christ and his church! If one drops away, another one comes immediately to maintain the old enmity. This was why, however, Joseph must not take the young Child into Judea. God will not thrust his children into the jaws of danger except when it is for his own glory and to test them.

3.2. They must settle in Galilee (v. 22). Philip now ruled there; he was a mild, quiet man. The providence of God commonly so orders things that his people will not lack a quiet retreat from the storm and tempest. The family were sent to Nazareth, a town on a hill at the center of the allotted territory of Zebulun. It was there that the mother of our Lord was living when she conceived that *holy thing*, and probably Joseph also lived there (Lk 1:26–27). It was there that they were sent; there they were well known and among their relatives, and so that was the most proper place for them to live in. There they remained, and it was from the name of that town that our Savior was called *Jesus of Nazareth*, which was to *the Jews a stumbling-block* (1Co 1:23), for, *Can any good thing come* out of *Nazareth?* (Jn 1:46). In this is said to

be fulfilled what was *spoken by the prophets, He shall be called a Nazarene* (v. 23), which may be looked on:

3.2.1. As a name of honor and position, though it primarily signifies nothing more than a *man of Nazareth*. There is an allusion or mystery in it, describing Christ to be:

3.2.1.1. The *Man, the Branch*, spoken of in Isa 11:1. The word there is *Netzer*, which means "a branch" but also sounds like *Nazareth*.

3.2.1.2. The *great Nazarite*. Not that Christ was, strictly, a *Nazarite*, for he drank wine and touched dead bodies, but he was eminently so, both because he was distinctively holy and because he was by a solemn designation and dedication set apart to the honor of God in the work of our redemption, as Samson was to save Israel. Or:

3.2.2. As a name of reproach and contempt. To be called *a Nazarene* was to be called *a despicable man*, a man from whom nothing good was to be expected and to whom no respect was to be shown. It stuck as a nickname for him and his followers. Let no name of reproach for religion's sake seem hard to us, since our Master was himself called *a Nazarene*.

CHAPTER 3

The Gospel begins with this chapter about the baptism of John. What went before is only an introduction; this is the beginning of the Gospel of Jesus Christ (Mk 1:1). Here is: 1. The glorious rising of the morning star (Rev 22:16), in the appearance of John the Baptist (v. 1). 2. The more glorious shining of the Sun of righteousness (Mal 4:2) immediately afterward.

Verses 1–6

We have here an account of the preaching and baptism of John:

1. The time when he appeared: *In those days* (v. 1), or, "after those days," long after what was recorded in the previous chapter, which left the child Jesus in his infancy; *in those days*, in the time appointed by the Father for the beginning of the Gospel, when the *fulness of time* (Gal 4:4) had come. Glorious things were spoken (Ps 87:3) about both John and Jesus at and before their births, which would have given cause to expect some extraordinary appearances of God's presence and power with them when they were very young, but things turned out quiet differently. Apart from Christ's conversing with the teachers at twelve years old, nothing remarkable appeared about either of them until they were about thirty years old.

1.1. This was to show two things. First, even when God is acting as the God of Israel, the *Saviour*, he is still *a God that hideth himself* (Isa 45:15). Second, our faith must look to Christ mainly in his office and undertaking, for it is there that we see the *display* of his power, but in his person is the *hiding* of his power.

1.2. Matthew says nothing about the conception and birth of John the Baptist — which is related in detail by St. Luke — but finds him at adult age, as if dropped from the clouds to preach in the desert. After Malachi there was no prophet, nor anyone who claimed to prophecy, until John the Baptist.

2. The place where he appeared first: *In the wilderness of Judea.* It was not an uninhabited desert, but a part of the country not so densely populated as other parts were. It was a desert that had six towns and their villages in it. John preached there too then towns and villages, for it was around there that he had lived up to that time. The *word of the Lord* found John here in a *wilderness*. No place

is so far away as to remove us from the help of divine grace. It was in this *wilderness* of Judah that David wrote Ps 63, a psalm that speaks much of the sweet fellowship he then had with God (Hos 2:14). John the Baptist was a priest of the order of Aaron, but we find him preaching in a *wilderness* and never *officiating* in the *temple*. Christ, however, who was not a son of Aaron, was often found in the temple, sitting there as one with authority (7:29), as was foretold (Mal 3:1): *The Lord whom ye seek shall suddenly come to his temple*—not the *messenger* who was to prepare his way. The Gospel's beginning in a desert speaks comfort to the deserts of the Gentile world. *The desert shall rejoice* (Isa 35:1–2).

3. His preaching. He made this his work. Christ's kingdom must be set up by *the foolishness of preaching* (1Co 1:21).

3.1. The doctrine he preached was that of repentance: *Repent ye* (v. 2). He preached it not in Jerusalem, but in the Desert of Judea, among the ordinary country people, for even those who think they are farthest from the way of temptation and farthest from the vanities and vices of the city cannot wash their hands in innocence (Ps 26:6), but must do so in repentance. John the Baptist's work was to call people to *repent* of their sins. "*Change your minds*; you have thought wrongly; think again, and think aright." A change of *mind* produces a change of *ways*. Those who are truly sorry for what they have done wrong will be careful to do so no longer. This repentance is a necessary duty, a part of obedience to the command of God (Ac 17:30), and it is a necessary preparation and qualification for the encouragement of the Gospel of Christ. The sore must be examined before it can be cured. *I wound* and *I heal* (Dt 32:39).

3.2. The argument he used to back up this call was, *For the kingdom of heaven is at hand* (v. 2). What Christ is the Sovereign of is *a kingdom*. It is a kingdom of *heaven*, not of this world (Jn 18:36). John preached that this was *at hand*; it was then at the door; it has now come to us.

3.2.1. This is a great incentive to us *to repent*. There is nothing like the consideration of divine grace to break the heart, both *for sin* and *from sin*. Kindness is conquering; abused kindness, humbling and melting. How wretched I was to sin against such grace, against the law and love of such a kingdom!

3.2.2. It is a great encouragement to us *to repent*. The declaration of pardon finds the evildoer who before had fled and run away, and then it draws them in. This is how we all are drawn to it by cords of human kindness and the bonds of love (Hos 11:4).

4. The *prophecy* that was fulfilled in him (v. 3). This was the one who was spoken of at the beginning of the part of the prophecy of Isaiah that is concerned with the Gospel and that points to Gospel times and Gospel grace; see Isa 40:3–4. John is here spoken about:

4.1. As the *voice of one crying in the wilderness*. John acknowledged it himself: "*I am the voice* (Jn 1:23), and that is all"; God was the Speaker who made known his mind through John, as a person does through their voice. John is called "the voice of one crying out," a voice that is startling and awakening. Christ is called *the Word*, which, being distinct and articulate, is more instructive. John, as the *voice*, roused people, and then Christ, as the *Word*, taught them.

4.2. As one whose work it was to *prepare the way of the Lord, and to make his paths straight* (v. 3). This was how John prepared the way of the Lord.

4.2.1. He himself did so among the people of that generation. In the Jewish church and nation at that time,

everything was in disorder. The people were, generally speaking, extremely proud of their privileges and unaware of their sin, and although they now suffered under the most humbling providences, having recently become a province of the Roman Empire, they were still unhumbled. John was now sent to level these mountains (Isa 40:4), to humble their high opinion of themselves.

4.2.2. His teaching of repentance and self-denial is still as necessary as it was then. There is a great deal to be done to make way for Christ into a soul, and nothing is more necessary to bring this about than the revelation of sin and a conviction of the inadequacy of our own righteousness. That which hinders will hinder until it is taken out of the way (2Th 2:7). The way of sin and Satan is *a crooked way* (Ps 125:5; Pr 2:15); to prepare a way for Christ, the paths must be *made straight* (Heb 12:13).

5. The garments he wore, his appearance, and his way of life (v. 4). He would be *great in the sight of the Lord* but lowly in the eyes of the world, just as Christ himself had *no form or comeliness* (Isa 53:2).

5.1. His *dress* was *plain*. This same John had *his raiment of camel's hair, and a leathern girdle about his loins* (leather belt around his waist), for he lived in the country and suited his clothing to his surroundings. It is good for us to adjust ourselves to the place and condition in which God, in his providence, has put us. John appeared in these clothes:

- To show that, like Jacob, he was *a plain man* and denied this world and its showy delights.
- To show that he was *a prophet*, for prophets wore *rough garments*, as those who were denying themselves (Zec 13:4).
- To show that he was determined; his belt was not *fine*, like those that were then commonly worn, but it was *strong*.

5.2. His *diet* was *plain*; his food was locusts and *wild honey*. Locusts were a kind of flying insect, very good for food and allowed as clean (Lev 11:22). *Wild honey* was what *Canaan* flowed with (1Sa 14:26). This suggests that he ate *sparingly*, that a little was enough for him; it would take a long time for a man to fill his stomach with locusts and wild honey. He was so completely preoccupied with spiritual things that he could rarely find time for a set meal. Those whose business is to call others to mourn for sin and put it to death should themselves live a serious life, a life of self-denial. Every day was *a fast day* with him. A conviction of the worthlessness of the world and everything in it is the best preparation to receive the kingdom of heaven in the heart. *Blessed are the poor in spirit* (Mt 5:3).

6. The people who attended him and flocked toward him: *Then went out to him Jerusalem, and all Judea* (v. 5). Very many people came to him both from the city and from all parts of the country. Now:

6.1. This was a great *honour* to John. Those who least court the shadow of real honor are frequently those who receive it most. People have a secret esteem and reverence for them, more than one would imagine.

6.2. This gave John a great opportunity to do good and was evidence that God was with him.

6.3. This was evidence that it was now a time of great expectation. It was generally thought that the *kingdom of God* would immediately *appear*. The people were ready to say about John that he was *the Christ* (Lk 3:15).

6.4. Those who wanted to enjoy the benefits of John's ministry must *go out* to him in the desert, sharing his scorn. Those who want to learn the teaching of repentance must *go out* from the hustle and bustle of this world and be still.

6.5. It appears from the outcome that of the many who came to John's baptism, only a few remained faithful to it. There may be many eager hearers where there are only a few true believers.

7. The ritual, or ceremony, by which he admitted disciples (v. 6). Those who received his teaching and submitted to his discipline were *baptized of him in Jordan*. They testified their repentance by *confessing their sins*. The Jews had been taught to *justify* themselves, but John taught them to *accuse* themselves. A penitent confession of sin is necessary to receive peace and pardon, and it is only those who are brought with sorrow and shame to acknowledge their guilt who are ready to receive Jesus Christ as their Righteousness (1Jn 1:9; Jer 23:6; 33:16; 1Co 1:30). The benefits of the *kingdom of heaven*, now *at hand*, were then sealed to them by baptism. He washed them with water as a sign of this—that God would *cleanse them* from all their sins (1Jn 1:9). It was *the baptism of repentance* (Ac 19:4). All Israel was baptized into Moses (1Co 10:2). The *ceremonial law* consisted in *divers washings or baptisms* (Heb 9:10), but John's baptism referred to the law intended to provide a remedy for sin, the law of repentance and faith. By baptism he obliged them to live a holy life, according to the profession they were making for themselves. Confession of sin must always be accompanied with holy resolutions.

Verses 7–12

The doctrine John preached was that of repentance. Here we have the application of that doctrine. Application is the life of preaching, and so it was of John's preaching. Notice to whom he applied it: the Pharisees and Sadducees who came to his baptism (v. 7). The Pharisees were zealots for ceremonies and the traditions of the elders; the Sadducees ran to the other extreme and were little better than deists, denying the existence of spirits and a future state. Many come to public services but do not come under their power. The application was plain and direct and addressed to their consciences. He spoke as one who came not to preach *before* them, but to preach *to* them. He was not shy when he appeared in public, nor did he fear anybody. Here is:

1. A word of conviction and awakening. He began with harsh words, not calling them rabbi, not giving them the titles—and much less the applause—they had been used to.

1.1. The title he gave them was *O generation of vipers.* Christ gave them the same title (12:34; 23:33). They were a *viperous brood*, the seed and offspring of those who had the same spirit; it was born and bred in their bones. They were a "viperous gang," as it may be read; they were all the same; although they were one another's enemies, they were united in causing trouble. It is befitting for ministers of Christ to be bold in showing sinners their true character.

1.2. The warning he gave them was, *Who has warned you to flee from the wrath to come?* This indicated that they were in danger of the wrath to come, that it would be close to a miracle to bring about anything hopeful among them. "What brings you here? Who ever thought we'd see you here? What shock have you been given, that you are looking for the kingdom of heaven?" This shows us:

1.2.1. There is *a wrath to come*.

1.2.2. It is the great concern of each one of us to flee from this wrath.

1.2.3. It is wonderful mercy that we are fairly warned to flee from this wrath: *Who has warned us?* God has warned us; he takes no pleasure in our ruin.

1.2.4. These warnings sometimes shock those who seemed to have been very much hardened in their self-confidence and the good opinion they had of themselves.

2. A word of exhortation and direction (v. 8): "*Bring forth therefore fruits meet for* (produce fruit in keeping with) *repentance.* Because you profess repentance and listen to the teaching and baptism of repentance, show that you are true penitents." Repentance is seated in the heart; it is there as a root. But it is futile for us to pretend to have it there if we do not produce its fruits. Those who say they are sorry for their sins but persist in them are not worthy of the name of penitents or their privileges. Those who profess repentance, as all who are baptized do, must be and act as befits penitents.

3. A word of warning not to trust in their external privileges: *Think not to say within yourselves, We have Abraham to our father* (v. 9). There is a great deal that worldly hearts tend to say within themselves to set aside the convincing and commanding power of the word of God. "Do not please yourselves with saying this," as some read it; "Do not lull yourselves to sleep with this; do not flatter yourselves into such a false sense of security." God takes notice of what we say *within* ourselves. Many hide in *their right hand* the lies that ruin them (Isa 44:20), and they roll them *under their tongue* (Job 20:12), because they are ashamed to acknowledge them. John now showed them:

3.1. What their pretense was; "*We have Abraham to our father*; we are not the sinners of the Gentiles; what has that got to do with us?" The word does us no good when we will not take it as spoken to us and belonging to us. "Do not think that because you are the descendants of Abraham, therefore:

3.1.1. "You *need not repent*, that there is no need for you to change your mind or way.

3.1.2. "You will *fare well enough* even if you do not *repent*." It is useless and presumptuous to think that we will be saved by having good relatives even if we are not good ourselves. What good will all that do us if we do not repent and live a life of repentance? Many people, by resting in the honors and advantages of their visible church membership, fall short of heaven.

3.2. How foolish and groundless this claim was; they thought that because they were the descendants of Abraham, they were the only people God had in the world. John showed them how foolish such a thought is; "*I say unto you*—whatever you say within yourselves—that *God is able of these stones to raise up children unto Abraham*." John was now baptizing in the Jordan at Bethabara (Jn 1:28; NIV: Bethany), "the house of passage," where, some think, the children of *Israel passed over* and where Joshua set up the twelve stones as a memorial, one for each tribe (Jos 4:20). It is not unlikely that he pointed to those stones, which God could raise to be—more than in representation—the *twelve tribes of Israel*. Whatever comes of the present generation, God will never lack a church in the world.

4. A word of terror to the careless and self-confident Pharisees and Sadducees and other Jews who did not know the signs of the times (16:3) or the day of God's coming to them (Lk 19:44) (v. 10). "Look around you, now that *the kingdom of God is at hand*, and become aware:

4.1. "How strict and short your time of testing is: *Now the axe is laid to the root of the tree.* Now you are marked out for ruin and cannot avoid it except by a speedy and sincere repentance. *Behold, I come quickly* (Rev 22:12)." Now they were subjected to their last time of testing; it was now or never.

4.2. "How harsh and severe your fate will be if you do not take this opportunity to repent." It was now declared that the ax was at the root, that *every tree*, however *high* it was in gifts and honors, however *green* in external professions and actions, if it did not produced fruits in keeping with repentance, would be *hewn down*, disowned as a tree in God's vineyard, unworthy to grow there, and *cast into the fire* of God's wrath, the most suitable place for barren trees. What else were they good for? If they were not fit for fruit, they were fit for fuel.

5. A word of instruction concerning Jesus Christ. Christ's ministers preach not themselves but him. Here is:

5.1. The dignity and supremacy of Christ above John. Notice in what lowly terms John spoke about himself in order to exalt Christ: "*I indeed baptize you with water*; that is the best I can do (v. 11). But *he that comes after me is mightier than I.*" John was truly great, great in the sight of the Lord—no one greater was born of a woman (11:11)—yet he still thought he was unworthy to be in the lowliest place to serve Christ, *whose shoes I am not worthy to bear*. He saw:

5.1.1. How powerful Christ was in comparison with him. It is a great encouragement to faithful ministers to think that Jesus Christ is more powerful than they are; their strength is made perfect in their weakness (2Co 12:9).

5.1.2. How lowly he was in comparison with Christ, unworthy to carry his sandals after him! Those whom God honors are made very humble and lowly in their own eyes; they are willing to be humbled as long as Christ may be everything.

5.2. The purpose and intention of Christ's appearing, which they were now to expect to come quickly. He would *sit as a refiner* (Mal 3:3), and the day on which he came would *burn like an oven* (Mal 4:1). Christ would come to make a distinction:

5.2.1. By the powerful working of his grace; "*He shall baptize you*, that is, some of you, *with the Holy Ghost and with fire.*" We can learn from this:

5.2.1.1. It is Christ's prerogative to baptize *with the Holy Ghost*. He did this in the extraordinary gifts of the Spirit given to the apostles. He does this in the graces, strengths, and encouragements of the Spirit given to those who ask him.

5.2.1.2. Those who are baptized with the Holy Spirit are baptized as *with fire*. Does fire enlighten? Then the Spirit is a Spirit of illumination. Does fire give heat? Then do not their hearts burn within them (Lk 24:32)? Does fire consume? Then does not the Spirit of judgment, as *a Spirit of burning* (Isa 4:4), consume the dross of their corruption? Does fire make everything it lays hold of like itself? Does it move upward? So does the Spirit make the soul holy like itself, and its tendency is toward heaven.

5.2.2. By the final decisions of his judgment (v. 12): *Whose fan is in his hand.* He sits now as a Refiner. Notice here:

5.2.2.1. The visible church is Christ's floor: The temple, a type of the church, was built on a threshing-floor (1Ch 21:28–22:1; 2Ch 3:1).

5.2.2.2. On this floor there is a mixture of wheat and chaff. True believers are like wheat, and hypocrites are like chaff; these are now mixed, good and bad, under the same external profession.

5.2.2.3. A day is coming when the floor will be swept clean and the wheat and chaff will be separated. However, it is the day of the final judgment that will be the great winnowing, distinguishing day, when saints and sinners will be separated forever.

5.2.2.4. Heaven is the barn into which Jesus Christ will soon gather all his wheat, and not a grain of it will be lost: there will be no chaff among them. They will be gathered not only into *the barn* (13:30) but into *the garner*, where they will be thoroughly purified.

5.2.2.5. Hell is the *unquenchable fire* that will burn up the chaff. As we now are in the *field*, we will then be on his *floor*.

Verses 13–17

Look, *the Sun of righteousness* rises in glory (Mal 4:2). *The fulness of time was come* (Gal 4:4; Eph 1:10), the time when Christ would enter on his prophetic work, and he chose to do it not at Jerusalem, but *where John was baptizing*, for those who *waited for the consolation of Israel* (Lk 2:25) turned to John, and to them alone Jesus would be welcome. Christ's coming from Galilee *to Jordan, to be baptized* teaches us not to shrink from pain and toil, so that we may have an opportunity of drawing near to God in the ordinances of worship. We should be willing to go far rather than fall short of fellowship with God. Those who want to find must first seek. In this account of Christ's baptism we may notice:

1. With what difficulty John was persuaded to allow it (vv. 14–15). It was an example of Christ's great humility that he offered himself *to be baptized of John.* As soon as Christ began to preach, he preached humility. Christ was intended to receive the highest honors, but in his first steps he humbled himself in this way. Those who want to rise high must begin low. Humility comes before honor. God will honor those who honor him (1Sa 2:30). We have here:

1.1. The objection that John raised to baptizing Jesus (v. 14). *John forbade him*, as Peter did when Christ was about to wash his feet (Jn 13:6, 8). Christ's gracious condescension is so surprising, so deep and mysterious, that even those who his mind well cannot sound the depths of its meaning. In his modesty, John thought this was an honor too great for him to receive. John had now gained a great reputation and was universally respected, but notice how humble he still was! God has further honors in reserve for those whose spirits continue to be low when their reputation rises.

1.1.1. John thought it necessary for him to be baptized by Christ: "*I have need to be baptized of thee* with the baptism of the Holy Spirit, a baptism that is like fire" (v. 11).

1.1.1.1. Although *John was filled with the Holy Ghost from the womb* (Lk 1:15), he still acknowledged that he needed to be baptized with that baptism. Those who have much of the Spirit of God see that they need more.

1.1.1.2. *John had need to be baptized* even though he was the *greatest that ever was born of woman* (11:11). The purest souls are most aware of their own remaining impurity, and they fervently seek spiritual washing.

1.1.1.3. He had *need to be baptized of* Christ. The best and holiest people *have need of* Christ, and the better they are, the more they see their need.

1.1.1.4. This was said in front of the crowds, who had great respect for John and were ready to embrace him as the Messiah. He acknowledged, however, that he *needed to be baptized of* Christ. It is not beneath the greatest person to confess that they are ruined without Christ and his grace.

1.1.1.5. John was Christ's forerunner, but he acknowledged that he *needed to be baptized of* Christ. Even those who were before Christ in time depended on him

1.1.1.6. While John was dealing with others about their souls, notice how consciously he spoke about his own soul: I *have need to be baptized of thee*. "Watch your own life and teaching closely; *save thyself*" (1Ti 4:16).

1.1.2. He therefore thought it absurd for Christ to be baptized by him: *Comest thou to me?* Christ's coming to us may well be wondered at.

1.2. The overruling of this objection (v. 15). *Jesus said, Suffer* (let) *it to be so now.* Christ accepted John's humility, but not his refusal. See:

1.2.1. How Christ insisted on it; it must *be so now.* Everything is beautiful in its season (Ecc 3:11). But *why now?* Why at this time?

1.2.1.1. Christ was *now* in a state of humiliation. He was not only *found in fashion as a man* (Php 2:8) but also *made in the likeness of sinful flesh* (Ro 8:3), and so he *was made sin for us,* even though he *knew no sin* (2Co 5:21).

1.2.1.2. John's baptism was now held in good repute; it was the means by which God was doing his work. When we see that God acknowledges something, we too must acknowledge it, and we must continue to acknowledge it as long as he does.

1.2.1.3. It must *be so now,* because now was the time for Christ's appearing in public, and this would be a fair opportunity for it.

1.2.2. The reason he gave for it: *Thus it becomes us to fulfil all righteousness* (v. 15).

1.2.2.1. There was a propriety in everything Christ did for us; it was all graceful, *lovely, and of good report* (Php 4:8).

1.2.2.2. Our Lord Jesus believed that *to fulfil all righteousness* was something that was *becoming* to him. *Thus it becomes* him to justify God and to prove his wisdom. *Thus it becomes us* to encourage and support everything good, by example as well as instruction. This is how Jesus began *first to do, and then to teach* (Ac 1:1), and his ministers must follow the same method. It was proper for Christ to submit to John's washing with water, because it was a divine appointment.

1.2.3. John was entirely satisfied with the will of Christ and this reason for it, and *then he suffered him* (consented). The same modesty that made him originally decline the honor Christ offered him now made him fulfill the service Christ asked him to perform. No pretense of humility must make us decline our duty.

2. How solemnly heaven was pleased to grace the baptism of Christ with a special display of glory (vv. 16–17): *Jesus, when he was baptized, went up straightway out of the water.* Other people who were baptized stayed to *confess their sins* (v. 6), but because Christ had no sins to confess, he *went up* immediately. *He went up straightway,* as one who entered on his work with the greatest cheerfulness and determination; he would lose no time. *How straitened* (distressed) *he was till it was accomplished!* (Lk 12:50).

2.1. *Lo! the heavens were opened unto him,* so as to reveal, at least to him, something above and beyond the stars of the sky. This was:

2.1.1. To encourage him to continue in his undertaking with the prospect of the glory and *joy that were set before him* (Heb 12:2).

2.1.2. To encourage us to receive him and submit to him. Sin closed heaven, putting an end to all friendly fellowship between God and human beings, but now Christ has opened the kingdom of heaven to all believers. Divine light and love are darted down onto people, and all this happens through Jesus Christ, who is the ladder that has its foot on earth and its top in heaven (Ge 28:12).

2.2. *He saw the Spirit of God descending like a dove,* or "as a dove," *and* coming or *lighting upon him.* Christ saw it (Mk 1:10), and John saw it (Jn 1:33–34), and all the bystanders probably saw it, for this was intended to be his public inauguration.

2.2.1. *The Spirit of God descended and lighted on him.* In the beginning of the old world, *the Spirit of God moved upon the face of the waters* (Ge 1:2), *hovered* as a bird on its nest. So here, at the beginning of this new world, *the Spirit of the Lord would rest upon him* (Isa 11:2; 61:1), and he did so here.

2.2.1.1. He was to be a Prophet, and prophets always spoke through the Spirit of God, who came on them.

2.2.1.2. He was to be the Head of the church. Christ *received gifts for men* (Ps 68:18), so that he might give gifts to men.

2.2.2. He *descended on him like a dove.* If there must be a physical form (Lk 3:22), it must not be that of a human being. No form, therefore, was more fitting than that of one of the birds of the sky—because heaven was now opened—and of all birds none was so significant as the dove.

2.2.2.1. The Spirit of Christ is a dovelike spirit. *The Spirit descended* not in the form of an eagle, which is, though a royal bird, still a bird of prey, but *in the shape of a dove,* than which no creature is more harmless and inoffensive. Christians must be *harmless as doves* (10:16). The dove mourns much (Isa 38:14). Christ wept often, and penitent souls are compared to *doves of the valleys* (Eze 7:16).

2.2.2.2. The dove was the only bird that was offered in sacrifice (Lev 1:14), and Christ *offered himself without spot to God* (Heb 9:14).

2.2.2.3. News of the falling of Noah's flood was brought by a dove, with an olive leaf in its beak (Ge 8:11); it is right that the good news of peace with God is brought by the Spirit as *a dove.* That God is in Christ reconciling the world to himself (2Co 5:19) is a joyful message that comes to us on the *wings of a dove* (Ps 68:13).

2.3. To explain and complete this ceremony, *there came a voice from heaven.* The Holy Spirit revealed himself in the likeness of a *dove,* but God the Father *by a voice.*

2.3.1. Notice here how God acknowledged our Lord Jesus: *This is my beloved Son.* See:

2.3.1.1. The Father's relation to Christ: "He *is my Son.*" He is the Son of God because he was specially designated for the work and office of the world's Redeemer. He was sanctified and sealed and sent on that errand, *brought up with* the Father for it (Pr 8:30).

2.3.1.2. The Father's devotion to him: he *is my beloved Son.* Particularly as Mediator, and in undertaking the work of human salvation, he was his *beloved Son.* Because Christ agreed to the covenant of redemption and delighted to do that *will of God, therefore the Father loved him* (Jn 3:35; 10:17). Now we know that God loved us, *seeing he has not withheld his Son, his only Son, his Isaac whom he loved* (Ge 22:16), but *gave him to be a sacrifice for our sin.*

2.3.2. Notice how ready he is to acknowledge us in him: "He *is my beloved Son,* not only *with* whom, but also *in* whom, *I am well pleased.*" He is pleased with all who are in Christ and are united to him by faith. Up to that time, God had been displeased with human beings, but now his anger is turned away and he has made *us accepted in the Beloved* (Eph 1:6). Apart from Christ, God *is a consuming fire* (Heb 12:29), but in Christ, he is a reconciled Father. This is the essence of the Gospel. We must by faith cheerfully submit and say that he *is our beloved* Savior, *in whom we are well pleased.*

CHAPTER 4

John the Baptist said about Jesus Christ, He must increase, but I must decrease *(Jn 3:30). He had done what he came to do. As the rising Sun advances, the morning star disappears. What we have concerning Jesus Christ in this chapter is: 1. The temptation he experienced (vv. 1–11). 2. The teaching he undertook, the places he preached in (vv. 12–16), and the subject he preached on (v. 17). 3. His calling of four of his disciples, Peter and Andrew and James and John (vv. 18–22). 4. His healing of diseases (vv. 23–24), and we see the great number of people who turned to him.*

Verses 1–11

We have here the account of a famous duel, fought hand to hand, between Michael and the dragon (Rev 12:7), the Seed of the woman and the seed of the Serpent (3:15), in fact, the Serpent himself, and in this duel, the seed of the woman suffers, being *tempted*, and so has his heel bruised, but the Serpent is completely thwarted in his temptations, and so has his head broken. Notice:

1. The time when it happened. It took place immediately after *the heavens were opened* to him and *the Spirit descended on him* (3:16). The next we hear of him was that he is *tempted*, because then he was most able to struggle with the temptation.

1.1. Great privileges and special signs of divine favor will not protect us from being *tempted*. In fact:

1.2. After great honors are put on us, we must expect something humbling.

1.3. God usually prepares his people for temptation before he calls them to it.

1.4. The assurance of our adoption as sons of God is the best preparation for temptation.

1.5. When he had been baptized, he was *tempted*. After we have been admitted into deeper fellowship with God, we must expect to be attacked by Satan. The enriched soul must redouble its guard. The Devil has his particular spite against useful people, those who not only are good but also give themselves to doing good, especially when they first set out. Let young ministers know what to expect and arm themselves accordingly.

2. The place where it happened: *in the wilderness*. After intimate fellowship with God, it is good to be private for a while, so that we do not lose in the crowd and in the rush of worldly business what we have received. Christ withdrew into the desert:

2.1. To gain advantage for himself. Withdrawing from the world provides an opportunity for meditation and fellowship with God; even those who are called to a very active life must still have their hours of contemplation and must find time to be alone with God. Those who have not first meditated on the things of God privately by themselves are not fit to speak about them to others in public.

2.2. To give the tempter an advantage. Although solitude is a friend to a good heart, Satan also knows how to use it against us. Those who, claiming sanctity and devotion, withdraw into their own haunts and deserts find that they are not out of the reach of their spiritual enemies and that there they lack the benefits of fellowship with other saints. Christ withdrew:

2.2.1. So that Satan could do his worst. To make his victory more glorious, he gave the enemy sun and wind on his side but still thwarted him.

2.2.2. So that he himself would have an opportunity to do his best, so that he would be exalted in his own power. Christ entered the battle without any help.

3. The two preparations for it:

3.1. He was led into the battle; he *was led up of the Spirit to be tempted of the Devil* (v. 1). The Spirit who *descended upon him like a dove* made him humble, but also made him bold. If God, through his providence,

directs us into circumstances of temptation to test us, we must not think it strange, but must redouble our guard: *Be strong in the Lord* (Eph 6:10), *resist steadfast in the faith* (1Pe 5:9), and all will be well. Wherever God leads us, we may hope he will accompany us and bring us off *more than conquerors* (Ro 8:37). Christ *was led to be tempted of the Devil*, and only by him. Others are tempted *when they are drawn aside of their own lust and enticed* (Jas 1:14), but our Lord Jesus had no corrupt nature, and so he was led, as a champion onto the field, *to be tempted* purely by *the Devil*. Christ's temptation is:

3.1.1. An example of his own condescension and humiliation. Christ submitted because he wanted to humble himself, *in all things to be made like unto his brethren* (Heb 2:17).

3.1.2. An occasion of Satan's confusion. There is no conquest without a combat. Christ was tempted so that he could defeat the tempter.

3.1.3. A matter of encouragement to all the saints. The temptation of Christ shows us that our enemy is not invincible. Although he is *a strong man armed* (Lk 11:21), the Captain of our salvation (Heb 2:10) is *stronger than he* (Lk 11:22). It is some encouragement to us to think that Christ suffered by being *tempted*, for it shows us that if temptations are not yielded to, they are not sins, but only afflictions. We have a High Priest who knows from his own experience what it is to be *tempted* and who therefore is more able to sympathize with *the feelings of our infirmities* in times of temptation (Heb 2:18; 4:15).

3.2. He lessened his food for the battle, as athletes do, who are *temperate in all things* (1Co 9:25), but Christ went beyond any other, for he *fasted forty days and forty nights*. Christ need not have fasted to deny himself—he had no corrupt desires to be subdued—yet he *fasted*. If good people are humbled, if they lack friends and help, it may encourage them to remember that their Master himself was similarly exercised. A person may lack bread but still be a favorite of heaven and be led by the Spirit. *When he fasted forty days, he was* never hungry; his contact with heaven took the place of food and drink for him. But *he was afterward an hungred*, to show that he was really and truly human. Adam fell by eating, and we often sin that way, so Christ became hungry.

4. The temptations themselves. Satan's aim in all his temptations was to bring Christ to *sin against God* and so make him forever incapable of being a Sacrifice for the sins of others. What he aimed at was to bring him to despair of his Father's goodness, to presume on his Father's power, and to seize his Father's honor and give it to Satan. The two first temptations were deceitful and required great wisdom to discern; the last one was a strong temptation and required great determination to resist.

4.1. He tempted Christ to despair of his Father's goodness and distrust his Father's care for him.

4.1.1. See how the temptation was managed (v. 3); *The tempter came to him. The tempter came to* Christ visibly. If ever the Devil *transformed himself into an angel of light* (2Co 11:14), he did so now, pretending to be a good spirit, a guardian angel. Notice the subtlety of *the tempter* in joining this first temptation with what had just happened, to make it stronger.

4.1.1.1. Christ began to be hungry, and so it seemed proper to suggest that he turn *stones* into *bread* to support himself with what he needed. Lack and poverty are a great temptation to discontent and unbelief; they also tempt us to use unlawful means for relief, pretending that "Necessity knows no law"—that rules are often broken at times of emergency or urgent need. Therefore, those who are reduced to difficulties need to redouble their guard; it is better to starve to death than live and prosper in sin.

4.1.1.2. Christ had recently been declared to be *the Son of God*, and here the Devil tempted him to doubt that: *If thou be the Son of God* (v. 3). "You now have occasion to question whether *thou be the Son of God* or not, for can it be that *the Son of God*, who is *Heir of all things* (Heb 1:2), should be reduced to such a difficulty? Either God is not your Father, or he is a very unkind one." Satan's great aim in tempting good people is to put an end to their relationship with God as a Father. Outward afflictions, needs, and burdens are the great arguments Satan uses to make the people of God question their adoption. Those who can say, with saintly Job, *"Though he slay me, though he* starve me, *yet I will trust in him* (Job 13:15) and love him as a Friend," know how to answer this temptation. The Devil aims to shake our faith in the word of God. *"Has God said* that you are his *beloved Son?* Surely he did not say so, or if he did, it is untrue" (compare Ge 3:1). The Devil carries out his purposes very much by giving people harsh thoughts about God, as if he were unkind or unfaithful. "You now have an opportunity to show that you are *the Son of God. If thou* art *the Son of God*, prove it by this: *command these stones*"—a pile of which probably now lay in front of him—"*to be made bread* (v. 3)." He did not say, *Pray to thy Father* to turn them into *bread*, but *command* it to be done; "your Father has forsaken you and left you to yourself; you therefore do not need to be indebted to him." The Devil wants nothing that is humbling, but everything that is arrogant.

4.1.2. Notice how this temptation was resisted and overcome.

4.1.2.1. Christ refused to submit to it. He would not *command these stones to be made bread*, not because he could not, but because he refused to. Why did he refuse? At first sight, it appears justifiable enough, and the truth is that the more plausible a temptation is, and the more good it appears to contain, the more dangerous it is. This matter would bear a dispute, but Christ was soon aware of the snake in the grass and would not do anything that looked like:

- Questioning the truth of the voice he heard from heaven.
- Distrusting his Father's care of him.
- Setting up as a freelance prophet and naming his own fee.
- Pleasing Satan by doing something at his suggestion.

4.1.2.2. He was ready to reply to it: *He answered and said, It is written* (v. 4). It is significant that Christ answered and refuted all the temptations of Satan with *It is written*. To set us an example, he honored the Scriptures by appealing to what was written in the Law. The Word of God is *the sword of the Spirit*, the only offensive weapon in all the Christian armory (Eph 6:17).

4.1.2.3. This answer, like all the rest, is taken from the book of Deuteronomy, which means "the second law," and in which there is little that is ceremonial; the Levitical sacrifices and purifications, though divine instituted, could not drive away Satan. Moral precepts and evangelical promises, mixed with faith (Heb 4:2), are *mighty, through God* (2Co 10:4), to defeat Satan. The reason given for God's feeding the Israelites with manna is that he wanted to teach them that *man shall not live by bread alone* (Dt 8:3). Christ applied this to his own situation.

4.1.2.3.1. The Devil wanted him to question his sonship, because he was in difficulties; "No," Christ said, "Israel was God's son (Ex 4:22)," and in the Scripture

Satan quoted, it follows, *As a man chasteneth his son, so the Lord thy God chasteneth thee* (Dt 8:5). Christ, *being a Son, learned obedience* (Heb 5:8).

4.1.2.3.2. The Devil wanted him to distrust his Father's love and care. "No," he said, "that would be to do as Israel did: *Can the Lord furnish a table in the wilderness?*" (Ps 78:19).

4.1.2.3.3. The Devil wanted him, as soon as he began to be hungry, to immediately look out for a supply, whereas God allowed Israel to hunger before he fed them, to humble them and test them (Dt 8:2). God wants his children, when they are in need, not only to wait on him but also to wait for him.

4.1.2.3.4. The Devil wanted him to supply himself with bread. "No," Christ said, "what need is there for that? People may live without bread, as Israel did in the desert, living for years on manna." *Any word proceeding out of the mouth of God*, anything that God will order and appoint for our sustenance, will be as good as bread and maintain us as well. Just as we may *have bread* and still not be nourished if God denies his blessing (Hab 1:6, 9; Mic 6:14)—for though bread is *the staff of life*, it is God's blessing that is *the staff of bread*—so we may *want* (lack) *bread* but still be nourished in some other way. Just as in our great abundance we must not think we may live *without* God, so in our greatest difficulties we must learn to live *upon* God. Let us learn from Christ to be at God's disposal rather than our own. *Jehovah jireh*; some way or other, *the Lord will provide* (Ge 22:14). It is better to live poorly on the fruits of God's goodness than to live plentifully on the products of our own sin.

4.2. He tempted him to presume on his Father's power and protection. Notice what a restless and unwearied enemy the Devil is! Now in this second attempt we may notice:

4.2.1. What the temptation was and how it was managed. In general, because Satan found Christ to be so confident of his Father's care of him in regard to nourishment, he tried to draw him to presume on that care in regard to his safety. No extremes are more dangerous than those of despair and presumption, especially in spiritual matters. Some who have obtained a persuasion that Christ is able and willing to save them *from* their sins are then tempted to presume that he will save them *in* their sins. In this temptation we may notice:

4.2.1.1. How Satan prepared the way for it. He did not take Christ by force and against his will, but moved him to go to Jerusalem and then accompanied him there. Whether by walking there and then climbing the steps or by being transported through the air, he was *set upon a pinnacle of the temple*. Notice:

4.2.1.1.1. How submissive Christ was in allowing himself to be rushed away like this, so that he might let Satan do his worst but still defeat him. It is a great encouragement that Christ, who let loose this power of Satan against himself, does not also let it loose against us, but restrains it, for he *knows our frame* (Ps 103:14)!

4.2.1.1.2. How subtle the Devil was in choosing the place for his temptations. He fixed him on a public place in Jerusalem, a populous city and *the joy of the whole earth* (Ps 48:2). Moreover, it was in the temple, one of the wonders of the world, continually gazed on with admiration by someone or other. There Christ could make himself significant and prove himself to be the Son of God not in the obscurity of a desert, but in front of crowds. Notice that:

4.2.1.1.2.1. Jerusalem is here called the *holy city*, for it was that in name and profession. There is no city on earth so holy that it will keep us exempt and safe from the Devil and his temptations. The *holy city* is the place where he tempts people to pride and presumption with the greatest advantage and success, but—God be blessed—nothing unclean will enter into the Jerusalem above, that Holy City (Gal 4:26; Rev 21:27); there we will be forever out of the reach of temptation.

4.2.1.1.*2.2.* He *set him upon a pinnacle of the temple.* Pinnacles of the temple are places of temptation. High places in general are so; they are slippery places. Yet God throws down so that he may raise up, whereas the Devil raises up so that he may throw down. High places *in the church* are especially dangerous. Those who excel in gifts, who are in eminent positions and have gained a great reputation, need to remain humble. Those who stand high should be concerned to stand fast.

4.2.1.2. How Satan suggested it: "*If thou be the Son of God*, show yourself to the world and prove that you are; *cast thyself down*, and then:

- "You will be admired as one who is under the special protection of heaven.
- "You will be received as one who has come with a special commission from heaven. All Jerusalem will see and acknowledge not only that you are more than a man but that you are that *Messenger*, that *Angel of the covenant*, who would *suddenly come to the temple* (Mal 3:1)."

4.2.1.3. How he said, *Cast thyself down.* The Devil could not throw him down. The power of Satan is limited; *hitherto he shall come, and no further* (Job 38:11). The Devil can only persuade; he cannot compel. He can only say, *Cast thyself down*; he cannot throw us down. Therefore let us not *hurt ourselves*, and then—God be blessed—no one else can hurt us (Pr 9:12).

4.2.1.4. How he backed up this suggestion with a Scripture: *For it is written, He shall give his angels charge concerning thee.* But *is Saul also among the prophets?* (1Sa 10:12). Is Satan so familiar with Scripture as to be able to quote it so readily? It seems that he is. It is possible for a person to have their head full of scriptural ideas and their mouth full of scriptural expressions while their heart is full of reigning enmity toward God and all goodness. In this quotation:

4.2.1.4.*1.* There was *something right.* It is true that there is such a promise of the ministry of the angels to protect the saints. The Devil knows it from experience. The angels guard the saints for Christ's sake (Rev 7:5, 11).

4.2.1.4.*2.* There was a great deal *wrong in it*, and perhaps the Devil had a particular spite against this promise; perhaps he perverted it because it often got in his way and thwarted his troublesome plans against the saints. Notice here:

4.2.1.4.2.*1.* How he misquoted it, and that was bad. The promise is that they will *keep thee*, but how? *In all thy ways*, not otherwise; if we go out of our way, out of the way of our duty, we lose the right to claim the promise and we put ourselves out of God's protection. It is good for us on all occasions to consult the Scriptures themselves: not to take things on trust, but to be like the noble *Bereans* (Ac 17:11).

4.2.1.4.2.*2.* How he misapplied it, and that was worse. This promise is firm and stands good, but the Devil misused it when he applied it as an encouragement to presume on God's care. But *shall we continue in sin, that grace may abound?* (Ro 6:1). Shall we throw ourselves down so that the angels may lift us up? By no means!

4.2.2. How Christ overcame this temptation; he resisted and overcame it, as he did the former, with *It is written.*

The Devil's abuse of Scripture did not prevent Christ from using it rightly; he immediately urged, *Thou shalt not tempt the Lord thy God* (Dt 6:16). In the place from which it is quoted, it is in the plural, *You shall not tempt*; here it is singular, *Thou shalt not.* We are likely to benefit from the word of God when we hear and receive general promises as speaking to us in particular. If Christ *cast himself down*, it would be putting God to the test, since it would be:

4.2.2.1. Requiring a further confirmation of what was already so well confirmed. Christ was already fully satisfied that God was his Father and that he took care of him.

4.2.2.2. Requiring a special preservation of him when he did what he had no call to do. We are tempting God if we expect that because God has promised not to abandon us, he will follow us when we leave the path of our duty, that because he has promised to supply our need, he should indulge us and please our fancies. This is presumption, tempting God. It is to insult the One whom we should honor. We must never promise ourselves any more than God has promised us.

4.3. He tempted him to the most *black and horrid idolatry*, with the offer of the *kingdoms of the world, and the glory of them.*

4.3.1. The worst temptation was reserved for the last. Whatever temptation we have been attacked by, we must still prepare for even worse. In this temptation, we may notice:

4.3.1.1. What the Devil *showed him*—*all the kingdoms of the world.* In order to do this, he took him to an *exceeding high mountain.* The pinnacle of the temple was not high enough; the prince of the power of the air (Eph 2:2) must take Christ further up into his territories. Blessed Jesus was taken here to be shown a great view—as if the Devil could show him more of the world than he knew already, since he had made it and he governed it. His taking Christ up to a high mountain was merely to provide a suitable setting, to add color to the delusion. Blessed Jesus did not allow himself to be deceived, but saw through the deception. Concerning Satan's temptations, notice here that:

4.3.1.1.*1.* They often enter through the eyes. The first sin began with the eyes (Ge 3:6). We therefore need to make a covenant with our eyes (Job 31:1) and pray that God would *turn them away from beholding vanity* (Ps 119:37).

4.3.1.1.*2.* Temptations commonly arise from the world and the things in it.

4.3.1.1.*3.* It is *a great deception* that the Devil puts on poor souls in his temptations. He deceives and so destroys; he deceives people with shadows and false colors; he shows the world and its glory, but he hides from people's eyes the sin and sorrow and death that stain the pride of all this glory.

4.3.1.1.*4.* The *glory of the world* is the most *charming* temptation to the *unthinking* and *unwary*, and it is what deceives people the most. The *pride of life* (1Jn 2:16) is the most dangerous snare.

4.3.1.2. What he *said to him* (v. 9): *All these things will I give thee, if thou wilt fall down and worship me.* See:

4.3.1.2.*1.* How worthless the promise was: *All these things will I give thee.* It seems he assumed that in the former temptations he had been partly successful. "Come," he said, "it seems that the God whose Son you think yourself to be deserts you and starves you—a sign that he is not your Father; but if you will be ruled by me, I will provide for you better; acknowledge me as your father and ask my blessing, and *all this will I give thee.*" Satan attacks people easily when he can persuade them to think they have been abandoned by God. The fallacy of this promise lies in the *All this will I give thee*. The Devil's attractive baits are all mere sham; the things he deceives them with are mere shows and shadows. The *nations of the earth* had been promised to the Messiah long before; if he was *the Son of God*, they belonged to him. We must beware of receiving anything at all out of Satan's hand, even what God has promised.

4.3.1.2.2. How contemptible the condition was: *If thou wilt fall down and worship me*. The Devil is fond of being worshiped. What temptation could be more hideous and more black? The best saints may be tempted to commit the worst sins. To be under such temptation is their affliction, but as long as they do not yield to it or approve of it, it is not their sin; Christ was tempted to worship Satan.

4.3.2. See how Christ fended off the attack. He rejected the proposal:

4.3.2.1. With abhorrence and detestation: "*Get thee hence, Satan*." It appeared detestable at first sight and so was rejected immediately. When Satan tempted Christ to cause himself trouble by throwing himself down, then even though he did not yield, he still heard it, but now that the temptation flew in the face of God, he could not bear it: *Get thee hence, Satan*. It is good to be *absolute* in resisting temptation, to *stop up our ears* to Satan's charms.

4.3.2.2. With an argument taken from Scripture. The argument was very suitable, fit the purpose exactly, and was taken from Dt 6:13; 10:20. *Thou shalt worship the Lord thy God, and him only shalt thou serve*. Our Savior went back to the fundamental law in this situation, which is indispensable and universally obligatory. Religious worship is due only to God. Christ quoted this law concerning religious worship, and he quoted it with application to himself:

- To show that in his condition of humiliation as man, he worshiped God, both publicly and privately. It was therefore proper for him to do so in order to fulfill all righteousness (3:15).
- To show that the law of religious worship has an eternal obligation.

5. We have here the end and outcome of this battle (v. 11).

5.1. The Devil was defeated and left the battlefield: *Then the devil leaveth him*, forced to do so by the power that accompanied the word of command, *Get thee hence, Satan*. He made a shameful and inglorious retreat and came off with disgrace. He despaired of moving Christ and began to conclude that he was the *Son of God* and that it was futile to tempt him anymore. If we resist the Devil, he will flee from us (Jas 4:7); if we stand our ground, he will yield. When the Devil left our Savior, he acknowledged he was beaten fairly. The Devil, though an enemy of all the saints, is a conquered enemy. The Captain of our salvation (Heb 2:10) has defeated and disarmed him (12:29); we have nothing to do but to follow up the victory.

5.2. The holy angels came and took care of our victorious Redeemer: *Behold, angels came and ministered unto him*. One angel might have been enough to bring him food, but here are many taking care of him, to show their respect for him and their readiness to receive his commands. Look at this! It is worth noticing that:

5.2.1. Just as there is a world of evil, malicious spirits that fight against Christ, his church, and all individual believers, so there is also a world of holy, blessed spirits engaged and employed for them.

5.2.2. Christ's victories are the angels' triumphs.

5.2.3. The angels ministered to the Lord Jesus by providing not only food but also whatever else he needed after this very tiring task. Although God may allow his people to be brought into need and difficulties, he will take effective care that their needs are supplied, and he will send angels to feed them rather than see them perish. Christ was helped after the temptation:

5.2.3.1. So that he might be encouraged to continue his undertaking

5.2.3.2. So that we might be encouraged to trust in him. We may expect, therefore, that he will not only sympathize with his people when they are tempted (Heb 4:15) but also come to them with timely relief.

Verses 12 – 17

We have here an account of Christ's preaching in the synagogues of Galilee. In the story of Christ's life as told in the other Gospels, especially in that of St. John, several passages intervene between his temptation and his preaching in Galilee. Matthew, however, having been a resident of Galilee, begins his story of Christ's public ministry with his preaching there. Notice:

1. The time: *When Jesus had heard that John was cast into prison, he went into Galilee* (v. 12). The cry of the saints' sufferings reaches the ears of the Lord Jesus. If John is thrown into prison, Jesus hears it, takes notice of it, and steers his course accordingly.

1.1. Christ did not go into the country till he heard of John's imprisonment, for John had to have time given him to *prepare the way of the Lord* (3:3) before the Lord himself appeared. John must be Christ's forerunner, but not his rival. The moon and stars are lost when the sun rises.

1.2. He did go into the country as soon as he heard of John's imprisonment, not only to provide for his own safety but also to fill the gap left by John the Baptist and to build on the good foundation he had laid. God will not leave himself without witness (Ac 14:17), nor his church without guides.

2. The place where he preached: in Galilee, a remote part of the country that lay farthest from Jerusalem and was looked on there with contempt, as primitive and uncivilized. The inhabitants of that country were reckoned to be strong, fit to be soldiers, but not polite or fit to be scholars. Notice:

2.1. The particular town he chose as his home: not Nazareth, where he had been brought up; no, particular notice is taken of the fact that he left Nazareth (v. 13). He left Nazareth with good reason, for the people of that town *thrust him out* from among them (Lk 4:29). Christ will not stay long where he is not welcome. Unhappy Nazareth! Instead, he *came and dwelt in Capernaum*, which was also a town of Galilee, but many miles away from Nazareth; it was a large town where many people went. It is said here to be *on the sea coast*, not the coast of the *great sea*, but that of the Sea of Tiberias (the Sea of Galilee). Here Christ came, and here he lived. However, he did not stay here constantly, for he went about doing good (Ac 10:38). Nevertheless, this was his headquarters for some time. The little rest he had was here. At Capernaum, it seems, he was welcome. If some people reject Christ, others will receive him and make him welcome. Capernaum is glad to see the One whom Nazareth rejected.

2.2. The prophecy that was fulfilled in this (vv. 14–16). It is quoted from Isa 9:1–2, but with some variation. The evangelist takes here only the latter clause, which speaks of the return of the light of liberty and prosperity to those countries that had been in the darkness of exile, and he applies it to the appearance of the Gospel among them. The places are spoken of in v. 15. When Christ came to Capernaum, the Gospel came to all those places around it; the Sun of righteousness spread such an influence so widely (Mal 4:2).

2.2.1. They were *in darkness*. Those who are without Christ are in the dark; in fact, they are darkness itself. The people of this land were *sitting* in this condition. Sitting is a continuing position; we intend to stay where we are sitting. It is a contented position; they were in the dark, and they loved darkness (Jn 3:19). Those who are in the dark because it is night may be sure that the sun will soon arise, but those who are in the dark because they are blind will not have their eyes opened so quickly. We have the light, but what good will that do us if we are not *light in the Lord* (Eph 5:8)?

2.2.2. When the Gospel comes, light comes; when it comes to any place, when it comes to any soul, it makes day there. Light is revealing and guiding, and so is the Gospel.

2.2.2.1. It is *a great light*, *great* in comparison with the light of the law, the shadows of which were now done away with. It is *a great light*, for it reveals great things, things that are very important; it will last long and spread far. That it *is sprung up* suggests that it is *a growing light*. It was only the *spring of day* with them; now was the dawn of the day that would *shine more and more* (Pr 4:18). The Gospel kingdom was like a grain of mustard seed (13:31–32) or the morning light, small in its beginning and gradual in its growth, but great in its perfection.

2.2.2.2. The light *sprang up to them*; they did not go out to seek it; it came on them before they were aware of it.

3. The text he preached on (v. 17): *From that time* he began to preach.

3.1. The subject Christ spoke about in his preaching— which was in fact the sum and substance of all his preaching—was the very same that John had preached on: *Repent, for the kingdom of heaven is at hand* (3:2); for the Gospel is substantially the same under various dispensations; it is the *everlasting Gospel* (Rev 14:6). *Fear God, and*, by repentance, *give honour to him* (Rev 14:6–7). Christ gave great respect to John's ministry when he preached on the same effect that John had preached for him. This is how God confirmed the word of his messenger (Isa 44:26). Christ chose this old, plain text, *Repent, for the kingdom of heaven is at hand.*

3.2. He preached this *first*; he began with this. We need not go up to heaven, nor down to the depths (Dt 30:14), for subjects or words in our preaching. Just as John the Baptist prepared Christ's way with the message of repentance, so with that same message Christ prepared his own way, making way for the further revelations he intended to give.

3.3. He preached *often* on this; wherever he went, this was his subject, and neither he nor his followers ever considered it worn out. What has been preached and heard before may still profitably be preached and heard again, but then it should be preached and heard better.

3.4. He preached this as Gospel. Not only the austere John the Baptist, who was looked on as a sad, morose man, but also the sweet and gracious Jesus, whose lips dripped with honey (SS 4:11), preached repentance.

3.5. The reason was still the same: the *kingdom of heaven is at hand*. Now that it was so much nearer, the argument was so much the stronger; now is the *salvation nearer* (Ro 13:11).

Verses 18–22

When Christ began to preach, he began to *gather disciples*, who would now be the hearers of his doctrine and later its preachers. In these verses, we have an account of the first disciples whom he called into fellowship with himself. This was an example of:

- The effectual calling of people to Christ. In all his preaching, Christ gave a common call to all the country, but here he gave a special and particular call to those who were given him by the Father (Jn 17:11). All the country was *called*, but these were *called out.*
- The ordaining and appointing of people to the work of the ministry. When Christ, as a Teacher, set up his great school, one of his first works was to appoint ushers, or subordinate teachers, to be employed in the work of instruction.

Now we may notice here:

1. Where they were called—by the *Sea of Galilee*, where Jesus was walking. He did not go to Herod's court—for few mighty or noble ones are called (1Co 1:26)—not to Jerusalem, among the chief priests and the elders, but to the Sea of Galilee; surely Christ does not see in the same way as we see (1Sa 16:7). Galilee was a remote part of the nation, the inhabitants were less cultivated and refined, their very language was broad and uncouth to the knowledgeable, and their *speech betrayed them* (26:73). Yet Christ went there to call his apostles, who were to be the prime ministers of state in his kingdom, for he *chooses the foolish things of the world, to confound the wise* (1Co 1:27).

2. Who they were. We have an account of the call of two pairs of brothers in these verses—Peter and Andrew, James and John. They had been disciples of John and so were disposed to follow Christ. Those who have submitted to the discipline of repentance will be welcome to the joys of faith. We may notice concerning them:

2.1. That they were *brothers*. It is the honor and comfort of a house when those who are of the *same* family are of *God's* family.

2.2. That they were *fishers*. Being fishermen:

2.2.1. They were poor men: if they had had possessions or any considerable goods, they would not have made fishing their business, though they might have made it their recreation. Christ does not despise the poor, and so neither must we.

2.2.2. They were unlearned men. This will not, however, justify the bold intrusion of *ignorant* and unqualified people into the work of the ministry.

2.2.3. They were men of business, who had been brought up to work hard. Diligence in an honest calling is pleasing to Christ and no hindrance to a holy life. Idle people are more open to the temptations of Satan than to the calls of God.

2.2.4. They were men who were used to hardships and hazards. The fisherman's trade, more than any other, is laborious and dangerous; fishermen must often get wet and cold; they must watch, wait, and toil and often be in peril from the waters in which they fish. Those who have learned to bear hardship and face danger are best prepared for the fellowship and discipleship of Jesus Christ. Good soldiers of Christ must endure hardship (2Ti 2:3).

3. What they were doing. Peter and Andrew were then using their nets in fishing, and James and John were *mending their nets*, which was an example of their diligence and good management. They did not go to their father for money to buy new nets, but made an effort to mend

their old ones. It is commendable to make what we have go as far, and last as long, as possible. James and John were *with their father Zebedee*, ready to help him. It is a happy and hopeful sign to see children taking care of their parents and behaving dutifully toward them. Notice:

3.1. They were all employed, all very busy, with no one idle. When Christ comes, it is good to be found active.

3.2. They were differently employed; two of them were fishing, and two of them *mending their nets*. Ministers should be always employed, either in teaching or in studying. *Mending their nets* is in its time as necessary work as fishing.

4. What the call was: *Follow me, and I will make you fishers of men* (v. 19). Even those who had been called to follow Christ needed to be called to *follow on* (Hos 6:3) and follow more closely. Notice:

4.1. What Christ intended them for: *I will make you fishers of men*. Let them not become proud of the new honor intended for them; they were still mere fishermen; let them not be afraid of the new work intended for them, for they had been used to fishing, and they were still fishermen.

4.1.1. Ministers are *fishers of men*, not to destroy them, but to save them by bringing them into another element.

4.1.2. It is Jesus Christ who makes them so: *I will make you fishers of men*. He is the One who qualifies people for this work; he calls them to do it, authorizes them in it, and gives them success in it.

4.2. What they must do, to this end: *Follow me*. They must detach themselves from their former way of life and conscientiously follow him.

4.2.1. Those whom Christ employs in any service for him must first be fitted and qualified for it.

4.2.2. Those who want to *preach Christ* (1Co 1:23; Php 1:15–16; etc.) must first *learn Christ* (Eph 4:20) and *learn from him* (11:29).

4.2.3. Those who want to know Christ must be diligent and constant in being with him. There is no learning comparable to what is obtained by following Christ.

4.2.4. Those who are to fish for people must follow Christ and do as he did with diligence, faithfulness, and tenderness.

5. What the result of this call was. Peter and Andrew *straightway left their nets* (v. 20), and James and John *immediately left the ship and their father* (v. 22), *and they all followed him*. Those who want to follow Christ rightly must leave all to follow him.

5.1. This example of the power of the Lord Jesus gives us good encouragement to depend on the sufficiency of his grace. How strong and effective is his word! *He speaks, and it is done* (Ps 33:9).

5.2. This example of the openness of the disciples gives us a good example of obedience to the commands of Christ. It is a good characteristic of all Christ's faithful servants that they come when they are called and that they follow their Master wherever he leads them. When these fishermen were called, they obeyed, and, like Abraham, *went out not knowing whither they went* (Heb 11:8), but knowing very well the One whom they followed.

Verses 23–25

See here:

1. What a diligent preacher Christ was: he *went about all Galilee, teaching in their synagogues, and preaching the Gospel of the kingdom*. Notice:

1.1. What Christ preached—the *Gospel of the kingdom. The kingdom of heaven*, that is, of grace and glory, is emphatically *the kingdom. The Gospel* is the charter

of that kingdom, containing the King's coronation oath, by which he has graciously obliged himself to pardon, protect, and save the subjects of that kingdom.

1.2. Where he preached—in *the synagogues*; not only there, but mainly there, because those were *the places of concourse*, where *wisdom* was to *lift up her voice* (Pr 1:21).

1.3. What effort he made in preaching; he *went about all Galilee, teaching*. He *waited to be gracious* (Isa 30:18) and came *to seek and save* (Lk 19:10). He *went about doing good* (Ac 10:38). Never was there such an itinerant preacher, such an indefatigable one, as Christ.

2. What a powerful physician Christ was (9:12); he *went about* not only *teaching* but also *healing*. See:

2.1. What diseases he healed—all without exception. He *healed all manner of sickness, and all manner of disease*. There are diseases that are called "the reproach of physicians," but *he healed them* all, however "incurable" they had been.

2.1.1. Three general words are used here to intimate this. He healed every *sickness*; every *disease*, or languishing; and all *torments*. None was too bad or too hard for Christ to heal by just speaking a word.

2.1.2. Three particular diseases are specified; *the palsy* (paralysis), which is the greatest weakness of the body; *lunacy* (seizures), which is the greatest illness of the mind; and *possession of the Devil*, which is the greatest misery and calamity of both. Christ healed all.

2.2. What patients he had. Notice how many flocked to him from everywhere; great crowds of people came, not only *from Galilee* and the surrounding country but even *from Jerusalem* and *from Judea*, which lay far away, for *his fame went throughout all Syria*. This is given as the reason why such multitudes came to him—that his fame had spread so widely. What we hear about Christ from others should invite us to come to him. The voice of fame says, "Come and see." Christ both *taught and healed*. It is good if anything will bring people to Christ, and those who come to him will find more in him than they expected. Concerning the cures that Christ did, let us, once for all, notice the *miracle*, the *mercy*, and the *mystery*, of them.

2.2.1. The *miracle* of them. They were performed in a way that clearly showed them to be the immediate products of a divine and supernatural power, and they were God's seal on his commission. Nature could not do these things. All this proved him to be *a Teacher come from God*, for otherwise no one could have done the works that he did (Jn 3:2). His healing and his preaching generally went together, for the former confirmed the latter; here he *began to do and to teach* (Ac 1:1).

2.2.2. The *mercy* of them. The miracles that Christ performed were mostly healings, and all of them—except the cursing of the barren fig tree—blessings and favors, for the Gospel era is based on, and built up in, love, grace, and sweetness. Christ intended his healings to win people and thereby draw them with the bonds of love (Hos 11:4). The miraculous nature of his healings proved his teaching to be *a faithful saying* and convinced the judgments of human beings; the mercy of his healings proved his teaching to be *worthy of all acceptation* (1Ti 1:15) and moved the affections of human beings. His healings were not only *great works* but *good works*, which he *showed them from his Father* (Jn 10:32).

2.2.3. The *mystery* of them. By healing physical diseases, Christ intended to show that his great mission into the world was to heal spiritual diseases. Sin is the *sickness, disease*, and *torment of* the soul; Christ *came to take away sin* and so to heal these. The particular accounts of the healings Christ performed are therefore to be explained and used in this way, to the honor and praise of that glorious Redeemer *who forgiveth all our iniquities, and so healeth all our diseases* (Ps 103:3).

CHAPTER 5

This chapter and the two that follow it are a sermon, the Sermon on the Mount. It is the longest and fullest continuous speech of our Savior that we have recorded. It is a practical message. After the circumstances of the sermon are explained (vv. 1–2), the sermon itself follows, the scope of which is not to fill our minds with ideas, but to guide and regulate our practice. 1. He proposes blessedness as the purpose and shows us the character of those who are entitled to blessedness in eight beatitudes, which may justly be called paradoxes (vv. 3–12). 2. He prescribes duty as the way and establishes rules for duty. He directs his disciples: 2.1. To understand what they are—the salt of the earth and the lights of the world (vv. 13–16). 2.2. To understand what they have to do—they are to be governed by the moral law. Here is: 2.2.1. A general confirmation of the Law and a recommendation of it to us as our rule (vv. 17–20). 2.2.2. A particular correction of various mistakes and an authentic explanation of various branches that most needed to be explained and upheld (v. 20). Here, particularly, is an explanation of the sixth commandment (vv. 21–26), of the seventh commandment (vv. 27–32), of the third commandment (vv. 33–27), of the law of retaliation (vv. 38–42), and of the law of mutual love (vv. 43–48).

Verses 1–2

We have here a general account of this sermon:

1. The Preacher was our Lord Jesus Christ, the Prince of preachers. The prophets and John had *done virtuously* in preaching, *but* Christ *excelled them all* (Pr 31:29). He is the eternal Word, through whom God *has in these last days spoken to us* (Heb 1:2). The many miraculous healings performed by Christ in Galilee were intended to incline people to receive instructions from the One in whom there appeared so much divine power and goodness, and this sermon was probably the summary of what he had preached in the synagogues. His text was, *Repent, for the kingdom of heaven is at hand* (4:17).

2. The place was a mountain in Galilee. Our Lord Jesus was poorly provided for; he had no convenient place to preach in, any more than he had a place *to lay his head* (8:20). Our Lord Jesus, the great Teacher of truth, was driven out to the desert and found no better pulpit than *a mountain*, and not one of the *holy mountains of Zion* (Ps 133:3), but a common *mountain*, by which Christ would show that it is *the will of God that men should pray* and preach *everywhere* (1Ti 2:8), anywhere, provided it is decent and convenient. Christ preached this sermon, which was an explanation of the Law, on a mountain, because the Law was given on *a mountain*. Notice the difference, however. When *the law was given*, the Lord *came down* on the *mountain* (Ex 19:20); now the Lord *went up*. Then, he spoke *in thunder and lightning* (Ex 20:18); now, *in a still small voice* (1Ki 19:12). Then the people were ordered to keep their distance; now they were invited to draw near. What a blessed change!

3. The listeners were *his disciples*. They followed him for love and learning, while others were present with him only to be healed. *He taught them* because they were will-

ing to be *taught*, because they would *understand* what he taught, and because they were to teach others. Although this speech was directed at the disciples, however, it was in the hearing of the *multitude*. No boundaries were set around *this mountain* to keep the people away, for through Christ, we have access to God. In fact, he had *the multitude* specifically in mind in preaching this sermon. It is an encouragement to a faithful minister to cast the net of the Gospel where there are a great many fish and where there is therefore hope that some will be caught. The sight of many people puts life into a preacher, but this must arise from a desire for their benefit, not for his own praise.

4. The solemnity of his sermon is suggested by the expression *when he was set*. This was a set sermon, one he preached when he had placed himself so as to be best heard. That phrase *He opened his mouth* is a Hebrew manner of speaking (Job 3:1). Some, however, think it suggests the solemnity of this speech; because the congregation was large, he raised his voice and spoke more loudly than usual. One of the old commentators remarks on it that Christ *taught* much without *opening his mouth*, that is, by his holy and exemplary life; in fact, he *taught* when, being *led as a lamb to the slaughter, he opened not his mouth* (Isa 53:7); but now *he opened his mouth, and taught*. He taught them what was the evil that they should hate and what was the good that they should do and abound in, for Christianity is intended to direct our attitudes and be the direction of our lives. The Gospel time is a time of reformation (Heb 9:10), and we must be reformed by the Gospel; we must be made good; in fact, we must be made better.

Verses 3–12

Christ began his sermon with blessings, for *he came into the world to bless us* (Ac 3:26). He began it *as one having authority* (7:29), as One who can *command the blessing, even life for evermore* (Ps 133:3). The Old Testament ended with a curse (Mal 4:6); the Gospel begins with a blessing.

1. Each of the blessings Christ declared here has a double intention:

1.1. To show who are to be counted truly happy.

1.2. To show what true happiness consists in.

1.2.1. This is intended to put right the terrible mistakes of a blind and corrupt world. Blessedness is what people are to pursue: *Who will make us to see good?* (Ps 4:6). However, most people make a mistake concerning their destination, forming a wrong idea of happiness, and then it is hardly surprising that they lose their way. The prevailing opinion is, *Blessed are they* who are rich, great, and honorable in the world; who spend their days in merriment and their years in pleasure; and who eat fine food, drink sweet beverages, and boldly sail through life. Our Lord Jesus came to give us a completely different idea of blessedness and blessed people. The beginning of the Christian way of life must be to take one's standard for happiness from these maxims and direct one's pursuits accordingly.

1.2.2. It is intended to remove the discouragements of the weak and poor who receive the Gospel. Even *the least* person *in the kingdom of heaven* whose heart is upright with God is happy in enjoying the honors and privileges of that kingdom.

1.2.3. It is intended to invite souls to Christ. Those who had seen the gracious healings he performed (4:23–24) and who now heard *the gracious words proceeding out of his mouth* (Lk 4:22) would say that he was all of a piece, all love and kindness.

1.2.4. It is intended to settle and sum up the articles of the agreement between God and human beings. The scope of divine revelation is to tell us what God expects from us and what we may then expect from him. Nowhere is this more fully set out in a few words than here. The way to happiness is opened up here and made *a highway* (Isa 35:8). Some of the wiser pagans had ideas of blessedness that were different from those of others and looked toward the idea of it that we have here from our Savior. When Seneca undertook to describe a blessed man, he thought that only an honest and good man could be so called, one "in whose opinions nothing is good or evil, except a good or evil heart" (*On the Happy Life*, ch. 4).

Our Savior gives us eight characteristics of blessed people here, which represent to us the principal graces of a Christian. On each of them a present blessing is pronounced: *Blessed are* they; and to each a future blessing is promised.

2. *The poor in Spirit* are happy (v. 3). There is a poor-spiritedness that is so far from making people blessed that it is a sin and a snare—cowardice and a corrupt fear. But this poverty of spirit is a gracious disposition of soul. To be *poor in spirit* is:

2.1. To be contentedly poor, willing to be empty of worldly wealth if God orders that for us. Many people are poor in the world but high in spirit, poor and proud, but we must come to terms with our poverty; we must *know how to be abased* (Php 4:12). To be rightly poor in spirit is to sit loose to all worldly wealth, not setting our hearts on it. It is not, in pride or pretense, to make ourselves poor by throwing away what God has given us. If we are rich in the world, we must be *poor in spirit*, that is, we must condescend to the poor and sympathize with them and their weaknesses. We must expect and prepare for poverty; we must not inordinately fear or shun it, but must welcome it, especially when it comes to us to help us maintain a good conscience (Heb 10:34). Job was *poor in spirit* when he blessed God in *taking away* as well as giving (Job 1:21).

2.2. To be humble and lowly in our own eyes. To be *poor in spirit* is to have lowly thoughts of ourselves, about what we are, have, and do. It is to be like little children in our own opinion of ourselves. Paul was rich in spiritual matters, exceeding most people in gifts and graces, yet *poor in spirit, the least of the apostles* (1Co 15:9), less than the least of all saints (Eph 3:8) and *having nothing* (2Co 6:10) in his own account. To be rightly poor in spirit is to be willing to make ourselves humble, lowly, and little in order to do good; it is to *become all things to all men* (1Co 9:22). It is to acknowledge that God is great and we are lowly, that he is holy and we are sinful, that he is all and we are nothing.

2.3. To be brought away from any confidence in our own righteousness and power, so that we may depend only on the merits of Christ and the spirit and grace of Christ. That *broken and contrite spirit* (Ps 51:17) with which the tax collector cried out for mercy for himself, a poor sinner, is this poverty of spirit. We must call ourselves poor because we are always in need of God's grace, always begging at God's door, always seeking his help.

2.3.1. This poverty in spirit is given first among the Christian graces. The philosophers did not reckon humility among their moral virtues, but Christ puts it first. The foundation of all other graces is humility. Those who want to build high must begin low. Those *who are weary and heavy laden* (11:28) are *the poor in spirit*, and they will find rest with Christ (11:29).

2.3.2. They are *blessed*. They are so even now, in this world. God looks graciously on them. Nothing comes to them wrongly, whereas arrogant spirits are always uneasy.

2.3.3. *Theirs is the kingdom of heaven.* The kingdom of *grace* is composed of such people; the kingdom of *glory* is prepared for them. The great, proud spirits go away with the glory of the kingdoms of the earth, but the humble, mild, submissive souls obtain the glory of *the kingdom of heaven.* The same happiness is promised to these who are contentedly poor as to those who are usefully rich. If I am not able to spend cheerfully for his sake, if I can only lack cheerfully for his sake, even that will be rewarded.

3. *They that mourn* are happy (v. 4). *Blessed are they that mourn.* This is another strange blessing. We tend to think, "Blessed are the *merry*," but Christ, who was himself a great mourner, said, "Blessed are the *mourners*." There is a sinful mourning that is an enemy of blessedness—the *sorrow of the world* (2Co 7:10). There is also a natural mourning that may prove a friend of blessedness by the grace of God working alongside it. However, there is a gracious mourning that qualifies for blessedness. This mourning is:

3.1. A penitential mourning for our own sins; this is *godly sorrow* (2Co 7:10), a sorrow according to God, sorrow for sin, looking to Christ (Zec 12:10). God's mourners are those who live a life of repentance and who, out of a regard for God's honor, also mourn the sins of others.

3.2. A sympathetic mourning for the suffering of others, the mourning of those who *weep with them that weep* (Ro 12:15), who look with compassion on souls who are perishing and *weep over* them, as Christ wept *over Jerusalem* (Lk 19:41). These gracious mourners:

3.2.1. *Are blessed.* Just as in worthless and sinful *laughter, the heart is sorrowful* (Pr 14:13), so in gracious mourning *the heart* has a serious joy, an inner, hidden satisfaction, which *a stranger does not intermeddle with* (Pr 14:10).

3.2.2. *Shall be comforted.* Light is sown for them (Ps 97:11), and it is certain that *they shall be comforted* in heaven, like Lazarus (Lk 16:25). The happiness of heaven consists in being perfectly and eternally comforted and in the *wiping away of all tears from their eyes* (Rev 7:17). Heaven will be true heaven for those who go mourning there; it will be a harvest of joy, the yield of what was sown in tears (Ps 126:5–6).

4. *The meek* are happy (v. 5); *Blessed are the meek.* The meek are those who quietly submit to God and are *gentle toward all men* (Tit 3:2). They are able to bear provocation without being inflamed by it and either are silent or respond with a soft answer (Pr 15:1). They can be cool when others are hot, and in their patience they maintain possession of their own souls, when they can scarcely keep possession of anything else. The meek are those who would rather forgive twenty wrongs than take revenge on one. These meek ones are represented here as happy, even in this world.

4.1. They are *blessed*, for they are like the blessed Jesus. They are *blessed*, for they have the most assured and undisturbed enjoyment of themselves, their friends, and their God; they are fit to live and fit to die.

4.2. *They shall inherit the earth.* Not that they will always have much of *the earth*, much less that they will be put off only with that, but this branch of godliness has, especially, *the promise of that life that now is* (1Ti 4:8). Meekness, however much it is ridiculed and criticized, has a real tendency to advance our health, wealth, strength, and security, even in this world. Or, "They shall inherit the land," as it may read, *the land of Canaan* (Ge 12:5; 17:8; etc.), a type of heaven. This means that all the blessedness of heaven above and all the blessings of earth below are the inheritance of the meek.

5. *They that hunger and thirst after righteousness* are happy (v. 6). Some understand this as a further example of outward poverty and a lowly condition in this world. People *hunger and thirst after* righteousness, but such is the power on the side of their oppressors that they cannot have it. But *blessed are they* if they suffer these hardships for and with a good conscience; let them hope in God. Those who contentedly bear oppression and quietly turn to God to plead their cause will in due time be abundantly satisfied in the wisdom and kindness that will be revealed when he comes to help them.

5.1. *Righteousness* stands for all spiritual blessings here. They are bought for us by *the* righteousness of Christ. To obtain righteousness is to become *a new man* (Eph 2:15; 4:24), bearing the image of God, and to enjoy privileges in Christ and his promises.

5.2. We must *hunger and thirst after* these. We must really and truly desire them. Our desires for spiritual blessings must be fervent and bold: "*Give me these, or else I die* (Ge 30:1); give me these, and I have enough, even though I have nothing else." *Hunger and thirst* are appetites that recur frequently and call for fresh satisfaction. The quickened soul calls for constant meals of righteousness, grace to accomplish the work of every day in its day. Those who *hunger and thirst* will labor to be supplied; we must not only desire spiritual blessings, therefore, but also make an effort to obtain them by using the appointed means. Those who *hunger and thirst shall be filled* with those blessings.

5.2.1. They are *blessed* in those desires. Although all desires for grace are not grace — false and faint desires are not — nevertheless, such a true desire is. It is evidence of something good and a pledge of something better. It is a desire that God himself has raised.

5.2.2. They *shall be filled* with those blessings. God will give them what they desire to their complete satisfaction. It is only God who can *fill a soul*, only God whose grace and favor are enough for its just desires. He *fills the hungry* (Lk 1:53), *satiates* them (Jer 31:25).

6. The *merciful* are happy (v. 7). This, like the others, is a paradox, for the merciful are not taken to be the wisest, nor are they likely to be the richest. Christ, however, declares that they are *blessed*. A person may be truly *merciful* even when they do not have the resources to be generous or liberal, and then God accepts the willing heart. We must not only bear our own adversities patiently but also, with Christian sympathy, share in the suffering of our brothers and sisters. Pity must be shown (Job 6:14), and *bowels of mercy* (compassion) *put on* (Col 3:12). We must have compassion on the souls of others and help them; we must pity the ignorant and instruct them, pity the careless and warn them, and pity those who are in their sin and snatch them as *brands out of the burning* (Am 4:11). In fact, *a good man is merciful to his beast* (Pr 12:10).

6.1. They are *blessed*; this is how they are described in the Old Testament: *Blessed is he that considers the poor* (Ps 41:1). Here, they are like God, whose goodness is his glory (Ex 33:18–19). One of the purest and most refined delights in this world is that of *doing good* (Ac 10:38). In this word, *Blessed are the merciful*, is included that saying of Christ that we do not otherwise find in the Gospels: *It is more blessed to give than to receive* (Ac 20:35).

6.2. *They shall obtain mercy.* They will obtain mercy *with men* when they need it — we do not know how

soon we may need kindness, and so we should be kind to others — but especially mercy *with God*, for *with the merciful he will show himself merciful* (Ps 18:25). The most *merciful* and charitable cannot pretend to merit anything, but must flee to God for mercy, whereas those who have *shown no mercy* will receive *judgment without mercy* (Jas 2:13).

7. The *pure in heart* are happy (v. 8). *Blessed are the pure in heart, for they shall see God.* This is the most comprehensive of all the beatitudes. Here is the most comprehensive:

7.1. Characterization of the blessed; they are *pure in heart*. True Christianity lies in the heart, in the *purity of the heart*, the *washing* of that *from wickedness* (Jer 4:14). We must lift up to God not only clean hands but also a pure heart (Ps 24:4–5; 1Ti 1:5). The heart must be *pure*, not alloyed — a heart that has integrity and aims well. It must be pure, opposing defilement, like wine that is unmixed or water that is unmuddied. The heart must be kept *pure* from all filthiness of flesh and spirit, all that comes *out of the heart* (15:19) and *defiles the man* (Mk 7:20). The heart must be *purified by faith* and kept complete for God. *Create in me such a clean heart, O God!* (Ps 51:10).

7.2. Comfort of the blessed; they will see God.

7.2.1. It is the perfection of the soul's happiness to *see God*. Seeing him in faith in our present state is a heaven on earth; seeing him as we will in the future state is the heaven of heaven.

7.2.2. The happiness of seeing God is promised only to those who are *pure in heart*. None but the *pure* are capable of *seeing* God. What delight could an unsanctified soul take in the vision of a holy God? All who are *pure in heart*, however, all who are truly sanctified, have desires produced in them that nothing but the sight of God will sanctify.

8. The *peacemakers* are happy (v. 9). The wisdom that is from above is first *pure*, and then *peaceable* (Jas 3:17); the blessed ones are *pure* toward God and *peaceable* toward others. The *peacemakers* are those who have:

8.1. A peaceable disposition. To make peace is to love, desire, and delight in peace, to be in our element when we are in peace.

8.2. A peaceable rule of conduct. To be peacemakers is to diligently preserve the peace, as far as we can, so that it is not broken, and to restore it when it is broken. The *making of peace* is sometimes a thankless task, and it is the fate of those who separate warring factions to receive blows on both sides. It is a good task, however, and we must be eager to undertake it.

8.2.1. Such persons are *blessed*. They are working together with Christ, who came into the world to slay all enmities and make known *peace on earth* (Lk 2:14).

8.2.2. *They shall be called the children of God.* God will acknowledge them as such. If the peacemakers are blessed, the peacebreakers are in a terrible state!

9. Those who are *persecuted for righteousness' sake* are happy. This is the greatest paradox of all, and it is distinctive to Christianity. This beatitude, like Pharaoh's dream, is doubled, because it is hard to believe; but *the thing is certain.*

9.1. The situation of suffering saints is described.

9.1.1. They are persecuted, hunted, hounded, and pursued like offensive animals, which people hunt in order to destroy them; they are abandoned as the *offscouring of all things* (1Co 4:13).

9.1.2. They are *reviled, and have all manner of evil said against them falsely.* Nicknames and names of reproach are directed at them, sometimes to make them seem formidable, so that they may be powerfully attacked. Those who have had no power in their hands to cause any trouble to the righteous directly still do this, and those who have had power to *persecute* have found it necessary to do this too, in order to justify themselves in their cruel treatment of them. *Reviling* the saints is *persecuting* them and will soon be found to be so, when *hard speeches* (harsh words) (Jude 15) and *cruel mockings* (Heb 11:36) must be accounted for. They will say all *manner of evil of you falsely*. There is no evil, no matter how black and horrible, that has not, at one time or another, been falsely spoken against Christ's disciples and followers.

9.1.3. All this is *for righteousness' sake* (v. 10), *for my sake* (v. 11). This excludes from this blessedness those who suffer *justly*, who are *truly* spoken of in an evil way for their real crimes. It is not suffering, but the cause, that makes the martyr. Those who suffer *for righteousness' sake* are those who suffer for doing good.

9.2. The encouragements that belong to suffering saints are established:

9.2.1. They *are blessed*; for they now, in their lifetime, receive *their evil things* (Lk 16:25), and receive them for good reason. They are *blessed*: it is an honor to them. It gives them an opportunity to glorify Christ and experience the special comforts and the signs of his presence.

9.2.2. They will be *recompensed* (Pr 11:31; Lk 14:14); theirs is *the kingdom of heaven*. They already are definitely entitled to it and its sweet foretastes, and before long they will actually possess it. *Great is your reward in heaven*, so great that it will far exceed the service. God will make sure that those who lose *for* him, even if they lose life itself, will not lose *by* him in the end. This is what has encouraged suffering saints throughout the ages—that this *joy is set before them* (Heb 12:2).

9.2.3. "*So persecuted they the prophets that were before you* (v. 12). They were *before you* in excellence, above what you have yet reached; they were *before you* in time, so that they would be examples to you of *suffering affliction* and *of patience* (Jas 5:10). Can you expect to go to heaven in a different way? It is an encouragement to see that the way of suffering is a road that is already well trodden; it is an honor to follow such leaders. That grace that was *sufficient for them* (2Co 12:9), to take them through their sufferings, will not be *deficient to you*."

9.2.4. Therefore, *rejoice and be exceeding glad* (v. 12). It is not enough to be patient and content under these sufferings; we must also rejoice. It is not that we must take pride in our sufferings—that would spoil everything—but we must take delight in them, knowing that Christ has gone before us on that same road and that he will not be slow to help us (1Pe 4:12–13).

Verses 13–16

Christ had just called his disciples, and he had told them that they would be *fishers of men* (4:19); here he told them what he intended them to be besides—*the salt of the earth* and *lights of the world*.

1. *Ye are the salt of the earth*. The prophets who went before them were the salt of the land of Canaan, but the apostles were the salt of the whole earth, for they must *go into all the world to preach the Gospel* (Mk 16:15). What could they do in such a large area as the whole earth? By force and violence, nothing; but because they were to work as silently as salt, one handful of that salt would spread its savor far and wide. It would go a long way and work as imperceptibly and irresistibly as yeast (13:33). The teaching of the Gospel is like *salt*; it is penetrating, it

reaches *the heart* (Ac 2:37). It is cleansing and flavoring and preserves from decay and rotting. An eternal covenant is called *a covenant of salt* (Nu 18:19), and the Gospel is an eternal Gospel. Salt was required in all the sacrifices (Lev 2:13). Christians, especially ministers, are the salt of the earth.

1.1. If they are such, they are like *good salt*, white, small, and broken into many grains, but very useful and necessary. Notice in this:

1.1.1. What they are to be in themselves—seasoned with the Gospel, with the salt of grace (Col 4:6). *Have salt in yourselves*, for otherwise you cannot spread it among others (Mk 9:50).

1.1.2. What they are to be to others: they must not only be good but also do good.

1.1.3. What great blessings they are to the world. Because the human race lies in ignorance and evil, it is a vast, unsavory heap that is ready to decay, but Christ sent out his disciples to season it by their lives and teaching with knowledge and grace, so making it acceptable to God.

1.1.4. How they must expect to be used. They must be scattered like salt on the meat, here a grain and there a grain. Some have noticed that whereas it is foolishly called an ill omen to have the salt fall toward us, it is really an ill omen to have this salt fall away from us.

1.2. If they are not, they are like *salt* that has *lost its savour*. If Christians—especially ministers—are like that, their condition is very sad, for:

1.2.1. They are irrecoverable: *Wherewith shall it be salted?* There is no remedy for tasteless salt.

1.2.2. They are unprofitable: *It is thenceforth good for nothing*. As a person without reason is useless, so is a Christian without grace.

1.2.3. They are doomed to ruin and rejection; they will be *cast out*. They will be *trodden under foot of men*.

2. *Ye are the light of the world* (v. 14). This also describes them as useful, as in the previous metaphor—nothing is more useful than sun and salt—but more glorious. *Truly the light is sweet* (Ecc 11:7); it is welcome. The light of the first day of the world was so. The morning light every day is welcome too, and so are the Gospel and those who spread it.

2.1. *As the lights of the world*, they are bright and conspicuous, with many eyes on them. A city that is *set on a hill cannot be hid*. They are like *signs* (Isa 8:18), *men wondered at* (Zec 3:8); all their neighbors keep their eyes on them. Some wonder at them, commend them, rejoice in them, and seek to imitate them; others envy them, hate them, criticize them, and seek to get rid of them. It should be their concern, therefore, to *walk circumspectly* (carefully) because *of their observers*.

2.2. *As the lights of the world*, they are intended to illuminate and give light to others (v. 15), and so:

2.2.1. They will be *set up* as lights. Because Christ has lit these candles, they will not be put under *a bushel*. The Gospel is such a strong light, and it carries with it so much of its own evidence, that, *like a city on a hill, it cannot be hid*; it must be clear that it comes from God. It will *give light to all that are in the house*, to all who will draw near to it and come where it is. Those to whom it does not give light have only themselves to blame; they have refused to be in the house with it.

2.2.2. They must *shine* as lights (v. 16):

2.2.2.1. By their *good preaching*. They must pass on the knowledge they have for the good of others, not putting it under a bowl, but spreading it. The disciples of Christ must not keep themselves to themselves in "a holy huddle," shrouded in privacy and obscurity, claiming to be deep in contemplation or humility.

2.2.2.2. By their *good living*. They must be *burning and shining lights* (Jn 5:35). Notice:

2.2.2.2.1. How our light must shine — by doing *good works* that people *may see*. We must do good works *that may be seen* to build up others, but not *so that* they may be seen, in order to make ourselves look important. Those around us must not only hear our good words but also see our good works.

2.2.2.2.2. For what purpose our light must shine — "so that those who see your good works may be brought to *glorify* not you, but *your Father which is in heaven*. The glory of God is the great thing we must aim at in everything we do in our religious faith (1Pe 4:11). We must do all we can to bring others to glorify him. The sight of our *good works* will do this, by providing them with matter for praise and with motives of godliness. The holy, regular, and exemplary lives of the saints may do much toward converting sinners. Examples of godly lives speak volumes and teach people. There is a winsome power in godly behavior.

Verses 17–20

Those to whom Christ preached looked:

- To the Scriptures of the Old Testament as their rule, and here Christ showed them they were in the right.
- To the teachers of the law and Pharisees as their example, and here Christ showed them they were in the wrong, for:

1. The rule that Christ came to establish corresponded exactly with the Scriptures of the Old Testament, called here *the law* and *the prophets*.

1.1. He objected to the thought of canceling and weakening the Old Testament: *Think not that I am come to destroy the law and the prophets*.

1.1.1. "Let not the godly Jews, who have an affection for the *law and the prophets, fear* that I have come to *destroy* them.

1.1.2. "Let not the worldly Jews, who have a disaffection for the Law and the Prophets and are weary of that yoke, *hope* that I have come to destroy them." The Savior of souls is the *destroyer* of nothing that comes from God, much less of those excellent decrees that we received from Moses and the prophets. No, he came to *fulfill* them, that is:

1.1.2.1. To obey the commands of the Law. He gave obedience to the Law in all respects; he never broke the Law in anything.

1.1.2.2. To fulfill the promises of the Law and the predictions of the prophets.

1.1.2.3. To fulfill the types of the law, revealing himself to be the Substance of all those shadows.

1.1.2.4. To fill up its defects and so complete and perfect it. As a picture that is roughly drawn first displays only some outlines of the intended piece, which are later filled in, so Christ filled in the Law and the Prophets by his additions and explanations.

1.1.2.5. To continue the same purpose. The Gospel is the *time of reformation* (Heb 9:10); it is not the repeal of the law, but the amendment and, consequently, the establishment of it.

1.2. He asserted that it would last forever: "*Verily I say unto you*—I, the Amen, the faithful Witness (Rev 1:5), solemnly declare—that *till heaven and earth pass, one jot, or one tittle, shall in no wise pass from the law till all be fulfilled." The word of the Lord endures for ever* (1Pe

1:25), both that of the Law and that of the Gospel. The concern of God for his Law extends even to those things that seem to be most insignificant in it, for whatever belongs to God and bears his stamp will be preserved, even if it is very small.

1.3. He gave his disciples the responsibility to carefully preserve the Law, and he showed them the danger of having contempt for it and neglecting it. *Whosoever therefore shall break one of the least commandments of the law of Moses, he shall be called the least in the kingdom of heaven* (v. 19). But *whosoever shall do and teach them* will be *called great in the kingdom of heaven*. We can learn from this:

1.3.1. That among the commands of God, there are some that are less important than others; none is totally insignificant, but some are comparatively so.

1.3.2. That it is dangerous, in teaching or practice, to revoke the least of God's commands. It is something more than disobeying the Law; it is *making void* the Law (Ps 119:126).

1.3.3. That the further such corruptions spread, the worse they are. It is arrogant enough to break the command, but it is far worse to teach people to do so. This clearly refers to those who at this time sat in Moses' seat (23:2) and corrupted and distorted the text by their comments. Those who teach in this way will be called *least in the kingdom of heaven*, in the kingdom of glory. On the other hand, however, people who both do and teach what is good are truly honorable and significant in the church of Christ. Those who do not do as they teach pull down with one hand what they build up with the other, but people who speak from experience, who live up to what they preach, are truly great; in the future they will shine as the *stars in the kingdom of our Father* (Da 12:3).

2. The righteousness that Christ came to establish by this rule must surpass that of the teachers of the law and Pharisees (v. 20). This was strange teaching to those who looked on the teachers of the law and Pharisees as having reached the highest level of religion. It therefore came as a great surprise to them to hear that they must be better than their leaders. The teachers of the law and Pharisees were the enemies of Christ and his teaching and were great oppressors, but it must also be acknowledged that there was something commendable in them. They were devoted to fasting and prayer and giving alms; they were prompt in observing the ceremonial appointments and made it their business to teach others. Our Lord Jesus here told his disciples, however, that the religion he came to establish not only excluded the badness of the teachers of the law and Pharisees but also excelled their goodness. We must do more than they and better than they. They were concerned with only the outside, but we must take care of inside godliness. They aimed at the *praise* and applause *of men* (Jn 12:43), but we must aim at acceptance with God. We, when we have done everything, must *deny ourselves* (16:24) and say that we are *unprofitable servants* (Lk 17:10) and are trusting only in the righteousness of Christ.

Verses 21–26

Christ proceeded to explain the Law in some particular instances. He did not add anything new; he only limited and restrained some permissions that had been abused, and as to the precepts, he showed their breadth, strictness, and spiritual nature. In these verses, he explained the law of the sixth commandment, according to its true intent and full extent. Here is:

1. The *command itself* set down (v. 21). The laws of God were not novel, newfangled laws, but had been delivered to them long ago; they were ancient laws, but of the kind that would never become *antiquated* or *obsolete*. *Killing is* forbidden here, killing ourselves, killing any other person, directly or indirectly, or being accessory to it in any way. The law of God, the God of life, is a hedge of protection around our lives (Job 1:10; Isa 5:5).

2. The explanation of this command that the Jewish teachers contented themselves with. Their comment on it was, *Whosoever shall kill shall be in danger of the judgment*. Their interpretation of this commandment was faulty, for it suggested that the law of the sixth commandment was only external, forbidding nothing more than the act of murder, imposing no restraint on sinful desires, from which *wars and fightings come* (Jas 4:1). This was indeed the fundamental error of the Jewish teachers, to think that the divine law prohibited only the sinful act, not the sinful thought.

3. The explanation that Christ gave of this commandment.

3.1. Christ told them that rash anger is heart murder: "*Whosoever is angry with his brother without a cause* breaks the sixth commandment" (v. 22). Anger is a natural passion; there are cases in which it is lawful and commendable. But it is *sinful* when:

3.1.1. It is without any just provocation, that is, for no cause, no good cause, or no great and proportionate cause, when we are angry on the basis of groundless suspicions or for trivial affronts not worth speaking of.

3.1.2. No good purpose is aimed at. Then it is in vain; then it is to do harm. If we are angry at any time, it should be to awaken the offender to repentance and prevent them from offending again.

3.1.3. It exceeds proper limits, when we are outrageous and troublesome, seeking to hurt those we are displeased with. This is disobedience to the sixth commandment, for those who are angry in this way would kill if they could and dared; they have taken the first step toward it.

3.2. He told them that abusing our brother or sister with words, calling them *Raca* and *Thou fool*, is tongue murder. When this is done with mildness and for a good purpose, to convince others of their pride and foolishness, it is not sinful. When it proceeds from anger and malice inside us, however, it is the smoke of the fire that is kindled from hell.

3.2.1. *Raca* is a scornful word and comes from pride: "You worthless fellow." *This people who knoweth not the law is cursed* is such language (Jn 7:49).

3.2.2. *Thou fool* is a spiteful word and comes from hatred, looking on the person addressed not only as lowly and not to be honored but also as despicable and not to be loved. *Raca* refers to a person without sense; *fool*, a biblical word, refers to a person without grace; the more an insult relates to the spiritual condition of the person at whom it is hurled, the worse it is. Malicious slanders and criticism are *poison under the tongue* (Job 20:12; Ps 10:7; 140:3; Ro 3:13), which kills secretly and slowly. Such words are evidence of a hatred toward our neighbor that would strike at their life if it were in our power.

3.3. He told them that however light they made of these sins, they would certainly be judged, for he *that is angry with his brother shall be in danger of the judgment* and anger of the council; he who calls him *Raca shall be in danger of the council*, of being punished by the Sanhedrin for reviling an Israelite; *but whosoever saith, Thou fool*, "you godless person, you child of hell," *shall be in danger of*

hellfire, to which he condemns his brother. Christ wanted to show which sin was most sinful by showing which had the most fearful punishment.

4. The inference that we should carefully preserve Christian love and peace with all our brothers and sisters, and that if at any time a rift occurs, we should seek reconciliation:

4.1. Because until this is done, we are completely unfit for fellowship with God in religious ceremonies (vv. 23–24). "If thou *have aught against thy brother*, make short work of it; nothing more is to be done than to forgive him (Mk 11:25) and forgive the injury. However, if the quarrel began on your side, if the fault, either at first or afterward, was yours, so *that thy brother* has a dispute with *thee*, *go* and *be reconciled to* him before thou *offer thy gift at the altar*, before you approach God solemnly." When we are about to take part in any religious exercises, it is good for us to use that occasion for serious reflection and self-examination. Religious exercises are not acceptable to God if they are performed when we are angry. Prayers made in wrath are written in bitterness (Isa 1:15; 58:4). Love is so much *better than all burnt offerings and sacrifice* (Mk 12:33) that God is content to wait for the gift rather than have it offered while we are under guilt and engaged in a quarrel. Yet even if we are made unfit for fellowship with God by our continual quarrel with a brother or sister, that can be no excuse for omitting or neglecting to do our duty. Many give this as a reason why they do not come to church or to communion: they have a dispute with a neighbor. And whose fault is that? One sin will never excuse another, but will rather double the guilt. A lack of love cannot justify a lack of godliness. We must *not let the sun go down upon our wrath* (Eph 4:26) any day, because we must go to prayer before we go to sleep; much less must we let the sun rise *upon our wrath* on a Sabbath day, because it is a day of prayer.

4.2. Because until this is done, we lie exposed to much danger (vv. 25–26):

4.2.1. For a temporal reason. If the offense we have committed against our brother or sister, whether in their body, goods, or reputation, is such that they could sue us for it, perhaps recovering considerable damages, we are wise, and it is our duty to our family, to prevent that by humbly submitting and seeking to make a just and peaceful satisfaction, for otherwise they may recover it by litigation, and, in an extreme case, put us in prison. It is futile to contend with the law, and we are in danger of being crushed by it. It is good to come to an agreement, for litigation is costly. Although we must be merciful to those we have an advantage against, we must still be just to those who have an advantage against us. A prison is an uncomfortable place for those who are brought to it by their own pride, extravagance, stubbornness, and foolishness.

4.2.2. For a spiritual reason. "*Go* and be *reconciled to thy brother*; be just and friendly toward him, because as long as the quarrel continues, just as thou art not ready to *bring thy gift to the altar*, to come to *the table of the Lord*, so also you are not ready to die." This may be applied to the great work of our reconciliation with God through Christ: *Agree with him quickly, whilst thou art in the way* (v. 25). We can learn from this:

- The great God is an Adversary to all sinners.
- It is our responsibility to *agree with him*.
- We would be wise to do this *quickly, while we are in the way*. While we are still alive, *we are in the way*; after death, it will be too late.

- Those who continue to be in a state of enmity toward God expose themselves continually to the arrests of his justice. Hell is the prison into which those who continue to be the enemies of God will be thrown (2Pe 2:4). Sinners must remain in hell for eternity; they will not *depart till they have paid the uttermost farthing* (v. 26), and that will not be to the farthest reaches of eternity.

Verses 27–32

We have here an explanation of the seventh commandment. It is the law against sexual immorality, which appropriately follows the one before it; that one placed a restraint on sinful passions, this one on sinful appetites.

1. The command is set down here (v. 27): *Thou shalt not commit adultery*, which includes a prohibition of all other acts of sexual immorality and all desire for them.

2. It is explained here in its strictness, in three aspects. We are taught here:

2.1. That there is such a thing as heart adultery, adulterous thoughts and attitudes that never proceed to the actual committing of adultery or other forms of sexual immorality. *Whosoever looketh on a woman*—not only another man's wife, as some think it refers to, but any woman—*to lust after her, has committed adultery with her in his heart* (v. 28). This command forbids not only the acts of sexual immorality and adultery but also:

2.1.1. All appetites toward them. Lust is the condition of a conscience that is biased or baffled: biased, if it says nothing against the sin; baffled, if it does not prevail in what it says.

2.1.2. All approaches toward them, feeding the eyes with looking at forbidden fruit. The eyes are both the inlet and outlet of much evil of this kind. Why do we have eyelids except to restrain corrupt glances and keep out defiling impressions? This command forbids also the using of any other sense to stir up lust. If ensnaring looks are forbidden fruit, then much more immoral speech and flirting, which fuel this fire of hell. These commands serve to protect the law of purity of the heart (v. 8). If looking is lustful, those who dress, decorate themselves, and expose themselves with the intention of being looked at and lusted after are no less guilty. People sin, but the devils tempt us to sin.

2.2. That such looks and flirting are very dangerous and destructive to the soul, that it is better to lose the eye and the hand that offend in this way than to give way to sin. Corrupt nature would soon object, claiming that it is impossible to be governed by this command: "*It is a hard saying; who can bear it?* (Jn 6:60). Flesh and blood must look with pleasure on a beautiful woman, and it is impossible not to look lustfully at such an object." Such pretenses will scarcely be overcome by reason and must therefore be argued against by reference to *the terrors of the Lord*.

2.2.1. It is a severe operation that is prescribed to prevent this sexual immorality: *If thy right eye offend thee*, or *cause thee to offend*, by immoral glances at or gazing on forbidden objects, *if thy right hand offend thee*, or *cause thee to offend*, by immoral flirting, and if there were no other way to restrain them—which, we bless God, through his grace there is—it would be better for us to *pluck out the eye* and *cut off the hand* than to allow them to sin and thereby destroy the soul. If this, which is shocking to the natural instincts, is to be submitted to, then much more must we be determined to keep a constant watch over our own hearts, suppressing the first

signs of lust and corruption there; to avoid the occasions of sin, resisting its beginnings and declining the company of those who may trap us, even though it is very pleasant; to keep out of harm's way, restraining ourselves in using lawful things when we find them to be temptations to us; to seek God for his grace, depending on that grace every day and thereby *walking in the Spirit* (Gal 5:16), so that we may not *fulfil the lusts of the flesh* (Ro 13:14). This will be as effective as *cutting off a right hand or pulling out a right eye*—and perhaps it goes against the grain of our flesh and blood just as much too; it is the destruction of the old self.

2.2.2. It is a shocking argument that is used to enforce this prescription (v. 29): *It is profitable for thee that one of thy members should perish, and not that thy whole body should be cast into hell.*

2.2.2.1. It is not unfitting for a minister of the Gospel to preach hell and damnation; in fact, they *must* do it, for Christ himself did it, and we are unfaithful to our trust if we do not give warnings of *the wrath to come* (3:7).

2.2.2.2. There are some sins from which we need to be *saved with fear* (Jude 23), particularly *fleshly lusts* (1Pe 2:11), which are wild animals that cannot be restrained except by being frightened. People who do not know what hell is like or do not believe what the Scriptures tell us of it have decided to risk their eternal ruin rather than deny themselves the gratification of their base and brute lusts.

2.2.2.3. Even those duties that are most unpleasant to flesh and blood are *profitable for us*, and our Master requires nothing from us except what he knows will be for our good.

2.3. That men's divorcing their wives because they dislike them, or for any reason except adultery, was an act against the seventh commandment, as it opened the door to adultery (vv. 31–32). Notice here:

2.3.1. How matters then stood with reference to divorce. "*Whosoever shall put away his wife, let him give her a bill of divorce*; let him not think he can do it by word of mouth, when he is in a fit of anger; let him do so solemnly." This was how the law prevented rash and hasty divorces.

2.3.2. How this matter was amended and put right by our Savior. He reduced the ordinance of marriage to its original institution: *They two shall be one flesh* (Ge 2:24; Eph 5:31), not to be easily separated, and so divorce is not to be allowed except in a case of adultery, which breaks the marriage covenant, and the man who divorces his wife for any other pretense *causeth her to commit adultery*, and so does the man who marries her when she is divorced in this way.

Verses 33–37

We have here an explanation of the third commandment. *God will not hold him guiltless*—however he may hold himself—who breaks this commandment by *taking the name of the Lord God in vain* (Ex 20:7).

1. It is agreed by everyone that this command forbids perjury, breaking oaths and vows (v. 33). Perjury is a sin condemned by the light of nature, as it is a combination of ungodliness toward God and injustice toward people and therefore renders a person greatly repugnant to divine wrath. And since it was thought that this wrath followed infallibly on that sin, the forms of swearing were commonly turned into curses or imprecations, such as, "God do so to me, and more also," and in our own society, "So help me God," expressing a desire that the swearer may never receive any help from God if they swear falsely.

Therefore, nations have arranged for people to curse themselves, thinking that God would curse the swearer if they lied against the truth when they had solemnly called God to witness it.

2. It is added here that the commandment forbids not only false swearing but also all rash, unnecessary swearing: *Swear not at all* (v. 34; Jas 5:12). It is not that all oath taking is sinful; far from that, if rightly done, it is part of religious worship, and we *give unto God the glory due to his name* in it (Ps 29:2; 96:8). In taking an oath, we offer the truth of something known as security to confirm the truth of something doubtful or unknown; we appeal to a greater knowledge, to a higher court. The mind of Christ in this matter is that:

2.1. We must *not swear at all* except when we are properly called to do so, when justice or love toward our brother and sister, or respect for the general welfare, make it necessary for *the end of strife* (Heb 6:16).

2.2. We must not swear lightly and irreverently, in ordinary speech: it is a very great sin to make an absurd appeal to the glorious Majesty of heaven. It is a sin that has no cloak, no excuse, and is therefore a sign of a graceless heart.

2.3. We must especially avoid promissory oaths, about which Christ spoke particularly here, for they are oaths that require action on our part. The frequent requiring and using of oaths in our society is a reflection on Christians, who should have such an acknowledged trustworthiness that their sober words should be as sacred as their solemn oaths.

2.4. We must not swear by any creature. It seems there were some who, out of politeness—or so they thought—toward the name of God, would not use that in swearing, but would swear *by heaven* or *earth*. There is nothing we can swear by that is not in some way or other related to God, who is the Fountain of all beings, and so it is as dangerous to swear by them as it is to swear by God himself. It is the truthfulness of the creature that is at stake, but that cannot be an instrument of testimony except as it has regard to God.

2.4.1. "*Swear not by the heaven*, which means saying, 'As surely as there is a heaven, this is true,' *for it is God's throne*, his home." You cannot *swear by heaven* except by swearing by God himself.

2.4.2. *Nor by the earth, for it is his footstool. The earth is the Lord's* (Ps 24:1), so that in swearing by it, you swear by its Owner.

2.4.3. *Neither by Jerusalem*, a place for which the Jews had such respect that they could not speak of anything more sacred to *swear by. It is the city of the great King* (Ps 48:2), *the city of God* (Ps 46:4), and he is therefore interested in it and in every oath taken by it.

2.4.4. "*Neither shalt thou swear by the head. It is* more God's than yours, for he made it and formed all its powers and their sources, whereas you yourself cannot, by any natural inner influence, change the color of *one hair*, so as to make *it white or black.* You cannot, therefore, *swear by thy head* except by swearing by the One who is *the Life of thy head* and *the Lifter up of it*" (Ps 3:3).

2.5. Therefore, in all our talk, we must content ourselves with our "Yes" being "Yes" and our "No" being "No" (v. 37). *Verily, verily* was our Savior's "Yes, yes." If we deny something, let it therefore be enough to say, "No." If our faithfulness is known, that will be enough for us to be believed. If it is questioned, then to back up what we say with swearing and cursing is only to render it more suspicious. They who can *swallow* a godless oath

will not *strain at a lie* (23:24). The reason is significant: *For whatsoever is more than these cometh of evil,* even though it does not amount to the sin of an oath. It comes from the deceitfulness that is in every human being: *All men are liars* (Ps 116:11); people use these declarations because they distrust one another and think they cannot be believed without them. An oath is medicine, and it presupposes a disease.

Verses 38–42

In these verses the law of retaliation is explained. Notice:

1. What the Old Testament permission was in cases of injury. It was not a command that everyone should necessarily require such satisfaction, but they could lawfully insist on it if they pleased: *an eye for an eye, and a tooth for a tooth* (v. 38). It was a direction to the judges of the Jewish nation and was enacted to be a terror to those who caused trouble and to restrain those who were caused it, so that they could not insist on a greater punishment than was proper. It was not *a life for an eye*, nor *a limb for a tooth*; the punishment must be in proportion to the crime. Now, this remains in force with us to the extent that it is an instruction to magistrates to use the sword of justice according to the good and wholesome laws of the land for the terror of evildoers and the vindication of the oppressed. It is also in force as a rule to lawgivers, requiring them to wisely apportion punishments to crimes.

2. What the New Testament command is with regard to the one lodging the complaint. Their duty is to *forgive the injury* as something done to them and to make no further insistence on its punishment than is necessary for the public good. Christ teaches us two things here:

2.1. We must not be vengeful (v. 39): *I say unto you, that ye resist not evil*—the evildoer who has injured you. We may avoid and *resist* evil so far as is necessary for our own security, but we must not *render evil for evil,* must not bear a grudge, nor avenge ourselves, nor seek to get even with those who have treated us unkindly, but must go beyond them by forgiving them (Pr 20:22; 24:29; 25:21–22; Ro 12:17). The law of retaliation must be made consistent with the law of love. We are not justified in hurting our brother or sister by saying that they began it, for it is the second blow that makes the quarrel. Our Savior specifies three things to show that Christians must patiently yield to those who act harshly toward them:

2.1.1. A blow on the cheek, which injures my body: "*Whosoever shall smite thee on thy right cheek*, which is not only a hurt but also an affront and an indignity, *turn to him the other cheek.*" Bear it patiently. Do not "give as good as you got." Ignore it and take no further notice of it: no bones are broken, no great harm done; forgive and forget. If proud fools think the worse of you and laugh at you for it, all wise people will esteem and honor you for it, as a follower of the godly Jesus. Although this may, with some corrupt spirits, expose us to similar insults another time and therefore is indeed, in effect, to *turn the other cheek*, let that not disturb us. Perhaps the forgiving of one injury may prevent another, whereas avenging it would have provoked another; some who would become angrier by resistance will be overcome by submission (Pr 25:22).

2.1.2. The loss of a coat, which wrongs me with regard to my possessions: *If any man will sue thee at the law, and take away thy coat* (v. 40). Even if judges are just and careful, it is still possible for bad people who have no scruples about oaths and fraud to go to court to force the tunic off a person's back. *Marvel not at the matter* (Ecc 5:8); *let him* even *take thy cloak also*. If the matter is small, it is good to submit to the loss for the sake of peace. "It will not cost you as much to buy another cloak as it will cost you by course of law to recover the costs of the one that was taken."

2.1.3. The going of a mile by force, which wrongs me with regard to my liberty: "*Whosoever shall compel thee to go a mile, go with him two miles* (v. 41)." Say, "I will do it, for otherwise there will be a quarrel"; it is better to serve him than to serve your own sinful desires of pride and vengefulness. The sum of all this is that Christians must not be fond of litigation and eager to go to court; small injuries must be submitted to, and no notice must be taken of them. If the injury is such that it requires us to seek reparation, it must be for a good end and without thoughts of revenge.

2.2. We must be kind and generous (v. 42); we must not only do no harm to our neighbors; we must seek to do them all the good we can.

2.2.1. We must be ready to give: "*Give to him that asketh thee*. If you are able, look on the request of the poor as giving you an opportunity to give to those in need." Nevertheless, the affairs of our charity must be *guided with discretion* (Ps 112:5), so that we do not give to the idle and unworthy what should be given to those who are in genuine need and are deserving. What God says to us is what we should be ready to say to our poor brothers and sisters: *Ask, and it shall be given you* (7:7).

2.2.2. We must be ready to lend. This is sometimes as great an act of charity as giving, as it not only relieves the present need but also obliges the borrower to be provident, diligent, and honest. "Make yourself easily accessible to him *that would borrow*; although he may be shy and not have the confidence to make his case known and beg the favor, yet you know both his need and his desire, and so you should offer him the kindness. It is good for us to be eager to commit acts of kindness, for before we call, God hears us and gives *us the blessings of his goodness* (Ps 21:3).

Verses 43–48

We have here, lastly, an explanation of that great fundamental law of the second table of the Ten Commandments, *Thou shalt love thy neighbour*. Notice:

1. How this law was corrupted by the comments of the Jewish teachers (v. 43). God said, *Thou shalt love thy neighbour*, and they understood *neighbour* to refer only to those whom they were pleased to look on as their friends. They were willing to infer what God never intended: *Thou shalt hate thine enemy*. They looked on whomever they wanted to as their enemies. Notice how willing corrupt passions are to draw support from the word of God, to *take occasion by the commandment* (Ro 7:8, 11) to justify themselves.

2. How it is clarified by the command of the Lord Jesus, who teaches us another lesson: "*But I say unto you, Love your enemies*" (v. 44). Even if people are very bad in themselves and act very corruptly toward us, that does not release us from the great debt of love we owe to them as members of our own race—indeed, of our own family. It is the great duty of Christians to *love their enemies*; even though we cannot delight in one who is openly evil and ungodly, nevertheless, we must take notice, with pleasure, of what is pleasant and commendable even in our enemies; we are to love those qualities in them even though they are our enemies. We must have compassion for them and goodwill toward them. We are told here that:

2.1. We must *speak* well of them: *Bless them that curse you*. When we speak to them, we must respond to their insults with polite and friendly words rather than *repay railing for railing*. Those *in whose tongues is the law of kindness* (Pr 31:26) can say good words to those who say bad words to them.

2.2. We must *do* well to them: *Do good to them that hate you*, and that will be a better proof of love than good words. Be ready to do them all the real kindness that you can, and be glad to have an opportunity to do so.

2.3. We must *pray for them: Pray for them that despitefully use you, and persecute you.* Christ himself was treated in that way. When we meet with such treatment, we have the opportunity to show our conformity to both the commands and the example of Christ by praying for those who so abuse us. We must pray that God will forgive them, that they may never fare the worse because of anything they have done against us, and that he would lead them to be at peace with us. This is *heaping coals of fire on their heads* (Ro 12:20). We must do it so that we may:

2.3.1. Be *like God our Father*: "so that you may be, may prove yourselves to be, *the children of your Father which is in heaven*." Can we follow a better example? God *maketh his sun to rise*, and *sendeth rain*, on *the just and unjust* (v. 45). *Sunshine* and *rain* are great blessings to the world, and they come from God. Common mercies must be valued as examples and proofs of the goodness of God, who shows himself in them to be a generous Benefactor. These gifts of common providence are dispensed indiscriminately to *good* and *evil, just* and *unjust*. The worst people share the comforts of this life in common with others, which is an amazing demonstration of God's patience and goodness. The gifts of God's goodness to evildoers who rebel against him teach us to *do good to those that hate us* (v. 44). Only those who seek to be like God, especially in his goodness, will be accepted as his children.

2.3.2. *Do*, here, *more than others* (vv. 46–47). *Publicans* (tax collectors) *love their friends.* Nature inclines them to do so; their own interests direct them to do so. To do good to those who do good to us is a common act of humanity. But we, as Christians, must love our enemies, so that we may exceed them. Christianity is something more than humanity. It is a serious question, one that we should frequently ask ourselves, "What do we do more than others? What surpassing thing do we do? God has done more for us, and so he justly expects more from us than from others, but what do we do more than others? In what aspects of life do we live above the ordinary ways of other people? We cannot expect the reward of Christians if we rise no higher than the goodness of tax collectors." Those who promise themselves a reward above others must seek to do more than others. Our Savior concludes this subject with this encouragement: *Be ye therefore perfect, as your Father which is in heaven is perfect* (v. 48). This may be understood:

2.3.2.1. In general, as including all those things in which we must be *followers of God as dear children* (Eph 5:1). It is the duty of Christians to seek, aim at, and press toward a perfection in grace and holiness (Php 3:12–14). Or:

2.3.2.2. In this particular, mentioned before: *doing good to our enemies*; see Lk 6:36. It is God's perfection to forgive injuries, to *entertain strangers* (Heb 13:2), and to do good to ungrateful evildoers, and it is our responsibility to be like him. We who owe so much, who owe our all, to God's goodness should follow his example as much as we can.

CHAPTER 6

In the previous chapter, Christ strengthened his disciples against the corrupt teachings and thoughts of the teachers of the law and Pharisees; in this chapter he comes to warn them against hypocrisy and worldly-mindedness, sins that, of all sins, those who profess a religious faith need to be most on their guard against. We are warned here: 1. Against hypocrisy: 1.1. In giving to the needy (vv. 1–4). 1.2. In prayer (vv. 5–8). We are taught here what to pray for and how to pray (vv. 9–13), and to forgive in prayer (vv. 14–15). 1.3. In fasting (vv. 16–18). 2. Against worldly-mindedness: 2.1. In what we choose, which is the destructive sin of hypocrites (vv. 19–24). 2.2. In our anxieties, which are the disturbing sin of many true Christians (vv. 25–34).

Verses 1–4

We must watch against hypocrisy, which was the yeast of the Pharisees, as well as against their teaching (Lk 12:1). Giving to the needy, praying, and fasting are three great Christian duties. We must not only *depart from evil* but also *do good*, do it well, and so *dwell for evermore* (Ps 34:14; 37:27). We are warned in these verses against hypocrisy in *giving alms. Take heed of it.* We are in great danger *of* it. It is a subtle sin; pride quietly worms itself into what we do before we are aware of it. We are also in great danger *by* this sin. Beware of hypocrisy, for if it reigns in you, it will ruin you. It is the dead fly that spoils the whole precious ointment. Two things are suggested here:

1. The *giving of alms* is a great duty, and a duty that all the disciples of Christ, according to their ability, must fulfill. The Jews called the poor's box, into which alms were put, "the box of righteousness." It is true that our good works do not deserve heaven, but it is as true that we cannot go to heaven without them. Christ assumes here that his disciples *give alms*; he will not acknowledge those who do not.

2. It is a duty that has a great reward accompanying it, which is lost if it is done hypocritically. In the resurrection of the just (Lk 14:14), it will be rewarded in eternal riches. "The riches you impart form the only wealth you will always retain" (Martial). Notice:

2.1. What the *practice of the hypocrites* was in fulfilling this duty. It is true that they did it, but not from any motive of obedience to God or love to other people, but out of pride and boasting; not out of compassion toward the poor, but purely for show. According to this intention, they chose to give their gifts to the needy *in the synagogues, and in the streets*, where the greatest number of people could observe them. Not that it is unlawful to give to the needy *when* people see us, but we must not do it *so that* people may see us. If the hypocrites gave gifts at their own houses, they *sounded a trumpet* to make known their kindness and get everyone talking about it. The condemnation Christ passes on this is significant: *Verily I say unto you, they have their reward.* Two words in it make it a threat:

2.1.1. It is a reward, but it is *their* reward; it is not the reward that God promises those who do good, but the reward they promise themselves, and it is a poor reward; they did it to be *seen of men*, and they *were* seen of men.

2.1.2. It is a reward, but it is *a present reward*; they *have* it, and there is none reserved for them in the future state. They now have all that they are likely to receive from God. It is payment in full. The world is merely a

provision for the saints; it is their spending money. But it is *pay* for hypocrites; it is their inheritance.

2.2. What the command of our Lord Jesus is about it (vv. 3–4). "*Let not thy left hand know what thy right hand doeth* when you are giving to the needy." The giving of alms with the *right hand* is a sign of readiness to do it and determination to do so; do it skillfully, but "whatever kindness your right hand shows to the poor, *let not thy left hand know it.* Conceal it as much as possible; be diligent about keeping it private. Do it because it is a good work, not because it will give you a good reputation." It is indicated:

2.2.1. That we must not let others know what we are doing.

2.2.2. That we must not notice it too much ourselves. Self-conceit and self-delight, the adoring of our own shadow, are branches of pride. We find that those who themselves had forgotten their good works had them remembered to their honor: *When saw we thee an hungered, or athirst?* (25:37).

2.3. What is the *promise to those who are thus sincere and humble* in giving to the needy. Let *thine alms be in secret*, and then *thy Father who seeth in secret will* notice them. When we take the least notice of our good deeds ourselves, God takes most notice of them. It is a comfort to sincere Christians that God *sees in secret.* Notice how emphatically it is expressed: *himself shall reward*; he himself will be the Rewarder (Heb 11:6). He will *himself be the Reward* (Ge 15:1), your *exceeding great reward.* He will reward you as your Father—not as a master who gives his servant just what he earns and nothing more, but as a father who gives abundantly more (Eph 3:20), and without any trace of meanness, to his son who serves him. If the work is not openly seen, the reward will be, and that is better.

Verses 5–8

In *prayer* we are even more obligated to be *sincere*, which is what we are directed to be here: *When thou prayest* (v. 5). It is assumed that all the disciples of Christ *pray.* You may as soon find a living person who does not breathe as a living Christian who does not pray. If we are without prayer, then we are without grace. The hypocrites were guilty of two great faults in prayer: boasting (vv. 5–6), and babbling (vv. 7–8).

1. We must not, in prayer, be proud and boastful or seek the commendation of other people. Notice here:

1.1. What the way and practice of the hypocrites was. In all their exercises of devotion, it was clear that their main aim was to be commended by their neighbors. When they seemed to *soar upwards* in prayer, then their eye was *downwards*, aiming at praise as their *prey.* Notice:

1.1.1. What places they chose for their devotion; they prayed in the *synagogues*, which were proper places for public prayer, but not for personal prayer. They prayed in *the corners of the streets*, "the wide streets," as the word means, those that were most frequented, so that they would be taken notice of.

1.1.2. The position they used in prayer; they prayed standing. This is a lawful and proper posture for prayer, but kneeling was the more humble and reverent gesture. Standing seemed to point to their pride and self-confidence (Lk 18:11).

1.1.3. Their pride in choosing those public places, which is expressed in two things:

1.1.3.1. They *loved* to pray there. They did not love prayer for its own sake, but because it gave them the opportunity of making themselves noticed.

1.1.3.2. They did it so that they might be *seen of men*; they did it not so that God would accept them, but so that people would wonder at and applaud them.

1.1.4. The product of all this: *they have their reward*; they had all the reward they must ever expect to receive from God for their service, and it was a poor reward. What good will it do us to receive the good word of our fellow servants if our Master does not say, *Well done* (25:21)? They did it to be *seen of men*; they were, and much good may it do them. What passes between God and our own souls must be out of sight. Public places are not the proper place for private, solemn prayer.

1.2. What the will of Jesus Christ is, in contrast to this. *Thou, when thou prayest,* do such and such—what is written in v. 6. Personal prayer is thought of here as the duty and practice of all Christ's disciples. Notice:

1.2.1. The guidance given here about it.

1.2.1.1. Instead of praying in *the synagogues* and in *the corners of the streets, enter into thy closet,* a private, secluded room. Isaac went into the field (Ge 24:63), Christ onto a mountain (14:23), Peter to a roof of a house (Ac 10:9). No place is wrong for ceremonial reasons, as long as it fulfills its purpose. If, however, the circumstances are such that we cannot possibly avoid being noticed, we must not for that reason neglect the duty, for such an omission would be a greater scandal than would be the observation of the fulfillment.

1.2.1.2. Instead of doing it to be *seen of men, pray to thy Father who is in secret.* The Pharisees prayed to people rather than to God. "When you pray to God, let that be enough for you. Pray to him as your Father, who is ready to listen and answer, graciously inclined to pity and help you. Pray to your Father, *who is in secret.* He is there in your room when no one else is there; he is especially near to you in what you *call upon him* for (Dt 4:7)."

1.2.2. The encouragements given us here to do it.

1.2.2.1. "Your Father *seeth in secret.*" There is not a single secret, sudden breathing after God that he does not see.

1.2.2.2. "He *will reward thee openly*; those who pray openly have their reward, and you will not lose yours simply because yours is done in secret." It is called *a reward,* but it is a reward *of grace,* not *of debt.* Sometimes secret prayers are rewarded openly in this world by significant answers, and by this means God reveals his praying people in the consciences of their adversaries.

2. We must not *use vain repetitions* in prayer (vv. 7–8). Although the life of prayer lies in *lifting up the soul* (Ps 25:1; 86:4; 143:8) and *pouring out* the heart (Ps 22:14), words have some importance in prayer, especially in joint prayer, for words are necessary in that. *Use not vain repetitions,* either alone or with others. Notice:

2.1. The *fault* that is rebuked and condemned here; it is paying mere lip service to the duty of prayer.

2.1.1. *Vain repetitions*—tautology. Not all repetition in prayer is condemned here, only babbling, *vain repetitions.* Christ himself prayed again *saying the same words* (26:44), out of an extraordinary fervor and zeal (Lk 22:44). It is displeasing to God, and to all who are wise, when we say much but cannot say much to the point.

2.1.2. *Much speaking,* a love of wordiness in prayer springing from a love of hearing oneself talk. Not that all long prayers are forbidden; Christ prayed all night (Lk 6:12). Nor is it much *praying* that is condemned—no, we are told to *pray always*—but much *speaking.* The danger of this error arises when we only *say* our prayers, not when we truly *pray* them.

2.2. The reasons that are given against this.

2.2.1. This is the way of the pagans; it is *as the heathen do*; it is not right that Christians should worship their God as the Gentiles worship theirs. Thinking God was altogether like them (Ps 50:21), they thought he needed many words to make him understand what was being said to him or to persuade him to agree to their requests. Lip service in prayer, even if it is hard service, if that is all it is, is merely lost service.

2.2.2. "That need not be the way you follow, *for your Father* in heaven *knoweth what things ye have need of before ye ask him,* and so there is no need for so many words. Yet it does not follow that therefore you do not need to pray, for God requires you to pray in order to acknowledge your need of him. Open up your situation, pour out your hearts before him, and then leave matters with him."

2.2.2.1. The God we pray to is our Father. Children do not make long speeches to their parents when they lack anything. They need not say many words, since they have been taught by the Spirit of adoption to say, rightly, *Abba Father* (Ro 8:15).

2.2.2.2. He is a Father who knows our situation and our needs better than we do ourselves: *He knows what things we have need of.* He often gives *before we call* (Isa 65:24), and *more than we ask for* (Eph 3:20). We need not be long or use many words to describe our situation, for God knows it better than we can tell him, but he wants to know it from us—*what will ye that I should do unto you?* (20:32). The most powerful intercessions are those that are made with *groanings that cannot be uttered* (Ro 8:26).

Verses 9–15

Because we do not know what to pray for as we ought, Christ helps our weaknesses here (Ro 8:26) by putting words into our mouths: *after this manner therefore pray ye* (v. 9). Not that we are to be tied to the use of only this form, or this one always, as if this were necessary for the consecrating of our other prayers. We are told here to pray like this, either with these words or to this effect. Without doubt, however, it is very good to use this prayer as a form, and its use is a pledge of the fellowship of saints, since it has been used by the church throughout the ages. It is used acceptably no further than it is used with understanding and without babbling in vain repetition.

The Lord's Prayer, as indeed every prayer, is a letter sent from earth to heaven. Here is the salutation of the letter, the addressing of the One to whom it is directed, *our Father*; the address, *in heaven*; its contents, consisting of several requests; the close, *for thine is the kingdom*; the seal, *Amen*; and, if you like, the date, too, *this day.* There are three parts:

1. The introduction, *Our Father who art in heaven.* Calling him *our Father* shows that we must pray not only alone and for ourselves but also with and for others. We are taught here *to whom to pray,* only to God, not to saints and angels. We are taught how to address God, what title to give him, a title that speaks of him as generous rather than magnificent, for we are to come boldly to the throne of grace (Heb 4:16). We must address him:

1.1. As *our Father,* and we must continually call him so. Nothing is more pleasing to God or pleasant to ourselves than to call God *Father.* In prayer, Christ generally called God *Father.* If he is our Father, he will pity us in our weaknesses (Ps 103:13), will spare us (Mal 3:17), will make the best of our actions even though they are defective, and will deny us nothing good for us (Lk 11:11–13). When we come repenting of our sins, we must look to

God as a Father, as the prodigal son did (Lk 15:18; Jer 3:19), as a loving, gracious, and reconciled Father in Christ (Jer 3:4).

1.2. As our Father *in heaven*. He is in heaven so as to be everywhere else, for heaven cannot contain him (1Ki 8:27); yet he is in heaven so as to reveal his glory there, for it is his throne (Ps 103:19), and it is a throne of grace to believers. It is there that we must direct our prayers. From there he has a full and clear view of all our needs, burdens, desires, and weaknesses. He is not only, like a Father, willing to help us, but also, like a heavenly Father, able to help us, able to do great things for us, more than we can ask or think (Eph 3:20). He has the resources to supply our needs, for every good gift comes from above (Jas 1:17). He is a Father, and so we may come to him with boldness, but he is also a Father in heaven, and so we must come to him with reverence (Ecc 5:2). By prayer, we send before us a message to the place where we profess to be going.

2. *The petitions*, and there are six, the three first relating more directly to God and his honor, and the last three to our own concerns. The method of this prayer teaches us to seek first the *kingdom of God and his righteousness*, and then to hope that *other things shall be added* (v. 33).

2.1. *Hallowed be thy name*. In these words:

2.1.1. We give glory to God. We should give glory to God before we expect to receive mercy and grace from him. Let him be praised for his perfections, and then let us benefit from them.

2.1.2. We settle our purpose, and it is the right purpose: that God may be glorified; all our other requests must be subordinate to this and in pursuit of it. "*Father, glorify thyself* (Jn 12:28) in giving me my daily bread and forgiving my sins." Since all comes from him and is through him, all must be to him and for him. In prayer more than at any other time, our thoughts and devotion should be pursued to the glory of God. "Do this for me *for the glory of thy name*, and as far as it is for its glory."

2.1.3. We desire and pray that the name of God — that is, God himself, in everything by which he has made himself known — may be sanctified and glorified by us and others, and especially by himself. "Father, may your name be glorified as a Father, and a Father in heaven; glorify your goodness and your eminence, your majesty and your mercy."

2.2. *Thy kingdom come*. This request has a clear reference to the doctrine that Christ preached at this time: *the kingdom of heaven is at hand* (10:7). "The kingdom of your Father, who is in heaven, is at hand; pray that it may come." We should turn the word we hear into prayer; our hearts should echo to it. Does Christ promise, *Surely I come quickly?* Our hearts should answer, *Even so, come* (Rev 22:20). We must pray for what God has promised, for promises are given not to replace prayer, but to encourage it.

2.3. *Thy will be done in earth as it is in heaven*. We pray that because God's kingdom is coming, we and others may be brought into obedience to all its laws and ordinances. We treat Christ as only a Prince in name if we call him King but do not do his will. Having prayed that he may rule us, we pray that we may in everything be ruled by him. Notice:

2.3.1. The thing prayed for: *thy will be done*. It was in this sense that Christ prayed, *not my will, but thine be done*. "Enable me to do what is pleasing to you; give me the grace that is necessary for the right knowledge of your will and an acceptable obedience to it, so that I may neither displease God in anything I do nor be displeased with anything God does."

2.3.2. The pattern according to which we wish for his will to be done: that it *may be done on earth* — for our work must be done here, or it will never be done — *as it is done in heaven*. We pray that earth may be made more like heaven by observing God's will.

2.4. *Give us this day our daily bread*. Because our natural existence is necessary for our spiritual well-being in this world, therefore, after the things of God's glory, kingdom, and will, we pray for the necessary supports and comforts of this present life. Every word here contains a lesson:

2.4.1. We ask for *bread*; not delicacies or excess, but what is wholesome.

2.4.2. We ask for *our* bread; that teaches us honesty and diligence.

2.4.3. We ask for our *daily* bread, which teaches us not to *take thought for the morrow* (v. 34), but to constantly depend on divine providence.

2.4.4. We beg God to *give* it to us. The greatest person must be indebted to the mercy of God for their *daily bread*.

2.4.5. We pray, "Give it to *us*, not only to me but also to others, for us to share." This teaches us kindness and a compassionate concern for the poor and needy.

2.4.6. We pray that God would give it us *this day*, which teaches us to renew the desire of our souls toward God, just as the needs of our bodies are renewed. We could as well go a day without food as without prayer.

2.5. *And forgive us our debts, as we forgive our debtors*. This is connected with the previous petition. Our daily bread only feeds us as lambs for the slaughter if our sins are not pardoned. We must therefore pray for daily *pardon* as much as we pray for daily *bread*. Here we have:

2.5.1. A request: "*Father in heaven, forgive us our debts*, our debts to you." Our sins are our debts; there is a debt of duty that, as creatures, we owe to our Creator. We do not pray to be discharged from that, yet upon its nonpayment, a debt of punishment arises. Our hearts' desire and prayer to our heavenly Father every day should be that he would *forgive us our debts*, that we may be discharged and enjoy the encouragement of knowing pardon.

2.5.2. An argument in support of this petition: *as we forgive our debtors*. This is not a plea of merit, but a plea of grace. Our responsibility is to *forgive our debtors*. We must forbear, forgive, and forget the insults thrown at us and the wrongs done to us, and this is a moral qualification for pardon and peace. The very praying of this petition encourages us to hope that God will *forgive us*. That he has produced the condition of forgiveness in us will be evidence to us that he has forgiven us.

2.6. *And lead us not into temptation, but deliver us from evil*. This petition begins negatively: *not into temptation*. Having prayed that the guilt of sin may be removed, we pray, as is right, that we may never return again to foolishness, that we may not be tempted to it. The petition concludes positively: *But deliver us from evil*, "from the Evil One," the Devil, the tempter; keep us so that we may not be attacked. Or "from the evil thing," sin, the worst of evils, the only evil, the evil that God hates and that Satan tempts people to and destroys them by.

3. The conclusion: *For thine is the kingdom, and the power and the glory, for ever. Amen*.

3.1. It is a form of plea to support the foregoing requests. It is our responsibility to plead with God in prayer, to fill our mouth with arguments (Job 23:4), not to move God, but to move ourselves; to encourage our faith, excite our fervency, and give evidence of both. The best pleas in prayer are those that are taken from God himself, and from what he has made known of himself. We must wrestle with God in his own strength. *"Thine is the kingdom"*; God gives and saves like a king. *"Thine is the power*, to maintain and support that kingdom and to fulfill all your commitments to your people. *Thine is the glory*, as the end of all that is given to and done for the saints in answer to their prayers."

3.2. It is a form of praise and thanksgiving. The best pleas with God are his praises; it is the way to obtain further mercy, as it qualifies us to receive it. We praise God and give him glory not because he needs it—he is praised by a world of angels—but because he deserves it. Praise is the work and happiness of heaven, and everyone who wants to go to heaven in the future must begin their heaven now. It is right that we should be full in praising God. True saints never think they can speak honorably enough of God. Ascribing glory to God *for ever* shows an acknowledgment that it is eternally due and a fervent desire to do it eternally, with the angels and saints above (Ps 71:14).

3.3. To all this we are taught to attach our *Amen*, "so be it." God's *Amen* is a grant: "It shall be so." Our *Amen* is only a summary desire: "Let it be so." Our saying *Amen* is a sign of our desire and assurance that we will be heard. It is good to conclude religious duties with some warmth and vigor, so that we may go out from them with a *sweet savor* on our spirits (Ge 8:21; Ex 29:18; Lev 1:9; 2Co 2:15; Eph 5:2; etc.).

Most of the petitions in the Lord's Prayer, or words to the same effect, had been commonly used by the Jews in their devotions; but that clause in the fifth petition, *as we forgive our debtors*, was completely new, and so our Savior shows here why he added it, namely, from the need and importance of the thing itself. In forgiving us, God particularly considers our forgiving those who have wronged us, and so when we pray for pardon, we must mention our concern for that duty, not only to remind ourselves of it but also to bind ourselves to it. Selfish nature is reluctant to comply with this, and so it is inculcated here (vv. 14–15):

3.3.1. In a promise. *If ye forgive, your heavenly Father will also forgive*. It is not as if this were the only condition required; there must also be repentance and faith and new obedience. Those who relent toward their brother or sister show that they repent toward their God. It is a good sign, and a good aid to our forgiving others, to give an extenuating, excusing name to the wrongs done to us. Do not call them deliberate injuries, but accidental inadvertencies; perhaps it was an oversight: therefore make the best of it. We must forgive others, as we hope to be forgiven; we must not rebuke our brother or sister for the injuries they have done us, nor rejoice in any harm that comes to them, but must be ready to help them and do them good, and if they repent and desire to be friends again, we must be free with them, as before.

3.3.2. In a threat. *"But if you forgive not"* those who have injured you, that is a bad sign, a sign that you have not fulfilled the other necessary conditions, but are completely unqualified for pardon, and so *your Father will not forgive you*. If other graces are sincere, but you are greatly deficient in forgiving, you cannot expect the assurance of your pardon. Those who want to find mercy with God must show mercy to their brothers and sisters. If we pray in anger, we have reason to fear that God will answer in anger. It has been said that prayers made in wrath are written in bitterness. Why should God forgive us the dollars we are indebted to him if we do not forgive our brothers and sisters the pennies they are indebted to

us? Christ came into the world as the great *Peacemaker*, *to reconcile us* not only *to God* but also to one another (Eph 2:14–16). For anyone to make light of what Christ emphasizes here is an act of significant presumption with dangerous consequences. Human passions will not frustrate God's word.

Verses 16–18

We are warned here against hypocrisy in fasting.

1. It is presumed that religious fasting is a duty that is required of the disciples of Christ when God, in his providence, calls people to it (Isa 22:12–13) and when the case of their own souls requires it for any reason. Fasting comes last here because it is not so much a duty for its own sake as a means to make us disposed toward other duties. Prayer comes between giving to the needy and fasting because it is the life and soul of both. It was not the Pharisee's fasting *twice in the week*, but his boasting about it, that Christ condemned (Lk 18:12). It is a commendable practice, and we have reason to lament its general neglect among Christians. It is an act of self-denial and self-humiliation under the hand of God. The most mature Christians must acknowledge that they are so far from having anything to be proud of that they are unworthy of their daily bread.

2. We are warned not to do this *as the hypocrites* did it, so that we may not lose its reward. Notice:

2.1. The *hypocrites* pretended to fast when they had none of that contrition or humility of soul that is the life and soul of the duty. Theirs were pretend fasts, mere show and shadow and no substance.

2.2. They made known their fasting, arranging it so that everyone who saw them would take notice that it was a day of fasting for them. On these days they came out onto the streets, so that people would see how often they fasted and praise them as being devout and humble. It is sad when people who have to some extent exercised self-control over the corrupt delights of human pleasure are ruined by their pride, which is a spiritual evil and no less dangerous. Here also *they have their reward*, and it is all they have.

3. We are instructed how to manage our own private fasts. Christ does not tell us how often we must fast; the Spirit in the word has left that to the Spirit in the heart. But we can take as a rule that whenever we undertake this duty, we are to seek to approve ourselves to God (2Ti 2:15) and not to commend ourselves to the good opinion of other people. Christ does not direct us to lessen the reality of the fast; he does not say, "Eat a little food, or take a little drink, or a little medicine." No; "let the body be humbled; set aside all show and pride in fasting. Look pleasant, *anoint thine head and wash thy face*, as you do on ordinary days, deliberately to hide your devotion, and you will not lose the commendation in the end, for although it will not be seen by people, it will be seen by God." Fasting is humbling the soul. Let that, therefore, be your main concern. If we are sincere and humble in our sacred fasts, if we trust in God's omniscience as our witness and his goodness as our reward, we will find both that he did *see in secret* and that he will reward openly. Religious fasts, if rightly kept, will soon be rewarded with an eternal feast.

Verses 19–24

Having warned us against coveting *the praise of men* (Jn 12:43), Christ proceeds next to warn us against coveting the wealth of the world. Here also we must beware, so that we do not become like the hypocrites and do as they do. The fundamental error they are guilty of is that they choose the world as *their reward*.

1. We must beware of hypocrisy and worldly-mindedness in choosing the *treasure* we *lay up* (v. 19). Everyone has something or other that they make their *treasure*, their portion, which their heart is set on. The soul will have something that it looks on as the best. Christ does not intend to deprive us of our treasure, but to guide us in choosing it. We have here:

1.1. A good warning against making *the things that are seen* (2Co 4:18; Heb 11:1), which are temporal, our best things and locating our happiness in them: *Lay not up for yourselves treasures upon earth*. Christ's disciples had left everything to follow him (Mk 10:28), and let them still follow the same good. Now we must *not lay up our treasures on earth*, that is:

1.1.1. We must not count these things the best things. We must not boast about them, but see and acknowledge that they have no glory in comparison with *the glory that excelleth* (2Co 3:10).

1.1.2. We must not seek an abundance of these things, nor continue to grasp at more and more of them, never knowing when we have enough.

1.1.3. We must not put our trust in them for the future; we must not say to the gold, *Thou art my hope* (Job 31:24).

1.1.4. We must not content ourselves with them as all that we need or desire. We should choose wisely, for we are choosing for ourselves (Pr 9:12) and will receive as we choose. If we know and consider what we are, what we are made for, how large our capacities are, and how long our lives are, and that our souls are ourselves (Ge 2:7; also Mt 16:25–26), we will see that it is a foolish thing to *lay up* our *treasures on earth*.

1.2. A good reason why we should not look on anything *on earth* as our *treasure*, because any such treasure is liable to loss and decay:

1.2.1. From corruption inside. What is treasure *upon earth, moth and rust do corrupt*. Manna itself bred worms. The *rust* breeds in the metal itself; the *moth* in the garment itself. Worldly riches contain in themselves their source of corruption and decay.

1.2.2. From violence outside. *Thieves break through and steal*. Every violent person will be aiming to enter the house where *treasure* is stored up; nothing can be stored up so safely that we cannot be robbed of it. It is foolish to make our *treasure* what we may so easily be robbed of.

1.3. Good advice, to make the joys and glories of the other world, those *things not seen* that *are eternal* (2Co 4:18), our best things, and to locate our happiness in them. *Lay up for yourselves treasures in heaven*. This shows us:

1.3.1. There are *treasures in heaven* as certainly as there are on this earth, and those in heaven are the only true *treasures*.

1.3.2. We would be wise to *lay up* our *treasure in* those *treasures*, to diligently make sure of our entitlement to eternal life through Jesus Christ, to depend on that as our happiness, and to look on everything here below with holy contempt. If we make those *treasures* ours, they are stored up, and we may trust God to keep them safe for us. Let us not burden ourselves with the cash of this world. The promises are bills of exchange by which all true believers return their *treasure* to *heaven*—bills that are payable in the future state.

1.3.3. Knowing that the *treasure we lay up in heaven* is safe is a great encouragement to us to *lay it up* there; there, *no moth* or *rust will corrupt* it; *thieves do not break*

through and steal. It is a happiness above and beyond the changes and chances of time, *an inheritance incorruptible* (1Pe 1:4).

1.4. A good reason why we should make this choice. *Where your treasure is*, on earth or in heaven, *there will you heart be* (v. 21). The *heart* follows the *treasure* as the needle follows the magnet, or the sunflower the sun. *Where the treasure is, there* the value and esteem are, *there* are love and affection. *Where the treasure is, there* are our hope and trust; our joys and delights will be *there*, and so will our thoughts. The *heart* is due to God, and so that he may have it, our *treasure* must be stored up with him. Our *treasure* is our gifts, prayers, and fasts and their rewards; if we have done these only to gain human applause, we have *laid up this treasure on earth*. Now it is foolish to do this, for *the praise of men* (Jn 12:43) that we covet so much is liable to corruption: a little foolishness, like a dead fly, will spoil it all (Ecc 10:1). Slander is one of the *thieves that break through and steal* it away. Hypocritical services store up nothing in heaven (Isa 58:3). However, if we have prayed, fasted, and given to the needy in truth and integrity, looking to God, we have stored up that treasure *in heaven*; *a book of remembrance is written in heaven* (Mal 3:16). Hypocrites are *written in the earth* (Jer 17:13), but God's faithful ones have their names *written in heaven* (Lk 10:2). His *well done* (25:21) will stand forever, and if we have stored up our *treasure* with him, our *hearts* will also be with him, and where can they be in a better place?

2. We must beware of hypocrisy and worldly-mindedness in choosing the *end we look at*. Our concern in this respect is represented by two kinds of eyes that people have, *a single* (good) *eye* and an *evil* (bad) *eye* (vv. 22–23).

2.1. *The eye* is the heart, according to some. If the heart *be single, free* and *bountiful* (Pr 22:9), if the heart is generously disposed to goodness and kindness, it will guide the person to Christian action; the whole way of life *will be full of light*, of good works, which are our *light shining before men* (5:16). If, however, *the heart be evil* (bad), greedy, harsh, and envious, griping and grudging, *the body will be full of darkness*; the whole way of life will be like that of the pagans, unchristian. *If the light that is in us be darkness*, if there is not even any good nature in a person, not even a kind disposition, *how great is the* corruption in that person, how great the *darkness* in which they sit (Lk 12:33; 2Co 9:7)!

2.2. *The eye* is the understanding, according to others, the practical judgment, the conscience, which is to the other faculties of the soul *as the eye* is to the *body*, to guide and direct their movements. Now, *if this eye be single*, if it makes true, right, and sound judgments, it will rightly guide the emotions and actions, which will all be *full of the light* of grace and encouragement. If, however, *this be evil* and corrupt, the heart and life must be *full of darkness*, and the whole way of life will be corrupt. An error in practical judgment proves fatal; it is what calls *evil good and good evil* (Isa 5:20).

2.3. *The eye* may refer to our aims and intentions; by *the eye* we set our goal in front of us. In everything we do in our religious faith, there is something that we have in our *eye*. If we aim purely and only at the glory of God, seeking his honor and favor and directing everything completely to him, then *the eye is single. The whole body will be full of light*; all its actions will be regular and gracious, pleasing to God and encouraging to ourselves. If, however, *this eye be evil*, if, instead of aiming only at the glory of God and our acceptance with him, we look aside at human applause and, claiming to honor God, contrive to honor ourselves, seeking our own things under a cover of *seeking the things of Christ*, this spoils everything. To be right in our goals is the most important aspect of religious faith. The hypocrite is like the boatman who looks one way but rows another; true Christians are like travelers who keep their destination in sight. The hypocrite soars up like the hawk, with his eye on the prey below; true Christians soar up like the lark, higher and higher, forgetting the things of life below.

3. We must beware of hypocrisy and worldly-mindedness in choosing the master we serve: *No man can serve two masters* (v. 24). Serving *two masters* is contrary to *the single eye*, for *the eye* will look to the master's hand (Ps 123:1–2). Our Lord Jesus exposes here the deception that people put on their own souls when they think that they can divide their allegiance between God and the world, having both *treasure on earth* and *treasure in heaven*, pleasing God and pleasing people too. Here is:

3.1. A general maxim set down; *No man can serve two masters*, much less two gods, for at one time or another, their commands will come into conflict or contradict each other. As long as *two masters* go together, a servant may follow them both, but when they part, you will see which he belongs to. This truth is clear enough in ordinary cases.

3.2. Its application to the task in hand: *Ye cannot serve God and Mammon. Mammon* is a Syriac word meaning "gain," so that whatever in this world is, or is counted by us to be, *gain* (Php 3:7) is *mammon*. Whatever in the world is *the lust of the flesh, the lust of the eye, and the pride of life* (1Jn 2:16) is *mammon*. Self, the unity in which the world centers—the worldly, secular self—is the *mammon* that cannot be served together with *God*. Christ does not say that we "must not" or "should not," but that we *cannot serve God and Mammon*; we *cannot* love both (1Jn 2:15; Jas 4:4), hold to both, or observe, obey, attend, trust, and depend on both, for each is in conflict with the other. Let us therefore not *halt between God and Baal*, but *choose ye this day whom ye will serve* (Jos 24:15; 1Ki 18:21), and remain faithful to your choice.

Verses 25–34

There is scarcely any one sin against which our Lord Jesus more fully and fervently warns his disciples than the sin of worry, having disturbing, distracting, and distrustful cares about the things of this life. Here is:

1. The prohibition set down. It is the advice and command of the Lord Jesus that we *take no thought* (do not worry) about the things of this world: *I say unto you.* He says it as our Lawgiver and the Sovereign of our hearts; he says it as our Comforter and the Helper of our joy. What is it that he says? *Take no thought,* "Be not concerned." It is the repeated command of the Lord Jesus to his disciples that they should not divide their minds and tear them to pieces with cares about the world. There is *a thought* concerning the things of this life that is not only lawful but is our duty, but the *thought* forbidden is here:

1.1. A disturbing, tormenting *thought,* which disturbs our joy in God, breaks our sleep, and hinders our enjoyment of ourselves, our friends, and what God has given us.

1.2. A distrustful, unbelieving *thought.* God has promised to provide all things that are necessary for life as well as godliness for those who are his, all things necessary for *the life that now is* (1Ti 4:8): food, shelter, and clothing, not the fine things we want, but the things we need. He never said, "They will be feasted," but, "*Verily, they shall be fed* (Ps 37:3)." An excessive worry about the future and

a fear of lacking those supplies spring from a disbelief of these promises and of the wisdom and goodness of divine Providence. As regards the future, we must *cast our care upon God* (1Pe 5:7) and *take no thought,* because worry looks like distrust of God, whereas he knows how to give what we want when we do not know how to obtain it. Let our souls rest in him! This gracious, carefree state is the same as that sleep that God gives to his beloved (Ps 127:2). *Take no thought for your life.* Life is our greatest concern in this world: *All that a man has will he give for his life* (Job 2:4). But do not worry about it. Submit to God to *lengthen* or *shorten* it as he pleases: *my times are in thy hand* (Ps 31:15), and so they are in good hands. Submit to God to make our lives bitter or sweet as he pleases. We must not worry about the necessary supports of this life, *food* and *raiment;* God has promised these. Do not say, *What shall we eat?* Though many good people have the prospect of little, there are few who do not have enough in the end. *Take no thought for the morrow,* for the future. Do not worry about the future. As we must not *boast of tomorrow* (Pr 27:1), so we must not be anxious about tomorrow.

2. The reasons and arguments to support this prohibition. To show how much the heart of Christ is set on it and what *pleasure he takes* in those who *hope in his mercy* (Ps 147:11), the command is backed up with very powerful arguments. To free us from anxious thoughts and to drive them out, Christ suggests to us encouraging thoughts here, so that we may be filled with them. It will be worthwhile to argue our hearts out of their worrying cares; our cares may be weakened by right reason. But it is only by an active faith that they can be overcome.

2.1. *Is not the life more than meat, and the body than raiment?* (v. 25). Yes, no doubt it is; the thing speaks for itself. Our life is a greater blessing than our livelihood. Food and clothing are given for life, and the end is more noble and excellent than the means. The most delicate food and finest clothes are from the earth, but life comes from the *breath of God* (Ge 2:7). This is an encouragement to us to trust God for food and clothes and so free ourselves from all worry about them. God has given us life, and he has given us the body; what can he not do for us, having done that? What *will* he not do for us? If we take care of our souls and eternity, which are more than the body and its life, we may leave it to God to provide for us food and clothing, which are less. The One who guards us against the evils we are exposed to will supply us with the *good things* we need (Ps 103:5).

2.2. *Behold the fowls of the air* and *consider the lilies of the field.* Here is an argument taken from God's ordinary providence toward the lower creatures. Fallen humanity has come to a sad state of affairs if they must learn from the *fowls of the air* what they have to *teach him* (Job 12:7–8)!

2.2.1. Look at the birds and learn to trust God *for food* (v. 26).

2.2.1.1. Notice the providence of God for them. There are various breeds of bird; they are numerous, some of them voracious, but they are all fed with the food they need. Just as the birds are least useful to human beings, so they are least within their care; people often feed on them, but they rarely feed them. They are, however, fed; it is *your heavenly Father that feeds them;* he *knows all the wild fowls of the mountains* better than you know the tame ones at your own barn door (Ps 50:11). However, what is noted especially here is that they are fed without any care or plan of their own: *they sow not, neither do they reap, nor gather into barns.* Every day, however, as regularly as the day comes, provision is made for them, and their *eyes wait on God* (Ps 145:15), that great and good House-keeper who *provides food for all flesh* (Ps 136:25).

2.2.1.2. Use this to encourage yourself to trust in God: *Are ye not much better than they?* Yes, certainly you are. The heirs of heaven are much better than the fowls of heaven; we are nobler and more excellent beings, and, by faith, we soar higher. God is their Maker and Lord, their Owner and Master, but to you, besides all this, he is a Father. You are his children, his firstborn; the One who feeds his birds will surely not starve his dear children. They trust in your Father's providence, and will you not trust in it? In dependence on that, they are not anxious about tomorrow, and because they are like that, they live the happiest lives of all creatures; they *sing among the branches*. If we were, by faith, as unconcerned about tomorrow as they are, we would sing as cheerfully as they do.

2.2.2. Look at the *lilies*, and learn to trust God for clothes. That is another part of our care, *what we shall put on*. This anxiety is as prevalent as that for our daily bread. *Consider the lilies of the field*; not only *look upon* them—every eye does that with pleasure—but *consider* them. There is a great deal of good to be learned from what we see every day, if only we would consider it (Pr 6:6; 24:32).

2.2.2.1. Consider how *frail* the lilies are; they are the *grass of the field*. *All flesh is grass* (Isa 40:6): although some endowments of body and mind are like lilies and much admired, they remain grass. This grass *today is*, and *tomorrow is cast into the oven* (thrown into the fire); soon the place that *knows us will know us no more* (Ps 103:16). We should not be anxious about what we will wear tomorrow, because perhaps by tomorrow we will need our graveclothes.

2.2.2.2. Consider how *free from care* the lilies are: they *toil not* as people do to earn money to buy clothing; *neither do they spin*, as women do, to make clothing. It does not follow that we must therefore neglect or do carelessly the proper business of this life. Idleness *tempts* God instead of *trusting* him.

2.2.2.3. Consider how *fair*, how *fine*, the lilies are, *how they grow*, what they grow from. The root of the lily is lost and buried underground in winter, but when spring returns, it appears and soon starts to grow. It is therefore promised to God's Israel that they will grow *as the lily* (Hos 14:5). Consider what they grow to. Out of that obscurity, in a few weeks they come to be very bright, so that even *Solomon, in all his glory, was not arrayed like one of these*. However finely Solomon dressed himself, he came far short of the beauty of the lilies, and a flowerbed of tulips far surpasses him. Let us, therefore, be ambitious to have the *wisdom* of Solomon rather than the glory of Solomon, in which he was surpassed by the lilies. Knowledge and grace are the perfections for which human beings were intended, not beauty, and much less fine clothes. God is said here to *clothe the grass of the field* in this way. All the excellences of the creation flow from God. It was he who gave the horse its strength (Ps 33:17) and the lily its beauty.

2.2.2.4. Consider how instructive all this is to us (v. 30).

2.2.2.4.1. As to *fine* clothing. This teaches us not to worry about it at all, neither to seek it nor to be proud of it, because after all our worry about this, the lilies will far surpass us. We cannot dress as finely as they do, so why should we try to compete with them? Their beauty will soon perish, as will ours.

2.2.2.4.2. As to necessary clothing. This teaches us to cast all our anxiety about it to God (1Pe 5:7). If he gives such fine clothes to the grass, then much more will he give fitting clothes to his own children. Notice the title Christ gives to his disciples: *O ye of little faith* (v. 30). This may be taken as:

2.2.2.4.2.1. An encouragement to true faith, even though it is weak. Great faith will be commended and will obtain great things, yet little faith will not be rejected. Sound believers will be provided for, even if they are not strong believers. The babies in the family are fed and clothed as well as the adults, and the babies are shown special care and tenderness. Or it is rather:

2.2.2.4.2.2. A rebuke to weak faith, even though that faith is true (14:31). If only we had more faith, we would worry less.

2.3. *Which of you*, the wisest, the strongest of you, *by taking thought, can add one cubit to his stature?* (v. 27).

2.3.1. We did not reach the height we are by our own worry or thought, but by the providence of God. An infant who is very short has grown up to be a man of six feet; he does not know how he grew, except that it is by the power and goodness of God. The One who made our bodies and made them of such a size will surely take care to provide for them. The time of growing is the thoughtless, careless age, but we still grow. Will not the One who brought us up to this point provide for us now that we are adults?

2.3.2. We could not alter the height that we are even if we wanted to. We are not all the same size, but the difference in height between one person and another is not significant or of any great account. Now we should regard our worldly possessions just as we do our physical stature. We should not seek an abundance of the wealth of this world, any more than we would seek to grow a cubit taller in stature. It is enough to grow by inches; great wealth acquired all at once would simply be unwieldy to us, making it awkward to move about and making us a burden to ourselves. We must come to terms with our state, as we do with our height; we must set the conveniences over against the inconveniences (Ecc 7:14) and so make a virtue out of necessity. We cannot change the ways Providence acts toward us.

2.4. *After all these things do the Gentiles seek* (v. 32). The pagans seek *these things* because they do not know *better things*. They are eager for the things of this world because they are strangers to a better one. They seek these things with anxiety because they are *without God in the world* (Eph 2:12) and do not understand his providence. They fear and worship their idols but cannot trust them to supply their needs. It is a shame for Christians, however, who build their lives on nobler principles, to walk as the pagans do, filling their minds and hearts with these things.

2.5. *Your heavenly Father knows ye have need of all these things*, these necessary things, food and clothes; he knows our needs better than we do ourselves. "You think that if such and such a good friend only knew your needs and difficulties, you would soon receive help; but your God knows them, and he is your Father, who loves you and pities you and is ready to help you." Although he already knows our needs, he wants to know them from us. We should relieve ourselves of the burden of anxiety by giving it to God, because it is he *that careth for us* (1Pe 5:7). If he cares, why should we be anxious?

2.6. *Seek first the kingdom of God, and his righteousness, and all these things shall be added unto you* (v. 33). Here is a double argument against the sin of anxiety; *take no thought* for your life, the life of the body, because:

2.6.1. You have greater and better things to be concerned about, the life of your soul, your eternal happiness; that is the *one thing needful* (Lk 10:42), about which you should occupy your thoughts.

2.6.2. You have a surer and easier, a safer and a briefer, way to obtain what you need in this life, and that better way is by *seeking first the kingdom of God*. Notice here:

2.6.2.1. The great duty required. It is the sum and substance of our whole duty: *"Seek first the kingdom of God."* Our duty is to seek; though we have not attained, but in many things fail and come short, sincere seeking is accepted. We must make heaven our goal, and holiness our way. We make nothing of our religious faith if we do not make heaven of it. Along with the happiness of this kingdom, seek its *righteousness, God's righteousness. Seek first the kingdom of God.* We must seek the things of Christ more than our own things. "Seek these things first. Seek them first in your days: let the morning of youth be dedicated to God. Seek them first every day: let your waking thoughts be of God." Let the One who is the First (Rev 1:11) have the first.

2.6.2.2. The gracious promise attached: *all these things*, the necessary supports of life, *shall be added unto you*; they will be given to you as well, just as the person who buys goods gets the package for free. *Godliness has the promise of the life that now is* (1Ti 4:8). When we begin with God, we are beginning at the right end of our work. As to all the things of this life, *Jehovah jireh*—the Lord will provide (Ge 22:14)—as much of them as he sees good to give us, and we would not wish for more. God's Israel were not only brought to Canaan eventually; they also had their expenses paid through the desert.

2.7. *The morrow shall take thought for the things of itself. Sufficient unto the day is the evil thereof* (v. 34). Every day brings with it its own burden of cares and grievances. It brings with it its own strength and supply. Let the morrow take thought for the things of itself. If needs and troubles are renewed by the day, helps and provisions are also renewed: compassions, which are new every morning (La 3:22–23). Therefore, let us look to tomorrow's strength to do tomorrow's work and bear tomorrow's burden. This does not forbid wise foresight and preparation, but it should put an end to a bewildering worry and a preoccupation with difficulties and adversities that may never come. The meaning is this: let us be concerned with our present duty, and then leave future events to God; do the work of the day in its day, and then let tomorrow bring its work along with it. *Sufficient unto the day is the evil thereof.* This present day has enough trouble attending it; we need not accumulate burdens by anticipating our trouble, nor borrow suffering from tomorrow's difficulties to add to those of today. Let us not take on ourselves all at once what Providence has wisely ordered to be borne one part at a time. We may use our daily prayers to obtain strength to help us endure our daily troubles and to arm us against the temptations that accompany them, and then let none of these things move us (Ac 20:24).

CHAPTER 7

This chapter continues and concludes Christ's Sermon on the Mount. Here are: 1. Some rules concerning criticism and rebuke (vv. 1–6). 2. Encouragements to pray to God for what we need (vv. 7–11). 3. The necessity of strictness in conduct (vv. 12–14). 4. A warning to watch out for false prophets (vv. 15–20). 5. The conclusion of the whole sermon (vv. 21–27). 6. The impression that Christ's message made on his hearers (vv. 28–29).

Verses 1–6

Our Savior here tells us how to behave with reference to the faults of others. We have here:

1. A warning *against judging* (vv. 1–2). The prohibition: *Judge not.* We must judge ourselves and judge our own acts, but we must not judge our brother. We must not sit in the judgment seat to make our word a law to everyone. We must not *despise him* or *set him at nought* (Ro 14:10). We must not judge rashly. We must not judge uncharitably, unmercifully, or with a spirit of revenge and a desire to cause trouble. We must not judge the hearts of others, or their intentions, for it is God's prerogative to try the heart (Ps 7:9; Pr 17:3; 1Th 2:4). Nor must we judge their eternal state, nor call them *hypocrites, reprobates*, and *castaways*; that is going beyond the limit; what right do we have to judge another person's servant in this way? Advise them, help them, but do not judge them. The reason to back up this prohibition: *That ye be not judged.* This suggests:

1.1. That if we presume to judge others, we may expect to be judged ourselves. Commonly, none are more criticized than those who themselves are most critical. No mercy will be shown to the reputation of those who show no mercy to the reputation of others (Jas 2:13). However, that is not the worst of it; they will also be judged by God: from him they will receive the *greater condemnation* (Jas 3:1). Both parties must appear before him (Ro 14:10), who will both relieve the humble sufferer and oppose the haughty scorner (Pr 21:24), and he will judge them well.

1.2. That if we are modest and charitable in our criticism of others, declining to judge them, judging ourselves instead, *we shall not be judged of the Lord.* Just as God will forgive those who forgive their brothers and sisters, so he will not judge those who refuse to judge their brothers and sisters; the *merciful shall find mercy* (5:7). The judging of those who judge others is based on the law of retaliation: *With what judgment ye judge, ye shall be judged* (v. 2). The righteous God, in his judgments, often observes the rule of proportion. *With what measure ye mete, it shall be measured to you again*, perhaps in this world, so that people may read their sin in their punishment. What would become of us if God were as exact and severe in judging us as we are in judging our brother or sister, if he weighed us in the same balances? This is what we may justly expect if we keep a record of what our brothers or sisters do wrong. In this, as in other matters, the violent acts of people return on their own heads.

2. Some warnings *about rebuking.* From the prohibition against judging others, which is a great sin, it does not follow that we must not rebuke others, which is a great duty and may be a means of *saving a soul from death* (Jas 5:20).

2.1. Not everyone is fit to rebuke. Those who are themselves guilty of the same faults of which they accuse others, or of worse faults, bring shame on themselves and are unlikely to do good to those they rebuke (vv. 3–5). Here is:

2.1.1. A just rebuke of the censorious person, who quarrels with his brother or sister for small faults while allowing himself great ones, who is quick to *spy a mote* (see the speck of sawdust) in his brother or sister's eye but is unaware of *a beam* (plank) *in his own.*

2.1.1.1. There are degrees of sin: some sins are comparatively small, like specks of sawdust; others are like planks. Some as small as *a gnat*, others as large as a *camel*. Not that there is really any sin that is little, for there is no little God to sin against.

2.1.1.2. Our own sins should appear greater to us than the same sins in others, for the sins of others must be lessened, but our own emphasized.

2.1.1.3. There are many people who have *beams in their own eyes* but do not consider it. They are under the guilt and power of very great sins but are not aware of it. Instead, they justify themselves, as if they did not need to repent or reform their ways. With great assurance, they say, *We see.*

2.1.1.4. It is common for those who are most sinful themselves and least aware of it to be most eager and free in judging and censuring others. Pride and lack of love are often *beams* in the eyes of those who pretend to be refined in censuring others. In fact, many people are guilty in secret of what they have the audacity to punish in others when it is revealed.

2.1.1.5. People's being so harsh toward the faults of others while they indulge their own is a mark of hypocrisy. *Thou hypocrite* (v. 5). Whatever such a person may claim, it is certain that they are no enemy to sin—if they were, they would be an enemy of their own sin—and so they are not worthy of commendation. This spiritual charity must begin at home: *"For how canst thou say*, how can you shamefully say to your brother or sister, *Let me help to reform thee*, when you take no care to reform yourself?"

2.1.1.6. The consideration of what is wrong in ourselves, though it should not keep us from administering friendly rebuke, should keep us from dictatorial censuring.

2.1.2. A good rule for rebukers (v. 5). Follow the right method: *first cast the beam out of thine own eye*. Our own badness, far from excusing us from rebuking, actually makes itself worse by making us unfit to rebuke. A person's offense will never become their defense; rather, I must first reform myself, so that I may help reform my brother or sister, having qualified myself to rebuke them. Those who blame others should be blameless and harmless themselves. The wick trimmers of the sanctuary were to be of pure gold (Ex 37:23).

2.2. Not everyone is fit to be rebuked: *Give not that which is holy unto the dogs* (v. 6). Our zeal against sin must be guided by discretion, and we must not go about giving instructions, advice, and rebukes, and much less encouragement, to hardened scoffers. If you throw a pearl to a pig, it will resent it, as if you were throwing a stone at it; so do not give holy things to dogs and pigs (unclean creatures). Good advice and rebukes are holy things, pearls: they are precious ordinances of God. Among the generation of evildoers, there are some who have *walked in the way of sinners* so long that they have sat down *in the seat of the scornful* (Ps 1:1); they professedly hate and despise instruction and defy it. Rebukes of instruction are badly given to such people, and they expose the rebuker to all the contempt and trouble that may be expected from dogs and pigs. People are to be reckoned as such when they *hate reproofs* and reprovers and defy those who, out of kindness to their souls, show them their sin and danger. Such people are sinning against the remedy; who will heal and help those who refuse to be healed and helped? It is *not meet to take the children's bread, and cast it to the dogs* (15:26). Yet we must be very careful about whom we condemn as dogs and pigs. Many a patient has been lost by being thought to be so when they could have been saved if proper means had been used. Our Lord Jesus is very sensitive toward the security of his people, and he

does not want them needlessly exposed to the fury of those who will *turn again and rend* them.

Verses 7–11

In the previous chapter, our Savior had spoken of prayer as a commanded duty, by which God is honored. Here he spoke about it as the appointed means of obtaining what we need. Here is:

1. A command given in three words to the same effect: *Ask, seek, knock* (v. 7); that is, in one word, "Pray, pray, and then pray again. *Ask*, as a beggar asks for gifts." Those who want to be rich in grace must go into the poor business of begging, and they will find that a thriving trade. "*Ask*; bring your needs and burdens to God. *Ask* as a traveler asks the way; to pray is to *inquire of God* (Eze 36:37). *Seek*, as when we look for something valuable that we have lost. *Seek by prayer* (Da 9:3). *Knock*, as a person knocks on a door when they want to enter a house." Sin has shut and barred the door against us. We knock on that door through prayer: *Lord, Lord, open to us* (25:11). Christ knocks at our door (Rev 3:20; SS 5:2), and he allows us to knock on his door, which is a favor we do not allow ordinary beggars. Seeking and knocking imply something more than asking and praying. We must not only *ask* but also *seek*; we must back up our prayers with effort; we must use the appointed means and *seek* what we *ask* for, for otherwise we are tempting God. We must not only *ask* but also *knock*. We must come to God's door and must *ask* boldly; we must not only pray but also plead and wrestle with God.

2. A promise attached: *our labour* in prayer, if we truly labor in it, *shall not be in vain* (1Co 15:58): where God finds a prayerful heart, he will be found to be a God who hears prayer; he will give you a favorable answer.

2.1. The promise is made, and it is made so that it exactly corresponds to the command (v. 7). God will meet those who listen to him; *Ask, and it shall be given you*: not lent to you, not sold to you, but *given you*; and what is more free than a gift? It is simply *ask* and have; *ye have not, because ye ask not*, or *ask not aright* (Jas 4:3): what is not worth asking for is not worth having, and then it is worth nothing. *Seek, and ye shall find*, and then you do not waste your effort. God himself is *found of those that seek* him (1Ch 28:9; Jer 29:13–14), and if we find him, we have enough. "*Knock, and it shall be opened*; the door of mercy and grace will no longer be closed against you as enemies and intruders, but opened up to you as friends and children. If the door is not *opened* at the first *knock*, continue to be faithful in prayer; it is an insult to a friend to *knock* at their door and then go away; although they may delay, continue to wait."

2.2. It is repeated (v. 8). It is to the same effect, but with some additions. It is extended to all who pray in the right way. *Everyone that asketh* receives, whether Jew or Gentile, high or low; they are all alike welcome to *the throne of grace* (Heb 4:16) if they come in faith: for God does not show partiality (Ac 10:34). It is made using words in the present tense and is therefore more than a promise for the future. *Everyone that asketh* not only *shall* receive but *receiveth*. The promises of God are so sure and inviolable that, in effect, they give present possession. What we have in hope, according to the promise, is as sure, and should be as sweet, as what we have in our hands. Conditional grants become absolute when the condition is fulfilled; similarly here, *he that asketh receiveth*.

2.3. It is illustrated by a comparison between earthly parents, with their innate readiness to give their children what they ask for, and our heavenly Father. Christ appeals to his hearers: *What man is there of you*, even if very morose and bad tempered, *whom if his son ask bread, will he give him a stone?* (vv. 9–10). He concludes from this (v. 11), *If ye then, being evil*, grant your children's requests, *much more will your heavenly Father give you the good things you ask*. Now this is useful:

2.3.1. To guide our prayers and expectations. We must come to God as children come to *a Father in heaven*. How naturally a child in need or distress runs to their father with their complaints! We must come to him for *good things*, for those he *gives to them that ask him*. He knows what is good for us; we must therefore leave that with him: *Father, thy will be done* (26:42). We often ask God for what would do us harm if we had it; he knows this, and so he does not give it to us. Denials in love are better than grants in anger; we would have been ruined before this if we had had everything we wanted.

2.3.2. To encourage our prayers and expectations. We have grounds for hoping that we will not be denied and disappointed: we will not be given *a stone* for *bread*, to break our teeth—even if we have a hard crust to employ our teeth—nor *a serpent* for *a fish*, to sting us. God has put into the hearts of parents a compassionate inclination to help and supply their children, according to their needs. No law was ever thought necessary to oblige parents to maintain their legitimate children. God has assumed the relationship of a Father to us, and he acknowledges us as his children. He compares his concern for his people to that of a father for his children (Ps 103:13)—in fact, to that of a mother, which is usually more tender (Isa 49:14–15; 66:13). However, it is imagined here that his love, tenderness, and goodness far surpass that of any earthly parent, and so it is argued with a *much more*. Our worldly fathers have taken care of us, and we have taken care of our children, but God will take care of his own children much more. Moreover:

2.3.2.1. God is more knowledgeable; parents are often foolishly fond, but God is infinitely wise.

2.3.2.2. God is kinder. If all the compassion of all the kind fathers in the world were compared *with the tender mercies of our God*, they would only be like a candle to the sun or a mere drop in the ocean. God is richer and more ready to give to his children than our human fathers can be.

Verses 12–14

Our Lord Jesus here urges on us the righteousness toward people that is an essential branch of true religious faith, and he urges on us the religious faith toward God that is an essential branch of universal righteousness.

1. We must make righteousness our rule and be ruled by it (v. 12). Set this down as your principle, to do as you would be done by so that you may benefit from the foregoing promises. It is right that the law of justice follows the law of prayer, for unless we are upright in our conduct, God will not hear our prayers (Isa 1:15–17; 58:6, 9; Zec 7:9, 13). We cannot expect to receive *good things from God* if we do not do *fair things*, what is *honest* and *lovely and of good report* (Php 4:8), among people. We have here:

1.1. The rule of justice set down: *Whatsoever ye would that men should do to you, do you even so to them*. Christ came to teach us not only what we are to know and believe but also what we are to do, and what we are to do not only toward God but also toward people. The golden rule of justice is to do to others as we want them to do to us. We must not do to others the evil they have done to us, nor the evil that they would do to us if it were in their

power, but what we want to be done to us. This is based on that great commandment, *Thou shalt love thy neighbour as thyself* (19:19). Just as we must show the same affection for our neighbor that we would like to have shown to us, so we must do the same good works. We must do to our neighbor what we ourselves acknowledge to be right and reasonable. We must put ourselves in their situation and imagine how we would want and expect to be treated—remembering that their situation may indeed become ours. Or at least, if the thought of this eventuality does not motivate us, we may fear that God by his judgments would do to us as we have done to others if we have not done as we would be done by.

1.2. A reason given to back up this rule: *This is the law and the prophets*. It is the summary of that second great commandment, which is one of the two *on which hang all the law and the prophets* (22:40). We have not read this in so many words either in *the law* or in *the prophets*, but it is the dominant language of the whole. Christ has taken it into this law here so that the Old Testament and the New Testament agree in prescribing that we do as we would be done by.

2. We must make religious faith our business and be intent on doing it. Notice:

2.1. The account that is given of the bad way of sin and the good way of holiness. There are only two ways, right and wrong, good and evil, the way to heaven and the way to hell. Each one of us is walking along one of these: there is no middle way in the future, no middle of the road now. Here is:

2.1.1. An account given us of the way of sin and sinners in both its best and its worst aspects.

2.1.1.1. What attracts many people into it and keeps them in it is that *the gate is wide, and the way broad*, and there are many travelers on that way.

2.1.1.1.1. "*You will* have much liberty in that way. You may take all your sinful desires with you when you enter at this gate; it does not restrain your appetites or your passions: you may *walk in the way of your heart* (Jer 3:17) *and in the sight of your eyes* (Ecc 6:9)." There is a choice of sinful ways, some being contrary to others, but all are paths on this *broad way*.

2.1.1.1.2. "You will have many people with you on that way: *many there be that go in* at this gate and walk on this way." If we *follow the multitude*, it will be *to do evil* (Ex 23:2): if we go with the crowd, it will be the wrong way. It is natural for us to incline to "go with the flow," to do as most other people do. If many perish, we should be all the more cautious.

2.1.1.2. What should frighten us all away from this path is that it *leads to destruction*. Whether it is the highway of open ungodliness or the back road of secret hypocrisy, if it is the way of sin, it will destroy us unless we repent.

2.1.2. An account given of the way of holiness. Let us see:

2.1.2.1. What it contains that frightens many people from it. Christ deals faithfully with us, and he tells us:

2.1.2.1.1. That *the gate is strait* (narrow). Conversion and regeneration are *the gate* by which we enter this way. We must pass out of a state of sin into a state of grace by the new birth (Jn 3:3, 5). This is a narrow gate, one that is hard to find and hard to pass through, like a passage between two rocks (1Sa 14:4). There must be *a new heart, and a new spirit* (Eze 36:26), and *old things must pass away* (2Co 5:17). The direction of the soul must be changed. We must swim against the stream; we must struggle with much opposition—from outside and from within—and break through it. It is easier to set a person against the whole world than against themselves, but this must happen in conversion. It is *a strait gate*, for we must stoop, or we cannot enter in by it; we must become as little children (18:3). We must deny ourselves, put off the world, *put off the old man* (Eph 4:22). We must be willing to abandon everything to follow Christ (19:27). *The gate is strait* to everyone, but it is *straiter* to some than others; for example, to the rich. *The gate is strait*; we bless God that it is not shut up or locked against us, or kept with a flaming sword (Ge 3:24), as it will be soon (25:10).

2.1.2.1.2. That *the way is narrow*. We do not arrive in heaven as soon as we have entered through *the strait gate*. No, we must go through a desert, must travel a *narrow way*, hedged in by God's law (Ps 89:39–40), which *is exceedingly broad* (Ps 119:96), and that makes *the way narrow*; self must be denied. Daily temptations must be resisted, and duties must be done that go against our inclination. We must endure hardship (2Ti 2:3), must wrestle and be in anguish; we must keep watch in all things (2Ti 4:5) and walk with care and circumspection. We must go *through much tribulation*. It is a way hedged about with thorns; we bless God that it is not hedged up; rather, as the understanding grows more and more sound, this way will open and enlarge and become more and more pleasant.

2.1.2.1.3. Because *the gate* is so *strait and the way so narrow*, it is not strange that there are only *a few that find it* and choose it. Many pass by and neglect it; they will not take the effort to find it. They think they are secure where they are and see no need to change their way. Others look at it but avoid it; it looks too restrictive and restrained for them. Those who are going to heaven are only few. This discourages many people: they are reluctant to be singled out and go it alone. But instead of stumbling at this, they should rather say, "If so few are going to heaven, there will be more room for me."

2.1.2.2. What there is in this way that, despite this, should encourage us all to it, namely, that it *leads to life*: to a present assurance of the favor of God, which is the life of the soul, and to eternal happiness at the end of our way, the hope of which should reconcile us to all the difficulties and inconveniences of the road. *The gate is strait and the way narrow* and uphill, but one hour in heaven will make up for it all.

2.2. The great concern and duty of each one of us, in consideration of all this: *Enter ye in at the strait gate.* The matter is stated fairly; life and death, good and evil, are set before us (Dt 30:15, 19), both the ways and both the ends. Choose this day which way you will follow (Jos 24:15). In fact, the matter determines itself and will not allow any debate. Do not delay, therefore; do not hold back any longer, but *enter ye in at the strait gate. Knock* on it by sincere and constant prayers and endeavors, *and it shall be opened.* It is true, *we* can neither go in nor go on without the help of divine grace, but it is equally true that grace is freely offered and will not be lacking to those who seek it and submit to it.

Verses 15–20

We have here a warning against *false prophets*, to make sure that we are not deceived by them. *Prophets* are properly those who foretell things to come; some of those mentioned in the Old Testament claimed to do that without authority, and the event disproved their claims. However, *prophets* also taught the people their duty, so that *false prophets* here are false teachers.

1. False teachers and *false prophets* are those:

1.1. Who produce false commissions, who claim that they have received direct authority and guidance from God to set themselves up as *prophets* and that they are divinely inspired, but are not.

1.2. Who preach false doctrine in those things that are essential to religious faith, who teach what is contrary to *the truth as it is in Jesus* (Eph 4:21). Watch out for them, suspect them, test them, and, when you have revealed their falsehood, avoid them, have nothing to do with them. Here is:

2. A good reason for this caution: *Beware of* them, for they are *wolves in sheep's clothing* (v. 15). We need to be very cautious:

2.1. Because their claims are very fair and plausible, and such as will deceive us if we are not on our guard. They *come in sheep's clothing,* wearing the clothes of *prophets.* We must watch out for being deceived by what people are wearing. Or it may be taken figuratively; they pretend to be sheep, and outwardly appear so innocent, harmless, humble, useful, and good that none could excel them. They and their errors are gilded with a veneer of sanctity and devotion. Satan himself turns *into an angel of light* (2Co 11:13–14).

2.2. Because under these claims their intentions are malicious and troublesome; *inwardly they are ravening* (ferocious) *wolves.* Every *hypocrite* is *a goat* in sheep's clothing, but *a false prophet* is *a wolf* in sheep's clothing. Those who want to deceive us away from any truth and make us take in an error intend trouble for our souls, whatever they claim. Paul calls them *grievous wolves* (Ac 20:29). Now since it is so easy, and also so dangerous, to be cheated, *Beware of false prophets.*

3. A good rule to follow in heeding this warning: we must *prove all things* (1Th 5:21): *ye shall know them by their fruits* (vv. 16–20). Notice:

3.1. The illustrating of this comparison between prophets and trees, according to which the fruit shows the nature of the tree. You cannot always distinguish trees by their bark and their leaves or by the spreading of their boughs, but *by their fruits ye shall know them.* The tree produces fruit according to its kind. Christ insists on this correspondence between the fruit and the tree. If you know what kind of tree it is, you may know what kind of fruit to expect. Never expect to gather *grapes from thorns, nor figs from thistles*; it is not in their nature to produce such fruits.

3.1.1. Corrupt, vicious, unsanctified hearts are like thorns and thistles, which came in with sin and are worthless, troublesome, and destined for the fire eventually.

3.1.2. Good works are *good fruit*, like grapes and figs, pleasing to God and useful to people.

3.1.3. This *good fruit* is never to be expected from bad people, any more than a *clean thing out of an unclean* (Job 14:4). On the other hand, if you know what the fruit is, you may recognize what the tree is by that. *A good tree cannot bring forth evil fruit*, and a *corrupt tree cannot bring forth good fruit.* Therefore, what the tree produces naturally must be reckoned as the fruit of the tree: what is plentifully, constantly, and usually produced. People are known not by individual acts, but by the general course and tendency of their lives, and by the more frequent acts.

3.2. The application of this to the false prophets.

3.2.1. By way of terror and threatening: *Every tree that brings not forth good fruit is hewn down* (v. 19). John the Baptist had used this very saying (3:10). Christ could have said the same thing in other words, but he did not think it beneath him to say the same thing John had said before him. To write and speak the same things must not be thought irksome, for it is a safeguard to those who hear (Php 3:1). Note the description of barren trees; they are trees that do *not bring forth good fruit*. Even if there is fruit, if it is not *good fruit* the tree is considered barren. Note also the fate of barren trees. *They are*, that is, certainly they will be, *hewn down, and cast into the fire*. God will deal with them as people deal with dry trees that take up land (Lk 13:7).

3.2.2. By way of testing: *By their fruits ye shall know them*.

3.2.2.1. *By the fruits* of their persons, their words and actions and the course of their conduct. If you want to know whether they are right or not, look at how they live; their works will testify for or against them. People have not been taught or sent by the holy God if their lives show that they are led by an evil spirit. God puts his treasure into jars of clay (2Co 4:7), but not into such corrupt jars.

3.2.2.2. *By the fruits* of their teaching, their fruits as prophets. What direction does their teaching lead? Into what affections and practices will it lead people who embrace it? If *the doctrine be of God* (Jn 7:17), it will tend to promote serious godliness, humility, holiness, and love, along with other Christian graces, but if, on the contrary, the doctrines these prophets preach have a clear tendency to make people proud, worldly, and contentious, unjust or unloving, and to take people away from governing themselves and their families by the strict rules of *the narrow way*, we may conclude that *this persuasion comes not of him that calleth us* (Gal 5:8). *This wisdom is not from above* (Jas 3:15). *Faith and a good conscience* are held together (1Ti 1:19; 3:9).

Verses 21–29

We have the conclusion of this long and excellent sermon here, the scope of which is to show the indispensable necessity of obedience to the commands of Christ.

1. He shows, by pleading directly, that an outer profession of religion, however remarkable, will not bring us to heaven unless there is a corresponding conduct (vv. 21–23). Notice here:

1.1. Christ's law set down (v. 21). *Not every one that saith, Lord, Lord, shall enter into the kingdom of heaven, into the kingdom of* grace and glory. Christ shows here that:

1.1.1. It will not be enough to say, *Lord, Lord*, to acknowledge Christ as our Master in word and tongue by speaking to him and professing him to others. We must indeed do this, but can we imagine that this is enough to take us to heaven or that the One who knows and requires the heart (Lk 12:20) would be so easily diverted from a true judgment by a substitution of show for substance? Compliments among people are acts of politeness that are returned with compliments, but they are never paid as real services, and can they then be significant with Christ? This is not to take us away from saying, *Lord, Lord*, from professing Christ's name and being bold in professing it, but it is to take us away from depending on these, in resting in the *form of godliness* without *the power* (2Ti 3:5).

1.1.2. It is necessary for our happiness that we *do the will of* Christ, which is indeed *the will of* his *Father in heaven*. And his will is that we believe in Christ, repent of our sin, live a holy life, and *love one another*. *This is his will, even our sanctification* (1Th 4:3). In the conduct of human beings, saying and doing are two things, often separated: one said, *I go, sir*, but did not move a step (21:30); but these two things *God has joined* in his command (19:6).

1.2. The hypocrite's plea against the strictness of this law, offering other things instead of obedience (v. 22). They make their plea with great boldness—*Lord,*

Lord—and with great confidence, appealing to Christ about it. "*Lord*, do you not know:

1.2.1. "That *we have prophesied in thy name?*" Yes, it may be so; Balaam (Nu 22–24) and Caiaphas (Jn 11:49–50; 18:14) were overruled by God so that they prophesied, and Saul, against his will, was *among the prophets*, but that did not save them. These *prophesied in* his *name*, but he did not send them; they only used his name to serve their own advantage.

1.2.2. "That *in thy name we have cast out devils?*" That may be true too; Judas *cast out devils* (Mk 3:14–15), but he was *a son of perdition* (Jn 17:12). A man could *cast devils out* of others but still have a demon, or could in fact be a demon himself.

1.2.3. "That *in thy name we have done many wonderful works?*" Gifts of tongues and healing would commend people to the world, but it is real holiness or sanctification that is accepted by God. Grace and love are *a more excellent way* than *removing mountains* or *speaking with the tongues of men and of angels* (1Co 13:1–2). Grace will bring a person to heaven without performing miracles, but performing miracles will never bring someone to heaven without grace. These hypocrites did not have many good works to plead; they could not pretend to have done many gracious works of godliness and love; one such deed would have added more credit to their account than *many wonderful works*. Miracles have now ceased, but this plea along with them, but do not ungodly hearts still encourage themselves in their unjustified hopes with similar worthless supports? Let us make sure we do not trust in external privileges and performances, so that *we* may not deceive *ourselves*.

1.3. The rejection of this plea as frivolous. The One who is the Lawmaker (v. 21) is the Judge according to that law here (v. 23). *I never knew you*, and so *depart from me, ye that work iniquity*. Notice:

1.3.1. Why, on what basis, he rejects them and their plea—because they were *workers of iniquity* (evildoers) (v. 23). It is possible for people to have a great name in devotion, but still be *workers of iniquity*; those who are will *receive the greater damnation* (23:14).

1.3.2. How it is expressed: *I never knew you*. This suggests that if he had ever known them, as *the Lord knows them that are his* (2Ti 2:19), if he had ever acknowledged them and loved them as his own, he would have known them, acknowledged them, and *loved them to the end*, but he *never* did *know* them, for he always knew them to be hypocrites. Christ does not accept those who go no further in his service than a mere profession, nor will he acknowledge them on the great day. See how people may fall from the heights of hope into the depths of misery: they may go to hell by a way that took them past the gates of heaven! In God's law court, a profession of religious faith will not allow anyone to practice and indulge in sin; therefore, *let every one that names the name of Christ depart from all iniquity* (2Ti 2:19).

2. He shows, by a parable, that listening to these sayings of Christ will not make us happy unless we are also careful to do them, but if we listen to them and do them, we are *blessed in our deed* (vv. 24–27).

2.1. Those who listen to Christ's word are divided into two kinds here, those who *do* what they *hear* and those who do not (Jas 1:22).

2.1.1. Some *hear his sayings and do them*: we bless God that there are any such people, though comparatively few. To listen to Christ is not simply to give him a hearing, but to obey him. It is a mercy that we *hear* his *sayings*: *Blessed are those ears* (13:16–17). However, if we do not put into practice what we hear, we *receive* that *grace in vain* (2Co 6:1). All the *sayings* of Christ—not only the laws he has enacted but also the truths he has revealed—must be obeyed by us. It is not enough to *hear* Christ's *sayings* and understand them, to *hear* them, remember them, talk about them, repeat them, and reason about them; we must *hear and do* them. *This do, and thou shalt live* (Lk 10:28). Only those *that hear and do* are *blessed* (Lk 11:28; Jn 13:17) and are related to Christ (12:50).

2.1.2. Others *hear* Christ's *sayings and do them not*; their religious faith stops at merely hearing and goes no further. *They hear* God's *words* as if they wanted to *know his ways*, like a people *that did righteousness, but they will not do them* (Eze 33:30–31; Isa 58:2). The seed is sown, but it never grows. Those who *hear* Christ's *sayings and do them not* sit down on the way to heaven, and that will never lead them to their destination.

2.2. The true character and situation of these two kinds of hearers are represented here by a simile comparing them to two builders. One was *wise* and *built upon a rock*, and his building stood in a storm; the other was *foolish* and *built upon the sand*, and his building fell down. The general scope of this parable teaches us that the only way to make sure work for our souls and eternity is to *hear and do the sayings of* the Lord Jesus. People make sure of the *good part* when, like Mary, upon hearing the word of Christ, they *sit at his feet* (Lk 10:39) in submission to it: *Speak, Lord, for thy servant heareth* (1Sa 3:9). The particular parts of the parable teach us various good lessons.

2.2.1. That everyone has a house to build, and that house is our hope for heaven. It should be our main and constant care that we *make our calling and election sure* (2Pe 1:10). Many never have any concern for this; it is the farthest thing from their thoughts. They are building only for this world, as if they will always be here and are not concerned to build for another world. All who take on themselves a profession of religious faith profess to ask what they will *do to be saved* (Ac 16:30), how they may finally get to heaven and, in the meantime, have a well-founded hope of it.

2.2.2. That *a rock* is provided for us to build this house on, *and that rock is Christ* (1Co 10:4). He *is our Hope* (1Ti 1:1). Christ in us is our hope (Col 1:27); we must base our hopes of heaven on the fullness of Christ's merit for the forgiveness of sin, on the power of his Spirit for the sanctification of our nature, and on the effectiveness of his intercession for the bringing to us of all the good that he has purchased for us. The church is *built upon this Rock* (16:18), as is every believer. He is strong and immovable as *a rock*; we may risk our all on him and will not be made *ashamed of our hope* (Ro 5:5).

2.2.3. That there is a remnant who, by hearing and doing the *sayings of* Christ, build their hopes *upon* this Rock. Those who make it their constant care to conform to all the rules of his holy religion *build upon* Christ. In doing that, they depend entirely on him for help from God and acceptance with him, *counting* every *thing but loss and dung that they may win Christ and be found in him* (Php 3:8–9). Building *upon a rock* requires care and effort: those who want to make their *calling and election sure* must *give diligence* (2Pe 1:10). Those who *begin to build* in such a way that they will be *able to finish* (Lk 14:30) are wise builders, and so they lay a firm foundation.

2.2.4. That there are many who profess that they hope to go to heaven but who despise this *Rock* and build their hopes *upon the sand*. Everything besides Christ is sand.

Some build their hopes on their worldly prosperity, as if that were a sure sign of God's favor (Hos 12:8). Others depend on their external profession of religion. They call themselves Christians, were baptized, go to church, hear Christ's word, say their prayers, and do no one any harm, but it is all mere sand, too weak to bear such a structure as our hope of heaven.

2.2.5. That a storm is coming, which will test our hopes and show us what they are made of. *Rain, and floods, and wind, will beat upon the house.* The time of testing is sometimes in this world; *when tribulation and persecution arise because of the word* (13:21), then we will see who only heard the word and who heard and put it into practice. However, when death and judgment come, then the storm comes indeed. Then everything will fail us except these hopes, and then, if ever, they will be turned into eternal fruition.

2.2.6. That those hopes that are built on Christ the Rock will stand; they will stand the builder in good stead when the storm comes. They will not fail; they will be his strength and song (Isa 12:2), *as an anchor of the soul, sure and steadfast* (Heb 6:19). When he comes to the final battle, those hopes will take away the terror of death and the grave; he will be approved by the Judge and will stand the test of the great day; he will be crowned with endless glory (2Co 1:12; 2Ti 4:7–8).

2.2.7. That those hopes that foolish builders base on anything except Christ will certainly fail them on the day of the storm. The foolish builder will *lean upon his house, but it shall not stand* (Job 8:14–15). The house in the parable came crashing down in the storm, when the builder needed it most and expected it to provide shelter. It was a great disappointment to the builder; the shame and loss were great. The higher people's hopes have been raised, the harder they fall. It is the most severe ruin of all that comes on those whose profession of religion is merely formal.

3. In the two last verses, we are told what impressions Christ's message made on the audience. *They were astonished at this doctrine;* it is to be feared that it brought few of them to follow him, but their immediate reaction was amazement and wonder. It is possible for people to admire good preaching and yet remain ignorant and unbelieving, to be amazed but not sanctified. The reason for their amazement was that he taught them *as one having authority, and not as the scribes*. The teachers of the law claimed to have as much authority as any other teachers, and they were supported by every possible external advantage. Yet they spoke as those who themselves had not learned what they preached: the word did not come from them with any life or power; they recited it as schoolchildren repeat their lessons. But Christ spoke his message as judges declare their verdict. His lessons were law; his word was a word of command. Christ showed more true authority on the mountain than the teachers of the law showed in Moses' seat (23:2). When Christ teaches through his Spirit in the soul, he teaches with authority. He says, *Let there be light, and there is light* (Ge 1:3).

CHAPTER 8

The evangelist proceeds to give some examples of the miracles Christ performed: 1. Christ's cleansing of a man with leprosy (vv. 1–4). 2. His curing of a paralyzed servant and a woman with a fever (vv. 5–18). 3. His talking with two who claimed they wanted to follow him (vv. 19–22). 4. His controlling the storm (vv. 23–27). 5. His driving out demons (vv. 28–34).

Verses 1–4

The people who heard him were *astonished at his doctrine*, and the effect was that *when he came down from the mountain, great multitudes followed him*. Those to whom Christ has revealed himself must want to know him more and more. Those who know much about Christ should seek to know even more. It is pleasing to see people so well disposed toward Christ that they think they can never hear enough of him. Some who gathered to him, however, did not remain faithful to him. Those who followed him closely and constantly were only few in number, compared with the crowds who were only casual followers. In these verses we have an account of Christ's *cleansing a leper*.

1. This is appropriately recorded with the first of Christ's miracles:

1.1. Because *leprosy* (The Greek word was used for various diseases affecting the skin—not necessarily leprosy [Ed.]) was looked on among the Jews as a particular sign of God's displeasure. Christ began with cleansing a leper, therefore, to show that he came to turn away the wrath of God by taking away sin.

1.2. Because it was thought that this disease both came directly from the hand of God and was removed directly by his hand, and doctors did not attempt to cure it. Instead, those with this disease were put under the inspection of the priests, the Lord's ministers, who waited to see what God would do. Christ proved himself to be God by restoring many people from leprosy and authorizing his disciples, in his name, to do so too (10:8). It is also included among the proofs of his being the Messiah (11:5). This healing also showed that he would save his people from their sins, for although every disease is both the fruit of sin and an image of sin, which is the disease of the soul, leprosy was especially so. It was therefore treated not as an illness but as uncleanness; the priest was to declare the party clean or unclean, according to the indications. However, the honor of making lepers clean was reserved for Christ. The law revealed sin—for by the law is the knowledge of sin (Ro 3:20)—and declared sinners unclean, but it could go no farther; it could not *make the comers thereunto perfect* (Heb 10:1). But Christ takes away sin; he cleanses us from it. Here are:

2. The words of the man with leprosy to Christ. We may presume that the man, though excluded by his disease from the towns of Israel, still got within hearing of Christ's sermon and was encouraged by it to turn to him, for the One who taught *as one having authority* (7:29) could heal also. His words were, *Lord, if thou wilt, thou canst make me clean*. The cleansing of him may be considered:

2.1. As a temporal mercy, a mercy to the body. This not only directs us to turn to Christ but also teaches us how we should turn to him: with assurance of his power, but with a submission to his *will*; *Lord, if thou wilt, thou canst*. God's power to give temporal blessings is unlimited, but his promise of them is limited by a consideration of his glory and our good. When we cannot be sure of his will, we may still be sure of his wisdom and mercy, to which we may cheerfully turn: *Thy will be done* (6:10).

2.2. As a type of a greater mercy. Sin is the leprosy of the soul; it excludes us from fellowship with God; we must be cleansed from this leprosy. Since Christ is the great Physician (9:12), when we turn to him, we are encouraged to expect that if he will, he can make us clean, and we should go to him with a humble, believing boldness and tell him so.

2.2.1. We must depend on his power; we must be confident that Christ *can* make us clean.

2.2.2. We must commend ourselves to his pity; we cannot demand it as a debt, but we must humbly request it as a favor: "*Lord, if thou wilt*. I throw myself at your feet, and if I perish, I will perish there (Est 4:16)."

3. Christ's response to these words, which was very kind (v. 3).

3.1. *He put forth his hand and touched him.* The leprosy was an offensive, loathsome disease, but Christ touched him. A ceremonial defilement was contracted by contact with a leper, but Christ wanted to show that when he dealt with sinners, he was in no danger of being infected by them.

3.2. He said, *I will, be thou clean*. He did not make him follow a tedious, troublesome, and expensive course of treatment from a doctor, but spoke the word and healed him. Here is:

3.2.1. A word of kindness, "*I will*; I am as willing to help you as you are to be helped." Christ is a Physician who does not need to be sought; he is always near. He does not need to be urged to come; while we are still speaking, he hears (Isa 65:24). He does not need to be paid; he heals freely, not for price or reward. He is as willing as he is able to save sinners.

3.2.2. A word of power: *Be thou clean*. Both the power of authority and the power of energy are exerted in this word. Christ heals by a word of command to us: *Be thou clean*. But along with this goes a word of command about us, a word that does the work: *I will that thou be clean*. The almighty grace that speaks healing will not be lacking to those who truly desire it.

4. The happy change it brought about: *Immediately his leprosy was cleansed*. Nature works gradually, but the God of nature works immediately; he speaks and it is done.

5. The follow-up directions Christ gave him. It is right that those who are healed by Christ should be ruled by him afterward.

5.1. *See thou tell no man*; "Tell no one until you have shown yourself to the priest and he has declared you to be clean, so that you have legal proof both that you were a leper before and that you are thoroughly cleansed now." Christ wanted his miracles to appear in their full light and evidence and not to be made known until they could be seen to be miracles.

5.2. *Go show thyself to the priest*, according to the Law (Lev 14:2). Christ was careful to make sure the Law was observed, so that he would not give offense, and to show that he wanted order to be maintained and good discipline and respect paid to those who hold office.

5.3. *Offer the gift that Moses commanded* as a sign of thankfulness to God and as a reward to the priest for his effort, and do this *for a testimony unto them*. It will be a testimony that there is One among them who does what the high priest cannot do. "Let it remain on record as a witness of my power and a testimony for me *to* them if they will use it, but let it be a testimony *against* them if they will not."

Verses 5–13

We have here an account of Christ's curing the centurion's paralyzed servant. This was done at Capernaum, where Christ now lived (4:13). Christ went about doing good (Ac 10:38), and he came home to do good too; every place he came to was better because of him.

1. The people Christ had to do with now were:

1.1. *A centurion*; it was a Gentile, a Roman, an officer of the army who came with his request. Although he was a soldier—and a little godliness usually goes a long way with people in that profession—he was nevertheless a godly man. God has his remnant among all kinds of people. No one's calling or place in the world will be an excuse for their unbelief and ungodliness. Sometimes where grace conquers the unlikely, it is more than a conqueror (Ro 8:37). Although he was a Roman soldier, and his very living among the Jews was a sign of their subjection to the Roman yoke, Christ, who was *King of the Jews*, nevertheless favored him. Here, he taught us to do good to our enemies. Although he was a Gentile, Christ nevertheless favored him. Now good old Simeon's word began to be fulfilled, that Christ would be *a light to lighten the Gentiles* as well as *the glory of his people Israel* (Lk 2:32). Christ touched and cured the leprous Jews, for he preached personally to them, but he healed the paralyzed Gentiles at a distance, for he did not go in person to them, but *sent his word and healed them* (Ps 107:20); in them, however, he was more greatly exalted.

1.2. *The centurion's servant.* Christ is as ready to heal the poorest servant as to heal the richest master, for he himself *took upon him the form of a servant* (Php 2:7), to show his regard to the lowliest.

Notice:

2. The grace of the centurion toward Christ. Can any good come from a Roman soldier (Jn 1:46)? Come and see, and you will find plenty of good coming from this centurion. Notice:

2.1. His affectionate words to Jesus Christ, which showed:

2.1.1. A godly regard for our great Master, as one who was able and willing to help and relieve poor petitioners. He came to him *beseeching him*, with "cap in hand," as one making a humble request. This shows that he saw more in Christ than appeared at first sight; he saw what commanded respect. The greatest people must become beggars when they have dealings with Christ. The centurion acknowledged Christ's sovereignty by calling him Lord, and he referred his situation to him and to his will and wisdom. He knew he was dealing with a wise and gracious Physician, to whom the telling of the illness was equivalent to the most fervent request. A humble confession of our spiritual needs and diseases will not fail to receive a favorable answer. Pour out your complaint, and mercy will be poured out to you.

2.1.2. A kind regard for his poor servant. We read about many who came to Christ for their children, but this is the only example of one who came to him for a servant: *Lord, my servant lieth at home sick.* It is the duty of masters to be concerned for their servants when they are suffering. The servant could not have done more for the master than the master did here for his servant. The centurion's servants were very dutiful toward him (v. 9), and here we see what made them so; he was very kind to them, and that made them more cheerfully obedient to him. Paralysis is a disease in which the physician's skill often fails; it was therefore great evidence of the centurion's faith in the power of Christ that he came to him for healing that was beyond the power of natural means to bring about. Notice how fervently he described his servant's situation; he was *sick of the palsy*, a disease that commonly makes the patient senseless of pain, but this person was *grievously tormented*. We should be just as concerned for the souls of our children and servants who are spiritually paralyzed, bringing them to Christ by faith and prayer, bringing them to the means of healing and health.

2.2. His great humility and self-abasement. After Christ had shown his readiness to come and heal his servant (v. 7), he expressed himself with greater humility. Humble souls are made more humble by Christ's gracious condescension to them. *Lord, I am not worthy that thou shouldst come under my roof* (v. 8), which showed lowly thoughts about himself and high thoughts about our Lord Jesus. He did not say, "My servant is not worthy that you should come into his room, because it is in the attic," but *I am not worthy that thou shouldst come into my house*. The centurion was a great man, but he acknowledged his unworthiness before God. Humility is very fitting in noble people. Christ was now insignificant in the world, yet the centurion paid him this respect. We should value and respect what we see of God even in those who, in their outward condition, are our inferiors in every way. Whenever we come to Christ, and to God through Christ, we should be humble ourselves, lying low in the sense of our own unworthiness.

2.3. His great faith. The more humility, the more faith. He had an assurance of faith not only that Christ could heal his servant but also that:

2.3.1. He could heal him from a distance. No physical contact was necessary, as in natural operations, nor any touching or treatment of the affected part. We read later about those who, with much difficulty, brought the *man sick of the palsy to Christ* (9:2) and set him before him, and Christ commended their faith as a working faith. This centurion did not bring his man *sick of the palsy*, and Christ commended his faith as a trusting faith. True faith is accepted by Christ no matter what form it appears in: Christ puts the best interpretation on the different ways of religious faith that people follow. Nearness and distance are all the same to him. Distance of place cannot obstruct either the knowing or the working of the One who *fills all places* (Eph 1:23).

2.3.2. He could heal him with a *word*, that he need not send him a medicine, much less a charm, but *"speak the word only*, and I know without question that *my servant shall be healed*." Here, the centurion acknowledged Christ to have divine power. With people, saying and doing are two different things, but not so with Christ.

2.4. His illustrating the faith he had in the power of Christ by describing the power he had as a centurion over his soldiers, which was the power of a master over his servants; he said to one, *Go, and he went*. They were all at his beck and call, so that he could use them to carry out his commands at a distance. Christ could speak in this way, and it would be done. The centurion had such command over his soldiers, even though he himself was a *man under authority*; and much more did Christ have this power, who is the supreme and sovereign Lord of all. We should all be such servants to God: we must go and come when he calls, according to the directions of his word and the disposals of his providence. When his will goes against our own, his must take priority, and our own will is to be set aside. Physical diseases are such servants to Christ. It is a matter of comfort to all who belong to Christ that every disease is made to serve the intentions of his grace. Those who see that sickness is in the hands of such a good Friend need not fear sickness or what it can do.

3. The grace of Christ appearing toward this centurion, for he will show himself gracious to those who are themselves gracious (Ps 18:26).

3.1. Christ complied with his words at the first opportunity. *I will come and heal him* (v. 7); not "I will come and see him," which would have shown him as a kind Savior, but, *I will come and heal him*, which showed him to be an all-powerful Savior. He has *healing under his wings* (Mal 4:2); his coming is healing. The centurion wanted Christ to heal his servant; Christ said, *I will come and heal him*, so expressing more favor than the centurion either asked or thought of (Eph 3:20). Christ often surpasses the expectations of poor petitioners. He would not go down to see the sick child of a royal official who insisted on his coming down (Jn 4:47–49), but he offered to go down to see a sick servant. Christ's humility in being willing to go gave the centurion an example and brought out his humility in acknowledging himself unworthy to have him come. Christ's gracious condescension to us should make us more humble and self-abasing to him.

3.2. Christ commended his faith and used the occasion to speak a kind word about the poor Gentiles (vv. 10–12).

3.2.1. As for the centurion himself, Christ not only approved him and accepted him—all true believers have that honor (Ps 149:9)—but also admired him and applauded him: great believers have that honor.

3.2.1.1. Christ was astonished not at his greatness but at his graces. *When Jesus heard it, he marvelled*; not as if it were something new and surprising to him, but it was great and excellent, rare and uncommon, and Christ spoke about it as wonderful in order to teach us what to admire: not worldly pomp and decorations, but the beauty of holiness (2Ch 20:21). The wonders of grace should affect us more than the wonders of nature or providence, and spiritual accomplishments more than any worldly achievements.

3.2.1.2. Christ *applauded* him in what he said to *them that followed. Verily, I have not found so great faith, no, not in Israel.* Now this speaks:

3.2.1.2.1. Honor to the centurion, who, though not a son of Abraham's body, was an heir of Abraham's faith (Ge 15:6). The thing that Christ seeks is *faith*, and wherever it is, he finds it, even if it is as small *as a grain of mustard seed* (17:20). We must be eager to give praise to those to whom it is due even if they are not within our own denomination or group.

3.2.1.2.2. Shame to Israel. When *the Son of man comes* (Lk 18:8), he *finds* little *faith*, and so he finds little fruit. Christ said this *to those that followed him.* They were Abraham's seed; to protect that honor, let them not allow themselves to be surpassed by a Gentile, especially in that grace for which Abraham was famous (Ge 15:6; Ro 4:3; Gal 3:6; Jas 2:23).

3.2.2. As to others, Christ told them two things, which must have been very surprising to those who had been taught that *salvation was of the Jews* (Jn 4:22).

3.2.2.1. That *a great many of the Gentiles would be saved* (v. 11). The faith of the centurion was an example of the conversion of the Gentiles. This was a subject our Lord Jesus spoke about often; he spoke with assurance: *I say unto you*, "I who know all people"; an intimation of this kind enraged the Nazarenes against him (Lk 4:27). Christ gives us here an idea:

3.2.2.1.1. Of the people who will be saved: many *from the east and the west*; he had said (7:14), *Few there be that find the way to life*, but here *many shall come.* Few at one time, and in one place, but when they all come together, they will be a great many. They will come *from the east* and *from the west*, places distant from each other, but they will all meet at the right hand of Christ, the Center of their unity. God has his remnant everywhere. Although the Gentiles were *strangers to the covenant of promise* now (Eph 2:12) and had been for a long time, who knows what *hidden ones* (Ps 83:3) God had among them then?

When we reach heaven, just as we will miss very many there who we thought had been going there, so we will also meet very many there whom we did not expect.

3.2.2.1.2. Of salvation itself. They will come together to Christ (2Th 2:1).

3.2.2.1.2.1. They will be admitted *into the kingdom of grace* on earth; they will be *blessed with faithful Abraham* (Gal 3:9). This makes Zacchaeus a son of Abraham (Lk 19:9).

3.2.2.1.2.2. They will be admitted into the *kingdom of glory in heaven.* They will sit down to rest from their work, having completed their day's labor. Sitting stands for continuance: while we stand, we are going; where we sit, we intend to stay, as *at a table*; that is the metaphor here. They will sit down to feast, which stands for both full communication and free and familiar communion (Lk 22:30). They will *sit down with Abraham.* Those who in this world were very distant from each other in time, place, or external condition will all meet in heaven. Holy society is a part of the happiness of heaven.

3.2.2.2. That a great many of the Jews would perish (v. 12). Notice:

3.2.2.2.1. A strange sentence passed: *The children of the kingdom shall be cast out. The kingdom of God*, which they boasted they were *the children* of, would be taken away from them. In the great day it will not do people any good that they have been *children of the kingdom*, either as Jews or as Christians, for people will then be judged not by what they were *called*, but by what they *were.* Being born to professing parents gives us the name of *children of the kingdom*, but if we depend on that and have nothing else to show for heaven except that, we will be *cast out.*

3.2.2.2.2. A strange punishment for *the workers of iniquity* described: *They shall be cast into outer darkness*, the darkness of those who are outside. *They shall be cast out* from God and all true comfort and *cast into darkness.* It is *utter darkness*, without any glimmer, point, or hope of light, not the slightest gleam or glimpse of it. It is darkness that results from their being excluded from heaven, the land of light.

3.3. He healed his servant. He granted him his request, which was a real answer (v. 13). Notice:

3.3.1. What Christ said to him: he said what made the healing as great a favor to him as it was to his servant, and much greater: *As thou hast believed, so be it done to thee.* The servant was healed of his disease, but the master received the confirmation and approval of his faith. Christ often gives encouraging answers to his praying people when they are interceding for others. It is kindness to us to be heard for others. *Be it done as thou believest.* What more could he have? Yet what was said to him is said to us all: *Believe, and ye shall receive* (Mk 11:24); *only believe* (Mk 5:36). Notice here the power of Christ and the power of faith. Just as Christ can do what he wants, so active believers may *have* what they want from Christ.

3.3.2. What was the effect of this saying: the prayer of faith was an effective prayer. It always was so and always will be so. The suddenness of the cure indicates that it was *miraculous: he spake, and it was done*, and this was proof of his almighty power, that he is strong to heal and save.

Verses 14–17

Here is:

1. A particular account of the healing of *Peter's wife's mother*, who was ill *of a fever*.

1.1. The *case*, which was nothing extraordinary; it is recorded as an example of the special care and kindness

Christ showed to the families of his disciples. We find here that:

1.1.1. Peter had *a wife*, and yet he *was called to be an apostle of Christ*. Christ supported the marriage state.

1.1.2. Peter had *a house*, though Christ did not (v. 20). The disciple was better provided for than his Lord.

1.1.3. He had a house in Capernaum, though he was originally from Bethsaida; he probably moved to Capernaum and made that his main home when Christ moved there. It is worthwhile changing where we live in order to be near Christ.

1.1.4. He had his *wife's mother* with him in his family, which is an example to marriage partners to be as kind to one another's relatives as they are to their own. Probably, this good woman was old but was still respected and taken care of, as old people should be, and with all possible tenderness.

1.1.5. She lay ill with a fever. Paralysis was a chronic disease, fever an acute disease, but both were brought to Christ.

1.2. The healing (v. 15).

1.2.1. How it was carried out: *He touched her hand*, not to identify the disease, as doctors do, by taking the pulse, but to heal it. This showed his kindness and tenderness. The Scripture *speaks the word*, the Spirit gives the touch: he touches the heart and hand.

1.2.2. How it was shown: the *fever left her, she arose, and ministered to them*. By this it is seen:

1.2.2.1. That the mercy was completed. Those who recover from fever by the power of nature are usually weak and feeble. She was immediately well enough to go about the business of the house.

1.2.2.2. That the mercy was sanctified. Although she was dignified by a special favor, she did not act self-important, but was as ready to wait at table, if need be, like any servant. Those whom Christ has honored must remain humble; being so restored, she sought how she might repay him. It is right that those whom Christ has healed should minister to him as his humble servants all their lives.

2. A general account of the many healings Christ performed. This healing of Peter's mother-in-law brought him many patients. "He healed so-and-so; then why not me? He healed so-and-so's friend; why not mine?" We are told here:

2.1. What he did (v. 16).

2.1.1. *He cast out devils*; he *cast out the* evil *spirits with his word*. About the time of Christ's coming in the world, there seems to have been an extraordinary unleashing of the Devil, enabling him to possess and trouble people's bodies. God wisely planned it this way so that Christ would have better and more frequent opportunities to demonstrate his power over Satan.

2.1.2. *He healed all that were sick*, all without exception, no matter how lowly the patient, and no matter how bad the illness.

2.2. How the Scripture was fulfilled in this (v. 17). Among other things, it was written about him: *Surely he hath borne our griefs, and carried our sorrows* (Isa 53:4). It is referred to in 1Pe 2:24, and there it is interpreted, *he hath borne our sins*; here it is referred to as well and is interpreted, *he hath borne our sicknesses*; our sins make our diseases our griefs. Christ took away sin by the merit of his death and took away sickness by the miracles of his life. We are subject to many diseases and adversities in the body, and there is more in this one line of the Gospels to support and encourage us in them than in all the writings of the philosophers. He carried them for us in his

passion, and he bears them with us in *compassion*, sympathizing with our weaknesses (Heb 4:15). He takes them away from us. Notice how emphatically it is expressed: *Himself took our infirmities, and bare our sicknesses*; he was both able and willing to intervene in that matter; as our Physician, he was concerned to deal with *our infirmities and sicknesses*.

Verses 18–22

Here is:

1. Christ's moving to *the other side of the sea of Tiberias*, having ordered his disciples, whose boats attended him, to get their vessels ready for that purpose (v. 18). He must go about doing good (Ac 10:38); the needs of souls called him: *Come over, and help us* (Ac 16:9); he moved *when he saw great multitudes about him*. Although this showed that they wanted to have him there, he knew that others wanted to have him with them just as much, and they must have their share of him. His being acceptable and useful in one place was no objection against, but rather a reason for, his going to another. Many would be glad to receive such help if they could have it next door but do not want to make the effort to follow it to *the other side*.

2. Christ's conversation with two men who, when he moved to *the other side*, were reluctant to stay behind and wanted to follow him. They were not like the others, who did not follow him closely; they wanted to come into close discipleship, which most people were unwilling to do. We have here Christ's managing of two different attitudes, one quick and eager, the other slow and heavy, and his instructions are adapted to each of them and are intended for our use.

2.1. Here was one man who was too hasty in promising, *a certain scribe* (v. 19), a scholar, a learned teacher of the law, one of those who studied and explained the law; we find that generally in the Gospels they are not men of good character. They very rarely followed Christ, but here was one who was a likely candidate for discipleship.

2.1.1. How he expressed his eagerness: *Master, I will follow thee whithersoever thou goest.* I do not know how anyone could have spoken better. His profession of self-dedication to Christ is:

2.1.1.1. Very ready. It seems to have come from an unbiased inclination: he was not called to it by Christ, but offered himself of his own accord to be a close follower of Christ; he was not a conscript, but a volunteer.

2.1.1.2. Very resolute; he seemed to make a point of this. "I am determined, *I will* do it."

2.1.1.3. Unlimited and without reserve: *I will follow thee whithersoever thou goest.* From Christ's answer, however, it is clear that his resolution was rash. Many decisions are made for religious faith that are produced by some sudden pangs of conviction and taken up without due consideration, and so they prove short lived and come to nothing: they quickly become ripe, and then quickly become rotten.

2.1.2. How Christ tested his eagerness to see whether it was sincere or not (v. 20). He let him know that this *Son of man*, whom he was so eager to follow, *had not where to lay his head* (v. 20). Now from this account of Christ's deep poverty, we notice that:

2.1.2.1. It is strange in itself that when the Son of God came into the world, he would put himself into such a low condition as to lack the convenience of a certain resting place. See here:

2.1.2.1.*1*. How well provided for the lower creatures are: *The foxes have holes*; their holes are their castles.

Although *the birds of the air* take no care for themselves, they are taken care of and *have nests* (Ps 104:17).

2.1.2.1.2. How poorly the Lord Jesus was provided for. He had no settlement, no place of rest, no house of his own to lay his head in, not even a pillow of his own to lay his head on. He and his disciples lived on the charity of well-disposed people, who *ministered to him of their substance* (Lk 8:3). Christ submitted to this to show us the worthlessness of worldly wealth and teach us to look on it with holy contempt, so that he might purchase better things for us (Heb 12:24) and so *make us rich* (2Co 8:9).

2.1.2.2. It is strange that such a declaration would be made on this occasion. One scribe might be able to do more to enhance Christ's reputation and service than twelve fishermen, but Christ looked at his heart, and he responded to the thoughts of that, and here he teaches all of us how to come to Christ.

2.1.2.2.1. The decision by the teacher of the law seems to have been sudden, and Christ wants us, when we take on a profession of faith, to *sit down and count the cost* (Lk 14:28). It is no advantage to religion to take people by surprise, before they are aware of what they are committing themselves to. Those who take up a profession when in pain will soon throw it off again when they become anxious; let the one who wants to follow Christ know the worst of it and be prepared for a life of hardship.

2.1.2.2.2. His decision seems to have been made from worldly, greedy motives. He saw how many healings Christ performed and concluded that he received large fees for them and would quickly amass great possessions. He did not want to follow Christ unless he could gain by him.

2.2. Here was another man who was too slow in performing. Delay in fulfilling a commitment is as bad as hastiness in entering into one; let it never be said that we left to be done tomorrow what we could have done today. Notice here:

2.2.1. The excuse this disciple made to delay following Christ (v. 21): "*Lord, suffer* (allow) *me first to go and bury my father.*" His father, some think, was now sick, dying, or dead; others think he was simply elderly and unlikely, given the course of nature, to continue to live long. This seemed a reasonable request, but it was not right. He did not have the zeal he should have had for the work, and that was why he pleaded in this way, because it seemed a plausible plea. An unwilling mind never lacks an excuse. Priority should have been given to Christ.

2.2.2. Christ's not allowing this excuse: *Jesus said to him, Follow me* (v. 22), and power no doubt accompanied this word to him, as it did Christ's word to others, and he did *follow Christ*. We are brought to Christ by the force of his call to us, not by the force of our promises to him. When Christ calls, he will overcome and make the call effective (1Sa 3:10). This disciple's excuse was set aside as insufficient: "*Let the dead bury their dead. Let* those who are *dead* spiritually *bury* those who are *dead* physically; let worldly duties be left to worldly people; do not get encumbered with them. Burying the dead, and especially a dead father, is a good work, but it is not your work at this time: you have something else to do and must not put that off." Devotion to God must be preferred over devotion to parents, even though that is a great and necessary part of our religious faith. We must comparatively neglect and regard lightly our nearest relatives when they compete with Christ, with either our actions for him or our suffering for him.

Verses 23–27

Christ had given sailing orders to his disciples (v. 18), that they should *depart to the other side of the sea of Tibe-*

rias. He chose to go by water. It would not have been much further if he had gone by land, but he chose to cross the lake. It is a comfort to those *who go down to the sea in ships* (Ps 107:23) and are often in dangers there to reflect that they have a Savior to trust in and pray to who knows what it is to be at sea and to be in storms at sea. *His disciples followed him*; the Twelve kept close to him. Only those who are willing to go to sea with Christ, to follow him into dangers and difficulties, will be found to be the true disciples. Many want to be content with following the land way to heaven, but those who want to rest with Christ in the future must follow him now wherever he leads them, whether into a boat or a prison or into a palace. Notice here:

1. The peril and perplexity of the disciples in this voyage. Those who follow Christ must count on difficulties (v. 20).

1.1. *There arose a very great storm* (v. 24). This storm was *for their sakes* (Jn 11:4), to confirm their faith. Christ wanted to show that those who are passing over the ocean of this world to the other side with him must expect storms on the way. It is only the upper region that enjoys a calm forever; this lower region is always disturbing and being disturbed.

1.2. Jesus Christ *was asleep in this storm*. We never read about Christ's sleeping except at this time; this was not a sleep of false security, like Jonah's in a storm, but one of holy peace and dependence on his Father. He had no guilt, no fear within, to disturb his rest. Those who can lay their heads on the pillow of a clear conscience may sleep quietly and sweetly in a storm (Ps 4:8), as Peter did (Ac 12:6). Christ slept at this time to test the faith of his disciples, to see whether they could trust him when he seemed to disregard them.

1.3. The poor disciples, though used to the sea, were in a panic, and in their fear they *came to* their Master (v. 25). Where else should they go to? It was good that they had him so near them. They *awoke him* with their prayers; *Lord, save us: we perish.* Those who want to learn to pray must go to sea. Imminent and perceptible dangers will drive people to the One who alone can help in time of need (Heb 4:16).

1.3.1. Their request was, *Lord, save us.* They believed he *could* save them; they begged that he *would*. Christ's mission into the world was *to save* (Lk 19:10), but only those *that call on the name of the Lord shall be saved* (Ac 2:21). They called him *Lord* and then prayed, *Save us.* Christ will save only those who are willing to take him as their Lord.

1.3.2. Their plea was, *We perish*, which was:

1.3.2.1. The language of their fear. They had received a sentence of death within themselves (2Co 1:9), and they pleaded this: "*We perish*, we're going to drown unless you save us; look on us with pity."

1.3.2.2. The language of their fervency. It is good for us to strive and wrestle in prayer in this way; Christ slept in order to draw out this boldness.

2. The power and grace of Jesus Christ shown to help them. Christ may sleep when his church is in a storm, but he will not sleep too long.

2.1. He rebuked the disciples: *Why are ye fearful, O ye of little faith?* (v. 26). He did not rebuke them for disturbing him with their prayers, but for disturbing themselves with their fears. Christ rebuked them first, and then he rescued them. Notice:

2.1.1. His dislike of their fears: "*Why are ye fearful?* You, my disciples?"

2.1.2. His revelation of the cause of their fears: *O ye of little faith.* Many who have true faith are weak in it, and it achieves only little. By faith we could see through the raging wind to the quiet shore and encourage ourselves with the hope that we will weather the storm.

2.2. *He rebuked the wind.* See:

2.2.1. How easily this was done, with the speaking of a word.

2.2.2. How effectively it was done. *There was* suddenly *a great calm.* Usually there is such a rage of waters after a storm that it is a long time before they settle down, but if Christ speaks the word, not only does the storm cease, but so do all its effects, along with all its remnants. Great storms of doubt and fear in the soul sometimes end in a wonderful calm.

2.3. This aroused their amazement: *The men marveled* (v. 27). They had long been familiar with the sea and had never seen a storm immediately become a perfect calm in all their lives. Notice:

2.3.1. Their reverence for Christ: *What manner of man is this!* Christ is incomparable; everything in him is wonderful: none so wise, so mighty, so pleasant as he.

2.3.2. The reason for it: *Even the winds and the sea obey him.* Christ is to be wondered at, because he has commanding power over even *winds and seas.* He who can do this can do anything. He can encourage our confidence and strength in him on the stormiest day, within or without (Isa 26:4).

Verses 28–34

We have here the story of Christ's driving out demons from two men who were possessed. The scope of this chapter is to show the divine power of Christ. Christ not only has all *power in heaven and earth* (28:18) and all deep places; he also has the keys of hell. It was observed in general (v. 16) that Christ *cast out the spirits with his word;* here we have a particular example of it. Although Christ was sent chiefly *to the lost sheep of the house of Israel* (15:24), he ventured among those who lived near its borders, as he did here to gain this victory over Satan. Notice what work this legion of devils did where they *were,* and notice where they *went.*

1. Let us see what work they did where they *were,* which is seen in the miserable condition of these two who were demon-possessed.

1.1. They lived among *the tombs;* they were coming from there when they met Christ. Conversing among the graves increased the sad frenzy of the poor demon-possessed creatures, and also made them more formidable to other people, who are generally deeply shocked at anything that stirs among *the tombs.*

1.2. They were *exceeding fierce,* not only uncontrollable within themselves but also violent toward others, frightening many and already having hurt some, *so that no man durst pass that way.* The Devil hates the human race, and he shows it by making people spiteful and malicious to one another. Mutual hostilities where there should be mutual helps and endearments, those sinful desires that make war in our bodies by pride, envy, malice, and revenge, make a person in whom Satan rules as unfit for human company, as unworthy of it, and as much an enemy to its comfort as these poor demon-possessed creatures were.

1.3. They defied Jesus Christ and denied all interest in him (v. 29). It shows the power of God over demons that they could not keep the men from meeting Jesus Christ. His chains could hold them when the chains that people made for them could not. But being brought before him, they protested against his jurisdiction, breaking out into a rage: *What have we to do with thee, Jesus, thou Son of God?* Here is:

1.3.1. One word that the Devil spoke like a *saint;* he addressed himself to Christ as *Jesus the Son of God*—a good word, and at this time, when it was a truth still being proved, it was *a great* word too. Even the demons know, believe, and confess that Christ is the *Son of God,* but they remain demons. It is not knowledge but love that distinguishes saints from devils.

1.3.2. Two words that he said like a *devil,* like himself.

1.3.2.1. A word of defiance: *What have we to do with thee?* It is true that the demons have nothing to do with Christ as a Savior. Oh the depth of this mystery of divine love (Ro 11:33), that fallen humanity has so much *to do with Christ,* when fallen angels have nothing *to do with* him! It is possible for people to call Jesus *the Son of God* but have nothing to do with him. It is just as true that the demons *desire* not to have anything *to do with Christ* as a Ruler; they hate him, they are filled with enmity against him. However, it is not true that the demons have nothing *to do with Christ* as a Judge, for they have, and they know they have.

1.3.2.2. A word of dread and a prayer that they not be tormented: *"Art thou come hither to torment us*—to drive us out from these people and restrain us from doing the harm we want to do?" To be turned out and tied up from causing trouble is a torment to the Devil. Should we not then count doing well as our heaven and reckon whatever hinders us from well-doing, whether internally or externally, as our torment?

2. Let us now see where they *went* when they were turned out of the demon-possessed men: into *a herd of swine* that *was a good way off* (v. 30). These *Gergesenes* (NIV: Gadarenes), though living on the other side of the Jordan, were Jews. What had they to do with *swine?* Notice:

2.1. How the demons seized the *swine.* Although these pigs were *a good way off,* the demons still looked to them.

2.1.1. They *asked* permission to enter *into the swine* (v. 31); *they besought* (begged) *him,* with great fervency: *If thou cast us out, suffer* (allow) *us to go away into the herd of swine.* Here:

2.1.1.1. They revealed how inclined they were to cause trouble and how much pleasure it gave them. If they were not to be allowed to hurt people in their bodies, they wanted to hurt them in their goods, and there too they intended to harm their souls, by making Christ a burden to them.

2.1.1.2. They acknowledged Christ's power over them, that without his permission they could not even hurt a *swine.* It is encouraging to all the Lord's people that although the Devil's power is very great, it is still limited and is not equal to his malevolence—what would become of us if it were?—and especially that it is under the control of our Lord Jesus Christ.

2.1.2. They *were given* permission. Christ said to them, *Go* (v. 32), as God said to Satan when Satan wanted permission to afflict Job. For his wise and holy purposes, God often allows the efforts of Satan's rage and lets him cause the trouble he wants. Christ allowed this destruction in order to punish the Gadarenes, who perhaps, though Jews, took the liberty of eating *swine's* flesh, contrary to the Law. Their keeping *swine* bordered on evil. In obedience to Christ's command, the demons came out of the men, and, having permission, *when they were come out, immediately they went into the herd of swine.* See how diligent an enemy Satan is, and how quick; he will lose no time in causing trouble.

2.2. Where they hurried the swine to when they had seized them. They made them *run violently down a* steep place into the sea, where they all perished, about two thousand in number (Mk 5:13). The possession that the Devil gains is for destruction. This is how the Devil rushes people to sin, rushes them to do what they have decided against doing and what they know will cause them shame and grief. In the same way, he rushes people to their ruin.

2.3. What effect this had upon the owners. News of it was soon brought them by those who looked after the pigs, who seemed more concerned for the loss of the pigs than anything else, for they did not go to tell *what was befallen to the possessed of the devils* until the pigs were lost (v. 33). Christ did not go *into the city*, but the news of his being there did. Now:

2.3.1. Their curiosity brought them to see Jesus. The *whole city came out to meet him*. This is how many go out, in profession, to meet Christ for company, but have no real affection for him and no desire to know him.

2.3.2. Their greed made them eager *to be rid of him*. Instead of inviting him into their town or bringing those who were ill to him to be healed, they wanted him to *depart out of their coasts*. Now the demons had what they aimed at in drowning the pigs; *they* did it, and then they made the people believe that *Christ* had done it and so made them prejudiced against him. This is how the Devil sows weeds in God's field (13:25). There are a great many people who prefer their pigs to their Savior; they therefore come short of Christ and his salvation.

CHAPTER 9

In this chapter we have remarkable examples of the power and compassion of the Lord Jesus. His power and compassion appear here in the good works he did: 1. To the bodies of people, by curing the paralytic (vv. 1–8), raising to life the ruler's daughter and healing a woman's bleeding (vv. 18–26), giving sight to two blind men (vv. 27–31), driving the demon out of a demon-possessed man (vv. 32–34), and healing all kinds of sickness (v. 35). 2. To the souls of people, by forgiving sins (v. 2), calling Matthew and associating freely with tax collectors and sinners (vv. 9–13), considering his disciples' frame (Ps 103:14) with reference to the duty of fasting (vv. 14–17), preaching the Gospel, and, in compassion to the crowds, providing preachers for them (vv. 35–38). In this way, he proved himself to be, as undoubtedly he is, the skillful, faithful Physician of both soul and body, who has sufficient remedies for all the illnesses of both.

Verses 1–8

The first words of this chapter make us look back to the close of the preceding chapter, where we find the Gadarenes so angry at the loss of their pigs that they were disgusted with Christ's company and pleaded with him to *depart out of their coasts* (8:34). It follows here, *He entered into a ship, and passed over*. They told him to go, and he took them at their word. Christ will not stay long where he is not welcome, but he remains with those who want and seek him to stay. He did not leave some destructive judgment behind him to punish them as they deserved for their contempt and stubbornness. He *entered into a ship, and passed over*. This was the day of his patience; he did not come to *destroy men's lives* (Lk 9:56), but to save them; not to kill, but to cure. He came *into his own city, Capernaum*, which was then the main place of his residence (Mk 2:1) and was therefore called *his own city*. When the Gadarenes pleaded with Christ to depart, the

people of Capernaum received him. If Christ is shown disrespect by some, he will be praised by others; if one will not receive him, then another will. Now the first event was the healing of the paralytic, in which we may notice:

1. The *faith of his friends* in bringing him to Christ. His illness was such that he could not come to Christ under his own power, but only by being carried. Even the lame may be brought to Christ, and they will not be rejected by him. Little children cannot go to Christ by themselves, but he will consider the faith of those who bring them, and it will not be in vain. *Jesus saw their faith*, the faith of the paralytic himself as well as that of those who brought him. Now their faith was:

1.1. A strong faith; they firmly believed that Jesus Christ both could and would heal him.

1.2. A humble faith; although the sick man was unable to move a step, they would not ask Christ to visit him, but brought him to Christ. It is fitter that we should wait on Christ than that he should wait on us.

1.3. An active faith: believing in Christ's power and goodness, they brought the sick man to him *lying on a bed*, which could not be done without a great deal of effort. A strong faith pays no attention to obstacles in seeking Christ.

2. The *favour of Christ*, in what he said to him: *Son, be of good cheer, thy sins be forgiven thee*. This was a sovereign medicine to a sick man. We do not read of anything said to Christ. They placed him in front of Christ; that was enough. It will not be in vain for us to present ourselves and our friends to Christ as the objects of his compassion. Misery as well as sin cries out, and mercy is no less quick to listen than justice. Here, in what Christ said, is:

2.1. A kind title: *Son*.

2.2. A gracious encouragement: *Be of good cheer*. Probably the poor man was afraid of being rebuked for being brought in so rudely, but Christ did not stand on ceremony. He told him to *be of good cheer*.

2.3. A good reason for that encouragement: *Thy sins are forgiven thee*. This may be considered:

2.3.1. As an introduction to the healing of his physical illness: "Your sins are *pardoned*, and so you will be healed." If we have the comfort of our reconciliation to God along with the comfort of our recovery from sickness, this makes it a true mercy to us, as it was to Hezekiah (Isa 38:17).

2.3.2. As a reason for the command to *be of good cheer*, whether he was healed of his disease or not; "Even if I do not heal you, you will not say you have sought me in vain if I assure you that *thy sins are pardoned*." Those who through grace have some evidence of the forgiveness of their sins have reason to take heart, whatever outward troubles or adversities they are suffering.

3. The objection of the teachers of the law at what Christ said (v. 3): they *said within themselves*, in their hearts, *among themselves*, in their secret whispers: *This man blasphemeth*. Notice how the greatest example of heaven's power and grace is branded with the blackest note of hell's enmity.

4. How Christ demonstrated to them the unreasonableness of this objection before he proceeded further.

4.1. He accused them of it. Although they only said it within themselves, he *knew their thoughts*. Our Lord Jesus has complete knowledge of everything we say within ourselves. Thoughts are secret and sudden, yet they lie open before Christ. The sins that begin and end in the heart, going no further, are as dangerous as any other.

4.2. He argued them out of it (vv. 5–6). Notice:

4.2.1. How he *asserted* his authority in the *kingdom of grace*. He undertook to prove that the *Son of Man*, the Mediator, has *power on earth to forgive sins*. What an encouragement this is to poor sinners to repent, that the power of forgiving sin is put into the hands of the *Son of Man*, who is human like us! If he had this *power on earth*, then much more now that he is exalted to the Father's right hand.

4.2.2. How he proved it by his power in the kingdom of nature. Is it not as easy to say, *Thy sins are forgiven thee*, as to say, *Arise and walk*? He who can heal the disease can forgive the sin. This was a general argument to prove that Christ had a divine mission. The power that appeared in his healings proved he was sent by God, and the compassion that appeared in them proved he was sent by God to heal and save. Paralysis was only a symptom of the disease of sin; he now made it clear by immediately removing the symptom that he could powerfully heal the original disease. The One who had power to remove the punishment no doubt had power to forgive the sin. His great mission in coming into the world was to *save his people from their sins* (1:21).

5. The immediate healing of the sick man. Christ turned from his discussion with the scribe and spoke healing to him. The most necessary discussions must not distract us from doing the good that our *hand finds to do* (Ecc 9:10). He said to *the sick of the palsy, Arise, take up thy bed, and go to thine house*, and a healing, quickening, and strengthening power accompanied this word: *he arose and departed to his house* (v. 7). He sent him to *his house*, to be a blessing to his family, where he had so long been a burden.

6. The impression this made on the crowd (v. 8): they *marvelled* (were filled with awe) and *glorified God*. They praised God for what he had done for this poor man. Others' mercies should be our praises, and we should give God thanks for them. Though few were led to believe in him, they still admired him, not as God, or the Son of God, but as a *man* to whom God *had given such power*. God must be praised in all the power that is *given to men* to do good, for all power is originally his; it is in him as the Fountain and in people as the vessels.

Verses 9–13

In these verses we have an account of the grace and favor of Christ shown to poor tax collectors, especially Matthew. Notice here:

1. The call of Matthew, the writer of this Gospel. Mark and Luke call him Levi. Some think Christ gave him the name Matthew when he called him to be an apostle, as he surnamed Simon *Peter. Matthew* means "the gift of God." Notice:

1.1. The position that Christ's call found Matthew in. He was *sitting at the receipt of custom*, the tax collector's booth, because he was a tax collector (Lk 5:27). He was in his calling, as were the others whom Christ called (4:18). Just as Satan chooses to come with his temptations to those who are idle, so Christ chooses to come with his calls to those who are working. Matthew's calling had a bad reputation among serious people, because so much corruption and temptation went along with it, and there were so few in that business who were honest. God has his remnant among all kinds of people. No one can justify themselves in their unbelief by their calling in the world, for *out of* every sinful calling some have been saved, and *in* every lawful calling some have been saved.

1.2. The effective power of his call. We do not find that Matthew looked for Christ or that he had any inclina-

tion to follow him. Christ is found by those who do not seek him (Isa 65:1). Christ *spoke first*; we have not chosen him; he has chosen us. He said, *Follow me*. The call was effective, for Matthew came at the call; *he arose, and followed him* immediately, neither denying nor delaying his obedience. The power of divine grace soon answers and overcomes all objections. He left his post and his hopes of advancement in that way of life, and although we find the disciples who were fishermen occasionally fishing again afterward, we never find Matthew at his tax collector's booth again.

2. Christ's dealings with tax collectors and sinners on this occasion; *Jesus sat at meat* (eating) *in the house* (v. 10). The other Evangelists tell us that Matthew held *a great feast* (Lk 5:29), which the poor fishermen, when they were called, were not able to do. However, when Matthew comes to speak about this himself, he tells us neither that it was his own house nor that it was a feast, but only that Christ *sat at meat in the house*. It is good to speak sparingly about our own good deeds. When Matthew invited Christ, he invited his disciples to *come along with him*. Those who welcome Christ must for his sake welcome all who are his and let them have room in their hearts. He invited many tax collectors and sinners to *meet him*. This was the chief thing Matthew aimed at in this meal, that he would have the opportunity of helping his old associates come to know Christ. Those who are effectively brought to Christ themselves must also want others to be brought to him, and they must be ambitious to contribute something toward it. True grace will not sit content to eat its morsels alone, but will invite others. Surely some of them *would follow him* as he *followed Christ*. This was what Andrew and Philip did (Jn 1:41, 45; 4:29).

3. The displeasure of the Pharisees at this (v. 11). They found fault with it: *Why eateth your Master with publicans and sinners?* Christ was quarreled with. It was not the least of his sufferings that he *endured the contradiction of sinners against himself* (Heb 12:3). Although he never spoke or did anything wrong, everything he said and did was objected to. He taught us to expect and prepare for reproach, therefore, and to bear it patiently (1Pe 2:20). Those who quarreled with him were the Pharisees. They were very strict in avoiding *sinners* but not in avoiding *sin*; no one was a greater zealot than they were for the *form* of godliness, nor greater enemies to its *power* (2Ti 3:5). They brought their objections not to Christ himself—they did not have the courage to face him with it—but to his disciples. Being offended at the Master, *they* quarreled with the disciples. Christians should be able to vindicate and justify both Christ himself and his teachings and laws, and they should be *ready always to give an answer to those that ask them a reason of the hope that is in them* (1Pe 3:15). While he is an Advocate for us in heaven, let us be advocates for him on earth, taking his reproach on ourselves (Heb 13:13). The complaint was against his *eating with publicans and sinners*: to associate closely with evildoers is against the law of God (Ps 1:1; 119:115). Perhaps by accusing Christ of this to his disciples, they hoped to tempt them away from him. To associate closely with tax collectors was against the *tradition of the elders*, and so they looked on it as detestable. They were angry with Christ for this:

3.1. Because they wished him harm. It is easy and very common to put the worst interpretations on the best words and actions.

3.2. Because they wished no good to tax collectors and sinners, but envied Christ's favor toward them. It may justly be suspected that those who begrudge others a share in the grace of God are those who have not known such grace themselves.

4. Christ's defense of himself and his disciples in their dealings with tax collectors and sinners (vv. 12–13). Leave him to vindicate himself, and to answer for us too. He urged two things in his defense:

4.1. The needs of the tax collectors, who called out for his help. It was the extreme need of poor, lost sinners that brought Christ from the pure regions above to this impure world, and it was the same need that brought him into this company that was thought impure.

4.1.1. He proved the needs of tax collectors: *they that be whole need not a physician, but they that are sick* (v. 12). The tax collectors were sick, and they needed someone to help and heal them, which the Pharisees thought they themselves did not need. Sin is the sickness of the soul. It is deforming, weakening, disturbing, wasting, and killing, but, we bless God, not incurable. Jesus Christ is the great Physician of souls. Wise and good people should be like physicians to everyone around them; Christ was so. Souls that are sick with sin need this Physician, for their disease is dangerous; nature will not help itself. No mortal can help us; we have such need of Christ that we are eternally ruined without him. There are many who think that they are sound and whole, that they have *no need of Christ*, that they can fend for themselves well enough without him, like the people in Laodicea (Rev 3:17). See Jn 9:40–41.

4.1.2. He proved that their need sufficiently justified his conduct, for that need made his associating with them *an act of charity*, which should always be preferred to the formalities of religious profession, and in which beneficence and *munificence* are much better than *magnificence*, just as substance is better than show or shadows. If to obey is in general better than sacrifice, as Samuel shows (1Sa 15:22–23), then much more so when our obedience does good to others. To further the conversion of souls is the greatest possible act of mercy; it is *saving a soul from death* (Jas 5:20). Notice how Christ quoted the saying of Samuel: *Go ye and learn what that meaneth.* It is not enough to be familiar with the letter of Scripture; we must also learn to understand its meaning. The meaning of the Scriptures has been learned best by those who have learned how to apply them to rebuke their own faults and to provide a rule for their own lives. This Scripture that Christ quoted served not only to vindicate him but also:

4.1.2.1. To show what true religion consists in: not in external observances, but in doing all the good we can to the bodies and souls of others in righteousness and peace.

4.1.2.2. To condemn the Pharisaical hypocrisy of those who put their religious faith in rituals rather than in morals (23:23).

4.2. The nature and purpose of his own commission. "*I am not come to call the righteous, but sinners to repentance, and so I must be with tax collectors.*" Notice:

4.2.1. What his mission was: it was to *call to repentance.* The Gospel call is a call to repentance, a call to us to change our mind and to change our way.

4.2.2. With whom his mission lay: not with *the righteous*, but with *sinners*. If people had not been *sinners*, there would have been no need for Christ's coming among them. His *greatest business* therefore lies with the *greatest sinners*. The more dangerous the sick person's case is, the more need for the physician's help. Christ came into the world to *save sinners*, but especially *the chief* (1Ti 1:15). Christ came not with expectations of success among *the righteous* — those who think they are and who there-fore will sooner be sick of their Savior than sick of their sins — but among the convinced, humble *sinners*. Christ will come to them, for he will be welcome to them.

Verses 14–17

The objections that were made against Christ and his disciples gave rise to some of the most useful of his discourses, and so the wisdom of Christ brings good out of evil. So here, from a reflection on the behavior of his family there arose a discussion about his kindness toward it. Notice:

1. The objection that the disciples of John raised against Christ's disciples for not fasting as often as they did, accusing them of this as another example of the laxity of their profession, besides that of eating with tax collectors and sinners. It appears from the other Evangelists (Mk 2:18; Lk 5:33) that the disciples of the Pharisees joined with the disciples of John in this, because the latter, being more in favor with Christ and his disciples, could raise the objection more plausibly. It is nothing new for evildoers to set good people at each other's throats: if the people of God differ in their attitudes, scheming adversaries will seize the opportunity to sow seeds of discord (Pr 6:14, 19). The complaint was, *Why do we and the Pharisees fast often, but thy disciples fast not?* It is a pity that the duties of religion, which should confirm holy love, cause strife and contention. Notice:

1.1. How the disciples of John boasted about their own fasting: *We and the Pharisees fast often.* In every age of the church fasting has been consecrated on special occasions to the service of religion; the Pharisees were very involved in it. The disciples of John *fasted often.* The more severe part of religion is often most followed by those who are still under the discipline of the Spirit as *a Spirit of bondage* (Ro 8:15), whereas, though these practices are good in their place, we must pass through them to that life of delight in God and dependence on him to which these should lead. There is a tendency in those who profess to be religious to boast about their own religious acts; they not only boast about them to people but also plead them to God, trusting in them as their righteousness (Lk 18:9–14).

1.2. How they blamed Christ's disciples for not fasting as often as they did: *Thy disciples fast not.* They must have known that Christ had taught his disciples to keep their fasts private and to control themselves in such a way that they would not *appear unto men to fast* (6:18). We must not judge a person's religious faith by what is visible to the world. It is common for worthless professors of faith to set themselves up as a standard in religious matters, as if all who did less than they did did too little, and all who did more did too much.

1.3. How they brought this complaint to Christ. If Christ's disciples, either by omission or commission, give offense, Christ himself will be sure to hear about it and be reflected on for it. "O Jesus, are these your Christians?" The quarrel with Christ was brought to the disciples (v. 11); the quarrel with the disciples was brought to Christ (v. 14). This is the way of sowing seeds of discord and killing love, to set people against ministers, ministers against people, and one friend against another.

2. Christ's defense of his disciples in this matter. When they had nothing to say for themselves, he had something ready to say for them. Christ will be sure to support us insofar as we are acting according to his commands and pattern. Christ pleaded two things in defense of their *not fasting.*

2.1. That it was not a proper season for that duty (v. 15): *Can the children of the bride chamber mourn, as long as the bridegroom is with them?* Christ's answer was framed in such a way that it would sufficiently justify the practice of his own disciples but not condemn the institution of John or the practice of his disciples. When at any time we are unjustly criticized, our concern must be only to clear ourselves, not to make recriminations or throw mud at others. His argument was taken from the common custom of joy and rejoicing during marriage festivities, when all displays of melancholy and sadness are looked on as improper and absurd. Now:

2.1.1. The disciples of Christ were the *children of the bride chamber*, invited to the wedding feast and welcome there. The faithful followers of Christ, who have the Spirit of adoption (Ro 8:15), enjoy a continual feast (Pr 15:15), while those who still have the spirit of slavery and fear cannot rejoice for joy as other people do (Hos 9:1).

2.1.2. The disciples of Christ had *the bridegroom with them*, which the disciples of John did not have; their master had now been thrown into prison, and so it was the right time for them *to fast often*. There would come to the disciples of Christ a day when the bridegroom would be taken away from them, and *then would they fast*. The thoughts of parting grieved them when he was going (Jn 16:6). Tribulation and suffering came on them when he was gone, which gave them occasion to *mourn* and *pray*, that is, to hold a religious fast. Whether the condition of the children of the bride chamber is joyful or sad depends on whether they have more or less of the bridegroom's presence. The presence and nearness of the sun makes day and summer; its absence and distance, night and winter. Christ is all in all to the church's joy. Every duty is to be done in its proper season. See Ecc 7:14; Jas 5:13. There is a time to mourn and a time to laugh (Ecc 3:4), to each of which we should adjust ourselves, producing fruit in the appropriate season.

2.2. That they did not have sufficient power for that duty. Christ explains this by comparing religious duties to two things: putting *new cloth into an old garment*, which simply pulls the old one to pieces (v. 16), and putting *new wine into old bottles* (wineskins), which bursts the skins (v. 17). Christ's disciples were not able to bear these severe exercises as well as those of John and of the Pharisees. Christ's disciples, being taken straight from their callings, had not been used to such religious austerities, were unfit for them, and would be unfitted for their other work by them.

2.2.1. Some duties of religious faith are harder and more difficult than others, and religious fasting and the duties that accompany it are of this sort.

2.2.2. The best of Christ's disciples pass through a state of infancy; all the trees in Christ's garden are not equally mature, nor have all his scholars advanced to the same level; there are *babes in Christ* (1Co 3:10), and there are adults.

2.2.3. The weakness of young Christians should be considered: just as the food provided for them must be such as is proper for their age (1Co 3:2; Heb 5:12), so also their work must be what is suitable for them. Christ would not speak to his disciples about what they could not then bear (Jn 16:12). Young beginners in religious faith must not be given the hardest duties first, or they become discouraged. Such was Jacob's care of his children and cattle; he did not drive them too hard (Ge 33:13). Christ's care of the little ones of his family is the same, and he gently leads the lambs of his flock (Isa 40:11). There may be excessiveness even in *well-doing*, being *righteous overmuch* (Ecc 7:16), and, through the

subtlety of Satan, such overdoing may prove to be a person's undoing.

Verses 18–26

We have here two events put together; the raising of Jairus's daughter to life and the healing, on the way to Jairus's house, of the woman who was subject to bleeding, which is introduced in parenthesis in the middle of the other account, for Christ's miracles were thickly sown and interwoven. He was called to do these good works while saying the foregoing things in answer to the objections of the Pharisees (v. 18). Jairus's request came *while he spake these things*, and we may suppose it was a pleasant interruption to that unpleasant work of disputing, which, though sometimes necessary, a good person will gladly leave to go about their works of love or devotion. We have here:

1. The ruler's words to Christ (v. 18). *A certain ruler*, a ruler of the synagogue, *came and worshipped him. Have any of the rulers believed on him?* (Jn 7:48). Yes, here was one. This ruler had a little daughter, twelve years old, just dead, and this shattering of the family well-being was the occasion of his coming to Christ. In trouble, we should seek God: the death of our relatives should drive us to Christ, who is our life (Dt 32:47; Pr 4:13). Notice, in what he said to Christ:

1.1. His humility. He came with his mission to Christ himself. It is not beneath the greatest rulers to personally come to the Lord Jesus. He *worshipped him*. Those who want to receive mercy from Christ must honor Christ.

1.2. His faith: *"My daughter is even now dead,"* and although any other physician would now be too late, Christ does not come too late. He is a Physician after death, for he is *the resurrection and the life* (Jn 11:25). *"O come then, and lay thy hand upon her, and she shall live."* This was completely above the powers of nature, but it was within the power of Christ, who has *life in himself, and quickeneth whom he will* (Jn 5:21). We cannot in faith bring him such a request; while there is life, there is hope and scope for prayer, but when our friends are dead, the case has already been decided. However, while Christ was here on earth working miracles, such a confidence was not only allowable but also very commendable.

2. The readiness of Christ to comply with his request (v. 19). *Jesus* immediately *arose*, left those he was with, *and followed him*; he was willing not only to grant him what he desired, by raising his daughter to life, but also to satisfy him so far as to come to his house to do it. Surely *he never said to the seed of Jacob, Seek ye me in vain* (Isa 45:19). Notice, too, when *Jesus followed him, so did his disciples*, whom he had chosen as his constant companions; it was not for show or in order to be given greater respect that he took his attendants with him, but so that those who were later to preach his doctrine could witness his miracles.

3. The healing of the poor woman's bleeding. I call her a poor woman not only because her case deserved pity but also because, though she had had something in the world, she had *spent it all upon physicians* to heal her illness, yet was no better. It doubly emphasized the misery of her condition that she had made herself poor seeking the recovery of her health, but now had neither her money nor her health. This *woman was diseased with a constant issue of blood twelve years* (v. 20), a disease that not only was weakening and wasting but also rendered her ceremonially unclean and excluded her from the courts of the Lord's house, but it did not cut her off from approaching

Christ. She turned to Christ and received mercy from him along the road. Notice:

3.1. The woman's great faith in Christ and in his power. Her disease was of such a nature that her modesty would not allow her to speak openly to Christ for healing, as others did, but she believed him to have such an overflowing fullness of healing power that the very *touch of his garment* (touching the edge of his cloak) would heal her. This, perhaps, had something of imagination mixed with faith, for she had no precedent for this way of turning to Christ. However, Christ overlooked any *weakness of understanding* that the gesture contained, and he accepted the sincerity and power of her faith. She believed she would be healed if she only *touched the* very *hem of his garment*, its extreme edge. There is power in everything that belongs to Christ. There is such a fullness of grace in Christ that *from it we may all receive* (Jn 1:16).

3.2. Christ's great favor to this woman. He did not stop his healing influences, but allowed this shy patient to take a cure without anyone else knowing it, even though she could not have thought it would be unknown to him. Now she was content to go, for she had what she came for, but Christ was unwilling to let her go. The triumphs of her faith must be to her praise and honor. He *turned about* to see her (v. 22), and soon he discovered her. Humble Christians may take great encouragement from knowing that those who hide themselves from human beings are known to Christ, who sees in secret when they turn to heaven most privately (6:6).

3.2.1. He put encouragement into her heart by the word, *Daughter, be of good comfort.* She had feared being rebuked for coming secretly, but instead she was encouraged. He called her *daughter*, for he spoke to her with the tenderness of a father, as he did *to the man sick of the palsy* (v. 2), whom he called *son*. He told her to *be of good comfort* (take heart). His telling her to *be comforted* brought comfort with it, as his saying, *Be ye whole*, brought health with it.

3.2.2. He honored her faith. That grace gives more honor to Christ than all others, and so he puts most honor on it: *Thy faith has made thee whole.* This woman had more faith than she thought she had. She was spiritually healed; she had received the kind of healing that is the proper fruit and effect of faith, namely, the forgiveness of sin and the work of grace. Her physical healing was the fruit of her faith, and that made it a truly fortunate and comfortable healing. The demons were driven out of the demon-possessed men by Christ's sovereign power; some are healed through the faith of others (v. 2). But in this case, "It is *thy faith that has made thee whole.*"

4. The condition in which he found the ruler's house (v. 23). He *saw the people and the minstrels*, or musicians (NIV: flute players), *making a noise*. There was much activity in the house: death makes such work when it comes to a family, and perhaps the necessary cares that arise at such a time, when our dead relative is to be decently buried out of our sight, provide some useful distraction to the grief that tends to overwhelm and control us. The people in the neighborhood came together to grieve the loss and comfort the parents and to prepare for and be present at the funeral, which the Jews did not delay long. The musicians were among them, according to the Gentile custom, with their melancholy tunes, to increase the grief and stir the mourning of those who were present on that occasion. This is how they indulged a passion that tends naturally to grow excessive on its own, and they stimulated the kind of *sorrow* that *those that had no hope* were subject to (1Th 4:13). Notice how religious faith

provides help where irreligion provides what destroys. Paganism worsens the grief that Christianity seeks to soften. The parents, who were directly affected by the affliction, were silent, while *the people and minstrels*, whose lamentations were forced, made such a noise. The loudest grief is not always the greatest; rivers are noisiest where they run shallow. The grief that shuns observation is most sincere.

5. The rebuke that Christ gave to this bustle and noise (v. 24). He said: *Give place* (go away). Sometimes, when *the sorrow of the world* is prevalent, it is difficult for Christ and his comforts to enter. Those who harden themselves in sorrow, who, like Rachel, *refuse to be comforted*, should think they hear Christ saying to their disturbing thoughts, "Go away." He gave a good reason why they should not so disturb themselves and one another: *The maid is not dead, but sleepeth*.

5.1. This was eminently true of this girl, who was to be raised to life immediately; she was really dead, but not so to Christ, who knew within himself what he would do and could do. This death was to last only a short time, and so it was only sleep, like one night's rest.

5.2. It is in a sense true of all who die, and chiefly true of those *that die in the Lord* (Rev 14:13).

5.2.1. Death is a sleep. All nations and languages, to soften what is so dreadful, and also so unavoidable, to reconcile themselves to it, have agreed to call it so. It is not the sleep of the soul — its activity does not cease — but the sleep of the body, which goes down in the grave still and silent. Sleep is only a short death, and death a long sleep. However, *the death of the righteous* is especially to be looked on as sleep (Isa 57:2). They sleep in Jesus (1Th 4:14); they not only rest from the toil and work of the day but also *rest in hope* (Ps 16:9) of a joyful waking again on the morning of the resurrection, when they will awake refreshed, to a new life, awake to sleep no more.

5.2.2. The consideration of this should lessen our grief at the death of our close relatives. Do not say, "They are lost." No, they have simply gone ahead of us. The apostle speaks of it as absurd to imagine that *they that are fallen asleep in Christ are perished* (1Co 15:18). Now could it be thought that such an encouraging word as this from the mouth of our Lord Jesus should be ridiculed as it was? *They laughed him to scorn.* That there are words and works of Christ that we cannot understand is not a reason to despise them. We must adore the mystery of divine sayings even when they seem to contradict what we are most confident of. Yet even this scorn of those in the house led to the confirmation of the miracle, for it seems she was so clearly dead that it was thought ridiculous to say otherwise.

6. The raising of the girl to life by the power of Christ (v. 25). *The people were put forth* (outside). Mockers who laugh at what they see and hear that is beyond them are not proper witnesses of the wonderful works of Christ, the glory of which lies not in their show but in their power. Christ went in and *took her by the hand*, to wake her up, as it were, and to help her up. The high priest, who was a type of Christ, was not to come near the dead (Lev 21:10–11), but Christ *touched the dead*. Christ, who has power to raise the dead, is above the infection and so is not shy about touching them. He *took her by the hand, and the maid arose.* The miracle was performed so easily and effectively — by a touch. Dead souls are not raised to spiritual life unless Christ *takes them by the hand.* He helps us up, or we lie still.

7. The general notice that was taken of this miracle, even though it was done in private (v. 26); *The fame*

thereof went abroad into all that land: it was the common subject of conversation. Christ's works are more talked about than considered and applied. Although we at this distance have not seen Christ's miracles, blessed *are they that have not seen, and yet have believed* (Jn 20:29).

Verses 27–34

In these verses we have an account of two more miracles performed together by our Savior.

1. The giving of sight to two blind men (vv. 27–31). Christ is the Fountain of light as well as of life. Notice:

1.1. The bold words of the blind men to Christ. He was returning from the ruler's house to his own lodgings, and these *blind men followed him*, as beggars do, with their incessant cries (v. 27). The One who healed diseases so easily and effectively, and also so cheaply, will have enough patients. Notice:

1.1.1. The title that these blind men gave to Christ: *Thou Son of David, have mercy on us*. The promise made to David that the Messiah would come out of his body was well known. At this time there was a general expectation of his appearing; these blind men knew, acknowledged, and declared in the streets of Capernaum that he had come, that this was the One. They who by the providence of God are deprived of physical sight may still by the grace of God have *the eyes of their understanding so enlightened* (Eph 1:18) as to discern those great things of God *which are hid from the wise and prudent* (11:25).

1.1.2. Their request: *Have mercy on us*. Whatever our needs and burdens are, we need no more than a share in *the mercy of our Lord Jesus* to supply and support us. Whether he heals us or not, if he *has mercy on us*, we have enough. Each of them did not say for himself, *Have mercy on me*; rather, both said for each other, *Have mercy on us*. Fellow sufferers should be joint petitioners. In Christ there is enough for everyone.

1.1.3. Their boldness in this request. They *followed him, crying*. It seems that he did not take notice of them at first, for he wanted to test their faith, which he knew to be strong; he wanted to stimulate their prayers, and to make his healing more valued because it did not always come when first asked for. He wants to teach us to *continue instant* (faithful) *in prayer* (Ro 12:12), *always to pray, and not to faint* (Lk 18:1). *When he came into the house*, they *followed him* there and *came to him*. Christ's doors are always open to believing and bold petitioners; it seemed rude to rush into the house after him when he wanted to withdraw, but such is the kindness of our Lord Jesus that they were not more bold than welcome.

1.2. The confession of faith that Christ drew from them on this occasion. When they came to him for mercy, he asked them, *Believe ye that I am able to do this?* Faith is the great condition of Christ's favors. Those who want to receive the *mercy* of Christ must firmly believe in the *power* of Christ. Whatever we want him to do for us we must be fully assured that he is *able to do*. Nature may produce fervency, but it is only grace that can produce faith. They had shown their faith in the role of Christ as *Son of David*, faith in his mercy, but Christ also demands a profession of faith in his power. *Believe ye that I am able?* This would amount to their belief in his being not only *the Son of David* but also *the Son of God*, for it is God's prerogative to *open the eyes of the blind* (Ps 146:8). The question is asked of us: *Believe we that Christ is able to do for us* what we need him to do? To believe in the power of Christ is not only to assure ourselves of it but also to commit ourselves to it and encourage ourselves

in it. They gave an immediate answer to this question, without hesitation. They said, *Yea, Lord*.

1.3. The healing that Christ performed on them: *he touched their eyes* (v. 29). He healed in response to their faith: *According to your faith be it unto you*. When they begged for healing, he asked about their faith (v. 28): *Believe ye that I am able?* He did not ask about their wealth, whether they were able to pay him for healing; he referred the matter to their faith, and now they had professed their faith: "The power you believe in will be exerted for you: *According to your faith be it unto you*." It is a great assurance to true believers that Jesus Christ knows their faith and that he is well pleased with it. Even if it is weak, even if others do not discern it, even if they themselves are ready to question it, it is still known to him. People who turn to Jesus Christ will be dealt with *according to their faith*, not according to their imagination or according to their profession. True believers may be sure that they will find all the favor that is offered in the Gospel. Our comforts ebb or flow according to whether our faith is stronger or weaker; we are not restricted in Christ, so let us not be restricted in ourselves.

1.4. The command he gave them to keep it private: *See that no man know it* (v. 30). In the good we do, we must not seek our own praise, but only the glory of God. We must be more concerned to be useful than to be widely known and observed to be so (Pr 20:6; 25:27). Some think that in keeping the miracle private, Christ showed his displeasure at the people of Capernaum, who had seen so many miracles but had not believed. It is just of Christ to deny the means of conviction to those who remain obstinate in their unfaithfulness and to shroud the light from those who have shut their eyes against it. He wished to keep it private also out of discretion, for his own preservation, because the more he was made known, the more jealous the rulers of the Jews would become of his growing influence among the people. However, honor is like the shadow: as it flees from those who follow it, so it follows those who flee from it: *They spread abroad his fame* (v. 31). Although it may be excused as honestly intended for the honor of Christ, it cannot be justified, being done against a particular command. Whenever we profess to direct our intention to the glory of God, we must see to it that the action is according to the will of God.

2. The healing of a mute man who was demon-possessed. Notice here:

2.1. His case, which was very sad. His particular case of muteness was caused by the power of the Devil (v. 32). See the disastrous state of this world and how various the adversities of those who suffer are! We have no sooner said farewell to *two blind men* than we meet with a mute man. How thankful we should be to God for our sight and speech! When the Devil gains possession of a soul, it is made silent as to anything that is good, mute in prayers and praises. *They brought* this poor creature *to Christ*, who welcomed not only those who came by themselves in their own faith but also those who were *brought to him* by their friends with the faith of others. They brought him in just as *the blind man went out*. Notice how untiringly Christ went about doing good (Ac 10:38); how closely one good work followed another! Treasures of mercy, wonderful mercy, are hidden in him; they may be continually shared, but can never be exhausted.

2.2. His healing, which was sudden: *When the devil was cast out, the dumb spake* (v. 33). Christ's healing strikes at the root; it removes the effect by taking away the cause. He opens the lips by breaking Satan's power in the soul.

2.3. The consequences of this healing.

2.3.1. *The multitudes marvelled*; they were amazed; though few believed, many wondered. The wonder of the ordinary people is sooner raised than any other emotion.

2.3.2. *The Pharisees* blasphemed (v. 34). When they could not contradict the convincing evidence of these miracles, they said that their author was the Devil, as if they had been performed by agreement and collusion: *he casteth out devils* (they say) by *the prince of the devils*. This breathes nothing but hatred and falsehood, and satanic enmity to the highest degree. It is sheer diabolism. Because the people were amazed, the Pharisees must say something to lessen the impact of the miracle, and this was all they could say.

Verses 35–38

Here is:

1. A conclusion of the foregoing account of Christ's preaching and miracles: *He went about all the cities teaching and healing* (v. 35). This is the same as we had before (4:23). There it ushers in the more detailed account of Christ's preaching (chs. 5–7) and of his healing (chs. 8–9); here it is admirably repeated at the close of these instances, as the *quod erat demonstrandum*, the "which was to be proved," as mathematicians put it — as if the Evangelist were to say, "Now I hope I have proved that Christ preached and healed." Notice how Christ in his preaching had concern for:

1.1. The poor places. He visited not only the great and wealthy cities but also the poor, obscure villages; he preached and healed there. The souls of those who are lowliest in the world are as precious to Christ, and should be to us, as the souls of those who are most significant.

1.2. The public worship. He taught *in their synagogues*, so that he could bear witness at their sacred meetings and have opportunity to preach there, where people were gathered with an expectation of hearing.

2. An introduction to the account in the following chapter of his sending out of his apostles. *He took notice of the multitude* (v. 36), not only of the crowds who *followed him* but also of the vast numbers of people with whom, as he passed along, he noticed the country to be populated. That nation had now grown so populous, and it was the effect of God's blessing on Abraham.

2.1. He pitied them and was concerned for them (v. 6). *He was moved with compassion on them*, not for temporal reasons, as he pitied the blind, the lame, and the sick, but for spiritual reasons; he was concerned when he saw that they were ignorant and careless and about to perish for lack of vision (Pr 29:18). It was pity for souls that brought him from heaven to earth, and then to the cross. Christ pities most those who pity themselves least; so should we. See what moved this pity:

2.1.1. *They fainted*; they were distressed, harassed, troubled, and wearied. They were helpless spiritually, with no one available who could help them. The teachers of the law and Pharisees filled them with idle notions. That was why *they fainted*, for what spiritual health, life, and vigor can there be in souls that are fed husks and ashes instead of *the bread of life* (Jn 6:35, 48)?

2.1.2. *They were scattered abroad, as sheep having no shepherd*. No creature is more inclined to go astray than a sheep, and none is more helpless, incapable, and exposed, or more disinclined to find its way home again when gone astray: sinful souls *are as lost sheep*; they need the care of shepherds to bring them back. The situation of those people who either have no ministers at all or have ministers who are as bad as none is very pitiable; they seek their own things, not *the things of Christ*.

2.2. He stirred his disciples to pray for them. It appears (Lk 6:12–13) that on this occasion, before he sent out his apostles, he himself spent a great deal of time in prayer. We should pray for those we pity. Christ prayed for his disciples and then told them:

2.2.1. What the situation was: *The harvest truly is plenteous, but the labourers are few*. There was a great deal of work to be done and a great deal of good likely to be done, but the hands to do it were lacking. It was an encouragement that *the harvest* was so *plenteous*. It was not strange that there were crowds who needed instruction, but what was indeed unusual — and still is now — was that those who needed it desired it. It is good to see people in love with good preaching. The valleys are then covered over with grain (Ps 65:13), and there are hopes that it may be gathered in well. A harvest day should be a busy one. It was a pity that *the labourers* would be so *few*, that the grain would spoil and rot on the ground for lack of reapers; there were many loiterers, but very *few labourers*.

2.2.2. What their duty was in this situation: *Pray ye therefore the Lord of the harvest* (v. 38). When things look discouraging, we should pray more, and then we would complain and fear less.

2.2.2.1. God is *the Lord of the harvest*; *my Father is the Husbandman* (Gardener) (Jn 15:1). It is for him and to him, and for his service and honor, that *the harvest* is gathered in. Those who wish the harvest work well are greatly encouraged to know that it is directed by God himself, who is sure to organize everything for the best.

2.2.2.2. Ministers are and should be *labourers* in God's *harvest*; the ministry is *a work* and must be acted on accordingly; it is harvest work, which is a necessary work, work that requires everything to be done in its season and requires diligence to do it thoroughly. It is also a pleasant work; the laborers *reap in joy* (Ps 126:5), and the joy of the preachers of the Gospel is likened to the *joy of harvest* (Isa 9:2–3); *he that reapeth receiveth wages* (Jn 4:36); *the hire of the labourers* who reap God's field will not be *kept back*, as was that of the laborers referred to by James (Jas 5:4). It is God's work to *send forth labourers*; Christ makes ministers (Eph 4:11); he appoints them, he qualifies them, and he calls them. All who love Christ and souls should show it by fervently praying to God, especially when *the harvest is plenteous, that he would send forth* more skilled, faithful, wise, and hardworking *labourers into his harvest*. Christ set his friends to pray this just before he sent apostles out to labor in *the harvest*. Notice, too, that Christ said this to his disciples, who were to be employed as *labourers*. They must pray that God *would send them forth. Here am I, send me* (Isa 6:8). Commissions given in answer to prayer are most likely to be effective; Paul is a chosen vessel, *for behold, he prays* (Ac 9:11, 15).

CHAPTER 10

This chapter is a sermon of ordination that our Lord Jesus Christ preached when he advanced his twelve disciples to the status and position of apostles. We have here: 1. The general commission given them (v. 1). 2. The names of the people to whom this commission was given (vv. 2–4). 3. The instructions given them, which are very detailed: 3.1. Concerning the services they were to fulfill: their preaching, their performing of miracles, to whom they must go, how they must behave, and with what method they must proceed (vv. 5–15). 3.2. Concerning the sufferings they were to experience. They were told what they would suffer, and from whom; they were advised what course to follow when persecuted, and encouragements were given them to bear their sufferings cheerfully (vv. 16–42).

Verses 1–4

We are told here:

1. Whom Christ ordained as his apostles or ambassadors; they were his disciples (v. 1). He had called them sometime before to be his disciples, and he then told them that they would be made *fishers of men* (4:19), a promise that he now fulfilled. Christ often confers honors and graces gradually. Christ had kept these twelve disciples all this time:

1.1. In a state of testing. Although he knows what people are like, although he knew from the start what was in them (Jn 6:70), he still used this method to give an example to his church. Because the ministry is a great trust, it is right that people be tested for a time before they are entrusted with it.

1.2. In a state of training. All this time he had been preparing them for this great work. He prepared them:

1.2.1. By *taking them to be with him*. The best preparation for the work of the ministry is friendship and fellowship with Jesus Christ. Those who want to *serve Christ* must first be *with him* (Jn 12:26). Paul had Christ revealed not only *to him* but also *in him* before he went to preach him among the Gentiles (Gal 1:16).

1.2.2. By *teaching them*, they were with him as his students or pupils. He opened up the Scriptures to them and opened their understandings (Lk 24:32, 45) to know the meaning of the Scriptures: to them it was given to *know the mysteries of the kingdom of heaven* (13:11), and to them they were *made plain*. Those who want to become teachers must first become learners; they must receive so that they may give. Christ *taught his disciples* before he sent them out (5:2), and later, when he enlarged their commission, he gave them fuller instructions (Ac 1:3).

2. What commission he gave them.

2.1. *He called them to him* (v. 1). He had called them to come *after* him before; now he called them to come *to* him; he admitted them to a greater familiarity with himself. The priests under the law were said to *draw near* (1Sa 14:36) and *approach* God (Lev 21:17–18), nearer than the people; the same may be said about Gospel ministers: they are called to draw near to Christ. It is significant that when the disciples were to be *instructed*, they *came unto* him of their own accord (5:1). But now that they were to be *ordained*, he *called them*. It is good for disciples of Christ to be more eager to learn than to teach. We must wait for a call, a clear call, before we take on ourselves the responsibility to *teach others*.

2.2. He *gave them power, authority* in his name, to command people to obedience, and to confirm that authority, he also gave them authority to command demons into submission. All rightful authority is derived from Jesus Christ. All power is given to him without limitation (Jn 3:34). He put some of his honor on his ministers, as Moses put some of his on Joshua. He gave them *power over unclean spirits* and over *all manner of sickness*. The purpose of the Gospel was to conquer the devil and to cure the world.

2.2.1. He gave them power over evil spirits, to drive them out. The power that is committed to the ministers of Christ is aimed directly against the Devil and his kingdom. Christ gave them power to drive him out of the bodies of people, but that was to show the destruction of his spiritual kingdom and of all the works of the Devil, which is the reason why the *Son of God* was *manifested* (1Jn 3:8).

2.2.2. He gave them power to *heal all manner of sickness*. He authorized them to perform miracles to confirm their teaching, to prove that it came from God, to prove that it is not only faithful but also *worthy of all acceptation* (1Ti 1:15), that the purpose of the Gospel is to heal and save. The aim of many of Moses' miracles was destruction, but the miracles that Christ performed and those that he appointed his apostles to work proved him to be not only the great Teacher and Ruler of the world but also its Redeemer. *They were to heal all manner of sickness* and *all manner of disease* without exception, even of those that were reckoned incurable and the discredit of physicians. In the grace of the Gospel there is lotion for every sore, a remedy for every illness. There is no spiritual disease so malignant, so hardened, that there are not sufficient resources in the power of Christ to heal it. Let no one, therefore, say there is no hope or that the breach is as wide as the sea and therefore cannot be healed.

3. The number and names of those who were commissioned; they were made apostles, that is, messengers. *Angel* and *apostle* mean the same thing—"one sent on an errand; an ambassador." All faithful ministers are sent by Christ, but those who were first, and directly, sent by him are notably called *apostles*, the prime ministers of state in his kingdom. Christ himself is called an apostle (Heb 3:1), for he was *sent by the Father* and so sent them (Jn 20:21). The prophets were called God's messengers (2Ch 36:16; Isa 42:19; Hag 1:13; Mal 3:1).

3.1. Their number was twelve, referring to the number of the tribes of Israel. The Gospel church must be the Israel of God; the Jews must be invited into it first; the apostles must be spiritual fathers, to beget descendants of Christ (Ps 22:30; Isa 53:10). Israel in the flesh was to be rejected for its unfaithfulness; these twelve, therefore, were appointed to be the fathers of another Israel. These twelve, by their doctrine, were to judge the twelve tribes of Israel (Lk 22:30). This was that famous jury—and to make it a "grand jury," Paul was added to it—that was impaneled to inquire into the matter between the King of Kings and the human race.

3.2. Their names are left on record here, and it is to their honor, but they had more reason to rejoice that their names were *written in heaven* (Lk 10:20).

3.2.1. About some of these twelve apostles, such as Bartholomew and Simon the *Canaanite* (Zealot), we know nothing more from the Scripture than their names. All the good ministers of Christ are not equally famous, nor are their actions equally celebrated.

3.2.2. They are named in twos, for originally they were sent out two by two, because *two are better than one* (Ecc 4:9); they would be useful to each other, and more useful together to Christ and souls; what one forgot the other would remember. Three twos were brothers: Peter and Andrew, James and John, and the other James and *Lebbeus* (Thaddaeus). It is excellent when brothers-by-nature are brothers-by-grace, those two bonds strengthening each other.

3.2.3. Peter is named first, because he was called first or because he was the most forward among them, always making himself the spokesman for the rest. However, that gave him no authority over the other apostles, nor was the slightest mark of any supremacy either given to him or ever claimed by him in this sacred college.

3.2.4. Matthew, the writer of this Gospel, is here connected with Thomas (v. 3), but here Matthew's account varies in two aspects from those of Mark and Luke (Mk 3:18; Lk 6:15). The latter two put Matthew first, but here, in Matthew's own listing, Thomas is put first. It is good for the disciples of Christ to honor others above themselves. By Mark and Luke he is called only Matthew, but here Matthew *the publican*. It is good for those who are advanced to honor with Christ to look *unto the rock whence they were hewn* (Isa 51:1), to remember often what they were before Christ called them, so that divine grace may be more glorified. Matthew the apostle was Matthew the tax collector.

3.2.5. Simon is called *the Canaanite*, or Simon the Zealot.

3.2.6. Judas Iscariot is always named last, and with that black mark against his name, *who also betrayed him*. There have been such spots on our love feasts, weeds among the wheat, wolves among the sheep, but a day of revelation and separation is coming, when hypocrites will be unmasked and discarded.

Verses 5–15

Here are the instructions that Christ gave to his disciples when he commissioned them. He *commanded them* in this. Christ commanded a blessing with these commands (Ps 133:3). Notice:

1. The people to whom he sent them.

1.1. Not to the Gentiles or the Samaritans. They must *not go into the way of the Gentiles*. As to the Samaritans, their country lay between Judea and Galilee, and so the apostles could not avoid *going into the way* of the Samaritans, but they must *not enter into any of their cities*. This restraint was on them only in their first mission; later, they were appointed to go *into all the world* and teach *all nations* (28:19).

1.2. But *to the lost sheep of the house of Israel*. The first offer of salvation must be made to the Jews (Ac 3:26). Christ had a particular and very tender concern for *the house of Israel*. He looked with compassion on them as *lost sheep* (9:36), whom he, as a shepherd, was to gather out of the byways of sin and error into which they had gone astray and in which, if not brought back, they would wander endlessly. Christ gave this description of those to whom the apostles were sent in order to incite them to diligence in their work. They were sent to the house of Israel—of which they themselves had recently belonged—whom they could not help pitying and wanting to help.

2. The preaching work that he appointed them to. He did not send them out without a mission; no, *As ye go, preach* (v. 7). They must declare the beginning of the Gospel (Mk 1:1), saying, *The kingdom of heaven is at hand* (compare Mk 1:15). Not that they must say nothing else, but this must be their text; they must speak about this subject. It is said that *they went out, and preached that men should repent* (Mk 6:12), which was the proper use and application of this message about the coming of the *kingdom of heaven*. The preaching of this message was like the coming of the morning light to announce the approach of the rising sun. This message declared that salvation was near, *nigh them that fear God; mercy and truth meet together* (Ps 85:9–10), that is, *the kingdom of heaven is at hand*, not so much the personal presence of the king—that must not be what they were devoted to—but a spiritual kingdom that was to be set up in the human heart when his physical presence was taken away. This was the same message that John the Baptist and Christ had preached before. People need to have good truths pressed on them again and again, and if they are preached and heard with a new affection, they come to us afresh. A kingdom of glory is still to come, and we must speak about that as being near and try to move people to diligence with a consideration of it.

3. The power he gave them to perform miracles to confirm their teaching (v. 8). When he sent them to preach the same doctrine he had preached, he gave them the power to confirm it by the same divine seals, which could never lie. This is not necessary now that the kingdom of God has come; to call for miracles now is to lay again the foundation when the building is already built (1Co 3:11). They were told here:

3.1. To use their power to do good: *Heal the sick, cleanse the lepers*. They were sent out as public blessings, to show the world that love and goodness were the spirit and heart of the Gospel they came to preach and of the kingdom that they were to set up. This shows that they were the servants of the God who is good and does good and whose mercy is *over all his works* (Ps 145:9). We do not read of their raising anyone to life before *the resurrection of Christ*, yet they were instrumental in raising many to *spiritual life*.

3.2. To do good freely: *Freely ye have received, freely give*. They must heal for free, to show further the nature of the Gospel kingdom, which is made up not only of grace but of free grace. The reason is that *freely you have received*. The consideration of Christ's freeness in doing good to us should make us free in doing good to others.

4. The provision that must be made for them in this mission. As to that:

4.1. They must make no provision for it themselves: *Provide neither gold nor silver* (vv. 9–10). Just as, on the one hand, they must not increase their possessions by their work, so, on the other hand, they must not spend the little they have of their own on it. Christ wanted to teach them:

4.1.1. To act under the direction of human wisdom. They were now to make only a short journey, so why should they burden themselves with what they would not need?

4.1.2. To act in dependence upon divine Providence. They must be taught to live without being anxious about their lives (6:25). Those who go on Christ's mission have, of all people, most reason to trust him for the food they need. Christ's hired servants will have *bread enough and to spare* (Lk 15:17); while we remain faithful to God and our duty and are careful to do our work well, we may cast all our other cares on God (1Pe 5:7).

4.2. They should expect that those to whom they were sent would *provide for them* what was necessary (v. 10). They must not expect to be fed by miracles, as Elijah was (1Ki 17:4–6), but they could depend on God to dispose the hearts of those they went among to be kind to them and provide for them. Ministers are and must be workers, laborers, and they are worthy of their keep. Christ wants his disciples not to distrust their God and not to distrust their compatriots so much as to doubt that they will be comfortably provided for. "If you preach to them and try to do good among them, they will surely give you enough food and drink for your needs, and if they do, never desire luxuries; God will pay you your wages later, and they will accumulate in the meantime."

5. The proceedings they were to observe in dealing with any place (vv. 11–15).

5.1. They were told here how to behave toward those who were foreigners to them.

5.1.1. In foreign towns and cities: "When you come to a town, *inquire who* in it *is worthy*."

5.1.1.1. It was presumed that there were some in every place who were more disposed than others to receive the Gospel and its preachers. In the worst times and places, we may charitably hope that there are some who swim against the tide, who are like wheat among the chaff (3:12). There were saints in Nero's household (Php 4:22). "Ask who is worthy, who there are who have some fear of God in their hearts." Previous dispositions to what is good are both directions and encouragements to ministers in dealing with people. There is most hope of the word being profitable to those who are already well disposed, to whom it is therefore acceptable; and one such person is to be found here and there.

5.1.1.2. They must seek out such people, not ask for the best inns. Public houses were not the proper places for them, since they neither took money with them (v. 9) nor expected to receive any (v. 8). Instead, they must look for accommodation in private houses, with those who would receive them well, and for this hospitality the hosts must expect no other reward than a prophet's reward (v. 41), an apostle's reward, their praying and preaching. Those who receive the Gospel must neither begrudge its expense nor promise themselves a profit from it in this world. Wherever Christ's disciples come, they should ask for the good people of the place and get to know them. When we took God as our God, we took his people as our people, and like will rejoice with like. It is implied that if they did ask who was worthy, they would be able to find them. Anyone could tell them where an honest, sober, good person lived, for this is a characteristic that, like the *ointment of the right hand* (Pr 27:16), reveals itself and fills the house with its fragrance.

5.1.1.3. They must stay in the house of those they found worthy. People who often change their living quarters are justly suspected of having wrong intentions. It is good for the disciples of Christ to make the best of the present situation, to remain faithful in it and not be constantly moving because of every dislike or inconvenience.

5.1.2. In the houses of those towns and cities. When they had found the house of a person they thought worthy, they must greet it at their entrance. "Be open and polite with people. Greet the family:

5.1.2.1. "To lead on to further conversation and so introduce your message." From matters of ordinary conversation, we may imperceptibly move on to talking that may be useful to build up others (Eph 4:29).

5.1.2.2. "To see whether you are welcome or not. Those who will not receive your greeting kindly will not receive your message kindly.

5.1.2.3. "To lead them to have a good opinion of you. *Salute the family*, so that they may see that although you are serious, you are not miserable." Religion teaches us to be polite and obliging to everyone with whom we have to do. The apostles' instructions required that when they came into a house, they must not *command it*, but to *salute* it; for *love's sake rather to beseech* (to appeal on the basis of love) is the way of the Gospel (Phm 8–9). Souls are first drawn to Christ with the *cords of a man* and then kept to him by the *bands of love* (Hos 11:4).

5.1.2.4. When they had greeted the family in a godly way, they must judge the family on their response. If *the house be worthy, let your peace come* and rest *upon it; if not, let it return to you* (v. 13). It seems that after they had asked for the *most worthy* (v. 11), it was possible they might come to those who were unworthy. Although it is wise to listen to common report and opinion, it is also foolish to rely on it; we should see for ourselves and judge with discretion. Now this rule was intended:

5.1.2.4.*1*. To give assurance to the apostles. The common greeting was, *Peace be unto you*. Christ told them that this Gospel prayer—for that was what it had now become—would be offered for all, just as the Gospel

offer was made to all generally, and that they should leave the matter to God to answer the prayer. "If the house is worthy, it will reap the benefit of your blessing. If it is not, no harm is done; you will not lose its benefit: *it shall return to you*." It befits us to judge all charitably, pray heartily for all, and to conduct ourselves politely to all, for that is our responsibility.

5.1.2.4.*2*. To guide them. "If, on your greeting, it appears that they are truly worthy, let them have more of your company, and so *let your peace come upon them*; preach the Gospel to them, peace through Jesus Christ. But if not, if they act rudely toward you and shut their doors on you, *let your peace*, as far as in you lies (Ro 12:18), *return to you*. Withdraw what you have said and turn your backs on them." Great blessings are often lost by a seemingly small and insignificant neglect.

5.2. They were told here how to act toward those who were refusers of them. Christ supposed the case of those who *would not receive them, nor hear their words* (v. 14). There would be those who would insult them and show contempt for them and their message. The best and most powerful preachers of the Gospel must expect to meet with some people who will not even listen to them or show them any sign of respect. Many people turn *a deaf ear* even to the *joyful sound* (Ps 89:15). Contempt of the Gospel and of its ministers often go together, and either of them will be interpreted as contempt for Christ and will be judged accordingly. In this situation we have:

5.2.1. The instructions given to the apostles; they must depart from that house or town. The Gospel will not wait long for those who put it away from them. When the apostles departed, they must *shake off the dust of their feet* in detestation of the evil of the place. They must not even take away the dust of the town with them. It was also a declaration of wrath against the inhabitants. It was to show that God would *shake them off*. Those who *despise* God and his Gospel will be *lightly esteemed* (1Sa 2:30).

5.2.2. The condemnation passed on such stubborn dissenters (v. 15). It will be *more tolerable in the day of judgment for the land of* Sodom, evil though that place was. Those who would not hear the message that would save them will be made to hear the sentence that will ruin them. There are different degrees of punishment on that day. Sodom and Gomorrah were exceedingly evil (Ge 13:13), and what filled up the measure of their sins (Ge 15:16; Mt 23:32) was that they *received not* the angels who were sent them, but abused them (Ge 19:4–5) and *hearkened not to their words* (v. 14). It will be more tolerable for them, however, than for those who do not receive Christ's ministers and who do not listen to their words. *Son, remember* (Lk 16:25) will sound most terribly in the ears of those to whom a fair offer of *eternal life* was made but who chose death instead.

Verses 16–42

All these verses relate to the sufferings of Christ's ministers in their work, which they were taught to expect and prepare for here. They were also told how to bear them and how to continue with their work in the midst of them. This part of the sermon looks further than to their present mission. They were forewarned here of the troubles they would encounter when, after Christ's resurrection, their commission would be enlarged. Christ told them that they must expect even greater suffering than they had previously been called to. It is good to be told what troubles we may meet with in the future, so that we may provide for them accordingly and may not boast as if we had put off the harness when we are still only putting it on (1Ki 20:11). We have here, interwoven, predictions of trouble, on the one hand, and prescriptions of advice and assurance with reference to it, on the other.

1. We have predictions of trouble that the disciples would face in their work. Christ foresaw *their* sufferings as well as his own, but nevertheless, he wanted them to continue, as he himself did. He foretold these troubles not only so that they would not come as a surprise to them and thereby shock their faith but also so that, being the fulfillment of a prediction, these troubles would confirm their faith. He told them what they would suffer and from whom.

1.1. What they would suffer: hard things certainly, for, *Behold, I send you forth as sheep in the midst of wolves* (v. 16). What may a flock of poor, helpless, unguarded sheep expect among a herd of ravenous wolves but to be harassed and torn? Christ's ministers are like *sheep among wolves*, and that is terrible, but Christ sends them out, and that is encouraging; the One who sends them out will protect them and support them.

1.1.1. They must expect to be hated (v. 22). *Ye shall be hated for my name's sake*: that is the root of all the other troubles, and it is a bitter root (Heb 12:15; Dt 29:18). Those whom Christ loves are hated by the world. *If the world hated Christ without a cause* (Jn 15:25), it is hardly surprising if it hated those who bore his image (Ro 8:29) and served his interests. It is painful to be *hated*, to be the object of so much ill will, but it is *for thy name's sake*, which, just as it speaks the true reason of the hatred, whatever is claimed, so it also speaks assurance to those who are hated in this way. It is for a good cause, and they have a good friend who shares with them in it and takes it on himself.

1.1.2. They must expect to be detained and accused as evildoers. The restless hatred of evildoers cannot be resisted, and "they will not only attempt but also succeed in *delivering you up to the councils*" (vv. 17–18). Much trouble is often caused to good people in the name of the law and justice. The apostles must look for trouble not only from lesser magistrates in local councils but also from governors and kings, the supreme magistrates. We find this often fulfilled in the Acts of the Apostles.

1.1.3. They must expect to be put to death: they would *be delivered to death* (v. 21). The hatred of their enemies raged so intensely as to inflict this; the faith and patience of the saints stood so firmly as to expect this. The wisdom of Christ would allow it, knowing how to make the blood of the martyrs the seal of the truth and "the seed of the church" (Quintus Tertullian). By this noble army's not loving their lives to the death, Satan has been defeated, and the kingdom of Christ and its interests greatly advanced.

1.1.4. They must expect, in the middle of these sufferings, to be called by the most terrible and shameful names and descriptions possible. Persecutors would be ashamed in this world if they did not first dress up in bearskins those whom they bait, describing them in such terms as may serve to justify such cruelty. The blackest of all the evil characterizations that persecutors give their victims is stated here; they call them *Beelzebub*, the name of the prince of the devils (v. 25). Since everyone thinks they hate the Devil, the persecutors try in this way to make their victims repugnant to the whole human race. Satan's sworn enemies are presented as his friends; the apostles, who demolished the Devil's kingdom, were called devils. On the other hand, Satan's sworn servants want to be thought of as his enemies, and they never do his work more effectively than when they claim to fight against him. Many times those who themselves are most closely related to the Devil tend most to call others his children.

1.1.5. These sufferings are represented here by a sword and division (vv. 34–35). *Think not that I am come to send peace*, temporal peace and outward prosperity. Christ came to give us *peace* with God, *peace* in our consciences, *peace* with our brothers and sisters, but *in the world ye shall have tribulation* (Jn 16:33). If all the world were to receive Christ, universal *peace* would follow, but while there are so many who reject him, the children of God, who are called out of the world, must expect to feel the fruits of their enmity.

1.1.5.1. Look not for *peace, but a sword*. Christ came to give *the sword of the word*, with which his disciples fight against the world (Rev 6:4; 19:21); he came also to give *the sword of persecution*, with which the world fights against the disciples, being *cut to the heart* with the sword of the word (Ac 7:54), and this sword made cruel work. Christ sent that Gospel that gives rise to the drawing of this sword, and so he may be said to send this sword.

1.1.5.2. Look not for *peace, but division* (v. 35): *I am come to set men at variance* (against one another). This effect of the preaching of the Gospel is not the fault of the Gospel, but of those who do not receive it. The faith of those who believe condemns those who do not believe, and that is why the latter are against the former. The most violent and implacable feuds have been those that have arisen from differences in religion; there is no enmity like that of persecutors, no determination like that of the persecuted. Christ has dealt fairly and faithfully with us by telling us the worst we may encounter in his service, and he wants us to deal with ourselves in the same way, by sitting down and counting the cost.

1.2. From whom and by whom they would suffer these hard things. Surely hell itself must be let loose, and demons must become incarnate, before there could be found such spiteful enemies to a teaching whose substance was *goodwill toward men* (Lk 2:14). No, would you believe it? All this trouble came to the preachers of the Gospel from those to whom they came to preach salvation. Christ's disciples must suffer these hard things:

1.2.1. From human beings: *"Beware of men* (v. 17). You will need to stand on your guard." Persecuting rage and enmity turn human beings into wild demons. It is a sad state of affairs that the world has come to when its best friends need to *beware of men*. The troubles of Christ's suffering servants are emphasized by the fact that they arise from those who *are bone of their bone* (Ge 2:23; 2Sa 19:12–13), blood relations. Unless human nature is sanctified, it is the worst nature in the world next to that of demons.

1.2.2. From people who claimed to *have a form of godliness* (2Ti 3:5) and made a show of religion. *"They will scourge you in their synagogues*, the places where they meet to worship God and to exercise their church discipline": the enemies of Christ looked on the scourging of Christ's ministers as a branch of their religion. Paul was *five times scourged in the synagogues* (2Co 11:24). Christ's disciples have suffered much from conscientious persecutors, who *scourge them in their synagogues*, drive them out, and kill them, and *think they do God good service* (Jn 16:2).

1.2.3. From great people, including people in authority. The Jews not only scourged them, which was the furthest their power could reach, but also handed them over to the Roman powers, as they did with Christ (Jn 18:30). *"Ye shall be brought before governors and kings* (v. 18), who, having more power, are able to cause more trouble."

1.2.4. From all people. *Ye shall be hated of all men* (v. 22), by all evildoers, and these are most people. There are so few who love, acknowledge, and support Christ's righteous cause that we may say that its friends are *hated of all men*. As far as apostasy from God goes, so far does enmity against the saints go; sometimes it appears more general than at other times, but there is something of this poison lurking in the hearts of all *the children of disobedience* (Eph 2:2).

1.2.5. From those of their own family. *The brother shall deliver up the brother to death* (v. 21). *A man shall be*, for this reason, *at variance with his own father. The persecuting daughter will be against the believing mother*, where one would have thought that natural affection and childlike duty would prevent or soon extinguish the quarrel. Then it is hardly surprising *if the daughter-in-law be against the mother-in-law*. In general, *a man's foes shall be they of his own household* (v. 36). Those who should be his friends would be angry with him for embracing Christianity, and especially for remaining faithful to it when he was persecuted, and would join with his persecutors against him. The strongest bonds of family love and duty have often been broken through by an enmity to Christ and his teaching. Sufferings from such people are more painful. Nothing is more cutting than this: *It was thou, a man, mine equal* (Ps 55:12–13); such enmity is often most implacable: *a brother offended is harder to be won than a strong city* (Pr 18:19).

2. With these predictions of trouble, we also have prescriptions of advice and encouragement for times of trial. Let us gather up what Christ said:

2.1. By way of advice and direction in several matters.

2.1.1. *Be ye wise* (shrewd) *as serpents* (snakes) (v. 16). This is a command, commending to us, as useful at all times, and especially in times of suffering, that wisdom of the prudent which consists in understanding their ways (Pr 14:8). It is the will of Christ that because his people and ministers are as exposed to the troubles in this world as they usually are, they should not unnecessarily expose themselves, but should use all fair and lawful means to secure their own preservation. In the cause of Christ we must not cling to this life and all its comforts, yet we must not squander them either. We must not *be wise* in such a way that we pull trouble down onto our own heads.

2.1.2. *Be ye harmless* (innocent) *as doves.* "Be mild, meek, and calm; not only do no one any harm, but also bear no one any ill will." We must not *be wise* in such a way that we wrong ourselves, yet we should prefer that over wronging anyone else; we must use the innocence of the *dove* to bear twenty injuries rather than the subtlety of the *serpent* to threaten or return even one. *The Spirit descended on Christ as a dove* (3:16), and all believers share in *the Spirit of Christ, a dovelike* spirit, made for love, not for war.

2.1.3. *Beware of men* (v. 17). "Be always on your guard and avoid dangerous company; be careful about what you say and do." Those who are gracious should also be cautious. We do not know whom we can safely put confidence in. Ever since our Master was betrayed with a kiss, by one of his own disciples, we need to *beware of men*.

2.1.4. *Take no thought how or what ye shall speak* (v. 19). "When you are brought before magistrates, behave decently, but do not burden yourselves with worry about what will happen to you. There must be wise thoughts, but not anxious, perplexing, disturbing thoughts; let this *care be cast upon God* (1Pe 5:7). Do not try to coin quaint expressions, flourishes of wit, or forced pauses, all of which are useful only to gild a bad cause; the gold of a good cause needs no gilding." The disciples of Christ must give more thought to doing well than to speaking

well, to keeping their integrity than to vindicating it. "Our lives, not boasting words," form the best defense.

2.1.5. *When they persecute you in this city, flee to another* (v. 23). "In this way, reject those who reject you and your teaching, and test whether others will receive you and it; and in this way, protect your own safety." In cases of imminent danger, the disciples of Christ may and must protect themselves by fleeing, when God in his providence opens to *them a door of escape* (1Co 10:13). Those who flee may fight again. It is not dishonorable for Christ's soldiers to abandon their ground, provided they do not abandon their flag: they may leave the way of danger, though they must not leave the way of duty.

2.1.6. *Fear them not* (v. 26), because *they can but kill the body* (v. 28). Those who truly fear God need not fear people, and those who are afraid of the least sin need not be afraid of the greatest trouble. *Yet will we not fear, though the earth be removed* (Ps 46:2), as long as we have such a good God, such a good cause, and such a *good hope through grace* (2Th 2:16). To strengthen us against this temptation, we have here:

2.1.6.1. A good reason against this fear, taken from the limited power of the enemies. They *kill the body*; that is the farthest their rage can go. *They are not able to kill the soul* or do it any harm, and the soul is the person. The soul is killed when it is separated from God and his love, which is its life; now this is out of reach of their power. *Tribulation, distress, and persecution* may separate us from all the world, but they cannot come between us and God (Ro 8:35); they cannot make us either not love him or not be loved by him (Ro 8:35, 37). If, therefore, we were more concerned about our souls, as our jewels, we would be less afraid of other people. They can only crush the cabinet.

2.1.6.2. A good remedy against it, and that is to fear God. *Fear him who is able to destroy both soul and body in hell. Hell* is the destruction of both *soul and body*, not of the existence of either, but of the well-being of both. This destruction comes from the power of God: he is *able to destroy*. God is to be feared, therefore, even by the best saints in this world. The fear of God and of his power reigning in the soul will be a sovereign antidote to the fear of human beings. It is better to fall under the frowns of the whole world than under God's frowns, and so, just as it is most right in itself, so it is also most safe for us, *to obey God rather than men* (Ac 4:19).

2.1.7. *What I tell you in darkness, that speak ye in light* (v. 27). "Whatever hazards you face, continue with your work, declaring the eternal Gospel throughout the world (Rev 14:6); that is your work, do that. The intention of enemies is not merely to destroy you but also to suppress that Gospel, and so, whatever the consequences, make that known." *What I tell you, that speak ye. Many things Christ spake openly, and* he said *nothing in secret* that varied from what he preached in public (Jn 18:20). They must communicate their message publicly, *in the light* and *upon the housetops*, for the teaching of the Gospel is what concerns us all (Pr 1:20–21; 8:2–3). The first indication of the admission of the Gentiles into the church was *upon a housetop* (Ac 10:9). There is no part of Christ's Gospel that needs to be concealed for any reason: *the whole counsel of God must be revealed* (Ac 20:27). Let it be clearly and fully communicated to people of every type everywhere.

2.2. By way of comfort and encouragement. Much is said here with that intention, and all little enough, considering the many hardships the apostles were to struggle with throughout the course of their ministry, and considering their present weakness. They could scarcely bear even the prospect of such treatment. Christ therefore showed them why they should be cheerful.

2.2.1. Here is one word that is distinctive to their present mission: *Ye shall not have gone over the cities of Israel, till the Son of man be come* (v. 23). It was an encouragement:

2.2.1.1. That what they said would be fulfilled: they said *the Son of man* was coming, and *behold, he comes. Christ will confirm the word of his messengers* (Isa 44:26).

2.2.1.2. That it would be fulfilled quickly. Christ's laborers can take encouragement from knowing that their time for work will be short, and soon over; the work and service will soon be accomplished.

2.2.1.3. That then they would be advanced to a higher position. "*When the Son of man comes*, you will be *endued with greater power from on high*" (Lk 24:49).

2.2.2. Here are many words concerning their work in general and the troubles they were to face in it, and *they are good words and comfortable words* (Zec 1:13).

2.2.2.1. That their sufferings were *for a testimony against them* (the Jews) *and the Gentiles* (v. 18). "When the Jewish councillors transfer you to the Roman governors to have you put to death, your being rushed from one judgment seat to another will help make your testimony more public. It will give you an opportunity to bring the Gospel to the Gentiles as well as to the Jews." God's people, especially God's ministers, are his witnesses not only in their work of doing but also in their work of suffering. They are therefore called *martyrs*, "witnesses," for Christ. Now if their sufferings were a testimony, then how cheerfully should they be borne.

2.2.2.2. That on every occasion they would have God's special presence with them and the direct help of his Holy Spirit. *It shall be given you* (said Christ) *in that same hour what ye shall speak* (v. 19). Christ's disciples were chosen *from among the foolish of the world* (1Co 1:27), unlearned and ignorant people, and so they could justly distrust their own abilities, especially when they were called before leaders. They were promised here that *what they should speak would be given them* not sometime before, but *in that same hour*. They would speak extemporaneously, but as much to the point as if they had thoroughly prepared for it. When God calls us to speak for him, we may depend on him to *teach us what to say* (Lk 12:12). They were here assured that the Holy Spirit would draw up their plea for them: *It is not ye that speak, but the Spirit of your Father which speaketh in you* (v. 20). They were not left to themselves on such occasions; God undertook for them. His Spirit of wisdom spoke *in* them. God gave them an ability not only to speak to the point but also to express their words with holy zeal. The same Spirit who assisted them in the pulpit also assisted them in the law court. They must come off well, since they had such an advocate.

2.2.2.3. That *he that endures to the end shall be saved* (v. 22). Here it is very encouraging to consider:

2.2.2.3.*1*. That there will be an *end* of these troubles; they may last a long time, but not forever. Christ comforted himself with this, and so may his followers: *The things concerning me have an end* (Lk 22:37). The troubles may seem tedious, but, we bless God, they are not eternal.

2.2.2.3.*2*. That while they continue, they can be *endured*; they can be endured *to the end*, because the sufferers will be supported in them, in his everlasting arms: *The strength shall be according to the day* (Dt 33:25, 27; 1Co 10:13).

2.2.2.3.*3*. Salvation will be the eternal reward of all those *that endure to the end*. The weather may be stormy, and the way difficult, but the pleasure of home will make up for everything. Those who *endure but awhile and in time of temptation fall away* (Lk 8:13) have run in vain and lose all they have achieved, but those, and only those, who persevere are sure of the prize. *Be faithful unto death*, and then you will receive *the crown of life* (Rev 2:10).

2.2.2.4. That whatever hard treatment the disciples of Christ face, it is nothing more than what their Master faced before: *The disciple is not above his master* (vv. 24–25). Here this was given as a reason why they should not stumble at the hardest sufferings. They are reminded of this saying in Jn 15:20. It is a proverbial expression: *The servant is not better than his master*, and so let them not expect to fare *better*. Jesus Christ, our Lord and Master, met with very harsh treatment from the world; they called him Beelzebub, "lord of flies," the name of the chief of the demons, with whom they said he was in league (12:24). It is hard to say which is more to be wondered at here, the evil of people who so abused Christ or the patience of Christ, who allowed himself to be so abused—that Satan's greatest Enemy and Destroyer should be called his ally and yet *endure such contradiction* (opposition) *of sinners* (Heb 12:3). Consideration of the harsh treatment that Christ faced in the world should make us expect and prepare for similar treatment and bear it patiently; nor let us think it hard if those who are soon to be made *like him in glory* are now made *like him in sufferings* (Ro 8:18). Christ took the first drink from the *bitter cup* (26:39), and so let us drink to him from the same cup, pledging our fidelity; his bearing the cross made it easy for us.

2.2.2.5. That *there is nothing covered that shall not be revealed* (v. 26). We understand this to refer to:

2.2.2.5.*1*. The revelation of the Gospel to the whole world. "You must proclaim it (v. 27), for it will be proclaimed. The truths that are now, as mysteries, hidden from people will all be revealed to all nations in their own language" (Ac 2:11). The *ends of the earth must see this salvation* (Isa 52:10). Those who are doing Christ's work may take great encouragement from knowing that it is a work that will certainly be done. There is an old English blessing, "God speed (prosper) the plow." Christ's work is a plow that God will prosper. Or:

2.2.2.5.*2*. The declaring of the innocence of Christ's suffering servants. However much their innocence and splendor are now *covered*, they *shall be revealed*. All their reproach will be rolled away (Jos 5:9), and their graces and services, which are now *covered, shall be revealed* (1Co 4:5). Let Christ's ministers faithfully reveal his truths and then leave it to him to reveal their integrity in due time.

2.2.2.6. That the providence of God is especially familiar to the lives of the saints in their suffering (vv. 29–31). It is good to go back to basic principles, especially to the doctrine of God's universal providence, extending to all creatures and all their actions, even the smallest and minutest. Notice here:

2.2.2.6.*1*. The general extent of providence, which reaches all creatures, even the least and least significant, even *sparrows* (v. 29). These small birds are so insignificant that one alone has no value; there must two of them to be worth *a farthing*—in fact, you can buy five for two farthings (Lk 12:6)—and yet they are not excluded from divine care: *One of them shall not fall to the ground without your Father*.

2.2.2.6.*1.1*. They do not fall to *the ground* for food, to pick up a kernel of grain, without *your* heavenly *Father*, in his providence, having prepared it for them. Now, the One who feeds the sparrows will not starve the saints.

2.2.2.6.*1.2.* They do *not fall to the ground* by death, either a natural or a violent death, without God noticing. Even their death comes within the notice of divine providence, and much more does the death of his disciples. "This is your God, who looks in this way on sparrows because they are his creatures, and how much more will he look on you, who are his children. If a sparrow does not die *without your Father*, surely a person does not, surely not a Christian, a minister, my friend, my child." There is enough in the doctrine of God's providence to silence all the fears of God's people: *Ye are of more value than many sparrows.*

2.2.2.6.*2.* The particular notice providence takes of the disciples of Christ, especially in their suffering: *But the very hairs of your head are all numbered* (v. 30). This is a proverbial expression, showing the account that God takes and keeps of all the concerns of his people, even of those who are least regarded and of least consequence. If God numbers their hairs, then much more does he number their heads, taking care of their lives, their comforts, and their souls. This assurance from Christ shows that God takes more care of his people than they do of themselves. God *numbers their hairs*, and *not a hair of their head shall perish* (Lk 21:18); not the least harm will be done them. God's saints are so precious to him, along with their lives and deaths (Ps 116:15).

2.2.2.7. That he will soon, on the day of triumph, acknowledge those who now, on the day of trial, acknowledge him; then those who denied him will be forever disowned and rejected by him (vv. 32–33).

2.2.2.7.*1.* It is our duty to *confess Christ before men*, and if we do it now, in the future it will be our indescribable honor and happiness to do it forever. It is our duty not only to believe in Christ but also to profess that faith, by suffering for him when called to it as well as by serving him. However much this may expose us to shame and trouble now, we will be abundantly rewarded for that *in the resurrection of the just.* Each of us will hear Christ say, "*I will confess him before my Father,* when it will do him the most service. I will present him; I will represent him to *my Father.*" Those who honor Christ he will honor in this way (1Sa 2:30). They honor him *before men*; that is poor. He will honor them *before* his *Father*; that is great.

2.2.2.7.*2.* It is dangerous for anyone to deny and disown *Christ before men*, for those who do so will be disowned by him *in the great day*, when they need him most. He will not acknowledge him as his servants those who would not acknowledge him as their Master: *I tell you, I know you not* (7:23).

2.2.2.8. That the foundation of their discipleship was laid in the giving to them of such a disposition as would make sufferings very light and easy to them (2Co 4:17), and it was on the condition of a readiness for suffering that Christ took them as his followers (vv. 37–39). He told them at the beginning that they were *not worthy of* him unless they were willing to part with everything for him. People do not hesitate at difficulties that are a necessary part of their work and that they counted on when they embarked on their profession. In the Christian profession, those who do not value their privileges in Christ before any other interests are reckoned unworthy of the dignity and happiness that attend such a profession. If they do not fulfill its terms, they cannot expect to benefit from it. If religious faith is worth anything, it is worth everything. Those who do not follow Christ on these terms may leave him at their peril. Whatever we part with for this pearl of

great price (13:46), we may comfort ourselves with the assurance that it is well worth what we give for it. The terms are that we must put Christ first:

2.2.2.8.*1.* Before our nearest and dearest relatives: *father or mother, son or daughter.* Children must love their parents, and parents must love their children, but if they love them more than Christ, they are unworthy of him. Just as we must not be deterred from Christ by the hatred of our relatives, which he spoke of earlier (vv. 21, 35–36), so also we must not be drawn away from him by their love.

2.2.2.8.*2.* Before our comfort and safety. We must *take up our cross* and *follow him*, for otherwise we are *not worthy* of him. Notice here:

2.2.2.8.*2.1.* Those who want to *follow Christ* must expect to *take up their cross.*

2.2.2.8.*2.2.* In taking *up the cross*, we must *follow Christ's* example, carrying it as he did.

2.2.2.8.*2.3.* When we meet with crosses, it is very encouraging to us that in bearing them we *follow Christ,* who has shown us the way, and that if we follow him faithfully, he will lead us through sufferings like his to the glory with him.

2.2.2.8.*3.* Before life itself: *He that findeth his life shall lose it* (v. 39). Those who think they have found it when they have saved it and kept it by denying Christ *shall lose it* in an eternal death, but *he that loseth his life for Christ's sake*, who will part with it rather than deny Christ, *shall find it*, to his overwhelming advantage, eternal life. Those who are best prepared for the life to come are the ones who cling least to things in this present life.

2.2.2.9. That Christ himself would so heartily embrace their cause as to show himself to be a friend to all their friends: *He that receiveth you receiveth me* (vv. 40–42).

2.2.2.9.*1.* It is implied here that although most people would reject them, they would meet with some who would receive them and welcome the message into their hearts, and who would welcome the messengers to their houses for its sake. Christ's ministers will not *labour in vain* (1Co 15:58).

2.2.2.9.*2.* Jesus Christ takes what is done to his faithful ministers, whether kindly or unkindly, as done to himself, and he considers himself treated as they are treated. *He that receiveth you receiveth me.* Notice how Christ may still be welcomed by those who want to show their respects to him; we always have his people and ministers with us (26:11), and he is *with them always*, even to the end of the world (28:20). In fact, the honor rises even higher: *He that receiveth me receiveth him that sent me.* By welcoming Christ's ministers, people do not entertain *angels unawares* (Heb 13:2), but Christ, and indeed God himself—and *unawares*, too, as is revealed in 25:37: *When saw we thee an hungered?*

2.2.2.9.*3.* Even if the kindness shown to Christ's disciples is very small, nevertheless, if there is the need for it and if there is no ability to do more, it will be accepted, even if it is only *a cup of cold water given to one of these little ones* (v. 42). Kind acts shown to Christ's disciples are valued by Christ not according to the cost of the gift, but according to the love and affection of the giver. By that reckoning, the widow's mite was not only judged authentic but also highly regarded (Lk 21:3–4). In this way, those who are truly rich in graces may be rich in good works, even though they are poor in things of this world.

2.2.2.9.*4.* The sort of kindness shown to Christ's disciples that he will accept will be that which is done with eyes toward Christ and for his sake. A prophet must be received *in the name of a prophet*, and *a righteous man* in the name of a *righteous man*, and one of those *little ones* in *the name of a disciple*, because they are righteous and so bear Christ's image. Christ does not interest himself in the matter unless we first interest him in it.

2.2.2.9.5. Kindnesses shown to Christ's people and ministers will not only be accepted but also be richly and suitably rewarded.

2.2.2.9.5.1. Those who show such kindness will *receive a reward*, and they will by no means lose it. He did not say that they *deserve a* reward; we cannot deserve anything as wages from the hand of God. But they will *receive a reward* from the free gift of God, and they will *in no wise lose it*. The reward may be delayed, but it will in no way be *lost*, nor will they be losers by the delay.

2.2.2.9.5.2. This is *a prophet's reward*, and *a righteous man's*, that is, either:

2.2.2.9.5.2.1. The reward that God gives to prophets and the righteous; the blessings given them will filter onto their friends. Or:

2.2.2.9.5.2.2. The reward he gives through prophets and the righteous, in answer to their prayers: *He is a prophet, and he shall pray for thee* (Ge 20:7); that is a prophet's reward. Prophets' rewards are spiritual blessings in heavenly things (Eph 1:3), and if we know how to value them, we will consider them good payment.

CHAPTER 11

In this chapter we have: 1. The constant and untiring diligence of our Lord Jesus (v. 1). 2. His conversation with John's disciples about whether he, Jesus, was the Messiah (vv. 2–6). 3. The honorable testimony Christ gave about John the Baptist (vv. 7–15). 4. The sad account he gave of that generation in general and of some places in particular with reference to the response received by both John's ministry and his own (vv. 16–24). 5. His thanksgiving to his Father for the wise and gracious way in which he had chosen to reveal the great mysteries of the Gospel (vv. 25–26). 6. His gracious call and invitation of poor sinners to come to him (vv. 27–30).

Verses 1–6

Some commentators attach the first verse of this chapter to the previous chapter, reading it—not inappropriately—as the close of that.

1. By way of introduction to the conversation related here, let us consider the following concerning vv. 1–2:

1.1. The ordination sermon Christ preached to his disciples in the previous chapter is called his *commanding* them here. They were not only allowed to preach the Gospel; they were also instructed to do so. *Necessity was laid upon them* (1Co 9:16).

1.2. When Christ had said what he had to say to his disciples, he *departed thence*. It seems they were very reluctant to leave their Master until *he departed* and left them alone, just as a nurse withdraws a hand so that the child may learn to walk on their own. Christ would now teach them how to live and work without his physical presence. It was *expedient for them* (Jn 16:7) that Christ go away for a while.

1.3. Christ departed *to teach and preach* in the towns to which he had sent his disciples before him to *work miracles* (10:1–8); the miracles would raise people's expectations and make way for his welcome. This was how the *way of the Lord was prepared*. When Christ empowered them to *work miracles*, he himself taught and preached, as if that were the more honorable of the two. The miracles were performed to make way for his teaching and preaching. The purpose of healing the sick was to save people physically, but preaching the Gospel was to save them spiritually. Christ had told his disciples to preach (10:7), but he did not stop preaching himself. How unlike Christ are those who put others to work so that they themselves may be idle! We should not make the increase and great number of laborers in the Lord's work an excuse for negligence, but an incentive to be conscientious. The busier others are, the busier we should be, and all that is little enough, because there is so much work to be done. He went to preach *in their cities*, which were well populated; he threw out the net of the Gospel where there were most fish to be caught.

1.4. Next is recorded a message from John the Baptist to Christ and Christ's response to it (vv. 2–6). We read before that Jesus heard about John's sufferings (4:12). We are now told that John, in prison, heard about Christ's actions. He *heard in the prison the works of Christ*, and no doubt he was glad to hear of them. Nothing is more encouraging to God's people in distress than to *hear of the works of Christ*, especially to experience them in their own souls. This turns a prison into a palace. One way or another, Christ will communicate the assurance of his love to those who are in trouble for conscience's sake. When John the Baptist heard about Christ's works, he sent two of his disciples to him, and here we have an account of what took place between them and Christ. Here is:

2. The question they asked him: *Art thou he that should come, or do we look for another?* This was a serious and important question.

2.1. It was assumed that the Messiah would come.

2.2. They indicated that if he was not the one, they would *look for another*. We must not become tired of looking for the One who is to come. Although he may be delayed, wait for him, because the One who is coming will certainly come, even though it may not be in our time.

2.3. They suggested that if they were convinced that he was the One, they would not be skeptical, but would be satisfied, and they would look *for no other*.

2.4. They therefore asked: *Art thou he?* John had said for himself, *I am not the Christ* (Jn 1:20).

2.4.1. Some think that John sent this question to satisfy himself. It is true that he had borne noble testimony to Christ; he had declared him to be the *Son of God* (Jn 1:34), *the Lamb of God* (Jn 1:29), and the One who *would baptize with the Holy Ghost* (Jn 1:33) and was *sent of God* (Jn 3:34), which were great things. However, he desired to be further and more fully assured. In matters relating to Christ and our salvation by him, it is good to be sure. Christ did not appear in that external pride and power in which it was expected he would appear; his own disciples stumbled at this point, and perhaps John did too. Christ showed that he saw something of this at the root of this question when he said, *blessed is he who shall not be offended in me*. It is hard even for good people to withstand general errors.

2.4.2. John's doubt might have arisen from his own present circumstances. He was a prisoner and might be tempted to think, "If Jesus is truly the Messiah, how is it that I, his friend and forerunner, have been brought into this trouble and been left so long in it?" No doubt there were good reasons why our Lord Jesus did not go to John in prison, but John interpreted his absence as neglect, and perhaps it greatly disturbed his faith in Christ. This shows us:

2.4.2.1. Where there is true faith, there may still be a mixture of unbelief. The best are not always equally strong.

2.4.2.2. Troubles for Christ, especially when they continue unrelieved for a long time, are tests to our faith that sometimes prove too hard to bear.

2.4.2.3. The remaining unbelief of good people may sometimes, in times of temptation, strike at the very roots of our life, calling into question the most fundamental truths, which we thought were well settled. The best saints need the best helps they can get to strengthen their faith and guard themselves against temptations to unfaithfulness.

2.4.3. Others think that John sent his disciples to Christ with this question not so much to satisfy himself as to satisfy them. Although he was a prisoner, they remained loyal to him and were with him; they loved him and refused to leave him.

2.4.3.1. They were weak in knowledge, wavering in their faith, and in need of instruction and confirmation. Here they were somewhat prejudiced; being jealous *for their* master, they were jealous *of our* Master. They were reluctant to acknowledge Jesus as the Messiah, because he surpassed John. Good people tend to have their judgments biased by their own personal interests. Now John wanted to have their mistakes put right, and he wanted them to be as satisfied as he himself was.

2.4.3.2. John had all along been diligent in turning his disciples over to Christ, as a teacher of grade school is concerned to prepare his students for college. Ministers' business is to direct everybody to Christ. Moreover, those who want to know the certainty of the teaching of Christ (Lk 1:4) must themselves turn to the One who has come to give understanding. Those who want to grow in grace must ask questions (2Pe 3:18).

3. Christ's answer to this question (vv. 4–6). It was a real and true answer. Christ wants us to spell out the convincing evidence of Gospel truths and to take pains in digging for knowledge.

3.1. He pointed them to what they heard and saw, which they must tell John. Christ refers us to the things we *hear and see*. "*Go and tell John*:

3.1.1. "What you see of the power of Christ's miracles; you see how, by the word of Jesus, *the blind receive their sight* and the *lame walk.*" Christ's miracles were done openly and in the view of all. Truth does not seek concealment. The miracles are to be considered:

3.1.1.1. As acts of a divine power. No one but the God of nature could overrule and outdo the power of nature in this way. It is especially spoken of as God's right to *open the eyes of the blind* (Ps 146:8). Miracles are therefore the authenticating seal of heaven, and the teaching that accompanies them must come from God. However much counterfeit miracles may be resorted to as proof of false teachings, true miracles are evidence of a divine commission. This is what Christ's miracles were like, and they leave no room for doubt that he was sent by God.

3.1.1.2. As the fulfillment of divine prediction. It was foretold that our God would come and that then *the eyes of the blind would be opened* (Isa 35:5–6).

3.1.2. "What you hear of the preaching of his Gospel." Although faith is confirmed by seeing, it comes by hearing (Ro 10:17). "Tell him that:

3.1.2.1. "*The poor have the Gospel preached to them.*" The Old Testament prophets were sent mostly to kings and rulers, but Christ preached to the *congregations of the poor* (Ps 74:19). Christ's gracious condescension and compassion to the poor showed that he was the One who would bring the tender mercies of our God to the world. Or, as we may understand it, he would be not so much the King of the *poor of the world* as the King of the *poor in*

spirit (5:3), and so that Scripture was fulfilled, *He hath anointed me to preach glad tidings to the meek* (Isa 61:1). Christ's mission is proved divine by the fact that his teaching is the true Gospel, good news to those who are truly humble in their self-denial; the Gospel comes to them, to those for whom God always declared he had mercy.

3.1.2.2. "The poor receive the Gospel and are persuaded by it; they receive and welcome the Gospel." The wonderful effectiveness of the Gospel proves its divine origin. The poor are persuaded by it. The Gospel of Christ made its way into their untaught minds.

3.2. He declared a *blessing* on those who *were not offended in him* (did not fall away on account of him) (v. 6). Those who are not willfully prejudiced against him — literally, "scandalized" in him — must receive his message and so be *blessed in him*. There are many things in Christ that those who are ignorant and unthinking tend to be offended by. The humbleness of his appearance, his upbringing in Nazareth, the poverty of his life, the insignificance of his followers, the insults that the leaders paid him, the strictness of his teaching, the challenge it gives to flesh and blood, and the sufferings that accompany the profession of his name: these are things that keep far away from him many people who otherwise see much of God in him. In this way, he is set *for the fall of many*, even in Israel (Lk 2:34). Those who overcome these stumbling blocks are happy. *Blessed are they.* The expression suggests that it is difficult to conquer these prejudices and dangerous not to conquer them.

Verses 7–15

Some of Christ's disciples might taken occasion from John's question to look down on him as weak and wavering, inconsistent with himself, and to prevent this, Christ characterized him in the following way. We must take every occasion, especially every occasion that reveals any weakness in others, to speak well of those who are praiseworthy. When John the Baptist was on the stage and Christ had withdrawn to private retirement, John testified to Christ; now that Christ appeared in public and John was under a cloud, he testified to John. John had denied himself to honor Christ (3:11; Jn 3:20, 30); he had made himself nothing so that Christ could be All (Col 3:11), and now Christ dignified him with this description. Those who humble themselves will be exalted (Lk 14:11), and Christ will honor those who honor him (1Sa 2:30). John had now completed his testimony, and now Christ commended him. Christ reserves honor for his servants when they *have done their work* (Jn 12:26). Notice concerning this commendation of John:

1. That Christ spoke so honorably about John not in the hearing of John's disciples, but *as they departed*, just after they had gone (Lk 7:24). He would not so much as seem to flatter John, nor would he have these commendations of him reported to him. Although we must be eager to give everyone due praise to encourage them, we must avoid everything that looks like flattery. Pride is a corrupt attitude, which we must not feed either in others or in ourselves.

2. What Christ said about John was intended not only to commend him but also to benefit the people, to revive the memory of John's ministry. "Now, consider, *what went ye out into the wilderness to see? Ask* yourselves this question."

2.1. John preached *in the wilderness*. If teachers are moved into corners, it is better to follow them than to be without them. If his preaching was worth taking so much effort over to hear, surely it was worth taking some care to remember. The greater the difficulties we have overcome to hear the word, the more we should be concerned to benefit from it.

2.2. They went out to him to see him out of curiosity rather than conscience. Many who listen to the word come to see and be seen rather than to learn and be taught, to have something to talk about rather than to be made wise to salvation (2Ti 3:15). Christ put it to them: *What went ye out to see?* We think that when the sermon is over, that is the end of the matter. No, it is then that the matter truly begins. *"What brought you thither?* Was it out of habit or for the company, or was it from a desire to honor God and gain good? *What have you brought thence?* What knowledge, grace, and comfort? *What went you to see?"*

3. The commendation itself. "Well," said Christ, "I will tell you what kind of a man John the Baptist was.

3.1. "He was firm and resolute, not *a reed shaken with the wind.* He did not waver in his principles; he was not inconsistent in his conduct." When the wind of popular applause on the one hand blew fresh and fair, when the storm of Herod's anger on the other hand grew fierce and blustering, John remained the same, calm in all kinds of weather. The testimony he had borne to Christ was not the testimony of *a reed*; it was not a fickle, changeable testimony. The people flocked to him because he was not like a reed. There is nothing lost in the long run by an unshaken resolution to continue with our work, neither seeking the smiles of others nor fearing the frowns.

3.2. "He was a self-denying man. Was he a man *clothed in soft raiment* (fine clothes)? If he had been, you would not have gone *into the wilderness* to see him, but to the court. You went to see one who had *his raiment of camel's hair* and had *a leathern girdle about his loins*; his clothing corresponded to the desert he lived in and to the doctrine he preached there, that of repentance. Now you cannot think that the one who was such a stranger to the pleasures of a court would be brought to change his mind by the terrors of a prison." Those who have lived a life of self-denial are least likely to be driven away from their religious faith by persecution. He was not clothed in fine garments; *there are* such people, but they are *in kings' houses*. It is good for people to make sure that their appearance is consistent with their character and their situation. Those who are preachers must not try to look like courtiers. Wisdom teaches us to be consistent.

3.3. His greatest commendation was his office and ministry.

3.3.1. He was *a prophet*, in fact, *more than a prophet* (v. 9). John said about himself that he was not *that prophet*, that great prophet, the Messiah himself, and now Christ — who was a very competent Judge — said about him that he was *more than a prophet.* The forerunner of Christ was not a king, but a prophet, a transcendent prophet, more than an Old Testament prophet; they *saw Christ's day* at a distance (Jn 8:56), but John saw the day dawn; he saw the sun rise (Mal 4:2). They spoke of Christ, but he pointed to him; he said: *Behold the Lamb of God!*

3.3.2. He was the same one who was predicted to be Christ's forerunner: *This is he of whom it is written* (v. 10). He was prophesied about by the other prophets and was therefore greater than they. Malachi prophesied about John: *Behold, I send my messenger* (Mal 3:1). In being made Christ's forerunner, John was greatly advanced above all the other prophets. He was *a messenger* sent on a great errand. He is *my messenger*, one sent *of God*, and he was sent before the *Son of God*. His business was to *prepare Christ's way*. He had said this about himself (Jn 1:23), and now Christ said it about him. Much of the

beauty of God's ways lies in their mutual connection and coherence and the reference they have to one another. What advanced John above the *Old Testament* prophets was that he came immediately before Christ. The nearer people are to Christ, the more truly honorable they are.

3.3.3. There *was not a greater born of women* than John the Baptist (v. 11). Christ knew how to value people according to their worth, and he raised John higher than all who went before him. John was the most eminent of all those whom God had raised up and called to any service in his church. Many had been born who were significant in the world, but Christ placed John above them. Greatness is not to be measured by outward appearances and splendor; rather, the greatest people are those who are the greatest saints and the greatest blessings, those who are, as John was, *great in the sight of the Lord* (Lk 1:15). *Notwithstanding* (yet), *he that is least in the kingdom of heaven is greater than he.* This is true in *the kingdom of heaven*, that is:

3.3.3.1. In the kingdom of *glory*. John was a *great* and *good* man, but he was still in a state of weak imperfection and therefore came short of glorified saints. There are degrees of glory in heaven, some who are less than others there; although every vessel is equally full, all are not equally large. The least saint in heaven is *greater*, knowing more, loving more, and doing more to praise God, and receiving more from him, than the greatest in this world.

3.3.3.2. In the *kingdom of grace*, which is how the *kingdom of heaven* should really be understood here, that is, in the Gospel era in the perfection of its power and purity. "He who is less" in that kingdom is *greater than John.* This should be understood to refer to the apostles and ministers of the New Testament, the evangelical prophets, and the comparison between them and John is not about their personal holiness, but about their office. John preached that Christ was coming, but they preached that Christ had not only come but also was *crucified* (1Co 2:2) and *glorified* (2Th 1:12). John came at the dawn of the Gospel day, but he was taken away before midday of that day, before the tearing of the veil (27:51), before Christ's death and resurrection and the outpouring of the Spirit. In this sense, therefore, because the least of the apostles and evangelists received greater revelations, they were employed in a greater mission and were *greater than John.* All true greatness in human beings comes from and takes its character from the gracious revelation of Christ to them. What reason we have to be thankful that our lot is cast in the days of the *kingdom of heaven*, under such advantages of light and love! However, the greater the advantages, the greater the account will be if we *receive the grace of God in vain* (2Co 6:1).

3.3.4. The great commendation of John the Baptist was that God acknowledged his ministry, making it wonderfully successful in breaking the ice and in preparing people for the *kingdom of heaven. From the days of* the first appearing of *John the Baptist* until now, *the kingdom of heaven suffereth violence*; like the violence of an army taking a city by storm or of a crowd bursting into a house, so is the *violence of those who take it by force.* Many people were persuaded by the ministry of John and became his disciples. It was:

3.3.4.1. An *improbable* multitude. Those who strove for a place in this kingdom were the ones who one would think had no right or entitlement to it and who therefore seemed to be intruders. When the *children of the kingdom* are excluded from it and many come into it *from the east and the west*, then it is forcibly entered. The tax collectors and prostitutes believed John, whom the teachers of the law and Pharisees rejected, and so these followers of John went into the kingdom of God before those leaders. It is no breach of good manners to go to heaven before our betters: it is a great commendation of the Gospel that from the days of its infancy it has brought many people to holiness who were thought to be unlikely recipients.

3.3.4.2. An *importunate* multitude. This violence denotes a strength, vigor, and fervent desire and endeavor in those who followed John's ministry. It shows us also what fervency and zeal are required of all those who intend to get to heaven through their religious faith. Those who want to *enter into the kingdom of heaven* must *strive to enter* (Lk 13:24); that kingdom suffers a holy violence; we must run, wrestle, fight, and be *in an agony*, and all is little enough to win such a prize and overcome such opposition from outside and from within us. *The violent take it by force.* Those who want to enjoy the privileges of this great salvation are carried out toward it with a strong desire. They want to have it upon any terms, they do not think the conditions are too hard, and they do not lose their grip without a blessing (Ge 32:26). The kingdom of heaven was never intended to indulge the ease of the frivolous, but to be the rest of those who work hard. Oh that we could see a greater number driving themselves into it with a holy contention!

3.3.5. The ministry of John was the *beginning of the Gospel* (Mk 1:1).

3.3.5.1. In John, the Old Testament era began to die (v. 13). The revelations of the Old Testament began to be superseded by the clearer revelation of the *kingdom of heaven* when it was *at hand* (4:17). When Christ said, *all the prophets and the law prophesied until John*, he showed us:

3.3.5.1.*1*. How the light of the Old Testament was set up; it was set up in *the law and the prophets*, who spoke, though unclearly, about Christ and his kingdom. We bless God that we have both the New Testament teaching to explain the Old Testament prophecies and the Old Testament prophecies to confirm and illustrate the New Testament teaching (Heb 1:1); like the two cherubim, they look at each other (Ex 25:20). The Scripture is teaching us to this day, though its writers have died. Moses and the prophets are dead, and the apostles and evangelists are dead (Zec 1:5), but *the word of the Lord endures for ever* (1Pe 1:25).

3.3.5.1.*2*. How this light was *laid aside*. Even before the sun rises, the morning light makes candles seem to shine dimly. Their prophecies of a Christ to come became out of date when John said: *He is come.*

3.3.5.2. In him the New Testament day began to dawn, because *this is Elias* (Elijah), *that was for to come* (v. 14). John was the link that coupled the two Testaments. The concluding prophecy of the Old Testament was, *Behold, I will send you Elijah* (Mal 4:5–6). Those words prophesied until John, and then, being turned into a history, they ceased to prophesy. Christ spoke about it as a great truth that John the Baptist was the Elijah of the New Testament, one who would come in the spirit and power of Elijah, and especially, as it was said in the prophecy, one who would *turn the hearts of the fathers to the children* (Lk 1:17). Christ surmised the kind of welcome this truth would receive: *if ye will receive it.* He was not implying that its truth depended in any way on whether they accepted it or not, but he rebuked them for their prejudices. Or, "If *you will receive him*, or if you will accept the ministry of John as that of the promised Elijah, he will be an Elijah to you, to turn you back to and to prepare you for the Lord." Christ is a Savior, and John an Elijah, to those who will

accept the truth about them. Our Lord Jesus closed this conversation with a solemn call to attention (v. 15): *He that hath ears to hear, let him hear.* This suggests that the things he had said were hidden and hard to understand (2Pe 3:16) and therefore needed attention, but were also of great concern and importance and therefore well deserved attention. The things of God are of great and common concern: everyone who has *ears to hear* anything should be concerned to listen to this. It also suggests that God requires no more from us than the right use of the faculties he has already given us. He requires those who have ears to hear. They do not hear because, like the deaf adder, they *stop their ears* (Ps 58:4).

Verses 16–24

Christ was continuing with the praise of John the Baptist and his ministry, but he suddenly stopped here, turning from that to rebuke those who had enjoyed both John's ministry and that of Christ and his apostles in vain. As to that generation, we may observe *to* whom he compares them (vv. 16–19), and as to the particular places he cites, we may observe *with* whom he compares them (vv. 20–24).

1. As to that *generation*, most continued in unbelief and obstinacy. John was a great and good man, but the generation in which he lived was very barren and unprofitable and unworthy of him (Heb 11:38). The badness of the places where good ministers live serves to contrast their beauty. Having commended John, Christ condemned those who had him among them but did not gain from his ministry. Our Lord Jesus set this out here in a parable: *Whereunto shall I liken this generation?* The comparison is taken from some common custom among Jewish children at play, who, as is usual with children, imitated the fashions of adults at their marriages and funerals, *rejoicing* and *lamenting*, but made fun of those practices and were no more impressed by them than the people of John the Baptist's generation were by either John's or Christ's ministry. The parable will be best explained if we examine it and its illustration in these five observations:

1.1. The God of heaven uses a variety of appropriate ways and means for the conversion and salvation of poor souls; the One who wants *all men to be saved* (1Ti 2:4) leaves no stone unturned in order to accomplish that. In the parable, this is called his *piping* and *mourning* to us; he has *piped to us* in the precious promises of the Gospel, which are appropriate to produce hope, and mourned to us in the dreadful threats of the Law, which are appropriate to produce fear. He has *piped to us* in gracious and merciful providences and *mourned to us* in calamitous, afflicting providences. In the explanation of the parable the various themes of John's ministry and of Christ's are set out.

1.1.1. On the one hand, John came *mourning to them, neither eating nor drinking*. Now one would have thought that this would have had an effect on them, for such an austere life of self-denial was very consistent with his teaching, and a minister whose way of life is consistent with his teaching is most likely to do good; but the preaching of even such a minister is not always effective.

1.1.2. On the other hand, *the Son of man came eating and drinking*, and so he could be said to have *gained unto them*. Christ had close relationships with many kinds of people, not showing any special strictness or austerity. Those who were not awed by the frowns of John might be attracted by the smiles of Christ, from whom the apostle Paul learned to become *all things to all men* (1Co 9:22). There may *be a great diversity of operations* even though *it is the same God that worketh all in all* (1Co 12:6), and these *various manifestations of the Spirit are given to every man to profit withal* (for the common good) (1Co 12:7). Notice especially that God's ministers are given various gifts. Some are Boanerges, "sons of thunder"; others, Barnabases, "sons of encouragement"; yet *all these worketh that one and the self-same Spirit* (that is, one and the same Spirit works all these [gifts]) (1Co 12:11), and so we should not condemn either, but praise both and praise God for both.

1.2. The various ways God uses for the conversion of sinners are fruitless and ineffective with many: *"Ye have not danced, ye have not lamented."* Now, if people will neither be awakened by the greatest things nor attracted by the sweetest things, they will not be startled by the most terrible things or woken up by the clearest things. If they will not listen to the voice of Scripture, reason, experience, providence, conscience, or interest, what more can be done? Faithful ministers who see small success from their labors can take encouragement from the realization that it is nothing new for the best preachers and the best preaching in the world to come short of the desired purpose. *Who has believed our report?* (Isa 53:1).

1.3. Usually those people who do not profit by the means of grace are corrupt. They do all the harm they can to others by raising and spreading prejudice against the word and its faithful preachers. This is what this generation did; because they were determined not to believe Christ and John, they set themselves to abuse them and represent them as the worst.

1.3.1. As for John the Baptist, they said, *He has a devil.* They attributed his strict and reserved nature to depression and some kind of satanic possession.

1.3.2. As for Jesus Christ, they attributed his free and pleasant way of life to self-indulgence: *Behold a gluttonous man and a wine-bibber.* No reflection could be more corrupt and invidious, yet none could be more false and unjust, for Christ *pleased not himself* (Ro 15:3), nor did anyone ever live such a life of self-denial and contempt for the world as he lived. The clearest innocence and the most unparalleled excellence will not always serve as protection against people's harsh words; in fact, a person's best gifts and actions may be turned into a reason to reproach them. Our best actions may be used against us in the worst accusations. It was true in some sense that Christ was *a Friend to publicans and sinners,* the best Friend they ever had, for he *came into the world to save sinners* (1Ti 1:15); yet this is and will be to eternity a reason to praise him, and those who turned it into a reason for reproach lost the right to benefit from it.

1.4. The cause of this great unfruitfulness and perverseness of people under the means of grace is that they are *like children sitting in the markets* (v. 16), foolish and naughty, mindless and playful; if only they would *show themselves men* in understanding (1Co 14:20), there would be some hope for them. *The market place they sit in* is to some a place of idleness (20:3), while it is a place of worldly business to others (Jas 4:13); it is a place of noise or diversion to all. Their heads, hands, and hearts are full of worldly cares, which *choke the word* (Mt 13:22) and ultimately choke their souls. And so they sit around in the marketplaces; their hearts rest in these things, and they have resolved to keep close to them.

1.5. Although the means of grace are insulted and abused by many—in fact by most—there is nevertheless a remnant who through grace make use of them. *But wisdom is justified of her children* (proved right by her actions) (v. 19). Christ *is* Wisdom (1Co 1:24, 30); in him *are hid treasures of wisdom* (Col 2:3). The Gospel is wis-

dom; it is *the wisdom from above* (Jas 3:17). True believers are born again by it, and also born from above (Jn 3:3, where the phrase translated "born again" also means "born from above" [Ed.]); they are wise *children.* These *children of wisdom justify wisdom;* they comply with the intentions of Christ's grace. *The publicans justified God, being baptized with the baptism of John* and afterward embracing the Gospel of Christ. Paul is *not ashamed of the Gospel of Christ,* because, whatever it is to others, *to them that believe it is the power of God unto salvation* (Ro 1:16). When *the cross of Christ,* which to others is *foolishness* and *a stumbling block, is to them that are called the wisdom of God and the power of God* (1Co 1:23–24), here *wisdom is justified by her children.* If the unbelief of some brings reproach to Christ by accusing him of lying, the faith of others will honor him by setting a seal to the affirmation that he is true and that *he also is wise* (1Co 1:25). Whether we justify him or not, he will be justified (Ps 51:4; Ro 3:4). That *generation is not passed away,* but is succeeded by similar ones, for as it was then, so it has been since and still is: *some believe the things which are spoken, and some believe not* (Ac 28:24).

2. As to the specific places in which Christ was best known, it is said that *then began he to upbraid* (denounce) *them* (v. 20). He began to preach to them long before (4:17), but he did not *begin to upbraid* till now. Rough and unpleasant methods must not be used until gentler means have been used first. Christ is not inclined *to upbraid.* *Wisdom* first invites, but when her invitations are turned down, she then *upbraids* (Pr 1:20, 24). Those who begin with finding fault do not follow Christ's method. Notice:

2.1. The sin they are accused of: the most shameful, unpleasant thing possible, that *they repented not.* Willful impenitence is the great condemning sin of many people who enjoy the Gospel. The great doctrine that John the Baptist, Christ, and the apostles preached was repentance; the great intention in both the *piping* and the *mourning* was to persuade people to change their minds and ways, to leave their sins and turn back to God, but they would not be brought to this. Christ rebuked them for their other sins in order to *lead them to repentance,* but when *they repented not, he upbraided them* for it, so that they would rebuke themselves, finally having seen that the folly of their ways was what alone made their sad case desperate and the wound incurable.

2.2. The emphasizing of the sin: they were *the cities in which most of his mighty works were done.* They should have been persuaded by Christ's *mighty works* not only to receive his teaching but also to obey his law; the healing of physical diseases should have led to the healing of their souls. But it did not have that effect. The stronger incentives we have to repent, the more dreadful is the impenitence and the more severe will the judgment be.

2.2.1. Korazin and Bethsaida are given here as examples (vv. 21–22); each had its woe: *Woe unto thee, Chorazin, woe unto thee, Bethsaida.* Christ came *into the world to bless us,* but if that blessing is scorned, he has woes in reserve, and his woes are the most terrible. These two cities were rich and well-populated places; Bethsaida had then recently been advanced to a city by Philip the tetrarch; Christ took at least three of his apostles from it: these places were highly favored! Soon after this they decayed and dwindled into mean, obscure villages. So fatal is the effect of sin on cities, and so certainly does the word of Christ take place! Christ here compared these two cities with Tyre and Sidon to convince and humble them, showing them:

2.2.1.1. That Tyre and Sidon would not have been as bad as Korazin and Bethsaida. If they had had the same word preached and the same miracles performed among them, *they would have repented*, and *long ago*, too, as Nineveh did, in *sackcloth and ashes* (Jnh 3:6). Christ, who knows the heart of everyone, knew that if he had gone and lived and preached in Tyre and Sidon, he would have done more good there than where he was. Nevertheless, he continued where he was for some time, to encourage his ministers to do so even if they did not see the success they desired. Our repentance is slow and delayed, but theirs would have been speedy; they would have repented long ago. Ours has been slight and superficial; theirs would have been deep and serious, in *sackcloth and ashes*.

2.2.1.2. That therefore Tyre and Sidon will not be so miserable as Korazin and Bethsaida; rather, it will be *more tolerable* for them in the *day of judgment* (v. 22). In that judgment, all the means of grace that were enjoyed in the state of testing in this life will certainly be brought into account, and it will be asked not only how bad we were but also how much better we might have been. If self-reproach is the torture of hell, it must truly be hell to those who had such a fair opportunity of reaching heaven.

2.2.2. Capernaum is emphatically condemned here (v. 23). *And thou, Capernaum*. Christ's miracles here were *daily bread* (6:11) and so, like the manna in former times, were despised and called *light bread* (Nu 21:5). Christ had read them many sweet and encouraging messages of grace, but with little result, and so he read out to them a fearful message of wrath. Here we have Capernaum's doom:

2.2.2.1. Expressed absolutely: You *which are exalted to heaven shalt be brought down to hell* (to the depths). Those who enjoy the Gospel in power and purity are *exalted to heaven*; they are lifted up *toward heaven*. If, however, they *cleave to the earth* despite that, they have only themselves to blame that they are not lifted up *into heaven*. Our external privileges will be so far from saving us that if our hearts and lives are inconsistent with them, they will only inflame the judgment: the higher the precipice, the more fatal is the fall from it.

2.2.2.2. Compared with the fate of Sodom. Christ tells us that Capernaum's means would have saved Sodom. If these miracles had been done among the Sodomites, bad as they were, they would have repented, and *their city would have remained unto this day* a memorial of sparing mercy. When there is true repentance through Christ, even the greatest sin will be pardoned and the greatest ruin prevented. *It shall be more tolerable for the land of Sodom than for that city.*

Verses 25–30

1. Christ gives thanks to God here for his favor to those *babes* who had the mysteries of the Gospel *revealed to them* (vv. 25–26). *Jesus answered and said*. It is called an answer because it is such an encouraging reply to the preceding sad thoughts. He refreshes himself with this thought, and to make it even more refreshing, he expresses it as a thanksgiving. We may take great encouragement in looking upward to God when all around us we see only discouragements. *Jesus answered and said, I thank thee*. Thanksgiving is a proper response to dark and disturbing thoughts and may be an effective means of silencing them. Songs of praise are sovereign comforts to drooping souls. When we have no other answer ready in response to suggestions of grief and fear, we may fall back on this: *I thank thee, O Father*; let us bless God that it is not worse with us than it is. Notice in this thanksgiving:

1.1. The titles Christ gives to God: *O Father, Lord of heaven and earth*. Whenever we approach God, in praise as well as in prayer, it is good for us to consider him as a Father. Mercies are doubly sweet and effective in releasing the heart in praise when they are received as signs of a Father's love. It is good for children to be grateful, to say, *Thank you, father*, as readily as, *Pray* (Please), *father*. When we come to God as a Father, we must also remember that he is *Lord of heaven and earth*. Remembering this makes us come to him with reverence but also with confidence, as One who is able to defend us from all evil and to provide us with all good.

1.2. What he gives thanks for: *Because thou hast hid these things from the wise and prudent, and* yet *revealed them to babes*. These *things*: the things that belong to our peace (Lk 19:42). This shows us:

1.2.1. The great things of the eternal Gospel have been and are hidden from many who were *wise and prudent* (learned), who were eminent in learning and worldly knowledge. *The world by wisdom knew not God* (1Co 1:21). People may dig deeply into the mysteries of nature and the intricacies of politics but remain ignorant of and mistaken about the mysteries of *the kingdom of heaven* for lack of experience of their power.

1.2.2. While *the wise and prudent* of the world are in the dark about Gospel mysteries, even the *babes in Christ* have the sanctifying, saving knowledge of them: *Thou hast revealed them unto babes* (little children). The learned in the world were not chosen to be the preachers of the Gospel; to this task *the foolish things of the world* were appointed (1Co 2:6, 8, 10).

1.2.3. This distinction between *the prudent* and *the babes* is by God's own choice. He is the One who has *hid these things from the wise and prudent* (learned); he gave them talents, learning, and much more human understanding than others, and they were proud of that, put their confidence in that, and looked no further. If they had honored God with the wisdom and learning they had, he would have given them the knowledge of these better things. He is the One who has *revealed them unto babes*. This is how *he resists the proud* and *gives grace to the humble* (Jas 4:6).

1.2.4. This dispensation must be considered in the light of divine sovereignty. Christ himself referred it to that: *Even so, Father, for so it seemed good in thy sight*. Christ here submits to the will of his Father in this matter: *Even so*. God may take whatever way he wishes to glorify himself. We can give no reason why Peter, a fisherman, should be made an apostle, but not Nicodemus, a Pharisee and a ruler of the Jews, even though he also believed in Christ—no reason except that *so it seemed good in God's sight*.

1.2.5. This way of giving divine grace is to be acknowledged by us with great thankfulness. We must thank God that *these things* are *revealed*, that they are *revealed to babes*, and that this honor is given to those whom the world shows contempt to. The mercy shown them is exalted in that *these things* are *hid from the wise and prudent*, and in this way divine power and wisdom are also caused to shine more brightly. See 1Co 1:27, 31.

2. Christ makes a gracious offer of the benefits of the Gospel to everyone here. Here is:

2.1. The solemn introduction that ushers in this call or invitation. Christ introduces his authority; he produces his credentials. He here lays two things before us (v. 27):

2.1.1. His commission from the Father: *All things are delivered unto me of* (have been committed to me by) *my Father* (v. 27). He is authorized to establish a new covenant between God and human beings and to offer peace and happiness to the apostate world on such terms as he thinks fit. We are encouraged to come to Christ by knowing that he is commissioned to receive us and give us what we come for and has all things committed to him for that purpose by the One who is *Lord of all*. All powers, all treasures, are in his hand. God has made him the great Mediator and Referee to place his hand on us both (Job 9:33); what we have to do is to submit to his arbitration in this unhappy disagreement and bind ourselves ahead of time to accept his judgment.

2.1.2. His intimacy with the Father: *No man knoweth the Son but the Father, neither knoweth any man the Father save* (except) *the Son*. It must be a great encouragement to us to be assured that they understood one another intimately in this matter: that the Father knew the Son, and the Son knew the Father, and both perfectly, so that there could be no mistake in establishing this matter, as there often is among people, with the result that contracts are canceled or promises gone back on because of misunderstanding between the parties. *None knows the Father save the Son*—and he adds, *and he to whom the Son will reveal him*. The happiness of people lies in knowing God; it *is life eternal* (Jn 17:3). Those who want to know God must turn to Jesus Christ, for the light of the knowledge of the glory of God shines in the face of Christ (2Co 4:6).

2.2. The offer itself that is made to us, with an invitation to accept it. We are invited here to come to Christ to be saved. He is our Priest, Prince, and Prophet.

2.2.1. We must come to Jesus Christ as our Rest, and we must depend on him: *Come unto me all ye that labour* (v. 28). Notice:

2.2.1.1. The description of the people invited: *all that labour, and are heavy laden* (who are weary and burdened). This is a word in season to someone who is weary (Isa 50:4). It is best understood as referring to the burden of sin, of both its guilt and power. All those, and only those, who are aware of sin as a burden and groan under it are invited to rest in Christ; they are not only convinced of the evil of sin, of their own sin, but also contrite in their soul about it. They are fed up with their sins. This is a necessary preparation for pardon and peace. The Comforter must first convict (Jn 16:8).

2.2.1.2. The invitation itself: *Come unto me*. See here how he holds out *the golden sceptre*, that we may touch the top of it and live (Est 5:2). It is the duty and the privilege of weary and burdened sinners to *come to Jesus Christ*. We must accept him as our Physician (9:12) and Advocate (1Jn 2:1), freely willing to be saved by him in his own way and on his own terms.

2.2.1.3. The blessing promised to those who do come: *I will give you rest*. Truly *rest is good* (Ge 49:15), especially to those *that labour and are heavy laden* (Ecc 5:12). Jesus Christ will give assured rest to those weary souls who come to him for it with a living faith. He gives *rest* in God, in his love.

2.2.2. We must come to Jesus Christ as our Ruler and submit to him: *Take my yoke upon you* (v. 29). The *rest* he promises is a release from the drudgery of sin, not from the service of God. Christ has *a yoke* for our necks as well as *a crown* for our heads (2Ti 4:8; Jas 1:12; 1Pe 5:4; Rev 2:10). To call those who are weary *and heavy laden* to *take a yoke upon* them looks like adding *affliction to the afflicted* (Ps 22:24; Php 1:16), but its significance lies in the word *my*: "You are under *a yoke* that makes you weary: shake off that yoke and try mine, which will give you rest." It is Christ's *yoke*, the *yoke* he has appointed, *a yoke* that he has himself taken on before us—*for he*

learned obedience (Heb 5:8)—and that he takes on with us through his Spirit, for *he helpeth our infirmities* (Ro 8:26). *A yoke* speaks of some hardship, but if the animal must draw, the *yoke* helps it. This is the hardest part of our lesson, and so it is qualified: "*My yoke is easy, and my burden is light* (v. 30); you need not be afraid of it." The *yoke* of Christ's commands is an *easy yoke*. There is nothing in it to make the submitting neck sore, nothing to harm us, but, on the contrary, much to refresh us. It is *a yoke* that is lined with love. Such is the nature of all Christ's commands, all summed up in one word, the sweet word *love*. It may be a little hard at first, but it soon becomes easy; the love of God and the hope of heaven will make it *easy*. The *burden* of Christ's cross is *a light burden*, very light. This *burden* in itself is *not joyous, but grievous* (Heb 12:11), but because it is Christ's, it is *light*. Paul knew as much about it as anyone, and he calls it a *light affliction* (2Co 4:17). Just as there is much suffering, and it lasts long, so there are also many encouragements, which also last long.

2.2.3. We must come to Jesus Christ as our Teacher and set ourselves to learn from him (v. 29). Christ has set up a good school, and he has invited us to be his students. We must enroll in his school, associate with our fellow students, and daily listen to the instructions he gives by his word and Spirit. We must so *learn of Christ* as to *learn Christ* (Eph 4:20), for he is both Teacher and Lesson, Guide and Way, and All in All (Eph 1:23; Col 3:11). Two reasons are given here why we must *learn of Christ*:

2.2.3.1. *I am meek and lowly in heart*. He *is meek*. He can have *compassion on the ignorant*. Many able teachers are impassioned and hasty, which is a great discouragement to those who are slow to learn, but Christ knows how to bear gently with such people and how to open up their understandings (Lk 24:32, 45). *He is lowly in heart*. He condescends to teach poor students, to teach his novice pupils. He teaches the basic principles, things that are like milk for babes; he stoops down to the lowliest level. His lowliness of heart is an encouragement to us to put ourselves in his school.

2.2.3.2. *You shall find rest to your souls*. Rest for the soul is the most desirable rest. The only sure way to find *rest for our souls* is to sit at Christ's feet and listen to his word. The understanding finds *rest* in the knowledge of God and Jesus Christ and is abundantly satisfied there. The emotions find rest in the love of God and Jesus Christ and enjoy in them what gives them abundant satisfaction: quietness and assurance forever. This rest is to be enjoyed with Christ by all those who learn from him.

CHAPTER 12

We have here: 1. Christ's clarifying the fourth commandment, about the Sabbath (vv. 1–13). 2. The wisdom, humility, and self-denial of our Lord Jesus in performing his miracles (vv. 14–21). 3. Christ's answer to the objections of the teachers of the law and Pharisees, who attributed his driving out of demons to a pact with the Devil (vv. 22–37). 4. Christ's reply to a demand of the teachers of the law and Pharisees, challenging him to show them a sign from heaven (vv. 38–45). 5. Christ's judgment about his family and relatives (vv. 46–50).

Verses 1–13

The Jewish teachers had corrupted many of the commandments by interpreting them more loosely than they were intended to be interpreted, but concerning the fourth commandment, they had erred to the opposite extreme and interpreted it too strictly. Now what our Lord Jesus laid down here was that the works of necessity and mercy are lawful on the Sabbath. It is usual to establish the meaning of a law by judgments given on actual cases, and that was how the meaning of this law was settled.

1. Christ showed that *works of necessity* are *lawful* on that day by justifying his disciples in picking heads of grain on the Sabbath. Notice here:

1.1. What the disciples did. They were following their Master through a grainfield one Sabbath, and *they were hungry*. Providence so ordered it that they *went through the corn* (grain), and there they were provided for. God has many ways of providing suitably for his people when they need it. Being in the grainfields, they began to *pluck the ears of corn*; the Law of God allowed this (Dt 23:25), to teach people to be neighborly and not insist on ownership of property in small matters where others may benefit. This was only a slender provision for Christ and his disciples, but it was the best they had, and they were content with it.

1.2. What offense the Pharisees took at this. It was only a dry breakfast, but the Pharisees would not allow them to eat that in peace. They did not quarrel with them for taking another person's grain, but for doing it *on the sabbath day*, for picking and hulling heads of grain on that day was expressly forbidden by the tradition of the elders, because they considered it a kind of reaping.

1.3. Christ's response to this objection of the Pharisees. The disciples could say little for themselves. However, Christ had something to say for them, and he justified what they did.

1.3.1. He justified them from precedents, which were allowed as good by the Pharisees themselves.

1.3.1.1. He urged an old example of David: "*Have ye not read* the story (1Sa 21:6) of David's eating the consecrated bread, which under the Law belonged to the priest?" What supported David in eating the consecrated bread was not his position but his hunger. The greatest people will not have their sinful desires indulged, but the lowliest will have their needs considered. Something may be done in a case of necessity that may not be done at another time; there are laws that necessity does not know, but it is a law to itself.

1.3.1.2. He urged a daily case of the priests, which they likewise *read in the law. The priests in the temple* did a great deal of menial work on the Sabbath day—which otherwise would *have been profaning the sabbath*—because the temple service required and justified it. This shows that those labors that are necessary not only to support life but also to serve the day, such as ringing a bell to call the congregation together, traveling to church, and similar actions, are lawful on the Sabbath day. Sabbath rest is to further, not hinder, Sabbath worship.

1.3.2. He justified them with forceful arguments:

1.3.2.1. *In this place is one greater than the temple* (v. 6). If the temple service would justify what the priests did in their ministry, the service of Christ would much more justify the disciples in what they did while with him. Christ, however, in a grainfield, was *greater than the temple*.

1.3.2.2. *God will have mercy and not sacrifice* (v. 7). This is quoted from Hos 6:6. It was used before to justify mercy to people's souls (9:13), and here it justifies mercy to people's bodies. The rest of the Sabbath was ordained for people's good. "*If you had known what this means,* had known what it is to have a merciful attitude, you would have been sorry that they were forced to do this to satisfy their hunger and would *not have condemned*

the guiltless." This shows us it is not enough for us to know the Scriptures; we must also work hard to *know the meaning* of them. *Let him that readeth understand* (Mk 13:14). Ignorance of the meaning of the Scriptures is especially shameful in those who take on the task of teaching others.

1.3.2.3. *The Son of man is Lord even of the sabbath day* (v. 8). That law, like all the others, was put into the hands of Christ to be altered, enforced, or dispensed with as he saw fit. He was authorized to alter that day in such a way that it would become the Lord's Day, the day of the Lord Jesus Christ.

1.4. After Christ had silenced the Pharisees and gotten clear of them (v. 9), he *departed* and *went into their synagogue*, the one in which these Pharisees presided and toward which he was going when they picked this quarrel with him. We can learn from this:

1.4.1. We must make sure we do nothing on our way to services of worship that makes us unfit for them or diverts us from our proper attendance at them.

1.4.2. We must not draw back from public worship for the sake of private feuds and personal quarrels. Satan wins a victory if by sowing discord among brothers and sisters (Pr 6:14, 19) he succeeds in driving them, or any of them, out of the synagogue and the fellowship of the faithful.

2. Christ showed that works of mercy are lawful and proper to be done on that day by *healing the man that had the withered hand on the sabbath day*. Here is:

2.1. The suffering of this poor man. Notice that he was in the synagogue: those who can do little for themselves, such as the aged or infirm, and those who have little to do with it, such as the rich, must do all the more for their souls.

2.2. A spiteful question that the Pharisees put to Christ at the sight of this man: *They asked him, saying, Is it lawful to heal?* We do not read here of any words this poor man spoke to Christ to ask for healing, but they noticed that Christ had seen him, and they knew it was usual for him to be *found of those that sought him not* (Isa 65:1), and so with their badness they anticipated his goodness. Did anyone ever ask whether it is lawful for God to heal, to send his word and heal? *Is it lawful to heal?* To inquire into the lawfulness and unlawfulness of actions is very good, and we cannot turn to anyone with such questions more appropriately than to Christ; the Pharisees, however, asked here not so that they would be instructed by him but so *that they might accuse him*.

2.3. Christ's answer to this question, in which he appealed to their own opinion and practice (vv. 11–12). If *a sheep* were to fall into a pit on the Sabbath, *would they not lift it out?* No doubt they could do it; the fourth commandment allows it. They must do it, for a *merciful man regardeth the life of his beast* (Pr 12:10). And on their part, they would do it, rather than lose a sheep. Does Christ take care of sheep? Yes, he does; he preserves and provides for both people and animals. Here, however, he said for our sakes (1Co 9:9–10)—and argued from it—*How much then is a man better than a sheep?* Human beings are inherently much better and more valuable than the best of the animals. Those who are more concerned for the education, preservation, and supply of their horses and dogs than of God's poor, or perhaps their own household, do not consider this. Christ deduced from this the truth that *it is lawful to do well on the sabbath days*; they had asked, *Is it lawful to heal?* Christ proved that it is lawful to *do well*. There are more ways of *doing well* on Sabbaths than by the direct duty of worshiping God:

looking after the sick, relieving the poor, and so on; this is *doing good*. All such work must be done from a motive of love and kindness; this is *doing well*, and it *shall be accepted* (Ge 4:7).

2.4. Christ's healing of the man despite the offense that he foresaw the Pharisees would take at it (v. 13). Duty is not to be left undone, nor opportunities of doing good neglected, for fear of giving offense. Christ said to the man, "*Stretch forth thy hand*; exert yourself as much as you can"; and the man did so, *and it was restored whole*. In order to heal us, Christ commands us to *stretch forth our hands*, to use our natural powers and do as much as we can, to stretch them out in prayer to God, to stretch them out to take hold of Christ by faith, to stretch them out in holy activities. This man could not stretch out his shriveled hand by himself, but Christ told him to do it. God's commands to us to do the duty that by ourselves we are unable to do are no more absurd or unjust than this command to the man with the shriveled hand *to stretch it forth*, because with the command there is a promise of grace given by the word.

Verses 14–21

We have here:

1. The cursed hatred of the Pharisees toward Christ (v. 14). Because they were angry at the convincing evidence of his miracles, they *went out, and held a council against him, how they might destroy him*. What angered them was not only that by his miracles his honor overshadowed theirs but also that the doctrine he preached was directly opposed to their pride, hypocrisy, and worldly interests. They pretended, however, to be displeased at his breaking the regulations of the Sabbath, which was a capital offense according to the law (Ex 35:2). They plotted not to imprison or banish him but to destroy him, to be the death of the One who came *that we might have life* (Jn 10:10). What an indignity our Lord Jesus was subjected to, that they pursued him as an outlaw and as the plague of his country when in fact he was the country's greatest blessing, the Glory of his people Israel (Lk 2:32)!

2. Christ's leaving on this occasion, and the privacy he chose, in order to decline not his work but his danger; because *his hour was not yet come* (v. 15), *he withdrew himself from thence*. He could have protected himself by a miracle, but he chose to do it in the ordinary way of escape and withdrawal. Here he humbled himself, by being driven to the common flight of those who are most helpless; here also he wanted to give an example of his own rule: *When they persecute you in one city, flee to another* (10:23).

2.1. Christ did not withdraw for his own comfort or seek an excuse to leave his work. Even when he was forced to flee, he continued to do good. Here he gave an example to his ministers, to do what they can when they cannot do what they want. The common people crowded after him; *great multitudes followed him* and found him. But it was really to his honor. Similarly, it was to the honor of his grace that the poor were evangelized (Lk 4:18), that when they received him, he received them and healed them all. Christ came into the world to be the Physician of the world, as the sun is the source of light to the world, *with healing in his wings* (Mal 4:2). Although the Pharisees persecuted Christ for doing good, he still continued doing it.

2.2. Christ sought to reconcile usefulness and privacy. He *healed them all*, but he also *charged them that they should not make him known* (v. 16). This was an act of wisdom. It was not so much the miracles themselves as the public discussions about them that enraged the Pharisees (vv. 23–24), so although Christ would not abandon doing good, he wisely took care to do it as quietly as possible. Wise and good people aim at God's acceptance, not human applause. Christ's withdrawal was also an act of righteous judgment on the Pharisees. By closing their eyes to the light, they had lost the right to benefit from it. Finally, his withdrawal was an act of humility and self-denial, to set us an example of humility and teach us not to make known our own goodness or usefulness or want to have it made known. Christ wanted his disciples to be the reverse of those who did all their works *to be seen of men* (6:5).

3. The fulfilling of the Scriptures in all this (v. 17). The Scripture said to be fulfilled here is Isa 42:1–4, which is quoted in detail (vv. 18–21). Its scope is to show how mild and quiet, and yet also how successful, our Lord Jesus would be in his undertaking. Notice:

3.1. The delight of the Father in Christ: *Behold my Servant, whom I have chosen; my Beloved, in whom my soul is well pleased* (v. 18). We may learn from this:

3.1.1. That our Savior was God's Servant in the great work of our redemption. As *a Servant*, he had a great work appointed for him and a great trust rested in him. In the work of our salvation he took on himself the form of a servant (Php 2:7). The motto of this Prince is, "I serve."

3.1.2. That Jesus Christ was chosen by God as the only fit and proper person to manage the great work of our redemption. He is *my Servant, whom I have chosen*. No one but him was able to fulfill the Redeemer's work or fit to wear the Redeemer's crown. Christ did not thrust himself into this work, but was fittingly chosen for it.

3.1.3. That Jesus Christ is God's Beloved, his beloved Son.

3.1.4. That Jesus Christ is the One in whom the Father is pleased. Moreover, he is well pleased with us in him, for he has *made us accepted in the Beloved* (Eph 1:6). All the privileges that fallen humanity have or can have in God are based on and owing to God's *well-pleasedness* in Jesus Christ.

3.2. The promise of the Father to him in two things.

3.2.1. That he would be well qualified for his undertaking in every way: *I will put my Spirit upon him*, as a Spirit of *wisdom and counsel* (Isa 11:2–3). Those whom God calls to any service will surely be fitted and qualified by him for it. He received the Spirit not in a limited way but *without measure* (Jn 3:34). Whomever God has chosen, whomever he is well pleased with, he will be sure to *put his Spirit upon*. Wherever he gives his love, he also gives something of his likeness.

3.2.2. That he would be abundantly successful in his undertaking. Those whom God sends he will certainly acknowledge.

3.2.2.1. He *shall show judgment to the Gentiles* (proclaim justice to the nations). In his own person, Christ preached to those who bordered on the nations (see Mk 3:6–8), and through his apostle, the apostle Paul, he revealed his Gospel, called here his *judgment*, to the Gentile world. The Gospel, since it has a direct tendency to reform human hearts and lives, would be declared to the Gentiles.

3.2.2.2. *In his name shall the Gentiles trust* (the nations will put their hope) (v. 21). He would proclaim justice to them in such a way that they would heed what he declared to them and be influenced by it to depend on him. The great purpose of the Gospel is to bring people to trust in the name of Jesus Christ, in his name *Jesus*, "Savior." The Evangelist here follows the Septuagint (a Greek version of the Old Testament)—or perhaps the later editions of the Septuagint follow the Evangelist; the Hebrew of Isa 42:4 is translated, *The isles shall wait for his law.* The law we wait for is the law of faith, the law of trusting in his name. This is now his great commandment, that we *believe in Christ* (1Jn 3:23).

3.3. The prediction about him, describing his mild and quiet management of his work (vv. 19–20).

3.3.1. That he would carry on his work quietly and without ostentation: *He shall not strive* (quarrel) *or make an outcry.* Christ and his kingdom *come not with observation* (Lk 17:20–21). He *was in the world, and the world knew him not* (Jn 1:10). He spoke in a still small voice (1Ki 19:22), which was attractive to everyone but terrifying to no one; he did not seek to make a noise, but came down silently, like dew (Dt 32:2; Hos 14:5).

3.3.2. That he would carry on his undertaking without severity and rigor: *A bruised reed shall he not break* (v. 20). Some understand this as referring to his patience in bearing with evildoers. Others prefer to understand it as referring to his power and grace in supporting the weak. In general, the intention of his Gospel is to establish a way of salvation that encourages sincerity, even though there is much imperfection. It does not insist on a sinless obedience, but accepts an upright, willing heart. As to particular individuals who follow Christ, notice:

3.3.2.1. How they are described—they are like *a bruised reed* and *smoking flax.* Young beginners in religious faith are weak as a bruised reed, and their weakness is offensive, like smoking flax. Christ's disciples were still very weak, and many are so who are in his family.

3.3.2.2. The compassion of our Lord Jesus toward them. He will not discourage them, much less reject them; the reed that is bruised will not be broken and trodden down, but will be supported and made as strong as a cedar or flourishing palm tree (Ps 92:12). The candle that is newly lit, even though it only smokes and does not burst into flame, will not be blown out, but fanned into flame. The *day of small things* is the day *of precious* things (Zec 4:10).

3.3.2.3. The good outcome and success of this, shown in the clause *till he send forth judgment unto* (leads justice to) *victory.* Both the preaching of the Gospel in the world and the power of the Gospel in the heart will be effective. Grace will gain the upper hand over corruption and ultimately be perfected in glory. Truth and victory are much the same, for *great is the truth, and will prevail* (1 Esd 4:41).

Verses 22–37

In these verses we have:

1. Christ's glorious conquest of Satan in the gracious healing of one under his power.

1.1. The man's life was very sad; he was demon-possessed. This poor man who was possessed was blind and mute, a truly miserable case. He could neither see to help himself nor speak to others to ask for help. Satan blinds the eye of faith and seals the lips of prayer.

1.2. Christ's healing was very strange, and all the more so because it was sudden: *he healed him.* When the cause is removed, immediately the effect ceases; the *blind and dumb both spake and saw.* When Satan's power is broken in the soul, the eyes are opened to see God's glory and the lips are opened to speak his praise.

2. The conviction this caused in the people, in *all the people:* they *were amazed.* They concluded from this, "*Is not this the Son of David?*" We may take this:

2.1. As an *inquiring* question. They started with a good question, but it seems it was soon lost and was not pur-

sued. Such convictions should be brought to a head, and then they are likely to be brought to the heart. Or:

2.2. As an *affirming* question: "*Is not this the Son of David?* Yes, it certainly is, it can be no other one." The way to this great truth that Christ is the Messiah and Savior of the world was so clear and easy to see that the ordinary people could not miss it: the *wayfaring men, though fools, could not err therein* (Isa 35:8). The world by wisdom did not know God, and the wise were confused by foolish things (1Co 1:21, 27).

3. The blasphemous objection of the Pharisees (v. 24). They were proud of the reputation they had among the people; that fed their pride, supported their power, and filled their purses. People who fix their happiness on human praise and applause expose themselves to a perpetual uneasiness about every favorable word that they hear said about anyone else. The shadow of honor followed Christ, who fled from it, and it fled from the Pharisees, who were eager to pursue it. Notice:

3.1. How scornfully they spoke about Christ: *this fellow.* It is bad to speak about good people with contempt because they are poor.

3.2. How blasphemously they spoke about his miracles. They could not deny the facts of the matter; it was as clear as daylight that demons had been driven out by the word of Christ. They had no way of avoiding the conclusion that *this is the Son of David* except by suggesting that *Christ cast out devils by Beelzebub,* that there was an agreement between Christ and Satan. If they thought that, the demon had not been driven out, but had voluntarily withdrawn.

4. Christ's reply to this evil insinuation (vv. 25–30). *Jesus knew their thoughts.* Jesus Christ knows what we are thinking at any time; he knows what is in us, and he *understands our thoughts afar off* (Ps 139:2). Christ's reply is said to be to their thoughts, because he knew that they had not spoken rashly, but from a deep-rooted malignity. Christ's reply to this accusation is full and significant.

4.1. It would be very strange and highly improbable that Satan would be driven out by such an agreement, because then Satan's *kingdom would be divided against itself* (vv. 25–26).

4.1.1. There is set down here a known rule that in all societies reciprocated quarrels result in general ruin: *Every kingdom divided against itself is brought to desolation.* Divisions commonly end in desolation; if we clash, we break up; if we separate from one another, we become an easy target to the common enemy. Churches and nations have come to know this by sad experience.

4.1.2. The rule is applied to this situation: *If Satan cast out Satan* (v. 26). If the prince of demons were to be in conflict with lesser demons, the whole kingdom and all its interests would soon be broken. In fact, if Satan were to come into an agreement with Christ, it would have to be to Satan's own destruction, for the clear intention and tendency of Christ's preaching and miracles was to overthrow the kingdom of Satan. If he did fall in with Christ, *how would then his kingdom stand?* He would himself contribute to its overthrow. This victory must be obtained by nobler methods. Even if the prince of demons gathers together all his forces, Christ will be too powerful for his united forces, and Satan's kingdom will not stand.

4.2. It was not at all strange or improbable that demons would be driven out by the Spirit of God, for:

4.2.1. *How* otherwise *do your children cast them out?* There are those among the Jews who, by invoking the name of the Most High God, or the God of Abraham, Isaac, and Jacob, sometimes drove out demons. Josephus speaks about some in his time who did it; we read about *Jewish exorcists* (Ac 19:13) and about some people who *in Christ's name cast out devils* even though they did not follow him (Mk 9:38). The Pharisees did not condemn these, but attributed their actions to the Spirit of God. It was merely out of spite and envy toward Christ, therefore, that they wanted to acknowledge that others drove out demons by the Spirit of God but suggested that he did it in alliance with Beelzebub. The judgments of envy are made not by reason but by prejudice.

4.2.2. This driving out of demons was a certain sign of the approach and appearance of the kingdom of God (v. 28); "But if it is true that I *cast out devils by the Spirit of God*, the kingdom of the Messiah is now about to be set up among you." Other miracles that Christ performed proved he was sent by God, but this one proved he was sent by God to destroy the Devil's kingdom and his works. If the Devil's interests in a soul are broken and sunk by the Spirit of God, as a Sanctifier, there is no doubt that *the kingdom of God*—that is, the kingdom of grace—*is come* to that soul, as a blessed pledge of the kingdom of glory.

4.3. The comparing of Christ's miracles with his teaching showed that he was far from being in league with Satan, that he was in open enmity and hostility toward him (v. 29): "*How can one enter into a strong man's house, and plunder his goods*, and take them away, *except he first bind the strong man? And then he* may do what he pleases with his goods." The world was in Satan's possession and under his power, and so is every unregenerate soul; Satan rules there. The purpose of Christ's Gospel was to despoil the Devil's house, which, as a strong man, he kept in the world. It was *to turn the people from darkness to light* (Ac 26:18), from sin to holiness. According to this purpose, he tied up the strong man when he drove out evil spirits by his word. When he showed how easily and powerfully he could drive demons out of people's bodies, he encouraged all believers to hope that whatever power Satan might usurp and exercise in human souls, Christ by his grace would break it. When some of the worst sinners were sanctified and justified and became the best saints, then Christ despoiled the Devil's house, and he will continue to do so more and more.

4.4. This holy war, which Christ pursued with vigor against the Devil and his kingdom, was such as would not admit neutrality: *He that is not with me is against me* (v. 30). In the minor differences that may arise between the disciples of Christ among themselves, we are taught to seek peace, by counting those who *are not against us, to be with* us (Lk 9:50). However, in the great quarrel between Christ and Satan, no peace is to be sought. Those who are not genuinely *for* Christ will be counted as *against* him: those who are detached from the cause are looked on as enemies. We must be entirely, faithfully, and immovably on Christ's side: it is the right side and will ultimately be the rising side. The latter clause has the same meaning: *He that gathereth not with me scattereth.* Christ's mission into the world was to gather in his harvest, to gather in those whom the Father had given him (Jn 11:52; Eph 1:10). Christ expects and requires from those who are with him that they gather with him and gather others to him. If we *gather not with Christ, we scatter*; it is not enough not to do harm; we must do good (Isa 1:16–17; Mk 3:4).

5. Christ's message on this occasion about sins of the tongue: *Wherefore I say unto you.* He warned the people concerning three sorts of sins of the tongue:

5.1. Blasphemous words against the Holy Spirit are the worst kind of sins of the tongue, and they are unpardonable (vv. 31–32). Here is:

5.1.1. A gracious assurance of the pardon of all sin under the terms of the Gospel. The greatness of sin will be no barrier to our acceptance with God if we truly repent and believe the Gospel: *All manner of sin and blasphemy shall be forgiven unto men.* Even though it *reaches up to the heavens* (2Ch 28:9), yet *with the Lord there is mercy that reacheth beyond the heavens* (Ps 36:5; 108:4). Mercy will be extended even to blasphemy, a sin directly affecting God's name and honor. Paul, who had *been a blasphemer*, obtained mercy (1Ti 1:13). We may well say: *Who is a God like unto thee, pardoning iniquity?* (Mic 7:18). Even *words spoken against the Son of man shall be forgiven*, as were those of the people who reviled him at his death, many of whom repented and found mercy.

5.1.2. The excepting of *the blasphemy against the Holy Ghost*, which is declared here to be the only unpardonable sin. Notice:

5.1.2.1. What this sin is; it is *speaking against the Holy Ghost*. Notice the evil in sins of the tongue: the only unpardonable sin is this. *But Jesus knew their thoughts* (v. 25). The sin named here does not include all speaking against the person or being of the Holy Spirit, or merely resisting his internal working in sinners themselves, for *who then would be saved?* None are excluded, either by name or by description, from the pardon granted to blasphemers except those *that blaspheme the Holy Ghost*. This blasphemy is excluded from the general pardon not because of any defect of mercy in God or merit in Christ but because it inevitably leaves the sinner in unfaithfulness and impenitence. Those who fear they have committed this sin show a good sign that they have not. Those, therefore, who blaspheme against this gift of the Spirit cannot possibly be brought to believe in Christ; those who believe he is in collusion with Satan, as the Pharisees believed concerning the miracles—what could convince them? This is such a stronghold of unbelief as can never be beaten out of a person, and it is unpardonable because it hides repentance from the sinner's eyes (Lk 19:42).

5.1.2.2. The sentence that is passed on it: *It shall not be forgiven, neither in this world nor in the world to come.* There is no healing for a sin that so directly opposes the remedy.

5.2. Christ spoke concerning other evil words here, the products of corruption reigning in the heart and breaking out from there (vv. 33–35). *Jesus knew their thoughts* (v. 25), and yet they tried to cover up by pretending they were just. Our Lord Jesus pointed to the springs, therefore, and healed them. Let the heart be sanctified, and it will appear in our words.

5.2.1. The heart is the root; the language is the *fruit* (v. 33). If the nature of the tree is good, it will produce fruit accordingly. Whatever sinful desire reigns in the heart, it will break out; diseased lungs make for offensive breath. A person's language reveals what country they come from. "*Either make the tree good, and then the fruit will be good*—purify your hearts, and then you will have pure lips and pure lives—or *the tree will be corrupt, and the fruit* accordingly." You can make a wild apple tree a good tree by grafting onto it a shoot from a good tree, and then the fruit will be good. If the tree remains the same, however, then wherever you plant it and however much you water it, the fruit will still be corrupt. Unless the heart is transformed, the life will never be thoroughly reformed. We should be more concerned to be good in reality than to appear good outwardly.

5.2.2. The heart is the fountain; the words are the streams (v. 34): *Out of the abundance of the heart the mouth speaks*, as the streams are the overflow of the spring. Evil words are the natural, genuine product of an evil heart. Nothing but the salt of grace, thrown into the spring, will heal the waters, *season the speech* (Col 4:6), and purify the *corrupt communications* (Eph 4:29). They lacked this, because they were evil, *and how can ye, being evil, speak good things?* The people looked on the Pharisees as a generation of saints, but Christ called them *a generation of vipers*. What could be expected from *a generation of vipers* except what was poisonous and malignant? Can a viper be anything else than venomous? Bad things may be expected from bad people. Christ wanted his disciples to know what kind of people they were to live among, so that they would know what to look for. They would be *among scorpions*, as Ezekiel had been (Eze 2:6), and must not think it strange if they were stung and bitten.

5.2.3. The heart is the *treasury*; the words are the things brought out of that treasury (v. 35). It is the character of a *good man* that he has a *good treasure in his heart* and *brings forth good things* from there as need be. Graces, encouragements, experiences, good knowledge, good affections, good decisions: these are a *good treasure in the heart*; the word of God hidden there, the law of God written there, divine truths living and ruling there are a valuable and suitable treasure, kept safe and secret like the stores of the good householder, available for use on all occasions. Some claim to have expensive goods that are not *good treasure*—such people will soon become bankrupt. Some hope they have it in them, and, thank God, whatever their words and actions are, they have good hearts. However, *faith without works is dead* (Jas 2:20), and some have a *good treasure* of wisdom and knowledge but do not share it; they have a talent but do not know how to use it. The complete Christian bears the image of God by both *being good and doing good*. It is the character of an *evil man* that he has an *evil treasure in his heart* and *bringeth forth* out of it *evil things*.

5.3. Christ spoke here about *idle words*, showing what evil they contain (vv. 36–37). *For every idle word*, or sentence or speech, *that men speak, they shall give account*. God notices every word we say, even what we ourselves do not notice. Careless and disrespectful talk displeases God; it is the product of a false and worthless heart. We must soon give account of these careless words; they will prove we are unprofitable servants (Lk 17:10), who have not used the faculties of reason and speech, which are part of the talents we have been entrusted with (25:24–28). *By thy words thou shalt be justified or condemned*. The overall tendency of our speech will be evidence either for us or against us, depending on whether it has been gracious or ungracious.

Verses 38–45

It is probable that these Pharisees were not the same as those who quibbled with him in v. 24, refusing to believe the signs he gave, but another group of them, who would not content themselves with the signs he gave unless he would give them further proof as they demanded. Here is:

1. Their speaking to him (v. 38). They complimented him using the title *Master*, pretending to have respect for him when they really intended to abuse him; not all who call Christ *Master* are his true servants. Their request was, *We would see a sign from thee*. It was highly reasonable for them to see a sign, for him to use miracles to prove his

divine mission, but it was highly unreasonable to demand a sign now, when he had given so many signs already. It is natural for proud people to dictate to God and then make that an excuse for not submitting to him, but a person's offense will never be their defense.

2. His answer to their demand:

2.1. He condemned the demand as the language of *an evil and adulterous generation* (v. 39). He directed the charge not only at *the scribes and Pharisees* but also at the whole nation of the Jews. Those who not only hardened themselves against the conviction of Christ's miracles but also set themselves to abuse him and show contempt for his miracles were a truly evil generation. They were *an adulterous generation* in the sense that they were adulterous children, who had so miserably degenerated from the faith and obedience of their ancestors that Abraham and Israel did not acknowledge them (Isa 63:16). They were also an adulterous wife, who had departed from the God to whom she had been promised in the covenant: they were guilty of all kinds of iniquity, and that is unfaithfulness; they did not look to gods that they themselves had made, but they looked for signs that they themselves had devised, and that was adultery.

2.2. He refused to give them any other sign than he had already given them, except *that of the prophet Jonas* (Jonah). Although Christ is always ready to listen to and answer holy desires and prayers, he will not satisfy corrupt, sinful desires and attitudes. Those who *ask amiss ask and have not* (Jas 4:3). Signs were given to those who wanted them to confirm their faith, as to Abraham and Gideon, but they were denied to those who demanded them as an excuse for their unbelief. Christ could justly have said that they would never see another miracle, but note his wonderful goodness. They would have one sign that was different from all these, and that was the resurrection of Christ from the dead by his own power, called here *the sign of the prophet Jonas*. That was a sign that surpassed all the others; it completed and crowned them. The unbelief of the Jews found a way to avoid that one too, however, by saying, *His disciples came and stole him away* (28:13), for none are so incurably blind as those who are determined not to see. He further explained this sign of the prophet Jonah: *As Jonas was three days and three nights in the whale's belly* (v. 40), so long would Christ be in the grave, and then he would rise again. Just as Jonah was discharged from his prison on the third day and came back to the land of the living, so on the third day Christ would return to life, rising from his grave to send out the Gospel to the Gentiles.

2.3. Christ used this occasion to describe the sad character and condition of that generation in which he lived, a generation that refused to be reformed. People and things now appear under false colors; characters and conditions are changeable here. Things are in reality what they are eternally. Now Christ described the Jewish people:

2.3.1. As a generation who would be condemned by *the men of Nineveh*, whose *repenting at the preaching of Jonas* would *rise up in judgment* against them (v. 41). Christ's resurrection would be the sign of the prophet Jonah to them, but it would not have such a happy effect on them as Jonah's had on the Ninevites, for the Ninevites were brought by it to such repentance as prevented their ruin. The Jews, however, would be hardened in an unbelief that would hasten their ruin. Christ renewed Jonah's calls, sitting and teaching in the synagogues. Besides the warning given us of our danger, Christ has shown us what we must repent of and has assured us of acceptance when we repent. Christ performed many miracles, and all were miracles of mercy. And yet the Ninevites *repented at the preaching of Jonas*, but the Jews were not persuaded by Christ's preaching. The goodness of those who have fewer helps and advantages for their souls will emphasize the badness of those who have much greater. Those who by the twilight discover *the things that belong to their peace* (Lk 19:42) will shame those who fumble at midday.

2.3.2. As a generation who would be condemned by the Queen of the South, the Queen of Sheba (v. 42). The Ninevites would shame them for not repenting; the Queen of Sheba, for not believing in Christ. She came from a far country to hear the wisdom of Solomon, but some people would not be, and even today some will not be, persuaded to come and hear the wisdom of Christ. The Queen of Sheba had no invitation to come to Solomon, nor any promise of being welcome, but we are invited to Christ, to sit at his feet and hear his word. She could not be sure that it would be worth her while to go so far on this errand; we, however, do not come to Christ with such uncertainties. *She came from the uttermost parts of the earth*, but we have Christ among us, and his word is very near us (Dt 30:14): *Behold, he stands at the door, and knocks* (Rev 3:20). It seems that the wisdom the Queen of Sheba came for was mere human philosophy and politics, but the wisdom that is to be found in Christ is wisdom to salvation. She could only *hear* Solomon's wisdom; he could not *give* her wisdom. Christ, however, will give wisdom to those who come to him (Pr 2:3–6; Jas 1:5).

2.3.3. As a generation who were determined to continue under the power of Satan. They are compared to one out of whom the Devil has gone but to whom he returns with double force (vv. 43–45).

2.3.3.1. The parable represents his possessing human bodies. Since Christ had just driven out a demon and they had said *he had a devil*, he used the occasion to show how much they were under the power of Satan. Christ's ejection of him was final and such as barred reentry: we find him commanding the evil spirit to *go out, and enter no more* (Mk 9:25).

2.3.3.2. Christ applied the parable so as to describe the situation of most of the Jewish church and nation: "*So it shall be with this wicked generation*, who now resist and will finally reject the Gospel of Christ." Let this be a warning to all nations and churches to beware leaving their first love (Rev 2:4), to beware setting aside a good work of reformation that has begun among them and returning to that evil that they seemed to have forsaken: *for the last state of such will be worse than the first.*

Verses 46–50

Many excellent, useful sayings came from the mouth of our Lord Jesus on particular occasions; even his digressions were instructive, as well as his set speeches, as here. Notice:

1. How Christ was interrupted in his preaching by *his mother and his brethren*, who stood outside, *desiring to speak with him* (vv. 46–47), conveying their desire through the crowd.

1.1. He was still *talking with the people*. Christ's preaching was *talking*; his was a plain, easy, and familiar style, suited to their capacity and needs. The opposition we encounter in our work must not drive us away from it. He stopped talking with the Pharisees, for he saw he could do no good with them, but he continued to talk to the common people.

1.2. His mother and brothers stood outside, asking to speak with him, when they should have been standing inside, asking to listen to him. They had the advantage of

his daily conversation in private and were therefore less concerned to listen to his public preaching. Familiarity and accessibility can breed contempt. There is too much truth in the common proverb "The nearer the church, the further from God." It is a pity that it should be so.

1.3. They not only would not listen to him themselves; they interrupted others who *heard him gladly* (Mk 12:37). We are often met with hindrances and obstructions in our work through our friends who are around us, and we are often taken away from our spiritual concerns by civil relationships. Those who really wish us and our work well may sometimes, by their indiscretion, prove to be false friends and impede our duty. Christ once said to his mother, *How is it that ye sought me? Wist ye not* (did you not know) *that I must be about my Father's business?* It was said then that she *laid up that saying in her heart* (Lk 2:49), but if she had remembered it now, she would not have interrupted him when he was about his Father's business. Many a good truth that seemed profitable to store up when we heard it is out of place when we want to use it.

2. How he resented this interruption (vv. 48–50).

2.1. He would not listen to it: *Who is my mother? And who are my brethren?* Not that natural affections are to be set aside, but *everything is beautiful in its season* (Ecc 3:11), and the lesser duty must be set aside while the greater is performed. The closest relatives must by comparison be hated; that is, we must love them less than we do Christ (Lk 14:26), and our duty to God must have priority. We must not take offense from our friends or think they are behaving corruptly if they prefer pleasing God over pleasing us. We must, in fact, deny ourselves and our own satisfaction rather than do anything that may divert or distract our friends from fulfilling their duty to God.

2.2. He used that occasion to put his disciples before his natural relatives; his disciples were his spiritual family. He would rather be profiting his disciples than pleasing his relatives. Notice:

2.2.1. The description of Christ's disciples. They are such as *do the will of his Father*, not only hear it, know it, and talk about it, but also *do it.*

2.2.2. The position of Christ's disciples: *The same is my brother, and sister, and mother.* His disciples, who had left everything to follow him (Mk 10:28) and embraced his doctrine, were dearer to him than any natural relative. It was very endearing and encouraging for Christ to say, *Behold my mother and my brethren.* It was not *their* privilege alone, however: *this honour have all the saints* (Ps 149:9). All obedient believers are closely related to Jesus Christ. He loves them and speaks freely with them as his relatives. He welcomes them to his table and sees that they lack nothing they need. He will never be ashamed of his poor relatives, but will confess them in front of other people, the angels, and his Father (10:32).

CHAPTER 13

In this chapter we have:

1. The favor Christ showed to his compatriots by preaching the kingdom of heaven to them (vv. 1–2). He preached to them in parables, and here he gave the reason why he chose that way of teaching (vv. 10–17). The Evangelist gives another reason (vv. 34–35).

1.1. Here is one parable to show how people are greatly hindered and even prevented from benefiting from the word of the Gospel, and that is the parable of the four kinds of ground, told in vv. 3–9 and explained in vv. 18–23.

1.2. Here are two parables intended to show that there would be a mixture of good and bad: the parable of the weeds, told in vv. 24–30 and explained at the request of the disciples in vv. 36–43, and that of the net let down into the lake (vv. 47–50).

1.3. Here are two parables intended to show that the Gospel church would be very small at first, but that in the course of time it would become significant: that of the mustard seed (vv. 31–32) and that of leaven (yeast) (v. 33).

1.4. Two parables intended to show that those who expect salvation through the Gospel must be willing to risk all: that of the treasure hidden in the field (v. 44) and that of the pearl of great price (vv. 45–46).

1.5. Here is one parable intended to lead the disciples to make use of the instructions Christ had given them for the benefit of others, and that is the parable of the good owner of a house (vv. 51–52).

2. The contempt his compatriots showed him on account of the humbleness of his parentage (vv. 53–58).

Verses 1–23

1. We have Christ preaching, and we may observe:

1.1. When Christ preached this sermon; it was the same day as he preached the sermon recorded in the previous chapter: he was so untiring in doing good (Ac 10:38). Christ spent both ends of the day in preaching. An afternoon sermon well listened to, far from driving out the morning sermon, will rather drive the point home even more securely. Although in the morning Christ had been opposed, disturbed, and interrupted, he continued with his work. Toward the end of the day, we do not find that he met such discouragements. Those who with courage and zeal break through difficulties in God's service will perhaps find them not so inclined to recur as they fear. Resist them, and they will flee (Jas 4:7).

1.2. To whom he preached; there were *great multitudes gathered together to him* (v. 2), and they were the audience. Sometimes there is the greatest power in religion where there is the least showiness. When Christ went to the side of the lake, *multitudes* were presently *gathered together to him*. Where the king is, there is the court; where Christ is, there is the church, even if it is by the side of the lake. Those who want to benefit from the word must be willing to follow it wherever it moves; when the ark is moved, follow it (Jos 3:3).

1.3. Where he preached this sermon. His meeting place was the side of the lake. He left the house to go into the open air, because there was no room for the audience. Just as he did not have his own house to live in, so he did not have his own chapel to preach in. This shows us that in external circumstances of worship we should not seek what is impressive but should make the best of the conveniences that God in his providence has allotted us. When Christ was born, he was crowded into the stable, and now he went to the lakeside, where everyone could freely come to him. His pulpit was a boat. Nowhere is out of place for such a Preacher, whose presence dignified and consecrated any site: let those who preach Christ not be ashamed, even if they have simple and inconvenient places to preach in.

1.4. What and how he preached. *He spoke many things unto them* (v. 3). He probably spoke many more things than have been recorded here. Christ did not speak about frivolous matters, but subjects of eternal consequence. What he spoke was in parables. It was a way of teaching that was used very often. It was found to be a very

profitable tool, all the more so because it was pleasing. Our Savior used it often, and by using it he stooped to the abilities of ordinary people and spoke to them in their own language.

2. We have here the general reason why Christ taught in parables. The disciples were a little surprised at it, for up to that time in his preaching, he had not used them much, and so they ask, *Why speakest thou to them in parables?* (v. 10). They asked this because they truly wanted the people to hear with understanding. They did not say, "Why are you speaking like this to *us*?"—they knew well enough how to have the parables explained—but "to *them*." Christ answered this question in detail (vv. 11–17), telling them that he preached by parables because that method made the things of God plainer and easier for those who were willing to be taught, and at the same time more difficult and obscure to those who were willingly ignorant. A parable, like the pillar of cloud and fire, turns a dark side toward Egyptians, which confounds them, but a light side toward the Israelites, which assures them (Ex 14:20).

2.1. This reason was set down: *Because it is given unto you to know the mysteries of the kingdom of heaven, but to them it is not given* (v. 11). That is:

2.1.1. The disciples had knowledge, but the people did not. "The people are ignorant; they are still babes and must be taught as such by clear comparisons." According to some: "Although they have eyes, they do not know how to use them." Or:

2.1.2. The disciples were well disposed toward the knowledge of Gospel mysteries and wanted to explore the parables; the worldly hearers who stopped at mere hearing would never be any wiser and would therefore justly suffer for their omissions. A parable is a shell that keeps good fruit *for* the diligent but keeps it *from* the lazy. There are mysteries concerning the kingdom of heaven. It was graciously given to the first disciples of Christ to come to know these mysteries. Knowledge is the first gift of God; it was given to the apostles because they were Christ's constant followers. The nearer we come to Christ, and the more we share our lives with him, the more we will know the mysteries of the Gospel. This knowledge is also given to all true believers, who have an experiential knowledge of the mysteries of the Gospel, and that is without doubt the best knowledge.

2.2. This reason was further illustrated by the rule God observes in distributing his gifts; he gives them to those who make use of them, but he takes them away from those who bury them. Here:

2.2.1. A promise was made to those who would have true grace and would use what they had: they would have an even greater abundance. God's favors are pledges of further favors; where he lays the foundation, he will build on it.

2.2.2. A threat was issued to those who would not have it, who would have something but not use what they had; what they had or seemed to have would be *taken away* from them. God would call in their talents, as a lender calls in a loan, and they would probably soon become bankrupt.

2.3. This reason was especially explained with reference to the two kinds of people Christ had to do with.

2.3.1. Some were willingly ignorant, and they were entertained by the parables: *because they seeing, see not* (v. 13). They had shut their eyes to the clear light of Christ's plain preaching and so were now left in the dark. God is just to take away the light from those who shut their eyes to it. Here the Scripture would be fulfilled (vv. 14–15). It is quoted from Isa 6:9–10, which is referred to no fewer than six times in the New Testament. What was spoken about the sinners in Isaiah's time was fulfilled in those in Christ's time, and it is still being fulfilled every day. Here is:

2.3.1.1. A description of sinners' willful blindness and darkness, which is their sin. *This people's heart is waxed gross;* "their heart is fattened," as it may also be rendered, indicating both sensuality and senselessness. When the heart is so heavy, it is hardly surprising that the ears can hardly hear. They shut both the learning senses, for they have also closed their eyes, deciding that they do not want to see light come into the world (Jn 1:9) when the Sun of righteousness arises (Mal 4:2).

2.3.1.2. A description of the judicial blindness that is the just punishment of this. "*By hearing, ye shall hear, and shall not understand;* whatever means of grace you have will be ineffective to you, although they will continue in mercy to be extended to others." The saddest condition a person can be in is to sit under the most lively services of worship with a dead, senseless, and untouched heart.

2.3.1.3. The terrible effects and consequence of this: *Lest at any time they should see. Lest they should be converted, and I should heal them.* This shows us that seeing, hearing, and understanding are necessary for conversion, because God, in working grace, deals with people as human beings, as rational agents; he draws with cords of human kindness (Hos 11:4), changes the heart by opening the eyes: he turns *from the power of Satan unto God* by turning first *from darkness to light* (Ac 26:18). All those who are truly converted to God will certainly be healed by him. "If they are converted, I will heal them. I will save them."

2.3.2. Others were effectively called to be the disciples of Christ and truly wanted to be taught by him. By these parables the things of God were made clearer and simpler, more intelligible and familiar, and more easily remembered (vv. 16–17). *Your eyes see, your ears hear.* Christ spoke about this:

2.3.2.1. As a blessing: "*Blessed are your eyes, for they see, and your ears, for they hear;* it is your happiness, and it is a happiness for which you are indebted to the special favor and blessing of God." The hearing ear and the seeing eye are God's work (Pr 20:12). They are the result of a blessed work, which will be fulfilled with power when those who *now see through a glass darkly shall see face to face* (1Co 13:12). The apostles were to teach others, and so they themselves were blessed with the clearest revelations of divine truth.

2.3.2.2. As a transcendent blessing, desired by but not given to many prophets and righteous people (v. 17). The Old Testament saints, who had some glimpses, some glimmers, of Gospel light, earnestly sought further revelation. Those who know something about Christ must want to know more. There was then, as there still is, *a glory to be revealed,* something in reserve, so *that they without us would not be made perfect* (Heb 11:40). It is good for us to consider how the means we enjoy and the revelations that are made to us under the Gospel surpass what God's people enjoyed under the Old Testament era.

3. We have here one of the parables that our Savior told, that of the *sower and the seed.* Christ's parables are taken from common, ordinary things, from the most obvious things, things observed in everyday life and within the reach of the lowest ability. Christ chose to express himself in this way so that:

3.1. Spiritual things would be made clearer and could be more easily assimilated into our understanding.

3.2. We could take occasion from those things that we see so often to meditate with delight on the things of God. So when our hands are busiest with matters of the world, we may, despite that—in fact, with the help of that—be led to have our hearts in heaven. This is how the word of God will talk in familiar terms to us (Pr 6:22). The parable of the sower is clear enough (vv. 3–9). We have its explanation from Christ himself, who knew best what he meant. "*Hear ye therefore the parable of the sower* (v. 18); you have heard it, but let us go over it again." We hear the word rightly and to good effect when we understand what we hear; it is not truly heard if it is not heard with understanding (Ne 8:2). It is God's grace that gives understanding, but it is our duty to give our minds to understand. Let us therefore compare the parable and its explanation.

3.2.1. The seed sown is the word of God, called here *the word of the kingdom* (v. 19), of the kingdom of heaven. This word is the seed that is sown; it seems dead and dry, but all the product is virtually in it. It is *incorruptible seed* (1Pe 1:23).

3.2.2. The sower who scatters the seed is our Lord Jesus Christ, either by himself or by his ministers; see v. 37. Preaching to a crowd is sowing the grain; we do not know where it must fall; our task is only to see that it is good and clean and be sure to spread enough seed.

3.2.3. The ground into which this seed is sown is the hearts of the people, which are differently qualified and disposed. The human heart is like soil, capable of bearing good fruit and capable of being improved; it is a pity for it to lie fallow. Just as it is with the earth—some ground is worked strenuously and sown with very good seed but still produces no good fruit, while good soil produces a plentiful crop—so it is with the human heart. Different characters are represented here by four kinds of ground, of which three are bad, and only one good. The number of fruitless hearers is very great, even of those who heard Christ himself. Notice the characters of these four kinds of ground.

3.2.3.1. The ground of the path, *by the way side* (vv. 4, 19). Farmers had paths through their grainfields (12:1), and the seed that fell on them never entered the ground, so the birds picked it up. Notice:

3.2.3.1.1. What kind of hearers are compared to the ground of the path: those who *hear the word and understand it not.* They pay no attention to it, do not take hold of it; they do not come with any intention to benefit from it. They pay no attention to what is said; it goes in one ear and out the other, making no impression at all.

3.2.3.1.2. How they come to be unprofitable hearers. The *wicked one,* that is, the Devil, *cometh and catcheth* (snatches) *away that which was* sown. Such mindless, careless, trifling hearers are an easy target for Satan. Because he is the great murderer of souls, he is the great thief of sermons. If we do not break up the fallow ground by preparing our hearts for the word, and if we do not cover the seed afterward by meditation and prayer, if we do not give a *more earnest heed to the things which we have heard* (Heb 2:1), we are like the ground on the path.

3.2.3.2. The *stony ground. Some fell upon stony places* (vv. 5–6), which represent the case of hearers who receive some good impressions from the word, but in whom they do not last (vv. 20–21). It is possible for us to be a great deal better than some yet not as good as we should be. Notice:

3.2.3.2.1. How far they go.

3.2.3.2.1.1. They *hear the word;* they turn neither their backs on it nor a deaf ear to it. Hearing the word will never by itself bring us to heaven.

3.2.3.2.1.2. They are *quick in hearing; forthwith it sprung up* (v. 5); it appeared sooner above ground than what was sown in the good soil. Hypocrites often get a head start on true Christians in their profession and are often too impulsive to hold back. He *receives it straightway*, without tasting it properly; he swallows it without chewing, and then it can never digest well.

3.2.3.2.1.3. They receive it with joy. There are many who are very glad to hear a good sermon but do not profit by it. Many *taste the good word of God* (Heb 6:5) and say they find it to be sweet, but still keep some beloved sinful desire to be *rolled under the tongue* (Job 20:12), with which the word disagrees, and so they spit it out again.

3.2.3.2.1.4. They *endure for a while*. Many endure for a while but do not endure to the end; they ran well, but something hindered them (Gal 5:7).

3.2.3.2.2. How they fall away, so that no fruit is brought to maturity. They have *no root in themselves*, no settled, fixed motives in their judgments, no firm determination in their wills. There may be the green shoots of a Christian faith where there is no root of grace. Where there is no firm foundation, even if there is a profession of faith, we cannot expect perseverance. Those who have no roots will endure only a while. Times of trial come, and then they come to nothing: *When tribulation and persecution arise because of the word, he is offended.* After a fair gale of opportunity usually comes a storm of persecution, as a test to see who has received the word sincerely and who has not. It is wise to prepare for such a day. When testing times come, those who have no roots soon stumble and fall away; they first quarrel with their faith and then abandon it. Persecution is represented in the parable by *the scorching sun* (v. 6); the same sun that warms and cherishes what was well rooted withers and burns up what lacked roots. Trials that shake some confirm others (Php 1:12). Notice how soon they fall away; a Christian faith taken up without consideration is commonly let fall without it. Easy come, easy go.

3.2.3.3. The thorny ground. *Some fell among thorns.* This went further than the seed along the path, for it had roots. Prosperity destroys the word in the heart as much as persecution does, and more dangerously, because it acts more silently: the stones spoiled the root, the thorns *spoil* the fruit. Now what are these choking thorns?

3.2.3.3.1. The cares of this world. Care for another world would stimulate the springing of this seed, but care for this world chokes it. Worldly cares are appropriately compared to thorns. They are entangling, troublesome, and scratching, and *their end is to be burned* (Heb 6:8). These thorns choke the good seed. Worldly cares are great hindrances to our profiting from the word of God. They consume that vigor of soul that should be spent on divine things. Those who *are careful and cumbered about many things* commonly neglect *the one thing needful* (Lk 10:40–42).

3.2.3.3.2. The deceitfulness of riches. Those who through their care and diligence have increased their possessions, and for whom the danger that arises from worry seems to be over, tend to promise themselves something that riches cannot provide them; they tend to rely on them, and this chokes the word as much as cares did. It is not so much riches as *the deceitfulness of riches* that causes this trouble. We put our confidence in them and raise our expectations from them, and it is then that they choke the good seed.

3.2.3.4. The good ground: *Others fell into good ground* (v. 18), and it is a pity that good seed does not always fall in good soil, for then there is no loss; such are *good hearers of the word* (v. 23). Now what distinguished this good ground from the rest was, in a word, fruitfulness. Christ did not say that this good ground contains no stones or thorns, but that none were effective in stopping it from being fruitful. Saints, in this world, are not completely free from the remains of sin, but they are happily freed from its reign. The hearers represented by the good ground are:

3.2.3.4.1. Intelligent hearers: they *hear the word and understand it.* They understand not only the sense and meaning of the word but also their own involvement in it; they understand it as business people understand their business.

3.2.3.4.2. Fruitful hearers, whose fruitfulness is evidence of their good understanding: which *also beareth fruit.* We bear fruit when we put the word into practice and do as we are taught to do. Yet:

3.2.3.4.3. Not all similarly fruitful; *some a hundredfold, some sixty, some thirty.* Among fruitful Christians, some are more fruitful than others. Where there is true grace, there are degrees of it; all Christ's students are not at the same level. However, if the ground is good and the fruit is right, those who produce only thirtyfold will be graciously accepted by God, and their fruit will be considered plentiful.

4. He closed the parable with a solemn call to attention: *Who hath ears to hear, let him hear* (v. 9). The sense of hearing cannot be used better than in hearing the word of God. Some want to hear music, a sweet melody: their ears are the *daughters of music* (Ecc 12:4); there is no melody like that of the word of God. Others want to hear *new things* (Ac 17: 21), and there is no news like that of the word of God.

Verses 24–43

In these verses, we have:

1. Another reason given why Christ preached by parables (vv. 34–35). *All these things he spoke in parables*, because the time had not yet come for clearer and plainer revelations of the mysteries of the kingdom. Christ tries by all possible ways to do good to people's souls. If people refuse to be instructed and influenced by direct preaching, he will see if parables have an effect on them. Here is:

1.1. What Christ preached. The mystery of the Gospel had been *hid in God*, in his purposes and decrees, *from the beginning of the world* (Eph 3:9).

1.2. How Christ preached; he preached using parables: wise sayings, but figurative ones, which help attract our attention and diligent seeking.

2. The parable of the *tares* (weeds) and its explanation. Notice:

2.1. The disciples' request to their Master to have this parable explained to them: *Jesus sent the multitude away* (v. 36), and it is to be feared that many of them went away no wiser than when they came. It is sad to think how many go away from sermons with the word of grace in their ears but not the work of grace in their hearts. Christ *went into the house* not so much for his own rest as to engage in a conversation with his disciples. The disciples seized hold of the opportunity and *came to him.* Those who want to be wise in everything must be wise in discerning and making the most of opportunities, especially opportunities for speaking with Christ. We lose the benefit of many sermons by worthless and unprofitable talk after them. See Lk 24:32; Dt 6:6–7. Private meetings would add much to our benefiting from public preaching. The disciples' request to their Master was, *Declare unto us the parable of the tares*. This implied an acknowledgment of their ignorance, which they were not ashamed to admit. People who are aware of their ignorance and sincerely want to be taught are rightly inclined toward Christ's teaching. Christ had explained the previous parable without being asked, but they ask him to explain this one. The first light and the first grace are given; further resources of light and grace must be prayed for daily.

2.2. The explanation Christ gave of this parable. Now the general sense of the parable is to describe to us the present and future state of the kingdom of heaven, the Gospel church: Christ's care of it, the Devil's enmity toward it, the mixture it contains of both good and bad in this world, and the separation between them in the other world. Let us consider the details of the explanation of the parable.

2.2.1. *He that sows the good seed is the Son of man.* Jesus Christ is the Lord of the field, *the Lord of the harvest* (9:38), the Sower of good seed. Whatever good seed there is in the world, it all comes from the hand of Christ and has been sown by him: truths preached, graces planted, and souls sanctified are good seed, and all are owing to Christ. Ministers are instruments in Christ's hand to sow good seed.

2.2.2. *The field is the world*, the world of the human race, a large field, capable of producing good fruit; it is to be greatly lamented, therefore, that it produces so much bad fruit. It is his field, and because it is his, he has taken care to sow it with good seed.

2.2.3. *The good seed are the children of the kingdom*, true saints, saints not only in profession, as the Jews were (8:12), but also sincerely. They are the good seed, precious as seed (Ps 126:6). The seed is scattered, as are the saints, dispersed, here one and there another, though sown in some places more thickly than in others.

2.2.4. *The tares are the children of the wicked one.* They are the children of the Devil. They are weeds in the field of this world. They do no good; they do harm. They are weeds in the garden, having the same rain, sunshine, and soil as the good plants, but are good for nothing.

2.2.5. *The enemy that sowed the tares is the devil.* He is an enemy of the field of the world, which he tries to make his own by sowing his weeds in it. Notice about the sowing of the weeds:

2.2.5.1. They were sown *while men slept*. Satan watches for every opportunity. We must therefore *be sober, and vigilant.*

2.2.5.2. When the enemy had sown the weeds, he *went his way* (v. 25), so that it would not be known who did it. When Satan is causing the greatest trouble, he seeks most to hide himself. If the enemy sows the weeds, even if he goes on his way, they will spring up by themselves and cause harm, whereas when good seed is sown, it must be nurtured, watered, and protected, for otherwise it will come to nothing.

2.2.5.3. The weeds did not appear until *the blade sprung up* (sprouted) *and brought forth fruit* (v. 26). There is a great deal of secret evil in the human heart, which lies hidden for a long time under the cloak of a plausible profession, but eventually it breaks out. When a time of testing comes, when fruit is to be produced, then if you return, you will be able to discern the sincere and the hypocrite: then you may say, "This is wheat, and that is weeds."

2.2.5.4. When the servants were aware of it, they complained to their master: *Sir, didst thou not sow good seed in thy field?* (v. 27). No doubt he did; we may well ask with wonder, concerning the seed that Christ sows, "Where could *these tares come* from?" It is sad to see such weeds in the garden of the Lord, to see the good soil go to waste, the good seed choked, and such shame brought to the name and honor of Christ.

2.2.5.5. The Master soon knew where it came from: *An enemy has done this* (v. 28). He did not lay the blame on the servants; they could not help it. Ministers of Christ who are faithful and conscientious will not be judged by Christ for the mixture of bad with good, hypocrites with those who are sincere, in the field of the church. *It must needs be that such offenses will come* (18:7), and we may not be accused of them if we are doing our duty.

2.2.5.6. The servants were very eager to have these weeds uprooted. "*Wilt thou that we go* and do it immediately?"

2.2.5.7. The Master very wisely prevented this: *Nay, lest while ye gather up the tares, ye root up also the wheat with them* (v. 29). No one can infallibly distinguish between weeds and wheat. Discipline can be either so mistaken in its rules or so fastidious in its application that it proves troublesome to many who are truly godly and conscientious. If the weeds continued under the means of grace, they might become good grain; it is good, therefore, to have patience with them.

2.2.6. *The harvest is the end of the world* (v. 39). This world will come to an end. At the harvest everything is ripe and ready to be cut down: both good and bad are ripe at the great day (Rev 6:11). At harvest everyone reaps as they have sown; every person's ground, seed, skill, and diligence will be revealed.

2.2.7. *The reapers are the angels*. The angels are servants of Christ, holy enemies of evildoers and the faithful friends of all saints, and so they are fit to be employed in this way.

2.2.8. The torments of hell are the *fire* into which the *tares* will then be thrown.

2.2.8.1. The weeds will then be pulled up: *The reapers*—whose primary work is to gather in the wheat—will be told first to *gather out the tares*. Although good and bad are indistinguishable while together in this world, they will be separated at the great day.

2.2.8.2. They will then be *bound in bundles* (v. 30). Those who have associated in sin will be together in shame and sorrow.

2.2.8.3. They *will be cast into a furnace of fire*; they are fit for nothing but fire. *There shall be weeping and gnashing of teeth*, comfortless sorrow and incurable indignation at God.

2.2.9. Heaven is the *barn. But gather the wheat into my barn*, as the parable puts it (v. 30). All God's wheat will be put together in God's barn. There will be sheaves of grain as well as bundles of weeds: they will then be secured, no longer exposed to the wind and weather, sin and sorrow. They will no longer be far away, in the field, but nearby, in the barn. In the explanation of the parable this is represented gloriously: *Then shall the righteous shine forth as the sun in the kingdom of their Father* (v. 43). The honor in reserve for them is that they *shall shine forth as the sun in that kingdom*. Here they are obscure and hidden (Col 3:3), their beauty eclipsed by their poverty and the humbleness of their outward condition; then they will shine brightly, as the sun shines from behind a dark cloud. They will shine like the sun, the most glorious of all visible beings. Those who shine as lights in this world so that God may be glorified will shine as the sun in the other world so that *they* may be glorified. Our Savior concludes, as before, with a call to attention: *Who hath ears to hear, let him hear.*

3. The parable of the *grain of mustard seed* (vv. 31–32). The scope of this parable was to show that the beginnings of the Gospel *would be small, but that its latter end would greatly increase* (Job 8:7). Notice about the work of the Gospel:

3.1. That it is commonly very weak and small at first: *like a grain of mustard seed, which is one of the least of all seeds*. In particular places, the first outbreak of the Gospel light is only as *the dawning of the day*. Young converts are like *lambs* that must *be carried in his arms* (Isa 40:11).

3.2. That it is nevertheless growing and increasing. *A grain of mustard seed* is small, but it is still a seed and contains a disposition to grow. Gracious habits are confirmed, and activities stimulated; knowledge will become clearer, faith more confirmed, and love more kindled; here the seed is growing.

3.3. That it will eventually become very strong and useful: *when it is grown to* some maturity, *it becomes a tree*. The church is like a great tree to which the birds of the air come and in whose branches they perch; God's people turn to it for food and rest, shade and shelter. In particular individuals, growing grace will be strong and will achieve much. Grown Christians must seek to be useful to others, as the mature mustard seed is to the birds.

4. The parable of the *leaven* (yeast) (v. 33).

4.1. *A woman took* this *leaven*; it was her work. Ministers are employed in leavening places and souls with the Gospel.

4.2. The yeast was *hid in three measures of meal* (flour). The heart, like flour, is soft and pliable; it is the tender heart that is likely to benefit by the word. It *is three measures of meal*, a great quantity, for *a little leaven leaveneth the whole lump*. The yeast must be *hid in the heart*. We must treasure it up, as Mary treasured the sayings of Christ (Lk 2:51).

4.3. The yeast hidden in the dough works there. The yeast works quickly, like the word, and yet gradually. It works silently and imperceptibly (Mk 4:26), yet strongly and irresistibly. We have only to hide the yeast in the dough, and all the world cannot stop it from spreading its flavor to it; no one sees how it is done, but gradually *the whole is leavened*.

4.3.1. This is how it was in the world. By their preaching, the apostles hid a handful of yeast in the great mass of the human race, and it had a strange effect; it put the world into ferment, in a sense turning it *upside down* (Ac 17:6). It was effective in this way not by outward force—and therefore not resistible and conquerable by any such force—but by *the Spirit of the Lord of hosts, who works, and none can hinder* (Job 11:10).

4.3.2. This is how it is in the heart. The Gospel produces a change not in the substance of the heart—the dough remains the same—but in its quality. It produces a universal change; it diffuses into all the powers and faculties of the soul. This change makes the soul share in the nature of the word, as the dough shares in the nature of the leaven. It is a word of faith and repentance, holiness and love, and these are produced in the soul by that word. When the dough has been worked through by the yeast, then it goes into the oven; trials and adversities commonly attend this change, but this is how saints are fitted to become bread for our Master's table.

Verses 44–52

We have four short parables in these verses:

1. That of the *treasure hid in the field*. Up to this time he had compared *the kingdom of heaven* to small things.

In this parable and the next he represented it as having great value in itself. It is likened here *to a treasure hid in the field* that, if we choose, we may make our own.

1.1. Jesus Christ is the true Treasure; in him there is an abundance of all that is rich and useful, and if we are united with him, it all belongs to us.

1.2. The Gospel is the field in which this treasure is hidden. It is hidden not *in a garden enclosed* (SS 4:12) but *in a field*, an open field. Whatever royal mines we find, they are all ours if we follow the right course.

1.3. It is a great thing to discover treasure hidden in this field and learn its inestimable value. The richest mines are often in ground that appears the most barren. How is the Bible any better than other good books? Those who have *searched the scriptures*, so as to find Christ and *eternal life* in them (Jn 5:39), have discovered such treasure in this field as makes it infinitely more valuable.

1.4. Those who discern this treasure in the field and therefore value it rightly will never be at peace until they have made it their own on any terms. The one who has found this treasure rejoices in it, even though as yet the bargain has not been made; he is glad there is such a bargain available. He decides to *buy this field*: those who embrace Gospel offers on Gospel terms buy this field. They make it their own for the sake of the unseen treasure it contains. The man in the parable is so intent on buying this field *that he sells all* in order to do so: those who want the precious salvation that is to be found in Christ must *count everything but loss, that they may win Christ, and be found in him* (Php 3:8).

2. That of *the pearl of price* (vv. 45–46).

2.1. All the people are busy *seeking goodly pearls*: one wants to be rich, another to be honorable, another to be learned, but most are deceived and settle for counterfeit pearls.

2.2. Jesus Christ is *a Pearl of great price*; in having him, we have enough to make us happy here and forever.

2.3. A true Christian is a spiritual *merchant* who seeks and finds this valuable pearl and who, as one determined to be spiritually rich, pays a high price: *He went and bought that pearl*. He not only bid for it but also bought it.

2.4. Those who want to have a saving interest in Christ must be willing to give up everything for him, leave everything to follow him (Mk 10:28). One can spend too much on gold, but not on this pearl of great value.

3. That of the *net cast into the sea* (vv. 47–49).

3.1. Here is the parable itself. The world is a vast sea; the preaching of the Gospel is the letting down of a net into this sea to catch something from it. This net gathers in every kind, as large dragnets do. In the visible church, there is a great deal of trash and rubbish, dirt, weeds, and vermin, as well as fish. A time is coming when this net will be full, and it will be drawn to the shore. The net is now being filled; sometimes it fills more quickly than at other times, but always it is filling. When the net is full and is drawn to the shore, the good and bad that are gathered in it will be separated. The good will be gathered into vessels as those who are valuable and are therefore to be kept carefully, but the bad will be thrown away. While the net is in the sea, it is not known what it contains; even the fishermen cannot tell. But they carefully draw it in to the shore, with everything that is in it, for the sake of the good that it contains.

3.2. Here is the explanation of the latter part of the parable. The first part is obvious and plain enough, but the latter part refers to what is still to come and is therefore explained in more detail (vv. 49–50). *So shall it be at the end of the world.* We must not look for the net full of all good fish; the vessels will be, but in the net the fish are mixed. Notice here:

3.2.1. The distinguishing of evildoers from the righteous.

3.2.2. The doom of evildoers when they have been separated in this way. They will be *cast into the furnace.*

4. That of the *good householder*, which is intended to drive all the others home.

4.1. Its occasion was the good proficiency that the disciples had acquired in learning, and the profit they had gained by this sermon in particular. He asked them: *Have ye understood all these things?* He was ready to explain what they did not understand. It is the will of Christ that all those who read and hear the word understand it, for otherwise how could they benefit from it? They answered him: *Yea, Lord.* When they did not understand, they asked for an explanation (v. 36). The explanation of that parable was a key to the others. Good truths mutually explain and illustrate one another.

4.2. The scope of the parable itself was to give his approval and commendation to their proficiency. Christ is ready to encourage willing learners in his school, even though they are weak, and to say: *Well done, well said* (25:21, 23).

4.2.1. He commended them as *scribes instructed unto the kingdom of heaven.* They were now learning so that they could teach. Those who are to instruct others must themselves be well instructed. The instruction of a Gospel minister must be in the *kingdom of heaven.* If not instructed in the kingdom of heaven, they will be a bad minister.

4.2.2. He compared such teachers to a good householder, who *brings forth out of his treasure things new and old,* fruits of last year's growth and this year's harvest, plenty and variety. Notice what a minister's equipment should be: *a treasure of things new and old.* Old experiences and new observations all have their use, and we must not be content with what we have found before, but must always be adding new finds. Let us live and learn. We store in order to give out, so that others may benefit. Christ himself received so that he could give (Ps 68:18; Eph 4:8–11); so must we, and we will receive more. In bringing things out, new and old go best together; old truths, but communicated using new methods and expressions.

Verses 53–58

Here we have Christ in his own country. His own compatriots had rejected him once, but he came to them again. Christ does not take those who refuse him at their first word; he repeats his offers to those who have often repelled them. He had a natural affection for his own country. The way he was treated this time was much the same as before, scornfully and spitefully. Notice:

1. How they expressed their contempt of him. When he *taught them in their synagogue, they were astonished* (v. 54); they thought him an unlikely teacher. They reproached him for two things:

1.1. His lack of an academic education. They acknowledged that he was wise and that he did mighty works, but they asked, "From where did he get this wisdom and this power to perform miracles?" Mean and prejudiced spirits tend to judge people by their education, and to ask more about their background than their motives. *Whence has this man these mighty works?* If they had not been stubbornly blind, they would have had to conclude he was divinely assisted and commissioned, since without the aid of education he gave such proof of extraordinary wisdom and power.

1.2. The insignificance and poverty of his relatives (vv. 55–56). They reproached him because of his father: *Is not this the carpenter's son?* What harm was there in that? It was not beneath him to be the son of an honest trader. This carpenter was *of the house of David* (Lk 1:27), *a son of David* (1:20); even though he was a carpenter, he was still a person of honor. Some corrupt spirits pay no attention to any branch, not even the Branch from the stem of Jesse (Isa 11:1), if it is not the top branch. They reproached him because of his mother. It was true that *his mother was called Mary,* which was a very common name, and they all knew her, and knew her to be an ordinary woman. They turned this into an insult, however, as if people could not be valued for anything but splendid titles, which are poor things to measure true worth by. They reproached him because of his brothers, whose names they knew, good but poor men, and therefore despised, as was Christ for their sakes. *His sisters,* too, *are all with us;* the people should for that reason have loved him and respected him even more, because he was one of themselves, but instead it was why they despised him. They were *offended in him.*

2. How he responded to this contempt (vv. 57–58).

2.1. It did not trouble his heart. He mildly imputed it to the common human attitudes that undervalue first-class people who are ordinary and local. It is usually so. *A prophet is not without honour, save in his own country.* This shows us that prophets should have honor paid them, and they usually do; men and women of God are great and honorable and deserve respect. Despite this, they are often least respected and revered in their own country. Familiarity breeds contempt.

2.2. It did, for the present, in effect—if we may say this reverently—tie his hands: *He did not many mighty works there, because of their unbelief.* Lack of faith is the great obstruction to Christ's favors. Therefore, if mighty works are not worked in us, it is not because of a lack of power or grace in Christ, but because of a lack of faith in us.

CHAPTER 14

Here is: 1. The martyrdom of John: his imprisonment (vv. 1–5) and his beheading (vv. 6–12). 2. The miracles of Christ: 2.1. His feeding five thousand men with five loaves and two fish (vv. 13–21). 2.2. His walking on the waves to his disciples in a storm (vv. 22–33). 2.3. His healing the sick when they touched the edge of his cloak (vv. 34–36).

Verses 1–12

We have here the account of John's martyrdom. Notice:

1. The occasion of relating this story (vv. 1–2). Here is:

1.1. The account brought to Herod of the miracles that Christ performed. Herod the tetrarch, or chief governor, of Galilee *heard of the fame of Jesus.* At that time, when Jesus' compatriots showed him disrespect because of his lowliness and obscure origins, he began to be famous at court. The Gospel, like the sea, gains in one place what it loses in another. It seems it was not until now that Herod even heard of him, much less heard reports about him. It is the misfortune of the great people in the world that they are most out of reach of hearing the best things (1Co 2:8).

1.2. The interpretation he put on this (v. 2): *He said to his servants, This is John the Baptist; he is risen from the dead.* While he lived, John *did no miracle* (Jn 10:41), but

Herod concluded that, having risen from the dead, John had now been given greater power than he had while he was alive. Notice about Herod here:

1.2.1. How he was disappointed in what he intended by beheading John. He thought that if he could get that troublesome fellow out of the way, he could continue in his sins undisturbed and uncontrolled. However, no sooner had he done that than he heard that Jesus and his disciples were preaching the same pure message that John preached. Ministers may be silenced, imprisoned, banished, and killed, but the word of God cannot be stopped. Sometimes God raises up many faithful ministers out of the ashes of one.

1.2.2. How he was filled with groundless fears, merely from the guilt of his own conscience. A guilty conscience suggests everything that is frightful and, like a whirlpool, draws into itself everything that comes near it. This is how *the wicked flee when none pursue* (Pr 28:1).

1.2.3. How he was hardened in his evil despite this. He still did not express the slightest remorse or sorrow for his sin of putting him to death. The demons believe and tremble (Jas 2:19), but they never believe and repent.

2. The story itself of John's imprisonment and martyrdom. If Christ's forerunner was treated in this way, let his followers not expect to be treated kindly by the world. Notice:

2.1. John's faithfulness in rebuking Herod (vv. 3–4). Herod was one of John's listeners (Mk 6:20), and so John could be more bold with him. The particular sin John rebuked Herod for was marrying his brother Philip's wife—not his widow, for that would not have been so criminal, but his wife. Philip was now still alive, but Herod took his wife from him and kept her as his own. John reproved him for this sin: *It is not lawful for thee to have her.* He accused him of sinning: it was not *lawful.* What by the law of God is unlawful to other people is by the same law unlawful to rulers, leaders, and other great people. There is no right, not even for the greatest and most despotic kings, to break the laws of God. If rulers and leaders break the law of God, it is right they be told about it by proper people in a proper way.

2.2. The imprisonment of John for his faithfulness (v. 3). *Herod laid hold on John, bound him, and put him in prison.* It was partly to satisfy his own desire for revenge and partly to please Herodias. Faithful rebukes, if they do not profit their hearers, often provoke them. It is nothing new for God's ministers to suffer harm for doing good. Troubles come most to those who are most conscientious and faithful in fulfilling their duty (Ac 20:20).

2.3. The restraint that Herod lay under from further expressing his rage against John (v. 5).

2.3.1. He would have put him to death. Perhaps that was not originally intended when he imprisoned him, but his revenge gradually reached that level.

2.3.2. What hindered him was his *fear of the multitude, because they counted John as a prophet.* It was not because he feared God—if he had feared God, he would not have imprisoned John—nor because he feared John, but because he feared the people. He was fearful for himself, for his own safety. Even tyrants have their fears. Evildoers are restrained from committing the most corrupt practices merely by their secular interests, and not from any regard for God. The danger of sin that appears to the senses, or only to the imagination, influences people more than what appears to faith. People fear being hanged for what they do not fear being damned for.

2.4. The means of bringing John to his death. Here we have an account of his release, but not by any other discharge than death, the end of all a good person's troubles. Herodias hatched the plot; her implacable revenge thirsted after John's blood and would not be satisfied with anything less. If you go against the appetites of the flesh, they turn into the most barbaric passions. Herodias worked out how to bring about the murder of John so artfully as to save Herod's reputation and thereby pacify the people. Here we have:

2.4.1. The indulging of Herod by the girl's dancing on a birthday. In honor of the day, there had to be the usual ball at his court. To grace the occasion, Herodias's daughter danced for them, which was more than she would ordinarily have done, because she was the queen's daughter. This young lady's dancing pleased Herod.

2.4.2. The rash and foolish promise that Herod made to this reckless girl, to give her whatever she asked for, and this promise was confirmed by an oath (v. 7). It was an extravagant obligation that Herod entered into here, and in no way becoming to a wise man.

2.4.3. The bloodthirsty demand the young lady made for John the Baptist's head (v. 8). She had earlier been instructed to do so by her mother. The case of children is very sad when their parents are *their counsellors to do wickedly.* After Herod had given the girl her commission and Herodias had given her her instructions, she required John the Baptist's head on a platter. John must be beheaded, then; that was the death by which he must glorify God. However, even this was not enough; the girl must also be indulged, and not only revenge but also fancy must be gratified. His head must be *given her here in a charger* (on a platter), served up in blood. His head must be given her, and she would consider it a reward for her dancing and desire nothing more.

2.4.4. Herod's granting of this demand (v. 9): *The king was sorry*—at least he pretended to be so—but *for the oath's sake, he commanded it to be given her.* Here is:

2.4.4.1. A pretended concern for John. *The king was sorry.* Many people sin with regret but never show true regret for their sin. He appeared to sin with reluctance but still carried on sinning.

2.4.4.2. A pretended conscientiousness toward his oath, with a counterfeit show of honor and honesty; he had to do something because of the oath. It is a great mistake to think that an evil oath will justify an evil action. No one can put themselves under an obligation to sin, because God has already so strongly committed every person against sin.

2.4.4.3. A real evil in agreeing with his wicked companions. Herod yielded not so much for the sake of the oath as because it was made in public and because he wanted to compliment *them that sat at meat* (feasting) *with him.* He granted the demand so that he would not seem to have broken his commitment in front of them. A point of honor goes much further with many people than a point of conscience.

2.4.4.4. A real hatred toward John at the root of this concession, for otherwise he might have found a way to get clear of his promise. *He commanded it to be given her.*

2.4.5. The execution of John, accordingly (v. 10): *He sent and beheaded John in the prison.* He must be beheaded with all speed, to satisfy Herodias. It was done at night. It was done in prison, not at the usual place of execution, for fear of uproar. A great deal of innocent blood, blood of martyrs, has accumulated in corners. And so that voice was silenced, that burning and shining light snuffed out (Jn 5:35); so that prophet, that Elijah, of the New Testament fell as a sacrifice to the feelings of an imperious prostitute.

2.5. The disposal of the poor remains of this blessed saint and martyr.

2.5.1. The girl brought the head triumphantly to her mother as a trophy of the victories of her hatred and revenge (v. 11).

2.5.2. The disciples *buried the body* and brought the news in tears to our Lord Jesus.

2.5.2.1. *They buried the body.* There is a respect that is due to the servants of Christ not only while they live but also, to their bodies and memories, when they have died.

2.5.2.2. *They went and told Jesus*, not so much for his own safety as to receive encouragement from him and be included among his disciples. When anything makes us suffer at any time, it is our duty and privilege to tell Christ about it. It will ease our burdened spirits to confide in a trusted friend, one whom we may be open with. When the shepherds are struck, the sheep need not be scattered (Zec 13:7; Mt 26:31) while they have the great Shepherd of the sheep to go to, who remains the same (Heb 13:8, 20). Encouragements that are otherwise highly valuable are sometimes taken away from us because they come between us and Christ and tend to take away the love and respect that are due only to him. It is better to be drawn to Christ by need and loss than not to come to him at all.

Verses 13–21

This passage about Christ's feeding *five thousand men with five loves and two fishes* is recorded by all four Evangelists. Notice:

1. The great number of people who turned to Christ when he withdrew *into a desert place* (v. 13). He withdrew privately not because he heard about John's death but because he heard about the thoughts Herod had concerning him, that Herod thought he was *John the Baptist risen from the dead.* Jesus went farther away to get out of Herod's jurisdiction. In times of danger, when God opens a door of escape (1Co 10:13), it is right to flee to preserve our own lives, unless we have some special call to expose ourselves. *He departed by ship.* But *when the people heard it, they followed him on foot* from all parts. Christ had such an influence on the crowds that his withdrawal from them only made them come after him even more eagerly. It seems there was more crowding toward Christ after John's martyrdom than before. Sometimes *the suffering of the saints* is used to further the Gospel (Php 1:12). When Christ and his word withdraw from us, it is best for us, whatever people may say to the contrary, to follow it. The presence of Christ and his Gospel makes a remote place not only tolerable but also desirable; it turns the desert into an Eden (Isa 41:19–20; 51:3).

2. The tender compassion of our Lord Jesus toward those who followed him (v. 14). He went out and appeared publicly among them. He went out from his seclusion when he saw that people wanted to hear him, as one who, for the good of souls, was willing both to exert himself and to give of himself. *When he saw the multitude, he had compassion on them* (v. 14). The sight of a vast crowd may justly move compassion. No one has pity for souls like Christ does: *his compassions fail not* (La 3:22). He not only pitied them but also helped them; many of them were *sick, and he, in compassion to them, healed them.* After a while, they were all hungry, *and he, in compassion to them, fed them.*

3. The disciples' suggestion that the crowds be dismissed and Christ's setting aside that suggestion. They thought a good day's work had been done and it was time to disperse. Christ's disciples are often more concerned to show their discretion than to show their zeal. Christ would

not dismiss them because they were hungry, but told his disciples to provide for them. All along, Christ expressed more tenderness toward the people than his disciples did. Notice how reluctant Christ is to part with those who are determined to stay with him! *They need not depart.* But if they are hungry, they need to depart, for hunger is a necessity that knows no law, and so he said to his disciples: *give you them to eat. The Lord is for the body* (1Co 6:13); it is *the work of his hands*; it is part of what he has purchased. He himself was clothed with a body, to encourage us to depend on him for our physical needs to be supplied. If we *seek first the kingdom of God*, making that our chief concern, we may depend on God to *add other things to* us (6:33), as far as he sees fit.

4. The slender provision that was made for this great multitude, and here we must compare the number of invited guests with the available food.

4.1. The number of the guests was *five thousand of men, besides women and children.* It was a vast audience whom Christ preached to here, and we have reason to think they were attentive, but it seems that most of them came to nothing; they went off and no longer followed him. We would rather see the acceptableness of the word in the conversion of its hearers than in their numbers, though the sight of vast crowds is a good sign.

4.2. The amount of food available was very disproportionate to the number of the guests, only *five loaves and two fishes.* The disciples carried this provision with them for the use of the immediate family, now that they *were retired into the desert.* There was no plenty or variety or delicacies here; a meal of fish was nothing rare for those of them who were fishermen. But it was all right for the Twelve. Here was no wine or alcohol; adequate water from the rivers in the desert was the best they had to drink with their food. But Christ wanted to use this to feed the crowd. When the need is urgent, those who have only a little must relieve others even if they have only a little to give, and that is the way to increase it (1Ki 17:12–16).

5. The generous distribution of this provision among the crowd (vv. 18–19): *Bring them hither to me.* The way to make our creature comforts truly encouraging to us is to bring them to Christ. What we put into the hands of our Lord Jesus is likely to prosper and do us good, so that he may use it as he pleases and we may take it back from him, and then it will be doubly sweet to us. Notice at this miraculous meal:

5.1. The seating of the guests (v. 19): *He commanded them to sit down.* But what would they all sit on? Let them *sit down on the grass.* Here not even a cloth was spread, no plates or napkins set out, no knives or forks, not even a bench to sit down on; instead, *he commanded them to sit down on the grass.* By doing everything in this way, without any pomp or splendor, he plainly showed *that his kingdom was not of this world* (Jn 18:36).

5.2. The seeking of a blessing. He himself *looked up to heaven, and blessed, and gave thanks.* He praised God for the provision they had, and he prayed to God to bless it to them. Here he has taught us that good duty of seeking a blessing and giving thanks at mealtimes: the good things God has created must be *received with thanksgiving* (1Ti 4:4). When Christ *blessed*, he *looked up to heaven*, to teach us that in our prayers, we too should look to God as *a Father in heaven*, and to teach us that when we receive our creature comforts we must look there, as those who receive them from God's hand and depend on him for a blessing.

5.3. The dividing of the food. The Master of the feast was himself the head carver, for *he brake, and gave the loaves to the disciples, and the disciples to the multitude.* Ministers can never fill people's hearts unless Christ first fills their hands, and what he has given to the disciples, they must pass on to the crowd. And we bless God that no matter how great the crowd, there is enough for all and enough for each.

5.4. The increase of the food. Only the increase itself is noticed here, not its cause or the way in which it was done. No mention is made of any word that Christ spoke. The purposes and intentions of his will and mind will take effect even if they are not spoken. Yet it is significant that the food was multiplied not when it was all together originally but when it was distributed. This shows us that grace grows by being acted on and that while other things perish when they are used, spiritual gifts increase as they are used. In this way, *there is that* which *scattereth, and yet increaseth* (Pr 11:24).

6. The abundant satisfaction of all the guests with this provision.

6.1. There was enough: *They did all eat, and were filled.* Those whom Christ feeds are filled by him. Just as there was enough for all, and so *they did all eat*, so also there was enough for each, and so *they were filled.* Although there was only a little, there was enough, and that is as good as a feast. The blessing of God can make a little go a long way.

6.2. There was to spare: *They took up of the fragments that remained, twelve baskets full*, one basket for each apostle. And so they received what they gave out, with a great deal more besides. This was to show that the provision Christ makes for those who are his is not bare and scanty, but rich and plentiful: an overflowing fullness. It is the same divine power that multiplies *the seed sown in the ground* every year and makes *the earth yield her increase*, so that what was brought out in handfuls is brought home in sheaves. *This is the Lord's doing* (Ps 118:23; Mk 12:11).

Verses 22–33

We have the story of another miracle here which Christ performed for the relief of his friends and followers, his *walking upon the water to his disciples.* Notice:

1. Christ's dismissing of his disciples and *the multitude* after he had fed them miraculously. He *constrained his disciples to get into a ship, and to go before him unto the other side* (v. 22). The apostle John gives a particular reason for the hasty breaking up of this meeting: the people were so affected by the miracle of the loaves that they were about to *take him by force, and make him a king* (Jn 6:15).

1.1. Christ sent the people away. He sent them away with a blessing, with some parting words of warning, advice, and encouragement.

1.2. He *constrained the disciples to go into a ship* (boat) first, for until they had gone, the people would not move. The disciples were reluctant to go and would not have gone if he had not *constrained* them.

2. Christ's withdrawal then (v. 23): *He went up into a mountain apart to pray.* Notice here that:

2.1. He was alone: *he went apart into a solitary place, and was there all alone.* He still chose to be alone sometimes, to set us an example. People who do not wish to be alone, who cannot enjoy themselves in solitude, when they have no one else to talk with, no one's company to enjoy except that of God and their own hearts, are not Christ's followers.

2.2. He was alone in prayer; the business of his solitude was to pray. Here, Christ has set us an example of private

prayer according to the rule he gave in 6:6. When the disciples went on the lake, their Master went to prayer.

2.3. He was alone for a long time; *there he was when the evening was come*, and it seems he was there until toward morning, *the fourth watch of the night. The night* came on, and it was a stormy night, but he continued *instant* (faithful) *in prayer* (Ro 12:12). When we find our hearts released, it is good to continue in private prayer for a long time.

3. The condition that the poor disciples were in at this time: *Their ship was now in the midst of the sea, tossed with waves* (v. 24).

3.1. They had reached the middle of the lake when the storm arose. We may have fair weather at the beginning of our voyage but meet with storms before we arrive at the port we are bound for. After a long calm, expect some storm or other.

3.2. The disciples were now where Christ sent them, but they still met with this storm. It is nothing new for Christ's disciples to meet with storms as they fulfill their duty, and to be sent to sea when their Master foresees a storm, but they are not to take it unkindly. Christ intends to reveal himself with more amazing grace to them and for them.

3.3. It was a great discouragement to them now that they did not have Christ with them as they did when they were in a storm before. And so we see how Christ first got his disciples used to small difficulties, and then to greater ones; he gradually trained them to live *by faith* (Gal 3:11).

3.4. Though *the wind was contrary* and they were tossed with waves, nevertheless, because they were ordered by their Master *to the other side*, they did not tack about and go back again, but made their way forward as best they could. Although troubles and difficulties may disturb us as we do our duty, they must not drive us away from it.

4. Christ's approach to them in this condition (v. 25), and here we have an example:

4.1. Of his goodness, that he went to them, as one who noticed their situation and was concerned for them. Christ considers the church's extremity his opportunity to come to them and appear on their behalf.

4.2. Of his power, that he *went unto them, walking on the sea.* This shows Christ's sovereign dominion over all created things. We need not ask how this was done. It is sufficient to say that what he did proved his divine power. Christ can use whatever method he wishes to save his people.

5. An account of what took place between Christ and his distressed friends as he came.

5.1. Between him and all the disciples. We are told here:

5.1.1. How their fears were raised: *When they saw him walking on the sea, they were troubled, saying, It is a spirit, it is a ghost* (v. 26). These disciples said, *It is a spirit*, when they should have said, "*It is the Lord*; it can be no one else."

5.1.1.1. Even the appearances and approaches of rescue are sometimes occasions of trouble and confusion for God's people, who are sometimes most afraid when they are least hurt.

5.1.1.2. The appearance of a ghost, or the thought of it, is always very frightening. Yet the more we know God, the Father of spirits (Heb 12:9), and the more careful we are to keep ourselves in his love, the better we will be able to deal with those fears. A little thing frightens us in a storm. Most of our danger from outward troubles arises from their potential for causing inward trouble.

5.1.2. How these fears were silenced (v. 27). He delayed his help while they wrestled with waves, but he hastened to help them overcome their fear, which was more dangerous; he immediately stilled that storm with his word: *Be of good cheer; it is I; be not afraid.* First, he put right their mistake, by making himself known to them: *It is I* (Ge 45:3). He did not name himself; it was enough to say to these disciples, *It is I.* They *knew his voice, as his sheep* (Jn 10:4), as Mary Magdalene did (Jn 20:16). To understand who it was that they saw was enough to make them at peace. Right knowledge, especially the knowledge of Christ, opens the door to true comfort. He encouraged them in their panic: *It is I,* and so: *Be of good cheer.* If Christ's disciples are not cheerful in a storm, it is their own fault; he wants them to be so. *Be not afraid:* "Be not afraid of me, now that you know it is I." Christ will not be a terror to those to whom he reveals himself; when they come to understand him rightly, the terror will be over. "*Be not afraid* of the storm, of the winds and waves; do not fear them, since I am so near you. I am the One who concerns himself for you, and I will not stand by and see you perish." Nothing need be a terror to those who have Christ near them and know he is theirs, not even death itself.

5.2. Between him and Peter (vv. 28–31). Notice:

5.2.1. Peter's courage, and Christ's encouraging of it.

5.2.1.1. It was very bold of Peter to want to venture out to Christ *upon the water: Lord, if it be thou, bid me come unto thee* (v. 28). Courage was Peter's characteristic grace, and that made him so much more eager than the others to express his love for Christ, even though others perhaps loved him as much.

5.2.1.1.1. That Peter wanted to come to Christ shows his devotion him. When he saw Christ, he was impatient to be with him. He did not say, *Bid me walk on the waters,* as if wanting it for the sake of a miracle, but, *Bid me come to me,* as if wanting it for Christ's sake. True love will break through fire and water to come to Christ. Those who want to gain benefits from Christ as a Savior must come to him in faith. When for a short time Christ has forsaken his people, his returns are welcome and are embraced most affectionately.

5.2.1.1.2. That he would not come without a command shows his caution and due observance of the will of Christ. Not, "If it is you, I will come," but *If it be thou, bid me come.* The boldest spirits must wait for a call to risky enterprises, and we must not rashly and presumptuously thrust ourselves into them.

5.2.1.1.3. That he ventured out on the water when Christ commanded him shows his faith and determination. What difficulty or danger could stand in the face of such a faith and such a zeal?

5.2.1.2. It was very kind of Christ to be willing to acknowledge him in it (v. 29). Christ knew that it came from a sincere and zealous affection for him, and he graciously accepted it. Christ is pleased with the expressions of his people's love, even though they are mixed with many weaknesses, and he makes the best of them. He told him to *come.* When Peter asked for a sign, he received it, because he did it with a determination to trust Christ. Then, Christ supported him when he did come: *Peter walked upon the water.* Elsewhere, the fellowship of true believers with Christ is represented by their being *quickened with him* and *raised up with him.* I think it is represented in this story by their *walking with him on the water.* Through the strength of Christ we are supported above the world, are kept from sinking into it and being overwhelmed by it, and obtain a victory over it (1Jn 5:4). Peter walked on the water not for show or entertainment

but to go to Jesus. Nor can we ever come to Jesus unless we are upheld by his power; and we must depend on that power, as Peter did when he *walked upon the water,* and there is no danger of sinking while *underneath are the everlasting arms* (Dt 33:27).

5.2.2. Peter's cowardice and Christ's rebuking him and helping him. Christ told him to come not only so that he would walk on the water and thereby know Christ's power but also so that he would sink and thereby know his own weakness. Notice:

5.2.2.1. Peter's great fear: *He was afraid* (v. 30). The strongest faith and the greatest courage contain a mixture of fear. Those who can say, *Lord, I believe,* must also say, *Lord, help my unbelief* (Mk 9:24). Peter was very bold at first, but afterward his heart failed him. The extending of a trial reveals the weakness of faith. Here is:

5.2.2.1.1. The cause of this fear: *He saw the wind boisterous.* While Peter kept his eyes fixed on Christ and on his word and power, he *walked upon the water* well enough, but when he also noticed the danger he was in, then he feared. Looking at difficulties with our physical eyes more than at the commands and promises with the eyes of faith lies at the root of all our excessive fears. When Peter *saw the wind boisterous,* he should have remembered what he had seen (8:27) when the winds and the sea obeyed Christ.

5.2.2.1.2. The effect of this fear: *He began to sink.* While his faith kept up, he kept above water, but when faith wavered, *he began to sink.* The sinking of our spirits is due to the weakness of our faith; we are upheld—just as we are saved—*through faith* (1Pe 1:5). It was Christ's great mercy to Peter that when his faith failed, Christ did not leave him to sink outright, to sink to the *bottom as a stone* (Ex 15:5), but gave him time to *cry, Lord, save me.* Christ has such care for true believers; though weak, they only begin to sink!

5.2.2.1.3. The remedy he applied in his distress, the old, tried and tested remedy: prayer. He cried out, *Lord, save me.* Notice how he prayed; it was bold and fervent: *He cried.* When our faith is weak, our prayer should be strong. What he prayed about was relevant and to the point: *he cried, Lord, save me.* Those who want to be saved must not only *come* to him but also *cry* to him for salvation. However, we are never brought to such a point until we find ourselves sinking; our sense of need will drive us to him.

5.2.2.2. Christ's great favor to Peter in this fear. He saved him: immediately *he stretched forth his hand, and caught him.* Christ's time to save is when we sink; he helps in a crisis. Christ's hand is still stretched out to all believers to keep them from sinking. Never fear, he will keep his own people. He rebuked Peter, for those he loves and saves are those he rebukes and disciplines (Pr 3:12; Heb 12:5–6): *O thou of little faith, wherefore didst thou doubt?* Faith may be true and yet weak; it may at first be like a mustard seed. Peter had enough faith to take him out onto the water, but because it was not enough to carry him through, Christ told him he had only a *little.* Our discouraging doubts and fears are all owing to the weakness of our faith: we *doubt* because we are *of little faith.* If only we believed more, we would doubt less. It is true that he does not reject weak believers, but it is also as true that he is not pleased with weak faith, especially not in those who are nearest to him. *Wherefore didst thou doubt?* What reason was there for it? There is no good reason why Christ's disciples should have a doubtful mind, not even on stormy days, because he is readily available to them, *a very present Help* (Ps 46:1).

6. *The ceasing of the storm* (v. 32). When Christ came into the boat, they were immediately at the shore. Christ *walked upon the water* till he came to the boat, and then went onto that, when he could as easily have walked to the shore. When Christ came into the boat, Peter came in with him. Companions with Christ in his patient endurance will be companions in his kingdom (Rev 1:9). Those who walk with him will reign with him (2Ti 2:12). *When they were come into the ship, immediately the storm ceased.* When Christ comes into a soul, he makes winds and storms peace. When we welcome Christ, *the noise of her waves will soon be quelled* (Ps 65:7; 89:9–10). The way to be still is to know that he is God (Ps 46:10), that he is the *Lord with us* (Mt 1:23).

7. The adoration then given to Christ: *They that were in the ship came and worshiped him, and said, Of a truth, thou art the Son of God* (v. 33). They made two good uses of this distress and rescue:

7.1. It was a confirmation of their faith in Christ. They knew before that he was the Son of God, but now they knew it better. Faith is sometimes more active after a conflict with unbelief, and it reaches greater degrees of strength by being exercised. Now they *knew it of a truth*. Faith grows when it reaches a full assurance, when it sees clearly and says, *Of a truth*.

7.2. They took it as an opportunity to *give him the glory due unto his name* (1Ch 16:29; Ps 96:8). *They worshiped Christ.* When Christ reveals his glory for us, we should return his glory to him (Ps 50:15). And so the disciples worshiped and adored Christ in this way: *Of a truth thou art the Son of God.* The matter of our beliefs may and must be made the matter of our praise. Faith is the proper motive in worship, and worship is the genuine product of faith.

Verses 34–36

Here is an account of miracles in great number that Christ performed on the other side of the lake, at Gennesaret. Wherever Christ went, he did good (Ac 10:38). Notice:

1. The eagerness and faith of *the men of that place*. These were more noble than the Gergesenes, their neighbors (Ac 17:11). Those *besought Christ to depart* from them (8:34); they had no need of him. These sought him to help them: they recognized their need of him. Christ reckons it the greatest honor we can do him to make use of him. We are told here:

1.1. How *the men of that place* were brought to Christ; they *had knowledge of* (recognized) *him* (v. 35). It is probable that his miraculous walking on the water helped make way for him to be welcomed in those parts. Perhaps that was one thing Christ intended in that miracle, for he has great purposes in what he does. Those who know Christ's name will turn to him: if Christ were better known, he would not be neglected as he is; he is trusted as far as he is known. They *had knowledge of him*, that is, of his being among them. The discerning of the day of our opportunities is a good step toward making the most of those opportunities. It is better to know that there *is* a prophet among us than that there *has been* one (Eze 2:5).

1.2. How they brought others to Christ: *They sent out into all that country.* Those who know Christ themselves should do all they can to bring others to come to know him too. We must not eat these spiritual morsels by ourselves; in Christ there is enough for us all, so that there is nothing to be gained by monopolizing him. When we have opportunities of obtaining good for our souls, we should bring as many others as we can to share with us. More people than we think of would take the opportunities if only they were called on and invited to share in them. Neighborhood is an advantage for doing good that must be made the most of.

1.3. What their business with Christ was: *They brought unto him all that were diseased.* If love for Christ and his teaching would not bring them to him, love for self would. If only we would rightly seek our own things, the things concerning our own peace and welfare (Lk 19:42), we would seek the things of Christ.

1.4. How they turned to him: *They besought* (begged) *him that they might only touch the hem of his garment* (v. 36). They turned to him:

1.4.1. With great boldness; they begged him. The greatest favors and blessings are to be obtained from Christ by seeking: *Ask, and it shall be given* (7:7).

1.4.2. With great humility. Their desiring to touch the edge of his cloak suggests they thought themselves unworthy even that he should be bothered with their case, much less that he should touch and heal them; they would look on it as a great favor if he would allow them to *touch the hem of his garment.*

1.4.3. With great assurance of the all-sufficiency of his power, not doubting that they would be healed even by touching the edge of his cloak. They were sure that there was in him such an overflowing fullness of healing power that they could not fail to be healed if only they could come near him. It was in this country and neighborhood that the woman who had been subject to bleeding was healed by *touching the hem of his garment* and was commended for her faith (9:20–22), and they were probably remembering that when they made their request. It is good to use those means and methods that others before us have found effective.

2. The fruit and success of their turning to Christ. It was not in vain, for as *many as touched were made perfectly whole.* Christ's healings are complete. Those whom he heals are healed perfectly. He does not do his work by halves. There is an abundance of healing power in Christ for all who turn to him, even if they are very many. The least of Christ's institutions, like the edge of his cloak, is constantly being refilled with the overflowing fullness of his grace. The healing power that is in Christ is spent for the benefit of those who touch him with a true and living faith. Christ is in heaven, but his word is near us (Dt 30:11–14), and he himself is in that word. When we combine faith with the word (Heb 4:2) and submit to its influences and commands, then we touch the edge of Christ's cloak. It is only by touching that we are made whole.

CHAPTER 15

In this chapter we have our Lord Jesus as the great Prophet teaching, as the great Physician healing, and as the great Shepherd of the sheep feeding (Heb 13:20). We also see him as the Father of spirits (Heb 12:9), instructing them; as the Conqueror of Satan, expelling him; and as One concerned for the bodies of his people, providing for them. Here is: 1. Christ's conversation with the teachers of the law and Pharisees about human traditions (vv. 1–9). 2. His conversation with the crowd about the things that defile (vv. 10–20). 3. His driving out the demon from the Canaanite woman's daughter (vv. 21–28). 4. His healing all who were brought to him (vv. 29–31). 5. His feeding four thousand men (vv. 32–39).

Verses 1 – 9

1. Here is the objection raised by the teachers of the law and Pharisees against Christ's disciples for eating with unwashed hands. These leaders were men of learning and also men of business, and they came from Jerusalem, the Holy City. They should have been better than others, therefore, but they were worse. External privileges, if not properly used, commonly swell people up with pride and hatred. Now if these great men were the accusers, then what was the accusation? Nonconformity to the canons of their church: *Why do thy disciples transgress the tradition of the elders?* (v. 2). They gave evidence for this accusation by citing one particular instance: *They wash not their hands when they eat bread.* Notice:

1.1. What the *tradition of the elders* was — that people should often wash their hands, and always when eating. The elders located much of their religion in this, thinking that the food they touched with unwashed hands would defile them. The Pharisees practiced this themselves, and they imposed it on others with a great deal of strictness. In fact, they would not eat food with another person who had not washed before eating.

1.2. What the breach of this tradition or injunction by the disciples was. It seems that they did not wash their hands when they ate bread. The custom was innocent enough and had a decency in its civil practice. When it came to be practiced and imposed as a religious ceremony, however, with such emphasis placed on it, the disciples, though weak in knowledge, were still so well taught as not to comply with it, observe it, or even notice when the teachers of the law and Pharisees had their eye on them. They had already learned St. Paul's lesson, "*All things are lawful for me*; no doubt it is lawful to wash before eating, *but I will not be brought under the power of* anyone (1Co 6:12)."

1.3. What the complaint of the teachers of the law and Pharisees against them was. They quarreled with Christ about this supposed infraction. "*Why do thy disciples transgress* the canons of the church?" It was good that the complaint was made to Christ, for the disciples themselves were perhaps not so able to give a reason for what they did as one would have wished.

2. Here is Christ's answer to this objection, his justification of the disciples. He replied to them in two ways:

2.1. By way of recrimination (vv. 3 – 6). They were seeing specks of sawdust in the eyes of his disciples, but Christ showed them a plank in their own (7:3). It was such a criticism of their tradition — and the authority of that was what they based their accusation on — as not only made it lawful not to submit but also made opposition a duty.

2.1.1. The charge in general was, *You transgress the commandment of God by your tradition.* They called it the *tradition of the elders,* emphasizing the antiquity of the custom and the authority of those who imposed it, but they *transgressed the commandment of God.* Those who are most zealous to impose their own ideas are usually most careless about God's commands.

2.1.2. The proof of this charge lay in a particular instance, that of their disobeying the fifth commandment.

2.1.2.1. Let us see what the command of God is (v. 4), what is the precept of the law and what is the incentive for obeying it. The command is, *Honour thy father and thy mother*; this is required by the Father of the whole human race. The whole of children's duty to their parents is included in this command to honor them, which is the spring and foundation of all the rest. The incentive for keeping this fifth commandment is a promise, *that*

thy days may be long (Ex 20:12), but our Savior waived that, so that no one would infer that it was something only commendable and profitable, and he insisted on the penalty attached to the breach of this commandment in another Scripture, which shows the duty to be highly and indispensably necessary: *He that curseth father or mother, let him die the death.* From our Savior's application of this law, it is clear that denying service or relief to parents is included in cursing them. Even if the language is respectful enough, containing nothing abusive, what good will it do if the deeds are not consistent with it?

2.1.2.2. Let us see how the tradition of the elders contradicted this command. It was not direct and downright, but implicit; their experts gave them rules that provided them with an easy way to avoid the obligation of this command (vv. 5 – 6). Notice:

2.1.2.2.1. What their tradition was: that a man could do no better with his worldly estate than give it to the priests, than devote it to the service of the temple, and that when anything was devoted in this way, not only was it unlawful to transfer it to someone else, but also all other obligations, no matter how just and sacred, were thereby superseded.

2.1.2.2.2. How they worked out the application of this to the situation of children. When their parents' necessities called for their help, they pleaded that all they could spare from themselves and their children was what they had devoted to the treasury of the temple: *It is a gift, by whatsoever thou mightest be profited by me* (whatever help you might otherwise have received from me is a gift devoted to God), and so their parents must expect nothing from them. The Pharisees taught that this was a good and valid plea, and many undutiful, unnatural children used it, and the Pharisees justified them in their actions, saying — our translation supplies these implied words, though they are not in the original — *He shall be free.* However, the absurdity and ungodliness of this tradition were very clear, for revealed religion was intended to improve, not overthrow, natural religion. One of the fundamental laws of natural religion is honoring our parents. This was *making the command of God of no effect.* To break the law is bad, but to *teach men so,* as the teachers of the law and Pharisees did, is much worse (5:19). Why is the command given, if it is not to be obeyed?

2.2. By way of reprehension. The other part of Christ's answer accused them of hypocrisy: *Ye hypocrites* (v. 7). It is the right of the One who searches the heart and knows what is in us (1Ch 28:9; Ro 8:27; Rev 2:23) to declare who is a hypocrite. We can notice open godlessness, but it is only the eye of Christ that can discern hypocrisy (Lk 16:15). Just as it is a sin that his eye discovers, so it is also a sin that his soul hates more than all others. Christ drew his rebuke from Isa 29:13. *Well did Esaias prophesy of you.* Isaiah spoke it about the people of the generation to which he prophesied, but Christ applied it to these teachers of the law and Pharisees. Threats that are directed against others belong to us if we are guilty of the same sins. Isaiah prophesied not only about them but also about all other hypocrites, against whom his word is still directed and stands in force. The prophecies of Scripture are being fulfilled every day.

2.2.1. The description of hypocrites, in two aspects:

2.2.1.1. In their own acts of worship (v. 8). When they *draw nigh to God with their mouth, and honour him with their lips, their heart is far from him.* Notice:

2.2.1.1.1. How far hypocrites go; they draw near to God and honor him; they are by profession worshipers of God. The *Pharisee went up to the temple to pray* (Lk 18:10); he did not stand as far away as those who *live without God in the world* (Eph 2:12). The people honored him; that is, they undertook to honor God, joining others who did so. God receives some honor even from the services of hypocrites.

2.2.1.1.*2*. What they do; their actions are done only with the mouth and lips. It is godliness only from the teeth outward; they show much love, but that is all. There is no true love in their hearts. Hypocrites are those who pay only lip service in their religious faith and worship.

2.2.1.1.*3*. What they fall short in; this is the main matter: *Their heart is far from me*, habitually separated from God (Eph 4:18), actually wandering and dwelling on something else. A hypocrite says one thing but thinks another. The great thing that God looks at and requires is the heart (Pr 23:26).

2.2.1.2. In what they prescribe to others. It shows their hypocrisy that *they teach for doctrines the commandments of men*. When human inventions are tacked onto God's institutions, and imposed accordingly, this is hypocrisy, a merely human religion. God wants his own work to be done by his own rules and does not accept what he himself did not appoint. Only what comes *from* him will be acceptable when it comes *to* him.

2.2.2. The condemnation of hypocrites; it is expressed briefly: *In vain do they worship me*. Their worship does not fulfill the purpose for which it was appointed; it will neither please God nor benefit them. If it is not *in spirit*, it is not *in truth* (Jn 4:23), and so it is all nothing. Lip service is lost service.

Verses 10–20

Notice:

1. The solemn introduction to this message: *He called the multitude* (v. 10). Christ considered the crowd. The humble Jesus, to humble the Pharisees, embraced those whom the Pharisees looked on with disdain. He turned away from the Pharisees, because they were stubborn and unteachable, and turned to the crowd, who, though weak, were humble and willing to be taught. He said to them, *Hear and understand*. What we hear from the mouth of Christ, we must seek to understand as thoroughly as possible. Not only scholars but even the crowd, the ordinary people, must apply their minds to understand the words of Christ.

2. The truth itself set down (v. 11), in two propositions.

2.1. *Not that which goes into the mouth defileth the man*. It is not the kind or quality of our food, or the condition of our hands, that pollutes or defiles the soul. *The kingdom of God is not meat and drink* (Ro 14:17). What defiles a person? By what is guilt contracted before God, and how is a person rendered repugnant to him and disqualified for fellowship with him? What we eat does not do this. Christ was now beginning to teach his followers to *call nothing common or unclean*, and if Peter, when he was told to *kill and eat*, had remembered this word, he would not have said, *Not so, Lord* (Ac 10:13–15, 28).

2.2. *But that which comes out of the mouth, this defiles a man*. We are defiled not by the food we eat with unwashed hands but by the words we speak from an unsanctified heart. It was not the disciples who defiled themselves with what they ate, but the Pharisees who defiled themselves with what they spoke spitefully and critically about them. Those who accuse others of breaking human commandments bring much greater guilt on themselves by breaking the law of God against rash judging.

3. The offense that was taken at this truth and the account brought to Christ of that offense: *The disciples said unto him, Knowest thou that the Pharisees were offended?* (v. 12).

3.1. It was not strange that the Pharisees should be offended at this plain truth. Sore eyes cannot bear clear light, and nothing is more offensive to proud deceivers than the undeceiving of those whom they have blindfolded and enslaved. Great contenders for the formalities of religion are often those who condemn its core beliefs.

3.2. The disciples thought it strange that their Master should say what he knew would cause so much offense; he should not do so. But he knew what he said and to whom he said it; he wanted to teach us that although we must be sensitive about giving offense in indifferent things, we must not, for fear of that, evade any definite truth or duty. Truth must be acknowledged, and duty done, and if anyone is offended by those, they are at fault; it is offense not given but taken. Perhaps the disciples themselves stumbled at the word Christ said; maybe they raised this objection with Christ so that they themselves could be better informed. Moreover, they seem to have had a concern for the Pharisees. They did not want the Pharisees to go away displeased with anything Christ had said, and so although they did not want him to retract his words, they hoped he would explain, correct, and modify them. Weak hearers are sometimes more concerned than they should be not to see evil hearers offended.

4. The condemnation passed on the Pharisees and their corrupt traditions. Christ foretold two things about them here.

4.1. The uprooting of them and their traditions: *Every plant which my heavenly Father hath not planted shall be rooted up* (v. 13). Their sect, ways, and constitution were plants that God had not planted. The rules of their profession were not his institutions, but owed their origin to pride and formality. In the visible church, it is not strange to find plants that our heavenly Father has not planted. Even if the farmer is very careful, their ground will produce weeds by itself, more or fewer, and an enemy is busy sowing them (13:25). What is corrupt, though permitted by God, has not been planted by him; he sows nothing but *good seed in his field*. Let us, therefore, not be deceived, as if all that we find in the church must be right and all those people and things that we find in our Father's garden are our Father's plants. *By their fruit you shall know them* (7:20). Those plants that are not planted by God will not be protected by him, but will undoubtedly be uprooted. What is not of God will not stand (Ac 5:38), but the Gospel of truth is great and will last (1 Esd 4:41). It cannot be uprooted.

4.2. Their ruin, together with that of their followers (v. 14).

4.2.1. Christ told his disciples to *let them alone*. "Have no dealings with them or concern for them; neither seek their favor nor dread their displeasure; they will follow their own ways, and let them come to terms with the outcome. They are wedded to their own imaginations and want everything to go their own way; leave them alone. Do not seek to please a generation who do not please God (1Th 2:15)." The case of those sinners whom Christ orders his ministers to leave alone is truly sad.

4.2.2. He gave them two reasons for it. "*Let them alone*, for:

4.2.2.1. "They are proud and ignorant," two bad qualities that often come together and make a person incurable in their foolishness (Pr 26:12). *They are blind leaders of the blind*. The Pharisees were grossly ignorant in the things of God but so proud that they thought they could see better and further than anyone else. They therefore undertook to lead others, to show others the way to heaven, when they themselves did not know one step of the way. They told everyone else the way but excluded those who would not follow them. Although they were blind, if they had acknowledged that fact and come to Christ for salve to put on their eyes (Rev 3:18), they could have seen. *Are we blind also?* They were confident that *they themselves were guides of the blind* (Ro 2:19–20), that they had been appointed to be so and were fit to be so, that everything they said was authoritative and a law.

4.2.2.2. "They are heading for destruction": *Both shall fall into the ditch.* This must necessarily be the outcome if both were so blind, but both so bold, venturing onward but unaware of danger. The blind leaders and the blind followers would die together. Those who by their craftiness draw others to sin and error will not, with all their wily cunning, escape ruin themselves. If *both fall together into the ditch,* the blind leaders will fall underneath and receive the worst of it. Those who have mutually increased each other's sin will mutually aggravate each other's ruin.

5. Instruction given to the disciples concerning the truth Christ had set down (v. 10). Although Christ rejected the willfully ignorant who did not want to be taught, he had compassion on the ignorant who wanted to learn (Heb 5:2). Here is:

5.1. Their desire to be better instructed in this matter (v. 15); in this request, as in many others, Peter was their speaker: *Declare unto us this parable.* What Christ said was clear, but they called it a parable because they could not understand it. This shows us that weak understanding tends to turn plain truths into parables, to seek difficulties where there are none. Where a weak head has doubts concerning any word of Christ, an upright heart and a willing mind will seek instruction. The disciples, though offended, sought assurance, attributing the offense not to the teaching they received but to the shallowness of their own capacity.

5.2. The rebuke Christ gave them for their weakness and ignorance: *Are ye also yet without understanding?* (v. 16). Christ rebukes as many as he loves and teaches (Pr 3:12; Heb 12:6). Two things emphasized their foolishness and dimness:

5.2.1. That they were the disciples of Christ: "Are *ye* also without understanding? You whom I have admitted into such a great intimacy with me, are you so unskillful in the word of righteousness?" The ignorance and mistakes of those who profess religious faith and enjoy the privileges of church membership are justly a grief to the Lord Jesus.

5.2.2. That they had been Christ's scholars for a long time: "Are ye *yet* so, after you have been so long under my teaching?" Had they come into Christ's school only yesterday, it would have been a different matter. Christ expects from us knowledge, grace, and wisdom in proportion to the time and means we have had. See Jn 14:9; Heb 5:12; 2Ti 3:7–8.

5.3. The explanation Christ gave them of this teaching on defilement. He shows us here:

5.3.1. What little danger we are in of defilement from what *entereth in at the mouth* (v. 17). An inordinate appetite, immoderation, and excess in eating come from the heart and are defiling, but food in itself is not so, as the Pharisees thought. What remains of defilement in our food can be eliminated in a way provided by nature—or rather the God of nature; *it goes in at the belly, and is cast out into the draught,* and nothing remains for us except pure

nutrition. By this means nothing defiles. If we eat with unwashed hands and, by that omission, anything unclean mixes with our food, nature will separate it and reject it, and it will not defile us. It may be an act of cleanliness, but it is not a point of conscience, to wash before eating.

5.3.2. What great danger we are in of defilement from what *proceeds out of the mouth* (v. 18). There is no defilement in the products of God's goodness; the defilement arises from the products of our corruption. We have here:

5.3.2.1. The corrupt fountain of what proceeds out of the mouth; it comes from the heart. It is the heart that is so desperately wicked (Jer 17:9), because there is no sin in word or deed that was not first in the heart. All evil words come out of the heart and defile.

5.3.2.2. Some of the corrupt streams that flow from this fountain are specified:

- *Evil thoughts*, sins against all the commandments. There is a great deal of sin that begins and ends in the heart and goes no further.
- *Murders*. These come from hatred in the heart against the life of our brother or sister, or contempt for it. The person who *hates his brother* is said to be a *murderer*; he is so in God's law court (1Jn 3:15).
- *Adulteries* and *fornications*. These come from the lustful, immoral, godless heart and the lust that reigns there. There is adultery in the heart first, and then in the act (5:28).
- *Thefts*, cheating, wronging, robbery, and all harmful contracts. The fountain of all these is in the heart. *Achan coveted, and then took* (Jos 7:20–21).
- *False witness.* If truth, holiness, and love, which God *requires in the inward parts*, reigned as they should, there would be no false testimony (Ps 64:6; Jer 9:8).
- *Blasphemies*, speaking evil of God and speaking evil of our neighbor. These are the overflowing of inner bitterness.

5.4. The conclusion of the sermon: *These are the things which defile a man* (v. 20). Sin defiles the soul, making it unlovely and detestable in the eyes of the pure and holy God and unfit for fellowship with him. These are the things, therefore, that we must carefully avoid, and we must avoid all approaches toward them, and not emphasize the washing of the hands, for, *To eat with unwashed hands—this defileth not a man.* If the people washed, they were no better before God; if they did not wash, they were not any worse.

Verses 21–28

We have here that famous story of Christ's casting the devil out of the daughter of the woman of Canaan. It contains something remarkable and surprising, looks favorably on the poor Gentiles, and was a pledge of the mercy Christ had in store for them. Here was a glimmer of that *light that was to lighten the Gentiles* (Lk 2:32).

1. *Jesus went thence;* he left that place. Justly is the light taken away from those who either play in it or rebel against it. Though Christ is patient for a long time, he will not always *endure the contradiction of sinners against himself* (Heb 12:3). Hardened prejudice against the Gospel and constant objections to it often cause Christ to withdraw (Ac 13:46, 51).

2. When he left there, he *departed into the coasts of Tyre and Sidon,* not to those cities but to the part of the land of Israel that lay in that direction. While he went about doing good (Ac 10:38), he never left his duty. The dark corners of the country, the remotest places, would

also receive their share of his kind influence. It was here that this miracle was performed. Notice:

2.1. The words of the Canaanite woman to Christ (v. 22). She was a Gentile, *a stranger to the commonwealth of Israel* (Eph 2:12). God will keep his remnant in all nations, his chosen ones in every place, even the most unlikely. If Christ had not now come to this area, she probably would never have come to him. A dormant faith and zeal are often stirred up when opportunities to come to know Christ come close to us. Her words were bold: she *cried* out to Christ, as one who was serious.

2.1.1. She described her misery: *My daughter is grievously vexed with a devil.* The troubles of children are the troubles of their parents. Caring parents feel acutely the miseries of those who are parts of themselves. "Although troubled by a demon, she is still my daughter." The greatest afflictions of our relatives do not dissolve our obligations to them and should not, therefore, remove our affections for them. It was the distress and trouble of the woman's family that now brought her to Christ. Because she came in faith, he did not reject her. Although it is need that drives us to Christ, we will not therefore be driven away from him.

2.1.2. She asked for mercy: *Have mercy on me, O Lord, thou Son of David.* Her petition was, *Have mercy on me.* She did not limit Christ to this or that instance of mercy, but mercy was what she begged. She did not plead any merit in herself, but depended only on mercy. Mercies to the children are mercies to the parents; favors to our families are favors to us. It is the duty of parents to pray fervently for their children. We must bring them to Christ in faith and prayer; only he is able to heal them.

2.2. The discouragement she met with in his words; in all the story of Christ's ministry we do not come across anything like this. It was his custom to welcome and encourage everyone who came to him, either *answering before they called* or *hearing while they were yet speaking* (Isa 65:24), but here was one who was treated differently, and what could be the reason for this? Some think that Christ showed himself to be reluctant to please this poor woman because he did not want to give offense to the Jews by being as free and as eager in his favor to the Gentiles as to them. Rather, Christ treated her in this way to test her; he knew what was in her heart, knew the strength of her faith, how able she was, by his grace, to break through such discouragements. He put them in her way so *that the trial of her faith might be found unto praise, and honour, and glory* (1Pe 1:6–7). Many of the dark and perplexing ways of Christ's providence, especially his grace in dealing with his people, may be explained with the key of this story. There may be love in Christ's heart while there are frowns in his face. Notice the particular discouragements given her:

2.2.1. When she cried out to him, *he answered her not a word* (v. 23). His ear was usually open and attentive to the cries of those who made humble requests, but he turned a deaf ear to this poor woman; she received neither alms nor an answer. But Christ knew what he was doing, and he declined to respond so that she would pray even more fervently. By seeming to draw away the desired mercy from her, he drew her on to be even bolder in asking for it. Not every accepted prayer is immediately answered. Sometimes God seems not to give his attention to the prayers of his people; it is to prove, and so increase, their faith.

2.2.2. When the disciples spoke a good word for her, he gave the reason why he refused her, which was even more discouraging.

2.2.2.1. It came as a little relief that the disciples intervened on her behalf; they said, *Send her away, for she crieth after us.* The disciples, though wishing she would receive what she came for, considered their own comfort rather than the poor woman's situation: "*Send her away* with a healing. *She cries after us* and is troublesome toward us, shaming us." Constant boldness may be uncomfortable, even to good people, but Christ loves to be sought.

2.2.2.2. Christ's answer to the disciples completely dashed her expectations: "*I am not sent but to the lost sheep of the house of Israel.*" Boldness rarely overcomes the settled reason of a wise person. He not only did not answer her; he also argued against her and silenced her with a reason. It is a great test for us when we find occasion to question whether we belong to those to whom Christ was sent. However, we bless God that no room is left for that doubt; the distinction between Jew and Gentile has been taken away; we are sure that he *gave his life a ransom for many* (20:28), and if for many, then why not for me?

2.2.2.3. When she continued to be bold, he insisted on her disqualification, not only repelling her but also seeming to reproach her: *It is not meet* (right) *to take the children's bread and to cast* (toss) *it to dogs* (v. 26). This seemed to cut her off from all hope, and it might have driven her to despair if she had not had a very strong faith. Gospel grace and miraculous healings—the accessories of that grace—were children's bread and were not on the same level as the rain from heaven and those fruitful seasons that God gave to the nations whom he allowed *to walk in their own ways* (Ac 14:16–17). No, these were special favors, to be taken up by his own distinctive people. The Gentiles were looked on by the Jews with great contempt; they were called and considered *dogs.* Christ here seemed to allow that designation of the Gentiles and to think it not right, therefore, for the Gentiles to share in the favors given to the Jews. Christ urged this against the Canaanite woman: "How can she expect to eat from the children's bread when she does not belong to the family?" We can learn from this:

2.2.2.3.*1.*Those whom Christ intends to honor most significantly he first humbles with a sense of their own lowliness and unworthiness. We must first see ourselves as dogs, *less than the least of all God's mercies* (Ge 32:10; Eph 3:8), before we are fit to be honored and privileged by them.

2.2.2.3.*2.* Christ delights to exercise great faith with great trials, and he sometimes reserves the sharpest for the last, so that, *being tried, we may come forth like gold* (Job 23:10).

2.3. The strength of her faith and resolution. Many people, if tested in this way, would have either sunk into silence or lost their temper. "This is cold comfort," she might have said, "for a poor, distressed woman. I might as well have stayed at home as come here, to be not only so pitifully insulted but also called a *dog!*" "*Is this the Son of David?*" she might have said: "Is this the One who has such a reputation for kindness, tenderness, and compassion? I am not a dog, I am a woman, an honest woman, and a woman in misery; moreover, I am sure it is not right to call me *dog*." But a humble, faithful soul that truly loves Christ accepts everything that he says and does and interprets it in the best way. She broke through all these discouragements:

2.3.1. With a fervent desire to pursue her petition. This appeared when she was deterred earlier: *Then came she, and worshiped him, saying, Lord, help me* (v. 25).

2.3.1.1. She continued to pray. What Christ said silenced the disciples. You hear no more of them; they accepted the answer. But the woman did not. The more we feel the burden, the more resolutely we should pray for it to be removed.

2.3.1.2. She made the most of her prayer. Instead of blaming Christ or accusing him of being unkind, she seems rather to have suspected herself. She feared that she had not been humble or reverent enough, and so now *she came, and worshipped him*; or she feared that she had not been serious enough, and so she now cried out, *Lord, help me*. When the answers of prayer are deferred, God is teaching us to pray more and pray better. Disappointments in prayer must stir us to pray further. In his agony, Christ *prayed more earnestly* (Lk 22:44).

2.3.1.3. She waived the question of whether she belonged to those to whom Christ was sent: "Whether I am an Israelite or not, I come to the Son of David for mercy, and *I will not let him go, except he bless me* (Ge 32:26)." Many weak Christians get confused with questions and doubts about their election; they would be better concerned with seeking God and being faithful in prayer for mercy and grace. It would be better to throw themselves by faith at the feet of Christ and say, *If I perish, I will perish here* (Est 4:16). If we cannot *reason* down our unbelief, then let us *pray* it down.

2.3.1.4. Her prayer was very brief but comprehensive and fervent: *Lord, help me*. We take this to be:

2.3.1.4.1. Her mourning her situation: It is not in vain for broken hearts to lament their own lives; God looks down on them then (Jer 31:18). Or:

2.3.1.4.2. Her begging for grace to help her in this hour of temptation. She found it hard to maintain her faith when it was frowned on, and so she prayed, "*Lord, help me*." Or:

2.3.1.4.3. Reinforcing her original request: "*Lord, help me*; Lord, give me what I came for." She believed that Christ could and would help her. She maintained good thoughts of him and would not let go her grip. *Lord, help me* is a good prayer if it is offered well, and it is a pity that it has become a cliché and that we take God's name in vain by it.

2.3.2. With a holy skillfulness of faith, suggesting a very surprising plea. Christ had placed the Jews with the children, *as olive plants round about* God's *table* (Ps 128:3), and he had put the Gentiles with the dogs, under the table. Nothing is gained by contradicting any word of Christ, even if it comes to us harshly. However, since this poor woman could not object to it, she decided to make the best of it: *Truth, Lord, yet the dogs eat of the crumbs* (v. 27). Notice here:

2.3.2.1. Her acknowledgment was very humble: *Truth, Lord*. You cannot speak in such a lowly way about a humble believer without her being ready to speak in such a lowly way about herself. "*Truth, Lord*; *I* cannot deny it; I am a mere dog, without any rights to eat the children's bread."

2.3.2.2. Her turning of this into a plea was very ingenious: *Yet the dogs eat of the crumbs*. It was by a special, unusual dexterity and by a spiritual alertness and discernment that she successfully made the substance of an argument out of what looked like an insult. A living, active faith will turn what seems to be against us into something for us. Faith can find encouragement even in what is discouraging and can draw nearer to God by laying hold of the hand that is stretched out to push it away. Her plea is, *Yet the dogs eat of the crumbs*. It is true that the full and regular provision is intended only for the children, but the small, accidentally dropped, and neglected crumbs are allowed to be given to the dogs, and the dogs are not grudged them. Surely, then, some of the bits of food may fall to a poor Gentile. "I beg to be healed by the crumbs that happen to fall; though small and insignificant compared with the loaves the children have, even such crumbs come from the same precious bread." When we are ready to gorge ourselves on the children's bread, we should remember how many people would be glad to receive merely the crumbs. The broken food of our spiritual privileges would be a feast to many people (Ac 13:42).

2.3.2.2.1. Her humility and necessity made her glad to receive the crumbs. Those who are aware that they deserve nothing will be thankful for anything. The least of Christ is precious to a believer, and even the crumbs are the bread of life (Jn 6:35, 48).

2.3.2.2.2. Her faith encouraged her to expect these crumbs. Why should she not eat at Christ's table, as at the table of someone great, where the dogs are fed as well as the children? She called it their *master's* table; if she was a dog, she was *his* dog. It is good to be in God's house, even if we lie at its threshold.

2.4. The happy outcome and success of all this. She came away with a great reputation and encouragement from this struggle, and though a Canaanite, she proved herself to be a true daughter of Israel, who, *like a prince, had power with God, and prevailed* (Ge 32:28). *Then Jesus said, O woman, great is thy faith*. He now began to speak like himself and to show what he was really like.

2.4.1. He commended her faith: *O woman, great is thy faith*.

2.4.1.1. It was her faith that he commended. Several other graces shone brightly in her conduct here—wisdom, humility, meekness, patience, perseverance in prayer—but these were the results of her faith. Because faith, of all graces, honors Christ the most, he honors faith more than any other grace.

2.4.1.2. It was the greatness of her faith. Although faith is equally precious in all the saints, it is not equally strong in all; all believers are not of the same size and stature. The greatness of faith consists much in a resolute faithfulness to Jesus Christ; it consists in loving him and trusting him as a Friend even when he seems to come out against us as an Enemy. Although weak faith, if true, will not be rejected, great faith will be commended.

2.4.2. He healed her daughter: "*Be it unto thee even as thou wilt*. I can deny you nothing; take what you came for." Great believers may receive what they want for the asking. When our will conforms to the will of Christ's command, his will agrees with the will of our desire. Those who will deny Christ nothing will find that he will deny them nothing finally, even though he seems to hide his face from them for a time. The event happened according to the word of Christ: *Her daughter was made whole from that very hour*; the mother's faith was effective in healing the daughter. *He spake, and it was done*.

Verses 29–39

Here is:

1. A general account of Christ's healings. The signs of Christ's power and goodness are neither scarce nor scanty, for there is an overflowing fullness in him. Notice:

1.1. The place where these healings were performed: it was *near the sea of Galilee*. We do not read about anything he did in the region of Tyre and Sidon except the driving out of the demon from the Canaanite woman's daughter, as if he took that journey deliberately with that in mind. Let ministers not grudge their effort to do good, even though it is only to a few people. The One who knows the value of souls would go a long way to help save one person from death and Satan's power. But *Jesus departed thence*. Having let that crumb fall under the table, he returned to prepare a full feast for the children here. We may occasionally do something for one person that we do not make a constant practice of. Christ stepped onto *the coasts* of Tyre and Sidon, but he *sat down by the sea of Galilee* (v. 29). He *sat down on a mountain*, so that everyone could see him and have free access to him, for he is an open Savior. He sat down there as one waiting to be gracious (Isa 30:18). He settled himself to this good work.

1.2. The crowds and illnesses that were healed by him (v. 30); *Great multitudes came to him*. We are soon aware of physical pain and sickness, but few are concerned about their souls and their spiritual diseases.

1.2.1. Such was the goodness of Christ that he received all kinds of people; the poor as well as the rich are welcome to Christ. He never looked down with contempt on the ordinary people, the *herd*, as they are sometimes called, for the souls of the lowliest are as precious to him as the souls of the leaders.

1.2.2. Such was the power of Christ that he healed all kinds of diseases; those who came to him brought their sick relatives and friends with them and *cast* (laid) *them down at Jesus' feet* (v. 30). We do not read about anything said to him by those who came, but they laid their dear ones down in front of him as objects of pity. Their illnesses spoke more eloquently for them than the voice of the most skilled orator could. Whatever our situation is like, the only way to find peace and relief is to lay it at Christ's feet, referring it to him for his decision. Here *lame, blind, dumb, maimed, and many others* were brought to Christ. Notice what terrible work sin has made! What a variety of diseases human bodies are subject to! Notice how the Savior works. He conquers those forces that are the enemies of the human race. *He sent his word, and healed them* (Ps 107:20). This shows Christ's power, which can strengthen us in all our weaknesses, and also his sympathy, which can comfort us in all our miseries.

1.3. The influence that this had on the people (v. 31).

1.3.1. They *wondered* (were amazed), and well they might. Christ's works should amaze us.

1.3.2. *They glorified the God of Israel.* Miracles, which we are amazed at, must be the subject of our praise, and blessings, which we should be joyful at, must be the subject of our thanksgiving. If he heals our diseases, all that is within us must bless his holy name (Ps 103:1, 3), and if we have been graciously preserved from blindness, lameness, and muteness, we have as much reason to bless God as if we had been healed; indeed, here even the bystanders glorified God. God must be acknowledged with praise and thankfulness in the mercies of others as much as in our own.

2. A particular record of his feeding *four thousand men* with *seven loaves, and a few little fishes*, as he had just fed *five thousand with five loaves*. The guests were now not quite so many as then, and the provision a little more; he performed his miracles as the occasion required. Both then and now he took as many people as needed to be fed, and he used all that was available to feed them. Whenever the farthest natural powers are exceeded, we must say, *This is the finger of God* (Ex 8:19), and it is not important how far they are surpassed. Here is:

2.1. Christ's pity: *I have compassion on the multitude* (v. 32). He told his disciples this both to test their compassion and to stir it. Notice in what he said to them:

2.1.1. The situation of the crowd: *They continue with me now three days, and have nothing to eat.* They showed their zeal and the strength of their devotion for Christ and his word by not only leaving their callings to listen to him on weekdays but also enduring a great deal of hardship to continue with him; they lacked necessary food and had scarcely enough to keep body and soul together. They paid greater respect to the words of Christ than to their necessary food (Job 23:12). Notice Christ's tenderness: *I have compassion on them.* It would have been better if they had had compassion on the One who took so much effort and care over them for three days—and it seems he, too, was fasting. Our Lord Jesus keeps an account of how long his followers continue to be with him, and he notices the difficulty they sustain in it. The need the people were reduced to serves to emphasize:

2.1.1.1. The mercy of supplying them: he fed them when they were hungry, and then food was doubly welcome.

2.1.1.2. The miracle of supplying them. If two hungry meals make the third a gluttonous one, what would three hungry days do? However, *they did all eat and were filled*. There is enough mercy and grace with Christ to fill the most fervent and enlarged desires abundantly: *Open thy mouth wide, and I will fill it* (Ps 81:10).

2.1.2. The care of our master for them: *I will not send them away fasting, lest they should faint by the way*. It is the misfortune of our present state that when our souls are elevated and enlarged to a certain extent, our bodies cannot keep pace with them in doing good works. The weakness of the flesh causes great trouble to the willingness of the spirit (26:41).

2.2. Christ's power. His pity toward their needs set his power at work to supply those needs. Notice:

2.2.1. How his power was distrusted by his disciples: *whence should we have so much bread in the wilderness?* (v. 33). They had been not only the witnesses but also the ministers of the earlier miracle; the multiplied bread had passed through their hands. They therefore showed their great weakness by asking, *Whence shall we have bread?* Could they be at a loss while they had their Master with them? Forgetting former experiences brings shadows of doubts into our present experience. Christ knew how slender the provision was, but he wanted to know it from them: *How many loaves have ye?* (v. 34). Before he was going to set to work, he wanted it to be seen how little he had to work with, so that his power would shine more brightly. What they had they had for themselves, and it was little enough, but Christ wanted them to give it all to the crowd. It is good for Christ's disciples to be generous; their Master was. What we have we should be free to share. Stinginess today prompted by concern for tomorrow makes a compound of corrupt attitudes that should be put to death. The disciples asked, *Whence should we have bread?* Christ asked, *How many loaves have ye?* We must not think so much of what we need as of what we have.

2.2.2. How his power was displayed to the crowd:

2.2.2.1. In the provision that was available: *seven loaves, and a few little fishes*. The fish were probably ones they themselves had caught. It is satisfying to *eat the labour of our hands* (Ps 128:2). What we have gained by God's blessing on our labor we should freely use and share, for we must labor so *that we may have to give* (Eph 4:28).

2.2.2.2. In the putting of the people into a position to receive it: *He commanded the multitude to sit down on the ground* (v. 35). They saw only a very little provision, but they must sit down in faith that they would receive a meal's food from it.

2.2.2.3. In the distributing of the provision among them. He first *gave thanks*. The word used in the former miracle was "he blessed." It all comes to the same thing; giving thanks to God is a proper way of seeking a blessing from God. He then *broke the loaves and gave to his disciples, and they to the multitude*. Although the disciples had distrusted Christ's power, he still made use of them now as he did before; he was not, as he might have been, provoked by the weakness of his ministers to set them aside, but continued to give to them, and they to give to his people, the word of life.

2.2.2.4. In the plenty there was among them: *They did all eat, and were filled* (v. 37). Christ fills those whom he feeds. While we work in the world, we work for what does not satisfy (Isa 55:2), but those who appropriately serve Christ will be *abundantly satisfied with the goodness of his house* (Ps 65:4). To show that they all had enough, Christ provided that there was a great deal *left — seven baskets full of broken meat* (pieces), enough to show that with Christ *there is bread enough, and to spare* (Lk 15:17), supplies of grace for more than seek it and for those who seek more.

2.2.2.5. In the account taken of the guests, not so that they could pay their share, but so that they would be witnesses of the power and goodness of Christ.

2.2.2.6. In the dismissal of the crowd and Christ's departure to another place (v. 39). He *sent away* the people. Although he had fed them twice, they must not expect miracles to be their daily bread. Let them now go home to their callings, back to their own tables.

CHAPTER 16

We have here: 1. A conversation with the Pharisees (vv. 1–4). 2. Another with his disciples about the yeast of the Pharisees (vv. 5–12). 3. Another with them about himself (vv. 13–20). 4. Another concerning his sufferings for them and theirs for him (vv. 21–28).

Verses 1–4

We have Christ's conversation with the Pharisees and Sadducees here, men at odds among themselves but in agreement in their opposition to Christ. Christ and Christianity meet with opposition on all sides. Notice:

1. Their demand and its intention.

1.1. Their demand was for a sign from heaven; in their demand, they pretended they were very willing to be satisfied and convinced.

1.1.1. What they claimed to want was some other sign than what they had already seen. They had received plenty of signs; every miracle Christ performed was a sign. However, this was not enough; they despised those signs that relieved the needs of the sick or sad, and they insisted that he give some sign that would satisfy the curiosity of the proud. The evidence given was enough to satisfy an unprejudiced understanding but was not intended to satisfy a vain whim. We show the deceitfulness of the heart when we think that we would be persuaded by the means and advantages that we do not have, while we show disrespect for those we already have.

1.1.2. It must be a sign from heaven. For proof of his commission, they wanted miracles like those performed at the giving of the Law on Mount Sinai: thunder, lightning, and the voice of words were the sign from heaven that they wanted.

1.2. Their intention was to test him, not to be taught by him but to trap him. If he were to show them a sign from heaven, they would attribute it to an alliance with

the *prince of the power of the air* (Eph 2:2). When they had signs from heaven, they tested Christ, saying, *Can he furnish a table in the wilderness?* (Ps 78:19). Now that he had spread a table in the desert, they tested him, saying: *Can he give us a sign from heaven?*

2. Christ's reply to this demand:

2.1. He condemned their overlooking of the signs they had (vv. 2–3). They were seeking the signs of the kingdom of God when it was already among them. To expose this, he pointed out to them:

2.1.1. Their skillfulness and knowledge in other matters, especially in natural weather forecasts. Common rules drawn from observation and experience make it easy to foretell what the weather will very probably be like. We *know not the balancing of the clouds* (Job 37:16), but we may discern something from their appearance.

2.1.2. Their foolishness and stupidity in the concerns for their souls: *Can ye not discern the signs of the times?* "Do you not see that the Messiah has come?" The miracles Christ performed and the gathering of the people to him were clear signs that the *kingdom of heaven was at hand* (Mk 1:15), that this was *the day of their visitation* (1Pe 2:12). We can learn from this that when we have slighted the signs that God has ordained, it is very hypocritical to seek signs that we ourselves prescribe. "Do you not foresee your own ruin coming for rejecting him?" It is the undoing of many people that they are unaware what will be the result of their refusing Christ.

2.2. He refused to give them any other sign (v. 4). He called them *an adulterous generation*, because while they professed to belong to the true church and be the bride of God, they were unfaithful and rebelled against him, departing from him and breaking their covenants with him. And so he refused to satisfy their desire. Christ will not be dictated to: *we ask, and have not, because we ask amiss* (Jas 4:3). He referred them to the sign of the prophet Jonah, which would be given them: his resurrection from the dead and his preaching by his apostles to the Gentiles. Although the imagination of proud people will not be gratified, the faith of the humble will be supported. This conversation was broken off abruptly: *he left them and departed*. Christ will not stay long with those who test him; he justly withdraws from those who want to quarrel with him.

Verses 5–12

We have Christ's conversation with his disciples about bread here, in which, as in many other conversations, he spoke to them about spiritual things using an illustration, and they misunderstood him as speaking literally. The occasion of it was that they forgot to take food on their boat. Usually they took bread with them; now, however, they forgot; we hope it was because their minds and memories were filled with better things. Christ's disciples are often the sort who give no great forethought to the things of this world. Here is:

1. The warning Christ gave them to *beware of the leaven of the Pharisees*. Disciples are in most danger from hypocrites; they stand on their guard against those who are openly immoral, but against such as the Pharisees and Sadducees, they are often unguarded. The warning was therefore doubled: *Take heed, and beware*. The corrupt principles and practices of the Pharisees and Sadducees are compared to *leaven* (yeast); they were fermenting wherever they went.

2. Their mistake concerning this warning (v. 7). They thought Christ was rebuking them for their lack of foresight and their forgetfulness. Or they took it as a warning

not to become on familiar terms with the Pharisees and Sadducees, not to eat with them. Yet the danger was not in the bread of the Pharisees and Sadducees—Christ himself ate with them (Lk 7:36; 11:37; 14:1)—but in their motives.

3. The rebuke Christ gave them for this.

3.1. He rebuked their distrust of his ability and readiness to supply them in this difficulty: "*O ye of little faith* (v. 8), why are you so bewildered because you have *taken no bread* that you can think of nothing else?" He did not rebuke them for their little forethought, as they expected he would. Parents and masters must not be angry at the forgetfulness of their children and servants more than is necessary to make them take more care the next time; we tend to forget our duty. Notice how easily Christ forgave his disciples' carelessness; we should be equally forgiving. What he rebuked them for was their little faith. This shows us:

3.1.1. He wanted them to depend on him to supply them. Although Christ's disciples are brought into great need and difficulty through their own carelessness and thoughtlessness, he still encourages them to trust in him to help them. We must not, however, use this as an excuse for showing them a lack of charity to those who are truly poor, telling them that they should have taken better care of their affairs and then they would not have been so needy. That may be so, but they must not be left to starve when they are in need.

3.1.2. He was displeased at their concern in this matter. The weakness and lack of concern of good people for their worldly affairs is something for which other people tend to condemn them, but to Christ it is not such an offense as their immoderate worry and anxiety about those things. We must try to keep the balance between the two extremes of carelessness and worry, but of the two, worry about the things of this world is worse for Christ's disciples.

3.1.3. What made their distrust even worse was the experience they had just had of the power and goodness of Christ in providing for them (vv. 9–10). They had with them the One who could provide bread for them. If they did not have the cistern, they had the Fountain: *Do ye not yet understand, neither remember?* Christ's disciples are often to be blamed for the shallowness of their understandings and the unreliability of their memories. "Remember *how many baskets ye took up.*" These baskets were intended to be the means of remembering the mercy; the One who could provide them with such a surplus then could surely provide them with what was necessary now. We are perplexed with our present cares and distrust because we do not properly remember the former experiences we have had of God's power and goodness.

3.2. He rebuked their misunderstanding of the warning he had given them: *How is it that you do not understand?* (v. 11). Christ's disciples may well be ashamed of the slowness and dullness of their grasp of divine things: *I spake it not unto you concerning bread.* He took it unfavorably:

3.2.1. That they should think he was as concerned about bread as they were, when his *meat* (food) *and drink were to do his Father's will* (Jn 4:34).

3.2.2. That they should be so unfamiliar with his way of preaching as to take literally what he spoke as a parable.

4. The putting right of the mistake by this rebuke: *Then understood they* what he meant (v. 12). He did not tell them expressly what he meant, but repeated what he had said, and so he compelled them to arrive at its sense from their own thoughts. This is how Christ teaches by the Spirit of wisdom in the heart, opening the understand-

ing to the Spirit of revelation in the word (Lk 24:45; Eph 1:17). Those truths that we ourselves have dug out are most precious.

Verses 13–20

We have here a private discussion that Christ had with his disciples about himself. It was in the region of Caesarea Philippi; there in that remote corner, perhaps, fewer people flocked to him than in other places, which gave him more opportunity to have this private conversation with his disciples.

1. He asked what were the opinions of other people about him: *Who do men say that I, the Son of man, am?*

1.1. He called himself the *Son of man*, which may be taken either:

1.1.1. As a title common to him with others. He was called, and rightly so, *the Son of God*, for he was (Lk 1:35), but he called himself the Son of Man, for he is really and truly *Man, born of a woman* (Job 14:1; 15:14). Or:

1.1.2. As a title distinctive to him as Mediator.

1.2. He asked what people's attitudes toward him were: "*Who do men say that I am?* The Son of Man?"—as I think it might better be read. "Do they acknowledge me as the Messiah?" He did not ask, "Who do the *scribes* and *Pharisees* say that I am?" but, "Who do *men* say that I am?" He was thinking of the ordinary people, whom the Pharisees despised. The ordinary people talked more familiarly with the disciples than they did with their Master, and so it would be from them that he would know better what the people said. Christ had not said plainly who he was; he left it to others to infer his identity from his works (Jn 10:24–25). Now he wanted to know what the people had inferred.

1.3. The disciples gave him an answer to this question: *Some say, thou art John the Baptist* (v. 14). People had different opinions; some said one thing, and others another. Truth is one, but those who vary from that commonly vary from one another. Since he was such a noted Person, everyone would be ready to judge him, and there are as many minds as there are people. The people's opinions, however, were honorable. It is possible for people to have good thoughts about Christ, but not the right ones, a high opinion of him, but not high enough. They all thought him to be *one risen from the dead*, which perhaps arose from a confused notion that the Messiah would rise from the dead. They were all false opinions, built on mistakes.

1.3.1. *Some say, thou art John the Baptist.* Herod said so (14:2), and those around him would tend to say as he said.

1.3.2. *Some, Elias* (Elijah). Those of this opinion no doubt based it on the prophecy of Malachi: *Behold, I will send you Elijah* (Mal 4:5).

1.3.3. *Others, Jeremias* (Jeremiah).

1.3.4. *Or, one of the prophets.* This shows what an honorable idea they had of the prophets, but they were *the children of them that persecuted and slew them* (23:29). Rather than allow the possibility that Jesus of Nazareth, one of their own country, could be such an extraordinary Person as his works showed him to be, they would say, "It was not he, but *one of the old prophets.*"

2. He asked what *their* thoughts were about him: "*But who say ye that I am?* (v. 15)."

2.1. The disciples had themselves been better taught than others; by their intimacy with Christ, they had greater advantages of gaining knowledge than others had. Those who know Christ more than others should have truer attitudes about him, and they should be able to give a better account of him than others.

2.2. The disciples were trained to teach others, and so it was necessary that they understand the truth themselves. This is a question each one of us should frequently put to ourselves: *"Who* do we say, *what* kind of person do we say, that *the Lord Jesus is?"* Things will go well or badly with us according to whether our thoughts are right or wrong about Jesus Christ. This is the question. Here is:

2.2.1. Peter's answer to this question (v. 16). Peter answered in the name of all the rest, they all agreeing to it. Peter's temperament led him to be forward in speaking on all such occasions, and sometimes he spoke well, sometimes badly. In all groups of people some people are passionate and bold, on whom the right to speak on behalf of others naturally falls. Peter was such a spokesperson. Peter's answer is brief, but it is full, true, and to the point: *Thou art the Christ, the Son of the Living God.* This is the conclusion of the whole matter (Ecc 12:13). The people called him *a Prophet, that Prophet* (Jn 6:14), but the disciples acknowledged him to be the Christ, "the Anointed One." It was very admirable to believe this about One whose outward appearance was so against the general idea the Jews had of the Messiah. He called himself the *Son of man,* but they acknowledged him to be *the Son of the living God.* They knew and believed him to be *the Son of the living God* and the Life of the world. Do we agree? Then let us then go to Christ and tell him so: "Lord Jesus, *thou art the Christ, the Son of the living God."*

2.2.2. Christ's approval of his answer (vv. 17–19). Christ replied to him both as a believer and as an apostle.

2.2.2.1. As a believer (v. 17). Christ showed himself to be very pleased with Peter's confession, that it was so clear and explicit. Christ showed Peter from where he received the knowledge of this truth. At the first revelation of this truth at the dawn of the Gospel day, it was a mighty thing to believe it. Peter had the joy of it: *Blessed art thou, Simon Bar-jona.* He reminded him of his rise and origin; he was *Bar jonas,* "The son of a dove." Let him remember *the rock out of which he was hewn* (Isa 51:1), so he might see that he was not born to this honor but had been advanced to it by God's favor; it was free grace that made him different. Having reminded him of this, Christ made him aware of his great blessedness as a believer: *Blessed art thou.* True believers are truly blessed, and those whom Christ declares blessed are truly blessed. All happiness accompanies right knowledge of Christ. If Peter had the joy of it, God must receive the glory for it: *"For flesh and blood have not revealed it to thee."* This light sprang neither from nature nor from education, but from my Father who is in heaven." This shows us that saving faith is the gift of God, and wherever it is, it is brought about by him. "You are blessed because *my Father has revealed it to thee."* Blessed are those who are so highly favored (Lk 1:28).

2.2.2.2. As an apostle or minister (vv. 18–19). Nothing is lost by being eager to confess Christ, for those who honor him in this way will be honored by him (1Sa 2:30).

3. On the occasion of this great confession Peter made of Christ, which is the church's honor and allegiance, Christ signed and declared this divine and royal charter by which that community is incorporated. The purpose of this charter was:

3.1. To establish the existence of the church: *I say also unto thee.* It was Christ who made the grant, the One who is the church's Head. The grant was put into Peter's hand: "I say it to you." The New Testament charter was delivered here to Peter as an agent, but for the use and benefit of the church in all ages, according to the purposes specified and contained in it. It was promised here that:

3.1.1. Christ would build his church on a rock. This community was incorporated under the title *Christ's church.* It is a number of people called out of the world, set apart from it, and dedicated to Christ.

3.1.1.1. The Builder and Maker of the church is Christ himself: *I will build it. Ye are God's building.* Building is a progressive work; the church in this world is like a house that is being built. It is a comfort that Christ, who has divine wisdom and power, undertakes to build it (Pr 9:1; 24:3).

3.1.1.2. The foundation on which it is built is *this Rock.* Even if the architect does his part very well, if the foundation is rotten, the building will not stand; let us see, therefore, what the foundation is.

3.1.1.2.*1.* The church is built on *a rock,* a firm, strong, and lasting foundation, which time will not ravage, nor will it sink under the weight of the building. Christ would not build his house on sand, for he knew that storms would arise (7:26–27).

3.1.1.2.*2.* It is built on *this* rock; you are *Peter,* which means "a stone or rock." Christ gave him that name when he first called him (Jn 1:42), and here he confirmed it. From the mention of this significant name, Christ took occasion for this metaphor of *building upon a rock.*

3.1.1.2.*2.1.* Some understand this rock to refer to Peter himself as an apostle. The church is built on the foundation of the apostles (Eph 2:20). The first stones of that building were laid in and by their ministry. Now because Peter was the apostle by whose hand the first stones of the church were laid, both in Jewish converts (Ac 2) and in the Gentile converts (Ac 10), he could in some sense be said to be the rock on which it was built.

3.1.1.2.*2.2.* Others understand this *rock* to refer to Christ. *"Thou art Peter,* you have the name of a *stone,* and *upon this rock"* —pointing to himself—*"I will build my church."* He took the example of Peter to speak of himself as the Rock. Christ is both the church's Founder and its Foundation; he draws souls, and he draws them to himself; they are united with him, and they rest on him and constantly depend on him.

3.1.1.2.*2.3.* Others understand this *rock* to be the confession that Peter made of Christ, and this comes to the same thing as understanding it as referring to Christ himself. "Now," Christ said, "this is the great truth *upon which I will build my church."* If you take away this truth, the universal church falls to the ground. If Christ is not the Son of God, Christianity is a deception. If you take away the faith and confession of this truth from any particular church, it ceases to be part of Christ's church. By the admission or the denial of this one article the church either rises or falls; it is the main hinge on which the door of salvation turns; those who let go of this do not hold to the foundation.

3.1.2. Christ would preserve and secure his church when it was built: *The gates of hell shall not prevail against it.*

3.1.2.1. This implies that the church has enemies who fight against it and try to bring about its ruin and overthrow, here represented *by the gates of hell,* that is, the city of hell, the Devil's interest among people; the city of hell is the direct opposite of this heavenly city, this *city of the living God* (Heb 12:22).

3.1.2.2. This assures us that the enemies of the church will not be victorious. While the world stands, Christ will keep a church in it. Somewhere or other the Christian faith will exist; it will not always be equally pure and splendid, and yet it will retain its essence, so that its inheritance will never be completely destroyed. The church may be thwarted in particular battles, but in the main war it will win as *more than a conqueror* (Ro 8:37).

3.2. To settle the government of the church (v. 19). A city without government is in chaos. This constituting of the government of the church is expressed here by the handing over of the keys and, with them, a power to bind and loose. This invests all the apostles and their successors with a ministerial power to guide and govern the church of Christ, as it exists in particular congregations or churches, according to the rules of the Gospel. The keys were first put into Peter's hand because he was the first *that opened the door of faith to the Gentiles* (Ac 10:28). Christ, having incorporated his church, has appointed the office of the ministry to maintain order and government and to see that his laws are duly served. He does not say, "The keys *shall* be given," but, "*I will give* them," for ministers derive their authority from Christ, and all their power is to be used in his name (1Co 5:4).

3.2.1. The power delegated here is a spiritual authority; it is an authority *pertaining to the kingdom of heaven* (Ac 1:3), that is, to the church, to the Gospel era.

3.2.2. It is the *power* of the keys that is given, alluding to the custom of investing people with authority in such and such a place by handing them the keys of the place. Or, Christ gives the keys to the church as the master of a house gives the keys to the steward, the keys to the rooms where the provisions are kept.

3.2.3. It is a power to *bind and loose*, that is—to keep with the metaphor of the keys—to shut and open.

3.2.4. It is an authority that Christ has promised to recognize proper administration of; *It shall be bound in heaven, and loosed in heaven.* The word of the Gospel in the mouth of faithful ministers is to be looked on not as a human word but as the word of God, and to be received as such (1Th 2:13; Jn 12:20). Now the *keys of the kingdom of heaven* are:

3.2.4.1. The key of doctrine, also called the key of knowledge. Now the apostles had an extraordinary power of this kind; some things forbidden by the Law of Moses were now to be allowed; some things allowed there were now to be forbidden, and the apostles were authorized to declare this to the world. When Peter was first taught himself, and then taught others, to call nothing *common or unclean* (Ac 11:8–9), this power was exercised. There is also an ordinary power conveyed here to all ministers, to tell people, in God's name and according to the Scriptures, *what is good, and what the Lord requires of them* (Mic 6:8). Christ gave his apostles authority to shut or open the book of the Gospel to people, as the situation required. When ministers preach pardon and peace to penitents, wrath and the curse to the impenitent, in Christ's name, they are acting according to this authority of binding and loosing.

3.2.4.2. The key of discipline, which is the application of the previous key to particular individuals, rightly assessing their characters and actions. The judge does not make the law, but only declares what is law and passes sentence accordingly. Christ's ministers have authority to admit members into the church: "Go, *teach all nations, baptizing them* (28:19); when people profess faith in Christ and obedience to him, admit them by baptism." Ministers are to let in to *the wedding feast those that are bidden* (22:3) and to keep out those who are clearly unfit for such holy fellowship. They also have authority to expel and drive out those who have forfeited their church membership, and then to restore and to receive again, on their repentance, those who had been driven out, to loose those whom they had bound. The apostles had a miraculous gift of *discerning spirits*, but even *they* went by the

rule of outward appearances (1Sa 16:7; see, for example, Ac 8:21; 1Co 5:1; 2Co 2:7; 1Ti 1:20), which ministers may still use as a basis for their decision making if they are skillful and faithful.

4. Here is Christ's command to his disciples to keep this matter private for the present: they must *tell no man that he was Jesus the Christ* (v. 20). What they had professed to him they must not yet declare to the world, for several reasons:

4.1. Because this was the time of preparation for his kingdom: the great thing now preached was that *the kingdom of heaven was at hand* (Mk 1:15). Everything is beautiful in its season (Ecc 3:1, 11), and it is good advice: *Prepare thy work, and afterward build* (Pr 24:27).

4.2. Christ wanted to have his messiahship proved by his works. He was so secure about the persuasiveness of his miracles that he waived other witnesses (Jn 10:25, 38).

4.3. Christ did not want to have the apostles preach this until they had the most convincing evidence ready to bring as confirmation of it. Great truths may suffer damage by being asserted before they can be sufficiently proved. Now the great proof of Jesus being the Christ was his resurrection (Ro 1:4).

4.4. It was necessary that the preachers of such a great truth be provided with a greater measure of the Spirit than the apostles then had. When Christ was glorified and the Spirit poured out, we find Peter declaring on the housetops what was here spoken in private (10:27). Just as there is a time to keep silence, so there is also a time to speak (Ecc 3:7).

Verses 21–23

We have Christ's conversation with his disciples about his own sufferings here, in which notice:

1. Christ's foretelling of his suffering. He had already given some hints of his suffering. Now, however, he began to *show* how he must suffer, to speak plainly and explicitly about it. Up to this time, he had not touched on this, because the disciples were weak, but now that they knew more and were stronger in their faith, he began to tell them this. Christ reveals his mind to his people gradually, letting in light as they can bear it and are fit to receive it (Jn 16:12; Mk 4:33). *From that time*, that is, when they had made that full confession of Christ; when he found they knew one truth, he taught them another. If they had not been well grounded in the belief that Christ was the Son of God, this new teaching would have greatly shaken their faith. All truths are not to be spoken to all people at all times, but such as are proper and suitable to their state at that time. Notice:

1.1. What he foretold about his sufferings, their details and circumstances, and all were surprising.

1.1.1. The place where he would suffer. He must go to Jerusalem, the capital city, the Holy City, and suffer there. There all the sacrifices were offered, and therefore there *he* must die, the One who is the great sacrifice.

1.1.2. The people at whose hands he would suffer: *the elders, and chief priests, and scribes.* Those who should have been most eager in acknowledging and worshiping Christ were the ones who persecuted him most bitterly.

1.1.3. What he would suffer: *he must suffer many things, and be killed.* His enemies' insatiable hatred and his own invincible patience appeared in the variety and great number of his sufferings—he suffered many things—and in their extreme nature; nothing less than his death would satisfy them: he must be killed.

1.1.4. What the happy outcome of all his sufferings would be: he would *be raised again the third day.* His rising again on the third day proved him to be the Son of God, despite his sufferings, and so he mentioned that to keep up their faith. This is how we must look on Christ's suffering for us, seeing in it the way to his glory, and this is how we must look on our suffering for Christ, looking through it to the reward. *If we suffer with him, we shall reign with him* (2Ti 2:12).

1.2. Why he foretold his sufferings.

1.2.1. To show that they were the product of an eternal plan and consent. They did not come on him as a snare; he had a clear and certain foresight of them, which greatly exalts his love (Jn 18:4).

1.2.2. To put right the mistakes that his disciples had taken in about the external pomp and power of his kingdom. Christ here read them another lesson: he told them about the cross and suffering. Those who follow Christ must be dealt with plainly; they must not be led to expect great things in this world.

1.2.3. To prepare them for the share of at least sorrow and fear that they must have in his suffering. When he suffered many things, the disciples would have to suffer some. Let them know it in advance and, being forewarned, be forearmed.

2. The offense that Peter took at this: he said, *Be it far from thee, Lord. He took him, and began to rebuke him.*

2.1. It was not good for Peter to contradict his Master or assume that he could advise him. When God's ways either are complex or go against our ways, we should silently accept them, not dictate to God what he should do; God knows what he is doing without our teaching him.

2.2. It suggested much worldly wisdom. It is the corrupt part within us that is so concerned to save ourselves from suffering. We tend to look on sufferings as they relate to this present life, in which they are uncomfortable, but there are other rules to measure them by. Peter wanted Christ to dread suffering as much as he did, but we are mistaken if we measure Christ's love and patience by our own.

3. Christ's displeasure with Peter for his suggestion (v. 23). We do not read about anything said or done by any of his disciples at any time that he was so much against as this. Notice how he expressed his displeasure: *Get thee behind me, Satan.* Just now, he had said, *Blessed art thou, Simon,* but here, *Get thee behind me, Satan,* and there was cause for both. A good man may be caught unexpectedly by a temptation and quickly become very unlike himself. It is the subtlety of Satan to send temptations to us by the unsuspected hands of our best and dearest friends. Even the kind actions of our friends toward us are often used wrongly by Satan, as temptations. We should learn to recognize the Devil's voice when he speaks in a saint as well as when he speaks in a serpent. We must be free and faithful in rebuking the dearest friend we have. We must not compliment mistaken courtesies, but rebuke them. Why did Christ respond so intensely against a suggestion that seemed not only harmless but even kind? Two reasons are given:

3.1. "You are my hindrance, you are a stumbling block to me, you are standing in my way." Christ was moving on with the work of our salvation, and his heart was so set on it that he took it badly to be hindered. Peter was not so sharply rebuked for disowning and denying his Master in his sufferings as he was for trying to dissuade him from them. Our Lord Jesus put our salvation before his own comfort and safety; he came into the world not to spare himself, as Peter advised, but to give himself. *Thou art an offence to me.* Those who are committed to any great and good work must expect to meet with hindrance and

opposition from friends and foes, from inside and outside. Those who hinder us from doing or suffering for God when we are called to it, whatever they are in other things, are *Satans* in that, our adversaries.

3.2. *Thou savourest not* (you do not have in mind) *the things that are of God, but those that are of men.* The things that are of God often come into conflict and interfere with *the things that are of men,* that is, our own wealth, pleasure, and reputation.

Verses 24–28

Having shown his disciples that he must suffer, Christ showed them here that they must suffer too.

1. Here the law of discipleship was established, and the terms on which we may have its honor and benefit were fixed (v. 24). Notice:

1.1. What it is to be a disciple of Christ; it is to come after him. A true disciple of Christ is one who follows him in duty and will follow him to glory. A disciple follows Christ and does not dictate to Christ, as Peter had tried to do. A disciple of Christ follows him as sheep follow the shepherd. Those who walk in the same way as he walked in *follow the Lamb, whithersoever he goes* (Rev 14:4).

1.2. What the great things required of those who want to be Christ's disciples are: *If any man* will come. This shows a deliberate choice and a cheerfulness and resolution in that choice. Christ wants his people to volunteer freely to follow him (Ps 110:3).

1.2.1. *Let him deny himself.* Peter had advised Christ to spare himself; Christ told them all that so far from *sparing* themselves, they must *deny* themselves. If self-denial is a hard lesson, one that goes against the grain of flesh and blood, nevertheless, it is nothing more than what our Master learned and practiced before us and for us. All the disciples and followers of Jesus Christ must deny themselves. It is the fundamental law of admission into Christ's school. It is the *strait* gate and the *narrow* way (7:14).

1.2.1.1. We must deny ourselves absolutely; we must not admire our own shadow, gratify our own whim, or seek our own things or our own ambition.

1.2.1.2. We must deny ourselves comparatively; we must deny ourselves for Christ; we must deny ourselves for our brothers and sisters, for their good. We must deny ourselves even for ourselves, deny our physical appetites to gain spiritual benefits.

1.2.2. *Let him take up his cross.* The cross stands for all suffering here, as human beings or as Christians: providential adversities, persecutions for righteousness' sake, every trouble that comes to us, either for doing good or for not doing wrong. It should reconcile us to our troubles and take the edge off their terror to know that they are what we bear in common with Christ and are the kind of sufferings that he has already borne before us.

1.2.2.1. Every disciple of Christ has their cross and must count on it; each has their special duty to fulfill, and everyone feels their own burden most. Crosses are the common lot of God's children, but of this common lot each has their individual portion. It is good for us to call the cross we are under our own and receive it accordingly. We tend to think we could bear another person's cross better than our own, but the best one is the one we carry, and we should make the best of it.

1.2.2.2. Every disciple of Christ must take up what the wise God has made their cross. We must not make crosses for ourselves, but must reconcile ourselves to the crosses that God has made for us. Our rule is that we should not go a step out of our duty either to meet a cross or to miss one. We must not by our rashness and indiscretion pull crosses down on our own heads, but must take them up when they are laid in our way. Whenever we find an adversity in our way, we must take it up out of our way and then continue with it on our way, even if it is heavy. What we have to do is not only to bear the cross but also *take up* the cross, use it to some good advantage. We should not say, "This is an evil, and I must bear it because I cannot help it," but, "This is an evil, and I will bear it, because it will work for my good." When we rejoice and glory in our afflictions, then we are taking up the cross.

1.2.3. *Let him follow me*, in this particular way, by taking up the cross. Do we carry the cross? We are to follow Christ as we do so; he carries it *before* us, carries it *for* us, and so carries it *from* us. He carried the heavy end of the cross, the end that had the curse on it, which was a heavy end, and so made the other end relatively light and easy for us. Or we may take the command more generally, that we must follow Christ in every instance of holiness and obedience. To do well and to suffer wrong is to follow Christ. Those who come after Christ must follow after him.

2. Self-denial and patient suffering are hard lessons that will never be learned if we *consult with flesh and blood* (Gal 1:16); let us therefore consult with our Lord Jesus about some proper considerations for the duties of self-denial and suffering for him. He gives us here:

2.1. Some proper considerations for the duties of self-denial and suffering for Christ. Consider:

2.1.1. The significance of the eternity that depends on our present choice (v. 25): *Whosoever will save his life* by denying Christ *shall lose it*, and whosoever is content to *lose his life* for acknowledging Christ *shall find it*. Here life and death, good and evil, the blessing and the curse, are set before us (Dt 30:15, 19). Notice:

2.1.1.1. The misery that attends the most plausible apostasy. *Whosoever will save his life* in this world, if it is by sin, *shall lose it* in another; the one who forsakes Christ to preserve a worldly life and avoid a physical death will certainly fall short of eternal life, be hurt by the second death, and be eternally held by it (Rev 2:11). The life saved is saved merely for a moment; the death avoided is like mere sleep; but the life lost is eternal, and the death that is met with is an endless separation from all good.

2.1.1.2. The advantage that attends the most risky and costly faithfulness: *Whosoever will lose his life for Christ's sake* in this world *shall find it* in a better. Many lives are lost for Christ's sake. Christ's holy faith is handed down to us sealed with the blood of thousands. Although many have been losers for Christ, even losing life itself, never has anyone been, and never will anyone be, a loser by him in the end. Suffering saints throughout the ages have found that an assurance of the life they would find in place of the life they risked has enabled them to triumph over death in all its terrors, to go smiling to the scaffold and stand singing as they were burned at the stake.

2.1.2. The value of the soul that is at stake and the worthlessness of the world in comparison to it: *What is a man profited, if he gain the whole world and lose his own soul?* (v. 26). This alludes to that common principle that whatever a person gets, if they lose their life, it will do them no good; they cannot enjoy their gains. But it looks higher, speaking of the soul as immortal and of a loss of it beyond death that cannot be compensated for by the gain of the whole world. We can learn from this:

2.1.2.1. Our souls are our own not with respect to power and ownership, but with respect to nearness and concern, for they are ourselves.

2.1.2.2. It is possible for the soul to be lost, and there is a great danger of that happening. The soul is lost when it is eternally separated from all good to do all the evil that a soul is capable of, when it is separated from the favor of God.

2.1.2.3. If the soul is lost, the sinner is the one who loses it. The *man loses his own soul*, for he does what is certainly destructive to it and neglects what alone would save it (Hos 13:9).

2.1.2.4. One soul is worth more than all the world; our own souls are more valuable to us than all the wealth, honor, and pleasures of this present time would be if we had them.

2.1.2.5. The winning of the world often means losing the soul. Many people have ruined their eternal interests by their excessive care to protect and advance their worldly concerns.

2.1.2.6. The loss of the soul is such a great loss that the gain of the whole world will not countervail it. The person who loses their soul, even though it is to gain the world, makes a very bad bargain. When that person comes to balance the accounts, to compare profit and loss, they will find that they are ruined to all intents and purposes, irreparably broken: *What shall a man give in exchange for his soul?* Once the soul is lost, it is lost forever. It is a loss that can never be repaired or retrieved. It is therefore good to be wise in time and do well for ourselves (Pr 9:11–12).

2.2. Some proper considerations to encourage us in self-denial and suffering for Christ.

2.2.1. The assurance we have of Christ's glory at his second coming to judge the world (v. 27). If we see things as they *will* appear then, we will see them as they *should* appear now. The great encouragement to being firm in our religious faith is taken from the second coming of Christ, considering it:

2.2.1.1. As his honor: *The Son of man shall come in the glory of his Father, with his angels*. To look on Christ in his state of humiliation would discourage his followers from taking any pains or running any risks for him; but looking with faith to see the Captain of our salvation (Heb 2:10) coming in his glory will motivate us and make us think that nothing is too much to do or too hard to suffer for him:

2.2.1.2. As our concern: *Then he shall reward every man according to his works*. Jesus Christ will come as a Judge to give rewards and punishments. People will then be rewarded not according to what they have gained in this world but according to their works, according to what they were and did, and the loyalty of faithful souls will be rewarded with a crown of life (Jas 1:12; Rev 2:10). The best preparation for that day is to *deny ourselves, and to take up our cross, and follow Christ* (v. 24), for this is how we will make the Judge our Friend. The rewarding of people according to their works is delayed until that day. Here good and evil seem to be dispensed indiscriminately; on that day, all will be set right.

2.2.2. The near approach of his kingdom in this world (v. 28). It was so near that there were some present with him who would live to see it. At the end of time, he will come in his Father's glory, but now, in the fullness of time (Gal 4:4; Eph 1:10), he was to come in his own kingdom, his kingdom as Mediator. Some small example of his glory was given a few days after this, in his transfiguration (17:1). However, this verse points to Christ's coming by the planting of the Gospel church. The apostles were employed in setting up Christ's kingdom; let them know, to their encouragement, that whatever opposition they met with, they would still be effective. It is a great encouragement to suffering saints to be assured not only of the security but also of the advancement of Christ's kingdom on earth, and not only despite their sufferings but also by their sufferings. This will be done soon, in the present age. The nearer the church's deliverances are, the more cheerful we should be in our sufferings for Christ. Those who would survive the present cloudy time were shown the favor of an assurance that they would see better days.

CHAPTER 17

We have here: 1. Christ in his splendor and glory, transfigured (vv. 1–13). 2. Christ in his power and grace, driving a demon out of a child (vv. 14–21). 3. Christ in his poverty and great humility: 3.1. Foretelling his own sufferings (vv. 22–23). 3.2. Paying tax (vv. 24–27). Here several demonstrations of Christ's gracious intentions are wonderfully interwoven.

Verses 1–13

We have here a record of Christ's transfiguration; he had said that the *Son of man would* shortly *come in his kingdom* (16:28), a promise with which the writers of all three of the Synoptic Gospels particularly connect this story. When Christ was here in his state of humility, though he was mainly humbled and afflicted, some glimpses of his glory were mixed in with that. However, because his public ministry was a state of continual humiliating circumstances, here, in its midst, came this revelation of his glory. Notice concerning Christ's transfiguration:

1. Its circumstances (v. 1):

1.1. The time: *six days* after he had the solemn meeting with his disciples (v. 21). Nothing is recorded that was said or done by our Lord Jesus for six days before his transfiguration. When Christ seems to be doing nothing for his church, we should expect to see something extraordinary before long.

1.2. The place; it was *on the top of a high mountain apart*. Christ chose a mountain:

1.2.1. As a private place. He went apart. Christ chose a secluded place to be transfigured in because his appearing publicly in his glory was not consistent with his present state, and this was how he wanted teach us that privacy is a great friend of our fellowship with God.

1.2.2. Yet also as a sublime place, elevated above things below. Those who want to maintain their fellowship with heaven must frequently withdraw. They will find themselves never less alone than when they are alone, for the Father is with them. Those who want to have a transforming fellowship with God must not only withdraw but also ascend; we are to lift up our hearts and *seek things above* (Col 3:1).

1.3. Its witnesses. He took with him Peter, James, and John. He took three, a competent number to testify what they were to see. Christ made his appearances certain enough, but not too common, so that those who did not see and yet believed would be blessed (Jn 20:29). He took these three because they were the chief of his disciples. They were later to be the witnesses of his agony, and this was to prepare them for that. A sight of Christ's glory while we are here in this world is a good preparation for our sufferings with him, just as these sufferings are preparations for the sight of his glory in the other world.

2. Its manner (v. 2): *He was transfigured before them.* The substance of his body remained the same; he was not turned into a spirit. But his body, which had appeared in weakness and dishonor, now appeared in power and

glory (1Co 15:43). In the days of his flesh he drew a veil over the glory of his Godhead (Heb 10:20), but now, in his transfiguration, he gave his disciples a glimpse of his glory, which must change his form. Now his transfiguration appeared in two things:

2.1. *His face did shine as the sun.* The face is the principal part of the body, by which we are known; that is why such brightness was put on Christ's face. It shone as the sun when it goes forth in all its brilliance (Rev 1:15; Ps 19:6), so clear, bright, and dazzling, even more perceptibly glorious because it suddenly broke out, as it were, from behind a black cloud.

2.2. *His raiment was white as the light.* The shining of the face of Moses was so weak that it could easily be concealed by a thin veil (Ex 34:33, 35), but such was the glory of Christ's body that his clothes were illuminated by it.

3. Its companions. There now *appeared unto them Moses and Elias talking with him* (v. 3). There were glorified saints with him, so that when there were three to testify on earth, Peter, James, and John, there would also be some to bear testimony from heaven. We see here that those who have fallen asleep in Christ do not perish (1Co 15:18). The Jews had great respect for the memory of Moses and Elijah, and so it was these two who came to witness to him. In them the Law and the Prophets honored and testified of Christ. Moses and Elijah appeared to the disciples; the disciples saw them, heard them talk, and knew them to be Moses and Elijah; glorified saints will recognize one another in heaven. The two of them talked with Christ. Christ has fellowship with the blessed.

4. The great pleasure and assurance that the disciples received from the sight of Christ's glory. Peter, as usual, spoke for the rest: *Lord, it is good for us to be here.* Peter expressed here:

4.1. Their delight in this conversation: *Lord, it is good to be here.* He said what his fellow disciples were thinking: "It is good not only for *me* but also for *us*." He did not seek to monopolize this favor, but gladly included them too. He said this to Christ. The soul that loves Christ and loves to be with him loves to go and tell him so: *Lord, it is good for us to be here.* All the disciples of the Lord Jesus count it as good for them to be with him on the holy mountain. It is good to be where Christ is; it is good to be here, withdrawn and alone with Christ, to be in a place where we may see the beauty of the Lord Jesus (Ps 27:4).

4.2. Their desire that this would continue: *Let us make here three tabernacles.* There was in this, as in many other of Peter's sayings, more zeal than discretion.

4.2.1. Here was a zeal for this contact with heavenly things. Those who by faith *behold the beauty of the Lord* in his house also want to *dwell there all the days of their life* (Ps 27:4). It is good to feel at home with holy worship, not like a traveler.

4.2.2. In this zeal, however, he betrayed a great deal of weakness and ignorance. What need did Moses and Elijah have of shelters? Christ had just foretold his sufferings; Peter forgot this, or, to prevent it, he wanted to build shelters on the glorious mountain, out of reach of trouble. There is a tendency in good people to expect the crown without the cross. We are not seeking rightly if we look for heaven here on earth. It is not for strangers and pilgrims to talk about building or to expect a continuing city (Heb 13:14). However, it is some excuse for the incongruity of Peter's proposal that *he knew not what he said* (Lk 9:33) and that he submitted the proposal to the wisdom of Christ: *If thou wilt, let us make tabernacles.*

Note that no reply was given to what Peter said; the disappearing of the glory would soon answer it.

5. The glorious testimony that God the Father gave to our Lord Jesus. Now concerning this testimony from heaven to Christ, notice:

5.1. How it came and was introduced. There was a cloud. We often find in the Old Testament that a cloud was the visible sign of God's presence. He took possession of the tabernacle, and later the temple, in a cloud; where Christ was in his glory, the temple was, and there God showed himself present. It was a bright cloud. Under the law it was commonly a dark, dense cloud that God made the sign of his presence. But *we are now come* (Heb 12:18) to the mountain that is crowned with a bright cloud. The former was an era of darkness, terror, and slavery; the latter is one of light, love, and liberty. The cloud overshadowed them. In revealing himself to his people, God considers how they are formed (Ps 103:14). This cloud was to their eyes as parables were to their understandings: to convey spiritual things by physical things, as they were able to bear them (Mk 4:33; Jn 16:12). *There came a voice out of the cloud*, and it was the voice of God. Here was no thunder, lightning, or voice of a trumpet, as there was when the Law was given through Moses, but only a still small voice (1Ki 19:11–12).

5.2. What this testimony from heaven was: *This is my beloved Son, hear ye him* (listen to him) (v. 5). Here we have:

5.2.1. The great Gospel mystery revealed: *This is my beloved Son, in whom I am well pleased*. This was the same as was spoken from heaven at his baptism (3:17). Moses and Elijah were great favorites of heaven, but they were only servants; Christ, on the other hand, is a *Son*, and God was always pleased with him. Moses was a great intercessor, and Elijah a great reformer, but in Christ God was reconciling the world (2Co 5:19). Christ's intercession is more effective than that of Moses, and his reformation more effective than that of Elijah. This repetition of the same voice that came from heaven at his baptism was to show that the thing was established. What God has *spoken once, yea twice* (Job 33:14), shows that he will no doubt stand by. Now it was repeated because he was entering his sufferings, to protect him from the terror of the cross and protect his disciples from the offense of it. When sufferings begin to flow into our lives, comforts are given more abundantly (2Co 1:5).

5.2.2. The great Gospel duty required: *Hear ye him*. God is pleased with no one in Christ except those who listen to him. It is not enough merely to hear him—what good will that do?—we must listen to him and obey him. Whoever wants to know the mind of God must listen to Jesus Christ, for God has in these last days spoken to us through him (Heb 1:2). Here God, as it were, turned us over to Christ for all the revelations of his mind. Christ now appeared in glory, and the more we see of Christ's glory, the more cause we will have to listen to him. Moses and Elijah—the Law and the Prophets—were now with Christ, and up to that time it was said: *Hear them* (Lk 16:29). "No," God now said, "*hear him*, and that is enough; *him*, not Moses and Elijah." Listen to Christ, and you will not lack the prophets."

6. The fright that the disciples were given by this voice, and the encouragement Christ gave them.

6.1. The disciples *fell on their faces, and were sore afraid*. The greatness of the light and their surprise at seeing it could have discouraged them. But that was not all; extraordinary appearances of God have always been terrible to human beings, who, knowing they have no rea-son to expect any good, have been afraid to hear anything directly from God. It is good for us that God speaks to us through people like ourselves (Ex 20:19), whose terror will not make us afraid (Job 33:7).

6.2. Christ graciously raised them up with much tenderness. Notice here:

6.2.1. What he did: *he came, and touched them*. His approaches banished their fears. Christ's touches often brought healing, and here they brought strength, comfort, and encouragement.

6.2.2. What he said: *Arise, and be not afraid*. It is Christ through his word, and the power of his grace accompanying it, that raises up good people from their dejection and silences their fears, and no one but Christ can do that: *Arise, be not afraid*. Fears that have no basis would soon disappear if we refused to give in to them. Considering what they had seen and heard, they had more reason to be joyful than to fear. Through the weakness of the flesh, we often frighten ourselves with the very things we should encourage ourselves with. After they had received an explicit command from heaven to listen to Christ, the first word they heard from him was, *Be not afraid*.

7. The disappearing of the vision (v. 8). They lifted themselves up, and then *lifted up their eyes*, and *saw no man, save Jesus only*. It is not wise to raise our expectations too high in this world, for the most valuable of our glories and joys here are fading. Even those of close fellowship with God are so; they are not a constant feast (Pr 15:15), but a rushed banquet. Two heavens are too much for those to expect who never deserve one. Now *they saw no man, save Jesus only*. Christ will stay with us when Moses and Elijah have gone.

8. The conversation between Christ and his disciples as they came down the mountain (vv. 9–13). *They came down from the mountain*. We must come down from the holy mountains where we have enjoyed close fellowship with God; even there we have no enduring city (Heb 13:14). When the disciples came down, Jesus came with them. When we return to the world after a time of worship, it must be our concern to take Christ with us. As they came down, they talked about Christ. When we are returning from services of worship, it is good for us to occupy ourselves with conversation that suits what we have been doing. Here is:

8.1. The command Christ gave the disciples to keep the vision private for the present: *Tell it to no man till the Son of man is risen* (v. 9). If they had declared it, its credibility would have been damaged by his sufferings, which were now coming quickly. Let its declaration be delayed until after his resurrection, and then that and his subsequent glory would greatly confirm it. Everything is beautiful in its season (Ecc 3:1, 11). Christ's time is the best and most suitable for him to reveal himself and to be listened to by us.

8.2. An objection that the disciples raised against something Christ had said: "*Why then say the scribes that Elias must first come?* (v. 10)." When the disciples could not reconcile what Christ said with what they had heard from the Old Testament, they wanted him to explain it to them. When we are puzzled with difficult passages of Scripture, we must turn to Christ in prayer for his Spirit to open our understandings and to lead us into all the truth (Lk 24:45; Jn 16:13).

8.3. The solving of this objection. *Ask, and it shall be given* (7:7); ask for instruction, and it will be given.

8.3.1. Christ acknowledged that the prediction was true: "*Elias truly shall first come, and restore all things* (v. 11); so far you are right." Christ did not come to change or invalidate anything foretold in the Old Testament. John the Baptist came to restore things spiritually, to revive the decay in religious faith, which means the same as *he shall restore all things*. John preached repentance, and that restores all things.

8.3.2. He asserted the fulfillment. "The teachers of the law say truly that *Elias shall come*, but *I say unto you*, what the teachers of the law could not say, that *Elias is come*" (v. 12). It often happens that God's promises are fulfilled and people do not realize that they have been, and so they ask, "Where is the promise?" when it has already been fulfilled. The teachers of the law were busy in critical discussion of the Scriptures, but they did not interpret the signs of the times (16:3) and recognize the fulfillment of the Scriptures. It is easier to explain the word of God than to apply it and use it rightly. Because they did not recognize him, *they have done to him whatsoever they listed* (wished); if they had known, they would not have crucified Christ or beheaded John (1Co 2:8). Christ added: *Likewise also shall the Son of man suffer of them*. When they had drenched their hands with the blood of John the Baptist, they were ready to do the same to Christ. As people deal with Christ's servants, so they would deal with him himself.

8.4. The disciples' satisfaction at Christ's reply to their objection: *They understood that he spake unto them of John the Baptist* (v. 13). He did not name John, yet he gave them such a description of him as would remind them of what he had said to them before about him: *This is Elias*. When we conscientiously apply the means of knowledge, how wonderfully mists are scattered and mistakes put right!

Verses 14–21

We have here the miraculous healing of a child who had seizures and was suffering greatly with a demon. Notice:

1. The sad description of this child's condition given to Christ by the afflicted father. This was immediately after Christ came down from the mountain where he was transfigured. Christ's glories do not make him neglect us, our needs, or our miseries. This poor man's words to him were bold; he came kneeling to Christ. A sense of misery will bring people to their knees. Christ delights to be so involved with people. The father of the child complained about two things:

1.1. The distress of his child: *Lord, have mercy on my son* (v. 15). If parents are concerned to pray for their children who are weak and cannot pray for themselves, how much more should they be concerned to pray for those who are evil and will not pray for themselves.

1.1.1. The nature of this child's disease was very sad: *He was lunatic and sore vexed* (had seizures and suffered greatly). This boy's disease lay in his brain. The child often had seizures, and the hand of Satan was in it. Satan afflicted those whom he gained possession of with those physical diseases that most affect the mind, for it is the soul that he aims to cause trouble to. In his complaint, the father said: *He is lunatic*, taking notice of the effect, but Christ, in his healing, rebuked the demon and so struck at the cause. This is how he heals spiritually.

1.1.2. The effects of the disease were deplorable: *He oft falls into the fire, and into the water.*

1.2. His disappointment with the disciples: *I brought him to thy disciples, and they could not cure him* (v. 16). Christ gave his disciples power to drive out demons (10:1, 8), and in general they were successful in that (Lk 10:17), but here they failed, even though there were nine of them

altogether. It is for the honor of Christ to come with help in a crisis when other helpers cannot help. Sometimes he keeps the cistern empty so that he may bring us to himself, the Fountain. However, the failures of instruments will not hinder the activity of his grace, which will be effective, if not *by* them, then *without* them.

2. The rebukes that Christ gave.

2.1. He rebuked those around him: *O faithless and perverse generation!* (v. 17). This is not spoken to the disciples, but to the people, perhaps especially to the teachers of the law. Christ himself could not do many mighty works among a people in whom there was little faith (Mk 6:5–6). It was here because of the faithlessness of this generation that they could not obtain those blessings from God that otherwise they might have had, just as it was because of the weakness of the disciples' faith that they could not do those works for God that otherwise they might have done. Christ rebuked the people for two things:

2.1.1. His presence with them for so long: "*How long shall I be with you?* Will you always need my physical presence, and never come to be so mature that you will be all right when left on your own? Must the child always be carried? Will it never learn to walk by itself?"

2.1.2. His patience with them for so long: *How long shall I suffer* (put up with) *you?* This shows us that the faithlessness and perverseness of those who enjoy the means of grace cause great sorrow to the Lord Jesus. He is God, not man, for otherwise he would not bear it for so long, or so much, as he does.

2.2. He healed the child and put him in his right mind again. He called out: *Bring him hither to me.* Though the people were perverse and Christ was provoked, he still took care of the child. Although Christ may be angry, he is never unkind. *Bring him to me.* When all other helps fail, we are welcome to Christ. Notice here the signs of Christ's work as our Redeemer.

2.2.1. He breaks the power of Satan: *Jesus rebuked the devil* (v. 18) as one having authority (Mk 1:25–27). Christ's victories over Satan are gained by the power of his word. Satan cannot stand in the face of the rebukes of Christ, even though his possession may have lasted a very long time.

2.2.2. He sets people's grievances right: *The child was cured from that very hour.* It was an immediate and complete healing. This is an encouragement to parents to bring their children to Christ. We are not only to bring them to Christ in prayer; we are also to bring them to the word of Christ. Christ's rebukes, brought home to the heart, will ruin Satan's power there.

3. Christ's conversation with his disciples.

3.1. They asked why they had not been able to drive out this demon: *They came to Jesus apart* (in private) (v. 19). Ministers, who are to work for Christ in public, need to keep up their private fellowship with him. We should freely use the access we have to come to Jesus in private, where we may be open and specific with him. When what is wrong is found out, it can be put right.

3.2. Christ gave them two reasons why they failed:

3.2.1. *Because of their unbelief* (v. 20). When he spoke to the father of the child and to the people, he accused them of unbelief; when he spoke to his disciples, he accused them of the same, for the truth was, there were faults on both sides. When the preaching of the word seems not to be so successful as it sometimes has been, the people tend to lay all the blame on ministers, and ministers on the people, whereas it is better if each side acknowledges their own faultiness, saying, "It is because of me." Although the disciples had faith, that faith was weak and ineffective. This shows us:

3.2.1.1. As far as faith falls short of its due strength, vigor, and activity, it may truly be said, "There is unbelief." Many may be accused of unbelief who are yet not to be called unbelievers.

3.2.1.2. It is because of our unbelief that we achieve so little in our faith and come short in what is good. Our Lord Jesus took this occasion to show them the power of faith: *"If ye have faith as a grain of mustard seed,* you will perform wonders" (v. 20). Some understand the comparison to refer to the quality of the mustard seed, which when bruised is sharp and penetrating; "If you have an active, growing faith, not dead, lifeless, or insipid faith, you will not be so disappointed." However, it refers rather to the quantity: "If you had only a grain of true faith, even as little as the smallest seed, you would do wonders." The faith required here was the faith that had as its object that particular revelation by which Christ gave his disciples power to work miracles in his name. It was a faith in this revelation that they were defective in. Perhaps their Master's absence with his three main disciples led them to doubt their power to perform this healing. It is good for us to be modest about ourselves and our own strength, but it displeases Christ for us to distrust any power derived from him or granted by him. "If you have even a very little genuine faith, *ye shall say to this mountain, Remove,"* This is a proverbial expression, referring to what follows and nothing more: *Nothing shall be impossible to you.* They distrusted the power they had received, and so they failed. To convince them of this, Christ showed them what they could have done. An active faith can move mountains, not by itself, but because of divine power engaged by a divine promise.

3.2.2. Because there was something in this kind of illness that made the cure especially difficult: *This kind goes not out but by prayer and fasting* (v. 21). The extraordinary power of Satan must not discourage our faith, but quicken us to a greater intensity in acting on it and a deeper fervency in praying to God for it to increase. Fasting and prayer are the proper means to draw in God's power to help us. Fasting is useful to give us an edge in prayer; it shows the humility we need in prayer. Fasting must be joined with prayer to restrain the body (1Co 9:27).

Verses 22–23

Christ foretold his own sufferings here; he had begun to do it earlier (16:21), and finding that his disciples thought it a hard saying to understand, he saw it as necessary to repeat it. Notice:

1. What he foretold about himself—that he would be betrayed and killed. He told them that:

1.1. He would *be betrayed into the hands of men,* people to whom he was related by nature and by whom he therefore could have expected to be treated with pity and tenderness; but these were his persecutors and murderers.

1.2. *They would kill him;* nothing less than that would satisfy their rage. They thirsted for his precious blood. If he was a Sacrifice of atonement, he must be killed; without the shedding of blood there is no forgiveness of sins (Heb 9:22).

1.3. *He would be raised again the third day.* When he spoke about his death, he gave a hint of his resurrection. This was an encouragement not only to him but also to his disciples, for if he rose on the third day, his absence from them would not be long and his return to them would be glorious.

2. How the disciples received this: *They were exceedingly sorry* (filled with grief). Here we see their love for their Master's person, but also their ignorance and mistakes concerning his undertaking.

Verses 24–27

We have an account of Christ's paying tax here. Notice:

1. How it was demanded (v. 24). Christ was now at Capernaum, where he lived most of the time, and he did not try to avoid paying the tax.

1.1. The tax demanded was not any civil payment to the Roman powers, but the church duties, which were required from every person for the service of the temple and the defraying of the expenses of the worship there.

1.2. The demand was very modest. Their question was, *Doth not your master pay tribute?* Some think that they sought a pretense for accusing Jesus. It seems rather that they asked with respect, indicating that if he had any privilege that made him exempt from paying this tax, they would not insist on it. Peter spoke for his Master: *"Yes, certainly, my Master pays tribute." He was made under the law* (Gal 4:4); it was for that reason that under this law a tax was paid for him at forty days old (Lk 2:22), and now he paid for himself. Now this tax paid to the temple is called *an atonement for the soul* (Ex 30:15). Christ paid it even though he had no sin to atone for, so that in everything he would *appear in the likeness of sinners* (Ro 8:3). He did this to set us an example of *rendering to all their due, tribute to whom tribute is due* (Ro 13:7), and of contributing to the support of the public worship of God in the places where we are. If we reap spiritual things, it is right that we should return earthly things. If Christ pays tax, who can claim to be exempt?

2. How it was discussed (v. 25). Christ discussed it not with the collectors themselves, but with Peter, so that he would be satisfied with the reason why Christ paid the tax. Peter brought the collectors into the house, but Christ anticipated him. The disciples of Christ are never attacked without his knowledge. First, Christ appealed to the way of the kings of the earth, which is to take tax from those who are not close to them. Then, he applied this to himself: *Then are the children free.* Christ is the Son of God and the Heir of all things (Heb 1:2), and so he is not obliged to pay this tax for the service of the temple. This was how Christ asserted his right. Yet God's children, though freed by grace and adoption from the slavery of sin and Satan, are not freed from their submission to civil magistrates in civil things; here the Law of Christ is explicit: *Render to Caesar the things that are Caesar's* (Mk 12:17).

3. How it was paid, nevertheless (v. 27). Notice:

3.1. Why Christ waived his privilege and paid this tax: *lest we should offend them.* Christ considered that if he refused this payment, it would increase people's prejudice against him and his teaching and alienate them from him, and so he decided to pay it. Christian wisdom and humility teach us to retreat from demanding our rights in many cases rather than give offense by insisting on them. We must never decline our duty for fear of giving offense, but we must sometimes deny ourselves in our earthly interests rather than give offense; we follow Paul's example (1Co 8:13; Ro 14:13).

3.2. What he did to pay this tax (v. 27), which shows:

3.2.1. The poverty of Christ; even though he healed very many people who were sick, it seems he did all this for free.

3.2.2. The power of Christ, in drawing money out of a fish's mouth for this purpose. It showed that he is God, the Lord of Hosts. Those creatures that are farthest from human beings are at the command of Christ: even the fish in the sea are under his feet (Ps 8:5; Heb 2:6–9). Notice:

3.2.2.1. Peter must catch the fish by fishing. Peter had something to do, and it was in his calling, too; Christ wants to teach us to be diligent in the employment we are called to and called in. Do we expect Christ just to give us something? Let us be ready to work for him for it.

3.2.2.2. The fish came with money in its mouth. Whatever work we do at Christ's command brings its own reward with it.

3.2.2.3. The coin was just enough to pay the tax for Christ and Peter. He wants to teach us not to seek too much, but, having enough for our present needs, to be content with that, and not to distrust God even if we have to live from hand to mouth. Peter fished for this money, and so part of it went for his use. Those who are *workers together with Christ* (2Co 6:1) in winning souls will be sharers with him in his glory. *Give it for thee and me* (v. 27). What Christ paid for himself was looked on as a debt; what he paid for Peter was out of courtesy to him. It is desirable, if God pleases, to have the resources of this world's goods not only to be just but also to be kind, not only to be kind to the poor but also to be pleasing to our friends.

CHAPTER 18

We have here instructions concerning: 1. Humility (vv. 1–6). 2. Offenses in general (v. 7), and particularly offenses given: 2.1. By us to ourselves (vv. 8–9). 2.2. By us to others (vv. 10–14). 2.3. By others to us. These last are of two kinds: 2.3.1. Scandalous sins (vv. 15–20). 2.3.2. Personal wrongs (vv. 21–35).

Verses 1–6

There never was a greater model of humility than Christ; he took every opportunity to command it and to commend it to his disciples and followers.

1. The occasion of this message about humility was an improper dispute among the disciples over rank: *Who is the greatest in the kingdom of heaven?* They did not mean, "Who, by character?" but "Who, by name?" They had heard much and preached much about the kingdom of heaven, but as yet they were so far from having any clear idea of it that they dreamed of a worldly kingdom with all its outward show and power. They expected that Christ's kingdom would commence when he rose from the dead, and now they thought it was time to apply for their places in it; it is good, in such cases, to speak up early. Instead of asking how they could have strength and grace to suffer with him, they asked him, "Who will be highest in reigning with you?" Many love to hear and speak about privileges and glory but want to forget all thoughts of work and trouble.

1.1. They thought that all who had a place in that kingdom would be great. Those who are truly good are truly great.

1.2. They thought that there were degrees of this greatness. All the saints are honorable, but not all are equally honorable.

1.3. They thought it must be some of them who would be the prime ministers of state.

1.4. They strove to see who it would be, each laying some claim or other to it. We tend all too often to amuse ourselves by foolishly imagining things that will never be.

2. The sermon itself was a just rebuke to the question *Who shall be greatest?* Christ taught them to be humble here:

2.1. By a sign: *He called a little child to him, and set him in the midst of them* (v. 2). Humility is a lesson so hard to learn that we need all possible ways to be taught it. When we look at a little child, we should be reminded of how Christ took this child. *He set him in the midst of them*, not so that they could play with him, but so that they could learn from him. Adults, even great adults, should not disdain the company of little children. They may either speak to them and give instruction to them or look at them and receive instruction from them.

2.2. By a sermon on this sign, in which he showed them and us:

2.2.1. The necessity for humility (v. 3). *Verily I say unto you, except ye be converted, and become as little children, ye shall not enter into the kingdom of heaven.* Notice here:

2.2.1.1. What he required and insisted on.

2.2.1.1.*1*. "You must be converted, you must be changed." Besides the first conversion of a soul, there are later conversions from particular ways of backsliding. Every step out of the way by sin must be a step back to it again by repentance.

2.2.1.1.*2*. *You* must *become as little children.* Converting grace makes us like little children. Like children, we must not worry about anything, but leave it to our heavenly Father to care for us (6:31). We must be humble like little children. The child of a gentleman is pleased enough to play with the child of a beggar (Ro 12:16). This is an attitude that leads to other good attitudes; the age of childhood is the age of learning.

2.2.1.2. What emphasis he placed on this: without this, *you shall not enter into the kingdom of heaven.* When the disciples put their question (v. 1), they thought they were sure of the kingdom of heaven. They were ambitious to be the *greatest in the kingdom of heaven*; Christ told them that if they did not have a different attitude, they would never reach there. Our Lord intends to show the great danger of pride and ambition here. Pride threw the angels who sinned out of heaven, and pride will keep us out too unless we are converted from it.

2.2.2. The honor and advancement that attend humility (v. 4). The person who humbles himself like a little child, *the same is greatest in the kingdom of heaven.* The humblest Christians are the best Christians; they are most like Christ and highest in his favor, and they are most qualified to serve God in this world and enjoy him in the next.

2.2.3. The special care Christ takes of those who are humble. Those who humble themselves in this way will be afraid:

2.2.3.1. That no one will receive them, but *Whoso shall receive one such little child in my name receiveth me* (v. 5). Whatever kindnesses are done to such people are taken by Christ as done to him. Even if it is only one such little child that is received in Christ's name, it will be accepted. The less those to whom we show kindness are in themselves, the more goodwill toward Christ there is in the kindness; the less we do it because of who they are and how we can profit from doing them kindness, the more we do it because of who he is, and he receives it accordingly.

2.2.3.2. That everyone will mistreat them. He dealt with this objection when he warned everyone not to offer any harm to one of his little ones. This word brings a protective wall of fire around the humble; anyone who touches them touches the apple of God's eye (Zec 2:8). Here:

2.2.3.2.1. The crime is imagined: *offending one of these little ones* (causing such a one to sin) *that believe in Christ.* Their trust in Christ unites them to him, so that as they share in the benefit of his sufferings, he also shares in the wrong of theirs. Among those who believe, the little ones have the same privileges as the great ones. The best people have often faced the worst treatment in this world.

2.2.3.2.2. The punishment of this crime is indicated by the words, *Better for him that he were drowned in the depth of the sea.* The sin is so terrible, and the ruin proportionately so great, that it would be better if he faced the most severe punishment inflicted on the worst evildoer, which can only kill the body (10:28).

Verses 7–14

Our Savior spoke here about *offences*, or stumbling blocks—things that cause people to sin:

1. In general (v. 7). An action is a stumbling block if it brings guilt and grief. Christ here told them:

1.1. That stumbling blocks would certainly come: *It must needs be that offences come*; they are sure to come. When we are sure there is danger, we should arm ourselves all the better. Not that Christ's word makes it necessary for anyone to cause another to sin, but this is a prediction in view of the causes. It is morally impossible for there not to be things that cause people to sin; let us therefore stand on our guard (24:24; Ac 20:29–30).

1.2. That they would be terrible things. Here is:

1.2.1. A woe to the careless and unguarded, to whom the cause to sin is given: *Woe to the world because of offences.* This present world is an evil world; it is so full of causes to sin, sins, snares, and sorrows; we travel a dangerous road that is full of stumbling blocks, precipices, and false guides. This world is in a desperate state. As for those whom God has chosen, they are preserved by the power of God and are helped to overcome all these stumbling blocks.

1.2.2. A woe to evildoers, who willfully cause sin: *But woe to that man by whom the offence comes.* Although causes to sin must come, that is not an excuse for those through whom they come. The guilt will be placed at the door of those who cause the sin, even though those who accept it also fall under a woe. God in his righteousness will judge those who ruin the eternal interests of precious souls and the earthly interests of precious saints. People will be judged not only for their *doings* but also for the *fruit of their doings* (Isa 3:10; Jer 17:10; Mic 2:7; etc.).

2. In particular, Christ spoke here about:

2.1. Ways in which we cause ourselves to sin, which are referred to as our hand or foot causing sin; in such cases, the hand or foot must be *cut off* (vv. 8–9). Christ had said this before (5:29–30). The hard sayings of Christ need to be repeated to us again and again, and all are still little enough. Notice:

2.1.1. What is commanded here. We must part with an *eye*, or *a hand*, or *a foot*, whatever is dear to us, when it makes us unavoidably commit sin. This shows us that many successful temptations to sin arise from within ourselves; if there were never a devil to tempt us, we would be drawn away by our own sinful desires (Jas 1:14). We must, as far as lawfully possible, part with what we cannot keep without being entangled in sin by it. It is certain that sinful desires must be put to death. Corrupt inclinations and appetites must be restrained and mortified. Outer occasions of sin must be avoided as far as possible, even though we would be doing to ourselves as great an act of violence as if we cut off a hand or plucked out an eye. We must think that nothing is too dear to part with in order to maintain a good conscience.

2.1.2. The reason why this is required: *It is better for thee to enter into life maimed than, having two hands, to be cast into hell.* The argument is the same as that of the apostle Paul (Ro 8:13). *If we live after the flesh, we shall die. If we through the Spirit mortify the deeds of the body, we shall live*; that is, we will *enter into life maimed*, with the body of sin injured, but it is injured for the best as long as we remain in this world. Those who are Christ's have nailed the sinful nature to the cross (Col 2:14), but it is not dead; yet though its life is prolonged, its *dominion* is *taken away* (Da 7:12).

2.2. Ways in which we cause others to sin (vv. 10–11). Notice:

2.2.1. The warning itself: *Take heed that ye despise not one of these little ones.* He will be displeased with the great ones of the church if they despise its little ones. We may understand it literally, as referring to little children; Christ was speaking about them in vv. 2, 4. Or it may be taken figuratively: true but weak believers are these little ones, who are like little children, the lambs of Christ's flock. We must not despise them, not look down on them. We must not make fun of their weaknesses, not look scornfully or disdainfully toward them, as if we did not care what became of them. We must not impose our own attitudes on the consciences of others. There is a respect that is due to the conscience of every person who appears to be conscientious. We must *take heed* that we do not despise them, being very careful about what we say and do so that we will not inadvertently cause Christ's little ones to sin.

2.2.2. The reasons to back up this warning. We must not look down on these little ones as contemptible. Let those whom God honors not be looked down on by us with disdain. To prove that the little ones who believe in Christ are worthy of respect, consider:

2.2.2.1. The ministry of the good angels for them: *In heaven their angels always behold the face of my Father.* Christ lets us know two things about these angels:

2.2.2.1.*1.* That they are the little ones' angels. God's angels are theirs; little ones can lay hold by faith on the heavenly hosts and call them theirs. It is bad being the enemies of those who are guarded in this way, and it is good to have God as our God, for then we have his angels as our angels.

2.2.2.1.*2.* That *they always behold the face of the Father in heaven.* This shows:

2.2.2.1.*2.1.* The angels' constant happiness and honor. The happiness of heaven consists in the vision of God, gazing on his beauty (Ps 27:4).

2.2.2.1.*2.2.* Their continual readiness to minister to the saints. They see the face of God, expecting to receive orders from him as to what to do for the good of the saints. If we want to see the face of God in glory in the future, we must see the face of God now, in readiness to fulfill our duty, as they do (Ac 9:6).

2.2.2.2. The gracious purpose of Christ concerning them: *For the Son of man is come to save that which was lost* (v. 11). This is a reason:

2.2.2.2.*1.* Why the little ones' angels have such responsibility for them and attend on them; it is according to Christ's purpose of saving them.

2.2.2.2.*2.* Why the little ones are not to be despised: because Christ came to save them, to save those who are lost. Our souls by nature are lost, as travelers who have lost their way are lost. Christ's mission to the world was *to save that which was lost*, to set us on the right path, the way that leads to our great destination. This is a good reason why the least and weakest believers should not be despised or offended. If Christ places such value on them, we are not to undervalue them.

2.2.2.3. Our heavenly Father's tender regard for these little ones and his concern for their welfare. This is illustrated by a comparison (vv. 12–14). Here is:

2.2.2.3.1. The comparison (vv. 12–13). The owner who loses one sheep out of a hundred diligently looks for it, is very pleased when he has found it, and has a deep joy in the sheep that he has found, more than in the ninety-nine that did not wander. Now this applies:

2.2.2.3.1.1. To the state of fallen humanity in general; we have strayed like lost sheep. A wanderer is looked for on the mountains, which Christ, in great fatigue, traversed in pursuit of him, eventually finding him, which is a matter of great joy. There is greater joy in heaven for returning sinners than for remaining angels (Lk 15:7).

2.2.2.3.1.2. To individual believers. God is graciously concerned not only for his flock in general but also for every lamb or sheep that belongs to it. Although they are many, of those many sheep he can easily miss one, for he is *a great* Shepherd (Heb 13:20), but he will not so easily lose it, for he is *a good* Shepherd (Jn 10:14).

2.2.2.3.2. The application of this comparison: *It is not the will of your Father that one of these little ones should perish* (v. 14). It is his will that these little ones should be saved; it is his intention and delight. This care extends to every particular member of the flock, even the lowliest. Later, Christ called God *my Father which is in heaven* (v. 19); here he called him *your Father which is in heaven* (v. 14), showing that he was not ashamed to call his poor disciples *brethren* (Heb 2:11). This also shows that the basis for the security of his little ones is that God is their Father. A father takes care of all his children, but he is particularly tender toward the little ones (Ge 33:13).

Verses 15–20

Having warned his disciples not to cause sin, Christ next undertook to instruct them as to what they must do when others sinned against them.

1. Let us apply it to quarrels that happen for any reason among Christians.

1.1. *Go and tell him his fault between thee and him alone.* Do not allow your anger to develop into a secret malice — like a wound, which is most dangerous when it bleeds inwardly — but express it in a mild and grave warning. Allow such emotions to be drained, and they will soon come to an end. If your fellow Christian has in fact wronged you significantly, try to make him aware of it, but let the rebuke be in private, between you and him alone; if you want to persuade him, do not expose him, for that will only make him angrier. "*If he shall hear thee,* well and good; *thou hast gained thy brother,*" you have won him over and have put an end to the dispute, and it is a happy conclusion; let no more be said about it, but let the falling out of friends become the renewing of friendship.

1.2. "*If he will not hear thee,* if he will not acknowledge that he is at fault, do not despair, but try to see what his response is if you take *one or two more,* not only to be witnesses of what takes place but also to reason the case further with him.

1.3. "If *he shall neglect to hear them,* refusing to refer the matter to their arbitration, then *tell it to the church;* do not immediately appeal to the magistrate or draw up a writ against him." This is fully explained by the apostle Paul in 1Co 6:1–20, where he rebukes those who take their disputes before the ungodly for judgment rather than before the saints (1Co 6:1). This rule was especially needed

when the civil government was in the hands of those who were not only foreigners but also enemies.

1.4. "If he will not *hear the church* but persists in the wrong he has committed toward you, *let him be to thee as a heathen man, and a publican.* You may, if you want to, break off your friendship with him; though you must by no means seek revenge, you may still choose whether or not to continue to have dealings with him. You wanted to preserve his friendship, but he did not want that, and so he has forfeited it." If someone cheats and mistreats me once, it is his fault; if twice, it is my own.

2. Let us apply it to sins that are truly *scandalous,* that is, ones that are stumbling blocks, causing *these little ones to sin* (the word translated *offence* in v. 7 is *skandalon* [Ed.]). Christ wanted to set up a church for himself in the world, and so here he took care to preserve both the church's purity and its peace and order. Now let us see:

2.1. The case that is discussed. *If thy brother trespass against thee.* Church discipline is for church members; *them that are without* (outside the church) *God judges* (1Co 5:12–13). The interests of Christ and believers are interwoven; what is done against them Christ takes as done against himself, and what is done against him they must take as done against themselves.

2.2. What is to be done in such situations.

2.2.1. Here are the rules prescribed (vv. 15–17).

2.2.1.1. "*Go and tell him his fault between thee and him alone.* Do not wait until he comes to you, but go to him, just as a doctor visits the patient. *Tell him his fault,* remind him of what he has done and its evil." People are reluctant to see their faults and need to be told them. Great sins often delight the conscience, and for the present they stupefy and silence it, and help is needed to wake it up. *Tell him his fault;* "argue the case with him," as it may also be read. Where the fault is plain and great, and we are the proper person to deal with it, we must with meekness and faithfulness tell people what is wrong in them. Christian rebuke is a sacred order of Christ to bring sinners to repentance. "Let the rebuke be in private, so that it may be clear that you do not seek his shame but his repentance." It is a good rule not to speak about the faults of our brother and sister to others until we have first spoken about them to our brother or sister. If we followed such a principle, it would make for less reproaching and more rebuking. An offender is likely to be influenced when he sees the rebuker showing concern not only for his salvation, by telling him hid fault, but also for his reputation, by telling him about it privately. "*If he shall hear thee, thou hast gained thy brother*; you have helped save him from sin and ruin, and it will be to your credit and comfort" (Jas 5:19–20). If the loss of a soul is a great loss, the gain of a soul is surely no small gain.

2.2.1.2. If that is not effective, *then take with thee one or two more* (v. 16). We must not become weary of doing good (Gal 6:9), even though we may not see any immediate success from our efforts. "If your brother will not listen to you, do not give him up as a desperate case. Continue to use other means. *Take with thee one or two more*:

2.2.1.2.1. "To assist you; they may speak some relevant, convincing word that you did not think of, and may manage the matter more wisely than you did." Christians should see that they need help in the good work of giving rebukes just as they need it in other good works.

2.2.1.2.2. "To have an effect on him; he will be more likely to be humbled for his fault when he sees it witnessed against by *two or three*" (Dt 19:15). Although it is rare to find one good person whom everyone speaks well of in such a world as this, it is even rarer to find one good person whom everyone speaks ill of.

2.2.1.2.*3*. "To be witnesses of his behavior, in case the matter is later brought before the church."

2.2.1.3. *If he neglect to hear them* and will not be humbled, *then tell it to the church* (v. 17). There are some stubborn spirits to whom the most likely means of conviction prove ineffective; yet such people must not be given up as incurable. Private warnings must always precede public criticism; if gentler methods are effective, rougher and severer ones must not be used (Tit 3:10). Those who will be reasoned out of their sins need not be shamed out of them. Let God's work be done effectively, but with as little noise as possible. Where private warning is not effective, however, public discipline must take place. *Tell it to the church.* The great question is, Which church must be told? The Sanhedrin? From what follows (v. 18), it is clear that he meant a Christian church, for, though not yet formed, the church did exist in embryo. "*Tell it to the church*, that particular church in the fellowship of which the offender lives. Tell it to the guides and governors of the church; let them examine the matter, and if they find the complaint frivolous and without basis, let them rebuke the one bringing the complaint; if they find it just, let them rebuke the offender and call him to repentance."

2.2.1.4. "*If he neglect to hear the church, let him be unto thee as a heathen man and a publican* (treat him as you would a pagan or a tax collector); let him be expelled from the fellowship of the church." Those who show contempt for the orders and rules of a society, bringing disgrace onto it, forfeit its honors and privileges. Notice, however, that Christ does not say, "Let that brother or sister be to you as a demon," but, "Let him be as a pagan or a tax collector, as one who is in a position to be received and restored." However, when by this means the brother is humbled and reclaimed, he must be welcomed back into fellowship, and all will be well.

2.2.2. Here is an executive order signed to authorize all the church's proceedings according to these rules (v. 18). What was said before to Peter is said here to all the disciples. As long as ministers preach the word of Christ faithfully and remain strictly faithful to his laws in their government of the church, they may be assured that he will acknowledge them and stand by them. He will acknowledge them:

2.2.2.1. In their sentence suspending the church member: *Whatsoever ye shall bind on earth shall be bound in heaven* (v. 18). If the discipline of the church duly follows the institution of Christ, his judgments will follow the discipline of the church, for Christ will not allow his own ordinances to be trampled on. Christ will not acknowledge as his or receive to himself those whom the church has duly delivered to Satan (1Ti 1:20), but if through error or envy the discipline of the church has been unjust, Christ will graciously find those who have been thrown out (Jn 9:34–35).

2.2.2.2. In their sentence of absolution: *Whatsoever ye shall loose on earth shall be loosed in heaven.* No church discipline binds so fast that a sinner cannot be loosed again on his repentance and reformation. Sufficient is the punishment that has fulfilled its purpose, and the offender must then be forgiven and encouraged (2Co 2:6). If those who have repented and been received back into fellowship by the church have their hearts upright with God, they may take encouragement from their absolution in heaven.

3. Now it is a great honor that Christ puts on the church here, and in the following verses we have two reasons for this.

3.1. God's readiness to answer the church's prayers: *If two of you shall agree* harmoniously *touching any thing that they shall ask, it shall be done for them* (v. 19). We may apply this:

3.1.1. In general, to all the requests of the faithful praying descendants of Jacob; they will not *seek God's face in vain* (Isa 45:19). We have many promises in Scripture of gracious answers to the prayers of faith, but this gives particular encouragement to prayer made jointly. No law of heaven limits the number of petitioners. If they join together in the same prayer or, though far apart, agree on some particular subject of prayer, they will be effective.

3.1.2. In particular, to those requests that are made to God about binding and loosing. The power of church discipline is not put into the hands of a single person; at least two are involved in it. Arguments and animosities among those whose work it is to take away offenses will be the greatest offense of all. Prayer must always accompany church discipline. We should pass no sentence that we cannot in faith ask God to confirm. Prayer must accompany all our endeavors for the conversion of sinners; see Jas 5:16. The unanimous requests of the church of God to confirm their just discipline will be heard in heaven. God especially acknowledges and accepts us when we are praying for those who have offended him and us. *The Lord turned the captivity of Job* (made him prosperous again) (Job 42:10) not when he prayed for himself but when he prayed for his friends who had wronged him.

3.2. The presence of Christ in the assemblies of Christians (v. 20). Assemblies of Christians for holy purposes are appointed, directed, and encouraged here.

3.2.1. They are appointed; the church of Christ in the world exists most visibly in religious meetings. It is the will of Christ that these should be set up and kept up. If there is no liberty and opportunity to gather in large and numerous assemblies, then it is the will of God that two or three should gather together. When we cannot do what we want to do in matters of our religious faith, we must do what we can, and God will accept us.

3.2.2. They are instructed to gather together in Christ's name. In the exercise of church discipline, they must *come together in the name of Christ* (1Co 5:4). In meeting for worship, we must look to Christ in fellowship with everyone in every place who calls on him. When we come together to worship God in dependence on the Spirit and the grace of Christ, having regard to him as our Way to the Father (Jn 14:6) and as our Advocate with the Father (1Jn 2:1), then we meet together in his name.

3.2.3. They are encouraged with an assurance of the presence of Christ: *There am I in the midst of them.* His sanctuary is where his people are, and he will dwell there. He is *in the midst of them*, that is, in their hearts. It is a spiritual presence, the presence of Christ's Spirit with their spirits, that is meant here. *There am I*; not only "I will be" there" but also "*I am* there," as if he came first and is ready before them, and they will find him there. Even if only two or three meet together, Christ is among them; this is an encouragement to the meeting of a few, whether it is:

3.2.3.1. By choice. There may sometimes be occasions for two or three to come together, either for mutual help in discussion or joint help in prayer. Christ will be present there. Or:

3.2.3.2. By constraint, when there *are not* more than two or three to come together or, if there are, they dare not. It is not the great number of worshipers, but their faith and sincere devotion, that invites the presence of Christ. Even if there are only two or three, the smallest number possible, nevertheless, if Christ, who is the main one, is one of them, then their meeting is as honorable and comfortable as if they were two or three thousand.

Verses 21–35

This part of the sermon about offenses is certainly to be understood as referring to personal wrongs, which it is in our power to forgive. Notice:

1. Peter's question about this matter: *Lord, how oft shall my brother trespass against me, and I forgive him?* (v. 21). Will it be enough to do it *seven times?* This shows us:

1.1. He assumed that he must forgive. He knew that he must not only not bear a grudge against his brother or sister, or think up how he could get revenge, but also be as good a friend as ever and forget the wrong.

1.2. He thought it was a great matter to forgive up to seven times; he did not mean *seven times a day*, as Christ said (Lk 17:4), but seven times in his life. Our corrupt nature makes us tend to be stingy in doing good—to do the smallest amount we can get by with—and to be afraid of doing too much in matters of our religious faith, especially of forgiving too much, even though we ourselves have been forgiven so much.

2. Christ's direct answer to Peter's question: *I say not unto thee, Until seven times,* but *Until seventy times seven,* a certain number to stand for an indefinite one, but nevertheless a large one. It does not make us look good to keep count of the offenses done against us by our brothers and sisters. There is something wrong in keeping a score of the wrongs we forgive, as if we would allow ourselves to take revenge when the limit had been reached. We must overlook injuries without reckoning how often we do so—forgive and forget. God's pardons are so many, and ours should be too. We should make it our constant practice to forgive wrongs and should get used to it until it becomes a habit.

3. A further message of our Savior's, by way of a parable, to show the necessity of forgiving the wrongs done to us. The parable is a comment on the fifth petition of the Lord's Prayer, *Forgive us our trespasses, as we forgive them that trespass against us* (6:12). Those, and only those, who forgive their brothers and sisters may expect to be forgiven by God. There are three things in the parable.

3.1. The master's wonderful mercy toward his servant who was indebted to him; he forgave him ten thousand talents out of pure compassion for him (vv. 23–27). Notice:

3.1.1. Every sin we commit is a debt to God, not like a debt to an equal, contracted by buying or borrowing, but one incurred with a superior, like a debt to a prince when a security is forfeited, or a penalty incurred by a violation of the law. We are all debtors; we owe payment and are exposed to the due process of law.

3.1.2. An account is kept of these debts. This king *would take account of his servants.* God now deals with us according to our own consciences; conscience is an auditor for God in the soul, to call us to account and settle accounts with us. One of the first questions that an awakened Christian asks is, *How much owest thou unto my Lord?* (Lk 16:5). Unless the heart has been bribed, it will tell the truth; it will not write fifty instead of a hundred.

3.1.3. The debt of sin is very large, and some are more in debt because of their sin than others. When he *began to reckon* (began the settlement), he saw that one of the first defaulters owed *ten thousand talents,* a vast sum, a king's ransom or a kingdom's subsidy. See what our sins are as regards:

3.1.3.1. Their detestable nature; they are talents, the greatest denomination ever used in accounting money or weight.

3.1.3.2. Their vast number; they are ten thousand, a myriad.

3.1.4. The debt of sin is so great that we are unable to pay it: *He had not to pay.* Sinners are bankrupt debtors.

3.1.5. If God dealt with us according to his strict justice, we would all be condemned as bankrupt debtors. Justice demands satisfaction. The servant had acquired this debt by his wastefulness and willfulness, and so he could justly have been left to "lie on the bed he had made" for himself. *His lord commanded him to be sold; his wife and children to be sold, and all that he had, and payment to be made.* We see here what every sin deserves; this is *the wages of sin* (Ro 6:23). In this way the king wanted *payment to be made,* that is, something to be done toward it, though it is impossible for the sale of someone so worthless to amount to such a great total as would repay such a great debt.

3.1.6. *The servant fell down* at the feet of his royal master *and worshiped him;* or, as some copies read it, "he besought him." His words to him were bold and submissive: *Have patience with me, and I will pay thee all* (v. 26). The servant knew beforehand that he was in so much debt, but he was not concerned about it until he was called to account. Sinners are usually careless about the forgiveness of their sins until they are arrested by some awakening word, some startling providence, or the approach of death. The bravest heart will fail when God sets outs its sins. He begged for time: *Have patience with me.* Patience is a great favor, but it is foolish to think that this alone will save us; a reprieve is not a pardon. He promised to pay: *Have patience* for a while, *and I will pay thee all.* The one who *had nothing to pay* with (v. 25) thought he could repay *all.* Notice how proud even awakened sinners are; they are convinced but not humbled.

3.1.7. The God of infinite mercy is very ready, out of pure compassion, to forgive the sins of those who humble themselves before him (v. 27). *The lord of that servant,* since he could not be satisfied by the payment of the debt, would be glorified by pardoning it. The servant's prayer was, *Have patience with me*; the master's grant was a full discharge. The pardon of sin is owing to the sheer tender mercy of God: *He was moved with compassion* (Lk 1:77–78). There is forgiveness with God for the greatest sins if they are repented of. Although the debt was immense, the king *forgave it all* (v. 32). The forgiving of the debt is the loosing of the debtor: *He loosed him.* The obligation was canceled, the judgment annulled. Yet although he discharged him from the penalty as a debtor, he did not discharge him from his duty as a servant. The pardon of sin does not lessen, but strengthens, our obligations to obey.

3.2. The servant's unreasonable severity toward his fellow servant, despite his master's mercy toward him (vv. 28–30). This represents the sin of those who are rigorous and unmerciful in demanding what is their own, insisting to the utmost on their rights, which sometimes proves a real wrong. To exact satisfaction for debts of wrong purely out of revenge—though the law may allow it—does not show a Christian spirit. Notice here:

3.2.1. How very small the debt was compared with the *ten thousand talents* that his master forgave him: the fellow servant *owed him a hundred pence.* Offenses done to people are nothing compared with those that are committed against God. It is not that we should make light of wronging our neighbor, for that is also a sin against God;

but we should make light of our neighbor's wronging us, not emphasizing it or seeking revenge.

3.2.2. How severe the demand was: *He laid hands on him, and took him by the throat.* What was the need for all this violence? The debt could have been insisted on without taking the debtor by the throat. How grandly this man struts about, but how corrupt and mean his spirit is! If he himself had been going to prison for his debt, he might have had some pretense for taking such an extreme measure in requiring what he was owed, but pride and hatred frequently prevail more to make people severe than the most urgent need would make them.

3.2.3. How submissive the debtor was: *His fellow servant fell down at his feet* and humbled himself to him for this tiny debt, as his creditor did to his own master for that great debt. The poor man's request was, *Have patience with me;* he honestly confessed the debt, only begging for time. Patience, though it is not acquittal, is sometimes an act of necessary and commendable charity. We must be neither harsh nor hasty in our demands, but remember how patient God is with us.

3.2.4. How implacable and furious the creditor was: *He would not have patience with him* (v. 30), but without mercy *cast him into prison.* How arrogantly he trampled on one as good as himself, who submitted to him!

3.2.5. How very concerned the other servants were: *They were very sorry* (distressed) (v. 31). The sins and sufferings of our fellow servants should be a matter of grief and trouble to us. To see a fellow servant either raging like a bear or trampled on like a worm must be a cause of great regret to everyone who has any regard for the honor of either their nature or their religious faith.

3.2.6. How notice of it was brought to the master: *They came and told their lord.* They dared not rebuke their fellow servant for it, because he was so unreasonable and outrageous, and so they went to their master. Let our complaints of both the evil of evildoers and the afflictions of the afflicted be brought to God and left with him.

3.3. The master's just anger at his servant. Notice:

3.3.1. How he rebuked his servant's cruelty: *O thou wicked servant* (vv. 32–33). Unmercifulness is a great evil. He rebuked the servant with the mercy the servant had found with his own master: *I forgave thee all that debt.* Those who want to accept God's favors will never be rebuked for them, but those who abuse them may expect to be rebuked (11:20). The greatness of sin exalts the riches of forgiving mercy: we should think *how much has been forgiven us* (Lk 7:47). The king showed the servant that the mercy he had received obligated him to be merciful to his fellow servant: *Shouldst not thou also have had compassion on thy fellow-servant, even as I had pity on thee?* It is rightly expected that those who have received mercy should also show mercy. He showed him:

3.3.1.1. That he should have been more compassionate toward the distress of his fellow servant, because he himself had experienced the same distress. What we have felt ourselves we can better feel with our brother or sister.

3.3.1.2. That he should have been more like the example of tenderness that his master had given him. The encouraging sense of forgiving mercy strongly inclines our hearts to forgive our brothers and sisters. We must have compassion on them, as God has on us.

3.3.2. How he revoked his pardon: *He delivered him to the tormentors, till he should pay all that was due unto him* (v. 34). Although the evil was very great, his master laid on him no other punishment than the payment of his own debt. Notice how the punishment corresponds to the sin; the one who refused to forgive would not be forgiven.

Our debts to God are never settled in part; either all is forgiven or all is exacted. Glorified saints in heaven are totally pardoned through Christ's complete atonement.

3.3.3. The application of the whole parable: *So likewise shall my heavenly Father do also unto you* (v. 35). If God's rule is fatherly, it follows that it is righteous, but from that it does not follow that it is not rigorous. When we pray to God as *our Father in heaven,* we are also taught to ask for *the forgiveness of sins, as we forgive our debtors* (6:12). Notice here:

3.3.3.1. The duty of forgiving: we must forgive *from our hearts.* We do not forgive our offending brother or sister rightly or acceptably if we do not forgive them from the heart, for the heart is what God looks at (1Sa 16:7). No hatred must be cherished there, nor any ill will to any person. Yet all this is not enough; we must desire from the heart and seek the welfare even of those who have offended us.

3.3.3.2. The danger of not forgiving: *So shall your heavenly Father do.* This is not intended to teach us that God reverses his pardons to anyone, but that he denies them to those who are unqualified for them. We have enough indications in Scripture of the loss of pardons to show that we should take them as warnings not to be presumptuous. However, we also have enough security in their continuance to encourage those who are sincere but fearful; let the one fear, and the other hope. Those who do not *forgive their brother's trespasses* never truly repented of their own, and so what is *taken away is* only what *they seemed to have* (Lk 8:18). This is intended to teach us that *they shall have judgment without mercy, that have showed no mercy* (Jas 2:13). It is vitally necessary for pardon and peace that we not only *do justly* but also *love mercy* (Mic 6:8).

CHAPTER 19

We have here: 1. Christ's changing the place where he is staying (vv. 1–2). 2. His dispute with the Pharisees on divorce and his conversation with his disciples on this occasion (vv. 3–12). 3. The kind reception he gave to some little children who were brought to him (vv. 13–15). 4. An account of what took place between Christ and a promising young man who turned to him (vv. 16–22). 5. His words to his disciples on that occasion (vv. 23–30).

Verses 1–2

We have here an account of Christ's move. Notice:

1. He left Galilee. He had been brought up there and had spent most of his life in that remote and insignificant part of the country. In this, as in other matters, he appeared in a lowly state so that he would be known as a Galilean, a north-countryman, one who was from the least well-bred and refined part of the country. Now, having *finished these sayings, he departed from Galilee,* and it was his final farewell, for he never came to Galilee again until after his resurrection.

2. *He came into the coasts* (region) *of Judea, beyond Jordan,* so that the people there as well as those in Galilee could receive him, for they also belonged *to the lost sheep of the house of Israel* (10:6).

3. *Great multitudes followed him.* When Christ departs, it is best for us to follow him. He *went about doing good* (Ac 10:38), for, as it follows, *he healed them there.* This shows the reason why they followed him—to have their sick healed—and they found him as able and ready to help here as he had been in Galilee.

Verses 3–12

We have the law of Christ in the case of divorce here, occasioned, as were some other declarations of his will, by a challenge from the Pharisees. Notice here:

1. The case suggested by the Pharisees: *Is it lawful for a man to put away his wife?* (v. 3). They asked this to test him, not to be taught by him. If he would declare himself now against divorce, they would use it to make the people of this country angrily prejudiced against him, make them look jealously on One who attempted to destroy one of the liberties they were fond of. If he said that divorces were not lawful, that would show he was an enemy of the Law of Moses, which allowed them. If, on the other hand, he said they were lawful, they would represent his teaching as not containing the perfection that was expected in the teaching of the Messiah, since though divorces were tolerated, they were looked on by the stricter people as disreputable. Their question was, *Is it lawful for a man to put away his wife for every cause?* That it could be done for some cause, namely, adultery, was granted, but could it be done, as now it commonly was done, by the permissive sort of people, for any reason that a man would think fit, even one that was very frivolous?

2. Christ's answer to this question; although the case was suggested to test him, he gave a full answer to the question—not a direct answer, but an effective one. His argument was this: "If husband and wife are by the will and appointment of God joined together in the strictest and closest union, then they are not to be lightly, and for just any reason, separated." He urged three things:

2.1. The creation of Adam and Eve, about which he appealed to their own knowledge of the Scriptures: "*Have ye not read? Ye have read*—but have not considered—*that he which made them at the beginning, made them male and female* (Ge 1:27; 5:2)." *He made them male and female,* one female for one male; this meant that Adam could not divorce his wife and take another woman, for there was no other woman to take. It also showed an inseparable union between them; Eve was a rib from Adam's side, which meant he could not put her away except by putting away a part of himself.

2.2. The fundamental law of marriage, which is that *a man shall leave father and mother, and shall cleave to his wife* (v. 5). The relationship between husband and wife is closer than that between parents and children; now, if the filial relationship may not be easily broken, much less may the marriage union be broken. May a child desert their parents, or may a parent abandon their children, for any cause, for every cause? No, certainly not.

2.3. The nature of the marriage contract; it is a union of human beings: *They twain* (the two) *shall be one flesh,* so that (v. 6) *they are no more twain* (no longer two), *but one flesh.* A man's children are parts of himself, but his wife is himself. As the marital union is closer than the relationship between parents and children, so it is in a way equivalent to that between one member and another in the natural physical body. From this he reasons: *What God hath joined together, let not man put asunder.* Husband and wife are joined together by God; "he has yoked them together" is the literal sense. God himself instituted the relationship between husband and wife. Although marriage is not distinctive to the church, but common to the world, nevertheless, it should be managed *after a godly sort* (2Co 7:11) and *sanctified by the word of God and prayer* (1Ti 4:5). Conscientious respect for God in this ordinance would have a good influence on the duty, and so on the encouragement, of that relationship. Because husband and wife are joined together by this ordinance of God, they are not to be separated by any human ordinance.

3. An objection raised by the Pharisees to this: "*Why did Moses command to give a writing of divorcement* (a certificate of divorce) (v. 7), in the event that a man did divorce his wife?" He urged scriptural reason against divorce; they alleged scriptural authority for it. The apparent contradictions that are in the word of God are great stumbling blocks to people with corrupt minds.

4. Christ's answer to this objection:

4.1. He set right their mistake about the Law of Moses. They called it a *command;* Christ called it only an allowance. Worldly hearts will take a mile if only an inch is given them. But Christ told them there was a reason for this toleration, not at all to their credit: "*It was because of the hardness of your hearts* that you were allowed to *put away your wives.*" Moses complained about the people of Israel in his time that *their hearts were hardened* (Dt 9:6; 31:27), hardened against God. Here the term referred to their being hardened against their relatives. There is no greater act of hardheartedness in the world than for a husband to be harsh and severe with his own wife. The Jews, it seems, were infamous for this, and that was why they were allowed to divorce their wives; better divorce them than to do worse. A little indulgence of someone who is mad or in a frenzy may prevent greater trouble. The Law of Moses considered the hardness of the human heart, but the Gospel of Christ heals it. Through the law came knowledge of sin (Ro 3:20), but through the Gospel came the conquest of sin.

4.2. He took them back to the original institution: but *from the beginning it was not so.* Corruptions that have crept into any ordinance of God must be cleansed by turning back to the original institution. If the copy is corrupt, it must be examined and corrected from the original.

4.3. He settled the point by an explicit law, beginning with *I say unto you* (v. 9), and it corresponds with what he said before (5:32). In both these places:

4.3.1. He allowed divorce in cases of adultery. The reason for the law against divorce was that *The two shall be one flesh.* If the wife is unfaithful and makes herself one flesh with an adulterer, the reason for the law ceases, and so does the law.

4.3.2. He disallowed it in all other cases: *Whosoever puts away his wife, except for fornication, and marries another, commits adultery.* This is a direct answer to their question: divorce is not lawful. There will be no need for divorces if we bear with one another and forgive one another in love (Eph 4:32; Col 3:13), as those who are and hope to be forgiven. There is no need for divorces if *husbands love their wives, and wives be obedient to their husbands* (Col 3:18–19), and they live together as heirs of the grace of life (1Pe 3:7).

5. A suggestion by the disciples against this law of Christ: *If the case of the man be so with his wife, it is better not to marry* (v. 10). It seems that the disciples themselves were reluctant to give up the liberty of divorce, thinking it a good way of preserving security in the married state. Unless they were free to divorce, they thought it good for a man not to marry in the first place. This shows us that corrupt nature is impatient with restraint. It is foolish and perverse for people to abandon the comforts of this life because of the crosses that they commonly experience. No; whatever our condition is, we must bring our minds to it, be thankful for its encouragements, be submissive to its adversities, and make the best of what is (Ecc 7:14).

If the yoke of marriage may not be rejected at pleasure, it does not follow that we must not come under it; rather, when we do come under it, we must be determined to go through with it in love, humility, and patience, which will make divorce the most unnecessary and undesirable thing possible.

6. Christ's answer to this suggestion (vv. 11–12). He allowed that it was good for some not to marry: *He that is able to receive it, let him receive it.* Christ allowed what the disciples said, *It is good not to marry*, as giving them a rule that those who have the gift of self-restraint do best if they continue to be single. The increase of grace is better than the increase of the family, and fellowship with the Father and with his Son Jesus Christ is to be put before any other fellowship. Yet he prohibited, as totally harmful, the forbidding of marriage, because *all men cannot receive this saying.* Christ spoke here of a twofold disinclination to marry:

6.1. What is an adversity by the providence of God, such as befalls those who are born eunuchs or are made so by people.

6.2. What is a virtue by the grace of God; such is the virtue of those who *have made themselves eunuchs for the kingdom of heaven's sake.* This is meant to refer to an unfitness to marry that comes not from the body but from the heart. Those who have made themselves eunuchs have reached a holy indifference to all the delights of the married state and are determined, in the power of God's grace, wholly to abstain from them. These are the people who *can receive* this saying. This affection for the single state must be given by God, for no one can receive it *save they to whom it is given.* Self-restraint is a special gift of God given to some people and not others. The single state must be chosen for the kingdom of heaven's sake. When it is for the sake of religious faith, then it is approved and accepted by God. The condition that is best for us and is therefore to be chosen and abided by is the one that is best for our souls and tends most to prepare and preserve us for the kingdom of heaven.

Verses 13–15

We have here the welcome that Christ gave to some little children who were brought to him. Notice:

1. The faith of those who brought them. The account given of it is that *there were brought unto him little children, that he should put his hands on them, and pray* (v. 13). Those who brought the children showed the respect they had for Christ and the value they put on his favor and blessing. They also showed kindness to their children. Others brought their children to Christ to be healed when they were sick, but these children were suffering no illness at that time; those bringing them wanted only a blessing for them. It is good to come to Christ ourselves and bring our children to him before we are driven to him by a particular need. They wanted him to place his hands on them and pray. The laying on of hands was a ceremony used especially in paternal blessings. It shows something of love and familiarity mixed with power and authority and speaks of an efficacy in the blessing. We cannot do better for our children than to commit them to the Lord Jesus to be prayed for and helped by him. We can only beg a blessing for them; it is only Christ who can command the blessing (Lev 25:21; Dt 28:8; Ps 133:3).

2. The fault of the disciples in rebuking them. They frowned on this errand as worthless and frivolous, and they rebuked those who came for being impertinent and troublesome. It is good for us that Christ has more love and tenderness in him than the best of his disciples has.

Let us learn from him not to discourage any willing, well-meaning souls from seeking, even though they may be weak. If *he* does not break the bruised reed (Isa 42:3; Mt 12:20), neither should *we.*

3. The favor of our Lord Jesus.

3.1. He rebuked the disciples (v. 14): *Suffer little children* (let the little children come to me), *and forbid them not*; and he put right the disciples' mistake: *Of such is the kingdom of heaven.*

3.1.1. The children of believing parents belong to the kingdom of heaven and are members of the visible church.

3.1.2. This is why they are welcome to Christ, who is ready to receive those who, when they cannot come by themselves, are brought to him. He is ready to receive children:

3.1.2.1. Out of respect to the little children themselves, whom he has on all occasions expressed concern for.

3.1.2.2. With an eye to the faith of the parents who bring them. Parents are trustees of their children's wills. Christ therefore accepts the parents' dedication of their children as the children's act and deed. He is displeased, therefore, when people forbid them, excluding those whom he has received.

3.2. *He received the little children* and did as those who brought them wanted him to do: *he laid his hands on them*; that is, *he blessed them.* The strongest believer does not live so much by taking hold of Christ as by being taken hold of by him (Php 3:12), and the smallest child is capable of this. If they cannot stretch out their own hands to Christ, he can still lay his hands on them, make them his own, and acknowledge them as his own.

Verses 16–22

Here is an account of what took place between Christ and a promising young man; he is said to have been a *young man* (v. 20), and we call him a gentleman, not only because he had great possessions but also because he was a ruler (Lk 18:18). Now concerning this young man, we are told how he sought heaven but came short of it. Notice:

1. How he sought heaven and how kindly and tenderly Christ treated him. Here is:

1.1. The man's serious address to Jesus Christ: *Good Master, what good thing shall I do, that I may have eternal life?* (v. 16). No better question could be asked, nor more earnestly.

1.1.1. He gave Christ an honorable title, "*Good Master.*" It means not a ruling master, but a teaching master. By calling him *Master*, the man showed his submissiveness and willingness to be taught, and by calling him *good Master*, he showed his affection and special respect for the Teacher. It is good when a person's achievement and advancement increase their civility and courtesy. It was gentlemanlike to give this title of respect to Christ. It was unusual among the Jews to speak to their teachers with the title *good*; doing so therefore showed the uncommon respect the man had for Christ.

1.1.2. He came to Christ on a serious matter—none could be more serious—and he did not come to test him, but sincerely wanted to be taught by him. His question was: *What good thing shall I do, that I may have eternal life?* He was convinced that there is a happiness prepared in the other world for those who are prepared for it in this world. It was rare for one of his age and quality to appear so concerned about the next world. Rich people tend to think it beneath them to ask such a question, and young people think there is plenty of time to ponder it, but here was a young man, and a rich man, concerned about his soul and eternity. He was aware that something must be done, something good, to reach this happiness. We must be active, doing what is good. The blood of Christ is the price that was paid for eternal life—he merited it for us—but obedience to Christ is the appointed way to it (Heb 5:9). Those who know what it is to have eternal life and what it is to come short of it will be glad to accept it on any terms. This is the sort of holy *violence* that the kingdom of heaven *suffers* (11:12). Since this world does not contain what will make us happy, our great question should be, *What shall we do that we may have eternal life?*

1.2. The encouragement that Jesus Christ gave to his words. It is not his way to dismiss without an answer anyone who comes to him on such a mission, for nothing pleases him more than to give an answer (v. 17).

1.2.1. He tenderly assisted his faith, for no doubt he did not mean it as a rebuke when he said, *Why callest thou me good?* The young man intended no more than to acknowledge and honor Christ as a good man, but Christ wanted to lead him on to acknowledge and honor him as a good God, for *there is none good but one, that is God*. Just as Christ is graciously ready to make the best that he can of what is said or done wrongly, so he is ready to make the most of what is said or done well. His interpretations are often better than our intentions. All crowns must lie before his throne (Rev 4:10). Only God is good. In our language we call him *God* because he is good.

1.2.2. He clearly directed his way of life. Christ's answer was, in brief, *If thou wilt enter into life, keep the commandments.*

1.2.2.1. The end that is aimed at is entering life. In his question, the young man spoke about eternal life. In his answer, Christ spoke about *life*; this teaches us that eternal life is the only true life. The young man wanted to know how he could *have* eternal life; Christ told him how he could *enter into it*. Christ directs us in the way of *entering into it*, that is, by obedience. Christ, who is our Life, is the Way to the Father (Jn 14:6). Christ is the only Way to the Father, but duty and the obedience of faith are the way to Christ.

1.2.2.2. The way prescribed is keeping the commandments. Keeping the commandments of God as they have been revealed and made known to us is the only way to life and salvation. *Keeping the commandments* includes *faith in Jesus Christ*, for that is the great commandment (1Jn 3:23). It is not enough for us to *know* the commandments of God; we must also *keep* them, keep in them as our way of life, keep to them as our rule.

1.2.2.3. At the man's further instance and request, Christ mentioned some particular commandments that he must keep: *The young man saith unto him, Which?* (vv. 18–19). In response to this, Christ specified several, especially the commandments of the second table of the Ten Commandments, which concern:

1.2.2.3.*1*. Our own and our neighbor's life: *Thou shalt do no murder.*

1.2.2.3.*2*. Our own and our neighbor's purity: *Thou shalt not commit adultery.*

1.2.2.3.*3*. Our own and our neighbor's wealth and outward possessions: *Thou shalt not steal.*

1.2.2.3.*4*. Truth and our own and our neighbor's good name: *Thou shalt not bear false witness.*

1.2.2.3.*5*. The duties of particular relationships: *Honour thy father and mother.*

1.2.2.3.*6*. The comprehensive law of love, that *royal law* (Jas 2:8), in which they are all fulfilled: *Thou shalt love thy neighbour as thyself* (Gal 5:14; Ro 13:9).

1.2.2.4. Our Savior here specified only second-table duties; not as if those of the first table were less significant, but:

1.2.2.4.*1*. Those who now sat in Moses' seat either wholly neglected or greatly corrupted these commands in their preaching. While they urged the tithing of *mint, anise, and cumin*, they overlooked "judgment, mercy, and faith," the summary of second-table duties (23:23). Their preaching was all ritual, and nothing moral.

1.2.2.4.*2*. He wanted to teach the young man, and all of us, that moral honesty is a necessary branch of true Christianity. Although a merely moral man falls short of being a complete Christian, an immoral man is certainly no true Christian. In fact, although first-table duties contain more of the essence of religion, second-table duties contain more of the evidence of it. Our light burns in love toward God, but it shines in love toward our neighbor.

2. How he came short and in what he failed.

2.1. In pride and a distorted view of his own goodness and strength. When Christ told him what commandments he must keep, he answered scornfully: *All these things have I kept from my youth up* (v. 20). Christ knew it, for he did not contradict him; in fact, it is said in Mark, *He loved him* (Mk 9:21), and so far he was very good and pleasing to Christ. The young man's observance of these commands was universal: *All these have I kept*. He began early in life and was faithful: *from my youth up*. A person may be free from gross sin and yet come short of grace and glory. It was also commendable that the man wanted to know more of what his duty was: *What lack I yet?* He was convinced that he lacked something to fill up his works before God, and he wanted to know it, for—if he was not mistaken about his own heart—he was willing to do it. Having not yet reached that point, he seemed to press forward. And it was commendable that he turned to Christ with his question. Who could make a better effort? But even in what he said, he revealed his ignorance and foolishness. If he had known the extent and spiritual meaning of the Law, then instead of saying, *All these have I kept; what lack I yet?* he would have said with shame and sorrow, "All these have I broken; what must I do to have my sins forgiven?" Whichever way you take it, what he said smacked of pride and boasting, and it contained too much of the boasting that is excluded by the law of faith (Ro 3:27). The words *What lack I yet?* were perhaps not so much a request for further instruction as a demand for praise of his present imagined perfection.

2.2. By an excessive love for the world and his enjoyment of it. This was the fatal rock on which he fell (Isa 8:14; 1Pe 2:8). Notice:

2.2.1. How he was tested in this matter: *Jesus said unto him, If thou wilt be perfect, go and sell that thou hast* (v. 21). Christ waived the matter of his boasted obedience to the law; he let that fall, because this would be a more effective way of revealing to the man his own true character than a dispute about the extent of the law. What Christ said to him he has said to us all, that if we want to show that we are true Christians, to be found on the last day to be the heirs of eternal life, we must do these two things:

2.2.1.1. We must in practice prefer heavenly treasures to all the wealth and riches of this world. Now, as evidence of this:

2.2.1.1.*1*. We must dispose of what we have in this world for the honor of God and in his service: "*Sell that thou hast, and give to the poor.* Sell what you can spare for godly use, all the things you don't really need; if you cannot otherwise do good with it, sell it. Don't cling to your possessions, but be willing to part with them for the honor of God and to bring relief to the poor." Those who have the resources must give to those in need in order to demonstrate their contempt for the world, and we must show compassion toward our brothers and sisters for the same reason. When we embrace Christ, we must let go of the things of this world, for we cannot serve God and Mammon (6:24). Christ knew that covetousness was the sin that most easily entangled this young man (Heb 12:1), that although he had gained honestly what he had, he could not cheerfully part with it, and by this he revealed his insincerity.

2.2.1.1.*2.* We must depend on what we hope for in the other world as an abundant reward for all we have left, lost, or laid out for God in this world: *Thou shalt have treasure in heaven.* We must trust God for a happiness that cannot be seen, which will make us rich and make up for all our expenses in God's service. Christ immediately attached this assurance of treasure in heaven. Christ's promises make his commands easy and make his yoke not only tolerable but also pleasant, sweet, and very comfortable (11:30).

2.2.1.2. We must devote ourselves entirely to the leadership and direction of our Lord Jesus: *Come, and follow me* (v. 21). It seems to refer to a close and constant attendance on his person here, the sort of *following* for which the selling of what he had in the world was necessary; but of us it is required that we follow Christ by conforming strictly to his pattern and keeping his laws. All this must be from a motive of love to him and dependence on him, and with a holy contempt of everything else in comparison with him. This is to follow Christ fully. To sell all and give to the poor will not be enough unless we come and follow Christ. If I give all my goods to feed the poor and have not love, I gain nothing (1Co 13:3).

2.2.2. How his weak spot was uncovered. This touched him at a tender point: *When he heard that saying, he went away sorrowful, for he had great possessions* (v. 22). He was a rich man and loved his riches, and that was why he went away. Those who have much in the world are in the greatest temptation to love it. Such is the captivating nature of worldly wealth that those who lack it least desire it most. A controlling love for this world keeps away from Christ many people who seem to have some good desires toward him. If we have many possessions, we have a choice: on the one hand, if we overcome the desire for more, it is a great furtherance on our way to heaven, but on the other, if we become entangled by the love of them, it is a great hindrance on our way there. There was, however, some honesty in the young man. He went away and would not pretend to have something that he could not find in his heart to reach the strictness of. Since he could not be a complete Christian, he would not be a hypocrite. Yet he was a thoughtful man, and well inclined, and so he *went away sorrowful.* He had some inclination to follow Christ and was reluctant to part with him. Many people have been ruined by the sin they commit with reluctance; they leave Christ sorrowfully but are never truly sorry for having left him, because if they were, they would return to him.

Verses 23–30

We have here Christ's conversation with his disciples on the occasion of the rich man's leaving him.

1. Christ used the occasion to show the difficulty of the salvation of rich people (vv. 23–26).

1.1. It is very hard for rich people to get to heaven. It is good for us to apply lessons from the difficulties and falls of others so as to infer warnings to us. Now:

1.1.1. This is passionately asserted by our Savior (vv. 23–24). He says this to his disciples, who are poor. The less they have of worldly wealth, the less hindrance they have on their way to heaven. Christ confirms this saying in v. 23: *Verily I say unto you.* He repeats it: *Again I say unto you* (v. 24). He *speaks once, yea twice* (Job 33:14), what people are reluctant to realize and even more reluctant to believe.

1.1.1.1. He says that it is hard for rich people to enter the kingdom of heaven, either here or in the future. The way to heaven is a narrow way to all, and the gate that leads into it is a narrow gate (7:14), but it is particularly so to rich people. Rich people are exposed to great, subtly penetrating temptations that are hard to resist, and it is difficult not to be charmed by a smiling world. It must be a great measure of divine grace that will enable someone to overcome these difficulties.

1.1.1.2. He says that the conversion and salvation of rich people is so extremely difficult that *it is easier for a camel to go through the eye of a needle* (v. 24). Nothing less than the almighty grace of God will enable a rich person to overcome this difficulty. It is very rare for a person to be rich and not set their heart on their riches, and it is completely impossible for someone who sets their heart on their riches to get to heaven. The way to heaven is appropriately compared to *a needle's eye,* which is hard to hit and hard to get through. A rich person is appropriately compared to *a camel,* a beast of burden, for they have riches, just as a camel has its load.

1.1.2. This truth is found astonishing by the disciples, who scarcely believe it: *They were exceedingly amazed, saying, Who then can be saved?* (v. 25). Christ has told them many surprising truths, which they have been astonished at and not known what to make of. It is not in contradiction to Christ, but to wake themselves up, that they say: *Who then can be saved?* When we think how good God is, it may seem amazing that so few are his, but when we think how bad people are, it is more amazing that so many are. *Who then can be saved?* Since so many people are rich and have great possessions, and so many more want to be rich and are well disposed to great possessions, who can be saved? This is a good reason why rich people should swim against the tide.

1.2. Although it is hard, it is not impossible for the rich to be saved. *Jesus beheld them;* he turns and looks thoughtfully at his disciples (v. 26), *and he says unto them, with men this is impossible, but with God all things are possible.* This is a great truth in general. Nothing is too hard for God (Ge 18:14; Nu 11:23). When people are at a loss, God is not. But this truth is applied here:

1.2.1. To the salvation of anyone. "*Who can be saved?*" ask the disciples. "None," Christ says, "by any created power. *With men this is impossible.*" It is an act of creation (Ps 51:10; Gal 6:15), a resurrection, and with human beings this is impossible; but *with God all things are possible.*

1.2.2. To the salvation of rich people especially. It is impossible for the rich to be saved, but with God even this is possible. The sanctification and salvation of rich people who are surrounded by the temptations of this world are not to be despaired of; they are possible. In this word of Christ there is an indication of the mercy Christ still had in store for this young man, who had now gone away sad; it was not impossible for God still to restore him.

2. Peter uses the occasion to ask what they will gain by having left everything to follow him (v. 27).

2.1. We have their expectations of Christ; *Behold, we have forsaken all, and have followed thee; what shall we have therefore?* Peter wants to know:

2.1.1. Whether they have sufficiently fulfilled those terms: they have not sold everything—for many of them had wives and families to provide for—but they have *forsaken all*. When we hear what is the character of those who will be saved, we should ask whether we, through grace, fulfill that description. "Lord," says Peter, "*we have forsaken all*." Unfortunately, it was a poor all they left. Notice, however, how Peter speaks about it, as if it were something great: *Behold, we have forsaken all*. We tend to make far too much of our service and suffering for Christ, our expenses and losses for him, and to think we have made him our debtor. However, Christ does not rebuke them for this. It was their all, like the widow's two very small copper coins, and it was as dear to them as if it had been more, and so Christ takes it kindly that they left it to follow him.

2.1.2. Whether, therefore, they can expect *that treasure* that the young man would have if he sold everything. All people are out for what they can gain, and Christ's followers are allowed to consider their own true interests and to ask, *What shall we have?* Christ encourages us to ask what we will gain by leaving all to follow him, so that we may see that he does not call us to our detriment, but indescribably to our advantage. It is the language of a confident, trusting faith to ask, "What will we *have*?" The disciples have not asked until now, *What shall we have?* They are so assured of his goodness that they know they will not lose by him in the end, and that is why they have been taken up with their work and have not asked what their wages will be. We honor Christ if we trust him and serve him, not bargaining with him.

2.2. We have Christ's promises to them here, and to all others who follow in the footsteps of their faith and obedience. He uses this occasion to give the assurance of a promise:

2.2.1. To his immediate followers (v. 28). He promises them not only treasure but also honor. *Ye which have followed me in the regeneration shall sit upon twelve thrones*. Notice:

2.2.1.1. The introduction to the promise, or the "in consideration of" clause of the grant, which, as usual, is a recital of their service: "You have followed me in the *regeneration* (the renewal of all things), and so I will do this for you." The disciples have followed Christ while the Gospel temple is being built. They now follow him with constant toil, while few do, and so it is to them that he will give special marks of honor. Christ has special favor for those who begin their lives with him, who trust him further than they can see him. Peter speaks of their forsaking all to follow him; Christ only speaks of their following him, which is the main matter.

2.2.1.2. The date of their honor, *when the Son of man shall sit in the throne of his glory*. All who share in the regeneration in grace will share in the renewal in glory. Now their waiting for their honor until the Son of Man is sitting on the throne of his glory indicates:

2.2.1.2.1. That they must wait for their advancement until then. As long as our Master's glory is delayed, it is right for ours to be so too. We must live, work, and suffer in faith, hope, and patience.

2.2.1.2.2. That they must share with Christ in his advancement. After they have suffered with a suffering Jesus, they must reign with a reigning Jesus (2Ti 2:12). The longest voyages make the richest returns.

2.2.1.3. The honor itself that is granted: *Ye also shall sit upon twelve thrones, judging the twelve tribes of Israel*. The general intention of this promise is to show the glory and position reserved for the saints in heaven, which will be an abundant reward for the disgrace they suffered here

in Christ's cause. There are higher degrees of glory for those who have done and suffered most. Here *bonds and afflictions and deaths did abide them* (Ac 20:23), but there they *shall sit on thrones of glory*. Will not this be a sufficient reward to make up for all their losses and expenses for Christ (Lk 22:29)? This grant is confirmed and certain; it is inviolably and unchangeably sure, for Christ has said: "*Verily I say unto you.*"

2.2.2. To all others who leave all to follow Christ. *This honour have all his saints* (Ps 149:9). Christ will take care that none of them will lose by him (v. 29).

2.2.2.1. Losses for Christ are considered here. Christ has told them that his disciples must deny themselves; he here goes into details, for it is good to consider the worst possible scenario. If they have not left all to follow Christ, still, they have left a great deal; for example, houses. Or they have left their close relatives who did not want to go with them. These are mentioned particularly, as the hardest for a sensitive, gracious spirit to part with: *brethren, or sisters, or father, or mother, or wife, or children*; and *lands* (fields) are added at the end, the profits of which were to support the family.

2.2.2.1.1. The loss of these things is presumed to be *for Christ's name's sake*, for otherwise he does not oblige himself to make them up. Many leave brothers and sisters, wife, and children, because of a changed attitude or anger; that is a sinful desertion. However, if we leave them *for Christ's sake*, because we must either leave them or leave our interest in Christ, if we leave our concern for them, our duty to them, or our comfort in them, rather than deny Christ, this is what will be rewarded. It is not the suffering, but the cause, that makes both the martyr and the confessor.

2.2.2.1.2. It is presumed to be a great loss, but nevertheless Christ undertakes to make it up.

2.2.2.2. A reward for these losses is guaranteed here. Thousands have entered into relationship with Christ and trusted him for much, but never has anyone lost by him; everyone has always received indescribable gains through him. They will receive:

2.2.2.2.1. *A hundredfold in this life*, sometimes in kind, in the things themselves that they have parted with. God will raise up for his suffering servants more friends, who will be friendlier to them for Christ's sake than those they have left, who were friends for their own sakes. Wherever the apostles came, they met some people who were kind to them, received them, and opened their hearts and doors to them. However, they *shall receive a hundredfold* in kindness. Their graces will increase, and their comforts will abound; they will have signs of God's love. Then they may truly say that they have received a hundred times more comfort in God and Christ than they could have in *wife or children*.

2.2.2.2.2. *Eternal life* at the end. The reward promised for this life would be enough if there were no more. But this comes over and above, into the bargain, as it were. Now if we could only have faith in this promise, trusting Christ for its fulfillment, we would surely think nothing too much to do, nothing too hard to suffer, nothing too dear to part with, for him.

3. In the last verse, our Savior disposes of a mistake some people make, when he says, *Many that are first shall be last, and the last, first* (v. 30). God will make an exchange. The heavenly inheritance is not given as earthly inheritances usually are, by seniority of age and priority of birth, but according to God's pleasure. This is the text of another sermon, which we will meet with in the next chapter.

CHAPTER 20

We have here: 1. The parable of the workers in the vine-
yard (vv. 1–16). 2. A prediction of Christ's approaching
suffering (vv. 17–19). 3. The rebuking of a request that
the mother of two of the disciples brought on their behalf
(vv. 20–28). 4. The granting of a request by two blind
men (vv. 29–34).

Verses 1–16

1. This parable of the workers in the vineyard is
intended:

1.1. To represent to us *the kingdom of heaven* (v. 1).
The laws of that kingdom are not wrapped up in parables,
but clearly set out, as in the Sermon on the Mount, but its
mysteries are communicated in parables. Its ideas need to
be illustrated more than its duties, and such illustration is
the intention of parables.

1.2. In particular, to represent to us what Christ had
said at the end of the previous chapter about the kingdom
of heaven, that *many that are first shall be last, and the*
last, first (19:30). The parable shows us:

1.2.1. That God is indebted to no one, which is a great
truth.

1.2.2. That many who begin last and promise little in
religious faith nevertheless reach, with the blessing of
God, greater accomplishments in knowledge, grace, and
usefulness than others whose entrance was earlier and who
promised greater things. John is swifter on his feet and
comes *first to the sepulcher*, but Peter has more courage
and goes *first into it* (Jn 20:4, 6). This is how *many that*
are last shall be first. Some consider Christ's words here
to be a warning to the disciples. Let them make sure that
they maintain their zeal, for otherwise their good beginnings will do them no good; those who seemed to be *first*
would be *last*. Sometimes those who are converted later in
their lives outstrip those who are converted earlier.

1.2.3. That *the recompence of reward* (Heb 10:35;
11:26) will be given to the saints not according to the time
of their conversion, and not according to their seniority,
but *according to the measure of the stature of the fulness*
of Christ (Eph 4:13). Sufferers for Christ in the last days
will receive the same reward as the martyrs and confessors in the early days, even though the latter are more
celebrated, and faithful ministers will receive the same
reward as the first church fathers.

2. We have two things in the parable: the agreement
made with the workers and the settling of accounts with
them.

2.1. Here is the agreement made with the workers
(vv. 1–7), and here it will be asked:

2.1.1. Who hires them? *A man that is a householder.*
God is the great Householder; as a householder, he has
work that he wants done and servants whom he wants to
do it. God hires workers out of kindness to them, to save
them from idleness and poverty, and he will pay them for
working.

2.1.2. Where are they hired? At *the market place*,
where, until they are hired into God's service, they *stand*
idle (v. 3), *all the day idle* (v. 6). This shows us that the
human soul stands ready to be hired into some service or
other; it was created, as all the creatures were, to work,
and is either a *servant to iniquity* or *a servant to righ-*
teousness (Ro 6:19). The Devil, by his temptations, is
hiring labourers into his field to *feed swine*. God, by his
Gospel, is *hiring labourers into his vineyard* (v. 1) *to dress*
it and keep it (Ge 2:15), a work of paradise. Until we are
hired into the service of God, we are standing around all

day. The Gospel call is given to those who *stand idle in*
the marketplace. The marketplace is *a place of concourse*
(Pr 1:21); it is also a place of fun, where the *children are*
playing (Zec 8:5; 11:16); it is a place of business, noise,
and hurry. "Come, come away from this marketplace."

2.1.3. What are they hired to do? To work in his
vineyard. The church is God's vineyard; he has planted,
watered, and fenced it. We are all called to be workers
in this vineyard. Each one of us has our own vineyard to
keep, our own soul; it belongs to God and is to be well
worked and taken care of for him. In this work we must
not be lazy or loiter around, but be *labourers*, working.
Work for God will not allow laziness. A person may go
idly to hell, but those who want to go to heaven must be
busy.

2.1.4. What will their wages be? He promises:

2.1.4.1. *A penny* (denarius) (v. 2), a day's wages for a
day's work, and the wages were enough for a day's maintenance. This does not prove that the reward of our obedience to God is *of works* or *of debt*. It is to show that a
reward is set before us, and it is a sufficient one.

2.1.4.2. *Whatsoever is right* (vv. 4–7). God will be
sure not to delay payment to anyone for the service they
do him: never has anyone lost by working for God.

2.1.5. How long are they hired for? *A day.* It is only
a day's work that is done here on earth. The time of life
is the day. It is a short time; the reward is for eternity,
but the work is only for *a day*. We should be stirred to
efficiency and diligence in our work when we remember
that we have only a little time to work in. We should also
be encouraged concerning the hardships and difficulties
of our work when we remember that it lasts only for *a*
day; the approaching *shadow* will bring with it rest and
the reward of our work (Job 7:2). Maintain your faith and
patience for a little while yet.

2.1.6. At what hours of the day were they hired? This
may be, and commonly is, applied to different ages of life
in which souls are converted to Christ. The effective call is
particular, and it is effective when we respond.

2.1.6.1. Some are effectively called and begin to work
in the vineyard when they are very young; they are sent
out early in the morning. Those who have such a journey
to go on need to set out early; the sooner the better.

2.1.6.2. Others are saved in middle age: *Go work in*
the vineyard, at the third, sixth, or ninth hour. In some
people, such as Paul, the power of divine grace is exalted
in a conversion when they are in the middle of their pleasures and worldly pursuits. God has work for people of all
ages; no time is wrong for us to turn to God. The time up
to that point in our lives is sufficient for serving sin: *Go*
ye also into the vineyard. God turns away no one who is
willing to be hired.

2.1.6.3. Others are hired into the vineyard in old age,
at *the eleventh hour*, when the day of life is far spent and
there is only one hour of the twelve remaining. "While
there is life, there is hope." There is hope for old sinners;
true repentance is never too late. There is hope for old sinners, that they may be brought to true repentance; nothing
is too hard for Almighty grace to do; it can set to work
those who have contracted idleness. Nicodemus can be
born again when he is old (Jn 3:4). Let no one misuse
this to presumptuously delay their repentance until they
are old. These were sent into the vineyard, it is true, at
the eleventh hour, but no one had hired them or offered
to hire them before.

2.2. Here is the settling of accounts with the workers.
Notice:

2.2.1. When the accounts were settled: *when the evening was come*, then, as usual, those who had worked during the day were called and paid. Evening time is the time of reckoning. Faithful workers will receive their reward when they die; it is delayed until then, so that they may wait for it with patience. Ministers call them into the vineyard to do their work; death calls them out of the vineyard to receive their pay. Those to whom the call into the vineyard is effective will find that the call out of it will be joyful. The workers in the parable did not come for their pay until they were called; we must wait patiently for God's time for our rest and reward. We must go by our master's clock.

2.2.2. What the accounts were, in which notice:

2.2.2.1. The general pay: *They received every man a penny* (vv. 9–10). Although there are degrees of glory in heaven, it will be complete happiness to everyone. In heaven, every vessel will be full to the brim, even though every vessel is not equally large and capacious. The giving of a whole day's wages to those who had not done the tenth of a day's work is intended to show that God distributes his rewards by grace and sovereignty, not according to debt. Because *we are under grace, not under the law* (Ro 6:14), even such defective service, if done in sincerity, will be accepted, and not only accepted but also richly rewarded by free grace.

2.2.2.2. The particular pleading with those who were offended by this distribution of payment. We have here:

2.2.2.2.1. The offense taken: *They murmured at the good man of the house* (vv. 11–12); not that there is or can be any discontent or murmuring in heaven, but there may be and often is discontent and murmuring about heaven and heavenly things while they are being viewed and promised in this world. These workers quarreled with their master not because they did not have enough but because others were made equal with them. They boasted about their good services: "*We have borne the burden and heat of the day. Now these last have worked but one hour*, and that in the cool of the day, but *thou hast made them equal with us.*" There is a great tendency in us to think that we have too little of the signs of God's favor, and others too much. We are all too ready to undervalue what others deserve and to overvalue what we deserve. Perhaps Christ was giving a hint to Peter here not to boast too much, as if, because he and the rest of the Twelve had borne the burden and heat of the day, they deserved a heaven for themselves. It is hard for those who do or suffer for God more than is ordinary not to be elevated too much with thinking about it (2Co 12:7).

2.2.2.2.2. The offense taken away. The master of the house urged three things:

2.2.2.2.2.1. The complainers had no reason at all to say that any wrong had been done to them (vv. 13–14). *Friend, I do thee no wrong.* He called him friend, for in reasoning with others we should use soft words and hard arguments. It is unquestionably true that God can do no wrong. Whatever God does to us or withholds from us, he does us no wrong. If God gives to others the grace that he denies to us, it is an act of kindness to them, but no injustice to us. And goodness to others, as long as it is no injustice to us, should draw no objection from us. To convince the grumblers that he was doing no wrong, the lord referred them to the terms on which they were hired: "*Didst not thou agree with me for a penny?* You will have the agreed-on payment." It is good for us often to consider what it was that we agreed with God for. Worldly people agree with God for their penny in this world; they choose *their portion in this life* (Ps 17:14). Believers agree with

God for their penny in the other world, and they must remember that they have agreed to that. He therefore bound him to his bargain: *Take that thine is* (Take what is yours), *and go thy way* (v. 14). If we understand *that thine is* as referring to what is ours by gift, the free gift of God, it teaches us *to be content with such things as we have* (Heb 13:5). If God is better in any respect to others than to us, we have no reason to complain as long as he is so much better to us than we deserve. The lord told the laborer that those he was jealous of would fare as well as he did: *I will give unto this last, even as unto thee.*

2.2.2.2.2.2. He had no reason to quarrel with the master, for what he gave was absolutely his own (v. 15). Just as earlier he asserted his justice, so now he asserted his sovereignty: *Is it not lawful for me to do what I will with my own?* God is the Owner of all good. He may therefore give or withhold his blessings as he pleases. What God has is his own, and this will justify him in all aspects of his providence. When God takes away from us what was dear to us, we must silence our discontent with this: *May he not do what he will with his own?* "He has taken away, but he originally gave" (Job 1:21). We are in his hand as clay is in the hands of a potter, and it is not for us to give orders to him or strive with him (Ro 9:21).

2.2.2.2.2.3. He had no reason to be angry that his fellow servant came into the vineyard no sooner—the reason he did not come sooner was that he was not called sooner—and he had no reason to be angry that the master had given him wages for the whole day. *Is thine eye evil, because I am good?* We see here the nature of envy; it is an evil eye. The eye is often both the inlet and the outlet of this sin. It is an evil eye that is displeased at the good of others and desires their harm. We also see the aggravation of envy: "You are envious because I am good." Envy is unlike God, who is good, does good, and delights in doing good. It is a direct violation of both of the two great commandments at once, both that of love for God, whose will we should accept, and love for our neighbor, in whose welfare we should rejoice.

3. Here is the application of the parable (v. 16), by the repetition of that observation that occasioned it (19:30): *the first shall be last, and the last first.* To deal with and silence their boasting, Christ told them:

3.1. That they might be surpassed by their successors in the faith; they might be found inferior to them in knowledge, grace, and holiness. Who knows whether the church may be richer and more flourishing in its old age than ever before? What *labourers* may still be *sent into the vineyard in the eleventh hour*, and what plentiful outpourings of the Spirit there may then be that are greater than those that have come so far? Who can tell?

3.2. That they had reason to fear that they themselves might be found to be hypocrites, for *many are called, but few chosen.* As to the outward call, *many are called* but refuse (Pr 1:24). There are only a few chosen Christians in comparison with the many who are only called Christians.

Verses 17–19

This was the third time that Christ gave his disciples notice of his approaching sufferings. Notice:

1. The privacy of this prediction: *He took the twelve disciples apart in the way.* His secret was with them (Ps 25:14; Pr 3:32), as his friends. It was a hard saying, and if anyone could bear it, they could (Jn 6:60). It was necessary that they should know about it, so that being forewarned, they might be forearmed. It was not the right time to speak it publicly yet, because many who were cool

toward him would have been driven to turn their backs on him and because many who were ardent in following him would be driven to take up arms in his defense, and it might have caused *an uproar among the people* (26:5). He never supported anything that would lead to the preventing of his suffering.

2. The prediction itself (vv. 18–19).

2.1. It was a repetition of what he had said twice before (16:21; 17:22–23). This shows that he not only saw clearly what troubles lay in front of him but also kept his heart set on his work of suffering; it filled him not with fear but with desire and expectation. He spoke so frequently about his sufferings because through them he was to enter into his glory.

2.2. He went into more detail here in foretelling his sufferings than he had before. He had said (16:21) that he *would suffer many things, and be killed.* Here he added that he would be *condemned, and delivered to the Gentiles,* that *they would mock him, and scourge him, and crucify him.* The more clearly he foresaw his sufferings, the more cheerfully he went out to face them. He foretold whose hands he would suffer at: *by the chief priests and the scribes*; he had said this before, but here he added, *They shall deliver him to the Gentiles.* He was to suffer for the salvation of both Jews and Gentiles; both had a hand in his death, because he was to reconcile both by his cross (Eph 2:16).

2.3. Here, as before, he mentioned his resurrection and his glory in addition to his death and suffering: *The third day he shall rise again.* He included this:

2.3.1. To encourage himself in his sufferings and to carry him cheerfully through them. *He endured the cross for the joy set before him* (Heb 12:2); he foresaw that he would rise again, and rise quickly, the third day. The reward was not only certain but very near.

2.3.2. To encourage his disciples and comfort them.

2.3.3. To direct us, under all *the sufferings of this present time,* to look at *the things that are not seen, that are eternal* (2Co 4:18), which will enable us to call our present afflictions light and momentary (2Co 4:17).

Verses 20–28

Here is the request of two disciples to Christ (vv. 20–23). The sons of Zebedee were James and John, two of the first three of Christ's disciples. Peter and they were his favorites; John was the disciple whom Jesus loved. But none was so often rebuked as they were; those Christ loves best he rebukes most (Rev 3:19).

1. Here is the ambitious request they made to Christ (vv. 20–21). They showed great faith by being so confident in his kingdom even though he now appeared in lowliness, but they also showed great ignorance by continuing to expect a temporal kingdom, with worldly show and power. They expected to have a high rank in his kingdom. They did not ask for employment in this kingdom, but only for honor. The final word in Christ's previous message, that on *the third day he would rise again,* probably gave rise to this request. And so they were puffed up by what was intended to encourage them. Some cannot bear comforts without turning them to a wrong purpose, just as sweetmeats in a sick stomach produce bile. Notice:

1.1. Shrewdness guided them in the management of their request. They asked their mother to present it so that it would be looked on as her request rather than theirs. She was one of those women who accompanied Christ and supported him, and they thought that he could deny her nothing. They therefore made her their advocate. It was their mother's weakness to become the instrument of

their ambition. Those who are wise and good should not be seen to be involved in a favor so wrongly motivated. In gracious requests, we should learn the wisdom of seeking the prayers of those who have an influence at the throne of grace; we should beg our praying friends to pray for us and count that as a real kindness.

1.2. Pride lay at its root. Pride is a sin that entangles us most easily and is hard to steer clear of. It is a holy ambition to strive to excel others in grace and holiness, but it is a sinful ambition to seek to exceed others in pomp and grandeur.

2. Here is Christ's answer to this request (vv. 22–23), directed not to the mother but to the sons who got her to ask that question.

2.1. He rebuked the ignorance and error in their request: *Ye know not what ye ask.*

2.1.1. They were very much in the dark about the kingdom they had their eye on. They did not know what it meant to sit at his right hand and at his left; they talked about it as blind people do about colors. Our concept of the glory that is yet to be revealed is like the ideas that a child has of the advanced thoughts of adults. For now, we can only ask for the good as it lies in the promise (Tit 1:2). What it will be like when the promise is fulfilled, no eye has seen, nor ear heard (1Co 2:9; Isa 64:4).

2.1.2. They were very much in the dark about the way to that kingdom. They did not know what they were asking; they asked about an end, but they overlooked the means to that end. The disciples thought that when they had left what little they had for Christ, all their service and sufferings were over, and it was now time to ask, *What shall we have?* They imagined their service had been completed when it had scarcely begun; so far, they had only *run with the footmen* (Jer 12:5). We do not know what we are asking when we ask for the glory of wearing the crown and do not ask for grace to bear the cross on our way to reach it.

2.2. He repressed the vanity and ambition of their request.

2.2.1. He led them to thoughts of their sufferings. They did not think about these things as they should, and so he thought it necessary to remind them of the hardships that lay in front of them, so that they would not be surprised or terrified by them. Notice:

2.2.1.1. How fairly he put the matter to them. "*Are you able to drink of the cup that I shall drink of?* Are you able to hold out to the end? Ask yourselves the question seriously." They did not know what kind of spirit they were of when they were lifted up by proud ambition (Lk 9:55). Christ sees the pride in us that we cannot discern in ourselves. We can learn from this:

2.2.1.1.1. To suffer for Christ is *to drink of a cup* and *to be baptized with a baptism.* It is supposed that it is a bitter cup, those waters of a full cup that *are wrung out* to God's people (Ps 73:10). It is supposed that it is a baptism, a washing with the waters of affliction: some are dipped in them; others have only a sprinkling of them. Both, however, are baptisms: some are overwhelmed by them, as in a deluge; others just soaked, as in a heavy shower. Yet even in this, *consolation doth also abound* (2Co 1:5). It is only a cup, a bitter one perhaps, but we will see its bottom; it is a cup in the hand of a Father (Jn 18:11). It is merely a baptism. If people are dipped in it, that is the worst it can do: they will not drown. They may be perplexed, but they will not be driven to despair.

2.2.1.1.2. It is to drink of the same cup that Christ drank and to be baptized with the same baptism that he was baptized with. Christ goes ahead of us in suffering.

The condescension of a suffering Christ is shown in that he would drink such a cup (Jn 18:11) and be baptized with such a baptism. The comfort of suffering Christians is shown in that they only share the bitter cup that is his, thereby pledging their loyalty.

2.2.1.1.3. It is good for us to ask ourselves often whether we are able to drink this cup and be baptized with this baptism. We must expect suffering. Are we able to suffer cheerfully? What can we afford to part with for Christ? The truth is that if religious faith is worth anything, it is worth everything, but if it is worth little, it is not worth suffering for. Let us sit down and count the cost of dying for Christ rather than denying him (Lk 14:28), and ask, "Will we follow him on these terms?"

2.2.1.2. How boldly they bound themselves; they said, *We are able*, yet fondly hoped they would never be brought to such a test. Just as earlier they did not know what they asked, so now they did not know what they answered. It is those who are least acquainted with the cross who are commonly the most confident.

2.2.1.3. How clearly and positively their sufferings were foretold: *Ye shall drink of my cup* (v. 23). Sufferings foreseen will be more easily borne. Christ wants us to know the worst, so that we may make the best of our way to heaven: *Ye shall drink*, that is, "You will suffer."

2.2.2. He left them in the dark about the degrees of their glory. To carry them cheerfully through their sufferings, it was enough to assure them that they would have *a place in his kingdom*. The lowest seat in heaven is an abundant reward for the greatest suffering on earth. "*To sit on my right hand and on my left is not mine to give*, and so it is not right for you to ask for it or to know about it; *it shall be given to them for whom it is prepared of my Father*. It is not mine to give to those who seek and are ambitious to obtain it, but only to those who are prepared to receive it in great humility and self-denial."

3. Here are the rebuke and instruction that Christ gave to the other ten disciples for their displeasure at the request of James and John. Notice:

3.1. The anger of the ten disciples: *They were moved with indignation against the two brethren* (v. 24), not because James and John wanted to be advanced, but because they wanted to be advanced before the rest. Many seem to be indignant at sin, but it is not because it is sin, but because it affects them. These disciples were angry at their brothers' ambition even though they themselves — in fact, because they themselves — were as ambitious as the two. It is common for people to become angry at those sins in others that they allow and indulge in themselves. Nothing causes more trouble among brothers and sisters, or is the cause of more anger and strife, than ambition.

3.2. The restraint that Christ gave them. He had rebuked this very sin before (18:3), telling them they must become as humble as little children; they lapsed into it, however, and still he rebuked them for it so mildly. *He called them unto him*, which shows great tenderness and familiarity. He did not, in anger, tell them to leave his presence, but called them, in love, to come into his presence.

3.2.1. They must not be *like the princes of the Gentiles*. Christ's disciples must not be like Gentiles, not even like the rulers of the Gentiles. Notice what the way of the rulers of the Gentiles was: to *exercise dominion and authority* over their subjects (v. 25). What supported them in it was that they were great, and great people think they can do anything. See what the will of Christ is in this matter. "*It shall not be so among you*. You are to teach the subjects of this kingdom, to take pains with them and suffer with them; you are not to *lord it over God's heritage* (1Pe

5:3), but to labor in it." It is wrong for Christ's disciples to have the pride and grandeur of the rulers of the Gentiles. How then *shall* it be among the disciples of Christ? Christ himself had intimated that there could be some greatness among them, and he explained it here: "*He that will be* (wants to be) *great among you*, who *will be chief, let him be your minister, your servant*" (vv. 26–27). It is the duty of Christ's disciples to serve one another so that all may be built up. This includes both humility and usefulness. It is the honorable calling of Christ's disciples to faithfully discharge this duty. The way to be great and be the first is to be humble and useful, self-denying and always doing good. Those who are so are to be counted best and respected most. They honor God the most, and he will honor them (1Sa 2:30). Just as those who want to become wise must become fools (1Co 3:18), so those who want to be first must become servants.

3.2.2. They must be like the Master himself; the *Son of Man came not to be ministered to, but to minister, and to give his life a ransom for many* (v. 28). Our Lord Jesus here set himself before his disciples as a model of those two things that were commended before: humility and usefulness.

3.2.2.1. Never was there such an example of humility and condescension as there was in the life of Christ, who came not to be *ministered unto, but to minister* (v. 20). He was truly ministered to as a poor man; he was never ministered to as a great man. He once washed his disciples' feet, but we never read that they washed his feet. He came to minister help to everyone who was in distress; he made himself a servant to those who were sick and diseased. He was as ready to fulfill their requests as any servant was to come at the beck and call of their master, and took as great pains to serve them.

3.2.2.2. Never was there such an example of usefulness and generosity as there was in the death of Christ, who *gave his life a ransom for many*. He lived as a servant and went about doing good (Ac 10:38), but he died as a sacrifice, and in that death he did the greatest good of all. He came into the world deliberately to give his life as a ransom. He gives his honor, and his life too, as a ransom for his subjects. It was a ransom for many: sufficient for all, effective for many. And if for many, then, says the poor doubting soul, "Why not for me?" Now this is a good reason why we should not strive for precedence, because the cross is our banner, and our Master's death is our life. It is a good reason why we should seek to do good. The more closely we are all concerned with, and the more we benefit from, the humility and humiliation of Christ, the more ready and careful we should be to imitate it.

Verses 29–34

We have here an account of the healing of two poor blind beggars, in which we may notice:

1. What they said to Christ (vv. 29–30).

1.1. Its circumstances are significant. It was as Christ and his disciples departed from Jericho. In leaving that place, which had been devoted to destruction (Jos 6:17–18) and rebuilt under a curse (Jos 6:26; 1Ki 16:34), he left this blessing. It was in the presence of *a great multitude that followed him*; Christ had a numerous crowd who followed him, and he did good to them. This crowd who followed Christ was a *mixed multitude* (Ex 12:38). Some followed him for loaves, and some for love; some out of curiosity, but very few with the desire to be taught their duty. However, for the sake of these few, he confirmed his teaching by miracles performed in the presence of great crowds. Two blind men agreed in their request, for joint prayer pleases Christ (18:19). Sharing in the same trouble, they shared in the same request. It is good for those who are suffering the same adversity, or physical or mental weakness, to join together in offering the same prayer to God for relief, that they may encourage one another's fervency and faith. There is enough mercy in Christ for all who seek him. These blind men were *sitting by the wayside.* It is good for us to be near Christ, to be by the road he walks along. *They heard that Jesus passed by.* Although they were blind, they were not deaf. Seeing and hearing are the senses we use for learning. These blind men had heard about Christ by listening, but they wanted their eyes to see him. *When they heard that Jesus passed by,* they asked no more questions, but immediately *cried out.* It is good to make the most of present opportunities. These blind men did so, and they did wisely, for we do not find that Christ ever came to Jericho again. *Now is the accepted time* (2Co 6:2).

1.2. Their words themselves are even more significant: *Have mercy on us, O Lord, thou Son of David*; and they repeated them (v. 31–32). Four things are commended to us as an example in these words. Here is an example of:

1.2.1. Boldness in prayer. They cried out as those who were serious; people in need are serious. Cold desires call to be denied. When they were discouraged in their prayer, they cried out all the more. If the stream of their fervency was stopped, it would rise and swell higher. This is wrestling with God in prayer, and it makes us more fit to receive mercy, for the more it is striven for, the more it will be prized and thankfully acknowledged.

1.2.2. Humility in prayer, in those words, *Have mercy on us,* not specifying the favor or prescribing what God might do. "Only have mercy." They did not ask for silver and gold (Ac 3:6), even though they were poor, but only mercy, sheer mercy. This is what our hearts must be set on.

1.2.3. Faith in prayer; notice the title they gave to Christ, which was in the form of a plea: *O Lord, thou Son of David.* They confessed that *Jesus Christ is Lord* (Ro 10:9). And so in praying they took their encouragement from his power, as in calling him the Son of David they took encouragement from his goodness as the Messiah, about whom such many kind and tender things had been foretold. It is excellent, in prayer, to consider Christ in the grace and glory of his Messiahship, to remember that he is the Son of David, whose role is to help and to save.

1.2.4. Perseverance in prayer, despite discouragement. *The multitude rebuked them* and told them to *hold their peace.* In following Christ with our prayers, we must expect to meet hindrances and many discouragements. Such rebukes are permitted so that faith and fervency, patience and perseverance, may be tested. These poor blind men were rebuked by the crowd who followed Christ. But the two would not be beaten back in this way. In pursuing such mercy, they would not give up: *they cried the more. Men ought always to pray, and not to faint,* to *pray with all perseverance* (Lk 18:1).

2. The response of Christ to their request. The crowd rebuked them, but Christ encouraged them. It would be sad for us if the Master were not kinder and tenderer than the crowd. He will not allow his humble petitioners to be insulted or discouraged.

2.1. *He stood still, and called them* (v. 32). He was now going up to Jerusalem, eager to accomplish his work, and yet he stood still to heal these blind men. When we are in great haste in any business, we should still be willing to stand still and do good. *He called them.* Christ not only tells us to pray but also invites us to; he holds out

the golden scepter to us and instructs us to touch its top (Est 5:2).

2.2. He inquired further into their case: *What will ye that I shall do unto you?* "Here am I; let me know what you want, and you will have it." What more could we want? *Ask, and it shall be given you* (7:7). One would have thought this a strange question: anyone could tell what these men wanted. Christ knew well enough, but he wanted to know it from them, whether they begged only for alms, as from an ordinary person, or for healing, as from the Messiah. The waterman in the boat, who uses his hook to take hold of the shore, does not pull the shore to the boat, but the boat to the shore. So it is in prayer: we do not draw the mercy to ourselves, but draw ourselves to the mercy. They soon told him what their request was: *Lord, that our eyes may be opened.* We are all too aware of the needs and burdens of the body and can readily speak about them. Oh that we were so aware of our spiritual illnesses and could as feelingly complain about them, especially our spiritual blindness! Lord, open the eyes of our heart! If only we were aware of our darkness, we would soon turn to him: *Lord, that our eyes may be opened.*

2.3. He healed them. What he did showed:

2.3.1. His pity: *He had compassion on them.* Misery is the object of mercy. It was the tender mercy of our God that gave light and sight to people who sat in darkness (Lk 1:78–79).

2.3.2. His power. He did it easily; he touched their eyes. He did it effectively: *Immediately their eyes received sight.* When these blind men received their sight, they *followed him.* No one can follow Christ blindfolded. He first opens people's eyes by his grace, and so draws their hearts after him.

CHAPTER 21

The account of Christ's sufferings, even unto death *(Php 2:8), and his resurrection, are recorded in more detail by all the Evangelists than any other part of his life, and it is to this that this writer now moves quickly. Christ had finally come to Jerusalem. We have here: 1. His public entry into Jerusalem (vv. 1–11). 2. The authority he exercised there by cleansing the temple (vv. 12–16). 3. The sign he gave of the state of the Jewish church by cursing the barren fig tree, and his conversation with his disciples about that (vv. 17–22). 4. His justifying his own authority (vv. 23–27). 5. His shaming the chief priests and elders by reference to the repentance of the tax collectors, illustrated by the parable of the two sons (vv. 29–32). 6. The parable of the vineyard rented out to unthankful farmers (vv. 33–46).*

Verses 1–11

All four Evangelists record Christ's triumphal entry into Jerusalem five days before his death. He had stayed at Bethany, a village not far from Jerusalem, for some time; at supper there the night before, Mary had *anointed his feet* (Jn 12:3). Our Lord Jesus traveled much, and his custom was to travel on foot from Galilee to Jerusalem; he had taken many dusty steps as *he went about doing good* (Ac 10:38). Christians, therefore, should not be excessively concerned about their own comfort. Yet once in his life he rode in triumph, and that was now, when he went to Jerusalem to suffer and die. We have here:

1. The provision that was made for this ceremony, and it was very poor and ordinary.

1.1. The preparation was sudden and unceremonious, for his glory in the next world was the glory his heart was set on; he was dead to any glory in this world. They had come to Bethphage. A long, wandering road lay toward the Mount of Olives, and when he entered on that road, *he sent two of his disciples* to fetch a donkey for him.

1.2. It was very simple. He sent only for a donkey and its colt (v. 2). Donkeys were used much in that country for traveling; horses were kept only by wealthy people, and for war. In his state of humiliation, he *rode upon an ass.*

1.3. It was not his own donkey, but a borrowed one. He had nothing of this world's goods except what was given him or lent him. The disciples who were sent to borrow this donkey were told to say, *The Lord has need of him.* In the borrowing of this donkey:

1.3.1. We see Christ's knowledge. Christ could tell his disciples where they would find a donkey tied up, and a colt with it.

1.3.2. We see his power over the human spirit. Christ asserted his right to use the donkey by telling them to bring it to him; he foresaw some hindrance that the disciples might face in this service. *If any man say aught to you, ye shall say, The Lord hath need of him.* Christ will support us in doing what he sets out for us to do. *Straightway he will send them.*

1.3.3. We see his justice and honesty, in not using the donkey without the owner's consent.

2. The prediction that was fulfilled in this (vv. 4–5). In all that Christ did and suffered, he had this very much in mind: *That the scriptures might be fulfilled* (26:56), especially what was written about him in Zec 9:9, where a lengthy prediction of the kingdom of the Messiah is introduced: *Tell ye the daughter of Sion, Behold, thy King cometh,* must be fulfilled. Notice:

2.1. How the coming of Christ was foretold: *Tell ye the daughter of Sion, Behold, thy King cometh unto thee.* Jesus Christ is the church's King. Christ, the King of his church, came to his church, even in this lower world. Notice was given to the church in advance of the coming of her King: *Tell the daughter of Sion.* Christ wanted his coming to be looked for and waited for, and his subjects full of expectation for it.

2.2. How his coming was described. When a king comes, something great and magnificent is expected. But there was nothing of that here: *Behold, he cometh to thee, meek, and sitting upon an ass.* When it was thought that Christ was going to appear in his glory, he appeared in humility, not majesty. This shows us:

2.2.1. His attitude was very gentle. He was willing, in his humility, to suffer the greatest injuries and indignities for Zion's cause. He was approachable and easily sought. His government is mild and gentle, and his laws are not written in the blood of his subjects, but in his own. His yoke is easy (11:30).

2.2.2. As evidence of this, his appearance was very insignificant; he came sitting on a donkey, a creature not made for service on state occasions, but for battles and to carry loads; it is slow moving, but sure, safe, and constant. Zion's King came riding not on a prancing horse, which a timorous petitioner would not dare come near, or a running horse, which the slow-footed petitioner could not keep up with, but on a quiet donkey, so that the poorest subjects would not be discouraged from coming to him.

3. The procession itself, which, similarly, was devoid of worldly pomp but accompanied by spiritual power. Notice:

3.1. His equipage: *The disciples did as Jesus commanded them* (v. 6). Christ's commands must not be disputed, but obeyed, and those who sincerely obey them will not be ignored or shamed in their obedience: *They brought the ass and the colt.* The disciples did not even have a saddle for the donkey, but threw some of their cloaks on it, and that must serve in place of better trappings. We should not be refined or fussy or punctilious in external matters. A holy indifference or neglect is good for us in such things. The disciples, however, provided him with the best they had, not objecting to the use of their cloaks when *the Lord had need of them.* We must not think the clothes on our backs are too precious to give up for the service of Christ to clothe his poor, destitute, and afflicted members. Christ stripped himself for us.

3.2. His retinue; there was nothing in this that was stately or magnificent. He had those who were with him, *a very great multitude*; only the common people, the mob or rabble, graced the ceremony of Christ's triumphal entry. Christ is honored more by the numerousness of his followers than by their magnificence, for he values people by their souls, not by their advancement, names, or titles of honor. We are told here concerning this great crowd:

3.2.1. What they did; according to the best of their ability, they sought to honor Christ. *They spread their garments in the way*, so that he could ride on them. When Jehu was proclaimed king, the officers put their clothes under him as a sign of their submission to him (2Ki 9:13). Those who take Christ as their King must lay all they have under his feet, including their clothes, as a sign of the heart. How will we express our respect for Christ? What honor and what dignity will we give him? *Others cut down branches from the trees, and strewed them in the way*, as they used to do at the Feast of Tabernacles (Lev 23:40), as a sign of liberty, victory, and joy.

3.2.2. What they said: *They that went before and they that followed cried, saying, Hosanna to the Son of David* (v. 9). When they carried branches around at the Feast of Tabernacles, they used to cry out *Hosanna*, and from then on they called the bundles of branches their *hosannas. Hosanna* means, "Save now, we beseech you," referring to Ps 118:22–26. The hosannas with which Christ was presented showed two things:

3.2.2.1. The people's welcoming his kingdom. *Hosanna* suggests the same as *Blessed is he that cometh in the name of the Lord* (Ps 118:26). *All nations shall call him blessed* (Ps 72:17); these people began here to call him blessed, and all true believers in all ages agree with it and call him blessed; it is the genuine language of faith. Well may we say, *Blessed is he*, for it is in him that we are blessed. Well may we follow with our blessings the one who meets us with his.

3.2.2.2. Their wishing his kingdom well was intimated in their *Hosannas*—their fervently wishing that it be victorious. If they understood Christ's kingdom to be a temporal kingdom, they were mistaken, and a short time would put their error right; however, their goodwill was accepted. It is our duty to desire and pray fervently for the prosperity and success of Christ's kingdom in the world. We mean this when we pray, *Thy kingdom come.* They added, *Hosanna in the highest.* Let him have a name above every name (Php 2:9), a throne above every throne.

3.3. His reception in Jerusalem: *When he was come into Jerusalem, all the city was moved* (v. 10); everyone took notice of him: some were moved with wonder at the newness of the thing, others with laughter at its humbleness; some perhaps were moved with joy; others, of the Pharisees, were moved by envy and indignation. There are so many different responses in human hearts to the approach of Christ's kingdom! We are further told concerning this commotion:

3.3.1. What the citizens said: *Who is this?* It seems they were ignorant about Christ. The Holy One unknown in the Holy City! There is more ignorance than we are aware of in places where the clearest light shines and the greatest profession of religious faith is made. Yet they were curious about him. *Who is this King of glory?* (Ps 24:8).

3.3.2. How the crowd answered them: *This is Jesus* (v. 11). In the account they gave of him they were right in calling him *the Prophet, that great Prophet.* They missed the mark, however, in saying he was *of Nazareth,* and it helped confirm some of the citizens' prejudice against him. Some who are willing to honor Christ and testify of him still labor under mistakes about him.

Verses 12–17

When Christ came into Jerusalem, he went *into the temple,* for he rules in holy things; he exercises authority in the temple of God. Now, what did he do there?

1. He drove out from there the buyers and sellers. Abuses must first be cleansed before what is right can be established. We are told here:

1.1. What he did: *He cast* (drove) *out all them that sold and bought* (v. 12); he had done this once before (Jn 2:14–15). Buyers and sellers driven out of the temple will return and settle there again unless the first blow is followed up and often repeated.

1.1.1. The abuse was buying and selling and changing money in the temple. Lawful things, at the wrong time and in the wrong place, may become sinful. The merchants sold animals for sacrifice for the convenience of those who could more easily bring their money with them than their animals, and they changed money for those who needed a half-shekel. With some, this might pass as the external business of the house of God, but Christ would not allow it. Great corruptions and abuses come into the church by the practices of those whose *gain is godliness,* that is, who make worldly gain the aim of their godliness, and false godliness their way to worldly gain (1Ti 6:5).

1.1.2. Christ cleansed this abuse. He *cast* (drove) *them out that sold.* He did it before *with a scourge of small cords* (Jn 2:15); now he did it with a look, a frown, and a word of command. Some consider it not the least of Christ's miracles that he cleared out the temple in this way. It shows Christ's power over the spirits of human beings and the hold he has of them by their own consciences. *He overthrew the tables of the money-changers;* he did not take the money for himself, but scattered it, throwing it to the ground, the best place for it.

1.2. What he said, to justify himself and to convict them: *It is written* (v. 13). The eye must be on Scripture, and that must be held firmly as the rule, the pattern on the mountain (Ex 25:40).

1.2.1. He showed from a Scripture prophecy what the temple should be like, what it was intended to be: *My house shall be called the house of prayer;* he quoted from Isa 56:7. All the ceremonial institutions were intended to be subservient to moral duties; the house of sacrifices was to be a house of prayer, for that was the essence of all those services.

1.2.2. He showed how they had abused the temple and corrupted its intention: *Ye have made it a den of thieves.* Markets are too often dens of thieves: there are so many corrupt and fraudulent practices in buying and selling, but markets in the temple are certainly so, for they rob God of his honor and are the worst thieves (Mal 3:8).

2. There, in the temple, he healed the blind and the lame (v. 14). When he had driven the buyers and sellers out of the temple, he invited the blind and lame into it.

It is good to come into the temple when Christ is there, who, just as he shows himself to be jealous for the honor of his temple by expelling those who desecrate it, also shows himself to be gracious to those who humbly seek him. *The blind and the lame* were debarred from David's palace (2Sa 5:8) but were admitted into God's house. The temple was desecrated and abused when it became a marketplace, but it was graced and honored when it became a hospital; to do good in God's house is more honorable, and more consistent with what it is, than gaining money there. Christ's healing was a real answer to that question, *Who is this?* His works testified more about him than the hosannas. There he also silenced the offense that the chief priests and teachers of the law took at the acclamations with which he was greeted (vv. 15–16). Those who should have been most eager to give him honor were his worst enemies.

2.1. They were indignant at the wonderful things he did. If they had had any sense, they would have had to acknowledge that these deeds were miraculous, and if they had had any good nature, they would have had to love them because of their mercy, but they were determined to oppose him, for they envied him and bore him a grudge.

2.2. They openly quarreled with the children's hosannas; they thought that the hosannas gave him the honor that did not belong to him. Proud people cannot bear honor to be given to anyone but themselves, and they are uneasy at nothing more than at the just praises of those who deserve to be commended. When Christ is most honored, his enemies are most displeased.

3. Here we have him taking the part of the children against priests and teachers of the law (v. 16).

3.1. The children were in the temple. It is good to bring children to the house of prayer from an early age, *for of such is the kingdom of heaven* (19:14). Let children be taught to keep up the form of godliness; it will help lead them to its power (2Ti 3:5). Christ shows tenderness toward the lambs of his flock (Isa 40:11; Jn 21:15).

3.2. They were there *crying Hosanna to the Son of David.* They learned this from the adults. Little children say and do what they hear others say and see others do; they imitate so easily, and so great care must be taken to set them good examples, not bad ones. Children will learn from those who are with them either to curse and swear or to pray and praise.

3.3. Our Lord Jesus not only allowed it; he was also very pleased with it, quoting a Scripture that was fulfilled by it (Ps 8:2), or that at least may be reconciled to it: *Out of the mouth of babes and sucklings thou hast perfected praise.*

3.3.1. Christ is so far from being ashamed of the service of little children that he takes particular notice of them—and children love to be taken notice of—and is very pleased with them.

3.3.2. Praise is *perfected* out of the mouths of such; it has a distinctive tendency to give honor and glory to God when little children join in his praises. The praise would be accounted defective and imperfect if they had not shared in it, which is an encouragement for children to be good from an early age, and to parents to teach them to be so. In the psalm it is, *Thou hast ordained strength.* God *perfecteth praise* by *ordaining strength out of the mouths of babes and sucklings.* When great things are brought about by weak and unlikely instruments, God is greatly honored, for his *strength is perfected in weakness* (2Co 12:9).

3.3.3. Having silenced them in this way, Christ left them (v. 17). If we complain at Christ's praises, we drive him away from us. *He left them* and *went out of the city to Bethany*, a quieter, secluded place; he went there not so much to be able to sleep undisturbed as to be able to pray undisturbed.

Verses 18–22

Notice:

1. Christ *returned in the morning to Jerusalem* (v. 18). Having work to do there, he returned.

2. *As he went, he hungered.* Christ was human, and he submitted to the weaknesses of humanity, *yet without sin* (Heb 4:15). He was a poor man and had no available provisions. Christ was hungry so that he would have a reason to perform this miracle to show us his justice and his power.

2.1. Notice his *justice* (v. 19). He went to the tree expecting fruit because it had leaves, but finding none, he sentenced it to a perpetual barrenness. All Christ's miracles up to that time were performed for the good of people and proved the power of his grace and blessing. Now at last he was going to show the power of his wrath and curse; yet he did not show it on any man, woman, or child, but on an inanimate tree. This is given as an example.

2.1.1. This cursing of the barren fig tree represents the state of hypocrites in general, and so it teaches us that:

2.1.1.1. The fruit of fig trees may justly be expected from those who have the leaves. Christ looks for the power of religious faith from those who make a profession of it.

2.1.1.2. Christ's just expectations from flourishing professors are often frustrated and disappointed. Many people have the name of being alive but are not really.

2.1.1.3. The sin of barrenness is justly punished by the curse and plague of barrenness: *Let no fruit grow on thee henceforward for ever.* Just as one of the most important blessings, and the first, is *Be fruitful* (Ge 1:28), so one of the saddest curses is "Be no more fruitful."

2.1.1.4. A false and hypocritical profession commonly withers in this world; the fig tree that had no fruit soon lost its leaves. Hypocrites may look good for a time, but their profession of faith will soon come to nothing; their gifts wither, common graces decay, and the falseness and foolishness of the pretender are clear to everyone.

2.1.2. It represents the state of the nation and people of the Jews especially; they were a fig tree planted on Christ's way. They gave disappointment to our Lord Jesus. He came among them expecting to find some fruit, something that would please him. However, his expectations were frustrated; he found nothing but leaves. They claimed to expect the promised Messiah, but when he came, they did not receive and welcome him. So we see the condemnation he passed on them, *that never any fruit should grow upon them from henceforward for ever.* No good ever came from them—except the particular individuals among them who believed—after they rejected Christ; they became worse and worse. Blindness and hardness crept up on them. How soon their fig tree withered after they had said: *His blood be on us, and on our children* (27:25)!

2.2. Notice the power of Christ.

2.2.1. The disciples wondered at the effect of Christ's curse: *They marvelled* (v. 20). They wondered at the suddenness of the thing: *How soon is the fig tree withered away!*

2.2.2. Christ empowered them by faith to do likewise (vv. 21–22). Notice:

2.2.2.1. The description of this wonder-working faith: *If ye have faith, and doubt not.* Doubting the power and promises of God is the great thing that spoils the effectiveness and success of faith. Just as the promise is certain, so our faith should be confident.

2.2.2.2. The power and effectiveness of this faith expressed figuratively: *If ye shall say to this mountain, Be thou removed, it shall be done.* This is a proverbial expression, suggesting that we are to believe that nothing is impossible with God and that what he has promised will certainly be fulfilled, even though it seems impossible to us.

2.2.2.3. The way and means of exercising this faith: *All things whatsoever ye shall ask in prayer, believing, ye shall receive.* Faith is the soul, prayer is the body; both together make a complete person for any service. Faith, if it is right, will stimulate prayer, and prayer is not right if it does not spring from faith. This is the condition of our receiving—we must *ask in prayer, believing.* The requests of prayer will not be denied; the expectations of faith will not be frustrated. It is simply ask and have, believe and receive, and what more do we need? Notice how comprehensive this promise is: *all things whatsoever ye shall ask. All things*, in general; *whatsoever*, in particular. Our unbelief is so foolish that although we think we can assent to promises in general, we hesitate when it comes to a specific application, and so the promise is expressed fully: *All things whatsoever.*

Verses 23–27

Our Lord Jesus—like the apostle Paul after him—preached his Gospel *with much contention* (1Th 2:2), and here, just before he died, we have him engaged in controversy. The great contenders with him were the chief priests and the elders, the judges of two distinct courts. The chief priests presided in the ecclesiastical court; the elders of the people were judges of the civil courts. These joined together to attack Christ, thinking they would expose him to either the one or the other. Here we have them disturbing him when he was preaching (v. 23). They would neither receive his instructions themselves nor allow others to receive them.

1. As soon as he came into Jerusalem, even though he had been shown great disrespect there the day before, he went to the temple, among his enemies and into the mouth of danger.

2. In the temple he was teaching; he had called it *a house of prayer* (v. 13), and here we see him preaching there. Praying and preaching must go together, and neither must encroach on or jostle out the other. To make up fellowship with God, we must not only speak to him in prayer but also listen to what he has to say from his word; ministers must *give themselves both to the word and to prayer* (Ac 6:4).

3. When Christ was teaching the people, the priests and elders came on him and challenged him to produce his orders. Yet good was brought out of the evil, for it gave Christ the opportunity to dispel the objections that were brought against him, and while his enemies thought they had silenced him by their power, it was he who silenced them by his wisdom. Notice:

3.1. How he was assaulted by their arrogant demand: *By what authority doest thou these things, and who gave thee this authority?* If they had properly considered his miracles and the power by which he performed them, they would not have needed to ask this question. It is good for all who act with authority to ask themselves this question, "Who gave us that authority?" Those who exceed their warrant go without a blessing (Jer 23:21–22). Christ had often said, and had proved beyond contradiction, that he was *a teacher sent of God* (Jn 3:2); yet now, so late in the day, when that point had been so fully cleared up and settled, they still came to him with this question:

3.1.1. To show off their power. They asked proudly: *Who gave thee this authority?* suggesting that he could have no authority, because he had received none from them (1Ki 22:24; Jer 20:1). It is common for those who greatly abuse their power, who take pride and pleasure in anything that looks like exercising it, to be the ones who assert its most rigorously.

3.1.2. To try to trap him. If he were to refuse to answer this question, they would suggest to the people that by his silence he tacitly confessed he was a usurper. If he pleaded authority from God, they would, as before, demand a sign from heaven or accuse him of blasphemy because of it.

3.2. How he answered this demand with another, which would help them answer it themselves: *I also will ask you one thing* (vv. 24–25). He declined to give them a direct answer, for then they might take advantage of him, but he answered them with a question of his own. The question he asked was about John's baptism, which stood for his whole ministry here. "Was this *from heaven, or of men?* It must be one of the two." This question was not meant to be evasive, to avoid theirs; rather, if they answered this question, it would answer theirs. If they said, against their consciences, that John's baptism was of human origin, it would be easy to answer: *John did no miracle* (Jn 10:41); Christ did many miracles. However, if they said, as they must acknowledge, that John's baptism was from heaven, then their demand was answered, for he testified about Christ. If they refused to answer it, then that would be a good reason why he should not offer proofs of his authority; he need not answer those who were stubbornly prejudiced against the strongest conviction.

3.3. How they were confused and stranded by this. Notice:

3.3.1. How *they reasoned with themselves*, though not concerning the merits of the cause; no, their concern was how they could successfully defend themselves against Christ. They considered and discussed two things: their reputation and their safety, the same things that those who *seek their own things* chiefly aim at (Php 2:21).

3.3.1.1. They considered their own reputation, which they would put at risk if they acknowledged John's baptism to come from God, for then Christ would ask them, in front of all the people, *Why did ye not believe him?*

3.3.1.2. They considered their own safety, fearing the resentment of the people if they said that John's baptism was of human origin: *We fear the people, for all hold John as a prophet.* It seems, then, that:

- The people had truer responses to John than the chief priests and the elders had. This people, it seems, about whom the leaders said in their pride that they *knew not the law, and were cursed* (Jn 7:49), knew the Gospel and were blessed.
- The chief priests and elders stood in awe of the common people, which shows that things were confused among them. If they had kept their integrity and done their duty, they would have kept their authority and not needed to fear the people.
- It is usually the attitude even of ordinary people to be zealous for the honor of what they consider sacred and divine. That is why the most intense disputes are about holy things.
- The chief priests and elders were kept from openly denying the truth not by the fear of God, but purely

by the fear of the people. Many bad people would be much worse than they are if they dared.

3.3.2. How they replied to our Savior and so dropped the question. They confessed reasonably, *We cannot tell*; that is, "We will not." The more shame on them. When they would not confess their knowledge, they were forced to confess their ignorance. Notice, by the way, when they said, *We cannot tell*, they were lying, for they knew that John's baptism came from God. Many are more afraid of the shame of lying than of the sin of it, and therefore have no scruples about speaking what they know to be false about their own thoughts and understanding, because in those things they know no one can disprove them.

3.3.3. And so Christ avoided the trap they set for him and justified himself in refusing to humor them: *Neither tell I you by what authority I do these things.* They were not fit to discuss Christ's authority, for people of such a disposition could not be convinced of the truth. Those who imprison in unrighteousness the truths they know are justly denied the further truths they seek (Ro 1:18–19). Take away the talent from the one who buried it (25:28); those who refuse to see shall not see.

Verses 28–32

Just as Christ instructed his disciples by using parables, so he also sometimes convinced his enemies by using parables, which bring rebukes closer and make people, before they are aware, rebuke themselves. This was Christ's intention here, as can be seen from the first words: *But what think you?* (v. 28). Notice:

1. The parable itself, which represents two kinds of people: some who prove to be better than they promise, others who promise better than they prove to be.

1.1. They both had the same father. There are favors that all alike receive from God, and there are obligations that all alike lie under to him. But there is a vast difference between human characters.

1.2. They both received the same command: *Son, go work today in my vineyard.* God sets his children to work, even though they are all heirs.

1.2.1. The work of religious faith, which we are called to engage in, is vineyard work: praiseworthy, profitable, and pleasant. By the sin of Adam we were turned out to work on common land and eat the vegetables of the field, but by the grace of our Lord Jesus we are called to work again in the vineyard.

1.2.2. The Gospel call to work in the vineyard requires present obedience: *Son, go work* today. We were not sent into the world to be lazy, nor were we given daylight to play by.

1.2.3. The encouragement speaks to us *as unto children: Son, go work.* It is the command of a Father, which carries with it both authority and affection; it is the command of a Father who is very tender toward *his Son that serves him* (Mal 3:17).

1.3. Their behavior was very different.

1.3.1. One of the sons did better than he said, proving better than he promised. His answer was bad, but his actions were good.

1.3.1.1. Here is the perverse answer he gave his father; he said flatly and directly: *I will not.* Excuses are bad, but downright denials are worse; however, the calls of the Gospel often meet with such absolute refusals. Some people love their comforts and refuse to work. Their hearts are set so much on their own fields that they do not want to work in God's vineyard. They love the business of the world better than the business of their religious faith.

1.3.1.2. Here is the favorable change of both his mind and his way, on second thoughts: *Afterward he repented, and went.* Repentance is *metanoia*, "afterthought," and *metameleia*, "aftercare." Better late than never. When he repented, he went; that was his *fruit meet for repentance* (3:8). The only true evidence of our repentance of our former resistance is to immediately comply and set to work, and then what is past will be pardoned, and all will be well. Our God waits to be gracious (Isa 30:18), and despite our former foolishness, if we repent and mend our ways, he will favorably accept us. Praise God that we are under a covenant that leaves room for such a repentance.

1.3.2. The other son said better than he did; his answer was good, but his actions bad. The father *said likewise* to him (v. 30). The Gospel call, though in a sense very different for each person, is in effect the same to all. Notice:

1.3.2.1. How promising this other son was: *He said, I go, sir.* He gave his father a title of respect, *sir.* He professed a ready obedience: *I go*; not, "I will go soon," but, "I am ready, sir, now; you may depend on it; I am going now."

1.3.2.2. How he failed in fulfilling his promise: *He went not.* Saying and doing are two different things, and there are many who say but do not do. Many people show much love with their mouth but have their heart going in a different direction. Buds and blossoms are not the same as fruit.

2. A general appeal on the basis of the parable: *Whether of them twain* (Which of the two) *did the will of his father?* (v. 31). They both had their faults: one was rude, the other false. However, the question is, Which was the better of the two? Which was less at fault? It was soon answered: the first, because his actions were better than his words, and his end better than his beginning. The whole tenor of Scripture gives us to understand that those who are sorry for the ways in which they have failed to do their Father's will, and who then do better, are accepted as doing their Father's will.

3. A particular application of it to the matter in hand (vv. 31–32). The primary scope of the parable is to show how the tax collectors and prostitutes received the teaching and submitted to the discipline of John the Baptist, his forerunner, whereas the priests and elders insulted John the Baptist and went against the intentions of his mission. In Christ's application of this parable, notice:

3.1. How he proved that John's baptism was *from heaven, and not of men.* "If you *cannot* tell," says Christ, "you *could have* told":

3.1.1. By the scope of his ministry: "*John came unto you in the way of righteousness.* Remember the test: *By their fruits ye shall know them* (7:16), the fruits of their teachings, the *fruits of their doings*" (Isa 3:10; Jer 17:10; etc.). It was clear that John came *in the way of righteousness.* In his ministry, he taught people to repent and to do the works of righteousness.

3.1.2. By the success of his ministry: *The publicans* (tax collectors) *and the harlots* (prostitutes) *believed him.* If God had not sent John the Baptist, he would not have crowned his labors with such wonderful success. The people's benefit is the minister's best testimony.

3.2. How he rebuked them for their contempt of John's baptism. To shame them for it, he set before them the faith, repentance, and obedience of the tax collectors and prostitutes, which served only to emphasize their unbelief and impenitence.

3.2.1. The tax collectors and prostitutes were like the first son in the parable, from whom little religious faith was expected. They promised little good, and those who knew them promised themselves little good from them. However, many of them were persuaded by the ministry of John.

3.2.2. The teachers of the law and Pharisees, the chief priests and elders, and in fact the Jewish nation in general were like the other son, who replied with good words. A hypocrite is harder to convince and convert than a gross sinner. It emphasized their unbelief:

3.2.2.1. That John was such an excellent person. The better the means, the longer the account there will be if the means are not applied.

3.2.2.2. That when they saw the tax collectors and prostitutes go before them into the kingdom of heaven, they did not later repent and believe. They did not want to lose face; they refused to seek God and Christ (Ps 10:4).

Verses 33–46

This parable clearly sets out the sin and ruin of the Jewish nation. We have here:

1. The privileges of the Jewish church, represented by the renting of a vineyard to the tenants. Notice:

1.1. How God established a church for himself in the world. The kingdom of God on earth is compared here to a vineyard, provided with everything that is needed for its advantageous management and use.

1.1.1. He planted this vineyard. The church is *the planting of the Lord* (Isa 61:3). The earth by itself produces thorns and briars (Ge 3:18), but vines must be planted.

1.1.2. He put a wall around it. God's church in the world is taken under his special protection, which is *a hedge round about* (wall around it). He does not want to have his vineyard lie open to all, so that those who are outside may force their way into it whenever they want; he does not want it to be without restraint, so that those who are inside may strike out whenever they want.

1.1.3. He *digged a winepress and built a tower.* God instituted ordinances in his church to provide for its proper oversight and promote its fruitfulness.

1.2. How he entrusted these visible church privileges to the nation and people of the Jews; he rented it to them as tenants, because he wanted to test them and be honored by them. Then he *went into a far country.* When God had visibly settled the Jewish church at Mount Sinai, he withdrew in a way; they no longer had so many visions, but were left to the written word.

2. God's expectation of rent from these tenants (v. 34). It was a reasonable expectation.

2.1. His expectations were not hasty; he waited *till the time of the fruit drew near.* God waits to be gracious (Isa 30:18), so that he may give us time.

2.2. His expectations were not great. He did not require them to come to him; he sent his *servants to them*, to remind them of their duty and of the day when the rent was due, to help them gather the fruit and make a profit on it.

2.3. His expectations were not harsh; he wanted only to *receive the fruits.* He did not demand more than they could deliver, only some fruit of what he himself planted—an observance of the laws and statutes he had given them.

3. The tenants' evil in mistreating the messengers who were sent to them.

3.1. When he sent his servants to them, they abused them. If the calls and rebukes of the word do not engage those who hear them, they will only exasperate them. Notice here what has been the lot of God's faithful messengers all along, more or less:

3.1.1. To suffer: *so persecuted they the prophets* (5:12). They not only despised and scorned them but also treated them as the worst evildoers. If people who *live godly in Christ Jesus* themselves will *suffer persecution* (2Ti 3:12), then much more the people who urge others to do so.

3.1.2. To suffer from their Master's own tenants; Christ's listeners here were those tenants who treated the servants in this way. Now see:

3.1.2.1. How God persevered in his goodness to them. He sent other servants, more than the first time, even though the first group had not fared well—had in fact been abused.

3.1.2.2. How they persisted in their evil. They *did unto them likewise*. One sin makes way for another of the same kind.

3.2. Finally, he sent them his Son; we have seen God's goodness in sending the servants, and the tenants' evil in abusing them, but in the final instance these both exceed themselves.

3.2.1. Never did grace appear more gracious than in *sending the Son*. This was done *last of all*, for if nothing else would work on them, then surely this would. "*Surely they will reverence my Son*, and that is why I will send him. If they will only respect the Son, there will be success. *Surely they will reverence my Son*, for he comes with more authority than the servants could."

3.2.2. Never did sin appear more sinful than in the mistreating of him. Notice:

3.2.2.1. How it was plotted: *When they saw the Son* (v. 38). His arrival to collect the rent affected their rights as tenants, because he would either be paid the rent or seize their goods as payment, and so they decided to make one last bold attempt to preserve their wealth and grandeur by taking him out of the way. *This is the heir; come, let us kill him*. Pilate and Herod, *the rulers of this world, knew not* (1Co 2:8). But the *chief priests and elders* knew that *this was the heir*, and that was why they said: *Come, let us kill him*. Many are killed for what they have. The main thing they envied him for, the main reason they hated and feared him, was his influence among the people. "Therefore *let us kill him*, and then"—as if the legacy must of course go to the occupant—"*let us seize on his inheritance*." They thought that if only they could get rid of this Jesus, they could do whatever they wished. Yet while they thought they would kill him and so seize his inheritance, he went by his cross to his crown.

3.2.2.2. How this plot was executed (v. 39). It is hardly surprising that they soon *caught him, and slew him*. Indeed, considering his unworthiness to live to be equal to their unwillingness to let him live, *they cast him out of the vineyard*, the holy church, and out of the Holy City, for he was crucified *without the gate* (Heb 13:12), as if he had been the shame and scorn of his people Israel, though he was their greatest glory.

4. Their doom read out of their own mouths (vv. 40–41). He put it to them: *When the Lord of the vineyard cometh, what will he do unto these husbandmen?* He put it to the chief priests and elders themselves, to convict them more strongly. God's ways are so unexceptionable that there need be only an appeal to sinners themselves concerning the fairness of those ways. These sinners could readily answer, *He will miserably destroy those wicked men*. Many can easily forecast the sad consequences of other people's sins but refuse to foresee the end of their own.

4.1. Our Savior, in his question, supposed that *the lord of the vineyard will come* and reckon with them. Persecutors say in their hearts, he *delays his coming* (24:48). Yet though he is patient with them for a long time, he will not always be so.

4.2. In their answer, they supposed that it would be a terrible reckoning:

4.2.1. That the lord would *miserably destroy those wicked men*. Let people never expect to do wrong but fare well. This was fulfilled in the Jews, in the miserable destruction that was brought on them by the Romans.

4.2.2. That he would *let out his vineyard to other husbandmen*. God will have a church in the world. Human unbelief and corruption will not make the word of God null and void.

5. The further illustration and application of this by Christ himself, telling them, in effect, that they had judged rightly.

5.1. He illustrated it by referring to a Scripture fulfilled in this: *Did ye never read in the scriptures?* (v. 42). The Scripture he quoted is Ps 118:22–23, the same context from which the children drew their hosannas. The same word provides subject matter for praise and encouragement to Christ's friends and followers, and it speaks conviction and terror to his enemies. The word of God is such a two-edged sword (Heb 4:12).

5.1.1. The builders' rejecting the stone is the same as the tenants' mistreating the son who was sent to them. They would not allow Christ a place in their building. They set him aside as a despised, broken vessel (Jer 22:28), a stone that would serve only as a stepping stone, to be trampled on.

5.1.2. The advancing of this stone to be the head of the corner is the same as *letting out the vineyard to other husbandmen*. The One who was rejected by the Jews was embraced by the Gentiles, and to the church that includes them, *Christ is all, and in all* (Col 3:11).

5.1.3. The hand of God was in all this: *This is the Lord's doing. It is marvellous in our eyes*. The evil of the Jews who rejected him is a wonder. The honor shown him by the Gentile world is a wonder—that the One whom the nation despised and abhorred should be adored by kings! But *it is the Lord's doing*.

5.2. He applied it to them, and application is the life of preaching.

5.2.1. He applied the sentence that they had passed (v. 41); he turned it back on them; not its former part, about the miserable destruction of the tenants—he could not bear to speak about that—but the latter part, about *letting out the vineyard to others*. Let them know, then:

5.2.1.1. That the Jews would be dischurched: *The kingdom of God shall be taken from you*. The adoption and the glory had for a long time belonged to the Jews (Ro 9:4); to them had been committed the sacred trust of revealed religion and of bearing of God's name in the world, but now it would be so no more. They not only failed to produce fruit in the use of their privileges but also opposed the Gospel of Christ, and so lost the right to those privileges.

5.2.1.2. That the Gentiles would be taken in. If God's vine is plucked up in one place, he will find somewhere else to plant it. The fall of Israel was the riches of the Gentiles (Ro 11:12). The Gentiles would produce fruits better than the Jews had. When God exchanges one thing for another, he never loses..

5.2.2. He applied the Scripture that he had quoted (v. 42) to their terror (v. 44). We have here the doom of two kinds of people.

5.2.2.1. Some, through ignorance, stumble at Christ in his humiliation; through their blindness and carelessness, they fall on it and fall over it, and *they shall be broken*. The unbelief of sinners will be their ruin.

5.2.2.2. Others oppose Christ, defying him in his exaltation when this Stone is advanced to the head of the corner, and *it shall fall* on them, for they will pull it down onto their own heads, and *it will grind them to powder* (those on whom it falls will be crushed). Christ's kingdom will be a burdensome stone to all those who attempt to overthrow it or raise it out of its place (Zec 12:3). No one ever hardened their heart against God and prospered (Job 9:4)

6. The reception that this message of Christ met with among the chief priests and elders.

6.1. *They perceived that he spake of them* (v. 45) and that in what they said (v. 41) they had only read their own doom. A guilty conscience needs no accuser.

6.2. *They sought to lay hands on him.* When those who hear the rebukes of the word realize that it is speaking about them, if it does not do them a great deal of good, it will certainly do them a great deal of harm.

6.3. They dared not do it, *for fear of the multitude, who took him for a prophet.* God has many ways of restraining the survivors of wrath, as he has of making what happens contribute to his praise (Ps 76:10).

CHAPTER 22

This chapter is a continuation of Christ's messages in the temple. We have here: 1. Instruction given: 1.1. About the rejection of the Jews and the calling of the Gentiles, through the parable of the wedding banquet (vv. 1–10). 1.2. About the danger of hypocrisy in the profession of Christianity (vv. 11–14). 2. Debates about paying taxes to Caesar (vv. 15–22), about the resurrection of the dead and the future state (vv. 23–33), about the great commandment of the Law (vv. 34–40), and about the relation of the Messiah to David (vv. 41–46).

Verses 1–14

Here is the parable of the guests invited to *the wedding feast.* It is said *Jesus answered* (v. 1): he answered not what his opponents *said* but what they *thought.* Christ knows how to answer people's thoughts, for he discerns them (Heb 4:12). This parable represents the Gospel offer and the reception it meets with.

1. Preparations for the Gospel are represented here by a banquet that a king held *at the marriage of his son.*

1.1. Here is *a marriage* (wedding banquet) *made for his son:* Christ is the Bridegroom; the church is the bride. The Gospel covenant is a marriage covenant between Christ and believers.

1.2. Here is *a dinner prepared for this marriage* (v. 4): all the blessings of the new covenant, including forgiveness of sin, the favor of God, peace in the conscience, the promises of the Gospel, the assurance of the Spirit, and a well-founded hope of eternal life. These are the preparations for this banquet that we experience now, which are a heaven on earth; and soon we will have a heaven in heaven.

1.2.1. It was *a feast.* Oxen and fatlings (fattened cattle) *were killed* at this banquet; there were no delicacies, but substantial food, enough of the best food. A banquet was made for love (SS 2:4); it was a reconciliation banquet. It was made *for laughter:* it was a banquet of joy. It was made for fullness; the intention of the Gospel was to fill every *hungry soul with good things* (Lk 1:53). It was made for fellowship.

1.2.2. It was *a wedding feast.* Wedding banquets are usually rich, free, and joyful. The first miracle Christ performed was to make plentiful provision at a wedding banquet (Jn 2:7), and surely he will not be lacking in providing for his own wedding banquet.

1.2.3. It was *a royal wedding feast;* it was *the feast of a king,* for the wedding not of a servant but of a son. The provision made for believers in the covenant of grace is such as is right for *the King of glory* to give (Ps 24:7–10). He gives as he himself is, for he gives himself: a true banquet for the soul.

2. Gospel calls and offers are represented by the king's invitations to this banquet. Those who give a banquet want to have guests to grace the banquet with. God's guests are human beings. Lord, *what is man* (Job 7:17; Ps 8:4), that he should be honored in this way! Now:

2.1. The guests are called, invited to come to the wedding. All who are within hearing distance of the joyful sound of the Gospel (Ps 89:15) receive the message of this invitation. None are excluded except those who exclude themselves.

2.2. The guests are called on, for the Gospel contains not only gracious proposals but also gracious persuasions. Notice how much Christ's heart is set on the happiness of poor souls! He not only provides for them, in consideration of their needs, but also sends word to them, in consideration of their weakness and forgetfulness. When the invited guests were slack in coming, the king *sent forth other servants* (v. 4). One would have thought it would be enough to give people an indication that they had permission to come, that they would be welcome, that during the wedding ceremony the king kept open house; but because *the natural man* does not desire *the things of the Spirit of God* (1Co 2:14), we are urged to accept the call by the most powerful incentives. *Behold, the dinner is prepared, the oxen and fatlings are killed, and all things are ready.* Pardon is ready, peace is ready, encouragement is ready; the promises are ready; and heaven, in the end, is ready to receive us. Is all this ready, and are we not ready? Have all the preparations been made for us, and is there any room to doubt our welcome?

3. The cold reception that the Gospel of Christ often meets with among people is represented here by the cold treatment this message met with and the hot treatment the messengers met with.

3.1. The message was cruelly spurned: *They would not come* (v. 3). The reason why sinners do not come to Christ and to salvation by him is not that they cannot, but that they will not. This was not all, however: *they made light of it* (v. 5); they paid no attention to the call, thinking the banquet not worth coming for; they could feast as well at home. Many who do not have a direct aversion to spiritual matters perish eternally through mere carelessness, a basic indifference toward such matters. The reason why *they made light of the marriage feast* was that they had other things that they were more concerned about: *they went their ways, one to his farm, and another to his merchandise.* No one turns their back on the banquet without giving some plausible excuse or other (Lk 14:18). The country people have their farms to look after, on which there is always something to do; the town people must look after their shops, which require constant work. It is true that both farmers and business people must be diligent about their work, but not so as to keep them from making religious faith their main work. Both the city and the country have their temptations, business in one and farming in the other, so that whatever occupation we follow, our concern must be to keep it out of our hearts, so that it will not come between us and Christ.

3.2. The messengers were cruelly mistreated: *The remnant* (v. 6)—the teachers of the law, Pharisees, and chief priests—were the persecutors. They *took the servants, and treated them spitefully, and slew them.* Never could anyone be so rude and cruel to servants who came to invite them to a banquet, yet in the application of the parable, it was a matter of fact. The prophets and John the Baptist had already been cruelly mistreated, and the apostles and ministers of Christ must count on facing the same reception.

4. The complete destruction that was coming on the Jewish church and nation is represented here by the revenge that the king, in wrath, took on these arrogant rebels: *He was wroth* (enraged) (v. 7). Notice:

4.1. What was the notorious sin that brought this ruin; it was that they were murderers. Christ did not say that the king destroyed those despisers of his call, but *those murderers* of his servants. It is as if God were more jealous for the lives of his ministers than for the honor of his Gospel. Persecution of Christ's faithful ministers fills up the measure of guilt more than anything else does (Ge 15:16; Mt 23:32).

4.2. What was the ruin itself was that was coming: *He sent forth his armies.* The Roman armies were his armies, raised by him. God is *the Lord of* human *hosts,* and he makes what use he pleases of them to serve his own purposes. It was made known as an example to all who would oppose Christ and his Gospel.

5. The bringing in the Gentiles is represented here by the providing of guests *out of the highways* (v. 8–10). Here is:

5.1. The complaint of the master of the banquet about those who were originally invited: *The wedding is ready* (v. 8), except *they which were bidden,* that is, the Jews, *were not worthy;* they were completely unworthy and had forfeited all the privileges they were invited to. It is not because of God that sinners perish; the fault lies within sinners themselves.

5.2. The commission he gave to the servants to invite other guests. The inhabitants of the *city* (v. 7) had refused; *"Go into the highways,"* then, into *the way of the Gentiles"*—which at first they were to decline (10:5). This is how through the fall of the Jews salvation has come to the Gentiles (Ro 11:11–12; Eph 3:8). Christ will have a kingdom in the world, even though many reject the grace and resist the power of that kingdom. The offer of Christ and salvation to the Gentiles was:

5.2.1. Unlooked for and unexpected, the sort of surprise it would be to travelers on a road to be met with an invitation to a wedding banquet. It was all new to the Gentiles, something they had never heard about before (Ac 17:19–20), and therefore something they could not conceive of as belonging to them.

5.2.2. Universal and undistinguishing: *Go, and bid as many as you find.* The highways are public places. "Ask those who are walking along the road; ask anyone (Job 21:29), tell them all that they will be welcome. Whoever wishes may come, without exception."

5.3. The success of this second invitation: *They gathered together all, as many as they found* (v. 10). The intention of the Gospel was:

5.3.1. To gather souls together, not only the nation of the Jews but also *all the children of God* who were *scattered abroad* (Jn 11:52), *the other sheep that were not of that fold* (Jn 10:16).

5.3.2. To gather them together to the wedding banquet so that they might share in the privileges of the new covenant. Where gifts are given, the poor will gather together to receive them. The guests who were gathered were a multitude, *all, as many as they found,* so many that the room was full. They were a mixed multitude (Ex 12:38; Nu 11:4), *both bad and good.* There were some who before their conversion were sober and well inclined, and

others who had plunged into a flood of dissipation (1Pet 4:4), such as the Corinthians—*Such were some of you.* Or there were some who after their conversion proved bad, and others who were upright and sincere and proved to be of a high caliber. Ministers, in casting the net of the Gospel, enclose both good fish and bad.

6. The case of hypocrites, who are in the church but not of it, is represented by *the guest that had not on a wedding garment,* one of the bad who were gathered in. Notice about this hypocrite:

6.1. How he was found out (v. 11).

6.1.1. *The king came in to see the guests,* to welcome those who came prepared and to turn out those who were not prepared. Let this be a warning to us against hypocrisy, a warning that soon disguises will be stripped away. And let this be an encouragement to us in our sincerity, that God bears witness to it. This hypocrite was never found to be without *a wedding garment* until *the king himself came in to see the guests.* It is God's right to know those whose hearts are sound in their profession and those whose hearts are not. We may be deceived by other people, either one way or other, but he cannot be.

6.1.2. As soon as he came in, *He saw there a man which had not on a wedding garment.* There is no hope of being hidden in a crowd from the arresting power of divine justice. This guest was not wearing wedding clothes; he did not have his best clothes on. If the Gospel is the wedding banquet, then wedding clothes are an attitude of heart and a way of life that is consistent with the Gospel. This man was not naked or in rags; he was wearing some clothes; but they were not wedding clothes. Those, and only those, who *put on the Lord Jesus* (Ro 13:14), and to whom he is everything, are wearing wedding clothes.

6.2. His trial (v. 12). Notice:

6.2.1. How he was accused: *Friend, how camest thou in hither, not having a wedding garment?* (v. 12)—a startling question to one who prided himself on the place he had securely possessed at the banquet. *Friend*! That word was cutting: an apparent friend, under many ties and obligations to be a friend. *How camest thou in hither?* He did not rebuke the servants for letting him in, but he restrained the guest's presumption in crowding in on the feast, since he knew the man's heart was not upright. Despised Sabbaths and abused sacraments must be judged. "How did you come to be at the Lord's Table at such a time as this, when you are not humbled or sanctified? *How camest thou in?* Not by the door, but *some other way, as a thief and a robber* (Jn 10:1)." It is good for those who have a place in the church to ask themselves often, "How did I come in here? Am I wearing the wedding clothes?" If we would *judge ourselves* in this way, *we would not be judged* (1Co 11:31).

6.2.2. How he was convicted: *he was speechless:* the man stood mute at this accusation, convicted and condemned by his own conscience. Those who never heard a word about this wedding banquet will have more to say for themselves; their sin will be more excusable than that of those who come to the feast without wearing wedding clothes and thus sin against the clearest light and dearest love.

6.3. His sentence: *Bind him hand and foot* (v. 13).

6.3.1. He was ordered to be bound, as condemned evildoers are—to be manacled and shackled. Those who will not work and walk as they should may expect to be bound hand and foot. They can neither resist nor outrun their punishment.

6.3.2. He was ordered to be taken away from the wedding banquet: *Take him away.* This shows the punishment of loss in the other world; such guests will be taken away from the king, from the kingdom, from the wedding banquet. Those who walk unworthily of their Christian faith (Eph 4:1) forfeit all the happiness they arrogantly laid claim to.

6.3.3. He was ordered to be thrown into a grim dungeon: *Cast him into utter darkness*. Hell is utter darkness; it is darkness out of heaven, the land of light, or it is extreme darkness, darkness to the ultimate degree, without the least ray or spark of light, or hope of it. *There shall be weeping and gnashing of teeth* (v. 13). *Weeping* is an expression of great sorrow and anguish. The *gnashing of teeth* expresses the greatest rage and indignation.

6.3.4. The parable was concluded with the remarkable saying that we had before (20:16): *Many are called, but few are chosen* (v. 14). Many are called to the wedding banquet, but few are chosen to wear wedding clothes.

Verses 15–22

In these verses, we see Christ attacked by the Pharisees and Herodians with a question about paying taxes to Caesar. Notice:

1. Their purpose: *They took counsel to entangle him in his talk* (they laid plans to trap him in his words). Now he was attacked from another quarter; the Pharisees wanted to see whether they could trap him through their knowledge of the law. It is futile for the best and wisest people to think that by their ingenuity, influence, or industriousness, or even by their innocence and integrity, they can escape the hatred of evildoers or protect themselves from *the strife of tongues* (Ps 31:20). Notice how tireless the enemies of Christ and his kingdom are in their opposition!

1.1. *They took counsel.* The more conspiracy and plotting there is about sin, the worse it is. The more there is of evil in contriving sin, the more evil it contains in its commission.

1.2. What they aimed at was *to entangle* (trap) *him in his talk* (words). They saw that he was free and bold in speaking his mind, and they hoped to gain an advantage over him by that. It has been the old practice of Satan's agents and ambassadors to see if they can make someone offend by a word (Isa 29:21), a word misplaced, mistaken, or misunderstood; they pervert by strained innuendos a word spoken with innocent intentions. There are two ways by which the enemies of Christ could take revenge on him and be rid of him, either by law or by force. They could not do it by law unless they could make him intolerable to the civil government. Nor could they do it by force unless they could make him intolerable to the people; the people took Christ as a prophet, and so his enemies could not raise the mob against him. The plan was to bring him into such a dilemma that he must make himself liable to the displeasure of either the Jewish multitude or the Roman magistrates; whichever side he followed in his answer to the question, they would win their point and make his own words recoil on him.

2. The question they put to him (vv. 16–17). Notice:

2.1. The people they used. They did not go themselves; they sent their disciples, who would look less like tempters and more like learners. Evildoers will never lack evil instruments to be employed in carrying out their evil purposes. Along with their disciples they sent the Herodians, a group of Jews who made it their business to reconcile people to the Roman government and urged everyone to pay their taxes. They went with the Pharisees to Christ, under this pretext: although the Herodians demanded the tax and the Pharisees denied it, they were both willing to

refer the matter to Christ, as a proper Judge to decide the quarrel. Now, if Christ supported the paying of the tax, the Pharisees would enrage the people against him; if he discouraged or disallowed it, the Herodians would enrage the government against him. It is common for those who oppose one another to proceed to oppose Christ and his kingdom. Samson's foxes looked different ways, but they were joined in one *firebrand* (torch) (Jdg 15:3).

2.2. The introduction; it was highly complimentary to our Savior: *Master, we know that thou art true, and teachest the way of God in truth* (v. 16). It is common for the most spiteful plans to be covered by the most specious pretenses. If they had come to Christ with the most serious question and the most sincere intentions, they could not have expressed themselves better. What they said about Christ was right: Jesus Christ was a faithful Teacher. *Thou art true, and teachest the way of God in truth*. He is the Truth itself. As for his teaching, its subject matter was the way of God, which leads to happiness. The manner of his teaching was *in truth*; he showed people *the right way*. He was a bold Admonisher. In preaching, he *cared not for any*; he paid no attention to who they were, he valued no one's frowns or smiles, he did not seek, he did not dread, either the great or the many. He *reproved with equity* (Isa 11:4) and never with partiality. Yet although what they said was true as regards its subject matter, there was nothing but flattery and treachery in its intention. They called him *Master* (Teacher) but were plotting to treat him as the worst evildoer. They pretended to show respect for him but really intended to cause him trouble, and they insulted his wisdom when they imagined that they could deceive him with these pretenses.

2.3. The proposing of the case: *What thinkest thou?* It was as if they had said, "Many people have different opinions in this matter; it is a case that relates to practice and occurs daily; let us have your thoughts freely on this matter: *Is it lawful to give tribute to Caesar, or not?*" This implies a further question: Has Caesar a right to demand it? Now the question was whether it was lawful to pay these taxes voluntarily or whether they should insist on the ancient liberty of their nation, and instead allow their goods to be seized? However, they hoped to trap Christ by this question and, whichever way he resolved it, to expose him to the fury either of the jealous Jews or of the jealous Romans.

3. The breaking of this trap by the wisdom of the Lord Jesus.

3.1. He recognized it: *He perceived their wickedness* (v. 18). A temptation perceived is one that is half conquered, for our greatest danger lies from snakes under the green grass, *and he said, Why tempt ye me, ye hypocrites?* Whatever mask the hypocrite wears, our Lord Jesus sees through it. He cannot be deceived, as we often are, by flattery and clever pretense. *Why tempt ye me, ye hypocrites?* Those who presume to test Christ will certainly find that he is too hard for them, and that his eyes are too piercing not to see, and too pure not to hate (Hab 1:13), the disguised evil of hypocrites, who dig deep to hide their purposes from him.

3.2. He evaded it. Such crafty, evil questions deserve a reproof, not a reply, but our Lord Jesus gave a full answer to their question, introducing it by an argument that was sufficient to support it.

3.2.1. He forced them, before they were aware of it, to confess Caesar's authority over them (vv. 19–20). In dealing with those who are crafty in this way, it is good to give our reasons—powerful, convincing reasons, if possible—before we give our decisions. This is how the evidence of truth may unexpectedly silence those who bring opposition, while they stand on guard against the truth itself, not against the reasons for it: *Show me the tribute money.* The Romans demanded their tax in their own money, which was current among the Jews at that time; that was therefore called the *tribute money*—money used for paying the tax. They *brought him a penny,* a Roman silver denarius, the most common coin then in circulation: it was stamped with the emperor's portrait and inscription, which gave authority to the public for the value of the coins stamped in this way. Christ asked them, *Whose image is this?* They acknowledged it to be Caesar's.

3.2.2. He inferred from this the lawfulness of paying taxes to Caesar: *Render therefore to Caesar the things that are Caesar's* (v. 21); not "Give it to him," as they expressed it (v. 17)), but "*Render* it; restore it; if Caesar fills the purses, let Caesar command them. Once a relationship has been accepted, its duty must be fulfilled. *Render to all their due,* especially *tribute to whom tribute is due* (Ro 13:7)." By this answer:

3.2.2.1. No offense was given. He did not intervene as a Judge or an Arbiter in such matters. Christ did not discuss the emperor's entitlements, but he commanded a peaceful submission to *the powers that be* (Ro 13:1). The government, therefore, had reason not to take offense at his determination but to thank him, for it would strengthen Caesar's influence with the people, who held Christ to be a prophet. As to the people, the Pharisees could not accuse him to them, because they themselves, before they were aware, had submitted to the principle. Truth does not seek to prevent offense by fraudulent concealment, but it sometimes needs to use wise management.

3.2.2.2. His adversaries were rebuked. Many excuse themselves from what they must do by arguing whether they may do it or not. They all withheld from God his dues, and they were rebuked for that.

3.2.2.3. His disciples were instructed:

3.2.2.3.*1.* That the Christian faith is no enemy to civil government, but its friend.

3.2.2.3.*2.* That it is the duty of subjects to render to magistrates what is due to them according to the laws of their country. Because the higher powers are entrusted with the public welfare, they are entitled to a just proportion of the public wealth to cover the costs of that. It is no doubt a greater sin to cheat the government than to cheat a private person. My coat is my coat by human law, but the person who takes it from me is a thief by the law of God.

3.2.2.3.*3.* When we render to Caesar the things that are Caesar's, we must remember also to render to God the things that are God's. If our purses are Caesar's, our consciences are God's. We must give God what is his due out of our time and out of our possessions; he must have his share from them as well as Caesar his, and if Caesar's commands interfere with God's, *we must obey God rather than men* (Ac 5:29).

3.2.2.3.*4.* Notice how they were put at a loss by this answer; they *marvelled, and left him, and went their way* (v. 22). They were amazed at his wisdom in recognizing and evading a trap that they thought they had laid so craftily. One would have thought they would be amazed and follow him, but no, they were amazed and left him. There are many people in whose eyes Christ is amazing but not precious. They wondered at his wisdom but would not be guided by it. *They went their way,* as those who were ashamed, making an inglorious retreat. They abandoned the field. There is nothing to be gained by contending with Christ.

Verses 23–33

Here is Christ's dispute with the Sadducees about the resurrection. Notice:

1. The opposition that the Sadducees brought to a very great truth of religion; they said, *There is no resurrection.* They came in for intense criticism among the writers of their own nation, as those who led a corrupt and debauched way of life. They were the fewest in number of all the Jewish sects, but generally people of some rank. They said, "There is no future state, no life after death. When the body dies, the soul is annihilated and dies with it." They maintained that apart from God, there is no spirit (Ac 23:8). The Pharisees and Sadducees opposed each other, but they allied themselves against Christ.

2. The objection they raised against the truth, which was taken from a supposed case of a woman who had seven husbands successively; the Sadducees took it for granted that if there is a resurrection, it must be a return to such a state as the one we are now in. If this is so, it would be indisputably absurd for this woman to have seven husbands in the future state, and the question of which of them she would be married to was an insuperable difficulty: Would it be the man she married first, the man she had married last, the one she loved best, or the one she lived longest with?

2.1. They stated the Law of Moses in this matter (v. 24), that the next of kin must marry the widow of the man who died childless (Dt 25:5). It was a political law, to preserve the distinction of families and inheritances.

2.2. They proposed a case according to this statute. If it had not really occurred, it could have. Now this case supposes:

2.2.1. The devastation that death sometimes makes in families. It often sweeps away a whole family of brothers in a short time.

2.2.2. The obedience of these seven brothers to the law. Many would say that the seventh brother, who was the last to marry the widow, was a brave man. I would say that if he did it purely out of obedience to God, he was a good man, one who was careful to do his duty. But *last of all, the woman died also.* Survivorship is merely a reprieve. Death's sour cup goes around, and sooner or later we must all drink it (Jer 25:26).

2.3. They proposed a difficulty in this case: "*In the resurrection, whose wife shall she be of the seven?* (v. 28). You cannot tell whose, and so we must conclude *there is no resurrection.*" The Pharisees, who professed to believe in a resurrection, had corrupt and worldly ideas about the future state, expecting to find there the delights and pleasures of the animal life, which perhaps drove the Sadducees to deny the thing itself. While those who are in error deny the truth, those who are superstitious betray it to them. If truth is set in a clear light, it will then appear in its full strength.

3. Christ's answer to this objection.

3.1. He rebuked their ignorance: *Ye do err* (v. 29). Those who deny the resurrection and a future state are greatly in error in their judgment of Christ. Here Christ rebuked them with the humility of wisdom, and he was not so sharp with them—whatever the reason—as he sometimes was with the chief priests and elders. *Ye do err, not knowing.* Ignorance is the cause of error; those who are in the dark miss their way. Ignorance is the cause of error about the resurrection and the future state. *What* it is in its particular instances, the wisest and best people do not know: *it does not yet appear what we will be* (1Jn 3:2). It is a glory that is still to be revealed. But that it *is* is something about which we are not left in the dark; we bless God we are not. Notice:

3.1.1. The Sadducees *knew not the power of God*, the knowledge of which would lead people to infer that there *may be* a resurrection and a future state. Ignorance of, or disbelief or weak belief in, God's power lies at the root of many errors, especially of those who deny the resurrection. When we are told about the soul's existence and agency in a state of separation from the body, we are ready to say: *How can these things be?* (Jn 3:9). If a man dies, will he live again (Job 14:14)? Because worthless people cannot comprehend how this could be, they question its truth. We must therefore focus, in the first place, on the fact that God is omnipotent, that he can do whatever is his will. There is then no room left for doubting that he will do what he has promised. His power far exceeds the power of nature.

3.2.2. The Sadducees also *knew not the scriptures*, which affirm decisively that there *will be* a resurrection and a future state. Now the Scriptures say plainly that the soul is immortal and that there is another life after this. Christ rose again *according to the scriptures* (1Co 15:3), and so will we. Ignorance of the Scriptures is the cause of much trouble.

3.2. He put right their mistake (v. 30), correcting those corrupt ideas that they had of the resurrection and future state.

3.2.1. It is not like our present state on earth: *They neither marry, nor are given in marriage.* In our present state marriage is necessary. All civilized nations have had a sense of the obligation for the marriage covenant. However, in the resurrection, there will be no need for marriage. In heaven, *where there shall be no more deaths* (Rev 21:4), there need be no more births.

3.2.2. It is like the state that angels are now in, in heaven: *They are as the angels of God in heaven.* When mortals were created, they were *made a little lower than the angels* (Ps 8:5), but in their complete redemption and renewal they will be like the angels, as pure and spiritual as the angels, knowing and loving, always praising God like them and with them. We should want to try to do the will of God now as the angels do it in heaven, because we hope soon to be like the angels who always see our Father's face (18:10).

4. Christ's argument to confirm this great truth; because the matters are of great concern, he did not think it enough to reveal the false reasoning of the objections, but backed up the truth by a solid argument. Notice:

4.1. Where he drew his argument from—Scripture. *It is written* (4:4) is Goliath's sword; there is none like it (1Sa 21:9). *Have ye not read that which was spoken to you by God?* (v. 31). We can learn from this:

4.1.1. What the Scripture speaks is spoken by God.

4.1.2. What was spoken to Moses was spoken to us.

4.1.3. We should read and hear what God has spoken, because it has been spoken to us. The argument was taken from the books of Moses because the Sadducees accepted only them, as some think, as canonical Scriptures. The latter prophets have more explicit proofs of a future state than the Law of Moses has; no explicit revelation of it is made through the Law of Moses. The truth of this matter was kept implicit because so much of that law was distinctive to that people. Yet our Savior finds a very solid argument for the resurrection even in the writings of Moses. Much Scripture treasure lies underground and must be dug for.

4.2. What his argument was: *I am the God of Abraham* (v. 32). This was not an explicit proof, but it really was

a conclusive argument. Conclusions from Scripture, if rightly drawn, must be received as Scripture, for Scripture was written for those who have the use of reason. The thrust of the argument was to prove:

4.2.1. That there is a future state, another life after this one. This was proved from what God said: *I am the God of Abraham.*

4.2.1.1. For God to be anyone's God presupposes some extraordinary privilege and happiness. The God of Israel is a God to Israel (1Ch 17:24), a spiritual Giver, an all-sufficient, generous Giver, a God who is enough, a complete Good and an eternal Benefactor, for he himself is eternal and will be eternally good to those who are in covenant with him.

4.2.1.2. It is clear that these good men had no extraordinary happiness in this life that looked anything like the fulfillment of such a great word as, *I will be to thee a God.* They were strangers in the Land of Promise; they had no ground that they could call their own except a burial place (Ge 23), which directed them to look for something beyond this life (Heb 11:10–16). In present enjoyments they came far short of their neighbors who were strangers to this covenant. What benefit did they enjoy in this world to distinguish them from any other people? What was there that was in any way proportionate to the honor and distinction of this covenant?

4.2.1.3. There must, therefore, certainly be a future state, in which, just as God will always live to be the One who rewards eternally, so Abraham, Isaac, and Jacob will always live to be rewarded eternally.

4.2.2. That the soul is immortal and the body will rise again, so that they may be united; if the previous point is gained, these will follow, but they are also proved by considering the time when God spoke this. It was to Moses at the bush, long after Abraham, Isaac, and Jacob were dead and buried. However, God did not say "I was" or "have been," but *I am the God of Abraham* (Ex 3:15). Now *God is not the God of the dead, but of the living.* This proves that the soul of one who has died remains alive and in a state of bliss, and that, in turn, presupposes the resurrection of the body.

5. The outcome of this debate. The Sadducees were *put to silence* (v. 34), and so put to shame. However, the crowds *were astonished at his doctrine* (v. 33):

5.1. Because it was new to them. The teachers of the law were useless, or this would have been no news to the people.

5.2. Because it contained something very good and great. Truth often shines more brightly and is more wondered at when it is opposed.

Verses 34–40

Here is a conversation Christ had with a Pharisee-lawyer about the great commandment of the law. Notice:

1. The alliance of the Pharisees against Christ (v. 34). They heard *that he had put the Sadducees to silence.* Yet the Pharisees were gathered together not to thank him for effectively asserting and confirming the truth against the Sadducees, but to *tempt* (test) *him,* in the hope of enhancing their reputation by puzzling the One who had puzzled the Sadducees. They were more troubled by the fact that Christ was honored than pleased that the Sadducees were silenced. It shows pharisaical envy and malice if we are displeased at the maintaining of a confessed truth when it is done by those we do not like.

2. The question the lawyer put to Christ. The lawyers were students in and teachers of the Law of Moses, as the scribes were. This expert in the law *asked him a question,*

tempting him; he had no intention of trapping him, as can be seen from Mark's description of the story, where we find that this was the one to whom Christ said, *Thou art not far from the kingdom of God* (Mk 12:34); he wanted only to see what Christ would say and to draw him out in order to talk further with him, to satisfy his own and his friends' curiosity.

2.1. The question was, *Master* (Teacher), *which is the greatest commandment of the law?* It is true that some commands that are the principles of the oracles of God are more extensive and inclusive than others.

2.2. The intention was to test him — to test not so much his knowledge as his judgment. It was a question that was disputed among the critics of the Law. They now wanted to see what answer Christ would give to this question, and if he exalted one commandment, they would criticize him for reviling the rest. The question was harmless enough, and it appears by comparing this account with Lk 10:27–28 that it was a settled point among the lawyers that the *love of God* and our *neighbour* is the great commandment and the sum of all the rest.

3. Christ's answer to this question. Now Christ commends to us as the great commandments not those that exclude others but those that are great because they include others. Notice:

3.1. Which these great commandments were (vv. 37–39). They were the love of God and our neighbor, which are the spring and foundation of all the rest, for if these are supposed, the others will follow naturally.

3.1.1. All the Law is fulfilled in one word, and that is *love.* See Ro 13:10. All obedience begins in the heart, and nothing in religion is done rightly if it is not done there first. Love is the leading affection, and so that is the main fort and must be the first to be secured and garrisoned for God. Human beings are creatures designed to love; the law that is written on the heart, therefore, is a law of love (Dt 30:14; Pr 3:4; Jer 31:33). Love is a short and sweet word, and if that is *the fulfilling of the law* (Ro 13:10), surely the yoke of the command is very easy (Mt 11:30). Love is the rest and satisfaction of the soul; if we walk in this good old way, we will find rest for ourselves (Jer 6:16).

3.1.2. The love of God is the first and greatest commandment of all. Now because God is infinitely, originally, and eternally good, he is to be loved in the first place, and nothing is to be loved besides him except what is loved for him. Love is the first and great thing that God demands from us, and so it is the first and great thing that we should devote to him. We are instructed here:

3.1.2.1. To love God as ours: *Thou shalt love the Lord thy God* as yours. To love God as ours is to love him because he is ours and to conduct ourselves toward him as ours, in obedience to him and dependence on him.

3.1.2.2. To love him *with all our heart, and soul, and mind.* Some believe these mean one and the same thing, to love him with all our powers; others distinguish between them, asserting that the heart, soul, and mind are the will, affections, and understanding, respectively. Our love of God must be a sincere love, not only in word and tongue. It must be a strong love: we must love him most intensely. It must be a special and superlative love: we must love him more than anything else, the stream of our affections must flow entirely this way. The heart must be united to love God; it must resist being divided. All our love is too little to give him, and so all spiritual powers must be engaged for him and carried out toward him. *This is the first and great commandment,* for obedience to this one is the spring of obedience to all the rest, which is acceptable only when it flows from love.

3.1.3. *To love our neighbour as ourselves* is the second great commandment (v. 39): *It is like unto that first;* it includes all the commands of the second table, as the previous one includes all those of the first. It is like it, for it is based on it and flows from it. It is implied that we do and should love ourselves. There is a self-love that is corrupt, and it must be put aside and put to death, but there is also a self-love that is natural, the rule of the greatest duty, and it must be preserved and sanctified. We must love ourselves; that is, we must have due regard for the dignity of our own natures and a proper concern for the welfare of our own souls and bodies. It is set down that we are to *love our neighbour as ourselves.* We must honor and esteem all people and must wrong and injure no one, and as we have opportunity, we must do good to all. We must love our neighbor as ourselves, as truly and sincerely as we love ourselves, and in the same instances; in fact, in many cases we must deny ourselves for the good of our neighbor.

3.2. What the weight and greatness of these commandments is: *On these two commandments hang all the law and the prophets* (v. 40). All depend on the law of love; if you take this away, all falls to the ground and comes to nothing. Love is the more excellent way (1Co 12:31). This is the spirit of the Law, which animates it; it is the root and spring of all other duties, the summary of the whole Bible, not only of the Law and the Prophets but also of the Gospel. All depends on these two commandments. *Love never faileth* (1Co 13:8). Into these two great commandments, therefore, let our hearts be poured as into a mold; in the defense and proving of these let us spend ourselves in zeal, and not in disputing minor points or ideas. Let everything else be made to bow to the commanding power of these.

Verses 41–46

The Pharisees had asked Christ many questions, but now let him ask them a question, and he would do it when they were gathered together (v. 41). He took them all together, when they had joined in making plans against him. God delights to baffle his enemies when they consider themselves at their strongest; he gives them all the advantages they can wish for, but he still conquers them.

1. Christ asked them a question that was in their own catechism: *"What think ye of Christ? Whose Son is he?"* They could easily answer this: *The Son of David.* It was the common expression for the Messiah. *What think ye of Christ?* They had asked him questions, one after another, out of the Law, but he came and asked them a question on the promise. Many are so full of the law that they forget Christ, as if their duties would save them without his merit and grace. Each one of us should seriously ask ourselves, "What do we think about the Christ?" Some do not think about him at all, some think low thoughts of him, and some think harsh thoughts of him, but *to them that believe he is precious* (1Pe 2:7), and *how precious then are the thoughts of him!* (Ps 139:17).

2. He posed a problem to them that they could not solve so easily (vv. 43–45). Many people think they have enough knowledge to be proud of because they can readily affirm the truth, but when they are called to confirm the truth, they show they have enough ignorance to be ashamed of. The objection Christ raised was, *If Christ be David's son, how then doth David, in spirit, call him Lord?* He did not intend to trap them, as they did him, but to instruct them.

2.1. It is easy to see that David called Christ *Lord.* Now, to prove that David did so, speaking through the

Spirit, Jesus quoted Ps 110, a psalm that the teachers of the law themselves understood to refer to the Christ. It is a prophetic summary of the teaching of Christ. It describes him fulfilling the offices of a Prophet, Priest, and King. Christ quoted v. 1, which shows the Redeemer in his exaltation:

2.1.1. *Sitting at the right hand of God.* His sitting shows both rest and rule; his sitting at God's right hand shows superlative honor and sovereign power.

2.1.2. Subduing his enemies. He will sit there until they are all made either his friends or his footstool. However, this verse is quoted to show that David calls the Messiah *his Lord; the Lord,* Jehovah, *said unto my Lord* (v. 44).

2.2. If Christ is David's son, it is not so easy for those who do not believe in the Godhead of the Messiah to remove an absurdity from the statement that David calls him Lord. Yet if David calls him Lord, that Lordship is established (v. 45) as the more evident truth. We must hold firmly that he is David's Lord, and by that explain his being David's son.

3. We have the success of this gentle test of the Pharisees' knowledge, in two things.

3.1. It puzzled them: *No man was able to answer him a word* (v. 46). Either because of their ignorance they did not know the Messiah to be God, or because of their ungodliness they would not acknowledge it, and this truth was the only key to unlock this difficulty. Christ, as God, was David's Lord, and Christ, as Man, was David's son. He did not now himself explain this, but reserved it till the proof of it was completed by his resurrection. Christ, as God, was David's Root; Christ, as Man, was David's Offspring.

3.2. It silenced them, and all others who sought to take advantage of him: *Neither durst* (dared) *any man, from that day forth, ask him any more questions.* Many are convinced by the word yet not converted by it. If these people had been converted, they would have asked him more questions, especially that great question, *What must we do to be saved?* (Ac 16:30). However, since they could not win their point, they wanted to have nothing more to do with him.

CHAPTER 23

In the previous chapter we had our Savior's conversations with the teachers of the law and Pharisees; here we have his message about them. 1. He acknowledges their office (vv. 2–3). 2. He warns his disciples not to imitate their hypocrisy and pride (vv. 4–12). 3. He brings charges against them for high crimes and misdemeanors, introducing each article with a woe (vv. 13–33). 4. He passes sentence on Jerusalem (vv. 34–39).

Verses 1–12

In all Christ's preaching, we do not find him so severe with any kind of people as he was with these teachers of the law and Pharisees. Yet these men were the idols and favorites of the people, who thought that if only two men went to heaven, one would be a Pharisee. Now Christ directed his words here *to the multitude, and to his disciples* (v. 1), to put right their mistakes about these teachers of the law and Pharisees by painting them in their true colors. It is good to know what people's true character is, so that we may not be deceived by great and mighty names, titles, and claims to power. Even the disciples needed these warnings, for good people tend to have their eyes dazzled by worldly ostentation.

1. Christ acknowledged the office of these leaders as explainers of the Law: *The scribes and Pharisees sit in*

Moses' seat (v. 2), as public teachers and interpreters of the Law. They were like judges, or a bench of justices; teaching and judging seem to be equivalents (2Ch 17:7, 9; 19:5–6, 8). Or we may apply this statement not to the Sanhedrin but to the other Pharisees and teachers of the law, who explained the Law and taught the people how to apply it to individual cases. *Moses had those in every city*—as the expression is in Ac 15:21—who preached him; this was their profession, and it was just and honorable. It was necessary that there be some people from whose mouth the people could *seek the law* (Mal 2:7).

1.1. Many good positions are filled with bad people. Then, the leaders are not so much honored by the seat as the seat is dishonored by the leaders.

1.2. Good and useful positions and powers are not to be condemned and abolished because they fall sometimes into the hands of bad people, who abuse them. Christ reasoned from this, "*Whatsoever they bid you observe, that observe and do* (v. 3). As far as they *sit in Moses' seat,* that is, as far as they read and preach the Law that was given by Moses, you must listen to them." Christ wanted the people to make use of and put into practice the helps the Pharisees gave them to understand the Scripture. As long as their comments illustrated the text, making plain the commandment of God rather than making it void (15:6)—so far they must be observed and obeyed. We must not think the worse of good truths because they are preached by bad ministers, nor of good laws because they are executed by bad magistrates. Although it is most desirable to have our food brought to us by angels, nevertheless, if God sends it to us by ravens and it is good and wholesome (1Ki 17:4–6), we must accept it and thank God for it.

2. He condemned the teachers of the law and the Pharisees. He had ordered the crowd to practice what they taught, but here he added a warning not to do as they did, to stand on their guard against their yeast (16:6): *Do not ye after their works.* Just as we must not swallow corrupt teachings for the sake of any commendable practices of those who teach them, so we must not imitate any bad examples for the sake of the plausible teachings of those who set such examples. Our Savior here, and in the following verses, specified various details of their works in which we must not imitate them. In general, he charged them with hypocrisy, pretense, or double-dealing in religion. The Pharisees were charged with four things in these verses:

2.1. What they said and what they did were two different things. *They say, and do not* (v. 3). They did not practice what they preached; they taught what was good from the Law, but their way of life contradicted that teaching. Those who allow themselves to commit the sins they condemn in others, or do even worse, are of all sinners most inexcusable. This speaks especially to evil ministers, for what greater hypocrisy can there be than to urge on others something that they themselves disbelieve and disobey, to build up an action as commendable in their preaching but demolish it by not doing it themselves, to preach so well that you wish they wouldn't stop but to live so badly that you wish they would never preach again, to be like church bells, which call others to worship but are not part of it themselves? Christ's words here are applicable to all others who do not practice what they preach, who make a plausible profession of religious faith but do not themselves live up to that profession, who are great talkers but little doers.

2.2. They were very harsh in imposing on others those things that they themselves were not willing to submit to the burden of: *They bind heavy burdens, and grievous to be borne* (v. 4). They did this not only by insisting on the minute details of the law but also by imposing their own inventions and traditions, with the highest penalties if they were disobeyed. They loved to show their authority and to exercise their power, but notice their hypocrisy: *They themselves will not move them with one of their fingers* (are not willing to lift a finger to move them). They urged on the people a strictness in religious matters that they themselves declined to be bound by. They indulged their pride by laying down the law to others but followed their personal comfort in their own conduct. They would not relieve the people in these matters, nor lift a finger to lighten their burden when they saw they were in difficulties.

2.3. All they cared about in their religion was mere show, nothing substantial: *All their works they do to be seen of men* (v. 5). We must indeed do such good works that those who see them may glorify God (5:16), but we must not declare our good works with the purpose that others may see them and glorify us. The Pharisees' whole ambition was to be praised by people, and so all their efforts were to that end: to be seen by people. The form of godliness would provide them with a name to live by, which was all they aimed at, and so they did not bother with its power, which is essential to a true life (2Ti 3:5). Those who do everything to be seen do nothing effective. Christ specified two things they did in which they wanted to be seen by people.

2.3.1. *They made broad their phylacteries.* Phylacteries were small scrolls of paper or parchment on which were written with great refinement four paragraphs of the Law: Ex 13:2–11; 13:11–16; Dt 6:4–9; 11:13–21. These were sewn up in leather and worn on their foreheads and left arms. Now the Pharisees made these phylacteries wide, so that they would be thought holier, stricter, and more zealous for the Law than others. It is a gracious ambition to seek to be really holier than others, but it is a proud ambition to want to appear so. It is good to excel in real piety, but not to exceed others in its mere outward show.

2.3.2. *They enlarged the borders of their garments.* God appointed the Jews to make borders or *fringes* (tassels) on their garments (Nu 15:38), to remind them that they were a distinctive people, but the Pharisees were not content to have tassels like other people's; they must be larger than ordinary ones, so as to be noticed, as if they were more religious than others.

2.4. They made much of an affected preeminence and superiority. Pride was the favorite and dominant sin of the Pharisees.

2.4.1. Christ described their pride (vv. 6–7). They sought:

2.4.1.1. Places of honor and respect. In all public appearances, such as *at feasts and in the synagogues*, they expected and had, to their hearts' delight, *the uppermost rooms and the chief seats.* They took the most important seats, and precedence was given to them as people who were the most significant and most deserving. Yet it was not possessing the uppermost rooms or sitting in the chief seats that was condemned — someone has to sit there! — but loving them. What is that but making an idol of ourselves and then falling down and worshiping it — the worst form of idolatry! It is bad anywhere, but especially in the synagogues. To seek honor for ourselves in the place where we come to give glory to God and humble ourselves before him is truly to mock God instead of serving him. It smacks of great pride and hypocrisy when

people do not care to go to church unless they can look fine and be seen to be important there.

2.4.1.2. Titles of honor and respect. They *loved greetings in the markets*, loved to have people raise their hats to them and show them respect when they met them in the streets. This was food, drink, and a refined delicacy to them. The greetings would not have done them half so much good if they had not been in the markets, where everyone would see how much they were respected and how high they stood in the opinion of the people. For students of the word to respect their teachers is commendable enough in the students, but for teachers to love that respect, demand it, and show it off is sinful and detestable, and a teacher who does so, instead of teaching others, needs to go back to Christ's elementary school and learn his first lesson, which is humility.

2.4.2. He warned his disciples against being like the Pharisees in that respect: "But you are not to be called 'Rabbi,' for you must not *be of such a spirit*" (v. 8; compare Lk 9:55). Here is:

2.4.2.1. A prohibition of pride. They were forbidden:

2.4.2.1.1. To demand titles of honor and power for themselves (vv. 8–10). He repeated it: *Be not called Rabbi, neither be ye called Master* or Teacher. Christ's ministers must not presume to take the name of Rabbi or Master to distinguish themselves from other people; it is not consistent with the simplicity of the Gospel. Nor may they assume the authority and power implied in those names, for:

2.4.2.1.1.1. One is your Master, even Christ (vv. 8, 10). Only Christ is our Master and Teacher; ministers are simply ushers in the school.

2.4.2.1.1.2. "*All ye are brethren.* You are brothers and sisters, just as you are all disciples of the same Teacher." Fellow students are brothers and sisters and as such should help one another in learning their lessons, but no student is allowed to step into the teacher's seat and lay down the law to the school.

2.4.2.1.2. To ascribe such titles to others: "*Call no man your father upon the earth*" (v. 9); make no man the father of your religion." Only God must be allowed to be called the *Father of our spirits* (Heb 12:9). Our religious faith must not be derived from or made to depend on any other human being. We must not pin all our faith on any person for support and help, because we do not know how they will handle it. The apostle Paul calls himself a Father to those whose conversion he has been instrumental in (1Co 4:15; Phm 10), but he uses that title to show not authority but affection; he therefore calls them not his indebted sons but his beloved sons (1Co 4:14). The reason Christ gave for this command was that *One is your Father, who is in heaven.* He is the Fountain and Founder of our religious faith, its Life and its Lord, from whom alone, as the Origin, our spiritual life is derived, and on whom it depends. Because Christ has taught us to say, *Our Father, who art in heaven* (6:9), let us *call no man Father upon earth* (v. 9).

2.4.2.2. Teaching on humility and mutual submission (v. 11): *He that is greatest among you shall be your servant.* We may take it as a promise: "He who is most submissive and useful will stand highest in the favor of God." Or we may take it as a command: "The one who is advanced to any place of dignity, *let him be your servant* (20:27). *He that is greatest* is not a lord, but a minister/servant."

2.4.2.3. A good reason for all this (v. 12). Consider:

2.4.2.3.1. The punishment intended for the proud: *Whosoever shall exalt himself shall be abased.* If God gives them repentance (Ac 5:31; 11:18; 2Ti 2:25), they will be humbled in their own eyes and will hate themselves for their sin; if they do not repent, sooner or later they will be humbled in front of the world.

2.4.2.3.2. The advancement intended for the humble: *He that shall humble himself shall be exalted.* In this world, the humble have the honor of being accepted by the holy God and respected by all wise and good people, of being qualified for and often called to the most honorable services, because honor is like the shadow, which flees from those who pursue it and grasp at it but follows those who flee from it. In the next world, however, those who have humbled themselves in contrition for their sin will be exalted to inherit the throne of glory.

Verses 13–33

In these verses we have eight woes directed against the teachers of the law and Pharisees by our Lord Jesus Christ, like many thunderclaps or flashes of lightning from Mount Sinai — eight woes set opposite the eight beatitudes (5:3). These woes are the more remarkable because backed up by the humility and gentleness of the One who declared them. He came to bless, and he loved to bless, but if his wrath was kindled (Ps 2:12), there was surely a just cause for it. This was the "burden," or chorus, of the song, and it is a heavy burden: *Woe unto you, scribes and Pharisees*, hypocrites. The teachers of the law and Pharisees were hypocrites; it was this that summed up their bad character. A hypocrite is a playactor in religion — that is the primary meaning of the word — hypocrites impersonate or act the part of people that they neither are nor can be, or perhaps that they neither are nor want to be. To each of these woes against the teachers of the law and Pharisees there is attached a reason justifying the judgment of Christ on them, because his woes, his curses, are never without basis.

1. They were the sworn enemies of the Gospel of Christ, and so of human salvation: *They shut up the kingdom of heaven against men* (v. 13). Christ came to open up the kingdom of heaven in order to make people into subjects of that kingdom. Now the teachers of the law and Pharisees, who sat in Moses' seat and claimed to have the keys to knowledge, should have contributed and helped the people in this matter. Those who undertook to explain Moses and the Prophets should have shown the people how those writings testified of Christ. This is how they could have facilitated that great work and have helped thousands on their way to heaven, but instead they shut the kingdom of heaven in people's faces; they made it their business to beget and nourish in the minds of the people prejudices against Christ and his teaching.

1.1. They would not enter the kingdom themselves: *Have any of the rulers or Pharisees believed on him?* (Jn 7:48). No, they were too proud to stoop to his lowliness; they did not like a religious faith that insisted so much on humility. Repentance was the door of admission into this kingdom, and nothing could be more disagreeable to the Pharisees than to repent. Therefore, they did not go into the kingdom themselves, but that was not all.

1.2. They would not *suffer* (allow) *them that were entering to go in.* It is bad to keep away from Christ ourselves, but it is even worse to keep others away from him. Their not going in themselves prevented many others from doing so; many rejected the Gospel simply because their leaders did. They opposed both Christ's reception of sinners (Lk 7:39) and sinners' reception of Christ, and they used all their knowledge and power to express their hatred of him. This was how they *shut up the kingdom of heaven*, so that *they who would enter* into it must *suffer violence* (11:12) and *press into it* (Lk 16:16).

2. They made religion and the form of godliness (2Ti 3:5) a cloak and pretext for their covetous practices and desires (v. 14). Notice here:

2.1. What their evil practices were: they *devoured widows' houses*, either by demanding that they give these leaders and their attendants a place to stay or by worming their way into the widows' affections and so becoming the trustees of their estates, which they could make easy prey of. Their aim was to make themselves rich. No doubt they also did all this in the name of the law, for they did it so skillfully that it passed uncriticized.

2.2. What was the cover they used to disguise this evil practice: *For a pretense they made long prayers* — very long indeed, if what some of the Jewish writers tell us is true, that they spent three hours at a time in the formalities of meditation and prayer, three times every day. This was how they gained their wealth deceitfully and maintained their grandeur. Christ does not condemn long prayers here as hypocritical in themselves. Christ himself *continued all night in prayer to God* (Lk 6:12). Where there are many sins to be confessed, many needs to pray for the providing of, and many mercies to give thanks for, there is a need for long prayers. However, the Pharisees' long prayers were for *a pretense*; by them they gained the reputation of being pious and devout, men who loved prayer and were the favorites of heaven. This was the means by which people were made to believe that the Pharisees could not possibly cheat them. This was how, while they seemed to soar heavenward on the wings of a prayer, their eye, like the eagle's, was all the time focused on their prey on earth, some widow's house or other that lay convenient for them to swoop down on. It is nothing new for the show and form of godliness (2Ti 3:5) to be made a cover-up for the most terrible atrocities.

2.3. The condemnation passed on them for this: *Therefore ye shall receive the greater damnation* (you will be punished more severely). The pretenses of religion with which hypocrites disguise or excuse their sin now will soon aggravate their punishment.

3. They shut the kingdom of heaven against those who wanted to turn to Christ, but at the same time they *compassed* (traveled across) *sea and land to make proselytes* to themselves (v. 15). Notice:

3.1. Their commendable industry in making converts to the Jewish religion. For this, for one such person — even only one — they traveled across sea and land. Yet what was their aim in all this? Not the glory of God and the good of souls, but the credit of making converts for themselves. The making of converts, if it is to the truth and serious godliness and is done with a good intention, is a good work. Such is the value of souls that nothing must be thought too much to do to save a soul from death. The hard work of the Pharisees in this respect shows up the negligence of many who would be thought to act from better motives but will go to no effort or expense to spread the Gospel.

3.2. Their cursed ungodliness in mistreating their converts once they had been made: "*Ye make him twofold more the child of hell than yourselves.*" Hypocrites are called *children of hell* because of their deep-rooted enmity to the kingdom of heaven, which was the motivating principle of Pharisaism. Corrupt converts are usually the greatest bigots; the students surpassed their teachers:

3.2.1. In fondness of ritual. Weak heads commonly admire those shows and ceremonies that the wise cannot help despising.

3.2.2. In fury against Christianity. Paul, a disciple of the Pharisees, was *exceedingly mad against the Christians* (Ac 26:11), while his master, Gamaliel, seems to have been more moderate (Ac 5:34–39).

4. They led the people into dangerous mistakes, especially in the matter of oaths, which have been considered sacred by all nations (v. 16): *Ye blind guides.* Christ declared a woe to the blind guides who had the blood of so many souls to answer for.

4.1. He laid down the doctrine they taught. They distinguished between an oath *by the temple* and an oath by the *gold of the temple*, and between an oath by *the altar* and an oath by *the gift upon the altar*, making the latter oaths binding, but not the former. Here was a double evil:

4.1.1. That there were some oaths that they dispensed with and made light of, reckoning that such oaths did not bind a person to assert the truth or fulfill a promise. A teaching that supports the breach of faith in any case whatsoever cannot come from the God of truth. Oaths are tools with sharp edges and are not to be played with.

4.1.2. That they preferred the gold to the temple and preferred the gift to the altar in order to encourage people to bring gifts to the altar and gold to the treasures of the temple, which they hoped to gain from.

4.2. He showed the foolishness and absurdity of this distinction (vv. 17–19): *Ye fools, and blind.* To convict them of foolishness, he appealed to them themselves, *Whether* (which) *is greater, the gold, or the temple that sanctifies the gold? The gift, or the altar that sanctifies the gift?* Those who swore by the gold of the temple looked at it as holy, but what was it that made it holy except the holiness of the temple, in the service of which it was used? The temple, therefore, could not be less holy than the gold, but must be more so.

4.3. He put right the mistake (vv. 20–22), by reducing all the oaths they had invented to the true intent of an oath, which is, "By the name of the Lord." This meant that even if an oath by the temple, the altar, or heaven was formally bad, it was still binding. If a person swore by the altar, his oath would be interpreted as taken by the altar and by all things on it. Moreover, because the things on it were offered to God, to swear by it and them was, in effect, to call God himself to witness, because it was the altar of God, and those who went to that went to God (Ps 26:6; 43:4). The person who swore by the temple, if he understood what he was doing, must understand that the reason for such a respect of it was that it was the house of God, the place in which he had chosen to put his name (1Ki 11:36), and so when a person swore *by it,* he swore *by him that dwelt therein* (v. 21). If a person swears by heaven, he sins (5:34), but he will not therefore be discharged from the obligation of his oath. No; God will make him understand that the heaven he swears by is his throne (Isa 66:1), and one who swears by the throne appeals to the One who sits on it.

5. They were very strict and precise in the smaller details of the Law, but just as careless and loose in more important matters (vv. 23–24). They were *partial in the law.* Sincere obedience is universal, and those who obey from a right motive any of God's commands will respect them all (Ps 119:6). The partiality of the teachers of the law and Pharisees appeared in two instances here:

5.1. They observed smaller duties but omitted greater ones; they were very exact in paying tithes when it came to *mint, anise* (NIV: dill), and *cumin*; exactness in tithing such things would not cost them much, but would be praised and would quickly gain them a good reputation. The Pharisee boasted about this: *I give tithes of all that I possess* (Lk 18:12).

5.1.1. Paying tithes was their duty; Christ told them they should not leave it undone. Everyone should contribute to the support and maintenance of a standing ministry where they are. Those who *are taught in the word* and do not *communicate to* (share with) *them that teach them* (Gal 6:6), who love a cheap Gospel, come short of the Pharisees.

5.1.2. But what Christ condemned them for here was that they *omitted the weightier matters of the law, judgment* (justice), *mercy, and faith* (faithfulness). All the things of God's Law are significant, but those that most express inner holiness in the heart are the most significant. Justice and mercy toward people and faith and faithfulness toward God are the more significant matters of the law, the *good things* that the *Lord our God requires* (Mic 6:8), to act justly, to love mercy, and to walk humbly by faith with God. This is the obedience that is better than sacrifices or tithes (1Sa 15:22). Mercy also is preferred to sacrifice (Hos 6:6). Nor will justice and mercy be enough without faith in divine revelation, for God wants to be honored in his truths as well as in his laws.

5.2. They avoided lesser sins but committed greater ones: *Ye blind guides* (v. 24). He had called them this before (v. 16), because of their corrupt teaching; here he called them this because of their corrupt living. They were blind and partial; they *strained at a gnat, and swallowed a camel.* In their teaching they strained out gnats, warning people against every slight violation of the tradition of the elders. In their lives they strained out gnats, heaving at them with an apparent dread, as if they had a great hatred of sin and were afraid of its slightest instance, yet they had no difficulty committing those sins that, in comparison, were as a camel to a gnat. It was not the shunning of a little sin that Christ rebuked here—if it is a sin, though only a gnat, it must be strained out—but the doing of that and then swallowing a camel.

6. They were concerned only with the outside of religious faith and not at all with the inside. This is shown by two illustrations.

6.1. Christ compared them to a cup or dish that is washed clean on the outside but still dirty inside (vv. 25–26). Now, how foolish it is for a person to wash only the outside of a cup, which is to simply be looked at, and to leave the inside dirty, which is to be used. Yet this is what people do when they avoid scandalous sins, which would damage their reputation with those around them, but allow themselves to keep corruption in the heart, which renders them repugnant to God in his purity and holiness. In reference to this, notice:

6.1.1. The practice of the Pharisees: they cleaned the outside. In things that were observed by their neighbors, they seemed to be very precise; people generally took them to be very good people. But inside, they were *full of extortion and excess.* While they wanted to appear godly, they were in fact neither sober nor righteous, and we are really what we are inwardly.

6.1.2. The rule Christ gave in opposition to this practice (v. 26). In Christ's sight, those who are strangers, and not enemies, to the evil in their own hearts, who do not see and do not hate the secret sin that lodges there, are blind. Self-ignorance is the most shameful and hurtful form of ignorance (Rev 3:17). The rule is, *Cleanse first that which is within.* The main work of being a Christian lies within, to get cleansed from the *filthiness of the spirit* (2Co 7:1). We must conscientiously abstain from those sins that are witnessed only by the eye of God, who searches the heart (Jer 17:10; Rev 2:23). *Cleanse first that which is within;* not only that, but that first, because if due care is taken about that, then the outside will also be clean. If renewing, sanctifying grace makes the inside clean, that will also influence the outside, for the motivating principle is within us. If the heart is well kept, all is well, for *out of it are the issues of life* (Pr 4:23). First let us cleanse what is inside us; our cleansing work will be successful when we make our first work the cleansing of the heart.

6.2. He compared them to *whited sepulchers* (whitewashed tombs) (vv. 27–28).

6.2.1. Outwardly they looked nice, like tombs *which appear beautiful outward.* Some think this refers to the Jews' custom of painting tombs white to mark them out, so that people could avoid the ceremonial defilement contracted by touching a grave (Nu 19:16). The formality of hypocrites makes all wise and good people more careful to avoid them. But actually, it alludes to the custom of whitewashing the tombs of well-known people to make them beautiful. It is said here that they *garnished* (decorated) *the sepulchres of the righteous* (v. 29). The righteousness of the teachers of the law and Pharisees is likened to the decorations of a grave, which are merely for show. The aim of their ambition was to *appear righteous before men* and to be applauded and admired by them.

6.2.2. They were *foul* within, like tombs, *full of dead men's bones, and all uncleanness.* They were so full of hypocrisy and sin. It is possible for those who have their hearts full of sin to have their lives free from blame and to appear very good. However, what will it benefit us to receive praise from our fellow servants if our Master does not say, *Well done* (25:21)?

7. They pretended to keep fond memories of the prophets who had died and were gone, while they hated and persecuted those who were present with them. God jealously protects his honor in his laws and decrees, but he has often expressed an equally jealous protectiveness of his honor in his prophets and ministers. Therefore, when our Lord Jesus began to speak on this subject, he spoke more fully than about any of the others (vv. 29–37). Notice here:

7.1. The respect the teachers of the law and Pharisees pretended to have for the prophets who had died (vv. 29–30).

7.1.1. They honored the relics of the prophets, building their tombs and decorating their graves. *The memory of the just* will be *blessed* (Pr 10:7) when the names of those who hated and persecuted them will be covered with shame. Yet the honor that the teachers of the law and Pharisees paid to the dead prophets was an instance of their hypocrisy. Like hypocrites in every age, they could pay respect to the writings of the dead prophets, which told them what they should be, but not to the rebukes of the living prophets, which told them what they were.

7.1.2. They protested against the murder of them: *If we had been in the days of our fathers, we would not have been partakers* (not have taken part) *with them in the blood of the prophets* (v. 30). No, not they; they would sooner have lost their right hand than have done any such thing. However, they were at this time plotting to murder Christ, *to whom all the prophets bore witness* (Ac 10:43). The deceitfulness of sinners' hearts is seen very much in that while they follow the tide of the sins of their own day, they vainly think they would have swum against the tide of the sins of former times. They think that if they had had other people's opportunities, they would have used them more faithfully. We sometimes think that if we had lived when Christ was on earth, we would have followed him faithfully; we would not have despised and rejected him,

as they did then. But Christ, in his Spirit, in his word, in his ministers, is still treated no better.

7.2. Their enmity and opposition to Christ and his Gospel, nevertheless, and the ruin they were bringing on themselves and on that generation by that opposition (vv. 31–33). Notice here:

7.2.1. The accusation proved: *Ye are witnesses against yourselves.* Sinners cannot hope to escape the judgment of Christ for lack of proof against them, since it is easy to see that they testify against themselves. By their own confession, it was the great evil of their ancestors to kill the prophets. Those who condemn sin in others but allow the same or worse sin in themselves are of all people most inexcusable (Ro 1:32–2:1). By their own confession, these notorious persecutors were their ancestors: *Ye are the children of them.* Christ turned it back on them: they were the children of those persecutors not only by blood but also by spirit and disposition. "They were, as you say, your ancestors, and you take after your ancestors; it is the sin that runs in the blood among you."

7.2.2. The sentence passed on them. Christ proceeded here:

7.2.2.1. To give them up to sin as irreclaimable: *Fill ye up then the measure of your fathers* (v. 32). Christ knew that they were now plotting his death and in a few days would bring it about; "Very well," he said, "continue with your plot, follow the way of your heart and the sight of your eyes (Isa 11:3), and see what comes of it. You will only fill up the measure of your guilt.

7.2.2.1.1. There is a measure of sins to be filled up. God will be patient for a long time, but the time will come when he can *no longer forbear* (Jer 44:22).

7.2.2.1.2. If, when their ancestors have died, children persist in sins that are the same as or similar to those of their ancestors, they fill up the measure of their ancestors' sins. The national guilt that brings national ruin is made up of the sins of many people in several ages. God justly brings the punishment for the sins of the ancestors on the children who follow in their footsteps.

7.2.2.1.3. Persecuting Christ and his people and ministers is a sin that fills up the measure of a nation's guilt more quickly than any other.

7.2.2.1.4. When people stubbornly persist in indulging in their own hearts' sinful desires, it is just of God to give them up to those desires.

7.2.2.2. To give them up to ruin as irrecoverable, to a personal ruin in the other world: *Ye serpents, ye generation of vipers, how can ye escape the damnation of hell?* (v. 33). These are strange words to come from the mouth of Christ, into whose lips grace was poured (Ps 45:2). But Christ can and will speak words of terror. Here is:

7.2.2.2.1. His description of them: *Ye serpents.* Does Christ call people names? Yes, but this does not authorize us to do so. He infallibly knew what was in people. They were *a generation of vipers*; they and those who joined with them were a generation of embittered, enraged, and spiteful enemies of Christ and his Gospel. Christ called them *serpents* and *vipers* because he tells people what they are truly like and delights to show contempt to the proud.

7.2.2.2.2. Their doom. *How can ye escape the damnation of hell?* Christ himself preached hell and damnation, for which his ministers have often been rebuked by those who do not want to hear about it. Because this condemnation came from Christ, it was more terrible than if it had come from all the prophets and ministers who ever lived, for he is the Judge into whose hands the keys of hell and death are put (Rev 1:18). There is a way of escaping this condemnation to hell: repentance and faith are necessary for that escape. How will people who have the spirit of the teachers of the law and Pharisees be brought to repentance when they have such conceited thoughts of themselves as these leaders had and are so prejudiced against Christ and his Gospel as they were? Tax collectors and prostitutes, who were aware of their disease and turned to the great Physician, were more likely to escape the condemnation of hell than those who, though on the highway to it, were confident they were on their way to heaven.

Verses 34–39

We have left the blind leaders fallen into the ditch (15:14); let us now see what was to become of the blind followers, especially Jerusalem.

1. Jesus Christ intended to test them with the means of grace: *I send unto you prophets, and wise men, and scribes.* One would think it would follow, "Therefore you will never have a prophet sent to you anymore"; but no, "*Therefore I will send unto you prophets*, to see if you will finally be persuaded; otherwise, you will be left without excuse."

1.1. It was Christ who would send them: *I send.* By this he confirmed that he was God, who has the authority to endow prophets with gifts and to commission them. It was an act of his kingly position. After his resurrection he fulfilled this word when he said, *So send I you* (Jn 20:21).

1.2. He would send them to the Jews first: "I send them to you." They began at Jerusalem, and wherever they went, their rule was to make the first offer of the Gospel grace *to the Jews* (Ac 13:46).

1.3. Those he would send he would call *prophets, wise men,* and *scribes,* Old Testament names for New Testament officers. We may take the apostles and evangelists as the prophets and wise men, and the pastors and teachers as the scribes, *instructed to the kingdom of heaven* (13:52), for the position of a scribe was honorable until people dishonored it.

2. He foresaw and foretold the cruel treatment that his messengers would encounter among them: "*Some of them ye shall kill and crucify,* but I will still send them." Christ knows in advance how cruelly his servants will be treated, but he still sends them. He loves them no less, however, for he intends to glorify himself by their sufferings, and to glorify them after their sufferings; he will make up for their sufferings, though not prevent them. Notice:

2.1. The cruelty of these persecutors: *Ye shall kill and crucify them.* It was no less than the blood, the lifeblood, that they thirsted after. In this way, the members shared in the sufferings of the Head: he was killed and crucified, and so were they. Christians must expect to resist to the point of shedding blood (Heb 12:4).

2.2. Their unwearied diligence: *Ye shall persecute them from city to city.* As the apostles went from town to town to preach the Gospel, the Jews followed them stealthily, haunted them, and stirred up persecution against them (Ac 14:19; 17:13).

2.3. The pretense of religion in this matter; they flogged Christ's followers in their synagogues, doing it as an act of service to the church.

3. He imputed the sin of their ancestors to them, because they imitated it: *That upon you may come all the righteous blood shed upon the earth* (vv. 35–36). Although God is patient for a long time with a persecuting generation, he will not be patient always, and when patience is abused, it turns into the greatest wrath. Notice:

3.1. The extent of this imputation: it includes *all the righteous blood shed upon the earth,* that is, the blood

shed for righteousness' sake. He dated the record *from the blood of righteous Abel.* Notice how soon martyrdom came into the world! He extended *it to the blood of Zacharias, the son of Barachias* (v. 36), probably *Zechariah the son of Jehoiada,* who was *slain in the court of the Lord's house* (2Ch 24:20–21). His father is called *Barachias,* which means much the same as *Jehoiada,* and it was usual among the Jews for the same person to have two names. This Zechariah was one "*whom ye slew,* you of this nation, though not of this generation."

3.2. The effect of it: *All these things shall come*; all the guilt of shedding this blood, all its punishment, would *come upon this generation.* The destruction would be so dreadful that it would be as if God was once for all calling them to account for all the righteous blood shed in the world. It would *come upon this generation,* which suggested that it would come quickly; some here would live to see it. The severer and closer the punishment of sin is, the louder comes the call to repentance and reformation.

4. He mourned the evil of Jerusalem and justly rebuked them with the many kind offers he had made them (v. 37). Notice with what concern he spoke about that city: *O Jerusalem, Jerusalem!* The repetition is emphatic and shows great commiseration. A day or two earlier Christ had wept over Jerusalem; now he sighed and groaned over it. Jerusalem, "the vision of peace," as it means, must now be the seat of war and confusion. But why would the Lord do all this to Jerusalem? Why? *Jerusalem hath grievously sinned* (La 1:8).

4.1. She persecuted God's messengers: *Thou that killest the prophets, and stonest them that are sent unto thee.* Jerusalem was especially accused of this sin because it was there that the Sanhedrin, or great council, sat, who took notice of church matters, and so a prophet could not perish except in Jerusalem (Lk 13:33). They killed the prophets in popular disturbances, mobbed them, as they did with Stephen, and incited the Roman powers to kill them. At Jerusalem, where the Gospel was first preached, came the first persecution (Ac 8:1); that was the headquarters of the persecutors; and it was there that saints were brought bound (Ac 9:2). *Thou stonest* them. There was much other corruption in Jerusalem, but this was the sin that cried out the loudest and that God was more concerned with than with any other.

4.2. She refused and rejected Christ and the offer of the Gospel. The former was a sin without remedy (2Ch 36:16), with nothing to save them; this one was against the remedy, against the way of being saved. Here is:

4.2.1. The wonderful grace and favor of Jesus Christ toward them: *How often would I have gathered thy children together, as a hen gathers her chickens under her wings!* The favor proposed was their being gathered. Christ's intention is to gather poor souls, gather them in from their wanderings, gather them home to himself. It is illustrated here by a humble comparison: *as a hen gathers her chickens together.* Christ had longed to gather them:

4.2.1.1. With such a tenderness of affection as a hen does, who has an instinctive special concern for his young ones. Christ's gathering of souls comes from his love (Jer 31:3).

4.2.1.2. For the same end. The hen gathers her chicks under her wings for protection and safety and for warmth and comfort. When they are threatened by the birds of prey, chicks naturally run to the hen for shelter; perhaps Christ was referring to that promise in Ps 91:4: *He shall cover thee with his feathers.* There is *healing under Christ's wings* (Mal 4:2), which is more than the hen has for her chicks.

4.2.2. The eagerness of Christ to give this favor. His offers are very free: *I would have done it.* His offers are very frequent: *How often!* Christ often came up to Jerusalem, preached, and performed miracles there. Just as we have often heard the sound of the Gospel, just as we have often felt the strivings of the Spirit, so often Christ has longed to gather us.

4.2.3. Their stubborn refusal of this grace and favor: *Ye would not.* "I have longed for you, but you refused me." He longed to save them, but they were not willing to be saved by him.

5. He read out Jerusalem's condemnation (vv. 38–39): Therefore, *behold, your house is left unto you desolate.* Both the city and the temple, God's house and their own, would be laid waste. However, it refers especially to the temple, which they boasted about and trusted in.

5.1. Their house would be deserted: *It is left unto you desolate.* Christ was now departing from the temple, never to return to it. They doted on it, wanting it only for themselves; Christ must have no room or interest there. "Well," Christ said, "it is left to you; take it and make the best of it; I will never have anything more to do with it." Their city also was left to them, empty of God's presence and grace.

5.2. It would be desolate: *It is left unto you desolate.* In the eyes of all who understood, it was immediately a sad, depressing place when Christ left it. Christ's departure makes the best-provided, best-furnished place a wilderness. For what comfort can there be in a place where Christ does not live? This is what comes of people's rejection of Christ and driving him away from them. The temple was destroyed and ruined not long afterward, with *not one stone left upon another* (24:2). The temple, that holy and beautiful house, became desolate. When God leaves a place, all the enemies break in.

6. He bade them and their temple a final farewell: *Ye shall not see me henceforth, till ye shall say, Blessed is he that cometh.* This shows:

6.1. His departure from them. The time was at hand when he would *leave the world to go to his Father* (Jn 16:28), to be seen no more. After his resurrection he was seen only by a few *chosen witnesses* (Ac 10:41), and they did not see him for long; he soon moved to the invisible world and will be there *till the time of the restitution of all things* (Ac 3:21), when his welcome at his first coming will be repeated with loud acclamation: *Blessed is he that cometh in the name of the Lord* (v. 39). If we want to be with those who say *Blessed is he that cometh,* let us now join those now who truly worship and truly welcome Jesus Christ.

6.2. Their continued blindness and stubbornness: *Ye shall not see me,* that is, not see the light of the truth about me, nor *the things that belong to your peace* (Lk 19:42), *till ye shall say, Blessed is he that cometh* (v. 39). Willful blindness is often punished by judicial blindness. If they refused to see, they would be punished by not seeing. Christ concluded his public preaching with these words. When *the Lord comes with ten thousand of his saints* (Jude 14), he will convince all of them. Those who now scorn and ridicule the hosannas of the saints will soon have a different mind; it would be better if they had that mind now.

CHAPTER 24

In this chapter we have prophetic teaching, which was intended not to satisfy the curiosity of his disciples but to guide their consciences. Here is: 1. The occasion of this teaching (vv. 1–3). 2. The teaching itself, in which we have: 2.1. The prophecy of various events, referring especially to the destruction of Jerusalem; to the introductions to that destruction, the circumstances that would accompany it, and the effects that would follow it; and, looking even further, to Christ's second coming at the end of time and to the consummation of all things (vv. 4–31). 2.2. The practical application of this prophecy (vv. 32–51).

Verses 1–3

Here is:

1. Christ's leaving the temple at the end of his public work there. He had said, as recorded at the end of the previous chapter, *Your house is left unto you desolate* (23:38), and here he fulfilled his words: *He went out, and departed from the temple.* He departed from it, never to return to it, and then a prediction of its ruin followed immediately. The house that Christ leaves is left truly desolate. But Christ did not depart until they drove him out; he did not reject them until they first rejected him.

2. His private conversation with his disciples; he left the temple, but he did not leave the Twelve. When he left the temple, his disciples left it too and came to him. It is good to be where Christ is and to leave what he leaves.

2.1. *His disciples came to him, to show him the buildings of the temple.* It was an impressive, beautiful structure. It was richly furnished by gifts and offerings. They showed Christ these things and called his attention to them, either:

2.1.1. Because they were greatly pleased with them themselves and expected him to be so too. They had lived mostly in Galilee, far away from the temple, and had rarely seen it, and so they were the more struck with wonder at it, and they thought he should admire *all this glory* (Ge 31:1) as much as they did. Even good people tend to be too taken up with outward pomp and show and to overvalue it, even in the things of God. The temple was truly glorious, but its glory was sullied and stained with the sin of the priests and people, and its glory was eclipsed and surpassed by the presence of Christ in it. Or:

2.1.2. Because they were grieved that this house would be left desolate; they showed him the buildings, as if it might move him to reverse the sentence. Christ had just looked at *the precious souls* (Ps 49:8) *and wept for them* (Lk 19:41). The disciples looked at the magnificent buildings and were ready to weep for them. In this, as in other things, his thoughts are not like ours (Isa 5:8).

2.2. Christ then foretold the complete ruin and destruction that were coming on this place (v. 2). A believing foresight of the destruction of all worldly glory will help take us away from overvaluing it. *See ye not all these things?* They called Christ's attention to them and wanted him to be as much in love with them as they were; he wanted them to look at them and to be as dead to them as he was. There is such a sight of these things as will do us good, to see them so as to see through them and see to their end. Instead of reversing the decree, Christ ratified it: *Verily, I say unto you, there shall not be left one stone upon another.*

2.2.1. He spoke of it as a certain destruction: "I *say unto you.*" *I,* who know what I am saying.

2.2.2. He spoke of it as a total destruction. The temple would not only be stripped, plundered, and defaced but also completely demolished and laid waste: *Not one stone shall be left upon another.* Although when Titus took the city, he did all he could to preserve the temple, he could not restrain the enraged soldiers from destroying it completely, and it was done to such a degree that Turnus Rufus plowed up the ground on which it had stood.

2.3. The disciples asked for further details about the time when it would take place and about the signs of its coming (v. 3). Notice:

2.3.1. Where they asked this question: privately, *as he sat upon the mount of Olives.* Probably he was returning to Bethany and sat down there beside the road to rest; the Mount of Olives directly faced the temple, and from there he would have a full view of it at some distance.

2.3.2. What the question itself was: *When shall these things be, and what shall be the sign of thy coming, and of the end of the world?* Here are three questions.

2.3.2.1. Some think that these questions all point to one and the same thing—the destruction of the temple. Or they thought the destruction of the temple must be the end of the world.

2.3.2.2. Others think their question *When shall these things be?* refers to the destruction of Jerusalem, and the other two to the end of the world. The Twelve had confused thoughts about future events, and so perhaps it is not possible to put any certain interpretation on their question.

Verses 4–31

The disciples had asked about the time: *When shall these things be?* Christ gave them no answer to that. But they had also asked, *What shall be the sign?* He answered that question fully. The prophecy was primarily about the events close at hand. Just as the prophecies of the Old Testament, which have an immediate reference to the affairs of the Jews, also point further, typologically, to the Gospel church and the kingdom of the Messiah, and are explained in this way in the New Testament, so this prophecy, using Jerusalem's destruction as a type, looks as far forward as the general judgment. What Christ said to his disciples here tended more to engage their caution than to satisfy their curiosity, more to prepare them for the events that were to happen than to give them a distinct idea of the events themselves.

1. Christ began with a warning: *Take heed* (watch out) *that no man deceive you.* They expected to be told when these things would happen, to be let in on that secret, but this warning served to restrain their curiosity: *"What is that to you?* You should take care of your own business, follow me, and not be dissuaded from following me." Deceivers are more dangerous enemies to the church than persecutors. Three times in this discourse he mentioned the appearing of false prophets, which was:

1.1. A sign of Jerusalem's coming ruin. It would be just for those who killed the true prophets to be left to be caught in a trap by false prophets, and for those who crucified the true Messiah to be left to be deceived and broken by false Christs (v. 24).

1.2. A test for the disciples of Christ, and therefore corresponded to their state of testing in this world and to God's purpose *that they which are approved may be made manifest* (1Co 11:19). Notice about these deceivers:

1.2.1. The pretenses they would make. Satan brings great trouble when he appears as an angel of light (2Co 11:14): the color of the greatest good often covers up the greatest evil.

1.2.1.1. There would appear *false prophets* (vv. 11–24); the deceivers would claim divine inspiration, though it was all false. Some think that the deceivers pointed to here were people who had been settled teachers in the church but had turned to error; from such people the danger is greater, because least suspected. One false traitor in a garrison may do more harm than a thousand confirmed enemies outside.

1.2.1.2. There would appear *false Christs* (v. 24), *coming in Christ's name* (v. 5), taking to themselves his own special name and saying, *I am Christ.* They would be pseudochrists (v. 24). At that time there was a general expectation of the appearing of the Messiah; people spoke about him as *he that should come* (11:3). But when he came, most of the nation rejected him; those who were ambitious to make a name for themselves took advantage of this rejection and set themselves up as Christs.

1.2.1.3. These false Christs and false prophets would keep their agents and ambassadors busy everywhere to draw people to them (v. 23). When public troubles are great and threatening and people are willing to seize at anything that looks like a rescue, Satan will take advantage of their desperation and deceive them; then they will say, *Lo, here is a Christ,* or *there* is one. The true Christ did not strive or cry out (12:19; Isa 42:2); it was not said of him, *Lo, here!* or, *Lo, there!* (Lk 17:21). Christ is All in all, not here or there (Eph 1:23; Col 3:11), and he meets his people with a blessing *in all places where he records his name* (Ex 20:24).

1.2.2. The proof they would bring in defense of such pretenses: *They shall show great signs and wonders* (v. 24), not true miracles: those have a divine seal and are confirmed by the teaching of Christ. It was not said that these deceivers would work miracles, but that they would *show* great signs; they were merely a show.

1.2.3. The success they would have in these attempts: *They shall deceive many* (v. 5 and again v. 11). The Devil and his instruments may be effective in deceiving poor souls; few find the narrow gate, and many are drawn to the broad way (7:13–14). *They shall deceive, if it were possible, the very elect* (v. 24). This shows:

1.2.3.1 The strength of the delusion; it is such that many will be carried away by it; the tide will flow so strongly, catching even those who were thought to stand firm. Nothing but the almighty grace of God, according to his eternal purpose, will serve as a protection.

1.2.3.2. The safety of God's chosen ones in the midst of this danger, which is assumed in that expression in parenthesis, *if it were possible,* clearly implying that it is not possible, for they are *kept by the power of God* (1Pe 1:5). This expression was used proverbially by Galen, who, when he wanted to express something very difficult and morally impossible, said, "You may sooner draw a Christian away from Christ."

1.2.4. The repeated warnings that our Savior gave; he gave them these warnings so that they would watch (v. 25): *Behold, I have told you before* (ahead of time). Those who are told in advance where they will be attacked may save themselves. Christ's warnings are intended to engage our watchfulness. We are kept through faith, faith in Christ's word, which he has told us ahead of time. We must not believe those who say, *Lo, here is Christ,* or, *Lo, he is there* (v. 23). We believe that the true Christ is at the right hand of God and that his spiritual presence *is where two or three are gathered together in his name* (18:20). There is not a greater enemy to true faith than vain gullibility. Simple people believe every word and run after every cry. We must not go out after those who say, *He is in the desert,* or, *He is in the secret chambers* (v. 26). We must not follow everyone who tries to point us to a new Christ and a new Gospel. Many a person's vain curiosity to go out has led them into a fatal apostasy.

2. He foretold wars and great disturbances among the nations (vv. 6–7). When Christ was born, there was a

universal peace in the empire: the temple of Janus was shut (the Roman god Janus was guardian of gates and doors, and his temple in Rome was shut in times of peace [Ed.]), but *think not that Christ came to send* or continue such *a peace* (Lk 12:51). No; his city and his wall are to be built even in troublesome times, and even wars will forward his work. Here is:

2.1. A prediction of the event of the day: "You will now soon *hear of wars, and rumors of wars.*" When wars are raging, they will be heard. Notice how terrible war is. Even those who lead quiet lives in the land must hear rumors of war. Notice what comes of refusing the Gospel! Those who will not listen to messengers of peace will be made to listen to messengers of war.

2.2. A prescription of their responsibility on that day: *See that ye be not troubled.* Is it possible to hear such sad news and not be troubled? Yet, where the heart is steadfast, trusting in God (Ps 112:7), it is kept in peace and is not afraid (Isa 26:3). It is against the mind of Christ (Jn 14:1, 27) for his people to have troubled hearts, even in troublesome times. We must not be troubled, for two reasons:

2.2.1. Because we are told to expect this: the Jews must be punished. This is how the justice of God and the honor of the Redeemer must be asserted, and so *all those things must come to pass.* God is simply performing the thing that is appointed for us. Let us therefore accept his will. The old house must be demolished—though it cannot be done without noise, dust, and danger—before the new building can be erected: the things that are shaken—and they were shaken severely—*must be removed, that the things which cannot be shaken may remain* (Heb 12:27).

2.2.2. Because we are still to expect worse: *The end is not yet.* The end of the age has not yet come, and while this age lasts, we must expect trouble, or, "The end of these troubles has not yet come. Do not give way to fear and trouble, do not sink under the present burden, but gather all the strength and spirit you have in order to face up to what lies in front of you." If running with the footmen wearies us, how will we compete with horses? Moreover, if we are frightened at a little brook in our way, how will we cope with the flooding of the Jordan (Jer 12:5)?

3. He foretold other judgments more directly sent by God: *famines, pestilences, and earthquakes.* These were the three judgments that David was to choose from, and he was in great difficulty, for he did not know which was the worst. Besides war—and that is enough—there will be:

3.1. *Famine,* represented by the *black horse* under the *third seal* (Rev 6:5–6). There was the severest famine in Jerusalem during the siege.

3.2. *Pestilences,* represented by the *pale horse, and death upon him,* and *the grave at his heels,* under the *fourth seal* (Rev 6:7–8).

3.3. *Earthquakes in divers places.* Great desolation has sometimes been caused by earthquakes; they have caused the death of many people, and the terror of even more. However, here they are spoken of as fearful judgments, which are only *the beginning of sorrows.*

4. He foretold the persecution of his own people and ministers and a general apostasy and decay in religion immediately after that (vv. 9–10, 12). Notice:

4.1. The cross itself foretold (v. 9). It is as much in our interests—though we are not very interested—to know about our own sufferings as to know about any other future event. Christ had told his disciples what hard things they would suffer, but up to that time they had experienced little of it, and so he reminded them again.

They would be *afflicted* with bonds and imprisonment. They would be *killed.* They would be *hated of all nations for Christ's name's sake,* as he had told them before (10:22). The world was generally imbued with an enmity and hatred toward Christians. What shall we think of this world, when we consider that the best people received the worst treatment in it? It is the cause that both makes the martyrs and comforts them; it was for Christ's sake that they were hated in this way.

4.2. *The offense of the cross* (vv. 10–12). Three adverse effects of persecution were foretold here:

4.2.1. The apostasy of some. When the profession of Christianity began to cost people dearly, *then many would be offended*; they would first fall from their profession and then turn away from it. It is nothing new, though it is strange, for those who have known the way of righteousness to turn aside from it. Times of suffering are times of disturbance, and those who stood in fair weather fall in the storm. Many who will follow Christ in the sunshine will leave him to fend for themselves on days of cloud and darkness.

4.2.2. The hatred of others. Then *they shall betray one another*; that is, "Those who have betrayed their religious faith will hate and betray those who remain loyal to it." Apostates have commonly been the most bitter and violent persecutors. Persecuting times are times of revelation. Wolves in sheep's clothing will then throw off their disguise and show themselves for what they truly are: wolves; they will *betray one another and hate one another.*

4.2.3. The general cooling of most people (v. 12). These two things are to be expected:

4.2.3.1. The increase of sin; although the world always lies in evil, there are some times in which it may be said that evil especially increases.

4.2.3.2. The decrease of love; this is the consequence of the previous change: *Because iniquity shall abound, the love of many shall wax cold.* This may be understood to refer in general to true serious godliness, which is all summed up in love; it is too common for those who profess religious faith to grow cold in their profession when evildoers are hot in their wickedness. Or it may be understood to refer more particularly to the mutual love between believers. When evil increases, evil that deceives and persecutes, then this grace often grows cold. Christians begin to be shy and suspicious of one another, and so love comes to nothing. That there will be such a general decay of love gives a sad prospect of the times, but:

• It is of the love of many, not of all. In the worst of times, God still keeps his remnant who hold firmly to their integrity and keep their zeal, as in Elijah's days, when he thought he himself was alone (1Ki 19:10, 14).

• This love grows cold but is not dead. There is still life in the roots, which will show itself when the winter is past (SS 2:11–13).

4.3. Encouragement given in reference to the offense of the cross, to support the Lord's people under it: *He that endures to the end shall be saved* (v. 13). It is encouraging to those who wish the cause of Christ well in general that although many people will turn away, some will endure to the end. It is encouraging to those who do endure to the end in this way, who suffer for their faithfulness, that they will be saved. Perseverance wins the crown, through free grace, and will wear it. *They shall be saved.* The crown of glory will make up for everything. Choose rather to die at the stake with the persecuted than to live in a palace with persecutors (Ps 84:10).

5. He foretold the preaching of the Gospel throughout the world: *This Gospel shall be preached, and then shall the end come* (v. 14). It is called *the Gospel of the kingdom*, because it reveals the kingdom of grace, which leads to the kingdom of glory. This Gospel, sooner or later, is to be preached in all the world, to every creature (Mk 16:15). The Gospel is preached *for a witness to all nations*, that is, as a faithful declaration of the mind and will of God.

5.1. It was indicated here that the Gospel would be at least heard about — if not heard — throughout the then known world before the destruction of Jerusalem. Within forty years after Christ's death, the *sound* of the Gospel had *gone forth to the ends of the earth* (Ro 10:18). The apostle Paul *fully preached the Gospel from Jerusalem, and round about unto Illyricum* (Ro 15:19), and the other apostles were not idle. The persecuting of the saints at Jerusalem helped disperse them, so that they *went everywhere, preaching the word* (Ac 8:1–4).

5.2. It was also indicated that even in times of temptation, trouble, and persecution, the Gospel of the kingdom would force its way through the greatest opposition. Although the enemies of the church would show their hatred with great intensity, and the love of many of its friends would become cold, the Gospel would still be preached. Then the people who did know their God would be strengthened to perform the greatest exploits of all.

5.3. What seems chiefly to have been intended here is that the end of the world would come when the Gospel had completed its work in the world, and not until then. When the mystery of God is finished, the mystical body completed, *then shall the end come*, about which he had spoken before as *not yet* (vv. 6–7).

6. He foretold more particularly the ruin that was coming on the people of the Jews: on their city, temple, and nation (v. 15). What he said here would be useful to his disciples both for their conduct and for their comfort in reference to that great event. He described the various steps of that disaster:

6.1. The Romans *setting up the abomination of desolation in the holy place* (v. 15).

6.1.1. Some understand this to refer to an idol or statue set up in the temple by some of the Roman governors, which was very offensive to the Jews. Since the exile in Babylon, nothing was or could be more repugnant to the Jews than an idol in the Holy Place.

6.1.2. Others choose to explain it by the parallel reference: *when ye shall see Jerusalem compassed with armies* (Lk 21:20). Jerusalem was the Holy City, Canaan was the Holy Land, and Mount Moriah, which lay near Jerusalem, was, they thought, especially holy ground, because of its closeness to the temple. The Roman army was encamped on the country lying around Jerusalem, and their presence there, on this interpretation, was the abomination that caused desolation.

6.1.2.1. Now this was said to be *spoken of by Daniel, the prophet*, who spoke more clearly about the Messiah and his kingdom than any other Old Testament prophet did. Christ referred his listeners to that prophecy of Daniel so that they could see how the ruin of their city and temple was spoken about in the Old Testament, which would confirm his prediction. Just as Christ confirmed the law by his commands, so he confirmed the prophecies of the Old Testament by his predictions, and it will be useful to compare the two.

6.1.2.2. Because reference was made here to a prophecy, and prophecies are commonly mysterious and obscure, Christ inserted this note: *Whoso readeth, let him understand*. Those who read the Scriptures should seek to understand them, for otherwise their reading will not do much good; we cannot apply what we do not understand. See Jn 5:39; Ac 8:30. We must not despair of understanding even mystifying prophecies; the great New Testament prophecy is called a revelation, not a secret. *Now things revealed belong to us* (Dt 29:29; 1Pe 1:12), and so they must be humbly and diligently searched into.

6.2. The means of preservation that thinking people should apply (vv. 16, 20): *Then let them which are in Judea flee*. We may take this:

6.2.1. As a prediction of the ruin itself: that it would be irresistible, that it would be impossible for the boldest hearts to withstand it, but that they must resort to getting out of the way. To show how fruitless it would be to try to withstand it, Christ here told each one of them to make their way out as best they could.

6.2.2. As a direction to the followers of Christ as to what to do. Let them accept the decree that had been issued and leave the city and country as quickly as possible, just as they would abandon a falling house or a sinking ship, and as Lot left Sodom (Ge 19). He showed them:

6.2.2.1. Where they must flee to — from Judea *to the mountains*. In times of imminent peril and danger, it is not only lawful but also our duty to seek out our own preservation by all good and honest means, and if God opens a door of escape (1Co 10:13), we should make our escape; otherwise, we are not trusting God but tempting him. As long as we leave only danger, not our duty, we may trust God to provide. Those who flee live to see another day and may fight again.

6.2.2.2. How quickly they must escape (vv. 17–18). The life would be in danger, and so let those *that are on the housetop* when the alarm comes not *come down into the house*, but take the nearest way down to make their escape. Those who were *in the field would* find it their wisest course of action to run immediately, for two reasons:

6.2.2.2.1. The time that would be taken up in packing up their things would delay their escape. When death is at the door, delays are dangerous.

6.2.2.2.2. The taking of clothes and other personal effects with them would encumber their escape. The Syrians, in their flight, *cast away their garments* (2Ki 7:15). Those who took away the least would be safest in their flight. Those who have grace in their heart take all they need with them when they are stripped of all their earthly possessions. Now those to whom Christ said this directly did not live to see this sad day, none of the Twelve except John, but they left the direction to their successors in profession, who pursued it, and it was useful to them, for when the Christians in Jerusalem and Judea saw the ruin coming on, they all withdrew to a town called Pella, on the other side of the Jordan, where they were safe. The result was that of the thousands who perished in the destruction of Jerusalem, there was not so much as one Christian.

6.2.2.3. Whom it would go hard with at that time: *Woe to them that are with child* (pregnant women), *and to them that give suck* (nursing mothers) (v. 19). That saying of Christ at his death referred to this same event: *They shall say, Blessed are the wombs that never bare* (bore), *and the paps that never gave suck* (breasts that never nursed) (Lk 23:29). The famine would be the severest to them when they would see the *tongue of the sucking child cleaving to the roof of his mouth for thirst*. The sword would be most terrible to them, since it would be in the hands of worse than brutal rage. The escape would be most painful to them also. Pregnant women cannot move quickly or go far; the nursed child cannot be left behind, or if it is, *can a woman forget it, that she should not have compassion on it?* (Isa 49:15). If the child is taken along with the mother, it slows down the mother's escape and so makes her life vulnerable.

6.2.2.4. What they should pray against at that time — *that your flight be not in the winter, nor on the Sabbath day* (v. 20). In general, it is good for Christ's disciples to be prayerful in times of public trouble and adversity; that is a lotion for every sore, never out of season. "There is no remedy but flight; the decree has been issued. Seek to make the best of what is, and when you cannot in faith pray that you may not be forced to flee, still pray that the circumstances of your flight may be graciously ordered in such a way that, though the cup may not pass from you (26:39), the extremity of judgment may be prevented." God has the disposing of the circumstances of events, which sometimes makes a great difference one way or another, and so our eyes must always be toward him in those matters. Christ's telling them to pray for this favor indicated his intention of granting it to them, and in a general disaster we must see and acknowledge the ways in which it might have been worse. When trouble is in sight, at a great distance, it is good to make a store of prayers beforehand; they must pray:

6.2.2.4.1. *That their flight*, if it was the will of God, *might not be in the winter*, when the days are short, the weather cold, the roads dirty, and traveling therefore very uncomfortable, especially for whole families. Although physical comfort is not the main consideration, it should be given due consideration; although we must accept what God sends, and when he sends it, we may still pray against physical inconveniences, and are encouraged to do so.

6.2.2.4.2. That it would not be *on the Sabbath day*. Christ often showed a concern for the Sabbath. Here he showed that he wanted the Sabbath usually to be observed as a day of rest from travel and worldly labor, but that works of necessity were lawful on the Sabbath day, such as this work of fleeing from an enemy to save our lives. However, it also showed that it is very uncomfortable to good people to be taken away by any work of necessity from the solemn service and worship of God on the Sabbath. We should pray that we may have quiet, undisturbed Sabbaths, and may have no other work than Sabbath work to do on Sabbath days, so that we may attend the Lord's presence without distraction. To flee in the winter is uncomfortable to the body, but to flee on the Sabbath is uncomfortable to the soul.

6.3. The greatness of the troubles that would immediately follow: *Then shall be great tribulation* (v. 21); when the measure of sins has been filled up, then comes the distress. *There shall be great tribulation*. Truly great, when within the city plague and famine raged and, even worse, factions and divisions arose, so that everyone raised their sword against their fellows; it was then and there that the pitiful women skinned their own children. Josephus's *History of the Wars of the Jews* contains more tragic passages than perhaps any other history.

6.3.1. It was an unparalleled desolation, such as *was not since the beginning of the world, nor ever shall be.* Many cities and kingdoms have been made desolate, but there has never been any such desolation as this. It is hardly surprising that the destruction of Jerusalem was an unparalleled destruction, since the sin of Jerusalem was an unparalleled sin — namely, their crucifying Christ. The closer any people are to God in profession and privileges, the greater and harsher will be his judgments on them.

6.3.2. It was a desolation that, if it were to continue for a long time, would have been intolerable, so that *no flesh should be saved* (no one would survive) (v. 22). *No flesh shall be saved*; Christ did not say, "No soul will be saved," for the destruction of the flesh may be for *the saving of the spirit in the day of the Lord Jesus* (1Co 5:5). Here is one word of comfort, however, in the middle of all this terror — that *for the elect's sake these days shall be shortened*, not made shorter than what God had determined but shorter than what he might have decreed if he had dealt with them according to their sins. In times of general disaster, God reveals his favor to his chosen remnant, his treasured possession (Ex 19:5; Ps 135:4), which he will protect when the spoils have been plundered. The shortening of disasters is a kindness God often grants. If we considered our weaknesses, then instead of complaining that our adversities last so long, we would have reason to be thankful that they do not last forever. When things are going bad with us, it is good for us to say, "Praise God they are no worse." Now comes the repeated warning to beware being ensnared by false Christs and false prophets (v. 23). Times of great trouble are times of great temptation, and so we need to redouble our guard then. Pay no attention to these deceivers; it is all mere talk.

7. He foretold the sudden spreading of the Gospel in the world about the time of these great events (vv. 27–28): *As the lightning comes out of the east, so shall the coming of the Son of man be.*

7.1. It seems primarily to refer to his coming to establish his spiritual kingdom in the world. The Gospel would be remarkable in two ways:

7.1.1. Its swift speed: it would fly like lightning. The Gospel is light (Jn 3:19), yet not like lightning in that lightning is a sudden flash and is then gone; for the Gospel is sunlight and daylight. It is like lightning in these respects:

7.1.1.1. It is light from heaven, as lightning is. It is God, not human beings, who sends lightning; he calls it.

7.1.1.2. It is as visible and conspicuous as lightning. Truth seeks no hidden corners, however much it may sometimes be forced into them. Christ preached his Gospel openly (Jn 18:20), and his apostles preached on *the housetop* (10:27).

7.1.1.3. It came as suddenly and unexpectedly to the world as lightning. The powers of darkness were dispersed and defeated by the lightning of the Gospel.

7.1.1.4. It spread far and wide, quickly and irresistibly, like lightning, which comes, we suppose, from the east — Christ is said to ascend *from the east* (Rev 7:2; Isa 41:2) — and gives light to the west. The light of the Gospel rose with the sun and continued to rise so that its rays reached the ends of the world (Ro 10:18). Although the Gospel was fought against, it could never be cooped up in a desert or in a secret place, as the deceivers were, but according to the rule of Gamaliel, it proved itself to be *of God*: it *could not be overthrown* (Ac 5:38–39). How soon the Gospel lightning reached this land of Great Britain! Tertullian, who wrote in the second century, takes notice of it: "The fortresses of Britain, though inaccessible to the Romans, were occupied by Jesus Christ." This was the Lord's doing (Ps 118:23).

7.1.2. Its strange success in those places to which it spread; it gathered in multitudes. The *lifting up of Christ from the earth*, that is, the preaching of Christ crucified, which one would think would drive people away from him, would *draw all men to him* (Jn 12:32). Where should the soul go but to Jesus Christ, who *has the words of eternal life* (Jn 6:68)? Those who have their spiritual senses exercised will distinguish the voice of the good Shepherd from that of a thief and a robber. Saints will be where the true Christ is, not where the false Christs are. A living motivation of grace is a kind of natural instinct in all the saints, drawing them ever closer to Christ, to live on him.

7.2. Some understand these verses to refer to the coming of the Son of Man *to destroy Jerusalem* (Mal 3:1–2, 5). Here two things are intimated about that:

7.2.1. That to most people it would come as unexpectedly as a flash of lightning, which indeed gives warning of the thunderbolt that follows, but is itself surprising.

7.2.2. That it was as just to expect it as to expect that the eagle would fly to the carcasses. The desolation would come as certainly as birds of prey fall on a dead carcass. The Jews were so corrupt and degenerate that they had become a carcass, liable to the righteous judgment of God. The Romans were like an eagle, and the ensign of their armies was an eagle. The destruction would find the Jews wherever they were, just as eagles scent their prey.

7.3. It applies very much to the Day of Judgment, the coming of our Lord Jesus Christ on that day. Notice here:

7.3.1. How he will come: *as the lightning.* Those who ask after Christ, therefore, must not go into the desert or the secret places, nor listen to everyone who raises a finger to call them to see Christ; rather, let them look upward, for the heavens must contain him (1Ki 8:27), and it is from there that *we look for the Saviour* (Php 3:20).

7.3.2. How the saints will be gathered to him, with the greatest possible speed.

8. He foretold his second coming at the *end of time* (vv. 29–31). *The sun shall be darkened.*

8.1. Some think this is to be understood as referring only to the destruction of Jerusalem and the Jewish nation; the darkening of the sun, moon, and stars, on this view, the eclipse of the glory of that state, the *sign of the Son of man* (v. 30) means a significant appearance of the power and justice of the Lord Jesus in it, and the gathering *of his elect* (v. 31) represents the rescue of a remnant from this sin and ruin.

8.2. I think, however, it refers to Christ's second coming. The only objection against this is that it is said to be *immediately after the tribulation of those days*, but as to that:

8.2.1. It is usual in prophetic style to speak about things that are great and certain as close and near at hand, simply to express their greatness and certainty.

8.2.2. *A thousand years are in* God's sight *but as one day* (2Pe 3:8). It was urged by Peter with reference to this very thing, and so it could be said to be immediately after. It was foretold about Christ's second coming here:

8.2.2.1. That there will then be a great and amazing change in created things, especially the *heavenly bodies* (v. 29). *The sun shall be darkened, and the moon shall not give her light. The stars shall fall,* and *the powers of heaven shall be shaken.* This shows that:

8.2.2.1.1. It will be a great change, so that all things may be made new.

8.2.2.1.2. It will be a visible change, one that the whole world must take notice of, for the darkening of the sun and moon must have such an effect. It will also be an amazing change. *The days of heaven* (Ps 89:29) and the *enduring of the sun and moon* (Ps 72:5) are used to express what is lasting and unchangeable, and yet even they will be shaken in this way.

8.2.2.1.3. It will be a universal change. Nature will sustain a general shock and convulsion, but this will be no hindrance to the joy and rejoicing of heaven and earth *before the Lord, when he cometh to judge the world.*

8.2.2.1.4. The darkening of the sun, moon, and stars, which were *made to rule over the day, and over the night* (Ge 1:16–18), represents the *putting down of all rule, authority, and power* (1Co 15:24, 28). The sun was darkened at the death of Christ, for that was in one sense *the judgment of this world* (Jn 12:31).

8.2.2.1.5. The glorious appearance of our Lord Jesus will darken the sun and moon, as a candle is darkened in the rays of the midday sun.

8.2.2.1.6. The sun and moon will be darkened because there will be no more need for them. To the saints who had their treasure above, such light of joy and encouragement will be given as will supersede the light of the sun and moon and make it useless.

8.2.2.2. That *then shall appear the sign of the Son of man in heaven* (v. 30), and the Son of Man himself will appear, as it follows here: *They shall see the Son of man coming in the clouds.* At his first coming, he was *set for a Sign that should be spoken against* (Lk 2:34), but at his second coming, he will be a sign that is wondered at.

8.2.2.3. That *then all the tribes of the earth shall mourn* (v. 30). Some of all the peoples of the earth will mourn, while the chosen remnant will lift up their heads with joy, knowing that their redemption and their Redeemer draw near. Penitent sinners look to Christ and mourn with godly sorrow (2Co 7:10), and those who sow in tears will soon reap in joy (Ps 126:5).

8.2.2.4. That *then they shall see the Son of man coming in the clouds of heaven, with power and great glory.* This shows us:

8.2.2.4.1. The judgment of the great day will be committed to the Son of Man (Jn 5:22).

8.2.2.4.2. The Son of Man will come on the clouds of heaven on that day. Much of the physical interaction between heaven and earth is by clouds, which are drawn by heaven from earth and distilled by heaven on earth. Christ went to heaven on a cloud and *will in like manner come again* (Ac 1:9, 11).

8.2.2.4.3. He will *come with power and great glory*: his first coming was in weakness and great lowliness (2Co 13:4), but his second coming will be with power and glory.

8.2.2.4.4. The Son of Man will be the Judge, so that he may be seen, so that sinners may be even more confounded by that. "Is this the One whom we have insulted, rejected, and rebelled against, the One whom we have crucified for ourselves afresh, the One who might have been our Savior but is now our Judge?"

8.2.2.5. That *he shall send his angels with a great sound of a trumpet* (v. 31). The angels will be Christ's ministers at his second coming; they will be required to wait on him. They are now ministering spirits sent out by him (Heb 1:14), and so they will be then. Their ministry will be introduced by a great sound of a trumpet. According to the law, trumpets were to be sounded in proclaiming the Year of Jubilee (Lev 25:9); it is therefore most appropriate that a trumpet will be sounded at the last day, when the saints will enter their eternal jubilee.

8.2.2.6. That *they shall gather together his elect from the four winds.* At the second coming of Jesus Christ, there will be a general meeting of all the saints. The gifts of love to eternity follow the thoughts of love from eternity, and *the Lord knows them that are his* (2Ti 2:19). The angels, as Christ's servants and the saints' friends, will be used to bring the saints together. They *shall be gathered from one end of heaven to the other*; the ones chosen by God are scattered (Jn 11:52), but when that great day of gathering comes, not one of them will be missing; distance of place will keep no one out of heaven, if distance of affection does not.

Verses 32–51

Here is the practical application of the foregoing prediction; in general, we must expect and prepare for the events foretold.

1. We must expect them: *"Now learn a parable of the fig tree* (vv. 32–33). Learn how to apply the things you have heard, so that you may foresee what is right at the door and prepare for it accordingly." The parable of the fig tree is no more than that its budding and blossoming are signs that summer is coming. When God fulfills prophecies, he fulfills them from beginning to end (1Sa 3:12). After *the branch grows tender*, we expect March winds and April showers before summer comes; we are sure, however, that it is coming. "Similarly, when the Gospel day dawns, the perfect day will come (Pr 4:18). *Know that it is near."* When the trees of righteousness begin to bud and blossom (Isa 61:3), when God's people promise faithfulness, it is a happy sign of good times coming. In them God begins his work (Php 1:6); he first prepares their heart, and then he will continue his work. Now concerning the events foretold here, which we are to expect:

1.1. Christ assures us of their certainty: *Heaven and earth shall pass away, but my words shall not pass away* (v. 35). The word of Christ is more sure and lasting than heaven and earth. We may build with more assurance on the word of Christ than we can on the pillars of heaven or the strong foundations of the earth, for when they are no more, the word of Christ will remain. In God's time, which is the best time, and in God's way, which is the best way, it will certainly be fulfilled. Every word of Christ is very pure and therefore also very sure.

1.2. He enlightens us as to their time here (vv. 34–36).

1.2.1. As to this, there is a clear distinction between *these things* (v. 34) and *that day and hour* (v. 36), which will help to clarify this prophecy. As to *these things*, especially the ruin of the Jewish nation, *"This generation shall not pass away, till all these things be fulfilled* (v. 34); there are people now alive who will see Jerusalem destroyed. Because it might seem strange, he backs it up with a solemn affirmation: *"Verily, I say unto you. You may take my word for it, these things are right at the door."*

1.2.2. However, as to *that day and hour* that will put an end to time, *that knoweth no man* (v. 36). A certain day and hour have been fixed for the coming judgment; it is called *the day of the Lord.* That day and hour are a great secret. *No man knows it*: not the wisest person in their wisdom, not the best person by any divine revelation. No one *knows but my Father only* (v. 36). To those who are watchful, the uncertainty of the time of Christ's coming is *a savour of life unto life*, making them more watchful, but to those who are careless, it is *a savour of death unto death*, making them more careless (2Co 2:16).

2. We must therefore show that we are expecting these events by preparing for them (vv. 37–41). In these verses there is given us an idea of the Day of Judgment that may serve to startle us and wake us up. It will be a day that surprises and a day that separates.

2.1. It will be a day that surprises, as the Flood was to the old world (vv. 37–39). Besides his first coming to save, he has other comings to judge. He says, *For judgment I am come* (Jn 9:39), and he will come for judgment. Now here this applies to:

2.1.1. Temporal judgments, especially to what was now coming quickly on the nation and Jewish people; although they had received fair warning of this judgment, it found them self-confident, crying out, *Peace and safety* (1Th 5:3). Human unbelief will not cancel out God's threats.

2.1.2. The eternal judgment, as the judgment of the great day is called (Heb 6:2). Christ shows here what the attitude of people was in the old world when the Flood came.

2.1.2.1. They were worldly: *they were eating and drinking, marrying and giving in marriage.* All of them except Noah were fully engrossed in the world, paying no attention to the word of God, and this was their destruction. Universal neglect of religious faith is a more dangerous symptom in any people than particular instances here and there of daring irreligious acts. *Eating and drinking* are necessary to preserve human life; *marrying and giving in marriage* are necessary to preserve the human race. Yet those people were unreasonable in their actions, excessive and completely absorbed in pursuing worldly pleasures. They were in their element in these things, as if the sole reason for their existence was to *eat and drink* (Isa 56:12). They were also unreasonable in their actions; they were wholeheartedly set on the world and the flesh. They were eating and drinking when they should have been repenting and praying.

2.1.2.2. They were self-confident and careless: *they knew not* (knew nothing about what would happen), *until the flood came* (v. 39). Knew not! Surely they must have known. Had he not called them to repentance while he remained patient (1Pe 3:19–20)? Their not knowing is joined to their eating, drinking, and marrying, for:

2.1.2.2.1. They were worldly because they were self-confident.

2.1.2.2.2. They were self-confident because they were worldly; they were so preoccupied with things that are seen and present that they had neither the time nor the heart to be concerned with the things that are not seen yet (2Co 4:18; Heb 11:1–3), which they were warned about. *They knew not, until the flood came* (v. 39). The Flood did come, though they refused to foresee it. The evil day is never further away because people put it far away from them (Am 6:3). They did not know it was coming until it was too late to prevent it. Judgments are most terrible and fearful to the self-confident and those who have made fun of them. We have the application of this account of the old world in the words *So shall the coming of the Son of man be.* Self-confidence and worldliness are likely to be the epidemic diseases of the last days. All will be off their guard and taking their ease. Just as the flood took away the sinners of the old world irresistibly and irrecoverably, so will self confident sinners who mocked at Christ and his coming be taken away.

2.2. It will be a day that separates (vv. 40–41): *Then shall two be in the field.*

2.2.1. We may apply it to the success of the Gospel, especially when it was first preached. It divided the world: *some believed the things which were spoken,* and were taken to Christ; *others believed not* (Ac 28:24) and were left to perish in their unbelief. When ruin came on Jerusalem, a distinction was made by divine Providence, according to what had been made before by divine grace, for all the Christians among them were saved from perishing in that calamity. If we are safe when thousands are falling on our right hand and our left (Ps 91:7), if we are not consumed when others are consumed around us, so that we are like brands plucked out of the fire (Zec 3:2), we have good reason to say, *It is of the Lord's mercies* (La 3:22), and it is a great mercy.

2.2.2. We may apply it to the second coming of Jesus Christ and the separation that will be made on that day.

He had said before (v. 31) that the chosen ones will be *gathered together*. Here it is applied to people who will still be alive. Christ will come unlooked for; he will find people busy at their usual occupations, in the field, at the mill. This speaks much encouragement to the Lord's people. Are they lowly and despised in the world, like the servant in the field or the slave at the mill (Ex 11:5)? They will not be forgotten or overlooked on that day. Are they dispersed in distant and unlikely places, where you would not expect to find heirs of glory—in the field, at the mill? The angels will find them there; it will be a very great change from plowing and grinding to going to heaven. Are they weak and unable by themselves to move toward heaven? They will be *taken*. Christ will never lose his hold of those whom he has once caught hold of. Do they mix with others? Are they linked with them in the same homes, communities, or jobs? Let that not discourage any true Christian; God knows how to separate the wheat and chaff on the same floor.

3. Here is a general encouragement to us *to watch and be ready* (v. 42). Notice:

3.1. The duty required: *Watch, and be ready* (vv. 42, 44).

3.1.1. *Watch therefore* (v. 42). It is the great responsibility of all the disciples of Christ to watch, to be awake and to keep awake. Just as a sinful state or way is compared to sleep, a condition of unconsciousness and inactivity, so a gracious state or way is compared to watching and waking. We must watch for our Lord's coming. To watch implies not only to believe that our Lord will come but also to want him to come, to be often thinking about his coming. To watch for Christ's coming is to maintain that gracious attitude that we should be willing to have our Lord find us in when he comes. Watching is supposed to be at night, which is the time for sleeping; while we are in this world, it is night with us, and we must make sure we keep awake.

3.1.2. *Be ye also ready*. We are awake in vain if we do not also get ready. It is not enough to look for such things; we must also give them due *diligence* (2Pe 3:11, 14). There is an inheritance that we hope to enter on, and we must prepare ourselves to share in it (Col 1:12).

3.2. The two reasons to encourage us to be watchful:

3.2.1. The time of our Lord's coming is uncertain. Let us consider, then:

3.2.1.1. That *we know not what hour he will come* (v. 42). We cannot know that we have a long time to live. Nor can we know how little time we have left to live, for it may prove less than we expect.

3.2.1.2. That he *may come at such an hour as we think not* (v. 44). Although we do not know when he will come, we are sure he will come. *In such an hour as you think not*, that is, in such an hour as those who are not ready and not prepared do not expect him in (v. 50); in fact, at such an hour as the most lively expectants perhaps thought least likely.

3.2.1.3. That *the children of this world are so wise in their generation* (Lk 16:8) that when they know about a danger that is approaching, they will keep awake and stand on guard against it. He shows this in a particular example (v. 43). If the master of a house had notice that a thief would come on a certain night and at a certain watch in the night, then even if it was during the midnight watch, when he was sleepiest, he would still be up, listening for every noise in every room, and be ready for the thief. Although we do not know just when our Lord will come, nevertheless, knowing that he will come, we should always keep watch. The Day of the Lord comes unexpect-

edly, *as a thief in the night*. If when Christ comes he finds us asleep and not ready, our house will be broken into, and we will lose all we are worth. *Be ye ready*, as ready at all times as the owner of the house would be at the hour when he expected the thief.

3.2.2. The outcome of our Lord's coming will be very happy and encouraging to those who are found ready, but very sad and fearful to those who are not (v. 45). This is represented by the different state of good and bad servants when their master comes to judge them. Now this parable seems especially intended as a warning to ministers, for the servant spoken of is a steward. Notice what Christ says here:

3.2.2.1. About the good servant. He shows here what he is: *a ruler of the household*; he shows what, being such a *ruler*, he should be: faithful and wise; and he shows what, if he is faithful and wise, he will be: eternally blessed. We have here:

3.2.2.1.1. The minister's position and office. He is one *whom the Lord has made ruler over his household, to give them meat* (food) *in due season*. The church of Christ is his household, or family, and he is its Father and Master. Gospel ministers are appointed rulers in this household; not ruling as kings, but as stewards (managers), or other subordinate officers; not as lords but as guides. They are rulers through Christ; whatever power they have is derived from him. The work of Gospel ministers is to give to Christ's household their food at the proper time, as stewards. Their work is to give; it is not to keep for themselves, but to give to the family what the Master has bought, to give out what Christ has bought. It is to give food; they are not to give law—that is Christ's work—but to communicate to the church those teachings that, if properly digested, will give nourishment to their souls. They must give food that is sound and wholesome. It must be given *in due season* (v. 45), at the proper time, that is, whenever any opportunity offers itself; or time after time, according to the duty of each day.

3.2.2.1.2. Ministers' right fulfillment of their office. The good servant, if advanced, will be a good steward, because:

3.2.2.1.2.1. He is *faithful*; stewards must be so (1Co 4:2). Those who are trusted must be trustworthy, and the greater the trust, the more is expected from them. It is a great and good deposit that is committed to ministers (2Ti 1:14), and they must be faithful with it. Christ regards as his ministers only those who are faithful (1Ti 1:12). A faithful minister of Jesus Christ is one who sincerely wants his master's honor, not his own. He gives proper attention to the lowliest and rebukes the greatest without showing partiality.

3.2.2.1.2.2. He is wise, understanding his duty. In guiding the flock there is a need for not only integrity of heart but also skillfulness of hands. Honesty may be enough for a good servant, but wisdom is necessary for a good steward.

3.2.2.1.2.3. He is active. The ministry is a good work, and those whose office it is always have something to do; they must not indulge in idleness, but be active, working effectively; not talking, but doing.

3.2.2.1.2.4. He is *found doing* when his Master comes, which shows:

3.2.2.1.2.4.1. Faithfulness in his work. At whatever hour his Master comes, he is found busy doing the work of the day. Just as with a good God the end of one mercy means the beginning of another, so with good people, good ministers, the end of one duty ought to mean the beginning of another.

3.2.2.1.2.4.2. Perseverance in his work until the Lord comes.

3.2.2.1.3. The great reward intended for a minister for this (Heb 10:35; 11:26).

3.2.2.1.3.1. He will be taken notice of. This is suggested by the words "Who then is that *faithful and wise servant?*" This implies that there are only a few who fulfill this description. Those who now distinguish themselves in this way by humility, diligence, and sincerity in their work will be both dignified and distinguished by the glory given them by Christ on the great day.

3.2.2.1.3.2. He will be blessed. *Blessed is that servant.* All the dead who die in the Lord are blessed (Rev 14:13). But there is a special blessedness kept safe for those who show themselves to be faithful stewards, who are found *so doing.* Next to the honor of those who die on the battlefield, suffering for Christ as martyrs, is the honor of those who die in the field of service, plowing, sowing, and reaping for Christ.

3.2.2.1.3.3. He will be promoted: *He shall make him ruler over all his goods* (v. 47). Great people, if the stewards of their house behave well in that place, often promote them to be managers of their estates. However, the greatest honor that the kindest master ever did to his most tried and tested servants in this world is nothing compared to that weight of glory (2Co 4:17) that the Lord Jesus will give to his faithful, watchful servants in the world to come.

3.2.2.2. Concerning the *evil servant.* Here we have:

3.2.2.2.1. His description given (vv. 48–49). The vilest creature is an evildoer, the vilest person is an evil Christian, and the vilest of them is an evil minister. Here we see:

3.2.2.2.1.1. The cause of his evil. He *said in his heart, My Lord delays his coming,* and so he begins to think that his lord will never come. Although the delay in Christ's coming is a gracious example of his patience, it is greatly abused by evildoers. Those who walk by their own natural instincts are ready to say about the unseen Jesus, as the people did about Moses when he continued on the mountain, *We wot not* (do not know) *what is become of him,* and so "Let's get *up, make us gods*" (Ex 32:1), making the world a god, the belly a god (Php 3:19), anything but the One who should be.

3.2.2.2.1.2. The details of his evil. He is a slave to his sinful desires and appetites. He is here accused of:

3.2.2.2.1.2.1. Persecution. He begins to *smite* (beat) *his fellow servants.* It is nothing new to see evil servants beating their fellow servants, both individual Christians and faithful ministers. The evil servant beats them either because they rebuke him or because they will not submit to and revere him. When the evil steward beats his fellow servants, he does it in their Master's name, but he will be made to know that he could not insult his Master more greatly.

3.2.2.2.1.2.2. Worldliness and immorality: *He begins to eat and drink with the drunken.*

3.2.2.2.1.2.2.1. He associates with the worst sinners. The drunken are merry and jovial company, and he wants to keep company with them, and so he hardens them in their evil.

3.2.2.2.1.2.2.2. He acts like them: he *eats, and drinks, and is drunken.* This lets in all kinds of sin. Drunkenness is an evil that leads other evils behind it; those who are slaves to that never control themselves in anything else. This, tragically, is the description of an evil minister: he may still have the ordinary gifts of learning and speech more than others; he may, as has been said about some,

preach so well in the pulpit that it is a pity he should ever come out of it, but live so badly out of the pulpit that it is a pity he should ever enter it.

3.2.2.2.2. His fate read out (vv. 50–51). Notice:

3.2.2.2.2.1. The surprise that will accompany his fate: *The Lord of that servant will come* (v. 50). Our putting off the thoughts of Christ's coming will not put off his coming. Whatever fanciful thoughts the evil servant deludes himself with, his Lord will still come. The coming of Christ will be a most fearful surprise to self-confident, careless sinners, especially to evil ministers: *He shall come in a day when he looketh not for him.* See, he has told us ahead of time (v. 25).

3.2.2.2.2.2. The severity of his fate (v. 51). It is not more severe than righteous, but it is a fate that carries with it complete destruction:

3.2.2.2.2.2.1. Death. His Lord will *cut him asunder* (to pieces); "he will cut him off from the land of the living," from the assembly of the righteous (Ps 1:5); he will set him apart to evil. Death cuts off good people as a fine shoot is cut to be grafted onto a better stem, but it cuts off an evildoer as a withered branch is cut off for the fire. Or, as our translation reads it, he *shall cut him asunder,* that is, separate body and soul. The soul and body of a godly person part fairly at death, the one cheerfully lifted up to God, the other left to the dust, but the soul and body of an evildoer at death are cut to pieces, torn apart.

3.2.2.2.2.2.2. Damnation. He *shall appoint him his portion with the hypocrites,* and it will be a wretched inheritance, for *there shall be weeping.*

3.2.2.2.2.2.2.1. There is a place and state where there is nothing but *weeping and gnashing of teeth.* This speaks of the soul's anguish and distress under God's indignation and wrath.

3.2.2.2.2.2.2.2. The divine sentence will appoint this place and state as the inheritance of those who by their own sin were fitted for it. The One who is now the Savior will then be the Judge, and the eternal state of human beings will be as he appoints.

3.2.2.2.2.2.2.3. Hell is the proper place for hypocrites; it is their portion. They own real estate there; other sinners are merely their fellow residents. When Christ wanted to express the most severe punishment in the next world, he called it *the portion of* (a place with the) *hypocrites* (v. 51).

3.2.2.2.2.2.2.4. Evil ministers will have their inheritance in the next world with the worst sinners, namely, hypocrites, and justly so, for they are the worst hypocrites. *Son, remember* (Lk 16:25) will be as cutting a word to ministers if they perish as to any other sinner whatsoever. Let those who preach to others therefore fear, so that they themselves will not make a shipwreck of their faith.

CHAPTER 25

This chapter continues and concludes our Savior's teaching about his second coming and the end of the world. This was his farewell sermon of warning. The application of the teaching of ch. 24 was, "Watch, therefore (24:42), and also be ready (24:44)." Here we have three parables, the scope of which is these—to motivate us all to act with the greatest care and diligence in preparing for Christ's second coming: 1. So that we may be ready to serve him, and this is shown in the parable of the ten virgins (vv. 1–13). 2. So that we may be ready to give an account to him, and this is shown in the parable of the three servants (vv. 14–30). 3. So that we may be ready to receive from him our final sentence, and so that it may be to eternal life, and this is shown in a clear description of the process of the Last Judgment (vv. 31–46).

Verses 1–13

Here:

1. What is generally being illustrated is *the kingdom of heaven*. Some of Christ's parables, such as those in 13:1–52, have shown us what that kingdom is like now, in the reception it meets with. This tells us what it will be like when the mystery of God is accomplished and that kingdom is handed over to the Father.

2. What it is illustrated by is a marriage ceremony. It was sometimes a custom among the Jews in marriages that the bridegroom came late at night, accompanied by his friends, to the house of the bride, where she waited for him with her bridesmaids. When notice was given of the bridegroom's approach, the bridesmaids were to go out with lamps in their hands, to light his way to the house with ceremony and formality, so that the marriage might be celebrated with great happiness.

2.1. The *Bridegroom* is our Lord Jesus Christ. This image shows his special, superlative love toward and his faithful and unbreakable covenant with his bride the church.

2.2. The virgins are those who profess religious faith; they are the members of the church, though they are here represented as *her companions*.

2.3. The task of these virgins was to meet the bridegroom, which was as much their joy as their duty. They came to wait on the bridegroom when he appeared, and in the meantime to wait for him. As Christians, we profess ourselves to be:

2.3.1. Attendants on Christ, to do him honor. Hold high the name and hold forth the praise of the exalted Jesus—this is our task.

2.3.2. Expectants of Christ and of his second coming. The second coming of Christ is the center in which all the lines of our religious faith meet and to which the whole of the divine life constantly refers and leads.

2.4. Their chief concern was to have lights in their hands when they attended the bridegroom, thereby to give him honor and serve him. Christians are children of light (Jn 12:36; Eph 5:8; 1Th 5:5). Notice about these ten virgins:

2.4.1. Their different characters, with proof and evidence of the difference.

2.4.1.1. Their character was that *five were wise, and five foolish* (v. 2). Those who are of the same profession and denomination may still have vastly different characters in the sight of God. Those who are wise in spiritual matters are truly wise, and those who are foolish in spiritual matters are truly foolish. True religion is true wisdom; sin is foolishness.

2.4.1.2. The evidence of this character was in the very thing that they were to be concerned with.

2.4.1.2.1. The foolish virgins were foolish insofar as they *took their lamps* but *took no oil with them* (v. 3). They had just enough oil to make their lamps burn for now, to make a show with, as if they intended to meet the bridegroom, but they took no jar or bottle of oil with them so as to have fresh supplies if the bridegroom took a long time to come. This is what hypocrites are like.

2.4.1.2.1.1. They have no motivation within themselves. They have a lamp of profession in their hands but do not have in their hearts that stock of sound knowledge that is necessary to carry them through the services and trials of the present state.

2.4.1.2.1.2. They have no prospect of what is to come, and they make no provision for it. The foolish virgins took lamps as show for the present but not oil for later use. Hypocrites do not provide for the future, as the ant does (Pr 30:25); they do not *lay up for the time to come* (1Ti 6:19).

2.4.1.2.2. It was the wisdom of the wise virgins that *they took oil in their vessels with their lamps* (v. 4). They had a good motivation within themselves, which would maintain and keep up their profession of religious faith.

2.4.1.2.2.1. The heart is the *vessel*, which we are wise to have supplied, for if good treasure is there, good things will certainly be brought out (12:35), but if that root is rotten, the blossom will be mere dust (Isa 5:24).

2.4.1.2.2.2. Grace is the *oil* that we must have in this *vessel* (jar). Our light must shine before people in good works (5:16), but this cannot be, or cannot be for long, unless there is in the heart a settled and active motivation of faith in Christ and love toward God and our brothers and sisters. Those who took oil in their jars did it thinking that perhaps the bridegroom might not come for a long time. In looking forward it is good to prepare for the worst, to store up supplies for a long siege.

2.4.2. Their common fault during the bridegroom's delay: *They all slumbered and slept* (v. 5).

2.4.2.1. The bridegroom was late in coming; that is, he did not come as soon as they expected. We tend to think that what we look for as certain is very near. To us, Christ seems to be delaying, yet really he is not (Hab 2:3). Although Christ is late according to our timing, nevertheless, he will not arrive later than the proper time.

2.4.2.2. While he was delayed, those who waited for him became careless and forgot what they were waiting for: *They all slumbered and slept*, as if they had stopped looking for him. Those who inferred from the certainty of his coming that it would be soon, and who then found that expectation unfulfilled, tended to infer from the delay that it was uncertain. The wise virgins kept their lamps burning, but they themselves did not keep awake. Too many Christians, when they have professed faith for a long time, become negligent; their graces are not as active, nor their works complete before God, and although all love is not lost, they leave their first love (Rev 2:4).

2.4.3. The surprising summons given them to go out to meet the bridegroom: *At midnight there was a cry made, Behold, the bridegroom cometh* (v. 6).

2.4.3.1. Although Christ may not come for a long time, he will come eventually; although he seems slow, he is sure to come. His friends will find, to their encouragement, that *the vision is for an appointed time* (Hab 2:3). The year of the redeemed is appointed (Isa 63:4), and it will certainly come.

2.4.3.2. Christ's coming will be at our midnight, when we are least looking for him. He often comes to help and encourage his people when the intended good seems to be farthest away. Christ will come when he pleases, to show his sovereignty, and he will not let us know when, to teach us our duty.

2.4.3.3. When Christ comes, we must *go forth* (out) *to meet him*. *Go ye forth to meet him* is a call to those who are habitually prepared, to be actually ready.

2.4.3.4. Both the notice given of Christ's approach and the call to meet him will be awakening; *There was a cry made*. His first coming was not observed at all (Lk 17:20), nor did they say, *Lo, here is Christ*, or, *Lo, he is there* (24:23). *He was in the world, and the world knew him not* (Jn 1:10). But his second coming will be observed by all the world.

2.4.4. The response they all made to this summons: *They all arose, and trimmed their lamps* (v. 7); they trimmed the wicks, supplied the reservoirs with oil, and prepared themselves as quickly as possible to receive the bridegroom.

2.4.4.1. With the wise virgins, this shows an actual preparation for the Bridegroom's coming. Even those who are best prepared for death have work to do to get themselves actually ready, so that they may be *found in peace* (2Pe 3:14), *found doing* (24:46), and not *found naked* (2Co 5:3). It will be a day of searching and inquiry (Job 10:6), and we should think now about how we will then be found.

2.4.4.2. With the foolish virgins, it shows a worthless confidence and wrong thoughts about the goodness of their state and their readiness for another world.

2.4.5. The distress that the foolish virgins were in for lack of oil (vv. 8–9). This shows:

2.4.5.1. The apprehensions that some hypocrites have of the misery of their state, even on this side of death, when God opens their eyes to see their foolishness. Or:

2.4.5.2. The real misery of their state on the other side of death and in the judgment:

2.4.5.2.1. The foolish virgins' lamps went out. The lamps of hypocrites often go out in this life, as when those who have begun in the spirit end in the flesh. The profession withers; its reputation is lost. Hopes fail, and their encouragement is gone. The gains of a hypocritical profession will not follow a person to judgment (7:22–23).

2.4.5.2.2. They lacked oil to supply them when they went out. An external profession, performed convincingly, may take someone a fair distance; it may carry them through this world. But the damp patches of the valley of the shadow of death will extinguish it.

2.4.5.2.3. They would gladly have been indebted to the wise virgins for a supply from their jars: *Give us of your oil.* Those who now hate the strictness of religion will at death and judgment wish for its solid comforts. There are those who do not want to live the life of the righteous but want to die their death. *Give us of your oil*; that is, "Speak a good word for us," according to some, but there is no need for one person to vouch for another on the great day: the Judge knows everyone's true character. Those who will not see their need of grace now, when it would sanctify and rule them, will see their need of grace in the future, when it would have saved them. This request comes too late. The oil cannot be bought when the market is closed; there is no bidding when the auction is finished.

2.4.5.2.4. They were denied a share in their companions' oil. *The wise answered, Not so*; that conclusive denial *Not so* is not in the original, but has been supplied by the translators: these wise virgins would rather give a reason without a positive refusal than, as many do, give a positive refusal without a reason. They were well inclined to help their neighbors in distress, but, "We must not, we cannot, we dare not do it, *lest there be not enough for us and you.* Charity begins at home; *go, and buy for yourselves.*"

2.4.5.2.4.1. Those who want to be saved must have grace of their own. Although we benefit from the fellowship of saints and from their faith and prayers, our own sanctification is indispensably necessary for our own salvation. Everyone must give an account of themselves, for they cannot get another person to gather for them on that day.

2.4.5.2.4.2. Those who have the most grace have none to spare; all we have is little enough for ourselves to appear before God in. The best need to borrow from Christ, but they have none to lend to any of their neighbors. These wise virgins do not rebuke the foolish with their neglect, but give them the best advice the situation will bear: *Go ye rather to them that sell.* When ministers help those who have been mindless of God and their souls throughout their lives but are under conviction on their deathbed, and when they tell them to repent, turn to God, and accept Christ, such ministers act only as these wise virgins did to the foolish, to make the best of a bad situation. They can only tell them what has to be done. It is good advice now, if it is taken in time: *Go to them that sell, and buy for yourselves.*

2.4.6. The coming of the bridegroom and the outcome of these different characters.

2.4.6.1. *While they went out to buy, the bridegroom came* (v. 10). It is highly unlikely that those who put off their great work to the last have time to do it then. Gaining grace is a work that takes time, and it cannot be done in a hurry. While the poor, awakened soul addresses itself to repentance and prayer, in terrible confusion, on a sick bed, it scarcely knows at which end to begin. This is what comes of having oil to buy when we should be buying it, and having grace to gain when we should be using it. *The bridegroom came.* Our Lord Jesus will come to his people as a Bridegroom at the great day; he will come in rich and magnificent garments, with his friends.

2.4.6.2. *They that were ready went in with him to the marriage.* To be eternally glorified is to be in Christ's immediate presence, in the most intimate fellowship with him. Those, and only those, who are made ready for heaven here will go to heaven in the future.

2.4.6.3. *The door was shut*, as is usual when all the company has come. The door was shut:

2.4.6.3.1. To protect those inside. Adam was put into Paradise, but the door was left open, and so he went out again, but when glorified saints are put into the heavenly Paradise, they are shut in.

2.4.6.3.2. To exclude those outside. Now the gate is narrow (7:14), yet it is open, but then it will be shut and bolted, and *a great gulf fixed* (Lk 16:26).

2.4.6.4. The foolish virgins came when it was *too late* (v. 11): *Afterward came also the other virgins.* There are many who will seek admission to heaven when it is too late, like worldly Esau, who *afterward would have inherited* (wanted to inherit) *the blessing* (Heb 12:17). The worthless confidence of hypocrites will take them far in their expectations of happiness: they go all the way to the gates of heaven and demand entrance; yet they are shut out.

2.4.6.5. They were rejected, as Esau was (v. 12): *I know you not.* We all should *seek the Lord while he may be found* (Isa 55:6). Time was, when *Lord, Lord, open to us* would have been effective on the basis of the promise *Knock, and it shall be opened to you* (7:7); but now it comes too late.

2.4.6.6. Here is a practical inference drawn from this parable: *Watch therefore* (v. 13). We had it before (24:42), and here it is repeated as the most necessary warning. Our great duty is to watch. Be awake, and be watchful. A good reason for our watching is that the time of our Lord's coming is uncertain: *we know neither the day nor the hour.*

Verses 14–30

Here is the parable of the talents committed to three servants. This parable implies that we are to go about our work and business, as the former parable implies that we are to be expectant. That parable showed the need for consistent preparation; this parable, the need for actual diligence in our present work and service. The *Master* is Christ. The *servants* are Christians, his own servants, as they are called. We have three things, in general, in this parable:

1. The trust committed to these servants: their master *delivered to them his goods*: having appointed them to work—Christ keeps none of his servants idle—he left them with something to work on.

1.1. Christ's servants have and receive all they have from him, nor do they have anything they can call their own except their sin.

1.2. We receive from Christ in order that we might work for him.

1.3. Whatever we receive is to be used for Christ, although its ownership remains with him. Notice:

1.3.1. On what occasion this trust was committed to these servants: the master was *travelling into a far country. When he ascended on high, he gave gifts unto men* (Eph 4:8). When Christ went to heaven, he was as a man *travelling into a far country.* When he went, he took care to provide his church with everything it needed during his personal absence. This is how Christ, at his ascension, left his goods to his church.

1.3.2. In what proportion this trust was committed. He gave talents. This shows us that Christ's gifts are rich and valuable, the purchases of his blood inestimable, and none of them worthless. He gave to some more, to others less, and to everyone according to their different ability. When divine Providence has made a distinction in human ability, grace dispenses spiritual gifts accordingly, but the ability itself remains as coming from him. Everyone had one talent at least, and that is not a contemptible amount for a poor servant to begin with. A soul of our own is the one talent each one of us has been entrusted with, and it will give us work. It is our human duty that people should render themselves useful to those around them. The person who is useful to others may be reckoned to be giving good to all. Everyone did not have the same, for they did not all have the same abilities and opportunities. Some are cut out for a service of one kind, others another kind, just as the parts of our natural body perform different functions.

2. The differing application and management of this trust (vv. 16–18).

2.1. Two of the servants did well.

2.1.1. They were diligent and faithful: *They went, and traded.* As soon as their master had gone, they immediately got down to business. Those who have so much work to do—as every Christian has—need to set about it quickly and not lose time. *They went, and traded.* A true Christian is a spiritual trader. A trader is one who, having chosen a particular trade and having taken pains to learn it, makes it their business to pursue it, making all other areas of life bow to it and living off its profit. We have no stock of our own to trade with, but trade as agents with our master's goods. The endowments of the mind and the enjoyments of the world must be used for the honor of Christ. The ordinances of the Gospel and our opportunities of being present at them must be used for the purpose for which they were instituted, and fellowship with God must be maintained by them through the exercise of the gifts and graces of the Spirit.

2.1.2. They were successful; they doubled their stock. The hand of those who are diligent makes rich (Pr 10:4) in graces, encouragements, and treasures of good works. There is a great deal to be gained by hard work in religious faith.

2.1.3. The returns were in proportion to what they had received. The greater gifts anyone has, the more effort they should take, as those must do who have a large stock to manage. From those to whom he has given only two

talents, he expects only the use of two. If they give themselves to do good according to the best of their ability and opportunity, they will be accepted, even though they do not do as much good as others.

2.2. The third did badly: *He that had received one talent went and hid his lord's money* (v. 18). The unfaithful servant was the one who had only one talent: no doubt there are many who have five talents and bury them all—have great abilities and great advantages but do no good with them. Christ, however, would suggest to us:

2.2.1. That if the one who had only one talent is held to account for burying that one, then much more will those who have more, or many, and bury them be counted as offenders.

2.2.2. That those who have least to do for God frequently do least with what they have. Some make it an excuse, saying that because they do not have the resources to do what they say they would like to do, they will not do what we are sure they can do, and so they sit back and do nothing. It really emphasizes their laziness that when they have only one talent to look after, they neglect that one. *He digged in the earth, and hid the talent*, for fear that it might be stolen. Money is like manure, as Lord Bacon used to say: good for nothing when amassed in a heap; it must be spread. So it is with spiritual gifts; many have them but make no use of them for the purpose for which they were given. He hid his master's money; if it had been his own, he could have done with it as he pleased. His fellow servants were busy and successful in putting their talents to work, and their zeal should have provoked him to be similarly diligent. If others are active, will we remain idle?

3. The settling of accounts for this use (v. 19).

3.1. The accounting was deferred; it was not *till after a long time* that they were reckoned with.

3.2. Yet the day of account came at last: *The lord of those servants reckoneth with them.* We must all be brought to account, be required to show what good we have gained for our own souls and what good we have done to others. We have here:

3.2.1. The good account of the faithful servants, and notice here:

3.2.1.1. The servants giving account (vv. 20, 22): "*Lord, thou deliveredst to me five talents*"—"And to me two"—"And see, *I have gained five talents*"—"And I, two talents *more.*" This shows us:

3.2.1.1.1. Christ's faithful servants acknowledge with thankfulness his blessings to them: "*Lord, thou deliveredst to me* such and such things." It is good to remember what we have received, so that we may know what is expected from us and may give back to him according to the benefits we have received. We must never look on the use we have made of God's gifts without generally mentioning God's favor to us and the honor he has shown us in entrusting us with his goods. The truth is that the more we do for God, the more indebted we are to him for making use of us.

3.2.1.1.2. They produce what they have gained as evidence of their faithfulness. God's good stewards have something to show for their diligence: *Show me thy faith by thy works*, and as for the one who is good, *let him show it* (Jas 2:18; 3:13). It is also significant that the servant who had only two talents gave his account as cheerfully as the one who had five. This encourages us to expect that on the Day of Judgment we will be judged according to our faithfulness, our sincerity, not our success, according to the uprightness of our hearts, not according to the extent of our opportunities.

3.2.1.2. The master's acceptance and approval of their account (vv. 21, 23):

3.2.1.2.1. He commended them; *Well done, good and faithful servant.* Those who acknowledge and honor God now will soon be acknowledged and honored by him (1Sa 2:30).

3.2.1.2.1.1. Their persons will be accepted: *Thou good and faithful servant.* Christ will give them their just characterization: *good and faithful.*

3.2.1.2.1.2. Their performances will be accepted: *Well done.* Those, and only those, who have done well will be called good servants by Christ. If we do what is good, and do it well, we will have *praise of the same* (Ro 13:3). Some masters are so grumpy that they refuse to commend their servants; it is thought enough not to rebuke. Christ, however, will commend his servants who do well; whether they receive praise from other people or not, praise will surely come from him. If he says, *Well done,* we are happy.

3.2.1.2.2. He rewarded them. All the work and labor of love of Christ's faithful servants will be rewarded (Heb 6:10). This reward is expressed here in two ways:

3.2.1.2.2.1. In one expression that conforms to the parable: *Thou hast been faithful over a few things, I will make thee ruler over many things.* It is usual in the courts of rulers and in the families of leaders to advance to higher offices those who have been faithful in lesser ones. Christ is a master who will advance his servants who acquit themselves well. Christ has honor in store for those who honor him (1Sa 2:30). Here they are beggars; in heaven they will be rulers. Notice the disproportion between the work and the reward; there are only a few things in which the saints are useful to the glory of God, but there are many things in which they will be glorified with God. The responsibilities we receive from God, the work we do for God in this world, is only little — very little — compared with *the joy set before us* (Heb 12:2).

3.2.1.2.2.2. In another expression that slips out of the parable into the thing referred to by it: *Enter thou into the joy of thy Lord.* The state of the blessed is a state of joy. Where the vision and enjoyment of God are — possession of perfect holiness and the company of the blessed — there must be fullness of joy. This joy is the *joy of their Lord,* the joy that he himself has bought and provided for them, the joy of the redeemed, bought with the sorrow of the Redeemer. Christ admits his faithful stewards into his own joy, to be joint heirs with him. Glorified saints will enter into this joy, will have full and complete possession of it, as those who were ready went in to the marriage banquet. Soon they will enter it, and they will be in it to eternity and be completely at home in it.

3.2.2. The bad account of the lazy servant. We have here:

3.2.2.1. His apology for himself (vv. 24–25). Although he had received only one talent, he was called to give account for that one. No one will be called to account for more than they have received, but we must all give account for what we have received. Notice:

3.2.2.1.1. What he trusted in. *"Lo, there thou hast that is thine.* If I have not made it more, as the others have done, I can still say this: I have not made it less." He thought this would be enough to get him, if not commendation, then safety. Those who make a lazy profession of their faith, who are afraid of doing too much for God, still hope to come off as well as those who go to great lengths with their faith. This servant thought that this account would see him through well enough because he could say, *There thou hast that is thine.* Many who are called Chris-

tians build great hopes of reaching heaven on being able to give such an account, as if nothing more were required or could be expected.

3.2.2.1.2. What he confessed. He acknowledged the burying of his talent: *I hid thy talent in the earth.* He spoke as if that were no great fault; in fact, he spoke as if he deserved praise for his prudence in putting it in a safe place and running no risks with it.

3.2.2.1.3. What he offered as his excuse: *I knew that thou were a hard man, and I was afraid.* Good thoughts of God would produce love, and that love would make us diligent and faithful, but harsh thoughts of God produce fear, and that fear makes us lazy and unfaithful. His excuse shows:

3.2.2.1.3.1. The feelings of an enemy: *I knew thee, that thou art a hard man.* In this way, he made his defense his offense. Notice how confidently he spoke: *I knew thee to be so.* How could he have known him to be like that? Does not the whole world know the opposite, that God is far from being a hard master, that *the earth is full of his goodness* (Ps 33:5), that far from reaping where he had not sown, he sows a great deal where he reaps nothing? For he *causes the sun to shine, and his rain to fall, upon the evil and unthankful* (Mt 5:45) and *fills with food and gladness* (Ac 14:17) *the hearts of those who say to the Almighty, Depart from us* (Job 21:14). This suggestion shows the common criticism that evildoers direct to God, as if all the blame of their sin and ruin lay at his door because he denied them his grace. But if we perish, it is our own fault.

3.2.2.1.3.2. The spirit of a slave: *I was afraid.* This wrong attitude toward God arose from his false thoughts about him. Harsh thoughts of God drive us away from him and restrict us in serving him. Those who think that it is impossible to please him, that they serve him in vain (Ps 73:13; Isa 49:4; 65:23; 1Co 15:58), will do nothing effective in their religion.

3.2.2.2. His Lord's answer to this apology. His plea is made to turn against him, and he is struck speechless by it. Here is:

3.2.2.2.1. His conviction (vv. 26–27). He is convicted of two things:

3.2.2.2.1.1. Laziness: *Thou wicked and slothful servant.* Lazy servants are evil servants. Those who are careless in God's work are closely related to those who are busy doing the Devil's work. Omissions are sins and must be judged; laziness makes way for evil. When the house is empty, the evil spirit takes possession (12:43–45). When people sleep, the enemy sows weeds (13:25).

3.2.2.2.1.2. Self-contradiction (vv. 26–27): *Thou knewest that I reap where I sowed not: thou oughtest therefore to have put my money to the exchangers.* This may be taken in three ways:

3.2.2.2.1.2.1. "Suppose I were such a hard taskmaster: should you not therefore have been more diligent and careful to please me, if not out of love, then out of fear?

3.2.2.2.1.2.2. "If you thought I was such a hard taskmaster and for that reason dared not put the money to work yourself, for fear of incurring a loss by it, nevertheless, you could have put it on deposit with the bank, and then at my coming I would have received *my own with usury* (interest)." If we could not find it in our hearts to risk the more difficult and hazardous services, will that justify us in shrinking back from those that are safer and easier? Something is better than nothing; if we fail to show our courage in bold enterprises, we must not fail to testify our goodwill in honest endeavors.

3.2.2.2.1.2.3. "Suppose I did reap *where I sowed not*: that is nothing to you, for I had sowed on you, and the talent was my money that you were entrusted with not merely to keep but to invest."

3.2.2.2.2. His condemnation. The lazy servant was sentenced:

3.2.2.2.2.1. To be deprived of his talent (vv. 28–29): *Take therefore the talent from him.* The meaning of this part of the parable was given in the reason for the sentence: *To every one that hath shall be given* (v. 29). This may be applied:

3.2.2.2.2.1.1. To the blessings of this life — worldly wealth and possessions. These are entrusted to us to be used for the glory of God and the good of those around us. But *from him that hath not*, that is, who has these things as if he did not have them, those things *shall be taken away.*

3.2.2.2.2.1.2. To the means of grace. People who are diligent in making use of the opportunities they have will find that God will enlarge them.

3.2.2.2.2.1.3. To the common gifts of the Spirit. Those who have these and do good with them will have abundance; these gifts grow by being exercised and become brighter by being used; the more we do in religious faith, the more we can do. However, those who do not stir up the gift that is in them find that their gifts rust, decay, and go out like a neglected fire.

3.2.2.2.2.2. To be *cast into outer darkness* (v. 30).

3.2.2.2.2.2.1. His characterization was that he was an *unprofitable servant.* Lazy servants will be judged unprofitable. A lazy servant is a withered member of the body (Jn 15:6), good for nothing. In one sense, we are all *unprofitable servants* (Lk 17:10); we cannot *profit God* (Job 22:2). Yet it is not enough not to do harm; we must also do good; we must produce fruit; and although God is not profited by it, he is nevertheless glorified (Jn 15:8).

3.2.2.2.2.2.2. His punishment was to be *cast into outer darkness.* The state of those who are condemned to hell is:

3.2.2.2.2.2.2.1. Very dismal; it is *outer darkness.* In the dark *no man can work* (Jn 9:4), a fitting punishment for a lazy servant. It is outer darkness, far away from the light of heaven, far away from the feast, far away from the joy of their Lord into which the faithful servants were admitted.

3.2.2.2.2.2.2.2. Very sad; there is weeping and gnashing of teeth. This will be the inheritance of the lazy servant.

Verses 31–46

Here is a description of the process of the Last Judgment on the great day. It is, as it were, the explanation of the foregoing parables. We have here:

1. The placing of the judge on the judgment seat: *When the Son of man shall come* (v. 31). Notice here:

1.1. That there is a judgment to come, in which everyone will be sentenced according to what they have done in this world of testing.

1.2. The administration of the judgment of the great day is committed to the Son of Man (Jn 5:22). Here, as elsewhere, when the Last Judgment is spoken about, Christ is called *the Son of man*, because he is to judge human beings — and, being himself of the same nature, he is completely satisfactory.

1.3. Christ's appearing to judge the world will be splendid and glorious. Christ will come to the judgment seat in real glory, not with mere *great pomp* (Ac 25:23). All the world will then see what the saints now believe — that he is the radiance of his Father's glory (Heb 1:3). His first coming was under a dark cloud of obscurity; his second will be in a bright cloud of glory.

1.4. When Christ comes in his glory to judge the world, he will bring all his holy angels with him (Mk 8:38). This glorious person will have a glorious retinue, myriads of his holy angels.

1.5. He will then sit on the throne of his glory. He is seated with the Father on his throne now, and it is a throne of grace, to which we may boldly come (Heb 4:16). When he comes again, he will sit on the throne of glory, the throne of judgment. In the days of his flesh (Heb 5:7), Christ was brought as a prisoner to the bar, but at his second coming, he will sit as a judge on the bench.

2. The appearing of all people before him: *Before him shall be gathered all nations* (v. 32). The judgment of the great day will be general. Everyone must be summoned to appear before Christ's tribunal: all people, all nations, all those nations that are *made of one blood to live on all the face of the earth* (Ac 17:26).

3. The distinction that will then be made: *He shall separate them one from another*, as the weeds and wheat are separated at harvest (13:25–30), good fish and bad on the shore, the grain and chaff on the threshing floor. Evildoers and godly live together here and are not positively distinguishable from one another, but in that day they will be separated forever. They cannot separate themselves from one another in this world (1Co 5:10), nor can anyone else separate them (13:29), but the Lord knows those who are his (2Ti 2:19), and he can separate them. This is compared to a shepherd's dividing sheep and goats.

3.1. Jesus Christ is the great Shepherd (Heb 13:20); he feeds his flock like a shepherd now (Isa 40:11), and he will soon distinguish between those who are his and those who are not.

3.2. The godly are like sheep — innocent, mild, patient, useful; evildoers are like goats, a more corrupt kind of animal, unsavory and unruly. The sheep and goats feed all day long on the same pasture here but at night will be put into different folds. Having separated them in this way, the Shepherd will set the *sheep on his right hand* and the *goats on his left* (v. 33). Christ puts honor on the godly as we show respect to those we set on our right hand. All divisions and subdivisions will then be abolished except the great distinction of people into saints and sinners, sanctified and unsanctified, which will remain forever.

4. The process of the judgment concerning each of these groups:

4.1. Concerning the godly, on the right hand. Notice here:

4.1.1. The glory given to them: *The king shall say unto them* (v. 34). The One who was the Shepherd — which shows the care and tenderness with which he will make this examination — is the King here. Where the word of this King is, there is power (Ecc 8:4). This sentence contains two things:

4.1.1.1. The acknowledging of the saints to be the blessed of the Lord: *Come, ye blessed of my Father.* He declares them *blessed*, and his saying they are blessed makes them so. They are *blessed of his Father*, scorned and cursed by the world but blessed by God. All our blessings in heavenly matters flow to us from God, as the Father of our Lord Jesus Christ (Eph 1:3). Christ calls the saints *to come*: this "come" is, in effect, "Welcome, ten thousand welcomes, to the blessings of my Father. Come to me to be with me forever; you who followed me carrying the cross now come with me wearing the crown." We now come boldly to the throne of grace (Heb 4:16), but we will then come boldly to the throne of glory.

4.1.1.2. The admission of the saints into the blessedness and kingdom of the Father: *Inherit the kingdom prepared for you.* This shows us:

4.1.1.2.*1.* The happiness they will possess is very rich. It is *a kingdom,* and a kingdom is reckoned to be the most valuable possession on earth and includes the greatest wealth and honor. Those who are beggars here, prisoners, counted as the scum of all things (1Co 4:13), will then inherit a kingdom. It is a kingdom *prepared:* the happiness must be great, for it is the product of divine purposes. It is prepared *for them.* This shows the suitableness of this happiness. It is theirs; it is prepared deliberately for them: "not only for people like you, but for you yourself, you by name." It is prepared *from the foundation* (creation) *of the world.* This happiness was intended for the saints, and they for it, before time began, from all eternity (Eph 1:4).

4.1.1.2.*2.* The entitlement by which they will hold and possess it is very good; they will come and *inherit it.* It is God who makes heirs, heirs of heaven. We come into an inheritance because of our sonship, our adoption: *if children, then heirs* (Ro 8:17). A title received by inheritance is the sweetest and surest title. In this world, saints are like heirs under age, under guardians and trustees until the time appointed by the Father (Gal 4:1–2), and then they will be given full possession of what now through grace they are entitled to: *Come* and inherit it.

4.1.2. The basis of this (vv. 35–36): *For I was an hungered, and ye gave me meat* (food). We cannot reason from this that any good works of ours merit the happiness of heaven. It is clear, however, that Jesus Christ will judge the world by the same rule by which he governs it, and so he will reward those who have been obedient to that law. This happiness will be awarded to obedient believers on the basis of the promise of God bought by Jesus Christ. It is the purchase and promise that give the entitlement; obedience is only the qualification of the heir. The good works mentioned here are such as we commonly think of as works of kindness to the poor, and this teaches us in general that faith working through love is the essence of Christianity (Gal 5:6): *Show me thy faith by thy works* (Jas 2:18). The good works described here imply three things that must be found in all who are saved.

4.1.2.1. Self-denial and contempt for the world, counting the things of the world good only insofar as they enable us to do good with them. Those who do not have the resources to do good must show the same attitude by being contentedly and cheerfully poor.

4.1.2.2. Love for our brothers and sisters, which is the second great commandment (22:39). We must give proof of this love by our readiness to do good and to share with others; good wishes are a mockery without good works (Jas 2:15–16; 1Jn 3:17). Those who are unable to give must show the same attitude in some other way.

4.1.2.3. A faithful regard for Jesus Christ. What is rewarded here is the relieving of the poor for Christ's sake, out of love to him. Those good works that are done in the name of the Lord Jesus will be accepted (Col 3:17). *I was hungry,* and *you gave them meat* (food). This shows us:

4.1.2.3.*1.* It is nothing new for those who enjoy a feast of the fine things of heaven to go about hungry and thirsty and to lack daily food, for those who are at home with God live as strangers in a strange land (Ex 2:22). It is nothing new for those who have put on Christ (Gal 3:27) to lack clothes to keep them warm, for those who have healthy souls to have ill bodies, and for those whom Christ has set free to be in prison.

4.1.2.3.*2.* Works of kindness and generosity, according to our ability to give them, are necessary for salvation.

These must be the proofs of our love and of our professed submission to the Gospel of Christ (2Co 9:13). However, those who show no mercy will be judged without mercy (Jas 2:13). This reason is modestly objected to by the righteous but is explained by the Judge himself.

4.1.2.3.*2.1.* It is questioned by the righteous (vv. 37–39). It is not that they are reluctant to inherit the kingdom or ashamed of their good deeds, but:

4.1.2.3.*2.1.1.* The statements are expressed in the form of a parable and are intended to introduce and impress these great truths: that Christ has great regard for works of kindness and that he is especially pleased with kindnesses done to his people for his sake.

4.1.2.3.*2.1.2.* They show the humble wonder that glorified saints will be filled with when they find such poor and worthless services as theirs so highly celebrated and richly rewarded: *Lord, when saw we thee an hungered, and fed thee?* Gracious souls tend to have a low opinion of their own good deeds, considering them especially unworthy when compared with the glory to be revealed (Ro 8:18). Saints in heaven will wonder what brought them there and why God would consider them and their services. "*When saw we thee an hungered?* We have seen the poor in distress many times, but when did we see you?" Christ is among us more than we think.

4.1.2.3.*2.2.* It is explained by the Judge himself: *Inasmuch as ye have done it to these my brethren,* to the least, to one of the least of them, *ye have done it unto me* (v. 40). When the good works of the saints are produced on that great day, they will all be remembered, and not the least will be overlooked, not even the gift of a cup of cold water (Mt 10:42). And all their works will be interpreted as much to their advantage as possible. Just as Christ makes the best of their weaknesses, so he also makes the most of their services. But what will become of the godly poor, who did not have the resources to feed the hungry and clothe the naked? Must they be excluded? No:

4.1.2.3.*2.2.1.* Christ will acknowledge them, even the least of them, as his brothers and sisters; he will not be ashamed or think it beneath him *to call them brethren* (Heb 2:11). At the height of his glory, he will not disown his poor relatives.

4.1.2.3.*2.2.2.* He will take the kindness done to them as done to him: *Ye have done it unto me.* And in saying this, he will show respect to the poor who were helped as well as to the rich who helped them.

4.2. Concerning the evildoers, on the left hand. We have:

4.2.1. The sentence passed on them (v. 41). He will say to them, *Depart from me, ye cursed.*

4.2.1.1. To be so close to Christ was some satisfaction, even though they were under his frowns, but that will not be allowed: *Depart from me.* In this world they were often called to come to Christ, to come for life and rest, but they turned a deaf ear to his calls. They had said to the Almighty, *Depart from us* (Job 21:14); he will then say to them, *Depart from me.*

4.2.1.2. If they must depart, and depart from Christ, could they not be dismissed with a blessing, with at least one kind and compassionate word? No; *Depart, ye cursed.* Those who refused to come to Christ to inherit a blessing must depart from him under the burden of a curse. The righteous are called "the blessed of my Father" because their blessedness is owing purely to the grace of God and his blessing, but evildoers are called only "ye cursed," because their condemnation comes from themselves.

4.2.1.3. If they must depart, may they not go into some place of comfort, relief, and rest? Will it not be miserable enough for them to mourn their loss? No; they must depart into fire. This fire is the wrath of the eternal God.

4.2.1.4. If they are to fall into a prepared fire, then may it last for only a short time, may they only pass through fire? No; because the streams of mercy and grace are excluded forever, there is nothing to extinguish it.

4.2.1.5. If they must be condemned to such a state of endless misery, may they not have some good company there? No; none except *the devil and his angels.* They served the Devil while they lived, and so they are justly sentenced to be where he is, just as those who served Christ are taken to be with him where he is.

4.2.2. The reason for this assigned sentence.

4.2.2.1. All that they are accused of, the whole basis of the sentence, is omission. "When I was in these distresses, you were so selfish that you did not minister as you might have done to help and relieve me." Omissions are the ruin of thousands of people.

4.2.2.2. It is the omission of works of kindness to the poor and other important matters of the law, such as *judgment, mercy, and faith* (23:23). Uncharitableness to the poor is a sin that brings condemnation. *They shall have judgment without mercy, that have showed no mercy* (Jas 2:13). Sinners will be condemned on the great day for the omission of the good that was in the power of their hands to do. The reason for this sentence is:

4.2.2.2.1. Objected to by the prisoners: *Lord, when saw we thee an hungered, or athirst?* (v. 44). Although condemned sinners have no plea that will support them, they will try in vain to offer excuses. *When saw we thee hungry, or thirsty, or naked?* They are not interested in repeating the full charge, because they are conscious in themselves of their own guilt. The content of their plea shows their former inconsideration of what they might have known but refused to consider until now, when it is too late. They imagined it was only a company of poor, weak, foolish, and contemptible people that they insulted, but those who think this way will be made to know that it was *Jesus whom they persecuted* (Ac 9:5).

4.2.2.2.2. Justified by the Judge. He goes by this rule: *Inasmuch as ye did it not to one of the least of these, ye did it not to me* (v. 45). What is done against the faithful disciples and followers of Christ, even the least of them, he takes as done against himself. *In all their afflictions he is afflicted* (Isa 63:9). Those who distress them are touching the precious apple of his eye (Zec 2:8).

4.3. Here is the execution of both of these sentences (v. 46):

4.3.1. *The wicked shall go away into everlasting punishment.* Sentence will be executed speedily. It cannot be thought either that sinners could change their own natures or that God would give his grace to change them, since in this world the day of grace was misspent.

4.3.2. *The righteous shall go away into life eternal;* that is, they will *inherit the kingdom* (v. 34). Heaven is life; it is all happiness. It is eternal life. There is no death to put an end to life itself, nor old age to put an end to its comfort, nor any sorrow to make it bitter. This is how life and death, good and evil, the blessing and the curse, are set before us, that we may choose our way (Dt 30:15, 19), and our end will be according to that choice.

CHAPTER 26

The narrative of the death and sufferings of Christ is recorded in more detail and more fully by all the four Evangelists than any other part of his life. This chapter begins that memorable account. In this chapter

we have: 1. The introduction to Christ's sufferings: 1.1. The advance notice he gave of it to his disciples (vv. 1–2). 1.2. The rulers' plot against him (vv. 3–5). 1.3. The anointing of his head at a supper in Bethany (vv. 6–13). 1.4. Judas's bargain with the priests to betray him (vv. 14–16). 1.5. Christ's eating the Passover with his disciples (vv. 17–25). 1.6. His instituting the Lord's Supper and his conversation with his disciples afterward (vv. 26–35). 2. His entering into his sufferings, including some of the details: 2.1. His anguish in the garden (vv. 36–46). 2.2. The seizing of him by the officers, with Judas's help (vv. 47–56). 2.3. His trial before the high priest and his condemnation in his court (vv. 57–68). 2.4. Peter's denying him (vv. 69–75).*

Verses 1–5

Here is:

1. The notice Christ gave his disciples that his sufferings would soon come (vv. 1–2). He had often told them about his sufferings at a distance, but now he spoke of them as close: *after two days.* Notice:

1.1. The time when he gave this warning: *when he had finished all these sayings.* Christ's witnesses do not die until they have finished their testimony (Rev 11:7). He had told his disciples to expect sad times, bonds and suffering, and then he told them: *The Son of man is betrayed.* This was to show them that they would fare no worse than he would and that his sufferings would take the sting out of theirs.

1.2. The thing itself that he gave them notice of: *The Son of man is betrayed.* The thing was not only so sure but also so close that it was as good as done. It is good to consider sufferings that are still to come as being present with us.

2. The plot of the chief priests, teachers of the law, and elders of the people against the life of our Lord Jesus (vv. 3–5). Many plans had been made against the life of Christ, but this plot was laid deeper than any up to that time, for the leaders were all engaged in it. Notice:

2.1. The place where they met: *in the palace of the high priest.*

2.2. The plot itself: to *take Jesus by subtlety* (in some sly way), *and kill him*; nothing less than his lifeblood would be enough for them.

2.3. The plan of the plotters: *Not on the feast day, lest there should be an uproar among the people.* They were awed not by the fear of God but by the fear of the people; their only concern was for their own safety, not God's honor.

Verses 6–13

In this passage of the story, we have:

1. The special kindness of a good woman to our Lord Jesus in anointing him (vv. 6–7). It was *in Bethany,* a village near Jerusalem, and *in the house of Simon the leper.* Probably this Simon was one who had been miraculously cleansed from his skin disease by our Lord Jesus and wanted to express his gratitude to him by welcoming him; Christ did not disdain coming to him and eating with him. The woman who did this is thought to have been Mary, the sister of Martha and Lazarus. She had *a box of ointment very precious* (a jar of very expensive perfume), which she *poured upon the head* of Christ as he was reclining at the table. Among us, this would be a strange kind of compliment, but it was counted as the highest form of respect then. Now this act may be looked on:

1.1. As an act of faith in our Lord Jesus, the Christ, the Messiah, the Anointed One.

1.2. As an act of love and respect to him. Some think that this was the woman who *loved much* at first, and *washed Christ's feet with her tears* (Lk 7:38, 47), and that she had not left her first love (Rev 2:4). Where there is true love in the heart toward Jesus Christ, nothing will be thought too good — nor indeed good enough — to give to him.

2. The offense that the disciples took at this. They *had indignation* (vv. 8–9).

2.1. Notice how they expressed their offense at it. They said: *To what purpose is this waste?* Now this shows:

2.1.1. Lack of tenderness toward this good woman, by interpreting her excessive kindness — even supposing it was so — to be wasteful. Kindness and love teach us to give everything the best interpretation that it will bear. It is true that there may be overdoing in well-doing; we must not learn from that to be critical of others, however, but to be cautious ourselves, so that we do not run to extremes, because what we may attribute to a lack of wisdom, God may accept as an example of abundant love. We must not say, "Those people are doing too much in their religious faith," if they are doing more than we do, but rather aim to do as much as they do.

2.1.2. Lack of respect to their Master. It was not right for them to call it waste when they realized that he admitted and accepted it as a sign of his friend's love. We must beware of thinking anything given to the Lord Jesus is a waste, either by others or by ourselves.

2.2. Notice how they excused their offense at it: *This ointment might have been sold for much, and given to the poor.*

3. The rebuke Christ gave to his disciples for the offense they took at this good woman (vv. 10–11): *Why trouble ye* (why are you bothering) *the woman?* It is a great trouble to good people to have their good works criticized and misinterpreted, and it is a thing that Jesus Christ takes exception to. He took the side of the woman here against all his disciples; he embraces the cause of the *offended little ones* just as sincerely (18:10). Notice his reason: *You have the poor always with you.*

3.1. There are some opportunities to do and gain good that are constant and that we must continually seek to make the most of. Those who have a heart to do good never need complain of a lack of opportunity.

3.2. There are other opportunities of doing and gaining good that come more rarely and that should be preferred to the other: "*Me ye have not always,* so make the most of me while you have me with you." Sometimes special works of godly devotion should take the place of ordinary works of kindness.

4. Christ's approval and commendation of the kindness of this good woman. He called it *a good work* (v. 10) and said more in praise of it than could have been imagined, particularly:

4.1. That its meaning was mystical: *She did it for my burial* (v. 12). Some think that she intended this and that the woman better understood Christ's frequent predictions of his death and sufferings than the apostles did. Christ interpreted it so, and he is always willing to make the best of his people's well-meant words and actions.

4.2. That its memory would be honorable: *This shall be told for a memorial* (v. 13). This act of faith and love was so remarkable that the preachers of Christ crucified (1Co 2:2) and the inspired writers of the account of his suffering would have to take notice of this passage. None of all the trumpets of fame sound so loud and so long as the eternal Gospel. Although Christ is the One whom the Gospel is principally intended to honor, the honor of

his saints and servants is not altogether overlooked. The memory of this woman was to be preserved by mentioning her faith and devotion in the preaching of the Gospel, as an example to others (Heb 6:12).

Verses 14–16

Immediately after an example of the greatest kindness done to Christ comes an example of the greatest unkindness. There is such a mixture of good and bad among the followers of Christ.

1. The traitor was Judas Iscariot; he was said to be *one of the twelve*, to emphasize his treachery. When the *number of the disciples was multiplied* (Ac 6:1), it was hardly surprising if there were some among them who caused shame and trouble to them, but when there were only twelve, and one of them was a devil, surely we must never expect any community to be completely pure on this side of heaven. The Twelve were Christ's chosen friends, but one of them betrayed him. No bonds of duty or gratitude will hold those who are demon-possessed (Mk 5:3–4).

2. Here is the offer that Judas made to the chief priests; he *went to them, and said, What will ye give me?* (v. 15). They did not send for him or make the suggestion to him; they could not have thought that one of Christ's own disciples would have been false to him. We have here:

2.1. What Judas promised: "*I will deliver him unto you,* so that you may seize him without noise or danger of an uproar." In their conspiracy against Christ, it was this that they were at a loss about (vv. 4–5). They dared not interfere with him in public and did not know where to find him in private. Here the matter rested, and the difficulty was insuperable until Judas came and offered them his services. Those who give themselves up to be led by the Devil find him readier than they imagine to help them in such a critical situation. Although the rulers, by their power and influence, could have killed him when they had him in their hands, no one but a disciple could betray him. *I will deliver him unto you.* He did not offer himself to be a witness against Christ, though they lacked evidence (v. 59). It is evidence of the innocence of our Lord Jesus that his own disciple, who was false to him, could not accuse him of anything criminal, even though it would have served to justify his treachery.

2.2. What he asked for in consideration of this undertaking: *What will ye give me?* This was the only thing that made Judas betray his Master: he hoped to gain money by it. It was not the hatred of his Master, or any quarrel with him, but purely the love of money. *What will ye give me?* Why, what did he lack? Neither bread to eat nor clothes to put on; neither necessities nor luxuries. This covetous wretch could not be content, but came corruptly cringing to the priests with *What will ye give me?* It is not the lack of money but the love of money that is the root of all evil (1Ti 6:10).

3. Here is the bargain that the chief priests made with him: *they covenanted with him for thirty pieces of silver.* According to the law (Ex 21:32), thirty pieces of silver was the price of a slave — a fair price at which Christ was valued (Zec 11:13)! They *covenanted with him;* "they paid immediately," according to some; they paid him his wages in hand, to keep him sweet and encourage him.

4. Here is the diligence of Judas in fulfilling his end of the bargain: *he sought opportunity to betray him* (v. 16); he was still working out a way to do it effectively. It is extremely evil to seek an opportunity to sin and to cause trouble, for it shows the human heart is fully set on doing evil (Ecc 8:11). He still had time to repent, but now, because of his agreement, the Devil told him he must be

true to his word, even though he was being false to his Master.

Verses 17–25

Here is an account of Christ's celebration of the Passover.

1. The time when Christ ate the Passover was the usual time appointed by God and observed by the Jews: *the first day of the feast of unleavened bread* (v. 17).

2. The place was especially appointed by him and told to the disciples when they asked: *Where wilt thou that we prepare the Passover?* (v. 17).

2.1. They assumed that their Master would eat the Passover, though at that time he was being persecuted by the chief priests, who were seeking to take his life; they knew that he would not be sidetracked from his duty, either by frightenings from outside or by fears within.

2.2. They knew very well that preparation must be made for it and that it was their business. *Where wilt thou that we prepare?* Before we participate in sacred services of worship there must be solemn preparation.

2.3. They knew that he had no house of his own in which he could eat the Passover.

2.4. They would not choose a place without receiving directions from him, and they received such direction from him; he sent them to *such a man* (v. 18), who probably was one of his friends and followers, and the man invited Christ and his disciples to his house.

2.4.1. Tell him, *My time is at hand*; he meant the time of his death. He knew when it was near and was therefore busy. We *know not our time* (Ecc 9:12), and so we must never be off our guard; *our time is always ready* (Jn 7:6), and so we must always be prepared. When our Lord Jesus invited himself to this good man's house, he sent him the news that his time was at hand. Christ's secret is with those who receive him in their hearts (Ps 25:14).

2.4.2. Tell him, *I will keep the Passover at thy house.* This showed his authority as *the Master*; he did not beg for, but commanded, the use of the man's house for this purpose. This is how, when Christ comes into the heart through his Spirit, he demands admission, as the One to whom the heart belongs and who cannot be denied. His people will be willing (Ps 110:3), for he makes them so. I *will keep the Passover with my disciples.* Wherever Christ is welcome, he expects his disciples to be welcome also. When we take God as our God, we take his people as our people.

3. The preparation was made by the disciples: *They did as Jesus had appointed* (v. 19). *They made ready the Passover*; they got the lamb killed and everything set in readiness for such a sacred feast.

4. They ate the Passover according to the Law: *He sat down* (v. 20). His sitting down shows how calm his mind was when he turned to this feast: *He sat down with the twelve*, including Judas. Under the Law, they were to *take a lamb for a household* (Ex 12:3–4). Christ's disciples were his household (Mt 12:48–50). Those to whom God has given responsibility for their families must have their household with them in serving the Lord.

5. Christ taught his disciples at the Passover supper. The usual subject was the rescue of Israel from Egypt (Ex 12:26–27), but the great Passover was now ready to be offered, and the message of that swallowed up all talk of the other (Jer 16:14–15). Here is:

5.1. The general notice Christ gave his disciples of the treachery that would be among them: *One of you shall betray me* (v. 21).

5.1.1. Christ knew it. We do not know what troubles will befall us, nor from where they will come, but Christ

knew all about the troubles that would come to him. It magnifies his love that he knew all the things that would happen to him and yet did not draw back.

5.1.2. When there was need, he told those around him. He had often told them that the Son of Man would be betrayed; he now told them that one of them would do it.

5.2. The disciples' feelings on this occasion (v. 22).

5.2.1. *They were exceedingly sorrowful.* It troubled them very much to hear that their Master would be betrayed. When Peter was first told about it, he said, *Be it far from thee* (16:22). It troubled them more to hear that one of them would do it. Gracious souls grieve for the sins of others, especially of those who have made a greater than usual profession of faith (2Co 11:29). It troubled them most of all that they were left in uncertainty as to which of them it was.

5.2.2. *They began every one of them to say, Lord, is it I?* They were not inclined to suspect Judas. Although he was a thief (Jn 12:6), it seems he had led such a generally acceptable life that none of them even looked at him, much less said, "Lord, is it Judas?" It is possible for a hypocrite to go through the world not only undiscovered but also unsuspected, like counterfeit money so cleverly produced that no one questions its genuineness. They were inclined to suspect themselves: *Lord, is it I?* They feared the worst and therefore asked the One who knows us better than we know ourselves, *Lord, is it I?* We do not know how strongly we may be tempted, nor how far God may leave us to ourselves, and so we have reason *not to be high-minded* (arrogant), *but to fear* (Ro 11:20).

5.3. Further information given them about this matter in vv. 23–24, where Christ told them:

5.3.1. That the traitor was a familiar friend (Ps 41:9): *he that dippeth his hand with me in the dish*, that is, "one of you who are now with me at this table." It is a corrupt ingratitude to dip our hands with Christ in the dish and still betray him.

5.3.2. That this was according to the Scriptures, which would prevent him from taking offense at it. The more we see of the fulfilling of the Scriptures in our troubles, the better we can cope with them.

5.3.3. That it would cost the traitor dearly: *Woe to that man by whom the Son of man is betrayed.* Although God can serve his own purposes through human sins, that does not make the sinner's condition less terrible: *It had been good for that man if he had not been born.*

5.4. The conviction of Judas (v. 25). He asked, *Is it I?* to avoid coming under the suspicion of guilt by his silence. He knew very well that he was the one, but he wanted to appear a stranger to such a plot. Many people whose consciences condemn them work very hard to justify themselves in the sight of other people and to put a brave face on it with, *Lord, is it I?* Christ soon answered this question: *Thou hast said.* It was enough to convict him and—if his heart had not been wretchedly hardened—make him abandon his plot, when he saw that his Master knew of it.

Verses 26–30

Here is the institution of the great Gospel ordinance of the Lord's Supper. Notice:

1. The time when it was instituted—*as they were eating*, toward the end of the Passover meal but before the dishes were removed from the table, because it was to take the place of that ordinance. Christ is to us the Passover sacrifice by which atonement is made: *Christ our Passover is sacrificed for us* (1Co 5:7).

2. The institution itself. A sacrament must be instituted; it has both its existence and significance from its divine

institution. This is why the apostle, in his message about this ordinance, all along calls Jesus Christ *the Lord* (1Co 11:23), because as Lord, he appointed this ordinance.

2.1. The body of Christ is signified and represented by bread. He had said earlier, *I am the bread of life* (Jn 6:35). Just as physical life is supported by bread, so spiritual life is supported and maintained by Christ's mediation.

2.1.1. *He took bread*, "the loaf," some loaf that was available and suitable for the purpose. His taking the bread was a solemn action and was probably done in such a way as to be noticed by those who sat with him.

2.1.2. *He blessed it*, set it apart for this use by prayer and thanksgiving. We do not find any set form of words used by him on this occasion. Christ could command the blessing (Lev 25:21; Dt 28:8; Ps 133:3), and we, in his name, are made bold to seek the blessing.

2.1.3. *He broke it*, which shows:

2.1.3.1. The breaking of Christ's body for us, so that it was made fit for our use: *He was bruised for our iniquities* (Isa 53:5).

2.1.3.2. The breaking of Christ's body for us, just as the father of the family breaks the bread for the children.

2.1.4. *He gave it to his disciples*, as the Master of the family and of this feast. *To the disciples*, because all the disciples of Christ have a right to this ordinance. Those who are his true disciples will enjoy its benefit, but he gave it to the Twelve as he did the multiplied loaves, to be handed by them to all his other followers.

2.1.5. *He said, Take, eat; this is my body* (v. 26). He here told them:

2.1.5.1. What they were to do with it: "*Take, eat*; accept Christ as he is offered to you, receive the atonement, give your approval and agreement to it." Believing on Christ is expressed by *receiving him* (Jn 1:12) and *feeding upon him* (Jn 6:57–58). Food looked at, even if the dish has all the trimmings, will not feed us; the food itself must be eaten, as the teaching of Christ must be taken into our lives.

2.1.5.2. What they would have with it: *This is my body*, not "this bread," but "this eating and drinking." Believing brings us all the effectiveness of Christ's death to our souls. "*This is my body*, spiritually and sacramentally; this signifies and represents my body." He employed sacramental language. This is contrary to the Roman Catholic doctrine of transubstantiation, which says the bread is changed into the substance of Christ's body. We share in the sun by having the form and body of the sun put into our hands, but by receiving its rays on us; in the same way we share in Christ by sharing in his grace and in the blessed fruits of the breaking of his body.

2.2. The blood of Christ is signified and represented by the wine. After thanks had been given, according to the custom of the Jews at the Passover, *he took the cup* (vv. 27–28), the cup of grace, which was ready to be drunk, and made it the sacramental cup. *He gave thanks*, to teach us to look to God not only in every ordinance but also in every part of the ordinance. He gave this cup to the disciples:

2.2.1. With a command: *Drink ye all of it.* This is how he welcomes his guests to his table, making them all drink from his cup.

2.2.2. With an explanation: *For this is my blood of the New Testament.* Up to this time the blood of Christ had been represented by the blood of animals, real blood; but after it was actually shed, it was represented by the blood of grapes, metaphorical blood.

2.2.2.1. *It is my blood of the New Testament.* The covenant God is pleased to make with us, with all its benefits and privileges, is owing to the merits of Christ's death.

2.2.2.2. *It is shed*; it was not shed till the next day, but it was now on the point of being shed; it was as good as done.

2.2.2.3. *It is shed for many.* Christ came to confirm *a covenant with many* (Da 9:27). The blood of the Old Testament was shed for a few, but Jesus Christ is an atoning sacrifice *for the sins of the whole world* (1Jn 2:2).

2.2.2.4. *It is shed for the remission* (forgiveness) *of sins*, that is, to buy remission of sins for us. The new covenant that is obtained and confirmed by the blood of Christ is a charter of pardon and forgiveness, an act of indemnity, in order to bring about a reconciliation between God and human beings. The pardon of sin is the great blessing that is given to all true believers in the Lord's Supper; it is the foundation of all other blessings and the spring of eternal comfort (Heb 9:22–23). A farewell was now said to the fruit of the vine (v. 29). How good it was to be here (Mk 9:5)! There never was such a heaven on earth as at this table, but it was not intended to last forever.

2.2.2.4.1. He took leave of such communion: "*I will not drink henceforth of this fruit of the vine.* Farewell to this fruit of the vine, this Passover cup, this sacramental wine." Dying saints take their leave of sacraments and the other ordinances of fellowship that they enjoy in this world with comfort, because the joy and glory they enter into supersede them all; when the sun rises, we can say farewell to candles.

2.2.2.4.2. He assured them of a happy meeting again in the end. *Until that day when I drink it new with you.* Some understand this to refer to the meetings he had with them after his resurrection. Others understand it to refer to the joys and glories of the future state, which the saints will share in eternal fellowship with the Lord Jesus. Christ himself will share in these pleasures; it was *the joy set before him* (Heb 12:2), which he looked forward to and which all his faithful friends and followers will share with him.

2.2.2.4.3. They closed the ceremony with a hymn: *They sang a hymn* or psalm (v. 30). Singing of psalms is a Gospel ordinance. It is very proper after the Lord's Supper to express our joy in God through Jesus Christ and our grateful acknowledgment of the great love with which God has loved us in him. It is not inopportune, even in times of sorrow and suffering. Our spiritual joy should not be interrupted by outward sufferings.

2.2.2.4.4. When this was done, *they went out into the mount of Olives.* He would not stay in the house to be seized, for in so doing he might cause trouble for the master of the house; he withdrew into the adjacent country, the Mount of Olives. They had the benefit of moonlight for this walk, for the Passover was always at full moon. After we have received the Lord's Supper, it is good for us to withdraw for prayer and meditation and to be alone with God.

Verses 31–35

Here is Christ's conversation with his disciples on the way, in which we have:

1. A prediction of the trial that both he and his disciples were now to go through. He foretold them:

1.1. A sad scattering storm about to rise up (v. 31).

1.1.1. That they would *all be offended* (fall away) *because of Christ that very night*; they would not have the courage to remain faithful to him but would all dishonorably desert him. Causes to stumble will come among the disciples of Christ in times of testing and temptation; they must, simply because the disciples are weak. Even those whose hearts are upright may sometimes be caused to stumble. There are some temptations and enticements whose effects are general: *All you shall be offended.* Although there would be only one traitor, they would all desert Christ. We need to prepare for sudden trials, which may come to a head very quickly. Notice how quickly a storm may rise up! The cross of Christ is the great stumbling block to many people who pass as his disciples.

1.1.2. That in this the Scripture would be fulfilled: *I will smite* (strike) *the Shepherd.* It is quoted from Zec 13:7. Here is the striking of the Shepherd in the sufferings of Christ, and here is the scattering of the sheep when the disciples fled. Each took care to fend for himself, and happy the man who could get furthest from the cross.

1.2. The prospect of an encouraging reunion after the storm: *"After I am risen again, I will go before you* (v. 32). Although you will abandon me, I will not abandon you; although you fall away, I will take care that you will not fall finally. We will meet again in Galilee; *I will go before you,* as the shepherd goes before the sheep." The captain of our salvation knows how to rally his troops (Heb 2:10) when, through cowardice, they have been put into a state of confusion.

2. The presumption of Peter: *Though all men be offended* (fall away), *yet will I never be offended* (fall away) (v. 33). Peter had great confidence and was eager to speak on every occasion. Sometimes it did him good, but at other times it betrayed him, as it did here. Notice:

2.1. How he committed himself with a promise that he would never fall away from Christ. Before the Lord's Supper, Christ led his disciples to examine themselves with, *Lord, is it I?* for that is our duty of preparation for the ordinance. Afterward, he led them to engage themselves to walk with him closely, for that is our subsequent duty.

2.2. How he thought himself better armed against temptation than anyone else: *Though all men shall be offended, yet will not I.* Peter thought it possible that some — in fact, all others — would fall away, but that he would escape better than anyone. We should rather say, "If it is possible that others may fall away, there is a danger that I may do so too."

3. The particular warning Christ gave Peter of what he would do (v. 34). Peter imagined that in the hour of temptation he would come off better than any of them, but Christ told him that he would come off worse. *"Verily, I say unto thee;* take my word for it, I who know you better than you know yourself." He told Peter:

3.1. That Peter would deny him. Peter said, "Although all, yet not I," but he did it sooner than anyone else.

3.2. How quickly he would do it: *this night,* before tomorrow, in fact, *before cock-crowing.* Just as we do not know how close we may be to trouble, so also we do not know how close we may be to sin; if God leaves us to our own devices, we are always in danger.

3.3. How many times he would do it: three times. Christ told him that he would do it again and again, for once our feet begin to slip, it is hard to recover our standing position (Ps 73:2).

4. Peter's repeated assurances of his faithfulness: *Though I should die with thee* (v. 35). He knew what he should do — die with Christ rather than deny him. And he thought he knew what he would do — never be false to his Master, whatever it cost him. But it turned out that he was false. It is easy to talk boldly and carelessly about death when it is far away — "I would rather die than do such a thing" — but it is not done so quickly as it is said when the time comes and death shows itself in its true colors. What Peter said, the rest agreed to: *likewise also said all the disciples.* There is a tendency in good people to be too confident of their own strength and stability. Those who are most confident of themselves are often those who fall first and sin most corruptly. Those who are most self-confident are least safe.

Verses 36–46

In these verses we have the story of his agony in the garden. The clouds had long been gathering and appeared black. But now the storm began in earnest. Notice:

1. The place where he experienced this terrible anguish; it was *in a place called Gethsemane.* The name means "an olive press," like a winepress, where they *trod the olives* (Mic 6:15). There our Lord Jesus began his suffering; there it pleased the Lord to bruise him and crush him (Isa 53:10), so that fresh oil might flow to all believers from him.

2. The company he had with him when he was in this anguish.

2.1. He took all of the Twelve with him to the garden except Judas, who was at this time otherwise employed.

2.2. He took only Peter, James, and John with him into that corner of the garden where he suffered his anguish. He left the rest at some distance, telling them, *Sit ye here, while I go and pray yonder.* Christ went to pray alone, though he had just prayed with his disciples (Jn 17:1). He took these three with him because they had been the witnesses of his glory at his transfiguration (17:1–2), and that would prepare them to witness his agony. Those who have seen Christ's glory by faith are best prepared to suffer with him. If we hope to reign with him, why should we not also expect to suffer with him (2Ti 2:12)?

3. The anguish itself that he was in: *He began to be sorrowful, and very heavy* (troubled). It is called *agony* (Lk 22:44), anguish. He was not in any physical pain or torment; it was from within him; he was troubled within himself (Jn 11:33). The words used here are emphatic; he began "to be sorrowful and in anguish." He had a very heavy burden on his spirits. But what was the cause of all this? What was it that put him into this agony? *Why art thou cast down,* blessed Jesus, and *why disquieted?* (Ps 42:5, 7; 43:5). Certainly it was nothing of despair or distrust of his Father, much less any conflict or struggle with him. Just as the Father loved him because he laid down his life for the sheep (Jn 10:15, 17), so he was completely submissive to his Father's will in it. However:

3.1. He engaged in an encounter with the powers of darkness; he indicates this in Lk 22:53: *"As the Father gave me commandment, so I do.* No matter what, I must struggle with the enemy, so *arise, let us go hence,* let us move quickly to battlefield to face him." When Christ works salvation, he is described as a champion taking to the field (Isa 59:16–18).

3.2. He was now bearing the iniquities that the Father laid on him (Isa 53:6), and by his sorrow and dismay he adapted himself to this part of his work. The sufferings he was entering on were for our sins; they were all made to meet in him, and he knew it. As we are obliged to be sorry for our particular sins, so was he grieved for the sins of us all.

3.3. He had a full and clear view of all the sufferings that lay before him. He foresaw the betrayal of Judas, the unkindness of Peter, and the hatred and corrupt ingratitude of the Jews. Death in its most fearful appearances, death on show, accompanied by all its terror, looked him in the face, and this overwhelmed him with sorrow, especially because it was the wages of our sin (Ro 6:23), which he had undertaken to make atonement for. It is true that the martyrs have suffered for Christ without any such sorrow and anguish; they have faced death cheerfully. But then:

3.3.1. Christ was now denied the supports and comforts they had; that is, he denied them to himself. Their cheerfulness under the cross was owing to God's favor, which for the present was suspended from the Lord Jesus.

3.3.2. His sufferings were of another kind than theirs. On the saints' cross is declared a blessing that enables them to rejoice under it (5:10, 12), but to Christ's cross was attached a curse that overwhelmed him with sorrow under it. His sorrow under the cross was the foundation of their joy under it.

4. His complaint of this anguish. He went to his disciples (v. 38), and:

4.1. He told them his condition: *My soul is exceedingly sorrowful, even unto death.* It gives a little relief to a troubled spirit to have a friend ready to share one's innermost thoughts with and express its sorrows to. Christ here told them:

4.1.1. The basis of his sorrow; it was his soul that was now in anguish. Christ suffered in his soul as well as in his body.

4.1.2. The degree of his sorrow. He was *exceedingly sorrowful.* It was sorrow at its most intense, even to death; it was a killing sorrow, such sorrow as no mortal could bear and live.

4.1.3. Its duration; it would continue to death. He now began to be sorrowful, but never stopped being so until he said, *It is finished* (Jn 19:30). It was prophesied about Christ that he would be *a Man of sorrows* (Isa 53:3).

4.2. He asked them to be with him: *Tarry* (stay) *ye here, and watch with me.* Surely he was devoid of help when he sought the help of those who he knew would be miserable comforters (Job 16:2). It is good to have, and therefore good to seek, the help of our brothers and sisters when we are in anguish at any time.

5. What took place between him and his Father when he was in this anguish: *Being in an agony, he prayed* (Lk 22:44). Prayer is never untimely, but it is especially timely in anguish. Notice:

5.1. The place where he prayed: *He went a little further*; he withdrew from them. He withdrew for prayer; a troubled soul finds most relief when it is alone with God, who understands the broken sighs and groans. Christ has taught us that private prayer must be made in private.

5.2. His position in prayer: *He fell on his face.* His lying face down shows the anguish he was in, the intensity of his sorrow, and his humility in prayer.

5.3. The prayer itself, in which we may notice three things:

5.3.1. The title he gave to God: *O my Father.* Thick though the cloud was, he could still see God as Father through it. It is a pleasing string of the harp to pluck at such a time — *My Father*; where should children turn when anything grieves them but to their father?

5.3.2. The favor he begged: *If it be possible, let this cup pass from me.* He called his sufferings *a cup*; not a river or a sea, but a cup, which we will soon see the bottom of. When we are suffering troubles, we should make the best, the least, of them, not make them worse than they really are. He begged that this cup would *pass from him*, that is, that he would avoid the sufferings now at hand, or at least that they would be shortened. This shows nothing more than that he was really and truly Man, and as a Man he must be averse to pain and suffering. A prayer of faith against an affliction may very well be consistent with the patience of hope in the suffering. But notice the condition: *If it be possible.* If God could be glorified, human beings saved, and the purposes of his undertaking fulfilled without his drinking this bitter cup, he desired to be excused;

otherwise not. What we cannot do while securing our great purpose, we must consider to be in effect impossible; Christ did so.

5.3.3. His complete submission to and acceptance of the will of God: *Nevertheless, not as I will, but as thou wilt.* Although our Lord Jesus had a vivid sense of the extreme bitterness of the sufferings he was to experience, he was still freely willing to submit to them for our redemption and salvation. The reason for Christ's submission to his sufferings was his Father's *will: as thou wilt* (v. 39). He bases his own willingness on the Father's will. He did what he did, and did it with delight, simply because it was the will of God (Ps 40:8). He had often referred to this as what made him go through and what carried him through his whole undertaking. In conformity to this example of Christ, we must drink from the bitter cup that God puts into our hands, even if is very bitter; although nature struggles, grace must submit.

5.4. The repetition of the prayer: *He went away again the second time, and prayed* (v. 42), and again a third time (v. 44). Though we may pray to God to prevent and remove an adversity, our chief purpose must be that he will give us grace to bear it well. We should be more concerned to have our troubles sanctified in them and our hearts assured in them than to have them taken away. *He prayed, saying, Thy will be done.* Prayer is the offering to God not only of our desires but also of our submission. The third time he *said the same words.* It seems from v. 40 that he continued an hour in anguish and prayer, but whatever more he said, it was to this effect, praying that if possible he might be saved from the approaching suffering, yet submitting to God's will in it. What answer did he receive to this prayer, however? Certainly it was not made in vain; the One who heard him *always* (Jn 11:42) did not deny him now. It is true that the cup did not pass from him, but he did receive an answer to his prayer, for *he was strengthened with strength in his soul*, and that was a real answer (Lk 22:43). In answer to his prayer, God provided that he would not fail or be discouraged.

6. What took place between him and his three disciples at this time.

6.1. The fault they were guilty of: that when he was in his anguish, they were so little concerned that they could not even keep awake. He came and *found them asleep* (v. 40). Even more, their love and care for their Master should have made them watch him more closely and vigilantly, but they were so drowsy that they could not keep their eyes open. What would have become of us if Christ had now been as sleepy as his disciples? Christ wanted them to watch with him, as if he expected some help from them, but they slept; surely it was the unkindest thing they could do. His enemies, who watched for him, were awake enough (Mk 14:43), but his disciples, who should have watched with him, were asleep.

6.2. Christ's favor to them, nevertheless. People who are sorrowful often tend to be cross and bad tempered with those around them. Christ in his anguish remained as humble as ever and was not inclined to take offense. When Christ's disciples showed him this disrespect:

6.2.1. *He came to them*, as if he expected to receive some encouragement from them, but instead they added grief to his sorrow (Jer 45:3). However, he still came to them, more concerned for them than they were for themselves; when he was most occupied, he still came to look after them, for those who were given him (Jn 17:2, 6, 9, 24) were on his heart, whether he was living or dying.

6.2.2. He rebuked them gently. He directed his rebuke to Peter, who usually spoke for them; let him now hear for them. *What! could ye not watch with me one hour?* He spoke as one dismayed to see them so foolish. Consider:

6.2.2.1. Who they were. "Could you not watch—you, my disciples and followers? I expected better things from you."

6.2.2.2. Who he was. "Watch with me, your Master, who has long watched over you for good (Jer 24:6; 31:28)." He woke up from his sleep to help them when they were in distress (8:26); could they not keep awake, at least to show their goodwill to him?

6.2.2.3. How little the thing was that he expected from them—only to watch with him. If he had told them to do something great or to die with him, they thought they could have done it, but they could not do what he asked when it was only to watch with him (2Ki 5:13).

6.2.2.4. How short a time it was that he expected them to do it—only *one hour*; they were not to be on guard for a whole night, only one hour.

6.2.3. He gave them good advice: *Watch and pray, that ye enter not into temptation* (v. 41). An hour of temptation was approaching, was very near; the troubles of Christ were temptations to his followers to disbelieve and distrust him, to deny and desert him, and to renounce all relationship with him. There was danger of their entering into temptation, as into a snare or trap. He therefore encouraged them to watch and pray: *Watch with me, and pray with me.* While they were asleep, they lost the benefit of joining in Christ's prayer. "Watch yourselves, and pray yourselves. Pray that you may watch; beg God by his grace to keep you awake, now that there is need."

6.2.4. He kindly excused them: *The spirit indeed is willing, but the flesh is weak.* We do not read about one word they had to say for themselves, but he then had a tender word to say on their behalf; here he set us an example of the love that *covers a multitude of sins* (1Pe 4:8). He considered how they were formed (Ps 103:14) and did not rebuke them, for he remembered that they were only flesh and blood, *and the flesh is weak, though the spirit be willing* (Ps 78:38–39). It is the unhappiness and burden of Christ's disciples that their bodies cannot keep up with their souls in works of godliness and devotion; many times their bodies obscure and obstruct their souls. When the spirit is free and disposed to do what is good, the flesh is averse and indisposed. It is our comfort, however, that our Master graciously considers this, and accepts the willingness of the spirit and pities and pardons the weakness and infirmity of the flesh, for *we are under grace, and not under the law* (Ro 6:14).

6.2.5. Although they continued to be drowsy and sleepy, he did not rebuke them any further for it, for although we stumble daily, he will not always rebuke (Ps 103:9).

6.2.5.1. When he came to them the second time, we do not find that he said anything to them: *he found them asleep again* (v. 43). One would have thought that he had said enough to them to keep them awake, but it is hard to recover from a spirit of slumber (Ro 11:8). *Their eyes were heavy,* which shows that they fought against it as much as they could but were overcome by it, and so their Master looked on them with compassion.

6.2.5.2. When he came the third time, he left them to be frightened by the approaching danger: *Sleep on now, and take your rest* (vv. 45–46). "Sleep now if you dare; I would not disturb you if Judas and his band of men were not going to." Notice here how Christ deals with those who allow themselves to be overcome by self-confidence and will not be woken up out of it. Sometimes he gives them up to its power: *Sleep on now.* Let those who want to

sleep continue to do so. The curse of spiritual slumber is the just punishment of its sin (Ro 11:8; Hos 4:17). Many times he sends some startling judgment. People who will not be frightened by reasons and arguments are better off being frightened by swords and spears than being left to perish in their self-confidence. Let those who refuse to believe be made to feel something. As to the disciples here, their Master gave them notice of the approach of his enemies. *The Son of man is betrayed into the hands of sinners.* And again, *He is at hand that doth betray me.* Christ's sufferings came as no surprise to him. He called them to rise and be going: not, "Rise, and let us flee from the danger," but, "Rise, and let us go to meet it." He suggested to them how foolish they had been in sleeping away the time they should have spent in preparation; now the event found them unprepared and was a terror to them.

Verses 47–56

We are told here how Jesus was seized and taken into custody; this followed immediately after his anguish, *while he yet spake,* for from the beginning to the end of his suffering there was not the slightest interval or breathing space. Notice in the capture of the Lord Jesus:

1. Who the people were who were employed in it. Here was *Judas, one of the twelve,* leading this infamous guard: *he was guide to them that took Jesus* (Ac 1:16); without his help they could not have found him when he had withdrawn to a quiet place. Here was *with him a great multitude* (a large crowd). This crowd was made up partly of a detachment from the guards; these were Gentiles, sinners, as Christ calls them (v. 45). The rest were the servants and officers of the high priest, who were Jews. Those who were in conflict with one another were agreed on their opposition to Christ.

2. How they were armed for their task:

2.1. What weapons they came armed with: they came *with swords and staves* (clubs). They were not regular troops, but a disorderly rabble. But why all this fuss? Because his hour had come, the time when he was to give himself up, all this force was unnecessary. When a butcher goes out into the field to take a lamb to be slaughtered, does he raise a militia and come armed? No; he does not need them, yet all this force was used to seize the Lamb of God (Jn 1:29, 36).

2.2. What authority they came with: *They came from the chief priests and elders of the people.* He was taken by authority of the great Sanhedrin, as one who was to be subject to them. Pilate, the Roman governor, gave them no warrant. No; those who were active in this prosecution, the most spiteful enemies Christ ever had, were men who claimed to be religious, leading the affairs of the church. Pilate rebuked him for it: *Thine own nation and the chief priests delivered thee to me* (Jn 18:35).

3. The way in which it was done and what took place at that time.

3.1. How Judas betrayed him; he did his business effectively, and his resolution in this evil may shame all of us who fail in doing what is good. Notice:

3.1.1. The instructions he gave to the soldiers: (v. 48). He *gave them a sign,* so that they would not make a mistake and seize one of the disciples instead of him. What great care was needed to avoid missing him—*That same is he*—and when they had him in their hands, what great care was needed not to let him go—*Hold him fast.* By his kiss, Judas intended not only to single him out but also to detain him, while the others came on behind to seize him.

3.1.2. The deceptive compliment he gave his Master. He came up close to Jesus; surely when he came to look him in the face, he would be either awed by his majesty or charmed by his beauty. Dared he come into his very sight and presence and betray him? Peter denied Christ, but when *the Lord turned and looked* at him (Lk 22:61), he immediately repented; but Judas came up to his Master and betrayed him. Judas said, *Hail, Master, and kissed him.* A kiss is a sign of allegiance and friendship (Ps 2:12). But Judas, when he broke all the laws of love and duty, desecrated this sacred sign to serve his purpose.

3.1.3. The reception his Master gave him (v. 50). He called him *friend.* He wanted to teach us to avoid bitterness even under the greatest provocation. He called Judas friend because Judas furthered his sufferings, and so befriended him, whereas he called Peter Satan for attempting to prevent them. He asked Judas, "*Wherefore art thou come?* Is it peace, Judas? Explain yourself; if you come as an enemy, what does a kiss mean? If you come as a friend, what do these swords and clubs mean? Why are you present? Why did you not have enough shame to keep out of sight, which you could have done and still have told the officer where I was?"

3.2. How the officers and soldiers seized him: *Then came they, and laid hands on Jesus, and took him*; they took him prisoner. We may well imagine what cruel hands this barbaric crowd laid on Christ, and now they probably handled him more roughly to make up for having been so often disappointed in their previous attempts. They could not have taken him if he had not surrendered himself and been *delivered by the determinate counsel and foreknowledge of God* (Ac 2:23). Our Lord Jesus was taken prisoner because he wanted in all things to be treated like an evildoer being punished for our crimes. He became a prisoner in order to set us free, because he said, *If ye seek me, let these go their way* (Jn 18:8), and those whom he makes free are truly free (Jn 8:36).

3.3. How Peter fought for Christ and was rewarded for his effort by being restrained. It is said here only that the attacker was *one of them that were with Jesus in the garden*, but in Jn 18:10 we are told that it was Peter who distinguished himself on this occasion. Notice:

3.3.1. Peter's rashness: he *drew his sword* (v. 51). They had only two swords among them all (Lk 22:38), and one of them, it seems, fell to Peter's share, and now he thought he would do something great with it. However, all he did was cut off an ear from the high priest's servant; he probably wanted to cut off his head but missed his target. Peter had talked much about what he would do for his Master, declaring that he would *lay down his life for him* (Jn 13:37), and indeed he would have; now he would be true to his word, risking his life in rescuing his Master. He had a great *zeal* for Christ and for his honor and safety, but it was not *according to knowledge* (Ro 10:2) or guided by discretion, because:

3.3.1.1. He did it without authority. Before we draw the sword, we must see not only that our cause is good but also that our call is clear.

3.3.1.2. He indiscreetly exposed himself and his fellow disciples to the rage of the crowd, for what could they do with two swords against a crowd who were armed?

3.3.2. The rebuke that our Lord Jesus gave him: *Put up* (back) *again thy sword into its place* (v. 52). He commanded Peter to put back his sword. He did not rebuke him for what he had done, because it was done out of goodwill, but he stopped the progress of his taking up arms. Christ's mission in coming into the world was to make peace (Eph 2:15). Just as Christ forbade his disciples the sword of justice (20:25–26), so here he forbade the sword of war. Christ told Peter to put back his sword, and he never told him to draw it again. Christ gave Peter three reasons for this rebuke:

3.3.2.1. His drawing the sword would be dangerous for himself and his fellow disciples: *They that take the sword shall perish with the sword*; those who use violence fall by violence, and people quickly increase their own troubles by bullying tactics of self-defense that involve bloodshed. Grotius gives another, and a probable, meaning of this blow, thinking that those who took the sword were not Peter but the officers and soldiers who came with swords *to take Christ*; they will *perish with the sword*. They took the Roman sword to seize Christ with, and not long afterward, they, their place, and their nation were destroyed by the Roman sword.

3.3.2.2. It was unnecessary for him to draw his sword in defense of his Master, who if he pleased could summon to his service all the forces of heaven: "*Thinkest thou that I cannot now pray to my Father, and he shall send* from heaven effective help (v. 53)? Peter, if I wished to set aside this suffering, I could easily do it without your hand or your sword." God does not need us or our service, much less our sins, to bring about his purposes. God can do his work without us. Although Christ was crucified in weakness, it was a voluntary weakness; he submitted to death not because he could not fight against it, but because he would not. Christ here tells us:

3.3.2.2.1. What authority he had with his Father: *I can pray to my Father, and he will send me help.* It is a great encouragement to God's people, when they are surrounded by enemies on every side, that a way is open to them toward heaven; if they can do nothing else, they can still pray to the One who can do everything. Those who are much in prayer at other times have most encouragement in praying when troublesome times come. Christ said not only that God could help him but also that if he insisted on it, he would do it; he could still have been released from the service. But he loved it and therefore refused that way, and so it was only with the cords of his own love that he was bound to the altar (Ge 22:9).

3.3.2.2.2. What authority he had with the heavenly powers: *He shall presently give me more than twelve legions of angels.* There is an *innumerable company of angels* (Heb 12:2), who are all at the disposal of our heavenly Father and delight to do his will (Ps 103:20–21). These angelic hosts were ready to come to help our Lord Jesus in his sufferings, if he had needed or desired it. *He shall give me them*; angels are therefore not to be prayed to; the Lord of the angels is the One to be prayed to (Ps 91:11). He will *presently* (immediately) give them me. Notice how ready his Father was to hear his prayer.

3.3.2.3. It was no time to make any defense at all, nor to offer to avoid the stroke: *For how then shall the scriptures be fulfilled, that thus it must be?* (v. 54). It was written that Christ would be *led as a lamb to the slaughter* (Isa 53:7). In all difficult situations, the word of God must act conclusively against our own objectives, and nothing must be done, nothing attempted, that will militate against the fulfilling of Scripture. We should say, "May God's word and will take place, may his law be exalted and honored, whatever happens to us." This is how Christ restrained Peter when he set himself up as his champion and leader of his bodyguard.

3.4. We are next told how Christ argued the case with those who came to seize him (v. 55); although he did not resist them, he still reasoned with them. It is consistent with Christian patience in suffering for us to calmly plead with our enemies and persecutors. "*Are ye come out*:

3.4.1. "With rage and enmity, *as against a thief*, as if I were a robber or one leading a rebellion, who would deservedly suffer in this way?" If he had been the curse of his country, he could not have been pursued with more intense violence.

3.4.2. "With all this power and force, as against the worst robbers, who challenge the law, defy public justice, and add rebellion to their sin (Job 34:37)?" He further pleaded with them by reminding them how he had behaved toward them up to that time, and they toward him. *I sat daily with you in the temple teaching. Ye laid no hold on me.* How then did this change come about? They were very unreasonable in treating him as they did. He had given them no cause to look on him as a thief, because he had taught in the temple. The gracious words that came from his mouth were not the words of a robber or of one who was demon-possessed. Nor had he given them cause to look on him as one who absconded or fled from justice and therefore must be seized at night. They could have found him every day in the temple; there they could do as they pleased with him, because the chief priests had custody of the temple. To come to him in such a secret way, when he had withdrawn to a private place, was cowardly and dishonorable. The greatest hero may be villainously assassinated in a corner by a person who would tremble to look him in the face in an open field. *But all this was done*, as it follows in v. 56, *that the scriptures of the prophets might be fulfilled.* It is difficult to say whether these are the words of the sacred writer, as a comment on this account, or whether they are the words of Christ himself, given as a reason why he submitted to this treatment.

3.5. How, in the middle of this distress, he was shamefully deserted by his disciples: *They all forsook him, and fled* (v. 56).

3.5.1. This was their sin, and it was a great sin for them, who had left everything to follow him (Mk 10:28), now to leave him for they did not know what. It showed both unkindness and unfaithfulness, for they had solemnly promised to remain faithful to him and never to leave him.

3.5.2. It was a part of Christ's suffering, adding suffering to his bonds (Php 1:16), to be abandoned in this way. They should have stayed with him to minister to him and, if need be, testify for him at his trial. As a sacrifice for sins, Christ was abandoned in this way. The deer that is marked out to be hunted and run down by the gamekeeper's arrow is immediately deserted by the whole herd. As the Savior of souls, Christ stood alone in this way. He bore everything and did everything himself.

Verses 57–68

We have here the trial of our Lord Jesus in the ecclesiastical court, the great Sanhedrin. Notice:

1. The sitting of the court; the teachers of the law and the elders were assembled, even though it was in the dead of night. To satisfy their malice against Christ, to be ready to pounce on the prey, they sat up all night. See:

1.1. Who had gathered: the scribes, the principal teachers of the law; and the elders, the principal rulers of the Jewish church. These were the bitterest enemies of Christ, our great teacher and ruler.

1.2. Where they had gathered: *in the palace* (courtyard) *of Caiaphas the high priest*; they had gathered there two days before to contrive the plot (v. 3), and they now met there again to put it into action. His house should

have been the sanctuary of oppressed innocence, but it had become the throne of sin, and it is hardly surprising when even God's house of prayer had become a den of thieves (21:13).

2. The bringing of the prisoner to the court; those who had *laid hold on Jesus led him away*, hurried him, no doubt, with violence. He was brought to Jerusalem through what was called the sheep gate, for that was the way into the city from the Mount of Olives. It was so called because the sheep appointed for sacrifice were brought that way to the temple. It was very fitting, therefore, that Christ was led that way.

3. The cowardice and fearfulness of Peter (v. 58).

3.1. He followed Christ, but it was *afar off*. There were some sparks of love and concern for his Master within him, and so he followed him, but fear and concern for his own safety were more dominant, and so he followed him at a distance. It looks bad, and bodes worse, when those who are willing to be Christ's disciples are unwilling to be recognized as such. To follow him at a distance meant that he gradually shrank back from him. There is danger in drawing back—even, in fact, in looking back.

3.2. He followed him, but he *went in, and sat with the servants*. He went to a place where there was a good fire and sat with the servants, not to silence their criticism, but to protect himself. It was presumptuous of Peter to put himself in the place of temptation; those who do so thrust themselves out of God's protection.

3.3. He followed him, but it was only to *see the end* (outcome); he was led more by his curiosity than by his conscience; he was there as an idle spectator rather than as a disciple. He went in only to look around him. It is not unlikely that Peter went in expecting Christ to make a miraculous escape out of the hands of his persecutors, so that Peter, having just struck at those who came to seize Christ, could now strike dead those who sat to judge him; this, then, would be the *end* that Peter wanted to see. If so, it was foolish for him to think of seeing any other ending than the one Christ had foretold, that he would be put to death. We should be more concerned to prepare for the end, whatever it may be, than curiously to seek to know what the end will be. The outcome is with God, but the duty is with us.

4. The trial of our Lord Jesus in this court.

4.1. They brought witnesses against him. The crimes properly recognized in their court were false teaching and blasphemy; these, therefore, they tried to prove against him. Notice:

4.1.1. Their search for proof: *They sought false witness against him.* They had seized him, bound him, and abused him, and then they tried to find something to accuse him of, but they could find no cause for his being handed over. They declared that if anyone could give information against the prisoner at the bar, they were ready to receive it, and immediately many people gave false testimony against him (v. 60).

4.1.2. How they fared in this search. In several attempts they were frustrated; they looked for false testimonies among themselves, and others came along to help them, but they found none. However, they eventually met two witnesses who, it seems, agreed in their evidence, and so they listened to these two in the hope that now their point would be won. The witnesses swore that Christ had said, *I am able to destroy the temple of God, and to build it in three days* (v. 61). Now here they wanted to accuse him:

4.1.2.1. As an enemy of the temple, one who sought to destroy it.

4.1.2.2. As one who dealt in sorcery, or some other such unlawful magic arts, by the help of which he could rebuild such a structure in three days. Now, as to this:

4.1.2.2.1. The words were misquoted. He said, *Destroy ye this temple* (Jn 2:19). They came and swore that he said, *I am able to destroy* this temple, as if the intention to destroy it was his. He said, *In three days I will raise it up*, using a Greek word that properly described a living temple: *I will raise it to life.* They came and swore that he said, *I am able* "to build it," using a word that properly described a house temple.

4.1.2.2.2. The words were misunderstood. *He spoke of the temple of his body* (Jn 2:21), but they swore that he was referring to the temple of God, this Holy Place. There have been and still are people who distort the sayings of Christ *to their own destruction* (2Pe 3:16). He was accused so that we might not be condemned, and if at any time we suffer in such a way that we have all kinds of evil not only said but also *sworn against us falsely* (5:11), let us remember that we cannot expect to escape what our Master had to suffer.

4.1.3. Christ's silence in all these accusations, to the dismay of the court (v. 62). The high priest, the judge of the court, rose angrily and said, *"Answerest thou nothing* (Are you not going to answer)? Come, you prisoner at the bar, you have heard what has been sworn against you. What have you now got to say for yourself?" *But Jesus held his peace* (remained silent) (v. 63), not because he lacked something to say or did not know how to express it, but so that the Scripture would be fulfilled: *As the sheep is dumb before the shearer* (Isa 53:7), and before the butcher, *so he opened not his mouth.* He remained silent because *his hour was come*; he would not deny the charge, because he was willing to submit to the sentence. He stood silent in this court so that we would be able to have something to say in God's law court.

4.2. They examined our Lord Jesus himself on oath. They tried, contrary to the law of justice, to make him accuse himself.

4.2.1. Here is the question put to him by the high priest. Notice:

4.2.1.1.The question itself: *whether thou be the Christ, the Son of God?* That is, "whether you claim to be so," for they would by no means consider whether he really was or not. They only wished him to confess that he called himself this, so that they could use that as a basis to accuse him of being a deceiver. What steps will pride and hatred not lead people to take?

4.2.1.2. The solemnity of this suggestion: *I adjure thee by the living God, that thou tell us.* Not that he had any respect for the living God; he took his name in vain. His only desire was to gain a point over our Lord Jesus. If Jesus were to refuse to answer this question when he was put under oath in this way, they would have charged him with contempt of the blessed name of God.

4.2.2. Here is Christ's answer to this question (v. 64), in which:

4.2.2.1. He acknowledged himself to be *the Christ the Son of God. Thou hast said*; that is, "It is as you have said," because in Mark's Gospel it is, *I am* (Mk 14:62). Up to this time, he had rarely professed himself explicitly to be the Christ, the Son of God, but now he would not omit confessing it, because that would have looked like disowning the truth that he came into the world to bear witness to (Jn 18:37), and he would have seemed to be declining his suffering. He confessed himself in this way to give his followers an example and an encouragement to which they should look when they would be called to

confess him before men (10:32), whatever danger they may be in by it.

4.2.2.2. To prove this, he referred himself to his second coming. They probably looked on him with a scornful, disdainful smile when he said, "*I am.*" Jesus' *nevertheless* responded to their scorn: "Although you now see me in this low and miserable state, *nevertheless*, the day is coming when I will appear otherwise." *Hereafter ye shall see the Son of man sitting on the right hand of power, to judge the world*; and his coming soon to judge and destroy the Jewish nation would be a type and pledge of this judgment. Notice:

4.2.2.2.1. Whom they would see: *the Son of man.* Having acknowledged himself to be the Son of God even now in his state of humiliation, he spoke of himself as the Son of Man even in his state of exaltation, for he had these two distinct natures in his one person. He is *Emmanuel*, God with us (1:23).

4.2.2.2.2. In what position they would see him: *sitting on the right hand of power* and *coming in the clouds of heaven.* Although he now stood in the law court, they would soon see him seated on the throne. Although they now judged him, he would then judge them. He had spoken of this day to his disciples a while before to encourage them, and he had told them to *lift up their heads* for joy as they viewed it (Lk 21:27–28). Now he was speaking of it to his enemies, to their terror.

5. His conviction at this trial: *The high priest rent his clothes*, according to the custom of the Jews when they heard or saw anything done or said that they looked on as bringing reproach to God (Isa 36:22; 37:1; Ac 14:14). Notice:

5.1. The crime he was found guilty of: *blasphemy. He hath spoken blasphemy.* When Christ *was made Sin for us* (2Co 5:21), he was condemned as a blasphemer for the truth he told them.

5.2. The evidence on which they found him guilty: "*Ye have heard the blasphemy*; why should we trouble ourselves to examine witnesses any further?" This was how he was *judged out of his own mouth* (Lk 19:22) in their law court, because we were subject to judgment in God's law court. There is no need to bring witnesses against us; our own consciences testify against us in the place of a thousand witnesses.

6. His sentence passed on this conviction (v. 66). Here is:

6.1. Caiaphas's appeal to the bench; *What think ye?* When he had already judged the case in advance, declaring Christ a blasphemer, then, as if he were willing to be advised, he asked for the judgment of his brothers. He knew that by the authority of his position he could influence the rest, and so he declared his judgment and then presumed they all shared his mind.

6.2. Their agreement with him; they said, *He is guilty of death.* Perhaps they did not all agree: certainly Joseph of Arimathea, if he was present, disagreed (Lk 23:51); so did Nicodemus, and probably others with them. However, the majority agreed with him. The judgment was, "*He is guilty of death*; according to the law he deserves to die." Although they did not now have the power to put anyone to death, nevertheless, by such a judgment they made a man an outlaw among his people and so exposed him either to the rage of popular tumult, as Stephen was exposed, or to having an outcry raised against him before the governor, as Christ was.

7. The abuses and indignities done to him after sentence had been passed (vv. 67–68): when he had been found guilty, they *spat in his face.* Because they did not

have the power to put him to death and could not be sure that they would prevail with the governor to be their executioner, they would cause Christ as much trouble as they could, now that they had him in their hands. When they had passed sentence on our Lord Jesus, he was treated as if he were not only *worthy of death* but—that was too good for him—unworthy of the compassion shown to the worst evildoers. Notice how they abused him.

7.1. *They spat in his face.* It is an expression of the greatest possible contempt and indignation, showing that they looked on him as more despicable than the very ground they spat on. Christ submitted to it. This was how confusion was poured onto his face, so that ours would not be filled with eternal shame and contempt (Da 12:2).

7.2. *They buffeted him and smote him with the palms of their hands* (they struck him with their fists and slapped him). This added pain to the shame, for both came in with sin. Here the margin reads, "They smote him with rods," and he submitted to this.

7.3. They challenged him to tell them who struck him, having first blindfolded him: *Prophesy unto us, thou Christ, who is he that smote thee?* They made fun of him, as the Philistines did with Samson; it is painful to those who are in misery to see people around them having fun, but even worse to have them make fun of them and their misery. They had heard him called *a prophet*; they rebuked him for this and pretended to test whether it was true, as if God's omniscience must stoop to the level of children's play.

Verses 69–75

Here is the account of Peter's denying his Master, and it is included as part of Christ's sufferings. Notice how he fell and how he got up again through repentance.

1. Here is his sin. Notice:

1.1. The immediate occasion of Peter's sin. He sat out in the courtyard, among the servants of the high priest. Bad company causes many people to sin, and those who unnecessarily throw themselves into such a position are treading on the ground of the Devil. They can hardly come out of such company without guilt or grief, or both.

1.2. The temptation to sin. He was accused of being a follower of Jesus of Galilee. First one servant girl and then another, and then the rest of the servants, accused him of this: *Thou also wert with Jesus of Galilee* (v. 69); again: *This fellow was with Jesus of Nazareth* (v. 71); and again (v. 73): *Thou also art one of them, for thy speech betrayeth thee* to be a Galilean. Fortunate are those whose speech betrays them to be the disciples of Christ. Notice how scornfully they spoke about Christ—Jesus *of Galilee*, and *of Nazareth*, reproaching him for the country he came from; notice how disdainfully they spoke about Peter—*This fellow*, as if they thought it a disgrace to have such a person in their company.

1.3. The sin itself. When he was accused of being one of Christ's disciples, he denied it. He was ashamed and afraid to acknowledge he was.

1.3.1. On the first mention of it, he said, *I know not what thou sayest.* This was an evasive reply; he claimed he did not understand the charge. It is a fault to pretend that we do not understand or did not think of or remember what we do understand and did think of and remember. This is a form of lying that we are more prone to than any other, because here a person is not easily disproved. It is an even greater fault to be ashamed of Christ, to cover up our knowledge of him; it is, in effect, to deny him.

1.3.2. On the next attack, he flatly and plainly denied it: *I know not the man*; and he backed it up with an oath

(v. 72). This was to say, in effect, "I refuse to acknowledge him." Why, Peter? Can you look on the Prisoner at the bar in the law court and say you do not know him? Have you forgotten all the kind and tender looks you had from him and all the intimate fellowship you had with him? Can you still look him in the face and say that you do not know him?

1.3.3. On the third offensive, *he began to curse and to swear, saying, I know not the man* (v. 74). This was worst of all, for the way of sin is downhill. He cursed and swore:

1.3.3.1. To back up what he said, to give it credibility, yet what he said was false. We have reason to suspect the truth of what is backed up with rash oaths and curses. None but the sayings of the Devil need the proofs of the Devil.

1.3.3.2. By way of evidence that he was not one of Christ's disciples, for this was not their sort of language. This is written to warn us so that we do not sin as Peter did, so that we never, either directly or indirectly, deny Christ the Lord by concealing our knowledge of him and being ashamed of him and his words (Mk 8:38).

1.4. What made this sin even worse. Consider:

1.4.1. Who he was; an apostle, one of the first three. The greater the profession we make of religious faith, the greater our sin is if we walk unworthily in anything (Eph 4:1).

1.4.2. What fair warning his Master had given him of his danger.

1.4.3. How solemnly he had promised to be loyal to Christ in this night of trial; he had said again and again, "*I will never deny thee.*"

1.4.4. How soon he fell into this sin after the Lord's Supper. To receive there such an inestimable pledge of redeeming love and yet on the same night, before morning, to disown his Redeemer was indeed *turning aside quickly* (Ex 32:8).

1.4.5. How comparatively weak the temptation was; it was not the judge or any of the officers of the court who accused him of being a disciple of Jesus, but a foolish servant girl or two.

1.4.6. How many times he repeated it; even after the rooster had crowed once, he continued in the temptation, and a second and third time he fell into this sin. This was how his sin was made worse, but on the other hand there is this to mitigate it: what he said he said *in his haste* (Ps 116:11). He fell into the sin by surprise, not like Judas, with intention; his heart was against it.

2. Here is his repentance for this sin (v. 75). Notice now:

2.1. What brought Peter to repentance.

2.1.1. *The cock crew* (v. 74). The word of Christ can give significance to whatever sign it pleases him to choose. The crowing of a rooster for Peter takes the place of John the Baptist, the voice of one calling to repentance. Conscience should be to us like the crowing of the rooster, to remind us of what we had forgotten. Where there is a living spirit of grace in the soul, though it may for a while be overpowered by temptation, a little hint will serve, when God is active with it, to restore it from the byways of sin. Here the crowing of a rooster was made to be the happy occasion of the conversion of a soul. Christ sometimes comes in mercy *at cockcrowing* (Mk 13:35).

2.1.2. *He remembered the words of the Lord*; it was this that brought him to himself (Lk 15:17), a sense of his ingratitude to Christ. Nothing grieves penitents more than that they have sinned against the grace of the Lord Jesus and the signs of his love.

2.2. How his repentance was expressed: *He went out, and wept bitterly.*

2.2.1. His sorrow was private; he went out of the high priest's courtyard, exasperated with himself that he ever came into it. He went out into the gateway before (v. 71), and if he had gone completely away then, his second and third denials would have been prevented, but then he came in again. Now, however, he went out and did not reenter.

2.2.2. His sorrow was serious: *He wept bitterly.* Sorrow for sin must not be slight, but great and deep. Those who have sinned greatly must weep bitterly, for sooner or later sin will become bitterness. This deep sorrow is necessary to show that there is a real change of mind. Peter, who wept so bitterly for denying Christ, never denied him again, but confessed him often and openly, and in times of danger. True repentance for any sin will be best shown by our abounding in the opposite grace and duty. Some of the old commentators say that as long as Peter lived, he never heard a cock crow without being caused to weep. Those who have experienced true sorrow for sin will grieve at every remembrance of it, yet not so as to hinder, but rather to increase, their joy in God, his mercy, and his grace.

CHAPTER 27

In this chapter there is recorded a very moving story about the suffering and death of our Lord Jesus Christ. However, considering the intention and results of Christ's sufferings, it is good news, and there is nothing we have more reason to glory in than the cross of Christ (Gal 6:14). In this chapter, notice: 1. How he was prosecuted: 1.1. His being handed over to Pilate (vv. 1–2). 1.2. The despair of Judas (vv. 3–10). 1.3. The questioning and trial of Christ before Pilate (vv. 11–14). 1.4. The shouts of the people against him (vv. 15–25). 1.5. The passing of the sentence and the signing of the warrant for his execution (v. 26). 2. How he was executed: 2.1. He was cruelly mocked (vv. 27–30). 2.2. He was led to the place of execution (vv. 31–33). 2.3. There every possible indignity was done to him (vv. 34–44). 2.4. Heaven frowned on him (vv. 45–49). 2.5. Many remarkable things accompanied his death (vv. 50–56). 2.6. He was buried, and a guard was set on his tomb (vv. 57–66).

Verses 1–10

We left Christ in the hands of the chief priests and elders, condemned to die, but they could only show their hostility; the Romans had taken away from the Jews the power of capital punishment. They could put no one to death, and so early in the morning another council was held to consider what was to be done.

1. Christ was handed over to Pilate, so that he would carry out the sentence they had passed on him. Pilate was described by the Roman writers of that time as rough and proud, willful and implacable; the Jews felt great enmity toward him and were weary of his government, but they used him as the tool of their hatred toward Christ.

1.1. They *bound* Jesus. Having found him guilty, they tied his hands behind him, as is usually done with convicted criminals. He was already bound to us with the bonds of love, which he had put on himself; otherwise, he would soon have broken these bonds, as Samson did his (Jdg 16:9, 12).

1.2. *They led him away* in a kind of triumphal procession, *as a lamb to the slaughter.* It was nearly a mile (about two kilometers) from Caiaphas's house to Pilate's. All that way they led him through the streets of Jerusalem,

as they began to fill up with morning traffic, to make him a display to the world.

1.3. They *delivered him to Pontius Pilate*, according to the words Christ had often said, that he would be *delivered to the Gentiles* (Mk 10:33). Christ was to be the Savior of both Jews and Gentiles, and so he was brought under the judgment of both Jews and Gentiles, and both had a hand in his death.

2. The money that they had paid to Judas for betraying Christ was handed back by him to them, and Judas, in despair, hanged himself. The chief priests and elders supported themselves in their prosecution of Christ with the fact that his own disciple betrayed him to them, but now, in the midst of the prosecution, that line failed them, and even he was made a witness of Christ's innocence and a memorial to God's justice, which served:

2.1. To give glory to Christ in his sufferings and provide an example of his victory over Satan, who had entered Judas.

2.2. As a warning to his persecutors, and to leave them more inexcusable. Notice here:

2.2.1. The way in which Judas repented: not like Peter, who repented, believed, and was pardoned. No; he repented, despaired, and was ruined. See:

2.2.1.1. What motivated him to repent. It was *when he saw that he was condemned.*

2.2.1.1.1. Judas probably expected either that Christ would make his escape out of their hands or that he would plead his own cause in such a way that he would be acquitted, and then Christ would have had the honor, the Jews the shame, and Judas the money, and no harm would have been done. He had no reason to expect this, because he had so often heard his Master say that he must be crucified. Those who measure actions by their consequences rather than by divine law will find themselves mistaken in their actions. The way of sin is downhill, and if we cannot easily stop ourselves, then much less can we stop others whom we have set going in the ways of sin.

2.2.1.1.2. He *repented himself*. When he was tempted to betray his Master, the thirty pieces of silver looked very fine and glittering, like the *wine, when it is red, and gives its colour in the cup* (Pr 23:31). However, when the action had been done, and the money paid, the silver had become worthless. Now his conscience flew back in his face: "What have I done? How foolish, how wretched, I am, to have sold my Master for such a trifling sum! It is because of me that he is bound and condemned, spit on, and struck. I little thought it would have come to this when I made that evil bargain." The memory of his Master's goodness to him, which he had dishonorably repaid, steeled his convictions and made them more piercing. Now he found his Master's words had become true: *It were better for that man, that he had never been born* (26:24). Sin will soon change its taste.

2.2.1.2. What the signs of his repentance were.

2.2.1.2.1. He made restitution: *He brought again the thirty pieces of silver to the chief priests*, when they were all together in public. Now the money burned in his conscience, and he was as sick of it as he had ever been fond of it. Ill-gotten gains will never do good to those who obtain them (Jer 13:10; Job 20:15). If he had repented and brought the money back before he had betrayed Christ, he might have done it with some encouragement, but now it was too late; now he could not do it without horror. What is unjustly gained must not be kept, for that is a continuation in the sin by which it was gained. He brought it to those from whom he received it, to let them know that he had changed his mind about the bargain.

2.2.1.2.2. He made confession: *I have sinned, in that I have betrayed innocent blood* (v. 4).

2.2.1.2.2.1. To the honor of Christ, he declared his blood innocent, freely and without being urged to do it, and to the face of those who had declared him guilty.

2.2.1.2.2.2. To his own shame, he confessed that he had sinned in betraying this blood. He did not lay the blame on anyone else, but took it all on himself: "I have sinned in doing it." Judas went some way toward repentance, but it was not to salvation. He confessed, but not to God; he did not go to him and say, *I have sinned, Father, against heaven* (Lk 15:18).

2.2.2. The way in which the chief priests and elders received Judas's penitential confession; they said, *What is that to us? See thou to that* (that is your responsibility). See:

2.2.2.1. How carelessly they spoke about betraying Christ. *What is that to us?* Was it nothing to them that they had thirsted after this blood, hired Judas to betray it, and had now condemned it to be shed unjustly?

2.2.2.2. How carelessly they spoke about Judas's sin; he said, *I have sinned*, and they said, *"What is that to us? What has that got to do with us? How are we concerned in your sin, that you are telling us about it?"* It is foolish for us to think that the sins of others are nothing to us, especially those sins that we are in any way an accessory to or share in. The guilt of sin is not so easily transferred as some people think it is. If there was guilt in the matter, they said, Judas must *look to it*; he must *bear it* (Pr 9:12):

2.2.2.2.1. Because he had betrayed Jesus to them. Yet although his was indeed *the greater sin* (Jn 19:11), it did not therefore follow that they had no sin.

2.2.2.2.2. Because he knew and believed him to be innocent. "If he is innocent, see to it; that is more than we know. We have judged him guilty, and so we may justly pursue him as such." Evil practices are supported by evil principles, especially the principle that sin is sin only to those who think it is so, that it is not harmful to persecute good people if we think they are bad.

2.2.2.3. How carelessly they spoke about the conviction, terror, and remorse that Judas felt. They were glad to use him in the sin, and then they were very fond of him. But now that his sin had shocked him, they showed him great disrespect; they had nothing to say to him, but turned him over to his own terror. Stubborn sinners stand on their guard against convictions, and those who are determined to be impenitent look with disdain on those who repent. When they had brought him into the trap, they not only left him but laughed at him. Sinners under conviction will find their old companions in sin to be miserable comforters (Job 16:2). It is usual for those who love treason to hate the traitor.

2.2.3. The complete despair that Judas was driven to (v. 5).

2.2.3.1. He cast down the pieces of silver in the temple. The chief priests would not accept the money, for fear of taking the whole guilt onto themselves, which they were willing for Judas to bear the load of; Judas would not keep it, for it was too dangerous for him to hold; and so he threw it down in the temple, so that whether they wanted it or not, it would fall into the hands of the chief priests.

2.2.3.2. He went, and hanged himself.

2.2.3.2.1. He retired; he withdrew to some solitary place. Woe to the one who is in despair and alone. If Judas had gone to Christ or to some of the disciples, perhaps he could have gained some relief, bad though his situation was.

2.2.3.2.2. He became his own executioner: *He hanged himself.* Judas had a sight and sense of sin but no apprehension of the mercy of God in Christ. His sin, we may suppose, was not unpardonable, but he concluded, as Cain did, that his sin was greater than could be forgiven (Ge 4:13). Some have said that Judas sinned more in despairing of the mercy of God than in betraying his Master's blood. He threw himself into the fire to avoid the flames, but miserable is the situation of one who must go to hell for relief. Now in this account we see an example of:

2.2.3.2.2.1. The miserable end of those whom Satan enters (Jn 13:27), especially of those who are given up to the love of money.

2.2.3.2.2.2. The wrath of God. Just as in the account of Peter we see the goodness of God and the triumphs of Christ's grace in the conversion of some sinners, so in the account of Judas we see the severity of God.

2.2.3.2.2.3. The terrible effects of despair; it often ends in suicide. Let us think as badly as we can of sin, provided we do not think it unpardonable; let us despair of help in ourselves but not of receiving help from God. Suicide, though prescribed by some pagan moralists, is certainly a remedy worse than the disease, however bad the disease may be.

2.2.4. The disposal of the money that Judas brought back (vv. 6–10). It was spent to buy a field, called *the potter's field.* This field was to be a burial place for foreigners. It looks like an example of the Jews' humanity that they took care in the *burying of strangers,* but it was not an example of their humility that they would bury strangers in a place by themselves. Foreigners, they thought, must keep their distance, alive and dead, and that principle must go down with them to the grave. This buying of the potter's field took place not long afterward, for Peter speaks about it soon after Christ's ascension. However, it is recorded here:

2.2.4.1. To show the hypocrisy of the chief priests and elders. They hesitated to put into the treasury, or *Corban* (Mk 7:11), of the temple the money with which they had hired the traitor. They would not put into it money that was *the price of blood* (blood money) (v. 6). The hire of a traitor, they thought, paralleled the hire of a prostitute, and they thought the price of an evildoer—and they considered Christ such a person—equivalent to the price of a dog, and neither of these was to be *brought into the house of the Lord* (Dt 23:18). This was how they *swallowed a camel* and *strained at a gnat* (23:24). They thought they could atone for what they had done by this public good act of providing a burial place for foreigners, though not at their own expense.

2.2.4.2. To show the favor God intended to show to strangers and sinners of the Gentiles by the blood of Christ. Through the price of his blood, a resting place was provided for them after death. The grave is the potter's field, and Christ by his blood purchased it. He has changed its "property," as a purchaser does, so that now death is ours, the grave is ours, and it is a bed of rest for us.

2.2.4.3. To make the infamy of those who bought and sold the blood of Christ last forever. This field was commonly called *Aceldama,* "the Field of Blood," not by the chief priests—they hoped to bury the memory of their own crime in this burial place—but by the people. They remembered this name for the field forever.

2.2.4.4. To show us how the Scripture was fulfilled: *Then was fulfilled that which was spoken by Jeremiah the prophet* (vv. 9–10). The words quoted are found in the prophecy of Zechariah (Zec 11:12). What is meant here by saying that they were spoken by Jeremiah is a difficult question. The ancient Syriac version reads only, "It was spoken by the prophet," not naming any one prophet. The Jews used to say, "The spirit of Jeremiah was in Zechariah." What was expressed there only figuratively, however, was enacted here in reality. The sum of money is the same—*thirty pieces of silver*. They *weighed* this *for his price*, and this was *cast to the potter in the house of the Lord* (Zec 11:13); and this prophecy was literally fulfilled here in Matthew. The fact that here in Matthew the *price of the one who was priced* was given not for him but for the *potter's field* shows:

2.2.4.4.*1*. The high value that would be put on Christ. He cannot be *valued with the gold of Ophir* (Job 26:16); this indescribable Gift cannot be bought with money.

2.2.4.4.*2*. The low value that was put on him. *The people of the children of Israel* (v. 9) strangely undervalued him, setting his price only high enough to buy a potter's field, a pitiful, sorry plot of ground, not worth looking at. *Cast it to the potter*—as it is written in Zechariah—a contemptible petty trader, not the merchant who deals in valuable things. He gave kings' ransoms for them, but they gave a slave's ransom for him (see Ex 21:32), valuing him merely at the price of a potter's field. But all this was *as the Lord appointed*.

Verses 11–25

We have here an account of what took place in Pilate's law court. We have:

1. The trial Christ had before Pilate.

1.1. He was brought before the court: *Jesus stood before the governor*, as the prisoner before the judge. Because of our sins, we could not stand before God unless Christ had been made sin for us in this way (2Co 5:21). He was brought before the court so that we could be discharged.

1.2. He was accused: *Art thou the king of the Jews?* Now the Jews thought that whoever was the Christ must be the *king of the Jews* and would rescue them from the Roman powers and restore temporal power to them. They accused our Lord Jesus of making himself king of the Jews in opposition to the Roman yoke. They assured the governor that if Jesus claimed to be Christ, he was claiming to be king of the Jews, and so the governor assumed that Jesus was going around corrupting the nation and undermining the government. *Art thou a king?*

1.3. He made his plea: *Jesus said unto him, "Thou sayest.* It is as you say, though not as you mean; I am a king, but not such a king as you suspect me of being."

1.4. Evidence was given against him: he was *accused of* (by) *the chief priests* (v. 12). Pilate found *no fault in him*; whatever was said, nothing was proved, and so what was lacking in substance they made up for in noise and violence.

1.5. The prisoner was silent in response to the prosecutors' accusations: *He answered nothing* because there was no need; nothing was alleged except what carried its own refutation along with it. His hour had come, and he submitted to his Father's will: *Not as I will, but as thou wilt* (26:39). Pilate urged him to make some reply: *Hearest thou not how many things they witness against thee?* (v. 13). Because Pilate had no hatred at all toward him, he wanted him to clear himself and urged him to do it. He wondered at his silence, thinking it not so much contempt of court as contempt of himself. Pilate is not said to have been angry at it, therefore, but to have *marvelled greatly* (been greatly amazed) at it, as something very unusual. He thought it strange that Jesus did not have one word to say for himself.

2. The outrage and violence of the people in urging the governor to crucify Christ. By the power of the mob the chief priests succeeded where they would otherwise have failed. Here are two examples of the outrage of the people:

2.1. Their preferring Barabbas to Jesus, choosing to have him released rather than Jesus.

2.1.1. It seems it had become a custom with the Roman governors, in order to indulge the Jews, to grace the Feast of Passover with the release of a prisoner (v. 15).

2.1.2. The prisoner set up in competition with our Lord Jesus was Barabbas; he is called here a *notable* (notorious) prisoner (v. 16). Treason, murder, and felony are the three most outrageous crimes that are usually punished by the sword of justice, and Barabbas was guilty of all three (Lk 23:19; Jn 18:40). A person whose crimes were so complex was a truly notorious prisoner.

2.1.3. The proposal was made by Pilate the governor: *Whom will ye that I release unto you?* (v. 17). Pilate suggested to them that Jesus should be released, because he was convinced of his innocence and that the prosecution was malicious. However, he did not have the courage to acquit him by his own power, as he should have, but wanted him to be released by the people's choice, and in this way he hoped to satisfy both his own conscience and the people. However, such little tricks and contrivances are the common practice of those who seek more to please people than God (Ac 5:29). *What shall I do then*, said Pilate, *with Jesus, who is called Christ?* He reminded the people that this Jesus whose release he proposed was looked on by some of them as the Messiah. The reason why Pilate sought to have Jesus discharged in this way was that he knew that it was out of *envy that the chief priests had delivered him up* (v. 18). He knew that it was not his guilt but his goodness that offended them. Anyone who heard the hosannas with which Christ had been brought into Jerusalem just a few days earlier would have thought that Pilate could safely have referred this matter to the common people. But events proved otherwise.

2.1.4. While Pilate was pondering the matter, he was confirmed in his unwillingness to condemn Jesus by a message sent to him from his wife as a warning: *Have thou nothing to do with that just man, for I have suffered many things this day in a dream because of him* (v. 19). Notice:

2.1.4.1. The special providence of God in sending this dream to Pilate's wife; it is not likely that she had heard anything before about Christ. Perhaps she was one of the *devout and honourable women* who had some sense of religion. She *suffered many things* in this dream. It seems that it was a terrible dream, and her thoughts *troubled her* (Da 2:1; 4:5).

2.1.4.2. The tenderness and care of Pilate's wife in sending this warning to her husband: *Have nothing to do with that just man*. This was an honorable testimony to our Lord Jesus, that he was a just man. When his friends were afraid to speak up to defend him, God made even those who were strangers and enemies to speak in his favor. When Peter denied him, Judas confessed him; when the chief priests declared him guilty of death, Pilate declared he found no fault in him. When the women who loved him stood at a distance, Pilate's wife, who knew little about him, showed concern for him. It was a fair warning to Pilate: *Have nothing to do with him*. God has many ways of restraining sinners in their sinful pursuits, and it is a great mercy to receive such restraints. It is also our great duty to listen to them. Pilate's wife sent him this warning out of the love she had for him; she did not fear a rebuke from him for meddling with what did not belong to her; rather, no matter how he might respond, she was going to give him the warning. We show true love to our friends and relatives when we do what we can to keep them from sin, and the closer anyone is to us, and the deeper affection we have for them, the more careful we should be not to allow sin to come or lie on them (Lev 19:17). The best friendship is friendship to our soul.

2.1.5. The chief priests and the elders were busy all this time influencing the people in favor of Barabbas (v. 20). They *persuaded the multitude that they should ask Barabbas, and destroy Jesus*. This was how they controlled the crowd, who otherwise were well disposed to Jesus, and if they had not been so much at the beck and call of their priests, they would never have done such a preposterous thing as to prefer Barabbas to Jesus. We must look on these evil priests with indignation. They wretchedly abused this great power put into their hands, and the leaders of the people caused them to go astray. We must look on the deluded people with pity: "*I have compassion on the multitude* (15:32), seeing them rushed so violently into such a great evil."

2.1.6. Being overruled by the priests, they finally made their choice: *Whether of the twain* (which of the two), asked Pilate, *will ye that I release unto you?* (v. 21). He hoped that he would succeed in having Jesus released, but to his great surprise they said *Barabbas*. Were there ever people who claimed to have reason or religion and yet were guilty of such enormous madness, such terrible wickedness? This was what Peter accused them of: *Ye desired a murderer to be granted to you* (Ac 3:14).

2.2. Their earnest insistence on having Jesus crucified (vv. 22–23). Pilate was stunned at their choice of Barabbas, and so he asked them, *What shall I do then with Jesus? They all said, Let him be crucified.* They wanted him to die that death because it was looked on as the most shameful and most notorious, and they hoped to make his followers ashamed to acknowledge him. Their angry hatred made them forget all rules of order and decency, and turned a court of justice into a riotous, tumultuous, and seditious assembly. See what a change was made in the mind of the people in such a short time. When he *rode in triumph* into Jerusalem, the acclamations of praise were so general that one would have thought he had no enemies, but now when he was led in triumph to Pilate's judgment seat, the cries of enmity were so general that one would have thought he had no friends. This changeable world knows such revolutions, and yet our way to heaven lies through them, as did our Master's way, *by honour and dishonour, by evil report and good report*, alternating (2Co 6:8). Now, we are further told, concerning this demand:

2.2.1. How Pilate objected to it: *Why, what evil hath he done?* This was a proper question for a judge to ask before he passed a sentence of death. It is much to the honor of the Lord Jesus that although he suffered as an evildoer, neither his judge nor his prosecutors could find that he had committed any evil. This repeated assertion of his immaculate innocence clearly shows that he died to atone for the sins of others, for if it had not been for our transgressions that he was wounded (Isa 53:5), and for our offenses that he had been delivered up (Ro 4:25), and that he made atonement for them of his own volition, I do not see how these extraordinary sufferings of a person who had never thought, said, or done anything wrong could be reconciled with the justice of the Providence that governs the world and that at least permitted this to be done in it.

2.2.2. How they insisted on it: *They cried out the more, Let him be crucified.* They did not even set about to show

any evil he had committed; right or wrong, he must be crucified. This unjust judge was worn out by their insistence and had to pass an unjust sentence, just as the judge in the parable had to grant justice (Lk 18:4–5).

3. The transferring of the guilt of Christ's blood to the people and priests.

3.1. Pilate tried to transfer it from himself (v. 24).

3.1.1. He saw that it was useless to struggle. What he said:

3.1.1.1. Would do no good; he could not get them to change their minds. He could not convince them how unjust and unreasonable it was for him to condemn a man whom he believed innocent and whom they could not prove guilty. Notice how strong the flow of lust and rage sometimes is; neither authority nor reason will be effective in restraining it. In fact:

3.1.1.2. It was more likely to do harm: he saw that rather a *tumult was made* (an uproar was starting). This rude and cruel people turned to extreme language and began to threaten Pilate with what they would do if he did not satisfy them. This wild, tumultuous attitude of the Jews contributed more than anything to the destruction of that nation not long after, because their frequent insurrections provoked the Romans to destroy them and their inveterate quarrels among themselves made them an easy target to the common enemy. Their sin was their ruin. The priests were apprehensive that their attempts to seize Christ would cause uproar, especially *on the feast day* (26:5), but it turned out that Pilate's attempt to save him caused an uproar, and on the feast day; the feelings of the crowd are so uncertain.

3.1.2. This put him in a great dilemma: whether to preserve the peace of his own mind or the peace of the city. If he had steadily and resolutely remained faithful to the sacred laws of justice, he would not have been in any such perplexity. A man in whom no fault was found should not be crucified for any reason whatever, nor must injustice be done to satisfy anyone or any group of people in the world.

3.1.3. Pilate thought he had found a way to pacify both the people and his own conscience: by doing what they asked but at the same time disowning it. He endeavored to clear himself from the guilt:

3.1.3.1. By a sign. He *took water, and washed his hands before the multitude*. It was not as if he thought he would be purifying himself from any guilt contracted before God, but it was a sign to acquit himself before the people. He borrowed the ceremony from the law that appointed it to be used to clear the country of the guilt of an undiscovered murder (Dt 21:6–7), and he used it more to move the people with the conviction he was under of the prisoner's innocence.

3.1.3.2. By a saying. Here:

3.1.3.2.1. He cleared himself: *I am innocent of the blood of this just person.* What nonsense this was, to condemn Jesus but at the same time declare himself innocent of shedding his blood! To protest a deed and yet do it is only to declare that one is sinning against one's conscience.

3.1.3.2.2. He cast responsibility on the priests and people: "*See ye to it*; you are to answer for it to God and the world." Sin is a horror that no one is willing to own up to. Many people deceive themselves by thinking that they will bear no blame if they can only find someone else to pin the blame on, but it is not so easy to transfer the guilt of sin as many think. The priests threw the responsibility onto Judas: *See thou to it*; and now Pilate threw the responsibility onto them.

3.2. The priests and people agreed to take the guilt on themselves; they all said, *His blood be on us, and on our children.* They agreed to it in the heat of their rage, rather than lose the victim they had in their hands, crying out, *His blood be upon us.*

3.2.1. By this they intended to indemnify Pilate. However, those who are themselves bankrupts and beggars will never be accepted as security for others. No one could bear the sin of others except the One who had no sin of his own to answer for. It is a bold undertaking, and too great for any creature (Ps 49:7–8), to bear the responsibility for a sinner to almighty God.

3.2.2. In reality, they invoked wrath and vengeance on themselves and their descendants. Christ had just told them that *all the righteous blood shed upon the earth* (23:35) would come on them, from that of righteous Abel, but as if that were too little, they here invoked on themselves the guilt of the blood that was more precious than all the rest, the guilt that would lie heavier on them. Notice:

3.2.2.1. How cruel they were in their invocation. They invoked the punishment of this sin not only on themselves but also on *their children.* It was madness to pull it down on themselves, but it was the height of cruelty to pass it on to their descendants. Notice what enemies evildoers are to their own children and families.

3.2.2.2. How righteous God was in his retribution according to this invocation. From the time they invoked this blood on them, they were followed by one judgment after another. On some of them, however, and on some of their families this blood came not to condemn them but to save them. When they repented and believed, divine mercy cut off the inheritance of this curse, and then *the promise* was again fulfilled *to them, and to their children* (Ac 2:39). God is better to us and our families than we ourselves are.

Verses 26–32

Here is:

1. The sentence passed, and the warrant signed for Christ's execution. This was done immediately, the same hour.

1.1. Barabbas was released, to show that Christ was condemned so that sinners, even the chief of sinners (1Ti 1:15), could be released. He was *delivered up* so that we could be delivered. In this unparalleled instance of divine grace, the upright is a ransom for the transgressors (Isa 53:12), the just for the unjust (1Pe 3:18).

1.2. Jesus was *scourged*; this was an ignominious and cruel punishment, especially as it was inflicted by the Romans, who did not keep to the moderation of the Jewish law, which forbade scourging more than forty lashes.

1.3. He was then *delivered to be crucified*, a kind of death used only among the Romans; the way in which death by crucifixion was carried out was such that it seemed to be the result of a combination of cruelty and wit, to make death most terrible and miserable. A cross was set up in the ground, to which the hands and feet were nailed, and on the nails the weight of the body hung until it died of pain. It was a bloody, painful, shameful, and cursed death (Dt 21:23; Gal 3:13). It was such a miserable death that merciful rulers appointed those who were condemned to it by the law first to be strangled, and then nailed to the cross.

2. The barbaric way in which the soldiers treated him. When he was condemned, he should have had some time allowed him to prepare for death. A law was made by the Roman senate in Tiberius's time, perhaps prompted by a complaint concerning this and similarly hurried actions,

that the execution of criminals must be delayed by at least ten days after sentence. However, our Lord Jesus was scarcely allowed that many minutes; the storm continued without intermission. When he was delivered to be crucified, that was enough; those who kill the body admit there is nothing more that they can do (10:28), but Christ's enemies would do more if they could. Pilate's guards set themselves to abuse Jesus; perhaps it was not so much out of spite to him as to make sport for themselves that they abused him as they did. They understood that he claimed title to a crown; taunting him with that entertained them somewhat and gave them an opportunity for merriment. Notice:

2.1. Where this was done—in the *common hall* (Praetorium). The governor's house, which should have been a shelter to the wronged and abused, was made a stage for this barbarity. Those in authority will be held responsible not only for the evil they do or order but also for the evil they do not restrain.

2.2. Who were concerned in it. They gathered the *whole band*, the soldiers who were to be present at the execution.

2.3. What particular humiliation was done to him.

2.3.1. They *stripped him* (v. 28). The shame of nakedness came in with sin (Ge 3:7).

2.3.2. They *put on him a scarlet robe*, some old red cloak such as Roman soldiers wore, in imitation of the *scarlet robes* that kings and emperors wore, so rebuking him for being called a king. They covered him with this sham of majesty while he was still in his own clothes, to put him on display before the spectators, making him look all the more ridiculous.

2.3.3. They *platted* (twisted) *a crown of thorns, and put it upon his head* (v. 29). This was to continue the spirit of making him a mock king; yet if they had intended it only as an insult, they might have twisted a crown of straw, or rushes, but they wanted it to be painful for him. Thorns represent afflictions (2Ch 33:11). Christ put these onto a crown; he changed their nature to those who are his, giving them reason to *glory in tribulation* (Ro 5:3) and making it achieve for them an eternal weight of glory (2Co 4:17). Christ was crowned with thorns, to show that *his kingdom was not of this world* (Jn 18:36) and that its glory was not worldly glory, but was accompanied here by *bonds* and *afflictions* (Php 1:16), while its glory was, and is, still *to be revealed* (Ro 8:18).

2.3.4. They *put a reed in his right hand*; this was intended to be a mock scepter, another of the insignias of the majesty that they jeered at him with. It was as if this were a scepter that was good enough for such a King; just as the scepter was weak and wavering, withering and worthless, so, they thought, was the kingdom. They were completely mistaken, however, for his throne is *for ever and ever* (Ps 45:6).

2.3.5. They *bowed the knee before him, and mocked him, saying, Hail, King of the Jews!* Having made him a sham king, they made fun of giving him homage, so ridiculing his claims to sovereignty.

2.3.6. They *spit upon him*; this was how he had been abused in the high priest's hall (26:67). In giving homage, the subject kissed the sovereign as a sign of allegiance; for this reason Samuel kissed Saul, and we are told to *kiss the Son* (Ps 2:12); but they, in this mock homage, instead of kissing him, spat in his face. It is strange that the people should act so treacherously, and that the Son of God should ever have to suffer such disgrace and shame.

2.3.7. They *took the reed, and smote him on the head.* What they had made the mock ensign of his royalty they now made real instruments of their cruelty and his pain. They struck him probably on the *crown of thorns*, and so struck these into his head, to wound it more deeply, which made greater fun for them, to whom his pain brought the greatest pleasure. He experienced all this misery and shame so that he could buy eternal life, joy, and glory for us.

3. The taking of him to the place of execution. After they had mocked and abused him for as long as they thought fit, they *took the robe off from him*. This signified their divesting him of all the royal authority they had invested him with by putting it on him. They put his own clothes on him, because those were to become the share of the soldiers who were employed in the execution. They took off the robe, but no mention is made of their taking off the *crown of thorns*, from which it is commonly supposed, though not certain, that he was crucified with that on his head.

3.1. They *led him away* to be *crucified*. He was led *as a lamb to the slaughter* (Isa 53:7), as a sacrifice to the altar. We may well imagine how they moved him on hurriedly, dragging him along as quickly as possible. They led him away *out of the city*, for Christ *suffered without* (outside) *the gate* (Heb 13:12).

3.2. They compelled Simon of Cyrene *to bear his cross* (v. 32). It seems that at first Christ carried the cross himself. This was intended, like other things, to give him both pain and shame. But after a while they took the cross off him, either:

3.2.1. Out of compassion for him, because they saw it was too great a load for him. We can hardly think that they had any consideration of that. Or:

3.2.2. Because he could not go on as fast as they wanted him to with the cross on his back. Or:

3.2.3. From fear that he might faint under the load of his cross and die, preventing what their hatred further intended to do against him. Taking the cross from him, they *compelled* one Simon of Cyrene to carry it. It brought disgrace, and no one would do it except by compulsion. Some think that this Simon was a disciple of Christ, or at least one of his well-wishers, and that they knew it and put this on him for that reason. All who want to show themselves to be true disciples must follow Christ, *bearing his cross* (16:24).

Verses 33–49

We have here the crucifixion of our Lord Jesus. Notice:

1. The place where our Lord Jesus was put to death.

1.1. They came to a place called *Golgotha*, near Jerusalem, probably the common place of execution. In the same place where criminals were sacrificed to the justice of the government, our Lord Jesus was sacrificed to the justice of God. Some think that it was called *the place of a skull* because it was the common charnel house, where the bones and skulls of the dead were put together out of the way, so that people would not touch them and become defiled. Here were the trophies of death's victory over many people, and when by dying Christ destroyed death, he added to his victory the honor that he triumphed over death on death's own rubbish heap.

1.2. They *crucified* him there (v. 35), nailed his hands and feet to the cross and then set it up with him hanging on it, because this was how the Romans enacted crucifixion. Let our hearts be moved by the intense pain that our blessed Savior now endured, and let us look on him who was pierced in this way and mourn (Zec 12:10). Was there ever sorrow like his sorrow (La 1:12)? And when we see

how he died, let us consider with wonder with *what manner of love* he *loved us* (1Jn 3:1).

2. The barbaric and abusive way they treated him. As if death, so great a death (2Co 1:10), were not bad enough, they sought to add to its bitterness and terror:

2.1. By the drink they provided for him before he was nailed to the cross (v. 34). It was usual for those who were to be put to death to have a cup of spiced wine brought to drink from, but with the wine Christ was to drink from they mixed *vinegar and gall*, to make it sour and bitter. He *tasted thereof*, and so had its worst, as he took the bitter taste into his mouth; now he was tasting death in its full bitterness. Yet he *would not drink it*, because he did not want to have its best; he wanted nothing to lessen his pain, because he wanted to die so as to feel himself die.

2.2. By the dividing of his garments (v. 35). When they nailed him to the cross, they *stripped* him of his garments. If we are at any time stripped of our comforts for Christ, let us bear that patiently; he was stripped for us. Enemies may strip us of our clothes, but they cannot strip us of our best strengths and encouragements; they cannot take from us the *garments of praise* (Isa 61:3). The clothes of those who were executed were the executioner's fee. Four soldiers were employed in crucifying Christ, and each of them must receive his share: Christ's upper garment would be of no use to any of them if it was divided, and so they agreed to *cast lots* for it.

2.2.1. Some think that the garment was so fine and rich that it was worth fighting for, but that did not correspond with the poverty of Christ's appearance.

2.2.2. Perhaps they had heard of those who had been healed by touching the edge of his garment, and they thought it valuable for some power it contained. Or:

2.2.3. They hoped to obtain money from his friends for such a sacred relic. Or:

2.2.4. It was a form of amusement; they wanted to pass the time while they waited for his death; they would play a game with dice for the clothes. Whatever the intention, the word of God is fulfilled in this. In that famous psalm whose first words Christ spoke on the cross, it was said, *They parted my garments among them, and cast lots upon my vesture* (Ps 22:18). Christ stripped himself of his glories to divide them among us. They now *sat down, and watched* (kept watch over) *him* (v. 36). However, Providence so ordered things that those who were appointed to keep watch over him became satisfactory witnesses for him, having the opportunity to see and hear what drew from them that noble confession: *Truly this was the Son of God* (v. 54).

2.3. By the title set up over his head (v. 37). The crime of evildoers who were to be executed was usually made known not only by a crier proclaiming it before them as they were taken to be executed but also by an inscription over their heads describing it. They therefore set the written accusation over Christ's head, to give public notice of the charge against him: *This is Jesus the King of the Jews*. Here no crime was alleged against him. It was not said that he was a false Savior or a usurping King, but, *This is Jesus, a Saviour*; surely that was no crime. And it was said, *This is the King of the Jews*; that was no crime either, for they expected the Messiah to be so. Here a very glorious truth was asserted about him — that he was *Jesus the King of the Jews*, the King whom the Jews expected and should have submitted to. Pilate, instead of accusing Christ as a criminal, declared him to be a *King* three times, in three inscriptions (Lk 23:38). This is how God makes people serve his purposes, which are quite beyond their own.

2.4. By his companions with him in suffering (v. 38). There were *two thieves crucified with him* at the same time, in the same place, under the same guard; two highwaymen, or robbers. That day was probably appointed to be the day of execution; be that as it may, the Scripture was fulfilled in it: *He was numbered with the transgressors* (Isa 53:12).

2.4.1. It was a disgrace to him that he was *crucified with them*; he was made to share with the worst evildoers in what they suffered, as if he had shared with them in their sins. At his death, he was numbered with the transgressors (Isa 53:12) and shared his fate with evildoers, so that we, at our death, can be numbered among the saints.

2.4.2. It was an additional shame that he was crucified between them, as if he had been the worst of the three, the chief evildoer, for among three the center is the place for the chief. Every circumstance worked to his dishonor, as if the great Savior were the greatest sinner of all. It was also intended to ruffle and disturb him, in his last moments, with the shrieks, groans, and blasphemies of these evildoers. This, however, was how Christ wanted himself to be affected by the miseries of sinners when he was suffering for their salvation.

2.5. By the blasphemies and insults they hurled at him when he was hanging on the cross. One would have thought that when they nailed him to the cross, they would have done their worst. A dying man, even an infamous evildoer, should be treated with compassion. It seems that none of his friends, who only the other day had cried out *Hosanna* to him (21:9), dared now be seen to show him any respect.

2.5.1. The ordinary *people that passed by reviled him* (hurled insults at him). His extreme misery and exemplary patience in all this did not calm them down or make them repent; those who by their outcries brought him to this point now thought they were justified in shouting abuse, as if they did well to condemn him. Notice here:

2.5.1.1. The people who hurled abuse at him: *they that passed by*, the travelers who went along the road. They were possessed with prejudice against him by the reports and clamors of the high priest's underlings. It is difficult to maintain a good opinion of people and things that are criticized and spoken against everywhere. Everyone tends to follow the crowd and say as most other people say, and to throw a stone at what is given a bad name.

2.5.1.2. The gesture they used to show their contempt of him — *wagging their heads*, which signifies their gloating and scoffing at his fall.

2.5.1.3. The taunts and jeers they hurled, which are recorded here.

2.5.1.3.*1*. They rebuked him for saying he would *destroy the temple*. To make him repugnant, they diligently spread among the people the report that he intended to destroy the temple, which would anger the people against him more than anything. "*Thou that destroyest the temple*, that vast and strong fabric, test your strength now by plucking that cross out of the ground and pulling out those nails, and so *save thyself*. If you have the power you boasted about, then this is the right time to exert it and prove it." He was *crucified in weakness* (2Co 13:4); so it seemed to them, but in fact Christ crucified is the *Power of God* (1Co 1:24).

2.5.1.3.*2*. They rebuked him because he said that he was *the Son of God*. "If you really are," they said, "*come down from the cross*." Here they took the Devil's words out of his mouth, the words he tempted Jesus with in the desert (4:3, 6), and so they renewed the same attack: *If thou be the Son of God*. They thought that now or never he

must prove himself to be the Son of God. They forgot that he had proved it by the miracles he performed. They were unwilling to wait for its complete proof by his own resurrection, to which he had so often referred himself. This is what comes of judging things by their present appearance without properly remembering the past and patiently expecting what may further be produced.

2.5.2. The *chief priests and scribes*, the church rulers, and the *elders*, the state rulers, all mocked him (v. 41). They did not think it enough to invite the crowd to do so. They should have been in the temple at their devotions, for it was the first day of the Feast of Unleavened Bread, but they were here at the place of execution, spitting out their venom at the Lord Jesus. Did they do themselves a great indignity by treating Christ so contemptuously? Then how can we fear that we will do ourselves an indignity by joining the many to *do him honour*? The priests and elders scorned him with two things:

2.5.2.1. That he could not *save himself* (v. 42).

2.5.2.1.*1*. They took it for granted that he could not save himself and therefore did not have the power he claimed, when really he would not save himself, because he wanted to die to save us.

2.5.2.1.*2*. They wanted to imply that because he did not now save himself, all his claims to be able to save others were false delusions.

2.5.2.1.*3*. They ridiculed him for claiming to be *the King of Israel*. Many people would like the *King of Israel* well enough if he would only *come down from the cross*. However, the matter was settled; if there was no cross, then there could be no Christ and no crown. Those who want to reign with him must be willing to suffer with him (2Ti 2:12), for Christ and his cross are nailed together in this world.

2.5.2.1.*4*. They challenged him to *come down from the cross*. But his unchangeable love and determination set him above this temptation and strengthened him against it, so that he did not *fail, nor was discouraged* (Isa 42:4).

2.5.2.1.*5*. They promised that if he would *come down from the cross, they would believe him*. When they had formerly demanded a sign, he had told them that the sign he would give them would be not his coming down from the cross, but something that showed his power more greatly, his coming up from the grave. To promise ourselves that we would believe if we had such and such means and motives of faith as we ourselves would dictate is not only a sign of the corrupt deceitfulness of our hearts but also a poor refuge, or rather subterfuge, of a stubborn, destructive faithlessness.

2.5.2.2. That God, *his Father*, would *not save him* (v. 43). *He trusted in God*, for he said, *I am the Son of God*. Those who call God Father and call themselves his children profess to put their confidence in him (Ps 9:10). The chief priests and scribes now suggested that Jesus was only deceiving himself and others, for if he had been the Son of God, he would not have been abandoned to all this misery, much less abandoned in it. This taunt was intended:

2.5.2.2.*1*. To vilify him, to make the bystanders think he was a deceiver and an impostor.

2.5.2.2.*2*. To terrify him, driving him to distrust and despair of his Father's power and love.

2.5.3. To complete the scorn that was poured on him, the *thieves also that were crucified with him* not only were not insulted as he was, as if they had been saints compared with him, but *cast the same in his teeth* (heaped insults on him) (v. 44); that is, one of them did, who said, *If thou be the Christ, save thyself and us* (Lk 23:39). One would have thought that of all people, this robber had least cause, and should have had the least desire, to ridicule Christ.

2.5.4. Because our Lord Jesus had undertaken to satisfy the justice of God for the wrong done to his honor by sin, he did it by suffering in his honor, submitting to the greatest possible indignity that could be done to the worst evildoer. Because he was made sin for us (2Co 5:21), he was made a curse for us (Gal 3:13).

3. The disapproval of heaven that our Lord Jesus suffered in all these human shameful wrongs, about which notice:

3.1. How this was shown—by an extraordinary and miraculous eclipse of the sun, which continued for *three hours* (v. 45). An extraordinary light gave news of the birth of Christ (2:2), and so it was proper that an extraordinary darkness should announce his death, for he is the *Light of the world* (Jn 8:12). This surprising, terrifying darkness was intended to silence the mouths of those blasphemers who were hurling abuse at Christ as he hung on the cross. Although their hearts were not changed, they were silent and stood wondering what all this meant, until after *three hours* the darkness *scattered*, and then, as it appears from v. 47, like Pharaoh when the plague was over (Ex 8:15, 32), they hardened their hearts. However, this darkness was chiefly meant to show:

3.1.1. Christ's present conflict with the powers of darkness. He fought them on their own territory; by this darkness, he gave them all the advantage they could have against him; he let them take the wind and sun, but he still confounded them and so became more than a conqueror (Ro 8:37).

3.1.2. His present lack of heavenly comforts. This darkness represented the dark cloud that the human soul of our Lord Jesus was now under. God makes his sun shine on the just and the unjust (5:45), but even the light of the sun was withheld from our Savior when he was *made sin for us* (2Co 5:21). When earth denied him a drop of cold water, heaven denied him a ray of light; having to save us from total darkness, he himself walked in darkness, with no light in the depths of his own sufferings (Isa 50:10). During the three hours that this darkness continued, we do not find that he said one word; he spent this time in a silent retreat in his own soul. Never were there three such hours since the day that God created human beings on earth; never was there such a dark and terrible scene; this was the critical point of that great act of human redemption and salvation.

3.2. How he complained about it: *About the ninth hour*, when it began to clear, after a long and silent conflict, *Jesus cried, Eli, Eli, lama sabachthani?* (v. 46). The words are conveyed to us in a dialect of Aramaic, in which they were spoken, for the sake of the perverse interpretation that his enemies put on them, by understanding *Eli* as *Elias*, that is, *Elijah*. Notice here:

3.2.1. From where he took this complaint: Ps 22:1. This, and those other words, *Into thy hands I commit my spirit*, he drew from David's psalms (Ps 32:5; Lk 23:46), to teach us that we should use the word of God to guide us in prayer, which will *help our infirmities* (Ro 8:26).

3.2.2. How he spoke it—*with a loud voice*, which shows the extremity of his pain and anguish, the strength of nature remaining in him, and the great fervor in his spirit in this pleading.

3.2.3. What the complaint was—*My God, My God, why hast thou forsaken me?* This was a strange complaint to come from the mouth of our Lord Jesus, who, we are sure, was the One in whom the Father was always *well pleased* (3:17). The Father now loved him; in fact, he

knew that *his laying down his life for the sheep* was itself a reason that the Father *loved him* (1Jn 3:16). What? Had he been forsaken, abandoned, and deserted by his Father, and in the middle of his suffering, too! Surely there has never been a sorrow such as this (La 1:12), that drew such a complaint from One who, being sinless, could never be a terror to himself. It is hardly surprising that such a complaint made the earth quake and tore apart the rocks. We can learn from this:

3.2.3.1. That our Lord Jesus was, in his sufferings, for a time, forsaken by his Father. This is what he himself said, and we are sure he was not mistaken about his own situation. It was not as if there were any lessening in his Father's love for him or in his for his Father, but his Father forsook him. He handed him over to his enemies and did not appear to save him from their hands. No angel was sent from heaven to save him, nor any friend on earth raised up to appear for him. When *his soul* was first *troubled*, he had a *voice from heaven* to comfort him (Jn 12:27–28); when he was in anguish in the garden, an angel appeared from heaven to strengthen him; but now he had neither. Christ was made *Sin* for us (2Co 5:21) and became a *Curse* for us (Gal 3:13), and so although God loved him as a Son, he frowned on him as a Surety.

3.2.3.2. That Christ's being *forsaken* by his Father was the most painful of his sufferings. Here he laid the most sorrowful emphasis, for it was this that *put wormwood and gall* into the affliction and misery (La 3:19).

3.2.3.3. That our Lord Jesus, even when he was abandoned in this way by his Father, still kept hold of him as his God, nevertheless: "*My God, my God*. Although you forsake me, you are still mine." He was supported by the assurance that even in the depth of his sufferings, God was his God, and he was determined to keep hold of this.

3.2.4. How his enemies godlessly ridiculed this complaint: *They said, This man calleth for Elias* (v. 47). Some think that this was the ignorant mistake of the Roman soldiers, who had heard Elijah being talked about but did not know the meaning of *Eli, Eli*, and so made this mistaken comment on the words of Christ. Much of the contempt shown to the word of God and the people of God arises from gross mistakes. Those who hear incompletely pervert what they hear. However, others think that it was the deliberate mistake of some of the Jews, who knew very well what he said but were inclined to mistreat him, to give themselves and their companions a laugh, and to misrepresent him as One who, being abandoned by God, was driven to trust in created things. It is nothing new for the godliest devotions of the best people to be ridiculed and abused by worldly scoffers. Christ's words were so, even though he spoke as no one had ever spoken before.

4. The cold comfort that his enemies ministered to him in this anguish.

4.1. Some *gave him vinegar to drink* (v. 48). Instead of some refreshing water to revive him under this heavy burden, they tantalized him with this.

4.2. Others, with the same purpose of disturbing and insulting him, referred him to Elijah: "*Let be, let us see whether Elias will come to save him* (v. 49). Come, let him alone, his situation is desperate; he has appealed to Elijah, and to Elijah let him go."

Verses 50–56

We have here, finally, an account of the death of Christ and several remarkable events that accompanied it. Notice:

1. How he breathed his last (v. 50). Between the third and the sixth hour, that is, between nine and twelve

o'clock, by our reckoning, he was nailed to the cross, and soon after the ninth hour, that is, between three and four o'clock in the afternoon, he died. That was the time of the offering of the evening sacrifice and the time when the paschal lamb was killed. Christ our Passover was sacrificed for us. Two things are noted here about how Christ died:

1.1. That he *cried with a loud voice*, as before (v. 46). Now:

1.1.1. This was a sign that after all his pain and troubles, his life was still whole in him, and his constitution still strong. The voice of one who is dying is one of the first things that fail; with a panting breath and a faltering tongue, a few broken words are spoken with difficulty, and heard with more difficulty. But Christ, just before he expired, spoke like a man *in his full strength* (Job 21:23), to show that his life was not forced out of him, but freely delivered by him into his Father's hands.

1.1.2. It was significant. His crying out with a loud voice when he died showed that his death would be declared to the whole world. Christ's loud cry was like a trumpet blown over the sacrifices (Nu 10:10).

1.2. That then he *yielded up the ghost* (gave up his spirit). This is the usual way of expressing dying, used here to show that the Son of God on the cross truly and properly died by the violence of the pain he was in. His soul was separated from his body, and so his body was left really and truly dead. He had undertaken to make his soul an *offering for sin* (Isa 53:10).

2. The miracles that accompanied his death. So many miracles were performed by him in his life that we could well expect some to be performed around him at his death.

2.1. *Behold, the veil of the temple was rent in twain* (the curtain of the temple was torn in two). Just as our Lord Jesus expired, at the time of the offering of the evening sacrifice, the curtain of the temple was torn by an invisible power—the curtain that separated the Holy Place and the Most Holy Place. In this, as in other miracles of Christ, there was a mystery:

2.1.1. The temple corresponded to the temple of Christ's body, which was now being broken up. Death is the tearing of the curtain of flesh that comes between us and the Most Holy Place (Heb 10:20); the death of Christ was so; the death of true Christians is so.

2.1.2. It showed the revealing of the mysteries of the Old Testament. The *veil* of the temple was to provide concealment, and no one could look at the vessels of the Most Holy Place without incurring great punishment except the high priest, and he only once a year, with great ceremony and through a cloud of smoke. Now, however, at the death of Christ, everything was exposed, and the mysteries were unveiled, so that now a messenger can run, read, and announce its meaning (Hab 2:2).

2.1.3. It signified the uniting of Jews and Gentiles by the taking away of the dividing wall of hostility between them (Eph 2:14), which was the ceremonial law. In his death, Christ repealed the ceremonial law, took it out of the way, nailed it to his cross. He died to tear all dividing curtains and make all his people one (Jn 17:21).

2.1.4. It signified the consecrating and laying open of *a new and living way* to God (Heb 10:20). The curtain in the temple kept people from drawing near to the Most Holy Place, where the *Shechinah* was, the visible manifestation of God's glory. But its tearing showed that Christ opened a way to God through his death:

2.1.4.1. For himself. Now that his sacrifice had been offered in the outer court, its blood was to be sprinkled on the atonement cover within the curtain. Although he did not personally ascend to the Holy Place not made with hands (Heb 9:11, 24) until more than forty days later (Ac 1:3), he immediately acquired the right to enter and had virtual admission.

2.1.4.2. For us in him: this is how the writer to the Hebrews applies it (Heb 10:19–20). He died to *bring us to God* (1Pe 3:18) and, to that end, to tear down that curtain of guilt and wrath that came between us and him. We have free access through Christ to the throne of grace, or mercy seat, now, and to the throne of glory in the future (Heb 4:16; 6:20). As an old hymn put it, "when Christ had overcome the sharpness of death, he opened the kingdom of heaven to all believers." Nothing can obstruct or discourage our access to heaven.

2.2. The *earth did quake*; this earthquake showed two things:

2.2.1. The terrible evil of Christ's crucifiers. By trembling under such a load, the earth testified to the innocence of the One who was persecuted, and against the ungodliness of those who persecuted him.

2.2.2. The glorious achievements of Christ's cross. This earthquake showed the mighty shock—indeed, the fatal blow—given to the Devil's kingdom. God shakes all nations when the *Desire of all nations is to come* (Hag 2:6, 21).

2.3. The *rocks rent* (split); the hardest and strongest part of the earth was caused to feel this powerful shock. Christ had said that if the children were to stop crying out *Hosanna, the stones would immediately cry out* (Lk 19:40), and now, in effect, they did so, declaring the glory of the suffering Jesus. Jesus Christ is *the Rock* (1Co 10:4), and the splitting of these rocks showed the splitting of that rock:

2.3.1. So that in its cracks we may be hidden, as Moses was hidden in the cleft of the rock at Horeb, so that there we may *behold the glory of the Lord*, as he did (Ex 33:22).

2.3.2. So that from its crevices rivers of living water may flow and follow us in this desert (1Co 10:4). When we celebrate the memory of Christ's death, our hard and rocky hearts must be broken—the heart, and not the garments (Joel 2:13). The heart that will not yield or melt when it clearly sees Jesus Christ crucified (Gal 3:1) is harder than a rock.

2.4. The *graves were opened.* It seems the same earthquake that split the rocks also *opened the graves*, and many bodies of *saints which slept arose.* Death to the saints is simply the sleep of the body, and the grave the bed it sleeps in; they woke up by the power of the Lord Jesus and came *out of the graves after his resurrection, and went into Jerusalem, the holy city, and appeared unto many* (v. 53).

2.4.1. We may ask many questions about it, which we cannot resolve, such as:

2.4.1.1. Who these *saints* who *arose* were. Some think they were the ancient patriarchs, who were so concerned to be buried in the land of Canaan (Ge 49:29–32; 50:25). Others think that the people who were raised to life were modern saints, those who had been with Christ in the flesh but had died before him. What if we supposed that the people were the martyrs, those who in Old Testament times had sealed the truths of God with their blood? Christ especially pointed them out as his forerunners (23:35). Sufferers with Christ will reign with him first (2Ti 2:12).

2.4.1.2. Whether they were raised now or not until Jesus' own resurrection. Some think they were raised to life now at the death of Christ but stayed elsewhere, not *going into the city* until after his resurrection. Others think that they did not revive and rise until after Jesus' resurrection; on this view, for the sake of brevity their resurrection is only mentioned here at the reference to the *opening of the graves.*

2.4.1.3. Whether they died a second time. Some think that they were raised to life only to bear witness to Christ's resurrection to those to whom they appeared and that, having finished their testimony (Rev 11:7), they withdrew to their graves. But it is more in harmony with both Christ's honor and theirs to suppose, though we cannot prove, that they were raised to life as Christ was, not to die again. Surely a second death had no power over those who shared in his first resurrection.

2.4.1.4. To whom they appeared, whether enemies or friends, how they appeared, how often, what they said and did, and how they disappeared. All these are secret things that are not for us to know (Dt 29:29). The relating of this matter so briefly is a clear indication to us that we must not look that way to confirm our faith; we have a more certain word of prophecy. See Lk 16:31.

2.4.2. We may, however, learn many good lessons from it:

2.4.2.1. That even those who lived and died before the death and resurrection of Christ enjoyed saving benefits from those events, as well as those who have lived since.

2.4.2.2. That the death of Jesus Christ conquered, disarmed, and disabled death. These saints who were raised to life were the present trophies of the victory of Christ's cross over the powers of death.

2.4.2.3. That because of Christ's resurrection, the bodies of all the saints will rise again in the fullness of time. This resurrection of a few was a promise of the general resurrection at the last day.

3. The conviction of his enemies who were employed in the execution (v. 54). Notice:

3.1. The people who were convinced; *the centurion and they that were with him watching Jesus.*

3.1.1. They were *soldiers,* whose profession is commonly a hard one, and whose emotions are usually not so susceptible as those of others to the impressions of either fear or pity. However, there is no spirit too great, too bold, for the power of Christ to break and humble.

3.1.2. They were Romans, Gentiles, yet only they were convinced. Here the Gentiles were softened, and the Jews hardened.

3.1.3. They were the persecutors of Christ, those who just before had mocked him, as can be seen from Lk 23:36. How soon God can, by the power he has over the consciences of human beings, change their language.

3.2. The means of their conviction; they saw *the earthquake,* which frightened them, and the other *things that were done.* These fulfilled their purpose with these soldiers, whatever effect they had on others.

3.3. The expressions of this conviction, in two things:

3.3.1. The terror that struck them; they *feared greatly,* feared that they might be buried in the darkness or swallowed up by the earthquake. God can easily frighten his boldest enemies. Guilt makes people fear, whereas there are those who will not fear *though the earth be removed* (Ps 46:1–2?).

3.3.2. The testimony that was drawn from them. They said, *Truly this was the Son of God* (v. 54). It was the great matter now being disputed, the point on which he and his enemies had taken issue (26:63–64). His disciples believed it, but they dared not confess it at that time. Our Savior himself was tempted to question it when he said, *Why hast thou forsaken me?* (v. 46). Now that he was

dying on the cross, the Jews looked on the question as clearly determined against him: he was not the Son of God, because he did not come down from the cross. But now this centurion and the soldiers made this voluntary confession of the Christian faith: *Truly this was the Son of God.* The best of his disciples could not have said more at any time, and at this time they did not have enough faith and courage to say this much.

4. The presence of his friends with him, who witnessed his death (vv. 55–56). Notice:

4.1. Who they were: *many women who followed him from Galilee.* Not his apostles, though elsewhere we find John by the cross (Jn 19:26); no, their hearts failed them; they dared not appear. But here were a group of women—some would have called them foolish—who boldly stood by Christ when the other disciples had dishonorably deserted him. Even those of the weaker sex are often, by the grace of God, made strong in faith. There have been women martyrs, who have been famous for their courage and determination in Christ's cause. It is said about these women:

4.1.1. That they had *followed Jesus from Galilee* out of the great love they had for him; otherwise, only the males were obliged to come up to worship at the festival. Having followed him on such a long journey, they were resolved not to abandon him now. Our former services and sufferings for Christ should be an argument for us to faithfully persevere with him to the end.

4.1.2. That they had *ministered to him* on the way, providing for his subsistence from their resources. How gladly would they have ministered to him now, if they had been allowed to! When we are restrained from doing what we want to do in serving Christ, we must do what we can.

4.1.3. Some of them are named particularly. They were those we have met several times before, and it is to their honor that we meet them at the end.

4.2. What they did; they were *beholding afar off.*

4.2.1. They stood *afar off.* It emphasized the sufferings of Christ that his *lovers and friends stood aloof from his sore* (Ps 38:11; Job 19:13). Perhaps they could have come nearer if they had wanted to, but when good people are suffering greatly, they must not think it strange if some of their best friends are reluctant to be with them. If we are looked at strangely, we are to remember that our Master was looked at in the same way.

4.2.2. They were there watching. When they were prohibited from carrying out any other task of love to him, they looked with a look of love toward him. It was a sorrowful look. We may well imagine how it cut them to the heart to see him in this torment. Let us have the eye of faith, so that we may see Christ, and him crucified (1Co 2:2), and let us be moved by the great love with which he loved us. Yet it was no more than a look; they saw him, but they could not help him. When Christ was suffering, even his best friends were merely spectators and onlookers.

Verses 57–66

We have here an account of Christ's burial. Notice the kindness and goodwill of his friends who laid him in the grave, and also the hatred and ill will of his enemies, who were very concerned to keep him there.

1. His friends gave him a decent burial. Notice:

1.1. Jesus Christ was buried; when his precious soul had gone to paradise, his blessed body was placed in the chambers of the grave. He was buried to make his death more certain and his resurrection more distinguished. Pilate would not give his body to be buried until he was assured that he was really dead. He was buried so that he could take away the terror of the grave and make it acceptable to us, so that he might warm and perfume that cold, noxious bed for us, and so that we could be *buried with him* (Ro 6:4; Col 2:12).

1.2. The particular circumstances of his burial given here.

1.2.1. The time when he was buried was *when the evening was come*, the same evening that he died, before sunset, as is usual in burying evildoers. It was not delayed until the next day, because that was the Sabbath.

1.2.2. The person who took care of the funeral was Joseph of Arimathea. The apostles had all fled. The women who followed him dared not act; God therefore stirred this good man to do it, for whatever work God has to do, he will find instruments to do it. Joseph was suitable, for:

1.2.2.1. He had the resources to do it, being *rich*. Most of Christ's disciples were poor, but here was one who was a *rich man*, ready to be employed in an act of service that required a man with possessions. Worldly wealth is an advantage and opportunity in some services to be done for Christ, and those who have it will do well if they also have a heart to use it for God's glory.

1.2.2.2. He was well disposed toward our Lord Jesus, for he was himself *his disciple* and believed in him, even though he did not openly profess it. Christ has more secret disciples than we are aware of.

1.2.3. The dead body was obtained by a grant from Pilate (v. 58). Joseph went to Pilate, the proper person to be turned to on this occasion. Pilate was willing to give the body to a person who would lay it to rest decently. In Joseph's request and Pilate's ready grant of it, honor was done to Christ, and a testimony borne to his integrity.

1.2.4. The body was dressed in its graveclothes (v. 59); although he was an honorable councillor, he himself still took the body, it seems, into his own arms, from the infamous and accursed tree (Ac 13:29), for where there is true love for Christ, no service will be thought too lowly to stoop to for him. Having taken it, he wrapped it in a *clean linen cloth*, for burying in linen was then the custom. This common act of humanity, if done in a godly way, may be made an acceptable Christian action.

1.2.5. It was placed in the sepulcher (v. 60). A private funeral was most fitting to the One whose kingdom did not come with observation (Lk 17:20).

1.2.5.1. He was laid in a borrowed tomb, in Joseph's burial place; just as he did not have a house of his own in which to *lay his head* while he lived (8:20), so he did not have a grave of his own in which to *lay his body* when he died. The grave is the special heritage of a *sinner* (Job 24:19). There is nothing we can truly call our own except our sins and our graves. When we go to the grave, we go to our own place, but our Lord Jesus, who had no sin of his own, did not have a grave of his own; dying under imputed sin, it was right that he should be buried in a borrowed grave.

1.2.5.2. He was laid in a *new tomb*, which Joseph probably intended for himself; it would be none the worse, however, for Christ's lying in it, since he was to rise so quickly; indeed it would be a great deal better for having been lain in by the One who has altered the significance of the grave.

1.2.5.3. It was a tomb that was hewn (cut) *out of a rock*; Christ's grave would be in a solid, single rock, so that no room would be left to suspect that his disciples could have gained access to it by some underground passage or have broken through its back wall to steal the body, because

there was no access to it except by the entrance, which was watched.

1.2.5.4. A *great stone was rolled to the door of his sepulchre*; this also was according to the custom of the Jews in burying their dead, as can be seen by the description of the grave of Lazarus (Jn 11:38). If the grave were his prison, now the prison door was locked and bolted. The rolling of the stone to the entrance of the grave was for them what filling up the grave with soil is for us: it completed the funeral. The saddest circumstance in the funerals of our Christian friends comes when, having laid their bodies in the dark and silent grave, we go home and leave them behind. But alas, it is not we who go home and leave them behind; it is they who have gone to a better home and left us behind.

1.2.6. A very small and insignificant number of people attended the funeral. Here were some good women who were true mourners — *Mary Magdalene, and the other Mary* (v. 56). Just as they had gone with him to the cross, so they followed him to the grave. True love for Christ will take us through to the utmost in following him. Death itself cannot quench that divine fire (SS 8:6 – 7).

2. His enemies did what they could to prevent his resurrection; what they did, they did on *the next day that followed the day of the preparation* (v. 62). That was the seventh day of the week, the Jewish Sabbath. All that day, Christ lay dead in the grave. On that day, the *chief priests and Pharisees*, when they should have been at their devotions, asking forgiveness for the sins of the previous week, were dealing with Pilate about protecting the sepulcher. Notice here:

2.1. Their words to Pilate; they wanted a guard posted who would keep the tomb secure.

2.1.1. Their request stated that *that deceiver had said, After three days I will rise again*. He had said so, and his disciples remembered those very words to confirm their faith, but his persecutors remembered them to provoke anew their own rage and malice. This is how the same word of Christ was to one a fragrance of life but to another the smell of death (2Co 2:16).

2.1.2. It also showed their jealousy: *lest his disciples come by night, and steal him away, and say, He is risen*.

2.1.2.1. What they were really afraid of was his resurrection; what is most Christ's honor and his people's joy is the source of most terror of his enemies. Come, they say, let us *slay* (kill) *him*, and see *what will become of his dreams* (Ge 37:20). Similarly, the chief priests and Pharisees sought to defeat the predictions of Christ's resurrection; if he were to rise, that would destroy all their plans. Even when Christ's enemies have won their point, they are still in fear of losing it again. Perhaps the priests were surprised at the respect shown to Christ's dead body by Joseph and Nicodemus, two honorable people; nor could they forget his raising Lazarus from the dead, which had stunned them.

2.1.2.2. What they pretended to be afraid of was that otherwise *his disciples should come by night, and steal him away*, which was most improbable, for they did not have the courage to acknowledge him while he lived, and it was unlikely that his death would put courage into such cowards. What could they promise themselves by stealing away his body and making people believe he had risen? What good would it do them to continue to deceive themselves, to steal his body and say, *He is risen*? The chief priests realized that if the teaching of Christ's resurrection was once preached and believed, the *last error* (NIV: deception) *would be worse than the first*. Those who oppose Christ and his kingdom will see not only their attempts thwarted but also themselves miserably overwhelmed and confused, their errors each worse than the last, and the last of all the worst of all (Ps 2:4–5).

2.1.3. In consideration of these thoughts, they humbly suggested that a guard be set to keep the grave secure until the third day: *Command that the sepulchre be made sure* (v. 64). One would have thought that death's prisoners needed no other guard and that the grave would have been enough security in itself.

2.2. Pilate's answer to these words: *Ye have a watch* (take a guard), *make it sure* (make the tomb secure) (v. 65), as secure as possible. He was ready to satisfy Christ's friends by allowing them to have the body and to satisfy his enemies by setting a guard on it, wanting to please all sides, looking at the hopes of one side and the fears of the other as similarly ridiculous. *Ye have a watch*; but as if he was ashamed to have himself seen in such a thing, he left its management wholly to them. It seems to me that the words *Make it as sure as you can* look like ridiculing either:

2.2.1. Their fears: "Be sure to set a strong guard on the dead man." Or rather:

2.2.2. Their hopes: "Do your worst, but if he is of God, he will rise again, in spite of you and all your guards." Speaking about Pilate, Tertullian says, "In his conscience he was a Christian," and it is possible that he was under such convictions at this time, on the basis of the centurion's report, but never was thoroughly persuaded to be a Christian, any more than Agrippa (Ac 26:28–32) or Felix (Ac 24:24–27) was.

2.3. The amazing care they then took to secure the tomb: *They sealed the stone* (v. 66). However, because they did not trust that very much, they also *set a watch* to keep *his disciples* from coming to *steal him away*. This was their intention, but God brought this good out of it: those who were set to oppose his resurrection had an opportunity to see it, and they did so, telling the chief priests what they saw. To guard the sepulcher against the poor, weak disciples was foolish, because it was unnecessary, but to think they could protect it against the power of God was also foolish, because it was useless, and yet they thought they were dealing shrewdly (Ex 1:10).

CHAPTER 28

In the previous chapters we saw the Captain of our salvation (Heb 2:10) engaged in a battle with the powers of darkness; victory seemed to hover between the combatants; in fact, it finally inclined to the side of the enemy, and our Champion fell before them. But then the Lord awaked as one out of sleep *(Ps 78:65). In this chapter, our* Prince of Peace *(Isa 9:6) rallied, coming out of the grave as a Conqueror. Now because the resurrection of Christ is one of the main foundations of our faith, we need to have infallible proofs of it. Four such proofs are given in this chapter, which are only a few of many, for Luke and John give a fuller account of the proofs of Christ's resurrection than Matthew and Mark. Here is: 1. The testimony of the angel to Christ's resurrection (vv. 1–8). 2. Christ's appearance himself to the women (vv. 9–10). 3. The confession of the guards (vv. 11–15). 4. Christ's appearance to the disciples in Galilee and the commission he gave them (vv. 16–20).*

Verses 1–10

To prove Christ's resurrection, here is the testimony of the angel and of Christ himself. Let us not prescribe to Infinite Wisdom, who directed that the witnesses of his resurrection would see him risen but not see him rise. His incarnation was a mystery, as was this "second incarnation." We have here:

1. The coming of the loyal women to the sepulcher.

1.1. When they came: *in the end of the sabbath, as it began to dawn toward the first day of the week* (v. 1). This establishes the time of Christ's resurrection.

1.1.1. He arose the *third day* after his death (Mk 9:31). He was buried on the evening of the sixth day of the week, and he arose on the morning of the first day of the following week.

1.1.2. He arose *after the Jewish sabbath*, and it was the Passover Sabbath. On the sixth day Christ finished his work, saying, *It is finished*; on the seventh day he rested (Ge 2:2); and then on the first day of the following week he began, as it were, a new world and undertook a new work. The time of the saints' lying in the grave is a Sabbath to them, for there they *rest from their labours* (Job 3:17).

1.1.3. He arose on the *first day of the week*. On the first day of the first week God *commanded the light to shine out of darkness* (Ge 1:3; 2Co 4:6); on this day, therefore, the One who was the Light of the world shone out of the darkness of the grave, and because the seventh-day Sabbath was buried with Christ, it rose again as the first-day Sabbath, called the *Lord's day* (Rev 1:10), and no day of the week is from this time on mentioned in the whole New Testament other than this. The Sabbath was instituted in remembrance of the perfecting of the work of creation (Ge 2:1). Human beings by their rebellion broke that perfect work, which was never completely restored until Christ rose from the dead. The One who on that day rose from the dead is the same One by whom and for whom all things were at first created (Col 1:16) and are now created anew (Gal 6:15; Rev 21:5).

1.1.4. He arose *as it began to dawn* toward that day; as soon as it could be said that the third day had come, he arose. Christ rose *when the day began to dawn* because then *the dayspring from on high did again visit us* (the rising sun came to us from heaven) (Lk 1:78). His suffering began at night; when he hung on the cross, the sun was darkened; he was placed in the grave at dusk; but he rose up from the grave when the sun was about to rise, for he is the *bright and morning Star* (Rev 22:16), the *true Light* (Jn 1:9; 1Jn 2:8).

1.2. Who they were: *Mary Magdalene and the other Mary*, the same who were present at the funeral and *sat over against* (opposite) *the sepulcher* (27:61), as they had earlier *sat over against* (opposite) *the cross*. They continued to express their love for Christ. Their attending Christ not only on the way to the grave but also in the grave represents his similar care for those who are his. Just as Christ in the grave was loved by the *saints*, so the saints in the grave are loved by Christ, for death and the grave cannot loosen the bonds of love between them.

1.3. What they came to do: the other Evangelists say that they came to anoint the body; Matthew says they came to *see the sepulchre*. They went to show their goodwill, to pay another visit to the dear remains of their beloved Master. Visits to the grave are very useful to Christians, especially visits to the grave of our Lord Jesus, where we may see sin buried out of sight, and the great proof of redeeming love shining illustriously even in that *land of darkness* (Job 10:21–22).

2. The appearance of an angel of the Lord to them (vv. 2–4). We have here an account of how the resurrection of Christ took place.

2.1. There was *a great earthquake*. When he died, the earth that received him shook for fear; now that he rose, the earth relinquished him, leaping for joy in his exaltation. It was the signal of Christ's victory. Those who are sanctified, and so raised to a spiritual life, will find an earthquake within themselves while it is being done, as Paul did, who *trembled* and was *astonished* (Ac 9:6).

2.2. The *angel of the Lord descended from heaven*. The angels frequently came to our Lord Jesus, but on the cross we find no angel with him. When his Father *forsook him*, the angels withdrew from him, but now that he was taking up again his glory, see, the *angels of God worshiped him* (Heb 1:6).

2.3. He came, rolled back the stone from the door, and sat on it. The stone of our sins was rolled onto the door of the grave of our Lord Jesus, but to demonstrate that divine justice was satisfied, an angel was commissioned to roll back the stone. All the powers of death and darkness are under the control of the God of light and life. An angel from heaven has power to *break the seal* (Rev 5:2), even if it were the great seal of Israel, and is able to *roll away the stone*, no matter how great. The angel's *sitting on the stone* when he had *rolled it away* is significant. He sat there in defiance of all the powers of hell to roll the stone back onto the grave. The angel sat as a guard on the grave, having frightened away the enemies' attendants; he sat, expecting the women, and ready to give them an account of Christ's resurrection.

2.4. His *countenance* (appearance) *was like lightning, and his raiment* (clothes) *white as snow* (v. 3). His appearance to the guards was like flashes of lightning. The whiteness of his clothes was a sign not only of purity but also of joy and triumph. When Christ died, the court of heaven went into deep mourning, as represented by the darkening of the sun, but when he rose, they again put on the *garments of praise* (Isa 61:3). The glory of this angel represented the glory of Christ, to which he had now risen, for it is the same description as was given about him in his transfiguration (17:2), but when he spoke with his disciples after his resurrection, he drew a veil over it.

2.5. *For fear of him the keepers* (guards) *did shake, and became as dead men* (v. 4). They were soldiers, who thought themselves hardened against fear, but the very sight of an angel struck them with terror. Just as the resurrection of Christ is the joy of his friends, so it is also the terror and confusion of his enemies. *They did shake*; the word is the same as the one used for the earthquake (v. 2). When the earth shook, these children of the earth, who had their inheritance in it, shook too, whereas those who have their happiness in things above, *though the earth be removed, yet are without fear* (Ps 46:2). They were posted here to keep a dead man in his grave—surely as easy a service as they had ever been assigned—but it proved too hard for them.

3. The message this angel spoke to the women (vv. 5–7).

3.1. He encouraged them against their fears (v. 5). To come near to graves and tombs, especially in silence and solitude, has something frightening about it, and it was much more so to those women when they found an angel at the grave, but he soon put them at ease with the words, *Fear not*. The guards shook and became as dead men, but "*Fear not*. Let not the news I have to tell you come as any surprise to you; let it not be a terror to you, for his resurrection will be your comfort. *Fear not ye, for I know that ye seek Jesus*. I do not come to frighten you, but to encourage you." Those who *seek Jesus* have no reason to be *afraid*, for if they seek him diligently, they will *find him* (Jer 29:13; Heb 11:6). *Ye seek Jesus that was crucified*. He mentioned his being crucified to commend their

love for him; "You seek him still, even though he was crucified." True believers love and seek Christ not only *though* he was crucified but also *because* he was so.

3.2. He assured them of the resurrection of Christ, and there was enough in that to silence their fears (v. 6). To be told *He is not here* would not have been welcome news to those who sought him, if it had not been added, *He is risen*. We must not listen to those who say, *Lo, here is Christ, or, Lo, he is there* (24:23), because he is not here, he is not there, he is risen. We must seek him as One who is risen. Those who make pictures and images of Christ forget that *he is not here, he is risen*; our fellowship with him must be spiritual, by faith in his word (Ro 10:6–9). We must seek him with great reverence and humility and a fearful respect for his glory, because he is risen. We must seek him with a heavenly mind; when we are ready to make this world our home and say, *It is good to be here* (17:4), let us remember that our Lord Jesus *is not here, he is risen*, and so let our hearts not be here, but let them rise too.

3.3. The angel referred these women to two things to confirm their faith.

3.3.1. To Christ's word now fulfilled, which they could remember: "*He is risen, as he said*. He said he would rise; why should you be reluctant to believe what he told you would happen?" Let us never consider strange something about which the word of Christ has raised our expectations. If we remember what Christ has said to us, we will be less surprised at what he does with us.

3.3.2. To his now empty grave, which they could look into: "*Come, see the place where the Lord lay*. Compare what you have heard with what you see, and putting both together, you will believe." It may have a good influence on us to come and look with the eye of faith to *see the place where the Lord lay*. When we look into the grave, where we all must expect to lie, then to take away its terror, let us look into the grave where the Lord lay, the place where *our* Lord lay.

3.4. He told them to go take the news of it to his disciples: *go quickly, and tell his disciples* (v. 7). It was good to be here (17:4), but they had other work appointed for them. They must not keep a monopoly of the encouragement they had received, must not keep it to themselves. They must go and *tell the disciples*. Public usefulness to others must come before the delights of private fellowship with God by ourselves.

3.4.1. The disciples of Christ must first be told the news; not, "Go and tell the chief priests and the Pharisees, so that they may be confounded," but, "Tell the disciples, so that they may be comforted." God seeks the joy of his friends more than the shame of his enemies. "*Tell his disciples*:

3.4.1.1. "So that they may encourage themselves in their present sorrows and scattering." It was a sad time for them, caught between grief and fear; what a relief this would be to them now, to hear that their Master was risen!

3.4.1.2. "So that they may look further into it themselves." This was to set them to seek him and to prepare them for his appearance to them. General hints lead us to make closer searches. They would now hear about him, but very soon they would see him.

3.4.2. The women were sent to tell them. This was a reward for their constant, affectionate loyalty to him at the cross and in the grave, and it was a rebuke to the disciples who abandoned him. Just as *the woman was first in the transgression* (1Ti 2:14), so these women were the first to believe in the redemption from transgression by Christ's resurrection.

3.4.3. They were told to *go quickly* on this mission. Why was great speed necessary? Would the news not keep, and be welcome at any time? Yes, but the other disciples were now overwhelmed by grief, and Christ wanted them to receive this good news quickly. We must always be ready and eager to do good to our brothers and sisters and to take comfort to them; now, *go quickly*.

3.4.4. They were told to tell the disciples to meet him in Galilee. Now this general rendezvous was appointed in Galilee, some eighty miles (about 130 kilometers) from Jerusalem:

3.4.4.1. In kindness to those of his disciples who remained in Galilee and did not—perhaps they could not—come up to Jerusalem. Christ knows where his disciples live, and he will visit them there. Even to those who seem to enjoy little of the means of grace he will graciously *manifest himself* (Jn 14:21).

3.4.4.2. In consideration of the weakness of his disciples who were now at Jerusalem, who were still afraid of the Jews and dared not appear publicly. Christ knows our fears, and he considers how we are formed (Ps 103:14), and so he made his appointment where there was least danger of disturbance. The angel solemnly affirmed on his word the truth of what he had told them: "*Lo, I have told you*; you may be assured of it." This angel was sent now to confirm the resurrection of Christ to the disciples, and so leave it in their hands to be declared to the world (2Co 4:7). "I have done my errand, I have faithfully fulfilled my mission, *I have told you.*" Those messengers from God who discharge their trust faithfully may take comfort from that, whatever the result of their efforts may be (Ac 20:26–27).

4. The women's departure from the sepulcher to tell the disciples (v. 8). Notice:

4.1. What mood they were in; they *departed with fear and great joy*, a strange mixture, fear and joy at the same time, in the same soul. To hear that Christ was risen was a matter of joy, but to be led into his grave and then see an angel and talk with him about it must have caused fear. It was good news, but they were afraid that it was too good to be true. Notice, however, that it is said of their *joy* that it was *great*; that is not said of their fear. Holy fear has joy accompanying it. It is only perfect love and joy that will drive out all fear.

4.2. How quickly they went: *They did run.* The fear and joy together quickened their pace and added wings to their movement. Those who are sent on God's mission must not loiter or lose any time.

4.3. What mission they went on; they ran to *bring his disciples word.* They ran to comfort them with the same comforts with which they themselves had been comforted by God (Eph 2:4). The disciples of Christ should be eager to share their experiences with one another. They should tell others what God has *done for their souls* (Ps 66:16) and spoken to them. Joy in Christ Jesus *will betray itself* (Pr 27:16).

5. Christ's appearing to the women to confirm the testimony of the angel (vv. 9–10). These zealous good women not only heard the first news of him after his resurrection but also had the first sight of him. Jesus Christ is often better than his word, but never worse; he often comes before, but never frustrates, the faithful expectations of his people. Here is:

5.1. Christ's surprising appearance to the women: *As they went to tell his disciples, behold, Jesus met then.* God graciously comes to us usually as we are fulfilling our duty, and to those who use what they have for others' benefit, more will be given. This meeting with Christ was unexpected. Christ is closer to his people than they think. Christ was *nigh them*, and still in *the word is nigh us* (Ro 10:8; see also Dt 30:11–14).

5.2. The greeting with which he met them: *All hail.* We use the old English form of greeting when we wish "all health" to those we meet, for this is what *All hail* means. It shows:

5.2.1. The goodwill of Christ toward us and our happiness.

5.2.2. The freedom and holy intimacy that he had in fellowship with his disciples, for he called them *friends.* The Greek word here translated *All hail* means, *Rejoice ye.* They were moved with both fear and joy; what he said to them tended to encourage their joy—*Rejoice ye* (v. 9)—and to silence their fears: *Be not afraid* (v. 10). It is the will of Christ that his people should be a cheerful and joyful people, and his resurrection provides them with much cause for joy.

5.3. The affectionate respect they paid him: *They came, and held him by the feet, and worshipped him.* They expressed in this way:

5.3.1. The reverence and honor they wanted to show him.

5.3.2. The love and affection they had for him; they *held him, and would not let him go* (SS 3:4).

5.3.3. The state of joyful delight they were in, now that they had this further assurance of his resurrection.

5.4. The encouraging words Christ said to them (v. 10). We do not find that they said anything to him; their affectionate embraces and adoration spoke clearly enough. What he said to them was no more than what the angel had said (vv. 5–6). Notice here:

5.4.1. How he rebuked their fear: *Be not afraid.* The news, though strange, was both true and good. Christ arose from the dead to silence his people's fears, and there is enough in that to silence them.

5.4.2. How he repeated the message they were to bring: "*Go, tell my brethren* that they must prepare for a journey to Galilee, and there *they shall see me.*" If there is any fellowship between our souls and Christ, he is the One who appoints the meeting, and he will keep the appointment. What is especially significant here, however, is that he called his disciples *his brethren.* He never called them that till after his resurrection, here and in Jn 20:17. Christ did not now speak so constantly and familiarly with his disciples as he had before his death, but he gave them this endearing title. *Go to my brethren* (Ps 22:22). They had shamefully deserted him in his sufferings, but he not only held to his purpose to meet them but also called them brothers.

Verses 11–15

We have here the confession of the enemies who were on guard, and there are two things that strengthen this testimony: that they were eyewitnesses and that they were enemies, set there to oppose and obstruct his resurrection. Notice:

1. How this testimony was given to the chief priests (v. 11). *Some of the watch came into the city*, bringing the report of their failure to those who employed them. *They showed to the chief priests all the things that were done* (had happened); they told them about the earthquake, the descent of the angel, the rolling away of the stone, and the coming of the body of Jesus alive from the grave. The greatest means of conviction were given the chief priests. It might justly have been expected that they would now have believed in Christ, but they were stubborn in their faithlessness and therefore were sealed in it.

2. How it was thwarted and stifled by them. They called a meeting and considered what was to be done. For their own part, they were determined not to believe that Jesus had risen, but they were also concerned to keep others from believing. The result of their debate was that those soldiers must by all means be bribed and hired not to tell tales.

2.1. They *put money into their hands*. They *gave large* (a large sum of) *money to the soldiers*. These chief priests loved their money as much as most people did, and were as reluctant to part with it, but to pursue their malicious intentions against the Gospel of Christ, they were very extravagant with it. Here *large money* was given to advance what both parties knew to be a lie, but many people begrudge giving a little money to advance what they know to be the truth. Let us never starve a good cause when we see a bad one so generously supported.

2.2. They put a lie into their mouths (v. 13): *Say ye, His disciples came by night, and stole him away while we slept*; a sorry excuse is better than none, but this was a truly sorry one.

2.2.1. The sham was ridiculous and bore with it its own refutation. If the guards slept, how could they have known anything about the matter or said who had come? But even if it had been very plausible:

2.2.2. It was very evil for these priests and elders to hire those soldiers to tell a deliberate lie against their own consciences—even if it had been in a matter of very small importance. However:

2.2.3. This was in effect a blasphemy against the Holy Spirit (Mk 3:29), imputing to the dishonesty of the disciples what was accomplished by the power of the Holy Spirit. In case the soldiers raised the objection of the penalty they incurred by the Roman law for *sleeping upon the guard*, which was very severe (Ac 12:19), the chief priests promised to intervene with the governor: "*We will persuade* (satisfy) *him, and secure you* (keep you out of trouble)." If these soldiers had really slept and so had allowed the disciples to steal the body away, the priests and elders would certainly have been the ones who would have been most eager to ask the governor to punish them for their treachery, so their concern for the soldiers' safety clearly contradicted the story.

2.3. Well, this was how the plot was laid. Did it succeed?

2.3.1. Those who were willing to deceive took the money and did as they were told. They *took the money*; that was their aim, and nothing else. Money entices people to fall into the blackest temptation; mercenary tongues will sell the truth for money (Pr 23:23). The great argument to prove Christ to be the Son of God is his resurrection, and no one could have had more convincing proofs of that truth than these soldiers had. They saw the angel descend from heaven, the stone rolled away, and the body of Christ come out of the grave, and yet they were so far from being convinced by it themselves that they were hired to tell lies and hinder others from believing in him. The clearest evidence will not persuade people without the operation of the Holy Spirit accompanying that evidence.

2.3.2. Those who were willing to be deceived not only believed the report but also spread it; this *saying* (story) *is commonly reported among the Jews until this day*. The story was accepted well enough and fulfilled its purpose. When the Jews were pressed with the argument of Christ's resurrection, they had a reply ready: *His disciples came and stole him away*. Once a lie is raised, no one knows how far it will spread, how long it will last, or what trouble it will cause.

Verses 16–20

This Evangelist passes over several other appearances of Christ that are recorded by Luke and John and moves quickly on to this, the most solemn of all, because it was the one that was promised and appointed again and again before his death and after his resurrection. Notice:

1. How the disciples were present when he appeared, according to the appointment: *They went into Galilee* (v. 16), a long journey to have one sight of Christ, but it was worthwhile:

1.1. Because he told them to. Although it seemed unnecessary to go to Galilee, they had learned to obey Christ's commands and not object to them. Those who want to keep up their fellowship with Christ must be with him in the place where he has appointed.

1.2. Because that was to be a public and general meeting. The place was *a mountain in Galilee*, probably the same mountain on which he was transfigured. There they met for privacy, and perhaps to represent his exalted state.

2. How they were moved by the appearance of Christ (v. 17). Now was the time that he was *seen of above five hundred brethren at once* (1Co 15:6). We are told:

2.1. That they *worshipped him*. Many of them did—indeed, it seems they all did that; they gave him divine honor. All who see the Lord Jesus with the eye of faith must worship him.

2.2. But *some doubted*. Even among those who worship there are some who doubt. The faith of those who are sincere may still be very weak and wavering. *They* "hung in suspense," as in the scales of a balance, when it is hard to say which side is heavier. It led much to the honor of Christ that the disciples doubted before they believed. Having doubted, they could not be said to have been too ready to believe and willing to be deceived, for they first *questioned, proved all things*, and then *held fast* what was true, and what they found to be so (1Th 5:21).

3. What Jesus Christ said to them: *Jesus came, and spoke unto them* (vv. 18–20). He did not stand far away, but came near, and gave them such convincing proofs of his resurrection as would weigh down the hesitant scales and make their faith triumph over their doubts. *He came, and spoke* familiarly *to them*, as one friend speaks to another (Ex 33:11). Christ now handed to his apostles the great charter of his kingdom in the world; he was sending them out as his ambassadors, and he gave them their credentials here. In explaining this great paragraph, we may notice two things:

3.1. The commission that our Lord Jesus himself received from the Father. Because he was about to authorize his apostles, he told us here: *All power is given unto me in heaven and in earth*. Here, he was asserting his universal authority as Mediator. He has *all power* (authority). Notice:

3.1.1. From where he received this authority. It was *given* him by a grant from the One who is the Fountain of all being, and consequently of all authority. As God, equal with the Father, he had all authority originally and essentially, but as Mediator, as God-man, he had all power given him. He had this *power* (authority) given him *over all flesh* so that he could *give eternal life to as many as were given him* (Jn 17:2). He was now, after his resurrection, more significantly invested with this power (Ac 13:33).

3.1.2. Where he exercised this power: in *heaven and earth*, taking in the whole universe. He is *Lord of all* (Ac 10:36). He has all *power in heaven*. He has authority and power over the angels. He has power of intercession with his Father; he intercedes not as one who appeals but as One who desires: *Father, I will* (Jn 17:24). He has *all power on earth*, too; he succeeds with human beings and deals with them as One with authority, by the ministry of reconciliation (2Co 5:18). All souls belong to him, and to him *every* heart and *knee must bow*, and *every* tongue must *confess* him to be the *Lord* (Isa 54:23; Ro 14:11). Our Lord Jesus told them this also to take away the stumbling block of the cross; they had no reason to be ashamed of *Christ crucified* (1Co 1:23) when they saw him *glorified* (Jn 13:31).

3.2. The commission he gave to those whom he sent out: *Go ye therefore*. This commission was given:

3.2.1. To the apostles primarily, the master builders who laid the foundation of the church. It was not only a word of command, like "Son, go and work" (21:28), but also a word of encouragement: "Go, and fear not, have I not sent you?" (Jdg 6:14). They must go and bring the Gospel to the nations' doors: *Go ye. As an eagle stirs up her nest, flutters over her young*, to encourage them to fly (Dt 32:11), so Christ stirs up his disciples to disperse themselves throughout the world.

3.2.2. To their successors, the ministers of the Gospel, whose business it is to communicate the Gospel from age to age, to the end of the world in time. At his ascension, Christ gave not only apostles and prophets but also *pastors and teachers* (Eph 4:11). Notice:

3.2.2.1. How far his commission extends: to *all nations*. Go and disciple *all nations*. This clearly shows that it was the will of Christ:

3.2.2.1.*1.* That the covenant made distinctively with the Jews would now be canceled and annulled. Whereas the apostles, when first sent out, were forbidden to go *into the way of the Gentiles* (10:5), they were now sent to all nations.

3.2.2.1.*2.* That salvation by Christ would be offered to all, excluding none except those who by their unbelief and impenitence excluded themselves. The salvation they were to preach was a salvation for all.

3.2.2.1.*3.* That Christianity would be intertwined in their national constitutions, that the kingdoms of the world would become Christ's kingdoms (Rev 11:15), and their kings the church's foster fathers (Isa 49:23).

3.2.2.2. What is the main intention of this commission: to disciple all nations. "'Admit them as disciples'; do your best to make the nations Christian nations." Christ the Mediator is establishing a kingdom in the world: "Bring the nations as his subjects; set up a school and bring the nations to be his students. Raise an army; enlist the nations of the earth under his banner." The work that the apostles had to do was to set up the Christian faith in all places, and it was an honorable work; the achievements of the mighty heroes of the world were nothing compared to it. Those heroes conquered the nations for themselves and made them miserable; the apostles conquered them for Christ and made them happy.

3.2.2.3. Their instructions to carry out this commission.

3.2.2.3.*1.* They must admit disciples by the sacred rite of baptism. "Go into all nations, preach the Gospel to them, perform miracles among them, and persuade them both to come into the church of Christ themselves and to bring their children with them, and then admit them and their families into the church by washing them with water."

3.2.2.3.*2.* This baptism must be administered *in the name of the Father, and of the Son, and of the Holy Spirit*. That is:

3.2.2.3.*2.1.* By authority from heaven, and not by human authority, for his ministers act by authority from the three persons of the Godhead.

3.2.2.3.*2.2.* Calling upon the name of the Father, Son, and Holy Spirit. Everything is sanctified by prayer, especially the waters of baptism. But:

3.2.2.3.*2.3. Into the name* of the *Father, Son, and Holy Spirit*. This was intended as the summary of the basic principles of the Christian faith. By being baptized, we solemnly profess:

3.2.2.3.*2.3.1.* Our assent to the Scripture revelation of *God, the Father, Son, and Holy Spirit*.

3.2.2.3.*2.3.2.* Our consent to a covenant relationship with God, *the Father, Son, and Holy Spirit*. Baptism is a sacrament, that is, an oath. It is an oath of renunciation, by which we relinquish the world and the flesh as rivals with God for the throne of our hearts, and it is an oath of allegiance, by which we give ourselves to God, to be his, body, soul, and spirit, to be ruled by his will and made happy in his favor; "we become his men," as it says in our form for the oath of homage.

3.2.2.3.*2.3.2.1.* It is into the name of *the Father*, believing him to be both the *Father of our Lord Jesus Christ* (Ro 15:6) and our Father, as our Creator, Preserver, and Benefactor. To him, therefore, we are to give ourselves, so that he may rule us, as free agents, by his law; and it is he whom we are to consider our chief good and highest end.

3.2.2.3.*2.3.2.2.* It is into the name of *the Son*, the Lord Jesus Christ, the *Son of God* (Jn 20:31). In baptism we assent, as Peter did, *Thou art Christ, the Son of the living God* (16:16), and we consent, as Thomas did, *My Lord, and my God* (Jn 20:28). We take Christ to be our Prophet, Priest, and King and give ourselves to be taught, saved, and ruled by him.

3.2.2.3.*2.3.2.3.* It is into the name of *the Holy Spirit*. We give up ourselves to his leadership and guidance as our Sanctifier, Teacher, Guide, and Comforter.

3.2.2.3.*3.* Those who are baptized in this way, and thereby enrolled among the disciples of Christ, must be taught: *Teaching them to observe all things, whatsoever I have commanded you* (v. 20). This shows two things:

3.2.2.3.*3.1.* The duty of disciples, of all baptized Christians; they must observe all things that Christ has commanded, and to that end, they must submit to the teaching of those he sends. He enlists soldiers so that he may train them to serve him. All who are baptized are obliged:

3.2.2.3.*3.1.1.* To make the command of Christ their rule. We are committed by baptism and must obey.

3.2.2.3.*3.1.2. To observe* what Christ has commanded. Appropriate obedience to the commands of Christ requires a diligent observation.

3.2.2.3.*3.1.3.* To observe *all things* that he has commanded, without exception: all the moral duties and all the instituted ordinances.

3.2.2.3.*3.1.4.* To confine themselves to the commands of Christ, not taking away from them and not adding to them.

3.2.2.3.*3.1.5.* To learn their duty according to the law of Christ from those whom he has appointed to be teachers in his school.

3.2.2.3.*3.2.* The duty of the apostles of Christ, and his ministers, and that is to teach the commands of Christ. They must teach them, and Christians must be trained up in the knowledge of them (Pr 22:6). Until the heirs of heaven reach maturity, they must be under tutors.

3.3. The assurance he gave them of his spiritual presence with them as they fulfilled this commission: *And lo, I am with you always, even unto the end of the world.* Notice:

3.3.1. The favor promised them: *I am with you.* Not, "I will be with you," but, "I am." He was now about to leave them; his physical presence was now to be taken away from them, and this grieved them, but he assured them of his spiritual presence. *I am with you,* that is, "My Spirit is with you, the Comforter will *abide with you* (Jn 16:7). I am with you, and not against you. I am with you to take your side, to be at your side. I am *with you,* and not absent from you, not far away; I am a very *present help*" (Ps 46:1). Christ was now sending them to set up his kingdom in the world. Then, he promised, his presence would be always with them:

3.3.1.1. To lead them through the difficulties they were likely to face. "I am with you, to bear you up, to plead your cause, to be with you in all your service, in all your sufferings."

3.3.1.2. To give them success in this great undertaking. "*Lo, I am with you,* to make your ministry effective for the discipling of the nations." It was unlikely that they would persuade people to become the disciples of a crucified Jesus, but *lo, I am with you,* and so you will be triumphant.

3.3.2. The continuation of the favor, *always, even unto the end of the world.*

3.3.2.1. They would have his constant presence. They would have it *always,* "all days," every day. "I will be with you on Sabbaths and weekdays, fair days and foul days, winter days and summer days." Since his resurrection he had appeared to them from time to time. Now, however, he assured them that they would have his spiritual presence continually with them without intermission. The *God of Israel,* the *Saviour, is* sometimes *a God that hideth himself* (Isa 45:15), but never a God who absents himself; sometimes in the dark, but never at a distance.

3.3.2.2. They would have his perpetual presence, even to *the end of the world.* This world is moving quickly toward its end, and until then the Christian faith will, in one part of the world or another, be maintained, and Christ will continue to be present with his ministers. "I am with you *to the end of the world.*" That is:

3.3.2.2.1. "I will be with you and your writings." There is a divine power accompanying the Scriptures of the New Testament, not only preserving them in existence but also producing unusual effects through them, which will continue to the end of time.

3.3.2.2.2. "I will also be with you and your successors, with all who baptize and teach in the way I have instructed." This is an encouraging word to all faithful ministers of Christ, that what was said to the apostles was said to them all: *I will never leave thee, nor forsake thee.*

4. Our Lord Jesus giving two solemn farewells to his church, and his parting word at both of them is very encouraging. One was here: "*Lo, I am with you always;* I leave you, but I am still with you." The other was, "*Surely, I come quickly.* I leave you for a while, but I will be with you again soon" (Rev 22:20). This shows that he did not part in anger, but in love, and that it is his will that we should keep up both our fellowship with him and our expectation of him.

5. One further word remaining, which must not be overlooked, and that is *Amen,* which is not a mere formality, intended only as a conclusion, like "Finis" at the end of a book. It shows Christ's confirmation of this promise, *Lo, I am with you.* It is the *Amen* of the One in whom all *the promises are Yea and Amen* (2Co 1:20). It also shows the church's agreement with this promise, in their desire, prayer, and expectation. It is the evangelist's *Amen,* "'So be it,' blessed Lord." Our *Amen* to Christ's promises turns them into prayers.

A PRACTICAL AND DEVOTIONAL EXPOSITION OF THE GOSPEL OF

Mark

We have heard the evidence given by the first witness to the teaching and miracles of our Lord Jesus Christ, and now here another witness comes, calling for our attention. Now let us inquire:

1. About this witness. His name is *Mark*. *Marcus* was a very common Roman name, but we have no reason to think that Mark was not a Jew by birth. As Saul took the Roman name *Paul*, so this Evangelist took the Roman name *Mark*. We read of a John whose surname was Mark and who was the son of Barnabas's sister, and whom Paul was displeased with (Ac 15:37–38) but later showed great kindness to, not only ordering the churches to receive him (Col 4:10) but also sending for him to be his assistant, with this commendation: *He is profitable to me for the ministry* (2Ti 4:11). Paul also reckoned this John Mark among his fellow workers (Phm 24). We read about a Mark whom Peter called his son (1Pe 5:13); whether this Mark was the same as the one known to Paul is uncertain. It is a tradition passed down by the old commentators that St. Mark wrote this Gospel under the direction of St. Peter, and that it was confirmed by Peter's authority; this is Jerome's view: "Mark, the disciple and interpreter of Peter, being sent from Rome by the brothers, wrote a concise Gospel"; and Tertullian said: "Mark, the interpreter of Peter, delivered in writing the things that had been preached by Peter." It is true that Mark was not an apostle, but we still have good reason to think that both he and Luke belonged to the seventy disciples who received a commission like that of the apostles (16:18; Lk 10:19). St. Jerome says that after writing this Gospel, Mark went into Egypt, where he became the first to preach the Gospel at Alexandria, founding a church there, to which he was a great example of holy living.

2. About this testimony. Mark's Gospel:

2.1. Is short, much shorter than Matthew's, not giving as full an account of Christ's sermons as Matthew did, but insisting chiefly on his miracles.

2.2. Is very much a repetition of what we had in Matthew; many remarkable circumstances are added to the stories related there, but not many new matters. It was right that such great things as these be spoken and written *once, yea twice* (Job 33:14), because we are so disinclined to understand them and so inclined to forget them. Although it was written at Rome, it was written in Greek, as was St. Paul's letter to the Romans, because Greek was the more universal language.

CHAPTER 1

Mark's record does not start as early as those of Matthew and Luke do; it begins at the baptism of John the Baptist. We have here: 1. The work of John the Baptist illustrated by the prophecy about him (vv. 1–3) and the account of him (vv. 4–8). 2. Christ's baptism and his being acknowledged from heaven (vv. 9–11). 3. His temptation (vv. 12–13). 4. His preaching (vv. 14–15, 21–22, 38–39). 5. His calling disciples (vv. 16–20). 6. His praying (v. 35). 7. His working miracles: 7.1. His rebuking an evil spirit (vv. 23–28). 7.2. His healing Peter's mother-in-law, who was sick with a fever (vv. 29–31). 7.3. His healing all who came to him (vv. 32, 34). 7.4. His cleansing a man with leprosy (vv. 40–45).

Verses 1–8

We may notice here:

1. What the New Testament is. It is *the Gospel of Jesus Christ, the Son of God* (v. 1).

1.1. It is *Gospel* ("good news"). It is *a good word* and deserving of full *acceptance* (1Ti 1:15); it brings us good news.

1.2. It is the *Gospel of Jesus Christ*. The previous Gospel began with the *generation of Jesus Christ* (Mt 1:1), that was only preliminary. This one gets down to business immediately—the *Gospel of Christ*.

1.3. This Jesus is the *Son of God*. That truth is the foundation that the Gospel is built on and is written to demonstrate.

2. How the New Testament refers to the Old. The Gospel of Jesus Christ begins, and so we will find it goes on, just *as it is written in the prophets* (v. 2), which was most proper and powerful to convict the Jews, who believed the Old Testament prophets to have been sent by God. However, it is of use to us all to confirm our faith in both the Old Testament and the New. Quotations are taken here from two prophecies—that of Isaiah and that of Malachi, both of whom spoke to the same effect

about *the beginning of the Gospel of Jesus Christ* in the ministry of John.

2.1. Malachi spoke very plainly (Mal 3:1) about John the Baptist. *Behold, I send my messenger before thy face* (v. 2). Christ himself had taken notice of this and had applied it to John (Mt 11:10), who was God's messenger, sent to prepare Christ's way.

2.2. Isaiah, the most evangelical of all the prophets, begins the evangelical part of his prophecy with this quotation, which points to the *beginning of the Gospel of Christ* (Isa 40:3): *The voice of him that crieth in the wilderness* (v. 3). Matthew had taken notice of this and applied it to John as well (Mt 3:3). Such is the corruption of the world that there is something to do to make room for him. When God sent his Son into the world, he took care—and when he sends him into the heart, he takes effective care—to *prepare his way before him*. The mistakes of judgment are put right, and the crooked ways of the desires are straightened: then the way is made open to receive Christ's comforts. It is in a wilderness—for such is this world, like the desert Israel passed through on their way to Canaan—that Christ's way is prepared, and the way of those who follow him lies in similar terrain. Those who are sent to *prepare the way of the Lord* in such a vast, barren desert need to cry aloud.

3. What the beginning of the New Testament was. The Gospel began in John the Baptist. His baptism was the dawning of the Gospel day.

3.1. In John's way of living there was the beginning of a Gospel spirit, for that way showed great self-denial, a holy contempt of the world, and a nonconformity to it. The more we sit loose to the body and live above the world, the better we are prepared for Jesus Christ.

3.2. In John's preaching and baptizing there was the beginning of the Gospel teachings and ordinances:

3.2.1. He preached the *remission* (forgiveness) *of sins*, which is the great Gospel privilege.

3.2.2. He preached *repentance*, as what a person needs in order to know forgiveness of sins; he told people that there must be renewal in their hearts and reformation of their lives.

3.2.3. He preached Christ, and he told his hearers to expect him to appear quickly and to expect great things from him. He preached:

3.2.3.1. The great supremacy Christ was advanced to; Christ is so high and great that John thought himself unworthy to be employed in the lowliest work for him, even to *stoop down* and *untie his shoes* (the thongs of his sandals).

3.2.3.2. The great power Christ was invested with: "He comes *after me* in time, but he is *mightier than I*, for he is able to *baptize with the Holy Spirit.*"

3.2.3.3. The great promise Christ makes in his Gospel to those who have repented and had their sins forgiven them: they will be *baptized with* the Holy Spirit.

3.2.4. All those who received his teaching and submitted to his institution, he *baptized with water*, as the Jews did when they admitted proselytes, as a sign of their cleansing themselves by repentance and reformation and of God's cleansing them both by forgiveness and by sanctification.

3.3. In the success of John's preaching and in the admission of disciples by his baptism there was the beginning of a Gospel church. He baptized *in the wilderness* (desert region); *there went out unto him all the land of Judea, and they of Jerusalem*, and they *were all baptized of him*. They committed themselves to be his disciples and submitted to his discipline, and as a sign of this, they confessed their sins. He admitted them as his disciples, and as a sign of this, he baptized them. Many of these later became followers of Christ and preachers of his Gospel; this grain of mustard seed became a tree (4:31–32).

Verses 9–13

Here is a brief account of Christ's baptism and temptation, which were largely related in Mt 3–4.

1. His baptism took place at his first public appearance, after he had long lived in obscurity in Nazareth.

1.1. Notice how humbly he acknowledged God by coming to be *baptized of* (by) *John*. Although he was perfectly pure and unspotted, he was washed as if he had been defiled.

1.2. Notice how honorably God acknowledged him when he submitted to John's baptism.

1.2.1. He *saw the heavens opened*; this was how he was acknowledged to be the Lord from heaven. Matthew said, *The heavens were opened to him.* Mark says, *He saw them opened.* Many have the heavens opened to receive them but do not see it.

1.2.2. He *saw the Spirit like a dove descending upon him*. It is an ancient tradition that a great light shone around the place.

1.2.3. He heard a voice that was intended to give him encouragement to proceed in his undertaking, and so it is expressed here as directed to him: *Thou art my beloved Son*. God is *well pleased* with him, and so well pleased with him as to be well pleased with us in him.

2. His temptation. The *Holy Spirit* who descended on him *led him into the wilderness* (v. 12). Withdrawing from the world provides the opportunity for free fellowship with God, and so it must sometimes be chosen even by those who are busiest. Mark notices concerning Jesus' being *in the wilderness* that he was *with the wild beasts*. His Father showed his care for him by preserving him from being torn to pieces by the wild animals, and this encouraged him to believe that his Father would provide for him when he was hungry. Special forms of protection are pledges of timely supplies. In that desert:

2.1. The evil spirits were active in opposing him; he *was tempted of* (by) *Satan*. Christ himself was tempted, not only to teach us that it is not a sin to be tempted but also to direct us to where we should go for help when we are tempted, to the One who suffered when he was tempted (Heb 2:18; 4:15).

2.2. The good spirits were active with him; the *angels ministered to him*, supplying him with what he needed. This shows us that the ministry of the good angels around us is a matter of great comfort in reference to the harmful intentions of the evil angels against us.

Verses 14–22

Here is:

1. A general account of Christ's preaching in Galilee. Notice:

1.1. When Jesus began to preach in Galilee: *After that John was put in prison*. When John had finished his testimony (Rev 11:7), Jesus began his.

1.2. What he preached: *The gospel of the kingdom of God*. Christ came to establish the kingdom of God among human beings, and he set it up by preaching his Gospel, with power accompanying it. Notice:

1.2.1. The great truths Christ preached: *The time is fulfilled, and the kingdom of God is at hand*. Christ explained the prophecies and signs of the times to them: "The time established beforehand is now at hand; glorious revelations of divine light, life, and love are now to be given." God keeps his time; when *the time is fulfilled, the kingdom of God is at hand* (v. 15).

1.2.2. The great duties inferred from these. Christ helped them to understand the times so that they would know what Israel should do (1Ch 12:32); they fondly expected the Messiah to appear in a display of power. They thought, therefore, that when that *kingdom of God* was *at hand*, they must prepare for war and victory. Christ told them, however, that in the prospect of that approaching kingdom, they must *repent, and believe the gospel*. By repentance we must mourn and abandon our sins, and by faith we must receive forgiveness of them. These must go together; we must not think either that reforming our lives will save us without trusting in the righteousness and grace of Christ, or that trusting in Christ will save us without reformation of our hearts and lives. Christ has joined these two together, and so no one should think of separating them (10:9). This is how the preaching of the Gospel began, and this is how it continues; the call remains, "Repent and believe, and live a life of repentance and faith."

2. Christ's appearing as a teacher and his *calling of disciples* (vv. 16–20). Notice:

2.1. Christ wants to have followers. If he is going to set up a school, he wants students; if he sets up his flag, he wants soldiers; if he preaches, he wants listeners.

2.2. The instruments Christ chose to employ in setting up his kingdom were the *weak* and *foolish things of the world* (1Co 1:27); they were not called from the great Sanhedrin or the schools of the rabbis, but drawn from the fishermen by the seaside.

2.3. Although Christ does not need human help, he is nevertheless pleased to use it in setting up his kingdom.

2.4. Christ honors those who are diligent in their business and loving to one another, as those whom he called in the beginning were. He found them working, and working together. Diligence and unity are good and pleasant (Ps 133:1), and where they are, the Lord Jesus commands the blessing: *Follow me.*

2.5. The work of ministers is to fish for souls and win them for Christ. When ministers preach the Gospel, they should *cast the net* into the waters (Mt 13:47). Some fish are caught and brought to shore, but most of them escape. If after drawing up the net many times the fishers have brought up nothing, they must still continue.

2.6. Those whom Christ calls must *leave all* to follow him, and by his grace he inclines them to do so. We must not cling to the things of this world; we are to forsake everything that is inconsistent with our duty to Christ. Mark comments that James and John left not only *their father*—which we read in Matthew—but also *the hired servants*, who were their fellow laborers and pleasant companions; not only relatives but also old friends must be left for Christ.

3. A particular account of his preaching in Capernaum. Notice:

3.1. When Christ *came into Capernaum*, he immediately applied himself to his work there, taking the first opportunity to preach the Gospel. Those who consider how much work they still have to do and what little time remains to do it in will think they must lose no time.

3.2. Christ religiously observed the Sabbath.

3.3. Sabbaths are to be sanctified by attendance at religious assemblies, if we have opportunity; it is *a holy day.*

3.4. In religious meetings on Sabbath days, the Gospel is to be preached.

3.5. Christ was an incomparable preacher; he did not preach *as the scribes* (v. 22), who recited the Law of Moses by rote. Their teaching did not come from the heart and therefore did not come with authority. But Christ taught *as one that had authority.*

Verses 23–28

As soon as Christ began to preach, he began to perform miracles to confirm his teaching. Here we have:

1. Christ's *casting the devil* out of a man in the synagogue at Capernaum who was possessed. *There was in the synagogue a man with an unclean spirit*, "in an evil spirit," for the spirit possessed the man and led him captive at his will. This man *was in the synagogue*, yet he did not come either to be taught or to be healed. We have here:

1.1. The rage that the evil spirit expressed at Christ: *He cried out*, as one in anguish at the presence of Christ. We are told what he said (v. 24); he did not seek terms but spoke as one who knew his doom.

1.1.1. He called him *Jesus of Nazareth*; it may be that he was the first who called him that, and he did it to fill the minds of the people with low thoughts of Jesus, because no good thing was expected to come from Nazareth.

1.1.2. A confession was, however, extorted from him—that he was *the holy One of God*. Those who have only an idea of Christ but have no faith in him or love for him go no further than the Devil.

1.1.3. He in effect acknowledged that he could not stand before the power of Christ: "*Let us alone*; for if you take us to task, we are ruined, because you can *destroy us*."

1.1.4. He wanted to have nothing to do with Jesus Christ, for he despaired of being saved by him and dreaded being destroyed by him.

1.2. The victory that Jesus Christ gained over the evil spirit. It is futile for Satan to beg and pray, *Let us alone*; his power must be broken, and the poor man must be relieved.

1.2.1. Jesus commanded. Just as he taught *with authority*, so he also healed with authority. Jesus *rebuked him*; *Hold thy peace*; "be muzzled." Christ has a muzzle for that evil spirit when he fawns as well as when he barks. However, this was not all; the spirit must not only *hold his peace* but also *come out of the man*.

1.2.2. The evil spirit yielded, for there was no remedy (v. 26). He *tore him*, shook the man violently. He would not touch Christ, but he vented his fury by distressing this poor creature terribly. When Christ by his grace rescues poor souls from the hands of Satan, it is not without terrible turmoil in the soul. The spirit *cried with a loud voice* (with a shriek), to frighten the spectators and make himself seem terrible.

2. The impression this miracle had on the minds of the people (vv. 27–28).

2.1. It astonished those who saw it: *They were all amazed*. This was surprising to them and made them discuss the matter among themselves, asking one another, "*What is this new doctrine?* For it must certainly come from God, since it is confirmed in this way." The Jewish exorcists tried to use their charms or invocations to drive out evil spirits, but this was completely different; *with authority he commands them*. Surely it is in our interests to make the One who has control of evil spirits our Friend.

2.2. It built up Christ's reputation among all who heard it: *Immediately his fame spread abroad into the whole adjacent region of Galilee*. The story was soon on everyone's lips, together with the comment, *What new doctrine is this?* It was therefore generally concluded that he was a *Teacher come from God* (Jn 3:2). This was how he prepared his own way, now that John, who was his messenger, was in prison.

Verses 29–39

In these verses, we have:

1. A particular account of one miracle that Christ performed, the healing of Peter's mother-in-law.

1.1. When Christ had done what caused news about him to spread everywhere, he did not then sit back, as some do, who think that they can lie in bed when they become well known. No; he continued to do good (Ac 10:38). Those who enjoy a good reputation need to be busy and be careful to maintain their good deeds.

1.2. When he *came out of the synagogue*, where he had taught and healed with divine authority, he still spoke in a friendly way with the poor fishermen who were with him.

1.3. He went to Peter's house; he was probably invited there to be received with such hospitality as a poor fisherman could give him, and he accepted it.

1.4. He healed Peter's mother-in-law, who was sick. Wherever Christ comes, he comes to do good, and he will be sure to richly reward those who receive him. The same hand that healed her also strengthened her, so that she was able to serve them. Healings are performed so that we may be fit for action.

2. A general account of many healings he performed—diseases healed, demons driven out. It was on the evening of the Sabbath, when the *sun did set*, or had set; perhaps many had scruples about bringing their sick to him, thinking they should wait until the Sabbath was over, yet their weakness in that matter did not deter them. Notice:

2.1. How numerous the patients were: *All the city* (the whole town) *was gathered at the door*, like those who beg for charity. The one healing in the synagogue caused this crowd to come to him. The fact that others do well with Christ should motivate us to seek him. Many people flocked to Christ in a private house, as well as in the synagogue; wherever he is, let his servants, his patients, be.

2.2. How powerful the Physician was; he *healed all* who were brought to him, even though there were very many. Nor was it only one particular disease that Christ healed; he healed those who were *sick of divers* (various) diseases. He repeated in the house at night the miracle that he performed in the synagogue, because he *cast* (drove) *out many devils* and *suffered not the devils to* (would not let the demons) *speak*.

3. His withdrawal to his private devotion (v. 35): *He prayed* alone, to set us an example of private prayer. Although he was prayed to as God, he also prayed as a human being. He still found time to be alone with his Father. Notice:

3.1. The time when Christ prayed.

3.1.1. It was *in the morning*, the morning after the Sabbath day. We must go to the *throne of grace* (Heb 4:16) every day of the week. This morning was the morning of the *first day of the week*, which he later sanctified and made remarkable by another kind of *rising early* (16:9).

3.1.2. It was early, *a great while before day*. When others were still asleep in their beds, he was praying. When our spirits are at their most fresh and lively, then we should take time for devout exercises.

3.2. The place where he prayed: he *departed into a solitary place*. Private prayer must be made in private. Those who have the most business in public, even business of the best kind, must sometimes be alone with God.

4. His return to his public work. The disciples thought they were up early, but they found that their Master had already gotten up before them, and *followed him* to his solitary place and there *found him* at prayer (vv. 36–37). They told him that he was wanted by many people. *All men seek for thee*. They were proud that their Master had become so popular already, and they wanted him to appear in public, even more in that place, because it was their own city. "*No*," Christ said, "*Let us go into the next towns*, the villages, *that I may preach there also, for therefore came I forth*, to *go about doing good* (Ac 10:38)." He *preached in their synagogues throughout all Galilee*, and to illustrate and confirm his teaching, *he cast out devils*.

Verses 40–45

Here we have the record of Christ's *cleansing a leper* (a man with leprosy) (the Greek word was used for various diseases affecting the skin—not necessarily leprosy [Ed.]). This teaches us:

1. How to turn to Christ, to come, as this leper did:

1.1. With great humility. This leper came *beseeching him and kneeling down to him* (begging him on his knees) (v. 40); it teaches us that those who want to receive grace and mercy from Christ must approach him with humility and reverence.

1.2. With a firm belief in his power: *Thou canst make me clean*. He believed it with application to himself; he not only believed, in general, *Thou canst do every thing* (Jn 11:22), but also, *Thou canst make me clean*. What we believe about the power of Christ, we must bring home to our own particular situation: *Thou canst do this for me*.

1.3. With submission to the will of Christ: *Lord, if thou wilt*. With the modesty befitting a poor petitioner, he handed over his own particular situation to him.

2. What to expect from Christ: that it will be to us according to our faith (Mt 9:29). His words were not in the form of prayer, but Christ answered them as a request.

2.1. Christ was *moved with compassion*. This is added here in Mark to show that Christ's pity employs his power to help and relieve poor souls. Our misery makes us the objects of his mercy. Moreover, what he does for us he does with all possible tenderness.

2.2. He *put forth his hand, and touched him*. In healing souls, Christ *toucheth them* (1Sa 10:26). Christ *toucheth* and *healeth* too.

2.3. He said, *I will, be thou clean*. The poor leper put an *if* on the will of Christ: *If thou wilt*; but that doubt was soon put beyond doubt: *I will*. Christ most readily wills favors to those who most readily turn themselves to his will. The man was confident of Christ's power; you *can make me clean*; and Christ will show how much the faith of his people draws his power into action. *Be thou clean.* Power accompanied this word, and the healing was complete in a moment: *Immediately his leprosy* vanished, and no further sign remained of it (v. 42).

3. What to do when we have received mercy from Christ. Along with his favors, we must receive his commands. When Christ had healed him, *he strictly charged him*. It is possible that this refers not to the directions Christ gave him to conceal it (v. 44)—for those are mentioned by themselves—but that *strictly charged him* refers to the sort of command he gave to the invalid he healed: *Sin no more, lest a worse thing come unto thee* (Jn 5:14). He also instructed him:

3.1. To *show himself to the priest*.

3.2. Not to *say any thing* of it *to any man* until he had done that. He must not proclaim it, because that would very much increase the crowd that followed Christ, which he thought was too great already. Not that he was unwilling to do good to everyone, to as many who came, but he wanted to do it with as little noise as possible. I do not know what to think of the leper's talking about it freely and spreading the news. He should have observed Christ's orders; yet no doubt he meant well when he freely told about the healing, and the only adverse effect was that it increased the crowds who followed Christ to the extent that he *could no more openly enter into the city*. This made him go into *desert places*. This shows how necessary it was for us that Christ should go *away*, for he could be bodily present in only one place at a time. By his spiritual presence he is with his people wherever they are, coming to them everywhere.

CHAPTER 2

In this chapter we have: 1. Christ's healing a paralytic (vv. 1–12). 2. His calling Matthew from the tax collector's booth and his eating with tax collectors and sinners (vv. 13–17). 3. His justifying his disciples in not fasting as much as the disciples of the Pharisees did (vv. 18–22). 4. His justifying them in picking some heads of grain on the Sabbath (vv. 23–28).

Verses 1–12

Having preached in the country for some time, Christ returned to Capernaum, his headquarters. Notice:

1. How many sought him there. Although he was *in the house*, people still came to him as soon as it was reported that he was in town. *Straightway many were gathered together to him*. Where the king is, the court sits. There were so many people that *there was no room to receive them, no, not so much as about* (not even outside) *the door*. It is wonderful to see people rushing in this way, *like a cloud* (Isa 60:8), to Christ's house.

2. The good reception Christ gave them; he *preached the word unto them* (v. 2). Many of them perhaps came only for healing, and many perhaps only out of curiosity, to catch a glimpse of him, but when he had them all together, he *preached to them*. He did not think it at all wrong to preach in a house on a weekday, even though some might have considered it an improper place and an improper time.

3. The presenting of a poor paralytic to him to be helped by him. The patient was *sick of the palsy* (paralyzed), completely disabled, so that he was carried by four men on *a bed* (mat), as if he were on a bier. It showed his miserable condition that he needed to be carried in this way; the men carried him out of love and kindness. These kind relatives or neighbors thought that if they could only carry this poor man to Christ once, they would not need to carry him anymore, and so they made a great effort to get him to him. They *uncovered* (dug through) *the roof where he was* (v. 4). Probably, the house was so small and insignificant that it had no upper room, but had the ground floor open to the roof, and these petitioners for the poor paralytic, unable to get through the crowd at the door, got their friend onto the roof of the house by some means or other, took off some of the tiles, and so let him down on his mat with cords into the house where Christ was preaching. This showed both their faith and their fervency. Here it was made clear that they were serious and that they would neither go away nor *let* Christ *go without a blessing* (Ge 32:26).

4. The kind words Christ said to this poor patient: *He saw their faith*, the faith of those who brought him. He commended their faith, because they brought their friend through so much difficulty. True faith and strong faith may work in various ways, conquering sometimes the objections of reason, sometimes those of sense, but however it

reveals itself, it will be accepted and approved by Jesus Christ. Christ said, *Son, thy sins be forgiven thee*. The title is very tender: *Son*. Christ acknowledges true believers as his sons: sons, but also paralytics. The comfort and reassurance is great: *Thy sins are forgiven thee*. Christ's words were to take the paralytic's thoughts off the disease, which was the effect, and to lead them to the sin, which was the cause, so that he would be more concerned about that—to get that forgiven. Recovery from sickness is a true mercy when the way is made for it by the forgiveness of sin. The way to remove the effect is to take away the cause. Forgiveness of sin strikes at the root of all diseases, either curing them or altering their effect.

5. The objection of some teachers of the law to what Christ said. Their job was to explain the law, and their teaching was true, but their application was false. It was true that none *can forgive sins but God only*, but it was false that therefore Christ could not. However, Christ *perceived in his spirit that they so reasoned within themselves*, and this proved him to be God. God's royal powers are inseparable, and the One who could know thoughts could also forgive sins. Now he proved his power to forgive sin by demonstrating his power to heal the *man sick of the palsy* (vv. 9–11). He would not have claimed to do the one if he could not do the other. *That ye may know that the Son of man has power on earth to forgive sin, thou that art sick of the palsy, arise, take up thy bed*. He could not have healed the disease, which was the effect, if he could not take away the sin, which was the cause. The One who could accomplish the sign by a word could no doubt perform the thing signified. It was therefore appropriate enough for him to appeal to them as to whether it is easier to say, *Thy sins are forgiven thee*, or to say, *Arise, and walk?* The removing of the punishment as such was the forgiving of the sin; the One who could go so far in the healing could no doubt complete it.

6. The healing of the paralytic and the impression it made on the people (v. 12). He not only arose from his bed, perfectly well, but also *took up his bed and went forth before them all*, and *they were all amazed* and *glorified God* saying, *"We never saw it on this fashion* (we have never seen anything like this)." Christ's works were without precedent. When we see what he does in healing souls, we must acknowledge that we have never seen anything like it.

Verses 13–17

Here is:

1. Christ's preaching by the *sea side* (beside the lake) (v. 13), where he went for some room. On the beach, as many as wanted to could come to him. It seems by this that our Lord Jesus had a strong voice and could and did speak loudly.

2. His calling Levi, the same person as Matthew, who had a place in the tax collector's booth at Capernaum and was therefore called *a publican* (tax collector). His position required that he be by the waterside, and Christ went to meet him there. Matthew was probably a loose and extravagant young man, for otherwise, being a Jew, he would never have become a tax collector. Christ called him to follow him. With God, through Christ, there is mercy to forgive the greatest sins and grace to sanctify the greatest sinners. Matthew, who had been a tax collector, became an evangelist. Great sin and scandal before conversion are no barrier to great gifts, graces, and advancements after conversion; in fact, God may be even more glorified. In physical healings, usually Christ was sought after, but in these spiritual healings, he was *found of them* (2Pe 3:14) that *sought him not* (1Ch 15:13). For the great

evil and danger of the disease of sin is that those who are under it do not want to be made whole.

3. His close dealings with *publicans and sinners* (v. 15). We are told here:

3.1. That Christ *sat at meat in Levi's house*, Levi having invited *him and his disciples* to the farewell feast he gave for his friends when he left everything to be with Christ.

3.2. That *many publicans and sinners* sat with Christ in Levi's house, and *they followed him*. They followed Levi, as some understand it. I rather think that they followed Jesus, because of the news they had heard about him. They did not leave all to follow him for the sake of conscience, but came to Levi's feast out of curiosity to see him. The tax collectors here and elsewhere are ranked with the worst of sinners:

3.2.1. Because commonly they were the worst of sinners; so pervasive were the corruptions of those who held that office: oppressing, exacting, taking bribes or extortionate fees, and *accusing falsely* (Lk 3:13–14).

3.2.2. Because the Jews had a particular hatred toward them and their work. The collection of taxes from the Jews showed contempt to the liberty of their nation, and so it was thought scandalous to be seen in their company. Yet our blessed Lord was pleased to converse with such people when he appeared *in the likeness of sinful flesh* (Ro 8:3).

4. The offense that the teachers of the law and Pharisees took at this (v. 16). They refused to come to hear him preach, which they might have been convinced and built up by, but they were willing to come to see him sit with tax collectors and sinners, which they would be provoked by. They wanted to make the disciples dissatisfied with their Master, and so they put the question to them: *How is it that he eateth and drinketh with publicans and sinners?*

5. Christ's justification of himself in it (v. 17). He stood by what he did and would not withdraw. Those who decline to undertake a good work because to do so might harm their reputation with fastidious people are too concerned for their reputation. Christ was the opposite. The teachers of the law and Pharisees thought the tax collectors were to be hated. "No," Christ said, "they are to be pitied; they are *sick* and *need a physician*. They are sinners and need a Savior." These leaders thought Christ's character should separate him from them; "No," Christ said, "*I came not to call the righteous, but sinners to repentance.* I have been sent to a sinful world, and so my business lies most with those who are its greatest sinners." Or: "*I am not come to call the righteous,* the proud Pharisees, who think they are righteous, but poor tax collectors, who acknowledge themselves to be sinners and are glad to be invited and encouraged to repent." It is good to deal with those for whom there is hope.

Verses 18–28

Here Christ was called on to justify his disciples, and he would justify and support them in what they did according to his will, and he still does.

1. He justified them in their not fasting. Why did the Pharisees and the disciples of John fast? They *used to fast*; it was the custom of the Pharisees to fast *twice in the week* (Lk 18:12), and probably the disciples of John did so too. In this way, strict professors of faith tend to make their own practice a standard, and to criticize and condemn all who do not live up to it. The Pharisees and John's disciples invidiously suggested that even if Christ went among sinners to do them good, the disciples did it to indulge their appetites, for they never fasted. Ill will

always suspects the worst. Christ pleaded two things to excuse his disciples from fasting.

1.1. That these were easy days for them, days of relative comfort, and fasting was not then as appropriate as it would be later (vv. 19–20). There is a time for all things.

1.2. That these were early days for them, and they were not able to undergo the severe exercises of religious faith that they would later be subjected to. The Pharisees had long ago gotten used to such austerity, and John the Baptist himself came neither eating nor drinking (Mt 11:18). It was not so with Christ's disciples, however; their Master *came eating and drinking* (Mt 11:19), and had not yet taught them to endure the difficult services of religious faith. To call them to undergo such frequent fasting from the beginning would discourage them. It would be as damaging as *putting new wine into old casks* or sewing *new cloth* onto what has worn thin and threadbare (vv. 21–22). God graciously considers *the frame of* young Christians (Ps 103:14), who are weak and young, and so must we; nor must we expect more than the work of the day in its day, according to the strength given. Weak Christians must make sure they do not overtax themselves, making the yoke of Christ harder than it really is, when it is easy, sweet, and pleasant (Mt 11:30).

2. He justified them in *plucking the ears of corn on the sabbath day*, which I am certain a disciple of the Pharisees would not dare to do, because it went against an explicit tradition of their elders. The Pharisees criticized the discipline of Christ's school as too easy. It is common for those who deny the *power of godliness* to be jealous for its *form* and critical of those who do not follow *their* form of it (2Ti 3:5). Notice:

2.1. What a poor breakfast Christ's disciples had on a Sabbath morning, as they went to church (v. 23); they *picked the heads of grain*, and that was the best they had. They were so intent on the spiritual delicacies in store for them in worship that they forgot even their *necessary food* (Job 23:12).

2.2. How even this was grudged them by the Pharisees, who considered it unlawful to *pluck the ears of corn* on the Sabbath because that was work as much as *reaping* was (v. 24): *Why do they on the sabbath day that which is not lawful?* If Christ's disciples do what is unlawful, it will reflect badly on Christ. It is significant that when the Pharisees thought Christ did wrong, they told the disciples (v. 16), and now when they thought the disciples did wrong, they spoke to Christ.

2.3. How Christ defended them.

2.3.1. By example. They had a good precedent for it in David's eating the *showbread* (the consecrated bread) (1Sa 21:6): *Have ye never read?* (vv. 25–26). Ritual observances must give way to moral obligations, and there are things that may be done in a case of necessity that otherwise may not be done.

2.3.2. By argument. To reconcile them to the disciples' picking the heads of grain, let them consider:

2.3.2.1. Whom the Sabbath was made for: *it was made for man, and not man for the sabbath* (v. 27). The Sabbath is a sacred and divine institution, but we must receive and embrace it as a privilege and a benefit, not as a chore and a drudge.

2.3.2.1.1. God never intended it to be an imposition on us, and so we must not make it so to ourselves. People were made for God, for his honor and service, but people were not *made for the Sabbath*.

2.3.2.1.2. God did intend it to be a benefit to us. He made it for people. He had some regard to our bodies in instituting the Sabbath; he wanted them to be able to rest, not be exhausted by the constant business of this world. He had much more regard for our souls. The Sabbath was made to be a day of rest only so that it could be a day of holy work, a day of fellowship with God, a day of praise and thanksgiving. Rest from worldly business is necessary so that we may more closely turn to that work. See here:

2.3.2.1.*2.1*. What a good Master we serve, all of whose institutions are for our own benefit. It is not he, but we, who gain by our service.

2.3.2.1.*2.2*. What we should aim at in our Sabbath work. If the Sabbath was made for human beings, we should then ask ourselves at the end of a Sabbath, "In what ways am I better because of this Sabbath?"

2.3.2.1.*2.3*. What care we should take not to make religious exercises a burden to ourselves or others, since God ordained them to be blessings.

2.3.2.2. Whom the Sabbath was made by: *The Son of man is Lord also of the sabbath* (v. 28). The Sabbath days are *days of the Son of man* (Lk 17:22); he is the Lord of the day, and it must be observed to his honor. It would be moved one day forward to the first day of the week in remembrance of his resurrection, and that was why the Christian Sabbath was to be called *the Lord's day* (Rev 1:10).

CHAPTER 3

We have here: 1. Christ's healing a man with a shriveled hand on the Sabbath (vv. 1–6). 2. The widespread turning of people to him from everywhere to be healed (vv. 7–12). 3. His appointing his twelve apostles (vv. 13–21). 4. His answer to the teachers of the law, who attributed his power to drive out demons to an alliance with the prince of demons (vv. 22–30). 5. His acknowledging his disciples as his closest and most precious relatives (vv. 31–35).

Verses 1–12

Here, as before, we have our Lord Jesus busy at work, first in the synagogue, then by the lake. This teaches us that his presence should not be confined either to the one or to the other, but that wherever any are gathered in his name, he is there in their midst (Mt 18:20).

1. When he *entered again into the synagogue*, he used the opportunity to do good.

1.1. The patient's case was pitiful; he had a *withered* (shriveled) *hand*, which made him unable to work for his living. Let those who cannot help themselves be helped.

1.2. The spectators were very unkind, both to the patient and to the Physician; instead of interceding for a poor neighbor, they did what they could to stop him from being healed: they hinted that if Christ healed him now on the Sabbath, they would accuse him of being a Sabbath breaker.

1.3. Christ dealt very fairly with the spectators, and he dealt with them first, so that if possible he might prevent the offense.

1.3.1. He sought to convince their judgment. He told the man to *stand forth* (stand up in front of everyone) (v. 3), so that by seeing him they might be moved with compassion. He then appealed to their own consciences; "*Is it lawful to do good on the sabbath days, or to do evil? Which is better, to save life or to kill?*" What fairer question could be put? However, because they saw that it would turn out against them, *they held their peace*.

1.3.2. When they rebelled against the light, he mourned their stubbornness: *He looked round about on them with anger, being grieved for the hardness of their hearts*

(v. 5). The sin he saw was the hardness of their hearts. We hear what is said wrongly and see what is done wrongly, but Christ looks at the root of bitterness in the heart (Dt 29:18; Heb 12:15), the blindness and hardness of the heart. Notice:

1.3.2.1. How he was provoked by the sin; he looked *round upon them*. He looked *with anger*; his anger was probably apparent on his face. The sin of sinners is very displeasing to Jesus Christ, and the way to be angry and not sin (Ps 4:4) is to be angry, as Christ was, at nothing except sin.

1.3.2.2. How he pitied the sinners; he was *grieved for the hardness of their hearts*. It deeply distresses our Lord Jesus to see sinners intent on their own destruction, because he does not want anyone to perish (2Pe 3:9). This is a good reason why the hardness of our own hearts and of the hearts of others should make us deeply distressed.

1.4. Christ dealt very kindly with the patient; he told him to *stretch forth his hand*, and it was immediately *restored*. Christ teaches us here to continue to be resolved to do our duty, however violent the opposition we may encounter. We must not deny ourselves the satisfaction of serving God and doing good, even though offense may unjustly be taken at it. No one could be more considerate with regard to giving offense than Christ, but rather than send this poor man away unhealed, he would dare to offend all the teachers of the law and Pharisees who surrounded him. In this he has given us an example of the healing performed by his grace on poor souls. Our hands are spiritually shriveled: the powers of our souls are weakened by sin. Although our hands are shriveled, and we cannot by ourselves *stretch them forth*, we must try to do so; we must, as well as we can, *lift them up to* God in prayer (La 3:21), *lay hold* of Christ and eternal life (1Ti 6:19), and use them in good works. If we do this, power goes along with the word of Christ, and he brings about the healing. If we will not try to stretch out, it is our own fault that we are not healed.

1.5. The enemies of Christ dealt very cruelly with him. Such a work of mercy should have stirred their love for him, and such a miracle should have stirred their faith in him. But instead the Pharisees and the Herodians *took counsel together against him, how they might destroy him*.

2. When he withdrew *to the sea* (lake), he did good there (v. 7). Now that his enemies were trying to destroy him, he left that place, to teach us to provide for our own safety in troublesome times. Notice here:

2.1. How he was followed to the place he withdrew to. When some people were so hostile toward him that they drove him out of their country, others esteemed him so much that they followed him wherever he went. *Great multitudes* followed him from all parts of the nation. Notice:

2.1.1. What motivated them to follow him: the news they heard of the *great things he did*. Some wanted to see the person who had done such great things, and others hoped he would do great things for them. The consideration of the great things Christ has done should make us come to him.

2.1.2. What they followed him for: *they pressed upon him, to touch him, as many as had plagues* (those with diseases were pushing forward to touch him) (v. 10). Diseases are here called *plagues*; the Greek is *mastigas*, "corrections," "chastisements." Those who were suffering in this way came to Jesus; this is the mission for which sickness is sent, to make us seek Christ and turn to him as our Physician. The people pushed forward, each trying to get closest to him and be helped first. They wanted to be allowed simply to touch him, having faith that they would be healed not only if he touched them but even if they touched him.

2.1.3. What provision he made to be with them: *he spoke to his disciples* (v. 9), telling them to make *a small ship* (boat) ready for him, to carry him from place to place on the same coast without pushing through the crowds who followed him out of curiosity. Wise people avoid a crowd as far as is possible.

2.2. How much good he did when he had withdrawn. He did not draw back to be idle, nor did he send back those who rudely crowded after him when he withdrew; he took it kindly and gave them what they came for, because he never said to anyone who sought him diligently, *Seek ye me in vain* (Isa 45:19).

2.2.1. Diseases were healed powerfully: he *healed many*.

2.2.2. Demons were defeated powerfully; when those who were possessed by evil spirits *saw him*, they trembled at his presence, and they also *fell down before him*, not to seek his favor, but to pray to be saved from his wrath.

2.2.3. Christ did not seek to attract praise to himself in doing those great things, for *he strictly charged* those people for whom he did them *that they should not make him known* (v. 12), that they should not seek to publicize his healing, should not, as it were, put advertisements in the newspapers, but allow *his own works to praise him*, let news of them spread by itself and make its own way. Let the bystanders take away news of it.

Verses 13 – 21

In these verses, we have:

1. Christ's choosing of the twelve apostles to be with him as his constant followers. Notice:

1.1. The introduction to this call, or advancement, of disciples; Christ *went up into a mountain*, and his purpose there was *to pray* (Lk 6:12).

1.2. The rule he followed in his choosing, which was that he chose those he wanted: *He called unto him whom he would*; not those whom we would have thought fittest to be called, but those he thought fit to call, those he was determined to equip for the service to which he called them. Christ calls those *whom he will*.

1.3. The effectiveness of the call: he *called* them to separate themselves from the crowd and to stand by him, and they *came unto him*. He made willing to come those whom it was his will to call (Ps 110:3).

1.4. The purpose and intention of this call: he appointed them *that they should be with him* constantly, to be witnesses of *his doctrine, manner of life, and patience*, that they could *fully know it* (2Ti 3:10). They must be with him to receive instructions from him, so that they would be qualified to give instructions to others. It would require time to equip them for the purposes he intended them for. Christ's ministers must spend a lot of time with him.

1.5. The power he gave them to perform miracles. He appointed them to *heal sicknesses and to cast out devils*. This showed that Christ's power to work these miracles was an original power; he did not receive it *as a Servant*, but *as a Son in his own house* (Heb 3:6). Our Lord Jesus had *life in himself* (Jn 5:26) and the Spirit without limit (Jn 3:34), and so he could give this power even to the *weak* and *foolish things* of the world (1Co 1:27).

1.6. Their number and names; he *ordained twelve*, according to the number of the twelve tribes of Israel. They are named here not in exactly the same order as they were in Matthew, and yet here, as there, Peter comes first and Judas last. Here Matthew is put before Thomas, but in the list that Matthew himself drew up, he put himself after Thomas. However, what only Mark takes notice of in this list of the apostles is that Christ called James and John *Boanerges*, which means, *the sons of thunder*; perhaps they were remarkable for their loud, commanding voices — they were thundering preachers — or rather it showed the zeal and fervency of their spirits. Yet John, one of those *sons of thunder*, was full of love and tenderness — as can be seen from his letters — and was the disciple whom Christ especially loved.

1.7. Their withdrawal with their Master and their close loyalty to him: *They went into a house*. Now that this jury was enrolled, they stood together to listen to the evidence.

2. The constant crowds that were present wherever Christ went: *the multitude cometh together again* (v. 20), unsent for and pushing toward him at an inopportune time. The result was that he and his disciples could not get enough time even *to eat bread*. He did not shut his doors against those who sought him, however, but made them welcome. Those whose hearts are released in the work of God can easily bear great inconveniences in pursuing that work. It is beneficial when zealous hearers and zealous preachers meet in this way and encourage one another. This was a favorable wind of opportunity that was worth making good use of. It is good to strike while the iron is hot.

3. The concern of his relatives for him: *When his friends* in Capernaum heard how he was followed, they *went out to lay hold on him* and bring him home, for they said, *He is beside himself* (v. 21).

3.1. Some understand this as referring to an absurd and preposterous concern, which contained more contempt toward him than respect, and this is how we must take it, as our translation reads it: *He is beside himself*. His family was willing to listen to this misinterpretation that some gave to his great zeal, and to conclude that he had gone crazy.

3.2. Others understand this as showing a well-meaning concern, and then they translate *exeste* as, "He faints" — "He has no time to eat bread, and so his strength will fail him. He will suffocate in the crowd of people. We will therefore use friendly force with him and give him a little breathing space." Those who pursue the work of God with vigor and zeal must expect to meet hindrances, both from the unfounded dislike of their enemies and from the mistaken affections of their friends.

Verses 22 – 30

Here is:

1. The ungodly and arrogant smear the teachers of the law directed at Christ's driving out demons. These *scribes came down from Jerusalem* (v. 22). It seems they deliberately came on this long journey to slow down the progress of Christ's teaching. Coming from Jerusalem, which was the home of the most refined and learned teachers of the law, they were in a better position to cause trouble. The reputation of teachers of the law from Jerusalem would have an influence not only on the country people but also on the country scribes. They could not deny that he drove out demons, but they insinuated that *he had Beelzebub* on his side and by *the prince of the devils cast out devils*. "There is a deception in the case: Satan is not driven out; he only goes out by consent."

2. The reasonable answer Christ gave to this objection.

2.1. Satan is so subtle that he will never voluntarily give up his possession: *If Satan cast out Satan, his kingdom is divided against itself*, and it *cannot stand* (vv. 23 – 26). He *called them to him*; he condescended to reason with them, so *that every mouth may be stopped* (Ro 3:19). It was clear that the teaching of Christ made war on the Devil's kingdom and had a direct tendency to break his power, and it was just as clear that driving demons out of the bodies of people confirmed that teaching. Everyone knows that Satan is no fool, nor will he act so directly against his own interests.

2.2. Christ is so wise that being engaged in war with Satan, he will attack his forces wherever he meets them, whether in the bodies of people or in their souls (v. 27). It is clear that Christ's purpose is to *enter into the strong man's house* and *spoil his goods*. Therefore, it is natural to suppose that he will *bind the strong man*, so showing that he has gained a victory over him.

3. The terrible warning Christ gave them to beware of speaking such dangerous words. However much they made light of them, as only conjectures, the language of free-thinking people, if they persisted in such speech, it would have fatal consequences for them. It would be found to be a sin against the last possible remedy and therefore unpardonable. It is true that the Gospel makes promises, because Christ has purchased forgiveness for the greatest sins and sinners (v. 28). Many of those who reviled Christ on the cross found mercy, and Christ himself prayed, *Father, forgive them* (Lk 23:34). But this was *blaspheming the Holy Spirit*, because it was through the Holy Spirit that he drove out devils, and they said, "It was *by the unclean spirit*" (v. 30).

Verses 31–33

Here is:

1. The disrespect Christ's natural relatives showed him when he was preaching. They not only *stood without* (outside) but also sent a message in to *call him out to them* (vv. 31–32).

2. The respect Christ showed to his spiritual relatives on this occasion. Now, as at other times, he showed a comparative neglect toward his mother. He looked on those who sat around him, and he declared those of them who not only heard but also obeyed the will of God to be like *his brother, and sister, and mother*: as much respected, loved, and cared for as his closest relatives (vv. 33–35). We have good reason to honor those that fear the Lord, for if we do, we will share with the saints in receiving this honor (Ps 149:9) of belonging to his family.

CHAPTER 4

We have here: 1. The parable of the seed and the four kinds of ground (vv. 1–9), with its explanation (vv. 10–20) and its application (vv. 21–25). 2. The parable of the seed growing gradually (vv. 26–29). 3. The parable of the mustard seed (vv. 30–34). 4. The miracle of Christ's sudden stilling of a storm at sea (vv. 35–41).

Verses 1–20

The previous chapter began with Christ's *entering into the synagogue* (3:1); this chapter begins with Christ's *teaching again by the sea side* (lake). Here we see how he changed his method, so that if possible he might use all means and thereby persuade everyone. Here he seems to use a new and convenient strategy that had not been used before, standing in a boat while his hearers stood upon the land. Notice here:

1. The way of teaching that Christ used with the multitude: *he taught them many things* (v. 2), but it was *by parables*, which would attract them to listen, for people love to be spoken to in their own language, and careless hearers will catch hold of a plain comparison that uses ordinary things. Yet unless they took the pains to look into it, it would only amuse them: *seeing they would see, and not perceive* (v. 12). They deliberately shut their eyes against the light, and so Christ was just to put it into the dark lantern of a parable, which had a bright side toward those who applied it to themselves, but gave only an occasional flash of light to those who were only willing to play with it for a while, and it sent them away in the dark.

2. The way of explaining that he used with his disciples: *When he was alone* with not only the Twelve, but also others who were *about him with the twelve*, they took the opportunity to ask him the meaning of the parables (v. 10). He told them what a distinctive favor it was to them that they were familiar with the *mystery of the kingdom of God* (v. 11). What others were only amused by instructed them. Those who know the mystery of the kingdom of heaven must acknowledge that it is given to them; they receive both light and sight from Jesus Christ. We have here:

2.1. The parable of the sower, as we had it in Mt 13:3–9. He began with, *Hearken* (listen) (v. 3), and concluded with, *He that hath ears to hear, let him hear* (v. 9). The words of Christ call for attention. We must pay careful attention even to what we as yet do not thoroughly, or not rightly, understand. We will find more in Christ's sayings than at first there seemed to be.

2.2. Its explanation to the disciples. Here is a question Christ asked them before he explained the parable, a question that we did not have in Matthew: "*Know ye not this parable?* Do you not know what it means? *How then will ye know all parables?* (v. 13)." "If you do not know this, which is so clear, how then will you understand other parables, which will be more hidden and obscure?" This should motivate us both to prayer and to hard work, so that we may increase in knowledge. If we do not understand the plain truths of the Gospel, how then will we grasp those that are more difficult? "This parable is to teach you to be attentive to the word and affected by it, so that you may understand it. If you do not receive this, you will not know how to use the key by which you must be let into all the others." Before Christ explained the parable:

2.2.1. He showed them how sad was the case of those who were not let into the meaning of the teaching of Christ: *To you it is given, but not to them.* It will help us to value the privileges we enjoy as disciples of Christ if we consider the miserable state of those who lack such privileges, who are kept out of the ordinary path to conversion, *lest they should be converted, and their sins should be forgiven them* (v. 12). Only those who are converted have their sins forgiven.

2.2.2. He showed them what a shame it was that they did not understand the word they heard when they heard it, but needed such detailed explanations of it. Those who want to improve their knowledge must first be made aware of their ignorance. He gave them the interpretation of the parable of the sower, as we had it before in Matthew. Let us only notice here:

2.2.2.1. That in the great field of the church, the word of God is distributed to all without any discrimination: *The sower soweth the word* (v. 14), sows it generally, not knowing where it will fall or what fruit it will produce. He scatters it, so that it will *increase*. Christ sowed himself for a while, when he went about teaching and preaching; now he sends out his ministers, sowing by their hands.

2.2.2.2. That of the many people who hear the word of the Gospel, only comparatively few receive it in such a way that they produce fruits from it; here it is only one in four that is fruitful. It is sad to think how much of the precious seed of the word of God is lost and sown in vain, but a day is coming when lost sermons must be accounted for.

2.2.2.3. Many are very much moved by the word for a short time but receive no lasting benefit from it. They make slight spiritual waves, which correspond to what they hear but are merely a flash in the pan or the crackling of thorns under a boiling pot (Ecc 7:6). Those represented here by *stony ground* (rocky places) received the word *with gladness* but came to nothing (v. 16).

2.2.2.4. The reason why the word does not leave commanding, abiding impressions on the minds of the people is that their hearts are not suitably disposed and prepared to receive it. Some are careless, forgetful hearers, and these do not benefit at all by the word; it comes in one ear and goes out the other. Others have their convictions overcome by their corruptions, and they lose the good effects the word has made on them, so that they gain no lasting good by it.

2.2.2.5. The Devil is very busy with loose, careless hearers, just as birds swoop down on the seed that lies above ground. *Like the fowls*, he comes swiftly and takes away the word before we have time to notice. We must drive these birds away, so that, though we cannot keep them from hovering over our heads, we may not let them nestle in our hearts.

2.2.2.6. Many who do not openly stumble, so as to throw away their profession of faith, as those on rocky places did, still have its effectiveness secretly choked and stifled, so that it comes to nothing.

2.2.2.7. Impressions that are not deep will not last; many who keep their profession of faith in fair days lose it in the storms of life, like those who go to sea only for pleasure and come back again when the wind rises. Hypocrites are ruined because they *have no root* (v. 17); they do not act according to living, fixed principles. Those who are true Christians are Christians inwardly.

2.2.2.8. Many are hindered from benefiting from the word of God because they have so much of the world. Many good lessons are choked and lost by a powerful delight in the things of this world, a delight that those on whom the world smiles tend to have.

2.2.2.9. Those who are not loaded down with the cares of the world and the deceitfulness of riches may still lose the benefit of their profession by the *lusts of other things*; this is added here in Mark (v. 19); it refers to an excessive desire for those things that are pleasing to the senses or to the imagination. Those who have only a little of the things of this world may still be ruined by indulgence of the body.

2.2.2.10. Fruit is the thing that God expects and requires from those who enjoy the Gospel—fruit according to the seed: an attitude and integrity of life that are consistent with the Gospel. This is fruit, and it will richly add to our account.

2.2.2.11. No good fruit is to be expected except from good seed. If the seed is sown on good ground, if the heart is humble, holy, and heavenly, there will be good fruit, and it will produce a rich crop, sometimes even a hundredfold.

Verses 21–34

The lessons that our Savior wants to teach us here by parables and figurative expressions are these:

1. Those who are good should do good, that is, produce fruit. God expects a pleasing return on his gifts to us and a useful application of his gifts in us, for, *Is a candle brought to be put under a bushel, or under a bed?* (v. 21). No; it is brought so that it can be *set on a candlestick*. All Christians, as they have *received the gift*, must *minister the same* (use it to serve others) (1Pe 4:10). Gifts and graces make a person like a candle; the most eminent human beings are merely candles, poor lights, compared with the *Sun of righteousness* (Mal 4:2). A candle gives out light only a little way, and only for a little while. It is also easily blown out and continually burning down and wasting. Many who are lit like candles put themselves *under a bed, or under a bushel*: they neither show grace themselves nor minister grace to others. Like a candle in a vase, they burn only for themselves. Those who are lit like candles should set themselves *on a candlestick*, that is, make the most of every opportunity to do good. We are not born for ourselves. The reason given for this is that *there is nothing hid, which shall not be manifested* (v. 22). The treasure of gifts and graces in each of us is given so that we will share them with others. The Gospel was not made a secret for the apostles; it was to *come abroad*, out into the open, to be divulged to the whole world. Although Christ explained the parables to his disciples in private, it was with the intention of making them more widely useful; the disciples were taught so that they could teach others.

2. It is the concern of those who hear the word of the Gospel to note what they hear and make good use of it: *If any man have ears to hear, let him hear* (v. 23). It is added: *Take heed what ye hear* (v. 24); give it due regard. "Consider what you hear." What we hear does us no good unless we also consider it; those who are to teach others must themselves be especially observant of the things of God. We must also *take heed what we hear by proving* (testing) all things, so that we may *hold fast that which is good* (1Th 5:21). As we deal with God, so will God deal with us: "*With what measure ye mete* (you use), *it shall be measured to you.*" As we use the talents we are entrusted with, we will increase them. If we make use of the knowledge we have, it will grow, and we will see growth, as goods increase in manufacturing: *Unto that hath, shall more be given; to you that have, it shall be given* (v. 25). Gifts and graces multiply by being exercised. If we do not use what we have, we lose it: *From him that hath not shall be taken even that which he hath.* Burying a talent is betraying a trust and amounts to a forfeiture (Mt 25:24–30); gifts and graces rust if they are not used and worn.

3. When the good seed of the Gospel is sown in the world and sown in the heart, it gradually produces wonderful effects, but silently: *So is the kingdom of God* (v. 26).

3.1. It will come up; even though it seems lost and buried underground, it will find or make its way through them. The seed *cast into the ground will spring up.* How soon the surface of a field changes after it has been sown with grain! When it is covered with green, it looks very bright and pleasant.

3.2. The farmer cannot describe how the seed grows; it is one of the mysteries of nature. It *springs and grows up, he knows not how* (v. 27). Similarly, we do not know how the Spirit makes a change in the heart through the Word, any more than we can explain the blowing of the wind, which we hear the sound of, but cannot tell where it comes from or where it is going (Jn 3:8).

3.3. When the farmer has sown the seed, he does nothing toward making it spring up: *He sleeps and rises, night and day*, and perhaps never even thinks about the grain he has sown, but *the earth brings forth fruit of itself*, according to the ordinary course of nature. Similarly, the word of grace, when it is received in faith, is a work of grace in the heart.

3.4. It grows gradually: *first the blade, then the ear, after that the full corn in the ear* (v. 28). When it has sprung up, it will mature; nature will take its course, as will grace. Christ's influence is and will be a growing influence, and though *the beginning be small, the latter end will greatly increase* (Job 8:7). Although at first it is only a tender *blade* (stalk), which the frost may nip or the foot may crush, nevertheless, it will grow to *the ear*, and then to the *full corn* (grain) *in the ear*. God carries on his work imperceptibly and silently, but his ways cannot be overcome and will not fail.

3.5. It comes to maturity eventually: *When the fruit is brought forth*, then the farmer *puts in the sickle* (v. 29). From the fruit of the Gospel taking its place and working in the soul, Christ gathers a harvest. When those who receive the Gospel have finished their course in the right way, the harvest comes, when they will be gathered as *wheat into God's barn* (Mt 13:30).

4. The work of grace is small in its beginnings but eventually comes to be great and significant (vv. 30–32): *"Whereunto shall I liken the kingdom of God?* How will I make you understand its intended method?"* It is *like a grain of mustard seed*; he had compared it before to seed sown; here he compared it to this particular seed, intending to show:

4.1. That the beginnings of the Gospel kingdom would be very small, like *one of the least of all seeds*. The work of grace in the soul is at first only the *day of small things* (Zec 4:10); a *cloud* no *bigger than a man's hand* (1Ki 18:44). Never were such great things undertaken by such an insignificant handful of people as when the discipling of the nations was undertaken by the ministry of the apostles.

4.2. That its maturity will be very great: *When it grows up, it becomes greater than all herbs* (the largest of all garden plants). The Gospel kingdom in the world will increase and spread to the most distant nations on earth. The difference between *a grain of mustard seed* and a *great tree* is nothing compared with that between a young convert on earth and a glorified saint in heaven.

5. *With many such parables he spoke the word unto them* (v. 33). He spoke in parables, *as they were able to hear them*; he drew his comparisons from things that were familiar to them. His manner of expression was easy, so that they could later recall his sayings for their edification. *But* for the present, *without a parable spoke he not unto them* (v. 34). The disciples themselves understood later those sayings of Christ that at first they did not rightly grasp; these parables *he expounded to them when they were alone*. We cannot help wishing we had the explanation of those other parables, as we had that of the parable of the sower, but it was not so necessary, because when the church was enlarged, its enlargement would explain these parables to us without any further difficulty.

Verses 35–41

We had this miracle before, in which Christ relieved his disciples by stilling the storm (Mt 8:23–27), but it is related here more fully. Notice:

1. It was *the same day, when the even* (evening) *was come* (v. 35). When he had been working hard teaching all day, then instead of resting, he put himself in a vulnerable position. The end of a toil may be the beginning of a toss.

2. He himself suggested putting to sea at night, because he wanted to lose no time: *Let us pass over to the other side*; he had work to do there. Christ went about doing

good (Ac 10:38), and no difficulties in his way could hinder him.

3. They did not put to sea until *they had sent away the multitude*, that is, until they answered all their requests, for Christ sent no one home complaining that they had been with him and gained nothing.

4. They took him *even as he was*, without any cloak to throw over him, which he should have had to keep warm when he went to sea at night. We may learn from this not to be too fussy or overconcerned about the body.

5. The storm was so great that the boat was *full of water* (v. 37). Because the boat was small, the waves broke over the sides, nearly swamping it.

6. There were *with him other little ships* (boats), which no doubt shared in the same distress and danger. The multitude went away when he put to sea, but some who wanted to venture out on the water remained with him. You may boldly and cheerfully put to sea in Christ's company, even if a storm is forecast.

7. Christ was asleep in this storm. It was *in the hinder part* (stern) *of the ship*, the pilot's place: Christ lay at the helm. He had *a pillow* (cushion) there. He slept, to test the faith of his disciples and to stir them to pray: in the test, their faith appeared weak and their prayers strong. Sometimes when the church is in a storm, Christ seems as if he is asleep, as if he is unconcerned at the troubles of his people, paying no attention to their prayers. Yet when he sleeps, he does not sleep; the keeper of Israel does not even slumber (Ps 121:3–4); he slept, but his heart was awake.

8. His disciples encouraged themselves with the knowledge that he was with them, and they thought that their best course was to make the most of that, to appeal to that, to ply the oar of prayer rather than their other oars. Their confidence lay in knowing that they had their Master with them, and the boat that has Christ in it, though it may be tossed about, cannot sink. They *awoke Christ*. When Christ seems as if he is asleep in a storm, he is woken up by the prayers of his people. We may be at our wits' end, but we will not be at the end of our faith as long as we have such a Savior to turn to. Their words to Christ are expressed very emphatically here: *Master, carest thou not that we perish?* I confess that this sounds somewhat harsh, rebuking him for sleeping rather than begging him to wake up. I know no excuse for it, except the present distress they were in, which put them into such a panic that they did not know what they were saying. Those who suspect Christ of not caring for his people in distress do Christ a great wrong.

9. The word of command with which Christ rebuked the storm here, which we did not have in Matthew. He said, *Peace, be still* (v. 39); "be silent, be still, be mute." Let the wind no longer roar, nor the sea rage. "The noise is threatening and terrifying; let us hear no more of it." This is:

9.1. A word of command to us; when our corrupt and evil hearts are *like the troubled sea which cannot rest* (Isa 57:20), let us think we hear the law of Christ, saying, "Be still." Do not think confusedly, do not speak rashly, but be still.

9.2. A word of comfort to us, that even if the storm of trouble is very loud or very strong, Jesus Christ can still it by simply speaking a word. The One who made the seas can make them quiet.

10. The rebuke Christ gave them for their fears is taken further here than in Matthew. There it is, *Why are ye fearful?* Here, *Why are ye so fearful?* In Matthew, it is, *O ye of little faith*. Here it is, *How is it that ye have no faith?*

(Do you still have no faith?) Not that the disciples were without faith. But at this time their fears were so great that they seemed to have no faith at all. Their level of faith did not match what was called for by the event, and so it was as if they did not have it. Those who can harbor such a thought as that Christ does not care if his people perish may suspect their faith.

11. The impression this miracle had on the disciples is expressed here differently. In Matthew it is said, *The men marveled*; here it is said, *They feared greatly* (they were terrified). Now their fear was put right by their faith. When they feared the wind and the sea, it was for lack of the reverence they should have had for Christ. But now that they saw a demonstration of his power over the wind and sea, they feared them less, and him more. They feared the power and wrath of the Creator in the storm, and that fear contained stunned torment, but now they feared the power and grace of the Redeemer in the calm, and that had pleasure and satisfaction in it. They said, *What manner of man is this?* (Who is this?) Surely more than a man, *for even the winds and the seas obey him.*

CHAPTER 5

In this chapter we have: 1. Christ's driving out the legion of demons from a demon-possessed man and allowing them to enter a herd of pigs (vv. 1–20). 2. Christ's healing the woman who was subject to bleeding as he was going to raise Jairus's daughter to life (vv. 21–43).

Verses 1–20

We have Christ's disarming the strong armed man here (3:27). He did this when he came *to the other side*, to where he went through a storm; his business there was to rescue this poor creature out of the hands of Satan. Notice:

1. The miserable condition the man was in; he was under the power of an *unclean* (evil) *spirit*, raving mad; his condition seems to have been worse than that of any other demon-possessed patient of Christ's.

1.1. He had *his dwelling among the tombs*, among the graves, which were outside the cities, in *desolate places* (Job 3:14). Perhaps Satan drove him to the tombs. Contact with a grave was defiling (Nu 19:16). The evil spirit drives people into company that is defiling and so keeps possession of them. By rescuing souls from Satan's power, Christ saves the living from among the dead.

1.2. He was very strong, uncontrollable: *No man could bind him.* Not only would cords not hold him, but even *chains* and *fetters of iron* would not (vv. 3–4). This illustrates the sad condition of souls that the Devil controls. Some notoriously stubborn sinners are like this madman. The commands and curses of the Law are like chains and fetters, to restrain sinners from their evil ways, but they *break those bonds in sunder* (Ps 2:3).

1.3. He was a terror and torment to himself and to everyone around him (v. 5). The Devil is a cruel master. This wretched man was *night and day in the mountains and in the tombs, crying, and cutting himself with stones.* What is a human being, when reason is dethroned and Satan enthroned?

2. His turning to Christ: *When he saw Jesus afar off,* coming ashore, he *ran and worshipped him* (v. 6). He usually ran upon others with rage, but here he ran to Christ with reverence. What could not be done with chains and fetters was done by the invisible hand of Christ; the man's fury was suddenly all curbed. The poor man came and *worshipped* Christ, sensing his need of help, while the

power of Satan in and over him was suspended for a moment.

3. The word of command Christ gave: *Come out of him, thou unclean spirit* (v. 8). He made the man want to be relieved when he enabled him to *run and worship him,* and then he showed his power to help him. If Christ brings about in us a sincere desire to pray for deliverance from Satan, he will bring about that deliverance for us.

4. The Devil's dread of Christ. The *man ran* and *worshipped Christ,* but it was the demon in the man who *cried with a loud voice*—making use of the poor man's tongue—*What have I to do with thee?* (v. 7).

4.1. He called God the *most high God,* above all other gods.

4.2. He acknowledged Jesus to be the *Son of God.* It is not strange to hear the best words fall from the worst mouths. Outward piety from the mouth is relatively easy. The most fair-spoken hypocrite cannot say anything better than "Jesus, Son of God," but the demon did this too.

4.3. He disowned any intentions against Christ: "*What have I to do with thee?*"

4.4. He prayed to be saved from wrath; "*I adjure thee,* though you drive me out from here, don't torture me."

5. How Christ took account of this evil spirit's name. We did not have this in Matthew. Christ asked him, *What is thy name? My name is Legion, for we are many.* Now this shows that the demons are:

5.1. Military powers. The demons wage war against God and his glory, Christ and his Gospel, people and their holiness and happiness.

5.2. Numerous; the man acknowledged, or rather boasted—*We are many*; it was as if he hoped to be too many for Christ himself to deal with.

5.3. Unanimous; there are many devils, but only one legion engaged in the same evil cause.

5.4. Very powerful; who can stand before a legion? We are no match for our spiritual enemies in our own strength, but *in the Lord, and in the power of his might,* we will be able to *stand against them* (Eph 6:10–11).

6. The request of this legion that Christ would allow them to go into a herd of pigs that was *feeding nigh unto the mountains* (v. 11). Their request was:

6.1. That he *would not send them away out of the country* (v. 10), not only that he would not *torment them before the time* (Mt 8:29) but also that he would not banish them from that country. They seem to have had a particular devotion for that country, or rather a particular hatred for it.

6.2. That he would allow them to *enter into the swine.*

7. The permission Christ gave them to enter the herd of pigs, and the immediate destruction of the pigs: *He gave them leave* (v. 13). Immediately the *unclean spirits entered into the swine,* which according to the Law were unclean creatures. Those who, like the pigs, delight in the mire of sinful physical desires are suitable dwelling places for Satan. The consequence of the demons entering the herd of pigs was that they all immediately went crazy and ran headlong into the adjacent lake, where all two thousand drowned.

8. The report of all this immediately spread throughout the country. These who *fed the swine* ran quickly to the owners to report what had happened to the animals in their charge (v. 14). This drew the people together to see what had been done. When they saw how wonderfully the poor man had been healed, they began to respect Christ (v. 15). They saw the man who had been demon-possessed *sitting clothed and in his right mind*; when Satan was driven out, he came to himself (Lk 15:17), immediately was his own true self. Those who are serious, who live lives of integrity

with consideration, show that the Devil's power has been broken by the power of Christ in their souls. The sight of this *made them afraid*; it astonished them and forced them to recognize that Christ was powerful and worthy to be feared. When they found that their pigs were lost, however, they began to dislike Christ. They pleaded with him to *depart out of their coasts* (region), for they could not think he would do them sufficient good to make up for the loss of so many of their pigs, which were perhaps fat and ready for market. Now the demons had what they wanted, for there are no means by which evil spirits more powerfully manage sinful souls than by the love of the world. If these people would only part with their sins, he had life and happiness for them. However, being reluctant to abandon either their sins or their pigs, they chose rather to abandon their Savior. This is how people fare when, rather than give up a corrupt, sinful desire, they throw away their interest in Christ. They wished he would go away.

9. An account of what this poor man did after his deliverance.

9.1. He wanted to go along with Christ (v. 18).

9.2. Christ *would not suffer* (allow) *him* to go with him. He had other work for him to do; the healed man must go home to his friends and tell them what *great things the Lord had done for him*, so that his neighbors and friends would be built up and invited to believe in Christ. He must take particular notice of Christ's pity rather than his power; he must tell them what *compassion* the Lord had had on him in his miserable condition.

9.3. The man, ecstatic with joy, made known throughout the country what *great things Jesus had done for him* (v. 20). Notice the effect of this report: *All men did marvel* (all the people were amazed), but few of them went beyond that. Many wonder at Christ's works but do not, as they should, move on from that wonder and seek him.

Verses 21–34

Because the Gadarenes wanted Christ to leave their country, he did not stay there long to trouble them, but immediately went by water back *to the other side*, and there *much people gathered to him* (v. 21). If there are some who reject Christ, there are also others who receive him and make him welcome.

1. Here was one who came openly to beg for the healing of a sick child, and it was no less a person than one of the *rulers of the synagogue*. He was not named in Matthew, but he is here, *Jairus*, or *Jair* (Jdg 10:3). He spoke to Christ with great humility and reverence: *When he saw him, he fell at his feet*. He pleaded with him boldly and fervently. He had a little daughter, about twelve years old, the darling of the family, and she lay dying, but he believed that if Christ would only come and *lay his hands upon her*, she would come back even from the gates of the grave. When the ruler first came, he said, *She lies dying* (as in Mark), but later, *She is even now dead* (as in Matthew), but he still pursued his case. Christ readily agreed and went with him (v. 24).

2. Here is another, who comes secretly to pocket a healing—if we may put it this way—for herself, and she gained the relief she came for. This healing was performed as he walked along the road, as he was going to raise the ruler's daughter. Many of his messages, and some of his miracles, are recorded as taking place while he walked along the road to somewhere; we should be doing good not only when we *sit in the house* but also when we *walk by the way* (Dt 6:7). Notice:

2.1. The pitiful case of this poor woman. She had been subject to constant bleeding for *twelve years*. She had

sought the best advice that she could obtain from doctors, and had used the many medicines and methods they prescribed, but now that she had spent all her money on them, they gave her up as incurable. People usually do not turn to Christ until they have tried all other means of help in vain—until they have found them, as they certainly will, *physicians of no value* (Job 13:4). Christ, however, will be found a sure refuge, even to those who make him their last refuge.

2.2. The strong faith that she had in the power of Christ to heal her: *If I may but* (only) *touch his clothes, I shall be whole* (v. 28). A private healing was what she sought, and her faith suited her case.

2.3. The wonderful effect produced by it: *She came in the crowd behind* him and eventually managed to *touch his garment*, and immediately she felt the healing performed (v. 29). The flow of blood *dried up*, and she felt perfectly well all over in a moment. Those whom Christ heals of the disease of sin, that bloody, guilty *issue* (flow), must experience in themselves a universal change for the better.

2.4. Christ's seeking his hidden patient and encouraging her; Christ *knew in himself that virtue* (power) *had gone out of him* (v. 30). Because he wanted to see his patient, he asked, not in displeasure, as one insulted, but in tenderness, as one concerned, *Who touched my clothes?* The disciples almost laughed at the question: *The multitudes throng thee, and sayest thou, Who touched me?* (v. 31). Christ ignored that lack of respect and *looked around* to *see her that had done this thing*, not in order to blame her for her presumption, but so that he could commend and encourage her faith and, by his own action, justify and confirm the cure. Just as secret acts of sin are known to the Lord Jesus, so he also sees secret acts of faith; they are under his eye. The poor woman then presented herself to the Lord Jesus, *fearing and trembling* (v. 33), not knowing how he would react. Christ's patients often come to him trembling when they have reason to be triumphing. *Knowing what was done in her*, she could have come boldly, but instead the knowledge made her fear and tremble. It was a surprise, and was not yet, as it should have been, a pleasant surprise. However, she *fell down before him*. There is nothing better for those who fear and tremble than to throw themselves at the feet of the Lord Jesus. She then *told him all the truth*. We must not be ashamed to acknowledge the secret transactions between Christ and our souls, but, when called to do so, must mention what he has done for our souls, the experience we have had of healing power derived from him. What an encouraging word he spoke to her: *Daughter, thy faith hath made thee whole* (v. 34). God's grace will set the seal of its Amen to the prayers and hopes of faith, saying, "So be it, and so it will be, to you." Therefore, "*Go in peace.*"

Verses 35–43

Having healed an incurable disease, Christ went on to triumph over death here.

1. The sad news was brought to Jairus that his *daughter was dead*. While there is life, there is still hope, and opportunity to use means, but when life has gone, it is beyond recall: *Why troublest thou the Master any further?* (v. 35). Usually, the proper thought in such situations is, "The matter has already been determined, the will of God has been done, and I submit to it, I accept it; *The Lord gave, and the Lord hath taken away* (Job 1:21)." However, here the situation was extraordinary; here the death of the child did not, as is usual, mean the end of the story.

2. Christ encouraged the afflicted father to still hope. Christ had stopped to heal on the way, but the father

would not suffer for that, would not lose by another's gain: *Be not afraid, only believe.* We may imagine that Jairus paused to think whether it was worth asking Christ to go on or not, but have we not as much need for God's grace and comfort when death is in the house as when sickness is? Therefore Christ soon decided this matter: *"Be not afraid* that my coming will be useless; *only believe* that I will make it turn out for good." *Only believe.* Keep up your confidence in Christ, keep depending on him, and he will do what is best. Believe in the resurrection, and then do not be afraid.

3. He went with a chosen company to the house where the dead child lay. Now he shook off the crowd, *suffering* (allowing) *no man to follow him* except his three closest disciples, Peter and James and John.

4. He raised the dead child to life. Here we may notice:

4.1. That the child was extremely well loved, for the relatives and neighbors *wept and wailed greatly.*

4.2. That it was clear beyond dispute that the child had really and truly died. Their laughing Christ to scorn for saying, *She is not dead, but sleepeth,* proved this.

4.3. That Christ put outside those who were ignorant of the things of God, judging them unworthy to witness the miracle; they did not understand him when he spoke about death as a sleep, or they were so scornful as to ridicule him for it.

4.4. That he took the parents of the child to witness the miracle, intending it for their comfort, since they were the true mourners, the silent mourners.

4.5. That Christ raised the child to life by a word of power, which is recorded here, and recorded in Aramaic, the language Christ spoke, to emphasize its greater certainty: *Talitha, cumi; Damsel, I say unto thee, Arise*—"I command you to arise"; the dead do not have the power to get up, and so power accompanies this word to make it effective. Christ works while he commands, and he works according to the command, and so he may command what he wishes, even the dead to get up. Such is the Gospel call to those who are by nature dead in their trespasses and sins (Eph 2:1) and can no more rise from that death by their own power than this child could.

4.6. That the young girl, as soon as life returned, *arose, and walked* (v. 42). Spiritual life will appear by our rising from our bed of lethargy and carelessness and *walking up and down* (Zec 10:12) in Christ's name and strength.

4.7. That all who saw it and heard about it wondered at the miracle and the One who performed it: *They were astonished with a great astonishment* (they were completely astonished). They had to acknowledge that there was something about it that was extraordinary and great, but they did not know what to make of it or how to understand it.

4.8. That Christ tried to hide it: *He charged them straitly* (gave strict orders) *that no man should know it.* It was sufficiently known to enough people, but he did not yet want it to be more widely known.

4.9. That Christ made sure that something was *given her to eat.* That she had an appetite for food showed that she was raised not only to life but also to good health. Where Christ has given spiritual life, he will provide food to support and nourish it to eternal life, for he will *never forsake,* or fail, *the work of his own hands* (Ps 138:8; Heb 13:5).

CHAPTER 6

We have here: 1. Christ condemned by his compatriots because he was one of them (vv. 1–6). 2. The just power he gave his apostles over evil spirits (vv. 7–13). 3. A

strange idea that Herod and others had about Christ, and the account of the martyrdom of John the Baptist (vv. 14–29). 4. Christ's retreat to a quiet place, the crowds that followed him, and his feeding five thousand of them with five loaves and two fish (vv. 30–44). 5. Christ's walking on the sea to his disciples, and the many healings he performed on the other side of the water (vv. 45–56).

Verses 1–6

Here:

1. Christ visited *his own country,* Nazareth, where his relatives were. His life had been in danger among them (Lk 4:29), but he came back to them; from our perspective it is strange that he waits to be gracious (Isa 30:18).

2. He *began to teach* there in their *synagogue* on the *sabbath day* (v. 2). On Sabbaths, the word of God is to be preached, following Christ's example.

3. They had to acknowledge what was very honorable about him: he spoke with great *wisdom* and did *mighty works.* They acknowledged the two great proofs of the divine origin of his Gospel, its divine wisdom and its divine power, but although they could not deny the premises, they refused to accept the conclusion.

4. They ridiculed him. They thought all this wisdom and all these mighty works to be of no value: *Is not this the Carpenter?* In Matthew, they rebuked him for being the carpenter's son; it seems they could also say, *Is not this the Carpenter?* Our Lord Jesus was probably employed as a carpenter, at least before his public ministry. He did this:

4.1. To humble himself, as One who had taken on himself the form of a servant.

4.2. To teach us to hate idleness and find ourselves something to do in this world. Nothing is more harmful for young people than to get used to wandering aimlessly. The Jews had a good rule about this, that their young men who were intended to be scholars must also be brought up to pursue some trade—for example, Paul was a tentmaker—so that they had some business to occupy their time with.

4.3. To honor despised manual work and encourage those who live by the labor of their hands (Ps 128:2), even though some people look down on them with contempt.

5. They rebuked him for another thing, the lowliness of his relatives; *"He is the son of Mary;* his *brethren* and *sisters* are here *with us;* we know his family and relatives," and therefore, though they were astonished at his teaching (v. 2), they were still offended at his person (v. 3). That was why they would not receive his teaching. Let us see how Christ bore this contempt:

5.1. He partly *excused it: A prophet is not despised any where but in his own country* (v. 4). No doubt many have overcome this prejudice, but usually ministers are not as acceptable and successful in their own country as among foreigners; familiarity in the younger years breeds contempt, the advancement of one who was subordinate gives birth to envy, and people will hardly put among the guides of their souls those whose fathers were thought worthy only to *set with the dogs of their flock* (Job 30:1).

5.2. He did some good among them despite the insults they showed him, for he is kind even to unthankful evildoers: *He laid his hands upon a few sick folk, and healed them.*

5.3. Yet *he could there do no might work* as in other places, or at least not as many, because of the unbelief that prevailed among the people (v. 5). It is a strange expression, as if unbelief tied the hands of almighty God;

he would have done as many miracles there as he had done elsewhere, but he could not. The people forfeited the honor of having miracles performed for them. Unbelief and contempt of Christ put up a barrier over people's own doors and stop the flow of Christ's favors to them.

5.4. He *marvelled because of their unbelief* (v. 6). We never find Christ wondering except at the faith of the Gentiles, who were foreigners, such as the centurion (Mt 8:10) and the woman of Samaria, and at the unbelief of Jews, who were his own people.

5.5. He *went round about the villages, teaching*. If we cannot do good where we want to, we must do it wherever we can, even if it is in villages. Sometimes the Gospel of Christ is received better in the country villages than in the busy cities.

Verses 7–13

Here is:

1. The commission given to the twelve apostles to preach and work miracles. Up to that time they had been familiar with Christ, sat at his feet, heard his teaching, and seen his miracles. But they had received so that they could give to others; they had learned so that they could teach others. Now, therefore, he *began to send them forth*. They must not always be studying in the academy, to increase knowledge; they must now do good with the knowledge they had gained. Although they were not yet as accomplished as they were to be, nevertheless, according to their present abilities, they must be set to work, and make further improvements later. Notice here:

1.1. Christ sent them out *by two and two*; Mark notes this. They went two by two to each place so that they would be company for one another when they were among foreigners and could strengthen each other's hands (1Sa 23:16; Ne 2:18) and encourage each other's hearts. They could also help each other keep their composure if anything went wrong. It is an approved maxim, *Two are better than one* (Ecc 4:9). Christ wanted to teach his ministers to keep each other company, both giving and asking for help.

1.2. He *gave them power over unclean* (evil) *spirits*. He commissioned them to attack the Devil's kingdom by driving him out of the bodies of those who were possessed by him.

1.3. He *commanded them not* to take provisions along with them, neither food nor money, so that wherever they went, it would be clear that they were poor. When he later told them to *take purse and scrip* (bag) (Lk 22:36), that did not suggest that his care of them was less than it had been, but that they would encounter worse times and not such a good reception as they met with on their first mission. In Matthew and Luke they were forbidden to *take staves* (staffs) with them, that is, fighting staffs, but here in Mark they were told to take nothing except a staff, that is, a walking stick, such as pilgrims carried. They must not put on shoes, only sandals. They must go in the readiest and plainest clothes possible, and must not even have two coats. What they lacked would be happily given them by those they preached to.

1.4. He told them that whenever they entered a town, they should make the house that happened to be their first quarters their headquarters: *"There abide till ye depart from that place* (v. 10). Since you know you are coming on an errand sufficient to make you welcome, be so kind to your friends who first invited you as to believe they do not think you a burden."

1.5. He declared severe condemnation on those who rejected the Gospel they preached: *"Whosoever shall not receive you*, or will not even *hear you, depart thence* and *shake off the dust under your feet, for a testimony against them* (v. 11)." That dust, like the dust of Egypt (Ex 9:9), would become a plague for them, and their condemnation on the great day will be more intolerable than *that of Sodom*.

2. The apostles' conduct in pursuit of their commission. Although they were conscious of their great weakness, nevertheless, in obedience to their Master's orders, and depending on his strength, they *went out*, as Abraham did, not knowing where they were going to (Heb 11:8). Notice:

2.1. The message they preached: *They preached that men should repent* (v. 12), that they should change their minds and reform their lives. The great purpose of Gospel preachers and the great aim of Gospel preaching should be to bring people to repentance, so that they will have a new heart and follow a new way. The apostles did not entertain the people with idle speculation, but told them that they must repent of their sins and turn back to God.

2.2. The miracles they performed. The authority Christ gave them over evil spirits was not ineffective, nor did they receive it in vain; they used it, for they *cast out many devils* (v. 13) and *anointed with oil many that were sick, and healed them.*

Verses 14–29

Here we see:

1. The foolish ideas the people had about our Lord Jesus Christ (v. 15). His compatriots could believe nothing great about him, because they knew his poor relatives, but others were willing to believe anything rather than the truth. They said, "He is Elijah," whom they expected, or, *He is a prophet*, one of the Old Testament prophets raised to life, or, *as one of the prophets*, a prophet now just raised up.

2. The opinion of Herod about him. He said, "It is certainly John the Baptist (v. 14). *It is John whom I beheaded* (v. 16). He is *risen from the dead*, he has come back with greater power, and *now mighty works do show forth themselves in him*." We can learn from this:

2.1. Where there is casual faith, there is often a lively imagination. The people said that a prophet had risen from the dead; Herod said, *It is John the Baptist risen from the dead*. It seems that they expected a prophet to rise from the dead and do mighty works, thinking it neither impossible nor improbable. It was now readily suspected when it was not true, but later, when it was true about Christ, it was obstinately contradicted and denied. Those who most willfully disbelieve the truth are commonly most gullible in believing errors and fanciful teachings.

2.2. Those who fight against God's cause will find themselves thwarted, even when they think they are conquerors.

2.3. A guilty conscience needs no accuser or tormentor but itself. *I beheaded him*. The terror of this self-accusation made him imagine that Christ was John risen. He feared John while he lived, and now, when he was dead, he feared him ten times more. One might as well be haunted by ghosts and avenging spirits as with the horrors of an accusing conscience.

2.4. There may be the terrors of strong conviction where there is no truth of a saving conversion.

3. An account of Herod's putting John the Baptist to death. Notice:

3.1. The great esteem and respect Herod had for John the Baptist for some time, which is related only by this Evangelist (v. 20).

3.1.1. He *feared John, knowing that he was a just man, and a holy.* A person can have great reverence for good people, especially their good ministers, and for what is good in them, yet be bad themselves.

3.1.1.1. John was *a just man, and holy*; to make a completely good person, both holiness and righteousness are necessary: holiness toward God and righteousness toward other people.

3.1.1.2. Herod knew this by personal acquaintance with him. Those who have only a little righteousness and holiness themselves may still discern it in others.

3.1.1.3. He therefore *feared* him; he honored him. Many who are not good in themselves have respect for those who are.

3.1.2. He took notice of him; he took notice of what was praiseworthy in him and commended it in the hearing of those around him; he made it clear that he took notice of what John said and did.

3.1.3. He heard him preach, which was a great condescension.

3.1.4. He did many of those things that John taught him in his preaching. He was not only *a hearer of the word* but also, partly, *a doer of the work* (Jas 1:22–23). But it will not be enough to do many things unless we have respect for all the commandments (Ps 119:6).

3.1.5. He *heard him gladly.* There is a brief, shallow joy that a hypocrite may have in hearing the word. The *stony ground received the word with joy* (Lk 8:13).

3.2. John's faithfulness to Herod in telling him of his faults. Herod had married his brother Philip's wife (v. 17). John *reproved* him (Lk 3:19), telling him plainly, *It is not lawful for thee to have thy brother's wife* (v. 18). This was Herod's own sin, which he could not abandon, even though he did many things that John taught him. Yet although he was a king, John would not spare him, any more than Elijah spared Ahab. Although it was dangerous to offend Herod, and much more to offend Herodias, John would rather run that risk than fail in his duty. Those ministers who want to be found faithful in the work of God must not be afraid of people.

3.3. Herodias's hatred toward John for this: she *had a quarrel with him, and would have him killed* (v. 19), but when she could not bring that about, she had him committed to prison (v. 17). Many who claim to honor prophesying want to hear only pleasant things; they love good preaching as long as it steers far enough away from their favorite sin. However, it is better that sinners persecute ministers now for their faithfulness than that they curse them eternally for their unfaithfulness.

3.4. The plot to cut off John's head. It is said to have happened *when a convenient day was come* (v. 21). There must be a ball at the royal court on the king's birthday. To make the ceremony even more beautiful, the daughter of Herodias must dance publicly, and Herod must make a show of being wonderfully charmed by her dancing. The king must then make her an extravagant promise to give her *whatever she would ask*, even up to *half the kingdom.* This promise was bound with an oath: *He sware unto her, Whatsoever thou shalt ask, I will give.* Being instructed by Herodias her mother, she asked for the *head of John the Baptist*, and she must have it brought her *in a charger* (on a platter), as something pretty for her to play with (vv. 24–25). There must be no delay, no time lost; she must have it *by and by* (right now). Herod granted it, and the execution was immediately carried out while the company were still together. However, he claimed:

3.4.1. To be very reluctant to do it, and that he would not have done it for all the world if he had not been sur-

prised into making such a promise: *the king was exceeding sorry.* He could not do it except with much regret and reluctance; natural conscience will not allow people to sin easily.

3.4.2. To be very sensitive about the obligation of his oath. The promise was made rashly and could not commit him to do something unrighteous. Sinful oaths must be repented of and therefore not fulfilled. Probably he was rushed into doing it by those around him, only to pursue this indulgence, for he did it *for their sakes who* (for the sakes of those who) *sat with him.* In this way, rulers often make themselves slaves to those whose respect they covet. The king sent an executioner, a soldier of his guard. Bloody tyrants have executioners ready to obey their most cruel and unrighteous decrees.

3.5. The effect of this was that Herod's evil court was all triumphant, and the head was given as a present to the girl and then given by her to her mother (v. 28). And John the Baptist's sacred college was all tearful. When they *heard of it*, they came and took up the neglected *corpse* and *laid it in a tomb.*

Verses 30–44

In these verses, we have:

1. The return to Christ of the apostles whom he had sent out (v. 7). They *gathered themselves together* and came back to Jesus to report what they had done. They *told him all things*, both *what they had done and what they had taught.* Ministers are accountable for both what they do and what they teach. Let them neither do anything nor teach anything except what they are willing to have reported to the Lord Jesus.

2. The tender care Christ took for their rest after their hard work: *He said unto them, Come ye yourselves apart into a desert* (quiet) *place, and rest awhile* (v. 31). It seems that John's disciples came to Christ with the sad news of their master's death about the same time that his own disciples came to him. Christ takes notice of the fears of some of his disciples and the hard work of other disciples, and he provides suitable help for both, rest for those who are tired and refuge for those who are afraid. Notice the compassion and kindness with which Christ said to them, *Come, and rest!* The most active servants of Christ cannot always be exerting themselves in their work; they, like everyone else, have bodies that need some relaxation, some breathing space. The Lord understands our body, he knows how we are formed (Ps 103:14), and he not only allows us time to rest but also reminds us that we need rest. Those who work diligently and faithfully may cheerfully withdraw to rest.

2.1. Christ called them to come *themselves apart*; if they must rest, they must be alone.

2.2. He invited them not to some pleasant country house, but *into a desert place.* It is not surprising that the One who had only a boat as a place for preaching had only a desert as a resting place.

2.3. He called them only to rest *awhile*, only to catch their breath, and then to go back to work.

2.4. The reason given for this was, *for there were many coming and going, and they had no leisure so much as to eat.* If proper times are set and kept for everything, a great deal of work may be done with relative ease, but if people are continually coming and going, a little work will not be done without much trouble.

2.5. They withdrew, therefore, in a boat (v. 32). Going by water was much less arduous than going by land would have been. They went away privately. The most public people wish to be on their own sometimes.

3. The diligence of the people in following him. They were not blamed for it, nor told to go back, but were made welcome. A failure in good manners will easily be excused in those who follow Christ if it is made up for by overflowing warm feelings. They followed him from all the towns, leaving their houses and shops, their callings and livelihoods. They followed him on foot, even though he had gone by sea; they stuck with him. They ran on foot, so quickly that they *out-went* (got ahead of) the disciples. They followed him even though it was to a desert place. The presence of Christ will turn a desert into a paradise.

4. The reception Christ gave them (v. 34). *When he saw much people*, instead of being moved with displeasure, he was *moved with compassion toward them*, because *they were as sheep having no shepherd.* They seemed to be well disposed and as manageable as sheep. But they had *no shepherd*, no one to lead and guide them in the right way, and so, out of compassion to them, he not only *healed their sick*, as it is in Matthew, but also *taught them many things.*

5. The provision he made for them all; he generously made all his hearers his guests and treated them to a magnificent reception — as it could truly be called, because it was miraculous.

5.1. The disciples suggested that the people be *sent home.* When *the day was now far spent*, they said, *This is a desert place*, and *much time is now past; send them away to buy bread* (vv. 35 – 36). The disciples suggested this to Christ, but we do not find that the crowd themselves did. The disciples thought it would be kind to the people if he dismissed them. Willing minds will do more and hold out longer on the path of good than one would expect them to.

5.2. Christ ordered that they all be fed: *Give ye them to eat* (v. 37). To teach us to be kind to those who are rude to us, he ordered that provision be made for them. He ordered that the people share in the bread that Christ and his disciples took with them into the quiet place to eat as a quiet meal by themselves. See how much he was given to hospitality. They listened to the spiritual food of his word, and then he made sure they did not lack physical food. Just as the way of duty is the way of safety, so it is also the way to be supplied. Providence, not tempted, but duly trusted, has never yet failed any of God's faithful servants, but has refreshed many with timely and unexpected relief.

5.3. The disciples objected to this suggestion as impracticable: *Shall we go and buy two hundred pennyworth of bread, and give them to eat?* Instead of waiting for instructions from Christ, they confused matters with plans of their own. Christ wanted to let them see their foolishness in forecasting for themselves, so that they would place greater value on his provision for them.

5.4. Christ made it happen, to everyone's satisfaction. They had brought with them *five loaves* and *two fishes*: that was the menu. This was only a little for Christ and his disciples, but they must give this away. We often find Christ received at other people's tables, but here we have him feeding very many at his own expense.

5.4.1. The provision was ordinary. Here were no delicacies. If we have what we need, it does not matter if we do not have elaborate treats. The promise to those who fear the Lord is that *verily they shall be fed* (Ps 37:3); he does not say they will enjoy a feast.

5.4.2. The guests were orderly, for they *sat down by companies on the green grass* (v. 39), *in ranks by hundreds and by fifties* (v. 40). God is the God of order, not of confusion (1Co 14:33, 40).

5.4.3. A blessing was sought on the food: *He looked up to heaven, and blessed.* Christ did not call one of his disciples to ask a blessing; he did it himself (v. 41), and by the power of this blessing the bread strangely multiplied, as did the fish, for they *all ate and were filled*, even though there were *five thousand* of them (vv. 42, 44). Christ came into the world to be the One who feeds people as well as heals them. In him there is enough for all who come to him. No one is sent away empty from Christ (Lk 1:53) except those who come to him full of themselves.

5.4.4. Care was taken of the pieces that were left over; the disciples filled *twelve baskets* with them. Although Christ had enough bread at his command, he wanted to teach us not to waste.

Verses 45 – 56

We read this account in Mt 14:22 – 36, though what was related there about Peter is omitted here. Here:

1. The the crowd was dispersing: Christ made his disciples go on ahead of him by boat to Bethsaida. The people were reluctant to scatter. Now that they had eaten a good meal, they were in no hurry to leave him.

2. Christ departed *to a mountain to pray.* He was still prayerful; he prayed often and long. He went alone to pray, to set us a good example and to encourage us in our private turning to God. A good person is never less alone than when they are alone with God.

3. The disciples were in distress at sea: *The wind was contrary* (against them) (v. 48), so that they *toiled in rowing* (were straining at the oars). This was an example of the hardships they were to expect when he later sent them out to preach the Gospel. The church is often like a ship at sea, *tossed with tempests, and not comforted* (Isa 54:11); we may have Christ for us and yet have wind and tide against us; nevertheless, it is encouraging to Christ's disciples in a storm that their Master is on the heavenly mountain, interceding for them.

4. Christ paid them a kind visit on the water. He chose to help them in the most endearing manner possible, by coming to them himself.

4.1. He did not come until the *fourth watch of the night*, not until after three o'clock in the morning, but then he came. Though Christ's visits to his people may be delayed a long time, he will finally come.

4.2. He came walking on the water. The sea was now tossed about with waves, but Christ came walking on it. No difficulties can obstruct Christ's gracious appearances for his people. He will either find or force a way through the stormiest sea to rescue them (Ps 42:7 – 8).

4.3. He *would have passed by them.* When Providence is acting intentionally and directly to help God's people, it sometimes seems as if it were ignoring them. They thought that he was going to pass by them, but we may be sure that he would not have done so.

4.4. They were frightened at the sight of him, supposing he was a ghost: *They all saw him, and were troubled* (v. 50). We often perplex and frighten ourselves with weird fantasies, the figments of our own imagination.

4.5. He encouraged them and silenced their fears by making himself known to them: *Be of good cheer, it is I; be not afraid.* We do not know Christ until he reveals himself to us. "*It is I*, your Master, your friend." The knowledge of Christ, as he is in himself and as he is near to us, is enough to make the disciples of Christ cheerful even in a storm, and no longer afraid. Christ's presence with us on a stormy day is enough to give us courage, even if clouds and darkness are around us. He did not tell them who he was: they knew his voice, just as the sheep know the voice of their own shepherd (Jn 10:4). When Christ said to those who came to take him by force, *I am he*, they were struck down by it (Jn 18:6). When he says to those who come to take him by faith, *I am he*, they are raised up by it and comforted.

4.6. He *went up to them into the ship*. Let them only have their Master with them, and all was well. As soon as he had come into the boat, *the wind ceased*. The wind died down suddenly. Although we do not hear the command being given, if the wind dies down and we have the comfort of a calm, we say that it is because Christ is in the boat.

4.7. They were more surprised and stunned at this miracle than was becoming. *They were sore* (completely) *amazed in themselves*, perplexed, as if it were something new and inexplicable. But why were they so confused about it? It was because they *considered not* (had not understood) *the miracle of the loaves*. If they had given that its due importance, they would not have been so surprised at this miracle, for Christ's multiplying the bread was as great a demonstration of his power as his walking on the water was. It is because we lack a right understanding of Christ's former works that we are astonished by his present works, as if there had never been the like before.

5. When they came to the land of Gennesaret, the people made them very welcome: *The men of that place knew* (recognized) *Jesus* (v. 54), and they knew what miracles he performed wherever he came. They also knew that he usually stayed only a little while in one place, and so *they ran through that whole region round about*, as fast as possible, and *began to carry about in beds* (on mats) *those that were sick*; there was no danger of their getting cold when they hoped to get a cure (v. 55). Wherever he went, he was crowded with patients: they *laid the sick in the streets*, to be in his way, and begged him to let them touch even *the border of his garment* (the edge of his cloak), and *as many as touched were made whole*. We do not find that they wanted to be taught by him, only that they wanted to be healed. If ministers could now heal people's physical diseases, what great numbers would listen to them! However, it is sad to think how much more concerned most people are about their bodies than about their souls.

CHAPTER 7

We have here: 1. Christ's dispute with the teachers of the law and Pharisees about eating food with unwashed hands (vv. 1–13), and the necessary instructions he gave to the people on that occasion (vv. 14–23). 2. His healing of the woman of Canaan's daughter (vv. 24–30). 3. The healing of a man who was deaf and could hardly talk (vv. 31–37).

Verses 1–23

One great purpose of Christ's coming was to set aside and bring to an end the ceremonial law that God made. To make way for this, he began with the ceremonial law that people had made and had added to the law that God had made. These Pharisees and teachers of the law with whom he had this discussion are said to have *come from Jerusalem* to Galilee—80 or 100 miles (about 150 kilometers)—to criticize our Savior there. Notice:

1. What the tradition of the elders was: all were instructed to *wash their hands* before eating food—a hygienic custom, with no harm in it, but the Pharisees and teachers of the law placed their religion in this matter. They intervened with their authority and commanded everyone to do it on penalty of excommunication; they kept this up as *a tradition of the elders* (v. 3). We have here an account of the practice of the Pharisees and *all the Jews* (vv. 3–4).

1.1. They *washed their hands oft*.

1.2. They particularly washed before they *ate bread*, because that was the rule. They must be sure to wash before they ate the bread on which they asked a blessing; otherwise they were thought to be *defiled* ("unclean").

1.3. They took special care to wash their hands when they came in *from the markets*. It refers to any meeting place where all kinds of people were present, where, it might be thought, by coming near to some pagans or Jews under a ceremonial defilement, they would become defiled. It is said that the rule of the rabbis was that if they washed their hands well in the morning, if it was the first thing they did, it would be enough for the whole day, provided they kept by themselves, but if they went into company and returned, they must neither eat nor pray until they had washed their hands.

1.4. They added to this the washing of *cups* and *pots* and *brazen* (copper) *vessels*; in fact, they washed even the *tables* on which they ate their food. The Law of Moses appointed washings in many cases, but these leaders added to them, enforcing observance of their own impositions as much as of God's institutions.

2. What the practice of Christ's disciples was; they knew what the law was, and the common custom, but they would not be bound by it: they ate bread with *defiled*, that is, with *unwashen hands* (v. 2). The disciples probably knew that the Pharisees were looking at them, yet they would not humor them by complying with their traditions. Here, *their righteousness*, however much it might seem to come short, really did *exceed that of the scribes and Pharisees* (Mt 5:20).

3. The offense the Pharisees took at this; they *found fault* (v. 3). They brought a complaint against the disciples to their Master, expecting him to restrain them and order them to conform. They did not ask, "Why do not your disciples *do as we do?*" but, "Why do they not *walk according to the tradition of the elders?*" (v. 5).

4. Christ's justifying his disciples in this, in which:

4.1. He argued with the Pharisees about the authority by which this ceremony was imposed. However, he did not speak about this publicly to the crowd—as can be seen by his *calling the people* to him (v. 14)—so that he would not seem to stir them up into a splinter group; instead, he rebuked the people concerned.

4.1.1. He rebuked them for their hypocrisy in pretending to honor God when really they had no such intention in their religious observances (vv. 6–7): "*They honour me with their lips*, claiming it is for the glory of God, but really *their heart is far from God.*" They depended on the externals of their religious exercises, and their hearts were not right with God in them, and this was worshiping God in vain, for such false devotions neither pleased him nor profited them.

4.1.2. He rebuked them for locating their religion in the inventions and injunctions of their elders and rulers; they taught for doctrines *the traditions of men*. They were enforcing the canons of their church, and they judged whether people were Jews or not on the basis of whether they did or did not conform to those canons, not considering at all whether they lived in obedience to God's laws. Instead of providing the substance, they arrogantly added to the ceremony and were very fussy about *washing pots and cups*. Notice, he added, *Many other such like things ye do* (v. 8). Superstitions are endless!

4.1.3. He rebuked them for *laying aside the commandment of God*, overlooking it and, in their discipline, turning a blind eye to the violation of it, as if it were no longer in force (v. 8). The trouble caused by rules that are imposed by human beings is that too often those who are zealous for them have little zeal for the essential duties of religious faith.

4.1.3.1. The Pharisees, in fact, *rejected the commandment of God* (v. 9). *Ye do fairly disannul and abolish the commandment of God*, by your traditions *making the word of God of no effect* (v. 13). They were entrusted with explaining the law and enforcing it, and yet, claiming to apply that power, they broke the law and dissolved its bonds.

4.1.3.2. Christ gave them a particular example of this, and it was a flagrant one. God commanded children to *honour their parents*, not only by the Law of Moses but also by the law of nature, and whoever *revileth* or *speaketh evil of* father or mother, *let him die the death* (v. 10). It is the duty of children, if their parents are poor, to relieve them according to their ability, and if those children who curse their parents are worthy to die, much more those who starve them. However, the Pharisees would find a way to release them from this obligation (v. 11). If a person's parents were in need and that person had the resources to help them, but would rather not, they could swear by *Corban*, that is, by the *gold of the temple* and the *gift upon the altar* (Mt 23:16–22), that their parents would not profit by them; and if the parents asked anything of them, it would be enough to tell their parents this. It was as if by the obligation of this evil vow they had released themselves from fulfilling the obligation.

4.1.3.3. He concluded, *And many such like things do ye.* Where will it all stop, once people have made the word of God give way to their traditions? These eager imposers of such ceremonies at first only made light of God's commandments in comparison with their traditions, but later they *made void* God's commandments, as if the ceremonies stood in competition with the commandments.

4.2. He instructed the people about the principles on which this ceremony was based. It was necessary that this part of his message be in public. He therefore *called the people unto him* (v. 14) and told them to *hear and understand*. It is not enough for the ordinary people to hear; they must also understand what they hear. Corrupt customs are best healed by putting right corrupt ideas. Now what he did to put them right was to tell them what the defilement is that we are in danger of being damaged by (v. 15).

4.2.1. Not by the food we eat; that is merely from outside and passes through a person. But:

4.2.2. By the breaking out of the corruption that is in our hearts; we become repugnant in the sight of God by what comes out of us. Our corrupt thoughts, attitudes, words, and actions defile us, and only these. We must therefore be concerned to *wash our heart from wickedness* (Jer 4:14).

4.3. He gave his disciples, in private, an explanation of the instructions he gave the people. They *asked him concerning the parable* (v. 17), and in response to their question:

4.3.1. He rebuked their dullness: *"Are ye so without understanding also?"* He did not expect them to understand everything; "but are you so weak that you do not understand this?"

4.3.2. He explained this truth to them, so that they could understand it, and then they would believe:

4.3.2.1. That what we eat and drink cannot make us "unclean," so as to call for any religious washing. It *goes into the stomach*, and anything that may be in it that is impure is gotten rid of and goes out.

4.3.2.2. That it is what comes out of the heart, the corrupt heart, that makes us "unclean." What comes out from the mind of a person is what defiles that person before God and calls for religious washing: *From within, out of the heart of men* (v. 21)—what defiles proceeds from that, causing all the trouble. Just as a contaminated fountain spurts out contaminated water, so a deceitful heart pours out deceitful thinking, corrupt emotions, and evil words and actions. Various details are given, as in Matthew; we had one there that is not here, and that is giving *false witness* (Mt 15:19), but seven are mentioned here to be added to those we had there.

4.3.2.2.1. *Covetousnesses*, for it is plural: immoderate desires for more of the wealth of the world and physical gratifications, and more and more, always crying out, *Give, give* (Pr 30:15).

4.3.2.2.2. "Wickedness": malice and hatred, a desire to cause trouble and a delight in trouble caused.

4.3.2.2.3. *Deceit*, which is wickedness covered up and disguised, so that it may be more safely and effectively committed.

4.3.2.2.4. *Lasciviousness* (sexual immorality): the filthiness and foolish talking that the apostle condemns, eyes full of adulterous thoughts, and all immoral and indecent behavior, including flirting.

4.3.2.2.5. The *evil eye* (sensuality): the envious eye and the covetous eye, grudging others the good we give them or grieving at the good they do or enjoy.

4.3.2.2.6. "Pride": exalting ourselves above others in our own opinion and looking down with scorn and contempt on others.

4.3.2.2.7. "Foolishness": imprudence, inconsiderateness; some understand this to mean especially boasting.

5. Wrong thinking is put first, as what is the spring of all our sins of *com*mission, and *unthinking* is put last, as what is the spring of all our sins of omission. Concerning all of these he concluded (v. 23) that they *come from within*, from the corrupt nature, and that they *defile the man*. They make a person unfit for fellowship with God, bringing a stain on the conscience.

Verses 24–30

Notice here:

1. How humbly Christ was willing to hide himself. Never was a person so praised as he was in Galilee, and so, to teach us not to be fond of popular applause, he left there and *went into the borders of Tyre and Sidon*, where he was little known. There he entered *into a* private *house* and *would have no man to know it* (did not want anyone to know). Just as there is a time to appear, so there is also a time to withdraw. Or, the reason he did not want to be known was that he was among the Gentiles, to whom he would not be so eager to show himself as to the tribes of Israel.

2. How graciously he was willing to reveal himself, nevertheless. Although he would not take a harvest of miraculous healings to those parts, he let fall this one that we have an account of here. *He could not be hid*, for although a candle may be put under a bowl (4:21), the sun cannot be (Ps 19:6). Christ was too well known to hide anywhere for long. Notice here:

2.1. The request made to him by a poor woman in distress and trouble. She was a Gentile, a Greek, *an alien to the covenant of promise* (Eph 2:12). She was by background a Syrophoenician, and she had *a daughter, a young* daughter, who was possessed by an evil spirit. Her request was:

2.1.1. Very humble, urgent, and bold: *She heard of him* and *came and fell at his feet.* Christ never drove away from him anyone who fell at his feet, which a poor trembling soul may do if it does not have the boldness and confidence to throw itself into his arms.

2.1.2. Very precise. She told him what she wanted. She begged him to *cast forth the devil* (drive the demon) *out of her daughter* (v. 26). The greatest blessing we can ask of Christ for our children is that he would break the power of Satan, that is, the power of sin, in their souls.

2.2. The discouragement he gave to this request (v. 27). He said to her, "*Let the children first be filled*; let the Jews have performed for them all the miracles that they need. Let not what was intended for them be thrown to those who do not belong to God's family, who are like *dogs in comparison to them*, and *dogs to them*, snarling at them and ready to attack them." When Christ knows the faith of poor beggars to be strong, he sometimes delights to draw it out in order to test it. However, his saying *Let the children first be filled* suggests there was mercy in reserve for the Gentiles, and that was not far away, because the Jews had already nearly had their fill of the Gospel of Christ, and some of them had wanted him to *depart out of their coasts* (5:17). The children began to play with their food, and their leftovers would be a feast for the Gentiles.

2.3. The response she gave to this declaration of Christ against her, how she made it work for her (v. 28). She said, "*Yes, Lord,* I acknowledge it is true that the *children's bread* should not be thrown to the dogs, but the dogs were never denied the *crumbs*, and they are allowed a place *under the table* so that they may be ready to receive them. I do not ask for a loaf, not even for a morsel, only for a crumb; do not refuse me that." She said this to exalt the abundance of miraculous healings that she had heard the Jews enjoyed, in comparison with which a single healing was a mere crumb. Perhaps she had just heard about Christ's feeding the five thousand, after which there must have been some crumbs left over for the dogs.

2.4. The favorable answer Christ then gave to her request. "*For this saying, Go thy way;* you will have what you came for; *the devil is gone out of thy daughter* (v. 29). This encourages us to pray and not to give up (Lk 18:1), not doubting that our prayers will eventually be answered. Christ's saying here that it *was* done was as effective as his saying at other times, *Let it be done,* for she *came to her house,* depending on the word of Christ, and that was what she *found*: the *devil was gone out* (v. 30). Christ can defeat Satan at a distance. She found her daughter not tossing about or agitated, but very quietly *lying on the bed,* resting, waiting for her mother's return to rejoice with her that she was so completely well.

Verses 31–37

Our Lord Jesus seldom stayed long in one place. When he had healed the daughter of the Canaanite woman (as she is called in Mt 15:22), he had done what he had to do in that place and returned *to the sea of Galilee.* He did not go there directly, but went around *through the midst of the coasts* (region) *of Decapolis,* which lay mostly on the other side of the Jordan. Here we have the account of a healing by Christ that is not recorded by any other of the Evangelists, the healing of a man who was deaf and mute.

1. His case was sad (v. 32). Some people brought to Christ *one that was deaf* and had an *impediment in his*

speech. He was completely unfit for ordinary conversation, deprived both of its pleasure and benefits; he did not have the satisfaction of either hearing other people talk or speaking his own mind. Let us use this as an opportunity, therefore, to thank God for preserving our sense of hearing, especially so that we may be able to hear the word of God; and let us thank him for preserving the faculty of speech, especially so that we may be able to speak God's praises. Those who brought this poor man to Christ begged him to *put his hand upon him.* It is not said that they begged him to heal him, but that they begged him to *put his hand upon him,* to take notice of his case and show his power to do to him as he pleased.

2. His healing was solemn, and some of its circumstances were remarkable.

2.1. Christ *took him aside from the multitude* (v. 33). Usually, he performed his miracles in public, but he did this one privately. Let us learn from Christ to do good where no one is looking except the One who sees everything.

2.2. He used more significant actions than usual in performing this healing.

2.2.1. He *put his fingers into his ears.*

2.2.2. He spit on his own finger and then *touched his tongue,* and as if to loosen whatever was tying his tongue. In no way could these actions contribute in the slightest to the healing; they were only signs to encourage the man's faith and the faith of those who brought him.

2.3. He *looked up to heaven.* This is how he showed that it was by a divine power. He also by this gesture instructed his patient—who could see although he could not hear—to look to heaven for help.

2.4. He sighed. Not as if he found any difficulty in working this miracle, but this was how he expressed his pity for the miseries of human life and his sympathy with those who were suffering, as One who was himself *touched with the feeling of their infirmities* (Heb 4:15).

2.5. He said, *Ephphatha*; that is, *Be opened. Be opened* served both parts of the healing: "Let the ears be opened, and let the lips be opened; let him hear and speak freely." And the effect corresponded to the words spoken: *Straightway his ears were opened, and the string of his tongue was loosed* (v. 35). Fortunate was the one who, as soon as he had his senses of hearing and speech given, had the blessed Jesus so near to talk with. This healing was:

2.5.1. Proof that Christ was the Messiah, because it was foretold that by his power the *ears of the deaf would be unstopped* and the *tongue of the dumb* be made to *sing* (Isa 35:5–6).

2.5.2. An example of the action of his Gospel on the minds of human beings. The great command of the Gospel, and the grace of Christ to poor sinners, is *Ephphatha,* "Be opened." He opens the heart, and so he opens the ears to receive the word of God and opens the mouth in prayer and praises.

2.6. He ordered that it be kept very private, but it was made very public. It was because of his humility that he *charged them they should tell no man* (v. 36). Most people will make known their own goodness, or at least they want others to make it known. We should take pleasure in doing good, but not in its becoming known. It was because of the zeal of these witnesses that they declared what Christ had done before he wanted it to be widely known. However, their intentions were sincere, and so it is to be reckoned as an act of indiscretion rather than an act of disobedience (v. 36). Those who told it and those who heard it were *beyond measure astonished.* Everyone said—it was the common verdict—*He hath done all things well* (v. 37). They were ready to witness for him not only that he had done no evil but also that he had done a great deal of good, and done it well, and all freely, *without money and without price* (Isa 55:1). He *maketh both the deaf to hear, and the dumb to speak*, and that is good, and so those who want to speak badly of him are without excuse (Ro 2:1).

CHAPTER 8

We have here: 1. Christ's miraculous feeding of four thousand with seven loaves and a few small fish (vv. 1–9). 2. His refusing to give the Pharisees a sign from heaven (vv. 10–13). 3. His warning his disciples to watch out for the yeast of Pharisaism and Herodianism (vv. 14–21). 4. His giving of sight to a blind man at Bethsaida (vv. 22–26). 5. Peter's confession of him (vv. 27–30). 6. The notice he gave to his disciples of his own approaching suffering (vv. 31–33), and the warning he gave them to prepare for similar suffering (vv. 34–38).

Verses 1–9

We had the story of a miracle very like this one before in this Gospel (6:35–44), and of this same miracle in Mt 15:32–39.

1. Our Lord Jesus was followed by many: *The multitude was very great* (v. 1). The ordinary people, who had greater sincerity than their leaders, and therefore more true wisdom, kept their high opinion of him. Notice with whom Christ had dealings, and with whom he was familiar; this encouraged the lowliest to come to him for life and grace.

2. *They were with him three days, and had nothing to eat*; that was hard service. Let the Pharisee never say that Christ's *disciples fast not* (2:18). However, they remained with Christ; they did not speak of leaving him till he spoke of dismissing them. True zeal makes nothing of hardships on the path of duty. It was an old saying among the Puritans, "Brown bread and the Gospel are good food."

3. Christ said, *I have compassion on the multitude*. The humble Jesus looked with pity and tenderness on those whom the proud Pharisees looked on with disdain. What he chiefly considered, however, was, *They have been with me three days, and have nothing to eat*. Whatever losses we sustain and whatever hardships we go through for Christ's sake and because of our love for him, he will make sure that they are made up to us in one way or another. Notice the sympathy with which Christ spoke: *If I send them away fasting to their own houses, they will faint by the way* (v. 3). He considered that *many of them came from afar* and had a long way to go home. When we see crowds listening to the preaching of the word, it is encouraging to think that Christ knows where they all come from, even though we do not. Christ did not want them to go home hungry, for it is not his way to *send empty away* (Lk 1:53) from him those who have rightly been with him.

4. The doubts of Christians are sometimes made to work for the exalting of the power of Christ. The disciples could not imagine from where so many people could be *satisfied with bread* in this remote place (v. 4). Since the disciples thought it impossible to do this, Christ's doing it would have to be wonderful.

5. Christ's time to act to help his people is when things are brought to their extremity. So that they did not follow him merely for food, he did not supply it until they came to the end of their own resources, and then he sent them away.

6. The goodness of Christ is inexhaustible. Christ repeated this miracle. His favors are renewed, just as our needs are. In the previous miracle of feeding, Christ used all the bread he had, which was five loaves, and fed all the guests he had, who were five thousand. He could have said now, "If five loaves would feed five thousand, four may feed four thousand," but he took all the seven loaves and fed them to the four thousand, because he wanted to teach us both to use what we have and to make the best of what is available.

7. In our Father's house *there is bread enough, and to spare* (Lk 15:17). Those who have Christ to live on need not fear that they will lack anything.

8. It is good for those who follow Christ to keep together. Christ fed them all. Christ's sheep must remain in the flock, and *verily they shall be fed* (Ps 37:3).

Verses 10–21

Christ continued on the move; he now visited the region of Dalmanutha. Meeting with hostility there, and with no opportunities to do good, he *entered into the ship* (boat) *again* (v. 13) and came back. We are told here:

1. How he refused to satisfy the Pharisees, who challenged him to give them *a sign from heaven*. They came out deliberately to *question with him*, in order to trap him.

1.1. They demanded *a sign from heaven* from him, as if the signs he gave them on earth were not sufficient. They demanded this sign, *tempting him* (to test him), not in the hope that he would give it them, but so that they could imagine they had a pretext for their unfaithfulness.

1.2. He denied them their demand; he *sighed deeply in his spirit* (v. 12). He "groaned," according to some, grieved at the *hardness of their hearts* (3:5). It troubles him that sinners stand in their own light in this way and put a barrier up over their own door.

1.2.1. He pleaded with them about this demand: "*Why doth this generation seek after a sign*—this generation, who are so unworthy to have the Gospel brought to them, much less to have any accompanying sign; this generation, who have received so many perceptible signs of mercy in the healing of their sick? How absurd it is to ask for a sign!"

1.2.2. He refused to answer their demand: *Verily, I say unto you, there shall no sign be given to this generation*. He denied them and then left them, as people unfit to talk to; if they refused to be convinced, they would not be; let them be left to their own strong delusions (2Th 2:11).

2. How he warned his disciples against the yeast of the Pharisees and of Herod. Notice here:

2.1. What the warning was: "*Take heed, beware*, or you may share in the *leaven* (yeast) *of the Pharisees* (v. 15)." Matthew adds, *and of the Sadducees*; Mark adds, *and of Herod*. The yeast of both was the same; they were unsatisfied with the signs they had, and they wanted to have others that they themselves had devised. "Watch out for this leaven," Christ said; "be convinced by the miracles you have seen."

2.2. How they misunderstood this warning. It seems that when they put out to sea at this time, they had *forgotten to take bread* and *had not in their ship* (boat) *more than one loaf* (v. 14). They *reasoned among themselves* what this warning meant and concluded, "*It is because we have no bread*." They *reasoned it*, they *disputed about it*; one said, "It was because of you," and the other said, "It was because of you that we are so badly provided for on this voyage." This is how distrust of God makes Christ's disciples quarrel among themselves.

2.3. The rebuke Christ gave them for their uneasiness in this matter. The rebuke was given with some heat, for he knew their hearts, and knew they needed to be rebuked so soundly: "*Perceive ye not yet, neither understand? Have ye your hearts yet hardened? Having eyes, see ye not? Having ears, hear ye not?* How strangely foolish you are! *Do ye not remember when I broke the five loaves among the five thousand,* and soon afterward, the *seven loaves among the four thousand?* Do you not remember *how many baskets full ye took up* of the pieces left over?" Yes; they did remember, and they could tell him that they took up twelve basketfuls one time, and seven another; "Why, then," he said, "*how is it that ye do not understand?* As if the One who multiplied five loaves and the seven could not multiply one." They seemed to suspect that one was not enough to work on, as if it were not all the same to the Lord to save by means of many or few (1Sa 14:6), as if it were not as easy to make one loaf feed five thousand as it was to make one loaf feed five. It was therefore right to remind them not only of the sufficiency but also of the excess of the former meals. The experiences we have had of God's goodness to us in our duty make our distrust of him worse. Our not understanding the true intention and meaning of God's favors to us is equivalent to our not remembering them. We are overwhelmed with present cares and distrusts because we do not understand and remember what we have known and seen of the power and goodness of our Lord Jesus. When we *forget the works of God* (Ps 78:7) in this way and distrust him, we should rebuke ourselves severely for it, as Christ did his disciples here.

Verses 22–26

This healing is related only by this Evangelist, and there is something remarkable in its circumstances. We have here:

1. A *blind man* brought to Christ by his friends, with a desire that he would *touch him* (v. 22). Here the faith of those who brought him is apparent, but the man himself did not show the fervency for or expectation of a healing that other blind men did. If those who are spiritually blind do not pray for themselves, let their friends and relatives pray for them, so that Christ will *touch them.*

2. Christ leading this blind man (v. 23). He did not tell his friends to lead him; he himself *took him by the hand, and led him.* Never had a poor blind man had such a Leader. He led him *out of the town.* Had he intended only privacy by this, he could have led him into a house, into an inner room, and have healed him there. Perhaps Christ took the blind man out of the town so that he would have a larger view of the open fields to test his sight on than he could have in the narrow streets.

3. The healing of the blind man. Notice in this healing:

3.1. Christ used a sign; he *spat on his eyes* and *put his hand upon him.* He could have healed him by a word, as he did others, but this was how he wished to help the man's weak faith, to help him against *his unbelief* (9:24).

3.2. The healing was performed gradually, which was not usual in Christ's miracles. He *asked him if he saw aught* (anything) (v. 23). He *looked up* and said, *I see men as trees walking.* He was not able to distinguish people from trees, except that he could discern them moving. He had some glimmerings of sight, and between him and the sky he could see someone standing upright like a tree.

3.3. It was soon completed. Christ never does his work by halves. He *put his hands again upon his eyes* to disperse the remaining darkness, and then told him to look up again, and he *saw every man clearly* (v. 25). Christ used this method:

3.3.1. Because he did not want to limit himself to one way. He did not heal according to a certain fixed pat-

tern. Providence achieves the same end in different ways, so that people may watch its processes with an implicit faith.

3.3.2. Because it would be according to the patient's faith, and perhaps this man's faith was at first very weak but later gathered strength, and his healing came about accordingly.

3.3.3. Because this was how Christ wanted to show how those who are *spiritually blind* by nature are healed by his grace; at first their knowledge is confused, and they see *men as trees walking,* but like the light of the morning, their knowledge *shines more and more to the perfect day,* and then they *see all things clearly* (Pr 4:18).

4. The instructions Christ gave the man he had healed not to *tell it to any in the town of Bethsaida,* nor even to *go into the town.* Let those who would not move one step out of town to see this healing performed not be satisfied with the sight of this blind man when he was healed. Christ did not forbid him to tell it to others, but he must not tell it to *any in the town.* Showing disrespect to Christ's favors is forfeiting them, and if people refuse to know the worth of their privileges, Christ will make them know that worth by the lack of them. Bethsaida refused to see, and so they would not see.

Verses 27–38

We have read a great deal about the doctrine Christ preached and the miracles he performed. It is now time for us to pause a little and consider what these things mean. What do we think of them? Is the record of those things intended only to entertain us or to give us something to discuss? No; certainly *these things are written that we may believe that Jesus is the Christ, the Son of God* (Jn 20:31). We are taught here three things that the miracles of Christ did.

1. They proved that he was the Son of God and Savior of the world. Here his disciples, who were the eyewitnesses of those miracles, professed their belief in him.

1.1. Christ asked them, *Who do men say that I am?* (v. 27). Although it is a comparatively small thing for us to be judged by other people, it may sometimes do us good to know what people say about us, not so that we may seek our own glory, but so that we may hear about our faults.

1.2. The account they gave him clearly showed the high opinion the people had of him. Although they came short of the truth, they were still convinced by his miracles that he was an extraordinary person with a divine commission. None of the people said that he was a Deceiver (Mt 27:63); some said *he was John Baptist,* others *Elias* (Elijah), others *one of the prophets* (v. 28). All agreed that he was someone risen from the dead.

1.3. The account the disciples gave him of their own attitude toward him showed how glad they were to have left everything to follow him. *But who say ye that I am?* They had a ready response to this: *Thou art the Christ,* the Messiah who had often been promised and long expected (v. 29). They knew this, and they would soon make it widely known, but at the moment they must keep it secret (v. 30), until its proof was completed and they were completely qualified to make it known.

2. These miracles of Christ take away the offense of the cross and assure us that in it Christ was not conquered, but a Conqueror. Now that the disciples were convinced that Jesus was the Christ, they could bear to hear about his sufferings (v. 31).

2.1. Christ taught his disciples that he must *suffer many things.* Although they had gotten past the common error that the Messiah was a worldly Ruler, they still retained it so far as to expect that he would soon *restore the king-dom to Israel* (Ac 1:6). Christ here showed them the con-trary, that he must be *rejected of the elders, and the chief priests,* and *the scribes,* that instead of being crowned, *he must be killed*—crucified—and *after three days must rise again* to a heavenly life, to be *no more in this world* (Jn 17:11). He spoke this *openly* (v. 32). He said it freely and clearly, not wrapping it up in ambiguous terms. He spoke it cheerfully and without any terror, wanting them to hear it in that way; he spoke it boldly, as One who not only knew he must suffer and die but also had determined he would, making it his own action.

2.2. Peter opposed it: *he took him, and began to rebuke him.* Here Peter showed more love than discretion, a zeal for Christ and his safety, but not according to knowledge (Ro 10:2). He "took hold of him," as it were, to stop and hinder him, "took him in his arms" and embraced him, as some understand it. Or he "took him aside," privately, and *began to rebuke* him. This was not the language of the least authority, but of the greatest affection. Our Lord Jesus allowed his disciples to be free with him, but Peter here took too great a liberty.

2.3. Christ restrained him for his opposition (v. 33): he *turned about* and *looked on his disciples,* to see if the rest of them shared that opinion and agreed. He said, *Get thee behind me, Satan.* Peter little thought he would receive such a sharp rebuke; perhaps he expected as much com-mendation now for his love as he had just had for his faith. Christ knows what kind of spirit we are of (Lk 9:55), even when we ourselves do not.

2.3.1. Peter spoke as one who did not rightly understand the purposes of God. The most powerful enemies could not defeat the One whom diseases and deaths, winds and waves and demons, were forced to obey and submit to. Yet Peter looked on Christ's death only as a martyrdom, which he thought could be prevented. He did not know that the thing was necessary for the glory of God, the destruction of Satan, and human salvation, that the Captain of our salvation must be *made perfect through sufferings* (Heb 2:11). Human wisdom is complete foolishness when it claims to advise God's purposes. The cross of Christ was a stumbling block to some and foolishness to others (1Co 1:23–24).

2.3.2. Peter spoke as one who did not rightly under-stand the nature of Christ's kingdom; he took it to be tem-poral and human, whereas it is spiritual and divine. *Thou savourest not* (you do not have in mind) *the things that are of God, but those that are of men.* Peter seemed more concerned with the things relating to this lower world than with those that concern the upper world and the life to come. Setting one's mind on the *things of men* more than on divine things, more than on God's glory and kingdom, is a very great sin, and the root of much sin, and is very common among Christ's disciples. "You are not wise," as it may read, *in the things of God,* but in the *things of men.* It seems advisable to avoid trouble, but if when we do that we avoid fulfilling our duty, it will lead to even greater foolishness.

3. These miracles of Christ should encourage us all to follow him, whatever it may cost us, not only because they confirmed his mission but also because they explained his purpose. They clearly showed that through his Spirit he would do for our blind, deaf, lame, leprous, diseased, possessed souls what he did for the bodies of those many people who came in their distress to him. This is written so that we may believe (Jn 20:31) that he is the great Phy-sician of souls and so that we may become his patients. He *called all the people to him* to hear this. This is what

all who expect Christ to heal their souls should know and consider.

3.1. They must not indulge physical comforts, because, "*Whosoever will come after me, let him deny himself* (v. 34) and live a life of self-denial. Let him not pretend to be his own doctor, and let him *take up his cross.* Let him continue to *follow me* in this way." Those who want to be Christ's patients must be with him, share their lives with him, receive teaching and rebuke from him, and decide they will never leave him.

3.2. They must not be concerned for *the life of the body* when they cannot keep it without leaving Christ (v. 35). Are we called by the words and works of Christ to follow him? Let us sit down and count the cost (Lk 14:28), to see whether we can put our benefits from Christ before life itself. When Satan is drawing away disciples and servants to follow him, he conceals the worst of it, but Christ tells us in advance about the troubles and dangers involved in serving him; he is not afraid to have us know the worst, because the advantages of serving him abundantly out-weigh the discouragements, if we will only impartially set one over against the other.

3.2.1. We must not dread the loss of our lives in the cause of Christ (v. 35); *Whosoever will save his life,* by declining Christ or by disowning him after professing to come to him, will *lose it,* and all hopes of eternal life; he will make a bad bargain for himself. But whosoever *shall lose his life,* whoever is truly willing to lose it when he cannot keep it without denying Christ, will *save it,* will gain indescribably. It is thought that those who lose their lives in serving their king and country are rewarded to some extent by having their memories honored and their families provided for, but what is that compared with the reward Christ gives in eternal life to all who die for him?

3.2.2. We must dread the loss of our souls (vv. 36–37), *for what shall it profit a man, if he should gain the whole world,* by denying Christ, and *lose his own soul?* "It is true," said Bishop Hooper, the night before he suffered martyrdom, "that life is sweet, and death is bitter, but eter-nal death is bitterer, and eternal life is sweeter." The gain of the whole world in sin is not enough to make up for the ruin of the soul by sin. He tells us here what it is that people do to save their lives and gain the world: *Whoso-ever therefore shall be ashamed of me, and of my words, in this adulterous and sinful generation, of him shall the Son of man be ashamed* (v. 38). The disadvantage that the cause of Christ labors under in this world is that it is to be acknowledged and professed in an *adulterous and sinful generation.* Some ages and some places are more especially sinful, such as the one in which Christ lived; in such a generation the cause of Christ is opposed and oppressed, and those who acknowledge it are exposed to scorn and contempt and are ridiculed and *spoken against everywhere* (Ac 28:22). There are many who, though they must acknowledge that the cause of Christ is righteous, are *ashamed* of it. They are *ashamed* of their relation-ship with Christ. They cannot bear to be frowned on and despised, and so they throw away their profession of faith. A day is coming when the cause of Christ will appear as bright and glorious as it now appears lowly and contempt-ible. Those who are not willing to share with him in his disgrace now will not share with him in his glory then.

CHAPTER 9

We have here: 1. Christ's transfiguration on the mountain (vv. 1–13). 2. His driving the evil spirit out of a child when the disciples could not do it (vv. 14–29). 3. His prediction of his own sufferings and death (vv. 30–32). 4. His restraining of his disciples for arguing who should be greatest (vv. 33–37), and of John for rebuking someone who drove out demons in Christ's name but did not follow them (vv. 38–41). 5. Christ's discourse to his disciples about the danger of causing one of his little ones to sin (v. 42) and of indulging in ourselves what is an offense and causes us to sin (vv. 43–50).

Verses 1–13

Here is:

1. A prediction that Christ's kingdom was now coming near (v. 1). What was foretold was that the *kingdom of God* would come, and would come so as to be seen; that it would come *with power* and overcome the opposition raised against it; and that it would come while some now *present were alive*. There were some *standing there that would not taste of death* until they saw it.

2. An example of that kingdom in the transfiguration of Christ *six days* after Christ spoke that prediction. He gave them this glimpse of his glory to show that his sufferings were voluntary and to prevent the *offense of the cross* (Gal 5:11). Notice:

2.1. It was on the top of a *high mountain*. Tradition has it that it was on the top of Mount Tabor that Christ was transfigured.

2.2. The witnesses of it were Peter, James, and John; these were the three who were to bear record on earth, corresponding to Moses, Elijah, and the voice from heaven. Just as some distinctive favors are given to disciples and not to the world, so also some are given to certain disciples and not to others. All the saints are a people near to Christ, but some are closest to him. James was the first of all the Twelve who died for Christ, and John survived them all, to be the last eyewitness of this glory; he testified: *We saw his glory* (Jn 1:14), as did Peter (2Pe 1:16–18).

2.3. How it happened: *He was transfigured before them.* See what a great change human bodies are capable of when God honors them. His *raiment* (clothes) *became shining* (dazzling white), *exceeding white as snow*, beyond the whitest that could be bleached.

2.4. His companions in this glory were Moses and Elijah (v. 4); they appeared *talking with him*, to testify to him. Moses and Elijah lived many years apart, but that is not important in heaven, where the *first shall be last, and the last first* (Mt 19:30), that is, where all are one in Christ.

2.5. The great delight that the disciples took in seeing this sight and hearing this message was expressed by Peter. *He said, Master, it is good for us to be here* (v. 5). Although Christ was transfigured and was speaking to Moses and Elijah, he still allowed Peter to speak to him. Many people, when they become great, want their friends to keep their distance from them, but true believers have access to come with boldness even to the glorified Jesus (Eph 3:12). Even in this heavenly conversation there was room for Peter to put in a word, and it is this: *"Lord, it is good to be here, and let us make tabernacles."* Gracious souls consider it good to be in fellowship with Christ, good to be on the mount with him. If it is good to be with Christ transfigured, on a mountain with only Moses and Elijah, how good it will be to be with Christ glorified, in heaven with all the saints! But notice too that while Peter wanted to stay there, he forgot the need of the presence of Christ among the people. At this very time, the other disciples greatly missed their presence (v. 14). When things are going well with us, we tend to forget others. It was a weakness in Peter to put private fellowship with God

before public usefulness. Peter talked about making three distinct shelters, one each for Moses, Elijah, and Christ, which was not a good idea. One tabernacle would have held them all; they live together in unity. However, whatever inconsistency there may have been in what he said, he may be excused, for they were all *sore afraid* (frightened), and he, for his part, *wist not* (did not know) *what to say* (v. 9).

2.6. The voice that came from heaven confirmed Christ as mediator (v. 7). *There was a cloud that overshadowed them.* Peter had talked about making shelters for Christ and his friends, but *while he yet spoke*, God created his shelter *not made with hands* (2Co 5:11). Now out of this cloud, it was said, *This is my beloved Son, hear him.* God acknowledges and accepts Christ as his beloved Son.

2.7. The vision disappeared: *Suddenly when they had looked round about* (v. 8), all was gone; *they saw no man any more*. Only Jesus remained with them, and he was not transfigured, but had his usual appearance. Christ does not leave the soul when extraordinary joy and encouragements leave it. Christ's disciples have, and will have, his ordinary presence with them always, even to the end of the world (Mt 28:20). Let us thank God for our daily bread and not expect to have a continual feast (Pr 15:15) this side of heaven.

2.8. The conversation between Christ and his disciples as they came down from the mountain.

2.8.1. He commanded them to keep this matter private until he had *risen from the dead* (v. 9). Because he was now in a state of humiliation, he did not want anything publicly taken notice of that might seem to be inconsistent with such a state. His telling his disciples to remain silent would also be useful to them to prevent their boasting. It is humbling to a person to be restrained from telling about their advancements, and it may help to keep them from pride.

2.8.2. The disciples were at a loss as to what the *rising from the dead* meant. Here was another thing that perplexed them (v. 11). *Why say the scribes, Elias must first come?* Elijah had gone, and Moses too. The teachers of the law had taught them to expect the person of Elijah, whereas the prophecy referred to one *in the spirit and power of Elias* (Lk 1:17).

2.8.3. Christ gave them a key to the prophecy about Elijah (vv. 12–13): "It is true that it is prophesied that Elijah will come and *restore all things*. It is also prophesied that the *Son of man* must *suffer many things* and be *set at nought.* Though the teachers of the law do not tell you so, the Scriptures do, and you have as much reason to expect that as to expect the coming of Elijah. As for Elijah, I tell you *he is come*, and if you stop and think about it for a moment, you will understand whom I mean, that it is the one to whom they have *done whatsoever they listed* (wished)." The true Elijah, as well as the true promised Messiah, has come, and we are to look for no other (Mt 11:3–6). He has come, has been, and has done according to what was *written of him*.

Verses 14–29

Here is the account of Christ's driving the evil spirit out of a child, somewhat more fully related than it was in Mt 17:14–21. Notice here:

1. Christ returned to his disciples and found them in confusion. Christ's glory above does not make him forget the concerns of his church below (v. 14). He came very promptly when the disciples were floundering. A child possessed by an evil spirit had been brought to them, and they could not drive out the spirit, and so the teachers

of the law were gloating as if they had won the battle. Christ *found the scribes questioning with them.* His return was very welcome to the disciples, no doubt, but it was unwelcome to the teachers of the law. Particular notice is taken of its being very surprising to the people. When they *beheld him* coming to them again, they were *greatly amazed*, and *running to him*, they greeted him. It is easy to give a reason why they should be glad to see him, but why were they *greatly amazed* (overwhelmed with wonder) when they saw him? Probably some unusual appearance remained on his face. Instead of seeming tired, his face seemed wonderfully lively, which amazed them.

2. A case that perplexed the disciples was brought to him. He asked the teachers of the law, "*What question ye with them?* What is the quarrel now?" The teachers of the law gave no answer, for they were confounded at his presence; the disciples gave no reply either, for they were comforted, and now left everything to him. However, the father of the child spoke up (vv. 17–18).

2.1. His child was possessed by a spirit that had robbed him of his speech, and in his fits he could not speak. Whenever the seizure took him, the spirit *tore* him, that is, threw him into convulsions so violent that they almost tore him to pieces, and *he foamed* at the mouth and *gnashed his teeth.* Although the fits soon subsided, they still left him so weak that he *pined away,* was worn down to a skeleton.

2.2. The disciples could not help him: "*I desired they would cast him out,* but *they could not,* and so you could not have come at a better time. *Master, I have brought him to thee.*"

3. He rebuked them all: *O faithless generation, how long shall I be with you? How long shall I suffer* (put up with) *you?* (v. 19). He called them *a faithless generation* and spoke as one who was weary of *being with them* and of *bearing with them.* "How long will I be among these faithless people? How long must I put up with them?"

4. When the child was brought to Christ, he was in a deplorable condition; we see it and then hear the father's sad description of it. When the child saw Christ, he fell immediately into a convulsion: *The spirit straightway tore him,* as if to defy Christ, hoping to be too hard for him too, hoping to keep possession in spite of him. The child *fell* on the *ground, and wallowed foaming.* Christ asked, *How long since this came to him?* It seems the disease was long standing; it had been with the boy since childhood (v. 21), which made the case even sadder and the healing more difficult.

5. The father communicated his child's need for healing with urgency: *Ofttimes it hath cast him into the fire, and into the waters, to destroy him* (v. 22). But *if thou canst do anything, have compassion on us, and help us.* The leper was confident of Christ's power but put an "if" on his will (Mt 8:2): *If thou wilt, thou canst.* This poor man referred himself to his goodwill but put an "if" on his power.

6. Christ answered his request: *If thou canst believe, all things are possible to him that believeth* (v. 23). He tacitly rebuked the weakness of the father's faith. The sufferer questioned Christ's power — *If thou canst do anything* — but Christ turned the question back to him and made him question his own faith; he wanted the father to attribute the disappointment to a lack of faith: *If thou canst believe.* Yet he graciously encouraged the strength of his desire: "*All things are possible to him that believes* the almighty power of God, to which all things are possible." In dealing with Christ, great importance is placed on our believing, and very much is promised according to

it. "*Canst thou believe?* Dare you believe? *If thou canst believe,* it is possible that your hard heart may be softened, that your spiritual diseases may be healed, and that, weak as you are, you may be able to hold out to the end."

7. The poor man then professed his faith (v. 24): he cried out, "*Lord, I believe;* my healing will not be prevented by the lack of faith: *Lord, I believe.*" He added a prayer for grace to enable him to rely more firmly on Christ to save: *Help thou my unbelief.* Those who complain about their own unbelief must look to Christ for grace to help them against it, *and his grace* will be *sufficient for them* (2Co 12:9). "*Help mine unbelief*; make up what is lacking in my faith with your grace, the strength of which is made perfect in our weakness (2Co 12:9)."

8. The child was healed. Christ *saw the people come running together,* and so he kept them in suspense no longer, but *rebuked the foul* (evil) *spirit.* Notice:

8.1. The command Christ spoke to this evil spirit: "*Thou dumb and deaf spirit, come out of him* immediately, and *enter no more into him.* Not only let him be brought out of this fit, but let his fits never return." Those whom Christ heals are completely healed by him. Satan may go out of his own accord and later regain possession, but if Christ drives him out, he will keep him out.

8.2. How the evil spirit took it; he become even more outraged; he *cried* and *rent him sore,* convulsed him so violently that he was *as one dead. Many said, He is dead.*

8.3. How the child was perfectly restored: *Jesus took him by the hand,* "took hold of him firmly" (v. 27), strongly lifted him up, and he got up and recovered, and all was well.

9. Christ told his disciples why they could not drive out this evil spirit. They *inquired* of him privately *why they could not,* and he told them: *This kind can come forth by nothing* except *prayer and fasting* (v. 29). The disciples must not think they can always do their work with a similar ease, but Christ can do by speaking a word what they must seek *by prayer and fasting.*

Verses 30–40

Here:

1. Christ foretold his own approaching suffering. He *passed through Galilee* and *would not that any man should know of it* (v. 30). The time of his sufferings was drawing near, and so he was willing to speak only with his disciples, to prepare them for the approaching time of testing. He said to them, *The Son of man is delivered into the hands of men* (v. 31), and *they shall kill him.* It is inexplicable that human beings, who have reason and should have love, would be so hateful toward the Son of Man, who came to redeem and save them. However, it is still significant that when Christ spoke about his death, he always spoke about his resurrection. But they *understood not that saying* (did not understand what he meant) (v. 32). The words were clear enough, but they could not be reconciled to events, and they were *afraid to ask him.* Many remain ignorant because they are ashamed to ask.

2. He rebuked his disciples for elevating themselves. When he came to Capernaum, he privately asked his disciples what they *disputed among themselves by the way* (v. 33). Everything we say among ourselves throughout our life will be recalled, and especially our disputes, and we will be called to account for them. Of all disputes, Christ will be sure to judge his disciples for those about precedence and superiority: that was the subject of the discussion here, *who should be the greatest* (v. 34). Nothing could go more against the two great laws of Christ's kingdom, which are humility and love, than desiring

advancement in the world and arguing about it. He took every occasion to restrain this bad attitude. They wanted to cover up this fault: they *held their peace* (v. 34). Just as they would not ask (v. 32) because they were ashamed to confess their ignorance, so here they would not answer because they were ashamed to confess their pride. Christ, on the other hand, wanted to put right this fault in them, and so he *sat down*, in order to talk seriously and fully to them. He *called the twelve to him* and told them:

2.1. That ambition, instead of gaining them advancement in his kingdom, would only postpone their advancement: *If any man desire* and aim *to be first*, he will *be last*; those who exalt themselves will be abased (Mt 23:12).

2.2. That no advancement is to be gained under him except an opportunity for and an obligation to much more labor and humility.

2.3. That those who are most humble and self-denying are most like Christ and will be most tenderly acknowledged by him. *He took a child in his arms.* "Look," he said; "*whosoever shall receive* a person such as this child *receives me.* Those who have a humble and gentle disposition are those I will acknowledge and support, and so will my Father, for he who *receiveth me receiveth him that sent me.*"

3. While they were arguing which of them was the greatest, they would not allow those who did not belong to their fellowship to be anything. Notice:

3.1. The account that John gave him of their restraining a person from using the name of Christ because he did not belong to their group. *Master*, John said, *we saw one casting out devils in thy name, but he followeth not us* (v. 38).

3.1.1. It was strange that someone who was not a professed disciple and follower of Christ would still have power to drive out demons in his name, for that seemed to be a distinctive feature of those whom he called (v. 7). Yet it seems likely that he used the name of Jesus because he believed him to be the Christ, as the other disciples did. Why, then, could he not receive that power from Christ — whose *Spirit*, like the wind, *bloweth where it listeth* (wills) (Jn 3:8) — without an outward call such as the apostles had? Moreover, perhaps there were many more such people, for Christ's grace is not limited to the visible church.

3.1.2. It was strange that someone who drove out demons in the name of Christ did not join the apostles and follow him with them, but continued to act separately from them. We know of nothing that could stop him from following them, unless it was that he was reluctant to leave everything to follow them. The matter did not look good, and so the disciples forbade him to use Christ's name as they did unless he followed him as they did. We tend to think that those who do not follow Christ with us are not following Christ at all, and that those who do not follow our ways are doing nothing well, but the *Lord knows them that are his* (2Ti 2:19), however dispersed they are.

3.2. The rebuke Christ gave them for this: *Jesus said, Forbid him not* (v. 39). What is good and does good must not be prohibited, even if there may be some defect or irregularity in how it is done. If Christ is preached, Paul rejoices in that, even though he is eclipsed by it (Php 1:18). Christ gave two reasons why such people should not be forbidden:

3.2.1. Because we cannot suppose that anyone who uses Christ's name in performing miracles blasphemes his name, as the teachers of the law and Pharisees did.

3.2.2. Because as long as those who differed in fellowship agreed to fight against Satan under the banner

of Christ, they should look on one another as on the same side. *He that is not against us is on our part* (v. 40). As to the great dispute between Christ and Beelzebub, he had said, *He that is not with me is against me* (Mt 12:30). Those who will not acknowledge Christ acknowledge Satan. But as to those who acknowledge Christ, who follow him, though not with us, we must consider them to be not against us, and therefore on our side.

Verses 41–50

Here:

1. Christ promises a reward to all those who are in any way kind to his disciples: *Whosoever shall give you a cup of water because ye belong to Christ, he shall not lose his reward* (v. 41). It is the honor and happiness of Christians that they belong to Christ. They wear his uniform and are his servants; in fact, they are more closely related: they are *members of his body* (Eph 5:30). The relieving of Christ's poor in their distress is a good deed; he accepts it and will reward it. Whatever kindness is done to Christ's poor must be done them for his sake and because they belong to him, because that is what sanctifies the kindness. This is a reason why we must not discourage those who are serving the interests of Christ's kingdom, even if they are not doing everything as we would. If Christ counts kindness to us as services to him, we should count services to him as kindnesses to us, and we should encourage them even if they are done by those who do not follow us.

2. He threatens those who *offend* his *little ones* (v. 42). Whoever grieves any true Christians, even the weakest, either restraining them from doing good or drawing them to commit sin, it would be *better for him that a millstone were hanged about his neck, and he were cast into the sea.* His punishment will be very great.

3. He warns all his followers to watch that they do not ruin their own souls. This charity must begin at home; if we must make sure we do nothing that hinders others from doing good, we must be much more careful to avoid everything that will take us away from doing our duty or lead us to sin; and if it belongs to us, or we to it, we must part with it, even if it is very dear to us. Notice:

3.1. The situation considered: that our own hand, eye, or foot may offend us, that the sin we indulge is as precious to us as an eye or a hand. Suppose that what is loved has become a sin, or the sin has become loved. Suppose we must either part with it or part with Christ and a good conscience.

3.2. The duty prescribed in such a case: *Pluck out the eye, cut off the hand and foot*, put to death the much-loved sinful desire; kill it, crucify it. Let the idols that have been *delectable things* (Isa 44:9) be rejected as *detestable things* (Eze 37:23). The part that has become affected by gangrene must be cut off to preserve the whole. Self must be denied so that it may not destroy.

3.3. The necessity of doing this. The flesh, the sinful nature, must be put to death, so that we may *enter into life* (vv. 43, 45), into the kingdom of God (v. 47). Although by abandoning sin we may make ourselves feel, for the present, as if we were *halt* (crippled) and *maimed*, yet it is for life that we abandon it. People will give everything they have for their lives (Job 2:4). These *haltings* and *maimings* will be the *marks of the Lord Jesus* on us (Gal 6:17); they will be scars of honor in that kingdom.

3.4. The danger of not doing this. The matter is brought to a head: either sin must die, or we must die. If we are ruled by sin, we will inevitably be ruined by it. Note the emphasis of terror in the repeating of those words three times here. It is a place *where their worm dieth not, and the fire is not quenched!* The reflections and disgrace of the sinner's own conscience are the *worm that dieth not.* The wrath of God directed on a guilty and defiled conscience is the fire that is not quenched, because it is the wrath of the living God, into whose hands it is fearful to fall (Heb 10:31). Philo says that the punishment of evildoers is "to live forever dying."

4. The last two verses are somewhat difficult, and interpreters do not agree on their sense: *for everyone* will be *salted with fire, and every sacrifice shall be salted with salt.* Therefore *have salt in yourselves.* It was appointed by the Law of Moses that every sacrifice must be salted with salt, not to preserve it, but because it was the food of God's table. Our chief concern is to present ourselves as *living sacrifices* to the grace of God (Ro 12:1), and to that end the nature of human beings, being corrupt, and as such being called *flesh*, must somehow be salted. We must have the fragrance of grace in our souls. Those who have the salt of grace must show they have it; they must show that they *have salt in themselves* (v. 50), a living motive of grace in their hearts, which roots out all corrupt dispositions. Our *speech* must be *always with grace, seasoned with* this salt (Col 4:6), so that no corrupt words may come out of our mouths (Eph 4:29), but instead may be loathed as much as we would loathe putting rotting meat into our mouths. Just as this gracious salt will keep our own consciences free of offense, so it will also keep our conversation with others so, so that we may not cause any of Christ's little ones to sin. We must not only have this salt of grace; we must always retain its flavor and aroma, for if this *salt lose its saltiness, wherewith will ye season it?* Those who will not be salted with the salt of divine grace will be *salted with fire.* The pleasures they have lived in *shall eat their flesh, as it were with fire* (Jas 5:3). Now since this will certainly be the fate of those who do not crucify the flesh with its sinful desires (Gal 5:24), let us, knowing this *terror of the Lord*, be persuaded to do it (2Co 5:11).

CHAPTER 10

We have here: 1. Christ's discussion with the Pharisees about divorce (vv. 1–12). 2. The kind welcome he gave to the little children who were brought to him to be blessed (vv. 13–16). 3. His testing of the rich young man who asked what he must do to get to heaven (vv. 17–22). 4. His discussion with his disciples on that occasion (vv. 23–27) about the advantage of being poor for his sake (vv. 28–31). 5. The repeated notice of his sufferings and approaching death (vv. 32–34). 6. The advice he gave James and John to think about suffering with him (vv. 35–45). 7. The healing of Bartimaeus (vv. 46–52).

Verses 1–12

Our Lord Jesus did not stay for long in one place, because the whole land of Canaan was his parish, and so he wanted to visit every part. Here we have him in the eastern *coasts* of Judea; not long before, we saw him at the western border, near Tyre and Sidon. And so his circuit was like that of the sun, from whose light and heat nothing is hidden (Ps 19:6). We have him:

1. Turned to by the people (v. 1). They came to him again, and *as he was wont* (as was his custom), *he taught them again.* He did *as he was wont.* In Matthew it is said that he healed them; here it is said that he taught them. His *teaching* was *healing* to poor souls. He *taught them again.* Such is the fullness of Christian doctrine that there is always more to be learned, and such is our forgetfulness that we need to be reminded of what we do know.

2. Being drawn into an argument with the Pharisees. Here is:

2.1. A question they asked about divorce: *Is it lawful for a man to put away his wife?* (v. 2). They proposed it to *tempt* (to test) *him*, seeking a pretext for accusing him, whichever way he answered the question. Ministers must stand on their guard; otherwise, under the pretense of being asked for advice, they may become ensnared.

2.2. Christ's reply to them with a question: *What did Moses command you?* (v. 3). He asked this of them to show that he respected the Law of Moses and did not come to destroy it.

2.3. The reasonable account they gave of what they found in the Law of Moses explicitly about divorce (v. 4). Christ asked, *What did Moses command you?* They acknowledged that Moses only *suffered* (permitted) a man to write his wife a certificate of divorce and to *send her away* (Dt 24:1).

2.4. The answer that Christ gave to their question, in which he was faithful to the teaching he had formerly set down in this matter, *that whosoever puts away his wife, except for fornication, causeth her to commit adultery* (Mt 5:32). He showed here:

2.4.1. That the reason why Moses, in his law, permitted divorce, was only *for the hardness of their hearts* (v. 5).

2.4.2. That the account that Moses, in his history, gave of the institution of marriage afforded such a reason against divorce as amounted to its prohibition. Moses tells us God made human beings *male and female*, one male and one female, so that Adam could not divorce his wife and take another woman. The law stated that a man must *leave his father and mother, and cleave* (be united) *to his wife* (v. 7). This shows not only the intimacy of the relationship but also the fact that it lasts forever. The result of the relationship is that although they are two, they are one, *one flesh* (v. 8). The union between them is a sacred thing that must not be violated. God himself has *joined them together*, to live together in love until death separates them. Marriage is not a human invention, but a divine institution. The bond that God himself has tied is not to be lightly untied.

2.5. Christ's discussion with his disciples in private about this matter (vv. 10–12). It was an advantage to them that they had opportunity for personal conversation with Christ, and not only about Gospel mysteries but also about moral duties. Nothing is related here about this private meeting besides the Law Christ set down in this case—that it is adultery for a man to divorce his wife and marry another woman; it is adultery *against the wife* he divorces (v. 11). He added, *If a woman shall put away her husband* and *be married to another*, she *commits adultery* (v. 12). Wisdom and grace, holiness and love, reigning in the heart will make easy those commands that may be like a heavy yoke to the sinful heart.

Verses 13–16

It is looked on as a sign of a kind and sensitive disposition to take notice of little children, and such a disposition was observed in our Lord Jesus, which is an encouragement not only to little children to turn to Christ, but also to adults who are conscious of their own weak and childish ways and of being helpless and useless, like little children. We have here:

1. Little children brought to Christ (v. 13). It does not appear that they needed any special physical healing, nor were they capable of being taught. Those who cared for

them were mostly concerned about their souls, their better part. They believed that Christ's blessing would do the children's souls good, and so they brought them to him, so that he might touch them, knowing that he could reach their hearts when nothing their parents could say to them or do for them would reach them. We may still present our children to Christ, now that he is in heaven; we may have faith in the fullness and extent of his grace and in the promise *to us and to our children* (Ac 2:39).

2. The discouragement the disciples gave to the bringing of children to Christ: *They rebuked them that brought them.*

3. The encouragement Christ gave to it. He was indignant that his disciples would keep them away: *When he saw it, he was much displeased* (v. 14). Christ is very angry with his own disciples if they discourage anyone either from coming to him themselves or from bringing their children to him. He ordered that the children be *brought to him*: *Suffer* (let the) *little children come to me.* Little children are welcome at an early age to come to the throne of grace with their hosannas. Christ came to set up the kingdom of God on earth, and he took this occasion to declare that that kingdom admitted little children to be its subjects. Something of the attitude and disposition of little children must be found in all whom Christ will acknowledge and bless. We must *receive the kingdom of God as little children* (v. 15); that is, we must stand disposed to Christ and his grace as little children are to their parents, teachers, and all who care for them. We must be inquisitive, as children are; we must learn as children do, and in our learning we must believe: "A learner must believe." The mind of a child is a *tabula rasa*, "a pristine blank"; you may write on it whatever you want to; this is the condition our minds must be in to receive the writing of the pen of the Holy Spirit. Children are to be instructed; so must we be. Little children depend on their parents' wisdom and care, and they are carried in their arms and accept what they provide for them; this is how we must receive the kingdom of God, with a humble submission of ourselves to Jesus Christ and a clear, straightforward dependence on him. He received the children and gave them what was desired: *He took them up in his arms, put his hands upon them, and blessed them* (v. 16). Their parents begged that he would touch them, but he did more than that. He *took them in his arms. He shall gather the lambs in his arms, and carry them in his bosom* (Isa 40:11). There was a time when Christ himself was taken up in old Simeon's arms (Lk 2:28). Now he took up these children, not complaining about the burden, but pleased with it. He *put his hands upon them*. He *blessed* them. Our children are fortunate if they only have the Mediator's blessing as theirs.

Verses 17–31

Here is:

1. A promising meeting between Christ and a *young man*; so he is called in Mt 19:20, 22, and in Luke, *a ruler* (Lk 18:18).

1.1. He came running up to Christ; he set aside the seriousness and grandeur of a ruler, showing his fervency and boldness; he ran as one in haste. He now had the opportunity of seeking advice from this great Prophet, and he would not allow the opportunity to pass by.

1.2. He came to him when he was walking along the road with others.

1.3. He kneeled to him, as a sign of the great esteem and respect he had for him and his sincere desire to be taught by him. He fell on his knees, as one who submitted to him.

1.4. His address to him was serious and significant: *Good Master, what shall I do, that I may inherit eternal life?* He thought it possible to *inherit eternal life*, looking on it as not only set before us but also offered to us. Most people ask for good to be enjoyed in this world, but he asked for good to be *done* in this world; not, "Who will make us see good?" (Ps 4:6), but, "Who will make us do good?" He asked for happiness in doing his duty. Now this was:

1.4.1. A very serious question. There begins to be some hope for people when they begin to ask with great concern about what they need to do to get to heaven.

1.4.2. Asked to the right person, one who was in every way fit to answer it, being himself *the Way, the Truth, and the Life* (Jn 14:6), the One who came from heaven with the deliberate purpose to first make the way to heaven, and then to make it known. It is a distinctive feature of the Christian faith that it both reveals eternal life and reveals the way to it.

1.4.3. Proposed with a good intention—that he might be instructed. We find this same question put by a lawyer with a bad intention; he *tempted* (tested) *him, saying, Master, what shall I do?* (Lk 10:25). It is not so much the good words as their good intention that Christ looks at.

1.5. Christ encouraged the young man's inquiry by helping his faith (v. 18). The man called him *good Master*. Christ wanted him to mean by that that he looked on Christ as God, since there is no one who is good except One, God himself. Our English word *God* no doubt has some affinity with the word *good*. Further, he guided the man's actions: *Keep the commandments* (v. 19). He mentioned the six commandments of the second table of the Ten Commandments, which prescribe our duty to our neighbor. The fifth commandment is given last here, as what should especially be remembered and observed in order to keep us to all the rest.

1.6. The young man was a promising candidate for heaven, having been free from any open and gross violations of the divine commands. *Master, all these have I observed from my youth.* He thought he had, and his neighbors thought so too. He who could say he was free from notorious sin was going further than many people on the way to eternal life.

1.7. Christ felt kindness toward him: *Jesus, beholding him, loved him* (v. 21). Christ particularly loves to see young people and rich people asking the way to heaven, with their lives set on that goal.

2. A sorrowful parting between Christ and this young man.

2.1. Christ gave him a command to test him. Had he really set his heart on it? Let him be tested. Could he find it in his heart to part with his riches to serve Christ? Let him know the bad news now; if he would not fulfill these terms, let him quit his claims now; it would be better for him to do it sooner than later. "*Sell whatsoever thou hast,*" and be *a father to the poor* (Job 29:16). Everyone, according to their ability, must relieve the poor. Worldly wealth is given us as a talent (Mt 25:14–30), to be used for the glory of our great Teacher in the world, who has so ordered matters that the poor, whom we will always have with us (Dt 15:11; Mk 14:7), should receive from him. Could the young man find it in his heart to go through the hardest, costliest services he might be called to undertake as a disciple of Christ, and could he depend on him for a reward in heaven? Did he really believe there was a treasure in heaven that was enough to make up for all he might leave, lose, or lay out for Christ? Was he willing to deal with Christ on trust? Could he trust him for all he was worth, and was he willing to bear a present cross in expectation of a future crown?

2.2. Hearing this, he went away: *He was sad at that saying* (v. 22). He was sorry that he could not be a follower of Christ on any easier terms, that he could not lay hold of eternal life and keep hold of his worldly possessions as well. But since he could not fulfill the terms of discipleship, he was reasonable enough not to pretend to do it: *He went away grieved.* Here the truth of the saying in Mt 6:24 is seen: *Ye cannot serve God and mammon.* While he held onto Mammon, he was in effect despising Christ. He bid for what he wanted in the market, but went away sad, leaving it, because he could not have it at his own price.

3. Christ's discussion with his disciples. We are tempted to wish that Christ had softened his approach to lessen its harshness, but he knew what the human heart is like. He would not seek the young man to be his follower because he was rich and a ruler; if he wanted to go, then let him go. Christ will keep no one against their will. Jesus then taught:

3.1. The difficulty of the salvation of those who have many goods of this world, because there are few who have a great deal to leave who can be persuaded to leave it all for Christ.

3.1.1. Christ first asserted this here; he looked around at his disciples and said, "*How hardly shall they* (how hard it is for those) *who have riches enter into the kingdom of God!* (v. 23). They have many temptations to grapple with and many difficulties to overcome that do not come in the path of poor people. Then, he explained himself (v. 24), calling the disciples children, because it was as children that they must be taught by him. Though he had just said, "How hard it is for those who have riches to get to heaven," he told them here that the danger arose not so much from their having riches as from trusting in them. Those who put the wrong value on the wealth of the world will never be brought to rightly value Christ and his grace. Those who have great riches but do not trust in them have overcome the difficulty and can easily part with them for Christ, but those who have very little, if they set their hearts on that little, will keep it from Christ. Finally, he backed up this assertion with, *It is easier for a camel to go through the eye of a needle, than for a rich man to enter into the kingdom of God* (v. 25). Some have sought to bring the camel and the eye of the needle a little closer together.

3.1.1.1. Some people think there might have been some wicket gate or other entrance into Jerusalem that was commonly known as the Needle's Eye for its narrowness, through which a camel could not pass unless it was unloaded. In the same way, on this view, the rich cannot get to heaven unless they are willing to part with the burden of their worldly wealth and stoop to the duties of a humble religion.

3.1.1.2. Others suggest that the word we translate *a camel* sometimes refers to a strong, thick rope. The rich, on this view, when compared with the poor, are like a thick rope compared with a single thread, and this rope will not go through the eye of a needle unless it is untwisted. In the same way, the rich must be loosed and disentangled from their riches, so that thread by thread they may pass through the eye of the needle; otherwise they are good for nothing and will fall to earth.

3.1.2. This truth was very surprising to the disciples: *They were astonished at his words* (v. 24). *They were astonished out of measure* (were even more amazed) (v. 26), *and said among themselves, Who then can be*

saved? They knew how many promises there were in the Old Testament of temporal good things. They also knew that those who are rich have so many greater opportunities to do good, and so they were amazed to hear that it was so hard for rich people to go to heaven.

3.1.3. Christ reconciled them to it by indicating that the need of even rich people for help to overcome the difficulties that lie in the way of their salvation must be referred to the almighty power of God (v. 27). "He *looked upon them and said, With men* (people) *it is impossible,* but the grace of God can do it, for *with him all things are possible.*"

3.2. The greatness of the salvation of those who have only a little of this world and leave it for Christ. He spoke about this when Peter mentioned what he and the other disciples had left to follow him: *Behold*, Peter said, *we have left all to follow thee* (v. 28). "You have done well," Christ replied. "You will be abundantly rewarded, and not only will you who have left a little be reimbursed, but also those who have left very much, even if it is as much as this young man had."

3.2.1. The loss was imagined to be very great. Christ specified:

3.2.1.1. Worldly wealth. Houses are listed here first, and lands last: he wanted them to consider a person who leaves his house, which should be his home, and his land, which should maintain him. This has been the choice of suffering saints.

3.2.1.2. Dear relatives, *father and mother, wife and children, brethren and sisters.* Without these people, the world would be a wilderness to us. However, when we must forsake either these or Christ, we must remember that we stand in a closer relationship to Christ than we do to any created thing. The greatest test of a good person's faithfulness is when their love for Christ comes to stand in competition with a love that is lawful or is their duty. It is easy for such a person to forsake a sinful desire for Christ, but to forsake *a father, a brother, a wife* for Christ, that is, to forsake those whom they know they must love, is hard. But they must do that rather than deny or disown Christ. It is not the suffering, but the cause, that makes the martyr. Therefore:

3.2.2. The benefits will be great. *They shall receive a hundredfold in this time, houses, and brethren, and sisters.* They will have great encouragements while they live that are enough to make up for all their losses. Suffering Christians will have *a hundredfold* in the comforts of the Spirit sweetening their creature comforts. *With persecutions* is added here in Mark. Even when they gain through Christ, they are still to expect to suffer for him. They will receive *eternal life in the world to come.* If they receive a hundred times as much in this present world, one would think they would not be encouraged to expect any more. Yet, as if that were something small, they will have eternal life as well. However, because the disciples talked so much—and really more than they should have—of leaving all for Christ, he told them that although they were called first, there would be disciples called after them who would be advanced above them. Then the *first* would be *last,* and the last *first* (v. 31).

Verses 32–45

Here is:

1. Christ's prediction of his own sufferings. Notice here:

1.1. How bold he was; when they were going up to Jerusalem, *Jesus went before them* (v. 32). Now that the time was at hand, more than ever, he pressed forward:

Jesus went before them, and they were amazed. They began to consider now what imminent danger they were running into by going to Jerusalem, and they were ready to tremble at the thought of it. To encourage them, therefore, Christ *went before them.* When we see ourselves entering on suffering, it is encouraging to see our Master go before us. Or, *He went before them,* and that was why they were amazed; they admired his zeal and cheerfulness as he went. Christ's courage and faithfulness is and will remain the wonder of all his disciples.

1.2. How timid and cowardly his disciples were: *As they followed, they were afraid.* Their Master's courage should have encouraged them.

1.3. How he silenced their fears. He did not try to make matters seem better than they were, but told them again the *things that should happen to him.* He knew the worst of it, and that was why he went on so boldly, and he wanted to let them know the worst of it. "Come, do not be afraid: *He shall rise again*; the outcome of his sufferings will both be glorious to him and bring great benefits to all who are his (vv. 33–34)." The method and details of Christ's sufferings are foretold here in greater depth than in any other of the predictions. Christ had perfect foresight not only of his own death but also of all its aggravating circumstances, and yet he went out to face it.

2. The reprimand Christ gave to two of his disciples for their ambitious request. This story is much the same here as we had in Mt 20:20–28. There it is said that they made their request through their mother; here it is said that they made it themselves. This shows us:

2.1. As, on the one hand, there are some who do not use the great encouragements Christ has given us in prayer, so, on the other hand, there are some who abuse those encouragements. It was irresponsible presumption of these disciples to make such a limitless demand on their Master: *We would that thou shouldest do for us whatsoever we shall desire.* We would do much better to leave it to him to do for us what he sees fit, and he will do more than we can desire (Eph 3:20).

2.2. We must be careful how we make general promises. Christ would not commit himself: *What would ye that I should do for you?* He wanted them to continue their request, so that they would be made ashamed of it.

2.3. Many have been led into a trap by thinking that Christ's kingdom is of this world (Jn 18:36). James and John concluded that if Christ was to rise again, he must be a king, and if he was a king, his apostles must be lords, and either James or John would willingly be the highest lord in the land, and the other would be glad to be next to him.

2.4. Worldly honor has often dazzled the eyes of Christ's own disciples. We should seek to be good, however, rather than to look great or have supremacy.

2.5. Our weakness and shortsightedness appear as much in our prayers as in anything. It is foolish of us to give orders to God, and it is wise to submit to him.

2.6. It is the will of Christ that we prepare for suffering and leave it to him to reward us for it. Our concern must be that we may have wisdom and grace to know how to suffer with him, and then we may trust him to provide in the best way how we will reign with him (2Ti 2:12).

3. The reprimand he gave the rest of the disciples for their uneasiness at it. *They began to be much displeased* (to be indignant) *with James and John* (v. 41). They were angry at them for seeking precedence, because each of them hoped to have it for himself. Here we see the disciples showing their own ambition, in their indignation at the ambition of James and John, and Christ used this

occasion to warn them against it (vv. 42–44). He *called them to him,* in a familiar way, to give them an example of condescension. He showed them:

3.1. That dominion was generally abused in the world: *"They that seem to rule over the Gentiles exercise lordship over them* (v. 42); that is all they seek. Their concern is what they can get out of their subjects to support their own pride and grandeur, not what they can do for them.

3.2. That dominion, therefore, should not be admitted into the church: *"It shall not be so among you;* those who will be given to you as your responsibility must be like sheep under the charge of the shepherd, who is to look after them and feed them, to be their servant, not like horses under the command of the driver, who works them and beats them to get his money's worth out of them. The one who wants to be great and important *shall be servant of all.* The one who wants to be truly great and important must spend their life in doing good to all. Those who are most useful will not only be the most honored later but also the most honorable now." To convince them of this, he set before them his own example (v. 45): he took on himself *the form of a servant* (Php 2:7), coming not to be *ministered to* and waited on, but *to minister*; and he became *obedient to death* (Php 2:8), by *giving his life a ransom for many.*

Verses 46–52

This passage agrees with Mt 20:29–34. The difference is that there we were told about two blind men, whereas here and in Lk 18:35–43 we are told of only one, but if there were two, there was one, and he is named here. He was called *Bartimaeus,* that is, the *son of Timaeus.*

1. This blind man sat *begging.* Those who are unable to gain a livelihood by their own labor are the most proper objects of charity, and special care should be taken of them.

2. He cried out: *Have mercy on me, O Lord, thou Son of David.* Misery is the object of mercy.

3. Christ encouraged him: he *stood still and commanded him to be called.* We must never consider it a hindrance to us in our life to stand still when the reason is that we have a good work to do. Those around Bartimaeus, who had discouraged him at first, were perhaps now the people who told him about the gracious call of Christ: *Be of good comfort, rise, he calls thee.* The gracious invitations Christ gives us to come to him are great encouragements to our hope that we will have what we come for.

4. The poor man then *cast away* (threw aside) *his garment* (cloak) and came to Jesus (v. 50); he threw away everything that might hold him back or in any way hinder him. Those who want to come to Jesus must throw away the cloak of their own sufficiency, and they must throw off the sin that, like long clothing, *most easily besets them* (Heb 12:1).

5. The particular favor he begged was that his *eyes might be opened,* so that he would be able to work for his living and would no longer be a burden to others.

6. This favor he received; his eyes were opened (v. 52). *"Thy faith hath made thee whole.* It was not your boldness, but your faith, setting Christ to work, or rather Christ setting your faith to work." Those supplies that are drawn in by our faith are the most encouraging. When he had *received his sight,* he *followed Jesus in the way.* He showed by this that he was thoroughly healed, that he no longer needed anyone to lead him. He also showed his gratitude, by using his sight to follow Christ. It is not enough to come to Christ for spiritual healing; when we

are healed, we must continue to follow him. Those who have spiritual eyesight see a beauty in Christ that will effectively draw them to *run after him* (SS 1:4).

CHAPTER 11

We have now come to Passion Week and the great events of that week. We have here: 1. Christ's triumphal entry into Jerusalem (vv. 1–11). 2. His cursing the barren fig tree (vv. 12–14). 3. His driving out of the temple those who turned it into an exchange (vv. 15–19). 4. His message to his disciples on the occasion of the withering of the fig tree that he cursed (vv. 20–26). 5. His reply to those who questioned his authority (vv. 27–33).

Verses 1–11

We have here the account of Christ's public entry into Jerusalem.

1. He came into town publicly:

1.1. To show that he was not afraid of the power and hatred of his enemies in Jerusalem. He did not enter the city incognito, as one who dared not show his face.

1.2. To show that he was not downcast or disturbed at the thoughts of his approaching sufferings. He came not only publicly but also cheerfully.

2. The appearance of this triumph was very humble; he rode on a donkey's colt, and a borrowed one at that. Christ went out on the lake in a borrowed boat, ate the Passover in a borrowed room, was buried in a borrowed sepulcher, and here rode on a borrowed donkey. Let not Christians scorn at being indebted to one another, nor let them think it beneath them to borrow, as our Master did not think such acts beneath him. He had no rich trappings; they threw their cloaks on the colt, and so he *sat upon him* (v. 7). All the show the disciples could put on was by *spreading their garments in the way* and *strewing branches of trees in the way* (v. 8), as they usually did at the Feast of Tabernacles. These circumstances are instructions to us not to *mind high things*, but to *condescend to them of low estate* (Ro 12:16). How unbecoming it is for Christians to become proud, since Christ was so far from it!

3. The meaning of this triumph was very great:

3.1. Christ showed his knowledge of distant things and his power over the human will when he sent his disciples to fetch the colt (vv. 1–3).

3.2. He showed his power over animals by riding on a colt that had never been ridden. Perhaps Christ, by riding on the donkey's colt, wanted to express a shadow of his power over the spirit of human beings, who are born as *the wild ass's colt* (Job 11:12).

3.3. The colt was brought from a place *where two ways met* (v. 4), as if Christ wanted to show that he came to direct onto the right way those who had two ways in front of them and were in danger of taking the wrong one.

3.4. Christ received the joyful hosannas of the people. It was God who put it into the hearts of these people to shout *Hosanna*.

3.4.1. They welcomed his person: *Blessed is he that cometh* (v. 9), the One promised so often and expected so long; he came *in the name of the Lord*. *Blessed is he:* may he receive our praise and our love; he is *a blessed* Savior and brings blessings to us. And may the One who sent him be blessed.

3.4.2. They wished his cause well (v. 10). They believed that he had *a kingdom*, that it was the kingdom of *their father David*, a kingdom that came *in the name of the Lord*. *Blessed be this kingdom*; may it come in power. May

it go on *conquering, and to conquer* (Rev 6:2). *Hosanna* to this kingdom; may all happiness come to it!

4. Christ, applauded by those present, came into the city and went directly *to the temple*. He came to the temple and looked at its present state (v. 11). He *looked round about upon all things* but did not yet say anything. He let things be as they were for this night, intending to return the next morning to carry out the necessary reformation. We may be confident that God sees all the evil in the world, even though he does not immediately judge it or reject it. Christ, having taken note of what he saw in the temple, withdrew in the evening to a friend's house at Bethany.

Verses 12–26

Here is:

1. Christ's cursing the fruitless fig tree. He returned in the morning, at the time for work. He was so intent on his work that he left Bethany without eating breakfast: he *was hungry* (v. 12). He went to *a fig tree*, which, being well adorned with green leaves, he hoped to find enriched with some fruit. However, he *found nothing but leaves*; he hoped to find some fruit, for although *the time* (season) of gathering figs *was not yet* come, it was near. Yet there was not even one fig to be found on it, even though it was so full of leaves. Christ therefore made an example of it, not for the sake of the trees, but for the sake of the people of that generation, and he cursed it. He said to it, *Never let any man eat fruit of thee hereafter for ever* (v. 14). This was intended to be a type of the condemnation that came on the Jewish church, to which he came *seeking fruit, but found none* (Lk 13:6–7). The disciples heard the sentence Christ passed on this tree and took notice of it. Woes from Christ's mouth, as well as his blessings, are to be observed and remembered.

2. His clearing the temple of the businesspeople who frequented it and of those who made it a highway. He came, hungry as he was, to Jerusalem, and going straight to the temple, he began to reform those abuses that he had noticed the day before. He did not come, as he was falsely accused of saying he had, to destroy the temple (Mt 26:61), but to purify and refine it.

2.1. He drove out the *buyers* and *sellers, overthrew the tables of the money changers*—throwing the money to the ground, the better place for it—and threw down the *seats of them that sold doves*. He did all this unopposed, because what he did was seen to be right and good, even in the consciences of those who had turned a blind eye to it and encouraged it because they gained money from it. It may be some encouragement to zealous reformers to know that the frequent cleansing of corruption and the correcting of abuses turn out to be an easier work than was thought. Sometimes wise attempts prove successful beyond our expectations.

2.2. He *would not suffer* (allow) *that any man should carry any vessel through the temple* (v. 16). The Jews themselves acknowledged that the honor due to the temple required that the *mountain of the house*, or the court of the Gentiles, not be made a road or ordinary thoroughfare, and that no one come into it with any goods.

2.3. He gave a good reason for this, namely, that *it was written, My house shall be called of all nations the house of prayer* (v. 17). It was to be spoken of among all people by that name. *It shall be the house of prayer to all nations;* it was like that when it was first instituted. Christ wanted the temple to be:

2.3.1. A *house of prayer.* After he had turned out the cattle and doves, which were things for sacrifice, he revived its appointment as a *house of prayer*, to teach us that only the spiritual sacrifices of prayer and praise would continue and remain forever.

2.3.2. A house of prayer *to all nations*, and not only to the Jews, for *whosoever shall call on the name of the Lord shall be saved* (Ac 2:21). When Christ drove out the buyers and sellers at the beginning of his ministry, he accused them only of making the temple *a house of merchandise* (Jn 2:16), but now he accused them of making it a *den of thieves*. Those who allow worthless thoughts to remain within them when they are at their devotions turn the *house of prayer* into a *house of merchandise*, but those who offer long prayers as a pretence for devouring widows' houses (12:40) turn it into *a den of thieves*.

2.4. The teachers of the law and the chief priests were extremely annoyed at this (v. 18). They hated him, but they *feared him*, feared that he might next overthrow their seats and expel them. They found that *all the people were astonished at his doctrine*, and that everything he said was authoritative and a law to them, and what dared he not attempt when he was supported in this way? They sought, therefore, not how they could make their peace with him, but *how they might destroy him*. They did not care what they did as long as it supported their own power and grandeur.

3. His conversation with his disciples on the occasion of the fig tree's withering. When evening came, as usual, he *went out of the city* (v. 19), to Bethany. The next morning, as they *passed by*, they noticed the *fig tree dried up from the roots* (v. 20). The curse was no more than that it would never bear fruit again, but the effect went further: it was *dried up from the roots*. If it bore no fruit, it would bear no leaves to deceive people. Notice:

3.1. How the disciples were moved by it. Peter remembered Christ's words and said, with surprise, *Master, behold, the fig tree which thou cursedst is withered away* (v. 21). Christ's curses have wonderful effects, and he can bring about the immediate withering of those who have flourished like the green bay tree (Ps 37:35). This seemed very strange to the disciples. They could not imagine how that fig tree could wither away so soon, but this was what came of the Jews' rejecting Christ and being rejected by him.

3.2. The good instructions Christ gave them from it; the withered tree was at least fruitful in this way.

3.2.1. Christ taught them from this to pray in faith: *Have faith in God* (v. 22). They wondered at the power of Christ's word of command. "Why," said Christ, "a lively, active faith would put just as great a power into your prayers (vv. 23–24). *Whosoever shall say to this mountain, Be removed, and be cast into the sea, and shall not doubt in his heart, but shall believe that those things which he saith shall come to pass, he shall have whatsoever he saith.*" Through the strength and power of God in Christ, the greatest difficulty will be overcome, and the thing will be carried out. Therefore, *"Whatsoever things ye desire, when ye pray, believe that ye shall receive them* (v. 24); in fact, believe that you *do receive them*, and the One who has power to give them says, *Ye shall have them. I say unto you* that you will (v. 24). *Verily* I say to you, You will" (v. 23). This should be applied:

3.2.1.1. To that faith of miracles that the apostles and first preachers of the Gospel were endowed with, which enabled them to perform wonders in natural things.

3.2.1.2. To that miracle of faith that all true Christians are endowed with. *It justifies* us (Ro 5:1) and so moves away mountains of guilt and throws them into the *depths of the sea*. It *purifies* the heart (Ac 15:9) and so

moves away mountains of corruption. It is by faith that the world is conquered, Satan's fiery arrows are quenched (Eph 6:16), and a soul is crucified with Christ (Ro 6:6; Gal 2:20) but still lives.

3.2.2. To this he added here the necessary qualification of effective prayer, that we must freely forgive and be loving to all (vv. 25–26): *When ye stand praying*, forgive. When we are praying, we must remember to pray for others, especially our enemies and those who have wronged us. If we have wronged others before we pray, we must go and *be reconciled to them* (Mt 5:23–24). But if they have wronged us, we are to go to work more deeply, and must immediately forgive them from our hearts:

3.2.2.1. Because this is a good step toward obtaining forgiveness of our own sins: *Forgive*, so that *your Father may forgive you*.

3.2.2.2. Because the lack of this is a certain barrier to our obtaining the forgiveness of our sins: "*If ye do not forgive, neither will your Father forgive your trespasses.*" We should remember this condition of forgiveness when we pray, because one great mission we have at the throne of grace is to pray for the forgiveness of our sins. And our Savior often insisted on this duty of forgiveness, for it was his great intention to make his disciples committed to loving one another.

Verses 27–33

Here Christ was examined by the great Sanhedrin concerning his authority. They came to him when he was *walking in the temple*, teaching the people. The cloisters of the temple courts were fitted for this purpose. The great men came to him and, as it were, accused him in court with this question: *By what authority doest thou these things?* (v. 28). Notice:

1. How they intended to embarrass him and make him fail. If they could make a case in front of the people that he did not have a legal mission, that he had not been properly ordained, they would tell the people that they should not hear him. This was the last refuge of their stubborn unbelief. They had decided to find some flaw or other in his commission. This is indeed a question for which all who act either as magistrates or as ministers should have a good answer prepared: "By what authority do I these things?" For *how can men preach except they be sent?* (Ro 10:15).

2. How he effectively embarrassed them and made them fail, with this question: "What are your thoughts about *the baptism of John? Was it from heaven, or of men* (of human origin)*? Answer me*" (v. 30). By answering their question in this way, our Savior showed how closely related his teaching and baptism were to John's; they had the same intention and tendency—to introduce the Gospel kingdom. His questioners knew what they thought about this question; they must have thought that John the Baptist was a man sent by God. But the difficulty was what they should say to it now.

2.1. If they acknowledged that the baptism of John came from heaven, they shamed themselves, because Christ would immediately turn the question back on them. "Why did you not believe him, then?" They could not bear to have Christ say this, though they could bear to have their own consciences say so.

2.2. If they said, "*It is of men* (of human origin)," he was not sent by God," they would make themselves vulnerable; the people would be ready to cause them trouble, for *all men counted John, that he was a prophet indeed*. There is a worldly, slavish fear that not only evil subjects but also evil rulers are liable to. Now in their dilemma:

2.2.1. They were confounded and forced to make a dishonorable retreat. They had to pretend ignorance—we *cannot tell*. What Christ did by his wisdom, we must seek to do by our doing well: *put to silence the ignorance of foolish men* (1Pe 2:15).

2.2.2. Christ justified himself in refusing to respond to their imperious demands: *Neither tell I you by what authority I do these things.* They did not deserve to be told, nor did he need to tell them, since no one could do the miracles he did unless God was with them.

CHAPTER 12

We have here: 1. The parable of the vineyard rented out to ungrateful farmers (vv. 1–12). 2. A question about paying taxes to Caesar (vv. 13–17). 3. Christ's silencing of the Sadducees (vv. 18–27). 4. His discussion with a teacher of the law about the most important command of the Law (vv. 28–34). 5. A question about Christ's being the Son of David (vv. 35–37). 6. The warning he gave the people to watch out for the teachers of the law (vv. 38–40). 7. His commendation of the poor widow who put two copper coins into the treasury (vv. 41–44).

Verses 1–12

Christ had formerly used parables to show how he intended to set up the Gospel church; he now began to use parables to show how he would set aside the Jewish church. Notice:

1. Those who enjoy the privileges of the visible church have a vineyard rented out to them. Rent is justly expected from the vineyard's occupants. Members of the church are God's tenants, and they have both a good Landlord and a good bargain, and they may live well on it unless they fall into sin.

2. Those whom God rents his vineyard out to, he sends his servants to, to remind them of his just expectations of them (v. 2).

3. It is sad to think what cruel treatment God's faithful ministers have met with in all ages. The Old Testament prophets were persecuted. The tenants *beat them, and sent them empty away* (v. 3); that was bad enough. They *wounded them* and *sent them away shamefully entreated* (v. 4); that was worse. Eventually, they reached such a level of evil that they *killed* them (v. 5).

4. It is hardly surprising if those who abused the prophets abused Christ himself. God finally sent them his Son, his *well-beloved Son*. It might be expected that they would respect and love the one whom their Master loved: *They will reverence* (respect) *my son* (v. 6). But instead of respecting him because he was the son and heir, they made that a reason to hate him (v. 7). Because Christ called them to repentance and reformation with more authority than the prophets did, the tenants were all the angrier with him, and all the more determined to put him to death, so that they could command all the respect and obedience of the people: *The inheritance shall be ours.* There is an inheritance that, if they had properly respected the Son, would have been theirs: a heavenly inheritance. But they *took him, and killed him*; and they *cast him out of the vineyard*.

5. For such sinful and wrathful actions nothing can be expected but a fearful condemnation (v. 9): *What shall therefore the Lord of the vineyard do?*

5.1. He would come and destroy the tenants. When they killed his servants and his Son, he determined to destroy them; this was fulfilled when Jerusalem was devastated.

5.2. He would *give the vineyards to others*. This was fulfilled when the Gentiles were taken in and the *Gospel*

brought forth great fruit in all the world (Col 1:6). If some from whom we expected good turn out bad, there will certainly be others who are better.

5.3. Their opposition to Christ's exaltation would not obstruct it (vv. 10–11): *The stone which the builders rejected is become the Head of the corner*. God will set Christ as *his King* on his *holy hill of Zion* (Ps 2:6). All the world will see and confess this to be *the Lord's doing* (Ps 118:23).

6. What effect did this parable have on the chief priests and teachers of the law? They knew *he spoke this parable against them* (v. 12). They must have seen their own faces in the mirror.

6.1. They *sought to lay hold on him* and take him prisoner immediately, to fulfill what he had just now said they would do to him (v. 8).

6.2. The only thing that restrained them from doing so was their awe of the people; they did not respect Christ, nor did they have any *fear of God before their eyes* (Ro 3:18).

6.3. They *left him and went their way*; if they could not harm him, they had resolved to prevent him from doing them any good, and so they got out of earshot of his powerful preaching. If people's prejudices are not conquered by the evidence of truth, those prejudices are only confirmed. If the Gospel is not a *savour of life unto life*, it will be a *savour of death unto death* (2Co 2:16).

Verses 13–17

Here the enemies of Christ tried to trap him with a question about the lawfulness of paying taxes to Caesar.

1. The people they used were the Pharisees and the Herodians (v. 13). The Pharisees greatly insisted on the liberty of the Jews, and if Christ said that it was lawful to pay taxes to Caesar, the Pharisees would enrage the ordinary people against him. The Herodians insisted greatly on Roman power, and if Christ discouraged the paying of taxes to Caesar, they would enrage the governor against him. It is nothing new for those who are in conflict in other matters to join together against Christ.

2. The pretense they made was that they wanted him to determine a case of conscience (v. 14). They complimented him highly, calling him Master, acknowledging him as a Teacher of the way of God, a Teacher of it in truth, who would not be swayed one step away from the rules of justice and goodness by others' approval or disapproval: "*Thou carest for no man*, nor *regardest the person of men* (nor pay any attention to who they are); *thou art right* (you are a man of integrity), and you rightly declare good and evil, truth and falsehood." They knew that he taught the way of God in truth, but they rejected the purposes of God against themselves.

3. The question they asked was, *Is it lawful to give tribute to Caesar, or not?* They wanted it thought that they wished to know their duty. In reality they only wanted to know what he would say, hoping that whichever side he took in answering the question, they could take advantage of it to accuse him. They seemed to refer the settling of this matter to Christ. They asked the question fairly: *Shall we give, or shall we not give?* They seemed determined to stand by his answer. Many seem to want to know their duty but are in no way inclined to do it.

4. Christ settled the question and evaded the trap (vv. 15–17). He *knew their hypocrisy*. Hypocrisy, even if skillfully managed, cannot be hidden from the Lord Jesus. He sees the *potsherd* that is *covered with silver dross* (Pr 26:23). He knew their intention was to trap him, and so he made things work so that they trapped themselves. He

made them acknowledge that the currency of their nation was Roman money, that it had the emperor's image on one side and his *superscription* (inscription) on the other, and if so:

4.1. Caesar could command their money for the public benefit: *Render to Caesar the things that are Caesar's.* The circulation of the money came from him as the fountain, and so it must return to him.

4.2. Caesar could not command their consciences, but he did not claim to. "Pay your taxes, therefore, without complaining, but be sure to *render to God the things that are God's."* Many who seem careful to give other people their due are not concerned to give God *the glory due to his name* (Ps 29:2). *All* who heard Christ *marvelled* (were amazed) at the discretion of his answer, but I doubt it brought anyone to give themselves and their devotion to God, as they should have. Many people will comment favorably on the lighter side of a sermon but will not obey the divine laws that were preached.

Verses 18–27

Here the Sadducees, the deists of that age, attacked our Lord Jesus. They were not bigots and persecutors, but skeptics and unbelievers, and their plot was against his teaching. They denied the resurrection, any spiritual world, and any state of rewards and punishments on the other side of death. Christ had made it his business to establish and prove these great fundamental truths that they denied, and so they set themselves the task of confusing his teaching. Notice here:

1. How they tried to entangle it; they quoted the old law, which required that if a man died without children, his brother must marry his widow (v. 19). They proposed a situation in which, in accordance with that law, seven brothers were successively the husbands of one woman (v. 20). These Sadducees probably intended to pour scorn on that law. Those who deny divine truths commonly set themselves up to disparage divine laws and ordinances. Their aim was to expose the teaching of the resurrection, because they supposed that if there was a future state, it must be like this one, and then the teaching, they thought, was obstructed either by an invincible absurdity, that a woman in that state must have seven husbands, or else by this unsolvable difficulty: whose wife she must be? Notice the subtlety with which these heretics undermined the truth. They did not deny it; they did not seem to doubt it. They pretended to acknowledge the truth, as if they were not Sadducees. They assumed there was a resurrection and gave the air of wanting to be taught about it, whereas in reality they were trying to deal it a death blow, and they thought they would achieve that. It is a common trick of heretics and Sadducees to try to confuse and entangle the truth that they do not have the impudence to deny.

2. How Christ followed a clear way of establishing this truth. This was a significant matter, and so Christ did not pass over it lightly, but enlarged on it.

2.1. He charged the Sadducees with error and attributed their error to their ignorance. *"Do ye not therefore err* (are you not in error)*?* You must be aware of it yourselves, and the cause of your error is:

2.1.1. "That you do not *know the scriptures."* Not that the Sadducees had not read the Scriptures, and perhaps become familiar with them, and yet it could be truly said that they did not really know the Scriptures, because they did not know their sense and meaning, but misinterpreted them. A right knowledge of Scripture, as the fountain from which all revealed religion now flows and as the

foundation on which it is built, is the best protection against error. Keep the truth, the truth of Scripture, and it will keep you.

2.1.2. "That you *know not the power of God."* They had to acknowledge that God is almighty, but they would not apply that teaching to this subject; they gave up the truth, handing it over to the objection that it could not be true. The power of God, seen in the return of the spring (Ps 104:30), in the reviving of the kernel of wheat (Jn 12:24), in the restoring of an abject people to their prosperity (Eze 37:12–14), in the raising of so many to life, miraculously, both in the Old Testament and in the New, and especially in the resurrection of Christ (Eph 1:19–20)—all these things were signs and promises of our resurrection by the same power, *according to the mighty working whereby he is able to subdue all things to himself* (Php 3:21).

2.2. He set aside all the power of their objections, by setting the doctrine of the future state in its true light: *When they shall rise from the dead, they neither marry, nor are given in marriage* (v. 25). It was foolish to ask which of the seven men she would be married to. No wonder we confuse ourselves with endless absurdities if we measure our ideas of the spiritual world by the affairs of this physical world.

3. He based the doctrine of the future state and of the blessedness of the righteous in that state on the covenant of God with Abraham, which God acknowledged after Abraham's death (vv. 26–27). He appealed to the Scriptures: *Have ye not read in the book of Moses?* Notice what he refers them to, what God said to Moses at the burning bush: *I am the God of Abraham* (Ex 3:6); not only "I was so" but *"I am* so." It is absurd to think that God's relationship with Abraham would be continued and so solemnly recognized if Abraham was destroyed, or that the living God would be the happiness and reward of a man who was dead and must remain so forever. Therefore, you must conclude that:

3.1. Abraham's soul exists and acts in a state of separation from the body.

3.2. At some time or other, the body must rise again. On the whole matter, he concluded, *Ye therefore do greatly err* (you are totally mistaken). Those who deny the resurrection are greatly mistaken, and they should be told so.

Verses 28–34

Here we have an account of one of them, a teacher of the law, who was so polite as to notice Christ's answer to the Sadducees and to acknowledge that he had *answered well* and to the point (v. 28). Here we have him turning to Christ for instruction, and the way he addressed Christ was becoming to him as a teacher of the law; he wanted to know Christ more.

1. He asked, *Which is the first commandment of all?* (v. 28). He did not mean first in order, but first in importance and honor. Not that any commandment of God is small, but some are greater than others; moral precepts are greater than rituals, and about some we may say that they are the greatest of all.

2. Christ gave him a direct answer to this question (vv. 29–31). Those who sincerely desire to be taught concerning their duty will be *guided* by Christ *in judgment* and *taught his way* (Ps 25:9). He told this teacher:

2.1. That the most important commandment, which indeed includes them all, is that of *loving God with all our hearts.* Where this is the leading motivation in the soul, there is a disposition to every other responsibility. Love is the leading affection of the soul; the love of God is the leading grace in the renewed soul. Where this is not the leading motivation in the soul, nothing else good is done. Loving God with all our heart will effectively take us away from all those things that are rivals with him for the throne in our souls. No commandment will be overwhelming where this motivation is strongest. Now here in Mark, our Savior introduces this command by the great doctrinal truth on which it is built: *Hear, O Israel, The Lord our God is one Lord* (v. 29); if we firmly believe this, it will follow that we will love him with all our heart. If he is one, our hearts must be one with him, and since there is no God besides him, no rival must be admitted beside him on the throne.

2.2. That the second great commandment is to *love our neighbour as ourselves* (v. 31), and we must show it by doing as we would be done by. Just as we must love God better than ourselves because he is a being infinitely better than we, so we must *love our neighbour as ourselves* because our neighbor is of the same nature as we, and if a neighbor is a fellow Christian, of the same holy community as we are, then the obligation is even stronger. *Hath not one God created us?* (Mal 2:10). Has not one Christ redeemed us? Well might Christ say, *There is no other commandment greater than these*, for in these the whole law is fulfilled, and if we are conscientious about doing these, all other kinds of obedience will naturally follow.

3. The teacher of the law agreed with what Christ said (vv. 32–33).

3.1. He commended Christ's judgment on this question: *Well, Master, thou hast said the truth* (well said, Teacher, you are right). It will be brought as evidence against those who persecuted Christ as a deceiver (Mt 27:63) that one of their own confessed that Christ *said the truth* and said it *well*. This is how we must submit to Christ's sayings; we must add our seal, affirming that they are true.

3.2. He commented on it. Christ had quoted the great teaching that *the Lord our God is one Lord*, and the teacher of the law not only assented to this but also added, *There is none other but he*. This teaching excludes all rivals to him and keeps the throne of the heart entirely for him. Christ had set down the great law of loving God with all our hearts, and the teacher also explains this—that it is loving him with the understanding. Just as our love for God must be wholehearted, so it must also be an intelligent love; we must love him with all our understanding. Our rational powers and faculties must all be set to work to lead the devotion of our souls toward God. Christ had said, "To love God and our neighbor is the greatest commandment of all"; "Yes," the teacher of the law said, "it is *more than all whole burnt offerings and sacrifices*, more acceptable to God." There were those who held the opinion that the law of sacrifices was the greatest commandment of all, but this teacher of the law readily agreed with our Savior that the law of love to God and our neighbor is greater than that of sacrifice, even than that of burnt offerings.

4. Christ approved of what the teacher said and encouraged him to continue questioning him (v. 34).

4.1. He acknowledged that the teacher understood well, as far as he went; so far, so good. *Jesus saw that he answered discreetly*, and he was all the more pleased with it because he had just met so many who answered unwisely. This teacher answered as "one who had a mind," as one who had his wits about him, whose judgment was not biased. He answered as one who allowed himself liberty and time to consider and had in fact considered.

4.2. He acknowledged that he was in a good position to make further progress: "*Thou art not far from the kingdom of God*, the kingdom of grace and glory." For those who make good use of the light they have, going as far as that will carry them, there is hope that by the grace of God they will be led further. We are not told what became of this teacher of the law, but we hope that he took the hint Christ gave him, and that he proceeded to ask him what was the great commandment of the Gospel as well. Yet if he did not, we are not to think it strange, for there are many who are *not far from the kingdom of God* but never reach there. *No man, after that, durst* (dare) *ask him any question*. Those who wanted to learn were ashamed to ask, and those who wanted to raise objections were afraid to ask.

Verses 35–40

Here:

1. Christ showed the people how weak and defective the teachers of the law were in their preaching, and how unable they were to solve the difficulties of the Scriptures of the Old Testament. He gave an example of this, which is not so fully related here as it was in Matthew.

1.1. They told the people that the Messiah was to be the *Son of David* (v. 35), and they were right. The people took it as what the teachers of the law said, whereas the truths of God should be quoted from our Bibles rather than from our ministers, because the Bible is their origin.

1.2. But they could not tell the people how the Messiah could be David's son, though it was very proper for David, in the spirit of prophecy, to call him *his Lord*, as he does (Ps 110:1). They had taught the people the truth about the Messiah that would be for the honor of their nation, that he would be a branch of their royal family, but they had not taken care to teach them what was for the honor of the Messiah himself, that he would be the Son of God and—as such, and not otherwise—*David's Lord*. If anyone should raise the objection, *How then doth David himself call him Lord?* they would not know how to avoid the force of the objection. Those who, though able to preach the truth, are not to some extent able to defend it when they have preached it and to convince those who contradict it are unworthy to sit in Moses' seat (Mt 23:2). It annoyed the teachers of the law to have their ignorance exposed in this way, but the *common people heard him gladly* (with delight) (v. 37). What he preached was surprising and moving, and they had never heard such preaching. There was probably some extraordinarily commanding and charming in his voice and delivery that commended him to the affections of the ordinary people, for wherever any were persuaded to believe in him and follow him, he was to them like a *lovely song of one that could play well on an instrument* (Eze 33:32). Perhaps some of these later cried out, *Crucify him*, as Herod heard John the Baptist gladly, and yet cut off his head.

2. He warned the people to watch out so that they would not be deceived by the teachers of the law. *He said unto them in his doctrine, Beware of the scribes* (v. 38).

2.1. They tried to appear very important, going about in *long clothing*, as rulers or judges. Their going around wearing such clothes was not sinful, but their loving to go around in them was a result of their pride. Christ prefers his disciples to go with *their loins girt* (the belt of truth buckled around their waist) (Eph 6:14).

2.2. They tried to appear very good, speaking *long prayers*. They took care to make sure it was known that they prayed and that they prayed long. But all this was merely for show; they did it so that they would appear to love prayer.

2.3. They sought applause and were fond of it; they loved *salutations in the market places, and the chief seats in the synagogues, and the uppermost rooms at feasts.* To have these given them, they thought, expressed the esteem that those who knew them had for them, and gained them respect from those who did not know them.

2.4. They aimed to enrich themselves. They *devoured widows' houses.* It was to screen themselves from suspicion of dishonesty that they put on the mask of piety. They wanted not to be thought as bad as the worst, and so they were careful to seem as good as the best. Let not prayers — not even long prayers, if offered humbly and sincerely — be thought the worse of because they have been abused by some. Iniquity disguised by a show of piety is double iniquity, and its doom will be doubly heavy: *These shall receive greater damnation.*

Verses 41 – 44

This passage was not in Matthew, but it is here and in Luke; it is Christ's commendation of the poor widow who put *two mites* into the treasury.

1. There was a public fund for charity. Contributions to this fund were put in a box, and that box was in the temple, because works of love and works of godliness go well together. We often find prayers and giving to the needy going together (Ac 10:2, 4). It is good for people to *lay by as God has prospered them* (1Co 16:2), so that when a need becomes apparent, they are ready to give, having dedicated resources to such use ahead of time.

2. Jesus Christ had *an eye* on it: *He sat over against* (opposite) *the treasury, and beheld how the people cast money into it.* Our Lord Jesus notices what we contribute to godly and charitable uses: whether we give liberally or sparingly, whether we do it *as to the Lord* (Col 3:23) or only to be seen by other people.

3. He saw *many that were rich cast in much,* and it was a good sight to see rich people so kind and to see them put in much. Those who are rich should give richly; if God has given abundantly to us, he expects us to give abundantly.

4. There was *a poor widow that cast in two mites, which make a farthing* (v. 42). Our Lord Jesus commended her highly; he *called his disciples* to him and told them to take notice of it (v. 43). He told them that she could hardly spare what she had given; it was *all her living.* He thought it was more than all that the rich people had given put together — because they had *cast in of their abundance, but she of her want* (v. 44). Many people would have been ready to criticize this poor widow; why should she give to others when she had little enough for herself? Charity begins at home. It is rare to find anyone who would not blame this widow, so we cannot expect to find anyone who will imitate her, but our Savior commended her. We must learn:

4.1. That giving to the needy is excellent and highly pleasing to the Lord Jesus. He will graciously accept it, even though in some circumstances it may not be the wisest thing in the world.

4.2. Those who have only a little should give to the needy out of their little. We should in many cases limit what we spend on ourselves so that we may supply the needs of others; this is loving our neighbors as ourselves.

4.3. Public charities should be encouraged, and although there may be some mismanagement in them, that is not a good reason why we should not bring our gifts to them.

4.4. Though we can give only a little in charity, it will be accepted by Christ, who requires *according to what a man has, and not according to what he has not* (2Co

8:12); if given in the right way, two copper coins will be noted and counted as if they had been two pounds or dollars.

4.5. It is much to the praise of charity when we give not only according to our ability but even beyond it, as the Macedonian churches did, whose *deep poverty abounded to the riches of their liberality* (2Co 8:2 – 3), and when we trust God to provide for us some other way, then this is commendable and worthy of thanks (1Pe 2:19).

CHAPTER 13

Here is the prophetic sermon our Lord Jesus preached, pointing to the destruction of Jerusalem and the consummation of all things. It was preached only to four of his disciples. Here is: 1. The occasion of his prediction — his disciples' admiring the buildings of the temple (vv. 1 – 2) and their asking about the time of its destruction (vv. 3 – 4). 2. The predictions themselves: 2.1. Of the rise of deceivers (vv. 5 – 6, 21 – 23). 2.2. Of the wars of the nations (vv. 7 – 8). 2.3. Of the persecution of Christians (vv. 9 – 13). 2.4. Of the destruction of Jerusalem (vv. 14 – 20). 2.5. Of the end of the world (vv. 24 – 27). 3. Some general indications about the timing of these events (vv. 28 – 32). 4. Some practical applications of all this (vv. 33 – 37).

Verses 1 – 4

We may see here:

1. How inclined many of Christ's own disciples are to idolize things that look great and have been long viewed as sacred. Here one of them said to him, "Look, Master, *what manner of stones, and what buildings are here* (v. 1). We never saw anything like this in Galilee; do not leave this fine place."

2. How little Christ values external show where there is no real purity: "*Seest thou these great buildings?*" he said. "I tell you the time is near when *there shall not be left one stone upon another, that shall not be thrown down*" (v. 2). He looks with pity on the ruin of precious souls, and he weeps over them, for he has put great value on them, but we do not find him looking with pity on the ruin of a magnificent house when he is driven out of it by sin. Notice with what little concern he said, *Not one stone shall be left on another!* While any part remained standing, there might be some hope of its restoration, but what hope is there when not one stone is *left upon another*?

3. How natural it is for us to want to know about future things and their times; we tend to be more curious about them than we are about our duty. His disciples did not know how to take in this teaching. They wanted to get him alone, therefore, to get him to tell them more about this matter. As he was returning to Bethany, therefore, he *sat upon the mount of Olives, over against* (opposite) *the temple.* Four of them agreed to *ask him privately* what he meant by the destruction of the temple. Christ's sermon in reply to it was probably given in the hearing of the other disciples, but still *privately,* that is, away from the crowd. Their question was, *When shall these things be?* They would not question whether the events Jesus had predicted would take place or not — they were willing to hope it was a long way away. "Tell us *what shall be the sign when all these things shall be fulfilled?*"

Verses 5 – 13

In reply to the disciples' question, our Lord Jesus set himself not so much to satisfy their curiosity as to guide their consciences; he gave them the warnings they needed concerning the events that would then soon come to pass.

1. They must be careful not to be deceived by the seducers and impostors who would now soon arise (vv. 5–6): *"Take heed lest any man deceive you.* Many will come *in my name,* saying, *I am Christ."* After the Jews had rejected the true Christ, they were deceived by many false Christs. Those false Christs deceived many; therefore, take heed in case they deceive you. When many people are deceived, we should be woken up to look to ourselves.

2. They must be careful not to be disturbed by the noise of wars, which they would be alarmed by (vv. 7–8). At some times, nations are more troubled and devastated by wars than at other times; so it would be now. Christ was born into the world at a time of general peace, but soon after he left the world there were general wars: *Nation shall rise against nation, and kingdom against kingdom.* "But *be not troubled* at it.

2.1. "Let it not be a surprise to you; such things must happen.

2.2. "Let it not be a terror to you; you have no concern in them, and so you need not fear any damage from them." Those who despise the approval of the world and do not seek that may also despise the disapproval of the world and need not fear that.

2.3. "Let it not be looked on as a sign of the approaching end of the world, for the *end is not yet* (v. 7). Do not think that these wars will bring the world to an end.

2.4. "Let it not be looked on as if in those wars God had done his worst. Do not be troubled at the wars you will hear of, for they are only *the beginnings of sorrows,* and so you should prepare for worse, for there will also be *earthquakes in divers* (various) *places,* and there *shall be famines* and *troubles.* The world will be full of troubles, but *be ye not troubled;* do not fear them." The disciples of Christ may enjoy a holy security and peace of mind when everything around them is in the state of greatest disorder.

3. They must be careful not to be drawn away from Christ by the sufferings they would encounter for Christ's sake. Again, he said, *"Take heed to yourselves* (v. 9). Although you may escape the sword of war better than some of your neighbors, nevertheless, do not think you are safe; you will be exposed to the sword of justice more than others. Take heed, therefore, that you do not deceive yourselves with the hope of outward prosperity, since it is *through many tribulations* that *you must enter into the kingdom of God* (Ac 14:22). Take heed what you say and do, because many eyes will be watching at you." Notice:

3.1. What trouble they must expect. They will be *hated of all men;* there will be enough trouble! The thought of being hated is a burden to a sensitive spirit; those who are malicious will be troublesome. It was not because of anything wrong in them or that they had done wrong that they were hated, but for Christ's name's sake. The world hated them because he loved them. Their own relatives would *betray them,* those to whom they were most closely related and on whom they therefore depended for protection. Their church rulers would inflict their judgment on them; "You will be *delivered up* and *beaten in the synagogues* with forty lashes at a time, as offenders against the law." It is nothing new for the church's weapons, through the treachery of its officers, to be turned against some of its own best friends. *Rulers* and *kings* would use their power against Christ's disciples. They will *cause them to be put to death* as enemies of the empire. They must resist to the point of blood (Heb 12:4), and then still resist.

3.2. What they would have to comfort themselves with.

3.2.1. That the work they were called to would be carried on and prosper (v. 10): *"The Gospel* will, for all this, be *published* (preached) *among all nations,* and the *sound* of it will *go forth into all the earth* (Ro 10:18)." It is encouraging to those who suffer for the Gospel that although they may be crushed and oppressed, the Gospel cannot be; it will stand its ground and win the day.

3.2.2. That their suffering, instead of obstructing their work, would forward it. "Your being *brought before governors and kings* will be for *a testimony against them* (as witnesses to them) (v. 9); it will give you an opportunity to preach the Gospel *to* those before whom you are brought as criminals." Or, as our translation reads it, it will be as a testimony *against* them, against both the judges and the persecutors. The Gospel is a testimony to us about Christ and heaven. If we receive it, it will be a testimony for us: it will justify and save us; if not, it will be a testimony against us in the great day.

3.2.3. That when they were brought before kings and governors for Christ's sake, they would receive special assistance from heaven: *"Take no thought beforehand what ye shall speak* (v. 11), but *whatsoever shall be given you in that hour,* that *speak ye,* and do not be afraid it will not succeed because it is spoken off the cuff, for *it is not ye that speak,* but *the Holy Spirit."* When we are engaged in the service of Christ, we may depend on the help of the Spirit of Christ.

3.2.4. That heaven would ultimately make up for everything; *he that shall endure to the end, the same shall be saved"* (v. 13). Perseverance will win the crown. The salvation promised here is more than a deliverance from evil; it is an eternal blessedness.

Verses 14–23

In rebelling against the Romans and in persecuting the Christians, the Jews were setting both God and people against them. Here we have a prediction of the ruin that came on them within forty years after this. Notice:

1. What was foretold about it.

1.1. That the Roman armies would attack Judea and besiege Jerusalem, the Holy City. These were the *abomination of desolation.* The Jews had rejected Christ as an abomination, though he would have been their salvation, and now God brought on them an abomination that would be their desolation. This army stood *where it ought not,* in and about the Holy City, which the nations should not have approached. Sin made the breach at which the glory went out, and the abomination of desolation broke in and *stood where it ought not.*

1.2. That when the Roman army came into the country, there would be no safety except by leaving the country—as fast as possible. A person would just about be able to escape by *fleeing to the mountains* out of Judea; let him pay attention to the first warning of danger and make his way as best he can. If he is *on the house-top* and sees them coming, let him not *go down to take anything out of the house,* for it would make him lose time. If he was in the field, let him rush away just as he was, not even *turning back to take up his garment* (v. 16). If he could save his life, let him reckon it a good bargain, even though he could save nothing else. Let him be thankful to God that although he was cut short, he was not cut off.

1.3. That things would go very hard at that time for poor mothers and nurses: *"Woe to them that are with child* (v. 17), who cannot fend for themselves or move as quickly as others can. And *woe to them that give suck,* who do not know either how they could leave weak infants behind them or how they could take them along with them." The time may come when the greatest comforts may turn out to be the greatest burdens. It would also be very uncomfortable if they were forced to flee *in the winter* (v. 18). If there is no way to avoid trouble, we may still desire and pray that circumstances may be so ordered as to lessen the trouble, and when things are bad, we should remember that they might have been worse.

1.4. There would be destruction and desolation unparalleled in history (v. 19): *In those days shall be affliction, such as was not from the beginning of the creation which God created unto this day, neither shall be.* The destruction of Jerusalem by the Romans threatened a universal slaughter of all the Jews; so barbaric was their devouring of one another and the Romans' devouring of them all that if their wars had continued a little longer, *no flesh could have been saved.* In the midst of wrath, however, God remembered mercy (Hab 3:2). He *shortened the days.* Many individuals escaped with their lives because the storm subsided when it did. It was *for the elect's sake* that those days were shortened; many among the Jews fared better for the sake of the few among them who believed in Christ. There was a promise that *a remnant* would be saved (Isa 10:22). God's own *elect cry day and night to him,* and their prayers must be answered (Lk 18:7).

2. What directions were given to the disciples with reference to this.

2.1. They must provide for their own safety: "When you see the country invaded and the city besieged, do not delay or think about it anymore—just go! Run for your lives—*let them that are in Judea flee to the mountains* (v. 14). Abandon the sinking ship."

2.2. They must provide for the safety of their souls: *Then, if any man shall* say to you, *Lo, here is Christ,* or, *Lo, he is there, believe them not, for false Christs* and *false prophets shall arise* (v. 22). False Christs will appear, together with false prophets who will preach them—or those who set themselves up as prophets—and they will *show signs* and counterfeit *wonders.* They *shall seduce, if it were possible, the very elect*; their claims will be so plausible that they will draw away many who were eager and zealous professors of religion, many who would very likely have persevered. They *shall seduce, if it were possible, the very elect,* but it is not in fact possible. In thinking about this, let the disciples be cautious whom they believe: *take ye heed* (v. 23). Christ knew that they belonged to the elect, but he still told them to take heed. An assurance of persevering and warnings against apostasy go very well together. God would keep them, but they must also keep themselves. "*I have foretold you all things,* so that, being forewarned, you may be forearmed."

Verses 24–27

These verses seem to point to Christ's second coming to judge the world; in their question, the disciples had confused the destruction of Jerusalem and the *end of the world* (Mt 24:3), and this confusion was built on a mistake, the supposition that the temple must stand as long as the world stands. Christ put right this mistake. Here he foretold:

1. The final dissolution of the present structure of the world. *The sun shall be darkened,* and the *moon* will no more *give her light* (v. 24). The *stars of heaven* will fall like leaves in autumn, and the *powers that are in heaven shall be shaken* (v. 25).

2. The visible appearance of the Lord Jesus, to whom the judgment of that day will be committed (Jn 5:22): *Then shall they see the Son of man coming in the clouds* (v. 26). He will come with *great power and glory. Every eye shall then see him* (Rev 1:7).

3. The gathering of all his chosen ones to him (v. 27): he will *send his angels* and *gather together his elect* to him. They will be taken from *the uttermost parts* (the ends) *of the earth,* farthest from the place where Christ's tribunal will be set, and will be brought to the *uttermost part* (the ends) *of heaven.* A faithful Israelite will be taken safely, even though from the farthest border of the land of slavery to the farthest border of the Land of Promise.

Verses 28–37

Here is the application of this prophetic sermon; *now learn* to look forward rightly.

1. "As for the *destruction* of Jerusalem, expect it to come very soon, as you expect summer to come soon when the *branch of the fig tree becomes soft* and the *leaves sprout forth* (v. 28). When *ye see these things come to pass,* when you see the Jewish nation embroiled in wars, distracted by false Christs and false prophets and drawing onto themselves the displeasure of the Romans, then say that their *ruin is nigh, even at the door,* and provide for yourselves." In fact, all the disciples except John were taken away from the evil to come, but the next generation would live to see it. "*This generation* that is now rising will not all be worn away before *all these things* come to pass. Just as this destruction is near and within sight, so it is sure." Christ did not speak these things merely to frighten them. No; they were the declarations of God's fixed purposes: "*Heaven and earth shall pass away,* but *my words shall not pass away* (v. 31)."

2. "As for the *end of the world,* do not ask when it will come, for *of that day* and *that hour knoweth no man.* It has not been revealed by any word of God, either to *men* on earth or to *angels in heaven.*" But it follows, *neither the Son*; is there anything that the Son is ignorant of? There were those in earlier times who taught from this text that there were some things that Christ, as man, was ignorant of. They said, "It is no more absurd to say that than to say that his human soul suffered grief and fear." Archbishop Tillotson says, "Christ, as God, could not be ignorant of anything, but the divine wisdom which dwelt in our Savior communicated itself to his human soul, according to the divine pleasure, so that his human nature would sometimes not know some things; therefore, Christ is said to grow in wisdom (Lk 2:52)."

3. "As to both, your duty is to *watch and pray* (v. 33): *Take ye heed* of everything that would make you indisposed for your Master's coming. Watch for his coming, so that no matter when it comes, it may not be a surprise to you, and pray for the grace that is necessary to qualify you for it, for *ye know not what the time is,* and you must prepare yourself to be ready every day for what may come any day." He illustrated this, at the close, by a parable:

3.1. Our Master has gone away and has left us something that we must give account of (v. 34). He is *as a man taking a far journey*: he has *left his house on earth* and left his servants each to do their assigned task, having given authority to some and work to others. Those who had authority given them have work assigned to them, because those who have the greatest power are involved in the most business, and to those to whom he gave work he gave authority to do that work. When he took his final leave, he *appointed the porter to watch,* to be sure to be ready to open the door to him when he returned. This is how our Lord Jesus, when he *ascended on high* (Eph 4:8), left something for all his servants to do. All are appointed to work, and some are authorized to rule.

3.2. We should always be watching in expectation of his return (vv. 35–37). Our Lord *will come* as the *Master of the house* to take account of his servants. We do not know *when he will come*. This may be applied to his coming to us in particular, at our death, as well as to the general judgment. Our present life is a night, a dark night, compared with the other life; we do not know in which watch of the night our Master will come, whether in the days of youth, middle age, or old age, but as soon as we are born, we begin to die, and so as soon as we are capable of expecting anything, we must expect death. Our great concern must be that whenever our Lord comes he will not *find us sleeping*, self-confident in ourselves, off guard, ready to say he will not come, and unready to meet him. His coming will truly *come suddenly*. It is the indispensable duty of all Christ's disciples, therefore, to watch, to be awake and keep awake: "*What I say unto you* four (v. 37), *I say unto all*. What I say to you in this generation, I say to all who will believe in me in every age: *Watch, watch*, expect my second coming, prepare for it, so that you may be found in peace, without spot, and blameless (2Pe 3:14)."

CHAPTER 14

This chapter sees the beginning of the account of the sufferings and death of our Lord Jesus Christ. We have here: 1. The plot of the chief priests and teachers of the law against Christ (vv. 1–2). 2. The anointing of Christ's head at a supper in Bethany (vv. 3–9). 3. The agreement Judas made to betray him (vv. 10–11). 4. Christ's eating the Passover with his disciples, his instituting of the Lord's Supper, and his words with his disciples (vv. 12–31). 5. Christ's anguish in the garden (vv. 32–42). 6. Judas's betrayal of Christ and the capture and arrest of Christ by the chief priests' agents (vv. 43–52). 7. His trial before the high priest, his conviction, and the indignities to which he was subjected (vv. 53–65). 8. Peter's denying him (vv. 66–72).

Verses 1–11

We have here examples:

1. Of the kindness of Christ's friends. Even in and around Jerusalem he had some friends, people who loved him and never thought they could do enough for him.

1.1. Here was one friend who was kind enough to invite him to eat with him (v. 3). Although he saw his death approaching, he did not abandon himself to a sad retreat from all company.

1.2. Here was another friend who was kind enough to anoint his head with very precious ointment as he *sat at meat* (eating). This was an extraordinary act of respect shown him by a good woman who thought nothing too good to give to Christ. If he poured out his soul to death for us, shall we think any jar of ointment too precious to pour out on him? It is significant that she took care to pour it all out on Christ's head; she *broke the box*. Christ must be honored with all we have. Do we give him the precious ointment of our best devotion? Let him have all; we are to love him *with all the heart* (12:30).

1.2.1. There were those who gave this action a worse interpretation than it deserved. They called it a *waste of the ointment* (v. 4). The *liberal* and *bountiful* should not be called *wasteful* (Isa 32:5). The objectors claimed that the perfume could have been sold and that the money could then have been given to the poor (v. 5). Yet common kindness to the poor will not be an excuse from a particular act of devotion to the Lord Jesus.

1.2.2. Our Lord Jesus interpreted it as something better, as far as we can tell, than it actually was intended to be. Christ considered it an act of *great faith* as well as *great* love (v. 8): "*She is come aforehand* (beforehand) *to anoint my body for the burying*." Notice how Christ's heart was filled with the thoughts of his death, how familiarly he spoke about it on every occasion. It is usual for those who are condemned to die to have their coffins prepared and other provisions made for their funerals while they are still alive, and so Christ accepted this. Christ never rode in triumph into Jerusalem except when he came there to suffer; nor was his head ever anointed except for his burial.

1.2.3. He commended this act of bold devotion for all ages: *Wherever this Gospel shall be preached, it shall be spoken of for a memorial of her* (v. 9). This was how this good woman was repaid for her jar of perfume. "She lost neither her oil nor her labor." She gained from it the good name that is *better than precious ointment* (Ecc 7:1). Those who honor Christ will be honored by him (1Sa 2:30).

2. Of the malice of Christ's enemies.

2.1. The chief priests, his open enemies, discussed how they might *put him to death* (vv. 1–2). The Feast of the Passover was now near, and he must be crucified at that feast so that:

2.1.1. His death and sufferings would be more public.

2.1.2. The fulfillment would correspond to the type. Christ, our Passover, was sacrificed for us (1Co 5:7) at the same time that the paschal lamb was sacrificed and Israel's rescue out of Egypt was commemorated. Now see:

2.1.2.1. How spiteful Christ's enemies were, for they aimed not only to silence him but to take revenge on him for all the good he had done.

2.1.2.2. How subtle they were: *Not on the feast-day, lest there should be an uproar* (v. 2), lest the people riot and rescue him. Those who desired nothing more than human commendation dreaded nothing more than human rage and displeasure.

2.2. Judas, his disguised enemy, made an agreement with them to betray him (vv. 10–11). He *went to the chief priests* to offer his services in this matter.

2.2.1. What Judas proposed to the chief priests and the teachers of the law was to betray Christ to them without causing an *uproar among the people*, which they were afraid of. Did the chief priests and teachers of the law know that he had thought about helping them and deceiving Jesus? No; they could not imagine that any of his intimate companions would be so evil. The spirit that works in all the children of disobedience (Eph 2:2) knows how to bring them to help one another in an evil project.

2.2.2. What he proposed to himself was to get money through the agreement he made; *they promised to give him money*. Greed was Judas's controlling sinful desire. Perhaps it was Judas's greed that brought him at first to follow Christ, when he was promised that he would be cash keeper, or treasurer, of the society; in his heart he loved handling money. Now that there was money to be gained "on the side," he was as ready to betray Christ as he had ever been to follow him.

2.2.3. Having gained the money, he set himself to fulfill his side of the bargain; he sought how he might conveniently betray him. Notice how careful we must be that we do not get trapped in sinful commitments. It is a rule in our law, as well as in our religion, that an obligation to commit evil is null and void; it requires repentance, not fulfillment. Notice how the way of sin is downhill: when people walk into it, they are drawn to go on in it.

Verses 12–31

In these verses we have:

1. Christ's eating the Passover with his disciples the night before he died. No apprehension of trouble that has come or is coming should either stop us from attending services of holy worship or put us out of spirits to attend them.

1.1. Christ ate the Passover at the usual time when the other Jews did. It was on the first day of that feast that was called *the feast of unleavened bread*, that day when they *killed the Passover* (v. 12).

1.2. He told his disciples how to find the place where he intended to eat the Passover. "*Go into the city*, and *there shall meet you a man bearing a pitcher of water. Follow him, go in* where he *goes*, ask for his master, *the good man* (owner) *of the house* (v. 14), and ask him to show you a room." No doubt the inhabitants of Jerusalem had rooms fitted for letting out on such occasions to those who came from the country to celebrate the Passover, and Christ used one of those. Probably he went where he was not known, so that he would be undisturbed with his disciples. Perhaps he designated the place by this particular sign to show that he chooses to live in the clean heart, that is, one that is washed, as with pure water (Heb 10:22). Where he intends to come, a jar of water must go before him.

1.3. He ate the Passover in an *upper room furnished*. In eating his common meals, he chose what was ordinary—for example, he sat down on the grass (6:39)—but when he was to celebrate a sacred feast, then, in honor of that, he would go to the expense of obtaining as good a room as possible.

1.4. He ate it *with the twelve*. If Christ came with the Twelve, then Judas was with them, even though he was at this time seeking to betray his Master, and it is clear from what follows (v. 20) that he was there. He did not absent himself, for then he might be suspected. Christ did not exclude him from the feast, though he knew his evil, because that evil had not yet become public.

2. Christ's words to his disciples as they were eating the Passover.

2.1. They were pleasing themselves with the company of their Master, but he told them that they must now soon lose him: "*The Son of man is betrayed*. If he is betrayed, the next news you will hear of him is that he has been crucified and killed. *The Son of man goes, as it is written of him*" (v. 21).

2.2. They were pleasing themselves with one another's company, but Christ put a damper on their joy by telling them, *One of you that eateth with me shall betray me* (v. 18). Christ said this to startle Judas's conscience—if it were possible—and to awaken him to repent of his evil and draw back from the brink of the abyss. But it seems that the one who was most implicated in the warning was least concerned about it. All the others were affected by it. They began to be *sorrowful*. Here were the *bitter herbs* (Ex 12:8) with which this Passover feast was celebrated. They began to be suspicious of themselves; they said *one by one, Is it I? And another said, Is it I?* They were more anxious about themselves than about one another. It is the law of charity to *hope the best* (1Co 13:5–7), because we know with certainty more evil about ourselves than about our brothers and sisters and therefore may justly suspect ourselves more. They trusted more in his words than in their own hearts, and so they did not say, "I am sure it is not I," but, "*Lord, is it I?*" Now, in response to their questions, Christ said:

2.2.1. What would give them peace: "It is not *you*, nor *you*; it is this one who now *dips with me in the dish*."

2.2.2. What one would have thought would make Judas very uneasy. If he went on in his undertaking, he would be under the pressure of a threat, for "*woe to that man by whom the Son of man is betrayed*; it would be *better for him that he had never been born*." Very probably Judas encouraged himself with the thought that his Master had often said he must be betrayed: "And if it must be done, then surely God *will not find fault* with the one who does it." But Christ told him that this would be no shelter or excuse for him. In fact, Christ was betrayed by *the determinate counsel and foreknowledge of God*, but despite that, it was *with wicked hands that he was crucified and slain* (Ac 2:23).

3. The institution of the Lord's Supper.

3.1. It was instituted at the close of a supper. In the Lord's Supper no physical nourishment is intended. It is only spiritual food, and so a very little of what is for the body, as much as will serve as a sign, is enough.

3.2. It was instituted by the example of Christ himself, by his own practice, because it was intended for those who are already his disciples.

3.3. It was instituted with a blessing and thanksgiving. This is how the gifts of common providence are to be received; much more the gifts of special grace. He *blessed* (v. 22) and *gave thanks* (v. 23).

3.4. It was instituted to be a memorial of his death; he therefore broke the bread to show how it *pleased the Lord to bruise him* (Isa 53:10), and he called the wine, which is the blood of the grape (Ge 49:11), the *blood of the New Testament*. Frequent mention is made of the *precious blood* (1Pe 1:19) as the price of our redemption. It is called the *blood of the New Testament* (v. 24) because the covenant of grace became a testament, a will, that came in force through the death of Christ, the testator (Heb 9:16). It is said to be *shed for many*, to bring *many* sons to glory (Heb 2:10). It was sufficient for many, being of infinite value; we read of a great crowd that no one could number, who had all *washed their robes, and made them white in the blood of the Lamb* (Rev 7:9–14), and still it is *a fountain opened* (Zec 13:1). How encouraging it is that the blood of Christ is *shed for many*! Moreover, if for many, then why not for *me*? If for sinners, sinners of the Gentiles, the chief of sinners (1Ti 1:15), then why not for *me*?

3.5. It was a sign of the conveying to us of those benefits that were bought for us by his death. He therefore broke the bread *to them* (v. 22) and said, "*Take, eat* of it," and he gave the cup *to them* and told them to *drink of it* (v. 23).

3.6. It was instituted with an eye to the happiness of heaven, and it was to be a pledge and foretaste of that, so making us lose our appetites for all worldly pleasures and delights (v. 25): *I will drink no more of the fruit of the vine*. "Lord, let the day come quickly when I will *drink* it anew and afresh *in the kingdom of God*."

3.7. It was closed with *a hymn* (v. 26). This was Christ's "swan song," which he sang just before he entered his anguish; it was probably what was usually sung (Pss 113–118).

4. Christ's words to his disciples as they returned to Bethany by moonlight. When they had *sung the hymn*, they immediately *went out*. The Israelites were forbidden to leave their houses the night they ate the first Passover, for fear of the sword of the destroying angel (Ex 12:22–23), but because Christ, the *great shepherd*

(Heb 13:20), was to be struck, he went out deliberately to expose himself to the sword, as a champion; the Israelites evaded the destroyer, but Christ conquered him.

4.1. Christ foretold here that in his sufferings he would be deserted by all his disciples: "*You will all be offended* (fall away) *because of me this night.*" Christ knew this before, but he still welcomed them to his table. Nor should we be discouraged from coming to the Lord's Supper from the fear of lapsing back into sin afterward; rather, the greater our danger, the greater our need to strengthen ourselves by the diligent, conscientious use of holy ordinances. Christ told them that they would fall away because of him. Up to that time, they had continued with him in his temptations; although they had sometimes stumbled, they had not fallen away because of him. But now the storm would be so great that they would all allow their anchors to slip and would be in danger of shipwreck. The striking of the shepherd often leads to the scattering of the sheep (v. 27; Zec 13:7): the whole flock suffers for it and is put at risk by it. But Christ encouraged them with a promise that they would rally; they would return both to their duty and to their comfort (v. 28): *After I am risen, I will go before you into Galilee.*

4.2. He foretold that he would be denied especially by Peter. When they went out to go to the Mount of Olives, we may presume that they left Judas — he stole away from them. However, Christ told them that they would still have no reason to boast of their faithfulness. Although God keeps us from being as bad as the worst, we may still be ashamed to think that we are not better than we are.

4.2.1. Peter was confident that he would not do as badly as the rest of the disciples: *Though all should be offended* (fall away), *yet will not I* (v. 29). He thought himself able to withstand the shock of temptation and then stand up against it, all alone, to stand even though no one else stood by him. It is bred in the bone with us to think well of ourselves and trust in our own hearts.

4.2.2. Christ told him that he would do worse than any of them. They would all desert him, but Peter *would deny* him, not once, but three times, and that very soon, too: "*This day, even this night before the cock crow twice,* you will *deny* that you ever knew me."

4.2.3. Peter stood by his promise: *If I should die with thee, I will not deny thee,* and no doubt he thought as he said. Judas said nothing like this when Christ told him he would betray him. He sinned according to plan; Peter, when he was taken by surprise; Peter was *overtaken in this fault* (Gal 6:1). It was wrong of Peter to contradict his Master. If he had said, with fear and trembling, "Lord, give me grace to keep me from denying you," it might have been prevented. They were all, however, just as confident as Peter; those who said, *Lord, is it I?* now said, "It shall never be me." Being acquitted from their fear of betraying Christ, they were now self-confident. But those who think they are standing must learn to watch out that they do not fall (1Co 10:12).

Verses 32–42

Here Christ was beginning to suffer, and the first form of suffering was the most severe, that in his soul. Here we have him in anguish.

1. He withdrew to pray. "*Sit ye here,*" he said to his disciples, "while I go a little farther and *pray.*" He had just prayed *with them* (Jn 17:1–26), and now he asked them to withdraw while he went to his Father on his own distinctive mission.

2. He took with him to that retreat *Peter and James and John* (v. 33), three good witnesses of this part of his

humiliation. These three had boasted the most about their ability and willingness to suffer with him; Peter here, in this chapter, and James and John earlier (10:39). Christ therefore took them with him so that they could see what a struggle he had, to convince them that they had not known what they were saying (10:38). It is right that people who are most confident should be tested first, so that they may be made aware of their foolishness and weakness.

3. There he was in tremendous anguish (v. 33): *He began to be sore amazed* (deeply distressed), a word not used in Matthew, but very significant; it speaks of something like that *horror of great darkness* that *fell upon Abraham* (Ge 15:12). Never was there sorrow like that which he suffered at this time (La 1:12). There was not the slightest disorder or irregularity in this commotion of his spirits, however, for he had no corrupt nature to mix with his feelings, as we have. If water has a sediment at the bottom, though it may be clear while it stands still, when shaken it becomes muddy; so it is with our feelings. Pure water, however, in a clean glass, even when it is stirred much, remains clear, and so it was with Christ.

4. He made a sad complaint of this anguish. He said, *My soul is exceeding sorrowful* (overwhelmed with sorrow). He was *made sin for us* (2Co 5:21), and that was why he was so sorrowful; he fully knew the evil of the sins he was to suffer for. As he had the greatest love for God, who was offended by those sins, and had the greatest love for people, who were damaged and endangered by them, it is hardly surprising that *his soul* was *exceeding sorrowful.* He was *made a curse* for us (Gal 3:13); the curses of the Law were transferred to him as our surety and representative. He now *tasted death,* as in Heb 2:9 he is said to have done: he drank up even the dregs of the cup, tasting all its bitterness. The consideration of Christ's sufferings in *his soul,* of his *sorrows* for us (Isa 53:3, 10–11), should be useful to us:

4.1. To make our sins bitter to us. Can we ever entertain a favorable — or even a slight — thought of sin when we see what effect sin had on the Lord Jesus Christ? Shall what sat so heavily on him sit light on our souls? If Christ was in such anguish for our sins, shall we never be in anguish for them? If Christ suffered for sin in this way, let us strengthen *ourselves with the same mind* (1Pe 4:1).

4.2. To make our sorrows sweet to us. If our souls are *exceeding sorrowful* at any time, let us remember that our Master was so before us, and the *disciple is not greater than his Lord* (Mt 10:24). Why should we seek to drive away sorrow, since Christ for our sakes submitted to it, not only taking its sting out of it but putting goodness and power into it and making it profitable — in fact, even putting sweetness into it and making it acceptable. The apostle Paul was *sorrowful,* yet *always rejoicing* (2Co 6:10).

5. He ordered his disciples to stay with him. He said to them, *Tarry ye here and watch.* He had said to the other disciples nothing but, "Sit here" (v. 32), but he asked these three to stay there *and watch,* as if expecting more from them than from the rest.

6. He turned to God in prayer: *he fell on the ground, and prayed* (v. 35). It was only a little before this that he had in prayer *lifted up his eyes* (Jn 17:1), but here, being in anguish, he *fell upon his face.* As Man, he prayed that he could be saved from his sufferings, that *if it were possible, the hour might pass from him* (v. 35). We have his very words (v. 36), *Abba, Father.* The Aramaic word that Christ used, which means "Father," is kept here to show what emphasis our Lord Jesus, in his sorrows, placed on it, and wants us too to place on it as well. Father, *all things*

are possible to thee. Even what we cannot expect to be done for us, we should still believe that God is able to do, and when we submit to his will, it must be with a faithful acknowledgment of his power, that *all things are possible to him.* As Mediator, Christ accepted the will of God concerning his sufferings: *Nevertheless, not what I will, but what thou wilt.*

7. He woke up his disciples, who had fallen asleep while he was praying (vv. 37–38). He came to look after them, since they did not look after him, but he *found them asleep.* Their neglect was a sign of their further offense in deserting him. He had just commended them for continuing with him in his temptations, even though they had not been without faults; and they had just promised they would not fall away because of him. Could they indeed have so little concern for him? He particularly rebuked Peter for his drowsiness; *Simon, sleepest thou? Couldest thou not watch one hour?* Christ did not require him to watch all night with him, only for one hour. He does not overtax us or weary us. Just as Christ *rebukes* those who *loves* when they do wrong (Rev 2:19), so he also counsels and comforts those whom he rebukes. It was a very wise and faithful word of advice that Christ here gave to his disciples: *Watch and pray, lest ye enter into temptation* (v. 38). It was bad to sleep when Christ was in his anguish, but if they did not stir themselves and draw resources of grace and strength from God through prayer, they would do worse, and so they did, when they all forsook him and fled. It was a very kind and sensitive excuse that Christ made for them: *"The spirit truly is willing*; you would willingly keep awake, but you cannot." This may be taken as a reason for the exhortation, *Watch and pray*: "Watch and pray, for although *the spirit is willing*, if you do not use the means of perseverance, you may be overcome nevertheless." The consideration of the weakness of our flesh should stir and engage us to prayer and watchfulness.

8. He repeated his prayer to his Father: *He went again, and prayed*, saying "the same word" (v. 39); he spoke to the same effect. And again *the third time.* This teaches us that *men ought always to pray, and not to faint* (Lk 18:1). Although answers to our prayers may not come quickly, we must still keep making our requests. When Paul was *buffeted by a messenger of Satan*, he *besought the Lord thrice*, as Christ did here, before he obtained a favorable answer (2Co 12:7–8). Christ here had to come before the Father a second and a third time, for the visits of God's grace in answer to prayer come either sooner or later, according to the pleasure of his will.

9. He repeated his visits to his disciples. Here he showed how he continues to care for his church on earth even when it is half asleep. He came the *second time* to his disciples, and he *found them asleep again* (v. 40). Notice how the weaknesses of Christ's disciples return to them despite their resolutions and overpower them despite their resistance. See what hindrances these bodies of ours are to our souls. Christ spoke to them this second time as before, but *they wist not* (did not know) *what to answer him.* Perhaps, like those who are between sleeping and waking, they did not know where they were or what they were saying. The third time, however, they were told to sleep if they wanted to: "*Sleep on now, and take your rest* (v. 41)." *It is enough*; we did not have that word in Matthew. "You had enough warning to keep awake, and you would not accept it. Now *the hour is come* in which I knew you would all forsake me." The Son of Man was now *betrayed into the hands of sinners.* "Come, *rise up. Let us go*, for *lo, he that betrayeth me is at hand.*"

Verses 43–52

Here we have the capture and arrest of our Lord Jesus Christ by the officers of the chief priests. He began first to suffer in his soul (Isa 53:10–11), but later he suffered in his body.

1. Here is a band of coarse wretches employed to take our Lord Jesus, *a great multitude with swords and staves* (clubs). At the head of this rabble was Judas, *one of the twelve.* It is nothing new for a very good and plausible profession to end in a shameful and fatal apostasy.

2. People of no less significance than the *chief priests and the scribes* and *the elders* sent them and set them to work. These leaders claimed to expect the Messiah and to be ready to welcome him, but when he came, they set themselves against him and resolved to seize him.

3. Judas betrayed him *with a kiss.* He called him *Master, Master, and kissed him.* Judas's using the title in this way is enough to take away any appeal there might be in being called *Rabbi, Rabbi* (Mt 23:7).

4. They arrested him and took him prisoner: *They laid their hands on him*, coarse and violent hands, and *took him* into custody (v. 46).

5. Peter set about defending his Master and wounded one of the assailants. Peter here is called *one of them that stood by*, one of those who were with him. He *drew a sword* and aimed, probably, to cut off the head of a servant of the high priest, but missed and only *cut off his ear* (v. 47). It is easier to fight for Christ than to die for him, but Christ's good soldiers overcome not by taking away other people's lives but by laying down their own (Rev 12:11).

6. Christ showed those who arrested him the absurdity of their actions against him.

6.1. They came out *against him as* if he were *a thief*, whereas he was innocent of any crime; he *taught daily in the temple*, and if he had been developing any evil plot, it would at some time or other have been discovered there. By his fruits he was known to be a good tree (Mt 7:16); why then did they come out against him as a thief?

6.2. They came to seize him privately, whereas he was neither ashamed nor afraid to appear publicly in the temple. He was not one of those evildoers who *hate the light*, who do not come *to the light* (Jn 3:20). To come to him in this way at midnight, in a place of retreat, was base and cowardly. But this was not all.

6.3. They came *with swords and staves* (clubs), as if he had wielded arms against the government. There was no need for those weapons, but they went to this bother:

6.3.1. To protect themselves from the rage of some; they came armed because they were afraid of the people.

6.3.2. To expose him to the rage of others. By coming *with swords and staves to take him*, they represented him to the people as dangerous and violent.

7. He reconciled himself to all this injurious, ignominious treatment by referring to the Old Testament predictions of the Messiah. "I am cruelly abused, but I submit, because *the scriptures must be fulfilled*" (v. 49). Notice what a high regard Christ had for the Scriptures; he would bear anything rather than let the least *jot or tittle* of the word of God fall empty to the ground (Mt 5:18; 1Sa 3:19; Isa 55:11). Notice what use we are to make of the Old Testament; we must seek Christ, the true *treasure hid in that field* (Mt 13:44).

8. All Christ's disciples then deserted him: *They all forsook him, and fled* (v. 50). They were very confident that they would be faithful to him, but even good people do not know what they would do until they are tested. If their *continuing with him* up to that time in his lesser

trials (Lk 22:28) was such a comfort to him as he had just intimated, we may well imagine how sorrowful it was for him now that they deserted him in his greatest trial. Let those who suffer for Christ not think it strange if they are deserted in this way, if the whole herd shuns the wounded deer. When the apostle Paul was in danger, no one *stood by him; all men forsook him* (2Ti 4:16).

9. The noise disturbed the neighborhood (vv. 51–52). We do not have this part of the account in any other Gospel. Here is an account of a *certain young man* who, it seems, was not a disciple of Christ; he probably lived near the garden. Notice about him:

9.1. How he was frightened out of his bed to view Christ's sufferings. Such a crowd, so armed, must have made a great noise. This alarmed the young man. He was curious to go and see what the matter was, and he was in such a haste to find out that he did not even wait to get dressed, but threw a sheet around himself. When all Christ's disciples had deserted him, this young man continued to follow him, to hear what he would say and see what he would do.

9.2. How he was frightened back into bed when he was in danger of having to share in Christ's sufferings. Christ's own disciples had run away from him, but this young man thought he could safely be with him, especially because he was so far from being armed that he was not even clothed, but the Roman soldiers who were called to help *laid hold of the young man*. Finding himself in danger, he *left the linen cloth* by which they had *caught hold of him*, and he *fled away naked*. This passage is recorded to show how narrowly the disciples escaped the hands of the gang that seized Christ; nothing could have kept them safe but their Master's care of them: *If ye seek me, let these go their way* (Jn 18:8). The passage also suggests there is no holding those who are led to follow Christ only by curiosity, and not by faith and conscience.

Verses 53–65

We have here Christ's indictment, trial, conviction, and condemnation before the great Sanhedrin, of which the high priest was president, the same Caiaphas who had just judged it better that Christ be put to death, guilty or not guilty (Jn 11:50), and who therefore could justly be objected to as biased.

1. Christ was hurried away to Caiaphas's *house*. There, though it was the dead of night, *all the chief priests and elders and scribes* who had met in private were *assembled*, ready to receive their victim; they were so sure of it.

2. *Peter followed* at a distance (v. 54). When he came to the high priest's courtyard, he *sat with the servants*. The high priest's fireside was not a proper place for Peter, nor were the high priest's servants proper company for him; rather, it was his entrance into temptation.

3. The Council worked hard to obtain, for love or money, false witnesses against Christ. They had seized him as an evildoer, and now that they had him, they had no indictment to raise against him, but they *sought for witnesses against him*, offering bribes if they *would accuse him* (vv. 55–56). The chief priests and elders were entrusted with the prosecuting and punishing of false witnesses according to the law (Dt 19:16–17). It is time to cry out, *Help, Lord* (Ps 12:1), when the leaders of a land are those who trouble it, when those who should keep the peace and equity corrupt both.

4. He was finally charged with words that, as represented by the witnesses, seemed to threaten the temple (vv. 57–58), but the witnesses did not agree (v. 59). "Their testimony was not sufficient," not equal to the charge of a

capital crime (Dr. Hammond); they did not accuse him of anything on which a sentence of death could be based.

5. He was urged to be his own accuser: *the high priest stood up* and said, *Answerest thou nothing?* (v. 60). He said this under pretense of justice and fair dealing, but his real intention was to trap Christ in order to *accuse him* (Lk 11:53–54; 20:20). We may well imagine with what arrogance and disdain this proud high priest brought our Lord Jesus to this question. He was pleased to think that the one who had so often silenced those who had picked quarrels with him seemed silent. Still Christ *answered nothing*, to set us an example:

- Of patience when we are slandered or falsely accused.
- Of the prudence that is needed when a person will be made an *offender* because of *a word* (Isa 29:21), when our defense is made our offense.

6. When he was asked *whether he was the Christ*, he confessed, and did not deny, that *he was* (vv. 61–62). Caiaphas asked, *Art thou the Son of the Blessed?*—that is, the Son of God? To prove that he was the Son of God, he referred them to his second coming: "*Ye shall see the Son of man sitting on the right hand of power*; that Son of Man who now appears so lowly—you will soon see and *tremble before* him." Now, one would have thought that such a word would have startled the court and that, at least in the opinion of some of them, it would have amounted to a reason for stopping the legal action. When Paul reasoned in court about the *judgment to come*, the judge *trembled* and adjourned the trial (Ac 24:25).

7. The high priest, on this confession of Christ, convicted him as *a blasphemer* (v. 63); he *rent* (tore) *his clothes*. If Saul's tearing Samuel's robe stood for the tearing of the kingdom away from him (1Sa 15:27–28), then much more did Caiaphas's tearing his own clothes mean the tearing of the priesthood from him, as the tearing of the curtain at Christ's death meant the throwing open of everything.

8. They agreed that he was a blasphemer and that as such he was guilty of a capital offense (v. 64). So they *all condemned him* to be *guilty of death*; whatever friends he had in the great Sanhedrin did not appear: they had probably not been told about it.

9. They set themselves to mistreat him and make fun of him (v. 65). It seems that some of the priests themselves forgot the dignity of their position, as well as their duty and the seriousness that befitted them, to such an extent that they helped their servants play the fool with a condemned prisoner. They amused themselves with this while they waited for the morning. If they did not think it beneath them to mistreat Christ, shall we think it beneath us to do anything by which we may honor him?

Verses 66–72

We have the account of Peter's denying Christ here.

1. It began in keeping a distance from Christ. Peter had followed *afar off* (v. 54). Those who are shy of Christ are likely to deny him.

2. It was brought about by his associating with the high priest's servants. Those who think it dangerous to be in the company of Christ's disciples because they think they may be drawn to suffer for him will find it much more dangerous to be in the company of his enemies, because there they may be drawn to sin against him.

3. The temptation was his being charged with being a disciple of Christ: *Thou also wert with Jesus of Nazareth* (v. 67). *This is one of them* (v. 69), *for thou art a*

Galilean; "one can tell from your thick accent" (v. 70). It does not appear that he was really being accused with this remark, only that he was mocked for it and in danger of being ridiculed as a fool. Sometimes the cause of Christ seems to fall so much on the losing side that everyone has a stone to throw at it. Yet, all things considered, the temptation could not be called very great; it was only a servant girl who casually looked at him and said, *Thou art one of them*, to which he need not have replied.

4. The sin was very great; he *denied Christ before men* (Mt 10:33), at a time when he should have confessed and acknowledged him. Christ had often told his disciples about his own sufferings, but when they came, they were as great a surprise and terror to Peter as if he had never heard of them before. When Christ was admired and flocked after, Peter would readily acknowledge him, but now that Christ had been deserted, despised, and seized, Peter was ashamed of him and would acknowledge no relationship with him.

5. His repentance was very prompt. He repeated his denial three times, and the third was the worst of all, because then he *cursed* and *swore* to confirm his denial. Then the *cock crew* the second time, which reminded him of his Master's words, the warning he had given him, with that particular detail of the cock crowing twice; and when he thought about that, he wept. Some notice that this Evangelist, who wrote, as some have thought, at the apostle Peter's direction, speaks as fully about Peter's sin as any of them, but more briefly of his sorrow, which Peter, in modesty, did not want to have magnified, because he thought he could never grieve enough for such a great sin. Or, as we understand it, "Fixing his mind upon it, *he wept*." A brief thought about what is humbling is not enough; we must dwell on it.

CHAPTER 15

Here we have Christ: 1. Prosecuted and accused before Pilate, the Roman governor (vv. 1–5). 2. Shouted at by the common people (vv. 6–14). 3. Condemned to be crucified immediately (v. 15). 4. Mocked and abused by the Roman soldiers (vv. 16–19). 5. Led out to the place of execution (vv. 20–24). 6. Nailed to the cross between two thieves (vv. 25–28). 7. Reviled and abused by all who passed by (vv. 29–32). 8. Forsaken for a time by his Father (vv. 33–36). 9. Dying, and tearing the curtain (vv. 37–38). 10. Affirmed and witnessed to by the centurion and others (vv. 39–41). 11. Buried in the sepulcher of Joseph of Arimathea (vv. 42–47).

Verses 1–14

Here we have:

1. A discussion held by the great Sanhedrin as to how they could successfully prosecute our Lord Jesus. They met *early in the morning* on this matter; they lost no time, but followed up their first blow with a second. The tireless diligence of evildoers in doing evil should shame us for our backwardness and reluctance in doing good.

2. The handing over of him as a prisoner to Pilate: they *bound him*. Christ was bound to make our bonds easy for us, and to enable us, like Paul and Silas, to sing even when we are in chains. It is good for us to *remember* often the *bonds* (Col 4:18) of the Lord Jesus, to remember that we are bound with the One who was bound for us. They led him through the streets of Jerusalem, to expose him to contempt, and we may well imagine how wretched he looked after such a night's cruelty as he had suffered.

They voluntarily betrayed the One who was Israel's crown to those who were Israel's yoke.

3. Pilate's interrogation of him: "*Art thou the king of the Jews?* (v. 2)." "Yes," Christ said, "it is as *thou sayest*; I am that Messiah."

4. The charges against him stated, and his silence in response. The chief priests turned informers, personally *accusing Christ of many things* (v. 3) and witnessing against him (v. 4). Evil priests are generally the worst people. The better anything is, the worse it is when it is corrupted. These priests were very eager and noisy in their accusations, but Christ *answered nothing* (v. 3). When Pilate urged him to clear himself, and wanted him to (v. 4), he remained silent (v. 5); he *answered nothing*, which Pilate thought very strange. He gave Pilate a direct answer (v. 2), but would not answer the prosecutors and witnesses, because their allegations were notoriously false, and he knew Pilate himself was convinced they were so. Christ provoked amazement both when he spoke and when he remained silent.

5. The suggestion Pilate made to the people that Jesus be released to them, since it was the custom at the feast to honor the ceremony with the release of one prisoner. The people, indeed, expected and demanded that he do *as he had ever done to them* (v. 8). Now Pilate realized that the chief priests had handed Jesus over out of envy (v. 10). It was easy to see that it was not his guilt but his goodness that they were offended by. Pilate thought that he could safely appeal to the people. If they would demand that Christ be released, Pilate would be ready to do it. There was indeed another prisoner, *one Barabbas*, who had influence and would get some votes, but Pilate had no doubt that Jesus would get more.

6. The unanimous, outraged clamors of the people to have *Christ put to death*—specifically, to have him crucified. It came as a great surprise to Pilate to find that they all agreed to ask that Barabbas be released (v. 11). Pilate opposed it as much as he could: "*What will ye that I shall do to him whom ye call the King of the Jews?*" (v. 12). They said, *Crucify him*. When Pilate objected, *Why, what evil has he done?* they did not pretend to answer it, but *cried out more exceedingly, Crucify him, crucify him*. The priests promised themselves that the clamor would influence Pilate in two ways to condemn him.

6.1. He might be inclined to believe Christ guilty because the outcry against him seemed so emphatically unanimous. "Surely," Pilate might think, "he must be a bad man, since the whole world is weary of him." It has been a common trick of Satan to cause people to speak ill of Christ and his religion and thereby give them a bad reputation. Let us judge people and things by their merits, and not prejudge them by what we commonly hear about them and by the cries of the people.

6.2. The clamor might induce him to condemn Christ to please the people, and indeed for fear of displeasing them. Although Pilate was not so weak as to be coerced by their opinion into believing him guilty, he was so evil as to be swayed by their outrage to condemn him, even though he believed him innocent. Because our Lord Jesus died as a sacrifice for the sins of many, he fell as a sacrifice to the rage of many.

Verses 15–21

Here:

1. To satisfy the Jews' hatred, Pilate handed Christ over to be *crucified* (v. 15). Wanting to satisfy the people, he *released Barabbas unto them* and *delivered Jesus* to be *crucified*. Although he had scourged Jesus before, hoping

that would satisfy them, and then not intending to crucify him, he scourged him again; the One who could persuade himself to punish one who was innocent (Lk 23:16) could gradually persuade himself to crucify him. Christ was crucified because that was:

1.1. A bloody death, and *without the shedding blood* there is *no remission* of sins (Heb 9:22). Christ was to lay down *his life for us* (1Jn 3:16), and so he shed his blood (Ge 9:4; Lev 17:11–14).

1.2. A painful death. Christ died in such a way that he would feel himself die. Christ would meet death in its greatest terror and so conquer it.

1.3. A shameful death, the death of slaves and the worst evildoers. The cross and the shame go together. Christ makes atonement by submitting to the greatest reproach and ignominy. But even this was not the worst of it.

1.4. A cursed death. This was how it was considered under the Jewish law (Dt 21:23). Now that Christ has submitted to being *hanged upon a tree* (Dt 21:23; Gal 3:13), the reproach and curse of that kind of death are completely rolled away (Jos 5:9).

2. To satisfy the mocking humor of the Roman soldiers, Pilate handed him over to them to be abused and treated spitefully. They called together *the whole regiment* who were then waiting, and they went into an inner hall, where they ignominiously abused our Lord Jesus as a king.

2.1. Do kings wear robes of purple or scarlet? They *clothed him with purple.*

2.2. Do kings wear crowns? They *platted* (twisted) *a crown of thorns* and *put it on his head.* A crown of straw or rushes would have been mocking enough, but this was also painful. He wore the crown of thorns that we had deserved, so that we could wear the crown of glory that he merited.

2.3. Are kings attended with the praise of their subjects—*O king, live for ever* (Da 3:9)? That also was mimicked; they greeted him with, "*Hail, King of the Jews.*"

2.4. Kings have scepters put into their hands, signs of power. To imitate this, they put *a reed in his right hand.* Those who despise the authority of the Lord Jesus in effect *put a reed in his hand;* indeed, like these here, they *smite him on the head* with it.

2.5. When subjects swore allegiance, they used to kiss their sovereign (Ps 2:12), but instead of a kiss, these soldiers *spit upon him.*

2.6. Kings used to have subjects address them by kneeling, and the soldiers also made fun of this, *bowing the knee, and worshiping him.* They did this in scorn, to make themselves and one another laugh. He was mocked not in his own clothes but in another's, to show that he did not suffer for his own sin; the crime was ours, but the shame was his. Those who bow the knee to Christ but do not bow the soul are throwing at him the same insult that these did here.

3. At the appointed hour, the soldiers led him away from Pilate's judgment hall to the place of execution (v. 20). They compelled a man named Simon of Cyrene to carry his cross for him. He *passed by, coming out of the country,* not thinking about any such matter. We must not think it strange if crosses come on us suddenly and we are surprised by them. The cross was a very difficult, unwieldy load, but the one who carried it for only a few minutes had the honor of having his name on record in the book of God. The result is that wherever this Gospel is preached, this will be told to remember him (14:9).

Verses 22–32

We have the crucifixion of our Lord Jesus here. Notice:

1. The place where he was crucified; it was called *Golgotha,* "the place of a skull." It was the common place of execution, because he was in all respects numbered with the transgressors (Isa 53:12).

2. The time when he was crucified. At the *third hour* (v. 25), according to the Jews' reckoning, that is, at about nine o'clock in the morning, or soon after, they nailed him to the cross.

3. The indignities to which he was subjected when he was nailed to the cross.

3.1. Because it was the custom to give wine to people who were to be put to death, they *mingled his with myrrh* (v. 23), which was bitter; he tasted it but would not drink it; he was willing to admit its bitterness but not its benefit.

3.2. Because the clothes of those who were crucified were, as they are with us, the executioners' fee, the soldiers *cast lots* for his garments (v. 24), so amusing themselves at his misery.

3.3. They set a notice above his head: *the king of the Jews* (v. 26). No crime was alleged here; rather, his sovereignty was acknowledged. Perhaps Pilate meant to mock Christ as a disgraced king, or to mock the Jews, as a people who deserved no better king. However, God intended by it to proclaim Christ the *king of Israel* even on the cross, though Pilate did not know what he was writing any more than Caiaphas knew what he was speaking (Jn 11:51). Whenever we look to Christ crucified, we must remember the title over his head, that he is a king.

3.4. They crucified *two thieves* with him, *one on his right hand, the other on his left,* and him between them as the worst of the three (v. 27). While he lived, he had associated with sinners to do them good. When he died, he was joined with them for the same purpose, for he both *came into the world* and went out of it to *save sinners* (1Ti 1:15). However, this Evangelist takes particular notice of the fulfillment of the Scriptures in it (v. 28). In that famous prediction of Christ's sufferings in Isaiah, it was foretold that he would be *numbered with the transgressors* (Isa 53:12).

3.5. The spectators, instead of sympathizing with him in his misery, added to it by gloating over him.

3.5.1. Even those who *passed by railed on* (hurled insults at) *him* (v. 29). They taunted him and expressed the most intense detestation of him and indignation at him. The chief priests no doubt put this sarcasm into their mouths: "*Thou that destroyest the temple, and buildest it in three days, now,* if you can, *save thyself* and *come down from the cross.*"

3.5.2. Even the chief priests, who, being *taken from among men and ordained,* should have been compassionate toward those who were suffering and dying (Heb 5:1–2), *mocked him, saying, He saved others; himself he cannot save.* They challenged him to *come down from the cross,* if he could (v. 32). Let them only see that, and they would believe.

3.5.3. Even those who were crucified with him hurled insults at him (v. 32).

Verses 33–41

Here is an account of Christ's dying.

1. There was a thick *darkness* over *the whole land* for three hours. The Jews had often demanded from Christ *a sign from heaven* (Mt 16:1), and now they had one, but one that represented the blinding of their eyes. It was a sign of the darkness that had come, and was coming, on the nation. This showed them that *the things that belonged to their peace* were now *hid from their eyes* (Lk 19:42). It

was the power of darkness that they were now under, and it was the works of darkness that they were now doing.

2. Toward the close of this darkness, our Lord Jesus, in anguish of his soul, cried out, *My God, my God, why hast thou forsaken me?* (v. 34). The darkness represented the present cloud that Christ's human soul was under when he was making it an *offering for sin* (Isa 53:10). Our Lord Jesus was denied the light of the sun when he was suffering, and this represented the withdrawal of the light of God's face. He complained about this more than anything; he did not complain about his disciples' forsaking him, but about his Father's:

2.1. Because this *wounded his spirit*, and that is something *hard to bear* (Pr 18:14).

2.2. Because in this especially he was *made sin for us* (2Co 5:21). These symptoms of divine wrath were like that fire from heaven that had sometimes been sent to consume the sacrifices and was always a sign of God's acceptance. The fire that would have fallen on the sinner if God had not been pacified fell on the sacrifice as a sign that he was so; therefore, it now fell on Christ. When Paul was to be *offered as a sacrifice for the service of saints*, he could *rejoice* (Php 2:17), but it is another thing to be offered as a sacrifice for the sin of sinners.

3. Christ's prayer was mocked by those who stood by (vv. 35–36); because he cried out, *Eli, Eli*, or (as Mark has it, according to a dialect of Aramaic) *Eloi, Eloi*, they said, *He calls for Elias* (Elijah), though they knew very well what he said and that it meant *My God, My God*. One of them *filled a sponge with vinegar* and extended it to him on a stick (v. 36). This was intended as a further insult and abuse to him, and whoever restrained the one who did it only added to the scorn: "*Let him alone; let us see whether Elias will come to take him down*, and if not, we may conclude that he also has abandoned him."

4. Christ again *cried with a loud voice*, and so *gave up the ghost* (v. 37). He was now commending his soul into his Father's hand (Lk 23:46; Ps 31:5). Even if speech fails us, so that we cannot cry out with a loud voice, as Christ did, nevertheless, if *God is the strength of the heart* (Ps 73:26), that strength will not fail. Christ was really and truly dead, for *he gave up the ghost*; his human soul departed to the world of spirits and left his body a breathless lump of clay.

5. Just at the moment that Christ died upon Mount Calvary, the curtain of the *temple* was *rent in twain* (torn in two) *from the top to the bottom* (v. 38). This was cause for a great deal:

5.1. Of terror to the unbelieving Jews, for it was a sign of the complete destruction of their church and nation, which followed not long afterward.

5.2. Of encouragement to all believing Christians, for it signifies the consecrating and laying open to us of a *new and living way into the holiest* by the *blood of Jesus* (Heb 10:19–20).

6. The centurion who commanded the unit that had oversight of the execution was convinced and confessed that this Jesus was the *Son of God* (v. 39). One thing that satisfied him was that Jesus *so cried out, and gave up the ghost*. He said, to the honor of Christ and the shame of those who abused him, *Truly this man was the Son of God.* But what reason did he have to say this?

6.1. He had reason to say that Christ suffered unjustly; this was clear from all the circumstances of his suffering. Since he suffered unjustly, and what he suffered for was his saying that he was *the Son of God*, what he said was true and he was really the *Son of God*.

6.2. He had reason to say that Christ was a favorite of heaven, since at his death Heaven did him the honor

of frowning on his persecutors. "Surely," this soldier thought, "this must be some divine person, greatly loved by God." Our Lord Jesus, even in the depth of his sufferings and humiliation, was the Son of God, and he was declared to be so *with power* (Ro 1:4).

7. Some of his friends, especially the good women, were with him (vv. 40–41): *There were women looking on afar off.* The men dared not show themselves at all. The women dared not come near, but stood far away, overwhelmed by grief. Some of these women are named here. *Mary Magdalene* was one; she owed all her strength and comfort to his power and goodness, which rescued her from the possession of seven demons (16:9), in gratitude for which she thought she could never do enough for him. *Mary the mother of James the little* (the younger) also was there. This Mary was the wife of Clopas or Alphaeus and sister of the Virgin Mary. These women had followed Christ from Galilee, though they were not required to attend the feast as the men were. Now to see him on a cross, the One whom they had wanted to see on a throne, must have been a great disappointment to them. Those who follow Christ in expectation of receiving great things in this world through him will probably live to see themselves sadly disappointed.

Verses 42–47

We are present at the funeral of our Lord Jesus here. Notice:

1. How the body of Christ was asked for. It was at the disposal of the government. We are told here:

1.1. When the body of Christ was asked for, and why such haste was made with the funeral: *The even* (evening) *was come*, and it was *the preparation* (the Preparation Day), that is, *the day before the Sabbath* (v. 42). The Jews were stricter in observing the Sabbath than in observing any other feast, and so although this day was itself a feast day, they still observed it more religiously as the evening of the Sabbath. The day before the Sabbath should be a day of preparation for the Sabbath. In fact, the whole week should be divided between making the most of the previous Sabbath and preparing for the following Sabbath.

1.2. Who asked for the body; it was *Joseph of Arimathea*, who is called here an *honourable counsellor* (a prominent member of the Council) (v. 43), a person of character and distinction; he was one of the great Sanhedrin. However, a more excellent prominence is given him here: he was one who *waited for the kingdom of God*. Those who *wait for the kingdom of God* and hope to enjoy its privileges must show it by their eagerness to acknowledge Christ's cause. God raised up this man for this necessary service when none of Christ's disciples could, or dared, undertake it. *Joseph went in boldly to Pilate*; though he knew how much it would disturb the chief priests, he put on courage; perhaps at first he was a little afraid.

1.3. What a surprise it was to Pilate to hear that Christ was dead, especially that he was *already dead*. Pilate doubted—as some understand it—whether Christ was then dead or not, fearing that he might be deceived, that the body might have been taken down alive. He called the centurion, his own officer, therefore, and asked him *whether he had been any while dead* (v. 44). The centurion could assure him of this, because he had observed in detail how Jesus *gave up the ghost* (v. 39). There was a special providence in the strictness of Pilate's examination, so that no one could claim that Christ was buried alive and thereby cast doubt on the truth of his resurrection. This is how the truth of Christ sometimes gains confirmation even from its enemies.

2. How the body of Christ was buried. Pilate gave Joseph permission to take the body and do what he pleased with it.

2.1. Joseph *bought fine linen* to wrap the body in, though in such a case old linen might have been thought sufficient.

2.2. He *took down* the body, mangled and emaciated as it was, and *wrapt it in the linen* as a very valuable treasure.

2.3. He *laid it in a sepulchre* of his own, in a private place. This sepulcher belonged to Joseph. When Abraham had no other possession in the land of Canaan, he still had a burial place (Ge 23), but Christ did not even have that. This sepulcher was *hewn out of a rock*, because Christ died to make the grave a refuge and shelter to the saints.

2.4. He *rolled a stone to the door of the sepulchre*, as this was the custom of burying with the Jews.

2.5. Some of the good women were present at the funeral and *beheld where he was laid*, so that they could come after the Sabbath to anoint the dead body, because they did not have enough time to do it when he was buried. When our great Mediator and Lawgiver was buried, special notice was taken of his sepulcher, because he was to rise again. The care taken of his body shows the care that he himself will take for his body, the church. Our meditations on Christ's burial should lead us to think about our own, so that the grave becomes familiar to us and we become at ease with the bed that we must soon make in the darkness.

CHAPTER 16

We have here a short account of the resurrection and ascension of the Lord Jesus: 1. Christ's resurrection told by an angel to the women who came to the grave to anoint him (vv. 1–8). 2. His appearance to Mary Magdalene (vv. 9–11). 3. His appearance to the two disciples going to Emmaus (vv. 12–13). 4. His appearance to the Eleven (vv. 14–18). 5. His ascension to heaven (vv. 19–20).

Verses 1–8

Since the Sabbath was first instituted, there was never such a Sabbath as this; during all of this Sabbath our Lord Jesus lay in the grave. It was to him a Sabbath of rest, but a silent Sabbath; to his disciples it was a sad Sabbath, spent in tears and fears. This Sabbath was now over, and the first day of the week was the first day of a new world. We have here:

1. The loving visit that the good women who had cared for Christ now made to his sepulcher. They set out from their lodgings *very early in the morning*, so that it was sunrise by the time they reached the grave. They had *bought sweet spices*, too, and came not only to moisten the dead body with their tears but also to perfume it with their *spices* (v. 1). Nicodemus had bought a very large quantity of *dry spices, myrrh* and *aloes* (Jn 19:39), but these admirable women did not think that enough; they too bought spices—perhaps some perfumed oils—to *anoint him*. The respect that others have shown to Christ's name should not stop us from showing our respect to it too.

2. Their concern about rolling away the stone, and the overcoming of that concern (vv. 3–4): *They said among themselves*, as they were coming along and now drew near the sepulcher, *Who shall roll us away the stone from the door of the sepulcher? For it was very great*, more than they could move together. There was a further difficulty

greater than this to be overcome, which they knew nothing about, namely, a guard of soldiers set to watch over the sepulcher, who, if the women had come before the soldiers themselves had been frightened away, would have frightened them away themselves. But their gracious love for Christ took them to the sepulcher, and notice how by the time they came there, both of these difficulties were removed, both the stone, which they knew about, and the guard, which they did not know about. They saw *that the stone was rolled away*. Those who diligently seek Christ will find that the difficulties that lie in their path strangely vanish and that they themselves are helped through their difficulties beyond their expectations.

3. The assurance an angel gave them that the Lord Jesus had risen from the dead and left him there to tell those who came there to seek him.

3.1. They *entered into the sepulchre* and saw that the body of Jesus was not there. He who by his death undertook to pay our debt secured our release in his resurrection, for it was by his release from death's prison that the matter in dispute was undeniably settled by incontestable evidence that he was the Son of God.

3.2. They saw a *young man sitting on the right side* of the sepulcher. The angel appeared in the likeness of a young man, because angels do not grow old. This angel was *sitting on the right hand* as they went into the sepulcher, *clothed with a long white garment*, a robe down to the feet. The sight of him might justly have encouraged them, but they were *affrighted* (alarmed). We see here how what should encourage us often proves a terror to us through our own mistakes and misapprehensions.

3.3. He silenced their fears by assuring them that there was enough reason for triumph, and none for trembling: *He saith to them, Be not affrighted* (don't be alarmed) (v. 6). "Do not be alarmed, because:

3.3.1. "You faithfully love Jesus Christ, and so, instead of being confounded, you should be comforted. Ye seek *Jesus of Nazareth, which was crucified*." He spoke of Jesus as One who *was* crucified: "The thing is past, that scene is over, you must not dwell so much on the sad circumstances of his crucifixion that you are incapable of believing the joyful news of his resurrection." He was crucified, but he is glorified, and that glory completely wipes away all the shame of his sufferings. After his entrance to his glory, he never drew any veil over his sufferings, nor was he unwilling to have his cross spoken of.

3.3.2. "It will therefore be good news to you to hear that instead of anointing him as one who is dead, you may now rejoice in him as one who is alive. *He is risen, he is not here*, not dead, but alive again. And you may see here *the place where they laid him*. You see he has gone from here, not stolen either by his enemies or by his friends, but risen."

3.4. He instructed them to tell his disciples this soon. And so they were made the apostles to the apostles, and were thereby rewarded for the devotion they had shown him in following him to the cross, to the grave, and into the grave. The first who came were the first who served; none of the other disciples dared come near his sepulcher. No one came near him except a few women, who were unable even to *roll away the stone*.

3.4.1. They must tell the disciples that he was risen. It was a sad time for them, because their dear Master had died, and all their hopes and joys were buried in his grave, so that no spirit remained in them. They were completely at their wits' end. "Go quickly to them," said the angel. "Tell them that their Master is risen; this will keep them from sinking into despair." Christ is not ashamed to acknowledge his poor disciples; his advancement does not make him withdraw from them: he took care to have the news told them. Christ does not keep a record of the wrongs (Ps 130:3) of those whose hearts are upright with him.

3.4.2. They must be sure to tell Peter. This is particularly taken notice of by this Evangelist, who is thought to have written at Peter's direction. He is named particularly: "*Tell Peter*, because:

3.4.2.1. "It will be good news to him, more welcome to him than to any of them, since he is grieving for his sin.

3.4.2.2. "He will be afraid that the joy of this good news does not belong to him." If the angel had said only, *Go, tell his disciples*, poor Peter would have been ready to sigh and say, "But I doubt I can look on myself as one of them, because I disowned him and deserve to be disowned by him (Mt 10:33)." To avoid that, the angel said, "Go to Peter by name and tell him he will be as welcome as any of the rest to see his Master in Galilee." A sight of Christ will be very welcome to a true penitent, and a true penitent will be very welcome to a sight of Christ, for there is joy in heaven for him (Lk 15:7).

3.4.3. They must appoint them all, including Peter by name, to meet him at Galilee, as *he said unto you* (Mt 26:32). All the meetings between Christ and his disciples are appointed by him, Christ never forgets his appointment, and in all meetings between Christ and his disciples, he goes on ahead. *He goes before you.*

4. The account of this that the women brought to the disciples: *they went out quickly, and ran from the sepulchre, trembling and amazed* (v. 8). Christ had often told them that on the third day he would rise again, and if they had given proper attention to that and truly believed it, they would have come to the sepulcher, expecting to find him risen, and would have received news of it with a joyful assurance, not with great terror and amazement. They told nothing of it to anyone they *met by the way, for they were afraid*, afraid the news was too good to be true.

Verses 9–13

We have here a very short account of two of Christ's appearances.

1. He appeared to Mary Magdalene, to her first, in the garden, which we have a detailed account of in Jn 20:14. It was she *out of whom he had cast seven devils*, and she *loved much* (Lk 7:47). Christ did her the honor of making her the first who saw him after his resurrection. The closer we are to Christ, the sooner we may expect to see him, and the more we may expect to see of him.

1.1. She told the disciples what she had seen; she told not only the Eleven but also the others who had followed him; she told them *as they mourned and wept* (v. 10). Christ had told them that they would *mourn and lament* (Jn 16:20), and their doing so showed their great love for him. But when their *weeping had endured a night* or two (Ps 30:5), comfort returned, as Christ had promised them: *I will see you again, and your heart shall rejoice* (Jn 16:22). To disciples in tears there cannot be brought better news than that of Christ's resurrection.

1.2. They could not believe the report she brought them: *They heard that he was alive* and had been seen by her, but *they believed not*. They feared that she had been deceived and had seen him in her imagination. If they had believed the frequent predictions of his resurrection from his own mouth, they would not now have been so incredulous at reports of it.

2. He appeared to two of the disciples *as they went into the country* (v. 12). This no doubt refers to what took place

between Christ and the two disciples going to Emmaus, which is related more fully in Lk 24:13–35. He is said here to have appeared to them in *another form*, wearing different clothes from his usual ones.

2.1. These two witnesses gave their testimony to this proof of Christ's resurrection: *They went and told it to the residue* (rest) (v. 13). Being convinced themselves, they wanted to convince their brothers and sisters, so that they too would be comforted and encouraged.

2.2. This did not convince them: *Neither believed they them*. We can see the wisdom of providence in the gradualness with which the proofs of Christ's resurrection were given and the caution with which they were admitted. We have more reason to believe those who themselves believed slowly; if the apostles had swallowed the testimony immediately, they might have been thought gullible, and their testimony less reliable, but their disbelieving at first showed that they later believed it with full conviction.

Verses 14–18

Here is:

1. The conviction Christ gave his apostles of the truth of his resurrection (v. 14): he *appeared to them* himself when they were all together, *as they sat at meat* (eating), which gave him the opportunity to *eat and drink with them*, to convince them completely; see Ac 10:41. Nevertheless, when he appeared to them, he *upbraided them with their unbelief and hardness of heart*. The evidence of the truth of the Gospel is so full that those who do not receive it may justly be rebuked for their unbelief, since it is due to the *hardness of their heart*, its foolishness and stubbornness. Although they had not until now seen him themselves, they were justly blamed *because they believed not them who had seen him after he was risen*. It will not be allowed as an excuse of our unfaithfulness on the great day to say, "We did not see him after he was risen," for we should have believed the testimony of those who did see him.

2. The commission he gave them to set up his kingdom on earth by the preaching of his *gospel*. Notice:

2.1. To whom they were to preach *the gospel*. Up to that time they had been sent only to *the lost sheep of the house of* Israel; they had been forbidden to go into the *way of the Gentiles* (Mt 10:5–6) or into any town of the Samaritans. But now they were authorized to *go into all the world* and to *preach the Gospel* of Christ to *every creature*, to the Gentiles as well as to the Jews, to every human creature who was capable of receiving it. These Eleven could not themselves preach it to all the world, much less to every creature in it, but they and the other disciples, together with those who would later be added to them, must disperse themselves in different directions and take the Gospel along with them wherever they went. They must make it the business of their lives to send that good news throughout the world with all possible faithfulness and care, not as an amusement or entertainment, but as a serious message from God to human beings and as an appointed means of making them joyful.

2.2. What was the summary of the Gospel that they were to preach (v. 16): "Set before the world life and death, good and evil (Dt 30:15, 19). Go and tell them:

2.2.1. "That if they believe the Gospel and give themselves to be Christ's disciples, if they renounce the Devil, the world, and the flesh and are devoted to Christ, they will be saved from the guilt and power of sin; it will not rule them; it will not ruin them. Those who are true Christians will be saved through Christ." Baptism was appointed as the inaugurating ceremony, by which those who embraced Christ acknowledged him.

2.2.2. *"If they believe not, they shall be damned*, by the sentence of a Gospel they have despised as well as of the law they have broken." Even this is *gospel*; it is good news that nothing but unbelief will condemn people; they will be condemned only if they sin against the way out that God has provided.

2.3. What power they would be endowed with to confirm the doctrine they were to preach (v. 17): *These signs shall follow them that believe.* They would do wonders in Christ's name — the same name into which they were baptized — because of the power derived from him and brought in by prayer. Some particular signs are mentioned:

2.3.1. They would *cast out devils*; this power was more common among Christians than any other.

2.3.2. They would *speak with new tongues*, which they had never learned and were not familiar with, and this was both a miracle to confirm the truth of the Gospel and also a means of spreading the Gospel among those nations who had not heard it.

2.3.3. They would *take up serpents* (pick up snakes). This was fulfilled in Paul, who was not hurt by the *viper* that *fastened on his hand*, and his escaping harm in this situation was acknowledged as a great miracle by the indigenous people (Ac 28:5–6).

2.3.4. If they were compelled by their persecutors to *drink any deadly* poison, *it would not hurt them.*

2.3.5. They would not only be preserved from harm themselves but also be enabled to do good to others: *They shall lay hands on the sick*, and the sick *shall recover*. Many of the elders of the church had this power, as appears from Jas 5:14, where they are said to *anoint* the sick *with oil in the name of the Lord*. With what assurance of success they could go about executing their commission, since they had such credentials to produce!

Verses 19–20

Here is:

1. Christ welcomed into the upper world (v. 19): *After the Lord had spoken* what he had to say to his disciples, he *went up into heaven* in a cloud, which we have a particular account of in Ac 1:9. He was received, and he *sat on the right hand of God*. He was now glorified with the glory he had before the world (Jn 17:5).

2. Christ welcomed in this lower world.

2.1. We have here the apostles working diligently for him; they *went forth, and preached every where*, far and near. Although the message they preached was directly hostile to the spirit of the world, although it met with much opposition, those who preached it were neither afraid nor ashamed.

2.2. We have here God working powerfully with them to make their labors successful by *confirming the word with signs following*, partly by the miracles that were performed on the bodies of people, and partly by the influence that Christian doctrine had on the minds of people. These were properly called *signs following* (accompanying) the word — the reformation of the world, the destruction of idolatry, the conversion of sinners, and the encouragement of saints. These signs still accompany the word, and so that they may do so more and more, for the honor of Christ and the good of the human race, the Evangelist concludes by praying, thereby teaching us to pray: *Amen.* "Father in heaven, may your name be hallowed, and may your kingdom come" (Mt 6:9).

A Practical and Devotional Exposition of the Gospel of

Luke

We are now entering into the labors of another Evangelist; his name was Luke. Some think he was the only one of all the writers of Scripture who was not a descendant of Israel. He was a Jewish convert, they say, and some think he was converted to Christianity by the ministry of the apostle Paul at Antioch. And from the time Paul left for Macedonia (Ac 16:10), Luke was his constant companion. He worked as a doctor, and so Paul calls him *Luke, the beloved physician* (Col 4:14). Some of the commentators that are alleged to be ancient say that he was a painter and that he drew a picture of the Virgin Mary. He is thought to have written this Gospel under the direction of the apostle Paul while traveling with him. Some think that Luke is *the brother* whom Paul speaks of (2Co 8:18), *whose praise is in the Gospel throughout all the churches of Christ.* His way of writing is accurate and exact, and his style polite and elegant, yet also clear. He expresses himself in a purer Greek style than is found in the other writers of the holy record. He relates various things more fully than the other Evangelists, and he especially deals with those things that relate to the priestly office of Christ. It is uncertain when, even approximately, this Gospel was written. Some think it was written at Rome shortly before he wrote his record of the *Acts of the Apostles* (which is a continuation of this), when he was there with Paul while Paul was a prisoner and preaching in *his own hired house* (Ac 28:30), with which the record of Acts concludes, and at that time Paul said that *only Luke was with him* (2Ti 4:11). When Luke was in that voluntary confinement with Paul, he had time to compile these two records — and the church has been indebted to a prison for many excellent writings. Jerome says that Luke died when he was eighty-four years old and never married.

CHAPTER 1

The account that this Evangelist gives us of the life of Christ begins earlier than either Matthew or Mark. We have here: 1. Luke's introduction to his Gospel (vv. 1–4). 2. The prophecy and account of the conception of John the Baptist (vv. 5–25). 3. The annunciation to the Virgin Mary (vv. 26–38). 4. The meeting of Mary the mother of Jesus and Elizabeth the mother of John (vv. 39–56). 5. The birth and circumcision of John the Baptist (vv. 57–66). 6. Zechariah's song of praise (vv. 67–79). 7. A short account of John the Baptist's infancy (v. 80).

Verses 1–4

Complimentary introductions and dedications, the language of flattery and the food and fuel of pride, are justly condemned by the wise and good, but it does not therefore follow that texts of this sort that are useful and instructive should be condemned. This is such a useful dedication. It is not certain who Theophilus was; the name means "a friend of God." Some think that it does not refer to any particular person, but to everyone who loves God. But it should rather be understood as referring to some particular person, probably a magistrate, because Luke gives him the same title of respect here that the apostle Paul gave to Festus the governor (Ac 26:25). Religion does not destroy politeness and good manners, but teaches us to *give, according to the customs of our country, honour to them to whom honour is due* (Ro 13:7). Notice:

1. Why St. Luke wrote this Gospel. It is certain that he was moved by the Holy Spirit not only *to* write it but also *in* writing it, but in both he was moved as a rational being, not as a mere machine, and he was led to consider:

1.1. That the things he wrote about were things that were most surely believed among all Christians and were therefore things that they should be instructed in. He would not write about disputable matters, but about the things that are and should be most surely believed. Although it is not the foundation of our faith, it is a support to it that the articles of our creed are things that have long been most surely believed. The teaching of Christ is what thousands of the wisest and best people have risked their souls upon.

1.2. That it was necessary that there be a *declaration made in order* of those things, that the record of the life of Christ should be arranged in order. When things are put in order, we know better where to find them for our own use and how to keep them for the benefit of others.

1.3. That many had undertaken to publish records of the life of Christ. Others' service for Christ must not be considered as superseding ours, but rather should encourage ours.

1.4. That the truth of the things he had to write was confirmed by the concurring testimony of those who were competent and satisfactory witnesses of them. What he was now about to make known agreed with what had been communicated by word of mouth again and again by those who *from the beginning were eyewitnesses and ministers of the word* (v. 2).

1.4.1. The apostles were ministers of the word of Christ or of the teaching of Christ; having received it for themselves, they ministered it to others (1Jn 1:1). They did not receive a Gospel to make them masters, but a Gospel for them to preach as ministers, that is, servants.

1.4.2. The ministers of the word were eyewitnesses. They themselves heard the teaching of Christ and saw his miracles; they did not receive them by report, at second hand.

1.4.3. They were so from the beginning of Christ's ministry (v. 2). He had his disciples with him when he performed his first miracle (Jn 2:11). They accompanied him all the time he went in and out among them (Ac 1:21).

1.4.4. The written Gospel, which we have to this day, corresponds exactly with the Gospel that was preached in the first days of the church.

1.4.5. *From the first*, Luke himself had a perfect understanding of the things he wrote about (v. 3). He asserted his ability to undertake this work: "It seemed good to me, having reached the exact knowledge of all things." He had diligently investigated these things. He had made it his work to discover for himself the precise details. He had received his information not only by tradition but also by revelation. He wrote of things reported by tradition, but they were ratified by inspiration. He could say, therefore, that he had *perfect understanding* of these things. He knew them "accurately, exactly."

2. Why he sent it to *Theophilus*: "I am writing these things to you *in order*, so *that thou mayest know the certainty of those things wherein thou hast been instructed.*" It is implied that Theophilus had been *instructed* in these things either before his baptism or since, or both, according to the rule set forth in Mt 28:19–20. The last phrase could be translated, "about which you have been catechized"; the most knowledgeable Christians began by being catechized. It was intended that he come to *know the certainty of those things*. There is a certainty in the Gospel of Christ; it contains something that we may build on, and we who have been well instructed in the things of God should be diligent in making sure that we know the certainty of those things, that we know not only what we believe but also why we believe it, so that we may be able to give *a reason of the hope that is in us* (1Pe 3:15).

Verses 5–25

The two preceding Evangelists begin the Gospel with the baptism of John and his ministry. This Evangelist wanted to give a more detailed account of our Savior's conception and birth than had been given by the others, and he decided to give such an account of John the Baptist as well. Notice here:

1. The account given of his parents (v. 5): they lived in *the days of Herod the king*, a foreigner and a deputy for the Romans, who had just made Judea a province of the empire. This is noted to show that the scepter had completely departed from Judah (Ge 49:10). Israel is enslaved, but then the glory of Israel comes. Now the father of John the Baptist was a priest, a son of Aaron; his name was *Zacharias* (Zechariah). No families in the world were ever so honored by God as those of Aaron and David; with one was made the covenant of priesthood, and with the other that of royalty. Christ came from David's house, John the Baptist from Aaron's. This Zechariah was *of the course*

(priestly division) *of Abia* (Abijah). When in David's time the family of Aaron was multiplied, he divided them into twenty-four priestly divisions, to give greater regularity to the procedures of their office. The eighth of those was that of Abijah (1Ch 24:10), who was descended from Eleazar, Aaron's eldest son. The wife of this Zechariah was a descendant of Aaron too, and her name was Elizabeth, the same name as *Elisheba*, the wife of Aaron (Ex 6:23). The priests were very careful to marry within their own family. Notice what is mentioned about Zechariah and Elizabeth:

1.1. That they were a very religious couple (v. 6): *They were both righteous before God*. They were sincerely upright. They *approved themselves to him* (2Ti 2:15). It is good when those who are married to each other are both joined to the Lord. *They walked in all the commandments and ordinances of the Lord, blameless*. They showed it not by their talk but by their life, by the way in which they *walked* and the principles by which they were guided. They walked not only in the ordinances of the Lord, which related to divine worship, but also in the commandments of the Lord, which refer to all the aspects of a good life. Not that they never did anything that came short of their duty, but it was their constant care and aim to fulfill it. Although they were not sinless, they were blameless; nobody could accuse them of any open, scandalous sin; they lived honestly and inoffensively.

1.2. That they had long been childless (v. 7). Children are *a heritage from the Lord* (Ps 127:3). They are valuable, desirable blessings, but there are many who are righteous before God and yet are not blessed in this way. Elizabeth was *barren*, and they began to despair of ever having children, because they were both now *well stricken* (advanced) *in years*. Many eminent persons, such as Isaac, Jacob, Joseph, Samson, Samuel, and here John the Baptist, were born of women who had long been childless, so that their births would be more remarkable and the blessing of their births even more valuable to their parents.

2. The appearing of an angel to his father, Zechariah, as he was ministering in the temple (vv. 8–11). Notice:

2.1. How Zechariah was employed in the service of God (v. 8): he *executed the priest's office before God in the order of his course* (the appointed order of his division); it was his week of regular service, and he was on duty. Now Zechariah was chosen by lot to burn incense morning and evening for that week of his waiting on the Lord, just as other services fell to other priests by lot. He was burning the daily incense at the *altar of incense* (v. 11), which was *in the temple* (v. 9), not in the Most Holy Place, into which only the high priest entered. The Jews say that no priest burned incense twice in his whole life—there were so many of them—at least never more than one week. While Zechariah was burning incense in the temple, *the whole multitude of the people were praying without* (outside) (v. 10). These were all attending to their devotions—in silent prayer, for their voices were not heard—when by the tinkling of a bell they were informed that the priest had gone in to burn incense. Notice here:

2.1.1. That the true Israel of God were always a praying people.

2.1.2. That at the time when ceremonial appointments, such as this of burning incense, were in full force, moral and spiritual duties were still required to accompany them. David knew that when he was far away from the altar, his prayer would be heard without incense, but that when he was going around the altar (Ps 26:6), the incense could not be accepted without prayer, any more than a shell is useful without its kernel.

2.1.3. That it is not enough for us to be in the place where God is worshiped if our hearts do not join in the worship.

2.1.4. That all the prayers we offer to God here in his courts are acceptable and effective only because of the incense of Christ's intercession in the temple of God above. We cannot expect to enjoy the privileges of Christ's intercession if we do not pray, and pray *with our spirits* (1Co 14:15), and continue faithfully in prayer (Ro 12:12).

2.2. How, when he was employed in this way, he was honored with a messenger sent to him from heaven (v. 11): *There appeared unto him an angel of the Lord.* This angel stood *on the right side of the altar of incense*, on Zechariah's right hand. Compare this with Zec 3:1, where Satan stands at the *right hand* of Joshua the priest to *resist him*; Zechariah the priest had a good angel standing at his right hand to encourage him.

2.3. What effect this had on Zechariah: *When Zacharias saw him*, he was *troubled, and fear fell upon him* (he was gripped with fear) (v. 12). Although he was *righteous before God* and *blameless* in his life (v. 6), he could not be completely free of apprehension. Ever since the first human beings sinned, our minds have been unable to bear the glory of such revelations, and our conscience is afraid they will bring bad news. This is why God chooses to speak to us through people like ourselves, whose *terror* will *not make us afraid* (Job 33:7).

3. The message that the angel had to give him. He began his message, as angels generally did, with *Fear not* (v. 13). Perhaps when Zechariah saw the angel, he was afraid that he had come to rebuke him for some mistake or failure. "No," the angel said, "*Fear not*, but compose yourself so that you may have a calm and steady spirit to receive the message I have to give to you." Let us see what that was.

3.1. The prayers he had often offered would now receive a favorable response: *Fear not, Zacharias, for thy prayer is heard.* If the angel was referring to Zechariah's particular prayer for a son, his prayers for that mercy must have been made long ago, when he was likely to have children. God would now, in giving this mercy, look a long way back to the prayers that Zechariah had spoken long before for and with his wife. Prayers of faith are filed in heaven and are not forgotten, even though the thing prayed for is not given immediately. If, on the other hand, the angel was referring to the prayers Zechariah was now offering, we may presume that those were the prayers required of him as a priest, prayers for the Israel of God and their well-being and for the fulfillment of the promises made to them about the Messiah and the coming of his kingdom: "This prayer of yours is now heard, because your wife will soon conceive the one who is to be the Messiah's forerunner." Some of the Jewish writers themselves say that when the priest burned incense, he prayed for the salvation of the whole world; and now that prayer would be heard. In general, "The prayers you are now making, and all your prayers, are accepted by God, and this will be the sign that you are accepted by God: Elizabeth will *bear thee a son*."

3.2. He would have a son in his old age, by Elizabeth his wife, who had long been barren. He was told what to name his son: *Call him John*, in Hebrew *Johanan*, a name we often met in the Old Testament: it means "gracious."

3.3. This son would be the joy of his family and of all his relatives (v. 14). He would be a welcome child. "*You, for your part, shall have joy and gladness*" (Isa 35:10; 51:11). When long-awaited mercies finally come, they are even more acceptable. "He will be a son you will have

great reason to rejoice in; many parents, if they could foresee what their children will turn out to be, instead of rejoicing at their birth, would wish they had never been born. However, I will tell you what your son will be, and then you will not need to *rejoice with trembling* (Ps 2:11) at his birth, as the best must do, but may rejoice with triumph at it." In fact, many would rejoice at his birth; all the family's relatives and all its well-wishers would rejoice in the birth, because it was for the honor and comfort of the family (v. 58).

3.4. This son would be a distinguished favorite of heaven and a distinguished blessing to the earth. The honor of having a son is nothing compared to the honor of having such a son.

3.4.1. He would be great in the sight of the Lord. God would watch over him and be with him continually. He would be a prophet—indeed, more than a prophet (Mt 11:9). He would be great, significant, in the sight of the Lord.

3.4.2. He would be a Nazarite, set apart for God from everything that is defiling; as a sign of this, according to the law of Naziriteship, he must drink neither wine nor strong drink. He must be a Nazarite for life. This suggests that those who want to be eminent servants for God and be employed in eminent services must learn to live a life of humility and self-denial; they must be dead to worldly pleasures and keep their minds from everything darkening and disturbing.

3.4.3. He would be abundantly qualified for those great and eminent services. *He will be filled with the Holy Ghost, even from his mother's womb* (v. 15).

3.4.3.1. Those who want to be filled with the Holy Spirit must be sober and temperate and very moderate in the use of wine and strong drink. *Be not drunk with wine, but be filled with the Spirit* (Eph 5:18).

3.4.3.2. Even infants can be used by the Holy Spirit, even from their mother's womb, for even then John the Baptist was filled with the Holy Spirit. God had promised to pour out his Spirit on the offspring of believers (Isa 44:3).

3.4.4. He would be instrumental in converting many souls to God and in preparing them to receive and welcome the Gospel of Christ (vv. 16–17).

3.4.4.1. He would be sent to the children of Israel, not to the Gentiles, yet he would be sent to the whole nation, not only to the family of the priests.

3.4.4.2. He would *go before* (ahead of) the Lord their God, that is, ahead of the Messiah, a little ahead of him, to announce his approach and prepare people to receive him.

3.4.4.3. He would *go in the spirit and power of Elijah*. That is:

3.4.4.3.*1*. He would be the kind of man Elijah was and do the kinds of works Elijah did. Like him, he would preach the necessity of repentance and reformation to a very corrupt and degenerate age. Like him, he would be bold and zealous in rebuking sin and witnessing against it even in the greatest people, and he would be hated and persecuted for it. He would also, like Elijah, be given power to carry on his work by a divine spirit, who would crown his ministry with wonderful success. He would introduce the Gospel era by preaching the substance of the Gospel message and duty: "Repent, with an eye to the kingdom of heaven."

3.4.4.3.*2*. He would be the very person who was prophesied of by Malachi under the name of Elijah (Mal 4:5), who was to be *sent before the coming of the day of the Lord.*

3.4.4.4. He would *turn many of the children of Israel to the Lord their God.* Whatever tends to turn us away from sin will turn us to Christ as our Lord and our God, for those who through grace are persuaded to shake off the yoke of sin will soon be persuaded to take on themselves the yoke of the Lord Jesus.

3.4.4.5. In doing this, John would *turn the hearts of the fathers to the children,* that is, turn the hearts of the Jews to the Gentiles. He would help conquer the deep-rooted prejudices the Jews had against the Gentiles; this conquest was made by the Gospel, and it was begun through John, who baptized and taught Roman soldiers (3:14) as well as Jewish Pharisees (Mt 3:7, 11), and who healed the pride and self-confidence of those Jews who gloried in having Abraham as their father, telling them that God would *out of stones raise up children unto Abraham* (Mt 3:9). When the Jews who embraced the faith of Christ were brought to join in fellowship with the Gentiles who did so too, then the hearts of the parents were turned to the children. The effect of this would be that hostilities would be put to death and discord brought to an end, and those who were at variance would, when united in his baptism, be better reconciled to one another. This agrees with the account Josephus gives of John the Baptist (*Antiquities,* bk. 18, ch. 7): "He was a good man and taught the Jews how to practice virtue through devotion toward God and righteousness toward one another." Josephus also said, "The people flocked to him and greatly delighted in his teaching." And so he turned the hearts of parents and children to God and one another by *turning the disobedient to the wisdom of the just.* Notice:

3.4.4.5.1. True religion is *the wisdom of the just.* It is both our wisdom and our duty to be religious; there is both justice and wisdom in it.

3.4.4.5.2. It is not impossible for those who have been unbelieving and disobedient to be turned to the *wisdom of the just;* divine grace can conquer the greatest ignorance and prejudice.

3.4.4.5.3. The great purpose of the Gospel is to bring people back to God and bring them closer to one another. In so doing, he will *make ready a people prepared for the Lord.* All who are to be devoted to the Lord and made happy in him must first be prepared and made ready for him. Nothing leads more directly to prepare people for Christ than the teaching of repentance. When sin is made so distressing, Christ will become very precious.

4. Zechariah's unbelief at the angel's prediction, and the rebuke he was given. We are told here:

4.1. What his unbelief said (v. 18). *Whereby shall I know this?* There are many examples in the Old Testament of those who had children when they were old, but he could not believe that he himself would have this promised child: "*For I am an old man,* and my wife is now also well advanced in years." He must therefore have a sign given him, or he would not believe. Although he had this announced to him in the temple, although it was given him when he was praying and burning incense, and although he firmly believed that God has almighty power and nothing is impossible with him (v. 37), nevertheless, giving too much consideration to his own body and his wife's, unlike a son of Abraham, he *staggered at the promise* (Ro 4:19–20).

4.2. How his unbelief was silenced and how he was silenced for it.

4.2.1. The angel *stopped his mouth* (Ro 3:19) by asserting his authority. Did he ask, *Whereby shall I know this?* Let him know it by this: *I am Gabriel* (v. 19). The angel attached his name to his prophecy. *Gabriel* means

"the power of God" or "the mighty one of God." He was Gabriel, who *stood in the presence of God.* "Although I am now talking with you here, I still *stand in the presence of God. I am sent to speak to thee,* sent with the deliberate purpose of *showing thee these glad tidings,* which, since they deserve full acceptance (1Ti 1:15), you should have received cheerfully."

4.2.2. The angel literally *stopped his mouth* by exerting his power: "So that you may raise no further objections, *behold, thou shalt be dumb* (v. 20). If you want to have a sign to support your faith, it will be one that will also be the punishment of your unbelief; *thou shalt not be able to speak till the day that these things shall be performed* (v. 20). "You will be both dumb and deaf"; the same word signifies both, and it is clear that he lost his hearing as well as his speech, because his friends *made signs* to him (v. 62), as well as he to them (v. 22). Now, in striking Zechariah silent, God dealt justly with him, because he had objected to God's word. Yet God was also dealing kindly, tenderly, and graciously with him, because:

4.2.2.1. In this way he was prevented from speaking any more such distrustful, unbelieving words. It is better not to speak at all than to speak evil.

4.2.2.2. In this way God confirmed his faith; being disabled from speaking, he was enabled to think better.

4.2.2.3. In this way he was kept from revealing the vision and boasting about it.

4.2.2.4. It was a great mercy that God's words would be fulfilled at the proper time, despite Zechariah's sinful distrust. He would not be dumb forever, but only till the day that these things would be performed, and then "your *lips* will be *opened,* so that your *mouth* may *show forth God's praise*" (Ps 51:15).

5. The return of Zechariah to the people, and eventually to his family, and the conception of this promised child.

5.1. The people remained, expecting Zechariah to come out of the temple, because he was to pronounce the blessing on them in the name of the Lord. Although he stayed beyond the usual time, they did not rush off without the blessing, but *waited* for him, marveling that he *tarried so long in the temple* and concerned that something might be wrong (v. 21).

5.2. When he came out, he was *speechless* (v. 22). He was now supposed to dismiss the congregation with a blessing, but he was mute and unable to do it.

5.3. He tried to make them understand that he had *seen a vision;* he *beckoned to them* and remained *speechless* (v. 22). The Old Testament speaks by signs; it beckons to us but remains speechless. It is the Gospel that speaks to us articulately, giving us a clear view of what was seen *through a glass darkly* (1Co 13:12) in the Old Testament.

5.4. He stayed there for his time of service, because his lot was to burn incense, and he could do that even though he was mute and deaf. When we cannot perform the service of God as well as we want, if we perform it as well as we can, God will accept us in it.

5.5. He then returned to his family, and his *wife conceived. She hid herself five months;* she kept the matter private (vv. 23–24), to avoid hurting herself and to avoid contracting any ceremonial defilement that might violate the Nazariteship of her child. Some think it was her excessive modesty that made her remain in seclusion. Or perhaps she did it out of humility, to avoid seeming to boast of the honor God had put on her. She *hid herself* for devotion. She gave this reason for her withdrawal: "*For thus hath the Lord dealt with me;* he has *taken away my reproach among men.*" Fruitfulness was looked on as such a great blessing among the Jews that it was a great disgrace to be barren, and those who were so were thought by some to have been guilty of some great unknown sin. Elizabeth now rejoiced, because not only had this disgrace been taken away, but also that great glory had been given to her instead: *Thus hath the Lord dealt with me in the days wherein he looked on me.*

Verses 26–38

Here we are told everything that it is fitting for us to know about the incarnation and conception of our blessed Savior. The same angel, Gabriel, who was employed in making known to Zechariah God's purpose concerning his son was employed in this task also, because the same glorious work of redemption that was begun in that birth was carried on in this one. We have here:

1. An account given of the mother of our Lord.

1.1. Her name was Mary, the same name as Miriam, the sister of Moses and Aaron; the name means "exalted."

1.2. She was a daughter of the royal family, descended from David's line, and she herself and all her friends knew it, because she included *the house of David* in her name. By God's providence and by her concern as a Jew for keeping her genealogy, she was enabled to reproduce it, and as long as the promise of the Messiah was to be fulfilled, it was worth keeping, but now, the noble ancestry of one who has been brought low in the world is not worth mentioning.

1.3. She was a virgin, pledged to be married to a man who was of the same royal stock, yet, like her, of low position. His name was Joseph; he also came from the house of David (Mt 1:20). Christ's mother was a virgin, because he was to be born miraculously; but he was born of a *virgin espoused*, one who was promised in marriage, to honor the married state.

1.4. She lived in Nazareth, a town in Galilee, a remote corner of the country, which had no reputation for religion or learning but bordered on the nations and was therefore called *Galilee* of the Gentiles. The angel was sent to her in Nazareth. No distance or disadvantage of place will harm those for whom God has favors in store.

2. The message of the angel to her (v. 28). He surprised her with this greeting: *Hail* (greetings), *thou that art highly favored.* This was intended to raise in her:

2.1. An esteem for herself. In some, who, like Mary, think only about their humble position, there is a need for such encouragement.

2.2. An expectation of great news, not from abroad, but from above. "Greetings; rejoice"; it was the usual form of greeting.

2.2.1. She was honored: "You are *highly favoured*. In choosing you as the mother of the Messiah, God has put distinctive honor on you."

2.2.2. She had the presence of God with her: "*The Lord is with thee*." Nothing is to be despaired of, not the fulfillment of any service, not the obtaining of any favor, even if it is very great, if we have God with us.

2.2.3. She had the blessing of God on her: "*Blessed art thou among women*; not only will you be counted so by people, but you will be so. You who are so *highly favoured in* this instance may expect to be *blessed* in other things." She explained this herself: *All generations shall call me blessed* (v. 48).

3. The dismay she was in at these words (v. 29). When she saw him, she was puzzled at it, unaware of anything in herself that either deserved or promised such great things. She *cast* (wondered) *in her mind what manner of salutation this should be.* Was it from heaven or from human

beings (20:4)? Her thoughtfulness on this occasion gives young people of her sex a very useful instruction, that when they are addressed, they should wonder what kind of greeting this might be.

4. The message itself that the angel had to communicate to her. He continued his mission (v. 30). She made no reply to what he had said; he therefore confirmed it: "Do not be afraid, Mary; you have found favor with God more than you think, as there are many who think they are more favored by God than they really are." Does God favor you? Is he for you? Then it does not matter who is against you (Ro 8:31).

4.1. Although she was a virgin, she would have the honor of being a mother: "You will conceive in your womb and give birth to a son, and you will *call his name Jesus*" (v. 31).

4.2. Although she lived in poverty and obscurity, she would still have the honor of being the mother of the Messiah; her son would be named *Jesus*—a Savior. He would be very closely related to the upper world. He would be truly great, for he would be called *the Son of the Highest*. He would be called, not miscalled, the *Son of the Highest*. Those who are the children of God are truly great and should therefore be concerned to be very good (1Jn 3:1–2). He would be very highly advanced in the lower world, for although he would appear in the form of a servant, the Lord God would give him the throne of his father David (v. 32). His people would not give him that throne; the Lord God would give him a right to rule them and would set him as his king on *the holy hill of Zion* (Ps 2:6). The angel assured her:

4.2.1. That his kingdom would be spiritual: he would reign *over the house of Jacob*, not Israel according to the flesh, but Israel *according to the promise* (Gal 3:29).

4.2.2. That it would be eternal: he would reign *for ever*, and *of his kingdom there would be no end.* Other crowns do not last to every generation, but Christ's does (Pr 27:24).

5. The further information given her upon her inquiry.

5.1. It was a just question that she asked: *How shall this be?* (v. 34). She knew that the Messiah must be born of *a virgin*, and if she must be his mother, she wanted to know how. This was not the language of distrust, but of wanting to be taught further.

5.2. A satisfactory answer was given to it (v. 35).

5.2.1. She would conceive by *the power of the Holy Spirit*. A divine power would undertake it, the power of the Holy Spirit himself.

5.2.2. She must ask no questions about how it would be performed, because the Holy Spirit, as the *power of the Highest*, would *overshadow* her. The formation of every baby in the womb and the entrance of the spirit of life into it is a mystery of nature. We were *made in secret* (Ps 139:15–16). Much more was the formation of the child Jesus a mystery.

5.2.3. The child she would conceive would be *a holy thing* and must therefore not be conceived by ordinary generation. He is spoken of emphatically, as *That Holy Thing*, One such as has never been, and he would be called *the Son of God.* His human nature must be produced in a way that befitted a human nature that was to be united with a divine nature.

5.3. It was a further encouragement to her faith to be told that *her cousin* (relative) *Elisabeth*, though advanced in years, was also *with child* (v. 36). "Here an age of wonders is beginning. *This is the sixth month with her that was called barren.*" The angel assured Mary of this to encourage her faith and then concluded with that great truth, which is absolutely certain and universally useful: *For with God nothing shall be impossible* (v. 37), and if nothing, then not even this. No word of God must be unbelievable to us as long as no work of God is impossible to him.

6. Her acceptance of God's will for her (v. 38). She declared herself to have:

6.1. A believing submission to divine authority: "*Behold, the handmaid of the Lord.* Lord, I am at your service." She left the outcome with God and submitted completely to his will.

6.2. A believing expectancy of divine favor. She not only was content to have it so but humbly desired that it would be so: *Be it unto me according to thy word.* We, like Mary here, must guide our desires by the word of God and base our hopes on it. Be it to me *according to thy word*; just so, and not otherwise.

7. *The angel's departure from her* (v. 38); having completed the mission on which he was sent, he returned.

Verses 39–56

Here we have a meeting between the two joyful mothers, Elizabeth and Mary. Sometimes we may do a greater service than we think by bringing good people together to compare notes. Here is:

1. The visit Mary made to Elizabeth (v. 39). She *arose* and left to see to this greater matter: *in those days, at that time*, as it is commonly explained (Jer 33:15; 50:4), a day or two later. She went "with care, diligence," and *haste*. She went *to a city of Judah in the hill country*; she went there quickly, even though it was a journey of many miles. It is generally presumed that she went there to strengthen her faith by seeing the sign that the angel had told her of, her favorite relative's pregnancy, and to rejoice with her. Besides that, she may also have gone there to withdraw from company, or to have more pleasant company than she could have in Nazareth. She probably did not tell any of her neighbors in Nazareth about the message she had received from heaven, yet longed to talk it over—she had thought it over a thousand times—and knew no one else in the world with whom she could talk freely about it except Elizabeth. It is very good and encouraging for those who have a good work of grace begun in their souls to talk with those who are in a similar situation. They will find that just as you see a reflection when you look into water, so the heart of one human being, of one Christian, reflects another.

2. The meeting between Mary and Elizabeth. Mary entered the house of Zechariah, *saluted* (greeted) *Elisabeth* (v. 40), and told her that she had come to visit her and *rejoice with her* in her joy.

2.1. The baby *leaped in* Elizabeth's *womb* (v. 41). She had probably been feeling the baby move for several weeks, but this movement of the child was more than ordinary, which told her to expect something extraordinary. The *babe leaped*, as it were, to give a signal to his mother that the one who was to come after him was now soon to be born.

2.2. Elizabeth herself was *filled with the Holy Spirit*, or a Spirit of prophecy, by which she was given to understand that the Messiah was near. The uncommon movement of the baby in her womb was a sign of the extraordinary emotion of her spirit under divine impulse.

3. The welcome that Elizabeth, by the Spirit of prophecy, gave to Mary, the mother of our Lord.

3.1. She congratulated her on her honor. She *spoke with a loud voice*. She said, *Blessed art thou among women*, the same greeting as the angel had given (v. 28). However, Elizabeth added a reason: *Blessed art thou, because blessed is the fruit of thy womb.* Elizabeth was the wife of a priest and was advanced in years, but she did not begrudge her relative, who was many years younger than she, the honor of conceiving in her virginity and being the mother of the Messiah, whereas the honor shown Elizabeth was much less. No; she rejoiced in it. As long as we must acknowledge that we are more favored of God than we deserve, let us in no way become envious of others when they are more highly favored than we.

3.2. She acknowledged Mary's condescension in visiting her (v. 43): *Whence is this to me, that the mother of my Lord should come to me?* She called the Virgin Mary the *mother of her Lord*. She not only welcomed her to her house but also considered this visit a great favor, one that she was unworthy of. *Whence is this to me?* Those who are filled with the Holy Spirit have low thoughts of their own merits and high thoughts of God's favors.

3.3. She told her the baby in her womb had concurred in this welcome to her (v. 44): "*As soon as the voice of thy salutation sounded in my ears*, not only did my heart leap *for joy*; the *babe in my womb did so* too." He leaped, as it were, for joy that the Messiah, whose messenger he was to be, would himself come so soon after him. The faith of the Virgin would be very much strengthened by knowing that such assurances were given to others.

3.4. She commended her faith and encouraged it (v. 45): *Blessed is she that believed.* Believing souls are blessed souls. Those who believe the word of God are blessed, because that word will not fail them; *there shall*, without doubt, *be a performance of those things which are told her from the Lord* (what the Lord has said to her will be accomplished) (v. 45). The faithfulness of God is the blessedness of the faith of the saints. Those who have experienced the fulfillment of God's promises themselves should encourage others to hope that he will be as good as his word to them too.

4. Mary's song of praise on this occasion. Elizabeth's prophecy was an echo of the Virgin Mary's greeting, and this song is an even stronger echo of that prophecy. We may presume that the Blessed Virgin arrived very tired from her journey; she forgot that, however, and was inspired with new life, vigor, and joy on the confirmation of her faith that she encountered here.

4.1. Here are the expressions of joy and praise, and God alone is the object of the praise and the center of the joy. Notice how Mary spoke about God here:

4.1.1. With great reverence for him, as the Lord: *My soul doth magnify the Lord.* Those, and only those, who are led to think more highly and honorably of God are advanced in blessing. The more honor God has shown us in any way, the more honor we must seek to give him. We are accepted in exalting the Lord when our souls glorify him, when all that is within us does so (Ps 103:1). Praising work must be a work of the soul.

4.1.2. With great delight in him as her Savior: *My spirit rejoiceth in God my Saviour.* This seems to refer to the Messiah, whom she was to be the mother of. She called him *God her Saviour* because the angel had told her that he would be the *Son of the Highest* and that his name would be *Jesus, a Saviour.* She focused on this, applying it to herself: *He is God my Saviour.* Even the mother of our Lord needed to know the privileges of having him as her Savior and would have been ruined without it.

4.2. Here are just causes given for this joy and praise.

4.2.1. On her own account (vv. 48–49). Her *spirit rejoiced in the Lord*, because of the kind things he had done for her. *He has regarded the low estate* (humble state) *of his handmaiden* (servant). "He has chosen me for this honor despite my great lowliness, poverty, and obscurity." Moreover, if God *regards her low estate*, he is not only showing an example of his favor to the whole human race, whom he remembers in their humble state, but he is also securing a lasting honor for her, for such is the honor that God gives—it is an unfading honor: "From now on all generations will call me blessed." Elizabeth had twice called her blessed. "But that is not all," Mary said; "all generations of Gentiles as well as Jews will also call me that." Her soul glorified the Lord (v. 49): *He that is mighty hath done to me great things.* It was truly something great that a Virgin should conceive. It was truly something great that the Messiah should now eventually be born. It was the power of the Highest that appeared in this. She added, "*and holy is his name*. He that is mighty, whose name is holy, has done great things for me." Glorious things may be expected from the One who is both mighty and holy, from the One who can do everything, and will do everything well and for the best.

4.2.2. On behalf of others. As the mother of the Messiah, the Virgin Mary had become a kind of public person, and she therefore looked out and around her; she looked in front of her and took notice of God's various dealings with other people (v. 50).

4.2.2.1. It is a certain truth that God has mercy in store for all who have a reverence for him. However, this never appeared so fully as when he sent his Son into the world to save us. *His mercy is on them that fear him* (v. 50); it has always been so. But he has revealed this mercy as never before in sending his Son to bring in eternal righteousness and work an eternal salvation for those who fear him, and to do this from generation to generation, because some Gospel privileges are transmitted by inheritance and intended to last forever. In him, mercy is settled on all who fear God. This mercy forgives, heals, accepts, and crowns from generation to generation, as long as the world stands.

4.2.2.2. It has often been observed that God in his providence shows contempt to the proud and honor to the humble. Just as God had, in showing *mercy* to her, also shown himself to be *mighty* (vv. 48–49), so he had also, with his *mercy on them that fear him, shown strength with his arm.* In the course of his providence, it is his usual way to thwart human expectations. Proud people expect to overcome everything in their path, but *he scatters them in the imagination of their hearts* (in their inmost thoughts) and brings them low. Powerful people think they can protect themselves by the power they establish, but he humbles them. On the other hand, those who are humble are wonderfully exalted. This observation about honor is also true of riches; many who were so poor that they did not have bread for themselves and their families come to be filled with good things by some surprising turn of providence in their favor. In contrast, those who were rich are strangely impoverished and sent away empty. God takes pleasure in disappointing the expectations of those who promise themselves great things in the world and in surpassing the expectations of those who promise themselves only a little. As a good God, he glories in exalting those who humble themselves and in speaking assurance to those who fear him. The Gospel grace is shown:

4.2.2.2.1. In the spiritual honors it gives. He scattered the proud and *put down the mighty but exalted them of low degree* when the proud Pharisees were rejected and tax collectors and sinners entered the kingdom of heaven before them; when the Jews, who followed the law of righteousness, did not reach it, and the Gentiles, who never

thought about it, obtained righteousness (Ro 9:30–31); and when God did not choose the wise in themselves, nor the mighty nor the noble, to preach the Gospel and plant Christianity in the world, but the foolish and weak things of the world and things that were despised (1Co 1:26–27).

4.2.2.2.2. In the spiritual riches it gives (v. 53). Those who see their need of Christ are *filled* with *good things* by him, with the best things; he gives liberally to them, and they are *abundantly satisfied* (Ps 36:8). Those who are weary and burdened will find rest with Christ (Mt 11: 28), and those who thirst are called to *come to him and drink* (Jn 7:37). Those who are rich—who, like Laodicea, think they need nothing, who are full of themselves and think they are *sufficient in themselves* (Rev 3:14–18)—he sends away from his door. He sends them away empty; they come full of themselves and are sent away empty of Christ.

4.2.2.3. It was always expected that the Messiah would be the strength and glory of his people Israel, and so he was in a special way: *He has helped his servant Israel* (v. 54). He had taken them by the hand and had helped those who had fallen and could not help themselves. The sending of the Messiah, *on whom help was laid* for poor sinners (Ps 89:19)—help for him and for them through him—was the greatest kindness that could be done, and what exalts it is:

4.2.2.3.1. That it was in remembrance of God's mercy. While this blessing was deferred, his people were often ready to ask, "Has God forgotten to be gracious?" But now he had made it clear that he had not forgotten, had remembered, his mercy. He remembered days of long ago (Ps 143:5).

4.2.2.3.2. That it was in fulfillment of God's promise. It was a mercy not only intended but also declared (v. 55). It was what *he spoke to our fathers*, especially to Abraham, that in his descendants all the families of the earth would be blessed with the blessings that last forever (Ge 12:3). What God has promised, he will fulfill; what he has spoken to the parents will be fulfilled to their children and to their children's children.

5. Mary's return to Nazareth (v. 56) after she had stayed with Elizabeth for about three months. Those in whose hearts Christ is formed (Gal 4:19) take more delight than they used to in sitting alone and keeping silent.

Verses 57–66

We have here:

1. The birth of John the Baptist (v. 57). *Elisabeth's full time came, that she should be delivered,* and then she *brought forth* (gave birth to) *a son.* Promised mercies are to be expected when their full time has come, not before.

2. The great joy that was among all the relatives on this extraordinary occasion (v. 58): *Her neighbours and her cousins heard of it.* These relatives and neighbors then revealed:

2.1. A devout regard for God. They acknowledged that the Lord had "magnified his mercy to her," as it may be translated. Many things worked together to make the mercy great—that she had been barren for a long time, that she was now old, but especially that the child would be *great in the sight of the Lord* (v. 15).

2.2. A friendly regard for Elizabeth. When she rejoiced, they *rejoiced with her.* We should take delight in the prosperity of our neighbors and friends and be thankful to God for their comforts as much as for our own.

3. The dispute that arose among them about his name (v. 59): *On the eighth day* they *came together to*

circumcise the child. Those who rejoiced in the birth of the child came together to circumcise him. The greatest comfort we can take in our children is in giving them to God. The baptism of our children should give us greater joy than their birth. Now it was the custom that when they circumcised their children, they named them, and it was not unfitting that they be left nameless until they were given up to God by name.

3.1. Some people suggested that he should be called by his father's name, *Zacharias.* They intended to honor the father, who was unlikely to have another child.

3.2. The mother opposed it and wanted him called *John,* having learned that God had appointed this as his name: *He shall be called John* (v. 60), "Gracious," because he would introduce the Gospel of Christ, in which God's grace shines more brightly than ever.

3.3. The relatives objected to that: "*There is none of thy kindred that is called by that name* (v. 61), and so let him have the name of some relative of his father's."

3.4. They appealed to the *father,* for it was his task *to name the child* (v. 62). *They made signs* to him, by which it appears that he was deaf as well as dumb. In any case, they gave him to understand what the dispute was and that only he could determine it, and then he made signs to them to give him a writing tablet. He wrote, *His name is John* (v. 63). Not "It will be so" or "I want it to be so," but "It is so." The matter had already been determined. When Zechariah could not speak, he wrote. When ministers have their mouths closed, so that they cannot preach, they may still do good as long as their hands are not tied, so that they cannot write. Zechariah's choice of the same name that Elizabeth had chosen was a great surprise to the company: *They marvelled all* (were astonished).

3.5. He then regained the use of his speech: *His mouth was opened immediately* (v. 64). The time that had been determined for his being silenced was *till the day that these things shall be fulfilled* (v. 20). That time had now elapsed, and so the restraint was lifted, and God opened his mouth again. Infidelity closed his mouth, and now believing opened it again. His mouth was opened, and he spoke and praised God. When God opens our lips, our mouths must declare his praise (Ps 51:15). It would be as good to be without our speech as not to use it to praise God.

3.6. These things were told throughout the country, to the great amazement of all who heard them (vv. 65–66). We are told here:

3.6.1. That *these sayings were discoursed of;* they were the common talk of everyone around the hill country of Judea.

3.6.2. That most people who heard about these things were dismayed by them: *Fear came on all them that dwell round about.*

3.6.3. That it raised the people's expectations for this child. They stored these thoughts in their hearts. This shows us that we should treasure up what we hear that may be useful to us, so that we may be able to bring out, for the benefit of others, both new things and old (Mt 13:52) and, when things come to perfection, may be able to look back and say, "It was what we could have expected." They said within themselves, and said among themselves, "*What manner of child will this be?* What is this child going to become? What will be the fruit when this is the blossom?"

4. It said, *The hand of the Lord was with him;* that is, he was taken under the special protection of the Almighty from his birth, as one intended for something great. God works on children in their infancy in ways that we cannot

explain. God never made a soul without knowing how to make it holy.

Verses 67–80

We have here the song with which Zechariah praised God when his mouth was opened; it is said that in it he *prophesied* (v. 67). Notice:

1. How he was qualified for this: *He was filled with the Holy Ghost;* he was divinely inspired. God not only forgave him his unbelief and distrust; he also filled him with the Holy Spirit.

2. What the subject of his song was. Here nothing was said about the private concerns of his own family, the rolling away of disgrace from it (Jos 5:9). In this song he was completely taken up with the kingdom of the Messiah. The Old Testament prophecies are often expressed in praises and *new songs* (Ps 33:3; 40:3; 96:1; etc.), like this one that begins New Testament prophecy: *Blessed be the Lord God of Israel.* Zechariah, speaking of the work of redemption, called God the *Lord God of Israel* because the prophecies, promises, and types of the redemption had been given to Israel up to that time, and it was to them that it was first offered and proposed. Zechariah here blessed God:

2.1. For the work of salvation that was to be undertaken by the Messiah himself (vv. 68–75).

2.1.1. In sending the Messiah, God had made a gracious visit to his people. He *visited* (came to) *them* as a friend, to take notice of their situation.

2.1.2. He had worked redemption for them: *He has redeemed his people.* This was why Christ came into the world, to redeem those who were sold for sin and as a slave to sin (Ro 7:14). Christ redeems them out of the hands of God's justice by paying the price, and he redeems them out of the hands of Satan's tyranny by exerting his power.

2.1.3. He had fulfilled the covenant of royalty made with the most famous Old Testament ruler, that is, David. Glorious things had been said about his family: that on him, as *a mighty one, help* would be *laid,* help for him and for others through him; and that his *seed,* his line, would endure forever (Ps 89:19–20, 24, 29). But that family had long been, in a way, *cast off.* Now here it was glorified in that, according to the promise, the *horn* of David would again be *made to bud.* He *hath raised up a horn of salvation for us in the house of his servant David* (v. 69), where it was promised and expected to arise. There is *salvation for us* in Christ, and only in him, and it is a *horn of salvation.* It is an honorable salvation, *raised up* above all other forms of salvation, none of which are to be compared with it. It is a plentiful salvation, a cornucopia, "a horn of plenty." It is a powerful salvation, which will demolish our spiritual enemies and protect us from them.

2.1.4. He had fulfilled all the precious promises made to the church by the most famous Old Testament prophets (v. 70): *As he spoke by the mouth of his holy prophets.* His doctrine of salvation by the Messiah is confirmed by an appeal to the prophets. God was now doing what he had spoken of long ago. See:

2.1.4.1. How sacred the prophecies of this salvation were. The prophets who spoke them were *holy prophets,* and it was the holy God himself who spoke through them.

2.1.4.2. How ancient they were: ever *since the world began.* Because God promised when the world began that the *Seed of the woman would break the serpent's head* (Ge 3:15), that promise echoed in the names Eve, "Living"; *Cain,* about whose birth Eve said, *I have gotten a man from the Lord* (Ge 4:1); Seth, "settled"; and Noah, "rest" (Ge 5:29).

2.1.4.3. What a wonderful harmony and agreement we notice among them. God spoke the same thing through them all. Now what is this salvation that was prophesied?

2.1.4.3.*1*. It is a rescue from the malice of *our enemies*; it is "a salvation from our enemies," from among them, and *out of the power of them that hate us* (v. 71); it is a salvation from sin. Christ would *save his people from their sins*, so that their sins would not have power over them (Mt 1:21).

2.1.4.3.*2*. It is a restoration to the favor of God; it is to *perform* (show) *the mercy promised to our forefathers* (v. 72). The Redeemer would reinstate us in the mercy of God and reestablish us in his covenant, which was represented by the promises made to the patriarchs and by the *holy covenant* made with them, *the oath which he sware to our father Abraham* (v. 73). Notice:

2.1.4.3.*2*.*1*. What was promised to the ancestors and is shown to us is *mercy*, pure mercy; nothing in it is because of what we would have deserved. He loved us because he wanted to.

2.1.4.3.*2*.*2*. God was here considering his *holy covenant*, the covenant with Abraham: *I will be a God to thee and thy seed* (Ge 17:7). His descendants had *really* forfeited this covenant by their disobedience; he *seemed* to have forgotten this in the disasters brought on them; but he would now remember it.

2.1.4.3.*3*. It is a qualification for and an encouragement to the service of God. "This was *the oath he sware to our Father Abraham*, that he would give us power and grace to serve him, in a way acceptable to him and encouraging to us." The great purpose of Gospel grace is not to release us from the service of God, but to engage us in it and encourage us in it. We are saved from the iron burden of sin so that our necks may be put under the sweet and easy yoke of the Lord Jesus (Mt 11:30). The very chains that he has freed us from bind us more closely to him (Ps 116:16). We are then enabled:

2.1.4.3.*3*.*1*. To serve God *without fear*. We are put into a state of holy peace so that we can serve God with a holy security and peace of mind, as those who are released from the fears of evil. God must be served with a childlike awe, a reverent, obedient wonder, an awakening and quickening fear, not with a slavish fear, like that of the lazy servant, who represented his master to himself as hard and unreasonable (Mt 25:24).

2.1.4.3.*3*.*2*. To serve him in *holiness and righteousness*, which includes the whole human duty toward God and our neighbor.

2.1.4.3.*3*.*3*. To serve him, serve *before him*, in the duties of worshiping him directly, to serve him as those who always look to him and see him always looking at us, at our inner self.

2.1.4.3.*3*.*4*. To serve him *all the days of our life*. Christ *loved us to the end*, and knowing this should encourage us to love him to the end (Jn 13:1).

2.2. For the work of preparing for this salvation, which was to be done by John the Baptist (v. 76): *Thou child shalt be called the prophet of the Highest*. Jesus Christ is *the Highest*. John the Baptist was *his prophet*. Prophecy had long ceased, but in John it revived. John's work was:

2.2.1. To prepare people for the salvation: *Thou shalt go before the face of the Lord* to *prepare his ways*. Let everything that might obstruct or prevent his progress or hinder people from coming to him be taken away: see Isa 40:3–4.

2.2.2. To give people a general idea of the salvation, because the message he preached was that the *kingdom of heaven is at hand* (Mt 3:2). You must know that this salvation consists in two things:

2.2.2.1. The forgiveness of what we have done wrong. It is salvation *by the remission of sins* (v. 77). John the Baptist gave the people to understand that although their situation was sad, it was not desperate, for forgiveness could be obtained *through the tender mercy of our God*: there was nothing in us except our pitifulness to commend us to God's great compassion.

2.2.2.2. Direction to do better in the future. The Gospel salvation sets up a clear and true light, by which we may walk in the right way. In it *the dayspring* (the rising sun) *hath visited us from on high* (v. 78), and this also is because of the *tender mercy of our God*. Christ is "the morning Light," the *rising Sun* (Mal 4:2). The Gospel brings *light* with it; it does not leave us to wander around either in the darkness of pagan ignorance or in the moonlight of the Old Testament types or figures, but brings the dawn of a new day with it. In John the Baptist daylight began to break, but it increased quickly and *shone more and more to the perfect day* (Pr 4:18). We who enjoy the Gospel day have as much reason to welcome it as those who have long awaited the morning have to welcome that.

2.2.2.2.*1*. The Gospel reveals; it is to *give light to them that sit in darkness*, the *light of the knowledge of the glory of God in the face of Jesus Christ* (2Co 4:6).

2.2.2.2.*2*. The Gospel revives. It brings light to those who sit *in the shadow of death*, as condemned prisoners in the dungeon; it brings them the news of pardon, at least of a reprieve and opportunity of a pardon. How pleasant is that light!

2.2.2.2.*3*. The Gospel directs; it is to *guide our feet in the way of peace*. It shows us the way to make our peace with God, that *way of peace* that as sinners we have wandered from and *have not known*, nor could ever have known by ourselves.

3. In the last verse, a brief account of the younger years of John the Baptist. We are here told:

3.1. Of his eminence in his inner being (2Co 4:16): the *child grew* in the capacities of his heart and mind, so that he *waxed* (became) *strong in spirit*; he had a strong judgment and strong resolution. Those who are strong in the Lord are *strong in spirit*.

3.2. Of his obscurity in his outward circumstances: he *was in the deserts*. He spent most of his time there, in contemplation and devotion, and did not have his education in schools or at the feet of the rabbis. Many people are qualified for great usefulness and yet are, as it were, buried alive, and in many of these, a longer time of being so buried seems to indicate that they were intended by God, and were therefore being prepared, for much greater usefulness in the end, as John the Baptist was, who was in the desert continually until the day of his public appearance to Israel. There is a time fixed to show to Israel publicly those favors that are reserved for it.

CHAPTER 2

In this chapter we have an account of the birth and infancy of our Lord Jesus: 1. The place and circumstances of his birth (vv. 1–7). 2. The announcement of his birth to the shepherds in that neighborhood by an angel, and the spreading of the news by the shepherds (vv. 8–20). 3. The circumcision and naming of Christ (v. 21) and the presenting of him in the temple (vv. 22–24). 4. The testimonies of Simeon and Anna about him (vv. 25–39).

5. *Christ's growth and abilities (vv. 40–52).* 6. *His observing the Passover at twelve years old and his discussions with the teachers in the temple (vv. 41–51).*

Verses 1–7

The *fulness of time* had now come (Gal 4:4), when God would send his Son, and it was foretold that he would be born in Bethlehem. Here we have an account of the time, place, and manner of this birth:

1. The time when our Lord Jesus was born.

1.1. He was born at the time when *the fourth kingdom* (Da 2:40) was at its height. Christ was born *in the days of Augustus Caesar,* when the Roman Empire had extended farther than ever before or since, from Parthia in the east to Britain in the west, so that it was then called *terrarum orbis imperium,* "the empire of the whole earth." Here that empire is called *all the world* (v. 1), as there was scarcely any part of the civilized world that did not depend on it.

1.2. He was born when Judea had become a province and tributary of the empire, as appears clearly from the fact that when the whole Roman Empire was taxed, the Jews were taxed. Jerusalem had been taken by the Roman general Pompey about sixty years before this. Judea was ruled by *Cyrenius* (Quirinius), the Roman governor of Syria (v. 2). This was the first census for taxes that was taken in Judea, a sign of their subjection to Rome.

1.3. Another circumstance as to the time is implied in this general enrollment of all the subjects of the empire, namely, that there was now universal peace (the *Pax Romana,* "the Roman peace") in the empire. The temple of Janus was now shut, which it never was if any wars were afoot, and so now the time was right for the Prince of Peace (Isa 9:6) to be born.

2. The place where our Lord Jesus was born, which is significant. He was born at *Bethlehem,* as it was foretold (Mic 5:2); the teachers of the law understood it in this way (Mt 2:5–6), as did the ordinary people (Jn 7:42). The name of the place was significant. *Bethlehem* means "the house of bread," and so it was a proper place for the One who is the Bread of life to be born, the Bread that *came down from heaven* (Jn 6:33, 35). Bethlehem was the town of David, where he was born, and so the One who was the *Son of David* (Mt 1:1) must be born there too. Zion was also called *the city of David* (2Sa 5:7), but Christ was not born there. Bethlehem was that town of David where he was born in humble circumstances, to be a shepherd, and so when our Savior humbled himself, he chose this as the birthplace rather than Zion, where David ruled in power and prosperity. When the Virgin Mary was with child and near her time to give birth, Providence so arranged it that by order from the emperor all the subjects of the Roman Empire were to be taxed. This meant they were to be "registered and enrolled" according to their families, which is the meaning of the word used here. Augustus, in ordering this census, was motivated either by pride, wanting to declare to the world how many people he ruled, or by politics, wanting to strengthen his interests and make his government appear even stronger; but Providence had another purpose for it. The whole world would go to the trouble of being enrolled only so that Joseph and Mary would do so. This took them up from Nazareth in Galilee to Bethlehem in Judea, because they were *of the stock and lineage of David* (vv. 4–5). Various purposes in Providence were fulfilled by this.

2.1. It brought the Virgin Mary, *great with child,* to Bethlehem, to be *delivered* there, according to the prediction. See how "man proposes and God disposes" (Thomas à Kempis, *Imitation of Christ,* 1.19).

2.2. It showed that Jesus Christ was a descendant of David, for what brought his mother to Bethlehem now except that she *was of the stock and lineage of David?*

2.3. It showed that he was *made under the law* (Gal 4:4), because he became a subject of the Roman Empire as soon as he was born. Instead of having kings bring tribute to him, when he came into the world he himself paid tribute.

3. The circumstances of his birth, which were very humble. He was indeed a *firstborn son,* but it was poor honor to be the firstborn of such a poor woman as Mary, who could give him no inheritance but the title *firstborn.*

3.1. He was humbled in the same ways as other children; he was *wrapped in swaddling clothes,* as other children are when they are newly born—as if he could be bound or needed to be held straight. The Ancient of Days (Da 7:9, 13, 22) became an infant of *a span long* (La 2:20).

3.2. He was humbled in some ways that were distinctive to him.

3.2.1. He was born *at an inn.* Christ was born in an inn to show that he came into the world only to stay here for a while, as in an inn. An inn receives all guests, and so does Christ. He hangs out the banner of love as his sign (SS 2:4), and whoever comes to him he will in no way drive out (Jn 6:37), except that, unlike other inns, he welcomes those who come *without money and without price* (Isa 55:1).

3.2.2. He was born in a stable; this is what some people think the word that we translate as *manger* means. Because there was no room in the inn, and for lack of any other convenient place—indeed, for lack of necessities—he was laid in the manger instead of a cradle. His being born in a stable and laid in a manger showed:

3.2.2.1. The poverty of his parents. If they had been rich, room would have been ready for them.

3.2.2.2. The bad manners of that age. If there had been any common humanity among them, they would not have made a woman in labor stay in a stable.

3.2.2.3. The humiliation of our Lord Jesus. By our sin, we had become like outcast infants, helpless and forlorn, and Christ was such.

Verses 8–20

The lowliest circumstances of Christ's humiliation were all along accompanied by some revelations of his glory to balance them out. When we saw him *wrapped in swaddling clothes* and *laid in a manger,* we were tempted to say, "Surely this cannot be the Son of God." But let us see his birth accompanied by a choir of angels, and we will say, "Surely it can be no one other than the Son of God." In Matthew we read how the announcement was given to the wise men, who were Gentiles, by a star; here we are told of its announcement to the shepherds, who were Jews, by an angel. God chose to speak to each in the language they were most familiar with. Notice:

1. How the shepherds were employed; they were *abiding in the fields* and *keeping watch over their flocks by night* (v. 8). The angel was not sent to the chief priests or the elders but to a group of poor shepherds. The patriarchs were shepherds, and this showed that God still had favor for those who were employed in such innocent jobs. The shepherds were not sleeping in their beds when this news was brought to them, but *abiding in the fields* and *watching.* They were wide awake and so could not have been deceived in what they saw and heard, as people may be when they are half asleep. They were employed now not in acts of devotion but in the work of their calling;

they were *keeping watch over their flock*. We do not miss divine visits when we are well employed in fulfilling an honest calling and remain faithful to God in it.

2. How they were surprised by the appearance of an angel (v. 9): *Behold, an angel of the Lord came upon them*, suddenly. The angel's *coming upon them* suggests that they little thought of such a thing or expected it. Gracious visits are made us from heaven *or ever* (before) *we are aware* (SS 6:12). They saw and heard the *glory of the Lord round about them*; this made the night as bright as day and made them *sore afraid*, as if fearing some bad news. As long as we are aware of much guilt in ourselves, we have reason to fear that every messenger from heaven is a messenger of wrath.

3. The message that the angel had for the shepherds (vv. 10–12). "*Fear not*; you need not fear your enemies and should not fear your friends." He provided them with a great reason for joy: "See, I bring you good news of—'I evangelize to you'—*great joy*. It will bring *joy to all people* that *unto you is born this day a Saviour which is Christ the Lord, in the city of David*" (v. 11). "The Savior *is born this day*, and since it is matter of *great joy to all people*, you may proclaim it. He is born in the place where it was foretold he would be born, in the *city of David*, and he is born *to you*; he is sent in the first place to you Jews, to *bless you*, and to you *shepherds*, though you are poor and insignificant in the world." This refers to Isa 9:6: *Unto us a child is born, unto us a son is given*. This is a matter of true and great joy to all people. The One who had long been looked for had finally come. The angel gave them a sign to confirm their faith in this matter. "You will find him by this sign: he is lying in *a manger*, where surely never any newborn infant has been laid before. You will find him there, wrapped in *swaddling clothes*."

4. The angels' doxology to God and expression of goodwill to people on this solemn occasion (vv. 13–14). The message was no sooner given by one angel than suddenly there was with that angel *a multitude of the heavenly hosts praising God*.

4.1. Let God have the honor of this work: *Glory to God in the highest. Glory to God*, whose kindness and love planned to bestow this favor and whose wisdom planned it in such a way that one divine attribute would not be glorified at the expense of another. Other works of God are for his glory, but the redemption of the world is for his *glory in the highest*.

4.2. Let people have the joy of it: *On earth peace, goodwill toward men*. If God is at peace with us, all peace results from it. Peace here stands for all good. All the good we have or hope for is because of God's goodwill, and if we have encouragement from it, he must receive the glory for it. Here peace was made known with great ceremony; whoever will, let them come and take its benefits. It is peace on earth to "men of goodwill," as some read it, to those who have goodwill toward God or to those whom God has goodwill toward. This is *a faithful saying that deserves full acceptance* (1Ti 1:15): the *goodwill* of God *toward men* is *glory to God in the highest, and peace on the earth* (v. 14).

5. The visit that the shepherds paid to the newborn Savior.

5.1. They discussed it (v. 15). While the angels were singing their song of praise, the shepherds could only listen to that, but *when they were gone away from them into heaven, the shepherds said one to another, Let us go to Bethlehem*. It is no reflection on the testimony of angels, nor on divine testimony itself, to have it corroborated by observation and experience. These shepherds did not speak doubtfully, saying, "Let us go see whether it is so or not," but with assurance, saying, *Let us go see this thing which is come to pass*, for what room was left to doubt it when *the Lord had made it known to them*?

5.2. They paid the visit immediately (v. 16). They lost no time, but *came with haste* to the place, and there *they found Mary and Joseph*, and *the babe lying in the manger*. The poverty and humble conditions in which they found *Christ the Lord* (v. 11) were no shock to their faith, since they themselves knew what is to live a life of assured fellowship with God in very poor and humble circumstances. We have reason to think that the shepherds told Joseph and Mary about the vision of angels that they had seen and the song of angels they had heard, which was a great encouragement to the new parents, more than if a visit had been paid them by the best women in town.

6. The care that the shepherds took to spread this news (v. 17): *When they had seen it*, they made *known abroad* (spread the word) the whole story that had been *told them* both by the *angels* and by Joseph and Mary *concerning this child*, that he was the Savior, *Christ the Lord*, and that in him there is *peace on earth*. They told everybody this, agreeing in their testimony about it. What impression did it make on people? Why truly, *All they that heard it wondered at those things which were told them by the shepherds* (v. 18). They wondered, yet they never inquired any further about the Savior, but let the thing drop as a nine days' wonder.

7. The use that was made of these things by the people who did believe them.

7.1. The Virgin Mary made them the matter of her private meditation. She said little, but *kept all these things and pondered them in her heart* (v. 19). Just as she had silently left it to God to make her purity known when that was in doubt, so she here silently left it to him to make her honor known now that that was veiled, and it was satisfying enough to find that if no one else took notice of the birth of her child, angels did. The truths of Christ are worth keeping, and the way to keep them safe is to ponder them. Meditation is the best help to memory.

7.2. The shepherds made them the matter of their more public praises. Even if others were not moved by those things, they themselves were (v. 20): They *returned, glorifying and praising God*. God would accept the thanksgiving they offered him. They praised God for what *they had heard* from the angel and for what *they had seen*, the baby in *the manger*, as they had been told. They thanked God that they had seen Christ. As with the cross of Christ later (1Co 1:23), so with his manger now: it was to some foolishness and a stumbling block, but others saw in it, wondered at, and praised the *wisdom of God* and the *power of God* (1Co 1:24).

Verses 21–24

Our Lord Jesus, being *made of a woman*, was *made under the law* (Gal 4:4). As the son of a daughter of Abraham, he was made under the Law of Moses. Here we have two expressions of his being made under that law and submitting to it.

1. He was *circumcised* on the very day that the Law appointed (v. 21): *When eight days were accomplished*, they *circumcised* him.

1.1. Even though it was a painful operation, Christ would undergo it for us.

1.2. Even though it presupposed he was a foreigner (Ge 17:14; 1Ch 29:15), who was by that ceremony admitted into covenant with God, he still submitted to it. Even though it presupposed he was a sinner, he still submitted to it. In fact, this alienation and sin were a reason why he submitted to it; he wanted be made in the likeness not only of flesh but even of *sinful flesh* (Ro 8:3).

1.3. Even though in submitting to this ceremony he made himself *a debtor to the whole law* (Gal 5:3), he still submitted to it. Christ was circumcised in order to:

1.3.1. Acknowledge that he was a descendant of Abraham.

1.3.2. Acknowledge himself to be a surety for our sins and a guarantor of our safety.

1.3.3. Justify the dedication of the infant seed of the church to God by the ordinance that is the instituted seal of the covenant; circumcision was that seal (Ro 4:11), and now baptism is. At his circumcision he had his name given him; he was called *Jesus* or *Joshua*, for *before he was conceived in the womb*, the angel told Mary to give him that name (1:31), and the same name was told to Joseph afterward (Mt 1:21). It was a common name among the Jews, and here he would be made *like unto his brethren* (Heb 2:17). It was the name of two eminent types of him in the Old Testament, Joshua the successor of Moses and Joshua the high priest; the latter prefigured Christ as a *priest upon his throne* (Zec 6:11, 13). His name said much about his work. Jesus means "a Savior." He *bringeth salvation* (Tit 2:11).

2. He was *presented* in the temple. This was done at the time appointed by the Law, when he was forty days old, *when the days of her purification were accomplished* (v. 22). Now according to the Law:

2.1. The child Jesus, being a firstborn son, was *presented to the Lord*. The law is repeated here: *Every male that opens the womb shall be called holy to the Lord* (v. 23). Christ was the firstborn among many brothers and sisters, and he was *called holy to the Lord* as no one else ever had been; he was still, however, *presented to the Lord* as other firstborn males were, and not in any special way. And in accordance with the Law, he was *redeemed* (Nu 18:15). *The firstborn of man shalt thou redeem*, and *five shekels* was the value (Lev 27:6; Nu 18:16). Probably in cases of poverty the priest was allowed to take less, or perhaps nothing, for no mention is made of it here.

2.2. The mother brought her offering (v. 24). So *it is said in the law of the Lord*, the law that was still in force: she must offer *a pair of turtledoves* or *two young pigeons*. If she had been able to, she would have brought a *lamb for a burnt offering* and a *dove for a sin offering*, but because she was poor and unable to afford the price of a lamb, she brought *two doves*, one for *a burnt offering and the other for a sin offering* (see Lev 12:6, 8). Christ was not conceived and born in sin, as others are, but because he was born under the Law (Gal 4:4), he submitted to it. *Thus it became him to fulfil all righteousness* (Mt 3:15).

Verses 25–40

Even when he humbles himself, Christ still has honor shown him. Simeon and Anna now gave him honor by the inspiration of the Holy Spirit.

1 A very honorable testimony was given to him by Simeon. Notice here:

1.1. The account that is given us of this Simeon. He lived in Jerusalem and was well known for his righteous devotion and fellowship with God. Some learned men who have been familiar with the Jewish writers find that there was at this time a certain Simeon in Jerusalem who was a notable man and the son of Hillel. The Jews say that he was endowed with a prophetic spirit. One objection against this conjecture is that Hillel, the father of this Simeon, was still alive at this time and that this Simeon

himself lived many years after this, but as to that, Simeon is not here said to be old, and although his saying *Now let thy servant depart* shows that he was willing to die now, it does not necessarily mean that he did actually die quickly. Another objection is that the son of Simeon was Gamaliel, a Pharisee and an enemy of Christianity, but as to that, it is nothing new for a faithful lover of Christ to have a son who is a bigoted Pharisee. The account given of him here is:

1.1.1. That he was just and devout, *just* toward people and *devout toward* God; these two must always go together, and each will be a friend of the other, but neither will make up for the defects of the other.

1.1.2. That he *waited for the consolation of Israel*, that is, for the coming of the Messiah. Christ is not only the author of his people's comfort but also its substance and basis. He was a long time coming, and those who believed he would come continued waiting, desiring his coming and hoping for it with patience—I almost said, with some degree of impatience. The consolation of Israel is to be waited for, and it is worth waiting for, and it will be very welcome to those who have waited for it and continue to wait.

1.1.3. That the *Holy Spirit* was on him, not only as a Spirit of holiness but also as a Spirit of prophecy; he was *filled with the Holy Spirit*.

1.1.4. That a gracious promise had been made to him that before he died he would see the Messiah (v. 26). He received *this oracle*—because this is the sense—*that he should not see death before he had seen* the Messiah, *the Lord's Anointed*. Those, and only those, who have seen Christ by faith can look death in the face with courage and without terror.

1.2. The timely coming of Simeon into the temple just at the time when Christ was presented there (v. 27). When Joseph and Mary brought the child, Simeon came into the temple by the direction of the Spirit. The same Spirit who had provided for the support of his hope now provided for the rapture of his joy. Those who want to see Christ must go to his temple, for there *the Lord, whom ye seek* (Mal 3:1), will suddenly come to meet you, and there you must be ready to meet him.

1.3. The deep satisfaction with which he welcomed this sight: *He took him up in his arms* (v. 28), embracing him and holding him to himself, as close as possible to his heart, which was as full of joy as it could be. He *took him up in his arms* to present him to the Lord. When we receive with a living faith the record of Christ that the Gospel gives us, and receive with love and submission the offer of Christ it presents to us, then we *take Christ in our arms*. It had been promised to Simeon that he would see Christ, but more was performed than was promised: he had him in his arms.

1.4. The solemn declaration he then made: *He blessed God* and said, *Lord, now let thou thy servant depart in peace* (vv. 29–32).

1.4.1. He had a pleasant prospect concerning himself; he had arrived at a state of holy contempt of life and at a desire for death: *"Lord, now let thou thy servant depart, for my eyes have seen the salvation I was promised a sight of before I died."* Here is:

1.4.1.1. An acknowledgment that God had been as good as his word. Never has anyone who hoped in God's word been made ashamed of their hope (Ro 5:5; 9:33; 10:11).

1.4.1.2. Thanksgiving for it. He *blessed God* that he saw that salvation in his arms.

1.4.1.3. A confession of his faith that this child in his arms was the Savior—was in fact salvation itself; *"thy salvation*, the salvation that you appointed, the salvation *which thou hast prepared*."

1.4.1.4. A farewell to this world: *Now let thy servant depart*. The eye is not satisfied with seeing (Ecc 1:8) until it has seen Christ, and then it is. This world looks poor to one who has Christ in his arms and salvation in his eye!

1.4.1.5. A welcome to death: *Now let thy servant depart*. Simeon had been promised that he would not *see death* until he had *seen Christ* (v. 26), and he was willing to interpret what was expressed as an indication that when he had seen Christ, he would die: *Lord, be it so*, he said; *now let me depart*. Notice here:

1.4.1.5.*1*. How encouraging the death of a good man is; he departs as God's servant from the place of toil to that of rest. He departs in peace, peace with God, peace with his own conscience, peace with death.

1.4.1.5.*2*. What is the basis of this encouragement? *For mine eyes have seen thy salvation*. This shows a confident expectation of a happy state on the other side of death, through this salvation he now had seen, which not only takes away the terror of death but also makes it gain (Php 1:21). Those who have welcomed Christ may welcome death.

1.4.2. He had a pleasant prospect of the world and the church. This salvation would be:

1.4.2.1. A blessing to the world. It was *prepared before the face of all people*, to be a *light to lighten* (for revelation to) *the Gentiles* who now sat in darkness. This refers to Isa 49:6, *I will give thee for a light to the Gentiles*, because Christ came to be the light of the world—not a candle in the Jewish lampstand, but the *Sun of righteousness* (Mal 4:2).

1.4.2.2. A blessing to the church: *the glory of thy people Israel*. He was truly *the glory of* those who were true Israelites, of the spiritual Israel, and will be so forever (Isa 60:19). They will glory in him. When Christ told his apostles to preach the Gospel to all nations (Mt 28:19), he made himself a light for revelation to the Gentiles, and when he added, *beginning at Jerusalem* (Lk 24:47), he made himself *the glory of his* people Israel.

1.5. The prediction he gave Joseph and Mary concerning this child when he blessed him. They *marvelled at those things* that were more and more fully and plainly spoken about this child (v. 33). Because what was said to them both moved them and strengthened their faith, more was said to them.

1.5.1. Simeon showed them what reason they had to rejoice. He *blessed them* (v. 34): he prayed that God would bless them, and he wanted others to do so too. This child was set *for the rising again of many in Israel*, that is, he was destined to convert to God many who were dead and buried in sin, and he was destined to bring comfort in God to many who were sunk and lost in sorrow and despair. Those whom he was set *for the fall of* may be the same as those whom he was set for the *rising again of*. He was set "for their fall in order for them to rise again." He wounds and then heals (Dt 32:39); Paul falls, and rises again (Ac 9:4, 8).

1.5.2. He also showed them what reason they had to *rejoice with trembling* (Ps 2:11). In case Joseph, and especially Mary, should be lifted up with the abundance of the revelations, a *thorn in the flesh* was given to them (2Co 12:7), and sometimes that is what we need. It was true that Christ would be a blessing to Israel, but there were those in Israel whom he was *set for the fall of*, who would be prejudiced and enraged against him and would take offense at him. Just as it is pleasant to think how many there are to whom Christ and his Gospel are a fragrance of

life, so also it is sad to think how many there are to whom he is the smell of death (2Co 2:16). He is *set as a sign*, to be wondered at by some but spoken against by others, by many. He had many eyes upon him; he was a sign. But he also had many tongues against him. The effect of this would be that the *thoughts of many hearts would be revealed* (v. 35). The secret devotion and good attitudes of some would be revealed by their embracing Christ and coming to know him; the secret corruptions and evil attitudes of others would be exposed by their hostility toward Christ and their rage against him. People will be judged by the thoughts of their hearts, their thoughts about Christ. The *word of God is a* discerner of the *thoughts* and *intents of the heart* (Heb 4:12). It was true that Christ would be a comfort to his mother, but she was not to become too proud of it, for *a sword shall pass through thine own soul also*. Jesus would suffer.

1.5.2.1. "You will suffer with him, by sympathy, because of the closeness of your relationship with him and the strength of affection for him." When he was mistreated, it was *a sword in her bones* (Ps 42:10). When she stood by his cross and saw him dying, we may well think her inner grief was such that it might truly be said, *A sword pierced through her soul*; it cut her to the heart.

1.5.2.2. "You will suffer for him." Many understand it as a prediction of her martyrdom.

2. He was noticed by one *Anna, a prophetess*. Here is:

2.1. The account given here of this Anna, who she was. She was *a prophetess*. Perhaps no more is meant than that she was one who had more understanding of the Scriptures than other women and made it her business to instruct the younger women in the things of God. God *left not himself without witness* (Ac 14:17). She was *the daughter of Phanuel*, and her name means "gracious." She was of *the tribe of Asher*, which was in Galilee. She was of *a great age*, a widow about eighty-four years old. Having become a widow after seven years of marriage, she never remarried, but remained a widow to her dying day, which is mentioned in praise of her. She was a constant resident in the temple, or at least an attendant there. Some think she had lodgings in the courts of the temple; others think her not *departing from the temple* means nothing more than that she was constantly there at the time of divine services; when any good work was to be done, she was ready to join in it. She *served God with fastings and prayers night and day*. She gave herself wholly to her devotion, spending in religious exercises the time that others spent eating, drinking, and sleeping. In these she *served* God; her serving him with them was what put value on them and gave them excellence. She *served God* and aimed at his honor in *fasting and praying*. Other duties are opportune now and then, but we must *pray always* (18:1). It is pleasant to see elderly Christians still full of acts of devotion, to see that they are not *weary of well-doing* (Gal 6:9), but take more and more pleasure in it. Anna was now at long last abundantly rewarded for her attendance in the temple for so many years.

2.2. The testimony she bore to our Lord Jesus (v. 38): *She came in at that instant*. The one who was so faithful in the temple could not miss the opportunity. She *gave thanks likewise to the Lord*, just as Simeon did, and perhaps, like him, wishing now to depart in peace. We should be encouraged to the duty of thanksgiving by the praises and thanksgiving of others; why should we not *give thanks likewise*, as well as they? As a prophet, she instructed others about him: she *spoke of him to all them* who believed the Messiah would come, and, with Simeon, she *looked for redemption in Jerusalem*. There were some in Jerusalem who *looked for redemption*, but only a few, because Anna, it seems, knew all who shared her expectation of the Messiah. She knew where to find them, or they knew where to find her, and she told them all the good news that she had seen the Lord (Jn 20:18). Those who know Christ themselves should do all they can to bring others to know him.

2.3. A short account of the infancy and childhood of our Lord Jesus.

2.3.1. Where he spent it (v. 39). They *returned to Galilee*. Luke writes no more about them until they returned to Galilee, but it appears from St. Matthew's Gospel (Mt 2) that from Jerusalem they returned to Bethlehem and that they remained there until they were told to flee into Egypt. Returning from there when Herod had died, they were told to go to their old quarters in Nazareth, which is here called *their own city*.

2.3.2. How he spent it (v. 40). In all things *it behoved him* (he had) *to be made like unto his brethren* (Heb 2:17), and so he passed through infancy and childhood as other children did. As other children, he grew in physical stature and increased in understanding in his human mind. Whereas other children are weak in understanding and determination, he was *strong in spirit*. By the Spirit of God, his human soul was endowed with extraordinary vigor. Whereas other children have *foolishness bound in their hearts* (Pr 22:15), he was *filled with wisdom*. Everything he said and did was wisely said and wisely done, above his years. Whereas other children show that the corruption of nature is in them, and *the tares* (weeds) of sin grow up with *the wheat* of reason (Mt 13:25–30), he made it clear that nothing but *the grace of God was upon him*. He was *greatly beloved* (Da 10:11), and highly favored by God.

Verses 41–52

We have here the only record of our blessed Savior from his infancy to the day of his public ministry to Israel, and so we want to make the most of this, because it is no good wishing we had more. Here is:

1. Christ's going with his parents to Jerusalem at the Feast of the Passover (vv. 41–42). It was their constant practice to attend there, according to the Law, even though it was a long journey and they were poor. Public ceremonies of worship must be attended frequently, and we must not *forsake the assembling of ourselves together*. They *went up* there *after the custom of the feast*. At *twelve years old*, the child Jesus went up with them. The Jewish teachers say that at twelve years old children must begin to fast from time to time, and that at thirteen years old a child begins to be "a son of the commandment," having been from his infancy, because of his circumcision, a son of the covenant. Those children who are forward in other things should be put forward in religious matters. When children who are dedicated to God in their infancy have grown up, they should be called on to come to the Gospel Passover, to the Lord's Supper, so that they may commit themselves to the Lord by their own action.

2. Christ's staying behind in Jerusalem when his parents left, without telling them.

2.1. His parents did not return until they had *fulfilled the days* (v. 43); they had stayed there all the seven days at the feast, although it was not absolutely necessary that they stay longer than the first two days. It is good to stay to the conclusion of a ceremony of worship, as befits those who say, "It is good to be here" (9:33), and not to rush away quickly.

2.2. The child *tarried* (stayed) *behind in Jerusalem*, not because he was reluctant to go home or averse to his parents' company, but because he had business to do there and wanted to let his parents know that he had *a Father in heaven* whom he was to be observant of more than of them, and that respect to him must not be interpreted as disrespect to them. It is good to see young people willing to *dwell in the house of the Lord* (Ps 27:4); they are then like Christ.

2.3. His parents went the *first day's journey* without any suspicion that he was left behind, as they *supposed him to have been in the company* (v. 44). On these occasions, the crowd was very great. They concluded that he must be coming along with some of their neighbors, and they *sought him among their kindred and acquaintance*. "Have you seen our Son?" or, "Have you seen him?" They *found him not* (v. 45). There are too many of our relatives and friends whom we cannot avoid talking with but among whom we find little or nothing of Christ. When Joseph and Mary did not hear of him from those whom they asked on the road, they hoped they would meet with him at the place where they stayed that night, but they could find no news of him there either.

2.4. When they did not find him where they were staying that night, the next morning they *turned back again* to *Jerusalem, seeking him*. Those who want to find Christ must *seek till they find*, because he will eventually be found by those who seek him (Jer 29:13). Those who have lost their assurance in Christ must ask themselves when and how they lost it and must *turn back again* to the place where they last had it.

2.5. The *third day* they found him *in the temple*. They found him there *sitting in the midst of* the teachers of the law (v. 46). He was not standing, as a new convert, to be taught or examined by them; they allowed him to sit among them as a fellow or member of their society. This shows that he was not only *filled with wisdom* (v. 40) but also both eager to increase it and ready to share it. Here, is an example to children and young people, who should learn from Christ to delight in the company of those they may gain good by and to choose to *sit in the midst of* the teachers rather than in the midst of the players. Many a young person at Christ's age in Christ's time would have been playing with other children in the temple, but he was sitting with the *doctors in the temple*.

2.5.1. He *heard* them. Those who want to learn must be swift to hear (Jas 1:19).

2.5.2. He *asked them questions*. I do not know whether he did this as a teacher—he had authority to ask in that way—or as a learner—he had the humility to ask in this way.

2.5.3. He gave *answers* to them, which were very surprising and satisfactory (v. 47). Moreover, his wisdom and *understanding* were as apparent in the questions he asked as in the answers he gave, so that all those who heard him *were astonished*: they had never heard one so young, nor indeed any of their greatest teachers, talk sense as much as he did. He "gave them a taste," according to Calvin, of his divine wisdom and knowledge. *They understood not*; they were only *astonished*.

2.6. His mother talked with him privately about it (v. 48). Joseph and Mary were both amazed to find him there, and to find that he was respected so much that he was admitted to *sit among the doctors* (teachers). His mother told him how badly they took it: "*Son, why hast thou thus dealt with us?* Why did you give us such a fright?" *Thy father and I have sought thee, sorrowing* (anxiously searching for you)." Those who think they have lost Christ may be allowed to complain about their losses. Yet Joseph and Mary did not sorrow and sit down in despair, but sorrowed and sought. Those who seek Christ in sorrow will find him, at length, with even greater joy. He gently rebuked their excessive concern for him (v. 49): *"How is it that you sought me?* Did you not know that I ought to be *about my Father's businesses?"* Some read the last phrase, "in my Father's house?" "By right, I should be:

2.6.1. *"Under my Father's care* and protection, and so you should have cast your anxiety for me on him (1Pe 5:7).

2.6.2. "At my Father's work; I must be *about my Father's business,* and so I could not go home as soon as you wanted. *Did you not know this?"* It was his mission into the world and his food and drink in the world (Jn 4:34) to do his Father's will and complete his work, but at that time his parents *understood not this saying* (v. 50).

2.7. Here is their return to Nazareth. He did not urge his parents either to come and settle at Jerusalem or to settle him there, but very willingly withdrew to obscurity at Nazareth, where for many years he was, as it were, buried alive. But here we are told:

2.7.1. That he was obedient to his parents. It seems he worked with his father at the carpenter's trade. Here he has given an example to children to be dutiful and obedient to their parents in the Lord (Eph 6:1). Although his parents were poor and insignificant, although he was *strong in spirit* and *filled with wisdom,* he was still obedient to his parents. If ordinary children, then, though foolish and weak, are disobedient to their parents, what account will they give of themselves?

2.7.2. That his mother, though she did not perfectly understand her son's sayings, still *kept them in her heart.* However much we may neglect the sayings of human beings because they are obscure, we must not neglect God's sayings. What at first is mystifying, so that we do not know what to make of it, may later become plain and easy. We may find a use another time for something that we do not see how we can make use of now.

2.7.3. That he improved, progressed, and was thought well of: *He increased in wisdom and stature* (v. 52). This is referring to his human nature: his body increased in height and weight, and he grew as young people do, and his soul increased in wisdom and in all the endowments of the human spirit. As the faculties of his human life grew more and more capable, the gifts it received from the divine nature were communicated more and more. He also increased in *favour with God and man.* The image of God shone more brightly in him when he grew up to be a youth than it did or could while he was an infant and a child.

CHAPTER 3

Nothing is said about our Lord Jesus from his twelfth year to the beginning of his public ministry in his thirtieth year. In this chapter we have: 1. The beginning of John's baptism (vv. 1–6), with his encouragements and warnings to the crowds (vv. 7–9) and the particular instructions he gave to those who wanted to be told their duty (vv. 10–14). 2. The announcement he gave them of the approach of the Messiah (vv. 15–18), to which is added the mention of John's imprisonment (vv. 19–20). 3. Christ coming to be baptized by John (vv. 21–22), along with a record of Christ's background and genealogy as far back as Adam (vv. 23–38).

Verses 1–14

Because John's baptism introduced a new era, it was necessary that we have a detailed account of it. Glorious

things were said about John (1:15, 17), but we lost him in the desert, and he remained there until *the day of his showing unto Israel* (1:80). Notice:

1. The date of the beginning of John's baptism; this is noted by Luke, though not by the other Evangelists, so that the truth of the thing could be confirmed by the exact fixing of the time. It is dated:

1.1. By reference to the government of the Gentiles whom the Jews were under.

1.1.1. It is dated by the reign of the Roman emperor; it was in the fifteenth year of Tiberius Caesar, the third of the twelve Caesars, a very bad man. After a long struggle, the Jewish people had recently been made a province of the Roman Empire, an insignificant, contemptible part of it, and were under the power of this Tiberius.

1.1.2. It is dated by the governments of the viceroys who ruled in the different parts of the Holy Land under the Roman emperor, which was another sign of their subjection, for these officials were all foreigners. Pilate is said here to have been the governor, or president or procurator, of Judea. Some other writers describe him as an evil man who had no scruples about telling lies. He reigned badly and was in the end displaced and sent to Rome to answer for his maladministration. The other three are called *tetrarchs. Tetrarch* means "fourth ruler," and some think these officials were given this title because of the countries they had command of, each of them being over a fourth part of what had been completely under the government of Herod the Great.

1.2. By reference to the government of the Jews among themselves (v. 2). Annas and Caiaphas were the high priests. God had appointed that there be only one high priest at a time, but here were two, for some bad purpose or another.

2. The origin and purpose of John's baptism.

2.1. Its origin was from heaven: *The word of God came unto John* (v. 2). It is the same expression that is used with the Old Testament prophets (Jer 1:2), because John was a prophet—indeed, more than a prophet (Mt 11:9). John was called *the son of Zacharias* here, to refer us to what the angel said to his father. The word of the Lord came to him *in the wilderness,* for those whom God fits he will find, wherever they are. Just as the word of the Lord is not bound in a prison, so it is not lost in a wilderness. John was the *son of a priest* and was now beginning his thirtieth year, and so, according to the custom of the temple, he was now to be admitted into the temple service. However, God had called him to a more honorable ministry.

2.2. Its purpose was to bring all the people of his country away from their sins and home to their God (v. 3). *He came* first *into all the country about Jordan,* the part of the country that Israel took possession of first; there the banner of the Gospel was first displayed. John lived in the loneliest part of the country, but when the word of the Lord came to him, he left his deserts and came into the inhabited country. Those who are most pleased to be in a place of retirement must cheerfully give it up when God calls them to places where they will meet many people. *He came into all the country, preaching* a new *baptism.* This sign, or ceremony, *washing with water,* was often used among the Jews in the admission of converts; its meaning was *repentance for the remission of sins.* All who submitted to John's baptism:

2.2.1. Were obliged to *repent of their sins,* to be *sorry* for what they had done wrong and to *do so no more.* Repentance was what they professed, and they were eager to be sincere in their professions; to sin no more was what they promised, and they were eager to fulfill what they promised. He required them to change their mind and change their ways, and to get new hearts (Eze 18:30) and live new lives.

2.2.2. Were assured of forgiveness of their sins when they repented. Just as the baptism John administered required them not to submit to the power of sin, so it also sealed them with a gracious discharge from the guilt of sin, a discharge that they could plead before God.

3. The fulfilling of the Scriptures in the ministry of John. The other Evangelists referred us to the same text that is referred to here, Isa 40:3: It is *written in the book of the words of Esaias the prophet.* Among those words it is found that there would be *the voice of one crying in the wilderness,* and John was that voice; he cried out, *Prepare ye the way of the Lord, and make his paths straight.* Luke goes further with the quotation, applying to John's ministry also the words of Isaiah that follow those quoted by Matthew and Mark (vv. 5–6): *Every valley shall be filled.*

3.1. The humble would be enriched with grace by the Gospel.

3.2. The proud would be humbled by it: *Every mountain and hill shall be brought low.*

3.3. Sinners would be converted to God (Ps 51:13): *The crooked ways* and the *crooked* spirits would be *made straight.* God by his grace can make straight what sin has made crooked.

3.4. Difficulties that were hindering and discouraging on the way to heaven would be removed: *The rough ways shall be made smooth.* The Gospel has made the way to heaven plain and easy to find, smooth and easy to walk on.

3.5. The great salvation would be more fully revealed than ever, and its revelation would spread further (v. 6): *All flesh shall see the salvation of God;* not only the Jews but also the Gentiles would see it. All would see it, and some of all kinds of people would see it, enjoy it, and benefit from it.

4. The general warnings and exhortations that he gave to those who submitted to his baptism (vv. 7–9). In Matthew he is said to have preached these same things to *many of the Pharisees and Sadducees* who *came to his baptism* (Mt 3:7–10), but here he is said to have spoken them *to the multitude* (crowds) *that came forth to be baptized of him* (v. 7). This was the purpose of his preaching to all who came to him. Just as he did not flatter the great, he did not compliment the many, but gave the crowds the same rebukes for sin and warnings of wrath that he gave the Sadducees and Pharisees, for if the crowds did not have the same faults, they had others that were as bad. Notice here:

4.1. That the guilty and corrupt human race has become *a generation of vipers,* not only poisoned but also poisonous, hateful to God and hating one another.

4.2. This brood of vipers is fairly warned to *flee from the wrath to come,* which is certainly before them if they remain as they are. Yet if we look around us in time, we are not only warned of this wrath but put in a position to escape it.

4.3. There is no way of *fleeing from the wrath to come* except by *repentance.*

4.4. Those who profess repentance have a great obligation to live like penitents (v. 8): *Bring forth therefore fruits meet for* (in keeping with) *repentance,* for otherwise you cannot escape *the wrath to come.* The change of our mind must be shown by the change of our ways.

4.5. If we are not really holy, both in heart and in life, our profession of faith will do us no good at all: *"Begin not* now to think up excuses to get out of this great duty of

repentance, *saying within yourselves, We have Abraham to* (as) *our father.*

4.6. We have no reason, therefore, to depend on our external privileges and professions of faith, because God can effectively ensure his own honor and interests without us. If we were cut off and ruined, he could raise up for himself a church out of what is most unlikely, *children to Abraham* even *out of stones.*

4.7. The greater professions we make of repentance, and the greater helps and encouragements are given us for repentance, the nearer and harsher will our destruction be if we do not produce fruit in keeping with repentance. Now that the kingdom of heaven is at hand (Mk 1:15), now that the *axe is laid to the root of the tree,* threats to evildoers and the impenitent are more terrible than before, just as encouragements to the penitent are now more comforting.

4.8. Barren trees will eventually be thrown onto the fire; that is the best place for them: *Every tree* that does not produce fruit, *good fruit, is hewn down* and *cast into the fire.*

5. The particular instructions he gave to several kinds of people who asked him about their duty: the *people,* the *publicans* (tax collectors), and the *soldiers.* Some of the Pharisees and Sadducees came to his baptism, but we do not find them asking, *What shall we do?* They thought they knew. But the *people,* the tax collectors, and the *soldiers,* who knew that they had done wrong and were aware of their great ignorance and unfamiliarity with the divine law, were particularly curious: *What shall we do?* Those who are baptized must be taught. Those who profess and promise repentance in general must show it by particular expressions of reformation. Those who want to do their duty must want to know their duty. These here do not ask, *What shall this man do?* (Jn 21:21) but, *"What shall we do?"* What fruit in keeping with repentance are we to produce?" Now John gave an answer to each one, according to their place and position.

5.1. He told the *people* their duty, and that was to be kind (v. 11): *"He that has two coats,* let him *give,* or *lend* at least, *to him that has none,* to keep him warm." The Gospel requires mercy, not sacrifice (Hos 6:6; Mt 9:13), and its intention is to encourage us to do all the good we can. Food and clothing are the two necessary supports of life; if anyone has food to spare, let them give to a person who does not have daily food. What we have we are merely stewards of, and so we must use it as our Master directs.

5.2. He told the tax collectors, the collectors of the emperor's revenue, their duty (v. 13): *Exact no more than that which is appointed you.* They must act justly between the government and the merchant, not oppressing the people in levying taxes. They must not think that because it was their responsibility to take care that the people did not defraud the ruler, they could therefore, by the power they had, come down hard on the people; those who have even a little power tend to abuse it, and so: "Collect for Caesar the things that are Caesar's (20:25), and do not make yourselves rich by taking more." Public revenue must be applied to public services and not be used to satisfy the greed of private people. He did not tell the tax collectors to give up their positions; the job in itself was lawful and necessary. But let them be just and honest in it.

5.3. He told the *soldiers* their duty (v. 14). Some think that these soldiers were Romans, and if so, their asking to be told their duty was an early example of Gentiles embracing the Gospel and submitting to it. Few soldiers seem inclined to have a religious faith, but these submitted even to John the Baptist's strict profession and wanted to receive the word of command from him: *What must we do?* In answer to this question, John did not tell them to lay down their arms, but warned them against the sins that soldiers were commonly guilty of. They must not wrong the people among whom they were quartered: "*Do violence to no man.* Your business is to keep the peace, and so do not *do violence* to any yourselves." "Shake no one" is the sense; "do not make people frightened, because the sword of war, as well as that of justice, is to be a terror only to evildoers (Ro 13:3); to those who do well it is a protection." Nor must they *accuse any falsely* to the government in order to make themselves feared and gain bribes. They must not wrong their fellow soldiers, for some think the warning not to *accuse falsely* has special reference to them: "Be not forward in complaining about one another to your superior officers so that you may take revenge on those whom you are angry with." They must not be given to mutiny or argue with their generals about their pay: "*Be content with your wages.* As long as you have what you agreed for, do not complain that it is not more." What makes people oppressive and harmful is discontent with what they have. It is wise to make the best of what is.

Verses 15–20

We see here:

1. How the people used the occasion of the ministry and baptism of John to think about the Messiah and to think of him as near. The way of the Lord was prepared, for when people's expectations are raised, what they are expecting becomes doubly acceptable. Now when they noticed what an excellent doctrine John the Baptist preached:

1.1. They soon began to think that now the time had come for the Messiah to appear. Never did the corrupt state of the Jews need a reformation more, nor their distressed state need rescuing more, than now.

1.2. Their next thought was, "Is not this the One who would come (Ps 118:26; Lk 7:19)?" All thinking *men mused*, wondered or reasoned *in their hearts*, about John, *whether he were the Christ or not*. His life was holy and strict, his preaching powerful and with authority, and so "why may we not think that he is the Messiah?" What makes people wonder and reason with themselves prepares the way for Christ.

2. How John disowned all pretensions to the honor of being the Messiah, but confirmed the people in their expectation of the One who really was the Messiah (vv. 16–17). John's work as crier or herald was to announce that the *kingdom of God was at hand* (Mk 1:15), and so when he had told all kinds of people each what they must do, he told them one more thing that they must all do: they must expect the Messiah to appear soon. This served as an answer to their wondering and discussion about John.

2.1. He declared that the most he could do was to *baptize* them *with water*. He could only encourage them to repent and assure them of forgiveness when they repented.

2.2. He consigned them, turned them over, as it were, to Jesus Christ, whom he was sent to *prepare the way* for. He wanted them no longer to discuss whether John was the Messiah or not, but to look for the One who really was.

2.2.1. John acknowledged that the Messiah had greater honor than he; the Messiah was One the *latchet of whose shoe* (the thong of whose sandals) he did not think he was *worthy to loose*. John was *a prophet*—no, *more than a*

prophet, more a prophet than any of the Old Testament prophets—but Christ was a prophet more than John. This was a great truth that John came to preach, but the way in which he expressed it showed his humility, and in it he not only did justice to the Lord Jesus but honored him. This is how highly we should speak about Christ and how humbly we should speak about ourselves.

2.2.2. He acknowledged that the Messiah had a greater power than he: "He is *mightier than I*." They thought that a wonderful power accompanied John, but what was that compared with the power that Jesus would come clothed with?

2.2.2.1. John could do no more than *baptize with water*, as a sign that those who were baptized should purify and cleanse themselves, but Christ could and *would baptize with the Holy Spirit*. He can give the Spirit to cleanse and purify the heart.

2.2.2.2. John could only preach a distinctive message; by word and sign he could distinguish *between the precious and the vile* (the worthy and the worthless) (Jer 15:19). But Christ would have his *fan* (winnowing fork) *in his hand*, with which he could and would completely separate the wheat and the chaff. He *will thoroughly purge his floor*.

2.2.2.3. John could only speak encouragement to those who received the Gospel; Jesus Christ would give them encouragement. John could only promise them that they would be safe, but Christ would actually make them safe.

2.2.2.4. John could only threaten hypocrites, telling the *barren trees* that they would be *hewn* (cut) *down* and *cast into the fire*, but Christ could carry out that threat; those who are like *chaff*, who are light and worthless, *he will burn with fire unquenchable*.

3. How the Evangelist concludes his account of John's preaching with an *etc.* (v. 18): *Many other things in his exhortation preached he unto the people*. This shows us:

3.1. John was a passionate preacher. He was "exhorting," warning and encouraging; he pressed things home to his hearers, as one who was serious.

3.2. He was a practical preacher. Much of his preaching was exhortation, encouraging them to do their duty and guiding them in it, not entertaining them with matters of idle speculation.

3.3. He was a popular preacher. He addressed himself *to the people*, "to the laity," and adjusted his way of speaking to their level, promising himself great success among them.

3.4. He was an evangelical preacher; "he preached the Gospel" to the people; in all his warnings and encouragements, he directed people to Christ and stirred up and encouraged their expectations of him.

3.5. He was a copious preacher: *Many other things he preached*, "many things, and different." He varied his preaching, so that those who were not reached, touched, and persuaded by one truth might be reached by another.

4. How an end was put to John's preaching. When he was in the middle of his usefulness, he was imprisoned by the hatred of Herod (vv. 19–20): *Herod the tetrarch, being reproved by him*, not only for living in incest with his brother Philip's wife but also for the many other *evils which Herod had done*—those who are evil in one way are often so in many others—could not *bear it*, and so he *added* this evil to all the others: he *shut up* (locked) *John in prison*. Because he could not bear John's reproofs, others would be deprived of the benefit of his instructions and advice. Must the one who is the *voice of one crying in the wilderness* be silenced? But this was how the faith

of his disciples must be tested; this was how the unbelief of those who rejected him must be punished; and in this way John must be Christ's forerunner in suffering as well as in preaching. He must now give way to Christ. Now that the Sun had risen, the Morning Star must of course disappear.

Verses 21–38

The Evangelist mentioned John's imprisonment before Christ's being baptized, even though it was nearly a year after it, because he wanted to conclude the account of John's ministry before introducing the ministry of Christ. We have here:

1. A short account of Christ's baptism. Jesus came to be baptized by John, and he was (vv. 21–22).

1.1. It is said here that *when all the people were baptized,* then *Jesus was baptized.* Christ wanted to be baptized last, among the common people, and at their rear. He also considered their desire for him: he saw what crowds were prepared to receive him, and then he appeared.

1.2. It is noted here, though not in Matthew, that Christ prayed when he was baptized: *being baptized, and praying.* He prayed, as others did, because he wanted to maintain his fellowship with his Father in this way. He prayed for the revelation of his Father's favor to him and for the descent of the Spirit. What was promised to Christ, he must obtain by prayer: *Ask of me, and I will give thee* (Ps 2:8).

1.3. When he prayed, *the heaven was opened.* Sin had locked heaven, but Christ's prayer opened it up again. Prayer is an ordinance that opens heaven: *Knock, and it shall be opened unto you* (Mt 7:7).

1.4. *The Holy Spirit descended in a bodily shape* (form) *like a dove upon him.* When he began to preach, *the Spirit of the Lord was upon him* (4:8). Now this presence of the Spirit was expressed here by physical evidence to encourage him in his work and to satisfy John the Baptist, because John had been told earlier that by this sign he would be shown who was the Christ (Jn 1:32–34).

1.5. There came *a voice from heaven,* from the *excellent glory,* as it is expressed in 2Pe 1:17: *Thou art my beloved Son.* Here and in Mark it is expressed as spoken to Christ; in Matthew it is expressed as spoken of him: *This is my beloved Son.* It all comes to the same thing. It was foretold about the Messiah, *I will be his Father, and he shall be my Son* (2Sa 7:14). It was also foretold that he would be God's *elect, in whom his soul delighted* (Isa 42:1), and so it was declared here, *Thou art my beloved Son, in whom I am well pleased.*

2. A long account of Christ's genealogy, which was related more briefly by St. Matthew. Here is:

2.1. His age: *He now began to be about thirty years of age.* At this age the priests came into the full responsibility of their office (Nu 4:3).

2.2. His genealogy (vv. 23–38). Matthew gave us something of this but went no further back than Abraham; Luke takes it as far back as Adam. Matthew intended to show that Christ was the son of Abraham, in whom all the families of the earth are blessed (Ge 12:3), and that he was heir to the throne of David, and so he began with Abraham and brought the genealogy down to Jacob, who was the father of Joseph, who was therefore a male heir of the house of David. Luke, however, wanting to show that Christ was the Seed of the woman, who would break the Serpent's head (Ge 3:15), traces his genealogy as far back as Adam, and begins it with Eli, or Heli, who was the father not of Joseph but of the Virgin Mary. Matthew draws the genealogy from Solomon, but since Solomon's

natural line ended in Jechonias (Jeconiah or Jehoiachin), the legal right was transferred to Salathiel (Shealtiel), who was of the house of Nathan, another son of David, and Luke here follows that line, thus leaving out all the kings of Judah. It is good for us that our salvation does not depend on our being able to solve all these difficulties. It is further worthy of observation that when those records of the Jewish genealogies had continued for thirty or forty years after these extracts from them, they were all lost and destroyed with the Jewish state and nation, because now there was no longer any need for them. The genealogy concludes with this: *who was the son of Adam, the son of God.* He was both the *Son of Adam* and the *Son of God,* so that he could be a proper Mediator between God and the sons of Adam and make the sons of Adam, through him, the *sons of God.*

CHAPTER 4

In this chapter we have: 1. Christ's further preparation for public ministry by being tempted in the desert (vv. 1–13). 2. His entrance on his public ministry in Galilee (vv. 14–15), particularly: 2.1. At Nazareth (vv. 16–30). Of this part of his ministry we had no account in Matthew. 2.2. At Capernaum, where, having amazed the people by his preaching (vv. 31–32), he drove out a demon from a man who was possessed (vv. 33–37), healed Peter's mother-in-law of a fever (vv. 38–39), and restored many others who were sick and possessed (vv. 40–41), and then went and did the same in other towns in Galilee (vv. 42–44).

Verses 1–13

In this record of Christ's temptation, notice:

1. How he was prepared and fitted for it.

1.1. He was *full of the Holy Spirit,* who had *descended* on him *like a dove* (3:22). Those who are *full of the Holy Spirit* are well armed against the strongest temptations.

1.2. He had just returned from the Jordan River, where he had been baptized and been acknowledged by a voice from heaven to be the beloved Son of God. When we have had the most assured fellowship with God and the clearest revelations of his favor to us, we may expect Satan to attack us—the richest ship is the prize for pirates—and that God will allow him to do so, so that the power of his grace may be revealed and exalted.

1.3. He was led by the Spirit into the desert. His being led into the desert gave some advantage to the tempter, because there he had Christ alone. When we are alone, we are in an unfortunate situation! If he had relied on his own strength, he might have given Satan the advantage; when we know our own weakness, we must not give him such an advantage. Yet Christ gained some benefits for himself during his forty days' fast in the desert. We may imagine that he was wholly taken up in proper meditation, that he spent all his time in direct and intimate fellowship with his Father, as Moses did on the mountain. This prepared and strengthened him for Satan's attacks.

1.4. He continued to fast (v. 2): *In those days he did eat nothing.* Just as by withdrawing into the desert he showed himself completely indifferent to the world, so by his fasting he showed himself completely indifferent to his physical needs. Satan cannot easily take hold of those who do not cling onto, and are dead to, the world and the flesh.

2. How he was attacked by one temptation after another and how he defeated the intention of the tempter in every attack. *During the forty days,* he was *tempted of the devil* (v. 2). However, at the end of the forty days, when the

Devil realized Christ was hungry, he, as it were, grappled with Christ (v. 2).

2.1. He tempted him to distrust his Father's care of him and fend for himself (v. 3): *If thou be the Son of God, command this stone to be made bread.*

2.1.1. "I advise you to do it, because if God really is your Father, he has forgotten you." If we begin to think we can live solely according to our own thoughts, without depending on divine Providence, we must look on it as a temptation of Satan and reject it accordingly; it is Satan's idea to think we can live independently from God.

2.1.2. "I challenge you to do it, if you can; if you do not do it, I will say you are not the Son of God." Christ did not give in to the temptation, because:

2.1.2.1. He would not do what Satan told him to do. We must not do anything that looks like giving a foothold to the Devil. Miracles were performed to confirm faith, and the Devil had no faith to be confirmed.

2.1.2.2. He performed miracles to confirm his teaching, and so he would not begin to work miracles until he began to preach.

2.1.2.3. He would not perform miracles for himself and his own provision. He would rather turn water into wine to help his friends in their believing and in their wedding than turn stones into bread to supply his own necessities.

2.1.2.4. He would reserve the proof of his being the Son of God for later.

2.1.2.5. He would not do anything that looked like distrust of his Father. He would, like the other children of God, lead a life of dependence on God's providence and promises. He responded with an answer from Scripture (v. 4): *It is written.* This is the first word recorded as spoken by Christ after his inauguration into his office as prophet, and it is a quotation from the Old Testament. The word of God is our *sword* (Eph 6:17), and faith in that word is our shield; we should therefore be *mighty in the scriptures* (Ac 18:24). The text of Scripture he used was quoted from Dt 8:3: "*Man shall not live by* bread alone. I need not turn the stone into bread; people can live on every word of God, by whatever God appoints for them to live on." God has many ways of providing for his people without the ordinary means of subsistence, and so he is not to be distrusted at any time; he may be depended on at all times when we are walking in the way of duty. She who said that she had made many a meal's food from the promises when she lacked bread was an active believer.

2.2. He tempted him to accept the kingdom from him, which Christ expected to receive from God and to pay him homage for (vv. 5–7). This Evangelist puts this temptation second, though Matthew put it last and though it seems it really was the last. Notice:

2.2.1. How Satan arranged this temptation.

2.2.1.1. He gave him a view of *all the kingdoms of the world in a moment of time.* He *took him up* for this purpose *into a high mountain.* This view must have been a fantasy presented by the Devil, because he showed it *in a moment of time,* whereas, ordinarily, if a person is to view a whole country, it must be done successively, one part at a time. This is how the Devil thought he could deceive our Savior with a fallacy and, by making him believe that he could *show him all the kingdoms of* the world, would draw him into the thought that he, the Devil, could give him all those kingdoms.

2.2.1.2. He boldly alleged that these kingdoms were *all delivered* (given) *to him,* that he had authority to dispose of them and all their splendor and to give them to *whomsoever he would* (v. 6). However, the offer was encumbered by the condition that Christ must *fall down and worship him.*

2.2.1.3. He demanded homage and adoration of him: *If thou wilt worship me, all shall be thine* (v. 7). He wanted Christ himself to worship him, and he also wanted to contract with Christ that when he had gained possession of the kingdoms of this world, he would make no changes of religion in them. Then he could take all the authority and splendor of the kingdoms if he pleased. As to the wealth and splendor of this earth, let anyone who wants it take it; Satan has everything he wants if only he can have people's hearts and adoration.

2.2.2. How our Lord Jesus triumphed over this temptation. He rejected it decisively and with abhorrence (v. 8): *Get thee behind me, Satan.* Such a temptation was not to be reasoned with, but refused immediately, and so it was immediately knocked on the head with the words, "*It is written, Thou shalt worship the Lord thy God,* and not only that, but you must worship *only him,* and *no other.*" People must be *turned from the power of Satan unto God* (Ac 26:18), from the worship of devils to the worship of the only living and true God. This was the great divine law that Christ would reestablish among people and make them obey, *that God only is to be served and worshiped.*

2.3. He tempted him to a presumptuous confidence in his Father's protection. Notice:

2.3.1. What the Devil intended in this temptation: *If thou be the Son of God, cast thyself down* (v. 9). He wanted Christ to seek a new proof that he was the Son of God, as if what his Father had already given him by the voice from heaven and the descent of the Spirit on him were not enough. He wanted him to seek a new way of declaring and proclaiming this to the world. If he now declared from *the pinnacle of the temple* that he was the Son of God, among all the great people who were present at the temple service, and then, as proof of it, threw himself down and was unhurt, he would immediately be received by everyone as a messenger sent from heaven. Or the fall might be to his death, and then the Devil would have finally gotten him out of the way.

2.3.2. How he backed up and strengthened this temptation. He suggested, *It is written* (v. 10). Christ had quoted Scripture against the Devil, and the Devil thought he would get even with him and show that he could quote Scripture as well as Christ. *He shall give his angels charge over thee,* and *in their hands they shall bear thee up* (Ps 91:11). It is true that God has promised the protection of angels, to encourage us to trust him, not to test him: just as far as the promise of God's presence is with us, so far does the promise of the angels' ministry go, but no further.

2.3.3. How he was defeated and thwarted in the temptation (v. 12). Christ quoted Dt 6:16, where it is said, *Thou shalt not tempt the Lord thy God* by asking for a sign to prove divine revelation when he has already given what is sufficient.

3. What was the outcome of this battle (v. 13). Our victorious Redeemer stood his ground and came off as conqueror not only for himself but also for us.

3.1. The Devil emptied his quiver: *He ended all the temptation.* Did Christ suffer, being tempted (Heb 2:18), until all the temptation had finished? Must not we expect to pass through tests also, to go through the hour of temptation assigned for us?

3.2. He then left the battlefield: *He departed from him.* He saw that it was useless to attack him; Christ had no blind spot, no weak or unguarded part in his defense. If we resist the Devil, he will flee from us (Jas 4:7).

3.3. He nevertheless held on to his hatred against him; he left only *for a season*, until the time when he was again to be let loose on him, not as a tempter but as a persecutor, to make him suffer. He left now until the time Christ called the *power of darkness* (22:53); then the prince of this world would again come (Jn 14:30).

Verses 14–30

Having defended himself against the Devil's attacks, Christ now went on the offensive with his preaching and miracles, attacks that the Devil could neither resist nor repel. Notice:

1. What is said here in general about his preaching and the reception it met with *in Galilee*. He went there *in the power of the Spirit*. He was not to wait for a human call, because he had light and life in himself (Jn 1:4). He *taught* there *in their synagogues*, their places of public worship, where they met not for ceremonial services, as in the temple, but for devotion. These meetings came to be more frequent after the exile, when the ceremonial worship was coming to an end. He did this in such a way that he gained a great reputation. *A fame of* (news about) *him went through all that region* (v. 14), and it was good fame, because he *was glorified of all* (v. 15). Now, at first, he met with no contempt or contradiction; all glorified him, and there were none as yet who hurled insults at him.

2. What is said here about his preaching at Nazareth, the town where he was brought up. Here we are told how he preached there and how he was persecuted.

2.1. How he preached there. Notice:

2.1.1. The opportunity he had for it: *He came to Nazareth* when he had gained a reputation in other places. He took the opportunity to preach there:

2.1.1.1. In the *synagogue*, the proper place. It had been *his custom* to attend there when he was a private individual (v. 16), but now that he had entered his public ministry, he preached there.

2.1.1.2. On the Sabbath, the proper time, which the godly Jews spent not in a mere ceremonial rest from worldly labor but in the duties of God's worship.

2.1.2. The call he had to it. He *stood up to read*. In their synagogues they had seven readers every Sabbath, the first a priest, the second a Levite, and the other five Israelites from that synagogue. We often find Christ preaching in other synagogues, but never reading except in this synagogue at Nazareth, of which he had been a member for many years. The *book of the prophet Esaias* (Isaiah) was *delivered to him*. Because the second lesson for that day came from the prophecy of Isaiah, they gave him that scroll to read.

2.1.3. The text he preached on. He *stood up to read*. When the book was *delivered to him*:

2.1.3.1. He *opened* it. The books of the Old Testament were, in a way, shut up until Christ opened them (Isa 29:11).

2.1.3.2. He *found the place* that was appointed to be read that day. Now his text was taken from Isa 61:1–2, which is here quoted in detail (vv. 18–19). There was a providence in the reading of that Scripture on that day, a Scripture that speaks so very clearly about the Messiah. This text gives a full account of Christ's undertaking and of the work he came into the world to do. Notice:

2.1.3.2.1. How he was qualified for the work: *The Spirit of the Lord is upon me*. All the gifts and graces of the Spirit were conferred on him, not in a limited way, as on other prophets, but without limit (Jn 3:34).

2.1.3.2.2. How he was commissioned: *Because he has anointed me and sent me*. His being anointed shows

both his being fitted for the undertaking and his calling to it.

2.1.3.2.3. What his work was. He was qualified and commissioned:

2.1.3.2.3.1. To be a great prophet. He was *anointed to preach*; that is mentioned here three times. Notice:

2.1.3.2.3.1.1. To whom he was to preach: *to the poor*, to those who were poor in the world, to those who were poor in spirit (Mt 5:3), to the lowly and humble, and to those who were truly sorrowful for sin.

2.1.3.2.3.1.2. What he was to preach. In general, he must *preach the Gospel*. He was sent to evangelize them, not only to preach to them but also to make that preaching effective, to bring it not only to their ears but also to their hearts. He was to preach three things:

2.1.3.2.3.1.2.1. *Deliverance to the captives*. The Gospel is a declaration of liberty, like the one given to Israel in Egypt and in Babylon. It is a rescue from the worst form of slavery, which all those who are willing to make Christ their Head will enjoy the benefits of.

2.1.3.2.3.1.2.2. *Recovering of sight to the blind*. He came not only through the word of his Gospel to bring *light* to those who sat *in darkness* (Mt 4:16), but also by the power of his grace to give sight to those who were blind. Christ came to tell us that he has a lotion for our eyes (Rev 3:18), which we may have if we ask for it, to tell us that if our prayer is, *Lord, that our eyes may be opened* (Mt 20:33), his answer will be, *Receive your sight* (Lk 18:42).

2.1.3.2.3.1.2.3. *The acceptable year of the Lord* (v. 19). He came to tell the world that the God whom they had offended was willing to be reconciled to them and to accept them on new terms. The phrase alludes to the *year of release* (Dt 15:9), or that of *jubilee* (Lev 25:10), which was an acceptable year. It was an acceptable time because it was a day of salvation.

2.1.3.2.3.2. To be a great Physician, because he was sent to *heal the broken-hearted*: to give peace to those who were troubled and humbled on account of sins and to give rest to those who were weary and under the burden of guilt and corruption (Mt 11:28).

2.1.3.2.3.3. To be a great Redeemer. He not only declares freedom to the prisoners but also sets free those who are bruised. The prophets could only *proclaim liberty*, but Christ, as One with authority (Mk 1:22), as One who had *power on earth to forgive sins* (5:24), came to *set at liberty*, and so that was what he said of himself here.

2.1.4. His application of this text to himself (v. 21): when he had read it, he *rolled up the book* (scroll), gave it back *to the minister*, or attendant, and *sat down*, according to the custom of the Jewish teachers. Now he *began* his address with, *This day is this scripture fulfilled in your ears*. It now began to be fulfilled in Christ's admission to his public ministry: now, in the report they heard of his preaching and miracles in other places, now, in his preaching to them in their own synagogue. He spoke many other gracious words, which these were only the beginning of, because Christ often preached long sermons, which we have only a short account of. This was enough to introduce a great deal: *This day is this scripture fulfilled*. The works of God are the fulfillment not only of his hidden word but also of his revealed word, and it will help us understand both the Scriptures and the providences of God to compare them with each other.

2.1.5. The attention and amazement of the listeners.

2.1.5.1. Their attention (v. 20): *The eyes of all them that were in the synagogue were fastened on him*. It is good, in hearing the word, to keep our eyes fixed on the minister through whom God is speaking to us, because just as the eye affects the heart, so, usually, the heart follows the eye, wandering when the eye wanders and remaining fixed when the eye is fixed.

2.1.5.2. Their amazement (v. 22): *They all bore him witness* and *wondered at the gracious words that proceeded out of his mouth*, but as can be seen from what follows, they did not believe in him. What they were amazed at was the *gracious words which proceedeth out of his mouth*. Christ's words are words of grace and are to be *wondered at*. Christ's name was Wonderful (Isa 9:6), and in nothing was he more wonderful than in his grace, in the words of his grace and in the power that accompanied those words. Their amazement increased when they considered his origin: *They said, Is not this Joseph's son?* Some were perhaps led by this suggestion to wonder all the more at his *gracious words*, concluding that he must have been *taught of* (by) *God*. Others who had this thought may have corrected their wonder at his gracious words, concluding that there could be nothing truly amazing in them, however amazing they seemed, because he was the *Son of Joseph*.

2.1.6. Christ's anticipating an objection that he knew to be in the minds of many of his hearers. Notice:

2.1.6.1. What the objection was (v. 23): *"You will surely say to me, Physician, heal thyself. You will* expect that I will perform miracles among you, as I have done in other places." Most of Christ's miracles were healings; "now why should not the sick in your own town be healed as well as those in other towns?" His miracles were intended to heal people of their unbelief; "now why should not the disease of unbelief be healed in those of your own town as well as in those of others? *Whatsoever we have heard done in Capernaum, do here also in thine own country."* They were pleased with *Christ's gracious words* only because they hoped they were the introduction to some wondrous works of his. They thought their own town as worthy to be the stage of miracles as any other. Moreover, why should not his neighbors and acquaintances have the benefit of his preaching and miracles, rather than any other?

2.1.6.2. How he answered this objection.

2.1.6.2.1. By a plain and positive reason why he would not make Nazareth his headquarters (v. 24), namely, that in general, *no prophet is accepted in his own country*. Experience seals this. "Familiarity breeds contempt," and we tend to have low thoughts about people we have known for a long time. What is imported and expensive is thought more valuable than what is home-grown, even if the latter is really better. Christ refused to work miracles or do anything extraordinary at Nazareth because of the deep-rooted prejudices against him there.

2.1.6.2.2. By relevant examples of two of the most famous prophets of the Old Testament.

2.1.6.2.2.1. Elijah supported a *widow of Sarepta* (Zarephath), *a city of Sidon*, one who was a stranger to the citizenship of Israel (Eph 2:12), when there was *a famine in the land* (vv. 25–26; 1Ki 17:9). Just as God wanted to show himself to be a *Father of the fatherless and a Judge of the widows* (Ps 68:5), so he wanted also to show that he was rich in mercy to all (Eph 2:4), even to the Gentiles.

2.1.6.2.2.2. Elisha cleansed Naaman the Aramean of his leprosy, even though he was an Aramean and therefore not only a foreigner but an enemy of Israel (v. 27). *Many lepers were in Israel in the days of Eliseus* (Elisha). However, we do not find that Elisha cleansed them, but only this Aramean, because no one besides him had faith to turn to the prophet for healing. Christ himself often met with greater faith among Gentiles than in Israel (7:9; Mt 15:21–28). Yet

Christ performed his miracles among Israelites—though not among his own townsmen—whereas these great prophets performed theirs among Gentiles.

2.2. How he was persecuted at Nazareth.

2.2.1. What offended them was his taking notice of the favor that God showed to the Gentiles through Elijah and Elisha: *When they heard these things, they were filled with wrath* (v. 28). A great change had come about since v. 22, when they *wondered at the gracious words that proceeded out of his mouth*; so fickle and uncertain are the opinions and attitudes of the crowd. If they had had faith in those gracious words of Christ that they were amazed at, they would have been woken up by his later words. But those earlier words only pleased the ear and went no further, and so these grated on the ear. But what exasperated them especially was that he showed that God had some kindness in store for the Gentiles. Their devout ancestors pleased themselves with the hope of adding the Gentiles to the church, but this degenerate race hated to think that any others would be taken in.

2.2.2. They were offended so much that they made an attempt on his life. They *rose up* in turmoil against him. They *thrust* (drove) *him out of the city*. They drove from them both the Savior and the salvation. They *led him to the brow of the hill* to *throw him down headlong*. Although they had heard such good reports of him and had only just now themselves *admired his gracious words*, they still rushed him away in a popular fury, or rather frenzy, to try to kill him in a most barbaric manner.

2.2.3. He escaped, however, because his hour had not yet come: he *passed through the midst of them*, unhurt. They drove him away from them, and he *went his way*. He would have gathered Nazareth, but they *would not*, and so their house was *left to them desolate* (13:34–35). But now, though they *received him not* (Jn 1:11), there were those who did.

Verses 31–44

When Christ was expelled from Nazareth, he came to Capernaum, another town of Galilee. We have here:

1. His preaching: *He taught them on the sabbath days* (v. 31). Christ's preaching affected the people very much (v. 32); they were *astonished at his doctrine*, for there was weight in every word he said, and wonderful revelations were made to them by it. *His word was with power*; it had a commanding force in it, and an active power accompanied it to human consciences.

2. His miracles.

2.1. Two miracles are mentioned particularly, showing Christ to be:

2.1.1. A controller and conqueror of Satan by his power to drive him out of the bodies of those he had taken possession of.

2.1.1.1. The Devil is an *unclean* (evil) *spirit*; his nature is directly opposite that of the pure and holy God.

2.1.1.2. This evil spirit works in people.

2.1.1.3. It is possible for those who are very much under the power and activity of Satan to be found *in the synagogue*.

2.1.1.4. Even the demons *know and believe* that *Jesus Christ is the Holy One of God* (v. 34).

2.1.1.5. They *believe and tremble* (Jas 2:19). This evil spirit *cried out with a loud voice*, apprehensive that Christ had now come to destroy him.

2.1.1.6. The demons have nothing to do with Jesus Christ, nor do they want to have anything to do with him.

2.1.1.7. Christ restrained the demon: *He rebuked him*, saying, *Hold thy peace*; this word he spoke *with power*; it may be translated, "Be muzzled." Christ did not only tell him to be silent; he also stopped his mouth.

2.1.1.8. In the breaking of Satan's power, the conquered enemy showed his hatred, and Christ, the conqueror, showed his overruling grace. The demon showed what he would have done. He *threw the man in the midst*, as if he would have dashed him to pieces. Christ showed what power he had over him, by forcing him not only to leave him but to leave him without even hurting him. Those whom Satan cannot destroy, he will harm as much as he can, but they may take encouragement in knowing that he can harm them no further than Christ permits; in fact, he will not do them any real harm. He *came out* and *hurt him not*.

2.1.1.9. Christ's power over demons was universally acknowledged and acclaimed (v. 36). They were *all amazed, saying, What a word is this!* Those who claimed to drive out demons did it with many charms and spells; Christ commanded them *with authority and power*.

2.1.1.10. This, as much as anything, gained Christ a reputation and spread his fame. This example of his power was exalted and was looked on as greatly exalting him (v. 37). On account of this, *the fame of him went out*, more than ever, *into every place of the country round about*. When our Lord Jesus set out at first in his public ministry, he was greatly talked about, more than later, when people's admiration wore off with the novelty of the thing.

2.1.2. *A healer of diseases*. In conquering Satan, he struck at the root of human misery, which was Satan's enmity; in healing diseases, he struck at one of the most spreading branches of that misery, one of the most common adversities of human life, and that is physical diseases. Our Lord Jesus came to take away the sting of these. Of all physical diseases, none are more common or fatal to grown people than fevers. Now here we have Christ's healing a fever by speaking a word; the place was in Simon's house, and his patient was Simon's mother-in-law (vv. 38–39). Notice:

2.1.2.1. Christ is a guest who will pay well for his reception; those who welcome him into their hearts and houses will not lose by him; he comes with healing.

2.1.2.2. Even families that Christ visits may experience sickness; houses that are blessed with his special favors are liable to the same common adversities of this life. Simon's mother-in-law was *ill with a fever*.

2.1.2.3. Even good people may sometimes be exercised with the sharpest afflictions; she was *taken with a great fever*, acute, high, and threatening. Nor is any age exempt from illness.

2.1.2.4. When our relatives are sick, we should turn to Christ in faith and prayer for them: *They besought him for* (they asked Jesus to help) *her*.

2.1.2.5. Christ has a tender concern for his people when they are ill and in distress: *He stood over her*, as one concerned for her.

2.1.2.6. Christ had and still has sovereign power over physical diseases: *He rebuked the fever*, and *it left her*.

2.1.2.7. Christ proved his healings to be miraculous by doing them in a moment: *Immediately she arose*.

2.1.2.8. Where Christ gives a new life, he intends and expects that it will be a truly new life, given more than ever in his service. If illnesses are rebuked, and we get up from our sickbed, we must set ourselves to minister to Jesus Christ.

2.1.2.9. Those who minister to Christ must be ready to minister for his sake to all who are his: *She ministered to them*, not only to the One who had healed her but also to those who had asked him to help her.

2.2. A general account is given of the many other miracles that Christ performed.

2.2.1. He *cured many that were diseased*, and it was *when the sun was setting* (v. 40), on the evening of that Sabbath that he had spent in the synagogue. It is good to do much spiritual work on that day, engaging in some good work or other even till sunset, as those who call the Sabbath and its work *a delight* (Isa 58:13). He healed *all that were sick of divers* (various kinds of) *diseases*, for he had a remedy for every illness. The sign he used in healing was *laying his hands* on the sick. He healed by his own power.

2.2.2. He drove out the demon from many who were possessed (v. 41). They said, *Thou art Christ the Son of God*. Christ *rebuked them* and did not *suffer* (allow) *them to say that they knew him to be the Christ*.

2.3. Here is his move from Capernaum (vv. 42–43).

2.3.1. He withdrew for a while to a place of *solitude*. He allowed himself only a little while for sleep. *When it was day*, he went *into a desert place*, because sometimes he wanted to be *alone with God*, as those who are most engaged in public work should be and should seek to be. They will find themselves never less alone than when alone with God.

2.3.2. He returned to the places where the people were and to the work he had to do there. Although a desert may be a convenient retreat, it is not a convenient residence, because we were not sent into this world to live for ourselves.

2.3.2.1. He was earnestly asked to stay at Capernaum. The people were very fond of him. They sought him, and although it was in a solitary place, they came to him. A desert is no desert if we are with Christ there. They detained him so that he would not leave him. It should not discourage the ministers of Christ that some reject them, because they will meet with others who will welcome them and their message.

2.3.2.2. He chose to spread the light of his Gospel to many places rather than to establish it in only one. Although he was welcome at Capernaum, he was sent to preach the Gospel to other towns too. Those who enjoy the benefit of the Gospel must be willing for others to share in that benefit and must not seek to monopolize it. Although Christ did not preach in vain in the synagogue at Capernaum, he still did not want to be limited to that, but preached in the synagogues of Galilee (v. 44). It is good for us that our Lord Jesus has not limited himself to any one place or people, but has promised that wherever two or three are gathered in his name, he will be there among them (Mt 18:20).

CHAPTER 5

In this chapter we have: 1. Christ's preaching to the people from Peter's boat (vv. 1–3). 2. The miraculous catch of fish with which he rewarded Peter (vv. 4–11). 3. His cleansing the leper (vv. 12–15). 4. A short account of his private devotion and public ministry (vv. 16–17). 5. His healing the paralyzed man (vv. 18–26). 6. His calling Levi the tax collector, and his close association with tax collectors on that occasion (vv. 27–32). 7. His justifying his disciples in not fasting as frequently as the disciples of John and the Pharisees (vv. 33–39).

Verses 1–11

These events are the same that are more briefly related by Matthew and Mark in their account of Christ's calling Peter and Andrew to be *fishers of men* (Mt 4:18 and

Mk 1:16). Matthew and Mark did not relate this miraculous catch of fish, having in mind only the calling of his disciples, but Luke includes it as one of the many signs Jesus did that *had not been written* in the previous books. Notice:

1. What vast crowds listened to Christ's preaching: *The people pressed upon* (crowded around) *him to hear the word of God* (v. 1). The people "flocked around him"; they showed respect to his preaching, though in *pressing upon him* they were somewhat rude to his person, which was very excusable. Some would have considered it a discredit to him to be praised so highly by the ordinary people when none *of the rulers or of the Pharisees believed in him* (Jn 7:48), but to Christ, the souls of ordinary people were as precious as the souls of the grand people, and it is his aim to bring not so much the mighty (1Co 1:26) as *many sons* to God (Heb 2:10). Notice how much the people relished good preaching: they crowded around him to *hear the word of God*; they realized it was the word of God, and so they sought to hear it.

2. What poor facilities Christ had for preaching: *He stood by the lake of Gennesareth* (v. 1), on a level with the crowd, so that they could neither see him nor hear him; he was lost among them and in danger of being crowded onto the water. What must he do? *There were two ships*, or fishing boats, on the shore, one belonging to Simon and Andrew, the other to Zebedee and *his sons* (v. 2). At first, Christ saw Peter and Andrew fishing at some distance—as Matthew tells us (Mt 4:18)—but he waited until they reached land and the *fishermen*, that is, the servants, had *gone out of them*. Christ got into Simon's boat, asked him if he would lend it to him as a pulpit, and *prayed* (asked) *him* that he would *thrust* (put) *out a little from the land*. This would make it harder for him to be heard, but Christ wanted it done in this way so that he could be seen better, and it is his being *lifted up* that *draws men to him*. This shows that Christ had a strong voice—indeed, strong enough to make even the dead hear it. He *sat down* there and *taught the people* the good knowledge of the Lord (2Ch 30:22).

3. What a special friendship then developed between Christ and these fishermen. They had had some dealings with him before, which began at John's baptism (Jn 1:40–41); they were with him at *Cana of Galilee* (Jn 2:2) and in Judea (Jn 4:3); but as yet they had not been called to be with him constantly. It was now that they were called into a more intimate fellowship with Christ.

3.1. When Christ had finished preaching, he told Peter to apply himself to the work of his calling again: *Launch out into the deep, and let down your nets* (v. 4). It was not the Sabbath, and so as soon as the sermon was over, he set them to work. Notice how cheerfully we may go about the duties of our ordinary calling when we have been on the mount with God. It is our wisdom and duty to manage our religious exercises so that they may be friends with our worldly business, and to manage our worldly business so that it may not be an enemy of our religious exercises.

3.2. After Peter had attended to Christ in his preaching, Christ would accompany him in his fishing. He stayed with Christ on the shore, and now Christ would *launch out* with him *into the deep*.

3.3. Christ told Peter and his boat's crew to *cast their nets into the sea*, which they did, in obedience to him, even though they had been hard at the work all night and had *caught nothing* (vv. 4–5). We may notice here:

3.3.1. How sad their business had been: *Master, we have toiled all the night and have taken nothing*. One would have thought that this would excuse them from

listening to the sermon, but it was more refreshing and reviving to them than the softest slumbers. But they mentioned their disappointment to Christ when he told them to go fishing again. We can learn from this:

3.3.1.1. Some callings are much more wearying than others, and more dangerous, but Providence has so ordered things for the common good that there is no useful calling so discouraging that someone or other does not have an inclination for it. Those who follow their business and gain an abundance from it with a great deal of ease should think with compassion about those who cannot follow their line of business except with great tiredness and can barely make a living by it.

3.3.1.2. If the calling is very laborious, it is still good to see people diligent in it. Christ singled out these hardworking fishermen as his favorites.

3.3.1.3. Even those who are most diligent in their business often meet with disappointments; those who *toiled all night* still *caught nothing*. We must do our duty, and then leave the outcome with God.

3.3.1.4. When we are tired of our worldly business and frustrated in our worldly affairs, we are welcome to come to Christ and lay out our situation before him.

3.3.2. How ready their obedience was to the command of Christ: *Nevertheless, at thy word, I will let down the net*.

3.3.2.1. Even though they had *toiled all night*, still, if Christ told them, they would renew their toil. For every fresh service they would receive a fresh supply of *grace sufficient* (2Co 12:9).

3.3.2.2. Even though they had caught nothing, if Christ told them to *let down for a draught* (catch), they would hope to catch something. We must not abruptly quit the callings to which we are called (Eph 4:4) because we do not have the success in them that we promised ourselves. Ministers of the Gospel must continue to let down that net even if they have toiled long and caught nothing; to continue tirelessly in our labors even when we do not see success in them is commendable (1Pe 2:19).

3.3.2.3. They looked to the word of Christ in this: *At thy word, I will let down the net*. We are likely to be successful when we follow the guidance of Christ's word.

3.4. Their catch of fish was so far beyond what had ever been known that it amounted to a miracle (v. 6): they *enclosed a great multitude of fishes*, so that *their net broke*. It was such a great catch that they did not have enough hands to draw it in, and they had to signal to their partners to come and help them (v. 7). However, the greatest sign of the great size of the catch was that they filled both of the boats with fish, so much that they overloaded them and the boats *began to sink*. By this vast catch of fish:

3.4.1. Christ intended to show his power over the seas as well as the dry land, over its wealth as well as over its waves.

3.4.2. He intended to confirm the doctrine he had just now preached from Peter's boat. We may presume that the people on the shore stayed around there to see what he would do next, and because this miracle immediately followed his preaching, it would confirm their faith that he was at least *a teacher come from God* (Jn 3:2).

3.4.3. He intended to repay Peter for the loan of his boat. Christ's rewards for services done for his name are abundant; indeed, they are superabundant.

3.4.4. He intended to give those who were to be his ambassadors to the world an example of the success of their mission would have, to show them that although they might for a time toil and catch nothing in one particular place, they would be instrumental in bringing many to Christ and would catch many in the Gospel net.

3.5. The impression this made on Peter was remarkable.

3.5.1. Everyone concerned was astonished, and they were all the more astonished because they were concerned. All the boat's crew were *astonished at the draught* (catch) *of fishes which they had taken* (v. 9); they were all surprised. *So were also James and John, who were partners with Simon* (v. 10). They were more affected by it because they understood it better than others did. Those who were familiar with this lake had never seen such a catch of fish taken out of it, and so they could not be tempted to detract from it by suggesting that it was what might as well have happened at any time. It greatly supports the evidence for Christ's miracles that those who were most familiar with them were the ones who most admired them. They were also more affected by it because they had the most interest in it and received the most benefit from it. Peter and his joint owners gained from this great catch of fish, and so their joy helped their faith. When Christ's miracles are works of grace especially for us, they especially command our faith in his teaching.

3.5.2. Peter was so amazed that he *fell down at Jesus' knees*, right where he was, in the stern of his boat, and said, *Depart from me, for I am a sinful man, O Lord* (v. 8). He thought himself unworthy of the favor of Christ's presence in his boat. It was the language of Peter's humility and self-denial and had not the least tinge of the talk of the demons who said, *What have we to do with thee, Jesus, thou Son of God?* (4:34).

3.5.2.1. His acknowledgment was very just, and a good one for us all to make: *I am a sinful man, O Lord.* Even the best people are sinful, and they should be ready to confess it on all occasions, and especially to confess it to Jesus Christ.

3.5.2.2. His conclusion from this was what might have been just, even though it really was not so. If I am a sinful person, as indeed I am, I should say, "Come to me, O Lord, or let me come to you, or I am ruined forever." Yet Peter may well be excused if, out of a sense of his own sinfulness and corruption, he cried out suddenly, *Depart from me.* Those whom Christ intends to admit to his most intimate friendship he first makes aware that they deserve to be set farthest away from him. We must all acknowledge that we are sinners and that Jesus Christ could therefore justly *depart from us*, but we must therefore fall down at his knees to pray that he would not depart.

3.6. Christ took this as an opportunity to tell Peter (v. 10), and soon afterward James and John (Mt 4:21), his purpose in making them his apostles. He *said unto Simon*, "You will both see and do greater things than these. *Fear not; henceforth thou shalt catch men.* That will be a more amazing miracle, and infinitely more advantageous than this."

3.7. The fishermen bade farewell to their calling in order to be with Christ constantly (v. 11): *When they had brought their ships to land*, they *forsook all and followed him.* It is significant that they *left all to follow Christ* when their calling prospered in their hands more than it ever had. When riches increase and we are therefore most tempted to set our hearts on them, to leave them for the service of Christ deserves commendation (1Pe 2:19).

Verses 12–16

Here is:

1. The cleansing of a leper (vv. 12–14). We had this account in both Matthew and Mark. Here it is said to have been *in a certain city* (v. 12); it was in Capernaum. This man is said to be *full of leprosy* (The Greek word was used for various diseases affecting the skin—not necessarily leprosy [Ed.]); he had a severe case. Let us learn from this:

1.1. What we must do when we recognize our spiritual leprosy.

1.1.1. We must seek Jesus.

1.1.2. We must humble ourselves in his presence as this leper did, who, seeing Jesus, *fell on his face.* We must be ashamed of our defilement and blush to lift up our faces in the presence of the holy Jesus.

1.1.3. We must fervently seek to be cleansed.

1.1.4. We must firmly believe in Christ's ability and sufficiency to cleanse us: "Lord, *thou canst make me clean*, even though I am *full of leprosy.*" We must have no doubts about the merit and grace of Christ.

1.1.5. We must be bold in prayer: *He fell on his face and besought him*; those who want to be cleansed must consider it a favor worth wrestling for.

1.1.6. We must turn to the goodwill of Christ: *Lord, if thou wilt, thou canst.* This is not so much the language of his diffidence or his distrust of the goodwill of Christ as of his submitting to his will, which is a good will.

1.2. What we may expect from Christ if we turn to him in this way.

1.2.1. We will find him very eager to notice our situation (v. 13): *He put forth his hand and touched him.* His touching the leper showed his wonderful condescension, but it is much greater to us when he is himself *touched with the feeling of our infirmities* (Heb 4:15).

1.2.2. We will find him very compassionate and ready to relieve us; he said, "*I will.* Whoever comes to me to be healed, *I will in no wise cast him out* (Jn 6:37)."

1.2.3. We will find him all-sufficient, able to heal and cleanse us even though we are full of this loathsome leprosy. One word, one touch, from Christ did the work: *Immediately the leprosy departed from him.*

1.3. What he requires from those who are cleansed (v. 14).

1.3.1. We must be very humble (v. 14): *He charged him to tell no man.* He must not tell it for his own honor. The people Christ has healed and cleansed must know that he has done it, and they must know in a way that forever excludes boasting (Ro 3:27).

1.3.2. We must be very thankful: *Go, and offer for thy cleansing.* Christ did not require him to give him a fee, but to bring the sacrifice of praise to God (Heb 13:15).

1.3.3. We must keep close to our duty: *Go to the priest.* The man whom Christ had made whole was *found in the temple* by him (Jn 5:14). If we have been detained from public services of worship by any form of suffering, then when the affliction is removed, we should attend them more diligently and more faithfully than before.

2. Christ's public usefulness to people and his private fellowship with God (vv. 15–16).

2.1. Even though no one ever had so much delight in his retreats as Christ had, he was *much in a crowd*, to do good (v. 15). Although the leper should have kept complete silence, the thing could not be hidden, and *so much the more went there a fame abroad of him.* Honor is like a shadow, which flees from those who pursue it but follows those who decline it. The less people say in favor of themselves, the more good others will say about them. But Christ counted it a small honor to him that his *fame went abroad*; he counted it a much greater honor that in this way crowds were brought to benefit from him by his preaching and by his miracles: they came together to *hear* him, and they came *to be healed by him of their infirmities.*

2.2. Even though no one ever did so much good in public, he still found time to retreat for his devotions (v. 16): *He withdrew himself into the wilderness, and prayed.* We, too, would be wise to arrange our lives so that our public work and our *secret* work (Mt 6:6) may neither encroach on nor interfere with one another. Private prayer must be performed in private, and those who are very busy even with the most admirable business in this world must maintain their regular constant times for it.

Verses 17–26

Here is:

1. A general account of Christ's preaching and miracles (v. 17).

1.1. He was *teaching on a certain day*, not on the Sabbath, but on a weekday. Preaching and hearing the word of God—if done well—are good works on any day of the week. It was in a private house, because it is not improper to give and receive good instruction even in the place where we ordinarily chat with our friends.

1.2. There he taught and healed (as before, v. 15): *And the power of the Lord was to heal them.* It was mighty to heal them, to heal their souls, to give them a new life, a new nature. Or the clause may be meant, as it is generally taken, to refer to the healing of those who were diseased in body, who came to him for healing. Whenever there was a need, Christ did not have to seek his power; it was already *present to heal.*

1.3. Some great people were present: *There were Pharisees, and doctors of the law, sitting by;* they were not sitting *at his feet*, to learn from him, but *sitting by* as spectators, critics, and spies, to pick up something on which to base some rebuke or accusation. How many there are in the midst of our assemblies who do not sit under the word, but sit back to find fault with it! To them it is merely a tale that is told to them, not a message that is sent to them; they are willing to have us preach in their presence but not to have us preach to them. These Pharisees and teachers of the law *came out of every town of Galilee, and Judea, and Jerusalem*; they came from all parts of the nation. Christ continued with his work of preaching and healing, even though he saw these Pharisees *sitting by* and knew that they despised him and were watching for an opportunity to trap him.

2. A particular account of the healing of the man *sick of the palsy* (paralyzed man). The previous Evangelists related it in much the same way; let us therefore only notice in brief:

2.1. The doctrines that are taught us and confirmed to us by the story of this healing.

2.1.1. That sin is the fountain of all sickness and that the forgiveness of sin is the only foundation on which a recovery from sickness can probably be built. They presented the sick man to Christ, and he said, *"Man, thy sins are forgiven thee* (v. 20); that is the blessing you are most to prize and seek." The cords of our sin are the bonds of our affliction.

2.1.2. That Jesus Christ has power on earth to *forgive sins.* This was what he intended to prove (v. 24): *"That ye may know* and believe *that the Son of man hath power to forgive sins (he said to the sick of the palsy), Arise, and walk,"* and he was healed immediately. Christ claimed one of the rights of the King of Kings when he undertook to forgive sin, and it was justly expected that he would produce good proof of it. "Well," he said, "I will put this to the test: here is a man who is paralyzed, and it is for his

sin; if I do not heal his disease by speaking a word, then you may say that I am not entitled to claim the right to forgive sin. If I do, however, you must acknowledge that *I have power to forgive sins.*" This was how it was put to a fair test, and one word of Christ determined it. He only said, *Arise, take up thy couch*, and that chronic disease was healed instantaneously: *immediately he arose before them.* They all had to acknowledge that there could have been no deception or trickery in it.

2.1.3. That Jesus Christ is God. He proved that he is:

2.1.3.1. *By knowing the thoughts* of the teachers of the law and Pharisees (v. 22).

2.1.3.2. By doing what their thoughts acknowledged no one but God could do (v. 21): *Who can forgive sins*, they said, *but only God?* "I will prove," Christ said, "that I can forgive sins," and what follows then but that he is God?

2.2. The duties that are taught us and commended to us by this account.

2.2.1. When we turn to Christ, we must be bold and persistent. The friends of this sick man tried to work out how they could bring him to Christ (v. 18), and when they were frustrated in their attempts, unable to get in by the door because it was so crowded, they did not give up their cause, but took the tiles off the house and let the poor patient down through the roof into the presence of Jesus (v. 19). Here, Jesus Christ saw their faith (v. 20). When the centurion and the woman of Canaan were not concerned to bring the patients they interceded for into Christ's presence, but believed that he could heal them at a distance, he commended their faith. But although these men seemed to have a different idea of what was required for a healing, that the patient had to be brought into his presence, he did not censure them and condemn their weakness; he did not ask them, "Are you so unfaithful as to think I could not have healed him, even if he had been outdoors?" Rather, he made the best of matters as they were and even saw the men's faith in this. It is an encouragement to us that we serve a Master who is willing to make the best of us.

2.2.2. When we are ill, we should be more concerned to have our sins forgiven than to have our sickness removed.

2.2.3. God must have the praise for the mercies we have comfort from. The man departed to his own home, praising God (v. 25).

2.2.4. The miracles that Christ performed were amazing to those who saw them, and we should praise God for them (v. 26). They said, *We have seen strange things today*, and *they glorified God*, who had sent such a benefactor into their country, *and they were filled with fear*, with reverence for God.

Verses 27–35

All these verses except the last appeared before in Matthew and Mark; it is not the record of any miracle in nature performed by our Lord Jesus, but an account of some of the wonders of his grace.

1. It was a wonder of his grace that he would call a tax collector from the tax collector's booth to be his disciple and follower (v. 27). By this he exposed himself to opposition and acquired a reputation as a friend of tax collectors and sinners.

2. It was a wonder of his grace that the call was made effective (v. 28). This tax collector, though those of that employment commonly had little inclination toward religion, got up and followed Christ. No heart is too hard for the Spirit and grace of Christ to work on, nor are any difficulties in the way of a sinner's conversion too great to be conquered by his power.

3. It was a wonder of his grace that he would not only admit a converted tax collector into his family but also associate with unconverted tax collectors. Here is a true wonder of grace, that Christ undertakes to be the Physician of souls diseased by sin and ready to die of the disease—he is a Healer by profession (v. 31)—that he came to call sinners, the worst of sinners, to repentance, and to assure them of pardon when they repented (v. 32). This is good news of great joy indeed (2:10)!

4. It was a wonder of his grace that he patiently endured the hostility of sinners (Heb 12:3) against himself and his disciples (v. 30). He did not express his resentment toward the objections raised by the teachers of the law and Pharisees, but answered them with reason and humility.

5. It was a wonder of his grace that in the discipline in which he trained his disciples, he considered how they were formed (Ps 103:14) and adjusted their service in proportion to their strength. It was raised as an objection that he did not make his disciples fast as often as those of the Pharisees and John the Baptist did (v. 33). He insisted most on what is at the heart of fasting, the living of a life of self-denial, which is as much better than fasting and physical penances as mercy is better than sacrifice (Hos 6:6).

6. It was a wonder of his grace that Christ reserved the tests of his disciples for their later times, when by his grace they were better prepared and fitted for them. Now they were as *the children of the bride chamber* (guests of the bridegroom) when the bridegroom is with them, when they have a joyful feast and every day is a festival. But this would not last forever: *The days will come when the bridegroom shall be taken away from them* (v. 35). When Christ left them with their hearts full of sorrow, their hands full of work, and the world full of enmity and rage against them, then they would fast.

7. It was a wonder of his grace that he adjusted their exercises in proportion to their strength. He would not put *new cloth upon an old garment* (v. 36), nor *new wine into old bottles* (vv. 37–38). He would not put them through the strict rigors and austerities of discipleship as soon as he had called them out of the world, for then they might be tempted to run away. Christ wanted to train his followers gradually to the discipline of his family, because no one, having *drunk old wine*, will suddenly, immediately want a new wine, nor will they relish it if served some of it; rather, they will say, *The old is better*, because they have been used to it (v. 39). The disciples would be tempted to think their old way of living was better until they were gradually trained to this way to which they were called. Although Christ's disciples did not have as much of the *form of godliness* as others, they had more of its *power* (2Ti 3:5).

CHAPTER 6

Here is: 1. A proof of the lawfulness of works of necessity and mercy on the Sabbath, necessity justifying his disciples' picking heads of grain, mercy justifying Christ in healing a man with a shriveled hand on that day (vv. 1–11). 2. His retreat for private prayer (v. 12). 3. His calling his twelve apostles (vv. 13–16). 4. His healing the crowds of various diseases (vv. 17–19). 5. The sermon he preached to his disciples and the crowd, instructing them in their duty both to God and to people (vv. 20–49).

Verses 1–11

We had these two passages in both Matthew and Mark, and they were put together there (Mt 12:1–14; Mk 2:23–27; 3:1–6), because although they happened some time apart from each other, both were intended to put right the mistakes of the teachers of the law and Pharisees about the Sabbath, because they laid greater stress on the bodily rest of that day, and required greater strictness in observing that rest, than the Lawgiver intended. Here:

1. Christ justified his disciples in a necessary work for themselves on that day, and that was *plucking the ears of corn* (grain) when they were hungry on that day. This record has a date, which we did not have in the other Gospels; it was *on the second sabbath after the first* (v. 1), that is, the first Sabbath after the second day of unleavened bread, from which day they counted the seven weeks to the Feast of Pentecost. We may notice:

1.1. Christ's disciples should not be fussy about what they eat, but accept what is gained most easily and be thankful. These disciples *plucked the ears of corn, and did eat* (v. 1); a little—and it was no delicacy—was enough for them.

1.2. Many are forward in censuring others for the most innocent and inoffensive actions (v. 2). The Pharisees quarreled with the disciples as doing what *was not lawful to do on the sabbath days*, even though it was their own practice to feed on fine food on Sabbaths.

1.3. Jesus Christ will justify his disciples, and he will acknowledge and accept them in many things that other people tell them it is not lawful for them to do.

1.4. Ceremonial appointments may be dispensed with in cases of necessity (vv. 3–4). Moreover, if God's own appointments can be set aside in this way for a greater good, then much more may human traditions be.

1.5. Works of necessity are particularly allowable on the Sabbath day.

1.6. Although Jesus Christ allowed works of necessity on the Sabbath, he wants us, nevertheless, to know and remember that it is his day: *The Son of man is Lord also of the Sabbath* (v. 5). In the kingdom of the Redeemer, the Sabbath is to be turned into a *Lord's day* (Rev 1:10). As a sign of this, it will not only have a new name, the *Lord's day*, but also be transferred to a new day, the first day of the week.

2. He justified himself in doing works of mercy for others on the Sabbath.

2.1. On the Sabbath day Christ *entered into the synagogue*. This shows us that whenever we have opportunity, it is our duty to keep Sabbaths holy by attending religious meetings. Our seat must not be empty except with a very good reason.

2.2. When he was in the synagogue on the Sabbath day, *he taught them*. Christ took every opportunity to teach not only his disciples but also the crowd.

2.3. Christ's patient here was one of his hearers. *A man whose right hand was withered* came. Those who want to be healed by the grace of Christ must be willing to learn the doctrine of Christ.

2.4. Among those who listened to Christ's excellent teaching and were the eyewitnesses of his miracles were some who came with no other intention than to pick a quarrel with him (v. 7). The teachers of the law and Pharisees *watched him* closely, as a lion watches its prey, to see whether he would *heal on the sabbath day, that they might find an accusation against* (find a reason to accuse) *him*.

2.5. Jesus Christ was neither ashamed nor afraid to acknowledge the purposes of his grace. He told the man to *rise, and stand forth*, to test the patient's faith and boldness.

2.6. He appealed to his opponents themselves as to whether it was the intention of the fourth commandment to restrain people from doing good on the Sabbath, the good that their hands find to do (Ecc 9:10) and that cannot very well be put off to another time: *Is it lawful to do good, or evil, on the sabbath days?* (v. 9).

2.7. He healed the poor man, even though he knew that his enemies would not only take offense at it but also try to take unfair advantage of him for it (v. 10).

2.8. His opponents were then enraged even more against him (v. 11). Instead of being brought to love him as One who was so generous to people, they were *filled with madness*, furious that they could not frighten him away from doing good. They were furious with Christ, furious with the people, and furious with themselves. When they could not prevent him from performing this miracle, they *communed* (discussed) *one with another what they might do to Jesus*, how they might be able to defeat him.

Verses 12–19

In these verses we have our Lord Jesus in private, in his family, and in public, and in all three acting like himself.

1. In private we have him praying to God (v. 12). This Evangelist takes frequent notice of Christ's retreats, to give us an example of private prayer, without which it is impossible for the soul to prosper. *In those days*, when his enemies were filled with fury against him, *he went out to pray.* He was alone with God; he *went out into a mountain, to pray*, where he would not be disturbed or interrupted. He was alone for a long time with God: *He continued all night in prayer.* We think half an hour is a long time, but Christ continued a whole night in meditation and private prayer. We have a great deal of business at the throne of grace, and we should take great delight in fellowship with God, and by both of these we may sometimes be kept at prayer for a long time.

2. We have him choosing those who would be with him most closely, who would constantly listen to his teaching and be eyewitnesses of his miracles, so that later they could be sent out as apostles, his messengers to the world (v. 13). After he had *continued all night in prayer*, one would have thought that *when it was day*, he would have slept. No; as soon as anyone was up and about, he *called unto him his disciples*. In serving God, our great concern should be not to lose time, but to make the end of one good duty the beginning of another. Ministers are to be ordained with prayer that is extraordinarily sacred. The number of apostles is twelve. Their names are recorded here; it is the third time that we have met with them, and in each of the three places their order is different. Never were men so privileged, but one of them had a devil (Jn 6:70) and turned out to be a traitor (v. 16), though when Christ chose him, he was not deceived by him.

3. In public we have him preaching and healing, the two great works between which he divided his time (v. 17). He came down with the Twelve from the mountain and *stood in the plain*, and immediately there were gathered around him not only the *company of his disciples* but also a great *multitude of people*, many others *out of all Judea and Jerusalem*. They came also from the *sea-coast of Tyre and Sidon*. Although those bordered on the Canaanites, some of them, dispersed throughout all parts, one here and one there, were well disposed to Christ. They *came to hear him*, and he preached to them. It is worth going a long way to hear the word of Christ, and it is worth going out of the way of other business to seek it. They came to be cured by him, and he healed them. Some were troubled in body, and some in mind; some had diseases, some had demons, but both the one and the other were *healed*, because he has power over illnesses and demons (vv. 17–18). In

fact, it seems that those who had no particular diseases to complain about still found it a great confirmation and renewal to their physical health and strength to share in the *virtue* (power) *that went out of him*, because *the whole multitude sought to touch him* (v. 19), and they were all, one way or another, better off because of him. He *healed them all*, and who is there who does not need, in one way or another, to be healed? There is a fullness of grace in Christ that is enough for all and enough for each.

Verses 20–26

Here begins a practical sermon of Christ, most of which is found in the Sermon on the Mount (Mt 5–7). We have:

1. Blessings declared on suffering saints (v. 20): he *lifted up his eyes upon his disciples*, not only on the Twelve but also on the whole *company of them* (v. 17), and directed his words to them from the mountainside. There he *sat* (Mt 5:1), as one with authority (Mt 7:29), and there *they came to him* (Mt 5:1).

1.1. "You are poor, you have *left all to follow me* (Mk 10:28). But you are blessed in your poverty; in fact, you are blessed for it, for *yours is the kingdom of God*, all the comforts and graces of his kingdom here and all the glories and joys of his kingdom in the future; it shall be yours; in fact, it is yours.

1.2. "*You hunger now* (v. 21); you are not well fed as others are, and you are glad to have a few heads of grain to eat at a meal (6:1). And so you hunger now in this world, but in the other world *you shall be filled*.

1.3. "*You weep now*. But *blessed are you*; your present sorrows will not harm your future joy, but are preparations for it: *You shall laugh*. You are only *sowing in tears*, and will soon *reap in joy*" (Ps 126:5–6). God was storing up comforts for them. The day was coming when their *mouth would be filled with laughing and their lips with rejoicing* (Job 8:21).

1.4. "You are now experiencing the world's hatred. You must expect all the evil treatment that a spiteful world can give you for Christ's sake, because you serve him and his interests. Evildoers *will hate you*: your teaching and life will convict and condemn them. *They will reproach you*; charge you with the worst crimes, which you are completely innocent of; describe you in the blackest terms, which you do not deserve; and *cast out your name as evil* (v. 22). *Blessed are you* when you are treated in this way. It is an honor to you, as it is an honor to brave heroes to serve in a war in the service of their ruler, and so *rejoice you in that day, and leap for joy* (v. 23). Do not only bear it, but triumph in it. You are treated as the prophets were before you, and so you not only need not be ashamed of it, but may justly rejoice in it. You will be greatly rewarded for this: *Your reward is great in heaven.* Although you lose earthly goods for Christ, you will not lose by him in the end."

2. Woes declared against prosperous sinners, as those who are miserable even though the world envies them. We did not have these in Matthew. It seems that the best explanation of these woes, when compared with the foregoing blessings, is the parable of the rich man and Lazarus (16:19–31). Here is:

2.1. A *woe* to those *who are rich* (v. 24), that is, who *trust in riches* (Mk 10:24). How terrible it will be for them, *for they have received their consolation*, what they placed their happiness in. In their lifetime, they received *their good things* (16:25), which, as they thought, were the best things. "You who are rich are in a place where you are tempted to set your hearts on a smiling world and to say, *Soul, take thine ease* in its embraces (12:19)."

2.1.1. It is the folly of worldly people that they make the things of this world their comfort, whereas those things were intended only for their convenience. They please themselves with them; the benefits and encouragements of God are small and insignificant to them.

2.1.2. It is their misery that they are put off with them as their comfort.

2.2. A *woe* to those who *are full* (v. 25), who have *more than heart could wish* (Ps 73:7). They are full of themselves but are without God and Christ. How terrible it will be for such people, for *they shall hunger*; they will soon be stripped and emptied of all the things they are so proud of.

2.3. A *woe* to those who *laugh now*, who always have a merry attitude, always have something to be merry about, and are always entertaining themselves with foolish laughter. *Woe unto such* people, because it is only now that they laugh, for a little while; they will *mourn and weep* soon.

2.4. A *woe* to those *whom all men speak well of*, that is, who make it their great and only aim to gain the praise and applause of other people (v. 26): "*Woe unto you*; it would be a sign that you were not faithful to your trust and to the souls of other people if you preached so that nobody would be displeased, since your business is to tell people their faults. There were false prophets who flattered your ancestors in their evil ways and were treated very nicely and spoken well of." We should desire to have the approval of those who are wise and good, but just as we should despise the insults of fools in Israel, so we should also despise their praises.

Verses 27–36

These verses agree with Mt 5:38–48: "*I say unto you that hear* (v. 27), to all you who hear, because these are lessons of universal concern." *He that has an ear, let him hear* (Rev 2:7). The lessons Christ teaches us here are:

1. That we must give to all what is due to them and be honest and just in all our dealings (v. 31): *As ye would that men should do to you, do ye also to them likewise*; this is *loving your neighbour as yourselves* (10:27). We must put ourselves in our neighbor's place and then pity and help them, just as we ourselves would want and justly expect to be pitied and helped.

2. That we must be free in giving to those who are in need (v. 30): "*Give to every man that asketh of thee*, who lacks necessities that you have the resources to supply out of your surplus. Give to those who are unable to help themselves." Christ wants his disciples to be ready to distribute and willing to share as much as they are able in ordinary cases and even beyond their ability in extraordinary ones (2Co 8:3).

3. That we must be generous in forgiving those who have in any way wronged us.

3.1. We must not be extreme in demanding our rights when they are denied us: "*Him that taketh away thy cloak, forbid him not to take thy coat also* (v. 29). Let him have that too, rather than fight for it. And 'from him that takes your goods' (v. 30) do not demand them back. If Providence has made such people insolvent, do not use the law to take advantage of them, but prefer to lose what they owe you rather than *take them by the throat* (Mt 18:28)."

3.2. We must not be rigorous in avenging a wrong when it is done to us: "*To him that smiteth thee on the one cheek* (v. 29), rather than strike him, be ready to receive another blow from him; that is, "leave it to God to plead your cause, and stay silent under the insult."

3.3. In fact, we must do good to those who do us evil. This is what our Savior chiefly intends to teach us, as a law that is distinctive to his religion and as a branch of its perfection (vv. 27–36). We must be loving to those from whom we have received wrongs. We must not only love our enemies and bear them goodwill; we must do good to them. We must seek to make it clear by positive acts that we bear them no hatred and seek no revenge. Do they curse us, speak evil of us, and wish us harm? Do they treat us badly in word or action? Do they try to make us look contemptible or repugnant? Let us bless them, pray for them, speak well of them—the best we can—wish them well, and intercede with God for them. This is repeated (v. 35): *Love your enemies, and do* them *good*. To commend this difficult duty to us, it is represented as something generous, and an achievement few reach. To love those who love us is not unusual; it is not a distinctive feature of being Christ's disciples, because sinners love those who love them. It is simply following nature; it does not make our nature uncomfortable at all (v. 32). "And *if you do good to them that do good to you* (v. 33), *what thanks have you*? What credit are you to the name of Christ, or what reputation do you bring to it? For *sinners also do even the same*. But it befits you to do something more excellent and outstanding, to do what sinners will not do: you must *render good for evil*"; if we do, then we are *to our God for a name and a praise* (Jer 13:11; Zep 3:20), and he will receive the thanks. We must love those from whom we expect no kind of benefit (v. 35): *Lend, hoping for nothing again*. We must lend even if we have reason to suspect that we will lose what we lend, lend to those who are so poor that they probably will not be able to repay us. Here are two motives for this loving and generous action.

3.3.1. It will lead to our profit, for our *reward shall be great* (v. 35). What is lent and lost on earth from a true motive of charity will be made up to us. "You will be not only repaid but greatly rewarded; it will be said to you, Come, ye blessed, inherit the kingdom (Mt 25:34)."

3.3.2. It will lead to our honor, because in such actions we are like God in his goodness, which is the greatest glory (Ex 33:18–19): *Ye shall be the children of the Highest*. It is the glory of God that he is *kind to the unthankful and to the evil*. Christ infers from this (v. 36), *Be merciful, as your Father is merciful*; this explains Mt 5:48: "*Be perfect, as your Father is perfect*. Imitate your Father in those things that are his brightest qualities." Those who are merciful as God is merciful, even to the evil and the unthankful, are perfect as God is perfect. This should make us strongly committed to being merciful to our brothers and sisters: not only that God is so to others but also that he is so to us even though we have been and are evil and unthankful; it is because of his mercies *that we are not consumed* (La 3:22).

Verses 37–49

We had all these sayings of Christ before in Matthew. They were sayings that Christ often spoke. We need not be critical here in seeking coherence: they are golden sentences, like Solomon's proverbs or parables.

1. We should be very fair in our criticism of other people, because we ourselves need allowances made for us: "Do not *judge* others, because then *you* yourselves *shall not be judged*; do not *condemn* others, because then *you* yourselves *shall not be condemned* (v. 37). God will not judge and condemn you, and people will not." Those who are merciful to other people will find that others are merciful to them.

2. If we have a giving and forgiving spirit, we will reap the benefit of it ourselves: *Forgive, and you shall be*

forgiven. If we forgive the wrongs done to us by others, others will forgive our inadvertent acts or omissions. If we forgive others' sins against us, God will forgive our sins against him. He will be no less mindful of the *liberal* person *who devises liberal things* (Isa 32:8) (v. 38): *Give, and it shall be given to you. Men* will *return it into your bosom* (pour it into your lap), because God often uses people as his just instruments not only to avenge but also to reward. God will dispose the hearts of others to give liberally to us, *good measure pressed down and shaken together.* Those whom God rewards are rewarded abundantly.

3. We must expect to be dealt with ourselves as we deal with others: *With the same measure that ye mete* (use) *it shall be measured to you again* (v. 38). Those who treat others harshly may expect to be paid back in their own coin. However, those who treat others kindly have reason to hope that God will raise up for them friends who will treat them kindly.

4. Those who put themselves under the guidance of the ignorant and weak are likely to perish with them (v. 39): *Can the blind lead the blind? Shall not both fall* together *into the ditch?* How can they expect anything else to happen? Those who are led by the common opinion, course, and ways of this world are themselves blind and are led by the blind.

5. Christ's followers cannot expect better treatment in the world than their Master received (v. 40). Let them not promise themselves more honor or pleasure in the world than Christ received. Let each live a life of hard work and self-denial as their Master did, becoming a servant of all; let them stoop, toil, and do all the good they can, and then they will be mature.

6. Those who take on themselves the task of rebuking and reforming others should make sure they themselves are without fault (vv. 41–42). It is absurd for anyone to pretend to be so quick-sighted as to see small faults in others, like a *mote* (speck) in the eye, when he himself is so entirely past feeling as not to notice *a beam* (plank) *in his own eye.* How can you offer your service to your brother, to *pull out the mote from his eye,* which requires a good eye as well as a good hand, when you yourself have a *beam in thine own eye?* To help pull the speck out of our brother's eye is good, we must qualify ourselves for it by beginning with ourselves, reforming our own lives.

7. We may expect that people's words and actions will be according to their character.

7.1. The heart is the tree, and the words and actions are fruit that are consistent with the nature of the tree (vv. 43–44). If a person is really good, then even if they do not produce much fruit, and even if they are sometimes like a tree in winter, still, they do not *bring forth corrupt fruit.* Although they may not do you all the good they should, nevertheless, they will not do you any harm. Even if they cannot reform their bad character, they will not corrupt their good character. If the fruit they produce is corrupt, you may be sure that they are not a good tree. On the other hand, *a corrupt tree doth not bring forth good fruit,* even though it may produce green leaves. So neither can you expect any good conduct from those who have a truly bad character. If the fruit is good, you may conclude that the tree is too, since *every tree is known by its fruit.*

7.2. The heart is the treasure, and the words and actions are the return it yields on investment (v. 45). The controlling love of God and Christ in the heart is a *good treasure* in the heart: it enriches a person. It provides them with a good store to spend for the benefit of others. Out of such a *good treasure* a person may produce what is good. But where the love of the world and the flesh reign, an evil treasure is in the heart, out of which an evildoer is continually producing evil. *Out of the abundance of the heart the mouth speaks*; what the mouth usually speaks generally agrees with what is innermost and uppermost in the heart. Not that a good person will never speak a bad word or that an evildoer may never use a good word for bad purposes, but generally the heart is as the words are, worthless or serious; we should seek to have our hearts filled, therefore, not only with good but with an abundance of good.

8. It is not enough to hear the sayings of Christ; we must also do them.

8.1. We show him disrespect if we call him Lord, Lord but are not careful also to seek to conform to his will. We are mocking Christ, like those do who scornfully said, *Hail, King of the Jews* (Mt 27:29), if we often call him *Lord, Lord* but continue to walk in the way of our own hearts.

8.2. We deceive ourselves if we think that hearing the sayings of Christ will bring us to heaven without doing them. He illustrates this by a comparison (vv. 47–49), which shows:

8.2.1. That only those who not only come to Christ as his students and *hear his sayings* but also put them into practice can be sure of doing what is right for their souls and eternity. They are like a *house built on a rock.* These are the people who make an effort in their religious faith, who *build on a rock,* who begin low and *dig deep,* who establish their hope on Christ, who is the Rock of ages (Isa 26:4)—and no one can lay another foundation (1Co 3:11). People who do this are doing well for themselves, because they will maintain:

8.2.1.1. Their integrity in times of temptation and persecution; when others *fall from their own stedfastness* (2Pe 3:17), these will *stand fast in the Lord.*

8.2.1.2. Their encouragement, peace, hope, and joy in the midst of the greatest distress. The storms and streams of adversity will not shock them, because their feet are *set upon a rock* (Ps 27:5; 40:2).

8.2.1.3. Their eternal welfare. Obedient believers are *kept by the power of* Christ, *through faith, unto salvation, and will never perish* (1Pe 1:5).

8.2.2. That those who rest in a mere listening to the sayings of Christ and do not live up to them are only preparing for a fatal disappointment: *He that heareth and doeth not* is like a man that *built a house without a foundation.* His hopes will fail him when he most needs strength and encouragement from them. When the *stream beats vehemently* on his house, it collapses; the sand that it is built on is washed away, and *immediately it falls.*

CHAPTER 7

We have here: 1. Christ confirming the doctrine he had preached with two glorious miracles, the healing of the centurion's servant at a distance (vv. 1–10) and the raising from the dead of the son of the widow at Nain (vv. 11–18). 2. Christ confirming the faith of John the Baptist, who was in prison, in response to a question from him (vv. 19–23). Having answered the question, he added an honorable testimony about John (vv. 24–35). 3. Christ comforting a poor penitent who turned to him. He assured her that her sins were forgiven, and then he justified himself in the favor he showed her (vv. 36–50).

Verses 1–10

There are some differences between this account of the healing of the centurion's servant and the one we had in Mt 8:5–13. It was said there that the centurion came to

Christ; here it is said that he sent to him some of the *elders of the Jews* (v. 3), and later some other *friends* (v. 6). This miracle is said here to have been performed by our Lord Jesus when he had completed all his sayings in the hearing of the people (v. 1). What Christ said he said publicly: *In secret have I said nothing* (Jn 18:20). Notice:

1. The centurion's servant who was sick was *dear* to (valued highly by) his master (v. 2). The servant deserved praise because by his diligence and faithfulness he commended himself to his master's respect and love. Servants should seek to commend themselves to their masters. The master, on the other hand, deserved praise because when he had a good servant, he knew how to value him. Many masters think they are doing their best servants a favor if they do not scold them, whereas they should be kind and considerate toward them and concerned for their welfare and comfort.

2. The master, *when he heard of Jesus* (v. 3), asked *Christ to come and heal his servant.*

3. He sent some of the *elders of the Jews* to Christ, thinking that that would show greater respect to Christ than if he came himself. That was why he sent Jews, and not ordinary Jews either, but *elders of the Jews*, so that the status of the messengers would honor the One to whom they were sent.

4. The elders of the Jews were sincere intercessors for the centurion: *They besought him instantly* (v. 4), pleaded earnestly with him, in a way that the centurion would never have pleaded for himself, *that he was worthy for whom he should do this.* The centurion said, "*I am not even worthy* of a visit (Mt 8:8)," but the elders of the Jews thought him worthy of the healing. What they insisted on in particular was that although he was a Gentile, he still sincerely wished the Jewish nation and religion well (v. 5). *He loveth our nation* — which few Gentiles did. Even conquerors and those in power should maintain an affection for the conquered and those they have power over. He was well disposed toward the worship of the Jews: *He built them a* new *synagogue* at Capernaum. Here, he showed his respect for the God of Israel, and his desire to have an interest in the prayers of God's Israel (Ezr 6:10). Building places of meeting for religious worship is a very good work; those who do such good works are *worthy of double honour* (1Ti 5:17).

5. Jesus Christ was very ready to show kindness to the centurion. He immediately *went with them* (v. 6), even though the centurion was a Gentile. The centurion did not think he himself was worthy to visit Christ (v. 7), but Christ thought him worthy to be visited by him.

6. The centurion gave further proofs of both his humility and his faith. *When* Christ *was now not far from the house*, the centurion *sent friends* to meet him with fresh expressions:

6.1. Of his humility: "*Lord, trouble not thyself*, because I am unworthy of receiving such an honor." This shows not only his low thoughts of himself, despite his prestige, but also his high thoughts of Christ, despite the lowliness and relative obscurity of Christ in the world.

6.2. Of his faith: "*Lord, trouble not thyself*; you can heal my servant without coming under my roof: *Say in a word, and my servant shall be healed.*" He illustrated his faith by a comparison taken from his own profession, and he was confident that Christ could as easily command the disease to go as he, the centurion, could command any of his soldiers (v. 8).

7. Our Lord Jesus was wonderfully pleased with the faith of the centurion, and was more surprised at it because he was a Gentile; and now notice how, having

been thus honored by the centurion's faith, he honored that faith (v. 9): *He turned him about* (turned around) and *said to the people that followed him, I have not found so great faith, no, not in Israel.* Christ wants those who follow him to notice and observe the great examples of faith, especially when those examples are found among people who do not follow Christ as closely as they do in profession — so that we may be shamed out of our weakness and wavering by the strength of their faith.

8. The healing was carried out immediately and completely (v. 10): *They that were sent* went back and found the servant well. Christ will take notice of the distressed case of poor servants, because he does not show favoritism. Nor are the Gentiles excluded from benefiting from his grace.

Verses 11–18

Here is the account of Christ's raising from the dead the son of a widow at Nain, which Matthew and Mark did not mention. Notice:

1. Where and when this miracle was performed. It was the day after he had healed the centurion's servant (v. 11). It was done at the gate of a small town called Nain, not far from Capernaum.

2. Who its witnesses were. It was done in the sight of two crowds that met in or near the town gate. A crowd of *disciples* and other *people* were *with* Christ (v. 11), and a crowd of relatives and neighbors were attending the funeral of the young man (v. 12).

3. How it was performed by our Lord Jesus.

3.1. The person raised to life was *a young man*. This young man was the *only son of his mother*, and *she* was *a widow*. She depended on him to support her in her old age, but he proved to be a broken reed (2Ki 18:21); everyone, even in their best state, is so. We may well think how deep the sorrow of this poor mother was for her only son, and it was all the deeper because she was a widow. *Much people of the city was with her*, expressing their condolences at her loss, trying to comfort her.

3.2. Christ showed both his pity and his power in raising him to life.

3.2.1. See how tender his compassions are toward the afflicted (v. 13): *When the Lord saw* the poor widow following her son to the grave, *he had compassion on her.* No one turned to him for help. He was troubled for her purely from the goodness of his nature. The situation was pitiful, and Christ looked on it with pity. He *said unto her, Weep not.* What a pleasant idea this gives us of the compassion of the Lord Jesus and the greatness of his loving-kindness. Christ said, *Weep not*, and he could give her a reason that no one else could: "Do not weep for a dead son, because he will soon become a living one." This reason was specific to her case, but there is a reason common to all who sleep in Jesus, that they will rise again in glory. We must not, therefore, *sorrow as those that have no hope* (1Th 4:13). Moreover, let our passion at such times be checked and calmed by the consideration of Christ's compassion.

3.2.2. See how triumphant his commands are over even death itself (v. 14): *He came and touched the bier.* He indicated to those who were carrying the coffin that they should not proceed any farther. *They that bore him stood still*, and then, with solemnity, as One who had authority (Mt 7:29), he said, *Young man, I say unto thee, Arise.* Power accompanied that word to put life into him. Christ's power over death was shown by the immediate effect of his word (v. 15): *He that was dead sat up.* Have we received grace from Christ? Let us show it. Another sign of life was that he *began to speak*, because whenever Christ gives us spiritual life, he opens the lips in prayer and praise (Ps 51:15). He *delivered him to his mother*, to be with her as befitted a dutiful son. Now she was comforted for as long as she had suffered (Ps 90:15), and much more.

4. What influence this miracle had on the people (v. 16): *There came a fear on all*; they were all struck with wonder at this miracle and *glorified God*. The Lord and his goodness, as well as the Lord and his greatness, are to be feared (Ex 33:18–23). The conclusion they drew from this was, "*A great prophet is risen up among us*, and in him *God hath visited his people*." This would be truly *life from the dead* (Ro 11:15) to all of those who waited for the consolation of Israel (Lk 2:25). The report of this miracle was taken:

4.1. In general, throughout Judea and the surrounding country (v. 17): *This rumour* (news) *of him went forth through all Judea*, which was a long way off, and throughout all Galilee, which was the *region round about*. Many people have the news of Christ's Gospel ringing in their ears but do not enjoy it in their souls.

4.2. In particular, carefully, to John the Baptist, who was now in prison (v. 18): *His disciples came* and gave him an account of all things, so that he would know that although he was bound, the word of the Lord was not bound (2Ti 2:9); God's work was continuing, even though he was set aside.

Verses 19–35

1. We have here the message John the Baptist sent to Christ and the response Christ gave to it. Notice:

1.1. The great thing we are to seek concerning Christ is whether he is the One who was to come, or whether we are to look for another (vv. 19–20). We are sure that God has promised that a Savior will come; we are as sure that he will fulfill what he has promised. If this Jesus is that promised Messiah, we will receive him, but if he is not, we will hold on to our expectations and continue to wait for the Messiah.

1.2. The faith of John the Baptist himself needed to be confirmed in this matter. The leaders of the Jewish church had not acknowledged Jesus. There had not been seen in him any of that power and grandeur that were expected to attend the Messiah when he appeared, and so it was not strange that John's messengers would ask, *Art thou the Messiah?*

1.3. Christ left it to his own works to praise him. While John's messengers were with him, he performed many miraculous healings, *in that same hour* (v. 21)! *He cured many of their infirmities and plagues in* body and cast out *evil spirits*, and *unto many that were blind he gave sight*. His healings were very many, so that there remained no basis whatsoever for suspecting fraud, and then (v. 22) he told them *go and tell John what they had seen*. And both John and they could easily argue, as even the common people did (Jn 7:31), "*When Christ cometh, will he do more miracles than these which this man hath done?* You see that Jesus does this to people's bodies, and so you must conclude this is the One who was to come to do it to people's souls, and you are to *look for no other*." He added miracles in the kingdom of grace to his miracles in the kingdom of nature: *To the poor the Gospel is preached* (v. 22), which they knew was to be done by the Messiah. "Judge, therefore, whether you can look for any other one who will more fully fulfill the character of the Messiah."

1.4. He gave them an indication of the danger people were in of being prejudiced against him: "*Blessed is he*

whosoever shall not be offended in me (v. 23), who does not fall away on account of me." Christ's education at Nazareth, his residence at Galilee, the insignificance of his family and relatives, his poverty, and the unimpressiveness of his followers—these and the like were stumbling blocks to many people. Those who are not overcome by these prejudices are blessed, because they are good, wise, and humble. It is a sign that God has blessed them, *and they shall be* really *blessed* in Christ (Ps 72:17).

2. We have here the high commendation that Christ gave of John the Baptist *when* John's disciples *were departed* (v. 24). Let the people now consider *what they went out into the wilderness to see*. "Come," Christ says, "I will tell you."

2.1. John the Baptist was a man of integrity, steadiness, and faithfulness. He was not *a reed shaken with the wind*; he was as firm as a rock, not as fickle as a reed.

2.2. He was a man of unparalleled self-denial. He was not *a man clothed in soft raiment* (fine clothes), nor did he *live delicately* (indulge in luxury) (v. 25); on the contrary, he lived in a desert and was clothed and fed accordingly.

2.3. He was *a prophet*. In fact, he was *more, much more than a prophet* (v. 26), more than any of the Old Testament prophets, because they spoke about Christ as at a distance, and he spoke of him as at the door.

2.4. He was the harbinger and forerunner of the Messiah and was himself prophesied of in the Old Testament (v. 27): *This is he of whom it is written, Behold, I send my messenger* (Mal 3:1) *before thy face*. Before God sent the Master himself, he sent a messenger to announce his coming. It was a clear enough sign of the spiritual nature of Christ's kingdom that the messenger he sent before him to *prepare his way* did it by preaching repentance and reformation. Certainly the kingdom that was ushered in in this way was not of this world.

2.5. He was so great that really there was not a *greater prophet* than he. Prophets were the greatest to whom women gave birth, and John was the greatest of all the prophets. However, *he that is least in the kingdom of God is greater than he*. The lowliest of those who *follow the Lamb* (Rev 14:4) far excel the greatest of those who went before him. Therefore, those who live under the Gospel era have even more to answer for.

3. We have here the just censure of the people of that generation.

3.1. Christ showed how John the Baptist was treated with contempt while he was preaching and baptizing. Those who did show him any respect were only the common, ordinary people (v. 29). *The people*, the common masses, about whom it was said, *This people, who know not the law, are cursed* (Jn 7:49), and the tax collectors—these were *baptized with* John's *baptism* and became his disciples. By their repentance and reformation they *justified God* in appointing one such as John the Baptist to be the forerunner of the Messiah. They also made it clear in this way that sending John was the best way by which the Messiah could have been introduced, because it was not in vain to them, whatever it was to others. The leaders of their church and nation, it is true, heard him, but they were not *baptized of him* (v. 30). The Pharisees and the lawyers *rejected the counsel of God against themselves* (rejected God's purpose for themselves); if they had submitted to the counsel of God, it would have been for themselves, but they rejected it, and it was *against themselves*, to their own ruin.

3.2. He showed how the objections the people of that generation raised and the prejudices they conceived against both John and Christ revealed a strange perverseness.

3.2.1. They laughed at God's ways of doing them good (v. 31): "*Whereunto shall I liken the men of this generation?* They are *like children sitting in the marketplace,* who are not occupied with anything serious, but are as full of play as possible. It is as if God were having fun with them, as children play with one another in the marketplace (v. 32). They take everything as a joke." This is the ruin of many people: they can never persuade themselves to be serious about spiritual matters. How desperately sad it is to see the foolishness and worthlessness of this blind and ungodly world! May the Lord wake them up out of their self-confidence.

3.2.2. They still found something or other to complain about.

3.2.2.1. John the Baptist was a reserved and austere man, living very much by himself, and should have been listened to as a man of thought and contemplation, but what he should have been commended for was turned to his reproach. "Because he came *neither eating nor drinking, you say, 'He has a devil';* he is gloomy, he is possessed.'"

3.2.2.2. Our Lord Jesus had a freer, more open character; he *came eating and drinking* (v. 34). He would go and eat with Pharisees, and he would eat with tax collectors. In the hope of doing good to each, he was on familiar terms with both. This shows that ministers of Christ may have very different characters and dispositions; there are very different styles of preaching and living, but all are good and useful. Therefore, no one must make themselves a standard to all others, nor judge harshly those who do not do things exactly as they do. John the Baptist bore witness to Christ, and Christ commended John the Baptist, although they were the opposites of each other in their way of living. However, their common enemies reproached them both. The very same people who had described John as crazy described our Lord Jesus as corrupt; *he is a gluttonous man, and a wine-bibber.* Ill will never speaks well.

3.3. He showed that, despite this, God would be glorified in the salvation of a chosen remnant (v. 35): *Wisdom is justified of* (proved right by) *all her children.* Wisdom's children are agreed on this one point: they all take delight in the ways of grace that divine wisdom follows, and they never think the worse of them just because they are laughed at by some.

Verses 36–49

When and where this event took place is not mentioned, but it is included here, when Christ is scorned as being *a friend to publicans and sinners,* to show that it was only for their good and to bring them to repentance that he had dealings with them. Who this woman was who showed such a great devotion for Christ is not mentioned. Notice:

1. The courteous reception that a Pharisee gave to Christ (v. 36): *One of the Pharisees desired him that he would eat with him.* It appears that this Pharisee did not believe in Christ, because he did not acknowledge Christ to be *a prophet* (v. 39), but our Lord Jesus still accepted his invitation, *went into his house, and sat down to meat* (at the table). People who have the wisdom and grace to explain and argue about spiritual matters should socialize with those in authority who are prejudiced against Christ.

2. The great respect a poor, penitent sinner showed him. It was a woman in the town *who was a sinner,* a notorious prostitute. She knew that Jesus was dining at

the Pharisee's house, and she came to acknowledge her obligation to him, having no opportunity of doing it in any other way than by washing his feet and pouring on them some sweet perfume that she brought with her for that purpose. Now this woman did not look Christ in the face, but came *behind him* and fulfilled the role of a female servant. Notice in this good woman's actions:

2.1. Her deep humiliation for her sin. She stood behind him weeping; her eyes had allowed sin to come in and go out, and now she made them fountains of tears. Her face, which perhaps used to be covered with makeup, was now soiled from her tears. She used her hair, which before had been plaited and adorned, as a towel. We have reason to think that she had already grieved for her sin earlier, but now that she had an opportunity of coming into the presence of Christ, her sorrow was renewed.

2.2. Her strong devotion for the Lord Jesus. This was what our Lord Jesus took special notice of, that she *loved much* (vv. 42, 47). She *washed his feet*; she washed them with her tears of joy; she was in such ecstasy that she found herself so close to her Savior, whom her soul loved (SS 1:7; 3:1–4). She *kissed his feet.* It was a kiss of adoration as well as affection. *She wiped them with her hair.* Her eyes would provide water to wash them, and her hair was a towel to wipe them, and she *anointed* his feet *with the ointment.* All true penitents dearly love the Lord Jesus.

3. The offense that the Pharisee took at Christ's accepting the respect this poor penitent showed him (v. 39): "*He said within himself, 'This man, if he were a prophet, would know that this woman is a sinner.* He would also be so holy that he would therefore not allow her to come so close to him.'" Notice how proud and narrow souls tend to think that others should be as proud and as censorious as they themselves are.

4. Christ's justification of the woman in what she did to him and his justification of himself in accepting it. Christ knew what the Pharisee was saying *within himself,* and he responded to it: *Simon, I have something to say unto thee* (v. 40). Simon was willing to listen to him: He saith, *Master, say on.* In his answer to the Pharisee, Christ reasoned in this way: It was true that this woman had been a sinner: he knew it. But she was a pardoned sinner, which implied that she was a penitent sinner. What she had done to him was therefore an expression of her great love for her Savior. If she, who had been so great a sinner, was forgiven, it might reasonably be expected that she would love her Savior more than others, and if this was the fruit of her love and flowed from an assurance of the forgiveness of her sins, he was right to accept it, and it was wrong of the Pharisee to be offended by it.

4.1. He used a parable to make Simon acknowledge that the greater sinner this woman had been, the greater love she should show Jesus Christ when her sins were pardoned (vv. 41–43). A man had two debtors who were both insolvent, but one of them owed him ten times as much as the other. He very freely forgave them both, rather than using the law to take advantage of them. Now they were both aware of the great kindness they had received, but *which of them would love him most?* Certainly, the Pharisee said, the one to *whom he forgave most.* Learn from this the duties that debtors and creditors owe each other.

4.1.1. If a debtor has anything to pay with, they should pay their debt.

4.1.2. If God in his providence has made the debtor unable to pay their debt, the creditor should not be severe with them, but forgive them freely.

4.1.3. The debtor who has found their creditors merciful should be very grateful to them and should love them.

Some insolvent debtors, instead of being grateful, are spiteful to their creditors and cannot speak a good word about them, only because the creditors complain, even though it is the creditors who have lost something by the relationship and therefore have a right to complain. However, this parable speaks about God, or rather about the Lord Jesus himself, because he is the One who forgives, and sinners are the debtors, and so we may learn here:

4.1.3.1. That sin is a debt, and sinners are debtors to God Almighty. As creatures, we owe a debt of obedience. We have not paid our rent; in fact, we have wasted our Lord's goods, and so we have become debtors.

4.1.3.2. That some are deeper in debt to God because of their sin than others are: one debtor in the parable owed 500 denarii, and the other fifty. The Pharisee was the lesser debtor, but he was still a debtor, which was more than he thought himself. This woman was the greater debtor.

4.1.3.3. That whether our debt is greater or less, it is more than we can repay: the debtors in the parable had no money to pay their debts, nothing at all. No righteousness of our own will repay our debt, not even our repentance and obedience for the future, because it is what we are already bound to.

4.1.3.4. That the God of heaven is ready to freely forgive poor sinners. If we repent and believe in Christ, our sin will not be charged to our account. God has declared his name to be gracious and merciful and ready to forgive sin (Ex 34:6).

4.1.3.5. That those who have their sins pardoned are obliged to love the One who pardoned them, and the more that is forgiven them, the more they should love him. The greater sinners that people have been before their conversion, the greater saints they should be afterward. When a persecuting Saul became a preaching Paul, he worked even harder (1Co 15:10).

4.2. He applied this parable to the different attitudes and behavior of the Pharisee and the sinner. Christ seemed ready to accept the Pharisee as one who was forgiven, though forgiven of less. It was true that he showed some love to Christ, but that was nothing compared with what this poor woman showed. "Notice," Christ said to him, "she is the one who has had much forgiven her, and so she should love much more than you do, and so it appears. Do you see this woman (v. 44)? Consider how much kinder a friend she is to me than you have been; should I then accept your kindness and refuse hers?

4.2.1. "You did not even arrange for me to have a bowl of water to wash my feet in, but she has done much more: she has washed my feet with tears and wiped them with the hairs of her head as a sign of her great love to me.

4.2.2. "You did not even kiss my cheek, but this woman has not stopped kissing my feet (v. 45).

4.2.3. "You did not provide me a little ordinary oil, as is usual, to put on my head, but she has poured out a jar of precious ointment on my feet (v. 46)." The reason why some people find fault with the pains zealous Christians take and the expense they go to is that they themselves are not willing to exert themselves in this way, but want to sit back with a cheap and easy faith that makes no demands on them.

4.3. He silenced the Pharisee's objection: "*I say to thee, Simon, her sins, which are many, are forgiven*" (v. 47). He acknowledged that she had been guilty of many sins: "But she has been forgiven them, because she loved much." It should be rendered, "therefore she loved much," because it is clear that her loving much was not the cause, but the effect, of her forgiveness. We love God because he loved us first; he did not forgive us because we loved him first.

"But one who has been forgiven little, as you have, loves only a little, as you do." Instead of grudging greater sinners the mercy they find with Christ, we should be stirred by their example to examine ourselves to see whether we are truly forgiven and love Christ.

4.4. He silenced her fears. Christ said to her, *Thy sins are forgiven* (v. 48). She was dismissed with this word from Christ, *Thy sins are forgiven!* And this would be an effective way of making sure she would not return to her sin! Although some who were present quarreled with Christ in their own minds for presuming to forgive sin and declare sinners pardoned (v. 49), he still stood by what he had said. He would now show that he had pleasure in forgiving sin. He loves to speak words of pardon and peace to penitents. He said to the woman, *Thy faith hath saved thee* (v. 50). All these expressions of sorrow for sin and love for Christ were the effects and products of faith. As faith honors God more than all other graces, so Christ honors faith more than all other graces.

CHAPTER 8

Most of this chapter is a repetition of various passages that we had before in Matthew and Mark. Here is: 1. A general account of Christ's preaching (vv. 1–3). 2. The parable of the sower (vv. 4–18). 3. The preference Christ gave to his obedient disciples over his closest relatives (vv. 19–21). 4. His stilling a storm on a lake (vv. 22–25). 5. His driving a legion of demons out of a man (vv. 26–40). 6. His healing of the woman who was subject to bleeding and his raising Jairus's daughter to life (vv. 41–56).

Verses 1–3

We are here told:

1. What Christ made the constant work of his life: preaching; he was tireless in that work as he went about doing good (Ac 10:38) (v. 1). Notice:

1.1. Where he preached: *He went about.* He was an itinerant preacher; he did not confine himself to one place, but spread the rays of his light. He went from one town and village to another, so that no one could plead ignorance. Here he set an example to his disciples; they must cross the nations of the earth, as he did the towns of Israel. Nor did he confine himself to the cities, but also went into the villages, among the ordinary country people.

1.2. What he preached: *He showed the glad tidings* (news) *of the kingdom of God.* News of the *kingdom of God* is good news, and Jesus Christ came to bring it. It was good news to the world that there was hope of its being reformed and reconciled.

1.3. Who was with him: *The twelve were with him* to learn from him what and how to preach later.

2. From where he received the necessary support for life: he lived on the kindness of his friends. There were *certain women* who *ministered to him of their substance* (helped to support him out of their own means) (vv. 2–3). Some of them are named, but there were *many others.*

2.1. They were mostly those who were the memorials to his power and mercy; they had been *healed by him of evil spirits and infirmities.* We are bound by our own interests to stay close to him, so that we may be ready to turn to him for help when we relapse; and we are bound by gratitude to serve him and his Gospel, because he is the One who has saved us by his Gospel.

2.2. One of them was Mary Magdalene, out of whom had been *cast seven devils.* Some think that she had been very wicked, and if so, we may suppose she *was* the *sinner* mentioned just before (7:37). On her repentance and reformation she found mercy and became a zealous disciple of Christ. The worse anyone has been before their conversion, the more they should seek to do for Christ afterward. This Mary Magdalene was at Christ's cross and his grave.

2.3. Another of them was *Joanna the wife of Chuza, Herod's steward* (Cuza, the manager of Herod's household). Her husband, though advanced in Herod's court, had received the Gospel and was very willing for his wife to both listen to Christ and support him.

2.4. There were many of them who *ministered to Christ of their substance* (their own means). Although *he was rich, yet for our sakes he became poor* (2Co 8:9) and lived on the gifts of others. Christ would rather be indebted to his known friends for support for himself and his disciples than be a burden to strangers. It is the duty of those who are taught in the word to *communicate to* (share with) *them who teach them in all good things* (Gal 6:6).

Verses 4–21

The foregoing paragraph began with an account of Christ's diligence in preaching (v. 1); this one begins with an account of the people's diligence in listening (v. 4). He *went into every city* to preach; there were those who came *to him out of every city* (town), who would not wait until he came to them and would not think that they had had enough when he left them, but met him when he was coming toward them and followed him when he was going away from them. *Much people were gathered together*, plenty of fish to cast his net among, and he was as ready and willing to teach as they were to be taught. Now here:

1. In the parable of the sower and its explanation, we have necessary and excellent rules and warnings for hearing the word. When Christ had spoken this parable:

1.1. The disciples asked about its meaning (v. 9). They asked him, *What might this parable be?* We should sincerely seek to know both the true intent and the full extent of the word we hear.

1.2. Christ told them what a great benefit it was to them to have the opportunity of acquainting themselves with the mystery and meaning of his word, which others did not have: *Unto you it is given* (v. 10). We are truly happy and fortunate, and forever indebted to free grace, if the same thing that is a parable to others, with which they are only entertained, is a clear truth to us. Now from the parable and its explanation, notice:

1.2.1. The human heart is like soil to the seed of God's word; it is capable of receiving it and producing its fruits, but unless that seed is sown in it, it will produce nothing valuable. Our concern, therefore, must be to bring seed and soil together.

1.2.2. The success of the sowing is very much according to the nature of the soil. As we are in ourselves, so the word of God is to us: either *a savour of life unto life* or *of death unto death* (2Co 2:16).

1.2.3. The Devil is a subtle and spiteful enemy. He takes the word out of the hearts of careless hearers, *lest they should believe and be saved* (v. 12). This is added here to what the other Evangelists recorded, to teach us that we cannot be saved unless we believe. That is why the Devil does all he can to keep us from believing, to make us not believe the word when we read and hear it, or, if we pay attention to it for the present, to make us forget it later, so that we drift away (Heb 2:1), or, if we remember it, to create prejudice in our hearts against it or distract us from it so that we think about something else. All this is *lest we should believe and be saved*.

1.2.4. Where the word of God is heard carelessly, contempt is usually shown to it. To what the other Evangelists wrote, it is added here that the seed that fell by the wayside was trampled on (v. 5). Those on whom the word makes some impression, but not a deep and durable one, will show their hypocrisy in a time of testing, like the seed sown on the rock, where it does not put down roots (v. 13).

1.2.5. These believe for a while; their profession of faith promises something, but in times of temptation they fall away from their good beginnings.

1.2.6. *The pleasures of this life* are like dangerous and troublesome thorns that choke the good seed of the word. This phrase is added (v. 14) to what the other Evangelists wrote. The soul may be ruined by worldly pleasures, even by lawful delights, if they are indulged and delighted in too much.

1.2.7. It is not enough for fruit to be produced; it must be brought to perfection; it must be fully ripened and mature. If it is not, it is as if no fruit at all had been produced, because what in Matthew and Mark is said to be unfruitful is what is said here to produce no mature fruit.

1.2.8. The good ground, which produces *good fruit*, is an honest and good heart (v. 15), a heart firmly established on God and duty, an upright heart, a tender heart, a noble and good heart, which, having heard the word, *understands* it (as it is in Matthew), *receives* it (as it is in Mark), and *keeps* it (as it is here), as the soil not only receives but also keeps the seed.

1.2.9. Where the word is kept well, fruit is produced *with patience* (perseverance). This also is added here. There must be both patience to suffer tribulation and persecution and patience to continue doing good to the end.

1.2.10. In consideration of all this, we should *take heed how we hear* (v. 18), consider those things that will prevent us from benefiting from the word we listen to, so that we may not listen carelessly and disrespectfully. We must take note of the condition of our spirits after we have heard the word, so that we do not lose what we have gained.

2. We have necessary instructions given both to those who are appointed to preach the word and to those who have heard it.

2.1. Those who have received the gift must minister with it (1Pe 4:10) (v. 16). People who have benefited by the word must look on themselves as lighted candles. *A candle* must not be *covered with a vessel* (in a jar) nor *put under a bed*. Ministers and Christians are to be lights in the world (Mt 5:14). Their light must shine in the presence of people; they must not only be good but also do good.

2.2. We must expect that what is now done *in secret will* soon be *manifested* and *made known* (v. 17). What is committed to you in secret should be disclosed by you, because your Master did not give you talents to be buried, but to be used (Mt 25:24–30).

2.3. The gifts we have will either remain with us or be taken away from us, depending on whether we do or do not make use of them for the glory of God: *Whosoever hath, to him shall be given* (v. 18). He who has gifts and does good with them will receive more; he who buries his talent will lose it. From him who does not have, even *that which he hath* will be taken away, as it says in Mark; what he *seemeth to have*, as it says in Luke. The grace that is lost was only apparent grace; it was never true. People only seem to have what they do not use.

3. In a particular example of Christ's respect to his disciples, his preferring them over even his closest relatives (vv. 19–21), we see the great encouragement given

to those who prove themselves faithful *hearers of the word* by being *doers of the work* (Jas 1:22) (vv. 19–21). Notice:

3.1. How people crowded around Christ. There was no getting near him because of the great throng.

3.2. Some of his closest relatives were least concerned to listen to him preach. Instead of going inside, wanting to hear him, they stood outside, wanting to see him.

3.3. Jesus Christ would rather be busy working than talking with his friends.

3.4. Christ is pleased to acknowledge as his nearest and most precious relatives those who *hear the word of God and do it.*

Verses 22–39

We have two memorable proofs of the power of our Lord Jesus here: his power over the winds and his power over demons. See also Mk 4:1–5:20.

1. We see his power over the winds.

1.1. Christ told his disciples to go over to the other side of the lake: *He went into a ship* (boat) *with his disciples* (v. 22). If Christ sends out his disciples, he goes with them, and people that have Christ accompanying them may safely and boldly venture anywhere. *He said, Let us go over unto the other side.*

1.2. Those who go out on the lake in a calm, even at Christ's word, must still prepare for a storm. A squall came down on the lake (v. 23), and immediately their boat was so tossed about that it was filled with water, and their lives were in danger.

1.3. Christ was asleep in the storm (v. 23). He needed some physical refreshment. The disciples of Christ may really have his gracious presence with them at sea, and in a storm, even though he may seem to be asleep. He may not appear immediately to relieve them. In this way he will test their faith and patience and make their rescue more welcome when it finally comes.

1.4. A complaint to Christ of our danger is enough to make him wake up and help us (v. 24). They cried out, *Master, master, we perish!* The way to have our fears silenced is to bring them to Christ. Those who sincerely call on him as their Master may be sure that he will not let them die.

1.5. Just as it is Satan's business to raise storms, it is Christ's business to still them. He delights to do it, because he came to proclaim peace on earth (2:14). He *rebuked the wind and the raging of the water,* and immediately, suddenly, *they ceased* (v. 24), and *there was a great calm.*

1.6. When our dangers have passed, we should become ashamed of our own fears and give Christ the glory of his power. Christ rebuked the disciples for their excessive fear: *Where is your faith?* (v. 25). Many who have true faith have to go looking for it when they most need it at hand. A little thing discourages them, and where is their faith then? They give him the glory of his power: *They, being afraid, wondered* (they had fear and amazement). Those who had feared the storm now feared the One who had stilled it, and they *said one to another, What manner of man is this!*

2. We see his power over the Devil. Immediately after the winds were stilled, they came to their desired destination, *the country of the Gadarenes,* and went ashore there (vv. 26–27). We may learn a great deal from this account about the world of the fiendish, evil spirits.

2.1. These spirits are numerous. Those that had taken possession of this one man called themselves *Legion* (v. 30), because *many devils were entered into him:* he

had *had devils a long time* (v. 27). They were, or at least wanted to be thought to be, a legion.

2.2. They have a hardened hostility toward people. Being under the influence of these demons, this man *wore no clothes, neither abode in any house* (v. 27). They forced him to *abide in the tombs,* to make him so much more a terror to himself and to everyone around him.

2.3. They are very strong, fierce, and unruly, and hate and scorn all restraint: *He was kept bound with chains and in fetters,* but he *broke the bands* (v. 29). Those who refuse to be ruled show that they are under Satan's rule. *He was driven of* (by) *the devil.* Those who are under Christ's rule are led sweetly with bands of love (Hos 11:4); those who are under the Devil's rule are driven furiously (2Ki 9:20).

2.4. They are intensely angry with our Lord Jesus and have a great dread and horror of him: *When the man saw Jesus,* he *roared out* and *fell down before him* and acknowledged him to *be the Son of God most high* (v. 28), who was infinitely above him and too powerful for him. He also protested against being in league with him at all: *What have I to do with thee?* The demons have neither inclination to serve Christ nor any expectation to receive benefits from him. Rather, they dread his power and wrath: *I beseech thee, torment me not.* They did not say, "I beg you, save me," but only, *Torment me not.* Notice whose language is spoken by those who have only a dread of hell, and no desire for heaven as a place of holiness and love.

2.5. They are perfectly at the command and under the power of our Lord Jesus, and these here knew it, for they *besought* (begged) *him that he would not command them to go* into the deep. What an encouragement it is to the Lord's people that all the powers of darkness are under the restraint and control of the Lord Jesus! He can send them to their own place when he pleases.

2.6. They delight in causing trouble. When they found there was no way out except by abandoning their grip on this poor man, they begged to be allowed to take possession of a *herd of swine* (v. 32). When Satan could not destroy the man, he wanted to destroy the pigs. If he could not harm people in their bodies, he would harm them in their goods, which sometimes prove a great temptation to people and draw them away from Christ, as here. Christ *suffered* (allowed) *them to enter into the swine.* They entered the pigs, and no sooner had they entered them than the herd ran violently *down a steep place into the lake* and were *drowned.*

2.7. When the Devil's power is broken in any soul, that soul recovers: *The man out of whom the devils were departed sat at the feet of Jesus* (v. 35). While he was under the Devil's power, he was ready to fly in the face of Jesus, but now he sat at his feet. If God has possession of us, he preserves our control and enjoyment of ourselves, but if Satan has possession of us, he robs us of both. We are never more our own than when we are Christ's.

2.8. Let us now see what the effect of this miracle was.

2.8.1. On the people of that country, the effect it had was that *the swineherds went and told it* both *in city and country* (v. 34). They told *by what means he that was possessed of the devils was healed* (v. 36), that it was by sending the devils into the pigs, as if Christ could not have delivered the man out of the demons' hands except by delivering the pigs into their hands. *The people came out to see what was done,* and *they were afraid* (v. 35); they were *taken with* (overcome with) *great fear* (v. 37). They thought more about the destruction of the pigs than about the deliverance of their poor afflicted neighbor, and so *the whole multitude besought* (begged) *Christ to depart from them.* No one who is willing to abandon their sins and give themselves to Christ need be afraid of him. But Christ took them at their word: *He went up into the ship, and returned back again.* People who love their pigs better than their Savior and their hopes in him will lose their Savior.

2.8.2. On the poor man, the effect was that he wanted Christ's company as much as the others dreaded it: he begged Christ that *he might be with him,* as others who *had been healed by him of evil spirits and infirmities* were (v. 2). He was reluctant to stay among those bad-mannered and senseless Gadarenes who wanted Christ to depart from them. However, Christ sent him home to declare among those who knew him the great things God had done for him, so that he could be a blessing to his country as much as he had earlier been a burden to it. We must sometimes deny ourselves the satisfaction even of spiritual benefits and encouragements to gain an opportunity of being useful to the souls of others.

Verses 40–56

Christ was driven away by the Gadarenes. However, when he returned to the Galileans, they *gladly received him;* they had waited for his return, and they welcomed him with all their hearts (v. 40). He returned and found fresh work to do in the place he came from. The needy are always with us (Dt 15:11). We have two miracles interwoven here, as they were in Matthew and Mark. We have:

1. A public request to Christ by *a ruler of the synagogue* named *Jairus* on behalf of his little daughter, who was very ill. Though a ruler, Jairus *fell down at Jesus' feet.* He *besought* (pleaded) *him* to *come into his house,* not having the faith of the centurion, who wanted Christ only to *speak the* healing *word* at a distance (Mt 8:8). However, Christ agreed to his request; *he went along* with him. Strong faith will be commended, but even weak faith will not be rejected. When Christ was going, *the people thronged* (crushed) *him.* Let us not complain about a crowd, a throng, or a need for hurry as long as we are doing our duty and doing good, though otherwise these situations are the sort that wise people will keep themselves out of as much as possible.

2. A secret request to Christ by a woman who had *an issue of blood,* who was subject to bleeding, which had wasted her body and used up all her money too: *she had spent all her living upon physicians* but had gotten no better (v. 43). The nature of her disease was such that she did not want to tell others about it publicly—and so she took this opportunity to come to Christ in a crowd. Her faith was very strong, for she did not doubt that if she could only *touch the hem of his garment* (the edge of his cloak), she would derive healing power from him. She looked on him as such a full fountain of mercies that she could take some healing and he would not miss it. Many poor souls who are lost in a crowd are healed, helped, and saved by Christ. The woman found an immediate change for the better in herself; her disease was healed (v. 44). Believers have assured fellowship with Christ *privately.*

3. The revealing of this secret healing.

3.1. Christ took notice that a healing had been performed: *Virtue is gone out of me* (v. 46). Those who have been healed by power from Christ must acknowledge it, because he knows it. He was delighted that power had gone out of him to do any good, and he did not grudge it to the lowliest person; they were as welcome to share in it as they were to share in the light and heat of the sun.

3.2. The poor patient acknowledged her case and the benefit she had received: *When she saw that she was not hid, she came and fell down before him* (v. 47). *She came trembling,* but *her faith saved her* (v. 48). There may be trembling where there is also saving faith. She *declared before all the people for what cause she had touched him,* namely, that she believed that a touch would heal her; and she declared that it had done so.

3.3. The great Physician confirmed her healing and sent her away with encouragement: *Be of good comfort: thy faith hath made thee whole* (v. 48). Her healing was gained surreptitiously and underhandedly, but it was secured and supported honorably. She was healed, and she would be healed (Ge 27:33).

4. An encouragement to Jairus not to distrust the power of Christ, even though his daughter was now dead and the people who brought him the news advised him not to give *the Master any further trouble* about her (v. 49): *Fear not,* Christ said; *only believe.* Our faith in Christ should be bold and daring. "Although the child is dead, still believe, and all will be well."

5. The preparations for raising her back to life.

5.1. Christ's choice of the witnesses who would see the miracle performed. A crowd followed him, but perhaps they were bad mannered and noisy. However, it was not right to let such a crowd come into a house, especially now that the family were all grieving, and that was why he sent them back. He took no one with him except Peter, James, and John, intending that these three, with the parents, would be the only ones who would see the miracle.

5.2. His restraining of the mourners. *They all wept, and bewailed* (mourned for) *her.* But Christ told them *not to weep; for she is not dead, but sleepeth.* He meant that in her particular case, death was not forever; to her friends it would seem as if she had been asleep for a few hours. However, the phrase may also be applied to all who die in the Lord; that is why we should not grieve for them as those *who have no hope* (1Th 4:13), because death is merely a sleep. This was a word of encouragement that Christ spoke to these mourners, but they cruelly ridiculed it, *laughing him to scorn.* They *knew* that she was dead; they were certain of it, and so nothing less than divine power could restore her to life. But he *put them all out* (v. 54). They were unworthy to witness this miracle.

6. Her return to life: *He took her by the hand*—as we do to a sleeping person whom we want to wake up and help up—and he called, saying, *Maid* (my child), *arise* (v. 55). Here is expressed what was only implied in the other Evangelists, that *her spirit came again.* We are not told where this child's soul was in this interval; it was in the hand of the *Father of spirits* (Heb 12:9). When *her spirit came again,* she got up, making it clear that she was alive by her movement, as she did also by her appetite, for Christ told them to give her something to eat. In the last verse, we need not wonder to find *her parents astonished.*

CHAPTER 9

Here is: 1. The commission Christ gave to his twelve apostles (vv. 1–6). 2. Herod's terror at the growing greatness of our Lord Jesus (vv. 7–9). 3. The apostles' return to Christ, his retreat with them, the great turning of people to them despite that, and his feeding five thousand men (vv. 10–17). 4. His conversation with his disciples about himself and his own sufferings for them (vv. 18–27). 5. His transfiguration (vv. 28–36). 6. The healing of a boy with an evil spirit (vv. 37–42).

7. The repeated announcement of his approaching suffering (vv. 43–45). 8. His restraint on the ambition of his disciples (vv. 46–48) and on their desire to monopolize power over demons (vv. 49–50). 9. The rebuke he gave them for their excessive anger at the disrespect shown him by a Samaritan village (vv. 51–56). 10. The answers he gave to several who were inclined to follow him (vv. 57–62).

Verses 1–9

We have here:

1. The method Christ took to spread his Gospel. He himself had traveled around, but he could be in only one place at a time, and so now he sent his twelve disciples out. Let them disperse, some one way and some another, to *preach the kingdom of God*. To confirm their teaching, he empowered them to perform miracles (vv. 1–2): he *gave them authority over all devils*, to drive them out. He also authorized and appointed them to *cure disease* and *heal the sick*, which would not only convince people's judgments but also win their affections. This was their commission. Notice:

1.1. What Christ told them to do in fulfillment of this commission.

1.1.1. They must not be concerned to commend themselves to people's respect by their outward appearance. They must go as they were, not changing their clothes or even putting on a new pair of shoes.

1.1.2. They must depend on Providence and the kindness of their friends. They must not take with them *either bread or money*. Christ does not want his disciples to be shy of receiving the kindnesses of their friends, but rather to expect them.

1.1.3. They must not change their lodgings, as if suspecting that those who lodged them were tired of them. *"Whatsoever house ye enter into, there abide* (v. 4), so that people may know where to find you. *Abide there* until you *depart* from that town; stay with those you are used to."

1.1.4. They must use the authority given them to speak a warning to those who refused them as well as to speak encouragement to those who received them (v. 5). "If there is any place that will not receive you, put them under the judgment of God for it; *shake off the dust of your feet* as a *testimony against them.*"

1.2. What they did in fulfillment of this commission (v. 6): *They departed* from their Master's presence; they *went through the towns, preaching the Gospel, and healing everywhere*. Their work was the same as their Master's, doing good to both souls and bodies.

2. Herod's perplexity and displeasure at this. The giving of Christ's authority to those who were sent out in his name was an amazing and convincing proof that he was the Messiah. His power not only to perform miracles himself but also to empower others to perform them spread his fame more than anything. *They had been with Jesus* (Ac 4:13). When the country saw such people healing the sick in the name of Jesus, it sounded the alarm. Notice:

2.1. The various speculations that the disciples' ministry raised among the people, who, although they did not think rightly, must have thought honorably about our Lord Jesus, that he was One who had come from the other world. They thought that either John the Baptist or *one of the old prophets* had *risen again*, or that Elijah *had appeared* (vv. 7–8).

2.2. The great confusion it created in the mind of Herod: *When he had heard of all that was done by* Christ, he was ready to conclude, along with the people, that John

was risen from the dead. "What should I do now?" Herod said. "John *have I beheaded, but who is this?* Is he carrying on John's work, or has he come to avenge John's death?" Those who oppose God will find themselves more and more uncomfortable. Herod *desired to see him*, and why did he not go and see him? He wanted to see him, but we do not find that he ever did until Christ was sent to him by Pilate.

Verses 10–17

We have here:

1. The account that the Twelve gave their Master of the success of their ministry. *When they returned, they told him all that they had done.*

2. Their retreat, to gain a little breathing space: *He took them, and went aside privately into a desert place.* The One who has appointed our *manservants and maidservants to rest* (Ex 20:10) wants his servants to rest as well. Those in the most public positions must sometimes withdraw privately, both to give rest to their bodies and to equip their minds for further public work by meditation.

3. The many people who turned to him and the kind reception he gave them. They followed him, even though it was into a remote place. And although they disturbed the rest he had planned, he still welcomed them (v. 11). Godly zeal may excuse a little rudeness; it did with Christ, and it should also with us. Although they came at the wrong time, Christ still gave them what they came for. He spoke to them about the kingdom of God, and he healed those of them who needed healing. Christ still has a power over physical diseases, and he heals his people who need healing. Yet sometimes he sees that we need the sickness for the good of our souls more than the healing for the relief of our bodies. Death is the servant to heal the saints of all diseases.

4. The plentiful provision Christ made for the crowd who were with him. He fed five thousand men with five loaves of bread and two fish. We had this narrative twice before, and we will meet with it again; it is the only miracle of our Savior's that is recorded by all four Evangelists. Let us observe from it here:

4.1. Those who are with Christ diligently doing their duty and who, in so doing, deny or expose themselves are taken under his special care. He will not allow those who fear him and serve him faithfully to lack any good thing (Ps 34:10).

4.2. Our Lord Jesus had a free and generous spirit. His disciples said, "Send them away, so that they may provide themselves with food," but Christ said, "No, you give them something to eat; let what we have go as far as it will reach, and they are welcome to enjoy it." In this way, he has taught both ministers and Christians in general to offer *hospitality without grudging* (1Pe 4:9). Let those who have only a little do what they can with that little, and that is the way to make it more.

4.3. Jesus Christ has not only medicine but also food. He not only heals those who need healing but also feeds those who need feeding. Christ has provided not only to save the soul from perishing by its diseases but also to nourish the soul to eternal life.

4.4. All the gifts of Christ are to be received in a regular and orderly manner: *Make them sit down by fifties in a company* (v. 14).

4.5. When we are receiving our creature comforts, we must look to heaven. Christ did so to teach us to do so. We receive them from God, and we depend on God's blessing on them to make them useful to us, and we must seek that blessing.

4.6. The blessing of Christ will make a little go a long way.

4.7. Those whom Christ feeds he fills; just as there is in him enough for all, so there is also enough for each. Here fragments were taken up, to assure us that in our Father's house there is bread enough and to spare (15:17). We are not starved or restricted in him.

Verses 18–27

1. One circumstance of this conversation is noted here that we did not have in the other Evangelists' accounts: that when Christ began to say this, he was *alone praying*, and his *disciples with him* (v. 18). Notice:

1.1. He still found some time to be alone in private, to have fellowship with himself, his Father, and his disciples.

1.2. When Christ was alone, he was *praying*. It is good for us to use our solitude for devotion, so that when we are alone, we may not be alone, but may have the Father with us.

1.3. When Christ was alone, praying, his *disciples were with him*, to join him in praying.

1.4. Christ prayed with them before he asked them questions. We should pray with and for those whom we instruct. We talked with them:

2. About himself; he asked:

2.1. What the people said of him: *Who say the people that I am?* (v. 18). They told him what thoughts about him they had heard in their conversations with the ordinary people. Ministers would know better how to adjust their instructions, rebukes, and advice to the case of ordinary people if only they spoke more frequently and informally with them. The better doctors know their patients, the better they will know what treatment to give them. Some said that he was John the Baptist, who had been beheaded only the other day; others said he was Elijah or *one of the old prophets*; they said he was anyone but who he really was.

2.2. What the Twelve themselves said about him. Peter said, "We know that you are *the Christ of God*, the Anointed One of God." Now one would have expected that Christ would command his disciples to make this truth known to everyone they met with, but no, he *strictly charged them to tell no man that thing* as yet (v. 21). After his resurrection, which completed the proof of his Messiahship, Peter made the temple ring with its news, that *God had made this same Jesus both Lord and Christ* (Ac 2:36), but at this time the evidence was not ready to be summed up, and so it must be concealed.

3. About his own sufferings and death. Now that his disciples were well established in the belief that he was the Christ and were able to bear it, he spoke about his own sufferings and death explicitly (v. 22). They must not yet preach that he was the Christ, because the miracles that would accompany his death and resurrection would be the most convincing proof that he was *the Christ of God*.

4. About his sufferings for him.

4.1. We ourselves must get used to all kinds of self-denial and patience (v. 23). We must not indulge our comforts and appetite, because then it will be hard to bear toil, weariness, and need for Christ. We frequently meet with adversities as we fulfill our duty, and although we must not bring them down onto our own heads, nevertheless, when they are there for us, we must take them up, carry them after Christ (Mk 8:34), and make the best of them.

4.2. We must put the salvation and happiness of our souls before any worldly concern whatever. Depend on it:

4.2.1. Whoever wants to keep his freedom or possessions or to save his life, whoever denies Christ and his truths, will not only not be a saver; he will be an unspeakable loser. *He that will save his life* upon these terms *will lose it* (v. 24), will lose what is infinitely more valuable, his precious soul.

4.2.2. If we lose our life because we remain faithful to Christ, we will save it to our indescribable advantage. We will have it again as a new and eternal life.

4.2.3. The gain of the whole world, if we were to forsake Christ, would be so far from making up for the eternal loss and ruin of the soul that it would not be in any way proportionate to it (v. 25). If we could possibly gain all the wealth, honor, and pleasure of the world by denying Christ, when by so doing we would *lose ourselves* to all eternity and be *cast away* in the end, what good would our worldly gain do us? In Matthew and Mark the terrible issue is a person's *losing his own soul*, whereas here it is *losing himself*, which clearly shows that our souls are ourselves. "The soul is the person," and things go well or badly with us according to whether things are going well or badly with our souls. The body cannot be happy if the soul is miserable in the other world, but the soul may be happy even though the body may be greatly afflicted and oppressed in this world.

4.3. We must never, therefore, be ashamed of Christ and his Gospel (v. 26): *For whosoever shall be ashamed of me and of my words, of him shall the Son of man be ashamed*, and justly. That person can expect nothing else than that on the great day, when his case calls for Christ's appearance on his behalf, Christ will be ashamed to acknowledge such a cowardly, worldly, sneaking spirit and will say, "That one does not belong to me." Just as Christ had a state of humiliation and of exaltation, so does his cause. Those, and only those, who are willing to suffer with his cause when it suffers will reign with it when it reigns (2Ti 2:12). Notice here how Christ, to support himself and his followers in their present disgrace, speaks magnificently of the shining of his second coming.

4.3.1. He will come *in his own glory*. This was not mentioned in Matthew and Mark.

4.3.2. He will come in *his Father's glory*.

4.3.3. He will come in *the glory of the holy angels*. What a glorious appearance the blessed Jesus will make on that day! If we really believed it, we would never be ashamed of him or his words now.

4.4. To encourage them in suffering for him, he assured them that *the kingdom of God* would now soon be set up (v. 27). "The kingdom of God will come in its power in the present age, while some who are present here are alive." They *saw the kingdom of God* when the Spirit was poured out, when the Gospel was preached to the whole world and nations were brought to Christ by it.

Verses 28–36

We have here the account of Christ's transfiguration, which was designed to show his glory, about which he had just been speaking; his disciples' witnessing of this transfiguration would therefore be an encouragement to them to suffer for him and never to be ashamed of him. We had this account before in Matthew and Mark.

1. Here is one circumstance of the narrative that seems to differ from those of the other two Evangelists. They said that it was *six days* after the previous sayings; Luke says that it was *about eight days after*. No doubt this means that it was on the same day of the week, one week later; six whole days intervened, and it was the eighth day.

2. Here are added and explained various significant circumstances.

2.1. We are told here that Christ had this honor given him when he was praying: he *went up into a mountain to pray* (v. 28), and *as he prayed* he was *transfigured.* When Christ humbled himself to pray, he was exalted (14:11; 18:14; Php 2:8–9). Christ himself had to seek the favors that were intended for him and promised to him. Moreover, this was how he intended to honor the duty of prayer and commend it to us. Prayer is a transfiguring, transforming duty, and by it we draw in resources of his wisdom, grace, and joy, which *make the face to shine* (Ecc 8:1).

2.2. Luke does not use the word *transfigured* (which Matthew and Mark used), but he uses an equivalent phrase: *the fashion of his countenance was altered,* "was another thing than what it had been" (the appearance on his face changed), and his clothes were white and glistening. It was bright as a flash of lightning—the word is used only here—so that he seemed to be completely arrayed with light; he seemed to *cover himself with light as with a garment* (Ps 104:2).

2.3. It was said in Matthew and Mark that Moses and Elijah appeared to them; here it is said that they appeared in glory. Because he was in glory, they appeared with him in glory.

2.4. We are told here what was the subject of the talk between Christ and the two great prophets of the Old Testament: *They spoke of his decease, which he should accomplish at Jerusalem.* "They spoke of his exodus, his departure," that is, his death.

2.4.1. The death of Christ is called here his exit, his going out, his leaving the world. The death of the saints is their exodus from the Egypt of this world, their release from a land of slavery.

2.4.2. He *must accomplish* (bring to fulfillment) this departure, because it had been determined by the purposes of God that he must, and those purposes could not be changed.

2.4.3. He must accomplish it at Jerusalem.

2.4.4. Moses and Elijah spoke about this to show that Christ's sufferings and his *entrance into his glory* were what Moses and *the prophets* had *spoken of*; see 24:26–27; 1Pe 1:11.

2.4.5. Our Lord Jesus, even in his transfiguration, was willing to talk about his death and sufferings. In our greatest glories on earth, let us remember that here *we have no continuing city* (Heb 13:14).

2.5. We are told here, though not in the other Gospels, that the disciples were *heavy with sleep* (very sleepy) (v. 32). Perhaps it was because of a sinful carelessness: when Christ was praying with them, they did not consider his prayer as they should have, and, to punish them for that, he left them to sleep for now, and so they lost the opportunity of seeing how that miracle was performed. These three were asleep now, when Christ was in his glory, and again later, when he was in his anguish. One would have thought that nothing could be more moving to these disciples than the glories and the anguish of their Master, and that both would have been most intensely moving, but neither the one nor the other could keep them awake. This shows us how much we need to pray to God for reviving grace, to make us not only alive but lively! After a while they recovered, and then they had a precise view of all those glories, and that they were able to give a detailed account—as we find one of them does (2Pe 1:18)—of all that took place when they were with Christ on the holy mountain.

2.6. It is noted here that it was when Moses and Elijah were about to depart that Peter said, *Lord, it is good to be here; let us make three tabernacles* (shelters). We are often not aware of the worth of our mercies until we are

about to lose them; nor do we care whether they continue until they are about to leave. Peter said this without knowing what he said.

2.7. It is added here about the cloud that overshadowed them that *they feared as they entered into the cloud.* This cloud was a sign of God's special presence, and so it is hardly surprising that the disciples were afraid to enter it (Ex 40:34–35; 2Ch 5:14). But no one should be afraid to enter a cloud with Jesus Christ, because he will be sure to bring them safely through it.

2.8. What was said by the voice that came from heaven is not related so fully here and in Mark as it is in Matthew, where the voice says, *This is my beloved Son, hear him.* Although those words, *in whom I am well pleased,* which we have both in Matthew (Mt 17:5) and in Peter (2Pe 1:17), are not expressed, they are implied in *This is my beloved Son.*

2.9. The apostles are said here to have kept this vision private. They told no one in those days. Just as there is a time to speak, so there is also a time to keep silence. Everything is beautiful and useful in its season (Ecc 3:1, 7, 11).

Verses 37–42

In Matthew and Mark this account immediately follows that of Christ's transfiguration and his talk with his disciples after it, but here it is said to be *on the next day, as they were coming down from the hill.* It was not until the next day that they *came down from the hill,* and it was then that he found things in some disorder among his disciples. Notice:

1. How eager the people were to receive Christ at his return to them. *Much people met him,* as at other times many people followed him.

2. How boldly the father of the boy with an evil spirit came to Christ to ask for help (v. 38): *I beseech* (beg) *thee, look upon my son*; this was his request. One compassionate look from Christ is enough to set everything right. Let us bring ourselves and our children to Christ to be looked upon. His plea is, *He is my only child.* Those who have many children may balance out their affliction in one with their comfort in the others, but the suffering of an only child may be balanced out with the love of God in giving his Only-begotten Son for us.

3. How deplorable the case of the child was (v. 39). He was under the power of an evil spirit, which *took* (seized) *him.* When the fit seized him, he suddenly *cried out,* and many times his shrieks had pierced the heart of his tender father. This evil spirit *tore him* (threw him into convulsions) and *bruised* (was destroying) him and *departed not from him* except with great difficulty. What trouble Satan causes where he gains possession! But happy are those who have access to Christ!

4. How deficient the disciples were in their faith. Although Christ had given them *power over unclean spirits,* they *could not* drive out this *evil spirit* (v. 40). Either they distrusted the power from which they were to draw strength, or they did not exert themselves in their prayers as they should have; and Christ rebuked them for this.

5. How effective was the healing that Christ performed on this child (v. 42). Christ can do for us what his disciples cannot: *Jesus rebuked the unclean spirit.* The demon *threw the child down, and tore him,* as if he were going to pull him to pieces. But one word from Christ *healed the child,* making good the damage the demon had caused. He *delivered him again* (gave him back) *to his father.* When our children have recovered from sickness, we must receive them as given back to us, as raised from the dead.

It is encouraging to receive them from the hands of Christ: "Here, take this child, and be thankful; take him and bring him up for me, because you have his life back from me." With such cautions parents should receive their children from Christ's hands, and then with assurance put them back into his hands.

Verses 43–50

Notice here:

1. The impression that Christ's miracles made on all who saw them (v. 43): *They were all amazed at the mighty power of God*. Their wonder was general: everyone marveled. Its causes were general: they marveled at *all things which Jesus did*; all his actions had something uncommon and surprising about them.

•2. The announcement Christ gave his disciples of his approaching sufferings: *The Son of man shall be delivered into the hands of men*. What is expressed by the other Evangelists—*They shall kill him* (Mt 17:23; Mk 9:31)—is implied here. However, what is distinctive here is:

2.1. The connection of this with what came immediately before, the wonder with which the people were struck at seeing Christ's miracles (v. 43): *While they all wondered at all things which Jesus did, he said this to his disciples*. They had a fond notion that he had a temporal kingdom and that he would reign in worldly pomp and power, and now they thought that this mighty power of his would easily establish this kingdom. Christ, therefore, used this occasion to tell them again that, far from having people delivered into his hands, he must be *delivered into the hands of men*.

2.2. The solemn introduction with which this announcement was presented: *"Let these sayings sink down into your ears*. Admit what I say and submit to it." "Let it sink down into your hearts" is the reading of the Syriac and Arabic. The word of Christ does us no good unless we allow it to sink down into our heads and hearts.

2.3. The unaccountable dullness of the disciples. It was said in Mark, *They understood not that saying*. It was clear enough, but they refused to understand it literally, and in fact they could not understand it in any way at all, *and they were afraid to ask him*, for fear that they might be put right and rescued from their pleasing dream. However, it is added here that *it was hidden from them, that they perceived it not*. We cannot think that it was hidden from them in mercy, so that they would not be swallowed up with excessive sorrow at its prospect; rather, it was a puzzle, because they made it so to themselves.

3. The rebuke Christ gave his disciples for disputing among themselves who should be the greatest (vv. 46–48). We had this passage before, and, sadly, we will meet with similar ones again. Notice here:

3.1. Ambition for honor and striving for superiority and precedence are the sins that most easily entangle the disciples of our Lord Jesus (Heb 12:1). They flow from a corruption that his disciples should be very anxious to subdue and put to death (v. 46). Those who expect to be great in this world commonly aim high, and nothing will be enough for them except being the greatest; this exposes them to a great deal of temptation and trouble, which those who are content to be little, to be least, to be less than the least are safe from.

3.2. Jesus Christ is perfectly familiar with the thoughts and intents of our hearts (Heb 4:12): he *perceived their thoughts* (v. 47). Thoughts are words to him, and whispers are loud cries.

3.3. Christ wants his disciples to aim at the honor that is to be obtained by a quiet humility, and not at what is to be obtained by a restless and aspiring ambition. Christ *took a child, and set him by him* (v. 47)—he always expressed a tenderness and kindness for little children.

3.3.1. Let them have the attitude of this child, being humble and quiet and at ease with themselves. Let them be willing to be the least, if that would lead in any way to their usefulness.

3.3.2. Let them assure themselves that this was the way to advancement. Those who loved Christ would receive them *in his name*, because they were most like him. And Christ would take the kindnesses done to children as done to himself: *Whosoever shall receive one such child receiveth me*, and *whosoever receiveth me, receiveth him that sent me*. What greater honor can anyone reach in this world than to have God and Christ acknowledge themselves to have been received and welcomed in him?

4. The rebuke Christ gave to his disciples for discouraging one who honored him and served him but did not belong to their fellowship. It was someone who only occasionally listened to Christ, believed in him, and used his name with faith and prayer in a serious manner to drive out demons.

4.1. They *rebuked and restrained* this man. They would not allow him to pray and preach, even though it was to the honor of Christ. He did not *follow Christ with them*.

4.2. Jesus Christ rebuked them for what they did: *"Forbid him not* (v. 50), but rather encourage him, for he is carrying out the same purpose as you are. He will meet you at the same end, even though he does not accompany you on the same road. *He that is not against us is for us* and should therefore be supported by us." We need not lose any of our friends as long as we have so few, and so many enemies. People may be found to be faithful followers of Christ and, as such, may be accepted by him, even though they do not follow us.

Verses 51–56

We do not have this passage in any other of the Evangelists' accounts. Here the disciples wanted to put unbelievers to death, and Christ reprimanded them, because a spirit of bigotry and persecution is directly hostile to the spirit of Christ. Notice:

1. The readiness and resolution of our Lord Jesus in pursuing his great undertaking for our redemption and salvation. Of this we have an example in v. 51: *When the time was come that he should be received up, he steadfastly set his face to go to Jerusalem*. A time was fixed for the sufferings and death of our Lord Jesus, and he knew well enough when it was, and yet now he appeared most publicly of all, and was most active, knowing that his time was short. When he saw his death and sufferings approaching, he looked through them and beyond them to the time when he would be *received up into glory* (1Ti 3:16). All true Christians may have in themselves the same idea of death as their Lord had: they may call it their being received up to be with Christ where he is (Mk 16:19; Php 1:23). He *steadfastly* (resolutely) *set his face to go to Jerusalem* with this prospect of the joy set before him (Heb 12:2). He was fully determined to go and would not be dissuaded from going; he went directly to Jerusalem. He went there cheerfully and courageously. He did not fail and was not discouraged, but *set his face as a flint*, knowing that he would be not only justified but also glorified (Isa 50:7; Ro 8:30), not only not overwhelmed, but received into glory. How this should shame us for, and shame us out of, our reluctance to act and suffer for Christ!

2. The rudeness of the Samaritans in a certain village who would *not receive him*. Notice:

2.1. How polite he was to them: *He sent messengers before his face* to find out whether he and his disciples would be allowed to stay among them and, if so, to secure lodgings. He sent some ahead to *make ready for him* so that his coming would not be a surprise.

2.2. How impolite they were to him (v. 53). They did not *receive him*, would not allow him to come into their village. He would have been the greatest blessing that had ever come to their village, but they forbade him from entering. Now the reason was that *his face was as though he would go to Jerusalem*. The great dispute between the Jews and the Samaritans was about the proper place of worship, whether it was Jerusalem or Mount Gerizim near Sychar; see Jn 4:20. The controversy between them was so intense that the *Jews would have no dealings with the Samaritans*, nor the Samaritans with them (Jn 4:9). However, these Samaritans were particularly angry with Christ, who was a celebrated teacher, for being loyal to and acknowledging the temple at Jerusalem. They would not show him the common civility that they probably used to show him on his journeys to Jerusalem.

3. The resentment that James and John expressed at this insult (v. 54). When these two heard this message, they immediately lost their temper, and nothing would be enough for them but the condemnation of Sodom on this village.

3.1. Here surely was something commendable, because they showed:

3.1.1. A great confidence in the power they had received from Jesus Christ. They could by speaking a word draw down *fire from heaven*. "Do you want us to speak the word?" And then the thing would be done.

3.1.2. A great zeal for the honor of their Master. They took it very badly that the One who did good wherever he went (Ac 10:38) and who generally found a hearty welcome should be denied free access to the road by a little group of Samaritans.

3.1.3. A submission, nevertheless, to their Master's goodwill and pleasure. They would not offer to do such a thing unless Christ allowed it: *Wilt thou that we* (do you want us to) do it?

3.1.4. Consideration given to the examples of the prophets who went before them. Was it doing *as Elias did* (2Ki 1:10, 12)? They thought that this precedent would authorize them; we are so inclined to misapply the examples of good people.

3.2. Although there was something right in what they said, much more was wrong, because:

3.2.1. This was far from the first time that our Lord Jesus had been insulted in this way, yet he never called for any judgment on any of those other occasions, but patiently endured the wrong done to him.

3.2.2. These were Samaritans, from whom better was not to be expected, and perhaps they had heard that Christ had forbidden his disciples to *enter into any of the cities of the Samaritans* (Mt 10:5), and so their offense was not as bad as that of others who knew more of Christ.

3.2.3. Perhaps it was only a few people in the town who sent that bad-mannered message to him, while, for all the disciples knew, many others in the town would have gone out to meet him and welcome him.

3.2.4. Their Master had never up to that time on any occasion called for *fire from heaven*. James and John were the two disciples whom Christ had called *Boanerges*, "sons of thunder" (Mk 3:17). Was that not enough for them—must they be sons of lightning too?

3.2.5. The example of Elijah did not match the situation. Elijah was sent to display the terrors of the Law; the

era now being introduced was an era of grace, to which such a terrible display of divine justice would not be at all suitable.

4. The rebuke he gave James and John (v. 55): he *turned* and *rebuked them*, because *as many as he loves, he rebukes and chastens* (Rev 3:19), especially when, under the guise of zeal for him, they do anything that is irregular and inconsistent with what they truly are.

4.1. He showed them their mistake in detail: *Ye know not what manner of spirit ye are of*.

4.1.1. "You are not aware how much there is of pride, passion, and personal revenge covered up by this false zeal for your Master." There may be much corruption still lurking—indeed, stirring—in the hearts of good people without their being aware of it.

4.1.2. "You do not consider what a good spirit you should have. Certainly you have still to learn what the spirit of Christ is. Have you not been taught to *love your enemies* and *bless them that curse you* (Mt 5:44), and to call down on them grace from heaven, not fire from heaven? You are in the era of love, liberty, and grace, which was introduced by the proclamation of *peace on earth* and *good will toward men* (2:14)."

4.2. He showed them the general intention and tendency of his religion (v. 56): *The Son of man has not himself come to destroy men's lives, but to save them*. He wanted to spread his holy religion by love and sweetness and by everything welcoming and endearing, not by fire and sword; by miracles of healing, not by plagues and miracles of destruction, as Israel was brought out of Egypt. Christ came to put to death all enmities, not to foster them. Christ came to save not only the souls of human beings but also their lives. Christ wants his disciples to do good to all. He wanted them to hurt no one; he wanted them to draw people into his church with the *cords of a man and the bands of love* (Hos 11:4) rather than driving them into it with a rod of violence or the lash of the tongue.

5. His withdrawal from this village. Christ would not only not punish them for their rudeness; he would go quietly and peaceably *to another village*, where they were not so mean. If some people are very rude, then instead of taking revenge, we should see whether others will not be more polite.

Verses 57–62

Here is an account of three people who separately offered to follow Christ:

1. Here is one who was extremely eager to follow Christ immediately but who seems to have been too rash and not to have sat down and counted the cost.

1.1. He made Christ a very big promise (v. 57): *As they went in the way*, one man said to him, *Lord, I will follow thee whithersoever thou goest*. This must be the resolution of all who will be found to be Christ's true disciples; they *follow the Lamb whithersoever he goes* (Rev 14:4).

1.2. Christ gave him a necessary warning, that he must not promise himself great things in the world in following Christ, because *the Son of man has not where to lay his head*. We may look on this:

1.2.1. As showing the lowly condition our Lord Jesus had in this world. He not only lacked the delights and ornaments that great rulers usually have; he even lacked basic accommodation, a simple necessity that *foxes* and *birds of the air* have. The One who made everything did not even make a place for himself to live, not even a house of his own to lay his head in. He called himself the *Son of man* here, a Son of Adam, One who shared in our flesh and blood. He glories in his condescension toward us, to show his love for us and to teach us to have a holy contempt of the things of this world and a constant affection for the other world. Christ was poor in order to sanctify and sweeten poverty to his people. We may well be content to live as Christ did.

1.2.2. As proposing this for the consideration of those who want to be his disciples. If we seek to follow Christ, we must not count on getting anything more than heaven as a reward for our religious faith. Christ told this man what he must count on if he followed him: he would lie cold and uneasy, living a life of hardship, a life of contempt. If he could not submit to this, let him not attempt to follow Christ. This word sent him back, it seems, but it will be no discouragement to anyone who knows what there is in Christ and heaven to put in the scales to balance it out.

2. Here is another man who seems to have decided to follow Christ but to have begged that he might first have one day's break (v. 59). Christ first gave the call to this man; he said to him, *Follow me*. The one who himself proposed to follow Christ ran off when he heard about the difficulties involved, but this man whom Christ called, though he hesitated at first, seems to have yielded afterward. It is not *of him that willeth, nor of him that runneth*—like that forward young fellow in the previous verses—*but of God* who shows mercy (Ro 9:16), who gives the call.

2.1. The excuse he made: "*Lord, suffer* (allow) *me first to go and bury my father*. I have an elderly father at home, who cannot live long and will need me while he is still alive; let me go and be with him until he has died, and then I will do anything." We may see three temptations here.

2.1.1. We are tempted to stay in an easy form of discipleship, in which we may remain loosely attached to Christianity but do not commit ourselves.

2.1.2. We are tempted to put off to a later date what we know to be our duty. When we have gotten clear of such and such a care and difficulty, then we will begin to think about being religious, and so we are cheated out of all our time by being cheated out of the present.

2.1.3. We are tempted to think that our duty to our relatives will give us an excuse for not fulfilling our duty to Christ. But the *kingdom of God and his righteousness* (Mt 6:33) must be sought and taken care of in the first place.

2.2. Christ's response to this (v. 60): "*Let the dead bury their dead*. You have other work to do; *go thou, and preach the kingdom of God.*" It is not that Christ wants his followers or his ministers to be unnatural; our religion teaches us to be kind and good in every relationship. But we must not make such actions an excuse from fulfilling our duty to God. If the closest and most precious relationship we have in the world stands in the way and keeps us from Christ, we must have a zeal that will make us forget *father and mother*. No excuses must be accepted against a present obedience to the call of Christ.

3. Here is another man who was willing to follow Christ but must have a little time to talk with his friends about it. Notice:

3.1. His request for special consideration (v. 61). He said, "*Lord, I will follow thee*, but *let me first go bid them farewell that are at home*." "Let me go and put my household affairs in order," as some understand it. Now what was wrong in this was:

3.1.1. That he looked on his following Christ as something sad, troublesome, and dangerous. Following Christ seemed to him like going to die, and so he must take leave

of all his friends, whereas in following Christ, he could be more of a comfort and blessing to them than if he had remained with them.

3.1.2. That he seemed to have his heart set on his worldly concerns more than would be consistent with a faithful fulfillment of his responsibilities as a follower of Christ. He seemed to yearn for his relatives and family matters; they clung to him. Maybe he had said farewell to them once, but "Loath to depart bids oft farewell," and so he must go home and say farewell to them once more.

3.1.3. That he was willing to be tempted away from his focused purpose of following Christ. To go and say farewell to those who were at his house would be to expose himself to the strongest possible requests to change his mind, because they would all beg and pray that he would not leave them. Those who decide to follow their Redeemer must be determined that they will not even enter into negotiations with their tempter.

3.2. The rebuke Christ gave him for this request (v. 62): "*No man, having put his hand to the plough*, will *look back*, or look behind him, because then he will carelessly miss a piece of ground with his plow, and the ground he plows will *not be fit* to be sown. In the same way, if you want to follow me, and yet you *look back* to a worldly life and hanker after that, *thou art not fit for the kingdom of God*. You are not a sower who is fit to scatter the good seed of the kingdom if you cannot hold the plow any better." Plowing is done in order to make way for sowing. Those who do not know how to break up the fallow ground, but, having *laid their hand to the plough*, look back on every occasion and think of abandoning it, are not fit to be employed in sowing. Looking back leads to drawing back, and drawing back leads to destruction. Those who turn around after they have set their faces toward heaven are not fit for heaven. But those, and only those, who *endure to the end shall be saved* (Mt 10:22).

CHAPTER 10

We have here: 1. The detailed commission Christ gave to the seventy disciples to preach the Gospel and confirm it by miracles (vv. 1–16). 2. The report of the seventy and his message to them (vv. 17–24). 3. Christ's talk with an expert in the law about the way to heaven, and the instruction Christ gave him through a parable to look on everyone as his neighbor (vv. 25–37). 4. Christ's reception at Martha's house, the rebuke he gave her for her excessive concern for the world, and his commendation of Mary (vv. 38–42).

Verses 1–16

We have here the sending out of seventy disciples, two by two. This is not noted by the other Evangelists, but the instructions given the seventy are much the same as those given to the Twelve. Notice:

1. Their number: they were seventy. Just as in the choice of twelve apostles Christ had in mind the twelve tribes and the twelve patriarchs, the rulers of those tribes, so here he seems to have had in mind the seventy elders of Israel (Ex 24:1, 9).

1.1. We are glad to find that Christ had so many followers who were suitable to be sent out; his labor was not completely in vain, though he met with much opposition. These seventy, though they were not with him as closely and constantly as the Twelve were, nevertheless constantly listened to his teaching, witnessed his miracles, and believed in him. These seventy were those of whom Peter spoke as *the men who companied with us all the time that the Lord Jesus went in and out among us*, and they were part of the 120 spoken about there (Ac 1:15, 21). We may presume that many of those who were the companions of the apostles and whom we read about in Acts and the Letters belonged to these seventy disciples.

1.2. We are glad to find there was work for so many ministers, and that there were listeners for so many preachers; this was how the grain of mustard seed began to grow (13:19) and how the fragrance of the yeast began to spread throughout the dough (13:21).

2. Their work and business: he sent them out two by two, so that they could strengthen and encourage one another. He sent them not to all the towns of Israel, as he did the Twelve, but only *to every city and place whither he himself would come* (v. 1), as his forerunners. They were told to do two things, the same as Christ did wherever he went:

2.1. They must *heal the sick* (v. 9), heal them *in the name of Jesus* (Ac 3:6), which would make people long to see this Jesus—eager to receive the One whose name was so powerful.

2.2. They must declare the approach of the kingdom of God: *the kingdom of God is come nigh to you.* It is good to be made aware of our advantages and opportunities, so that we may grasp them. When the *kingdom of God comes nigh us*, we should go out to meet it.

3. The instructions he gave them.

3.1. They must set out with prayer (v. 2). They must be properly moved by the needs of people's souls. They must look around them and see how great the harvest was. There was grain ready for harvest, and it would be lost if no hands were found to gather it in. They must also be concerned that *the labourers were so few.* It is common for traders not to care how few there are of their own trade, but Christ wants to have the laborers in his vineyard consider it a cause for complaint that the *labourers are few.* They must fervently seek to receive their mission from God, that he would send them out as *labourers into his harvest* and that he would send others out, because if God sent them out, they could hope that he would accompany them and give them success.

3.2. They must set out with an expectation of trouble and persecution: "*Behold, I send you forth as lambs among wolves.* Your enemies will be like wolves. But you must be like lambs, peaceable and patient, even though you realize you can easily be attacked." It would have been very hard to be sent out as *sheep among wolves* if he had not endowed them with his spirit and courage.

3.3. They must not burden themselves, as if they were going on a long journey, but must depend on God and their friends to provide: "Carry neither *a purse* for money, nor *a scrip* (bag) or knapsack for your clothes or food, nor new *shoes*"—as he had said before to the Twelve (9:3)—"and *salute no man by the way.*"

3.3.1. They must go quickly, must not hinder themselves or slow themselves down by unnecessary ceremonies or gifts.

3.3.2. They must go out as business people, on business that related to another world, and so they must not get caught up with secular affairs.

3.3.3. They must go as people who are serious.

3.4. They must show everyone to whom they came not only their goodwill but also God's goodwill (vv. 5–6).

3.4.1. The command given them was that to whatever *house* they *entered*, they must say, *Peace be to this house.* Here:

3.4.1.1. It was presumed that they would enter private houses, because, not being admitted to the synagogues, they would be forced to preach where they were free to.

Since their public preaching was driven into houses, they took it there. Christ's church was at first very much a house church.

3.4.1.2. They were taught to say, "*Peace be to this house. Salute no man by the way* in compliment, but when you enter a house, say, *Peace be to you*, with seriousness and in reality." Christ's ministers go into the whole world to say, in Christ's name, "Peace be to you." We are to offer peace to everyone, to preach peace through Jesus Christ, peace on earth (2:14), and to invite the people to come and receive its benefits. We are to pray for peace to all.

3.4.2. The response to their preaching would be different in different places, according to the different dispositions of those whom they preached to and prayed for. Whether their peace rested or did not rest on that house would depend on whether the head of the house loved peace or not. "You will meet with some who are *the sons of peace*, who are ready to accept the word of the Gospel in its light and love. As to those, *your peace* will find them and *rest upon them*; your prayers for them will be heard, and the promises of the Gospel will be confirmed to them. You will meet with others who are in no way disposed to listen to your message, whole houses that do not have one *son of peace* in them." Now it is certain that our peace will not come on such people. It will return to us again; that is, we will have the encouragement of having done our duty to God and having discharged our trust. Our peace will return to us, not only to be enjoyed by ourselves but also to be communicated to others, those who are *sons of peace.*

3.5. They must accept the kindnesses of those who would receive them and make them welcome (vv. 7–8). "Those who receive the Gospel will receive you who preach it.

3.5.1. "Do not be shy; do not doubt that you will be welcome, and do not be afraid that you will be troublesome, but *eat and drink* heartily *such things as they give.* You will deserve it, *for the labourer is worthy of his hire. Let those who are taught in the word communicate to* (share with) *those who teach them* (Gal 6:6), for this is not an act of love but of justice.

3.5.2. "Do not be fussy about what you eat: *Eat and drink such things as they give* (v. 7), *such things as are set before you* (v. 8). Be thankful for plain food, and do not object to it, even if it is not presented elegantly." It is not good for Christ's disciples to want luxuries. Christ is probably referring here to the traditions of the elders about their food. Christ did not want the seventy to consider those things, but to eat what was given them, asking no question for conscience's sake.

3.6. They must declare the judgments of God against those who rejected them and their message: "If you enter into a town and they do not receive you, leave them (v. 10). If they will not welcome you into their houses, warn them in their streets." He told them to do as he had told the apostles to do (9:5). "Say to them, '*Even the dust of your city, which cleaveth on* (sticks to) *us, we do wipe off against you* (v. 11).' Do not receive any kindnesses at all from them; do not be indebted to them in any way." That Christ's messengers had followed their Master's orders and brought their message would be a witness for them; offer and refusal were part of fulfilling their trust. "But tell them clearly, and make them sure of it, *The kingdom of God is come nigh to you.* Here a fair offer has been made to you; if you do not benefit from it, it is your own fault. Now that the kingdom of God has come near to you, if you will not enter it, your sin will be inexcusable." The fairer the offer we have of grace and life through Christ, the more we will have to answer for another day if we reject these offers: *It shall be more tolerable for Sodom than for that city* (v. 12). Indeed, the Sodomites rejected the warning given them by Lot, but rejecting the Gospel is a more detestable crime. On this occasion, the Evangelist repeats:

3.6.1. The particular condemnation of those towns in which most of Christ's mighty works were done, which we had before (Mt 11:20).

3.6.1.1. They enjoyed greater privileges. Christ's *mighty works were done in them*. They were hereby *exalted to heaven* (lifted up to the skies). They were brought as close to heaven as external means could possibly bring them.

3.6.1.2. God's intention in favoring them in this way was to bring them to repentance and reformation of life, so that they would *sit in sackcloth and ashes* (v. 13).

3.6.1.3. They thwarted this intention, receiving the grace of God in vain. It is implied that they did not repent; they did not produce fruits consistent with the advantages they enjoyed (3:8).

3.6.1.4. There was reason to think, morally speaking, that if Christ had gone to Tyre and Sidon, Gentile towns, their repentance would have been so speedy that they would have repented long ago; their repentance would have been so deep that they would have repented in *sackcloth and ashes*.

3.6.1.5. The condemnation of those who received the grace of God in vain (2Co 6:1) will be fearful. Those who were lifted up in this way but who did not make use of their elevation will *be thrust down to hell*.

3.6.1.6. On the Day of Judgment, Tyre and Sidon will fare better than these towns; for those Gentiles it will be more tolerable.

3.6.2. The general rule that Christ would follow in judging those to whom he would send his ministers: he would consider himself treated as his ministers were treated (v. 16). "*He that heareth you heareth me. He that despiseth you* is in effect *despising me*; in fact, he *despiseth him that sent me*." Those who despise the faithful ministers of Christ and turn their backs on their ministry will be counted as those who despise and reject God and Christ.

Verses 17–24

Christ sent out the seventy disciples as he was going to Jerusalem to the Feast of Tabernacles, when he *went up, not openly*, but *as it were in secret* (Jn 7:10), having sent out such a great part of his ordinary retinue. Dr. Lightfoot thinks that these disciples — or at least some of them — returned to Christ before his return from that feast, while he was still at Jerusalem, or at Bethany, which was close by — soon he would stay with Mary and Martha (v. 38; compare Jn 12:1–3). Now we are told here:

1. What account they gave him of the success of their expedition: *They returned again with joy* (v. 17), not complaining about how tired they were after the journey, but rejoicing in their success, especially in driving out evil spirits: *Lord, even the devils are subject unto us through thy name*.

1.1. They gave Christ the glory for this: it is *through thy name*. All our victories over Satan are obtained by power derived from Jesus Christ. We must join battle with our spiritual enemies in his name. If the work is done in his name, the honor is due to his name.

1.2. They encouraged themselves with the assurance of it, speaking of it with excitement: *Even the devils are subject to us*. If demons are subject to us, what can remain standing before us?

2. How he received this account.

2.1. He confirmed what they said, noting that it agreed with his own observation (v. 18): *I saw Satan fall as lightning from heaven*. Satan and his kingdom fell in the presence of the preaching of the Gospel. He falls *as lightning falls from heaven*, so suddenly and irrecoverably. Satan *falls from heaven* when he falls from the throne in people's hearts (Ac 26:18). Christ foresaw that the preaching of the Gospel would tear down Satan's kingdom wherever it went. *Now is the prince of this world cast out* (Jn 12:31).

2.2. He repeated, confirmed, and enlarged their commission: *Behold, I give you power to tread on serpents* (v. 19). They had used their authority strongly against Satan, and now Christ entrusted them with even greater authority. He gave them:

2.2.1. An offensive power, authority to tread on snakes and scorpions, demons and evil spirits, the old Serpent (Rev 12:9; 20:2). "Just as the demons have now been subject to you, so they will continue to be."

2.2.2. A defensive power: "Nothing will hurt you by any means, not even snakes or scorpions. If evildoers are like serpents to you, and you live among those scorpions, you may despise their rage and tread on them. They may hiss at you, but they cannot harm you."

2.3. He instructed them on how to channel their joy in the right way (v. 20): "Despite your success, do not rejoice that the spirits are subject to you. Do not rejoice in this only, or even chiefly, but rather rejoice because your names are written in heaven, because you are the children of God through faith." Christ could tell them that their names were written in heaven because it is the Lamb's book of life that they are written in. The right to become the children of God (Jn 1:12) is to be valued more highly than the right to work miracles, because we read of those who drove out demons in Christ's name but who will be disowned by Christ on the great day. However, those whose names are written in heaven will never perish; they are Christ's sheep, to whom he will give eternal life. Holy love is a more excellent way than speaking in tongues (1Co 12:31–13:1).

2.4. He offered a sacred prayer of thanksgiving to his Father (vv. 21–22). We had this before (Mt 11:25–27), except that here it is introduced by a statement that Jesus *rejoiced in that hour*. In the hour in which he saw Satan fall, he *rejoiced in that hour*. Christ's joy was solid, substantial, and inward: he rejoiced in spirit. Before he addressed his Father in thanksgiving, he stirred himself up to rejoice, for just as thankful praise is the genuine language of holy joy, so holy joy is the root and spring of thankful praise. He gave thanks for two things:

2.4.1. For what was revealed by the Father through the Son: *I thank thee, O Father, Lord of heaven and earth* (v. 21). Now what he gave thanks for was:

2.4.1.1. That the purposes of God concerning the reconciliation of human beings to him were revealed to some people, who could be equipped to teach them to others; to them he had revealed what had been *kept secret from the foundation of the world* (Mt 13:35).

2.4.1.2. That they were revealed to *babes* (little children), to those who were merely children in understanding until God raised their abilities by his Spirit. We have reason to thank God not so much for the honor he has put on little children as for the honor he has done himself in perfecting strength out of weakness (Ps 8:2; Mt 21:16; 2Co 12:9; Heb 11:34).

2.4.1.3. That at the same time as he revealed them to little children, he *hid them from the wise and prudent* (learned), the Gentile philosophers, the Jewish rabbis. He did not reveal the things of the Gospel to them, nor use them in preaching his kingdom. It is true that Paul was brought up as a scholar among the wise and learned, but when he became an apostle, he became a child, making neither show nor use of any other knowledge than that of *Christ and him crucified* (1Co 2:2, 4).

2.4.1.4. That God here was acting in his sovereignty: *Even so, Father, for so it seemed good in thy sight.* If God gives his grace and the knowledge of his Son to some who are less likely, and if he does not give it to others whom we might think better able to communicate it well, we must take comfort in the assurance that this is what pleases God. He chooses to entrust the communication of his Gospel to the hands of those who will use divine power to give it an impetus, rather than to the hands of those who will use their mere human skill to hinder its advance.

2.4.2. For what was secret between the Father and the Son (v. 22). We see here:

2.4.2.1. The immense confidence that the Father puts in the Son: *All things are delivered to me of my Father.* All fullness must dwell in him (Col 1:19), and it must be derived from him; he is the great Trustee who manages all the concerns of God's kingdom.

2.4.2.2. The good understanding that there is between the Father and the Son: *No man knows who the Son is* except the Father. Nor does anyone know *who the Father is* except the Son and whomever the Son by the Spirit chooses to reveal him to.

2.5. He told his disciples how good it was for them that they had these things revealed to them (vv. 23–24). He turned to his disciples, intending to make them aware of how much it was for their happiness that they knew the mysteries of the kingdom and were employed in leading others into the knowledge of them, considering:

2.5.1. What a step it was toward something better. Although the bare knowledge of these things is not saving, it still puts us in a favorable position to receive the way of salvation: *Blessed are the eyes which see the things which we see.*

2.5.2. What a step it was above those who went before them: "*Many prophets and righteous men*" — as it is in Mt 13:17 — "*many prophets and kings*" — as it is here — "*have desired to see* and *hear those things*" that you are daily and intimately familiar with but *have not seen* and *heard* them." The honor and happiness of the New Testament saints far exceed even those of the prophets and kings of the Old Testament. The general ideas that the Old Testament saints had of the graces and glories of the Messiah's kingdom made them wish a thousand times that they could see the substance of those things of which they saw only faint shadows.

Verses 25–37

We have here Christ's conversation with a lawyer about some points of conscience, which we are all concerned to be rightly informed about, and here we are so informed by Christ.

1. It is our concern to know what good we should do in this life in order to obtain eternal life. A question to this effect was put to our Savior by a *certain lawyer*, only with the intention of testing him (v. 25). The lawyer *stood up* and *asked him, Master, what shall I do to inherit eternal life?* If Christ had anything special to prescribe, the lawyer would draw it out of him by this question, and perhaps expose him for it. If Christ had nothing special to prescribe, the lawyer would expose his teaching as useless. Or perhaps he had no malicious intentions against

Christ, but only wanted to have a little talk with him, just as people go to church out of curiosity, to hear what the minister will say. The lawyer asked a good question, but it lost all its goodness when it was asked with an evil intention. It is not enough to speak and ask about the things of God; we must also obey him with a suitable concern. Notice:

1.1. How Christ turned the lawyer to the divine law. Although he knew the thoughts and intentions of his heart (Heb 4:12), he did not answer him according to that folly (Pr 26:4), but according to the wisdom and goodness of the question he asked. Christ responded with a question: *What is written in the law? How readest thou?* (v. 26). Christ would teach him and make him understand himself. The studies of his profession would inform him; let him practice according to his knowledge, and he would not come short of eternal life. It will be very useful to us on our way to heaven to consider *what is written in the law* and *what we read* there. We must turn to our Bibles, to the law as it is now, in the hands of Christ, and walk in the way that is shown us there (Lev 18:4; Jdg 2:22). Having it written down, we have the duty of reading it with understanding so that when we need to, we may be able to tell *what is written in the law* and *how we read*.

1.2. What a good account he gave of the law, of the law's main commandments. He did not, like a Pharisee, refer to the tradition of the elders, but focused on the two first and great commandments of the law, which included all the others (v. 27). We must *love God with all our hearts*, must look on him as the best of beings, the One who in himself is most precious and is infinitely good and perfect. Our love for him must be sincere and fervent; it must be a superlative love, a love that is as strong as death (SS 8:6), but also an intelligent love. It must be a whole love; he must have all our souls, and we must serve him with all that is within us (Ps 103:1). We must love *our neighbor as ourselves*, which we will easily do if we love God better than ourselves, as we should do. We must do all the good we can in the world and no harm, and we must settle it as a rule to ourselves to do to others as we want them to do to us, and this is loving our neighbor as ourselves.

1.3. Christ's approval of what he said (v. 28). What the lawyer said that was good was commended by Christ: *Thou hast answered right.* Christ himself focused on these as the two great commandments of the law (Mt 22:37). The lawyer was right as far as he went, but the hardest part of this work still remained: "*This do, and thou shalt live*; you will *inherit eternal life.*"

1.4. His concern to avoid the conviction that was now ready to come on him. When Christ said, *This do, and thou shalt live*, he began to be aware that Christ intended to draw from him an acknowledgment that he had not done this. He was *willing to justify himself*, and so he did not want to continue this conversation. Many people ask good questions with the intention of justifying themselves rather than informing themselves, to show proudly what is good in them rather than to see humbly what is bad in them.

2. It is our concern to know who is our neighbor. This is another of this lawyer's questions. As to loving God, he was willing to say no more about it, but as to his neighbor, he was sure that there he had met the standard, because he had always been very kind and respectful to everyone around him. Notice:

2.1. What a corrupt idea the Jewish teachers had in this matter. "Where he says, 'Thou shalt love thy neighbor,' he excludes all Gentiles, because they are not our neighbors, but we are to love only those who belong to our own nation and religion." If they saw a Gentile in danger of death, they thought themselves under no obligation to help save his life.

2.2. How Christ corrected this inhuman idea, showing by a parable that anyone whom we may need kindness from must be looked on as our neighbor. Notice:

2.2.1. The parable itself, which describes to us a poor Jew in distressed circumstances who was helped and relieved by a good Samaritan. Let us see here:

2.2.1.1. How he was abused by his enemies. The honest man was traveling peacefully on his lawful business down the road, a main road leading from Jerusalem to Jericho (v. 30). Probably the events happened just as they are related here. This poor man *fell among thieves*. They were very cruel. They not only took his money but also stripped him of his clothes, and they *wounded him* and left him *half dead*, ready to die of his wounds. What reason we have to thank God for being kept from the dangers of robbers!

2.2.1.2. How he was shown disrespect by those who should have been his friends, one a priest and the other a Levite, men of professed sanctity, whose offices obliged them to show tenderness and compassion (Heb 5:2), who should have taught others their duty in such a case as this. Many of the priestly divisions had their residence in Jericho and came up from there to Jerusalem, and then went back again, which meant that many priests went back and forth that way, with the Levites as their attendants. This priest and Levite came this way and saw the poor wounded man. The Levite not only saw him but also *came and looked on him* (v. 32). But both *passed by on the other side*; when they saw his situation, they got as far away from him as possible.

2.2.1.3. How he was helped and relieved by a stranger, *a certain Samaritan*, of the nation that the Jews despised and detested more than all others and would have no dealings with. This man had some humanity in him (v. 33). The priest had his heart hardened against one of his own people, but the Samaritan had his heart opened toward one of another people. *When he saw him he had compassion on him.* Although the injured man was a Jew, he was still a man, a man in misery, and the Samaritan had learned to honor all people; and so he pitied him, as he himself would desire and expect to be pitied in a similar case. The compassion of this Samaritan was not idle; when he *drew out his soul*, he also *reached forth his hand* to this poor, needy creature (Isa 58:7; Pr 31:20). Notice how friendly this good Samaritan was.

2.2.1.3.1. He *went to* the poor man, whom the priest and Levite kept far away from.

2.2.1.3.2. He fulfilled the surgeon's role, for lack of anyone better to perform it. He *bound up his wounds*, probably using his own cloths for that purpose, and he poured *in oil and wine*, wine to wash the wound and oil to soothe it and close it up. He did all he could, as one whose heart went out to him.

2.2.1.3.3. Going on foot himself, he *set him on his own beast* (donkey) and *brought him to an inn*. We presume the Samaritan went on business, but he understood that both his own business and God's sacrifice must give way to such an act of mercy.

2.2.1.3.4. He *took care of him* in the inn: he got him to bed, got suitable food for him, and duly attended him; maybe he prayed with him. In fact:

2.2.1.3.5. As if the wounded man had been his own child, when he left him the next morning, he left money with the innkeeper and gave his word that he would repay

any extra expense he might incur. *Two pence* of their money would have gone a long way; however, here it was a pledge that he would pay back in full all the additional costs. All this was kind and generous, and as much as one could have expected from a friend or a brother, but here it was done by a stranger and foreigner.

2.2.2. The application of the parable.

2.2.2.1. The truth contained in it was drawn from the lawyer's own mouth. Christ said, "*Which of these three was neighbour to him that fell among thieves* (v. 36). Which of these fulfilled the neighbor's part?" The lawyer would not answer this with, "No doubt, the Samaritan," but, "*He that showed mercy on him*; he was without doubt a good neighbor to him."

2.2.2.2. The duty inferred from it was pressed home to the lawyer's own conscience: *Go, and do thou likewise.* If a Samaritan does well when he helps a distressed Jew, then certainly a Jew does not do well if he refuses to help a distressed Samaritan. "Therefore go and do as the Samaritan did, whenever the need arises: show mercy to those who need your help. Do it freely and with concern and compassion, even though they do not belong to your own nation." This lawyer thought he had confounded Christ himself, but Christ sent him to school to a Samaritan to learn his duty: "Go and do as he did." It is the duty of each one of us to help and relieve all who are in distress and need, and it is especially the duty of experts in the law.

2.2.2.3. This parable may also be applied to another purpose than that for which it was originally intended; it sets out magnificently the kindness and love of God our Savior toward sinful, miserable humans. We were like this poor, distressed traveler. The Law of Moses passes by on the other side, having neither pity nor power to help us, but then the blessed Jesus comes along, that good Samaritan, and he has compassion on us. He takes care of us. This exalts the riches of his love and makes us all say, "How much we are indebted to him, and how can we ever repay him?"

Verses 38–42

We may notice here:

1. The reception Martha gave to Christ and his disciples at her home (v. 38). Notice:

1.1. Christ's coming to the village where Martha lived: *As they went, he entered into a certain village.* This village was Bethany, near Jerusalem. Christ honored the country villages with his presence and favor, not only the great and well-populated towns and cities, because just as he chose privacy, so he also supported poverty.

1.2. His reception at Martha's house: *A certain woman named Martha received him into her house* and made him welcome. Christ's had close friends, whom he loved more than his other friends and visited more frequently. He loved this family (Jn 11:5) and often invited himself to their house. It is called Martha's house probably because she was a widow and was the householder. Although at this time it had become dangerous to receive him, especially somewhere so close to Jerusalem, she still did not care what risks she ran for his name's sake. Although many rejected him and would not receive him, there was one who would make him welcome.

2. The attention that Mary, the sister of Martha, gave to the word of Christ (v. 20). She heard his word. It seems that as soon as our Lord Jesus came into Martha's house, he turned to his great work of preaching the Gospel. A good sermon is never the worse because it is preached in a house. Since Christ is eager to speak, we should be quick to listen. Mary sat down to listen, which shows the

close attention she gave him. Her mind was calm, and she was determined that she would not just catch a word every now and then, but receive everything that Christ spoke. If we sit with him at his feet now, we will soon sit with him on his throne.

3. The concern of Martha about her domestic affairs: *But Martha was cumbered about much serving* (v. 40), and that was the reason why she was not where Mary was. Housekeepers know how much hustle and bustle there is to prepare for a great reception. Notice here:

3.1. Something commendable, which must not be overlooked. Here was a commendable respect to our Lord Jesus. It was not for ostentation, but purely to show her goodwill to him, that she made all these preparations. Here was a commendable concern for household affairs. It is the duty of those who have the charge of families to *look well to the ways of their household* (Pr 31:27). A hankering for grand living and a love of ease lead to the neglect of many families.

3.2. Something blameworthy. She was distracted by *much serving*. Her heart was set on providing lavish and splendid hospitality. She was worried because so much had to be done. It is not good for the disciples of Christ to take on themselves great preparations; what need is there of elaborate preparations, when much less will be enough? She was *cumbered* about it; "she was distracted by it." Whatever cares the providence of God puts on us, we must not be *cumbered* with (distracted by) them. Care is good and dutiful, but distraction is sin and foolishness. She was distracted by all the preparations she had to make, when she should have been with her sister, sitting at Christ's feet and listening to his word.

4. The complaint that Martha made to Christ against her sister Mary (v. 40): "*Lord, dost thou not care that my sister has left me to serve alone? Ask her to come and help me.*"

4.1. Martha's complaint may be considered as revealing her worldliness; it was the language of her excessive concern and worry. Excessive worldly cares and pursuits are often the cause of disturbance in families and of strife and contention among relatives. Being angry with her sister, Martha appealed to Christ, wanting him to say that she *did well to be angry* (Jnh 4:9). *Lord, dost thou not care that my sister has let me to serve alone?* When Martha was working away, she wanted Mary, too, and Christ and everyone, to be concerned, or else she would not be pleased. Those who are most forward in appealing to God are not always right; we must therefore be careful not to expect Christ to embrace our unjust and unwarranted quarrels. The concerns that he puts on us we may cheerfully cast on him (1Pe 5:7), but not those that we foolishly draw on ourselves.

4.2. It may be considered as a discouragement of Mary's godliness and devotion. Her sister should have commended her for it; instead she condemned her as failing in her duty. It is not strange for those who are zealous in religious faith to meet not only with opposition from enemies but also with blame and criticism from their friends.

5. The reproof that Christ gave Martha for her excessive care (v. 41). *Martha, Martha, thou art careful and troubled about many things*, whereas only *one thing is needful.*

5.1. He reproved her even though he was her guest at this time. *As many as Christ loves, he rebukes and chastens* (Rev 3:19). Even those who are precious to Christ will be sure to hear about it if anything is wrong in them.

5.2. When he rebuked her, he called her by her name, *Martha*. He repeated her name, *Martha, Martha*; he spoke

as one who was serious and deeply concerned for her welfare. Those who are entangled in the cares of this life (2Ti 2:4) are not easily disentangled from them.

5.3. What he rebuked her for was her being *careful and troubled* (worried and upset) *about many things*. Christ rebukes her both for the excessiveness of her care—"You are *careful and troubled*, inwardly divided and disturbed by all your care"—and for its extensiveness: "about *many things*. Poor Martha, you have many things to be anxious about, and this is making you tense, whereas less hustle and bustle would be all right." Excessive concern or trouble about many things in this world is a common fault among Christ's disciples. If they are worried for no just cause, Christ is just to give them something to worry about.

5.4. What emphasized the sin and foolishness of her concern was that only *one thing is needful. The one thing needful* is certainly meant to refer to what Mary made her choice—sitting at Christ's feet, listening to his word. Martha was troubled about many things, whereas she should have applied herself to one; godliness unites the heart, which the world had divided. The many things she was troubled about were unnecessary, while the one thing she neglected was necessary. Martha's concern and work were good in their proper time and place, but now she had something else to do, which was inexpressibly more necessary. She expected Christ to blame Mary for not doing as she did, but he blamed Martha for not doing as Mary did. The day would come when Martha would wish she had sat where Mary did.

6. Christ's approval and commendation of Mary for her serious devotion: *Mary hath chosen the good part.*

6.1. She had justly preferred what was most deserving, the *one thing is needful*, this one thing that she had done. Serious godliness is necessary; it is the *one thing needful*. Nothing but this will go with us into another world.

6.2. She had wisely done well for herself. Christ justified Mary against her sister's complaints. Sooner or later, Mary's choice will be justified, along with that of all those who make that choice and remain faithful to it. But this was not all; he also praised Mary for her wisdom: *She hath chosen the good part*, because she chose to be with Christ. By receiving his word into her heart, she took a better way of honoring Christ and of pleasing him than Martha did by providing for him to be received in her home. Notice:

6.2.1. A part with Christ is *a good part*; it is a part for the soul and eternity.

6.2.2. It is a part that will never be taken away from those that have it. Nothing *shall separate us from the love of Christ* (Ro 8:35, 38–39) and our share in that love. People and demons cannot take it away from us, and God and Christ will not.

6.2.3. It is the wisdom and duty of each of us to choose this *good part*. Mary had the choice whether she would share with Martha in her preparations and gain the reputation of being a fine housekeeper or sit at the feet of Christ and show herself to be a zealous disciple, and by her choice in this matter, Christ judged her general choice.

CHAPTER 11

In this chapter: 1. Christ teaches his disciples to pray (vv. 1–13). 2. He fully answers the blasphemous accusation of the Pharisees, who accused him of driving out demons because of an alliance with Beelzebub (vv. 14–26). 3. Christ shows the honor of obedient disciples to be greater than that of his own mother (vv. 27–28). 4. He rebukes the people of that genera-tion for their stubborn unfaithfulness (vv. 29–36). 5. He severely rebukes the Pharisees and experts of the law (vv. 37–54).

Verses 1–13

Prayer is one of the great guiding principles of natural religion. One great purpose of Christianity, therefore, is to help us pray, to urge the duty on us, to instruct us in it, and to encourage us to expect to benefit by it.

1. We find Christ himself *praying in a certain place* (v. 1). This Evangelist took particular notice of Christ's praying often, more than any other of the Evangelists: when he was baptized (3:21), he was *praying*; he *with-drew into the wilderness, and prayed* (5:16); he *went out into a mountain to pray, and continued all night in prayer* (6:12); he was *alone praying* (9:18); soon afterward, he *went up into a mountain to pray*, and *as he prayed he was transfigured* (9:28–29); and here he was *praying in a certain place.*

2. His disciples asked him for guidance regarding prayer. When he was praying, they asked, *Lord, teach us to pray.* They came to him with this request *when he ceased*, because they did not want to disturb him while he was praying. *One of his disciples* said, *Lord, teach us.* Although Christ is *apt to teach* (1Ti 3:2; 2Ti 2:24), this is something about which he wants to *be enquired of* (Eze 36:37).

2.1. Their request was, *"Lord, teach us to pray."* It is good for the disciples of Christ to turn to him for instruc-tion on prayer. *Lord, teach us to pray* is itself a good prayer, and a necessary one, because it is hard to pray well. It is only Jesus Christ who can teach us, by his word and Spirit, how to pray. "Give me *mouth and wisdom* (21:15) in prayer, that I may speak as I should; *teach me what I shall say* (12:12)."

2.2. Their plea was, *"As John also taught his disciples.* John was careful to teach his disciples this necessary duty, and we want to be taught as they were." Whereas the Jews' prayers were generally adorations, praises of God, and doxologies, John taught his disciples prayers that were more filled with petitions and requests. "Now, Lord, teach us this, to be added to those blessings of the name of God that we have been used to from our childhood." Christ taught them a prayer consisting wholly of petitions, even omitting the doxology and *Amen* at the end, with which prayers were usually concluded.

3. Christ taught them, much the same as he had before in his Sermon on the Mount (Mt 6:9). They would find all their requests expressed in these few words and would be able, in words of their own, to enlarge on them.

3.1. There are some differences between the Lord's Prayer in Matthew and in Luke.

3.1.1. There is a difference in the fourth petition. In Matthew we pray, "Give us daily bread *this day*"; here, "Give us daily bread *day by day*; give us each day the bread that our bodies need, as they call for it." "Let us have bread today for today, and tomorrow for tomorrow." In this way, we may be kept continually depending on God, as children depend on their parents, and may find ourselves under fresh obligations to do the work of each day on that day, according to the duty the day requires, because we have received from God the supplies every day for that day, according to the needs of that day.

3.1.2. There is also some difference in the fifth peti-tion. In Matthew it is, *Forgive us our debts, as we forgive*: here it is, *Forgive us our sins, for we forgive.* This is a very necessary qualification for forgiveness, and if God

has worked it in us, we may plead that work of his grace to support our petitions for the forgiveness of our sins: "Lord, forgive us, because you yourself have inclined us to forgive others." There is another addition here; we plead not only in general that we forgive our debtors but also in particular that "we profess *to forgive everyone that is indebted to us*, without exception." The doxology at the close is completely omitted, and so is the Amen. He left a space here, to be filled by a doxology more distinctive to the Christian structure, giving glory to *Father, Son, and Holy Spirit.*

3.2. Yet it is substantially the same, and we will there-fore only gather some general lessons from it here.

3.2.1. That in prayer we should come to God as chil-dren to a Father, a common Father to us and the whole human race.

3.2.2. That in the same petitions that we address to God for ourselves, we should include the whole the human race with us. A deep-rooted principle of general love should accompany us throughout this prayer, which is so worded as to be adjusted to that noble principle.

3.2.3. That in order to confirm the habit of heavenly-mindedness in us, we should look toward heaven with faith and view the God we pray to as our Father in heaven.

3.2.4. That in prayer we must *seek first the kingdom of God and the righteousness thereof* (Mt 6:33), by ascrib-ing honor to his holy name and power to his rule, both the rule of his providence in the world and that of his grace in the church. Oh that both the one and the other might be revealed more!

3.2.5. That the principles and practices of the unseen world, which we are aware of only by faith, are the great original to which we should try to make the principles and practices of this lower world more comparable. The words *As in heaven, so on earth* refer to all the first three petitions.

3.2.6. That those who are faithfully and sincerely con-cerned for the kingdom of God may humbly hope that *all other things shall be added to them* (12:31), and they may in faith pray for them. If our first and main desire and concern is that God's name will be sanctified, his kingdom come, and his will be done, then we may come boldly to the throne of grace for our daily bread (Heb 4:16).

3.2.7. That in our prayers for physical blessings we must moderate our desires, confining them to what is nec-essary. Some think that *epiousios*, here translated "daily," should be translated "necessary," referring to the bread that is suitable to our natural longings.

3.2.8. That sins are debts that we contract daily and that we should therefore pray every day to be forgiven of. Every day adds to the total of our guilt, and it is a miracle of mercy that we have so much encouragement given us to come every day to the throne of grace to pray for the forgiveness of the sins of our daily weakness. God *multiplies to pardon* (Isa 55:7) more than seventy times seven (Mt 18:22).

3.2.9. That we have no reason to expect God to forgive our sins against him if we do not sincerely forgive those who have at any time insulted us or wronged us.

3.2.10. That we should fear and pray to be saved from temptations to sin, knowing they will ruin us. We must pray as earnestly to God that we may not be led into temp-tation as that we may not be led by it to sin, and so to ruin.

3.2.11. That God is to be depended on for our deliver-ance from all evil; we should pray not only that we may not be left to ourselves to fall into evil but also that we may not be left to Satan to bring evil on us.

4. He stirred up and encouraged boldness, fervency, and faithfulness in prayer by showing:

4.1. That importunity will go far in our dealings with other people (vv. 5–8). Suppose a man is in an emergency and goes to borrow a loaf or two of bread from a neighbor at an unreasonable time of night, not for himself but for a friend who has unexpectedly called on him. His neighbor will be reluctant to oblige him, because he has woken him up with his knocking and put him in a bad mood, and so the neighbor has good reasons to excuse himself. But the one with the emergency will not take no for an answer; he continues to knock and tells him he will do so until he receives what he has come for. The neighbor must, therefore, give him the bread, to get rid of him: *He will rise and give him as many as he needs, because of his importunity.* Our importunity is effective with people because they are displeased with it, but it is effective with God because he is pleased with it. This parable may be of use to us:

4.1.1. To guide us in prayer.

4.1.1.1. We must come to God for what we need with boldness and confidence, as a man comes to the house of his neighbor or friend, who he knows loves him and is inclined to be kind to him.

4.1.1.2. We must come for bread, for what is necessary.

4.1.1.3. We must come to him through prayer for others as well as for ourselves. This man did not come for bread for himself, but for his friend. We cannot come to God on a more pleasing mission than when we come to him for grace to enable us to do good.

4.1.1.4. We may come with greater boldness to God in a difficulty if it is not a difficulty that we have brought on ourselves by our own foolishness and carelessness, but one that Providence has led us into. This man would not have needed bread if his friend had not come unexpectedly. We may cheerfully cast on Providence the concerns that Providence puts on us (1Pe 5:7).

4.1.2. To encourage us in prayer. If importunity could be so effective with a man who was angry at it, then it will be much more effective with a God who is infinitely more kind and who is not angry at our boldness, but accepts it. If he does not answer our prayers immediately, he will do so in due time if we continue to pray.

4.2. That God has promised to give us what we ask him for. We can take encouragement not only from the goodness of nature but also from the word that he has spoken (vv. 9–10): *"Ask, and it shall be given you." I say unto you*: we have it from Christ's own mouth. We must not only ask but also seek; we must back up our prayers with work. In asking and seeking, we must continue to press on, continue to knock on the same door, and we will eventually *prevail* (Ge 32:28). *Every one that asketh receiveth*, even the most insignificant saint who asks in faith. When we ask God for those things that Christ has here told us to ask for, so that his name may be sanctified, that his kingdom may come, and his will be done, we must be bold in these requests.

5. He gave us both instruction and encouragement in prayer, based on a consideration of our relationship with God as a Father. Here is:

5.1. An appeal to the compassion of human fathers: "Let any of you who *is a father* tell me, if his son *asks for bread, will he give him a stone? If he asks for a fish, will he for a fish give him a serpent? Or, if he shall asks for an egg* for his supper—an egg before going to bed—*will he offer him a scorpion?* You know you would not be so unnatural to your own children" (vv. 11–12).

5.2. An application of this to the blessings of our *heavenly Father* (v. 13): *If ye then, being evil, give good gifts to your children, much more shall God give you the Spirit.* Matthew has *give good things*. Notice:

5.2.1. The guidance Christ gives us as to what to pray for. We must ask for the Holy Spirit, not only because we need the aid of the Holy Spirit in order to pray well, but also because his presence includes all the good things we are to pray for: we need nothing more to make us happy.

5.2.2. The encouragement he gives us to hope that we will be effective in this prayer: *Your heavenly Father will give.* It is in his power to give the Spirit; he has all good things to give, wrapped up in that one gift. But that is not all. Giving us the Spirit is also included in his promise. If our earthly parents, though evil, are still so kind, if they, though weak, are still so knowledgeable, that they not only give but give wisely, give what is best, then much more will our heavenly Father give us his Holy Spirit.

Verses 14–26

We had the substance of these verses in Mt 12:22–37. Christ here gave a general proof of his divine mission by a particular proof of his power over Satan. In the same act, he also gave a pledge of the success of that undertaking. He provided this proof and pledge by driving out a demon that made the poor possessed man mute. In Matthew we are told that he was blind and mute. When the demon was forced out by the word of Christ, the man who had been mute spoke immediately, and his lips were opened to declare God's praise (Ps 51:15).

1. Some were moved by this miracle. The people *wondered*; they were amazed at the power of God.

2. Others were offended by it and suggested that it was because of an alliance with Beelzebub, the prince of demons, that he had done this (v. 15). To confirm this accusation and oppose the evidence of his miraculous power, some people challenged Christ to *give them a sign from heaven* (v. 16) to confirm his teaching, as if a sign from heaven could not just as well have been given them by an alliance and collusion with *the prince of the power of the air* (Eph 2:2) as the driving out of a devil had been. Stubborn unfaithfulness will never be at a loss for something to say to excuse itself, though it may be very frivolous and absurd. Christ responded here with a full and direct answer, in which he showed:

2.1. That it can by no means be imagined that such a subtle ruler as Satan would ever agree to measures that had such a direct tendency to lead to his own overthrow (vv. 17–18). Jesus *knew their thoughts* even when they worked hard to conceal them, and he said, "You yourselves must surely see the groundlessness of this accusation, because it is an assured principle that no interest that is divided against itself can stand, not the more public interests of a kingdom, not the private interests of a house or family. If either the one or the other is *divided against itself*, it cannot stand. Now, if Satan were *divided against himself* in this way, he would quicken his own overthrow."

2.2. That it was biased and ill natured of them to attribute his work to an alliance with Satan even though they had praised and admired the work of driving out demons in other fellow Israelites (v. 19): "*By whom do your sons cast them out?* Some of your own kindred, some of your own followers, have undertaken, in the name of the God of Israel, to drive out demons, and they were never accused of such a satanic alliance." It is gross hypocrisy to condemn in those who rebuke us what we allow in those that flatter us.

2.3. That in opposing the conviction that this miracle was intended to bring about in them, they were their own enemies, because they were thrusting the kingdom of God away from themselves (v. 20): "*If I with the finger of God cast out devils, no doubt the kingdom of God is come upon you,* and if you do not receive it, your lives are in danger." In Matthew it is *by the Spirit of God,* here *by the finger of God.* He did not need to show all his eternal power; when God wishes, that roaring lion (1Pe 5:8) is crushed like a moth with a touch of a finger.

2.4. That his driving out demons was really the destruction of them and their power (vv. 21–22). When Christ drove out demons, he was stronger than they and could do it by force and in such a way as to ruin Satan's power. Now this may be applied to Christ's victories over Satan both in the world and in the hearts of particular individuals. We may therefore notice here:

2.4.1. The miserable condition of unconverted sinners. In their hearts, which were fitted to be a dwelling place for God, the Devil has his home, and all the powers and faculties of the soul are his goods. The heart is a house, a noble dwelling place, but the unsanctified heart is the Devil's home. The Devil, like *a strong man armed* (v. 21), guards this house. All the prejudices with which he hardens people's hearts against truth and holiness are the strongholds that he sets up to guard his house. There is a kind of peace in the home of an unconverted soul while the Devil, like a *strong man armed,* guards it. Sinners have a good opinion of themselves; they are self-confident and cheerful. They flatter themselves and think they are completely secure. Before Christ appeared, everything was quiet, because everything went in one direction, but the preaching of the Gospel disturbed the peace of the Devil's house.

2.4.2. The wonderful change that is made in conversion. *Satan is a strong man armed,* but our Lord Jesus *is stronger than he* (v. 22). See the manner of this victory: *He comes upon him* by surprise, when *his goods are in peace* (safe), and *overcomes him.* See the signs of this victory:

2.4.2.1. He *takes from him all his armour wherein he trusted.* Christ disarms him. When the power of sin and corruption in the soul is broken, Satan's armor is taken away.

2.4.2.2. He *divides the spoils;* he takes possession of them for himself. All the endowments of mind and body are now converted to Christ's service. This is not all, however; he distributes them among his followers, giving to all believers the benefits of that victory. From this Christ inferred, since the whole purpose of his teaching and miracles was to break the power of the Devil, that it was the duty of all to join him, to receive his Gospel and heartily join the Gospel cause, because otherwise they would justly be reckoned as siding with the enemy: *He that is not with me is against me* (v. 23).

2.5. That there was a vast difference between the Devil's going out by agreement and his being driven out by force. Those out of whom Christ drove him he never entered again, because this was Christ's command (Mk 9:25), whereas if the Devil had gone out freely, he would have reentered whenever he saw fit. Christ gives a total and final defeat to the enemy. Here we have:

2.5.1. The condition of a recognized hypocrite, his bright side and his dark side. His heart still remains the Devil's house, but:

2.5.1.1. The *unclean* (evil) *spirit is gone out.* He was not driven; He just withdrew for a time, so that the person seemed not to be under the power of Satan as before.

2.5.1.2. The *house is swept* from common defilements by a partial reformation. The house is *swept* but not washed; the house must be washed, or it does not belong to Christ. Sweeping takes away only the loose dirt, while the sin that entangles the sinner (Heb 12:1) is untouched. It is swept of the filth that lies open to the eyes of the world, but it is not searched and ransacked for hidden filthiness (Mt 23:25). It *is swept,* but the *leprosy is in the house* (Lev 14:34).

2.5.1.3. The house is *garnished* (decorated) with common gifts and graces. It is not furnished with true grace, but *garnished* with the pictures of all graces. It is all paint and varnish, nothing real or lasting. The house is decorated, but its owner has never changed; it was never surrendered to Christ.

2.5.2. The condition of a final apostate, into whom the demon returns after he has gone out: *Then goes he, and takes seven other spirits more wicked than himself* (v. 26). These *enter in* without any difficulty or opposition; they are welcomed, and they live there; and the *last state of that man is worse than the first.* Hypocrisy is the highway to apostasy. Where secret haunts of sin are maintained, the conscience is defiled, and the private hypocrite commonly turns out to be an open apostate. The last state of such a person is *worse than the first,* with respect to both sin and punishment. Apostates are usually the worst people; their consciences are seared, and their sins will be judged more severely than anyone else's. In the other world they will *receive the greater damnation* (20:47).

Verses 27–28

We did not have this passage in the other Evangelists' accounts. We have here:

1. The praise that an affectionate, honorable, well-meaning woman gave to our Lord Jesus on hearing his excellent discourses. As he spoke these things (v. 27), a *certain woman of the company* was so pleased that she could not stop herself from crying out, "*Blessed is the womb that bore thee.* Fortunate is the woman who has you for her son. I would have thought myself very fortunate to be the mother of one who *speaks as never man spoke,* who has in him so much of the grace of heaven and is such a blessing to this earth." The person of Christ is precious to all who believe the word of Christ.

2. The occasion Christ took from this to declare that those who are his faithful and obedient followers are more fortunate than the woman who gave him birth and nursed him. *Yea, rather, blessed are they that hear the word of God, and keep it* (v. 28). This was intended partly as a restraint on her for devoting herself so much to his physical presence, and partly as an encouragement to her to hope that she could be as happy as his own mother if she would *hear the word of God and keep it.* Only those who hear it and keep it are truly blessed.

Verses 29–36

Christ's teaching in these verses shows two things:

1. The sign we may expect from God to confirm our faith. The great and most convincing proof that Christ was sent by God was Christ's resurrection from the dead. Here is:

1.1. A rebuke to the people for demanding other signs than those that had already been given them in abundance. *The people were gathered thickly together* (v. 29), a vast crowd of them. Christ knew what brought such a crowd together; they came *seeking a sign,* they came to gaze, so that they would have something to talk about when they went home—"Did you see …?"

1.2. A promise that there would still be one more sign given them, the *sign of Jonas the prophet*, which in Matthew is explained as referring to the resurrection of Christ. But if this did not affect them, let them look for nothing but complete ruin: *The Son of Man shall be a sign to this generation* (v. 30), a sign speaking to them, though a sign spoken against by them (2:23).

1.3. A warning to them to make the most of this sign. The *queen of Sheba* would *rise up in judgment against them* and condemn *their unbelief* (v. 31). She was a stranger to the citizenship of Israel (Eph 2:12), but she came from the ends of the earth to *hear Solomon's wisdom*, not only to satisfy her curiosity but also to inform her mind. See, *a greater than Solomon is here*. These miserable Jews, however, would pay no attention to what Christ said to them, even though he was among them. The Ninevites, too, would rise up in judgment against them (v. 32): they *repented at the preaching of Jonas*, but here was preaching that far exceeded that of Jonah, yet none were startled by it into *turning from their evil way*, as the Ninevites did (Jnh 3:10).

2. The sign God expects from us as evidence of our faith: the sincere practice of the religion that we profess to believe.

2.1. That generation had *the light*. God, having *lighted the candle* of the Gospel, did not put it in *a secret place* or *under a bushel* (v. 33); Christ did not preach in hidden corners. It is a great privilege that the light of the Gospel is put on a lampstand, so that all who enter may see it and see by it.

2.2. Having the light, they had the task of seeing. Even if an object is very clear, if the organ of sight is not right, we are no better off: *The light of the body is the eye* (v. 34). So the light of the soul is its power of discerning between good and evil, truth and falsehood. Now, whether we benefit from the light of divine revelation depends on whether understanding and judgment enlighten the soul.

2.2.1. If this eye of the soul is good and sees things clearly, if it aims only at truth and seeks it for its own sake, then the whole body, that is, the whole soul, is full of light. If our understanding accepts the Gospel in its full light, the Gospel fills the soul, and it has enough to fill it. Moreover, if the soul is so filled, having no dark parts, then the whole soul will be full of light. That soul was darkness itself, but it is now light in the Lord (Eph 5:8), *as when the bright shining of a candle doth give thee light* (v. 36). The Gospel will come into those souls whose doors and windows are thrown open to receive it.

2.2.2. If the eye of the soul is evil, it is hardly surprising if the whole body, the whole soul, is full of darkness (v. 34). The conclusion is, therefore, "*Take heed that the light which is in thee be not darkness* (v. 35). Be sincere in your seeking after truth, and be ready to receive its light, love, and power, and not as the people of this generation to whom Christ preached, who never sincerely desired to know God's will nor intended to do it and therefore, not surprisingly, continued walking in darkness.

Verses 37–54

Christ said here to a Pharisee and his guests in a private conversation at the table many of those things that he later said in a public sermon in the temple (Mt 23); what he said in public and private was consistent. Here is:

1. Christ's going to dine with a Pharisee who very politely invited him to his house (v. 37. *As he spoke, a certain Pharisee* interrupted him with a request to him to come and *dine with him*. We do not know the mind of this Pharisee, but whatever it was like, Christ knew what it

was: if he meant harm, he would know Christ did not fear him; if he meant well, he would know Christ was willing to do him good: so Christ *went in, and sat down to meat*. Christ's disciples must learn from him to be conversational, not morose. Although we need to be cautious about the company we keep, we need not be rigid about it.

2. The exception that the Pharisee took at Christ for not *washing before dinner* (v. 38). He was amazed that a man of Christ's sanctity would sit down to eat without washing his hands first. The Pharisee himself and all his guests were no doubt washing, and so Christ would not stand out as different if he washed. All the preparations had been made, and yet he had not washed his hands? The ceremonial law consisted in *divers washings* (Heb 9:10), but this was not one of them, and so Christ would not practice it, though he knew that offense would be taken because he had omitted it.

3. The sharp rebuke that Christ gave to the Pharisees.

3.1. He rebuked them for so emphasizing those aspects of religion that are merely external and visible to the human eye, while those that concern the soul and come under the eye of God were not only made secondary but even completely wiped out (vv. 39–40). Notice here:

3.1.1. The absurdity they were guilty of: "*You Pharisees make clean the outside* only. You wash your hands with water, but you do not wash your hearts from wickedness." Those who wash only the *outside of the cup* or the *platter* can never be counted as true servants. A person's attitude in every religious service is like the inside of the cup and dish; the impurity of the attitude infects the services. To live under the control of spiritual evil is as great an insult to God as it would be for a servant to put into his master's hand a cup wiped clean from all the dirt on the outside but full of cobwebs and spiders inside. *Ravening* and *wickedness* are the dangerous, condemning sins of many people who have cleaned the *outside of the cup* from the more gross, scandalous, and inexcusable sins of sexual immorality and drunkenness.

3.1.2. A particular instance of its absurdity: "*Ye fools, did not he that made that which is without make that which is within also?* (v. 40). Did not the God who in the Law of Moses appointed various ceremonial washings appoint also that you should cleanse and purify your hearts? The One who made laws for what is outside—did he not even in those laws further intend something inside?" Did not God, who gave us these bodies, make us these souls also? Now if he made both, he justly expects us to take care of both, and so we should not only wash the body but also wash the spirit, which he is the Father of (Heb 12:9), and get the disease cleansed from the heart. He added to this a rule for making our creature comforts clean to us (v. 41): "Instead of washing your hands before you eat, *give alms of such things as you have*. Let the poor have their share of them, and then *all things are clean to you*, and you may be comfortable in using them." Here is a clear allusion to the Law of Moses, by which it was provided that certain portions of the harvest of their land must be given *to the Levite, the stranger, the fatherless, and the widow*, and when that had been done, what was reserved for their own use was *clean to them* (Dt 26:12–15). We can comfortably enjoy the gifts of God's goodness when we *send portions to them for whom nothing is prepared* (Ne 8:10). What we have is not our own unless God receives his dues from it, and it is by liberality to the poor that we are free to make use of our creature comforts.

3.2. He rebuked them for emphasizing what was not important and neglecting the more significant aspects of the Law (v. 42). They were very exact in observing the laws that related only to the means of religion: "*Ye pay tithe of mint and rue*, pay it in kind and to the full." By this they would gain a reputation with the people as strict observers of the Law. Now Christ did not condemn them for being so exact in paying tithes—*these things ought ye to have done*—but for thinking that this would make up for their neglect of their greater duties. They made nothing of those laws that concern the essentials of religion: "*You pass over judgment and the love of God*, not in the slightest concerned to give people their dues and God your hearts."

3.3. He rebuked them for their pride and vanity (v. 43): "*Ye love the uppermost seats in the synagogues*, and you love greetings in the markets." It was not sitting in the most important seats or being greeted that was rebuked, but loving it.

3.4. He rebuked them for their hypocrisy (v. 44): "You are like graves overgrown with grass, which the living, not seeing, walk over without knowing it, thereby contracting the ceremonial defilement that, according to the Law, arises from touching a grave." On the inside, these Pharisees were full of detestable things, as a grave is full of rottenness, but they concealed their defilement so skillfully that it was not apparent. Therefore, those who talked with them and followed their teaching were infected with their corruptions and ill morals and yet feared no harm from them. The contagion wormed its way into their lives and caught on without their being aware of it, and they caught it without knowing and therefore thought themselves no worse off.

4. The testimony that he bore also against the experts or teachers of the law, who made it their business to explain the Law, as the Pharisees made it theirs to observe the Law.

4.1. One member of that profession was angry with what Christ said against the Pharisees (v. 45): "*Master, thus saying thou reproachest* (insult) *us also.*" It is the foolishness of those who are united to their sins, who are determined not to part with them, to make bad use of the faithful and friendly warnings given them that come from love and to have their passions provoked by them as if they were intended as insults. This lawyer embraced the Pharisee's cause and so made himself share in his sins.

4.2. Our Lord Jesus took them to task for this (v. 46): *Woe unto you also, ye lawyers*, and again (v. 52), *Woe unto you, lawyers.* They blessed themselves for the reputation they had among the people. Christ declared woes against them because he saw what people cannot see. Those who quarrel with the rebukes of others and suspect them of insulting them are only earning woes of their own by doing so.

4.2.1. The experts in the law were rebuked for making the duties of religious faith more burdensome to others, but more comfortable to themselves, than God had made them (v. 46): "*You lade* (load) *men with burdens grievous to be borne*, but *you yourselves touch them not with one of your fingers.*" That is:

4.2.1.1. "You will not burden yourselves with them, nor will you be bound by those restraints with which you hold others back."

4.2.1.2. "You will not relieve them; *you will not touch them*, that is, either repeal them or dispense with them when you find they have become a heavy burden to the people." They would use both hands to give up a command of God, but not lift a finger to lessen the harshness of any of the traditions of the elders.

4.2.2. They were rebuked for pretending to respect the memory of the prophets whom their ancestors killed,

even though they still hated and persecuted those in their own day who were sent to them on the same mission (vv. 47–49).

4.2.2.1. These hypocrites *built the sepulchres of the prophets*; that is, they set up monuments over their graves in honor of them. They were not so superstitious as to enshrine the relics of the prophets or to think their devotions were more acceptable to God because they were offered at the tombs of the martyrs. Rather, as if they thought themselves the *children of the prophets* (Ac 3:25), they repaired and beautified the monuments sacred to their godly memory.

4.2.2.2. Despite this, they had a hardened hostility toward those in their own day who came to them in the spirit and power of those prophets. The *Wisdom of God*—that is, Christ—said that they would *slay* (kill) and *persecute* the prophets and apostles who would be sent to them. The *Wisdom of God* would test them by sending them prophets, who would rebuke them for their sins and warn them of the judgments of God. "*I will send them prophets* under the title *apostles*. And the Jews will not only contradict and oppose these; they will even *slay* and *persecute* them and put them to death."

4.2.2.3. Therefore God would justly give to their building the tombs of the prophets a different interpretation from the one they wanted imputed to them; it would be interpreted as their *allowing the deeds of their fathers* (v. 48). The building of the prophets' sepulchers would be interpreted as showing that the builders were determined to keep in their graves those whom their ancestors had driven there.

4.2.2.4. They must expect nothing other than to be judged as those who *were filling up the measure* of persecution (Mt 23:32) (vv. 50–51). It would all be *required of this generation*, whose sin in persecuting Christ's apostles would exceed any of their ancestors' sins of that kind. Their destruction by the Romans was so terrible that it could well be considered the completion of God's vengeance on that persecuting nation.

4.2.3. They were rebuked for opposing the Gospel of Christ (v. 52). They had not, according to the duty of their place, faithfully explained to the people those Scriptures of the Old Testament that pointed to the Messiah. Instead they had corrupted those texts by their corrupt interpretations: this is called *taking away the key of knowledge.* Instead of using that key for the people and helping them to use it rightly, they hid it from them; in Matthew this is called *shutting up the kingdom of heaven against men* (Mt 23:13). They themselves did not embrace the Gospel of Christ, even though by their acquaintance with the Old Testament they must have known that the *time was fulfilled* and the *kingdom of God was at hand* (Mk 1:15). They themselves would not *enter into it*, and they did all they could to hinder and discourage those who, without any guidance or help from them, wanted to enter in. They threatened to drive them out of the synagogue. It is bad for people to be disinclined toward revelation, but even worse to be hostile toward it.

4.3. At the end of the chapter we are told how spitefully and maliciously the teachers of the law and Pharisees sought to draw Christ into a trap (vv. 53–54). They could not bear those incisive rebukes, which they had to acknowledge to be just, and so, as if the heat of his reproofs led them to hope that they could stir him up to some intemperate anger and thereby put him off guard, they *began to urge him vehemently* and to *provoke him to speak of many things, laying wait* for something that might serve their intention of making him either odious to the people or obnoxious to the government, or both. Those who faithfully rebuke sin must expect to have many enemies. Let us *consider him who endured such contradiction of sinners against himself* (Heb 12:3), so that we may endure such tests with patience and overcome them with wisdom.

CHAPTER 12

In this chapter we have various excellent discourses our Savior gave on various occasions, many of which are to the same effect as those we had in Matthew. We need to be constantly taught with God's commands and instructions. 1. Christ warned his disciples to watch out for hypocrisy and cowardice (vv. 1–12). 2. He warned against all kinds of greed, illustrating it by a parable of a rich man who was suddenly destroyed by death (vv. 13–21). 3. He encouraged his disciples to cast all their cares on God (1Pe 5:7) (vv. 22–34). 4. He stirred them up to watch out for their Master's coming (vv. 35–48). 5. He told them to expect trouble and persecution (vv. 49–53). 6 He warned the people to observe and make the most of the day of their opportunities (vv. 54–59).

Verses 1–12

We have here:

1. A vast audience that had gathered to hear Christ preach. The teachers of the law and Pharisees tried to accuse him, but the people were still amazed at him; they were with him and honored him. *In the meantime* (v. 1), while he was in the Pharisee's house, the people got together for an afternoon sermon, a sermon after dinner, after dinner with a Pharisee (11:37); and he did not disappoint them. Although in the morning sermon, when they had *gathered thickly together* (11:29), he had rebuked them severely, they still came back to be with him; the people could bear their reproofs so much better than the Pharisees could bear theirs. The more the Pharisees tried to drive people away from Christ, the bigger the crowds that flocked to him. Here was an *innumerable multitude* (many thousands) *of people gathered together, so that they trode one upon* (trampled upon one) *another*. It is good to see people so eager to listen to the word. When the net is cast where there is such a multitude of fish, it may be hoped that some will be caught up in it.

2. The instructions he gave his followers.

2.1. He began with a warning against *hypocrisy*. He said this *to his disciples first of all*. These were his special responsibility, and so he warned them particularly as his *beloved sons* (1Co 4:14); they made a greater profession of religious faith than the others, and hypocrisy in that was the sin they were most in danger of. Hypocrisy would be worse in them than in others. Christ's disciples were, for all we know, the best men then in the world, but even they needed to be warned against hypocrisy. Christ said this to the disciples *in the hearing* of this great crowd, to add greater emphasis to the warning and to let the world know that he would not support hypocrisy, not even in his own disciples. Notice:

2.1.1. The description of the sin that he warned them against: *It is the leaven of the Pharisees.*

2.1.1.1. It is *leaven* (yeast); it spreads like yeast, insinuating itself into the whole being, into all that a person does; it swells and sours like leaven, puffing people up with pride and thereby making them bitter with malice and making their service unacceptable to God.

2.1.1.2. It is the *leaven of the Pharisees*: "It is the sin that most of them fall into. Be on your guard about imi-

tating them; do not be hypocritical in Christianity as they are in Judaism."

2.1.2. A good reason against it: *"For there is nothing covered that shall not be revealed* (vv. 2–3). Sooner or later the truth will come out. If you *speak in darkness* what does not befit you and your public profession, *it shall be heard in the light*; some way or other it will be found out, and your foolishness and falsehood will be *made manifest."* If people's religious faith is not effective in conquering and healing the evil of their hearts, nonetheless, it will not serve as a cloak forever. The day is coming when hypocrites will be stripped of their fig leaves (Ge 3:7).

2.2. He added a charge to them to be faithful to the trust vested in them, not to betray it through cowardice or fear. "Whether people will listen or fail to listen (Eze 2:5, 7; 3:11), tell them the truth, the whole truth, and nothing but the truth; what has been spoken to you privately, you are to preach publicly, no matter who is offended." The cause of Christ was likely to involve suffering, even though it would never fail; let them therefore strengthen themselves with courage. Various arguments were provided here to make them strong with a holy determination to do their work.

2.2.1. "The power of your enemies is limited (v. 4): *I say unto you, my friends"*—Christ's disciples are his friends, for he calls them friends and gives them this friendly advice—*"be not afraid."* Those whom Christ acknowledges as his friends need not fear any enemies. "*Be not afraid*, not even of those who *kill the body*; *after that there is no more that they can do."* Those who can only *kill the body* can do Christ's disciples no real harm, because they only send the body to its rest, and the soul to its joy, more quickly.

2.2.2. God is to be feared more than the most powerful people: "*I will forewarn you whom you shall fear* (v. 5). By acknowledging Christ you may incur the wrath of other people, but by denying Christ and disowning him you will incur the wrath of God, who has power to send you to hell. Therefore *I say unto you, Fear him."* "It is true," said the godly martyr, Bishop Hooper, "life is sweet, and death bitter, but eternal life is sweeter, and eternal death bitterer."

2.2.3. The lives of good Christians and good ministers are the special care of divine Providence (vv. 6–7). Providence takes notice of the most insignificant creatures, even *sparrows*. "Although they are so insignificant that *five* of them are sold for *two farthings*, yet *not one of them is forgotten by God. Now, you are of more value than many sparrows*, and so you may be sure you *are not forgotten."* Providence takes notice of the most insignificant interests of the disciples of Christ: "*Even the very hairs of your head are all numbered* (v. 7); then much more are your sighs and tears numbered, and the drops of blood that you shed for Christ's name's sake."

2.2.4. "Whether you are acknowledged or disowned by Christ on the great day depends on whether you now acknowledge or disown him" (vv. 8–9).

2.2.4.1. To encourage us to *confess Christ before men*, however much it may cost us, we are assured that those who confess Christ now will be acknowledged by him on the great day *before the angels of God*. Jesus Christ will confess not only that he suffered for them but also that they suffered for him, and what greater honor can be given them?

2.2.4.2. To deter us from denying Christ, we are here assured concerning those who deny Christ and treacherously depart from him that whatever they may save by it, even if it is life itself, and whatever they may gain by it, even if it is a kingdom, they will lose everything in the end, because they will be *denied before the angels of God*. Christ will not know them; he will not acknowledge them.

2.2.5. The mission they were soon to be sent out on was of the highest and greatest importance (v. 10). Let them be bold in preaching the Gospel, because a severer and heavier fate would come on those who rejected them—after the Spirit was poured out on them, which was to be the last method of conviction—than on those who now rejected Christ himself. "*Whosoever shall speak a word against the Son of man* has a plausible excuse: *Father, forgive them, for they know not what they do* (23:34). But to those who *blaspheme the Holy Spirit*, the privilege of the *forgiveness of sins* will be denied; they will have no benefit through Christ and his Gospel."

2.2.6. Whatever times of testing they were called to, they would be sufficiently provided for and honorably brought through them (vv. 11–12). The faithful martyr for Christ has not only sufferings to undergo but also a testimony to bear and a good confession to make (1Ti 6:13), and should therefore be concerned to do that well, so that the cause of Christ may not suffer, even if they suffer for it, and if this is their concern, let them cast their concerns about it on God (1Pe 5:7): "When they *bring you into the synagogues* or before *magistrates and powers* to be examined about what you believe, *take no thought what ye shall answer*:

2.2.6.1. "So that you may save yourselves. If it is the will of God that you should go free, and your time has not yet come, he will bring it about effectively.

2.2.6.2. "So that you may serve your Master; aim at this, but do not worry yourselves about it, because *the Holy Spirit*, as the Spirit of wisdom, *shall teach you what* is for the honor of God and his cause."

Verses 13–21

We have in these verses:

1. The appeal to Christ by one of his listeners, asking him to intervene *between him and his brother* in a matter concerning the family's estate (v. 13): "*Master, speak to my brother that he* (tell my brother to) *divide the inheritance with me.*" Some think that the man's brother was doing him wrong and that he was appealing to Christ to make his brother do what was right. There are such brothers in the world, who have no sense at all either of natural justice or natural affection. Those who are wronged in this way have a God they may turn to, who will administer justice for those who are oppressed. Others think that the man wanted to do his brother wrong and wanted Christ to help him do so—that whereas the law gave the elder brother a double share of the estate, this man wanted Christ to change that law and make his brother to *divide the inheritance* equally *with him*. I suspect that this was the case, that it was not a lawful desire to get his own, but a sinful desire to get more than his own.

2. Christ's refusal to intervene in this matter (v. 14): *Man, who made me a judge or divider* (arbiter) *over you?* Christ will not assume either a legislative authority or a judicial authority. He corrected the man's mistake. If the man had come to Christ for help in his pursuit of a heavenly inheritance, Christ would have helped him as much as he could, but he had nothing to do with this matter. Whatever Christ did, he could tell by what authority he did it and who gave him that authority (Mt 21:23). Now this shows us what the nature and constitution of Christ's kingdom is. It is a spiritual kingdom, and not one of this world (Jn 18:36).

2.1. It does not interfere with civil powers. As to civil powers, Christianity leaves the matter as it found them.

2.2. It does not interfere with civil rights; it obliges everyone to act justly, according to the settled rules of justice.

2.3. It does not encourage us to expect worldly benefits from our religious faith.

2.4. It does not encourage us to dispute with our brothers and sisters or be rigorous and excessive in our demands.

3. The necessary warning Christ gave his hearers on this occasion.

3.1. The warning itself (v. 15): *Take heed and beware of covetousness*. "*Take heed*; that is, watch out; consider yourselves; keep a protective eye on your own hearts, so that principles of greed may not steal into them. And *beware*; that is, preserve yourselves; keep a strict hand on your own hearts, so that principles of greed may not rule and control them."

3.2. An argument to support this warning: *For a man's life consisteth not in the abundance of the things which he possesseth*; that is, "our happiness and comfort do not depend on our having a great deal of the wealth of this world." The life of the soul certainly does not depend on it. The things of the world do not suit the nature of a soul, supply its needs, or satisfy its desires. Even the life of the body and its happiness do not consist of an abundance of these things; many people who have only a little of the world's wealth—*a dinner of herbs with holy love* (Pr 15:17) is better than a feast of rich food—live with great contentment, and, on the other hand, many people who have a great deal of the things of this world live very miserably.

3.3. The illustration of this by a parable, which is intended to strengthen that necessary caution to us all to *take heed of covetousness*. The parable gives us the life and death of a rich man and leaves us to judge whether he was happy or not.

3.3.1. Here is an account of his worldly wealth and abundance (v. 16): *The ground of a certain rich man brought forth plentifully*. His wealth consisted largely of the crops of the earth. He had a great deal of ground, and his ground was fruitful; the more people have, the more they want, and he had more.

3.3.2. Here are the thoughts of his heart. We are told here what *he thought within himself* (v. 17). The God of heaven knows and observes everything we think, and we are responsible to him for it. Notice:

3.3.2.1. What his cares and concerns were. When he saw an extraordinary crop on his land, instead of thanking God for it or rejoicing in the opportunity it would give him to do more good, he afflicted himself with this thought: *What shall I do, because I have no room where to bestow my fruits* (store my crops)? He spoke as one who was at a loss and perplexed—*What shall I do now?* The poorest beggar in the country, who did not know where to get their next meal, could not have said anything more anxious. Even the abundance of the rich will not allow them to sleep (Ecc 5:12), because they are thinking about what they will do with what they have. The rich man seems to speak with a sigh: *What shall I do?* If you were to ask him, "Why, what is the matter?" actually, he has an abundance of wealth and wants a place to store it; that is all.

3.3.2.2. What his plans and purposes were (v. 18): "*This will I do: I will pull down my barns and build greater* (bigger ones), *and there will I bestow* (store) *all my fruits and my goods*, and then I will be at peace."

3.3.2.2.*1*. It was foolish of him to call the crops of the ground "his" fruits and his goods. What we have is only lent us for our use; it is still owned by God (Lev 25:23; 2Ch 29:15). We are merely stewards of our Lord's goods.

3.3.2.2.*2*. It was foolish of him to hoard what he had and then to think it was well stored. "There will I store it all"—as if none must be given to the poor and *the stranger*, the *fatherless and the widow* (Dt 14:29), but all must be stored up for him himself in a larger barn.

3.3.2.2.*3*. It was foolish of him to let his mind rise with his condition, to talk of larger barns, as if the next year must be as fruitful as this, and even more abundant (Isa 56:12), whereas the barn might be as much too large the next year as it was too small this year.

3.3.2.2.*4*. It was foolish of him to think he would relieve his worries by building new barns, because building them would only increase his worry; those who know anything about the spirit of building know this all too well.

3.3.2.2.*5*. It was foolish of him to contrive and resolve to do all this absolutely and without reserve. "*I will* do this; I will do it without even a thought of that necessary condition, *If the Lord will, I shall live* (Jas 4:13–15)." Plans made dogmatically and arrogantly are foolish, because our times are in God's hand (Ps 31:15); they are not in our own, and we do not even *know what shall be on the morrow* (Jas 4:14).

3.3.2.3. What he pleasantly hoped and expected. "Then *I will say to my soul, Soul, thou hast much goods laid up for many years*; now *take thine ease, eat, drink, and be merry*" (v. 19). Here, too, we see his foolishness.

3.3.2.3.*1*. It was foolish of him to delay enjoying the comfort of his abundance until he had fulfilled his plans for it. When he had built bigger barns, then he *would take his ease*; could he not as well have done that now?

3.3.2.3.*2*. It was foolish of him to be confident that his goods were *laid up for many years*; for all he knew, in an hour's time they might be burned down with everything stored in them. They might be struck by lightning. A few years may see great changes: *moth and rust may corrupt, or thieves break through and steal* (Mt 6:19).

3.3.2.3.*3*. It was foolish of him to count on a life of ease, since many things may make people uneasy in the midst of their greatest abundance. One dead fly may spoil a whole jar of precious ointment, and one thorn a whole bed of feathers. Pain and sickness of body, broken relationships, and, especially, a guilty conscience may rob a person of their peace, even if they have very much of the wealth of this world.

3.3.2.3.*4*. It was foolish of him to think of using his abundance only to *eat, drink, and be merry*, to indulge his sinful nature and satisfy his physical appetite without any thought of doing good to others, as if we lived to eat rather than ate to live.

3.3.2.3.*5*. It was most foolish to say all this to his *soul*. If he had said, "Body, *take thine ease, for thou hast goods laid up for many years*," there might have been some sense in it, but the soul was in no way interested in a barn full of grain or a bag full of gold. If he had had the soul of a pig, he might have blessed it with the satisfaction of eating and drinking. The children of this world are guilty of something most absurd when they make the wealth of the world and physical pleasures their souls' inheritance.

3.3.3. Here is God's sentence on all this. The man said to himself, *Take thine ease*. If God had said so too, the man would have been happy. But God spoke quite differently; God said the man had done badly for himself: *Thou fool, this night thy soul shall be required of thee* (v. 20). *God said to him*, that is, decreed this about him.

This was said when he was *in the fulness of his sufficiency* (Job 20:22), when his eyes were kept awake on his bed with his cares and plans about enlarging his barns. When he was forecasting this, and then lulled himself to sleep again with a pleasant dream of many years' enjoyment, then God said this to him. Notice:

3.3.3.1. The description God gave him: *Thou fool*, you *Nabal*, alluding to the story of Nabal, that *fool*—Nabal is his name, and he is foolish (1Sa 25:25). Worldly people are fools, and the day is coming when God will call them by their own name, *Thou fool*, and they will call themselves so.

3.3.3.2. The sentence he passed on him, a sentence of death: *This night thy soul shall be required of thee*, and then *whose shall those things be which thou hast provided?* He thought he had goods that would last him for many years, but he must be parted from them that night; he thought he would enjoy them himself, but he must leave them to people he did not know (Ecc 2:18–21).

3.3.3.2.*1*. It is a force, an arrest; it is the *requiring of the soul*. "What have you to do with a soul, you who cannot use it any better? Your soul will be required of you." When a good man dies, he cheerfully submits his soul and gives it up, but a worldly man has it torn from him forcefully. God will require it; he will require an account of it. "Man, woman, what have you done with your soul? How have you spent your life? Give an account of your stewardship." It could also be read, "They shall require your soul"; that is, evil angels, as the messengers of God's justice, shall.

3.3.3.2.*2*. It is a surprise, something unexpected. It is at night. The time of death is daytime to a good person; it is their morning. But it is night to a worldly person, a dark night. It is *this night*, this present night, with no delay. "This pleasant night, when you are promising yourself so many years of a life of ease in the future, now, you must die." In the middle of it all here comes an end to it all (Isa 21:4).

3.3.3.2.*3*. It is the leaving behind of all those things that they have provided. All that they have placed their happiness in and built their hopes on, they must leave behind.

3.3.3.2.*4*. It is leaving them to—who knows? "Then *whose shall those things be?* Not yours, to be sure, and you do not know how those for whom you intended them will turn out—your children and relatives, whether they will be wise or fools (Ecc 2:18–19), whether they will bless your memory or curse it, whether they will be a credit to your family or a blemish, do good or harm with what you are leaving them." If many people could have foreseen to whom their house would pass after their death, they would have burned it down rather than made it beautiful.

3.3.3.2.*5*. It shows his foolishness. *At his end he shall be a fool* (Jer 17:11), because then it will be clear that he tried to store treasure in a world he was moving quickly out of, but was not careful to lay it up in the world he was moving quickly to (Mt 6:19–20).

3.4. The application of this parable (v. 21): *So is he who layeth up treasure for himself, and is not rich toward God.* This is the way, and this is the end, of such a person.

3.4.1. The description of a worldly person: he stores up treasure for himself, for the body, for this world, for himself in opposition to God, for that self that is to be denied (9:23).

3.4.1.1. He is in error in considering his flesh to be all he is, as if the body were the whole person (Ge 2:7).

3.4.1.2. He is in error in making it his sole business to store up for the flesh, which he calls storing up for himself.

3.4.1.3. He is mistaken in counting as his treasure those things that are stored up in this way for the world, the body, and *the life that now is* (1Ti 4:8).

3.4.1.4. His greatest error of all is that he is not concerned to be *rich toward God*, rich in the *things of God*. Many people who have an abundance of this world are completely devoid of what will make their souls rich, which will make them rich toward God, rich for eternity.

3.4.2. The foolishness and misery of worldly people: *So is he.* Our Lord Jesus Christ has told us here what the end of worldly people will be. It is the unspeakable foolishness of most people to pursue what is merely for the body and for time more than what is for the soul and eternity.

Verses 22–40

"Therefore, because there are so many who are ruined by all kinds of greed, *I say unto you,* my disciples, beware of it." *Thou, O man of God, flee these things,* as well as you, man of the world (1Ti 6:11).

1. He told them not to afflict themselves with disturbing, perplexing concerns about the necessary supports of life: *Take no thought for* (do not worry about) *your life* (v. 22). In the foregoing parable he had warned us against that kind of greed that rich people are most in danger of. He warned them against another kind of greed here, with which those who have only a little of this world are most tempted. The temptation was to have an anxious concern about the necessary supports of life: "Do not worry about your life, what you are to eat or what clothes you are to wear." This is the warning he had insisted on at some length in Mt 6:25–33, and the arguments used here are much the same.

1.1. God, who has done for us what is greater, may be depended on to do what is less. He has given us life and a body, and so we may cheerfully leave it to him to provide food for the support of that life and to provide clothes to protect that body.

1.2. God, who provides for the lower creatures, may be depended on to provide for good Christians. "Trust God for food, because he feeds the ravens (v. 24); they neither sow nor reap, but they are fed. Now consider how much better you are than the birds, than the ravens. Trust God for clothing, because he clothes the lilies (vv. 27–28); they *toil not, they spin not,* but as the flower grows, it appears wonderfully beautiful. Now, if God has clothed the flowers in this way, will he not much more clothe you?" Then let none of them have little faith. Our excessive cares are owing to the weakness of our faith, for a powerful, practical belief in the all-sufficiency of God would be *mighty* enough, through God, *to pull down the strongholds* of these disturbing, perplexing, and anxious thoughts (2Co 10:4).

1.3. Our cares are fruitless, worthless, and insignificant. They will not gain for us what we want, and so we should not let them disturb us (v. 25): "*Which of you by taking thought can add to his stature one cubit?* Now if you are not able to do what is least, if it is not in your power to alter your height, why should you become perplexed about other things, which are just as much out of your power?" Just as in our stature, so also in our state, we are wise to take things as they are and make the best of them, because becoming anxious, complaining, and overconcerned will not make things any better.

1.4. An excessive, anxious pursuit of the things of this world, even things that are necessary, is unbecoming to the disciples of Christ (vv. 29–30): "*Seek not ye what ye shall eat, or what ye shall drink.* Do not afflict yourselves with worries that disturb you. The disciples of Christ should not seek their food in this way; they are to ask God for it day by day. Let them not be *of doubtful mind,* gusting in every direction. Be even and steady, and have your hearts settled and fixed (Ps 57:7; 108:1; 112:7); do not lead lives of a constant uncertainty, anxiety, and apprehension. Don't let your minds be continually perplexed between hope and fear, always stressed and worried." Let the children of God not make themselves constantly restless, because:

1.4.1. This is making themselves like the children of this world: "*All these things do the nations of the world seek after* (v. 30). Those who provide only for life in this world and not life in the other look no further than what they will eat and drink. But it is not right for you to do so. When excessive worries get the better of us, we should ask ourselves, "What am I, a Christian or a pagan? If a true Christian, shall I join the Gentiles in their pursuits?"

1.4.2. It is unnecessary for them to disturb themselves with concerns about the necessary supports of life: "*Your Father knows that you have need of these things*; he will supply your needs *according to his riches in glory* (Php 4:19), because he is your Father. He will take care that you *want* (lack) *no good thing* (Ps 34:10)."

1.4.3. They have better things to be concerned with and pursue (v. 31): "*But rather seek ye the kingdom of God*—you, my disciples, who are to *preach the kingdom of God.* Let all who have souls to save *seek the kingdom of God,* the only kingdom in which they can be safe. Then *all these things shall be added to you.* Be concerned for spiritual matters with diligence and care, and then trust God with all other aspects of your life."

1.4.4. They have better things to expect and hope for: *Fear not, little flock* (v. 32). When we are frightened with thoughts of evil to come, we make ourselves tense with trying to work out how we can avoid that evil, when after all it is perhaps only the figment of our own imagination. Therefore, *fear not, little flock, for it is your Father's good pleasure to give you the kingdom.* We did not have this word of encouragement in Matthew. We can learn from this:

1.4.4.1. Christ's flock in this world is a little flock. The church is a vineyard (Isa 5:1–2; Lk 20:9–16), a garden (Ge 2:8; SS 4:12, 16; 5:1; etc.), a small plot of land, compared with the desert of this world.

1.4.4.2. Although it is a little flock, completely outnumbered by its enemies, it is the will of Christ that they should not be afraid: "*Fear not, little flock,* but see that you are safe under the protection and leadership of the great and good Shepherd (Jn 10:14; Heb 13:20)."

1.4.4.3. God has a kingdom in store for all who belong to Christ's little flock, a crown of glory (1Pe 5:4).

1.4.4.4. The kingdom is given according to the good pleasure of the Father: *It is your Father's good pleasure.* It is given not to repay a debt, but freely, from his grace.

1.4.4.5. The faithful hopes and prospects of the kingdom should silence and suppress the fears of Christ's little flock in this world. "Fear no trouble, because although it may come, it will not come between you and the kingdom." There is no point in trembling at the thought of what cannot separate us from the love of God (Ro 8:39).

2. He told them to make their souls secure by storing up their treasure in heaven (vv. 33–34).

2.1. "*Sell that ye have,* and *give alms*"; that is, "rather than lack resources with which you could relieve those who are truly needy, sell what you have that is superfluous, and give it *to the poor. Sell what you have* if you find it a hindrance from or an encumbrance in the service of Christ. Do not sell to hoard up the money, or because you can make more of it by lending at interest, but *sell and give alms*; what is rightly given to the poor is invested at the best interest and with the best security.

2.2. "Set your hearts on the other world. *Provide yourselves bags that wax not* (do not grow) *old.*" Grace will go with us into another world, because it is woven in the soul, and our good works will follow us (Rev 14:13). These will be *treasures in heaven*, and such treasure will make us rich for eternity.

2.2.1. It is treasure that will not be exhausted; we may spend it to eternity; there is no danger of seeing the end of this treasure.

2.2.2. It is treasure that we are in no danger of being robbed of; what is stored in heaven is out of the reach of enemies.

2.2.3. It is treasure that will not spoil with keeping, any more than it will dissipate with spending; the moth does not destroy it (Mt 6:19–20). We have stored up our treasure in heaven if our hearts are there while we are here (v. 34). However, if your hearts are set on the earth and the things of this world, it is to be feared that you have your treasure and inheritance in that and that you will therefore be ruined when you leave it.

3. He told them to get ready and stay ready for Christ's coming (v. 34).

3.1. Christ is our Master, and we are his servants, not only working servants but also waiting servants. We must be people who wait for their Lord, who sit up late when he stays out late, to be ready to receive him when he returns.

3.2. Christ our Master, though now gone away from us, will return. Christ's servants are now in a state of expectation, looking for their Master's *glorious appearing* (Tit 2:13). He will come to identify and acknowledge his servants, and they will either stay with him or be turned out of doors, depending on what they are found doing on that day.

3.3. The time of our Master's return is uncertain; it will be far into the night, when he has long delayed his coming: in the *second watch*, just before midnight, or in the *third watch*, beginning at midnight (v. 38). *The Son of Man cometh at an hour that ye think not* (v. 40). This shows the prevalent self-confidence of most people, who are unthinking, so that whenever he comes, it is *in an hour that they think not.*

3.4. What he expects and requires from his servants is that they be *ready to open to him immediately* (v. 36), that is, that they be found as his servants, with their *loins girded about*; the phrase alludes to servants who are ready to go wherever their master sends them and do what their master tells them, having fastened a belt or girdle around their long, loose robes, which would otherwise hang loosely about them and hinder their movement, and having *their lights burning*, so as to light their master's way into the house.

3.5. Those servants who are found ready when their Lord comes will be happy (v. 37): *Blessed are those servants* who, having waited long, are found awake and aware of his first approach, of his first knock. Again in v. 38: *Blessed are those servants.* He *will make them sit down to meat* (recline at table) *and will serve them.* For the bridegroom to wait on his bride at the table is not uncommon, but to wait on his servants is not the ordinary human way, and yet Jesus Christ, to show his condescension, once *girded himself* and *served them* by *washing their feet* (Jn 13:4–5).

3.6. We are kept uncertain about the precise time of his coming so that we may always be ready: *The good man*

(owner) *of the house, if he had known what hour the thief would have come*, even if he was very careless, *would still have watched* (v. 39). But we do not know at what time the alarm will sound for us, and so we should be careful never to be off our guard. Or this may point to the miserable case of those who are careless and unbelieving in this great matter. We have received notice that the day of the Lord's coming will be *as a thief in the night* (1Th 5:2), and yet we do not *watch* as we should. If people will take such good care of their houses, let us be so wise for our souls: *Be ye therefore ready also*, as ready as the owner of the house would be *if he knew what hour the thief would come.*

Verses 41–53

Here is:

1. The question Peter asked Christ on the occasion of the foregoing parable (v. 41): "*Lord, speakest thou this parable to us, or also to all*, to all who listen to you?" Peter was now, as often, the spokesman for the disciples. We have reason to bless God that there are some people who are so eager; let those who have such a gift watch out that they do not become proud. Now Peter wanted Christ to explain himself. "Lord," Peter said, "was it intended for us, or for all?" Christ gave a direct answer to this in Mk 13:37: *What I say unto you, I say unto all.* But here he seems to show that the apostles were primarily concerned in it. *Speakest thou this to us?* "Is this word for me? Speak it to my heart."

2. Christ's reply to this question, directed to Peter and the rest of the disciples. What follows, however, is especially suited to ministers, who are the stewards in Christ's house. Here, our Lord Jesus told them:

2.1. What duty they had as stewards and what trust was committed to them (1Ti 1:11; 6:20).

2.1.1. Ministers are made rulers in God's household, under Christ, whom the house belongs to; they derive authority from Christ.

2.1.2. Their business is to give God's children and servants their share of food, what is proper for them, convictions and encouragement to those to whom they belong.

2.1.3. They must give it to them at the right time, *a word in season to him that is weary* (Isa 50:4).

2.1.4. Here, they must show themselves faithful and wise: faithful to both their Master and their fellow servants, and wise in order to make the most of every opportunity. Ministers must be both skillful and faithful.

2.2. How happy they would be if they showed themselves faithful and wise (v. 43): *Blessed is that servant*:

2.2.1. Who is active, not lazy.

2.2.2. Who is as active as he should be, by public preaching and personal application.

2.2.3. Who is found active when his Lord comes. Now his happiness is illustrated by the advancement of a *steward* (manager) who has proved himself within a lower and narrower service; such a manager will be promoted to larger and higher responsibilities (v. 44): *He will make him ruler over all that he has.* Ministers who obtain mercy from the Lord to be faithful will obtain the further mercy of an abundant reward for their faithfulness on the day of the Lord.

2.3. What a fearful reckoning there would be if they were unfaithful and disloyal (vv. 45–46). We had all this before in Matthew, and so will notice here only:

2.3.1. That *he saith in his heart, My Lord delays his coming.* Christ's patience is very often misinterpreted as delay, to the discouragement of his people and the encouragement of his enemies.

2.3.2. That the persecutors of God's people are commonly abandoned to worldly self-confidence; they beat their fellow servants and then eat and drink with drunkards, completely unconcerned about either their own sin or the suffering of their brother or sister.

2.3.3. Death and judgment will be very terrible to all evildoers, but especially to evil ministers. It will come as a surprise to them, *at an hour when they are not aware.*

2.4. Their sin and punishment are even worse because they knew their duty but did not do it (vv. 47–48): *That servant that knew his lord's will* and did not do it *shall be beaten with many stripes,* and the one who did not know will be beaten with few; his punishment will be less. This seems to allude to the law, which distinguished between sins committed through ignorance and presumptuous sins (Lev 5:15; Nu 15:29–30).

2.4.1. Ignorance of our duty extenuates sin. The servant who did not know his master's will and did things deserving blows will be beaten, because he could have known his duty better, but he will be beaten with fewer blows; his ignorance is a partial excuse, but not a whole one. Through ignorance the Jews put Christ to death (Ac 3:17; 1Co 2:8), and Christ pleaded that ignorance in their excuse: *They know not what they do* (23:34).

2.4.2. The knowledge of our duty emphasizes our sin: *That servant that knew his lord's will will be beaten with many stripes.* God is just to inflict more on him, because to sin against knowledge shows greater willfulness and contempt. A good reason for this is added: *To whomsoever much is given, of him shall be much required.* To those who have greater mental capacities than others, more knowledge and learning, more familiarity with and knowledge of the Scriptures, much has been given, and they will be held responsible accordingly.

3. A further message about his own suffering and the sufferings of his followers. In general (v. 49): *I am come to send fire on the earth.* Some understand this to mean the preaching of the Gospel and the outpouring of holy fire of the Spirit, and this fire was already kindled. However, from what follows, it seems to be understood as referring to the fire of persecution. Christ is not the author of this fire, because it is the sin of the persecutors, but he allows it as a refining fire to test the persecuted.

3.1. He himself must suffer many things; he must pass through this fire that was already kindled (v. 50): *I have a baptism to be baptized with.* Afflictions are compared to both fire and water (Ps 66:12; 69:1–2). Christ's sufferings were both. He called them a baptism (Mt 20:22) because he had them poured or sprinkled on him like water, and because he was dipped into them, as Israel was baptized in the sea (1Co 10:2). Notice here:

3.1.1. Christ's foresight of his sufferings: *I am to be baptized with a baptism.* He called his sufferings by a name that lessened them; they were a baptism, not a deluge. "I must be dipped in them, not drowned in them." And he called them by a name that sanctifies them, because baptism is a sacred ceremony.

3.1.2. Christ's eagerness to undergo his sufferings: *How am I straitened* (distressed) *till it be accomplished!* He longed for the time when he would suffer and die, looking to the glorious outcome of his sufferings. Christ's sufferings were the "labor pains" of his soul, which he submitted to cheerfully. His heart was set so much on human redemption and salvation.

3.2. He told those around him that they also must undergo hardships and difficulties (v. 51): "Do you suppose that I came to give peace on earth?" It is suggested that they relied on this supposition, that they thought that

the Gospel would meet with a universal welcome, that people would unanimously embrace it, and that Christ would give them at least peace, if not pride and power. "But," Christ said, "you are mistaken. The outcome will declare the opposite, and so do not flatter yourselves into a fool's paradise. You will find:

3.2.1. "That the effect of the preaching of the Gospel will be division." This is not to deny that the intention and proper tendency of the Gospel are to unite human beings to one another, to knit them together in holy love (Col 2:2); and if all received the Gospel, this would be its effect. However, many people not only will not receive the preaching of the Gospel but will actively oppose it, and so it will prove to be the occasion of division, though not its cause. While the *armed strong man kept his palace* in the Gentile world, his goods were safe (11:21); the sects of philosophers agreed well enough, as did the worshipers of different gods. But when the Gospel was preached and many were *turned from the power of Satan to God* (Ac 26:18), then there was a disturbance. Some set themselves apart by embracing the Gospel, and others were angry that they did so. Indeed, among those who received the Gospel there would be division, and Christ allows these for his holy ends (1Co 11:18), so that Christians may learn and practice patience with one another (Ro 14:1–2).

3.2.2. "That this division will reach into private families" (v. 53): *The father will be divided against the son, and the son against the father,* when one becomes a Christian and the other does not, because the one who does become a Christian will zealously try to persuade the other by arguments and endearments to turn to Christ (1Co 7:16). The person who continues in unbelief will be provoked and will hate and persecute the one who by faith and obedience witnesses against and condemns their unbelief and disobedience. Even mothers and daughters fall out over religion, and those who do not believe are ready to deliver those who believe into the hands of the bloodthirsty persecutors, even though those believers are otherwise very near and dear to them. We find in Acts that wherever the Gospel went, persecution was stirred up; the Gospel was *everywhere spoken against* (Ac 28:22), and there was *no small stir about that way* (Ac 19:23). Therefore, let the disciples of Christ not promise themselves *peace upon earth* (v. 51).

Verses 54–59

Having in the previous verses given his disciples their lesson, Christ here turned to the people and gave them theirs (v. 54). In general, he wanted them to be as wise in spiritual matters as they were in outward matters of life.

1. Let them learn to discern the way of God toward them, so that they might prepare for it accordingly. They understood the weather; they could forecast when it would rain and when hot weather would come (vv. 54–55). Even in regard to changes in the weather God warns us what is coming, and human skill has invented the barometer to enhance the announcements nature gives us. From what has happened we work out what will happen. We see the benefits of experience; by taking notice we may learn to give notice. Whoever is wise will observe and learn. Notice:

1.1. The details of the signs: "*When you see a cloud arising out of the west,* perhaps it is at first *no bigger than a man's hand* (1Ki 18:44), but you say that a shower of rain is about to fall, and so it does. When you *observe* the *south wind blow,* you say, *There will be heat,* and it usually *comes to pass*"—though nature has not limited itself to such a track, and sometimes we are mistaken in our forecast.

1.2. The inferences he drew from them (v. 56): "*Ye hypocrites*, who claim to be wise but really are not so, *how is it that you do not discern this time?* Why are you not aware that you now have the opportunity that you will not have long and that you may never have again?" *Now is the accepted time* (2Co 6:2); it is now or never. People are foolish and miserable if they do not *know their time* (Ecc 9:12). This was the ruin of the people of that generation, that they *knew not the day of their visitation* (19:44). He added, *Yea, and why even of yourselves, judge ye not what is right?* (v. 57). If people would allow themselves the liberty of *judging what is right*, they would soon find that all of Christ's commands about all things are right and that there is nothing more just in itself than to submit to them and be ruled by them.

2. Let them quickly *make their peace with God*, before it is too late (vv. 58–59). We had this on another occasion (Mt 5:25–26).

2.1. We count it our wisdom in our temporal affairs to settle with those with whom we cannot dispute. "*When thou goest with thine adversary to the magistrate* and you are in danger of being thrown into prison, you know it is the wisest course to settle the matter between you; *as thou art in the way, give diligence to be delivered from him.*" Wise people will not allow their quarrels to go to an extremity, but will settle them in time.

2.2. Let us act in the same way in spiritual matters. By our sin, we have made God our adversary, and he has both right and might on his side. Christ, to whom all judgment is committed (Jn 5:22), is the judge before whom we are soon to appear. If we stand on trial before him, the cause will certainly go against us; the *Judge will deliver* us to the *officer*, and we will be *cast* (thrown) *into* the *prison* of hell *till the last mite* (penny) *be paid*, which will not be to all eternity. Christ's sufferings were short, yet because of their value they made full satisfaction. Now, in consideration of this, let us be diligent to make sure we are delivered out of the hands of God the Adversary and into the hands of God the Father, and let us do this *as we are in the way*, on which the emphasis is placed here. While we are still alive, we are *in the way*, and now is the time for us, by repentance and faith, to have the quarrel settled, now, while it can be done, before it is too late. Let us take hold of the arm of the Lord that is stretched out in this gracious offer, so that we may make peace.

CHAPTER 13

In this chapter we have: 1. The good use Christ made of news that was brought to him about some Galileans who had recently been massacred by Pilate (vv. 1–5). 2. The parable of the unfruitful fig tree (vv. 6–9). 3. Christ's healing a poor ill woman on the Sabbath (vv. 10–17). 4. A repetition of the parables of the mustard seed and of the leaven (yeast) (vv. 18–22). 5. His answer to the question about the number of people saved (vv. 23–30). 6. The contempt he expressed toward Herod's malice and threats, and his reading of the fate of Jerusalem (vv. 31–35).

Verses 1–5

We have here:

1. News brought to Christ of the recent death of some Galileans, whose blood *Pilate had mingled with their sacrifices* (v. 1). Let us consider:

1.1. What this tragic story was. It is briefly related here and is not dealt with by any of the historians of those times. Because the Galileans were Herod's subjects, this outrage committed on them by Pilate probably brought about the quarrel between Herod and Pilate that we read about in 23:12. We are not told how many they were, perhaps only a few, but the circumstance noted is that he *mingled their blood with their sacrifices*. Although they perhaps had good reason to fear Pilate's hatred, they would not keep away from Jerusalem, where the law required them to go with their sacrifices. Neither the holiness of the place nor the holiness of the work would protect them from the rage of an unjust judge, *who neither feared God nor regarded man* (18:2). The altar, which used to be a sanctuary and place of shelter, had now become a trap, a place of danger and slaughter.

1.2. Why it was related to our Lord Jesus at this time.

1.2.1. Perhaps it was merely news that they thought he had not yet heard and that they thought he would lament just as they did.

1.2.2. Perhaps it was intended to confirm what Christ had said at the end of the previous chapter about the necessity of making our peace with God in time. "Master, here is a fresh example of some people who were very suddenly *delivered to the officer*, who were taken away by death when they little expected it, and so we all need to be ready." It will be very useful to us both to explain the word of God and to impose it on ourselves by observing the providences of God.

1.2.3. Perhaps, since he himself was from Galilee and was a prophet, they wanted to stir him up to find a way to avenge the death of these Galileans on Herod.

1.2.4. Perhaps this was told to Christ to dissuade him from going to Jerusalem to worship (v. 22), for fear that Pilate would treat him as he had treated those Galileans. So that Pilate, having set his hand to the task, might not proceed any further, they thought it advisable for Christ to keep out of the way for the present.

1.2.5. Christ's answer suggests that they told him this with a spiteful overtone, that without doubt these Galileans had secretly been evildoers, for otherwise God would not have allowed Pilate to cut them off so barbarically. Such an insinuation was very malicious; rather than presume that those who died were martyrs, those who here reported their deaths would without any proof assume them to be evildoers. Yet this fate of theirs was capable not only of a favorable interpretation but of an honorable one.

2. Christ's reply to this report.

2.1. He added another story, which, like it, was an example of people being taken away by sudden death. It had not been long since *the tower of Siloam fell*, killing and burying eighteen people in its ruins. It was a sad story, but sadly we often hear about such tragic accidents. Towers, which were built for safety, often turn out to destroy people.

2.2. He warned his listeners not to make wrong use of these and similar events; they must not, for instance, take occasion from them to censure great sufferers as if their suffering proved them to be great sinners: *Suppose ye that these Galileans were sinners above all the Galileans, because they suffered such things? I tell you nay* (vv. 2–3). Perhaps those who told him the story of the Galileans were Jews and were glad to have any information that reflected badly on the Galileans, and so Christ replied to them with the story of the *men of Jerusalem* who came to an untimely end. "Now do you suppose that those eighteen who met with their death when the tower of Siloam fell on them, while perhaps they were expecting their healing from the pool of Siloam, were debtors to divine justice *above all men that dwelt at Jerusalem?*

I tell you nay." We cannot judge people's sins by their sufferings in this world, because many are thrown into the furnace as gold to be purified (Job 23:10; Isa 1:25), not as dross and chaff to be consumed. We must not, therefore, be harsh in our criticism of those who suffer more than their neighbors, so that we may not add further sorrow to the sorrowful. If we want to judge, we have enough to do in judging ourselves. We might as justly conclude that the oppressors on whose side are power and success are the greatest saints as conclude that the oppressed are the greatest sinners. Let us, in our censures of others, do as we would have done to us, because as we do, so we will have done to us: *Judge not, that ye be not judged* (Mt 7:1).

2.3. He used these stories as a foundation for a call to repentance, adding to each of them this awakening word, *Except ye repent, ye shall all likewise perish* (vv. 3–5). This shows that:

2.3.1. We all deserve to perish as much as they did. Our censures must be lessened by the knowledge that we are not only sinners, but as great sinners as they, that we have as much sin to repent of as they had to suffer for.

2.3.2. Therefore we should all repent, that is, be sorry for what we have done wrong and do so no more. The judgments of God on others are loud calls toward us to repent.

2.3.3. Repentance is the way of escape from perishing, and it is a sure way.

2.3.4. If we do not repent, we will certainly perish, as others have before us. Unless we repent, we will perish eternally, as they perished out of this world. The same Jesus who calls us to *repent because the kingdom of heaven is at hand* (Mt 4:17) tells us to repent because otherwise we will perish; that is why he has set before us life and death, good and evil (Dt 30:15, 19), giving us the choice.

Verses 6–9

This parable is intended to back up that warning that came immediately before: *"Except ye repent, ye shall all likewise perish."*

1. This parable refers primarily to the Jewish people and nation. God chose them as his own and made them a people close to him, expecting from them a response of duty and obedience, which he would have counted as fruit. They did not live up to his expectations, however. They were a disgrace rather than a credit to their profession. He justly decided to abandon them, therefore, but upon Christ's intercession, he graciously gave them further time and further mercy. He tested them, as it were, for another year, by sending his apostles among them to call them to repentance and offer them pardon in Christ's name. Some of them were persuaded to repent and produce fruit, and all was well with them, but most of the nation continued to be impenitent and unfruitful, and ruin without any remedy came on them.

2. Yet it has a further reference: it is designed to wake up all who enjoy the means of grace to see to it that the attitude of their hearts and minds and the whole tenor of their lives correspond to their opportunities, because that is the fruit that is required. Notice:

2.1. The advantages this fig tree had. It was *planted in a vineyard,* in better soil than other fig trees, and where it had more care taken of it, for fig trees commonly grew by the *way-side* (road) (Mt 21:19). This fig tree belonged to *a certain man.* The church of God is his vineyard (Isa 5:1–2). We are fig trees planted in this vineyard, and our being placed there is a special favor.

2.2. The owner's expectation of it: *He came, and sought fruit thereon.* He did not send someone else, but came himself. Christ came into this world, *came to his own* (Jn 1:11), seeking fruit. The God of heaven requires and expects fruit from those who have a place in his vineyard. It is not enough to produce leaves, to cry out, *Lord, Lord* (Mt 7:21); nor to produce blossoms, to begin well and promise much; there must be real fruit. Our thoughts, words, and actions must be according to the Gospel, light and love.

2.3. The disappointment of his expectation: *He found none,* not one fig. It is sad to think how many people enjoy the privileges of the Gospel but do nothing at all to honor God.

2.3.1. He complained about it to the man who took care of the vineyard: "I come *seeking fruit* but am disappointed—*I find none."*

2.3.2. He emphasized his disappointment, on two considerations:

2.3.2.1. That he had waited long but was still disappointed. Just as he did not have great expectations—he expected only fruit, not much fruit—so he was not hasty: *he came three years,* year after year. In general, the parable teaches us that the patience of God is stretched out toward many people who enjoy the Gospel and do not produce fruits from it. How many times in three years has God come to many of us *seeking fruit* but *found none?*

2.3.2.2. That this fig tree not only did not produce fruit; it also caused harm; it *cumbered the ground* (used up the soil); it took up the space that a fruitful tree could have occupied, and it was harmful to everything around it. Those who do not do good commonly do harm by the influence of their bad example. The trouble caused is the greater, and the land is more obstructed, if the tree is tall, large, old, and spreading.

2.4. The sentence passed on it: *Cut it down.* For barren trees, one can expect no other end than for them to be cut down, and with good reason, for *why cumbers it the ground?* What reason is there for it to have a place in the vineyard if it is useless?

2.5. The intercession for it by the man who took care of the vineyard. Christ is the great Intercessor. Ministers are intercessors; we should pray for those we preach to. Notice:

2.5.1. What it was that he prayed for, namely, a reprieve: *Lord, let it alone this year also* (v. 8). He did not pray, "Lord, let it never be cut down," but, "Lord, not now." It is desirable to have a barren tree reprieved. Some do not yet have grace to repent (Ac 5:31; 11:18), but it is a mercy to them to have opportunity to repent. We owe it to Christ, the great Intercessor, that barren trees are not cut down immediately. We are encouraged to pray to God for the merciful reprieve of barren fig trees: "Lord, let them alone; bear with them a little longer, and wait to be gracious (Isa 30:18)." This is how we must stand in the gap to turn away wrath (Eze 22:30). Yet reprieves of mercy are only for a time: *Let it alone this year also.* When God has been patient for a long time, we may hope he will be patient a little longer, but we cannot expect him always to be patient. The prayers of others for us may obtain reprieves for us, but not pardons; there must be an individual personal faith, repentance, and prayer.

2.5.2. How he promised to make the most of this reprieve: *Till I shall dig about it, and dung it* (spread manure around it). This shows us:

2.5.2.1. In general, our prayers must always be backed up by our endeavors. We must seek God's grace in all our prayers with a humble resolution to do our duty; otherwise we mock God and show that we do not rightly value the mercies we pray for. The one looking after the vineyard committed himself to do his part, and this teaches ministers to do theirs.

2.5.2.2. In particular, when we pray for grace, we must follow up our prayers by diligently using the means of grace. The one looking after the vineyard would dig around the tree and spread manure around it. Unfruitful Christians must be woken up by the terrors of the law, which *break up the fallow ground*, and then encouraged by the promises of the Gospel, which are warming and enriching, as manure is to the tree. Both methods must be tried; the one prepares for the other, and it is all little enough.

2.5.3. How he left the matter: "Let us see what we can do with it for one more year, *and if it bear fruit, well* (fine) (v. 9)." The word *well* is not in the original in v. 9; the expression is abrupt: *If it bear fruit—*. Finish the sentence as you wish, so as to express how wonderfully pleased both the owner and one looking after it would be. If unfruitful people who profess religious faith repent after a long time of unfruitfulness, putting things right and producing fruit, they will find all is well. God will be pleased; ministers' hands will be strengthened. In fact, there will be joy in heaven because of it (15:7); the ground will no longer be occupied by something useless, but will be put to better use; the vineyard will be made more beautiful, and its good trees improved. As for the tree itself, it is *well*; it will also *receive blessing from God* (Heb 6:7); it will be *purged* and *bring forth more fruit*. But he added, *If not, then after that thou shalt cut it down*. Although God is patient for a long time, he will not always be patient. Barren trees will certainly be cut down in the end and *cast into the fire* (Rev 20:15). The longer God has waited, the greater their destruction will be: to be cut down after that will be truly sad. Cutting down, though a work that must be done, is a work that God does not take pleasure in. If barren trees persist in their unfruitfulness, those who now intercede for them will even be content to see them cut down. Their best friends will accept the righteous judgment of God.

Verses 10–17

Here is:

1. The miraculous healing of a woman who had long been under a *spirit of infirmity* (crippled by a spirit). Our Lord Jesus spent *his Sabbaths* in the *synagogues* (v. 10). We should be careful to do so and not think we can spend the Sabbath as well at home in reading a good book. Moreover, when he was in the synagogues on the Sabbath, "he was teaching there." He was at home when he was teaching. Now to confirm the doctrine he preached, he performed a miracle of mercy.

1.1. The one who was to receive Christ's love was a woman in the synagogue who had *a spirit of infirmity eighteen years* (v. 11). By divine permission, an evil spirit had crippled her, so that she was *bowed together* and could *in no wise lift up herself*: she could not stand up straight. Although she suffered much under this infirmity, she still went to the *synagogue on the sabbath day*. Even physical weaknesses, unless they are very painful indeed, should not keep us from public worship on the Sabbath, because God can help us beyond our expectation.

1.2. The offer of this healing to someone who did not seek it shows the forwardness of the mercy and grace of Christ: *When Jesus saw her, he called her to him* (v. 12). Before she called, he answered (Isa 65:24). She came to him to be taught, to receive good for her soul, and then

Christ gave this relief to her physical infirmity. Those whose first and chief concern is their souls are doing the best thing they can to befriend the true interests of their bodies as well.

1.3. The effectiveness and immediacy of the healing show his almighty power. He *laid his hands on her* and said, "*Woman, thou art loosed from thine infirmity.*" Although *she could in no wise lift up herself*, Christ could both lift her up and enable her to lift herself up. This woman who had been crooked was immediately made straight. This healing represents the work of Christ's grace on the souls of people:

1.3.1. In the conversion of sinners. Unsanctified hearts are under this *spirit of infirmity*; they are distorted. They cannot at all *lift up themselves* to God and heaven; in its natural state, the bent of the soul, its tendency, is completely away from heaven. Such crooked souls do not seek Christ, but he calls them to himself, speaking a healing word to them, by which he releases them from their infirmity. He makes the soul straight. The grace of God can make straight what human sin has made crooked.

1.3.2. In the comfort of good people. Many of the children of God are suffering long under *a spirit of infirmity*, a spirit of bondage. But Christ, by his Spirit of adoption (Ro 8:15), releases them from this weakness at the appropriate time.

1.4. This healing had an immediate effect on the soul of the patient as well as on her body. She *glorified* God. When crooked souls are straightened, they will show it by glorifying God.

2. The offense that was taken at this by the *ruler of the synagogue*. He was indignant at it, because it was performed *on the sabbath day* (v. 14). What light can shine so clearly and strongly that a spirit of bigotry will not serve to shut people's eyes against it? He said *to the people, There are six days in which men ought to work: in them therefore come and be healed, and not on the sabbath day*. Notice here how lightly he took the miracles Christ performed, as if they were things that happened as a matter of course: "You may come and be healed any day of the week." Christ's healing had become, in his eyes, cheap and common. This was clearly the work of God, and when God prohibited us from working on that day, did he prohibit himself too (Jn 5:17)? The same word in Hebrew, *chesed*, signifies both "godly" and "merciful," to show that works of mercy and love are in a way works of piety (1Ti 5:4) and are therefore very proper to do on the Sabbath.

3. Christ's justification of himself in what he had done (v. 15): *The Lord then answered him, Thou hypocrite*. We *must* judge charitably and *can* judge only according to outward appearance (1Sa 16:7). Christ knew that the synagogue ruler had a real hostility to him and his Gospel, that he was only cloaking this hostility with a pretended zeal for the Sabbath day. Christ could have told him this, but he condescended to reason the case with him.

3.1. He appealed to the Jews' practice—which was common to them all and never disallowed—of watering their cattle on the Sabbath day. Cattle that were kept in the stable were constantly *loosed from the stall on the sabbath day, and led away to watering*. It would be cruel not to do it. If letting the cattle rest on the Sabbath day meant imposing a fast on them, such rest would be worse than work.

3.2. He applied this to the present situation (v. 16): "Must the ox and the donkey have compassion shown them on the Sabbath, and shall not this woman be set free from much greater suffering? She is a *daughter of*

Abraham; she is your sister, and shall she be denied a favor that you give to an ox or a donkey? She is *a daughter of Abraham* and so is entitled to receive the Messiah's blessings. She is one whom Satan *has bound*, and so to break the power of the Devil and thwart him was not only an act of love to this poor woman but also an act of devoutness to God. She has been in this deplorable condition, *lo, these eighteen years*, and so, now that there is an opportunity to deliver her, it should not be put off a day longer. Any of you would have thought eighteen years' affliction was long enough."

4. The various effects that this had on those who heard him.

4.1. What confusion this caused his persecutors as a recompense for their malice: *When he had said these things, all his adversaries were ashamed* (v. 17). It was a shame that brought not repentance, but rather indignation.

4.2. What confirmation this gave to the faith of his friends: *All the people rejoiced for all the glorious things that were done by him*. The humiliation of his enemies was the joy of his followers. The things Christ did were glorious things, and we should rejoice in them.

Verses 18–22

1. The Gospel's progress is here foretold in two parables, which we had before (Mt 13:31–33). Christ undertakes here to show *what the kingdom of God is like* (v. 18): *"Whereunto shall I liken the kingdom of God?* (v. 20). It will be completely different from what you expect. You expect it to appear great and to reach its perfection suddenly, but you are mistaken. *It is like a grain of mustard-seed*, something that is small, looks insignificant, and promises little, but which, when sown, *waxes* (grows into) *a great tree"* (v. 19). Many people were perhaps prejudiced against the Gospel because its beginning was so small. Christ wanted to set aside this prejudice by assuring them that although *its beginning was small, its latter end would greatly increase* (Job 8:7), so that many people would *fly* to it *as a cloud* (Isa 60:8) to rest in its branches. "You expect it to grow by external means, but it will work *like leaven* (yeast), silently and imperceptibly, without any force or violence (v. 21). *A little leaven leaveneth the whole lump* (1Co 5:6). In the same way, the message of Christ will strangely diffuse its fragrance into the whole human race. But you must give it time, and you will find it has worked wonders. Gradually *the whole will be leavened."*

2. Christ's progress toward Jerusalem is recorded: *He went through the cities and villages, teaching and journeying* (v. 22). Here we find Christ making his way toward Jerusalem, to the Feast of Dedication, which was in winter, when traveling was uncomfortable.

Verses 23–30

We have here:

1. A question put to our Lord Jesus. We are not told who asked it, whether it was a friend or foe. The question was, *Are there few that are saved?* (v. 23). Perhaps it was a trick question. If he said that many would be saved, they would censure him as too lax; if he said few, they would censure him for being too rigorous and narrow. In nothing do people show their ignorance more than in judging the salvation of others. Perhaps it was asked inquisitively, as a sophisticated speculation. Many people are more inquisitive about who will be saved and who will not than about what they need to do to be saved themselves. Perhaps it was asked in wonder. The questioner had noticed how

strict the law of Christ was and how bad the world was and, comparing these, cried out, "How few there are who will be saved!" We have reason to be amazed that of the many to whom the word of salvation is sent there are so few to whom it is indeed a saving word. Perhaps it was asked to find out more. It may be translated this way: "If the saved be few ..." That is, "If the saved are few, what then? What effect should this have on me? What should I do about it?"

2. Christ's answer to this question. Our Savior did not answer the question directly, because he came to guide people's consciences, not to gratify their curiosity. Not, "What will become of such and such a person?" But, "What shall I do, and what will become of me?" Notice:

2.1. A stimulating exhortation and direction: *Strive to enter in at the strait gate* (make every effort to enter through the narrow door). This is directed not only to the one who asked the question, but to all: *Strive ye*. All who wish to be saved must *enter in at the strait gate* and submit to a strict discipline. Those who want to enter through the narrow door must *strive to enter*. It is hard to get to heaven, and one will not get there without a great deal of worry and pains. It may be read, "Be in anguish"; strive as those who run for a prize (1Co 9:24; Php 3:14); we must stir and exert ourselves to the utmost."

2.2. Various rousing considerations.

2.2.1. Think how many people take some effort for salvation but perish because they do not take enough. *Many will seek to enter in, and shall not be able*; they seek, but they do not strive. The reason why many come short of grace and glory is that they seek lazily. They have a mind for happiness and a good opinion of holiness and take some good steps toward both, but their convictions are weak; their desires are cold, and their endeavors feeble, and there is no strength or steadiness in their determination. They therefore *come short* (Ro 3:23).

2.2.2. Think of the day of separation that is coming, and think of the decisions of that day: the *Master of the house will rise up, and shut to the door* (v. 25). Now he seems to have left things open, but the day is coming when he will *rise up, and shut to the door*. What door is this?

2.2.2.1. A door of division. Now, within the temple of the church there are worldly professors of faith who worship in the outer court, and spiritual professors of faith who worship *within the veil* (Heb 6:19); between these the door is now open. But when the *Master of the house is risen up*, the door will be shut between them, so that those who are in the outer court may be kept out. As to those *that are filthy* (Rev 22:11), the door is shut on them, so that those who are inside may be kept in and those who are holy may remain holy. The door is shut to separate the worthy and the worthless (Jer 15:19).

2.2.2.2. It is also a door of denial and exclusion. The door of mercy and grace has long stood open for them, but they refused to come in through it. They hoped they could get to heaven by their own merits, and so when the Owner of the house has gotten up, he will justly *shut that door*.

2.2.3. Think how many who were so confident that they would be saved will be rejected in the day of testing, and you will say that there are few who will be saved and that we all ought to strive. Consider:

2.2.3.1. How far their hope will carry them, even to heaven's gate. They will stand there and knock, knocking as those who belong to the house, saying, "Lord, Lord, open up to us, because we think we have a right to enter." Many are ruined by an ill-founded hope of heaven that they never distrusted or called into question. They call

Christ "Lord"; they now want to enter through the door that they formerly made light of.

2.2.3.2. What reasons they will have for their self-confidence. Let us see what their plea is (v. 26). They have been Christ's guests and shared in his favors: "*We have eaten and drunk in thy presence*, at your table." And they have been Christ's hearers: "*Thou hast taught in our streets.* Would you teach us and not save us?"

2.2.3.3. How their self-confidence will fail them. Christ will say to them, *I know you not whence you are* (I don't know where you came from) (v. 25). And again (v. 27), *I tell you, I know you not; depart from me*.

2.2.3.3.1. He will disown them: "*I know you not*; you do not belong to my family." The Lord knows those who are his, but he does not know those who are not his, those who do not belong to him—he has nothing to do with them.

2.2.3.3.2. He will discard them: *Depart from me*. "Depart from my door. There's nothing for you here."

2.2.3.3.3. He will describe them in a way that shows the reason for this condemnation: *You are workers of iniquity*. This is their ruin, that under a pretense of piety they did the Devil's work wearing Christ's uniform.

2.2.3.4. How terrible their punishment will be (v. 28): *There will be weeping and gnashing of teeth*, the greatest possible grief and indignation: *You will see Abraham and Isaac and Jacob and all the prophets in the kingdom of God, and yourselves thrust out*. The Old Testament saints are in the kingdom of God; they saw Christ's day at a distance, and it brought comfort to them (Jn 8:56). New Testament sinners will be thrown out of the kingdom of God. They will be thrown out covered in shame, not having any part or share in the matter (Ac 8:21). The sight of the saints' glory will emphasize the sinners' misery.

2.2.4. Think about those who will be saved nevertheless: *They shall come from the east and the west, and the last shall be first* (vv. 29–30). From what Christ said here, it is clear that of those whom we think most likely to be saved, only *few shall be saved*. However, do not then say that the Gospel has been preached in vain. Many will come from all parts of the Gentile world and be admitted. When we come to heaven, we will meet very many there whom we little thought we would, and we will miss very many whom we truly expected to see. Those who *sit down in the kingdom of God* are those who made an effort to get there, coming from far, *from the east and from the west, from the north and from the south*. This shows that those who want to enter that kingdom must strive. Many who are likely to go to heaven fall short, and others who seemed behind will win and wear this prize, and so we should *strive to enter*. Will I, who started out first and stood closest, miss out on heaven, when others, who are less likely, enter it? If it is gained by striving, why should not I strive?

Verses 31–35

Here is:

1. A suggestion to Christ that he was in danger from Herod now that he was in Galilee, within Herod's jurisdiction (v. 31): "*Certain of the Pharisees came* to Christ and said, '*Get thee* out of this country; otherwise *Herod will kill thee*.'" Some think that these Pharisees had no reason at all to say this, but that they made up this lie to drive him out of Galilee and into Judea, where they knew there were those who really sought his life. However, because Christ's answer was directed to Herod himself, it seems that the Pharisees had a reason for what they said, and that Herod was very angry with Christ and wanted to cause

him trouble; indeed, he wanted to rid his dominions of Christ, and he hoped to frighten him away by sending him this threatening message.

2. His defiance of Herod's rage: *Go you, and tell that fox so* (v. 32). In calling Herod a fox, Christ described his true character, because Herod was as subtle as a fox, noted for his craft, treachery, and evil. Although it is a black and ugly characterization, it was not wrong of Christ to describe him in this way. Christ was a prophet, and prophets always had freedom of speech in rebuking rulers and leaders. That was why he could rightfully call this proud king by his own name. "Go and tell that fox that I do not fear him, because:

2.1. "I know that I must die, and soon. I expect it *the third day*," that is, "very soon; my hour is at hand. If Herod were to kill me, he would not take me by surprise.

2.2. "I know that death will be my advancement, and so I do not fear him. When I die, *I shall be perfected* (I will reach my goal); I will have completed my work; I shall be consecrated." It is said that when Christ died, he *sanctified himself* (Heb 10:29); he consecrated himself to his priestly office with his own blood.

2.3. "I know that neither he nor anyone else can kill me until I have done my work. *I will cast out devils, and do cures, today and tomorrow*, despite him and all his threats. It is not in his power to hinder me. I must *go about* preaching and healing, *today, and tomorrow, and the day following*." It is good for us to look on the time we have left to us as only a little, so that we may be stirred to *do the work of the day in its day* (Lev 23:37; 1Ch 16:37). It is encouraging to us to know that the power and hatred of our enemies is powerless to take us away as long as God still has any work for us to do.

2.4. "I know that Herod can do me no harm, not only because *my time is not yet come* (Jn 7:6) but also because the place appointed for my death is Jerusalem, which is not within his jurisdiction: *It cannot be that a prophet perish out of Jerusalem*." No one except the great Sanhedrin, which always sat at Jerusalem, undertook to try prophets; and so if a prophet was put to death, it must be at Jerusalem.

3. His mourning for Jerusalem and his declaration of wrath against that city (vv. 34–35). We had this in Mt 23:37–39.

3.1. The evil of people and places that profess a relationship with God more eminently than others is especially provocative and grieving to the Lord Jesus. How passionately he spoke about the sin and ruin of that holy city! *O Jerusalem! Jerusalem!*

3.2. If those who enjoy great plenty of the means of grace do not benefit by them, they are often prejudiced against them. If human sins are not conquered, they are provoked.

3.3. Jesus Christ has shown himself willing to receive poor souls who come to him: *How often would I have gathered thy children together, as a hen gathers her brood under her wings*, with such care and tenderness!

3.4. The reason why sinners are not protected is that they do not want to be: "I *would*, I often would, but ye *would not*." Christ's willingness emphasizes sinners' unwillingness.

3.5. The house that Christ leaves *is left desolate*. The temple is desolate if Christ has deserted it. He left it to them; let them take it to themselves and make the best of it; Christ would trouble it no more.

3.6. Christ justly withdraws from those who drive him away from them. They would not be gathered by him, and so he said, "*You shall not see me* anymore."

3.7. The judgment of the great day will powerfully convince unbelievers who would not now be convinced: "Then you will say, *Blessed is he that cometh.* You will not see me to be the Messiah till the time when it is too late."

CHAPTER 14

We have here: 1. The healing that our Lord Jesus performed on the Sabbath on a man whose body was badly swollen (vv. 1–6). 2. A lesson on humility (vv. 7–11). 3. A lesson on love (vv. 12–14). 4. The success of the Gospel offer foretold in the parable of the guests invited to a feast (vv. 15–24). 5. The great law of discipleship set down (vv. 25–35).

Verses 1–6

In this account we find that:

1. *The Son of man came eating and drinking* (7:34), conversing familiarly with all kinds of people. He *went into the house of one of the chief Pharisees to eat bread on the sabbath day* (v. 1). See how favorable God is to us, that he allows us time even on his own day for physical refreshment, and consider how careful we should be not to abuse that liberty. Christ went only to eat bread, to take such refreshment as was necessary on the Sabbath. Our Sabbath meals must be shown special care to guard against all kinds of excess.

2. He *went about doing good* (Ac 10:38). Here was *a certain man before him who had the dropsy* (whose body was badly swollen). Christ took the initiative and came to him with the blessings of goodness; *before* the man *called*, Christ answered him (Isa 65:24). It is good to be where Christ is. This man had the *dropsy*, probably very badly.

3. He *endured the contradiction of sinners against himself* (Heb 12:3). *They watched him* (v. 1). It seems that the Pharisee who invited him did it with the intention of picking a quarrel with him. When Christ asked them whether they thought it *lawful to heal on the Sabbath*, they would say neither yes nor no, since their intention was to inform on him, not to be informed by him. They would not say it was lawful to heal, and they could not for shame say it was not lawful. Good people have often been persecuted for doing what even their persecutors must acknowledge to be lawful and good. Christ did many good works, for which they threw stones at him and his name (Jn 10:32).

4. Christ would not be hindered from doing good by the opposition and contradiction of sinners. He *took him, and healed him, and let him go* (v. 4). *He took him,* that is, laid hands on him, to heal him; "he embraced him," took him in his arms, big and unwieldy as he was—people suffering from dropsy usually are—and restored him to a normal shape in a moment. He then let him go, so that the Pharisees could not attack him for being healed: what absurdities would such people as these Pharisees not be guilty of?

5. Our Lord Jesus did nothing but what he could justify (vv. 5–6). Those who before had remained silent in order to be subtle were now forced to remain silent out of shame, as he continued to answer their thoughts, appealing to their own practice. "*Which of you shall have an ass or an ox fallen into a pit, and will not pull him out on the Sabbath day*—and do it immediately, not putting it off until the end of the Sabbath, in case it perishes?" It was not so much out of compassion for the poor creature that they did it as out of a concern for their own interests. It was their own ox and their own donkey, which was worth

money, and they would dispense with the law of the Sabbath to save that. Many people can easily dispense with something for their own interests even though they cannot dispense with it for God's glory and the good of their brothers and sisters. This question silenced them: *They could not answer him again to these things* (v. 6). Christ will be justified when he speaks (Ps 51:4; Ro 3:4).

Verses 7–14

Our Lord Jesus here sets us an example of the profitable, edifying speech we should have at our tables when we are with our friends. When he was with strangers—indeed, when he was with enemies who *watched him* (v. 1), he took the opportunity to rebuke what he saw wrong in them and to instruct them. We must not only not allow any corrupt speech at our tables; we must also go beyond common harmless talk and use the occasion of God's goodness to us at our tables to speak well of him, learning to spiritualize common things. Our Lord Jesus was among people of quality, and yet, as one who did not show favoritism:

1. He used the occasion to rebuke the guests for striving to sit in the place of honor.

1.1. He noticed how these lawyers and Pharisees desired the places of honor (v. 7). He had already spoken about that kind of people in general (11:43). Here he brought home the command to particular individuals. He *marked* how they *chose out the chief rooms*; everyone, as he came in, got as close to the best seat as he could. Even in the common actions of life, Christ's eye is on us, and he notices what we do.

1.2. He noticed how those who were so aspiring often exposed themselves and were turned away in disgrace, whereas those who were modest and seated themselves in the lowest seats often gained respect by it.

1.2.1. Those who take up the highest seats may be forced to yield them to someone *more honourable* (vv. 8–9) and take a lower seat. It should restrain our high thoughts of ourselves to think how many there are who are *more honourable* than we are, not only with respect to worldly honor but also in personal merits and achievements. The host of the feast will marshal his guests and will not allow the more honorable to be kept out of the seats that they are due, and so he will boldly direct to a lower seat the one who usurped the honorable one: *Give this man place.* Pride will suffer humiliation and will eventually lead to a fall (Pr 16:18).

1.2.2. Those who content themselves with the lowest seats are likely to be advanced (v. 10): "Go and *seat thyself in the lowest room*, taking it for granted that your friend has guests to come who are of a higher rank and quality than you are; and yet perhaps not, and then it will be said to you, *Friend, go up higher.*" The way to rise high is to begin low: "*Thou shalt have honour and respect before those that sit with thee.*" They will see you to be an honorable person. Honor stands out more brightly when it shines out of obscurity. They will also see you to be a humble person, which is the greatest honor of all." A parable from one of the rabbis has a similar theme: "Three men were invited to a feast; one sat in the highest position, because, he said, 'I am a prince'; the second sat in the seat just below the first, because, he said, 'I am a wise man'; and the third sat in the lowest position, because, he said, 'I am a humble man.' The king then seated the humble man in highest position and put the prince in the lowest."

1.3. He applied this generally, so that we might all learn not to *mind high things* (Ro 12:16). Pride and ambition are disgraceful in people, but humility and self-denial are truly honorable; for *whosoever exalteth himself shall be abased*, but *he that humbleth himself shall be exalted* (v. 11).

2. He used the occasion to rebuke the host of the meal for inviting so many rich people, when he should rather have invited the poor. Our Savior teaches us here that our wealth is better used in works of love than in splendid housekeeping.

2.1. "Do not long to give a banquet to the rich; don't invite your friends, brothers and sisters, and neighbors, who are rich" (v. 12). This does not prohibit the entertaining of such people in order to cultivate friendship among relatives and neighbors, but:

2.1.1. "Do not make it your ordinary custom. One banquet for the rich will cost the same as very many meals for the poor.

2.1.2. "Don't become proud of it." Many people put on a banquet for show, and so they rob their families merely to satisfy their whims.

2.1.3. "Don't aim at being paid back in your own coin." This is what our Savior blames in putting on such receptions: "You commonly do it in the hope that you will be invited back by them, and so you will be rewarded."

2.2. "Be eager to relieve the poor (vv. 13–14): When you give a banquet, invite the poor and *maimed* (crippled), those who have nothing to live on and are unable to work for their living. These are to be the objects of your love. They lack necessities; provide for them, and they will reward you with their prayers. They will go away and thank God for you. Don't say that you have lost something because they cannot reward you, for you will be rewarded *at the resurrection of the just*." Works of love may not be rewarded in this world, for the things of this world are not the best things, and so God does not pay the best people in those things; and yet such people will in no way lose their reward (Mt 10:42). It will be found that the longest voyages make the richest returns.

Verses 15–24

Here is another teaching of our Savior's, in which he spiritualized the banquet he was invited to, which is another way of maintaining good conversation during ordinary events. Here we have:

1. The opportunity given by one of the guests, who said to him, *Blessed is he that shall eat bread in the kingdom of God* (v. 15).

1.1. What was the man's purpose in saying this?

1.1.1. Perhaps, fearing Christ would displease the company, he mentioned it to try to move the discussion on to something else. Or:

1.1.2. Admiring the good rules that Christ had now given, but despairing of seeing them lived out, he longed for the kingdom of God, and so he declared blessed those who will have a place in that kingdom. Or:

1.1.3. Christ having mentioned the resurrection of the just, the man confirmed here what Christ had said. "Yes, Lord, those who will be rewarded in the resurrection of the just will eat bread in the kingdom."

1.1.4. Noticing that Christ was silent, he was willing to draw him into further discussion. He knew that nothing was more likely to engage Jesus than to mention the kingdom of God. Even those who are unable to continue a good discussion among themselves should put in a word now and then to help it forward.

1.2. Now what this man said was a clear and acknowledged truth, and it was quoted very appositely now that they had sat down to eat. To us, too, this thought will be very fitting when we share in physical refreshment:

Blessed are they that will eat bread in the kingdom of God:

1.2.1. In the kingdom of grace. Christ promised his disciples that they would eat and drink with him in his kingdom.

1.2.2. In the kingdom of glory. Blessed are those who will sit down at that table, from which they will never get up.

2. The parable that our Lord Jesus gave on this occasion (v. 16). "But who are those who will enjoy that privilege? You Jews will generally reject it, and the Gentiles will be the greatest sharers in it." Notice in the parable:

2.1. The free grace and mercy of God shining out in the Gospel of Christ. It appears:

2.1.1. In the rich provision he has made for poor souls (v. 16): *A certain man made a great supper.* It is called a supper because in those countries supper time was the chief time for a banquet.

2.1.2. In the gracious invitation given us to come and share in this provision.

2.1.2.1. A general invitation was given: he *bade many*. Christ invited the whole nation and Jewish people to share in the benefits of his Gospel. Christ, in the Gospel, keeps both a good house and an open house.

2.1.2.2. A particular message was given; the servant was sent around to remind them of it: *Come, for all things are now ready* (v. 17). This is the call now given to us: "*All things are now ready; now is the accepted time* (2Co 6:2); and so come now. Don't delay; accept the invitation now. Believe you are welcome."

2.2. The cold reception that the grace of the Gospel meets with. The invited guests declined to come. They *all with one consent* (all alike) *began to make excuse* (v. 18). They all found some excuse or other to put off their attendance. This shows how the Jewish nation generally neglected to accept Christ's offer. It also suggests the reluctance there is in most people to respond to the Gospel call. For fear of shame, those invited in the parable could not openly confess their refusal, but they desired to be excused. They were unanimous in it; they all spoke alike, with one voice.

2.2.1. Here were two who had made purchases. One had *bought a piece of ground* (field) that was described to him as a good bargain, and he must go and check it out, see whether it really was or not, and so, *I pray thee, have me excused.* What a frivolous excuse this was! He could have put off going to see his land until the next day, and it would have been in the same place and condition it was in now. Another had bought livestock for his land. "*I have bought five yoke of oxen* for plowing, and I must now go and *prove them* (try them out), and so excuse me this time." The first person's excuse suggests excessive delight in the things of this world; this second excuse suggests excessive care and concern about the world, which keep people from Christ and his grace. When we are called to do any duty, it is criminal to make excuses for neglecting it. It is a sign that we are convicted that it is a duty but have no inclination to do it. These things here were:

2.2.1.1. Little things. It would have been better for them to say, "I am invited to eat bread in the kingdom of God and must therefore be excused from going to see the ground or the oxen."

2.2.1.2. Lawful things. Things lawful in themselves prove to be fatal hindrances in religious faith when the heart is set too much on them.

2.2.2. Here was one man who was newly married (v. 30): *I have married a wife, and therefore*, in short, *I cannot come.* He pretended that he could not when the truth was he that he would not. Many people pretend to be unable to undertake the duties of religious faith when really they have an aversion to them. Our affection for our relatives often proves a hindrance to us in fulfilling our duty to God. He could have gone and taken his wife along with him; they would both have been welcome.

2.3. The account that was brought to the master of the feast concerning the insult shown him by his friends, who now showed how little they valued his friendship (v. 21): *That servant came, and showed his lord these things*, told him with surprise that he was likely to eat alone. He made the matter neither better nor worse, but told it just as it was. Ministers must give an account of the effectiveness of their ministry. They must do it now at the throne of grace. If they *see of the travail of their soul* (Isa 53:11), they must go to God with their thanks; if they *labour in vain* (Gal 4:11), they must go to God with their complaints. The apostle urges this as a reason why people should listen to the word of God sent them by his ministers: *they watch for your souls, as those that must give account* (Heb 13:17).

2.4. The master's just resentment at this insult: *He was angry* (v. 21). The ingratitude and contempt shown to the God of heaven by those who show disrespect to the offers of the Gospel are a very great provocation to him, and justly so. Abused mercy turns into the greatest wrath. *None of the men that were bidden* (invited) *shall taste of my supper.* Grace despised is grace forfeited, like Esau's birthright (Ge 25:34; 27:1–40). Those who refuse to receive Christ when they can have him will not have him when they want him.

2.5. The care that was taken to supply the table with guests as well as food. "Go," he said to the servants, "first into the streets and alleys of the town, so that you may invite those who will be glad to come. Bring in here the poor and the crippled, the blind and the lame; fetch the ordinary beggars." They soon gathered many such guests: *Lord, it is done as thou hast commanded.* Many of the Jews were brought in, yet not from among the teachers of the law and Pharisees, but from among tax collectors and sinners; these were the poor and the crippled. However, there was still room for more guests. "Go, then, secondly, out into the *highways and hedges* (country lanes). Go out into the country and fetch the vagrants, or those who are returning now in the evening from working in the field, and *compel them to come in*, not by force of arms, but by force of arguments. Be serious with them; plead with them, because it will be necessary to convince them that the invitation is sincere. They will hardly believe that they are welcome, and so do not leave them until you have persuaded them." This refers to the calling in of the Gentiles; the church was filled with them.

2.5.1. The provision made for precious souls in the Gospel of Christ will be seen not to have been made in vain, for if some reject it, others will thankfully accept its offer.

2.5.2. Those who are very poor and insignificant in the world will be as welcome to Christ as the rich and great. Christ clearly referred here to what he had said just before, that we are to invite to our tables the poor and crippled, the lame and blind (v. 13). His condescension and compassion toward them should make us respond similarly to them.

2.5.3. The Gospel is often most effective among those who are least likely to benefit from it. The tax collectors and prostitutes went into the kingdom of God before the teachers of the law and Pharisees (Mt 21:31–32); so the last will be first, and the first last (13:30). Let us not be

confident about those who are most forward, and let us not despair of those who are least promising.

2.5.4. Christ's ministers must be both very prompt and very bold in inviting people to the Gospel banquet: "*Go out quickly* (v. 21); lose no time, because all things are now ready."

2.5.5. Although many have been brought in to share in the benefits of the Gospel, there is still room for more. There is in him enough for all and enough for each. The Gospel excludes none who do not exclude themselves.

2.5.6. Although Christ's house is large, it will be filled in the end.

Verses 25–35

In these verses, Christ was directing his words to the crowds who followed him, and his exhortation to them was to understand the terms of discipleship. See here:

1. How zealous people were in following Christ (v. 25): *There went great multitudes with him*, many out of love and more for the company. Here was a *mixed multitude* (Ex 12:38; Nu 11:4).

2. How considerate he wanted them to be in their zeal. Those who undertake to follow Christ must count on the worst situation and prepare accordingly.

2.1. He told them the worst things that they must expect to happen. He assumed that they wanted to be his disciples. They expected him to say, "If anyone comes to me and is my disciple, he will have great wealth and honor." But here he told them completely the opposite.

2.1.1. They must be willing to abandon what was dear to them rather than abandon their relationship with Christ (v. 26). A person cannot be Christ's disciple without *hating father, and mother, and his own life*. He is not sincere; he will not be faithful and persevering unless he loves Christ more than anything in this world. No mention is made here of houses and lands (Mt 19:29); philosophy will teach a person to look on these with contempt, but Christianity takes the contempt for earthly things higher.

2.1.1.1. Every good person loves his relatives, but if he is a disciple of Christ, he must hate them by comparison. Not that the persons of our relatives must be actually hated in any way, but our comfort and satisfaction in them must be lost and swallowed up in our love for Christ. When our duty to our parents comes to compete with our clear duty to Christ, we must give Christ the priority. If we must either deny Christ or be banished from our families and relatives—as many of the first Christians were—we must lose their company rather than his favor.

2.1.1.2. Every person loves *his own life*; no one ever yet hated it (Eph 5:29). And we cannot be Christ's disciples if we do not love him more than our own lives. Our experience of the pleasures of the spiritual life and our faithful hopes and prospects of eternal life will make this hard saying easy. When trouble and persecution come because of the word (Mt 13:21), then what is chiefly being tested is whom we love more: Christ, or our relatives and our lives. Even in days of peace, however, this matter is sometimes brought to a test. Those who are ashamed to confess him for fear of displeasing a relative or friend or losing a customer give cause to suspect that they love these people more than Christ.

2.1.2. They must be willing to bear what was very heavy (v. 27): *Whosoever doth not bear his cross* and so *come after me cannot be my disciple.* Although the disciples of Christ are not all crucified, they all still *bear their cross.* They must be content to be given a bad name, for no name is more ignominious than *Furcifer*, "the bearer of the gibbet." Christ's true disciples must bear their cross and *come after Christ*; that is, whenever they find it lying in the path of duty, they must carry it along that path. They must carry it when Christ calls them to do so, and they must live in hope of a reward from him.

2.2. He asked them to expect these things and then consider them. It is better not to begin than not to proceed, and so before we begin we must consider what it means to proceed. This is to act rationally and as befits human beings. The cause of Christ will stand up to scrutiny. Satan shows the best but hides the worst. Consideration of the situation is necessary for us to persevere. Our Savior here used two comparisons to illustrate the need to count the cost.

2.2.1. We are like someone who undertakes to *build a tower* and so must consider how much it will cost (vv. 28–30): *Which of you, intending to build a tower, sitteth not down first, and counteth the cost?* Let him compare the cost with what he can afford, so that he will not be ridiculed when, having *begun to build*, he is *not able to finish*. All who take on themselves a profession of religious faith undertake to *build a tower*. Begin small, lay a deep foundation, build it on rock, and make unshakeable work of it, and then aim as high as heaven. Those who intend to build this tower must first *sit down and count the cost*. Let them consider that it will cost them a life of self-denial and watchfulness. It may cost them their reputation among other people and all that is dear to them in this world, even life itself. On the other hand, if it were to cost us all this, what is that in comparison with what it cost Christ? Many who begin to build this tower do not go on with it or persevere in it, and they are foolish. It is true that none of us have within ourselves *sufficient to finish* this tower, but Christ has said, *My grace is sufficient for thee* (2Co 12:9). Nothing is more shameful than for those who have begun well in their religious faith to give it up.

2.2.2. When we undertake to be Christ's disciples, we are like a king who *goes to war* and must therefore consider its dangers (vv. 31–32). A king who thinks of declaring war on a neighboring ruler first considers whether he has the strength to win, and if not, he will set aside thoughts of war. Is not the Christian life one of warfare? We must fight every step we take: our spiritual enemies are so restless in their opposition. Before enlisting under Christ's banner, we should consider whether we can endure the hardship that a good soldier of Jesus Christ must expect and count on (2Ti 2:3). Of the two, Christ and the world, it is better to negotiate the best terms possible with the world than to pretend to renounce it and afterward return to it. That young man who could not find it in his heart to give up his possessions for Christ did better to go away from Christ sorrowing than he would have by staying with him pretending (Mt 19:22).

2.3. This parable may be applied in another way, as intended to teach us to begin to be religious quickly rather than cautiously; it may mean the same as Mt 5:25: *Agree with thine adversary quickly*.

2.3.1. Those who persist in sin are at war with God.

2.3.2. The proudest and most daring sinner is no match for God. In consideration of this, it is in our interests to make our peace with him. We need not send messengers to *desire conditions of peace* (v. 32); conditions are offered to us, and they are satisfactory. Let us become familiar with them and be at peace, and let us do this in time, *while the other is yet a great way off*.

2.4. However, the way the parable is applied here (v. 33) shows also the consideration that should be exercised when we take on ourselves a profession of religious faith. Be well advised before you begin a life of religious

faith, as those who know that *except you forsake all you have, you cannot be Christ's disciples.*

2.5. He warned them against apostasy, for that would make them utterly useless (vv. 34–35).

2.5.1. Good Christians, especially good ministers, are *the salt of the earth* (Mt 5:13), and this salt is good and very useful.

2.5.2. Corrupt Christians, who, rather than give up what they have in the world, will throw away their life of faith, are like *salt that has lost its savour*, the most useless and worthless thing in the world; it has no kind of goodness left in it.

2.5.2.1. It can never be restored: *Wherewith shall it be seasoned?* You cannot make it salty again. This shows that it is extremely difficult—indeed, next to impossible—to restore an apostate (Heb 6:4–6).

2.5.2.2. It is useless. It is *not fit*, as manure is, *for the land*, to build fertility, nor will it be any better if it is put on the manure pile to rot. A professor of religious faith whose mind and manners have become corrupt is the most wishy-washy creature possible.

2.5.2.3. It is abandoned: *Men cast it out* as something they want nothing more to do with. Such scandalous professors of faith should be put out of the church, because others may become infected by them. Our Savior concluded this discourse with a call to everyone to sit up and take notice of it and to accept the warning: *He that hath ears to hear, let him hear.*

CHAPTER 15

The murmuring of the teachers of the law and Pharisees at the grace and favor Christ showed to tax collectors and sinners led to a fuller revelation of that grace, in the three parables in this chapter, than perhaps we would otherwise have had. The scope of all three parables is the same, namely, to show not only what God had said and sworn in the Old Testament, that he has no pleasure in the death and ruin of sinners (Eze 18:32; 33:11), but also that he has great pleasure in their return and repentance. Here is: 1. The offense that the Pharisees took at Christ for keeping company with pagans and tax collectors and preaching his Gospel to them (vv. 1–2). 2. His justifying himself in these actions by reference to their purpose and natural tendency, which was to lead people to repent and reform their lives; and no more pleasing and acceptable service could be offered to God than this, as Christ showed in the parable of the lost sheep that was brought home with joy (vv. 4–7); that of the lost coin that was found with joy (vv. 8–10); and that of the lost son who had been a prodigal but returned to his father's house and was received with great joy, though his elder brother, like these teachers of the law and Pharisees, was offended by it (vv. 11–32).

Verses 1–10

Here is:

1. The persevering presence of the tax collectors and sinners with Christ. *Great multitudes* of Jews *went with him* (14:25) with such an assurance of admission into the kingdom of God that he found he had to say to them something that would shake their vain hopes. Here many *publicans* and *sinners* drew near to him, with a humble, modest fear of being rejected by him, and he found it necessary to give them this encouragement. Perhaps some of the tax collectors were bad, but they were all given a bad name, because of the prejudice of the Jewish nation against their work. They are sometimes spoken of in the

same breath as *harlots* (Mt 21:32); here and elsewhere they are linked with *sinners*. They drew near to him not, like some, out of curiosity to see him, nor, like others, to seek healing, but to listen to his wonderful teaching. In all our approaches to Christ we must have this in mind, to hear him, to listen to the instructions he gives us and to his answers to our prayers.

2. The offense that the teachers of the law and Pharisees took at this. They *murmured* (muttered), *This man receiveth sinners, and eateth with them* (v. 2).

2.1. They were angry that tax collectors and pagans were allowed to have the means of grace and were encouraged to hope for forgiveness when they repented.

2.2. They thought it inconsistent with the honor of Christ's role as a rabbi to be friendly toward such people and *eat with them*. They could not, out of shame, condemn him for preaching to them, and so they criticized him for eating with them, which was more expressly against the tradition of the elders.

3. Christ's justifying himself in it by showing that the worse the people were, the more glory would be given to God and the more joy there would be in heaven if they were brought to repentance by his preaching. It would be more pleasant for those in heaven to see tax collectors and sinners begin to live an orderly life than to see teachers of the law and Pharisees continue to lead such lives. He illustrated this by two parables here.

3.1. The parable of the *lost sheep*. We had something like this in Mt 18:12–14. There it was intended to show the care God takes for the preservation of saints; here it is intended to show the pleasure God takes in the conversion of sinners. We have here:

3.1.1. The case of a sinner who continues in sinful ways. Such a person is like *a lost sheep*, a sheep *gone astray*; they are lost to God, lost to the flock, and lost to themselves. They do not know where they are, and they wander around endlessly, continually exposed to the wild animals, subject to fears and terrors, taken away from the shepherd's care, lacking green pastures, and unable to find the way back to the fold by themselves.

3.1.2. The care the God of heaven takes of poor wandering sinners. Particular care is to be taken of this lost sheep, and even though the shepherd has a hundred sheep, he will not lose that one, but goes after it and shows great care in finding it. God follows backsliding sinners until they are finally persuaded to think of returning. Although the shepherd finds the sheep weary and unable to bear being driven home, he does not leave it to die, but *lays it on his shoulders* and, with much tenderness and labor, brings it back to the fold. God sends his Son to *seek and save that which was lost* (19:10). Christ is said to *gather the lambs in his arms, and carry them in his bosom* in Isa 40:11, showing his pity and tenderness. Here he is said to put them *upon his shoulders*; those he carries on his shoulders can never perish.

3.1.3. The pleasure that God takes in repenting sinners who return to him. The shepherd *lays* the sheep *on his shoulders, rejoicing*, and his joy is greater because he began to give up all hope of ever finding it. He *calls his friends and neighbours, saying, Rejoice with me*. Notice that he calls the sheep his sheep, even though it is a stray, wandering sheep. He has a right to it; that was why he looked for it himself, and now, *I have found it.* He did not send a servant, but his own Son, the great and good Shepherd (Heb 13:20; Jn 10:14), who will find what he seeks and will be found by those who do not seek him (Isa 65:1).

3.2. The parable of the *lost piece* (coin) *of silver*.

3.2.1. The person who lost the coin is a woman. She has *ten pieces* (coins) *of silver*, and she loses only one of them. Let us maintain high thoughts of divine goodness despite the sinfulness and misery of the human race, considering that there are nine to one—indeed, in the previous parable there are ninety-nine to one—who retain their integrity, in whom God is praised and was never dishonored. Oh the countless beings who were never lost!

3.2.2. What is lost is a piece of silver. The soul is silver, of intrinsic worth—not base metal, such as iron or lead, but silver. It is a silver coin. It is stamped with God's *image and superscription* (20:24). This silver was lost in the dirt. A soul plunged in the world is like a coin in the dirt; anyone would say, "What a shame."

3.2.3. The loss arouses great concern, and great pains are taken in seeking lost thing. The woman *lights a candle, sweeps the house*, and *seeks diligently till she finds it*. This represents God's various ways of bringing lost souls home to himself: he has *lighted the candle* of the Gospel not to show himself the way to us, but to show us the way to him. His heart is set on bringing lost souls back to himself.

3.2.4. There is a great deal of joy at finding it: *Rejoice with me, for I have found the piece which I had lost* (v. 9). Those who rejoice want others to rejoice with them. The pleasant surprise of finding it put her, for the present, into a kind of ecstasy. "I have found it!"—the language of joy.

3.3. The explanation of these two parables is to the same effect (vv. 7, 10): *There is* more *joy in heaven, joy in the presence of the angels of God, over one sinner that repenteth* than over a great number of *just persons, who need no repentance.*

3.3.1. The repentance and conversion of sinners on earth is a matter of joy and rejoicing in heaven. The greatest sinners may be brought to repentance. While there is life there is hope, and the worst people are not to be despaired of. God will be overjoyed to show them mercy. There is always *joy in heaven*; God *rejoiceth in all his works* (Ps 104:31). But especially in the works of his grace. He rejoices to do good to penitent sinners. He rejoices not only in the conversion of nations but even over *one sinner that repenteth*, even though it is only one. The good angels, too, will be glad that mercy is shown them. The redemption of the human race was a matter of joy in the presence of the angels, for they sang, *Glory to God in the highest* (2:14).

3.3.2. There is more joy over *one sinner that repenteth* than there is *over ninety-nine just persons, who need no repentance*:

3.3.2.1. More joy at the conversion of the Gentile sinners and of those tax collectors who now heard Christ preach than at all the praises and devotions and all the *God I thank thee* (18:11) of the Pharisees and other self-justifying Jews who thought that they needed no repentance. God derived more praise and pleasure from the penitent broken heart of one of those despised, envied sinners, said Christ, than from all the long prayers offered by the teachers of the law and Pharisees, who could not see anything wrong in themselves.

3.3.2.2. More joy at the conversion of one such great sinner than at the regular conversion of one who had always behaved decently and well and who, by comparison, needed no repentance. Not that it is best to go astray, but the grace of God is revealed more in the subduing of great sinners than in the leading of those who never went astray. Often those who have been great sinners before their conversion prove to be more eminently and zealously good afterward. Those who are forgiven much will love much (7:47). We are moved by a deeper joy at the recovery of what we had lost than at the continuation of what we had always enjoyed; we rejoice more in health after sickness than in health without sickness. A constant way of religious faith may be more valuable in itself, but a sudden return from an evil way of sin may yield a more surprising pleasure.

Verses 11–32

We have here the parable of the prodigal son, the scope of which is the same as that of the previous two. However, the circumstances of the parable set out the riches of Gospel grace much more fully, and to poor sinners ever since it has been indescribably useful, and so it will be as long as the world exists.

1. The parable represents God as a common Father to the whole human race. He is our Father because he educates us and provides for us. Our Savior showed the proud Pharisees here that these tax collectors and sinners, whom they despised, were their brothers, and that the Pharisees should therefore be glad to see any kindness shown them.

2. It represents human beings as having different characters. The father in the parable had two sons, one of them a solid, serious young man, reserved and austere, sober in himself, but not at all good humored to those around him; such a person would follow his education and not be easily drawn aside from it. But the other was fickle and volatile and impatient with any restraint, wanting to leave home and travel, willing to try his luck, and, if he fell into bad company, likely to become loose and immoral. This second character represents the tax collectors and sinners and the Gentiles. The elder brother represents the Jews in general, especially the Pharisees. The younger son is the prodigal son. Notice:

2.1. The riotous way of life he fell into when he was a prodigal, both his extravagance and his misery. We are told:

2.1.1. What his request to his father was (v. 12): *He said to his father, "Father, give me"* — he might have expanded that slightly and said, "Please give me," or, "Sir, if you please, give me," but he demanded imperiously — *"give me the portion of goods that falleth to me* (my share of the estate), what falls to me as my due." It is bad, and the beginning of worse, when people look on God's gifts as debts. "Give it all to me as a lump sum, and I will renounce all my future rights in the estate." The great foolishness of sinners is being content to have their share now, to receive *their good things* in this lifetime (16:25). They look only at the things that are visible and seek satisfaction only for the present, unconcerned for their future happiness. Why did he want to have his share now in his own hands?

2.1.1.1. He was tired of his father's control. He wanted his so-called — and wrongly called — freedom. Notice the foolishness of many young people, who never think they have gained their rightful independence until they have broken and thrown off all God's bonds (Ps 2:3) in order to replace them with the cords of their own sinful desires. Here is the origin of the apostasy of sinners from God: they will not be tied to the rules of God's authority; they will themselves *be as gods*, knowing no other *good and evil* (Ge 3:5) than what pleases them.

2.1.1.2. He wanted to get away from under his father's eye. A wariness of God and a willingness to deny his omniscience lie at the root of the evil of evildoers.

2.1.1.3. He distrusted his father's management. He wanted to have his share of the estate himself, because he

thought that his father would limit what he spent at present, and he did not like that.

2.1.1.4. He was proud of himself and had an inflated opinion of his own abilities. He thought that if only he had his share in his own hands now, he could manage it better than his father did and make better use of it. More young people are ruined by pride than by any other vice.

2.1.2. How kind his father was to him: *He divided unto them his living* (his property). He worked out what he had to dispose of between his two sons and gave the younger son his share. He offered the elder son his, but it seems he wanted his father to keep it himself, and we can see what he gained by it (v. 31): *All that I have is thine.* He gave the younger son what he asked for. He had as much as he expected, and perhaps more.

2.1.2.1. In this way he could see his father's kindness, how willing he was to please him and make him comfortable.

2.1.2.2. In this way he would in a short time be made to see his own foolishness, and that he was not such a wise manager for himself as he thought.

2.1.3. What he did when he got hold of his share. He set out to spend it as fast as he could and made himself a beggar in a short time: *not many days after* (v. 13). What the younger son decided was to go away immediately, and so he *gathered all together* (got together all he had). The condition of the prodigal son in his going astray represents to us a sinful state, into which human beings have fallen.

2.1.3.1. A sinful state is a state of departure and distance from God. The sinfulness of sin is that it turns away from God. He *took his journey* from his father's house. Sinners have fled from God. They get as far away from him as possible. The world is the far country in which they live. The misery of sinners is that they are far from God, and they are going farther and farther from him. What is hell itself, except being far from God?

2.1.3.2. A sinful state is a spending state: there he *wasted his substance with riotous living* (v. 13); he squandered it on prostitutes (v. 30) and in a short time *had spent all* (v. 14). He bought fine clothes and associated with those who helped him use up all he had in a short time. However, this may also be applied spiritually. Willful sinners waste their inheritance by misusing their thoughts and all the powers of their souls. They not only bury but also steal the talents they are entrusted with to use for their Master's honor, and the gifts of Providence, which were intended to enable them to serve God and do good with, are made the food of their sinful desires. The soul is made a slave either to the world or to the flesh and squanders its wealth in wild living.

2.1.3.3. A sinful state is a needy state: *When he had spent all, there arose a mighty famine in that land*, and he *began to be in want* (v. 14). Deliberate waste brings terrible need. In time, perhaps in a short time, wild living brings people down to a crust of bread, especially when bad times accelerate the effects of bad management. This represents the misery of sinners, who have thrown away *their own mercies* (Jnh 2:8). They give these away in the pursuit of physical pleasure and the wealth of their world, and then are about to perish for lack of them. Sinners lack what they need for their souls; they have neither food nor clothes for them, nor any provision for the future. A sinful state is like a land where a great famine reigns. Sinners are wretchedly and miserably poor, and, what makes matters worse, they have brought themselves into that condition.

2.1.3.4. A sinful state is a worthless, servile state. When this young man's wild living had led to want, his want brought him to slavery. *He went, and joined himself to a citizen of that country* (v. 15). The same evil life that before was represented by riotous living is here represented by servile living. The Devil is the *citizen of that country*; sinners *join themselves* to him. How this young man degraded himself when he hired himself out into the service of such a master as this! This master *sent him into the fields* not to feed sheep but to *feed swine* (pigs). The business of the Devil's servants is to *make provision for the flesh, to fulfil the lusts thereof* (Ro 13:14), and there is no better way of doing this than by feeding greedy, dirty, noisy pigs, and how can rational, immortal souls disgrace themselves more?

2.1.3.5. A sinful state is a state of constant dissatisfaction. *He would fain* (longed to) *have filled his belly with the husks which the swine did eat* (v. 16). This young man had gotten himself into a fine condition, to eat with the pigs! What sinners promise themselves satisfaction in when they go away from God will certainly disappoint them: they are *labouring for that which satisfieth not* (Isa 55:2). Pods are food for pigs, not for human beings. The wealth of the world and the physical delights will be enough for our bodies, but what are these for precious souls? They neither suit the soul's nature, satisfy its desires, nor supply its needs.

2.1.3.6. A sinful state is a state that cannot expect to receive relief from anybody. When the prodigal son could not earn his bread by working, he took to begging, but *no man gave unto him*. Those who depart from God cannot be helped by anybody. It will be futile to cry out to the world and the flesh; they have what will poison a soul, but they have nothing to feed and nourish it.

2.1.3.7. A sinful state is a state of death: *This my son was dead* (vv. 23, 32). Sinners are not only dead in law, since they are under a sentence of death, but also dead in trespasses and sins, devoid of spiritual life; no union with Christ, no living to God, and therefore dead. The prodigal son in the far country was dead to his father and his family, and he had brought this death upon himself.

2.1.3.8. A sinful state is a lost state: *This my son was lost*—lost to everything good, lost to his father's house. Souls that are separated from God are lost souls, lost like travelers who have lost their way, and if infinite mercy does not intervene, they will soon be lost irrecoverably.

2.1.3.9. A sinful state is a state of madness and frenzy. This is suggested in the expression (v. 17) *when he came to himself*, which shows that before then he had been beside himself. He was surely beside himself when he left his father's house, and even more so when he hired himself out to a citizen of that country. Sinners, like those who are mad, destroy themselves with foolish sinful desires, but at the same time they deceive themselves with foolish hopes.

2.2. His return from this wandering. Notice here:

2.2.1. What was the reason for his return and repentance. It was his suffering; when he was in need, then he *came to himself*. When sufferings are sanctified by divine grace, they prove to be a good means of turning sinners away from the error of their ways. When we find the insufficiency of the creation to make us happy and have tried all other ways to relieve our poor souls in vain, then it is time to think of returning to God. When we see what miserable comforters (Job 16:2), what physicians of no value (Job 13:4), all except Christ are, and when *no man gives unto us* what we need, then surely we will turn to Jesus Christ.

2.2.2. What was the preparation for it; it was *consideration*. He said within himself when he came to his right

mind (8:35), *How many hired servants of my father's have bread enough!* Consideration is the first step toward conversion (Eze 18:28). He considered how bad his condition was: *I perish with hunger.* Not only, "I am hungry," but, "*I perish with hunger.*" Sinners will not come to the service of Christ until they are led to see themselves as just about to perish in the service of sin. Yet even though we are driven to Christ in this way, he will not think himself dishonored by our being forced to come to him, but rather honored by our being turned to in such a desperate case. The prodigal considered how much better it would be if only he returned: "*How many hired servants of my father's have bread enough, and to spare*; such a good house he keeps!" In our *Father's house* (Jn 14:2) there is bread for all his family. There is *enough* and to *spare*, enough for all and enough for each, enough and to spare for charity. There are crumbs that fall from his table that many would eat gladly and thankfully. Even the *hired servants* in God's family are well provided for. The consideration of this should encourage sinners who have gone astray from God to think about returning to him.

2.2.3. What its purpose was. His consideration eventually led to this conclusion: *I will arise, and go to my father.* Good purposes are good things, but good actions are everything.

2.2.3.1. He decided what to do: *I will arise and go to my father.* Although he was in *a far country*, a long way from his father's house, he would still return; every step of backsliding from God must be a step back again to return to him. Notice with what determination he spoke: "*I will arise, and go to my father*; I have firmly decided that I will, whatever the outcome."

2.2.3.2. He decided what to say. True repentance is rising and coming back to God. But what words will we take with us (Hos 14:2)? Whenever we speak to God, it is good to think beforehand what we are going to say, so that we may *order our cause before him* (Job 23:4). Let us notice what he intended to say:

2.2.3.2.1. He would confess his fault and folly: *I have sinned.* Since we have all sinned, we must all admit that we have sinned. The confession of sin is required and insisted on as a necessary condition of peace and pardon. If we plead "Not guilty," we put ourselves on trial. If we plead "Guilty," we turn to the covenant of grace with a contrite, penitent, and obedient heart, and we find that that covenant offers forgiveness to those who confess their sins.

2.2.3.2.2. He would be so far from extenuating the matter that he would lay a burden on himself for it: I have sinned *against heaven* and *before thee.* Let those who are undutiful to their earthly parents think about this; they sin *against heaven and before* God. Offenses against parents are offenses against God. Sin is committed:

2.2.3.2.2.1. In contempt of God's authority over us: we *have sinned against heaven.* The evil of sin has a high aim; it is *against heaven.* It is powerless evil, however, since we cannot hurt the heavens. In fact, it is foolish evil; what is shot against the heavens will return on the head of the one who shoots it (Ps 7:16).

2.2.3.2.2.2. In contempt of God's watching over us: "I have sinned *against heaven*, and yet also *before thee.*"

2.2.3.2.3. He would acknowledge that he had lost the right to all the privileges of the family: *I am no more worthy to be called thy son* (v. 19). He did not deny the relationship—that was all he could trust in—but he acknowledged that his father could justly deny that relationship. At his own demand, he had received the share of the estate that belonged to him, and he had reason to expect no more. It is good for sinners to acknowledge themselves unworthy to receive any favor from God.

2.2.3.2.4. He would nevertheless seek admission into the family, though into its lowest position: *"Make me as one of thy hired servants; that is good enough, and too good, for me."* If he had to sit with the servants to humble himself, he would not only submit to it but count it an advancement in comparison with his present state. *"Make me as a hired servant,* so that I may show I love my father's house as much as I ever insulted it."

2.2.3.2.5. In all this he would look to his father as a father: *"I will arise, and go to my father, and will say unto him, Father.* Viewing God as a Father, and our Father, will be very useful in our repentance and return to him. It will make our sorrow for sin genuine and our resolutions against it strong, and it will encourage us to hope for pardon. God delights to be called "Father" by both penitents and petitioners.

2.2.4. What the fulfillment of this purpose was: *He arose, and came to his father.* He put his good decision into practice without delay; he struck while the iron was hot. Have we said that we will get up and go? Then let us immediately get up and come. He did not go halfway and then pretend that he was tired and could go no further, but, weak and weary as he was, made a thorough business of it.

2.3. His reception by his father here: *He came to his father,* but was he welcome? Yes; he was heartily welcome. And by the way, this is an example to parents whose children have been foolish and disobedient: if they repent, parents should not be harsh and severe with them, but guide and encourage them by the wisdom that comes from above, which is *gentle and easy to be entreated* (Jas 3:17). However, it is chiefly intended to show the grace and mercy of God to poor sinners who repent and return to him, how ready he is to forgive them. Notice here:

2.3.1. The great love and affection with which the father received the son: *When he was yet a great way off, his father saw him* (v. 20). He expressed his kindness even before the son expressed his repentance. Even *before we call, he answers* (Isa 65:24), because he knows what is in our hearts. What vivid images are presented here!

2.3.1.1. Here were eyes of mercy, and those eyes were quick-sighted: *When he was yet a great way off, his father saw him,* as if from the top of some high tower he had been looking down the road by which his son had gone, thinking something like, "Oh that I could see there my wretched son coming home!" This shows God's desire for the conversion of sinners and his readiness to meet those who are coming toward him. He is aware of their first inclination toward him.

2.3.1.2. Here was a heart of mercy, yearning at the sight of his son: *He had compassion.* Misery is the object of pity, even the misery of a sinner; even though sinners have brought their misery on themselves, God still has compassion.

2.3.1.3. Here were feet of mercy, and those feet were swift: *He ran.* The prodigal son came slowly, weighed down by a burden of shame and fear, but the loving father ran out to meet him with his encouragements.

2.3.1.4. Here were arms of mercy, and those arms were stretched out to embrace him: *He fell on his neck.* Although the son was guilty and deserving to be beaten, although dirty and just come from feeding the pigs, his father took him in his arms and held him close. This is how precious penitents are to God, and they are just as welcome to the Lord Jesus.

2.3.1.5. Here were lips of mercy: *He kissed him.* This kiss not only assured him of his welcome but also sealed

his pardon; his former folly would be totally forgiven, nor was one word of rebuke spoken.

2.3.2. The poor prodigal's penitent submission to his father (v. 21): He *said unto him, Father, I have sinned.* Just as it commends the good father's kindness that he showed it before the prodigal expressed his repentance, so it also commends the prodigal's repentance that he expressed it after his father had shown him so much kindness. When he had received the kiss that sealed his pardon, he still said, *Father, I have sinned.* Even those whose sins are pardoned must be sincerely contrite in their hearts. The more we see of God's readiness to forgive us, the more difficult it should be to us to forgive ourselves.

2.3.3. The splendid provision this kind father gave to the returning prodigal. One thing he wanted to say (v. 19) was something he did not actually say (v. 21), and that was, *Make me as one of thy hired servants.* We cannot think that he forgot it, much less that he changed his mind; his father interrupted him, stopping him from saying it: "Hold on, son, you are heartily welcome, and although you are not worthy to be called a son, you will be treated as *a dear son.*" The one who is received in this way as soon as he arrives does not need to ask to be made a hired servant. It is strange that here is not one word of rebuke: "You made your own bed — you'll just have to lie on it. You could never have found your way home until you'd been beaten here with your own rod." No; there is nothing like this. This shows that when God forgives the sins of true penitents, he forgets them; he *will remember them no more* (Jer 31:34). But this was not all; rich and royal provision was made for him, far beyond what he expected or could expect. He would have thought it enough if his father had only taken notice of him and told him to go to the kitchen and eat his dinner with the servants, but for those who throw themselves on his mercy, God does far more than they are able to even ask or think (Eph 3:20). The prodigal son came home between hope and fear, fear of being rejected and hope of being received, and yet his father was not only better to him than his fears but also better to him than his hopes.

2.3.3.1. He came home in rags, and his father not only clothed him but also adorned him. He *said to the servants,* "Bring out the best robe and put it on him." The worst old clothes in the house would have served, and yet the father did not call for a coat, but for a robe, the best robe. In the Greek there is a double emphasis: "that robe, that main robe, you know the one I mean. Bring out that robe, and put it on him. He will be ashamed to wear it and will think that it is not good for the one who comes home in such a dirty state, but put it on him. Put a ring on his hand, too, a signet ring, with the family coat of arms, as a sign of his being acknowledged as a member of the family." The son had come home barefoot, his feet perhaps sore with travel, and so, "Put sandals on his feet." This is how the grace of God provides for true penitents.

2.3.3.1.1. The righteousness of Christ is the robe with which they are clothed; they *put on the Lord Jesus Christ* (Ro 13:14). A new nature is this best robe; true penitents are clothed with this.

2.3.3.1.2. The promise of the Spirit is the *ring on the hand.* "*Put a ring on his hand,* to be a constant reminder of his father's kindness to him, so that he may never forget it."

2.3.3.1.3. The *preparation of the Gospel of peace* is like *shoes for our feet* (Eph 6:15). The image shows that converts will continue cheerfully and with determination on the path of religious faith, as people can walk further wearing shoes than they can when barefoot.

2.3.3.2. He came home hungry, and his father not only fed him but feasted him (v. 23): *"Bring hither the fatted calf* and *kill it,* so that my son may be satisfied with the best we have." The fattened calf could never be put to a better use. It was a great change for the prodigal, who just before had longed to have filled his stomach with pods. How sweet the supplies of the new covenant will be to those who have been working in vain for satisfaction in created things! Now the prodigal found his own words fulfilled; *In my father's house there is bread enough and to spare.*

2.3.4. The great joy and rejoicing brought about by his return. The bringing of the fattened calf was intended to be not only a feast for him but also a festival for the family: *"Let us all eat, and be merry,* for it is a good day; *for this my son was dead.* We thought he had died, but look, he lives. He *was lost*—we gave him up as lost—but he *is found."* The conversion of a soul from sin to God is the raising of that soul from death to life and the finding of what seemed to be lost: it is a great, wonderful, and happy change. It is a change like that which comes on the face of the earth when spring returns. The conversion of sinners is greatly pleasing to the God of heaven, and all who belong to his family should rejoice in it; those in heaven do, and those on earth should. It was the father who began the joy, and he set all the others rejoicing. The family agreed with the master: *They began to be merry.* God's children and servants should be affected by things as he is.

2.4. The resentment of the elder brother, which is described by way of rebuke to the teachers of the law and Pharisees. Christ represented the elder brother's attitude so as not to make matters worse, but only to acknowledge that they still had the privileges of elder brothers. When Christ rebuked them for their faults, he still spoke to them mildly, to smooth them into a good attitude toward the poor tax collectors. However, we may understand the elder brother here to represent those who are really good and never went astray, who—by comparison—need no repentance. It is to such people that these words at the close, *Son, thou art ever with me,* can be applied without any difficulty, but not to the teachers of the law and Pharisees. Notice concerning the elder brother:

2.4.1. How foolish and fretful he was at his brother's reception, how displeased he was at it. It seems he was out *in the field* when his brother came home, and by the time the elder brother had returned home, the celebration had begun: *When he drew nigh to the house, he heard music and dancing* (v. 25). He asked *what these things meant* (what was going on) (v. 26) and was told that his brother had come home and been welcomed by his father with a feast. He was also told that there was great joy because his father had received the younger son *safe and sound* (v. 27). *Safe and sound* translates only one word in the original, a word meaning "in health," both physically and mentally well. He received him not only well in body but also as a penitent, returned to his right mind, healed of his corruption, for otherwise the prodigal would not have been received safe and sound. Now this offended the elder brother most intensely: *He was angry, and would not go in* (v. 28), because he wanted to show his father that he should have kept his younger brother out. This shows up a common fault:

2.4.1.1. In people's families. Those who have always been a comfort to their parents think they should have a monopoly of their parents' favors, and they tend to be too sharp toward those who have disobeyed.

2.4.1.2. In God's family. Those who are comparatively innocent seldom know how to be compassionate toward those who are clearly penitents. We have the language of such people here in what the elder brother said (vv. 29–30).

2.4.1.2.1. He boasted about himself and his own goodness and obedience. *Lo, these many years do I serve thee, neither transgressed I at any time thy commandment.* It is too common for those who are better than their neighbors to boast about it. I am inclined to think that this elder brother said more than was true when he said that he had never *transgressed his father's commands,* because if this were true, I believe he would not have been so stubborn as he now was in response to his father's pleading. Those who have served God for a long time and have been kept from gross sins have a great deal to be humbly thankful for, but nothing to proudly boast about.

2.4.1.2.2. He complained about his father: *Thou never gavest me a kid* (young goat), *that I might make merry with my friends.* He was in a bad mood now, for otherwise he would not have made this complaint, because if he had requested such a favor at any time, he would doubtless have had it immediately. The *killing of the fatted calf* made him think in this perverse way. When people have lost their temper, they tend to think in ways they would not think if they were in their right mind. He had many times celebrated at his father's table, but his father had never given him so much as a young goat, which was only a small sign of love compared with the fattened calf. Those who think highly of themselves and their services tend to think harshly of their master and have a low opinion of his favors. We should acknowledge ourselves completely unworthy of the mercies God has thought fit to give us, and so we must not complain. The elder brother wished he had had a young goat to celebrate with his friends away from home, whereas the fattened calf was given to his brother to celebrate with his family at home: the happiness of God's children should be with their father and his family, not with any other friends.

2.4.1.2.3. He was very bad tempered toward his younger brother. Some good people tend to be caught up in this fault; they look down on those who have not kept their reputation as clean as they have, even when those who have soiled themselves in this way have given good evidence of their repentance and reformation. This is not the Spirit of Christ, but of the Pharisees. Notice what happened.

2.4.1.2.3.1. He *would not go in;* one house would not hold both him and his brother, not even his father's house. Although we are to avoid the company of those sinners by whom we are in danger of being defiled, we must still not be shy of the company of penitent sinners, by whom we may benefit. The elder brother saw that his father had taken his younger son in, but he still refused to go in to him. We have too high an opinion of ourselves if we cannot find it in our hearts to receive those whom God has received and who are taken into friendship and fellowship with him.

2.4.1.2.3.2. He would not call him brother, but *this thy son,* which sounds arrogant and reflected badly on his father. Let us give our relatives the titles that belong to them. Let the rich call the poor their brothers and sisters, and let the innocents call the penitents this too.

2.4.1.2.3.3. He emphasized his brother's faults, making the worst of them: he is *thy son, who hath devoured thy living with harlots.* The prodigal had spent his share of the inheritance foolishly enough—whether on prostitutes or not, we were not told before, and perhaps that was only the language of the elder brother's jealousy and resentment—but that he had squandered all *his father's living* was false; the father still had a good estate. Now this shows how we tend to make the worst of everything and to paint the picture in the darkest colors, which is not doing as we would have other do to us, nor as our heavenly Father does to us.

2.4.1.2.3.4. He begrudged him the kindness that his father showed him: *Thou hast killed for him the fatted calf.* It is wrong to envy penitents the grace of God. Just as we must not envy those who *are* the worst of sinners the gifts of common providence, so we must not envy those who *have been* the worst of sinners the gifts of covenant love when they repent. We must not envy them any extraordinary gift that God may give them. Before his conversion, Paul had been a prodigal son; however, when after his conversion he had greater resources of grace given him than the other apostles, who were the elder brothers, they did not envy him his more extensive usefulness, but *glorified God in him* (Gal 1:24), which should be an example to us to do the opposite of this elder brother.

2.4.2. How favorable and friendly his father was in his behavior toward him when he was so sour and bad tempered. This is as surprising as the elder son's behavior toward his father. I think the mercy and grace of our God in Christ shine almost as brightly in his tender and gentle attitude and actions toward perverse saints as they shine earlier in his reception of them when they repent as prodigal sinners. The disciples of Christ themselves had many weaknesses and were as human as others, but Christ was patient with them.

2.4.2.1. When he would not come in, his *father came out, and entreated* (pleaded with) *him*, spoke to him mildly, with good words (Zec 1:13), asking him to come in. He could justly have said, "If he will not come in, let him stay out. Isn't this my house? Can't I do what I want in it? Isn't the fattened calf my own? Can't I do what I want with it (Mt 20:15)?" No; just as he went out to meet the younger son, so now he went to seek the elder one. This is intended to represent to us the goodness of God; how strangely gentle and winning he has been toward those who were strangely perverse and provocative. It is to teach all who are over others to be mild and gentle with their subordinates even when their subordinates are at fault and passionately justify themselves in it. Even in such a case, let fathers *not provoke their children to more wrath* (Eph 6:4), and let *masters forbear threatening* (Eph 6:9), and let both show great humility.

2.4.2.2. His father assured him that the kind reception given him younger brother was neither any reflection on him nor any harm to his interests (v. 31): "*Son, thou art ever with me*; my reception of him does not mean a rejection of you. Nor does my spending on him mean any lessening of what I have for you; *all that I have is thine*, by unassailable title." Even though the father had not *given him a kid to make merry with his friends*, he had allowed him to eat bread at his table continually, and it is better to be happy with our Father in heaven than to amuse ourselves with any friend we have in this world.

2.4.2.2.1. It is the indescribable happiness of all the children of God that they are and always will be with him. All that he has is theirs, because *if children, then heirs* (Ro 8:17).

2.4.2.2.2. We should not envy others God's grace to them, for we will never have any less because they share in it. If we are true believers, all that God is and all that he has are ours, and if others come to be true believers, all that he is and all that he has are theirs too, and yet we have no less, just as those who walk in the light and warmth of the sun have all the benefit they are capable of receiving from it, and have no less because others have as much.

2.4.2.3. His father gave him a good reason: *It was meet* (fitting) *that we should make merry and be glad* (v. 32). He could have insisted on his own authority, saying, "It was my will that the family celebrate and be glad." However, it is not good for those who have authority to appeal to their authority on every occasion, because that only makes it cheap and common. It is better to give a convincing reason, as the father does here: "*It was meet*, fitting and right, *that we should make merry* at the return of a prodigal son," more than for the perseverance of a dutiful son, because although the latter is a greater blessing to a family, the former is a greater pleasure. Any family would be much more taken up with joy at the raising of a dead child to life than at the continued life and health of many children. We do not find that the elder brother made any reply to what his father said, which shows that he was reconciled to his prodigal brother; and his father reminded him that he was his brother: *This thy brother.* Although a good person does not have a strong enough command of himself at all times to keep his temper, yet he will, with the grace of God, recover his temper; although *he fall, yet shall he not be utterly cast down* (Ps 37:24).

CHAPTER 16

The scope of Christ's teaching in this chapter is to wake us all up and stimulate us so that we manage all our possessions and enjoyments here in such a way that they may work for us and not against us in the other world. 1. If we do good with them, we will reap the benefits of it in the next world, and he shows this in the parable of the unjust steward. We have the parable itself (vv. 1–8); its explanation and application (vv. 9–13); and the Pharisees' contempt for the message that Christ preached to them, for which he rebuked them sharply, adding some other significant sayings (vv. 14–18). 2. If instead of doing good with our worldly enjoyments we make them the fuel of our self-indulgence and deny relief to the poor, we will certainly perish eternally. He showed this to the Pharisees in the parable of the rich man and Lazarus (vv. 19–31).

Verses 1–18

We are mistaken if we think that the purpose of Christ's teaching and holy religious faith was either to entertain us with ideas of divine mysteries or merely to give us ideas of divine mercies. No; the divine revelation of both of these in the Gospel is intended to stir and inspire us to actually do our Christian duties, and in particular our duty to do good to those who are in need of anything that we either have or can do for them. We are simply *stewards of the manifold grace of God* (1Pe 4:10); we would be wise to think how we may make what we have in the world turn to good account. If we want to act wisely, we must use our riches as diligently and skillfully in acts of godliness and love, in order to promote our future and eternal welfare, as worldly people use theirs to earn the greatest temporal profit. Consider:

1. The parable itself, in which all people are represented as *stewards* (managers) of what they have in this world. Whatever we have, it is owned by God; we have only the use of it. Here is:

1.1. The dishonesty of this manager. He *wasted his lord's goods*, and he was *accused to his lord* for this (v. 1). We are all subject to the same charge. We have not made proper use of what God has entrusted us with in this world. We should judge ourselves so that we may not be judged by our Lord for this.

1.2. His discharge from his position. His master *called for him* and said, *How is it that I hear this of thee?* He spoke as one who was sorry to be disappointed in his steward. It troubled him to hear it, but the manager could not deny it, and so there was no remedy: the manager must settle his accounts and be gone in a short time (v. 2). Now this is intended to teach us:

1.2.1. That all of us must soon be discharged from our *stewardship* (management) in this world. Death will come and send us away from our stewardship, and others will come in our places.

1.2.2. That our discharge from our stewardship at death is just and deserved, because we have wasted our Lord's goods.

1.2.3. That when our stewardship is taken away from us, we must *give an account* of it to our Lord.

1.3. His second thoughts, his later wisdom. He now began to consider, *What shall I do?* (v. 3). It would have been better if he had considered this before, but it is "better late than never" to have such thoughts. He must live; how would he get a livelihood?

1.3.1. He knew that he was not industrious enough to gain a living by work: *I cannot dig*. But why could he not dig? The truth was, he was lazy. When he said he *could not*, what he really meant was that he *would not*; it was not a natural but a moral inability that he was under. He *could not dig* because he had never been used to it.

1.3.2. He knew that he had not enough humility to gain a livelihood by begging: *To beg I am ashamed*. This expressed his pride, as the previous statement expressed his laziness. This manager had more reason to be ashamed of cheating his master than of begging for his bread.

1.3.3. He decided, therefore, to make friends of his master's debtors: "*I am resolved what to do* (v. 4). I know my master's tenants; I have helped them on many occasions, and now I will do them one more favor, which will so please them that they will make me welcome to their houses. Until I can work things out better for myself, I will stay with them, going from one good house to another." Accordingly, he sent for one debtor who owed his master *a hundred measures of oil. Take thy bill*, he said, and *sit down quickly, and write fifty* (v. 6). And so the steward reduced the tenant's debt by a half. "*Sit down* and do it *quickly*, for otherwise we may be caught by surprise in our negotiations and suspected." He took another debtor, who owed his master *a hundred measures of wheat*, and told him to write *fourscore* (eighty) (v. 7). Notice here how insecure our worldly possessions are; they are most insecure to those who have most of them, who delegate to others all the concern for them and thereby put it in their power to cheat them. Notice, too, what treachery is to be found even among those in whom trust is put. Although this manager was turned out for dealing dishonestly, he still continued to do so. It is so rare for people to put right a fault, even when they suffer for it.

1.4. The approval of this: *The lord commended the unjust steward, because he had done wisely* (v. 8). The *lord* may refer to the lord, or master, of that servant, who, though he must have been angry, was still pleased with the steward's shrewdness, but even if we read it that way, the end of the verse must be the words of *our* Lord, and so I think the whole may refer to him. He did not commend the steward because he had acted dishonestly toward his master, but because he had acted shrewdly for himself. Yet perhaps he did well for his master too, and did for the tenants only what was fair. He knew what hard bargains the master had driven with his tenants, so that they could not pay their rent. Now, as he left, considering this, he did

as he ought to do, both in justice and in love. He had been wholly on his master's side, but now he began to consider the tenants, so that he might have their favor when he had lost his master's. Now his plan for a comfortable livelihood in this world shames our improvidence for another world: *The children of this world are wiser for their generation*, are more shrewd concerning their worldly interests and advantages, than the *children of light* (v. 8) are in *their generation*, that is, in the concerns of their souls and eternity.

1.4.1. The wisdom of worldly people in the concerns of this world is to be imitated by us in spiritual matters: they are motivated to make the most of every opportunity, to do first what is most necessary. Oh that we were so wise in our spiritual lives!

1.4.2. The children of light are commonly surpassed by the children of this world. Not that the children of this world are truly wise; it is only *in their generation*. It is in that that they are *wiser* (more shrewd) *than the children of light in theirs*. We live as if we were to be here always and as if there were not another life after this. Although as *children of the light* we must see another world before us, we still do not prepare for it, do not send our best possessions and loyalties there, as we should.

2. The application of this parable and the conclusions drawn from it (v. 9): "*I say unto you*, you my disciples" — because this parable was directed to them (v. 1) — "although you have only a little in this world, consider how you may do good even with the little you have." Notice:

2.1. What our Lord Jesus exhorts us to do here: "*Make to yourselves friends of the mammon of unrighteousness* (worldly wealth)." It is the shrewd stewards of this world who administer their financial affairs so that they may benefit from them in the future, not only for the present. Now we should learn from them to use our money in such a way that we may be better off because of it in the next world, as they manage theirs in the hope of being better off because of it in this world. Although whatever goods are ours are our Lord's goods, nevertheless, as long as we dispose of them among our Lord's tenants and for their advantage, it is so far from being reckoned as doing wrong to our Lord that it is a duty to him as well as shrewd management for ourselves.

2.1.1. The things of this world are the *mammon of unrighteousness*, or the false *mammon*. Riches are perishable and will disappoint those who allow their expectations to be raised by them.

2.1.2. Although this *mammon of unrighteousness* is not to be trusted in for happiness, it may and must be used in our pursuit of what is our happiness. Although we cannot find true satisfaction in it, we may still *make to ourselves friends* of it.

2.1.3. At death we must all *fail. Hotan eklipete*, "when you suffer an eclipse." Death eclipses us. Traders are said to fail when they become bankrupt. We must all fail in this way soon. Death shuts up the shop; it *seals up the hand* (Job 37:7).

2.1.4. We should make sure that *when we fail* at death, we may be *received into everlasting habitations* (dwellings) in heaven. Christ has gone before us to prepare a place for those who are his (Jn 14:2–3), and he is there ready to receive them. See also 1Ti 6:17–19.

2.2. What arguments he uses to urge this exhortation on us.

2.2.1. If we do not use the gifts of God's providence in the right way, how can we expect from him the gifts of his spiritual grace? Our unfaithfulness in using the things of this world may be justly reckoned as a loss of the right to the grace that is necessary to bring us to glory (vv. 10–14).

2.2.1.1. The riches of this world are the lesser gifts; grace and glory are the greater. If we are unfaithful in what is less, it may justly be feared that we would also be so in the gifts of God's grace, and that therefore they will be denied us: *He that is faithful in that which is least is faithful also in much* (v. 10). Those who serve God and do good with their money will serve God and do good with the more noble and valuable talents of wisdom and grace, but those who bury the one talent of this world's wealth will never make the most of the five talents of spiritual riches (Mt 25:24–30).

2.2.1.2. The riches of this world are deceitful and uncertain; they are the *unrighteous mammon* that is moving quickly away from us, and if we want to take any advantage of it, we must move quickly. If we do not, how can we expect to be entrusted with spiritual riches, which are the only *true riches* (v. 11)? Let us be convinced that those people who are *rich in faith* (Jas 2:5) and *rich toward God* (12:21), rich in Christ, in the *kingdom of God and the righteousness*, are truly rich—indeed, very rich. If other things are added to us, by using them well we may take a firmer hold on the true riches and be qualified to receive even more grace from God. To those who are *faithful in the unrighteous mammon* he gives the *true riches*.

2.2.1.3. The riches of this world are *another man's* (v. 12). They are not our own, because they belong to God. They are *another man's*; we have received them from others. We use them for others. We must soon leave them to others. Spiritual and eternal riches, however, are our own, inseparably; they are the good part that will never be taken away from us (10:42). If we make Christ, the promises, and heaven our own, we have what we may truly call our own. But how can we expect God to enrich us with these if we do not serve him with our worldly possessions, of which we are merely the stewards?

2.2.2. We have no other way to show that we are the servants of God than by giving ourselves so completely to his service that we make all our worldly wealth useful to us in his service (v. 13): *No servant can serve two masters.* If a person loves the world and holds to that, he must hate God and despise him. But if a person loves God and remains faithful to him, he will comparatively hate the world. The things of the world will be made to help him serve God and work out his salvation (Php 2:12). The matter is set out clearly before us here: *Ye cannot serve God and mammon.* Their interests are so divided that their services can never be reconciled.

2.3. How Christ's teaching was received by the Pharisees.

2.3.1. They wickedly sneered at him (v. 14). *The Pharisees, who were covetous, heard all these things* and could not contradict him, but *they derided him.* Let us consider this:

2.3.1.1. As their sin, as the fruit of their love for money, which was their prevailing sin. Many who make a great profession of religion and are full of exercising their devotion are ruined by the love of the world. These Pharisees who loved money could not bear to have touched what was their favorite desire, their Delilah; this was why they sneered at him; it could be read, "they turned up their noses at him," or sniffed at him. It is an expression of the most intense scorn and disdain. They laughed at him for going so against the opinion and ways of the world. Those who are determined not to be ruled by the word of God often make fun of it.

2.3.1.2. As his suffering. Our Lord Jesus endured not only the contradiction of sinners (Heb 12:3) but also their contempt. The One who spoke as no one else had ever spoken before was mocked and ridiculed, so that his faithful ministers, whose preaching is unjustly sneered at, may not be discouraged by it. It is not a disgrace to be laughed at, but it is if we deserve to be laughed at.

2.3.2. He justly rebuked them for deceiving themselves with a mere show of godliness (v. 15). Here is:

2.3.2.1. Their empty exterior.

2.3.2.1.1. They *justified themselves before men*; they denied whatever evil they were accused of. They claimed to be looked on as especially holy and devout: "*You are they that* make it your business to seek people's good opinion and are intent on justifying yourselves before the world; you are notorious for this."

2.3.2.1.2. They were *highly respected among people.* People not only acquitted them but also applauded them, not only as good but also as the best.

2.3.2.2. Their odious interior, which was under the eye of God: "He *knows your heart*, and it is detestable in his sight."

2.3.2.2.1. It is foolish to *justify ourselves before men* and think that in the judgment of the great day others' ignorance of anything bad about us will be enough to acquit us, because God, who knows our hearts, knows the wrong in us that no one else knows. That *God knows our hearts* should restrain our self-esteem and self-confidence; it gives us good reason to humble and distrust ourselves.

2.3.2.2.2. It is foolish to judge people and things by the opinions of others about them, to follow the stream of popular judgment, because what is *highly esteemed among men* is perhaps *an abomination in the sight of God*, who sees things as they really are. Some who are despised and condemned by human beings are still accepted and approved by God (2Co 10:18).

2.3.3. He turned from them to the tax collectors and sinners, since they would be more likely to be persuaded by his Gospel than those money-loving, arrogant Pharisees (v. 16): "The *law and the prophets were* indeed *until John*; since John the Baptist appeared, *the kingdom of God is preached. Every man presses* into the Gospel kingdom, Gentiles as well as Jews. It is not so much a political and national kingdom as the Jewish society was when it was under the Law and the Prophets, when *salvation was of the Jews* (Jn 4:22); it has now been made an individual, personal concern, and so everyone who is convinced they have a soul to save is trying very hard to get in, so that they may not fall short." Some interpret it in this way: the Pharisees sneered at Christ for speaking in contempt of riches, because they thought, "Are there not many promises of riches and other temporal good things in the *law and the prophets*?" "It is true," Christ said. "That is what it was like, but now that the kingdom of God has begun to be preached, blessed are the poor, the mourners, and the persecuted (Mt 5:3–4, 10). Now that the Gospel is preached, the eyes of the people are opened, and they press into the kingdom of God with a holy violence (Mt 11:12)." Those who want to go to heaven must make an effort, must go against the flow, must force their way against the crowd who are going in the opposite direction.

2.3.4. He still denied any intention to invalidate the law (v. 17): *It is easier for heaven and earth to pass than for one tittle of the law to fail.* The moral law is confirmed; the duties imposed by it remain duties; the sins that it forbids remain sins. The ceremonial law is made perfect in the Gospel, and its obscure areas are filled in with the

Gospel colors; not *one tittle* of it fails, because it is found printed in the Gospel. Some things that were condoned by the law to prevent greater harm are prohibited by the Gospel, but without any detriment or disparagement to the law, as in the case of divorce (v. 18), which we had before (Mt 5:32; 19:9). The Gospel is intended to strike at the bitter root of corrupt human appetites and passions, to kill them and uproot them, and so they must not be indulged even to the extent that that permission did indulge them, since the more they are indulged, the more impetuous and headstrong they become.

Verses 19–31

The parable of the prodigal son set out the grace of the Gospel; this one sets before us the *wrath to come* (3:7), to wake us up. The tendency of the Gospel of Christ is both to reconcile us to poverty and suffering and to arm us against temptations to worldliness. This parable goes a long way in fulfilling those two great intentions. This parable is not like Christ's other parables, in which spiritual things are represented by comparisons with worldly things, like that of the sower and the seed. Here, instead, the spiritual things themselves are represented in a narrative or description of the different states of good and bad persons in this world and the other. We need not, however, call it an account of a particular occurrence; rather, it is something that happens every day: poor, godly people, whom others neglect and trample on, are released from their miseries by death and go to heavenly bliss and joy, and rich self-indulgent people, who live in luxury and are unmerciful to the poor, die and go to a state of terrible torment. Is this a parable? What comparison is there in this? The conversation here is only an illustration of the description of the two states. Our Savior came to make us familiar with another world, and here he did so. In this description—for that is what I will call it—we may notice:

1. The different conditions of a wicked *rich man* and a godly *poor man* in this world. The Jews in former times were ready to make prosperity one of the marks of a good person, and so they could hardly have any favorable thoughts of a poor man. Christ used this opportunity, among others, to correct this mistake, and he did so fully. We have here:

1.1. An evildoer in the height of his prosperity, though he was destined to be miserable forever (v. 19): *There was a certain rich man.* We commonly call him *Dives*, Latin for "a rich man," but no name is given to him by Christ, though the poor man is given a name. We are told about this rich man that:

1.1.1. He was *clothed in purple and fine linen* and that these enhanced his appearance. He had fine linen for pleasure, and no doubt it was clean every day, one set for the day and one for the night. He had purple for show. Whenever he went out, he appeared in magnificent clothes.

1.1.2. He lived a life of luxury; he *fared sumptuously every day.* His main table was supplied with the widest range of fine delicacies that could possibly be provided; his side table was richly decorated with silver or gold; his servants, who waited at table, wore rich uniforms, and no doubt the guests at his table enhanced it, or so he thought. Well, what harm was there in all this? It is not a sin to be rich, not sinful to wear purple and fine linen, nor to keep a full table, if you can afford it. Nor are we told that he gained his estate by fraud, oppression, or extortion, nor that he was drunk or made others drunk. Christ wanted to show here that:

1.1.2.1. A person may have a great deal of the wealth but still lie under and perish forever under God's wrath

and curse. We cannot conclude from a person's grand living either that God's giving them so much shows he loves them or that they love God for giving them so much.

1.1.2.2. Plenty and pleasure are very dangerous. This man might have been happy if he had not had such great possessions and enjoyments.

1.1.2.3. Indulgence of the body and worldly pleasures are the ruin of many a soul. Eating fine food and wearing fine clothes are lawful, but they often become the food and fuel of pride and self-indulgence and so become a sin for us.

1.1.2.4. Feasting ourselves and our friends while forgetting the distresses of the poor and suffering are very offensive to God and condemning to the soul.

1.2. A godly man in the depths of adversity and distress, though he is destined to be happy forever (v. 20): *There was a certain beggar, named Lazarus.* This poor man was reduced to the most critical state; as to outward things, he was as miserable as you can imagine a person to be in this world.

1.2.1. His body was *full of sores*, like Job's. To be sick and weak in body is a great affliction, but sores are even more painful, and more loathsome to those around the one afflicted with them.

1.2.2. He was forced to beg for his bread. He was so sore and lame that he could not walk by himself, but was carried by some compassionate hand or other, and in this way he was *laid at the rich man's gate.* Those who are unable to help the poor with their money should help them with their effort; those who cannot lend them a dollar should lend them a hand. In his distress, Lazarus had nothing of his own to live on. Notice:

1.2.2.1. His expectations from the rich man's table: *He desired to be fed with the crumbs* (v. 21). He did not expect a bowl of soup from his table, though he should have had one; he would have been thankful for the crumbs from under the table—indeed, he would have been glad to have the leftovers of the rich man's dogs. This is taken notice of to show:

1.2.2.1.1. The poor man's distress and disposition. He was poor, but he was *poor in spirit* (Mt 5:3), contentedly poor. He did not lie at the rich man's gate complaining, crying out, but silently and modestly wanted to be *fed with the crumbs.* Here was a child of wrath and an heir of hell sitting in the house, living in luxury, and a child of love and an heir of heaven lying at the gate, perishing for hunger. Is their spiritual state to be judged by their outward condition?

1.2.2.1.2. The rich man's attitude toward him. We are not told that he abused him, but it is suggested that he showed him no respect. Here was a real object of charity, and a very moving one, which spoke for itself; it was presented to the rich man at his own gate. A little thing would have been a great kindness to the poor man, yet the rich man took no notice of his situation, but let him lie there. It is not enough not to oppress and trample on the poor; we will be found unfaithful stewards of our Lord's goods if we do not help and relieve them. The reason given for the most fearful doom is *I was hungry, and you gave me no meat* (Mt 25:42). I wonder how those rich people who have read the Gospel of Christ and say that they believe it can be so unconcerned as they often are about the needs and miseries of the poor and suffering.

1.2.2.2. The treatment he had from the dogs: *The dogs came and licked his sores.* The rich man may have kept a kennel of hounds or other dogs, and these were fed to the full, but poor Lazarus could not get enough to keep him alive. Those people who feed their dogs but neglect the poor will have a great deal to answer for on the Day of Judgment. Those who pamper their dogs and horses but let the families of their poor neighbors starve offend God; in fact, they show contempt for human nature. Now those dogs *came and licked the* sores of poor Lazarus. This may be taken:

1.2.2.2.*1*. As emphasizing his misery. His sores were bleeding, which tempted the dogs to come and lick them. The dogs were like their master, thinking they lived luxuriously when they were licking human gore. Or:

1.2.2.2.*2*. As some relief to him in his misery; the master was hardhearted toward him, but the dogs *came and licked his sores*, which somewhat relieved them. The dogs were kinder to the poor man than their master was.

2. The different conditions of this godly *poor man* and this wicked *rich man* at and after death.

2.1. They both died (v. 22): the *beggar died*; the *rich man also died*. Death is the common lot of rich and poor, godly and ungodly; they meet together there (Pr 22:2). Saints die so that they may bring their sorrows to an end and may enter their joys. Sinners die so that they may go to give an account. Both the rich and the poor should prepare for death, because it waits for them both.

2.2. The beggar died first. God often takes godly people out of the world and leaves evildoers to flourish. Since the poor man could find no other shelter or resting place, he was *hid in the grave* (Job 14:13).

2.3. The rich man *died and was buried*. Nothing is said about the burial of the poor man. They dug a hole anywhere and dropped his body in. However, the rich man had an ostentatious funeral. A funeral oration was probably given in praise of him, of his generous way of living and the good table he kept; those who had feasted at his table would praise him for this. How foreign is the ceremony of a funeral to the happiness of the person!

2.4. The beggar died and was *carried by angels into Abraham's bosom*. How much did the honor given to his soul exceed the honor given to the rich man on earth when the poor man's soul was taken to its rest and the rich man's body was taken with so much magnificence to its grave! Notice:

2.4.1. His soul existed separately from the body. It did not die or fall asleep with the body.

2.4.2. His soul moved to another world; it returned to God, who gave it, to its native country. The spirit of a person goes upward (Ecc 3:21).

2.4.3. Angels took care of it; it was *carried by angels*. Angels are ministering spirits to the heirs of salvation (Heb 1:14) not only while they live but also when they die. The human soul, if not chained to this earth and obstructed by it, as unsanctified souls are, has in itself a spontaneity by which it springs upward as soon as it gets clear of the body; but Christ will not trust those who are his to that, and so he will send special messengers to take them to himself. Saints will be brought home not only safely but also honorably. Who were the bearers at the rich man's funeral—though they were probably persons of the highest rank—compared with Lazarus' bearers?

2.4.4. It was carried *into Abraham's bosom*. Abraham was the father of the faithful, and where should the souls of the faithful be gathered except to him? Lazarus was carried *to his bosom* (side), that is, to enjoy his presence. The *saints in heaven* sit *down with Abraham, and Isaac, and Jacob* (Mt 8:11). Abraham was a great and rich man, but in heaven he does not think it beneath him to lay poor Lazarus at his side. Rich saints and poor saints meet in heaven. The poor man was laid at the side of Abraham. Such was the destiny of the one whom the rich glutton

scorned so much that he would not *set* him *with the dogs of his flock* (Job 30:1).

2.5. The next news you hear of the rich man is that *in hell he lifted up his eyes, being in torment* (v. 23).

2.5.1. His state was very miserable. He was in hell, in Hades, in the state of separate souls, and there he was suffering the greatest misery and anguish. Just as the souls of the faithful are in joy and blessing immediately after they are delivered from the burden of the flesh, so evil and unsanctified souls are in endless, useless, remediless misery and torment immediately after they are taken away from the pleasures of the flesh by death. This rich man had given himself completely to the pleasures of this world, and so he was completely unfit for the pleasures of the world of spirits. They would not be any pleasure to such a worldly mind as his, and so, not surprisingly, he was excluded from them.

2.5.2. The misery of his state was made worse by his knowledge of the happiness of Lazarus: he *lifted up his eyes* and *saw Abraham afar off*, and *Lazarus in his bosom*. He now began to consider what had become of Lazarus. He did not find him where he himself was; in fact, he clearly saw him far away at Abraham's side.

2.5.2.1. He saw *Abraham afar off*. We would have thought seeing Abraham would have been pleasant, but to see him far away was tormenting.

2.5.2.2. He saw Lazarus at Abraham's side. The sight of him brought to his mind his own cruel behavior toward him, and the sight of him in that happiness made his own misery even more painful.

3. An account of the conversation between the rich man and Abraham in the separate state. Notice:

3.1. The rich man's request to Abraham that his present misery be lessened (v. 24). Seeing Abraham far away, *he cried to him*. The one who used to command aloud now begged aloud. The songs of his dissipation and self-indulgence had all turned into weeping (Am 8:10). Notice here:

3.1.1. The title he gave to Abraham: *Father Abraham*. Many in hell can call Abraham father. Perhaps this rich man, in his worldly merriment, had laughed at Abraham and the story of Abraham, as the scoffers of the last days will do (2Pe 3:3), but now he gave him a title of respect, *Father Abraham*. The day is coming when evildoers will be desperate to have any acquaintance with the righteous, to claim they are related to them even in the smallest way, though they now insult them.

3.1.2. The description he gave him of his present deplorable condition: *I am tormented in this flame*. It was the torment of his soul that he complained about, and so it was the sort of fire that will come on condemned souls. The wrath of God is such a fire directed at a guilty conscience. Horrors of the mind are such a fire, as are the rebukes of a self-accusing and self-condemning heart.

3.1.3. His request to Abraham in consideration of this misery: *Have mercy on me*. The day is coming when those who make light of divine mercy will beg desperately for it. The One who had no mercy on Lazarus expected Lazarus to have mercy on him, "for," he thought, "Lazarus is better natured than I ever was." The particular favor he begged was, *Send Lazarus, that he may dip the tip of his finger in water, and cool my tongue*.

3.1.3.1. Here he complained especially about the torment of *his tongue*. The tongue is one of the organs of speech, and by its torment he was reminded of all the evil words he had spoken against God and other people, all his harsh and filthy speech; he was condemned by his words, and so he was tormented in his tongue. The tongue is also one of the organs of tasting, and so its torments would remind him of his excessive enjoyment of worldly delights.

3.1.3.2. He wanted *a drop of water to cool his tongue*. He asked for something as small as possible, *a drop of water* to cool his tongue for one moment.

3.1.3.3. He asked that Lazarus might bring it. He named him because he knew him and thought Lazarus would not be unwilling to do him this good work for old times' sake. A day is coming when those who now hate and despise the people of God would gladly receive kindness from them.

3.2. Abraham's reply to this request. In general, he did not grant it. Notice how justly this rich man was paid back in his own coin. The one who denied a crumb was denied a drop. Now we are told, *Ask, and it shall be given you* (11:9), but if we allow this accepted time to pass (2Co 6:2), we may ask, but it will not be given us.

3.2.1. Abraham called him *Son*, a kind and civil title. The rich man had been a son, but a rebellious one, and now he was an abandoned, disinherited son.

3.2.2. He reminded him of his own former condition and that of Lazarus during their lifetimes: *Son, remember*; this is a powerful word. Sinners are called on to remember already now, but they do not. They refuse to; "*Son, remember now your Creator* (Ecc 12:1), your Redeemer, remember your end (Isa 47:7)"—but they forget why they have their memories. "*Son, remember* the many warnings given you. Remember the offers made to you of eternal life and glory, which you would not accept!" But what the rich man was reminded of here was:

3.2.2.1. *Thou in thy life-time receivedst thy good things*. Abraham did not tell him that he had abused them, but that he had received them: "Remember how generous God has been to you; you cannot, therefore, say he owes you anything, not even *a drop of water*. What he gave thee *thou receivedst*, and that was all. You have been the grave of God's blessings, in which they were buried (Mt 25:18, 24–30), not their field, in which they were sown (Mt 13:1–23). Thou receivedst *thy good things, thine*: they were the things thou chosest for *thy good things*, that were in your eyes the best things. You wanted the good things of your lifetime and had no thought of better things in another life. The day of your good things has past and gone.

3.2.2.2. "Remember, too, what *evil things Lazarus received*. Think what a large share of miseries he had *in his lifetime*. You have as much good as one could imagine coming to such a bad man, and he as much evil as one could imagine coming to such a good man. He received his bad things; he received them as treatment prescribed for the cure of his spiritual diseases, and the cure was brought about." Just as evildoers have good things only in this life, godly people have bad things only in this life. Now Abraham awakened the rich man's conscience to remind him how he had behaved toward Lazarus. He could not forget that in his lifetime he would not help Lazarus, and so how could he expect Lazarus to help him now?

3.2.3. He reminded him of Lazarus' present happiness and his own misery: *Now he is comforted, and thou art tormented*. Heaven is comfort, and hell is torment; heaven is joy, and hell is weeping and wailing. Heaven will be truly heaven to those who go there through many and great adversities in this world. When they have fallen asleep in Christ, you may truly say, "Now they are comforted (v. 25); now all their tears are wiped away (Rev 7:17)." In heaven, there is eternal comfort. On the other hand, hell will truly be hell to those who go there from the midst of enjoying all worldly delights and pleasures.

3.2.4. He assured him that it was useless to think of having any relief by the ministry of Lazarus, because (v. 26), *Besides all this, between us and you there is a great gulf fixed*, a great, impassable chasm. The kindest saint in heaven cannot visit the assembly of the dead and condemned to bring any comfort or relief to anyone there who was once their friend. *They that would pass hence to you cannot*. The most daring sinner in hell cannot force their way out of that prison. *They cannot pass to us that would come thence*. In this world, thank God, there is no chasm fixed between nature and grace, and we may pass freely from one to the other, from sin to God. It was now too late for any change of the rich man's condition; it might have been prevented in time, but now it could not be remedied in eternity. A stone was rolled over the door of the pit, which cannot be rolled back.

3.3. The rich man's further request to his father Abraham. Having an opportunity to speak to Abraham, he would now use it for his relatives whom he had left behind.

3.3.1. He begged that Lazarus be *sent to his father's house* on an errand: *I pray thee therefore, father* (v. 27). Again he called on Abraham. "Surely you will be so compassionate as not to deny me this one favor. Send him back *to my father's house*; he knows well enough where it is, having been there many times. He knows I have *five brethren* there; they will know him and will listen to what he says. Let him *testify to them*; let him tell them what condition I am in. Let him warn them not to follow in my steps, *lest they also come into this place of torment* (v. 28)." He did not say, "Allow me to go to them, so that I may testify to them." His going would frighten them out of their wits; rather, "Send Lazarus, whose words will be less terrible, but whose testimony will be sufficient to frighten them out of their sins." He wanted to prevent their ruin out of tenderness toward them, since he had a natural affection for them.

3.3.2. Abraham denied him this favor too. No request is granted in hell. Abraham left the brothers the testimony of Moses and the prophets. This was their privilege: *They have Moses and the prophets*; and it was their duty: "*Let them hear them* and have faith in them, and that will be enough to keep them out of this place of torment."

3.3.3. The rich man urged his request even further (v. 30): "*Nay, father Abraham*. True, they have Moses and the prophets, but they do not give them due regard. It may be hoped, however, that *if one went to them from the dead, they would repent*, that that would be a conviction they might take more notice of. They are used to Moses and the prophets, but this would be something new and more startling; surely this would bring them to repent." Foolish people tend to think any method of conviction better than the one God has chosen and appointed.

3.3.4. Abraham insisted on denying the request, with a conclusive reason (v. 31): *If they hear not Moses and the prophets, neither will they be persuaded though one rose from the dead.*

CHAPTER 17

In this chapter we have: 1. Conversations Christ had with his disciples, in which he taught them to avoid giving offense and to forgive the wrongs done them (vv. 1–4), encouraged them to pray for their faith to increase (vv. 5–6), and taught them humility (vv. 7–10). 2. His healing ten men who had leprosy and receiving thanks from only one of them, a Samaritan (vv. 11–19). 3. His teaching concerning when the kingdom of God would come (vv. 20–37).

Verses 1-10

We are taught here:

1. That the giving of *offences*—the word means "things that cause people to sin," or stumbling blocks—is *a great sin* (Ex 32:21, vv. 1–2). We can confidently expect that stumbling blocks will come, and so we should provide for that, but *woe to him through whom they come*, for his condemnation will be heavy (v. 2). He perishes under a load of guilt heavier than that of millstones. This includes a woe:

1.1. To persecutors who cause any injury to the least of Christ's *little ones*.

1.2. To deceivers, who corrupt the truths of Christ and so trouble the minds of the disciples.

1.3. To those who lead disgraceful lives and so weaken the hands and sadden the hearts of God's people.

2. That the forgiving of offenses that come by way of *trespasses* is an important duty (v. 3): *Take heed to yourselves*. This may refer either to what goes before or to what follows. On the one hand, it may mean, *Take heed that you offend not one of these little ones*. On the other hand, it may mean, "When *your brother trespasses against you, take heed to yourselves* at such a time, so that you will not lose your temper."

2.1. "If you are allowed to *rebuke him*, you are advised to do so. Do not smother the resentment, but express it: *Tell him his faults*, and perhaps you will realize that you mistook him, that it was not a *trespass against you*, but an oversight, and then you will beg his pardon for misunderstanding him.

2.2. "You are commanded to forgive him when he repents: *If he repent, forgive him*; forget the wrong, never think of it again. And even if he does not repent, you must not therefore bear ill will toward him or think how you can get revenge.

2.3. "You are to repeat this every time he repeats his sin (v. 4). If he could be supposed to be either so negligent or so arrogant as to *trespass against thee seven times in a day*, and if he then professes himself sorry for his fault just as many times, continue to *forgive him*." Christians should have a forgiving spirit and be willing to make the best of everybody, and they should seek as much to show that they have forgiven a wrong as others seek to show that they resent it.

3. That we all need to have our faith strengthened, because as that grace grows, all other graces grow. Notice:

3.1. How the disciples turned to Christ for their faith to be strengthened (v. 5). *The apostles* themselves still acknowledged the weakness of their faith and saw their need of Christ's grace to make it stronger; they *said unto the Lord, Increase our faith*. The increase of our faith is what we should earnestly seek. They offered this prayer to Christ when he urged on them the duty of forgiving wrongs: "*Lord, increase our faith*, or we will never be able to practice such a difficult duty as this." Faith in God's forgiving mercy will enable us to overcome the greatest difficulties that lie in the way of our forgiving our brother or sister.

3.2. The assurance Christ gave them of the wonderful effectiveness of true faith (v. 6): "*If ye had faith as a grain of mustard seed*, as small as mustard seed—or as 'sharp or pungent' *as a mustard seed*, by its sharpness stimulating all other graces—then nothing that was fitting to be done for the glory of God would be too hard for you, even the transplanting of a tree from the earth to the sea." Just as *nothing is impossible* with God, so all *things are possible to him that can believe* (Mk 9:23).

4. That whatever we do in the service of Christ, we must be very humble. Even the apostles themselves, who worked so much more for Christ than others, must not think they had made him indebted to them.

4.1. We are all God's servants. Our whole strength and our whole time are to be employed for him.

4.2. As God's servants, we should do what we can to occupy our time with fulfilling our duty; we should make the end of one service the beginning of the next. The servant who has been *ploughing* or *feeding cattle* in the field still has work to do when he comes home at night; he must wait at table (vv. 7–8). When we have been working for God, we must continue to wait on God.

4.3. Our main concern here on earth must be to do the duty entailed by our relationship with God, and we should leave it to our Master to encourage us for it. No servants expect their master to say to them, *Go and sit down to meat*; there is time enough to do that when we have done our day's work. Let us be eager to complete our work, and then the reward will come at the appropriate time.

4.4. It is right that Christ be served before us: *Make ready wherewith I may sup* (prepare my supper), *and afterward thou shalt eat and drink*.

4.5. When Christ's servants are to wait on him, they must *gird themselves* (get themselves ready), must free themselves from everything entangling and encumbering. When we have prepared for Christ's reception, we must then prepare ourselves to be with him. This is expected from servants, and Christ could require it from us, but he does not insist on it. He was *among his disciples as one that served* (22:27), and did not come *to be ministered unto, but to minister* (Mt 20:28), as can be seen in his washing his disciples' feet.

4.6. Christ's servants do not even deserve his thanks for any service they do him: *Does he thank that servant?* No good works of ours can deserve anything from the hand of God.

4.7. Whatever we do for Christ, it is no more than our duty. Although we should *do all things that are commanded us*—and unfortunately we come short of this in many things—it is only what we are bound to by the first and great commandment of *loving God* with *all our heart and soul* (10:27).

4.8. The best servants of Christ must humbly acknowledge that they are simply *unprofitable servants*. God cannot gain anything by our services, and so he cannot be made a debtor by them. We should therefore call ourselves *unprofitable servants* but call his service a profitable service.

Verses 11-19

Here we have an account of the healing of ten men who had leprosy; we did not have this narrative in any other of the Evangelists' accounts. The Jews thought this disease was a clearer sign of God's displeasure than any other, and so Christ, who came to take away sin, took particular care to heal the lepers who came his way. Christ was now on his way to Jerusalem, about midway. He was now in the border country between Samaria and Galilee. Notice:

1. The way these lepers turned to Christ. There were ten of them; although those who were diseased in this way were excluded from associating with others, they were free to be with one another.

1.1. They met Christ as he entered a certain village. They did not wait until he had refreshed himself, but met him as he entered town. Weary as he was, he did not put them off.

1.2. They stood far away. A sense of our spiritual leprosy should make us very humble whenever we approach Christ. Who are we, that we should draw near to the One who is infinitely pure?

1.3. Their request was unanimous and very bold (v. 13): *They lifted up their voices* and cried out, *Jesus, Master, have mercy on us*. People who expect help from Christ must take him as their Master. If he is Master, he will be Jesus, a Savior. The lepers did not ask specifically to be healed of their leprosy, but asked, *Have mercy on us*, and it is enough for us to turn to the *compassions* of Christ, because they *fail not* (La 3:22).

2. Christ sent them to the priests to be inspected. He did not tell them positively that they would be healed, but told them to go and show themselves to the priests (v. 14). This was a test of their obedience. Those who expect Christ's favors must follow them in this way. The lepers all went to the priests. Because the ceremonial law was still in force, Christ took care to observe it.

3. As they went, they were cleansed. We may expect God to meet us with mercy when we are found fulfilling our duty. If we do what we can, God will not fail to do for us what we cannot do. Although the means will not heal you by themselves, God will heal you as you diligently use those means.

4. One of them—only one!—returned to give thanks (v. 15). When he saw that he was healed, he turned back toward the Author of his healing, whom he wished to have the glory for it. He appears to have been very sincere and warm in his thanksgiving: *With a loud voice he glorified God* (v. 13). Those who have received mercy from God should make it known to others. However, the leper also gave a special word of thanks to Christ (v. 16): *He fell down at his feet* and *gave him thanks*. We should give thanks for the favors Christ gives us, especially when we recover from sickness. It is good for us to be very humble in our thanksgiving as well as in our prayers.

5. Christ took notice of this one man who had distinguished himself in this way, since it seems he was a Samaritan, whereas the others were Jews (v. 16). The Samaritans did not have the pure knowledge and worship of God among them that the Jews had, but it was one of them who glorified God, whereas the Jews forgot. Notice:

5.1. The special notice Christ took of this leper's grateful response and of the ingratitude of those who shared with him in the mercy—that the one who was a foreigner was the only one who returned to give glory to God (vv. 17–18). See here:

5.1.1. How rich Christ is in doing good: *Were there not ten cleansed?* Here was a general healing, a whole hospital healed with the speaking of one word. We will never have less grace because others share in it.

5.1.2. How poor we are in our response: *Where are the nine?* Ingratitude is a very common sin. Of the many who receive mercy from God, only very few return to give thanks.

5.1.3. How those from whom gratitude is least expected often prove most grateful. A Samaritan gives thanks, but a Jew does not. This serves here to emphasize the ingratitude of those Jews about whom Christ speaks.

5.2. The great encouragement Christ gave him (v. 19). The rest had their healing; it was not revoked. But the one who returned to give thanks had his healing confirmed particularly: *Thy faith hath made thee whole*. The others were made whole by the power of Christ, in compassion to their distress, but the one who gave thanks was made whole through his faith, by which Christ saw that the man was set apart from the others.

Verses 20–37

Here is a message of Christ about the *kingdom of God*, that is, the kingdom of the Messiah, which was now soon to be set up and which people expected great things of. Here is:

1. The demand of the Pharisees about it that gave rise to this talk. They asked when the kingdom of God would come. They understood, perhaps, that Christ had taught his disciples to pray for it to come, and they, the Pharisees, had long preached that it was near. "Now," they said, "when will that glorious view open up?"

2. Christ's reply to this demand, directed first to the Pharisees and later to his own disciples (v. 22); what he said to both, he says to us.

2.1. That the kingdom of the Messiah was to be a spiritual kingdom. They asked when it would come. "You do not know what you are asking," Christ said; "when it comes, you may not be aware of it." He said this because this kingdom has no external show, as other kingdoms have, whose advancements and revolutions fill the newspapers. "No," Christ said:

2.1.1. "It will enter silently; *it cometh not with observation*." They wanted to have their curiosity satisfied about its timing; Christ wanted to have their mistakes put right about its nature. When *Messiah the Prince* (Da 9:25) comes to establish his kingdom, people will not say, *Lo here*, or *Lo there*, as when a ruler goes in a procession to visit his territories. Christ will not come with all this talk; his kingdom will not be set up in this or that particular place. Those who confine Christianity and the church to this place or that group cry, *Lo here*, or *Lo there*; this is the talk of those who consider prosperity and external show marks of the true church.

2.1.2. "It has a spiritual influence: *The kingdom of God is within you*." It is not of this world (Jn 18:36). Its glory does not strike people's imagination, but it affects their spirits, and its power is over their souls and consciences. The kingdom of God will not change people's outward condition, but it will change their hearts and lives. It comes when it takes people who were proud, arrogant, and worldly and makes them humble, sincere, and heavenly; so look for the kingdom of God in the revolutions of the heart. The kingdom of God is "among you," as some read it. "You ask when it will come because you are not aware that it has already begun to be set up in your midst. It is in your nation, though not in your hearts." It is the folly of many who curiously inquire about the times to come that what they look for ahead of them is already among them.

2.2. That the setting up of this kingdom was a work that would meet with a great deal of opposition and interruption (v. 22). The disciples thought they would defeat everything in their path; Christ told them it would be otherwise: "*The days will come when you shall desire to see one of the days of the Son of man* but will not see it. At first, it is true, you will have wonderful success"—as they had, when thousands were added to the church in a day—"but do not think it will always be so. People will grow cool toward it." This looks ahead to the times of his disciples in later ages; they must expect much disappointment.

2.2.1. Ministers and churches would sometimes be under outward restraints. Then they would wish to see such days of opportunity as they had enjoyed formerly. God teaches us to know the value of such mercies by their lack.

2.2.2. Sometimes they would be under inward restraints. The Spirit would be withdrawn from them.

Then they would wish to see such victorious, triumphant days as they had sometimes seen. We must not think that Christ's church and cause are lost because they are not always equally visible and effective.

2.3. That Christ and his kingdom were not to be looked for in this or that particular place; rather, his appearance would be general, in all places at once (vv. 23–24): "*They will say to you, See here, or, See there. Go not after them, nor follow them.* The kingdom of God was not intended to be the glory of only one people, but to give light to the Gentiles (2:32), for like *the lightning that lightens out of one part under heaven, and shines* suddenly and irresistibly *to the other part under heaven, so shall also the Son of man be in his day.* The Gospel that is to set up Christ's kingdom in the world will fly like lightning through the nations. The kingdom of the Messiah is not to be something local, but is to be dispersed far and wide over the face of the whole earth." The intention of setting up Christ's kingdom was not to make one nation great, but to make all nations good—some people, at least, out of all nations.

2.4. That the Messiah must suffer before he must reign (v. 25): "*First must he suffer many things* and *be rejected of this generation,* and if he is treated in this way, his disciples must expect nothing else than to suffer and be rejected too, for his sake. We must go to the crown by way of the cross. The *Son of man must suffer many things* (9:22). Pain, shame, and death are those many things. He must be *rejected by this generation* of unbelieving Jews before he is embraced by another generation of faithful Gentiles."

2.5. That the setting up of the kingdom of the Messiah would introduce the destruction of the Jewish nation. Notice:

2.5.1. How things had gone with sinners formerly. Look at the old world, when the *earth was filled with violence* (Ge 6:11), and remember the people of Sodom, *sinners before the Lord exceedingly* (Ge 13:13). Notice:

2.5.1.1. That they had fair warning given them. Noah was *a preacher of righteousness* (2Pe 2:5) to the old world, as was Lot to the people of Sodom.

2.5.1.2. That they did not pay any attention to the warning given them. They were very self-confident. They were all very merry and very busy. When they should have been—as the people of Nineveh were—fasting and praying, repenting and reforming (Jnh 3:7), they carried on in their secure self-confidence, *eating flesh* and *drinking wine.*

2.5.1.3. That they continued in their self-confidence and worldliness until the threatened judgment came.

2.5.1.4. That God took care for the preservation of those who were his. Noah entered *into the ark* (v. 27) and was safe there; Lot went out of Sodom and so went out of harm's way.

2.5.1.5. That they were surprised by the ruin that they would not fear. The *flood came* and destroyed all the sinners of the old world; *fire and brimstone* came and *destroyed* all the sinners of Sodom. However, what is especially intended here is to show what a terrible surprise destruction will be to those who are self-confident and worldly.

2.5.2. How it will be with sinners still (v. 30): *Thus shall it be in the day when the Son of man is revealed.* They had a warning from Christ, and it would be repeated to them by the apostles after him, but it would be all in vain. One would have thought that this message of our Savior's, which was made in public, would wake them up, but it did not.

2.6. That his disciples and followers should set themselves apart from the unfaithful Jews in that day, fleeing at the signal they were directed to watch for. This flight of theirs from Jerusalem must be prompt, not slowed down by any concern about their worldly affairs (v. 31): "*He that shall be on the house-top, let him not come down, to take his stuff* (belongings) *away.*" It would be better to leave his things behind than to stay to look after them and perish with those who did not believe. He should do as Lot and his family were commanded to do: *Escape for thy life* (Ge 19:17). *Save yourselves from this untoward generation* (Ac 2:40). When they had made their escape, they must not think of returning (v. 32): "*Remember Lot's wife* and do not *look back* as she did. Do not be reluctant to leave a place marked out for destruction." Let them not look back, so that they may not be tempted to go back; indeed, looking back might be interpreted as going back in heart or as evidence that the heart was left behind. There would be no other way of saving their lives (v. 33): "*Whosoever shall seek to save his life* will *lose it,* but whoever is willing to risk his life will *preserve* it, because he will make sure of eternal life."

2.7. That all good Christians would certainly escape, but many of them just barely (vv. 34–36). When God's judgments are devastating everything, he will make sure to preserve those who are his: *two in a bed, one taken and the other left.* Sooner or later it will be made clear that the Lord knows those who are his and those who are not (2Ti 2:19).

2.8. That this distinguishing, dividing, and discriminating work would be done in all places, as far as the kingdom of God would extend (v. 37). *Where, Lord?* The Pharisees had asked about the time, and he would not satisfy their curiosity; they therefore tested him with another question: "*Where, Lord?*" The answer is proverbial: *Wheresoever the body is, thither will the eagles be gathered together.*

2.8.1. Wherever evildoers are, they will be found by the judgments of God, just as the birds of prey will swoop down on a dead carcass wherever it is. The judgments of God will be directed at them as eagles come on their prey.

2.8.2. Wherever the godly are, who are marked out for preservation, they will be found happily enjoying Christ. Wherever Christ is, believers will flock to him and meet in him, by the instinct of the new nature, as eagles go to their prey. *Wherever the body is* (v. 37), wherever the Gospel is preached, godly souls will turn there and find Christ. Wherever Christ records his name, he will meet his people and bless them (Jn 4:21; 1Ti 2:8).

CHAPTER 18

We have here: 1. The parable of the persistent widow (vv. 1–8). 2. The parable of the Pharisee and the tax collector, which is intended to teach us that when we pray, we must humiliate ourselves for sin (vv. 9–14). 3. Christ's favor to little children who were brought to him (vv. 15–17). 4. The test of a rich man who wanted to follow Christ, to see whether he loved Christ more than his riches (vv. 18–30). 5. Christ's foretelling his own suffering and death (vv. 31–34). 6. His restoring sight to a blind man (vv. 35–43).

Verses 1–8

This parable has its key hanging on the door. Christ spoke it to teach us that *men ought always to pray and not to faint* (v. 1). It supposes that all God's people are praying people; all God's children send messages to him both according to discipline and in emergencies. It is our privilege and honor that we may pray. It is our duty; we should pray. It is to be our constant work; we should always pray. We must pray and never become tired of praying until our prayer is swallowed up in eternal praise. However, what seems to be particularly intended here is to teach us faithfulness and perseverance in our requests for any spiritual blessings that we seek, relating either to ourselves or to the church of God. When we are praying for strength against our spiritual enemies, our sinful desires and corruptions, we must continue to be faithful in prayer (Ro 12:12), must *pray and not faint*, because we will not *seek God's face in vain* (Isa 45:19).

1. Christ shows by a parable the power of persistence among human beings. He gives us an example of an honest cause that was successful before an unjust judge not because it was just or deserved pity but purely because of persistence. Notice:

1.1. The bad character of the judge who lived in a certain town. He *neither feared God nor regarded man*; he took no trouble to do his duty either to God or to people; he was a perfect stranger to both godliness and honor. It is not strange for those who have rejected the fear of their Creator to be completely unconcerned about their fellow creatures; where there is no fear of God, no good is to be expected. Such a prevalence of indifference to religion and heartlessness to people is bad in anyone, but exceptionally bad in a judge. Instead of doing good with his power, he will be in danger of doing harm.

1.2. The distressed case of a poor widow. She clearly had right on her side, but it seems she did not tie herself to the formalities of the law, but personally applied to the judge every day, continuing to cry out, *Avenge me of mine adversary*; that is, "Grant me justice against my adversary." Magistrates are particularly commanded not only not to do *violence to the widow* (Jer 22:3) but also to *judge the fatherless* and *plead for the widow* (Isa 1:17).

1.3. The difficulty and discouragement she met with in presenting her case: *He would not for a while* (for some time he refused). According to his usual practice, he took no notice of her case because she could not pay him a bribe.

1.4. Her eventual winning by continually nagging this unjust judge (v. 5): *"Because this widow troubleth me*, I will hear her case and grant her justice, for fear that by her shouting at me she may wear me out, for she is determined that she will give me no rest until it is done. I will do it, therefore, to save myself any further trouble." And so she was shown justice because of her continual asking.

2. He applies this to encourage God's praying people.

2.1. He assures them that God will finally be gracious to them (v. 6): *Hear what the unjust judge saith, and shall not God avenge his own elect?* Notice:

2.1.1. What they want and expect: that God would *avenge his own elect*. This shows us:

2.1.1.1. There is a people in the world who are God's people, his own elect, and he has this relationship in mind in everything he does for them.

2.1.1.2. God's own chosen ones meet with a great deal of trouble and opposition in this world; there are *many adversaries*.

2.1.1.3. What is needed and waited for is God's preserving and protecting them.

2.1.2. What is required of God's people: they must *cry day and night to him* (v. 7). He has made this their duty, and he has promised mercy for this. We should be detailed in praying against our spiritual enemies, as this persistent

widow was. "Lord, put to death this corruption." "Lord, strengthen me against this temptation." We should be concerned for the persecuted and oppressed churches and pray that God would do them justice. We must cry out from the heart; we must cry out day and night; we must wrestle with God. God's praying people are told to *give him no rest* (Isa 62:6–7).

2.1.3. What discouragements they may encounter in their prayers. He may *bear long with them*. It may be read, "He exercises patience toward them," that is, toward the adversaries of his people; and he exercises the patience of his people.

2.1.4. What assurance they have that mercy will eventually come, even if it is delayed; if this widow is successful by being persistent, then much more will God's elect succeed.

2.1.4.1. This widow was a stranger, but God's praying people are his own chosen ones, those whom he knows and loves.

2.1.4.2. She was only one, but the praying people of God are many. Saints on earth besiege the throne of grace with their united prayers.

2.1.4.3. She came to a judge who told her to keep her distance; we come to a Father who tells us to come boldly to him.

2.1.4.4. She came to an *unjust judge* (v. 6); we come to *a righteous Father* (Jn 17:25).

2.1.4.5. She came to this judge purely on her own account, but God is himself committed in the cause that we are seeking.

2.1.4.6. She had no friend to speak up for her; we have an *Advocate with the Father* (1Jn 2:1), his own Son, who *ever lives to make intercession* for us (Heb 7:25).

2.1.4.7. She had no encouragement given her to ask, but we have a promise that it will be given to us (Mt 7:7).

2.1.4.8. She could have access to the judge only at certain times, but we may cry out to God *day and night*, at all times of the day and night.

2.1.4.9. Her persistence was offensive to the judge, but our persistence is pleasing to God and therefore, we may hope, will be effective if it is offered as an *effectual fervent prayer* (Jas 5:16).

2.2. He intimates to them that, despite this, they will begin to become tired of waiting for him (v. 8): *Nevertheless, when the Son of man cometh, shall he find faith on the earth?* The question implies a strong negative reply: No, he will not; he himself foresees it.

2.2.1. This presumes that faith is the great thing that Jesus Christ looks for. He does not ask, "Is there innocence?" but, "Is there faith?"

2.2.2. It presumes that if there were faith, even if it was very little, he would find it.

2.2.3. It is foretold that when Christ comes, he will find only *little faith* (12:28).

2.2.3.1. In general, he will find only a few good people. He will find many who have the form and fashion of godliness, but few who have faith, few who are sincere and honest.

2.2.3.2. In particular, he will find few who have faith about his coming. It suggests that Christ may and will delay his coming until:

- Evildoers will begin to defy it, and his delay will harden them in their evil (Mt 24:48).
- Even his own people will begin to despair of it. However, our comfort is that when the appointed time comes, it will be seen that human unbelief has not nullified the promises of God.

Verses 9–14

The scope of this parable, too, is given before it. Christ intended it to convict some who *trusted in themselves that they were righteous, and despised others.*

- They were those who had a high opinion of themselves; they thought they were as holy as they needed to be and holier than all their neighbors.
- They were self-confident before God. They *trusted in themselves as being righteous*; they thought that God was indebted to them.
- They despised others. This is called a parable even though there is nothing comparative in it. It happens every day.

1. Here are both of these men taking up the duty of prayer at the same place and time (v. 10): *Two men went up into the temple to pray.* It was not the hour of public prayer; they went there to offer their personal devotions. The *Pharisee* and the *publican* (tax collector) both went *to the temple to pray.* Among the worshipers of God there is a mixture of good and bad people. The Pharisee, proud as he was, could not think himself above prayer; nor could the tax collector, humble as he was, think himself excluded from its benefit. The Pharisee went to the temple to pray because it was a public place, where many people would be looking at him. The description Christ gave of the Pharisees, that *all their works they did to be seen of men* (Mt 23:5), gives us cause for this suspicion. There are many whom we see every day at the temple who, it is to be feared, will not be seen in the great day at Christ's right hand. The Pharisee came to the temple to pay a compliment, the tax collector on business; the Pharisee went to make his appearance, the tax collector to make his request. God sees what our attitudes and intentions are when we come to look to him.

2. Here is the Pharisee's address to God—we cannot call it a prayer: he *stood* and *prayed thus with himself* (vv. 11–12); "standing by himself, he prayed in this way," as some read it; he was wholly intent on himself, had nothing in mind except himself, not God's glory. What is thought to say here shows:

2.1. That he considered himself righteous. He said very many good things about himself, which we suppose were true. He was not an *extortioner.* He was not *unjust* in any of his dealings; he did no one any wrong; he was no *adulterer.* But this was not all: he *fasted twice in the week.* This is how he glorified God with his body; yet even that was not all: he *gave tithes of all that he possessed* and so glorified God with his worldly possessions. But he was not accepted, and why not?

2.1.1. His giving God thanks for this seems to have been a mere formality. He did not say, *By the grace of God I am what I am* (1Co 15:10), as Paul did, but spoke offhandedly: *God, I thank thee.*

2.1.2. He boasted as if all his duty in the temple were to tell God Almighty how very good he was.

2.1.3. He trusted in it as his righteousness.

2.1.4. There is not one word of prayer in anything he said. He went *up to the temple to pray*, but forgot why he went. He thought he needed nothing, not even the favor and grace of God, which it seems he did not think worth asking for.

2.2. That he despised others.

2.2.1. He thought disapprovingly of everyone except himself: *I thank thee that I am not as other men are.* We may have reason to thank God that we are not as some people are, but to speak as if only we were good is to judge indiscriminately.

2.2.2. He thought especially disapprovingly of this tax collector. He knew that he was a tax collector, and so he had concluded, very uncharitably, that he was an *extortioner, unjust,* and all that is wrong. Suppose it had been so: what business had he to take notice of it? Could he not say his prayers without rebuking his neighbors? Was he as much pleased with the tax collector's badness as with his own goodness?

3. Here is the tax collector's prayer to God, which was the opposite of the Pharisee's, as full of humility and humiliation as the Pharisee's was of pride and ostentation, as full of repentance for sin and desire toward God as the Pharisee's was of confidence in himself.

3.1. He expressed his repentance and humility in what he did.

3.1.1. He *stood afar off.* The tax collector *kept at a distance* out of a sense of unworthiness to draw near to God. Here he acknowledged that God could justly *behold him afar off*, and that it was a great favor that God was willing to allow him to come so close.

3.1.2. He *would not lift up so much as his eyes to heaven.* He did lift up his heart to God in the heavens, in holy desires, but out of great shame and humiliation he did not lift up his eyes in holy confidence and courage. The dejection of his looks showed the dejection of his heart and mind at the thoughts of his sin.

3.1.3. He *smote upon his breast* (beat his chest). First, the sinner's heart strikes him in a penitent rebuke (2Sa 24:10). "Sinner, what have you done?" Then he strikes his heart with penitent remorse: *O wretched man that I am* (Ro 7:24).

3.2. He expressed it in what he said. His prayer was short. Sighs and groans swallowed up his words, but what he said was to the point: *God, be merciful to me a sinner.* Thank God that we have this prayer on record as an answered prayer.

3.2.1. He acknowledged himself to be a sinner by nature and by practice, guilty before God. The Pharisee denied he was a sinner, but the tax collector gave himself no other description than that of a sinner.

3.2.2. He depended on nothing except the mercy of God. The Pharisee had insisted on the merit of his fasting and tithes, but the poor tax collector disclaimed all thought of merit and fled directly to mercy as his city of refuge (Nu 35:6). "Justice condemns me; nothing will save me except sheer mercy."

3.2.3. He fervently prayed to receive the benefit of that mercy: *"O God, be merciful*, be favorable, *to me."* He came as a beggar who seeks alms when he is about to die for hunger. Probably he repeated this prayer with renewed devotion; this was the chorus of his song: *God, be merciful to me a sinner.*

4. Here is the tax collector's acceptance with God. Some would praise the Pharisee and look down with contempt on this sneaking, whining tax collector. However, our Lord Jesus assures us that this poor, penitent, broken-hearted tax collector *went to his house justified, rather than the other.* The Pharisee thought that if one of them must be justified and not the other, certainly it would be he rather than the tax collector. "No," Christ said, *"I tell you,* it is the tax collector rather than the Pharisee." The proud Pharisee went away rejected by God; he was not justified. He was not accepted as righteous in God's sight, because he was so righteous in his own sight, but the tax collector obtained forgiveness of his sins; the one whom the Pharisee would not put *with the dogs of his flock* (Job 30:1) was put by God with the children of his

family. Proud people, who exalt themselves, are rivals with God, and so they shall certainly be humbled. Humble people, who abase themselves, are subject to God, and they will be exalted. Notice how the punishment corresponds to the sin: *He that exalteth himself shall be abased.* Notice how the reward corresponds to the duty: *He that humbles himself shall be exalted* (v. 14). Notice, too, the power of God's grace in bringing good out of evil; the tax collector had been a great sinner, and out of the greatness of his sin he was brought the greatness of his repentance. It was good that the Pharisee was not an extortioner or unjust, but the Devil made him proud of this, to his destruction.

Verses 15–17

1. Those who are themselves blessed in Christ should want to have their children also blessed in him. People here brought to him *infants,* very young children, not able to walk, still drinking their mothers' milk, as some think. No one is too little or too young to be brought to Christ.

2. One gracious touch of Christ's will make our children happy. They *brought infants to him, that he might touch them.*

3. It is not strange for those who turn to Jesus Christ—for themselves or for their children—to meet with discouragement: *When the disciples saw it, they rebuked them.*

4. Many whom the disciples rebuke are invited by the Master: *Jesus called them unto him.*

5. It is the desire of Christ that *little children* be brought to him: "*Suffer* (let) *little children to come to me, and forbid them not;* let nothing be done to hinder them, because they will be as welcome as anyone."

6. The children of those who belong to the kingdom of God also belong to that kingdom, just as the children of freemen are freemen also.

7. Those adults who have within them the clearest disposition and attitude of children are the most welcome to him: *Whosoever shall not receive the kingdom of God as a little child* (v. 17). That refers to those who receive its benefits with humility and thankfulness, gladly acknowledging themselves indebted to free grace for them. Unless a person is brought to this self-denying attitude, they will *in no wise enter* that kingdom.

Verses 18–30

In these verses we have:

1. Christ's conversation with a ruler, who had a good intention to be directed by him on the way to heaven. Here we may notice:

1.1. Luke notices that he was a ruler. Few of the rulers had any respect for Christ, but here was one who did.

1.2. The great thing that each of us should be concerned to seek is *what we shall do to inherit eternal life.*

1.3. Those who want to inherit eternal life must turn to Jesus Christ as their *Master,* as both their teaching Master and their ruling Master. There is no way of learning the way to heaven except in the school of Christ.

1.4. Those who come to Christ as their Master must believe that he has not only a divine mission but also divine goodness (v. 19): "*Why callest thou me good?* You know *there is none good but one, that is, God.*"

1.5. Our Master, Christ himself, has not changed the way to heaven from what it was before his coming, but has only made it plainer, easier, and more assured. "*Thou knowest the commandments.* Do you want to inherit eternal life? Live your life according to the commandments."

1.6. The duties of the second table of the Ten Commandments must be conscientiously observed. Nor is it enough to keep ourselves free from gross violations of these commandments; we must know these commandments in their full extent and spiritual nature.

1.7. People think they are innocent because they are ignorant; this was the mistake of this ruler. He said, *All these have I kept from my youth up* (v. 21). He boasted that he began to be good early in life, that he had continued to lead such a life to this day, and that he had not disobeyed in any instance. If he really knew the nature of the divine law and the workings of his own heart, if he had really been one of Christ's disciples for a while, he would have said completely the opposite: "*All these have I* broken from my youth up."

1.8. The great things by which we are to test our spiritual state are our attitudes toward Christ and our brothers and sisters, toward this world and toward the next. If the ruler had a true love for Christ, he would *come and follow him,* whatever it might cost him. No one will inherit eternal life who is unwilling to follow the Lamb wherever he goes (Rev 14:4). If he had a true love for his brothers and sisters, he would *distribute to the poor.* If he had a low opinion of this world, he would not stop short of *selling what he had* to relieve God's poor. If he thought highly of the next world, he would desire no more than to have *treasure in heaven.*

1.9. There are many who have a great deal in them that is very commendable but who perish for lack of some one thing; so it would be with this ruler here. He left Christ because of this one condition that would come between him and his wealth.

1.10. Many who are reluctant to leave Christ still do leave him. Their corruptions win. If either God or mammon must be left, it will be their God.

2. Christ's talk with his disciples on this occasion, in which we may notice:

2.1. Riches are a great hindrance to many people on their way to heaven. Christ *saw that* the ruler *was very sorrowful,* and he was sad for him, but he concluded from this, *How hardly* (With what difficulty) *shall they that have riches enter into the kingdom of God!* (v. 24). Having great wealth, he was greatly influenced by it, and he preferred to leave Christ rather than put himself under the obligation of disposing of his wealth for charitable use. Christ emphatically asserted the difficulty of the salvation of rich people: *It is easier for a camel to go through a needle's eye than for a rich man to enter into the kingdom of God* (v. 25).

2.2. It is really very hard for anyone to reach heaven. If we must either *sell all* or break away from Christ, *who then can be saved?* (v. 26). The disciples did not find fault with what Christ required, calling it hard and unreasonable. However, they knew how closely the hearts of most people cling to this world, and so they were ready to despair of ever being brought to this.

2.3. There are difficulties in the way of our salvation that could never be overcome except by God's almighty grace. The *things which are impossible with men are possible with God.* His grace can work on the soul so as to change its inclination and bias and give it an opposite leaning.

2.4. There is a tendency in us to speak too much about what we have left and lost for Christ. This appears in Peter: *Lo, we have left all, and followed thee* (v. 28). When he had a chance, he could not stop exalting the love he and his brothers' had shown for Christ by leaving everything to follow him.

2.5. Whatever we have left for Christ will without fail be abundantly made up to us in this world and the world to come (vv. 29–30): *No man has left* the comfort of his possessions or relatives *for the kingdom of God's sake, who shall not receive manifold more in this present time,* in the delights of fellowship with God and of a good conscience, advantages that will abundantly make up for all his losses. In the world to come he *shall receive life everlasting,* which is what that the ruler seemed to have his eye and heart set on.

Verses 31–34

Here is:

1. The notice Christ gave to his disciples of his sufferings and approaching death and of the glorious outcome of these events. Two things are stated here that we did not have in the other Evangelists' accounts:

1.1. The sufferings of Christ are spoken of here as the fulfilling of the Scriptures: *All things that are written by the prophets concerning the Son of man shall be accomplished* (fulfilled). That the Scriptures are the word of God is proven by the fact that they were completely fulfilled, and that Jesus Christ was sent from God was proven by the fact that they were fulfilled in him. This makes the *offence of the cross to cease* (Gal 5:11) and gives it honor. *Thus it was written, and thus it behoved* (was necessary for) *Christ to suffer* (24:46).

1.2. The shame and disgrace shown to Christ in his sufferings are insisted on very much here. The other Evangelists had said that he would be mocked, but here it is added, *He shall be spitefully treated,* insulted in every possible way. Here, however, as always, when Christ spoke about his sufferings and death, he foretold his resurrection as what took away both the terror and the shame of his sufferings: *The third day he shall rise again.*

2. The confusion that the disciples were put into by this. This went so much against the ideas they had of the Messiah and his kingdom that *they understood none of these things* (v. 34). Their prejudice was so strong that they would not understand them literally, and they could not understand them in any other way, and so they did not understand them at all. This saying was *hidden from them;* they could not receive it. They were so intent on those prophecies that spoke about his glory that they overlooked those that spoke of his sufferings. People run into mistakes because they read their Bibles incompletely, and they are as limited in their reading of the Prophets as in their reading of the Law. In this way we become too inclined, in reading the prophecies that are still to be fulfilled, to have our expectations raised concerning the glorious state of the church in the last days, and so we overlook its desert sackcloth state and are willing to think that that is over.

Verses 35–43

Christ came not only to bring light to a dark world, and so to set before us the objects we are to look at, but also to give sight to blind souls, to enable them to view those things. Here is an account of one man to whom he gave sight near Jericho. Mark gives us an account of one whom he healed *as he went out of Jericho,* and he names him (Mk 10:46). Matthew speaks of two whom he healed *as they departed* from Jericho (Mt 20:30). Luke says it was "when he was near" Jericho. Notice:

1. This poor blind man *sat by the wayside, begging* (v. 35). It seems that he was not only blind but also poor, a very apt picture of the human race that Christ came to heal and save. He sat begging because he was blind

and could not work for his living. Such objects of charity along the road should not be overlooked by us. Christ looks favorably on *a common beggar* here.

2. Hearing the noise of a crowd of people passing by, he asked *what it meant* (v. 36). We did not have this before. It teaches us that it is good to be inquisitive and that those who are so will at one time or another benefit from it. Those who lack their sight should make better use of their hearing; when they cannot see with their own eyes, they should make use of other people's eyes by asking questions. This was what this blind man did, and that was how he came to understand that *Jesus of Nazareth passed by* (v. 37).

3. His prayer contains a great deal of both faith and fervency: *Jesus, thou Son of David, have mercy on me* (v. 38). He believed Jesus could help him, and he sincerely begged his favor: "*Have mercy on me.*" It is enough to pray, *Have mercy on us,* because Christ's mercy includes everything.

4. Those who are serious about seeking Christ's favors and blessings will not be put off from pursuing them even if they meet with opposition and rebuke. People who walked along rebuked the blind man as causing trouble to the Master, as being noisy and cheeky, and told him to *hold his peace.* But the restraint imposed on him was merely like a dam to a full river, which makes it swell even more: he *cried the louder, Thou Son of David, have mercy on me.*

5. Christ encourages poor beggars and invites them to come to him: *He commanded him to be brought to him.* Christ has more tenderness and compassion for distressed petitioners than any of his followers have. Those who had restrained the blind man must now lend him their hands to help him go to Christ.

6. Although Christ knows all our needs, he wants to know them from us (v. 41): *What wilt thou that I shall do unto thee?* This man poured out his soul to Christ when he said, *Lord, that I may receive my sight.*

7. The prayer of faith will not be offered in vain (v. 42). Christ said, *Receive thy sight; thy faith hath saved thee.* True faith will produce zeal in prayer, and both together will bring in many fruits of Christ's favor.

8. The grace of Christ should be thankfully acknowledged (v. 43).

8.1. The poor beggar himself, who had his sight restored, *followed Christ, glorifying God.* Those whom Christ healed pleased him best when they *praised God,* as those who praise Christ and give him honor will please God best.

8.2. The *people that saw it* could not stop *giving praise to God.* We must give praise to God for his mercies to others as well as for mercies to ourselves.

CHAPTER 19

In this chapter we have: 1. The conversion of Zacchaeus the tax collector at Jericho (vv. 1–10). 2. The parable of the king who entrusted pounds (minas) to his servants and had rebellious subjects (vv. 11–27). 3. Christ's riding in triumph into Jerusalem and mourning as he viewed the prospect of the ruin of that city (vv. 28–44). 4. His teaching in the temple and driving the buyers and sellers out of it (vv. 45–48).

Verses 1–10

No doubt many people of whom no account is kept in the Gospels were converted to the faith of Christ, but the conversion of some whose cases were extraordinary are recorded, such as this of Zacchaeus. Christ passed through Jericho (v. 1). This city was built under a curse (Jos 6:26; 1Ki 16:34), but Christ still honored it with his presence, because the Gospel takes away the curse. Notice:

1. Who and what this Zacchaeus was. His name shows he was a Jew. Consider:

1.1. His calling and his job: *He was the chief among the publicans.* We often read of tax collectors coming to Christ, but here one sought him who was chief of the tax collectors. God has his remnant among all kinds of people. Christ came to save even the chief sinners (1Ti 1:15), and therefore even the chief tax collectors.

1.2. His circumstances in the world were very considerable: *He was rich.* Christ had just shown how hard it is for rich people to enter the kingdom of God, but immediately he produced an example of one rich man who had been lost and was found, and not as the prodigal son had been found, by being reduced to great need (15:11–32).

2. How he came in Christ's path.

2.1. He was very curious to see Jesus (v. 3). It is natural for us to want to see those whose fame we have heard much about; at least we will be able to say later that we have seen such and such famous people. We should now seek to see Jesus with the eye of faith, to see who he is: *We would see Jesus* (Jn 12:21).

2.2. He could not have his curiosity satisfied in this way, because he was short and the crowd was large. Christ did not seek to show himself, but, like one of us, was lost in a crowd. Zacchaeus was *low of stature* and overshadowed by others, so that he could not see Jesus. Many people who are short have large souls and are spiritually dynamic.

2.3. Determined not to be disappointed in his curiosity, he forgot his dignity, ran out like a boy, and climbed up into a sycamore-fig tree to see Jesus. Those who sincerely want to see Christ will use the proper means to see him. Those who find themselves little must take every advantage they can get to lift themselves up to see Christ. Let short people not despair: if they have good help and aim high, they will be able to reach high.

3. The notice Christ took of him, the call he gave him to come to know him further (v. 5), and the effectiveness of that call (v. 6).

3.1. Christ invited himself to Zacchaeus's house. Christ looked up into the tree and saw Zacchaeus. Zacchaeus came to look at Christ, but he little thought of being taken notice of by Christ. Notice how Christ went before him with the blessings of his goodness, surpassing his expectations; notice, too, how he encouraged very small beginnings. Zacchaeus, who had a mind to know Christ, would be known by him; the one who only wanted to catch a glimpse of him would be allowed to speak to him. Sometimes those who come to hear the word of Christ only out of curiosity, as Zacchaeus did, have their consciences woken up and their hearts changed. Christ called him *by name, Zaccheus.* He told him to *make haste, and come down.* Zacchaeus must not hesitate, but hurry. He must come down, because Christ intended this day to stay at his house, to spend an hour or two with him.

3.2. Zacchaeus was overjoyed to have such an honor shown to his house (v. 6): *He made haste, and came down, and received him joyfully,* and his receiving him into his house was a sign of his receiving him into his heart. How often, when Christ has said to us, *Open to me,* have we made excuses (SS 5:2–3)! Zacchaeus's eagerness to receive Christ will shame us.

4. The offense that the people took. Those narrow-souled, ungenerous, critical Jews *murmured,* saying that he had *gone to be a guest with a man that is a sinner;* and yet were they not sinners themselves? Was it not Christ's mission to seek and save sinners? Now it was very unjust to blame Christ for going to Zacchaeus's house.

4.1. Even though he was *a tax collector,* and many of the tax collectors were bad, it did not follow that they were all like that. We must be careful not to condemn people generally, because in God's law court everyone will be judged as they are.

4.2. Even though he had been a sinner, it did not follow that he was now as bad as he had been. God allows opportunity for repentance, and so must we.

4.3. Even though he was now a sinner, they should not blame Christ for going to him. Where should the doctor go to but to those who are sick?

5. The proofs that Zacchaeus gave publicly that he was now a penitent (v. 8). By his good works he would show the sincerity of his faith and repentance. He stood, which showed his saying it deliberately and seriously, as a vow to God. He spoke it to Christ, not to the people but to the Lord. He made it clear that there was a change in his heart—repentance—by a change in his ways.

5.1. Zacchaeus had great wealth, but he now decided that for the future he would live wholly for God and do good to others with it: *Behold, Lord, the half of my goods I give to the poor.* "I give it now," Zacchaeus said; "although up to this time I have been uncharitable to the poor, I will now relieve them, giving all the more because I have neglected the duty so long—even *half of my goods.*" Zacchaeus would give one half to the poor, which would make him cut down on all his extravagant expenses. He mentioned this here as a fruit of his repentance.

5.2. Zacchaeus knew that he had not gained all he had honestly and fairly. He promised to make restitution: "If *I have taken anything from any man by false accusation,* exacting more than was appointed, I promise to pay them back *four-fold.*"

5.2.1. He clearly acknowledged, it seems, that he had done wrong. True penitents will not only acknowledge themselves guilty before God in general; they will also reflect on what has been their particular sin, what has entangled them most easily, because of their business and employment in the world.

5.2.2. He admitted that he had done wrong *by false accusation.* Tax collectors had the ear of the government, which gave them an opportunity to satisfy their revenge if they bore anyone ill will.

5.2.3. He promised to restore *four-fold.* He did not say, "If I am sued and compelled to make payment, I will make restitution"—some are honest when they cannot help it—but that he would do so voluntarily. Those who are convinced that they have done wrong can show evidence of the sincerity of their repentance only by making restitution. Zacchaeus did not think that his giving half his wealth to the poor would atone for the wrong he had done. It is no act of love, but hypocrisy, to give what does not belong to us, and we are not to count as our own what we have not come by honestly.

6. Christ's approval and acceptance of Zacchaeus's conversion (vv. 9–10).

6.1. Zacchaeus was declared to be now a happy man. *This day is salvation come to this house.* Now that he had been converted, he was in effect saved. Christ had come to his house, and where Christ comes, he also brings salvation with him. This is not all, however. On this day salvation came *to his house.*

6.1.1. When Zacchaeus became a convert, he would be, more than he had been, a blessing to his house. He would bring the means of grace and salvation to his house. He who is loving to the poor does a kindness to his own house and brings a blessing on it.

6.1.2. When Zacchaeus himself was brought to Christ, his family also became related to Christ, and so *salvation came to his house*. By coming to Christ, he became *a son of Abraham*, and so the blessing given to Abraham that God would be a God *to him and to his children* came on Zacchaeus through faith. Zacchaeus was by birth a son of Abraham, but, being a tax collector, he was regarded as a pagan. By being a true penitent, he had become as good a son of Abraham as if he had never been a tax collector.

6.2. What Christ had done was consistent with the great purpose of his coming into the world (v. 10). He had used the same argument before to justify his associating with tax collectors (Mt 9:13). He pleaded there that he came to *call sinners to repentance* (5:32); now he pleaded that he came to *seek and save that which was lost*. Notice:

6.2.1. The deplorable case of human beings: they were lost. The whole human race, through the Fall, has become a lost world: as travelers are lost when they have lost their way in a desert, as the sick are lost when their disease is incurable.

6.2.2. The gracious intention of the Son of God: he came to *seek and save*, to seek in order to save. He took the long journey from heaven to earth to seek what was lost — what had *wandered and gone astray* — and to bring it back (Mt 18:11 – 12); and he came to save what was lost, what was perishing. Christ undertook the cause when it was given up as lost. Christ came into this lost world to seek and save it. His intention was to save. In pursuit of that plan, he *sought*; he used all probable means to bring about that salvation. He seeks those who did not seek him (Isa 65:1; Ro 10:20) or ask for him, like Zacchaeus here.

Verses 11 – 27

Our Lord Jesus was now on his way to Jerusalem, to his last Passover. We are told:

1. How the expectations of his friends were raised on this occasion: *They thought that the kingdom of God would immediately appear* (v. 11). The Pharisees expected it about this time (17:20), and it seems Christ's own disciples did too. The disciples thought that their Master would introduce it, but with real pride and power. They concluded that Jerusalem must be the seat of his kingdom, and so, now that he was going directly there, they did not doubt that in a short time they would see him on the throne there. Even good people are subject to mistakes about the kingdom of Christ.

2. How their expectations were restrained, and their mistakes rectified. He did this in three things:

2.1. They expected him to appear in his glory without any delay now, but he told them that he must not be publicly installed in his kingdom for a great while yet. He was like *a certain nobleman* who *went into a far country to receive for himself a kingdom*. He must receive the kingdom and then *return*. Christ returned when the Spirit was poured out, and again when Jerusalem was destroyed. However, what is chiefly meant here is his return at the great day, which we are still expecting.

2.2. They expected his apostles and immediate followers to be promoted to positions of dignity and honor, that they would all be made rulers and peers, privy councillors and judges, and have all the pomp and advancement of the court and of the city. But Christ told them here that instead he intended them to be businesspeople; they must expect no other promotion in this world than promotion to a trade. He would set them up with stock, and they

themselves must use it to serve him and the interests of his kingdom on earth. The true honor of a Christian and a minister is the kind that will enable us to look on all temporal honors with holy contempt. The apostles had dreamed of *sitting on his right hand and on his left in his kingdom* (Mt 20:21), and they were pleasing themselves with this dream, but Christ told them what would fill them with serious thoughts instead of those aspiring ones.

2.2.1. They had a great work to do now. Their Master would soon leave them, and as they parted he would give each of them *a pound*. This stands for the same thing as the talents in the parable that is parallel to this (Mt 25:14 – 30). However, perhaps the gift was represented in the parable as a mere *pound* to make them more humble; their honor in this world was only that of traders, not that of high-quality merchants. The master gave these pounds to his servants with this charge: *Occupy till I come*. Or, as it might much better be translated, "Do business with this till I come; be busy; put this money to work. Take care of your business, and make a business out of it; set about it seriously, and stick at it."

2.2.1.1. All Christians, especially ministers, have work to do for Christ in this world; the former were not baptized, nor the latter ordained, to be idle.

2.2.1.2. He provides those who are called to work for him with the necessary gifts for their business, and, on the other hand, he expects service from those he gives power to. He hands over the *pounds* with this command: "Do business with them."

2.2.1.3. We must continue to take care of our business *till our Master comes*.

2.2.2. They had an important account to give soon. These servants were *called to him that he might know what every man had gained by trading*.

2.2.2.1. Those who trade diligently and faithfully in the service of Christ will be gainers. Many hardworking traders have lost money, but those who trade for Christ will be gainers.

2.2.2.2. The conversion of souls is winning them; every true convert is a clear gain for Jesus Christ. Ministers are merely agents for him, and they must give an account to him of what fish they have caught in the Gospel net, that is, what they have gained by trading. Notice:

2.2.2.2.1. The good account that was given by some of the servants, and notice also the master's approval of them. Examples are given of two such people (vv. 16, 19):

2.2.2.2.1.1. They had both made a considerable profit, but not both the same; one had gained ten pounds by his trading, and another five. All who are equally faithful are not equally successful. Perhaps, although they were both faithful, one of them worked harder and applied himself more closely to his business than the other, and was therefore more effective.

2.2.2.2.1.2. They both acknowledged their obligations to their Master: "Lord, it is not my diligence but *thy pound that has gained ten pounds*." God must receive all the glory for all our gains.

2.2.2.2.1.3. They were both commended for their faithfulness and diligence: *Well done, thou good servant* (v. 17). He spoke to the other similarly (v. 19). If he says "Well done," it does not matter so much who says otherwise.

2.2.2.2.1.4. They were promoted in proportion to the return they had made on what had been given them: "Because you have been faithful in a very little, take charge of ten cities." Those who are likely to rise far are those who are content to begin low. Two things were promised to the apostles:

2.2.2.2.1.4.1. That when they worked hard to plant many churches, great respect would be shown them and they would have a great share in the love and respect of good Christians.

2.2.2.2.1.4.2. That when they had served their generation according to the will of Christ (Ac 13:36), in the next world they would reign as kings with Christ. The happiness of heaven will be a much greater advancement to a good minister or Christian than being made governor of ten cities would be to a poor trader. The one who gained only *five pounds* had authority over *five cities*. There are degrees of glory in heaven; every vessel will be full, but not all equally large. The degrees of glory there will be according to the degrees of usefulness here.

2.2.2.2.2. The bad account that was given by one of them and the sentence passed on him (v. 20).

2.2.2.2.2.1. He acknowledged that he had not traded with the pound with which he had been entrusted (v. 20): "*Lord, behold, here is thy pound;* it is true, I have not made it more, but neither have I made it less; I have kept it safely *laid up in a napkin* (piece of cloth)." This represents the carelessness of those who have gifts but never give themselves to do any good with them. It is all the same to them whether the interests of Christ's kingdom sink or swim, go backward or forward; for their part, they are unconcerned about it. Those who think it enough to say that they have done no harm in the world, but who have not done any good either, are the servants who store their pound in a piece of cloth.

2.2.2.2.2.2. He justified himself with a plea that made matters worse, not better (v. 21): *I feared thee, because thou art an austere man,* a stern man: *Thou takest up that which thou laidst not down.* This servant thought his master *reaped where he did not sow,* whereas in reality he reaped where he had sown. The servant had no reason to fear his master's sternness. This excuse was complete sham, a frivolous, unjustified excuse for his laziness.

2.2.2.2.2.3. His excuse was turned back on him: *Out of thine own mouth will I judge thee, thou wicked servant* (v. 22). He would be condemned by his crime, but self-condemned by his plea. "If you had had any regard for my interest at all, you could at least have put my money *into the bank,* so that I might have had not only *my own* money but also my own *with usury* (interest)." If he dared not trade for fear of losing the capital sum, nevertheless, that would be no excuse for not putting it on deposit with a bank, where it would be safe and still earn interest. Whatever lazy professors of the faith may claim to excuse their laziness, the true reason for it is a prevalent indifference to the interests of Christ and his kingdom. They do not care whether religious faith gains ground or loses ground, as long as they can live in comfort.

2.2.2.2.2.4. His pound was taken from him (v. 24). It is right for those who will not use their gifts to lose them. *Take from him the pound.*

2.2.2.2.2.5. The pound was given to the one who had the *ten pounds.* When this was objected to because he had so much already — *Lord, he has ten pounds* (v. 25) — it was answered (v. 26), *Unto everyone that hath shall be given.* It is the rule of justice:

2.2.2.2.2.5.1. That those who have worked the hardest should be most encouraged. More will be given to the one who has made a profit, so that he may be in a position to gain even more.

2.2.2.2.2.5.2. That those who have their gifts as if they did not have them should be deprived of them. To those who try to increase the grace they have, God will give more; those who neglect it and allow it to become less can expect nothing other than that God will do so too.

2.3. Another thing they expected was that when the kingdom of God appeared, most of the Jewish nation would immediately fall in with it, but Christ told his disciples that after his departure most of the Jews would persist in their stubborn rebellion. This is shown here:

2.3.1. In the message the subjects sent after the man who was to be made king (v. 14). When he had gone to be invested in his kingdom, they then continued their hostility toward him, saying, *We will not have this man to reign over us.*

2.3.1.1. This was fulfilled in the great unfaithfulness of the Jews after the ascension of Christ. They would not submit themselves to his yoke.

2.3.1.2. It speaks the language of all unbelievers; they were content for Christ to save them, but they did not want him to reign over them.

2.3.2. In the sentence passed on them at his return: *Those mine enemies bring hither* (v. 27). When his faithful subjects were promoted and rewarded, he would then take vengeance on his enemies. The kingdom of God appeared when vengeance was taken on those irreconcilable enemies to Christ and his government; they were brought out and put to death before him. However, this is applicable also to all others who persist in their unfaithfulness. Complete destruction will certainly be the fate of all Christ's enemies. "Bring them here, to have their frivolous pleas overruled and to receive sentence according to what they have deserved." Those who *will not have Christ to reign over them* will be considered enemies and dealt with as such. We are ready to think that only those who persecute Christianity are Christ's enemies; however, those who will not submit to Christ's discipline, but want to be their own masters, will be considered his enemies too. Whoever will not be ruled by the grace of Christ will inevitably be ruined by the wrath of Christ.

Verses 28 – 40

We have here the same account of Christ's riding in triumph into Jerusalem that we had before in Matthew and Mark.

1. Jesus Christ was eager and willing to suffer and die for us. He went forward *to Jerusalem;* he knew very well the things that would happen to him there, but *he went before, ascending up to Jerusalem* (v. 28). He led the way. Was he so eager to suffer and die for us, and will we draw back from any service we are able to do for him?

2. It was in no way inconsistent either with Christ's humility or with this present state of humiliation to make a public entry into Jerusalem shortly before he died. By attracting more attention, he would make the shame of his death appear greater.

3. Christ is entitled to power over all creatures. Christ sent disciples to fetch a donkey and its colt from their owner and master's crib when he needed them for their service.

4. Christ has the hearts of all people both under his eye and in his hand. He could influence those to whom the donkey and the colt belonged so that they would agree to let them be taken away as soon as they were told that the Lord needed them.

5. Those who go on Christ's missions are sure to be successful (v. 32). It is encouraging to Christ's messengers that if the Lord really has a use for something, they will certainly return with it when they are sent for it.

6. The disciples of Christ, who take what he needs from others, should not think that is enough; they should be

ready to serve him with whatever they themselves have, anything with which he may be served. Those disciples not only took the donkey's colt for him but also *cast their own garments upon the colt.*

7. Christ's triumphs are the matter of his disciples' praises. When Christ came near Jerusalem, God suddenly put it into the hearts of a *whole multitude of the disciples,* not only of the Twelve, *to rejoice and praise God* (v. 37) and to *spread their clothes in the way* (v. 36), which was a common expression of joy. Notice:

7.1. What was the cause or occasion of their joy and praise. They praised God *for all the mighty works they had seen,* especially the *raising of Lazarus,* which is mentioned specifically in John's account of the same events (Jn 12:17–18).

7.2. How they expressed their joy and praise (v. 38): *Blessed be the king that cometh in the name of the Lord* (Ps 118:26). Christ is *the king;* he *comes in the name of the Lord. Blessed be he.* Let us praise him; may God prosper him. *Peace in heaven.* May the God of heaven send peace and bring success to his undertaking, and then there will be *glory in the highest.* Compare this song of the saints on earth with that of the angels (2:14). The two choirs agreed to give *glory to God in the highest.* The angels said, *On earth peace.* The saints said, *Peace in heaven.* Such is the fellowship we have with the holy angels that just as they rejoice in the peace on earth, so we also rejoice in the peace in heaven.

8. Christ's triumphs and his disciples' joyful praises of them troubled the proud Pharisees. There were some Pharisees among the crowd who were enraged at those who praised Christ. Having heard of his humility, they thought that he would not accept such acclamations as these, and so they expected him to rebuke his disciples (v. 39). But just as he despises the contempt of the proud, so he also accepts the praises of the humble.

9. Whether human beings praise Christ or not, he will and must be praised (v. 40): *If these should hold their peace, the stones would immediately cry out,* rather than let Christ go without praise. Pharisees tried to silence the praises of Christ, but they could not win their point, because just as God can raise up children to Abraham out of stones (Mt 3:9), so he can also *perfect praise out of the mouths* of those children (Ps 8:2; Mt 21:16).

Verses 41–48

The great Ambassador from heaven is here making his public entry into Jerusalem, not to be respected there, but to be rejected. See here two examples of his love and concern for that place:

1. The tears he shed for the approaching ruin of the city (v. 41): *When he was come near, he beheld the city, and wept over it.* It was probably when he was coming down from the Mount of Olives, where he had a full view of the city, and his eye moved his heart, and his heart moved his eye again. Notice here:

1.1. What a tender spirit Christ had; we never read that he laughed, but we often find him in tears.

1.2. That Jesus Christ wept when everyone around him was rejoicing, to show how little he was lifted up by the applause and acclamation of the people.

1.3. That he *wept over Jerusalem.* There are cities to be wept over, and none to be more lamented than Jerusalem. But why did Christ weep at the sight of Jerusalem? He himself gives us the reason for his tears.

1.3.1. Jerusalem had not made the most of the day of her opportunities. He wept and said, *If thou hadst known, even thou at least in this thy day, the things that belong to thy peace—but* thou *dost not know the day of thy visitation* (v. 44). The expression is abrupt: *If thou hadst known!* "Oh that you had" is how some read it. Or, "If you had borne fruit, fine! (13:9). How beneficial it would have been for you." What he said put all the blame for Jerusalem's impending ruin on herself. This shows us:

1.3.1.1. There are things that *belong to our peace,* that we are all obligated to know and understand. The things that belong to our peace are those things that concern our present and future welfare; we must know these with conviction.

1.3.1.2. There is a *time of visitation* when the things that *belong to our peace* can be known by us. When we enjoy the means of grace in great plenty and have the word of God powerfully preached to us, then is *the time of visitation.*

1.3.1.3. With those who have long neglected the time of God's coming to them, if at last their eyes are opened and they come to themselves (15:17), all will still be well. Those who come into the vineyard *at the eleventh hour* (Mt 20:6, 9) will not be refused.

1.3.1.4. It is the amazing foolishness of many who enjoy the means of grace that they do not make the most of the day of their opportunities. The things that would bring them peace are revealed to them, but they do not want to pay any attention to them; they shut their eyes to them. They are not aware of the *accepted time* and the *day of salvation* (2Co 6:2) and therefore let it slip, and so they perish through sheer carelessness. There are none so blind as those who will not see.

1.3.1.5. The sin and foolishness of those who persist in showing their contempt for Gospel grace are a source of great grief to the Lord Jesus, and should also be so to us. He looks with weeping eyes on lost souls, those that remain impenitent. He would rather have them *turn and live* (Eze 18:32) than go on and die, because he is not willing that any should perish (2Pe 3:9).

1.3.2. Jerusalem could not escape the day of her destruction. The *things of her peace* were now in a way hidden from her eyes. This is not to say that after this the Gospel was not preached to them by the apostles; indeed, many were convinced and converted. But as to most of the nation, and its leading part, they were sealed in their unbelief. They were justly given up to judicial blindness and hardness. Neglecting the great salvation (Heb 2:3) often brings temporal judgments on a people; it brought them on Jerusalem.

1.3.2.1. The Romans besieged the city, *cast a trench* (built an embankment) *about it, compassed it round* (encircled it), and *kept their* inhabitants in *on every side.*

1.3.2.2. They *laid it even with the ground.* Titus commanded his soldiers to dig up the city, and the whole area of it was leveled except three towers. Not only the city but also the citizens were leveled to the ground—*thy children within thee*—by the cruel slaughter carried out on them, and scarcely one stone was *left upon another.* This was because they *knew not the day of their visitation.*

2. The zeal he showed for the present purification of the temple.

2.1. Christ cleared it of those who desecrated it. He went straight to the temple and *began to cast* (drive) *out the buyers and sellers* (v. 45). Its purity was more its glory than its wealth was. Christ gave a reason for his removing the temple merchants (v. 46). The temple was *a house of prayer,* set apart for fellowship with God: the *buyers* and *sellers* made it *a den of thieves* by the fraudulent bargains they made there. It would be a distraction to those who came there to pray.

2.2. He put it to the best use that it was ever put to, because he *taught daily in the temple* (v. 47). When Christ preached in the temple, notice here:

2.2.1. How spiteful the church rulers were toward him (v. 47): *The chief priests and scribes, and the chief of the people, sought to destroy him.*

2.2.2. How respectful the common people were to him. They were *very attentive to hear him* (they hung on his words). The people paid him great respect, listening to his preaching attentively. Some read it, "All the people, as they heard him, took his side," and so his enemies *could not find what they might do* against him. Until his hour came, his influence on the ordinary people protected him, but when his hour had come, the chief priests' influence on the common people handed him over.

CHAPTER 20

We have here: 1. Christ's answer to the chief priests' question about his authority (vv. 1–8). 2. The parable of the vineyard that was rented out to unjust and rebellious tenants (vv. 9–19). 3. Christ's answer to the question he was asked about the lawfulness of paying taxes to Caesar (vv. 20–26). 4. His upholding of that great, fundamental teaching, the resurrection of the dead and the future state (vv. 27–38). 5. His puzzling the teachers of the law with a question about the Messiah's being the Son of David (vv. 39–44). 6. The warning he gave his disciples to watch out for the teachers of the law (vv. 45–47).

Verses 1–8

Nothing is added here to what we had in the other Evangelists' accounts, except in the first verse, where we are told:

1. That he was now *teaching the people in the temple* and *preaching the Gospel.* Christ preached his own Gospel. He not only purchased salvation for us but also proclaimed it to us. This confirms the truth of the Gospel. It also honors the preachers of the Gospel. In particular, it honors the popular preachers of the Gospel; Christ condescended to the level of the people in preaching the Gospel and *taught them.*

2. That his enemies are said here to have *come upon him.* The Greek word is used only here in the New Testament, and it shows that they thought they would:

2.1. Surprise him with this question; they *came upon him* suddenly.

2.2. Frighten him with this question. We may learn from this account that:

2.2.1. We must not think it strange if even what is clearly a display of Christ's authority is disputed and called into question by those who shut their eyes to the light. Christ's miracles clearly showed *by what authority he did these things.*

2.2.2. If those who question Christ's authority are themselves catechized, their foolishness will be revealed to all people. Christ answered these priests and teachers of the law with a question about the baptism of John: *Was it from heaven or of men?* They all knew it was *from heaven.* This is the question that made them founder and shamed them before the people.

2.2.3. It is not strange if those who are controlled by their concern for their reputation and secular interests imprison the clearest truths (Ro 1:18), as these priests and teachers of the law did, who would not acknowledge that John's baptism was *from heaven* but had no reason for not saying it was *of men* except that they *feared the people.* What good can be expected from people who have such a spirit?

2.2.4. Those who bury the knowledge they have are justly denied further knowledge (vv. 7–8).

Verses 9–19

Christ spoke this parable against those who were determined not to acknowledge his authority.

1. The parable has nothing more than what we had in Matthew and Mark. Its theme is to show that the Jewish nation had caused God to abandon them to destruction. It teaches us:

1.1. That those who enjoy the privileges of the visible church are like tenants and farmers who have a vineyard to look after and rent to pay for it. By setting up revealed religion, God has planted a vineyard, which he rents out (v. 9). The tenants have the work of a vineyard to do, necessary and constant work, but also pleasant and profitable. They also have the fruits of the vineyard to present to the Lord of the vineyard. There is rent to be paid and service to be done.

1.2. That the work of God's ministers is to call on those who enjoy the privileges of the church to produce fruit accordingly. Ministers are those who gather God's rent (v. 10).

1.3. That God's faithful servants have often been wretchedly abused by his own tenants. Those who have decided not to do their duty to God cannot bear to be called on to do it.

1.4. That God sent his Son into the world to gather the fruits of the vineyard. The prophets spoke as servants; Christ spoke *as a Son* (Heb 3:6). One would have thought that the honor of having the Son sent to them would persuade them.

1.5. That those who reject Christ's ministers would reject Christ himself. The tenants said, *This is the heir; come, let us kill him.* When they killed the servants, other servants were sent; "but," they thought, "if we can only bring about the death of the son, there is no other son to be sent; we would then have quiet possession of the vineyard for ourselves." Therefore they took the bold step of *casting* (throwing) *him out of the vineyard and killing him.*

1.6. That the putting of Christ to death filled up the measure of Jewish sins (Mt 23:32). Nothing else could be expected but that God would destroy those evil tenants. They had begun by not paying their rent, and they ended by killing the Son. Those who neglect their duty to God do not know how much sin and destruction they are running into.

2. To the application of the parable is added something we did not have before, namely, their deploring of the judgment declared at the end (v. 16): *When they heard it, they said, God forbid* (May this never be). Notice how they deceived themselves: they thought they could avoid the punishment by a cold *God forbid*, but they did nothing toward preventing it. Notice what Christ said.

2.1. *He beheld them.* This is taken notice of only by this Evangelist (v. 17). Christ looked on them with pity and compassion. He looked directly at them, to see if they would be ashamed of their own foolishness.

2.2. He referred them to Scripture: "*What is this then that is written? The stone that the builders rejected is become the head of the corner* (Ps 118:22)." The Lord Jesus will be exalted to the Father's right hand. Even those who stumble at him *shall be broken*—it will be their ruin; but as to those who not only reject him but also hate and persecute him, he will fall on them and crush them to pieces—he *will grind them to powder.*

2.3. We are told how the chief priests and teachers of the law were enraged by this parable (v. 19): *They perceived that he had spoken this parable against them.* They fell into a rage at him and looked for a way to arrest him. The only reason they did not seize him and take him by the throat now was that they were afraid of the people. They were ready to fulfill his words: *This is the heir; come, let us kill him.* Christ told them that instead of kissing the Son of God (Ps 2:12), they would kill him. They, in effect, said: "We will do that: go for him now." Although they wanted to avoid the punishment of their sin, in the next breath they were planning to commit the sin.

Verses 20–26

We have here Christ's avoiding a trap that his enemies set for him by asking him a question about paying taxes. Here is:

1. The trouble they wanted to cause him. The plot was to *deliver him unto the power and authority of the governor* (v. 20). They could not themselves put him to death by the normal course of the law, nor in any other way than by a popular uprising. But they hoped to win their point by incensing the governor against him. By this cursed deception of theirs Christ's word that he would be *delivered into the hands of the Gentiles* (Ac 21:11) must be fulfilled.

2. The people they used. They were *spies, who should feign themselves just men* (who pretended to be honest). It is nothing new for evildoers to pretend to be honest. A spy must go in disguise. These spies pretended to value Christ's judgment and therefore need his advice in a case of conscience.

3. The question they asked.

3.1. Their introduction was very polite: *Master, we know that thou sayest and teachest rightly* (v. 21). In this way they thought they could flatter him into being off his guard so that he would speak with incautious freedom and openness. They were very much mistaken if they thought they could deceive the humble Jesus in this way. He *accepts not the person of any* (does not show partiality) (Mt 22:16), but it is also as true that he knows the hearts of everyone, and he knew theirs, even though they seemed honest in their words. It was certain that he *taught the way of God truly*, but he knew that those who came to *take hold of his words* (v. 20), not to be taken hold of by them, were unworthy to be taught by him.

3.2. Their question was difficult and dangerous: "Is it lawful *for us*—*for us* is added here in Luke—"*to give tribute to Caesar?*" Their pride and covetousness made them reluctant to pay taxes, and so they wanted to ask whether it was lawful or not. Now if Christ were to say that it was lawful, the people would take it badly. However, if he were to say that it was not lawful—as they expected he would—then they would have something to accuse him of to the governor.

4. His avoiding the trap they set for him: *He perceived their craftiness* (saw how they were trying to trick him) (v. 23). He did not give them a direct answer, but rebuked them for trying to deceive him—*Why tempt ye me? Show me a penny.* He asked them whose money it was, whose portrait and inscription it bore, who coined it. They acknowledged, "It is Caesar's money." "Why then," he said, "you should first have asked whether it was lawful to pay and receive Caesar's money among yourselves, to accept that as legal tender for your trade. But having granted this, you have answered your question by your own actions, and you must, therefore, *render to Caesar the things that are Caesar's.* But in sacred things, only God is your King. You must *render to God the things that are God's.*"

5. The confusion they were put into by this (v. 26). The trap was broken: *They could not take hold of his words*

before the people. They *marvelled at his answer*, that it was so discreet and satisfactory. Their mouths were silenced; they *held their peace.* They dared ask him no more questions, for fear that he would shame and expose them.

Verses 27–38

We read this discussion with the Sadducees before, just as it is here, except that the description Christ gives of the future state is somewhat fuller and more detailed here. Notice:

1. In every age there have been people with corrupt minds who have tried to subvert the fundamental principles of revealed religion. The Sadducees denied that *there was any resurrection*, any *future state*, any spiritual world, any state of reward and retribution for what was done in the body (2Co 5:10). If you take this away, all religion falls to the ground.

2. It is common for those who want to undermine any truth of God to confuse it. This is what these Sadducees did when they wanted to weaken people's faith in the teaching of the resurrection. The case may have been a matter of actual fact; at least it could be. "A woman," they said, "had *seven husbands.* Now in the resurrection *whose wife shall she be?*"

3. There is a great deal of difference between the state of people on earth and that of the people of God in heaven.

3.1. The people in this world *marry, and are given in marriage.* Much of our business in this world is to raise and build up our families and to provide for them. Much of our pleasure in this world is in our relatives, especially our wives and children; this is the way of nature. Marriage is instituted for the comfort of human life.

3.2. The world to come is completely different; it is called *that world* (v. 35), to emphasize it and indicate its eminence. Notice:

3.2.1. Who will live in that world: those who will be *accounted worthy to obtain it.* They do not have a legal worthiness, but an evangelical worthiness. The worthiness by which we are glorified is an imputed worthiness, just as the righteousness by which we are justified is an imputed righteousness. By grace some are made and *counted worthy to obtain that world*; the phrase shows that there is some difficulty in reaching it and some danger of falling short. We must *so run as that we may obtain* it (1Co 9:24). These who are counted worthy will obtain the *resurrection from the dead*, that is, the blessed resurrection, because the resurrection of *condemnation*—as Christ calls it (Jn 5:29)—is a resurrection *to* death—a second death (Rev 2:11; 20:6, 14).

3.2.2. What the happy state of those who live in that world will be we cannot express or conceive (1Co 2:9). Notice what Christ here says about it.

3.2.2.1. They *neither marry nor are given in marriage.* Those who have entered into the joy of their Lord (Mt 25:21) are entirely taken up with that. Nothing that defiles enters the *new Jerusalem* (Rev 21:27).

3.2.2.2. They cannot *die any more*, and this is given as a reason why they do not marry. Where there are no burials, there is no need for weddings. The happiness of that world is crowned by the freedom from death. Death reigns here, but it is forever excluded from there.

3.2.2.3. They are *equal unto the angels.* In the other Evangelists' accounts it was said that they are *as the angels*, but here they are said to be *equal to the angels*, their peers; they have a glory and happiness that is in no way inferior to that of the holy angels. When saints come to heaven, they will be naturalized. They will in all respects have privileges equal to the privileges of those who were freeborn, the angels who are the indigenous residents of that country.

3.2.2.4. They *are the children of God*, and so they are like the angels. Already *now are we the sons of God* (1Jn 3:2), having the nature and disposition of sons, but that will not be perfected until we reach heaven.

3.2.2.5. They are the *children of the resurrection*; that is, they are made capable of receiving the employments and enjoyments of the future state. They are the *children of God*, since they are the *children of the resurrection*.

4. It is an undoubted truth that there is another life after this one (vv. 37–38): *Moses showed this* when he *called the Lord* the *God of Abraham, and the God of Isaac, and the God of Jacob*. Abraham, Isaac, and Jacob were then dead with respect to our world. They had left it many years before; how then could God say, not "I was," but *I am the God of Abraham*? We must conclude that they were then in existence in another world, because *God is not the God of the dead, but of the living*. Luke also adds, *For all live unto him*, that is, all who, like those men, are true believers; although they are dead, they still live (Jn 11:25). But there is even more in this: when God called himself *the God* of these patriarchs, he meant that he was their happiness and inheritance, their *exceeding great reward* (Ge 15:1). Yet he never did for them in this world what would completely fulfill that great commitment, and so there must be another life after this, in which he will do so.

Verses 39–47

The *scribes* were students of the law, and they explained it to the people; they had a reputation for wisdom and honor, but most of them were enemies of Christ and his Gospel.

1. We have them here commending the reply Christ gave to the Sadducees: *Certain of the scribes said, Master, thou hast well said* (v. 39). Even the *scribes*, the teachers of the law, commended his performance and acknowledged that he had spoken well. Many who call themselves Christians come short even of this spirit.

2. We see them struck with reverence for Christ's wisdom and authority (v. 40): *They durst* (dared) *not ask him any questions at all*. His own disciples, who were still willing to receive his message, dared *ask him any question*, but the Sadducees dared not ask him any more.

3. We have them puzzled and foundering at a question about the Messiah (v. 41). It was clear from many Scriptures that Christ was to be the *Son of David*; even the blind man knew this (18:39). And yet it was also clear that David called the Messiah *his Lord* (vv. 42, 44): *The Lord said to my Lord* (Ps 110:1). Now if the Messiah is David's Son, why does David call him his Lord? If the Messiah is David's Lord, why do we call him David's Son? They could not reconcile this apparent contradiction; thank God that we can, that we know that Christ, as God, was David's Lord, but Christ, as man, was David's Son.

4. We have them described in their black colors here (vv. 45–47). Christ told his disciples to *beware of the scribes*. That is:

4.1. "Watch out that you are not drawn into sin by them; watch out that you do not have the kind of spirit they are controlled by.

4.2. "Watch out that you are not brought into trouble by them," in the same sense that he said in Mt 10:17, "*Beware of men, for they will deliver you up to the councils*; beware of the teachers of the law, for they will do so. Beware of them; they are proud and arrogant. They like

to walk around the streets in *long robes*, as those who are above manual work and who are proud and seeking attention." In their hearts, they loved to have people pay them homage *in the markets*. They *loved the highest seats in the synagogues* and *the chief rooms at feasts*, and they looked on themselves very proudly and looked down on everyone around them with great contempt. "They are *covetous and oppressive* and use their religion as a cover for crime." They *devour widows' houses. For a show they make long prayers*. Christ spoke their fate in a few words: these *shall receive greater damnation*, a double condemnation. Hypocritical godliness is double iniquity.

CHAPTER 21

We have here: 1. The notice Christ took of a poor widow who put two very small copper coins into the temple treasury (vv. 1–4). 2. Various predictions in answer to his disciples' questions (vv. 5–7). He foretold: 2.1. What would happen between that time and the destruction of Jerusalem (vv. 8–19). 2.2. The destruction itself (vv. 20–24). 2.3. The second coming of Jesus Christ to judge the world (vv. 25–33). 3. A practical application of this (vv. 34–36) and an account of Christ's preaching and the people's listening to it (vv. 37–38).

Verses 1–4

We had this short passage before in Mark. It is recorded twice to teach us:

1. That loving acts to the poor are an important matter in religious faith. Our Lord Jesus took every opportunity to commend such acts.

2. That Jesus Christ looks on us to examine what we give to the poor. Although intent on his preaching, Christ looked up to see what *gifts were cast* (put) *into the treasury* (v. 1). He notices whether we give much and generously, in proportion to what we have, or whether we are mean and give as little as possible. He watches to see whether we give charitably and with a willing mind, or grudgingly and with reluctance. This should encourage us to be generous in our giving. He sees in secret, and he will reward openly (Mt 6:4, 6, 18).

3. That Christ notices and accepts the love of the poor especially. Those who have nothing to give may still show a great deal of love by ministering to the poor, helping them. However, here was one woman who was herself poor but still gave what little she had to the temple treasury. It was only *two mites*, two very small copper coins, which make a fraction of a penny, but Christ praised it as an act of charity that exceeded all the others: *She has cast in more than they all*. Christ did not blame her for indiscretion, but commended her generosity, which proceeded from her belief in and dependence on God's providence to take care of her.

4. That whatever may be called *the offerings of God* should be respected and contributed to by us cheerfully according to our power, and even beyond our power.

Verses 5–19

Notice here:

1. With what wonder some people spoke of the external beauty and magnificence of the temple. They spoke to him about *how it was adorned with goodly stones and gifts* (v. 5). They thought their Master would be moved by those things as much as they were. When we speak of the temple, it should be of the presence of God in it.

2. Christ spoke of its all being destroyed very soon (v. 6): "*As for those things which you behold, the days*

will come in which there shall not be left one stone upon another. This building will be completely ruined."

3. With what curiosity those around him asked about the time when this great destruction would take place: *Master, when shall these things be?* (v. 7). It is natural for us to seek to know future things, whereas we should be more concerned to ask what is our duty as we see these things, and how we may prepare for them. They asked *what sign there shall be when these things shall come to pass.* They did not ask for an immediate sign, to confirm the prediction itself, but what would be the future signs of the approaching fulfillment of the prediction.

4. With what clarity and fullness Christ answered their questions.

4.1. They must expect to hear of false Christs and false prophets appearing (v. 8): *Many shall come in my name,* usurping the title and role of the Messiah. To encourage people to follow them, they would add, *"The time draws near* when the kingdom will be restored to Israel." Now as to this, he gave them a necessary warning.

4.1.1. *Take heed that you be not deceived.* When they eagerly and anxiously asked, *Master, when shall these things be?* the first word Christ said was, *Take heed that you be not deceived.* Those who are most inquisitive about the things of God—though it is very good to be so—are in most danger of being deceived.

4.1.2. *Go you not after them.* If we are sure that Jesus is the Christ and that his message is the *gospel of God* (Ro 15:16), we must be deaf to all suggestions of another Christ and another Gospel (2Co 11:4).

4.2. They must expect to hear about great commotions in the nations. There will be bloody wars (v. 10): *Nation shall rise against nation.* There will be *earthquakes in divers* (various) *places.* There will *be famines* and *pestilences* (plagues). God has various ways of punishing an offensive people. Although spiritual judgments are more commonly inflicted in Gospel times, God still makes use of physical judgments. There will be *fearful sights* and *great signs from heaven. "Be not terrified.* Others will be frightened at them, but you are not to be frightened (v. 9). As to the *fearful sights,* let them not be fearful to you. You fall into the hands of God (2Sa 24:14). Trust in him and do not be afraid. It is in your interests to make the best of what is happening, since all your fears cannot change matters: *these things must first come to pass.* There is worse to come: *The end is not by and by,* not suddenly. Do not be terrified, because if you begin to get discouraged so quickly, how will you cope with what is still ahead of you?"

4.3. They must expect that they themselves would be signs and wonders in Israel: *"Before all these, they shall lay their hands on you.* This must be considered not only as the suffering of the persecuted but also as the sin of the persecutors." The ruin of a people is always introduced by their sin.

4.3.1. Christ told them what hardships they would suffer for his name's sake: they should *sit down and count the cost.* Because the Christians were originally Jews, they might expect mercy from the Jews, but Christ told them not to expect it:

4.3.1.1. *"They shall deliver you up to the synagogues* to be scourged there.

4.3.1.2. "They will *deliver you into prisons, that* you may be *brought before kings and rulers for my name's sake.*

4.3.1.3. "Your own relatives will betray you (v. 16), *your parents, brethren, kinsfolks* (brothers, sisters, and relatives), *and friends.*

4.3.1.4. *"You* will be called to *resist unto blood* (Heb 12:4). *Some of you shall they cause to be put to death.*

4.3.1.5. *"You shall be hated of all men for my name's sake."* This is worse than death itself. They were hated by everyone, that is, by everyone bad, who could not bear the light of the Gospel because it revealed their evil. The evil world, which hated to be reformed, hated Christ, the great Reformer, and for his sake hated all who belonged to him.

4.3.2. He encouraged them to endure these trials and to persevere in their work.

4.3.2.1. God would bring glory both to himself and to them out of their sufferings: *"It shall turn to you for a testimony* (v. 13). Because you are set up as a mark and are publicly persecuted, you will be noticed more. Your being brought *before kings and rulers* will give you an opportunity to preach the Gospel to them. Your suffering such harsh things and being so hated by the worst people will be a testimony that you are good. Your courage, cheerfulness, and faithfulness in suffering will be a testimony for you that you believe what you preach, that you are supported by God's power.

4.3.2.2. "God will stand by you, acknowledge you, and help you, and you will be well provided for with instructions (vv. 14–15). *Settle it in your hearts, not to meditate before what you shall answer.* Do not depend on your own cleverness and ingenuity, and do not distrust or despair of the immediate and extraordinary help of divine grace. I promise you the special help of divine grace: *I will give you a mouth and wisdom."* This shows us:

4.3.2.2.1. *A mouth* and *wisdom* together completely fit a person both for service and suffering; wisdom tells them what to say, and a mouth enables them to say it.

4.3.2.2.2. Those who plead Christ's cause may depend on him to give them *a mouth* (words) *and wisdom* to enable them to answer for themselves.

4.3.2.2.3. When Christ gives his witnesses words and wisdom, they are enabled to say, both for him and themselves, what *all their adversaries are not able to gainsay* (contradict) *or resist* (Ac 4–6).

4.3.2.3. "You will suffer no real injury by all the hardships they will subject you to (v. 18): *There shall not a hair of your head perish."* Will some of them lose their heads, but not lose a hair? Take it figuratively, in the same sense as Christ said, *He that loseth his life for my sake shall find it* (Mt 10:39). "Not a hair of your head will perish unless:

4.3.2.3.1. "I take notice of it." It was with this in mind that he said, *The hairs of your head are all numbered* (Mt 10:30).

4.3.2.3.2. "It is for a valuable consideration." We do not reckon something lost or perishing if it is spent for a good purpose. If we lose the body itself for Christ's name's sake, it does not perish, but is well given.

4.3.2.3.3. "It is abundantly rewarded." Although we may lose some things for Christ, we will not, we cannot, lose by him in the end.

4.3.2.4. "It is therefore your duty and in your interests to maintain a holy sincerity and peace of mind, which will keep you always at rest (v. 19): *In your patience* (endurance) *possess ye your souls."*

4.3.2.4.1. It is our duty and in our interests at all times, especially in dangerous times, to gain possession of our own souls, so that they are not diseased and our possession of them is not disturbed and interrupted. *"Possess your souls,* be your own people. Keep under control the turmoil of passion, so that neither grief nor fear may rule over you."

4.3.2.4.*2.* It is by *patience* (endurance), true Christian persistence, that we keep possession of our own souls. "Be patiently on your guard, and keep out all those influences that would disturb or unsettle you."

Verses 20–28

Now he would show them what would be the final outcome of all those things, namely, the destruction of Jerusalem. This would be a small day of judgment, a type and figure of Christ's second coming.

1. He told them that they would see Jerusalem surrounded, *compassed with armies* (v. 20), and when they saw this, they could conclude that *its desolation was nigh.*

2. He warned them that when they saw this signal, they must fend for their own safety (v. 21): "*Then let them that are in Judea flee to the mountains; let them that are in the midst of it depart out*, and those who are in the surrounding towns and villages should not enter the city. Abandon the city and country that you see God has abandoned and given over to destruction."

3. He foretold the terrible havoc that would be made of the Jewish nation (v. 22): "*Those are the days of vengeance* so often spoken about by the Old Testament prophets." All their predictions would now be fulfilled. *All things that are written must* finally *be fulfilled.* Reprieves are not pardons. The greatness of that destruction is described by reference to:

3.1. Its inflicting cause. It was the wrath of God on this people that would kindle this fire.

3.2. The particular terror it would be for pregnant women and poor mothers who were nursing their babies.

3.3. The general confusion that there would be throughout the nation.

4. He described the outcome of the struggles between the Jews and the Romans. Many of the Jews *would fall by the edge of the sword.* The siege of Jerusalem was, in effect, a military execution. The rest would be *led away captive*, not into one nation, but *into all nations.* Jerusalem itself was *trodden down of* (trampled down by) *the Gentiles.* The Romans ravaged it completely.

5. He described the great panic that people would generally be in. Many fearful sights would be *in the sun, moon, and stars*, and also here in this lower world, the *sea and the waves roaring.* The effect of this would be universal confusion and fear *upon the earth, distress of nations with perplexity* (v. 25). *Men's hearts shall fail them for fear* (v. 26); they would be dying for fear, sinking under what lay on them, but still trembling for fear of even worse to come and *looking after those things which are coming upon the world.* The *powers of heaven shall be shaken*, and then the pillars of the earth have to tremble (Job 9:6). Just as that day was all terror and destruction to the unfaithful Jews, so will the great day be to all unbelievers.

6. He represented this as a kind of appearing of the Son of Man: *Then shall they see the Son of man coming in a cloud, with power and great glory* (v. 27). The destruction of Jerusalem was especially an act of Christ's judgment. It could justly be looked on, therefore, as *a coming of the Son of man, in power and great glory*, yet not visibly, but *in the clouds.* Now this was:

6.1. Evidence of the first coming of the Messiah. Those who did not want to have him reign over them would have him triumph over them (19:14, 27).

6.2. A promise of his second coming.

7. He encouraged all the faithful disciples (v. 28): "*When these things begin to come to pass*, then you are

to *look up*, look toward heaven in faith, hope, and prayer, and *lift up your heads, for your redemption draws nigh.*" When Christ came, he came to redeem the Christians who were persecuted and oppressed. When he comes to judge the world at the last day, he will redeem all who are his from all their grievances. When they see that day coming, they can *lift up their heads with joy*, knowing that *their redemption draws nigh.*

8. Here is one word of prediction that looks further than the destruction of the Jewish nation, a word that is not easily understood; it is in v. 24: *Jerusalem shall be trodden down of the Gentiles, till the times of the Gentiles be fulfilled.*

8.1. Some understand this to refer to what is past. The Gentiles would keep possession of the city, and it would be completely Gentile until a great part of the Gentile world had become Christian.

8.2. Others understand it as referring to what is still to come. Jerusalem will be possessed by the Gentiles until the kingdoms of this world become Christ's kingdoms (Rev 11:15), and then all the Jews will be converted.

Verses 29–38

At the end of this message:

1. Christ appointed his disciples to take note of the signs of the times, by which they could discern the approach of the kingdom of God, as they could discern the approach of summer by the budding of trees (vv. 29–31). Just as there is a chain of cause and effect in the kingdom of nature, so in the kingdom of providence one event follows as a consequence of another. When we see the ruin of persecuting powers coming on quickly, we may conclude that *the kingdom of God is nigh at hand.*

2. He told them to look on those things as definite and very near. The destruction of the Jewish nation:

2.1. Was near (v. 32): *This generation will not pass away till all be fulfilled.* Some who were then alive would see it.

2.2. Was definite; the decree had been issued (v. 33): "*Heaven and earth shall pass away* sooner than any of my words. *My words shall not pass away.*"

3. He warned them against self-confidence and worldliness (vv. 34–35): *Take heed to yourselves.* This is the word of command given to all Christ's disciples. We cannot be safe if we are self-confident. At all times, but especially at certain times, we should be very cautious. Notice here:

3.1. What our danger is: that the day of death and judgment may come upon us unawares, when we do not expect it and are not prepared for it, that it may *come upon us as a snare.*

3.2. What our duty is: we must *take heed lest our hearts be overcharged* (be careful so that our hearts are not weighed down). We must watch against two things so that our hearts are not weighed down by them:

3.2.1. Indulging our physical appetites: *Take heed lest you be overcharged with surfeiting and drunkenness* (be careful so that your hearts are not weighed down by wasteful living and drunkenness), excessive eating and drinking. They numb the conscience and cause the mind to be unmoved by those things that are most disturbing.

3.2.2. Pursuing the good things of this world immoderately. The heart is weighed down by the *cares of this life.* This is the snare of businesspeople who want to be rich.

4. He advised them to get ready for this great day (v. 36). Notice here:

4.1. What our aim should be: that we may be *accounted worthy to escape all these things.* However, we must aim not only to escape condemnation but also to *stand before the Son of man*, not only to stand acquitted before him as our Judge but also simply to *stand before him*, to be with him as our Master, serving him day and night, always *beholding his face*. The saints are here, as before, said to be *accounted worthy* (20:35). By the goodwill of his grace toward them, God *accounts them worthy* of it. A great part of our worthiness lies in acknowledging our unworthiness.

4.2. What our actions should be in pursuing these aims: *Watch therefore, and pray always.* Watching and praying must go together (Ne 4:9). Those who want to make sure of the joys to come must watch and pray. They must make it the constant business of their lives:

4.2.1. To keep a guard on themselves. "Watch against sin, watch in every duty. Be alert and stay alert."

4.2.2. To maintain their fellowship with God: *Pray always.* Those who live a life of prayer in this world will be counted worthy to lead a life of praise in the next world.

5. In the last two verses we have an account of what Christ did during those three or four days between his triumphal entry into Jerusalem and the night on which he was betrayed.

5.1. He was *all day teaching in the temple.* He was a tireless preacher; he preached in the face of opposition, among those who he knew were trying to take advantage of him.

5.2. At night he went out to stay at a friend's house on the Mount of Olives.

5.3. Early in the morning he was back in the temple, and the people were eager to hear One who was obviously eager to preach (v. 38). *They all came early in the morning to hear* him. Sometimes the taste for and enjoyment of good preaching that serious, honest, and plain people have are to be valued more highly than the opinion of the so-called experts and learned people.

CHAPTER 22

All the Evangelists give us a detailed account of the death and resurrection of Christ; this Evangelist does so as fully as any, and with many details and passages added that we did not have before. We have here: 1. The plot to seize Jesus and Judas's agreement to betray him (vv. 1–6). 2. Christ's eating the Passover with his disciples (vv. 7–18). 3. The instituting of the Lord's Supper (vv. 19–20). 4. Christ's speaking to his disciples after supper (vv. 21–38). 5. His anguish in the garden (vv. 39–46). 6. His capture (vv. 47–53). 7. Peter's denial of him (vv. 54–62). 8. The indignities done to Christ, and his trial and condemnation in the ecclesiastical court (vv. 63–71).

Verses 1–6

Christ was here handed over, *when the feast of unleavened bread drew nigh* (v. 1). Here we have:

1. His sworn enemies plotting it (v. 2), *the chief priests* and the teachers of the law *seeking how they might kill him*. If they could have had their wish, it would have been carried out earlier, but they *feared the people*.

2. A treacherous disciple joining them, Judas surnamed *Iscariot*. He is said here to have been *of the number of the twelve*. One wonders how one of that number, who must have known Christ, could be so evil as to betray him. And yet he did: *Satan entered into Judas* (v. 3). It was the Devil's work. Whoever betrays Christ, or his truths or ways, it is Satan who puts them up to it. Judas knew how much the chief priests wanted to get Christ into their hands. He

went, therefore, and made the suggestion to them himself (v. 4). When we see Judas in discussion with the chief priests, we can be sure they are plotting some trouble.

3. The outcome of the agreement between them.

3.1. Judas must *betray Christ to them*, and they would be *glad of* this.

3.2. They must give him a sum of money for doing it, and he would be glad to receive this (v. 5). *They covenanted to give him money.* Judas watched for an *opportunity to betray him.* He gained the advantage he sought, and he fixed the time and place where it could be done *in the absence of the multitude* and without disturbance.

Verses 7–20

We have here:

1. The preparation that was made for Christ to eat the Passover with his disciples on the very *day of unleavened bread, when the passover must be killed* according to the law (v. 7). He sent Peter and John to *prepare the passover*. He told those he employed where they should go (vv. 9–10): *they must follow a man bearing a pitcher of water*, and he must be their guide to the house. Christ directed them in this way to teach them to depend on the guidance of Providence and to follow it step by step. Having come to the house, they must ask the owner of the house to show them a room (v. 11), and he would readily do so (v. 12). The disciples found their guide, the house, and the room just as Christ had said to them (v. 13). They got everything ready for *the passover* (v. 11).

2. The celebration of the Passover. When the time had come, he sat down, and the twelve apostles with him, including Judas. Although Judas was already guilty of an overt act of treason, yet because it was not publicly known, Christ allowed him to sit down with the others at the Passover. Notice:

2.1. How Christ welcomed this Passover (v. 15): *With desire I have desired to eat this Passover with you before I suffer.* He knew it was to introduce his sufferings, and so he desired it, because it was for his Father's glory and human redemption. Shall we be reluctant to do any service for the One who was so eager to undertake the work of our salvation? Notice the love he had for his disciples; he wanted to eat the meal with them, so that he and they would have a little time together for private conversation. He was now about to leave them, but he wanted very much to *eat this Passover with them before he suffered*, as if the comfort of that would carry him more cheerfully through his sufferings.

2.2. How Christ took his leave of all Passovers in it (v. 16): *I will not any more eat thereof until it be fulfilled in the kingdom of God.*

2.2.1. The Passover was fulfilled when Christ our Passover was sacrificed for us (1Co 5:7).

2.2.2. It was fulfilled in the Lord's Supper, an ordinance of the Gospel kingdom, in which the Passover's purpose was accomplished. The disciples ate the Lord's Supper, and Christ could be said to eat with them, because of the spiritual fellowship they had with him in that ordinance.

2.2.3. The complete fulfillment of that commemoration of liberty will be in the kingdom of glory. What Christ had said concerning his eating the paschal lamb, he repeated concerning his drinking of the Passover wine, the *cup of blessing* (1Co 10:16), or of thanksgiving. This *cup he took*, according to the custom, and *gave thanks*, and then he said, *Take this, and divide it among yourselves* (v. 17). This is not said later about the sacramental cup, which, being the *New Testament in his blood*, he could give into everyone's hand, to teach them to apply it particularly to their own souls, but as for the paschal cup, it was enough to say, "*Take* it and *divide it among yourselves* (v. 18). *I will not drink of the fruit of the vine any more, till the kingdom of God shall come.*" Christ's dying the next day opened up that kingdom.

3. The institution of the Lord's Supper (vv. 19–20). The Passover and the rescue from Egypt were types and prophetic signs of a Christ to come, who by dying would save us from sin and death and the tyranny of Satan. The Lord's Supper is instituted to be a commemorative sign or memorial of a Christ who has already come, who has rescued us by dying.

3.1. The breaking of Christ's body as a sacrifice for us is commemorated here by the *breaking of bread* (Ac 2:42): *This is my body which is given for you.* This bread that was given for us is given to us as food for our souls. The bread that was broken and given *for* us to satisfy the guilt of our sins is broken and given *to* us to satisfy the desire of our souls. We do this in remembrance of what he did for us when he died for us, and we do it as a memorial of what we do by making ourselves *partakers of him* (Heb 3:14) and joining ourselves to him in an eternal covenant.

3.2. The shedding of Christ's blood by which the atonement was made is represented by the wine in the cup. It commemorates the purchase of the covenant by the blood of Christ and confirms the promises of the covenant. In all our commemorations of the shedding of Christ's blood, we must consider it as shed for us; we commemorate Christ, *who loved me, and gave himself for me* (Gal 2:20).

Verses 21–38

We have here Christ's talk with his disciples after supper, much of which is new, and in John's Gospel we will find further additions.

1. He spoke to them about the one who would betray him.

1.1. He told them that the traitor was now among them and was one of them (v. 21). From the placing of this after the institution of the Lord's Supper—although in Matthew and Mark it is placed before it—it seems clear that Judas received the Lord's Supper, did *eat of that bread* and *drink of that cup,* because after that ceremony was over, Christ said, *Behold, the hand of him that betrayeth me is with me on the table.*

1.2. He foretold that the act of treason would take effect (v. 22): *Truly the Son of man goes as it was determined,* because he is handed over according to the purpose and foreknowledge of God (Ac 2:23). Christ was not driven to his sufferings, but cheerfully went to them.

1.3. He declared woe to the traitor: *Woe to that man by whom he is betrayed.* Although God had determined that Christ would be betrayed, and Christ himself had cheerfully submitted to it, neither Judas's sin nor his punishment was any less.

1.4. He frightened the other disciples into suspecting themselves, by saying that the traitor was one of them (v. 23): *They began to inquire among themselves who it was that should do this thing.*

2. He spoke to them about the dispute that had arisen among them over priority or supremacy.

2.1. Notice what the dispute was: *Which of them should be accounted* (considered) *the greatest.* How inconsistent this is with verse 23! There they were questioning who would be the traitor, and here which would be the ruler. The human heart is so self-contradictory!

2.2. Notice how Christ responded to this dispute. He was not sharp with them, but mildly showed them how sinful and foolish it was.

2.2.1. To dispute in this way was to make themselves like the *kings of the Gentiles* (v. 25), who *exercise lordship* over their subjects. The *exercising of lordship* is more suitable for the *kings of the Gentiles* than for ministers of Christ. *They that exercise authority* are called *Benefactors;* they call themselves that, and that is what their flatterers call them. However much they really serve themselves, they want to be thought to be serving their country. One of the Ptolemies was surnamed "The Benefactor." By taking notice of this, our Savior showed:

2.2.1.1. That to do good is much more honorable than to look great. By their own confession, one who is a benefactor to his country is much more valued than one who is a ruler of his country.

2.2.1.2. That to do good is the surest way to become great. Christ, therefore, wanted to have his disciples believe that their greatest honor would be to do all the good they could in the world. If they had what was confessedly the greater honor of being benefactors, let them despise the lesser one of being rulers.

2.2.2. To dispute in this way was to make themselves unlike Christ himself: *You shall not be so* (vv. 26–27). "It was never intended that you would rule in any other way than by the power of truth and grace, than by serving." Notice here:

2.2.2.1. The rule Christ gave to his disciples is, "The one who is *greater among you,* who is senior, let him *be as the younger.*" Let elders, as well as those who are younger, make an effort. Their age and honor, instead of guaranteeing them their ease, obligate them to do double the work. In addition, let the one who is chief be *as he that* serves.

2.2.2.2. The example that he himself gave of this rule: *Whether is greater, he that sitteth at meat* (the one who is at table) *or he that serveth?* He was ready to do any act of kindness and service for them, as can be seen from his washing their feet (Jn 13:5).

2.2.3. They should not seek worldly honor and grandeur, because he had better honor in store for them: a kingdom, a feast, a throne, in which they would all share alike. Notice:

2.2.3.1. Christ's commendation of his disciples for their faithfulness to him. It is spoken with praise: "*You are they who have continued with me in my temptations* (trials), who have stood by me and been faithful to me." His disciples remained loyal to him and suffered with him in all his hardships. They could give him only a little help; nevertheless, he took it kindly that they *continued with him* (v. 28), and here he acknowledged their kindness. Christ's disciples had been very deficient in fulfilling their duty; we find them guilty of many mistakes and weaknesses. But their Master passed everything by and forgot it. *You are they who have continued with me.* This was how he praised them at his parting, to show how willing he is to make the best of those whose hearts he knows are upright with him. Notice:

2.2.3.2. The reward he intended to give them for their faithfulness: *I appoint unto you a kingdom.*" We may understand this:

2.2.3.2.1. As what would be done for them in this world. God gave his Son a kingdom among human beings, the Gospel church. The Son conferred this kingdom on his apostles and their successors in the ministry of the Gospel. "This is the honor reserved for you." Or:

2.2.3.2.2. As what would be done for them in the next world. God would give them the kingdom. They would *eat and drink at Christ's table in his kingdom,* about which he had spoken (vv. 16, 18). They would share in those joys and pleasures that were the reward of his services and sufferings. They would have the highest positions: "You will *sit down with me on my throne* (Rev 3:21)."

3. He spoke to them about Peter's denying him. Here we may observe:

3.1. The general notice Christ gave to Peter of the Devil's intention toward him and the rest of the apostles (v. 31): *The Lord said, Simon, Simon, Satan hath desired to have you, that he may sift you as wheat.* Peter, who was used to being the mouthpiece for the others in speaking to Christ, was here made the ear of the rest, and what was intended as a warning to them all—*all you shall be offended, because of me*—was directed at Peter, because he would be struck at by the tempter in a particular way: *Satan has desired to have you.* "Allow me to test them," Satan had said, "especially Peter." He had asked to have them so *that he might sift them,* so that he could show them to be chaff, not wheat. Satan could not sift them unless God allowed him to: he *desired to have them.* "He has challenged you in order to prove you to be a company of hypocrites, especially Peter, the most forward of you."

3.2. The particular encouragement he gave to Peter: "*I have prayed for thee:* you will suffer the most violent attack, *but I have prayed for thee, that thy faith fail not.*" Although there may be many weaknesses in the faith of true believers, their faith will not fail totally and finally. It is because of the mediation and intercession of Jesus Christ that the faith of his disciples, though at times sadly shaken, has not completely collapsed. They are *kept by the power of God* (1Pe 1:5) and the prayer of Christ.

3.3. The command he gave Peter to help others: "*When thou art converted, strengthen thy brethren*; when you have found that your faith has been kept from failing, seek to confirm the faith of others; when you have found mercy with God yourself, encourage others to hope that they too will find mercy." Those who have fallen into sin must be *converted* from it. Those who through grace are converted from sin must do what they can to strengthen and prevent the falling of their brothers and sisters who stand; see Ps 51:11–13; 1Ti 1:13.

3.4. Peter's declared determination to remain faithful to Christ, no matter what it cost him (v. 33): *Lord, I am ready to go with thee, both into prison and to death.* These were great words, and yet I believe that at this time they were no more than he meant and thought he would fulfill. All true disciples of Christ sincerely desire and want to *follow him, whithersoever he goes* (Rev 14:4).

3.5. Christ's explicit prediction that Peter would deny him three times (v. 34): "*I tell thee, Peter, the cock shall not crow this day before thou even deny that thou knowest me.*" Christ knows us better than we know ourselves. It is good for us that Christ knows where we are weak better than we do, and that he therefore knows where he is to come to us with grace that is sufficient for our needs (2Co 12:9).

4. He spoke to them about the condition of all the disciples.

4.1. He appealed to them about what had been (v. 35). He had acknowledged that they had been faithful servants to him (v. 28). Now he expected them to acknowledge that he had been a kind and careful Master to them. *When I sent you without purse, lacked you any thing?*

4.1.1. He acknowledged that he had sent them out in a very poor and bare condition. If God sends us out in this way into the world, let us remember that better people than we have begun as low.

4.1.2. However, he wanted them to acknowledge that despite this, they had *lacked nothing*; they readily acknowledged, *Nothing, Lord.* It is good for us often to look back on the providences of God and to notice how we have gotten through the difficulties we have faced. Christ is a good Master, and his service is good, because although his servants may sometimes be brought low, he will still help them. We must consider ourselves as having received much if we have received the necessary supports of life, even though we have lived from hand to mouth. The disciples had lacked nothing.

4.2. He announced to them that a very great change in their circumstances was now approaching.

4.2.1. The One who was their Master was now beginning his sufferings, which he had often foretold (v. 37): "*Now that which is written must be fulfilled in me. He was numbered among the transgressors* (Isa 53:12). This is still to be fulfilled, and then *the things concerning me* will have an end; I will then say, *It is finished.*" It may be the comfort of suffering Christians, as it was of a suffering Christ, that their sufferings were foretold. Those sufferings will have an end, and will end eternally well.

4.2.2. They must therefore expect troubles. They must now suffer to some extent with their Master, and when he had gone, they must expect to suffer like him.

4.2.2.1. They must expect that their friends would no longer be as kind and generous to them as they had been, and so, *He that has a purse, let him take it.*

4.2.2.2. They must now expect their enemies to be fiercer toward them than they had been, and they would need weapons as well as provisions: *He that has no sword* will find a great need for one and will wish that he had sold his clothes to buy one. But the *sword of the Spirit* (Eph 6:17) is the sword that the disciples of Christ must supply themselves with. Now that *Christ has suffered for us,* we must *arm ourselves* with the same mind (1Pe 4:1), with a holy submission to the will of God. We will then be better prepared for it than if we had sold a coat to buy a sword. The disciples then asked what weapons they had, and they found they had among them *two swords* (v. 38), of which one was Peter's. However, Christ showed how little he wanted them to depend on this when he said, *It is enough.* Two swords are sufficient for those who need none, having God himself to be *the shield of their help and the sword of their excellency* (Dt 33:29).

Verses 39–46

We have here the terrible account of Christ's agony in the garden. In it Christ joined battle with the powers of darkness, but he conquered them.

1. What we have in this passage that we had before is:

1.1. That when Christ went out, *his disciples*—eleven of them, because Judas had given them the slip—*followed him.* Having continued with him up to this time in his trials, they would not leave him now.

1.2. That he went to the place *where he was wont* (went usually) to be in private, which shows that Christ was often alone, to teach us also to be so.

1.3. That he encouraged his disciples to pray that although the approaching trial could not be avoided, they would not *enter into temptation* to sin in it.

1.4. That he withdrew from them and prayed by himself. He withdrew about *a stone's cast,* and there he *kneeled down* (v. 41)—the other Evangelists say that later he *fell on his face*—and there *prayed* (Mt 26:39) that if it was the will of God, this cup of suffering might be *removed from him* (v. 42).

1.5. That, knowing it was his Father's will that he suffer and die, he withdrew that request and submitted himself to his heavenly Father's will: "*Nevertheless not my will* be done, not the will of my human nature, but the will of God—let that be done" (Ps 40:7–8).

1.6. That his disciples were asleep when he was praying—and when they should have been praying themselves (v. 45). When he *rose from prayer, he found them sleeping*. See what a favorable interpretation is put on it here, which we did not have in the other Gospels: they were *sleeping for sorrow*. This teaches us to make the best of the weaknesses of our brothers and sisters; if it makes them look better to attribute their weaknesses to one cause rather than another, we should do so.

1.7. That when he awoke them, he encouraged them to pray (v. 46): "*Why sleep ye? Rise and pray.*" When we find ourselves entering temptation, we should *rise and pray*, "Lord, help me in this time of need."

2. There are three things in this passage that we did not have in the other Gospels:

2.1. That when Christ was in anguish, *there appeared to him an angel from heaven, strengthening him* (v. 43).

2.1.1. It showed the deep humiliation of our Lord Jesus that he needed the help of an angel.

2.1.2. When he was not rescued from his sufferings, he was still strengthened and supported in them, and that amounted to the same thing. If God makes the shoulders fit for the burden, we have no reason to complain, whatever he wishes to lay on us.

2.1.3. The angels ministered to the Lord Jesus in his sufferings. He could have had legions of angels to rescue him, but he used this angel's ministry only to *strengthen him*.

2.2. That, *being in an agony, he prayed more earnestly* (v. 44). As his sorrow and trouble became more intense, he became bolder in prayer. Prayer, though never out of season, is especially seasonable when we are in anguish, and the more intense our anguish, the more lively and frequent our prayers should be.

2.3. That in this anguish, *his sweat was as it were great drops of blood falling down to the ground*. There is some dispute among the commentators whether this sweat is only compared to drops of blood or had real blood mingled with it, so that it was like blood in color and could truly be called a bloody sweat; the matter is not significant. Every pore was like a bleeding wound, and his blood stained all his clothes. This showed the *travail of his soul* (Isa 53:11).

Verses 47–53

We have here:

1. Jesus' being marked out by Judas. A numerous crowd appeared, with Judas at their head, because he was *guide to them that took Jesus* (Ac 1:16); they did not know where to find Jesus, but Judas brought them to the place. When they were there, they did not know which one Jesus was, but Judas told them that whoever he kissed was the man. He *drew near to him to kiss him*, therefore. Luke takes notice of the question Christ asked him, which we do not have in the other Gospels: *Judas, betrayest thou the Son of man with a kiss?* Must one of his own disciples betray him? Must he be betrayed with a kiss? Was ever such a token of love so desecrated and abused?

2. The effort that his disciples made for his protection (v. 49): *When they saw what would follow*, they said, "*Lord, shall we smite* (strike) *with the sword?* You allowed us to have two swords: should we now use them?" But they were in too much of a hurry and in too much of a passion to wait for an answer. Peter, aiming at the head of one of the servants of the *high priest*, missed and *cut off his right ear*. The other Evangelists tell us how Christ restrained Peter from it. Luke tells us:

2.1. How Christ excused the blow: *Suffer ye thus far* (v. 51). He said this to pacify his enemies who had come to take him, so that they would not be provoked by it to attack the disciples: "Overlook this wrong and insult; it was without authority from me, and another blow will not be struck." He spoke to them in fair terms, begging their pardon, as it were, for an attack made on them by one of his followers, to teach us to speak good words even to our enemies.

2.2. How he healed the wound: *He touched his ear, and healed him*, fastened his ear on again. Christ proved to them here:

2.2.1. His power. The One who could heal could destroy if he pleased.

2.2.2. His mercy and goodness. Christ here gave a good example of his own rule of *doing good to them that hate us* (6:27), as later he gave an example of *praying for them that despitefully use us* (6:28). Those who repay good for evil do as Christ did.

3. Christ's pleading with the officers to show them how absurd it was for them to make all this fuss and noise (vv. 52–53). Luke tells us that Jesus spoke here to the *chief priests and captains of the temple*, indicating that all who were employed in this hateful service were ecclesiastical people, attached to the temple. Notice:

3.1. How Christ reasoned with them about their proceedings. What need was there for them to come out at dead of night, and *with swords and staves* (clubs)? They knew that he was One who would not resist. "Why then *are ye come out as against a thief?*" They knew he was One who would not run away, because he was among them every day in the temple.

3.2. How he reconciled himself to their actions; and we did not have this before: "*But this is your hour, and the power of darkness.* However harsh it may seem that I should be exposed in this way, I still submit, because this is what has been determined. Now the *power of darkness*, Satan, *the ruler of the darkness of this world*, is allowed to do his worst. Let him do his worst." It is *the power of darkness* that reigns, but darkness must give way to light, and the power of darkness be made to submit to the prince of light.

Verses 54–62

We have here the sad record of Peter's denying his Master. No notice is taken here, as was in the other Gospels, of Christ's now being examined in front of the high priest, only of his being brought into *the high priest's house* (v. 54). But the expression is significant. They *took him, and led him, and brought him*, which to me seems to show that they were still confused. Struck with inner terror at what they had seen and heard, they took him the longest way around. Maybe they did not know which way they were hurrying him, because they were in such a hurry within themselves. We have here:

1. Peter's falling.

1.1. It began with sneaking. He followed Christ; this was good, but he followed *afar off* (v. 54). He thought he would make things easier for himself by, on the one hand, following Christ and thereby satisfying his conscience, and, on the other, following him at a safe distance and thereby saving his reputation—and his skin.

1.2. It proceeded in associating with the high priest's servants. The *servants kindled a fire in the midst of the hall* and *sat down together. Peter sat down among them*, as if he had been one of them.

1.3. His fall itself was disowning all acquaintance with Christ, because he was now in distress and danger. He was accused of being a follower of this Jesus by a poor, simple servant girl. She looked thoughtfully at him as he *sat by the fire*, and she said, *This man was with him.* Just as Peter did not have the courage to acknowledge the charge, so he also did not have the wit and presence of mind to deflect it, and so he denied it point blank: *Woman, I know him not.*

1.4. His fall was repeated a second time (v. 58): *After a little while another saw him* and said, *"Even thou art one of them." Not I,* said Peter; *Man, I am not.* And *a third* time, *about the space of an hour after, another* strenuously asserted, *"Of a truth* (certainly) *this fellow also was with him.* Let him deny it if he can, because you can all tell *he is a Galilean."* Peter now denied not only that he was a disciple of Christ but even that he knew anything of him (v. 60): *Man, I know not what thou sayest.*

2. Peter's getting up again. Notice how blessedly he recovered himself.

2.1. The *cock crew*, and this startled him and made him start thinking. Small accidents may lead to great consequences.

2.2. *The Lord turned and looked upon him.* We did not have this detail in the other Gospels, but it is significant. Although Christ now had his back to Peter and was being tried, he knew all that Peter said. Christ takes more notice of what we say and do than we think he does. When Peter disowned Christ, Christ did not disown him. It is good for us that Christ does not deal with us as we deal with him. Christ turned and *looked upon Peter*, because he knew that although Peter had denied him with his lips, his eye was still toward him. He only gave Peter a look, which no one but Peter would understand the meaning of.

2.2.1. It was a convicting look. Peter said that he did not know Christ. Christ *turned, and looked upon him,* as if to say, "Do you not know me, Peter?"

2.2.2. It was a rebuking look.

2.2.3. It was a pleading look: "What, Peter, are you the one who disowns me now? You who were the most eager to confess me to be the Son of God and who solemnly promised you would never disown me?"

2.2.4. It was a compassionate look; he looked at him with tenderness. "Poor Peter! How you are fallen and ruined unless I help you!"

2.2.5. It was a directing look. Christ guided him with his eye to withdraw and think things over a little.

2.2.6. It was a significant look: it conveyed grace to Peter's heart. The crowing of the rooster would not have brought him to repentance without this look. Power to change Peter's heart accompanied this look.

2.3. *Peter remembered the words of the Lord.*

2.4. Then *Peter went out, and wept bitterly.* One look from Christ melted him into tears of godly sorrow for sin.

Verses 63–71

We are here told, as before in the other Gospels:

1. How our Lord Jesus was mistreated by the servants of the high priest. Those who *held Jesus mocked him* and *smote* (beat) *him* (v. 63). They made fun of him; this sad night for him would be a merry night for them. They blindfolded him, and then they *struck him on the face,* continuing to do so until he named the person who had beat him (v. 64), intending to insult his prophetic role. *Many other things blasphemously spoke they against him* (v. 65).

2. How he was accused and condemned by the great Sanhedrin, the council of the *elders of the people, the chief priests, and the scribes,* who had all risen early and gathered *as soon as it was day* to pursue the mat-

ter. They would not have been up so early to pursue any good work.

2.1. They ask him, *Art thou the Christ?* They could not prove that he had ever said so explicitly, and so they urged him to acknowledge it to them (v. 67). If they had asked him this question with a willingness to admit that he was the Christ, it would have been good, but they asked it with a determination not to believe in him and with the intention of trapping him.

2.2. He justly complained about their unfair and unjust treatment of him (vv. 67–68). They should have examined him as a candidate for messiahship. "But," he said, "*if I tell you* that I am the Christ, *you will not believe.* Why should the cause be brought before you when who have already judged it in advance? Yet *if I ask you* what objections you will raise against the proofs I produce, *you will not answer me. You will neither answer me nor let me go*; if I am not the Christ, you should answer the arguments with which I prove I am; if I am, you should let me go. But you will do neither."

2.3. For the full proof that he was the Christ, he referred them to his second coming (v. 69): "*Hereafter* will the Son of Man sit at the right hand of the power of God, and then you will not need to ask whether he is the Christ or not."

2.4. They inferred from this that he had set himself up as the Son of God, and so they asked him whether he was or not (v. 70): *Art thou then the Son of God?* He called himself the Son of Man, referring to Daniel's vision of the *Son of man* (Da 7:13–14), but they understood enough to know that if he was that Son of Man, he was also the Son of God.

2.5. He acknowledged himself to be the Son of God: *Ye say that I am*; that is, "you are right in saying I am."

2.6. They based his condemnation on this (v. 71): *What need we any further witness?* It was true, they needed no further testimony to prove that he said he was *the Son of God*; they had it from *his own mouth.* But they could not think it possible for him to be the Messiah if he did not appear in worldly show and grandeur, as they had expected.

CHAPTER 23

This chapter continues and concludes the account of Christ's suffering and death. We have here: 1. His trial before Pilate the Roman governor (vv. 1–5). 2. His examination before Herod (vv. 6–12). 3. Pilate's struggle with the people to release Jesus and his finally submitting and condemning him to be crucified (vv. 13–25). 4. An account of what happened as they led him out to be crucified, and the words he spoke to the people who followed (vv. 26–31). 5. An account of what happened at the place of execution (vv. 32–38). 6. The conversion of one of the thieves as Christ was hanging on the cross (vv. 39–43). 7. The death of Christ (vv. 44–49). 8. His burial (vv. 50–56).

Verses 1–12

Our Lord Jesus was condemned as a blasphemer in the spiritual court. When they had condemned him, they knew they could not put him to death, and so they followed another course.

1. They accused him before Pilate. The *whole multitude* (assembly) *of them arose, and led him unto Pilate.* They demanded justice against him not as a blasphemer—that was not a crime that Pilate recognized—but as one who was disloyal to the Roman government, though in their

hearts Jesus' accusers did not look on this as any crime at all. Here is:

1.1. The accusation drawn up against him (v. 2). They misrepresented him:

1.1.1. As making the people rebel against Caesar. It was true, and Pilate knew it, that there was a general uneasiness among the people under the Romans. Jesus' accusers now wanted Pilate to believe that this Jesus was active in stirring up the general discontent. *We have found him perverting* (subverting) *the nation.* Christ had especially taught that they should pay taxes to Caesar, but he was falsely accused of *forbidding to give tribute to Caesar* here. Innocence is no protection against slander.

1.1.2. As making himself a rival with Caesar, though the very reason why they rejected him was that he did not offer to do anything against Caesar. This, however, was what they accused him of, that he was *saying he himself is Christ a king*.

1.2. His plea in response to this accusation: *Pilate asked him, Art thou the king of the Jews?* (v. 3), to which Christ answered, *Thou sayest it*; that is, "It is as you say." Christ's kingdom is wholly spiritual and therefore will not interfere with Caesar's jurisdiction. All who knew him knew that he never claimed to be the king of the Jews, never set himself up in opposition to Caesar's supremacy.

1.3. Pilate's declaration of his innocence (v. 4): He *said to the chief priests and the people, I find no fault in this man*.

1.4. The continued fury and outrage of the prosecutors (v. 5). Instead of being moderated by Pilate's declaration of Jesus' innocence, they were even more infuriated and vicious. We do not find that they were armed with any particular statement of fact, but they had resolved to continue loudly and confidently: *He stirs up the people, teaching throughout all Judea, beginning from Galilee to this place.* He did stir up the people, but it was for everything good and commendable. He did teach, but they could not charge him with teaching anything that tended to disturb the public peace.

2. They accused him before Herod.

2.1. Pilate moved Jesus and his case to Herod's court. The accusers mentioned Galilee. "Well," said Pilate, "does he come from that country? Is he a Galilean?" (v. 6). "Yes," they said. "Let's send him to Herod then," Pilate said, "since he belongs to Herod's jurisdiction." Pilate was already sick of the case and wanted to get it off his hands.

2.2. Herod was very willing to question him (v. 8): *When he saw Jesus, he was exceedingly glad.* He had *heard many things of him* in Galilee, and he longed to see him, but purely out of curiosity. It was only to satisfy this that he *hoped to have seen some miracle done by him.* To this end, he *questioned with him in many things.* But Jesus *answered him nothing*; nor would he satisfy him even with performing one miracle. The poorest beggar who asked a miracle to relieve his needs was never denied, but this proud ruler was denied. He could have seen Christ and his wonderful works many times in Galilee, but he refused, and now that he wanted to see them, he would be refused, because he had not recognized the day of God's coming to him (19:42, 44). Miracles must not be made cheap; almighty God is not at the beck and call of even the greatest human power.

2.3. His prosecutors appeared against him before Herod. *They stood, and vehemently accused him* (v. 10); "vigorously and arrogantly" is the meaning of the word.

2.4. Herod was very abusive toward him: he, with *his men of war, set him at nought.* They considered him a nobody; they treated him with contempt; they ridiculed him. They laughed at him as One who had lost his power and had become weak as other people (Jdg 16:7, 11, 17). Herod was more abusive toward Christ than Pilate was. Herod dressed Christ in *a gorgeous robe*, as a make-believe king, and so he taught Pilate's soldiers later to do him the same indignity.

2.5. Herod sent him back to Pilate, and it proved to be the occasion of a new friendship between them. Herod would not condemn Jesus as an evildoer, and so he *sent him again to Pilate* (v. 11), returning Pilate's polite respect. This mutual obligation contributed to their having a better understanding of one another (v. 12). They had been *at enmity between themselves.* Notice how those who quarreled with one another could still unite against Christ. Christ is the great peacemaker; both Pilate and Herod acknowledged his innocence, and their agreeing in this healed their disagreements in other matters.

Verses 13–25

We have here the righteous Jesus abused by the mob and rushed to the cross in the storm of popular noise and tumult.

1. Pilate solemnly declared that he believed Jesus had done nothing worthy of death or of chains. If he really believed that, he should have immediately released him. However, because Pilate himself was a bad man who lacked integrity, had no kindness for Christ, and was afraid of displeasing the people, he *called together the chief priests, and rulers, and people* and wanted to hear what they had to say. "'*You have brought this man to me*,' he said, 'and *I have examined him before you* and listened to all your allegations against him, but I can make nothing of it: *I find no fault in him.*'"

2. He appealed to Herod concerning him (v. 15): "*I sent you to Herod*, and he has *sent him back*. In his opinion, the crimes of the accused are not capital offenses. He has laughed at Jesus as someone who is weak but has not stigmatized him as dangerous." Herod thought the psychiatric hospital a more suitable place for Jesus than the place of hanging.

3. He proposed to release him if they would only agree to it. He should have done it without asking their permission. However, the fear of other human beings brings many into this trap: they would rather act unjustly than risk any trouble to themselves. To please the people:

3.1. He would release him as an evildoer, because *of necessity he must* (he was obliged to) *release one* at the time of the feast (v. 17).

3.2. He would punish him and then release him. Yet if there was no basis for the charges against him, why should he be punished?

4. The people chose to have Barabbas released instead. He was imprisoned for *a sedition* (insurrection) *made in the city* and for *murder*, but it was this criminal who was preferred over Christ: *Away with this man, and release unto us Barabbas* (vv. 18–19).

5. When Pilate urged a second time that Christ should be released, they cried out, *Crucify him, crucify him* (vv. 20–21). Nothing would be enough for them except that he be crucified: *Crucify him, crucify him.*

6. When Pilate reasoned with the people a third time, they were all the more imperious and outrageous (v. 22): "*Why? What evil hath he done?* Name the crime he has committed. *I have found no cause of death* (no grounds in him for the death penalty); *I will chastise him and let him go.*" But they were *instant with loud voices* (they insistently demanded), not requesting but demanding *that he*

might be crucified, as if they had as much right to demand the crucifying of One who was innocent as to demand the release of one who was guilty.

7. Pilate eventually gave in. The voice of the people and that of the *chief priests prevailed*. He *gave sentence that it should be as they required* (decided to grant their demand) (v. 24). This is repeated in v. 25, with the additional terrible record of the release of Barabbas: *He released unto them him that for sedition and murder was cast into prison*, because *him they had desired*, but he *delivered Jesus to their will*, and he could not have dealt more cruelly with him than to hand him over to their will.

Verses 26–31

The speed with which they conducted his trial is very strange. He was brought before the chief priests at daybreak (22:66), after that to Pilate, then to Herod, then back to Pilate, and there seems to have been a long struggle between Pilate and the people about him. He was scourged, crowned with thorns, and treated scornfully, and all this was done in the space of four or five hours, or six at the most, because he was crucified between nine o'clock and twelve. Never was anyone so *chased out of the world* as Christ was (Job 18:18). Now as they led him away to death, we find:

1. One who was made to carry his cross, *Simon* by name, *a Cyrenian*. They put Christ's cross on him and made him carry it behind Jesus (v. 26), so that Jesus would not faint under it and die. It was pity, but a cruel pity, that gave him this relief.

2. Many who were mourners. The ordinary people were moved with compassion toward him, because they had reason to think he was suffering unjustly. This drew a great crowd to follow him, as is usual at executions: *A great company of people followed him*, especially of women (v. 27), and they *bewailed and lamented him*. Although there were many who despised and insulted him, there were some who valued and pitied him. Many mourn Christ who do not believe in him, and many mourn for him but do not love him above all. He was not wholly taken up with his own concerns; he still found time and heart to notice their tears. Christ died lamented. He *turned to them* and told them *to weep not for him, but for themselves*.

2.1. He gave them a general direction concerning their mourning: *Daughters of Jerusalem, weep not for me*. They must not weep only for him—but rather let them *weep for themselves and for their children*. When we look on Christ crucified with the eye of faith, we should weep not for him but for ourselves. The death of Christ was something unique; it was his victory and triumph over his enemies; it was our salvation and the purchase of eternal life for us. Let us weep, therefore, not for him but for our own sins and the sins of our children, which were the cause of his death.

2.2. He gave them a particular reason why they should *weep for themselves and for their children*: "For behold, sad times are coming on your city." He had just wept over Jerusalem himself (19:42–44), and now he told them to weep over it. Christ's tears should set us weeping. Now the destruction of Jerusalem was foretold here by two proverbial sayings to show that this destruction would be terrible. People would then desire what they usually dread, to die childless (Jer 22:30) and to be buried alive.

2.2.1. They would wish to die childless. They would envy those who had no children, and they would say, *Blessed are the barren, and the wombs that never bare*.

2.2.2. They would wish to be buried alive: *They shall begin to say to the mountains, Fall on us, and to the hills,*

Cover us (v. 30). They would wish to be hidden in the darkest caves, so that they would be unable to hear anything of these disasters. They would be willing to be sheltered on any terms, even if it brought the risk of being crushed to pieces.

2.3. He showed how natural it was for them to infer from his sufferings that this desolation would come: *If they do these things in a green tree, what shall be done in the dry?* (v. 31). Christ was a green tree, fruitful and flourishing; now, if such things were done to him, we may conclude from that what would have been done to the whole human race if he had not intervened, and what will be done to those who continue to be dry trees despite all that is done to make them fruitful. The consideration of the bitter sufferings of our Lord Jesus should make us stand in awe of the justice of God. The best saints, compared with Christ, are dry trees; if he suffers, why should they not expect to suffer?

Verses 32–43

In these verses we have:

1. Various passages that we had before in Matthew and Mark about Christ's sufferings.

1.1. That *two others, malefactors* (criminals), *were led with him* to the place of execution.

1.2. That he was crucified at a place called *Calvary*, "skull." This was a more painful and shameful death than any other kind.

1.3. That he was crucified between two thieves. He was not only treated as a transgressor but also *numbered with* them (Isa 53:12).

1.4. That the soldiers who were employed in the execution seized his garments as their payment and divided them among themselves by lot: *They parted his raiment and cast lots*.

1.5. That he was jeered at and rebuked: *The people stood beholding. The rulers* stood among the crowds *and derided him*, saying with the people, *He saved others; let him save himself*. They challenged him to save himself from the cross, whereas he was saving others through the cross: "*If he be the Christ, the chosen of God*, let him save himself." They *mocked him* (vv. 36–37); they made fun of him, joking about his sufferings. And they said, *If thou be the king of the Jews, save thyself*.

1.6. That the written notice over his head, setting out his crime, was *This is the King of the Jews* (v. 38). He was put to death for claiming to be the king of the Jews, but God intended it as a declaration of who he really was. He is *the king of the Jews*, and his cross was the way to his crown. This was written in three learned languages, *Greek, and Latin, and Hebrew*. It was written in these three languages so that it could be known and read by all people. In these three languages Jesus Christ is proclaimed king.

2. Two passages that we did not have before, which are remarkable:

2.1. Christ's prayer for his enemies (v. 34): *Father, forgive them*. Christ spoke seven remarkable sayings while nailed to the cross, and this is the first. As soon as he was fastened to the cross, or while they were nailing him, he prayed this prayer, in which notice:

2.1.1. The petition: *Father, forgive them*. The sin they were now guilty of could justly have been made unpardonable. But no, they were especially prayed for. He now made intercession for transgressors (Isa 53:12). Now the sayings of Christ on the cross as well as his sufferings had a larger purpose than they seemed to have. He spoke this word as Mediator, which explained the meaning and purpose of his death: "*Father, forgive them*, not only these but all who will repent and believe the Gospel." The great thing that Christ died to purchase and obtain for us is the forgiveness of sin. His *blood speaks* this (Ge 4:10; Heb 12:24): *Father, forgive them.* Although they were his persecutors and murderers, he still prayed, "Father, forgive them."

2.1.2. The plea: *For they know not what they do*, because *if they had known*, they would not have crucified him (1Co 2:8). This shows us:

2.1.2.1. The crucifiers of Christ *know not what they do*.

2.1.2.2. There is a kind of ignorance that partly excuses sin: ignorance through lack of the means of knowledge or lack of an ability to receive instruction. The crucifiers of Christ were kept in ignorance by their rulers; they had prejudices against him instilled into them, so that in what they did against Christ and his message they thought they were doing God a service (Jn 16:2). Such people are to be pitied and prayed for. This is written also to give us an example.

2.1.2.2.1. In prayer we must call God Father, coming to him with reverence and confidence.

2.1.2.2.2. The great thing we must beg from God, both for ourselves and others, is the forgiveness of sins.

2.1.2.2.3. We must pray for our enemies, those who hate and persecute us, and we must pray fervently to God for the forgiveness of their sins, their sins against us. This is Christ's example of his own rule: *Love your enemies* (Mt 5:44–45). If Christ loved and prayed for such enemies, what enemies can we have whom we are not obliged to love and pray for?

2.2. The conversation with the thief on the cross. Christ was crucified between two thieves, and in them were represented the different effects the cross of Christ would have on people. Now the cross of Christ is to some *a savour of life unto life*, to others of *death unto death* (2Co 2:16).

2.2.1. Here was one of these criminals who was hardened to the end. Being near the cross of Christ, he hurled insults at him, as others did (v. 39). He said, *If thou be the Christ*, save yourself and us. Although he was now in pain and anguish, this did not humble his proud spirit, nor teach him to speak good words, not even to his fellow sufferer. He challenged Christ to save both himself and them. There are some who have the impudence to hurl insults at Christ and yet have the confidence to expect to be saved by him.

2.2.2. Here was the other one, who softened at the end. This criminal was snatched as a brand out of the burning (Am 4:11; Zec 3:2) and made a trophy of divine mercy and grace. This gives no encouragement to any to delay their repentance, for although it is certain that true repentance is never too late, it is just as certain that late repentance is seldom true. He had never had any offer of Christ, nor day of grace, before now: he was intended to be made a special example of the power of Christ's grace. Having conquered Satan in the destruction of Judas and the preservation of Peter, Christ set up this further memorial of his victory over Satan. We will see the case to be extraordinary if we notice:

2.2.2.1. The extraordinary activity of God's grace on this thief, which appeared in what he said.

2.2.2.1.1. Notice what he said to the other criminal (vv. 40–41).

2.2.2.1.1.1. He rebuked him for hurling insults at Christ, suggesting that this showed the insulter to be devoid of the fear of God: *Dost not thou fear God?* This question implies that it was the fear of God that restrained the questioner from following the crowd to commit this

evil. "If you had any humanity in you, you would not gloat over one who is suffering with you; *thou art in the same condition*; you are a dying man too."

2.2.2.1.1.2. He acknowledged that he deserved what was done to him: *We indeed justly. We received the due reward of our deeds.* True penitents acknowledge the justice of God in all the punishments of their sin. God *has done right*, but we *have done wickedly* (Ne 9:33).

2.2.2.1.1.3. He believed Christ had suffered wrongfully. This penitent thief was convinced by how Christ was behaving in his suffering that *he had done nothing amiss*. The chief priests wanted him crucified between the two criminals, as one of them, but this thief had more sense than they.

2.2.2.1.2. Notice what he said to our Lord Jesus: *Lord, remember me when thou comest into thy kingdom* (v. 42). This is the prayer of a dying sinner to a dying Savior. It was the honor of Christ to be prayed to in this way. It was the happiness of the thief to pray in this way; perhaps he had never prayed before, but now he was heard and saved in his last gasp.

2.2.2.1.2.1. Notice his faith in this prayer. In his confession of sin (v. 41) he revealed *repentance toward God*. In this request he showed his *faith toward our Lord Jesus Christ* (Ac 20:21). He acknowledged that he was Lord, that he had a kingdom, that he was going to that kingdom, and that those whom he favored would be happy; and to *believe* and *confess* all this (Ro 10:9) was a great thing at this time of the day, at the eleventh hour of his life (Mt 20:6). He believed in another life after this one and wanted to be happy in that life, not to be happy as the other thief wanted to be, by being saved from the cross, but to be well provided for when the cross had done its worst.

2.2.2.1.2.2. Notice his humility in this prayer. All he begged was, *Lord, remember me*, leaving it to Christ as to how he would remember him. And Christ did remember him.

2.2.2.1.2.3. Notice the hint of boldness and fervency in this prayer. He, as it were, breathed out his soul in it: "*Lord, remember me*; I desire nothing more; I commit my case into your hands." To be remembered by Christ now that he is in his kingdom is what we should fervently seek and pray for, and it will be enough to secure our welfare both in our living and in our dying.

2.2.2.2. The extraordinary gifts of Christ's favor to him: *Jesus said unto him, "Verily I say unto thee*—I the *Amen*, the faithful Witness—I say *Amen* to this prayer (Rev 3:14). In fact, you will have more than you asked for: *This day thou shalt be with me in paradise*" (v. 43). Notice:

2.2.2.2.1. To whom this was spoken: to the penitent thief. Although Christ himself was now experiencing the greatest struggle and anguish, he still had a word of encouragement to speak to a poor penitent. Through Christ, even great sinners, if they are true penitents, will obtain not only the pardon of their sins but also a place in the Paradise of God (Heb 9:15).

2.2.2.2.2. By whom this was spoken. This was another word that Christ spoke as Mediator, to explain the true meaning and purpose of his sufferings. Just as he died to purchase the *forgiveness of sins* for us (v. 34), so he died also to purchase eternal life for us. By this word we are given to understand that Jesus Christ died to open the kingdom of heaven to all penitent obedient believers.

2.2.2.2.2.1. Christ lets us know here that he was going to Paradise himself. He went through the cross to the crown, and we must not think of going any other way.

2.2.2.2.*2.2*. He lets all penitent believers know that when they die they will go to be with him there. Notice here how the happiness of heaven is described to us. It is *paradise*, a garden of pleasure, the *paradise of God* (Rev 2:7). It is being with Christ there. That is the happiness of heaven. It is immediate upon death: "*This day shalt thou be with me*, tonight, before tomorrow."

Verses 44–49

In these verses we have three things:

1. Christ's dying exalted by the wonderful signs that accompanied it.

1.1. The darkening of the sun at noon. It was now about the *sixth hour*, that is, twelve noon, and there was *a darkness over all the earth until the ninth hour*.

1.2. The tearing *of the veil* (curtain) *of the temple*. The sign of darkness was in the heavens, and this sign was in the temple, since both of these are the houses of God. This tearing of the curtain signified the taking away of the ceremonial law and of all other difficulties and discouragements in our approaches to God, so that now we may *come boldly to the throne of grace* (Heb 4:16).

2. Christ's dying explained (v. 46) by the words with which he breathed out his spirit. Jesus had cried out with a loud voice when he said, *Why hast thou forsaken me?* We are told so in Matthew and Mark. And it seems it was with *a loud voice*, too, that he said, *Father, into thy hands I commend my spirit*. He borrowed these words from his father David (Ps 31:5). Christ died with Scripture on his lips. In this prayer to God he called him *Father*. When he complained about being forsaken, he cried, *Eli, Eli, My God, my God*, but, to show that that terrible anguish of his soul was now past, he here called God Father. Christ used these words in a sense that was distinctive to himself as Mediator. He was now to *make his soul an offering for our sin* (Isa 53:10), to *give his life a ransom for many* (Mt 20:28). Now by these words he offered up the sacrifice; he, as it were, laid his hand on its head and surrendered it (Ex 29:10; Lev 4:4). "I deposit it"; "I pay it into your hands. Father, accept my life and soul instead of the lives and souls of the sinners I die for." The goodwill of the one bringing the offering was necessary for the acceptance of the offering. He commended his spirit into his Father's hand to be received into Paradise and returned the third day. Christ has made those words of David correspond to the purpose of dying saints; he has, as it were, sanctified them for their use. We must show that we are freely willing to die, that we firmly believe in another life after this, by saying, *Father, into thy hands I commend my spirit*.

3. Christ's dying applied by the impressions it made on those who were with him.

3.1. The centurion who had command of the guard was very moved by what he saw (v. 47). He was a Roman, a Gentile, but he *glorified God*. He also bore testimony to the patient sufferer: *Certainly this was a righteous man*. His testimony in Matthew and Mark goes further: *Truly this was the Son of God* (Mt 27:54; Mk 15:39).

3.2. The disinterested spectators were troubled. This is taken notice of only here (v. 48). They had come together to see an execution, but when they had seen what actually took place, they had to be very somber when they left. *They smote* (beat) *their breasts, and returned*. They took the thing very much to heart for the present. These very people probably belonged to those who had cried out, *Crucify him, crucify him* (v. 21), and had jeered at and blasphemed him when he was nailed to the cross, but the unusual way in which he died not only stopped their mouths but also startled their consciences. It seems, how-

ever, that the impression quickly wore off: *They smote their breasts, and returned*. They did not show any further sign of respect for Christ, but went home, and we have reason to fear that they forgot about it quickly and completely. This is how many who see Christ clearly as crucified among them in the word and sacraments are moved slightly for the present but receive no lasting impression. They see Christ's face and wonder at him briefly, but then they go away and immediately forget what kind of man he is and why they have to love him.

3.3. His own friends and followers had to keep their distance, but they got as close as they could and dared in order to see what was happening (v. 49): *All his acquaintance stood afar off*. This was part of his sufferings. And *the women who followed him from Galilee were beholding these things*. Now Christ was set as a sign that would be spoken against, as Simeon had foretold, so that the thoughts of many hearts would be revealed (2:34–35).

Verses 50–56

Here is an account of Christ's burial. Notice:

1. Who buried him. Those who knew him *stood afar off*; God raised up a *man named Joseph* (v. 50). He is characterized as *a good man and a just*, of unspotted reputation for goodness and godliness, not only just to all but good to everyone who needed him. He was a person of quality, a counselor, a member of the Sanhedrin, one of the elders of the Jewish church. Although he belonged to that group of men who had put Christ to death, he *had not consented to their counsel and deed* (v. 51). In fact, he not only dissented openly from those who were Christ's enemies but also agreed secretly with those who were his friends: *He himself waited for the kingdom of God*. There are many who, though they do not make a show of their outward profession of faith, will be more ready to do him an act of real service than others who appear more significant and make a louder noise.

2. What he did toward burying him.

2.1. He *went to Pilate* and *begged* (asked for) *the body of Jesus*.

2.2. He *took it down*, it seems, with his own hands and *wrapped it in linen*. It was the custom of the Jews to roll the bodies of the dead, as we wrap little children in their swaddling cloths. He bought a large piece of fine linen cloth and cut it into many pieces for this purpose.

3. Where he was buried: *In a sepulchre that was hewn in stone*. But it was *a sepulchre in which never man before was laid*.

4. When he was buried: on the Day of Preparation, when the Sabbath was about to begin. This is given as a reason why they were in such a hurry with the funeral. Weeping must not prevent sowing. Although they were weeping tears for the death of Christ, they must still apply themselves to the sanctifying of the Sabbath.

5. Who attended the funeral; not any of the disciples, only the women who came with him from Galilee (v. 55), who, just as they stayed by him while he hung on the cross, also followed him. They saw the sepulcher and how his body was laid in it. They were led to this not out of curiosity but out of devotion for the Lord Jesus.

6. What preparation was made for embalming his body after he was buried (v. 56): *They returned, and prepared spices and ointments* (perfumes), which was clearer evidence of their love than of their faith, because if they had remembered and believed that he would rise again on the third day, they would have spared their expense and effort in this. However, busy as they were in this preparation, they rested on the Sabbath.

CHAPTER 24

Our Lord Jesus went gloriously to his death, and he rose again even more gloriously. The evidence of Christ's resurrection is more fully related by this Evangelist than it was by Matthew and Mark. Here is: 1. Assurance given by two angels to the women who visited the tomb (vv. 1–7), and the report of this to the apostles (vv. 8–11). 2. Peter's visit to the tomb (v. 12). 3. Christ's meeting with the two disciples on the way to Emmaus (vv. 13–35). 4. His appearing to the eleven disciples themselves that same evening (vv. 36–49). 5. His farewell to them, his ascension into heaven, and the joy and praise of the disciples whom he left behind (vv. 50–53).

Verses 1–12

The *infallible proofs* of Christ's resurrection (Ac 1:3) are *things revealed which belong to us and to our children* (Dt 29:29). We have some of them here in these verses. We have:

1. The love and respect that the good women who had followed Christ showed him after he was dead and buried (v. 1). As soon as they could, after the Sabbath was over, they *came to the sepulchre* to embalm his body, to anoint his head and face, and perhaps his wounded hands and feet, and to scatter sweet spices on and around the body, as we usually scatter flowers around the dead bodies and graves of our friends. The zeal of these good women for Christ continued. Having prepared the spices on the evening before the Sabbath, they brought them to the tomb on the morning after the Sabbath, very early. Let what is prepared for Christ be used for him. Notice is taken of the names of these women: *Mary Magdalene, and Joanna, and Mary the mother of James.* Notice is also taken of certain others with them (v. 1 and again v. 10). These, who had not joined in preparing the spices, would still accompany them to the tomb; it was as if the number of Christ's friends increased when he died (Jn 12:24, 32).

2. Their surprise at finding the stone rolled away and the grave empty (vv. 2–3). They were *much perplexed* (v. 4) that *the stone was rolled away from the sepulchre* and that they *found not the body of the Lord Jesus.* Good Christians are often confused about things they should comfort and encourage themselves with.

3. The clear account that they had of Christ's resurrection from two angels, who appeared to them *in shining garments*. When the women saw the angels, they *were afraid* that the angels might have some bad news; but instead of asking them, they *bowed down their faces to the earth* to look for their dear Master in the grave. They would rather find him in his graveclothes than angels in their shining garments.

3.1. The angels rebuked the women for the absurdity of their search: *Why seek ye the living among the dead?* (v. 5). By this question the angels testified that Christ was living. It is the assurance of all the saints, *I know that my Redeemer liveth* (Job 19:25), and because he lives we also will live. However, those who look for him *among the dead* are rebuked.

3.2. They assured them that he had risen from the dead (v. 6): "*He is not here, but is risen*; he has left his grave."

3.3. They referred them to his own words: *Remember what he spoke to you when he was yet in Galilee.* If they had properly believed and taken notice of the prediction of his resurrection, they would have easily believed the thing itself when it came true. The angels repeated to them what Christ had often said in their hearing: *The Son of man must be delivered into the hands of sinful men.* He

must then *be crucified.* And would not this always remind them of what followed, that on *the third day he shall rise again?* These angels from heaven did not bring any new Gospel, but reminded the women of the sayings of Christ and taught them how to use and apply them.

4. Their satisfaction in this account (v. 8). They *remembered his words* when they were reminded of them in this way, and they concluded that if he had risen, it was no more than they had reason to expect. A timely remembrance of the words of Christ will help us come to a right understanding of his providence.

5. The report they brought of this to the apostles: *They returned from the sepulchre, and told all these things to the eleven, and to all the rest* of Christ's disciples (v. 9). In a short time, that morning, they all heard the announcement. But we are also told how the report was received (v. 11): *Their words seemed to them as idle tales* (like nonsense), *and they believed them not.* The hearers thought it was only the women's imagination, because they too had forgotten Christ's words. One has to wonder at the stupidity of these disciples, who had themselves professed so often that they believed Christ to be the Son of God, who had been told so often that he must die and rise again and then enter into his glory, who had seen him more than once raise the dead — that they should so hesitate to believe.

6. The investigation that Peter then made (v. 12). It was Mary Magdalene who brought the news to him, as is clear from Jn 20:1–2, where this story of his running to the tomb is told in more detail.

6.1. Peter ran quickly to the tomb when he heard the news. Perhaps he would not have been so ready to go there now if the women had not told him that the guard had fled. Many who run swiftly when there is no danger are cowardly when there is.

6.2. He looked into the tomb and noticed how orderly the strips of linen in which Christ had been wrapped had been taken off, folded up, and laid by themselves, but the body had gone. He was very particular in making his observations, as if he would rather believe his own eyes than the testimony of the angels.

6.3. He went away *wondering in himself at that which was come to pass.* He did not believe; he was only amazed at the thing; he did not know what to make of it. Many things that are puzzling and perplexing to us would be both clear and useful if we only rightly understood the words of Christ.

Verses 13–35

This appearance of Christ to the *two disciples* going to Emmaus was mentioned, but only mentioned, before (Mk 16:12); here it is related in detail. It happened the same day that Christ rose, the first day of the new world that rose with him. One of these two disciples was *Cleopas*; who the other was is not certain. It was one of those who were associated with the Eleven, mentioned in v. 9. Notice:

1. The walk and talk of these two disciples: *They went to a village called Emmaus*, which is reckoned to be about two hours' walk from Jerusalem. The accounts brought to them that morning of their Master's resurrection seemed to them *as idle tales*. However, as they traveled, they *talked together of all those things which had happened* (v. 14). They talked over these things, reasoning with themselves concerning the probability of Christ's resurrection.

2. The good company they met with on the road, when Jesus himself came and joined them (v. 15): *They communed together, and reasoned.* And then *Jesus himself*

drew near, as a stranger who, seeing them walking the same way as he was going, told them that he would be glad of their company. Where only two are well employed together in such a work, Christ will come to them and be a third. Two intertwined in faith and love become a *threefold cord, not easily broken* (Ecc 4:12). In their talk and discussion, they were together searching for Christ, and now Christ came to them. Those who seek Christ will find him. However, although they had Christ with them, they were not aware of it at first (v. 16): *Their eyes were held* (kept), *that they should not know* (recognize) *him*. Christ arranged matters in this way so that they could more freely converse with him, and he with them.

3. The discussion that took place between Christ and them when he recognized them but they did not recognize him. As is usual when friends meet incognito, or in disguise, Christ and his disciples were all asking questions.

3.1. Christ's first question to them was about their present sadness: *What manner of communications are these that you have one with another* (what are you discussing together) *as you walk, and are sad?* (v. 17). Notice:

3.1.1. They were sad. They had lost their dear Master and been sorely disappointed in their expectations of him. They had given up the cause and did not know what they could do to revive it. Although he had risen from the dead, they either did not know it or did not believe it, and so they were still sad. Christ's disciples are often sad and sorrowful even when they have reason to rejoice. They had *communications with one another* about Christ. It is good for Christians to talk about Christ, not only about God and his providence but also about Christ, his grace, and his love. Good company and good conversation are excellent antidotes to long-lasting sadness. Expressing grief may perhaps relieve the grieving. Joint mourners should comfort one another; comfort sometimes comes best from fellow mourners.

3.1.2. Christ came up to them and asked them what they were talking about together: *What manner of communications are these?* Although Christ had now entered into his state of exaltation, he still continued to be sensitive toward his disciples' needs. Our Lord Jesus notices the sorrow and sadness of his disciples, and in their distress, he is distressed (Isa 63:9). Christ has taught us to be conversational. It is not good for Christians to be morose and shy; they should be sociable. He has also taught us to be compassionate. When we see our friends sad and sorrowful, we should, like Christ here, notice their grief.

3.2. In answer to this, they asked him if he was a visitor. *Art thou only a stranger in Jerusalem, and hast not known the things that are come to pass there in these days?* Cleopas replied to him politely. We should be civil to those who are civil to us. It was a dangerous time now for Christ's disciples, but Cleopas was not suspicious that this stranger intended to inform on them. He himself was full of thoughts of Christ and of his death and sufferings, and he was amazed that everyone else was not so too: "What! Are you the only visitor to Jerusalem who does not know what has been done to our Master there?" He was very willing to inform this visitor about Christ. He did not want anyone to be ignorant of Christ. It is significant that these disciples, who were so eager to instruct the visitor, were instructed by him; to those who have, and use what they have, more will be given (Mk 4:25). It appears from what Cleopas said that the death of Christ was talked about greatly in Jerusalem, so that it could not be imagined that anyone would visit the city without knowing about it.

3.3. By way of reply, Christ asked about their knowledge (v. 19): *He said unto them, What things?* so making

himself seem even more of a stranger. Jesus Christ made light of his own sufferings, in comparison with the joy set before him (Heb 12:2). Notice how unconcerned he was as he looked back on his sufferings. He had reason to know what things they were talking about, because they were a bitter burden to him, and yet he asked, *What things?* They must tell him what things they knew, and then he would tell them the meaning of these things and lead them into their mystery.

3.4. They then gave him a detailed account of Christ. Notice the story they told (v. 19):

3.4.1. Here is a summary of Christ's life and character. The things they were full of were about *Jesus of Nazareth*, who *was a prophet*, a teacher come from God. He confirmed it by many glorious miracles of mercy, so that he was *mighty in deed and word before God and all the people*. He was greatly accepted by God and had a great reputation in the country. Many who are great before all the people are not so before God. Christ was mighty *before God and all the people*. Those who did not know this were strangers in Jerusalem.

3.4.2. Here is a modest account of his suffering and death (v. 20). "The *chief priests and our rulers delivered him to be condemned to death*, and *they have crucified him*." It is strange that they did not place a greater burden on those who had been guilty of crucifying Christ.

3.4.3. Here is an indication of their disappointment in him as the reason for their sadness: *We trusted that it had been he who should have redeemed Israel* (v. 21). Great things were expected from him by those who *looked for redemption*, and in it for the consolation of Israel (2:25). Now, if *hope deferred makes the heart sick* (Pr 13:12), hope disappointed, especially such a hope, kills the heart. *We trusted* (they said) *that it had been he that should have redeemed Israel*. Is it not he who does redeem Israel? In fact, was he not by his death paying the price of their redemption? So now, since that most difficult part of his undertaking was over, they had more reason than ever to trust that *this was he that should deliver Israel*.

3.4.4. Here is an account of their present wonder: "*This is the third day* since he was crucified and died, and that was the day when it was expected, if ever, that he would rise again and show himself as publicly in honor as he had been shown three days before in disgrace; but we see no sign of it. Everything is silent." They acknowledged that there was a report among them that he had risen, but they seemed to think it insignificant (vv. 22–23). "*Certain women also of our company made us astonished*. The went *early to the sepulchre* and found the body gone, and they said that they had *seen a vision of angels, who said that he was alive*, but we are ready to think it was only their imagination. Women are easily deceived." They acknowledged that some of the apostles had visited the tomb and found it empty (v. 24). "But *him they saw not*, and so we have reason to fear that he has not risen, because if he had, then surely he would have shown himself to them. We therefore have no great reason to think that he has risen. Our hopes were all nailed to his cross and buried in his grave."

3.4.5. Our Lord Jesus, though not recognized by them, made himself known to them through his word.

3.4.5.1. He rebuked them for the weakness of their faith in the Old Testament Scriptures: *O fools, and slow of heart to believe* (v. 25). Christ called them fools not in the sense of "evildoers," but in the sense of "people who are weak." What was condemned in them as their foolishness was:

3.4.5.1.1. Their slowness to believe. Christ tells us that those who are *slow of heart to believe*, who are kept from belief by prejudices that have never been examined impartially, are *fools*.

3.4.5.1.*2*. Their slowness to believe the writings of the prophets. If only we were more familiar with the Scriptures, and the divine purposes as far as they are made known in Scripture, we would not be subject to the perplexities we often get caught up in.

3.4.5.2. He showed them that the sufferings of Christ were really the appointed way to his glory and that he could not reach it any other way (v. 26): *"Ought not the Christ to have suffered* (did not the Messiah have to suffer) *these things, and to enter into his glory?"* The cross of Christ was something to which they could not reconcile themselves; now here he showed them two things that take away the offense of the cross (Gal 5:11):

3.4.5.2.*1*. That the Messiah had to suffer these things, and so his sufferings were not only no objection to his being the Messiah; they were really a proof of it. He could not have been a Savior if he had not been a sufferer.

3.4.5.2.*2*. That when he had suffered these things, he would *enter into his glory*, which he did at his resurrection. It is called *his* glory because he was entitled to it; it was the glory he had before the world was (Jn 17:5). It was also his because he had to enter into it. We are told to expect the crown of thorns and then that of glory.

3.4.5.3. He opened up to them the Scriptures of the Old Testament and showed them how they were fulfilled in Jesus of Nazareth (v. 27): *Beginning at Moses*, he went in order through all the prophets *and expounded to them the things concerning himself*, showing that the suffering he had now experienced was the fulfillment of all the prophecies of Scripture.

3.4.5.3.*1*. There are things dispersed throughout all the Scriptures about Christ that are very useful. You cannot go far in any part of Scripture without coming across something that refers to Christ, some prophecy, some promise, some prayer, some type or other. A golden thread of Gospel grace runs through the whole Old Testament.

3.4.5.3.*2*. The things about Christ need to be *expounded* (explained). They were delivered in darkness, according to that era, but now that the veil has been taken away (2Co 3:14–16), the New Testament explains the Old.

3.4.5.3.*3*. Jesus Christ is himself the best One to explain Scripture, especially the Scriptures about himself.

3.4.5.3.*4*. In studying the Scriptures, it is good to be methodical, because the Old Testament light shone gradually until *the perfect day* (Pr 4:18), and it is good to notice how at different times and in various ways God spoke to our ancestors concerning his Son, through whom he has now spoken to us (Heb 1:1–2). Some begin their Bible at the wrong end, studying Revelation first.

4. The revelation Christ eventually made of himself to them. One would have paid a great deal of money for a copy of the sermon Christ preached to them on the road, of that explanation of the Bible that he gave them, but it is not thought fit that we have it. The disciples were so charmed by it that they thought they had come to their destination too soon, but so it was: *They drew nigh to the village whither they went* (v. 28). At that point:

4.1. They asked him to stay with them: *He made as though he would have gone further*; he did not say that he would, but he seemed to them to be going farther. He would have gone farther if they had not urged him to stay. Those who want to have Christ live with them must invite him and be importunate with him. If he seems to draw away from us, it is only to draw out our importunity, as he did here: *they constrained him* (urged him strongly) with a kind and friendly insistence, saying, *Abide with us*. Those

who have experienced the pleasure and profit of fellowship with Christ want to do nothing but seek more of his company, and so they beg him not only to walk with them all day but also to stay with them at night. Christ gave in to their importunity: *He went in to tarry with them*. He has promised that if any *man open the door* to welcome him, he will *come in to him* (Rev 3:20).

4.2. He revealed himself to them (vv. 30–31). We may suppose that he continued with them the discussion that he had begun on the road. While supper was being prepared, which perhaps happened quickly, because the provision was small and ordinary, he probably continued to speak with them. Still they little thought it was Jesus himself who had been talking with them all this while; it was not until he eventually threw off his disguise that they began to suspect it was Jesus, as they sat down to eat: *He took bread, and blessed it*, and *broke, and gave* to them. This was not a miraculous meal like the feeding of the 5,000 with five loaves, nor a sacramental meal like that of the Eucharist, but an ordinary meal, and yet Christ did the same here as he did in those, to teach us to maintain our fellowship with God through Christ in ordinary providences as well as in special ceremonies. Wherever we sit down to eat, let us set Christ at the higher end of our table, take our food as blessed to us by him, eat and drink to his glory, and receive contentedly and thankfully what he wishes to give us, even if the food is very hastily prepared and ordinary. Then *their eyes were opened* and they recognized him. The mists scattered, the veil was taken away, and they knew for certain that it was their Master. He could take on another form, but no one else could assume his form, and so it had to be he. Notice how Christ by his Spirit and grace makes himself known. The work was completed by the opening of the eyes of their mind. If the One who gives revelation does not also give understanding, we remain in the dark.

4.3. He immediately disappeared: *He vanished out of their sight*. He "became not visible by them." As soon as he had given his disciples one glimpse of himself, he went immediately. We have such short and transient views of Christ in this world; we see him, but in a little while we lose sight of him.

5. The reflections these disciples had on this meeting, and the report they gave of it to their brothers at Jerusalem:

5.1. The thoughts each of them had on the influence that Christ's talk had had on them (v. 32): *They said one to another, Did not our hearts burn within us?* They did not so much compare notes as compare hearts as they looked back on the sermon Christ had preached to them. They had found his preaching powerful even when they did not know who the preacher was. It made things very clear to them, and, what was more, brought a divine heat with a divine light into their souls. They took notice of this to confirm their belief that it was truly, as at last they saw, Jesus himself who had been talking with them all along. Notice here:

5.1.1. What kind of preaching is likely to do good, namely, such as Christ's was, plain preaching: *he talked with us by the way*. Also scriptural preaching: *he opened to us the scriptures*. Ministers should show people their religious faith in their Bibles. They must show that they have made the Bible the fountain of their knowledge and the foundation of their faith.

5.1.2. What kind of hearing is likely to do good, namely, what makes the heart burn; when we are very moved by the things of God, especially by the love of Christ in dying for us, so having our hearts drawn out in love to him and drawn up in holy desires and devotions, then our hearts burn within us.

5.2. The report they brought of this to their brothers and sisters at Jerusalem (v. 33): *They rose up the same hour.* They were so ecstatic at Christ's revelation of himself to them that they could not wait to finish their supper, but returned as fast as possible to Jerusalem, even though it was toward evening. Now that they had seen Christ, they could not rest until they had brought the good news to the disciples, both to confirm their trembling faith and to encourage their sorrowful spirits. It is the duty of those to whom Christ has revealed himself to let others know what he has done for their souls. These disciples were full of this matter themselves, and so they had to go to their brothers and sisters to express their joys. Notice:

5.2.1. How, at the very moment they arrived, they found them talking about another proof of the resurrection of Christ. They found the Eleven and their usual companions *gathered together* late at night, and they found them saying among themselves—and when these two came in, they repeated to the two with joy and triumph—*The Lord is risen indeed, and hath appeared to Simon* (v. 34). That Peter had seen Christ before the other disciples had is seen from 1Co 15:5, where it is said, *He was seen of Cephas, then of the twelve.* Because the angel had ordered the women to tell Peter about it especially (Mk 16:7), to encourage him, it is highly probable that our Lord Jesus himself appeared the same day to Peter, even though we have no particular account of it. He had told this to his brothers, but notice that Peter did not declare it here himself; he did not boast about it, but the other disciples spoke of it with delight: *The Lord is risen indeed.* He had appeared not only to the women but also to Simon.

5.2.2. How they supported their evidence with an account of what they had seen (v. 35): *They told what things were done in the way.* The words spoken by Christ to them along the road are called here the *things* that were *done in the way.* The words Christ speaks are not empty sounds; wonderful things are done by them. And they are done along the way, casually, as it were, where they are unexpected. The two also told how Christ was eventually *known to* (recognized by) *them in the breaking of bread.*

Verses 36–49

Christ was seen five times the same day that he rose: by Mary Magdalene alone in the garden (Jn 20:14), by the women as they were going to tell the disciples (Mt 28:9), by Peter alone, by the two disciples going to Emmaus, and now at night by the Eleven. Notice:

1. The great surprise his appearance gave them. He came in among them at just the right time, as they were comparing notes about the proofs of his resurrection. *As they thus spoke, Jesus himself stood in the midst of them* and put it beyond question. Notice:

1.1. The encouragement Christ spoke to them: *Peace be unto you.* This shows in general that it was a kind visit that Christ now paid them, a visit of love and friendship. They did not believe those who had seen him; he therefore came himself. He had promised that after his resurrection he would see them in Galilee, but he wanted so much to see them that he made ahead of that appointment and saw them in Jerusalem. Christ is often better than his word, but never worse. Now his first word to them was, *Peace be to you.* With his very first word, Christ would show them that he had not come to quarrel with Peter for denying him or with the rest for running away from him; no, he came peaceably, to show them that he had forgiven them.

1.2. The fear they put themselves into because of his appearance (v. 37): They were *terrified,* supposing that *they had seen a spirit* (ghost), because he was among them before they were aware of it (SS 6:12). The word used (Mt 14:26) when they said *It is a spirit* is one that means "specter, apparition," but the word used here properly means "spirit"; they thought it was a spirit not clothed with a real body.

2. The great assurance they received from his message, in which we have:

2.1. The rebuke he gave them for their unjustified fears: *Why are you troubled, and why do thoughts* (doubts) *arise in your hearts?* (v. 38). Notice here:

2.1.1. That when at any time we are troubled, thoughts that do us harm tend to arise in our hearts. Sometimes the trouble is the effect of the thoughts. Sometimes the thoughts are the effect of troubles: outside there is conflict, and then inside there are fears (2Co 7:5).

2.1.2. That many of the troublesome thoughts with which our minds are disturbed arise from our mistakes about Christ. The disciples here thought that they had seen a spirit, whereas in reality they saw Christ. When Christ is convincing and humbling us through his Spirit, when he is testing and converting us through his providence, we make a mistake if we think he intends to harm us and if this then troubles us.

2.1.3. That all the troublesome thoughts and doubts that arise in our hearts at any time are known to the Lord Jesus. He rebuked his disciples for such thoughts to teach us to rebuke ourselves for them.

2.2. The proof he gave them of his resurrection, both to silence their fears and to strengthen their faith. He gave them two proofs:

2.2.1. He showed them his body, especially *his hands and his feet.* "Behold my hands and my feet; you see I have hands and feet, and so I have a real body. You can also see the marks of the nails in my hands and feet, and so it is my own body, the same one that you saw crucified, not a borrowed one." He stated the principle that a *spirit has not flesh and bones.* Now he inferred from this, "*It is I myself,* whom you have known so closely and have had such familiar dealings with; it is *I myself,* whom you have reason to rejoice in and not to be afraid of."

2.2.1.1. He appealed to their sight, showing them *his hands* and *his feet,* which had been pierced with the nails. Christ kept the marks of them in his glorified body so that they would be proofs that it really was he, and he was willing for them to be seen. He later showed them to Thomas, because he is not ashamed of his sufferings for us; we then have little reason to be ashamed of them, or of our sufferings for him.

2.2.1.2. He appealed to their sense of touch: *Handle* (touch) *me, and see.* He would not allow Mary Magdalene to touch him when he appeared to her (Jn 20:17), but the disciples were entrusted with that privilege here, so that those who were to preach his resurrection, and to suffer for doing so, would themselves be completely convinced of it. He told them to touch him so that they would be certain he was not a spirit. There were many heretics in the early days of the church who said that Christ never had any substantial body, that he neither was really born nor truly suffered. Thank God that these heresies have long since been buried, and we know and are certain that Jesus Christ was not a spirit or apparition, but had a true and real physical body, even after his resurrection.

2.2.2. He ate with them, to show that he had a real and true physical body. Peter emphasizes this: we *did eat and drink with him after he rose from the dead* (Ac 10:41).

2.2.2.1. When they *saw his hands and his feet, they yet believed not for joy, and wondered* (v. 41). In their weakness they did not believe—*yet* they did not believe. The truth of Christ's resurrection is very much corroborated by the fact that the disciples were so slow to believe it. Instead of stealing away his body and saying, "He is risen," when he was not, as the chief priests suggested they would do, they were ready to say again and again, "He is not risen," when really he was. When they did believe it later and risked their lives on it, it was only after the most comprehensive demonstration possible. However, although that was their weakness, it was excusable, because they did not disbelieve out of any contempt for the evidence offered them; rather, they *believed not for joy*. They thought the news was too good to be true. They *wondered*; they thought it not only too good, but also too great, to be true.

2.2.2.2. For their further assurance and encouragement, he *called for some meat* (food). It is not said that he ate with the disciples at Emmaus, but he did actually eat with them and the others here, to show that his body really and truly had returned to life. They gave him *a piece of a broiled fish, and of a honeycomb* (v. 42). This was ordinary food, but if it was food for the disciples, their Master would share in it as they did, because in the kingdom of our Father they will be provided for as he is.

2.3. The insight he gave them into the word of God.

2.3.1. He referred them to the words that they had heard from him when he was with them (v. 44): *These are the words which I said unto you while I was yet with you.* We would understand better what Christ does if only we remembered better what he has said.

2.3.2. He referred them to the words they had read in the Old Testament: *All things must be fulfilled which were written.* Whatever they found written about the Messiah in the Old Testament must be fulfilled in him, what was written about his sufferings as well as what was written about his kingdom. All things must be fulfilled, even the hardest, even the heaviest. The various parts of the Old Testament are mentioned here, since each contains things about Christ: *The law of Moses*, the *prophets*, the *Psalms* (v. 44). See in what various ways of writing God then revealed his will.

2.3.3. By a direct and immediate work on their minds he enabled them to grasp the true meaning and intention of the Old Testament prophecies of Christ: *Then opened he their understanding, that they might understand the scriptures* (v. 45). When he talked with the two disciples, he took the veil from the text, by opening the Scriptures; here he took the veil from the heart, by opening the mind. Notice here:

2.3.3.1. Jesus Christ by his Spirit operates on the minds of people. He has access to our spirits and can influence them directly.

2.3.3.2. Even good people need to have their understandings opened, because although they are not darkness, in many things they are still in the dark.

2.3.3.3. Christ's way of working faith in the soul is by opening the understanding. He comes into the soul by the door (Jn 10:1–2).

2.3.3.4. The intention of opening the understanding is that we may understand the Scriptures; not that we may be wise above what is written (1Co 4:6), but that we may be wiser *in* what is written. Christ's students never learn beyond their Bibles in this world, but they need to learn more and more from their Bibles.

2.4. The instructions he gave them as apostles: *"You are* to be *witnesses of these things* (v. 48), to announce them to the whole world. You are fully assured of these things yourselves; you are eyewitnesses and ear witnesses of them. Go and assure the world of them." Notice:

2.4.1. What they must preach. They must preach the Gospel. They must take their Bibles along with them and show people how the Messiah and the glories and graces of his kingdom were written about in the Old Testament, and then they must tell them how all this was fulfilled in the Lord Jesus.

2.4.1.1. The great Gospel truth about the death and resurrection of Jesus Christ must be declared to people (v. 46): *Thus it was written*, and so *thus it behoved* (was necessary for) *Christ to suffer.* "Go and tell the world:

2.4.1.1.1. "That Christ suffered, as it was written of him. Go, preach *Christ crucified* (1Co 1:23); do not be ashamed of his cross, do not be ashamed of a suffering Jesus. Tell them that it *behoved him to suffer*, that it was necessary for the taking away of the sin of the world.

2.4.1.1.2. "That he rose from the dead on the third day. In this also the Scriptures were fulfilled. Go and tell them that the One who *was dead is alive* and *lives for evermore* and *has the keys of death and the grave* (Rev 1:18)."

2.4.1.2. The great Gospel duty of repentance must be urged on people. *Repentance for sin* must be preached in *Christ's name* and by his authority (v. 47). "Go and tell all people that they must turn to the service of God in Christ. Their hearts and lives must be changed."

2.4.1.3. The great Gospel privilege of the *remission of sins* must be offered to all, and assured to all who *repent* and *believe the Gospel* (Mk 1:15). "Go and tell a guilty world that there is hope for them."

2.4.2. To whom they must preach.

2.4.2.1. They must preach this *among all nations.* They must scatter themselves and take this light along with them wherever they go. The prophets had preached repentance and remission to the Jews, but the apostles must preach them to the whole world. No one is exempt from the obligations the Gospel puts on people to repent, nor are any excluded from the immeasurable benefits of forgiveness.

2.4.2.2. They must *begin at Jerusalem*. There the Gospel day must dawn. Why must they begin there?

2.4.2.2.1. Because *thus it was written*: *The word of the Lord must go forth from Jerusalem* (Isa 2:3).

2.4.2.2.2. Because there the events on which the Gospel was based took place, and so they were first attested there. The first shining of the glory of the risen Redeemer was so strong and bright that it dared to face those daring enemies of his who had put him to death; it defied them.

2.4.2.2.3. Because he wanted to give us a further example of forgiving our enemies. The first offer of Gospel grace was made to Jerusalem, and thousands there were soon brought to share in that grace.

2.4.3. What help they would have in preaching. *Behold, I send the promise of my Father upon you*, and *you shall be endued* (clothed) *with power from on high* (v. 49). He assured them here that in a short time the Spirit would be poured out on them in greater measures than ever, and they would thereby be supplied with all the gifts and graces that were necessary for them to discharge this great trust. Those who receive the Holy Spirit are *endued with a power from on high*. Christ's apostles could never have planted his Gospel and set up his kingdom in the world as they did if they had not been given such power. This power from on high was the *promise of the Father*. Moreover, if it is the *promise of the Father*, we may be sure that the promise cannot be broken and that the thing promised is invaluable. Christ's ambassadors must wait until they have their powers. Although one would have thought that there was never such reason for haste in the preaching of the Gospel as now, nevertheless, the preachers must still wait until they were clothed with power from heaven.

Verses 50–53

His ascension into heaven, of which we have a very brief account in these verses. Notice:

1. How solemnly Christ took leave of his disciples. He had business to do in both worlds, and so he came from heaven to earth in his incarnation to fulfill his business here, and, having finished this, he returned to heaven to reside there. Notice:

1.1. Where he ascended from: from *Bethany*, near Jerusalem, by *the Mount of Olives*. That was the location of the garden in which his sufferings began; there he was in anguish, and Bethany means "the house of sorrow." Those who want to go to heaven must ascend from the house of sufferings and sorrow. It was here also that he began his triumphant entry into Jerusalem a while before (19:22).

1.2. Who the witnesses of his ascension were: *He led out his disciples* to see him ascend. The disciples did not see him rise up from out of the grave, because his resurrection was capable of being proved by their seeing him alive afterward, but they saw him ascend into heaven, because they could not otherwise have a visible demonstration of his ascension.

1.3. The farewell he gave them: *He lifted up his hands, and blessed them.* He did not go away in displeasure, but in love; he left a blessing behind him. He blessed them to show that having loved his own who were in the world, he loved them to the end (Jn 13:1).

1.4. How he left them: *While he was blessing them, he was parted from them,* to show that his being parted from them did not put an end to his blessing them. He began to bless them on earth, but he went to heaven to continue it.

1.5. How his ascension is described.

1.5.1. He *parted from them.* Those who love us, pray for us, and instruct us must be parted from us. Those who knew him physically must from now on no longer know him in this way.

1.5.2. He was *carried up into heaven.* No chariot of fire or horses of fire were needed (2Ki 2:11); he knew the way.

2. How cheerfully his disciples continued to serve him. They worshiped him at his departure (v. 52). He blessed them, and in gratitude for the blessing, they worshiped him. The cloud that received him from their sight did not cut off them or their services from his sight. They *returned to Jerusalem with great joy.* They went there and stayed there *with great joy.* This was a wonderful change. When Christ told them that he must leave them, sorrow filled their hearts, but now that they had seen him go, they were filled with joy. They performed many acts of devotion while they continued to expect the promise of the Father (v. 53). They attended the temple service at the hours of prayer. *They were continually in the temple,* as their Master was when he was at Jerusalem. They knew temple sacrifices had been superseded by Christ's sacrifice, but they joined in the temple songs. Nothing better prepares the mind to receive the Holy Spirit than holy joy and praise. Fears are silenced, sorrows sweetened and softened, and hopes maintained. *Amen.* May he be praised and blessed continually!

A Practical and Devotional Exposition of the Gospel of

John

The question of when and where this Gospel was written does not matter; we are sure that it was given to John, the brother of James, one of the twelve apostles, who was distinguished by the honorable characterization *that disciple whom Jesus loved.* The old commentators tell us that John lived the longest of all the twelve apostles and was the only one of them who died naturally. Some of them say that he wrote this Gospel at Ephesus, in opposition to the heresy of the Ebionites, who held that our Lord was merely human. It is clear that he wrote as the last of the four Evangelists, and comparing his Gospel with theirs, we may notice: 1. That he relates what they omitted; he brings up the rear, gleans what the others passed by. 2. That he gives us more of the mystery of what the other Evangelists gave us only the history of. Some of the old commentators observe that the other Evangelists wrote more of the physical things of Christ, but that John writes of the spiritual things of the Gospel, its life and soul.

CHAPTER 1

The scope and purpose of this chapter is to confirm our faith in Christ as the eternal Son of God, the true Messiah and Savior of the world. To this end, we have: 1. An account given of him by the inspired writer himself, laying down fairly, in the beginning, what he intended his whole book to prove (vv. 1–5, 10–14, 16–18). 2. The testimony of John the Baptist about him (vv. 6–9, and again v. 15, and especially vv. 19–37). 3. His own revelation of himself to Andrew and Peter (vv. 38–42) and to Philip and Nathanael (vv. 43–51).

Verses 1–5

Let us ask what there is in these strong lines. The Evangelist lays down here the great truth he is to prove, that Jesus Christ is God, one with the Father. Notice:

1. About whom he speaks—the *Word.* This is an idiom that is distinctive in John's writings. Even the common Jews were taught that the *Word of God* was the same as God. The Evangelist, at the close of this introduction (v. 18), clearly tells us why he calls Christ *the Word: because he is the only begotten Son, who is in the bosom of the Father, and has declared him. Word* is twofold: "word conceived" and "word uttered."

1.1. There is the word conceived, that is, thought, which is the first and only immediate product and conception of the soul. Therefore, the second person in the Trinity is rightly called *the Word,* because he is the *first-begotten of the Father.* There is nothing we are surer of than that we think, but nothing we are more in the dark about than how we think. Surely, then, generations of the Eternal Mind may well be allowed to be great mysteries of godliness (1Ti 3:16), the bottom of which we cannot fathom, while we continue to adore the depths.

1.2. There is the word uttered, and this is speech, the chief and most natural indication of the mind. In this way,

too, Christ is *the Word,* because *by him* God has in *these last days spoken to us* (Heb 1:2). He has made known God's mind to us, as a person's word or speech makes known their thoughts. John the Baptist was the voice, but Christ the Word.

2. What he says about him. He asserts:

2.1. His existence in the beginning: *In the beginning was the Word.* This shows that he existed not only before his incarnation but also before all time. The world was from the beginning, but the Word was in the beginning. The Word existed before the world had a beginning. The One who was in the beginning never began, and so always was.

2.2. His coexistence with the Father: *The Word was with God, and the Word was God.* It is repeated in v. 2: *the same* was *in the beginning with God;* that is, he was with God from eternity. In the beginning, the world was from God, and the Word was with God, since he was always with him. The Word was with God:

2.2.1. With respect to essence and substance, the *Word was God.*

2.2.2. With respect to delight and happiness. There was a glory and happiness that Christ had *with God* before the world was (17:5).

2.2.3. With respect to purposes and intentions. This grand matter of human reconciliation to God was agreed on between the Father and the Son from eternity.

2.3. His agency in making the world (v. 3).

2.3.1. This is here explicitly asserted: *All things were made by him.* He was with God, active in the divine work at the beginning of time. God made all things *by* him not as a worker cuts by means of an ax, but as the body sees by the eye.

2.3.2. The opposite is denied: *Without him was not anything made that was made,* from the highest angel to the lowliest worm. God the Father did nothing in that work without the Word. This proves that he is God, which in turn proves the excellence of the Christian religion—its author and founder is the same One who was the author and founder of the world. The verse also shows how well qualified he was for the work of our redemption and salvation. The One who is appointed the author of our happiness was the author of our being.

2.4. The origin of life and light that is in him: *In him was life* (v. 4). This further proves that he is God.

2.4.1. He has *life in himself*; he is not only the true God but also *the living God* (Jer 10:10).

2.4.2. All living creatures have their life in him, and all the life that is in the creation is derived from him. He is that Word by which people live more than on bread (Mt 4:4; Dt 8:3).

2.4.3. Reasonable creatures have their light from him; that *life* which is *the light of men* comes from him. Life in human beings is something greater and nobler than it is in other creatures; it is rational, not merely animal. The *spirit of a man is the candle of the Lord* (Pr 20:27), and it was the eternal Word who lit this candle. The light of reason, as well as the life of sense, is derived from him. From whom may we better expect the light of divine revelation than from the One who gave us the light of human reason?

2.5. The revelation of him to human beings. Why is it that he has been so little noticed and regarded? John answers this: *The light shines, but the darkness comprehends it not* (v. 5). Notice:

2.5.1. The revelation of the eternal Word to this fallen world, even before he was revealed in the flesh: *The light shineth in darkness.*

2.5.1.1. The eternal Word, as God, shines in the darkness of natural conscience. The whole human race has an innate sense of something of the power of the divine Word. See Ro 1:19–20.

2.5.1.2. The eternal Word shone in the darkness of the Old Testament prophecies and promises. The One who had commanded the light of this world to shine out of darkness (2Co 4:6) was himself a light shining in darkness for a long time.

2.5.2. The inability of the corrupt world to receive this revelation: *The darkness comprehended it not.* The darkness of error and sin overcame and completely eclipsed this light. The Jews, who had the light of the Old Testament, did not comprehend Christ in it. It was necessary, therefore, for Christ to come, both to put right the errors of the Gentile world and to apply the truths of the Jewish church.

Verses 6–14

The Evangelist here brings in John the Baptist giving honorable testimony to Jesus Christ. Now in these verses, before he does this:

1. He gives us an account of the witness he is about to produce. His name was John, which means "gracious."

1.1. We are here told about him, in general, that he was *a man sent from God* (v. 6). He was a mere man. God is pleased to speak to us through people like ourselves. He was *sent from God*; he was God's messenger. God gave him both his mission and his message. John performed no miracle; the strictness and purity of his life and message were clear indications that he was sent of God.

1.2. We are here told what his role and work were (v. 7): *The same came for* (as) *a witness*, "as a testimony." The legal institutions had long been a testimony for God in the Jewish church, but now divine revelation was to be directed into another channel. There was a profound silence about the Redeemer until John the Baptist came as a witness to him. Notice:

1.2.1. The subject of his testimony: *He came to bear witness to the light.* Light is something that witnesses for itself. Christ's light does not need human testimony, but the world's darkness does. John was like the night watchman who goes around town declaring the approach of morning light to those who have closed their eyes. He was sent by God to declare that the era that would bring life and immortality to light was near (2Ti 1:10).

1.2.2. The purpose of his testimony: *That all men through him might believe*—not in him, but in Christ. He taught people to look and pass through him, to look to Christ. If they would only receive this human witness, they would soon find that the witness of God was greater (1Jn 5:9). It was intended that through him all might believe, none being excluded except those who excluded themselves.

1.3. We are warned here not to mistake John the Baptist for the light, since he came only to testify to it (v. 8): *He was not that light.* He was a star, like the one that guided the wise men to Christ, a morning star, but he was not the Sun. The Evangelist here, while speaking very honorably of him, nevertheless shows that he had to give way to Christ. He was great as the prophet of the Highest God but was himself not the Highest. We must be careful neither to overvalue ministers nor to undervalue them; they are not our lords, but ministers by whom we believe. Those who usurp the honor of Christ lose the right to the honor of being the servants of Christ, but John was very useful as a witness to the light, even though he was not that light. Those who shine the light of the Gospel on us may be very useful to us, even though their light is borrowed.

2. Before he continues with John's testimony, he returns to give us a further account of this Jesus to show the graces of his incarnation.

2.1. Christ was the *true Light* (v. 9). Christ is the great light that deserves to be called so (Ge 1:16). Other lights are only figuratively and equivocally called so: Christ is *the true light*. But how does Christ enlighten everyone who comes into the world?

2.1.1. By his creating power he enlightens everyone with the light of reason; all the beauty it puts on us is from Christ.

2.1.2. By the declaration of his Gospel to all nations he in effect enlightens every person. John the Baptist was a light, but he enlightened only Jerusalem and Judea, as a candle illuminates only one room. Christ, however, is the true light, because he is a light to enlighten the Gentiles (Lk 2:32). Divine revelation was not now to be confined, as it had been, to one people, but was to be spread to all people (Mt 5:15). Whatever light any person has, they are indebted to Christ for it, whether it is natural or supernatural.

2.2. Christ *was in the world* (v. 10). This speaks of his being in the world when he took our nature on him and lived among us: *I am come into the world.* He left a world of happiness and glory and was here in this sad and miserable world. *He was in the world*, but not of it (17:14, 16). The greatest honor that was ever put on this world was that the Son of God was once in the world. It should reconcile us to our present living in this world that Christ was once here. Notice here:

2.2.1. What reason Christ had to expect the most affectionate and respectful welcome possible in this world, namely, that *the world was made by him.* He came to save a lost world because it was a world that he himself had made. The world was made by him and should therefore praise him.

2.2.2. What a cold reception he met with nevertheless: *The world knew him not.* The *ox knows his owner* (Isa

1:3), but the crueler world did not. They did not acknowledge him, did not welcome him, because they did not *know* (recognize) *him*. When he comes as a Judge, the world will recognize him.

2.3. He *came to his own* (v. 11), not only to the world, which was his own, but also to the people of Israel, who were especially his own. He was sent to them first (Mt 10:6; 15:24; Mk 7:27). He came to his own people, to seek and save them, because they were his own (Lk 19:9–10). Notice:

2.3.1. That most rejected him: *His own received him not*. He had reason to expect that those who were his own would welcome him. He came among them himself, introduced with signs and wonders, himself the greatest of those wonders, and it is not said of them, therefore, as it was of the world, that they *knew him not* (v. 10); rather, *his own*, though they recognized him, still *received him not* (v. 11). Many who profess to be Christ's own do not receive him, because they will neither part with their sins nor agree to have him reign over them (Lk 19:14).

2.3.2. That even so, there was a remnant who acknowledged him and were faithful to him. There were those who received him (v. 12): *But as many as received him*. Many of them were persuaded to submit to Christ, and so were many more who *were not of that fold* (10:16). Notice here:

2.3.2.1. The true Christian's description and right: that a Christian is someone who receives Christ and *believes on his name*. Believing in Christ's name is receiving him as a gift from God. We must receive his message as true and good, and we must receive the image of his grace and impressions of his love as the motive of our affections and actions.

2.3.2.2. The true Christian's honor and privilege are twofold:

2.3.2.2.1. The privilege of adoption: *To them gave he the power to become the sons of God*. Up to that time, the adoption concerned only the Jews, but now, by faith in Christ, Gentiles are the *children of God* (Gal 3:26). To them he gave a right; all the saints have this power. It is the indescribable privilege of all true Christians that they have become the children of God. If they are the children of God, they have become so; they have been made so. *Behold what manner of love is this* (1Jn 3:1). God calls them his children; they call him Father. The privilege of adoption is entirely owing to Jesus Christ; he gave this right to those who believe on his name. The Son of God became a Son of Man, so that the sons and daughters of men could become the sons and daughters of God Almighty.

2.3.2.2.2. The privilege of regeneration (v. 13): *Which were born*. All the children of God are born again (3:3); all who are adopted are regenerated. Now here we have an account of the origin of this new birth:

2.3.2.2.2.1. Negatively: it is *not* brought about *of blood, not of the will of the flesh*, nor of *corruptible seed* (1Pe 1:23). We do not become the children of God as we become the children of our natural parents. Grace does not run in the blood, as corruption does. It is not produced by the natural power of our own will. Just as it is not of *blood*, nor of *the will of the flesh*, so neither is it of the *will of man*. It is the grace of God that makes us willing to be his.

2.3.2.2.2.2. Positively: it is *of God*. This new birth comes about by the word of God as the means (1Pe 1:23) and by the Spirit of God as the great and sole author. True believers are *born of God* (1Jn 3:9; 5:1).

2.4. The *word was made flesh* (v. 14). This expresses Christ's incarnation more clearly than what went before. Now that the right time had come (Gal 4:4; Eph 1:10), he

was sent out in a different way, *made of a woman* (Gal 4:4). Notice here:

2.4.1. The human nature of Christ with which he was veiled (Heb 10:20), and that is expressed in two ways.

2.4.1.1. *The word was made flesh*. Forasmuch as the *children* who were to become the sons of God were *partakers of flesh and blood, he also himself likewise took part of the same* (Heb 2:14). The Socinians said that he was man and was "made a god" (compare Ex 7:1), whereas John here says that *he was God* but *was made flesh*. Compare v. 1 with this. Christ subjected himself to the miseries and adversities of human nature. *Flesh* refers to human beings as tainted with sin (Ge 6:3), and Christ appeared *in the likeness of sinful flesh* (Ro 8:3), was made *sin for us* (2Co 5:21), and *condemned sin in the flesh* (Ro 8:3). The *Word of the Lord*, who was made flesh, *endures for ever* (1Pe 1:25); when made flesh, he did not stop being the Word of God.

2.4.1.2. He *dwelt among us*. Having taken on himself human nature, he put himself into the place and condition of other human beings. Having taken a body of the same mold as ours, he came in it and lived in the same world as we. He *dwelt among us*, us worms of the earth (Job 17:14; 25:6; Isa 41:14), us who were corrupt and depraved and who rebelled from God. When we look to the upper world, how insignificant and contemptible this flesh, this body, that we carry about with us appears, and this world in which our lot is cast. By being made flesh and living in this world as we do, the eternal Word has honored them both, and this should make us willing to remain in the flesh as long as God has any work for us to do. He lived *among* the Jews. Although the Jews were unkind to him, he continued to live among them. He *dwelt among us*. He was not in the world as a traveler who stays at an inn for a night, but *dwelt* among us. The original word is significant: he lived *as in a tabernacle*, which shows that he lived here in very humble circumstances, like shepherds who live in tents. Yet his stay among us would not last forever. He lived here as in a tent, not as at home. As God formerly lived in the tabernacle of Moses, so now he lived in the human nature of Christ. And we are to offer all our prayers to God through Christ.

2.4.2. The rays of his divine glory that penetrated this veil of flesh: *We beheld his glory, the glory as of the only begotten of the Father, full of grace and truth* (v. 14). As the sun is still the fountain of light even when it is eclipsed or clouded over, so Christ remained the brightness of his Father's glory. There were those who saw through the veil. Notice:

2.4.2.1. Who were the witnesses of this glory: *we*, his disciples and followers, we among whom he lived. Other people reveal their weaknesses to those with whom they have even a casual acquaintance, but it was not so with Christ; those who associated with him most closely saw most of his glory. They saw the glory of his divinity, while others saw only the veil of his human nature.

2.4.2.2. What evidence they had of it: *we saw* it. They did not receive their evidence by report, secondhand, but were themselves eyewitnesses (Lk 1:2). *We saw* it. The word refers to a fixed, enduring sight. This apostle himself explains this: *What we declare unto you* of the Word of life is what we have *seen with our eyes* and what we *have looked upon* (1Jn 1:1).

2.4.2.3. What the glory was: *the glory as of the only begotten of the Father*. The glory of the *Word made flesh* was such a glory as was fitting for *the only begotten Son of God* and could not be the glory of any other. Jesus Christ is the *only begotten of the Father*. Believers are the children of God by the special favor of adoption and the special grace of regeneration. They are in a sense *of a like nature* to the divine nature (2Pe 1:4) and have the image of God's perfections, but Christ is *of the same nature* as God. He was clearly declared to be the *only begotten of the Father* by what was seen of his glory when he lived among us. His divine glory appeared in the holiness and heavenliness of his message, in his miracles, and in the purity, goodness, and kindness of his whole way of life. God's goodness is his glory (Ex 33:18–19), and Christ went about doing good (Ac 10:38). Perhaps the Evangelist especially had in mind the glory of Christ's transfiguration, of which he was an eyewitness.

2.4.2.4. What advantage those he lived among had from this. The law was in the old tabernacle in which God lived; in this tabernacle was grace. In that old tabernacle were types; in this one was truth. Christ was *full of grace and truth*, the two great things that fallen humanity stands in need of. He was full of grace and therefore completely qualified to intercede for us, and he was full of truth and therefore fit to instruct us. He had a fullness of knowledge and a fullness of compassion.

Verses 15–18

In these verses:

1. The Evangelist again begins to give us John the Baptist's testimony about Christ (v. 15). Notice:

1.1. How he expressed his testimony: he cried out, according to the prophecy that he would be *the voice of one crying*. The Old Testament prophets cried out to show people their sins; this New Testament prophet cried out to show people their Savior. It was an open, public testimony that was declared so that all kinds of people could take notice of it. He was free and sincere in testifying. He cried out as one who was both very much assured by the truth to which he witnessed and very much moved by it.

1.2. What his testimony was. He appealed to what he had said at the beginning of his ministry, when he had directed them to expect One who would *come after him*, whose forerunner he was. What the Baptist said then, he applied now to this Jesus whom he had just baptized: *This was he of whom I spoke*. He went beyond all the Old Testament prophets here by particularly pointing out the person:

1.2.1. He said that Jesus surpassed him: "*He that comes after me* is more important than I, just as the ruler or peer who follows is more important than the messenger or usher who makes way for them." Jesus Christ, who was to be called the *Son of the Highest* (Lk 1:32), was more important than John the Baptist, who was to be called only the *prophet of the Highest* (Lk 1:76). John was a great man, but he was still eager to say that Jesus was far greater than he. All ministers of Christ must declare him to be more important than themselves and their own personal interests. "He comes after me but is more important than I." God dispenses his gifts according to his good will, and he crosses hands many times, as Jacob did (Ge 48:13–14). Paul far surpassed those who were in Christ before him.

1.2.2. He gave a good reason for it here: *For he was before me.* Christ was before John with respect to seniority because he was before Abraham (8:58): "I was born only recently, in comparison; he is from eternity." He was also before John with respect to supremacy: "He is my Master; I am his minister and messenger."

2. The Evangelist returns to speak about Jesus Christ; he cannot continue with John the Baptist's testimony until v. 19. V. 16 has a clear connection with v. 14, where the incarnate Word was said to be *full of grace and truth*. He has a fountain of overflowing fullness: *we all have*

received. "All we believers"; as many as received him (v. 16) received from him. All true believers receive from Christ's fullness; the best and greatest saints cannot live without him, and the weakest and most insignificant can live through him. Because we have nothing except what we have received, proud boasting is excluded (Ro 3:27), and because there is nothing we lack that we cannot receive, our perplexing fears are silenced. We have received:

2.1. *Grace for grace.* What we have received through Christ is all summed up in the one word *grace*; it is "even grace," so great a gift, so rich, so invaluable. We have received no less than grace. It is repeated, *grace for grace.* Notice:

2.1.1. What the blessing is that we have received. It is grace, the goodwill of God toward us and the good work of God in us. God's goodwill produces the good work, and then the good work qualifies us for further signs of his goodwill. Just as the cistern receives water from the fullness of the fountain, the branches receive sap from the fullness of a root, and the air receives light from the fullness of the sun, so we receive grace from the fullness of Christ.

2.1.2. How we receive this blessing: *Grace for grace.* The phrase is distinctive, and interpreters give it different senses, each of which is useful to illustrate the unsearchable riches of the grace of Christ (Eph 3:8). *Grace for grace* shows us:

2.1.2.1. The freeness of this grace. It is grace for the sake of grace. We receive grace not for our own sakes, but for the sake of Jesus Christ.

2.1.2.2. The fullness of this grace. *Grace for grace* is an abundance of grace, grace on grace. It is a blessing poured out, such that there will not be room to receive it: one grace promises even more grace.

2.1.2.3. The usefulness of this grace. *Grace for grace* is grace to advance further grace. Gracious favors received are to lead to gracious acts performed. Grace is a talent to be used.

2.1.2.4. The substitution of New Testament grace for Old Testament grace. This sense is confirmed by what follows (v. 17), because the Old Testament had grace in a type, whereas the New Testament has grace in truth. This is grace instead of grace.

2.1.2.5. It shows the growth and continuation of grace. *Grace for grace* is one grace to apply, confirm, and perfect another grace.

2.1.2.6. *Grace for grace* is grace in us corresponding to grace in him, just as the impression on wax corresponds to the seal line for line. The grace we receive from Christ *changes us into the same image* (2Co 3:18).

2.2. *Grace and truth* (v. 17). The Evangelist earlier said (v. 14) that Christ was *full of grace and truth*; here he says that through him *grace and truth* came to us. From Christ we receive grace; this is a theme John delights to harp on; he cannot leave it. He further observes two things in this verse about this grace:

2.2.1. It is more important than the Law of Moses: *The law was given by Moses*, and it was a glorious revelation, but the Gospel of Christ is a much clearer revelation. What was given by Moses was purely terrifying and threatening; what is given by Jesus Christ has all the beneficial uses of the law, but not its terror, because it is grace. The attractive winsomeness of love, not the fears of law and the curse, is the genius of the Gospel.

2.2.2. It is linked with truth: *grace and truth*. In the Gospel we have the revelation of the greatest truths to be embraced by the mind as well as of the richest grace to be embraced by the heart and will. It is grace and truth with reference to the law that was given by Moses. It is:

2.2.2.1. The fulfillment of all the Old Testament promises.

2.2.2.2. The substance of all the Old Testament types and shadows. Christ is the true paschal lamb (1Co 5:7), the true scapegoat (Lev 16:8, 10), the true manna (6:49, 58). Israel had grace in the picture; we have grace in person. *Grace and truth came*, or "was made"; the word translated *came* is the same word that was translated *were made* and *was made* in v. 3. By him this *grace and truth* hold together (Col 1:17).

2.3. A clear revelation of God to us (v. 18): he has *declared* God to us, whom *no man hath seen at any time*. Notice:

2.3.1. The insufficiency of all other revelations: *No man hath seen God at any time*. This shows:

2.3.1.1. That because the nature of God is spiritual, he is invisible to physical eyes. We, therefore, need to live by faith, by which we see the One who is invisible (Heb 11:27).

2.3.1.2. That the revelation that God made of himself in the Old Testament was very short and imperfect in comparison with what he has now made known through Christ: *No man hath seen God at any time*.

2.3.1.3. That Christ's holy religion is commended to us by its having been founded by One who had seen God and who knew more of his mind than anyone else ever did.

2.3.2. The all-sufficiency of the Gospel revelation proved from its author: *the only begotten Son, who is in the bosom of the Father, he has declared him*. Notice here:

2.3.2.1. How fit Christ was to make this revelation.

2.3.2.1.1. He is the only-begotten Son. Who is more likely to know the Father than the Son? In whom is the Father better known than in the Son (Mt 11:27)?

2.3.2.1.2. He is *in the bosom of the Father*, that is:

2.3.2.1.2.1. In the bosom of his special love, dear to him, precious to him, in whom he was pleased (Mt 3:17; 12:18; 17:5).

2.3.2.1.2.2. In the bosom of his secret purposes. No one was so fit as the Son to make God known, because no one knew his mind as he did.

2.3.2.2. How free he was in making this revelation: *he has declared*. The Son has declared the revelation of God that no one had seen or known at any time, not only what was hidden of God but also what was hidden in God (Eph 3:9). It refers to a plain, clear, and full revelation. The message, the will, of God and the way of salvation are now clear for all to see. This is the grace, this the truth, that came through Jesus Christ.

Verses 19–28

We have here the testimony of John that he gave to the messengers who were sent from Jerusalem to ask about him. Notice:

1. Who sent to him and who were sent.

1.1. Those who sent to him were *the Jews at Jerusalem*. One would have thought that those leaders of the Jewish church would have understood the times (1Ch 12:32; Mt 16:3) well enough to know that the Messiah was near and that they would therefore have recognized the one who was his forerunner, but instead they sent messengers to cross-examine him. Secular learning, honor, and power seldom make people's minds ready to receive divine light.

1.2. Those who were sent were:

1.2.1. *Priests and Levites*. John the Baptist was himself a priest of the descendants of Aaron, and so it was not right that he be examined by anyone except priests.

1.2.2. Some *of the Pharisees*, who thought they did not need to repent.

2. Why they were sent; it was to ask about John and his baptism. They did not send for John to come to them; they thought it was good to keep him at a distance. They asked about him:

2.1. To satisfy their curiosity. The message of repentance was foreign to them.

2.2. To show their authority.

2.3. To suppress him and silence him.

3. What answer he gave them, his account of both himself and his baptism. Here is his testimony:

3.1. About himself. They asked him, *Thou, who art thou?* John's appearing in the world was surprising. His spirit, his way of life, and his message contained something that commanded and gained respect, but he did not say that he himself was great. He was more concerned to do good than to look great. He answered their question:

3.1.1. Negatively. He was not that great One who some thought he was. God's faithful witnesses are more on their guard against undue respect than against unjust contempt.

3.1.1.1. John denied that he was *the Christ* (v. 20): *He said, I am not the Christ*. Notice how emphatically this is expressed about John here: he *confessed, and denied not, but confessed*; he confessed this freely, passionately, and faithfully. "*I am not the Christ, not I*; another is at hand, who is the One, but I am not he." His disclaiming that he was the Christ is called his confessing and not denying Christ.

3.1.1.2. He denied that he was Elijah (v. 21). The Jews expected the person of Elijah to return from heaven. Hearing about John's character, message, and baptism and noticing that he appeared as one who seemed to have dropped from heaven, it is not surprising that they were ready to take him for Elijah, but he disowned this honor too. It was true that he had been prophesied about under the name of Elijah (Mal 4:5), and he came in the *spirit and power of Elias* (Lk 1:17) and was the Elijah who was to come (Mt 11:14), but he was not the person of Elijah himself. He was the Elijah that God had promised, not the Elijah they foolishly dreamed about. Elijah did come, and *they knew him not* (Mt 17:12), because they had promised themselves such an Elijah as God had never promised them. John denied that he was *that prophet*.

3.1.1.2.1. He was not *the* prophet that Moses said *the Lord* would *raise up to them of their brethren* (Ac 3:22).

3.1.1.2.2. He was not such a prophet as they expected and wished for, who would intervene in public affairs and rescue them from the Roman yoke.

3.1.1.2.3. He was not one of the former prophets raised from the dead.

3.1.2. Positively. The committee sent to examine him pressed him to give a positive answer (v. 22), urging the authority of *those that sent them*: "*Tell us, What art thou?* that we may *give an answer* to those who sent us." John was looked on as sincere, and so they believed he would be fair and honest, giving a clear answer to a clear question: *What sayest thou of thyself?* He did so: *I am the voice of one crying in the wilderness*.

3.1.2.1. He gave his answer using Scripture, to show that the Scripture was fulfilled in him.

3.1.2.2. He gave his answer in very humble, modest, and self-denying expressions. He chose to apply to himself the Scripture that showed him to be small: *I am the voice*, a mere voice.

3.1.2.3. He gave an account of himself that might awaken them to listen to him, because he *was the voice* (see Isa 40:3), a voice to alarm, an articulate voice to teach. Ministers are simply the voice by which God shares his thoughts.

3.1.2.3.*1.* He was a human voice. The people were prepared to receive the law by the sound of thunder, but they were prepared for the Gospel by the voice of a man like ourselves, *a still small voice* (1Ki 19:12).

3.1.2.3.*2.* He was the voice of *one crying*, which shows:

3.1.2.3.2.*1.* His seriousness and boldness; he *cried aloud, and did not spare* (Isa 58:1). Ministers must preach as those who are serious. Words are not likely to thaw the hearers' hearts if they freeze between the speaker's lips.

3.1.2.3.2.*2.* His open declaration of the message he preached.

3.1.2.3.*3.* It was in the desert that this voice was calling out, in a place of silence and solitude, far away from the noise of the world and the rush of its business.

3.1.2.3.*4.* What he called out was, *Make straight the way of the Lord.* He came to put right the mistakes of human beings about the ways of God. The teachers of the law and Pharisees had perverted them; now John the Baptist called people to return to the original rule.

3.2. About his baptism. Notice:

3.2.1. The question that the committee asked about it: *Why baptizest thou, if thou be not the Christ, nor Elias, nor that prophet?* (v. 25).

3.2.1.1. They realized that baptism was rightly and properly used as a sacred ceremony, to stand for their being cleansed from the defilement of their former state. That sign was used in the Christian church so that it might be more acceptable. Christ did not insist on using the latest innovation, and neither should his ministers.

3.2.1.2. They expected that it would be used in the days of the Messiah. It was assumed that Christ and Elijah and *that prophet* would all baptize when they came to cleanse a defiled world. Divine grace has provided for the cleansing of this new world from its filth.

3.2.1.3. They wanted to know, therefore, by what authority John baptized. His denying that he was Elijah or *that prophet* subjected him to this further question: *Why baptizest thou?*

3.2.2. The account he gave of it (vv. 26–27).

3.2.2.1. He acknowledged himself to be only the minister of the outward sign: "I baptize with water, and that is all. I cannot confer the spiritual grace signified by it."

3.2.2.2. He directed them to One who was greater than he, who would do for them what he could not do. John gave the same account to this committee that he had given to the people (v. 15): this *was he of whom I spoke.*

3.2.2.2.*1.* He told them that Christ was among them now: *There stands one among you, whom you know not.* Christ stood among the ordinary people and was as one of them. Much true worth lies hidden in this world; obscurity is often the place of real excellence. God himself is often closer to us than we are aware of. The kingdom of God was already around them and among them (Lk 17:21).

3.2.2.2.*2.* He told them Christ would surpass him: *He comes after me, and yet is preferred before me, whose shoe latchet* (the thongs of whose sandals) *I am not worthy to unloose."* If such a great man as John counted himself unworthy of the honor of being near Christ, how unworthy should we then count ourselves! Now, one would have thought that these chief priests and Pharisees would immediately have asked who and where this excellent person was. No; they came to bother John, not to receive any instruction from him. They could have known Christ, but they refused to.

4. The place where all this was done: *In Bethabara beyond Jordan* (v. 28). *Bethabara* means "the house of passage"; there the way was opened up into the Gospel territory by Jesus Christ. John made this confession in the same place where he was baptizing, so that all who were present at his baptism would witness it.

Verses 29–36

In these verses we have an account of the testimony about Jesus Christ that John gave to his own disciples who followed him. As soon Christ was baptized, he was immediately rushed into the desert to be tempted, and he stayed there forty days. During his absence, John continued to testify of him, but now at last he *saw Jesus coming to him.* Now here are two testimonies given by John of Christ, but they agree with each other.

1. Here is his testimony of Christ on the day he saw him coming out of the desert, and four things were witnessed by him about Christ.

1.1. He was *the Lamb of God which taketh away the sin of the world* (v. 29). Let us learn here that:

1.1.1. Jesus Christ is the *Lamb of God*, which shows he is the great sacrifice by which atonement is made for sin, reconciling human beings to God. Of all the legal sacrifices, he chose to allude to the lambs that were offered, with special reference to:

1.1.1.1. The *daily sacrifice*, which was offered every morning and evening and was always *a lamb* (Ex 29:38).

1.1.1.2. The *paschal lamb*, the blood of which kept the Israelites safe from the stroke of the destroying angel. Christ is *our Passover* (1Co 5:7). Christ, who was to make atonement for sin, is called *the Lamb of God.*

1.1.2. Jesus Christ, as the *Lamb of God, takes away the sin of the world.* John the Baptist had called people to repent of their sins so that they would be forgiven. Now here he showed how and by whom that forgiveness was to be expected. The basis of our hope is that Jesus Christ is *the Lamb of God.*

1.1.2.1. He takes away sin. He came to take away the guilt of sin by the merits of his death and to take away the power of sin by the Spirit of his grace. The phrase translated *which taketh away* could also be translated *who is taking away*; it refers to a continued act. He is always taking away sin.

1.1.2.2. He takes away the *sin of the world*; he purchases forgiveness for all, whichever country, nation, or language they are of. The Lamb of God was offered to be an atoning sacrifice for the *sin of the whole world*; see 1Jn 2:2. If Christ takes away the sin of the world, then why not *my* sin?

1.1.2.3. He does this *by taking it upon himself.* He is the Lamb of God who "bears the sin of the world," as the margin reads. He bears it away from us; he bore the sin of many, as the scapegoat had the sins of Israel put on its head (Lev 16:21). God has found a way of abolishing sin but sparing the sinner, by making his Son *sin for us* (2Co 5:21).

1.1.3. It is our duty to *behold* the Lamb of God taking away the *sin of the world.* See him taking away sin, and let that increase our hatred of sin and increase our love for Christ.

1.2. He was the One about whom John had spoken before (vv. 30–31): *This is he of whom I said, After me cometh a man.*

1.2.1. John had this honor above all the prophets, that whereas they spoke about the Messiah as One who would come, he saw him as already come. There is such a difference between present faith and future vision.

1.2.2. He referred to what he himself had said about him before: *This is he of whom I said.* Although Christ did not appear in any external show or grandeur, John was not ashamed to confess, *This is he whom I* meant, who *is preferred before* (who has surpassed) *me.* It was necessary for John to show them the person; otherwise they would not have believed that the person who seemed so insignificant could be the One about whom John had spoken such great things.

1.2.3. He protested against any suspicion that he had an alliance or arrangement with this Jesus: *And I knew him not.* There was no acquaintance at all between them; John had no personal knowledge of Jesus until he saw him come to his baptism. Those who are taught believe and confess One whom they have not seen, and *blessed are they that have not seen yet have believed* (Jn 20:29).

1.2.4. The great intention of John's ministry and baptism was to introduce Jesus Christ: *that he should be made manifest to Israel, therefore am I come baptizing with water.* Although John did not know Jesus by appearance, he knew that he would be revealed. We may know the certainty (Lk 1:4) of what we do not fully know the nature and intention of. The general assurance John had that Christ would be revealed was enough to carry him through his work with diligence and determination: *Therefore am I come.* God reveals himself to his people gradually. At first, John knew nothing more about Christ than that he would be revealed, and now he was favored with seeing him.

1.3. He was the One *upon whom the Spirit descended from heaven like a dove.* To confirm his testimony about Christ, John appealed here to the extraordinary sign at Christ's baptism, in which God himself testified to him. We are told here (vv. 32–34):

1.3.1. That John the Baptist saw the sign: he *bore record* (testified); he told it as the truth, with all the seriousness and solemnity of testifying. He gave it as an affidavit: *I saw the Spirit descending* from heaven. John could not see the Spirit, but he saw the dove that was a sign and representation of the Spirit. God's children are revealed by their graces; their glories are reserved for their future state. The Spirit descended *like a dove*—a sign of humility, mildness, and gentleness. The dove brought the olive branch of peace after the Flood (Ge 8:11). The Spirit that descended on Christ rested on him. The Spirit did not *move him at times* (Jdg 13:25), but at all times.

1.3.2. That he had been told to expect it. It was an instituted sign that he was told of beforehand so that he would definitely recognize it (v. 33): *I knew him not.* He *that sent me to baptize* gave me this sign: *Upon whom thou shalt see the Spirit descending, the same is he.*

1.3.2.1. Notice here on what a firm basis John carried out his ministry. He did not run without being sent: God *sent him to baptize.* He had authority from heaven for what he did. When a minister's call is clear, their assurance is sure, even though their success is not always so. Nor did he run without succeeding: when he was sent to *baptize with water,* he was directed to One who would *baptize with the Holy Spirit.* It is a great assurance to Christ's ministers that the One whose ministers they are can put life, soul, and power into their ministry; he can speak to the heart what they speak to the ear; he can breathe on the dry bones to which they *prophesy* (Eze 37:4).

1.3.2.2. Notice on what sure ground he stood in pointing to Jesus as the Messiah. God had given him a sign before: "The One on whom you will see the Spirit descend, *that same is he.*" This not only prevented any mistakes but also gave John boldness in his testimony.

When he had such assurance given him, he could speak with assurance.

1.4. He was *the Son of God.* This was the conclusion of John's testimony, the center of everything: *I saw, and bore record, that this is the Son of God* (v. 34). The truth asserted was *that this is the Son of God.* This was the distinctive Christian creed, that Jesus is the Son of God (Mt 16:16), and here is its first outlining. Notice John's testimony to it: "*I saw, and bore record.*" What he saw he was eager to testify about. What he testified was what he saw. Christ's witnesses were eyewitnesses.

2. Here is John's testimony of Christ on the following day (vv. 35–36), in which notice:

2.1. He took every opportunity to lead people to Christ. *John stood looking upon Jesus as he walked.* It seems that while he was in close conversation with two of his disciples, he saw Jesus walking. He was *looking upon Jesus,* fixing his eyes on him. Those who want to lead others to Christ must be diligent and frequent in contemplating him themselves.

2.2. He repeated the same testimony he had given of Christ the day before. Christ's sacrifice for the taking away of the sin of the world should especially be insisted on by all good ministers: Christ, the Lamb of God, *Christ and him crucified* (1Co 2:2).

2.3. He intended this especially for his two disciples who stood with him; he wanted to turn them to Christ. He did not reckon that he lost those disciples who went from him to Christ, any more than the schoolteacher reckons as lost those students who go to college. John gathered disciples not for himself but for Christ. Humble and generous souls will give others their due praise without fear of diminishing themselves by it.

Verses 37–42

We have here the turning of two disciples from John to Jesus, and one of them drawing in a third; these are the firstfruits of Christ's disciples.

1. Andrew and another with him were the two whom John the Baptist had directed to Christ (v. 37). Who the other was we are not told. Here is:

1.1. Their readiness to follow Christ. They heard John speak about Christ as the *Lamb of God, that takes away the sin of the world,* and this made them follow him.

1.2. The kind notice Christ took of them (v. 38). He was soon aware of them and *turned* and *saw them following.* Christ quickly notices the first movements of a soul toward him. He did not wait until they asked to speak to him; he spoke first. When there is fellowship between a soul and Christ, it is he who begins the conversation. He said to them, *What seek ye* (what do you want)? It is a kind invitation for them to come to know him: "Come, what have you to say to me?" Those whose business it is to instruct people in spiritual matters should be humble and approachable. The question Christ asked them is one we would all do well to ask ourselves when we begin to follow Christ: "*What seek ye?* What do we want? Do we seek a teacher, ruler, and reconciler? In following Christ, do we seek the favor of God and eternal life?"

1.3. Their modest question about where he was staying: *Rabbi, where dwellest thou?*

1.3.1. In calling him *Rabbi,* they showed that their intention in coming to him was to be taught by him. *Rabbi* means "Teacher." They came to Christ to be his students, as must all those who turn to him.

1.3.2. In asking where he lived, they showed a desire to come to know him more. They wanted to be with him at some suitable time, which he would appoint. Politeness and good manners are good qualities for those who follow Christ. They hoped to gain more from him than they could have now along the road. They decided to make conversing with Christ their vocation, not a mere avocation. Those who have had some fellowship with Christ must want further fellowship with him, more settled fellowship with him, the privilege of sitting at his feet (Lk 10:39) and abiding by his instructions. It is not enough to follow Christ now and then; we must stay with him.

1.4. The polite invitation Christ gave them to come to where he was staying: *He saith unto them, Come and see.* He invited them to come to where he was staying: the closer we come to Christ, the more we see of his beauty. Deceivers maintain their influence over their followers by keeping them far away, but what Christ desired in order to commend himself to the respect and affections of his followers was that they would *come and see.* He invited them to come immediately and without delay. There is never a better time. It is best to take people when they are in a good frame of mind, to "strike while the iron is hot." It is wise to take up the opportunities that present themselves now: *Now is the accepted time* (2Co 6:2).

1.5. Their cheerful, and no doubt thankful, acceptance of his invitation: *They came and saw where he dwelt,* and they *abode with him that day.* They readily went along with him. Gracious souls cheerfully accept Christ's gracious invitations. It is good to be where Christ is, wherever it is. They *abode with him that day* (they spent that day with him) — "Master, it is good to be here" (Mk 9:5) — and he made them welcome. It was about the tenth hour.

2. Andrew brought his brother Peter to Christ. Andrew had the honor of being the first to know Christ and being the instrument of bringing Peter to him. Notice:

2.1. The information Andrew gave to Peter.

2.1.1. *He first finds his own brother Simon*; his finding implies his seeking him. *He first findeth Simon,* who came only to be with John but had his expectations surpassed; he met with Jesus.

2.1.2. He told him whom they had found: *We have found the Messias.* Andrew spoke:

2.1.2.1. Humbly; not, "I have found," but "We have," rejoicing that he had shared with others in it.

2.1.2.2. Joyfully: *"We have found* that pearl of great price (Mt 13:46)." He did not keep it to himself, but proclaimed it, knowing that he would never have any less in Christ because others shared in him.

2.1.2.3. Intelligently: *We have found the Messias,* which was more than had been said up to that time. He spoke more clearly about Christ than *his teacher* ever had (Ps 119:99).

2.1.3. He *brought him to Jesus,* brought him to the fountain. Now this was:

2.1.3.1. An expression of true love for his brother. We should exert ourselves with a particular concern and diligence in seeking the spiritual welfare of those who are related to us, because their relationship to us adds both to the obligation and to the opportunity of doing good to their souls.

2.1.3.2. An effect of his day's conversation with Christ. That Andrew had *been with Jesus* (Ac 4:13) was clear from his being so full of him that his face shone (Ex 34:29). He knew there was enough in Christ for all, and having tasted that he is gracious (1Pe 2:3), he could not rest until those he loved had also tasted it. True grace hates to have a monopoly of Christ and does not enjoy eating its treats alone.

2.2. The reception Jesus Christ gave Peter (v. 42).

2.2.1. Christ called him by name: *When Jesus beheld him, he said, Thou art Simon, the son of Jona* (NIV: John). Some take note of the meaning of these names: *Simon,* "obedient," and *Jona,* "a dove." An obedient, dovelike spirit qualifies us to be the disciple of Christ.

2.2.2. He gave him a new name: *Cephas.* Christ's giving him a name shows his favor to him. By this Christ also adopted Simon into his family as one of his own. The name he gave him shows his faithfulness to Christ: *Thou shalt be called Cephas* (Hebrew for "stone"), *which is by interpretation Peter.* Peter's natural attitude was solid, tough, and determined, which we take to be the main reason why Christ called him *Cephas,* "a stone." When Christ later prayed for him that his faith would not fail, so that he could be firm for Christ, then he made him what he here called him, *Cephas,* "a stone." Those who come to Christ must come with a determination to be firm and faithful to him, like a stone, and it is by his grace that they are so.

Verses 43–51

Here is the call of Philip and Nathanael.

1. Philip was called directly by Christ himself, not like Andrew, who was led to Christ by John the Baptist, or like Peter, who was invited by his brother. God uses various ways to bring his chosen ones home to himself.

1.1. Christ took the initiative: *Jesus findeth Philip.* Christ sought us and found us before we sought him. The name *Philip* is of Greek origin and was much used among the Gentiles, but Christ did not change Philip's name.

1.2. Philip was called on the *day following.* When tasks are to be done for God, we must not lose a day.

1.3. Jesus decided to leave for Galilee to call him. Christ will find all those who are given to him.

1.4. Philip was brought to be a disciple by the power of Christ accompanying that word, *Follow me.*

1.5. We are told that Philip came from Bethsaida and that Andrew and Peter did too (v. 44). Bethsaida was an evil place (Mt 11:21), but even in Bethsaida there was a remnant, according to the election of grace (Ro 11:5).

2. Nathanael was invited to Christ by Philip. Notice:

2.1. What took place between Philip and Nathanael. Here is:

2.1.1. The joyful news that Philip brought to Nathanael (v. 45). Though he had just come to know Christ himself, Philip went off to find Nathanael. Philip said, *we have found him of whom Moses and the prophets did write.* Notice:

2.1.1.1. How delighted Philip was about having come to know Christ: "We have found the One whom we have so long wished and waited for; at last he has come, he has come, and we have found him!"

2.1.1.2. What an advantage it was to him to be so familiar with the Old Testament Scriptures, which prepared his mind to receive the light of that Gospel.

2.1.1.3. What mistakes and weaknesses he suffered. It was his weakness to say, *We have found him,* for Christ found them before they found Christ. He did not yet understand, as Paul did, how he had been *apprehended of Christ Jesus* (Php 3:12).

2.1.2. The objection that Nathanael raised against this: *Can any good thing come out of Nazareth?* (v. 46).

2.1.2.1. His caution was commendable; we should *prove all things* (1Th 5:21).

2.1.2.2. His objection arose from ignorance. If he meant that the Messiah, that great good person, could not come out of Nazareth, he was right as far as he went — but then he was ignorant of the fact that this Jesus had been born in Bethlehem; the mistake Philip made in calling him *Jesus of Nazareth* brought about this objection.

2.1.3. The short response Philip gave to this objection: *Come and see.*

2.1.3.1. It was Philip's weakness that he could not give a satisfactory answer to the objection. We may know enough to satisfy ourselves but not be able to say enough to silence a subtle enemy.

2.1.3.2. It was his wisdom and zeal that when he could not answer the objection himself, he suggested that Nathanael go to One who could: *Come and see.* Not "Go and see," but, "*Come*, and I will come with you." Many people are kept from the ways of religious faith by the unreasonable prejudices they have against religion, on account of some strange circumstances that have nothing to do with the merits of the case.

2.2. What took place between Nathanael and our Lord Jesus. Nathanael came and saw, and not in vain.

2.2.1. *Jesus saw him* coming. He said about him to those around him, *Behold an Israelite indeed* (Here is a true Israelite). Notice:

2.2.1.1. He commended him, not to flatter him, but perhaps because he knew him to be modest. Nathanael had raised an objection against Christ, but Christ showed that he excused it, because he knew Nathanael's heart was upright.

2.2.1.2. He commended him for his *integrity.*

2.2.1.2.1. *Behold an Israelite indeed. All are not Israel that are of Israel* (Ro 9:6); here, however, was *a true Israelite*, that is:

2.2.1.2.1.1. A sincere follower of the good example of his father Israel, a genuine son of honest Jacob.

2.2.1.2.1.2. A sincere professor of the faith of Israel, really as good as he seemed, his practice consistent with his profession. A true Jew is one who is inwardly so (Ro 2:29), as is a true Christian.

2.2.1.2.2. He was one *in whom was no guile.* A true Christian has no guile toward people; they are someone that people can trust. And they have no guile toward God; they are sincere in repentance for sin. Christ did not say "without guilt," but "without guile," a true Israelite, a miracle of divine grace.

2.2.2. Nathanael was very surprised at this.

2.2.2.1. Here is Nathanael's modesty: *"Whence knowest thou me,* who am unworthy of your notice?" It was evidence of his sincerity that he accepted the praise. Does Christ know us? Let us seek to know him.

2.2.2.2. Here is Christ's further revelation of himself to him: *Before Philip called thee, I saw thee.*

2.2.2.2.1. He gave Nathanael to understand that he knew him, so showing his divinity.

2.2.2.2.2. Before Philip called Nathanael, Christ saw him under a fig tree. Christ knows us before we have any knowledge of him. He had looked at Nathanael when he was *under the fig tree*; this was a private sign that nobody understood except Nathanael: "When you had retreated *under the fig tree*, I had my eye on you and saw what was acceptable." Nathanael was probably meditating, praying, and enjoying fellowship with God under the fig tree. Sitting under the fig tree shows quietness and calmness of spirit, which are very much friends of fellowship with God.

2.2.3. Nathanael gained full assurance of faith in Jesus Christ here (v. 49): *Rabbi, thou art the Son of God; thou art the king of Israel*; that is, to put it concisely, "You are the true Messiah." Notice here how firmly Nathanael believed with the heart. Now he did not ask anymore, *Can any good thing come out of Nazareth?* See how freely he confessed with the mouth (Ro 10:9). He confessed

Christ's prophetic office by calling him *Rabbi*. He confessed his divine nature and mission by calling him the Son of God. He confessed, *Thou art the king of Israel.* If he is the Son of God, he is king of the Israel of God.

2.2.4. Christ then raised the hopes and expectations of Nathanael to something further and greater than all this (vv. 50–51).

2.2.4.1. He showed here his acceptance of and, it seems, his wonder at the ready faith of Nathanael: *Because I said, I saw thee under the fig tree, believest thou?* It was a sign that Nathanael's heart was prepared beforehand, for otherwise the work would not have been done so suddenly.

2.2.4.2. He promised Nathanael much greater help to confirm and increase his faith.

2.2.4.2.1. In general: *Thou shalt see greater things than these*, namely, the miracles of Christ and his resurrection. This shows us that those who truly believe the Gospel will find that its evidence grows on them. Whatever revelations Christ makes of himself here in this world, he has even greater revelations than these to make known to them.

2.2.4.2.2. In particular: "Not only you, but you, all you my disciples, *you shall see heaven opened.*" *Verily, verily I say unto you*—which commands both a fixed attention to what is said, as significant, and a full agreement to it, as undoubtedly true. No one used this expression at the beginning of a sentence except Christ, though the Jews often used it at the end of a prayer. It is a solemn oath. Now see what it is that Christ assured them of: *Hereafter*, or "before long," *ye shall see heaven opened.*

2.2.4.2.2.1. It was a humble title that Christ took to himself here: *the Son of man.* It is a title frequently applied to him in the Gospel, but always by himself. Nathanael had called him the *Son of God* and *king of Israel*: Christ called himself *Son of man*, to express his humility and to teach his humanity.

2.2.4.2.2.2. The things that he foretold here were great things: *You shall see heaven opened* and *the angels of God ascending and descending upon the Son of man.* This was fulfilled in the many services of the angels to our Lord Jesus, especially at his ascension, when heaven was opened to receive him and the angels ascended and descended—and this in the sight of the disciples. Christ's ascension was the great proof of his mission, and it very much confirmed the faith of his disciples (6:62). We may also understand this prediction as referring to Christ's miracles. Christ was now beginning an era of miracles, and immediately after this, he began to perform them (2:21).

CHAPTER 2

In this chapter we have: 1. The account of the first miracle that Jesus performed, at Cana of Galilee (vv. 1–11), and his appearance at Capernaum (v. 12). 2. The account of the first Passover he kept at Jerusalem after he began his public ministry; his driving the buyers and sellers out of the temple (vv. 13–17); and the sign he gave to those who quarreled with him for it (vv. 18–22), with an account of some almost-believers (vv. 23–25).

Verses 1–11

Here is the story of Christ's miraculous conversion of water into wine at a wedding at Cana in Galilee. He could have performed miracles before, but because miracles were intended as the sacred and solemn seals of his message, he did not begin to perform any until he began to preach. Notice:

1. The occasion of this miracle. Maimonides observes it to be to the honor of Moses that all the signs he did in the desert he did because he had to: "We needed food; he brought us manna"—and so did Christ.

1.1. The time: the *third day* after he came to Galilee. The Evangelist keeps a journal of events. Our Master occupied his time better than his servants do, never lying down at night complaining that he had lost a day.

1.2. The place: it was at Cana in Galilee. Christ began to work miracles in an obscure part of the country. His message and miracles would not be opposed as much by the plain and honest Galileans as they would be at Jerusalem.

1.3. The occasion itself, a wedding. The *mother of Jesus* is said to have been there. Notice the honor Christ gives the ordinance of marriage here, that he graced a wedding ceremony not only with his presence but also with his first miracle. There was *a marriage feast* to grace the wedding ceremony. Marriages were usually celebrated with festivals.

1.4. The main guests at this reception: Christ, his mother, and his disciples. *The mother of Jesus was there*; no mention is made of Joseph, and so we conclude he had died before this. Jesus was *called*, and he came and enjoyed the reception with them. Christ came in a way that was different from that of John the Baptist, who came *neither eating nor drinking* (Mt 11:18–19).

1.4.1. There was a marriage, and Jesus was invited. When there is a wedding, it is very good to invite Jesus Christ to be present at it, to have the marriage recognized and blessed by him; the marriage is then truly honorable. Those who want to have Christ with them in their marriage must invite him in by prayer; that is the messenger that must be sent to heaven for him, and he will come; he will turn the water into wine.

1.4.2. The disciples were also invited. They had placed themselves under his protection, and they soon found that although he had no wealth, he had good friends. Those who follow Christ will feast with him; they will eat as he eats. Love for Christ is shown by a love for those who are his.

2. The miracle itself:

2.1. They lacked wine (v. 3).

2.1.1. There was a lack at a banquet; although much was provided, all was consumed. While we are in this world, we sometimes find ourselves in need, even when we think we have everything we need. If we are always spending, perhaps everything is spent before we are aware of it.

2.1.2. There was a lack at a marriage banquet.

2.1.3. It seems that Christ and his disciples were the cause of this lack; however, those who restrict themselves for Christ's sake will not lose by him.

2.2. The *mother of Jesus* asked him to help her friends. We are told (vv. 3–5) what took place between Christ and his mother.

2.2.1. She told him about the difficulty they had (v. 3): *She saith unto him, They have no wine*. Some think that she did not expect any miraculous supply from him, because he had not up to that time performed any miracle. But most probably she looked for a miracle. The bridegroom could have sent out for more wine, but she wanted to go directly to the fountain. We should be concerned for the needs of our friends. In our own and our friends' difficulties, it would be wise to apply ourselves to Christ in prayer. Yet when we speak to Christ, we must not tell him what to do, but humbly spread out our case before him (2Ki 19:14).

2.2.2. He rebuked her for it. Here is:

2.2.2.1. The rebuke itself: *Woman, what have I to do with thee?* Christ disciplines and rebukes as many as he loves (Heb 12:6; Pr 3:11–12). He called her *woman*, not *mother*. When we begin to have too high an opinion of ourselves, we should be reminded of what we are, men and women, frail, foolish, and sinful individuals. His response was intended to be:

2.2.2.1.1. A restraint on his mother for intervening in a matter that was the act of his Godhead, which did not depend on her in any way and which she was not the mother of. Great advancement must not make us forget ourselves and our place, nor should the familiarity into which the covenant of grace welcomes us breed contempt, irreverence, or any kind of presumption.

2.2.2.1.2. An instruction to his other relatives—that they must never expect him to show any favoritism for his natural relatives in his performing miracles, since in this matter they meant no more to him than any other people. In the things of God we must not show favoritism.

2.2.2.2. The reason for this rebuke: *Mine hour is not yet come*. Everything that Christ did and that was done to him had its hour, the fixed time and the best time. "My time for performing miracles has not yet come." He later performed this miracle, before his appointed hour, because he foresaw that it would confirm the faith of his new disciples (v. 11). This was a pledge of the many miracles he would work when his hour had come. His mother urged him to help them when the wine "began to fail," as v. 3 may be read, but his time had not yet come until it had been completely consumed. This teaches us that "man's extremity is God's opportunity." His time has come when we are reduced to the greatest difficulty and do not know what to do. Delays of mercy are not to be interpreted as denials of prayer.

2.2.3. Despite this, she encouraged herself with the expectation that he would help, and so she told the servants to follow his orders (v. 5).

2.2.3.1. She took the rebuke very submissively and did not respond to it. It is best not to deserve rebuke from Christ, but it is next best to be humble and quiet under it, and to count it as a kindness (Ps 141:5).

2.2.3.2. She kept up her hope in Christ's mercy. When we come to God in Christ for any mercy, two things discourage us: a sense of our own foolishness and weakness, and a fear of our Lord's disapproval and rebukes. Sufferings continue, rescue is delayed, and God seems angry with our prayers. This was the situation of the mother of our Lord here, but she still encouraged herself with hope that he would eventually respond favorably to her, to teach us to wrestle with God even when he seems in his providence to act against us.

2.2.3.3. She told the servants to look to him immediately, and not to turn to her. Let their souls *wait only* on him (Ps 62:5).

2.2.3.4. She told them to follow his orders promptly: *Whatsoever he saith to you, do it*. Those who expect Christ's favors must carry out his orders with an implicit obedience. The way of duty is the way to mercy, and Christ's methods must not be objected to.

2.2.4. Christ did eventually supply them miraculously, as he is often better than his word, but never worse.

2.2.4.1. The miracle itself was turning water into wine; the substance of water acquired a new form, with all the appearance and qualities of wine. By this Christ showed himself to be the God of nature, who makes the earth bring forth wine (Ps 104:14–15). The beginning of Christ's miracles was turning water into wine; the blessing of the Gospel turns water into wine. Christ was showing in this that his mission into the world was both to increase creature comforts to all believers and to make them true comforts.

2.2.4.2. The circumstances of it are exalted and freed from all suspicion of deception:

2.2.4.2.1. It was done in water jars (v. 6): *There were set there six waterpots of stone.* Notice:

2.2.4.2.1.1. For what use these water jars were intended: for the legal purification commanded by the Law of God, and many more by the tradition of the elders. They used a lot of water in washing, which is why six large water jars were provided. There was a saying among them, "Those who use much water in washing will gain much wealth in this world."

2.2.4.2.1.2. For what purpose Christ used them; to be the containers for the miraculous wine. Christ came to bring in the grace of the Gospel, which is like wine, to replace the shadows of the law, which were like water. These were water jars, which had never been used for containing wine; they were made of stone, which does not tend to keep the scent of former liquids, if they had ever contained wine. They contained *two or three firkins apiece,* from twenty to thirty gallons (about 75 to 115 liters). Christ gives according to his nature and according to his riches in glory (Eph 1:18): abundantly.

2.2.4.2.2. The water jars were filled *up to the brim* by the servants at Christ's word (v. 7).

2.2.4.2.3. The miracle was performed suddenly, and in such a way as greatly exalted it.

2.2.4.2.3.1. As soon as they had filled the water jars, he said, *Draw out now* (v. 8), and it was done without any ceremony, in full view of the spectators. He sat still in his place, saying not a word, but willing the thing, and so it happened. Christ does great and marvelous things silently, working great changes in a hidden way, without any hesitation or uncertainty within himself. With the greatest possible assurance, even though it was his first miracle, he commended the wine to the master of the banquet. Just as he knew what he wished to do, so he also knew what he could do. Everything was very good, even from the beginning (Ge 1:1, 31).

2.2.4.2.3.2. Our Lord Jesus instructed the servants:

2.2.4.2.3.2.1. To draw the wine out to be drunk. Christ's works are all to be used. Has he turned your water into wine, given you knowledge and grace? It is for the common good, and so draw it out now. Those who want to know Christ must actually do what he says.

2.2.4.2.3.2.2. To present it to *the governor of the feast* (master of the banquet). Although he was not treated as the Master of the banquet, he kindly showed himself to be a friend of the banquet, to be, if not its founder, then its best benefactor. Some think that this *governor* was the monitor of the banquet, whose task it was to see that each had enough, that no one drank too much, and that there was no indecent or disorderly behavior. Banquets need masters, because too many people at banquets do not control themselves. Some think that this master of the banquet was a priest or Levite who asked a blessing and gave thanks, and that Christ wanted the cup to be brought to him so that he would bless it and bless God for it, because the extraordinary signs of Christ's presence and power were not to replace or jostle out the ordinary rules and ways of godliness and devotion.

2.2.4.2.4. The wine that was so miraculously provided was the best and finest. This was acknowledged by the master of the banquet (vv. 9–10). It was certain that:

2.2.4.2.4.1. This was wine. The master knew this when he drank it, though he did not know where it came from;

the servants realized where it came from, but they had not yet tasted it.

2.2.4.2.4.2. It was the best wine. Christ's works commend themselves even to those who do not know their author. The products of miracles were always the best of their kind. The master of the banquet commented on this to the bridegroom with an air of pleasantness, as something rare.

2.2.4.2.4.2.1. The usual way was the opposite. Good wine is usually brought out to the best advantage at the beginning of a banquet, but *when they have well drunk* (have had too much to drink), good wine is wasted on them, and worse will be all right for them. Notice the worthlessness of all physical pleasures; they soon surfeit, but never satisfy; the longer they are enjoyed, the less pleasant they become.

2.2.4.2.4.2.2. This bridegroom pleased his friends with a reserve of the best wine for the end: *Thou hast kept the good wine until now.* Not knowing to whom they were indebted for this good wine, the master thanked the bridegroom.

2.2.4.2.4.2.2.1. In providing so plentifully for the guests, Christ, though he hereby allows us a sober and good use of wine, especially in times of joy (Ne 8:10), does not invalidate his own warning, which is that our hearts must not *at any time,* not even at a wedding banquet, be *overcharged with surfeiting and drunkenness* (Lk 21:34). Temperance when there is no other choice is a thankless virtue, but if divine Providence gives us many physical delights, and divine grace enables us to use them moderately, this self-denial is commendable. Two considerations, drawn from this story, may be sufficient at any time to strengthen us against temptations to intemperance. First, our food and drink are the gifts of God's goodness to us. It is therefore ungrateful and ungodly to abuse them. Second, wherever we are, Christ looks at us.

2.2.4.2.4.2.2.2. He has given us an example of the way he deals with those who deal with him, which is to reserve the best for the last, and so they must deal on the basis of trust. The pleasures of sin give their color to the cup, but in the end they will bite (Pr 23:31–32); but the pleasures of religion will be *pleasures for evermore* (Ps 16:11).

3. The conclusion of this account (v. 11), in which we are told:

3.1. That this was *the beginning of miracles* that Jesus did. He himself was the greatest miracle of all, but this was the first performed by him. He had power, but there was *a time of the hiding of his power* (Hab 3:4).

3.2. That here he *manifested* (revealed) *his glory;* here he proved he was the Son of God.

3.3. That *his disciples believed on him.* Those whom he had called (1:35–51) now saw this, shared in it, and had their faith strengthened by it. Even the faith that is true is only weak at first. The strongest people were once babies, as it is with the strongest Christians.

Verses 12–22

Here we have:

1. The short visit Christ made to Capernaum (v. 12). It is called *his own city* (Mt 9:1), because he made it his headquarters in Galilee, and the little rest he had was taken there. It was a place where people met, and that was why Christ chose it, so that the high reputation of his teaching and miracles would spread further from there. Notice:

1.1. The company who went with him there: *his mother, his brethren, and his disciples.* Wherever Christ went:

1.1.1. He would not go alone, but took with him those who had put themselves under his guidance.

1.1.2. He could not go alone, without them following him, because they liked the sweetness either of his teaching or of his wine (6:26). His mother still followed him, not to intercede with him, but to learn from him. He was followed by his brothers, who were at the marriage, as well as by his disciples, were with him wherever he went. It seems people were more moved by Christ's miracles at first than they were later, when they had become more routine and less strange.

1.2. His stay there, which was at this time *not many days*. Christ was continually moving about; he did not want to confine his usefulness to one particular place, because many people needed him. He did not stay long at Capernaum because the Passover was near, and he must be present at Jerusalem.

2. His keeping of the Passover at Jerusalem; it was the first one after his baptism. Being *made under the law* (Gal 4:4), Christ observed the Passover at Jerusalem. He went up to Jerusalem when *the passover was at hand*, so that he would be there with the first. Christ had kept the Passover at Jerusalem every year ever since he was twelve years old, but now that he had begun his public ministry, something more could be expected from him than before, and he did two things there:

2.1. He cleansed the temple (vv. 14–17).

2.1.1. The first place we find him at Jerusalem was the temple, and it seems he did not make any public appearance till he came there.

2.1.2. The first work we find him doing in the temple was cleansing it. He first cleansed what was wrong and then taught them to do what was right. He expects all who come to him to reform their hearts and lives (Ge 35:2). He has taught us this by cleansing the temple. Notice here:

2.1.2.1. What corruptions were to be cleansed. He found a market in one of the courts of the temple, the one called the *court of the Gentiles*. There:

2.1.2.1.1. People sold *oxen, and sheep, and doves* for sacrifice; these were not for common use, but for the convenience of those who came from the country and could not bring their sacrifices in kind along with them. This market was admitted into the temple by the chief priests for dishonest gain. Great corruption in the church owes its rise to the love of money (1Ti 6:5, 10).

2.1.2.1.2. People *changed* (exchanged) *money* for the convenience of those who had to pay the half-shekel poll tax for the service of the tabernacle, and no doubt the money changers profited by it.

2.1.2.2. How our Lord cleansed such corruption. He did not complain to the chief priests, because he knew they supported such corruption.

2.1.2.2.1. He himself *drove out the sheep and oxen* and those who sold them. He never used force to drive anyone into the temple, but only to drive out those who desecrated it. He made a whip out of *small cords*, which the owners of the sheep and oxen had probably led them in with. Sinners themselves prepare the scourges with which they will be driven out of the temple of the Lord.

2.1.2.2.2. He *poured out the changers' money* (scattered the coins). In scattering the money, he showed his contempt toward it. In overthrowing the tables, he showed his displeasure toward those who make religion a matter of worldly gain. Money changers in the temple are its scandal.

2.1.2.2.3. He *said to them that sold doves* (sacrifices for the poor), *Take these things hence*. The sparrows and swallows, which were left to God's providence (Ps 84:3), were welcome, but not the doves, which were taken for profit. God's temple must not be made a house of pigeons.

2.1.2.2.4. He gave them a good reason for what he did: *Make not my Father's house a house of merchandise* (market).

2.1.2.2.4.1. Here is a reason why they should not defile the temple: it was the *house of God*. Stock is a good thing in a market, but not in a temple. To defile the temple was sacrilege, robbing God. It was defiling and making common what was solemn and should inspire awe. It was making the business of religion subservient to worldly interests. God's house is made a market by people whose minds are filled with cares about worldly business when they are participating in religious services—as were the minds of those in Am 8:5; Eze 33:31—and by people who perform divine services for dishonest gain.

2.1.2.2.4.2. Here is a reason why he was concerned to cleanse it: it *was his Father's house*. He had authority to purge it, as a Son has authority *over his own house* (Heb 3:5–6). He was also zealous to purge it: "It is my Father's house, and so I cannot bear to see it defiled and him dishonored." We must be saddened to see God's name defiled; Christ's cleansing the temple may therefore justly be reckoned among his *wonderful works* (Ps 40:5), considering:

2.1.2.2.4.2.1. That he did it without the help of any of his friends.

2.1.2.2.4.2.2. That he did it without the resistance of any of his enemies. The corruption was too plain to be justified; sinners' own consciences are reformers' best friends. That was not all, however; a divine power was displayed in this cleansing, a power over human spirits.

2.1.2.2.5. His disciples reacted to it (v. 17): *They remembered that it was written, The zeal of thine house hath eaten me up.* There came to their minds one Scripture that taught them to reconcile this action with both the humility of the Lamb of God and the majesty of the King of Israel, for David, speaking about the Messiah, took notice that his *zeal for God's house* was so great that it even consumed him. Notice:

2.1.2.2.5.1. The disciples came to understand the meaning of what Christ did by remembering the Scriptures: *They remembered* now *that it was written*. The word of God and the works of God mutually explain and illustrate each other. Notice how useful it is for the disciples of Christ to be thoroughly familiar with the Scriptures and to have their memories well stocked with Scripture truths.

2.1.2.2.5.2. The Scripture they remembered was very relevant: *The zeal of thine house hath eaten me up.* All the graces that were to be found among the Old Testament saints were eminently seen in Christ, especially this grace of zeal for the house of God. Zeal for the house of God forbids us to consider our own reputation, comfort, and security when they come to compete with Christ's service, and sometimes this zeal carries our souls along so far and so fast as we do our duty that our bodies cannot keep up with them.

2.2. Having purged the temple, Christ gave a sign to those who demanded it to prove his authority for doing so. Notice:

2.2.1. Their demand of a sign: *Then answered the Jews,* that is, the many people with their leaders. When they could raise no objection against the thing itself, they questioned his authority to do it: *What sign showest thou unto us?* What business was it of his to undertake it, since it seemed he had no authority there? But was not the thing itself enough of a sign?

2.2.2. Christ's answer to this demand (v. 19): he gave them a sign in something to come, the truth of which must appear later.

2.2.2.1. The sign that he gave them was his own death and resurrection. He referred them to what would happen.

2.2.2.2. He foretold his death and resurrection not directly but in figurative expressions: *Destroy this temple, and in three days I will raise it up.* He spoke in parables to those who were willingly ignorant, so that *they might not perceive* (Mt 13:13–14). Those who refuse to see will not see. In fact, the figurative speech used here proved such a stumbling block to them that it was produced in evidence against him at his trial (Mt 26:60–61).

2.2.2.2.1. He foretold his death by the Jews' hatred in these words: *Destroy you this temple.* Even at the beginning of his ministry, Christ had a clear foresight of all his sufferings at the end of it, but he continued cheerfully with it.

2.2.2.2.2. He foretold his resurrection by his own power: in *three days I will raise it up.* There were others who were raised, but Christ raised himself.

2.2.2.3. He chose to express this by the image of destroying and rebuilding the temple because he was now to justify himself in cleansing the temple, which they had defiled. "You who defile one temple will destroy another, and I will prove my authority to cleanse what you have defiled by raising what you will destroy."

2.2.3. Their objection to this answer: "*Forty and six years was this temple in building* (v. 20). Temple work was always slow work, and can you make such quick work of it?" Here they showed some knowledge; they could tell how long the temple took to be built. Yet they showed more ignorance, ignorance of the meaning of Christ's words and of his almighty power—as if he could do no more than any other person.

2.2.4. A vindication of Christ's answer to their objection. *He spoke of the temple of his body* (v. 21). Some think that when he said, "Destroy this temple," he pointed to his own body; be that as it may, it is certain that he *spoke of the temple of his body.* Like the temple, his body was built by direct divine instruction. Like the temple, it was a holy house; it is called *that holy thing* (Lk 1:35). It was, like the temple, the dwelling place of God's glory, there the eternal Word lived. He is *Emmanuel,* "God with us" (Mt 1:23). Worshipers looked toward the temple (1Ki 8:30, 35); in the same way, we must worship God by looking to Christ.

2.2.5. A reflection that the disciples made on this, long after (v. 22): *When he was risen from the dead, his disciples remembered that he had said this.* The memories of Christ's disciples should be like the treasure of the good householder, furnished with things both *new* and *old* (Mt 13:52). Notice:

2.2.5.1. When *they remembered* that saying: *when he was risen from the dead.* They stored up the saying in their hearts, and it later became both intelligible and useful. Juniors in years and profession should treasure up those truths of which at present they do not understand either the meaning or the application very well, because those truths will be useful to them later. This saying of Christ was recalled in the memories of his disciples *when he was risen from the dead,* and why then?

2.2.5.1.1. Because it was then that the Spirit was poured out to remind them of the things that Christ had said to them. That very day that Christ rose from the dead, he *opened their understandings* (Lk 24:45).

2.2.5.1.2. Because this saying of Christ was fulfilled then. When the temple of his body had been destroyed and was raised again, on the third day, they then remembered this.

2.2.5.2. What use they made of it: *They believed the scripture, and the word that Jesus had said.* They were slow of heart to believe (Lk 24:25), but they were sure. The Scripture and the words of Christ are put together here, because they mutually illustrate and strengthen each other.

Verses 23–25

Here is an account of the success—the poor success—of Christ's preaching and miracles at Jerusalem while he celebrated the Passover. Notice:

1. When he was in Jerusalem for the Passover, our Lord Jesus preached and performed miracles. The time was a holy time, *the feast day,* when many people met together, and Christ took that opportunity to preach.

2. Many were brought to *believe in his name,* to acknowledge him to be *a teacher come from God,* as Nicodemus did (3:2).

3. But *Jesus did not commit himself unto them* (v. 24): Christ did not see cause to put any confidence in these new converts at Jerusalem, either:

3.1. Because they were false, at least some of them. He had more disciples that he could trust among the Galileans than among those who lived at Jerusalem. Or:

3.2. Because they were weak.

3.2.1. They were timid and lacked zeal and courage. In times of difficulty and danger, cowards are not fit to be trusted. Or:

3.2.2. They were turbulent and lacked discretion and prudence.

4. The reason he did not *commit himself* to them was that *he knew* them (v. 25), knew the wickedness of some and the weakness of others. The Evangelist uses this occasion to assert Christ's omniscience.

4.1. He *knew all men,* not only their names and faces, as it is possible for us to know many people, but also their nature, characters, attitudes, and intentions, as we do not know any person, scarcely ourselves. He knows those who are truly his (2Ti 2:19), knows their integrity and their weaknesses too.

4.2. He *needed not that any should testify of man* (he did not need human testimony about them). His knowledge came not merely from information from others but through his own infallible intuition. He *knew what was in man.* We know what is done by people; Christ knows what is in them. How fit Christ is to be the Savior of human beings, how fit to be the physician, who has such perfect knowledge of the patient's case, attitudes, and illnesses; he knows what is in us! How fit he is also to be the *Judge of all* (Heb 12:23)! The Lord comes to his temple, and no one comes to him except a small group of weak, simple people that he can neither have credit from nor put confidence in.

CHAPTER 3

In this chapter we have: 1. Christ's conversation with Nicodemus, a Pharisee (vv. 1–21). 2. John the Baptist's conversation with his disciples about Christ (vv. 22–36), in which he fairly and faithfully submits all his honor and influence to Christ.

Verses 1–21

At the end of the previous chapter, we found that few were brought to Christ at Jerusalem, but here was one, an important person. Notice:

1. Who this Nicodemus was. Not many who are mighty and noble are called (1Co 1:26), but some are, and here

was one. Not many of the *rulers, or of the Pharisees* (7:48) were called, but this was *a man of the Pharisees*, brought up to be a learned scholar. Let it not be said that all Christ's followers are *unlearned and ignorant men* (Ac 4:13). Nicodemus was *a ruler of the Jews* and a member of the great Sanhedrin, a man of authority in Jerusalem. Bad though things were, there were some rulers who were well inclined. Nicodemus, while continuing in his position, did what he could do, since he could not do all he wanted to.

2. His solemn words to our Lord Jesus Christ (v. 2). Notice here:

2.1. When he came: *He came to Jesus by night.* He did not think it enough to hear him speaking in public. He decided to talk with him by himself, where he could speak freely. He went to Christ *by night*, which may be thought of:

2.1.1. As an act of wisdom and discretion. Christ was engaged all day in public work, and Nicodemus did not want to interrupt him then; he waited until Christ was freely available to speak to him. Christ had many enemies, and so Nicodemus came to him incognito, to avoid being recognized by the chief priests and thereby provoking them to become even more enraged against Christ.

2.1.2. As an act of zeal. He would rather take time from the diversions of the evening, or from his rest at night, than not talk with Christ. When others were asleep, he was acquiring knowledge. He did not know how soon Christ might leave the town, nor what might happen between that feast and the next, and so he wanted to lose no time. At night his conversation with Christ would be freer and less likely to be disturbed.

2.1.3. As an act of fear and cowardice. He was afraid or ashamed to be seen with Christ, and that was why he came at night. Although he came at night, Christ still welcomed him, accepting his integrity, and pardoning his weakness, hereby teaching his ministers to encourage good beginnings, even if they are weak. Although Nicodemus came at night now, afterward he confessed Christ *publicly* (7:50; 19:39). The grace that is at first as small as a grain of mustard seed may grow to be a large tree (Mt 13:31–32).

2.2. What he said. He got down to business right away. He called Christ *Rabbi*, which means "a great man." There are hopes for those who have respect for Christ, who think and speak honorably of him. He told Christ how far he had reached: We *know that thou art a teacher*. Notice:

2.2.1. His assertion about Christ: "*Thou art a teacher come from God*, supported by divine inspiration and divine authority." The One who came first to be a teacher would rule by the power of truth, not by the power of the sword.

2.2.2. His assurance of it: "*We know*, not only I but also others." He took this for granted, as clear and self-evident.

2.2.3. The basis for this assurance: *No man can do those miracles that thou doest, except* (unless) *God be with him.* Here was Nicodemus, who was wise, sensible, and curious, one who had all possible reason and opportunity to examine Christ's miracles, and he was so fully satisfied they were real that he was persuaded by them to go against the tide of those of his own rank. In Nicodemus's statement here, we are directed to the conclusion we ought to draw from Christ's miracles: that he is a *teacher come from God* and that we are to receive him as such.

3. The conversation between Christ and Nicodemus that then took place (v. 11–12). Our Savior spoke about four main things.

3.1. He spoke about the necessity and nature of regeneration, or the new birth (vv. 3–8).

3.1.1. We must consider this as a relevant response to Nicodemus's words. Jesus *answered* (v. 3). It was not enough for Nicodemus to wonder at Christ's miracles and acknowledge his mission; he must be *born again*. It is clear that he expected the kingdom of heaven now to appear soon. He was aware early on of the dawning of that day. However, Christ told him that he could have no benefit of a change of state unless there was a change of the spirit, equivalent to a new birth. When Nicodemus acknowledged Christ to be a *teacher come from God*, he clearly showed a desire to know what this revelation was, and Christ declared it.

3.1.2. We must consider this as a positive and vehement assertion by our Lord Jesus: *Verily, verily, I say unto thee, except a man be born again, he cannot see the kingdom of God.* Notice:

3.1.2.1. What is required: to be *born again*. We must live a new life. Birth is the beginning of life; to be born again is to begin a new life. We must not think we can just patch up an old building; we must begin a new building from the foundation. We must have a new nature, a new driving force in our lives, fresh affections, fresh aims. We must be born both "again" and "from above"; the word here means both. We must be born *anew*; our souls must be formed and given life again. And we must be born *from above*; this new birth has its origin from heaven. To be born in this way is to be born to a divine and heavenly life.

3.1.2.2. The indispensable necessity of this: "Except a *man be born again, he cannot see the kingdom of God.*" Unless we are born from above, we cannot see this kingdom. We cannot understand its nature. We cannot receive comfort from it. Regeneration is absolutely necessary for our happiness here and in the future. It will be seen by the nature of the thing that we must be born again, because it is impossible for us to be happy if we are not holy.

3.1.3. Now that this great truth of the necessity of regeneration had been so solemnly laid down, it was objected to by Nicodemus (v. 4): *How can a man be born when he is old? Can he enter the second time into his mother's womb, and be born?* We see here:

3.1.3.1. His weakness in knowledge; what Christ spoke spiritually he seems to have understood in a physical, worldly way, as if there were such a link between the soul and the body that there could be no making the heart again except by forming the bones again. It came as a great surprise to him to hear of being born again. Could he have been better born and brought up than to have been born and brought up as an Israelite? Those who are proud of their first birth are brought to a new birth with difficulty.

3.1.3.2. His willingness to be taught. He did not turn his back on Christ because of his difficult saying, but honestly acknowledged his ignorance. "Lord, make me understand this, as it is a puzzle to me. I am so foolish as to know no other way for a man to be born again than for his mother to give birth to him." When we meet with divine things that are mysterious and hard to understand, we must continue to share in the means of knowledge.

3.1.4. It was opened up and further explained by our Lord Jesus (vv. 5–8). He took Nicodemus's response as an opportunity:

3.1.4.1. To repeat and confirm what he had said (v. 5): "*Verily, verily I say unto thee,* the very same as I said before." Although Nicodemus did not understand the mystery of regeneration, Christ still asserted its necessity as positively as he did before. It is foolish to think of evading the obligation of the commands of the Gospel by pleading they are unintelligible (Ro 3:3–4).

3.1.4.2. To explain and clarify what he had said about regeneration. To this end:

3.1.4.2.1. He revealed the author of this blessed change, who works it. To be born again is to be *born of the Spirit* (vv. 5–8). The change is not brought about by any wisdom or power of our own, but by the power and influence of the blessed Spirit of grace.

3.1.4.2.2. He revealed the nature of this change, what is to be done; it is *spirit* (v. 6). Those who are regenerated are made spiritual. The dictates and interests of the rational and immortal soul have regained the power they should have over the flesh.

3.1.4.2.3. He revealed the necessity of this change.

3.1.4.2.3.1. Christ showed here that it is necessary in the nature of the thing: *That which is born of the flesh is flesh* (v. 6). We are here told:

3.1.4.2.3.1.1. What we are: flesh. The soul is still a spiritual substance, but it is so wedded to the flesh, so captivated by the will of the flesh, that it is justly called flesh. What fellowship can there be between God, who is a spirit, and a soul in this condition?

3.1.4.2.3.1.2. How we came to be so: by being *born of the flesh*. It is a corruption that is bred in the bone with us. The corrupt nature, which is flesh, arises from our first birth, and so the new nature, which is spirit, must arise from a second birth. Nicodemus spoke of entering again into his mother's womb and being born again, but if he could do so, what purpose would it fulfill? If his mother gave birth to him a hundred times, that would not put matters right, because still that *which is born of the flesh is flesh*. Corruption and sin are woven into the very fabric of our being; we are *shapen in iniquity* (Ps 51:5). It is not enough to put on a new coat or wear new makeup; we must put on the new self (Eph 4:24; Col 3:10).

3.1.4.2.3.2. Christ made it additionally necessary by his own word: *Marvel not that I said unto thee, You must be born again* (v. 7).

3.1.4.2.3.2.1. Christ has said it. The One who is the great Physician of souls knows what they are like, and what is needed to heal them, has said, *You must be born again.*

3.1.4.2.3.2.2. We are not to *marvel* at it, because when we consider the holiness of the God with whom we have to deal (Heb 4:13) and the depravity of our nature, we should not think it strange that being born again is emphasized as the one thing needed (Lk 10:42).

3.1.4.2.4. He illustrated the change by two comparisons. He compared the regenerating work of the Spirit to:

3.1.4.2.4.1. *Water* (v. 5). To be born again is to be *born of water* and of the Spirit. What is primarily intended here is to show that the Spirit, in sanctifying a soul, cleanses and purifies it as water cleanses a body, taking away its filth. The Spirit also cools and refreshes the soul, as water refreshes the hunted hart and the weary traveler. Christ was probably thinking of the ceremony of baptism, which John had used and he himself had begun to use. "You must be born again of the Spirit," and this regeneration by the Spirit would be represented by washing with water, as the outward, visible sign of the working of inner spiritual grace.

3.1.4.2.4.2. Wind: *The wind bloweth where it listeth; so is every one that is born of the Spirit* (v. 8). The same word means both "wind" and "Spirit." The Spirit, in regeneration, works as a free agent where he wishes; the Spirit gives his influences where, when, on whom, and in what measure he pleases. He works powerfully and with clear effects: *Thou hearest the sound thereof;* although its causes are hidden, its effects are clear. He works mysteriously and in secret, hidden ways: *Thou canst not tell whence it comes, nor whither it goes.* How the wind gathers its force and how it exhausts its strength is a puzzle to us; likewise, the ways of the Spirit's working are a mystery.

3.2. Here Christ took occasion from the weakness of Nicodemus to speak about the certainty and sublimity of Gospel truths. Here is:

3.2.1. The objection Nicodemus still raised (v. 9): *How can these things be?* Christ's explanation of the teaching of the necessity of regeneration made it no clearer to him, it seems. The corruption of nature that makes it necessary and the way of the Spirit that makes it practicable were as mysterious to him as the thing itself. Many will neither believe the truths of Christianity nor submit to its laws further than they want to. They will let Christ be their teacher, provided they can choose the lesson. Nicodemus acknowledged himself ignorant of what Christ meant, after all: "How can these things be? These are things I do not understand; my abilities do not reach that far." Because this teaching was unintelligible to him, he questioned its truth. Many think that something they cannot believe cannot be proved.

3.2.2. The rebuke Christ gave him for his slowness and ignorance: "*Art thou a master in Israel* and yet not only unfamiliar with the teaching of regeneration but also incapable of understanding it?" This remark is a rebuke:

3.2.2.1. To those who undertake to teach others but who remain ignorant and *unskillful in the word of righteousness* themselves (Heb 5:13).

3.2.2.2. To those who spend their time in religious ideas and ceremonies, scriptural details and criticism, and neglect what is practical. Two words in the rebuke are emphatic:

3.2.2.2.1. The place where Nicodemus's lot was cast: *in Israel*, where divine revelation was. He could have learned this from the Old Testament.

3.2.2.2.2. The things he was so ignorant of: *these things*, these necessary, great, and divine things.

3.2.3. Christ's message, then, on the certainty and sublimity of Gospel truths (vv. 11–13). Notice here:

3.2.3.1. The truths Christ taught were certain and what we may depend on (v. 11): *We speak that we do know.* The truths of Christ are of undoubted certainty. We have all the reason in the world to be assured that the sayings of Christ are *faithful sayings* (Rev 22:6), ones that we may rest our souls on. Whatever Christ spoke, he spoke of his own knowledge. The things are so sure and clear, but *you receive not our witness.*

3.2.3.2. The truths Christ taught, though communicated in expressions taken from ordinary and earthly things, were nevertheless most sublime and heavenly; this is indicated in v. 12: "If I have told them earthly things, that is, have told them the great things of God in comparisons taken from earthly things—such as the comparison between the new birth and the wind—to make them easier to understand, if I have in this way adjusted my teaching to your level, lisping to you in your own language, and still cannot make you understand my message, what would you do if I adjusted my language to the real nature of things, speaking with the tongues of angels, languages that mortals cannot speak?" We may learn from this:

3.2.3.2.1. To wonder at the height and depth of the teaching of Christ. The things of the Gospel are heavenly things, out of the normal channels of human reason, and much more out of the reach of what that reason can find out by itself.

3.2.3.2.2. To acknowledge with thankfulness the condescension of Christ. He considers how we are formed (Ps 103:14), that we are of the earth, and where we live, that we are on the earth, and so he speaks to us about earthly things, making physical things the medium by which he explains spiritual things, to make them the easier for us to grasp.

3.2.3.2.3. To mourn our great disinclination to receive and welcome the truths of Christ. Earthly things are despised because they are common, and heavenly things are despised because they are obscure, and so whatever method is followed, some fault or other is found with it.

3.2.3.3. Our Lord Jesus, and only he, was fit to reveal to us a teaching that was so certain and sublime: *No man hath ascended up into heaven but he* (v. 13).

3.2.3.3.1. No one except Christ was able to reveal to us the will of God for our salvation. Nicodemus spoke to Christ as a prophet, but he must know that Christ was greater than all the Old Testament prophets, because none of them had *ascended into heaven.* No one has reached the certain knowledge of God and heavenly things that Christ has. It is not for us to send to heaven for instructions; we must wait to receive whatever instructions heaven wants to send to us.

3.2.3.3.2. Jesus Christ is able to reveal the will of God to us because he is the One who came down from heaven and is in heaven. He had said (v. 12), *How shall ye believe, if I tell you of heavenly things?* Now here:

3.2.3.3.2.1. He gave the Jews an example of those heavenly things when he told them about One who came down from heaven and yet was the Son of Man. If the regeneration of the human soul is such a mystery, what then is the incarnation of the Son of God? We have here an indication of Christ's two distinct natures in one person.

3.2.3.3.2.2. He gave them a proof of his ability to speak to them about heavenly things by telling them:

3.2.3.3.2.2.1. That he came down from heaven. The relationship settled between God and human beings began above. We love him and go to him because he first loved us and came to us. Now this shows:

3.2.3.3.2.2.1.1. Christ's divine nature.

3.2.3.3.2.2.1.2. His intimate acquaintance with divine purposes.

3.2.3.3.2.2.1.3. The revelation of God. The New Testament shows us God coming down from heaven to teach and save us. Here he commended his love.

3.2.3.3.2.2.2. That he is *the Son of man,* which the Jews always understood to refer to the Messiah.

3.2.3.3.2.2.3. That he is *in heaven.* Now, when he was talking with Nicodemus on earth, still, as God, he was in heaven.

3.3. Christ spoke here about his great intention in coming into the world and about the happiness of those who believe in him (vv. 14–18). Here we have the very heart and essence of the whole Gospel, that Jesus Christ came to seek and to save (Lk 19:11) people from death and restore them to life. Now sinners are dead in two ways. They are dead as those who are mortally wounded or sick and as those who are justly condemned to die for an unpardonable crime. Thus saving is here set opposite both kinds of death (vv. 16–18).

3.3.1. Jesus Christ came to save us by healing us, just as the children of Israel who were bitten by venomous snakes were healed and lived by looking to the bronze snake. Now in this type of Christ we may notice:

3.3.1.1. The deadly and destructive nature of sin, which is implied here. The guilt of sin is like the pain of a venomous snakebite; the power of corruption is like the

venom diffused. The curses of the law are like venomous snakes, and so are all the signs of divine wrath.

3.3.1.2. The powerful remedy provided against this fatal illness. The case of poor sinners is deplorable, but is it desperate? Thank God, it is not. The *Son of man is lifted up,* as the *serpent of brass* was lifted up by Moses (Nu 21:19).

3.3.1.2.1. It was a bronze snake that healed them. It was made in the shape of *a fiery serpent* (Nu 21:8) but had no poison, no sting, fitly representing Christ; it was as harmless as a bronze snake.

3.3.1.2.2. It was lifted up on a pole, and so must the Son of Man be lifted up. Christ was lifted up:

3.3.1.2.2.1. In his crucifixion. He was lifted up on the cross. His death is called his being *lifted up* (12:32–33).

3.3.1.2.2.2. In his exaltation. He was lifted up to the Father's right hand. He was lifted up to the cross to be further lifted up to the crown.

3.3.1.2.2.3. In the proclaiming and preaching of his eternal Gospel (Rev 14:6).

3.3.1.2.3. Being lifted up in this way, the serpent was appointed for the healing of those who had been bitten by the venomous snakes. The One who sent the plague provided the remedy. It was God himself who *found the ransom.* The One whom we have offended is himself *our peace* (Eph 2:14).

3.3.1.3. The way of applying this remedy, and that is by believing. Everyone who looked at the bronze serpent was made well (Nu 21:9). Christ has said, "Look, and be saved" (Isa 45:22), "look and live."

3.3.1.4. The great encouragements given us by faith to look at him.

3.3.1.4.1. To be looked at was why he was lifted up, so that his followers would be saved.

3.3.1.4.2. The offer of salvation that is made by him is general; it is made to whoever believes, without exception.

3.3.1.4.3. The salvation offered is complete: they will not perish; they will have eternal life.

3.3.2. Jesus Christ came to save us by pardoning us (vv. 16–17). Here is true Gospel, good news, the best that ever came from heaven to earth.

3.3.2.1. Here is God's love in giving his Son for the world, in v. 16. In this account of that love, we have three things:

3.3.2.1.1. The great Gospel mystery revealed: *God so loved the world that he gave his only-begotten Son.* Jesus Christ is the *only-begotten Son of God.* Now we know that God loves us, since he has given his only begotten Son for us. In order to accomplish human redemption and salvation, it pleased God to give his only begotten Son. He gave him, that is, he gave him up to suffer and die for us. His enemies could not have taken him if his Father had not given him. Here God has commended his love to the world; *God so loved the world,* so really, so richly. Look in wonder, that the great God should love such a worthless world, that the holy God should love such an evil world. The Jews vainly thought that the Messiah would be sent only in love for their nation, but Christ told them that he came out of love for the whole world, Gentiles as well as Jews (1Jn 2:2). Through him a general offer of life and salvation is made to all. God loved the world so much that he sent his Son with this fair offer, that whoever believes in him will not perish. Salvation had been *of the Jews* (4:22), but now Christ would be known as salvation to the ends of the earth.

3.3.2.1.2. The great Gospel duty, and that is to believe in Jesus Christ.

3.3.2.1.*3.* The great Gospel benefit: *That whosoever believes in Christ* will not perish. God has taken away their sin; they will not die. A pardon has been purchased. They are entitled to the joys of heaven: they will *have everlasting life.*

3.3.2.2. Here is God's intention in sending his Son into the world: it was *that the world through him might be saved.* He came into the world with salvation in his mind, with salvation in his hand (v. 17): God sent his Son into the world; he sent him as his agent or ambassador, as a resident. We should ask why he comes: *Is it in peace?* (2Ki 9:17–19). This Scripture returns the answer, "Peaceably."

3.3.2.2.*1. He did not come to condemn the world.* We had enough reason to expect that he would, because it is a guilty world; it is convicted. Justly may such a world as this be condemned. He came with full powers indeed to *execute judgment* (5:22, 27), and yet he did not begin with a judgment of condemnation, but put us on a new trial before a throne of grace.

3.3.2.2.*2.* He came *that the world through him might be saved.* God was in Christ *reconciling the world to himself* (2Co 5:19), and so saving it. This is good news to a convicted conscience, healing to broken bones and bleeding wounds, that Christ, our judge, came not to condemn, but to save.

3.3.3. From all this the happiness of true believers is inferred: *he that believeth on him is not condemned* (v. 18). This denotes more than a reprieve; they are not condemned, that is, they are acquitted, and if they are not condemned they are discharged. Who is the One who condemns? It was Christ who died (Ro 8:34). Whoever believes will suffer, but they will not be condemned. The cross perhaps lies heavy on them, but they are saved from the curse: they will be condemned by the world, maybe, but not condemned with the world (Ro 8:1; 1Co 11:32).

3.4. Christ, at the end, spoke about the deplorable condition of those who persist in unbelief and willful ignorance (vv. 18–21).

3.4.1. We read about the fate of those who refuse to believe in Christ here: they are *condemned already.* Notice:

3.4.1.1. How great the sin of unbelievers is: they *believe not in the* name of the only begotten Son of God, who is infinitely true and deserves to be believed, who is infinitely good and deserves to be accepted. God sent One to save us who was dearest to himself, and will he not be dearest to us?

3.4.1.2. How great the misery of unbelievers is: they *are condemned already.* The condemnation is certain and present. They are already condemned, because their own hearts condemn them. They receive a condemnation based on their former guilt: *He is condemned already, because he has not believed.* Unbelief is a sin against the remedy.

3.4.2. We also read about the fate of those who refused even to know him (v. 19). And *this is the condemnation, that light is come into the world, and they loved darkness rather.* Notice here:

3.4.2.1. That the Gospel is light, and when the Gospel came, *light came into the world.* Light gives evidence of itself, and so does the Gospel; it proves its own divine origin. Light reveals, and *truly the light is sweet* (Ecc 11:7); the world would truly be a dark place without it.

3.4.2.2. That it is the unspeakable folly of most people that they loved darkness rather than this light. Sinners who were devoted to their sinful desires loved their ignorance and mistakes rather than the truths of Christ. Wretched humanity is in love with its sickness, in love with its slav-ery, and so does not want to be set free, does not want to be made whole.

3.4.2.3. That the true reason why people love darkness rather than light is that *their deeds are evil.* Their case is sad, and because they are determined they will not put it right, they are determined they will not see it.

3.4.2.4. That willful ignorance is so far from excusing sin that it will be found to emphasize the condemnation: *This is the condemnation,* that they close their eyes to the light and will not even begin to think about Christ and his Gospel. We must give an account in the judgment not only for the knowledge we sinned against but also for the knowledge we sinned away.

3.4.2.4.*1.* It is not strange if those who are determined to persist in evil hate the light of Christ's Gospel; it is a common observation that *everyone that doeth evil hateth the light* (v. 20). Evildoers seek concealment out of a sense of shame and fear of punishment. *They come not to this light,* but keep as far away from it as possible, *lest their deeds should be reproved.* The light of the Gospel is sent into the world to reprove the evil deeds of sinners, to show people their transgressions, to show to be sin what they thought was not, so *that sin by the* new *commandment* might be seen to be *exceeding sinful* (Ro 7:13). The Gospel has to do its convicting work to make way for its work of comfort. This is why evildoers *hate the light of* the Gospel. There were those who had done evil and were sorry for it, who welcomed this light, such as the tax collectors and prostitutes. However, those who do evil and are determined to continue in it *hate the light.* Christ is hated because sin is loved. Those who do not *come to the light* show a secret hatred of the light.

3.4.2.4.*2.* On the other hand, upright hearts welcome this light (v. 21): *He that doeth truth cometh to the light.* Just as it convinces and terrifies evildoers, so it also confirms and comforts those who conduct their lives in integrity. Notice here:

3.4.2.4.*2.1.* The character of good people.

3.4.2.4.*2.1.1.* They are those who *do truth.* Although sometimes they fall short of doing good, the good they want to do, they still live by truth; their aims are honest. They have their weaknesses, but they hold firmly to their integrity.

3.4.2.4.*2.1.2.* They are those one who *come to the light.* Those who live by the truth are willing to know the truth about themselves and to *have their deeds made manifest.* They are concerned to know what the will of God is and are determined to do it, even though it may go against their own will and interests.

3.4.2.4.*2.2.* The description of a good work: it is *wrought in God.* Our works are good when they are guided by the will of God and when their aim is the glory of God, when they are done in his strength and for his sake. Nicodemus, though puzzled at first, later became a faithful disciple of Christ.

Verses 22–36

In these verses we have:

1. Christ's move into the Judean countryside (v. 22). After our Lord Jesus began his public work, he traveled much and moved often. He took many weary steps to do good to souls. The *Sun of righteousness* (Mal 4:2) took a large circuit to spread his light and heat (Ps 19:6). He did not usually stay long in Jerusalem. *After these things,* after he had had this conversation with Nicodemus, he came into the Judean countryside, not so much to give himself greater privacy as to be more useful. His preaching and miracles, perhaps, attracted most attention at Jerusalem,

the fountain of news, but they did least good there. When he came into Judean countryside, his *disciples came with him*. There he *tarried with them*. Those who are ready to go with Christ will find him as ready to stay with them. There *he baptized*. John began to baptize in the land of Judea (Mt 3:1), and so Christ began there. He did not baptize with his own hands, but his disciples baptized under his orders and directions, as can be seen from 4:2. Holy ceremonies are Christ's, even though they are administered by weak people.

2. John's continuation in his work, as long as opportunities lasted (vv. 23–24). Here we are told:

2.1. That *John was baptizing*. Christ's baptism was substantially the same as John's, and so they did not clash or interfere with one another in any way.

2.1.1. Christ took up the work of preaching and baptizing before John laid it down, so the wheels would be kept moving. When useful people are leaving the stage, it is an encouragement to them to see the rise of those who are likely to fill their places.

2.1.2. John continued the work of preaching and baptizing even though Christ had taken it up. There was still work for John to do, as Christ was not yet generally known, nor were the minds of people thoroughly prepared for him by repentance. He went on with his work until Providence set him aside. The greater gifts of some do not make the labors of others who come short of them unnecessary and useless; there is enough work for everyone to do. Those who sit down and do nothing when they see themselves eclipsed are really bad tempered.

2.2. That he baptized in Aenon near Salim; neither place is mentioned anywhere else. Wherever this Aenon was, it seems that John moved from place to place. Ministers must follow the opportunities they see. John chose a place where there was *much water*, that is, many streams of water, so that wherever he met anyone who was willing to submit to his baptism, water was nearby to baptize.

2.3. That people *came to him* there and *were baptized*. Some refer this both to John and to Jesus: some came to John, some to Jesus, and as their baptism was one, so were their hearts.

2.4. That *John was not yet cast into prison* (v. 24). John never stopped pursuing his work as long as he was free to.

3. An argument between *John's disciples and the Jews about purifying* (ceremonial washing) (v. 25). Notice:

3.1. Who argued: *some of John's disciples and the Jews* who had not submitted to his baptism of repentance. This sinful world is divided into penitents and impenitents.

3.2. What was being argued about: *purifying*, ceremonial washing. We may presume that John's disciples praised his baptism, his purifying, and gave preference to it as perfecting and superseding all the purifications of the Jews, and they were right. No doubt the Jews were just as sure in applauding the ceremonial washings in use among them. It is very likely that when the Jews in this argument could not deny the excellent nature and purpose of John's baptism, they raised an objection against it by referring to Christ's baptism, which gave rise to the complaint that came here (v. 26). This is how objections are raised against the Gospel by reference to the advancement and application of the light of the Gospel, as if childhood and adulthood were opposed to each other, and as if the superstructure were against the foundation.

4. A complaint by John's disciples to their master about Christ and his baptizing (v. 26). They came to their master and told him, "*Rabbi, he that was with thee*, he *baptizeth, and all men come to him*."

4.1. They suggested that Christ's setting up his own baptism was an act of presumption; it was as if John, having first set up this ceremony of baptizing, must have, as it were, a patent for it as his invention: *He that was with thee beyond Jordan, behold, the same baptizes*.

4.2. They suggested that it was an act of ingratitude toward John. "*He to whom thou barest witness baptizes*"—as if Jesus owed all his reputation to the honorable characterization John gave of him. However, Christ did not need John's testimony (5:36). He reflected more honor on John than he received from him. John was just toward Christ in testifying to him, and Christ's fulfilling his testimony enriched rather than impoverished John's ministry.

4.3. They concluded that it would mean John's baptism was completely eclipsed: *All men come to him*. Seeking a monopoly of honor and respect has been the bane of the church throughout all ages, to the shame of its members and ministers. We are mistaken if we think that the excelling gifts and graces and the works and usefulness of one person lessen and belittle those of another who has obtained mercy to be faithful (1Co 7:25). We must leave it to God to choose, use, and honor his own instruments as he pleases.

5. John's answer. It did not disturb him, but was what he wished for. He therefore refused to go along with the complaint, and used this occasion to confirm the testimonies he had formerly given to Christ as superior to him.

5.1. John here humbled himself in comparison with Christ (vv. 27–30).

5.1.1. John accepted the divine arrangement (v. 27): *A man can receive nothing except* (unless) *it be given him from heaven*. Different jobs are given according to the direction of divine Providence, different gifts given according to the distribution of divine grace (1Co 7:17). We should not envy those who have a larger share of gifts than we have, or who move in a larger sphere of usefulness. John reminded his disciples that Jesus would not have excelled him as he did *except he had received it from heaven*, and if God gave him *Spirit without measure* (v. 34), would they begrudge him that? We should not be discontented if we are inferior to others in gifts and usefulness and are surpassed by their excellencies. John was ready to acknowledge that it was God who gave him the influence and privilege of enjoying the love and respect of the people, and if now that influence declined, may God's will still be done! When he had fulfilled his ministry, he could contentedly watch his term expire.

5.1.2. John appealed to the testimony he had earlier given about Christ (v. 28): "I said again and again, *I am not the Christ, but I am sent before him*." Neither the disapproval of the chief priests nor the flattery of his own disciples could make him change his tune. This served here:

5.1.2.1. To convict his disciples about the unreasonableness of their complaint. "Now," John said, "do you not remember the testimony that I gave? Did I not say, *I am not the Christ*? Did I not say, *I am sent before him*? Why then does it seem strange to you that I stand by and give way to him?"

5.1.2.2. To comfort himself with the assurance that he had never given his disciples any occasion to set him up in competition with Christ, but, on the contrary, had particularly warned them against making this mistake. John had not only not encouraged them to hope that he was the Messiah; he had also clearly told them the opposite. Those who have undue honor paid them often try to excuse themselves by saying, "If the people want to be deceived, let them be," but that is a poor maxim for those whose business is to tell people the truth.

5.1.3. John professed the great assurance he had in the advancement of Christ; he rejoiced in it. He expressed this (v. 29) by an apt comparison. He compared our Savior to the bridegroom: "*He that hath the bride is the bridegroom. Do all men come to him? It is his right.*" As far as individual souls are devoted to him in faith and love, so far does the bridegroom have the bride. John compared himself to the *friend of the bridegroom*, who helps him pursue the match, speaking a good word for him, and rejoices when the bridegroom has the bride. *The friend of the bridegroom stands and hears him*; he *rejoices with joy because of the bridegroom's voice.* Faithful ministers are friends of the bridegroom, who are to commend him to the people, bringing letters and messages from him, since the bridegroom courts by proxy. The friends of the bridegroom must *stand and hear the bridegroom's voice*; they must receive instruction from him and listen to his orders. The betrothing of souls to Jesus Christ in faith and love is the fulfilling of the joy of every good minister. Surely they have no greater joy (3Jn 4).

5.1.4. He acknowledged it to be highly fitting and necessary that the reputation and interests of Christ be advanced, and his own diminished (v. 30): *He must increase, but I must decrease.* John spoke about Christ's increase and his own decrease also as highly just and agreeable, and giving him complete satisfaction. He was very pleased to see the kingdom of Christ gain ground: *He must increase.* The kingdom of Christ is and will be a growing kingdom, like the light of the morning (Pr 4:18), like the grain of mustard seed (Mt 13:31–32). He was not at all displeased that the effect of this was the diminishing of his own interests: *I must decrease.* The shining out of the glory of Christ eclipses the brightness of all other glory. As the light of the morning increases, the light of the morning star decreases. We must be cheerfully content to be anything—in fact, to be nothing—so that Christ may be everything.

5.2. John the Baptist here advanced Christ and instructed his disciples about him. John instructed them about:

5.2.1. Christ's rank (v. 31): *He that cometh from above is above all.* John described Christ's divine origin. He *came from above*, from heaven. No one but the One who came from heaven was qualified to show us the will of heaven or the way to heaven. John inferred from this Christ's sovereign authority: *he is above all*, above all things and all people. When we come to speak about the honors of the Lord Jesus, we can say only this: *He is above all.* John further illustrated this by reference to the lowliness of those who stood in competition with him: *He that is of the earth is earthly*; he has his contact with earthly things, and his concern is for them. The prophets and apostles were of the same mold as other people; they were merely *earthen vessels* (2Co 4:7), even though rich treasure was deposited in them.

5.2.2. The excellence and certainty of Christ's teaching.

5.2.2.1. John, for his part, spoke from the earth, as do all those who are from the earth. The prophets were human beings; they could only speak from the earth (2Co 3:5). The preaching of the prophets and of John was lowly and flat compared with Christ's preaching; just as heaven is high above the earth, so his thoughts were far above theirs (Isa 55:8–9).

5.2.2.2. The One who came from heaven, however, is above all the prophets that ever lived on earth. The teaching of Christ is commended to us here:

5.2.2.2.1. As infallibly trustworthy and certain, and to be received accordingly (v. 32): *What he hath seen and heard, that he testifieth.* Notice here:

5.2.2.2.1.1. Christ's divine knowledge; he testified nothing except *what he had seen and heard*. What he revealed of the divine nature was what he had seen; what he revealed of the mind of God was what he had heard directly from him. The prophets testified what was made known to them in dreams and visions, but not what they had seen and heard. The Gospel of Christ is not a matter of doubt, like some scientific hypothesis or philosophical idea. It is a revelation of the mind of God, which is eternally true in itself.

5.2.2.2.1.2. His divine grace and goodness, in revealing to us what was very important for us to know. Christ's preaching is called here his testifying, to show:

5.2.2.2.1.2.1. How convincing it was as evidence; it was not reported as news by hearsay, but given as testimony in court.

5.2.2.2.1.2.2. The passionate earnestness of its delivery. From the certainty of Christ's teaching, John took the opportunity:

5.2.2.2.1.2.2.1. To mourn the unfaithfulness of most people. They did not accept it; they refused to listen to it and did not believe it. He spoke about this not only as a matter of wonder but also as a matter of grief. John's disciples grieved that *all men came to Christ* (v. 26); they thought his followers were too many. But John grieved that *no man came to him*; he thought them too few. The unbelief of sinners is the grief of saints.

5.2.2.2.1.2.2.2. To commend the faith of the chosen remnant (v. 33): *He that hath received his testimony* has *set to his seal that God is true.* God is true even if we do not *set our seal to it*; God's truth does not need our faith to support it; but by faith we do ourselves the honor and justice of submitting to his truth. God's promises are all *yea and Amen* (2Co 1:20); by faith we put our Amen to them (Rev 22:20). By believing in Christ we *set to our seal* (certify) both that God is true to all the promises he has made *concerning* Christ and that he is true to all the promises he has made *in* Christ. Being satisfied that he is true, we are willing to deal with him on trust.

5.2.2.2.2. As a divine doctrine (v. 34): *For he whom God hath sent speaketh the word of God, for God giveth not the Spirit by measure unto him.*

5.2.2.2.2.1. Christ spoke the *words of God.* Both the substance and the language were divine. He proved himself *sent of God* (v. 2), and so his words are to be received as the words of God.

5.2.2.2.2.2. He spoke as no other prophet did, for *God giveth not the Spirit by measure to him.* The Old Testament prophets had the Spirit, and in different degrees (2Ki 2:9–10), but whereas God gave them the Spirit *by measure* (1Co 12:4), he gave him to Christ *without measure* (without limit). The Spirit was not in Christ as in a container, but as in a fountain, as in a bottomless ocean.

5.2.3. The power and authority he was invested with.

5.2.3.1. He is the beloved Son of the Father (v. 35): *The Father loveth the Son.* The prophets were faithful as servants, but Christ is faithful as a Son (Heb 3:5–6). The Father continued his love for Christ even in his humiliation, never loving him any less because of his poverty and suffering.

5.2.3.2. He is Lord of all. The Father *hath given all things into his hand.* Love is generous. Having given him the Spirit without measure, he gave him all things, that is:

5.2.3.2.1. *All power*, as it is explained in Mt 28:18. He has *power over all flesh* (17:2), the nations given him as his inheritance (Ps 2:8). Both the golden scepter and the iron rod are put into his hands.

5.2.3.2.2. All grace, as the channel through which he gives the good things God intended to give to human beings. We are unworthy to have the Father put those things into our hands. The things he intended for us he puts into the hands of the One who is worthy. They are put into his hands by the Father in order to be put into ours. The riches of the new covenant are deposited in such a faithful, kind, and good hand, the hand of the One who purchased them for us.

5.2.3.3. He is the object of the faith that is made the great condition of eternal happiness: *He that believeth on the Son hath life* (v. 36). This is the conclusion of the whole matter (Ecc 12:13). Just as God offers and gives good things to us through the testimony of Jesus Christ, so we receive and share in those favors by believing the testimony. This way of receiving corresponds to that way of giving. We have here the essence of the Gospel that is to be preached to the whole creation (Mk 16:16). Here is:

5.2.3.3.1. The blessed state of all true Christians: *He that believes on the Son hath everlasting life.* We must not only believe him, that what he says is true, but also believe *on* him and trust in him. The benefit of true Christianity is nothing less than eternal life. True believers have eternal life even now. They have the Son of God, and in him they have life. Grace is glory begun.

5.2.3.3.2. The wretched and miserable condition of unbelievers: *He that believeth not the Son* is ruined. The word translated *believeth not* includes both disbelief and disobedience. Unbelievers cannot be happy either in this world or in the world to come: *He shall not see life,* the life that Christ came to give, and so he must be miserable: *The wrath of God abides upon* an unbeliever.

CHAPTER 4

In this chapter we have Christ: 1. Departing from Judea (vv. 1–3). 2. Passing through Samaria. We read of: 2.1. His coming to Samaria (vv. 4–6). 2.2. His conversation with the Samaritan woman at the well (vv. 7–26). 2.3. The information the woman gave about him to the town (vv. 27–30). 2.4. Christ's talk with his disciples in the meantime (vv. 31–38). 2.5. The good effect of this on the Samaritans (vv. 39–42). 3. Staying for some time in Galilee (vv. 43–46) and healing an official's son there (vv. 46–54).

Verses 1–3

Now Christ left Judea four months before harvest (v. 35).

1. He *made disciples.* His ministry was successful despite the opposition it met with (Ps 110:2–3). It is Christ's right to make disciples, to form and fashion them according to his will. "Christians are made, not born."

2. He *baptized* those whom he made disciples. He himself did not baptize them; he did it by the ministry of his disciples (v. 2), because he wanted to distinguish between his baptism and that of John, who baptized everyone himself. He also wanted to honor his disciples by empowering and employing them to do it, and so train them up to further service. And he wanted to teach us that he acknowledges as done by himself what is done by his ministers according to his direction.

3. He made and baptized *more disciples than John.* Christ's work was more winning than John's.

4. The Pharisees were informed about this. When the Pharisees thought they had gotten rid of John, Jesus

appeared. What grieved them was that Christ made so many disciples. The success of the Gospel exasperates its enemies.

5. Our Lord Jesus knew very well what information had been given against him. No one can dig so deeply as to *hide their counsels from the Lord* (Isa 29:15).

6. Then our Lord Jesus *left Judea* and *departed again* to go to Galilee.

6.1. He *left Judea* because he was likely to be persecuted there even to death. He left the country and went where his actions would be less offensive than under the immediate gaze of the Pharisees. For:

6.1.1. His hour had not yet come (7:30). He had not completed his testimony (Rev 11:7) and therefore would not surrender or make himself vulnerable.

6.1.2. The disciples he had gathered in Judea were not able to bear hardships, and so he did not want to expose them.

6.1.3. He wanted to give an example of his own rule: *When they persecute you in one city, flee to another* (Mt 10:23). We are not called to suffering as long as we can avoid it without sin, and so we may still change our place.

6.2. He departed to Galilee because there he had work to do and had many friends and fewer enemies.

Verses 4–26

Here we have an account of the good Christ did in Samaria. The Samaritans, both in blood and religion, were half Jews. They worshiped only the God of Israel, but they set up a temple to him on Mount Gerizim, in competition with that at Jerusalem. There was great enmity between them and the Jews. The Samaritans would not welcome Christ when they saw him going to Jerusalem (Lk 9:53); the Jews thought they could not give him a worse name than to say, *He is a Samaritan* (8:48). Now notice:

1. Christ's coming into Samaria. He told his disciples not to enter any town of the Samaritans (Mt 10:5), nor did he preach publicly or work any miracle here in the town of Sychar, because his eye was on the lost sheep of the house of Israel (Mt 10:6; 15:24). The kindness he did them here was only a crumb of the children's bread that casually fell from the master's table (Mt 15:27).

1.1. His road from Judea to Galilee lay through the country of Samaria (v. 4): *He must needs go through Samaria.* There was no other way unless he made a detour to the other side of the Jordan, a long way around. We should not go into places of temptation except when we have to, and then we should not live in them, but pass quickly through them. It was fortunate for Samaria that it lay on Christ's route.

1.2. His resting place happened to be in a town of Samaria. Now notice:

1.2.1. How the place is described. It was called Sychar; it was probably the same as *Sichem,* or *Shechem.* Shechem saw the first convert who ever came into the church of Israel (Ge 34:24), and now it was the first place where the Gospel was preached outside of the community of Israel. Abimelech was made king there (Jdg 9:6); it was Jeroboam's royal seat (1Ki 12:25), but the Evangelist notes Jacob's influence there, which was more his honor than its crowned heads. Jacob's ground lay there (Ge 33:18–19), the plot of ground that Jacob gave to his son Joseph (Ge 48:21–22). Here was Jacob's well: *Being wearied with his journey,* Jesus *sat thus on the well.*

1.2.2. The condition of our Lord Jesus at this place: *Being wearied with his journey.* We have our Lord Jesus here:

1.2.2.1. Laboring under the ordinary tiredness of travelers. He was *wearied with his journey*, because it was the sixth hour, the time of the heat of the day. He was truly human, subject to the ordinary weaknesses of human nature. He was a poor man, for otherwise he might have traveled on horseback or in a carriage. When we travel in comfort, let us think about the tiredness of our Master. It seems he did not have a very strong constitution; his disciples apparently were not tired, because they went into the town without any difficulty. Bodies of the finest form are the most sensitive to tiredness and least able to bear it.

1.2.2.2. Availing himself of the usual relief for travelers here: *Being wearied, he sat thus on the well*. He sat down uncomfortably.

2. His conversation with a Samaritan woman. This conversation may be considered under four headings:

2.1. They spoke about water (vv. 7–15).

2.1.1. Notice is taken of the circumstances that gave rise to this conversation. A *woman* of Samaria came to *draw water*. She had no servant to be a *drawer of water* (Dt 29:11); she wanted to do it herself. Notice here how divine Providence brings about glorious purposes by events that seem to us accidental. Christ's disciples had *gone away into the city to buy meat* (food). Christ did not go into the town to eat, but sent his disciples to get his food there, not because he had scruples about eating in a Samaritan town, but:

2.1.1.1. Because he had a good work to do at that well.

2.1.1.2. Because it was more private and secluded, cheaper and more homely, to have his meal brought to him there than to go into town for it. Christ could eat his dinner as acceptably at a deep well as in the best inn in town. He often preached to many people, but here he stooped to teach one individual, a poor woman, a foreigner, a Samaritan. This teaches his ministers to do likewise, as those who know what a glorious achievement it is to help to save souls from death—even only one soul.

2.1.2. Let us notice the particulars of this conversation.

2.1.2.1. Jesus began with a modest request for a drink of water: *Give me to drink*. The One who *for our sakes became poor* (2Co 8:9) here became a beggar. Christ asked for it not only because he needed it and needed her help to reach it but also because he wanted to draw her on to further conversation. Christ is still begging by way of his poor members, and *a cup of cold water* (Mt 10:42) given to them in his name will not lose its reward.

2.1.2.2. The woman quarreled with him because he did not display the attitude of his own nation (v. 9): *How is it?* Notice:

2.1.2.2.1. What a deadly feud existed between Jews and Samaritans: *The Jews have no dealings with the Samaritans*. Quarrels about religion are usually the most implacable of all quarrels. If people's worshiping at different temples causes them to refuse to love one another, and this in the name of religious zeal, they clearly show that however much they think their religion may be true, they are not truly religious.

2.1.2.2.2. How ready the woman was to rebuke Christ for the pride and ill nature of the Jewish nation: *How is it that thou, being a Jew, askest drink of me?* Moderate people of different sides are *men wondered at*. This woman was amazed:

2.1.2.2.2.1. That he would ask this kindness, because the Jews were so proud that they would endure any hardship rather than be indebted to a Samaritan. Even if the spirit of our country or the attitude of those around us is very miserable and bad tempered, we must exercise

goodness and kindness, as our master did. This woman expected Christ to be like the other Jews, but every rule has its exceptions.

2.1.2.2.2.2 That he would expect to receive this kindness from her, a Samaritan.

2.1.2.3. Christ used the opportunity to instruct her in divine things: *If thou knewest the gift of God, thou wouldst have asked* (v. 10).

2.1.2.3.1. He brushed aside her objection concerning the feud between Jews and Samaritans. Some differences are best healed by avoiding all occasions of entering into dispute about them. Christ wanted to convert this woman, showing her her need of a Savior.

2.1.2.3.2. He filled her with a perception that she now had an opportunity to gain what would benefit her indescribably. He told her explicitly that she now had a season of grace.

2.1.2.3.2.1. He hinted to her what she ought to have known but was ignorant of: *If thou knewest the gift of God, who it is that saith, Give me to drink*. She saw him as a Jew, a poor, weary traveler, but he wanted her to know something more about him. Jesus Christ is the *gift of God*, the richest sign of God's love to us. It is an indescribable privilege to have this gift of God offered to us. "It is he who says, *Give me to drink*; this gift is being offered to you."

2.1.2.3.2.2. He said what he had hoped she would do if she had known him: *Thou wouldst have asked*. Those who want to receive any benefit from Christ must ask him for it. Those who have a right knowledge of Christ will seek him. Christ knows what those who lack the means of knowledge would do if they had it (Mt 11:21).

2.1.2.3.2.3. He assured her of what he would have done for her if she had turned to him: He *would have given thee living water*. This living water means the Spirit, who is not like the water at the bottom of the well, but like living, or running, water. The Spirit of grace is like *living water*. Jesus Christ can and will give the Holy Spirit to those who ask him.

2.1.2.4. The woman raised an objection to the gracious sign Christ gave her (vv. 11–12): "*Thou hast nothing to draw with*, and besides, *Art thou greater than our father Jacob?*" What Christ spoke figuratively, she took literally; Nicodemus did so too (3:4).

2.1.2.4.1. She did not think he was capable of supplying her with any water: *Thou hast nothing to draw with*, and *the well is deep*. He who *causeth the vapours to ascend from the ends of the earth* (Ps 135:7) needs nothing to draw with, but there are those who will not believe his promises unless the means of fulfilling the promises are visible—as if he said, "He could not draw water without our buckets. She asked scornfully, "*Whence hast thou this living water?* I do not see where you can get it from." The fountain of life is hidden with Christ. Christ has enough for us, even though we cannot see where he gets it from.

2.1.2.4.2. She did not think he could supply her with any better water: *Art thou greater than our father Jacob, who gave us the well?*

2.1.2.4.2.1. We will suppose that the tradition was true, that Jacob *himself, and his children, and cattle, did drink of this well*. We may notice from this the power and providence of God in the continuation of the fountains of water from generation to generation.

2.1.2.4.2.2. Yet even allowing that to be true, she was mistaken in several matters:

2.1.2.4.2.2.1. In calling Jacob *father*. What authority did the Samaritans have to consider themselves from the descendants of Jacob?

2.1.2.4.*2.2.2.* In claiming this well as Jacob's gift; he gave it no more than Moses gave the *manna* (6:32). But we tend to call the messengers of God's gifts the donors of them, and to look so much at the hands those gifts pass through that we forget the hand they come from.

2.1.2.4.*2.2.3.* In speaking of Christ as unworthy to be compared with *our father Jacob.* Excessive respect for former times shows disrespect for God's grace in the good people of our own time.

2.1.2.5. Christ answered this objection, telling her that the *living water* he had to give was far better than that of Jacob's well (vv. 13 – 14). Christ did not reject her, but encouraged her. He showed her:

2.1.2.5.*1.* That the water of Jacob's well gave only a transient satisfaction: "*Whoso drinketh of this water shall thirst again.* It is no better than other water; it will quench the present thirst, but the thirst will return." This shows:

2.1.2.5.*1.1.* The frailty of our bodies in this present state; they are always craving. Life is a fire, a lamp, which will soon go out unless it is continually supplied with fuel, with oil.

2.1.2.5.*1.2.* The flaws in all our comforts in this world; they do not last. Yesterday's food and drink do not do today's work.

2.1.2.5.2. That the living waters he would give would yield a lasting satisfaction and happiness (v. 14). Whoever shares in the Spirit of grace:

2.1.2.5.2.*1.* Will *never thirst.* He has a desiring thirst for nothing more than God, for still more and more of God, but not a despairing thirst.

2.1.2.5.2.*2.* Will never thirst because the water that Christ gives *shall be in him a well of water.* Those who have in themselves a fountain of supply and satisfaction can never be reduced to extremity. Such water will be:

2.1.2.5.2.2.*1.* Always ready, because it will be in him. He does not need to look to the world for comfort.

2.1.2.5.2.2.*2.* Never failing, for it will be in him a *well of water,* overflowing, ever flowing:

2.1.2.5.2.2.2.*1. Springing up,* always moving. If good truths stagnate in our souls, like stagnant water, they do not fulfill the purpose of our receiving them.

2.1.2.5.2.2.2.*2. Springing up to everlasting life.* The phrase shows three things: (1) The aims of the workings of grace. Spiritual life springs up toward its own perfection in eternal life. (2) The constancy of those workings: it will continue to spring up until it reaches perfection. (3) The crown of those workings, which is to finally have eternal life. Is this water not better than that of Jacob's well?

2.1.2.6. The woman begged him to give her some of this water (v. 15): *Give me this water, that I thirst not.*

2.1.2.6.*1.* Some think that she spoke tauntingly, ridiculing what Christ had said as worthless: "A novel idea! It will save me a great deal of discomfort if I am not thirsty, and a great deal of effort if I never *come hither to draw.*"

2.1.2.6.*2.* Others think that it was a well-intentioned but weak and ignorant wish. "Whatever it is, let me have it." Comfort, or the saving of labor, is a valuable good to poor, hardworking people. This shows us that even those who are weak and ignorant may still have some faint and fluctuating desires toward Christ and his gifts.

2.2. The next subject of conversation with this woman was *her husband* (vv. 16 – 18). Christ brought up this topic not to drop the subject of the water of life, but with a gracious intention. He found that what he had said about his grace and eternal life had had little effect on her; therefore, setting aside the conversation about living water, he set himself to awaken her conscience, and then she would more easily take hold of the answer through grace. This

is the way to deal with souls; this is the way to administer spiritual medicine: they must first be made weary and burdened under the weight of sin, and then brought to Christ for rest (Mt 11:28). Notice:

2.2.1. How discreetly and decently Christ introduced this subject (v. 16): *Go, call thy husband, and come hither.* The order Christ gave her looked very good: "*Call thy husband,* so that he may teach you, help you understand these things: *Call thy husband,* so that he may learn with you, so that then you may be *heirs together of the grace of life* (1Pe 3:7)." Just as it looked good, so it also had a good purpose, namely, to give him an occasion to remind her of her sin. There is a need for skill and wisdom in rebuking people.

2.2.2. How determinedly the woman sought to evade the conviction, and yet imperceptibly convicted herself. She said, *I have no husband.*

2.2.3. How closely our Lord Jesus brought home the conviction to her conscience. He probably said more than is recorded here, because she thought he had told her all that she ever did (v. 29). Here is:

2.2.3.1. A surprising account of her past life: *Thou hast had five husbands.*

2.2.3.2. A severe rebuke of her present life: *He whom thou now hast is not thy husband.* In short, she lived in adultery. Notice, however, how mildly Christ told her about it; *He with whom thou livest is not thy husband.* And then he left it to her own conscience to say the rest.

2.2.3.3. A better interpretation of her evasive statement than it would very well bear: *Thou hast well said, I have no husband,* and again, *In that saidst thou truly.* What she intended as a denial of the fact, he interpreted favorably, as a confession of the fault. Those who want to win souls should make the best of people, thereby giving themselves a hope of influencing their good nature, because if they make the worst of them, they certainly exasperate their bad nature.

2.3. The next subject of conversation with this woman was *the place of worship* (vv. 19 – 24). Notice:

2.3.1. The question of conscience that the woman put to Christ concerning the place of worship (vv. 19 – 20). Notice:

2.3.1.1. She revealed her incentive for asking about this matter: *Sir, I perceive that thou art a prophet.* She did not deny the truth of what he had charged her with. Nor was she provoked by it to lose her temper, as many are when they are touched in a sore place; she could bear to be told her fault, which is rare. She went further:

2.3.1.1.*1.* She spoke respectfully to him, calling him *Sir.* This was the effect of Christ's humility in rebuking her; he did not use abusive language with her, and so she did not use such language with him.

2.3.1.1.*2.* She acknowledged him to be a *prophet.*

2.3.1.1.*3.* She wanted some further guidance from him.

2.3.1.2. The matter itself that she asked about was the place of religious worship in public. She knew she must worship God, and she wanted to do so in the right way, and therefore, meeting with a prophet, she begged for his guidance. It was agreed between the Jews and the Samaritans that God is to be worshiped — even those who were such fools as to worship false gods were not so senseless as to worship none. However, the matter in dispute was where they should worship God. Notice how she stated the case:

2.3.1.2.*1.* As for the Samaritans, *Our fathers worshiped in this mountain*; the Samaritan temple was built there by Sanballat II, a governor of Samaria in the fourth century B.C. She insinuated:

2.3.1.2.*1.1.* That whatever the temple was, the place was holy; it was Mount Gerizim, the mountain on which the blessings were declared (Dt 11:29; 27:12; Jos 8:30–35).

2.3.1.2.*1.2.* That the Samaritans could plead precedence in defense of their worshiping there: *Our fathers worshiped here.* She thought they had antiquity, tradition, and succession on their side.

2.3.1.2.2. As to the Jews: *You say* that *in Jerusalem is the place where men ought to worship.* The Samaritans governed themselves by the five books of Moses. Now, although they found frequent mention there of the place God would choose, they did not find it named there, and they so thought themselves free to set up another place.

2.3.2. Christ's response to this question (v. 21).

2.3.2.1. He passed over the question, as she had asked it (v. 21): "*Woman, believe me.* What you have been taught to emphasize so much will be set aside as unimportant. *The hour comes when you shall neither in this mountain nor yet at Jerusalem worship the Father.*" An end would come to all the details and all the differences about the place of worship. It would be completely immaterial whether people worshiped God in either of these places or any other, because they would not be limited to any one place; neither here nor there, but both, and anywhere, in fact, everywhere.

2.3.2.2. He emphasized other things. When he made so light of the place of worship, he did not intend to lessen our concern about worship itself.

2.3.2.2.1. As to the present state of the dispute, he decided against Samaritan worship. He told her:

2.3.2.2.*1.1.* That the Samaritans were certainly in the wrong, because they were mistaken in the object of their worship: *you worship you know not what.* Ignorance is so far from being the mother of devotion that it is its murderer.

2.3.2.2.*1.2.* That the Jews were certainly in the right. For:

2.3.2.2.*1.2.1.* "*We know what we worship.* We are on a sure footing in our worship." Those who have obtained some knowledge of God by the Scriptures may worship him with assurance for themselves and with acceptance before him, because they know what they worship. Worship may be true where it is not pure and wholehearted. Our Lord Jesus considered himself to be among the worshipers of God: *We worship.* Let not the greatest people think the worship of God below them, since the Son of God himself did not.

2.3.2.2.*1.2.2. Salvation is of the Jews,* and that is the reason why they know what they worship and on what grounds they do what they do in their worship. The author of eternal salvation came from the Jews, and he was sent to bless them first. The means of eternal salvation are offered to them. The *word of salvation* (Ac 13:26) was through the Jews.

2.3.2.2.2. He described worship under the Gospel. Having shown that the place was not important, he came to show what is necessary and essential—that we worship God *in spirit and in truth* (vv. 23–24). The emphasis is on the state of heart in which we worship him. We should be anxious to be right not only in the object of our worship but also in its manner, and this is what Christ teaches us about here. Notice:

2.3.2.2.*2.1.* The revolution that would introduce this change: *The hour cometh, and now is.* The perfect day was coming (Pr 4:18), and now it dawned.

2.3.2.2.*2.2.* The wonderful change itself. *True worshipers shall worship the Father in spirit and in truth.*

As creatures, we worship the Father of all: as Christians, we worship the Father of our Lord Jesus. Now the change would be:

2.3.2.2.*2.2.1.* In the nature of the worship. Christians would worship God not in the ceremonial observances of the Mosaic institution, but in spiritual ordinances.

2.3.2.2.*2.2.2.* In the attitude of the worshipers: all *would,* Jesus said—and they will—*worship God in spirit and in truth.* It is spoken of as their character (v. 23) and as their duty (v. 24). It is required of all who worship God that they worship him in spirit and in truth. We must worship God *in spirit* (Php 3:3), with fixed thought and ardent devotion, with *all that is within us* (Ps 103:1), depending on God's Spirit for strength and help. And we must worship him *in truth,* that is, sincerely. We must be more concerned with power than with form (2Ti 3:5).

2.3.2.2.*2.3.* He intimated the reasons why God must be worshiped in this way.

2.3.2.2.*2.3.1.* Because in Gospel times those, and those only, who worship in this way are counted as the true worshipers. The Gospel sets up a spiritual way of worship, so that those who profess the Gospel do not live up to the Gospel light and laws unless they worship God *in spirit and in truth.*

2.3.2.2.*2.3.2.* Because the *Father seeketh such worshipers of him.* Such worshipers are very rare. The gate of spiritual worshiping is narrow (Mt 7:14). Yet such worship is necessary and is what the God of heaven insists on. God is greatly pleased with and graciously accepts such worship and such worshipers. His seeking such worshipers implies his making them such. Christ came to *declare God* to us (1:18), and he has declared this about him; he declared it to this poor Samaritan woman, since even the lowliest should know God.

2.3.2.2.*2.3.3.* Because God is a spirit. It is easier to say what God is not than to say what he is. The spirituality of the divine nature is a very good reason for the spirituality of divine worship. If we do not worship God, who is a spirit, in the spirit, we miss the purpose of worship (Mt 15:8–9).

2.4. The last subject of conversation with this woman was the Messiah (vv. 25–26). Notice:

2.4.1. The faith of the woman, by which she expected the Messiah: *I know that Messias cometh—and he will tell us all things.* She had no objections to raise against what Christ had said; his teaching was, for all she knew, such as would befit the Messiah who was then expected, but for now she was willing to receive it from Jesus and thought it best to suspend her belief. Many have no desire for a profit *in their hand* now (Pr 17:16) because they think they have a prospect of getting more later. Notice here:

2.4.1.1. Whom she expected: *I know that Messias cometh.* The Jews and Samaritans were agreed on the expectation of the Messiah and his kingdom. Those who knew least knew that the Messiah was to come. The one who was to come was *Messias, who is called Christ.* Although the Evangelist retained the Hebrew word *Messias,* he took care to provide the Greek word with the same meaning: *who is called Christ,* "the Anointed One."

2.4.1.2. What she expected from him: "*He will tell us all things.* He will tell us the mind of God fully and clearly, keeping nothing back." This implies an acknowledgment:

2.4.1.2.*1.* Of the imperfection of both the revelation of God's will and the rule for divine worship that both Samaritans and Jews now had. They therefore expected some great advance or improvement.

2.4.1.2.*2*. Of the sufficiency of the Messiah to bring about this change: "*He will tell us all things* we want to know, all the things about which we are fumbling in the dark."

2.4.2. The favor of our Lord Jesus in making himself known to her: *I that speak to thee am he* (v. 26). Christ never made himself known so explicitly to anyone as he did here to this poor Samaritan and to the blind man (9:37). But:

2.4.2.1. He wanted to honor the poor and despised.

2.4.2.2. This woman may have never had the opportunity of seeing Christ's miracles, which were then the ordinary method of conviction. God can make the light of grace shine *into the heart* (2Co 4:6) even where he does not make the light of the Gospel shine in the face (Ecc 8:1).

2.4.2.3. This woman was better prepared to receive such a revelation than others were. Christ will reveal himself to those who have an honest, humble heart and want to come to know him more: *I that speak to thee am he*. Notice how close Jesus Christ was to her, and yet she did not know who he was (Ge 28:16). Many people mourn Christ's absence and long for his presence when all the time he is speaking to them. Christ makes himself known to us by speaking to us: *I that speak unto thee, I am he*.

Verses 27–42

Here we have:

1. The interruption of this conversation by the coming of the disciples. Just when the conversation was brought to a head, *then came the disciples*. They were amazed at Christ's dealings with this woman: that he talked so seriously with a woman, that he talked with a strange woman alone, and especially that he talked with a Samaritan woman. They were amazed that he would condescend to talk to such a poor, contemptible woman, forgetting how despicable they themselves had been when Christ first called them. Yet they accepted it; they knew it was for some good reason, and so none of them asked, "What are you looking for?" or, "Why were you talking to her?" All that Jesus Christ says and does is good. Whatever they were thinking, they said nothing.

2. The news the woman passed on to her neighbors (vv. 28–29). Notice here:

2.1. How she forgot why she had come to the well (v. 28). She *went her way*. She withdrew out of politeness to Christ, so that he would have time to eat his dinner. She delighted in his talk, but she did not want to be rude. But she was also expecting Jesus to continue on his journey, and so she was quick to tell her neighbors. See how she made the most of the time. When opportunities to receive good things come to an end, we should seek opportunities to do good. Mention is made of her *leaving her water pot*. She left it out of kindness for Christ, so that he would have water to drink with his dinner, and she left it in order to go more quickly to the town. She left it as one who no longer thought about it, being wholly taken up with better things.

2.2. How she was anxious to take her experience to the town. She *went into the city* and said to *the men*, that is, to every person she met on the streets: *Come, see a man who told me all things that ever I did. Is not this the Christ?* Notice:

2.2.1. How concerned she was to have her friends and neighbors come to know Christ. When she had found that treasure, she *called together her friends and neighbours* (Lk 15:9) not only to *rejoice with her* but also to share with her. Has he done us the honor of making himself

known to us? Let us do him the honor of making him known to others; we can do ourselves no greater honor. This woman became an apostle, one who was "sent away" to tell the good news to others. I have most opportunity, and so lie under the greatest obligation, to do good to those who live near me.

2.2.2. How fair and frank she was in what she told them about the stranger.

2.2.2.1. She told them plainly what made her admire him: *He has told me all things that ever I did*. No more is recorded than what he had told her about her husbands, but it is not improbable that he had told her about more of her faults. Two things affected her:

2.2.2.1.*1*. The extent of his knowledge. We ourselves cannot tell *all things that ever we did*.

2.2.2.1.*2*. The power of his word. It made a great impression on her that he told her her *secret sins* (Ps 90:8). "*Come see a man* who has told me about my sins." She focused on that part of Christ's conversation that one would have thought she would have been most shy of repeating. The knowledge of Christ into which we are led by the conviction of sin and humiliation is most likely to be sound and saving.

2.2.2.2. She invited them to *come and see* the One. Not merely, "Come and look at him"—she was not inviting them to come to look at him as if he were a show—but "Come and talk with him; come and hear his wisdom, as I have." She would not undertake to marshal the arguments that had convinced her so as to convince others; not all who see the evidence of the truth themselves can make others see it. Jesus was now on the outskirts of the town. "Now come and see him." Will we not cross the threshold to see the One whose day the prophets and kings wanted to see (8:56; Lk 10:24)?

2.2.2.3. She decided to appeal to their own hearts: *Is this not the Christ?* She did not say in a dogmatic way, "He is the Messiah." She did not want to impose her faith on them, but only offer it to them. By such fair but effective appeals as these, people's judgments and consciences are sometimes taken hold of *ere* (before) *they are aware* (SS 6:12).

2.2.3. What success she had in this invitation: *They went out of the city, and came to him* (v. 30). They *came unto him*; they did not send for him to come into the town to them; they went out to him. Those who want to know Christ must meet him where he *records his name* (Ex 20:24).

3. Christ's conversation with his disciples while the woman was absent (vv. 31–38). Notice how diligent our Lord Jesus was to redeem the time, to use every minute wisely. It would be good if we could gather up the fragments of time in this way. Two things are significant in this conversation:

3.1. How Christ expressed the delight that he himself had in his work. That he was wholly taken up with this work is apparent here.

3.1.1. He neglected his food and drink to undertake his work. When he sat down by the well, he was weary and needed refreshment, but this opportunity to save souls made him forget his tiredness and hunger. He was so little concerned for his food that:

3.1.1.1. His disciples were forced to encourage him to eat: *They prayed him, Master, eat*. It showed their love for him that they pressed him, but greater than their love for him was his love for souls, reflected in the fact that he would not eat without being urged by them.

3.1.1.2. They suspected he had had food brought to him in their absence (v. 33): *Has any man brought him aught to eat?* He had so little appetite for his dinner that they were ready to think he had already eaten.

3.1.2. He made his work his *meat* (food) *and drink.* The work he had done in instructing the woman, the work he had to do among the Samaritans, this was *meat* (food) *and drink* to him. Never did a hungry man, or an epicure, expect a plentiful feast with so much desire or feed on its delicacies with so much delight as the desire and delight with which our Lord Jesus expected and grasped an opportunity to do good to souls. He said about this:

3.1.2.1. That it was such *meat* (food) as the disciples *knew not of.* This may be said of good Christians too, that they have food to eat that others know nothing about, joy no stranger can share (Pr 14:10). Now this comment made them ask, *Has any man brought him aught to eat?*

3.1.2.2. That the reason why his work was his food and drink was that it was his Father's work, his Father's will: *My meat* (food) *is to do the will of him that sent me* (v. 34). We can learn from this:

3.1.2.2.1. The salvation of sinners is the will of God, and instructing them in order to bring about this salvation is his work.

3.1.2.2.2. Jesus made this work his business and delight. When his body needed food, his mind was so taken up with this that he forgot both his hunger and thirst, both food and drink.

3.1.2.2.3. He was eager and concerned to pursue it and finish every part of it. He was determined never to abandon it or lay it down until he could say, *It is finished* (19:30). Many people have the zeal to begin a work but not the zeal to complete it.

3.2. How Christ motivated his disciples to be diligent in their work; they were *workers with him* (2Co 6:1) and so should be workers like him. The work they had to do was to preach the Gospel. He compared this work here to harvest time (vv. 35–38). Harvest time is a busy time; all hands must then be set to work. Harvest time is an opportunity, a short and limited time, and harvest work is a work that must be done then or not at all. Now he suggested here three things to them to stir them to be conscientious:

3.2.1. That it was a necessary work, and that the occasion for it was very urgent and pressing (v. 35): *"You say, It is four months to harvest,* but I say, *The fields are already white."* Here is:

3.2.1.1. A saying of Christ's disciples concerning the grain harvest: there *are yet four months, and then comes harvest.* "You say, for the encouragement of the sower at the time of sowing, that it will be only four months to harvest." God has not only promised us a harvest every year but also appointed the weeks of harvest, so that we know when to expect it.

3.2.1.2. A saying of Christ's about the Gospel harvest: *Look, the fields are already white* for harvest.

3.2.1.2.1. Here, in this place, there was harvest work for him to do. They wanted him to eat (v. 31). "Eat!" he said. "I have other work to do, which is more necessary. Look at the crowds of Samaritans coming who are ready to receive the Gospel." People's eagerness to hear the word is a great incentive to ministers' diligence and liveliness in preaching it.

3.2.1.2.2. In other places, all over the country, there was enough harvest work for them all to do. "There are many people as ready to receive the Gospel as a field of fully ripe grain is ready to be reaped." The fields were now made *white to the harvest.* If we understand from the signs of the times that it is the proper season to do a particular work for God, we will be greatly encouraged to engage in that work. John the Baptist had *made ready a*

people prepared for the Lord (Lk 1:17). Since he began to preach the kingdom of God, *every man pressed into it* (Lk 16:16). This, therefore, was a time to *thrust in their sickle.* It was necessary to work now. If ripe grain is not reaped, it will drop and be lost. If souls who are under conviction are not helped now, their promising beginnings will come to nothing.

3.2.2. That it was useful and beneficial work, which they themselves would gain by (v. 36): *"He that reapeth receiveth wages."* Christ's reapers never have cause to say they serve a hard Master. His work is its own wages.

3.2.2.1. Christ's reapers have fruit: *he gathereth fruit unto life eternal*; that is, they will save both themselves and those who hear them (1Ti 4:16). This is the encouragement of faithful ministers, that their work leads to the eternal salvation of precious souls.

3.2.2.2. They have joy: *that he that sows and they that reap may rejoice together.* The minister who is the happy instrument of beginning a good work is *he that sows*; those who are employed to continue it and complete it are those who reap, and both will rejoice together. The reapers share in the joy of harvest, even though the profits belong to the master (1Th 2:19).

3.2.3. That it was easy work, and work partly done for them by those who had gone before them: *One soweth, and another reapeth* (vv. 37–38). Moses, the prophets, and John the Baptist had paved the way for the Gospel. *I send you to reap that whereupon you bestowed no labour* (Isa 40:3–5).

3.2.3.1. This suggests two things about the Old Testament ministry:

3.2.3.1.1. That it came very much short of the New Testament ministry. Moses and the prophets sowed, but they could not be said to reap. Their writings have done much more good since they left us than their preaching ever did.

3.2.3.1.2. That it was very useful to the New Testament ministry and made way for it. Had it not been for the seed sown by the prophets, this Samaritan woman could not have said, *We know that Messias cometh.*

3.2.3.2. This also suggests two things about the ministry of the apostles of Christ.

3.2.3.2.1. It was a fruitful ministry: they were reapers who gathered in a great harvest.

3.2.3.2.2. It was very much facilitated by the writings of the prophets. The prophets *sowed in tears* (Ps 126:5), crying out, "We have *laboured in vain*" (Gal 4:11); the apostles *reaped in joy,* saying, *Thanks be to God, who always causeth us to triumph* (2Co 2:14). From the labors of ministers who are dead and gone such good fruit may be reaped by the people who survive them and the ministers that succeed them. See what reason we have to bless God for those who have gone before us. We have *entered into their labours.*

4. The good effect this visit of Christ had on the Samaritans (vv. 39–42). Notice:

4.1. What impressions were made on them by the woman's testimony concerning Christ; although the testimony was no more than, *He told me all that ever I did,* it still had a good influence. The Samaritans were brought to two things:

4.1.1. To believe Christ's word (v. 39): *Many of the Samaritans of that city believed on him for the saying* of the woman. Note who believed: *Many of the Samaritans,* who were not from the household of Israel. Their faith was a pledge of the faith of the Gentiles. Note, too, what encouraged them to believe: *because of the saying of the woman.* See here:

4.1.1.1. How God sometimes uses very weak and unlikely instruments to begin and carry on a good work.

4.1.1.2. How a great forest may be set on fire by a small spark. By instructing one poor woman, our Savior spread instruction to a whole town. Let ministers neither be careless in their preaching nor become discouraged in it because their hearers are few and humble, for in the doing of good to them, good may be conveyed to more. How good it is to speak about our experience of Christ. Those who can tell what God has done *for their souls* (Ps 66:16) are most likely to do good.

4.1.2. To beg him to stay among them (v. 40): *When they were come to him, they besought* (urged) *him that he would tarry with them.* On the woman's report, they believed him to be a prophet and came to him, and when they saw him, they still respected him as a prophet. They begged him to stay with them, so that:

4.1.2.1. They could show their respect for him. Compare this with the account of Lydia in Ac 16:15.

4.1.2.2. They could receive instruction from him. Many people would have flocked to a person who would tell them their fortune, but these flocked to One who would tell them their faults. The Jews drove him away from them, while the Samaritans invited him to them. The degree of success that the Gospel meets with is not always according to the probability, nor is what is experienced always according to what is expected. Finding a welcome among them, Christ granted their request. He *abode there.* When he had an opportunity to do good, he stayed there.

4.2. What impressions were made on them by Christ's own word (vv. 41–42). What he said and did there is not related, but whatever it was, it convinced them that he was the Christ; and the hard work of a minister is best seen by its good fruit. Now their eyes saw him, and the effect was:

4.2.1. That their number grew (v. 41): *Many more believed.*

4.2.2. That their faith grew. Those who had been persuaded by the report of the woman now saw reason to say, *Now we believe, not because of thy saying* (v. 42). Here are three things in which their faith grew:

4.2.2.1. In its substance. On the testimony of the woman, they believed him to be a prophet, but now that they themselves had spoken with him, they believed he was *the Christ,* the Anointed One, and that, being the Christ, he was the *Saviour of the world.* They believed him to be the Savior not only of the Jews but of the world, which they hoped would include them, even though they were Samaritans.

4.2.2.2. In its certainty; their faith now grew to full assurance: *We know* that this is *indeed* the *Christ.*

4.2.2.3. In its grounds: *Now we believe, not because of thy saying, for we have heard him ourselves.* They had believed before because of what she said, but "*Now we believe* because we have *heard him ourselves.* We are abundantly satisfied and assured that *this is the Christ.*" In this instance we may see how *faith comes by hearing* (Ro 10:17).

4.2.2.3.1. Faith comes to its birth by hearing a human report. The instructions of parents and preachers make the teaching of Christ familiar to us.

4.2.2.3.2. Faith comes to its growth by hearing the testimony of Christ himself, and this goes further and makes his message acceptable to us. We were stirred to look into the Scriptures by the testimony of those who told us that in them they had found eternal life, but we now believe *not for their saying* but because we have searched them ourselves, and our faith *stands not in the wisdom of men,* but in the power of God* (1Co 2:5; 1Jn 5:9–10).

5. How the seed of the Gospel was sown in Samaria. Four or five years later, when Philip preached the Gospel in Samaria, *the people with one accord gave heed unto those things which Philip spoke* (Ac 8:6).

Verses 43–54

In these verses we have:

1. Christ's coming into Galilee (v. 43). *After two days* he left them because *he must preach to other cities* (Lk 4:43). *He went into Galilee.* Notice here:

1.1. Where Christ went; *into Galilee,* but not to Nazareth, which was, strictly speaking, his own country. He went among the villages but declined to go to Nazareth, for a reason given here by Jesus himself: *that a prophet has no honor in his own country.* The honor due to the Lord's prophets has very often been denied them. This rightful honor is more frequently denied them in their own country. Christ's close relatives spoke most disrespectfully of him (7:5). Human pride and envy make people scorn instruction from those who were once in the same class at school or whom they played with. It is just of God to deny his Gospel to those who despise its ministers. Those who mock the messengers lose the benefits of the message (Mt 21:35, 41).

1.2. The reception he met with among the Galileans in the country (v. 45): *They received him.* Christ and his Gospel are not sent in vain; if they are not honored by some, they will be by others. Now the reason given why these Galileans were so ready to receive Christ is that they had seen the miracles he performed at Jerusalem (v. 45). Notice:

1.2.1. They went up to Jerusalem at the Passover Feast, and there they came to know Christ. Those who are conscientious and constant in attending public services of worship will at one time or another meet with more spiritual benefit than they expect.

1.2.2. At Jerusalem they saw Christ's miracles. The miracles were performed for the benefit of those at Jerusalem, but the Galileans gained more advantage from them than did those for whom they were chiefly intended. The word preached to a mixed audience may edify occasional hearers more than the usual audience.

1.3. What town he went to. He chose to go to Cana of Galilee, where he had turned the water into wine (v. 46; 2:1–11). The Evangelist mentions this miracle here to teach us to remember what we have seen of the works of Christ.

2. His healing the *nobleman's* (royal official's) son. This account is not recorded by any of the other Evangelists. Notice:

2.1. Who brought the petition and who was the patient: the petitioner was *a nobleman* (a royal official); the patient was his son. The father was a royal official, but the son was sick; dignities and titles of honor are no security from the attacks of sickness and death. It was fifteen miles (about twenty kilometers) from Capernaum to Cana, where Christ now was, but this suffering in the official's family sent him that far to seek Christ.

2.2. How the petitioner submitted his request to the physician. He *went to him* himself and *besought* (begged) *him to come and heal his son* (v. 47). See here:

2.2.1. His tender love for his son. When the son was sick, the father would spare no effort to get help for him.

2.2.2. His great respect for our Lord Jesus. He would personally bring his request, begging him, when, as a man in authority, he could have ordered Christ to come to his house. When the greatest people come to God, they must become beggars. As to why the official came, we may consider what was in his faith. There was sincerity in it; he believed that Christ could heal his son. There was also a lack in it; he thought Christ could not heal him at a distance, and so he begged him to come and heal him. We are encouraged to pray, but we are not allowed to give orders to the Lord: "Lord, heal me, but, whether it is by a word or a touch, *thy will be done* (Mt 26:42)."

2.3. The gentle rebuke he met with in his request (v. 48): *Jesus said to him, Except* (unless) *you see signs and wonders, you will not believe.* Even though the man was a royal official and was now grieving over his son, Christ still rebuked him. Christ first showed him his sin and weakness, to prepare him for mercy, and then he granted his request. Those whom Christ intends to honor with his favors he first humbles with his frowns. Like Herod, this official longed to see some miracle (Lk 23:8), as did most of the people. Now their fault was:

2.3.1. That, whereas they had heard plausible and undeniable reports of the miracles he had performed in other places, they would not believe unless they saw them with their own eyes (Lk 4:23). They must be honored and humored or they would not be convinced.

2.3.2. That, whereas they had seen various miracles that sufficiently proved Christ to be a teacher who had come from God (3:2), they would go no further in believing than the point they were driven to by signs and wonders. The spiritual power of the word did not affect them; it did not attract them; only the visual power of miracles did.

2.4. His continued importunity in his address (v. 49): *Sir, come down ere my child die.* In the official's reply we have:

2.4.1. Something that was good. He accepted the rebuke patiently; he spoke to Christ respectfully. Just as he did not take offense at the rebuke, so he did not take it as a denial of his request, but continued to pursue his request, continued to *wrestle* until he *prevailed* (Ge 32:24, 28).

2.4.2. Something that was bad.

2.4.2.1. He seems to have taken no notice of the rebuke Christ gave him. He was so wholly taken up with concerns about his child that he could think about nothing else.

2.4.2.2. He still showed the weakness of his faith in the power of Christ. He believed that Christ must come down with him, that he could not otherwise help the child. He thought Christ could heal a sick child but not raise a dead child: "*O come down, ere* (before) *my child die*" — as if Christ would be too late if he arrived after the child died. The official forgot that Elijah and Elisha had raised dead children, and was Christ's power inferior to theirs? Notice what a hurry the man was in: *Come down, ere my child die* — as if there were danger of Christ's missing his opportunity.

2.5. The favorable answer Christ gave (v. 50): *Go thy way; thy son liveth.* Christ shows us here:

2.5.1. His power, that he not only could heal, but could heal with so much ease. Here nothing was said, nothing done, nothing ordered to be done, but the healing was performed. This royal official wanted Christ to *come down and heal his son*; Christ would heal his son, but not come down. In this way, the healing was performed the sooner, the royal official's mistake was put right, and his faith was confirmed, so that the thing was done better in Christ's way. When he denies what we ask, he gives what is much more to our advantage.

2.5.2. His pity; he noticed the pain the royal official felt for his son, and so he dropped his rebuke and assured him that his child would recover, because he knows how *a father pities his children* (Ps 103:13).

2.6. The royal official's belief in the word of Christ: he *believed, and went away.* He was satisfied with the method Christ used. Now he saw no sign or wonder, but he believed that the wonder was done. Christ said, *Thy son liveth,* and the man believed him. Christ said, *Go thy way,* and as evidence of the sincerity of his faith, he *went his way.*

2.7. The further confirmation of his faith by his comparing notes with his servants when he returned. His servants met him with the great news of the child's recovery (v. 51). Christ said, *Thy son liveth,* and now the servants said the same. Good news will meet those who hope in God's word. The father asked what time the child began to recover (v. 52). He wanted to have his faith confirmed. The diligent comparison of the works of Christ with his word will be very useful to us to confirm our faith. This was the course the royal official took: *He inquired of the servants the hour when he began to amend,* and they told him, *Yesterday at the seventh hour the fever left him.* The boy did not merely begin to recover then; he was perfectly well suddenly. *The father knew that it was at the same hour* when Jesus had said to him, *Thy son liveth.* Two things helped confirm his faith:

2.7.1. That the child's recovery was sudden, not gradual. The servants named the exact time, to the hour: *Yesterday,* not "about the seventh hour," but *at the seventh hour the fever left him.* The word of Christ did not work like a course of medicine, which needs time to take effect, and perhaps heals only because it is expected to. No; with Christ it was, *he spoke and it was done* (Ps 33:9), not, "he spoke and it was set in motion."

2.7.2. That it was at precisely the same time that Christ spoke to him: *at that very hour.* The fact that two events happen at precisely the same time adds very much to the beauty and harmony of Providence. In human works, distance of place means a delay in time and the slowing down of business, but it is not so with the works of Christ.

2.8. The happy outcome of this. The bringing of healing to the family brought salvation to it.

2.8.1. The royal official *himself believed.* He had believed the word of Christ before, but now he believed in Christ. Christ has many ways of gaining the heart, and by the gift of a physical mercy he may make way for better things.

2.8.2. His *whole house* (all his household) believed as well:

2.8.2.1. Because of the benefit they all gained in the miracle, which preserved the blossom and hopes of the family; this affected them all, endeared Christ to them.

2.8.2.2. Because of the influence the master of the family had on them all. This was *a nobleman* (v. 49), and he probably had a great household, but when he came into Christ's college, he brought all his students with him. What a wonderful change in this house was occasioned by the sickness of the child! We should be reconciled to our sufferings by the knowledge that we do not know what good may follow from them.

2.9. the Evangelist's remark on this healing (v. 54): *This is the second miracle;* he alludes to 2:11. In Judea he had performed many miracles (3:2; 4:45); they had the first offer. But, being driven away from there, he performed miracles in Galilee. Somewhere or other Christ will find a welcome. People may, if they want to, shut the sun out of their own houses, but they cannot shut it out of the world. This is noted as the second miracle to remind us of the first. Fresh blessings should recall the memories of former ones, just as former blessings should encourage our hope of further ones. Since the patient was the son of a high-ranking person, the healing probably brought Christ many other patients. When this royal official himself turned to Christ, many others followed. How much good may great people do, if they are good!

CHAPTER 5

We have in the Gospels a faithful record of all that Jesus began both to do and to teach (Ac 1:1). These two are interwoven, because what he taught explained what he did, and what he did confirmed what he taught. We have in this chapter, therefore, a miracle and a message. 1. The miracle was the healing of a man who had been an invalid for thirty-eight years (vv. 1–16). 2. The message was Christ's vindication of himself when he was prosecuted as a criminal for healing the man on the Sabbath. He asserted his authority as Messiah (vv. 17–30). 3. He proved it and condemned the Jews for their unbelief (vv. 31–47).

Verses 1–16

This miraculous healing is not recorded by any of the other Evangelists, who confine themselves mostly to the miracles performed in Galilee. John relates those performed in Jerusalem. Notice:

1. The time when this healing was performed: it was at a *feast of the Jews*, that is, the Passover, which was the most celebrated feast. Although Christ was living in Galilee, he still *went up to Jerusalem* at the feast (v. 1). It was an opportunity to do good. There were very many people gathered there at that time; it was a general meeting place for people from all parts of the country, besides converts from other nations. It was to be hoped that they were in good spirits, because they came together to worship God. Now a mind inclined to devotion lies very open to the further revelations of divine light and love.

2. The place where this healing was performed: at the pool of *Bethesda*, which had a miraculous healing power in it (vv. 2–4). We are told:

2.1. Where it was situated: *At Jerusalem, by the sheep-market.* Some think this was near the temple, and if so, it offered a sad but profitable spectacle to those who went to the temple to pray.

2.2. What it was called: it was *a pool which is called in Hebrew, Bethesda,* "the house of mercy," because much of the mercy of God to the sick and diseased appeared there. In a world of so much misery as this, it is good that there are some *Bethesdas.*

2.3. How it was equipped: it had *five porches* in which the sick lay. In this way, human love agreed with the mercy of God to relieve the distressed. Nature has provided remedies, but people must provide hospitals.

2.4. How it was frequented by the sick and the disabled (v. 3): *In these lay a great multitude of impotent* (disabled) *folks.* How great the distress of the sufferers in this world is! It may do us good to visit hospitals sometimes, so that we may have cause to thank God for our benefits when we look at the adversities others suffer. The Evangelist specifies three kinds of diseased people who lay here: *blind, halt* (lame), and *withered* (paralyzed). These are mentioned because they are least able to help themselves into the water, and so they lay longest waiting in the colonnades. Oh that people were as wise for their souls, and as concerned to have their spiritual diseases healed!

2.5. What power it had for healing these disabled people (v. 4): *An angel went down* and *troubled* (stirred up) *the water,* and *whoso first stepped in was made whole.* The power of this pool was supernatural. Notice:

2.5.1. The preparation of the medical treatment by an angel, who *went down into the pool* and *troubled* (stirred up) *the water.* Notice what humble work the holy angels stoop to. If we want to do the will of God as the angels do it, we must think nothing beneath us except sin. The disturbing of the waters was the sign that the angel had come down. The waters of the sanctuary are healing when they are put in motion (Eze 47:1, 8–12). Ministers must *stir up the gift* that is in them (2Ti 1:6). When they are cold and dull in their ministry, the waters settle and tend not to heal. The angel came down to stir up the water *at a certain season.*

2.5.2. The operation of this treatment: *Whoever first stepped in was made whole.* Whatever disease it was, this water healed it. The power of miracles takes effect where the power of nature falls down. The first one who stepped in had the benefit, not those who lingered and came in later. This teaches us to take notice of and make the most of our opportunities, so that we do not allow a season to go by that may never return. Now this is all the account we have of this continual miracle. It was a sign of God's goodwill to that people and an indication that although they had long been without prophets and miracles, God had not rejected them. It was a type of the Messiah who arises *with healing under his wings* (Mal 4:2).

3. The patient on whom this healing was performed (v. 5): one who *had been infirm thirty-eight years.* His disease was severe: he was an invalid; he had lost the use of his limbs. It is sad to have the body so disabled that instead of being the soul's instrument, it has become, even in the affairs of this life, its burden. We have great reason to thank God for physical strength, and we should use it for him. The disease had lasted a very long time: *thirty-eight years.* He had been lame for longer than many people live. Will we complain about one wearisome night, or one bout of illness, when we perhaps have scarcely known for many years what it means to have a day when we are sick, when many others who are better than we are have scarcely known what it means to be well for a day?

4. The healing and its circumstances briefly related (vv. 6–9).

4.1. *Jesus saw him lie* (lying there). When Christ came to Jerusalem, he visited not the palaces but the hospitals, a sign of his great intention in coming into the world, which was to seek and save (Lk 19:10) the sick and wounded. There were very many poor, disabled people here at Bethesda, but Christ focused his eyes on one. Christ delights to help the helpless. The man had often failed to be healed; Christ therefore took him as his patient: it is his honor to be on the side of the weakest.

4.2. He knew and considered *how long he had lain* in this condition.

4.3. He asked him, *Wilt thou be made whole?* This was a strange question to ask someone who had been ill for so long. It is true that some do not want to be healed, because their sores give them reason to beg; yet Christ asked him this question:

4.3.1. To express his own pity and concern for him. Christ tenderly probes the desires of those who are suffering.

4.3.2. To teach him to value the mercy and to stimulate in him a desire for it. In spiritual cases, people are not willing to be healed of their sins. If people were willing to be *made whole,* the work would be half done, because Christ is willing to heal if we are simply willing to be healed (Mt 8:3).

4.4. The poor disabled man took this opportunity to set out the misery of his case: *Sir, I have no man to put me into the pool* (v. 7). He complained of a lack of friends to help him in: "*I have no man*, no friend to do me that kindness." One would have thought that some of those who themselves had been healed would have lent him a hand. To the sick and disabled it is as true an act of love to work for them as to relieve them. He mourned his unhappiness, that very often when he was coming, *another stepped in before him*. There was only one step between him and healing, but he remained disabled. There is no overcoming the old maxim, "Everyone for himself." Having been disappointed so often, he had begun to despair, but now came Christ's time to come to his relief. Notice further, to the man's credit, that although he had waited so long in vain, he still continued lying by the poolside, hoping that sometime or other help would come (Hab 2:3).

4.5. Our Lord Jesus healed him here by a word. We have here:

4.5.1. The word he said: *Rise, take up thy bed* (v. 8).

4.5.1.1. The man was told to *rise and walk*—a strange command to give to someone who had been so long disabled. He must get up and walk, that is, attempt to do it, and as he tried, he would receive strength to do it. If he had not attempted to help himself, he would not have been healed. It does not follow, however, that when he did get up and walk, it was through his own strength. No; it was by the power of Christ.

4.5.1.2. He was told to *take up his bed* (pick up your mat). This was to:

4.5.1.2.1. Make it clear that it was a complete healing, and purely miraculous, because he did not recover his strength gradually, but from his extreme weakness and disability suddenly stepped into the greatest physical strength. He who one minute could not turn himself over on his mat was the next minute able to carry it.

4.5.1.2.2. Declare the healing. Because it was the Sabbath, whoever carried a load through the streets stood out, and everyone would ask what it meant.

4.5.1.2.3. Witness against the tradition of the elders. The case may be such that it may become a work of necessity or mercy to carry a mat on the Sabbath, but here it was more: it was a work of godly devotion.

4.5.1.2.4. Test the faith and obedience of his patient. By carrying his mat publicly, he made himself vulnerable to the censure and punishment of the ecclesiastical court. Those who have been healed by Christ's word should be ruled by his word.

4.5.2. The effectiveness of this word (v. 9): *Immediately he was made whole*. What a joyful surprise this was to the poor cripple, to find himself suddenly so well, so strong, so able to help himself! What a new world he was in, in a moment! *He took up his bed and walked*, not worrying for a moment about who blamed him or threatened him for it.

5. What happened to the poor man after he was healed. We are told:

5.1. What took place between him and the Jews who saw him carry his mat on the Sabbath.

5.1.1. The Jews quarreled with the man, telling him that *it was not lawful* (v. 10). They were commendable to the extent that, not knowing *by what authority* the healed man did these things (Lk 20:2), they were jealous to protect the honor of the Sabbath.

5.1.2. The man justified himself in what he did by an authority that would support him (v. 11). "I do not do it in contempt of the law and the Sabbath. The One who could work such a miracle as to heal me no doubt can give me such a command as to carry my mat. The One who was so kind as to heal me would not be so unkind as to tell me to do what is sinful."

5.1.3. The Jews went on to ask who gave him that authority (v. 12): *What man is that?* How carefully they overlooked what might have been a basis for their faith in Christ. They were determined to look on Christ as a mere man: *What man is that?* They had resolved that they would never acknowledge him to be the *Son of God* (10:36). And they were determined to look on him as a bad man: he who told this man to carry his mat was certainly a criminal.

5.1.4. The poor man was unable to give them any explanation of Christ: *He wist not* (did not know) *who he was* (v. 13). Christ was unknown to him when he healed him. Christ does many good deeds for those who do not know him (Isa 45:4–5). He enlightens, strengthens, enlivens, and comforts us, and we do not know who he is. For the present Christ kept himself unknown; as soon as he had performed the healing, he *conveyed himself away, a multitude being in that place*. This is mentioned to show either:

5.1.4.1. How Christ *conveyed himself away*—by withdrawing into the crowd, so that he could not be distinguished from the ordinary people. Or:

5.1.4.2. Why he *conveyed himself away*, because there was *a multitude* there, and he actively avoided both the applause of those who would be amazed at and praise the miracle and the censure of those who would condemn him for breaking the Sabbath. Christ left the miracle to commend itself, and he left the man on whom it was performed to justify it.

5.2. What took place at their next meeting (v. 14).

5.2.1. Where Christ found him: *in the temple*. Christ and the man who was healed both *went to the temple*, and there Christ found him. The man went there right away:

5.2.1.1. Because his infirmity had long prevented him from going there (Lev 21:18). Perhaps he had not been there for thirty-eight years, and so his first visit would be to the temple.

5.2.1.2. Because his recovery was a good reason to go there; he went to the temple to give thanks to God for his recovery.

5.2.1.3. Because he wanted to show that he honored the Sabbath, since by carrying his mat he had seemed to show contempt for it. Works of necessity and mercy are allowed, but when they have been completed, we must "go to the temple."

5.2.2. What he said to him. He now turned to healing the man's soul.

5.2.2.1. He reminded him of his healing: *Behold, thou art made whole*. Christ called his attention to it. "Let the impressions of it remain with you and never be lost (Isa 38:9)."

5.2.2.2. He warned him against sinning: *Being made whole, sin no more*. This implied that the man's disease was the punishment of sin. As long as those chronic diseases lasted, they prevented many outward sins, and so watchfulness was even more necessary when the disability was taken away. When the trouble that only dammed up the flow is over, the waters will return to their old ways. It is common for people to promise much when they are sick, then to fulfill part of their promise when they have just recovered, but to forget the whole promise soon after that.

5.2.2.3. He warned him of his danger so that he would not return to his former sinful ways: *Lest a worse thing come to thee*. Christ knew that the man was one of those who must be frightened from sin. Something worse would come to him if he fell into sin after God had rescued him in such a way.

6. Now after this, see in vv. 15–16:

6.1. The information that this poor, simple man gave to the Jews about Christ (v. 15). He told them it was Jesus who had *made him whole.*

6.2. The rage and enmity of the Jews toward him: *Therefore did the* rulers of the Jews *persecute Jesus.* See:

6.2.1. How absurd and unreasonable their enmity toward Christ was. Because he had made a poor sick man well, because he did good in Israel, they persecuted him.

6.2.2. How bloodthirsty and cruel this was: *They sought to slay him.*

6.2.3. How it was covered over with a veneer of zeal for the honor of the Sabbath, for violation of the Sabbath was the supposed crime: *Because he had done these things on the sabbath day.* This is how hypocrites often cover up their real enmity against the power of godliness with a pretended zeal for its form (2Ti 3:5).

Verses 17–30

We have here what Christ said on the occasion of his being accused of breaking the Sabbath. Notice:

1. The doctrine by which he justified what he did on the Sabbath (v. 17): *He answered them.* This presupposes that either he was accused of something or he knew of their private suggestions to one another (v. 16). Whichever it was, his answer was, *My Father worketh hitherto* (until now), *and I work.* Waiving all other pleas, he insisted on and stood by the one that stood for all the others: *The Son of man is Lord even of the sabbath day* (Mt 12:8).

1.1. He pleaded that he was the Son of God, which was clearly shown in his calling God his Father.

1.2. He pleaded that he was a *worker together with God* (2Co 6:1).

1.2.1. *My Father worketh hitherto* (until now). After creating the cosmos, God rested only from such work as he had done the six days before; otherwise he is always at work, upholding and governing the whole creation.

1.2.2. "Like him, *I work.* I also work with him." Just as God created all things through Christ, so he also supports and governs everything through him (Heb 1:3). The One who does all is Lord of all, and so he is *Lord of the sabbath* (Mk 2:28).

2. The offense that was taken at his teaching (v. 18): *The Jews sought the more to kill him.* His defense was made his offense. They sought to kill him:

2.1. Because he had broken the Sabbath.

2.2. Because he had said that God was his Father. They now claimed to protect God's honor, accusing Christ of the detestable crime of making himself equal with God. Now:

2.2.1. This was justly concluded from what he said, that he was the Son of God and that God was his Father. He had also said that he worked with his Father, and in this, too, he had made himself equal with God.

2.2.2. Yet his making himself equal with God was unjustly reckoned to him as an offense, because he was and is God. Christ, therefore, in answer to this charge, argued his claim and proved he is equal with God in power and glory.

3. Christ's sermon on this occasion. In these verses he explained, and in those following he confirmed (vv. 31–47), his commission as Mediator. Moreover, as the honors he was thereby entitled to were such as it is not fit for any creature to receive, so the work he was entrusted with was such as it is not possible for any creature to go through with, and so he is God.

3.1. In general, he is one with the Father in all he does as Mediator. He ushered in this claim with a solemn introduction (v. 19): *Verily, verily, I say unto you.* This suggests

that the things declared are fearful and great, trustworthy, and purely of divine revelation, things that we could not otherwise have come to know. He said two things in general about the Son's oneness with the Father in working:

3.1.1. That the Son conforms to the Father (v. 19): *The Son can do nothing of himself but what he sees the Father do; these things does the Son.* The Lord Jesus, as Mediator, is:

3.1.1.1. Obedient to his Father's will. Christ was so completely devoted to his Father's will that it was impossible for him to act separately in anything.

3.1.1.2. Observant of his Father's purposes; he can and will do nothing *but what he sees the Father do.* No one can find out the work of God (Job 9:10; Ro 11:33) except the only begotten Son, who sees what the Father does, knows his purposes intimately, and has the plan for carrying them out always before him. What the Father did in his purposes, the Son had always in his view, always had his eye on. Yet he is equal with the Father in working, because whatever the Father does the Son also does (v. 19). He did the same things; not "such things," things of the same sort, but the *same things.* He also did them in the *same manner,* with the same authority, the same energy and effectiveness.

3.1.2. That the Father communicates to the Son (v. 20). Notice:

3.1.2.1. The inducement to communicate to his Son: *the Father loveth the Son.* Christ was now hated by people; but he comforted himself with the assurance that his Father loved him.

3.1.2.2. The expressions of this communication. They appear:

3.1.2.2.1. In what the Father does communicate to the Son: *He shows him all things that himself doeth.* He shows him all things *which he does,* that is, that the Son does; all that the Son does is by direction from the Father.

3.1.2.2.2. In what he will communicate; he will *show him,* that is, will appoint and direct him to do, *greater works than these.* They will be works of greater power than the healing of the disabled man, because Christ would raise the dead and would himself rise from the dead. Many are brought to wonder at Christ's works, by which he gains the honor of them, but are not brought to believe, by which they would benefit from them.

3.2. In particular, he proved his equality with the Father by specifying some of the works he did that are the distinctive works of God. This is enlarged on in vv. 21–30.

3.2.1. Notice what was said here about the Mediator's power to raise the dead and give life.

3.2.1.1. He has authority to do it (v. 21): *As the Father raiseth up the dead, so the Son quickeneth* (gives life to) *whom he will.*

3.2.1.1.1. It is God's right to raise the dead and give life. A resurrection from the dead never lay on the ordinary path of nature, nor ever fell within the thought of those who studied only the range of nature's power. It is purely the work of a divine power, and knowledge of it comes purely by divine revelation.

3.2.1.1.2. The Mediator is invested with this right: *He quickens whom he will.* He does not give life to things by natural necessity, as the sun does, whose rays naturally revive, but acts as a free agent. Just as he has the power, so he also has the wisdom and sovereignty, of a God; he has the *key of the grave and of death* (Rev 1:18).

3.2.1.2. He has ability to do it, because *he has life in himself, as the Father has* (v. 26).

3.2.1.2.1. It is certain that the Father has life in himself. He is also a sovereign giver of life; he has the disposal of life and of all good—*life* sometimes refers to all that is good. He is to his creatures the fountain of life and of all good.

3.2.1.2.*2*. It is as certain that he has given the Son life in himself. The Son, as Redeemer, is the origin of all spiritual life and good. The Son is to the church what the Father is to the world. The kingdom of grace, and all the life in that kingdom, are as fully and absolutely in the hand of the Redeemer as the kingdom of providence is in the hand of the Creator.

3.2.1.3. He acts according to this authority and ability. Two resurrections are performed by his powerful word, both of which are spoken of here:

3.2.1.3.*1*. A present resurrection (v. 25), a resurrection from the death of sin to the life of righteousness. The hour is coming and has now come. It is a resurrection that has already begun. This is plainly distinguished from the resurrection referred to in v. 28, the one at the end of time. Some think this verse was fulfilled in those he miraculously raised to life. I understand it rather to refer to the power of the message of Christ to give life to and restore those who were dead in trespasses and sins (Eph 2:1). The *hour was coming* when dead souls would be made alive by the preaching of the Gospel; in fact, this hour of resurrection *then was*, when Christ was on earth. This is to be applied to all the wonderful success of the Gospel, among both Jews and Gentiles; it is an hour that continually is and continually is coming. Sinners are spiritually dead, wretched, but neither aware of their misery nor able to help themselves out of it. The conversion of a soul to God is its resurrection from death to life; it begins to live when it begins to live to God. It is through the *voice of the Son of God* that souls are raised to spiritual life. *The dead shall hear* the *voice of the Son of God.* The voice of Christ must be heard by us, so that we may live by it.

3.2.1.3.*2*. A future resurrection; this is spoken of in vv. 28–29. Notice:

3.2.1.3.*2.1*. When this resurrection will be: *The hour is coming.* It has not yet come; it is not the hour spoken of at v. 25, *which is coming, and now is.* Yet it will certainly come; it is coming nearer each day. We do not know how far off it is.

3.2.1.3.*2.2*. Who will be raised: *all that are in the graves.* Christ tells us here that all must appear before the Judge, and so all must be raised. The grave is the prison of dead bodies, where they are detained. Having the prospect of their resurrection, however, we may call it their bed, where they will sleep until they are woken up.

3.2.1.3.*2.3*. How they will be raised. The cause of this resurrection will be that *they shall hear his voice.* Divine power will accompany the voice to put life into them and enable them to obey it. The effect of this resurrection will be that *they shall come forth* out of their graves and appear before Christ's tribunal.

3.2.1.3.*2.4*. To what they will be raised: to a state of happiness or misery, depending on their character.

3.2.1.3.*2.4.1*. They that have done good shall come *forth to the resurrection of life*; they will live again, to live forever. It will be good on the great day only for those who have done good. They will also be admitted into the presence of God, and that is life (Ps 16:11)—indeed, it is better than life (Ps 63:3).

3.2.1.3.*2.4.2*. They that have done evil to the resurrection of damnation; they will live again to be dying forever.

3.2.2. Notice what is said here about the Mediator's authority to execute judgment (vv. 22–24, 27). Just as he has almighty power, so he also has sovereign jurisdiction. Here we read of:

3.2.2.1. Christ's commission or delegation to the office of judge, which is spoken of twice here: *He hath committed all judgment to the Son* (v. 22); *He hath given him authority* (v. 27).

3.2.2.1.*1*. The *Father judges no man*; he is pleased to govern through Jesus Christ. He does not rule us by the mere right of creation. Having made us, he may do what he pleases with us, as the potter does with the clay, but he does not take advantage of this. Because the Mediator has undertaken to make a substitutionary atonement, the matter is referred to him.

3.2.2.1.*2*. He has *committed all judgment to the Son.* It is God in Christ who reconciles the world (2Co 5:19), and he has given Christ power to confer eternal life. The Book of Life is the Lamb's book (Rev 21:27); we must stand or fall by what is awarded us by him. He is constituted sole manager of the judgment on the great day. The final and universal judgment is committed to the Son of Man.

3.2.2.1.*3*. He has *given him authority to execute judgment also* (v. 27). He who executes judgment on them is the same One who would have saved them. The Father gave him that authority. All this leads very much to the honor of Christ and very much to the comfort of all believers, who may with the greatest assurance depend on him for everything.

3.2.2.2. The reasons—kingdom reasons—for which this commission was given him.

3.2.2.2.*1*. Because he is the Son of Man, which shows these three things:

3.2.2.2.*1.1*. His humiliation and gracious condescension. He stooped to this lowly condition. Because he condescended to be the Son of Man, his Father made him *Lord of all* (Php 2:8–9).

3.2.2.2.*1.2*. His relationship and alliance to us. Being the Son of Man, he shares the same human nature as those whom he is set over.

3.2.2.2.*1.3*. His being the promised Messiah. He is the Messiah and so is given all this power. Christ usually called himself the Son of Man, which was a more humble title and showed he was a ruler and Savior not only to the Jewish nation but to the whole human race.

3.2.2.2.*2*. So *that all men would honour the Son* (v. 23). The honoring of Jesus Christ is spoken of here as the great purpose of God and as the great duty of human beings. We must honor the Son. We must *confess that he is Lord* (Php 2:11) and worship him; we must honor him who was dishonored for us. *Even as they honour the Father.* This supposes it to be our duty to honor the Father and directs us to honor the Son. To enforce this law, it is added, *He that honours not the Son honours not the Father* who has sent him. Some pretend to have reverence for the Creator and speak honorably about him but make light of the Redeemer and speak contemptibly about him. Indignity done to the Lord Jesus reflects on God himself. The Father counts himself struck at through the Son, because the *Father hath sent him.* Insults spoken to an ambassador are justly resented by the sending ruler.

3.2.2.3. The rule by which the Son executes this commission (v. 24): *He that heareth and believeth* has *everlasting life.* Here we have the substance of the whole Gospel. Notice:

3.2.2.3.*1*. The character of a Christian: *He that heareth my word and believeth on him that sent me.* To be a Christian is actually to *hear the word* of Christ. It is not enough to be within hearing of it. We must hear and obey it; we must remain faithful to the Gospel of Christ as the established rule of our faith and practice. And to be a Christian is to *believe on him that sent* him, because Christ's purpose is to *bring us to God* (1Pe 3:18). Christ is our way; God is our rest.

3.2.2.3.*2*. The contract of a Christian. It is:

3.2.2.3.*2.1*. A contract of pardon: *He shall not come into condemnation.* The grace of the Gospel is a full discharge from the curse of the law.

3.2.2.3.*2.2*. A contract of privileges: he has *passed out of death to life.* Hear and live, believe and live, is what we may rest our souls on.

3.2.2.4. The righteousness of his proceedings (v. 30). *My judgment is just.* His judgments are certainly just, because they are directed:

3.2.2.4.*1*. By the Father's wisdom: "*I can of myself* do nothing; rather, *as I hear, I judge.* As he had said before (v. 19) that the Son *can do nothing but what he sees the Father do,* so here he said that he would judge nothing except what he heard the Father say: "*As I hear*:

3.2.2.4.*1.1*. "From the secret, eternal purposes of the Father, *so I judge.*" Do we want to know what we can depend on in our relationship with God? Hear the word of Christ. What Christ has judged is an exact copy or equivalent to what the Father has decreed.

3.2.2.4.*1.2*. "From the published records of the Old Testament." In all the execution of his undertaking, Christ had an eye to Scripture. *As it was written in the volume of the book* (Ps 40:7).

3.2.2.4.*2*. By the Father's will: *My judgment is just, because I seek not my own will,* but that of *him who sent me.* It is not as if the will of Christ were against the will of the Father. Christ, as man, had the natural and innocent affections of the human nature, a sense of pain and a sense of pleasure, an inclination to life and an aversion to death. He *pleased not himself* (Ro 15:3), however, but completely accepted the will of his Father. What he did as Mediator was not the result of any special or exclusive purpose and intention of his own; rather, he was guided by his Father's will.

Verses 31–47

In these verses we learn how our Lord Jesus proved and confirmed the commission he had produced and how he showed that he was sent by God to be the Messiah:

1. He set aside his own testimony of himself (v. 31): "*If I bear witness of myself,* even though it is infallibly true (8:14), you will not admit it."

2. He produced other witnesses who testify to his being sent by God.

2.1. The Father himself testified to who he was (v. 32) *There is another that beareth witness.* I take this to refer to God the Father. Notice:

2.1.1. The seal that the Father gave to his commission: "he *beareth witness of me*; not only has he done so by a voice from heaven; he still does so by the signs of his presence with me.

2.1.2. The assurance Christ had from this testimony: "*I know that the witness which he witnesseth of me is true* (I know that his testimony about me is valid)."

2.2. John the Baptist witnessed to who Christ was (v. 33). John came to testify about the light (1:7).

2.2.1. Now the testimony of John was a solemn and public testimony: "You sent an embassy of priests and Levites to John, which gave him the opportunity to declare what he had to say." It was also a true testimony: *He bore witness to the truth.* Christ did not say, "He bore witness to me," but that, like an honest man, John *bore witness to the truth.*

2.2.2. Two things were added about John's testimony:

2.2.2.1. That it was an abundant testimony, more than was needed (v. 34): *I receive not testimony from man*

(not that I accept human testimony). Christ needs no testimonials or certificates, except what his own worth and excellence bring with him. Why then did Christ urge the testimony of John here? Why, *these things I say, that you may be saved.* His aim throughout this message was to save not his own life, but the souls of others. Christ wants and plans for the salvation even of his enemies and persecutors.

2.2.2.2. That it was a personal testimony, because John the Baptist was one whom they respected (v. 35). Notice:

2.2.2.2.*1*. The character of John the Baptist: *He was a burning and a shining light.* He was a light; he was not a light source, like Christ, but a luminary, a derived, subordinate light. He was a burning light, which stands for sincerity; painted fire may be made to shine, but what burns is true fire. It also stands for his activeness, zeal, and fervency. Fire is always working on itself or something else, as is a good minister. He was a shining light, which stands either for his exemplary conduct—in our conduct our light should shine (Mt 5:16)—or a great and diffusive influence.

2.2.2.2.*2*. The affections of the people for him: *You were willing for a season to rejoice in his light.*

2.2.2.2.*2.1*. They were delighted at the appearance of John: "You enjoyed his light; you were very proud that you had such a man among you. You were willing to exult and were excited about this light, as children are around a bonfire."

2.2.2.2.*2.2*. It lasted only a short time: "You were fond of him for a season, as little children are fond of something new, but you soon grew tired of him and said that he had a demon, and now you have him in prison." It is common for those who make an eager and noisy profession of faith to cool off and fall away. These here rejoiced in John's light but never walked in it. Christ mentioned their respect for John to condemn them for their present opposition to himself, to Christ. If they had continued their respect for John, they would have accepted Christ.

2.3. Christ's own works witnessed to him (v. 36): *I have a greater witness than that of John,* because if we believe human witnesses, then the witness of God is greater (1Jn 5:9). We must be glad to have all the supports that offer themselves to confirm our faith, even though they may not amount to a conclusive proof; we need them all. Now this greater testimony was that of the works his Father had given him to finish. In general, it was the whole course of his life and ministry, all the work about which he said when he died, *It is finished* (19:30). All he said and did was holy and heavenly, and a divine purity, power, and grace shone in it, proving abundantly that he was sent by God. In particular, the miracles he performed to prove his divine mission witnessed of him. Now it is said here:

2.3.1. That these works were given him by the Father, that is, that he was both appointed and empowered to perform them.

2.3.2. That they were given to him to finish, and his completing them proved his divine power.

2.3.3. That these works testified about him; they proved he had been sent by God. The Father had sent him as a Father, not as a master sends his servant on an errand, but as a father sends his son to take possession for himself.

2.4. He produced, more fully than before, his Father's testimony about him (v. 37): *The Father that sent me hath borne witness of me.* God was pleased to testify about his Son, by a voice from heaven at his baptism (Mt 3:17), *This is my beloved Son.* Those whom God sends he will testify to; where he gives a commission, he will not fail to seal it. On the other hand, where God demands belief, he will not fail to give sufficient evidence, as he has done with Christ. If God himself testified about Christ in this way, why was he not universally accepted by the Jewish nation and their rulers? Christ answered that it was not to be thought strange, nor could their unfaithfulness weaken his credibility, for two reasons:

2.4.1. Because they were not familiar with such extraordinary revelations of God and his will: "*You have neither heard his voice at any time* nor seen his form or appearance." They showed themselves to be as ignorant of God as we are of a person we never saw or heard. Ignorance of God is the true reason why people reject the record he has given of his Son.

2.4.2. Because they were not moved by the ordinary ways by which God had revealed himself to them: *You have not his word abiding in you* (v. 38).

2.4.2.1. The word of God was not in them; it was among them but not in them, in their hearts. It did not rule their souls, but only shone in their eyes and sounded in their ears. What good did it do them to have the very words of God entrusted to them (Ro 3:2), when they did not have these very words commanding them? If they had, they would readily have accepted Christ.

2.4.2.2. It did not *abide*, or dwell, in them. Many people have the word of God coming into them and making some impressions for a time, but not abiding in them; it is not constantly in them, as someone is in their home; it is like a traveler who is only now and then at home. But how was it clear that they did not have the word of God remaining in them? By this: *Whom he hath sent, him ye believe not* (v. 38). The indwelling of the word, Spirit, and grace of God in us is best tested by its effects, particularly by our response to what he sends, especially Christ, whom he has sent.

2.5. He appealed to the witness of the Old Testament (v. 39): *Search the scriptures.*

2.5.1. This may be read either:

2.5.1.1. As a statement: "You *search the scriptures,* and you do well to do so." Christ acknowledged that they truly searched the Scriptures, but what they were really searching for was their own glory. It is possible for people to diligently study the letter of Scripture but still be strangers to its power and influence. Or:

2.5.1.2. As a command: *Search the scriptures.*

2.5.1.2.1. It was spoken to them as an appeal. When appeal is made to the Scriptures, they must be searched. Search the whole book of Scripture from beginning to end, compare one passage with another, and explain one by another. We must also study particular passages fully, so as to see not what they seem to say but what they truly say.

2.5.1.2.2. It is a word of advice. All those who want to find Christ must search the Scriptures, which stands for:

2.5.1.2.2.1. Diligence in seeking, careful application of mind.

2.5.1.2.2.2. Desire and intention to find. We must often ask, "What am I now searching for?" We must search as those who mine gold or silver, or who dive for pearls (Job 28:1–11).

2.5.2. We are here told that when we search the Scriptures, we must have two things within ourselves: heaven, our end, and Christ, our way.

2.5.2.1. We must search the Scriptures for heaven as our great destination: *For in them you think you have eternal life.* Scripture assures us of the eternal state set before us and offers us an eternal life in that state. But to the Jews Christ said only, *You think you have eternal life in the scriptures.* They looked for it by merely reading

and studying the Scriptures. It was a common but corrupt saying among them, "He that has the words of the law has eternal life."

2.5.2.2. We must search the Scriptures for Christ, as the new and living way leading to this destination (Heb 10:20). *These are they that testify of me.* The Scriptures, even those of the Old Testament, testify of Christ, and by them God bears witness to him. The Jews knew very well that the Old Testament testified of the Messiah, and they were analytical in their remarks on the passages that pointed in that direction; they were careless and wretchedly mistaken, however, in applying them. We must *search the scriptures* because they testify about Christ; this is *life eternal, to know him.* Christ is the treasure hidden in the field of the Scriptures (Mt 13:44), the water in those wells.

2.5.3. He added to this testimony a rebuke of their unfaithfulness and evil in four instances.

2.5.3.1. Their neglect of Christ and his message: "*You will not come to me, that you might have life* (v. 40)." Their separation from Christ was the fault not so much of their understandings as of their wills. Christ offered life, but that offer was not accepted. There is life to be gained with Jesus Christ for poor souls. Life is the perfection of our being and includes all happiness: Christ is our life. Those who want to have this life must come to Jesus Christ for it; we may have it if we come for it. The only reason why sinners die is that they refuse to come to Christ, not that they cannot but that they will not. They will not be healed, because they refuse to pay attention to the methods of healing. The words (v. 41) *I receive not honour from men* are a parenthesis, to forestall a potential objection that by requiring everyone to come to him and praise him he was seeking his own glory. He did not seek human applause; he did not receive human praise. Instead of receiving honor from people, he received much disrespect and disgrace from them. Nor did he need human applause; it did not add to his glory.

2.5.3.2. Their lack of love for God (v. 42): "*I know you, that you have not the love of God in you.*" The reason why people treat Christ with disrespect is that they do not love God. Christ had just now charged the Jews with ignorance of God (v. 37), and here he charged them with lack of love for him; people do not love God because they do not want to know him. Notice:

2.5.3.2.1. The offense they were accused of: *You have not the love of God in you.* They claimed a great love for God, and they thought they proved it by their zeal for the law, but they were really without love for God. Many people who make a great profession of religious faith show they lack the love of God by their neglect of Christ. They hate his holiness and underrate his goodness. It is the love of God *in* us, that love seated in the heart, the love *shed abroad* there (Ro 5:5), that God will accept.

2.5.3.2.2. The proof of this charge, given by personal knowledge of Christ: *I know you.* Christ sees through all our disguises and can say to each of us, "I know you." Christ knows people better than their neighbors know them. Christ knows people better than they know themselves. We may deceive ourselves, but we cannot deceive him.

2.5.3.3. Their readiness to receive false Christs and false prophets (v. 43): *I am come in my Father's name, and you receive me not. If another shall come in his own name, him you will receive.* They refused to receive Christ, who came in his Father's name, but they listened to everyone who set himself up in his own name. They *forsook their own mercies,* which is bad enough, and it was for *lying vanities*, which is worse (Jnh 2:8). Those prophets who come in their own name are false. It is just of God to allow those who do not receive the truth to be deceived by false prophets. Those who shut their eyes to the true light are given up to wander endlessly after false lights, and to be led astray after every will-o'-the-wisp. They loathe manna (Nu 21:5), and at the same time feed upon ashes (Isa 44:20).

2.5.3.4. Their pride, boasting, and unbelief, and the effects of these (v. 44). They insulted and undervalued Christ because they admired and overvalued themselves. Here is:

2.5.3.4.*1*. Their ambition for worldly honor. Christ despised it (v. 41), but they set their hearts on it: "*You receive honour one of another.* You want to receive it, and you aim at this in all you do. You honor and praise others only so that they may honor and praise you. Whatever respect is shown to you, you receive it yourselves and do not pass it on to God."

2.5.3.4.*2*. Their neglect of spiritual honor, called here *the honour that comes from God only*. *This honour have all the saints* (Ps 149:9). All who believe in Christ receive through him the honor that comes from God. We must seek this honor that comes from God. We must count it our reward, as the Pharisees counted *the praise of men* (12:43).

2.5.3.4.*3*. The influence this had on their unfaithfulness. *How can you believe*, you who are affected in this way? The ambition and love of worldly honor are a great hindrance to faith in Christ. How can people believe when the summit of their ambition is to *make a fair show in the flesh* (make a good impression outwardly) (Gal 6:12)?

2.6. The last witness called here is Moses (v. 45). Christ showed them:

2.6.1. That Moses was a witness against the unbelieving Jews: *There is one that accuses you, even Moses.* This may be understood either:

2.6.1.1. As showing the difference between the Law and the Gospel. "Moses, that is, the Law, accuses you, because the knowledge of sin is through the Law; it condemns you." The intention of Christ's Gospel, however, is not to accuse us: *Think not that I will accuse you.* He came to be an advocate (1Jn 2:1), not an accuser; he came to reconcile God and people. Or:

2.6.1.2. As showing the clear unreasonableness of their unfaithfulness: "Do not think that I will appeal from your law court to God's and challenge you to answer there for what you do against me, as wronged innocence usually does." Instead of accusing his crucifiers to his Father, he prayed, *Father, forgive them* (Lk 23:34). And let the Jews not make a mistake about Moses, as if he would stand by them in rejecting Christ. No; *There is one that accuses you, even Moses, in whom you trust.* The Jews trusted in Moses, and they thought that having his laws and religious ceremonies would save them. Those who trust in their privileges will find that those very privileges will testify against them.

2.6.2. That Moses was a witness for Christ and his teaching (vv. 46–47): *He wrote of me.* The ceremonies of the Law of Moses were *figures of him that was to come* (Ro 5:14). Christ showed here that, far from writing against Christ, Moses wrote for him, and of him.

2.6.2.1. Christ here accused the Jews of not believing Moses. Christ had said (v. 45) that they trusted in Moses, but here he showed that although they trusted in his name, they did not receive his message in its true sense and meaning.

2.6.2.2. He proved this charge from their disbelief in him: *Had you believed Moses, you would have believed*

me. Many people say they believe, but their actions show the opposite. Those who rightly believe one part of Scripture will receive every part.

2.6.2.3. From their disbelief of Moses he also concluded that it was not strange that they rejected him, Christ: "*If you believe not his writings, how shall you believe my words?* If you do not believe sacred writings, those words written in black and white, which is the most dependable way of communicating, *how shall you believe my words*, since spoken words are usually less valued? If you do not believe what Moses spoke and wrote about me, how will you believe me and my mission?" If we do not accept the premises, how will we accept the conclusion? If, therefore, we do not believe that those writings were divinely inspired, how will we receive the message of Christ?

3. Thus ended Christ's plea. They were silenced for the present, but their hearts remained hardened.

CHAPTER 6

We have here: 1. The miracle of the bread and fish (vv. 1–14). 2. Christ's walking on water (vv. 15–21). 3. The people's flocking to him at Capernaum (vv. 22–25). 4. His talk with them—occasioned by the miracle of the bread (vv. 26–27)—showing them how they must work for spiritual food (vv. 28–29) and what that spiritual food is (vv. 30–59). 5. Their discontent at what he said (vv. 60–65). 6. Many turning away from him (vv. 66–71).

Verses 1–14

Here is an account of Christ's feeding five thousand men with five loaves and two fish. It is the only passage of the actions of Christ's life that is recorded by all four Evangelists. John relates this because of the reference the following discussion has to it. Notice:

1. The place and time of this miracle.

1.1. The part of the country that Christ was in (v. 1): *He went over the sea of Galilee.* Christ did not go directly across, but went along the coast to another place on the same side.

1.2. The people who were with him: *A great multitude followed him, because they saw his miracles* (v. 2).

1.2.1. While our Lord Jesus went about doing good (Ac 10:38), he lived continually in a crowd. Good and useful people must not complain about rushed business when they are serving God. There will be time enough to enjoy ourselves when we come to the world where we will enjoy God directly.

1.2.2. Christ's miracles drew many people after him who were not effectively drawn to him.

1.3. Christ's positioning himself advantageously to receive them (v. 3): *He went up into a mountain, and there he sat with his disciples.* Christ was now an open-air preacher, but his word was never the worse to those who continued to follow him not only when he went out to an isolated place but also when he went up a mountain, though that way was difficult. Whoever wanted to could come and find him there. He sat with his disciples.

1.4. The time when it took place: *After those things.* We are told that it was *when the passover was nigh* (v. 4):

1.4.1. Because the Jews had a custom of religiously observing the approach of Passover thirty days before.

1.4.2. Perhaps because the approach of the Passover, when everyone knew Christ would go to Jerusalem—and be absent for some time—made the crowds listen to him even more intently. The prospect of losing opportunities should motivate us to make the most of them with double the diligence.

2. The miracle itself.

2.1. The notice Christ took of the crowd that was with him (v. 5): He *lifted up his eyes* and *saw a great company come to him*. Christ showed that he was pleased with their presence and concerned for their welfare, to teach us to *condescend to those of low estate* (Ro 12:16) and not *set with the dogs of our flock* (Job 30:1) those whom Christ has put with his lambs.

2.2. The question he asked about how they would all be provided for. He spoke to Philip, who had been his disciple from the beginning and had seen all his miracles, especially that of turning water into wine (2:1–11). Those who have witnessed Christ's works and shared in their benefits are without excuse if they say, *Can he furnish a table in the wilderness?* (Ps 78:19). Philip came from Bethsaida, the town Christ was now near, and so he was likely to be able to help provide for them the best. Christ asked, *Whence shall we buy bread, that these* may eat?

2.2.1. He assumed they must all eat with him. One would have thought that when he had taught and healed them he had fulfilled his part. However, he wished to provide food for them. Those who will accept Christ's spiritual gifts as gifts instead of trying to pay for them will be paid for their acceptance of them.

2.2.2. His question was, *Whence shall we buy bread?* One would have thought he would have been more likely to ask, "Where shall we get the money to buy enough food for them?" He will buy to give, and we must labor so that we may give (Eph 4:28).

2.3. The intention of this question. It was only to test the faith of Philip, *for he himself knew what he would do* (v. 6). When we do not know what to do, Christ *himself knows what he will do*. When Christ perplexes his people, it is only with the intention of testing them.

2.4. Philip's answer to this question: *"Two hundred pennyworth of bread is not sufficient* (v. 7). The country will not have that much bread, nor can we afford to spend so much money." Christ could now have said to him, as he did afterward, *Have I been so long with you, and yet hast thou not known me, Philip?* (14:9). We tend to distrust God's power when visible and ordinary means fail; that is, we trust him no further than we can see him.

2.5. The information Christ received about the provision they had. It was Andrew who told Christ about what they had available. In this we may see:

2.5.1. The intensity of Andrew's love for those whom he saw his Master was concerned for, in that he was willing to bring out all that the Twelve had, even though he did not know how they would have enough for themselves, and anyone would have said, "Charity begins at home." He did not try to hide it. It was *five barley loaves* and two small fish.

2.5.1.1. The provision was inferior and ordinary; they were *barley loaves*. Christ and his disciples were glad to have barley bread. It does not follow that we should limit ourselves to such inferior food on the basis of our religious faith — when God brings what is finer into our hands, let us receive it and be thankful — but barley bread is what Christ had, and it is better than we deserve.

2.5.1.2. It was only small and insufficient; there were only *five loaves*, and those were so small that one small lad carried them all. There were only two fish, and those were small ones. The provision of bread was little enough, but that of the fish was even less, so that they would have had to eat many slices of dry bread before they could have made a meal. Well, Andrew was willing for the people to

have this, as far as it went. A distrustful fear of our own lack should not stop us from giving to others in need.

2.5.2. The weakness of his faith in that word: *But what are they among so many?* Philip and he did not consider the power of Christ as they should have.

2.6. The directions Christ gave the disciples to seat the guests (v. 10): *Make the men sit down*. This was like sending Providence to market, going to buy without money (Isa 55:1). Notice:

2.6.1. The furnishings of the dining room: *there was much grass in that place*. There was plenty of grass where Christ was preaching; the Gospel brings other blessings with it. This abundant grass made the place more comfortable for those who had to sit on the ground; it served them as cushions, and, considering what Christ said about the grass of the field (Mt 6:29–30), these surpassed those of Xerxes: nature's show is the most glorious.

2.6.2. The number of guests: *about five thousand*; it was a great reception, representing that of the Gospel, which is *a feast for all nations* (Isa 25:6), a feast for all comers.

2.7. The distribution of the provisions (v. 11). Notice:

2.7.1. It was done with thanksgiving: *He gave thanks*. We should give thanks to God for our food, because it is a mercy to have it. Even if our provisions are inferior and insufficient, even if we have neither plenty nor delicacy, we must still give thanks to God for what we have.

2.7.2. It was distributed from the hands of Christ by the hands of his disciples (v. 11). All our benefits come to us from the hand of Christ originally; whoever brings them, he is the One who sends them.

2.7.3. It was done to everyone's satisfaction. They did not each take a bite; rather, all had *as much as they would*. Considering how much more wonderful this miraculous food must have been than ordinary food, a little would not have satisfied them. Christ does not limit those whom he feeds with the bread of life (Ps 81:10). There were only *two small fishes*, but they all had as much as they wanted of them too. Those who say that feeding on fish is fasting scorn the reception Christ gave here, which was a complete feast.

2.8. The care that was taken of the pieces left over.

2.8.1. The orders Christ gave concerning them (v. 12): When they were filled, Christ said to the disciples, *Gather up the fragments*. We must always take care that we do not waste any of God's good creations, because the gift we have of them is given with this condition: exclude willful waste. God is just to bring us to a lack of what we waste. When we are filled, we must remember that others are lacking and that we may be in that situation one day too. Those who want to have the resources to be charitable must be provident. Christ did not order the leftovers to be gathered up until all had been filled; we must not begin to hoard and save until everything is spent that should be.

2.8.2. The observance of these orders (v. 13): *They filled twelve baskets with the fragments*, which was evidence not only of the truth of the miracle that they were fed but also of its greatness; not only were they filled, but there was all this left over. Notice how generous God's goodness is; there is enough bread and to spare in our Father's house (Lk 15:17). The leftovers filled twelve baskets, one for each disciple; they were repaid with interest for their willingness to give up what they had for public service.

3. The influence this miracle had on the people (v. 14): they said, *This is of a truth that prophet*. This shows us:

3.1. Even the ordinary Jews had a great assurance that the Messiah was to come into the world and would be a great prophet. The Pharisees despised them as not knowing the Law, but it seems the people knew more about the One who is the end of the law than the Pharisees did.

3.2. The miracles Christ performed clearly demonstrated that he was the promised Messiah, a teacher who had come from God (3:2), and the great Prophet (Dt 18:15). Many people were convinced he was *the prophet who would come into the world* (v. 14), but they did not receive his teaching into their hearts. It is possible for people to acknowledge that Christ is that prophet but still turn a deaf ear to him.

Verses 15–21

Here is:

1. Christ's withdrawal from the crowd. Notice:

1.1. What made him withdraw; he realized that those who acknowledged him to be the prophet would come and *take him by force, to make him a king* (v. 15). Here we have an example:

1.1.1. Of the misguided zeal of some of Christ's followers; their only desire was to make him a king. Now:

1.1.1.1. This was an act of zeal for the honor of Christ. They were concerned to see such a great benefactor to the world so little respected in it, and so they wanted to make him king. Those whom Christ has feasted with the royal delicacies of heaven should, in return for his favor, make him their king and set him on the throne of their souls. But:

1.1.1.2. It was a misguided zeal, for:

1.1.1.2.*1.* It was based on a mistake about the nature of Christ's kingdom, as if it were to be *of this world* (18:36) and he must appear with outward show. They wanted to make him such a king, but this would have been as great a disparagement to his glory as it would be to put lacquer on gold or to paint a ruby. Right ideas of Christ's kingdom would keep us using right methods to advance it.

1.1.1.2.*2.* It was stirred by the love of the flesh; they wanted to make him their king—the One who could feed them so abundantly without their having to work for it, which would save them from the curse of *eating their bread in the sweat of their face* (Ge 3:19).

1.1.1.2.*3.* It was intended to carry on a worldly purpose; they hoped this might provide them with a good opportunity to shake off the Roman yoke. This is how religion is often surrendered to worldly interests, and Christ is served only to give people a personal advantage (Ro 16:18). "Jesus is usually sought after for something else, not for his own sake."

1.1.1.2.*4.* It was against the mind of our Lord Jesus himself, because they wanted to make him king by force, whether he wanted to be king or not.

1.1.2. Of the humility of the Lord Jesus, that he departed; far from supporting the intention, he effectively quashed it. Here he has left a testimony:

1.1.2.1. Against ambition for worldly honor. Let us not, then, seek to be the idols of the crowd or be *desirous of vain glory* (Gal 5:26).

1.1.2.2. Against faction, rebellion, treason, and whatever tends to disturb the peace of rulers and provinces.

1.2. Where he withdrew to: *He departed again into a mountain*—into *the* mountain, the mountainside where he had preached (v. 3). He had come down from it to feed the people, and then he returned to it by himself to be private. Christ chose sometimes to be by himself to have freer, fuller, and deeper fellowship with God. We are never less alone than when we are alone.

2. The disciples' distress on the lake.

2.1. They *went down to the sea* in a boat (vv. 16–17): *When even was come* and they had completed their day's

work, it was time to look toward home, so they went aboard their boat and set sail for Capernaum.

2.2. The stormy wind arose (Ps 148:8). They had just enjoyed a feast at Christ's table, but after the sunshine of comfort a storm is to be expected. *It was now dark.* Sometimes the people of God are in trouble and cannot see a way out. They are in the dark about the cause of their trouble, about its purpose, where it is leading, and what the outcome will be. Jesus *was not come to them*. The absence of Christ aggravates the troubles of Christians. The *sea arose by reason of a great wind*. It was calm and fair when they started their voyage, but the storm blew when they were at sea. In times of tranquility we must prepare for trouble, because it may arise when we least think of it. Clouds and darkness sometimes surround the children of the light and of the day (1Th 5:5).

2.3. Christ promptly came to them (v. 19). *They had rowed about twenty-five or thirty furlongs* (three or three and a half miles; about five or six kilometers). When they had gone a good way at sea, they *saw Jesus walking on the sea*. We see here:

2.3.1. The power Christ has over the laws and customs of nature. Christ walked on the water as on dry land.

2.3.2. The concern Christ has for his disciples in their distress: *He drew nigh to the ship.* He will not *leave them comfortless* (14:18) when they seem to be tossed with tempests and uncomforted.

2.3.3. The relief Christ gives to his disciples in their fears. They *were afraid*, more afraid of a ghost—which they thought he was—than of the winds and waves. When they thought a demon haunted them, they were more terrified than they had been while they saw nothing in the sea but what was natural. Our real distresses are often much increased by our imaginary ones. We are often not only more frightened than hurt, but most frightened when we are about to be helped. Notice how affectionately Christ silenced their fears with his compassionate words (v. 20): *It is I, be not afraid!* Nothing is more powerful to comfort saints than this: "I am Jesus, whom you love; do not be afraid of me, nor of the storm." When trouble is near, Christ is also near.

2.4. They quickly arrived at the port they were bound for (v. 17). They welcomed Christ into the ship; they *willingly received him*. Christ departs for a time only so as to endear himself to his disciples all the more at his return. He brought them safely to the shore: *Immediately the ship was at the land whither they went.* The ship of the church may be broken and in distress, but it will still eventually arrive safely at the harbor. The disciples had rowed hard, but they could not row effectively until they had gotten Christ into the ship, and then the work was done suddenly. If we have received Christ Jesus the Lord, then, though the night is dark and the wind is high, we may still comfort ourselves with the knowledge that we will soon reach the shore and that we are nearer to it than we think we are.

Verses 22–27

In these verses we have:

1. The careful search the people made for Christ (vv. 23–24). Having seen him withdraw to the mountain, they lay in wait for his return, and the *day following*:

1.1. They were much at a loss as to where he was. They saw no boat there except the one in which the disciples went away. They also noticed that Jesus did not go with his disciples, but that they went alone.

1.2. They were very diligent in seeking him. They searched the places around there, and when they saw that neither Jesus nor his disciples were there, they decided to search elsewhere. People whom Christ has given the feast of the bread of life should have their souls carried ahead of them in fervent desire for him. A deep fellowship with Christ wants to be even deeper. They decided to go to Capernaum to look for him. His disciples had gone there, and the people knew he would not leave them for long. Providence favored the people with the opportunity to go there because other boats came from Tiberias, near the place where they had eaten bread. Those who sincerely seek Christ are commonly acknowledged and helped by Providence in that pursuit. The Evangelist adds, *after the Lord had given thanks* (v. 23). The disciples were so moved by their Master's giving thanks that they could never forget the impression it made on them by it. This was the grace and beauty of that meal, and made it remarkable; their hearts burned inside them (Lk 24:30–32).

1.3. They got into the boats and went to Capernaum looking for Jesus. Because their convictions were strong and their desires enthusiastic, they followed him. Good ideas are often crushed and come to nothing for lack of being pursued promptly. They came to Capernaum, and it seems they had a calm and pleasant passage, whereas his sincere disciples had a rough and stormy one. It is not strange if things go worst for the best people in this evil world. They came seeking Jesus.

2. The success of their search: *They found him on the other side of the sea* (v. 25). It is worthwhile crossing a sea to seek Christ if only we may find him eventually. These people appeared later to be unsound, not motivated by any good intentions, but they were zealous. If people have nothing more to show for their love to Christ than their running after sermons and prayers and their pangs of affection for good preaching, they have reason to suspect themselves as being no better than this eager crowd. However, although these people had no better motives, and Christ knew it, he was still willing to be found by them.

3. The question they asked him: *Rabbi, when camest thou hither* (when did you get here)? It seems from v. 59 that they found him in the synagogue. They found him there, and all they had to say to him was, *Rabbi, when camest thou hither?* Their question referred not only to the time, but also to the way, of his going there; not only, "When did you get here?" but also, "How did you get here?" They were curious about Christ's movements but not concerned to observe their own.

4. The answer Christ gave them, an answer that suited their situation.

4.1. He revealed the corrupt motive from which they followed him (v. 26): "*Verily, verily, I say unto you, You seek me*; that is good, but you are not doing so from good motives." Christ knows not only what we do but also why we do it. *Not because you saw the miracles.* It was for their own stomachs' sake: *Because you did eat of the loaves, and were filled*; they sought him not because he taught them but because he fed them. He had given them:

4.1.1. A filling meal: *They did eat, and were filled*, and some of them perhaps were so poor that it had been a long time since they had had enough to eat and been able to leave leftovers.

4.1.2. A cheap meal, indeed, a free meal. Many follow Christ for loaves, not for love. These people complimented Christ by using the term *Rabbi*, but he spoke to them faithfully about their hypocrisy. His ministers must learn from this not to flatter those who flatter them, but to give faithful rebukes where there is cause to do so.

4.2. He directed them to better motives (v. 27): *Labour for that meat which endures to everlasting life.* His purpose is:

4.2.1. To moderate our worldly pursuits: *Labour not for the meat that perishes* (do not work for food that spoils). We must not make the things of this world our chief aim and concern. The things of the world are *meat that perishes* (food that spoils). Worldly wealth, honor, and pleasure are food; they feed the imagination—and many times that is all they do—and fill the stomach. These are things that people hunger for as food. Those who have the largest share of them are not sure to have them while they live, but they are sure to leave them and lose them when they die. It is therefore foolish for us to work for them excessively. We must not make these perishable goods our chief good.

4.2.2. To encourage and stir our gracious pursuits: "*Labour for that meat* (food) that concerns the soul." It is indescribably desirable: it is food that *endures to everlasting life*; it is a happiness that will last as long as we must, a food that not only endures eternally but also will nourish us to eternal life. And it is undoubtedly attainable. It is that *which the Son of man shall give.* Notice:

4.2.2.1. Who gives this food: the *Son of man*, who has power to give eternal life, with all its means. We are told to *labour for it*, as if it were to be gained by our own diligence, as if it were to be sold to us for that valuable consideration. However, when we have worked so hard for it, we have not deserved it as our hire; the Son of Man gives it. What is freer than a gift?

4.2.2.2. What authority he has to give it: *for him has God the Father sealed.* God the Father has *sealed him* (put on him the seal of approval), that is, has given him full authority to deal between God and humanity, as God's ambassador to humanity and humanity's intercessor with God, and has proved his commission by miracles.

Verses 28–59

Christ allowed the people to ask him questions; he did not take offense at the interruption. Those who want to teach must be swift to hear and must learn how to answer questions.

1. They asked what work they must do, and he answered them (vv. 28–29).

1.1. Their question was relevant enough (v. 28): *What shall we do, that we may work the works of God?* A humble and sincere question, showing them to be, at least at that time, in a good state of mind and wanting to know and do their duty. They were convinced that those who wanted to obtain this eternal food:

1.1.1. Must aim to do something great. Those who look high in their expectations must aim high in their endeavors and seek to *work the works of God*, which are different from the works of worldly people in their worldly pursuits. It is not enough to speak the words of God; we must also do the works of God.

1.1.2. Must be willing to do anything: *What shall we do?* "Lord, I am ready to do whatever you appoint."

1.2. Christ's answer was clear enough (v. 29): *This is the work of God, that ye believe.* The work of faith is the work of God. They asked about the works of God—in the plural—being concerned about many things, but Christ directed them to the one thing that is needed (Lk 10:41): *that ye believe.* Without faith you cannot please God (Heb 11:6). The faith that accepts Christ, that depends on him and submits to him, is the work of God.

2. After Christ had told them that the Son of Man would give them this food, they asked about it.

2.1. Their inquiry was concerning a sign (v. 30): *What sign showest thou?* They were right as far as they went: since he required them to believe him, they asked that he produce his credentials. But their inquiry was off the mark in the following ways:

2.1.1. They overlooked the many miracles they had already seen him perform. Was this the time to ask, "What sign are you showing us?" Especially at Capernaum, where he had done so *many mighty works*? Were not these the very people who only the other day were miraculously fed by him? There are none so blind as those who will not see.

2.1.2. They preferred the miraculous feeding of Israel in the desert to all the miracles Christ performed (v. 31): *Our fathers did eat manna in the desert*. They quoted a Scripture for it: *He gave them bread from heaven* (Ps 78:24). What use can be made of this story to which they referred! Yet see how these people corrupted it and made wrong use of it.

2.1.2.1. Christ rebuked them for their fondness of the miraculous bread and told them not to set their hearts on food that spoils. "Why," they said, "food for the stomach was the great and good thing that God gave to our ancestors in the desert, and why then should we not work for that food?"

2.1.2.2. Christ had fed five thousand men with five loaves, but, claiming to exalt the miracles of Moses, they tacitly undervalued this miracle of Christ. Christ fed them only once, and then rebuked those who followed him in the hope of still being fed. Moses fed his followers for forty years, and miracles were not rare but were their daily bread. Christ fed them with bread from the earth, barley bread, and fish from the sea, but Moses fed Israel with bread from heaven, angel's food (Ps 78:25). These Jews talked big about the manna that their ancestors ate, but their ancestors had insulted it and called it *light bread* (Nu 21:5). We tend to disrespect and overlook the appearances of God's power and grace in our own times while claiming to admire the wonders about which our ancestors told us (Jdg 6:13).

2.2. Here is Christ's reply to this question. It was true that their ancestors ate manna in the desert, but it was not Moses who gave it to them; he was merely the instrument, and so they must look beyond him to God. Moses gave them neither that bread nor that water. Christ told them about the true manna: "*but my Father giveth you the true bread from heaven*; the bread from heaven is now given not to your ancestors but to you, for whom the better things were reserved. He is now giving you that bread from heaven that is truly so called."

3. Having replied to their questions, Christ continued, in response to their objection concerning the manna, to speak of himself using the metaphor of bread and to speak of believing using the comparison of eating and drinking. These images, combined in that of the eating of his flesh and drinking of his blood, and remarked on by the hearers, were the subject of the rest of this conversation.

3.1. After Christ had spoken about himself as the great gift of God and the *true bread* (v. 32), he explained and confirmed this at length.

3.1.1. He showed here that he is the *true bread*; he repeated this again and again (vv. 33, 35, 48–51). Notice:

3.1.1.1. That Christ is bread; he is to the soul what bread is to the body: *it is the staff of life*. Our bodies could better live without food than our souls without Christ.

3.1.1.2. That he is the *bread of God* (v. 33), divine bread, and the bread of God's family, his *children's bread* (Mt 15:26).

3.1.1.3. That he is *the bread of life* (v. 35); and again (v. 48), *that* bread of life. Christ is the bread of life

because he is the fruit of the *tree of life* (Ge 2:9). He is the living bread, as he himself explains (v. 51): *I am the living bread*. Bread itself is dead, but Christ himself is *living bread*, nourishing through his own power. Christ is always living. He is the eternal bread. The message of Christ crucified (1Co 1:22–23) is now as strengthening and comforting to a believer as it has ever been: *He gives life unto the world* (v. 33). The manna only preserved and supported life. Christ gives life to those who were dead in sin (Eph 2:1). The manna was ordained only for the life of the Israelites, but Christ is given for the *life of the world* (v. 51).

3.1.1.4. That he is the *bread which came down from heaven*; this is often repeated here (vv. 33, 50, 51, 58). This shows both the divinity of Christ's person and the divine origin of all the good that flows to us through him.

3.1.1.5. That he is that bread of which the manna was a type and figure (v. 58), the true bread (v. 32). There was *manna* enough for them all; in the same way, in Christ there is a fullness of grace for all believers (1:16). Those who gather much of this manna will have none to spare when they use it, and those who gather little will find that when their grace is perfected in glory, they will not lack.

3.1.2. He showed here what his work was, giving us an account of his work among human beings (vv. 38–40).

3.1.2.1. He assures us, in general, that he came from heaven to do his Father's work (v. 38): not to *do his own will, but the will of him that sent him*. He came from heaven. We may well ask with wonder, "What would him to undertake such an expedition?" Here he tells us that he came to do not his own will but the will of his Father. "I am come *to do the will of him that sent me*." He came into the world as God's great agent and the world's great doctor. The scope of his whole life was to glorify God and do good to people.

3.1.2.2. He tells us, in particular, about the will of the Father that he came to fulfill. Notice:

3.1.2.2.1. The private instructions given to Christ to save all the chosen remnant. This is the covenant of redemption between the Father and the Son (v. 38): *This is the Father's will, who hath sent me*, that *of all whom he hath given me I should lose none*. There is a certain number of people given by the Father to Jesus Christ to be his responsibility and thereby to be *to be to him for a name and a praise* (Isa 55:13). Those whom God chose to be the objects of his special love he entrusted to the hands of Christ. Jesus Christ has undertaken that he will lose none of those who were given him in this way by the Father. Christ's undertaking for those who are given him extends to the resurrection of their bodies. *I will raise it up again at the last day*. Christ's undertaking will never be completely fulfilled until the resurrection. The spring and origin of all this is the sovereign will of God.

3.1.2.2.2. The public instructions that were to be given to human beings, telling them on what terms they could gain salvation through Christ, and this is the covenant of grace between God and human beings. Who in particular were given to Christ is a secret. Yet, though their names are concealed, their characters are made known. An offer was made, so that by it those who were given to Christ would be brought to him (v. 40): "*This is the will of him that sent me*, that *every one* who *sees the Son, and believes on him*, may have *everlasting life*, and *I will raise him up*." Is it not reviving to hear this? *Eternal life* can be gained unless we reject it. The crown of glory is set before us (2Ti 4:8; 1Pe 5:4) as the prize of our high calling (Php 3:14), which we may run for and gain. Everyone can have it. This eternal life is guaranteed to all those who believe in Christ. *Everyone which seeth the Son and believes on him* will be saved. I understand *seeing* here to refer to the same as *believing*. *Everyone that sees the Son*, that is, *believes on him*, everyone who sees him with the eye of faith, will *have everlasting life*. It is not a blind faith that Christ requires; he does not require us to have our eyes removed and then follow him, but to see him, and see on what basis we continue in our faith. Those who believe in Jesus Christ will be raised up by his power at the last day. He had this responsibility as his Father's will (v. 39), and here he solemnly made it his own undertaking: *I will raise him up*.

3.2. Now let us see how Christ's hearers responded to his speaking in this way about himself, as the bread of life that came down from heaven.

3.2.1. When they heard of such a thing as the bread of God that gives life, they prayed sincerely for it (v. 34): *Lord, evermore give us this bread*. I take this request to have been made honestly, though ignorantly, and to have been well intentioned. General and confused ideas of divine things produce some kinds of desire toward them. Those who have an unclear knowledge of the things of God, who *see men as trees walking* (Mk 8:24), make, as we may call them, inarticulate prayers for spiritual blessings. They think the favor of God is good and heaven is a fine place, but they neither value nor desire at all that holiness that is necessary for both.

3.2.2. However, when they understood that by this bread of life Jesus meant himself, then they despised it. *They murmured at him*. This comes immediately after that sacred declaration Christ had made of God's will and his own undertaking concerning human salvation (vv. 39–40), which certainly were some of the most significant and gracious words that ever came from the mouth of our Lord Jesus. One would have thought that when they heard that God had visited them in this way, they would have *bowed their heads and worshipped* (Ex 4:31), but on the contrary, they murmured, grumbling and quarreling with what Christ said. Many who will not professedly contradict the teaching of Christ still say in their hearts that they do not like it. What offended them was Christ's asserting that his origin was *heaven* (vv. 41–42). "How is it that he says, *I came down from heaven?*" What they thought justified them in this was that they knew his background on earth: *Is not this Jesus the son of Joseph, whose father and mother we know?* They took offense that he would say that he came down from heaven, since he was one of them.

3.3. Christ, having spoken of faith as the great *work of God* (v. 29), discussed this work in detail.

3.3.1. He shows what it is to believe in Christ. V. 35 implies that *he that comes to* me is the same as he who *believes in me* (v. 35), and so the phrase has the same meaning in vv. 37, 44–45. Repentance toward God is *coming to him* (Jer 3:22) as our chief good and highest end, and so faith toward our Lord Jesus Christ is coming to him as our Prince and Savior and our way to the Father. Even when he was here on earth, coming to him meant more than merely coming to his geographical location, and even now it means more than coming to hear his word and observe his ordinances. It is to feed upon Christ (v. 51): *If any man eat of this bread. Coming* to Christ means applying ourselves to him; *eating of this bread* means applying Christ to ourselves.

3.3.2. He shows what is to be gained by believing in Christ. How will we be better off if we feed on him? Lack and death are the chief things we dread. These two are now secured here for true believers.

3.3.2.1. They will never lack anything they need: *never hunger, never thirst* (v. 35). They have desires, earnest desires, but these are so abundantly satisfied that they cannot be called hunger and thirst, which are uncomfortable and painful.

3.3.2.2. They will never die; that is, they will not die eternally. Those who believe on Christ *have everlasting life* (v. 47). Union with Christ and fellowship with God in Christ are everlasting life begun. Whereas those who ate manna died, Christ is such bread as a person can eat and never die (vv. 49–50). Notice here:

3.3.2.2.1. The insufficiency of the manna as a type: *Your fathers did eat manna in the wilderness, and are dead.* Those people who ate manna, angels' food (Ps 78:25), died like other people. Many of them died for their unbelief and grumbling. Their eating manna was no security to them from the wrath of God, as believing in Christ is to us. The rest of them died in the normal course of nature, and their carcasses fell in the desert where they ate manna (Nu 14:29). Let the Jews then not boast so much of manna.

3.3.2.2.2. The all-sufficiency of the true manna: *This is the bread that cometh down from heaven, that a man may eat thereof and not die.* Not die, that is, not perish, not fall short of the heavenly Canaan: *If any man eat of this bread, he shall live for ever* (v. 51). This is the meaning of never dying: although he dies, he will pass through death to the world where there will be *no more death* (Rev 21:4). To live forever is not merely to be forever, but to be happy forever.

3.3.3. He shows what encouragements we have to believe in Christ. Christ speaks here of some who *had seen him and yet believed not* (v. 36). Faith is not always the effect of sight; the soldiers were eyewitnesses of his resurrection, but instead of having faith in him, they told lies about him. Two things encourage our faith:

3.3.3.1. That the Son will welcome all those who come to him (v. 37): *Him that cometh to me I will in no wise cast out.* How welcome to our souls should this word be that makes us come to Christ!

3.3.3.1.1. The duty required is a pure Gospel duty: to come to Christ so that we may come to God through him. His beauty and love must draw us to him; a sense of need and fear of danger must drive us to him; anything to bring us to Christ.

3.3.3.1.2. The promise is a pure Gospel promise: *I will in no wise cast out.* There are two negatives: *I will not, no, I will not.* Much favor is expressed here. We have reason to fear that he might *cast us out* (drive us away). We may justly expect him to frown on us and close his doors to us. But he responds to these fears with the assurance that he will not do it; he will not reject us even though we are sinful. More favor is implied than is expressed; when it is said that he will not drive them away, the meaning is, "He will receive them and give them all they come to him for."

3.3.3.2. That the Father will without fail bring to Christ in due time all those who were given him.

3.3.3.2.1. Christ assures us that this will be done here: *All that the Father giveth me shall come to me* (v. 37). Christ spoke (v. 36) of those who have not believed in him even though they have seen him, and then he added this:

3.3.3.2.1.1. For their conviction and awakening. How can we think that God gave us to Christ if we give ourselves to the world and the flesh (2Pe 1:10)?

3.3.3.2.1.2. For his own comfort and encouragement. *All that the Father gives him shall come to him.* Here we have:

3.3.3.2.*1.2.1.* Election described. The elect are *all that the father giveth me* and all that belongs to them, all their service and all their interests. As all that he has is theirs, so all that they have is his. God was now about to *give him the heathen for* (nations as) *his inheritance* (Ps 2:8). Although the Jews who saw him did not believe on him, "These," he said, "will come to me; the other sheep, which are not of this fold, will be brought" (10:15–16).

3.3.3.2.*1.2.2.* The effect of election secured: they shall *come unto me*. This is spoken not as a promise but as a prediction. None of them will be forgotten; not a kernel of God's grain will be lost. The elect are by nature alienated from Christ and hostile to him, but they shall come. Not, "They will be driven to me," but, "They will come freely; they will be made willing" (Ps 110:3).

3.3.3.2.*2.* He here tells us how it will be done. How will those who are given to Christ be brought to him? Two things are to be done to this end:

3.3.3.2.*2.1.* Their understandings will be enlightened; this is promised in vv. 45–46. It is written in the prophets, *And they shall be all taught of God* (Isa 54:13); and, *They shall all know me* (Jer 31:34). This shows us:

3.3.3.2.*2.1.1.* In order to believe in Jesus Christ, it is necessary that we be *taught of God*, that is:

3.3.3.2.*2.1.1.1.* That a divine revelation be made to us. Some things are taught by nature, but to bring us to Christ a higher light is needed.

3.3.3.2.*2.1.1.2.* That a divine work be done in us. In giving us reason, God teaches us more than he teaches the animals, but in giving us faith he teaches more than we would learn naturally. All who are true Christians are *taught of God*; he has undertaken to teach them.

3.3.3.2.*2.1.2.* It follows then, that *every man* who has *heard and learned of the Father comes to Christ* (v. 45). It is implied here:

3.3.3.2.*2.1.2.1.* That no one will come to Christ except those who have heard and learned from the Father. Unless God by his grace enlightens our minds and not only tells us, so that we may hear, but also teaches us, so that we may learn the truth as it is in Jesus (Eph 4:21), we will never be brought to believe in Christ.

3.3.3.2.*2.1.2.2.* That this divine teaching so necessarily produces the faith of God's elect that we may conclude that those who do not come to Christ have never heard nor learned of the Father, for if they had, they would doubtless have come to Christ. It is in vain for people to claim to have been taught by God if they do not believe in Christ. In case anyone should dream of a visible appearance of God the Father, Christ adds (v. 46), *Not that any man hath seen the Father.* God, in enlightening people's eyes and teaching them, works in a spiritual way. The Father of spirits (Heb 12:9) can enter and influence human spirits undetected. Those who have not seen his face have felt his power. Those who *learn of the Father* must learn from Christ, who alone has seen his face.

3.3.3.2.*2.2.* Their wills will submit to God. In the corrupt soul of fallen humanity the will rebels against the right dictates of the understanding. A work of grace is therefore to be undertaken on the will, which is here called drawing (v. 44): *No man can come to me except the Father, who hath sent me, draw him.* The Jews grumbled at the teaching of Christ. Christ said (v. 43), "*Murmur not among yourselves*; do not lay the fault of your dislike of my teaching on one another. Your hostility to the truths of God is so strong that nothing less than divine power can overcome it. *No man can come to me except* (unless) *the Father, who hath sent me, draw him*" (v. 44). Notice here:

3.3.3.2.*2.2.1.* The nature of the work: it is drawing, which does not refer to a force imposed on the will, but to a change brought about in the will. A new tendency is given to the soul, by which it is inclined to God. The One who formed the human spirit knows how to mold the soul again.

3.3.3.2.*2.2.2.* The necessity of the work: *No man can come to* Christ in this weak and helpless state without it.

3.3.3.2.*2.2.3.* The author of the work: the *Father who hath sent me.* The Father would not send him on a fruitless errand. Having sent Christ to save souls, he sends souls to him to be saved by him.

3.3.3.2.*2.2.4.* The crown and perfection of this work: *and I will raise him up at the last day.* This is mentioned four times in this sermon. If Christ undertakes this, surely he can do anything. Let us extend our expectations toward a happiness reserved for the last day.

3.4. Christ now undertook to show in greater detail what part of him is this bread (vv. 51–58), namely, his flesh, and, still pursuing the metaphor of food, he shows that believing means eating of that. *The bread that I will give is my flesh* (v. 51), *the flesh of the Son of man and his blood* (v. 53). His *flesh is meat indeed, and* his *blood is drink indeed* (v. 55). We must *eat the flesh of the Son of man and drink his blood* (v. 53); and again (v. 54), *Whoso eateth my flesh and drinketh my blood*; and again (vv. 56–57), he that *eateth me.*

3.4.1. Let us see how Christ's message was open to mistake and misinterpretation.

3.4.1.1. It was misinterpreted by the worldly Jews (v. 52): *They strove* (argued) *among themselves, saying, How can this man give us his flesh to eat?* Christ had spoken (v. 51) of giving his flesh *for* us, to suffer and die, but they understood it as his giving it *to* us, to be eaten.

3.4.1.2. It is misunderstood by the many who conclude that if they take the sacrament when they die, they will certainly go to heaven.

3.4.2. Let us see how this message of Christ is to be rightly understood.

3.4.2.1. What is meant by the flesh and blood of Christ. It is called (v. 53) *the flesh of the Son of man, and his blood.* It is said to be *given for the life of the world*, that is:

3.4.2.1.*1.* Instead of the life of the world, which was forfeited by sin; Christ gives his own flesh as a ransom.

3.4.2.1.*2.* In order to give life to the world, to purchase a general offer of eternal life to the whole world. *The flesh and blood of the Son of Man* therefore refers to Christ and *him crucified* (1Co 2:2) and to the redemption brought by him. The covenant promises and eternal life are called the flesh and blood of Christ:

3.4.2.1.*2.1.* Because they are purchased by the breaking of his body and the shedding of his blood.

3.4.2.1.*2.2.* Because they are food and drink for our souls. He had earlier compared himself to bread, which is an essential food; here he compared himself to flesh, or meat, which is delicious. His flesh and blood are real meat and real drink, in contrast to the shows and shadows with which the world fobs off those who feed on it.

3.4.2.2. What is meant by eating this flesh and drinking this blood (v. 55). It is certain that it means neither more nor less than believing in Christ. Believing in Christ includes these four things, which eating and drinking also include:

3.4.2.2.*1.* An appetite for Christ. This spiritual eating and drinking begins with *hungering* and *thirsting* (Mt 5:6): "Give me Christ or else I die."

3.4.2.2.*2.* An application of Christ to ourselves. If we just look at food, it will not nourish us; we must take it into ourselves. We must accept Christ in such a way that he belongs to us.

3.4.2.2.3. A delight in Christ and his salvation. The message of Christ crucified must be food and drink to us, what is most pleasant and delightful.

3.4.2.2.4. A derivation of nourishment from him and a dependence on him to support and comfort our spiritual life and the strength, growth, and vigor of our new being. It is to live on him as we live on our food. When Christ later wanted to institute some outward physical signs by which to represent our sharing in the benefits of his death, he chose those of eating and drinking and made them sacramental actions.

3.4.3. Having explained in general the meaning of this part of Christ's message, we may reduce the details to two headings:

3.4.3.1. The necessity of our feeding upon Christ (v. 53): *Except* (unless) *you eat the flesh of the Son of man, and drink his blood, you have no life in you.*

3.4.3.1.1. "It is a certain sign that you have no spiritual life in you if you have no desire for or delight in Christ." If the soul does not hunger and thirst, it certainly does not live.

3.4.3.1.2. "It is certain that you can have no spiritual life unless you derive it from Christ by faith; apart from him you can do nothing" (15:5). Our bodies can live without food as well as our souls can without Christ.

3.4.3.2. The benefit and advantage of it, in two things:

3.4.3.2.1. We will be one with Christ (v. 56): *He that eats my flesh, and drinks my blood, he dwelleth in me, and I in him.* By faith we have a close and intimate union with Christ; he is in us, and we in him (17:21–23; 1Jn 3:24). Such is the union between Christ and believers that he shares in their griefs, and they share in his graces and joys; he *sups with them* (Rev 3:20) on their bitter herbs (Ex 12:8), and *they with him* on his luxurious food.

3.4.3.2.2. We will live eternally through him.

3.4.3.2.2.1. We will *live* by him (v. 57): *"As the living Father* hath sent me, and I live by the Father, so he who feeds on me will live through me."* True believers receive this divine life because of their union with Christ. He *that eateth me will live by me* (v. 57): those who live on Christ will live because of him. Because he lives, we will live also.

3.4.3.2.2.2. We will live *eternally* by him (v. 54): *Whoso eateth my flesh, and drinketh my blood, hath eternal life.* He will live forever (v. 58).

4. The writer concludes by telling us that Christ's message to the Jews took place *in the synagogue as he taught* (v. 59). He taught them many other things besides these, but this was something in his message that was new. Christ pleaded this at his trial (18:20): *I ever* (always) *taught in the synagogue.*

Verses 60–71

We have here an account of the effects of Christ's message.

1. To some it was *a savour of death unto death* (2Co 2:16); not only to the Jews, but even to many of his disciples. We have here:

1.1. Their murmurings at the teaching they heard (v. 60); not a few, but many of them, were offended by it. Notice what they said about it (*v.* 60): *This is a hard saying; who can hear it?*

1.1.1. They did not like it themselves. Now, when they found it a hard teaching, if they had humbly begged Christ to explain to them this parable to them (Mt 13:36), he

would have opened it up, and their understandings too (Lk 24:45).

1.1.2. They thought it impossible for anyone else to like it: "Who can bear it? Surely no one can." Those who mock religion are ready to think that all intelligent human beings agree with them. Thank God that thousands have heard these sayings of Christ and found them not only easy but also pleasant.

1.2. Christ's response to their grumbling.

1.2.1. He was aware of it (v. 61). Christ knew their objections; he saw them, he heard them, however hard the objectors tried to hide them. He knew them *in himself,* not by any information given him, but by his own divine omniscience. Thoughts are words to Christ; we should be careful, therefore, not only about what we say and do but also about what we think.

1.2.2. He knew well enough how to answer them: *Doth this offend you?* We may justly be amazed that so much offense would be taken at the teaching of Christ with so little reason. Christ spoke about it here with amazement: *Doth this offend you?*

1.2.2.1. He gave them a hint of his ascension to heaven, as what would be compelling evidence of the truth of his teaching (v. 62): *"What and if you shall see the Son of man ascend up where he was before?* If this is such a hard saying that you cannot hear it, how then will you digest my saying that I will return to heaven, from where I came?" Those who stumble at smaller difficulties should consider how they will overcome greater ones. "You think I take too much on myself when I say, *I came down from heaven,* and you quarreled with this (v. 42), but will you think so when you see me return to heaven?" Christ often referred in this way to later proofs.

1.2.2.2. He gave them a general key to this and all such messages spoken in parables, teaching them that the parables were to be understood spiritually: *It is the spirit that quickeneth; the flesh profiteth nothing* (v. 63).

1.2.2.2.1. Merely taking part in religious services counts for nothing unless the Spirit of God works with them and gives life to the soul through them. If the Spirit works with the word and ordinances of worship, they are like food to a living being; if not, they are like food to a dead corpse.

1.2.2.2.2. The doctrine of eating Christ's flesh and drinking his blood, if understood literally, counts for nothing. Its spiritual sense or meaning gives life to the soul, making it alive and lively: *The words that I speak unto you, they are spirit, and they are life.* To believe that Christ died for me, to derive strength and comfort from that teaching, this is the spirit and life of that teaching, and, interpreted in this way, it is an excellent teaching. The reason why people dislike Christ's sayings is that they misunderstand them. The literal sense of a parable does us no good; we are never any the wiser because of it. *The flesh profits* (counts for) *nothing,* but *the Spirit quickeneth.* They found fault with Christ's teachings, whereas the fault lay in themselves; it is only to worldly minds that spiritual things are foolish and useless; spiritual minds enjoy them; see 1Co 2:14–15.

1.2.2.3. He gave them an indication of his knowledge of them, and that he had expected nothing better from them, even though they called themselves his disciples (vv. 64–65). Referring to Isa 53:1, we may say that Christ took notice:

1.2.2.3.1. That they did not *believe his report.* Among those who are nominal Christians, there are many who are true unbelievers. The unbelief of hypocrites is naked and open to the eyes of Christ. He *knew from the beginning* who *believed* and who of the Twelve would betray him (v. 64), which of them were sincere, like Nathanael (1:47), and which were not. It is Christ's prerogative to know the heart (Rev 3:23); he knows who those are who do not believe but make a pretense of their profession. But if we try to judge people's hearts, we step onto Christ's throne. We are often deceived by people and see reason to change our attitudes toward them.

1.2.2.3.2. That the reason why they did not believe his report was that the *arm of the Lord* was not *revealed* (Isa 53:1) to them (v. 65): *Therefore said I unto you that no man can come to me, except it be given unto him of my Father*; here he referred to v. 44. He had said there that no one could *come to him, except the Father draw him*; here he said, *except it be given him of my Father*, which shows that God draws souls by giving them grace and strength, and a heart to come.

1.3. Their final apostasy from Christ: *From that time many of his disciples went back, and walked no more with him* (v. 66). Notice here:

1.3.1. The backsliding of these disciples. They had enrolled in Christ's school, but they went back. They did not merely play truant once; they took leave of him. Many turned back. It is often like this; when some backslide, many backslide with them; the disease is infectious.

1.3.2. The timing of this backsliding: *From that time*, from the time that Christ preached this encouraging message, that he is the bread of life and that those who by faith feed on him will live through him. The corrupt and evil human heart often turns something that is the source of the greatest comfort into an offense. What is the undoubted word and truth of Christ must be faithfully communicated, no matter who may be offended at it. People's attitudes must be captivated by God's word, and not God's word brought down to the level of human attitudes.

1.3.3. The extent of their apostasy: *They walked no more with him*, returned no more to him and were no longer with him in his ministry.

2. This message was *a savour of life unto life* to others (2Co 2:16). Many turned back, but thank God, not all did. Notice here:

2.1. The affectionate question that Christ asked the Twelve (v. 67): *Will you also go away?* He said nothing to those who turned back. Those whom he never truly had were no great loss: "Easy come, easy go." He took advantage of this occasion, however, to speak to the Twelve, to confirm them: *Will you also go away?*

2.1.1. "It is your choice whether you will or will not; if you are going to leave me, then now is the time, when many are doing so." Christ will detain none with him against their wills; his soldiers are volunteers, not conscripts. The Twelve had now had enough time to see how they liked Christ and his message. He allowed them the liberty to withdraw here.

2.1.2. "It is at your peril if you turn back. Those who have just left have not been so intimate with me as you have, nor received as many favors from me; they are gone, but will you also go?" The closer we have been to Christ and the longer we have been with him, and the more blessings we have received from him, the greater our sin will be if we abandon him.

2.1.3. "I have reason to think you will not. *I hope better things of you* (Heb 6:9), because *you are they that have continued with me*" (Lk 22:28). Christ and believers know one another too well to part for every grievance.

2.2. The confident response that Peter, in the name of the others, gave to this question (vv. 68–69). Peter was on all occasions the mouthpiece of the rest, not so much because he had more of his Master's ear than they, but because he was more outspoken, and what he said was sometimes approved and sometimes rebuked (Mt 16:17, 23)—the common fate of those who are quick to speak. Here is:

2.2.1. Their good decision to remain faithful to Christ: "*Lord, to whom shall we go?* No, Lord, we like our choice too much to change." Those who leave Christ would do well to consider to whom they will turn: "*Whither shall we go?* Shall we seek the favor of the world? It will certainly deceive us. Shall we return to sin? It will certainly destroy us. Shall we leave the *fountain of living waters* (Rev 7: 17) for *broken cisterns* (Jer 2:13)?" The disciples decided to continue to pursue life and happiness, and they would remain faithful to Christ as their guide. "If we ever find the way to happiness, it must only be in following you." Let those who find fault with this religion find a better one before they abandon it.

2.2.2. A good reason for this decision. It was not the inconsiderate decision of blind devotion, but the result of mature deliberation. The disciples were determined never to turn away from Christ:

2.2.2.1. Because of the advantages they promised themselves through him: *Thou hast the words of eternal life.* The words of his message showed the way to eternal life and told us what to do in order to inherit it. His having *the words of eternal life* is the same as his having *power to give eternal life*. In the previous message he had assured his followers of eternal life; these disciples focused on this clear teaching and so decided to remain faithful to him, while the others overlooked this, focused on the difficult teaching, and left him. Though we cannot explain every mystery, every obscurity, in Christ's teaching, we know that it is the word of eternal life, and so we must live and die by it.

2.2.2.2. Because of the assurance they had about him (v. 69): *We believe and are sure that thou art that Christ.* Notice:

2.2.2.2.1. The doctrine they believed: that this Jesus was the Messiah promised to the ancestors, not a mere man but the Son of the living God.

2.2.2.2.2. The degree of their faith. It rose to a full assurance: *We are sure.* When we have such a strong faith in the Gospel of Christ as to boldly rest our souls upon it, then, and not until then, will we be willing to risk everything else for it.

2.3. The sad remark our Lord Jesus made on this reply of Peter's (vv. 70–71): *Have not I chosen you twelve, and one of you is a devil?* The Evangelist tells us whom he meant: *he spoke of Judas Iscariot.* Peter had committed them all to be faithful to their Master. Now Christ did not condemn Peter's love—it is always good to hope for the best—but he tacitly corrected his confidence. We must not be too sure concerning anyone. God knows those who are his (2Ti 2:19); we do not. Notice here:

2.3.1. Hypocrites and betrayers of Christ are no better than devils. Judas, whose heart Satan entered (Lk 22:3) and filled, was called a devil.

2.3.2. Many who appear to be saints are really devils. It is strange and a source of amazement; Christ spoke of it with wonder: *Have not I chosen?* It is sad and a fact to be mourned.

2.3.3. However much the disguises of hypocrites may deceive people, they cannot deceive Christ. Christ's divine sight, far better than any second sight, can see spirits.

2.3.4. Some who are chosen by Christ to undertake special services prove false to him: "*I have chosen you, and one of you is a devil.*"

2.3.5. In the most exclusive groups of people on this side of heaven it is nothing new to meet with those who are corrupt. Of the Twelve who were chosen for intimate fellowship with an incarnate Deity, one was an incarnate devil. The writer emphasizes this, that Judas was *one of the twelve* (v. 71) who were so honored and dignified. Yet let us not reject the Twelve because one of them is a devil. There is a society within the veil (Heb 6:19) into which nothing unclean will enter (Rev 21:27).

CHAPTER 7

We have here: 1. Christ's declining to appear publicly in Judea for some time (v. 1). 2. His intention to go to Jerusalem to the Feast of Tabernacles, and his conversation with his relatives in Galilee about his going to this feast (vv. 2–13). 3. His preaching publicly in the temple at that feast. 3.1. In the middle of the feast (vv. 14–15). We have his talk with the Jews concerning: 3.1.1. His teaching (vv. 16–18). 3.1.2. The accusation of Sabbath-breaking that was brought against him (vv. 19–24). 3.1.3. Himself, both where he came from and where he was going (vv. 25–36). 3.2. On the last day of the feast: 3.2.1. His gracious invitation to poor souls to come to him (vv. 37–39). 3.2.2. The reception that it met: 3.2.2.1. Many of the people argued about it (vv. 40–44). 3.2.2.2. The chief priests wanted to get him in trouble over it (vv. 45–49) but were silenced by one of their own court (vv. 50–53).

Verses 1–13

We have here:

1. The reason given why Christ spent more of his time in Galilee than in Judea (v. 1): *because the Jews*, the people in Judea and Jerusalem, were waiting to kill him for healing the disabled man on the Sabbath (5:16). It is not said, "he dared not *walk in Jewry* (Judea)," but, "he *would not walk in Jewry*; it was not through fear and cowardice that he declined it, but out of wisdom, because his time had not yet come. Notice:

1.1. Christ will withdraw from those who drive him away from them.

1.2. In times when danger is near, it is not only allowable but also advisable to withdraw and choose the benefit of those places that are least dangerous (Mt 10:23).

1.3. If the providence of God drives people of merit into places of obscurity and insignificance, it must not be thought strange; it was the fate of our Master himself. Yet he did not sit still in Galilee, but walked; he went about doing good (Ac 10:38). When we cannot do what we want to do where we want to do it, we must do what we can where we can.

2. The approach of the Feast of Tabernacles (v. 2), one of the three ceremonies that called for the personal attendance of all the males at Jerusalem. It was still religiously observed. Divine institutions never go out of date by length of time; similarly, desert mercies must never be forgotten.

3. Christ's talk with his *brothers*. They intervened to advise him what to do. Notice:

3.1. Their ambition and boasting in urging him to make a more public appearance than he did: *Depart hence*, they said, *and go into Judea* (v. 3).

3.1.1. They gave two reasons for this advice:

3.1.1.1. That it would be an encouragement to those in and around Jerusalem. These brothers of our Lord wanted to have the disciples there supported particularly, and they thought the time he spent among his Galilean disciples

was wasted. They also thought that his miracles were useless unless the people at Jerusalem saw them.

3.1.1.2. That it would be for the advancement of his name. *There is no man that does anything in secret* (v. 4) if he seeks to be known openly. They assumed that Christ sought to make himself known: "If you do these things, if you are so able to gain applause, go farther afield and show yourself to the world. It is high time to think of becoming famous."

3.1.2. The Evangelist notes that it is evidence of their unfaithfulness: *For neither did his brethren believe in him* (v. 5). Those who hear his word and keep it are the family he values (Lk 8:21; Jas 1:22). There were those who were related to Christ naturally who believed in him, but there were also others who did not believe in him.

3.1.3. What was wrong in the advice they gave him?

3.1.3.1. In distrusting his ability to guide himself, they showed that they did not believe he could guide them.

3.1.3.2. They showed great carelessness about his safety when they suggested that he go to Judea, where they knew the Jews were trying to kill him.

3.1.3.3. Perhaps they were tired of his company in Galilee and this was, in effect, a desire that he would leave there vicinity.

3.1.3.4. They tacitly reproached him as lacking in self-confidence, that he dared not trust himself on the public stage, which he would do if he had any courage and greatness of soul, rather than sneak away in a corner.

3.1.3.5. They seemed to question the truth of the miracles he performed by saying, "If you really do these things, if they will bear the test of public scrutiny in the higher courts, then produce them there."

3.1.3.6. They thought Christ was altogether like themselves (Ps 50:21), as desirous as they were of making a good outward impression.

3.1.3.7. Self lay at the root of it all; if he would only make himself as great as he could, they, being his relatives, would share in his honor. Many go to public ceremonies only to show themselves, and their whole concern is to make a good appearance.

3.2. The wisdom and humility of our Lord Jesus (vv. 6–8). Although his brothers' advice contained so many corrupt insinuations, he answered them mildly. We should learn from our Master to reply with humility, and even where it is easy to find much that is wrong, we should seem not to see it and should ignore the disrespect.

3.2.1. He showed the difference between himself and them, in two things:

3.2.1.1. His time was set; theirs was not: *My time is not yet come, but your time is always ready.* Those who live useless lives have their time always ready; they can go and come when they please. But those whose time is filled up with duty will often find themselves restricted and lacking the time for what others can do at any time. The restriction of hard work is a thousand times better than the liberty of idleness. We, who are ignorant and shortsighted, tend to give him orders. The present time is our time, but he is best to judge the right time, and maybe *his time is not yet come*. Therefore, wait with patience for his time.

3.2.1.2. His life was sought, but theirs was not (v. 7). When they showed themselves to the world, they did not make themselves vulnerable: "*The world cannot hate you*, for you are *of the world*." See 15:19. The world, which lies in wickedness, cannot hate unholy souls, whom the holy God cannot love, but when Christ showed himself to the world, he laid himself open to the greatest danger, for *me it hateth*. Christ was not only shown great disrespect but hated. But why did the world hate Christ? "Because," he said, "*I testify of it, that the works of it are evil.*"

3.2.1.2.*1*. The works of an evil world are evil works; as the tree is, so are its fruits (Mt 7:16, 20).

3.2.1.2.*2*. It causes the world great uneasiness and offense to be convicted of the evil of its works.

3.2.1.2.*3*. Whatever is claimed, the real cause of the world's enmity toward the Gospel is the testimony the Gospel gives against sin and sinners. It is better to incur the world's hatred by testifying against its evil than to gain its goodwill by going along with its tide.

3.2.2. He dismissed them, with the intention of staying behind for some time in Galilee (v. 8): *Go you up to this feast; I go not up yet.* He allowed them to go to the feast, but he denied them his company. Those who go to religious celebrations to show off or to serve some worldly purpose go without Christ and will be rewarded accordingly. If the presence of Christ does not go with us, why should we go up (Ex 33:14–15)? When we are going to or coming from sacred services of worship, we should be careful what company we keep, so that the fires of good feelings may not be quenched by corrupt company. *I go not up yet to this feast*; he did not say, "I am not going at all," but "not yet." The reason he gave was, *My time is not yet fully come.*

3.3. Christ's continuing to stay in Galilee until the right time had come (v. 9). In saying these things to them, he *abode still in Galilee.* He would not depart from his own purpose. It is good for the followers of Christ to be stable and not make decisions lightly (2Co 1:17).

3.4. His going to the feast when his time had come. Notice:

3.4.1. When he went: *When his brethren were gone up.* He went up after them. His natural brothers went up first, and then he went. The question will not be, "Who comes first?" but, "Who comes fittest?" If we bring our hearts with us, it does not matter who gets there before us.

3.4.2. How he went, as if he were hiding himself: *not openly, but as it were in secret.* Provided the work of God is done effectively, it is best done when it is done with least fuss. We can do the work of God privately and yet not do it deceitfully.

3.5. The great expectation there was of him among the Jews at Jerusalem (v. 11–14).

3.5.1. They could not help thinking about him (v. 11): *The Jews sought him at the feast, and said, Where is he?* They did not think it worthwhile to go to him in Galilee, but they hoped the feast would bring him to Jerusalem, and then they would see him. If an opportunity to get to know Christ came to their door, they liked it well enough. Those who want to see Christ at a feast must seek him there. Perhaps it was his enemies who were waiting for an opportunity to seize him. They said, *Where is he?* It could be translated, "Where is that fellow?" This is how scornfully and contemptibly they spoke about him. When they should have welcomed the feast as an opportunity to serve God, they were glad to have it as an opportunity to persecute Christ.

3.5.2. The people differed much in their attitudes toward him (v. 12): *There was much murmuring,* or rather whispering, *among the people concerning him.* The rulers' enmity against Christ caused him to be all the more talked about. In this way, the Gospel of Christ has gained ground by the opposition raised against it. By being *every where spoken against* (Ac 28:22), it has come to be everywhere spoken about, and this has been the means of spreading it further. This whispering was not against Christ, but about him: some grumbled about the rulers because they did not support and encourage him; others grumbled about them because they did not silence and restrain him. Christ and his religion have been and will be the subject of much controversy and debate (Lk 12:51–52). The noise and encounter of liberty and business are surely preferable to the silence and conformity of a prison.

3.5.2.1. Some said, *He is a good man.* This was true, but it came far short of the whole truth. He was the Son of God. Many who have no wrong thoughts of Christ still have low thoughts of him; they do not say enough. It was to his honor, however, that even those who refused to believe he was the Messiah had to acknowledge he was a good man.

3.5.2.2. Others said, *Nay, but he deceiveth the people.* If this had been true, he would have had to be a very bad man. Yet it must be assumed, they thought, that there was some undiscovered deception at the root of his teaching and miracles, because the chief priests were anxious to oppose him.

3.5.2.3. Their superiors made them afraid to speak much about him (v. 13): *No man spoke openly of him, for fear of the Jews.* Either they dared not speak well of him openly, or they dared not speak at all about him openly. Because nothing could justly be said against him, they would not allow anything at all to be said about him.

Verses 14–36

Here is:

1. Christ's public preaching in the temple (v. 14): he *went up into the temple, and taught.* His sermon is not recorded, but what is significant here is that it was *about the midst of the feast,* the Feast of Tabernacles (v. 2). Yet why did he not go to the temple to preach sooner?

1.1. Because the people would have more opportunity to hear him when they had spent some days in their booths, as they did at this feast.

1.2. Because he chose to appear when both his friends and his enemies had stopped looking for him. But why did he appear so publicly now? Surely it was to shame his persecutors, by showing that he did not fear them and by taking their work out of their hands. Their work was to teach the people in the temple, but they taught human commandments, and so he went to the temple and taught the people.

2. His talk with the Jews, which may be discussed under three headings:

2.1. His teaching. Notice:

2.1.1. How the Jews were amazed at it (v. 15): *They marvelled,* saying, *How knoweth this man letters, having never learned* (how did this man get such learning without having studied)*?* Notice here:

2.1.1.1. Our Lord Jesus was not educated in the schools of the prophets or at the feet of the rabbis. Having received the Spirit without measure (3:34), he did not need to receive any knowledge either from human beings or through them.

2.1.1.2. Christ had learning even though he had never studied. Christ's ministers must have learning, and since they cannot expect to acquire it by inspiration, they must make an effort to get it in the ordinary way.

2.1.1.3. Because Christ had learning even though he had not been taught it, he became truly great and wonderful. Some of the Jews probably honored him for his learning. Others probably mentioned it in disparagement and to show their contempt of him: whatever he seemed to have, he could not really have any true learning, because he never went to university and never took a degree. Some perhaps suggested that he had gained his learning by magic. Since they did not know how he could have become a scholar, they thought he was a conjurer.

2.1.2. The three things he asserted about it:

2.1.2.1. That his doctrine was divine (v. 16): *My doctrine is not mine, but his that sent me.* They took offense because he undertook to teach even though he had never studied, in answer to which he told them that his teaching was a kind that could not be learned. It was a divine revelation. "*My doctrine is not mine,* but *his that* (that of him who) *sent me;* it does not center on me, nor lead ultimately to me, but to the One who sent me."

2.1.2.2. That the most competent judges were those who had a sincere and upright heart and desired and sought to do the will of God (v. 17): *If any man be willing to do the will of God, he shall know of the doctrine whether it be of God or whether I speak of myself.* Notice here:

2.1.2.2.1. What the question about the teaching of Christ is: *whether it be of God* or not. Christ himself was willing to have his teaching scrutinized, and much more should his ministers be willing.

2.1.2.2.2. Who is likely to succeed in this search: those who *do the will of God*, at least want to do it. Notice:

2.1.2.2.2.1. Who they are who *will do the will of God*: those who have decided that by the grace of God they will conform to the will of God once they know what that will is.

2.1.2.2.2.2. How it is that such a person will know the truth of Christ's teaching. Christ has promised to give knowledge to such people; he has said, *He shall know.* Those who apply the light they have will be kept by divine grace. Those who are inclined to submit to the rules of the divine law are disposed to accept the rays of divine light.

2.1.2.3. That this showed that Christ, as a teacher, did not *speak of himself* (v. 18).

2.1.2.3.1. Notice here the character of a deceiver: he *seeketh his own glory*, which is a sign that he *speaks of himself.* Here is the description of deceivers: what they say comes from themselves; they have received no commission or instructions from God. They have no authority but their own will, no inspiration but their own imagination. They are concerned only with their own glory; self-seekers are self-speakers. Those who speak from God will speak for God and for his glory.

2.1.2.3.2. Notice the opposite characterization Christ gave of himself and his teaching: *He that seeks his glory* (the glory of him) *that sent him, he is true.*

2.1.2.3.2.1. Christ was sent by God. Those teachers, and only those, who are sent by God are to be received and welcomed by us.

2.1.2.3.2.2. He sought the glory of God. It was both the subject of his teaching and the theme of his whole life to glorify God.

2.1.2.3.2.3. This was a proof that he was true. False teachers are most unrighteous; they are unjust toward God, whose name they abuse, and they are also unjust to the souls of the people they deceive. However, Christ made it clear that he was true, that he was really what he said he was.

2.2. The crime that he was accused of for healing the disabled man and telling him to carry his mat on the Sabbath.

2.2.1. He argued against them by way of recrimination (v. 19). How could they be so shameful as to criticize him for breaking the Law of Moses when they themselves disobeyed it so notoriously? *Did not Moses give you the law?* But they were so evil that none of them kept the law. Their neglect of the law was universal: *None of you keepeth* it. They boasted about the Law and pretended to

be zealous toward it, but none of them kept it. It is like those who say that it is good to go to church, but they themselves never go to church. This emphasized their evil in persecuting Christ: "*None of you keepeth the law.* Why then do you try to put me to death for not keeping it?" Those who are most at fault themselves are often most critical of others. Those who support themselves and their interests by persecution and violence, whatever they claim, do not keep the law of God. Here the people rudely interrupted him (v. 20): *Thou hast a devil; who goes about to kill thee?* This shows the good opinion they had of their rulers, who, they thought, would never attempt such an atrocious act as to kill him. It also shows the bad opinion they had of our Lord Jesus: "*Thou hast a devil;* you are possessed with a lying spirit, and your making this accusation shows that you are a bad man," according to some; or rather, "You are miserable and weak; you are afraid without cause." Not only open rage but also silent depression were then commonly attributed to the power of Satan. "You are crazy; you are insane." Let us not think it strange if the best people are described in the worst terms. Those who want to be like Christ must put up with insults; they must pay no attention to them, much less be angry with them, and least of all take revenge for them.

2.2.2. He argued by way of appeal and vindication.

2.2.2.1. He appealed to their own response to this miracle: "*I have done one work, and you all marvel* (v. 21). You have to be astonished at its greatness."

2.2.2.2. He appealed to their own practice in other situations: "*I have done one work* on the Sabbath, and you all are amazed, and you make a fuss of it, that a religious man should dare do such a thing. If it is lawful for you, indeed your duty—as no doubt it is—to circumcise a child on the Sabbath, it was much more lawful and good for me to heal a diseased man on that day." Notice:

2.2.2.2.1. The rise and origin of circumcision: *Moses gave you circumcision.* Circumcision was said to have *been given* (v. 22), and (v. 23) they were said to have *received* it. The laws of God, especially those that are seals of the covenant, are *gifts given to men* (Ps 68:18; Eph 4:8) and are to be received as such. Note that although it is said that Moses gave circumcision to them, really Moses did not give it to them; God did. In fact, it did not even come from Moses, but from *the fathers* (the patriarchs) (v. 22). It was ordained long before, for it was a seal of the righteousness of faith and was part of the blessing of Abraham that was to come on the Gentiles (Gal 3:14).

2.2.2.2.2. The greater respect paid to the law of circumcision than to that of the Sabbath. If a child was born one Sabbath, it was without fail circumcised on the next.

2.2.2.2.3. The conclusion Christ drew in justification of himself (v. 23): "*A man on the sabbath day receives circumcision, that the law of circumcision might not be broken.* Now, if you allow this, how unreasonable you are when you are *angry with me because I have made a man every whit whole* (healed a whole man) *on the sabbath day!*" The word translated *angry* refers to a spiteful anger, anger with gall. It is absurd and unreasonable of us to condemn others for something in which we justify ourselves. Notice the comparison Christ made here between their circumcising a child and his healing a man on the Sabbath.

2.2.2.2.3.1. Circumcision was only a ceremonial institution, but what Christ did was a good work by the law of nature.

2.2.2.2.3.2. Circumcision was painful, but what Christ did made whole.

2.2.2.2.3.3. When they had circumcised a child, their concern was to heal only the part that was circumcised, and so the child might be healed of that wound but still be unwell in other ways, whereas Christ had made this man *every whit whole.* "I have made the whole man healthy and sound." The whole body was healed. In fact, Christ healed not only his body but also his soul, by that warning, *Go, and sin no more,* and so he really did make the whole man sound. He concluded this argument with the rule (v. 24), *Judge not according to the appearance, but judge righteous judgment.* This may be applied either:

2.2.2.2.3.3.1. In particular, to this work. "Do not show partiality in your judgment." It may also be translated, "Do not judge according to face." Or:

2.2.2.2.3.3.2. In general, to Christ's person and preaching, which the Jews took offense at. Those things that are false commonly appear best when they are judged *according to the outward appearance* (1Sa 16:7): they appear most plausible at first glance. It was this that gained the Pharisees such an influence and reputation, that they appeared right to other people (Mt 23:27–28), and people judged them by outward appearance. "But," Christ said, "do not be too confident that all who appear to be saints are real saints." Those who judged whether he was the Son of God or not by his outward appearance were unlikely to judge correctly. If a divine power accompanied him, God testified to him, and the Scriptures were fulfilled in him, they should still receive him, judging by faith, not by the sight (2Co 5:7). We must not judge anyone merely by their outward appearance, not by their titles, by whether they look important in the world, or by their fluttering showiness, but by their intrinsic value and by the gifts and graces of God's Spirit in them.

2.3. Himself, where he came from and where he was going (vv. 25–36).

2.3.1. Where he came from (vv. 25–31). Notice:

2.3.1.1. The objection raised against this by some of the residents of Jerusalem, who seem to have been more prejudiced against him than others (v. 25). Our Lord Jesus has often met with the least welcome from those whom one would have expected the best from. It was not without some just reason that it became proverbial, "The nearer the church, the further from God." These people of Jerusalem showed their hatred toward Christ:

2.3.1.1.1. By complaining about their rulers because they did not arrest Christ: "*Is not this he whom they seek to kill?* Then why don't they do it? See, *he speaketh boldly,* and *they say nothing to him;* do *the rulers know indeed that this is the very Christ?*" (v. 26). Here they slyly and maliciously insinuated two things to enrage the rulers against Christ:

2.3.1.1.1.1. That by turning a blind eye to his preaching they brought their authority into contempt. "If our rulers will allow themselves to be trampled on in this way, they have only themselves to blame if no one stands in awe of them." The worst persecutions have often been carried on in the name of giving the necessary support to authority and government.

2.3.1.1.1.2. That in so doing they brought their judgment into suspicion. *Do they know that this is the Christ?* It is spoken ironically: "How did they come to change their mind?" When religion and the profession of Christ's name are unfashionable and have a poor reputation, many people are strongly tempted to persecute and oppose them, only so that they may not be thought to favor them and be well disposed toward them. It was strange that the rulers who were enraged in this way did not seize Christ, but his

hour had not yet come, and God can tie people's hands in wonder even when he will not turn their hearts.

2.3.1.1.2. By their objection to the claim that he was the Christ, in which appeared more venom than substance (v. 27). "We have the argument against it, that *we know this man, whence he is,* but *when Christ comes, no man knows whence he is.*" They despised him because they knew where he came from. Familiarity breeds contempt, and we tend to have no use for a leader whose origin we know. Christ's own people did not receive him, because he was one of their own, whereas that should rather have been a reason for them to love him.

2.3.1.2. Christ's answer to this objection (vv. 28–29).

2.3.1.2.1. He spoke freely and boldly; he *cried in the temple as he taught,* to express his fervency, being *grieved for the hardness of their hearts* (Mk 3:5). It is possible to be vehement in contending for the truth without immoderate heat or passion. It is possible to instruct with passion but also with humility those who contradict our message. Whoever has ears to hear, let them hear this (Mt 11:15).

2.3.1.2.2. His answer to their objection was:

2.3.1.2.2.1. By way of allowance: "*You both know me, and you know whence I am.* You know me — you think you know me; but you are mistaken; you take me to be the carpenter's son, born at Nazareth, but it is not so."

2.3.1.2.2.2. By way of negation, denying that what they did see in him and know about him was all that was to be known. He was going to tell them what they did not know, from whom he came:

2.3.1.2.2.2.1. He did *not come of himself.*

2.3.1.2.2.2.2. He had been sent by his Father; this is mentioned twice.

2.3.1.2.2.2.3. He *was* from his Father: *I am from him.* He was from him by essential emanation, as the rays come from the sun.

2.3.1.2.2.2.4. The Father *who sent him is true;* he had promised to give the Messiah. The One who made the promise is true and has fulfilled it. He is true and will fulfill the promise in the calling of the Gentiles.

2.3.1.2.2.2.5. These unfaithful Jews did not know the Father: *He that sent me, whom you know not.* There is much ignorance of God even with many who have *a form of knowledge* (Ro 2:20), and the true reason why people reject Christ is that they do not know God. Our Lord Jesus knew intimately the Father who sent him: *but I know him.* He was not in the slightest doubt about his mission from him, nor was he at all in the dark about the work he had to do.

2.3.1.3. The offense this gave his enemies (v. 30). *They sought to take him,* but nobody touched him, *because his hour was not yet come.* This shows us:

2.3.1.3.1. God has evildoers on a chain. The hatred of persecutors is impotent even when it is most impetuous, and when Satan fills their hearts, God still ties their hands.

2.3.1.3.2. God's servants are sometimes wonderfully protected by means that cannot be discerned or explained.

2.3.1.3.3. Christ had *his hour* set. All his people and all his ministers have this. Nor can all the powers of hell and earth overcome them until they have *finished their testimony* (Rev 11:7).

2.3.1.4. The good effect Christ's words had on some of his hearers (v. 31): *Many of the people believed on him.* Even where the Gospel meets opposition, a great deal of good may still be done there (1Th 2:2). Notice:

2.3.1.4.1. Who believed: not a few, but many, more than one would have expected when the tide was flowing so strongly in the opposite direction. But these *many* were *of the people*. We must not measure the prosperity of the Gospel by its success among the powerful people, nor must ministers say that they are working in vain, even if none but the poor receive the Gospel (1Co 1:26).

2.3.1.4.2. What persuaded them to believe: the *miracles which he did*.

2.3.1.4.3. How weak their faith was: they did not positively assert, as the Samaritans did, *This is indeed the Christ*; they only argued, *When Christ comes, will he do more miracles than these?* "Why can't this be the One?" They believed it but did not have the courage to confess it. Even weak faith may be true faith and therefore be accepted as such by the Lord Jesus.

2.3.2. Where he was going (vv. 32–36). Notice:

2.3.2.1. The plans of the Pharisees and chief priests to arrest him (v. 32).

2.3.2.1.1. What provoked them was that they had been brought information by their spies to the effect that *the people murmured such things concerning him*, that there were many who respected and esteemed him. Although the people only whispered these things, the Pharisees were still angry at it. The Pharisees were aware that if Christ was increasing, their influence would inevitably decrease.

2.3.2.1.2. The plan they then had was to seize Jesus and take him into custody: *They sent officers to take him*. The most effective way to disperse the flock is to *smite the shepherd* (Mt 26:31). The Pharisees as such had no power, and so they got the chief priests to join them. *As the world by wisdom knew not God* (1Co 1:21), so the Jewish church by their wisdom did not know Christ.

2.3.2.2. The words of our Lord Jesus that he then spoke (vv. 33–34): "*Yet a little while I am with you, and then I go to him that sent me*; *you shall seek me, and shall not find me, and where I am, you cannot come*." These words, like the pillar of cloud and fire, had a bright side and a dark side (Ex 14:20).

2.3.2.2.1. They had a bright side toward our Lord Jesus himself. Christ here comforted himself with three things:

2.3.2.2.1.1. That he had only a short time to remain here in this troubled world. His warfare would soon be completed (Isa 40:2). Whoever we are with in this world, friends or foes, we will be with them only for a little while. We must remain for a while with those who are *pricking briars and grieving thorns* (Eze 28:24), but, thank God, it is only a short time, and we will soon be out of their reach.

2.3.2.2.1.2. That he would *go to him that sent him*. "When I have completed my work with you, then — and not until then — I will go to the One who sent me." Let those who suffer for Christ comfort themselves with the knowledge that they have a God to go to and that they are going quickly to him, to be with him forever.

2.3.2.2.1.3. That none of their persecutions could follow him to heaven: *You shall seek me, and shall not find me*. It adds to the happiness of glorified saints that they are out of reach of the Devil and all his evil instruments.

2.3.2.2.2. These words had a black and dark side toward those who hated and persecuted Christ. They now longed to get rid of him, but let them know:

2.3.2.2.2.1. That their condemnation would be according to their choice. He would not trouble them for long; in a little while he would leave them. Those who are weary of Christ need nothing more to make them miserable than to have their wishes fulfilled.

2.3.2.2.2.2. That they would certainly repent of their choice when it was too late.

2.3.2.2.2.2.1. They would seek the presence of the Messiah in vain: *You shall seek me, and shall not find me*. Those who seek Christ now will find him, but the day is coming when those who now refuse him *shall seek him, and shall not find him*.

2.3.2.2.2.2.2. They would expect a place in heaven in vain: "*Where I am*, and where all believers will be with me, *thither* (there) *ye cannot come*." They would be rendered unable by their own sin and unfaithfulness: "*You cannot come* because you will not." Heaven would be no heaven to them.

2.3.2.3. Their comments on these words (vv. 35–36): *They said among themselves, Whither will he go?* (Where does he intend to go?). Notice:

2.3.2.3.1. Their willful ignorance and blindness. He had explicitly said where he would go — to the One who sent him, to his Father in heaven; but they asked, *Whither will he go?* and, *What manner of saying is this?*

2.3.2.3.2. Their daring contempt of Christ's threats. Instead of trembling at that terrible word, *You shall seek me, and not find me*, they laughed at it and made fun of it.

2.3.2.3.3. Their hardened hatred and rage against Christ. All they dreaded in his departure was that he would be out of reach of their power: *Whither will he go, that we shall not find him?*

2.3.2.3.4. Their proud contempt for the Gentiles, whom they call the *dispersed of the Gentiles*. Would he seek their favor? "Will he go and *teach the Gentiles*? Will he take his message to them?" It is very common for those who have lost the power of religion to seek very jealously to monopolize the name. His enemies now made a joke of his going to teach the Gentiles, but not long after this he taught them in earnest through his apostles and ministers.

Verses 37–44

In these verses we have:

1. Christ's message and its explanation (vv. 37–39). These are probably only short hints of what he spoke on at some length, but they have in them the substance of the whole Gospel; here is a Gospel invitation to come to Christ and a Gospel promise of comfort and happiness in him. Notice:

1.1. When he gave this invitation: *On the last day* of the Feast of Tabernacles, *that great day*. Many people had gathered together, and if the invitation was given to many people, it might be hoped that some would accept it (Pr 1:20). The people were now returning to their homes, and he wanted to give them something to take away with them as his parting word. When a great congregation are about to go to their own homes, it is moving to think that they will probably never all come together again in this world, and so, if we can say or do anything to help them to go to heaven, then this must be the time. It is good to be dynamic at the end of a service of worship. Christ made this offer on the last day of the feast. He would speak to them once more, and if they would now hear his voice (Ps 95:7; Heb 3:7, 15; 4:7), they would live. It would be half a year before the next feast, and in that time many of them would die. *Behold, now is the accepted time* (2Co 6:2).

1.2. How he gave this invitation: *Jesus stood and cried*, which showed:

1.2.1. His great fervency and boldness. Love for souls will make preachers dynamic.

1.2.2. His desire that everyone would take notice and accept this invitation. He *stood* and *cried*, so that he could be heard better. The pagan oracles were delivered in secret by those who *peeped and muttered* (Isa 8:19), but the oracles of the Gospel were declared by One who stood and spoke in a loud voice.

1.3. The invitation itself, which is very general: *If any man is thirsty, whoever he is, he is invited to Christ.* It is also very gracious: *"If any man thirst, let him come to me and drink.* If anyone wants to be truly and eternally happy, let him turn to me."

1.3.1. The people invited were those who *thirsted,* which may be understood as referring to either:

1.3.1.1. Their needs, either as to their outer condition— let their poverty and suffering draw them to Christ for the peace that the world can neither give nor take away—or as to their inner state: "If anyone lacks spiritual blessings, they will be supplied by me." Or:

1.3.1.2. The inclination of their souls and their desire for spiritual happiness. *If any man* hungers and *thirsts* for righteousness (Mt 5:6).

1.3.2. The invitation itself: *Let him come to me.* Let him go to Christ as the fountain of living waters.

1.3.3. The satisfaction promised: "Let him come *and drink*; he will have what will not only refresh but also replenish.

1.4. A gracious promise attached to this gracious call (v. 38): *He that believeth on me, out of his belly shall flow rivers of living water.* Notice here:

1.4.1. What it means to come to Christ: it is to believe on him *as the scripture hath said.* We must not construct a Christ according to our imagination, but believe in a Christ according to the Scripture.

1.4.2. How thirsty souls who come to Christ will be made to drink. Israel drank from the rock that followed them (1Co 10:4); believers drink from a rock in them, *Christ in them* (Col 1:27). Provision is made not only for their present satisfaction but also for their continual comfort forever. Here we read of:

1.4.2.1. *Living water,* running water, which the Hebrew calls *living* because it is continually moving. The graces and comforts of the Spirit are compared to *living water.*

1.4.2.2. *Rivers* of living water. The comfort flows both plentifully and constantly, like a river, and is therefore strong enough to overcome the opposition of doubts and fears.

1.4.2.3. Rivers flowing from the believer's *belly,* that is, their heart or soul. There springs of grace are planted, and out of the heart, in which the Spirit lives, flow the *issues of life* (Pr 4:23). Where there are springs of grace and comfort in the soul, they will send forth streams. Grace and comfort will be revealed. A holy heart will be seen in a holy life; a tree is known by its fruits, and the fountain is known by its streams. Those from whom such rivers flow will give themselves for the good of others; a good person is a source of good to many.

1.5. The words *as the scripture hath said,* which seem to refer to some promise in the Old Testament to this effect, and there are many. It was a custom of the Jews, accepted by tradition, to conduct on the last day of the Feast of Tabernacles a ceremony called "the pouring out of water." They took a golden jug of water from the pool of Siloam, brought it into the temple with the sound of a trumpet and other ceremonies, and, having ascended the altar, poured it out before the Lord with every possible expression of joy. It is also thought that our Savior might have been alluding to this custom here. Believers will have the comfort not of a jug of water taken from a pool but of a river flowing from themselves.

1.6. The Evangelist's explanation of this promise (v. 39): *This spoke he of the Spirit,* of the gifts, graces, and comforts of the Spirit. Notice:

1.6.1. It is promised to *all that believe* on Christ that they will *receive the Holy Spirit.* Some received his miraculous gifts (Mk 16:17–18); all receive his sanctifying graces.

1.6.2. The Spirit living and working in believers is like *a fountain of living,* running *water,* from which plentiful streams flow, cooling and cleansing as water, calming and moistening as water, making them fruitful, and others joyful.

1.6.3. This plentiful outpouring of the Spirit was still the matter of a promise, for *the Holy Spirit was not yet given, because Jesus was not yet glorified.* Notice here:

1.6.3.1. It was certain that he would be glorified, but he was still in a state of humiliation and contempt. If Christ must wait for his glory, let us not think it too much to wait for ours.

1.6.3.2. *The Holy Spirit was not yet given.* If we compare the clear knowledge and strong grace that the disciples of Christ themselves had after the day of Pentecost with their confusion and weakness before, we will understand in what sense the Holy Spirit had not yet been given; the promise and firstfruits of the Spirit were given, but the full harvest had not yet come. The Holy Spirit had not yet been given in such rivers of living water as would flow out to water the whole earth (Ge 2:10; Isa 55:10), including the Gentile world.

1.6.3.3. The reason why *the Holy Spirit was not given* was that *Jesus was not yet glorified.* The death of Christ is sometimes called his glorification (13:31), because in his cross he conquered and triumphed. The gift of the Holy Spirit was purchased by the blood of Christ: till this price was paid, the Holy Spirit was not given. There was not as much need of the Spirit while Christ himself was here on earth as there was when he was gone. Although the Holy Spirit had not yet been given, he was promised. Although the gifts of Christ's grace are delayed for a long time, nevertheless, as long as we are waiting for the fulfillment of the promise, we have the promise to live on.

2. The effects of this message. In general, it led to disagreements: *There was a division among the people because of him* (v. 43). There were various opinions, which people argued with passion; there were various attitudes, and those put people in conflict with one another. Do we think that Christ came to send peace? No; the effect of preaching of his Gospel would be division (Lk 12:51), because while some are drawn together for it, others will be drawn together against it. This is no more the fault of the Gospel than it is the fault of a wholesome medicine that it stirs up the unhealthy influences in the body in order to get rid of them.

2.1. Some were captivated by him: *Many of the people, when they heard this saying,* could not help thinking highly of him. Some of them said, *Of a truth this is the prophet,* the herald and forerunner of the Messiah. Others went further and said, *This is the Christ* (v. 41), the Messiah himself. We do not find that these people became his disciples and followers. A good opinion of Christ comes far short of a living faith in Christ; many speak a good word for Christ but nothing more.

2.2. Others were prejudiced against him. No sooner was this great truth stated—that Jesus *is the Christ*—than it was immediately contradicted and argued against. That his origin was, as they assumed, in Galilee was thought enough to answer all the arguments for his being the Christ. For, *shall Christ come out of Galilee?* Has not *the scripture said that Christ comes of the seed of David?* Notice here:

2.2.1. A commendable knowledge of Scripture. Even the common people knew this from the traditional explanations that their teachers of the law gave them. Many who embrace some corrupt ideas seem to be very familiar with the Scriptures, but in reality they know little more than those Scriptures they have been taught to corrupt.

2.2.2. A blameworthy ignorance of our Lord Jesus. They spoke of it as certain and beyond dispute that *Jesus was of Galilee*, whereas by asking they could have known that he was the Son of David and a native of Bethlehem.

2.3. Others were infuriated with him and *would have taken* (wanted to seize) *him* (v. 44). Although what he said was most sweet and gracious, they were still angry with him for it. They would have taken him, *but no one laid hands on him*, because his hour had not yet come. Just as the hatred of Christ's enemies is always unreasonable, so also its suspicion is sometimes inexplicable.

Verses 45–53

The chief priests and Pharisees were here conspiring as to how they could suppress Christ. Even though this was the *great day of the feast*, they were not present at the religious services of the day. They sat in the council chamber, expecting Christ to be brought in to them as a prisoner, since they had issued warrants to seize him (v. 32). We are told here:

1. What happened between them and their own officers, who returned without him.

1.1. The rebuke they gave the officers for not executing the warrant they had given them: *Why have you not brought him?* The leaders were troubled that those who derived their employment from them would disappoint them in this way.

1.2. The reason the officers gave: *Never man spoke like this man* (v. 46).

1.2.1. This was a very great truth, that *never any man spoke* with the wisdom, power, and grace, with that convincing clarity and that charming sweetness, with which Christ spoke.

1.2.2. Even the officers who were sent to seize him were captivated by him and acknowledged this. They simply had to prefer him to all those who sat in Moses' seat (Mt 23:2). And so Christ was preserved by the power God has on the consciences even of evildoers.

1.2.3. They said this to their lords and masters, who could not bear to hear anything that tended to honor Christ but who could not avoid hearing this. Their own officers, who could not be suspected of being biased in favor of Christ, were witnesses against them.

1.3. The Pharisees' attempt to secure their influence over their officers and to create in them a prejudice against Christ. They suggested that if the officers embraced the Gospel of Christ:

1.3.1. They would deceive themselves (v. 47): *Are you also deceived?* From its very beginning Christianity has been represented to the world as a great deception, and those who embraced it as people who are deceived, whereas they who were beginning to be undeceived. Notice what a compliment the Pharisees paid to these officers: "*Are you also deceived?* What! Men with your sense?" They tried to make them prejudiced against Christ by persuading them to have a high opinion of themselves.

1.3.2. They would devalue themselves. Most people, even in religious matters, are willing to be ruled by the example of those of the first rank; these officers, therefore, were asked to consider:

1.3.2.1. That if they became disciples of Christ, they would be going against people of high quality and reputation: *Have any of the rulers, or of the Pharisees, believed on him?* Some of the rulers accepted Christ (4:53; Mt 9:18), and more believed in him but lacked the courage to confess him (12:42), but when the influence of Christ is running low in this world, it is common for its adversaries to represent it as lower than it really is. The cause of Christ rarely has rulers and Pharisees on its side. Self-denial and the cross are hard lessons for rulers and Pharisees. Many people have been confirmed in their prejudice against Christ because the rulers and Pharisees have not been friends to him and it. If rulers and Pharisees do not believe in Christ, those who do believe in him will be the most unusual, unfashionable, unrefined people in the world. By thinking in this way, some people are foolishly willing to be condemned purely for the sake of fashion.

1.3.2.2. That they would align themselves with the contemptible, common sort of people (v. 43): *But this people, who know not the law, are cursed.* Notice:

1.3.2.2.1. How scornfully and disdainfully they spoke of them: *This people.* Just as the wisdom of God has often chosen corrupt things and things that are despised (1Co 1:28), so human foolishness has often corrupted and despised those whom God has chosen.

1.3.2.2.2. How unjustly they criticized them: *They know not the law.* Perhaps many of those whom they despised in this way knew the Law, and the Prophets too, better than they did. Many plain, honest, unlearned disciples of Christ have a clearer, sounder, and more useful knowledge of the word of God than some great experts with all their knowledge and learning. If the common people did not know the law, whose fault was it except that of the Pharisees, who should have taught them better?

1.3.2.2.3. How arrogantly they declared sentence on them: they are *cursed.* Here they usurped God's prerogative; we are unable to try a person in the heavenly court, and therefore we are unfit to condemn them there, and our rule is, *Bless, and curse not* (Ro 12:14). They used this terrible word *cursed* to express their own indignation and to frighten their officers from having anything to do with them.

2. What happened between them and Nicodemus (v. 50). Notice:

2.1. The just and rational objection Nicodemus raised against their actions. Notice:

2.1.1. Who appeared against them: Nicodemus, who *came to Jesus by night, being one of them* (v. 50). Although he had been with Jesus and taken him as his teacher, he still kept his place on the council and his vote among them. Some consider this to be his weakness and cowardice. But Christ never said to him, *Follow me,* and so it seems rather to have been his wisdom not to immediately abandon his place, because there he might have the opportunity to serve Christ and stop the tide of the Jewish anger. God has his remnant among all kinds of people, and many times he finds, puts, or makes some good in the worst places and societies. Although at first Nicodemus came to Jesus *by night,* for fear of being known, yet when need be, he boldly appeared in defense of Christ and opposed the whole council. Many believers who at first were afraid have finally, by divine grace, become courageous. Let no one justify the disguising of their faith by the example of Nicodemus, unless, like him, they are ready to appear openly in the cause of Christ, even if they stand alone in it, because this is what Nicodemus did here, and in 19:39.

2.1.2. What he alleged against their actions (v. 51): *Doth our law judge any man before it hears him* and knows what he is doing? He wisely argued from the principles of their own law, and an undeniable rule of justice, that no one is to be condemned without being given a hearing. Whereas the Pharisees had criticized the people as being ignorant of the law, Nicodemus tacitly turned the charge back on them here. The law is said here to judge, hear, and know. It is fitting that no one come under the sentence of the law until they have first had a fair trial in which they have submitted to the scrutiny of the law. Judges have two ears, to remind them to listen to both sides of the case. People are to be judged not by what is said about them but by what they do. Facts, without a shred of partiality, must be known in judgment, and the scales of justice must be used before the sword of justice.

2.2. What was said to this objection. Here no direct reply was given to it. What was lacking in reason they made up for in abuse and scolding. Whoever is against reason gives cause to suspect that reason is against them. Notice how they taunted him: *Art thou also of Galilee?* (v. 52). Notice:

2.2.1. How false the grounds of their argument were. They supposed that Christ came from Galilee. This was false. They supposed that because most of his disciples were Galileans, they were all such. They supposed that no prophet had risen out of Galilee. However, this was false too: Jonah and Nahum were both from Galilee.

2.2.2. How absurd their arguments themselves were. Is anyone of value and virtue ever less worthy or valuable because of the poverty and obscurity of their country? Even supposing no prophet had risen from Galilee, it was still not impossible that any would come from there.

2.3. The hasty adjournment of the court. They broke up the assembly in confusion, and hurriedly, and *every man went to his own house*. All the politics of their worldly intrigue were broken to pieces with one plain, honest word. They were unwilling to listen to Nicodemus, because they could not answer him.

CHAPTER 8

We have here: 1. Christ's avoiding the trap the Jews set for him by bringing him a woman caught in adultery (vv. 1–11). 2. Various discussions or meetings he had with the Jews. Here we have: 2.1. A discussion about his being the light of the world (vv. 12–20). 2.2. A discussion about the ruin of the unfaithful Jews (vv. 21–30). 2.3. A discussion about liberty and slavery (vv. 31–37). 2.4. A discussion about his Father and their father (vv. 38–47). 2.5. His message in response to their blasphemous criticism (vv. 48–50). 2.6. A discussion about the immortality of believers (vv. 51–59).

Verses 1–11

Although in the previous chapter Christ was cruelly abused by both the rulers and the people, here we have him at Jerusalem in the temple. *How often would he have gathered them* (Mt 23:37)! Notice:

1. His withdrawal from the town in the evening (v. 1): *He went unto the mount of Olives.* He went out of Jerusalem, perhaps because he had no friend there who had either enough kindness or enough courage to give him lodging for a night, while his persecutors had houses of their own to go to (7:53). In the daytime, when he had work to do in the temple, he willingly made himself vulnerable, but at night he withdrew into the country and sheltered there.

2. His return in the morning to the temple and to his work there (v. 2). Notice:

2.1. What a diligent preacher Christ was: *Early in the morning he came again, and taught.* Three things were noted about Christ's preaching here.

2.1.1. The time: *early in the morning.* When a day's work is to be completed for God and souls, it is good to take advantage of the day before us.

2.1.2. The place: *in the temple*, not so much because it was a consecrated place as because it was now *a place of concourse* (Pr 1:21)

2.1.3. His position: *he sat down* and taught, as one having authority (Mt 7:29).

2.2. How diligently his preaching was attended: *all the people came unto him.* Although the rulers were displeased with those who came to hear him, they still came; and *he taught them*, even though they were angry with him.

3. His dealing with those who, to test him, brought to him the *woman taken in adultery.* Notice here:

3.1. The situation proposed to him by the teachers of the law and Pharisees, who tried to pick a quarrel with him here (vv. 3–6).

3.1.1. They brought the prisoner to the bar in the court (v. 3): *they brought him a woman taken in adultery.* Those who were caught in adultery were to be put to death according to the Jewish law. The teachers of the law and Pharisees brought her to Christ and set her in the center of the assembly, as if they would leave her wholly to the judgment of Christ.

3.1.2. They brought a charge against her: *Master, this woman was taken in adultery* (v. 4). Here they called him Master—just a day after they had called him a deceiver—in the hope of flattering him and thereby trapping him. The crime for which the prisoner stood accused was nothing less than adultery. The Pharisees seemed to have a great zeal against the sin, whereas it later became clear that they themselves were not free from it. It is common for those who are indulgent toward their own sin to be harsh toward the sins of others. The evidence of the facts was undeniable proof. She had been caught in the act. Sometimes it proves a mercy to sinners to have their sin brought to light. It is better that our sin shame us than that it condemn us.

3.1.3. They came up with the ruling in this case on which she was accused (v. 5). "In the Law, Moses commanded that *such should be stoned.*" Moses commanded that they should be *put to death* (Lev 20:10; Dt 22:22), but not that they should be stoned, except in certain circumstances. Adultery is an exceedingly sinful sin. It is disobedience against a divine institution given in the age of our innocence, by the indulgence of one of our most sinful desires in the age of our corruption.

3.1.4. They asked for his judgment in the case: "But what do you say, you who claim to be a teacher who has come from God to repeal old laws and enact new ones?" If they had asked this question sincerely, it would have been very commendable. But they said this to tempt him, so that they would have a reason to accuse him (v. 6).

3.1.4.1. If he were to confirm the sentence of the law, they would censure him for being inconsistent with himself—since he had welcomed tax collectors and prostitutes—and with the role of the Messiah, who should be humble and offer salvation.

3.1.4.2. If he acquitted her, they would represent him as an enemy of the Law of Moses and a friend of sinners, and as One who favored sin, and to One who professed the strictness, purity, and work of a prophet, no reflection on him could be more invidious than this.

3.2. The method he took to determine this case and thereby break this trap.

3.2.1. He seemed to disregard it and turn a deaf ear to it: he *stooped down, and wrote on the ground*. It is impossible to tell, and therefore unnecessary to ask, what he wrote, but this is the only mention made in the Gospels of Christ's writing. By this, Christ teaches us that we should be slow to speak when difficult cases are offered to us, not in a hurry to shoot into the air. We should think twice before we speak once. But although Christ seemed not to hear them, he made it clear that he not only heard their words but also knew their thoughts.

3.2.2. He turned the conviction of the prisoner back on the prosecutors (v. 7).

3.2.2.1. They *continued asking him*, and his apparent disregard of them made them even more vehement, because now they were sure they had found his weak spot. They therefore pursued their appeal to him with even more vigor. They should instead have interpreted his disregard of them as a restraint on their purposes and as a sign that they should stop.

3.2.2.2. At last he put them all to shame and silence with one word: *He lifted up himself* and *said unto them, He that is without sin among you, let him first cast a stone at her.*

3.2.2.2.1. Here Christ avoided their trap. He neither disparaged the law nor excused the prisoner's guilt. Nor, on the other hand, did he encourage the prosecution or support their anger. When we cannot make our point by steering a direct course, it is good to follow an indirect one.

3.2.2.2.2. They came with the intention of accusing him, but they were forced to accuse themselves.

3.2.2.2.2.1. He referred here to the rule that the Law of Moses prescribed in the execution of criminals, that the *hand of the witnesses must be first upon them* (Dt 17:7), as in the stoning of Stephen (Ac 7:58). Christ asked them whether, according to their own law, they would dare be the executioners. Dared they take away with their hands that life which they were now taking away with their tongues?

3.2.2.2.2.2. He built on a recognized maxim in morality. Those who judge others when they themselves do the same thing are no better than self-condemned: "If there is any one of you who is *without sin*, let him throw the first stone at her." Whenever we find fault with others, we should reflect on ourselves, and be more severe against sin in ourselves than we are in others. We should be favorable not to the sins but to the person himself who has offended, considering ourselves and our own corrupt nature. Let this restrain us from throwing stones at our brothers and sisters. Those who are in any way obliged to criticize the faults of others should take a good look at themselves and keep themselves pure (Mt 7:5).

3.2.2.2.2.3. Perhaps he was alluding to the law requiring the trial of a suspected wife by the jealous husband with the waters of jealousy (Nu 5:11–31). Now the Jews believed that if the husband who brought his wife to that trial had himself been at any time guilty of adultery, the bitter water had no effect upon the wife. "Come then," Christ said. "If you are without sin, stand by the charge, and let the adulteress be put to death, but if you are not, then even though she is guilty, as long as you who present her are equally so, according to your own rule she must go free." He aimed not only to bring the prisoner to repentance by showing her his mercy but also to bring the prosecutors to repentance by showing them their sins. They sought to trap him; he sought to convince and convert them.

3.2.2.3. Having spoken these shocking words to them, he left them to consider them *and again stooped down* and

wrote on the ground (v. 8). The matter was lodged within them; let them make the best of it there. Some Greek copies here read, "he wrote on the ground the sins of every one of them." He does not write people's sins in the sand, however; no, they are written as with a *pen of iron* (Jer 17:1), never to be forgotten until they are forgiven.

3.2.2.4. The teachers of the law and Pharisees were so strangely thunderstruck by the words of Christ that they dropped their persecution of him, whom they no longer dared set traps for, and their prosecution of the woman, whom they no longer dared accuse (v. 9): *They went out one by one.*

3.2.2.4.1. Perhaps his writing on the ground frightened them as the handwriting on the wall frightened Belshazzar (Da 5:5–6). Happy are those who have no reason to be afraid of Christ's writing.

3.2.2.4.2. What he said frightened them by sending them to their own consciences; he had revealed them to themselves, and they were afraid his next word would reveal them to the world. They went out *one by one*, in order to go out quietly. They went away secretly, *as people being ashamed steal away when they flee in battle* (2Sa 19:3). The order of their departure is taken notice of: *beginning with the eldest*. If the eldest leave the field and retreat ingloriously, it is hardly surprising if the younger follow them. We see here:

3.2.2.4.2.1. The force of the word of Christ to convict sinners: *They who heard it were convicted by their own consciences.* Conscience is God's deputy in the soul, and one word from him will set it to work (Heb 4:12). Even teachers of the law and Pharisees are forced to withdraw with shame by the power of Christ's word.

3.2.2.4.2.2. The foolishness of sinners under these convictions. It is foolish for those who are under conviction to make it their chief care to avoid shame. Our concern should be more to save our souls than to save our reputation. The teachers of the law and Pharisees had the wound opened, and now they should have wanted to have it examined, and then it might have been healed. It is foolish for those who are under conviction to get away from Jesus Christ, because he is the only One who can heal the wounds of conscience. To whom then will they go (6:68)?

3.2.2.5. When the self-conceited prosecutors left the scene, the self-condemned prisoner stood her ground. *Jesus was left alone, and the woman standing in the midst* (v. 9), where they had placed her (v. 3). She did not try to run away. Her prosecutors had appealed to Jesus, and so to Jesus she would go. Those whose case is brought to our Lord Jesus will never need to move it to any other court. Our cause is lodged in the Gospel court; we are left alone with Jesus; it is only with him that we now have to deal. Let his Gospel rule us, and it will infallibly save us.

3.2.2.6. Here is the conclusion of the trial: *Jesus lifted up himself, and he saw none but the woman* (vv. 10–11). The woman probably stood trembling at the bar, as one who was very doubtful about what would happen next. Christ was without sin and could have thrown the first stone, but although no one is more severe than he is against sin, no one is more compassionate than he is to sinners, because he is infinitely gracious and merciful, and this poor evildoer found him so.

3.2.2.6.1. The prosecutors were called: *Where are those thine accusers? Hath no man condemned thee?* He asked so that he could shame them when they declined his judgment and so that he could encourage her, since she was determined to stand by it.

3.2.2.6.2. They did not appear when the question was asked: *Hath no man condemned thee?* She said, *No* man, Lord. She spoke respectfully to Christ, calling him "Lord," but she was silent about her prosecutors. She did not triumph in their retreat or gloat over them as witnesses against themselves or against her. But she answered the question that concerned her: *Has no man condemned thee?* True penitents find it enough to give an account of themselves to God and will not take it on themselves to give an account of other people.

3.2.2.6.3. The prisoner was therefore discharged: *Neither do I condemn thee*; *go, and sin no more.* Consider this:

3.2.2.6.3.1. As her discharge from temporal punishment: "If they do not condemn you to be stoned to death, neither do I." Christ would not condemn this woman:

3.2.2.6.3.1.1. Because it was none of his business; he would not interfere in worldly matters.

3.2.2.6.3.1.2. Because she had been prosecuted by those who were guiltier than she and who could not without shame insist on their demands for justice against her. But when Christ dismissed her, it was with this warning: *Go, and sin no more* (leave your life of sin). The more pleasing the escape, the more pleasing is the warning to go and not sin anymore. Those who help save the life of a criminal should, as Christ here, help save the soul with this warning.

3.2.2.6.3.2. As her discharge from eternal punishment. For Christ to say, *I do not condemn thee*, was in effect to say, "I do forgive you," and the *Son of man had power on earth to forgive sins* (Mt 9:6). He knew the tenderness and sincere repentance of the prisoner, and so he said what would comfort her. Those whom Christ does not condemn are truly happy. Christ will not condemn those who, though they have sinned, will *go and sin no more* (Ps 85:8; Isa 55:7). Christ's favor to us in the remission of the sins that are past should be a controlling argument with us to *go and sin no more* (Ro 6:1–2).

Verses 12–20

The rest of the chapter is taken up with discussions between Christ and sinners who contradicted him (Heb 12:3). There were still other Pharisees (v. 13) to confront Christ, and they were arrogant enough to challenge him. We see here:

1. A great teaching set down, with its application.

1.1. The teaching is that Christ is *the light of the world* (v. 12): *Then spoke Jesus again unto them.* They had turned a deaf ear to what he had said, but he *spoke again to them, saying, I am the light of the world.* He was expected to be a *light to enlighten the Gentiles* (Lk 2:32), and therefore the light of the world. The visible light of the world is the sun. One sun enlightens the whole world, as does one Christ, and so there need be no more. What a dungeon the world would be without the sun! This is what it would be like without Christ, by whom *light came into the world* (3:19).

1.2. The application of this teaching is, *He that followeth me shall not walk in darkness*, but *shall have the light of life.* It is our duty to follow him. Christ is the true light. It is not enough to look at this light, or even gaze on it; we must also follow it, believe in it, and walk in it, because it is a light to our feet, not only to our eyes. It is the happiness of those who follow Christ that they *shall not walk in darkness.* They *will have the light of life*, the light of spiritual life in this world and the light of eternal life in the other world. Let us follow Christ now, and then we will follow him to heaven.

2. The objection the Pharisees raised against this teaching: *Thou bearest record of thyself; thy record is not true*

(you are appearing as your own witness; your testimony is not valid) (v. 13). The objection was very unjust, because they made a crime out of that which was necessary and unavoidable in the case of One who introduced divine revelation. Did not Moses and all the prophets bear witness of themselves when they declared themselves to be God's messengers? Furthermore, they overlooked the testimony of all the other witnesses: his teaching was confirmed by more than *two or three* credible *witnesses*, enough to *establish every word* of it (Mt 18:16).

3. Christ's reply to this objection (v. 14). He is the light of the world, and one of the qualities of light is that it gives evidence of itself. First principles prove themselves. He urged three things to prove that his testimony, though of himself, was true and convincing.

3.1. That he was conscious of his own authority. He did not speak as One who was uncertain: *I know whence I came, and whither I go* (I know where I came from and where I am going). He knew that he had come *from the Father* and that he was going *to him* (16:28), that he had come *from glory* and was going *to glory* (17:5).

3.2. That they were incompetent to judge him:

3.2.1. Because they were ignorant: *You cannot tell whence I came, and whither I go.* He had told them about his coming from heaven and his returning to heaven, but it was *foolishness to them*; they *received it not* (1Co 2:14). They took it on themselves to judge what they did not understand.

3.2.2. Because they were biased (v. 15): *You judge after the flesh* (by human standards). The judgment cannot be right when the rules are wrong. The Jews judged Christ and his Gospel by outward appearances (1Sa 16:7), and they thought it impossible that he was the light of the world—as if the sun under a cloud were not a sun.

3.2.3. Because they were unjust and unfair toward him. He implied this when he said, "*I judge no man* (I pass judgment on no one); I have nothing to do with and I do not interfere with your political affairs." He passed judgment on no one. Now, if he did not do battle according to the flesh, it was very unreasonable for them to judge him according to the flesh.

3.3. That his testimony of himself was sufficiently supported and confirmed by the testimony of his Father with him and for him (v. 16): *And yet if I judge, my judgment is true* (my decisions are right). Consider him then:

3.3.1. As a judge. "*If I judge, my judgment is true.* If I judge, my judgment must be true, and then you would be condemned." Now what made his judgment satisfactory was:

3.3.1.1. His Father's concurrence with him: *I am not alone, but I and the Father.* He did not act separately, but in his own name and his Father's, and *by his authority* (5:17; 14:9–10).

3.3.1.2. His Father's commission to him: "It is the Father who sent me." No doubt his judgment was true and valid.

3.3.2. As a witness. As such he gave testimony that was true and satisfactory; he showed this in vv. 17–18, where:

3.3.2.1. He quoted a maxim of the Jewish law (v. 17): *That the testimony of two men is true.* Although many times hand has joined hand (Pr 11:21; 16:5) to give false testimony (1Ki 21:10), such testimony is allowed as sufficient evidence on which to base a decision, and if nothing appears to the contrary, it is assumed to be true.

3.3.2.2. He applied this to the matter in hand (v. 18): *I am one that bear witness of myself, and the Father that sent me bears witness of me.* Here are two witnesses! Now if the testimony of two distinct persons, who are human and can therefore deceive or be deceived, is conclusive, then much more should the testimony of the Son of God about himself, backed up by the testimony of his Father about him, command assent.

4. At the conclusion, how their tongues were let loose, and their hands tied.

4.1. Notice how their tongues were let loose (v. 19). They set themselves to cross-examine him. Notice:

4.1.1. How they evaded the conviction: *Then said they unto him, Where is thy Father?* They could easily have understood that when he spoke about his Father he was referring to none other than God himself, but they pretended to understand him as referring to an ordinary person. They challenged them, if he could, to produce his witness: *Where is thy Father?* This is how, as Christ had said about them (v. 15), they *judged after the flesh*. They dismissed his claim with a taunt.

4.1.2. How he avoided their objection with a further conviction; he charged them with willful ignorance: "*You neither know me nor my Father.* It is useless to discuss divine things with you, since you are talking about them as blind people talk about colors." He charged them with ignorance of God: *You know not my Father.* Their eyes were darkened in such a way that they could not see the light of the Father's glory shining in *the face of Jesus Christ* (2Co 4:6). The little children of the Christian church know the Father, but these rulers of the Jews did not know the Father, because they refused to know him as a Father. Christ showed them the true cause of their ignorance of God: *If you had known me, you would have known my Father also.* The reason why people are ignorant of God is that they do not know Jesus Christ. If we knew Christ, we would know the Father. If we knew Christ better, we would know the Father better.

4.2. Notice how their hands were tied, though their tongues were let loose. *These words spoke Jesus in the treasury.* Now the priests could easily, with the assistance of the guards who were at their command, either have seized him and exposed him to the rage of the mob or, at least, have silenced him. However, even in the temple, where they had him within their reach, *no man laid hands on him*, for *his hour was not yet come.* Notice:

4.2.1. The restraint laid on his persecutors by an invisible power. God can set bounds to human wrath (Ps 76:10), as he does to the waves of the sea (Job 38:11).

4.2.2. The reason for this restraint: *His hour was not yet come.* The frequent mention of this suggests how much the time of our departure from the world depends on the fixed purpose and decree of God. It will come, it is coming, but it has not yet come, though it is near. "My times are in your hands" (Ps 31:15), and better there than in our own.

Verses 21–30

Christ here gave fair warning to the foolish, unbelieving Jews to consider what would be the consequence of their unfaithfulness. Notice:

1. The wrath threatened (v. 21): *Jesus said again unto them.* He continued to teach, out of kindness to those few people who received his teaching, which is an example to ministers to continue with their work despite opposition, because a remnant will be saved (Ro 9:27; Isa 10:22). Here Christ changed his voice; he had *piped to them* in the offers of his grace, and they *had not danced* (Mt 11:17); now he mourned to them in the declarations of his wrath, to see if they would mourn. He said, *I go my way, and you shall seek me, and shall die in your sins. Whither I go, you cannot come.* Every word is terrible and speaks spiritual

judgments, which are the severest of all judgments. Four things were threatened against the Jews:

1.1. Christ's departure from them: *I go my way.* It is terrible for those from whom Christ departs! He often said farewell, as one who was reluctant to leave and willing to be invited.

1.2. Their enmity toward the true Messiah, and their ineffective inquiring about another Messiah when he had gone away. *You shall seek me*, which shows either:

1.2.1. Their enmity toward the true Christ: "You will seek to destroy my interests by persecuting my teaching and followers." Or:

1.2.2. Their seeking false Christs: "You will continue to confuse yourselves with expectations of the Messiah, a Christ to come, when he has already come."

1.3. Their final impenitence: *You shall die in your sins* (v. 21). The Greek is actually singular: *sin.* What is especially meant here is the sin of unbelief. Those who live in unbelief are ruined forever if they die in their unbelief. Many who have long lived in sin are, through grace, saved from dying in sin by their prompt repentance.

1.4. Their eternal separation from Christ. *Whither I go, you cannot come.* When Christ left the world, he went to Paradise. He took the penitent thief there with him, who did not die in his sins, but the impenitent not only shall not come to him; they cannot, because heaven would not be heaven to those who die unsanctified and unfit for it.

2. The mockery they made of this threat. They scorned it (v. 22): *Will he kill himself?* What trivial thoughts they had of Christ's threats; they could make themselves and one another merry with them. What harsh thoughts they had of Christ's meaning, as if he had an inhuman purpose against his own life. They had earlier given a much more favorable interpretation to his word (7:34–35): *Will he go to the dispersed among the Gentiles?* But notice how indulged hatred becomes increasingly malicious.

3. The confirmation of what he had said.

3.1. He had said, *Whither I go, you cannot come*, and here he gave the reason for this (v. 23): *You are from beneath; I am from above: you are of this world; I am not of this world.* "*You are* of those things which are beneath. You are devoted to these things. How can you come where I go, when your spirit and disposition are so directly against mine?" Notice:

3.1.1. What the spirit of the Lord Jesus was—not of *this* world, but from *above.* No one will be with him except those who are born from above (3:3, 7) and have their *conversation in heaven* (Php 3:20).

3.1.2. How contrary to this their spirit was: *You are from beneath.* What fellowship could Christ have with them?

3.2. He had said, *You shall die in your sins*, and here he stood by it. He also gave this further reason for it: *If you believe not that I am he, you shall die in your sins* (v. 24). Notice:

3.2.1. What we are required to believe: *that I am he*, the One who would come (Ps 118:26; Mt 11:3), the One whom you expect the Messiah to be. I do not only call myself so; *I am he.* True faith does not entertain the soul with an empty sound of words, but moves it as something real.

3.2.2. How necessary it is that we believe this. If we do not have this faith, *we shall die in our sins.* Without this faith we cannot be saved from the power of sin while we live, and so we will certainly continue in it to the end. No one but the Spirit of Christ's grace will be a powerful enough agent to turn us away from sin to God. If Christ does not heal us, our case is desperate, and we will die in our sins. And without this faith we cannot be saved from the punishment of sin when we die. This implies the great Gospel promise: if we believe that Christ is the one he claims to be, and if we receive him accordingly, we shall not die in our sins. Believers die in Christ, in his love, in his arms.

4. A further message about himself (vv. 25–29).

4.1. The question the Jews asked him (v. 25): *Who art thou?* He had said, "You must believe that *I am he*." When he did not say expressly who he was, they turned it to his discredit, as if he did not know what to say about himself: *Who art thou?*

4.2. His answer to this question, in which he directed them down three paths for information:

4.2.1. He referred them to what he had said all along: "Do you ask who I am? *Even the same that I said unto you from the beginning.*" "I am *the same that I said to you from the beginning* of time in the Old Testament Scriptures," or, "*from the beginning* of my public ministry." He was determined to abide by the account he had already given of himself. He therefore referred them to this as an answer to their question.

4.2.2. He referred them to his Father's judgment (v. 26): "*I have many things to say, and to judge of you. I speak to the world*—to which I am sent as an ambassador—*those things which I have heard of him.*"

4.2.2.1. He suppressed his accusation of them. He had many things to charge them with, but he had said enough for the present.

4.2.2.2. He entered his appeal against them to his Father: *He that sent me.* Here are two things that comforted him:

4.2.2.2.1. That he had been true to his Father and to the trust rested in him: *I speak to the world*—for his Gospel was to be preached to every creature (Mk 16:15)—*those things which I have heard of him.*

4.2.2.2.2. That his Father would be true to him. Although he would not accuse them to his Father, the Father, who sent him, would undoubtedly judge. Christ would not accuse them, "for," he said, "the One who sent me is true and will pass judgment on them." Here, the Evangelist has a sad comment to make on this part of our Savior's teaching (v. 27): *They understood not that he spoke to them of the Father.* Although Christ spoke so clearly of God as his Father in heaven, they still did not understand whom he meant. Day and night are the same to the blind.

4.2.3. He then referred them to *their own convictions* (vv. 28–29). Notice here:

4.2.3.1. What they would before long be convinced of: "*You shall know that I am he.* You will be forced to know it in your own consciences, the convictions of which, though you may stifle them, you cannot despise." They would be convinced of two things:

4.2.3.1.1. That he did nothing *of himself*, on his own, without the Father. It is said of false prophets that they prophesied *out of their own hearts* (Eze 13:2) and followed their own spirits.

4.2.3.1.2. That as *his Father taught him,* so he *spoke these things,* that he was not *self-taught,* but *taught of God.*

4.2.3.2. When they would be convinced of this: "*When you have lifted up the Son of man,* lifted him up on the cross, like the bronze snake on the pole" (3:14). On the other hand, the expression shows that his death was his exaltation. Those who put him to death lifted him up to the cross, but then he lifted up himself to his Father. Notice with what tenderness and mildness Christ here spoke to those who he certainly knew would put him to

death. Christ spoke about his death as what would be a powerful conviction of the unfaithfulness of the Jews. "When you have lifted up the Son of Man, then will you know this." Why then?

4.2.3.2.1. Because foolish and unthinking people are often taught the worth of blessings by the lack of them (Lk 17:22).

4.2.3.2.2. Because the guilt of the Jews' sin would so wake up their consciences that they would be made to seriously seek a Savior, and then they would know that Jesus was the One who alone could save them. And so it proved, when, being told that they had crucified and killed the Son of God with evil hands, they cried out, *What shall we do?* (Ac 2:36).

4.2.3.2.3. Because such signs and wonders would accompany his death as would give stronger proof that he was the Messiah than any proof that had been given up to that time.

4.2.3.2.4. Because by Christ's death he purchased the outpouring of the Spirit, who would convince the world that Jesus is the One he claimed to be (16:7–8).

4.2.3.2.5. Because the judgments the Jews brought on themselves by putting Christ to death were a visible proof to the most hardened among them that Jesus was the One he claimed to be.

4.2.3.3. What supported our Lord Jesus in the meantime (v. 29): "*He that sent me is with me.* The Father has not left me alone, because I always do those things that please him." Here is:

4.2.3.3.1. The assurance Christ had of his Father's presence with him. "The One who sent me is with me" (Isa 42:1; Ps 89:21). This gives boldness to our faith in Christ and our dependence on his word: the King of kings accompanied his own ambassador and never left him alone, either solitary or weak. This presence of the Father with him also emphasized the evil of those who opposed him.

4.2.3.3.2. The basis for this assurance: *For I do always those things that please him.* His whole undertaking is called the pleasure of the Lord (Isa 53:10). His management of that matter did not displease his Father in any way. Our Lord Jesus never offended his Father in anything; he fulfilled all righteousness (Mt 3:15). God's servants can expect God's presence with them when they choose and do those things that please him (Isa 66:4–5).

5. The good effect Christ's message had on some of his hearers (v. 30): *As he spoke these words, many believed on him.* There is still a remnant (Ro 11:5) *who believe to the saving of their souls* (Heb 10:39). If Israel, the whole body of the people, are not gathered to him, there are still those of them in whom Christ will be glorious (Isa 49:5). When Christ told them that if they did not believe, they would die in their sins, such people thought it was time to consider matters (Ro 1:16, 18). Sometimes a wide door is opened, an effective one, even where there are many enemies. The Gospel sometimes gains great victories where it meets with great opposition. Let this encourage God's ministers to preach the Gospel even if it meets with *much contention* (1Th 2:2), for they will not *labour in vain* (1Co 15:58). Many people may be secretly brought home to God by endeavors that are openly contradicted.

Verses 31–37

We have in these verses:

1. An encouraging teaching set down about the spiritual liberty of Christ's disciples. Knowing that his message was beginning to have an effect on some of his hearers, Christ addressed those weak believers. Notice:

1.1. How graciously the Lord Jesus looks on those who *tremble at his word* (Isa 66:5) and are ready to receive it; and if people place themselves in his path, he will not pass by them without speaking to them.

1.2. How carefully he cherishes the beginnings of grace. In what he said to them, we have two things that he said to all who would believe at any time. He described:

1.2.1. The character of a true disciple of Christ: *If you continue in my word, then are you my disciples indeed.* He laid it down as an established rule that he would acknowledge as his disciples only those who continued in his word. Those who are not strong in faith should make sure they are sound in the faith. Let those who have thoughts of making a covenant with Christ have no thoughts of keeping in reserve a power of revoking their agreement. Children are sent to school and committed as apprentices for only a few years, but only those who are willing to be committed to Christ for life are truly his. Only those who continue in Christ's word will be accepted as his. The verb translated *continue* means *to dwell*; we must dwell in Christ's word, as a person does at home, which is their center, rest, and refuge.

1.2.2. The privilege of a true disciple of Christ. Here are two precious promises (v. 32).

1.2.2.1. *You shall know the truth.* Even those who are true believers may be—and they are—very much in the dark about many things they should know. God's children are only children, and they understand and speak as children (1Co 13:11). If we did not need to be taught, we would not need to be disciples (that is, "learners"). It is a very great privilege to *know the truth.* Christ's students are sure to be well taught.

1.2.2.2. *The truth shall make you free,* that is:

1.2.2.2.1. The truth Christ teaches tends to make people free (Isa 61:1). It sets us free from our spiritual enemies, free to serve God, free to enjoy the privileges of sons.

1.2.2.2.2. Knowing, receiving, and believing this truth actually makes us free, free from prejudices, mistakes, and false ideas. We are set free from the controlling rule of sinful desires and passions; the soul is restored to govern itself. By accepting the truth of Christ, the heart is greatly released; it never acts with so true a liberty as when it acts under divine command (2Co 3:17).

2. The offense the worldly Jews took at this doctrine. They still found fault with it (v. 33). They answered him with much pride and envy, *"We Jews are Abraham's seed, and so are free-born; we were never in bondage to any man; how sayest thou then, You shall be made free?"* Notice:

2.1. What they were grieved at; it was the implication, in *You shall be made free,* that the Jewish nation were in some sort of slavery.

2.2. What they alleged against it.

2.2.1. "We are Abraham's descendants." It is common for a declining, decaying family to boast of the glory and dignity of its ancestors, and to take honor from the name to which they repay disgrace; this is what the Jews did here. It is the common fault and foolishness of those who have godly parents and education to trust in and boast of their privileges as if those would make up for a lack of real holiness. Saving benefits are not conveyed by inheritance to us and our children, nor can entitlement to heaven be made by descent. All who are descended from Israel are not Israel (Ro 9:6).

2.2.2. *We were never in bondage to any man.* Notice:

2.2.2.1. How false this claim was. I wonder how they could have had the assurance to say such a thing in the face of a congregation when it was so notoriously untrue. Were they not at this time subjects of the Romans, and,

though not in a personal, yet in a national, slavery to them, and groaning to be made free?

2.2.2.2. How foolish the application was. Christ had spoken of a liberty that the truth would lead them into, which must be taken as referring to a spiritual liberty, because just as the truth enriches the mind, so it also liberates the mind, releasing it from the captivity of error and prejudice. They, however, against the offer of spiritual liberty, pleaded that they were never held in physical slavery. Sinful hearts are aware of no grievances except those that hurt the body and harm their worldly affairs. If you speak to them about the being enslaved to sin, being held captive to Satan, and being at liberty in Christ, *you bring certain strange things to their ears* (Ac 17:20).

3. Our Savior's vindication of his teaching (vv. 34–37), in which he did four things:

3.1. He showed that it was still possible that they were enslaved (v. 34): *Whosoever commits sin is the servant of sin.* Christ further explained for their edification what he had already said.

3.1.1. The introduction was very solemn: *Verily, verily, I say unto you.* The style of the prophets was, *Thus saith the Lord,* for they were faithful as servants, but because Christ is a Son (Heb 3:5–6), he speaks in his own name: *I say unto you.* He rested his integrity on it.

3.1.2. The truth was of universal concern: "*Whosoever commits sin is the servant of sin* and sadly needs to be made free."

3.1.2.1. Notice on whom this mark is fastened, on the one who *commits sin.* There is not a *just man* on earth, who *lives, and sins not* (Ecc 7:20); yet not everyone who sins is a servant of sin, for then God would have no servants; but those who choose sin, who live according to the flesh and make sin their business, are servants of sin.

3.1.2.2. See what a mark Christ put on those who commit sin. He stigmatized them, giving them a mark of slavery. They are *servants of sin.* They do the work of sin, supporting its interest and accepting its wages (Ro 6:16).

3.2. He showed them that their having a place in the house of God would not entitle them to the inheritance of sons, for (v. 35) *the servant abideth not in the house for ever, but the son* of the family remains always.

3.2.1. This points primarily to the rejection of the Jewish church and nation. Israel had been God's son, his firstborn (Ex 4:22). Christ told them that having made themselves servants, they would not *abide in the house for ever.* "Do not expect to be made free from sin by the ceremonies of the Law of Moses, for Moses was merely a servant. But if the Son makes you free, it is good" (v. 36).

3.2.2. It looks further, to the rejection of all who are the servants of sin. Only true believers are counted free and will remain forever in the house.

3.3. He showed them the way of rescue. The case of those who are the servants of sin is sad, but, thank God, it is not helpless; it is not hopeless. He who is the Son has power of both release from slavery and adoption into his family (v. 36): *If the Son shall make you free, you shall be free indeed.*

3.3.1. Jesus Christ in the Gospel offers us our freedom. He has authority and power to make free, that is:

3.3.1.1. To discharge prisoners. He does this in justification, by making atonement for our guilt and our debts. As our surety, Christ settles matters with the creditor, fulfilling the demands of wronged justice with more than an equivalent.

3.3.1.2. To rescue slaves, and he does this in sanctification. By the powerful activity of his Spirit, he breaks the power of corruption in the soul and rallies the scattered forces of reason and goodness, and so the soul is made free.

3.3.1.3. To naturalize strangers and foreigners, and he does this in adoption. This is a further act of grace. There is a charter of privileges as well as a pardon.

3.3.2. Those whom Christ makes free are truly free. The word translated *indeed* in v. 31, in *disciples indeed*, means "truly"; the word here means "really." This shows:

3.3.2.1. The truth and certainty of the promise. The liberty that the Jews boasted of was an imaginary liberty; the liberty that Christ gives is certain; it is real. The servants of sin promise themselves liberty and think they are free, but they are deceiving themselves. None are really free except those whom Christ makes free.

3.3.2.2. The remarkable excellence of the promised freedom; it is a freedom that deserves the name. It is a glorious liberty (Ro 8:21). It is substance (Pr 8:21), while the things of the world are shadow.

3.4. He applied this answer to their boasts of their relationship with Abraham (v. 37): *I know that you are Abraham's seed, but now you seek to kill me, because my word hath no place in you.* Notice:

3.4.1. The honor of their extraction was admitted: *I know that you are Abraham's seed.* They boasted of their descent from Abraham as what made their names great (Ge 12:2), whereas it really only emphasized their offenses.

3.4.2. The inconsistency of their practice with this honor was shown: *But you seek to kill me.* They had tried to do so several times and were now intending to do so, as quickly became apparent (v. 58) when they *took up stones to cast at him.*

3.4.3. The reason for this inconsistency was that *my word hath no place in you.* Some of the critics understand it as, "My word does not penetrate you"; it descended as the rain (Dt 32:2), but it came on them like rain on rock, which it ran off, rather than soaking into their hearts like rain on plowed ground (Isa 55:10–11). Our translation is significant: *It has no place in you.* The words of Christ should have a place in us, the innermost and uppermost place, a place to live, like a person's home, not like the working place of a stranger or traveler. The word must have room to operate, to work sin out of us and work grace into us; it must have a ruling place, the throne of our hearts. Yet in many who profess religious faith, the word of Christ has no place; they will not allow it any place, because they do not like it. Other things take up the place it should have in us. Where the word of God has no place, no good is to be expected, because the room that is available is left there for all wickedness (Mt 12:43–45).

Verses 38–47

Here Christ and the Jews are still disputing.

1. He traced the difference between his attitude and theirs to a different origin (v. 38): *I speak that which I have seen with my Father,* and *you* do *what you have seen with your father.*

1.1. Christ's teaching came from heaven: *I speak that which I have seen.* The revelations Christ has made to us of God and of another world are not based on guess and hearsay. *It is that which I have seen with my Father.* The teaching of Christ is not a plausible hypothesis supported by probable arguments. It was not merely what he had heard from his Father; it was also what he had seen with him. It was Christ's right to have seen what he spoke and to speak what he had seen.

1.2. Their actions were from hell: *You do that which you have seen with your father.* Just as a son who is brought up with his father learns his father's words and ways, growing like him by imitation as well as by natural image, so these Jews made themselves as like the Devil as if they had carefully taken him as their model.

2. He answered their proud boasting that Abraham and God were their fathers.

2.1. They pleaded a relationship with Abraham: *Abraham is our father* (v. 39); and he replied to this plea. They intended this:

2.1.1. To honor themselves and make themselves look great.

2.1.2. To show their hatred for Christ, as if what he said reflected badly on the patriarch Abraham when he spoke of their father as one they had learned evil from. Christ overturned this plea by a plain and convincing argument: "Abraham's children will do the works of Abraham, but you do not do Abraham's works, and so you cannot be Abraham's children."

2.1.2.1. The major premise was clear: *If you were Abraham's children,* then you would *do the works of Abraham.* Only those who follow in the steps of his faith and obedience (Ro 4:12) are considered the descendants of Abraham. Those who want to prove themselves to be Abraham's descendants must not only have Abraham's faith but also do Abraham's works (Jas 2:21–22).

2.1.2.2. The minor premise was also clear: "*But you do not do the things Abraham did, because you seek to kill me, a man that has told you the truth, which I have heard of God; this did not Abraham*" (v. 40).

2.1.2.2.1. He showed them what their work was, what they were now doing: they *sought to kill him.* They were so unnatural as to seek the life of a man who had done them no harm nor provoked them in any way. They were so ungrateful as to seek the life of One who had told them the truth. They were so ungodly as to seek the life of One who told them the truth that he had heard from God.

2.1.2.2.2. He showed them that this did not befit the children of Abraham, because *this did not Abraham.* "He did nothing like this." He was famous for his humanity and godliness. *Abraham believed God* (Ro 4:3); they were obstinate in unbelief. "He would not have acted in this way if he had lived now, or if I had lived then."

2.1.2.3. The conclusion followed naturally (v. 41): "You are not Abraham's children, but betray yourselves as coming from another family (v. 41); there is *a father whose deeds you do.*" He did not yet say clearly that he was referring to the Devil. He tested them to see whether they would allow their own consciences to conclude from what he said that they were the Devil's children.

2.2. Far from acknowledging the unworthiness of their relationship to Abraham, they pleaded a relationship to God himself as their Father: "We are *not born of fornication; we have one Father, even God.*"

2.2.1. Some understand this literally. They were Hebrews of the Hebrews (Php 3:5). Being born in lawful wedlock, they could call God Father.

2.2.2. Others take it figuratively. They began to be aware now that Christ was speaking about a spiritual father, the father of their religion, and so:

2.2.2.1. They denied that they were a generation of idolaters: "We are *not born of fornication,* are not the children of idolatrous parents." If they meant no more than that they themselves were not idolaters, what then? A man may be free from idolatry and yet perish in another sin.

2.2.2.2. They boasted that they were true worshipers of the true God. "We do not have many fathers, as the pagans had. *The Lord our God is one Lord and one Father,* and so all is well with us." Now our Savior gave a full answer to this fallacious plea (vv. 42–43) and proved, by two arguments, that they had no right to call God Father.

2.2.2.2.1. They did not love Christ: *If God were your Father, you would love me.* He had disproved their relationship with Abraham by revealing that they were seeking to kill him, Christ (v. 40), but here he disproved their relationship with God by revealing that they did not love and confess Christ. All who have God as their Father have a true love for Jesus Christ. God has used various methods to test us, and this was one: he sent his Son into the world, concluding that all who called God Father would welcome his Son. Our adoption will be proved or disproved by this: did we love Christ, or not? If they were God's children, they would love him, because:

2.2.2.2.1.1. He was the Son of God. Now this must commend him to the affections of all who were *born of God* (1Jn 5:1).

2.2.2.2.1.2. He was sent by God. Notice the emphasis he laid on this: *I came from God; neither came I of myself, but he sent me.* He came to *gather together in one the children of God* (11:52). Would not all God's children embrace with both arms a messenger sent from their Father on such a mission?

2.2.2.2.2. They did not understand him. They did not understand the language and dialect of the family: *You do not understand my speech* (my language is not clear to you) (v. 43). Those who had made the word of the Creator familiar to them needed no other key to the language of the Redeemer. The reason they did not understand Christ's speech made the matter much worse: *Even because you cannot hear my word*; that is, "You cannot persuade yourselves to hear it without prejudice, as it should be heard." The meaning of this *cannot* is a stubborn "will not." They did not like it nor love it, and so they would not understand it. *You cannot hear my words* because you have *stopped your ears* (Ps 58:4–5).

3. He then told them plainly whose children they were: *You are of your father the devil* (v. 44). If they were not God's children, they were the Devil's. This is a terrible accusation, and it sounded very harsh and horrible, and so our Savior proved it fully:

3.1. By a general argument: *The lusts of your father you will do.*

3.1.1. "You do the Devil's desires, the desires he wants you to fulfill, and are led captive by him at his will." The distinctive desires of the Devil are spiritual wickedness: pride and envy, wrath and hatred, enmity toward good and enticing others to commit evil; these are the desires that Satan fulfills.

3.1.2. "You *will* do the Devil's desires." The more there is of the will in these desires, the more there is of the Devil in them. "You delight to carry out the desires of your father; they are rolled under the tongue like sweet tidbits" (Job 20:12).

3.2. By showing that they clearly resembled the Devil in two particular ways—murder and lying.

3.2.1. He was *a murderer from the beginning.* He hated human beings and was therefore their murderer in disposition. He tempted Adam and Eve to commit the sin that brought death into the world, and so he was effectively the murderer of the whole human race. The great tempter is the great destroyer. The Jews called the Devil "the angel of death." If the devil had not been very strong in Cain, he could not have done something so unnatural as to kill his own brother. Now these Jews here followed him and were murderers like him, murderers of souls, sworn enemies of Christ, now ready to be his betrayers and murderers: *Now you seek to kill me.*

3.2.2. He was and is a liar. He is:

3.2.2.1. An enemy of truth, and so of Christ. He is a deserter from the truth; he *abode not in* (did not hold to) *the truth*, the truth that Christ was now preaching and that the Jews opposed. Here they were like their father the Devil. He is therefore destitute of the truth: *There is no truth in him.* There is no truth, nothing you can trust in, in him, nor in anything he says or does.

3.2.2.2. A friend and patron of lying: *When he speaketh a lie, he speaketh of his own* (when he lies, he speaks his native language). Three things were said here about the Devil with reference to the sin of lying:

3.2.2.2.1. That he is a liar; his words have always been lying words, his prophets lying prophets. All his temptations are carried on by lies, calling evil good and good evil (Isa 5:20).

3.2.2.2.2. That when he speaks a lie, he speaks *of his own*, of his *idion*. It is the proper *idiom* of his language.

3.2.2.2.3. That he is *the father of it.* He is the author and founder of all lies, and he is the father of every liar. God made people with a disposition for truth; it is consistent with reason and natural light that we speak the truth. But the Devil, the author of sin, is the father of liars, who begot them, who trained them up to tell lies, whom they are like and obey.

4. Having proved all murderers and all liars to be the children of the Devil, Christ in the following verses helped them apply it to themselves. He accused them of two things:

4.1. That they would not *believe the word of truth* (v. 45).

4.1.1. This may be taken in two ways:

4.1.1.1. "Although I tell you the truth, you will not believe me." They still would not believe he told them the truth. Some people would not believe the greatest truths, because they *rebelled against the light* (Job 24:13). Or, as our translation reads it:

4.1.1.2. *Because I tell you the truth, you believe me not.* They would neither receive him nor welcome him as a prophet, because showing them their faces in a mirror would not flatter them. Those to whom the light of divine truth has become a torment are in a miserable state.

4.1.2. Now, to show them the unreasonableness of their unfaithfulness, he condescended to submit to a fair test (v. 46).

4.1.2.1. If he was in error, why did they not convince him? But Christ said, *which of you convinceth me of sin?* Their accusations were malicious, groundless slander, utterly false. Even the judge who condemned him acknowledged he *found no fault in him* (Lk 23:9). The only way not to be convicted of sin is not to sin.

4.1.2.2. If they were in error, why were they not convinced by him? *If I say the truth, why do you not believe me?* If you cannot convince me of error, you must acknowledge that I speak the truth, and then why do you not believe me?" It will be found that the reason we do not believe in Jesus Christ is that we are unwilling to leave our sins, deny ourselves, and serve God faithfully.

4.2. That they would not hear the words of God (v. 47). Here is:

4.2.1. A teaching set down: *He that is of God heareth God's words.* He is willing and ready to hear them, sincerely wants to know the will of God, and cheerfully embraces whatever he knows to be that will. He comprehends and discerns God's words; he hears them so as to recognize the voice of God in them, as those who belong to the family know the master's footsteps and the master's knock, as the sheep can distinguish the voice of their shepherd from the voice of a stranger (10:4–5; SS 2:8).

4.2.2. The application of this teaching: "*You therefore hear them not, because you do not belong to God.* That you are so deaf and dead to the words of God is clear evidence that you do not belong to God." Or, that they did not belong to God was the reason that they did not profitably hear the words of God that Christ spoke. If the word of the kingdom does not produce fruit, the blame is to be laid on the soil, not on the seed.

Verses 48–50

Here is:

1. The malice of hell breaking loose in the corrupt words of the unfaithful Jews. Up to that time they had found fault with his teaching, but, having shown themselves to be uneasy when he complained (vv. 43, 47) that they would not hear him, now at length they stooped to downright insulting (v. 48). The teachers of the law and Pharisees scornfully turned away the conviction with, *Say we not well that thou art a Samaritan, and hast a devil?* We see here:

1.1. The blasphemous description of our Lord Jesus commonly given among the evil Jews:

1.1.1. That he was a Samaritan. This was how they exposed him to the hatred of the people, to whom you could not describe someone worse than as a Samaritan. They had often enough called him "a Galilean," meaning "an insignificant man," but they wanted him to be known as a Samaritan, a bad man. Great efforts have been made throughout the ages to render good people repugnant by describing them in sinister terms, and it is easy to join the crowd and cry out against a group of people who are generally despised.

1.1.2. That *he had a devil*, that he was in league with the Devil, that he was possessed by a demon, that he was depressed, dim, or insane, that his mind was overexcited, and what he said was no more to be believed than the extravagant rambles of someone who was delirious.

1.2. How they tried to justify this description: *Say we not well* (aren't we right) *that thou art so?* Their hearts were even more hardened, and their prejudices more deeply confirmed. They prided themselves on their hostility toward Christ, as if they had never spoken better than when they spoke the worst they could about Christ. It is wrong to say and do bad things, but it is even worse to stand by them.

2. The humility and mercifulness of heaven shining in Christ's reply (vv. 49–50).

2.1. He denied their charge against him: *I have not a devil.* Their accusation was unjust; "I am neither motivated by a demon nor in alliance with one."

2.2. He asserted the sincerity of his own intentions: but *I honour my Father.* This proved that he *had not a devil*, because if he had, he would not honor God.

2.3. He complained about the wrong they did him by their slander: *You do dishonour me.* From this it was clear that, as man, he was sensitive to the disgrace and indignity he was subjected to. Christ honored his Father in a way that no one ever had, but he himself was dishonored in a way that no one had ever been, because although God has promised that he will honor those who honor him (1Sa 2:30), he has never promised that people would honor them.

2.4. He cleared himself from the imputation of boasting (v. 50). See here:

2.4.1. His contempt for worldly honor: *I seek not mine own glory.* He did not aim at his own glory or at advance-

ment in the world. "*You do dishonour me,* but you cannot shake me, because I *seek not my own glory.*" Those who are dead to commendation from human beings can safely bear their contempt.

2.4.2. His comfort under worldly dishonor: *There is one that seeketh and judgeth.* Christ showed two ways in which he declined to seek his own glory:

2.4.2.1. He did not seek respect from human beings. In reference to this, he said, *There is one that seeketh.* God will seek honor for those who do not seek their own, because humility comes before honor (Pr 15:33; 18:12).

2.4.2.2. He did not take revenge against the insults of human beings, and in reference to this he said, "*There is one that judgeth,* who will vindicate my honor." If we are humble and patient petitioners, we will find to our comfort that *there is one that judgeth.*

Verses 51–59

In these verses we have:

1. The teaching of the immortality of believers set down (v. 51). It was introduced with the usual solemn foreword: *Verily, verily, I say unto you*; and what he said was, *If a man keep my sayings, he shall never see death.* We have here:

1.1. The character of believers: they are those who *keep the sayings* of the Lord Jesus, who keep "my word." We must not only receive but also keep this, not only have it but also hold on to it. We must keep it in our minds and hearts, keep it in love and devotion, keep in it as our way and rule.

1.2. The privilege of believers: they "*shall* by no means *see death* forever." Not as if the bodies of believers are kept safe from the stroke of death. How then is this promise fulfilled that they *shall not see death*?

1.2.1. The quality of death is so changed to them that they do not see it as death; they do not see the terror of death. Their sight does not terminate in death; they look so clearly and comfortably through death and beyond it that they overlook death and do not see it.

1.2.2. The power of death is so broken that they will not see death *for ever.* The day will come when *death shall be swallowed up in victory* (1Co 15:54).

1.2.3. They are completely saved from eternal death. They will have their eternal inheritance where there will be *no more death,* where they *cannot die any more* (Lk 20:36).

2. The Jews' objection to this teaching. They used this occasion to abuse the One who made them such a kind offer: *Now we know that thou hast a devil. Abraham is dead.* Notice:

2.1. Their insult: *Now we know that thou hast a devil.* If he had not abundantly proved himself to be a teacher who had come from God (3:2), his promises of immortality to his credulous followers could justly have been ridiculed, and even a charitable listener would have attributed those promises to a crazy imagination, but his teaching was clearly divine, his miracles confirmed it, and the Jews' religion taught them to expect such a prophet and believe in him.

2.2. Their reasoning. They looked on him as guilty of an insufferable act of arrogance in claiming to be greater than *Abraham and the prophets*: "*Abraham is dead,* and *the prophets* are also dead." It was true that Abraham and the prophets were great, great in the favor of God and great in the respect of all good people. It was true that they kept God's sayings. It was true that they died; they never claimed to have, much less give, immortality. It was their honor that they *died in faith* (Heb 11:13), but they must die. Why should a good person be afraid to die when Abraham is dead and the prophets are dead? They followed their route through that dark valley, and this should reconcile us to death and help to take away its terror. Now the Jews thought Christ was talking madly when he said, *If a man keep my sayings, he shall never taste death.* Their argument was based on two mistakes:

2.2.1. They understood Christ to be referring to immortality in this world. God is still the *God of Abraham* (Ex 3:6) and the *God of the holy prophets* (Rev 22:6). God is not the God of the dead, but of the living (Mt 22:32). Abraham and the prophets were therefore still alive, and, as Christ meant it, they had neither seen nor tasted death.

2.2.2. They thought no one could be greater than Abraham and the prophets, whereas they must have known that the Messiah would be greater than Abraham or any of the prophets. Instead of concluding that Christ's calling himself greater than Abraham meant he had a devil, they should have concluded that he was the Christ; but their eyes were blinded. They scornfully asked, *Whom makest thou thyself?*

3. Christ's reply. He continued to condescend to reason with them. This was the day of his patience.

3.1. In his answer he did not insist on his own testimony about himself, but waived that as insufficient or inconclusive (v. 54): *If I honour myself, my honour is nothing.* Honor of our own creation is mere fancy; it is nothing, and so it is called worthless. Self-admirers are self-deceivers.

3.2. He referred himself to his Father, God, and to their father, Abraham.

3.2.1. He referred to his Father, God: *It is my Father that honoureth me.* He derived from his Father all the honor he now claimed. He depended on his Father for all the honor he further looked for. Christ and all who are his depend on God for their honor, and the One who is sure of honor where he is known is not concerned even if he is insulted where he is in disguise.

3.2.1.1. He took the opportunity here to show the reason for their unbelief, namely, that they did not know God. You *say of him that he is your God, yet you have not known him* (vv. 54–55). Notice here:

3.2.1.1.1. The profession they made of their relationship with God: *You say that he is your God.* Many claim to belong to God but have no just cause for their claim. What good will it do us to say he is our God if we are not sincerely his people?

3.2.1.1.2. Their ignorance of him: *Yet you have not known him.* "You do not know him at all." Or: "You do not know him rightly," and this is as bad as not knowing him at all, or even worse. People may be able to dispute the fine details about God and yet not know him. They have merely learned to talk about the name of God. The Jews did not know God, and so they did not recognize the image and voice of God in Christ. The reason why people do not receive the *Gospel of Christ* (Ro 1:16) is that they do not have the *knowledge of God.*

3.2.1.2. He gave them the reason for his assurance that his Father would honor him and acknowledge him (v. 55): *But I know him,* and again, *I know him.* This showed also his confidence in his Father. Notice:

3.2.1.2.1. How he professed his knowledge of his Father with the greatest certainty: *If I should say I know him not, I should be a liar like unto you.* He would not deny his relationship with God to humor the Jews. If he were to do so, he would be found to have been a false witness against God and himself.

3.2.1.2.2. How he proved his knowledge of his Father: *I know him and keep his saying,* or his word. He kept his Father's word, and he kept his own word with the Father. Christ requires (v. 51) that we *keep his sayings,* and he has set before us an example of obedience: he *kept his Father's sayings;* well could he who *learned obedience* teach it (Heb 5:8). Christ showed by this that he knew the Father.

3.2.2. He referred them to their father, and that was Abraham.

3.2.2.1. Christ asserted that Abraham had had a prospect of him and a respect for him: *Your father Abraham rejoiced to see my day, and he saw it, and was glad* (v. 56). He spoke here about two things as showing the patriarch's respect for the promised Messiah:

3.2.2.1.1. The ambition he had to *see his day*: *He rejoiced;* "he leaped at it, was overjoyed at it." Although the word commonly means "rejoice," here it must refer to an ecstasy of desire rather than of joy, because otherwise the end of v. 56—he *saw it, and was glad*—would be a tautology. The announcements Abraham had received of the future Messiah had raised in him an expectation of something great, which he fervently longed to know more about. Those who rightly know anything of Christ must fervently want to know him more. Those who discern the dawning of the light of the Sun of righteousness must wish to see his rising (Mal 4:2). Abraham desired to see Christ's day even though it was a long way away, but his corrupt descendants did not discern Christ's day, nor did they welcome it when it came.

3.2.2.1.2. The satisfaction he enjoyed in what he did see of it: *He saw it, and was glad.* Notice:

3.2.2.1.2.1. How God satisfied the godly desire of Abraham; he longed to see Christ's day, and he *saw it.* Although he did not see it as clearly as we now see it under the Gospel, he still saw something of it, more afterward than he did at first. To those who desire and pray to know Christ more, God will give more knowledge. But how did Abraham see Christ's day? Some understand it as referring to the sight he had of it in the other world. The longings of gracious souls for Christ will be fully satisfied when they come to heaven, but not until then. But it is more commonly understood of some sight he had of Christ's day in this world. Those who *received not the promises* nevertheless *saw them afar off* (Heb 11:13). There is room to think that Abraham had some vision of Christ and his day that is not recorded in the account of his life.

3.2.2.1.2.2. How Abraham received these revelations of Christ's day: *He saw, and was glad.* He was glad to see God's favor toward him and glad to foresee the mercy God had in store for the world. A faithful sight of Christ and his day will put only gladness into the heart. There is no joy like the joy of faith; we never know true pleasure until we know Christ.

3.2.2.2. The Jews objected to this and criticized him for it (v. 57): *Thou art not yet fifty years old, and hast thou seen Abraham?* They thought it absurd for him to claim to have seen Abraham, who had died so many ages before he was born. Now this gave them cause to *despise his youth* (1Ti 4:12), as if he were born only yesterday and knew nothing: *Thou art not yet fifty years old.*

3.2.2.3. Our Savior gave a powerful answer to this objection by solemnly asserting that he was more ancient than even Abraham himself (v. 58): *"Verily, verily, I say unto you;* I say it to your faces, take it however you wish: *Before Abraham was, I am."* It may be read, "Before Abraham *was made or born*, I am." The change in verb tense is significant, showing that Abraham was created, and he himself was the Creator. Before Abraham, Christ was God. *I am* is the name of God (Ex 3:14). He did not say "I was," but "I am," because he is the first and the last (Rev 1:8). He was the appointed Messiah long before Abraham.

3.2.2.4. This great statement ended the dispute abruptly. They could not bear to hear any more from him, and he needed to say nothing more to them. Their hardened prejudice against the holy, spiritual teaching and law of Christ defeated all methods of conviction. Notice here:

3.2.2.4.1. How they were enraged with Christ for what he said: *They took up stones to cast at him* (v. 59). Perhaps they looked on him as a blasphemer, and such were indeed to be stoned (Lev 24:16), but they must be first legally tried and convicted. We may say farewell to justice and good order if everyone claims to administer the law as they choose. Who would think that there would ever be such evil in people? Everyone has a stone to throw at Christ's holy religion (Ac 28:22).

3.2.2.4.2. How he made his escape out of their hands.

3.2.2.4.2.1. He absconded; Jesus *hid himself*. Not that Christ was afraid or ashamed to stand by what he had said, but his *hour was not yet come* (v. 20), and by his own example he wanted to support the decision of his ministers and people in times of persecution to flee when they were called to do so.

3.2.2.4.2.2. He departed; he *went out of the temple, going through the midst of them*, undiscovered, and *so passed by*. This was not a cowardly, inglorious escape, and it did not show guilt or fear. Rather:

3.2.2.4.2.2.1. It showed his power over his enemies that they could do no more against him than he allowed them to do. They now thought they had him for sure, but he *passed through the midst* of them and so he left them to be angry.

3.2.2.4.2.2.2. It showed his wise provision for his own safety. This is how he gave an example of his own rule, *When they persecute you in one city, flee to another* (Mt 10:23; 23:34).

3.2.2.4.2.2.3. It was a righteous deserting of those who stoned him away. Christ will not long stay with those who tell him to go. Christ now went through the middle of the Jews, and none of them tried to stop him or roused themselves to take hold of him; indeed, they were content to let him go. God never leaves anyone until they have first provoked him to withdraw and want to have nothing to do with him. When Christ left them, it is said that he passed by silently and unobserved, so that they were not aware of him; he slipped away from the temple grounds. Christ's departures from a church or from a particular soul are often secret. *As the kingdom of God comes not*, so it does not go, *with observation* (Lk 17:20). This is the situation of these Jews who had forsaken God: God left them, and sadly they never missed him.

CHAPTER 9

In this chapter we have: 1. The miraculous healing of a man who was born blind (vv. 1–7). 2. The discussions that now arose from that: 2.1. Among the neighbors and between them and the man (vv. 8–12). 2.2. Between the Pharisees and the man (vv. 13–34). 2.3. Between Christ and the poor man (vv. 35–38). 2.4. Between Christ and the Pharisees (vv. 39–41).

Verses 1–7

Here we have sight given to a poor beggar who had been blind from birth. See:

1. The notice our Lord Jesus took of the pitiful situation of this poor blind man (v. 1): *As Jesus passed by, he saw a man which was blind from his birth.*

1.1. Though the Jews had abused Jesus so cruelly, he did not miss any opportunity to do good among them. The healing of this blind man was a kindness to the public, enabling him to work for his living, whereas before he had been an expense and a burden to the neighborhood. It is noble, generous, and Christlike to be willing to serve the public.

1.2. Even though he was escaping from a threatening danger, fleeing for his life, he still willingly stopped and stayed awhile to show mercy to this poor man. We make more haste than speed when we miss out on opportunities to do good.

1.3. Christ took this poor blind man he met on his way and cured him *as he passed by*. We, like our Lord, should take opportunities to do good even as we pass by, wherever we are.

1.3.1. The condition of this poor man was miserable. He was blind and had been so *from his birth*. Those who are blind cannot enjoy the light, but those who are born blind have no idea of it. It seems to me that such a person would give a great deal to have his curiosity satisfied by being able to see, even for only one day, light and colors, shapes and figures, even though he would never see them again. Let us bless God that it was not so with us. The eye is one of the most intricate parts of the body, having a very complex structure. What a mercy it is that there was no failure in the way we have been made! Christ healed many who were blinded by disease or accident, but here he healed a person who was born blind, in order to show his power to help in the most desperate cases and give an example of the work of his grace on the souls of sinners, which gives sight to those who were by nature blind.

1.3.2. The compassion of our Lord Jesus toward him was very tender. He *saw him*; that is, he looked on him with great concern. Others saw him, but not as Jesus did. Christ is often found by those who are not seeking him, or who do not ask for him (Isa 65:1).

2. The conversation between Christ and his disciples about this man.

2.1. The question the disciples asked their Master (v. 2). When Christ looked at him, they looked at him too; Christ's compassion should kindle ours. But they did not ask Christ to heal him. Instead, they asked a very strange question about him: *Rabbi, who sinned, this man or his parents, that he was born blind?* Now this question of theirs was:

2.1.1. Uncharitably censorious. They assumed that this extraordinary adversity was the punishment of some uncommon evil. The people who suffer the most are not to be thought the greatest sinners solely on account of their suffering. The grace of repentance calls our own afflictions punishments, but the grace of love calls the afflictions of others trials.

2.1.2. Unnecessarily curious. They asked, Who were the criminals, *this man or his parents*? What business of the disciples was this? Or what good would it do them if they knew it? We tend to be more inquisitive about other people's sins than about our own. To judge ourselves is our duty, but to judge our brother or sister is our sin. They asked:

2.1.2.1. Whether this man was being punished because of some sin of his own, either committed or foreseen before his birth. Was this man's soul condemned to the dungeon of this blind body to punish it for some great sin committed in another body that the soul had given life to before? The Pharisees seemed to have had the same opinion of him when they said, *Thou wast altogether born in sin* (v. 34). Or:

2.1.2.2. Whether he was being punished because of the evil of his parents, which God sometimes *visits upon the children* (Ex 20:5). One good reason for parents to watch out for sin is that their children may have to suffer for their parents' sin when their parents have gone. Being at a loss as to how to interpret this providence, the disciples wanted to be informed. The fairness of God's ways is always certain, for *his righteousness is as the great mountains*, but it cannot always be explained, because his *judgments are a great deep* (Ps 36:6).

2.2. Christ's answer to this question.

2.2.1. He gave the reason for this poor man's blindness: *"Neither has this man sinned nor his parents*; rather, he was born blind so that now at last *the works of God would be made manifest in him* (that the work of God might be displayed in his life)" (v. 3). Here, Christ told them two things about such uncommon adversities:

2.2.1.1. That they are not always inflicted as punishments of sin. Many who are not at all more sinful than others are made more miserable than others in this life. It was not some exceptional guilt in either the man or his parents that God had in mind in inflicting blindness on the man.

2.2.1.2. Misfortunes are sometimes intended purely *for the glory of God*, to display his work. If God is glorified either by us or in us, our lives are not worthless. This man was born blind so *that the works of God might be manifest in him* (v. 3), that is:

2.2.1.2.1. So that the attributes of God could be displayed in him, and especially so that God's extraordinary power and goodness would be revealed in healing him. The difficulties of Providence, which are otherwise inexplicable, can all be resolved by affirming that in them God intends to show himself. Those who do not consider him in the ordinary course of things are sometimes alarmed by extraordinary things.

2.2.1.2.2. So that the purposes of God could be revealed in him. He was born blind so that our Lord Jesus would prove he was sent by God to be the true light to the world (1:9; 8:12; 9:5). It had now been a long time since this man was born blind, but until now no one knew why he was. Sometimes the sentences in the book of Providence are long, and we must read a long way into the book before we can grasp their sense.

2.2.2. He gave the reason for his own eagerness and readiness to help and heal him (vv. 4–5). *I must work the works of him that sent me while it is day. The night cometh, when no man can work.* It was the Sabbath, on which only essential work could be done, and he proved this to be an essential work.

2.2.2.1. It was his Father's will: *I must work the works of him that sent me.* Those whom God sends he employs, because he sends no one to be lazy. Christ was a worker together with God (2Co 6:1). He was pleased to put himself under the strongest obligations to undertake the business he was sent for: *I must work.* Christ fully and diligently set himself to undertake his work. He *worked the works* he had to do. It is not enough to look at our work and talk about it; we must also do it.

2.2.2.2. Now his opportunity came: "I must work *while it is day*, while the light given to work by lasts." Christ himself had his day. All the work he himself had to do here on earth was to be done before his death; the time of his living in this world was the day spoken about here. The time of our life is our day. Daytime is the proper time

for work; during the day of our lives we must be busy, not wasting time by playing around; there will be enough time to rest when our day is done.

2.2.2.3. The end of his opportunity was at hand, and so he wanted to be busy: "*The night comes, when no man can work.* It will undoubtedly come; it may come suddenly and is coming nearer and nearer." We cannot figure out how near our sunset is; the sun may set for us at noon; nor can we promise ourselves a dusk between the day of life and the night of death. When the night comes, we cannot work. When night comes, *call the labourers* (Mt 20:8); we must then show our work and receive according to the things done. We must seize every opportunity that presents itself.

2.2.2.4. His business in the world was to give it light (v. 5): *As long as I am in the world, I am the light of the world.* He had said this before (8:12). Christ was going to heal this blind man, the representative of a blind world, because he came to be the light of the world, not only to give light but also to give sight. Now this gives us a great encouragement to come to him. In which direction should we turn our eyes (6:68), except to the One who is the light? We share in the sun's light without money and without price, and so we may also share in Christ's grace on the same terms (Isa 55:1). Here is a good example of usefulness in the world. What Christ said about himself, he says about his disciples: *You are lights in the world,* and if so, *Let your light shine* (Mt 5:14, 16). What were candles made for but to burn?

3. The manner of the healing of the blind man (vv. 6–7). The circumstances of the miracle were special and were no doubt significant. *When he had thus spoken*, opening their understanding (Lk 24:45), he turned to the opening of the blind man's eyes. He did not delay it until the Sabbath was passed, when it would cause less offense. The good we have opportunity to do we should do quickly; those who will never do good until there are no objections to it will leave many good works undone forever (Ecc 11:4). In the healing, notice:

3.1. The preparation of the eye salve (Rev 3:18). Christ *spat on the ground, and made clay of the spittle.* He made some mud from his own saliva, because there was no water nearby and because he wanted to teach us to be willing to simply take what is readily available if it will do. Why should we go the long way around looking for something we can get just as easily nearby?

3.2. The application of it to the place: *He anointed the eyes of the blind man with the clay.* Like a sensitive doctor, he himself did it with his own hand, even though the patient was a beggar. Daubing clay on the eyes would close them up, but never open them. The power of God often works through opposites. The purpose of the Gospel is to *open men's eyes* (Ac 26:18). The salve that is now effective has been prepared by Christ. We must come to Christ for *the eyesalve* (Rev 3:18). He is the only One who is able, and the only One who is appointed, to make it up (Lk 4:18). The means used in this work are very weak and unlikely and are made effective only by the power of Christ. The way Christ uses is first to make people feel themselves blind and then to give them sight.

3.3. The directions given to the patient (v. 7). His doctor said to him, *Go, wash in the pool of Siloam.* Christ wanted to test his obedience, to see whether he would have the implicit faith to obey the orders of One whom he was so much a stranger to. He also wanted to test how he was disposed toward the tradition of the elders, which taught that it was not lawful to wash the eyes on the Sabbath. He wanted to describe the way of spiritual healing, in which, though the effect is owing purely to his power and grace, there is also a duty to be done by us. "Go and search the Scriptures, go and listen to the ministry, go and speak with wise people"—these are all ways that are like washing in the Pool of Siloam. Promised graces must be expected when we are present at organized services of public worship. Concerning the Pool of Siloam, notice that it was supplied with water from Mount Zion, living waters, which were *healing* (Eze 47:9). The Evangelist notes the meaning of the name, "sent." Christ is often called "the One sent by God," and so when Christ sent him to the Pool of Siloam, he was in effect sending him to himself, to Christ. "Go, wash in the *fountain opened* (Zec 13:1), a fountain of life, not a pool."

3.4. The patient's obedience to these directions: *He went his way therefore.* The man washed his eyes. Out of confidence in Christ's power as well as in obedience to his command, he went and washed.

3.5. The healing carried out: *He came seeing.* In the same way, when the pains and struggles of the new birth are ended, the bonds of sin fly off, and a glorious light and liberty come in their place (Ro 8:21). We see here the power of Christ. What could be impossible for the One who could do this, and do it in this way? This man let Christ do what he pleased, and he did what Christ appointed him to do, and so was healed. Those who want to be healed by Christ must be ruled by him. The man came back from the pool wondering and wondered at; he *came seeing.* This represents the benefit gracious souls find in being present at services of organized public worship, according to Christ's appointment: they have gone trembling and come away triumphing; they have gone blind and come away seeing, come away singing (Isa 52:8).

Verses 8–12

Such a miracle as the giving of sight to a man born blind must surely have been the talk of the town. Here, however, to confirm the facts, we are told what the neighbors said about it. What at first was not believed without scrutiny may later be accepted without scruple. Two things were debated:

1. Whether this was the same man who previously had been blind (v. 8).

1.1. The neighbors were staggered when they saw that he had gained his eyesight, and they said, *Is not this he that sat and begged?* When he could not work, then, because his parents were unable to maintain him, he begged. Those who cannot otherwise subsist must not be *ashamed to beg* (Lk 16:3); let no one be ashamed of anything except sin. There are some common beggars who are objects of charity, and these should be distinguished; we must not let the bees starve for the sake of the drones or wasps among them. In this man, who was well known and noticeable, the truth of the miracle was better confirmed, because there were more to witness against those unfaithful Jews who would not believe that he had been blind than if he had been looked after in his father's house. Note Christ's condescension. When it was for the advantage of his miracles that they be performed on those who were well known, he chose those who were made so by their poverty and misery, not by their high position.

1.2. Some said, *This is he*, the same man, and these were the witnesses of the truth of the miracle, because they had long known him to be completely blind. Others said, *He is not he, but is like him*, implying a confession that "if it is he, a great miracle has been performed on him." Think:

1.2.1. Of the wisdom and power of Providence in arranging such a universally wide range of faces of men

and women, so that no two are so alike that they cannot be distinguished, which is necessary for society, commerce, and the administration of justice.

1.2.2. Of the wonderful change that the converting grace of God makes on some who before were evil but are so universally and visibly changed that one would not think they were the same person.

1.3. This dispute was quickly decided by the man himself: *He said, I am he*; "I am the man who was blind, but now look, I am a memorial to the mercy and grace of God." Those who are savingly enlightened by the grace of God should be ready to acknowledge what they were like before.

2. How he came to have his eyes opened (vv. 10–12). They would now turn aside and *see this great sight* (Ex 3:3), and further inquire about it. These neighbors asked about two things:

2.1. How the healing happened: *How were thine eyes opened?* It is good to notice how God works; then his works will appear more wonderful. In answer to this question, the poor man gave them a direct and full account of the matter: *A man that is called Jesus made clay, and I received sight* (v. 11). Those who have experienced God's power and goodness, either in physical or in spiritual matters, should always be ready to share their experiences. It is a debt we owe to our God, who has given so generously to us, and also to our brothers and sisters. God's favors are lost on us when they are lost with us, going no further.

2.2. Who brought about the healing (v. 12): *Where is he?* Perhaps some asked this question out of curiosity. "Where is he, so that we can have a look at him?" Others, perhaps, asked out of ill will. "Where is he, so that we may seize him?" The unthinking crowd would have wrong thoughts about those who were given a bad name. Yet some, we hope, asked this question out of goodwill. "Where is the man who performed this miracle, so that we may come to know him?" In answer to this question, the man could say nothing: *I know not.* As soon as Christ had sent him to the Pool of Siloam, it seems, he immediately withdrew. The man had never seen Jesus, because by the time he had gained his sight he had lost his Doctor. None of all the new and surprising objects that presented themselves could be so delightful to him as one glimpse of Christ, but up to that time he knew no more about him than that he was called Jesus, "a Savior." We see the change brought about on the soul in the work of grace, but not the hand that has made that change.

Verses 13–34

One would have expected that such a miracle as Christ performed on the blind man would have silenced and shamed all opposition, but it had the opposite effect; instead of being embraced as a prophet for it, he was prosecuted as a criminal.

1. Here is the information given to the Pharisees: *They brought to the Pharisees him that aforetime* (before) *was blind* (v. 13). Some think that those who brought this man to the Pharisees did it with a good intention, to show them that this Jesus was not what they represented him as being but one who gave considerable proofs of his divine mission. It seems, however, they did it with a bad intention.

2. Here is the reason given for providing this information to the Pharisees. What is good has never been maligned except by being called evil. The crime objected to here (v. 14) was that *it was the sabbath day when Jesus made the clay, and opened his eyes.* The traditions of the Jews had made violations of the law of the Sabbath out of

actions that were far from being so. But it may be asked, "Why would Christ not only perform miracles on the Sabbath but also do them in such a way as he knew would give offense to the Jews? Could he not have healed this blind man without making mud?" I answer:

2.1. That he did not want to seem to give in to the usurped power of the teachers of the law and Pharisees. Christ was made under the law of God (Gal 4:4), but not under their law.

2.2. He did it so that he could explain the law of the fourth commandment by both word and action. Works of necessity and mercy are allowed, and the Sabbath rest is to be kept not so much for its own sake as in order to do the work of the Sabbath.

3. Here is the trial and examination of this matter by the Pharisees (v. 15). So much passion, prejudice, and hard feelings, and so little reason, appear here that the discussion is nothing but a cross-examination. Their enmity toward Christ had emptied them of all humanity and all sense of God. Let us see how they teased information out of this man.

3.1. They interrogated him about the healing itself.

3.1.1. They *did not believe* that he had been *born blind*. The Pharisees' disbelief sprang not from wise caution but from prejudiced faithlessness. However, they used a good way to clear up the matter: *They called the parents of the man who had received his sight*. They did this in the hope of disproving the miracle, but God so ordered and overruled their purposes as to turn it into further evidence of the miracle, leaving them obliged to be either convinced or confounded. In this part of the examination we have:

3.1.1.1. The questions that the Pharisees asked the parents (v. 19): "They *asked them, Is this your son? Do you say he was born blind? How then doth he now see?* That is impossible, and so you had better withdraw your claim that he can now see." Those who cannot bear the light of truth do all they can to overshadow it and prevent it from being discovered.

3.1.1.2. The parents' answers to these questions, in which:

3.1.1.2.1. They fully confirmed what they could safely say about this matter (v. 20): *"We know that this is our son*, and we know he was *born blind*." Their care had cost them many sad thoughts and many anxious, troublesome hours. Those who are ashamed of their children because of their physical weaknesses may take a rebuke from these parents, who freely acknowledged, "This is our son," even though he was born blind.

3.1.1.2.2. They cautiously declined to give any evidence about his healing. They had not been eyewitnesses to it and therefore could say nothing about it from their own personal knowledge.

3.1.1.2.2.1. Notice how cautiously they expressed themselves (v. 21): *By what means he now seeth, we know not; or who has opened his eyes, we know not*. Now these parents of the blind man were bound in gratitude to give their testimony to the honor of the Lord Jesus, who had done their son such a great kindness, but they did not have the courage to do so; they thought they could atone for not testifying in Jesus' favor by pointing out that they had said nothing against him. They referred themselves and the court to their son himself: *He is of age; ask him; he shall speak for himself*. Though born blind, the man seems to have had a quicker understanding than many others. By a kind providence, God often makes up in the mind what is lacking in the body (1Co 12:23–24). But the parents directed the Pharisees to their son only to save themselves from trouble.

3.1.1.2.2.2. Notice the reason why they were so cautious (vv. 22–23): *they feared the Jews*. They wanted to shift the burden of trouble away from themselves. My friend is dear to me, and so is my child, and perhaps my religious faith, but "dearer is myself." Here is:

3.1.1.2.2.2.1. The recent law that the Sanhedrin had enacted. If any man within their jurisdiction *confessed that Jesus was Christ, he would be put out of the synagogue* (v. 22). Notice:

3.1.1.2.2.2.1.1. The crime intended to be punished, and that was embracing and confessing Jesus of Nazareth as the promised Messiah. They themselves expected a Messiah, but they could by no means bear to think that this Jesus was the One, for two reasons. First, his precepts were all so contrary to their traditional laws. The spiritual worship he established overthrew their formalities. Humility, self-denial, and repentance were new lessons to them, and they sounded difficult and strange to their ears. Second, his promises and appearance were so contrary to their traditional hopes. To hear of a Messiah whose outward circumstances were humble and poor and who told his followers to expect the cross and count on persecution was more than they could accept. All this was such an insult and disappointment to all their hopes that they could never be reconciled to it. Rightly or wrongly, it must be crushed.

3.1.1.2.2.2.1.2. The penalty to be inflicted for this crime. If anyone acknowledged themselves to be a disciple of Jesus, they would be *put out of the synagogue* as one who had rendered themselves unworthy of the honors of their church and ineligible to share in its privileges. Nor was this simply an ecclesiastical censure. It in effect made a person an outlaw. From its origin, Christ's holy religion has been opposed by penal laws made against those who profess it. When the command of the church has fallen into the wrong hands, the church's artillery has often been turned against it. It is nothing new to see those who were the synagogue's greatest jewels and blessings thrown out of it. Note that the Jews had *already* agreed to enact this law. They were so quickly aware of Christ's growing influence and had already agreed to do their best to suppress it.

3.1.1.2.2.2.2. The influence this law had on the parents of the blind man. They declined to say anything about Christ, *because they feared the Jews*. Christ had incurred the disapproval of the government by helping their son, but they would not incur that disapproval by giving Jesus honor. We will now continue with the examination of the man himself.

3.1.2. The Pharisees asked him how the healing took place (vv. 15–16).

3.1.2.1. *Now again the Pharisees asked him* the same question that his neighbors had asked him, *how he had received his sight*. They did not ask this question with any sincere desire to find out the truth, but only with a desire to try to prove something against Christ.

3.1.2.2. He repeated here to the Pharisees, in effect, the same answer as he had given before to his neighbors: *He put clay upon mine eyes, and I washed, and do see*. In the previous account he said, *I washed, and received sight*, but in case they thought it was only a glimpse, he now said, "*I do see*; the healing is complete and lasting."

3.1.2.3. The remarks made on this story were very diverse and led to a discussion in the court (v. 16).

3.1.2.3.1. Some took advantage of this to criticize and condemn Christ. Some of the Pharisees said, *This man is not of God, because he keepeth not the sabbath day* (v. 16). The teaching on which this censure was based is true—that those who do not *keep the sabbath day are not of God*. Those who come from God will keep the commandments of God, and it is his commandment that we keep the Sabbath holy. The application of this teaching to our Savior, however, was very unjust, because he religiously observed the Sabbath; he never did anything but good on the Sabbath. He did not keep the Sabbath according to the tradition of the elders, but he kept it according to the command of God. Much unrighteousness and uncharitable judging is caused by people making the rules of religion stricter than God has made them, adding their own whims to what God has appointed. Not everything that we take as a rule of practice must immediately be made a rule of judgment.

3.1.2.3.*2*. Others spoke in his favor, urging very relevantly, *How can a man that is a sinner do such miracles?* There were some who were witnesses for Christ even among his enemies. The facts of the matter were plain: this was a true miracle. Such things could never be done by a man who was a sinner. Such a person may perhaps show some *signs and lying wonders* (2Th 2:9), but not such signs and true wonders as Christ performed. There was therefore *a division among them* (v. 16). This is how God defeats the purposes of his enemies by dividing them against one another.

3.2. They inquired about its author. Notice:

3.2.1. What the man said about him. They asked him (v. 17), *"What sayest thou of him, seeing that he has opened thine eyes?"* If he were to speak disrespectfully of Christ in response to this, as he might be tempted to do to please them, they would have triumphed in it. Nothing confirms Christ's enemies in their hostility toward him so much as the disrespect shown him by those who have passed as his friends. However, if the man were to speak honorably of Christ, they would prosecute him and make an example of him. Or perhaps Christ's friends suggested hearing the man's own thoughts and feelings about his doctor, since he appeared to be sensible. Those whose eyes Christ has opened know best what to say about him and have great reason to speak well of him. What do we think about Christ? The poor man gave a short, plain, direct answer to this question: *He is a prophet*. It seems this man had no idea that Jesus was the Messiah, the great Prophet. He thought well of Jesus according to the light he had, though he did not think well enough of him. This poor, blind beggar had a clearer judgment of the things concerning the kingdom of God than the *masters in Israel* (3:10).

3.2.2. What they said about Christ in reply to the man's testimony. Finding that a *notable miracle* had really been performed, which *they could not deny* (Ac 4:16), they did all they could to shake the good opinion the man had of the person who had opened his eyes, and to convince him that Christ was a bad man (v. 24): *Give God the praise; we know that this man is a sinner*. This is to be understood in two ways:

3.2.2.1. By way of advice, that the man should beware ascribing the praise of his healing to a sinful man, but should give it all to God. When God uses sinners as instruments of good to us, we must give God the glory, but there is gratitude owing to the instruments. It was a good charge, *Give God the praise*, but here it was used wrongly.

3.2.2.2. By way of a solemn charge to tell the truth. "We know that this man is a sinner. We are sure of this, and so give God the praise. In God's name, tell the truth." Notice how corruptly they spoke about the Lord Jesus: *We know that this man is a sinner*. Notice:

3.2.2.2.*1*. Their arrogance and pride. They knew very well that he was a sinner, and no one could convince them to the contrary. He had challenged them to their faces (8:46) to prove him guilty of sin, and they had had nothing to say, but now behind his back they spoke about him as an evildoer. False accusers make up in their confidence what is lacking in proof.

3.2.2.2.*2*. The injury and indignity done here to the Lord Jesus. When he became a human being, he took on himself not only the form of a servant but also the likeness of a sinner. Being *made sin for us* (2Co 5:21), he *despised even this shame* (Heb 12:2).

3.3. A debate arose between the Pharisees and this poor man about Christ. They said, "He is a sinner"; the man said, "He is a prophet." Those who are called out to witness for Christ are encouraged when they notice the wisdom and courage with which this man managed his defense, according to the promise, *It shall be given you in that same hour what you shall speak* (Mt 10:19). Now in the discussion we may notice three steps:

3.3.1. The man insisted on the truth of the evidence they tried to shake.

3.3.1.1. He abided by what, to him at least, was beyond dispute (v. 25): *"Whether he be a sinner or no I know not*, or, as it could better be rendered, *"If he be a sinner, I know it not*, because this *one thing I know, that whereas I was blind, now I see*, and so I say he is *a prophet*; I am both able and obliged to speak well about him." He tacitly rebuked their great assurance of the bad character they ascribed to the holy Jesus: "I, who know him as well as you do, cannot describe him in any such way." He boldly relied on his own experience of the power and goodness of the righteous Jesus, and decided to stand by that. There is no disputing experience. Just as Christ's mercies are most valued by those who have felt the lack of them, so the most powerful and long-lasting affections for Christ are those that arise from an experience of him (1Jn 1:1; Ac 4:20). In the work of grace in the soul, although we cannot tell when and how the blessed change was brought about, we may still take comfort from it if we can say, through grace, *"Whereas I was blind, now I see."*

3.3.1.2. They tried to confuse and stifle the evidence by a needless repetition of their questions about it (v. 26): *What did he to thee? How opened he thine eyes?* They asked these questions because they lacked something positive to say and preferred to speak arrogantly rather than appear to be silenced, and also because they hoped that by making the man repeat his evidence they could catch him changing his story.

3.3.2. He rebuked them for their invincible prejudices, and they hurled insults at him as a disciple of Jesus (vv. 27–29). Notice:

3.3.2.1. The man boldly rebuked them for their willful and unreasonable opposition to the evidence of this miracle (v. 27). He was not going to satisfy them by repeating the story. *I have told you already, and you did not hear; wherefore would you hear it again? Will you also be his disciples?* Some think that he spoke seriously, really expecting them to be convinced. However, it rather seems to be spoken ironically: *"Will you be his disciples?* No, I know you hate even the thought of it." Those who willfully shut their eyes to the light, as these Pharisees did:

3.3.2.1.*1*. Make themselves contemptible and corrupt.

3.3.2.1.*2*. Forfeit all benefits of further instructions. They have already been told once and have refused to listen, and so why should they be told it again (Jer 51:9)?

3.3.2.1.*3*. Are here *receiving the grace of God in vain* (2Co 6:1). This is implied in, *Will you be his disciples?*

One would have thought that those who would not see reason to accept Christ and join his followers would still see enough reason not to hate and persecute him and them.

3.3.2.2. They scorned him and hurled insults at him for this (v. 28). When they could not resist the wisdom and spirit with which he spoke (Ac 6:10), they lost their temper. Unreasonable people usually try to make up for a lack of truth and reason by an abundance of noisy insults.

3.3.2.2.1. They taunted this man for his devotion to Christ; they said, *Thou art his disciple.* They *reviled him.* The Vulgate reads, "they cursed him"; and what was their curse? It was this: *Be thou his disciple.* "May such a curse," Augustine says here, "ever be on us and on our children!" They had no reason to call this man a disciple of Christ—he had only spoken favorably of a kindness Christ had done him. But they could not bear this.

3.3.2.2.2. They boasted of their relationship with Moses as their Master: *We are Moses' disciples.* Before this, these Pharisees had boasted about their good parentage: *We are Abraham's seed* (8:33). Here they boasted about their good education: *We are Moses' disciples*—as if these boasts would be good enough to save them. Yet there was a perfect harmony between Christ and Moses; they could be disciples of Moses and also become the disciples of Christ. Here, however, they set the two teachers in opposition to each other. If we rightly understand the matter, we will see that the grace of God and the responsibility of human beings meet together and kiss and befriend each other (Ps 85:10).

3.3.2.2.3. They gave some sort of reason for their loyalty to Moses against Christ (v. 29): *We know that God spoke unto Moses; as for this fellow, we know not whence he is.* But did they not know that they must expect another prophet and a further revelation of the mind of God (Dt 18:15)? Yet when our Lord Jesus did appear, they not only forfeited but also abandoned *their own mercies* (Jnh 2:8). In their argument, notice:

3.3.2.2.3.1. How arrogantly they alleged what none of his followers ever denied: *We know that God spoke unto Moses*; and, thank God, we know it too.

3.3.2.2.3.2. How absurdly they urged their ignorance of Christ as a reason to justify their contempt for him: *As for this fellow.* See how scornfully they spoke of the blessed Jesus, as if they did not think it worthwhile to burden their memories with such an insignificant name. *"As for this fellow,* this sorry fellow, *we know not from whence he is."* Not long before this, the Jews had made the opposite objection to Christ (7:27): *We know this man whence he is, but when Christ comes, no man knows whence he is.* Here we see how they could with the greatest assurance either affirm or deny the same thing, depending on what would give them an advantage. Notice the absurdity of faithlessness. People do not know the message of Christ because they are determined not to believe it, and then they claim not to believe it because they do not know it.

3.3.3. He reasoned with them, and they threw him out.

3.3.3.1. When the poor man found he had reason on his side, he grew bolder. He wondered at their stubborn faithlessness (v. 30), but he answered bravely, *"Why, herein is a marvellous thing,* that *you know not whence he is,* but he has opened my eyes." He wondered at two things:

3.3.3.1.1. That they would be strangers to a man who was so famous. The One who could open the eyes of the blind must certainly be an important man and worth taking notice of. The fact that they would talk as if they thought it beneath them to be aware of such a man as this was very strange. Many who pretend to be learned and knowledgeable are not at all concerned—in fact, not even

curious—to become familiar with what the *angels desire to look into* (1Pe 1:12).

3.3.3.1.2. That they would question the divine mission of One who had undoubtedly performed a divine miracle. "Now this is strange," the poor man said, "that the miracle performed on me has not convinced you, that you would close your eyes against the light." If Christ had opened the eyes of the Pharisees, they would not have doubted that he was a prophet. The man argued strongly against them (vv. 31–33), proving not only that Christ was *not a sinner* (v. 31) but also that he was *of God* (v. 33).

3.3.3.1.2.1. He argued:

3.3.3.1.2.1.1. With great knowledge. Though he could not read a letter of the book, he was very familiar with the Scriptures; he had lacked the power of sight, but had made the most of his sense of hearing, *by which faith cometh* (Ro 10:17).

3.3.3.1.2.1.2. With great zeal for the honor of Christ.

3.3.3.1.2.1.3. With great boldness and courage. Those who are ambitious to enjoy the favors of God must not be afraid of the frowns of human beings.

3.3.3.1.2.2. His argument may be reduced to a simple syllogism, rather like the argument of David in Ps 66:18–20. David's major premise: *If I regard iniquity in my heart, God will not hear me.* Here: *God heareth not sinners.* David's minor premise: *But verily God hath heard me.* Here: "Truly God has heard Jesus; Jesus has been honored by being appointed to do what has never been done before." David's conclusion: *Blessed be God.* The conclusion here: "Jesus is *of God*" (v. 33).

3.3.3.1.2.2.1. He established it as an undoubted truth that none but the good are the favorites of heaven (v. 31): *Now we know that God heareth not sinners. If any man be a worshiper of God, and does his will, him he heareth.* The assertions, rightly understood, are true. Let it be said for the terror of evildoers, *God heareth not sinners.* This is no discouragement to repenting, returning sinners, but to those who continue in their sins. God will not *hear* them. Let it be said for the encouragement of the righteous: *If any man be a worshiper of God, and does his will, him he heareth.* We see here the complete characterization of a good person—he is one who worships God and does his will. Here also is the indescribable comfort of such a person: God hears him; he hears his prayers and answers them (Ps 34:15).

3.3.3.1.2.2.2. To strengthen his argument even more, he exalted the miracles that Christ had performed (v. 32): *Since the world began was it not heard that any man opened the eyes of one that was born blind.* It was a true miracle, beyond the power of nature. It had never been heard that anyone had healed a person blind from birth by natural means. It was also an extraordinary miracle, beyond the precedents of former miracles. Moses performed miraculous plagues, but Christ performed miraculous healings.

3.3.3.1.2.2.3. He therefore concluded, *If this man were not of God, he could do nothing.* What Christ did on earth sufficiently demonstrated what he was like in heaven. Each of us can know by this whether we come from God or not: *What do we?* What are we doing more than others?

3.3.3.2. The Pharisees clashed with him and rudely broke off the discussion (v. 34). We are told here:

3.3.3.2.1. What the Pharisees said. Having no answer to give to his argument, they argued ad hominem: *Thou wast altogether born in sin, and dost thou teach us?* Notice:

3.3.3.2.1.1. How they despised him: *"Thou wast not only born in sin,* as every person is, but completely so, and carrying with you in your body as well as in your soul the marks of that corruption; you were steeped in sin from birth." It was most unjust to take notice of his sin now that the healing had not only rolled away the reproach of his blindness (Jos 5:9) but also singled him out as a favorite of heaven.

3.3.3.2.*1.2.* How they disdained the thought of learning from him: *Dost thou teach us?* Very great emphasis must be put here on *thou* and *us.* "What! Will you, a foolish, sorry fellow, ignorant and illiterate—do you imagine you can teach us, who sit in Moses' seat (Mt 23:2)?" Proud people scorn being taught, especially by their inferiors, whereas we should never think ourselves too old, too wise, or too good to learn from others. Those who have a lot of money want to have more, and so why should not those who have a lot of knowledge desire more?

3.3.3.2.*2.* What they did: they *cast* (threw) *him out.* Some understand this to refer only to his rude and scornful dismissal from their council room. But it seems rather to be a judicial act; they excommunicated him.

Verses 35–38

In these verses we may notice:

1. The tender care that our Lord Jesus took of this poor man (v. 35): *When Jesus heard that they had cast him out,* he *found him,* which implies that he looked for him, so that he could encourage and strengthen him:

1.1. Because the man had spoken so well, so bravely, and so boldly in defense of the Lord Jesus. Jesus Christ will be sure to stand by his witnesses; he will acknowledge those who acknowledge him (1Sa 2:30), his truth, and his ways. Our testimonies for him will redound not only to our credit later but also to our comfort now.

1.2. Because the Pharisees had thrown him out. Here was one poor man who was suffering for Christ, and Christ took care that as his sufferings abounded, so his comfort would *much more abound* (2Co 1:5). Fortunate are those who have a friend whom human beings cannot prohibit them from seeing. Jesus Christ will graciously find and receive those who for his sake are unjustly rejected and thrown out by human beings.

2. The encouraging talk Christ had with him. Christ taught him further, for those who are faithful in a little will be entrusted with more (Mt 13:12).

2.1. Our Lord Jesus examined his faith: *"Dost thou believe on the Son of God?"* To give us an idea of his kingdom that is purely spiritual and divine, Christ called himself the *Son of God.*

2.2. The poor man carefully asked about the Messiah he was to believe in, professing his readiness to accept him (v. 36): *Who is he, Lord, that I may believe on him?* Some think he did know that Jesus, who healed him, was the Son of God, but that he did not know which of the people around him was Jesus, and therefore, supposing that the person who talked with him was a follower of Jesus, asked him to do him the favor of leading him to his master. Others think the man knew that this person talking with him was Jesus, whom he believed to be a great and good man and a prophet, but that he did not yet know that Jesus was the Son of God. "You who have given me physical sight, please tell me who and where this Son of God is." The question was rational and just: *Who is he, Lord, that I may believe on him?*

2.3. Our Lord Jesus graciously revealed himself to him as that Son of God: *Thou hast both seen him, and it is he that talketh with thee* (v. 37). We do not find that Christ revealed himself to any other person so expressly, and in so many words, as he did to the man here and to the

woman of Samaria (4:26). He left others to find out by arguments who he was. Christ described himself to this man in two ways here.

2.3.1. *Thou hast seen him.* The man was now made aware, more than ever, of what an indescribable blessing it was to be healed of his blindness, so that he could see the Son of God. The greatest comfort of physical eyesight is its usefulness to our faith and the interests of our souls. Can we say that we have seen Christ by faith, that we have seen him in his beauty and glory? Let us give him the praise, since he himself has opened our eyes.

2.3.2. *It is he that talketh with thee.* Great rulers are willing to be seen by some people whom they will not condescend to talk with. But Christ talks with those whose desires are toward him (SS 7:10), and he reveals himself to them, as he did to the two disciples when he talked and their hearts were warmed (Lk 24:32). This poor man was carefully inquiring after the Savior even as he saw him and was talking with him. Jesus Christ is often nearer to the souls who seek him than they themselves are aware of.

2.4. The poor man readily welcomed this surprising revelation and said, *Lord, I believe, and he worshipped him.*

2.4.1. He professed his faith in Christ: *"Lord, I believe you to be the Son of God."* He would not dispute anything that was said by the One who had shown such mercy to him and performed such a miracle for him. Believing with his heart, he confessed with his mouth (Ro 10:9), and now the bruised reed (Isa 42:3) had become a cedar (Ps 92:12; Eze 17:23).

2.4.2. He adored him: *He worshipped him.* In worshiping Jesus, he confessed him to be God. Those who believe in him will see every reason in the world to worship him. We read no more of this man, but he probably became a constant follower of Christ.

Verses 39–41

We have here:

1. The explanation Christ gave of his purpose in coming into the world (v. 39): *For judgment I am come.* What Christ spoke, he spoke not only as a preacher in the pulpit but also as a king on the throne and a judge on the bench.

1.1. His business in the world was great. He came *for judgment:* to preach a doctrine and a law that would try people, effectively revealing their true character and distinguish between them, by revealing the thoughts of many hearts (Lk 2:35).

1.2. He explained this great truth by a metaphor taken from the miracle he had just performed. He came so that *those who see not might see, and so that those who see might be made blind.*

1.2.1. This may be applied to nations and people. The Gentiles would see a great light, while blindness would come upon Israel, and their eyes would be darkened.

1.2.2. It may be applied to particular individuals. Christ came into the world:

1.2.2.1. Intentionally and deliberately to give sight to those who were spiritually blind, to reveal the object of sight by his word and to heal the organ of sight by his Spirit, so that many precious souls would be turned *from darkness to light* (Ac 26:18).

1.2.2.2. Eventually, at the last day, so *that those who see might be made blind,* so that those who have a high opinion of their own wisdom and set that in contradiction to divine revelation will be sealed in their ignorance. To those who through their so-called wisdom *knew not God,* the preaching of the cross seemed to be foolishness (1Co 1:18–21).

2. The Pharisees' objection to this. They said, *Are we blind also?* When Christ said that those who saw would be made blind by his coming, they realized he meant them, who were the "seers" of the people, who prided themselves on their insight and foresight. "We know that the common people are blind, but are we blind also?" Frequently those who most need and deserve a reproof have enough wit to discern an implied one but not enough grace to bear a just one. These Pharisees took this rebuke as pouring shame on them.

3. Christ's answer to this objection, which, if it did not convince them, at least silenced them: *If you were blind, you should have no sin, but now you say, We see; therefore your sin remaineth.* They gloried in their not being blind, in being able to see with their own eyes, having abilities—or so they thought—that were sufficient for their own guidance. The very thing they gloried in, Christ here told them, was their shame and ruin (Php 3:19).

3.1. *If you were blind, you would have no sin.* "If you were blind, you would have had comparatively no sin. If you had been really ignorant, your guilt would not have been so deeply aggravated." God ignored the times of ignorance. It will be more tolerable for those who perish for lack of vision (Pr 29:18) than for those who *rebel against the light* (Job 24:13). "If you had recognized your own blindness, you would soon have accepted Christ as your guide, and then you would have had no sin." Those who are convinced of their disease are on the way to being healed, for there is no greater hindrance to the salvation of souls than self-sufficiency.

3.2. "*But now you say, We see*; now that you have knowledge, being instructed from the law, now that you think you see your way better than anyone else can show it to you, *therefore your sin remains.*" Just as those who will not see are most blind, so the blindness of those who think they can see is the most dangerous blindness. *Seest thou a wise man in his own conceit?* Can you hear the Pharisees saying, *We see? There is more hope for a fool* (Pr 26:12), a tax collector or a prostitute, than for such people.

CHAPTER 10

We have here: 1. Christ's discourse about himself as the door of the sheepfold and the shepherd of the sheep (vv. 1–18). 2. The various responses of the people to that (vv. 19–21). 3. The discussion Christ had with the Jews in the temple at the Feast of Dedication (vv. 22–39). 4. His departure to the country after that (vv. 40–42).

Verses 1–18

The Pharisees defended their opposition to Christ by reference to their role as pastors or shepherds of the church. Because Jesus had not received a commission from them, he was an intruder and an imposter. The people were therefore bound by duty to stick with them and against him. In opposition to this, Christ described here those who were the false shepherds and those who the true ones were, leaving his listeners to conclude which they were.

1. Here the parable or comparison is set forth (vv. 1–5): *Verily, verily, I say unto you*; the word translated *verily* is *amen.* This strong affirmation shows the certainty and significance of what he said.

1.1. In the parable we have:

1.1.1. A thief and a robber, who comes to cause trouble to the flock and damage to the owner (v. 1). *He enters not by the door,* having no lawful reason to enter, but *climbs up some other way.* How hard evildoers work to cause trouble! This should shame us out of our laziness and cowardice in serving God.

1.1.2. The characterization that distinguishes the sheep's rightful owner: *He enters in by the door* (v. 2), coming to do them good. Sheep need human care, and in return for it they are useful to us (1Co 9:7); they clothe and feed those who look after and feed them.

1.1.3. The ready entrance that the shepherd finds: *To him the porter* (gatekeeper or watchman) *openeth* (v. 3).

1.1.4. The care he takes. The *sheep hear his voice,* and, what is more, he *calls his own sheep by name,* so exact is the notice he takes of them, and he leads them out of the fold to the green pastures (Ps 23:2). He does not drive them, but, as was the custom in those times, he goes in front of them (vv. 4–5), and they, being used to it, follow him and are safe.

1.1.5. The extraordinary way the sheep listen to the shepherd: *They know his voice,* and *a stranger will they not follow,* but will run away from him, not knowing his voice.

1.2. Let us notice from this parable:

1.2.1. Good people are appropriately compared to sheep. People, as creatures who depend on their Creator, are called the *sheep of his pasture* (Ps 100:3).

1.2.2. The church of God in the world is a sheep pen, into which the children of God who were scattered are *gathered together* (11:52).

1.2.3. This sheep pen is very exposed to thieves and robbers, wolves in sheep's clothing (Mt 7:15).

1.2.4. The great Shepherd of the sheep takes great care of the flock and of all who belong to it. God is the great Shepherd (Ps 23:1).

1.2.5. The undershepherds, who are entrusted to feed the flock of God, should be careful and faithful in discharging that trust. Ministers must serve the sheep in their spiritual interests, must feed their souls with the word of God. They must know the members of their flocks by name and watch over them; they must lead them into the pastures of public worship, serving as their mouthpiece to God and God's mouthpiece to them.

1.2.6. Those who are truly the sheep of Christ will be very alert for their Shepherd and very cautious and shy of strangers. *They follow their Shepherd,* since they *know his voice,* having both a discerning ear and an obedient heart. *They flee from a stranger* and dread following him, because they do not know his voice.

2. Here is the Jews' ignorance of the drift and meaning of this talk (v. 6): *Jesus spoke this parable* to them, *but they understood not what the things were which he spoke unto them.* The Pharisees had a high opinion of their own knowledge, and they did not have enough sense to understand the things that Jesus spoke of; those things were beyond their capacity. Frequently those who claim to have the greatest knowledge are the ones who are most ignorant in the things of God.

3. Here is Christ's explanation of this parable. In the parable, Christ had distinguished the shepherd from the robber by the fact that the shepherd *enters in by the door.* He identified himself as both the door by which the shepherd enters and the shepherd who enters by the door.

3.1. Christ is the door. He said it to the Jews, who wanted to be thought the only sheep God had, and to the Pharisees, who wanted to be thought the only shepherds the Jews had: "*I am the door* of the sheep pen."

3.1.1. In general, he is like a door that is closed to keep out thieves and robbers and those not fit to be admitted.

He is also like a door that is open to allow passage and communication. Through Christ, as the door, we are first admitted into the flock of God (14:6). Through him God comes to his church, that is, visits it and shares himself with it. Through Christ, as the door, the sheep are admitted into the heavenly kingdom (Mt 25:34).

3.1.2. In more detail:

3.1.2.1. Christ is the door of the shepherds, so that any who do not come in through him are not to be counted pastors, but rather *thieves and robbers*, because, though they claimed to be shepherds, *the sheep did not hear them* (v. 8). Note their description: they are *thieves and robbers*, and they were *all that went before him*, that is, all who assumed precedence and superiority above him. The Pharisees thought themselves the door through which all pastors must enter, and so they condemned our Savior as a thief and a robber, because he did not come in through them; but he showed that they should have been admitted by him. Note also the care taken to preserve the sheep from these thieves and robbers: *But the sheep did not hear them.* Those who were spiritual and heavenly could by no means approve of the traditions of the elders, nor enjoy their rules and regulations.

3.1.2.2. Christ is the door of *the sheep* (v. 9): *By me if any man enter into the sheepfold, he shall be saved, shall go in and out.* Here are:

3.1.2.2.1. Plain directions as to how to come into the fold: we must come in through Jesus Christ as the door. By faith in him we come into covenant and fellowship with God.

3.1.2.2.2. Precious promises (2Pe 1:4) to those who observe these directions. They *shall be saved* in the future; this is the privilege of their home. They will have found happiness forever. In the meantime they will *go in and out and find pasture*; this is the privilege of their life. True believers are at home in Christ; when they go out, they are not shut out as strangers, but are free to come in again when they please. When they come in, they are not shut in as trespassers, but are free to leave when they want to. They go out to the field in the morning and return to the pen at night. They find *pasture*, that is, food, in both: grass in the field, fodder in the pen.

3.2. Christ is the *shepherd* (v. 11). God has designated his Son Jesus to be our shepherd; here again and again Jesus acknowledged that relationship. He expects the church and every believer to serve and obey him just as the flocks in those countries served and obeyed their shepherds.

3.2.1. Christ is *a shepherd*, and not like the thief. Notice the troublesome intentions of the thief (v. 10): *The thief cometh not* only to *steal, and to kill, and to destroy.* Those whom thieves steal, whose hearts and affections they steal from Christ and his pastures, they kill and destroy spiritually. Deceivers of souls murder souls. Notice also the gracious intention of the shepherd. He has come:

3.2.1.1. To give life to the sheep. Christ said, *I am come*:

3.2.1.1.1. That *they might have life.* He came to put life into the flock, the church in general, which had seemed more like a valley full of dry bones (Eze 37:1–2) than a pasture covered with flocks. He came to give life to individual believers. Life includes all good.

3.2.1.1.2. That they might have it *more abundantly*, that they might have a life more abundant than could have been expected or than we are ever *able to ask or think* (Eph 3:20). However, it may also be interpreted "that they may have life to the full." Christ came to give life and *something more*, something better, life plus

something. Life in abundance is eternal life, life and much more.

3.2.1.2. To give his life for the sheep, so that he could give life to them (v. 11): *The good shepherd giveth his life for the sheep.* It is the responsibility of every good shepherd to risk and expose his life for the sheep. It was the privilege of the great Shepherd to give his life to purchase his flock (Ac 20:28).

3.2.2. Christ is *a good shepherd*, not a hired hand. Many of the Jews' shepherds were not thieves but were very careless in discharging their duty, and through their neglect the flock was greatly damaged. Christ here called himself *the good shepherd* (v. 11 and again v. 14). Jesus Christ is the best shepherd. There is no one so skillful, faithful, or tender as he is. He proves himself so, in contrast to all hired workers (vv. 12–14). Notice:

3.2.2.1. The carelessness of the unfaithful shepherd (vv. 12–13); the one who is a hired hand, *whose own the sheep are not, sees the wolf coming* and *leaves the sheep*, because he really *careth not for them.* Evil shepherds, judges, and ministers are described here both by their bad motives and their bad practices:

3.2.2.1.1. Their bad motives, the root of their bad practices. What makes those who have responsibility for souls in times of testing betray their trust, and what makes them neglect it in times of quiet? It is that they are *hirelings* and *care not for the sheep.* The wealth of the world is their main aim, because they are hired hands. They undertook the shepherds' job simply as a occupation to live by and to become rich from. It is the love of money and of their own stomachs that keeps them going. Those who love the wages more than the work are hired hands. The work involved is the least of their concerns. They do not value the sheep; they are unconcerned for the souls of others. They seek their own interests. What can be expected except that they will flee when the wolf comes? He *careth not for the sheep*, because he is one *whose own the sheep are not* (v. 12).

3.2.2.1.2. Their bad practices, the effect of these bad motives (v. 12). See how disgracefully the hired hand deserts his position; when he sees *the wolf coming*, he *leaves the sheep and flees.* Those who are more concerned for their safety than for their duty are an easy target for Satan's temptations. How fatal the consequences are! *The wolf catches the sheep* and *scatters them.*

3.2.2.2. The grace and tenderness of the Good Shepherd. The Lord Jesus is and always will be, as he has always been, *the good Shepherd.* Here are two great examples of the shepherd's goodness:

3.2.2.2.1. His knowing his flock:

3.2.2.2.1.1. He knows all who are now of his flock (vv. 14–15), as the Good Shepherd (vv. 3–4): *I know my sheep and am known of mine.* The sheep and shepherd know one another very well, and that relationship shows affection.

3.2.2.2.1.1.1. Christ knows his sheep. He knows those who are his sheep and those who are not. He knows the sheep with their many weaknesses, and the goats with their most plausible disguises. He knows them, that is, he approves of and accepts them (Ps 1:6; 37:18; Ex 33:17).

3.2.2.2.1.1.2. He is known by them. They look to him with faith. It is not so much our knowing him as our being known by him that is the basis of our happiness (Gal 4:9). On this occasion Christ mentioned (v. 15) the mutual relationship between his Father and himself: *As the Father knoweth me, even so know I the Father.* This may be considered:

3.2.2.2.*1.1.2.1*. As the basis for that intimate relationship between Christ and believers. The Lord Jesus *knows whom he hath chosen* and is sure of them (13:18), and they also *know whom they have trusted* and are sure of him (2Ti 1:12), and the basis of both is the perfect knowledge that the Father and the Son had of one another's mind.

3.2.2.2.*1.1.2.2*. As an apt analogy for the intimacy that is between Christ and believers. It may be connected with the previous words in this way: *I know my sheep, and am known of mine, even as the Father knows me, and I know the Father.* Just as the Father knew the Son and loved him, so Christ knows his sheep and looks watchfully and tenderly at them. Just as the Son knew the Father, loved him, and obeyed him, so believers know Christ.

3.2.2.2.*1.2*. He knows all those who will later belong to this flock (v. 16): *Other sheep I have, which are not of this fold; them also I must bring.* Notice:

3.2.2.2.*1.2.1*. How Christ considered the poor Gentiles. He had sometimes shown his special concern for *the lost sheep of the house of Israel* (Mt 15:24), but he said, *I have other sheep.* Those who in the course of time would believe in Christ from among the Gentiles are called sheep here. Christ has a right to many souls that he does not yet possess. Christ spoke about those other sheep to take away the contempt that was shown him as having only a *little flock* (Lk 12:32), with the implication that even if he was a good shepherd, he was still a poor shepherd: "But," he said, "I have more sheep than you can see."

3.2.2.2.*1.2.2*. The purposes of his grace for them: *Them also I must bring.* But why must he bring them? What was the need? The necessity of their situation required it. Like sheep, they would never come back by themselves. The necessity of his own commitment also required it; he must bring them, or he would not be faithful to his trust.

3.2.2.2.*1.2.3*. The beneficial effect of this. "They will hear my voice. It will be heard by them; I will speak and make them listen." Faith comes by hearing (Ro 10:17). *There shall be one fold and one shepherd.* Just as there is one shepherd, so there would be one fold. Both Jews and Gentiles would become part of one church. Being united to Christ, they would unite in him; two sticks would become one in the hand of the Lord (Eze 37:15–17).

3.2.2.2.*2*. Christ's offering up himself for his sheep (vv. 15, 17–18).

3.2.2.2.*2.1*. He declared his purpose of dying for his flock (v. 15): *I lay down my life for the sheep.* He laid down his life not only for the good of the sheep, but also in their place. Thousands of sheep had been offered in sacrifice for their shepherds, as sin offerings, but here, in a surprising reversal, the shepherd would be sacrificed for the sheep. Although for the present the striking of the shepherd meant the scattering of the flock (Zec 13:7), its purpose was that in the end they would be gathered in.

3.2.2.2.*2.2*. He took away the offense of the cross (Gal 5:11) by four considerations:

3.2.2.2.*2.2.1*. That his laying down his life for the sheep entitled him to the honors and powers of his exalted state (v. 17): *Therefore doth my Father love me, because I lay down my life.* He was loved by the Father because he undertook to die for the sheep. If he thought God's love was a sufficient reward for all his service and suffering, will we think it too little for ours, and seek the smiles of the world to make up for our suffering?

3.2.2.2.*2.2.2*. That he laid down his life in order to take it up again: *I lay down my life, that I may receive it again.* God loved him too well to leave him in the grave (Ps 16:10). He submitted to death as if he were struck down

before it, so that he would more gloriously conquer death and triumph over the grave.

3.2.2.2.*2.2.3*. That his sufferings and death were completely voluntary (v. 18): "I freely *lay it down of myself,* because I *have power to lay it down, and to take it again.*" Notice:

3.2.2.2.*2.2.3.1*. The power of Christ as the Lord of life. He had power *to keep his life* against the whole world. Although Christ's life seemed to be taken by storm, it really was surrendered, because it was impregnable in every way. *No man taketh my life from me.* He had power not only *to keep his life* but also to *lay it down.* On the one hand, he had the ability to do it. He could, when he pleased, slip the knot of union between soul and body. Having voluntarily taken up a body, he could voluntarily lay it down again. On the other hand, he also had authority to lay down his life. We are not free to do this, but Christ had sovereign authority to dispose of his own life as he pleased. He had power not only to keep his life and to lay it down but also to *take it again*; we do not have. Our life, once laid down, is *as water spilt upon the ground* (2Sa 14:14), but when Christ laid down his life, he still had it within reach and could resume it.

3.2.2.2.*2.2.3.2*. The grace of Christ; he *laid it down of himself* for our redemption. He offered himself to be the Savior.

3.2.2.2.*2.2.4*. That he did all this by the explicit order and appointment of his Father: *This commandment have I received of my Father,* not such a commandment as made what he did necessary, prior to his own voluntary undertaking, but the law of mediation, which he was willing to have written in his heart so as to delight in doing the will of God according to it (Ps 40:8).

Verses 19–21

We see here the people's different attitudes toward Christ. There was a division—it is the word from which we get "schism"—among them. They had been in such a ferment before (7:43; 9:16), and where there has been a division once, a little thing will make a division again. Splits are sooner made than mended. However, it is better that people be divided about the teaching of Christ than united in the service of sin (Lk 11:21).

1. Some Jews on this occasion spoke badly about Christ and his sayings. They said, *He has a devil, and is mad; why do you hear him?* They accused him of being demon-possessed. "He is mad, no more to be listened to than someone in a rage." They ridiculed his hearers: "*Why hear you him?*" People would not let themselves be laughed out of eating, but they let themselves be laughed out of what is even more necessary.

2. Others stood up to defend him; although the tide was strong, they dared to swim against it. They could not bear to hear him abused in that way. If they could say no more about him, they would at least maintain that he was still a man with his wits about him, that he was not demon-possessed, that he was neither without sense nor without grace. They pleaded two things:

2.1. The excellence of his teaching: "*These are not the words of him that hath a devil.* These are not the words of one who is either violently possessed by a demon or voluntarily in alliance with the Devil." There is so much holiness in the words of Christ that we may conclude they are *not the words of one that has a devil* and are therefore the words of One who was sent by God.

2.2. The power of his miracles: *Can a devil open the eyes of the blind?* Neither people who are mad nor people who are evil can work miracles. The Devil will sooner put out people's eyes than open them. Therefore Jesus did not have a devil.

Verses 22-38

It is hard to say which were stranger, the gracious words that came from his mouth or the spiteful ones that came from theirs. We have here:

1. The time when Christ met the Jews in the temple. *It was at the feast of dedication, and it was winter.* This feast was generally observed every year in remembrance of the dedication of a new altar and the cleansing of the temple by Judas Maccabaeus. The return of the Jews' liberty was to them like life from the dead (Ro 11:15), and in remembrance of it they kept an annual feast on the twenty-fifth day of the month Chislev, about the beginning of December, and seven days after. Its celebration was not confined to Jerusalem; everyone observed it in their own town, not as a holy time but as a joyful time.

2. The place where the meeting was held (v. 23): *Jesus walked in the temple in Solomon's porch* (Solomon's Colonnade). *He walked,* ready to listen to anyone who would turn to him, ready to offer them his services. Those who have anything to say to Christ may find him in the temple and walk with him there.

3. The meeting itself, in which notice:

3.1. A significant question that the Jews asked him (v. 24). They *came round* (gathered) *about him,* to provoke him. He was waiting for an opportunity to do them a kindness. Goodwill is often repaid by ill will. They gathered around him, pretending to undertake an impartial and bold inquiry for truth but intending to launch a general attack on our Lord Jesus: *How long dost thou make us to doubt? If thou be the Christ, tell us.*

3.1.1. They quarreled with him, as if he had unfairly held them in suspense up to that time. "How long will you keep us in suspense? How long are we to be kept debating whether you are the Christ or not?" It was the effect of their faithlessness and powerful prejudices. The struggle was between their convictions, which told them he was Christ, and their corruptions, which said he was not, because he was not such a Christ as they expected. They put the blame for their doubt on Christ himself, as if he made them doubt by being inconsistent with himself. Christ wants to make us believe; we make ourselves doubt.

3.1.2. They challenged him to give a direct and categorical answer: "*If thou be the Christ, tell us plainly,* clearly and explicitly, either that you are the Christ or, like John the Baptist, that you are not" (1:20). Now, their urgent query appeared good, but it was really bad, made with wrong intentions. Everyone knew the Messiah was to be a king, and so whoever claimed to be the Messiah would be prosecuted as a traitor, which was what they wanted.

3.2. Christ's answer to this question:

3.2.1. He justified himself, referring them:

3.2.1.1. To what he had said: *I have told you.* He had told them that he was the Son of God, the Son of Man. Is not this the Christ, then? *You believed not.* They pretended that they only doubted, but Christ told them that they did not believe. It is not for us to teach God how he should teach us, but to be thankful for the divine revelation we have.

3.2.1.2. To his works, that is, to the example of his life, and especially to his miracles. No one could do those miracles unless God were with him, and God would not be with him to confirm a fraud.

3.2.2. He condemned them for their stubborn unbelief: "*You believed not.*" The reason he gave is surprising: "*You believed not, because you are not of my sheep.* You are not disposed to be my followers. You will not come with my sheep; you refuse to come and see (1:39, 46), to come and listen to my voice." Deep-rooted hostility to the Gospel of Christ is the chain of sin and faithlessness.

3.2.3. He used this occasion to describe both the gracious disposition and the happy state of those who are his sheep.

3.2.3.1. To convince his listeners that they were not his sheep, he described to them the characteristics of his sheep. They *hear his voice* (v. 27), for they know it to be his (v. 4), and he has committed himself to make sure they will hear it (v. 16). They discern it, they delight in it, and they act according to it. Christ will not count as his sheep those who are deaf to his calls, deaf to his charms (Ps 58:5). His sheep follow him. The word of command has always been, *Follow me* (Mt 4:19). We must follow in his footsteps, *follow the Lamb whithersoever he goes* (Rev 14:4). We hear his voice in vain if we do not follow him.

3.2.3.2. To convince them that it was their great unhappiness and misery not to belong to Christ's sheep, he described here the blessed state and case of those who do.

3.2.3.2.1. Our Lord Jesus takes notice of his sheep: they *hear my voice,* and *I know them* (v. 27). He distinguishes them from others (2Ti 2:19); he has particular regard for every individual (Ps 34:6).

3.2.3.2.2. He has provided a happiness for them that is suited to them: *I give unto them eternal life* (v. 28). Human beings have a living soul (Ge 2:7); therefore, the happiness provided is life. Human beings have an immortal soul: therefore the happiness provided is eternal life. Life eternal is the happiness and chief benefit of an immortal soul. *I give it to them* (v. 28); it is given by the free grace of Jesus Christ. Not "I will give it," but "I do give it"; it is a gift now. He gives assurance of it, heaven in the seed, in the bud, in the embryo.

3.2.3.2.3. He has undertaken to keep them secure and preserved for this happiness.

3.2.3.2.3.1. They will be saved from eternal destruction. The words in v. 28 that are translated, *they shall never perish,* may also be translated, "They shall by no means perish forever." Just as there is an eternal life, so there is also eternal destruction. They will not *come into condemnation* (5:24). Shepherds who have large flocks often lose some of the sheep and allow them to perish, but Christ has given his word that not even one of his sheep will perish.

3.2.3.2.3.2. They cannot be kept away from their eternal happiness.

3.2.3.2.3.2.1. His own power is engaged for them: *Neither shall any man pluck them out of my hand.* The Shepherd is so protective of them that he has them not merely within his fold but in his hand, under his special protection. Their enemies are so daring that they attempt to snatch them out of his hand, but they cannot, they will not do it. Those who are in the hands of the Lord Jesus are safe.

3.2.3.2.3.2.2. His Father's power is also engaged to preserve them (v. 29). Notice:

3.2.3.2.3.2.2.1. The power of the Father: *My Father is greater than all,* greater than all the other friends of the church, all other shepherds, judges, or ministers. Those shepherds become drowsy and fall asleep; he keeps his flock day and night. He is also greater than all the church's enemies. He is greater than all the combined forces of hell and earth. The Devil and his angels have attempted many times to gain control, but they have never succeeded (Rev 12:7-8).

3.2.3.*2.3.2.2.2.* The involvement of the Father with the sheep: "It is my Father who *gave them to me.*" And so God will still look after them. All divine power is committed to fulfilling all the divine purposes.

3.2.3.*2.3.2.2.3.* From the Father's power and involvement, Christ inferred the security of the saints. *None* (neither people nor demons) *is able to pluck them out of the Father's hand.* Christ himself had experienced the power of his Father upholding and strengthening him, and so he put all his followers into his hand too. The One who secured the glory of the Redeemer will secure the glory of the redeemed. To confirm the security even further, Christ asserted, *I and my Father are one.* The Jews understood him as claiming to be God in this (v. 33), and he did not deny it. No one could snatch his sheep out of his hand because no one could not snatch them out of the Father's hand.

4. The rage of the Jews: *The Jews took up stones again* (v. 31). The word translated *took up* is different from the one used earlier in a similar situation (8:59), and the stones were "great stones"; "they carried heavy stones," such as they used in stoning evildoers. The absurdity of this insult will be seen if we consider that they had arrogantly, not to say impudently, challenged him to tell them directly whether he was the Christ or not, but now that he had said and proved that he was, they condemned him as an evildoer. If the preachers of the truth propose it modestly, they are branded as cowards; if boldly, then they are called arrogant. When they had made a similar attempt before, it was in vain; he *escaped through the midst of them* (8:59). But they now repeated their attempt. Daring sinners will throw stones at heaven, even though the stones may fall back down onto their own heads.

5. Christ's tender pleading with them (v. 32): *Jesus answered* what they did—we do not find that they had said anything. He replied mildly: *Many good works have I shown you from my Father; for which of those works do you stone me?* One would have thought that such tender words would melt a heart of stone. In dealing with his enemies, Christ still argued from his works—people show what they are by what they do—his good works, for the expression means both "great works" and "good works."

5.1. The divine power of his works convicted them of their stubborn faithlessness. They were works from his Father. He showed them these works; he did them openly in front of the people. He did not shine an artificial light on his works, like those who want only to make a show, but revealed them to the world at midday, openly (18:20). His works were an incontestable display of the validity of his commission.

5.2. The divine grace of his works convicted them of the worst ingratitude. The works he did among them were not only works of wonder that amazed them but works of love and kindness that would do them good, and so make them good. *"Now, for which of these do you stone me?"* If you want to pick a quarrel with me, it must be for some good work; tell me for which one." When he asked, *For which of these do you stone me?* he both showed the deep assurance he had of his own innocence and made his persecutors consider what was the true reason for their hostility by asking, "Why are we persecuting him?" (Ac 9:4).

6. Their vindication of the attempt they made on Christ (v. 33).

6.1. They did not want to be thought to be such enemies toward their country that they would persecute him for a good work: *For a good work we stone thee not.* Indeed, they would scarcely allow that any of his works were good. But even if he had done any good works, they

would not acknowledge that they were stoning him for them. And so, though they acted very absurdly, they could not be brought to confess their absurdities.

6.2. They wanted to be thought to be such friends of God that they would prosecute him for blasphemy: *Because that thou, being a man, makest thyself God.* They had:

6.2.1. A pretended zeal for the law. They seem greatly concerned for the honor of the divine majesty. A blasphemer was to be stoned (Lev 24:16). The most corrupt actions are often covered with a veneer of plausible excuses. Just as nothing is more courageous than a well-informed conscience, so nothing is more outrageous than a mistaken one.

6.2.2. A real hostility toward the Gospel, which they could not show greater disrespect to than by describing Christ as a blasphemer. It is nothing new for the best people to be described in the worst terms by those who are determined to treat them in the worst way. The crime he was charged with was blasphemy. The supposed proof of the crime was, *Thou, being a man, makest thyself God.* Just as it is God's glory that he is God, so it is his glory that there is no other besides him (Isa 46:9; Da 3:29). They were right as far are they went, that what Christ said about himself amounted to saying that he was God, because he had said that he was one with the Father and that he would give eternal life. And Christ did not deny it. Yet they were very much mistaken when they looked on him as a mere man, and on the Godhead he claimed as of his own making.

7. Christ's reply to their accusation and his fulfilling those claims that they had called blasphemous (v. 34), by two arguments:

7.1. By an argument taken from God's word. It is written (Ps 82:6), *I have said, You are gods.* "If they were gods, then much more am I." Notice:

7.1.1. How he explained the text (v. 35): *He called them gods to whom the word of God came, and the scripture cannot be broken.* We are sure that the Scripture *cannot be broken* or found fault with. Every word of God is right.

7.1.2. How he applied it. *Say you of him whom the Father hath sanctified, Thou blasphemest?* Notice:

7.1.2.1. The honor shown to the Lord Jesus by the Father: he *sanctified him, and sent him into the world.* Our Lord Jesus was himself the Word and had the Spirit without limit (3:34). He was sent into the world as Lord of all. The Father's sanctifying and sending him was given here as a sufficient authority for his calling himself the *Son of God.*

7.1.2.2. The dishonor shown him by the Jews in their calling him a blasphemer because he called himself the Son of God: "Do you say this about him? Dare you say this? Are you bold and arrogant enough to look the God of truth in the face and tell him that he is lying? Are you saying about the Son of God that he is a blasphemer?" If demons, whom he came to condemn, had said this about him, it would not have been so strange, but that human beings, whom he came to teach and save, would say this about him was appalling: *be astonished, O heavens, at this!* (Jer 2:12).

7.2. By an argument taken from his own works (vv. 37–38). Here he explained his own claims and proved that he and the Father are one (vv. 37–38): *If I do not the works of my Father, believe me not.* Notice:

7.2.1. What he argued from—from his works. Just as he proved himself to have been sent by God by the divinity of his works, so we must prove ourselves to be related to Christ by the Christianity of our works.

7.2.1.1. The argument is powerful, because the works he did were the *works of his Father*, which only the Father could do and which could not be done in the ordinary course of nature. The miracles that the apostles performed in his name confirmed this argument and continued supplying evidence for it when he was gone.

7.2.1.2. It was proposed as fairly as could be desired, and put to a simple test. *If I do not the works of my Father, believe me not.* He did not demand approval of his divine mission further than the proof he gave of it. Christ is not a hard taskmaster who expects to reap in approval where he has not sown in arguments (Mt 25:24). "But if I do *the works of my Father, though you believe not me, yet believe the works*; believe your own eyes, your own reason." The invisible things of the Redeemer were seen by his miracles and by all his works both of power and of mercy, so that those who were not convinced by these works were *without excuse* (Ro 1:20).

7.2.2. What he argued for—*that you may know and believe* that *the Father is in me, and I in him*, which is the same as what he had said before (v. 30): *I and my Father are one.* We must know this, not know and explain it, but know and believe it, acknowledging and adoring its depths, since we cannot find the bottom.

Verses 39–42

Here is the outcome of the meeting with the Jews. We are told here:

1. How they attacked him by force. *They sought again to take him* (v. 39). Because he persevered in the same testimony about himself, they persisted in their hatred toward him. They expressed the same resentment, justifying their attempt to stone him by another attempt to seize him.

2. How he avoided them by fleeing. He *escaped out of their hands* not by the intervention of a friend who helped him but by his own wisdom. The One who knew how to save himself no doubt also *knows how to deliver the godly out of temptation* (2Pe 2:9) and how to make *a way* for them *to escape* (1Co 10:13).

3. What he did in his retreat: he *went away again beyond Jordan* (v. 40). Notice:

3.1. What shelter he found there. He went into a private part of the country, and *there he abode* (stayed); he found some rest and quietness there, when in Jerusalem he could find none. Christ and his Gospel have often been better received among the plain country people than among *the wise, the mighty, the noble* (1Co 1:26–27).

3.2. What success he found there. He chose to go where John baptized in the early days (1:28), because some impressions of John's ministry and baptism must have remained there, which would make them likely to receive Christ. The outcome to some extent fulfilled the expectation, for we are told:

3.2.1. That they flocked after him (v. 41): *Many resorted to him.* The return of the means of grace to a place commonly causes a great stirring of affections.

3.2.2. That they reasoned in his favor as much as those at Jerusalem sought to raise objections against him. They said, *John did no miracle, but all things that John spoke of this man were true.* They considered two things;

3.2.2.1. That Christ far surpassed John the Baptist's power, for John had done no miracles, but Jesus did many, from which it was easy to conclude that Jesus was greater than John. How great then was this Jesus! Christ is best known and acknowledged by a comparison with others that sets him superlatively higher than others.

3.2.2.2. That Christ exactly fulfilled John the Baptist's testimony. All things that *John said of this man were true.*

John had said great things about him, which had raised their expectations. Now, they acknowledged that Christ was as great as John had said he would be. When we come to know Christ more, and come to know him in our own experience, we find that the reality far exceeds the report (1Ki 10:6–7). John the Baptist was now dead and gone, but his hearers profited by what they had heard him say, in two ways:

3.2.2.2.1. They were confirmed in their belief that John was a prophet, who foretold such things.

3.2.2.2.2. They were prepared to believe that Jesus was the Christ. The success and effectiveness of the preached words are not confined to the life of the preacher, nor do they die with his breath.

3.2.3. That *many believed on him there.* They gave themselves to him as his disciples (v. 42). And they were many. It was where John had had great success; there many believed on the Lord Jesus. Where the preaching of the message of repentance has had success, the preaching of the message of reconciliation is most likely to be effective. Where John has been acceptable, Jesus will not be unacceptable.

CHAPTER 11

We have here the raising of Lazarus to life, which is recorded only by this Evangelist. The other three confine themselves to what Christ did in Galilee and scarcely ever take their account to Jerusalem until Passion Week, whereas John's writings mainly concern what took place at Jerusalem. This miracle is recorded in more detail than any other miracle by Christ, because it was a pledge of what was to be the crowning proof of all—Christ's own resurrection. Here is: 1. The news sent to our Lord Jesus of the sickness of Lazarus (vv. 1–16). 2. Jesus' visit to Lazarus's relatives when he heard of his death (vv. 17–32). 3. The miracle (vv. 33–44). 4. The effect of this miracle on others (vv. 45–57).

Verses 1–16

We have in these verses:

1. A detailed account of the people mainly concerned in this story (vv. 1–2). They lived at Bethany, a village not far from Jerusalem, where Christ usually stayed when he came up to the festivals. It is here called *the town of Mary and Martha*. Here was a brother named Lazarus, and here were two sisters, Martha and Mary, who seem to have been the housekeepers. It was a decent, happy, and well-ordered family; they were a family Christ knew very well. One of the sisters is particularly described as *that Mary which anointed the Lord with ointment* (v. 2). This refers to the anointing of Christ that this Evangelist describes (12:3). It was this woman *whose brother Lazarus was sick*, and the sickness of those we love is our suffering. The more friends we have, the more frequently we suffer in this way through sympathy. The multiplying of our comforts is simply the multiplying of our cares and crosses.

2. The news that was sent to our Lord Jesus of the sickness of Lazarus (v. 3). Lazarus's sisters knew where Jesus was, and they sent a special messenger to him. In doing this, they showed:

2.1. Their love and concern for their brother. They showed their love for him now, when he was sick, because *a brother is born for adversity* (Pr 17:17), and so is a sister.

2.2. Their consideration for the Lord Jesus, to whom they were willing to tell all their worries. The message they sent was very brief, simply describing the situation with a tender, heartfelt plea: *Lord, behold, he whom thou lovest is sick.* They did not say, "Lord, see, he who loves you," but, "he whom you love." Our love for him is not worth speaking of, but his love for us can never be spoken of enough. It is nothing new for those loved by Christ to be sick: all things come alike to all (Ecc 9:2). When we are sick, it is very encouraging to us to have people around us who will pray for us. We have reason to love and pray for those whom we have reason to think Christ loves and cares for.

3. An account of how Christ received this news.

3.1. He forecast the event and outcome of the sickness. He forecast two things:

3.1.1. *This sickness is not unto death.* The illness turned out to be terminal, and there was no doubt that Lazarus was truly dead for four days. And yet it did not come, as a terminal illness usually does, as a call to the grave. That was not the final effect of this sickness. He died, but it could be said he did not die. Death is an eternal farewell to this world, and in this sense the illness was *not unto death*. The sickness of good people, however threatening, is not *unto death*. The body's death in this world is the soul's birth into another world.

3.1.2. *But it is for the glory of God.* The sufferings of the saints are intended for the glory of God. The sweetest blessings are those that God sends as a remedy for our trouble. Let this reconcile us to the darkest ways of Providence: they are all for the glory of God. If God is glorified, we should be satisfied (Lev 10:3). The illness came so *that the Son of God might be glorified thereby*, since it gave him an opportunity to perform that glorious miracle, the raising of Lazarus from the dead. Let those whom Christ loves encourage themselves in all their adversities and suffering by remembering that the intention of them all is that *the Son of God may be glorified thereby*.

3.2. He delayed visiting his patient (vv. 5–6). They had pleaded, *Lord, it is he whom thou lovest*, and the plea was accepted (v. 5): *Jesus loved Martha, and her sister, and Lazarus.* Now one would have thought it would follow, "When he heard that Lazarus was sick, he went to him as quickly as he could." However, he followed the opposite way to show his love. Instead of going quickly to him, he stayed *two days still in the same place where he was.*

3.2.1. He loved them and *therefore* he delayed his coming to them, in order to test them, so that their testing would in the end be *found to praise and honour* (1Pe 1:7).

3.2.2. He loved them, that is, he intended to do something great and extraordinary for them. That was why he delayed coming to them, so that Lazarus would be dead and buried before he came. Delaying his relief for so long, he had the opportunity to do more for him than for anyone. God has gracious intentions even in apparent delays (Isa 54:7–8; 49:14). Christ's friends at Bethany were not out of his thoughts, even though he did not go quickly to them.

4. The conversation he had with his disciples (vv. 7–16). He spoke about two things—his own danger and Lazarus's death.

4.1. He spoke about his own danger in going to Judea (vv. 7–10). Here is:

4.1.1. Christ notice that he would now enter Judea (v. 7): *Let us go into Judea again.* This may be considered:

4.1.1.1. As an intention motivated by his kindness to his friends at Bethany. When he knew they were in crisis, "Now," he said, "let's go to Judea." Christ will come to favor his people when *the time to favour them, yea, the set time, is come* (Ps 102:13), and the worst time is

commonly the appointed time. In the depths of suffering, therefore, let this keep us out of the depths of despair: that human extremity is God's opportunity.

4.1.1.2. As a test of the courage of the disciples, to see whether they would dare follow him there. *Let us go into Judea*, which had just become "too hot" for them, was a saying that tested them (6:6). Christ never brings his people into any danger without accompanying them in it.

4.1.2. Their objection to making this journey (v. 8): *Master, the Jews of late sought to stone thee, and goest thou thither again?* They reminded him of the danger he had been in there not long before. Christ's disciples tend to emphasize suffering more than their Master does. The memory of their panic was still fresh in their minds, and so they were amazed that he wanted to go there again. "Will you favor with your presence those who expelled you from their region? *Goest thou thither again*, where you have been so mistreated?" If Christ had been inclined to escape suffering, he did not lack friends to persuade him to do it. Yet their objection showed not only concern for his safety but also distrust of his power and a secret fear that they themselves would suffer, because they had to expect this if he suffered. They did not have faith that he could protect both himself and them in Judea now as well as he had before.

4.1.3. Christ's answer to this objection (vv. 9–10): *Are there not twelve hours in the day?* Divine providence has given us daylight to work by. The life of a human being is a day. This day is divided into various ages, states, and opportunities, as into hours, and consideration of this should make us not only very busy with the work of life but also relaxed about the dangers of life. Our day will be extended until our work is done and our testimony finished (Rev 11:7). Christ applied this to his case. To open this up:

4.1.3.1. He showed the comfort and assurance that people can have while they keep to the path of their duty: *If any man walk in the day, he stumbles not*: he does not hesitate in his own mind, but, walking uprightly, walks determinedly. Just as the person who walks in the day does not stumble, but continues steadily and cheerfully on his way, *because he sees the light of this world*, and by it sees the way ahead, so a good person relies on the word of God as his rule, and considers the glory of God as his aim, because he sees those two great lights. He has a faithful guide in all his doubts and a powerful guard in all his dangers (Gal 6:4; Ps 119:6). Wherever Christ went, he walked in the day, and so will we if we follow his steps.

4.1.3.2. He showed the pain and danger of someone who does not walk according to this rule (v. 10): *If a man walk in the night, he stumbles.* If *he walks in the way of his heart* (Ecc 11:9), according to the course of this world, he falls into temptations and snares. He stumbles, *because there is no light in him*, for light within us is to our moral actions what light around us is to our natural actions.

4.2. He and his disciples discussed the death of Lazarus (vv. 11–16). Here is:

4.2.1. Christ's announcement to his disciples of the death of Lazarus (v. 11). Having prepared them for the dangerous journey, he then gave them:

4.2.1.1. Clear information about the death of Lazarus: *Our friend Lazarus sleepeth.* Notice here how Christ describes a believer and a believer's death.

4.2.1.1.*1*. He describes a believer as his friend: *Our friend Lazarus.* Those whom Christ is pleased to confess as his friends should be accepted by all his disciples as their friends. Christ spoke about Lazarus as their common friend: *Our friend.* Even death itself does not break the bond of friendship between Christ and a believer. "Lazarus is dead, but he remains *our friend.*"

4.2.1.1.2. He describes the death of a believer as sleep: *he sleepeth.* It is good to call death by such names and titles as will help to make it more familiar and less formidable to us. Why should not the confident hope of the resurrection to eternal life make it as easy for us to take off the body and die as it is to take off our clothes and go to sleep? When true Christians die, they are merely asleep: they are resting from the work of the previous day and refreshing themselves for the following morning. To the godly the grave is a bed, and all its bonds are like the soft and downy fetters of a quiet and restful sleep. It is merely taking off our clothes to be mended and trimmed for our wedding day.

4.2.1.2. Particular indications of his favorable intentions toward Lazarus: *but I go, that I may awake him out of sleep.* Christ had no sooner said, *Our friend sleeps,* than he immediately added, *I go, that I may awake him.* When Christ tells his people at any time how bad their situation is, he lets them know in the same breath how easily and how quickly he can put matters right. Christ's telling his disciples that this was his work in Judea might help take away their fear of going there with him; besides, it was to do a kindness to a family to whom they were all obliged.

4.2.2. Their mistake, their blunder, concerning the meaning of this announcement (vv. 12–13): they said, *Lord, if he sleep, he shall do well.* This shows:

4.2.2.1. Some concern they had for their friend Lazarus; they hoped he would recover. Now that they heard he was sleeping, they concluded that the worst was past. Sleep is often nature's therapy. This is true of the sleep of death; if true Christians sleep in this way, they will do well.

4.2.2.2. A greater concern for themselves. It was now unnecessary, they thought, for Christ to go to Lazarus, exposing himself and them. If the good work we are called to is dangerous, we are willing to hope that it will do itself.

4.2.3. This mistake of theirs put right (v. 13): *Jesus spoke of his death.* Christ's disciples were still so slow to understand. Frequently death is called sleep in the Old Testament. They should have understood Christ when he spoke the language of Scripture. Whatever Christ undertakes to do is, we may be sure, something significant and uncommon and worthy of him. The Evangelist carefully corrects this error: *Jesus spoke of his death.*

4.2.4. Jesus' clear and explicit declaration to them of the death of Lazarus and his decision to go to Bethany (vv. 14–15).

4.2.4.1. He announced the death of Lazarus; what he had earlier said obscurely he now said clearly: *Lazarus is dead* (v. 14).

4.2.4.2. He then gave them the reason why he had delayed so long: *I am glad for your sakes that I was not there.* Healing Lazarus's disease would have comforted Lazarus's friends, but then Christ's disciples would have seen no further proof of his power than they had often seen, and so their faith would not have increased. His going now to raise him from the dead, however, led both to the conversion of many who previously had not believed on him (v. 45) and to a growth in the faith of those who already believed, which was Christ's aim: *To the intent that you may believe.*

4.2.4.3. He decided to go to Bethany now and take his disciples along with him: *Let us go unto him.* Death cannot separate us from the love of Christ (Ro 8:35–39) or put us beyond reach of his calls. Perhaps those who said,

"If he is asleep, there is no need to go," were ready to say, "If he is dead, it is useless to go."

4.2.5. Thomas's encouragement of his fellow disciples to go cheerfully with their Master (v. 16): He is referred to as *Thomas, who is called Didymus. Thomas* in Hebrew and *Didymus* in Greek mean "a twin." Probably Thomas was a twin. He very courageously said *to his fellow disciples, Let us also go, that we may die with him*; *with him*, that is:

4.2.5.1. With Lazarus, who was now dead, as some interpret it. Perhaps Thomas had a particularly close friendship with Lazarus.

4.2.5.1.1. "If we survive, we do not know how we will live without him." We are sometimes ready to think our lives are bound up with the lives of some who were dear to us, but God wants to teach us to live, and to live comfortably, in dependence on him when those whom we thought we could not live without have died. But also:

4.2.5.1.2. "If we die, we hope to be happy with him." Thomas had such a firm belief in happiness on the other side of death that he was willing for them all to go and die with Lazarus. The greater the number of our friends who are taken away from us to heaven, the fewer cords we have to tie us to this earth, and the more there are to draw our hearts toward heaven.

4.2.5.2. "With our Master," and this is the reading I incline toward. "If he will go into danger, let us also go, according to the command we received, *Follow me* (Mt 4:19)." Thomas knew so much of the Jews' hatred toward Christ that it was not strange that he supposed that Christ was now going to die. Thomas showed a gracious readiness to die with Christ, which flowed from his strong affection for Christ. And he had a zealous desire to help his fellow disciples in the same spirit: "Let us go and die with him; who would desire to survive such a Master?" In difficult times Christians should encourage one another.

Verses 17–32

The matter had now been decided: Christ would go to Judea with his disciples, and they prepared for their journey. Finally, he came near to Bethany, which is said to be about *fifteen furlongs* from Jerusalem (v. 18). In this way, it is noted that this miracle was in effect performed in Jerusalem and was therefore charged to her account. Notice:

1. What condition he found his friends in there. When we part from our friends, we do not know what changes may affect us or them before we meet again.

1.1. He found his friend Lazarus *in the grave* (v. 17). Lazarus had been buried four days. Although promised acts of salvation will definitely come, they often come slowly.

1.2. He found his surviving friends grieving. *Many of the Jews came to Martha and Mary to comfort them* (v. 19). Usually, with death there are mourners. Here was Martha's house, a house where the fear of God was, one on which his blessing rested, yet it was made a *house of mourning* (Ecc 7:2, 4). Grace will keep sorrow from the heart (14:1) but not from the house. Where there are mourners, there should be comforters. We owe it to those who are in sorrow to mourn with them and comfort them. These friends comforted the sisters *concerning their brother,* that is, by speaking to them about him, not only about the good name he left behind but also about the happy state he had gone to. We have reason to be comforted about those who have gone before us to a happiness in which they do not need us. This visit the Jews made to Martha and Mary is evidence that the sisters were distinguished people. There was also a providence in the coming together of so many Jews just at this time, for in this way, they would become satisfactory witnesses of the miracle.

2. What took place between him and his surviving friends. His departures make his returns precious, and his absences teach us how to value his presence. We have here:

2.1. The interview between Christ and Martha.

2.1.1. We are told that she *went and met him* (v. 20). It seems that Martha was eagerly expecting Christ's arrival and asking about it. However it happened, she heard about his coming before he came. When the good news came that Jesus had arrived, Martha set everything aside and *went and met him*. When Martha went to meet Jesus, Mary *sat still in the house*. Some think she did not hear the news, while Martha, who was busy with household matters, received early notice of it. Others think Mary did hear that Christ had come, but that she was so overwhelmed with sorrow that she did not want to move. Comparing this account with that in Lk 10:38, we may notice the different attitudes of the two sisters. Martha's natural personality was to keep active and busy; she loved to go here and there and be involved in everything. This had been a trap to her when it meant that she was not only overconcerned and distracted by many things but also kept from her devotions. Now, however, on a day of adversity, this active attitude was a favor to her, keeping the grief away from her heart and making her eager to meet Christ, and so she received comfort from him more quickly. On the other hand, Mary's natural personality was contemplative and reserved. This had formerly been an advantage to her, when it placed her at Christ's feet so that she might listen to his word, when it enabled her to be with him there without the distractions that Martha had succumbed to; but now, in the time of adversity, that same attitude proved to be a trap for her. It made her less able to deal with her grief and made her more likely to be depressed. Notice how much our wisdom in such situations will consist in watching carefully against the temptations, and making the most of the advantages, of our natural temperaments.

2.1.2. Here the conversation between Christ and Martha is fully related:

2.1.2.1. Martha's words to Christ (vv. 21–22).

2.1.2.1.*1*. She complained about Christ's long absence and delay. *Lord, if thou hadst been here, my brother had not died.*

2.1.2.1.*1.1*. Here is some evidence of faith. She believed in Christ's power, that he could have prevented Lazarus's death. She also believed in his pity, that if he had only seen Lazarus in his extreme illness, he would have had compassion.

2.1.2.1.*1.2*. Here are sad examples of unbelief. Her faith was true, but it was as weak as a bruised reed (Isa 42:3; Mt 12:20), because she limited the power of Christ when she said, *If thou hadst been here*. What she should have known was that Christ could heal from a distance. She also reflected on the wisdom and kindness of Christ, implying that he had not come quickly to them when they had sent for him, and now he might as well have stayed away.

2.1.2.1.*2*. Yet she corrected and comforted herself. At least, she blamed herself for blaming her Master, for suggesting that he had come too late, *for I know that even now, whatsoever thou wilt ask of God, God will give it to thee.* Notice:

2.1.2.1.*2.1*. How willing her hope was. She humbly commended the case to the wise and compassionate consideration of the Lord Jesus. When we do not know what to ask or expect in particular, let us turn in general to God.

2.1.2.1.*2.2*. How weak her faith was. She should have said, "Lord, you can do whatever you wish," but she said only, "You can obtain whatever you are praying for." His power is always eminent; his intercession always effective.

2.1.2.2. The comforting word Christ gave to Martha (v. 23): *Jesus saith unto her, Thy brother shall rise again.* In her complaint, Martha looked back. We tend in such cases to add to our own trouble by imagining what might have been. Christ told Martha, and us through her, to look forward and think what shall be: *Thy brother shall rise again.* This was true of Lazarus in a sense that was special to him: he was now about to be raised; it may also be applied to all the saints. Imagine that you hear Christ saying, "Your grandparent, your parent, your child, your marriage partner, will rise again."

2.1.2.3. The faith that Martha had in this word, and the unbelief with that faith (v. 24). She considered it *a faithful saying* (1Ti 1:15) that *he would rise again at the last day.* Yet she seems to have thought this saying not so worthy of complete acceptance as it really was. *I know that he shall rise again at the last day*—and is not that enough, Martha? She seems to have thought it was not. In the same way, when we are unhappy in our present adversities, we greatly undervalue our future hopes.

2.1.2.4. The further instruction and encouragement Jesus Christ gave her. He said to her, *I am the resurrection and the life* (vv. 25–26). Christ led her to believe in two things:

2.1.2.4.*1*. The sovereign power of Christ: *I am the resurrection and the life.* Martha believed that at Christ's prayer God would give anything, but he wanted her to know that by his word he could work anything. It is the indescribable comfort of all good Christians that Jesus Christ is the resurrection and the life, and will be so to them. Resurrection is a return to life; Christ is the author both of that return and of the life to which it is a return.

2.1.2.4.*2*. The promises of the new covenant. Notice:

2.1.2.4.*2.1*. To whom these promises are made—to those who believe in Jesus Christ. The condition of the latter promise is expressed: *Whosoever liveth and believeth in me*, which may be understood as referring to either:

2.1.2.4.*2.1.1*. Natural life: whoever lives in this world, whether Jew or Gentile, if they believe in Christ, they will live through him. Or:

2.1.2.4.*2.1.2*. Spiritual life. Those who live and believe are those who by faith have been born again (3:3) to a heavenly and divine life.

2.1.2.4.*2.2*. What the promises are (v. 25): *Though he die, yet shall he live*; in fact, *he shall never die* (v. 26). Provision is made for the happiness of both body and soul:

2.1.2.4.*2.2.1*. For the body. Here is the promise of a blessed resurrection. Although the body is dead because of sin, it shall live again. The body will be raised a glorious body.

2.1.2.4.*2.2.2*. For the soul. Here is the promise of a blessed immortality. Those who *live and believe in me shall never die.* That spiritual life will never be extinguished, but will be perfected in eternal life. The mortality of the body will finally be *swallowed up by life* (2Co 5:4), but the life of the soul will at death be immediately swallowed up by immortality. Christ asked her, "*Believest thou this?* Can you take my word for it?" Martha was thinking about her brother's being raised to life in this world; before Christ gave her hope of this, he directed her thoughts to another life and another world. The adversities and comforts of this present time would not make such an impression on us as they do if we only believed the things of eternity as we should.

2.1.2.5. Martha's heartfelt agreement with what Christ said (v. 27). We have here Martha's creed, the good confession she made. It is the *conclusion of the whole matter* (Ecc 12:13). Here is:

2.1.2.5.*1*. The guide of her faith, and that was the word of Christ. She took it completely as Christ had said it: *Yea, Lord*. Faith is an echo of divine revelation, responding with the same words.

2.1.2.5.*2*. The ground of her faith, and that was the authority of Christ. She turned to the foundation for the support of the superstructure. "I believe"—it may also be read, "I have believed"—"that you are the Christ, and so I do believe this." Notice here:

2.1.2.5.*2.1*. What she believed and confessed about Jesus: That he was *the Christ* (v. 27), that he was the *Son of God*, that it was *he who was to come* (Ps 118:26; Mt 11:3). She embraced the blessing of blessings as now being present.

2.1.2.5.*2.2*. What she concluded from this. If she accepted that Jesus was the Christ, there was no difficulty in believing that he was the resurrection and the life. He is the fountain of light and truth, and we may take all his sayings as faithful and divine. He is the fountain of life and blessedness, and we may therefore depend on his ability.

2.2. The interview between Christ and Mary.

2.2.1. The announcement Martha gave her of Christ's coming (v. 28): *When she had so said, she went her way* and *called Mary her sister.*

2.2.1.1. There had been a time when Martha would have drawn Mary away from Christ, to come and help her *in much serving* (Lk 10:40). Here she was diligent in drawing her to Christ.

2.2.1.2. She called her *secretly*. The saints are called into the fellowship of Jesus Christ by an invitation that is secret and distinctive.

2.2.1.3. She called her at Christ's request: *The Master is come, and calleth for thee.* Martha triumphed in his arrival: "*The Master is come.* The One whom we have long wished and waited for: he has come, he has come!" This was the best encouragement in the present distress. She invited her sister to go and meet him: *He calls for thee.* When Christ our Teacher comes, he calls for us. He calls for you in particular; he is calling you *by name* (Ps 27:8; Jn 10:3). If he is calling you, he will heal, encourage, and strengthen you.

2.2.2. The speed with which Mary came to Christ (v. 29): *As soon as she heard* that the *Master was come*, she *arose quickly* and came to him. She little thought how near he was to her; he is often nearer to those who mourn in Zion than they are aware of (Isa 61:3). The least indication of Christ's gracious approaches is enough to cause a dynamic faith, which stands ready to take the hint, to answer the first call. She did not consider her neighbors, the Jews who were with her, comforting her; she left them all to come to him.

2.2.3. Where she found the Master (v. 30): *in that place where Martha met him.* See here:

2.2.3.1. Christ's love for his work. He stayed near the place where the grave was, so that he was ready to go to it.

2.2.3.2. Mary's love for Christ; she still *loved much* (Lk 7:47). Although Christ had seemed unkind in his delays, she could not take offense at him.

2.2.4. The Jews' misinterpretation of her going away so quickly (v. 31): they said, *She goes to the grave, to weep there.* Martha coped better in this distress than Mary, who was a woman of tender and sorrowful spirit; such was her natural temperament. These comforters concluded, therefore, that when she went out, it was to go *to the grave and weep there.* See:

2.2.4.1. What the foolishness and fault of mourners often is; they seek how to emphasize their own grief and so make what is bad even worse. We tend to focus on those things that emphasize the adversity, whereas it is our duty to come to terms with the will of God in it.

2.2.4.2. What the wisdom and duty of comforters is, and that is to prevent as much as possible the resurgence of the sorrow and to redirect it. The Jews who followed Mary were led to Christ and became witnesses of one of his most glorious miracles. It is good to cling to Christ's friends in their sorrows, because that is how we may come to know him better.

2.2.5. Mary's words to our Lord Jesus (v. 32): she came and *fell down at his feet* and said with many tears, as can be seen from v. 33, *Lord, if thou hadst been here, my brother had not died*, as Martha said before. *She fell down at his feet*, which was more than Martha did, who had greater command of her emotions. This Mary had sat *at Christ's feet to hear his word* (Lk 10:39), and here we find her there on another errand. Those who on a day of peace place themselves at Christ's feet to receive instruction from him may with comfort and confidence on a day of trouble throw themselves at his feet with the hope of finding favor with him. Here Mary professed Christian faith as truly as Martha did, because by her actions she said in effect, *I believe that thou art the Christ.* She did this in the presence of the Jews who were with her, who, though friends of her and her family, were still the bitter enemies of Christ. Let them take offense at it if they wanted to—she would fall at his feet. Her address was very emotional: *Lord, if thou hadst been here, my brother had not died.* Christ's delay was intended for the best, and it proved so, but both the sisters unreasonably threw the same statement at him, in effect accusing him of the death of their brother. Mary did not, like Martha, add other words to this confession. She said less than Martha, but wept more, and tears of devout affection have a voice in the ears of Christ; there are no words like tears.

Verses 33–44

We have here:

1. Christ's tender sympathy for his suffering friends, which he showed in three ways:

1.1. By being deeply moved and troubled in his spirit (v. 33): *Jesus saw Mary weeping* and the *Jews that came with her weeping; he groaned in the spirit, and was troubled.* See here:

1.1.1. The griefs of human beings represented in the tears of Mary and her friends. What a sign this was of the world we live in, this vale of tears! Our religious faith teaches us to *weep with them that weep* (Ro 12:15), as these Jews wept with Mary. Those who truly love their friends will share with them in their joys and griefs, for what is friendship but encouraging, comforting, strengthening, and relieving our friends (Job 16:5)?

1.1.2. The grace of the Son of God and his compassion toward those who are miserable. *In all their afflictions he is afflicted* (Isa 63:9; Jdg 10:16). When Christ saw them all in tears:

1.1.2.1. He *groaned in the spirit.* This was an expression of his emotional response to the adversities of human life and the power of death. About to make a vigorous attack on death and the grave, he stirred up himself for the encounter. It also showed his kind sympathy for his friends who were grieving. Christ not only seemed concerned; he *groaned in the spirit*; he was inwardly and sincerely affected by the situation. Christ's was a deep and sincere sigh.

1.1.2.2. He was *troubled*. The expression means he "troubled himself." He was never troubled except when he troubled himself, as he saw cause to. He often composed himself for trouble, but he never lost his composure or was disturbed by trouble.

1.2. By his kind question (v. 34): *Where have you laid him?* He wanted to divert the grief of his mourning friends by raising their expectations of something great.

1.3. By his tears. Those around him wanted him to *come and see* (v. 34).

1.3.1. As he was going to the grave, *Jesus wept* (v. 35). This is a very short verse, the shortest in Scripture, but it provides many useful instructions. We can learn from this that Jesus Christ was really and truly human, susceptible to impressions of joy and grief. Christ gave this as a proof of his humanity, in both senses of the word, showing that as a man, he could weep, and as a merciful man, he would weep, before he gave this proof of his divinity. He was *a man of sorrows*, and *acquainted with grief*, as was foretold (Isa 53:3). We never read that he laughed, but we see him more than once in tears. Tears of compassion are good for Christians and make them most like Christ.

1.3.2. Different interpretations were made of Christ's weeping.

1.3.2.1. Some interpreted it kindly and honestly (v. 36): *Then said the Jews, Behold how he loved him!* They seem to have been amazed that he would have such a strong affection for a person to whom he was not related. It is good for us, according to this example of Christ, to show our love for our friends both when they are living and when they die. Although our tears do not benefit the dead, they embalm their memory. When he only dropped a tear over Lazarus, they said, *See how he loved him!* Much more reason have we, then, for whom he laid down his life, to say: *See how he loved us!*

1.3.2.2. Others reflected on it perversely (v. 37): "*Could not this man, who opened the eyes of the blind,* have prevented the death of Lazarus? If he could have prevented it, he would have"—and so because he did not, they were inclined to think that he could not. Therefore, they thought, it could justly be questioned whether he had truly *opened the eyes of the blind*. They thought that his failure to perform this miracle invalidated the former miracle. When, soon after this, Christ raised Lazarus from the dead, which was the greater work, he convinced these whisperers that he could have prevented his death.

2. Christ's approach to the grave.

2.1. Christ repeated his groaning (v. 38): *Again groaning in himself, he came to the grave.* He was deeply moved in his spirit:

2.1.1. Because he was displeased at the unbelief of those who spoke with doubt about his power and blamed him for not preventing the death of Lazarus. He never groaned so much over his own pains and sufferings as he did for the sins and foolish acts of human beings.

2.1.2. Because he was moved by the fresh grief that the mourning sisters probably poured out as they came near the grave; his tender spirit was deeply touched by their wailing. When ministers are sent to raise dead souls through the preaching of the Gospel, they should be deeply moved by the deplorable condition of those they

preach to and pray for, and they should groan inwardly when they think of it.

2.2. The grave in which Lazarus lay is described: it was a cave, and a stone lay across the entrance, and such was the grave in which Christ was buried. They considered the funeral ceremony ended when the stone was rolled over the grave or, as here, laid across the entrance.

2.3. Orders were given to remove the stone (v. 39): *Take away the stone.* Christ wanted to have this stone removed so that all the onlookers could see the body lying dead in the sepulcher and then see it coming out normally, through an opening, so that it would be recognized as a true body and not a ghost or specter. It is a good step toward the raising of a soul to spiritual life when prejudices are removed and overcome to make way for the word to enter the heart.

2.4. Martha objected to the opening of the grave: *Lord, by this time he stinketh, for he has been dead four days.* Probably Martha noticed the smell of the body as they were removing the stone, and so she cried out.

2.4.1. It is easy to note from this the nature of the human body: four days is only a short time, but this time will make a great change on the human body. Christ rose the third day because he was not to *see corruption* (Ps 16:10).

2.4.2. Some think she said this out of fitting tenderness toward the dead body. She did not want it to be on display so publicly and made a spectacle of. Others think she said it out of concern for Christ. If there was anything offensive, she did not want her Master to come near it. But he was not one of those people who are sensitive and delicate and cannot bear a bad odor; if he had been, he would not have come to this world of humanity, which sin had made a complete rubbish heap. Yet it seems from Christ's answer that she had spoken the language of unbelief and distrust: "Lord, it is too late now. It is impossible for this putrid carcass to live." She gave her brother up as a helpless and hopeless case. This distrusting comment of hers, however, served to make the miracle both more evident and more eminent. Her suggesting that it could not be done gave greater honor to the One who did it.

2.5. Christ gently rebuked Martha (v. 40): *Said I not unto thee that if thou wouldest believe, thou shouldest see the glory of God?* Our Lord Jesus has given us all possible assurances that a sincere faith will finally be crowned with a blessed vision. If we will take Christ's word and depend on his power and faithfulness, we will see the glory of God, and be happy as we do so. We often need to be reminded of these faithful blessings with which our Lord Jesus has encouraged us. We tend to forget what Christ has spoken and need him to remind us of it through his Spirit: "*Said I not unto thee* so and so? Do you think that I will ever take my words back?"

2.6. The grave was opened despite Martha's objection (v. 41): *Then they took away the stone.* If we want to see the glory of God, we must let Christ follow his own way. *They took away the stone,* and this was all they could do; only Christ could give life.

3. The miracle itself performed.

3.1. He turned to his *living Father in heaven* (6:17). The gesture he used was very significant: *He lifted up his eyes.* What is prayer except the ascent of the soul to God and the directing of its love and actions toward heaven? He lifted up his eyes, looking beyond the grave where Lazarus lay and overlooking all the difficulties that arose from that. He prayed to God with great assurance: *Father, I thank thee that thou hast heard me.*

3.1.1. He has taught us here, by his own example:

3.1.1.1. That in prayer we should call God Father.

3.1.1.2. That in our prayers we should praise him, and when we come to seek further mercy, we should thankfully acknowledge former blessings.

3.1.2. Our Savior's thanksgiving here, however, was intended to express the unshaken confidence he had in carrying out this miracle. He spoke of this as his own act (v. 11): *I go, that I may awake him.* He also spoke of it as what he had obtained by prayer because his Father heard him.

3.1.2.1. Christ spoke of this miracle as an answer to prayer because he wished to honor prayer, making it the key with which he unlocked the treasures of divine power and grace.

3.1.2.2. Being assured his prayer was answered, Christ professed:

3.1.2.2.*1.* His thankful acceptance of this answer: *I thank thee that thou hast heard me.* He triumphed before the victory. No other person can claim to have had such assurance as Christ had, yet we, by faith in the promise, may have a prospect of mercy before it is actually given and may give God thanks for it. Blessings in answer to prayer should be specially acknowledged with thankfulness. And we must value not only the gift of the blessing itself but also the great favor of having our poor prayers noticed. Just as God answers us with blessing even *before we call,* so we should answer him with praise even before he gives.

3.1.2.2.*2.* His cheerful assurance of a ready answer at any time (v. 42): *And I know that thou hearest me always.* "I gave thanks," he said, "for being heard in this matter because I am sure to be heard in everything." Notice here:

3.1.2.2.*2.1.* The influence our Lord Jesus had in heaven; the Father always heard him, which may encourage us to depend on his intercession and give all our petitions to him.

3.1.2.2.*2.2.* The confidence he had: *I know* it. We cannot have such a particular assurance as he had, but we know that *whatsoever we ask according to his will, he heareth us* (1Jn 5:14–15).

3.1.2.3. But why should Christ give this public indication of his obtaining this miracle by prayer? *Because of the people who stand by, that they may believe that thou hast sent me,* because prayer may preach.

3.1.2.3.*1.* It was to remove the objections of his enemies. It had been blasphemously suggested by the Pharisees that he performed his miracles because he was in alliance with the Devil. Now, to prove the opposite, he openly addressed God, using prayers, not charms, with his eyes lifted high and his voice professing his dependence on heaven.

3.1.2.3.*2.* It was to confirm the faith of those who were well disposed toward him: *That they may believe that thou hast sent me.* Christ proved his mission by raising to life one who had died.

3.2. He now turned to his dead friend. He *cried with a loud voice, Lazarus, come forth.*

3.2.1. He could have raised Lazarus by a silent exertion of his power and will, but he did it by a loud call:

3.2.1.1. To demonstrate the power then exerted to raise Lazarus. The soul of Lazarus, which was to be recalled, was at a distance; it was not hovering about the grave, as the Jews thought, but removed to Hades. It is natural to speak loudly when we call to people far away. And the body of Lazarus, which was to be called up, was asleep, and we usually speak loudly when we want to wake someone.

3.2.1.2. To make this miracle a type of other miracles that the power of Christ was to effect. This loud call was a picture:

3.2.1.2.*1.* Of the Gospel call, by which dead souls were to be brought out of the grave of sin.

3.2.1.2.*2.* Of the sound of the archangel's trumpet at the last day, with which those who sleep in the dust will be woken up when Christ will *descend with a shout* (1Th 4:16).

3.2.2. This loud call was only short, but it was *mighty through God* (2Co 10:4).

3.2.2.1. He called the dead man by name, *Lazarus,* as we call by name those we want to wake from a deep sleep.

3.2.2.2. He called him out of the grave: *come forth.* He did not say to him, "Live," but, "Move," because when we live spiritually by the grace of Christ, we must stir ourselves to move; the grave of sin and this world is no place for those whom Christ has given life to, and so they must *come forth.*

3.2.2.3. The result was according to Christ's intention: *He that was dead came forth* (v. 44). Power accompanied the word of Christ to reunite the soul and body of Lazarus, and then he came out. The miracle is described not by the invisible spring from which it arose, to satisfy our curiosity, but by its visible effects, to confirm our faith. If anyone were to ask whether Lazarus, once raised, could give an account or description of his soul's removal from the body or its return to it, or what he saw in the other world, I suppose both of those changes were so inexplicable to him that it was neither lawful nor possible to express it. Let us not seek to be wise beyond what is written (1Co 4:6), and this is all that is written about the resurrection of that Lazarus, that *he that was dead came forth.*

3.2.3. This miracle was performed:

3.2.3.1. Quickly. Nothing came between the command, *Come forth,* and the effect, *He came forth.*

3.2.3.2. Completely. He was so thoroughly revived that he got up from his grave as strongly as he had ever gotten up out of his bed, and he returned not only to life but to health. He was not raised to serve some temporary purpose, but to live as other people.

3.2.3.3. With this additional miracle, as some consider it: he came out of his grave even though he was hampered by his graveclothes (v. 44), *bound hand and foot* and with *his face bound about with a napkin* (a cloth)—because this was the burial custom of the Jews; he came out wearing the same clothes in which he was buried, so that it would be clear that it was he himself and not another person. When the onlookers unwrapped him, they would handle him and see that it was he himself and would thus witness the miracle. Notice how little we take with us when we leave the world—only a shroud and a coffin; there is no change of clothes in the grave, nothing but a single suit of graveclothes. Because Lazarus had come out, hampered and caught up in his graveclothes, we may well imagine that those around the grave were extremely surprised and frightened at the sight. To make the thing less shocking to the people, Christ set them to work: "*Loose him,* loosen his graveclothes, so that he can wear them until he comes to his house."

Verses 45–57

We have here an account of the effects of this glorious miracle.

1. Some found it inviting and were led to believe. When many of the Jews *saw the things that Jesus did, they believed on him.* They had often heard about his miracles

but evaded being convicted by them by calling into question the facts of the matter, but now that they themselves had seen this done, their unbelief was conquered. These were some of the Jews who came to Mary to comfort her. When we are doing good works for others, we put ourselves in the path of receiving favors from God.

2. Others were irritated and hardened in their unbelief by it.

2.1. The informers were so (v. 46): *Some of them went to the Pharisees and told them what things Jesus had done*, with the spiteful intention of exciting to greater rage those who needed no further reason to prosecute him more vigorously. We see here a most stubborn unfaithfulness, a refusing to give in to the most powerful means of conviction. We also see a most hardened hostility. If they would not be satisfied that he was to be believed in as the Christ, one would have thought they would nevertheless be pacified and persuaded not to persecute him.

2.2. The judges, the *blind leaders* (Mt 15:14), of the people were no less exasperated by the report given to them.

2.2.1. A special council was called and held (v. 47): *Then gathered the chief priests and Pharisees a council.* This council was called not only for mutual advising but also for mutual irritation, so that they exasperated and inflamed one another with their hostility and rage against Christ.

2.2.2. The case was proposed, and it was shown to be significant.

2.2.2.1. The matter to be debated was what course they should take with this Jesus; they said, *What do we? For this man doeth many miracles.*

2.2.2.1.1. They acknowledged that Christ's miracles were genuine and that he had performed many of them. They were witnesses against themselves, therefore, because they acknowledged his credentials but denied his commission.

2.2.2.1.2. They considered what was to be done, and they rebuked themselves for not having done something effective to crush him sooner. They did not consider at all whether they should receive him and acknowledge him as the Messiah, but assumed that he was an enemy and that, as such, he was to be struck down: "*What do we?* Shall we be always talking but never do anything?"

2.2.2.2. What made this matter significant was the danger they knew their church and nation were in from the Romans (v. 48). "If we do not silence him, *all men will believe on him*, and since this will mean the setting up of a new king, the Romans will *come* and *take away our place and nation.*" Notice what a high opinion they had of their own power. They spoke as if they thought Christ's progress depended on their condoning him, as if it were in their power to overcome the One who had conquered death.

2.2.2.2.1. They took it on themselves to prophesy that if he was allowed to go on, *all men would believe on him.* They now considered his influence formidable, though when it suited them these same men sought to make that influence contemptible: *Have any of the rulers believed on him?* (7:48). This was what they were afraid of, that people would believe on him.

2.2.2.2.2. They foretold that if most of the nation was drawn after him, the anger of the Romans would be drawn upon them. They *will come and take away our place.* Here cowardice appeared. If they had kept their integrity, they would not have needed to fear the Romans, but now they spoke like a discouraged people. When people lose their godliness, they also lose their courage.

2.2.2.2.2.1. It was false that there was any danger of the Romans' being enraged against their nation by the progress of Christ's Gospel. He taught people to pay taxes to Caesar and not to *resist evil* (Mt 5:39). At his trial, the Roman governor could *find no fault in him* (18:38). Claimed fears often cover up malicious intentions.

2.2.2.2.2.2. If there really had been some danger of displeasing the Romans by tolerating Christ's preaching, this still would not have justified their hating and persecuting a good man. The enemies of Christ and his Gospel have often covered their hostility with an apparent concern for the public good and the common safety and have branded his prophets and ministers as people who want to *turn the world upside down* (Ac 17:6). Worldly politics commonly pits national security against the rules of justice. The disaster that we seek to escape by sin is the disaster that we take the most effective course of action to bring down onto our own heads.

2.2.3. Caiaphas made a malicious but mystical speech in the council.

2.2.3.1. Its malice is obvious at once (vv. 49–50). Being the high priest, he took it on himself to decide the matter. "*You know nothing at all.* The matter is quickly determined if you consider the accepted maxim that *it is expedient for us that one man should die for the people.*"

2.2.3.1.1. The counselor was Caiaphas, who was *high priest that same year.*

2.2.3.1.2. The drift of his advice was, in short, that some way must be found to put Jesus to death. Caiaphas did not say, "Let him be silenced"; no, he must die.

2.2.3.1.3. This was plausibly insinuated with the subtlety and malice of the old Serpent (Rev 12:9; 20:2).

2.2.3.1.3.1. He implicitly invoked his own wisdom. How scornfully he said, "*You know nothing*, you who are merely common priests." It is common for those in authority to impose their corrupt dictates by virtue of their authority; because they should be the wisest and best, they expect everyone to believe they really are.

2.2.3.1.3.2. He assumed that the case was plain and beyond dispute. Reason and justice are often struck down high-handedly. *Truth is fallen in the streets*, and "when it is down, down with it!" And *equity cannot enter*, and "when it is out, out with it!" (Isa 59:14).

2.2.3.1.3.3. He insisted on the political maxim that the welfare of communities is to be put before that of specific individuals. *It is expedient for us* that *one man die for the people.* Caiaphas craftily insinuated that the greatest and best man should think his life well spent — in fact, well lost — if it is spent or lost to save his country from ruin. The case should have been put like this: was it expedient for them to bring on themselves and on their nation the guilt of blood to secure their civil interests? Worldly politics, though it thinks it can save everything by sin, ruins everything in the end.

2.2.3.2. The mystery that was contained in this advice of Caiaphas is not obvious at first view, but the Evangelist leads us into it (vv. 51–52): *This spoke he not of himself.* With these words, though he himself was not aware of it, Caiaphas prophesied that *Jesus would die for that nation.* Here is a precious comment on a deadly text. Love teaches us to put the most favorable interpretation on people's words and actions that they will bear, but godliness teaches us to apply them well. If evildoers are God's hand to humble and reform us, why may they not be God's mouthpiece to instruct and convince us? Just as the hearts of all people are in God's hand, so are their tongues.

2.2.4. The Evangelist explains and enlarges on Caiaphas's words.

2.2.4.1. He explains what Caiaphas said. He did not *speak it of himself*. To the extent that it was a way of stirring up the council against Christ, he spoke it from himself, but to the extent that it was an authoritative word, declaring the purpose and intention of God, he did not speak it from himself.

2.2.4.1.*1*. He prophesied, and those who prophesied did not, in their prophesying, *speak of themselves*. But was Caiaphas also among the prophets (1Sa 10:11–12; 19:24)? He was so on this one occasion. God can and often does make evildoers instruments that serve his own purposes, even contrary to their own intentions. Words of prophecy in the mouth are not infallible evidence of a spring of grace in the heart. *Lord, Lord, have we not prophesied in thy name?* (Mt 7:22) will be rejected as an empty plea.

2.2.4.1.*2*. He prophesied, *being high priest that year*. Not that his being high priest disposed or qualified him to be a prophet at all. Rather, since he was high priest, God wished to put this significant word into his mouth rather than into the mouth of any other person, so that it would be more observed, or rather, so that the nonobservance of it would be emphasized all the more.

2.2.4.1.*3*. The content of his prophecy was that Jesus would die for that nation. Caiaphas meant by *the nation* those in it who remained stubbornly loyal to Judaism, but God meant those in it who would receive the message of Christ and become followers of him. It is a great thing that is prophesied here: that Jesus would die for others, not only for their good but also in their place. If the whole nation of the Jews had unanimously believed in Christ and received his Gospel, they would have been not only saved eternally but also saved as a nation from their grievances.

2.2.4.2. The Evangelist enlarges on this word of Caiaphas (v. 52). The high priest, he said, had prophesied that Jesus must die *not for that nation only*, but *that also he should gather together in one the children of God that were scattered abroad*. Notice here:

2.2.4.2.*1*. The people Christ died for: *not for the nation* of the Jews *only*. He must die for *the children of God that were scattered abroad*. Some understand this to refer to the children of God who were then living but were scattered far and wide in the Gentile world, *devout men of every nation* (Ac 2:5) who *feared God* (Ac 10:2) and worshiped him (Acts 17:4). Christ died to join these together in one great community. Others include with these all who belong to the election of grace (Ro 11:5), who are called the children of God. There are those who *fear him throughout all generations* (Ps 72:5); he considered all these in the atonement he made. He both prayed and died for *all that would believe on him* (17:20).

2.2.4.2.*2*. The purpose and intention of his death: he died to gather in those who wandered and *to gather together in one* those *who were scattered*. Christ's dying is:

2.2.4.2.*2*.1. The great force that attracts our hearts, because this is why he was lifted up, to draw people to himself (12:32). His love in dying for us attracts our love.

2.2.4.2.*2*.2. The great center of our unity. He gathers them together in one (Eph 1:10). All the saints in all places and ages meet in Christ.

2.2.5. The result of this discussion was a decision to put Jesus to death (v. 53): *From that day they took counsel together* (they plotted) *to put him to death*. They now understood one another's minds, and so each had settled in his own that Jesus must die.

2.2.5.1. They now agreed on what they had earlier thought of separately, and so they strengthened one anoth-

er's hands in their evil plotting. Evildoers confirm and encourage themselves and one another in their evil practices by comparing notes; then the evil that before seemed impracticable appears not only possible but easy to effect.

2.2.5.2. They were now provided with a plausible pretense to justify themselves in what they had earlier wished to do but had lacked a reason for.

2.2.6. Christ then hid (v. 54).

2.2.6.1. He stopped appearing in public: *He walked no more openly among the Jews.*

2.2.6.2. He withdrew to an obscure part of the country, so obscure that the name of the town he withdrew to is scarcely met with anywhere else. He went to a country *near the wilderness* and entered a village called Ephraim. His disciples went there with him; they did not want to leave him alone, and he did not want to leave them in danger. But why would Christ leave now? It was not because he either feared the power of his enemies or distrusted his own power. He withdrew:

2.2.6.2.*1*. To show his displeasure toward Jerusalem and the Jewish people. They rejected him and his Gospel; he, therefore, justly took himself and his Gospel away from them. It was a sad sign of the thick darkness that was soon to come on Jerusalem because she did not recognize the time when God came to her (Lk 19:44).

2.2.6.2.*2*. To make the cruelty of his enemies more inexcusable. He would see whether their anger would be turned away by his retreat into privacy.

2.2.6.2.*3*. Because his hour had *not yet come* (7:30), and so he refused to take the dangerous path.

2.2.6.2.*4*. To make his return to Jerusalem even more remarkable and illustrious. This increased the acclamations of joy with which his well-wishers welcomed him when he rode triumphantly into the city.

2.2.7. A rigorous search was made for him during his retreat (vv. 55–57).

2.2.7.1. The occasion of it was the approach of the Passover, which they expected him to attend, according to the custom (v. 55): *The Jews' passover was nigh at hand*, a festival that shone brightly in their calendar. Because the Passover was now near, *many went out of* all parts of *the country to Jerusalem, to purify themselves*. This was either a necessary purification of those who had contracted any ceremonial defilement or a voluntary purification, by fasting and prayer and other religious exercises, which many spent some time in before the Passover.

2.2.7.2. The searchers were very anxious: *They said, What think you, that he will not come to the feast?* (v. 56). Some think this was said by those who wished him well and expected him to come. Those who came out of the country early so that they could cleanse themselves wanted very much to meet with Christ, and perhaps they came sooner with that expectation. They asked if there was any news of Christ. But it seems rather that his enemies made this search for him. When they should have been helping those who came to purify themselves, according to the duty of their place, they were plotting against Christ. Their asking, *What think you? Will he not come up to the feast?* implied:

2.2.7.2.*1*. An invidious reflection on Christ, as if he would neglect his attendance at the feast of the Lord for fear of exposing himself. It is sad to see holy services of worship corrupted to such unholy purposes.

2.2.7.2.*2*. A fearful apprehension that they would miss their victim: "*Will he not come up to the feast?* If he does not, all our plans will fail."

2.2.7.3. The orders to arrest him were very strict (v. 57). The great Sanhedrin issued a proclamation strictly charging and requiring that if anyone knew where he was, they must reveal it so that he could be arrested. Notice:

2.2.7.3.*1.* How set they were on this prosecution.

2.2.7.3.*2.* How willing they were to involve others in the guilt with them. It emphasizes the sins of evil rulers that they commonly make those who are under them the instruments of their unrighteousness (Ro 6:13).

CHAPTER 12

Let us see what honors were heaped on the head of the Lord Jesus even in the depths of his humiliation. 1. Mary honored him by anointing his feet at the dinner in Bethany (vv. 1–11). 2. The ordinary people honored him with their acclamations of joy when he entered Jerusalem in triumph (vv. 12–19). 3. The Greeks honored him by seeking him with a longing desire to see him (vv. 20–26). 4. God the Father honored him by a voice from heaven (vv. 27–36). 5. He had honor shown him by the Old Testament prophets (vv. 37–41). 6. He had honor shown him by some of the chief rulers, even though they did not have the courage to confess it (vv. 42–43). 7. He claimed honor for himself by asserting his divine mission (vv. 44–50).

Verses 1–11

In these verses we have:

1. The kind visit our Lord Jesus made to his friends at Bethany (v. 1). He came up from the country *six days before the Passover* and stayed at Bethany. He lodged here with his friend Lazarus, whom he had just raised from the dead. His coming to Bethany now may be considered:

1.1. As an introduction to the Passover he intended to celebrate, to which reference is made in assigning the date of his coming: *six days before the Passover.*

1.2. As a voluntary exposing of himself to the anger of his enemies; now that his hour was near, he came within their reach. Our Lord Jesus suffered willingly; his life was not forced from him; rather, he submitted to the Father's will. Just as the power of his persecutors could not defeat him, so their subtlety could not surprise him. Just as there is a time when we are allowed to run to save our own lives, so there is also a time when we are called to risk our lives in the cause of God.

1.3. As showing kindness toward his friends at Bethany, whom he loved. This was a farewell visit. Bethany is described here as the town *where Lazarus was, whom he raised from the dead.* The miracle performed here gave a new honor to the place and made it significant. Where he has sown plentifully, he looks to see whether plants are growing.

2. The kind reception his friends there gave him: they *made him a supper* (v. 2). It may be asked whether this was the same dinner as is recorded in Mt 26:6–13, in the house of Simon. Most commentators think it was, since the two stories have much in common. Yet the dates seem to be different (Mt 26:2), nor is it likely that Martha would serve in any house except her own, and so I am inclined to agree with Dr. Lightfoot and think they were different occasions. Let us see the account of this reception.

2.1. They *made him a supper,* because with them supper was usually the best meal. They did this as a sign of their respect and gratitude, for a feast is made for friendship; and they did it so that they would have the opportunity of free and pleasant conversation with him, for a feast is also made for fellowship (Ecc 10:19).

2.2. Martha served; she did not think it beneath her to serve when Christ sat down to eat; nor should we think it

a dishonor to stoop to any service in which Christ may be honored. Christ had formerly rebuked Martha for being *troubled with much serving* (Lk 10:40). She did not, however, for that reason stop serving, as some do, who, when they are rebuked for one extreme, run in a bad temper to the other. No, she continued to serve. Better to be a waiter at Christ's table than a guest at the table of a ruler.

2.3. Lazarus was *one of those that sat at the table.* It proved the truth of his resurrection, as it did of Christ's, that there were those who *ate and drank with him* (Ac 10:41). He sat at table as a memorial of the miracle Christ had performed. Those whom Christ has raised up to a spiritual life are seated together with him.

3. The particular respect that Mary showed him (v. 3). She had *a pound of ointment of spikenard* (a pint of pure nard), *very costly,* and with this she *anointed the feet of Jesus.* She *wiped them with her hair,* and *the house was filled with the odour of the ointment.* She intended this no doubt as a sign of her love for Christ. By this her love for Christ appears to have been:

3.1. A generous love. If she had anything that was more valuable than what others had, that must be brought out to honor Christ. Those who really love Christ love him so much more than this world that they are willing to spend the best they have on him.

3.2. A humble love. She not only gave her perfume to Christ but also used her own hands to pour it out on him. In fact, she did not, as usual, anoint his head with it, but his feet. True love for Christ spares neither expense nor effort to honor him.

3.3. A believing love. Her faith was working through this love (Gal 5:6), faith in Jesus as the Messiah, the Christ, the Anointed One. God's Anointed should be our Anointed. Let us pour out on him the perfume of our best love and devotion. The filling of the house with the pleasant fragrance of the perfume shows us that those who receive Christ into their hearts and homes bring a sweet fragrance into them.

4. Judas's dislike of Mary's sign of her respect for Christ (vv. 4–5). Notice:

4.1. The person who objected to it was Judas, *one of his disciples*; he was not one of their nature, only one of their number. Judas was an apostle, a preacher of the Gospel, but one who discouraged this expression of godly affection. It is sad to see the life of religious faith discouraged by those who according to their office should help and encourage it. However, he was the one who would betray Christ.

4.2. The pretense with which he covered up his dislike (v. 5): *Why was not this ointment sold for three hundred pence, and given to the poor?*

4.2.1. Here worldly wisdom criticized godly zeal. Those who pride themselves on their worldly political ways and undervalue others for their serious godliness have more in them of the spirit of Judas than they want to be thought to have.

4.2.2. Here the appearance of charity to the poor was secretly made a cloak for greed. Many people excuse themselves from spending on charity under pretense of saving for charity. Judas asked, *Why was it not given to the poor?* We must not conclude that those who do not do acceptable acts of service in the way we would are not acting satisfactorily. Proud people think everyone is ill advised who does not consult them.

4.3. The detection and revelation of Judas's hypocrisy in this (v. 6). *This he said, not that he cared for the poor, but because he was a thief and had the bag* (kept the money bag).

4.3.1. It did not come from a motive of love: *Not that he cared for the poor.* What did he care for the poor, except that by overseeing the care of the poor he could serve his own ends? Some people eagerly strive for the power of the church—as others do for its purity—when perhaps it is all the same to them whether its true interests sink or swim; they are interested only in advancing themselves.

4.3.2. It came from a motive of greed. The truth of the matter was that he would rather have had the value of the perfume in cash, to be put in the common store, and then he would know what to do with it. Notice:

4.3.2.1. Judas was treasurer of Christ's household.

4.3.2.1.*1.* See what resources Jesus and his disciples had to live on: only a money bag, in which they kept just enough for them to live on, giving the surplus, if any, to the poor. This money bag was supplied by the contributions of good people, and the Master and his disciples had everything in common (Ac 2:44; 4:32); *for our sakes he became poor* (2Co 8:9).

4.3.2.1.*2.* Notice who was the manager of the little they had: it was Judas; he kept the money bag. Perhaps he was appointed to this office because he was the least and lowest of all the disciples; it was not Peter or John who was made manager. To a minister of the Gospel, worldly employments are not only a distraction but also a degradation. Or perhaps he was given the position because he wanted it. In his heart he loved to handle money, and so the money bag was committed to him. He chose the bag, and the bag was his. Strong inward inclinations to sin are often justly punished by strong outward temptations to sin. We have little reason to be fond or proud of the money bag, for at best we are merely its managers.

4.3.2.2. Being entrusted with the money bag, Judas *was a thief.* The dominant love of money is theft in the heart as much as anger and revenge are murder committed in the heart. Those to whom the management and disposal of public money is committed need to be ruled by firm principles of justice and honesty, so that no stain will cling to their hands. Judas, who had betrayed his trust, soon after betrayed his Master.

5. Christ's justification of what Mary did (vv. 7–8). *Let her alone.* Here he showed his acceptance of her kindness. Since it was a sign of her goodwill, he showed he was pleased with it. Christ does not want those who sincerely want to please him censured or discouraged, even though in their honest endeavors there is not all the discretion there could be (Ro 14:3). To justify Mary:

5.1. Christ put a favorable interpretation on what she did, revealing something that those who condemned it were unaware of: *Against the day of my burying she has kept this.* "The day of my burial is now near, and she has anointed a body that is already as good as dead." Providence often opens a door of opportunity to true Christians so that the expressions of their godly zeal prove to be more timely and more beautiful than any foresight of their own could make them.

5.2. He gave a sufficient answer to Judas's objection (v. 8). Matters are so structured in the kingdom of providence that *the poor we have always with us* (Dt 15:11). Matters are so structured in the kingdom of grace that the church would not always have the physical presence of Jesus Christ: *Me you have not always.* Opportunities are to be taken advantage of, and those opportunities likely to pass soonest must be grasped first and most vigorously. The good duty that can be done at any time should give way to what cannot be done except right now.

6. The public notice that was taken of our Lord Jesus here at this supper at Bethany (v. 9): *Much people of the Jews knew that he was there,* and they came flocking there. They came to see Jesus, whose name was very much exalted by his recent miracle of raising Lazarus. They came not to hear him but to satisfy their curiosity by seeing him. Because it was known where Christ was, crowds came to him. They came to see Lazarus and Christ together, which was a very inviting sight. Some people came to have their faith in Christ confirmed; others, only to satisfy their curiosity, so that they would be able to say they had seen a man who had been dead and buried but who now lived again. And so, on these holidays, Lazarus served as a spectacle.

7. The anger of the chief priests at the growing influence of our Lord Jesus (vv. 10–11): they *consulted how they might put Lazarus also to death,* because *by reason of him many of the Jews went away, and believed on Jesus.* Notice here:

7.1. How ineffective and unsuccessful their attempts against Christ had been up to that time. They had done all they could to alienate the people from him, but many of the Jews were so overcome by the convincing evidence of Christ's miracles that they went away from the party of the priests *and believed on Jesus.* They did this because of Lazarus; his resurrection put life into their faith. What was impossible for One who could raise the dead?

7.2. How absurd and unreasonable it was that Lazarus must be put to death. It was a sign that they *neither feared God nor regarded man* (Lk 18:2). For:

7.2.1. If they had feared God, they would not have been so defiant toward him. God wanted Lazarus to live by a miracle, and they wanted him to die by malice. Lazarus was singled out to be the object of their special hatred because God had distinguished him by the signs of his special love. One would have thought that they would discuss how they could join in friendship with Lazarus and his family, and how by the mediation of that family they could reconcile themselves to this Jesus whom they had persecuted.

7.2.2. If they had respected human beings, they would not have committed such an act of injustice to Lazarus, an innocent man, whom they could not justly accuse of any crime.

Verses 12–19

This account of Christ's triumphal entry into Jerusalem is recorded by all the Evangelists as worthy of special comment, and here we may notice:

1. The respect shown to our Lord Jesus by the ordinary people (vv. 12–13). Notice:

1.1. Who gave him this respect: *much people,* "a great crowd" of those who came to the feast, not the residents of Jerusalem but the country people. The nearer people were to the temple of the Lord, the further they were from the Lord of the temple. These country people were the ones who came up to the feast. Perhaps they had heard Christ talking in the country and had become great admirers of him there, and so they were eager to show their respect for him at Jerusalem. Perhaps they were those more devout Jews who had come to the feast some time before to purify themselves, who were more inclined to religious faith than their neighbors, and they were the people who were so eager to honor Christ. It was not the rulers or the leaders who went out to meet Christ, but the ordinary people. But Christ is honored more by the numerousness of his followers than by the magnificence of some of them, because he values people by their souls, not their names and titles of honor.

1.2. When they expressed their respect: when *they heard that Jesus was coming to Jerusalem.* They had asked for him: *Will he not come up to the feast?* (11:55–56). When they heard he was coming, they roused themselves to welcome him.

1.3. How they expressed their respect: they gave him what they had, and even this insignificant crowd faintly resembled the glorious company that John saw *before the throne, and before the Lamb* (Rev 7:9–10). Although these people were not before the throne, they were before the Lamb. In John's vision, it is said of that heavenly choir:

1.3.1. That they held palm branches in their hands. The palm tree has always been a sign of victory and triumph. Christ was now coming to defeat principalities and powers through his death (Col 2:15). Although he was only putting on his armor, he could still boast as though he had taken it off (1Ki 20:11).

1.3.2. That they *cried with a loud voice, saying, Salvation to our God* (Rev 7:10), as did this crowd. They shouted, *Hosanna, blessed is the king of Israel, that comes in the name of the Lord—hosanna* meaning "Save."

1.3.2.1. They acknowledged our Lord Jesus to be the king of Israel, who was coming *in the name of the Lord* (Ps 118:26). They recognized him to be a king, which shows his position and his honor, which we must adore, and his power and his rule, to which we must submit. He was a rightful king, coming in *the name of the Lord* (Ps 2:6), the promised and long-expected king, *Messiah the prince* (Da 9:25), because he was *king of Israel*.

1.3.2.2. They sincerely wished his kingdom well, which is the meaning of *hosanna*. In crying hosanna they prayed three things: that his kingdom would come, in its light and knowledge and in its power and effectiveness; that it would conquer; and that it would continue. Hosanna, though literally it means "Save," is equivalent to saying, "Let the king live forever."

1.3.2.3. They welcomed him in Jerusalem: "*Welcome is he that cometh*; *come in, thou blessed of the Lord* (Ge 24:31)." This is how each one of us must welcome Christ into our hearts. Faith says, *Blessed is he that cometh.*

2. The position Christ put himself into to receive the respect given to him (v. 14): *When he had found a young ass,* he *sat thereon*. He appeared as an insignificant figure, alone on a donkey, with a crowd of people around him shouting *Hosanna*. This was a much more dignified form than he was used to taking; he was used to traveling on foot, but he now was mounted. Yet it was a much less dignified form than the famous people in the world usually take. His kingdom was not of this world (18:36), and so he did not come with outward pomp.

3. The fulfilling of the Scripture in this: *As it is written, Fear not, daughter of Sion* (v. 15). This is quoted from Zec 9:9.

3.1. It was foretold both that Zion's king would come and that he would come as he did, *sitting on an ass's colt*. Although he comes only slowly—a donkey moves slowly—yet he comes surely, and with such expressions of condescension as greatly encourage his loyal subjects. Humble petitioners can get close enough to speak to him.

3.2. The daughter of Zion is therefore called on to *behold her king*. She is also told, *Fear not*. In the prophecy, Zion is told to rejoice greatly and shout, but here it is rendered, *Fear not*. Unfaithful fears are enemies of spiritual joys; if they are healed, if they are conquered, joy will come naturally. If the situation is such that we cannot reach exultations of joy, we should still seek to obtain relief from the oppression of fear. *Rejoice greatly* (Zec 9:9); at least, *fear not*.

4. The Evangelist's remark about the disciples (v. 16): *They understood not at first*, but when *Jesus was glorified*, they remembered that *these things were written of him* and that they and others had *done these things to him*.

4.1. Notice here the imperfection of the disciples; *they understood not these things at first*. They did not consider that they were performing the ceremony of the inauguration of Zion's king. The Scripture is often fulfilled by the agency of those who themselves do not look to the Scripture in what they are doing (Isa 45:4). What later becomes clear was at first mysterious and doubtful. It is good for the disciples of Christ to reflect on the follies and weaknesses of their first beginnings, so that they may have compassion on the ignorant. *When I was a child, I spoke as a child* (1Co 13:11).

4.2. Notice here the improved knowledge of the disciples in their adulthood. Notice:

4.2.1. When they understood it: *When Jesus was glorified*. Until then they had not rightly understood the nature of his kingdom. Until then the Spirit had not been poured out, who was to lead them into all truth (16:13).

4.2.2. How they understood it: they compared the prophecy with the outcome. *Then remembered they that these things were written of him*. The memory of what is written will enable us to understand what has been done, and the observation of what has been done will help us understand what has been written.

5. The reason that led the people to show this respect to our Lord Jesus: it was the clear miracle he had just performed in raising Lazarus. Notice here:

5.1. What account and what assurance they had of this miracle; no doubt the city rang with news of it. Those who considered it proof of Christ's mission and a basis of their faith in him traced the report to those who were eyewitnesses of it so that they would *know the certainty* of it (Lk 1:4). *The people therefore that* stood by *when he called Lazarus* out of his grave *bore record* (continued to testify about him) (v. 17). They unanimously confirmed the miracle to be true, beyond all dispute or contradiction. The truth of Christ's miracles was proved by undeniable evidence.

5.2. What influence it had on them (v. 18): *For this cause the people met him*. Some went out to meet him out of curiosity; they wanted to see One who had performed such a wonderful act. Others, out of conscience, sought to give him honor, as One sent by God.

6. The anger of the Pharisees at all this.

6.1. They acknowledged they had gained no ground against him. Those who oppose Christ will be made to realize that they can gain nothing, that they are getting nowhere. God will fulfill his own purposes in spite of them and their little efforts of impotent malice. *You prevail nothing*, "you gain nothing" (v. 19). There is nothing to be gained by opposing Christ.

6.2. They acknowledged he had gained ground: *The world is gone after him*. Here, however, like Caiaphas, before they were aware of it, they prophesied that *the world would go after him*.

6.2.1. This was how they expressed their own irritation; their envy made them anxious. Considering how great these Pharisees were, one would have thought they did not need to begrudge Christ such an insignificant piece of honor as was now shown him, but proud people want to monopolize honor, to share it with no one.

6.2.2. This was how they motivated themselves and one another to a more vigorous pursuit of the battle against Christ. The enemies of religion are made more determined and active by being shamed; shall its friends, then, be discouraged at every disappointment, when they know its cause is righteous and will finally be victorious?

Verses 20–26

Honor was shown here to Christ by certain Greeks who asked for him. We are told:

1. Who gave this honor to our Lord Jesus: *Certain Greeks among* the people who *came up to worship at the feast* (v. 20). Some think they were "Jews of the dispersion," who had scattered among the Gentiles and were called Greeks. Others think they were Gentiles, those whom they called "proselytes of the gate," such as the Ethiopian eunuch (Ac 8:26–40) and Cornelius (Ac 10). There were devout worshipers of the true God even among those who were strangers to the citizenship of Israel (Eph 2:12). Although these Greeks, if uncircumcised, were not allowed to eat the Passover, they still came to *worship at the feast*. We must thankfully use the privileges we have, even though we may be excluded from others.

2. What honor they gave him: they wanted to come to know him (v. 21).

2.1. Wanting to see Christ, they were careful to use the proper means. They did not limit themselves simply to their bare wishes, but were determined to see what could be done.

2.2. They turned to Philip, one of his disciples. Some think that they had known him from before. It is good to know those who know the Lord. However, if these Greeks had been near Galilee, they would probably have been with Christ there. I think, therefore, that they turned to Philip only because they saw he was a close follower of Christ. Those who want to see Jesus by faith now that he is in heaven must turn to his ministers, whom he has appointed to guide poor souls in seeking him. The leading of these Greeks to know Christ by way of Philip showed that God had chosen the apostles as his agents, that he would use their ministry in the conversion of the Gentiles.

2.3. Their request to Philip was brief: *Sir, we would see Jesus.* They gave him a title of respect because he knew Christ. Their business was that they wanted to see Jesus; yet they wanted not only to see his face, so that they would be able to say when they arrived home they had seen the One so much talked about, but also to speak freely with him and be taught by him. Now that they had come to worship at the feast, they wanted to see Jesus. In our attendance at holy services of worship, especially the Gospel Passover, the great desire of our souls should be to see Jesus. We miss the purpose of our coming if we do not see Jesus.

2.4. Philip reported this to his Master (v. 22). First he told Andrew. They agreed that the suggestion must be made, but then Philip wanted Andrew to go along with him. Christ's ministers should help one another and agree to help souls come to Christ. It seems that Andrew and Philip brought this message to Christ when he was teaching in public, for we read of the *people that stood by* (v. 29).

3. How Christ accepted this honor (v. 23). He foretold both the honor he himself would have in being followed (vv. 23–24) and the honor that those who followed him would have (vv. 25–26).

3.1. He foresaw the plentiful harvest of which this was, as it were, the firstfruits (v. 23), namely, the conversion of the Gentiles (v. 23). *The hour is come when the Son of man shall be glorified.* Notice:

3.1.1. The purpose of the foretold events, which was the glorifying of the Redeemer: "And is it so? Are the Gentiles beginning to seek me? Then the hour has come for the glorifying of the Son of Man." This was no surprise to Christ, but it was a puzzle to those around him. This shows us:

3.1.1.1. The calling of the Gentiles led greatly to the glory of the Son of Man. The multiplying of the redeemed was the exalting of the Redeemer.

3.1.1.2. There was a set time for the glorifying of the Son of Man, and he spoke of its approach with exultation and triumph: *The hour is come.*

3.1.2. The strange way in which this end was to be reached, and that was by the death of Christ, which was shown by a parable (v. 24): "*Verily, verily, I say unto you, except* (unless) *a corn* (a kernel) *of wheat fall into the ground and die*, it *abideth alone* (remains only a single seed), and you never see any more of it, but *if it die* it *bringeth forth much fruit* (produces many seeds)." Now here:

3.1.2.1. The necessity of Christ's humiliation was shown. He would never have been the living, life-giving head and root of the church if he had not descended from heaven to this cursed earth and ascended from earth to the cursed tree, and so accomplished our redemption. He must *pour out his soul unto death* (Isa 53:12).

3.1.2.2. The advantage of Christ's humiliation was illustrated. He fell to the ground in his incarnation, but this was not all: he died. He lay in the grave like seed underground, but as the seed comes up again green, fresh, and flourishing, and with a great increase, so one dying Christ gathered to himself thousands of living Christians. The salvation of souls up to that time, and from that time on to the end of time, is all owing to the dying of this kernel of wheat.

3.2. He promised a great reward to those who would warmly embrace him and who wanted to show that they did so by their faithfulness:

3.2.1. In suffering for him (v. 25): *He that loves his life shall lose it*, but *he who hates his life in this world* will *keep it unto life eternal.* The great purpose of Christ's religion is to detach us from this world by setting before us another world.

3.2.1.1. Notice here the fatal consequences of an excessive love of life; many people hug themselves to death, losing their life by loving it too much. Those who so love their physical life will shorten their days; they will lose both the life they are so fond of and the infinitely better life. Those who are so much in love with the life of the body as to deny Christ will lose it; that is, they will lose a real happiness in the other world even as they think they are securing an imaginary one in this world. Those who give their soul, their God, their heaven, for it buy life too dear.

3.2.1.2. Notice, too, the blessed reward of a holy disregard for life. Those who hate the life of the body so much that they will risk giving it up to preserve the life of their soul will find both in eternal life. This shows us:

3.2.1.2.1. It is required of the disciples of Christ that they hate *their life in this world.* Our life in this world includes all the enjoyments of our present state. We must hate these; that is, we are to consider them as comparatively worthless and incapable of making us happy, and we must cheerfully part with them whenever they come to compete with the service of Christ (Ac 20:24; 21:13; Rev 12:11). Notice here the power of godliness—that it conquers the strongest natural affections; notice, too, the mystery of godliness—that it is the greatest wisdom, but it also makes people hate their own lives.

3.2.1.2.2. Those who for the love of Christ hate their own lives in this world will be abundantly rewarded in the resurrection of the just. *He that hateth his life shall keep it.*

3.2.2. In serving him (v. 26): *If any man* profess *to serve me*, let him *follow me*. Some read the next part, "*and where I am, there* let *my servant be*," indicating the servant's duty, which is to attend his master. Our translation reads it as part of the promise: "*there shall he be*, happy with me." Moreover, in case this should seem a small matter, he added, *If any man serve me, him will my Father honour*. The Greeks wanted to see Jesus (v. 21), but Christ let them know that it was not enough to see him; they must also serve him. In taking on servants, it is usual to settle both the work and the wages; Christ did both here.

3.2.2.1. Here is the work that Christ expects from his servants.

3.2.2.1.*1*. Let them follow their Master's movements: *If any man serve me, let him follow me.* Christians must follow Christ, doing the things that he says and walking as he walked. We must go where he leads us, and in the way he leads us.

3.2.2.1.*2*. Let them follow their Master's rest: "*Where I am, there let my servant be*, to wait on me." Christ is where his church is, and *there let his servants be*, to present themselves before him and receive instructions from him.

3.2.2.2. Here are the wages Christ promises to his servants:

3.2.2.2.*1*. They will be happy with him: *Where I am, there shall also my servant be.* No doubt he meant that his servants will be with him in Paradise. Christ spoke of heaven's happiness as if he were already in it—*where I am*—because he was sure of it and near it. The same joy and glory that he thought enough reward for all his services and sufferings are offered to his servants as the reward of theirs. Those who follow him along the path will be with him at the end.

3.2.2.2.*2*. They will be honored by his Father; he will make up to them all their hard work and loss by giving them honor far beyond what such worthless worms of the earth could expect to receive. The reward is honor—true, lasting honor, the highest honor; it is the honor that comes from God. God will honor those who wait on Christ. Those who serve Christ must humble themselves, and they are commonly insulted by the world, but they will be rewarded for both by being exalted in due time.

4. We are not told what became of those Greeks, but we are willing to hope that those who asked about the way to heaven as they did, with their faces set toward it, found it and walked along it.

Verses 27–36

Here Christ was shown honor by his Father in a voice from heaven, which gave rise to a further discussion with the people. In these verses we have:

1. Christ's prayer to his Father when trouble had seized his spirit: *Now is my soul troubled* (v. 27). This is a strange word to come from Christ's mouth, and it is surprising at this time, since it comes in the middle of various pleasing prospects, in which one would have thought he would say, "Now is my soul pleased." Trouble of soul sometimes follows great joys of spirit. Notice:

1.1. Christ's dread of his approaching suffering: *Now is my soul troubled.* Now came the first throes of the suffering of his soul (Isa 53:11). The sin of our soul was the trouble of Christ's soul. The trouble of his soul was intended to relieve the trouble of our souls. Christ was *now* troubled, but it would not always remain so; it would not last for long. The same is the comfort of Christians in

their troubles; they are only *for a moment* (2Co 4:17) and will be turned into joy.

1.2. The distress he seems to have been in here: *And what shall I say?* Christ spoke like one who was at a loss, as if he did not know what he should choose. There was a struggle between the work he had taken on him, which required suffering, and the nature he had taken on him, which dreaded it; between these two he here paused with, *What shall I say?*

1.3. His prayer to God in this distress: *Father, save me from this hour*; it could be translated "out of this hour"; he prayed not so much that it would not come as that he would be brought through it. This was the language of innocent nature, of its feelings poured out in prayer. Christ willingly experienced his suffering, but he also prayed to be saved from them. Prayer against a trouble may very well be consistent with patience in it and submission to the will of God in it. The time of his suffering was:

1.3.1. A set time.

1.3.2. A short time. An hour is soon over, and so were Christ's sufferings; he could see through them to the *joy set before him* (Heb 12:2).

1.4. His acceptance of his Father's will, nevertheless. *But for this cause came I to this hour.* Innocent nature spoke the first words, but divine wisdom and love spoke the last. Those who want to live by their principles must rely on their second thoughts. Christ checked himself with a second thought: *For this cause came I to this hour*: he did not silence himself by saying that he could not avoid it, but satisfied himself with the resolution that he would not avoid it. It should reconcile us to the darkest hours of our lives to know that we were destined for them all along.

1.5. His consideration of his Father's honor in this. *Father, glorify thy name*, he said, which is to the same effect as *Father, thy will be done* (Mt 26:42), because God's will is for his own glory. This expresses more than a bare submission to the will of God; it is a consecration of his sufferings to the glory of God. It was a word spoken as Mediator, spoken by him as our security, who had undertaken to satisfy divine justice for our sin. Our Lord Jesus intervened, undertaking to satisfy God's injured honor, and he did it by his humiliation. Now here he made an offer of this atonement as equivalent: "*Father, glorify thy name*; let the debt be paid by me." And so he restored what he did not take away.

2. The Father's answer to this prayer. Notice:

2.1. How this answer was given: by a voice from heaven.

2.2. What the answer was. Responding explicitly to that petition, *Father, glorify thy name*, the voice said, *I have glorified it* already, and *I will glorify it yet again.*

2.2.1. The name of God had been glorified in the life of Christ, in his message and miracles, and in all the examples he had given of holiness and goodness.

2.2.2. It would be glorified further in the sufferings and death of Christ. His wisdom and power, his justice and holiness, his truth and goodness, were greatly glorified. God accepted the atonement and declared himself pleased. What God has done to glorify his own name is an encouragement to us to expect that he will glorify it even further.

3. The opinion of the crowd who listened to this voice (v. 29). Some of them said that *it thundered*; others said that certainly *an angel spoke to him*. This shows:

3.1. That it was real.

3.2. That they were reluctant to admit such a clear proof of Christ's divine mission. They would say it was this, that, or anything rather than admit that God spoke to him in answer to his prayer.

4. The account our Savior himself gave of this voice.

4.1. Why it was sent (v. 30): "It came *not because of me, but for your sakes* (benefit), that all you who heard it may *believe that the Father hath sent me.*" What is said from heaven about our Lord Jesus is said for our benefit, so that we may be brought to depend on him. The voice came "so that you my disciples, who are to follow me in sufferings, may be assured in this with the same assurance that sustains me."

4.2. What its meaning was. God intended two things when he said he would *glorify his own name*:

4.2.1. That Satan would be conquered by the death of Christ (v. 31): *Now is the judgment.* He spoke with a divine joy and triumph. "Now the year of my redeemed has come (Isa 63:4): now that great work that has so long been thought of in the divine purposes is to be done." The subject of the triumph was:

4.2.1.1. That *now was the judgment of the world.* Some take it as a medical term: "Now is the crisis of this world." The sick and diseased world has now reached a turning point; this was the critical time when, as with a fever, the trembling scales would turn for life or death for the whole human race. Or, rather, it is a legal term, as our translation renders it: "Now, judgment has been entered." The death of Christ was the *judgment of this world.*

4.2.1.1.1. It was a judgment of revelation and distinction. Now the trial of this world had come, for people will be characterized according to how they have responded to the cross of Christ, and they will be judged by what they think of the death of Christ.

4.2.1.1.2. It is a judgment of favor and absolution. Christ on the cross came between a righteous God and a guilty world. It was, as it were, the judgment of this world, because an eternal righteousness was brought in not only for Jews but also for the whole world (1Jn 2:1–2; Da 9:24).

4.2.1.1.3. It was a judgment of condemnation declared against the powers of darkness; see 16:11. Satan's dominion was declared a usurpation. The judgment of this world was that it belongs to Christ, not to Satan.

4.2.1.2. That *now is the prince of this world cast out.* The Devil was called the *prince of this world* here because he rules over the people of the world by the things of the world. He was said to *be cast* (driven) *out,* to *be now* cast out. Christ's reconciling the world to God (2Co 5:19) by the merits of his death broke the power of death and drove Satan out as a destroyer. When Christ subdued the world to God by the message of his cross, he broke the power of sin and drove out Satan as a deceiver. Notice with what assurance Christ spoke here about the victory over Satan; it was as good as done, and even when he yielded to death, he triumphed over it.

4.2.2. That by the death of Christ souls would be converted, and this would be the driving out of Satan (v. 32): *If I be lifted up from the earth, I will draw all men unto me.* Notice here two things:

4.2.2.1. The great intention of our Lord Jesus, which was to *draw all men to him,* not only the Jews but also the Gentiles. Notice here how Christ himself is everything in the conversion of a soul. It is Christ who draws. He does not drive by force, but draws like a magnet; the soul *is made willing* (Ps 110:3). It is to Christ that we are drawn; those who were shy and distrustful of him are brought to love him and trust him; we are drawn to his terms, into his arms.

4.2.2.2. The strange way in which he chose to fulfill his purpose: by being *lifted up from the earth. This he spoke signifying by what death he should die,* the death of the cross. The One who was crucified was first nailed to the cross, and then lifted up on it. The word here translated *lifted up,* however, means an honorable advancement: *If I am exalted;* he reckoned his sufferings his honor. Now Christ's drawing all people to himself followed his being *lifted up from the earth.*

4.2.2.2.1. It followed after it in time. The great increase of the church came after the death of Christ.

4.2.2.2.2. It followed from it as its blessed effect. Although the cross of Christ is a stumbling stone to some, to others it is a loadstone (magnet). Some consider this an allusion to the lifting up of the bronze snake in the desert, which drew to it all those who were stung by venomous snakes (Nu 21:6). How many flocked to it! In the same way many flocked to Christ when salvation through him was preached to all nations; see 3:14–15. Perhaps it also has some reference to the position in which Christ was crucified, with his arms stretched out, to invite everyone to him and embrace all who would come.

5. The people's objection to what he said (v. 34). Although they had heard the voice from heaven, they still picked quarrels with him. Christ had called himself the *Son of man* (v. 23), which they knew to be one of the titles of the Messiah (Da 7:13). He had also said that the *Son of man must be lifted up,* which they understood to refer to his dying. Now in objection to this:

5.1. They put forward those Scriptures of the Old Testament that speak of the everlasting life of the Messiah, from all of which they concluded that the Messiah would not die. The people's perverseness in raising this in opposition to what Jesus had said will be seen if we consider:

5.1.1. That when they appealed to the Scripture to prove that the Messiah *abideth for ever,* they took no notice of the texts that speak of the Messiah's death and sufferings. Had they never heard from the Law that he would *pour out his soul unto death* (Isa 53:12), especially that his *hands and feet* would be pierced (Ps 22:16)? Why then did they think it so strange that the Son of Man would be lifted up?

5.1.2. That when they opposed what Christ said about the sufferings of the Son of Man, they took no notice of what he had said about his glory and exaltation. The message of Christ contains paradoxes, which are stumbling blocks to people with corrupt hearts.

5.2. They then asked, *Who is the Son of man?* "You are saying, *The Son of man must die;* we have proved that the Messiah must not, so where is your Messiahship?" They would rather have no Christ than have a suffering one.

6. What Christ said in response to this objection. If they had wanted to, they could have answered themselves: a human being dies and yet is immortal, enduring forever; so also the *Son of man.* He gave them a serious warning to make sure they did not waste their opportunities (vv. 35–36): "*Yet a little while is the light with you; therefore walk while you have the light.*"

6.1. In general, we may notice here:

6.1.1. Christ's concern for people's souls and his desire for their welfare. Notice the great tenderness he showed here when he told them to look to themselves when they were plotting against him!

6.1.2. The method he used with these objectors, *with meekness instructing those that opposed themselves* (2Ti 2:25).

6.2. We have here particularly:

6.2.1. The advantage they enjoyed in having Christ and his Gospel among them, and the shortness and uncertainty of their enjoyment of it: *Yet a little while is the light with you.* Christ is this light. His dying on the cross was as consistent with his remaining forever as the setting of the sun every night is with its rising again every morning. The Jews at this time had the light with them; they had Christ's physical presence. It was to be with them only a short time; Christ would leave them soon. It is good for us all to consider what a short time we have the light with us. Time is short, and opportunity may not be very long.

6.2.2. The warning given them to make the best of this privilege while they enjoyed it: "*Walk while you have the light,* like travelers who go as far as they can before nightfall." It is our business to walk, to press on toward heaven. The best time for walking is while we have light. The day is the proper time for work, just as the night is for rest. We must be greatly concerned to make the most of our opportunities, so that our day will not be finished before we have finished our day's work and our day's journey: "*Lest darkness come upon* you."

6.2.3. The sad condition of those who have sinned away the Gospel. *They walk in darkness,* knowing neither where they are going nor which way to go. If we set aside the instructions of the Christian message, we know little of the difference between good and evil. Those who have sinned away the Gospel are headed for destruction and unaware of the danger they are in, because they are either sleeping or dancing at the edge of the pit.

6.2.4. The great duty and privilege of each one of us inferred from all this (v. 36): *While you have light, believe in the light.* This was a warning to the people not to wait to buy until the market was closed, but to accept the offer when it was made to them. Christ says the same to all who enjoy the Gospel. It is the duty of each one of us to believe in the Gospel light and submit to the truths it reveals because it is a light to our eyes (Ps 19:8), and to follow its guidance because it is a light to our feet (Ps 119:105). We should do this while we have the light. Those who have God as their Father are children of light (Lk 16:8; Eph 5:8), because God is light (1Jn 1:5).

7. Christ's withdrawing from them: *These things spoke Jesus and departed, and did hide himself from them.* He did this:

7.1. To convict them and wake them up. If they would pay no attention to what he had said, he had nothing more to say to them. Christ justly takes away the means of grace from those who quarrel with him.

7.2. To preserve his own life. He hid himself from their rage and fury. What he said irritated and angered them, and they were made worse by what should have made them better.

Verses 37–41

We have here the honor shown to our Lord Jesus by the Old Testament prophets, who foretold and lamented the faithlessness of the many who did not believe in him. Two things are said about this hardened people, and both were foretold by the evangelical prophet Isaiah: that they did not believe, and that they could not believe.

1. They did not believe, *though he had done so many miracles before them* (v. 37). Notice:

1.1. The many means of conviction. He *did miracles, so many miracles;* both so many and so great. He insisted on two things about them here:

1.1.1. Their number; they were many, and every new miracle confirmed the reality of all that had gone before. Being all miracles of mercy, the more there were, the more good was done.

1.1.2. Their notoriety. He performed these miracles *before them,* not in a corner (Ac 26:26), but in front of many witnesses.

1.2. The ineffectiveness of these means: *Yet they believed not on him.* These people saw, but they did not believe.

1.3. The fulfilling of the Scripture in this (v. 38): *That the saying of Esaias* (Isaiah) *might be fulfilled.* The more improbable any event is, the more does a divine foresight appear in its prediction. One could not have imagined that the kingdom of the Messiah, supported by such powerful proofs, would have met with so much opposition among the Jews, and so their unbelief is called a *marvellous work, and a wonder* (Isa 29:14). Christ himself *marvelled at it,* but it was what Isaiah foretold (Isa 53:1). Notice:

1.3.1. The Gospel was here called *their report:* "*Who has believed* our message, which we have heard from God, and which you have heard from us?"

1.3.2. It was foretold that many would hear it but only a few would heed it and embrace it: *Who hath believed it?* Here and there one, but not many to speak of.

1.3.3. It was spoken of as something greatly to be lamented that so few believed the message of the Gospel.

1.3.4. The reason why people did not believe the message of the Gospel was that *the arm of the Lord* was not *revealed* to them (Isa 53:1). They saw Christ's miracles but did not see the arm of the Lord revealed in them.

2. They could not believe *because Esaias said, He hath blinded their eyes.* This is a hard saying, and who can explain it (6:60)? God condemns no one by mere sovereignty, and yet it is said, *They could not believe.*

2.1. They could not believe, that is, they would not; they were stubborn in their determination not to believe. This is a moral impotence, like that of one who is *accustomed to do evil* (Jer 13:23).

2.2. They could not because Isaiah had said, *He hath blinded their eyes.* It is certain that God is not the author of sin, but:

2.2.1. There is a righteous hand of God that is sometimes to be acknowledged in the blindness of those who persist in their impenitence and unbelief, by which they are justly punished for their former resistance of divine light. If God withholds abused grace and gives people over to their indulged lusts, then he blinds their eyes and hardens their hearts, and these are spiritual judgments. Notice the method of conversion implied here (v. 40). Sinners are led to *see with their eyes,* to discern the reality of divine things. Then they are led *to understand with their heart,* not only to assent and approve but also to agree and accept. Third, they are *converted,* effectively turned from sin to Christ. Finally, God will *heal them;* he will pardon their sins and put to death their corruptions, which are like hidden diseases.

2.2.2. Judicial blindness and hardness are threatened in the word of God against those who willfully persist in evil. All God's works are known to him (Ac 15:18), and all ours are too. Christ knew in advance who would betray him.

2.2.3. What God has foretold will certainly come to pass, and so it could be said that they could not believe. Such is the knowledge of God that he cannot be deceived in what he foresees, and such is his truth that he cannot deceive in what he foretells. However, it should be noticed that the prophecy did not name particular individuals. It pointed to the Jewish nation in general. Yet a remnant would be preserved, which would be enough to keep a door of hope open to particular individuals, for each one could say, "Why may not I belong to that remnant?"

2.3. Having quoted the prophecy, the Evangelist shows (v. 41) that its main reference was to the days of the Messiah: *These things said Esaias when he saw his glory, and spoke of him.*

2.3.1. We read in the prophecy that this was said to Isaiah (Isa 6:8–9), but here we are told that it was said by him. Nothing was said by him as a prophet that was not first said to him; nor was anything said to him that was not later said by him to those to whom he was sent.

2.3.2. The vision that the prophet had there of the glory of God is here said to be his seeing the glory of Jesus Christ: he *saw his glory*.

2.3.3. It is said that the prophet there *spoke of him*. The questions asked by Isaiah (v. 38) are said to be spoken by Christ, because all the prophets both testified about him and were types of him. It could be objected that if his message came from heaven, why did the Jews not believe it? It was not for lack of evidence, but because their *ears were heavy* (Isa 6:10). It was said of Christ that he would be glorified in the ruin of an unbelieving crowd as well as in the salvation of a distinguished remnant.

Verses 42–43

Some honor was given to Christ by these rulers, for they *believed on him* (v. 42), but they did not give him enough honor, because they did not have the courage to confess their faith in him. Many people professed more goodwill toward Christ than they really had; these had more goodwill toward him than they were willing to profess.

1. Notice the power of the word in the convictions felt by many of them. They believed on him as Nicodemus did, accepting him as a teacher who had come from God (3:2). Many people cannot help accepting in their hearts what they are outwardly shy about acknowledging. Perhaps there are more good people than we think. Some are really better than they seem to be. Their faults are known, but their repentance is not; a person's goodness may be concealed by a blameworthy yet pardonable weakness, which they themselves truly repent of. Nor do all who are good have the same ability to appear so.

2. Notice the power of the world in smothering these convictions. They believed in Christ, but because of the Pharisees they dared not confess him. Notice here:

2.1. In what they failed and were defective. They did not *confess* Christ. There is cause to question the sincerity of a faith that is either afraid or ashamed to show itself.

2.2. What they feared: being *put out of the synagogue*, which they thought would disgrace and harm them.

2.3. What lay at the root of this fear: *They loved the praise of men* (v. 43), chose it as a more valuable good *than the praise of God*. They set these two in the scales against each other.

2.3.1. They set human glory in one scale, considering how good it was to give praise to people and receive praise from people. They would not confess Christ for fear that they would both detract from the reputation of the Pharisees and lose their own. Besides, the followers of Christ were given a bad name and were looked down on with contempt, and those who had been used to honor could not bear the thought of being treated this way. Each one thought that if he were to declare himself in favor of Christ he would stand alone, whereas if anyone had had the determination to break the ice, he would have had more supporters than he thought.

2.3.2. They put God's glory in the other scale. They were aware that by confessing Christ they would both give praise to God and have praise from God, but:

2.3.3. They gave the preference to human glory, and this tipped the scales. Many fall short of the glory of God (Ro 3:23) by having too high a regard for human praise. Love of the praise of human beings as an ulterior motive for doing good will make a person a hypocrite when religion is in fashion, and love of the praise of human beings as a

corrupt motive for doing evil will make people turn away from their religious faith when religion is disgraced.

Verses 44–50

We have here the honor Christ asserted for himself—he did not assume it—as the honor that belonged to him, in the account he gave of his mission. As this Evangelist records it, it was his last public message; all that follows was in private with his disciples. He *cried and said*.

1. The raising of his voice and his crying out show:

1.1. His boldness in speaking. Although they did not have the courage to openly confess faith in his message, he had the courage to openly declare it. If they were ashamed of it, he was not.

1.2. His fervency in speaking. He cried out as One who was passionate, who spoke from the heart.

1.3. His desire that all would take notice of it. Because this was the last time he himself would declare his Gospel in person, he proclaimed, "Whoever will hear me, let them come now." Now what is this closing summary of all Christ's messages? It is much like Moses' conclusion: *See, I have set before you life and death* (Dt 30:15).

2. Christ took leave of the temple here with a solemn declaration of three things:

2.1. The privileges and honors of those who believe.

2.1.1. By believing in Christ we are brought into honorable friendship with God (vv. 44–45): *He that believes on me, believes on him that sent me. He that believes* in Christ:

2.1.1.1. Does not believe in him as a mere human being, but as One who is the Son of God.

2.1.1.2. Has a faith that does not end in Christ, but is carried through him to the Father. This is illustrated in v. 45: *he who sees me sees him that sent me*; in coming to know Christ, we come to know God; God reveals himself in the face of Christ (2Co 4:6). All who have a believing sight of Christ are led by him to know God. God deals with fallen human beings by proxy.

2.1.2. We are then brought into a comfortable enjoyment of ourselves (v. 46): *I am come a light into the world, that whoever believes in me should not abide in darkness*. Notice:

2.1.2.1. The description of Christ: *I am come a light into the world*, to be a light to it.

2.1.2.2. The assurance of Christians: they *do not abide in darkness*. They do not continue in the darkness in which they were by nature; they are *light in the Lord* (Eph 5:8). *Light is sown* for them (Ps 97:11). More importantly, they are saved from the darkness that lasts forever.

2.2. The danger of those who do not believe (vv. 47–48): "*If any man hear my words, and believe not, I judge him not*. Yet let unfaithfulness not think that it will therefore go unpunished, because *though I judge him not, there is one that judgeth him*." Notice:

2.2.1. Whose unbelief is condemned: that of those who hear Christ's words but do not believe them. Those people who never had nor could have the Gospel will not be condemned for their unfaithfulness; everyone will be judged according to the dispensation of light they were under.

2.2.2. What it is in their unbelief that constitutes evil: not receiving Christ's word, which is interpreted as rejecting Christ (v. 48). Where the banner of the Gospel is displayed, there can be no neutrality.

2.2.3. The wonderful patience of our Lord Jesus: *I judge him not*. He had work of another kind to do first, which was to save the world, that is:

2.2.3.1. To effectively save those who were given him (6:39).

2.2.3.2. To offer salvation to the whole world, thereby saving them to such an extent that it would be their own fault if they were not saved.

2.2.4. The certain and unavoidable judgment of unbelievers on the great day, the day of the revelation of the righteous judgment of God.

2.2.4.1. There is *one that judgeth them*. Nothing is more fearful than abused patience and trampled-on grace.

2.2.4.2. Their final judgment is reserved for the *last day*.

2.2.4.3. The word of Christ will judge them then: *The words that I have spoken, the same shall judge* the unbeliever *in the last day*. Christ's words will judge unbelievers. As the evidence of their crime, his words will convict them. As the rule of their doom, those words will condemn them.

2.3. The authority Christ had to demand our faith (vv. 49–50). In this declaration, notice:

2.3.1. The commission our Lord Jesus received from the Father (v. 49): *I have not spoken of myself; rather, the Father gave me a commandment what I should say*. This is the same as what he said in 7:16: *My doctrine is not mine*, for *I have not spoken of myself*. It was the teaching of the One who sent him. God the Father gave him his commission. His instructions are called *a commandment*. Our Lord Jesus learned obedience himself before he taught it to us, even though he was a Son (Heb 5:8). *The Lord God commanded* the First Adam (Ge 2:16), and he by his disobedience ruined us; he commanded the Second Adam, and he by his obedience saved us.

2.3.2. The scope of this commission: *I know that his commandment is life everlasting* (v. 50). The commission given to Christ referred to the eternal state of human beings and was given him so that he might bring about their eternal life and happiness. This was how the command given to him was eternal life. Christ said he knew this: "*And I know that* it is so." Those who disobey Christ despise eternal life; they renounce it.

2.3.3. Christ's exact adherence to the commission and instructions given him: *Whatsoever I speak*, it is as the *Father said unto me*. As the faithful witness saves souls (Pr 14:25), so did he, and he spoke the truth, the whole truth, and nothing but the truth. Now:

2.3.3.1. This is a great encouragement to faith; the sayings of Christ, rightly understood, are what we may dare to risk our souls on.

2.3.3.2. It is a great example of obedience. Christ said what he was told to say; he esteemed himself for this honor: that what the Father had said to him, he spoke. By a sincere belief in every word of Christ and a complete submission of ourselves to it, we must give him the glory due to his name (1Ch 16:29).

CHAPTER 13

Now that our Savior had finished his public sermons, he turned to a private conversation with his friends. From this time on, we have an account of what took place between him and his disciples. 1. He washed his disciples' feet (vv. 1–17). 2. He foretold who would betray him (vv. 18–30). 3. He instructed them in the great teaching of his own death and the great duty of mutual love (vv. 31–35). 4. He foretold Peter's denying him (vv. 36–38).

Verses 1–17

It has generally been assumed by commentators that Christ's washing his disciples' feet and his teaching of

them afterward took place on the same night on which he was betrayed and at the same sitting at which he ate the Passover and instituted the Lord's Supper. Because this Evangelist makes it his business to gather those passages that the others omitted, he meticulously omits those that the others recorded, which leads to some difficulty in putting them together. The foot-washing is here said to have been done *before the feast of the passover* (v. 1). But why would Christ do this? A wise man will not do something that looks odd and unusual except with very good cause and after much consideration. The transaction was solemn, and four reasons are suggested here why Christ did this: he did it to show his love for his disciples (vv. 1–2); to express his own willing humility (vv. 3–5); to show them a sign for spiritual washing, which is referred to in his discussion with Peter (vv. 6–11); and to set them an example (vv. 12–17).

1. Christ washed his disciples' feet in order to prove the great love with which he loved them (17:26) (vv. 1–2).

1.1. Our Lord Jesus, *having loved his own that were in the world, loved them to the end* (v. 1).

1.1.1. This is true of the disciples who were his immediate followers, especially the Twelve. These were *his own* in the world, his closest friends. He loved these; he called them into fellowship with him. He was always tender toward them. He allowed them to be very free with him and was patient with their weaknesses. He loved them *to the end*; he never took away his loving-kindness. Although some noble people embraced his cause, he did not set aside his old friends, but stuck to his poor fishermen. Although he rebuked them often, he never stopped loving them and taking care of them.

1.1.2. It is true of all believers.

1.1.2.1. Our Lord Jesus has a people in the world who are his own: his own, because they were given to him by the Father, he has purchased them and paid dearly for them, and he has set them apart for himself; his own, because they have devoted themselves to him as his distinctive people. Where *his own* who *received him not* were spoken of, the expression means "his own things," as a person's goods are their own and may be disposed of by them if they wish. But here the expression means "his own persons," as a man's wife and children are his own.

1.1.2.2. Christ has a warm love for his own people who are in the world. He was now going to his own people in heaven, but he seemed most concerned for his own people on earth, because they most needed his care: the ill child is looked after most.

1.1.2.3. Those whom Christ loves, *he loves to the end*. Nothing can separate a believer *from the love of Christ* (Ro 8:38–39). The expression translated *to the end* may also be read *to perfection*.

1.2. Christ revealed his love for them by washing their feet. This was how he wanted to show that his love for them was both devoted and condescending; he wanted to honor them in a way that was as great and surprising as it would be for a master to serve his servants. The disciples had just revealed the weakness of their love for him by begrudging the ointment that was poured on his head (Mt 26:8), but he immediately gave this proof of his love to them. Our weaknesses serve as foils to Christ's kindness.

1.3. He chose this time to do it for two reasons:

1.3.1. Because now *he knew that his hour was come when he should depart out of this world to the Father*. Notice:

1.3.1.1. The change that was to come on our Lord Jesus; he must *depart*. Just as with Christ himself, so also with all believers, when they depart from the world, they *go to the Father*. It is a departure out of the world, and it is a going *to the Father* and the fruition of him as ours.

1.3.1.2. The time of this change: *His hour was come*. It is sometimes called his enemies' hour (Lk 22:53), the hour of their triumph; sometimes his hour, the hour of his triumph.

1.3.1.3. His foresight of it: he *knew that his hour was come*; he knew from the beginning that it would come, but now he knew that it had come.

1.3.2. Because the *devil had now put it into the heart of Judas to betray him* (v. 2). These words in parenthesis may be considered:

1.3.2.1. As tracing Judas's treason to its origin. We cannot tell what access the Devil has to human hearts. However, there are some sins that are so exceptionally sinful that it is clear that Satan has hatched them in a heart that is ready to receive them.

1.3.2.2. As suggesting a reason why Christ now washed his disciples' feet.

1.3.2.2.*1*. Because Judas was now determined to betray him, the time of his departure could not be far away. The more malicious we perceive our enemies to be toward us, the more diligent should we be to prepare for the worst that may come.

1.3.2.2.*2*. Because Judas had now fallen into the trap, and the Devil was aiming at Peter and the rest of them (Lk 22:31), Christ would strengthen his own people against the Devil. If the wolf has seized one sheep from the flock, it is time for the shepherd to look carefully after the rest. Antidotes must be in preparation when the infection has begun.

1.3.2.2.*3*. Judas, who was now plotting to betray him, was *one of the twelve*. Now Christ would show that he did not intend to drive away all of them for the faults of one of them. Although one had a devil (6:70) and was a traitor, they would not all come off the worse for that. Christ was still kind toward his disciples even though a Judas was among them and he knew it.

2. Christ washed his disciples' feet in order to tell the whole world how low he could stoop in love to his own people. This is shown in vv. 3–5. *Jesus, knowing that the Father had given all things into his hand, rose from supper* and, to the great surprise of the company, *washed his disciples' feet*.

2.1. Here is the rightful advancement of the Lord Jesus.

2.1.1. *The Father had given all things into his hands*, given him power over them all. See Mt 11:27. He *is heir of all things* (Heb 1:2).

2.1.2. He *came from God*. This implies that he was in the beginning with God (1:2). He came from God as the Son of God and the One sent by God.

2.1.3. He *went to God*. What comes from God will go to God; those who are born from heaven are bound for heaven.

2.1.4. He *knew* all this; the situation was not like that of a prince in the cradle, who knows nothing of the honor he is born to. He knew full well all the honors of his exalted state, but he stooped so low. But why is this included here? His knowing these things:

2.1.4.1. Was an incentive to him now to leave quickly whatever lessons and legacies he had for his disciples, because his hour had come.

2.1.4.2. Was what supported him in his suffering. Judas was now betraying him, and he knew it, but knowing also *that he came from God and went to God*, he did not draw back.

2.1.4.3. Was a foil to his condescension. And so what should rather have been a reason for Christ to demand honor is given as a reason for Christ to stoop; but God's thoughts are not as ours (Isa 55:8).

2.2. Here is the willing abasement of our Lord Jesus. A well-founded assurance of heaven and happiness, instead of puffing a person up with pride, will make and keep them very humble. Now what Christ humbled himself to was to *wash his disciples' feet*.

2.2.1. The action itself was lowly and servile, a task performed by servants of the lowest rank. If he had washed their hands or faces, it would have been an act of great condescension, but for Christ to stoop to such an act of drudgery may well stir our wonder.

2.2.2. The condescension was so much the greater because he did this for his own disciples, who in themselves were of a low and despicable condition, not fussy about their bodies; their feet were probably seldom washed and were therefore very dirty. Moreover, they were his servants, and as such should have washed his feet. Many people of great strength of mind will sometimes perform a humble service to seek the favor of their superiors; they rise by stooping and climb by cringing. But for Christ to do this to his disciples could not possibly be a political act, but had to be pure humility.

2.2.3. He *rose from supper* to do it. Though our translation reads it (v. 2), *supper being ended*, it might better be read, "now that the supper was being served," because he sat down again (v. 12), and we find him *dipping a sop* (piece of bread) (v. 26), so that he washed their feet in the middle of his meal, teaching us:

2.2.3.1. Not to consider it a disturbance to be called from our meal to do God, our brother, or our sister any real service. Christ would not leave his preaching to please his closest relatives (Mk 3:33), but he left his supper to show his love for his disciples.

2.2.3.2. Not to be too fussy about our food. It would have turned many a squeamish stomach to wash dirty feet at supper time, but Christ did it, not so that we could learn to be rude and slovenly—cleanliness and godliness go well together—but to teach us not to indulge, but put to death, the refined preferences of appetite, giving good manners their due place, and no more.

2.2.4. He took on himself the clothes of a servant to do it: he *laid aside* his *garments*. We must address ourselves to duty as those who are serious about getting down to business.

2.2.5. He did it with all the humble ceremony possible. He *girded himself with the towel*; he *poured water into the basin* and then *washed their feet* and *wiped them*.

2.2.6. It appears that he washed the feet of Judas, for nothing is said to the contrary, and Judas was present (v. 26). Jesus washed the feet of a sinner here, the worst of sinners, who was at this time working out how to betray him.

3. Christ washed his disciples' feet in order to represent the cleansing of the soul from the defilement of sin. This is clearly shown in his conversation with Peter about it (vv. 6–11). Notice:

3.1. The surprise Peter felt (v. 6): *Then came he to Simon Peter* and told him to put out his feet to be washed. Probably when he went about this service—which is all that is meant by *began to wash* (v. 5)—he took Peter first, for the rest would not have allowed it if they had not first heard it explained in what was said between Christ and Peter. Peter was startled at the suggestion: "*Lord*—he said—*dost thou wash my feet?* What, you, our Lord and Master, whom we know and believe to be the Son of God, do this for me, a worthless worm of the earth, *a sinful man, O Lord* (Lk 5:8)? Will my feet be washed by those hands that have touched lepers to heal them, have given sight to the blind, and have raised the dead?" Peter would very willingly have taken the basin and towel and washed his Master's feet, and been proud of the honor (Lk 17:7–8). "But for my Master to wash my feet is a paradox I cannot understand."

3.2. The immediate assurance Christ gave. This was at least sufficient to silence Peter's objections (v. 7): *What I do, thou knowest not now, but thou shalt know hereafter.* Here are two reasons why Peter must submit:

3.2.1. Because he was at present in the dark about it and must not oppose what he did not understand. Christ wanted to teach Peter implicit obedience. "*What I do thou knowest not now*, and you are therefore not competent to judge it."

3.2.2. Because there was something significant in it that he would later understand: *Thou shalt know hereafter.* Our Lord Jesus does many things whose meaning even his own disciples do not know for the present, but they will know later. Subsequent providences explain preceding ones, and we see later the good influence of events that seemed most adverse to us when they took place; we see later that the way that we thought was in the wrong direction was the right way. We must let Christ take his own way, and we will find in the end that it was the best way.

3.3. Peter's positive refusal to let Christ wash his feet (v. 8): *Thou shalt by no means wash my feet*; "no, never." This is the language of a fixed resolution.

3.3.1. Here was an expression of humility and modesty. Peter here seemed to have, and no doubt he really had, a great respect for his Master.

3.3.2. Under this show of humility there was a real opposition toward the will of the Lord Jesus. It is not humility but unfaithfulness to turn away the offers of the Gospel as if they were too rich to be taken as ours, or as if they were news that is just too good to be true.

3.4. Christ's insistence in pursuing his offer: *If I wash thee not, thou hast no part with me.* This may be taken:

3.4.1. As a severe warning against disobedience: "*If I wash thee not*, if you continue to be stubborn, you will not be acknowledged as one of my disciples." If Peter wanted to dispute the commands he should obey, he was in effect renouncing his allegiance.

3.4.2. As a declaration of the necessity of spiritual washing: "*If I wash not* your soul from the defilement of sin, *thou hast no part with me.*" All those, and only those, who are spiritually washed by Christ share in Christ. It is the *good part* that is the *one thing needful* (Lk 10:42). It is necessary that Christ wash us if we are to have a part in Christ.

3.5. Peter's hypersubmission, his fervent request to be washed by Christ (v. 9). *Lord, wash not my feet only, but also my hands and my head.* Notice how quickly Peter changed his mind! Let us, therefore, not be dogmatic in our decisions, because we may soon need to withdraw them; rather, let us look carefully at any objectives we plan to hold firmly on to. Notice:

3.5.1. How ready Peter was to withdraw what he had said: "Lord, how foolish I was to speak so quickly!" Now that the washing of him was revealed as an act of Christ's grace, he accepted it; he only disliked it when it seemed merely an act of humiliation. When good people see their error, they will not be reluctant to admit it.

3.5.2. How bold Peter was in asking for the purifying grace of the Lord Jesus and its universal influence, even on his hands and head. Exclusion from sharing in Christ is the most terrible form of evil in the eyes of all who are

enlightened. For fear of this we should seek God passionately in prayer, asking that he will wash us: "*Lord, wash not my feet only* from the dreadful defilements that cling to them, *but also my hands and my head* from the spots they have contracted; wash even the unnoticed dirt that comes by perspiration from the body itself."

3.6. Christ's further explanation of this sign:

3.6.1. With reference to his disciples who were faithful to him (v. 10): *He that is washed* all over in the bath *needeth not save to wash his feet*, his hands and head having been washed, and he having gotten only his feet dirty in walking home. Peter had gone from one extreme to the other. At first he would not allow Christ to wash his feet; now he overlooked what Christ had done for him in his baptism and what was meant by that.

3.6.1.1. Notice here what is the privilege and comfort of those who are justified; they are washed by Christ and are *clean every whit* (completely clean). The heart may be swept and put in order and yet remain the Devil's palace (Mt 12:44), but, if it is washed, it belongs to Christ, and he will not lose it.

3.6.1.2. Notice what the daily objective of those who are justified through grace should be, and that is to wash their feet, to cleanse themselves from the guilt they contract daily through weakness and inadvertence by the renewed exercise of repentance. We must also wash our feet by constant watchfulness against everything defiling. The provision made for our cleansing should not make us presumptuous, but more cautious. From yesterday's pardon we should draw an argument to protect us from today's temptation.

3.6.2. With reflection on Judas: *And you are clean, but not all* (vv. 10–11). He washed them himself, and then he said, *You are clean*, but excluded Judas: *not all.* Many have the sign but do not have what is signified by it. Christ considered it necessary to tell his disciples that they were not all clean so that we would all watch ourselves closely—"*Is it I? Lord, is it I* who am among the clean but am not clean?"

4. Christ washed his disciples' feet to set before us an example. This is the explanation he gave of what he had done (vv. 12–17). Notice:

4.1. With what seriousness he explained the meaning of what he had done (v. 12): *After he had washed their feet*, he said, *Know you what I have done?*

4.1.1. He delayed the explanation until he had finished with the washing:

4.1.1.1. To test their submission and implicit obedience so that they would learn to accept his will even when they could not give a reason for it.

4.1.1.2. Because it was right to finish the riddle before he explained it.

4.1.2. Before he explained it, he asked them if they could interpret it: *Know you what I have done to you?* He asked them this question not only to make them aware of their ignorance but also to raise their desires and expectations of instruction.

4.2. On what he based what he said (v. 13): "*You call me Master* (Teacher) *and Lord*, and *you say well, for so I am.*" He who is our Redeemer and Savior is, to that end, our Lord and Teacher. He is our Teacher, our instructor in all necessary truths and rules. He is our Lord, our ruler and owner. It is right for the disciples of Christ to call him Teacher and Lord, not as a compliment, but to acknowledge reality, and not by constraint, but with delight. Our calling Christ Teacher and Lord obliges us to receive and carry out his instructions. We are bound in honor and honesty to do what he tells us to.

4.3. The lesson he taught by this: *You also ought to wash one another's feet* (v. 14).

4.3.1. Some, understanding this literally, have thought that Christians should solemnly and religiously *wash one another's feet* as a sign of their humble love for one another. St. Ambrose took it so, and practiced it in the church at Milan. Augustine said that those Christians who did not do it with their hands did—he hoped—practice it with their hearts in humility, but he said that it is much better to do it with the hands also. What Christ has done, Christians should not disdain to do.

4.3.2. However, it is no doubt to be understood figuratively. Our Teacher wanted to teach us three things by it:

4.3.2.1. Humility. We must learn from our Teacher to be *lowly in heart* (Mt 11:29). Christ had often taught his disciples humility, and they had forgotten the lesson, but now he taught them in such a way as they could surely never forget.

4.3.2.2. A humility that is useful. To wash one another's feet is to stoop down to the lowliest task of love for the real good and benefit of one another. We must not begrudge taking care and pains and spending time for the good of those to whom we are not under any particular obligations, even those who are our inferiors. The duty is mutual; we must both accept help from our brothers and sisters and give them help.

4.3.2.3. A usefulness to the sanctification of one another: *You ought to wash one another's feet* from the defilements of sin. We cannot make atonement for one another's sins—but we may help to purify one another from sin. We must wash ourselves in the first place; this charity must begin at home (Mt 7:5). But it must not end there; we must be sorry for the failings and foolishness of our brothers and sisters, must wash the defiled feet of our brothers and sisters with our tears.

4.4. The reinforcing of this command by the example of what Christ had now done: "*If I your Lord and Master have* done it to you, you should do it *to one another*.

4.4.1. "I am your Master, and you are my disciples, and so you should learn from me (v. 15), because in this *I have given you an example*, indicating that *you should do* to others *as I have done* to you." Notice:

4.4.1.1. What a good teacher Christ is. He teaches by example as well as doctrine, and this is why he came into the world, in order to set us a pattern, and it is a pattern without one false stroke.

4.4.1.2. What good students we must be. We must do as he has done because the reason he set us an example was so that we would follow it. Christ's example is to be followed especially by ministers, in whom the graces of humility and holy love should especially appear. When Christ sent his apostles out, it was with the responsibility of *becoming all things to all men* (1Co 9:22). "What I have done to your dirty feet, you are to do to the defiled souls of sinners: wash them." All Christians likewise are here taught to condescend to one another in love, and to do it unasked and unpaid; we must not be mercenary in the services of love.

4.4.2. "I am your Master, and you are my disciples (v. 16), and *the servant is not greater than his Lord, neither he that is sent greater than he that sent him*." Christ had urged this (Mt 10:24–25) as a reason why they should not think it strange if they suffered as he did; he here urged it as a reason why they should not think it a great burden to humble themselves as he did. What he did not think beneath him, they must not think beneath him. Christ reminded them of their position as his servants; they were not better than their Teacher. We need to be

reminded that we are not greater than our Lord. By humbling himself, Christ has honored humility. We sometimes say to those who disdain to do a certain act that, "Others who are as good as you have done it"; and as to washing one another's feet, this is true indeed if our Master has done it. When we see our Master serving, we must see how wrong it is for us to become proud.

5. Our Savior closed this part of his teaching with a reminder to obey: *If you know these things, happy are you if you do them*. Most people think, "Happy are those who rise and rule." Washing one another's feet will never get you more possessions or greater advancement, but Christ says, despite this, "Happy are those who are humble and obey." Since they had such excellent commands given them to complete their happiness, commands commended by such an excellent model, they must carry them out.

5.1. This may be applied to the commands of Christ in general. Although it is a great advantage to know our duty, we will come short of happiness if we do not do our duty. Knowing is for doing (Jas 4:17). It is knowing and doing that will demonstrate that we belong to Christ's kingdom and are wise builders (Mt 7:24–25).

5.2. It is to be applied especially to this command of humility. Nothing is better known than that we should be humble. Few will acknowledge themselves to be proud, because it is as inexcusable a sin, and as hateful, as any other, but how little do we see of true humility. Most people know these things so well as to expect others to act in this way to them, but they do not know them so well as to actually do them themselves.

Verses 18–30

We have here the revelation of Judas's plot to betray his Teacher. Christ knew it from the beginning, but now he revealed it to his disciples for the first time.

1. Christ gave them a general indication of it (v. 18): "*I speak not of you all*, for *I know whom I have chosen*, but the Scripture will be fulfilled: *He that eateth bread with me hath lifted up his heel against me* (Ps 41:9)." He indicated to them that:

1.1. They were not all right. He had said earlier (v. 10), *You are clean, but not all*. So here: *I speak not of you all*. What is said about the excellencies of Christ's disciples cannot be said about all who are called that. There is a mixture of bad and good in the best communities, a Judas among the apostles.

1.2. He himself knew who was right and who was not: *I know whom I have chosen*. Christ himself chose the ones who are chosen. Those who are chosen are known to Christ, because he never forgets any whom he has once had in his thoughts of love (2Ti 2:19).

1.3. The Scripture was fulfilled in his betrayal by the disciple who proved false to him. Christ took into his family one who he foresaw would be a traitor, so *that the scripture might be fulfilled*. Most expositors understand *He that eateth bread with me* to refer to Ahithophel (2Sa 15:12, 31). Our Savior applied this to Judas.

1.3.1. Judas, as an apostle, was admitted to the highest privilege: he shared Christ's bread. He was favored by him; he was one of those whom he knew intimately. Christ said, *he that eateth bread with me*; his disciples—including Judas—had their share of the bread, such as he had. Wherever he went, Judas was welcome with him; he sat at table with his Master and in all respects did as he had. He ate miraculous bread with him when the loaves were multiplied, and he ate the Passover with him. Not all who eat bread with Christ are his true disciples.

1.3.2. As an apostate, Judas was guilty of the most corrupt treachery: he *lifted up the heel* against Christ. He abandoned him (v. 30). He despised him. He became his enemy. It is nothing new for those who were Christ's apparent friends to turn out to be his real enemies.

2. He gave them a reason why he was telling them beforehand about the treachery of Judas (v. 19): "*Now I tell you before it come, that when it is come to pass you may* be confirmed in your *belief that I am he,* he who was to come (Ps 118:26)." By his clear and certain foresight of future things, of which he gave undeniable proof, he proved himself to be the true God. By applying the types and prophecies of the Old Testament to himself, he proved himself to be the true Messiah.

3. He gave a word of encouragement to his apostles, a word that continues to be addressed to all his ministers whom he employs in his service (v. 20): *He that receiveth whomsoever I send receiveth me.* Christ had told his disciples that they must humble themselves. "Now," he said, "although there may be those who will despise you for your humility, there will also be those who will honor you, and they will be honored for so doing." Those who know themselves to be honored by Christ's commission may be content to be despised in the world's opinion. Just as Christ would never think the worse of them for Judas's crime, so he would acknowledge them and would raise up people who would receive them. Those who had received Judas when he was a preacher were never the worse off, because he was one whom Christ sent, even though he later proved to be a traitor. We must receive those who appear to be sent by Christ until the opposite is apparent. Although some people, by entertaining strangers, have entertained robbers unawares, by that means some have entertained angels (Heb 13:2). The abuse hurled at our love will neither justify our lack of love nor lose us the reward of our love. We are encouraged here to receive ministers as sent by Christ: "*He that receiveth whomsoever I send* even if the one I send is weak and poor, because, though weak and poor, he communicates my message, will be acknowledged as my friend." To accept such a messenger is to receive Christ Jesus the Lord himself. We are encouraged here to accept Christ as sent by God: "*He that receiveth me* in this way accepts the Father also. *He that receiveth me* as his ruler and Savior accepts *him that sent me* as his portion and happiness."

4. Christ more particularly told them about the plot (v. 21): *When Jesus had thus said,* he was *troubled in spirit,* and *he testified*—he solemnly declared it—*One of you shall betray me.* This prediction did not force Judas to commit the sin by any fatal necessity, because although the event followed according to the prediction, it was not caused by the prediction. Christ is not the author of sin. As to this detestable sin that Judas committed:

4.1. Christ foresaw it. He knows what is in people better than they do themselves (2:25), and so he sees what will be done by them.

4.2. He foretold it, not only for the sake of the rest of the disciples but also for the sake of Judas himself, so that he could take the warning. Traitors do not proceed with their plots when they are found out; surely when Judas found that his Master knew his intentions, he would draw back in time.

4.3. He spoke about it with evident concern; he was *troubled in spirit* when he mentioned it. The falls of the disciples of Christ cause great trouble in the spirit of their Teacher; the sins of Christians are the grief of Christ. "What! One of you betray me?" This cut him to his heart,

just as the undutifulness of children grieves those who have *nourished and brought them up* (Isa 1:2).

5. The disciples quickly took notice of the distress, and so they *looked one upon another* with evident concern, *doubting of whom he spake* (v. 22). It struck such horror in them that they did not know which way to look or what to say. They saw that their Teacher was troubled, and so they were troubled. What grieves Christ is and should be a grief to all who are his people. On account of this they tried to reveal the traitor. And so Christ perplexed his disciples for a time, so that he could *humble them, and prove them* (Dt 8:16), could stir them to watch themselves. It is good for us sometimes to be the object of a gaze, to be forced to pause.

6. The disciples were anxious to get their Master to explain himself.

6.1. Of all the disciples, John was most fit to ask, because he was the favorite and sat next to his Master (v. 23): *There was leaning on Jesus' bosom one of the disciples whom Jesus loved.* A comparison of this passage with 21:20, 24 makes it clear that this was John. Notice:

6.1.1. The particular kindness that Jesus felt for him; he was *the disciple whom Jesus loved.* Jesus loved all his disciples (v. 1), but John was especially dear to him. His name means "gracious." Among the disciples of Christ, some are dearer to him than others.

6.1.2. His place at this time: he was *leaning on Jesus' bosom.* It seems to be an extraordinary expression of endearment. Those who lay themselves at Christ's feet, he will lay at his side.

6.1.3. However, John concealed his name. To show that he was pleased with his special relationship with Jesus, instead of his name he wrote that he was *the disciple whom Jesus loved*; it was his title of honor.

6.2. Of all the disciples, Peter was most eager to know (v. 24). Sitting at some distance, Peter motioned to John to ask which one Christ meant. Peter was generally the leading man. When people's natural dispositions lead them to be bold in answering and asking, they can be very useful, as long as they are restrained by the laws of humility and wisdom. God gives his gifts diversely (1Co 12:4), but it must be noted that it was not Peter but John who was the beloved disciple. The reason why Peter himself did not ask was that John had a much better opportunity to whisper the question into the ear of Christ and to receive a similarly private answer. It is good to make the most of our relationship with those who are close to Christ. Do we know anyone who we have reason to think lies at Christ's side? Let us beg them to speak a good word for us.

6.3. Accordingly, the question was asked (v. 25): *He then, lying at the breast of Jesus, saith unto him, Lord, who is it?* Now here John showed:

6.3.1. Regard for his fellow disciple. Those who lie at Christ's side can often learn from those who lie at his feet; they can be reminded of what they themselves had not thought of.

6.3.2. Reverence for his Teacher. Although he whispered this in Christ's ear, he still called him Lord; the familiarity he was admitted to did not at all lessen his respect for his Master. The more intimate the fellowship that gracious souls have with Christ, the more aware they are of his worthiness and their own unworthiness.

6.4. Christ gave a quick response to this question, but it seems he whispered it in John's ear, for it appears (v. 29) that the rest were still ignorant of the matter. *He it is to whom I shall give a sop, when I have dipped it.* Therefore, *when he had dipped the sop, he gave it to Judas.*

6.4.1. Christ revealed the traitor by a sign. He could have told John by name who he was. The false brothers and sisters we are to stand on guard against are not made known to us by words, but by signs; they are to be known to us by *their fruits* (Mt 7:16).

6.4.2. That sign was a piece of bread. Christ sometimes gives pieces of bread to traitors. Worldly riches, honors, and pleasures are pieces of bread—if we may express it in this way—that Providence sometimes puts into the hands of evildoers. We must not be outraged against those whom we know to be evil toward us. Christ gave food to Judas as kindly as he did to anyone at the table, even though he knew Judas was then plotting his death.

7. Judas, instead of being convinced of his evil by this, was even more confirmed in it.

7.1. The Devil then took possession of him (v. 27): *After the sop, Satan entered into him.* Satan entered him to possess him with a powerful contempt of Christ, to stir up in him greed for the wages of unrighteousness (2Pe 2:15) and a determination to stop at nothing to obtain them. Now, was Satan not in him before? Why then was it said that now *Satan entered into him*? Judas was all along a devil (6:70), but now Satan gained fuller possession of him. Although the Devil is in every corrupt person who does his works, he enters more clearly and more powerfully at some times than at others. How did Satan come to enter him after the piece of bread? Perhaps he was aware that the bread had revealed him, and it made him desperate in his determination. Many people are made worse by the gifts of Christ's goodness, confirmed in their impenitence by what should have led them to repentance.

7.2. Christ then dismissed him: *Then said Jesus unto him, What thou doest, do quickly.* This is to be understood either as:

7.2.1. Abandoning him to the guidance and power of Satan. Christ knew that Satan had entered him and had peaceable possession, and so now he gave him up as hopeless. The various ways Christ had used to convict him had been ineffective. When the evil spirit is willingly admitted, the good Spirit justly withdraws. Or:

7.2.2. Challenging him to do his worst: "I am not afraid of you; in fact, I am ready for you."

7.3. Those who were with him at table did not understand what he meant (vv. 28–29): *No man at table knew for what intent he spoke this to him.*

7.3.1. They did not suspect that Christ said it to Judas as a traitor, because it did not enter their heads that Judas was or would prove to be such a person. Christ's disciples were so well taught to love one another that they could not easily learn to suspect one another.

7.3.2. They assumed, therefore, that he said it to him as treasurer of the household, giving him orders to spend some of the money, either:

7.3.2.1. On works of devotion to God: *Buy those things that we have need of against the feast.* Or:

7.3.2.2. In works of love for others: *That he should give something to the poor.* Although our Lord Jesus lived on the gifts of others himself (Lk 8:3), he still gave gifts to the poor and needy, a little from a little. Although he could very well have been excused, not only because he himself was poor but also because he did so much good in other ways, healing so many freely, nevertheless, to set us an example, he gave for the relief of the poor. The time of a religious feast was thought to be a proper time for works of love. When he celebrated the Passover, he ordered something to be given to the poor. When we experience God's goodness to us, this should make us generous to the poor.

7.4. Judas then set himself to pursue his plan against him vigorously: he *went away.* Notice:

7.4.1. His quick departure: *He went out immediately* for fear of being revealed more plainly to the others. He went out as one who was tired of Christ's company and the community of his apostles. Christ did not need to expel him; he expelled himself. *He went out* to pursue his plan. Now that Satan had entered him, he rushed him on.

7.4.2. The time of his departure: *It was night.*

7.4.2.1. Although it was night, the coldness and darkness of the night presented no difficulties to him. That the Devil's servants are so serious and adventurous in his service should shame us out of our laziness and cowardice in serving Christ.

7.4.2.2. He went out now *because* it was night, which gave him the advantage of privacy and concealment. Those whose deeds are evil love darkness rather than light (3:19).

Verses 31–35

This and what follows, to the end of ch. 14, was Christ's informal conversation with his disciples. When supper was over, Judas went out, but the Master and his disciples applied themselves to useful conversation. Christ began this conversation. People who lead the community and to whom other people listen because of their position, reputation, and gifts should use the influence they have to do good. Christ spoke:

1. About the great mystery of his own death and sufferings, about which they were still very much in the dark; much less did they understand its meaning. Christ did not begin to tell them this until Judas had gone out. The presence of evildoers is often a hindrance to good discussion. When Judas *was gone out*, Christ said, *Now is the Son of man glorified.* Christ is glorified by the purifying of Christian communities: corruptions in his church bring disgrace on them. Or, *now* Judas had gone to set in motion the plans for Christ's execution: *Now is the Son of man glorified*, meaning, *Now he is crucified.*

1.1. Here is a comforting teaching about his sufferings:

1.1.1. That he himself would be glorified in them. Now the Son of Man was to be exposed to the greatest shame and dishonor both by the cowardice of his friends and by the arrogance of his enemies, yet *now he was glorified.* Now he was to win a glorious victory over Satan and all the powers of darkness. Now he was to bring about a glorious rescue for his people: by his death he would reconcile them to God and bring in an eternal righteousness and happiness for them. Now he was to give such a glorious example of self-denial and patience under the cross and of love for people's souls that he would be forever wondered at. Christ had been glorified in the many miracles he had performed, but now he spoke of being glorified in his sufferings as if that were more than all his other glories.

1.1.2. That God the Father would be glorified in them. The sufferings of Christ were the satisfaction of God's justice and the revelation of his holiness and mercy. God is love (1Jn 4:16), and here he has demonstrated his love (Ro 5:8).

1.1.3. That he himself would be greatly glorified after them, in consideration of God's being greatly glorified by them (v. 32). He was sure that:

1.1.3.1. God would glorify him. Hell and earth set themselves to abuse Christ, but God was determined to glorify him. He glorified him in his sufferings by the amazing signs and wonders that accompanied them, drawing even from his crucifiers an acknowledgment that he was the Son of God.

1.1.3.2. He would glorify him *in himself*, in Christ himself. He would glorify him in his own person. This implies his quick resurrection. Ordinary people may be honored after their death, in their memory or descendants, but Christ was honored in himself.

1.1.3.3. He would glorify him immediately. Christ looked on the joy and glory set before him (Heb 12:2) not only as great but as near. Good services done to earthly rulers often remain unrewarded for a long time, but Christ had his advancement immediately.

1.1.3.4. All this was in consideration of God's being glorified in and by Christ's sufferings: since *God was glorified in him*, God would glorify him in himself. Those who are concerned with the business of glorifying God no doubt will have the happiness of being glorified with him.

1.2. Here is an arousing teaching about his sufferings, because the disciples found them so hard to understand (v. 33). Christ here suggested two things to stir his disciples up:

1.2.1. That they would find his stay in this world to be very short. *Little children.* This form of address does not show so much their weakness as his tenderness. "Know this, then, that *yet a little while I am with you.*" Let them make the most of the advantage they now had. We must make the most of the helps we have for our souls while we still have them. Let the disciples not depend too much on his physical presence. They must think about living without it; they must not always remain like little children, but must grow up, learn to live without their nurses.

1.2.2. That they would find their following him to the next world to be very difficult. What he had said to the Jews (7:34) he said to his disciples. Christ told them here:

1.2.2.1. That when he was gone, they would feel their lack of him: *You shall seek me.* We are often taught the value of blessings by their lack. The presence of the Comforter (14:16, 26; 15:26; 16:7; NIV: Counselor) was not such a definite satisfaction as Christ's physical presence would have been. But notice that to the Jews Christ said, "You will seek me and *not find me* (7:34)," but to the disciples he said only, *You shall seek me.* They would find what was equivalent and would not seek in vain (Isa 45:19).

1.2.2.2. That where he went, they *could not come.* Christ told them that they could not follow him—only to stir them to even more diligence and care. They could not follow him to his cross, because they did not have the courage and determination. Nor could they follow him to his crown, because they did not have a power of their own, nor was their work or service finished.

2. About the great duty of mutual love (vv. 34–35): *You shall love one another.* Now that they must expect to be treated as their Master had been, they must have a mutual love for one another that would strengthen one another's hands. Three arguments for mutual love were urged here.

2.1. The command of their Master (v. 34): *A new commandment I give unto you.* He not only commended it, not only counseled it, but commanded it and made it one of the fundamental laws of his kingdom. It was a new commandment; that is:

2.1.1. It was a renewed commandment. It is like an old book in a new edition that has been corrected and expanded. This commandment had been so corrupted that when Christ revised it, it could well be called a new commandment. The law of mutual love had been forgotten as if it were obsolete and out of date. Therefore, when it came from Christ afresh, it was new to the people.

2.1.2. It was an eternal command; it was so strangely new that it would always be so; it will be new to eternity, when faith and hope are obsolete.

2.1.3. As Christ gave it, it was new. Before, the command was, *Thou shalt love thy neighbour* (Mt 5:43); now it was, "You shall love one another"; it was urged in a more appealing way when it was pressed as a mutual duty we owe to one another.

2.2. The example of their Savior: *As I have loved you.* What made it a new commandment was that it was now motivated by this rule and reason of love. We are to understand this as referring to:

2.2.1. All the expressions of Christ's love to his disciples. This was how he had loved them, and this was how they must love one another, and how they must *love to the end* (v. 1).

2.2.2. The special expression of love that he was now about to give by laying down his life for them. *Greater love hath no man than this* (15:13). Not that we are capable of doing what he has done for us (Ps 49:7), but we must love one another in the same manner in some respects; we must set this before us as our example. Our love for one another must be love for the souls of one another. We must also love one another from this motive, and for this reason: that Christ has loved us.

2.3. The reputation of their profession (v. 35): *By this shall all men know that you are my disciples, if you have love one to another.* We must have love, not only show love but have it in its root and habit; we must always be ready to show our love. Mutual love is the badge of Christ's disciples. This is the uniform that his family wear; he wants them noted for this quality, as something in which they excel all others—their loving one another. This was what their Master was famous for, and so if you see any people more affectionate for one another than what is common, say, "Certainly these are the followers of Christ; they have been with Jesus (Ac 4:13)." This shows us:

2.3.1. That the heart of Christ was very much set on his desire that his disciples love one another. In this they must be distinctive; whereas the way of the world is everyone for themselves, they should be sincerely loving toward one another. He did not say, "*By this shall men know* that you are my disciples—if you work miracles," for a worker of miracles is nothing without love (1Co 13:1–2).

2.3.2. That it is the true honor of Christ's disciples to excel in mutual love. Christians were known by their affection for one another. Their enemies took notice of it and said, "See how these Christians love one another." If the followers of Christ do not love one another, they give themselves just cause to suspect their own sincerity. When our brothers and sisters stand in need of help from us, when they are in any way rivals with or provoking to us, so that we have an opportunity to forgive, in such cases it will be known whether we show this badge of Christ's disciples or not.

Verses 36–38

In these verses we have:

1. Peter's curiosity.

1.1. Peter's question was bold and blunt (v. 36): *Lord, whither goest thou?* He was referring to what Christ had said in v. 33: *Whither I go, you cannot come.* It is a common fault among us to be more concerned to have our curiosity satisfied than to have our consciences guided. It is easy to notice in the conversation of Christians how quickly a discussion of what is clear and edifying is dropped, and nothing more is said about it—whereas disputable matters are discussed endlessly.

1.2. Christ's answer was instructive. He did not satisfy Peter's curiosity, but said what he had said before (v. 36): "Let this be enough: *thou canst not follow me now, but thou shalt follow me hereafter.*"

1.2.1. We may understand it as referring to Peter's following him to the cross: "You are not yet strong and faithful enough to drink from my cup." When Christ was seized, he provided for the safety of his disciples. *Let these go their way* (18:8), he said, because they could not *follow him now* (v. 36). Christ considered how his disciples were formed (Ps 103:14). The day will be as the strength is. Although Peter was destined for martyrdom, he could not follow Christ now; he would follow him later; in the end he would be crucified, like his Master. Let him not think that because he escaped suffering now, he would never suffer. We may be reserved for greater trials than we have yet known.

1.2.2. We may understand it as referring to his following him to the crown: "No," Christ said, "*thou canst not follow me now. Thou shalt follow me afterward,* after you have fought the good fight (2Ti 4:7)." There is a desert between the Red Sea and Canaan.

2. Peter's confidence.

2.1. Peter made a daring declaration of his loyalty. *Lord, why cannot I follow thee now? I will lay down my life for thy sake.* Having heard his Master speak so often about his own sufferings, he could not understand him in any other way than as referring to his going away through death, and he was determined, like Thomas, to *go and die with him* (11:16); better to die with him than to live without him. See here:

2.1.1. What an affectionate love Peter had for our Lord Jesus: "*I will lay down my life for thy sake.*" Peter spoke as he thought, and although he did not consider the matter properly, he was not insincere.

2.1.2. How badly he took the questioning of it: "*Lord, why cannot I follow thee now?* (v. 37). Do you suspect my loyalty to you?" (1Sa 29:8). It is with regret that true love hears its sincerity called into question (21:17). We tend to think that we can do anything and to take offense when we are told that we cannot do something, whereas the reality is that without Christ we can do nothing (15:5).

2.2. Christ gave him a surprising prediction of his disloyalty (v. 38).

2.2.1. He rebuked Peter for his confidence: *Wilt thou lay down thy life for my sake?* In this way Christ prompted Peter to second thoughts, so that he would insert into his resolution the necessary condition, "Lord, your grace enabling me, I will lay down my life for your sake." "Will you undertake to die for me? What! You who trembled to walk on the water to me? It was relatively easy to leave your boats and nets to follow me, but it is not so easy to lay down your life." It is good for us to shame ourselves out of our presumptuous self-confidence. "How foolish I am I to boast about what I can do."

2.2.2. He clearly foretold the cowardice Peter would show at the critical hour. Christ solemnly asserted it with *Verily, verily:* "*Verily, verily, I say unto thee, the cock shall not crow till thou hast denied me thrice: the cock shall not crow* — will not have stopped its final crowing — until you have again and again denied me." The crowing of the rooster was to be the occasion of his repentance. Christ foresaw not only that Judas would betray him even though he had only planned it in his heart; he also foresaw that Peter would deny him even though he did not plan to, and intended the opposite. He knows not only the evil of sinners but also the weakness of saints. Christ told Peter that he would deny him, that he would not only do this once by

a hasty slip of the tongue but would repeat it a second and third time. We may well imagine how humbling it must have been to Peter's confidence and courage to be told this. Those who think they are most secure are commonly the least safe, and those who most confidently presume on their own strength are the ones who most shamefully betray their own weakness (1Co 10:12).

CHAPTER 14

When Christ had convicted and rejected Judas, he set himself to reassure the rest of the disciples. The general scope of this chapter is in the first verse; it is intended to stop the disciples' hearts from being troubled. Let them consider: 1. Heaven as their eternal rest (vv. 2–3). 2. Christ himself as their way (vv. 4–11). 3. The great power they will be clothed with by the effectiveness of their prayers (vv. 12–14). 4. The coming of another Comforter (Counselor) (vv. 15–17). 5. The fellowship that would be between him and them after his departure (vv. 18–24). 6. The instructions that the Holy Spirit would give them (vv. 25–26). 7. The peace Christ left them (v. 27). 8. Christ's own cheerfulness in his departure (vv. 28–31).

Verses 1–3

In these verses we have:

1. A general warning that Christ gave his disciples against trouble in their hearts (v. 1): *Let not your hearts be troubled.* Note:

1.1. How Christ took notice of the trouble in their hearts. Perhaps it was apparent in their looks; in any case, it was intelligible to the Lord Jesus, who knows all our secret, undiscovered sorrows, along with the wound that bleeds inwardly. He takes notice of all the troubles that his people are at any time in danger of being overwhelmed by. Many things conspired to trouble the disciples at that time.

1.1.1. Christ had just told them about the unkindness he would receive from some of them, and this troubled them all. As to this, Christ comforted them. Although a godly watchfulness over ourselves is very useful to keep us humble and alert, it must not be so great that it disturbs our spirits and dampens our holy joy.

1.1.2. He had just told them about his own departure from them, that he would not only go away but go away under a cloud of suffering. When we now look at Christ pierced, we must *mourn and be in bitterness* (Zec 12:10), even though we see its glorious result and fruit; much more terrible must the sight have been to them, to those who could then look no further. If Christ departed from them:

1.1.2.1. They would think themselves shamefully disappointed, because they had wanted him to rescue Israel.

1.1.2.2. They would think they had been sadly deserted and exposed. Now, in reference to all these things, *Let not your hearts be troubled.* Here are three words, on any of which the emphasis may significantly be laid:

1.1.2.2.1. On the word *troubled.* "Do not be like the troubled sea in a storm. He did not say, "Let not your hearts be aware of grief," or, "Let not your hearts become sad at them," but, "Don't become disturbed and unsettled."

1.1.2.2.2. On the word *heart:* "Although nation and city are troubled, although your little family and flock are troubled, *let not your heart be troubled.* Keep possession of your own souls when you can keep possession of nothing else." The heart is the main fort; whatever you do, keep trouble out of this (Pr 4:23).

1.1.2.2.3. On the word *your*: "You who are my disciples and followers, make sure you are not troubled, for you know better." In times of trouble, Christ's disciples should do more than others; they should keep their minds quiet when everything else is unruly.

1.2. The remedy he prescribed; in general, *believe*.

1.2.1. Some read both parts as a command: "*Believe in God*, in his nature and providence; *believe also in me*, in my mediation."

1.2.2. Our translation reads the former as an acknowledgment that they did believe in God. "But if you want to prepare for stormy days, *believe also in me*." By believing in Christ as the Mediator between God and humanity, we can take comfort in our belief in God. Those who rightly believe in God will believe in Jesus Christ, and believing in God through Jesus Christ is an excellent means of keeping trouble from the heart. The joy of faith is the best answer to the griefs we suffer while in our bodies.

2. A particular instruction to have faith in the promise of eternal life (vv. 2–3). What must they trust God and Christ for? Trust them for a future happiness, for a happiness that will last as long as the immortal soul and the eternal world last. Believers have encouraged themselves in their greatest crises with the assurance that heaven would make amends for everything. Let us see how this was suggested here.

2.1. Let us believe and consider that there really is such a happiness: *In my Father's house there are many mansions; if it were not so, I would have told you* (v. 2).

2.1.1. Notice how the happiness of heaven was described here: as mansions.

2.1.1.1. Heaven is a house, not a tent or tabernacle.

2.1.1.2. It is a Father's house: *my Father's house*, and his Father is our Father (20:17). All true believers will be welcome to the happiness of their home.

2.1.1.3. There are mansions there, distinct dwelling places, a room for each. Our individuality will not be lost there. The dwelling places are durable, too. The house itself is lasting; we will possess it not for a term of years, but forever. Here we are staying as in a hotel; in heaven we will gain a settled residence.

2.1.1.4. There are many rooms, because there are many sons and daughters to be brought to glory (Heb 2:10).

2.1.2. Notice what assurance we have of the reality of the happiness itself: "*If it were not so, I would have told you.*" The assurance depends on the truthfulness of his word and the sincerity of his affection for them. Just as he is true and would not deceive them, so he is also kind and would not allow them to be deceived by others. He loves us too well, and is too well-meaning toward us, to disappoint the expectations that he himself raises.

2.2. Let us believe and consider that the intention of Christ's departure was to prepare a place in heaven for his disciples. He went to prepare a place for us, that is:

2.2.1. To take possession for us as our advocate or attorney and thereby keep our title secure so that it cannot be canceled.

2.2.2. To make provision. The happiness of heaven must be further fitted for humanity. Because it consists much in the presence of Christ there, it was necessary for him to go before. Heaven would be an unready place for a Christian if Christ were not already there.

2.3. They must believe and consider that he would certainly come again (v. 3): *If I go and prepare a place for you, I will come again, and receive you to myself, that where I am, there you may be also.* Now these are truly comforting words.

2.3.1. Jesus Christ will come again. It may also be translated, "I am coming," intimating its certainty. We say that we are coming when we are busy preparing to come, and so he is.

2.3.2. He will come again to receive all his faithful followers to himself. The coming of Christ is in order to gather us *together unto him* (2Th 2:1).

2.3.3. *Where he is, there they shall be also.* This shows that the essence of heaven's happiness is being with Christ there (17:24; Php 1:23; 1Th 4:17). "*That where I am*; where I am to be soon, where I am to be eternally, there you will be soon, there you will be eternally" — and not only as spectators of his glory but as sharers in it.

2.3.4. This may be concluded from his *going to prepare a place* for us, for his preparation will not be in vain. He will not build and furnish lodgings and then let them stand empty. If he has prepared the place for us, he will also prepare us for it, and in due time he will give us possession of it.

Verses 4–11

Here:

1. Having set the happiness of heaven before them as their end, Christ showed them himself as the way to it. *You know,* that is:

1.1. "You may know; it is not one of the secret things that do not belong to you, but one of the things revealed (Dt 29:29).

1.2. "You do know; you know what is the home and which is the way, though perhaps you do not know them as the home and as the way. You have been told about them and must surely know."

2. Thomas asked about the way (v. 5).

2.1. He said, *Lord, we know not whither thou goest, and how can we know the way?* Christ's testimony about their knowledge made them more aware of their ignorance and more inquisitive for further light. Thomas here showed more modesty than Peter. Peter was more concerned to know where Christ was going. Thomas here seemed more concerned to know the way.

2.1.1. His confession of his ignorance was commendable. Good people, if they are in the dark and know only in part (1Co 13:12), are willing to acknowledge their defects.

2.1.2. The cause of his ignorance was blameworthy. They did not know where Christ was going because they dreamed of a temporal kingdom. Their imagination ran on to his going to some significant town to be anointed king there. They could not tell where these castles in the air were to be built — east, west, north, or south? — and so they did not know the way to it. If Thomas had understood that Christ was going to the invisible world, he would not have said, *Lord, we do not know the way.*

2.2. Christ gave a full answer to this complaint of their ignorance (vv. 6–7). Thomas had asked both where Christ was going and what was the way, and Christ answered both these questions. They knew him, and he was the way; they knew the Father, and he was the end, and so, "*whither I go you know, and the way you know* (v. 4). Believe in God as the end and in me as the way" (v. 1).

2.2.1. He spoke of himself as the way (v. 6). *I am the way; no man comes to the Father but by me.* Christ here showed us:

2.2.1.1. The nature of his mediation: he is *the way, the truth, and the life.*

2.2.1.1.1. Let us consider each of these individually.

2.2.1.1.1.1. Christ is the way. In him God and humanity meet and are brought together. We could not reach the tree of life along the path of innocence, but Christ is another path to it. The disciples followed him, and Christ told them that while they continued following him, they would never be on the wrong path.

2.2.1.1.*1.2.* He is the truth, as truth contrasts with falsehood and error. When we ask for truth, we need learn no more than the truth as it is in Jesus. He is also the truth as truth contrasts with dishonesty and deceit. He is as true as truth itself (2Co 1:20).

2.2.1.1.*1.3.* He is the life, for we are *alive unto God* only in and *through Jesus Christ* (Ro 6:11). Christ is *the resurrection and the life* (11:25).

2.2.1.1.*2.* Let us consider these together: *the way, the truth, and the life.* He is the beginning, the middle, and the end. He is *the true and living way* (Heb 10:20); there are truth and life along the way as well as at its destination and end. He is the true way to life. Other ways may seem right, but the end of them is *the way of death* (Jer 21:8).

2.2.1.2. The necessity of his mediation: *No man cometh to the Father but by me.* Fallen humanity cannot come to him as a Father, except through Christ as Mediator.

2.2.2. He spoke about his Father as the end (v. 7): "*If you had known me, you would have known my Father also, and henceforth you know him and have seen him.*" Here is:

2.2.2.1. A tacit rebuke to them for their slowness and carelessness in not coming to know Jesus Christ more. *If you had known me.* They knew him, but they did not know him as well as they could and should have known him. Christ had said to the Jews (8:19), *If you had known me, you would have known my Father also,* and here he said the same to his disciples, for it is difficult to say which is stranger, the willful ignorance of those who are the enemies of the light, or the defects and mistakes of *the children of light* (1Th 5:5).

2.2.2.2. A favorable indication that he was well satisfied about their sincerity despite the weakness of their understanding: *And henceforth you know him, and have seen him,* because we see the glory of God in the face of Christ (2Co 4:6). Many of the disciples of Christ have more knowledge and more grace than they think they have. Those who know God do not know all at once that they know him (1Jn 2:3).

3. Philip asked about the Father (v. 8), and Christ answered him (vv. 9–11). Notice:

3.1. Philip's request for some extraordinary revelation of the Father. From a fervent desire for further light, he cried out, *Show us the Father.* "That is what we want, what we really want: *Show us the Father, and it sufficeth us.*"

3.1.1. This implied a strong desire to know God as a Father. The request was, *Show us the Father.* The plea is, "*It sufficeth us.* Give us just one glimpse of the Father, and we will have enough." The soul is satisfied in the knowledge of God as our Father; a sight of the Father is a heaven on earth. "Let us see the Father with our physical eyes, as we see you, *and it sufficeth us.*"

3.1.2. It revealed not only the weakness of his faith but also his ignorance of the Gospel way of revealing the Father. Christ's institutions have provided better for the confirmation of our faith than our own ideas would.

3.2. Christ's reply (vv. 9–11).

3.2.1. He referred him to what he had seen (v. 9). *Have I been so long time with you, and yet hast thou not known me, Philip?* Now, *he that hath seen me hath seen the Father, and how sayest thou then, Show us the Father?*

3.2.1.1. He corrected him for two things:

3.2.1.1.*1.* For not growing in his acquaintance with Christ toward a clear and distinct knowledge of him: *Hast thou not known me, Philip?* The first day Jesus came to him, Philip declared that he knew him to be the Messiah (1:45), but to this day he did not know the Father in him. Many know Christ but do not know what they could know of him, nor see what they should see in him. *I have been so long time with thee.* Christ expects our proficiency to be in some measure according to our standing, that we will not always remain babies in the faith.

3.2.1.1.*2.* For his weakness shown in the prayer, *Show us the Father.* Much of the weakness of Christ's disciples is apparent when they *know not what to pray for as they ought* (Ro 8:26), but often *ask amiss* (Jas 4:3).

3.2.1.2. He instructed him and gave him an answer that justified what he had said earlier (v. 7): *You know the Father, and have seen him*; and in saying this, he answered what Philip had asked: *Show us the Father. He that hath seen me hath seen the Father.* All who saw Christ in the flesh could have seen the Father in him. All who saw Christ by faith did see the Father in him, even though they were not immediately aware that they did. The holiness of God shone out in the spotless purity of Christ's life, and God's grace shone out in all the acts of grace Christ did.

3.2.2. He referred him to what he had reason to believe (vv. 10–11): "*Believest thou not that I am in the Father, and the Father in me, so that in seeing me you have seen the Father?*"

3.2.2.1. See here what it is that we are to believe: *That I am in the Father, and the Father in me*; that is, as he had said, *I and my Father are one* (10:30). In knowing Christ, we know the Father, and in seeing him we see the Father.

3.2.2.2. See here what two inducements we have to believe this. We must believe it:

3.2.2.2.*1.* For his word's sake: *The words that I speak to you, I speak not of myself.* What he said was inspired by the wisdom of God and enforced by the will of God. *He spoke not of himself* only, but also the mind of God according to God's eternal purposes.

3.2.2.2.*2.* For his works' sake: *The Father that dwelleth in me, he doeth them,* and so *believe me for their sake.* The Father was said to dwell in me. The Father lives in Christ in such a way that he can be found in Christ, as a man can be found where he lives. *Seek ye the Lord,* seek him in Christ, and *he will be found* (Isa 55:6), because he lives in him. *He doeth the works* (v. 10). Christ did many works of power and works of mercy, and the Father did them in him. We are bound to believe this *for the very works' sake.* Christ's miracles are proofs that he was sent on a divine mission both to convict unbelievers and to confirm the faith of his own disciples (2:11; 5:36; 10:37).

Verses 12–14

Just as the disciples were full of grief to think of parting with their Master, so they were also full of worry about what would happen to them when he was gone. If he left them, they would be as *sheep having no shepherd* (Mt 9:36). Christ assured them here that they would be clothed with sufficient powers to support them (Lk 24:49). They would have:

1. Great power on earth (v. 12): *He that believeth on me, the works that I do shall he do also.* It exalted his power more than anything that he not only performed miracles himself but also gave power to others to do so too.

1.1. He assured them of two things.

1.1.1. That they would be enabled to do works like those he had done. Did Christ heal the sick, cleanse lepers, raise the dead? So would they. Did he convince and convert sinners and draw crowds to him? So would they. Even though he would depart, the work would not come to an end, would not fall to the ground (1Sa 3:19; Isa 55:11), and it is still being done.

1.1.2. That they would do *greater works than these*. In the kingdom of nature they would perform greater miracles. No miracle is small, but some seem greater in our perception than others. Christ performed miracles for two or three years in one country, but his followers performed miracles in his name for many ages in various countries. In the kingdom of grace, they would obtain greater victories through the Gospel than had been obtained while Christ was on earth. The truth is, the captivating of such a great part of the world for Christ under such outward disadvantages was the greatest miracle of all.

1.2. The reason Christ gave for this: *Because I go unto my Father*. "*Because I go*, it will be necessary for you to have such power. *Because I go to the Father*, I will be able to provide you with such power."

2. Great power in heaven: *Whatsoever you shall ask, that will I do* (vv. 13–14). Notice:

2.1. How they were to derive power from him when he was gone to the Father: by prayer. When dear friends are a distance from one another, they keep in touch by correspondence; similarly, when Christ was going to his Father, he told his disciples how they could write to him on every occasion and send their letters by a safe and ready way. "Let me hear from you through prayer, and you will hear from me through the Spirit." Christ by his death has laid this way more open than it was before, and it is still open to us. Here:

2.1.1. Humility is directed: *You shall ask.* They could demand nothing of him as a debt, but must come as humble petitioners, beg or starve, beg or perish.

2.1.2. Liberty is allowed: "Ask anything, anything that is good and proper for you; anything, provided you know what you ask." Occasions vary, but Christ's disciples will be welcome to the throne of grace on every occasion.

2.2. In what name they were to present their requests: *Ask in my name.* They were to plead his merit and intercession and to depend on it. If we ask in our own name, we cannot expect success, for, being strangers, we have no name in heaven; being sinners, we have a bad name there, but Christ's is a good name, well known in heaven.

2.3. What success they would have in their prayers: "What you ask, *that will I do*" (v. 13), and again (v. 14), "*I will do it.* You may be sure I will: not only will it be done, but *I will do it*." Through faith in his name we may have what we want if we ask for it.

2.4. For what reason their prayers would be answered: *That the Father may be glorified in the Son. Hallowed be thy name* (Mt 6:9) is an answered prayer, and it comes first, because if the heart is sincere in this, in a way it consecrates all the other petitions. Christ would aim at this in granting what they asked, and he would do it for the sake of this. The wisdom, power, and goodness of God were exalted in the Redeemer when his apostles and ministers were enabled to do such great things, both proving their teaching and bringing about its success.

Verses 15–17

To impress these things on them, Christ promised here to send the Spirit, who would be their *Comforter* (Counselor).

1. He introduced this by reminding them of their duty (v. 15): *If you love me, keep my commandments.* We may expect strength and encouragement only when we are doing our duty. When they were concerned about what would become of them then, he told them to keep his commandments. In difficult times, our concern about the

events of the day should be swallowed up by a concern that we actually fulfill the duties of the day. When they were showing their love for Christ by grieving at the thought of his departure, and showing the sorrow that filled their hearts at that thought, he told them that if they wanted to show their love for him, they must do it not by these weak passions but by obeying all his commands; this is better than sacrifice (1Sa 15:22), better than tears. When Christ had given them precious promises, he set this down as a condition of the promises: "provided you keep my commandments from a motive of love for me."

2. He promised this great and overwhelming blessing to them (vv. 16–17).

2.1. He promised that they would have *another Comforter*. This is the great New Testament promise, a promise adapted to the present distress of the disciples, who were sorrowful and needed a comforter. Notice:

2.1.1. The blessing promised. The word here translated *Comforter* is used in the New Testament only here in these messages of Christ (vv. 16, 26; 15:26; 16:7) and in 1Jn 2:1, where it is translated *an advocate*. "You will have:

2.1.1.1. "Another *advocate*." The role of the Spirit was to be Christ's advocate with them and others, to plead his cause and take care of his concerns on earth. The Spirit would also be their advocate with those who opposed them. When Christ was with them, he spoke for them, but now that he was leaving them, the Spirit of the Father would speak in them (Mt 10:19–20). The cause cannot fail when it is pleaded by such an advocate.

2.1.1.2. "Another master or teacher, another exhorter." While they had Christ with them, he encouraged and stirred them to do their duty, but now he would leave with them One who would do that work just as effectively.

2.1.1.3. "Another *Comforter*." Christ comforted his disciples when he was with them, and now that he was leaving them in their greatest need, he promised them another Comforter.

2.1.2. The giver of this blessing: *The Father* would give him. The One who gave the Son to be our Savior would give his Spirit to be our Comforter.

2.1.3. How this blessing would be obtained—by the intercession of the Lord Jesus: *I will pray the Father.* Christ's saying, *I will pray the Father*, does not suggest that the Father was unwilling, but only that the gift of the Spirit is a fruit of Christ's mediation.

2.1.4. The continuation of this blessing: *That he may abide with you for ever*, that is, "with you as long as you live. You will never know the lack of a Comforter." Eternal comforts await us. The disciples must disperse, and so a Comforter would be with them all, everywhere; he would be the only One who was fit to be with them for ever. "And when you are gone, he will abide with your successors to the end of time."

2.2. This Comforter would be the *Spirit of truth, whom you know* (vv. 16–17).

2.2.1. The promised Comforter was *the Spirit*, One who would do his work in a spiritual way.

2.2.2. He is the *Spirit of truth*. "He will be true to you and to his undertaking for you. He will teach you the truth. The Spirit of truth will not only lead you into all truth but also lead others into all the truth through your ministry." Christ is the truth, and the Holy Spirit is the Spirit of Christ.

2.2.3. "He is One *whom the world cannot receive*, but *you know him. Therefore he* will remain *with you*."

2.2.3.1. The disciples of Christ are distinguished from the world here; they are the children and heirs of another world, not of this one.

2.2.3.2. It is the misery of those who are unshakably devoted to the world that they cannot receive the Spirit of truth. Where the spirit of the world is dominant, the Spirit of God is excluded.

2.2.3.3. People *cannot receive the Spirit of truth* because they *see him not, neither know him.* The comforts of the Spirit are *foolishness to them,* as much as the cross of Christ was (1Co 1:18). If you speak to the children of this world about the activity of the Spirit, it is as if you are speaking a foreign language to them.

2.2.3.4. The best knowledge of the Spirit of truth is what is gained by experience: *You know him, for he dwelleth with you.* Christ had lived with them, and they had come to know him in such a way that they knew *the Spirit of truth.* The experiences of the saints are the explanations of the promises. He *dwelleth with you, and shall be in you,* because the Holy Spirit does not move his home.

2.2.3.5. Those who know the Spirit in their own experience have a comfortable assurance that he will continue to be with them. They know how to invite him and welcome him; he, therefore, will be in them as the light is in the air, as the sap is in the tree, and their union with him is inseparable.

2.2.3.6. The gift of the Holy Spirit is a special gift, imparted to the disciples of Christ in a particular way — he is given to them, not to the world. No comforts are comparable to those that make no show or noise.

Verses 18–24

When friends are parting, they often say to each other, "Keep in touch as often as you can": Christ made such a commitment to his disciples, so they would know that although they would be out of sight, they would not be out of mind.

1. He promised that he would continue to care for them (v. 18): *"I will not leave you comfortless* (as orphans or fatherless); *I will come to you."* His departure from them was neither total nor final.

1.1. It would not be total. "Although I leave you without my physical presence, I do not leave you without comfort." Although the situation of true believers may sometimes be sorrowful, it is never without comfort, because they are never orphans: God is their Father.

1.2. It would not be final: *I will come to you.* "I will come quickly to you at my resurrection." He had often said, *The third day I will rise again* (Mt 20:19). But also, "I will be coming to you every day through my Spirit"; in the tokens of his love and the visits of his grace, he continues to come. Finally, "I will come certainly at the end of time." The consideration of Christ's coming to us saves us from being without comfort when he has moved away from us.

2. He promised that they would continue to know him (vv. 19–20): *Yet a little while, and the world sees me no more.* The evil world thought they had seen enough of him, and *cried, Away with him; crucify him* (19:15), and so will their doom be; they will see him no more. But his disciples have spiritual fellowship with him in his absence.

2.1. *You see me.* They saw him with their physical eyes after his resurrection. And *then were the disciples glad when they saw the Lord* (20:20). They saw him with the eye of faith after his ascension; they saw in him what the world did not see.

2.2. *Because I live, you shall live also.* What made them very sad was that their Master was dying, and they could think about nothing else except dying with them. "No," Christ said: *"I live."* Not only, "I will live," as he said about them, but also, "I do live." We are not left as orphans while we know that our Redeemer lives (Job

19:25). Therefore *you shall live also.* The life of Christians is bound up in the life of Christ; as surely and as long as he lives, those who are united to him through faith will also live. This life is hidden with Christ (Col 3:3); if the head and root are alive, the members and branches will also be alive.

2.3. "You will have the assurance of this" (v. 20): *At that day you shall know* that *I am in my Father, and you in me, and I in you.* These glorious mysteries will be fully known:

2.3.1. In heaven. Now we do not know *what we shall be,* but then we will seen what we were (1Jn 3:2).

2.3.2. After the outpouring of the Spirit on the apostles. At that day divine light would shine, and their eyes would see more clearly, like those of the blind man at the second touch of Christ's hand, who at first only *saw men as trees walking* (Mk 8:24).

2.3.3. By all who receive the Spirit of truth. They knew that Christ is in the Father and is one with the Father by their experience of what Christ had done for them and in them. Christ was in them, and they were in Christ, because the relationship was mutual. Christ was in them and they were in Christ, which speaks of an intimate and inseparable union. Union with Christ is the life of believers. The knowledge of this union is their inexpressible joy and satisfaction.

3. He promised that he would love them and reveal himself to them (vv. 21–24). Notice:

3.1. Whom Christ will accept as those who love him: those who *have his commandments, and keep them.* By this Christ showed that the kind things he said to his disciples here were intended not only for those who were now his followers but also for all who would *believe in him through their word* (17:20). Here is:

3.1.1. The duty of those who claim the honor of being disciples. Having Christ's commandments, we must keep them. Having them in our minds, we must also keep them in our hearts and lives.

3.1.2. The honor of those who fulfill the duty of disciples. It is not those who have the greatest knowledge and who know how to speak for him, or who have the greatest wealth to spend for him, but those who keep his commandments. The most certain evidence of our love for Christ is our obedience to the laws of Christ.

3.2. How he will respond to them for their love:

3.2.1. They will have the Father's love: *he that loveth me shall be loved of my Father.* We could not love God unless he first gave us his grace to love him, but a love of delight is promised to those who do love God (Pr 8:17). He loves them, and he lets them know he loves them. God so loves the Son as to love all those who love him.

3.2.2. They will have Christ's love: *"And I will love him.* God will love them as a Father, and I will love them as a brother, an elder brother." In the nature of God, nothing shines more brightly than that *God is love* (1Jn 4:8, 16). Moreover, in the work of Christ nothing appears more glorious than that he loved us. Christ was now leaving his disciples, but he promised to continue his love for them. He carries believers in his heart and always lives to intercede for them (Heb 7:25).

3.2.3. They will have the comfort of that love: *I will manifest myself to him.* Some understand this as Christ's showing himself alive to his disciples after his resurrection, but, being promised to all who *love him and keep his commandments,* this must be interpreted so as to extend to everyone who does love him and keep his commandments.

3.3. What occurred when Christ made this promise.

3.3.1. One of the disciples expressed his wonder and surprise at it (v. 22). Notice:

3.3.1.1. Who said this: *Judas, not Iscariot.* Two of Christ's disciples were of that name: one of them was the traitor; the other was the *brother* (son) *of James* (Lk 6:16). There were a very good man and a very bad man called by the same name, for names neither commend us to God nor make people worse. Judas the apostle was never the worse, nor Judas the apostate ever the better, for sharing the same name. This is probably the Judas who wrote the last of the New Testament letters, whom for the sake of clarity we call Jude. The Evangelist carefully distinguishes them. "Make sure you do not make a mistake; let us not confuse the noble and the worthless (Jer 15:19)."

3.3.1.2. What he said — *Lord how is it?* This shows:

3.3.1.2.*1.* The weakness of his understanding. He expected the temporal kingdom of the Messiah to appear in external pomp and power. The words rendered *how is it* may also be translated, "What is the matter?": "What is the matter now, that you will not show yourself openly as is generally expected?"

3.3.1.2.*2.* The strength of his affections: *Lord, how is it?* He was amazed at the humility of divine grace. What is there in us to deserve such a great favor? It is justly *marvellous in our eyes* (Mt 21:42), because it cannot be explained, except in the light of free and sovereign grace.

3.3.2. Christ explained and confirmed what he had said (vv. 23–24).

3.3.2.1. He further explained the condition of the promise, which was loving him and keeping his commandments. Love is the root; obedience is the fruit. Where a sincere love for Christ is in the heart, there will be obedience: "*If a man loves me* truly, *he will keep my words.*" Where love is, duty follows naturally; and not as a burden — it flows from a motive of gratitude. Where, on the other hand, there is no true love for Christ, there will be no concern to obey him: *He that loveth me not keepeth not my sayings* (teaching) (v. 24). Certainly those who do not believe his truths and do not obey his laws do not love him. Such people find Christ's sayings to be idle talk, which they pay no attention to, or hard sayings, which they do not like. Why should Christ be friendly with those who want to have nothing to do with him?

3.3.2.2. He further explained the promise (v. 23): *If a man thus love me, I will manifest myself to him. My Father will love him*; he had said this before (v. 21), and he repeated it here to confirm our faith. Jude was amazed that Christ would *manifest himself to them. We will come unto him, and make our abode with him.* Not only, *I will*, but, *We will, I and the Father.* Wherever Christ is formed (Gal 4:19), the image of God is stamped. Not only, "*I will show myself to him* at a distance," but also, "*We will come to him*, to be near him and to be with him." Not only, "I will give him a brief glimpse of me, or pay him a short and quick visit," but, *We will take up our abode* (will make our home) with him. God will not only love obedient believers; he will also rest in his love for them (Zep 3:17). He will be with them as at his home.

3.3.2.3. He gave a good reason both to commit us to observe the condition and to encourage us to depend on the promise. *The word which you hear is not mine, but his that sent me* (v. 24). He had often spoken to this effect (7:16; 8:28; 12:44).

3.3.2.3.*1.* In stating his command as our rule, he emphasized our duty.

3.3.2.3.*2.* In stating his promise, he emphasized our comfort. Now since, in dependence on that promise, we must leave everything (Mt 16:24), we should ask whether the security is sufficient to justify our risking all we are and have on what is promised; and what satisfies us that it is sufficient is that the promise is not merely Christ's word, but that of the Father, who sent him, and so we may well rely on it.

Verses 25–27

Christ comforted his disciples here with two things:

1. That they would be under the guardianship of his Spirit (vv. 25–26). Notice:

1.1. Christ wanted them to reflect on the instructions he had given them: *These things have I spoken unto you being yet present with you.* This shows that he did not retract what he had said. What he had spoken he had spoken, and he remained faithful to it.

1.2. Christ would find a way of speaking to them after his departure from them (v. 26). Notice:

1.2.1. On whose account this other teacher would be sent: "The Father will send him *in my name*, that is, for my sake." Christ had come in his Father's name: the Spirit would come in Christ's name to continue Christ's undertaking.

1.2.2. On what mission he would be sent: *He shall teach you all things.* He would teach them all the things they needed either to learn themselves or to teach others. Those who want to teach the things of God must first themselves be taught by God. *He shall bring all things to your remembrance whatsoever I have said unto you* (v. 26). Christ had taught them many good lessons, which they had forgotten. The Spirit would not teach them a new Gospel, but bring to their minds what they had been taught, by leading them to an understanding of it. The Spirit of grace is given to all the saints to be the One who reminds his people.

2. That they would be under the influence of his peace (v. 27): *Peace I leave with you.* When Christ was about to leave the world, he made his will. His soul he committed to his Father (Lk 23:46); his body he bequeathed to Joseph, to be buried decently; his clothes fell to the soldiers; he left his mother to the care of John; but what would he leave to his poor disciples, who had left everything for him? Silver and gold he did not have (Ac 3:6), but he left them what was infinitely better, his peace. "I leave you, but I am leaving my peace with you." He did not part in anger, but in love, because this was his farewell: *Peace I leave with you.* We are told:

2.1. The legacy that was bequeathed here: *Peace, my peace.* Peace stands for everything good. Peace stands for reconciliation and love; the peace he bequeathed is peace with God. Peace within ourselves seems to be meant especially. It is the peace on which the angels congratulated people at his birth (Lk 2:14).

2.2. To whom this legacy was bequeathed: "to you, my disciples and followers." This legacy was left to them and their successors, to them and all true Christians in all ages.

2.3. How it was left: *Not as the world giveth, give I unto you.* "I do not greet you with a merely formal 'Peace be unto you.' No, it is no mere formality, but a real blessing. The gifts I give to you are not like those the world gives." The world's gifts concern only the body and time; Christ's gifts enrich the soul for eternity. The peace Christ gives is infinitely more valuable than what the world gives. The difference between Christ's peace and the world's is like the difference between a deadly lethargy and a reviving, refreshing sleep.

2.4. What use they were to make of it: *Let not your heart be troubled, neither let it be afraid.* This comes here as the conclusion of the whole matter (Ecc 12:13); he had said (v. 1), *Let not your heart be troubled*, and he repeated it here as what he had now given sufficient reason for.

Verses 28–31

Christ gave his disciples here another reason why their hearts should not be troubled at his going away, and that was that his heart was not troubled. He comforted himself:

1. That although he was going away, he would come again: *You have heard how I have said, I go away, and come again.* Christ encouraged himself in his sufferings and death by remembering that he would come again, and the same encouragement should comfort us in our departure at death; we are going away to come back; the leave we take of our friends at that parting is only a good night, not a final farewell.

2. That he was going to his Father: "*If you loved me, you would rejoice*, because although I said I am leaving you, *I go unto the Father*, because *my Father is greater than I.*" Notice here:

2.1. It is a matter of joy to Christ's disciples that he has gone to his Father. His departure had a bright side as well as a dark side (Ex 14:19–20).

2.2. The reason this would be comforting was that *the Father is greater than he.* His state with his Father would be much more excellent and glorious than his present state. Christ raised the thoughts and expectations of his disciples to something greater than what they now thought all their happiness was bound up in. The kingdom of the Father will be even greater than the kingdom of the mediator.

2.3. The disciples of Christ would show they loved him by their joy in the glories of his exaltation. Many who love Christ allow their love to flow out along the wrong channel; they think that if they love him they must be continually in pain because of him, whereas really those who love him should *rejoice in Christ Jesus* (Php 3:3).

3. That his going away would confirm the faith of his disciples (v. 29): *I have told you before it come to pass, that, when it is come to pass, you might believe.* He gave this reason elsewhere (13:19; 16:4). Christ told his disciples about his death because it would later lead to the confirmation of their faith. He who foretold these things had a divine foreknowledge. The things foretold were according to the divine purpose. Let the disciples not be troubled at what would confirm their faith.

4. That he was sure of a victory over Satan (v. 30): *Henceforth I will not talk much with you.* He taught them a great deal after this (chs. 15–16), but in comparison with what he had said, it was not much. One reason why he would not talk much with them was that he now had other work to turn to: *The prince of this world comes.* He had called the Devil the *prince of this world* (12:31). Now, accordingly, he told them that the prince of this world was his enemy. But *he has nothing in me* (he has no hold on me). Notice:

4.1. The prospect Christ had of an approaching conflict, not only with human beings but also with the powers of darkness. The Devil had attacked him with his temptations (Mt 4:1–11), offering him the *kingdoms of this world. Then the devil departed from him for a season* (Lk 4:13). "But now," Christ said, "I see him rallying." Foresight of a temptation gives us a great advantage in resisting it, because being forewarned, we should be forearmed.

4.2. The assurance he had of good success in the conflict: *He hath nothing in me.*

4.2.1. There was no guilt in Christ, because Christ had done no evil. Satan, though successful in crucifying him, was not successful in terrifying him; although he pushed him toward death, he could not push him into despair. When Satan comes to disturb us, he has something in us to confuse us with, since we have all sinned, but when he wanted to disturb Christ, he could not take advantage of him.

4.2.2. There was no corruption in Christ. Such was the spotless purity of his nature that he was above the possibility of sinning.

5. That his departure was in obedience to his Father. He would die so *that the world may know that I love the Father* (v. 31). We may take this:

5.1. As confirming what he had often said, that his work as Mediator would show the world:

5.1.1. His submission to the Father. Just as his dying for our salvation was evidence of his love for humanity, so his dying for God's glory and the fulfilling of his purposes was evidence of his love for God.

5.1.2. His obedience to his Father: *As the Father gave me commandment, even so I did.* The best evidence of our love for the Father is our doing as he has commanded us. The command of God is sufficient to support us in what is most disputed by others, and it should therefore be sufficient to see us through in what we find most difficult.

5.2. As concluding what he had now said. "So *that the world may know that I love the Father*, you will see how cheerfully I can face up to the appointed cross." *Arise, let us go hence.* When we talk about troubles at a distance, it is easy to say, *Lord, I will follow thee whithersoever thou goest* (Mt 8:19). But when an unavoidable adversity lies across the path of our duty, to say at that time, "Arise, let us go to meet it"—instead of going out of our way to avoid it—this lets the world know that we love the Father. Now:

5.2.1. In these words he gave his disciples an encouragement to follow him. He did not say, "I must go," but, *Let us go.* He called them out to no hardships except what he himself has gone through before them as their leader.

5.2.2. He gave them an example, teaching them at all times to hold the things of this earth loosely, not to be tied to them, and to think and speak often of leaving them. When we sit down under Christ's shadow with delight and say, *It is good to be here* (Mt 17:4), we must still think about rising and leaving, about coming down the mountain.

CHAPTER 15

It is generally agreed that Christ's talk in this and the next chapter came at the end of the Last Supper. What he chose to speak about was very relevant for the present sad occasion of a farewell. His message in this chapter may be reduced to four words: fruit (vv. 1–8), love (vv. 9–17), hatred (vv. 18–25), the Comforter (vv. 26–27).

Verses 1–8

Here Christ spoke about the fruit, *the fruit of the Spirit* (Gal 5:22), using the metaphor of a vine. Notice:

1. The doctrine of this metaphor.

1.1. Jesus Christ is *the true vine.* He was pleased to speak of himself using lowly and humble metaphors.

1.1.1. He is the vine planted in the vineyard, not a spontaneous crop; he has been planted in the earth, because he is *the Word made flesh* (1:14). The vine is a spreading plant, and Christ will be known as *salvation to the ends of the earth* (Ac 13:47). The fruit of the vine honors God and cheers humanity (Jdg 9:13), and so does the fruit of Christ's mediation.

1.1.2. He is the true vine, as truth contrasts with what is false and deceitful. Unfruitful trees are said to "lie" (Hab 3:17, margin), but Christ is a vine that will not deceive.

1.2. Believers are branches of this vine, which presupposes that Christ is the root of the vine. The root supports the tree (Ro 11:18), circulates sap throughout it, and has everything it needs for flourishing and bearing fruit, and all our supports and supplies are in Christ. The vine has many branches, but, meeting in the root, they are all one vine. In the same way, all true Christians—however far from one another in place and opinion—still meet in Christ, the center of their unity.

1.3. The Father is the husbandman, the "land-worker." Although the earth is the Lord's (Ps 24:1), it produces no fruit for him unless he works the ground. God not only owns but also cares for the vine and all its branches. Never was any gardener so wise and watchful about his vineyard as God is about his church, which therefore must prosper.

2. The duty taught us by this metaphor.

2.1. We must be fruitful. We expect grapes from a vine, and we expect the Christian life from a Christian; the fruit of a Christian is a Christian attitude and a Christian way of living, honoring God and doing good. The disciples here, as Christians, must be fruitful in all the fruits of righteousness (Php 1:11), and as apostles they must be fruitful in spreading the fragrance of the knowledge of Christ (2Co 2:14). To persuade them, he pointed out:

2.1.1. The fate of the unfruitful (v. 2): they are taken away. It is shown here that many who pass for branches in Christ do not bear fruit. Being only tied to him by the thread of an outward profession, though they appear to be branches, they will soon be seen to be dry ones. Unfruitful professors of faith are unfaithful professors; they are mere professors and nothing more. It is threatened here that they will be taken away.

2.1.2. The promise made to the fruitful: He purgeth them, that they may bring forth more fruit. Further fruitfulness is the blessed reward of early fruitfulness. Even fruitful branches need to be purged (cleansed or pruned), to be even more fruitful. The best have in them something offensive, some thoughts, emotions, or attitudes that need to be pruned. These will be gradually taken away at the proper time. The pruning of fruitful branches is the concern and work of the great gardener.

2.1.3. The benefits that believers gain. Now you are clean (v. 3). Their community was clean now that Judas had been expelled. Until they were clear of him, they were not all clean (13:11). Each of them was clean, that is, sanctified, by the truth of Christ (17:17). This may be applied to all believers. The word of Christ is spoken to them; there is a cleansing power in the word. It cleanses as fire cleanses gold from dross, and as a doctor cleanses a wound.

2.1.4. The glory that will come to God from our fruitfulness (v. 8). If we bear much fruit:

2.1.4.1. Our Father will be glorified. The fruitfulness of all Christians is to the glory of God. By the renowned good works of Christians many are brought to glorify our Father who is in heaven (Mt 5:16).

2.1.4.2. We will show ourselves to be Christ's true disciples. We will both express our discipleship and adorn it, and we will be to our Master for a name and a praise (Jer 13:11). The more fruit we produce, that is, the more we overflow in what is good, the more he is glorified.

2.2. To be fruitful, we must remain in Christ. Here notice:

2.2.1. The duty commanded (v. 4): Abide in me, and I in you. Those who have come to Christ must remain in him: "Abide in me, and I in you. Abide in me, and then do not be afraid that I will not abide in you," because the fellowship between Christ and believers never fails on his side. The base of the branch remains in the vine, and the sap of the vine remains in the branch, and so there is a constant communication between them.

2.2.2. The necessity of our remaining in Christ in order to be fruitful (vv. 4–5): "You cannot bring forth fruit, except you abide in me, but if you do, you bring forth much fruit, for without me you can do nothing." Fruitfulness is so necessary for our happiness that the best argument to persuade us to remain in Christ is that there is no other way in which we can be fruitful. Remaining in Christ is necessary for us to do much good. Those who are constant in exercising faith in Christ and love toward him bring forth much fruit. A life of faith in the Son of God is incomparably the most excellent life a person can live in this world. It is necessary for our doing any good. It is the root and spring of all goodness: "Without me you can do nothing: not only no great thing, but nothing." Without Christ we can do nothing properly, nothing that will be fruit that pleases God or is useful for ourselves (2Co 3:5). We depend on Christ not only as the vine depends on the wall, for support, but also as the branch depends on the root, for sap.

2.2.3. The fatal consequences of abandoning Christ (v. 6): If any man abide not in me, he is cast forth as a branch. This is a description of the fearful state of hypocrites, who are not in Christ.

2.2.3.1. They are thrown away like dry, withered branches, which are cut off because they obstruct the growth of the tree. It is just for those who reject him to be rejected by him. Those who do not remain in Christ will be abandoned by him.

2.2.3.2. They are withered, like a branch broken off a tree. Those who do not remain in Christ wither and come to nothing in a short time. Those who bear no fruit will bear no leaves after a while.

2.2.3.3. Men gather them. Satan's agents and ambassadors pick them up and dispose of them easily.

2.2.3.4. They are burned; this follows as a matter of course, but it is added here emphatically, making the threat a terrible one.

2.2.4. The wonderful privilege that belongs to those who remain in Christ (v. 7): If my words abide in you, you shall ask what you will and it shall be done. See here:

2.2.4.1. How our union with Christ is maintained: If you abide in me; he had said before, and I in you; here he explained himself: and my words abide in you. It is in the word that we receive and embrace him, and so where the word of Christ dwells richly (Col 3:16), Christ dwells. If the word is at home in us, then we are remaining in Christ, and he in us.

2.2.4.2. How our fellowship with Christ is maintained: You shall ask what you will, and it shall be done to you. What can we want more than to have what we ask for? Those who remain in Christ, making him their heart's delight, will have, through Christ, their heart's desire. If we remain in Christ, and his word remains in us, we will not ask anything other than what is proper to be done for us. The promises are there for us, ready to be turned into prayers, and prayers that are so regulated will certainly be effective.

Verses 9–17

Christ, who is love itself, here discussed love under four headings.

1. The Father's love for him.

1.1. The Father loved him (v. 9): *As the Father hath loved me.* He was the Son of his love (Col 1:13, where "Son of his love" is an alternative translation to *his dear Son* [Ed.]). God *so loved the world* as to give his Son up for us all (3:16). Those whom God loves as a Father may spurn the hatred of the whole world.

1.2. He still remained in his Father's love. Because he continued to love his Father, he went cheerfully through his sufferings, and that was why his Father continued to love him.

1.3. He remained in his Father's love because he kept his Father's law: *I have kept my Father's commandments* and therefore *abide in his love.* Christ made atonement for us by obeying the law of redemption, and so he remained in God's love and restored us to it.

2. His own love for his disciples. Although he was leaving them, he still loved them. Notice here:

2.1. The pattern of this love: *As the Father has loved me, so have I loved you.* As the Father loved him, who was most worthy, so he loved them, who were most unworthy. The Father loved Christ as his Son, and Christ loved them as his children. The Father was pleased with him so that he could be pleased with us in him, and the Father loved him so that in him, as *the beloved*, he could *make us accepted* to himself (Eph 1:6).

2.2. The proofs and products of this love. We know that:

2.2.1. Christ loved his disciples by laying down his life for them (v. 13): *Greater love hath no man than this*, to *lay down his life for his friend.* This is the love with which *Christ hath loved us* (17:26). See the extent of the love of people for one another. The highest proof of it is laying down one's life for a friend to save their life. It is love at the highest level, which is *strong as death* (SS 8:6). See the excellence of the love of Christ. He has not only equaled but even exceeded the most noted love. Others have laid down their lives for their friends, but Christ laid down his for us *when we were enemies* (Ro 5:8, 10). "Those hearts that are not softened by such incomparable sweetness of divine love must be harder than iron or stone" (Calvin).

2.2.2. Christ loved his disciples by taking them into a covenant of friendship with him (vv. 14–15). The followers of Christ are the friends of Christ. Those who fulfill the duty of his servants are admitted and advanced to the honors of his friends. All Christ's servants have this honor. Christ takes believers to be his friends. Although they are often unfriendly toward him, he is a friend who loves at all times (Pr 17:17). He will not *call them servants*; he will *call them his friends.* He will not only love them but will let them know it. Although Christ called them his friends, they called themselves his servants: Peter, *a servant of Christ* (1Pe 1:1); also James (Jas 1:1). The more honor Christ puts on us, the more honor we should seek to give him; the higher we may be in his eyes, the lower we are to be in our own.

2.2.3. Christ loved his disciples by communicating his heart to them freely (v. 15). *All things that I have heard of my Father I have declared unto you.* Jesus Christ has faithfully handed to us what he received from the Father (1:18; Mt 11:27). Christ made known the great things about human redemption to his disciples so that they could make them known to others.

2.2.4. Christ loved his disciples by choosing and ordaining them (v. 16): *I have chosen you, and ordained you.* His love to them appeared in their:

2.2.4.1. Election to apostleship (6:70): *I have chosen you twelve.* It did not begin with them: "*You have not cho-*

sen me*; I first *chose you.*" It is right for Christ to be the One who chooses his own ministers; he continues to do it. Although ministers make that holy calling their own choice, Christ's choice comes before theirs and directs and determines it.

2.2.4.2. Ordination: *I have ordained you*; "*I have put you* into commission." He had great confidence in them. The treasure of the Gospel was committed to them:

2.2.4.2.1. So that it would be spread; *that you may go* from place to place throughout the world and *bring forth fruit* (v. 16). They were ordained not to sit back and do nothing but to be busy. They were ordained not to shadow-box but to be instrumental in bringing the nations to obey Christ (Ro 1:13). Those whom Christ ordains will find that their hard work is not in vain (1Co 15:58).

2.2.4.2.2. So that it would last forever. The church of Christ was not to be short-lived. It did not *come up in a night*, nor would it *perish in a night* (Jnh 4:10). As one generation of ministers and Christians has passed away, another has come. And so their fruit remains to this day and will remain as long as the earth.

2.2.4.3. Privileges that they enjoyed at the throne of grace: *Whatsoever you shall ask of my Father, in my name, he will give it you.* This probably refers firstly to the power of working miracles, which was to be drawn out by prayer. "Whatever help from heaven you need at any time, you have only to ask, and it will be yours." Three things are given us here to encourage us in prayer:

2.2.4.3.1. We have a God to go to who is a Father.

2.2.4.3.2. We come in a good name. Whatever reason we come to the throne of grace for, we may mention Christ's name in it with humble boldness.

2.2.4.3.3. A favorable answer is promised us. "What you come for will be given you."

3. The disciples' love for Christ. He encouraged them to do three things:

3.1. To remain in his love (v. 9). "Continue in your love for me, and in mine for you." All who love Christ should remain in their love for him. "*Continue in my love.* Keep up your love for me, and then all the troubles you meet with will be easy. Let not the troubles you meet with for Christ's sake quench your love for Christ, but rather let them stimulate it."

3.2. To let his joy remain in them and fill them (v. 11). He intended:

3.2.1. That his joy would remain in them. The words may be read either:

3.2.1.1. "That my joy in you may remain." If they produced a great deal of fruit and continued in his love, he would continue to rejoice in them as he had done. Fruitful and faithful disciples are the joy of the Lord Jesus. Or:

3.2.1.2. "That my joy, that is, your joy in me, may remain." It is the will of Christ that his disciples constantly and continually rejoice in him (Php 4:4). The joy of those who remain in Christ's love is a continual feast (Pr 15:15).

3.2.2. *That their joy might be full*—"not only that you may be full of joy but also that your joy in me and in my love may rise higher and higher until it reaches perfection." Those, and only those, who have Christ's joy remaining in them have their joy full; worldly joys soon surfeit but never satisfy. The intention of Christ in his word is to *fill the joy* of his people.

3.3. To show their love for him by keeping his commandments: *If you keep my commandments, you shall abide in my love* (v. 10). Notice here:

3.3.1. The promise: "*You shall abide in my love* as in a dwelling place, at home in Christ's love; you will remain in it as in a resting place, at ease in Christ's love; you will remain in it as in a stronghold, safe and secure in it. *You shall abide in my love*; you will have the grace and strength needed to persevere in loving me."

3.3.2. The condition of the promise: *If you keep my commandments.* The disciples were to keep Christ's commandments not only by constantly conforming to them themselves but also by faithfully passing them on to others; they were to keep them as trustees. To motivate them to keep his commandments, he urged:

3.3.2.1. His own example: *as I have kept my Father's commandments, and abide in his love* (v. 10).

3.3.2.2. The necessity of it to their share in him (v. 14): *"You are my friends if you do whatsoever I command you."* It is only those who prove themselves to be his obedient servants who will be counted as Christ's faithful friends, and it is only universal obedience to Christ that is acceptable obedience.

4. The disciples' love for one another. We must keep his commandments, and it is one of his commandments that we *love one another* (v. 12 and again v. 17). No one duty of religion is more frequently inculcated or more warmly urged on us by our Lord Jesus than that of mutual love.

4.1. It was commended here by Christ's example (v. 12): *as I have loved you. As*: we should love one another both in this way and from this motive. *Go you and do likewise* (Lk 10:37).

4.2. It is required by his command. Notice how differently it is expressed in v. 12 and v. 17, and both are emphatic.

4.2.1. *This is my commandment* (v. 12)—as if this were the most necessary of all the commandments. Christ, foreseeing the addiction of the Christian church to uncharitableness, has emphasized this command the most.

4.2.2. *These things I command you* (v. 17). He spoke as if he were about to ask them to do many things, but then he named only this one, *that you love one another*.

Verses 18–25

Here Christ spoke about hatred, which is the character and spirit of the Devil's kingdom, just as love is the hallmark of Christ's kingdom. Notice:

1. In whom this hatred is found—the world, the children of this world, as distinguished from the children of God. The fact that these are called "the world" shows:

1.1. Their number. There was a world of people who opposed Christ and Christianity. I fear that if an election were held between Christ and Satan, Satan would win decisively.

1.2. Their alliance. Jews and Gentiles who could agree on nothing else agreed to persecute Christ's ministers.

1.3. Their attitude and spirit. They are *men of the world* (Ps 17:13–14). Although the people of God are taught to hate the sins of sinners, they are not to hate their persons, but should love them and do good to everyone. A hateful, spiteful, and envious spirit is not the spirit of Christ, but of the world.

2. Against whom this hatred is directed—against the disciples of Christ, against Christ himself, and against the Father.

2.1. The world hates the disciples of Christ: *The world hateth you* (v. 19).

2.1.1. Notice how this is included here. Christ had expressed the great kindness he had for them as friends, but he gave them a *thorn in the flesh*, reproaches and persecutions for his sake (2Co 12:7, 10). He had appointed them to do their work, but he told them what hardships they would face in it. He had commanded them to *love*

one another, and they would certainly need to do so, since the world would hate them. Those who are among enemies should join together as one.

2.1.2. Notice what is included here.

2.1.2.1. The world's enmity toward the followers of Christ: it hated them. The world curses those whom Christ blesses. The favorites and heirs of heaven have never been the favorites of this world.

2.1.2.2. The results of that enmity (v. 20).

2.1.2.2.*1.* "One result of that enmity is that they will persecute you." It is the common fate of those who want to lead a godly life in Christ Jesus that they *suffer persecution* (2Ti 3:12). He sent them out as sheep among wolves.

2.1.2.2.*2.* Another result of their enmity was implied: that the world would reject their teaching. When Christ said, *If they have kept my sayings, they will keep yours*, he meant, "They will keep yours, and consider yours, no more than they have considered and kept mine."

2.1.2.3. The causes of that enmity. The world would hate them:

2.1.2.3.*1.* Because they did not belong to it (v. 19): "*If you were of the world, of its spirit, the world would love you* as its own." We are not to be surprised if those who are devoted to the world are treated by it as its friends. Nor are we to be surprised if those who are saved from the world are maligned by it as its enemies. The reason why Christ's disciples did not belong to the world was that Christ had chosen them out of it. The glory that all his disciples are intended for sets them above the world and so makes them the objects of its envy. The grace that they are endowed with sets them against the world. They testify against it and are not conformed to it. In all the disasters the world's hatred would bring on them, they would be supported by the knowledge that they were hated because they were the choice and the chosen ones of the Lord Jesus and did not belong to the world. Now:

2.1.2.3.*1.1.* Their having been chosen by Christ was no just cause for the world's hatred of them. If people hate us for something for which they should love and value us, then we have reason to pity them.

2.1.2.3.*1.2.* It was just cause for their own joy. Those whom the world hates may love themselves, because Christ loves them.

2.1.2.3.*2.* "Because you do belong to Christ" (v. 21): *For my name's sake.* Whatever is claimed, this is the basic point of the quarrel: the world hates Christ's disciples because they bear his name, and bear up his name in the world. It is the character of Christ's disciples that they stand up for his name. It has commonly been the fate of those who support Christ's name to suffer for it; they have to suffer *all these things. If you be reproached for the name of Christ, happy are you* (1Pe 4:14). *If we suffer with Christ*, and for Christ, *we shall reign with him* (2Ti 2:12).

2.1.2.3.*3.* It is the world's ignorance that is the true cause of its enmity toward the disciples of Christ (v. 21): *Because they know not him that sent me.* The world does not know God, and it does not know God as the One who sent our Lord Jesus. We do not rightly know God if we do not know him in Christ.

2.2. The world hates Christ himself. This was spoken of here for two purposes:

2.2.1. To lessen the trouble of his followers that arises from the world's hatred (v. 18): *You know that it hated me before you.* We read the phrase *before you* as showing priority of time, but it may be read as expressing his superiority over them: "You know that it hated me, the One who is before you, your 'first,' your leader and captain." If Christ was hated, can we expect that any good quality or merit of ours would protect us from hatred? If our Master, the One who founded our religion, met with so much opposition in establishing it, his servants and followers can expect nothing else in professing and spreading it. In this matter he referred them to his own word (v. 20): *Remember the word that I said unto you.* In this word there is:

2.2.1.1. A plain truth: *The servant is not greater than his Lord.* The servant is subordinate to his master. The clearest truths are sometimes the strongest arguments for the hardest duties.

2.2.1.2. A proper conclusion drawn from this: *"If they have persecuted me, they will also persecute you*; you may expect it because:

2.2.1.2.1. "You will do the same as I have done to provoke them; you will rebuke them for their sins and give them strict rules of holy living, which they will not listen to.

2.2.1.2.2. "You cannot do more than I have done to please them. Let no one wonder if they suffer harm for doing good." He added, *"If they have kept my sayings, they will keep yours also*; as there have been a few who have been persuaded by my preaching, so there will be a few who are persuaded by yours—a few."

2.2.2. To emphasize the evil of this unbelieving world and reveal its great sinfulness. The world generally has a bad name in Scripture, and nothing can give it a worse name than the fact that it hated Jesus Christ. He insisted on two things to emphasize the evil of those who hated him:

2.2.2.1. That there was the greatest possible reason why they should love him.

2.2.2.1.1. His words were those that deserved their love (v. 22): *"If I had not spoken unto them, they had not had* (they would not have been guilty of) *sin.* However, now they have no excuses for their sin." Notice here:

2.2.2.1.1.1. The advantage that those who enjoy the Gospel have: Christ comes and speaks to them in the Gospel; he spoke in person to the people of that generation, and he continues to speak to us. Every word of his carries with it a condescending tenderness, and one would have thought it would be capable of charming the deafest adder (Ps 58:4).

2.2.2.1.1.2. The excuse that those who do not enjoy the Gospel have: *"If I had not spoken to them, they had not had* (would not have been guilty of) *sin."*

2.2.2.1.1.2.1. Not this kind of sin. They would not have been accused of contempt for Christ. As *sin is not imputed where there is no law* (Ro 5:13), so unbelief is not imputed where there is no Gospel.

2.2.2.1.1.2.2. Not such a degree of sin. If they had not had the Gospel among them, their other sins would not have been so bad.

2.2.2.1.1.3. The greater guilt that lies on those to whom Christ has come and spoken in vain. *They have no cloak for their sin*; they are completely without excuse. The word of Christ strips sin of its cover-up, so that it may appear in its true colors as sin.

2.2.2.1.2. His works were those that deserved their love (v. 24): *"If I had not done among them* such works as *no other man ever did, they had not had* (would not have been guilty of) *sin*; their unbelief and enmity would have been excusable." But he produced satisfactory proofs of his divine mission, *works which no other man did.* This shows us:

2.2.2.1.2.1. As the Creator demonstrates his power and Godhead through his works (Ro 1:20), so does the

Redeemer. His miracles, his mercies, his works of wonder and his works of grace, proved he was sent by God on a kind mission.

2.2.2.1.2.2. Christ's works were such as *no man ever did.* No ordinary person, no one who did not have a commission from heaven and God with him, could perform miracles (3:2). And all his works were good works and works of mercy. One would have thought that a person who was so universally useful would have been universally loved, but even he was hated.

2.2.2.1.2.3. The works of Christ enhance the guilt of sinners' enmity to him. If they had only heard his words and not seen his works, unbelief might have pleaded lack of proof. But they saw that Christ sought to do them a kindness, and yet they hated him. We see in his word the great love with which he loved us (17:26) but are not persuaded by it.

2.2.2.2. That there was no reason at all why they should hate him (v. 25): *"This comes to pass that the word might be fulfilled which is written in their law, 'They hated me without a cause.'"*

2.2.2.2.1. Those who hate Christ hate him without any just cause; enmity toward Christ is unreasonable enmity. Christ was the greatest possible blessing to his country, but he was still hated. He did indeed testify that their works were evil, but he did it with the intention of making them good, and to hate him for this cause was to hate him without cause.

2.2.2.2.2. Here the Scripture was fulfilled. Those who hated Christ did not intend to fulfill the Scripture in their action, but God, in allowing it, had that in mind, and it confirms our faith in Christ as the Messiah that even this was foretold about him and, being foretold, was fulfilled in him. We must not think it strange or hard if it has a further fulfillment in us.

2.3. By hating Christ, the world hates God himself; this is said here twice (v. 23): *He that hateth me hateth my Father also.* Again in v. 24: they have *seen and hated both me and my Father.* This shows us:

2.3.1. There are those who hate God. Those who cannot bring themselves to deny that there is a God, but wish there were none, see and hate him.

2.3.2. Hatred of Christ will be judged to be hatred of God. Whatever reception the Son has, therefore, is what the Father has. Let an unbelieving world know that their enmity toward the Gospel of Christ will be looked on as enmity toward holy God himself, and let all who suffer for righteousness' sake take comfort from this; if God himself is hated in them, they need not be either ashamed of their cause or afraid of the outcome.

Verses 26–27

Christ had spoken about the great opposition his Gospel was likely to encounter; here he showed what effective provision would be made to support it, both by the main testimony of the Spirit (v. 26) and by the subordinate testimony of the apostles (v. 27).

1. He promised that the Holy Spirit would maintain the cause of Christ in the world: *When the Comforter is come, who proceedeth from the Father, and whom I will send, he shall testify of me.* We have more in this verse about the Holy Spirit than in any other verse in the Bible. Here is an account of him:

1.1. In his essence: he is *the Spirit of truth, who proceedeth from the Father.* He is spoken of as a distinct person, as a divine person, who *proceedeth from the Father.* The human spirit or breath, called the *breath of life* (Ge 2:7), may be said to proceed out of a human being; by modifying that breath into a voice, a person expresses their mind, and through it they sometimes exert their strength to blow out what they want to extinguish or blow up what they want to stir up. Similarly, the Holy Spirit is One who is released by divine light and whose source of energy is the divine power.

1.2. In his mission. He would come in a more plentiful outpouring of his gifts, graces, and power than he ever had before. *I will send him to you from the Father.* He had said (14:16), *I will pray the Father, and he shall send you the Comforter.* Here he said, *I will send him.* The Spirit was sent:

1.2.1. By Christ as Mediator, who now *ascended on high* to *give gifts unto men* (Eph 4:8).

1.2.2. From the Father: "Not only from heaven, my Father's house, but according to my Father's will and appointment."

1.2.3. To the apostles to instruct them in their preaching.

1.3. In his office and works, which are two:

1.3.1. One implied in the title given to him; he is the *Comforter* (Counselor or Advocate), an advocate for Christ, to maintain his cause against the world's faithlessness, and a comforter to the saints against the world's hatred.

1.3.2. Another expressed: *He shall testify of me.* He is not only an advocate but also a witness for Jesus Christ. The power of the ministry is derived from the Spirit, because he qualifies ministers, and the power of Christianity is also derived from the Spirit, because he sanctifies Christians, and in both he testifies about Christ.

2. He promised that the apostles, too, would have the honor of being Christ's witnesses (v. 27): "*And you also shall bear witness of me.*"

2.1. The apostles were appointed to be witnesses for Christ in the world. When he had said, *The Spirit shall testify,* he added, *And you also shall bear witness.* The Spirit's activity is not to replace ours, but to engage and encourage it. Although the Spirit testifies, ministers must also testify. This shows:

2.1.1. The work they were to undertake; they were to bear witness to the truth, the whole truth, and nothing but the truth about Christ. Although Christ's disciples fled at his trial before the high priest and Pilate, they were courageous in upholding the cause of Christ after the Spirit was poured out on them. The truth of the Christian religion was to be proved very much by the evidence of facts, especially by Christ's resurrection, of which the apostles were especially chosen witnesses (Ac 10:41). Christ's ministers are his witnesses.

2.1.2. The honor put on them in this—that they would be workers together with God (2Co 6:1). "The *Spirit shall testify of me,* and you also *shall bear witness.*" The fact that Christ had honored them might encourage them against the hatred and contempt of the world.

2.2. They were qualified to be so: *You have been with me from the beginning.* They not only heard his public sermons but also had been his constant private companions. Others saw the wonderful and merciful works that he did only in their own town and country; those who went around with him were witnesses of them all. Those who themselves have been with him through faith, hope, and love are best able to bear witness for Christ. Ministers must first *learn Christ* (Eph 4:20) and then preach him. Those who speak from their own personal experience speak best about the things of God. It is especially a great advantage to have known Christ from the beginning, to have been with him from the beginning of our lives. Coming to know Christ at an early

age in life and being with the Gospel of Christ constantly will make a person like a good householder, who brings out of his storehouse new and old things (Mt 13:52).

CHAPTER 16

1. Here are wounding words that announced the troubles that lay ahead of them (vv. 1–6). 2. Here are healing words that brought comfort and support to them—five healing words: 2.1. That he would send them the Comforter (vv. 7–15). 2.2. That he would come to them again at his resurrection (vv. 16–22). 2.3. That he would ensure a favorable response to all their prayers (vv. 23–27). 2.4. That he was now returning to his Father (vv. 28–32). 2.5. That whatever troubles they would meet, they would be sure of peace in him (v. 33).

Verses 1–6

Christ dealt faithfully with his disciples when he sent them out. He told them the worst, so that they would sit down and count the cost (Lk 14:28).

1. He gave them a reason why he had alarmed them in that way: *These things have I spoken unto you, that you should not be offended* (v. 1). The disciples of Christ tend to be offended by the cross; the offense of the cross is a dangerous temptation, even to good people, to turn their backs on the ways of God. By telling us about trouble in advance, our Lord Jesus intended to take away its terror, so that it would not come as a surprise to us. We can easily welcome a guest we expect, and because we are forewarned, we are forearmed.

2. He foretold particularly what they would suffer (v. 2): "Those who have power to do it will *put you out of their synagogues,* and *they shall kill you.*" Here are two swords drawn against the followers of the Lord Jesus:

2.1. The sword of church censure. "The Jewish leaders will *cast you out of their synagogues.*" At first, they flogged the disciples in their synagogues as those who despised the law (Mt 10:17), and finally they threw them out as incorrigible. Also, more generally: "They will drive you out of the congregation of Israel, and you will be pursued as an outlaw." Many good truths have been branded with a curse.

2.2. The sword of civil power. "When you are expelled as heretics, they *will kill you, and think they do God service.* You will find them truly cruel: they *will kill you.*" All the twelve apostles except John, it is said, were put to death. "You will find that they appear to be conscientious; they will think they are offering a service to God." It is possible for those who are real enemies of God's service to claim to have a great zeal for it. The Devil's work has many times been done by people wearing God's uniform, and it is common to support hostility to religion with a veneer of duty to God. God's people have suffered the greatest hardships from conscientious persecutors. This does not at all lessen the sin of the persecutors, but it does enhance the sufferings of the persecuted to die at the hand of an enemy of God.

3. He gave them the true reason for the world's enmity and rage against them (v. 3): "*These things will they do unto you, because they have not known the Father, nor me.*" Many who claim to know God are wretchedly ignorant of him. Those who are ignorant of Christ cannot have any right knowledge of God. Those who think it is acceptable to persecute good people are really very ignorant of God and Christ.

4. He told them why he was telling them about this now and had not told them sooner. He was telling them about it now (v. 4) not to discourage them, but so that, *when the time shall come, you may remember that I told you.*

When times of suffering come, it will be useful for us to remember what Christ has told us about suffering, so that the trouble may be less painful, not being a surprise. Why had he not told them about it sooner? *I spoke not this to you from the beginning because I was with you.* While he was with them, he bore the shock of the world's hatred and stood at the front in the battle.

5. He expressed a very warm concern about the present sadness of his disciples (vv. 5–6): "*Now I go my way to him that sent me,* and *none of you asketh me, Whither goest thou?* Instead of asking about what would comfort you, you ponder what looks sad."

5.1. He had told them that he was about to leave them: *Now I go my way.* He was not driven away forcefully, but departed voluntarily. He went *to him that sent him,* to give an account of his dealings with humanity.

5.2. He had told them what hard things they must suffer when he was gone. They would be tempted to think they had made a bad deal. Their master sympathized with them in this, but he still blamed them:

5.2.1. For neglecting the means of comfort: *None of you asks me, Whither goest thou?* Peter had introduced this question (13:36), and Thomas had seconded it (14:5), but they did not pursue it. Notice what a compassionate teacher Christ is. Many teachers will not be patient with learners who ask the same question twice; if a student cannot accept a matter quickly, let them go without it. But our Lord Jesus knows how to deal with infants, who must be taught with *precept upon precept* (Isa 28:10). Examining the intention and tendency of the darkest ways of Providence would help us to accept them. It will silence us if we ask, "Where do they come from?" but it will be very satisfactory if we ask, "Where are they going to?" for we know they *work for good* (Ro 8:28).

5.2.2. For being too intent on the occasions of their grief: *Sorrow had filled their hearts.* By looking only at what was against them and overlooking what was for them, they made themselves so full of sorrow that there was no room left for joy. It is the common fault and foolishness of melancholy Christians to dwell only on the dark side of the cloud (Ex 14:20). What filled the disciples' hearts with sorrow was too great an affection for this present life. They had great hopes of their Master's external kingdom and glory. Nothing spoils our joy in God more than the love of the world and—its consequence—the sorrow of the world.

Verses 7–15

Here are three things about the coming of the *Comforter* (Counselor):

1. Christ's departure was absolutely necessary to the Comforter's coming (v. 7). Christ saw that it was necessary to assert this with a more than usual solemnity: *I tell you the truth.*

1.1. "*It is expedient* not only for me but also *for you* (for your advantage) *that I go away.*" Our Lord Jesus always wants what is best for us, giving us the medicine we do not want to take, because he knows it is good for us.

1.2. It was good for them because it was so that the Spirit could be sent.

1.2.1. Christ's going was so that the Comforter could come. *If I go not away, the Comforter will not come.* The One who gives freely may recall one gift before he gives another, while we foolishly want to keep a firm grip on everything. The sending of the Spirit was to be the result of what Christ purchased, and that purchase was to be made through his death. It was to be an answer to his intercession in God's inner sanctuary. See 14:16. This gift must both be

paid for and prayed for by our Lord Jesus. The disciples must be weaned from his physical presence before they were properly prepared to receive the spiritual help and comforts of a new era. *If I depart, I will send him to you.* Even though he was departing, he would send the Comforter; in fact, he was departing deliberately to send him.

1.2.2. The presence of Christ's Spirit in his church is so much more desirable than his physical presence that it was really to our advantage that he go away. His physical presence could be only in one place at one time, but his Spirit is wherever *two or three are gathered in his name* (Mt 18:20). Christ's physical presence draws people's eyes; his Spirit draws their hearts.

2. The coming of the Spirit was absolutely necessary to continue Christ's interests on earth (v. 8): *And when he is come, he will reprove,* or, *he will "convince" the world,* about *sin, righteousness, and judgment.*

2.1. Notice here why he was sent.

2.1.1. To *reprove.* The Spirit, through the word and conscience, is One who rebukes.

2.1.2. To *convince.* This is a legal term, speaking of the work of the judge in summing up the evidence. He will convince, that is, "He will silence the enemies of Christ and his cause." The work of conviction is the work of the Spirit; people may open up a case, but only the Spirit can open up the heart. The Spirit is called the *Comforter* (v. 7), and here it is said, *He shall convince.* One would have thought that this would be cold comfort, but it is the Spirit's way first to convict and then to comfort, first to lay open the wound and then to apply healing medicines.

2.2. Notice whom the Spirit was to rebuke and convict: *the world.*

2.2.1. He would give the world the most powerful means of conviction, the Gospel, fully proved.

2.2.2. He would sufficiently provide for the silencing of the objections and prejudice of the world against the Gospel.

2.2.3. He would savingly convict many people in the world, some in every age, in every place. The Spirit will still work on this evil world, and the conviction of sinners is the comfort of faithful ministers.

2.3. Notice what the Spirit would convict the world of.

2.3.1. *Of sin, because they believe not on me* (v. 9). The Spirit is sent to convict sinners of sin, not merely to tell them about it. To convict them of it is to prove it to them and make them acknowledge it. The Spirit convinces them of the fact of sin, of the fault of sin, of the foolishness of sin, of the filth of sin, and, lastly, of the fruit of sin, that its end is death. The Spirit, in conviction, fastens especially on the sin of unbelief, of not believing in Christ:

2.3.1.1. As the great dominant sin. There was and is a world of people who do not believe in Jesus Christ, and they are not aware that it is their sin. When *God speaketh to us by his Son* (Heb 1:2), the people who *refuse him that speaketh* (Heb 12:25) break this law.

2.3.1.2. As the great destructive sin. Every sin is destructive in its own nature, but unbelief is a sin against God's remedy for sin.

2.3.1.3. As what lies at the root of all sin. The Spirit would convince the world that the true reason why sin reigned among them was that they were not united with Christ through faith.

2.3.2. *Of righteousness, because I go to my Father, and you see me no more* (v. 10). We may understand this as referring to:

2.3.2.1. Christ's personal righteousness. The Spirit would convict the world that Jesus of Nazareth was Christ the Righteous One, as the centurion acknowledged:

Certainly this was a righteous man (Lk 23:47). Now by what medium or argument would the Spirit convict people of the sincerity of the Lord Jesus? Their *seeing him no more* would contribute to some extent toward removing their prejudices. His *going to the Father* would mean full conviction. The coming of the Spirit, according to the promise, was proof of Christ's exaltation to God's *right hand* (Ac 2:33), and this demonstrated his righteousness.

2.3.2.2. Christ's righteousness that is communicated to us for our justification and salvation. The Spirit would convict people of this righteousness. Having shown them their need of a righteousness, in case this should drive them to despair, he would show them where it is to be found. It was hard to convict of this righteousness those who *went about to establish their own* (Ro 10:3), but the Spirit would do it. Christ's ascension is the great and proper argument that will convince people of this righteousness: *I go to the Father, and you shall see me no more.* Now that we are sure he is *at the right hand of God* (Mk 16:19), we are sure of being justified through him.

2.3.3. *Of judgment, because the prince of this world is judged* (v. 11). Notice here:

2.3.3.1. The Devil, *the prince of this world*, was judged, was revealed to be a great deceiver and destroyer. He was driven out of the souls of people by the grace of God working with the Gospel of Christ.

2.3.3.2. This was a good argument with which the Spirit would convince the world of judgment, that is:

2.3.3.2.1. Of indwelling holiness and sanctification (Mt 12:18). By *the judgment of the prince of this world*, it is clear that Christ is stronger than Satan.

2.3.3.2.2. Of a new and better dispensation of things. The Spirit would show that Christ's mission in coming into the world was to set things right in it. All would be well when the power of the one who caused trouble was broken. If Satan is subdued by Christ in this way, we may be sure no other power can oppose him.

3. The coming of the Spirit would be of inexpressible advantage to the disciples themselves. The Spirit has work to do not only on the enemies of Christ but also on his servants and agents, and so it was *expedient for them that he should go away* (v. 7).

3.1. He let them know how keenly he felt their present weakness (v. 12): *I have yet many things to say unto you, but you cannot bear them now.* Notice what a good teacher Christ is. There is no teacher like him (Job 36:22) for fullness. Treasures of wisdom and knowledge are hidden in him (Col 2:3). There is none like him for compassion; he wanted to tell them more about *the things concerning the kingdom of God*, but they could not bear it. It would have confused them and made them stumble rather than giving them any assurance.

3.2. He assured them of sufficient help. "*But when he, the Spirit of truth, is come*, all will be well." The Spirit would undertake to guide the apostles and glorify Christ.

3.2.1. To guide the apostles:

3.2.1.1. So that they did not lose their way: *He will guide you.* The Spirit is given to us to be our guide (Ro 8:14) to accompany us.

3.2.1.2. So that they did not come short of their destination: *He would guide them into all truth*, just as a skillful pilot guides a ship into the port it is bound for. To be led into a truth is more than to merely know it; it is to know it intimately and in personal experience. The expression refers to a gradual revelation of truth that shines more and more (Pr 4:18). But how into *all truth*?

3.2.1.2.1. Into the whole truth relating to their mission, whatever was necessary or useful for them to know.

The Spirit would teach them the truths they were to teach others.

3.2.1.2.2. Into nothing but the truth. All that *he shall guide you into* will be *truth* (1Jn 2:27).

3.2.1.2.2.1. "The Spirit will teach nothing but the truth, *for he shall not speak of himself*; rather, *whatsoever he shall hear, that*, and only that, *shall he speak*." The testimony of the Spirit in the word and by the apostles is what we may depend on. We may trust our souls to the Spirit's word. The testimony of the Spirit always agrees with the word of Christ, *for he does not speak of himself.* The word and spirit of a human being often disagree, but the eternal Word and the eternal Spirit never do.

3.2.1.2.2.2. "He will teach you all truth, because *he will show you things to come*." The Spirit was a Spirit of prophecy in the apostles. This brought a great assurance to the apostles' minds and was useful to them in their lives. We should not begrudge the fact that the Spirit does not show us things to come in this world now; let it be enough that the Spirit in the word has shown us things to come in the other world, which are our main concern.

3.2.2. To glorify Christ (vv. 14–15). Even the sending of the Spirit was the glorifying of Christ. It was the honor of the Redeemer that the Spirit was both sent in his name and sent on his mission, to continue and perfect his undertaking. All the gifts and graces of the Spirit, all the preaching and all the writing of the apostles, all the tongues and miracles, were to glorify Christ. The Spirit glorified Christ by leading his followers into *the truth as it is in Jesus* (Eph 4:21).

3.2.2.1. The Spirit would communicate the things of Christ to them: *He shall receive of mine, and shall show it unto you.* All that the Spirit shows us, all that he gives us for our strengthening and renewing, all belonged to Christ and was from him. The Spirit came not to set up a new kingdom, but to advance and establish the same kingdom that Christ had set up.

3.2.2.2. In doing so, he would communicate the things of God to us. *All things that the Father hath are mine.* All the grace and truth that God intended to show us he put into the hands of the Lord Jesus (Col 1:19). Spiritual blessings in heavenly things are given by the Father to the Son for us (Eph 1:3), and the Son entrusts the Spirit to convey them to us.

Verses 16–22

To encourage his sad disciples, our Lord Jesus promised here that he would come to them again. Notice:

1. The indication he gave them of the encouragement he intended for them (v. 16).

1.1. He told them that they would now soon lose sight of him: *A little while, and you shall not see me*, and so if they had any good question to ask him, they must ask quickly. It is good to consider how near to an end seasons of grace are, so that we may be prompted to make the most of them. They lost sight of Christ, first, at his death. The most that death does to our Christian friends is to remove them from our sight, only out of sight, but not out of mind. Christ also withdrew from them at his ascension, *out of their sight*; a cloud received him, and *they saw him no more* (Ac 1:9–10; 2Ki 2:12).

1.2. He told them that they would, however, quickly regain sight of him: *Again a little while, and you shall see me.* His farewell was not a final one. They would see him again:

1.2.1. At his resurrection, soon after his death, when *he showed himself alive* by many infallible proofs.

1.2.2. By the outpouring of the Spirit, soon after his ascension. The Spirit's coming was Christ's visit to his disciples, not a short-lived visit but a permanent one.

1.2.3. At his second coming.

1.3. He assigned the reason: *Because I go to the Father.* This refers to his going away at death and his return at his resurrection rather than his going away at his ascension and his return at the end of time, for it was his death that was their grief, not his ascension. This is what we may say about our ministers and Christian friends: *Yet a little while, and we shall not see them.* It is certain that we must part soon, but it will not be forever. It is only a "goodnight" to those whom we hope to see with *joy in the morning* (Ps 30:5).

2. The bewilderment of the disciples. They were at a loss as to what to make of it (vv. 17–18). *Some of them said among themselves, What is this that he saith to us?* Although Christ had often spoken to this effect before, they were still in the dark. Notice:

2.1. The disciples' weakness, in that they could not understand such a plain saying. Even though he had told them so often in clear terms that he would *be killed, and the third day rise again* (Mt 20:19), they still said, *We cannot tell* (understand) *what he saith*, for:

2.1.1. *Sorrow had filled their heart* (v. 6) and made them unready to receive the sense of comfort. Mistakes cause griefs, and griefs confirm mistakes, and so the cycle continues.

2.1.2. The idea of Christ's physical kingdom was so deeply rooted in them. When we think Scripture must be made to agree with the false ideas we have taken in, it is not surprising that we complain about its difficulty, but when our reasonings are captivated by revelation, the matter becomes easy.

2.1.3. It seems what puzzled them was the *little while.* They still could not conceive how he would leave them quickly. It is hard for us to appreciate that a change is close even when we know it will certainly come, and may come suddenly.

2.2. Their willingness to be instructed. When they were at a loss about the meaning of Christ's words, they discussed the matter together. Mutual conversation about divine things provides light from others so that we can improve our own understanding. We must ponder what we cannot explain, and wait *till God shall reveal even this unto us* (Php 3:15).

3. The further explanation of what Christ had said.

3.1. Notice here why Christ explained it (v. 19): because he *knew they were desirous to ask him.* We must bring to him the knots we cannot untie. Christ knew they wanted to ask him but were shy and ashamed to ask. Christ instructed those who he knew wanted to ask him, even though they did not ask. This show us what kind of people Christ will teach: the humble, who confess their ignorance, and the diligent, who use the means they already have at their disposal. "Are you asking questions? You will be taught."

3.2. Notice here how he explained it. He explained it in terms of their sorrow and joy, because we often measure things according to how they affect us (v. 20): *You shall weep and lament, but the world shall rejoice; and you shall be sorrowful, but your sorrow will be turned into joy.* Believers have joy or sorrow according to whether they have or have not seen Christ.

3.2.1. What Christ said here and in vv. 21–22 about their sorrow and joy is primarily to be understood as concerning the present state of the disciples, and so we have:

3.2.1.1. Their grief foretold: *You shall weep and lament, and you shall be sorrowful.* They wept for him because they loved him; the pain of our friends is painful to us too. They wept for themselves, because of their own loss. Christ has told his disciples in advance to expect sorrow so that they may treasure up comforts accordingly.

3.2.1.2. The world's joy: *But the world shall rejoice.* What is the grief of saints is the joy of sinners. Those who are strangers to Christ will continue in their worldly merriment. Those who are enemies to Christ will rejoice because they hope they have conquered him. Let it not come as a surprise to us if we see others triumphing when we are *trembling for the ark* (1Sa 4:13).

3.2.1.3. The return of joy to them in due time: *But your sorrow shall be turned into joy.* The sorrow of the true Christian *is but for a moment* (Job 20:5). *The disciples were glad when they saw the Lord* (20:20). His resurrection was life from the dead to them, and their sadness at Christ's sufferings was turned to joy. They were *sorrowful, and yet always rejoicing* (2Co 6:10); they had sad lives but also joyful hearts.

3.2.2. It may be applied to all the faithful followers of the Lamb.

3.2.2.1. Their condition and disposition are both mournful. Those who know Christ must be, as he was, *acquainted with grief* (Isa 53:3). They mourn with sufferers who mourn, and they mourn for sinners who do not mourn for themselves.

3.2.2.2. The world, at the same time, goes on with its merriment. Worldly happiness and pleasure are surely not the best things, for then the worst people would not have such a large share of them, and the favorites of heaven would not be such strangers to them.

3.2.2.3. Spiritual mourning will soon be turned to eternal rejoicing. Their sorrow will not only be followed by joy; it will be turned into joy. Christ illustrated this, for their encouragement, by the metaphor of a woman in labor, because it is the will of Christ that his people be an encouraged people.

3.2.2.3.1. Here is the metaphor itself (v. 21): *A woman, when she is in travail, hath sorrow because her hour is come, but as soon as she is delivered of the child, she remembers no more the anguish, for joy that a man is born into the world.* Notice:

3.2.2.3.1.1. The fruit of the curse according to the sentence: *In sorrow shalt thou bring forth* (Ge 3:16). Notice what this world is; all its roses are surrounded by thorns. This is the result of sin.

3.2.2.3.1.2. The fruit of the blessing: in *the joy there is for a child born into the world.* The fruit of a blessing is a matter of joy; the birth of a living child is the parents' joy. Although children bring great worries and uncertain comforts and often prove to be the greatest crosses, it is still natural for us to rejoice at their birth. Now this sets out:

3.2.2.3.1.2.1. The sorrows of Christ's disciples in this world; they are certain and sharp, but they do not last long, and they lead to joy.

3.2.2.3.1.2.2. Their joys after these sorrows, which will *wipe away all tears.* When disciples reap the fruit of all their services and sorrows, the toil and anguish of this world will not be remembered anymore.

3.2.2.3.2. Here is the application of this metaphor (v. 22): *You now have sorrow, but I will see you again.*

3.2.2.3.2.1. He again told them about their sorrow: "*You now therefore have sorrow*, because I am leaving you." Christ's withdrawal is a just cause of sadness to his disciples. When the sun sets, the sunflower will hang its head.

3.2.2.3.*2.2*. He assured them, in more detail than before, of a return of joy (Ps 30:5, 11). Three things commend the joy:

3.2.2.3.*2.2.1*. Its cause: *I will see you again.* Christ will graciously return to those who wait for him. When people are exalted, they scarcely look at their inferiors, but the exalted Jesus will come to his disciples. Christ's returns are returns of joy to all his disciples.

3.2.2.3.*2.2.2*. Its comfort: *Your heart shall rejoice.* Joy in the heart is solid, and not short-lived; it is special, sweet, guaranteed, and not easily interrupted.

3.2.2.3.*2.2.3*. Its continuation: *Your joy no man taketh from you.* People would attempt to take their joy away from them, but they would not be successful. Some understand this as referring to the eternal joy of those who are glorified. We are liable to be robbed of our joy on earth by a thousand events, but heavenly joys are eternal. I rather understand it as referring to the spiritual joys of those who are sanctified. The evil world could not rob them of their joy, because it could not *separate them from the love of Christ* (Ro 8:35); it could not rob them either of their God or of their *treasure in heaven* (Mt 19:21).

Verses 23–27

An answer to their questions was promised here. There are two ways of asking: asking by way of inquiry, which is the way those who are ignorant ask, and asking by way of request, which is the way those who are needy ask. Christ here addressed both their ignorance and their need.

1. By way of inquiry, they would have no need to ask (v. 23): *"In that day you shall ask me nothing."* You will not need to inquire." In the account of the Acts of the Apostles we rarely find them asking questions, because they were constantly under divine guidance. Asking questions implies that we are at a loss, or at least at a standstill. The best of us need to ask questions. Christ gave a reason why they would ask him nothing (v. 25): *"These things have I spoken unto you in proverbs* (figuratively), *but the time cometh when I shall show you plainly of the Father,* so that you will not need to ask any more questions."

1.1. The great thing Christ wanted to lead them into was the knowledge of God: *I will show you the Father.* When Christ wanted to express the greatest favor intended for his disciples, he told them that he would *show them plainly of the Father,* for what is the happiness of heaven except to see God directly and eternally?

1.2. He had spoken about this up to this time in proverbs. Christ had spoken many things very clearly to them, sometimes explaining his parables privately to the disciples (Mk 4:34), but:

1.2.1. Considering how slow and unwilling they were to receive what he said to them, he could be said to speak in proverbs; what he said to them was like words sealed in a scroll (Isa 29:11).

1.2.2. Comparing the revelations he had made to them with what he would give them, everything up to that time had been proverbial.

1.2.3. Confining the reference of the verse to what he had said about the Father, we may say that what he had said was relatively obscure compared with what would soon be revealed (Col 2:2).

1.3. He would speak to them *plainly* of the Father. When the Spirit was poured out, the apostles reached a much greater knowledge of divine things than they had before. However, this promise will have its complete fulfillment in heaven, where we will see the Father as he is. While we remain here, we have many questions to ask, but in that day we will see all things clearly and ask no more questions.

2. By way of request, they would ask nothing in vain. He assumed that all his disciples would give themselves to prayer. Their instruction, direction, strength, and success must be drawn in through prayer.

2.1. Here is an explicit promise of a gift (v. 23). The introduction to this promise leaves no room to question it: *Verily, verily, I say unto you.* The golden scepter is held out to us here, with the words, "What is your petition? It shall be granted" (Est 5:6; 7:2; 9:12). He said, *Whatsoever you shall ask the Father in my name, he will give it to you.* What more could we want? The promise is as clear as we could want.

2.1.1. We are here taught how to seek: we must ask the Father in Christ's name. Asking things of the Father indicates a sense of spiritual need and a desire for spiritual blessings, with a conviction that they are to be received only from God. Asking in Christ's name indicates an acknowledgment of our own unworthiness and a complete dependence on Christ.

2.1.2. We are told here how we will be successful: *He will give it to you.* What more can we wish for? Christ had promised them great enlightenment through the Spirit, but they must pray for it. They must continue to pray. Perfect possession is reserved for the land where we will rest; asking and receiving are the encouragement of the land where we are pilgrims.

2.2. Here is an invitation to them to submit their requests. It is thought enough if great people allow their inferiors to address them at all, but Christ calls on us to ask for things (v. 24).

2.2.1. He looked back on what they had done up to that time: *Hitherto have you asked nothing in my name.* This referred either:

2.2.1.1. To the subject of their prayers: "You have asked nothing comparatively, nothing compared with what you could have asked for." Notice what a generous giver our Lord Jesus is; he gives freely and generously, and is so far from finding fault with us for the frequency and generosity of his gifts that he rather rebukes us for the rarity and restrictiveness of our requests. Or:

2.2.1.2. To the name in which they prayed. They prayed many prayers but never prayed so expressly in the name of Christ as he was now instructing them to do, for he had not as yet offered up that great sacrifice because of which our prayers were to be accepted, the incense of which was to perfume all our devotions.

2.2.2. He looked forward to what they would do in the future: *Ask, and you shall receive, that your joy may be full.* He told them to ask for all that they needed and he had promised, and he assured them that they would receive. What we ask for from a gracious motive God will graciously give. Christ assured them that when they had asked and received, their *joy would be full.* This shows:

2.2.2.1. The blessed effect of the *prayer of faith* (Jas 5:15); it helps to fill up the *joy of faith* (Php 1:25). When we are told to *rejoice evermore,* it follows immediately, *Pray without ceasing* (1Th 5:16–17). Notice how high we are to aim in prayer—not only at peace but also at joy. Or:

2.2.2.2. The blessed effects of the favorable answer: "Ask, and you will receive what will fill your joy."

2.3. Here are the reasons why they could hope to be successful (vv. 26–27), which are summed up in short by the apostle (1Jn 2:1): *We have an advocate with the Father.*

2.3.1. We have an advocate: *I say not unto you that I will pray the Father for you.* He spoke as if they needed no further favors when he had effectively given them the gift of the Holy Spirit to make intercession within them, as if they had no further need for him to pray for them now, but we will find that he does more for us than he says he will.

2.3.2. We are dealing with a Father: *For the Father himself loveth you.* The disciples of Christ are loved by God himself. Notice that this is emphasized: *"The Father himself loveth you.* The Father himself, whose favor you have lost the right to, and with whom you need an advocate, he himself now loves you!" Notice:

2.3.2.1. Why the Father loved the disciples of Christ: *because you have loved me, and have believed that I came from God,* that is, "because you are my true disciples." Notice the character of Christ's disciples: they love him because they *believe he came from God.* Faith in Christ expresses itself in love for him (Gal 5:6). If we believe he is our Savior, we must love him as the One who is very kind to us. Notice with what respect Christ spoke about his disciples' love for him; he spoke about it as what commended them to his Father's favor. What an advantage Christ's faithful disciples have: the Father loves them because they love Christ.

2.3.2.2. What encouragement this gave them in prayer. They did not need to fear how they would fare when they came to the One who loved them. This warns us against having harsh thoughts of God. When we are taught that in prayer we must plead Christ's merit and intercession, it is not as if all the kindness were only in Christ. We owe Christ's merit to God's mercy in giving him for us. Let this promote and confirm in us good thoughts of God. Believers, who love Christ, should know that God loves them.

Verses 28–33

Christ here comforted his disciples with two things:

1. With an assurance that although he was leaving the world, he was returning to his Father (vv. 28–32), and in this assurance we have:

1.1. A clear declaration of Christ's mission from the Father and his return to him (v. 28): *I came forth from the Father, and am come into the world. Again, I leave the world and go to the Father.* This is the conclusion of the whole matter (Ecc 12:13).

1.1.1. These two great truths are here:

1.1.1.1. Contracted. Brief summaries of Christian teaching are very useful to beginners. The creeds and catechisms in which the principles of divine revelation are summarized have, like the beams of the sun concentrated in a magnifying glass, conveyed divine light and heat with a wonderful power.

1.1.1.2. Compared. There is a wonderful harmony in divine truths; they both confirm and illustrate one another; Christ's coming and his going do so. Christ had commended his disciples for believing that he came from God (v. 27), and he inferred from this the necessity of his returning to God. Making good use of what we already know and confess would help us to understand what seems difficult and doubtful.

1.1.2. If we ask where the Redeemer came from and where he went to, we are told:

1.1.2.1. That he *came from the Father* and came into this world, to this human race. His business was here, and he came here to attend to it. He left his home for this foreign country, his palace for this cottage.

1.1.2.2. That when he had completed his work on earth, he left the world and returned to his Father, though he is still spiritually present with his church and will be to the end.

1.2. The assurance the disciples felt at this declaration (vv. 29–30): *Lo, now speakest thou plainly.* It seems this

one word of Christ did them more good than all the rest. They improved in two matters:

1.2.1. In knowledge: *Lo, now speakest thou plainly.* Divine truths are most likely to do good when they are spoken clearly (1Co 2:4). When Christ speaks clearly to our souls, we have reason to rejoice in it.

1.2.2. In faith: *Now are we sure.* Notice:

1.2.2.1. What the object of their faith was: *We believe that thou camest forth from God.* He had said (v. 27) that they believed this; "Lord," they said, "we do believe it."

1.2.2.2. What was the motive of their faith—his omniscience. This proved he was a teacher who had come from God (3:2) and was more than a prophet (Mt 11:9), that he knew all things. Those who know Christ by experience know him the best; they can say about his power, "It works in me"; they can say about his love, "He has loved me." This confirmed the faith of the disciples here.

1.2.2.3. The words *and needest not that any man should ask thee* may show either:

1.2.2.3.1. Christ's aptness to teach. He comes before us with his instructions; he does not need to be harassed into speaking. Or:

1.2.2.3.2. His ability to teach. Even the best teachers can only answer what is spoken, but Christ can answer also what is thought.

1.3. The gentle rebuke Christ gave the disciples (vv. 31–32). Observing how they triumphed in what they had reached, he said, *"Do you now believe?* Unfortunately, you do not know your own weakness; you will very soon *be scattered every man to his own."* We have here:

1.3.1. A question intended to make them think: *"Do you now believe?* If now, then why not sooner?" Those who after many instructions and invitations are finally persuaded to believe have reason to be ashamed that they held out for so long. "If now, then why not always? When the hour of temptation comes, where will your faith be then?"

1.3.2. A prediction of their fall. In a short while they would all abandon him; this prediction was fulfilled that very night. They were scattered:

1.3.2.1. From one another; everyone fended for his own safety.

1.3.2.2. From him: *You shall leave me alone.* They should have been his witnesses at his trial, but they were *ashamed of his chain* (2Ti 1:16) and afraid of sharing with him in his sufferings, and left him completely alone. Many a good cause is deserted by its friends when it is damaged by its enemies. Those who are tested do not always prove to be trustworthy. If we find our friends unkind to us at any time, let us remember that Christ's friends were unkind to him. When they left him alone, they were scattered *every man to his own.* Everyone went his own way, where he thought he would be safest. Notice here:

1.3.2.2.1. Christ knew in advance that his disciples would abandon him at the critical moment, but he was still loving toward them. We are ready to say about some, "If we could have foreseen their ingratitude, we would not have been so generous in showing our favors to them." Christ did foresee theirs, but he was still kind toward them.

1.3.2.2.2. He told them about it: *"Do you now believe?* Do not have high thoughts about yourselves, but fear." Even when we are taking encouragement from our graces, it is good to remember the danger we are in from our corrupt hearts. When our faith is strong, and our love is aflame, and the evidence of our lives is clear, we cannot conclude from that that *tomorrow shall be as this day* (Isa 56:12). Even when we have most reason to think we are standing, we still have enough reason to watch out that we do not fall (1Co 10:12).

1.3.2.2.3. He spoke of it as very close. *The hour was already come* (v. 32) when they would be as ashamed of him as they had ever been fond of him.

1.3.3. An assurance of his own comfort nevertheless: *Yet I am not alone. The Father is with me.* We may consider this:

1.3.3.1. As a privilege distinctive to the Lord Jesus. The divine nature did not desert the human nature, but supported it. Even when he complained that his Father had forsaken him, he still called him *My God* (Mt 27:46), and he was so assured of God's favorable presence with him as to commit his Spirit into his hand (Lk 23:46). He had encouraged himself with this all along: *He that sent me is with me; the Father hath not left me alone* (8:29).

1.3.3.2. As a privilege common to all believers. When they are alone, they are not alone; the Father is with them. When solitude is their choice, when they are alone like Nathanael under the fig tree (1:48) or Peter on the roof (Ac 10:9–16), meditating and praying, the Father is with them. Those who speak with God in solitude are never less alone than when alone. A good God and a good heart are good company at any time. When solitude is the affliction of believers, on the other hand, even then they are not so much alone as they think they are, because the Father is with them. While we have God's favorable presence with us, we are happy, even if the whole world abandons us.

2. With a promise that they would have peace in him because of his victory over the world, whatever troubles they might encounter in it (v. 33): *"These things have I spoken, that in me you might have peace. In the world you shall have tribulation* (trouble), *but I have overcome the world."* Notice:

2.1. The purpose Christ aimed at: *That in him they might have peace.* His departure from them was really for the best. It is the will of Christ that his disciples have peace within themselves, no matter what their troubles may be outside. Peace in Christ is the only true peace. Through him we have peace with God, and so in him we have peace in our own minds. The word of Christ aims at giving believers peace.

2.2. The reception they were likely to meet with in the world. It has been the lot of Christ's disciples to have more or less trouble in this world. People persecute them because they are so good, and God corrects them because they are no better than they are. So between both *they shall have tribulation.*

2.3. The encouragement Christ gave them: *"But be of good cheer,* take heart, all will be well." In the middle of the troubles of this world it is the duty and privilege of Christ's disciples to remain cheerful. They should be truly sorrowful because of what the world is like, yet always rejoicing, always cheerful, even *in tribulation* (Ro 5:3).

2.4. The basis of that encouragement: *I have overcome the world.* Christ's victory is a Christian triumph. When he sends out his disciples to preach the Gospel to the whole world, he says, "Be *of good cheer; I have overcome the world."* He overcame the evil things of the world by submitting to them; he endured the cross, despising it and its shame (Heb 12:2). And he overcame the good things of the world by being wholly dead to them. Never was there such a conqueror of the world as Christ was, and we should be encouraged by it. Christ has overcome the world before us, and so we may look on it as a conquered enemy. He has conquered it for us, as the captain of our salvation (Heb 2:10). By his cross the world is *crucified to us* (Gal 6:14), which shows that it has been completely

conquered. Because Christ has overcome the world, believers have nothing to do but to make the most of that victory, and we do this by faith (1Jn 5:4). *We are more than conquerors through him that loved us* (Ro 8:37).

CHAPTER 17

This chapter is a prayer, the Lord Christ's prayer. This was properly and especially his, and it is also useful to us both to instruct and to encourage us in prayer. Notice: 1. The circumstances of the prayer (v. 1). 2. The prayer itself. 2.1. He prayed for himself (vv. 1–5). 2.2. He prayed for those who were his. See here: 2.2.1. The general pleas with which he introduced his requests for them (vv. 6–10). 2.2.2. His particular requests on their behalf: that they might be protected (vv. 11–16), that they might be sanctified (vv. 17–19), that they might be united (vv. 20–23), and that they might be glorified (vv. 24–26).

Verses 1–5

Here we have:

1. The circumstances of this prayer (v. 1). None of his prayers is recorded so fully as this one. Notice:

1.1. The time when he prayed this prayer: when he had *spoken these words,* had given the foregoing farewell message to his disciples.

1.1.1. It was a prayer after a sermon; when he had spoken from God to them, he turned to speak to God for them. Those we preach to we must also pray for. The word preached should be prayed over, for God *gives the increase* (1Co 3:7).

1.1.2. It was a prayer after the sacrament. He closed the ceremony with this prayer that God would preserve the good impressions of the ceremony on them.

1.1.3. It was a family prayer. Christ's disciples were his family, and to set a good example to heads of families, he blessed his household, praying for them and with them.

1.1.4. It was a parting prayer. When we and our friends are parting, it is good to part with prayer (Ac 20:36).

1.1.5. It was a prayer that introduced his sacrifice, which he was now about to offer on earth. Christ prayed, then, as a priest now offering a sacrifice whose merit would be the basis on which all prayers were to be offered.

1.1.6. It was a prayer that was an example of his intercession, which he always lives to make for us in the inner sanctuary behind the curtain (Heb 7:25).

1.2. The outward expression of passionate desire he used in this prayer: he *lifted up his eyes to heaven.* He consecrated this gesture to those who use it and justified it against those who mock it. *Sursum corda,* "Lift up your hearts [to heaven]," has been used since ancient times as a call to prayer.

2. The first part of the prayer itself, in which Christ prayed for himself.

2.1. He prayed to God as a Father: he *lifted up his eyes, and said, Father.* If God is our Father, we have free access to him and great expectations from him. Christ called him here *holy Father* (v. 11) and *righteous Father* (v. 25). It will be very useful to us in prayer to call God what we hope to find him to be.

2.2. He prayed for himself first. Although Christ, as God, was prayed to, Christ, as man, prayed. What he had purchased he must ask for; can we, then, expect to have what we have never deserved, but have lost the right to a thousand times, if we do not pray for it? Prayerful people may take encouragement in knowing that prayer was the messenger Christ sent on his own errands. There was a time when the One who is the advocate for us (1Jn 2:1) had his own cause to plead, and he was to seek this in the same way that is prescribed to us, *by prayers and supplications* (Heb 5:7). Christ began with prayer for himself and later prayed for his disciples; this charity must begin at home, though it must not end there. Christ was much shorter in his prayer for himself than in his prayer for his disciples. Our prayers for the church must not be crowded into a corner of our prayers. Now here are two petitions that Christ offered for himself, and these two were one petition, *Glorify thou me*, made twice because it has a double reference. It refers, first, to the further pursuit of his undertaking: *Glorify me, that I may glorify thee* (vv. 1–3). It refers, second, to the fulfillment of his work up to that time: *"Glorify me, for I have glorified thee.* I have done my part, and now, Lord, do yours" (vv. 4–5).

2.2.1. Christ prayed here to be glorified so that he might glorify God (v. 1): *Glorify thy Son, that thy Son may glorify thee*. Notice:

2.2.1.1. What he prayed for—that he would be glorified in this world. The Father glorified the Son on earth:

2.2.1.1.*1*. Even in his sufferings, by the signs and wonders that accompanied them.

2.2.1.1.*2*. Even by his sufferings; when he was crucified, he was exalted; he was glorified (13:31). It was in his cross that he conquered Satan and death; his thorns were a crown.

2.2.1.1.*3*. Much more after his sufferings, when he *raised him from the dead* (Ac 3:15).

2.2.1.2. What he pleaded to support this request.

2.2.1.2.*1*. Relationship: *Glorify thy Son*. Those who have received the adoption of sons may pray in faith for the inheritance of sons (Ro 8:15); if they are sanctified, then they are glorified.

2.2.1.2.*2*. The time: *The hour is come*. He had often said his hour had not yet come, but now it had come, and he knew it. Earlier he had called it *this hour* (12:27); here he called it *the hour*. The hour of the Redeemer's death, which was also the hour of the Redeemer's birth, was the most significant and remarkable hour, and without doubt the most critical, that there has ever been since the clock of time was first set in motion.

2.2.1.2.*2.1*. "*The hour is come* during which I need to be acknowledged." The decisive battle between heaven and hell was now to be fought. "*Now glorify thy Son*; now give him victory, now let your Son be upheld in such a way that he will neither fail nor be discouraged." The Father glorified his Son when he made the cross his triumphant chariot.

2.2.1.2.*2.2*. "*The hour is come* when I am to *be glorified*." Good Christians in the hour of testing, especially the hour of death, may plead in this way: "Now that the hour has come, stand by me, now or never: now that *the earthly tabernacle is to be dissolved* (2Co 5:1), *the hour is come that I should be glorified*."

2.2.1.2.*3*. The Father's own concern in him: *that thy Son may also glorify thee*. He desired to glorify the Father two ways:

2.2.1.2.*3.1*. By *the death of the cross* (Php 2:8). *Father, glorify thy name* expressed the great intention of his sufferings. "Father, acknowledge me in my suffering, so that I may honor you by them."

2.2.1.2.*3.2*. By *the teaching of the cross*, now soon to be declared to the world. If God had not glorified the crucified Christ by raising him from the dead, Christ's whole undertaking would have been crushed; therefore, *glorify me, that I may glorify thee*. Now he has taught us here:

2.2.1.2.*3.2.1*. What to consider and aim at in our prayers, that is, the honor of God. "Do this and that for

your servant so that your servant may glorify you. Give me health so that I may glorify you with my body; give me success so that I may glorify you with my possessions." *Hallowed be thy name* must be our first petition (Mt 6:9), which must determine our aim in all other petitions (1Pe 4:11).

2.2.1.2.*3.2.2*. What to expect and hope for. If we sincerely set ourselves to glorify our Father, he will give us the grace that he knows is sufficient for us and the opportunity that he considers convenient. However, if we secretly honor ourselves more than him, then instead of honoring ourselves, we will shame ourselves.

2.2.1.2.4. His commission (vv. 2–3). he desired to glorify his Father in conformity to the commission given him. Notice here the power of the Mediator:

2.2.1.2.*4.1*. The origin of his power: *Thou hast given him power*; he had received it from God, to whom all power belongs (Ps 62:11). The church's king is no usurper, as the prince of this world is (12:31; 14:30; 16:11); Christ's right to rule is incontestable.

2.2.1.2.*4.2*. The extent of his power: he has *power over all flesh*.

2.2.1.2.*4.2.1*. Over the whole human race. He has power over the world of spirits, but now, mediating between God and humanity, he pleaded his power over all flesh. Those whom he was to subdue and save were human beings; it was out of the human race that he had a remnant given him; and so all of that rank of beings were *put under his feet* (Heb 2:8).

2.2.1.2.*4.2.2*. Over the human race considered as corrupt and fallen. If humanity had not been flesh in this sense, we would not have needed a Redeemer. The Lord Jesus has all power over this sinful race, and *all judgment is committed to him* (5:22). Those whom he does not rule, he overrules (3:35; Ps 22:28; 72:8; Mt 28:18).

2.2.1.2.*4.3*. The grand intention and purpose of this power: *That he should give eternal life to as many as thou hast given him* (v. 2).

2.2.1.2.*4.3.1*. Here is the Father making over the chosen ones to the Redeemer and giving them to him as the crown and reward of his undertaking.

2.2.1.2.*4.3.2*. Here is the Son undertaking to protect the happiness of those who were given him so that he would *give eternal life to them*. He has lives and crowns to give: eternal lives that never die, immortal crowns that never fade (1Pe 5:4). Now consider how great and gracious the Lord Jesus is.

2.2.1.2.*4.3.2.1*. He sanctifies his people in this world, giving them spiritual life, which is eternal life in embryo (4:14). Grace in the soul is heaven in that soul.

2.2.1.2.*4.3.2.2*. He will glorify them in the other world; their happiness will be completed in the vision and full enjoyment of God. We are *called to his kingdom and glory* (1Th 2:12) and given new life for the inheritance (1Pe 1:3). What is executed last was its first intention, and that is eternal life.

2.2.1.2.*4.3.3*. Here is the subordination of the Redeemer's universal authority to this. Christ's power over human beings is in order to bring about the salvation of the children of God. The administration of the kingdoms of providence and grace are put into the same hands, so that all things may be made to work together for the good of those who have been called (Ro 8:28).

2.2.1.2.*4.4*. A further explication of this grand intention (v. 3): *This is life eternal, to know thee the only true God*. Here is:

2.2.1.2.*4.4.1*. The great purpose the Christian religion sets before us, and that is eternal life. He was to reveal this to all and to protect all who were given him. Through the Gospel *life and immortality are brought to light*, are brought to hand (2Ti 1:10).

2.2.1.2.4.4.2. The sure way of fulfilling this blessed end, which is by the right knowledge of God and Jesus Christ: *This is life eternal, to know thee*, which may be taken two ways:

2.2.1.2.4.4.2.1. *Life eternal* lies in the knowledge of God and Jesus Christ. Those who are brought into union with Christ and lead a life of fellowship with God in Christ will say, "If this is heaven, then heaven is sweet."

2.2.1.2.4.4.2.2. The knowledge of God and Christ leads to eternal life. The Christian religion shows us the way to heaven. Firstly, it points us to God, because Christ died to *bring us to God* (1Pe 3:18). He is the true God, the only true God; serving him is the only true religion. Secondly, it points us to Jesus Christ: *Jesus Christ, whom thou hast sent.* If people had continued to be innocent, the knowledge of the only true God would have been eternal life to them, but now that they are fallen, there must be something more. It is our concern, therefore, to know Christ as our Redeemer. It is eternal life to believe in Christ, and he has undertaken to give this. Those who know God and Christ are already in the city of eternal life.

2.2.2. Christ prayed here to be glorified in consideration of his having glorified the Father up to that time (vv. 4–5). The meaning of the former request was, "Glorify me in this world"; the meaning of this request was, "Glorify me in the other world." Notice:

2.2.2.1. With what comfort Christ reflected on the life he had lived on earth: *I have glorified thee, and finished my work.* He pleased himself by reviewing the service he had given his Father. This is recorded here:

2.2.2.1.1. For the honor of Christ, showing that his life on earth completely fulfilled in every respect the purpose of his coming into the world. Our Lord Jesus had work given him to do. His Father gave him his work, both appointing him to do it and helping him in it. He finished the work that was given him to do. It was as good as done; he was giving it its finishing touches. He glorified his Father in this. It is the glory of God that *his work is perfect* (Dt 32:4), and the same is the glory of the Redeemer; he will be the finisher of what he is the author of.

2.2.2.1.2. As an example to everyone, so that we may follow his example. We must make it our business to fulfill the work God has appointed for us to do. We must aim at the glory of God in everything. We must persevere in this to the end of our lives; we must not sit down until we have finished our work.

2.2.2.1.3. As an encouragement to all those who rest in him. If he has finished the work that was given him to do, then he is a complete Savior, One who did not do his work by halves.

2.2.2.2. With what confidence he expected *the joy set before him* (Heb 12:2) (v. 5): *Now, O Father, glorify thou me.*

2.2.2.2.1. See here what he prayed for: *Glorify thou me*; he had prayed this a moment ago (v. 1). What his Father had promised him he must still pray for; promises are not intended to replace prayers, but to be the guide of our desires and the basis of our hopes. See how the glory he prayed for is described.

2.2.2.2.1.1. It was a glory with God; not only, *Glorify my name on earth*, but also, *Glorify me with thine own self.* The prayers of the lower world draw out grace and peace *from God our Father and our Lord Jesus Christ* together (Gal 1:3), and this is how the Father has glorified him with himself.

2.2.2.2.1.2. It was the glory he had with God before the world was.

2.2.2.2.1.2.1. Jesus Christ, as God, existed *before the world was* (v. 5). Our religion acquaints us with One who *was before all things, and by whom all things consist* (Col 1:17).

2.2.2.2.1.2.2. His glory with the Father is from eternity. Christ undertook the work of redemption not because he needed glory—for he had a glory *with the Father before the world*—but because we needed glory.

2.2.2.2.1.2.3. Jesus Christ in his state of humiliation divested himself of this glory. He was *God manifested in the flesh* (1Ti 3:16), not in his glory.

2.2.2.2.1.2.4. In his exalted state he resumed this glory. He did not pray to be glorified with the rulers and leaders of the earth. No; the One who knows both worlds chose his advancement in the glory of the other world, as a world far exceeding all the glory of this one. *Let the same mind* be in us (Php 2:5). *Father, glorify thou me with thine own self.*

2.2.2.2.2. Notice what he pleaded here: *I have glorified thee*, and now, *glorify thou me.*

2.2.2.2.2.1. There was justice in it, and a wonderful harmony, *that if God was glorified in him*, God *would glorify him in himself.* If the Father was a gainer in his glory by the Son's humiliation, it was fitting that the Son be no loser by it, in the long run, in his glory.

2.2.2.2.2.2. It was according to the covenant between them. It was *for the joy set before him* that *he endured the cross* (Heb 12:2). He still expects the completing of his exaltation, because he perfected his undertaking (Heb 10:13).

2.2.2.2.2.3. It was the most proper evidence of his Father's accepting and approving the work he had finished. By the glorifying of Christ we are assured that God was satisfied, and in that a real demonstration was given that his Father was pleased with him as his dearly loved Son (Mt 3:17; 12:18; 17:5).

2.2.2.2.2.4. In this way we must be taught that only those who glorify God on earth will be glorified with the Father when they come to leave this world.

Verses 6–10

Having prayed for himself, Christ came next to pray for those who were his. Notice:

1. Whom he did not pray for (v. 9): *I pray not for the world.* This does not refer to the world of the human race in general—he prayed for that in v. 21: *That the world may believe that thou hast sent me.* If we take the world as the mass of unwinnowed grain on the threshing floor, and God loves it, and Christ prays for it and dies for it, *for a blessing is in it* (Isa 65:8), nevertheless, *the Lord perfectly knows those that are his* (2Ti 2:19), and so Christ considered especially those that were given him out of the world (v. 6). Then if we take the world as the remaining chaff, Christ did not pray for these; there are some things that he intercedes with God for on their behalf, as the gardener does for the reprieve of the barren tree (Lk 13:8–9), but he did not pray for them in this prayer. He did not say, "I am praying against the world," but, I *pray not for them*: "I pass them by and leave them to themselves." We who do not know who are chosen and who are passed by must *pray for all men* (1Ti 2:1, 4). While there is life, there is hope, and scope for prayer.

2. Whom he did pray for: his people. He prayed for those who had been given him, who received and believed the words of Christ (vv. 6, 8). He prayed also for all who would believe on him (v. 20). Not only the requests that

follow but also those that preceded must be interpreted to extend to all believers in every place and every age.

3. The general pleas with which he introduced his requests for them. They are five:

3.1. The commission he had received for them: *Thine they were, and thou gavest them me* (v. 6), and again (v. 9), *those whom thou hast given me.* Now:

3.1.1. This refers primarily to the disciples who then were. They were given him so that they would declare his Gospel and plant his church. When they left everything to follow him, this was the secret spring of that strange decision: they were given to him, for otherwise they would not have given themselves to him. The apostleship and ministry, which are Christ's gift to the church, were first the Father's gift to Jesus Christ. Christ received this gift for people so that he could give it to people (Ps 68:18; Eph 4:8, 11). This lays on ministers of the Gospel a great obligation to devote themselves completely to Christ's service, as those who have been *given to him.*

3.1.2. However, it is intended to extend to all the chosen ones, because they are elsewhere said to be given to Christ (6:37, 39). He showed here:

3.1.2.1. That the Father had authority to give them: *Thine they were,* his own in three ways:

3.1.2.1.*1.* They were creatures, whose lives and existence were therefore derived from him.

3.1.2.1.*2.* They were sinners, whose lives and existence had therefore been forfeited to him. It was a remnant of fallen humanity that was given to Christ to be redeemed, a remnant who could have been made a sacrifice to justice as easily as chosen to be the monuments of mercy.

3.1.2.1.*3.* They were chosen for him; they were set apart for God and were given to Christ as his agent. He insisted on this again (v. 7): "*All things whatsoever thou hast given me are of thee*; they all come from you, and so, Father, I bring them all to you, so that they may be all for you."

3.1.2.2. That he accordingly gave them to the Son. "*Thou gavest them to me,* as sheep are given to the shepherd, to be kept, as patients to the doctor, to be cured, as children to a teacher, to be educated." They were delivered to Christ so that the election of grace (Ro 11:5) would not be thwarted, so *that not one,* no, not *of the little ones, might perish* (Mt 18:14), and so that the work of Christ would not be fruitless. And he would *see of the travail of his soul and be satisfied* (Isa 53:10–11).

3.2. The care he had taken of them in order to teach them (v. 6): *I have manifested* (revealed) *thy name to them. I have given to them the words which thou gavest to me* (v. 8). Notice here:

3.2.1. The great purpose of Christ's message, which was to reveal God's name, to declare him so that he would be better loved and worshiped.

3.2.2. His faithful fulfillment of this work: "I have done it." His faithfulness appears:

3.2.2.1. In the truth of his teaching. It corresponded exactly to the instructions he received from his Father. In wording their message, ministers must consider *the words which the Holy Spirit teaches* (1Co 2:13).

3.2.2.2. In the tendency of his teaching, which was to reveal God's name. He did not seek things for himself, but aimed to exalt his Father. This shows us:

3.2.2.2.*1.* It is Christ's right to reveal God's name to the souls of his people. Only he knows the Father and is therefore able to open up the truth, and only he has access to human spirits and is therefore able to open up people's understanding. Ministers may *publish the name of the Lord,* but only Christ can reveal that name. Ministers may

speak the words of God to us, but only Christ can *give us* his words, can put them in us.

3.2.2.2.*2.* Sooner or later, Christ will reveal God's name to all who were given him.

3.3. The good effect of the care he had taken of them (v. 6): *They have kept thy word* (v. 7); *they have known that all things are of thee* (v. 8); *they have received thy words, and have known surely that I came out from thee, and have believed that thou didst send me.* Notice here:

3.3.1. What success the teaching of Christ had among those who were given to him.

3.3.1.1. "They have received the words that I gave them, as the ground receives the seed and as the earth drinks in the rain." The word was an engrafted word to them (Jas 1:21).

3.3.1.2. "*They have kept thy word*; they have conformed to it." Christ's commandment is kept only when it is obeyed. It was necessary that these disciples *keep what was committed to them* (2Ti 1:14), because it was to be passed on by them to every place for every age.

3.3.1.3. "They have understood the word; they have been aware *that all things whatsoever thou hast given me are of thee.*" All Christ's work and powers, all the gifts of the Spirit, all his graces and comforts—all came from God; they were designed by his grace and for his own glory in human salvation. We may trust even our lives, therefore, to Christ's mediation. If the righteousness is appointed by God, we will be justified; if the grace has been dispensed by him, we will be sanctified.

3.3.1.4. They had set their seal to it: *They have known surely that I came out from God* (v. 8). See here:

3.3.1.4.*1.* What it is to believe: to know with certainty that something is true. We may know with certainty what we neither do nor can know fully. *We walk by faith,* which knows surely, but *not* yet *by sight* (2Co 5:7), which knows clearly.

3.3.1.4.*2.* What we are to believe: *that Jesus Christ came out from God* and that God sent him. All the teachings of Christ are therefore to be received as divine truths, and all his promises depended on as divine securities.

3.3.2. How Jesus Christ spoke about this here:

3.3.2.1. As One who was pleased with it himself. The disciples' constant loyalty to him, their gradual improvements, and finally their great achievements were his joy. Christ is a teacher who delights in the proficiency of his students. He accepts the sincerity of their faith and graciously passes over its weakness.

3.3.2.2. As One who was pleading it with his Father. He was praying for those who were given to him, and he pleaded that they had given themselves to him. When people keep Christ's word and believe in him, leave it to him to commend them, and, what is more, to recommend them to his Father.

3.4. The Father's own interest in them (v. 9): *I pray for them, for they are thine. All mine are thine, and thine are mine.* Notice:

3.4.1. The plea particularly urged for his disciples: *They are thine.* The giving of the chosen ones to Christ was so far from making them less the Father's that it was in order to make them even more so. Christ has *redeemed us* not only to himself but also *to God* (Rev 5:9–10). This is a good plea in prayer, and Christ here pleaded it: *They are thine.* We may plead for ourselves, "I am thine, save me" (Ps 119:94), and for others, as Moses did, "*They are thy people*" (Ex 32:11). They are yours. Will you not protect them, so that they may not be defeated by the Devil and the world? They are yours; acknowledge them as yours."

3.4.2. The foundation on which this plea was based: *All mine are thine, and thine are mine* (v. 10). This shows that the Father and Son are one in essence and one in interest.

3.4.2.1. What the Father has as Creator is handed over to the Son. *All things are delivered to him* (Mt 11:27); and nothing and no one is excluded except the One who himself *put all things under him* (1Co 15:27).

3.4.2.2. What the Son has as Redeemer is intended for the Father. All the benefits of redemption purchased by the Son are intended for the Father's praise: *All mine are thine.* The Son acknowledges none as his who are not devoted to the service of the Father. In a limited sense, every true believer may say, *All thine are mine.* In an unlimited sense every true believer does say, Lord, *all mine are thine*; all is laid at his feet, to be useful to him. "Lord, take care of what I have, because it is all yours."

3.5. His own interest in them: *I am glorified in them.*

3.5.1. *I have been glorified in them.* What little honor Christ had in this world was among his disciples, and that was why he said, *I pray for them.*

3.5.2. "*I am to be glorified in them*; they are to lift up my name. *I am glorified in them*, and that is why I concern myself for them. That is also why I commit them to the Father, who has committed himself to glorify the Son and, on this account, will look graciously at those in whom the Son is glorified."

Verses 11–16

After the general pleas came the particular requests he made for them. Let us consider:

1. Three general observations concerning these requests:

1.1. They all related to spiritual blessings in heavenly things (Eph 1:3). The prosperity of the soul is the best form of prosperity.

1.2. These blessings were such blessings as were suited to their present situation. Christ's intercession is always relevant. Our *advocate with the Father* (1Jn 2:1) knows all the details of our needs.

1.3. He was generous and comprehensive in the petitions, to teach us to be fervent and bold in prayer, wrestling like Jacob—*I will not let thee go, except thou bless me* (Ge 32:26).

2. The first request he made for his disciples, which was for their preservation (vv. 11–16), and to this end he committed them all to his Father's custody: *Keep them from the world. Keep* implies that there is danger, and their danger arose from the world; he begged that they would be protected from the evil of this. There were two ways of their being saved from the world:

2.1. By taking them out of it, and he did not pray that they would be saved in such a way: *I pray not that thou shouldest take them out of the world.*

2.1.1. "I do not pray that they may be quickly removed by death." If the world would be troublesome to them, the most certain way to protect them would be to move them quickly out of it. Send chariots and horses of fire for them to take them to heaven (2Ki 2:11–12). Christ did not want to pray that for his disciples, for two reasons:

2.1.1.1. Because he came to conquer those excessive passions that make people impatient with life and seek death. It is his will that we take up our cross (Mt 16:24), not leave it behind.

2.1.1.2. Because he had work for them to do in the world, and so the world could hardly spare them. Out of pity to this dark world, Christ did not want to have these lights removed from it, therefore, especially for the sake

of those in the world who were to *believe in him through their word* (v. 20). They must each in his own order die a martyr, but not until they had finished their testimony (Rev 11:7). The taking of good people out of the world is by no means to be desired. Although Christ loves his disciples, he does not immediately send for them to come to heaven, but leaves them for some time in this world, so that they may be ready for heaven. Many good people are spared for life because they can hardly be spared to die.

2.1.2. "I do not pray that they may be exempt from the troubles of this world and taken out of its toil and terror." "Not that, being freed from all trouble, they may bask in luxurious ease, but that by the help of God they may be protected in scenes of danger" (Calvin). Not that they may be kept from every conflict with the world, but that they may not be overcome by it. It is more the honor of a Christian soldier to overcome the world by faith than to take a monastic vow and retreat from it; it is more for the honor of Christ to serve him in a city than to serve him in a cell.

2.2. By keeping them from the corruption that is in the world (vv. 11, 15). Here are three aspects of this petition:

2.2.1. *Holy Father, keep those whom thou hast given me.*

2.2.1.1. Christ was now leaving them. He committed them here to the care of his Father. It is the inexpressible comfort of all believers that Christ himself has committed them to the care of God. Those the almighty God protects must remain safe, and he must protect those whom the Son of his love (Col 1:13) commits to him.

2.2.1.1.*1.* He put them under divine protection here. The wonderful preservation of the Gospel ministry and the Gospel church in the world to this day is owing to this prayer.

2.2.1.1.*2.* He put them under the divine teaching. We need God's power not only to put us into a state of grace but also to keep us in it.

2.2.1.2. The titles he gave to the One he prayed to and to those he prayed for reinforced the petition.

2.2.1.2.*1.* He spoke to God as a *holy Father* (v. 11). If he is a holy God and hates sin, he will make his people holy and keep them from sin, which they also hate and dread as the greatest evil. If he is a Father, he will take care of his own children; who else would?

2.2.1.2.*2.* He spoke about the disciples as those whom the Father had *given him.* What we receive as our Father's gifts, we may comfortably give to our Father's care.

2.2.2. *Keep* them *through thine own name*: "keep them for your name's sake." Those who are really more concerned for the honor of God's name than for any interests of their own may plead this with assurance. Or, "Keep them in your name. Keep them in the knowledge and fear of your name; keep them in the profession and service of your name, whatever it may cost them." Or, "Keep them by or through thy name. Keep them by your own power, in your own hand. Let your name be their strong tower (Pr 18:10)."

2.2.3. *Keep them from the evil.* He had taught them to pray daily, *Deliver us from evil* (Mt 6:13), and this would encourage them to pray. "Keep them from the evil one. Keep them from Satan as a tempter, so that their faith may not fail (Lk 22:31–32). Keep them from him as a destroyer. Keep them from the evil thing, that is, sin. Keep them, so that they will not commit evil or do anything wrong. Keep them from both the evil of the world and the evil of their trouble in it, so that it may have no sting in it." He did not pray that they might be protected from suffering, but that they might be protected through it.

3. The reasons with which he backed up these requests, which are five:

3.1. He pleaded that up to that time he had kept them (v. 12): "*While I was with them in the world, I have kept them in thy name*; they are all safe, and none of them is missing, except *the son of perdition*; he is lost, so that the Scripture may be fulfilled." Notice:

3.1.1. Christ's faithful discharge of his work: while he was with them, he kept them, and his care concerning them was not in vain. Many people who followed him for a while fell away for some reason or other, but he kept the Twelve so that they did not go away (6:66–69). *While he was with them*, he kept them visibly. When he had gone from them, they must be kept in a more spiritual manner. Comforts and supports are sometimes given and sometimes withheld, but when they are withdrawn, his people are not *left comfortless* (14:18). What Christ said here is true of all believers as long as they are in this world; Christ keeps them in God's name. They were weak, he said, and could not keep themselves, yet in God's account they were valuable and worth protecting; they were his treasure, his jewels. Their salvation was intended, because this was the reason for which they were kept (1Pe 1:5). The righteous are preserved for the day of bliss. The disciples were the responsibility of the Lord Jesus; he kept them as the good shepherd keeps the sheep.

3.1.2. The satisfying account he gave of his undertaking: *None of them is lost*. Jesus Christ will certainly protect all who were given to him; they may think they are lost, and may be nearly lost when they are in imminent danger, but it is the Father's will that he lose none, and he will lose none.

3.1.3. A mark put on Judas, as not belonging to those whom Christ had undertaken to keep. He was among those who were given to Christ but did not belong to them. However, the apostasy and ruin of Judas were no disgrace at all to his Teacher or his Teacher's family. He was *the son of perdition* and therefore did not belong to those who were given to Christ to be kept. It is a fearful thought that one of the apostles proved to be a son of perdition. No one's place or name in the church will protect them from ruin if their heart is not right with God. The Scripture was fulfilled; the sin of Judas was foreseen and foretold, and the event would certainly follow the prediction as a consequence, though it cannot be said necessarily to follow it as an effect.

3.2. He pleaded that he now had to leave them (v. 11): "Keep them now. Keep them, so *that they may be one* with us *as we are* with each other." Notice:

3.2.1. With what delight he spoke about his own departure (see Lk 9:31). He expressed himself about it with an air of triumph and exultation, with reference both to the world he was leaving and to the world he was moving to. "*Now I am no more in the world*. I am now saying farewell to this offensive, troublesome world. Now the welcome hour has come when I will be *no more in it*." It should be a delight to those who have their home in the other world to think of being in this world no more. What is there here that we should stay for? *Now I come to thee*. Yet to get clear of this world is only one half of the comfort of a dying Christ, of a dying Christian; the far better half is to think about going to the Father. Those who love God must be pleased to think about coming to him, even though it is through the valley of the shadow of death (Ps 23:4). When we go to be *absent from the body*, it is to be *present with the Lord* (2Co 5:8), like children brought from school to their parents' home.

3.2.2. With what a tender concern he spoke about those whom he left behind: "*But these are in the world. Holy*

Father, keep them; they will miss my presence, so let them have yours. They now have greater need than ever to be protected, and will be lost if you do not protect them." When our Lord Jesus was going to the Father, he still kept with him a tender concern for his own who were in the world. When he is out of their sight, they are not out of his sight, and much less out of his mind. When Christ wanted to express the greatest need his disciples had of divine protection, he said only, *They are in the world*; this shows enough danger to those who are destined for heaven.

3.3. He pleaded what assurance it would be to them to know they were safe and secure and what assurance it would be to him to see them at peace: *I speak this, that they may have my joy fulfilled in themselves* (v. 13).

3.3.1. Christ passionately desired fullness of joy for his disciples, because it is his will that they always rejoice. When they thought their joy in him had come to an end, it was then advanced closer to perfection than it had ever been, and they were fuller of it. We are taught here to base our joy in Christ. Christ is a Christian's joy, their *chief joy* (Ps 137:6). Joy in the world is withering; joy in Christ is eternal, as he is. We are taught to build up our joy with diligence—no part of the Christian life is urged on us more passionately (Php 3:1; 4:4)—and to aim at the perfection of this joy.

3.3.2. To this end, he solemnly committed them into his Father's care and keeping: *These things I speak in the world*. His intercession in heaven would have been as effective, but saying this in the world would be a greater assurance and encouragement to them and would enable them to *be joyful in tribulation* (2Co 7:4). This shows us:

3.3.2.1. Christ has not only treasured up strength and assurance for his people; he has also given strength and assurance to them. He condescended here to declare his last will and testament, and—what many people who make a will are reluctant to do—told them what legacies he had left them and how well they were protected.

3.3.2.2. Christ's intercession for us is enough to make our joy in him full; nothing will more effectively silence all our fears and mistrust than knowing that he always appears in the presence of God for us. See Heb 7:25.

3.4. He pleaded the mistreatment they were likely to face in the world for his sake (v. 14): "*I have given them thy word, and they have received it*, and that is why *the world hath hated them*, because they are *not of the world*, any more than I am." We have here:

3.4.1. The world's hostility toward Christ's followers. Even though as yet they had given only a little opposition to the world, it still hated them, and it would do so much more when by their more extensive preaching of the Gospel they would *turn the world upside down* (Ac 17:6). "Father, stand by as their friend," said Christ. "Let them have your love, for the world's hatred is passed on as an inheritance to them." It is God's honor to take the part of the weaker side and to help the helpless.

3.4.2. The reasons for this hostility, which strengthened the plea.

3.4.2.1. One reason was that the disciples had accepted the word of God by the hand of Christ when most of the world rejected it. Those who receive Christ's goodwill and good word must expect the world's ill will and adverse words. Gospel ministers have been especially hated by the world, because they call people out of the world, separate them from it, and so condemn the world. "*Father, keep them*; they are sufferers for you." Those who keep Christ's command to endure patiently are entitled to special protection in the hour of temptation (Rev 3:10). The cause that makes a martyr may well make a joyful sufferer.

3.4.2.2. Another reason was more explicit; the world hated them because they *were not of the world*. Those to whom the word of Christ comes in power do not belong to the world, and that is why the world bears a grudge against them.

3.5. He pleaded that they had conformed to him by a holy nonconformity to the world (v. 16): "Father, protect them; *they are not of the world, even as I am not of the world*." Those who may commit themselves in faith to God's care are all those:

3.5.1. Who are *as Christ was in this world*. God will love those who are like Christ.

3.5.2. Who do not commit themselves to the world's interests. Notice:

3.5.2.1. Jesus Christ did not belong to this world; he never had belonged to it. This shows:

3.5.2.1.1. His state: he was not one of the world's favorites or darlings; he had no worldly possessions, not even a place to lay his head (Mt 8:20), no worldly power.

3.5.2.1.2. His Spirit: he was completely dead to the world; the prince of this world *had nothing in him* (14:30).

3.5.2.2. That is why true Christians do not belong to this world. They are bound to be despised by the world; they are not in favor with the world any more than their Teacher before them was. They have the privilege of being saved from the world. It is their duty and character to be dead to the world. Christ's first disciples were weak and had many failings, but he could say this for them: they were not part of this world; and that was why he commended them to the care of heaven.

Verses 17–19

The next thing he prayed for them was that they would be sanctified, not only protected from evil but also made good.

1. Here is the petition (v. 17): *Sanctify them through thy truth; thy word is truth*. He wanted them to be sanctified, to be made holy:

1.1. As Christians (1Th 5:23). Notice:

1.1.1. The grace desired—sanctification. He prayed, "*Father, sanctify them*. Confirm the work of sanctification in them; reinforce their good resolutions. Carry on that good work in them; let the light shine more and more (Pr 4:18). Complete it; sanctify them throughout and to the end." Out of shame, he could not acknowledge them as his, either here or in the future, or present them to his Father, if they were not sanctified. Those who through grace are sanctified need to be sanctified more and more. Not going forward is going backward; *he that is holy must be holy still*, more holy still (Rev 22:11). It is God who sanctifies as well as God who justifies (2Co 5:5).

1.1.2. The means of giving this grace—*through thy truth; thy word is truth*. Divine revelation, as it now stands in the written word, is not only pure truth with nothing else mixed in; it is also whole truth without deficiency. This word of truth would be the outward and ordinary means of our sanctification. It is the seed of the new birth (1Pe 1:23) and the food of the new life (1Pe 2:1–2).

1.2. As ministers. "*Sanctify them*; let their call to apostleship be confirmed in heaven. Qualify them for the office with Christian graces and gifts of ministry. Set them apart for that work. I have called them, and they have agreed to undertake it; Father, say Amen to it. Recognize them in that work; let your hand accompany them. Sanctify them to your truth, to preach your truth to the world." Jesus Christ intercedes for his ministers with special concern, commending to his Father's grace those stars

he carries in his right hand (Rev 1:20). The great thing to be asked from God for Gospel ministers is that they may be sanctified, completely devoted to God and knowing in their own experience the influence of the word on their own hearts that they preach to others.

2. We have here two pleas to support the petition:

2.1. The mission the disciples had from him (v. 18): "*As thou hast sent me into the world*, so now *I have sent them into the world*."

2.1.1. Christ spoke with great assurance of his own mission: *Thou hast sent me into the world*. He was sent by God to say what he said, do what he did, and be what he is to those who believe on him.

2.1.2. He spoke of the commission he had given his disciples: "*So have I sent them* on the same mission," to preach the same message that he preached. He gave them their commission (20:21) with reference to his own, and it exalted their work that it came from Christ and that there was some similarity between the commission given to the ministers of reconciliation and the one given to the Mediator. The difference was that they were sent as servants, whereas he was sent as a Son (Heb 3:5–6). Christ was so concerned for them because he himself had put them into a difficult work, which required great abilities to be properly fulfilled. Christ will stand by those he sends. He will equip us to do the work he calls us to, and he will support us as we fulfill that work. He committed them to his Father because he was concerned for their cause, since their mission was in pursuit of his. The Father *sanctified him* when *he sent him into the world* (10:36). Now, because they were sent as he was, let them also be sanctified.

2.2. The merit he had for them (v. 19): *For their sakes I sanctify myself*. Notice:

2.2.1. Christ's designation of himself to the work of Mediator: *I sanctified myself*. He devoted himself wholly to this work and every aspect of it, especially now that he was now about to *offer up himself without spot unto God, by the eternal Spirit* (Heb 9:14). He pleaded this with his Father, for his intercession was made on the basis of his atonement.

2.2.2. Christ's intention of kindness toward his disciples in this. It was for their sakes, that *they might be sanctified*, that is, "so that they may be martyrs," according to some. However, I prefer to take it more generally, as meaning "so that they may be saints and ministers, duly qualified and accepted by God." The office of the ministry was purchased by Christ's blood; it was one of the blessed fruits of his atonement. The real holiness of all true Christians is the fruit of Christ's death. He *gave himself for his church*, to *sanctify it* (Eph 5:25–26). The One who intended the purpose also intended the means, so that they would be sanctified by the truth. The word of truth receives its sanctifying power from the death of Christ. Christ has prayed for this for all who are his people, because *this is his will, even their sanctification* (1Th 4:3), which encourages them to pray for it.

Verses 20–23

After praying for their purity, he prayed for their unity. Notice:

1. Who were included in this prayer (v. 20): "*Not these only*, but *for those also who shall believe on me through their word*. I pray for them all." Only those who believe in Christ enjoy the privilege of sharing the benefits of his mediation. Those who lived then *saw and believed*, but those in later times *have not seen* and yet *have believed* (20:29). It is through the word that souls are brought to

believe on Christ. He did not pray randomly here. Christ knew very well whom he prayed for. Jesus Christ intercedes not only for great and famous believers but also for the most insignificant and the weakest. The Good Shepherd looks even to *the poor of the flock* (Zec 11:11). In his mediation, Jesus Christ considered those who were still unborn, the *other sheep* that he *must yet bring* (10:16).

2. What is intended in this prayer (v. 21): *That they all may be one.* The same was said before (v. 11): *that they may be one as we are*; and again in v. 22. Christ's heart was very much set on this. "Let them be not only of one heart but also of one mouth, speaking the same thing." The unity prayed for in v. 21 concerns all believers. The prayer of Christ for all who are his is *that they all may be one*, one in us (v. 21), one *as we are one* (v. 22), made *perfect in one* (v. 23). It includes three things:

2.1. That they would all be joined together in one body. "Father, look on them all as one. Although they live in distant places and in several ages, let them still be united in me as their common head." Christ both died and prayed to *gather them all in one* (11:52; Eph 1:10).

2.2. That they would all be enlivened by one Spirit. This is clearly implied in *that they may be one in us.* "Let them all be stamped with the same image and title and influenced by the same power."

2.3. That they would all be bound together in love, all of one heart. *That they all may be one*:

2.3.1. In judgment and attitude; not in every tiny detail in life—that is neither possible nor necessary—but in the great things of God; in those things, by the effectiveness of this prayer, they are all agreed.

2.3.2. In temperament and inclination. They all have a new heart, and it is one heart.

2.3.3. In their intentions and aims.

2.3.4. In their desires and prayers; although they differ in words and expressions, they pray for the same things in effect.

2.3.5. In love and affection. What Christ prayed for here was the communion of saints that we profess to believe. However, this prayer of Christ will not have its complete fulfillment until all believers come to heaven, for then, and not until then, they will be *perfect in one* (v. 23; Eph 4:13).

3. What is indicated by way of plea to reinforce this petition.

3.1. The unity between the Father and the Son, which is mentioned again and again (vv. 21–23). Christ assumed that the Father and he were one, one in mutual affection. The *Father loveth the Son*, and the Son always pleased the Father. They are one in purpose. The intimacy of this oneness is expressed in the words *thou in me, and I in thee.* This was insisted on in Christ's prayer for his disciples' unity:

3.1.1. As the model of that unity. In some measure, believers are one as God and Christ are one; they are united by a divine nature, by the power of divine grace, according to the divine purposes. It is a holy union for holy purposes, not a body politic for any worldly purpose. It is a complete union.

3.1.2. As the center of that unity: "that they may be *one in us.*" There is *one God* and *one Mediator* (1Ti 2:5). Any joining together that does not center on God as the aim and Christ as the way is a conspiracy, not a union. All who are truly united to God and Christ, who are one, will soon be united one to another.

3.1.3. As a plea for that unity. The Creator and Redeemer are one in interests and intentions, but to what purpose are they united in this way if all believers are not one body with Christ and do not jointly receive grace after grace from him (1:16), just as he has received it for them? Those words, *I in them*, and *thou in me*, show what that union is that is so necessary not only to the beauty of his church but also to its very being.

3.1.3.1. Union with Christ: *I in them.*

3.1.3.2. Union with God through him: *Thou in me*, so as to be in them through me.

3.1.3.3. Union with one another, resulting from these: *that they may be made perfect in one.* We are complete in him.

3.2. The intention of Christ in all his sharing of light and grace with them (v. 22): "*The glory which thou gavest me I have accordingly given them, that they may be one, as we are one*, and so those gifts will be in vain if those people you have given me are not one." Now these gifts are either:

3.2.1. Those that were given to the apostles. The glory of being God's ambassadors to the world and of setting up the throne of God's kingdom on earth—this glory was given to Christ, and he put some of the honor on them when he sent them to disciple all nations (Mt 28:19). Or:

3.2.2. Those that are given in common to all believers. The glory of being in covenant relationship with the Father was the glory the Father gave to the Redeemer, and he has confirmed it to the redeemed. Christ said he *had given them* this honor because he had intended it for them, and so it already belonged to them. He gave it to them so *that they might be one*, that is:

3.2.2.1. To entitle them to the privilege of unity. The gift of the Spirit, the great glory that the Father gave to the Son, to be given by him to all believers, makes them one.

3.2.2.2. To commit them to fulfill the duty of unity, so that in consideration of what they had in one God and one Christ, and of what they hoped for in one heaven, they might be of one mind and one mouth. Worldly glory sets people in conflict with one another, because if some are advanced, others are overshadowed. The more Christians are taken up with the glory Christ has given them, the less they will want to boast and, therefore, the less disposed they will be to quarrel.

3.3. The beneficial influence their unity would have on others. This was urged twice (v. 21): *that the world may believe that thou hast sent me*, and again, *that the world may know it* (v. 23). Believers must know what they believe and why they believe it. Those who believe without due thought will get sidetracked. Christ here showed:

3.3.1. His goodwill to the human race in general. Here, he is of his Father's mind, desiring that all people be saved. It is his will, therefore, that no stone be left unturned for the conviction and conversion of the world. We must do all we possibly can where we are to further people's salvation.

3.3.2. The good fruit of the church's unity; it will be evidence of the truth of Christianity and a means of bringing many to embrace it.

3.3.2.1. In general, it will commend Christianity to the world. The embodying of Christians in one community will greatly promote Christianity. When the world sees so many of those who were its children changed from what they *sometimes* were (Eph 2:13; 5:8; Col 1:21; 3:7), they will be ready to say, *We will go with you, for we see that God is with you* (Zec 8:23). The uniting of Christians in love and kindness is the beauty of their profession and invites others to join them. When Christianity, instead of causing quarrels about itself, makes all other battles come to an end, when it disposes people to be kind and loving, seeking to preserve and promote peace, this will commend it to all who have anything either of natural religion or of natural affection in them.

3.3.2.2. In particular, it will produce good thoughts in people:

3.3.2.2.1. Concerning Christ: they will know and believe that *thou hast sent me* (v. 23). That Christ was sent by God will be clear when it is seen that his religion persuades people to join when they have so many different abilities, personalities, and interests in other matters, and when it is seen that the people so joined are not only by faith one body but also by love one heart.

3.3.2.2.2. Concerning Christians: they will *know that thou hast loved them as thou hast loved me*. Here is:

3.3.2.2.2.1. The privilege of believers: the Father himself loves them with a love that resembles his love for his Son, because they are loved in the Son with an eternal love.

3.3.2.2.2.2. The evidence of their sharing in this privilege, and that is their being one. What will show that God loves us will be that we *love one another with a pure heart* (1Pe 1:22). Notice how much good it would do to the world to know better how dear to God all true Christians are. Those who have so much of God's love should have more of ours.

Verses 24–26

Here is:

1. A petition for the glorifying of all those who were given to Christ (v. 24): *Father, I will that they may be with me*. Notice:

1.1. The connection of this request with the previous ones. Christ had prayed that God would sanctify them; now he prayed that God would crown all his gifts with their glorification. We, too, are to pray first for *grace* (favor) and then for *glory* (honor), because this is how God gives.

1.2. The manner of the request: *Father, I will*. Here, as before, he addressed God as Father, and we must do likewise; but when he said, *I will*, he spoke a language that is not suited to ordinary petitioners. This shows the authority of his intercession in general; his word had influence in heaven as well as on earth. It also shows his particular authority in this matter; he had power to *give eternal life* (v. 2), and, according to that power, he said, *Father, I will*.

1.3. The request itself—that all the chosen ones might come to be with him in heaven in the end. Notice:

1.3.1. With what ideas we are to hope for heaven. What does that happiness consist of? Three things make heaven:

1.3.1.1. It is to be where Christ is: *"where I am,* am to be soon, am to be eternally." In this world we are merely in transit; there we truly are where we are to be forever.

1.3.1.2. It is to be with him where he is. The happiness of that place will consist of being in his presence. The very heaven of heaven is to be with Christ.

1.3.1.3. It is to *behold his glory, which the Father* has given him. The glory of the Redeemer is the brightness of heaven. The Lamb is the light of the New Jerusalem (Rev 21:23). God shows his glory there through Christ, just as he shows his grace here through him. The happiness of the redeemed consists very much in seeing this glory. They will see into those springs of love from which all the streams of grace flow. They will *be changed into the same image, from glory to glory* (2Co 3:18).

1.3.2. On what basis we are to hope for heaven: only through the mediation of Christ, because he has said,

Father, I will. Our sanctification is our evidence, but it is the will of Christ that is our entitlement. Christ spoke here as if he did not count his own happiness complete unless he had his chosen ones to share with him in it.

1.4. The argument to support this request: *for thou lovedst me before the foundation of the world*. This is a reason:

1.4.1. Why he expected this glory himself. "You will give it to me, *for thou lovedst me*." The *Father loves the Son*, is infinitely pleased with his work, and *therefore has given all things into his hands*. The Father is said to have loved the Son as Mediator *before the foundation of the world*. Or:

1.4.2. Why he expected that those who were given to him would be with him to share in his glory: *"Thou lovedst me*, and them in me, and cannot deny me anything I ask for them."

2. The conclusion of the prayer. Notice:

2.1. The respect he had for his Father (v. 25). Notice:

2.1.1. The title he gave to God: *O righteous Father*. When he prayed that they would be sanctified, he called God *Holy Father*; when he prayed that they might be glorified, he called him *righteous Father*.

2.1.2. The description he gave of the world: *the world has not known thee*. Ignorance of God pervades the human race; this is the darkness people sit in (Lk 1:79). These disciples needed the help of special grace, both because of the necessity of their work and because of the difficulty of their work; therefore: "Keep them." They were qualified for further special favors because they had the knowledge of God that the world did not have.

2.1.3. The plea he insisted on for himself: *but I have known thee*. Christ knew the Father as no one else ever did, and so in this prayer he could come to the Father with confidence, as we come to the one we know. One would have expected that when he had said, *the world has not known thee*, he would then say, "but my disciples have known thee." But no, their knowledge was not to be boasted of; he said, instead, *but I have known thee*. There is nothing in us to commend us to God's favor; our fellowship with him and all the privileges we enjoy in him result from Christ's privileges and fellowship. We are unworthy, but he is worthy.

2.1.4. The plea he insisted on for his disciples: *and they have known that thou hast sent me*.

2.1.4.1. In this they were distinguished from the unbelieving world. To know and believe in Jesus Christ in a world that persists in ignorance and faithlessness will certainly be crowned with a distinctive glory. Special faith qualifies for special favors.

2.1.4.2. In this they shared in the benefits of knowing the Father: *"I have known thee, and these have known that thou hast sent me."* Knowing Christ as sent by God, they had, in him, known the Father. "Father, look after them for my sake."

2.2. The respect he had for his disciples (v. 26): "I have led them into the knowledge of you, so *that the love wherewith thou hast loved me may be in them, and I in them*." Notice here:

2.2.1. What Christ had done for them: *I have declared unto them thy name*. He had done this both for those who were his immediate followers and for all who would believe in him. We are indebted to Christ for all the knowledge we have of the Father's name. Those whom Christ commends to the favor of God he first leads to knowing God.

2.2.2. What he intended to do even further for them: *I will declare it*. He intended to give the disciples further instructions after his resurrection (Ac 1:3), by the out-pouring of the Spirit after his ascension; and to all believ-ers, into whose hearts he has shone, he shines more and more (Pr 4:18).

2.2.3. What he aimed at in all this: to protect and advance their real happiness in two things:

2.2.3.1. Fellowship with God: "That is why I have given them the knowledge of your name, so *that thy love, wherewith thou hast loved me, may be in them.* Let the Spirit of love, with which you have filled me, be in them." Christ declares his Father's name to believers, so that along with that divine light darted into their minds a divine love may be *shed abroad in their hearts* (Ro 5:5), so that they may share in the divine nature. When God's love to us comes to be in us, it is like the power that a magnet gives to the needle in a compass, inclining it to move toward the North Pole; that love draws out the soul toward God. "Let them not only know the privilege of the love of God but also enjoy the assurance of that privilege, so that they not only know God but *know that they know him.* It is when *the love of God* is *shed abroad in the heart* that that love fills the heart with joy (Ro 5:3, 5). We can not only be satisfied with his unfailing love but also be deeply assured of it. We must seek this with all our hearts; if we have it, we must thank Christ for it; if we lack it, we only have ourselves to blame.

2.2.3.2. To that end, union with Christ: *and I in them.* There is no way of gaining access to the love of God except through Christ, nor can we keep ourselves in that love except by remaining in Christ. It is *Christ in us* that *is the* only *hope of glory* that *will not make us ashamed* (Col 1:27). All our fellowship with God, the reception of his love to us along with our response of love to him, passes through the hands of the Lord Jesus. Christ had said only a little while before, *I in them* (v. 23), and here he repeated it and ended the prayer with it, to show how much the heart of Christ was set on it. "*I in them*; let me have this, and then I desire nothing more." Let us, therefore, make sure of our union with Christ, and then take the assurance of his intercession. This prayer came to an end, but he always lives to bring that prayer (Heb 7:25).

CHAPTER 18

Up to now this Evangelist has recorded little of the life of Christ, including only what was needed to introduce his messages, but now he goes into detail in describing the circumstances of Christ's sufferings. This chapter relates: 1. How Christ was arrested in the garden (vv. 1–12). 2. How Christ was mistreated in the high priest's courtyard and how Peter, in the meantime, denied him (vv. 13–27). 3. How Christ was brought before Pilate and then put before the people so that they could vote whether to show favor to him or to Barabbas, and how Christ lost this election (vv. 28–40).

Verses 1–12

The hour had now come that *the captain of our salva-tion,* who was to be *made perfect by sufferings* (Heb 2:10), would fight the enemy. *Let us turn aside now, and see this great sight* (Ex 3:3).

1. Our Lord Jesus, like a bold champion, took to the field first (vv. 1–2): *When he had spoken these words,* he wanted to lose no time, and so he *went forth with his disciples over the brook Cedron* (Kidron), *where was a garden.*

1.1. Our Lord Jesus began his sufferings *when he had spoken these words* (v.1), as in Matthew they began *when*

he had finished all these sayings (Mt 26:1). Christ had said all he had to say as a prophet, and now he turned to fulfilling his work as a priest, to *make his soul an offering for sin* (Isa 53:10), and when he had gone through this, he began his kingly role. Having prepared his disciples for this hour of testing by his sermon and prepared himself for it by his prayer, he courageously went out to meet it. When he had put on his armor, he entered the battle, but not until then. Christ will not engage those who are his in any conflict without first doing what is necessary to prepare them for it. We may go through the greatest hard-ships with unshaken resolution as we follow the path of our duty.

1.2. *He went forth with his disciples.*

1.2.1. When his hour had come, he wanted to do as he usually did, not changing his ways either to meet the cross or to miss it. It was his custom that when he was in Jerusalem, he would withdraw at night *to the mount of Olives* (Lk 23:39). Because this was his custom, he would not be forced to vary his routine by the foresight of his sufferings.

1.2.2. He was as unwilling for there to be *an uproar among the people* as his enemies were (Mt 26:5). If he had been seized in the city and there had been a tumult, trouble might have been caused, with much bloodshed, and that was why he withdrew. When we find ourselves involved in trouble, we should be afraid of involving oth-ers. It is not a disgrace to the followers of Christ to fall tamely. Those who aim at honor from other people pride themselves on a decision to sell their lives for the highest possible price, but those who know that their blood is pre-cious to Christ need not insist on such terms.

1.2.3. He wanted to set us an example by his with-drawal from the world. We must both set aside and leave behind the crowds, cares, and comforts of cities—even holy cities—if we want to cheerfully take up our cross.

1.3. He went *over the brook Cedron* (Kidron). He must go over this to go to the Mount of Olives, but the men-tion of it suggests something significant. It points, on the one hand, to David's prophecy about the Messiah, that *he shall drink of the brook in the way* (Ps 110:7), the brook of suffering. This was represented by *the brook Cedron,* "the black brook," so called either from the darkness of the valley it ran through or from the color of the water, made dirty by the refuse of the city. The godly kings of Judah had burned and destroyed the idols they found at *the brook Cedron.* Detestable things were thrown into that valley. Christ began his suffering in the same valley.

1.4. He entered a garden. That Christ's sufferings began in a garden is noticed only by this Evangelist. Sin began in the Garden of Eden; there the Redeemer was promised (Ge 3:15). Christ was also buried in a garden. Let us, therefore, when we walk around in our gardens, use the occasion to meditate on Christ's sufferings in a garden, to which we owe all the pleasure we have in our gardens. When we are enjoying our possessions, we must also expect troubles, because our gardens of delight are in this vale of tears.

1.5. He had his disciples with him. They must be wit-nesses of his sufferings and of his patience in them, so that they could preach those sufferings to the world with greater assurance and warmth (Lk 24:48) and be prepared to suffer themselves. He also wanted to take them into the danger to show them their weakness. Christ sometimes brings his people into difficulties so that he may exalt himself in saving them.

1.6. Judas the traitor *knew the place.* A solitary garden is an appropriate place for meditation and prayer, so that we may pray over the impressions made and the vows renewed, and drive home what we have learned. Mention is made of Judas's knowing the place:

1.6.1. To emphasize Judas's sin, that he would betray his Master, that he made use of his familiarity with Christ to provide himself with the opportunity to betray him. A generous mind would have scorned to do something so evil.

1.6.2. To exalt the love of Christ, that although he knew where the traitor would seek him, he still went there to be found by him. This is how he showed that he was willing to suffer and die for us. It was late in the evening—probably eight or nine o'clock—when Christ went out into the garden. When others were going to bed, he was going to prayer, going to suffer.

2. When *the captain of our salvation* (Heb 2:10) had taken the field, the enemy attacked him (v. 3): Judas came to the grove. This Evangelist does not comment on Christ's anguish, because the other three had related it fully. Notice:

2.1. The people employed in this action—a *band of men and officers from the chief priests, with Judas.*

2.1.1. Here are many people against Christ—a *band of men.* Christ's friends were few, but his enemies were many.

2.1.2. Here was a *mixed multitude* (Ex 12:38; Nu 11:4); the band of men were Gentiles, Roman soldiers, the *officers of the chief priests.* The officers of their courts were Jews. These two groups were hostile toward each other but united against Christ.

2.1.3. It was a commissioned group who had received orders *from the chief priests,* and it is likely that the priests had obtained a warrant to arrest him, *for they feared the people* (Mk 11:32). Notice what enemies Christ and his Gospel have had and are likely to have: numerous and powerful ecclesiastical and civil powers combined against them (Ps 2:1–2).

2.1.4. They were all under the direction of Judas. He *received* this *band of men.* He thought himself wonderfully advanced, coming from behind the contemptible Twelve to be placed at the head of these formidable hundreds.

2.2. The preparation they had made for an attack: they came *with lanterns, and torches, and weapons.*

2.2.1. If Christ were to try to escape, even though they had the light of the moon, they would need their lights. Yet he would not hide like the First Adam (Ge 3:8); it was foolish to light a candle to seek the sun by.

2.2.2. If he were to resist, they would need their weapons. The weapons of his warfare were spiritual (2Co 10:4), and with these weapons he had often beaten them, so they now turn to other weapons, swords and sticks.

3. Our Lord Jesus gloriously repelled the first attack of the enemy (vv. 4–6). Notice:

3.1. How he received them.

3.1.1. He met them with a mild and humble question (v. 4): *Knowing all things that should come upon him,* undisturbed and undaunted, he *went forth* to meet them and asked softly, *Whom seek you?* Notice here:

3.1.1.1. Christ's foresight of his sufferings. He *knew all those things that would come upon him.* We should not seek to know what will happen to us; it would only make us anticipate our pain; *sufficient unto the day is the evil thereof* (Mt 6:34). It will do us good, however, to expect sufferings in general. "It is only the cost we sat down and counted (Lk 14:28)."

3.1.1.2. Christ's eagerness to undergo his sufferings. When the people wanted to force him to wear a crown, he withdrew and hid himself (6:15), but when they came to force him to take up a cross, he offered himself, because

he came into this world to suffer and went to the other world to reign. This does not give us authority to expose ourselves needlessly to trouble; we are called to suffering when we have no way of avoiding it except by sin.

3.1.2. He met them with a very calm and mild answer when they told him whom they were seeking (v. 5). They said, *Jesus of Nazareth,* and he said, *I am he.*

3.1.2.1. It seems *their eyes were held* (Lk 24:16). It is probable that at least the officers of the temple had often seen him, and Judas knew him well enough, yet none of them could claim to say, "You are the man we seek."

3.1.2.2. In their seeking him, they called him *Jesus of Nazareth.* It was a name of reproach, to darken the evidence that he was the Messiah. This shows that they did not really know him and where he came from.

3.1.2.3. He answered them fairly: *I am he.* Although they called them Jesus of Nazareth, he answered the name, because he scorned the shame (Heb 12:2). He could have said, "I am not he," because he was Jesus of Bethlehem. He has taught us in this to acknowledge him, whatever it may cost us; we are not to be *ashamed of him or his words* (Mk 8:38).

3.1.2.4. Particular notice is taken *that Judas stood with them.* The one who used to stand with those who followed Christ now stood with those who fought against him. This is mentioned to show the arrogance of Judas. One would wonder where he got the confidence with which he now faced his Master—that he *was not ashamed* (Jer 8:12). It also shows that Judas was particularly aimed at in the power that accompanied those words, *I am he,* to foil the aggressors.

3.2. How he terrified them and made them withdraw (v. 6): *They went backward and fell to the ground.* These words, "I am he," had revived his disciples and raised them up, but the same words struck his enemies down. Here, he showed clearly:

3.2.1. What he could have done with them. When he struck them down, he could have struck them dead, but he would not do so. He wanted only to show that his life was not forced from him, but that he laid it down himself, as he had said he would do (10:17). He wanted to show his patience and his compassionate love even for his enemies. In striking them down, but doing nothing more, he gave them both a call and an opportunity to repent.

3.2.2. What he will do in the end with all his implacable enemies, *who will not repent to give him glory* (Rev 16:9); they will flee, they will fall, before him.

4. Having repelled his enemies, he protected his friends (vv. 7–9).

4.1. He continued to expose himself to his enemies' anger (v. 7). One would have thought that when they were down, Christ would have escaped, and that when they got up again, they would have dropped their pursuit. Yet:

4.1.1. They were as eager as ever to seize him. They could not imagine what had happened to them but would attribute to it anything rather than Christ's power. There are hearts so hardened in sin that nothing will work on them to subdue and reclaim them.

4.1.2. He was as willing as ever to be seized. When they had fallen before him, he asked them the same question, *Whom seek you?* And they gave him the same answer, *Jesus of Nazareth.* In repeating the same answer, they showed a stubbornness in their evil ways; they still called him Jesus of Nazareth, with as much disdain as ever, and Judas was as unrelenting as any of them.

4.2. He contrived to protect his disciples from their anger. When he showed his courage with reference to himself—*I have told you that I am he*—he showed his care for his disciples: *Let these go their way* (v. 8). This emphasized the sin of the disciples in abandoning him, especially Peter's in denying him. When Christ said, *Let these go their way*, he intended:

4.2.1. To show his affectionate concern for his disciples. When he made himself vulnerable, he excused them, because they were not yet ready to suffer. It would have been as much as their souls, and the lives of their souls, were worth to bring them into sufferings now. Besides, they had other work to do; they must go their own way, because they were to go into the whole world to preach the Gospel. Now here:

4.2.1.1. Christ gives us a great encouragement to follow him. He still considers how we are formed (Ps 103:14), and he will wisely time the laying on us of our cross and make the burden of it in proportion to our strength.

4.2.1.2. He gives us a good example of love to our brothers and sisters. We must not consider only our own comfort and safety, but that of others' as well (Php 2:4), and in some cases more than our own.

4.2.2. To give an example of his undertaking as Mediator. When he offered himself to suffer and die, it was so that we could escape.

4.3. He confirmed the word he had spoken a little before (17:12): *Of those whom thou gavest me, I have lost none.* Although Christ's *keeping* them referred especially to the preservation of their souls from sin, it is also applied here to the preservation of their natural lives. Christ will preserve the natural life for the service for which it is intended. It will be held in life as long as any use is to be made of it. This preservation of the disciples was a spiritual preservation. They were now so weak in faith and resolution that if they had been called to suffer at this time, some of them, at least the weaker of them, would probably have been lost, and that was why he would not expose them, so that he would lose none.

5. He rebuked the rashness of one of his disciples and repressed the violence of all of them (vv. 10–11). We see here:

5.1. Peter's rashness. They had two swords among them (Lk 22:38), and because Peter was entrusted with one, he drew it. *He smote* (struck) *one of the high priest's servants and cut off his right ear. The servant's name* is recorded to give greater certainty to the account; it *was Malchus.*

5.1.1. We must here acknowledge Peter's goodwill; he showed honest zeal for his Master, though he was misguided. He had just promised to risk his life for him, and now he wanted to keep his word.

5.1.2. We must also, however, acknowledge Peter's wrongful conduct; though his good intention excused him, it would not justify him.

5.1.2.1. He had no authority from his Master for his action. Christ's soldiers must wait for the word of command, and not act before it.

5.1.2.2. He resisted the official powers, which Christ had never encouraged, but forbidden (Mt 5:39).

5.1.2.3. He opposed his Master's suffering. While seeming to fight for Christ, he fought against him.

5.1.2.4. He broke the surrender his Master had just made to the enemy. When Christ said, *Let these go their way*, he in effect gave his word for their good behavior. Peter heard this but would not be bound by it.

5.1.2.5. He foolishly exposed himself and his fellow disciples to the fury of this enraged crowd. Many have been guilty of self-destruction in their zeal for self-preservation.

5.1.2.6. Peter acted cowardly so soon after this, denying his Master, that we have reason to think his courage

failed him. The true Christian hero, however, will support the cause of Christ not only when it is winning but also when it seems to be failing; that person will be on the right side even though it may not be the rising side.

5.1.3. We must acknowledge God's overruling providence in giving Christ an opportunity to show his power and goodness in healing the injury (Lk 22:51).

5.2. The rebuke his Master gave him (v. 11): *Put up thy sword into the sheath.* It is a gentle rebuke, because it was Peter's zeal that took him beyond the bounds of discretion. Many think that being in grief and distress will excuse them for being vehement and hasty with the people around them, but Christ has set us an example here of humility in suffering.

5.3. The reason for this rebuke: *The cup which my Father has given me, shall I not drink it?* Christ gives us:

5.3.1. A full proof of his own submission to his Father's will. Of everything that was wrong in what Peter did, Christ seemed to resent nothing so much as that Peter wanted to hinder Christ's sufferings now that his hour had come. He was willing to drink from this cup, even though it was a bitter cup. He drank it, so that he could put the cup of salvation into our hands (Ps 116:3). He was willing to drink it because *his Father put it into his hand* (3:35).

5.3.2. A good pattern to us of submission to God's will. We must follow Christ in the cup that he drank from (Mt 20:23). It is only *a cup*, a comparatively small amount. It is a cup that is given us; sufferings are gifts. It is given to us by a Father, who has a Father's affection and means us no harm.

6. He calmly surrendered and yielded himself as prisoner, not because he could not have made his escape, but because he would not. Notice:

6.1. How they seized him: *They took Jesus.* Only a few of them could lay hands on him, but they are all mentioned as arresting him, because they were all aiding and abetting. In treason there are no accessories; all are the principal causes. They had been frustrated so often in their attempts to take him that now we may imagine they attacked him with much more violence.

6.2. How they kept him secure: *They bound him.* This detail of his suffering is noted only by this Evangelist. As soon as he was arrested, he was bound, restrained, and handcuffed.

6.2.1. This shows the spitefulness of his persecutors. They bound him so that they could torment him, disgrace him, and prevent his escape. They bound him as One already condemned, because they had determined to prosecute him to death. Christ had bound the consciences of his persecutors with the power of his word, which infuriated them, and to get their revenge on him, they bound him.

6.2.2. Christ's being bound was very significant. Before they bound him, he had bound himself to fulfill the work of a Mediator. He was already bound to the horns of the altar (Ex 29:12) with the cords of his own love to humanity and duty to his Father. Guilt binds the soul to the judgment of God; corruption binds the soul to the power of Satan. Christ freed us from these bonds by submitting himself to be bound for us. We owe our liberty to his bonds. This is how the Son makes us free (8:36). Christ was bound so that he could bind us to duty and obedience. His bonds for us are bonds on us, by which we are obliged to love him and serve him forever. Christ's bonds for us were intended to make our bonds for him easy for us, to sanctify and sweeten them; Christ's bonds enabled Paul and Silas to sing in the stocks (Ac 16:24).

Verses 13–27

We have here an account of Christ's being brought before the high priest, including some details of that trial that were omitted by the other Evangelists; we also have, interwoven with the other passages, an account of Peter's denying him, of which the other Evangelists gave us the whole account all at once. Because the crime Christ was accused of related to religious matters, the judges of the spiritual court took it to fall directly under their jurisdiction. Both Jews and Gentiles seized him, and so both Jews and Gentiles tried and condemned him, because he died for the sins of both.

1. Having arrested him, they *led him away to Annas first* (v. 13).

1.1. They *led him away*, led him in triumph, as a trophy of their victory. They rushed him away forcefully, as if he had been the worst evildoer. We would have been led away by our own impetuous, sinful desires and taken captive by Satan at his will; so that we could be rescued, Christ was led away, taken captive by Satan's agents and instruments.

1.2. They led him away to their masters, who had sent them. It was now about midnight, and one would have thought they would put him in custody until it was the proper time to call a sitting of the court, but he was rushed away immediately, not to be consigned to the justices of peace, but to be condemned by the judges; the prosecution was so violent.

1.3. They led him to Annas first. I suppose Annas was old and infirm and could not be present at the council at that time of night, but still passionately wanted to see the victim. To satisfy him, therefore, with the assurance of their success, they produced their prisoner before him. Christ, the great sacrifice, was presented to him, and then he was sent away bound, as a sacrifice approved of by the high priest and ready for the altar according to the law. This Annas was the father-in-law of Caiaphas the high priest. Acquaintance and alliance with evildoers are a great confirmation to many people in their evil ways.

2. Annas, being as willing as any of them to move the prosecution on, sent him bound to Caiaphas. We have here:

2.1. The power of Caiaphas shown (v. 13). He was *high priest that same year*. The high priest's commission was for life, but there were now such frequent changes that it had become almost an annual office. While they were undermining one another, God was overturning them all. Caiaphas was high priest in the year when the Messiah was to be *cut off* (Isa 53:8). When a bad thing was to be done by a high priest, Providence so ordered it that a bad man would be in the chair to do it. It was the ruin of Caiaphas that he was high priest that year and so became a ringleader in putting Christ to death. Many a person's advancement has lost them their reputation; many a person would not have been dishonored if they had not been promoted.

2.2. The hatred of Caiaphas, which is indicated (v. 14) by repeating what he had said some time before, that *it was expedient that one man should die for the people*. This was the Caiaphas who governed himself and the church by rules of politics, in defiance of rules of justice. Christ's case was judged even before it had been heard; they had already decided what to do with him: he must die. Christ's trial was therefore a mockery. Caiaphas's words were a testimony to the innocence of our Lord Jesus from the mouth of one of his worst enemies, who acknowledged that he fell as a sacrifice to the public good and that it was not just that he die, but only expedient.

2.3. The share Annas had in the prosecution of Christ. He himself shared in the guilt:

2.3.1. With the commander and the officers, by continuing to have him bound when he should have set him loose. It was more excusable for the uneducated soldiers to bind him than for Annas, who should have known better, to keep him bound.

2.3.2. With the chief priest and council. This Annas was not present with them, but he shared in their evil deeds.

3. In the house of Caiaphas, Simon Peter began to deny his Master (vv. 15–18).

3.1. It was with much fuss that Peter got into the hall where the court was sitting. We have an account of his being admitted in vv. 15–16. Notice:

3.1.1. Peter's kindness to Christ, which, though it did not turn out to be a kindness, appeared in two things:

3.1.1.1. That he *followed Jesus* when Jesus was *led away*; although at first Peter fled with the others, later he took heart a little and followed at a distance, remembering his promises to be loyal no matter what the cost. Those who truly love and value Christ will follow him in all weathers and every day.

3.1.1.2. When he could not get in where Jesus was among his enemies, he *stood at the door without*, wanting to be as close to him as possible and waiting for an opportunity to get nearer. Yet as events turned out, he only put himself into a trap. Christ, who knew him better than he knew himself, had clearly told him, *Whither I go thou canst not follow me now* (13:36). Christ had told Peter again and again that Peter would deny him, and Peter had just experienced his own weakness when he abandoned Christ.

3.1.2. The other disciple's kindness to Peter, which, as events turned out, was no kindness either. Because the apostle John speaks several times in this Gospel about himself as another disciple, many interpreters have been led by this to think that the other disciple here was John. I, however, see no reason to think that this other disciple was John or any other of the Twelve; Christ had other sheep that did not belong to that fold (10:16). As there are many who seem to be disciples and are not, so there are also many who are disciples but seem not to be. There are good people hidden in courtyards, even in Nero's (Php 4:22), as well as hidden in crowds. This other disciple showed respect for Peter by introducing him, not only to satisfy affection but also to give him an opportunity to be useful to his Master during his trial. However, this kindness turned out not to be a kindness; in fact, it was a great unkindness. By letting Peter into the high priest's courtyard, he let him into temptation, and the effects were bad.

3.2. Having gained access, Peter was immediately attacked by the temptation (v. 17). Notice:

3.2.1. How slight the attack was. It was merely a foolish girl — so insignificant that she was set to guard the door — who challenged him, and she only asked him carelessly, *Art not thou one of this man's disciples?* Peter would have had some reason to be alarmed if Malchus had accosted him with, "This is the one who cut off my ear, and I will have his head for it."

3.2.2. How quickly he surrendered. Without taking time to gather himself together, he hastily answered, *I am not*. Because he was only concerned for his own safety, he thought he could protect that only by a flat denial.

3.2.3. How he went even further into the temptation: *And the servants and officers stood there, and Peter with them* (v. 18).

3.2.3.1. Notice how the servants made much of themselves; because the night was cold, they made a fire in the courtyard. They did not care what happened to Christ; their only concern was to be able to sit down and warm themselves (Am 6:6).

3.2.3.2. Notice how Peter herded with them. *He sat and warmed himself.* It was bad enough that he was not with his Master, that he did not support him at the upper end of the courtyard. If he had been there, he could have been a witness for his Master. Or at least he could have been a witness *to* him. He could have learned from his Master's example what to do when his turn came to suffer in this way; yet neither his conscience nor his curiosity could bring him into the courtyard. It was much worse that he attached himself to his Master's enemies: *He stood with them, and warmed himself.* Those who can be drawn into bad company by the love of a good fire are weak indeed. If Peter's zeal for his Master had not frozen, but had continued as it had seemed to be only a few hours before, he would have had no need to warm himself now. Peter was much to be blamed:

3.2.3.2.1. Because he associated with these evildoers. No doubt they were amusing themselves with this night's expedition, mocking Christ. But what kind of entertainment would this have been to Peter? If Peter did not have enough courage to appear publicly for his Master, he could still have had enough devotion to withdraw into a corner and weep in secret at his Master's sufferings, and at his own sin in abandoning him.

3.2.3.2.2. Because he wanted to be thought of as one of them. Was this Peter? It is bad to warm ourselves with those with whom we are in danger of burning ourselves (Ps 141:4).

4. As Peter, Christ's friend, began to deny him, the high priest, his enemy, began to accuse him (vv. 19–21). It seems the first attempt was to prove Christ a teacher of false doctrine, and we learn of this from John; and when they failed to prove this, then, as related by the other Evangelists, they accused him of blasphemy. Notice:

4.1. The headings under which Christ was examined (v. 19): *his disciples and his doctrine.* Notice here:

4.1.1. The irregularity of the process; it was against all law and justice. Now that he was their prisoner, they had nothing to charge him with. Against all reason and justice, he was called on to be his own accuser.

4.1.2. The intention. The *high priest then* examined him with those questions that would determine whether he lived or died, questions:

4.1.2.1. About his disciples, in an attempt to accuse him of sedition. Some think Caiaphas's question about Christ's disciples was, "What has now become of them all? Why do they not appear?" rebuking him for their cowardice in abandoning him, and so adding to its suffering.

4.1.2.2. About his teaching, in an attempt to accuse him of heresy. This was a matter properly within the jurisdiction of that court, and so a prophet could die only at Jerusalem, where that court sat. They said nothing to him about his miracles, by which he had done so much good, because they were sure they could not make use of these.

4.2. The appeal Christ made in answer to these questions.

4.2.1. As to his disciples, he said nothing, because it was an arrogant question. His having disciples was no more than what was practiced and allowed by the Jews' own teachers. If Caiaphas intended to trap them, it was out of kindness to them that Christ said nothing about them, because he had said, *Let these go their way* (v. 8).

If Caiaphas meant to rebuke Christ for their cowardice, it is hardly surprising that he said nothing. He would say nothing to condemn them, and could say nothing to justify them.

4.2.2. As to his teaching, he said nothing in particular, but in general he referred himself to those who had heard him (vv. 20–21).

4.2.2.1. He tacitly charged his judges with illegal proceedings. He appealed to the settled rules of their own court as to whether they were dealing fairly with him. *Why ask you me?* he said, which implied two absurdities in judgment:

4.2.2.1.1. "*Why ask you me now* concerning my teaching, when you have already condemned it?" They had made an order of court to excommunicate everyone who acknowledged him (9:22), and now they came to ask what his teaching was!

4.2.2.1.2. "*Why ask you me?* Must I accuse myself?"

4.2.2.2. He insisted that he had dealt fairly and openly with them in declaring his message. Christ cleared himself very fully:

4.2.2.2.1. As to the manner of his preaching. He *spoke openly,* with freedom and plainness of speech. Christ explained himself fully, with, *Verily, verily, I say unto you.*

4.2.2.2.2. As to the people he preached to: *He spoke to the world,* to all who had *ears to hear* (Mk 4:9) and were willing to hear him, high or low, learned or unlearned, Jew or Gentile, friend or foe.

4.2.2.2.3. As to the places he preached in. When he was in the country, he usually preached in synagogues; when he came to Jerusalem, he preached the same message in the temple. Although he often preached in private houses and on mountains and by the seaside, what he preached in private was the same as what he spoke publicly. The message of Christ need not be ashamed to appear in the most populous gathering, because it carries its own power and beauty with it.

4.2.2.2.4. As to the teaching itself. *In secret have I said nothing.* He sought no hidden corners, because he feared no foes, nor did he say anything he needed to be ashamed of. What he did speak in private to his disciples he told them to make known from the roofs (Mt 10:27).

4.2.2.3. He appealed to those who had heard him, and he asked that they be examined: *Ask those that heard me what I said unto them.* He was not referring to his friends and followers, who might be presumed to speak in his favor, but, "Ask any impartial hearer." The teaching of Christ may safely appeal to all who know it. Those who judge impartially must witness to it.

5. While the judges were examining him, the servants who stood by were mistreating him (vv. 22–23).

5.1. One of the officers wickedly insulted him; this arrogant fellow *struck him with the palm of his hand,* saying, *Answerest thou the high priest so?*

5.1.1. He *struck him;* it may be read, "he gave him a blow." It was unjust to strike One who neither said nor did anything wrong, it was cowardly to strike One who had his hands tied, and it was cruel to strike a prisoner at the bar. Here was a breach of the peace in the face of the court, but the judges supported it.

5.1.2. He rebuked him proudly and imperiously: *Answerest thou the high priest so?* He spoke as if the blessed Jesus were not good enough to speak to his master, but, like a rude and ignorant prisoner, must be controlled by the jailer and taught how to behave. The man did this to please the high priest and seek his favor, because what he said implied a jealousy for the dignity of the high priest. Evil rulers will not lack evil servants, who will *help forward the affliction* (Zec 1:15) of those whom their masters persecute.

5.2. Christ bore this insult with wonderful humility and patience (v. 23): "*If I have spoken evil* (something wrong), *bear witness of the evil* (testify to what is wrong). But if I spoke well, *why smitest thou me?*" Christ did not here *turn the other cheek*, which makes it clear that the rule requiring such a response to injustice (Mt 5:39) is not to be understood literally. Comparing Christ's command with his example, we learn that in such cases we must not be our own avengers, nor judges in our own cause, and our anger at injuries done to us must always be rational, never passionate.

6. While the servants were mistreating him in this way, Peter continued to deny him (vv. 25–27).

6.1. He repeated the sin (v. 25). While he was warming himself with the servants, they asked him, *Art not thou one of his disciples?* He, perhaps fearing he would be arrested if he acknowledged it, flatly denied it and said, *I am not.*

6.1.1. It was very foolish of him to thrust himself into the temptation by staying with those who were unsuitable for him. He stayed to warm himself, but those who warm themselves with evildoers grow cold toward good people and good things, and those who are fond of the Devil's fireside are in danger of the Devil's fire.

6.1.2. It was his great unhappiness that he was again attacked by the temptation. Notice:

6.1.2.1. The subtlety of the tempter in pursuing and overwhelming one whom he saw falling; now he used not a girl, but all the servants. Yielding to one temptation invites another, and perhaps a stronger one. Satan redoubles his attacks when we give way.

6.1.2.2. The danger of bad company. We commonly seek to approve ourselves to those whom we choose to associate with. As we choose our people, we choose our praise; we should therefore be anxious to make the first choice well.

6.1.3. It was his great weakness to yield to the temptation, saying, "I am not one of his disciples," as one who was ashamed of what was his honor. When Christ was admired and treated with respect, Peter prided himself in being a disciple of Christ. Many people who seem fond of the reputation of religion when it is fashionable are ashamed of its shame.

6.2. He committed the sin a third time (vv. 26–27). Here he was attacked by one of the servants who was a relative of Malchus, who exposed his lie with great assurance: *Did not I see thee in the garden with him?* Peter then denied it again.

6.2.1. Before this, his relationship with Christ was only suspected; here it was proved against him by a person who saw him with Jesus. Those who by sin think they can help themselves out of trouble only get caught up in it even more. Dare to be brave, for truth will out. Notice is taken of this servant's being related to Malchus because this circumstance would make it more of a terror to Peter. We should not make anyone in particular our enemy if we can help it. Those who may need friends should not make enemies. Although here was sufficient evidence against Peter to prosecute him, he still escaped harm. We are often drawn into sin by baseless fears, which a small amount of wisdom and determination would make nothing of.

6.2.2. His yielding to it was no less corrupt than his doing so before: *He denied again.* We see here the nature of sin in general: *the heart is hardened by the deceitfulness of it* (Heb 3:13). *The beginning of* sin, as of *strife, is as the letting forth of water* (Pr 17:14); once the fence is

broken, people easily go from bad to worse. We also see the nature of the sin of lying in particular; it is a fruitful, multiplying sin; one lie needs another to support it, and that one another, and so on. *Immediately the cock crew*, and this is all that is said here about his repentance, because it is recorded by the other Evangelists. To others, the crowing of the rooster was accidental and had no significance, but to Peter it was the voice of God.

Verses 28–40

We have here an account of Christ's indictment before Pilate, the Roman governor, in the *hall of judgment*, his palace. The Jews rushed him there to have him condemned in the Roman court and executed by the Roman power.

1. They followed this course so that he could be:

1.1. Put to death more legally and regularly, not stoned in a popular uprising, as Stephen was, but put to death with the present formalities of justice.

1.2. Put to death more safely. If they could engage the Roman government in the matter, there would be little danger of an uproar.

1.3. Put to death with more shame on him. Because *the death of the cross* (Php 2:8) was the most shameful of all deaths, they wanted to use that method to mark him indelibly with infamy. The chorus of their chant was, *Crucify him* (19:6).

1.4. Put to death with less shame to them. It was shameful to put to death someone who had done so much good, and that was why they wanted to throw the odium onto the Roman government. Many people are more afraid of the scandal of a bad action than of its badness. Notice:

1.4.1. Their persistence in the prosecution: *It was early*, when most people were in bed. Now that they had him in their hands, they would lose no time till they had him on the cross.

1.4.2. Their superstition and evil hypocrisy: *The chief priests and elders went not into the judgment hall lest they should be defiled*, but stayed outside, so *that they might eat the Passover*. They had scruples about this, but they had no scruples about breaking all the laws of justice to persecute Christ to the death.

2. Pilate met with the prosecutors. They were called first, and they stated what they had to say against the prisoner (vv. 29–32).

2.1. The judge called for the indictment. Because they would not come into the hall, *he went out to them*. We may commend three things in him:

2.1.1. His diligent and close application to business. People in positions of public trust must not love their rest.

2.1.2. His condescending to the mood of the people. He could have said, "If they are so fastidious that they will not come in to me, let them go home as they came," but he did not insist on it; he went out to them.

2.1.3. His faithfulness to the rules of justice in demanding the accusation: "*What accusation bring you against this man?* What is the crime you charge him with, and what proof have you got of it?"

2.2. The prosecutors demanded judgment against him on the general suspicion that he was a criminal (v. 30): *If he were not a malefactor, we would not have delivered him to thee.* This shows they were:

2.2.1. Very rude and impolite to Pilate. He put the most reasonable question possible to them, but even if they had tried to be more absurd, they could not have answered him with greater disdain.

2.2.2. Very spiteful and malicious toward our Lord Jesus. They were set on presuming guilty the One who could prove he was innocent. They said, "He is an evildoer." An evildoer who *went about doing good* (Ac 10:38)! It is nothing new for the best and most generous people to be branded and maligned as the worst evildoers.

2.2.3. Very proud and conceited concerning their own judgment and sense of justice.

2.3. The judge remanded him to their own court (v. 31): *"Take you him, and judge him according to your* own *law."*

2.3.1. Some think Pilate was complimenting them in this, acknowledging the remains of their authority and allowing them to exert it. "Go as far as your own law will allow you to go, and if you go further, no notice will be taken." He was willing to do the Jews a favor but unwilling to do them the service they required.

2.3.2. Others think he was rebuking them for their present weakness and submission: "You have found him guilty by your own law; condemn him, if you dare, by your own law." Some think Pilate was reflecting on the Law of Moses here, as if it allowed them what the Roman law would by no means allow—the judging of a person without hearing the case.

2.4. They disowned any authority as judges: *It is not lawful for us to put any man to death.* Some think they had lost their power to administer judgment in matters of life and death only by their own carelessness; not, *It is not lawful for us*, but, "It is not in our power; if we do put anyone to death, we will have the mob around us immediately." Others think their power was taken away from them by the Romans. They intended by their acknowledgment of this to compliment Pilate and atone for their rudeness (v. 30). In any case, there was a providence in this state of affairs; it came about so *that the saying of Jesus might be fulfilled, which he spoke, signifying what death he should die* (v. 32). Even those who intended to defeat Christ's sayings were made useful in fulfilling them by the overruling hand of God. Those sayings of Christ that he had spoken about his own death in particular were fulfilled. Two sayings of Christ about his death were fulfilled by the Jews' declining to *judge him according to their law* (v. 31).

2.4.1. He had said that he would be *delivered to the Gentiles* and that *they would put him to death* (Mt 20:19; Mk 10:33; Lk 18:32–33).

2.4.2. He had said that he would be crucified (Mt 20:19; 26:2), *lifted up* (3:14; 12:32). Now if they had judged him by their law, he would have been stoned. It was necessary, therefore, for Christ to be put to death by the Romans. As the Roman power had caused him to be born at Bethlehem, so now it caused him to die on a cross, and both according to the Scriptures.

3. Pilate met with the prisoner (v. 33).

3.1. The prisoner stood at the bar. After Pilate had conferred with the chief priests at his door, he entered the hall and called for Jesus to be brought in. Pilate entered into judgment with him so that God would not enter into judgment with us.

3.2. He was examined. The other Evangelists tell us that his accusers had charged him with perverting the nation by forbidding to give tribute to Caesar (Lk 23:2).

3.2.1. Here a question was put to him to find something on which to base an accusation: *"Art thou the king of the Jews?"* Some think Pilate asked this question with an air of scorn and contempt: "What! *Art thou a king? Art thou the king of the Jews*, by whom you are so hated and persecuted?" Since it could not be proved that Christ ever said this, Pilate wanted to force him to say it now, so that he could proceed on the basis of Christ's own confession.

3.2.2. Christ answered this question with another question to indicate that Pilate should consider what he was doing (v. 34): *"Sayest thou this thing of thyself, or did others tell it thee of me?"*

3.2.2.1. "It is clear that you have no reason to *say this of yourself.*" Pilate was bound by his office to take care of the interests of the Roman government, but he could not say that that government was in any danger or suffered any damage from anything our Lord Jesus had ever said or done.

3.2.2.2. "If others *tell it of me*, you should consider whether those who represent me as an enemy to Caesar are not really such themselves." If Pilate had been as inquisitive as he should have been in this matter, he would have found that the true reason why the chief priests were so outraged against Jesus was that he did not set up a temporal kingdom in opposition to the Roman power. Because he did not fulfill this expectation of theirs, they accused him of what they themselves were most notoriously guilty of—discontentment with and plotting against the present government.

3.2.3. Pilate was angry with Christ's answer and took it very badly (v. 35). This was a direct answer to Christ's question (v. 34).

3.2.3.1. Christ had asked him whether he had spoken from himself. "No," he said; *"am I a Jew?"* Notice the disdain with which Pilate asked, *Am I a Jew?* A man of sense and honor counted it a scandal to be considered a Jew.

3.2.3.2. Christ had asked him whether others told him. "Yes," he said, "and they were *thine own people* and *the priests*, and that is why I have nothing to do but to proceed on their information."

3.2.3.3. Christ had declined answering that question, *Art thou the king of the Jews?* Pilate therefore asked, *"What hast thou done?"* Surely there cannot be all this smoke without some fire; what is going on?"

3.2.4. In his next reply, Christ gave a fuller answer to Pilate's first question, *Art thou a king?* explaining in what sense he was a king (v. 36). Here is:

3.2.4.1. An account of the nature and constitution of Christ's kingdom: It *is not of this world*. Christ is a king and has a kingdom, but not of this world.

3.2.4.1.*1*. Its origin is not from this world.

3.2.4.1.*2*. Its nature is not worldly; it is a kingdom within human beings, set up in their hearts and consciences (Ro 14:17), its riches and powers being spiritual.

3.2.4.1.*3*. Its guards and supports are not worldly; its weapons are spiritual (2Co 10:4).

3.2.4.1.*4*. Its tendency and purpose are not worldly.

3.2.4.1.*5*. Its subjects, though in the world, *are not of the world* (17:16). They are neither the world's students nor its favorites, neither ruled by its wisdom nor enriched by its wealth.

3.2.4.2. Evidence of the spiritual nature of Christ's kingdom produced. If *my kingdom were of this world, then would my servants fight, that I should not be delivered to the Jews* (v. 36). His followers did not attempt to fight; there was no uproar, no bid to rescue him. He did not order them to fight; in fact, he forbade them, knowing that what would have been the destruction of any worldly kingdom would lead to the advancement and establishment of his. *"Now* you can see that *my kingdom is not from hence*; it is in the world but not of it."

3.2.5. In answer to Pilate's further query, he replied even more directly (v. 37). Here we have:

3.2.5.1. Pilate's plain question: *"Art thou a king then?* You are speaking about a kingdom you have; are you then, in any sense, a king? Explain yourself."

3.2.5.2. The *good confession* our Lord Jesus *witnessed before Pontius Pilate* (1Ti 6:13): *Thou sayest that I am a king*; that is, "It is as you say; I am a king."

3.2.5.2.1. He granted he was a king, though not in the sense that Pilate meant. Although Christ *took upon him the form of a servant* (Php 2:7), even then he justly claimed the honor and authority of a king.

3.2.5.2.2. He explained himself, showing how he was a king, since he came to *bear witness to the truth*; he rules in human minds by the power of truth. He came to be a witness, a witness for the God who made the world and against sin, which ruins the world, and by this word of his testimony he set up and keeps up his kingdom. Christ's mission into the world and his work in the world were *to bear witness to the truth*, that is:

3.2.5.2.2.1. To reveal to the world what otherwise could not have been known about God and his *goodwill to men* (1:18; 17:26).

3.2.5.2.2.2. To confirm it (Ro 15:8). By his miracles *he bore witness to the truth* of religion, so *that all men through him might believe* (1:7). Now in doing this he was a king and set up his kingdom. The spirit and character of Christ's kingdom is divine truth. When he said, *I am the truth* (14:6), he said, in effect, "I am a king." He conquers by the convincing evidence of truth; he rules by the commanding power of truth. He came as *a light into the world* (12:46), and he rules as the sun by day (Ge 1:16, 18; Ps 136:8). The subjects of this kingdom are those who are *of the truth*. All who are in love with the truth will hear the voice of Christ, because nowhere can there be found greater, better, surer, and sweeter truths than those that can be found in Christ. It is through Christ that *grace and truth came* (1:17).

3.2.6. Pilate then asked Christ a good question, but he did not wait for an answer (v. 38). He said, *What is truth?* and *immediately went out again.*

3.2.6.1. It is certain this was a good question. Truth is the *pearl of great price* (Mt 13:46) that the human understanding seeks, for that understanding can rest only in what is, or at least is perceived as, truth. But many ask this question who do not have enough patience to persevere in their search for truth, or who do not have enough humility and sincerity to receive it when they have found it (2Ti 3:7).

3.2.6.2. It is uncertain with what intention Pilate asked this question. Perhaps he spoke it as a learner, as one who was beginning to think well of Christ. Some think he spoke it as a judge, probing further into the cause: "Tell me what its truth is, the true state of this matter." Others think he spoke it as a scoffer: "You are talking about truth; can you tell what truth is, or give me a definition of it?" Just as people of no religion take pleasure in laughing at all religions, Pilate ridiculed both sides, and that was why Christ gave him no reply. Although Christ would not tell Pilate what is truth, however, he had told his disciples, and through them he has told us (14:6).

4. The result of both of these meetings, one with the prosecutors and the other with the prisoner (vv. 38–40), were as follows:

4.1. The judge appeared to be his friend.

4.1.1. He publicly declared him innocent (v. 38): *I find in him no fault at all.* Nothing criminal could be found in him. This solemn declaration of Christ's innocence was:

4.1.1.1. To justify and honor the Lord Jesus. Although he was treated as the worst evildoer, he had never merited such treatment.

4.1.1.2. To explain the purpose and intention of his death, that he did not die for any sin of his own, and so he

died as a sacrifice for our sins, and because, even in the judgment of the prosecutors themselves, *one man should die for the people* (11:50).

4.1.1.3. To emphasize the sin of the Jews who prosecuted him with so much violence. Although our Lord Jesus was found not guilty, he was still pursued as an evildoer, and his blood was thirsted for.

4.1.2. He proposed a way out to have him released (v. 39): "*You have a custom, that I should release to you a prisoner at the passover*; will it be this king of the Jews?" This was an appeal not to the chief priests but to the people, as can be seen in Mt 27:15. He had probably heard how this Jesus had been praised only the other day with the hosannas of the common people, and so he had no doubt they would demand the release of Jesus.

4.1.2.1. He allowed their custom, which was in honor of the Passover, which in turn was a memorial of their release.

4.1.2.2. He offered to release Jesus to them, according to the custom. Yet if he found no fault in him, he was bound in conscience to release him, regardless of the custom. But he was willing to make things easier all round, being guided more by worldly wisdom than by rules of justice.

4.2. The people appeared as his enemies (v. 40): *They cried all again, Not this man, but Barabbas.* Notice how fierce and outrageous they were. Pilate proposed the matter to them calmly, but they decided the matter in a moment of passion and announced their decision with clamor and noise. There is cause to suspect a deficiency of reason and justice on the side that calls for the help of the popular uprising. How foolish and absurd they were is seen in the short account given here of the other candidate: *Now Barabbas was a robber*, and therefore:

4.2.1. A breaker of the Law of God. However, he was the one who was spared.

4.2.2. An enemy of the public security and personal property. The clamor of the town is usually set against robbers, but here it was on the side of one. This is what people do when they prefer their sins to Christ. Sin is a robber that is foolishly chosen rather than Christ, who would truly enrich us.

CHAPTER 19

When he comes to the sufferings and death of Christ, this Evangelist repeats what was related before, with considerable additions, as one who wants to know nothing except Christ and him crucified (1Co 2:2). We have here: 1. The remainder of Christ's trial before Pilate (vv. 1–15). 2. Sentence passed, and execution carried out on it (vv. 16–18). 3. The inscription over his head (vv. 19–22). 4. The dividing up of his garments (vv. 23–24). 5. The care he took of his mother (vv. 25–27). 6. The giving to him of wine vinegar to drink (vv. 28–29). 7. His dying word (v. 30). 8. The piercing of his side (vv. 31–37). 9. The burial of his body (vv. 38–42).

Verses 1–15

Here is a further account of the unfair trial given to our Lord Jesus. The prosecutors carried it out with great confusion among the people, and the judge with great confusion within himself.

1. The judge abused the prisoner even though he declared him to be innocent, hoping that this would pacify the prosecutors.

1.1. He ordered him to be flogged as a criminal (v. 1). *Pilate*, having been prevented from carrying out his plan to release Jesus through the people's choice, *took Jesus, and scourged him.* Matthew and Mark mention his flogging after his condemnation, but here it appears to have been before. Luke speaks about Pilate's offering to *chastise him, and let him go,* which must have been before his sentence. This flogging of him was intended only to pacify the Jews. Flogging among the Romans was usually very severe, not limited, as among the Jews, to *forty stripes* (Dt 25:3), but Christ submitted to this pain and shame for our sakes:

1.1.1. So that the Scripture would be fulfilled, which spoke of *the chastisement of our peace* being *upon him* (Isa 53:5). He himself had foretold it (Mt 20:19; Mk 10:34; Lk 18:33).

1.1.2. So that *by his stripes we might be healed* (1Pe 2:24). The physician was flogged, and so the patient was healed.

1.1.3. So that wounds received for his sake might be sanctified and made beneficial to his followers. Christ's wounds take the sting out of those of his followers.

1.2. He turned him over to his soldiers to be ridiculed and made fun of as a fool (vv. 2–3): *The soldiers put a crown of thorns upon his head; they put on him a purple robe* and complimented him with, *Hail, king of the Jews;* and then they *smote him with their hands.*

1.2.1. See here the corruption and injustice of Pilate. He did this:

1.2.1.1. To satisfy his soldiers' appetite for merriment, and perhaps his own too. *Herod,* as well as *his men of war,* had just before done the same thing (Lk 23:11). It was like a play in a theater to them, now that it was a festival time.

1.2.1.2. To satisfy the Jews' appetite for doing ill.

1.2.2. Notice here the rudeness and arrogance of the soldiers. Christ's holy religion, like Christ himself, has been corruptly misrepresented, dressed up by evildoers at their pleasure, and so exposed to contempt and ridicule.

1.2.2.1. They clothed him with a mock robe. Just as Christ was represented here as a king in name only, so his religion was represented as a concern in name only, and to many people, God and the soul, sin and duty, heaven and hell, are all myths.

1.2.2.2. They crowned him with thorns, as if to submit to the control of God and conscience were to thrust one's head into a thicket of thorns; but this is an unjust assertion: *thorns and snares are in the way of the froward* (Pr 22:5), but roses and laurels are along the paths of religious faith.

1.2.3. Notice here the wonderful condescension of our Lord Jesus. Great and generous minds can bear anything better than disgrace, but the great and holy Jesus submitted to this for us. Notice in wonder the invincible patience of a sufferer and the invincible love and kindness of a Savior. He was committed in love: he not only died for us; he died like a fool for us.

1.2.3.1. He endured the pain, and not only the pain of death; as if that were too little, he submitted to those previous pains. Since Christ humbled himself to bear those thorns in the head, and those torments, to save and teach us, shall we complain of a thorn in the flesh, and of being buffeted about by adversity?

1.2.3.2. He despised the shame (Heb 2:12), the shame of the clothes of a fool and of the false respect shown him with, *Hail, king of the Jews.* The One who bore these false honors was rewarded with real honor, as we will be too if we patiently suffer shame for him.

2. Pilate presented him to the prosecutors in the hope that they would now be satisfied (vv. 4–5). He proposed two things for their consideration here:

2.1. That he had not found anything in Jesus that made him repugnant to the Roman government (v. 4): *I find no fault in him.* If he found no fault with him, why then did he bring him out to his prosecutors, and not immediately release him, as he should have? Wanting to do what was expedient, wanting to please the people by flogging Christ and to save his own conscience by not crucifying him, he did both. Those who think they can keep themselves from greater sins by risking lesser sins commonly run into both.

2.2. That he had done to him what would make him less dangerous to them and their government (v. 5). He brought him out to them wearing the crown of thorns, his head and face all bloody, and said, *Behold the man,* treating him as a slave and exposing him to contempt, after which he supposed the people would never look on Christ with any respect. Little did Pilate think with what respect even this suffering of Christ would later be commemorated by the best and greatest people. Notice here:

2.2.1. Our Lord Jesus showed himself dressed in all the marks of shame. He came out willing to be made a spectacle. Did he go out bearing our shame? Let us go out to him *bearing his reproach* (Heb 13:13).

2.2.2. How Pilate presented him: Pilate said to them, with the intention of appeasing them, *Behold the man.* He said this not so much to move them to pity — "Behold a man worthy of your compassion" — as to silence their jealousy: "Behold a man not worthy of your suspicion." The words, however, are very moving: *Behold the man.* It is good for each of us to look at the man Christ Jesus (1Ti 2:5) in his sufferings. "Look at him and mourn because of him. Look at him and love him; be continually *looking unto Jesus* (Heb 12:2)."

3. The prosecutors were actually even angrier (vv. 6–7). Notice:

3.1. Their clamor and outrage. *The chief priests cried out,* and their officers joined them in shouting, *Crucify him, crucify him.* The common people perhaps would have accepted Pilate's declaration of his innocence, but their leaders *caused them to err* (Am 2:4). The malice of the mob against Christ was:

3.1.1. Unreasonable and most absurd, in that they did not offer to substantiate their charges against him, but, even though he was innocent, demanded that he be crucified.

3.1.2. Insatiable and very cruel. Neither the extremity of his flogging nor his patience in suffering it could pacify them in the slightest.

3.1.3. Violent and most determined; they wanted their own way. Shall not we be as vigorous and zealous in crying out, *Crown him, Crown him,* if they were so violent in trying to defeat our Lord Jesus, and in shouting, *Crucify him, crucify him*? And shall not our love for him quicken our attempts to glorify him and his kingdom?

3.2. The rebuke Pilate imposed on their fury: *Take you him and crucify him.* He knew they could not, they dared not, crucify him, but it was as if he said, "You will not make me a drudge to your hatred." This was a good decision, if he had only stuck by it. He had found no basis for charges against Christ, and so he should not have continued to negotiate with the prosecutors. Those who want to be kept safe from sin should be deaf to all temptation. In fact, he should have secured the prisoner from their insults. But Pilate did not have enough courage to act according to his conscience.

3.3. The further pretext that the prosecutors gave to their demand (v. 7): *We have a law, and by our law we ought to die, because he made himself the Son of God.* Notice here:

3.3.1. They *made their boast of the law* (Ro 2:23). They had a truly excellent law, but they boasted about their law in vain when they abused it for such corrupt purposes.

3.3.2. They revealed a restless and hardened hatred toward our Lord Jesus. They urged that he claimed he was a God. They turned every stone to remove him.

3.3.3. They perverted the law and made it the instrument of their malice. It was true that blasphemers were to be put to death. Whoever falsely claimed to be the Son of God was guilty of blasphemy (Lev 24:16). But it was false that Christ merely claimed to be the Son of God; he really was. What was his honor, and might have been their happiness, they imputed to him as a crime for which he should die; and yet even if he should die by their law, he should not be crucified, for this was not a death inflicted by their law.

4. The judge brought the prisoner again to his trial, on the basis of this new suggestion. Notice:

4.1. The concern Pilate had when he heard this alleged (v. 8): when he heard that his prisoner claimed not only royalty but also deity, he was *more afraid*.

4.1.1. There was more danger of offending the people if he released him. Although he might hope to pacify their rage against a false king, he could never reconcile them to a false God.

4.1.2. There was even more danger of offending his own conscience if he were to condemn him. "Is he one," Pilate thought, "who claims to be *the Son of God*? What would happen if it turned out that he really is? What would become of me then?"

4.2. His further examination of our Lord Jesus (v. 9). He resumed the debate, going into the palace and asking Christ, *Whence art thou?* Notice:

4.2.1. The place he chose for this examination: He *went into the judgment hall* (palace) for privacy, so that he would be away from the noise and clamor of the crowd. Those who want to find the truth as it is in Jesus (Eph 4:21) must get away from the noise of prejudice and withdraw, as it were, into the judgment hall to speak with Christ alone.

4.2.2. The question he asked him: "*Whence art thou?* Where do you come from? From below or from above? Are you from the human realm or heaven?"

4.2.3. The silence of our Lord Jesus: *But Jesus gave him no answer.* This was not a sullen silence, in contempt of court, nor was it because he did not know what to say. It was a patient silence. This silence showed loudly his submission to his Father's will in his present suffering. He was silent because he would say nothing to prevent his sufferings. It was also a wise silence. When the chief priests asked him, *Art thou the Son of the Blessed?* (Mk 14:61), he answered, *I am*, but when Pilate asked him, he knew Pilate did not understand his own question, having no conception of the Messiah or of the Messiah's being the Son of God. Why should he reply to one whose head was filled with pagan theology?

4.2.4. The arrogant rebuke Pilate gave him for his silence (v. 10): *Speakest thou not unto me? Knowest thou not that I have power to crucify thee, and have power to release thee?* Notice here how Pilate exalted himself and boasted about his own authority. People in power tend to be puffed up with a sense of their power, and the more absolute and arbitrary it is, the more it satisfies and humors their pride. Notice how he trampled on our blessed Savior: *Speakest thou not unto me?* He reflected on Jesus as if he were undutiful and disrespectful to those in authority or as if he were ungrateful to one who had been considerate toward him, as if he were unwise for

himself. If Christ had in fact sought to save his life, now would have been his time to speak up.

4.2.5. Christ's relevant answer to this rebuke (v. 11).

4.2.5.1. He boldly reprimanded Pilate's arrogance: *Thou couldest have no power at all against me, except it were given thee from above.* Although Christ did not see fit to answer Pilate when he was impertinent, he did see fit to answer him when he was imperious. When Pilate used his power, Christ silently submitted to it, but when he became proud of it, he made him understand his position: "All the power you have has been given you from above." His power in general, as a judge, was limited, and he could do no more than God would allow him to do. Let the proud oppressors know that there is *a higher than they*. Let this silence the murmurings of the oppressed; let it comfort them to know that their persecutors can do no more than God will allow them to. Pilate never thought he looked so great as he did now, when he sat in judgment over such a prisoner, who was looked on by many as the Son of God and king of Israel. But Christ let him know that even in this he was only an instrument in God's hand.

4.2.5.2. He mildly excused Pilate's sin in comparison with the sin of the ringleaders: "*Therefore he that delivered me unto thee* lies under greater guilt." It is clearly shown that what Pilate did was sin, that he committed a great sin, and that the force that the Jews exerted on him would not justify him. The guilt of others will not acquit us, nor will it do us any good on the great day to say that others were worse than we were. The sin of those who handed him over to Pilate was the greater. This shows that all sins are not equal; some are more detestable than others. *He that delivered Christ to Pilate* was:

4.2.5.2.1. The Jewish people, who cried out, *Crucify him, crucify him.* They had seen Christ's miracles, which Pilate had not. Their sin in appearing against Christ was much worse, therefore, than Pilate's. Or:

4.2.5.2.2. Caiaphas in particular, who first advised that he be put to death (11:49–50). The sin of Caiaphas was much greater than the sin of Pilate. Caiaphas prosecuted Christ out of pure hostility and with cold premeditation. Pilate condemned him purely out of fear of the people, and it was a hasty decision that he did not give himself time to calmly consider. Or, some think:

4.2.5.2.3. Judas. The sin of Judas was, on many accounts, greater than the sin of Pilate. The sin of Judas was a leading sin, which opened the door to everything that followed. He was *a guide to them that took Jesus* (Ac 1:16).

5. Pilate struggled with the Jews to rescue Jesus out of their hands, but in vain.

5.1. Pilate seems to have been more zealous now than before to have Jesus released (v. 12): *Thenceforth*, though Christ found fault with him, he still found no fault in Christ, but *sought to release him.* If Pilate's politics had not prevailed over his justice, he would not have been trying to release him for long, but would simply have done it.

5.2. The Jews were all the more violently set on having Jesus crucified. They still pursued their plan with noise and clamor, as they had done before. They worked hard to get him decried by the crowd—and it is not difficult to gather a mob. A few mad people may shout down many wise people, and then the former fancy that they are speaking sense—when it is really nonsense—for a nation, but it is not so easy to change the sense of the people as it is to misrepresent it. In their outcry they sought two things:

5.2.1. To describe the prisoner as an enemy of Caesar. They would have it thought that he *speaks against Caesar*. It has always been the trick of the enemies of religion to describe it as harmful to kings and provinces, when it would in fact be highly beneficial to both.

5.2.2. To frighten the judge, as no friend to Caesar: "If you *let this man go thou art not Caesar's friend.*" They insinuated a threat that they would inform on him, and here they touched him at a very tender and sensitive spot. A claimed zeal for what is good often serves to cover up real hatred of what is better.

5.3. Pilate tried to some extent to mock them out of their fury, but in doing this, he betrayed himself to them, yielding to the rapid stream (vv. 13–15). Having seemed just now as if he would vigorously resist this attack (v. 12), he cruelly surrendered. Notice:

5.3.1. What it was that shocked Pilate (v. 13): *When he heard that saying*, that he could not be sure of Caesar's favor if he did not put Jesus to death, then he thought it was time to look around him. Those who have their happiness bound up in the favor of people make themselves an easy target to the temptations of Satan.

5.3.2. What preparation was made for a definitive sentence on this matter: *Pilate brought Jesus forth* and then *sat down in the judgment* (on the judge's) *seat*. Christ was condemned with all possible ceremony. Notice is taken here of the place and time. The place where Christ was condemned was in *a place called the Pavement, but in Hebrew, Gabbatha*, probably the place where Pilate customarily sat to judge between litigants and try criminals. The time was the day of Preparation for the Passover (v. 14), *about the sixth hour*. Notice:

5.3.2.1. The day: it was the day of Preparation for the Passover, that is, for the Passover Sabbath. This took place when the Jews should have been cleansing and removing the old yeast to get ready for the Passover; but the better the day, the worse the deed.

5.3.2.2. The hour: *It was about the sixth hour.* Some ancient Greek and Latin manuscripts read that it was "about the third hour," which corresponds with Mk 15:25, and it appears from Mt 27:45 that he was on the cross before the sixth hour. This expression seems to have been included here to give additional emphasis to the sin of his prosecutors: they were pursuing the prosecution not only on a solemn day, the *day of the preparation*, but also from the third to the sixth hour—the time of their religious service—on that day they were employed in this wickedness; for that day, then, though they were priests, they dropped the temple service.

5.3.3. The encounter Pilate had with the Jews, trying in vain to stem the tide of their rage.

5.3.3.1. He said to them: *"Behold your king*, that is, the One whom you accuse as a pretender to the crown. Is this man likely to be dangerous to the government?" It seems as if Pilate was the voice of God to them, though he was far from meaning to be so. Christ, now crowned with thorns, was, like a king at his coronation, offered to the people: *Behold your king.*

5.3.3.2. They cried out with the greatest indignation, *"Away with him, away with him. Take him*; he has nothing to do with us; we disown him; *away with him* out of our sight." This shows:

5.3.3.2.1. How we deserved to be treated at God's tribunal. If Christ had not been so rejected by people, we would have been rejected forever by God.

5.3.3.2.2. How we should treat our sins. In Scripture we are often said to crucify sin (Ro 6:6; Gal 5:24; 6:14) in conformity to Christ's death. We should defeat sin in ourselves with a godly indignation, just as they had an ungodly indignation and defeated the One who was made sin for us (2Co 5:21).

5.3.3.3. Pilate, willing to have Jesus released, asked them, *Shall I crucify your king?* He intended either:

5.3.3.3.1. To silence their mouths, showing them how absurd it was for them to reject one who offered himself to them to be their king. Although Pilate saw no reason to fear Christ, they might see cause to hope for something from him. Or:

5.3.3.3.2. To silence the mouth of his own conscience. "If this Jesus is a king," Pilate thought, "he is only king of the Jews. If they refuse him and want to have their king crucified, what is that to me?"

5.3.3.4. The chief priests cried out, *We have no king but Caesar.* They knew this would please Pilate, and so they hoped to win their point, though at the same time they hated Caesar and his rule. It was righteous of God to bring on them through the Romans the ruin that followed not long afterward. They were faithful to Caesar, and to Caesar they would go (Ac 25:12). God soon gave them enough of their Caesars. From that time on, they were rebels to the Caesars, and the Caesars were tyrants to them, and their hostility ended in the overthrow of their city and nation. It is just of God to make a scourge and plague to us out of what we prefer before Christ.

Verses 16–18

Here the sentence of death was passed on our Lord Jesus, and execution carried out soon afterward. Pilate had had a mighty struggle within him, but finally his conviction gave in and his corruptions won, the fear of human beings having greater power over him than the fear of God.

1. Pilate declared judgment against Christ and signed the warrant for his execution (v. 16). We may see here:

1.1. How Pilate sinned against his conscience; he had again and again declared Christ innocent, but finally he condemned him as guilty. Pilate had displeased the Jewish nation often, because he was a man of a proud and implacable spirit. Fearing, therefore, that he would be complained about, he was willing to satisfy the Jews in this matter. Now this made the matter even worse. For a man who was so willful in other things and had such fierce resolution to be overcome in something like this showed him to be a truly bad man, who could better bear the wronging of his conscience than the crossing of his mood.

1.2. How he tried to transfer the guilt onto the Jews. He delivered Christ to the prosecutors, the chief priests and elders, so excusing the wrong to his own conscience by calling it merely a permissive condemnation, telling himself that he had not put Christ to death but only turned a blind eye to those who did.

2. No sooner was judgment given than the prosecutors, having won their point, resolved to lose no time for fear that Pilate might change his mind and there might be *an uproar among the people.* We would do well to be as quick in doing good as they were in doing evil, not waiting around for greater difficulties to arise.

2.1. They immediately rushed the prisoner away. The chief priests greedily pounced on the victim they had long been waiting for. Or *they*, that is, the soldiers, took him and led him away. Both the priests and the soldiers joined in leading him away. According to the Law of Moses, the prosecutors were to be the executioners (Dt 17:7), and the priests here were proud of the office. He was led out for us so that we could escape.

2.2. To add to his misery, they forced him to carry his cross (v. 17), according to the custom among the Romans. Their crosses did not stand up constantly, because the evildoer was nailed to the cross as it lay on the ground.

Everyone who was crucified had a cross of his own. Christ's carrying his cross may be considered:

2.2.1. As a part of his sufferings; he endured the cross literally. The blessed body of the Lord Jesus was tender; it had now just been harassed and tired out; his shoulders were sore from the flogging they had given him; every jog of the cross would renew the sting from this and also tend to strike the thorns he was crowned with deeper into his head. But he patiently underwent all this. He was made a curse for us, and so the cross was on him.

2.2.2. As fulfilling the type that had gone before him: Isaac (Ge 22:6).

2.2.3. As very instructive to us. Our Master was teaching all his disciples here to take up their cross and follow him (Mt 16:24). Whatever cross he calls us out to bear at any time, we must remember that he bore the cross first. He carried that end of the cross that bore the curse on it; this was the heavy end, and so all who are his are enabled to call their sufferings for him *light* (2Co 4:17).

2.3. They brought him to the place of execution: he *went forth*; he was not dragged against his will, but was voluntary in his sufferings. He went outside the city, because he was *crucified without the gate* (Heb 13:12). Moreover, to put greater infamy on his sufferings, they led him to the common place of execution, a place called *Golgotha, the place of a skull*. Christ suffered there because he was *made sin for us* (2Co 5:21).

2.4. *There they crucified him*, and the other evildoers with him (v. 18). Notice:

2.4.1. What death Christ died: the death of the cross, a bloody, painful, shameful death, a cursed death. He was lifted up like the bronze snake (Nu 21:9). His hands were stretched out to invite and embrace us.

2.4.2. In what company he died: *Two others with him.* This exposed him much to the contempt and hatred of the people, who would be likely to judge individuals according to those they were associated with, and not to be interested in discerning differences between them. They would conclude not only that he was an evildoer because he was yoked with evildoers, but also that he was the worst of the three because he was put between the other two. But this was how the Scripture was fulfilled: *He was numbered among the transgressors* (Isa 53:12). He died among the criminals and mixed his blood with those who were sacrificed to public justice. Now let us pause for a while and look at Jesus with the eye of faith. Was ever sorrow like his sorrow (La 1:12)? See him bleeding, see him struggling, see him dying, see him and love him, love him and live for him, and seek what *we shall render to the Lord* (Ps 116:12).

Verses 19–30

Here are some remarkable details of Christ's dying that are related more fully than before.

1. The notice set over his head. We have here:

1.1. The inscription itself that Pilate wrote and ordered to be fastened to the top of the cross, declaring the reason that he was crucified (v. 19). It was this: *Jesus of Nazareth, the King of the Jews.* Pilate intended this as a reproach to Jesus, that he, being *Jesus of Nazareth*, had claimed to be king of the Jews and set himself up to compete with Caesar. However, God overruled in this matter so that:

1.1.1. The inscription would bear further testimony to the innocence of our Lord Jesus, because here was an accusation that, as it was worded, contained no crime.

1.1.2. It would display his position and honor. This was Jesus, a Savior, dying for the good of his people, as Caiaphas had foretold (11:50).

1.2. The notice taken of this inscription (v. 20): *Many of the Jews read it*, not only those from Jerusalem but also those from other countries who came to worship at the feast. Very many people read it, and it brought a wide range of reflections and speculations. Christ himself was *set as a sign* (Lk 2:34). The inscription was read so much:

1.2.1. Because the place where Jesus was crucified, though outside the gates of the city, was still near the city. It is an advantage to have the means of knowing Christ brought close to our doors.

1.2.2. Because it was written in Hebrew, Greek, and Latin; they all understood one or another of these languages. Everyone would be curious to ask what it was that was so meticulously made known in the three most well-known languages. In each of these Christ was declared king; this showed that Jesus Christ would be a Savior to all nations, not only to the Jews, and also that every nation would hear *in their own tongue the wonderful works* (Ac 2:8, 11) of the Redeemer. It teaches us that the knowledge of Christ should be spread throughout every nation in their own language, so that people may converse as freely with the Scriptures as they do with their neighbors.

1.3. The offense the prosecutors took at it (v. 21). They did not want it written, *the king of the Jews*, but that he claimed, *I am the king of the Jews.* Here they showed themselves:

1.3.1. Very spiteful and malicious toward Christ. To justify themselves they were concerned to describe him as a usurper of honors and powers he was not entitled to.

1.3.2. Foolishly jealous of the honor of their nation. Although they were a conquered and enslaved people, they scorned to have it said that this was their king.

1.3.3. Very arrogant and troublesome toward Pilate. They must have been aware that they had forced him against his will to condemn Christ, and yet in such a trivial matter as this, they continued to tease him; nor had they proved their charge that Christ had claimed to be king of the Jews.

1.4. The judge's decision to stand by what he had written: *What I have written I have written.*

1.4.1. Here Pilate insulted the chief priests. By this inscription he insinuated:

1.4.1.1. That despite their pretense, they were not sincere in their affection for Caesar and his government.

1.4.1.2. That such a king, so humble and contemptible, was good enough to be the king of the Jews.

1.4.1.3. That they had been very unjust in prosecuting this Jesus when there was no basis for bringing charges against him.

1.4.2. Here Pilate honored the Lord Jesus. Pilate insisted with determination that Jesus was the king of the Jews. When the Jews rejected Christ, Pilate, a Gentile, insisted that he was a king, which was a pledge of what took place soon afterward, when the Gentiles submitted to the kingdom of the Messiah.

2. The dividing of his garments among the executioners (vv. 23–24). Four soldiers were employed, who, *when they had crucified Jesus*, when they had nailed him to the cross and lifted it up with him on it, and there was nothing more to do but wait for him to die, went to divide up his clothes. They *made four parts*, as nearly of the same value as they could, *to every soldier a part*, but *his coat, without seam, woven from the top throughout*, they *cast lots for.* Notice:

2.1. The shame they put on our Lord Jesus. The shame of nakedness came in with sin (Ge 3:7, 10). Therefore the One who was made sin for us (2Co 5:21) bore that shame.

2.2. The wages with which these soldiers paid themselves for crucifying Christ. They were willing to do it for his old clothes. Whenever something bad is to be done, there will always be evildoers who are bad enough to do it for a petty sum.

2.3. The game they played with his seamless coat. We do not read of anything about him that was valuable or remarkable except this. Tradition says that his mother wove it for him, and adds that it was made for him when he was a child and it never wore out. But this is a thought without basis. The soldiers thought it a pity to tear it, because it would then unravel; they *therefore cast lots for it*. While Christ was in his dying anguish, they were merrily dividing his spoils. The preserving of Christ's seamless garment is commonly alluded to to show the care all Christians should take that they do not tear apart the church of Christ with strife and division.

2.4. The fulfilling of the Scripture in this. David, in the Spirit, foretold this very detail of Christ's sufferings in Ps 22:18. *These things therefore the soldiers did—therefore*, that is, so that the Scripture would be fulfilled.

3. The care that he took of his poor mother.

3.1. His mother was with him to his death (v. 25): *There stood by the cross his mother*, and some of his relatives and friends with her. At first they stood near, as it is said here, but later the soldiers probably forced them to stand at a distance, as it is said in Matthew and Mark.

3.1.1. Notice here the caring love of these godly women. When all his disciples except John had forsaken him, these women stayed with him. They were not deterred by the fury of the enemy or the horror of the sight; they could not rescue him nor relieve him, but they were still with him.

3.1.2. We may easily suppose what suffering it was for these poor women to see him mistreated as he was, especially to the Blessed Virgin. Now Simeon's word was fulfilled: *A sword shall pierce through thy own soul* (Lk 2:35). His torments tortured her, and her heart bled with his wounds.

3.1.3. We may justly wonder at the power of divine grace in supporting these women, especially the Virgin Mary. We do not find his mother wringing her hands or crying out loudly, but standing by the cross, her friends with her. Surely she and they had such patience because they were strengthened by God's power. We do not know what we can bear until we are tested, and then we know the One who has said, *My grace is sufficient for thee* (2Co 12:9).

3.2. He tenderly provided for his mother. It is probable that Joseph had died long before and that her son Jesus had supported her, and now that he was dying, what would become of her? He saw her standing by, and he saw John standing not far away, and so he settled a new relationship between his dearly loved mother and his dearly loved disciple, saying, *Woman, behold thy son*, and to him, *Behold thy mother*. So *from that hour that disciple took her to his own home*. Notice:

3.2.1. The care Christ took of his dear mother. He was not taken up with a sense of his own suffering so much that he forgot his friends. He had no other way of providing for his mother than through his relationship with a friend, which he did here.

3.2.1.1. He called her *woman*, not mother, because "Mother" would have been a cutting word to her when she was already wounded to the heart with grief.

3.2.1.2. He told her to look on John as her son. This was an expression of divine goodness. Sometimes, when God removes one comfort from us, he raises up another for us, perhaps where we were not looking for it. Let no

one, therefore, consider everything lost when one cistern has dried up, for another can be filled from the same fountain. His words here were also an example of the duty of children to show respect for their parents. Christ has here taught children to provide for the comfort of their aged parents. Children should provide, according to their ability, that if their parents survive them and need their kindness, their needs will be supplied.

3.2.2. The confidence he put in the disciple he loved. He said to him, *Behold thy mother*. This was an honor given to John and a testimony to both his wisdom and his faithfulness. It is a great honor to be employed for Christ, to be entrusted with any of his concerns in the world. It would be a care and a great responsibility for John, but he accepted it cheerfully *and took her to his own home*. Those who truly love Christ and are loved by him will be glad to have an opportunity to do any service for him or his people.

4. The fulfilling of the Scripture in the giving of wine vinegar to him to drink (vv. 28–29). Notice:

4.1. How much respect Christ showed the Scriptures (v. 28): *Knowing that all things were accomplished, that the scripture might be fulfilled, he saith, I thirst.*

4.1.1. It was not at all strange that he was thirsty. Well might he thirst after all his toil and rushing around, and because he was now in the anguish of death, he was about to expire purely from the loss of blood and the extremity of his pain.

4.1.2. However, his complaining about it is somewhat surprising; it is the only word he spoke that looked like a complaint about his outward sufferings. When flogged, he did not cry out, "Oh, my back!" Yet now he cried out, *I thirst*. He did this because:

4.1.2.1. He wanted to express in this way *the travail of his soul* (Isa 53:11). He thirsted for the fulfillment of the work of our redemption.

4.1.2.2. He wanted to make sure the Scripture was fulfilled. Up to this time, all had been fulfilled, and he knew it. The Scripture had foretold his thirst, and so he himself spoke about it—because it could not be known otherwise—saying, *I thirst*. The Scripture had foretold that in his thirst he would have wine vinegar given him to drink (Ps 69:21).

4.2. How little respect his persecutors showed to him (v. 29): *There was set a vessel* (jar) *full of vinegar*, probably according to the custom at all executions of this kind, and *they filled a sponge* with this, *and they put it upon hyssop*, a stalk of hyssop, and used this to lift it to his mouth. A drop of water would have cooled his tongue better than a draft of vinegar. When heaven denied him a ray of light, earth denied him a drop of water and put wine vinegar in its place.

5. The dying word with which he gave up his spirit (v. 30): *When he had received the vinegar, he said, It is finished*, and with that, *bowed his head, and gave up the ghost*. Notice:

5.1. What he said, and we may imagine he said it with triumph and exultation: *It is finished*.

5.1.1. *It is finished*, that is, the hatred and enmity of his persecutors have now done their worst.

5.1.2. *It is finished*, that is, the purpose and command of his Father concerning his sufferings were now fulfilled. He had said when he began his sufferings, *Father, thy will be done* (Mt 26:42), and now he said with pleasure, *It is done*.

5.1.3. *It is finished*, that is, all the types and prophecies of the Old Testament, which pointed to the sufferings of the Messiah, were fulfilled and answered.

5.1.4. *It is finished*, that is, the ceremonial law was abolished. The substance had now come, and all the shadows were done away with (Col 2:17; Heb 8:5; 10:1).

5.1.5. *It is finished*, that is, sin is finished, and transgression brought to an end. *The Lamb of God was sacrificed to take away the sin of the world* (1:29), and it was done (Heb 9:26).

5.1.6. *It is finished*, that is, his sufferings were now finished. The storm was over, the worst was past, and he was entering *the joy set before him* (Heb 12:2). Let all who suffer for Christ and with Christ comfort themselves with the assurance that in a little while they too will say, "It is finished."

5.1.7. *It is finished*, that is, his life was now finished, and he was ready to breathe his last. We must all come to such a point soon.

5.1.8. *It is finished*, that is, the work of human redemption and salvation had now been completed, a fatal blow given to the power of Satan, and a fountain of grace opened that will always flow. *He that has begun a good work will perform it* (Php 1:6); the mystery of God will be finished (Rev 10:7).

5.2. What he did: *He bowed his head, and gave up the ghost. He gave up the ghost* (his spirit). His life was not forcibly extorted from him; he freely gave it up. He had said, *Father, into thy hands I commit my spirit* (Lk 23:46), and accordingly, he gave up his spirit, paid the price of pardon and life at his Father's hands. *He bowed his head.* When those who were crucified were dying, they stretched up their heads to gasp out for breath, not dropping their heads until they had breathed their last, but Christ bowed his head first, composing himself, as it were, to fall asleep.

Verses 31–37

This passage about the piercing of Christ's side after his death is recorded only by this Evangelist. Notice:

1. The superstition of the Jews that brought it about (v. 31): *Because it was the preparation for the sabbath, and because that sabbath day was a high day*, they would *not have the dead bodies to remain on the crosses on the Sabbath day*, but *besought Pilate that their legs might be broken*, and then they could be buried out of sight. Notice:

1.1. The respect they wanted to be thought to have for the approaching Sabbath. Every Sabbath is a holy day, and a good day, but this was a special day, "a great day." Sacrament days, Supper days, Communion days are special days, and there should be more than an ordinary preparation for them.

1.2. The insult they reckoned it would be to that day if the dead bodies were left hanging on the crosses. Dead bodies were not to be left at any time, but in this case, the Jews would have allowed the Roman custom to take place if it had not been an extraordinary day, when it would have offended those visiting for the feast; nor could they bear the sight of Christ's crucified body, because it would cause their consciences to rebuke them.

1.3. Their request to Pilate that their bodies, now as good as dead, be finished off by breaking their legs, which would end their lives in the most excruciating pain. The false sanctity of hypocrites is detestable. These Jews had no hesitation about putting an innocent and good person on the cross, but had scruples about letting a dead body hang on the cross.

2. The dealing with the *two thieves that were crucified with him* (v. 32). Pilate gave orders as they wanted, *and the soldiers came and broke the legs of the two thieves.*

One of these thieves was a penitent and had received from Christ an assurance that he would soon be with him in Paradise, but he still died in the same pain and misery that the other thief did. The extremity of dying anguish is no obstruction to the living comforts that wait for holy souls on the other side of death.

3. The examination that was made to see whether Christ was dead or not.

3.1. They thought he was dead, and so they *did not break his legs* (v. 33). Jesus died in less time than people crucified usually did. This was to show that he laid down his life by himself. Although he yielded to death, he still was not defeated. His enemies were satisfied that he really was dead.

3.2. Yet because they wanted to be sure he was dead, they would put it beyond dispute. *One of the soldiers with a spear pierced his side, and forthwith came there out blood and water* (v. 34).

3.2.1. The soldier wanted to settle the question whether he was dead or not, and by this honorable wound in his side he would replace the ignominious method they used with the other two. Tradition says that this soldier was healed of a disease in his eyes by blood from Christ's side that fell on them.

3.2.2. However, God had a further intention in this matter:

3.2.2.1. To give evidence of the truth of his death, in order to prove his resurrection. He was certainly dead, because this spear broke open the true fountains of life.

3.2.2.2. To illustrate the intention of his death. His death contained much mystery, and its being so solemnly affirmed (v. 35) shows there was something miraculous in it. It was remarkable; this same apostle refers to it as significant (1Jn 5:6, 8).

3.2.2.2.1. The opening of his side was significant. When we want to declare our sincerity, we wish there were a window in our hearts, so that their thoughts and intentions might be visible to all. Through this window that opened up in Christ's side, you may look into his heart and see love aflame there, love strong as death (SS 8:6).

3.2.2.2.2. The blood and water that flowed out of it were significant. They represented the two great benefits that all believers share in through Christ—blood for atonement, water for purification. Guilt contracted must be atoned for by blood; stains contracted must be done away by *the water of purification* (Nu 19:9). These two must always go together. Christ has joined them together, and we must not think to separate them (Mt 19:6). They both flowed from the pierced side of our Redeemer. They represented the two great decrees of baptism and the Lord's Supper. It is not the water in the font that will be *the washing of regeneration* (Tit 3:5) to us, but the water from the side of Christ; it is not the blood of the grape that will refresh the soul, but the blood from the side of Christ.

4. The affirmation of the truth of this by an eyewitness (v. 35), the Evangelist himself. Notice:

4.1. What a competent witness of the facts he was.

4.1.1. What he gave testimony to he saw; he was an eyewitness of it.

4.1.2. What he saw he faithfully gave testimony to; he told not only the truth but the whole truth. His record is undoubtedly true, because he wrote from the inspiration of the Spirit of truth. He had full assurance of the truth of what he wrote himself: *He knows that he saith true* (v. 35).

4.1.3. He witnessed these things so *that we might believe*; he did it to draw people to believe the Gospel for their eternal welfare.

4.2. What care he showed in this particular instance. Let this silence the fears of weak Christians and encourage their hopes. Both water and blood flowed out of Christ's pierced side, so that they might be both justified and sanctified. If you ask, "How can we be sure of this?" you may be sure because *he that saw it bore record.*

5. The fulfillment of the Scripture in all this (v. 36): *that the scripture might be fulfilled.*

5.1. The Scripture was fulfilled in the preserving of his legs from being broken. In this those words were fulfilled, *A bone of him shall not be broken* (Ps 34:20). A promise of this was indeed made to all the righteous, but it pointed mainly to *Jesus Christ the righteous* (1Jn 2:1). There was a type of this in the paschal lamb (Nu 9:12): *You shall not break any bone of it.* Christ is *the Lamb of God* (1:29), and since he was the true Passover, his bones were kept unbroken. There was a significance in it; the strength of the body is in the bones, and the Hebrew word for *bones* means "strength." Although *he was crucified in weakness* (2Co 13:4), his strength to save was not broken at all. Sin breaks our bones, but it did not break Christ's bones; he stood firm under the burden, powerful to save (Isa 63:1).

5.2. The Scripture was fulfilled in the piercing of his side (v. 27): *They shall look on me whom they have pierced,* as it is written (Zec 12:10). It was implied here that the Messiah would be pierced, and here it had a more complete fulfillment than in the piercing of his hands and feet. It was promised that *when the Spirit was poured out, they would look on him and mourn* (Zec 12:10). This was partly fulfilled when many of those who were his betrayers and murderers *were pricked to the heart* (Ac 2:37) and brought to believe in him. We have all been guilty of piercing the Lord Jesus, and we should all be anxious to look at him with appropriate feelings.

Verses 38–42

We have here an account of the burial of the body of our Lord Jesus. Come and see a burial that conquered the grave and buried it, a burial that made beautiful the grave and softened it for all believers. Here is:

1. The body asked for (v. 38). This was done by *Joseph of Arimathea,* of whom no mention is made in the whole New Testament except in the narrative each of the Evangelists gives us of Christ's burial. Notice:

1.1. The character of this Joseph. He was a secret disciple of Christ, a better friend of Christ than he would willingly be known to be. It was his honor that he was a disciple of Christ, and there are some such people, who themselves are great but are unavoidably linked with bad people. But it was his weakness that he acted so secretly. Christ may have many who are his sincere disciples but who keep their faith secret. Better secret than not at all, especially if, like Joseph here, they grow stronger and stronger. Some who have been afraid in times of small testing have been very courageous in greater ones, as was Joseph here. He went boldly to Pilate the governor, but feared the Jews. The powerless hatred of those who can only censure and insult is sometimes more formidable even to wise and good people than one would think.

1.2. The part he had in this matter. Having access to Pilate, he asked permission from him to dispose of the body. Christ's disciples had gone; if no one appeared, the Jews or soldiers would bury him with the thieves. When God has work to do, he can find the proper people to do it and make them bold to undertake it. It shows the humiliation of Christ that his dead body lay at the mercy of a pagan judge and must be begged for before it could be buried.

2. The embalming prepared (v. 39). This was done by Nicodemus, another person of high status and a holder of a public position. He brought *a mixture of myrrh and aloes.* We see here:

2.1. The character of Nicodemus, which was much the same as that of Joseph; he was a secret friend of Christ. He originally *came to Jesus by night* (3:2), but now he confessed him publicly, as before (7:50–51). The grace that is at first like a bruised reed may later become like a strong cedar. It is a wonder that Joseph and Nicodemus, men of such influence, did not appear on the scene sooner and ask Pilate not to condemn Christ. Begging for his life would have been a nobler act of service than begging for his dead body.

2.2. The kindness of Nicodemus. Joseph served Christ with his influence; Nicodemus with his financial resources. They probably made an agreement as to what each would do, because they were pressed for time. But why did they make such a fuss about Christ's dead body? Some think it showed the weakness of their faith. What need was there for such furnishings of the grave for One who, like a traveler, only turned aside there to stay for a night or two? However, we may clearly see in it the strength of their love. Here they showed the value they had for his person and teaching, and that it was not lessened by the shame of the cross. They showed not only the charitable respect of committing his body to the earth but also the honorable respect shown to great people. They could do this and yet believe and look for his resurrection. Since God intended honor for this body, they would honor it.

3. The body prepared (v. 40). They *took it* and, having washed the blood and dust from it, *wound it in linen clothes* with the spices, as *the manner of the Jews is to bury.*

3.1. Here care was taken of Christ's body: it was *wound in linen clothes.* As a human being, Christ wore clothes just as we do, even graveclothes, to make them comfortable for us and enable us to call them our wedding clothes. Dead bodies and graves are repulsive and offensive, but because Christ's sacrifice is like a *sweet-smelling savor to God* (Eph 5:2), it has taken away our defilement. No ointment or perfume can make the heart so joyful as the grave of our Redeemer does, when the heart has faith to recognize the sweet fragrance of that grave.

3.2. In conformity to this example, we should respect the dead bodies of Christians, not to enshrine and adore their relics, but carefully to deposit them, dust in dust, as those who believe the dead bodies of the saints are still united to Christ. The resurrection of the saints will be owing to Christ's resurrection, and so in burying them we should look to Christ's burial.

4. The grave being chosen, in a garden that belonged to Joseph of Arimathea, very near the place where Jesus was crucified. There was a new, unused tomb. Notice:

4.1. Christ was buried outside the city, as was the custom of the Jews. In those days there was a special reason for this prohibition, namely, that by touching a grave one contracted ceremonial defilement; but now that the resurrection of Christ has changed the nature of death, we need not keep so far away from it. Those who want to visit the holy tomb by faith, not superstitiously, must leave the noise of this world.

4.2. Christ was buried in a garden. Joseph had his tomb in his garden so that it would be a reminder:

4.2.1. To himself while living. The garden is a proper place for meditation, and a tomb there may provide us with a proper subject for meditation.

4.2.2. To his heirs and successors when he was gone. It is good to come to know the *place of our fathers' sepulchres* (Ne 2:3), and perhaps we would make our own graves less formidable if we were more familiar with theirs. Christ's body was laid in a tomb in a garden. In the Garden of Eden death and the grave first received their power, and now in a garden they were conquered.

4.3. He was buried in a new tomb. This was ordered:

4.3.1. To honor Christ. The One who was born from a virgin's womb must rise from a virgin tomb.

4.3.2. To confirm the truth of his resurrection, so that it could not be suggested that it was not he, but some other person, who rose. The One who has *made all things new* (Rev 21:5) has made the grave new for us.

5. The funeral ceremony held (v. 42): *There laid they Jesus*. They laid him there because it was the day of Preparation. Notice:

5.1. The respect the Jews showed to the Sabbath and the day of preparation. This day had been poorly kept by the chief priests, who called themselves the church, but was well kept by the disciples of Christ, who were branded as dangerous to the church; and so it often is. They would not delay the funeral until the Sabbath, because the Sabbath is to be a day of holy rest and joy. Nor would they delay it too late on the day of Preparation for the Sabbath.

5.2. That they used a tomb nearby, *nigh at hand*. It was so ordered:

5.2.1. Because he was to lie there for only a short while, as in an inn, and so he took the first tomb that presented itself.

5.2.2. Because this was a new tomb. Those who prepared it little thought who would use it for the first time.

5.2.3. To teach us not to be too fussy about the place where we are buried. Where the tree falls, why should it not lie (Ecc 11:3)? Christ was buried in the tomb that was closest, without any pomp or solemnity. Here death itself lay, put to death, and the grave was defeated. *Thanks be to God, who giveth us the victory* (1Co 15:57).

CHAPTER 20

Although this Evangelist did not begin his Gospel as the others did, he concludes it as they did, with an account of Christ's resurrection. He does not write about the resurrection itself but about its proofs and evidence. The proofs of Christ's resurrection that we have in this chapter are: 1. Those that occurred immediately at the tomb. 1.1. The tomb was found empty (vv. 1–10). 1.2. Two angels appeared to Mary Magdalene at the tomb (vv. 11–13). 1.3. Christ himself appeared to her (vv. 14–18). 2. Those that occurred later, at the meetings of the apostles. 2.1. At one on the same evening that Christ rose, when Thomas was absent (vv. 19–25). 2.2. At another a week later, when Thomas was with them (vv. 26–31).

Verses 1–10

1. There was no one thing that the apostles were more concerned to produce substantial proof for than the resurrection of their Master:

1.1. Because it was what he himself appealed to as the last and most powerful proof that he was the Messiah. That was why his enemies were most concerned to stifle this announcement.

1.2. Because it was on this that the fulfillment of his commitment to redeem and save us depended.

1.3. Because he never showed himself alive after his resurrection to all the people (Ac 10:40–41). The demonstrations of his resurrection were to be reserved as a favor

for his special friends, and by them its message was to be declared to the world, so that those who have not seen but have believed would be blessed (v. 29).

In these verses we have the first step toward the proof of Christ's resurrection: the tomb was found empty.

2. When Mary Magdalene came to the tomb, she found the *stone taken away*. This Evangelist does not mention the other women who went with Mary Magdalene, but only her. She had been forgiven much, and that was why she loved much (Lk 7:47). She had shown her affection for him while he lived, listening to his teaching and ministering to him out of her resources (Lk 8:2–3). The continued expressions of her respect for him at and after his death prove the sincerity of her love. If love for Christ is sincere, it will be constant. Her love for Christ was *strong as death* (SS 8:6), the death of the cross, because it stood by the cross.

2.1. She *came to the sepulchre* to *wash* the dead body *with her tears*, because she went to the grave *to weep there* and to *anoint* his body *with the ointment* she had prepared (Lk 7:38; 24:1). Only an extraordinary love for a person will endear their grave to us. The grave is especially terrible to women. Love for Christ will take the edge off the terror of death and the grave. If we cannot come to Christ except through that dark valley, then even in that, if we love him, we will *fear no evil* (Ps 23:4).

2.2. She came as soon as she could, on the *first day of the week*, as soon as the Sabbath had passed. This was the first Christian Sabbath, and she began it accordingly, with seeking Christ. She came *early, while it was yet dark*. Those who want to seek Christ so as to find him must seek him early (Pr 8:17), seek him with great concern; we are to be up and about early for fear of missing him. We are to seek him diligently and seek him early. The day that is begun in this way is likely to end well. Those who diligently seek Christ while it is still dark will be given a light concerning him that will shine *more and more* (Pr 4:18).

2.3. She found the stone taken away, which she had seen *rolled to the door of the sepulchre* (Mt 27:60–61). Now notice this:

2.3.1. A surprise to her. But Christ crucified is the fountain of life. His grave is one of the wells of salvation; if we come to it in faith, we will find the stone rolled away and free access to its strengths and encouragements. Surprising comforts are the frequent encouragements of early seekers.

2.3.2. The beginning of a glorious discovery; the Lord had risen, even though she did not grasp this at first. Those who are most faithful in following Christ are commonly aware of the first and sweetest signs of divine grace. Mary Magdalene, who followed Christ to the last in his humiliation, met him at the beginning in his exaltation.

3. Finding the stone taken away, she quickly ran back to Peter and John: "*They have taken the Lord out of the sepulchre, and we know not where they have laid him.*" Notice here:

3.1. What idea Mary had of the situation. One would have expected that when she found the grave empty, her first thought would be, "Surely the Lord is risen," because whenever he had told them that he was going to be crucified, he added in the same breath that *the third day he would rise again* (Mt 20:19). Could she now see the grave empty but have no thought of the resurrection enter her mind? When we come to reflect on our own behavior *in a cloudy and dark day* (Eze 34:12), we will stand amazed at our dullness and forgetfulness, that we could miss thoughts that later appear obvious. She suggested,

They have taken away the Lord. Whatever her suspicion, it seems it troubled and disturbed her greatly that the body was gone, whereas if she had understood it rightly, nothing could be happier. Weak believers often make the substance of their complaint what is really the just basis of their hope and a matter for their joy.

3.2. What she told Peter and John about it. She did not stand poring over the grief herself, but told her friends about it. The communication of sorrows is one good way we can benefit from the communion of saints. Although Peter had denied his Master, he had not deserted his Master's friends; this shows the sincerity of his repentance. Moreover, the disciples' keeping up their relationship with him as before teaches us to restore gently those who have been caught in sin (Gal 6:1). If God has received them on their repentance, why should not we?

4. Peter and John went as fast as they could to the tomb (vv. 3–4). Some think that the other disciples were with Peter and John when the news came, because the women *told these things to the eleven* (Lk 24:9). But none of them went to the tomb except Peter and John, who were often distinguished from the rest by special favors. It is good when those who are more honored with the enjoyment of the privileges of being disciples than others are more active than others in fulfilling the responsibility of being disciples, more willing to take pains and risks. Notice:

4.1. What use we should make of the experience of others. When Mary told them what she had seen, they wanted to go and see with their own eyes. Do others tell us about the comfort and benefit of God's services of worship? Let that lead us to try them out.

4.2. How ready we should be to share with our friends in their problems and fears. Peter and John went quickly to the tomb.

4.3. How quickly we should set about a good work. Peter and John considered neither their comfort nor their dignity, but ran to the tomb.

4.4. What a good thing it is to have good company as we undertake a good work.

4.5. That it is a commendable ambition among disciples to strive for excellence in doing good. It was no breach of manners for John, though he was the younger, to run faster than Peter. We must do our best, and neither envy those who can do better nor despise those who do what they can, even though they come after us. The one who came first in this race was *the disciple whom Jesus loved* (v. 2). A sense of Christ's love toward us, kindling love in us as a warm response to him, will make us excel in goodness. The one who was left behind was Peter, who had denied his Master and was sad and ashamed of it. When our conscience is offended, we lose ground.

5. Peter and John, having come to the tomb, pursued their quest.

5.1. John went no further than Mary Magdalene had. He had the curiosity to look into the tomb and saw it was empty. He *stooped down* and *looked in*. Those who want to find the knowledge of Christ must stoop down and look in. But he did not have the courage to go into the tomb. The warmest affections are not always accompanied by the boldest resolutions.

5.2. Peter went in first and therefore saw more than John had (vv. 6–7). While John was looking in with great caution, Peter came and *went into the sepulchre* with great courage.

5.2.1. Notice the boldness of Peter, and how God distributes his gifts diversely. John could run faster than Peter, but Peter could take greater risks than John. Some disciples are quick, and they are useful to quicken those who are slow; others are bold, and they are useful to embolden those who are shy. Those who are serious about seeking Christ must not frighten themselves with imaginary and foolish fears. Good Christians need not be afraid of the grave, since Christ has lain in it. Let us not, therefore, indulge, but conquer, the fears we tend to conceive when we see a dead body, or when we are alone among the graves. We must be willing to go through the grave to Christ; he went that way to his glory, and so must we. If we cannot see God's face and live (Ge 32:30; Ex 33:20), it is better to die than never see it.

5.2.2. Notice the position in which he found things in the tomb. Christ had left his graveclothes behind him there. He put them aside because he arose to die no more. Lazarus came out wearing his graveclothes, since he was to use them again. When we rise from the death of sin to the life of righteousness, we must leave our graveclothes behind us; we must put off all corruption. Christ left graveclothes in the grave, as it were, for our use; if the grave is a bed to the saints, this is how he has put sheets on that bed and made it ready for the saints. The graveclothes were found in good order, which serves as evidence to show that his body was not stolen away while people slept.

5.2.3. See how Peter's boldness encouraged John; he now took heart and dared to go in (v. 8), and *he saw and began to believe* that Jesus had risen to life again.

5.2.3.1. John followed Peter in daring to go in. He would not have dared to go into the tomb if Peter had not gone in first. It is good to be made bold in a good work by the boldness of others. The dread of difficulty and danger will be taken away by taking note of the courage and determination of others. Perhaps John's quickness had made Peter run faster, and now Peter's boldness made John risk more. John not only associated with Peter; he also did not think it beneath him to follow him.

5.2.3.2. John got a head start on Peter in believing. Peter saw and wondered (Lk 24:12), but John saw and believed. A mind disposed to contemplation may receive the evidence of divine truth sooner than a mind disposed to action. But why were they so slow of heart to believe (Lk 24:25)? The Evangelist tells us (v. 9), *as yet they knew not the scripture* that he must *rise again from the dead.* Notice:

5.2.3.2.1. How disinclined the disciples themselves were, at first, to believe the resurrection of Christ, which confirms the testimony they later gave with so much assurance about it, because by their reluctance to believe it they showed they were not gullible in believing it and were not simpleminded people who believe every word. It was strange to them, and one of the things furthest from their thoughts. Peter and John were so hesitant about believing it at first that nothing less than the most convincing proof could bring them to testify about it later with so much assurance. This shows they were not only honest people, who would not deceive others, but also cautious people, who would not be deceived themselves.

5.2.3.2.2. What was the reason for their slowness to believe: *as yet they knew not the scripture.* This seems to be the Evangelist's acknowledgment that he shared this fault with the rest.

5.3. Peter and John pursued their inquiry no further, hovering between faith and unbelief (v. 10): *The disciples went away to their own home*:

5.3.1. For fear of being arrested on the suspicion that they had conspired to steal away the body, or for fear that now that it was gone, they would be arrested on suspicion of having stolen it. In times of difficulty and danger, it is hard even for good people to continue their work with the appropriate determination.

5.3.2. Because they were at a loss and did not know what to do next or what to make of what they had seen, which shows their weakness at that time.

5.3.3. To return to the rest of the disciples, who were probably together, and tell them about what they had discovered. It is significant that Peter and John saw no angel at the tomb. Before they came to the tomb, an angel had appeared there, rolled away the stone, frightened the guard, and comforted the women; as soon as they had left the tomb, Mary Magdalene saw two angels in the tomb (v. 12); but Peter and John came to the tomb, went into it, and saw none. Why? Angels appear and disappear at will, according to the orders and instructions given them. They may be and really are in places where they are not visible. It is presumptuous of us to ask how. But notice that the favor of the angels' appearance was shown to those who were early and constant in seeking Christ; it was the reward of those who came first and stayed last, but was denied to those who made a quick visit.

Verses 11–18

Mark tells us that Christ appeared first to Mary Magdalene (Mk 16:9); that appearance is related in detail here, and in this account we may notice:

1. The constancy and fervency of Mary Magdalene's devotion to the Lord Jesus (v. 11).

1.1. She stayed at the tomb when Peter and John had gone, because her Master had lain there. Although this good woman had lost him, she would remain by his grave for his sake, remaining in his love even when she lacked the comfort of it.

1.2. She stayed there weeping, and these tears showed her great affection for her Master. Those who have lost Christ have cause to weep. Those who seek Christ must weep not for him but for themselves (Lk 23:28).

1.3. *As she wept, she looked into the sepulchre.* When we are seeking something we have lost, we look again and again in the place where we last left it and expected to find it. Weeping must not prevent seeking. Although she wept, she *stooped down and looked in.*

2. The vision she had of two angels in the tomb (v. 12). Notice:

2.1. The description of the persons she saw. They were *two angels in white, sitting*—one *at the head* of the grave, the other at the *feet.* Here we have:

2.1.1. Their nature. They were angels, messengers from heaven, deliberately sent to honor the Son. Now that the Son of God was to be brought back into the world, the angels had a responsibility to be present with him, as they were at his birth (Heb 1:6). They came also to comfort the saints, to prepare them for seeing the Lord by announcing that he had risen.

2.1.2. Their number, which was two: not *a multitude of the heavenly host,* to sing praise (Lk 2:13), only two, to testify.

2.1.3. Their appearance: they were *in white,* showing their purity and holiness. Glorified saints, when they become like the angels (Mt 22:30), will walk with Christ in white.

2.1.4. Their position and place: they sat in Christ's grave. These angels went into the grave to teach us not to be afraid of it. Matters are so arranged that the grave is not much out of our way to heaven. These angelic guards kept possession of the tomb when they had frightened away the guards, so representing Christ's victory over the powers of darkness. Their sitting to face each other, one at his

head and the other at his feet, may also remind us of the two cherubim, placed one at either end of the atonement cover, looking at each other (Ex 25:18). Christ crucified was the great atoning sacrifice, at the head and feet of which were these two cherubim, not with flaming swords, to keep us from the way of life (Ge 3:24), but as welcome messengers, to direct us to it.

2.2. Their compassionate question about the cause of Mary Magdalene's grief (v. 13): *Woman, why weepest thou?* This was:

2.2.1. A rebuke to her weeping: *"Why weepest thou* when you have cause to rejoice?" Many of the floods of our tears would dry away when faced with such a search into their origin.

2.2.2. Intended to show how much angels are concerned at the griefs of the saints. Christians should sympathize in this way with one another.

2.2.3. Only to give an opportunity to inform her of what would turn her mourning into rejoicing.

2.3. The sad account of her present distress: *"Because they have taken away* the precious body I came to embalm, *and I know not where they have laid it."* This showed:

2.3.1. The weakness of her faith. We often perplex ourselves unnecessarily with imaginary difficulties, which faith would reveal to us as real advantages.

2.3.2. The power of her love. Mary Magdalene was not distracted from her questions by the unexpectedness of the vision, nor satisfied with its honor, but continued to harp on the same string: *They have taken away my Lord.* A vision of angels and their smiles will not be enough without a vision of Christ and God's smiles on him. In fact, the vision of angels is merely an opportunity to seek Christ. The angels asked her, *Why weepest thou?* "I have reason enough to cry," she said, "for *they have taken away my Lord."* None know, except those who have experienced it, the sorrow of a deserted soul, who has felt a deep assurance of the love of God in Christ but has now lost it, only to walk in darkness.

3. Christ's appearing to her while she was talking with the angels. Christ himself stepped in. Mary wanted to know where her Lord is, and see—he was at her right hand (Ps 16:8)! Those who will be content with nothing short of seeing Christ will be put off with nothing less. In revealing himself to those who seek him, Christ often surpasses their expectations. Mary longed to see the dead body of Christ, and now she saw him alive. This is how he does more for his praying people than they are able to ask or even think (Eph 3:20). Notice:

3.1. How he at first concealed himself from her.

3.1.1. He stood by as an ordinary person, and she looked on him accordingly (v. 14). She *turned herself back* from talking with the angels and *saw Jesus himself* standing there, but she *knew not that it was Jesus.* We can learn from this:

3.1.1.1. *The Lord is nigh unto them that are of a broken heart* (Ps 34:18), nearer than they are aware. Those who seek Christ may be sure he is not far from them even if they do not see him.

3.1.1.2. To seek the Lord diligently is to look everywhere for him. *Mary turned herself back* in the hope of making some discovery. It was her energetic desire in seeking that made her turn in every direction.

3.1.1.3. Christ is often near his people without their knowing it. She *knew not that it was Jesus.*

3.1.2. He asked her an ordinary question, and she answered him accordingly (v. 15).

3.1.2.1. The question he asked her was what anyone would have asked her: *Woman, why weepest thou? Whom seekest thou?* It seems this was the first word Christ spoke after his resurrection: *Why weepest thou?* Christ is aware of his people's griefs, and asks, *Why weep you?* He is also aware of his people's worries, and asks, *Whom seek you, and what would you have?* When he knows they are seeking him, he still wants to know it from them.

3.1.2.2. The reply she gave him is natural enough. *Supposing him to be the gardener,* she replied, *Sir, if thou hast carried him hence,* then *tell me where thou hast laid him, and I will take him away.* This showed:

3.1.2.2.1. The error of her understanding. She supposed our Lord Jesus to be the gardener. On a cloudy and dark day, troubled spirits tend to misrepresent Christ to themselves.

3.1.2.2.2. The truth of her devotion. Notice how her heart was set on finding Christ. She asked the question of everyone she met. When she spoke about Christ, she did not name him, but said simply, *If thou have borne him hence,* assuming that this gardener was as full of thoughts about this Jesus as she was. Further evidence of the strength of her devotion was that wherever he was laid, she would undertake to move him. Such a body was much more than she could hope to carry, but true love thinks it can do more than it can and makes nothing of difficulties. Christ need not stay where he is thought to be a burden.

3.2. How Christ finally made himself known to her, giving her infallible assurances of his resurrection. Notice:

3.2.1. How Christ revealed himself to this good woman (v. 16): *Jesus saith unto her, Mary.* He said it with that air of kindness with which he usually spoke to her. Now he changed his voice and spoke like himself, not like the gardener. Christ's *sheep know his voice* (10:4). This one word, "Mary," was like the words spoken to the disciples in the storm, *It is I* (Mt 14:27).

3.2.2. How readily she received this revelation. She turned and said, *Rabboni, My Master.* Notice:

3.2.2.1. The title of respect she gave him: *My Master; didaskale,* "Teacher"—a teaching Master. *Rabboni* was a more honorable title with them than *Rabbi,* and that was why Mary chose that, with the suffix *-i* indicating that she took him as hers: "*My* great Master." Notwithstanding the freedom of fellowship that Christ allows us, he is still our Teacher.

3.2.2.2. With what ardent devotion she gave this title to Christ. She turned from the angels to look to Jesus. We must turn our eyes away from all creatures, even the brightest and best, to fix them on Christ. When she thought he was the gardener, she looked another way while speaking to him, but now that she recognized the voice of Christ, she turned.

3.2.3. The further instructions Christ gave her (v. 17): *"Touch me not,* but go and take the news to the disciples."

3.2.3.1. He deterred her from expecting familiar association and conversation with him at this time: *Touch me not, for I am not yet ascended.* Mary was ready to express her joy by affectionately embracing him, but Christ here forbade it at this time.

3.2.3.1.1. "*Touch me not,* because I am to ascend to heaven." He told the disciples to touch him to confirm their faith. Mary must believe him and adore him but must not expect to be as familiar with him as she had been. He forbade her to be devoted to his physical presence and led her to the spiritual fellowship she would have with him after he had ascended to his Father. Although *I am not yet ascended, go to my brethren, and tell them, I am to ascend.* As before his death, so now after his resurrec-

tion, he still spoke of his going away and being *no more in the world* (17:11), and so they must look higher than his physical presence and look further than the present state of things.

3.2.3.1.2. "*Touch me not;* do not now stay to ask any further questions or give any further expressions of joy, because *I am not yet ascended.* The best service you can do now is to take the news to the disciples; lose no time in doing this; go as fast as you can." Mary must not stay to talk with her Teacher, but must pass on his message, for it was a day of good news.

3.2.3.2. He told her what message to take to his disciples: *But go to my brethren, and tell them* that *I ascend.* Notice:

3.2.3.2.1. To whom this message was sent: *Go to my brethren* with it. He was now entering his glory, but he acknowledged his disciples as his brothers. He had called them friends (15:13–14), but never brothers until now. Although Christ is high, he is not haughty. Despite his advancement, he does not disdain to acknowledge his poor relatives. He had not seen them together since *they all forsook him and fled* (Mt 26:56), but he forgave, forgot, and did not rebuke them.

3.2.3.2.2. By whom it was sent: by *Mary Magdalene, out of whom had been cast seven devils* (Mk 16:9). This was her reward for her constancy in following Christ; she became an apostle to the apostles.

3.2.3.2.3. What the message itself was: *I ascend to my Father.*

3.2.3.2.3.1. Our joint relation to God resulting from our union with Christ is an inexpressible comfort. Christ said, "He is *my Father, and your Father; my God, and your God.*" It is the great distinction of believers that the Father of our Lord Jesus Christ is, in him, their Father. He is ours by gracious adoption, but even this warrants us to call him, as Christ did, *Abba, Father* (Mk 14:36; Ro 8:15; Gal 4:6). It is the great condescension of Christ that he acknowledges the believer's God as his God. "God is *my God, and your God:* mine so that he may be yours, the God of the Redeemer, to support him (Ps 89:26), so that he may be the God of the redeemed, to save them."

3.2.3.2.3.2. Christ's ascension to heaven is also an inexpressible encouragement: "Tell them I must soon ascend." Here is:

3.2.3.2.3.2.1. A word of warning to these disciples that they should not expect his physical presence to remain on earth. "I have risen not to stay with them but to go on their mission to heaven." Those who are raised to spiritual life must reckon that they rise to ascend. Let them not think that this earth is to be their home and rest. No; being born from above (3:3, 7), from heaven, they are bound for heaven. "I ascend, and so I must seek things above."

3.2.3.2.3.2.2. A word of comfort to them and to all *that shall believe in him through their word* (17:20); he was then ascending, and he has now ascended, to his Father and our Father. He said it with triumph, so that those who love him may rejoice (Ps 105:3). He ascended as our forerunner (Heb 6:20), *to prepare a place for us* (14:2) and be ready to receive us. Some understand those words, *I ascend to my God and your God,* to include a promise of our resurrection. *Because I live, you shall live also* (14:19).

4. Mary Magdalene's faithful report to the disciples (v. 18): *She came and told the disciples that she had seen the Lord.* Peter and John had left her seeking him dejectedly with tears and would not seek him with her. She had asked about a dead body; now she found it was a living and glorified body. She had found what she sought,

and what was infinitely better; she had joy at seeing the Master herself. When God encourages us, it is with the intention that we may encourage others. She told them not only what she had seen but also what she had heard: *that he had spoken these things unto her* as a message to be passed on to them.

Verses 19–25

The infallible proof of Christ's resurrection was *his showing himself alive* (Ac 1:3). In these verses we have an account of his first appearance to the company of his closest disciples on the day on which he rose from the dead. He had sent them the news of his resurrection, but to confirm their faith in him, he himself came, so that they would not hear it only as a rumor, but would themselves be eyewitnesses that he was alive. Notice:

1. When and where this appearance took place (v. 19). It was *the same day, being the first day of the week*. There are three secondary ordinances—as we may call them—instituted by our Lord Jesus to continue in his church; these are the Lord's Day, sacred meetings, and a regular ministry. The thinking of Christ about each of these is clearly shown us in these verses; we see his thinking concerning the first two here in the circumstances of this appearance; concerning the third, in v. 21.

1.1. Here is a Christian Sabbath observed by the disciples and acknowledged by our Lord Jesus. Christ came to his disciples on *the first day of the week*. The first day of the week is—I think—the only day of the week, month, or year that is ever mentioned by number in the whole New Testament, and this is spoken of several times as a day that is religiously observed. In this way Christ, in effect, blessed and sanctified that day.

1.2. Here is a Christian meeting held by the disciples and acknowledged by the Lord Jesus. The disciples probably met here for some religious exercise, to pray together. They met to discover one another's thoughts, strengthen one another's hands, and agree on the proper measures to be taken at this critical time. This meeting was private, because they dared not appear publicly. They met in a house, but they kept the door locked, so that they would not be seen together and so that no one could come among them except those they knew, because they were afraid of the Jews. Those *sheep of the flock were scattered* (Mt 26:31) in the storm, but sheep are sociable and will come together again. It is nothing new for the assemblies of Christ's disciples to be driven into corners and forced into the desert (Rev 12:14; Pr 28:12). God's people have often been obliged to *enter into their chambers, and shut their doors* (Isa 26:20), as here, *for fear of the Jews*.

2. What was said and done in this visit Christ paid to his disciples. When they had assembled, Jesus came among them. *Where two or three are gathered together in his name, he will be in the midst of them* (18:20). He came even though the doors were shut. It is an encouragement to Christ's disciples that when they have to hold their religious meetings in private, no doors can shut out Christ's presence from them. Here are five things in this appearance of Christ:

2.1. His kind and familiar greeting to his disciples: *He said, Peace be unto you*. The phrase was common, but the sense was now distinctive. From Christ, *Peace be unto you* meant, "May all good be given to you, all peace always by all means." Christ had left them his peace as their legacy (14:27). He promptly paid the legacy here: "*Peace be unto you*. Peace with God, peace in your own consciences, peace with one another. May all this peace be with you; not peace with the world, but peace in Christ." His sudden

appearing in the middle of them must have confused them and made them afraid, but he stilled the stormy noise of their fears with his words *Peace be unto you*.

2.2. The clear and undeniable revelation of himself to them (v. 20). Notice here:

2.2.1. The method he used to convince them of the truth of his resurrection. No one could ask for further proof than the scars or marks of the wounds on his body. The marks of the wounds remained on the body of the Lord Jesus even after his resurrection, so that they would demonstrate its truth. Conquerors glory in the marks of their wounds. On earth Christ's wounds would speak the message that it really was he, and that was why he rose from the dead with them. In heaven they were to speak in the intercession he must always live to make (Heb 7:25), and that was why he ascended with them. He showed these marks to his disciples for their conviction. They not only had the satisfaction of seeing him look with the same face and hearing him speak with the same voice; they also had the further evidence of these distinctive marks. He opened his hands to them so that they could see the marks of the wounds on them; he showed them his breast, as a nurse shows hers to an infant, to show them the wound there. The exalted Redeemer will always show himself to be openhanded and openhearted to all his faithful friends and followers.

2.2.2. The impression it made on them. They were convinced that they were seeing the Lord; their faith was confirmed in this way. Many true believers who, while weak, feared that their strengths and encouragements were only imaginary later find them, through grace, real and substantial. *Then they were glad*. The Evangelist seems to write it with a note of delight and triumph. "Then! then *were the disciples glad, when they saw the Lord!*" If it *revived the spirit of Jacob* to hear that *Joseph was yet alive* (Ge 45:27–28), how much more would it revive the heart of these disciples to hear that Jesus is again alive! It was life from the dead to them. Now that word of Christ was fulfilled (16:22), *I will see you again, and your heart shall rejoice*. This wiped away all tears from their eyes (Rev 7:17; 21:4).

2.3. The commission he gave them to be his ambassadors in planting his church (v. 21). Notice:

2.3.1. The introduction to their commission, which was the sacred repetition of the foregoing greeting: *Peace be unto you*. The purpose of the greeting had been to still the turmoil of their fears so that they could calmly take in the proofs of his resurrection; this commission was to calm the ecstasy of their delight, either to enable them to hear what he had further to say to them or to encourage them to accept the commission he was giving them. It would lead to their peace. Christ was now sending out the disciples to declare peace to the world, and he not only conferred it on them here but committed it to them as a trust to be passed on by them.

2.3.2. The commission itself: *As my Father hath sent me, even so send I you*.

2.3.2.1. It is easy to understand how Christ sent them; he appointed them to continue with his work on earth. He sent them authorized with a divine warrant, armed with divine power. That was why they were called *apostles*, "the sent ones."

2.3.2.2. But how Christ sent them *as the Father sent him* is not so easily understood. Certainly their commissions and powers were infinitely inferior to his, but:

2.3.2.2.1. Their work was of the same kind as his, and they were to continue where he left off. Just as he was sent to bear witness to the truth, so were they. Was he sent *not to be ministered to, but to minister* (Mt 20:28), *not to do his own will, but the will of him that sent him* (6:38), *not to destroy the law and the prophets, but to fill them up* (Mt 5:17)? So were they. As the Father sent him *to the lost sheep of the house of Israel* (Mt 10:6), in the same way he sent them into the whole world.

2.3.2.2.2. He had a power to send them equal to the power with which the Father had sent him. "I send you by the same authority that the Father sent me." Did he have an undeniable authority and an irresistible power for his work? So did they for theirs. Or, *As the Father hath sent me* may be read as a reference to his power: by virtue of the authority given him as a Mediator, he gave them authority to act for him and in his name. Those who received them or rejected them received or rejected Christ and the One who sent him (13:20).

2.4. The qualifying of them (v. 22): *He breathed on them, and said, Receive ye the Holy Spirit.* Notice:

2.4.1. The sign he used: *He breathed on them,* not only to show them by this breath of life that he himself was really alive but also to represent to them the spiritual life and power they would receive from him. As the breath of the Almighty gave life to human beings and began the old world (Ge 2:7), so the breath of the mighty Savior gave life to his ministers and began a new world (Job 33:4). The Spirit is the breath of Christ, "proceeding from the Son," as the Nicene Creed put it. *The breath of God* stands for the power of his wrath, but the breath of Christ represents the power of his grace; the breathing of threats (Ac 9:1) is changed into the breathings of love by the mediation of Christ. The Spirit is also the gift of Christ. The apostles communicated the Holy Spirit by the laying on of hands, because they could only carry it as messengers, but Christ conferred the Holy Spirit by breathing, because he is the author of the gift.

2.4.2. The sacred gift he made: *Receive ye the Holy Spirit.*

2.4.2.1. Christ here assured them of the Spirit's help in their future work: "*I send you,* and you will have the Spirit to go along with you." Christ will clothe with his Spirit those he employs, and he will supply them with all necessary powers.

2.4.2.2. He gave them here an experience of the Spirit's influence in their present situation. He had shown them his hands and his side to convince them of the truth of his resurrection, but the clearest evidence will not produce faith by itself. "Therefore *receive ye the Holy Spirit,* to produce faith in you." They were now in danger from the Jews: "Receive the Holy Spirit, to bring about courage in you." What Christ said to them he says to all true believers: *Receive ye the Holy Spirit* (Eph 1:13).

2.5. One branch of the power given them was mentioned in particular (v. 23): "*Whosesoever sins you remit* (If you forgive anyone their sins), they are forgiven, *and whosesoever sins you retain* (if you do not forgive them), *they are retained.*" Now this followed from their receiving the Holy Spirit, because if they had not had an extraordinary spirit of discernment, they would not have been fit to be entrusted with such authority. It must be understood, however, as a general charter to the church and its ministers, encouraging the faithful stewards of the mysteries of God (1Co 4:1) to stand by the Gospel they were sent to preach, because God himself will stand by it. Being raised for our justification (Ro 4:25), Christ sent out his Gospel heralds to declare that the act of indemnity had now been passed. Those whom the Gospel acquits will be acquitted, and those whom the Gospel condemns will be condemned, which puts immense honor on the ministry

and should put immense courage into ministers in two ways, and both have authority:

2.5.1. By sound doctrine. They are commissioned to tell the world that salvation is to be found on the terms of the Gospel, and no other.

2.5.2. By a strict discipline, applying the general rule of the Gospel to particular individuals.

3. The incredulity of Thomas, which introduced Christ's second appearance. Here is:

3.1. Thomas's absence (v. 24). He is said to have been *one of the twelve,* who were now eleven. One of them was missing. Christ's disciples will never be all together until the general assembly on the great day. By his absence, Thomas missed out on the satisfaction of seeing his Master risen and of sharing with the disciples in their joy on that occasion.

3.2. The account the other disciples gave him (v. 25). They *said unto him, We have seen the Lord.* It seems that although Thomas was then not with them, he was not away from them long; those who are absentees for a time must not be condemned as apostates forever: Thomas was not Judas. With what joy they said it: "*We have seen the Lord,* and we wish you had been here to see him too." The disciples of Christ should try to *build up one another in their most holy faith* (Jude 20), both by repeating what they have heard to those who were absent and by communicating what they have experienced. Those who have seen the Lord by faith and tasted that he is gracious (1Pe 2:3) should tell others what God has done for their souls (Ps 66:16); only let boasting be excluded (Ro 3:27).

3.3. The objections Thomas raised against the evidence. "*Except* (unless) *I shall* not only see *in his hands the print of the nails,* but put my finger into it, *and thrust my hand* into the wound *in his side, I will not believe.*" Some think he was a man of a rough, morose temper, one who tended to speak ill-temperedly, for all good people are not equally happy in their temperament. There was certainly much that was wrong in his behavior.

3.3.1. He had either not paid attention to or not taken proper notice of what Christ had said so often, that he would *rise again the third day* (Mt 20:19).

3.3.2. He did not show just respect to the testimony of his fellow disciples; all ten of them agreed on the testimony with great assurance, but he could not persuade himself to say that *their record was true* (19:35). It was not, however, their truthfulness that he called into question, but their good sense; he feared they were too gullible and naïve.

3.3.3. He tested Christ by saying he would be convinced by his own method or not at all. Thomas restricted his faith to this evidence. Either he would be indulged and have his imagination satisfied, or he would not believe.

3.3.4. His open confession of this in the presence of the disciples was an offense and discouragement to them. As one coward makes many more, so does one believer, one skeptic. His declaring his faithlessness so openly and conclusively might have an adverse effect on the others.

Verses 26–31

Here is a record of another appearance of Christ, when Thomas was with them. We have here:

1. When it was: *After eight days,* which must therefore have been, as that earlier day was, *the first day of the week* (v. 19).

1.1. He delayed his next appearance for some time, to show his disciples that he belonged to another world and visited this world only now and then, when there was need. At the beginning of his ministry, he had been tempted by the Devil, unseen, for forty days (Mt 4:1–2). At the beginning of his glory, he was attended by good spirits for forty days, for the most part unseen.

1.2. He delayed it for as long as seven days:

1.2.1. So that he could rebuke Thomas for his skepticism. Thomas would not be allowed another such opportunity for several days. Those who miss one tide must wait awhile for another. Thomas had a very sad week, while the other disciples were full of joy.

1.2.2. So that he could test the faith and patience of the rest. They had triumphed greatly when they were satisfied that they had seen the Lord. He would test them to see whether they could keep the ground they had gained. He would gradually wean them from his physical presence, which they had depended too much on.

1.2.3. So that he could honor the first day of the week and give a clear indication of his will that it should be observed in his church as the Christian Sabbath. The religious observance of that day has been passed down to us through every age of the church.

2. Where and how Christ visited them. It was at Jerusalem, because the doors were locked now, as before, for fear of the Jews. Notice:

2.1. Thomas was with them; although he had withdrawn once, he did not do so a second time. When we have lost one opportunity, we should be more serious about grasping the next. It is a good sign if such a loss whets our desires, and a bad sign if it cools them. The disciples accepted Thomas among them. They did not receive him to dispute the matter, but made him welcome to come and see (1:39, 46). Christ did not appear to Thomas until he found him with his other disciples. He wanted all the disciples to be witnesses of the rebuke he gave to Thomas, but also to notice the tender care he showed him.

2.2. Christ came in among them and *stood in the midst.* See the condescension of our Lord Jesus. For the benefit of his church, he remained on earth and visited the little private meetings of his poor disciples, *standing in the midst of them.*

2.3. He greeted them all in a friendly way, as before: *Peace be unto you.* This was no vain babbling, but was a sign of the abundant peace Christ gives and of the continuation of his blessings.

3. What took place between Christ and Thomas at this meeting; only that is recorded. Notice:

3.1. Christ's gracious condescension to Thomas (v. 7). He singled him out from the rest: *"Reach hither thy finger* and *behold my hands,* the *print of the nails; reach hither thy hand* and *thrust it into my side."* Here is:

3.1.1. An implicit rebuke of Thomas's incredulity, in the clear reference to what Thomas had said, answering it word for word. There is not an unbelieving word on our tongues, nor even such a thought in our minds, that is not known to the Lord Jesus (Ps 139:4; see also 78:21).

3.1.2. A clear condescension to his weakness. Christ allowed his wisdom to be dictated to. Christ was here willing to come down to the level even of Thomas's whim about something unnecessary, rather than allow him to remain in his unbelief. He allowed his wounds to be searched, even allowed Thomas to push his hand into his side, if that was what it would take to make him believe. This is why, for the confirmation of our faith, he has instituted a ceremony to deliberately maintain the memory of his death. In that ceremony in which we *show the Lord's death* (1Co 11:26) we are called, as it were, to put our finger into the print of the nails. Reach out your hand to him, who reaches out his inviting, giving, helping hand. It

was with moving words that Christ closed what he had to say to Thomas: *Be not faithless, but believing.* This warning is given to us all: *Be not faithless,* because if we are without faith, we are without Christ and without grace, hope, and joy.

3.2. Thomas's believing submission to Jesus Christ. He was now ashamed of his incredulity and cried out, *My Lord and my God* (v. 28). We are not told whether he did put his finger into where the nails had been; it seems not, since Christ said (v. 29), *Thou hast seen, and believed;* seeing was enough. Now faith came away as a conqueror.

3.2.1. Thomas was now fully satisfied of the truth of Christ's resurrection. His slowness and reluctance to believe may help strengthen our faith.

3.2.2. He therefore believed Christ to be Lord and God, and we are to believe he is too. We must believe:

3.2.2.1. His deity—that he is God, not a human being who was made God, but God made human.

3.2.2.2. His mediation—that he is Lord, the one Lord (1Co 8:6; 1Ti 2:5), to settle the great concerns between God and humanity and establish the living relationship that was necessary for our happiness.

3.2.3. He accepted him as *his* Lord and *his* God. We must accept Christ as being to us what the Father has appointed him to be. This is the vital act of faith: *He is mine* (SS 2:16).

3.2.4. He made an open profession of this. He said to Christ, "You are *my Lord and my God,"* or, speaking to his brothers, "This is *my Lord and my God."* Do we accept Christ as our Lord God? We must go to him and tell him so and tell others that we have, as those who glory in our relation to Christ. Thomas spoke with an ardent devotion, as one who took hold of Christ with all his power: *My Lord* and *my God.*

3.3. The judgment of Christ on the whole matter (v. 29): *Thomas, because thou hast seen me, thou hast believed,* but *blessed are those that have not seen, and yet have believed.*

3.3.1. Christ acknowledged Thomas as a believer. Sound and sincere believers, even if they are slow and weak, will be graciously accepted by the Lord Jesus. No sooner did Thomas consent to Christ than Christ gave him the assurance of it, letting him know that he did indeed believe.

3.3.2. He rebuked him for his former incredulity. Well might Thomas be ashamed to think:

3.3.2.1. That he had been so reluctant to believe and had come so slowly to his own assurance. Those who have sincerely accepted Christ see a great deal of reason to lament their not having done so sooner.

3.3.2.2. That it was not without a lot of fuss that he was brought to finally believe. If no evidence must be accepted except that of our own senses, and we must believe nothing except what we ourselves are eyewitnesses of, how must the world be converted to the faith of Christ? Thomas was therefore justly blamed for emphasizing this so much.

3.3.3. He commended the faith of those who believe on simpler terms. As a believer, Thomas was truly blessed, but more *blessed are those that have not seen. Have not seen* is meant to refer not to the objects of faith (see Heb 11:1; 2Co 4:18) but to motives of faith—Christ's miracles, especially his resurrection; blessed are those who do not see these but still believe in Christ. This may look either backward, to the Old Testament saints, who had not seen the things the disciples now saw but still believed the promise made to their ancestors and lived by that faith, or forward, to those who would later believe, the Gentiles. This faith is more commendable than that of those who saw and believed.

3.3.3.1. It is evidence of a better attitude in those who do believe. Those who believe upon seeing have their resistance conquered by a sort of violence, but those who believe without it are nobler (Ac 17:11).

3.3.3.2. It is a greater example of the power of divine grace. Flesh and blood contribute more to the faith of those who see and believe than to the faith of those who do not see but still believe.

4. The comment the Evangelist makes on this account, like a historian drawing toward a conclusion (vv. 30–31).

4.1. He assures us that many other things took place that are *not written in the book*: *many signs*.

4.1.1. We may apply this general affirmation to confirm our faith. Those who recorded the resurrection of Christ were not required to fish around for evidence, to grasp hold of any small and scanty pieces of proof that they could find and make up the rest with mere conjecture. No, they had enough evidence; in fact, they had evidence to spare. The disciples, in whose presence these other signs were done, were to preach Christ's resurrection to others, and that was why they needed abundant proofs.

4.1.2. We need not ask why they were not all written down, or why more than these were not written down. If this account had been a merely human composition, it would have been swollen with many of formal statements and affidavits to prove the contested truth of Christ's resurrection, but because it is a divine account, the writer wrote with a noble security, sufficient to convince those who were willing to be taught and to condemn those who remained stubborn in their unbelief; if this did not satisfy, then more would not. People produce all they have to say in order to be believed, but God does not, because he can give faith. If this history had been written to entertain the curious, it would have been fuller; it was written to bring people to believe, and enough is said to fulfill that intention.

4.2. He instructs us in the purpose of recording what we find here (v. 31): "*That you might believe* on this evidence, that you may believe that Jesus is the Christ, the Son of God." Here is:

4.2.1. The purpose of those who wrote down the Gospel. The Evangelists wrote their Gospels without any view of temporal benefits for themselves or others; they did it simply to bring people to Christ and heaven and, to that end, to persuade people to believe.

4.2.2. The duty of those who read and hear the Gospel. It is their duty to believe — to take to themselves — the message of Christ. Notice:

4.2.2.1. What the great Gospel truth is that we are to believe: that *Jesus is that Christ*, that *Son of God*. He is the Christ, "the anointed One" of God, anointed to be a ruler and a Savior. He is the Son of God, endowed with the power of God and entitled to the glory of God.

4.2.2.2. What the great Gospel blessing is that we are to hope for: *That believing we shall have life through his name*. This is:

4.2.2.2.1. To direct our faith. Life through Christ's name is what we must see as the fullness of our joy.

4.2.2.2.2. To encourage our faith. People will venture far on the prospect of gaining some great advantage; there can be no greater advantage than what is offered by the *words of this life* (Ac 5:20). *This life* includes both spiritual life and eternal life. Both are through Christ's name, and both are absolutely certain for all true believers.

CHAPTER 21

The Evangelist seems to have concluded his account, but then new matter then occurs to him, and he starts again. He said there were many other signs that Jesus did (20:30). In this chapter he mentions one, Christ's appearance to some of his disciples by the Sea of Tiberias. Here we have: 1. His revelation of himself to them as they were fishing, how he filled their net and then very informally came and had breakfast with them, eating what they had caught (vv. 1–14). 2. The talk he had with Peter after breakfast: 2.1. About himself (vv. 15–19). 2.2. About John (vv. 20–23). 3. The solemn conclusion of this Gospel (vv. 24–25).

Verses 1–14

1. We have here an account of Christ's appearance to his disciples by the Sea of Tiberias.

1.1. Let us compare this appearance with those that went before. In those, Christ showed himself to his disciples when they met on a Lord's Day, when they were all together, but here he showed himself to some of them on a weekday, when they were fishing. Christ has many ways of revealing himself to his people; sometimes he visits them through his Spirit when they are employed in their ordinary business.

1.2. Let us compare it with what followed at the mountain in Galilee, where Christ had told them to meet him (Mt 28:16). Now this appearance took place while they were waiting for that meeting, so that they would not become tired of waiting. Notice:

2. Whom Christ now showed himself to (v. 2): not to all the Twelve, but only to seven of them. Nathanael is mentioned as one of them, whom we have not met since 1:45–51, though some think he was the same person as Bartholomew. It is good for the disciples of Christ to spend much time together in ordinary conversation and ordinary business. Christ chose to reveal himself to them when they were together so that they would jointly witness the same facts. Thomas was one of them and is named immediately after Peter, as if he was now more conscientious in being present at the meetings of the apostles than ever.

3. How they were employed (v. 3).

3.1. They agreed to go fishing. "As for me," Peter said, "*I will go a fishing.*" The others then said, "*We will go with thee* then." Although two who ply the same trade usually do not agree about how it is to be done, here they did. They did it:

3.1.1. To redeem the time and avoid being idle. The hour for entering into action was still to come. Now, in the meantime, rather than do nothing, they would go fishing — and not for recreation, but for a living. It is also an example of their conscientiousness, showing that they were good managers of their time. While they were waiting, they would not be lazy. Those who want to give an account of their time with joy should seek to fill up its gaps.

3.1.2. To support themselves and not be a burden to anyone.

3.2. They were disappointed in their fishing. They caught nothing that night. The hand of the diligent often returns empty (in spite of Pr 10:4; 12:24). Even good people may come short of desired success in their honest work. Providence so arranged things that all that night they caught nothing, so that the miraculous catch of fish in the morning would be even more acceptable. In those disappointments that are very painful to us, God often has intentions that are very gracious.

4. How Christ revealed himself to them. It is said (v. 1), *He showed himself.* We may notice four things in this appearance of Christ to them:

4.1. He showed himself to them at the right time (v. 4): *When the morning was now come,* Jesus *stood on the shore.* Christ's time of revealing himself to his people is when they are most at a loss. When they think they are completely lost, he will let them know that they have not lost him. Christ appeared to them not *walking upon the water* (Mt 14:25), but standing upon the shore, because now they were to make their way toward him. When our passage is rough and stormy, it is encouraging to us to know that our Master is on the shore and we are moving quickly toward him.

4.2. He showed himself to them gradually. The disciples *knew not* (did not realize), all at once, *that it was Jesus.* Christ is often closer to us than we think he is.

4.3. He showed himself to them by expressing his compassion (v. 5). He called to them, *Children* (NIV: friends), *have you any meat* (food)?

4.3.1. The name was very familiar; he spoke to them with the care and tenderness of a father: *Children.* They were not children in age, but they were still his children, the children whom God had given him (Isa 8:18; Heb 2:13).

4.3.2. The question was very kind: *Have you any meat* (food)? *The Lord is for the body* (1Co 6:13). Christ takes notice of the physical needs of his people, and he has promised them not only sufficient grace (2Co 12:9) but also enough food. Christ looks at the cottages of the poor and asks, *Children, have you any meat?* Christ takes care of them; he looks after them. Christ has set us an example of compassionate concern for our brothers and sisters here. There are many poor householders who are unable to work or who are unsuccessful in their work, who are in difficulties, of whom the rich should ask, *Have you any meat?* Often it is the neediest who make least noise and fuss. The disciples gave a short answer. They said, *No.* Christ asked them the question not because he did not know their needs but because he wanted to know them from them. Those who want to receive supplies from Christ must acknowledge they are empty and needy (Ps 40:17; 70:5).

4.4. He showed himself to them by showing his power (v. 6): he ordered them to *cast the net on the right side of the ship.* And then they, who were going home empty-handed, were enriched with a great catch of fish. Notice:

4.4.1. The orders Christ gave them and the promise attached to those orders: "*Cast the net* in such and such a place, and *you shall find.*" Divine Providence extends itself to the minutest things, and people who know how to take hints from there in the conduct of their affairs are blessed.

4.4.2. Their obedience to these orders and the good success they had as a result. As yet *they knew not that it was Jesus*; however, they were willing to be advised by anybody. In being so attentive to strangers, they were obedient to their Teacher without knowing it (Heb 13:2). Moreover, they succeeded wonderfully as a result; now they had a catch that repaid all their hard work. Nothing is lost by observing Christ's orders. Now the catch of fishes may be considered:

4.4.2.1. As a miracle in itself. Christ reveals himself to his people by doing for them what no one else can do.

4.4.2.2. As a mercy to them. When their own skill and diligence failed them, the power of Christ came in time to help them.

4.4.2.3. As the memorial of a former mercy, with which Christ had rewarded Peter for the loan of his boat (Lk 5:4).

Both that miracle and this one affected him very much, since they met him in his own element, in his own sphere of employment. Later favors are intended to remind us of former favors, so that we may not become an example of the proverb, "Eaten bread is soon forgotten."

4.4.2.4. As a mystery, clearly pointing to the work to which Christ was now sending them out. When, soon after this, three thousand were converted in one day (Ac 2:41), then the net was *cast on the right side of the ship.* Christ's ministers are encouraged when they continue diligently in their work. One final happy catch may be enough to repay many years of toil at the Gospel net.

5. How the disciples received this revelation (vv. 7–8):

5.1. John was the most intelligent and quick-sighted disciple. The one whom Jesus loved was the first who said, *It is the Lord.* His secret is with his favorites (Ps 25:14). When John himself was aware that it was the Lord, he shared his knowledge with those with him; those who know Christ themselves should try to bring others to know him. We need not keep him to ourselves; there is enough in him for us all. John told Peter in particular that it was the Lord, knowing he would be gladder to see Christ than any of others.

5.2. Peter was the most zealous and warmhearted disciple, because as soon as he heard that it was the Lord, the boat could not hold him; he threw himself into the sea so that he could be the first to come to Christ.

5.2.1. He showed his respect for Christ by *girding his fisher's coat* (wrapping his outer garment) around him, so that he would appear before his Master in the best clothes he had. Perhaps the *fisher's coat* kept out the wet, and so he wrapped it around himself so that he could go as quickly as possible through the water to Christ.

5.2.2. He showed the strength of his devotion to Christ by jumping into the water and either wading or swimming to the shore to reach Christ. *He cast himself into the sea* quickly; sink or swim, he would show his goodwill and aim to be with Jesus. Peter had been forgiven for much, and he had made it seen that he loved much by his willingness to take risks to come to Christ (Lk 7:47). Those who have been with Jesus will be willing to swim through a stormy sea to come to him.

5.3. The rest of the disciples were careful and sincere. They went quickly in the boat to the shore, making their way as best they could (v. 8). This shows us:

5.3.1. How diversely God distributes his gifts (1Co 12). Some excel, like Peter and John; they are eminent in gifts and graces; others are only ordinary disciples, who quietly get on with their duty and remain faithful to him. Both the one and the other, however, the eminent and the obscure, will sit down together with Christ in glory; in fact, perhaps *the last shall be first* (Mt 19:30). Some, like John, are very contemplative, with great gifts of knowledge, and serve the church with those gifts; others, like Peter, are very active and courageous and very useful to their generation in this way (Ac 13:36). Some are useful as the church's eyes, others as the church's hands, and all serve the good of the body (1Co 12:19–21).

5.3.2. What a great difference there may be between some good people and others in the way each honors Christ, and yet both are *accepted of him* (2Co 5:9). Peter should not be criticized for jumping into the sea, but commended for his zeal and the strength of his devotion, and so must those be who, out of love for Christ, leave the world, with Mary, to *sit at his feet* (Lk 10:39). Others serve Christ more in worldly affairs. They continue in the boat, dragging the net and bringing the fish to the shore, as the other disciples did here. They should not be criticized as worldly, because they, in their place, are as truly serving Christ as the other ones, even in serving at tables. Christ was very pleased with both, and so must we be.

6. What reception the Lord Jesus gave them.

6.1. He had provisions ready for them. When they came to the land, wet and cold, weary and hungry, they found a good fire already blazing to warm and dry them, and fish and bread. We need not be curious in asking where this fire, fish, and bread came from. There was nothing stately or refined here. We should be content with simple things, for Christ was. We may be comforted in this expression of Christ's care for his disciples. He kindly provided for those fishermen when they came in weary from their work. It is encouraging to Christ's ministers that they may depend on the One who employs them to provide for them. Let them be content with what they have here; they have better things in reserve.

6.2. He called for some of what they had caught (vv. 10–11). Notice:

6.2.1. Christ's command that they bring their catch of fish to the shore: "Bring here some of the fish you have now caught."

6.2.1.1. He wanted them to eat the fruit of their labor (Ps 128:2). What is gained by God's blessing on our own hard and honest work has a particular sweetness about it. Christ wants to teach us here to use what we have.

6.2.1.2. He wanted them to taste the gifts of his miraculous goodness. The benefits Christ gives us are not to be buried and hoarded, but used and spent.

6.2.1.3. He wanted to give an example of the spiritual reception he has for all believers: *he sups with them, and they with him* (Rev 3:20). Ministers, who are *fishers of men*, must bring all they catch to their Master.

6.2.2. Their obedience to this command (v. 11). It was said (v. 6), *They were not able to draw the net to shore, for the multitude of fishes*. Similarly, the fishers of men, when they have enclosed souls in the Gospel net, cannot bring them to shore and complete the good work begun without the continuous influence of divine grace. Notice who was most active in landing the fish: Peter, who, just as he had earlier (v. 7) shown a more zealous devotion to his Master's person than any of the others, now showed a readier obedience to his Master's command; but not all who are faithful are equally eager. Notice the number of the fish that were caught. They were in all *a hundred and fifty three*, and all *great fishes*. Here is a further expression of Christ's care for them: *For all* (Even though) *there were so many*, and *great fishes* too, *yet was not the net broken*, so that they lost none of their fish, nor damaged their net. The net of the Gospel has enclosed very many people, three thousand in one day (Ac 2:41), but still it is not broken; it is still as powerful as it ever was to bring souls to God.

6.3. He invited them to eat. Noticing that *they were afraid to ask him, Who art thou?* because they *knew* it *was their Lord*, he called to them in very friendly terms: *Come and dine*.

6.3.1. Notice here how free Christ was with his disciples; he treated them as friends: "*Come and dine* with me." We may refer to this invitation to illustrate:

6.3.1.1. The call Christ gives all his disciples into communion with him in grace. Christ is your friend; come and eat with him, and he will welcome you (SS 5:1).

6.3.1.2. The call he will give them into the full enjoyment of him in glory in the future. Christ has the resources to give a feast to all his friends and followers; there is room and enough provision for them all.

6.3.2. Notice how reverent the disciples were in Christ's presence. They were rather shy about using the freedom he invited them to. *None of them durst* (dare) *ask him, Who art thou?* They were reluctant either:

6.3.2.1. Because they did not want to be so bold with him. Although perhaps he appeared now in something of a disguise, they still had very good reason to think it was he and could not be anyone else. Or:

6.3.2.2. Because they did not want to go so far as to betray their own foolishness. They would have had to be truly stupid if they questioned whether or not it was he. We should be ashamed of our distrust. Doubts that have no basis must be silenced, not stated.

6.4. He served them, as the master of the feast (v. 13). *He came, and took bread himself*, and *gave them, and fish likewise*. The reception here was ordinary; it was only a breakfast of fish; it was plain and simple. Hunger is the best sauce. Christ *showed himself* to be *alive* by eating (Ac 1:3) rather than showing himself to be a ruler by feasting. He wanted to show that he had a true body that was capable of eating. The apostles produced this as one proof of his resurrection, that *they had eaten and drunk with him* (Ac 10:41). He shared the food with all his guests. He not only provided it for them; he himself also divided it among them and put it into their hands. Similarly, we owe the application as well as the purchase of the benefits of redemption to him. The Evangelist leaves them at breakfast, with this remark (v. 14): *This is now the third time that Jesus showed himself alive to his disciples*. Although he had appeared to Mary, to the women, to the two disciples, and to Cephas, he had still only twice before this appeared to any group of them together. This is taken notice of:

6.4.1. To confirm the truth of his resurrection; the vision was doubled (Ge 41:32), was trebled, because the thing was certain.

6.4.2. To show Christ's continued kindness to his disciples; he came to them once, again, and a third time. It is good to keep an account of Christ's gracious visits. *This is now the third*; have we made good use of the first and second? This is the third, and perhaps it will be the last.

Verses 15–19

We have here Christ's discussion with Peter after breakfast:

1. Christ examined Peter's love toward him, giving him a command about his flock (vv. 15–17). Notice:

1.1. When Christ entered into this discussion with Peter. It was after they had all eaten. Christ foresaw that what he had to say to Peter would make him uneasy. Peter was aware that he had incurred his Master's displeasure and could expect nothing but to be rebuked for his ingratitude. He had seen his Master twice, if not three times, since his resurrection, and the Lord had not said a word to him about his fault. We may imagine that Peter was full of doubts as to what terms he stood on with his Master, sometimes hoping for the best, yet not without some fears. But now, at last, his Master relieved his pain. *When they had dined* together, as a sign of reconciliation, then he discussed the matter with him as one speaks with a friend. Peter had reproached himself for his denial of Christ, and so Christ did not reproach him for it. Satisfied that Peter was sincere, he not only forgave the offense but forgot it, and let him know that he was as dear to him as ever. Here he has given us an encouraging example of his tenderness toward penitents.

1.2. The discussion itself. Here the same question was asked three times, the same answer given three times, and the same reply made to that answer three times. The same thing was repeated by our Savior again and again in order to move Peter. It is repeated by the Evangelist to move us and all who read it.

1.2.1. Christ asked Peter three times whether Peter loved him or not. The first time the question was, *Simon, son of Jonas, lovest thou me more than these?* He spoke to him by name, to move him more effectively, as when he said to him, *Simon, Simon* (Lk 22:31). He did not call him *Cephas*, nor *Peter*, the name he had given him, but used his original name, *Simon*. However, he did not use harsh language with him, but used the same name as when he had declared him blessed: *Simon Bar-jona* (Mt 16:17). Notice how he taught Peter: *Lovest thou me more than these?*

1.2.1.1. *Lovest thou me?* If we want to establish whether we are truly Christ's disciples, this must be the question: "Do we love him?"

1.2.1.1.*1.* Peter's fall had given cause to doubt his love: "Peter, I have cause to suspect your love for me, for if you had loved me, you would not have been ashamed and afraid to acknowledge me in my suffering." We must not be offended by the questioning of our sincerity if we ourselves have done what makes it questionable. The question is moving: "Do you love me? Just give me proof of this, and the way you dishonored me will be overlooked, and nothing more will be said about it." Peter had declared himself to be a penitent, as can be seen from his tears; he was now "on probation" as a penitent. And yet the question was not, "Simon, how much have you wept?" but, "Do you love me?" It is this that will make the other expressions of repentance acceptable. *Much was forgiven her* not because she wept much, but because *she loved much* (Lk 7:47).

1.2.1.1.*2.* The task that lay before Peter would give him occasion to exercise his love. Before Christ would commit his sheep to Peter's care, he asked him, *Lovest thou me?* Christ has such a tender regard for his flock that he will not trust it to any but those who love him. Those who do not truly love Christ will never truly love people's souls; nor will ministers love their work if they do not love their Master. Nothing except love for Christ will compel ministers to cheerfully go through all the difficulties and discouragements they have to face in their work (2Co 5:13–14). But this love will make their work easy and make them serious about it.

1.2.1.2. *Lovest thou me more than these?*

1.2.1.2.*1.* "Lovest thou me more than thou lovest these? Do you love me more than you love James or John, or Andrew?" Those who do not love Christ better than their best friend in the world do not love Christ rightly.

1.2.1.2.*2.* "Lovest thou me more than these love me, more than any of the other disciples love me?" If this is the meaning, the question is intended to rebuke Peter for boasting, *Though all men should be offended because of thee, yet will I not deny thee* (Mt 26:33, 35). Or perhaps Christ meant to show Peter that he now had more reason to love Christ than any of the others had, since he had been forgiven of more than any of them (Lk 7:47). It is no breach of the peace to compete with each other for the title of the one who loves Christ the best.

1.2.1.3. *The second and third time* that Christ asked this question, he asked it differently:

1.2.1.3.*1.* Both the second and the third time, he left out the comparison *more than these*, because Peter modestly left it out, not willing to compare himself with his brothers, much less to put himself above them. Even though we cannot say, "We love Christ more than others do," we will still be accepted if we can say, "We truly love him."

1.2.1.3.*2.* The third time, he changed the verb. In the first two questions, the original verb means "feel kindness": "Do you feel kindness toward me?" In answer to this, Peter used another word, a more emphatic one, meaning "love dearly": "I love you dearly." In asking the question the last time, Christ used Peter's word: "Do you truly love me dearly?"

1.2.2. Peter gave the same answer three times to Christ: *Yea, Lord, thou knowest that I love thee.*

1.2.2.1. Peter did not claim to love Christ more than the other disciples did. Although we must aim to be better than others, we must, *in lowliness of mind, esteem others better than ourselves* (Php 2:3), because we know more evil in ourselves than we do in any of our brothers and sisters.

1.2.2.2. He professed again and again, however, that he loved Christ: *Yea, Lord,* surely *I love thee.* He had a grateful awareness of Christ's kindness; his desire was toward him (SS 7:10), and his delight was in him, as one he would be inexpressibly happy with. This amounts to a profession of repentance for his sin, for it grieves us to have dishonored one we love; and it amounts to a promise of future loyalty to him: "Lord, I love you and will never leave you." Christ had *prayed that* Peter's *faith might not fail* (Lk 22:32), and because his faith did not fail, his love did not, because faith will work through love (Gal 5:6). Christ's test of Peter's repentance was this question: *Dost thou love me?* Peter accepted the test: *Lord, I love thee.*

1.2.2.3. He appealed to Christ himself for proof of it: *Thou knowest that I love thee*; and *the third time* he put it even more emphatically: *Thou knowest all things; thou knowest that I love thee.* He called Christ himself to witness. Peter was certain Christ knew all things, especially that he knew what was in his heart. Peter was satisfied that Christ, who knew all things, knew the sincerity of his love for him and would affirm it in his favor. It is a terror to hypocrites to think that Christ knows all things. But it is an encouragement to sincere Christians. Christ knows us better than we know ourselves. Even though we do not know our own uprightness, he knows it.

1.2.2.4. *He was grieved* when Christ asked him the *third time, Lovest thou me?* (v. 17). It reminded him that he had denied Christ three times. Every remembrance of past sins, even pardoned sins, renews the sorrow of a true penitent. It made him fear that his Master foresaw some further failure he would make. "Surely," Peter thought, "my Master would not torment me in this way unless he saw some cause to do so. What would become of me if I were tempted again?"

1.2.3. Christ committed the care of his flock to Peter three times: *Feed my lambs*; *feed my sheep*; *feed my sheep.*

1.2.3.1. Those whom Christ committed to Peter's care were his lambs and his sheep. In this flock, some are lambs, others sheep. The Shepherd here took care of both, and first of all of the lambs, for he showed a particular tenderness for them on every occasion.

1.2.3.2. The command he gave Peter about them was to feed them. The word used in vv. 15 and 17 strictly means "to give them food," but the word used in v. 16 refers, more generally, to fulfilling all the responsibilities of a shepherd for sheep. It is the duty of all Christ's ministers to feed his lambs and sheep. "Feed them," that is, teach them. "Feed them," that is, "Lead them to green pastures" (Ps 23:2), minister all the services of worship to them. Feed them by personal application to their respective situations; not only lay food in front of them but also feed those who are willful and will not eat, or who are weak and cannot feed themselves."

1.2.3.3. Why, however, did he give this charge especially to Peter? The particular application to Peter here was intended:

1.2.3.3.1. To restore him to his apostleship, now that he had repented. This commission given to Peter was evidence that Christ was reconciled to him, for otherwise he would never have put such confidence in him. When Christ forgave Peter, he trusted him with the most valuable treasure he had on earth.

1.2.3.3.2. To stir him to diligently fulfill his work as an apostle. Peter was always eager to speak and act, and in case he should be tempted to take on himself the directing of the shepherds, he was charged to feed the sheep. If he wanted to be active, let him be active in this and claim nothing more.

1.2.3.3.3. To be heard by all his disciples; he commanded them all not only to be fishers of human beings through the conversion of sinners but also to be those who would feed the flock, by building up the saints.

2. Having confirmed to him the honor of an apostle, he now told him of the further advancement intended for him — the honor of a martyr. Notice:

2.1. How Peter's martyrdom was foretold (v. 18): *Thou shalt stretch forth thy hands*, and *another shall gird thee* (as a prisoner who is bound) *and carry thee whither thou wouldest not*.

2.1.1. Christ introduced the announcement he gave to Peter about his suffering with a solemn affirmation, *Verily, verily, I say unto thee*. He spoke of it not as something probable, but as something certain: *I say it to thee*. Just as Christ foresaw all his own suffering, so he also foresaw the sufferings of all his followers. Having charged Peter to feed his sheep, he told him not to expect comfort and honor in it, but trouble and persecution.

2.1.2. He especially foretold that Peter would die by the hands of an executioner. The ancient tradition tells us that Peter was crucified in Rome under Nero. The pomp and ceremony of an execution add much to the terror of death. In these horrid shapes, death has often been the lot of Christ's faithful ones. It was a violent death that he would be led to, such a death as even innocent nature could not think of without dread. Those who become Christians do not stop being human. Christ himself prayed to be saved from the bitter cup. A natural aversion to pain and death is reconcilable to a holy submission to the will of God in both.

2.1.3. He compared this with Peter's former freedom. "There was a time when *thou girdest thyself and walkedst whither thou wouldest*." When trouble comes, we tend to be anxious about the grievances of restraint, sickness, and poverty, because we have known the sweet ways of liberty, health, and plenty (Job 29:2; Ps 42:4). However, we may turn things the other way around: "How many years of prosperity have I enjoyed more than I have deserved and used? Having received such good, will I not also receive evil (Job 2:10)?" What a change may occur to our condition in this world! What a change may quickly come to those who leave all to follow Christ! They must no longer walk where they want to, but where he wants.

2.1.4. Christ told Peter he would suffer in this way in his old age. His enemies would want to rush him out of the world when he was about to withdraw from it peacefully. Yet God would shelter him from the rage of his enemies until he came to be old, so that he would be better equipped for suffering and the church could enjoy his services for longer.

2.2. The explanation of this prediction (v. 19): *This spoke he* to Peter, *signifying by what death he should glo-rify God*. It is not only *appointed to all once to die* (Heb 9:27); it is also appointed to each person what kind of death they will die. There is one way into the world, but there are many ways out of it, and God has determined which way we will go. It is the great concern of every good person, whatever death they die, to glorify God in it. When we die patiently, cheerfully, and usefully, we glorify God in dying. The deaths of the martyrs were especially glorifying to God. The blood of the martyrs has been the seed of the church: he will honor those who give their lives in honoring him (1Sa 2:30).

2.3. The word of command Christ then gave him: *When he had spoken thus, he saith unto him, Follow me*. This command, *Follow me*, was:

2.3.1. A further confirmation of Peter's restoration to his Master's favor, because *Follow me* was the first call.

2.3.2. An explanation of the prediction of his sufferings. *Follow me:* "Expect to be treated as I have been, *for the disciple is not greater than his Lord* (13:16)."

2.3.3. To encourage him in faithfulness and diligence in his work as an apostle. Christ had told Peter to *feed his sheep* and to keep his Master in mind as an example. They had followed Christ while he was here on earth, and now he still preached the same duty to them: *Follow me*. What greater encouragement, in both service and suffering, could they have than to know:

2.3.3.1. That in serving him and suffering for him, they would follow him and thus bring themselves honor? Who would be ashamed to follow such a leader?

2.3.3.2. That in the future they would follow him in his death and resurrection, and that would be their joy? Those who faithfully follow Christ in grace will certainly follow him to glory.

Verses 20–25

In these verses, we have:

1. The meeting Christ had with Peter about John.

1.1. Peter looked at John (v. 20): Peter followed him, and *turning about, he saw the disciple whom Jesus loved following* as well. Notice:

1.1.1. How John is described. He does not name himself, but gives a description of himself that tells us enough to know whom he meant. *He was the disciple whom Jesus loved.* Probably the reason it is mentioned that John had *leaned on Jesus' breast* and had asked about the traitor — which he did at Peter's instigation (13:24) — is to indicate why Peter asked the following question about him: he asked it to repay John for that kindness. At that time John had been in the favorite's place and had used the opportunity to please Peter. Now that Peter was in the favorite's place and was called to take a walk with Christ, he thought himself bound in gratitude to ask such a question about John as he thought would please John, because we all want to know about things to come. Since by grace we have a right to come boldly to the throne of grace, we should use that right for the benefit of one another. This is the communion of saints.

1.1.2. What John did: he also followed Jesus; where Jesus was, his servant would be also (12:26). What Christ said to Peter, John took as being said to him, as the word of command *Follow me* was given to all the disciples.

1.1.3. The notice Peter took of it: *He, turning about, seeth him.* This may be looked on as:

1.1.3.1. A blameworthy distraction from following his Master. The best people find it hard to *attend upon the Lord without distraction* (1Co 7:35). An unnecessary and untimely regard for our brothers and sisters often distracts us from fellowship with God. Or:

1.1.3.2. A commendable concern for his fellow disciples. He was not so elevated with the honor his Master showed him as to deny a kind look to one who followed.

1.2. Peter asked a question about John (v. 21): *"Lord, and what shall this man do?* What will be his work and his lot?" This may be taken as the language:

1.2.1. Of concern for John and kindness toward him. "Here comes the disciple you love especially; have you nothing to say to him? Will you not tell him how he must be employed, and how he must be honored?" Or:

1.2.2. Of uneasiness at what Christ had said to him about his suffering: "Lord, must I alone be *carried whither I would not*? Must this man have no share in the cross?" Or:

1.2.3. Of curiosity and a fond desire to know future things. It seems from Christ's answer that there was something wrong in the question.

1.2.3.1. Peter seemed more concerned about someone else than about himself. We are so inclined to be busy about other people's matters but negligent in the concerns of our own souls—quick sighted outside ourselves but dim sighted at home.

1.2.3.2. He seemed more concerned about outcomes than about duty. We need not ask, "What will be the lot of those who come after us?" Scripture predictions should be considered as a guide to our consciences, not as a way to satisfy our curiosity.

1.3. Christ replied to this question (v. 22): *If I will that he tarry till I come, what is that to thee? Follow thou me.*

1.3.1. Christ seems here to indicate his purposes for John: that he would not die a violent death, as Peter did, but would wait until Christ himself came to draw him to himself by a natural death. The most credible of the ancient historians tell us that John was the only one of the Twelve who did not actually die as a martyr. He finally died in his bed at a good old age (Ge 25:8; Jdg 8:32; 1Ch 29:28). Although the crown of martyrdom is bright and glorious, the disciple whom Christ loved came short of it.

1.3.2. Others think that it is only a rebuke to Peter's curiosity: "Suppose I intended that John would never die: what concern is that of yours? I have told you how you must die; it is enough for you to know that. *Follow thou me.*" It is the will of Christ that his disciples be concerned for their own present duty and not be curious about future events for either themselves or others.

1.3.2.1. We tend to be concerned about many things that have nothing to do with us. What other people are like is of no concern to us; we are out of line if we judge them (Ro 14:4). Other people's affairs are nothing for us to interfere in. "What do you think will become of so and so?" is a common question, which may easily be answered with another: "What is that to me?" To his own Master he stands or falls (Ro 14:4). Secret things are not for us to know (Dt 29:29).

1.3.2.2. The great thing that is most important for us is that we do our duty and do not worry about how things will turn out. Outcomes belong to God; duty belongs to us. All our duty is summed up in the one duty of following Christ. If we pay close attention to that, we will find neither the heart nor the time to interfere with what has nothing to do with us.

1.4. A mistake arose from this saying of Christ, that *that disciple would not die*. Notice:

1.4.1. How easily a mistake arose in the church through a misinterpretation of the sayings of Christ. Because John would not die a martyr, they concluded he would not die at all.

1.4.1.1. They were inclined to expect it because they could not help desiring it. They thought that for John to continue in the world until Christ's second coming would be a great blessing to the church. We tend to devote ourselves too much to people and means, instruments and external helps, whereas God will change his workers but carry on his work. There is no need for immortal ministers to be the guides of the church, as long as it is being led by the eternal Spirit.

1.4.1.2. Perhaps they were confirmed in their expectations when they now found that John survived all the rest of the apostles. However, it arose from a saying of Christ's that was misunderstood and then made a saying of the church. From this we may see:

1.4.1.2.1. The uncertainty of human tradition and the foolishness of building our faith on it. Here was a tradition, an apostolic tradition, a saying that *went abroad among the brethren* (v. 23). It was early, common, and public, but false. Let Scripture be its own interpreter and explain itself.

1.4.1.2.2. The human tendency to misinterpret the sayings of Christ. The Scriptures themselves have been perverted by the ignorant and unstable (2Pe 3:16).

1.4.2. The easy putting right of such mistakes by remaining faithful to the word of Christ. The Evangelist here corrects the saying among the believers by repeating the exact words of Christ. Christ said, *If I will that he tarry till I come, what is that to thee?* He said that and nothing more. Let the words of Christ speak for themselves. The best purpose of human controversies would be to keep to the clear words of Scripture. Scripture language is the safest and most proper agent of Scripture truth. Just as the Scripture itself is the best weapon with which to deal effectively with all dangerous errors, so also Scripture itself is the best lotion to heal the wounds that are inflicted by different expressions about the same truths. Those who cannot agree on the same logic and metaphysics may still agree on the same terms in Scripture, and then they may agree to love one another.

2. The conclusion of this Gospel (vv. 24–25).

2.1. This Gospel concludes with an account of its writer (v. 24): *This is the disciple which testifies of these things* to the present age and *wrote these things* for the benefit of all future generations. Notice:

2.1.1. Those who wrote the history of Christ were not ashamed to put their names to it. John here is in effect signing his name. The record of Christ's life and death was drawn up by men of known integrity, who were ready to seal it with their blood.

2.1.2. Those who wrote the account of Christ wrote from their own knowledge. The writer of this record was a disciple, one who had leaned back against Christ, who had himself heard his sermons and seen his miracles and the proofs of his resurrection. This was the one who testified what he was certain of.

2.1.3. Just as those who wrote the account of Christ testified what they had seen, so they also wrote what they had first testified. It was made known by word of mouth with the greatest assurance before it was committed to writing. What they wrote they wrote as an affidavit, which they would stand by.

2.1.4. It was graciously appointed that the account of Christ would be recorded in writing, so that it could spread to every place and last to every age.

2.2. It concludes with an affirmation of the truth of what has been related here: *We know that his testimony is true.* This may be taken:

2.2.1. As expressing the common sense that people have in matters of this nature, which is that the testimony of one who is an eyewitness, who has a spotless reputation, and who solemnly states what he has seen and writes it down to give it greater certainty is evidence that cannot be objected to. *We know*, that is, "The whole world knows that the testimony of such a person is valid. The truth of the Gospel comes confirmed by all the evidence we can reasonably desire or expect. So let the message commend itself, and let the miracles prove it to have come from God.

2.2.2. As expressing the assurance of the churches at that time about the truth of what is related here. It is not as if an inspired writing needed any human confirmation; they commended it to the notice of the churches. Or:

2.2.3. As expressing the Evangelist's own assurance of the truth of what he wrote. The Evangelists themselves were completely satisfied about the truth of what they testified to and passed on to us. They risked both this life and the other on it; they threw away this life and depended on another.

2.3. It concludes with an "etc.," a reference to *many other things* said and done by our Lord Jesus (v. 25). If they were to be fully written down, even the world itself could not contain the books that could be written. If the question is asked why the Gospels are not any longer, it may be answered:

2.3.1. It was not because the writers had exhausted their subject and had nothing more to write that was worth writing. Everything that Christ said and did was worth our notice. He performed very many miracles of many different kinds, and the same kinds were repeated often. The repetition of the miracles before a wide range of witnesses helped very much to prove they were true miracles. Every new miracle made the report of the previous one more credible, and the large number of them makes the whole report undeniable. When we speak about Christ, we have a plentiful subject before us; the reality exceeds the report, and, in the end we must confess, *the one half is not told us*

(2Ch 9:6). The apostle Paul quotes one of Christ's sayings that is not recorded by any of the evangelists (Ac 20:35), and no doubt there were many more.

2.3.2. Rather, it was for these three reasons:

2.3.2.1. It was unnecessary to write more. What is written is a sufficient revelation of the message of Christ and the proof of that message. If we do not believe and make use of what is written, neither would we if there had been much more.

2.3.2.2. It was not possible to write everything down. It would be a history so large and overgrown that it could not be contained; it would jostle out all other writings and leave no room for them. A complete record would have been endless.

2.3.2.3. It was not advisable to write much, because *the world*, in a moral sense, *could not contain the books that should be written. The world could not contain.* It is the word Christ used in 8:37, when he said, "My word *has no place* in you." There would have been so many words that the church would have found no room for them. All people's time would have been spent in reading, and other duties would have been crowded out. Much of what is written is overlooked, much is forgotten, and much made the matter of dispute; this would have been even more the case if there had been such a world of books, especially since it was necessary that what was written down be meditated on and explained, which God wisely thought fit to leave room for. Let us be thankful for the books that have been written, and not prize them any less because of their plainness and brevity. We must long to be above, where our capacities will be so advanced and enlarged that there will be no danger of their being overloaded. The Evangelist concludes with *Amen*, so setting his seal to his testimony, and let us set ours to it too, an *Amen* of our faith, which is all true. Let us speak out a sincere *Amen* of satisfaction at what is written, since it can make us wise for salvation (2Ti 3:15). *Amen*, "so be it."

A PRACTICAL AND DEVOTIONAL EXPOSITION
OF THE

Acts of the Apostles

W ith abundant satisfaction, we have now seen the foundation of our holy religious faith laid in the account of our blessed Savior. The Christian church is built on this rock (Mt 16:18). We next turn to the account of how it began to be built on this rock. Now:

1. This account may be considered as looking back to the foregoing Gospels.

1.1. We find here the fulfillment of the promises made there, especially the great promises of the descent of the Holy Spirit. The powers that were vested in the apostles there are here found being exerted in miracles performed on people's bodies: miracles of mercy, miracles of judgment, and much greater miracles performed on people's hearts and minds.

1.2. The proofs of Christ's resurrection with which the Gospels closed are abundantly confirmed here according Christ's prediction that his resurrection would be the most convincing proof of his divine mission. Christ had told his disciples that they would be his witnesses, and this book sees them witnessing for him.

1.3. But that *day-spring from on high* (rising sun from heaven) (Lk 1:78) whose first appearance we discerned in the Gospels is seen shining out more and more (Pr 4:18) here. *The kingdom of heaven*, which was then *at hand* (Mt 4:17), is now set up. Christ's predictions of the intense persecutions that the preachers of the Gospel would suffer are here abundantly fulfilled, and so are the assurances he gave them of extraordinary support, strength, and encouragement in their suffering.

1.4. This later part of the history of the New Testament exactly corresponds to the word of Christ in its earlier part, and so the two parts mutually confirm and illustrate each other.

2. It may be considered as looking forward to the following letters. This book introduces them and is a key to them. We are members of the Christian church, that *tabernacle of God among men* (Rev 21:3). This book gives us an account of the setting up of that tabernacle. The four Gospels showed us how the foundation of that house was laid; this book shows us how the superstructure began to be erected:

2.1. Among the Jews and Samaritans.

2.2. Among the Gentiles.

3. Two further matters are to be observed concerning this book:

3.1. Its writer. It was written by Luke, who wrote and gave his name to the third of the four Gospels. This Luke was very much a companion of Paul in his service and suffering. *Only Luke is with me* (2Ti 4:11). We may know from his style in the latter part of this book when and where Luke was with Paul, because then he writes, "*We* did such and such" (e.g.,16:10; 20:6).

3.2. Its full title: The Acts of the Apostles.

3.2.1. It is the record of the apostles, but it also contains the record of Stephen, Barnabas, and some other apostolic men; and of those who were apostles, only Peter and Paul have their ministries recorded here. Peter was the apostle to the Jews, and Paul the apostle to the Gentiles (Gal 2:7).

3.2.2. It is called their *acts*, or "doings." The apostles were active, and although the wonders they did were performed by the word, they are still appropriately called their acts; they *spoke, and it was done* (Ps 33:9).

CHAPTER 1

The inspired writer begins his narrative of the Acts of the Apostles: 1. With a reference to his Gospel, dedicating this account, as he had his earlier one, to his friend Theophilus (vv. 1–2). 2. With a summary of the proofs of Christ's resurrection, an account of his meet- *ing with his disciples, and the instructions he gave them during the forty days of his stay on earth (vv. 3–5). 3. With a detailed account of Christ's ascension to heaven (vv. 6–11). 4. With a general idea of the embryo of the Christian church (vv. 12–14). 4. With a detailed account of the filling, by the election of Matthias, of the vacancy that was brought about in the sacred college of apostles by the death of Judas (vv. 15–26).*

Verses 1–5

1. Theophilus is reminded, and we in him, about Luke's Gospel, which it will be useful for us to consider briefly.

1.1. Luke's patron, to whom he dedicates this book, is Theophilus (v. 1). The directing of some of the books of Scripture to particular persons or groups is an indication to each of us that we ought to receive them as if they were directed to us in particular, to us by name.

1.2. His Gospel is called here *the former treatise which he had made.* He wrote the former book, and now he was divinely inspired to write this one, for Christ's students must *go on toward perfection* (Heb 6:1), not thinking that their past labors will excuse them from further labor. Because Luke had laid the foundation in a former book, he would build on it in this one. Let not new sermons and new books make us forget old ones, but let them remind us of them and help us make good use of them.

1.3. The contents of his Gospel were *all that Jesus began both to do and teach.*

1.3.1. Christ both did and taught. Those who both do and teach, whose lives are a constant sermon, are the best ministers.

1.3.2. *He began both to do and teach*; he laid the foundation. His apostles were to continue what he began. Christ put them in the office and then left them to continue, but he sent his Spirit to empower them. Those who are trying to continue the work of the Gospel can take comfort in knowing that Christ himself began it.

1.3.3. The four Evangelists, especially Luke, have handed down to us *all that Jesus began both to do and to teach*; not all the details, but all the headings, so that we may judge the rest by them.

1.4. The end of the Gospel record is fixed as *the day in which he was taken up* (v. 2). It was then that he left this world and was no longer physically present in it.

2. The truth of Christ's resurrection is maintained and proved (v. 3). The great evidence of his resurrection was that *he showed himself alive to his apostles* and *was seen of them.*

2.1. There were infallible proofs both that he was *alive*—he walked and talked with them, he ate and drank with them—and that it was he himself, not another: he showed them again and again the marks of the wounds in his hands, feet, and side.

2.2. The proofs were many and repeated often: *He was seen by them forty days*, not constantly living with them, but frequently appearing to them.

3. A general hint is given of the instructions he gave his disciples.

3.1. He instructed them about the work they were to do: *he gave commandments to the apostles whom he had chosen.* Those whom he elected to the apostleship expected him to promote them, but instead he gave them commandments. *He gave them commandments through the Holy Spirit.* In giving them the Holy Spirit, he gave them his commandments, because the *Comforter* (Jn 14:26; NIV: Counselor) will be a commander.

3.2. He instructed them in the message they were to preach: *He spoke to them of the things pertaining to* (about) *the kingdom of God.* He had given them a general idea of that kingdom, but here he instructed them more in its nature, as a kingdom of grace in this world and of glory in the other, to prepare them to receive the Holy Spirit and to go through what they were intended for. This instruction was one of the proofs of Christ's resurrection; the

disciples, to whom *he showed himself alive*, knew that it was he not only by what he showed them but also by what he said to them. No one but him could speak so clearly, so fully, *of the things pertaining to the kingdom of God.*

4. He gave them a specific assurance that they would now soon receive the Holy Spirit (vv. 4–5). Notice:

4.1. The command he gave them to wait. This was to raise their expectations.

4.1.1. They must wait until the appointed time, which was now *not many days hence* (v. 5). Those who by faith hope promised mercies will come must wait with patience until they come.

4.1.2. They must wait in the appointed place, *in Jerusalem.* It was there that Christ was put to shame, and so there he would have this honor shown him, and this favor was done to Jerusalem to teach us to forgive our enemies and persecutors. The apostles were now to be public figures. Jerusalem was the most suitable lampstand (Rev 1:12–13, 20) for those lights to be set up on.

4.2. The assurance he gave them that they would not wait in vain.

4.2.1. The blessing intended for them would come: *You shall be baptized with the Holy Spirit.* They had already been breathed on with the Holy Spirit (Jn 20:22), and they had found the benefit of such a breathing, but now they would receive larger measures of his gifts, graces, and comforts. "You will be cleansed and purified by the Holy Spirit," as the priests were baptized and washed with water when they were consecrated to the sacred function: "They had the sign; you will have the thing represented by the sign. You will be committed more powerfully than ever to your Master. You will be tied so firmly to Christ that you will never abandon him again."

4.2.2. Now he spoke about this gift of the Holy Spirit:

4.2.2.1. *As the promise of the Father, which they had heard of him* and could therefore depend on.

4.2.2.1.1. The Spirit was given by promise. The Spirit of God is not given as the human spirit is given us, but by the word of God, so that the gift may be more valuable, be more certain, be through grace, and be received by faith. As Christ is received by faith, so is the Spirit.

4.2.2.1.2. It was *the promise of the Father*: of Christ's Father, of our Father. He will give the Spirit, as *the Father of mercies* (2Co 1:3); it is *the promise of the Father.*

4.2.2.1.3. This promise of the Father they had heard from Christ many times. He had assured them again and again that *the Comforter* (Counselor) would come. That we have heard a promise from Jesus Christ confirms it as the promise of God.

4.2.2.2. As the prediction of John the Baptist (v. 5): "You have heard it not only from me but also from John; he said, *I indeed baptize you with water, but he that comes after me shall baptize you with the Holy Spirit* (Mt 3:11)." It was a great honor that Christ now did to John. This is how *he confirmeth the word of his servants, his messengers* (Isa 44:26). However, Christ can do more than any of his ministers. It is an honor of theirs to be employed in sharing the means of grace, but it is his prerogative to give *the Spirit of grace* (Heb 10:29).

4.2.3. Now this gift of the Holy Spirit that Christ promised in this way is what we find that the apostles received in the next chapter, because this promise had its complete fulfillment then. Other Scriptures speak of *the gift of the Holy Spirit* (2:38) to ordinary believers; this Scripture speaks of the particular power that the first preachers of the Gospel were endowed with. Because of this promise we receive the New Testament as divinely inspired.

Verses 6–11

Here the disciples met together to be the witnesses of Christ's ascension. Notice:

1. They asked him a question at this meeting. *Lord, wilt thou at this time restore again the kingdom to Israel?* This may be taken in either of two ways:

1.1. "Surely you will not in any way restore the kingdom to the present rulers of Israel. What! Will those who hate and persecute you and us be trusted with power?" Or rather:

1.2. "Surely you will now restore the kingdom to the Jewish nation, as far as that nation will submit to you." Two things were wrong in this question:

1.2.1. Their expectation of the thing itself. They thought Christ would *restore the kingdom to Israel.* The reality, however, was that Christ came to establish his own kingdom, the kingdom of heaven, not to restore the kingdom to Israel, a worldly kingdom. See here:

1.2.1.1. How even good people tend to define the success of the church too much in terms of external power and show. We are told to expect the cross in this world (Mt 16:24) and to wait for the kingdom in the other world.

1.2.1.2. How we tend to hang on to what has been instilled in us, how hard it is to overcome the prejudices of our education. It took a long time for the disciples to understand that Christ's kingdom was spiritual.

1.2.1.3. How naturally we tend to be biased in favor of our own people. The kingdoms of this world were to become Christ's (Rev 11:15) whether Israel sank or swam.

1.2.1.4. How we tend to misunderstand Scripture and to explain Scripture according to our own plans, whereas in reality we should form our plans from the Scriptures.

1.2.2. Their question about its timing: "*Lord, wilt thou do it at this time?*" They inquired into what their Master had never encouraged them to inquire into. They were impatient to see the setting up of the kingdom in which they promised themselves such a great share. Christ had told them that they would *sit on thrones* (Lk 22:30), and now they could not wait to sit on them.

2. Christ rebuked this question (v. 7): *It is not for you to know the times and seasons.* Their mistake in expecting that the kingdom would be restored to Israel would soon be put right by the outpouring of the Spirit, after which they never had any more thoughts of the worldly kingdom. And there was, in fact, a sense in which their expectation about the setting up of the Gospel kingdom in the world would be fulfilled. But he restrained their question about the time.

2.1. This knowledge was not allowed to them: *It is not for you to know.*

2.1.1. Christ was now leaving them, and he gave them this rebuke as a warning to his church to make sure that his people are careful not to break themselves on the rock that was fatal to our first parents, namely, an excessive desire for forbidden knowledge.

2.1.2. Christ had given his disciples more knowledge than he had given others. Here he told them that there were some things that it was not for them to know. We will see how little reason we have to be proud of our knowledge when we consider how many things we are ignorant of.

2.1.3. Christ had given his disciples enough instructions to enable them to fulfill their duty, and he wanted them to be satisfied with this knowledge.

2.1.4. Christ himself had told his disciples *the things pertaining to the kingdom of God* (v. 3), and he had prom-

ised that the Spirit would *show them things to come.* He had also given them *signs of the times.* But they must neither expect nor desire to know either all the details of future events or their exact times. As to the times and seasons of the year, we know in general that summer and winter will come and go, but we do not know what the weather with be like on any particular day—which day will be fine or which stormy, either in summer or in winter. We cannot tell what any particular *day will bring forth* (Pr 27:1), but must accept it, whatever it is, and make the best of it.

2.2. This knowledge was reserved to God; it is what *the Father hath put in his own power* (v. 7). No one besides him can reveal the future times and seasons. "He has not thought fit to let you know the times and seasons. He has not said he will not allow you to know something more than you do of the times and seasons, but he has reserved the right to do it or not, as he thinks fit."

3. He appointed them to do their work and assured them with authority that they would succeed in it. "Know this (v. 8): you will receive a spiritual *power* by the *descent of the Holy Spirit upon you,* and *you shall be witnesses unto me.* Your testimony will be received here in Jerusalem, in the surrounding country, and all over the world" (v. 8). If Christ makes us useful to his honor in our own day and generation, let this be enough for us. Christ told them here:

3.1. That their work would be honorable and glorious: *You shall be witnesses unto me.* They would make him known as king. They must openly and solemnly preach his Gospel to the world. They would confirm their testimony not as witnesses do, with an oath, but with the divine seal of miracles and supernatural gifts: *You shall be* "martyrs" *to me*—the word translated *witnesses* is *martures*—for they affirmed the truth of the Gospel with their suffering, even to death.

3.2. That their power for this work would be sufficient. They did not have strength of their own for it, nor enough wisdom or courage. "But you shall receive the power of the Holy Spirit coming upon you. You will have power to preach the Gospel and to confirm it both by miracles and by suffering." He will equip for his service those he employs.

3.3. That their influence would be great and very extensive: "*You shall be witnesses to Jerusalem*; you must begin there. Your light will shine from there throughout all Judea. From there you will proceed *to Samaria.* And your usefulness will reach *to the uttermost part of the earth.*"

4. Having left these instructions with them, he left them (v. 9): *When he had spoken these things, he blessed them,* as we were told in Lk 24:50, and *while they beheld him, he was taken up, and a cloud received him out of their sight.* He began his ascension in the sight of his disciples, *while they beheld.* They saw him go up toward heaven, and actually had their eyes on him with so much care and seriousness that they could not have been deceived. He *vanished out of their sight* (Lk 24:31), in *a cloud.* It was a bright cloud that overshadowed him at his transfiguration, and most probably this was so now (Mt 17:5). A kind of communication is kept up by the clouds between the upper and lower world; in them vapors are sent up from the earth (Ps 135:7), and dew sent down from heaven (Dt 32:28; Pr 3:20; Zec 8:12). It is appropriate, therefore, that the One who ascends in a cloud is *the Mediator between God and man* (1Ti 2:5), through whom God's mercies come down on us and our prayers come up to him. This was the last that was seen of him.

5. When he had gone out of the disciples' sight, they continued *looking up steadfastly to heaven* (v. 10).

5.1. Perhaps they hoped that Christ would come back to them immediately. They were still so devoted to his physical presence, even though he had told them that *it was expedient for them that he should go away* (Jn 16:7).

5.2. Perhaps they expected to see some change in the visible heavens after Christ's ascension. Christ had told them that in the future they would *see heaven opened* (Jn 1:51), and why should not they expect it to happen now?

6. Two angels appeared to them. To show how much Christ had the concerns of his church on earth at heart, he sent back to his disciples two of those who came to meet him, who appeared as *two men in white apparel*. We are told here what the angels said to them:

6.1. To curb their curiosity: "*You men of Galilee, why stand you gazing up into heaven?* What do you want to see? You have seen all you were called together to see, and so why are you looking any longer? *Why stand you gazing?*" Christ's disciples should never stand around looking, because they have a sure rule to follow.

6.2. To confirm their faith about Christ's second coming. Their Master had often told them about this: *This same Jesus, who is taken up from you into heaven, will come in like manner thence, as you have seen him go thither.*

6.2.1. "*This same Jesus* who came once in disgrace to be judged will come again in glory to judge.

6.2.2. "He *shall come in like manner*. He is gone away in a cloud. You have now lost sight of him in the clouds. *Whither he is gone you cannot follow him now* (Jn 13:36). But you will when he returns." When we stand around gazing and toying with this and that, consideration of our Master's second coming should give us life and wake us up, and when we stand gazing and trembling, consideration of it should comfort and encourage us.

Verses 12–14

We are told here:

1. Where Christ ascended: *from the mount of Olives* (v. 12). He began his suffering there, and so it was there that he rolled away the reproach (Jos 5:9) of his suffering by his glorious ascension. And so he would enter into his kingdom in the sight of Jerusalem. This mount is here said to have been near Jerusalem, *a sabbath day's journey* from it, no further than devout people used to walk on a Sabbath evening for meditation after public worship. It is about three-quarters of a mile, about 1,100 meters. The principle of a Sabbath day's journey is to be a rule for us to the extent that we ought not to journey on the Sabbath any further than we need to in order to fulfill Sabbath work, and we are not only allowed but also commanded to undertake this as is necessary (2Ki 4:23).

2. Where the disciples returned to: they went back to Jerusalem, according to their Master's instruction. It seems, however, that although immediately after Christ's resurrection they were watched, after it was known that they had gone to Galilee, no notice was taken of their return to Jerusalem. God can find hiding places for his people among their enemies. At Jerusalem the disciples *went up into an upper room, and there abode*; they assembled there every day, expecting the descent of the Spirit. Some think it was one of the upper rooms in the temple, but the chief priests would not have allowed this. *They were* indeed *continually in the temple* (Lk 24:53), but that was in the courts of the temple, *at the hours of prayer* (3:1), where they could not be stopped from attending. It seems, therefore, that this upper room was in a private house.

3. Who the disciples were who stayed together. The eleven apostles are named here (v. 13), as is Mary the mother of our Lord (v. 14), and it is the last time that any mention is ever made of her. There were others who are here said to have been the *brethren* of our Lord, and, to make up *the hundred and twenty* spoken of (v. 15), we may suppose that all or most of the *seventy disciples* (Lk 10:1) were with them.

4. How they spent their time: *They all continued with one accord in prayer and supplication.*

4.1. *They prayed and made supplication.* All God's people are praying people. It was now a time of trouble and danger, and, *Is any afflicted? Let him pray* (Jas 5:13). They had a new work before them, and before they embarked on it, *they were instant* (faithful) *in prayer to God* (Ro 12:12). Before they were first sent out, Christ spent time praying for them, and now they spent time praying for themselves. Those who are in a prayerful attitude are in the best attitude to receive spiritual blessings. God wants to be asked for promised mercies, and the closer the appearance seems to be, the more serious we should be in praying for it.

4.2. *They continued in prayer.* It is said in Lk 24:53, *They were praising and blessing God*; here, *They continued in prayer and supplication.* Praise for the promise is a proper way to seek its fulfillment, and praise for former mercies a proper way to seek further mercy.

4.3. They did this *with one accord.* Those who keep *the unity of the Spirit in the bond of peace* (Eph 4:3) are best prepared to receive the assurance of the Holy Spirit.

Verses 15–26

The sin of Judas opened up a vacancy in the sacred college of the apostles. If they were only eleven, everyone would ask what had become of the twelfth; care was taken, therefore, to fill that vacancy. We have here:

1. The people concerned in this matter. The group consisted of *about a hundred and twenty*. This was *the number of the names*, that is, people. This was the beginning of the Christian church: these 120 were the grain of mustard seed that grew into a tree, the yeast that leavened the whole lump (Mt 13:31–33). The speaker was Peter, who had been and still was the most forward. Because Peter was intended to be the apostle to the Jews, he is brought in here, while the sacred story continues to focus on the Jews, just as later, when the record comes to speak about the Gentiles, it keeps to the story of Paul.

2. The proposal Peter made for choosing another apostle. He *stood up in the midst of the disciples* (v. 15). Notice:

2.1. The account he gave of the vacancy left by the death of Judas. In this account, Peter was very detailed and took notice of the fulfilling of the Scriptures in this matter. Here is:

2.1.1. The power to which Judas had been advanced (v. 17): *He was numbered with us, and had obtained part of this ministry.* What good will it do us to be added to the number of Christians if we do not share in the spirit and nature of Christians?

2.1.2. The sin of Judas. He was *guide to those that took Jesus.* He not only told Christ's persecutors where to find him; he also had the arrogance to appear openly at the head of the party that arrested him and give the word of command: *That same is he, hold him fast* (Mt 26:48). Ringleaders in sin are the worst sinners.

2.1.3. The ruin of Judas by this sin. Realizing that the chief priests were seeking to take the life of Christ and his disciples, Judas thought he would save his own skin by going over to their side; and not only that: he hoped that they would provide him with an estate.

2.1.3.1. He lost his money shamefully enough (v. 18): *He purchased a field* with the *thirty pieces of silver*, which were the *reward of his iniquity*. He thought he would buy a field for himself, but it turned out to be the purchase of a field as a burial place for foreigners, and how was he or any of his family better for this act?

2.1.3.2. He lost his life even more shamefully. We were told earlier (Mt 27:5) that he *went away* in despair; it is added here, *fell headlong*. He *burst asunder in the midst, so* that *all his bowels gushed* (his intestines spilled) *out.* Disembowelling is part of the punishment of traitors.

2.1.4. The public notice that was taken of this: *It was known to all the dwellers in Jerusalem.* It was, as it were, put into the newspapers, and was the talk of the town, as a remarkable judgment of God on the one who betrayed his Master (v. 19). It was on everybody's lips, and nobody disputed the truth of the fact. *It was known*, that is, it was known to be true. Here is one proof of the notoriety of the thing mentioned, that the field was called *Aceldama,* "the field of blood," because it was bought with the *price of blood* (Mt 27:6).

2.1.5. The fulfilling, in this matter, of the Scriptures, which had clearly said *that it must needs be fulfilled* (v. 16). Let no one be surprised or stumble when they see that this was the exit of one of the Twelve, because David had foretold not only Judas's sin but also:

2.1.5.1. His punishment: *Let his habitation be desolate.*

2.1.5.2. The substitution of another in his place. His *bishopric,* or "his office," *shall another take.* We are not to think the worse of any office that God has instituted either because of the evil of any who are in that office or because of the ignominious punishment of that evil; nor will God allow any purpose of his to be frustrated, or any work of his to be undone, because of the failures of those who are entrusted with them. Judas is hanged, but his place of leadership is not lost. Christ's cause will never be lost for lack of witnesses.

2.2. The suggestion he made for the choice of another apostle (vv. 21–22). Notice:

2.2.1. How the person who filled that vacancy must be qualified. It must be one of *these men that have companied with* (accompanied) *us all the time that the Lord Jesus went in and out among us, beginning from the baptism of John, unto that same day that he was taken up from us.* Those who have been diligent in discharging their duty in a lower work are best suited to be advanced to a higher one; those who have been faithful in a little will be entrusted with more (Lk 19:17). No one will be an apostle except one who has continually been with the apostles.

2.2.2. The work of the one who would be called: he must be *a witness with us of his resurrection.* This shows that other disciples were with the Eleven when Christ appeared to them after his resurrection. The great matter the apostles were to declare to the world was Christ's resurrection. Notice what the apostles were ordained to, not to worldly honor and power, but to preach Christ and the power of his resurrection (Php 3:10).

3. The naming of the person who was to succeed Judas.

3.1. Two who were known to have been constantly with Christ were proposed as candidates for the place (v. 23): *They appointed two.* The two they named were Joseph and Matthias, about neither of whom we have read elsewhere. These two were both so well qualified for the office that the gathered disciples could not tell which of them was more suitable, but all agreed it must be one of these two.

3.2. The believers turned to God in prayer for his direction as to which of these two it was to be (vv. 24–25).

3.2.1. They appealed to God as the One who searches hearts (1Ch 28:9; Jer 17:10): "*Thou, Lord, who knowest the hearts of all men.*" When an apostle was to be chosen, he must be chosen according to his heart and its attitude. It is an encouragement to us, in our prayers for the well-being of the church and its ministers, that the God to whom we pray *knows the hearts of all men;* he can make them fit for his purpose: he gives them another spirit (1Sa 10:9).

3.2.2. They asked to know which of these God had chosen: "*Lord*, show us this." It is right that God choose his own servants.

3.2.3. They were ready to receive as a brother the one whom God had chosen to *take part of this ministry and apostleship from which Judas by transgression fell*—from which, indeed, he had thrown himself, so that he would go *to his own place,* the place of a traitor, the most suitable place for him. Those who betray Christ fall *from* the dignity of knowing him and fall *into* complete misery. Our Savior had said that Judas's own place would be such that *it would have been better for him that he had never been born* (Mt 26:24).

3.2.4. The doubt was resolved by lot (v. 26), which is an appeal to God and is lawful to use for determining matters that cannot be determined in any other way, provided it is done in a sacred and religious manner and with the prayer of faith. This is how the number of the apostles was made up.

CHAPTER 2

Between the promise of the Spirit and his coming there were only a few days, and during those days the apostles were detained and did not attempt to preach. However, in this chapter the north wind and the south wind awake (SS 4:16), and when they do, we immediately find them preaching. Here is: 1. The descent of the Spirit on the Day of Pentecost (vv. 1–4). 2. The various speculations among the people who had now met in Jerusalem from all parts (vv. 5–13). 3. The sermon Peter preached, in which he showed that this outpouring of the Spirit fulfilled an Old Testament promise (vv. 14–21), confirmed Christ as the Messiah (vv. 22–32), and was a fruit and evidence of his ascension into heaven (vv. 23–36). 4. The good effect this sermon had in the conversion of many to faith in Christ (vv. 37–41). 5. The outstanding devotion and love of those first Christians (vv. 42–47).

Verses 1–4

Here is an account of the coming of the Holy Spirit on the disciples of Christ. Notice:

1. When and where this was done.

1.1. It was *when the day of pentecost was fully come.*

1.1.1. The Holy Spirit came at the time of a sacred festival, because that was the time of a great meeting of people in Jerusalem from all parts, which would make the news of the Spirit's coming spread more quickly and further. Now, as earlier at the Passover, the Jewish festivals served to toll the bell for Gospel services.

1.1.2. This feast of Pentecost was celebrated in remembrance of the giving of the Law on Mount Sinai. It was appropriate, therefore, that the Holy Spirit was given at that festival, and that he was given in fire and in tongues, to declare the Gospel law not to one nation but to the whole creation (Mk 16:15).

1.1.3. This feast of Pentecost took place on the *first day of the week,* which confirmed it as the Christian

Sabbath and as a constant memorial of those two great blessings—the resurrection of Christ and the outpouring of the Spirit. On every Lord's Day in the year, I think, full and particular notice should be taken of these two blessings in our prayers and praises.

1.2. It was when *they were all with one accord in one place*. We are not told what place it was exactly. But it was in Jerusalem, because this had been the place God chose (2Ch 6:6), and the prophecy was that from there the word of the Lord would go out (Isa 2:3). Here God had promised to meet them and bless them; here, therefore, he met them with this blessing of blessings. He still did Jerusalem this honor, to teach us not to quarrel with places, because God has his remnant everywhere; he had this remnant in Jerusalem. Here the disciples were together in one place. Here they were *with one accord*. They had prayed more together recently than they had before (1:14), and this made them love one another better. By his grace he had prepared them in this way for the gift of the Holy Spirit, because that holy dove does not come where there is noise and clamor; he moves on the face of the still waters (Ge 1:2; Ps 23:2), not the stormy ones. Do we want the Spirit to be *poured out upon us from on high* (Isa 32:15)? Let us all be of one mind; let us agree to love one another.

2. How the Holy Spirit came on them. We often read in the Old Testament of God's coming down in a cloud (Ex 40:34–35; 2Ch 7:1–2). Christ went up to heaven in a cloud (1:9). But the Holy Spirit did not descend in a cloud, for he was to dispel and scatter the clouds that spread over people's minds.

2.1. Here is an audible call given to them to wake up their expectations (v. 2). It came *suddenly*; it was at its peak immediately. It came sooner than they expected, startling even those who were now together waiting. It was *a sound from heaven*. It was the sound of a wind, for the way of the Spirit is like that of the wind (Jn 3:8): *thou hearest the sound thereof, but canst not tell whence it comes nor whither it goes*. It was like *a rushing mighty wind*; it was strong and violent and came with great force, as if it would overthrow everything in its path. This was to represent the powerful influence and activity of the Spirit of God. *It filled* not only the room but *all the house where they were sitting*. This wind filling the house would strike awe on the disciples and help to put them into a very serious attitude, to receive the Holy Spirit. This is how the convictions of the Spirit make way for his assurance, and the rough blasts of that blessed wind prepare the soul for its soft and gentle breeze.

2.2. Here is a visible sign of the gift. They saw *cloven tongues like as of fire* (v. 3), and *it sat*—not *they sat*, for the verb is singular, and should really be translated "he, that is, the Holy Spirit, sat"—the Holy Spirit rested on each of them. There is an atmospheric phenomenon called "St. Elmo's fire," which is a luminous discharge sometimes seen in stormy weather and is also called *ignis lambens*, "a gentle flame," not a devouring fire; such was this.

2.2.1. There was an outward, physical sign to confirm the faith of the disciples themselves.

2.2.2. The sign given was fire, so that John the Baptist's saying about Christ would be fulfilled: *He shall baptize you with the Holy Spirit and with fire* (Mt 3:11). They were now remembering the giving of the Law on Mount Sinai, and as that Law was given in fire, so is the Gospel. The Spirit, like fire, melts the heart, burns up the dross, and kindles godly and devout affections in the soul. This is the fire that Christ came to send on the earth (Lk 12:49).

2.2.3. This fire appeared in tongues that separated. The activities of the Spirit were many; that of speaking in dif-

ferent kinds of tongues was one, and this sign referred to that. The flames were tongues. Christ wants to speak to the world through the Spirit. He gave the Spirit to the disciples also, to clothe them with a power (Lk 24:49) to declare to the world what they knew. These tongues were divided, but the believers continued to be all *with one accord*, for there may be a sincere unity of affections where there is a diversity of expressions.

2.2.4. This fire rested on them to show the constant residence of the Holy Spirit with them. The disciples of Christ had the gifts of the Spirit always with them, though the sign, we may assume, soon disappeared.

3. What was the immediate effect of this.

3.1. *They were all filled with the Holy Spirit.* They were filled with the graces of the Spirit and were more than ever under his sanctifying influence. They were more filled with the assurance of the Spirit and rejoiced more than ever in the love of Christ and the hope of heaven. They were also filled with the gifts of the Holy Spirit. They were clothed with miraculous powers for the furtherance of the Gospel. It seems clear that not only the twelve apostles but also all the 120 disciples were *filled with the Holy Spirit* at this time. The *all* here must refer to the all who were together (v. 1; 1:14–15).

3.2. *They began to speak with other tongues*, besides their native language. They did not talk about matters of ordinary conversation, but spoke the word of God and the praise of his name, *as the Spirit gave them utterance*. We may suppose that they understood not only themselves but also one another. They spoke not from any previous thought or meditation, but *as the Spirit gave them utterance*; he supplied them with the content as well as the language. Now this was:

3.2.1. A very great miracle; it was a miracle on the mind, for words are framed in the mind. They had not only never learned these languages before; it seems they had never even heard these languages spoken. They were neither students nor travelers. Peter, indeed, was forward enough to speak in his own tongue, but the rest of them were no spokesmen. The One who made the human mouth (Ex 4:11) made theirs afresh.

3.2.2. A very proper, necessary, and useful miracle. The language the disciples spoke was Aramaic, a dialect of Hebrew, yet they had been commissioned to *preach the Gospel to every creature* (Mk 16:15), to disciple all nations (Mt 28:19), and here was an insuperable difficulty at the threshold. And so, to prove that he could give authority to preach to the nations, Christ gave an ability to preach to them in their own language. This may well be reckoned, all things considered, as a greater work than the miraculous healings Christ performed. It was the first effect of the *pouring out of the Spirit* on the believers.

Verses 5–13

Here is an account of the public notice taken of this extraordinary gift. Notice:

1. The great throng of people now in Jerusalem. *There were dwelling at Jerusalem* Jews who were *devout men, out of every nation under heaven*; the phrase indicates that there were some from most of the then known parts of the world. Jerusalem at that time was a rendezvous of religious people.

1.1. We may see here what some of those countries were from which those foreigners came (vv. 9–11). Some were from the eastern countries, such as the *Parthians, Medes, Elamites, and dwellers in Mesopotamia*. Then we come to Judea. Next come the inhabitants of Cappadocia, Pontus, and the specific region then called *Asia*. Next come those who lived in *Phrygia and Pamphylia*, which lay westward, and the *strangers of Rome*. There were some also who lived in the southern parts of *Egypt, in the parts of Libya about Cyrene*. There were also some from the island of Crete and some from the deserts of Arabia. But they were all either Jews originally or *proselytes* to the Jewish religion. The Jewish writers about this time speak of the Jews as "dwelling everywhere through the whole earth," and they say that "there is not a people upon earth among whom some Jews do not dwell."

1.2. We may ask what brought all those Jews and converts together to Jerusalem at this time, for they are said to have been *dwelling* there. They took lodgings there because at this time there was a general expectation of the appearing of the Messiah. This brought those who were most zealous and devout to Jerusalem to stay there.

2. The amazement with which these foreigners were seized when they heard the disciples speak their own languages.

2.1. They noticed that the speakers are all Galileans, who knew nothing other than their native language (v. 7). God chose the weak and foolish things of the world to confound the wise and mighty (1Co 1:27).

2.2. They acknowledged that these Galileans spoke intelligibly and readily their own — the foreigners' — language. *We hear every man in our own tongue wherein we were born* (v. 8). *We do hear them speak in our tongues the wonderful works of God.* It was not only a surprise, but a pleasant surprise, to them to hear the language of their own country being spoken.

2.2.1. The things they heard the apostles speaking about were the *wonderful works of God*, "the great things of God." It is probable that the apostles spoke about Christ, redemption by him, and the grace of the Gospel, and these are truly the *great things of God*.

2.2.2. They heard them both praise God for these great things and teach the people about these things *in their own tongue*. Now although, perhaps, these foreigners had so mastered the Jewish language that they could have understood the meaning of the disciples if they had spoken that language, this was stranger, and helped convince their judgment that this teaching came from God. It was also kinder and thus helped move their emotions. To us, this is a clear indication of the mind and will of God, that the Scriptures would be read, and public worship performed, in the common languages of the nations.

2.3. They wondered at it (v. 12): *They were all amazed*; they were in doubt as to what it meant. They asked themselves and one another, *What meaneth this?* or, "What is the tendency of this?" They would *turn aside, and see this great sight* (Ex 3:3).

3. The scorn with which some responded to it, probably the teachers of the law, Pharisees, and chief priests; they said, "*These men are full of new wine*; they have drunk too much at this festival time" (v. 13). Because these scorners were native Jews, they did not know, as others did, that what was being spoken really was the languages of other nations, and so they thought it was gibberish and nonsense, such as drunkards speak. If they called the Master of the house *a wine-bibber* (drunkard) (Mt 11:19), it was hardly surprising if they called those who belonged to him the same.

Verses 14–36

Here are the firstfruits of the Spirit in the sermon Peter preached immediately, which was directed to the Jews, even to those who mocked. He began with their blasphemous slander (v. 15), addressing his message (v. 14) *to the men of Judea and the inhabitants of Jerusalem*. It was not by Peter's preaching only, but also by the speaking of all the believers, *that three thousand souls were* converted that day (v. 41), but only Peter's sermon is recorded, as evidence of his restoration. He was now just as courageous in openly declaring Christ as he had been cowardly in denying him. We have here:

1. His introduction: *Peter stood up* (v. 14) *with the eleven*. Those who had the greatest authority stood up to speak to the mocking Jews. Among Christ's ministers, similarly, some with greater gifts are called out to take hold of sword and spear, that is, to instruct those who bring opposition. *Peter lifted up his voice*, as one who was both certain of what he said and neither afraid nor ashamed to acknowledge it. He addressed himself to the *men of Judea*, "Fellow Jews, especially you *that dwell at Jerusalem, be this known unto you, and hearken* (listen) *to my words*."

2. His answer to their blasphemous slander (v. 15): "*These men are not drunken, as you suppose.*" These disciples of Christ, who now *speak with other tongues*, are speaking sense. They know what they are saying. You cannot think they are drunk, since *it is but the third hour of the day*," nine o'clock in the morning; on Sabbaths and sacred festivals, the Jews did not eat or drink before this time.

3. His account of the miraculous outpouring of the Spirit. He analyzed the matter into two parts: this miracle was both the fulfilling of Scripture and the fruit of Christ's resurrection and ascension.

3.1. It was the fulfillment of the prophecies of the Old Testament. He specified one, that of *the prophet Joel* (v. 28). It is significant that although Peter *was filled with the Holy Spirit*, he did not set aside the Scriptures, nor think himself above them. Christ's students never go beyond the Bible. Notice:

3.1.1. The text itself that Peter quoted (vv. 17–21). It refers to *the last days*, that is, the times of the Gospel, which are called *the last days* because the age of God's kingdom that the Gospel sets up is the last age of divine grace. "It was prophesied and promised, and so you should expect it and not be surprised at it; you should desire it and welcome it." The apostle quoted the whole paragraph, because it is good to take Scripture in its whole context. It had been foretold:

3.1.1.1. That there would be a more plentiful and extensive outpouring of the Spirit of grace from heaven than there had ever been. "Now *the Spirit shall be poured out* not only on the Jews but *upon all flesh*, Gentiles as well as Jews." The Jewish teachers taught that the Spirit came only on the wise and rich, and only on those of them who were the descendants of Israel, but God would not restrict himself to their rules.

3.1.1.2. That the Spirit would be a Spirit of prophecy in them. This power would be given without distinction of sex — "now only *your sons*, but then also *your daughters, shall prophesy*"; it would be given without distinction of age — "both *your young men and your old men shall see visions, and dream dreams*, and the *servants and handmaids* will receive of *the Spirit, and shall prophesy*" (v. 18). Or, in general, this power would be given to both men and women, whom God calls his servants. The mention of *the daughters* (v. 17) and *the handmaidens* (v. 18) makes one think that the women mentioned in 1:14, as well as the men, received the extraordinary gifts of the Holy Spirit.

3.1.1.3. That the one great thing they would prophesy would be the judgment that was coming on the Jewish nation. Those who would not submit to the power of God's grace would fall and lie under the outpourings out of the bowls of his wrath (Rev 16:1). Those who will not bend will be broken.

3.1.1.3.*1.* The destruction of Jerusalem, which was about forty years after Christ's death, was called here *that great and notable day of the Lord.* The desolation itself was such as was never brought on any place or nation, either before or since. It was *the day of the Lord* because it was the day of his vengeance on that people for crucifying Christ. It was a little day of judgment, *a notable day.* The destruction of the Jews meant the rescue of the Christians.

3.1.1.3.*2.* The terrible signs that would herald such destruction were foretold (v. 19–20): *There shall be wonders in heaven above, the sun turned into darkness and the moon into blood*; *and* there would be *signs in the earth beneath*, too, *blood and fire.* In his introduction to his history of the wars of the Jews, Josephus speaks of the extraordinary signs that preceded those wars: there was terrible thunder, lightning, and earthquakes; a fiery comet hung over the city for a year, and a flaming sword was seen pointing down on it. *The fire and vapor of smoke* literally came to pass in the burning down of their cities, towns, synagogues, and the temple at the end.

3.1.1.3.*3.* The significant preservation of the Lord's people was promised (v. 21): *Whosoever shall call upon the name of the Lord Jesus shall be saved.* In the destruction of Jerusalem by the Romans not one Christian perished. The saved remnant were a praying people: *they called on the name of the Lord.* And *the name of the Lord* that *they called upon* was *their strong tower* (Pr 18:10).

3.1.2. The application of this prophecy to the present event (v. 16): *This is that which was spoken by the prophet Joel.* This was the expected outpouring of the Spirit on all people, and we are to look for no other similar event. This Spirit of grace, the Advocate or Comforter (Jn 14:26; 1Jn 2:1), who was given now according to the promise, will, according to the same promise, remain with the church on earth to the end.

3.2. It was the gift of Christ. Peter used this gift of the Holy Spirit to preach Jesus to them (v. 22): *You men of Israel, hear these words.* Here is:

3.2.1. A summary of the life of Christ (v. 22). Peter called him *Jesus of Nazareth*, but Jesus was also *a man approved of God among you*, criticized and condemned by people but approved by God: "a man marked out by God." "You yourselves are witnesses to how he became famous by *miracles, wonders, and signs, which God did by him*; *for no man could do such works unless God were with him.*" Notice how Peter emphasized Christ's miracles. The facts of the matter were not to be denied: "They were done *in the midst of you, as you yourselves also know.* You have been eyewitnesses of his miracles." The conclusion could not be disputed: certainly God had *approved him*, had declared him to be *the Son of God* (Jn 5:25) and *the Saviour of the world* (Jn 4:42).

3.2.2. An account of his sufferings and death. This was the greatest miracle of all, that a man approved by God would seem to have been abandoned by him as Jesus was, and that a man so approved of among the people would be so completely abandoned by them as well. But both of these mysteries were explained here (v. 23), and his death was considered:

3.2.2.1. As God's act, and in Jesus it was an act of wonderful grace and wisdom. *He delivered him to death.* But there was nothing in this that showed God's disapproval of him, because it was done by *the determinate counsel*

(set purpose) *and foreknowledge of God.* This reconciled Christ to the cross: *Father, thy will be done* (Lk 11:2), and *Father, glorify thy name* (Jn 12:28).

3.2.2.2. As the people's act, and in them it was an act of monstrous sin and foolishness. It was their voluntary action, from a motive that was morally evil, and so, "the hands *with which you have crucified and slain* him were *wicked hands.*" Probably, some of those who had shouted, *Crucify him, crucify him*, were present there (Lk 23:21). Peter charged them, in particular, with the crime, to bring them to faith and repentance more powerfully.

3.2.3. An affirmation of his resurrection (v. 24): *Whom God raised up*; the same One who delivered him to death delivered him from death.

3.2.3.1. Peter described Christ's resurrection: God *loosed the pains of death, because it was impossible that he should be holden* (held) *of it.* The Father released him from these pains and sorrows of soul when at his death Christ said, *It is finished* (Jn 19:30). However, most people refer this verse to the resurrection of Christ's body. Christ was imprisoned for our debt; he was thrown into the chains of death. But it was not possible for him to be detained there, because he had life in himself (Jn 10:18) and had conquered the prince of death.

3.2.3.2. He affirmed the truth of his resurrection (v. 32): *God hath raised him up, whereof we all are witnesses.* They received power by the descent of the Holy Spirit upon them, with the deliberate intention that they would be skillful, faithful, and courageous witnesses.

3.2.3.3. He showed it to be the fulfillment of the Scripture: "*it was impossible that he should be holden* (held) by *death* and *the grave*, because David speaks of his being raised." Here is:

3.2.3.3.*1.* The text quoted fully (vv. 25–28), because it shows us:

3.2.3.3.*1.1.* Our Lord Jesus' constantly looking to his Father: *I foresaw the Lord before me continually.* He placed before him his Father's glory as his purpose in everything, because he saw that his sufferings would lead greatly to the honor of God.

3.2.3.3.*1.2.* The assurance he had of his Father's presence and power: *He is on my right hand, that I should not be moved* (v. 25). If God is at our right hand, we will not be moved.

3.2.3.3.*1.3.* The cheerfulness with which our Lord Jesus fulfilled his work: "Being assured *that I shall not be moved, my heart doth rejoice, and my tongue is glad*" (v. 26). It was a constant pleasure to our Lord Jesus to look to the end of his work. It did his heart good to think how the outcome would fulfill the purpose.

3.2.3.3.*1.4.* The happy outcome of his death and suffering: *My flesh shall rest*, and *it shall rest in hope, because thou wilt not leave my soul in hell*; what follows is the matter of his hope. He was assured:

3.2.3.3.*1.4.1.* That his soul would not continue in a state of separation from the body: "*Thou wilt not leave my soul in hell*" (in Hades, the Greek word for the realm of the dead).

3.2.3.3.*1.4.2.* That his body would lie only a short time in the grave: *Thou wilt not suffer thy Holy One to see corruption.* He must die, but he must not *see corruption.*

3.2.3.3.*1.4.3.* That his death and sufferings would be a way into blessed immortality: "*Thou hast made known to me the ways of life* (v. 28), and by me made them known, and laid them open, to the world."

3.2.3.3.*1.4.4.* That all his sorrows and sufferings would end in complete happiness: *Thou shalt make me full of joy with thy countenance.* The reward set before him was *joy* (Heb 12:2), a fullness of joy (Ps 16:11), joy in God's *countenance* (presence). That is the joy of our Lord into which all his people will enter and in which they will be happy forever.

3.2.3.3.2. The comment on this text. He addressed himself to them with respect: *Men and brethren* (v. 29). "Allow me *freely to speak to you concerning the patriarch David*. David cannot be understood here as speaking about himself, but about the Christ to come." When we read Psalm 16, we must consider:

3.2.3.3.2.1. That David could not have said the words of that psalm of himself, because *he was dead, and buried, and* even till now, when Peter spoke this, *his sepulchre remained* in Jerusalem. He could never have said of himself that he *would not see corruption*, for it was clear that his body did decay.

3.2.3.3.2.2. Therefore, certainly he spoke it as a prophet, looking to the Messiah.

3.2.3.3.2.2.1. David knew that the Messiah would descend from his body (v. 30), *that God had sworn to him, that of the fruit of his loins, according to the flesh, he would raise up Christ to sit on his throne*. When our Lord Jesus was born, it was promised *that the Lord God would give him the throne of his father David* (Lk 1:32). According to the spirit, and by his divine nature, the Messiah was *to be David's Lord*, not his son (v. 34; Ps 110:1; Mt 22:41–46).

3.2.3.3.2.2.2. Therefore, when David said that *his soul would not be left in its separate state, nor his flesh see corruption*, without doubt he must be understood to have been speaking of the resurrection of Christ (v. 31). Moreover, as Christ died according to the Scriptures, so he rose again according to the Scriptures (1Co 15:3–4), and *we are witnesses* that he did so.

3.2.3.3.2.2.3. Here is a consideration of his ascension too. Just as David did not rise from the dead, so neither did he *ascend into the heavens* (v. 34). Furthermore, in another psalm he clearly showed that he was speaking about another person, and that that other person was his Lord (Ps 110:1): *The Lord said unto my Lord, Sit thou at my right hand until I make thy foes thy footstool* (v. 35).

3.2.4. The application of this message.

3.2.4.1. These verses from the Psalms, said Peter, explained the meaning of the present wonderful outpouring of the Spirit. Some of the people had asked (v. 12), *What meaneth this?* "I will tell you the meaning of this," said Peter. "This Jesus, being exalted to the right hand of God and *having received of the Father the promise of the Holy Spirit, hath shed forth this which you now see and hear*." The gift of the Holy Spirit was a fulfillment of divine promises already made; this was the promise that included all the others. It was a promise of all future divine favors that were further intended: "What you now see and hear is simply a pledge of greater things to come."

3.2.4.2. "This proves that Christ Jesus is the true Messiah and Savior of the world." Peter closed his sermon with this: *Therefore let all the house of Israel know assuredly that God has made that same Jesus whom you have crucified both Lord and Christ*. The Twelve had been commanded to *tell no man that he was Jesus the Christ* until after his resurrection (Mt 16:16–20; 17:9), but now it must be *proclaimed*. It was not suggested as probable, but set down as certain: *Let them know assuredly*:

3.2.4.2.1. That God had glorified the One *whom they had crucified*, and the dishonor they had shown him had served as a foil to his brightness.

3.2.4.2.2. That he had glorified him so much as to make him *both Lord and Christ*. This is the great truth of the Gospel: *that that same Jesus that was crucified* at Jerusalem is the *Lord and Christ*.

Verses 37–41

We have seen the wonderful effect of the outpouring of the Spirit in its influence on the preachers of the Gospel. We are now to see another blessed fruit of the outpouring of the Spirit in its influence on the hearers of the Gospel. From the first communication of that divine message, it was clear that a divine power accompanied it. Here are the firstfruits of that vast harvest of souls who were gathered by it to Jesus Christ. Let us see how it worked.

1. They were made to ask a serious question (v. 37): *When they heard, they were pricked to the heart* and, deeply concerned, turned to the preachers with this question: *What shall we do?* It was very strange that such impressions would suddenly be made on such hard hearts. Peter had accused them of having a hand, *a wicked hand*, in his death (v. 23), which was likely to anger them against Peter, but when they heard this plain scriptural sermon, they were very moved by it.

1.1. It gave them pain: *They were pricked in their hearts*. Peter awakened their consciences, cutting them to the quick. When sinners' eyes are opened, they must be *pricked to the heart* for sin.

1.2. It made them ask a question. Notice:

1.2.1. To whom they spoke: *to Peter and to the rest of the apostles*. By the apostles they had been convinced, and so it was by the apostles that they expected to be counseled and comforted. They called the apostles *men and brethren*, as Peter had called them (v. 29); here, however, it expressed friendship and affection rather than honor. Ministers are spiritual physicians, and it is good for people to be free and familiar with those ministers who work for the souls of the flock as for their own; they should speak to such ministers as *men and their brethren*.

1.2.2. What they asked: *What shall we do?*

1.2.2.1. They spoke as people who had come to a standstill in life, who did not know what to do: "Is that Jesus whom we have crucified both *Lord and Christ*? Then what will become of us who crucified him?" There is no way to be happy except by seeing how miserable we are. When we find ourselves in danger of being lost forever, there is hope of our being saved forever.

1.2.2.2. They spoke as people who had come to a turning point, who were determined to do immediately anything they would be directed to. Those who are convicted of sin would gladly know the way to peace and pardon (9:6; 16:30).

2. Peter and the other apostles guided them briefly in what they must do (vv. 38–39). Convicted sinners must be encouraged; although their case is sad, it is not desperate; there is hope for them.

2.1. Peter showed them here the course they must follow:

2.1.1. *Repent*; this was a plank to take hold of after shipwreck. To do so was the same duty that John the Baptist and Christ had preached, and here it was still insisted on: "*Repent*, change your mind, change your ways."

2.1.2. *Be baptized every one of you in the name of Jesus Christ*; that is, "firmly believe the message of Christ, make an open and sacred profession of this, and renounce your unfaithfulness." They must be baptized *in the name of Jesus Christ*, believing in the name of Jesus, and that he is the Christ, the Messiah promised to the ancestors. They must be baptized *in his name* for the *remission of sins*. This was urged on each particular individual: *every one of you*. "Even those of you who have been the greatest sinners, if you repent and believe, are welcome to be baptized. There is enough grace in Christ for each and every one of you, even though you are very many, and Christ's grace will be enough for everyone."

2.2. He gave them encouragements for following this course:

2.2.1. "It will be for *the remission* (forgiveness) *of sins.* Repent of your sin, and it will not be your ruin; be baptized into the faith of Christ, and you will truly be justified. Aim at this, depend on Christ for it, and you will have this.

2.2.2. "You will *receive the gift of the Holy Spirit,* just as we have." All who receive the forgiveness of sins *receive the gift of the Holy Spirit.*

2.2.3. "Your children will still have an interest in the covenant, because the promise of the forgiveness of sins and the gift of the Holy Spirit is *to you and to your children*" (v. 39). Now it is proper for an Israelite to ask, "What must be done with my children? Must they be rejected, or may they be taken in with me?" "Taken in," Peter said, "by all means, for the promise is now as much to you and to your children as it ever was.

2.2.4. "Although the promise is still extended to your children, it is not confined to you and them; its benefit is intended for *all that are afar off.*" To this general promise, the following limitation must refer: *even as many of them,* as many particular individuals in each nation, *as the Lord our God shall call.* God can make his call reach those who are very distant.

3. These directions were followed with a necessary warning (v. 40): *With many other words did he testify.* He had said much in a short time (vv. 38–39); he still had more to say. When we have heard words that have done our souls good, we wish to hear more. Among other things, he said, *Save yourselves from this untoward generation.*

3.1. "Be diligent in saving yourselves from their ruin. *Repent, and be baptized,* and then you will not share in the destruction of those with whom you have shared in sin.

3.2. "To that end, do not continue with them in their sin. *Save yourselves* from this *untoward generation.* Don't share with them in their sins, so that you do not share with them in their punishment." The only way to save ourselves from corrupt people is to separate ourselves from them. If we consider the destiny toward which they are quickly moving, we will see that it is better to have the trouble of swimming against their stream than the danger of being carried down their stream. Those who repent of their sins and give themselves to Jesus Christ must show their sincerity by breaking off all intimate association with evildoers.

4. Here is the blessed success and outcome of this (v. 41). The Spirit worked with the word and performed wonders by it. These same people who—many of them—had been eyewitnesses of the death of Christ were now persuaded by the preaching of the word.

4.1. They received the word, and it is only when we receive the word, when we embrace it and make it welcome, that it does us good.

4.2. They *gladly* received it. Herod heard the word gladly (Mk 6:20), but these gladly accepted it.

4.3. They were baptized and enrolled among the disciples of Christ by the sacred ceremony he had instituted. Those who accept the Christian covenant should receive Christian baptism.

4.4. There were added to the disciples about *three thousand souls that same day.* All those who had received the Holy Spirit had their tongues at work to preach and their

hands at work to baptize, because when there was such a harvest to be gathered in, it was time to be busy. The conversion of these 3,000 with these words was a greater work than the feeding of 4,000 or 5,000 with a few loaves. These were *added to them.* When we take God as our God, we must take his people to be our people.

Verses 42–47

In these verses we have the account of the first days of the early church. This was, indeed, its state of infancy, but it was also, like infancy, the state of its greatest innocence.

1. They kept close to holy rules and ceremonies. Christianity will incline the soul to have fellowship with God in all those ways in which he has appointed us to meet him and promised to meet us.

1.1. They were conscientious and faithful in their attendance at the preaching of the word. They *continued in the apostles' doctrine.* Those who have given themselves to Christ must be conscientious about hearing his word.

1.2. They kept up the fellowship of saints. They continued *in fellowship* (v. 42) and *continued daily with one accord in the temple* (v. 46). They were very much together. Wherever you saw one disciple, you would see more, like birds of a feather. See how these Christians loved one another. They had fellowship with one another in religious worship. They met *in the temple:* that was their meeting place, because joint fellowship with God is the best fellowship we can have with one another (1Jn 1:3). They met *daily* in the temple. Worshiping God is to be our daily work. They were *with one accord;* there was not only no discord nor strife; there was a great deal of holy love among them.

1.3. They frequently joined in the ceremony of the Lord's Supper. They continued *in the breaking of bread.* They broke bread *from house to house;* they administered that ordinance in private houses. They moved from one to another of these little synagogues or domestic chapels, celebrating the Eucharist there with those who usually met there to worship God.

1.4. They continued *in prayers.* After the Spirit was poured out, as well as before, they continued to be faithful in prayer, because prayer will never be superseded until it comes to be swallowed up in eternal praise.

1.5. They were full of thanksgiving; they were continually *praising God* (v. 47). This should be part of every prayer, and not be crowded into a corner.

2. They were loving to one another, and their joining together in holy ordinances very much endeared them to one another.

2.1. They met frequently for Christian fellowship (v. 44): *All that believed were together.* They associated together and thereby both expressed and increased their mutual love.

2.2. They had *all things common.* There was such a readiness to help one another that it could be said that they had everything in common, according to the law of friendship.

2.3. They were very cheerful. They did *eat their meat with gladness and singleness of heart.* They brought the comforts of God's table along with them to their own, and their doing so:

2.3.1. Made them very pleasant and filled their hearts with a holy joy. No one has such reasons to be cheerful as true Christians have; it is a pity that they do not always have the hearts to be so.

2.3.2. Made them very generous to their poor brothers and sisters. They did *eat their meat with singleness of heart*, "with glad, generous, and sincere hearts." They did not eat their small portions of food by themselves, but welcomed the poor to their table. It is good for Christians to be openhearted and openhanded.

2.4. They raised funds for charity (v. 45): they *sold their possessions and goods* and gave the money to their brothers and sisters, as anyone had need. This was to destroy not property rights but selfishness. Here, they probably had in mind the command Christ gave to the rich man as a test of his sincerity: *Sell that thou hast, and give to the poor* (Mt 19:21). Not that this was intended as an example of a constant, obligatory rule. The case was an extraordinary one here. They were under no obligation of a divine command to do this, as is clear from what Peter said to Ananias (5:4): *Was it not in thine own power?* And yet it was a very commendable expression of their love for their brothers and sisters, their compassion toward the poor, and their great zeal to encourage Christianity and nurture it in its infancy. Our rule is to give according to what God has blessed us with.

3. God acknowledged them and gave them special signs of his presence (v. 43): *Many wonders and signs were done by the apostles.* However, the Lord's giving them power to perform miracles was not all he did for them; he also *added to the church daily.* The word in their mouths did wonders, and God blessed their endeavors.

4. The people were influenced by it.

4.1. They feared and respected the believers (v. 43): *Fear came upon every soul.* Although the apostles made no great external parade, they had many spiritual gifts that were justly honorable, which made people revere them inwardly. The souls of people were strangely influenced by their extraordinary preaching and living.

4.2. They favored the believers. Although we have reason to think there were those who despised them, most of the ordinary people were kind to them, and so it is said that they *had favour with all the people.* Here we find them *in favour with them all,* which shows that people's prosecuting Christ had been the result of a kind of coercion by the deception of the priests; the people now returned to their right minds (Mk 5:15). True godliness and love will command respect, and cheerfulness in serving God will commend religious faith to outsiders (Col 4:5; 1Th 4:12; 1Ti 3:7).

4.3. They showed great eagerness to come to the believers. Someone or other came in daily, and they were those who *should be* (were to be) *saved* (v. 47).

CHAPTER 3

In this chapter we have a miracle and a sermon. 1. The miracle was the healing of a man who had been crippled from birth (vv. 1–8), and the impression this made on the people (vv. 9–11). 2. The aim of the sermon was to bring people to Christ, to lead them to repent of their sin of crucifying him (vv. 12–19) and believe in the One who was now glorified (vv. 20–26).

Verses 1–11

We were told in general (2:43) that *many signs and wonders were done by the apostles.* Here we have one given us as an example.

1. The people through whose ministry this miracle was performed were Peter and John. Each had a brother among the Twelve, but now, it seems, they were knit together more closely than either of them had been to his brother, because the bond of friendship is sometimes stronger than that of blood relation. Peter and John seem to have had a special closeness after Christ's resurrection, greater than they had before (Jn 20:2). That Christ's favorite was made Peter's closest friend was a good sign of Peter's acceptance with God upon his repentance.

2. The time and place are established here. It was in *the temple,* to which *Peter and John went up together.* There were the shoals of fish among which the net of the Gospel was to be thrown out. It is good to go to the temple, to be present at public services of worship, and it is encouraging to go together to the temple. The best fellowship is that which we have in worshiping God with others. It was *at the hour of prayer.* There must be a house of prayer and an hour of prayer. It is useful for individual Christians to have such hours of personal prayer as may serve, though not to bind them, nevertheless to remind their consciences.

3. The patient on whom this miraculous healing was performed (v. 2) was a poor crippled beggar at the temple gate.

3.1. He was a cripple not by accident but from birth. He was *lame from his mother's womb.* Such pitiful cases show us what we all are by nature spiritually: *without strength* (Ro 5:6), crippled from birth, unable to work or walk in God's service.

3.2. He was a beggar. Being unable to work for his living, he must live on gifts of money from others; these are God's poor. He was *laid daily* at *one of the gates of the temple* to *ask alms of those that entered into the temple.* Those who are in need and cannot work must not be ashamed to beg (Lk 16:3). Our prayers and our gifts should go together. Objects of charity should be especially welcome to us when we go to the temple to pray; it is a pity that any common beggars at church doors should be of such a character as to discourage charity, but even if there are some who are such, they should not be overlooked always. There are surely some who deserve our help, and it is better to feed ten dronelike sluggards—indeed, even some wasps as well—than let one bee starve. The gate of the temple at which the man was laid is named here: it was called *Beautiful.* It was no lessening of the beauty of this gate that a poor man lay there begging.

3.3. He begged Peter and John for alms (v. 3); this was the most he expected from them. He *asked an alms,* and received healing.

4. We have here the way in which this healing was carried out.

4.1. His expectations were raised. Peter, instead of turning his eyes away from him, *fastened his eyes upon him* (v. 4). John did so too, and they said, *Look on us.* This gave the man cause to expect that he would *receive something from them,* and that was why he *gave heed to them* (v. 5). We must come to God with our hearts fixed and our expectations raised. We must look to heaven and expect to receive.

4.2. His expectation of a gift of money was disappointed. *Peter said, Silver and gold have I none.* It is not often that Christ's friends and favorites have much of the wealth of this world. Peter and John had much money laid at their feet, but this was used to support the poor of the church. Public trusts should be strictly and faithfully managed. Many who are well disposed toward works of charity are still not able to do anything significant, while others, who have the resources to do much, do not have the heart to do anything.

4.3. His expectations were completely surpassed. Peter had no money to give him, but:

4.3.1. He had what was better, a power from heaven to heal his disease. Those who are poor in the world may still be rich—in fact very rich—in spiritual gifts.

4.3.2. He gave him what was better: he healed him of his disease. This would enable him to work for his living so that he would not have needed to beg anymore; in fact, he would now have money to give to those in need. When Peter had no silver and gold to give, he still said, *such as I have I give thee*. Those who do not have silver and gold have their limbs and senses, and with these they can be useful to the blind, crippled, and sick, and if they are not, then neither would they give them silver and gold if they had that. Notice how the healing was carried out.

4.3.2.1. Christ *sent his word, and healed him* (Ps 107:20). Peter's telling a lame man to *rise up and walk* would have been a mockery to him if Peter had not introduced it by *in the name of Jesus Christ of Nazareth*. He told the cripple to *rise up* and walk. If he tried to get up and walk, depending on God's power to enable him to do it, then he would be enabled to do it, and by standing and walking he must show the power that had done this for him. Let him then take comfort, and let God have all the praise.

4.3.2.2. Peter lent a hand by helping him up (v. 7): *He took him by the right hand and lifted him up*. When God through his word commands us to rise and walk in the way of his commandments (Ps 119:35), he will give his Spirit to lead us by the hand and lift us up. If we set ourselves to do what we can, God has promised his grace to enable us to do what we cannot. *His feet and ankle bones received strength*. He did his part, and Peter did his, but it was Christ who really did everything: it was he who put strength into him.

5. Here is the impression this healing made on the patient himself.

5.1. He leaped up, in obedience to the command, *Arise*. He sprang up as one refreshed from sleep, who did not question his own strength. The incoming rush of strength was so sudden, and he was no less sudden in displaying its effects.

5.2. He stood, and he walked. He walked with a firm, strong, steady tread, which revealed the healing. Those who have had experience of the working of divine grace on them should give evidence of what they have experienced. Has God put strength into us? Let us stand up resolutely for him and walk cheerfully with him.

5.3. He *held* on to *Peter and John* (v. 11). We need not ask why he held on to them. I believe he scarcely knew himself, but we can imagine the ecstasy of joy with which he embraced them. This is how he testified to his affection for them; he held on to them, refusing to let them go. Those whom God has healed love those whom he made instruments of their healing, and they see the need of their further help.

5.4. He *entered with them into the temple*. His strong affection for them held them, but it could not hold them so firmly as to keep them out of the temple. He was determined to go with them, especially because they were going into the temple. Like the disabled man whom Christ healed, he was immediately found in the temple (Jn 5:14). He was there *walking, and leaping, and praising God*. The strength God has given us, both in our mind and in our body, should be used to his praise. As soon as this man could jump, he leaped for joy in God and praised him. All true converts walk and praise God, but perhaps young converts leap more in his praises.

6. We are told how the people who were the eyewitnesses of this miracle were influenced by it.

6.1. They were completely satisfied with the truth of the miracle. *They knew it was he that sat begging at the beautiful gate of the temple* (v. 10). He had sat there for so long that they all knew him. They now saw him *walking and praising God* (v. 9). He was now as loud in praising God as he had been before in begging relief. Mercies are perfected when they are sanctified.

6.2. They were astonished at it: they were *filled with wonder and amazement* (v. 10); they ran to Peter and John, *greatly wondering* (v. 11). This seems to have been the effect of the outpouring of the Spirit, that the people were much more moved by the miracles the apostles performed than they had been by those performed by Christ himself.

6.3. They gathered around Peter and John: *All the people ran together unto them in Solomon's porch* to see this great sight.

Verses 12–26

We have here the sermon Peter preached. *When Peter saw it*, he preached. When he saw the people getting together in a crowd, he took that opportunity to preach Christ to them. When he saw the people moved by the miracle, he sowed the Gospel seed in the ground that was prepared to receive it. When he saw the people ready to worship him and John, he diverted their respect away from them so that it would be directed only to Christ.

1. He humbly disclaimed the honor of the miracle. He addressed himself to them as *men of Israel*, those to whom belonged not only the law and the promises but also the Gospel and its fulfillments. He asked them two things:

1.1. Why they were so surprised at the miracle itself: *Why marvel you at this?* It was really marvelous, but it was no more so than what Christ had done many times. It was only a short time before that Christ had raised Lazarus from the dead (Jn 11:43); why then should this seem so strange? Foolish people consider strange what might have been familiar to them if they had not culpably refused to pay attention to it. Christ had just risen from the dead himself; why did they not wonder at that?

1.2. Why they gave so much of the praise for it to them, Peter and John, who had been only instruments: *Why look you so earnestly on us?*

1.2.1. It was certain that Peter and John *had made this man to walk*, which showed that the apostles were not only sent by God but sent to be blessings to the world.

1.2.2. But they did not do it by any *power or holiness of their own*. The power they did it through came wholly from Christ. They had not deserved the power Christ gave them to do it by. It was not because of their own godliness; Peter recognized he was a sinful man (Lk 5:8). And yet he performed miracles in Christ's name.

1.2.3. It was the people's fault that they attributed the miracle to Peter and John's power and godliness. The instruments of God's favor to us must not be idolized.

1.2.4. It was commendable of Peter and John that they would not take the honor of this miracle for themselves, but carefully passed it on to Christ. Useful people must make sure that they remain very humble.

2. He preached Christ to them.

2.1. He preached Christ as the true Messiah promised to their ancestors (v. 13).

2.1.1. He is Jesus, the Son of God. He is *his Son Jesus*; to God, dear as a Son (Col 1:13); to us, Jesus, a Savior.

2.1.2. God has glorified him by raising him up.

2.1.3. He has glorified him as *the God of our fathers, the God of Abraham, of Isaac, and of Jacob*. God sent him into the world according to the promises made to those patriarchs. The Gospel the apostles preached was the revelation of the mind and will of the God of Abraham.

2.2. He accused them plainly and directly of the murder of this Jesus.

2.2.1. "*You* of the common people *delivered him up* to your chief priests and elders and were influenced to shout against him, as if the public had a legitimate grievance against him.

2.2.2. "*You denied him*, disowned him, and could not look on him as the Messiah, because he did not come in external show and power; *you denied him in the presence of Pilate*. You were worse than Pilate, for he would have released him if you had let him follow his own judgment. *You denied the Holy One and the Just* (v. 14)." The holiness and justice of the Lord Jesus, which are something more than his innocence, greatly emphasized the sin of those who put him to death.

2.2.3. "*You desired a murderer to be released*, and you demanded that Christ be crucified.

2.2.4. "*You killed the prince of life*. You preserved a murderer, a destroyer of life, but you destroyed the Savior, the author of life. You killed the prince of life, and so not only rebelled against your own mercies but also abandoned them (Jnh 2:8)."

2.3. He affirmed his resurrection as before (2:32). "You thought *the prince of life* could be deprived of his life, but *we are all witnesses* of his resurrection."

2.4. He attributed the healing of this crippled man to the power of Christ (v. 16): *His name, through faith in his name, has made this man strong.* He repeated it: *The faith which is by him hath given him this soundness.*

2.4.1. He appealed to them about the truth of the miracle; the man on whom it had been performed was one *whom you see and know*. The miracle was performed publicly, *in the presence of you all*, in the gate of the temple. The healing was complete; it was perfectly sound; "you see the man walking and jumping around."

2.4.2. He told them about the power by which it was done.

2.4.2.1. It was done by the name of Christ, "by the power he has invested us with, which derives from the name Christ has that is above every name (Php 2:9). Christ's authority, his command, has done it, as a king is said to do something that he orders to be done in his name, even though it is a subordinate officer who executes it."

2.4.2.2. The power of Christ is obtained *through faith in his name*, and it is obtained for his sake, so that he may have the glory of it. Those who performed this miracle by faith derived power from Christ to work it, and so they gave all the glory to him. Peter both confirmed the great Gospel truth they were to preach to the world—that Jesus Christ is the fountain of all power and grace, and also the great healer and Savior—and commended the great Gospel duty of faith in him as the only way of receiving benefits through him. In this way, Peter preached Jesus to them, and him crucified (1Co 2:2).

3. He encouraged them to hope that they might still find mercy; he did all he could to convince them, but he was careful not to drive them to despair.

3.1. He lessened their crime by candidly imputing it to their ignorance. He considered it necessary to lessen slightly the rigors of the charge by calling them *brethren*. Well might he call them that, because he himself had been a brother with them in this iniquity: he had *denied the Holy One and the Just* (v. 14), swearing that he did not know him (Lk 22:57). *I know that through ignorance you did it, as did also your rulers* (v. 17). This was the language of Peter's kindness, which teaches us to think the best of those whom we want to make better. He had the example of his Master's praying for his crucifiers and pleading on their behalf that they did not know what they were doing. Perhaps some of the rulers and some of the

people did it out of malice, but most of them did it out of ignorance, going with the flow.

3.2. He lessened the effects of their crime; it was *according to the scriptures* (v. 18). This was what he himself said: *Thus it is written, and thus it behoved Christ to suffer* (Lk 24:46). "You fulfilled the Scripture and did not know it; God, by your hands, *hath fulfilled what he showed by the mouth of all his prophets, that Christ would suffer*; this was his intention, but you had your own views and were completely ignorant of this intention. God was fulfilling the Scripture when you were satisfying your own passions." This is no mitigation at all of their sin in hating and persecuting Christ to the death, but it was an encouragement to them to repent and hope for mercy. The death and sufferings of Christ were for *the remission of sins* (2:38) and were therefore the basis of that display of mercy that Peter now encouraged them to hope for.

4. He encouraged them all to become Christians.

4.1. He told them what they must believe.

4.1.1. They must believe that Jesus Christ was the promised offspring (v. 25). Jesus was of *the seed of Abraham, according to the flesh*, and *in him all the families of the earth are blessed*, and not only the families of Israel.

4.1.2. They must believe that Jesus Christ was a prophet, *that prophet like unto Moses* whom God had promised to *raise up to them from among their brethren* (v. 22; Dt 18:18). Christ is a prophet because God speaks to us through him.

4.1.2.1. He was *a prophet like unto Moses*. He rescued his people from slavery like Moses. Moses was *faithful as a servant*, Christ *as a Son* (Heb 3:5–6). Moses was a model of humility (Nu 12:3) and patience, as is Christ. *There was no prophet like unto Moses*, but a greater One than Moses was here (Mt 12:41–42).

4.1.2.2. He was a prophet of God's raising up. He was raised up to Israel first. They had the first offer of divine grace made to them, and that was why he was *raised up from among them*. One would have thought that when he came to his own, they would receive him (Jn 1:11). The Old Testament church was blessed with many prophets: *from Samuel, and those that follow after* (v. 24); but because these servants were all mistreated, last of all God sent them his Son (Mt 21:33–39).

4.1.3. They must believe *that times of refreshing will come from the presence of the Lord* (v. 19) and that these times will be *the times of the restitution of all things* (v. 21). The absence of the Lord gives rise to the self-confident boasts of sinners and the distrusting complaints of the saints, but his presence is coming quickly, which will silence both forever. The presence of the Lord will introduce:

4.1.3.1. *The restitution of all things* (v. 21), the renewal of the whole creation, that *end of all things which God hath spoken of by the mouth of all his holy prophets since the world began*. This was more clearly revealed in the New Testament than it had been before.

4.1.3.2. With this, *the times of refreshing* (v. 19), like a cool shade to those *that have borne the burden and heat of the day* (Mt 20:12). All Christians look for *a rest that remains for the people of God* (Heb 4:9) after the travail and toil of their present state. The refreshing that *comes from the presence of the Lord* will continue eternally in the presence of the Lord.

4.2. He told them what they must do. They must *repent*; they must begin anew. Peter, who had himself denied Christ, repented, and he wanted them to do so too. They must *be converted*, must turn around; they must return to the Lord their God. It is not enough to repent of sin; we must also be turned away from it and not return to it. They must listen to Christ, the great prophet: "*Him shall you hear in all things whatsoever he shall say unto you* (v. 22). Listen to him with a divine faith, as prophets should be listened to: *Hear him in all things*; let his laws direct all your actions. Whatever he says to you, welcome it." Our lives will be in danger if we turn a deaf ear to his call (v. 23): *Every soul that will not hear that prophet shall be destroyed from among the people.* Those who will not be advised by the Savior can expect nothing but to fall into the hands of the destroyer.

4.3. He told them what they could expect.

4.3.1. That their sins would be forgiven (v. 19): *Repent and be converted, that your sins may be blotted out.*

4.3.1.1. To have one's sins forgiven is to have them blotted out. When God forgives sin, he does not hold it against the sinner anymore; it is forgotten, like what is wiped out.

4.3.1.2. We cannot expect our sins to be forgiven unless we repent of them and turn away from them and to God. If there is no repentance, there is no forgiveness.

4.3.1.3. Hopes of the forgiveness of sin upon repentance should be a powerful incentive to us to repent. This was the first and great argument: *Repent, for the kingdom of heaven is at hand* (Mk 1:15).

4.3.1.4. The most encouraging fruit of the forgiveness of our sins will be *when the times of refreshing shall come.* During these times of toil and conflict — in which we know doubts and fears within us and troubles and dangers outside us — we cannot enjoy the full assurance of our forgiveness that we will know when times of refreshing come, which will wipe away all our tears (Isa 25:8; Rev 7:17; 21:4).

4.3.2. That they would have the comfort of Christ's coming (vv. 20–21): "*He shall send Jesus Christ, that before was preached unto you.* If you *repent and be converted*, you will find no lack of him; in some way or other you will see him."

4.3.2.1. We must not expect Christ's personal presence with us in this world, for the heavens, which received him out of the sight of the disciples, must keep him until the end of time. We must live by the faith in him that is *the evidence of things not seen* (Heb 11:1).

4.3.2.2. It is promised, however, that he will be sent to all who repent and are converted (v. 20): "*He shall send Jesus Christ, who was preached to you.* You will have his spiritual presence. The One who is sent into the world will be sent to you; you will have the encouragement of his being sent. The sending of Christ to judge the world at the end of time will be a blessing to you." This is what it seems to refer to, for until then *the heavens must receive him* (v. 21).

4.4. He told them what reason they had to expect these things if they were converted to Christ.

4.4.1. As Israelites, they were, above any other people, God's favorite nation: *You are the children of the prophets and of the covenant.* This was a double privilege:

4.4.1.1. They were *the children of the prophets.* "You belong to that people from among whom prophets were raised up and to whom prophets were sent." Those who lived in the later ages of the Old Testament church, when prophecy had ceased, could still fitly be called *the children of the prophets*, because they heard *the voices of the prophets, which were read in their synagogues every sabbath day* (13:27). Now this, Peter said, should stir them to accept Christ. Those who are blessed with prophets and prophecy — as all are who have the Scriptures — should not receive the grace of God in them in vain (2Co 6:1).

4.4.1.2. They were *the children*, that is, the heirs, *of the covenant which God made with our Fathers.* "The promise of the Messiah was made to you, and so you may hope it will be fulfilled to you." If all the people of the earth were to be blessed in Christ, then much more those descendants, *his kinsmen according to the flesh* (Ro 9:3).

4.4.2. As Israelites, they had the first offer of the grace of the New Testament. The Redeemer was sent first to them, which was an encouragement to them to hope that if they did repent and were converted, he would be sent to them again for their comfort (v. 20): "*He shall send Jesus Christ, for he has sent him to you first* (v. 26). *Unto you first, God, having raised up his Son Jesus from the dead, sent him, to bless you*, especially with that great blessing of *turning every one of you from his iniquities.*" We are told here:

4.4.2.1. From where Christ received his mission: *God raised up his Son Jesus, and sent him.* God raised him up when he constituted him a prophet. He sent him to bear witness to the truth and thereby to seek and save lost souls (Lk 19:10). Some refer *the raising of him up* to the resurrection. Although, once raised, he seemed to be taken away from us immediately, God really did send him afresh to us in his Gospel and Spirit.

4.4.2.2. To whom he was sent: "*Unto you first*, you who are *the children of the prophets, and of the covenant.*" The personal ministry of Christ, like that of the prophets, was confined to the Jews, *to the lost sheep of the house of Israel* (Mt 15:24), and he forbade the disciples he then sent out to go any further. After his resurrection, he was, it is true, to be preached to all nations, but they must *begin at Jerusalem* (Lk 24:47). And when they went to other nations, even there they first preached to the Jews they found. So far were the Jews from being excluded because they put Christ to death that when he had risen, he was sent first to them.

4.4.2.3. On what mission he was sent: "*He is sent to you first, to bless you*; not to condemn you, as you deserve, but to justify you." Christ's mission to the world was to bless us, and when he left the world, he left a blessing behind him, because it is said that he was *parted from the disciples as he blessed them* (Lk 24:51). It is through Christ that God sends blessings to us, and only through him can we expect to receive them. The great blessing was to turn us away from our sins so that we might be qualified to receive all the other blessings. Sin is something we naturally cling to; the purpose of divine grace is to turn us away from it — indeed, to turn us against it, so that we may not only abandon it but even hate it. "Therefore, fulfill your part; *repent and be converted*, because Christ is ready to fulfill his part by *turning you from your iniquities* and thereby blessing you."

CHAPTER 4

Here: 1. Peter and John were arrested and put in jail (vv. 1–4). 2. They were examined by a committee of the great Sanhedrin (vv. 5–7). 3. They bravely affirmed what they had done, and they preached Christ to their persecutors (vv. 8–12). 4. Their persecutors commanded them to be silent and sent them away (vv. 13–22). 5. They turned to God in prayer for the further activity of the grace they had already experienced (vv. 23–30). 6. God acknowledged them by clear signs of his presence (vv. 31–33). 7. The believers had their hearts knit together in holy love (Col 2:2), and the church flourished more than ever (vv. 33–37).

Verses 1–4

We have here the powers of darkness rising up against the interests of the kingdom of God to try to stop them. No matter how determined Christ's servants are, Satan's agents will be spiteful, and so, no matter how spiteful Satan's agents are, let Christ's servants remain determined.

1. The apostles Peter and John continued with their work, not laboring in vain (1Co 15:58).

1.1. The preachers faithfully communicated the message of Christ: *They spoke unto the people* (v. 1). *They taught the people* (v. 2); they taught those who did not yet believe, for their conviction and conversion, and they taught those who did believe, for their encouragement and establishment. *They preached through Jesus the resurrection from the dead.*

1.1.1. The teaching of the resurrection of the dead was verified in Jesus. He had been the first One to rise. They preached the resurrection of Christ as their authority for what they did.

1.1.2. This teaching is obtained and kept safe by him for all believers. *They preached* this *through Jesus Christ,* as something that was achievable through him (Php 3:10–11) and only through him. They did not interfere in political matters, but kept to their own business, preaching to the people heaven as their ultimate destination and Christ as their way.

1.2. The hearers cheerfully received the message (v. 4): *Many of those who heard the word believed, to the number of about five thousand.* Although the preachers were persecuted, the word won through, for sometimes the days of the church's suffering have been the times in which it has grown: the days of its infancy were like that.

2. The chief priests and their group did what they could to crush them; the apostles' hands were tied for a while, but their hearts were not changed in the least. Notice:

2.1. Who opposed the apostles. They were *the priests. The captain of the temple* came with them, who, it is thought, was a Roman officer. Both Jews and Gentiles were still allied against Christ. *The Sadducees* also, who denied the existence of spirits and the future state, were zealous against them.

2.2. How they felt about the apostles' preaching: *They were grieved that they taught the people* (v. 2). It grieved them both that the Gospel message was preached and that the people were so ready to listen to it. It now vexed them to see that his Gospel gained ground instead of losing it. Those to whom the glory of Christ's kingdom is a cause of grief are truly miserable. They were disturbed that the apostles *preached through Jesus the resurrection from the dead.* The Sadducees were disturbed that the resurrection from the dead was preached, because they opposed that teaching. The chief priests were disturbed that they preached the resurrection of the dead through Jesus; they would rather have given up that important belief than have it preached and proved to be through Jesus.

2.3. How far they took their opposition (v. 3): *They laid hands on them* and *put them in hold* (jail) until the next day. See how God gradually trains his servants for suffering; they now resisted only to the point of chains, but later to blood (Heb 12:4).

Verses 5–14

Here is the trial of Peter and John before the judges of the ecclesiastical court.

1. The court was set. It was an extraordinary court session, it seems, one that was deliberately called on this occasion. Notice:

1.1. The time when the court sat (v. 5): *on the morrow.* They adjourned the trial to the next day, but no longer, because they were impatient to have the apostles silenced.

1.2. The place: Jerusalem (v. 6). Where there were so many people who looked for redemption before it came, there were more people who would not look at it when it did come.

1.3. The judges of the court.

1.3.1. Their general characterization: they were *rulers, elders,* and *scribes* (v. 5). The scribes were learned men; the rulers and elders were the men in power. The Gospel of Christ had both the learning and the power of the world against it.

1.3.2. The names of some of them, who were the most significant. Here were Annas and Caiaphas, ringleaders in this persecution: Annas, the president of the Sanhedrin, and Caiaphas, the high priest—although Annas is called that here. They were equally hateful toward Christ and his Gospel. There were also others who were *of the kindred* (family) *of the high priest,* who, because they depended on him, would be sure to say as he said. Relatives who are great but not good have been a trap to many people.

2. The prisoners were called to answer the charges against them (v. 7). They were brought to the court; the leaders *set them in the midst,* for the Sanhedrin sat in a circle. The question they asked the apostles was, "*By what power, or by what name, have you done this?* Who commissioned you to preach such a message? Where did you get the power to perform such a miracle?" They knew very well that the apostles preached Jesus (v. 2), but they asked them in order to provoke them, to see if they could get anything out of them that looked criminal.

3. They entered their plea, not so much to clear themselves and make themselves safe as to advance the name and honor of their Master. Notice:

3.1. By whom this plea was drawn up: it was dictated by the Holy Spirit. The apostles set themselves to preach Christ, and then Christ fulfilled his promise to them that the Holy Spirit would *give them in that same hour what they should speak* (Mt 10:19). Christ's faithful advocates will never lack instructions (Mk 13:11).

3.2. To whom it was given: Peter addressed the judges of the court as the *rulers of the people, and elders of* Israel, because the evil of those in power does not rob them of their power, but the consideration of the power they are entrusted with should effectively rob them of their wickedness.

3.3. What the plea was:

3.3.1. What they did had been done in the name of Jesus Christ, which was a direct answer to the question the court asked them (vv. 9–10): "*If we this day be examined* for *a good deed done to the impotent* (crippled) *man,* if we are asked *by what means,* or by whom, *he is made whole,* we have a ready answer. *Be it known to you all,* and not only to you, but also *to all the people of Israel, that by the name of Jesus Christ, whom you crucified, and whom God hath raised from the dead, even by him doth this man stand here before you whole,* a memorial to the power of the Lord Jesus."

3.3.1.1. He justified what he and his colleague had done in healing the lame man. It was *a good deed.* "Now, if we are to be judged for this good deed, we have no reason to be ashamed of it (vv. 14, 16; 1Pe 2:20). Let those who bring us into trouble for it be ashamed." It is nothing new for good people to suffer wrong for doing good.

3.3.1.2. He gave all the praise and glory for this good deed to Jesus Christ. "It is through him, not through any power of ours, that this man has been healed. May only the Lord be exalted; it doesn't matter what happens to us."

3.3.1.3. He accused the judges themselves of having murdered this Jesus: "It is he *whom you crucified*." He tries to convict them of sin, of the sin that was the one most likely to stir their conscience—their putting Christ to death. Peter would not miss the opportunity to tell them about it.

3.3.1.4. He declared the resurrection of Christ as the strongest testimony for him and against his persecutors: "God *raised him from the dead*; you took away his life, but God gave it back to him."

3.3.1.5. He preached this to all the people standing by: "*Be it known to you all*, to *all the people of Israel*, that wonders are performed in the name of Jesus, not by simply repeating that name as a charm, but by believing in it as a divine revelation of grace and goodwill to humanity.

3.3.2. The name of this Jesus is the only name by which we can be saved. It is not something that people can take or leave; rather, it is of paramount necessity that people believe in this name and call on it.

3.3.2.1. We are obliged to do so out of duty to God and in compliance with his purposes (v. 11): "*This is the stone which was set at nought of you builders, you* who are *the rulers of the people and the elders of Israel*, who should be the builders of the church. Here a stone was offered you, to be put in the chief place of the building, but you rejected it, threw it aside as good for nothing; yet this stone is *now become the head of the corner*." Peter probably chose to use this quotation from Ps 118:22 here because Christ himself had used it not long before this (Mt 21:42). Scripture is a tried and tested weapon in our spiritual conflicts: let us therefore stand by it.

3.3.2.2. We are obliged to do so for our own interests. We can be saved only by Jesus Christ (v. 12): *Neither is there salvation in any other.* Just as there is no other name by which diseased bodies can be healed, so there is no other name by which sinful souls can be saved. Notice:

3.3.2.2.*1.* Our salvation is our chief concern.

3.3.2.2.*2.* Our salvation is not in ourselves; we can destroy ourselves, but we cannot save ourselves.

3.3.2.2.*3.* The the honor of Christ's name is that it is the only name through which we must be saved: *there is no other name under heaven given among men whereby we must be saved.* This name is *given*; God has appointed it for our benefit. It is given *under heaven*; Christ has all power in both the higher and the lower world (Mt 28:18). It is given *among men*, who need salvation. We can be saved by his name, and we cannot be saved by any other name. It is not our responsibility to try to work out how far God's favor may be found by people who do not know Christ but live up to the light they have received. Whatever saving favor such people may receive, it is on account of Christ and only for his sake, so that still *there is no salvation in any other.*

4. The prosecution was brought to a standstill by this plea (vv. 13–14).

4.1. The Sanhedrin could not deny that the healing of the lame man was both a good deed and a miracle. They had *nothing to say against it* (v. 14).

4.2. They could not challenge Peter and John. Here was a miracle that was not inferior to the healing of the lame man. They saw *the boldness of Peter and John* (v. 13), who appeared not only undaunted by the rulers, but even courageous and daunting to them. The courage of Christ's faithful confessors has often confounded their cruel persecutors. Notice:

4.2.1. What made the persecutors' wonder increase: *They perceived that they were unlearned and ignorant men.* They asked about the apostles and found that they were born in Galilee, brought up as fishermen, and without formal schooling, but the moment you started talking to them about the Messiah and his kingdom, you found that they spoke so relevantly and so fluently, and had the Scriptures concerning this topic so ready on their tongues, that the most learned judge on the bench was not able to answer them. They were *ignorant men*—men who had no public persona or employment, which made the persecutors marvel to see the liberty they had.

4.2.2. What made their wonder largely come to an end: they *took knowledge of them that they had been with Jesus.* When they understood that *they had been with Jesus*, they knew what to attribute their boldness to. Those who have been with Jesus should behave in every aspect of their lives in such a way that those who are with them may *take knowledge of them that they have been with Jesus.* You may know that they have been on the mountain from the shining of their faces (Ex 34:29–30).

Verses 15–22

We have here the outcome of the trial. The apostles came off now with flying colors.

1. Here is the consultation of the court, how they then proceeded.

1.1. The prisoners were ordered to withdraw from the Sanhedrin (v. 15): They *commanded them to go aside out of the council.* The Sanhedrin were willing enough to get rid of the apostles—the apostles brought home to their consciences hard truths. Christ's enemies pursue their designs in small groups, as if they want to hide their plans from the Lord.

1.2. A debate arose on this matter: *They conferred among themselves.* The question asked was, *What shall we do to these men?* (v. 16). If they had yielded to the convincing and commanding power of truth, it would have been easy for them to say what they should do to these men. But when people refuse to be persuaded to do what they should do, it is hardly surprising that they are always at a loss as to what to do.

1.3. They eventually resolved:

1.3.1. That it was not safe to punish the apostles. They could not work out how to do it, *because of the people* (v. 21). They knew it would be unrighteous to punish them, and so they should have been restrained from doing it by the fear of God, but they considered it only as something dangerous and were therefore restrained from it only by the fear of the people.

1.3.1.1. The people were convinced of the truth of the miracle; it was *a notable miracle*, "a known, or outstanding, miracle." This was a known example of the power of Christ and a proof of his teaching. That it was a great miracle, and one performed to confirm the message they preached, was *manifest to all that dwelt in Jerusalem*; it was reported throughout the city, and throughout the city it was recognized as a sign. The Sanhedrin themselves, even with all their crafty scheming and arrogance, *could not deny it* to be a true miracle; everyone would have laughed at them if they had. They could easily deny it to their own consciences, but not to the world.

1.3.1.2. All the people *glorified God for that which was done.* Even those who were not persuaded by it to believe in Christ had to praise God for it.

1.3.2. That it was nevertheless necessary to silence them for the future (vv. 17–18). The Sanhedrin's whole concern was to make sure that the message of Christ *spread no further among the people* — as if that healing institution were a new plague whose contagion must be stopped. To prevent this message from spreading further:

1.3.2.1. They commanded the apostles never to preach it again, that *no man speak at all nor teach in the name of Jesus* (v. 18). "We command not only that you do not preach this message publicly but also that you *speak henceforth to no man*, not to any particular individual privately, *in this name*" (v. 17). No greater service is done for the Devil's kingdom than the silencing of faithful ministers and the putting under a bowl of those who are the lights of the world (Mt 5:14–15).

1.3.2.2. They threatened to punish them if they did; their lives would be in danger. Christ had not only commanded them to preach the Gospel to the whole creation (Mk 16:15) but also promised to support them in it. Those who know how to justly value Christ's promises know how to show just contempt for the world's threats.

2. Here is the courageous determination of the prisoners to continue with their work, and their declaration of this determination (vv. 19–20). Peter and John jointly answered: "*Whether it be right in the sight of God to hearken* (listen) *unto you more than unto God, judge you; for we cannot but speak the things which we have seen and heard.*" The wisdom of the serpent would have told them to be silent. However, the boldness of the lion told them to defy their persecutors in this way. They justified themselves in their defiance with two things:

2.1. The command of God: "You command us not to preach the Gospel; he has commanded us to preach it; now whom must we obey, God or you?" Nothing can be more absurd than to listen to weak and fallible men more than to a God who is infinitely wise and holy. "The case is so plain and self-evident that we will dare to leave it to you yourselves to judge it. Can you think it *right in the sight of God* to break a divine command in obedience to a human injunction?"

2.2. The convictions of their consciences. They still *could not but speak those things which they had seen and heard*, that is, Christ's doctrine.

2.2.1. They felt its influence on them, what a wonderful change it had brought about in them. Those who have felt the power of the teaching of Christ are the ones who speak out its message best.

2.2.2. They knew the importance of it for others. They looked with concern on souls that were perishing, and they knew that those souls could not escape eternal ruin except through Jesus Christ. They therefore wanted to be faithful to them by warning them. "They are things which we have seen and heard, and of which we are therefore completely sure; if we, then, do not make them known, who will? Who can?"

3. Here is the release of the prisoners (v. 21): *They further threatened them*, and then *let them go*:

3.1. Because they dared not contradict the people, who *glorified God for that which was done*. Just as rulers are made a terror and restraint to evildoers by the decree of God (Ro 13:3), so people are sometimes made a terror and restraint to evil rulers by the providence of God.

3.2. Because they could not contradict the miracle: *For the man was above forty years old on whom this miracle of healing was shown* (v. 22).

3.2.1. The miracle was so much the greater because the man had been lame *from his mother's womb* (3:2). If those who have long been used to evil are healed of their spiritual disability and enabled to do good, then the power of divine grace is so much more exalted.

3.2.2. The truth of it was so much better affirmed because *the man, being above forty years old*, was able to *speak for himself* (Jn 9:21) when he was questioned.

Verses 23–31

We hear no more for now about the chief priests, but must remain with these two witnesses. We have here:

1. The apostles' return to their brothers and sisters (v. 23): *Being let go, they went to their own company.* As soon as they were free, they went back to their old friends.

1.1. Although God had honored them highly by calling them to be his witnesses, they were not puffed up with the honor shown them, but *went to their own company*. No advancement in gifts or usefulness should make us think ourselves above either the duties or the privileges of the fellowship of saints.

1.2. Although their enemies had threatened them severely, they still went back to their own people. Christ's followers do best in company, provided it is in their own company.

2. The account they gave them of what had passed: They *reported all that the chief priests and elders had said to them*. They related it to them:

2.1. So that they would know what to expect both from people and from God. They could expect from people everything that was terrifying, but from God everything that was encouraging.

2.2. So that they would have it recorded to confirm our faith as it concerns the resurrection of Christ. These apostles told the chief priests to their faces that God had *raised up Jesus from the dead*. The chief priests did not have the confidence to deny it, but, in the most despicable and foolish way possible, commanded the apostles not to tell anyone about it.

2.3. So that they could now join with them in prayer and praise.

3. The believers' prayer to God on this occasion: *When they heard that, they lifted up their voice to God with one accord* (v. 24). One, in the name of the others, *lifted up his voice to God* and the rest joined with him "with one mind"; the hearts of all joined with the voice of the one, and so, though only one person spoke, they all prayed. In this prayer we have:

3.1. Their adoration of God as the Creator of the world (v. 24). They *said, "O Lord, thou art God*, sovereign Lord; you are the God *who has made heaven and earth, and the sea.*" The nations worship gods they have made; we worship the God who made us and the whole world. It is very proper to begin our prayers, as well as our creed, by acknowledging that God is the "Father almighty, Maker of heaven and earth, and of all things visible and invisible." The Christian faith was intended to confirm and apply, not overshadow or jostle out, the truths and dictates of natural religion. It is a great encouragement to God's servants that they serve the God who made all things and who is able to strengthen them in all their difficulties.

3.2. Their reconciling themselves to the present ways of Providence by reflecting on the Old Testament (vv. 25–26). *Thus he spoke by the mouth of his servant David.* Let this opposition to the Gospel not, therefore, come as a surprise to them, because the *scripture must be fulfilled*. It was foretold (Ps 2:1–2):

3.2.1. That the *heathen would rage* (nations would conspire) at Christ and his kingdom.

3.2.2. That the *people would imagine against it all the things they could.*

3.2.3. That the kings of the earth, particularly, would stand up in opposition to the kingdom of Christ.

3.2.4. That the rulers would gather together against God and Christ. Where power was vested in many rulers, councils, and senates, those bodies would *gather together against the Lord and against his Christ*. What is done against Christ, God takes as done against himself. Christianity was opposed and fought against by these forces, but it made its way.

3.3. Their representing those predictions as fulfilled in the present (vv. 27–28). It is *of a truth that Herod and Pilate*, the two Roman governors, with the *people of Israel*, were *gathered together against thy holy child Jesus whom thou has anointed*. Notice:

3.3.1. The wise and holy intentions God had for Christ.

3.3.1.1. He is called here the *child Jesus*. The word is *paida* and means both "a son" and "a servant." He was the Son of God, but in the work of redemption he acted as his Father's servant.

3.3.1.2. He was the One whom God anointed, and that was why he was called the Lord's Christ (v. 26). God, who anointed Christ, determined what would be done to him.

3.3.1.3. He was anointed to be a Savior, and therefore it was determined he would be a sacrifice to make atonement for sin. He must die, and therefore he must put to death, but not by his own hands, and therefore God wisely determined beforehand by what hands it would be done. He must be *delivered into the hands of sinners*.

3.3.1.4. God's *hand and his counsel determined it* (v. 28). His hand and his purpose always agree, for *whatsoever the Lord pleased, that did he* (Ps 135:6).

3.3.2. The evil and unholy instruments that were employed in carrying out these intentions. Herod and Pilate, Gentiles and Jews, who had been in conflict with each other, united against Christ. Sin is no less evil because God brings good out of it, but he is more glorified by this.

3.4. Their request with reference to their situation at this time.

3.4.1. That God would take note of the hatred of their enemies: *Now, Lord, behold their threatenings* (v. 29). *And now, Lord*; there is an emphasis on the *now*. God's time to appear for his people is when the power of their enemies is at its most daring and threatening. The believers did not dictate to God what he must do, but referred themselves to him: "We appeal to you. Consider their threats, and either tie their hands or turn their hearts." It is an encouragement to us that if we are unjustly threatened, we may make ourselves more at ease by spreading our situation out before the Lord and leaving it with him (Isa 37:14).

3.4.2. That God, by his grace, would keep up their spirits: *Grant unto thy servants that with all boldness they may speak thy word*. Their prayer was not, "*Lord, behold their threatenings*, and frighten them," but, "*Behold their threatenings*, and enliven us." They did not pray, "Lord, give us a good opportunity to withdraw from our work, now that it has become dangerous," but, "Lord, give us grace to continue in our work and not be afraid." Those who are sent on God's missions should communicate their message with boldness, not doubting either what they say or that they will be supported by God in saying it. God is to be sought for an ability to speak his word with boldness. The threats of our enemies should stir us up to even more courage. Are those who fight against Christ defiant? Let us not be ashamed or slow in speaking up for him.

3.4.3. That God would continue to give them power to perform miracles to confirm the message they preached: *Lord, grant us boldness, by stretching forth thy hand to heal*. Nothing makes faithful ministers bolder in their work than the signs of God's presence with them. They prayed *that signs and wonders might be done by the name of the holy child Jesus*, which would convince the people and confound the believers' enemies. It was the honor of Christ that they aimed at, that the wonders might be done in the name of Jesus.

4. The gracious answer God gave.

4.1. God gave them a sign of the acceptance of their prayers (v. 31): *When they had prayed, the place was shaken where they were assembled together.* This shaking of the place was intended to wake them up, raise their expectations, and give them a physical sign that God was truly with them, to show them why they had to fear God more, and then they would fear people less. The place was shaken so that their faith would be established and unshaken.

4.2. God gave them a greater measure of his Spirit. Their prayer, without doubt, was accepted, because it was answered: *They were all filled with the Holy Spirit.* This not only encouraged them but also enabled them to speak the word of God with boldness. The Holy Spirit taught them not only what to speak (Lk 12:12) but also how to speak. They had been *filled with the Holy Spirit* in the court of law (v. 8), and now they were *filled with the Holy Spirit* in the pulpit. We have here an example of the fulfillment of that promise *that God will give the Holy Spirit to those that ask him* (Lk 11:13), because it was in answer to prayer that they were filled with the Holy Spirit. We also have an example of the application of that gift; have it and use it, use it and have more of it. *They spoke the word with all boldness.* Talents must be put to good use, not buried in the ground (Mt 25:14–30).

Verses 32–37

In these verses we are given a general idea—and it is a very beautiful one—of the spirit and state of the early church; it is a view of that age of infancy and innocence.

1. The disciples loved one another dearly. *The multitude of those that believed were of one heart, and of one soul* (v. 32).

1.1. There were many who believed; even in Jerusalem *there were three thousand* (2:41) converted on one day, and *five thousand* on another (v. 4), and besides these, *there were added to the church daily* (2:47). The increase of the church is its glory.

1.2. They *were all of one heart, and of one soul.* Although there were many, in fact, very many, of different ages, attitudes, and conditions in the world, they were agreed, and in their faith in Christ they were of one heart and mind; being all joined to the Lord, they were joined to one another in holy love. This was the blessed fruit of Christ's dying command to his disciples to *love one another* (Jn 13:34), and of his dying prayer for them *that they all might be one* (Jn 17:11). *They were all of one heart, and one soul.* This is how it was then, and we must not despair of seeing it so again.

2. The ministers continued in their work with great vigor and success (v. 33). *With great power gave the apostles witness of the resurrection of the Lord Jesus.* The resurrection of Christ, rightly understood, will let us into the great mysteries of religious faith. The great power with which the apostles affirmed the resurrection may refer to:

2.1. The great vigor, spirit, and courage with which they declared this message; they did not declare it softly and diffidently, but with liveliness and resolution. Or:

2.2. The miracles they performed to confirm their message. God himself, in them, *bore witness* (Heb 2:4).

3. The beauty of the Lord our God (Ps 90:17) shone on them: *Great grace was upon them all; grace* that had something great in it—something magnificent and very extraordinary—*was upon them all*. Christ poured out plentiful *grace upon them*. There were clear fruits of this grace in all they said and did. Some think this grace includes the favor in which they were held by the people (2:47). Everyone saw a beauty and excellence in them and respected them.

4. They were very generous to the poor.

4.1. They did not insist on holding on to their own property, which even children seem to have a sense of and a jealousy for, and which worldly people triumph in. *No man said that aught of the things which he possessed was his own* (v. 32). They did not take away property; rather, they were indifferent toward it. They did not call it their own, because they had, in affection, forsaken everything for Christ. We can call nothing our own but sin. *No man said that what he had was his own* because each one was willing to share with others. Those who had lands and possessions were not anxious to hoard what they had, but were very willing to give to others; they were willing to restrict themselves to help their brothers and sisters. They did not call things "mine" and "yours," which produces great conflicts. When people hang on too tightly to what is their own and grasp for more than their own, they cause wars and other conflicts.

4.2. They were very loving to one another, so that, in effect, *they had all things common*, because *there was not any among them that lacked* (v. 34). Just as there were many poor who received the Gospel, so there were some rich who were able to maintain them, and the grace of God made them willing to do so. The Gospel has put *all things common*, which means not that the poor are allowed to rob the rich, but that the rich are appointed to relieve the poor.

4.3. Many of them sold their lands or possessions: *As many as had possession of lands or houses sold them* (v. 34).

4.3.1. We are told here what they did with the money that was raised in that way: they *laid it at the apostles' feet*—they left it to the apostles to be disposed of as they thought fit. *Distribution was made unto every man according as he had need*. In the distribution of public charity, great care should be taken that it is given to those who have a real need, and above all to those who are reduced to need because of their well-doing. Care should be taken also that it is given to *every man according as he has need*, without discrimination or favoritism.

4.3.2. One particular individual is mentioned as an example: *Barnabas*, who was later Paul's colleague. Notice:

4.3.2.1. The description of him given here (v. 36). His name was *Joses*; he was of *the tribe of Levi*. He was born in Cyprus, a long way away from Jerusalem. As he associated with the apostles, he came to be respected by them, and to show how much they valued him, they changed his name to *Barnabas*. He was *a son of consolation*, one who, walking very much in strengths and encouragements of the Holy Spirit, was a cheerful Christian, and this released his heart to give to the poor. He was well known as one who had a wonderful gift for encouraging the Lord's people. Two among the apostles were called *Boanerges*, "sons of thunder" (Mk 3:17), but here *a son of consolation* was with them. Each had his particular gift. Let the one probe or examine the wound, and then let the other heal it and bind it up.

4.3.2.2. The account given of his great generosity. This is particularly remarked on here because of the impor-

tance of his service later in the church of God. Or perhaps this is mentioned because it was an outstanding feature of his character and therefore an example to others: *He, having land, sold it, brought the money, and laid it at the apostles' feet*. By doing so, he lost nothing in the balancing of accounts, since he himself was, in effect, numbered among the apostles by that word of the Holy Spirit, *Separate me Barnabas and Saul for the work whereunto I have called them* (13:2). And so, for the respect he showed to the apostles as apostles, he received an apostle's reward (Mt 10:41).

CHAPTER 5

We have here: 1. The sin and punishment of Ananias and Sapphira (vv. 1–11). 2. The flourishing state of the church (vv. 12–16). 3. The imprisonment of the apostles and their miraculous release from prison (vv. 17–26). 4. Their being brought before the Sanhedrin (vv. 27–33). 5. Gamaliel's advice about them, and the council's agreement with this advice for the present (vv. 34–40). 6. The apostles' cheerful continuance in their work (vv. 41–42).

Verses 1–11

The chapter begins with a sad *but*. Both every human being and every church, even in their best state, have their *buts*. The disciples all seemed to be exceedingly good, but there were hypocrites among them. There is a mixture of bad with the good in the best communities this side of heaven; weeds grow among the wheat until harvest (Mt 13:25–30). They reached the perfection that Christ recommended to the rich young ruler—they *sold what they had, and gave to the poor* (Mt 19:21), but even that proved to be a cover-up to their hypocrisy. The signs and wonders the apostles performed were miracles of mercy up to that time, but now came a miracle of judgment, so that God might be feared as well as loved. Notice here:

1. The sin of Ananias and Sapphira, his wife.

1.1. They were ambitious to be thought eminent disciples when really they were not even true disciples. They *sold a possession* (a piece of property) *and brought the money to the apostles' feet*, so that they would not seem to be lagging behind the best believers. It is possible for hypocrites to deny themselves in one matter, but if they do, it is to serve their own ends in another. Ananias and Sapphira wanted to take on themselves a profession of Christianity and make a good outward impression with it, since they knew they could not continue with a real Christian profession. Going to greater lengths in profession than one's heart will support often brings fatal consequences.

1.2. They were greedy to gain worldly wealth and distrustful of God and his providence: *They sold their land* and, in a fit of zeal, intended to dedicate the whole of the proceeds of the sale for godly uses, but when the money was received, their hearts failed them and *they kept back part of the price* (v. 2), because they loved money. They could not take God at his word that they would be provided for, but thought they would be wiser than the others and set something aside for a rainy day, as if there were not an all-sufficiency in God to make up the whole to them. If they had been thoroughbred worldlings, they would not have sold their possession, and if they had been thoroughbred Christians, they would not have kept back part of the proceeds.

1.3. They thought they would deceive the apostles by making them believe that they had brought all the money they had received for the sale. They came and *laid the money at the apostles' feet*, as if it were all they had.

2. The charge brought against Ananias, which proved to be both his condemnation and his execution for this sin. When he brought the money, Peter took him to task about it. Without any investigation, Peter positively accused him of the crime, showing it in its true colors (vv. 3–4). The Spirit of God in Peter not only revealed the fact but also discerned the motive of controlling unfaithfulness in Ananias's heart, which lay at the root of the sin. If it had been a sin of weakness, and he had been caught unawares by temptation, Peter would have told him to go home and repent of his foolishness.

2.1. He showed him the origin of his sin: *Satan filled thine heart*; Satan had not only suggested it to Ananias, not only put it into his mind, but also rushed him on to do it with determination.

2.2. He showed him the sin itself: Ananias had *lied to the Holy Spirit*, a sin that was so detestable that he could not have been guilty of it unless Satan had filled his heart. *Thou hast not lied unto men, but unto God.*

2.2.1. Ananias had told a lie; he had told Peter that he had sold a property and that this was all the proceeds. He acted like the others who brought the whole proceeds, and he wanted it to be thought he had done so, expecting the praise received by those who had done so. Many are brought to corrupt lying by a controlling pride and a desire for human praise, especially in works of charity to the poor. Those who boast about good works they never did, or promise good works they never do, or who pretend they do more good works than they really do, or better ones, come under the guilt of Ananias's lie.

2.2.2. He had told this *lie to the Holy Spirit*. It was not so much to the apostles as to the Holy Spirit in them that the money was brought, and that was why Peter said what he said (v. 4): *Thou hast not lied unto men, but unto God.*

2.3. He showed him what made the sin even worse (v. 4): *While it remained, was it not thine own? And, after it was sold, was it not in thine own power?*

2.3.1. "You were under no temptation *to keep back part of the price*; before it was sold, it was your own, and when it was sold, it was in your own power to dispose of the money as you wished." Or:

2.3.2. "You were under no obligation to sell your land at all; you didn't have to bring any money to the apostles' feet. You could have kept the money if you had wanted to, along with the land." It is better not to vow than to vow and not pay (Ecc 5:5), so it would have been better for him if he had not pretended to do the good work than to do it incompletely. *"When it was sold, it was in thine own power*, but it was not so once it was vowed." In giving our hearts to God, we are not allowed to divide them. Satan, like the mother to whom the child did not belong (1Ki 3:26), would be satisfied with a half, but God wants all or nothing.

2.4. Ananias was accused of all this guilt, and it was emphasized: *Why hast thou conceived this thing in thine heart?* He was said to have conceived it in his own heart, which shows that we cannot mitigate our sins by laying the fault of them on the Devil; he tempts, but he cannot force. The closing part of the accusation is very great, but also very just: *Thou hast not lied unto men, but unto God.* If we think we can deceive God, we will prove in the end to have deceived our own souls.

3. The death and burial of Ananias (vv. 5–6).

3.1. He died on the spot: *Ananias, hearing these words, was speechless* (Mt 22:12); he had nothing to say for him-

self. But this was not all. He *fell down, and gave up the ghost.* Notice the power of the word of God in the mouth of the apostles. Just as there are those whom the Gospel justifies, so there are also those whom it condemns. This punishment of Ananias may seem severe, but we are sure it was just.

3.1.1. It was intended to uphold the honor of the Holy Spirit. Ananias's lie was a great insult to the Holy Spirit, implying that he thought the Holy Spirit could be deceived.

3.1.2. It was intended to deter others from similar presumptions. The performance of this action by the ministry of Peter, who himself had denied his Master with a lie, shows that it was not an expression of resentment for a wrong done to Peter, for then he would have forgiven this disrespect and tried to bring the offender to repentance; rather, it was the act of the Spirit of God in Peter. The dishonor was done to the Spirit of God, and the punishment was inflicted by him.

3.2. He was buried immediately, for this was the custom of the Jews (v. 6): *The young men wound up* the dead body in graveclothes, *carried it out*, and *buried it.*

4. The judgment of Sapphira, the wife of Ananias. *She came in about three hours after*, because *she knew not what had been done.*

4.1. She was found guilty, by a question that Peter asked her, of sharing with her husband in his sin (v. 8): *Tell me whether you sold the land for so much?* She said, "We had no more; this was all we received." Ananias and his wife agreed to tell the same story; they thought they could safely stand by the lie and thereby be credited with great generosity. It is sad to see those relatives who should stir one another up to do good harden one another in doing evil.

4.2. She was sentenced to share in her husband's condemnation (v. 9).

4.2.1. Her sin was examined: *How is it that you have agreed together to tempt the Spirit of the Lord?* Before Peter passed sentence, he showed her the evil of her sin.

4.2.1.1. Ananias and Sapphira had tested the Spirit of the Lord. They saw that the apostles had the gift of tongues, but did they have the gift of distinguishing between spirits (1Co 12:10)? Those who expect safety and impunity in sin are testing the Spirit of God.

4.2.1.2. They had agreed together to do it. It is hard to say which is worse between marriage partners and other relatives—disagreement in good or agreement in evil.

4.2.2. Her condemnation was read out: *Behold, the feet of those who have buried thy husband are at the door, and they shall carry thee out.*

4.3. The sentence was carried out. *Then she fell down straightway at his feet.* God makes quick work with some sinners, while he is patient with others for a long time; no doubt there are good reasons for the difference, but he is not accountable to us for them. There are many sudden deaths that are not to be looked on as the punishment of some gross sin, as this one was. We must not think that all who die suddenly are greater sinners than others; to some, perhaps, a sudden death is a favor, a quick passage. To all, however, the witnessing of a sudden death is a forewarning always to be ready. But here it is clear that it was a judgment. Some ask about the eternal state of Ananias and Sapphira, inclining to the view that the flesh was destroyed so that *the spirit might be saved in the day of the Lord Jesus* (1Co 5:5). However, secret things are not for us to know (Dt 29:29). It is said, *She fell down at Peter's feet.* The *young men* came in and *found her dead. They carried her out and buried her by her husband.* Some ask whether the apostles kept the money the couple did bring. I am inclined to think they did. What they brought was not defiled to those to whom they brought it, but what they kept back was defiled to those who kept it back.

5. The impression this made on the people. Notice is taken of this in the middle of the story (v. 5): *Great fear came upon all that heard these things.* It is also mentioned in v. 11: *Great fear came upon all the church, and upon as many as heard these things.* Those who had joined the church were struck with an awe of God and his judgments. It did not restrain or spoil their holy joy, but taught them to be serious about it, and to rejoice with trembling (Ps 2:11).

Verses 12–16

Here is an account of the progress the Gospel made despite this terrible judgment inflicted on two hypocrites.

1. Here is a general account of the miracles the apostles performed (v. 12): *By the hands of the apostles were many signs and wonders wrought among the people.* God had come out to punish; he now returned to his mercy seat (Ex 25:22; Lev 16:2; Nu 7:89). The miracles the apostles performed proved their divine mission. They were *signs and wonders,* such wonders as were generally acknowledged to be signs of a divine presence and power.

2. We are here told about the effects of these miracles.

2.1. The church was kept together: *They were all with one accord in Solomon's porch.* They met in the temple, in the part called Solomon's Colonnade. Shame prevented those who allowed buyers and sellers there from prohibiting such preachers and healers there. The believers all met in public worship; they were there with *one accord.* The separation of hypocrites should make the sincere cling so much closer to one another.

2.2. The miracles gained the apostles great respect. *Of the rest* of their company *no man durst* (dare) *join himself to them,* as their equal or associate. All *the people magnified them.* Although the chief priests did all they could to make the apostles seem disreputable, this did not prevent the people from exalting them. The apostles were far from exalting themselves, but the people exalted them, because those who humble themselves will be exalted (Mt 23:12), and those who honor only God will be honored (1Sa 2:30).

2.3. The church increased in numbers (v. 14): *Believers were the more added to the Lord;* in fact, *multitudes both of men and women* joined. Far from being deterred by the example that was made of Ananias and Sapphira, they were encouraged by it to enter into a community that kept such strict discipline. Many people have been brought to the Lord, but there is still room for many others to be added to him, added to the number of those who are united to him. Women as well as men are converted. Just as among those who followed Christ while he was on earth, so also among those who believed in him after he went to heaven, great notice was taken of the good women.

2.4. The apostles had many patients, and they elevated their reputation by healing them all (vv. 15–16). So many *signs and wonders were wrought by the apostles* that all kinds of people came asking to benefit from them, in both the city and the country, and they received it.

2.4.1. In the city, people *brought forth their sick into the streets.* They *laid them on beds and couches* (mats), so that at least the shadow of Peter, passing by, might overshadow (fall on) *some of them,* even though it could not reach them all. It had the desired effect, just as the wom-

an's touch of the edge of Christ's cloak had (Mt 9:20), and here the word of Christ was fulfilled, *Greater works than these shall you do* (Jn 14:12). If such miracles were performed by Peter's shadow, we have reason to think miracles were performed in the same way by the other apostles, as they were, for example, by the handkerchiefs that Paul had touched (19:12).

2.4.2. Very many people also came from the country towns. They came to Jerusalem from *the cities round about, bringing sick folks* and *those that were vexed with unclean spirits,* and these were *healed every one;* diseased bodies and diseased minds were healed. And so by these miracles the apostles were given opportunities both to convince people's judgments of the heavenly origin of the message they preached and to engage people's affections both for them and it.

Verses 17–25

Never did any good work continue with any hope of success without meeting opposition. It would have been strange if the apostles had gone on teaching and healing in this way with no restraint. In these verses we read of the hatred of hell and the grace of heaven struggling around them, the one to drive them away from this good work, and the other to encourage them in it:

1. The priests were jealous of them and shut them up in prison (vv. 17–18). Notice:

1.1. Who their enemies and persecutors were. The high priest was the ringleader, either Annas or Caiaphas. Those who were most eager to join the high priest in their opposition were the *sect of the Sadducees,* who were particularly hostile toward the Gospel of Christ because it confirmed the resurrection of the dead and the future state, all of which they denied.

1.2. How these enemies felt toward them: exasperated. They *rose up* in a passion, being *filled with indignation* at the apostles for preaching the message of Christ and healing the sick. They were also angry at the people for hearing the apostles and bringing the sick to them to be healed.

1.3. How they proceeded against them (v. 18): *They laid their hands on them* and *put them in the common prison* (public jail), among the worst evildoers:

1.3.1. To restrain them. While they held them in prison, they kept them from continuing with their work, and they reckoned this at least a partial success.

1.3.2. To make them afraid and thereby drive them away from their work. The last time the council had the apostles before them, they only threatened them (4:21), but now they imprisoned them, to make them afraid of them.

1.3.3. To disgrace them, and that was why they chose to put them up in the public jail.

2. God sent his angel to release them from prison. The powers of darkness fought against them, but the Father of lights (Jas 1:17) fought for them. The Lord will never desert his witnesses, his advocates; he will certainly stand by them.

2.1. The apostles were released from their imprisonment (v. 19): *The angel of the Lord by night opened the prison doors* and, in spite of the guards who stood at the doors, brought out the prisoners (v. 23). There is no prison so dark, so strong, that God cannot both visit his people in it and bring them out of it.

2.2. They were charged to continue with their work. The angel told them, *Go, stand, and speak in the temple to the people all the words of this life* (v. 20). When they were miraculously set free, it was so that they could continue with their work with even more boldness. Recovery from sickness, release from trouble, are given us not so that we may enjoy the comforts of our life, but so that God may be honored with the service of our life. Notice:

2.2.1. Where they must preach: *Speak in the temple.* One would have thought it would be wise to continue their preaching in a more private place. No, "Speak in the temple courts, for this is where people are; this is your Father's house." It is not for the preachers of Christ's Gospel to withdraw into hidden corners, as long as they have any opportunity to preach in the great assembly.

2.2.2. To whom they must preach: "*Speak to the people,* who are willing and want to be taught, and whose souls are as precious to Christ as the souls of the greatest.

2.2.3. How they must preach: *Go, stand, and speak*—which shows not only that they must speak publicly but also that they must speak boldly and resolutely. They must speak *all the words of this life.* "Go and preach the same message to the world, so that others may be comforted with the same comforts with which you yourselves are comforted by God (2Co 1:4). "Preach the words of *this* life"—emphatically—"this heavenly, divine life, in comparison with which the present earthly life does not deserve the name of life." The Gospel is about matters of life and death, and ministers must preach it and people must listen to it accordingly. The apostles must speak *all the words of this life,* the full message of this new life, not keeping back anything. Christ's witnesses are sworn to speak the whole truth.

3. They continued with their work (v. 21): *When they heard this,* they *returned to Solomon's porch* (v. 12).

3.1. It was a great joy and assurance to them to have received these fresh orders. Now that the angel ordered them to go and preach in the temple courts, their way was plain, and they went out without compunction or fear into the temple courts. If we may only be assured of our duty, our business is to remain close to it, and then we may cheerfully trust God with our safety.

3.2. They set themselves immediately to carry out these orders. They *entered into the temples early in the morning* and taught the people the Gospel of the kingdom; they were not afraid in the slightest what people might do to them. The whole treasure of the Gospel was put in their hands; if they were silent now, the springs would shut up, and the whole work would fall to the ground and come to an end. When God gives an opportunity to do good, even though we may be under the restraint and terror of human powers, we should dare to go far rather than allow such an opportunity to drop.

4. The high priest and his associates continued with their prosecution (v. 21). They *called the council together,* the Sanhedrin, and it was a great and extraordinary meeting of the council, because they summoned *all the senate of the children of Israel.* Notice:

4.1. How the council was prepared to crush the Gospel of Christ and its preachers: they convened the whole assembly. The last time they had the apostles in custody, they brought them before only a committee of those who belonged to the family of the high priest, but now they called together the full assembly of the elders of Israel. This is how God arranged it, so that the enemies' confusion and the apostles' testimony against them would be more public, and so that those who would not hear the Gospel otherwise than in the assembly would hear it.

4.2. How they were disappointed and their faces were covered with shame. An officer was immediately dispatched to bring the prisoners to the court.

4.2.1. The officers came and told the court that the prisoners were not to be found in the prison (vv. 22–23).

They had gone, and the report that the officers made was, "*The prison door truly found we shut with all safety* (we found the jail securely locked), *the keepers* standing at the doors, but when we went in, *we found no man* in the jail." We are not told which way the angel took them; however it happened, they had gone. The Lord knows how to rescue the godly out of temptation (2Pe 2:9) and how to loose those who are in chains for his name's sake, even though we do not, and he will do it, as here, when he has a use for them (v. 24): *When the high priest, and the captain of the temple,* and the *chief priests, heard these things,* they were all puzzled and looked at one another, *doubting what this thing should be.* They were at their wits' end, having never been so disappointed in all their lives about anything they were so sure of. Those who think they can distress and embarrass the cause of Christ often end up distressing and embarrassing themselves.

4.2.2. Another messenger partly resolved their doubt but also increased their trouble, bringing them word that their prisoners were preaching in the temple courts (v. 25): "*Behold, the men whom you put in prison are now standing in the temple,* under your nose and in defiance of you, *teaching the people.*" Now this perplexed them more than anything. Common evildoers may have enough skill to break out of prison, but it is uncommon for them to have enough courage to affirm that they have done so.

Verses 26–42

We are not told what it was that the apostles preached to the people, but we have here an account of what took place between them and the council, because in their sufferings there appeared more of a divine power and energy than even in their preaching. We have here:

1. The seizing of the apostles a second time.

1.1. The council's officers brought the apostles without violence. One would have thought that reverence for the temple and fear of the apostles, who might strike them down as they had Ananias, would give these officers enough reason for restraint, but all that restrained their violence was their fear of the people, who had such a respect for the apostles that they would have stoned the officers if they had abused them in any way.

1.2. Yet they brought them to those who they knew would do violence to them (v. 27). They *brought them, to set them before the council.* The powers that should have been a terror to evil works and evildoers became a terror to the good.

2. Their trial. The high priest told them what they were accused of (v. 28):

2.1. They had disobeyed the commands of authority (v. 28): "*Did not we* strictly command you *that you should not teach in this name?* But you have disobeyed our clear commands." *Did not we command you?* Yes; they did, but did not Peter at the same time tell them that God's authority was superior to theirs, and his commands must take precedence over theirs (4:19)? They had forgotten this.

2.2. They had spread false teaching among the people. "*You have filled Jerusalem with your doctrine,* and so have disturbed the public peace."

2.3. They had a malicious intention against the government; they aimed to represent it as having made itself justly repugnant both to God and to people: "*You intend to bring this man's blood,* its guilt before God, the shame of it before people, *upon us.*" Notice here how those who will do evil with a great deal of presumption nevertheless cannot bear to hear about it afterward. When the chief priests and the elders were in the fires of persecution, they could cry out daringly enough, *His blood be upon us and upon our children* (Mt 27:25). But now they took it as a great affront to be held responsible for the shedding of his blood.

3. Their answer to the charge leveled against them: *Peter and the other apostles* all spoke in the same vein. They spoke as one and the same Spirit enabled them to speak (2:4).

3.1. They justified themselves in their disobedience (v. 29): *We ought to obey God rather than men.* God had commanded them to teach in the name of Christ, and that was why they should do it, even though the chief priests forbade them. Those rulers who punish people for disobeying them in order to do their duty to God have a great deal to answer for.

3.2. They justified themselves in doing what they could to fill Jerusalem with the message of Christ, and if in so doing they brought his blood on his enemies, those enemies had only themselves to blame.

3.2.1. The chief priests were told to their faces the indignity they had done to this Jesus: *You slew him and hanged him on a tree* (v. 30). People's reluctance to hear their own faults is no good reason why they should not be faithfully told them. It is a common excuse for not rebuking sin that the times will not bear it. However, those whose job it is to rebuke must not be put off by this; the times must bear it, and will bear it.

3.2.2. They were also told what honors God put on this Jesus, and then let them judge who was in the right, the persecutors of his message or its preachers. Peter called God the *God of our fathers.* The God of *Abraham, Isaac,* and *Jacob* (Ex 3:6) is the *God and Father of our Lord Jesus Christ* (1Pe 1:3); notice what honor God gave to Christ.

3.2.2.1. He *raised him up.* "You put him to death, but God has restored him to life, so that God and you are clearly disputing this Jesus, and which must we side with?"'

3.2.2.2. He *exalted him with his right hand* (v. 31). "You loaded him down with shame, but God has crowned him with honor, and should we not honor the One whom God honors? God has *given him a name above every name* (Php 2:9)."

3.2.2.3. "He has appointed him to be *a prince and a Saviour.*" We cannot have Christ as our Savior unless we are also willing to take him as our Prince. We cannot expect to be redeemed and healed by him unless we give ourselves to be ruled by him. Faith accepts a whole Christ, who came not to save us in our sins but to save us from our sins.

3.2.2.4. He was appointed to *give repentance to Israel and remission of sins.* That was why they must preach in his name to the people of Israel, for his favors were intended primarily and principally for them. Why should the rulers and elders of Israel oppose One who came with no less a blessing to Israel than repentance and forgiveness? However, repentance and forgiveness of sins were blessings they neither valued nor saw their need of. Repentance and forgiveness go together; wherever repentance is worked, forgiveness is always granted. On the other hand, there is no forgiveness without repentance. It is Jesus Christ who gives both repentance and forgiveness. Are we appointed to repent? Christ is appointed to give repentance. The new heart is his work, and the broken spirit a sacrifice that he has provided (Ps 51:17), and if he were not to give remission when he has given repentance, he would *forsake the work of his own hands* (Ps 138:8).

3.2.2.5. All this was well affirmed:

3.2.2.5.1. By the apostles themselves. "*We are his witnesses,* and if we were to be silent, as you want us to be, we would betray that trust." When a case is being tried,

witnesses should not be silenced, because the outcome of the cause depends on their testimony.

3.2.2.5.2. By the Spirit of God. *The Holy Spirit is witness* (Heb 10:15), a witness from heaven; "We must preach in Christ's name, because this is why we have been given the Holy Spirit, whose activity we cannot suppress." The giving of the Holy Spirit to obedient believers, not only to bring them to the obedience of faith but also to make them eminently useful in the faith, is a very strong proof of the truth of Christianity.

3.2.2.5.3. The giving of the Holy Spirit to those who obey Christ is clear evidence that it is the will of God that Christ should be obeyed. "Judge, then, whether we should obey you in opposition to him."

4. The impression the apostles' defense of themselves made on the court. Surely such fair reasoning must clear the prisoners and convert the judges. Yet instead the judges were enraged against it, filled:

4.1. With indignation: they were *cut to the heart* (v. 33), angry at seeing their own sin set out before them, furious to find that the Gospel of Christ had so much to say for itself. When a sermon to this effect was preached to the people, they were *pricked to the heart* in remorse and godly sorrow (2:37), but these here were *cut to the heart* with fury and anger.

4.2. With hatred toward the apostles themselves. Since they saw that they could not silence the apostles in any other way than by stopping them from breathing, they *took counsel to slay them.* While the apostles continued in their service of Christ with a holy security and peace of mind, their persecutors continued their opposition to Christ with a constant perplexity and disturbance in their minds, being a trouble to themselves.

5. The solemn advice that Gamaliel gave on this occasion. This Gamaliel is here said to have been *a Pharisee* by profession and sect and *a doctor of the law* by occupation. Paul was brought up at his feet (22:3). He is said here to have been *in reputation among all the people.* He was a moderate man, and one inclined to be restrained. People of moderation and kindness are justly held in high reputation for restraining the agitators who otherwise would set the world on fire. Notice:

5.1. The necessary caution he gave to the council: *He commanded to put the apostles forth* (that the apostles be put out of the room) *a little while.* "*You men of Israel,* he said, *take heed to yourselves,* consider what you are doing, or *intend to do, as touching these men*" (v. 35). He called them *men of Israel* to back up this caution: "You are men, who should be governed by reason. You are men of Israel, who should be governed by revelation. *Take heed to yourselves.*" The persecutors of God's people had best look to themselves, in case they fall into the pit they are digging (Ps 7:15; 9:15).

5.2. The cases he cited. He gave two examples of subversive, rebellious men whose attempts came to nothing all by themselves, and from the ends to which these other rebels had come, he concluded that if these men were truly as the Sanhedrin represented them, their cause would sink under its own weight.

5.2.1. There was one *Theudas, boasting himself to be somebody.* Gamaliel remarked here (v. 36) about how far Theudas was successful: "*A number of men, about four hundred* in all, joined him." Then he remarked on how soon Theudas's claims were all dashed: "When *he was slain, all, as many as obeyed him, were scattered.* Now compare that case with this. You have killed Jesus, the ringleader of this faction. Now if he was an impostor and pretender, his death will mean the death of his cause."

5.2.2. The case was the same with *Judas of Galilee* (v. 37). Notice:

5.2.2.1. The attempt he made. It is said to be *after this*, which some read, "besides this." It is not easy to determine particularly when these events happened. They were probably cases that had just happened and were fresh in people's memory. This *Judas drew away much people after him.*

5.2.2.2. His attempt was defeated: *He also perished, and all, even as many as obeyed him,* were dispersed.

5.3. His opinion on the whole matter.

5.3.1. That they should not persecute the apostles (v. 38): *Now I say unto you, Refrain from these men* (leave these men alone); *let not our hand be upon them.* It is uncertain why he spoke this. Perhaps it was purely for political ends. The apostles did not attempt anything using outward force. Why should any external force be used against them? Or perhaps it was only the language of a mild, quiet spirit. Or perhaps God put this word into Gamaliel's mouth beyond Gamaliel's own intention. We are sure there was an overruling providence in it so that the servants of Christ would not only come out of it, but come out of it honorably.

5.3.2. That they should leave this matter to Providence: "Wait to see what happens. *If it be of men* (of human origin), *it will come to nought* (will fail) by itself; *if of God, it will stand* in spite of all your powers and politics." What is clearly evil and immoral must be suppressed, but if a thing appears good, and it is doubtful whether its origin is divine or human, it is best to leave it alone and let it take its course. Christ rules by the power of truth, not by the power of the sword.

5.3.2.1. "If this *counsel, and this work* (this purpose or activity), *be of men, it will come to nothing.* If it is the purpose and activity of foolish crackpots, they will run out of breath; they will make themselves look ridiculous. If it is the purpose and activity of political schemers, leave them alone for a while, and their foolishness will be clear to everyone. Providence will never support it. *It will come to nothing* in a short time: there is no need to kill what will die by itself if you give it a little time. The unnecessary use of power is a misuse of it. But:

5.3.2.2. "If it should prove that these plans and this work are of God, then what do you think of persecuting them, of this attempt of yours (v. 33) *to slay them?* You must conclude it to be:

5.3.2.2.1. "A fruitless attempt against them: *If it be of God, you cannot overthrow it.*" All who are sincerely on God's side may take comfort in knowing that whatever comes from God cannot be overthrown totally and finally, even though it may be vigorously opposed; it may be attacked, but it cannot be defeated.

5.3.2.2.2. "An attempt that is dangerous to you. I say to you, leave it alone, *lest haply you* (or you might even) *be found even to fight against God.*" Those who hate and abuse God's faithful people, who restrain and silence his faithful ministers, are fighting against God. Well, this was the advice of Gamaliel: we wish it were duly considered by those who persecute for conscience's sake.

6. The decision of the council on the whole matter (v. 40). They agreed with Gamaliel to the extent that they dropped their intention of putting the apostles to death. They could not, however, refrain from expressing their rage to some extent. *They beat them,* flogged them as evildoers, and notice is taken of the shame of this (v. 41). In this way they thought they would make them ashamed of preaching, and the people ashamed of listening to them. *They* also *commanded them that they should not speak* anymore *in the name of Jesus.*

7. The wonderful courage and faithfulness of the apostles. *They departed from the council,* and we do not find they said one word against the court, *but committed their cause to him* to whom Gamaliel had referred it (1Pe 2:23).

7.1. They endured their suffering with an invincible cheerfulness (v. 41): when *they went out,* instead of being ashamed of Christ, *they rejoiced that they were counted worthy to suffer shame for his name.* They were men who had never done anything to make themselves despicable, and so they could not help feeling the shame that had been heaped on them, which was more hurtful to them than the pain, as it usually is to trusting hearts, but they considered that it was for the name of Christ that they had been so mistreated, and that their sufferings would be made to contribute to the further advancement of his name.

7.1.1. They reckoned it an honor *that they were counted worthy to suffer shame;* it could be translated, "they were honored to be dishonored for Christ." Suffering disgrace for Christ is true advancement.

7.1.2. They rejoiced in this, remembering what their Master had said to them when they first set out (Mt 5:11–12): *When men shall revile you, and persecute you, rejoice and be exceedingly glad.* They rejoiced not only though they suffered shame but also *that they suffered shame.* If we suffer wrong for doing good, provided we suffer it well, we should rejoice in the grace that enables us so to do.

7.2. They continued their work with indefatigable diligence (v. 42): they were commanded *not to preach,* and yet *they ceased not to teach and preach.* Notice:

7.2.1. When they preached—every day; every day, as regularly as the day came.

7.2.2. Where they preached—both publicly *in the temple* and privately *in every house.* Although in the temple they were under the eye of their enemies, they did not confine themselves to their own houses, but dared to venture into dangerous places, and although they had the freedom of the temple, they had no scruples against preaching in houses, in every house, even the most humble cottage.

7.2.3. The subject matter of their preaching: *They preached Jesus Christ.* They did not preach themselves, but Christ. This was the preaching that caused most offense to the priests, but they would not change what they preached about simply to please the priests. It should be the constant business of Gospel ministers to preach Christ: *Christ, and him crucified* (1Co 2:2); Christ, and him glorified (2Th 1:12).

CHAPTER 6

We have here: 1. The discontent among the disciples about the distribution of relief funds (v. 1). 2. The election and ordination of seven men to take care of that matter (vv. 2–6). 3. The increase of the church (v. 7). 4. A particular account of Stephen: 4.1. His great activity for Christ (v. 8). 4.2. The opposition he encountered from the enemies of Christianity (vv. 9–10). 4.3. His being brought before the great Sanhedrin (vv. 11–14). 4.4. God's acknowledging him in his trial (v. 15).

Verses 1–7

Having seen the church's struggles with her enemies and triumphed in her victories, we now come to consider the administration of her affairs at home, and we have here:

1. A sad disagreement among some of the church members, which was wisely dealt with in time (v. 1):

When the number of the disciples was multiplied, there arose a murmuring.

1.1. It does our hearts good to find *that the number of the disciples was multiplied*; the priests and Sadducees, on the other hand, were no doubt troubled to see it. The opposition that the preaching of the Gospel met with contributed to its success. The preachers were beaten, threatened, and mistreated, but the people accepted their message and were encouraged to join them by the disciples' wonderful patience and cheerfulness in their trials.

1.2. However, it grieves us to find that the multiplying of the disciples proved to be an occasion of discord. Now that they had multiplied, they began to complain: *There arose a murmuring*, not an open falling out, but a hidden grumbling.

1.2.1. The ones making the complaints were *the Grecians* — the Jews who were scattered in Greece and other parts, many of whom accepted the faith of Christ at the festival in Jerusalem. These Grecian Jews complained *against the Hebrews*, the Hebraic Jews, the native Jews. Some of each of these groups became Christians, and their joint acceptance of the faith of Christ did not effectively extinguish the little jealousies they had of one another before their conversion. All alike are welcome to Christ, and for his sake they should be dear to one another.

1.2.2. The complaint of these Grecian Jews was *that their widows were neglected in the daily administration.* The first contention in the Christian church was about a financial matter. A great deal of money was gathered for the relief of the poor, but, as often happens in such cases, it was impossible to please everyone with the way in which it was distributed. The apostles no doubt intended to do it with the greatest impartiality, and yet here they were complained to — and tacitly complained about — *that the Grecian widows were neglected.* Now:

1.2.2.1. Perhaps this complaint was unjust and without basis, but those who are in any way disadvantaged — as the Grecian Jews were, in comparison with those who were the Hebrews of the Hebrews — tend to be jealous and feel ill treated when really they have not been. It is also a common fault of poor people that instead of being thankful for what they have been given, they tend to complain noisily that they have not been given more. Jealousy and greed may be found among the poor as well as the rich.

1.2.2.2. But let us suppose there was some cause for the Grecian Jews' complaint. Just as those entrusted with the administration of public justice should especially protect widows from wrong, so those entrusted with the administration of financial distribution should especially provide widows with what is necessary. In the best-ordered church in the world there will still be something wrong, some grievances, or at least some complaints; yet the best churches have the least and the fewest.

2. The satisfactory settlement of this matter. Up to that time, the matter had been managed by the apostles. Now, to manage the matter properly, some people must be chosen who had more time to deal with it than the apostles had. Notice

2.1. How the apostles proposed to deal with the matter: they *called the multitude of the disciples unto them.* The Twelve themselves would not decide anything without them. Those who were more familiar with the affairs of this life than the apostles were would be best able to advise.

2.1.1. The apostles could by no means accept such a great diversion from their great work (v. 2): *It is not reasonable that we should leave the word of God and serve*

tables. This was foreign to the business the apostles were called to. They were to preach the word of God. Although they did not need to prepare by studying as much as we do, they still thought preaching was work enough for their whole being. If they served tables, they must to some extent leave the word of God. They would no more be drawn from their preaching by the money laid at their feet than they would be driven away from it by the lashes struck on their backs. Preaching the Gospel is the best work a minister can be employed in. Ministers must not get involved in civilian affairs, not even in the outward business of the house of God (Ne 11:16).

2.1.2. They therefore wanted *seven men* to be chosen whose work it would be *to serve tables* (v. 2). The business must be dealt with, and it must be dealt with better than it had been, better than the apostles could deal with it, and so proper people must be chosen. These men would not be so completely devoted to the word and prayer as the apostles were, and so they would be able to attend to all those things that were necessary for the spiritual disciplines, so that everything would be done decently and in order (1Co 14:40), and no person or thing neglected.

2.1.2.1. The persons chosen must be properly qualified. The people were to choose, and the apostles to ordain: *Look out seven men.* These must be:

2.1.2.1.*1. Of honest report* (of good reputation), free from scandal, men who were looked on by their neighbors as men of integrity, who could be trusted, well spoken of in regard to everything that is virtuous.

2.1.2.1.*2. Full of the Holy Spirit.* They must be not only honorable but also able and courageous, hereby being seen to be *full of the Holy Spirit.*

2.1.2.1.*3. Full of wisdom.* It was not enough for them to be honest and good; they must also be discreet and judicious, those who could not be deceived. They must be *full of the Holy Spirit and wisdom*, that is, of the Holy Spirit as a Spirit of wisdom. Those who are entrusted with public money must be full of wisdom, so that it may be disposed of not only with faithfulness but also with frugality.

2.1.2.2. The people must nominate the persons: *Look you out among yourselves seven men.* The people could be presumed to know better than the apostles, or at least were more suitable to ask, what character the men among them had.

2.1.2.3. The apostles would ordain them to the service; they would be *men whom we*, the apostles, *may appoint over this business*, to take responsibility for it and see that there is neither waste nor want.

2.1.3. The apostles committed themselves to be wholly devoted to their work as ministers, if only they could be relieved of this problematic role (v. 4): *We will give ourselves continually to prayer, and to the ministry of the word.* Notice here:

2.1.3.1. What the two great Gospel ordinances are — the *word and prayer.* By these two means the kingdom of Christ must be advanced, and additions made to it.

2.1.3.2. What the great work of Gospel ministers is — to give themselves continually to prayer and the ministry of the word. They must be God's mouthpiece to the people in the ministry of the word, and the people's mouthpiece to God in prayer. In order to convict and convert sinners, and build up and encourage the saints, we must not only offer our prayers for them but also minister the word to them. Nor must we only minister the word to them; we must also pray for them. God's grace can do everything without our preaching, but our preaching can do nothing without God's grace. Those ministers who commit themselves continually to prayer and the ministry of the word are without doubt the successors of the apostles, in that they are doing the best and most excellent of the apostolic works.

2.2. How this proposal was agreed to by the disciples. It was not imposed, but proposed. *The saying pleased the whole multitude* (v. 5).

2.2.1. They chose the persons. The majority of votes fell on the people named here, and the rest of the candidates and the electors accepted. An apostle was chosen by lot (1:26; Pr 16:33), but the overseers of the poor were chosen by the vote of the people, which is still to be regarded as the providence of God. We have a list of the people chosen. We may presume, concerning these seven:

2.2.1.1. That they were those who had sold their possessions and land and brought the money into the common fund. Those who had been most generous in contributing to the fund were the most suitable to be entrusted with its distribution.

2.2.1.2. That these seven all came from the Grecian Jews, because all had Greek names, and this would be most likely to silence *the murmurings of the Grecians.* Nicolas clearly was one of them, for he was *a proselyte of Antioch* (v. 5).

2.2.1.2.1. The first to be named is Stephen, *a man full of faith and of the Holy Spirit;* he was full of faithfulness and full of courage, according to some, because he was full of the Holy Spirit, of his gifts and graces. He was an extraordinary man and excelled in everything good; his name means "a crown."

2.2.1.2.2. Philip comes next. He was later ordained to the office of evangelist, and as such became a companion and assistant to the apostles, because he is expressly called that later in Acts (21:8). His preaching and baptizing, which we read about in 8:12, were certainly not done by him as a deacon, but as an evangelist.

2.2.1.2.3. The last to be named is Nicolas, who some say later went astray — like a Judas among these seven — and was the founder of *the sect of the Nicolaitans,* which we read about in Rev 2:6, 15 and which Christ said there, again and again, was something he hated. However, some of the old commentators clear Nicolas of this charge, telling us that although that vile, impure sect named themselves after him, they had done so unjustly, and that, merely because he insisted very much *that those that had wives should be as though they had none* (1Co 7:29), they corruptly concluded that those who had wives should have them in common; Tertullian, when he speaks about the community of goods, therefore particularly excludes this practice: "All things are in common among us, except our wives" (*Apology,* ch. 39).

2.2.2. The apostles appointed them to do this work of serving at tables for the present (v. 6). They prayed with them and for them. All who are employed in serving the church should be committed to the guidance of divine grace by the prayers of the church. *They laid their hands on them.* Having through prayer sought a blessing on them, by laying on hands they assured them that the blessing was given in answer to prayer, and in this way they gave them authority to fulfill that office.

3. The advancement of the church. When things were put into such good order in the church, then religion gained ground (v. 7).

3.1. *The word of God increased.* Now that the apostles had decided to stick more closely than ever to their preaching, it spread the Gospel further. Ministers who disentangle themselves from worldly employments, who devote themselves entirely to their work, will contribute very much, as a means, to the success of the Gospel.

3.2. Christians became numerous: *The number of the disciples multiplied in Jerusalem greatly.* When Christ was on earth, his ministry had least success in Jerusalem, but now that city yielded the most converts. God has his remnant even in the worst places.

3.3. *A great company of the priests were obedient to the faith.* The word and grace of God are greatly exalted when those who were least likely are persuaded by it. It seems they came as a group; in order to keep up one another's credibility and strengthen one another's hands, many of them agreed to join together in giving their names to Christ: *polis ochlos,* a "great crowd" of priests, by the grace of God, were helped to overcome their prejudices and *were obedient to the faith.*

3.3.1. They accepted the message of the Gospel; their understandings were captivated by the power of the truths of Christ.

3.3.2. They showed the sincerity of their belief in the Gospel of Christ by a cheerful submission to all the rules and commands of the Gospel.

Verses 8 – 15

Stephen, no doubt, was diligent and faithful in fulfilling his office. Because he was called to that office, he did not think it beneath him to do the duty that it entailed. Moreover, being faithful in a little, he was entrusted with more (Lk 19:17). We find him here called to very honorable services, and acknowledged in them.

1. He proved the truth of the Gospel by performing miracles in Christ's name (v. 8). He was *full of faith and power.* Those who are full of faith are also full of power, because through faith the power of God is committed for us. Through faith we are emptied of self and so are filled with Christ. Because Stephen was like this, *he did great wonders and miracles among the people,* openly and in the sight of everybody; Christ's miracles were not afraid of the strictest scrutiny.

2. He pleaded the cause of Christianity against those who opposed it (vv. 9 – 10); he served the interests of religious faith as a public debater, on the high places of the field, while others were serving them as vinedressers and gardeners.

2.1. We are told here who his opponents were (v. 9). They were Jews, but Grecian Jews. It was with difficulty that they retained the practice of their faith in the country where they lived, and they kept up their attendance at Jerusalem with great expense and toil, which made them more active sticklers for Judaism than those whose profession of their religion was relatively cheap and easy.

2.1.1. They were *of the synagogue which is called the synagogue of the Libertines* (Freedmen); the Romans gave the name *Liberti* or *Libertini* to those who either were foreigners by birth and were naturalized or had been slaves from birth and were released. Some think these Freedmen were some of the Jews who had obtained the Roman *freedom,* as Paul had (22:27 – 28).

2.1.2. Others were there who belonged to the synagogue of the Cyrenians and Alexandrians, and others came from Cilicia and Asia. The Jews who were born in other countries, and had interests in them, had frequent occasion also to reside in Jerusalem. Each nation had its synagogue, as in London there are, for example, French, Dutch, and Danish churches.

2.1.3. Now those who were in these synagogues, because they were confident of the goodness of their cause and their own ability to direct it, were determined to defeat Christianity by sheer force of argument. It was a fair and rational way of dealing with it, and one that religion is always ready to accept. But why did they dispute with Stephen? Why not with the apostles themselves?

2.1.3.1. Some think it was because they despised the apostles as *unlearned and ignorant men*, but Stephen had been brought up as a scholar, and they thought it honorable to fight with one who was an even match for them.

2.1.3.2. Others think it was because they stood in awe of the apostles.

2.1.3.3. Perhaps, the synagogue having issued a public challenge, Stephen was chosen by the disciples to be their champion. Stephen, who was only a deacon in the church, but a very sharp young man, of bright personal qualities, was appointed to this service.

2.1.3.4. Probably it was because he was zealous to argue with them and convince them, and this was the service to which God had called him.

2.2. We are told here how he won this dispute (v. 10): *They were not able to resist the wisdom and the Spirit by which he spoke.* They could neither support their own arguments nor answer his. Although they were not convinced, they were overcome. It is not said, "They were not able to resist him," but, "They were not able to resist the *wisdom and the Spirit by which he spoke.*" They thought they had only disputed with Stephen, but they were disputing with the Spirit of God in him, for whom they were an unequal match.

3. In the end, he sealed his testimony with his blood. When they could not answer his arguments as a debater, they prosecuted him as a criminal, secretly persuading witnesses to say they had heard him speak words of blasphemy. They secretly instigated some men and instructed them as to what to say, and then hired them to swear it. Notice:

3.1. How they enraged both the government and the mob against him (v. 12): *They stirred up the people* against him, so that if the Sanhedrin still thought fit to leave him alone, the synagogue might still be able to defeat him by a popular uprising. They also found means to stir up the elders and teachers of the law against him, so that if the people did support him, they, the synagogue, would win by the authority of their leaders. They did not doubt that they would win a victory, since they had two strings to their bow.

3.2. How they got him to the court: *They came upon him and caught him and brought him to the council.* They came on him together, flying on him as a lion attacks its prey.

3.3. How they were ready with evidence against him. They had *heard him speak blasphemous words against Moses and against God* (v. 11): against this *holy place and the law* (v. 13), because they heard him say what Jesus would do to their place and their customs (v. 14). Those who swore it against him are called *false witnesses*, because although there was some element of truth in their testimony, they interpreted what he had said wrongly and maliciously and perverted it to suit their own purposes. Notice:

3.3.1. What the general charge directed against him was—that he *spoke blasphemous words*, and, to make matters worse, "He *ceases not to speak blasphemous words.*" The statement also suggests some rebellious stubbornness and contempt of admonition. "He has been warned against it, but he still carries on talking like this." Stephen's persecutors wanted it thought that they had a deep concern for the honor of God's name and were persecuting him out of protective jealousy for that. He was said to have spoken blasphemous words *against Moses and against God.* But did Stephen blaspheme against

Moses? By no means; neither Christ nor the preachers of his Gospel ever said anything that looked like blasphemy against Moses. It was very unjust, therefore, that Stephen was accused of this.

3.3.2. How this charge was supported. All they could accuse him of was speaking *blasphemous words against this holy place and the law.* This was how the charges dwindled when it came to the actual evidence.

3.3.2.1. He was charged with speaking against *this holy place.* Christ was condemned as a blasphemer for words that he was alleged to have uttered against the temple, which they claimed to honor, even though by their evil they had defiled it.

3.3.2.2. He was charged with speaking against *the law.* The charges dwindled again, because all they could accuse him of was that they had heard him say that *this Jesus of Nazareth shall destroy this place, and change the customs which Moses delivered to us.* He could not be accused of having said anything disparaging about either the temple or the law. But, they alleged:

3.3.2.2.1. He had said, *Jesus of Nazareth shall destroy this place,* destroy the temple, destroy Jerusalem. Perhaps he did say so—and what blasphemy was it against the Holy Place to say that it would not last forever? Was Stephen a blasphemer, then, because he told them that Jesus of Nazareth would bring about a just destruction of their place and nation, and they would have only themselves to blame?

3.3.2.2.2. He had said, *This Jesus shall change the customs which Moses delivered to us.* Christ *came not to destroy* the law, *but to fulfill* it (Mt 5:17), and if he changed some customs, it was to introduce and establish those that were much better.

4. We are told here how God acknowledged him (v. 15): *All that sat in the council, looking stedfastly on him, saw his face as it had been the face of an angel.* It is usual for a judge to notice the prisoner's face, which sometimes shows either guilt or innocence. Stephen looked as if he had never been more pleased in his life than he was now, when he was likely to receive the crown of martyrdom. His face contained such an undisturbed peace, such undaunted courage, and such an inexplicable mixture of mildness and majesty that everyone said he looked like an angel. There was a miraculous splendor and brightness about his face, since God intended to honor his faithful witness and to overwhelm his persecutors and judges. *All that sat in the council saw it,* and it was a great shame that when they did, they did not call him from standing at the bar to sit in the chief seat on the bench. Wisdom and holiness make a person's face shine (Ecc 8:1), but they will not protect a person from the greatest indignities.

CHAPTER 7

In this chapter we have the martyrdom of Stephen. He was the first martyr of the Christian church, and so his sufferings and death are related in greater detail than those of any other. Here is: 1. His defense of himself before the council; the scope of his defense was to show that it was no blasphemy against God to say that the temple would be destroyed and the customs of the ceremonial law changed. 1.1. He showed this by going over the record of the Old Testament. The Holy Place and the law simply prefigured good things to come, and it was not belittling them at all to say that they must give way to better things (vv. 1–50). 1.2. He applied this to those who prosecuted him and sat in judgment on him (vv. 51–53). 2. His execution by stoning and his patient, cheerful, godly submission to it (vv. 54–60).

Verses 1–16

Stephen was now at the bar of the court before the Sanhedrin, accused of blasphemy. We had an account of what the witnesses swore against him in the previous chapter: that he spoke blasphemous words against Moses and God, because he spoke against this holy place and the law. Now here:

1. The high priest called on him to answer for himself (v. 1). "You hear what is sworn against you. *Are these things so? Guilty or not guilty?*"

2. He began his defense, and it was long.

2.1. In this speech he showed himself to be well read and knowledgeable about the Scriptures. He was *filled with the Holy Ghost*, not so that new things would be revealed to him, but so that the Spirit would bring to his memory the Scriptures of the Old Testament and teach him (Lk 12:12) how to apply them. Those who are full of the Holy Spirit will be full of Scripture, as Stephen was.

2.2. He quoted the Scriptures according to the *Septuagint* (a Greek version of the Old Testament), which shows he was one of the Grecian Jews. Notice:

2.2.1. His introduction: *Men, brethren, and fathers, hearken.* He gives them titles that, though not flattering, were civil and respectful. They were ready to look on him as an apostate from the Jewish church and therefore their enemy, but he addressed them as *men, brethren, and fathers*, determined to look at himself as one of them, even though they would not look on him in that way. He sought their attention: *Hearken* (Listen).

2.2.2. The beginning of the speech: it was all to the point, to show them that just as God had a church in the world many ages before that holy place was founded and the ceremonial law given, so he would have one when both had come to an end.

2.2.2.1. Stephen began with the call of Abraham, the father of the Old Testament church. His native country was an idolatrous country: Mesopotamia (v. 2), *the land of the Chaldeans* (v. 4); God brought him out of there. He first brought him out of the land of the Chaldeans to *Charran*, or Haran, and from there, five years later, when his father had died, he *removed him into* the land of *Canaan, wherein you now dwell.*

2.2.2.1.1. We may notice from this call of Abraham:

2.2.2.1.1.1. We must acknowledge God in all our ways (Pr 3:6), paying attention to the directions of his providence. *God removed* (sent) *him into this land wherein you now dwell*, and Abraham simply followed his Leader.

2.2.2.1.1.2. Those whom God takes into covenant with himself must not cling to the things of this world; they must live above it and everything in it, even what is dearest to them in it. God's chosen ones must follow him with an implicit faith and obedience.

2.2.2.1.2. Let us see how this applies to Stephen's case.

2.2.2.1.2.1. The people of the synagogue had accused him of blaspheming against God; he showed, therefore, that he was a true son of Abraham, who prided himself on being able to say, *Our father Abraham*, and that he was a faithful worshiper of the God of Abraham, whom he therefore called here *the God of glory*.

2.2.2.1.2.2. They were proud of being circumcised, and so he showed that Abraham was taken under God's guidance and into fellowship with him before he was circumcised.

2.2.2.1.2.3. They were very jealous for *this holy place*, which may refer to the whole land of Canaan. "Now," Stephen said, "you need not be so proud of it, for you came

originally from *Ur of the Chaldees*, and you were not the first settlers in the Land of Promise. Think of the humbleness of your beginnings, and how you are completely indebted to divine grace, and then you will see that any boasting is forever excluded (Ro 3:27). God appeared in his glory to Abraham far away in Mesopotamia, before he came near Canaan, and so you must not think God's visits are confined to this land."

2.2.2.2. He proceeded to the unsettled state of Abraham and his descendants for many years after he was called out of Ur of the Chaldeans. God did indeed promise that he would *give the land of Canaan to him for a possession, and to his seed after him* (v. 5). But:

2.2.2.2.1. *As yet he had no child*, nor did he have any by Sarah for many years afterward.

2.2.2.2.2. He himself was only a stranger and a sojourner in that land, and God *gave him no inheritance in it, no, not so much as to set his foot on*; he was there as a foreigner.

2.2.2.2.3. His descendants did not come into possession of the land for a long time: "*After four hundred years* they will come *and serve me in this place*, but not till then" (v. 7).

2.2.2.2.4. They would have to experience a great deal of hardship before they would be given possession of that land: they would be brought into slavery and mistreated in a strange land. *At the end of four hundred years that nation to whom they shall be in bondage will I judge, saith God.* Now this teaches us:

2.2.2.2.4.1. That *known unto God are all his works* beforehand (15:18). When Abraham had neither inheritance nor heir, he was told he would have both.

2.2.2.2.4.2. That although God's promises are slow, they are certain. They will be fulfilled, though perhaps not as soon as we expect.

2.2.2.2.4.3. That although the people of God may be in distress and trouble for a time, God will eventually rescue them and judge those who have oppressed them. But let us consider how this served Stephen's purpose.

2.2.2.2.4.3.1. The Jewish nation was very insignificant in its beginning; just as their common father, Abraham, was taken out of obscurity in Ur of the Chaldeans, so also their tribes were taken out of slavery in Egypt. The One who brought them out of Egypt could bring them back into it, but he would lose nothing in doing so, since he can raise up children for Abraham out of stones (Mt 3:9).

2.2.2.2.4.3.2. The slow steps by which the promise made to Abraham progressed toward its fulfillment clearly show that it had a spiritual meaning, and that the land principally intended to be conveyed by that promise was the *better country, that is, the heavenly* (Heb 11:9–10, 16). It was not blasphemous, therefore, to say, *Jesus shall destroy this place* (6:14), when at the same time we say, "He will lead us to the heavenly Canaan."

2.2.2.3. He related the building up of Abraham's family.

2.2.2.3.1. God committed himself to be a God to Abraham and his descendants, and as a sign of this, he appointed that Abraham and his male descendants must be circumcised (Ge 17:9–10). He *gave him the covenant of circumcision*. When Abraham had a son, therefore, he *circumcised him the eighth day* (v. 8). Then his descendants began to multiply: *Isaac begat Jacob, and Jacob the twelve patriarchs.*

2.2.2.3.2. Joseph, the favorite and blessing of his father's house, was mistreated by his brothers; they envied him because of his dreams and *sold him into Egypt.*

2.2.2.3.3. God acknowledged Joseph in his troubles and was with him by the influence of his Spirit, both on his heart, giving him assurance, and on the hearts of those he had to deal with, giving him favor in their eyes. So finally he *delivered him out of his afflictions.*

2.2.2.3.4. Jacob was compelled to go to Egypt by a famine so great that *our fathers found no sustenance* in Canaan (v. 11). When they heard there was *corn* (grain) *in Egypt*—treasured up by the wisdom of Jacob's own son—he *sent out our fathers first* to fetch grain (v. 12). The second time they went, Joseph made himself known to them, and Pharaoh was told they were Joseph's family (v. 13). Then *Joseph sent for his father Jacob to him into Egypt,* with *all his kindred and family, to* the number of *seventy-five souls* (v. 14).

2.2.2.3.5. Jacob and his sons died in Egypt (v. 15) but were taken to be buried in Canaan (v. 16). Let us now see how this served Stephen's purpose.

2.2.2.3.5.1. He continued to remind the court of the humble beginnings of the Jewish nation. It was by a miracle of mercy that the Jews had been raised up out of nothing to what they then were. If they did not fulfill the intentions of their being raised up in this way, they could expect nothing else than to be destroyed. The prophets had frequently reminded them that they had been brought out of Egypt, to emphasize their contempt for the law of God. Here it was urged on them as emphasizing their contempt for the Gospel of Christ.

2.2.2.3.5.2. He also reminded them how evil they had been in their jealousy of their brother Joseph, selling him into Egypt; and the same spirit was still working in them toward Christ.

2.2.2.3.5.3. Their ancestors were kept for a long time from possessing their Holy Land, which the Jews were now so devoted to; let them not, therefore, think it strange if, having been defiled with sin for so long, it was finally destroyed.

Verses 17–29

Stephen here went on to relate:

1. The wonderful increase of the people of Israel in Egypt; it was by a great miracle of Providence that in a short time they advanced from being a family to become a nation.

1.1. It was *when the time of the promise drew nigh*—the time when they were to be formed into a people. The movement of Providence is sometimes at its quickest when it comes closest to the center. God knows how to redeem the time that seems to have been lost, and *when the year of the redeemed is* at hand (Isa 63:4), he can do a double work in a single day.

1.2. It was in Egypt, where they were oppressed. Times of suffering have often been times of growth for the church.

2. The extreme hardship they experienced there (vv. 18–19). Stephen commented on three things:

2.1. The Egyptians' corrupt ingratitude: the Israelites were oppressed by *another king that knew not Joseph.* Those who wrong good people are very ungrateful, because good people are the blessings of the age and place they live in.

2.2. Their diabolical treachery: *They dealt subtly with our kindred. Come on,* they said, *let us deal wisely* (Ex 1:10), thinking they would protect themselves. People are greatly mistaken if they think they deal wisely for themselves when they deal deceitfully or unmercifully with their brothers and sisters.

2.3. Their barbaric cruelty. *They cast out* the Israelites' *young children, to the end they might not live.* What the Jews were now doing against the Christian church in its infancy was as ungodly, and would be as fruitless, as what the Egyptians did against the Jewish church in its infancy. "In spite of your malice, Christ's disciples will increase and multiply."

3. The raising up of Moses to be their deliverer.

3.1. Moses was born when the persecution of Israel was at its most intense: *At that time, Moses was born* (v. 20), and he himself was in danger of falling as a sacrifice to that bloody decree. When the way of God's people is darkest, and their distress deepest, God is preparing for their rescue.

3.2. He *was exceedingly fair.* He was sanctified from the womb (Jdg 13:5, 7; Lk 1:15), and this made him beautiful in God's eyes.

3.3. He was wonderfully preserved in his infancy, first by the care of his tender parents, who *nourished him three months in their own house,* and then by a favorable providence that set him *into the arms of Pharaoh's daughter, who took him up, and nourished him as her own son* (v. 21). Those whom God intends to make special use of he will take special care of.

3.4. He became a great scholar (v. 22): *He was learned in all the wisdom of the Egyptians.*

3.5. He became a prime minister in Egypt and was *mighty in words and deeds.* Although he did not have a ready way of expressing himself, but stammered, he still spoke admirably good sense, and everything he said commanded approval. Now, from all this, Stephen would show that he had as high and honorable thoughts of Moses as his accusers and judges had.

4. The attempts Moses made to save Israel, which they spurned. Stephen insisted very much on this, and it serves as a key to this story, introducing the public service Moses would be called to (v. 23). *When he was full forty years old, it came into his heart*—God put it there—*to visit his brethren the children of Israel* and see how he could help them. He showed himself:

4.1. As Israel's savior. He gave an example of how he would save them when he avenged an oppressed Israelite, killing the Egyptian who mistreated him (v. 24). *Seeing one of his brethren suffer wrong, he avenged him that was oppressed, and smote* (killed) *the Egyptian. He supposed that his brethren would have understood that God by his hand would deliver them.* If they had only understood the signs of the times, they might have taken this as the dawning of the day of their rescue, but *they understood not.*

4.2. As Israel's judge. He gave an example of this the very next day, when he offered to settle matters between two Hebrews who were fighting (v. 26): *He showed himself to them as they strove,* and *he would have set them at one again, saying, Sirs, you are brethren; why do you wrong one to another?* He had noticed that, as in most conflicts, there were faults on both sides, and so there must be a mutual forgiveness and deference. However, the contending Israelite who was most in *the wrong thrust him away* (v. 27); he would not bear the rebuke, but was ready to fly in his face with, *Who made thee a ruler and a judge over us?* Proud and contentious spirits are impatient with those who try to restrain or control them. The wrongdoer was so enraged at the rebuke that he reprimanded Moses for the service he had done to their nation by killing the Egyptian: *Wilt thou kill me as thou didst the Egyptian yesterday?* (v. 28). Thus he charged Moses with a crime for what was really the hanging out of the flag of defiance to the Egyptians and the raising of the banner of love and rescue to Israel. Then *Moses fled into the land of Midian*. He settled as a stranger in Midian, married, and had two sons by Jethro's daughter (v. 29). Notice how this served Stephen's purpose.

4.2.1. They had accused him of blaspheming against Moses, and in answer to this he told them about the indignities their fathers did to Moses, which they should be ashamed of, instead of picking quarrels with one who had as great a respect for him as any of them had.

4.2.2. They persecuted him for disputing in defense of Christ and his Gospel. They set up Moses and his law: "But," Stephen said, "you had better watch out:

4.2.2.1. "In case you refuse and reject one *whom God has raised up to be to you a prince and a Saviour* (5:31). Through this Jesus, God will rescue you from a worse form of slavery than that in Egypt. Make sure you do not thrust him away.

4.2.2.2. "In case you suffer as your fathers suffered. You put away the Gospel from you, and it will be sent to the Gentiles; you will not accept Christ, and so you will not have him."

Verses 30–41

Stephen here continued his account of the life of Moses. Here is:

1. The vision Moses saw of the glory of God at the burning bush (v. 30): *When forty years had expired*, now, at eighty years old, he entered into that honorable position to which he was born. Notice:

1.1. Where God appeared to him: *in the wilderness of Mount Sinai* (v. 30). When he appeared to him there, that was holy ground (v. 33), which Stephen noted as a restraint to those who prided themselves on the temple, as if there were no fellowship to be had with God except there. They were deceiving themselves if they thought God was confined to any one place; he can bring his people into a desert, and even there he can speak words of assurance to them.

1.2. How he appeared to him: *in a flame of fire in a bush*; but *the bush was not consumed*.

1.3. How Moses was affected by this:

1.3.1. *He wondered at the sight* (v. 31). At first he had the curiosity to look into it: *I will turn aside now, and see this great sight*; but the closer he came, the more he was struck with amazement.

1.3.2. *He trembled, and durst* (dared) *not behold*, because he was soon aware that it was *the angel of the Lord*. This made him tremble.

2. The declaration he heard of the covenant of God (v. 32): *The voice of the Lord came to him. I am the God of thy fathers, the God of Abraham, the God of Isaac, and the God of Jacob*, and so:

2.1. "I am the same that I was." The covenant God made with Abraham was, *I will be to thee a God* (Ge 17:7). "Now," God said, "that covenant is still in full force; I am, as I was, the God of Abraham." All the favors and all the honors God showed Israel were founded on this covenant with Abraham.

2.2. "I will be the same that I am." He would be a God:

2.2.1. To the souls of these patriarchs, which were now separated from their bodies. Our Savior proved the future state by this (Mt 22:31–32). Abraham is dead, but God is still his God, and so Abraham is still alive. Now this is the life and immortality that are brought to light by the Gospel (2Ti 1:10). Those, therefore, who stood up in defense of the Gospel were so far from blaspheming

against Moses that they in fact gave the greatest possible honor to Moses.

2.2.2. To their descendants. In declaring himself to be the God of their ancestors, God showed his kindness to their descendants, that they would be *beloved for the fathers' sakes* (Ro 11:28; Dt 7:8). Now the preachers of the Gospel preached this covenant, *the promise made of God unto the fathers* (26:6–7). Would they, Stephen's accusers and judges, claiming to support the Holy Place and the law, oppose the covenant that was made with Abraham before the law was given and long before the Holy Place was built? God wants our salvation to be by promise, not by the law; therefore the Jews who persecuted the Christians, claiming that the Christians blasphemed against the law, in fact blasphemed against the promise themselves.

3. The commission God gave him to rescue Israel from Egypt. When God had declared himself to be the God of Abraham, he proceeded:

3.1. To order Moses into a reverent posture: *"Put off thy shoes from thy feet*. Do not be hasty and rash when you come into God's presence; tread softly."

3.2. To order Moses into a very eminent service. He was commissioned to demand permission from Pharaoh for Israel to leave his land (v. 34). We have here:

3.2.1. The notice God took of both their sufferings and their sense of their sufferings: *I have seen, I have seen their affliction, and have heard their groaning*. Their rescue arose from his pity.

3.2.2. His determination to redeem them by the hand of Moses: *I am come down to deliver them*, and Moses was the one who must be employed. *Come, and I will send thee into Egypt*, and if God sent him, he would give him success.

4. His acting in pursuit of this commission.

4.1. God honored the one whom the Israelites showed contempt to (v. 35): *This Moses whom they refused, saying, Who made thee a ruler and a judge? did God send to be a ruler and a deliverer, by the hand of the angel which appeared to him in the bush*. Now, by this example, Stephen wanted to show the council that this Jesus whom they now rejected, *saying, Who gave thee this authority?* had been advanced by God *to be a prince and a Saviour*, just as the apostles had told them a while before (5:30–31) *that the stone which the builders refused was become the headstone in the corner* (4:11).

4.2. God showed favor to them through him. God could justly have refused them Moses' service, but it was all forgotten (v. 36). *He brought them out after he had shown wonders and signs in the land of Egypt, in the Red Sea and in the wilderness forty years*. Far from blaspheming against Moses, Stephen admired him as a glorious instrument in the hand of God. It did not detract in any way from Moses' just honor to say that he was merely an instrument and that he was outshone by this Jesus, whom he encouraged these Jews to accept. The people of Israel were rescued by Moses even though they had once refused him.

5. His prophecy of Christ and his grace (v. 37). Moses spoke of Christ (v. 37): *This is that Moses who said unto the children of Israel, A prophet shall the Lord your God raise up unto you of your brethren*. Stephen here spoke of this as one of the greatest honors God showed Moses, that through him he announced to the children of Israel the coming of the great prophet into the world. In asserting that Jesus would change the customs of the ceremonial law, Stephen was so far from blaspheming against Moses that he really showed him the greatest possible honor.

Christ himself told them, *If they had believed Moses, they would have believed me* (Jn 5:46).

5.1. Moses told them that a prophet would be raised up among them, one of their own nation, who would therefore have authority to change the customs that Moses had delivered and to bring in a better hope, since he would be *the Mediator of a better testament* (Heb 7:22).

5.2. He commanded them to listen to that prophet. "This will be the greatest honor you can do to Moses and to his law, since Moses said, *Hear you him*."

6. The very important services Moses continued to do for the people of Israel after he had been instrumental in bringing them out of Egypt (v. 38). It was the honor of Moses:

6.1. That *he was in the church in the wilderness*; he presided in all the affairs of that assembly for forty years. It would have been destroyed many times if Moses had not been in it to intercede for it. But Christ is the president and guide of a more excellent and glorious church, and is in it more, as its life and soul, than Moses could be in that earlier church.

6.2. That *he was with the angel that spoke to him in the mount Sinai, and with our fathers. Moses was in the church in the wilderness*, but it was *with the angel that spoke to him in mount Sinai*. That angel was his guide, for otherwise Moses could not have been a guide to Israel. Christ, on the other hand, is himself the angel—Michael, our prince (1Co 10:4; see also commentary on Rev 12:1–11, 3.2.)—and so has authority above Moses.

6.3. That *he received the lively oracles to give unto them*, not only the Ten Commandments but also other instructions *the Lord spoke unto Moses*.

6.3.1. The words of God are *oracles*, certain and infallible, and all disputes must be settled by them.

6.3.2. They are *lively oracles*. The word that God speaks is spirit and life; the Law of Moses could not give life, but it showed the way to life.

6.3.3. Moses received them from God, and he delivered nothing except what he had first received from God (1Co 11:23).

6.3.4. He faithfully communicated to the people the living words he received from God. The One who gave them those customs through his servant Moses could change the customs through his Son Jesus, who received more living words to give to us than Moses did.

7. The contempt that was shown him by the people. Those who accused Stephen of speaking against Moses followed in their ancestors' steps.

7.1. *They would not obey him, but thrust* (rejected) *him from them* (v. 39). *In their hearts they turned back again into Egypt*, preferring their garlic and onions there (Nu 11:5) to the manna they had under Moses' leadership, or to the milk and honey they hoped for in Canaan (Ex 3:8, 17). Many people who pretend to be going forward toward Canaan are at the same time turning back in their hearts to Egypt. Now, if the customs that Moses passed on to them would not change them, it is hardly surprising that Christ came to change the customs.

7.2. *They made a golden calf*, which was also a great indignity to Moses, for they made the calf because, *as for this Moses, who brought us out of the land of Egypt, we know not what is become of him*—as if a calf would have been enough to make up for the lack of Moses, as if that idol would be as capable of going before them into the Promised Land. *So they made a calf in those days, and offered sacrifices unto the idol, and rejoiced in the work of their own hands* (v. 41). All this shows there was a great deal that the law could not do. It was necessary, there-

fore, for this law to be perfected by a better hand, and the one who said that Christ had done it was no blasphemer against Moses.

Verses 42–50

We have two things in these verses:

1. Stephen rebuked them for the idolatry of their ancestors, which God gave them over to because they had worshiped the golden calf. This was the saddest punishment of all for that sin, *that God gave them up to a reprobate mind* (Ro 1:28) (v. 42): *Then God turned, and gave them up to worship the host of heaven* (the heavenly bodies). For this, Stephen quoted a passage from Am 5:25–27, because it would be less invidious to tell them their own character and condemnation from an Old Testament prophet, who rebuked them:

1.1. For not sacrificing to their own God in the desert (v. 42): *Have you offered to me slain beasts, and sacrifices, by the space of forty years in the wilderness?* No, during all that time sacrifices to God had been suspended; they did not even keep the Passover after the second year. This rebuke was also a restraint on the Jews' zeal for the customs that Moses passed on to them and their fear of having them changed by this Jesus—immediately after they were rescued, they left these customs unused for forty years, considering them unnecessary.

1.2. For sacrificing to other gods after they came to Canaan (v. 43): *You took up the tabernacle of Moloch*. Molech was the idol of the children of Ammon, to which they barbarically offered their own children in sacrifice. However, the Israelites arrived at this unnatural idolatry when *God gave them up to worship the host of heaven*. "*Yea, you took up the tabernacle of Moloch*; you submitted even to that, and to the worship of *the star of your god Remphan* (Rephan)." Some think *Remphan* referred to Saturn, since that planet is called *Remphan* in Aramaic. The Septuagint (a Greek version of the Old Testament) substitutes *Remphan* for *Chiun*. They had idols representing this *star of their god* (Am 5:26)—like the *silver shrines for Diana* (Ac 19:24)—and these idols are here called *the figures which they made to worship*. A poor thing to make an idol of, but better than a golden calf! Now God's threat against them for this idolatry was, *I will carry you away beyond Babylon*. Let it not seem strange to Stephen's accusers and judges, therefore, to hear about the destruction of this place, because they had heard about it many times from the Old Testament prophets.

2. He specifically answered the charge concerning the temple, *that he spoke blasphemous words against that holy place* (vv. 44–50). He was accused of saying that Jesus would destroy this Holy Place: "And what if I did say so?" Stephen said. "The glory of the holy God can be preserved untouched even if the glory of this place is laid in the dust," because:

2.1. "It was not until our ancestors came into the desert that they had any fixed place of worship. The One who was worshiped without a Holy Place in the first, best, and purest ages of the Old Testament church can and will still be worshiped when this Holy Place is destroyed.

2.2. "The Holy Place was at first only a tabernacle, humble and movable, not intended to last forever. Why cannot this Holy Place, like that one, be decently brought to its end?

2.3. "That tabernacle was *a tabernacle of witness* (Nu 17:7), or of Testimony. The glory of both the tabernacle and temple was that they were built as a testimony.

2.4. "That tabernacle was formed *according to the fashion which Moses saw in the mount* (v. 44). It referred to good things to come." That is why it was no lessening at all of its glory to say that this temple made with hands would be destroyed so that *another made without hands* might be built.

2.5. "That tabernacle was first pitched in the desert; it was not indigenous to this land of yours, but was brought in by our ancestors; it was *brought into the possession of the Gentiles, whom God drove out before the face of our fathers* (v. 45)." And why should God not set up his spiritual temple in those countries that were now the possession of the Gentiles? That first tabernacle had been brought in by those who came *with Jesus*, that is, Joshua. So the New Testament Joshua would bring the true tabernacle *into the possession of the Gentiles.*

2.6. "That tabernacle continued *even to the days of David* before there was any thought of building a temple (v. 45). Then David, having *found favour before God*, did indeed desire the further favor of being allowed to build God a constant, settled tabernacle, or dwelling place. Those who have found favor with God should be eager to advance the interests of his kingdom on earth.

2.7. "God had his heart set so little on a temple that when David wanted to build one, he was forbidden to do so; God was in no hurry to have one. It was not David, but his son Solomon, some years later, who built God a house.

2.8. "God often declared that temples made with human hands were not his delight." Solomon acknowledged that God *dwelleth not in temples made with hands* (v. 48). The whole world is his temple, in which he is present everywhere, and he fills it with his glory; what need does he have for a temple? The one true and living God needs no temple, because *the heaven is his throne*, in which he rests, *and the earth is his footstool*, over which he rules (vv. 49–50), and so, *"What house will you build me; what is the place of my rest?* What need do I have of a house, either to rest in or to show myself in? *Hath not my hand made all these things?"* Just as the world is God's temple in the sense that he reveals himself there, so it is also God's temple in the sense that it is where he chooses to be worshiped. Just as the earth is full of his glory, so the earth is, or will be, full of his praise, and it is his temple for this reason. It was no reflection at all on this Holy Place, therefore, to say *that Jesus would destroy this temple* and set up another one, into which all nations would be admitted (15:16–17).

Verses 51–53

From the train of thought evident in Stephen's speech, it seems he was aiming to show that just as the temple must come to an end, so must the temple service. But he noticed that they could not bear it. They would not even give him so much as a hearing. He broke off abruptly and, by the spirit of wisdom, courage, and power with which he was filled, sharply rebuked his persecutors. If they would not accept the testimony of the Gospel to them, it would become a testimony against them (Mk 6:11).

1. They, like their ancestors, were stubborn and willful and would not be persuaded by the various means God used to restore and reform them.

1.1. They were *stiff-necked* (v. 51), refusing to submit to the sweet and easy yoke of God's direction. They would not submit even to God himself, would not humble themselves before him.

1.2. They were *uncircumcised in heart and ears*. "In name and appearance you are circumcised Jews, but in your hearts and ears you remain uncircumcised pagans, paying no more respect to the authority of your God than they do (Jer 9:26)."

2. They, like their ancestors, were not only not influenced by the means God used to reform them; they were enraged against them: *You do always resist the Holy Spirit.*

2.1. They resisted the Holy Spirit speaking to them through the prophets. *Which of the prophets have not your fathers persecuted?* Their ancestors had resisted the Holy Spirit in the prophets, and they themselves, Stephen's accusers and judges, resisted the Holy Spirit in Christ's apostles and ministers.

2.2. They resisted the Holy Spirit striving with them in their own consciences. There is something in the sinful hearts of human beings that always resists the Holy Spirit, but in the hearts of God's chosen ones, this resistance is overcome, and after a struggle the throne of Christ is established in the soul. The grace that brings about this change, therefore, could more appropriately be called "victorious" grace than "irresistible."

3. They, like their ancestors, persecuted and killed those whom God sent to them.

3.1. Their ancestors had been the cruel and constant persecutors of the Old Testament prophets (v. 52): *Which of the prophets have not your fathers persecuted?* More or less, at one time or another, they had attacked them all. What made the sin of persecuting the prophets even worse was that the work of the prophets was to *show before of the coming of the just One*, to announce God's kind intention to send the Messiah among them. Those who were the messengers of such good news should have been treated very well and kindly, but instead they were treated as the worst evildoers.

3.2. They themselves, Stephen's accusers and judges, had been the *betrayers and murderers of the just One* himself, as Peter had told them (3:14–15; 5:30). They had hired Judas to betray him and had forced Pilate to condemn him; that was why they were charged with being his betrayers and murders. By killing him, they showed that they themselves would have killed those prophets if they had lived when they did, and this was how they brought on themselves the guilt of the blood of all the prophets. If they had no regard for the Son of God himself, which of the prophets would they have shown any respect for?

4. They, like their ancestors, showed contempt for divine revelation. Just as God had given their ancestors his law in vain, he had now given them, the descendants, his Gospel in vain.

4.1. Their ancestors received the law but paid no attention to it (v. 53). God wrote for them the great things of his law, but they regarded his law as strange or foreign. The law is said to have *been received by the disposition of angels*, because angels were employed in the sacred ceremony of giving the Law, in the thunder and lightning and with the sound of the trumpet (Ex 19:16; 20:18). However, those who received the law in this way did not keep it; by making the golden calf, they broke it immediately and terribly.

4.2. They, of the synagogue, received the Gospel now, which was put into effect not by angels, but by the Holy Spirit, but they did not accept it. They refused to submit to God in either his Law or his Gospel.

Verses 54–60

We have here the death of the first martyr of the Christian church. Here we see both the fire and darkness of hell and the light and brightness of heaven, and these serve as contrasts to each other. It is not said here that the votes of the council were taken on his case, that the majority found him guilty and then condemned him to be stoned to death, but probably he was not put to death merely by the violence of the people, without an order from the council, because we have here the usual ceremony of standard executions: he was dragged out of the city, and the hands of the witnesses were first to stone him.

1. See the strength of corruption in the persecutors of Stephen.

1.1. *When they heard these things, they were cut to the heart* (v. 54); the verb is similar to that used in Heb 11:37, where it is translated *they were sawn asunder.* Stephen's hearers were tortured in their minds as much as the martyrs were tortured in their bodies. They were not cut to the heart with sorrow, as were those about whom the same is said in 2:37, but cut to the heart with rage and fury, as they themselves had been earlier (5:33). Enmity toward God cuts the heart; faith and love heal the heart. They heard how the one who *looked like an angel* (6:15) before he began his speech talked like an angel before he concluded it, and, despairing of knowing how to overwhelm a cause that had been pleaded so bravely, they were nevertheless determined not to yield to it.

1.2. They *gnashed upon him with their teeth.* This shows:

1.2.1. Their great hatred and rage against him. They snarled at him, as dogs do at those they are enraged at. Enmity toward the saints turns people into wild beasts.

1.2.2. Their great vexation within themselves. They were furious to see in him such clear signs of a divine power. Gnashing the teeth is often used to express the horror and torments of the condemned in hell. Those who have the malice of hell must also have some of the pain of hell with it.

1.3. *They cried out with a loud voice* (v. 57). When he said, *I see heaven opened,* they cried out with a loud voice, so that his voice would not be heard. When a righteous cause is being advanced, it is very common for an attempt to be made to overwhelm it by noise and clamor; what is lacking in reason is made up for in uproar.

1.4. They *stopped* (covered) *their ears,* pretending they could not bear to listen to his blasphemies. These *stopped their ears* when Stephen said, *I now see the Son of man standing in glory.* Their covering their ears was a clear example of their willful stubbornness; they were determined they would not hear. It was also a fatal omen of the judicial hardness to which God would give them over. They covered their ears, and then God, by way of righteous judgment, covered them.

1.5. They *ran upon him with one accord;* they all rushed on him like wild animals attacking their victim. They rushed on him all together, hoping that would put him into confusion, envying him his composure and the assurance he had in his soul. They did all they could to disturb him.

1.6. They *cast* (dragged) *him out of the city, and stoned him,* claiming in this to be carrying out the Law of Moses (Lev 24:16): *He that blasphemeth the name of the Lord shall surely be put to death; all the congregation shall certainly stone him.* They dragged him out of the city; they treated him as the scum of all things (1Co 4:13). The witnesses against him were the leaders in the execution, in accordance with the law. This is how they confirmed their testimony. The witnesses took off their upper garments, *and they laid them down at a young man's feet, whose name was Saul.* It is the first time his name is mentioned; we will know it and love it better when we read of it being changed to Paul. This little example of his agency in Stephen's death he later reflected on with regret (22:20): *I kept the raiment* (clothes) *of those that slew* (killed) *him.*

2. Notice the power of grace in Stephen. Just as his persecutors were full of Satan, so he was *full of the Holy Spirit.* When he was chosen for public service, he was described as *full of the Holy Spirit* (6:5), and now that he was called to martyrdom, he still had the same character. Those who are full of the Holy Spirit are equipped for anything, either to act for Christ or to suffer for him. When the followers of Christ are for his sake *killed all the day long, and accounted as sheep for the slaughter* (Ps 44:22), does this separate them from the love of Christ? Do they love him any less? No, not at all (Ro 8:35–39)! This is shown by this account, in which we may notice:

2.1. Christ's gracious revelation of himself to Stephen. When his enemies were cut to the heart and gnashed their teeth at him, Stephen himself then had a view of the glory of Christ.

2.1.1. He, *being full of the Holy Spirit, looked up steadfastly into heaven* (v. 55).

2.1.1.1. He looked above the power and fury of his persecutors, despising them, as it were. They had their eyes fixed on him, full of hatred and cruelty, but he looked up to heaven, hardly noticing them. He looked up to heaven; it was only from there that his help would come (Ps 121:1–2), and his way was still open there. His persecutors could not interrupt his fellowship with heaven.

2.1.1.2. He directed his sufferings to the glory of God, appealing, as it were, to heaven for them. Now that he was ready to be offered, he looked up intently to heaven, as one willing to offer himself.

2.1.1.3. In lifting his eyes toward God in heaven, he lifted up his soul toward him too (Ps 25:1), calling on God for wisdom and grace to help him endure this trial. God has promised that he will be with his servants whom he calls to suffer for him, but he wants to be asked for such help.

2.1.1.4. He longed for the heavenly country (Heb 11:16), to which he saw that the fury of his persecutors would soon send him. It is good for dying saints to look up steadfastly to heaven: "And then, *O death! where is thy sting?* (1Co 15:55)."

2.1.1.5. He made it clear that he was full of the Holy Spirit. Those who are full of the Holy Spirit will look up intently to heaven, because that is where their hearts are. If we expect to hear from heaven, we must look up unwaveringly to heaven.

2.1.2. He saw the glory of God (v. 55), for he *saw the heavens opened* (v. 55). The heavens were opened to give him a view of the happiness he was going to, so that he would go cheerfully through death, such a great death (2Co 1:10). If we were to look by faith unwaveringly, we could see the heavens opened by the mediation of Christ. We may also see the glory of God in his word, and the sight of this will take us through all the terrors of sufferings and death.

2.1.3. He *saw Jesus standing on the right hand of God* (v. 55); that is, he saw *the Son of man,* as v. 56 makes clear. When the Old Testament prophets saw the glory of God, it was attended with angels. But here no mention is made of the angels. The glory of God shines most brightly in the face of Jesus Christ (2Co 4:6).

2.1.3.1. Here is a proof of the exaltation of Christ. Stephen saw Jesus at the right hand of God. Whatever God's right hand gives to us or receives from us or does for us, it is by Christ, because Christ is God's right hand.

2.1.3.2. Stephen saw him not sitting, as he is usually represented, but *standing* there. He stood ready to receive Stephen and crown him, and in the meantime he gave him a prospect of the joy before him (Heb 12:2).

2.1.3.3. This was intended to encourage Stephen. He saw that Christ was for him, and then it did not matter who was against him (Ro 8:31). When our Lord Jesus was in his anguish, an angel appeared to support him (Lk 22:43), but Stephen had Christ himself appearing to him. There is nothing so comforting or inspiring as to see Jesus at the right hand of God; we may see him there by faith.

2.1.4. He told those around him what he saw (v. 56): *Behold, I see the heavens opened.* He declared what he saw, and let them make whatever use of it they wished. If some were enraged by it, others might be persuaded to consider this Jesus and believe in him.

2.2. Stephen's godly addresses to Jesus Christ. *They stoned Stephen, calling upon God* (v. 59). Although Stephen called on God, they still proceeded to stone him; although they stoned him, he still called on God. It is the comfort of those who are unjustly hated and persecuted by human beings that they have a God to turn to. People cover their ears, as they did here (v. 57), but God does not. Stephen had now been dragged out of the city, but he was not rejected by his God. He was now taking leave of the world, and that was why he called on God. It is good to die praying. Stephen offered up two short prayers to God in his dying moments.

2.2.1. Here is a prayer for himself: *Lord Jesus, receive my spirit.* Similarly, Christ himself had given his spirit directly into the hands of the Father (Lk 23:46). We are taught here to give our spirit into the hands of Christ as Mediator. Notice:

2.2.1.1. The soul is the real person, and our great concern, living and dying, must be for our souls. "Lord," he said, "let my spirit be secure; let it go well with my poor soul."

2.2.1.2. Our Lord Jesus is God, whom we are to seek, and in whom we comfort ourselves in both living and dying. Stephen here prayed to Christ, and so must we; we dare not go into another world except under his conduct; there are no living comforts in dying moments except those that come from him.

2.2.1.3. Christ's receiving our spirits at death is the great thing we are to comfort ourselves with. Moreover, if this has been our concern while we live, it can be our comfort when we come to die.

2.2.2. Here is a prayer for his persecutors (v. 60).

2.2.2.1. The circumstances of this prayer are significant. He *knelt down*, which showed his humility in prayer. He *cried with a loud voice*, which expressed his boldness. In his prayer for his enemies—since that goes against the grain of corrupt nature so much—it was necessary for him to prove he was being serious.

2.2.2.2. The prayer itself was, *Lord, lay not this sin to their charge.* Here, he followed the example of his dying Master, and he has set an example to all later sufferers for the cause of Christ. Prayer may preach, and this prayer preached to those who stoned Stephen. He wanted them to learn:

2.2.2.2.1. That what they were doing was a great sin.

2.2.2.2.2. That despite their hatred and fury against him, he loved them. Let them take notice of this, and when their thoughts were calm, they would surely not forgive themselves easily for putting to death one who could so easily forgive them. Although the sin was detestable, they must not despair of receiving forgiveness for it when they repented. If they would take it to their hearts, God would not add it to their debt.

2.3. His dying with these words: *When he had said this, he fell asleep.* Death is simply a sleep to good people. Stephen's death was hurried as much as anyone's ever

was, but when he died, he fell asleep. He fell asleep when he was praying for his persecutors; it is expressed as if he thought he could not die in peace until he had done this. If he sleeps in this way, he will do well; he will wake up on the morning of the resurrection.

CHAPTER 8

It was strange, but true, that the more the disciples of Christ suffered, the more they multiplied. 1. Here we see the church suffering (vv. 1–3). 2. Here we see the church spreading. We have here: 2.1. The Gospel being brought to Samaria, preached there (vv. 4–5), and accepted there (vv. 6–8), even by Simon the sorcerer (vv. 9–13); we also see the gift of the Holy Spirit given to some of the believing Samaritans (vv. 14–17), and the severe rebuke given by Peter to Simon the sorcerer (vv. 18–25). 2.2. The Gospel sent to Ethiopia through the eunuch. He was returning home in his chariot from Jerusalem (vv. 26–28). Philip, being sent to him, preached Christ to him in his chariot (vv. 29–35), baptized him (vv. 36–38), and then left him (vv. 39–40).

Verses 1–3

In these verses we have:

1. Something more about Stephen and his death, how people were affected by it. Here is:

1.1. Stephen's death rejoiced in by one person in particular, and that was Saul, who was later called Paul; he was *consenting to his death.* We have reason to think that Paul ordered Luke to insert this, to bring shame on himself and give glory to free grace.

1.2. Stephen's death mourned by others (v. 2)—*devout men.* Some of the church gathered up the poor crushed and broken remains and gave them a decent burial. They buried him solemnly and mourned him greatly. Something is seriously wrong if the taking away of such people is not taken to heart. Those godly men paid their last respects to Stephen to show that they were neither ashamed of the cause for which he suffered nor afraid of the wrath of those who were its enemies, and to show the great value and respect they had for this faithful servant of Jesus Christ. They sought to honor the one whom God honored.

2. An account of the persecution of the church that began with the martyrdom of Stephen. One would have thought that Stephen's dying prayers and dying comforts would have overcome them and melted them into a better opinion of Christians and Christianity, but it seems that did not happen. As if they hoped to be too strong for God himself, they were determined to follow through their blows. Notice:

2.1. Against whom this persecution was raised: it was *against the church in Jerusalem.* Christ had particularly foretold that Jerusalem would soon be made too uncomfortable for his followers, because that city had been famous for killing the prophets and stoning those who were sent to it (Mt 23:37).

2.2. Who was active in it; no one was as zealous or busy as the young Pharisee Saul (v. 3). As for Saul, *he made havoc of the church*; he did all he could to destroy it and ruin it. He aimed at nothing less than destroying the Gospel Israel. Saul was brought up as a scholar and gentleman, but he did not think it beneath him to be employed in such evil work. He *entered into every house.* No one could be safe in their own house, even though they thought of it as their castle. He dragged away both men and women, without any regard for the weaker sex.

He committed them to prison, so that they might be put on trial and put to death.

2.3. What was the effect of this persecution: *They were all scattered abroad* (v. 1). They remembered our Master's rule, *When they persecute you in one city, flee to another* (Mt 10:23), and so they dispersed *throughout the regions of Judea and of Samaria*. Their work was pretty well finished in Jerusalem, and now the time had come for them to think about the needs of other places. Although persecution must not drive us away from our work, it may send us to work elsewhere. The preachers were all scattered *except the apostles*. They waited in Jerusalem so that they would be ready to go where their help was most needed by the other preachers, who were sent to break the ice.

Verses 4 – 13

Christ had said, *I am come to send fire on the earth* (Lk 12:29), and the persecutors thought that by scattering the ones who were kindled with that fire they would put the fire out, but instead they helped spread it.

1. Here is a general account of what was done by them all: *They went everywhere, preaching the word* (v. 4). They went everywhere, both into the places frequented by the Gentiles and into the towns of the Samaritans, which before they had been forbidden to enter (Mt 10:5). They scattered to all parts, not to take life easy but to find work. They were now in a country where they were not foreigners, for Christ and his disciples had had many dealings with the regions of Judea, and so they already had a foundation that had been laid there for them to build on.

2. Here is a specific account of what was done through Philip, not Philip the apostle, but Philip the deacon. Stephen was advanced to the work of a martyr, and Philip to the work of an evangelist. Notice:

2.1. What wonderful success Philip had in his preaching.

2.1.1. The place he chose: the town of Samaria, the central town of that country. Some think it was the same as Sychem or Sychar, that town of Samaria where Christ was when we spoke with the woman at the well (Jn 4:5). The Jews wanted to have no dealings with the Samaritans, but Christ sent his Gospel to put to death all hostility.

2.1.2. The message he preached: he *preached Christ to them*. The Samaritans expected the Messiah, as can be seen from Jn 4:25. Now Philip told them that the Messiah had come and that the Samaritans were welcome to him.

2.1.3. The proofs he produced: miracles (v. 6). The miracles were undeniable; the people heard and saw the miracles he performed.

2.1.3.1. He was sent to break the power of Satan, and as a sign of this, when evil spirits were commanded in the name of the Lord Jesus to leave many people, they *came out of many that were possessed with them* (v. 7). Wherever the Gospel is accepted and submitted to as it should be, evil spirits are dislodged. This was shown by the driving out of these evil spirits from the bodies of people; it is said here that the spirits came out *crying with a loud voice*. They came out with great reluctance, but were forced to acknowledge themselves defeated by a superior power (Mk 1:26; 3:11; 9:26).

2.1.3.2. He was sent to heal a diseased world. As a sign of this, *many that were taken with palsies* (many paralytics), *and that were lame, were healed*. The grace of God in the Gospel is intended to heal those who are spiritually crippled and paralyzed and who cannot help themselves (Ro 5:6).

2.1.4. The acceptance that Philip's message met with in Samaria: *The people with one accord gave heed to those things which Philip spoke* (v. 6), motivated to do so by the miracles, which at first captured their attention and then gradually gained their assent. The ordinary people paid close attention to Philip; they were "the crowds," not one here and there, but all together; they were all of one mind.

2.1.5. The success of Philip's preaching with many of them: they felt satisfied when they listened to him (v. 8): *There was great joy in that city*, because many *believed Philip, and were baptized* (v. 12), *both men and women*.

2.1.5.1. Philip preached *the things concerning the kingdom of God*, and he preached the name of Jesus Christ as king of that kingdom.

2.1.5.2. The people not only paid close attention to what he said but also eventually believed it, being fully convinced that it came from God and was not of human origin.

2.1.5.3. When they believed, *they were baptized*. It was only males who were capable of being admitted into the Jewish church, but, to show that *in Jesus Christ there is neither male nor female* (Gal 3:28), the initiating ceremony is one that women can undergo, because they are counted in God's spiritual Israel.

2.1.5.4. This brought great joy. The bringing of the Gospel to any place is a good reason for great joy in that place. The Gospel of Christ does not make people sad, but fills them with joy, because it is *glad tidings of great joy to all people* (Lk 2:10).

2.2. What there was at this city of Samaria that made the success of the Gospel extraordinarily wonderful.

2.2.1. That Simon the sorcerer had been busy there and had gained a great influence among the people. To unlearn what is bad often proves much more difficult than to learn what is good. These Samaritans had recently been drawn to follow this sorcerer, later known as Simon Magus, who had strangely captivated and amazed them. Notice:

2.2.1.1. How strong Satan's deception is. Simon had been for a *long time, in this city, using sorceries*.

2.2.1.1.*1*. He claimed to be someone significant: *He gave out that he himself was some great one*. He had no intention to reform their lives, only to make them believe that he was some divine person, the Great Power of God. Pride, ambition, and claims of grandeur have always been the cause of much trouble in both the world and the church.

2.2.1.1.2. The people gave him what he wished.

2.2.1.1.*2.1. They all gave heed to him, from the least to the greatest. To him they had regard* (vv. 10 – 11).

2.2.1.1.*2.2.* They said about him, *This man is the great power of God*. Notice how ignorant, inconsiderate people mistake what is done by the power of Satan for something done by the power of God.

2.2.1.1.*2.3.* They were brought to it by his sorcery: *He bewitched the people of Samaria* (v. 9), *bewitched them with sorceries* (v. 11). By his magic arts he bewitched the minds of the people. By God's permission, Satan filled their hearts so that they followed Simon. When they knew no better, they were influenced by his sorcery, but when they were familiar with Philip's real miracles, they clearly saw that those were real and Simon's were false. When they saw the difference between Simon and Philip, they abandoned Simon.

2.2.1.2. How strong the power of divine grace is. By the grace working with the word, those who had been taken captive by Satan *were brought into obedience to Christ* (2Co 10:5). Let us not, therefore, despair of the salvation of even the worst people, because even those whom Simon the sorcerer had captivated were brought to believe.

2.2.2. That — and this was even more wonderful — *Simon himself believed also* (v. 13). He was convinced that Philip preached a true message, because he saw it confirmed by real miracles, which he was more able to judge than others were because he was aware of the tricks of his own false miracles. The present conviction went so far that *he was baptized*. We have no reason to think that Philip acted wrongly in baptizing him. When prodigals return, they must be welcomed home joyfully, even though we cannot be sure they will not play the prodigal again. It is God's prerogative to know the heart. The church and its ministers must judge according to love. "We must hope the best for as long as we can." The present conviction lasted as long as he continued to be with Philip. The one who had claimed to be someone great was content to sit at the feet of a preacher of the Gospel. Even bad people, or very bad ones, may sometimes be in a very good frame of mind. The present conviction was brought about and maintained by miracles. Many are amazed at the proofs of divine truths but never experience their power.

Verses 14–25

The Twelve stayed together in Jerusalem (v. 1), and the good news was brought to them there *that Samaria had received the word of God* (v. 14). The word of God was not only preached to them but also received by them. *When the apostles at Jerusalem heard it, they sent unto them Peter and John*. Two apostles were sent, the two most outstanding ones, to Samaria to encourage and support Philip and to continue the good work that had begun. Notice:

1. How those of them who were sincere advanced and improved. It is said (v. 16), *The Holy Spirit was as yet fallen upon none of them*; that is, he had not fallen on them with those extraordinary powers that were conveyed by the outpouring of the Spirit; *only they were baptized in the name of the Lord Jesus*, and they had joy and satisfaction (v. 8). Those who have truly given themselves to Christ, who have experienced the sanctifying influences of the Spirit of grace, have great reasons to be thankful and no reason to complain, even though they do not have those gifts that are more ostentatious and would make them stand out. However, it was intended that they go on to the perfection of the present era.

1.1. *The apostles prayed for them* (v. 15). This example should encourage us, in our praying, to ask God to give the renewing graces of the Holy Spirit to those whose spiritual welfare we are concerned for: our children, friends, and ministers.

1.2. They laid their hands on them; this sign was used, and *they received the Holy Spirit*. The laying on of hands was used in former times as a blessing. The apostles blessed these new converts.

2. How they discovered and rejected Simon the sorcerer. Notice:

2.1. The evil proposal Simon made, by which his hypocrisy was revealed (vv. 18–19): *When he saw that through laying on of the apostles' hands the Holy Spirit was given*, it gave him the idea that Christianity was nothing other than an superior act of sorcery. He was ambitious to have the honor of an apostle, but was not at all concerned to have the spirit of a Christian. He was more concerned to gain honor for himself than to do good to others.

2.1.1. He showed great disrespect to the apostles, as if they were mercenaries, who would do anything for money.

2.1.2. He showed great disrespect for Christianity, as if the miracles were done by magic.

2.1.3. He showed that he aimed at the rewards of divination.

2.1.4. He showed that he had a very high opinion of himself. No less a place would be enough for him than to be entrusted with a power that only the apostles had and that Philip himself did not have.

2.2. The just rejection of his proposal (vv. 20–23).

2.2.1. Peter showed him his crime (v. 20): *Thou hast thought that the gift of God may be purchased with money*. Simon had put too high a value on the wealth of this world, as if it would purchase the forgiveness of sin, the gift of the Holy Spirit, and eternal life. And he had put too low a value on the gift of the Holy Spirit. He thought the power of an apostle could as well be obtained for a good fee as the advice of a doctor or a lawyer could.

2.2.2. He showed him what he was really like, inferring his character from his crime. Peter told Simon frankly:

2.2.2.1. That his heart was *not right in the sight of God* (v. 21). We are as our hearts are; if they are not right, we are wrong. They lie open to the sight of God, who knows them, judges them, and judges us by them. Our great desire should be to show ourselves as those who are approved by him in our integrity (Ps 26:1; 2Ti 2:15), because otherwise we are deceiving ourselves, to our own ruin. Simon was not aiming at the glory of God or the honor of Christ in it, but at a profit for himself.

2.2.2.2. That he was *in the gall* (full) *of bitterness, and in the bond of iniquity* (captive to sin): *I perceive that thou art* so (v. 23). This is plain speaking, and plain speaking is best when we are dealing with souls and eternity. *I perceive it*, Peter said. The disguises of hypocrites many times are quickly seen through; the nature of the wolf shows itself despite the cover of the sheep's clothing. Now the description here given of Simon is really the description of all evildoers. They are *in the gall of bitterness* — repugnant to God, as bitter as gall is to us. And they are *in the bond of iniquity*, bound over to the judgment of God by the guilt of sin and bound under the power of Satan to the power of sin.

2.2.3. He read him his fate in two matters:

2.2.3.1. Simon would sink with his worldly wealth: *Thy money perish with thee*. Peter rejected Simon's offer with the greatest disdain and indignation: "Away with you and your money! We won't have anything to do with either." When we are tempted to do evil with money, we should see what a perishable thing money is. Peter warned him that he was in danger of total destruction if he continued in this way: "Your money will perish, and you will lose it. However, this is not the worst of it: *thou wilt perish with it, and it with thee*."

2.2.3.2. He would fall short of the spiritual blessings, which he valued too little (v. 21): "*Thou hast neither part nor lot in this matter*; you have nothing to do with the gifts of the Holy Spirit, because *thy heart is not right in the sight of God* if you think that Christianity is a trade to live by in this world."

2.2.4. He gave him good advice, nevertheless (v. 22). Although he was angry with him, he still did not abandon him. Notice:

2.2.4.1. What Peter advised Simon to do.

2.2.4.1.*1*. He must *repent*; he must see his error and withdraw it. His repentance must be specific: "Repent of this; acknowledge you are guilty in this." He must not play it down by calling it a mistake or misguided zeal, but must see it in its true colors, calling it wickedness. Those people who have said and done wrong must, as far as they can, withdraw their actions and words in repentance.

2.2.4.1.*2.* He must *pray* that God would give him repentance (5:31; 11:18; 2Ti 2:25) and then forgive him when he repented. Penitents must pray, which implies a desire for God and a confidence in Christ. Simon the sorcerer would not be favored by the apostles' fellowship on any terms but those on which other sinners are admitted—repentance and prayer.

2.2.4.2. What encouragement he gave him to do this: *If perhaps the thought of thy heart may be forgiven thee.* There may be a great deal of evil in the thoughts of the heart that must be repented of; otherwise we are ruined. Even though the thoughts of the heart are evil, they will be forgiven when we repent. When Peter here put a *perhaps* on it, the doubt was about the sincerity of Simon's repentance, not about whether he would be forgiven if his repentance was sincere.

2.2.4.3. Simon's request to them to pray for him (v. 24). *Pray you to the Lord for me, that none of the things which you have spoken come upon me.* Here was:

2.2.4.3.*1.* Something good: he was moved by the rebuke and therefore begged the prayers of the apostles for him.

2.2.4.3.*2.* Something lacking. He begged them to pray for him, but he did not pray for himself. His concern was more that the judgments he had exposed himself to would be prevented than that that his heart, by divine grace, would be put right in the sight of God.

3. The return of the apostles to Jerusalem when they had completed the business they came for.

3.1. There, in the town of Samaria, they were preachers: *They testified the word of the Lord,* confirming what the ministers preached.

3.2. On their way home they were itinerant preachers; they preached the Gospel as they passed through many Samaritan villages. God cares for the inhabitants of his villages in Israel (Jdg 5:11), and so should we.

Verses 26–40

We have here the account of the conversion of an Ethiopian eunuch to faith in Christ.

1. Philip the evangelist was sent onto the road where he would meet this Ethiopian (v. 26). Here we have:

1.1. Instructions given Philip by an angel as to which way to go: *Arise, and go toward the south.* No doubt there is a special providence of God that is familiar with the moves and settlements of ministers. He will send those who sincerely want to follow him along the way in which he will acknowledge them. Philip must *go southward, to the way that leads from Jerusalem to Gaza,* through the desert of Judah. He would never have thought of going there, into a desert; what a useless place to find work! Yet that was where he was sent. Sometimes God opens a door of opportunity to his ministers in very unlikely places.

1.2. His obedience to these instructions (v. 27): *He arose and went,* without objecting.

2. An account is given of this eunuch (v. 27).

2.1. He was a foreigner, *a man of Ethiopia.* The Ethiopians were looked down on; their skin was dark, as if it might be thought that nature had stigmatized them, but the Gospel was sent to them, and divine grace looked on them.

2.2. He was a person of high rank, a significant person in his own country, *a eunuch,* lord chamberlain or steward of the household. He was *of great authority* and was important *under Candace queen of the Ethiopians.* He *had charge of all her treasure* (was in charge of all the treasury); that was how much she trusted him. *Not many mighty, not many noble, are called,* but some are (1Co 1:26).

2.3. He was a convert; we know this because *he came to Jerusalem to worship.* Some think that there were remnants of the knowledge of the true God in this country from the time of the queen of Sheba.

3. Philip and the eunuch were brought together, and now Philip would find out why he was sent into a desert.

3.1. Philip was ordered to join this traveler. The eunuch had been in Jerusalem, where the apostles had been preaching the Christian faith, but there he had taken no notice of it. The grace of God pursued him, however, caught up with him in the desert, and there overwhelmed him. Philip had this order by the Spirit whispering it in his ear (v. 29): *Go near, and join thyself to this chariot.* We should seek to do good to those we are in company with when we travel. We should not be so shy of all strangers as some are. Even if we know nothing else about a person, we know at least that they have a soul.

3.2. He found him reading his Bible as he sat in his chariot (v. 28): he *ran to him, and heard him read* (v. 30). By reading, he not only relieved the tediousness of the journey but also redeemed the time; and he redeemed it all the better by reading the Scriptures, *the book of Esaias* (Isaiah). It is the duty of each and every one of us to have a great deal of contact with the Holy Scriptures. People of high rank should give more of their time to exercises of devotion than others, because their example will influence many. It is wise for business people to redeem time for holy duties, to fill every minute with something useful. Those who search the Scriptures diligently are in a favorable position to increase in knowledge and apply it.

3.3. He asked the eunuch a fair question: *Understandest thou what thou readest?* When we read and hear of the word of God, we should often ask ourselves whether we understand it or not. We cannot gain from the Scriptures unless we in some measure understand them (1Co 14:16–17).

3.4. The eunuch sensed his need of assistance and requested Philip's company (v. 31): *"How can I understand,* he said, *except some one guide me?"* He spoke as one with very humble thoughts of his own abilities. He took the question kindly, replying very modestly, *How can I?* Those who want to learn must see their need to be taught. He spoke as one who very much wanted to be taught, to have someone guide him. Although there are many things in the Scriptures that are mysterious and hard to understand, we must not therefore throw them all aside, but must study them for the sake of those things that are relatively easy. Knowledge and grace grow gradually. He invited Philip to *come up and sit with him.* To correctly understand the Scripture, we need someone to guide us; we need some good books and some good people, but above all we need the Spirit of grace to lead us into all truth (Jn 16:13).

4. We learn what portion of Scripture the eunuch was reading, with some hints of Philip's comments on it.

4.1. The chapter he was reading was Isaiah 53, two verses of which are quoted here (vv. 32–33; Isa 53:7–8). They are quoted from the Septuagint (a Greek version of the Old Testament), which differs in some matters from the original Hebrew. The greatest variation appears in the part of Isa 53:8 where our translation, based on the original Hebrew, reads, *He was taken from prison and from judgment.* Here in Acts, in the quotation from the Septuagint, the same passage from Isaiah reads, *In his humiliation his judgment was taken away.* He appeared so contemptible and despicable in the eyes of his accusers and judges that they denied him common justice. They declared him innocent but condemned him to die. "He is down, and so down with him!" This is how *in his humiliation his judgment was taken away*. These verses, therefore, foretold about the Messiah:

4.1.1. That he would die, would be *led to the slaughter*, like the sheep that were offered in sacrifices.

4.1.2. That he would die wrongfully, would be rushed out of his life, and *his judgment would be taken away*.

4.1.3. That he would die patiently. Like *a lamb dumb before the shearer*—indeed, and in the presence of the butcher too—*so he opened not his mouth*. Never was there such an example of patience as our Lord Jesus. When he was accused, when he was abused, he remained silent.

4.1.4. That he would live forever, to ages that cannot be numbered, because this is how we understand *Who shall declare his generation? His life was taken* only *from the earth*; in heaven he will live for endless and innumerable ages.

4.2. The eunuch's question about this was, *Of whom speaketh the prophet this?* (v. 34). He asked a significant and very sensible question: "Is the prophet speaking this about himself, in expectation of being treated—mistreated—as the other prophets were? Or is he speaking it *of some other man?*" He asked the question to draw Philip into talking. The way to receive good instructions is to ask good questions.

4.3. Philip used the occasion to open up to him the great mystery of the Gospel about *Jesus Christ, and him crucified* (1Co 2:2). He *began at this scripture* and *preached too unto him Jesus* (v. 35). This is all the account we are given of Philip's sermon. Here we have an instance of speaking the things of God, and speaking of them to good effect, not only as we *sit in the house* but also *as we walk by the way* (Dt 6:7; 11:19).

5. The eunuch was baptized in the name of Christ (vv. 36–38). Here we have:

5.1. The eunuch's own modest suggestion that he be baptized (v. 36): *As they went on their way*, they *came unto a certain water*, the sight of which made the eunuch think of being baptized. This is how God, by hints of providence that seem accidental, sometimes reminds his people of their duty, which otherwise they perhaps would have thought of. The eunuch did not know how much longer Philip would be with him, and so if Philip thought it right, he would take advantage of the present opportunity to be baptized: *"See, here is water; what doth hinder me to be baptized?"* He did not demand baptism; he did not say, "Here is water, and I have decided to be baptized here." But he did desire it, and unless Philip could show good reason why not, he wanted it now. In the solemn dedicating and devoting of ourselves to God, it is good to be speedy and not delay, for the present is the best time (Ps 119:60). The eunuch feared that the good devotion now at work within him might cool off and abate, and that was why he was willing to bind his soul immediately to the Lord.

5.2. Philip's fair declaration to him (v. 37): *If thou believest with all thy heart, thou mayest.* He must believe with all his heart, because with the heart we believe; we do it not only with the head, by an assent to Gospel truths in our understanding, but also with the heart, by a consent of the will to the terms of the Gospel. "If you truly believe with all your heart, then you are united to Christ by that, and you may be joined to the church by baptism."

5.3. The confession of faith that the eunuch made. It was very short, but it was comprehensive and very much to the point: *I believe that Jesus Christ is the Son of God.* He had been a worshiper of the true God before, and so all he had to do now was to receive Christ Jesus the Lord. He

believed that Jesus is *the Christ*, the true Messiah promised, and that Christ is *Jesus*, "a Savior," the only Savior of his people from their sins. He also believed that this Jesus Christ is the *Son of God*, that he has a divine nature, for the Son is of the same nature as the Father.

5.4. The baptizing of him. The eunuch *commanded the chariot to stand still*. It was the best stopping place he had ever come to on any of his journeys. *They went down both into the water.* They went barefoot, according to the custom, perhaps up to their ankles or mid-leg into the water, and Philip sprinkled water on the new convert. Although Philip had just been deceived by Simon the sorcerer, that was not a reason for him to hesitate to baptize the eunuch immediately upon his profession of faith. If some hypocrites crowd into the church, who later prove a grief and scandal to us, we must not therefore make the door of admission any narrower than Christ made it; they will answer for their apostasy, not we.

6. Philip and the eunuch went their own ways immediately, and this is as surprising as the other parts of the story. As soon as they had *come up out of the water, the Spirit of the Lord caught away Philip* (v. 39). The performing of this miracle on Philip was as great a confirmation of his message as the performance of a miracle by him would have been. He was *caught away, and the eunuch saw him no more*, but, having lost his minister, he returned to using his Bible again. Notice:

6.1. How the eunuch felt: he *went on his way rejoicing.* Business called him home, and he must pursue it quickly, because it was in no way inconsistent with his Christianity, which is a religious faith that people can and should carry around with them into the affairs of this life. But he went on his way rejoicing. He was never more pleased in all his life. He rejoiced:

6.1.1. That he himself was joined to Christ.

6.1.2. That he had this good news to bring to his compatriots and had the prospect of bringing them also into fellowship with Christ.

6.2. Where Philip was found (v. 40): *He was found at Azotus*, or *Ashdod*. Philip, wherever he was, would not be lazy: *Passing through, he preached in all the cities*, until he came to Caesarea and settled there. In 21:8 we find him in a house of his own at Caesarea. The one who had been faithful in working for Christ as an itinerant preacher finally acquired a settled home.

CHAPTER 9

We have here: 1. The famous account of the apostle Paul's conversion. We read here: 1.1. How he was first awakened and persuaded by an appearance of Christ himself to him, and we read of the condition he was in while he lay under the power of those convictions and terrors (vv. 1–9). 1.2. How he was baptized by Ananias (vv. 10–19). 1.3. How he immediately became a teacher, preaching faith in Christ and proving what he preached (vv. 20–22). 1.4. How he was persecuted (vv. 23–25). 1.5. How he was admitted among the brothers and sisters at Jerusalem and was persecuted there (vv. 26–30). 1.6. The rest and quietness the churches enjoyed for some time after this (v. 31). 2. The healing performed by Peter on Aeneas (vv. 32–35). 3. The raising of Tabitha in response to Peter's prayer (vv. 36–43).

Verses 1–9

We have already had mention of Saul two or three times in the account of Stephen's life and death. His name in Hebrew was *Saul*, "desired"; his Roman name was *Paul*, "little." He was born in Tarsus, a city of Cilicia, a free city of the Romans, and he himself was a freeman of that city. His father and mother were both indigenous Jews, and that is why he called himself a *Hebrew of the Hebrews*; he was of the tribe of Benjamin. His education was first in the schools of Tarsus, which, for learning, was a little Athens. From there he was sent to Jerusalem to study divinity and the Jewish law. His tutor was Gamaliel (22:3). He had extraordinary natural talents. He also had a handicraft trade, having been brought up to be a tent-maker, which was common among the Jews who were brought up as scholars. We are told:

1. How very bad he was before his conversion; he was a hardened enemy of Christianity. In other respects he was good enough; as *touching the righteousness which is of the law*, he was *blameless* (Php 3:6), a man of no bad morals, but a persecutor of Christians. His conscience was so ill informed that he thought that he was serving God in that. We have here:

1.1. His general enmity and rage against the Christian religion (v. 1): He *yet breathed out threatenings and slaughter against the disciples of the Lord*. The people he persecuted were the disciples of the Lord; he hated and persecuted them because they were so. The substance of the persecution was *threatenings and slaughter*. There is persecution in threats (4:17, 21); they terrify and break the spirit. But those whom Saul threatened were killed by him if he was not successful in frightening them away from Christ. His *breathing out* threatenings and slaughter shows that it was natural to him. Even his breath, like that of some venomous creatures, was deadly. He breathed death to the Christians wherever he went.

1.2. His particular plots against the Christians at Damascus. Saul could not rest as long as he knew a Christian was at peace. Therefore, hearing that the Christians in Damascus were so, he decided to disturb them. He applied to the high priest for a commission to go to Damascus (vv. 1–2). The high priest did not need to be stirred up to persecute the Christians, but it seems the young persecutor drove more furiously than the old one (2Ki 9:20). The converts that the teachers of the law and Pharisees make often prove seven times more the children of hell than those leaders themselves had been (Mt 23:15). Now the commission authorized him to ask among the synagogues at Damascus whether there were any who tended to favor this heresy or who believed in Christ, and if he found any such, whether men or women, he must take them as prisoners to Jerusalem. Notice:

1.2.1. The Christians are here said to have been *those of this way*. Perhaps the Christians sometimes called themselves that, from Christ, *the Way* (Jn 14:6).

1.2.2. The Jews of all synagogues, even those who were not in the jurisdiction of the civil government of the Jewish nation, respected the authority of the Sanhedrin.

1.2.3. According to this authority, all who worshiped God in this way that the Sanhedrin called heretical were to be prosecuted. Even the women, who might deserve to be excused, or who at least might have deserved compassion, would not find that with Saul.

1.2.4. He was ordered to take them to Jerusalem as criminals. This is how Saul was employed when the grace of God brought about that great change in him. Let us not despair, therefore, of renewing grace for the conversion of the greatest sinners, and let such people not despair of the pardoning mercy of God for the greatest sin, because Paul himself obtained mercy.

2. How suddenly and strangely a wonderful change was brought about in him. Here is:

2.1. The place and time of it: *As he journeyed, he came near to Damascus*, and Christ met him there.

2.1.1. He was on his way, traveling on his journey. The work of conversion is not restricted to the church. Some are reclaimed when they are traveling on the road alone. Even there the Spirit may step into our lives, for that wind blows where it pleases (Jn 3:8).

2.1.2. He was near Damascus, almost at the end of his journey; the one who was to be the apostle of the Gentiles was converted to the faith of Christ in a Gentile country.

2.1.3. He was set on his evil way, pursuing his murderous threats against the Christians in Damascus. Sometimes the grace of God works on sinners when they are at their worst, which contributes much to the glory both of God's pity and of his power.

2.1.4. The cruel decree was about to be carried out, and now it was happily prevented. It was:

2.1.4.1. A great kindness to the poor saints at Damascus, who had notice of his coming, as is clear from what Ananias said (vv. 13–14). Christ has many ways of rescuing the godly from temptation, and sometimes he does it by a change brought about in their persecutors.

2.1.4.2. A very great mercy to Saul himself. A special sign of divine favor has been shown us, and must be valued as such, if God prevents us from pursuing and carrying out sinful purposes (1Sa 25:32).

2.2. The appearance of Christ to him in his glory. Here it is said only that there *shone round about him a light from heaven*, but what follows reveals (v. 17) that the Lord Jesus was in this light. This light shone on him *suddenly*. Christ's revelations of himself to poor souls are often sudden and surprising, and he anticipates them with the blessings of his goodness. It was a light from heaven. It was a light brighter than the sun (26:13), because it was visible at midday. It shone *round about him*, not only in his face but on every side of him. The devil comes to the soul in darkness; this is how he gains and keeps possession of it. But Christ comes to the soul in light, because he himself is the light of the world (Jn 8:12; 9:5). The first thing in this new creation, as in that of the world, is light (2Co 4:6).

2.3. The arresting of Saul. *He fell to the earth* (v. 4). It appears (26:14) that all who were with him fell to the earth as well as he, but Saul was the main object of the plan. This fall may be considered:

2.3.1. As the effect of Christ's appearing to him and of the light that shone around him. Christ's revelations of himself to poor souls are humbling; they make them feel very low.

2.3.2. As a step toward his intended advancement. Those whom Christ intends for the greatest honors are commonly first laid low. Those whom God will employ are first struck by a sense of their unworthiness to be employed.

2.4. The accusation against Saul. He heard a voice saying to him—and it was a discriminating voice, addressed only to him, because although those who were with him heard a sound (v. 7), they did not understand the words spoken to him (22:9)—*Saul, Saul, why persecutest thou me?*

2.4.1. Saul not only saw a light from heaven but also heard a voice from heaven. God's revelations of himself were never silent shows, because he exalts *his word above all his name* (Ps 138:2), and what was seen was always intended to make way for what was said. Saul heard a voice. Faith comes by hearing (Ro 10:17). The voice he heard was the voice of Christ. The word we hear is likely to do us good when we hear it as the voice of Christ; no voice except his can reach the heart.

2.4.2. What he heard was very awakening.

2.4.2.1. He was called by his name, which was repeated: *Saul, Saul.* Christ's calling him by name brought the conviction home to his conscience and put it beyond dispute whom the voice was speaking to. What God speaks in general is likely to do us good when we insert our own names into the commands and promises, as if God were speaking to us by name. The doubling of the name — *Saul, Saul* — shows the tender concern Jesus had for him and for his recovery. He spoke as one who is serious. He spoke to Saul as to one in imminent danger, at the edge of the pit and just about to fall in.

2.4.2.2. The charge directed against him was, *Why persecutest thou me?* Notice here:

2.4.2.2.1. Before Saul was made a saint, he was made to see himself as a sinner. Now he was made to see the evil in himself that he had never seen before. A humbling conviction of sin is the first step toward a saving conversion from sin.

2.4.2.2.2. He was convinced of one particular sin, which he had justified himself in, and thus the way was opened up for his conviction of all the rest.

2.4.2.2.3. The sin he was convinced of was persecution: *Why persecutest thou me?* It is a very affectionate form of pleading. Notice:

2.4.2.2.3.1. The person sinning: "It is you; you who have good gifts and accomplishments, who know the Scriptures, which, if you properly considered them, would show you how foolish you are. It is worse in you than in another."

2.4.2.2.3.2. The person sinned against: "It is I, who was not long ago crucified for you. Must I be crucified by you afresh?"

2.4.2.2.3.3. The kind of sin and its continuation. It was persecution, and he was at this time engaged in it. In God's account, those who are intending to cause trouble are actually causing trouble.

2.4.2.2.3.4. The question he was asked: "Why are you doing it?"

2.4.2.2.3.4.1. It is complaining language. Christ never complained so much about those who persecuted him in his own person as he did here about those who persecuted him in his followers. The sins of sinners are a very distressing burden to the Lord Jesus.

2.4.2.2.3.4.2. It is convincing language: "Why are you doing this?" It is good for us to often ask ourselves why we are doing a certain action, so that we may discern how unreasonable sin is. *Why persecutest thou me?* Saul thought he was persecuting only a company of poor, weak, foolish people, little imagining that it was the One in heaven that he was insulting all the time. Those who persecute the saints are persecuting Christ himself, and he takes what is done against them as done against himself.

2.5. Saul's question in response to this accusation (v. 5).

2.5.1. He asked about Christ: *Who art thou, Lord?* He gave no direct answer to the charge leveled against him, being convicted by his own conscience. If God accuses us of our own sins, we are unable to answer one time out of a thousand (Job 9:3). When convictions of sin are brought home powerfully on the conscience, they silence all excuses and all forms of self-justification. However, Saul wanted to know who his judge was. The one who had been a blasphemer of Christ's name now spoke to him as his Lord. The question was proper: *Who art thou?* This implied Saul's present unfamiliarity with Christ. He wanted to come to know him, and that was why he said, *Lord, who art thou?* There is some hope for people when they begin to ask about Jesus Christ.

2.5.2. He received an answer immediately, in which we see:

2.5.2.1. Christ's gracious revelation of himself to Saul. *I am Jesus whom thou persecutest.* The name of Jesus was not unknown to him, and he would gladly have buried it in oblivion. Little did he think that he would hear it from heaven. He said:

2.5.2.1.1. *I am Jesus, a Saviour; I am Jesus of Nazareth,* in the account Paul gave in 22:8. Saul used to call him this when he blasphemed him.

2.5.2.1.2. *I am that Jesus whom thou persecutest.* There is nothing more effective to wake up and humble the soul than to see that sin is against Christ.

2.5.2.2. His gentle rebuke of Saul: *It is hard for thee to kick against the pricks,* or goads. Those who stifle and smother the convictions of conscience are kicking against the goads. Those who rebel more and more when they are affected by the word or rod of God are kicking against the goads.

2.6. His surrender of himself to the Lord Jesus eventually (v. 6). Notice here:

2.6.1. The attitude he was in when Christ was dealing with him. He trembled. Strong convictions, brought home by the Holy Spirit, will make an awakened soul tremble. He was stunned, as one who was brought into a new world and did not know where he was.

2.6.2. His words to Jesus Christ: *Lord, what wilt thou have me to do?* This may be taken:

2.6.2.1. As a serious request for Christ's teachings: "You have revealed my sin to me; reveal to me the way of pardon and peace." A serious desire to be instructed by Christ about the way of salvation is evidence of a good work that has begun in the soul. Or:

2.6.2.2. As a sincere submission of himself to the direction and government of the Lord Jesus. This was the first word that grace spoke in Paul, and a spiritual life began with this: *What wilt thou have me to do?* The great change in conversion is brought about in the will and consists in the submission of that to the will of Christ.

2.6.3. The general direction Christ gave him: *Arise, go into the city of Damascus, and it shall be told thee what thou must do.* It was enough encouragement to have further instruction promised him:

2.6.3.1. He would not receive it yet. Let him consider for a while what he had done in persecuting Christ; let him be deeply humbled for that, and then he would be told the next steps that he had to take.

2.6.3.2. He must not have it in this way, by a voice from heaven, as it was clear that he could not bear it. He would be told what he must do, therefore, by a man like himself. Christ reveals himself to his people gradually.

2.7. How far his fellow travelers were moved by this. *They stood speechless,* as if confused, and that was all (v. 7). We do not find that any of the others were converted, even though they saw the light and were struck speechless by it. No external means will by themselves produce a change in the soul, apart from the Spirit and grace of God. None of them said, *Who art thou, Lord?* or, *What wilt thou have me to do?* as Paul did. *They heard a voice, but saw no man;* they heard Paul speaking, but did not see the One to whom he was speaking, nor did they hear distinctly what was being said to Paul. And so those who went there to be the instruments of Paul's anger against the church served as witnesses of the power of God over him.

2.8. What condition Saul was in after this (vv. 8–9). *He arose from the earth* when Christ commanded him. *When his eyes were opened, he saw no man.* It was not so much this glaring light, but the sight of Christ, that had this effect on him. This is how a believing sight of the glory of God in the face of Christ (2Co 4:6) dazzles the eyes, making them blind to all things here below. *They led him by the hand into Damascus.* And so the one who thought he would take the disciples of Christ as prisoners to Jerusalem was himself led captive to Christ into Damascus. He lay *without sight, neither did eat nor drink for three days* (v. 9). He was in the dark about his own spiritual state and was so wounded in his spirit because of his sin that he could enjoy neither food nor drink.

Verses 10–22

A good work was begun in Saul when he was brought to Christ's feet with the words, *Lord, what wilt thou have me to do?* Christ has never left anyone who was brought to such a point. The One who has convinced will also comfort.

1. Ananias was here ordered to go and look after him.

1.1. The person employed was *Ananias, a certain disciple at Damascus,* not lately driven there from Jerusalem, but a native of Damascus, because it is said (22:12) that he *had a good report of all the Jews who dwelt there, as a devout man according to the law.*

1.2. The directions given him were to go and ask at such and such a house for one *Saul of Tarsus.* Christ called Ananias by name in a vision (v. 10), probably not for the first time, for Ananias readily answered, without terror or confusion, *"Behold, I am here, Lord." Go then,* Christ said, *into the street which is called Straight, and inquire in the house of Judas—for one called Saul of Tarsus.* Christ knows very well where to find those in distress who are his; they have a friend in heaven who knows what street they are on and what house they are in; in fact, even more, he knows how they feel.

1.3. Ananias was given two reasons why he must go:

1.3.1. Because the stranger was praying, and Ananias's coming to him must be an answer to his prayer. This was a reason:

1.3.1.1. Why Ananias did not need to be afraid of him, as we find he was (vv. 13–14). There was no question, Christ said, that this stranger was not a true convert, *for, behold, he prayeth. Behold* shows its certainty: "Go and look for yourself." It also shows its strangeness: "Look in wonder." But was it so strange for Saul to pray? Was he not a Pharisee? Yes, but now he began to pray differently than before: then he had said his prayers; now he prayed them. You may as soon find a living person without breath as a living Christian without prayer; if breathless, then lifeless, and so, if without prayer, then without grace.

1.3.1.2. Why Ananias must go to him as quickly as possible. Now was no time to linger, *for behold, he prayeth.* Saul was under conviction of sin. Conviction should drive us to prayer. He was suffering a physical problem, was blind and sick. Christ had promised him that he would be told later what he was to do (v. 6), and Saul prayed that someone would be sent to him to instruct him. We must pray for what God has promised.

1.3.2. Because the stranger had had a vision, and in the vision he had seen such a man as Ananias coming to him, and Ananias's coming to him must be the answer to his dream, because it came from God (v. 12): *He hath seen in a vision a man named Ananias coming in and putting his hand on him that he might receive his sight.* Now the vision Paul had may be considered:

1.3.2.1. As a direct answer to his prayer and as the maintaining of that fellowship with God that he had entered in prayer.

1.3.2.2. As intended to raise his expectations, making Ananias's coming more welcome to him. Notice what a great thing it is to bring a spiritual doctor and patient together: here were two visions for this purpose.

2. Ananias objected to going to him.

2.1. Ananias pleaded that this Saul was a notorious persecutor of the disciples of Christ (vv. 13–14). *"Lord, I have heard by many of this man, how much evil he hath done to thy saints in Jerusalem.* There was no one they were more afraid of. His mission to Damascus at this time is to persecute us Christians: *Here he has authority from the chief priests to bind* (arrest) *all that call on thy name."* Now, why did Ananias object to this? He should not have said, "Therefore I do not owe him so much help." No; Christ has taught us another lesson, to repay good for evil and pray for our persecutors (Mt 5:44). Yet would it be safe for Ananias to go to him? If he got himself into trouble in this way, he would be blamed for his indiscretion. Would it serve any purpose to go to Saul? Could such a hard heart ever be softened?

2.2. Christ overruled his objection (vv. 15–16): "Go on your way as fast as possible, *for he is a chosen vessel* of mine. You need not be afraid of him." He was a vessel in which the Gospel treasure would be lodged; he was an *earthen vessel* (2Co 4:7), but a chosen vessel. Saul was intended:

2.2.1. To be *an earthen vessel* (2Co 4:7). He was designed for eminent service: *He is to bear my name before the Gentiles.* Saul must be a standard bearer. He must bear Christ's name before kings, King Agrippa and Caesar himself; in fact, he must take that name to the children of Israel, too, even though many were already doing so.

2.2.2. To suffer greatly (v. 16): *I will show him how great things he must suffer for my name's sake.* The one who had been a persecutor would himself be persecuted. Those who bear Christ's name must expect to bear the cross for his name, and those who do most for Christ are often called to suffer most for him. It is simply like telling soldiers with a bold and brave spirit that they will go on the battlefield and soon see military action. It was no discouragement to Saul to be told how he must suffer great things for Christ's name's sake.

3. Ananias went on Christ's errand to Saul. He had started to raise an objection against going to him, but he dropped it and did not insist on it. When difficulties are removed, what have we to do but to continue with our work and not hang on to objections?

3.1. Ananias spoke his message to Saul (v. 17).

3.1.1. *He put his hands on him.* Saul came to lay violent hands on the disciples at Damascus, but here a disciple laid a helping and healing hand on him.

3.1.2. He called him *brother.* His readiness to acknowledge Saul as a brother showed Saul God's readiness to acknowledge him as a son, even though he had been a blasphemer of God and a persecutor of his children.

3.1.3. He produced his commission. "That *same Jesus that appeared unto thee in the way as thou camest* has now sent me to you." The hand that had wounded would now heal (Hos 6:1). "His light struck you blind, but he *hath sent me to thee that thou mightest receive thy sight."* Caustic medicine would no longer be applied, but softening ones.

3.1.4. He assured him that he would not only have his sight restored but also be filled with the Holy Spirit.

3.2. Ananias saw the good outcome of his mission:

3.2.1. In Christ's favor to Saul. At the word of Ananias, Saul was released from his confinement and delivered from the spirit of bondage by the restoring of his sight (v. 18), which was represented by the falling of scales from his eyes. The cure was sudden, to show that it was miraculous. This showed his restoration:

3.2.1.1. From the darkness of his unconverted state. Christ often told the Pharisees they were blind, but he could not make them aware of it. Saul was saved from his pharisaical blindness by being made aware of it. Converting grace opens the eyes of the soul. This was what Saul was sent among the Gentiles to do, and that was why he must first experience it in himself.

3.2.1.2. From the darkness of his present terrors. Now the scales fell from his eyes, clouds scattered, and the Sun of righteousness rose on his soul, with healing in his wings (Mal 4:2).

3.2.2. In Saul's submission to Christ: he was baptized, so submitting to Christ's rule and throwing himself on the grace of Christ. Saul was now a disciple of Christ, not only ceasing to oppose him but devoting himself completely to his service.

4. The good work that was begun in Saul was continued wonderfully.

4.1. He received his physical strength (v. 19). He had continued fasting for three days, which had made him very weak, but *when he had received meat, he was strengthened* (v. 19). The Lord is for the body (1Co 6:13), and that is why care must be taken of it, so that it may be fit to serve the soul in God's service.

4.2. He associated with the disciples who were in Damascus. He had just been breathing out murderous threats against them, but now he breathed out love and affection to them. Those who take God as their God take his people for their people. This was how he made a profession of his Christian faith, openly declaring himself to be a disciple of Christ.

4.3. *He preached Christ in the synagogues* (v. 20). He was so full of Christ himself that *the Spirit within him constrained him* to preach him to others. Notice:

4.3.1. Where he preached—in the synagogues of the Jews. There they used to preach against Christ and punish his disciples. It was there, therefore, that he wanted to face the enemies of Christ; in a place where they had been most daring in their opposition to Christianity, he would openly profess it.

4.3.2. What he preached: *He preached Christ.* When he began to be a preacher, he established this as his principle, which he stuck by forever after: nothing but *Christ, and him crucified* (1Co 2:2). He preached about Christ *that he is the Son of God*, with whom God is pleased, and that he is pleased with us in Christ.

4.3.3. How people were moved by it (v. 21): *"All that heard him were amazed, and said, Is not this he that destroyed those who called on this name in Jerusalem? Did he not come here to arrest all the Christians he could find and to bring them bound to the chief priests?* Who then would have thought that he would preach Christ as he is now doing?" This miracle in the heart of such a man surpassed the miracles on people's bodies, and giving a man such a different heart was more than giving people the gift of speaking in tongues.

4.4. He disproved and confounded those who opposed the message of Christ (v. 22).

4.4.1. He increased in strength. He became more intimately acquainted with the Gospel of Christ, and his godly love grew stronger and stronger. He grew more daring and resolute in defending the Gospel, and he became increasingly powerful despite the censures he was subjected to (v. 21), his new friends rebuking him for having been a persecutor and his old friends rebuking him for having betrayed the cause.

4.4.2. He baffled his antagonists: he *confounded the Jews who dwelt in Damascus*; he silenced them and shamed them. He was instrumental in converting many people to the faith of Christ and in building up the church at Damascus, the very city where he had intended to destroy the church.

Verses 23–31

Luke makes no mention of Paul's journey to Arabia here, which Paul himself tells us he made immediately after his conversion (Gal 1:16–17). As soon as God *had revealed his Son in him, that he might preach him, he went not up to Jerusalem,* but to Arabia. From there he returned to Damascus, and there, three years after his conversion, the events that are recorded here took place.

1. He met with difficulties at Damascus and narrowly escaped being killed. Notice:

1.1. What his danger was (v. 23): *The Jews took counsel* (conspired) *to kill him.* He had been such a remarkable deserter, and his being a Christian was a testimony against them. It is said, *The Jews watched the gates day and night to kill him* (v. 24). Now Christ showed Paul *what great things he must suffer for his name* (v. 16). Saul was no sooner a Christian than a preacher, and no sooner a preacher than a sufferer. Where God gives great grace, he usually exercises that grace with great times of testing.

1.2. How he was rescued. The plot against him was discovered: *Their lying in wait was known of Saul,* and the disciples managed to help him get away at night. They *let him down by the wall, in a basket,* as he himself relates (2Co 11:33).

2. He met with difficulties at Jerusalem the first time he went there (v. 26). This is thought to be the journey to Jerusalem about which he himself speaks: *After three years I went up to Jerusalem to see Peter, and abode with him fifteen days* (Gal 1:18). But I am rather inclined to think that this was a journey before that one, because *his coming in* and *going out, his preaching and disputing* (vv. 28–29), seem to be more than would have been consistent with a fifteen days' stay. Nevertheless, it might have been the same one. Notice:

2.1. How wary of him his friends were (v. 26): *When he came to Jerusalem, he assayed* (tried) *to join himself to the disciples.* Wherever he went, he acknowledged himself as belonging to that despised and persecuted people. But they looked on him as a stranger, shutting the door against him. *They were afraid of him.* The Jews had abandoned and persecuted him, and the Christians would not receive him.

2.1.1. Notice what the cause of their anxiety about him was: *They believed not that he was a disciple,* but that he was only pretending to be so, and that he came among them as a spy or an informer. The disciples of Christ need to be cautious as to whom they admit into their fellowship. They need the wisdom of the serpent (Mt 10:16), to keep a happy medium between the extremes of suspicion on the one hand and gullibility on the other. Yet it seems to me that it is safer to err on the side of charity.

2.1.2. Notice how it was resolved (v. 27): *Barnabas took him to the apostles* themselves *and declared to them:*

2.1.2.1. What Christ had done for Saul: *He had shown himself to him in the way* and spoken to him.

2.1.2.2. What Saul had done for Christ since: *He had preached boldly at Damascus in the name of Jesus.* We are not told how Barnabas became aware of this, but however he came to know it, he himself was satisfied concerning Saul's account of his conversion, and so he satisfied the apostles about it.

2.2. How sharp his enemies were with him.

2.2.1. He was admitted into the fellowship of the disciples. It troubled the unfaithful Jews to see Saul become a trophy of Christ's victory, to see him *coming in and going out with the apostles* (v. 28).

2.2.2. He represented the cause of Christ vigorously, and this was even more offensive to them (v. 29): *He spoke boldly in the name of the Lord Jesus.* The Grecian, or Hellenist, Jews were most offended by him, because he had been one of them, and they drew him into a dispute, in which he was no doubt too strong for them. That same natural quickness and fervor of spirit that had made him a furious, bigoted persecutor of the faith now made him a most zealous and courageous defender of the faith.

2.2.3. This put his life in danger: *the Grecians went about to slay him.* However, when the believers heard about this conspiracy too, care was taken to protect this young champion (v. 30): *When the brethren knew, they brought him down to Cesarea.* The one who flees may live to fight again. The one who fled from Jerusalem could do service at Tarsus, the place where he was born, and that was where they wanted him to go. Yet it was also by direction from heaven that he left Jerusalem at this time, as he himself tells us (22:17–18): Christ now appeared to him and ordered him to *go quickly out of Jerusalem*, for he must be sent *to the Gentiles* (v. 15).

3. The churches had now a comforting glimmer of liberty and peace (v. 31): *Then had the churches rest.* Then, when Saul was converted, those whom he used to attack were quiet.

3.1. *The churches had rest.* After a storm comes a calm. A breathing space was allowed them to prepare them for the next encounter.

3.2. They made good use of this quiet interval.

3.2.1. They *were edified*, were built up in their most holy faith (Jude 20).

3.2.2. They *walked in the fear of the Lord.* They lived in such a way that all could have said, "Surely the fear of God reigns in these people."

3.2.3. They *walked in the comfort of the Holy Spirit*—they were not only faithful in their religious faith but also cheerful in it; they remained faithful to the ways of the Lord and sang in those ways (Ps 138:5). They applied the strength and encouragements of the Holy Spirit, and they lived on that not only in times of danger and suffering but also in times of rest and prosperity. When they walked *in the fear of the Lord*, they walked *in the comfort of the Holy Spirit.* Those who walk carefully are most likely to walk cheerfully.

3.3. God blessed these things to them by increasing their numbers: they *were multiplied.* Sometimes the church multiplies more in times of adversity, but if it were always so, the saints of the Most High (Da 7:18) would be worn out. At other times its rest contributes to its growth.

Verses 32–35

Here we have:

1. The visit Peter made to the churches that had been newly planted (v. 32). He *passed through all quarters* (traveled about the country). As an apostle, he was not the resident pastor of any one church. He was, like his Master, always on the move, and *went about doing good* (10:38), but his headquarters remained at Jerusalem, for it is there that we will later find him imprisoned (12:4).

He came to the saints at Lydda. The Christians are called saints; every sincere believer in Christ is a saint. These are the saints on earth (Ps 16:3).

2. The healing Peter performed on Aeneas (v. 33).

2.1. Aeneas's case was terrible: *He was sick of the palsy* (was a paralytic). The disease was extreme: *he kept his bed*; it was a chronic illness, for it had kept him bedridden for *eight years.* Probably both he and everyone around him despaired of his ever being helped. Such were the patients Christ chose, those whose disease was incurable in the course of nature. When we were without strength, as this poor man was, Christ sent his Word to heal us (Ro 5:6).

2.2. His healing was wonderful (v. 34). Peter involved Christ in his life. *Eneas: Jesus Christ maketh thee whole.* Peter declared it to be Christ's action and assured Aeneas of an immediate cure: not, "He will make you whole," but, "He makes you whole." And he assured him that it was a perfect cure: not, "He makes you comfortable," but, "He makes you whole." Peter ordered Aeneas to move: "*Arise and make thy bed.*" Let no one say that because it is Christ who performs all our works in us, we need not to undertake any work or duty. Although Jesus Christ heals you, you must still get up and use the power he gives you: "*Arise and make thy bed*, which will no longer be a sickbed to you, but a bed of rest." Power accompanied this word: Aeneas got up immediately.

3. The good effect this had on many people (v. 35): *All that dwelt at Lydda and Saron saw him, and turned to the Lord.* They all inquired about the truth of the miracle and saw that it was a miraculous cure that had been performed on Aeneas by the power of Christ. They all *turned to the Lord*, to the Lord Jesus. They turned themselves to him to be ruled, taught, and saved.

Verses 36–43

Here we have another miracle performed by Peter to confirm the Gospel, a miracle that surpassed the previous one: the raising of Tabitha to life when she had been dead for some time. Here is:

1. The life, death, and character of Tabitha (vv. 36–37). She lived at Joppa, and her name in Greek was *Dorcas*; both names mean "a doe," a pleasant creature.

1.1. She was a disciple well known for her works of kindness and love. She showed her faith by her good works (Jas 2:17–18). She was *full of good works* as a tree is full of fruit. Many people are full of good words but are empty and barren in good works, but Tabitha was a great doer, not a great talker.

1.1.1. She was remarkable for her *almsdeeds which she did*, not only her works of devotion but also works of charity and beneficence, flowing from love to her neighbor.

1.1.2. She is commended not only for the gifts she gave but also for the deeds she did. Those who do not have great possessions that they can give in charity can still do charitable deeds, working with their hands or walking with their feet for the benefit of the poor, and those who will not do a charitable deed—whatever they may claim they *would* do if they were rich—would not bestow a charitable gift even if they had the means to give one.

1.1.3. She was full of good works *which she did*; her doing them is emphasized because what her hand found to do of this kind she did with all her strength (Ecc 9:10), persevering in it. This is the life and character of a certain disciple, and it should be that of all the disciples of Christ.

1.2. She was taken away in the middle of her usefulness (v. 37): *In those days she fell sick, and died.*

1.3. Her friends and those around her did not bury her immediately. Instead, they *washed the dead body*, according to their custom, probably with warm water, which it was thought would restore a person if there were any life left in them. They *laid her out* in her graveclothes *in an upper chamber*.

2. The request her Christian friends made to Peter to come to them as quickly as possible. The disciples at Joppa had heard that Peter was there and that he had raised Aeneas from his sickbed. They therefore *sent to him two men, desiring him* (urging him) *that he would not delay to come to them*. Their friend was dead, and it was too late to send for a doctor, but not too late to send for Peter.

3. The position in which he found the survivors (v. 39): *Peter arose and went with them*. Let faithful ministers not begrudge being at everybody's beck and call, since the great apostle *made himself the servant of all* (1Co 9:19). Peter found the corpse laid out in the upstairs room, with widows present. They were:

3.1. Commending the deceased: this is a good work when it is done modestly, soberly, and without flattery. The commendation of Tabitha was like her own goodness: in actions, not words. *The widows showed the coats and garments which she made while she was with them*. It is much more honorable to clothe a group of poor widows with necessary clothing than to clothe a group of lazy footmen with rich uniforms, who perhaps will curse those who clothe them behind their backs, for goodness is true greatness and will be seen to be better on the Day of Judgment, shortly. Notice:

3.1.1. Into what channels Tabitha channeled most of her good deeds. It seems that with her own hands she *made coats and garments* for poor widows. This is an excellent act of charity: *If thou seest the naked, that thou cover him* (Isa 58:7), and not think it enough to say, *Be ye warmed* (Jas 2:15–16).

3.1.2. What a grateful sense of her kindness the poor had: *They showed the coats*. Those who have kindness shown them but will not make the slightest acknowledgment of it by showing the evidence of it are truly most ungrateful. Those who receive gifts are not obliged to conceal it as carefully as those are who give gifts to those in need. The widows' showing the coats and garments that Dorcas made led to the praise not only of her charity but also of her hard work.

3.2. Mourning their loss of her here: *the widows stood by Peter, weeping* (v. 39). They did not need to weep for her; *she rested from her labours, and her works followed her* (Rev 14:13). But they wept for themselves and their children (Lk 23:28), who would soon feel the lack of such a good woman. They took notice of what good Dorcas did *while she was with them*, but now that she had gone away from them, this was their grief. The widows wept in front of Peter to move him to have compassion on them, so that he would restore to them one who used to have compassion on them. When charitable people are sick, this act of gratitude is due them, to pray for their recovery, so that they may be spared to live, since they can hardly be spared to die.

4. How she was raised to life.

4.1. In private: *Peter put them all forth* (sent them all out of the room). Peter declined everything that looked like boasting and show; they came to see, but he did not come to be seen.

4.2. By prayer. In his healing of Aeneas there was an implied prayer, but in this greater work he addressed himself to God in sacred prayer. Peter prayed with the submis-

sion of a servant (Heb 3:5–6), and so he *knelt down and prayed*.

4.3. By the word, a life-giving word. When he had prayed, he *turned to the body* and spoke in his Master's name: *Tabitha, arise*. Power accompanied this word, and she came to life; she *opened her eyes*, which death had closed. When she saw Peter, she sat up; *he gave her his hand and lifted her up* (v. 41). He welcomed her back to life, as it were, giving her the right hand of fellowship among the living (Gal 2:9), from whom she had been cut off. Lastly, he *called the saints and widows* and *presented her alive* to them.

5. The good effects of this miracle.

5.1. By it, many were convinced of the truth of the Gospel and believed in the Lord (v. 42). The thing was *known throughout all Joppa*; although some took no notice of it, many were persuaded by it. This was the purpose of miracles, to confirm a divine revelation.

5.2. Peter was stirred by this to remain some time in this town (v. 43). Finding that a door of opportunity had been opened up for him there, he stayed for some time, until he was sent on business to another place. He took up lodgings with one Simon, a tanner. Although Peter might seem to have been buried in obscurity here in the house of a poor tanner by the seaside, it was from here that God took him to perform a valuable service, which is recorded in the next chapter.

CHAPTER 10

In this chapter, the Acts of the Apostles takes a new and remarkable direction. Lo, we turn to the Gentiles (13:46), and to them the door of faith is opened up here. The apostle Peter was the man first employed to admit uncircumcised Gentiles into the Christian church, and Cornelius, a Roman centurion, with his family and friends, was the first one to be admitted. We are told here: 1. How Cornelius was instructed in a vision to send for Peter (vv. 1–8). 2. How Peter was instructed in a vision to go to Cornelius, even though he was a Gentile (vv. 9–23). 3. The beneficial meeting between Peter and Cornelius at Caesarea (vv. 24–33). 4. The sermon Peter preached in the house of Cornelius (vv. 34–43). 5. The baptizing of Cornelius and his friends, first with the Holy Spirit and then with water (vv. 44–48).

Verses 1–8

We should notice carefully all the circumstances of the beginning of this great work, this part of the *mystery of godliness—Christ preached to the Gentiles, and believed on in this world* (1Ti 3:16). The Gospel had never up to this time been intentionally preached to the Gentiles, nor had any of them been baptized—Cornelius was the first. We have here:

1. An account given to us of this Cornelius, who was the firstborn of the Gentiles to Christ. We are told here that he was a great man and a good man—two characteristics that seldom meet in the same person. Where they meet, they brighten each other: goodness makes greatness really valuable, and greatness makes goodness much more useful.

1.1. Cornelius was an officer in the army (v. 1). Here there was a regiment, or cohort, of the Roman army, which is called here *the Italian band* because they were all indigenous Romans or Italians. Cornelius had command of this part of the army. He was an officer of considerable rank and impressive appearance, a centurion. We read about one of that rank in our Savior's time whom he greatly commended (Mt 8:10). When a Gentile was to be chosen as the first to receive the Gospel, it was a Gentile soldier, who was a man of freer thought; those who really are freethinking cannot help receiving and welcoming the Christian message when it is properly set out for them. Let soldiers and officers of the army not plead that because their calling keeps them from settling down at one residence, they may be excused from settling on a religion. It was a mortification to the Jews that not only were the Gentiles taken into the church, but also the first one taken in was an officer of the Roman army.

1.2. He was a religious man. He is characterized as a very good man (v. 2). He had a godly reverence for the true and living God. He was *a devout man and one that feared God*. Although he was a soldier, it was no discredit to his courage that he trembled before God. He kept up religion in his family. He *feared God with all his house*. He took care that not only he but also all his family served the Lord. Every good person will make sure as much as they can that those around them are good too. He was very charitable: he *gave much alms to the people*. He was very often in prayer: He *prayed to God always*. Wherever the fear of God rules in the heart, it will appear both in works of charity and in godly devotion.

2. The orders given him from heaven to send for Peter. Notice:

2.1. How these orders were given him. He had a vision in which an angel gave them to him about the *ninth hour of the day*. Because it was the time of offering the evening sacrifice in the temple, devout people made it an *hour of prayer* (3:1), and Cornelius was now praying, as he tells us himself (v. 30). An angel of God *came in to him*, and he *saw* the angel *evidently* (distinctly) with his physical eyes, not in a dream presented to his imagination, but in a vision presented to his sight. The angel called him by his name, *Cornelius*, to show the special notice God took of him. This put Cornelius for the present into a state of some confusion (v. 4): *When he looked on him, he was afraid*. Then, as one who wanted to know the mind of God and was ready to submit to it, Cornelius cried, "*What is it, Lord*? What is the matter?"

2.2. What the message was.

2.2.1. He was assured that God accepted him (v. 4): *Thy prayers and thine alms are come up for a memorial before God*. Prayers and gifts to the poor must go together. We must follow our prayers with giving *alms* to those in need *out of such things as we have*, and then everything will be clean for us (Lk 11:41). We must also follow our alms with our prayers that God would graciously accept them. Cornelius prayed and gave to those in need sincerely, as to God, and he was told here that they had *come up for a memorial before God*. Prayers and gifts to the poor are our spiritual offerings, which God is pleased to respond to.

2.2.2. He was appointed to seek a further revelation of divine grace (vv. 5–6). He must "*send* immediately *to Joppa, and inquire for one Simon Peter; he lodgeth at the house of one Simon, a tanner; his house is by the sea side*, and when he comes, *he shall tell thee what thou oughtest to do*." Now here are two very surprising things:

2.2.2.1. Cornelius prayed and gave gifts to the poor in the fear of God; he himself was religious, and he kept up religion in his family; yet there was something further that he should do—he should accept the Christian religion. Not, "You may do it if you wish," but, "You must do it." The one who believed the promise of the Messiah must now believe the fulfillment of that promise. Neither our prayers nor our gifts to the poor can come up as a memorial offering before God unless we believe in Jesus Christ.

2.2.2.2. Cornelius now had an angel from heaven talking to him, but he must not receive the Gospel of Christ from this angel; all that the angel had to say was, "Send for Peter, and he will tell you." Just as it was an honor to the apostle that he must preach what an angel could not, so it was a further honor that an angel was sent to arrange for him to be sent for. To bring a faithful minister and a willing people together is a work worthy of an angel.

3. His immediate obedience to these orders (vv. 7–8). Notice:

3.1. When he sent: as soon as possible, as soon as the *angel which spoke unto him had departed*, he sent two of his servants to Joppa to bring Peter to him. He did not delay to fulfill this commandment (Ps 119:60). It is good for us to lose no time in any spiritual matter that concerns us.

3.2. Whom he sent: *two of his household servants, and a devout soldier, that waited on him continually*. A devout centurion had devout soldiers. A little devotion commonly goes a long way with soldiers, but there would be more in the soldiers if only there were more of it in their commanders. When this centurion had to choose some of his soldiers to be always with him, he chose those who were devout.

3.3. What instructions he gave them: *He declared all these things unto them* (v. 8). He told them not only where to find Peter but also on what mission Peter was to come, so that they would urge him.

Verses 9–18

Cornelius had received positive orders from heaven to send for Peter, but here another difficulty was put in the way of bringing them together—would Peter come to Cornelius? It was a point of conscience for Peter: Cornelius was a Gentile, uncircumcised. God in his Law had forbidden his people to associate with idolatrous nations, and the Jews took the matter so far that they considered even the involuntary touch of a Gentile as contracting ceremonial uncleanness (Jn 18:28). Since Peter had not overcome this narrow, bigoted idea of his compatriots, he would be reluctant to come to Cornelius. Now, to deal with this difficulty, he had a vision to prepare him to receive the message sent to him by Cornelius. Christ ordered his disciples to *teach all nations* (Mt 28:19), but even Peter himself could not understand it until it was revealed here by a vision. Notice:

1. The circumstances of this vision.

1.1. It was when the messengers were *nigh* (near) *the city* (v. 9). Peter knew nothing about their coming, and they knew nothing about his praying, but the One who knew both him and them was preparing things for the meeting. He often brings to the minds of his ministers things that they had not thought of, just when they need to use them.

1.2. It was when *Peter went up upon the house-top to pray*. Peter did a lot of praying, and he was now praying *about the sixth hour*; he prayed not only in the *morning and evening* but also *at noon* (Ps 55:17). We would think that from morning to night is too long to go without food, but who thinks it is too long to go without prayer? He prayed *upon the house-top*. He had this vision immediately after he had prayed. The rising of the heart to God in prayer is an excellent preparation to receive the revelations of divine grace.

1.3. It was when he became *very hungry* (v. 10) and *would have eaten* (wanted to eat). Now this hunger was a proper inlet to the vision about food, as Christ's hunger in the desert was a proper inlet to Satan's temptation to turn stones into bread (Mt 4:1–3).

2. The vision itself.

2.1. He *fell into a trance*. He lost himself completely to this world and so had his mind entirely free for contact with divine things. The more we get clear of the world, the closer we get to heaven.

2.2. He *saw heaven opened*, so that he could be sure that his authority to go to Cornelius really came from heaven.

2.3. He saw *a great sheet full of all manner of living creatures, which descended from heaven, and was let down to him to the earth*. Here were placed at his feet not only animals of the earth but also birds of the air. There were no fish of the sea, because none of them were particularly unclean. Some think this sheet, filled in this way, represents the church of Christ. In this we find people from all countries without any distinction of Greek or Jew. The net of the Gospel encloses all, *both bad and good* (Mt 22:10), those who previously were clean and unclean. Or it may be applied to the goodness of divine Providence. Such a vision should double our enjoyment in animals and our sense of obligation to serve God in our use and treatment of them—to see them let down to us from heaven in this way!

2.4. He was ordered by a voice from heaven to use this plenty and variety that God had sent him (v. 13): *Rise, Peter, kill and eat*. It would be difficult for Jews to dine with Gentiles, because Gentiles would place before them food they were not allowed to eat. Now Jews could fare as the Gentiles fared, eating with them and sharing with them.

2.5. He stood by his principles and would not listen to such a suggestion at all (v. 14): *Not so, Lord*. Although hunger will break through stone walls, God's laws should be to us a stronger fence than stone walls. Temptations to eat forbidden fruit must not be considered even for a moment, but conclusively rejected. The reason he gave was, *"For I have never eaten any thing that is common or unclean*; up to this time I have kept my integrity in this matter, and I will still keep it." His conscience could witness for him that he had never indulged his appetite with any forbidden food.

2.6. God, by a second voice from heaven, proclaimed the repeal of the law in this case (v. 15): *What God hath cleansed, that call thou not common*. The One who made the law could change it when he pleased. He has now taken away that restraint; he has cleansed what was before ceremonially unclean to us. We should welcome this as a great mercy, not so much because we gain the use of the meat of pigs, hares, rabbits, and other pleasant and wholesome food for our bodies, but chiefly because our conscience is freed from a yoke in such matters.

2.7. *This was done thrice* (v. 16), with the same call to him and the same reason. The instructions given us in the things of God need to be repeated often. At last *the vessel was received up into heaven*. Those who believe this sheet represents the church, which includes both Jews and Gentiles, very aptly represent this lifting up of the sheet as referring to the admission of believing Gentiles into the church, and into heaven too. They are those whom God has cleansed.

3. The providence that explained this vision (vv. 18–19).

3.1. Peter *doubted within himself what this vision which he had seen should mean*. He had no reason to doubt its truth; all his doubt was concerning its meaning. Christ reveals himself to his people gradually, leaving them to doubt for a while, to ponder a matter and think it over before he clarifies it to them.

3.2. However, he would understand it in a moment, because *the men who were sent from Cornelius* were *at the gate* inquiring whether Peter lodged there, and from their mission the meaning of this vision would become apparent. God knows what services are before us and therefore knows how to prepare us for them, and we know better the meaning of what he has taught us when we find what need we have to use it.

Verses 19–33

Here is the meeting between Peter and Cornelius. Although Paul was destined to be the apostle of the Gentiles, and Peter to be the apostle to the Jews, matters were so arranged that Peter would break the ice and reap the firstfruits of the Gentiles, so that the faithful Jews would be more easily reconciled to the admission of the Gentiles into the church, since they were first brought in by the Jews' own apostle.

1. Peter was instructed by the Spirit to accompany Cornelius's messengers (vv. 19–20). Now the riddle was explained, *while Peter thought on the vision*; he was pondering it, and then it was opened up to him. Those who want to be taught the things of God must think about those things. Notice:

1.1. From where he received direction. The Spirit told him what he should do. It was not spoken to him by an angel, but spoken in him by the Spirit.

1.2. What the instruction was. He was told that three men below wanted to speak to him (v. 19), and he must get up from his thoughts and go down to them (v. 20). Those who are investigating the meaning of the words of God and the visions of the Almighty (Nu 24:4, 16) should not always be poring over them, nor even always praying, but should sometimes look around them. Peter was told to *go along with the messengers to Cornelius, doubting nothing* (not hesitating to go), not doubting either whether he could go or whether he should go, because it was his duty. *Go with them, for I have sent them*. When we see that our call to any service is clear, we should not allow ourselves to be confused with doubts and hesitations or to fear censure by other people.

2. He received both them and their message: *He went down to them* (v. 21).

2.1. He received the message favorably. He asked what their business was: *What is the cause wherefore you are* (why have you) *come?* And they told him their reason (v. 22): *"Cornelius*, an officer of the Roman army, *was warned from God* by an angel, and he is a man *who fears God above many* (Ne 7:2), *of good report among all the people of the Jews*. He was ordered to send for you to come to his house, *and* he was ordered *to hear words of thee*." These words, Peter later tells us more fully, are *words whereby thou and all thy house shall be saved* (11:14).

2.2. He received the messengers kindly (v. 23): *He called them in, and lodged them*. They would be welcome to share in what was being prepared for him (v. 10); he had little thought what company he would have when he ate his dinner, but God foresaw it. Peter kept them even though they were Gentiles, to show how readily he submitted to the vision's intention that he eat with Gentiles. Although two of them were servants, and the other an ordinary soldier, Peter did not think it beneath him to take them into his house.

3. He *went with them* to Cornelius. Peter was *accompanied by certain brethren from Joppa* (v. 23). Six of them went along with him, as we find in v. 12. This was one way in which the first Christians very much showed their

respect for their ministers: they accompanied them on their journeys. It is a pity that those who have the skill and will to do good to others by their speech would ever forgo an opportunity to do so by traveling alone. Cornelius *had called some friends together of Cesarea*. Now when they came into the house of Cornelius, Peter found:

3.1. That he was expected, and this was an encouragement to him. *Cornelius waited for them*, and such a guest was worth waiting for; nor can I blame him if he waited with some impatience.

3.2. That he was expected by many, and this was a further encouragement to him. Just as Peter brought some with him to share in the spiritual gift he had to give now, so *Cornelius had called together* not only his own family but also *kinsmen and near friends*. We should not seek to eat our spiritual bread alone (Job 31:17). When we invite our relatives and friends to join with us in religious activities, to go with us to hear a sermon, the invitation should be both given and taken as an act of kindness and respect.

4. Here is the first interview between Peter and Cornelius. We have here:

4.1. The deep respect and honor that Cornelius paid to Peter (v. 25): *He met him as he was coming in*, and *he fell down at his feet and worshiped him*. His worshiping a man was indeed wrong, but considering his present ignorance, it was excusable. No wonder if, till better informed, he worshiped the one he was ordered to send for by an angel from heaven.

4.2. Peter's modest refusal of the honor shown him (v. 25): *He took him up, saying, Stand up, I myself also am a man*. The good angels of the churches (Rev 1:20, where *angelos*, "messenger," may refer either to angels or to ministers) cannot bear to be shown the least honor that is due only to God. Christ's faithful servants could better bear to be insulted than to be deified. Let the centurion know that Peter was a man, that *the treasure is in earthen vessels* (2Co 4:7), so that he might value the treasure for its own sake.

5. Here is the account Peter and Cornelius gave to each other and to the group with them of how the hand of heaven had brought them together: *As he talked with him, he went in* (v. 27). When Peter came in, *he found many that were come together*, which both added solemnity to the occasion and increased his opportunity to do good in this service.

5.1. Peter told them about the instructions God gave him to come to those Gentiles (vv. 28–29). They knew that such an encounter had never been allowed by the Jews, since it had always been looked on as *unlawful for a man that is a Jew to keep company* (associate) *or come unto* (visit) *one of another nation*, an uncircumcised Gentile. It was not made unlawful by the law of God, but by the decree of their wise men. Those leaders did not forbid them to talk or have dealings with Gentiles on the street, in a shop, or in the marketplace, but they did forbid them to eat with them, or even to come into the house of a Gentile. This is how scornfully the Jews looked on the Gentiles, who, for their part, did not lack contempt for the Jews. *But now*, Peter said, *God hath shown me that I should not call any man common or unclean*. Peter, who had taught his new converts to *save themselves from the untoward generation of wicked men* (2:40), was now himself taught to join himself with the pure generation of devout Gentiles. He now assured them, therefore, of his readiness to do them all the good he could. He had kept far away only because he had lacked permission from heaven; having now received that permission, he was at

their service and wanted to know how he could be useful to them: *Therefore came I unto you without gainsaying* (without raising any objection), *as soon as I was sent for. I ask, therefore, for what intent you have sent for me?*

5.2. Cornelius told them about the instructions God gave him to send for Peter.

5.2.1. Cornelius gave an account of the angel's appearing to him and ordering him to send for Peter. He told how this vision found him employed (v. 30): *Four days ago I was fasting until this hour; and at the ninth hour I was praying in my house*. He was praying not in the synagogue, but at home. *At the ninth hour of the day*, three o'clock in the afternoon, when most people were traveling or trading, working in the fields, visiting their friends, entertaining themselves, or napping after dinner—then Cornelius was spending time with God in his devotions, which shows how important religion was to him. He described the messenger: *There stood a man before me in bright clothing*. He repeated the message that was sent to him (vv. 31–32), just as we had it before (vv. 4–6), except here he reported that the angel said, *thy prayer is heard*. We are not told what his prayer was, but if this message was its answer, we may suppose that he had prayed that God would further reveal to him both himself and the way of salvation.

5.2.2. Cornelius told of his own and his friends' readiness to receive the message Peter had to deliver (v. 33): *Immediately therefore I sent to thee, and thou hast well done that thou hast come*. Faithful ministers do well to come to a people who want to receive instruction from them; to come when they are sent for is as good an action as any they can do. Notice:

5.2.2.1. Their religious attention and readiness: "*We are all here present before God. Therefore*, because you have come to us by such authority and on such a mission, *we are present* and ready to come at a call. *We are all present*, all who were invited." The whole of the person must be present; not the body here while the heart, with the *eyes of a fool*, is *in the ends of the earth* (Pr 17:24).

5.2.2.2. The intention of this attendance: *We are present to hear all things that are commanded thee of God*. Peter was there to preach all the things that had been commanded him by God. They were ready to listen—not to whatever he wished to say, but to what he was commanded by God to say. "We are ready to hear all that you have been commissioned to preach, no matter how unpleasant and contrary to our former ideas or our present worldly interests. We are ready to hear everything, and so let nothing that is profitable for us be kept back."

Verses 34–43

Here is Peter's sermon. In that phrase, *he opened his mouth, and spoke* (v. 34), it is suggested that he expressed himself with great intensity and seriousness, but also with freedom and exuberance.

1. Because those to whom he preached were Gentiles, it was a new sermon. He showed that there was a share for them in the Gospel of Christ and that they were entitled to enjoy benefits of it on an equal footing with the Jews. He set down as an undoubted principle that *God is no respecter of persons*. He does not declare justice in a person's favor for the sake of any external advantage foreign to the merits of the cause. Rather, *in every nation he that fears God and works righteousness is accepted of him* (v. 35). God never did and never will justify and save an evil Jew who lived and died impenitent; such a person's privileges and professions, instead of protecting them from the judgment of God, will only aggravate

their guilt and condemnation. He never did and never will reject or refuse an honest Gentile who, like Cornelius, fears God and worships him, undertaking acts of righteousness and living up to the light they have received. A person's nationality, whatever it is, will not prejudice them. God judges people by their hearts, not according to what country they come from or what their background is. Wherever God finds someone who is *upright* (blameless), he will be found to be an *upright* (blameless) God (Ps 18:25). Fearing God and working righteousness must go together. But where these are predominant, acceptance with God is not in doubt. Those who do not know Christ and therefore cannot have an explicit regard for him may still, for his sake, receive grace from God *to fear God and to work righteousness*. Wherever God gives grace to do so, as he did to Cornelius, he will, through Christ, accept the work of his own hands (Ps 138:8). It was always a truth, long before Peter perceived it, *that God respecteth no man's person*. God will not ask on the Day of Judgment what country people came from, but what they were like. Yet now it was made clearer than it had been in the past. Peter came to realize it here by comparing the vision that he had with the one Cornelius had.

2. Because they were Gentiles living in a place within the confines of the land of Israel, he referred them to what they themselves must have known of our Lord Jesus, for these were things that were reported as they spread into every corner of the nation (v. 37).

2.1. They knew, in general, *the word which God sent to the children of Israel: That word, I say, you know* (v. 37). Although the Gentiles had not been admitted to hear it, they could not help hearing it. We are often told in the Gospels how the fame of Christ went into every part of Canaan (Mk 1:28). "That word of power and grace *ye know*; you know what the effect of this word was." Through it, God "published the glad tidings of peace by Jesus Christ," as it should read. It is God himself who declares peace, who justly could have declared war. The word was first sent *to the children of Israel* (v. 36).

2.2. They knew several factual matters about this word of the Gospel sent to Israel. They knew the baptism of repentance that John preached by way of introduction to it. They knew how extraordinary John was, and that the direct aim of his preaching was to *prepare the way of the Lord* (Mt 3:3). They knew that immediately after John's baptism the Gospel of Christ, that word of *peace, was published throughout all Judea*, and that it had its origin in Galilee. They knew that Jesus of Nazareth *went about doing good*. They knew how generous he was to that nation, how he made it his business to do good to everyone. He was not lazy, but continued to do good, going from place to place and doing good wherever he went. Here, he showed *that he was sent of God*. They knew especially that he *healed all that were oppressed of the devil*. This showed that he was sent to *destroy the works of the devil* (1Jn 3:8), because by healing people in this way, he obtained many victories over him. They knew that the Jews put Jesus to death; they, to whom he had done and intended so much good, *slew* (killed) him by *hanging him on a tree*. Peter's congregation knew all this, but in case they thought it was only an exaggerated report, Peter affirmed it for himself and the rest of the apostles (v. 39): *We are witnesses of all things which he did, both in the land of the Jews and in Jerusalem.*

2.3. They could know from all this that Jesus had received a commission from heaven to preach and act as he did. This Jesus *is Lord of all*; not only as *God over all, blessed for evermore* (Ro 9:5), but also as Mediator, he

has had *all power both in heaven and on earth* put into his hands (Mt 28:18) and all judgment committed to him (Jn 5:22). *God anointed him with the Holy Spirit and with power* (v. 38), which is why he was called Christ, "the Messiah, the Anointed One." He was full of power both in preaching and in performing miracles, which were the seal of his divine mission. *God was with him* (v. 38). God not only sent him but also was present with him all along. Those whom God anoints he will accompany; he himself will be with those to whom he has given his Spirit.

3. Because they had had no more certain information about this Jesus, Peter told them about his resurrection from the dead and the proofs of it. At Caesarea they had probably heard some talk of his having risen from the dead, but it was soon silenced by that vile suggestion of the Jews that *his disciples came by night and stole him away* (Mt 28:13).

3.1. The power by which he arose was undeniably divine (v. 40): *Him God raised up the third day.* He did not break out of prison, but was legally discharged. *God raised him up.*

3.2. The proofs of his resurrection were undeniably clear, for God *showed him openly.* It was such an appearance of him as amounted to a demonstration of the truth of his resurrection. He showed himself not publicly, but clearly: *not to all the people* (v. 41). By resisting all the evidence he had given them of his divine mission, the people in general had forfeited the favor of being eyewitnesses of the great proof of that mission. Those who immediately made and furthered that lie that he had been stolen away were justly given up to strong delusions to believe it (2Th 2:11). A sufficient number saw him to affirm the truth of his resurrection. The resurrection of Christ was proved in the presence sufficient witnesses. They were not so by chance, but were *chosen before of God* to witness it. They had not had a sudden, short-lived view of him, but had a great deal of free conversation with him: *They did eat and drink with him after he rose from the dead.* This was not all; they also saw him without any fear or terror, which might have made them incompetent witnesses; he spoke to them so familiarly that *they did eat and drink with him.*

4. Peter concluded by inferring from all this that what they all should do was to believe in this Jesus: he was sent to tell Cornelius what he must do, and it was this. One thing he lacked (Mk 10:21): he must believe in Christ. Notice:

4.1. Why he must believe in him. The Christian faith is *built upon the foundation of the apostles and prophets* (Eph 2:20), on the testimony given by them.

4.1.1. By the apostles. Peter spoke for the rest, telling the group that *God commanded them to preach to the people, and to testify* about Christ. Their testimony was God's testimony, and they were his witnesses to the world.

4.1.2. By the prophets of the Old Testament (v. 43): *To him give all the prophets witness.* Out of the mouth of these two clouds of witnesses (Heb 12:1) *this word was established* (2Co 13:1).

4.2. What they must believe about him.

4.2.1. That we are all responsible to Christ as our Judge. This Jesus is *ordained of God to be the Judge of the quick and dead* (v. 42). He is empowered to set down the terms of salvation, the rule by which we must be judged. God has assured us of this, *in that he hath raised Jesus from the dead* (17:31), so that it is the great concern of each of us to make Christ our friend.

4.2.2. That if we believe in him, we will all be justified by him as our righteousness (v. 43). The prophets witnessed *that through his name, whosoever believeth in him shall receive remission of sins.* This is the great thing we need, without which we are ruined. The forgiveness of sins lays a foundation for all other favors and blessings. If sin is pardoned, all is well, and will end eternally well.

Verses 44–48

We have here the effect and outcome of Peter's sermon. They were all brought home to Christ. We have here:

1. God's acknowledging Peter's word by conferring the Holy Spirit on those who heard it (v. 44): *While Peter was yet speaking these words, the Holy Spirit fell on all those who heard the word*, even as he did on the apostles at Pentecost; this is what Peter says (11:15). Notice:

1.1. When the Holy Spirit fell on them—while Peter was preaching. This is how God witnessed what he said and accompanied it with divine power. The Holy Spirit fell on others after they were baptized, to confirm them, but he fell on these Gentiles before they were baptized, to show that God is not restricted to one method and does not confine himself to external signs.

1.2. How it was seen that the Holy Spirit had fallen on them (v. 46): *They spoke with tongues.* When they spoke in tongues, they *magnified God*; they spoke about Christ and the benefits of redemption, which Peter had been preaching. Whatever gift we are endowed with, we should honor God with it, especially the gift of speaking and all its uses.

1.3. What impression it made on the faithful Jews who were present (v. 45): *Those of the circumcision who believed were astonished,* because *upon the Gentiles also was poured out the gift of the Holy Spirit.* If they had understood the Scriptures of the Old Testament, it would not have been so astonishing to them.

2. Peter's acknowledging God's work by baptizing those on whom the Holy Spirit fell. Notice:

2.1. Although they had received the Holy Spirit, they still needed to be baptized; although God is not limited to instituted ordinances, we are.

2.2. Although they were Gentiles, nevertheless, having received the Holy Spirit, they could be admitted to baptism (v. 47): *Can any man forbid water, that these should not be baptized, who have received the Holy Spirit as well as we?* The argument is conclusive; can we deny the sign to those who have received the thing signified by that sign? It is good for us to follow God's signs, to take into fellowship with us those whom he has taken into fellowship with himself. Now it was clear why the Spirit had been given them before they were baptized—because otherwise Peter could not have persuaded himself to baptize them. In this way, we see one unusual step after another taken by divine grace to bring the Gentiles into the church. How good it is for us that the grace of a good God is so much more extensive than the charity of some good people!

2.3. Peter did not baptize them himself, but *commanded them to be baptized* (v. 48). The apostles received the commission to *go and disciple all nations by baptism* (Mt 28:19), but they were to *give* themselves to prayer and the ministry of the word (6:4). The work of baptizing, therefore, was ordinarily delegated to lesser ministers; these acted on the orders of the apostles.

3. The congregation's desire to benefit further from Peter's ministry: *They prayed him to tarry* (stay with them) *certain days.* They did not want him to go away immediately, and so they passionately begged him to stay some time among them, so that they could be taught by him further. Those who know Christ a little must want to

know him more. Even those who have received the Holy Spirit must see their need of the ministry of the word.

CHAPTER 11

In this chapter we have: 1. Peter's necessary vindication of what he had done in receiving Cornelius and his friends into the church (vv. 1–18). 2. The success of the Gospel at Antioch (vv. 19–21). 3. The continuation of the good work begun at Antioch, and the lasting name of Christian first given to the disciples there (vv. 22–26). 4. A prediction of an approaching famine, and the contribution to help the poor saints in Judea (vv. 27–30).

Verses 1–18

Because the preaching of the Gospel was such a great surprise to the believing as well as the unbelieving Jews, it is worthwhile asking how it was received.

1. Information about it was immediately brought to the church in Jerusalem and the surrounding area. Before Peter himself had returned to Jerusalem, *the apostles and* the *brethren* there and *in Judea heard that the Gentiles also had received the word of God*, that the Gentiles themselves, with whom it had up to that time been thought unlawful to associate, had *received the word of God.* That is:

1.1. The word of God was preached to them, and in this way a greater honor was shown them than the Jews had expected. But the prejudices of pride and bigotry often hold out firmly against the clearest revelations of divine truth.

1.2. It was received and submitted to by them, and in this way a better work was done in them than the Jews had expected. The Jews looked on the Gentiles as not having any inclination toward religion; they were therefore surprised to hear that the Gentiles had accepted the word of the Lord. We sometimes tend to despair of doing good to those who, when tested, prove to be very amenable.

2. Offense was taken at it by the faithful Jews (vv. 2–3): *When Peter had himself come up to Jerusalem, those that were of the circumcision contended with him.* They thought it a crime that he *went in to men uncircumcised, and did eat with them,* and so they thought he had stained, if not forfeited, the honor of his apostleship.

2.1. It is a blight and damage to the church to monopolize it, excluding from it those who are not like us in everything.

2.2. Christ's ministers must not think it strange if they are censured not only by their professed enemies but also by their professing friends. However, if we have proved our own work, we may have joy in ourselves, as Peter had, whatever censures we may receive from our fellow believers. Those who are zealous and courageous in serving Christ must expect to be censured by those who, claiming to be cautious, are in reality cold and indifferent. Those who have generous, charitable motives must expect to be criticized by those who are conceited and narrow-minded.

3. Peter gave an account of the facts of the matter that was sufficiently full and reasonable to justify him and to satisfy them (v. 4): *He rehearsed* (began speaking and explaining) *the matter from the beginning.*

3.1. He assumed that if they had correctly understood how the matters were, they would not have argued with him. We should be moderate in our criticism, because if we correctly understood what we are so eager to criticize, we might see good reason to go along with it.

3.2. He wanted very much for them to agree with his opinion. He was ready to *give a reason of the hope that is in him* about the Gentiles (1Pe 3:15) and why he had retreated from his former attitudes, which had been the same as theirs.

3.2.1. He was instructed by a vision that he must no longer maintain the distinctions that had been made by the ceremonial law; he related the vision here (vv. 5–6), as we had it before (10:9). The sheet that in his earlier account was said to have been *let down to the earth*, he here said came *even to him*. We, similarly, should see all God's revelations of himself as coming directly to us, and we should apply them by faith to ourselves. When the sheet *came to him, he fastened his eyes upon it and considered it* (v. 6). If we want to be led into the knowledge of divine things, we must fix our minds on them and consider them. He told the believers what orders he received to eat all kinds of meat without distinction, asking no questions for conscience' sake (v. 7). He pleaded that he had been as averse to the thoughts of associating with Gentiles as they, his fellow believers, could be, and that was why he refused the liberty given him: *Not so, Lord; for nothing common or unclean has at any time entered into my mouth* (v. 8). But he was told that God had cleansed those persons and things that had previously been unclean, and that was why he must no longer call them *common* (v. 9), and so he was not to be blamed for changing his thoughts when God had changed the thing he thought about. So that the believers could be sure he was not deceived in this matter, he told them it was done three times (v. 10), and that to confirm to him even further that it was a divine vision, the things he saw did not vanish into the air, but *were drawn up again into heaven*.

3.2.2. He was specifically told by the Spirit to accompany the messengers Cornelius had sent. Peter told his listeners what time it was when the messengers came—immediately after he had that vision; but in case this was not sufficient to clear his way, the Spirit told him to *go with the men, nothing doubting* (vv. 11–12). He must not hesitate at all.

3.2.3. He took with him some of his brothers who were circumcised, so that they would be satisfied as well as he. He did not act alone, but with advice; not rashly, but after due deliberation.

3.2.4. Cornelius had a vision too (v. 13): *He showed us how he had seen an angel in his house*, who told him to *send to Joppa for one Simon, whose surname is Peter*. Peter was more confirmed in the truth of his vision by Cornelius's, and Cornelius by Peter's. Here something was added to what the angel said to Cornelius; before it was, *Send for Peter, and he shall speak to thee; he shall tell thee what thou oughtest to do* (10:6, 32), but here it is, *He shall tell thee words whereby thou and thy house shall be saved* (v. 14). The message of the Gospel consists of words by which we may be eternally saved, not by merely hearing them, but by believing and obeying them. They open up the way of salvation to us. Those who accept the Gospel of Christ will have salvation brought by it to their families: "*Thou and all thy house shall be saved*; your household, even to your lowliest servant, will be as welcome to the benefits of the salvation as you yourself." Now salvation was brought to the Gentiles.

3.2.5. What put the matter beyond all dispute was the falling of the Holy Spirit on the Gentile hearers.

3.2.5.1. The facts were clear and undeniable (v. 15): *As I began to speak, the Holy Spirit fell on them as on us at the beginning*. This was how God affirmed what was done and declared his approval of it.

3.2.5.2. Peter was reminded of a saying of his Master's (1:5): *John baptized with water*, but *you shall be baptized with the Holy Spirit* (v. 16). The Holy Spirit was the gift of Christ, and it was the result and fulfillment of that great promise that he left them when he went to heaven. It was therefore beyond doubt that this gift came from him. Just as it was promised by his mouth, so it was fulfilled by his hand. The gift of the Holy Spirit was a kind of baptism.

3.2.5.3. When the question was raised whether these people should be baptized or not, Peter compared that promise of Christ's, so worded, with this gift just now conferred, and he concluded that the question was determined by Christ himself (v. 17): "*Forasmuch then as God gave them the like gift as he did to us*—gave it to us as *believing in the Lord Jesus Christ*, and to them upon their believing in *him—What was I, that I could withstand God?* Could I refuse to baptize with water those whom God had baptized with the Holy Spirit?" When people work out how to exclude from their fellowship those whom God has taken into fellowship with himself, they usurp his authority.

4. This account that Peter gave of the matter satisfied them. Some people, when they have focused their criticism on a person, will stand by it even when later it is seen very clearly to have been unjust and baseless. It was not so here. When the believers heard this, they held their peace and said nothing more against what Peter had done. They not only held their peace from quarreling with Peter; they opened their mouths to glorify God. They were thankful that God had shown more mercy to the poor Gentiles than they were inclined to show them, saying, *Then hath God also to the Gentiles granted repentance unto life!* He had granted them the grace of repentance by giving them his Holy Spirit, who first gives a sight of sin and sorrow for it, and then gives a sight of Christ and joy in him. We can learn from this:

4.1. If repentance is true, it leads to life. Those who by repentance die to sin live from that time on for God (Ro 6:2, 10), and then, and not till then, we begin to really live as God intended, and it will lead to eternal life.

4.2. Repentance is God's gift; not only does his free grace accept it, but also his mighty grace produces it in us.

4.3. Wherever God intends to give life, he gives repentance. God has exalted his Son Jesus to *give repentance and the remission of sins* not only *to Israel* (5:31) but also to the Gentiles.

Verses 19–26

We have here an account of the planting and nurturing of a church at Antioch, the chief city of Syria, later considered to be the third most significant city in the empire, after Rome and Alexandria. It has been suggested that Luke, the writer of this account, as well as Theophilus, to whom he dedicates it, came from Antioch, which may be the reason that Luke takes more particular notice of the success of the Gospel at Antioch.

1. The first preachers of the Gospel there were those who had been dispersed from Jerusalem by persecution, the persecution that arose at the time of Stephen's death (v. 19): *They travelled as far as Phenice* (Phoenicia) *preaching the word*. What was intended to harm the church was made to work for its good. The enemies wanted to scatter and lose the believers, but Christ wanted to scatter and use them. Notice:

1.1. Those who *fled from persecution* did not flee from their work. Those who persecuted the preachers of the Gospel hoped that persecution would prevent them from taking the Gospel to the Gentile world, but instead it hastened the spread of the Gospel. Those who were persecuted in one city fled to another, but they took their religious faith along with them.

1.2. They pressed forward in their work. When they had preached successfully in Judea, Samaria, and Galilee, they traveled into Phoenicia, to the island of Cyprus, and to Syria. Although the further they traveled, the more they exposed themselves to persecution and danger, they still traveled on: "further still" was their motto.

1.3. They *preached the word to none but to the Jews only* (v. 19) who were dispersed throughout all those parts. They did not yet understand that the Gentiles were to be fellow heirs, but left the Gentiles either to become Jews or to remain as they were.

1.4. They especially addressed the Hellenist Jews, here called the Greeks. Many of the preachers were natives of Judea and Jerusalem, but some of them, such as Barnabas himself (4:36) and Simon (Mk 15:21), came by birth from Cyprus and Cyrene. Because these were Greek Jews themselves, they had a particular concern for those of their own background and devoted themselves especially to them at Antioch. They preached the Lord Jesus to them. This was the constant subject of their preaching; what else should the ministers of Christ preach but Christ?

1.5. They had wonderful success in their preaching (v. 21).

1.5.1. Their preaching was accompanied by divine power. *The hand of the Lord was with them* to bring home to the hearts and consciences of people what the human preachers could only speak to the outward ear. These were not apostles, but ordinary ministers, yet they had the hand of the Lord with them and performed wonders.

1.5.2. Much good was done: *A great number believed, and turned unto the Lord.* They believed; they were convinced of the truth of the Gospel. The effect of this was that they *turned unto the Lord*. They turned from trusting in the righteousness of the law to depending only on the righteousness of Christ, the righteousness that is through faith (Ro 3:22). They turned to the Lord Jesus, and he became *all in all* to them (Eph 1:23; Col 3:11). Whatever we profess or claim, we do not really believe the Gospel if we do not sincerely accept Christ as he is offered to us in the Gospel.

2. The good work begun in this way in Antioch was continued to perfection through the ministry of Barnabas and Saul.

2.1. The church at Jerusalem sent Barnabas to Antioch.

2.1.1. They heard the good news that the Gospel had been received at Antioch (v. 22). News *of these things came to the ears of the church that was in Jerusalem.*

2.1.2. They *sent Barnabas forth* to them as an ambassador from them. He must *go as far as Antioch*. Barnabas probably had a special talent for such work and was therefore the most suitable person to be employed in it. God gives different gifts for different services.

2.1.3. Barnabas was wonderfully pleased to find that the Gospel had gained ground and that some of his own compatriots, people of Cyprus, were instrumental in it (v. 23): *When he came, and had seen the grace of God, he was glad.* He saw the grace of God among them. Whenever we see anything good in anyone, we must call that God's grace in them. We must be glad to see the grace of God in others, and all the more so when we see it where we did not expect it.

2.1.4. He did what he could to confirm in the faith those who were converted to the faith. He *exhorted them.* The word translated *exhorted* is the same that was used to translate Barnabas's Aramaic name into Greek (4:36), in the phrase *hyios parakleseos*, which may be

translated into English as "Son of Exhortation"; he had a talent for exhortation, and he used it. Or, being *a son of consolation* — for this is how our translation renders his name in 4:36 — he encouraged *them to*, or comforted them so that they would, *cleave* (remain true) *to the Lord with purpose of heart.* Barnabas was glad because of what he saw of the grace of God among them, and that was why he earnestly urged them to persevere, that is:

2.1.4.1. To *cleave* (remain true) *to the Lord.* They were not to fall away from following him, nor flag and tire in following him, and they must not only hold him firmly but also be held firmly by him.

2.1.4.2. To remain true to him with all their hearts, with an intelligent, firm, and deliberate resolution.

2.1.5. Here, he gave proof of his good character (v. 24): *He was a good man, and full of the Holy Spirit, and of faith.* He was not only righteous but also good tempered. Ministers who are like that commend themselves and their message very much to the good opinion of outsiders (1Ti 3:7). He was a good man, that is, he was kind; he had proved himself to be so when he sold a field he owned and gave the money to the poor (4:37). Yet he was also richly endowed with the gifts and graces of the Spirit, and the goodness of his natural disposition would not have qualified him for this service unless he had been *full of the Holy Spirit.* And he was full of faith; he was full of the grace of faith and full of the fruits of the faith that works by love (Gal 5:6).

2.1.6. He was instrumental in doing good by bringing in outsiders as well as by building up those who were already within: *Much people were added to the Lord.*

2.2. Barnabas went to find Saul. He traveled to Tarsus to tell him what a great door of opportunity had opened up in Antioch and to express his desire that Saul come and spend some time with him there (vv. 25–26). Here, too, it is shown that Barnabas was a good person, in two matters:

2.2.1. He would take so much effort to bring an active, useful man out of obscurity, to bring him out of the corner into which he was driven and into a more public position. It is a very good work to take a candle out from under a bowl and put it on a lampstand (Mt 5:15).

2.2.2. He would bring Saul to Antioch, since Paul, being a *chief speaker* (14:12), would probably eclipse him there by outshining him. Barnabas brought Saul to Antioch even though it might lessen his own reputation.

2.3. We are also told here:

2.3.1. What service was now done for the church at Antioch. Paul and Barnabas continued there for a whole year, leading their religious gatherings and preaching the Gospel (v. 26). *Teaching the people* is one part of the work of ministers. They are to be not only the people's mouthpiece to God in prayer and praise but also God's mouthpiece to the people in opening up the Scriptures and teaching the good knowledge of the Lord (2Ch 30:22). It is a great encouragement to ministers to have opportunity to teach many people, to throw open the net of the Gospel where there is a large shoal of fish. Yet preaching is undertaken not only to convert outsiders but also to teach and build up those within the church.

2.3.2. What honor was now shown to the church at Antioch: *There the disciples were first called Christians.* Because two such great men as Paul and Barnabas stayed there so long and met with large numbers of followers, Christian meetings became more significant there than anywhere else, which was the reason they were first called Christians there. Up to that time those who gave their names to Christ were called disciples, which means "learners" or "scholars," but from that time on they were called Christians. In this way:

2.3.2.1. The disrespectful names their enemies had branded them with up to that time would perhaps be superseded. Their enemies called them *Nazarenes* (24:5), *the men of that way* (9:2), that byway that had no name, and this was how they made people prejudiced against the believers. To take away the prejudice, the believers gave themselves a name that their enemies could not help saying was proper.

2.3.2.2. Those who before their conversion had been distinguished by the names *Jew* and *Gentile* would now be called by one and the same name. Let not one say, "I was a Jew," nor the other, "I was a Gentile," since both the one and the other must now say, "I am a Christian."

2.3.2.3. They tried to honor their Master and showed that they were not ashamed to acknowledge their relationship to him. They took their name not from the name of his person, *Jesus*, but from his office, *Christ*, "the Anointed One," so making their names express their creed *that Jesus is the Christ* (Jn 20:31). Their enemies would turn this name into an accusation and impute it to them as their crime, but they would glory in it.

2.3.2.4. They now acknowledged their dependence on Christ.

2.3.2.5. They laid on themselves, and on all who would profess that name, a strong and lasting obligation to follow the example of Christ and to devote themselves completely to the honor of Christ. Are we Christians? Then we should do nothing to bring disgrace to that worthy name by which we are called. Just as we must look on ourselves as Christians and live accordingly, so we must also look on others as Christians and behave toward them accordingly. Christians who do not share our opinion in everything should still be loved and respected for the sake of the One whose name they bear, because they belong to Christ.

Verses 27–30

When our Lord Jesus *ascended on high, he gave gifts unto men*, not only gifts to be *apostles and evangelists* but also gifts to be *prophets* (Eph 4:8, 11). We have here:

1. A visit some of these prophets made to Antioch (v. 27): *In these days came prophets from Jerusalem to Antioch.*

1.1. They came from Jerusalem. Jerusalem had been notorious for killing the prophets and mistreating them, and so the city was now justly deprived of these prophets.

1.2. They came to Antioch. Barnabas came to encourage the believers at Antioch, and because they received the encouragement well, prophets were now sent them to *show them things to come.*

2. A particular prediction of an approaching famine, spoken by one of these prophets, *Agabus*; we read about him again, prophesying Paul's imprisonment (21:10–11). Here he stood up and prophesied (v. 28). Notice:

2.1. From where he received his prophecy. *He signified* (predicted) *by the Spirit that there should be* a famine.

2.2. What the prophecy was: *There would be great dearth throughout all the world*, so that many of the poor would die for lack of bread. This would be not in any one particular country, but *through all the world*, that is, the entire Roman Empire. Christ had foretold in general *that there would be famines*. Agabus foretold one very significant famine that was now at hand.

2.3. Its fulfillment: *It came to pass in the days of Claudius Caesar*; it began in the second year of his reign

and continued to the fourth, if not longer. Several of the Roman historians mention it, as does Josephus.

3. The good use the believers at Antioch made of this prediction. When they were told about an approaching famine, they did not store grain for themselves, but, as befitted Christians, set aside for charity to relieve others. Notice:

3.1. What they decided—that *every man, according to his ability*, should *send relief to the brethren that dwelt in Judea* (v. 29).

3.1.1. The people who were commended to them as objects for their charity were *the brethren that dwelt in Judea*. Although we must, as we have opportunity, *do good to all men*, we must have a special regard *to the household of faith* (Gal 6:10). No poor must be neglected, but God's poor must be remembered especially. However, the fellowship of saints was extended here, and provision was made by the church at Antioch to provide help for the poor in Judea, whom they called their *brethren*. Now we may suppose that the greatest part of those who became Christians in that country were poor. If a famine came, things would be very hard for them. If any of them were to die of starvation, it would bring great disgrace to the Christian profession, and so care was taken quickly to send them a stock in advance, so that it would not be delayed until the famine came and therefore be too late.

3.1.2. The disciples agreed that that *every man* should contribute *according to his ability* to this good work. Merchants earn a profit by sending goods to distant countries, and so we should be eager to give gifts to the needy who are far away when we are called on to do it. What may be said to be according to our ability we must judge for ourselves, but we must be careful that we judge rightly.

3.2. What they did—they did as they determined (v. 30): *Which also they did.* They not only talked about it; they did it. Many a good idea of that kind has been made and commended but not pursued, and so comes to nothing. The collection was taken, and it was so considerable that they thought it worthwhile *to send Barnabas and Saul to Jerusalem.* They sent the collection *to the elders of the churches in Judea* to be distributed by them according to the needs of those who received it, just as it had been contributed according to the ability of the givers. It was sent *by Barnabas and Saul.* It is not beneath ministers of the Gospel, in extraordinary situations, to be messengers of the church's charity.

CHAPTER 12

We have here: 1. The martyrdom of James the apostle and the imprisonment of Peter by Herod Agrippa (vv. 1–4). 2. The miraculous rescue of Peter from prison in answer to the prayers of the church for him (vv. 5–19). 3. The destruction of Herod at the height of his pride (vv. 20–23), and this was done while Barnabas and Saul were at Jerusalem. At the close of the chapter we have an account of their return to Antioch (vv. 24–25).

Verses 1–4

Since the conversion of Paul, we have heard nothing about the priests' persecuting of the saints at Jerusalem. Here, however, the storm arose from another point. The civil power acted by itself in the persecution. And yet Herod Agrippa, though from an Edomite family, seems to have been a convert to the Jewish religion, for Josephus says he was zealous for the Mosaic rituals and ceremonies. He was not only, as Herod Antipas was, tetrarch of Galilee, but also charged by Claudius the emperor with governing Judea, and he lived mostly in Jerusalem, where he was at this time. We are told here about three things he did:

1. He *stretched forth his hands to vex certain of the church* (v. 1). Herod "laid hands on some of the church to mistreat them," as some read it. Notice how he advanced gradually. He began with some of the members of the church, first hunted small game, and then moved on to the apostles themselves. He began by troubling them or mistreating them. Afterward he proceeded to greater expressions of cruelty.

2. He killed James the brother of John with the sword (v. 2). We are to consider here:

2.1. Who the martyr was: it was *James the brother of John*, so called to distinguish him from the other James, the brother of *Joses* (Joseph). The one who was crowned here with martyrdom was one of the first three of Christ's disciples (Lk 5:8–11). He was one of those whom Christ called *Boanerges*, "Sons of Thunder," and perhaps by his powerful, arousing preaching he had provoked Herod, as John the Baptist had provoked the other Herod. He was one of those sons of Zebedee whom Christ told *that they would drink of the cup that he was to drink of, and be baptized with the baptism that he was to be baptized with* (Mt 20:23). Now those words of Christ were fulfilled in him. The apostle died a martyr, to show the rest of them what they must expect.

2.2. What kind of death he suffered: his head was cut off with a sword, a more disgraceful way of being beheaded than with an ax. It is strange that we do not have a fuller account of the martyrdom of this great apostle, as we had of that of Stephen, but even this brief mention is enough to inform us that the first preachers of the Gospel were so well assured of its truth that they sealed it with their own blood.

3. He imprisoned Peter. Notice:

3.1. When Herod had beheaded James, *he proceeded further to take Peter also*. In the bloodthirsty, shedding blood only increases bloodthirst, and the way of persecution, as of other sins, is downhill; when the bloodthirsty are set on that path, they find they must continue on it. Those who take one bold step on the path of sin are giving Satan an advantage over them in his tempting them to take another. We would be wise, therefore, to be on our guard against the beginnings of sin.

3.2. He did this *because he saw it pleased the Jews*. The Jews made themselves guilty of the blood of James by showing themselves pleased with it afterward. Those who take pleasure in others' persecution will be counted as persecutors. Although Herod had no reason to fear displeasing the Jews if he did not imprison Peter, he hoped to please them by doing it, and so make up for displeasing them in something else. Those who make it their business to please human beings make themselves an easy target to Satan.

3.3. *Then were the days of unleavened bread*. At the Passover, when the Jews came from all parts to Jerusalem to keep the feast, they stirred one another up against the Christians, acting more violently then than at other times.

3.4. Here is an account of Peter's imprisonment (v. 4): *When he* had seized him, *he put him in prison*. Peter *was delivered to four quaternions* (squads) *of soldiers*, that is, to sixteen soldiers in all, who were to keep guard of him four at a time. And so they thought they held him securely.

3.5. Herod's intention was that *after Easter* he would *bring him forth unto the people*, making a spectacle of him. Herod would satisfy them with the sight of Peter

in chains, of Peter being beheaded, so that they could feed their eyes on such a pleasing spectacle. And he who was *willing to please the people* (Mk 15:15) in this way must indeed have been very ambitious to please them! He would do this *after Easter*; actually, "after the Passover" is a better reading. After the rush of the festival was over and the town was empty, he would entertain them with Peter's public trial and execution. Both Herod and the people longed to have the feast over so that they could indulge themselves in this barbaric form of entertainment.

Verses 5–19

Here is an account of Peter's rescue from prison:

1. It was a significant answer to prayer (v. 5): *Peter was kept in prison, but prayer was made without ceasing of the church unto God for him*. Prayers and tears are the church's weapons; she fights with them not only against her enemies but also for her friends.

1.1. The delay of Peter's trial gave them time for prayer. James must be offered as the sacrifice and service of their faith, but Peter must remain with them, and so prayer for him was encouraged, and time was given for it by Herod's delaying of the prosecution.

1.2. They were very specific in their prayers for Peter; they prayed that it would please God to defeat Herod's purpose. The death of James alarmed them to an even greater passion in their prayer for Peter. Although the death and sufferings of Christ's ministers may be made to serve the interests of Christ's kingdom greatly, it is still the duty and concern of the church to pray earnestly for their life, freedom, and peace.

1.3. *Prayer was made without ceasing*. It was an extended prayer. Times of public distress and danger should be times of prayer with the church; we must always pray, but especially then.

2. Let us notice when his deliverance came.

2.1. It was the very night before Herod intended to bring him to trial. Herod was determined that Peter would die, and now God opened a door of escape for him. God's time to help is when things are brought to crisis.

2.2. It was when he *was fast bound with two chains, between two soldiers*; and besides this, to make it foolproof, the *keepers before the door kept the prison*, so that no one could even try to rescue him. Never could human skill have done more to secure a prisoner. But when people think they can be too strong for God, God will make it clear that he is too strong for them.

2.3. It was when he was *sleeping between the soldiers*, when he was:

2.3.1. Not terrified about his danger. There was only a step between him and death (1Sa 20:3), but he could still lie down in peace and sleep (Ps 4:8) — sleep in the middle of his enemies! Even in prison, between two soldiers, God gave him sleep.

2.3.2. Not expecting his rescue; he did not stay awake, and was totally surprised by his deliverance.

3. An *angel was sent from heaven* deliberately to rescue him.

3.1. *The angel of the Lord came upon him*; it may be translated, "He stood next to him." Peter seemed to have been abandoned by people, but he was not forgotten by his God. Gates and guards kept all his friends away, but those impediments could not keep the angels of God away from him. Wherever the people of God are, there is always a way open toward heaven; nothing can interrupt their fellowship with God.

3.2. *A light shone in the prison*. Although it was a dark place, and at night, Peter would see his way clear.

3.3. The angel woke Peter up by giving him *a blow on his side*, a gentle touch, enough to rouse him from sleep. When good people sleep in times of danger, let them expect to be struck on the side by some sharp adversity; better to be raised up in that way than left asleep. The language of this tap was, *Arise up quickly*.

3.4. *His chains fell off from his hands.* Those who had arrested him had handcuffed him to keep him secure, but God loosed his chains.

3.5. He was ordered to get dressed immediately and follow the angel, and he did so (vv. 8–9). When Peter was awake, he could not think of doing anything but what the angel told him. He must *gird himself*, that is, fasten his belt; *bind on his sandals* so that he could walk in them; *cast his garments* (wrap his cloak) *about him*; and follow the angel. He could go with great courage and joyfulness when he had a messenger from heaven as his guide and guard. He *went out, and followed him*. Those who are rescued from spiritual imprisonment must follow their deliverer, as Israel did; they *went out, not knowing whither they went* (Heb 11:8), but the One whom they followed knew. When Peter followed the angel, *he knew not that it was true which was done by the angel, but thought he saw a vision*. He thought the news was too good to be true.

3.6. He was led to safety by the angel (v. 10). Guards were kept at two points, which the angel and Peter had to make their way past, and they did so with no opposition—without, it seems, even being discovered. The angel and Peter safely *passed the first and second ward* (guards). But there was still an iron gate, after all the others, that would stop them; the prisoner and the angel, however, marched up to that gate, and it *opened to them*. They did not even put their hand to it; it opened *of its own accord*, by itself, by an invisible power. When God works salvation for his people, no difficulties that lie in their way are insuperable; even gates of iron are made to open by themselves. This iron gate led Peter out of the castle or tower and into the city, so that when he and his companion were through this one, they were on the street. This rescue of Peter represents to us our redemption by Christ, which is often spoken of as the setting free of prisoners, as not only the declaration of liberty to the captives but also the *bringing of them out of the prison-house* (Isa 42:7).

3.7. When this was done, *the angel departed from him* and left him to himself. He was out of danger from his enemies and needed no guard. He knew where he was and how to find the way to his friends, and so he needed no guide. Miracles are not to be expected when ordinary means are to be used.

4. Having seen how glorious his rescue was, we next see how it was seen both by him and by others. Notice:

4.1. How Peter came to himself and so came to know what had happened (v. 11). To this man who had just been asleep, so many strange and surprising things came all at once that he was confused for a while, but finally Peter *came to himself* and found that it was not a dream and the real thing: "*Now I know of a surety*, now I know that it is truth, *that the Lord Jesus hath sent his angel* and *delivered me* by him *out of the hands of Herod*, and so has disappointed *all the expectation of the people of the Jews*." When Peter came to himself, he *perceived of a truth* what great things God had done for him, which at first he could not believe because he was so overjoyed. Similarly, souls that are rescued from spiritual slavery are not at first aware of what God has done in them. Many have the truth of grace but lack evidence of it. But *when the Comforter came*, he would let them know certainly what a blessed change had been brought about in them.

4.2. How Peter came to his friends and told them of his rescue.

4.2.1. He *considered the thing* (v. 12), considered how imminent his danger had been and how great his rescue, and now what was he to do? God's providence leaves room for us to use our minds wisely, and although he has undertaken to perform and complete what he has begun (Php 1:6; Ps 138:8), he still expects us to consider matters for ourselves.

4.2.2. He went directly to a friend's house; it was the house of Mary, a sister of Barnabas and the mother of John Mark. A church in a house makes the house a little sanctuary.

4.2.3. There he found *many* who were *gathered together praying* at the dead of night, praying for Peter.

4.2.3.1. They continued in prayer as a sign of their boldness. As long as we are kept waiting for a mercy, we must continue praying for it.

4.2.3.2. It seems that now, when the matter came to a crisis, they were more fervent in prayer than they had been before, and it was a good sign that God intended to rescue Peter when he stirred up a spirit of prayer for his rescue.

4.2.3.3. They gathered together for prayer. They knew what an encouragement Christ had given to joint prayer (Mt 18:19–20). It was always the practice of God's praying people to unite in prayer.

4.2.3.4. Many of them had joined together for this work. No doubt there were many ordinary Christians who knew how to pray, how to pray relevantly and for a long time.

4.2.3.5. Peter came to them when they were praying in this way. It was as if God had said, "You are praying that Peter may be restored to you—now here he is."

4.2.4. He knocked at the outer entrance, and it took a lot of fuss to get those inside to let him in (vv. 13–16): *Peter knocked at the door of the gate*.

4.2.4.1. *A damsel came to hearken* (a girl came to answer the door); she would not open the door until she knew who was there and what their business was. Her being named suggests that she was noted among the Christians and was more zealously disposed toward spiritual things than most who were of her age.

4.2.4.2. She knew Peter's voice, but instead of letting him in out of the cold immediately, *she opened not the gate for gladness*. Sometimes, even while carried away with affection for our friends, we do what is unkind.

4.2.4.3. She ran in and told them that Peter was definitely at the outer entrance. But they said, "*Thou art mad*; it is impossible, because he is in prison." We are sometimes most reluctant to believe what we most fervently wish for, because we are afraid of being deceived. She, however, stood by her statement that it was he. Then said they, *It is his angel* (v. 15). "It is *a messenger* from him, who is using his name," according to some. When the girl was confident it was Peter because she recognized his voice, they thought it was because the man who was standing at the entrance had called himself Peter, and so they proposed this solution: "It is a man who has come on a mission from him, and you have mistaken him for Peter himself." Or: "It is his guardian angel." Some think they supposed that Peter's angel had appeared as a sign of his approaching death. If this was what the gathered believers meant by their response to the girl, they must have concluded that this visitor was an ill omen and that the language of the apparition was, "Let it be enough for you to know that Peter must die." Others think they took this to be an angel from heaven who was sent to bring them a favorable answer to their prayers.

4.2.5. They finally let him in (v. 16): *He continued knocking*, and they eventually admitted him. The iron gate had opened by itself, but the door of his friend's house that was to welcome him must be knocked on for a long time. However, *when they saw him, they were astonished*, filled with wonder and joy in him, as much as they had been sad and afraid for him only a short time before.

4.2.6. Peter told them about his rescue. When he came to the group, they gathered around him to congratulate him on his rescue. And they were so noisy in doing this that he could not make them hear him, but was forced to *beckon to them with the hand to hold their peace* while *he declared unto them how the Lord Jesus had brought him out of prison*. Very probably he did not leave them until he and they had together solemnly given thanks to God for his release. What is obtained in prayer must be acknowledged with praise.

4.2.7. Peter sent the account to his other friends: *Go, show these things to James, and to the brethren with him*. He wanted James and his friends to know about his rescue, not only so that they would be saved from their fears for Peter but also so that they would give thanks to God with him and for him. Although Herod had killed one James with the sword, here was another James, and in Jerusalem too, who stood up in his place to lead among the brothers and sisters there.

4.2.8. Peter had nothing more to do for the present than to fend for his own safety: he *departed, and went into another place*. Even the Christian law of suffering for Christ has not repealed the natural law of self-preservation, as far as God gives an opportunity to provide for it.

5. Having seen the triumph of Peter's friends in his rescue, let us now notice the confusion of his enemies at this time.

5.1. The guards were in the greatest consternation about it (v. 18): *As soon as it was day*, there was *no small stir among the soldiers* concerning *what had become of Peter*. They thought themselves as sure as they could be that he had been with them the previous night, but now the bird had flown. The persecutors of the Gospel of Christ have often been greatly disturbed when they have seen its cause conquering.

5.2. Houses were searched in vain for the rescued prisoner (v. 19): *Herod sought for him, and found him not*. Who can find the one whom God has hidden? All believers have God as *their hiding place* (Ps 119:114). The powerless world cannot reach them.

5.3. The guards were punished: *Herod examined the keepers* and then he *commanded that they should be put to death*.

5.4. Having punished the guards but been thwarted in his purpose, Herod himself withdrew: *He went down from Judea to Cesarea, and there abode*. He was deeply angry, like a lion that has been disappointed in pursuit of its prey, and all the more so because he had so much raised the *expectation of the people of the Jews* about Peter. It made him ashamed to be robbed of this boast and to see himself prevented from fulfilling his words. This was such a humiliation to his proud spirit that he could not bear to stay in Judea, but went away to Caesarea.

Verses 20–25

We have in these verses:

1. The death of Herod. God judged him not only for putting James to death but also for his plan to put Peter to death, because sinners will be held responsible for both the trouble they have caused and the trouble they wanted to do. Notice:

1.1. How the limit of his sins was reached (Mt 23:32): it was pride that did it. The example here is significant, showing how God *resists the proud* (Jas 4:6).

1.1.1. The men of Tyre and Sidon, it seems, had offended Herod. Some very small matter would have been enough to provoke such a man as Herod. He was greatly displeased with this people.

1.1.2. The offenders decided to submit. They were willing to make peace with him on any terms. Notice:

1.1.2.1. The reason they wanted to have the matter settled: *their country was nourished by the king's country* (they depended on the king's country for their food supply). Tyre and Sidon were trading cities and were always supplied with grain from the land of Canaan. Now if Herod were to make a law to prohibit the export of grain to Tyre and Sidon, their country would be ruined. Would it not be wise for us, then, to make our peace with God, humbling ourselves before him, since we depend on him in a much more constant and necessary way than one country can depend on another?

1.1.2.2. What they did to prevent such a breach: *They made Blastus the king's chamberlain their friend*. Blastus had Herod's ear and knew how to soften his anger, and a time was fixed for the ambassadors of Tyre and Sidon to come and submit publicly, to beg his majesty's pardon and promise never to offend again. Feeding his pride in this way would cool his passion.

1.1.3. Herod appeared in all the show and grandeur possible: he was *arrayed in his royal apparel* (v. 21) *and sat upon his throne*. Foolish people value others by their outward appearance (1Sa 16:7), and those who, like Herod, pride themselves on having the high opinion of such people are no better; he thought he could make up for the lack of a royal heart by wearing *royal apparel* and *sitting upon his throne*.

1.1.4. He made a speech to the people of Tyre and Sidon, a fine public address. He probably kept them in suspense as to what their fate would be until he gave this speech to them, so that the act of grace would come to them as a more pleasant surprise.

1.1.5. The people applauded him. They *gave a shout*: *It is the voice of a god, and not of a man* (v. 22). Perhaps it was not from any real impression made on their minds, any high or good thoughts they had conceived of him, but because they were determined to get on his good side, to strengthen the newly made peace between him and them. Great people are made an easy prey to flatterers if they lend an ear to them. This is not only a great insult to God but also a great wrong to those who are flattered, since it makes them forget what they are really like and makes them so proud that they are in the greatest possible danger of falling into the condemnation of the Devil (1Ti 3:6).

1.1.6. He greedily seized these undue praises. This was his sin and his fault: he said nothing; he neither rebuked their flattery nor *gave God the glory* (v. 23), but was very willing to be thought a god and paid divine honor.

1.2. How his sin was punished (v. 23): *Immediately the angel of the Lord smote him because he gave not God the glory*. Herod was eaten by worms *and gave up the ghost*. Now he was judged for persecuting the church of Christ, killing James, imprisoning Peter, and all the other trouble he had caused.

1.2.1. It was no less than an angel that was the agent of Herod's destruction—*the angel of the Lord*. Those ministering spirits (Heb 1:14) are the ministers of either divine justice or divine mercy, employed however God wishes to employ them. The angel struck him down just at that moment when he was proud of the applause of the people, and adoring his own shadow. The angel *smote him, because he gave not the glory to God.*

1.2.2. It was nothing greater than a worm that was the instrument of Herod's destruction: he was *eaten of worms;* it may be read, "he became worm-eaten"; he was rotten, and he became like a piece of rotten wood. See here what repulsive bodies we carry around with us. We should not, therefore, be proud of our bodies; nor should we spoil them, because this is simply feeding the worms, and feeding our bodies for the worms. Notice what weak and contemptible creatures God can make the instruments of his justice. Notice, too, how God delights not only to humble proud people, but also to do it in the most humiliating way. Herod was not only destroyed, but destroyed by worms, so that the pride of his glory might be thoroughly stained.

2. The progress of the Gospel after this.

2.1. *The word of God grew and multiplied* (v. 24). The courage and comfort of the martyrs and God's acknowledging them did more to invite people to Christianity than their sufferings did to deter them from it. After the death of Herod, the word of God gained ground.

2.2. Barnabas and Saul returned to Antioch: *When they had fulfilled their ministry,* they *returned from Jerusalem.* Although they had very many friends in Jerusalem, at present their work lay at Antioch, and where our business is, there we should be. When Barnabas and Saul went to Antioch, they *took with them John, whose surname was Mark,* at whose mother's house they had met for the prayer we read about in v. 12. John Mark's mother was Barnabas's sister. Barnabas probably stayed in her house while in Jerusalem, and perhaps Paul with him, and their close relationship with that family gave rise to their taking a son of that family with them when they returned, so that he could be trained under them. Educating young people for the ministry and inducting them into it is a very good work for older ministers to take care of.

CHAPTER 13

We have not yet read anything about the spreading of the Gospel to the Gentiles that bears any proportion to the greatness of that commission, Go, and disciple all nations *(Mt 28:19), though the door was opened up in the baptizing of Cornelius and his friends. However, here in this chapter that work is revived. We have here: 1. The solemn ordination of Barnabas and Saul to the great work of spreading the Gospel among the surrounding nations (vv. 1–3). 2. Their preaching the Gospel in Cyprus and encountering opposition there from Elymas the sorcerer (vv. 4–13). 3. A summary of a sermon Paul preached to the Jews at Antioch in Pisidia (vv. 14–41). 4. The preaching of the Gospel to the Gentiles at their request (vv. 42–49). 5. The trouble the unfaithful Jews gave to the apostles (vv. 50–52).*

Verses 1–3

We have here the divine commission given to Barnabas and Saul to go and preach the Gospel among the Gentiles:

1. An account of the present state of the church at Antioch. Notice:

1.1. How well provided it was with good ministers; there were *certain prophets and teachers* (v. 1), men who were eminent in gifts, graces, and usefulness. Agabus seems to have been a prophet and not a teacher, and many were teachers who were not prophets, but these men were both. Antioch was a great city, and there were many Christians there; they therefore needed many teachers. Barnabas is named first, and Saul last, but afterward the last became first, and Saul became more famous. Three others are mentioned: *Simeon,* or Simon, who for the sake of distinction was called *Niger,* Simon the Black; *Lucius* of Cyrene; *Manaen,* a person of some standing, it seems, because he was *brought up with Herod the tetrarch,* was his companion and friend, which gave him good prospects of advancement at court, but for Christ's sake he left all hopes of it. It is better to be a fellow sufferer with a saint than a fellow persecutor with a tetrarch.

1.2. How well employed they were (v. 2): *They ministered to the Lord, and fasted.* Conscientious, faithful teachers truly minister to the Lord. Those who instruct Christians serve Christ. Ministering to the Lord, in one way or another, should be the clear business of churches and their teachers. Religious fasting is useful in our ministering to and worship of the Lord. Although it was not so much practiced by the disciples of Christ *while the bridegroom was with them* (Mt 9:15), nevertheless, after the bridegroom was taken away, they practiced this discipline often and regularly.

2. The orders given by the Holy Spirit: *Separate me Barnabas and Saul for the work whereunto I have called them.* The Spirit did not specify the work, but referred to an earlier call that they themselves knew the meaning of. It had been settled at Jerusalem earlier that, as Peter, James, and John had given themselves to Jews, so Paul and Barnabas would *go to the heathen* (Gentiles) (Gal 2:7–9). The orders were, *Separate me Barnabas and Saul.* Notice:

2.1. Christ through his Spirit names his ministers. There are some whom the Holy Spirit has set apart to serve Christ, and directions are given about them to those who are competent judges: *Separate* them.

2.2. Christ's ministers are set apart for him and the Holy Spirit: *Separate them to me;* they are to be employed in Christ's work and under the Spirit's guidance.

2.3. All who are set apart for Christ as his ministers are set apart to work; Christ keeps none of his servants idle. They are set apart to work hard, not to become proud of their positions.

2.4. The work of Christ's ministers is work that all Christ's ministers have always been called to.

3. Their ordination, which was not to the ministry in general but to a particular service in the ministry. Simeon, Lucius, and Manaen, *when they had fasted and prayed, laid their hands on Barnabas and Saul, and sent them away* (v. 3).

3.1. They prayed for them. When good people are being sent out to undertake a good work, they should be solemnly and specifically prayed for.

3.2. They added fasting to their prayers (v. 3), as they did in their other forms of service. They laid their hands on Paul and Barnabas, showing:

3.2.1. That they were discharging them from their present service in the church of Antioch, acknowledging that they were leaving not only justly and with the church's approval but also honorably and with a good report.

3.2.2. That they sought a blessing on them in their present work, asking God fervently to be with them and give them success. They were not jealous of Barnabas and Saul for the honor to which they were advanced, but cheerfully committed the commission to them and *sent them away* with all speed, out of a concern for those countries where they were to break up fallow ground.

Verses 4–13

We have here:

1. A general account of the arrival of Barnabas and Saul on the famous island of Cyprus. Barnabas was born

in that country (4:36), and he wanted them to have the firstfruits of his labors. The apostles' being sent on their way by the Holy Spirit was the great thing that encouraged them in this work (v. 4). They came to Seleucia, and from there crossed the sea to Cyprus, and the first town they came to was Salamis (v. 5). When they had sown good seed there, they went on *through the isle* (v. 6) until they reached Paphos. *They preached the word of God in the synagogues of the Jews*; far from excluding the Jews, they gave them priority. They did not work in secret, but boldly exposed their message to the censures of the rulers of the synagogues. *They had John* Mark *for their minister*, not as their servant in ordinary things, but as their helper in the things of God. Such a person could be very useful to them in many ways, especially in a strange country.

2. A detailed account of their encounter in Paphos with *Elymas the sorcerer* (v. 6).

2.1. There the *deputy* (proconsul) *of the country*, a Gentile, *Sergius Paulus* by name, encouraged the apostles. He was governor under the Roman emperor. He had the reputation of being *a prudent man*, one who was ruled by reason, not passion or prejudice, as was evident from his having sent for Paul and Barnabas *and desired to hear the word of God*. Those who seek the mind and will of God are wise, however much they may be ranked among the foolish of this world. If Paul and Barnabas had a message from God, let him know what it was; he was ready to receive it.

2.2. There Elymas, a Jew, *a sorcerer*, opposed them.

2.2.1. This Elymas claimed to have *the gift of prophecy*; he was *a sorcerer, a false prophet*—one who wanted to be taken as a "divine"—a minister—because he was skilled in the art of divination. His *name was Bar-jesus*, "the son of Joshua"; it means the "son of salvation," but the Aramaic commentary on this passage calls him *Bar-shoma*, "the son of pride."

2.2.2. He *was with the deputy* (proconsul) of the country; that is, he was a hanger-on in the court.

2.2.3. He made it his business to oppose Barnabas and Saul. *He sought to turn away the deputy from the faith* (v. 8), to keep him from receiving the Gospel. Satan is especially busy with leaders and powerful people, to keep them from having a religious faith, because he knows that their example, whether good or bad, will influence many others.

2.2.4. Saul—who is called Paul here for the first time—rebuked Elymas for this opposition with a holy indignation. *Saul, who is also called Paul* (v. 9). Saul was his name as a Hebrew; Paul was his name as a citizen of Rome. Up to this time we have had him dealing mostly with Jews, and so he has been called by his Jewish name, but now, in the account of his being sent among the Gentiles, he is called by his Roman name. It is said of Paul:

2.2.4.1. That he was *filled with the Holy Spirit* on this occasion, filled with power to declare the wrath of God against Elymas. What Paul said did not come from any personal resentment, but from the strong impressions the Holy Spirit made on his spirit.

2.2.4.2. That he *set his eyes upon* Elymas in opposition to his evil arrogance.

2.2.4.3. That he gave him his true characterization (v. 10), describing him as:

2.2.4.3.1. An agent for hell. Although this Elymas was called *Bar-jesus*, "a son of Jesus," he was really a *child of the devil*. He was like the Devil in deceit: though devoid of all wisdom, he *was full of all subtlety*. He was like the Devil in evil, *full of all mischief*, spiteful and ill tempered.

A fulness of subtlety and mischief together makes a person a true child of the Devil.

2.2.4.3.2. An adversary of heaven. If he was a child of the devil, it followed naturally that he was *an enemy to all righteousness* (everything that is right).

2.2.4.4. That he accused him of his present crime. *Wilt thou not cease to pervert the right ways of the Lord?* The ways of the Lord are right; they are the only right ways to heaven and happiness. There are those who pervert these right ways, who not only wander away from them themselves but also mislead others, suggesting to them unjust prejudices and making the right ways seem corrupt. Those who pervert the right ways of the Lord are commonly so hardened in that perversion that they will not turn away from it in spite of the most powerful evidence.

2.2.4.5. That he declared the judgment of God against him to be blindness for the present (v. 11): *And now, behold, the hand of the Lord is upon thee*; *thou shalt be blind, not seeing the sun for a season.* Elymas had shut his eyes, the eyes of his heart, against the light of the Gospel, and so the eyes of his body were justly shut against the light of the sun. He had tried to blind the proconsul, and so he himself was struck blind. Yet it was a moderate punishment: he was blind only *for a season*; if he would repent and give glory to God, his sight would be restored; in fact, it seems that even if he did not, his sight would be restored.

2.2.4.6. That this judgment was immediately executed: *There fell on him mist and a darkness.* Let him no longer claim to be a guide to the proconsul's conscience, since he *went about seeking some to lead him by the hand.* Where now was all his skill in sorcery?

2.3. Despite all the attempts of Elymas *to turn away the deputy* (proconsul) *from the faith*, the proconsul was brought to believe, and this miracle contributed to it. The proconsul was very perceptive, and he noticed something that was uncommon and indicated a divine origin:

2.3.1. In Paul's preaching: he was *astonished at the doctrine of the Lord.* The teaching of Christ contains a great deal that is amazing, and the more we know it, the more reason we will see to wonder and stand amazed at it.

2.3.2. In this miracle: *When he saw what was done*, he believed. It is not said that he was baptized, but he probably was.

3. Their departure from the island of Cyprus. They left the country and *went to Perga*. Those who went were *Paul and his company*. Then John *Mark departed from them, and returned to Jerusalem*, without the agreement of Paul and Barnabas. He was at fault, and we will hear about it again (15:37–39).

Verses 14–41

Perga in Pamphylia was a significant place, but nothing at all is related of what Paul and Barnabas did there except that they came there (v. 13) and departed from there (v. 14). The next place we find them in is another Antioch, called Pisidian Antioch to distinguish it from the Antioch in Syria, from which they were sent out. Many Jews lived there, and the Gospel was to be preached to them first. We have in these verses Paul's sermon to them.

1. We have here the appearance Paul and Barnabas made in a religious assembly of the Jews at Antioch (v. 14). *When they came to Antioch*, they turned to the Jews, which is further proof of their strong affection for the Jews.

1.1. The apostles observed the Jews' time of worship, *the sabbath day*, the Jewish Sabbath. Among themselves, Paul and his company observed *the first day of the week* as a Christian Sabbath, but if they wanted to meet the Jews, it must be on the seventh-day Sabbath.

1.2. They met them at their place of worship, *in the synagogue*. Paul and Barnabas were strangers, but wherever we go, we must seek out God's faithful worshipers and join them. Although Paul and Barnabas were strangers, they were still admitted into the synagogue and allowed to sit down there. We should make sure to accommodate strangers, even the poorest, in places of public worship.

2. We have here the invitation given them to preach.

2.1. The usual service of the synagogue was carried out (v. 15): *The law and the prophets were read*, a portion of each, the lessons for the day.

2.2. When that was done, the apostles were asked by *the rulers of the synagogue* to give them a sermon (v. 15). They sent a messenger to the apostles, saying, *Men and brethren, if you have any word of exhortation for the people, say on.* Whether or not they were well disposed to receive the Gospel, at least they were curious to hear Paul preach, and so they begged his favor to speak a *word of exhortation to the people*. The bare reading of the Scriptures in public assemblies is not enough; they need to be explained, and the people need to be encouraged from them. Those who lead and have authority in public gatherings should provide for a message of encouragement for the people. Sometimes a message of encouragement from a strange minister may be very useful to the people. These synagogue rulers were nobler, more generous, than the persons holding that office generally were.

3. We have here the sermon Paul preached. He gladly welcomed the opportunity given him to preach Christ to his compatriots, the Jews. He *beckoned* (motioned) *with his hand*. He waved his hand as an orator trying to stir their emotions, showing himself to be a passionate yet serious speaker. Everything is touched on in this sermon that might convince the judgment of the Jews, to win them over to receive and accept Christ as the promised Messiah.

3.1. Paul acknowledged that:

3.1.1. They were God's favorite people, whom he had taken into a special relationship with himself, and for whom he had done great things.

3.1.2. *The God of the whole earth* was particularly *the God of this people Israel*, a God in covenant with them.

3.1.3. God had *chosen their fathers* to be his friends—Abraham was called *the friend of God* (2Ch 20:7; Isa 41:8; Jas 2:23). Paul reminded them of this to let them know that the reason why God favored them was that he wanted to remain faithful to his choice of *their fathers* (Dt 7:7–8).

3.1.4. God had *exalted that people*, had advanced them to become a people and raised them up from nothing *when they dwelt as strangers in the land of Egypt*. They should remember this and infer from it that God was not indebted to them. They were indebted to him, however, and were obliged to receive such further revelations as he would make to his church.

3.1.5. God had *with a high arm* (with his mighty power) *brought them out of Egypt*, had rescued them at the expense of very many miracles, both in mercy toward them and in judgment to their oppressors.

3.1.6. *He had suffered their manners forty years in the wilderness* (v. 18). God provided for them greatly for forty years in the desert: miracles were their daily bread (Ex 16). He exercised a great deal of patience with them, allowing his anger to be turned away many times by the prayer and intercession of Moses. We must acknowledge

that God has been like a tender father to us over all the years each of us has lived in this world; he has taken care of us. He has been a God of forgiveness. We have tried his patience, but we have not yet exhausted it.

3.1.7. God had given them possession of the land of Canaan (v. 19): *When he had destroyed seven nations in the land of Canaan, he divided their land to them by lot.*

3.1.8. God had raised up those people to save them from the hands of those who oppressed them after they had settled in Canaan (vv. 20–21).

3.1.8.1. He *gave them judges*. Even though they were an offensive people, nevertheless, when they sought help, a deliverer was raised up.

3.1.8.2. He ruled them through *a prophet, Samuel.*

3.1.8.3. He *afterward*, at their request, *set a king over them* (v. 21), *Saul, the son of Cis* (Kish).

3.1.8.4. Eventually, he made David their king (v. 22). *When God had removed Saul, he raised up unto them David to be their king*, and made a covenant of royalty with him and his descendants. Paul quoted the testimony God gave about David.

3.1.8.4.1. The choice of David was divine: *I have found David* (Ps 89:20). Finding implies seeking; it was as if God had ransacked all the families of Israel to find a man fit for his purpose, and this was the one.

3.1.8.4.2. His character was divine: *"a man after my own heart* (1Sa 13:14), the kind of man I want, one on whom the image of God is stamped."

3.1.8.4.3. His behavior was under divine direction: "*He shall fulfil all my will.* He will want and seek to do the will of God, and he will be enabled to do it." The changes of their government showed that it *made nothing perfect* (Heb 7:19) and must therefore give way to the spiritual kingdom of the Messiah, which was now being established, and so they need not be jealous because of the preaching of the Gospel.

3.2. He gave them a full account of our Lord Jesus, showing that this Jesus was David's promised descendant (v. 23): "*Of this man's seed*, from that *man after God's own heart, hath God, according to his promise, raised unto Israel a Saviour, Jesus*, who brings salvation in his name."

3.2.1. How welcome the preaching of the Gospel of Christ should have been to the Jews, and how they should have accepted it, as *well worthy of all acceptation* (1Ti 1:15), when it brought them the good news of a Savior:

3.2.1.1. To *save them from their sins* (Mt 1:21), their worst enemies.

3.2.1.2. Whom God had raised up *to be a Saviour unto Israel*, to them first; far from intending the Gospel to cause the rejection of Israel, it was intended for their gathering.

3.2.1.3. Who was raised up *of the seed of David*, that ancient royal family, which the people of Israel gloried so much in—raised up *according to his promise*, the promise to David. Was this the promise *which the twelve tribes hoped to come* (26:7)? Why then did they receive it so coldly, now that it had come to them?

3.2.2. He told them about this Jesus:

3.2.2.1. That John the Baptist was his forerunner, that great man whom everyone acknowledged to be a prophet (Mk 11:32). Let them not say that the Messiah's coming was a surprise to them, because they had sufficient warning from John, who *preached before his coming* (v. 24).

3.2.2.1.1. He made way for the Messiah to come by preaching *the baptism of repentance to all the people of Israel*. He showed them their sins, *called them* both *to repent* and *to bring forth fruits meet for repentance*.

3.2.2.1.2. He announced his approach (v. 25): "*As he fulfilled his course*—when he was pursuing his work vigorously and had established his influence—*Now*, he said, *Whom think you that I am? You may be thinking that I am the Messiah*, whom you expect, but you are mistaken. *I am not he*, but he is at the door; *behold, there cometh one* immediately *after me whose shoes of his feet I am not worthy to loose*, and you may guess who that must be."

3.2.2.2. That the rulers and people of the Jews, who should have welcomed him, were his persecutors and murderers. When the apostles preached Christ as the Savior, they were so far from concealing his ignominious death that they always *preached Christ crucified* (1Co 1:23), and even crucified by his own people, *by those that dwelt in Jerusalem*, crucified by *their rulers* (v. 27).

3.2.2.2.1. Their sin was *that though they found no cause of death* (no proper ground for a death sentence) *in him, they desired* (asked) *Pilate that he might be slain* (v. 28). They compelled Pilate to crucify him not only against his inclination but also against his conscience. They condemned him to *so great a death* (2Co 1:10), though they could not convict him of the slightest sin. Those who had so abused him could justly have been cut off from all benefit by the Messiah. However, they were not cut off; despite all this, the preaching of this Gospel had begun at Jerusalem.

3.2.2.2.2. The reason they did this was that *they knew him not* (did not recognize him) (v. 27). Christ acknowledged this as a mitigation of their crime: *They know not what they do*; and so did Peter: *I wot* (know) *that through ignorance you did this* (3:17). They did it also because they did not recognize the voice of the prophets even though they heard them read every Sabbath. They did not understand or consider that it was foretold that the Messiah would have to suffer. Many who read the prophets do not recognize the voice of the prophets. They have the sound of the Gospel in their ears but not its sense in their minds.

3.2.2.2.3. God overruled them to fulfill the prophecies of the Old Testament: *Because they knew not the voice of the prophets, they fulfilled them in condemning him*. People may fulfill Scripture prophecies even when they are breaking Scripture commands.

3.2.2.2.4. All that was foretold about the suffering of the Messiah was fulfilled in Christ (v. 29): "*When they had fulfilled all* the rest *that was written of him*, they fulfilled what was foretold about his being buried. They *took him down from the tree, and laid him in a sepulchre*." This was noted here as what made his resurrection more outstanding. They laid him in a tomb and thought they held him securely.

3.2.2.3. That he *rose again from the dead*. This was the great truth that was to be preached, because it is the central pillar by which the whole structure of the Gospel is supported.

3.2.2.3.1. Christ rose by God's approval: *God raised him from the dead* (v. 30). His enemies laid him in a tomb with the intention that he would always lie there, but God said, "No."

3.2.2.3.2. There was sufficient proof of his having risen (v. 31): "*He was seen many days*. Those who knew him very closely *came up with him from Galilee to Jerusalem*, and *they are his witnesses unto the people*." They had affirmed the matters many times and were ready to confirm it even if they had to die for it. Paul said nothing of his own seeing of Christ, because it was in a vision, which was more convincing to himself than it could have been to others.

3.2.2.3.3. The resurrection of Christ was the fulfillment of the promise made to the patriarchs. It was not only truthful news but good news: "In declaring this, we *declare unto you glad tidings* (vv. 32–33), which should be especially acceptable to you Jews. The message we preach, if you receive it rightly, brings you the greatest possible satisfaction, because it is in the resurrection of Christ that *the promise which was made to your fathers is fulfilled to you*." The great promise of the Old Testament was that of the Messiah, *in whom all the families of the earth would be blessed* (Ge 12:3), not only the family of Abraham. This shows us:

3.2.2.3.3.1. God has *raised up Jesus, raised* him *again*, meaning "from the dead."

3.2.2.3.3.2. This is the fulfilling of the promises made to the ancestors, the promise of sending the Messiah and the promise of all the benefits and blessings. "This is the One who would come (Ps 118:26; Mt 11:3), and in him you have all that God promised in the Messiah, though not everything you promised yourselves." Paul included himself among the Jews, to whom the promise was fulfilled: *To us their children*. Now if those who preached the Gospel brought the Jews this good news, then they should welcome their message with both arms, because if they valued the promise, then much more should they value its fulfillment. Moreover, the preaching of the Gospel to the Gentiles, which was the great thing that the Jews were grieved about, was so far from violating the promise made to them that the promise itself that *all the families of the earth* would be blessed in the Messiah could not be fulfilled in any other way.

3.2.2.3.4. The resurrection of Christ was the great proof that he was the Son of God, confirming what was written in Psalm 2: *Thou art my Son; this day have I begotten thee. He was declared to be the Son of God with power by the resurrection* (Ro 1:4). When he was first raised up out of obscurity, God declared by a voice from heaven, *This is my beloved Son* (Mt 3:17), which clearly referred to the statement in the second psalm, *Thou art my Son* (Ps 2:7), which was declared at Christ's baptism and again at his transfiguration and was undeniably proved by his resurrection. The decree that was declared so long before was then confirmed: "This day have I made it clear that I have begotten you."

3.2.2.3.5. His being raised the third day so as not to see decay (Ps 16:10) and his being raised to a heavenly life so as to never return to decay further confirmed that he was the promised Messiah.

3.2.2.3.5.1. He arose never to die again. Lazarus came out of the grave with his graveclothes on, because he was to use them again, but since Christ had no further need for them, he left them behind. Now that Scripture was fulfilled, *I will give you the sure mercies of David* (Isa 55:3). They are beyond doubt *sure mercies* (faithful love), because the One who is entrusted with dispensing them has risen, never to die again. If Christ had either died and not risen again or risen to die again, we would have come short of the faithful blessings, or at least could not have been sure of them.

3.2.2.3.5.2. He rose so soon after he was dead that his body did not see decay (Ps 16:10); this was one of *the sure mercies of David*, because it was said to him, *Neither wilt thou suffer thy Holy One to see corruption* (v. 35). This promise could not have been fulfilled in David, but looked forward to Christ.

3.2.2.3.5.2.1. It could not have been fulfilled in David himself (v. 36), because *David, after he had served his own generation, by the will of God, fell asleep, and was laid to his fathers, and saw corruption.* Here we have a short account of the life, death, and burial of the patriarch David, and his remaining under the power of death:

3.2.2.3.*5.2.1.1.* His life: *He served his own generation by the will of God.* David was useful and good; he did good in the world *by the will of God.* He *served his own generation* so as to serve God in them. He served the good of people, but did not serve human will. David was a great blessing to the age in which he lived; he was the servant of his generation, in contrast to many people who are the curse, plague, and burden of their generation. Those who want to do good in the world must make themselves *servants of all* (1Co 9:19). We were not born for ourselves, but are members of the communities we live and work in, to which we must seek to be useful. Here is the difference between David and Christ, however: David was to serve only his own generation, but Christ was to serve all generations. He always lives and will reign for all time, as long as the sun and moon last (Ps 89:29, 36–37).

3.2.2.3.*5.2.1.2.* His death: *He fell asleep.* Death is a sleep, a quiet rest, to those who during their lifetimes worked hard in the service of God and their generation. David did not fall asleep until he had completed the work for which God raised him up. God's witnesses never die until they have finished their testimony (Rev 11:7), and then *the sleep of the labouring man will be sweet* (Ecc 5:12).

3.2.2.3.*5.2.1.3.* His burial: *He was laid to his fathers.*

3.2.2.3.*5.2.1.4.* His remaining in the grave: *He saw corruption.* We are sure he did not rise again. His body decayed, and so that promise could not have been fulfilled in him.

3.2.2.3.*5.2.2.* It was fulfilled in the Lord Jesus Christ (v. 37): *He whom God raised again saw no corruption.* The promise must, therefore, be understood as referring to him, and no one else.

3.3. Having given them this account of the Lord Jesus, Paul applied it.

3.3.1. In the middle of his speech he had told his hearers they were concerned in all this (v. 26): "*To you is the word* (message) *of this salvation sent.* It is sent to you as a message of salvation; if it turns out not to be so for you, it is your own fault." He therefore spoke to them with tenderness and respect: "you are *men and brethren.*" Those to whom Paul brought the message of salvation were:

3.3.1.1. The native Jews, Hebrews of the Hebrews (Php 3:5), as Paul himself was: "*Children of the stock of Abraham,* this message of salvation is sent to you; indeed, it is sent to you to save you from your sins." It is an advantage to be of a good family, because although salvation does not always follow the children of godly parents, the message of salvation does.

3.3.1.2. The converts, who were Gentiles by birth: "*Whosoever among you that feareth God, to you is the word of this salvation sent;* you need the further revelations and directions of revealed religion, and you will welcome them, and so you will certainly be welcome to benefit from them."

3.3.2. At the end of his speech, he applied what he had said about Christ to his hearers. Now they would be ready to ask, "What does all this mean to us?" He told them clearly, therefore, what it meant to them.

3.3.2.1. It would be to their indescribable advantage if they accepted Jesus Christ and believed this message of salvation. "*Be it known unto you therefore, men and brethren*—we are authorized to declare this message to you, and you are called to take notice of it." He did not stand up just to preach before them, but to preach to them,

and not without hope of persuading them. They were brothers and sisters, spoken to and dealt with by people like themselves, from the same nation. It is right for the preachers of the Gospel to call their hearers brothers and sisters, to show an affectionate concern for their welfare and a recognition that they, the preachers, are equally involved with them in the Gospel they preach. Let all who hear the Gospel of Christ know these two things:

3.3.2.1.*1.* That it is an act of indemnity granted to all human beings. It is because of the mediation of Christ that this act of grace has been passed and declared (v. 38): "*Through this man is preached unto you the forgiveness of sins.* It is *through this man:* it was purchased by his merits, and it is offered in his name. We preach to you *the forgiveness of sins.* That is the salvation we bring you."

3.3.2.1.*2.* That it does for us what the Law of Moses could not do. "Let it be known that it is only through Christ that *those who believe in him* are *justified from all things from which you could not be justified by the law of Moses* (v. 39). That is why you should receive and accept the Gospel and not remain loyal to the Law in opposition to it." This shows us:

3.3.2.1.*2.1.* The great concern of sinners is to be justified and accepted as righteous in God's sight.

3.3.2.1.*2.2.* Those who are truly justified are acquitted from all their guilt.

3.3.2.1.*2.3.* It was impossible for a sinner to be justified by the Law of Moses.

3.3.2.1.*2.4.* Through Jesus Christ we obtain a complete justification, because complete atonement was made for sin by him.

3.3.2.1.*2.5.* All who believe in Christ and give themselves to him to be ruled by him are justified by him.

3.3.2.2. Their lives were in danger if they rejected the Gospel of Christ. "Make sure not only that you do not come short of the blessings and benefits spoken of in the prophets, but also that you do not fall under the condemnation spoken about in the prophets: *lest that come upon you which is spoken of.*" The threats are warnings intended to wake us up so that we make sure it does not come on us. The apostle follows the Septuagint (a Greek version of the Old Testament), which reads *Behold, you despisers* where our translation renders the Hebrew of Hab 1:5 as *Behold, you among the heathen.*

3.3.2.2.*1.* "Take care that the guilt spoken of in the prophets does not come on you. Take care that it may not be said to you, *Behold, you despisers.*" It is the ruin of many people that they despise religion, looking on it as beneath their dignity and being unwilling to stoop to it.

3.3.2.2.*2.* "Take care that the judgment spoken of in the prophets does not come on you: that *you shall wonder and perish.*" Those who will not wonder and be saved will wonder and perish. Those who enjoyed the privileges of the church and flattered themselves by thinking these would save them will be amazed when they find that their privileges only make their condemnation even more intolerable. Let the unbelieving Jews expect that God *will work a work in their days which you shall in no wise believe, though a man declare it unto you.*

3.3.2.2.2.*1.* This may be understood as a prediction of their sin, that they would be disbelieving, that even though that great work of God, the redemption of the world by Christ, would be most solemnly declared to them, they would still *in no wise believe it.* Those who had the honor and advantage of having this work performed in their days did not have the grace to believe it.

3.3.2.2.2.*2.* Or it may be understood as a prediction of their destruction, a work that one would not have believed possible, considering how much they had been the favorites of heaven. There is indeed a *strange punishment to the workers of iniquity*, especially to the despisers of Christ.

Verses 42–52

Since the purpose of this account was to vindicate the apostles, especially Paul, it is noted here that he proceeded with them with all possible caution.

1. Some of the Jews were so angry at the preaching of the Gospel that they could not bear to listen to it, but *went out of the synagogue*. Now this showed:

1.1. Their open unfaithfulness. They publicly expressed their contempt for Christ and his message, trying to instill prejudice in the minds of others.

1.2. Their stubborn unfaithfulness. They went out of the synagogue to show that they did not believe the Gospel; they were determined they would not. The Gospel was therefore justly taken away from them, since they first took themselves away from it. It is certainly true that God never leaves anyone until they first leave him.

2. The Gentiles were as willing to hear the Gospel as those Jews were to get out of its hearing: *They besought* (begged) *that these words might be preached to them the next Sabbath*. They begged:

2.1. That the same offer would be made to them that was made to the Jews, that forgiveness of sins through Christ would be preached to them. What the Jews left—indeed, what they loathed—was what these people longed for. This justified Paul in preaching to them, that he was invited to do so. Who could refuse to break the bread of life to those who begged so much for it? Who could refuse to give to the poor at the door what the children at the table threw under their feet (Mt 15:26–27)?

2.2. That the same instructions would be given to them. They had heard the message of Christ, but did not understand it when they first heard it, and so they begged to have it preached to them again. What we have heard we should want to hear again, so that it may take deep root in us, and so that the points made may be driven home. It emphasizes the bad disposition of the Jews that the Gentiles wanted to hear often what the Jews were not willing to hear once.

3. There were many, both of Jews and converts, who were persuaded by the preaching of the Gospel. *Many of the Jews and religious proselytes* (devout converts to Judaism) *followed Paul and Barnabas*.

3.1. They submitted to the grace of God and were admitted to its benefits, strengths, and encouragements. They *followed Paul and Barnabas*; they became their disciples, or rather the disciples of Christ. Those who join themselves to Christ will join themselves to his ministers and follow them. Paul and Barnabas welcomed those Jews who were willing to submit to their instructions.

3.2. They were encouraged to persevere: *Paul and Barnabas, speaking to them, persuaded them to continue in the grace of God*. The grace of God will not be lacked by those who continue in it.

4. The preaching was cheerfully listened to the *next sabbath day* (v. 44): *Almost the whole city came together to hear the word of God*. This brought a vast gathering of people to the synagogue on the Sabbath. Some came out of curiosity; others longed to see what the Jews would do. Many who had heard something of the word of God came to hear more, to listen to it *not as the word of men but as the word of God*. Now because Paul met with the most encouraging audience among the Gentiles, he was justified in preaching to them.

5. The Jews were enraged at this; not only would they not receive the Gospel themselves, but they were filled with indignation at the crowds who followed it (v. 45): *When the Jews saw the multitudes*, it *filled them with envy*. They begrudged the influence the apostles had on the people. This was the same spirit that worked in the Pharisees toward Christ; they were cut to the heart when they saw *the whole world go after him* (Jn 12:19). They opposed the message the apostles preached: *They spoke against those things that were spoken by Paul*, finding some fault or other with everything he said, *contradicting and blaspheming*. They contradicted for the sake of contradiction, and when they could find no reason to raise an objection, they broke out into slander against Christ and his Gospel, *blaspheming* him and it. Those who begin with contradicting often end up blaspheming.

6. The apostles then solemnly declared themselves released from their obligations to the Jews and free to take the message of salvation to the Gentiles. The Jews had received the offer of the Gospel, but they refused it, and so they should not say anything against the Gentiles' having it. It is said that in declaring this (v. 46), *Paul and Barnabas waxed* (became) *bold*. There is a time for the preachers of the Gospel to show the boldness of a lion as well as the wisdom of the serpent and the innocence of the dove (Mt 10:16). When the enemies of Christ's cause begin to be bold, it is not the time for its advocates to be timid. The arrogance of the enemies of the Gospel should not frighten its friends, but embolden them, because they know whom they have trusted to support them. Now having made the Jews a fair offer of the grace of the Gospel, Paul and Barnabas gave them here fair notice that they were taking it to the Gentiles.

6.1. They acknowledged that the Jews were entitled to the first offer: "*It was necessary that the word of God should first have been spoken to you*, to whom the promise was made, whom Christ counted himself as being sent to first."

6.2. They charged them with refusing it: *You put it from you*. If people put the Gospel far away from them, God justly takes it away from them. Here, they *judged themselves unworthy of everlasting life*. In one sense we must all judge ourselves unworthy of eternal life, since there is nothing in us by which we can claim to deserve it. Here, however, the meaning is, "You make it clear that you are not fit to receive eternal life. *You* in effect *pass this judgment* on yourselves, and *out of your own mouth you shall be judged* (Lk 19:22). You will not receive it through Christ, through whom alone it is to be obtained, and so your condemnation will be that you will not have it at all."

6.3. On this they based their preaching the Gospel to the Gentiles: "*Lo, we turn to the Gentiles*. If one group will not receive it, another group will."

6.4. They justified themselves in this by a divine authority (v. 47): *For so hath the Lord commanded us*. This was according to what was foretold in the Old Testament. When the Messiah, at the prospect of the Jews' unfaithfulness, was about to say, *I have laboured in vain*, he was told that although *Israel were not gathered*, nevertheless, *he would be glorious* (Isa 49:4–5). For *I have set thee* to be *a light of the Gentiles, that thou shouldst be for salvation unto the ends of the earth* (Isa 49:6). He is set up as a light; he gives light to the understanding and so saves the soul. He is, and is to be, light and salvation to the Gentiles, to the ends of the earth. All nations will finally become his kingdom (Rev 11:15).

7. The Gentiles joyfully accepted what the Jews scornfully rejected (vv. 48–49). Notice how the Gentiles welcomed this happy turn of events in their favor:

7.1. They took encouragement from it: *When they heard this, they were glad.* It was good news to them that they were as welcome to enjoy the benefits of the Messiah's kingdom as the Jews themselves, and could share in the Jews' promise. When the Gentiles only heard that the offers of grace would be made them, *they were glad.* Many grieve under doubts as to whether they benefit from Christ or not, when they really should be rejoicing that they do benefit from him.

7.2. They gave God praise for it: *They glorified the word of the Lord,* that is, the Gospel; the more they knew it, the more they were in wonder at it. Oh, what light, what power, what a treasure, this Gospel brings! They glorified the word of the Lord:

7.2.1. Because now the knowledge of it was spread; it was not confined only to the Jews. It is the glory of the word of the Lord that the further it spreads, the brighter it shines. This shows that it is not like the light of the candle, but like the light of the sun when it shines very brightly.

7.2.2. Because now the knowledge of it had been brought to them. Those who have themselves been subdued by its power and comforted by its sweetness speak best of the honor of the word of the Lord.

7.3. Many of them became sincerely obedient to the faith: *As many as were ordained to eternal life believed.* Those whom God gave grace to believe were the ones who believed. Those whom the Father drew came to Christ (Jn 6:44); they were those to whom the Spirit made the Gospel call effective. God gave this grace to believe to all those among them who were appointed for eternal life, or as many as were destined to eternal life, all who were concerned about their eternal state and aimed to make sure of eternal life; and it was the grace of God that brought it about in them.

7.4. When they believed, they did what they could to spread the knowledge of Christ (v. 49): *And the word of the Lord was published throughout all the region.* Those new converts were ready to communicate to others what they were so full of themselves. Those who have come to know Christ for themselves will do all they can to help others come to know him. Those in great and rich cities who have received the Gospel should not think they can monopolize it, but should do all they can to have it declared in the country among the ordinary people, who have souls to be saved as well as they.

8. Having sown the seeds of a Christian church there, Paul and Barnabas left the place and went to do similar work elsewhere. We do not read anything about their performing miracles here to confirm their message. Although God usually used that method of conviction then, producing faith by the direct influence of his Spirit was itself the greatest miracle to those in whom it was performed. We are told:

8.1. How *the unbelieving Jews* expelled the apostles from that region. They *raised persecution against Paul and Barnabas.* Satan and his agents are angriest with the preachers of the Gospel when they see that they are successful. It has been the common lot of the best people in the world to suffer harm for doing good. Notice:

8.1.1. How the Jews gave them trouble: *They stirred up the devout and honorable women against them* (v. 50). It is sad when, claiming devotion to God, *devout and honorable women* conceive enmity toward Christ, as did those mentioned here. What? Women persecutors! Could they forget their natural tenderness and compassion? What? Respected women staining their honor! But, strangest of all, God-fearing women! Would they kill Christ's servants and think they were performing a service for God? Through these

God-fearing and respected women, the apostles' enemies stirred up *the chief men of the city,* the magistrates and the rulers, and set them against the apostles.

8.1.2. How far they carried their opposition, so far that *they expelled them out of their coasts* (region); they banished them. It was not by fear, but downright violence, that they were driven out. This was a way God used to make those who were well disposed toward the apostles even more warmly disposed toward them, because seeing people persecuted arouses our pity and makes us more ready to help them. The expelling of the apostles from the region perhaps gave them more friends than paying no attention to them would have.

8.2. How the apostles abandoned and rejected the unbelieving Jews (v. 51): *They shook off the dust of their feet against them.*

8.2.1. They declared that they would have nothing more to do with these Jews.

8.2.2. They expressed their detestation of their unfaithfulness. If Jews and Gentiles believe, they are equally acceptable to God and good people; it is just as true that if they do not believe, they are equally detestable.

8.2.3. They defied them, expressing their contempt for them and their hatred.

8.2.4. They left behind them a testimony that the Jews had received a fair offer of the grace of the Gospel. Christ had commanded the apostles to do this as a testimony against those who rejected their message (Mt 10:14; Lk 9:5). When *they left them, they came to Iconium,* not so much for safety as for work.

8.3. What attitude they left the new converts in at Antioch (v. 52): *the disciples* also continued with their work.

8.3.1. They were very cheerful. One would have expected that when Paul and Barnabas were expelled from the region, the disciples they left behind would have been full of grief and fear. But no, *they were filled with joy* in Christ. All their fears were swallowed up in their believing joy.

8.3.2. They were courageous, wonderfully encouraged by a holy determination to remain faithful to Christ. The more we enjoy the comforts and encouragements we meet with in the power of godliness, the better prepared we are to face the difficulties we meet with both in professing our faith and in leading godly lives.

CHAPTER 14

In this chapter we have a further account of the progress of the Gospel through the ministry of Paul and Barnabas among the Gentiles. Here is: 1. Their successful preaching of the Gospel for some time at Iconium and their being driven from there by the violence of their persecutors (vv. 1–7). 2. Their healing a lame man at Lystra (vv. 8–18). 3. The outrage of the people against Paul, the effect of which was that they stoned him—so they thought—to death (vv. 19–20). 4. Paul and Barnabas's visit to the churches they had planted (vv. 21–23). 5. Their return to Antioch and their report to the church concerning their journey (vv. 24–28).

Verses 1–7

In these verses we have:

1. The preaching of the Gospel at Iconium. Just as the blood of the martyrs has been the seed of the church, so the banishment of the confessors has helped scatter that seed.

1.1. The apostles made the first offer of the Gospel *to the Jews in their synagogues.* Although the Jews at Antioch had mistreated them, they did not therefore decline to preach the Gospel to the Jews at Iconium. Let not those of any denomination be condemned wholesale, nor some suffer for others' faults.

1.2. The apostles agreed in this work. *They went both together into the synagogue* to show their unanimity and mutual affection.

2. The success of their preaching there: *They so spoke that a great multitude, both of the Jews and also of the Greeks*, that is, the Gentiles, *believed*.

2.1. The Gospel was now preached to Jews and Gentiles together. At the end of the previous chapter it was preached first to the Jews and then to the Gentiles; here they were put together. The Jews had not so lost their preference as to be totally thrown out, but the Gentiles were brought to stand on the same terms as they did, and both together were admitted into the church, without distinction.

2.2. There seems to have been something significant in the way the apostles preached here: *They so spoke that a great multitude believed*—they spoke so plainly, so convincingly, so warmly and affectionately. What they spoke came from their hearts and therefore was likely to reach the heart. They spoke so boldly and courageously that the people who heard them could not help saying that *God was with them of a truth* (1Co 14:25).

3. The opposition their preaching met with there.

3.1. Unbelieving Jews were the first cause of their trouble here, as elsewhere (v. 2): they *stirred up the Gentiles*. When many Gentiles were influenced by the Gospel and accepted it, some of the Jews developed a holy jealousy and were stirred up to receive the Gospel (Ro 11:14), but others were provoked to a corrupt jealousy and enraged against the Gospel.

3.2. Discontented Gentiles, incited by the unbelieving Jews, were the instruments of their trouble. The Jews, by false suggestions, made the Gentiles' *minds evil affected* (poisoned their minds) *against the brethren*. They made their spirits sour and bitter against both the converters and the converted. It is hardly surprising if those who are ill disposed toward good people wish them harm and plan unkind things against them; it is all because of ill will. *They embittered* the minds of the Gentiles; they were continually taunting them. Those who allow themselves to be the tools of persecutors lead a dog's life, being harassed continually.

4. Their persistence in their work there and God's acknowledging them in it (v. 3). We have here:

4.1. The apostles working for Christ. Because the minds of *the Gentiles were evil affected against them*, one would have thought that they would withdraw. But on the contrary, that was why *they abode there a long time, speaking boldly in the Lord*. The more they saw of the spite against the new converts, the more they were encouraged to pursue their work. *They spoke boldly* and were not afraid of causing offense to the unbelieving Jews. But notice what gave them strength: *They spoke boldly in the Lord*, in his power, not depending on anything in themselves.

4.2. Christ working with the apostles according to his promise, *Lo, I am with you always* (Mt 28:20). He did not fail to give testimony to the message of his grace.

4.2.1. The Gospel is a message of grace, the assurance of God's goodwill to us. It is the message of Christ's grace, for it is only in him that we can find favor with God.

4.2.2. Christ himself has affirmed this message of grace. He has assured us that it is the message of God. It is also said especially of the apostles here *that the Lord*

confirmed their testimony, in granting signs and wonders to be done by their hands (v. 3)—in the miracles they performed in the kingdom of nature—as well as in the greater miracles brought about on human hearts by the power of divine grace. The Lord was with them as long as they were with him.

5. The division this brought about in the city (v. 4): *The multitude of the city was divided*. It seems that this work of preaching the Gospel was so widely noticed that every person, even of the *multitude of the city*, was either for it or against it; no one was neutral. We see here the meaning of Christ's prediction that he *came not to send peace upon earth, but rather division* (Lk 12:51–53). If everyone had unanimously submitted to his plans, there would have been universal peace; because they disagreed here, the breach was as wide as the sea. It was better that part of the city go to heaven than that everyone go to hell. Let us not think it strange if the preaching of the Gospel brings about division. It is better to be persecuted as those who bring about division, because we swim against the stream, than to yield and be carried down the stream that leads to destruction.

6. The attempt made on the apostles by their enemies. Their enemies' evil attitude against them broke out eventually into violent outrage (v. 5). Notice:

6.1. Who was behind the plot: *Both the Gentiles and the Jews, with their rulers*. The Gentiles and Jews were at enmity with one another, but they were united against the Christians. If the church's enemies can unite in this way for its destruction, will not its friends unite for its preservation?

6.2. What the plot was. Their plan *was to use the apostles despitefully*, exposing them to disgrace, and then *stone them*.

7. The rescue of the apostles (vv. 6–7). They got away when they found about the plot against them, and they made an honorable retreat—not a dishonorable flight—to *Lystra and Derbe*. They found safety: God shelters his people in a storm. They found work, and this was what they went for. They went to these cities, and there, and *in the region that lieth round about, they preached the Gospel*. In times of persecution, ministers may have reason to abandon a place, but they do not abandon their work.

Verses 8–18

In these verses we have:

1. A miraculous healing performed by Paul at Lystra on a man who had been lame from birth. Notice:

1.1. The miserable situation of the poor cripple (v. 8): he was *impotent in his feet*, disabled. It was well known that he had been so *from his mother's womb, never had walked*, and could not *stand up*.

1.2. The expectation that was raised in him of healing (v. 9): he heard Paul preach, and he was probably very much affected by what he heard. Paul was aware of this by the spirit of discernment; perhaps the look on the man's face partly witnessed for him: *Paul perceived that he had faith to be healed*.

1.3. The healing performed: *Paul, perceiving that he had faith to be healed*, brought *the word and healed him* (Ps 107:20). Paul spoke to him with a loud voice, so that the people around would be led to expect that this voice would have some remarkable effect. It is said only that the man *sat* (v. 8), not that he sat begging, and yet we may imagine how welcome Paul's words were to him, *"Stand upright on thy feet*; help yourself, and God will help you." *He leaped and walked*; he jumped up and not only *stood upright* but also walked back and forth before them all.

Those who through the grace of God are healed of their spiritual lameness must show it by leaping with holy joy and walking in a holy life.

2. The impression this healing made on the people: they were amazed at it. The performing of this one miracle was enough to make Paul and Barnabas truly great and honorable in the eyes of this people, even though the large number of Christ's miracles could not protect him from the greatest contempt among the Jews.

2.1. The people thought the apostles were gods (v. 11): *They lifted up their voices in the speech of Lycaonia, The gods are come down to us in the likeness of men.* This idea corresponded well enough with the fabled account they had of the visits their gods had made to this lower world. They were proud enough to think that they should have been visited. They took this idea so far here that they claimed to know which of their gods they were (v. 12): *They called Barnabas Jupiter*, for if they wanted to have him as a god, it was easy to make him the ruler of their gods as not. *Paul they called Mercury*, who was the messenger of the gods, for Paul was *the chief speaker*.

2.2. The priest then prepared to offer sacrifices to them (v. 13). The temple of Jupiter was in front of the gate of their city, as its protector and guardian, and when the priest heard the people cry out, he thought it was time for him to do his duty. If Jupiter was among them himself, the priest should do all he could to honor him. When Christ appeared in human likeness and performed very many miracles, the people were so far from offering sacrifices to him that they offered him as a sacrifice. But after Paul and Barnabas had performed only one miracle, they were immediately thought to be gods. The people *brought oxen* to be sacrificed *to them and* brought *garlands* with which to crown the sacrifices.

3. Paul and Barnabas's protest at this: they immediately tried to stop it. Many of the pagan emperors called themselves gods and took pride in having divine honor paid them, but Christ's ministers refused those honors when they were offered. Notice:

3.1. The holy anger Paul and Barnabas had at this: *When they heard this, they rent* (tore) *their clothes.* We do not find that they tore their clothes when the people insulted and abused them; they could bear that without being disturbed. When the people thought they were gods, however, and spoke of worshiping them, they could not bear it.

3.2. The effort they took to prevent it: they did not turn a blind eye to it. Christ had put enough honor on them by making them apostles; they did not need to assume the honor of either rulers or gods. Let us see what they did to prevent it.

3.2.1. *They ran in among the people* as soon as they heard about it (v. 14). They did not stand still, expecting honors to be shown them, but clearly declined them by thrusting themselves into the crowd.

3.2.2. They reasoned in this manner, "*crying out, Sirs, why do you do these things?* (v. 15). Why are you going about making gods of us?

3.2.2.1. "Our nature will not accept it: *We also are men of like passions with you.* You are wronging God if you give to us or any other person the honor that is to be given only to God. We are not only human, but also sinners and suffers, and so we are not to be considered as gods.

3.2.2.2. "Our teaching goes directly against it. Must we, whose work it is to abolish the gods you have, be added to your many gods? *We preach unto you that you should turn from these vanities unto the living God.*" When they preached to the Jews, they had nothing to do but preach the grace of God in Christ; when they preached

to the Jews, they had no need to preach against idolatry; but when they associated with the Gentiles, they must put right their mistakes in natural religion. Notice here what they preached to the Gentiles:

3.2.2.2.1. The gods they and their ancestors worshiped, and all the ceremonies of their worship, were worthless, idle, unreasonable, and unprofitable. "Therefore *turn from these vanities.*"

3.2.2.2.2. The God to whom the apostles wanted them to turn is *the living God.* Up to that time they had worshiped dead idols, which were completely unable to help them. Now they had been urged with arguments to worship the living God, who has life in himself (Jn 5:26) and life for us, and *lives for evermore* (Rev 1:18).

3.2.2.2.3. This God is the creator of the world, the fountain of all being and power: "He *made heaven and earth, and the sea, and all things therein.* We call you to worship *the God that made you and all the world*; worship the true God."

3.2.2.2.4. The world owed it to his patience that he had not destroyed them long before for their idolatry (v. 16): "*In times past* he *suffered* (allowed) *all nations to walk in their own ways.* Your serving gods tested God's patience, and it was a miracle of mercy that you were not destroyed for it. Now that he has sent his Gospel into the world, if you continue in your idolatry, he will not continue to be patient with you as he has been. Now that God has sent into the world a revelation that is to be made known to all nations, the situation is changed. Now you will no longer be excused in these worthless lies, but must turn away from them." God's patience with us up to this time should *lead us to repentance* (Ro 2:4), not encourage us to presume. Our having done wrong while we were still in ignorance will not support us in doing wrong when we have been better taught.

3.2.2.2.5. Even when they were not under the direction and correction of the word of God, they still should have known to do better through the works of God (v. 17). *He left not himself without witness.* Besides the witness for God within them, namely, the dictates of natural conscience, they had witnesses for God all around them, namely, the goodness of common providence. Their having no Scriptures partially excused them. It did not, however, wholly excuse them. There were other witnesses for God. God had *not left himself without witness*; he has not left us without a guide, and so he has left us without excuse.

3.2.2.2.5.1. The goodness of common providence witnesses to us that there is a God. The *rain and fruitful seasons* could not come about by chance. All the powers of nature witness to us of a sovereign power in the God of nature. It is not the sky that gives rain, but God who gives us rain from the sky.

3.2.2.2.5.2. The benefits we have through this goodness witness to us that we should acknowledge the Creator. *He left not himself without witness in that he did good.* God seems to consider the expressions of his goodness to be more significant, convincing proofs of his title to our praise than the evidence of his greatness; for his goodness is his glory (Ex 33:18–19). Because the most clearly perceptible expression of the goodness of Providence is that of the daily provision made of food and drink for us, the apostle chose to insist on that, and he showed how God does us good:

3.2.2.2.5.2.1. In preparing this provision for us. He does us good by giving us rain from above—both rain to drink and rain for our land to drink, for we have our food as well as drink from the rain. In giving us this, he *gives us fruitful seasons*. Of all the common actions of Providence, the nations chose to form their idea of the supreme God from that which calls forth terror, and this was the thunder. However, the apostle sets before us his generosity, so that we may have good thoughts of him, so that we may love him and delight in him as one who does good by giving *rain from heaven and fruitful seasons*.

3.2.2.2.5.2.2. In giving us its comforts. He is the One who *fills our hearts with food and gladness*. God is a very generous giver: *He fills our hearts with food*, not merely what we need, but a plentiful and wide range of delicacies. The Gentiles who had *lived without God in the world* (Eph 2:12) still lived on God. Those people had *their hearts filled with food*; *these things will not*, of course, *fill the soul* (Eze 7:19), nor will those who know how to value their own souls be satisfied with them. Yet we must all acknowledge that God fills our hearts with food and gladness, not only food, so that we may live, but also gladness, so that we may live cheerfully. We must thank God not only for our food but also for our joy. And if *our hearts be filled with food and gladness*, they should also be filled with love and thankfulness.

3.3. The success of this prohibition that the apostles gave to the people (v. 18): by *these sayings, they restrained the people from doing sacrifice to them*. They could scarcely restrain them from it. Paul and Barnabas had healed a lame man, and so the people thought them gods, which should make us very careful not to give to any other or take for ourselves the honor due only to God.

Verses 19–28

Here is a further account of the service and suffering of Paul and Barnabas. We see here:

1. How Paul was stoned and left for dead (vv. 19–20). They attacked Paul rather than Barnabas, because Paul, being the chief speaker, troubled them much more than Barnabas. Notice here:

1.1. How the people were enraged against Paul; *there came certain Jews from Antioch*, and they enraged the people against Paul and Barnabas. Notice how restless the rage of the Jews was against the Gospel of Christ; they could not bear it to gain a foothold anywhere.

1.2. To what extent they were enraged by these cruel Jews: they arose as a mob and *stoned Paul*, then *drew him out of the city, supposing he had been dead*. Just as it is with great difficulty that people are restrained from committing evil on one side, so it is with great ease that they are persuaded to commit evil on the other side. Notice how fickle worldly people are. Those who only the other day would have treated the apostles as more than human now treat them as worse than animals. Today "Hosanna" (Mk 11:1–11), but tomorrow "Crucify" (Mk 15:12–14); today sacrificed to, but tomorrow sacrificed. Popular breath turns like the wind.

1.3. How he was rescued by the power of God: when he was *drawn out of the city, the disciples stood round about him* (v. 20). It seems there were some at Lystra who became disciples, and even these new converts had enough courage to acknowledge Paul when he was stoned. They stood around him to guard him; they stood around him to see whether he was alive or dead; and suddenly *he rose up*. Although God's faithful servants may be brought within a step of death (1Sa 20:3), they will not die as long as he has work for them to do.

2. How the apostles continued with their work. All the stones the people threw at Paul could not stop him from pursuing his work: they *drew him out of the city* (v. 19), but he *came into the city* again. However, the persecution

the apostles had faced was a sign to them that they should seek opportunities to be useful elsewhere, and so they left Lystra for the present.

2.1. They went to break up and sow fresh ground at Derbe. The next day *Paul and Barnabas departed to Derbe*. There they preached the Gospel; they taught many there (v. 21). Nothing that happened at Derbe is recorded.

2.2. They returned and went over their work again; having stayed as long as they thought fit at Derbe, they came back to Lystra, Iconium, and Antioch (v. 21).

2.2.1. They *confirmed* (strengthened) *the souls of the disciples* (v. 22). Young converts tend to waver, and a little thing shocks them. These new converts were tempted to think of retreating after a little while, but the apostles came and told them that *this was the true grace of God wherein they stood* (1Pe 5:12). There was no danger like that of losing their union with Christ, no advantage like that of keeping their hold of him. Whatever trials they might face, they would have strength from Christ to endure them, and whatever their losses might be, they would be abundantly rewarded. This *confirmed the souls of the disciples*. We can learn from this:

2.2.1.1. Those who are converted need to be *confirmed*, strengthened; those who are planted need help to become rooted. Ministers' work is to establish saints as well as to wake up sinners.

2.2.1.2. True strengthening is a strengthening of the soul. It is the grace of God and nothing less that can effectively *confirm* (strengthen) *the souls of the disciples*.

2.2.2. *They exhorted them to continue in the faith*, or they encouraged them. They told them it was both their responsibility and in their interests to persevere. Those who are in the faith should be concerned to *continue in the faith*. They need to be encouraged to do so often.

2.2.3. What they insisted on most was *that we must through much tribulation enter into the kingdom of God*. But was this the way to *confirm the souls of the disciples* and engage them to *continue in the faith*? One would have thought it would rather shock them and make them tired. No, the matter was stated realistically: it would help strengthen them. It was true that they would meet with hardships. But then:

2.2.3.1. It had been appointed. They must go through them; there was no way out. All who want to *live godly in Christ Jesus shall suffer persecution* (2Ti 3:12). All who want to be Christ's disciples must *take up their cross* (Mt 16:24). When we gave up our names to Jesus Christ, it was what we agreed to; when we sat down and counted the cost (Lk 14:28, 33), if we calculated correctly, it was what we counted on.

2.2.3.2. It is the lot of the leaders in Christ's army as well as of the soldiers. It is not only "you" but also "we" who are subject to it. As Christ did not make the apostles go through any harder service than what he experienced before them, so neither did the apostles insist that ordinary Christians go through any harder service than they, the apostles, went through.

2.2.3.3. It is true that we must count on *much tribulation*, but it is encouraging that we will get through it. And we will not only get through it, but also get through it *into the kingdom of God*. It is true that we must go via the cross, but it is also as true that we will go to the crown.

2.2.4. *They ordained them elders in every church*. Now, at this second visit, they settled the churches in some order, put them under the guidance of a settled ministry.

2.2.4.1. Every church had its governors or leaders. Every congregation should have one or more such leaders.

2.2.4.2. Those governors were then elders. They were given authority to see that the laws Christ made were properly observed and carried out.

2.2.4.3. These elders were *ordained*. Having devoted themselves, they were solemnly set apart for the work of the ministry.

2.2.4.4. These elders were ordained *to them*, to serve the believers for their good. Those who are in the faith need to be build up in it; they need the elders' help in that matter.

2.2.5. *By prayer* accompanied by *fasting* they *commended them to the Lord on whom they believed*.

2.2.5.1. Even when people are brought to believe, ministers' care for them is not finished. There is still something lacking in their faith that needs to be perfected (1Th 3:10).

2.2.5.2. Even the ministers who take most care of those who believe must ultimately commend them to the Lord. Believers must commit themselves to his custody, and their ministers must commit them.

2.2.5.3. It is through prayer that believers must be commended to the Lord.

2.2.5.4. It is a great encouragement to us ministers that we can say, "They have believed in him; we commit to him those who have committed themselves to him."

2.2.5.5. It is good to add fasting to prayer to show our shame for our sin and to add power to our prayers.

2.2.5.6. When we part from our friends, the best kind of farewell is to commend them to the Lord and leave them with him.

2.3. They continued to preach the Gospel in other places where they had been. From Antioch they *passed through Pisidia*. From there they went into the province of *Pamphylia*, whose capital city was *Perga*, where they had been before (13:13). Now they returned to that city and *preached the word* (v. 25) there again. From there they *went down to Attalia*, on the coast of Pamphylia. They did not stay long in one place, but wherever they went, they tried to lay a foundation that could be built on later. They tried to sow the seeds that would in time produce a great harvest.

3. How they finally came back to Syrian Antioch, from which they had been sent out. From Attalia they went by sea to Antioch (v. 26). Notice:

3.1. Why they went there: because *thence they had been recommended* (committed) *to the grace of God*. Because it was there that the brothers and sisters had commended the apostles to the grace of God for the work *which they fulfilled*, the apostles thought they owed them an account of how they had fared so that the brothers and sisters could help them by their praises just as they had helped them by their prayers.

3.2. What account they gave the believers at Antioch of the work they had done and the reactions they had met with (v. 27). They *gathered the church together* and gave them an account of two things:

3.2.1. Of the signs they had had of God's presence with them in their work: *They rehearsed* (reported) *all that God had done with them*. They did not tell what they had done, but what God had done, because he is not only the One who works in us both to will and to do (Php 2:13), but also the One who then works with us to make what we do effective. God's grace can do anything without ministers' preaching, but ministers' preaching can do nothing without God's grace.

3.2.2. Of the fruit of their work among the Gentiles. They told how *God had opened the door of faith unto the Gentiles*. There is no entering into the kingdom of Christ except through the door of faith, and it is God who opens this door. We have reason to be thankful that God has *opened the door of faith to the Gentiles*. This was how the Gospel was spread, and it shone more and more brightly (Pr 4:18), and no one was able to close this door that God had opened (Isa 22:22).

3.3. What they did with themselves for the present: *There they abode a long time with the disciples* (v. 28), not because they feared their enemies, but because they loved their friends.

CHAPTER 15

In this chapter we find the apostles had other work cut out for them that was not so pleasant. The Christians and ministers were engaged in controversy. When they should have been making war on the Devil's kingdom, they had much to do to keep the peace in Christ's kingdom. Here is: 1. A disagreement raised in Antioch by the Judaizing teachers (vv. 1–2). 2. A consultation held with the church at Jerusalem about this matter (vv. 3–5). 3. An account of what took place at the synod that was convened on this occasion (v. 6). Here we have: 3.1. What Peter said (vv. 7–11). 3.2. What Paul and Barnabas spoke about (v. 12). 3.3. What James proposed to settle this matter (vv. 13–21). 4. The result of this debate, and the circular letter that was written to the Gentile converts (vv. 22–29). 5. The delivering of this decision to the church at Antioch (vv. 30–35). 6. The beginning of a second journey by Paul and Barnabas to preach to the Gentiles, in which a quarrel about their assistant led to their separation (vv. 36–41).

Verses 1–5

Even when things go very smoothly and pleasantly, it is foolish to rest secure. There will arise some uneasiness or other that is unforeseen. If ever there was a heaven on earth, surely it was in the church at Antioch at this time. But here their peace was disturbed by the arising of differences. Here is:

1. A new teaching that was started among them, which called for the Gentile converts to submit to circumcision and the ceremonial law (v. 1).

1.1. The people who urged this were *certain men who came down from Judea*. They came to Antioch because that was both the headquarters of those who preached to the Gentiles and the meeting place of the Gentile converts, and if these men from Judea could only gain influence there, this yeast would soon spread throughout all the churches of the Gentiles. They welcomed the Gentiles, but told them that *yet one thing they lacked* (Mk 10:21): they must be circumcised. Even those who are very well taught need to stand on their guard against being untaught or badly taught.

1.2. The position they set forth was that unless the Gentiles who had become Christians were *circumcised after the manner of Moses, they could not be saved*.

1.2.1. Many of the Jews who accepted the faith of Christ still continued to be very *zealous for the law* (21:20). They knew it had come from God and that its authority was sacred, and they had been brought up to observe it. Their following of these practices was overlooked for the present, because the prejudices of upbringing and background are not all overcome immediately. However, it was not enough for them to indulge in these practices themselves; they must have the Gentile converts brought under the same obligations. There is a strange tendency in us to make our own personal opinion and practice the basis of rule and law for everybody else, and to conclude that because we are doing something right, everyone else is doing wrong just because they are not doing as we do.

1.2.2. Those Jews who believed that Christ was the Messiah could not get clear of their idea of the Messiah, that he would set up a temporal kingdom in favor of the Jewish nation. It was a disappointment to them that as yet nothing had been done toward this, and now they heard that the message of Christ had been received among the Gentiles and that his kingdom was beginning to be set up among them. If they could only persuade those who accepted Christ also to accept the Law of Moses, they hoped that their point would be won, that the Jewish nation would become as significant as they could wish for, though following a different path. It is hardly surprising if those who have wrong ideas about the kingdom of Christ follow wrong ways to advance it.

1.2.3. The great stress these Jews laid on this requirement is significant; they did not say merely, "You ought to be circumcised after the manner of Moses," but, *Except you be circumcised, you cannot be saved.* If you do not follow our mind and way in this matter, you will never go to heaven, and so of course you will go to hell." Gentile believers, though otherwise good people and believers in Christ, could not be saved, said these Jews, unless they were members of the Jewish church and conformed to the ceremonies of their worship; without that, salvation itself could not save them. No one was in Christ except those who belonged to their little group.

2. The opposition that Paul and Barnabas raised against this schismatic idea (v. 2): *They had no small dissension and disputation* (sharp dispute and debate) *with them.* They would in no way yield to this teaching.

2.1. As faithful servants of Christ, they refused to see his truths betrayed. They knew that Christ came to free us from the burden of the ceremonial law, and so they could not bear to hear of circumcising the Gentile converts, since their instructions were only to baptize them.

2.2. As spiritual fathers to the Gentile converts, they would not see their liberties infringed. They had told the Gentiles that if they believed in Jesus Christ, they would be saved. To be told now that this was not enough would discourage them. The apostles, therefore, set themselves against it.

3. The way the believers at Antioch chose to prevent this dangerous idea from spreading and causing further trouble. They decided that Paul and Barnabas and some others from Jerusalem should *go to Jerusalem to the apostles and elders.* They sent the matter to Jerusalem:

3.1. Because those who taught this teaching came from Jerusalem and claimed to have received directions from the apostles there. It was therefore proper to go to Jerusalem to discuss it, to find out if these Judaizers had any such instructions from the church there, and what had claimed to be apostolically right was soon found to be all wrong. It was true that these men had *gone out from them* (v. 24), but they had never received any such orders from them.

3.2. Because those who were taught this teaching would be more confirmed in their opposition to it if they were sure that *the apostles and elders at Jerusalem* were against it.

3.3. Because the apostles at Jerusalem were the most suitable people to consult about a point that was not yet fully settled, and so their decision would be likely to end the controversy.

4. The journey of Paul and Barnabas and their company to Jerusalem on this mission (v. 3), where we find:

4.1. That they were honored when they departed: *They were brought on their way by the church.* This is how the church showed their favor to those who stood up for them.

4.2. That they did good as they went along. They visited churches on their way; they passed through Phoenicia and Samaria, and as they went they *declared the conversion of the Gentiles,* which *caused great joy to all the brethren.* The progress of the Gospel is and should be a matter of great joy. All the brethren in Christ's family rejoice when more are born into the family, because the family will never be any poorer because of the vast numbers of its children. In Christ and heaven there is enough room, and enough inheritance, for them all.

5. The enthusiastic welcome they received at Jerusalem (v. 4).

5.1. The good reception their friends gave them: they were *received of the church, and of the apostles and elders,* with every possible expression of sincere love and friendship.

5.2. The good reception they gave their friends: they *declared all things that God had done with them,* telling them about the success of their ministry among the Gentiles. As they had traveled, they had planted, and as they had come back, they had watered, but in both they were the first to acknowledge that it was God who gave the growth (1Co 3:6).

6. The opposition they encountered from the same party at Jerusalem (v. 5). *There rose up certain of the sect of the Pharisees* who believed in Christ but thought it necessary that the Gentiles be circumcised. Notice here:

6.1. Sometimes even those who have been most prejudiced against the Gospel have been captivated by it. When Christ was here on earth, few or none of the rulers and of the Pharisees believed in him (Jn 7:48), but now there were those who belonged to the party of the Pharisees who believed, and many of them, we hope, did so sincerely.

6.2. It is very hard for people to suddenly get rid of all their prejudices: those who had been Pharisees kept some of the old yeast even after they became Christians. All did not do so, as can be seen from the example of Paul, but some did.

Verses 6–21

Here we have an account of the council that was called to discuss this question (v. 6): *The apostles and presbyters came together to consider this matter.* They did not give their judgment rashly, but considered the matter. Although they were clear about it in their own minds, they still took time to consider it and to hear what might be said by the other party. Here is a direction to the pastors of the churches: when difficulties arise, they should come together in formal and godly meetings, so that they may know what one another thinks and strengthen one another. We have here:

1. Peter's speech. He was a faithful member of this assembly, and he offered what was very much to the point and would be better to hear from him than from another, because he himself had been the first to preach the Gospel to the Gentiles. *There had been much disputing* regarding this question, both for and against, and liberty of speech had been allowed, as it should be in such cases. When both sides had been heard, *Peter rose up.*

1.1. He reminded them of the commission he had received some time before *to preach the Gospel to the Gentiles.* "You know that from a good while ago God made *choice* of one person to preach the Gospel to the Gentiles, and I was the one, so *that the Gentiles by my mouth would hear the word and believe* (v. 7). Everybody rejoiced that *God had granted to the Gentiles repentance unto life,* and no one said a word about circumcising them." See 11:18. "Why then should the Gentiles who hear the word of the Gospel from Paul's mouth be compelled to submit to circumcision any more than those who heard it from my mouth?"

1.2. He reminded them how God had significantly acknowledged him in his preaching to the Gentiles (v. 8): "*God, who knows the hearts, bore them witness* by *giving them the Holy Spirit even as he did unto us* apostles." See 11:15–17. When God gives the Holy Spirit to people, he bears witness that they belong to him; we are sealed with that Holy Spirit of promise (Eph 1:13)—marked for God. "God has *put no difference between us and them* (v. 9); although they are Gentiles, they are as welcome to receive the grace of Christ and come to the throne of grace as we Jews are." We should not set any conditions on our brothers' and sisters' acceptance with us except those that God has set as the conditions of their acceptance with him (Ro 14:3). "Now the Gentiles were fit for fellowship with God because they had *had their hearts purified by faith.* Why should we think, therefore, that they are not fit for fellowship with us unless they submit to the ceremonial purifying commanded by the law to us?" By faith the heart is purified. The faith of all the saints is equally precious and has equally precious effects. Those who are united to Christ by faith are to look on themselves as joined to one another in such a way that all distinctions, even that between Jew and Gentile, are swallowed up by it.

1.3. He sharply rebuked those teachers who wanted to bring the Gentiles under the obligation of the Law of Moses (v. 10): *Now therefore, why tempt you* (why do you try to test) *God to put a yoke upon the neck of the disciples, a yoke which neither our fathers nor we were able to bear?* Here he demonstrated that:

1.3.1. They were showing God great disrespect. "By calling into question what he has already settled by no less a sign than the gift of the Holy Spirit, you are in effect asking, 'Did God know what he was doing?' Or, 'Was he serious about it?'" Those who try to dictate terms to God, saying that people cannot be saved except on certain terms that God never appointed, are testing him.

1.3.2. They were proposing to do a great deal of wrong to the disciples: Christ came to declare *liberty to the captives* (Lk 4:18), and they were trying to enslave those whom he had set free. Christ came to ease us of this burden. For these teachers to go about laying on the shoulders of the Gentiles that load from which Christ came to free even the Jews was the most harmful thing that could be done to them.

1.4. Whereas the Jewish teachers had urged circumcision as necessary to salvation, Peter showed that both Jews and Gentiles were to be saved purely *through the grace of our Lord Jesus Christ,* and in no other way (v. 11): *We believe we shall be saved through that grace* only. It may also be translated, "We believe to be saved": "We who are circumcised believe in order to be saved, just as those who are uncircumcised do. We must depend on the grace of Christ for salvation just as they do. There is not one way of salvation for the Jews and another for the Gentiles. Why should we burden them with the insistence that the Law of Moses is necessary for their salvation, when it is not that, but the Gospel of Christ, that is necessary for both our salvation and theirs?"

2. A summary of what Barnabas and Paul said, which was what has been recorded in the previous chapters: *what*

miracles and wonders God had wrought among the Gentiles by them* (v. 12). They had given such a report to the church *at Antioch* (14:27), and now they gave it again to the synod, and it was right that they gave it again here to show, by clearly relating the facts of the matter, that God acknowledged the preaching of the pure Gospel to those who were outside the law. Notice:

2.1. What account they gave; they declared what signs and wonders *God had wrought among the Gentiles by them,* what confirmation he had given by miracles performed in the kingdom of nature, and what success by miracles performed in the kingdom of grace. What need had they of any other advocate when God himself pleaded their cause?

2.2. What attention was given to them: *All the multitude kept silence, and gave audience to Paul and Barnabas.* It seems they took more notice of the apostles' account than they had of all the arguments that had been offered. As in physics and medicine nothing is so satisfactory as experiments, so also in the things of God the best explanation of the word of grace is the accounts given of the activity of the Spirit of grace. Those who fear God will most readily listen to those who can tell them *what God has done for their souls,* or by their action (Ps 66:16).

3. The speech that James gave to the synod (v. 13). *After they had held their peace,* then James stood up. The hearing of a range of ministers may be useful to us when one truth does not drive out, but firmly drives home, another.

3.1. He addressed himself respectfully to those present: "*Men and brethren, hearken unto me.* We are all brothers, equally concerned that nothing be done to dishonor Christ or disturb Christians."

3.2. He referred to what Peter had said about the conversion of the Gentiles (v. 14): "*Simeon hath declared how God at the first did visit the Gentiles* by visiting Cornelius and his friends, who were the firstfruits of the Gentiles." James observed here:

3.2.1. That the grace of God was the origin of the Gentiles' conversion; it was *God that visited the Gentiles.* The friendship began on his side; he not only *visited and redeemed his people* (Lk 1:68) but also visited and redeemed those who were *Lo-ammi,* not his people (Hos 1:9–10; 2:23).

3.2.2. That the glory of God was the purpose of their conversion: he had visited them to take from them a people for his name, who would glorify him, and in whom he would be glorified. As in former times he took the Jews, so now he took the Gentiles.

3.3. He confirmed this with a quotation from the Old Testament. It was foretold in the Old Testament, and so it must be fulfilled (v. 15). The words of the prophets agreed with this; most of the Old Testament prophets spoke more or less about the calling of the Gentiles. It was the general expectation of the devout Jews that the Messiah would be a light to enlighten the Gentiles (Lk 2:32), but James set aside such better-known prophecies and chose one that seemed more obscure, one written in Am 9:11–12, where there is foretold:

3.3.1. The setting up of the kingdom of the Messiah (v. 16): *I will raise up the tabernacle of David, that is fallen.* This tabernacle was ruined and fallen down; there had not been a king from the family of David for many years. But God would return and would rebuild it, would raise it up from its ruins, a phoenix out of its ashes, and this had now just been fulfilled when our Lord Jesus was raised up from that family. The church of Christ may be called the tabernacle of David. The church may sometimes be brought very low and seem to be in ruins, but it will be rebuilt, and its withering interests will revive.

3.3.2. The inclusion of the Gentiles as the effect and result of this (v. 17): *That the residue of men* (rest of humanity) *might seek after the Lord*, not only the Jews but also the rest of humanity, who had been left out of the visible church up to that time. They must now be led to seek the Lord. The Septuagint (a Greek version of the Old Testament), which is the translation James quotes, reads, *that the residue of men might seek, and all the Gentiles on whom my name is called*; that is, "that the residue of men, all the Gentiles on whom my name is called, might seek." (To the Septuagint text, after *seek*, James adds: *after the Lord*.) The Lord's name would be declared among them, and they would be led both to know his name and to call on it. They would call themselves the people of God, and he would call them that, and so, by the agreement of both parties, they would bear his name. "This promise is now beginning to be fulfilled, because it is added, *saith the Lord, who doeth this*"; "who does all these things," according to the Septuagint. It was said by the One who does it — who is determined to do it. Although saying and doing are two different things with us, they are not so with God. The uniting of Jews and Gentiles in one body, and all those things that were done to that end, were:

3.3.2.1. What God did, whatever instruments were employed in it.

3.3.2.2. What God was pleased with, because he is the God of the Gentiles as well as the Jews.

3.4. He saw it in the light of the purposes of God (v. 18): *Known to God are all his works from the beginning of the world*. God not only foretold the calling of the Gentiles through the prophets but also foreordained it in his eternal purposes. Whatever God does, he intended and determined to do before. He not only does whatever he determined, which is more than we can do — our purposes are frequently thwarted, and our actions unsuccessful — but also determined whatever he does. What we will do in such and such a case we cannot tell until it is time to do it, but all God's works are known to him. We are poor and shortsighted; the wisest among us can see only a little way ahead, and nothing at all with any certainty, but we may be encouraged by the assurance that there is infallible certainty in the divine foreknowledge: *known unto God are all his works*.

3.5. He gave his advice with reference to the Gentiles (v. 19), beginning with, *My sentence is*. The phrase means, "I give it as my opinion, or judgment"; he gave it not as one with authority over the others, but as an adviser to them. His advice was:

3.5.1. That circumcision and the observance of the ceremonial law should in no way be imposed on the Gentile converts. "I am clearly set on treating them with every possible consideration and putting no kind of discouragement on them. I am determined not to trouble them or make it difficult for them." Great care must be taken not to discourage or disturb young converts by debating doubtful matters. First let the essentials of religious faith be impressed deeply on them, and these will satisfy them and give them peace.

3.5.2. That it would be good, nevertheless, if the Gentiles would comply with the Jews in some areas where noncompliance would give most offense. It would please the Jews — and if a small matter would please them, it was better to follow that than to go against them — if the Gentile converts abstained:

3.5.2.1. *From pollutions of idols* (food polluted by idols) *and from fornication* (sexual immorality), which are two bad things, and always to be abstained from. Nor did the apostles neglect to warn against these things. Christians should have no kind of fellowship with idolaters in their idolatrous worships, especially not in the feasts they held on the occasions of their sacrifices. See 1Co 10:14; 2Co 6:14. And Paul is very urgent and insistent in his warnings against *Fornication* (sexual immorality) (1Co 6:9–15; Eph 5:3). But the Jews suggested that the Gentiles, even after their conversion, allowed themselves these things, and that the apostle to the Gentiles took no notice of it. Now, to make this suggestion unnecessary, James advised that the Gentiles should also be publicly warned *to abstain from pollutions of idols and from fornication*.

3.5.2.2. *From things strangled* (from the meat of strangled animals) *and from blood*, which had been forbidden before the giving of the Law of Moses (Ge 9:4).

3.6. He gave a reason for his advice, that great respect should be shown to the Jews, since they had been used to the formal injunctions of the ceremonial law for so long that they must be borne with patiently if they could not immediately do without them (v. 21): *For Moses hath of old those that preach him in every city, being read in the synagogues every sabbath day*.

3.6.1. "Moses is continually preached to them, and they are called on *to remember the Law of Moses*." Even the word of God that is written to us should also be preached.

3.6.2. "His writings are read *in their synagogues* and on *the sabbath day*, so that from their childhood they have been trained to have a high regard for the Law of Moses.

3.6.3. "This has been done *of old time*; they have received from their fathers a great respect for Moses.

3.6.4. "This has been done *in every city*, so that none of them can be ignorant of the emphasis the law places on these matters. They should not be blamed if they are reluctant to part with these laws and cannot suddenly be persuaded to look on them as unnecessary and indifferent. We must give them time, therefore; they must be borne with patiently for a while, and brought on gradually." In this way this apostle showed a spirit of moderation, seeking, as far as possible, to please both sides and provoke neither.

Verses 22–35

We have here the result of the consultation. The advice that James gave was unanimously approved. Letters were sent, therefore, by messengers from the Jerusalem church to the Gentile converts, which would strengthen the latter greatly against the false teachers. Notice:

1. The choice of delegates to be sent with Paul and Barnabas on this errand.

1.1. The leaders in Jerusalem thought it right *to send men of their own company to Antioch with Paul and Barnabas* (v. 22). This was agreed to by *the apostles and elders, with the whole church*. They sent these messengers:

1.1.1. To show their respect to the church at Antioch as a sister church and to find out more about how they were doing.

1.1.2. To encourage Paul and Barnabas and make their journey home more pleasant.

1.1.3. To give a good reputation to the letters they carried, so that more attention would be given to the message, which would probably meet with opposition from some people.

1.1.4. To maintain the communion of the saints, showing *that, though they were many, yet they were one* (1Co 12:20).

1.2. Those they sent were not unimportant people, who could serve merely to carry the letters; *they were chosen men, and chief men among the brethren*. They are named here: *Judas*, who was called *Barsabas, and Silas*.

2. The drawing up of the letters by which the churches would be notified of the synod's decision in this matter. Here is:

2.1. A very obliging introduction to this decree (v. 23), which contains:

2.1.1. What suggests the humility of the apostles, that they considered *the elders and brethren*, the ministers and ordinary Christians, as sharing in their commission, and had taken advice from them in this matter. Here, they remembered the instructions their Master gave them (Mt 23:8).

2.1.2. What shows their respect: they *sent greeting* and called the Christians at Antioch *brethren of the Gentiles*, so giving them the right hand of fellowship (Gal 2:9): "You are our brothers, though Gentiles." Now that *the Gentiles were fellow-heirs and of the same body* (Eph 3:6), they were to be encouraged and called brothers and sisters.

2.2. A just and severe rebuke to the Judaizing teachers (v. 24): "*We have heard that certain who went out from us have troubled you with words*. It was true that they *went out from us*, but as for their urging the Law of Moses on you, we *gave* them *no such commandment* (authorization)." These teachers had done a great deal of wrong to the Gentile converts by saying, *You must be circumcised, and you must keep the law*.

2.2.1. It confused them: "*They have troubled you with words*. You depended on those who told you, *If you believe in the Lord Jesus Christ, you shall be saved*, and now you have been startled by those who tell you *you must keep the Law of Moses, or you cannot be saved*. They trouble you with words—mere words—sounds, but no substance." How much the church has been troubled by words, by the pride of people who loved to hear themselves talk!

2.2.2. It put them in danger; these teachers *subverted* (troubled) the souls of the Gentile believers, unsettling them, and pulling down what had been built up.

2.3. An honorable testimony given of the messengers:

2.3.1. Of Paul and Barnabas, whom these Judaizing teachers had criticized as having done their work incompletely because they had brought the Gentile converts only to Christianity and not to Judaism.

2.3.1.1. "These men are precious to us; they are *our beloved Barnabas and Paul*." Sometimes it is good for those who are eminent to express their esteem not only for the despised truth of Christ but also for the despised preachers and defenders of that truth.

2.3.1.2. "They have distinguished themselves in serving Christ. They *have hazarded* (risked) *their lives for the name of our Lord Jesus Christ* (v. 26). They have risked everything for Christ, have engaged in the most dangerous forms of service as good soldiers of Christ." It was improbable that such faithful confessors would be unfaithful preachers.

2.3.2. Of Judas and Silas: "*They are chosen men* (v. 25), and they are those who have listened to our debates and will *tell you the same things by mouth* (v. 27)." What is useful for us is good to have both in writing and by word of mouth, so that we may have the advantage of both reading and hearing it.

2.4. The instructions as to what to require from the Gentile converts. Notice here:

2.4.1. The content of the injunction, which is according to the advice given by James.

2.4.1.1. They should never eat anything they knew had been offered in sacrifice to an idol, but should look on it as defiled to them. This is an obsolete case to us.

2.4.1.2. *They should not eat blood. That they should not eat anything that was strangled* or had not had the blood drained out.

2.4.1.3. They should be very strict in censuring those who *were guilty of fornication*. "These things are especially offensive to the Jews, and so do not displease them in this matter."

2.4.2. How it was worded.

2.4.2.1. The council expressed themselves with a note of authority: *It seemed good to the Holy Spirit, and to us*, that is, "to us under the guidance of the Holy Spirit." They would not order anything because *it seemed good to them* without them first knowing it *seemed good to the Holy Spirit*.

2.4.2.2. They expressed themselves with much tenderness and fatherly concern.

2.4.2.2.1. They were afraid of imposing heavy burdens on them: we will *lay upon you no greater burden*. They dreaded nothing so much as imposing too much on them and thereby discouraging them as they set out on their lives as believers.

2.4.2.2.2. They imposed on them *no other than necessary things*. Church rulers should impose only necessary things, matters Christ has made our duty. They do not have the authority to make new laws, but only to see that the laws of Christ are properly carried out.

2.4.2.2.3. They reinforced their order with a commendation of those who would comply with it rather than with the condemnation of those who would disobey it: *From which if you keep yourselves you will do well*. It was all sweetness, love, and good humor. The difference in the style between the true apostles and the false apostles is significant. Those who wanted to impose the ceremonial laws were positive and imperious: *Except you keep it, you cannot be saved* (v. 1). The apostles of Christ, who only commended what was necessary, were mild and gentle: "*From which if you keep yourselves, you will do well. Fare ye well*; we sincerely wish you well, to your honor and peace."

3. The delivering of the letters.

3.1. *When they were dismissed, they then came to Antioch*. They stayed no longer at Jerusalem than until their business was completed, and then they came back.

3.2. As soon as they came to Antioch, *they gathered the multitude together, and delivered the epistle to them* (vv. 30–31), so that they would all know what was forbidden them. However, this was not all; it was so that they would know that no more than this was forbidden them.

3.3. The people were very pleased (v. 31): *They rejoiced for the consolation* (for its encouraging message). They were confirmed in their freedom from the burden of the ceremonial law. Those who troubled their minds with an attempt to force circumcision on them were silenced. The Gentiles were encouraged to receive the Gospel, and those who had received it remained faithful to it. The peace of the church was restored.

3.4. They got the visiting ministers who came from Jerusalem to give them each a sermon (v. 32). Judas and Silas, *being prophets also themselves, exhorted the brethren with many words* and *confirmed them*. Even those who had the constant task of preaching, Paul and Barnabas, were still glad of the help of Judas and Silas; the diversity of the gifts of ministers is useful to the church. Notice what the work of ministers is toward those who are in Christ:

3.4.1. To confirm them, to confirm their choice of Christ and their determination to follow Christ.

3.4.2. To encourage them to persevere, to stir them to do what is good and tell them how to do it. They encouraged the brothers and sisters, and this strengthened them, because the joy of the Lord will be our strength (Ne 8:10). One word would affect one person and a different one would affect another. What they had to say might have been summed up in a few words, but it was for the edification of the church that they used *many words*.

3.5. The Jerusalem ministers were sent away (v. 33). When they had spent some time among them, the brothers and sisters at Antioch let them go in peace, to return to the apostles at Jerusalem.

3.6. Silas, Paul, and Barnabas, however, stayed at Antioch.

3.6.1. When it was time to go, Silas chose rather to *abide still at Antioch* (v. 34). We do not know why, but we have no reason to blame him.

3.6.2. Although the work of Paul and Barnabas lay chiefly among the Gentiles, they stayed for some time in Antioch. They remained there not for their own personal enjoyment but to *teach and preach the word of God*. Many Gentiles probably went there from all parts, so that in preaching there they were in effect preaching to many nations. So it was that they were not only not idle in Antioch, but were fulfilling their main intention.

3.6.3. There were *many others also* there. That there are many workers in Christ's vineyard does not discharge us from fulfilling our duty. There may still be opportunities for us; the zeal and usefulness of others should excite us, not put us to sleep.

Verses 36–41

Having seen the good outcome of a public disagreement among Christians, here we have a private quarrel between two ministers, no less than Paul and Barnabas. Though it was not settled, it still ended well. Here is:

1. A good suggestion that Paul made to Barnabas to go and review and renew their work among the Gentiles. Antioch was now a safe and quiet harbor for them, but Paul remembered that they were put there only to re-equip and refresh themselves, and that the work appointed him was far away among the Gentiles, and so now he began to think of putting out to sea again, on a second journey. He did this *some days after*; his active spirit could not bear to be out of work for long, nor could his bold and daring spirit long be out of danger. Notice:

1.1. To whom he proposed this—to Barnabas, his old friend and coworker. We need one another, and may be useful to one another in many ways. We should be eager, therefore, both to seek and to give help. Every soldier needs a comrade.

1.2. For whom the visit was intended: "Let us not begin a new work; let us look at the fields we have already sown. *Let us go again and visit our brethren in every city where we have preached the word of the Lord*." He called all the Christians *brethren*. He had a concern for them in *every city*. Wherever we have *preached the word of the Lord*, let us go and nurture the seed that has been sown. Those who have preached the Gospel should visit those to whom they have preached it. Just as we must look after our praying and must listen for God's response to that, so we must also look after our preaching to see what success that has.

1.3. What was intended in this visit: "Let us *see how they do*." He wanted to visit them so that he could get to know their situation. He was like a doctor who visits a patient who is recovering, to prescribe what is necessary

to complete the patient's cure and prevent a relapse. "Let us see how they are doing," that is:

1.3.1. *What spirit they were of* (Lk 9:55), their attitude and behavior.

1.3.2. What state they were in, "so that we may rejoice with them if they are rejoicing, weep with them if they are weeping, and know better how to pray for them."

2. The disagreement between Paul and Barnabas about an assistant.

2.1. Barnabas wanted to take his nephew John, also called Mark, with them (v. 37). He decided to take him because he was his relative. We should be suspicious of showing favoritism and should guard against it in advancing our relatives.

2.2. Paul opposed it (v. 38): *He thought not good to take him with them*, since John Mark had *departed from them* from Pamphylia (13:13) and had *not gone with them to the work*. He had deserted just as they were about to engage in battle. He now probably promised that he would not do so again, but Paul thought it was not right that he be honored in this way, at least not until he had been tested for a longer period. If someone deceives me once, it is their fault, but if twice, it is my fault for trusting them.

3. The outcome of this disagreement: they separated because of it. The conflict was so intense that they *departed asunder one from the other* (they parted company). Neither would give in, and so there was no way out except to part company. We see here something that is just cause for regret, but also very instructive, because we see:

3.1. That the best people are still only human, *subject to like passions* as we are (Jas 5:17); these two good men had explicitly acknowledged this about themselves (14:15), and now it was shown to be only too true. I suspect there was a fault on both sides, as there usually is in such disagreements. They were certainly both at fault to be so passionate as to allow the disagreement to become *sharp*, and also to be so stubborn that each one stuck resolutely to his opinion and neither would yield. It is a pity that some friend did not intervene to prevent it from coming to such an open break. We must acknowledge that they acted as they did out of human weakness. We must not, of course, use this account to excuse our own immoderate passions, and yet it must restrain and moderate our criticism of other people. Repentance teaches us to have harsh thoughts about ourselves, but charity teaches us to be kind and fair in our thoughts about others. It is only Christ's example that is a copy without errors, a perfect image of God.

3.2. That we are not to think it strange if differences arise between wise and good people. Even those who are united to one and the same Jesus, who are sanctified by one and the same Spirit, see things differently. We will never all be completely in harmony until we reach heaven.

3.3. That these differences often go so far that they bring about a separation. Paul and Barnabas, who were not separated either by the persecutions of the unbelieving Jews or by the impositions of the believing Jews, were still separated by an unhappy disagreement between themselves.

4. The good that was brought out of this evil. It was strange that even the sufferings of the apostles would lead to the *furtherance of the Gospel of Christ* (Php 1:12), but even stranger that the quarrels of the apostles would do so. Yet God would not allow such things to exist if he did not know how to make them serve his own purposes.

4.1. More places were visited. Barnabas went one way; he sailed to Cyprus (v. 39), where they began their work

(13:4), and where he would be in *his own country* (4:36). Paul went another way, to Cilicia, which was *his own country* (21:39). Each seems to have been influenced by his affection for his native soil, as is usual. Yet God served his own purposes by it.

4.2. More hands were used in the ministry of the Gospel among the Gentiles. John Mark, who had been unfaithful, was not rejected, and for all we know, he proved very useful and successful. Silas, who was a new hand, was brought in.

5. Occasion for us to observe, further:

5.1. That the church at Antioch seems to have supported Paul in what he did. Barnabas sailed with his nephew to Cyprus, and no notice was taken of him. However, when Paul departed, he was *recommended by the brethren to the grace of God*. They prayed publicly for Paul and for the success of his ministry. They transferred the matter to the grace of God, leaving it to that grace both to work on him and to work with him. People who are enabled to behave themselves in such a way that they do not lose the right to the influence of the love and prayers of good people are happy at all times.

5.2. That later, however, when John Mark had been further tested, Paul seems to have developed a better opinion of him, for he writes to Timothy (2Ti 4:11): *Take Mark and bring him with thee, for he is profitable to me for the ministry*.

5.2.1. Even those we justly condemn we should condemn moderately, because we do not know whether later we may have cause to think better of them. We should so regulate our attitude that if this happens we may not later be ashamed of how we treated them earlier.

5.2.2. Even those whom we have justly condemned should be cheerfully received by us if they later prove more faithful; we must then forgive and forget, and even, if the opportunity arises, speak a good word to them.

5.3. That Paul continued with his work cheerfully (v. 41): *He went through Syria and Cilicia, confirming the churches*. Ministers are well employed when they are used to strengthen those who believe as well as to convert those who do not believe.

CHAPTER 16

It is a rebuke to Barnabas that after he left Paul we hear nothing more about him. But Paul's services for Christ after this are recorded in detail. We have here: 1. The beginning of his friendship with Timothy (vv. 1–3). 2. His visit to the churches to establish them (vv. 4–5). 3. His call to Macedonia and his coming to Philippi (vv. 6–13). 4. The conversion of Lydia there (vv. 14–15). 5. The driving out of an evil spirit from a slave girl (vv. 16–18). 6. The accusing and abusing of Paul and Silas for this exorcism, and their imprisonment (vv. 19–24). 7. The miraculous conversion of the jailer (vv. 25–34). 8. The honorable discharge of Paul and Silas (vv. 35–40).

Verses 1–5

Paul was a spiritual father, and we see him here in that role adopting Timothy, and he appears to have been a wise and tender father in everything. Here is:

1. His taking Timothy into his friendship and teaching him. We are told here:

1.1. That Timothy was a disciple, one who belonged to Christ. Paul took him to be brought up for Christ.

1.2. That his mother was originally a Jew, *but believed in Christ*; her name was *Eunice*, and Timothy's grand-

mother was named *Lois*. Paul speaks about them both with great respect and commends them especially for their genuine faith (2Ti 1:5).

1.3. That his father was a Greek, a Gentile. Now because his father was not a Jew, Timothy had not been circumcised and was neither obliged nor even entitled to be circumcised, unless when he grew up he himself wanted it. Although his mother could not get him circumcised in his infancy, she still brought him up in the fear of God, so that although he lacked the sign of the covenant, he did not lack what it stood for.

1.4. That he had gained a very good reputation among the Christians: he was *well reported of by the brethren* at Lystra and Iconium. He had a name for good things with good people.

1.5. That Paul wanted him *to go forth with him*.

1.6. That Paul *took him and circumcised him*. This was strange. Had not Paul opposed as far as he could those who wanted to impose circumcision on the Gentile converts? He had, and yet he circumcised Timothy, not to make him keep the ceremonial law, but only to render his ministry acceptable among the Jews, of whom there were many in that area. He took him and circumcised him so that the Jews would not shun him as one who was unclean because he was uncircumcised. He was against those who made circumcision necessary to salvation. Although he did not follow the letter of the decree in this instance, he followed its spirit, which was a spirit of tenderness toward the Jews. Paul had no difficulty in taking Timothy as his companion, even though he was uncircumcised, but the Jews would not listen to him if he remained uncircumcised, and so Paul would accommodate them in this matter.

2. His confirming the churches he had planted (vv. 4–5): *He went through the cities* where he had *preached the word of the Lord*. We are told:

2.1. That Paul and his company gave the churches copies of the decrees of the Jerusalem synod. All the churches were concerned in that decree, and so they all needed to have it well attested.

2.2. That this was very useful to them.

2.2.1. The churches were *established in the faith* (v. 5). They were strengthened especially in their opinion against the imposing of the ceremonial law on the Gentiles. When they saw that the testimony not only of the apostles and elders but also of the Holy Spirit was against that imposition, they were strengthened. This shows us that although testimonies to truth may not convince those who oppose the truth, they may be very useful to strengthen those who have doubts about it. Besides that, the spirit of tenderness that appeared in these letters clearly showed that the apostles and elders were under the guidance of the One who is love itself.

2.2.2. They *increased in number daily*. The imposing of the burden of the ceremonial law on the church's converts was enough to frighten people away from them. However, if people found there was no danger of being enslaved in this way, they were ready to accept Christianity, and this was how the church *increased in numbers daily*. And to those who have a sincere goodwill toward human souls, it is a joy to see such an increase.

Verses 6–15

In these verses we have:

1. Paul's travels throughout the area to do good.

1.1. He and Silas, his colleague, went throughout Phrygia and the region of Galatia.

1.2. They were forbidden at this time to preach the Gospel in Asia, the country properly so called. At this time Christ wanted to use Paul in a new work, which was to preach the Gospel to a Roman colony at Philippi, for up to that time the Gentiles to whom he had preached were Greeks. The Romans were hated more by the Jews than other Gentiles were. It was the Holy Spirit who forbade them to go to Asia. The moving of ministers is especially under divine guidance and direction. We find an Old Testament minister forbidden to preach at all (Eze 3:26), but these New Testament ministers were forbidden to preach only in one place, while they were directed to another where there was greater need.

1.3. They would have gone into Bithynia but were not permitted to: *the Spirit suffered them not* (did not allow them) (v. 7). They came to Mysia; although their judgment and inclination drew them toward Bithynia, they were overruled. We must now follow Providence, and if this does not allow us to do what we seek to do, we should accept the situation and believe it to be for the best. "The Spirit of Jesus did not allow them" is how many ancient copies read. The servants of the Lord Jesus should always be under the restraint and guidance of the Spirit of the Lord Jesus.

1.4. They *passed by Mysia*, or passed "through it," according to some, probably sowing good seed as they went along, and they came to Troas, the city of Troy. Here a church was planted, for we find one in existence here in 20:6. At Troas Luke joined Paul and his company, for from now on, when he speaks about Paul's journeys, he includes himself in their number: *we* (v. 10).

2. Paul's particular call to Macedonia, that is, to Philippi, which was inhabited mostly by Romans, as is stated here (v. 21). Notice:

2.1. The vision Paul had (v. 9). An angel appeared to him to indicate to him that it was the will of Christ that he go to Macedonia. Although he would not go where he intended to, he would go where God had a work for him to do.

2.1.1. The person Paul saw. There stood by him *a man of Macedonia*. Christ wanted Paul to be directed to Macedonia not as the apostles were at other times, by a messenger from heaven who sent him there, but by a messenger sent from the place to which he was being called. Paul would be called to Macedonia by a man of Macedonia, and by him speaking in the name of his fellow residents. He was *a man* of Macedonia, not a magistrate of the country, and much less a priest; he was an ordinary inhabitant of that country, a plain man, who did not come to waste Paul's time, but seriously sought his help.

2.1.2. The invitation given him. This honest Macedonian *prayed him, saying, Come over into Macedonia, and help us;* that is, "Come and preach the Gospel to us. You have helped many; now come and help us. It is your work and your delight to help poor souls; come and help us. We need your help as much as any people. Therefore, come to us as quickly as you can. Do not only help us with your prayers here; you must come over and help us personally." People have a great need of spiritual help, and it is their duty to look out for it and invite to come to them those who can help them in such matters.

2.2. The interpretation Paul's company gave to the vision (v. 10): They *gathered assuredly from this that the Lord had called them to preach the Gospel* there. We can sometimes discern a call from God in a human call. If a man of Macedonia says, *Come and help us,* Paul concludes that God says, "Go and help them."

3. Paul's voyage to Macedonia: he *was not disobedient to the heavenly vision* (26:19), but followed this divine direction with greater assurance than that with which

he would have followed any thoughts or inclination of his own.

3.1. He turned his thoughts there. *Immediately we endeavoured to go into Macedonia.* Paul shared the vision with his companions, and they all decided to go to Macedonia. As Paul would follow Christ, so all his people would follow Paul, or rather follow Christ with him. God's calls must be complied with immediately. Do it today, in case your heart becomes hardened (Heb 3:7, 13, 15; Ps 95:7–8). They could not immediately go into Macedonia, but they immediately tried to do so. If we cannot be as quick as we want to be in our actions, we can still be so in our attempts.

3.2. He steered his course there. They *set sail from Troas.* They *came with a straight course,* a successful voyage, *to Samothracia;* the *next day they came to Neapolis,* and they finally landed at *Philippi.* It is said (v. 12) to have been:

3.2.1. *The chief city of that part of Macedonia,* or, as some read it, "the first city." They began with the first city, because if the Gospel was received there, it would more easily spread throughout all the country from there.

3.2.2. A colony. Not only did the Romans have a garrison, but also the inhabitants of the city were Romans.

4. The cold reception Paul and his companions met with at Philippi. One would have expected that because they had such a particular call from God there, they would have been joyfully welcomed there. Where was the man of Macedonia who begged Paul to come there as quickly as possible? Why did he not stir up his compatriots to go and meet him? Nothing like this happened.

4.1. It was a long time before he was noticed at all: *We were in that city abiding certain days.* They had gone there as quickly as they could, but now that they were there, they were almost tempted to think they might as well have stayed where they were. People who are eminent and useful are not fit to live in this world when they do not know how to be dishonored and overlooked. Let ministers not think it strange if they are first enthusiastically invited to a place, and then looked on reluctantly when they arrive.

4.2. When they had an opportunity to preach, it was in an obscure place (v. 13). There was no Jewish synagogue there, but they discovered a small meeting of good women. The place of this meeting was outside the city. It was a place *where prayer was wont to be made.* Those who worshiped the true God and refused to worship idols met there to pray together. Each of them prayed in solitude every day, but besides this, *they came together on the sabbath day.* Although they were only few in number and discouraged by the rest of the town, the worshipers of God must still have a religious gathering on the Sabbath. When we cannot do as we want to do, we must do as we can; if we do not have synagogues, we must be thankful for more private places and turn to them. This place is said to have been *by a river side,* which perhaps was chosen because it aided contemplation. Paul, Silas, and Luke went there and *sat down.* They *spoke unto the women who resorted thither,* and they led them on further in their knowledge of Christ.

5. The conversion of *Lydia.* In this story of Acts, we have recorded not only the conversion of places but also the conversion of many individual people, because such is the value of souls that the conversion of one of them to God is significant. Nor do we have only the conversions that were brought about miraculously, like Paul's, but also some that were brought about by the ordinary methods of grace, like Lydia's. Notice:

5.1. Who this convert was. Four things are recorded about her:

5.1.1. Her name, *Lydia*. It is an honor to her to have her name recorded in the book of God. We cannot have our names recorded in the Bible, but if God opens our hearts, we will find them *written in the book of life* (Php 4:3; Lk 10:20).

5.1.2. Her calling. She was *a seller of purple*. She had an honest calling, which the writer takes notice of to commend her. It was humble calling. She was *a seller of purple*, not one who wore purple, for few people of that sort are called (1Co 1:26). Although she had a job to do, she was still a worshiper of God. The business of our particular work may be made to coexist well alongside the life of faith and will therefore not entitle us to excuse ourselves by saying, "We have shops to look after and a business to take care of," for have we not also a God to serve and a soul to look after?

5.1.3. The place she came from—*the city of Thyatira*, which was a long way from Philippi. Providence brought Lydia to Philippi to be under Paul's ministry, and there, where she met with it, she made good use of it.

5.1.4. Her faith before the Lord opened her heart.

5.1.4.1. She worshiped God according to the knowledge she had; she was one of the devout women. Sometimes the grace of God acted on those who before their conversion were corrupt and evil; sometimes it was directed to those who had a good character. It is not enough to be worshipers of God; we must also be believers in Jesus Christ. Christ would be welcome to them, for those who know what it is to worship God see their need of Christ.

5.1.4.2. She heard the apostles. Here, where prayer was practiced, *the word was preached*. Can we expect God to listen to our prayers if we will not listen to his word? Those who worshiped God according to the light they had looked for further light.

5.2. The work that was done in her: *whose heart the Lord opened*.

5.2.1. The author of this work was *the Lord*. The work of conversion is God's work; he is the One who *works in us both to will and to do* (Php 2:13); not as if we had nothing to do, but by ourselves, without God's grace, we can do nothing. The salvation of those who are saved must be wholly attributed to him.

5.2.2. The home of this work is in the heart. The work of conversion is a work in the heart; it is a renewing of the heart.

5.2.3. The nature of the work is such that Lydia had her heart not only touched but also opened. An unconverted soul is closed and fortified against Christ. In dealing with the soul, Christ knocks at the door that is shut against him (Rev 3:20), and when a sinner is effectively persuaded to accept Christ, then the heart is opened for *the King of glory to come in* (Ps 24:7).

5.3. The effects of this work on the heart.

5.3.1. She took great notice of the word of God. Her heart was so *opened that she attended to the things that were spoken by Paul*. She "applied to herself," as some read it, *the things that were spoken by Paul*, and the word does us good only when we apply it to ourselves.

5.3.2. She gave her name to Jesus Christ. *She was baptized*, and *her household* was also baptized with her.

5.3.3. She was very kind to the ministers and wanted very much to be further instructed by them: *She besought us saying, If you have judged me to be faithful to the Lord, come into my house, and abide there*. She sought an opportunity to show her gratitude to those who had been the instruments of divine grace in this wonderful

change in her. When her heart was open to Christ, her house was open to his ministers for his sake. In fact, not only were they welcome to her house, but also she was extremely insistent and bold with them: *She constrained us*; which shows that Paul was unwilling to go. However, Lydia would not take no as an answer. She wanted to have an opportunity to receive further instruction. In her own house she could not only hear them but also ask them questions, and they could pray with her daily and bless her household.

Verses 16–24

Paul and his companions now began to be noticed.

1. *A damsel* (slave girl) *that had a spirit of divination* caused them to be noticed. Here is:

1.1. The account that is given of this girl: she was *possessed with a spirit of divination*, as that girl was by whom the oracles of Apollo at Delphos were delivered. In those times of ignorance and idolatry, the Devil led people captive at his will, and he could not have gained such adoration from them as he had if he had not claimed to give oracles to them. This slave girl *brought her masters much gain by soothsaying*; many people came to consult this witch. Everyone had to pay for that service, of course.

1.2. The testimony that this girl gave to Paul and his companions: she *met them in* the street as they were going to prayer (v. 16). They went publicly; everybody knew where they were going. Notice how subtle Satan is in taking the opportunity to distract us when we are going about our religious activities, and to make us uncomfortable when we need most to be composed. When she met them, she followed them, crying out, "*These men are the servants of the most high God, who show unto us the way of salvation*."

1.2.1. This witness is true:

1.2.1.1. "They are *the servants of the most high God*; they are his servants, are employed by him; they come to us on his mission; the message they bring comes from God. The gods we Gentiles worship are inferior beings, not gods, but these men belong *to the most high God*, who is over all people, over all gods. They are his servants, and that is why we should listen to them, and our lives will be in danger if we show them disrespect.

1.2.1.2. "They *show unto us the way of salvation*." Even the pagans had some idea of the miserable and deplorable state of the human race and their need for salvation. "Now," she said, "these people are the ones who show us what we have sought in vain."

1.2.2. How did this testimony come from the mouth of one who had a spirit of divination? Is Satan divided against himself (Mt 12:26)? We may take it either:

1.2.2.1. As extorted from this spirit of divination for the honor of the Gospel by the power of God, as the Devil was forced to say about Christ: *I know thee who thou art, the Holy One of God* (Mk 1:24). The truth is sometimes exalted by the confession of its enemies, in which they are witnesses against themselves. Or:

1.2.2.2. As intended by the evil spirit to dishonor the Gospel. Those who were most likely to receive the apostles' message were those who were prejudiced against these spirits of divination; by this testimony, therefore, they would be prejudiced against the Gospel, and as for those who took notice of these diviners, the Devil thought himself sure of them.

2. Christ caused them to be noticed by giving them power to drive the demon out of this girl. She continued *many days* shouting (v. 18), and it seems Paul took no notice of her at first, but finding perhaps that her shouting

harmed them rather than helped them, he soon silenced her by driving the demon out of her.

2.1. He was *grieved.* It disturbed him to hear a sacred truth desecrated so much. Perhaps the girl spoke in an ironic, bantering way, and if so, Paul could justly be troubled, as any good person's heart would be, to hear any good truth of God bawled out in the streets in a mocking and jeering way.

2.2. He commanded the evil spirit to come out of her. *He turned and said, I command thee in the name of Jesus Christ to come out of her*, and by this he would show, without her testimony, *that these men were the servants of the living God* (v. 17). Her silence would demonstrate it more than her speaking could. Power accompanied the word of Christ (Lk 4:32), in whose presence Satan could not stand, but was forced to abandon his hold. *He came out the same hour.*

3. The masters of the girl who was dispossessed caused them to be noticed by bringing them before the magistrates for performing this exorcism.

3.1. What provoked the girl's masters was that they *saw that the hope of their gain was gone* (v. 19). See here what evil *the love of money is the root of* (1Ti 6:10)! The power of Christ and the great kindness done to her in rescuing her from Satan's hand made no impression on them when they realized that it meant they would lose money.

3.2. The method they used was to enrage the higher powers against them: *They caught them* and *dragged them into the market place*, where public justice was administered. They brought them *to the rulers*, their justices of peace. From them they rushed them *to the magistrates*, the governors of the city.

3.3. The charge they leveled against them was that they were the troublers of the land (v. 20). They assumed that these men were Jews, and the general charge against them was *that they troubled the city*, sowing discord and disturbing the public peace. If they troubled the city, it was only like the angel's troubling the water of Bethesda's pool (Jn 5:7), in order to bring healing. The evidence offered for this accusation was the apostles' teaching customs that it was unlawful to admit into a Roman colony (v. 21). The Romans were always very jealous of innovations in religion. Rightly or wrongly, they would remain faithful to what they had received by tradition from their ancestors. No foreign deity or upstart god must be allowed.

4. The magistrates caused them to be noticed.

4.1. By supporting the persecution, they provoked the mob against them (v. 22): *The multitude rose up together against them.* It has been the trick of Satan to make God's ministers and people odious by representing them as dangerous people who aim to destroy the constitution and who advocate changes in customs.

4.2. By punishing them, they further represented them as the worst evildoers: *They rent off their clothes* so that they could be flogged. This was one of those three occasions when Paul was beaten with rods, according to the Roman custom, which was not under the compassionate restriction that the number of lashes was not to exceed forty, which was provided by the Jewish law (Dt 25:3). It is here said that *they laid many stripes upon them* (v. 23), without counting how many. One would have thought this might have satisfied their cruel lusts; if the prisoners had to be flogged, surely they would then be released. But no; they were imprisoned. The judges made their commitment very strict: they *charged the jailer to keep them safely*, as if they were dangerous men, who either would risk breaking out of prison themselves or had allies who would try to rescue them. The jailer made their confinement very

severe (v. 24): *Having received such a charge, he thrust them into the inner prison.* When magistrates are cruel, it is hardly surprising that the officers under them are as well. *He put them into the inner prison*, the inner cell or dungeon, into which only condemned evildoers were usually put. As if this were not enough, *he made their feet fast in the stocks.* They were not the first of God's messengers who had their feet in the stocks (Jer 20:2; Ps 105:18). Oh how cruelly God's servants have been treated, both in ancient times and in more recent times.

Verses 25–34

Here we see the intentions of Paul and Silas's persecutors thwarted and wrecked.

1. The persecutors intended to dishearten and discourage the preachers of the Gospel, but here we find them both hearty and heartened.

1.1. They themselves were hearty. Let us consider their situation. The many wounds on their bodies were very sore, and one might have reason to hear them complaining about them. This was not all, however; they had reason to fear the axes next. In the meantime they were in the inner cell, their feet in the stocks, which both held and hurt them, and yet, *at midnight* they *prayed and sang praises to God.*

1.1.1. They prayed together that God would support them and comfort them in their suffering; they prayed that even their chains and wounds would further the Gospel. They prayed for their persecutors, that God would forgive them and turn their hearts. This was not an official hour for prayer, but midnight; it was not in a house of prayer, but in a dungeon. Nevertheless, it was the right time to pray, and the prayer was acceptable. Both in the dark and out of the depths we may cry out to God (Ps 130:1). No trouble, however painful, should make us unwilling to pray.

1.1.2. *They sang praises to God.* We never lack things to praise God for unless we lack the heart to praise him, and what should put the heart of a child of God out of tune for this duty if a dungeon and a pair of stocks will not do it? In fact, *they not only praised God but sang praises to him.* Our rule is that those facing adversity should pray (Jas 5:13), and so in their suffering they prayed; it is also our rule that those who are happy should sing psalms (Jas 5:13), and so, being joyful in their suffering, *they sang psalms.*

1.1.3. Notice is taken here of a particular circumstance: *the prisoners heard them.* If the prisoners did not hear them pray, *they heard them sing praises.*

1.1.3.1. The apostles sang so loudly that even though they were in the dungeon, they were heard throughout the whole prison. We should sing psalms with all our heart.

1.1.3.2. Although they knew the prisoners would hear them, they still sang out loud, as those who were not ashamed of their Master. If those who want to sing psalms in their families omit that duty, shall they excuse the omission by pleading that they are afraid their neighbors would hear them, when those who sing worldly songs roar them out, not caring who hears them?

1.1.3.3. The prisoners were made to hear the prison songs of Paul and Silas so that they would be prepared for the miraculous favor that would be shown to them all for the sake of Paul and Silas when *the prison-doors were thrown open* (v. 27).

1.2. God encouraged them wonderfully through his significant appearances from heaven (v. 26). A great earthquake struck immediately; *the very foundations of the prison were shaken.* The Lord was in these earthquakes, to show his anger at the disrespect shown to his servants. The prison doors were thrown open, and the prisoners' chains knocked away: *Every man's bands were loosed.* Just as God later gave Paul *all those that were in the ship with him* (27:24), so now he gave him all those who were in the prison with him.

2. The persecutors intended to stop the progress of the Gospel, but here we find converts made in the prison, the trophies of the Gospel's victories set up there, and the jailer, their own servant, turned into a servant of Christ.

2.1. He was afraid he would lose his life, and Paul put him at ease as to this concern (vv. 27–28).

2.1.1. He *awoke out of his sleep.* The shock of the earthquake probably woke him up, and to this disturbance were added the prisoners' expressions of stunned joy when in the dark they found their bands loosened. This was enough to wake up the jailer, whose job required that he not be hard to wake up.

2.1.2. He saw the prison doors open and supposed that the prisoners had escaped, and then what would become of him? He knew the Roman law in such cases.

2.1.3. In his panic *he drew his sword* and was going *to kill himself* to prevent an even more terrible death, which he knew he would have to suffer for letting his prisoners escape. The philosophers generally allowed suicide. This jailer thought there was no harm in anticipating his own death, but Christianity proves itself to have come from God by holding us to the law of our creation, obliging us to be just toward our own lives, teaching us to submit them cheerfully to our graces but courageously withhold them from our corruptions.

2.1.4. Paul stopped him (v. 28): he *cried with a loud voice,* saying, *Do thyself no harm.* All the warnings of the word of God against sin lead to this: "*Do thyself no harm.* Do not harm yourself, and then no one else can harm you; do not sin, because nothing else can hurt you." The jailer did not need to fear being held responsible for the escape of his prisoners, for *they were all here.* It was strange that some of them did not slip away when the prison doors were opened and they were set loose from their chains. God showed his power by binding their spirits as much as by setting loose their feet.

2.2. He was afraid he would lose his soul, and Paul put him at rest concerning this too. One worry led him to another, and a much greater one. The jailer began to think about where death would have taken him to and what would have become of him on the other side of death.

2.2.1. Whatever the cause, he was put into a state of great fear. The Spirit of God, who was sent to convict first in order to be the Comforter (Jn 14:16, 26) afterward, struck terror on him. He *called for a light, sprang* (rushed) *in, and came trembling to Paul and Silas.* When this jailer was made to tremble in this way, he could not have turned to a better person than Paul, for the jailer's situation had once been Paul's own; he had once been a persecutor of good people and had thrown them into prison, and that was why he was able to speak more feelingly to the jailer.

2.2.2. In his fear, he turned to Paul and Silas for help. Notice:

2.2.2.1. How reverent and respectful he was toward them: *He called for a light. He fell down before them.* He probably had heard what the girl had said about them, that they were *the servants of the living God, who showed to them the way of salvation.* He fell down before them to beg forgiveness for the dishonor he had shown them and to beg their advice as to what he should do. He gave them a title of respect, *Sirs,* "Lords," "Masters." Only a short time before they had been rogues and villains, and he was

their master, but now, "Sirs, lords," and they were his masters. Converting grace changes people's language.

2.2.2.2. How serious his question was: *What must I do to be saved?*

2.2.2.2.1. His salvation was now his great concern; what earlier was farthest from his mind was now closest to his heart.

2.2.2.2.2. He did not ask about other people, what they must do, but about himself, "What must I do?" It was his own precious soul that he was concerned about.

2.2.2.2.3. He was convinced that something must be done, and done by him too, to obtain salvation; it was not a thing that would happen by itself. He did not ask, "What can be done for me?" but, "What shall I do?"

2.2.2.2.4. He was willing to do anything: "Tell me what I must do, and I am ready to do it. Sirs, put me on the right way; even if it is narrow, thorny, and uphill, I will still walk in it." Those who are thoroughly convicted of their sin and truly concerned about their salvation will be glad to have Christ on his own terms, Christ on any terms.

2.2.2.2.5. He wanted to know what he should do and asked those who were likely to tell him. Those who set their faces toward Zion must ask the way there (Jer 50:5). We cannot know it by ourselves, but God has made it known to us through his word; he has appointed his ministers to help us and has promised *to give his Holy Spirit to those that ask him* (Lk 11:13), to be their guide in the way of salvation.

2.2.2.2.6. He *brought them out.* He brought them out of the cell in the hope that they would bring him out of a much worse situation.

2.2.3. They told him what he must do (v. 31). Although they were cold, sore, and sleepy, they did not delay this opportunity to a more convenient time and place; they struck while the iron was hot, took him now when he was in a good frame of mind, before the conviction wore off. Now that God began to work, it was time for them to set in as *workers together with God* (2Co 6:1). They were as glad to show him the way to heaven as to show their best friend. They gave him the same directions they gave others: *Believe in the Lord Jesus Christ.* Here is the summary of the whole Gospel, the covenant of grace in a few words: *Believe in the Lord Jesus Christ, and thou shalt be saved, and thy house.* Here is:

2.2.3.1. The happiness promised: "*Thou shalt be saved,* not only rescued from eternal destruction but also brought to eternal life and blessedness. Although you are a persecutor, your terrible sins will all be forgiven. Your hard and bitter heart will be softened and made sweet by the grace of Christ."

2.2.3.2. The condition required: *Believe in the Lord Jesus Christ.* We must agree with the method God has taken of reconciling the world to himself through a Mediator, and we are to accept Christ as he is offered to us. This is the only guaranteed way to salvation. There is no way of salvation except through Christ, and no danger of falling short if we follow this way. It is the Gospel that is to be preached to every creature (Mk 16:15): *Believe in the Lord Jesus Christ, and thou shalt be saved.*

2.2.3.3. The extension of this to his family: *Thou shalt be saved, and thy house.* Even if there were very many, let them believe in Jesus Christ, and they would be saved.

2.2.4. They proceeded to instruct him and his family in the teaching of Christ (v. 32): *They spoke unto him the word of the Lord.* He was, or so it seems, a complete stranger to Christ, and so it was necessary to tell him who this Jesus was so that he could believe in him. Christ's ministers should have the word of the Lord so readily available to them and so richly living in them that they are able to give instructions immediately to anyone who wants to hear and receive them. They spoke the word to *all that were in his house.* Heads of families should make sure that everyone they are responsible for shares in the opportunity for knowledge and grace, that the word of the Lord is spoken to them, because the souls of the poorest servants are as precious as those of their masters and have been bought with the same price.

2.2.5. The jailer and his family were immediately baptized. He was *baptized, he and all his, straightway.* The Spirit of grace worked such a strong faith in them, suddenly, that it superseded further debate, and Paul and Silas knew through the Spirit that it was a work of God that had been performed in them.

2.2.6. The jailer was then very respectful toward Paul and Silas. He *took them the same hour of the night,* would not let them lie a minute longer in the inner cell. He *washed their stripes* (wounds) to cool them and lessen their pain. He *brought them into his house* and made them welcome. Now nothing was thought to be too good for them, as before nothing had been too bad. He *set meat before them,* and they were welcome to eat it. They had broken the bread of life to him and his family, and he, having reaped such an abundance of spiritual things, thought it was only reasonable that they reap of his material things (1Co 9:11). What have we houses and tables for except to use them, as we have opportunity, to serve God and his people?

2.2.7. The voice of joy with that of salvation (Ps 118:15) was heard in the jailer's house; never had there been such a truly happy night there before: *He rejoiced, believing in God, with all his house.*

2.2.7.1. His believing in Christ is called believing in God, which shows that Christ is God, and the Gospel leads us directly to God.

2.2.7.2. His faith produced joy. Those who by faith have given themselves up to God in Christ and made him theirs have many reasons to be joyful. Believing in Christ is rejoicing in Christ.

2.2.7.3. He showed his joy to everyone around him. One joyful Christian should cause many to be joyful.

Verses 35–40

In these verses we have:

1. Orders sent for the release of Paul and Silas (vv. 35–36). The magistrates who had so cruelly mistreated them the day before gave the orders, and their doing it so early, *as soon as it was day,* suggests that they had been tossing and turning on their beds in a mental anguish, complaining about the lashes on their consciences, and were now more concerned to give the apostles a quick release than the apostles were to ask for one. The magistrates sent *sergeants, those that had the rods,* those who had been employed in beating them. The order was, *Let those men go.* The jailer brought them the news (v. 36): *The magistrates have sent to let you go: now therefore depart.* Not that he wanted to part with them as his guests; he wanted them to depart as his prisoners; they would still be welcome to his house, but he was glad they were free to leave his stocks.

2. Paul's insistence that the magistrates had violated his rights as a Roman citizen (v. 37). Paul said to the sergeants, *"They have beaten us openly, uncondemned, being Romans, and have cast us into prison* against all law and justice, and *now do they thrust us out privily* (quietly)? *Nay verily, but let them come themselves and fetch us out* (escort us out) and acknowledge they have done us wrong."

2.1. Paul did not plead this before he was beaten, for then he might have seemed afraid of suffering for the truth that he had preached. He had nobler things than this to comfort himself with in his suffering.

2.2. He did plead it later, to honor the cause he suffered for, to tell the world that the preachers of the Gospel deserved to be treated better. He did it also to soften the magistrates toward the Christians at Philippi and to lead the people to have a higher opinion of the Christian religion.

2.2.1. Paul told the magistrates how many ways they had fallen into a predicament.

2.2.1.1. They had beaten those who were Romans. Roman historians provide examples of cities that had their charters removed for showing contempt to Roman citizens. To tell the magistrates that they had beaten those who were the messengers of Christ would have had no influence on them, but to tell them they had mistreated Roman citizens would make them panic: it is common for people to be more afraid of Caesar's wrath than of Christ's.

2.2.1.2. They had beaten them uncondemned. They had not calmly examined what had been said against the apostles, much less what the apostles had to say for themselves. Christ's servants would not have been mistreated as they have been if they and their cause had only received an impartial trial.

2.2.1.3. It was worse that they had done this openly.

2.2.1.4. They had *cast them into prison* without showing any cause for their punishment.

2.2.1.5. They now *thrust them out privily*; they did not have the arrogance to stand by what they had done, but neither did they have the honesty to acknowledge themselves to be at fault.

2.2.2. He insisted that the magistrates acknowledge their error and discharge them publicly, since they had disgraced them publicly. *"Let them come themselves and fetch us out* and testify that we have done nothing worthy of being lashed or put in chains." It was not a point of honor that Paul stood on so stiffly, but a point of justice, and not for himself so much as for his cause.

3. The reversal of the judgment declared against Paul and Silas (vv. 38–39).

3.1. The magistrates were frightened when they were told that Paul was a Roman. The proceedings of persecutors have often been illegal, even according to international law, and often inhuman, against natural law, but always sinful and against God's Law.

3.2. They *came and besought* (appealed to) *them* not to take advantage of the law against them; they *brought them out* of the prison, acknowledging that they had wrongfully put them into it and asking them to peacefully and quietly *depart out of the city.* If the repentance of these magistrates had been sincere, however, they would not have wanted the apostles to leave their city, but would have begged them to continue in their city to show them the way of salvation. However, many who are convinced that Christianity is not to be persecuted are not convinced that it should be accepted. They are compelled to honor Christ and his servants, but they do not go so far as to actually benefit themselves from Christ.

4. The departure of Paul and Silas from Philippi (v. 40). They went out of the prison when they were legally released.

4.1. They took leave of their friends: they *went to the house of Lydia, saw the brethren,* and *comforted them.* Young converts should have a great deal said to them to encourage them, for *the joy of the Lord will be* very much *their strength* (Ne 8:10).

4.2. They left the town. *They departed*. Paul and Silas had an extraordinary call to Philippi, but when they arrived there, they found that all their hard work did not bear much fruit, and they were soon driven away. They did not go there in vain, however. They laid the foundation of a church at Philippi, which became very famous and had people who were more generous to Paul than any other church, as can be seen from his letter to the Philippians (Php 1:1; 4:15). Let not ministers be discouraged, even though they do not see immediate fruit from their hard work; the seed sown seems to be lost underground, but it will come up again in an abundant harvest.

CHAPTER 17

Here is a further account of Paul's travels. He was not like a lamp on a table (Mt 5:15), which gives light only to one room, but like the sun, which moves around and gives light to many (Ps 19:6). We have him here: 1. Preaching and persecuted at Thessalonica (vv. 1–9). 2. Preaching at Berea, but driven from there also by persecution (vv. 10–15). 3. Challenging and debating at Athens (vv. 16–21), and there giving an account of natural religion to lead them to the Christian religion (vv. 22–31); and we read of the variety of responses this sermon met with (vv. 32–34).

Verses 1–9

Paul's two letters to the Thessalonians give such a shining account of that church that we are very glad to meet with an account of the founding of the church there. Here is:

1. Paul's coming to Thessalonica.

1.1. Paul continued with his work despite the mistreatment he had faced at Philippi. He comments on this in his first letter to the church there (1Th 2:2). The opposition and persecution that he met with made him even more determined. He could never have held out, and held on, as he did unless he had been inspired by a spirit of power from heaven.

1.2. He only *passed through Amphipolis and Apollonia*. We may imagine that although he is said to have only passed through these towns and cities, he stayed in them long enough to make the Gospel known and prepare the way for the arrival of other ministers.

2. His preaching to the Jews first, in their synagogue at Thessalonica. He found a synagogue of the Jews there (v. 1), and he used it to launch his ministry.

2.1. It was always his way to begin with the Jews, so that the Jews' mouths would be silenced from shouting against him because he preached to the Gentiles, because if they accepted the Gospel, they would cheerfully accept the new converts, but if they refused the Gospel, they would have only themselves to blame if the apostles took it to those who would welcome it.

2.2. He met them in their synagogue on the Sabbath, in their place and at their time of meeting. It is good to be in the house of the Lord on his day. This was Christ's way and Paul's way, and has also been the way of all the saints.

2.3. He *reasoned with them out of the scriptures*. They agreed with him in accepting the Scriptures; so far they were in agreement. However, they accepted the Scripture and thought they had reason to reject Christ; Paul accepted the Scripture and saw great reason to accept Christ. He must reason with them, therefore, to convince them that his conclusions from Scripture were right and theirs were wrong. The preaching of the Gospel should be both Scriptural and rational; such was Paul's, for he *reasoned out of the scriptures*. We must reason from the Scriptures and on the basis of them. Reason must not be set up to compete with Scripture, but must be used in explaining and applying the Scripture.

2.4. He continued to do this *three sabbath days* successively. God waits for sinners' conversion; all the laborers did not come into the vineyard at the first hour (Mt 20:1–16), nor is everybody persuaded as suddenly as the jailer (16:27–34).

2.5. The theme of his arguing was that *Jesus is the Christ*; this was what he *opened*, or explained, and *alleged*, that is, proved (v. 3). He first explained his thesis, opened up the terms, and then he proved it, establishing it. He opened it up as one who knew it, and he proved it as one who believed it. He showed them:

2.5.1. That it was necessary for the Messiah to *suffer, and die, and rise again*, because the Old Testament prophecies of the Messiah made it necessary. Paul here proved undeniably not only that it was possible for Jesus to be the Messiah even though he suffered but also that because he was the Messiah, it was necessary for him to suffer. He could not be made perfect except by suffering (Heb 2:10), because if he had not died, he could not have risen again from the dead. He had to suffer for us, because he could not otherwise have purchased redemption for us, and he had to rise again because he could not otherwise apply that redemption to us.

2.5.2. That Jesus is the Messiah: "*This Jesus whom I preach unto you is Christ*, is the Christ, the One who would come (Ps 118:26; Mt 11:3). God has borne witness to him through both the Scriptures and miracles." Gospel ministers should preach Jesus; he must be the main subject. And what we are to preach about Jesus is that he is Christ.

3. The success of his preaching there (v. 4).

3.1. Some of the Jews believed, and they *consorted with* (joined) *Paul and Silas*. Those who believe in Jesus Christ come into fellowship with his faithful ministers and associate with them.

3.2. Many more of the devout Greeks and the prominent women accepted the Gospel. These were "the worshiping Gentiles," as in America those of the indigenous people who are converted to Christianity are called "praying Indians." Of these *a great multitude believed*. Also *not a few of the chief women* of the city embraced Christianity. Particular notice is taken of this as an example to the prominent women of all times and places, that they should submit themselves to the commanding power of Christ's holy religious faith, for this account shows how acceptable their devotion will be to God and what a great influence it may have on many. No mention is made here of the apostles preaching the Gospel to the Gentile idolaters at Thessalonica, but it is certain that they did, for in writing to the Christians there, Paul notes that they have *turned to God from idols* (1Th 1:9), and that they did so when the apostles first came to them.

4. The trouble that was made for Paul and Silas at Thessalonica. Notice:

4.1. Who the authors of their trouble were: the *Jews who believed not, who were moved with envy* (v. 5). Some of the Jews believed the Gospel and pitied and prayed for those who did not, while those who did not were jealous of and hated those who did.

4.2. Who the instruments of the trouble were: the Jews made use of *certain lewd persons of the baser sort* (some evildoers). All wise and sober people looked on the apostles with respect, and no one would appear against them except those who were the scum of the city. It is the honor of religion that those who hate it are generally the *lewd fellows of the baser sort*.

4.3. How these Jews and their mob proceeded to act against them.

4.3.1. They *set the city in an uproar.* They began a riot, and then the mob was soon aroused. Notice how the Devil pursues his intentions: he sets cities in uproar, sets souls in uproar, and then fishes in troubled waters.

4.3.2. They *assaulted the house of Jason*, where the apostles were staying, with the intention of *bringing them out to the people*, whom they had incited against the apostles. The proceedings here were completely illegal. If people have offended, magistrates are appointed to look into the offense and judge it, but to make the rabble judges and executioners was to make truth fall in the street (Isa 59:14), to get rid of all equity and enthrone fury.

4.3.3. When they could not get the apostles into their hands, they fell on an honest citizen of their own, one Jason, a converted Jew, and brought him out with some others of *the brethren* to the rulers of the city.

4.3.4. They accused the apostles to the rulers, representing them as dangerous men. The crime Jason was accused of was receiving and harboring the apostles (v. 7). Two very bad descriptions were given of the apostles here.

4.3.4.1. That they were enemies to the public peace and threw everything into disorder wherever they went: *Those that have turned the world upside down are come hither also.* In one sense it is true that whenever the Gospel comes in its power to any place, to any soul, it works such a change there that it may be said to turn the world upside down. The love of the world is uprooted from the heart, and the way of the world contradicted in the life, so that the world is turned upside down there. But these enemies of the apostles wanted it thought that the preachers of the Gospel were troublemakers wherever they went. Because they persuaded people to turn from idols to the living and true God, from malice and envy to love and peace, they were accused of turning the world upside down, whereas it was only the kingdom of the Devil in the world that they overturned. Their enemies *set the city in an uproar* and then blamed the apostles for it. If Christ's faithful ministers are so invidiously misrepresented, let them not think it strange. We are no better than Paul and Silas, who were also mistreated in this way. The accusers cried out, "They have *come hither also*; it is therefore time for us to move."

4.3.4.2. That they were enemies of the established government (v. 7): "They all *do contrary to the decrees of Caesar*, because they say, *There is another king, one Jesus.*" It is true that the Roman government was very jealous of any governor under their power taking on himself the title of king, and it was true that Jesus' followers said, "Jesus is a king," but he was not an earthly king. There was nothing in the message of Christ that led to the dethroning of rulers. The Jews knew this very well, it did not befit the Jews, of all people, to bring such an accusation, since they so hated Caesar and his government. They expected a Messiah to be a temporal ruler, who would overturn the thrones of kingdoms, and so opposed our Lord Jesus because he did not appear as that sort of ruler.

4.4. The great uneasiness that this gave to the city (v. 8): *They troubled the people and the rulers of the city, when they heard these things.* The people and the rulers had no bad opinion of the apostles or their message, but if the apostles were represented to them by the prosecutors as enemies of Caesar, they would be obliged to sup-

press them. It troubled the magistrates to have to disturb good men.

4.5. The outcome of this troublesome affair. The magistrates did not want to prosecute the Christians. Care was taken to keep the apostles safe; they fled and kept out of the hands of their enemies, so that nothing was to be done but to discharge Jason and his friends on bail (v. 9). So they *took security of Jason and the other* (made Jason and the others post bond). Among the persecutors of Christianity, just as there have been examples of the madness and rage of wild beasts, so there have also been examples of the prudence and moderation of human beings.

Verses 10–15

In these verses we have:

1. Paul and Silas moving to Berea and being employed in preaching the Gospel there (v. 10). They had proceeded so far at Thessalonica that the foundations of a church were laid, and so when the storm arose, they withdrew. That command of Christ to his disciples, *When they persecute you in one city, flee to another* (Mt 10:23), intended that their flight be not so much for their own safety — "flee to another so that you can hide there" — as for continuing their work — "flee to another so that you can preach there." The Devil was outshot by his own bow; he thought that by persecuting the apostles he would stop the progress of the Gospel, but his intention was overruled in such a way that the persecution furthered that progress. See here:

1.1. The care that the believers took of Paul and Silas; they *immediately sent them away by night to Berea*. They sent them away under the cover of night, as if they had been evildoers.

1.2. The faithfulness of Paul and Silas in their work. Although they fled from Thessalonica, they did not flee from the service of Christ. When *they came to Berea, they went into the synagogue of the Jews.* They did not decline paying their respect to the Jews, either out of revenge for the wrongs already done them or for fear of more that might be done them. If others will not do their duty to us, we still should do ours to them.

2. The good character of the Jews in Berea (v. 11): *These were more noble*, "better brought up," *than those in Thessalonica.*

2.1. Their thinking was freer. They were willing to listen to reason and admit its force, even though it was contrary to their former sentiments. This was nobler.

2.2. They had a better attitude. Just as they were ready to unite with those whom they were brought to agree with, so they continued in love with those they saw cause to differ with. This was nobler.

2.2.1. *They received the word with all readiness of mind.* They were very willing to listen to it and did not shut their eyes to the light. They did not pick quarrels with the word or seek to take unfair advantage of its preachers, but welcomed it. This was true nobility. The Jews thought they were well born and that they could not have been better born. But they were told here who were the noblest and best-brought-up among them — those who were most disposed to receive the Gospel. These were the noblest, and, if I may put it this way, the most gentleman-like.

2.2.2. *They searched the scriptures daily whether those things were so.* Their readiness of mind to receive the word was not such that they took things on trust. Rather, since Paul reasoned from the Scriptures, referring his listeners to the Old Testament to prove what he said, they too turned to their Bibles, examining whether Paul's arguments were convincing, and acted accordingly. Notice:

2.2.2.1. The teaching and message of Christ does not fear scrutiny.

2.2.2.2. The New Testament is to be examined in the light of the Old. The Jews accepted the Old Testament, and those of them who did so could not help seeing good reason to accept the New, because in it they saw all the prophecies and promises of the Old completely and exactly fulfilled.

2.2.2.3. Those who read and receive the Scriptures must *search them* (Jn 5:39). They must study them, so that they may find the whole truth contained in them and may have an intimate acquaintance with the mind of God revealed in them.

2.2.2.4. Searching the Scriptures must be our daily work.

2.2.2.5. Those who make the Scriptures their authority and touchstone are truly noble and are set to be more and more noble. Those who rightly study the Scriptures and *meditate therein day and night* (Jos 1:8) have their minds filled with noble thoughts. *These are more noble.*

3. The good effect of the preaching of the Gospel at Berea (v. 12). Many of the Jews believed. At Thessalonica only *some of them believed* (v. 4), but at Berea, where they heard with unprejudiced minds, many believed. God gives grace to those whom he first inclines to make a diligent use of the means of grace, especially to search the Scriptures. Many of the Greeks also believed, both many of *the honourable women and of men not a few*; from their being mentioned with the honorable women, it seems they were men of the highest rank. The wives first accepted the Gospel, and then they persuaded their husbands to accept it.

4. The persecution that was raised up against Paul and Silas at Berea.

4.1. *The Jews at Thessalonica* were the troublemakers at *Berea*. They *had notice that the word of God was preached at Berea*, and they came there *and stirred up the people*, inciting them against the preachers of the Gospel. Notice how restless Satan's agents are in opposing the Gospel of Christ and the salvation of human souls.

4.2. This led to Paul's move to Athens. Paul stayed at Berea long enough, and had such success there, that there were brothers and sisters there — and sensible, active ones, too, which can be seen from the care they took of Paul (v. 14). They were aware of the coming of the persecuting Jews from Thessalonica, and, fearing what it would come to, they lost no time, but *immediately sent Paul away*, while they still kept Silas and Timothy there, who might be enough to continue the work without exposing them to danger. They *sent Paul to go as it were to the sea.* He went out from Berea on the road that went to the coast; he went by land to Athens. *Those that conducted Paul brought him to Athens.* The Spirit of God directed him to that famous city, famous for its power and the extent of its rule since ancient times, famous later for learning. Those who wanted learning went there to obtain it, because those who had learning went there to show it. It was a great university, and so Paul was sent there. He was not ashamed or afraid to show his face among the philosophers there and to preach Christ crucified there.

4.3. He instructed *Silas and Timothy to come to him to Athens* when he found there was a prospect of doing good there, or because, there being no one there whom he knew, he was lonely and dejected without them.

Verses 16–21

A scholar who is familiar with and loves the learning of ancient peoples would imagine that they would be very happy if they were where Paul now was, at Athens. Yet Paul, though brought up as a scholar, did not make it any part of his business at Athens to improve himself in their philosophy. He had other work in mind; his business was, in God's name, to turn them away from serving idols to the *service of the true and living God* in Christ (1Th 1:9). Here is:

1. The impression that the superstition of the Athenians made on Paul's spirit (v. 16). Notice:

1.1. The account given here of that city: it was *wholly given to idolatry.* This agrees with the account that the pagan writers give of it, that there were more idols in Athens than there were in the rest of Greece. Whatever foreign gods were commended to them were accepted by them and given a temple and an altar. It is significant that in the place where human learning flourished most, idolatry abounded most too. *The world by wisdom knew not God* (1Co 1:21). The greatest claimants to reason were the greatest slaves to idols: so necessary was it that there should be a divine revelation, and one that centered on Christ.

1.2. How disturbed Paul was at the sight of this. *His spirit was stirred within him.* He was greatly distressed in his concern for the glory of God, which he saw given to idols, and he had compassion on human souls, which he saw so enslaved to Satan.

2. His testimony against their idolatry and his attempts to bring them to the knowledge of the truth. He *went to the synagogue of the Jews*, who, though enemies of Christianity, were free from idolatry, and took the opportunity given him there to argue for Christ (v. 17). He *disputed with the Jews*, reasoned fairly with them, asking them what reason they could give — since they expected the Messiah — for not accepting Jesus. There he met with the devout people who had left the idol temples, and he talked with them to lead them to the Christian church, to which the Jews' synagogue was simply a porch. He entered into conversation with all who came his way about religious matters: *In the market, he disputed daily with those that met with him*, who were pagans and therefore never came to the Jews' synagogue. Zealous advocates for the cause of Christ will be ready to plead on its behalf in every group of people, as opportunities offer themselves.

3. The questions some of the philosophers asked. Notice:

3.1. Who entered into discussions with him: *He disputed with all that met him, in the places* where they met. Most took no notice of him, but some philosophers thought he was worth commenting on. There were:

3.1.1. *The Epicureans*, who *thought God altogether such a one as themselves* (Ps 50:21). They would not acknowledge either that God made the world or that he rules it. The Epicureans indulged themselves in all worldly and sensual pleasures, putting their happiness in those things — in what Christ has taught us to begin by denying ourselves.

3.1.2. *The Stoics*, who thought themselves wholly as good as God; they thought their virtuous human beings to be in no way inferior to God himself. Christianity is directly opposite to this, for it teaches us to turn away from all confidence in ourselves, so that Christ may be all in all (Eph 1:23; Col 3:11).

3.2. What their different attitudes toward him were (v. 18).

3.2.1. *Some called him a babbler*; the name they called him means literally "this scatterer of words," one who goes around throwing out one idle word or story here and another there; or, "this picker up of seeds." Some say the term is used for a certain small, worthless kind of bird "that picks up the seeds that are uncovered, either in the field or by the wayside, and hops here and there for that purpose." They took Paul to be such a pitiful and contemptible creature, supposing that he went from one place to another place expressing his ideas to obtain money, a few cents here and a few cents there, as that bird picks up a grain here and there. They looked on him as idle and regarded him as nothing more than a poor ballad singer.

3.2.2. *Others* called him *a setter forth of strange gods*, and if he had foreign gods to talk about, he could not have brought them to a better marketplace than that of Athens. He did not promote new gods openly, but they thought he seemed to promote them, *because he preached unto them Jesus, and the resurrection*. Although he did not call these gods, they thought he meant to make them so. Jesus they took as a new god, and *anastasis*, the word translated "resurrection," they took as the name of a new goddess—as if believing in Jesus and looking for the resurrection were the worshiping of new demons.

3.3. The proposal they made to give him a public hearing (vv. 19–20). They had heard some snatches of his message and wanted to have a better-developed knowledge of it.

3.3.1. They looked on it as strange and surprising. "It is a new teaching. *Thou bringest certain strange things to our ears*, which we never heard about before and do not now know what to make of." By this it seems that, among all the learned books they had, they either did not have, or had paid no attention to, the books of Moses and the prophets. There was only one book in the world that was divinely inspired, and that was the only book they were strangers to.

3.3.2. They wanted to know more about it, only because it was new and strange: "*May we know what this new doctrine is? We would gladly like to know what these things mean.*" It was right for them to know what this message was before they accepted it, and they were fair enough not to condemn it until they had had some account of it.

3.3.3. The place they brought him to was the *Areopagus*, the same word that is translated (v. 22) *Mars' Hill*. It was the town hall, or guildhall of their city, where the magistrates met on public business and the learned met to talk about their ideas. The court of justice that sat here was famous for its equity. No new god could be admitted without their approval. They brought Paul there to be tried, then, not as a criminal but as a candidate.

3.4. The general characterization given of the people of that city (v. 21): *All the Athenians spent their time in nothing else but either to tell or to hear some new thing.* They were curious about Paul's message not because it was good but because it was new.

3.4.1. They wanted to talk about things. It is true that good company is very useful and will polish a person who has had a good foundation in study, but knowledge gained only by conversation will be very showy and superficial.

3.4.2. They loved the latest things; they were for *telling and hearing some new thing*. They were chiefly interested in new schemes and new ideas. They wanted change.

3.4.3. They interfered in other people's business, never minding their own. Gossips are always *busybodies* (1Ti 5:13).

3.4.4. *They spent their time in nothing else.* Time is precious, and time is marching quickly on to eternity, but much of it is wasted in useless talk. To set ourselves up as those who are only interested in the latest choice piece of news, and to spend our time doing nothing else, is to lose what is very precious to gain what is worth little.

Verses 22–31

Here is the apostle Paul's sermon at Athens. We have had various sermons that the apostles preached to the Jews or to those Gentiles who were worshipers of the true God, and all the apostles had to do with those listeners was to explain and prove *that Jesus is the Christ* (1Jn 5:1). Here, however, we have a sermon to pagans, who worshiped false gods, and the theme of their message to them was quite different from what it was to the others. Their task with those others was to lead them by prophecies and miracles to a knowledge of the Redeemer and faith in him; here it was to lead their listeners by the common works of Providence to a knowledge of the Creator and the worship of him.

1. He laid down as the scope of his message that he aimed to bring them to *the knowledge of the only living and true God.* He was obliged here to instruct them in the basic principle of all religion, that there is a God and that God is one. When he preached against the gods they worshiped, he had no intention of drawing them to atheism, but to the service of the true God, by declaring that he did not seek to introduce any new gods, but to bring them to the knowledge of one God.

1.1. He showed them that by worshiping the false gods they had made, they had lost the knowledge of the true God who made them. *I perceive that in all things you are too superstitious* (NIV: very religious) (v. 22). The crime he accused them of was that they feared and worshiped demons, spirits that they thought lived in the idols. "It is time for you to be told that *there is but one God.* You easily accept everything that claims to be religion, but it is what corrupts it more and more; I bring you what will reform it." They accused Paul of offering new demons: "No," he said, "you already have enough demons; I will not add to their number."

1.2. He showed them that they themselves had given him a good occasion for declaring this one true God to them, *by setting up an altar To the Unknown God.* It is sad to think that at Athens, a place that was thought to have the monopoly of wisdom, the true God was an unknown God, the only God who was unknown. Where we are aware we are defective and come short, there, and just there, the Gospel takes us up and carries us on.

1.2.1. The expert commentators have had various thoughts about this *altar dedicated to the unknown God.* Some think that the meaning is, "to the God whose honor it is to be unknown," and that the Greeks meant the God of the Jews, whose name is beyond words and whose nature is unsearchable. The pagan nations called the Jews' God "the God without name." *This God*, according to Paul, *I now declare unto you.* Others think the meaning is, "To the God whom it is our unhappiness not to know," which implies that they would think it their happiness to know him.

1.2.2. Notice how modestly Paul mentioned this. He told them that he noticed it *as he passed by, and saw their devotions.* It was public, and he could not stop himself from seeing it. Notice how he used this occasion to bring in his message about the true God. He told them that the God he preached to them was One they already worshiped. He was One whom they ignorantly worshiped. "Now," he said, "I come to take away *that reproach*, so that you may worship with understanding. And it must surely be acceptable to have your blind devotion turned into an intelligent service so that you may not worship what you do not know."

2. He confirmed his message of the one living and true God from God's works of creation and providence: "The God whom I call you to worship is *the God that made the world.*" The Gentiles in general, and the Athenians in particular, were ruled in their devotions not by their philosophers, but by their poets and their light fiction. Now Paul here set himself, first, to reform their philosophy, and then to give them right ideas of *the one only living and true God*, and, finally, to take them away from their idolatry. Notice what glorious things Paul here said about the God he served and wanted them to serve.

2.1. *He is the God that made the world, and all things therein; the Father almighty, the Creator of heaven and earth.* Paul here maintained that God, by the activity of an infinite power, according to the contrivance of infinite wisdom, made the world and all things in it, so that the origin of the cosmos was owing not, as they supposed, to an eternal matter, but to an eternal mind.

2.2. He is therefore *Lord of heaven and earth.* If he created everything, without doubt it is all his to administer, and where he gives existence, he has indisputable right to give law.

2.3. He is the Creator, specifically, of all people (v. 26): *He made of one blood all nations of men.* He made the first human being; he makes every person. He has made *nations of men*, not only all the people in the nations but also the nations in their political capacity. He is their founder, having placed human beings in communities. He made them all from one blood, from one and the same nature, so that they may be committed to one another in mutual affection and help, as fellow creatures and brothers and sisters. *He hath made them to dwell on all the face of the earth.* He made them not to live in one place, but to be spread over all the earth; therefore, one nation should not look down with contempt on another, as the Greeks did, and this proud thought about themselves was humbled by the apostle.

2.4. He is the One who is generous to the whole creation (v. 25): *He giveth to all life, and breath, and all things.* He not only breathed into the first man the breath of life (Ge 2:7); he continues to breathe it into every person. He gave us these souls; he formed the human spirit within us. He gives to all the human beings *their life and breath*, because as the most humble people live on him, so also the greatest, the wisest philosophers and most powerful leaders, cannot live without him. *He gives to all*, not only to all people but also to the lesser creatures, to all animals. They receive their life and breath from him, and where he gives life and breath, he gives all things necessary to support life.

2.5. He is the sovereign administrator of all human affairs (v. 26): *He hath determined the times before appointed, and the bounds of their habitation.* Notice:

2.5.1. The sovereignty of God's dealing with us: he *hath determined* every event; the workings of providence are incontestable and must not be disputed.

2.5.2. The wisdom of what he does; he has *determined* what was *before appointed* (v. 26). The decisions of the Eternal Mind are not sudden ones, but the counterparts of an eternal purpose.

2.5.3. The realms in which his providence operates; these are time and place.

2.5.3.1. *He has determined the times* that are ours. Our times are in his hands (Ps 31:15). Whether the times are prosperous or difficult, he is the One who has determined them.

2.5.3.2. He has also *determined and appointed the bounds of our habitation.* The One who appointed the earth to be a place for human beings to live in has determined where they should live on earth. The particular homes in which our lot is cast are appointed by God, which is a reason why we should come to terms with the homes we are in and make the best of them.

2.6. *He is not far from every one of us* (v. 27). He is present everywhere. He is an infinite Spirit, one who *is not far from any of us.* He is near us both to receive the worship we give him and to give the mercies we ask of him, wherever we are, even though we are near no altar, idol, or temple. Whether we are in a palace or in a cottage, in a crowd or in a corner, in a city or in a desert, in the depths of the sea or high in the skies, it is certain that *God is not far from every one of us.*

2.7. *In him we live, and move, and have our being* (v. 28). We necessarily and constantly depend on his providence, just as the streams depend on their spring and rays of light depend on the sun.

2.7.1. *In him we live.* Not only are our forfeited lives not destroyed because of his patience and pity; our frail lives are prolonged because of his power, goodness, and fatherly care. If he were to suspend the positive acts of his goodness, we would die by ourselves.

2.7.2. *In him we move.* It is through him as well that our souls move our bodies; just as he is the first cause, so he is also the first mover.

2.7.3. *In him we have our being*; not only did we receive it from him in the beginning, but also we have it in him still; and in him we have *our* being, *this being*, that we were and still are of such a noble rank of beings, capable of knowing and enjoying God, and are not thrust into the lowliness of wild animals or the misery of demons.

2.8. The sum of the whole matter is that we are *God's offspring.* The apostle quoted here a saying of one of the Greek poets, Aratus (c. 315 – c. 245 B.C.), a native of Cilicia, Paul's compatriot, who, speaking of the pagan Jupiter — that is, in the poetic language, the supreme God — says of him, "for we are also his offspring." This shows not only that Paul was himself a scholar but also that human learning is both enhancing and useful to a Gospel minister, especially to convince outsiders, because it enables the minister to defeat people using their own weapons, to cut off Goliath's head with his own sword (1Sa 17:51). How can the enemies of truth be beaten out of their strongholds by those who do not know them? Since we live in God, we should live for him; since we move in him, we should move toward him; and since we have in him our being, we should consecrate our lives to him.

3. On the basis of all these great truths about God, he inferred the absurdity of their idolatry.

3.1. God cannot be represented by an idol. If we are *the offspring of God* (v. 29), then certainly the One who is *the Father of our spirits* (Heb 12:9) is himself a Spirit, and we should not think the Godhead is *like unto gold, or silver, or stone, graven by art and man's device* (v. 29). God honored human beings by making their soul in his own likeness, but we dishonor God if we make him in the likeness of our bodies.

3.2. *He dwells not in temples made with hands* (v. 24). A temple brings him no nearer to us, nor does it keep him farther away from us. A temple is a good place for us to come together to worship God, but God does not need any place of rest or residence.

3.3. He is *not worshiped with men's hands, as though he needed any thing* (v. 25). The One who maintains everything cannot benefit from any of our services, nor does he need them. What need can God have of our services, or what benefit can he gain from them, since he has all perfection in himself, and we have nothing that is good except what we receive from him?

3.4. We should all seek after God (v. 27): *That they should seek the Lord.* We have clear indications of God's presence among us and his goodness to us, and these indications are given us so that we will ask, *Where is God our Maker?* Nothing, one would think, could be more powerful with us to convince us there is a God than the consideration of our own nature, especially the noble powers and faculties of our own souls. In comparison with divine revelation, however, this discovery is so dim that only those who have no other god could perhaps reach out for God and find him.

3.4.1. It was very uncertain whether human beings could by this searching *find out God* (Job 11:7); it is only a perhaps: *if haply* they might.

3.4.2. If they did find out something about God, it was only some confused ideas of him; they only felt after him, like people wandering around in the dark, or like the blind. It is true that by the knowledge of ourselves we may be led to the knowledge of God, but it is a very confused knowledge. We have reason, therefore, to be thankful that through the Gospel of Christ we do not now feel after him, but *with open face behold, as in a glass, the glory of God* (2Co 3:18).

4. He proceeded to call them all to repent of their idolatry (vv. 30–31). This is the practical part of Paul's sermon to his university audience; having declared God to them (v. 23), he then duly urged them to *repentance toward God* (20:21). Having shown them the absurdity of their worshiping other gods, he tried to persuade them to return from it to the living and true God. Notice:

4.1. The way of God toward the Gentile world before the Gospel came among them: *The times of this ignorance God winked at* (overlooked).

4.1.1. These were times of great ignorance. In the things of God the Gentiles were grossly ignorant. Those who either do not know God or worship him ignorantly are truly ignorant; idolatry was owing to ignorance.

4.1.2. These times of ignorance God overlooked. We understand this as an act of divine patience and forbearance. He overlooked these times, but he gave them the gifts of his providence (14:16–17). He was not harsh and severe with them, but patient, because they acted in ignorance (1Ti 1:13).

4.2. The command God brought to the Gentile world through the Gospel: *He now commandeth all men everywhere to repent*—to change their mind and their ways. To repent is to turn with sorrow and shame from every sin and undertake every duty with cheerfulness and resolution.

4.2.1. This is God's command. He comes in with his own authority for our good, and he has made our privilege our duty.

4.2.2. It is his command to *all men, every where.* Everyone has to repent, and each has enough reason to repent; all people are invited to repent, and all who do repent will enjoy the benefits of repentance. Now the way of remission was opened up more than it had been, and the promise was more fully confirmed; "he therefore now expects us all to repent."

4.3. The great reason that supported this command. God commands us to repent *because he hath appointed a day in which he will judge the world in righteousness* (v. 31).

4.3.1. The God who made the world will judge it. The God who now rules the world will reward the faithful friends of his government and punish the rebels.

4.3.2. A day has been appointed for this general review of all that people have done in time, a day of decision, a day of reward, a day that will put an end to all the days of time.

4.3.3. The world will be judged in righteousness, because God is not unrighteous (Ro 3:5).

4.3.4. God will judge the world *by that man whom he hath ordained,* who can be no other than the Lord Jesus Christ, to whom all judgment is committed (Jn 5:22).

4.3.5. God's raising Christ from the dead is the great proof that he has been appointed and ordained to be the Judge of the living and the dead. God has *given assurance unto all men,* sufficient basis for their faith to build on, both that there is a future judgment and that Christ will be their Judge. Let all his enemies be assured of this and tremble before him; let all his friends be assured of it and triumph in him.

4.3.6. The consideration of the future judgment and of the great hand Christ will have in that judgment should lead us all to repent of our sins and turn away from them to God.

Verses 32–34

We have here a short account of the outcome of Paul's preaching at Athens.

1. Few were better off for it: the Gospel had as little success in Athens as anywhere.

1.1. Some mocked Paul and his preaching. They heard him patiently until he began to speak of the resurrection of the dead (v. 32), and then they *mocked.* If he spoke of a *resurrection of the dead,* even though it was the resurrection of Christ himself, it was completely unbelievable to them. They had deified their heroes after their death, but they never thought of them being raised from the dead. How was this possible? This great teaching, which is the saints' joy, was what Paul's listeners here made their joke. We are not to think it strange if sacred truths are made the scorn of worldly wits.

1.2. Others were willing to take time to consider it; they said, *We will hear thee again of this matter.* They did not want to agree with what Paul said at that time, but neither did they oppose it. Many lose out on the benefits of the practical message of Christianity by wading beyond their depth into controversies. Those who refused to yield to the present convictions of the word thought they would get clear of them by putting them off to a later opportunity (Ac 24:25). And so Satan deceived them out of all their time by deceiving them at the present time.

1.3. For the present, then, Paul left them to consider it (v. 33): *He departed from amongst them.*

2. There were some, however, who were persuaded (v. 34). Some of the people joined him and believed. When he departed from them, they would not part with him. Two are named particularly. One was well known, *Dionysius the Areopagite,* one of that high court that sat in the Areopagus, one of those before whom Paul had been summoned to appear; Paul's judge became his convert. Another convert was a *woman named Damaris.* Although not so great a harvest was gathered at Athens, nevertheless, because these few were persuaded there, Paul had no reason to say he had *laboured in vain* (Php 2:16).

CHAPTER 18

We have here: 1. Paul's coming to Corinth, his private conversation with Aquila and Priscilla, and his public reasoning with the Jews, from whom he turned to the Gentiles after they rejected him (vv. 1–6). 2. The great success of his ministry there, and the encouragement Christ gave him to continue his labors there (vv. 7–11). 3. The attack from the Jews, which he got through pretty well because of the coldness of Gallio, the Roman proconsul (vv. 12–17). 4. Paul's travels—after a long stay in Corinth—through many countries to build up and nurture the churches he had founded and planted; in making this circuit he briefly visited Jerusalem (vv. 18–23). 5. An account of Apollos's usefulness in the church (vv. 24–28).

Verses 1–6

We do not find that Paul was persecuted much in Athens, nor that he was driven from there by any harsh treatment, but because his reception was cold, with little prospect of doing good there, he left Athens. From there he came to Corinth. We have here:

1. Paul working for his living (vv. 2–3).

1.1. Although he was brought up a scholar, he was also skilled in a trade. He was a tentmaker. It was the custom of the Jews to bring up their children to pursue some trade, even though they gave them learning or estates. An honest trade, by which a person may earn their bread, is not to be looked on with contempt by anyone. Having learned in his youth to make tents, Paul did not lose the skill even when he did not practice it for a time.

1.2. Although he was entitled to receive maintenance from the churches he had planted, he still worked at his calling to earn his living, and he deserves praise for not asking for support when those who should have supplied his needs without being asked did not do so. Notice how humble and hardworking Paul was. The one who had so much to do with his mind did not think it beneath him to work with his hands. Notice how careful Paul was to commend his ministry. He maintained himself with his own labor so that he did not make the Gospel of Christ *burdensome* (2Co 11:7; 2Th 3:8–9).

1.3. Although we may imagine he was skilled at his trade, he still did not disdain to work at menial tasks: he *wrought* (worked) *with Aquila and Priscilla, who were of that same craft*, so that he earned no more than wages by the day, a bare subsistence.

1.4. Although he himself was a great apostle, he still chose to work with Aquila and Priscilla, because he found them to be very intelligent in the things of God (v. 26), and in Romans he acknowledges that they have been his *helpers in Christ Jesus* (Ro 16:3). It is good to choose to work with those who are likely to help us know and serve Christ Jesus more. Aquila was a Jew, born in Pontus (v. 2). He had just come from Italy to Corinth. The reason he left Italy was that all Jews had been banished from Rome by a recent decree of the emperor Claudius Caesar. Although a Christian, Aquila was banished because he had been a Jew. If Jews persecute Christians, it is not strange if pagans persecute them both.

2. Paul preaching to the Jews, both the native *Jews and the Greeks*.

2.1. He *reasoned with them in the synagogue every sabbath*. Notice how the apostles spread the Gospel, not by force and violence, but by fair reasoning. Paul was a rational as well as a Scriptural preacher.

2.2. *He persuaded them* (tried to persuade them). This shows:

2.2.1. The urgency of his preaching. He followed up his arguments with warm persuasion, appealing to them not to refuse the offer of salvation.

2.2.2. The good effect of his preaching: he persuaded them, that is, he prevailed with them. Some of them were convinced by his reasoning and gave their lives to Christ.

2.3. He was even more serious in this matter when his fellow laborers came with him (v. 5): *When Silas and Timothy had come from Macedonia*, ready to help him here, then Paul was more than before *pressed in spirit*, devoting himself more than ever to his preaching. Therefore, being urged in this way, he *testified to the Jews that Jesus is the Christ* (Jn 20:31).

3. Paul abandoning the unbelieving Jews and turning from them to the Gentiles (v. 6).

3.1. Many of the Jews persisted in contradicting the Gospel of Christ; they *opposed themselves* to it and *blasphemed*; "they set themselves in battle array" against the Gospel. They could not argue against it, but what was lacking in reason they made up for in abusive language: they *blasphemed*.

3.2. Paul then declared himself free to move on from them and left them to perish in their unbelief. The one who had been *pressed in spirit to testify to them* (v. 5) was *pressed in spirit* to testify against them (v. 6). He *shook his raiment* (shook out his clothes), shaking off the dust as a testimony against them. Thus he cleared himself of responsibility for them but threatened the judgments of God against them. He had fulfilled his part and was clean from the blood of their souls; like a faithful watchman, he had given them warning, so that if they perished in their unbelief, their blood was not to be required at his hands. It is a great encouragement to ministers to have the testimony of their conscience for them that they have faithfully discharged their trust by warning sinners. The Jews would certainly perish if they persisted in their unbelief, and the blame would lie wholly on them: *Your blood be upon your own heads*. If anything would frighten them eventually into compliance with the Gospel, then surely this would.

3.3. Having given them up, he did not give up his work. *Henceforth I will go unto the Gentiles*. The guests who were first invited would not come; guests must be welcomed, therefore, *from the highways and the hedges* (Lk 14:23). This was how the fall of the Jews became the riches of the Gentiles (Ro 11:12).

Verses 7–11

We are told here:

1. Paul changed where he lived. He left the synagogue and *entered into a certain man's house, named Justus* (v. 7). It seems he went to this man's house not to stay—he continued to live with Aquila and Priscilla—but to preach. This honest man opened his doors to him. When Paul did not have the freedom to preach in the synagogue, he preached in a house.

1.1. The man was next door to being a Jew; he was one who *worshipped God*; he was not an idolater, even though he was a Gentile.

1.2. The house was next door to the synagogue; it *joined close to it*. Paul probably chose this location out of goodwill, to show that he would come as near to the Jews as he could and that he was ready to return to them if only they would be willing to receive his message.

2. Paul immediately saw the good fruit of his labors among both Jews and Gentiles. *Crispus*, a Jew, an eminent one, *the chief ruler of the synagogue, believed on the Lord Jesus, with all his house* (v. 8). This would leave the Jews without excuse, that the ruler of their synagogue believed the Gospel, even though they opposed and abused it. Not only he but also his house believed. Many of the Corinthians who were Gentiles, *hearing, believed, and were baptized*. Some people perhaps came to listen to Paul because they were under some conviction of conscience, but most

probably came only out of curiosity. In any case, hearing, *they believed*, and then, *believing*, they were *baptized*, and so established in Christ.

3. Paul was encouraged by a vision to continue with his work at Corinth (v. 9): *The Lord Jesus spoke to Paul in the night by a vision.*

3.1. Christ renewed his commission and charge to preach the Gospel: "*Be not afraid of the Jews.* Do not be afraid of the magistrates of the city either. It is the cause of heaven you are pleading; do so boldly. Do not speak timidly and cautiously, but clearly, fully, and courageously. Speak out."

3.2. He assured him of his presence with him, which was sufficient to inspire and encourage him: "*Be not afraid, for I am with thee* to support you, to rescue you from all your fears, to work with you, and to confirm the word by signs following (Mk 16:20)." Those who have Christ with them need not fear and therefore should not cower.

3.3. He guaranteed that Paul would be protected: *No man shall set on thee to hurt thee.* Christ did not promise that no one would attack Paul, for the next news we hear is that he was attacked and *brought to the judgment-seat* (v. 12); rather, "*No man shall set on thee to hurt thee.* No one will do you evil. Whatever trouble they may make against you, there is no real evil, or harm, in it."

3.4. He gave him a prospect of success: "*For I have much people in this city.* That is why you are to pursue your work vigorously and cheerfully, for there are many in this city who are to be effectively called by your ministry." The Lord knows those who are his (2Ti 2:19). "I have them, even though they do not yet know me, for the Father has given them to me, and I will lose none of those who were given me (Jn 17:9–12, 24). *In this city*, even though it is a very worldly, evil city, full of impurity, and the more so because it has a temple of Venus, nevertheless, in this mass, which all seems to be chaff, there is wheat; in this ore, which all seems to be dross, there is gold." Let us not despair of any place, since even in Corinth Christ had many people.

4. After this encouragement, Paul stayed there a long while (v. 11): he *continued at Corinth a year and six months, teaching the word of God among them.* He stayed that long:

4.1. To bring in those who were outsiders. God works in different ways. The people Christ had at Corinth must be called in gradually. Let Christ's ministers continue with their duty, even though their work is not done all at once.

4.2. To build up those inside the church. Those who were converted still needed to be *taught the word of God.* No sooner was the good seed sown in that field than the enemy came and sowed weeds (Mt 13:24–30), *the false apostles* (2Co 11:13) about whom Paul complains so much in his letters to the Corinthians. Soon after Paul came to Corinth, he probably wrote the first letter to the Thessalonians, and the second letter to the same church was written not long afterward. Ministers may serve Christ by writing good letters as well as by preaching good sermons.

Verses 12–17

We have here an account of some disturbance at Corinth, but no great harm done.

1. Paul was accused by the Jews before the Roman governor (vv. 12–13). The governor was *Gallio, deputy of Achaia.* This Gallio was the elder brother of the famous Seneca and was a man of great ingenuity and integrity, and of a wonderfully sweet temper; he was called "Sweet Gallio," and he is said to have been universally loved. Notice:

1.1. How rudely Paul was apprehended and brought before Gallio: *The Jews made insurrection with one accord against* (made a united attack on) *Paul.* They were the ringleaders. They were unanimous in it: they attacked him *with one accord.* They did it with violence and fury: *They made an insurrection* and rushed Paul off *to the judgment seat* (court).

1.2. How falsely Paul was accused before Gallio (v. 13): *This fellow persuades men to worship God contrary to the law.* They could not accuse him of persuading people not to worship God at all, but only to worship God in a way that was against the law. But the charge was unjust. Those Jews at Corinth could not observe the law concerning the temple service, and there was no part of their synagogue worship that Paul contradicted. Even today, when people are taught to worship God in Christ and to worship him in the Spirit, they are ready to quarrel, as if they were taught to worship him against the law.

2. Gallio dismissed the case and would not take any notice of it (vv. 14–15). Paul was about to make his defense, but the judge, having decided not to pass sentence on this case, would not even trouble himself with examining it.

2.1. He showed himself very ready to fulfill the role of a judge in any matter that it was proper for him to take notice of. "He *said to the Jews, If it were a matter of wrong, or wicked lewdness* (if you were making a complaint about some misdemeanor or serious crime), I would think myself bound *to bear with you.*" It is the duty of magistrates to set right those who have been wronged and to censure those who have committed the wrong, and if the complaint is not made with all possible decorum, they should still hear it out.

2.2. He would by no means allow them to complain to him of something that was not within his jurisdiction (v. 15): *If it be a question of words and names, and of your law, look you to it; I will be no judge of such matters.* Therefore, *he drove them from the judgment-seat* (ejected them from the court) (v. 16). Here was:

2.2.1. Something right and commendable in Gallio's conduct—that he would not claim to judge things he did not understand, that he left the Jews to themselves in matters of their own religion. He would not himself be the instrument of their hatred. But:

2.2.2. It was certainly wrong to speak so disrespectfully about a law and religion that he might have known to have come from God, and with which he should have become familiar. He spoke as if he wanted to boast about his ignorance of the Scriptures, as if it were beneath him to take notice of the law of God.

3. Sosthenes was mistreated, and about this, too, Gallio was unconcerned (v. 17).

3.1. Great contempt was shown to the court by those who *took Sosthenes and beat him before the judgment-seat.* There are many thoughts about this matter, because it is uncertain who this Sosthenes was and who the Greeks were who mistreated him.

3.1.1. It seems most probable that Sosthenes was a Christian. It is certain that there was a Sosthenes who was a friend of Paul and well known in Corinth; Paul calls him his brother and joins him with himself in his first letter to the church at Corinth (1Co 1:1). He is said to be a *ruler of the synagogue.*

3.1.2. As for the Greeks who mistreated him, they were probably either Hellenist Jews or Jewish Greeks, those who joined the Jews in opposing the Gospel (vv. 4, 6).

They were so angry with Paul that they beat Sosthenes, and they were so angry with Gallio that they beat Sosthenes before the court, by which they showed that they had no respect for Gallio; if he would not be their executioner, they would take judgment into their own hands.

3.2. The court showed no less contempt to the case, and to the people too. But *Gallio cared for none of these things.* If he meant that he was not worried about the insults of evildoers, it was commendable. But if he meant that he himself was not concerned about the mistreatment of good people, then he carried his indifference too far. Gallio, as judge, should have protected Sosthenes and restrained and punished the Greeks who attacked him. Those who see and hear about the suffering of God's people but have no sympathy with them or concern for them, because it is all the same to them whether the interests of religion sink or swim, have the spirit of Gallio here, who, when a good man was mistreated before him, *cared for none of these things.*

Verses 18–23

Here we have Paul on the move, as we had him in Corinth at rest for some time, but in both he was very busy. Here is:

1. Paul's departure from Corinth (v. 18).

1.1. He did not go away until sometime after the trouble he met with there; he had departed from other places when the storm arose, but not from Corinth, because there it had no sooner risen than it fell again. *After this he tarried there yet a good while* (v. 11). As long as he found that he was not working in vain (1Co 15:58), he continued to work.

1.2. When he went, he took leave of the believers solemnly and with much affection.

1.3. He took *with him Priscilla and Aquila.* They seemed to like to be on the move and to be disinclined to stay long at a place, a disposition that may arise from a good principle and have good effects and should therefore not be condemned in others, even though we should be suspicious when we find it in ourselves.

1.4. At Cenchrea, the port where those who went to sea from Corinth took ship, either Paul or Aquila—the original does not state which—had his head shaved to release himself from the vow of a Nazarite: *Having shorn his head at Cenchrea; for he had a vow.* Those who lived in Judea were, in such cases, bound to do it at the temple, but those who lived in other countries could do it in other places. I see no harm in admitting that it happened to Paul, for we must admit that he did the same thing later (21:24, 26), complying for a time with the Jews, to whom he *became as a Jew* (1Co 9:20), so *that he might win upon them.*

2. Paul's calling *at Ephesus,* which was the capital of Asia Minor.

2.1. *There he left Aquila and Priscilla.* They might be useful to the interests of the Gospel at Ephesus. Paul intended shortly to settle there for some time, and Aquila and Priscilla might be able to incline the minds of many to favorably receive Paul when he came to them.

2.2. There he preached *to the Jews in their synagogue. He entered into the synagogue* not as a hearer but as a preacher, for *there he reasoned with the Jews.* Although he had abandoned the Jews at Corinth, he did not, because of them, decline to go to the Jewish synagogues in other places, but still made the first offer of the Gospel to the Jews. We must not condemn a whole body or denomination of people for the sake of some who conduct themselves badly.

2.3. The Jews at Ephesus wanted him to stay with them (v. 20): *They desired him to tarry longer with them.* These were nobler and better brought up than those Jews at Corinth, and this desire of theirs was a sign that God had not completely rejected his people, but had a remnant among them.

2.4. Paul would not stay with them now: *He consented not* (declined to stay longer), but *bade them farewell.* He *must by all means keep this feast at Jerusalem.* We are not told which of the feasts this was.

2.5. He indicated that after this journey he intended to come and spend some time at Ephesus. It is good to have opportunities in reserve, to have another good work to apply ourselves to when the one we are engaged in is over: *I will return again to you.* But he added that necessary condition, *if God will.* Our times are in God's hand (Ps 31:15); we propose, but he disposes (Thomas à Kempis, *The Imitation of Christ,* 1.19), and that is why we must make all our promises submit to the will of God.

3. Paul's visit to Jerusalem; it was only a short visit.

3.1. He went by sea to the port closest to Jerusalem. *He sailed from Ephesus* (v. 21) *and landed at Caesarea* (v. 22).

3.2. He went *up, and saluted* (greeted) *the church,* which I think clearly refers to the church at Jerusalem.

3.2.1. It was a very friendly visit that he paid to them, out of pure kindness, to show his sincere goodwill toward them. The increase of our new friends should not make us forget our old ones; it should be a pleasure to good people to revive former friendships. He was careful to maintain good relations with them, so that he and they could congratulate one another on successes and wish one another well.

3.2.2. It was only a short visit. He went *up, and saluted them* but did not stay with them long. It was intended to be a short meeting. God's people are dispersed and scattered, but it is good to see one another sometimes.

4. His return through those regions where he had formerly preached the Gospel.

4.1. He went and spent some time in *Antioch* (v. 22), where he had been first sent out from to preach among the Gentiles (13:1). He went down to Antioch to refresh himself with the sight of the ministers there, and it is very refreshing for a faithful minister to have the company of close believing friends for a while.

4.2. From there he went over the country of *Galatia and Phrygia,* where he had preached the Gospel and planted churches. These country churches—for this is what they were (Gal 1:2), and we do not read of any city in Galatia where a church was—Paul visited *in the order* (successively) in which they lay, nurturing what he had been instrumental in planting, and *strengthening all the disciples.* Paul's supporting them with his presence was an encouragement to them, but that was not all he did: what he preached to them then strengthened them even more. Disciples need to be strengthened. Ministers must do what they can to strengthen them by pointing them to Christ, whose strength is perfected in their weakness (2Co 12:9).

Verses 24–28

The sacred history leaves Paul on his travels, and here goes to meet Apollos at Ephesus.

1. Here is an account of Apollos's character.

1.1. He was *a Jew, born at Alexandria* in Egypt, but of Jewish parents.

1.2. He was a man well suited to public service. He was *an eloquent* (a learned) *man, and mighty in* (with a thorough knowledge of) *the scriptures.* He had a great command of language. "He *came to Ephesus,* being *mighty in the scriptures,*" as it is in the original word order; he came having an excellent faculty for explaining Scripture. He was not only familiar with the Scriptures, able to quote texts off the top of his head and tell you where to find them, but truly *mighty in the scriptures.* He understood their sense and meaning, and he knew how to make use of them and apply them, how to reason from the Scriptures, and reason strongly.

1.3. He *was instructed in the way of the Lord.* That is, he was to some extent familiar with the teaching of Christ; he had obtained some good general ideas of the Gospel and the principles of Christianity. He was taught something of Christ and the way of salvation through Christ. Those who want to teach others must first be taught the word of the Lord themselves, not only to talk about it but also to walk in it. It is not enough to have our tongues tuned to the word of the Lord; we must also have our feet directed to the way of the Lord.

1.4. He *knew only the baptism of John,* however. He knew *the preparing of the way of the Lord* rather than the way of the Lord itself. He himself had been baptized *only with the baptism of John,* not with the Holy Spirit.

2. We have here the employment and improvement of his gifts at Ephesus.

2.1. He made a very good use of his gifts in public there. He was willing to be employed: *Being fervent in the Spirit, he spoke and taught diligently the things of the Lord* (v. 25). Although he did not have the miraculous gifts of the Spirit, he still made use of the gifts he had. We have seen how Apollos was qualified with a good head and a good tongue: he was *an eloquent man, and mighty in the scriptures.* Let us now see what he had further to commend him as a preacher, and his example is commended for the imitation of all preachers.

2.1.1. He was a lively, passionate preacher, one who had a good heart and was *fervent in Spirit.* He had in him a great deal of divine fire as well as divine light (Jn 5:35). This appeared both in his eagerness to preach when he was called to it and in the enthusiasm of his preaching. He preached as one who was serious, who put his heart into his work. Many people are fervent in spirit but weak in knowledge. On the other hand, many people are eloquent enough and well versed in the Scriptures but have no life, passion, or enthusiasm. Here was a complete *man of God,* full of both divine knowledge and divine feeling.

2.1.2. He worked hard as a preacher. *He spoke and taught diligently.* He took great pains over his preaching; he would not offer to God or to the synagogue what cost nothing, or even what cost *him* nothing. He *taught diligently,* "accurately, exactly"; everything he said had been weighed carefully.

2.1.3. He was an evangelical preacher. Even though he knew only the baptism of John, that was the beginning of the Gospel of Christ, and he kept close to that, for he taught the things of the Lord Christ, the things that tended to make way for him.

2.1.4. He was a courageous preacher: *He began to speak boldly in the synagogue,* as one who, having put his confidence in God, did not fear what other people might say or think. He preached the things of God *in the synagogue,* where the Jews were not only present but also in power.

2.2. In private, on the other hand, he enhanced his gifts well there. *Aquila and Priscilla expounded to him the way of God more perfectly.*

2.2.1. They heard him preach in the synagogue, and they encouraged his ministry by attending it diligently

and constantly. Young ministers who are promising should be supported by more mature Christians.

2.2.2. Finding him deficient in his knowledge of Christianity, *they took him to them* and *expounded to him the way of God more perfectly.* They neither despised him themselves nor disparaged him to others. They did not call him a young, raw preacher, one who was unfit to come into the pulpit. Rather, they communicated what they knew to him and gave him a clear, methodical account of the things that previously he had had only confused ideas about.

2.2.2.1. See an instance of truly Christian love and kindness in Aquila and Priscilla. Aquila did not undertake to speak in the synagogue, because he did not have such gifts for public work as Apollos had, but he provided Apollos with content and then left him to clothe it with acceptable words. Instructing young Christians and young ministers privately in conversation is an act of very good service.

2.2.2.2. See an instance of great humility in Apollos. He was a very bright young man, one with great gifts and learning, greatly praised and followed by many, but when he found Aquila and Priscilla, who, though mere artisans, could speak intelligently and from their own experience about the things of God, he was glad to receive instruction from them, to have them show him his defects and mistakes. Young students may gain a great deal by talking with older Christians, as young students in law may by talking to older practitioners. Although Apollos *was instructed in the way of the Lord,* he did not rest in the knowledge he had already reached. Those who know a great deal should seek to know more.

2.2.2.3. Here is an instance of a good woman who used the knowledge God had given her to do good in private conversation.

3. Here is his advancement in the service of the church of Corinth. Paul had set the wheels in motion at Corinth. Many were stirred up by his preaching to receive the Gospel, and they needed to be strengthened. Paul was gone; and now Apollos, who was more suited to water than to plant (1Co 3:6), had a good opportunity to fill this vacancy. Here we have:

3.1. His call to this service: he himself was inclined to go: *He was disposed to pass into Achaia.* Apollos thought there might be some work for him, and God inclined his mind that way. His friends encouraged him to go; they gave him letters of recommendation. Although those at Ephesus would feel a great loss without his ministry, they did not begrudge those in Achaia the benefit of it, but, on the contrary, used their influence in those churches to introduce him.

3.2. His success in this service.

3.2.1. Believers were greatly edified: *He helped those much who had believed through grace.* Those who believe in Christ believe through grace; it is *not of themselves, it is God's gift to them* (Eph 2:8). Those who through grace do believe still need help. Faithful ministers are capable of helping in many ways those who through grace believe, and it is their business to help them.

3.2.2. Unbelievers were greatly mortified. Their objections were fully answered, their mouths silenced, and their faces filled with shame (v. 28): *He mightily convinced the Jews, and that publicly.* He did it *earnestly*; he took pains to do it. He did it effectively and to everyone's satisfaction. If the Jews would only be convinced that Jesus is Christ, even their own law would teach them to listen to Apollos. The business of ministers is to preach Christ. The way he took to convince them was *by the scriptures*; he drew his arguments from there. Ministers must be able not only to preach the truth but also to prove it and defend it, and to convince its opponents with humility and yet with power.

CHAPTER 19

We left Paul on his missionary journey visiting the churches (18:23), but we have not forgotten, and neither has he, his promise to his friends at Ephesus that he would return to them. Now this chapter shows us his fulfillment of that promise. We see here: 1. How he worked there, how he taught some weak believers who had gone no further than John's baptism (vv. 1–7), how he taught for three months in the Jewish synagogue (v. 8), how he taught the Gentiles for a long time in a public school (vv. 9–10), and how he confirmed his message by miracles (vv. 11–12). 2. What was the result of his labor, especially among the sorcerers: some were conquered (vv. 13–17), but others were converted (vv. 18–20). 3. What projects he had in mind in order to continue to be useful (vv. 21–22), what trouble he finally met with at Ephesus from the silversmiths, how a riot was created by Demetrius to praise Diana (vv. 23–34), and how it was suppressed and dispersed by the town clerk (vv. 35–41).

Verses 1–7

Ephesus was a notable city in Asia, famous for a temple built there to Diana (Artemis), which was one of the wonders of the world: *Paul came to preach the Gospel there while Apollos was at Corinth* (v. 1). While Apollos was watering there, Paul was planting here, and he continued the new work that was cut out for him at Ephesus with greater cheerfulness and satisfaction because he knew that such an able minister as Apollos was now at Corinth continuing the good work there. Having gone through the region of Galatia and Phrygia and *passed through the upper coasts* (interior), he *came to Ephesus*, where he had left Aquila and Priscilla, and he found them there. He met with some disciples there who professed faith in Christ as the true Messiah but were still in the first and lowest class in the school of Christ, under his usher, John the Baptist. They were *about twelve* in number (v. 7). Notice:

1. How Paul taught them.

1.1. They did believe in the Son of God, but Paul asked whether they had *received the Holy Spirit*, whether they were familiar with and had accepted this revelation. This was not all; extraordinary gifts of the Holy Spirit had been conferred on the apostles and other disciples after Christ's ascension. Had these believers participated in those gifts? *"Have you received the Holy Spirit since you believed?* Have you received that seal of the truth of Christ's message in yourselves?"* Graces of the Spirit are given to all believers, and these graces are pledges to them (2Co 1:22; 5:5; Eph 1:13–14). Many are deceived in this matter, however, thinking they have received the Holy Spirit when really they have not. As there are those who only claim to have the gifts of the Holy Spirit, so there are those who only claim to enjoy his grace and comfort. We should strictly examine ourselves, therefore: did we receive the Holy Spirit when we believed? The tree will be known by its fruits (Mt 7:15–20). Are we producing the fruit of the Spirit? Do we walk by the Spirit (Gal 5:16–26)?

1.2. They acknowledged their ignorance in this matter: *"Whether there be a Holy Spirit* is more than we know. We know from the Scriptures that there is a promise of the Holy Spirit, and we do not doubt that this promise will be fulfilled at the appropriate time. We have not even

heard whether the Holy Spirit has indeed been given."* The Gospel light, like that of the morning, shone out more and more brightly (Pr 4:18), but gradually; not only was it clearer and clearer, but also it shone further and further.

1.3. Paul asked how they came to be baptized if they knew nothing of the Holy Spirit: *"Unto what then were you baptized?* This is strange and inexplicable. What! Baptized, but know nothing of the Holy Spirit?"* Ignorance of the Holy Spirit is as inconsistent with a sincere profession of Christianity as ignorance of Christ is. Let us often consider what we were baptized for, so that we may live up to our baptism.

1.4. They acknowledged that they were baptized *unto John's baptism,* that is, that they were baptized in the name of John, by some disciple of his, who ignorantly kept up his name as the head of a party. As it is here expressed, they were baptized *unto John's baptism.*

1.5. Paul explained to them the true intention and meaning of John's baptism, that it referred especially to Jesus Christ. Those who have been left in ignorance or led into error by any unfortunate gaps in their education should be compassionately instructed and better taught, as these disciples were by Paul.

1.5.1. He acknowledged that John's baptism was very good as far as it went: *John verily baptized with the baptism of repentance.*

1.5.2. He showed them that John's baptism had a further reference. They should believe in the One who was to come after him, that is, in Christ Jesus, for John's baptism of repentance was intended only to prepare the way of the Lord, whom John directed them to: *Behold the Lamb of God* (Jn 1:29). John was only the messenger; Christ is the Ruler. "John's baptism was the porch you were to pass through, not the house you were to live in."

1.6. When they were shown their error, they thankfully accepted the revelation and *were baptized in the name of the Lord Jesus* (v. 5). Unlike Apollos (18:25) and Christ's first disciples, these believers had received John's baptism only looking to John and no further, as if he were their savior; their error was therefore so fundamental that it was as fatal to that baptism as the error of anyone who was baptized in the name of Paul would be to theirs (1Co 1:13). When they came to understand things better, they wanted to be *baptized in the name of the Lord Jesus,* and were. It does not follow, therefore, that there was not an agreement between John's baptism and Christ's, for those who were baptized here *in the name of the Lord Jesus* had never been baptized in this way before.

2. How Paul conferred the extraordinary gifts of the Holy Spirit on them (v. 6).

2.1. Paul solemnly *prayed to God, laying his hands on them.*

2.2. God granted the thing he prayed for: *The Holy Spirit came upon them, and they spoke with tongues and prophesied.* They had the Spirit of prophecy so that they could understand the mysteries of the kingdom of God themselves, and they had the gift of tongues so that they could preach those mysteries to every nation and in every language. Oh, what a wonderful change suddenly came upon these men here! Those who so recently had *not so much as heard that there was any Holy Spirit* were now themselves filled with the Holy Spirit.

Verses 8–12

Here Paul was very busy at Ephesus.

1. He began, as usual, in the Jews' synagogue. Notice:

1.1. Where he preached to them: in their synagogue (v. 8). Where there were no Christian churches yet formed, he frequently went to the Jewish meetings. Paul went into the synagogue because that was where he would find them together and, it might be hoped, in a good mood.

1.2. What he preached to them: *The things concerning the kingdom of God*, the great things that concerned God's rule over human beings and his favor to them, and their submission to God and joy in God. Or, more particularly, *the things concerning the kingdom of the Messiah*. He gave them a right idea of this kingdom and showed them their mistakes about it.

1.3. How he preached to them. He preached argumentatively: he disputed, giving reasons and answering objections, so that they might not only believe but also see cause to believe. He also preached passionately: he tried to persuade. Paul was a moving preacher and was master of the art of persuasion. And he preached undauntedly and with a holy resolution: he spoke boldly.

1.4. How long he preached to them: *For the space of three months*, enough time for them to consider it.

1.5. What results his preaching had among them. Some were persuaded to believe in Christ. Yet many continued to be stubborn and were confirmed in their prejudice against Christianity. Now that he settled among them and his word came closer to their consciences, they soon became tired of him. They had an invincible aversion to the Gospel of Christ themselves: they were *hardened, and believed not*. They also did all they could to raise and keep up a dislike for the Gospel in others. *They spoke evil of that way before the multitude*, to make them prejudiced against it. Although they could not show that it contained any kind of evil, they still said all kinds of bad things about it.

2. When he had taken matters as far as he could in the Jewish synagogue, he left. They had driven him away from them by their public maligning of those things he spoke *concerning the kingdom of God*. They hated to be reformed, hated to be instructed, and so *he departed from them*.

2.1. When Paul departed from the Jews, he took the disciples with him and thus *separated them*. So that they would not be defiled with the poisonous tongues of those blasphemers, he took those who believed with him to be the foundation of a Christian church. When Paul departed, nothing more was needed to separate the disciples: let him go wherever he would—they would follow.

2.2. When Paul separated from the synagogue, he *disputed* (had discussions) *daily in the school of one Tyrannus*. He gained a double advantage from this separation, because now:

2.2.1. His opportunities were more frequent. In the synagogue he could preach only every Sabbath (13:42), but now he held discussions daily.

2.2.2. They were more open. Only Jews or converts could come to the Jewish synagogue; Gentiles were excluded. In the *school* (lecture hall) of Tyrannus, on the other hand, both Jews and Greeks came to attend his ministry (v. 10). Some think this school of Tyrannus was a school of divinity of the Jews, of the sort they commonly had in their great cities besides their synagogue; they called it *Beth midrash*, "the house of inquiry." But others think it was a Gentile school of philosophy belonging to one Tyrannus; it was some convenient place that Paul and the disciples could use, either for love or for money.

2.3. He continued his labors here for *two years*. These two years begin from the end of the *three months* he spent in the synagogue (v. 8); he could justly reckon it, therefore, to have been three years in all, as he did later (20:31).

2.4. The Gospel then spread near and far (v. 10): *All those that dwelt in Asia heard the word of the Lord Jesus*, not only all who live in Ephesus but also all who live in that large province called Asia, of which Ephesus was the leading city. A great number of people came to Ephesus from throughout the country, which gave Paul opportunity to make the Gospel known to all the towns and villages of that region. They all heard the *word of the Lord Jesus*. Some from all groups, from all parts of both city and country, embraced this Gospel and took it in, and it was communicated by them to others.

3. God confirmed Paul's message by miracles (vv. 11–12). Why did he not work miracles at Thessalonica, Berea, and Athens? Or, if he did, why are they not recorded? But here at Ephesus we have the proofs of this kind that he gave of his divine mission. They were *special miracles*. God exerted powers that were not according to the ordinary course of nature. Or, they were not only, as all miracles are, out of the ordinary, but were uncommon even as miracles. God performed miracles that were beyond the ordinary. Yet it was not Paul who performed them, but God who *wrought them by the hand of Paul* (v. 11). Paul was merely the instrument. Not only did he heal the sick who were brought to him, or to whom he was brought, but *from his body were brought to the sick handkerchiefs or aprons*. We read of one woman who was cured by touching the edge of Christ's garment, and he knew that *virtue went out of him* (Lk 6:19), but here people were cured by Paul's garments when they were taken from him. Christ gave his apostles power *against unclean spirits and against all manner of sickness* (Mt 10:1); those to whom Paul sent relief had it in both cases: *for the diseases departed from them*, and the *evil spirits went out of them*.

Verses 13–20

We have here in these verses two remarkable instances of the conquest of Satan, not only in those who were violently possessed by him, but also in those who were voluntarily devoted to him. Here is:

1. The confusion of some of Satan's servants, some *vagabond* (itinerant) *Jews*, who were *exorcists*, who used Christ's name in their satanic chants. Notice:

1.1. The general character of those who were guilty of this presumption. They were Jews, but itinerant Jews. They strolled about telling people their fortunes, claiming that by spells and charms they could heal diseases and restore those who were depressed or insane. The superstitious Jews, to give a good reputation to these magic arts, wickedly attributed their invention to Solomon. Christ seems to refer to this in Mt 12:27: *By whom do your children cast them out?*

1.2. A particular account of some at Ephesus who followed this way of life. They were *seven sons of one Sceva, a Jew, and chief of the priests* (v. 14). Their father was a chief of the priests, a leader of one of the twenty-four divisions of priests. One would have thought that the temple would find both enough employment and enough encouragement for the sons of a chief priest.

1.3. The corruption they were guilty of: *They took upon them to call over evil spirits the name of the Lord Jesus*, not as those who respected Christ and trusted in his name—as we read of some who drove out demons in Christ's name but did not follow his disciples (Lk 9:49)—but as those who were willing to try all methods to pursue their evil trade. They said, *We adjure you by Jesus whom Paul preaches*; not, "whom we believe in and depend on," but *whom Paul preaches*; as if they had said, "We will see what that name will do."

1.4. The confusion they were put in while performing their ungodly operations. The evil spirit replied sharply,

"*Jesus I know, and Paul I know*, but *who are you?* (v. 15). What power have you to command us in his name, or who gave you any such power (Mt 21:23)? What right have you to declare the power of Jesus, since you hate his instruction?" (Ps 50:16–17). *The man in whom the evil spirit was* gave them a hostile reception: he *leaped upon them, overcame them*, and *prevailed against them*. The result was that *they fled out of the house* not only *naked* but also *wounded*. This is a warning to all those who name the name of Christ but do not depart from sin. The same enemy who overcomes them with his temptations will overcome them with his terrors. If we resist the Devil by a true and living faith in Christ, he will flee from us (Jas 4:7), but if we think we can resist him by merely using Christ's name as a spell or charm, he will overwhelm us.

1.5. The general notice that was taken of this (v. 17): *This was known to all the Jews and Greeks also dwelling at Ephesus*. It was the common talk of the town. People were terrified: *fear fell on them all*. Here they saw the hatred of the Devil they served and the power of Christ, whom they opposed. God was glorified; *the name of the Lord Jesus was the more magnified*, since now it was seen to be a name above every name (Php 2:9).

2. The conversion of other servants of Satan.

2.1. Those who had been guilty of evil practices confessed them (v. 18). Many who had believed and were baptized, but had not then been as specific as they might have been in confessing their sins, came to Paul and confessed what evil lives they had led and what a great deal of secret wickedness their own consciences accused them of. *They showed their deeds*, were ashamed of themselves, and gave glory to God and a warning to others (Jos 7:19). Where there is true contrition for sin, there will be a frank confession of sin to God and to other people whom we have offended when the case requires it.

2.2. Those who had dealings with evil books burned them (v. 19). There were *many also of those who used curious arts*, whose business was the study of magic and divination. These people, their consciences now more awake than ever, *brought their books together, and burnt them before all men*. Ephesus was notorious for the use of these magic arts. It was therefore much to the honor of Christ and his Gospel to have such a noble testimony given against those arts in a place where they were so fashionable.

2.2.1. In this way they showed holy indignation at the sins they had been guilty of. Those very things were now as detestable to them as they had previously been delightful to them.

2.2.2. In this way they showed their determination never to return to sorcery. Having firmly decided never to use the books again, they burned them.

2.2.3. In this way they put far away from them a temptation to return to sorcery. Those who truly repent of their sin will keep themselves as far as possible from any temptations that might cause them to sin.

2.2.4. In this way they prevented the books from causing trouble to others. It was the safest course to commit them all to the flames. Those who are restored from sin themselves will do all they can to keep others from falling into it.

2.2.5. In this way they showed contempt for the wealth of this world, for the price of the books was added up and was found to be *fifty thousand pieces of silver* (*drachma*). Probably they had cost the owners a lot; yet because the books were Satan's, the new converts did not think the books' monetary value would justify them in being so corrupt as to sell them again.

2.2.6. In this way they testified in public of their joy at their conversion from these evil practices. These converts joined together in making this bonfire, and they made it in front of everyone. They chose to do it together, by common agreement, and to do it in the town center, so that Christ and his grace in them would be exalted even more.

3. A general account of the progress and success of the Gospel (v. 20): *So mightily grew the word of God, and prevailed*. It is wonderful to see the word of God growing powerfully, to see it:

3.1. Grow extensively by the addition of many people to the church. When more and more people are persuaded by the Gospel, then it grows. When those who had been most hardened in their opposition to it are brought into obedience to it, then it may be said to grow mightily.

3.2. Prevail extensively. When strong corruptions are put to death, long-standing evil traditions broken, and attractive, profitable, fashionable sins abandoned, then the Gospel spreads widely and is growing in power, and in it Christ goes on *conquering and to conquer* (Rev 6:2).

Verses 21–41

1. Paul got into trouble here at Ephesus just when he was expecting to leave. Notice:

1.1. How he established his purpose of going to other places (vv. 21–22). He was a man who had vast plans for God and wanted to spread his influence as widely as possible.

1.1.1. He wanted to visit the churches of Macedonia and Achaia (v. 21). He had planted churches there, and now he was eager to visit them. He *purposed in the spirit*, either in his own spirit or by the direction of the Holy Spirit, who was his guide in all his actions. He wanted to go and see how the work of God was faring in those places.

1.1.2. He intended to go from there to Jerusalem, to visit the brothers and sisters there, and from there he intended to visit Rome, to go and *see Rome*. It was an expression people often used—that they would go and see Rome, would look around them there; Paul, on the other hand, intended to see the Christians there. The good people at Rome were the glory of the city that he longed to visit.

1.1.3. He sent Timothy and Erastus into Macedonia to give the churches there notice of the visit he intended to pay them, while he, for the present, stayed in Asia.

1.2. How he was supported in his purpose and obliged to pursue it by the troubles that he finally met with at Ephesus. It was strange that things had been quiet there for him for so long, but it seems he had met with trouble there that was not recorded in this story. In his letter he speaks of his having *fought with beasts at Ephesus* (1Co 15:32). He also speaks about the trouble that came on them in Asia, near Ephesus, when he *despaired of life* (2Co 1:8–9).

2. However, in the trouble that is related here, he was more frightened than hurt. In general, *there arose no small stir* (a great disturbance) *about that way* (v. 23). Let us consider its details. Here is:

2.1. A serious complaint made against Paul for drawing people away from the worship of Diana (Artemis), so spoiling the trade of the silversmiths who worked for Diana's temple.

2.1.1. The one bringing the complaint was Demetrius, a silversmith. The most profitable part of his work was *making silver shrines for Diana* (v. 24). Some think these were medals stamped with the effigies of Diana; others think they were representations of the temple, including a picture of Diana in miniature, all in silver. Those who came from far away to perform their devotions at the temple of Ephesus took these little temples or shrines home with them. Notice how skilled workers, including skilled workers higher than the rank of silversmiths, take advantage of people's superstitions.

2.1.2. The people he appealed to were not the magistrates, but the mob; he called the *craftsmen* together, *with the workmen of like occupation*, and he tried to incite them against Paul.

2.1.3. His complaint and representation are described in detail.

2.1.3.1. He established it as a principle that the making of silver shrines for the worshipers of Diana must be kept up: *You know that by this craft we have our wealth* (v. 25). It is natural for people to be jealous for whatever they gain their wealth by, and many have set themselves against the Gospel of Christ, because it calls people away from that work which is unlawful, however much wealth is gained by them.

2.1.3.2. He accused Paul of dissuading people from worshiping idols. He had asserted, *Those are no gods which are made with hands* (v. 26). Could any truth be more plain and self-evident than this: *The workman made it, therefore it is not God* (Hos 8:6)? By the people of Ephesus, however, this must be looked on as a heretical and atheist idea, and Paul as a criminal for maintaining it. The consequence of this idea was that not only at Ephesus, but almost throughout the whole of Asia, Paul had *persuaded and turned away much people* from the worship of Diana. There are those who will argue stubbornly for what is most grossly absurd and unreasonable if it has merely human laws and worldly interests on its side.

2.1.3.3. He reminded them of the danger their trade was in of going into decline. "If this teaching gains in reputation, we are all ruined, and may even have to shut up shop; *this our craft will be set at nought.*"

2.1.3.4. He claimed a great zeal for Diana: *Not only this our craft is in danger.* All his concern was that *the temple of the great goddess Diana* might *be despised, and her magnificence destroyed*; he would not see the diminishing of the honor of that goddess *whom all Asia and the world worship.* See what the worship of Diana had to plead for itself. It had magnificence on its side; the splendor of the temple was what charmed them. It had numbers on its side: *All Asia and the world worshiped* it; it must surely, therefore, be the right way of worship, whatever Paul might say to the contrary.

2.2. The popular reception of this complaint. The craftsmen showed:

2.2.1. Great displeasure against the Gospel and its preachers: *They were full of wrath* (v. 28). The craftsmen went wild with anger when they were told that their trade and their idol were both in danger.

2.2.2. Great jealousy for the honor of their goddess: "*They cried out, Great is Diana of the Ephesians.* Whatever Paul may say to prove that things made with human hands are not gods, we will maintain that *Great is Diana of the Ephesians.* We must and will stand up for the religion of our country." Much more should the servants of the true God do so.

2.2.3. A great disturbance among themselves (v. 29): *The whole city was full of confusion* — the common and natural effect of excessive zeal for a false religion.

2.3. What went on in the mob under the power of these strong feelings.

2.3.1. They laid hands on some of Paul's companions and rushed them off to the theater (v. 29). They seized

Gaius and Aristarchus. Gaius was of Derbe, and both he and *Aristarchus* are referred to in 20:4; *Aristarchus* is also spoken of in Col 4:10. They had come with Paul *from Macedonia*, and their only crime was that they were Paul's companions.

2.3.2. When Paul — who had escaped being seized — saw that his friends were in distress for his sake, he *would have entered in unto the people* (wanted to appear before the crowd). It was evidence that he had a generous spirit and loved his neighbor as himself.

2.3.3. Paul was dissuaded from doing so by the kindness of his friends.

2.3.3.1. *The disciples suffered him not* (would not allow him), because it better befitted him to offer to appear than it would have befitted them to allow it.

2.3.3.2. Other friends of his intervened to prevent him from throwing himself into the mouth of danger in this way (v. 31). They were *certain of the chief of Asia.* We are not told whether they were converts to the Christian faith or whether they were only people who wished Paul well because he was an honest, good man; we know only that they were Paul's friends. It is very good natured to take more care of the lives and comforts of good people than they do of themselves. Paul's friends overruled him so that he would obey the law of self-preservation, and so teaching us to keep out of the way of danger as long as we can without leaving the path of duty. We may be called to lay down our lives, but not to throw them away.

2.3.4. The mob was in complete confusion (v. 32): *Some cried one thing, and some another*, and *the assembly was confused.* The truth was that *the greater part knew not wherefore they had come together.* On such occasions, most of the people come only to see what is going on: they follow the cry, follow the crowd, which grows like a snowball, and where there are many, there will be more.

2.3.5. The Jews would have involved themselves in this disturbance, but now at Ephesus they did not have enough influence to raise the mob, and yet when it was raised, they had enough hatred to join in with it: *They drew Alexander out of the multitude* (19:33), calling on him to speak out on behalf of the Jews against Paul and his companions: "You have heard what Demetrius and the silversmiths have to say against these men, as enemies of their religion; now let us tell you what we have to say against this Paul as an enemy of our religion." The Jews thought they had to do this to defend themselves, and so what he intended to say is called his apologizing — *ethelen apologeisthai*, "he wished to apologize," that is, *make his defense* — to the people, not for himself in particular, but for the Jews in general. Now the Jews wanted these Greeks to know that they were as much Paul's enemies as the worshipers of Diana were. *Alexander beckoned with the hand*, asking to be heard against Paul, because it would have been strange if a persecution had been carried on against the Christians and Jews were not involved in it somewhere along the line; if they could not begin the trouble, they would help move it along. Some think this Alexander had been a Christian but had turned away to Judaism, and so was chosen as the best person to accuse Paul, and that he was that *Alexander the coppersmith* who caused Paul so much trouble (2Ti 4:14) and whom he had *delivered unto Satan* (1Ti 1:20).

2.3.6. This led the prosecutors to drop the prosecution of Paul's friends and to turn it into acclamations in honor of their goddess (v. 34): *When they knew that he was a Jew* and, as such, an enemy of the worship of Diana, they were determined not to listen to him, and so they set the mob shouting, "*Great is Diana of the Ephesians*;

whoever runs down her name, whether Jew or Christian, we are determined to praise her." They shouted this for about *two hours*, which was thought a sufficient denial of Paul's message *that those are not gods which are made with hands.* The most sacred truths are often vilified with nothing other than noise, clamor, and popular fury.

2.4. The suppressing and dispersing of these rioters by the wisdom and vigilance of *the town clerk.* Eventually, with great difficulty, he stilled the noise, so as to make himself heard, and then he gave a speech that quieted them.

2.4.1. He indulged them by acknowledging that Diana was the celebrated goddess of the Ephesians (v. 35). They had no need to be so loud and strenuous in asserting a truth that no one denied. "Everyone *knows that the city of the Ephesians is a worshiper of the great goddess Diana.*" The temple of Diana at Ephesus was a very rich and lavish structure, but the image of Diana in the temple was held in greater respect than the temple, because the image was thought to sanctify the temple; and the Ephesians claimed that that image had *fallen down from Jupiter* and was therefore no god made with human hands. Because this idol of Diana had been set up so many years ago that no one could remember when, and no one knew who had made it, the leaders made people believe it had fallen from heaven, from Jupiter. "Now *these things*," said the town clerk very seriously, "*cannot be spoken against;* they have gained such a universal reputation that you need not fear contradiction."

2.4.2. He warned them against all violent and disorderly proceedings, which their religion did not need: *You ought to be quiet, and to do nothing rashly* (v. 36). This is a very good rule that should be observed at all times, both in private and in public affairs: not to be hasty and precipitate in our actions, but to be calm and composed, always keeping reason on the throne and passions restrained. *We ought to be quiet and to do nothing rashly,* do nothing in haste, which we may repent of at leisure.

2.4.3. He wiped away the odium that had covered Paul and his associates (v. 37): "*You have brought hither these men.* What can you prove against them? They have not robbed churches. They have done no violence to Diana's temple or its treasures; nor are they *blasphemers of your goddess.* Why should you prosecute with all this violence those who do not denounce you bitterly? Since they are calm, why should you be so angry?" It was the idol in the heart that the apostles directed all their force against, and they did so by reason and argument; if only they could demolish that, the idol in the temple would fall by itself. Those who preach against idolatrous churches have truth on their side, but let them instruct with humility those who oppose them, not rebuke them with anger and foul language, because God's truth does not need immoderate human anger.

2.4.4. He told them to pursue the regular channels of the law. It is a great mercy to live in a country where provision is made for the keeping of the peace and the administration of public justice, and in this nation we are as fortunate in this respect as any people.

2.4.4.1. If the complaint concerned a matter of private wrong, let them turn to the judges and law courts. If Demetrius and his fellow silversmiths considered themselves aggrieved, let them bring their action before the court, and the case would be tried fairly, and justice would be done. *The law is open, and there are deputies,* whose business it is to listen to both sides, and all parties must accept their determination and not be their own judges or appeal to the people.

2.4.4.2. If the complaint was of a public grievance, it must be redressed not by a confused riot but by a formal meeting (v. 39): "*If you inquire anything concerning other matters, it shall be determined in a lawful assembly* called together in a regular way by those in authority." Private people should not interfere in public matters; we have enough to do to take care of our own business.

2.4.5. He made them aware of the danger they had fallen into by this riot (v. 40): "It will be good if we are not *called in question for this day's uproar,* because *there is no cause whereby we may give an account of this concourse.* Let the matter go no further, as it has gone too far already." Most people stand in awe of human judgment more than they do of the judgment of God. How good would it be if we would still the agitation of our disorderly appetites and passions by considering the account we must soon give to the Judge of heaven and earth for all such disorders! We must be eager to control ourselves *as those that must give account* (Heb 13:17).

2.4.6. When he had shown them the absurdity of their riotous gathering, he advised them to disperse as quickly as they could (v. 41): he *dismissed the assembly.* See here how the overruling providence of God preserves the public peace by an inexplicable power over human spirits. This is how the world is kept in some order, and people are restrained from being like the fish of the sea, where the greater devour the smaller. Considering what an uncontrollable, untamable wild beast the mob is when it is aroused, we have good reason to acknowledge God's goodness for providing that we are not always under its tyranny. Notice how many ways God has of protecting his people. Perhaps this town clerk was no friend at all of Paul, yet his human wisdom was made to serve God's purpose.

CHAPTER 20

We have here: 1. Paul's travels through Macedonia, Greece, and Asia, and his eventual arrival at Troas (vv. 1–6). 2. A detailed account of his spending a Lord's Day in Troas and his raising Eutychus from the dead there (vv. 7–12). 3. His journey to visit the churches he had planted, after which he intended to go to Jerusalem (vv. 13–16). 4. The farewell sermon at Ephesus (vv. 17–35). 5. The very sad parting of him and them (vv. 36–38).

Verses 1–6

If everything in Paul's travels that was memorable and worthy of being written down in letters of gold had been recorded, *the world would not contain the books that would have been written* (Jn 21:25). We are therefore given only some general hints of what took place, which should make them more precious. Here is:

1. Paul's departure from Ephesus. He had stayed there longer than anywhere else. Now it was time to think of moving on, for he must *preach in other cities also* (Mk 1:38). However, after this we never find him breaking fresh ground again, because at the end of the next chapter we find him taken prisoner, and he continued to be so at the end of this book. Paul left Ephesus soon after the uproar had come to an end (v. 1).

1.1. His move might somewhat appease the rage of his adversaries and gain mercy for the Christians there. Some think that before he left Ephesus he wrote the first epistle to the Corinthians, and that his fighting with beasts at Ephesus, which he mentions in that letter (1Co 15:32), was a figurative description of this uproar.

1.2. He did not leave them abruptly, but took leave of them in an orderly manner: *He called unto him the disciples* and "embraced them, taking leave of them with the kiss of love," according to the Aramaic paraphrase. Loving friends do not realize how much they love one another until they come to part, and then it emerges how close they were to one another's hearts.

2. His visit to the churches in Greece, which he had planted and which seem to have been very close to his heart. He went first *to Macedonia* (v. 1), as he planned before the riot (19:21); there he visited the churches of Philippi and Thessalonica and *gave them much exhortation* (v. 2). He had many words of encouragement to say to them and was not stingy with his time. He stayed *three months in Greece* (vv. 2–3), that is, in Achaia, because he also decided to go to Corinth and thereabouts (19:21).

3. The changing of his plans. *Paul was about to sail into Syria, to Antioch.* He changed his mind and decided *to return to Macedonia* by the same way he had come, because the Jews, expecting him to go to Antioch, had organized a plot against him to kill him.

4. His companions on his travels when he went to Asia; they are named here (v. 4). *Sopater of Berea* was probably the same person as *Sosipater*, who is mentioned in Ro 16:21. Timothy is counted among them. When Paul left Ephesus (v. 1), he had left Timothy there, but Timothy soon followed him and accompanied him along with the others named here. Now one would have thought that this was not good management, to have all these experienced people accompanying Paul, but matters were organized in this way so that they could:

4.1. Help him teach people who were woken up and startled by his preaching. Wherever Paul went, the waters were stirred, and then many hands were needed to help the disabled come in (Jn 5:6–7).

4.2. Be trained up and equipped by him for future service.

5. His coming to Troas for a general meeting of his friends.

5.1. They went ahead and waited for him at Troas (v. 5). We should not think it hard to stay awhile with good company on a journey.

5.2. Paul made his way there as best he could, and Luke was now with him, for Luke says, *We sailed from Philippi* (v. 6), and the first time we found Luke in Paul's company was here at Troas (16:11). *The days of unleavened bread* are mentioned only to describe the time. He *came to them to Troas* by sea *in five days*, and then he stayed there only *seven days*. Those who go around doing good (10:38) will find they cannot avoid losing a great deal of time traveling back and forth, but it will not be charged against their account as lost time. Paul thought it worthwhile to give five days to go to Troas, even though it was only for an opportunity to stay there seven days.

Verses 7–12

Here is an account of what took place at Troas on the last of the seven days that Paul stayed there.

1. There was a solemn religious assembly of the Christians who were there.

1.1. *The disciples came together* (v. 7). Although they read, meditated, prayed, and sang psalms separately, so keeping up their fellowship with God, that was not enough; they must also gather together to worship God, so maintaining their fellowship with one another. There should be regular times for disciples of Christ to come together; even though they cannot all do so in one place, as many as can should do so.

1.2. They *came together upon the first day of the week*, which they called *the Lord's day* (Rev 1:10). This is said here to be the day when it was their practice to meet together in all the churches. The first day of the week is to be religiously observed by all the disciples of Christ, and it is a sign between Christ and them.

1.3. *They were gathered together in an upper chamber* (v. 8); they had no large, stately chapel, but met in a private house, in an attic. Because they were few and did not need a large meeting place, they were also poor and could not build one, but they came together in that unimposing and inconvenient place. We will not be excused for absenting ourselves from religious gatherings because the meeting place is not as decent or convenient as we would like.

1.4. They *came together to break bread*, that is, to celebrate the ceremony of the Lord's Supper. In the breaking of the bread, there is not only a commemoration of the breaking of Christ's body *for* us as a sacrifice for our sins, but also a sign of the breaking of Christ's body *to* us as food and a feast for our souls. It was the custom of many churches to share the Lord's Supper every Lord's Day, together, in a formal meeting, to show that the two are in agreement, expressing the same faith and worship.

2. In this meeting Paul preached them a sermon, a long sermon, a farewell sermon (v. 7).

2.1. He *preached to them*. The preaching of the Gospel should accompany the sacraments.

2.2. It was a farewell sermon, he being *ready to depart on the morrow.* When he had gone, they would be able to have the same Gospel preached, but not as he preached it, and so they must make the best possible use of him that they could while they still had him with them.

2.3. It was a very long sermon: he *continued his speech until midnight*, because he had a great deal to say and did not know whether he would ever have another opportunity to preach to them. There may be occasions for ministers to preach not only in *season but* also *out of season* (2Ti 4:2). We know some people who would have rebuked Paul for being a long-winded preacher who exhausted his listeners, but they were willing to listen. He saw that they were, and so he continued speaking. We wish we had an outline of this long sermon, but we may imagine it was substantially the same as what he wrote in his letters. Because the meeting went on until midnight, candles were lit, *many lights* (v. 8), so that the censures of their enemies, who said they met at night for works of darkness, might be prevented.

3. *A young man* in the congregation, who fell asleep during the sermon, was killed by a fall *out of the window, but raised to life again.* His name, *Eutychus*, means "one who had good fortune," and he lived up to his name. Notice:

3.1. The weakness with which he was overtaken. He presumptuously *sat in the window*, perhaps one without glass, and so put himself in danger, whereas if he had been content to sit on the floor, he would have been safe. He slept; in fact, he *fell into a deep sleep when Paul was preaching*, which was a sign he was not giving proper attention to the things that Paul spoke of. The particular notice taken of his sleeping makes us willing to hope none of the others slept, even though it was after supper and time for bed.

3.2. The disaster that then seized him: *He fell down from the third loft* (story), *and was taken up dead.* Some think that the hand of Satan was in it, and that he intended it to disturb this assembly and rebuke Paul. Others think that God intended it as a warning to all people to make sure they do not sleep when they are listening to the word preached. We must look on such inattention as a bad sign of our little respect for the word of God. We must do what we can to prevent our being sleepy, having our hearts so moved by the word we hear that sleep may be driven far away.

3.3. The miraculous mercy shown him in his recovery *to life again* (v. 10). It turned out to be an occasion of great confirmation to Paul's preaching.

3.3.1. *Paul fell on the dead body, and embraced* (put his arms around) the boy, so expressing great compassion and affectionate concern for him. Such kindhearted spirits as Paul's are very much affected by sad events of this kind, and are far from judging and censuring those who fall under them. It was a sign representing the descent of divine power on the dead body to put life into it again, which at the same time Paul inwardly, fervently, and in faith prayed for.

3.3.2. He assured them that Eutychus had returned to life. This bad accident had caused various forms of speculation in the congregation, but Paul put an end to them all: *Trouble not yourselves, for his life is in him.*

3.3.3. Paul returned to his work immediately after this interruption (v. 11): *He came up again* to the meeting, they *broke bread* together in a love-feast, and *they talked a long while, even till break of day.* Paul did not now continue with his unbroken speech, as before, but he and his friends fell into a free conversation. They did not know when they would have Paul with them again, and so they made the best use they could of him while he was with them, and considered a night's sleep well lost for that purpose.

3.3.4. Before they parted, *they brought the young man alive* into the congregation, and *they were not a little comforted* (v. 12). It was a matter of great joy among them, not only to the relatives of the young man but to the whole group.

Verses 13–16

Paul was moving quickly toward Jerusalem. He had called at Troas, and now he made a kind of journey near the coast, no doubt trying to make every place he came to better because of his visit.

1. He sent his companions by sea to Assos, but he himself was *minded to go afoot* (had decided to go on foot) (v. 13). He would go on foot to Assos, and if the way across land that Paul took was the shorter way, it is remarked on by the ancients as a rough way. Paul would take that way so that he could:

1.1. Call on his friends on the way. Or:

1.2. Be alone and have greater freedom to speak with God and his own heart in solitude. Or:

1.3. Get used to hardship and not seem to indulge his ease. We should all get ourselves used to self-denial.

2. At Assos he went on board with his friends. There they *took him in.*

3. He made his way as best he could to Jerusalem. His ship passed by *Chios* (v. 15), touched *Samos*, stayed awhile at *Trogyllium*, the port next to Samos, *and the next day* came *to Miletus*, the port that lay next to Ephesus, because he had resolved not to go to Ephesus at this time (v. 16), *for he hasted* (was in a hurry), *if it were possible for him, to be at Jerusalem on the day of pentecost.* He had been at Jerusalem about four or five years before (18:21–22), and now he was going there again to renew his expressions of respect to that church. He aimed to be there by the festival of Pentecost because it was a time of meeting, and the festival of Pentecost had been made

famous among the Christians especially by the outpouring of the Spirit. Businesspeople must equip themselves, and they will help themselves do so if they set times for their various tasks—in submission to Providence—and seek to keep them, not allowing themselves to be distracted from the task at hand. It is a pleasure to us to be with our friends; it diverts us—nothing occupies us more pleasantly—but we must not be diverted from our work by it. When Paul had a call to go to Jerusalem, he would not fritter away his time in Asia, even though he had more and kinder friends there.

Verses 17–35

When Paul reached Miletus, he went ashore and stayed there long enough to send for the elders of Ephesus to come to him there; if he had gone to Ephesus, he could never have gotten away from them. Paul sent for them so that he could instruct and encourage them to continue in the work they had gotten involved in. It was a very moving and practical speech with which Paul took leave of these elders here, and it contained much of the excellent spirit of this good man.

1. He appealed to them about both the way he had lived and the message he had preached all the time he had been in and around Ephesus (v. 18): *You know after what manner I have been with you.* They all knew him to be a man of a serious, gracious, and heavenly spirit, that he was not someone who intended to draw attention to himself. He could not have been carried along with so much evenness and faithfulness in his service and suffering except by the power of divine grace. His whole attitude and the tendency of both his preaching and his conduct were such as clearly proved that God was truly with him. He also used this reference to his own behavior as an instruction to them to follow his example: *"You know after what manner I have been with you;* you are to act similarly toward those who are committed to your charge when I have gone."

1.1. His spirit and conduct had been excellent and exemplary.

1.1.1. He had behaved well all along, *from the very first day that he came into Asia.* From the day they met him it was clear that he was a man who aimed not only to do well but also to do good. He was a man who was consistent within himself, who had integrity. He did not change with the wind or the weather, but was as uniform as a die, which always falls on a square side, no matter which way you throw it.

1.1.2. He had made it his business to serve the Lord. He never served himself or made himself a servant of people. He did not "blow hot and cold"—become zealous one week and then apathetic the next.

1.1.3. He had done his work *with all humility of mind.* He never became proud. He was not aloof from people, but was able to converse as freely and familiarly with the weakest, for their good, as if he stood on the same level as they. He was willing to stoop down to perform any service.

1.1.4. He had always been very warm, affectionate, and compassionate among them; he had *served the Lord with many tears.* Paul was like his Master here, often in tears. In his preaching, what he had told them before he told them again, *even weeping* (Php 3:18). They were so close to his heart that he *wept with those that wept* (Ro 12:15), which was very endearing.

1.1.5. He had struggled with many difficulties among them. He continued his work in the face of much opposition, *many temptations*, tests of his patience and courage. These temptations came to him *by the lying in wait of the*

Jews (v. 19), who still were plotting some trouble or other against him. Those who continue to serve the Lord in the middle of troubles and perils are his faithful servants; they are not concerned with what enemies they make, as long as they can show themselves to be approved by their Master (2Ti 2:15) and make him their friend.

1.2. His preaching was also as it should be (vv. 20–21).

1.2.1. He was a clear and direct preacher: he communicated his message so as to be understood. He expressed this by saying, *I have shown you, and have taught you.* He did not entertain them with fine speculations or lose them in the clouds of lofty ideas and expressions, but showed them the clear truths of the Gospel and taught them as children are taught.

1.2.2. He was a powerful preacher, which is shown in his *testifying* to them; he preached as one who was on oath. He preached the Gospel not as a newspaper seller shouts out news on the street—it is all the same to them whether it is true or false—but as a conscientious witness gives evidence at the bar.

1.2.3. He was a helpful preacher. He sought what was *profitable unto them*, what would tend to make them wise and good, wiser and better, to reform their hearts and lives. He preached things that brought with them divine light, passion, and power to their souls. It is not enough not to preach what is harmful; we must preach what is helpful. Paul aimed to help people.

1.2.4. He was a careful preacher; he preached *publicly, and from house to house.* He was neither afraid nor ashamed to preach the Gospel publicly, nor was he reluctant to take pains privately for a few when there was need for it. Ministers should make private visits, and as they go from house to house, they should discuss the things they have taught publicly. They should also especially help people apply the truths to themselves and their own situations.

1.2.5. He was a faithful preacher. He preached everything he thought might be helpful; he kept back nothing. He did not refuse to preach whatever he thought might be helpful, even though it was unfashionable and was unacceptable to some. He did not keep back rebukes when they were necessary, for fear of offending; nor did he keep back the preaching of the cross, even though he knew it was a stumbling block to the Jews and foolishness to the Greeks (1Co 1:23).

1.2.6. He was a general preacher. He *testified both to the Jews and also to the Greeks.* Though born and brought up as a Jew and trained in their prejudice against the Gentiles, he did not therefore confine himself to the Jews and avoid the Gentiles, but preached as readily to the Gentiles as to the Jews. On the other hand, though called to be the apostle to the Gentiles and implacably hated by the Jews for that reason, he did not therefore abandon the Jews as reprobates. Ministers must preach the Gospel without favoritism, because they are ministers of Christ for the whole church.

1.2.7. He was a true Christian preacher, a Gospel preacher. He did not preach philosophical ideas, nor did he preach politics; he preached faith and repentance. On all occasions he urged:

1.2.7.1. *Repentance toward God.* He preached repentance as God's great command (17:30)—*that men should repent, and turn to God, and do works meet for repentance,* as he explains it in 26:20—and he preached it as Christ's gift given for the *remission of sins* (5:31).

1.2.7.2. *Faith toward our Lord Jesus Christ.* In repentance we must look toward God, and through faith we are

to turn toward Christ as our way to God. Our repentance toward God is not sufficient; we must also have a true faith in Christ as our Redeemer and Savior. There is no way to return to God, as penitent prodigals return to their Father, except in the strength of Jesus Christ as Mediator.

2. He declared his expectation that he would suffer on his present journey to Jerusalem (vv. 22–24).

2.1. Let them not think that he was now leaving Asia for fear of persecution. No; he was now like a hero moving quickly to where the battle would be most intense: *Now, behold, I go bound in the spirit to Jerusalem,* which may be understood as referring to either:

2.1.1. The certain foresight he had of trouble before him. He fully expected trouble, and he made it his daily business to prepare for it. Or:

2.1.2. The strong compulsion he sensed to go on this journey: "*I go bound in the spirit,* that is, firmly resolved to proceed. And not because of any mood or idea of my own; I go led by the Spirit, bound to follow him wherever he leads me."

2.2. He did not know in detail the things that would happen to him at Jerusalem. God had not thought fit to reveal those to him. It is good to be kept in the dark concerning future events, so that we may constantly trust in God and wait for him. We do not know what will happen to us, nor what a day, a night, or an hour, may bring forth (Pr 27:1; Jas 4:14), and so we must turn to God, letting him do with us as seems good in his eyes (1Sa 3:18; 2Sa 10:12; 15:26).

2.3. He did know, however, that in general a storm lay in front of him, for the prophets in every city he passed through told him, through the Holy Spirit, that *bonds and afflictions* (prison and hardship) awaited him.

2.4. He had a brave and heroic determination to continue with his work. It was a sad peal that rang in his ears in every city, that *bonds and afflictions did abide him*; yet through the grace of God he was enabled to continue with his work. Let us take it from his own mouth here (v. 24): *None of these things move me.* Paul was an example here:

2.4.1. Of holy courage and resolution. He made nothing of difficulties and oppositions: "*None of these things move me*; I take no account of them. I consider my life worth nothing." He did not take these things to heart: Christ and heaven were uppermost there. None of these things moved him.

2.4.1.1. They did not distract him from his work; he did not wander off and go back to where he came from when he saw the storm rise, but continued resolutely.

2.4.1.2. They did not deprive him of his strength and encouragement. In the middle of troubles he was like one who was unconcerned. Those who have their citizenship (Php 3:20) in heaven can look down not only on the common troubles of this earth but also on the threatening rage and malice of hell itself, saying that none of these things move them, knowing that none of these things can harm them.

2.4.2. Of a holy contempt for life: *Neither count I my life dear to myself.* Life is sweet and is naturally dear to us. *All that a man has will he give for his life* (Job 2:4). Yet it is comparatively abhorrent to the eye of faith; it is not so dear that it cannot be cheerfully parted with for Christ.

2.4.3. Of a holy desire to continue with the work of life, which should be much more our concern than to protect either its outward comforts or its encouragements. Two things this great and good man was concerned about, and if he gained them, it did not matter to him what became of life:

2.4.3.1. That he might be found faithful to the trust placed in him, that he might *finish the ministry which he had received of the Lord Jesus*, might do the work that he was sent into the world for, or, rather, that he was sent into the church for, and might not do his work incompletely. Notice:

2.4.3.1.*1*. The apostleship was a ministry both to Christ and to human souls, and those who were called to it considered the ministry — the service — of it more than its honor or power.

2.4.3.1.*2*. This ministry was *received from the Lord Jesus*. He entrusted them with it, and they received their commission from him; they did their work for him, in his name, and in his strength.

2.4.3.1.*3*. The work of this ministry was to *testify the gospel of the grace of God*. The Gospel is a proof of God's goodwill to us and a means of his good work in us; it shows him to be gracious toward us and tends to make us gracious, and that is why it is the Gospel of the grace of God. Paul did not want to live a day longer than he could be instrumental in spreading the knowledge of this Gospel.

2.4.3.2. That he might finish well. He was not concerned about when the end of his life would come, nor how, as long as he could *finish his course with joy* (v. 24).

2.4.3.2.*1*. He looked on his life as *a course*, "a race." This shows that we have both our labors and our limits appointed for us, because we were not sent into the world to be here always, but to pass through the world — in fact, to run through it, and it is soon run through.

2.4.3.2.*2*. He counted on finishing his race and spoke of that as something definite and near. Dying is the end of our race, when we come away with either honor or shame. He was full of the desire to finish well.

2.4.3.2.*3*. He thought nothing was too much to do or too hard to suffer, as long as he could finish well and with joy. We must look on it as the business of our life to provide for a joyful death, not only a safe death but a comfortable death.

3. He realized that this was the last time they would see him, and so he appealed to their consciences about his integrity.

3.1. He told them that he was now taking his final leave of them (v. 25): "*I know that you all, among whom I have lived, preaching the kingdom of God*, will never see my face again." Paul said here with assurance that these Ephesians would *see his face no more*, and we cannot think that the one who spoke so doubtfully about what he was not sure of — *not knowing the things that shall befall me there* (v. 22) — would say this with so much confidence unless he had received special authority from the Spirit to say it. He would never have said this so solemnly, *Now, behold, I know* it, if he had not known it for certain. We should often consider that those who are now preaching to us the kingdom of God will soon be taken away, and we will not see their faces anymore. Their light is with us only for a short while; we should therefore make the most of it while we have it, so that when we do not see their faces anymore on earth, we may still hope to look them in the face with joy on the great day.

3.2. He appealed to them about the faithful discharge of his ministry among them (v. 26).

3.2.1. He challenged them to prove he had been unfaithful: *I am pure from the blood of all men*, the blood of souls. "You cannot say that I have not given you a warning, and so I cannot be held responsible for anyone's blood." If a minister has been faithful, they may have the joy of being able to say, *I am pure from the blood of all men*.

3.2.2. He therefore left the blood of those who perished on their own heads, because they had been given a fair warning, which they would not accept.

3.2.3. He commanded these ministers to make sure that they took care and pains, as he had done. *I take you to record this day*. Just as sometimes heaven and earth are appealed to, so here this day would be a witness, this parting day.

3.3. He proved his own faithfulness with this: *For I have not shunned to declare unto you all the counsel of God* (v. 27).

3.3.1. He had preached to them nothing but the counsel, the will or purpose, of God, and had not added any inventions of his own; "it was pure Gospel, and nothing else." The Gospel is the will of God. It is this will of God that ministers are to declare as it is revealed, and not otherwise.

3.3.2. He had preached to them the whole will of God. Just as he had preached the pure Gospel to them, so he had also preached it to them completely.

3.3.3. He had not *shunned to* do it; he had not willfully nor intentionally avoided declaring any part of the will of God. He had not declined to preach either on the most difficult parts of the Gospel or on its clearest and easiest parts; he had not avoided preaching the doctrines that he knew would provoke the watchful enemies of Christianity or displease its careless professors. In this way he kept himself innocent of the blood of everyone.

4. He charged them as ministers to be diligent and faithful in their work.

4.1. To these elders he committed the care of the church at Ephesus, who, though doubtless so numerous that they could not all meet in one place, were still here called one flock because they not only agreed on one faith but in many instances also maintained fellowship with one another. To these elders or presbyters the apostle committed the government of this church, telling them that not he, but *the Holy Spirit, had made them overseers*. The word translated *overseers* is the origin of our word *bishops*; they were to be bishops of the flock. "You who are elders are bishops of the Holy Spirit's making." Now that they began to be fledged, they must learn to fly by themselves and act without him, because the Holy Spirit had made them overseers. The Holy Spirit in them qualified them for and enriched them with this great undertaking; the *Holy Spirit fell upon them* (19:6). The Holy Spirit also directed those who called and ordained them to this work in answer to prayer.

4.2. He commanded them to take care of the work to which they were called. High position calls for duty; if the Holy Spirit had made them *overseers of the flock*, they must be true to their trust.

4.2.1. They must keep watch over themselves in the first place; they must walk very carefully. "Many eyes are watching you, some for an example and others for a reason to quarrel, and so you should *take heed to yourselves*." Those who do not keep their own vineyard are unlikely to be skillful or faithful keepers of those of others.

4.2.2. *Take heed to the flock*. Ministers must not only keep watch over their own souls; they must also have a constant concern for the souls of those who are their responsibility: "*Take heed to all the flock*, so that none of them go astray from the fold or are seized by wild animals; make sure that none of them go missing."

4.2.3. They must feed the church of God. They must lead the sheep of Christ into green pastures (Ps 23:2). They must lay food before them, feeding them with wholesome teaching. They must see that the sheep have all the nourishment they need to bring them to maturity and prepare them for eternal life. Pastors must not only gather the church of God but also to feed it by building up those already within the fold.

4.2.4. They must *watch* (v. 31), as shepherds keep watch over their flocks by night (Lk 2:8); they must watch against everything that would harm the flock, and they must see to everything that would benefit it.

4.3. He gave them several good reasons why they should take care of the work of their ministry:

4.3.1. Let them consider their Master's interests, his concern for the flock. It *is the church which he has purchased with his own blood* (v. 28).

4.3.1.1. "It is his own; you are simply his servants to take care of it for him. It is your honor that you are employed for God, but then your carelessness and treachery are so much worse if you neglect your work, for then you wrong God. If it is the church of God, he expects you to show your love for him by feeding his sheep and lambs (Jn 21:15–17)."

4.3.1.2. He has bought it. It should be dear to us because it was dear to him—because it cost him dearly—and we cannot respond in any better way than by feeding his sheep and his lambs.

4.3.1.3. This church of God is what God has bought *with his own blood.* Calling Christ's blood God's blood proves that Christ is God. In consideration of this, therefore, *feed the church of God,* because it was purchased at such a high price. Since Christ laid down his life to buy it, will his ministers withhold anything necessary for the care of it?

4.3.2. Let them consider the danger that the flock might be attacked by its enemies (vv. 29–30). "You must keep watch on both yourselves and it." Here are reasons for both.

4.3.2.1. *Take heed to the flock,* because there are wolves who seek to devour it (v. 29): *I know this, that after my departure grievous wolves shall enter in among you.*

4.3.2.1.1. Some understand this as referring to persecutors. Because while Paul was with them, the rage of the Jews was directed mostly against him, the elders thought that when he had left the country, the persecutors would be quiet: "No," he said, *"after my departure* you will find the persecuting spirit still at work." Ministers must take extraordinary care of the flock in times of persecution.

4.3.2.1.2. It should rather be understood to refer to deceivers and false teachers. Probably Paul was thinking of those of the circumcision (Tit 1:10), who praised the ceremonial law; he called these people *grievous wolves.* While Paul was at Ephesus, they kept away because they dared not face him, but when he had gone, then they came among the Christians there.

4.3.2.2. *Take heed to yourselves,* because some shepherds will turn away and commit apostasy: *"Also of your own selves shall men arise speaking perverse things* (v. 30). They will twist some sayings of the Gospel to make them support their errors (2Pe 3:16). They will do this to *draw away disciples after them,* to make a little group for themselves." They would *draw away disciples after them;* those who were already disciples of Christ would be drawn from him to follow them. However, although there were some such deceivers in the church at Ephesus, it seems from Paul's letter to that church that they were not so much infested with false teachers as some other churches were. The peace and purity of the church at Ephesus were preserved by the blessing of God on the care and watchfulness of these elders.

4.3.3. Let them consider the great effort Paul had taken in planting this church: *"Remember that for the space of three years I ceased not to warn everyone night and day with tears"* (v. 31).

4.3.3.1. Paul, like a faithful watchman, had warned them, and through the warnings he gave people, he won them over to accept Christianity.

4.3.3.2. He warned everyone; besides the public warnings he gave in his preaching, he also applied himself to particular individuals when he saw that he had something helpful to say to their life and situation.

4.3.3.3. He warned constantly; he *warned night and day;* his time was filled with his work.

4.3.3.4. He was indefatigable in it; he *ceased not* to warn. He continued to warn those who were righteous not to turn away from their righteousness, as he had warned them when they were evil to turn from their wickedness (Eze 3:18–21).

4.3.3.5. He spoke to them about their souls with much affection and concern: he *warned them with tears.* He had served them, as he had served the Lord, *with many tears.* He had given himself completely to them; why then should they not give themselves as completely as he had, now that the baton was being passed on to them?

5. He commended them to divine direction and influence (v. 32): *"And now, brethren, I commend you to God."* Paul told them to look to God with the eye of faith and begged God to look down on them with his eye of favor.

5.1. Notice here to whom he commended them.

5.1.1. He commended them to God; that is, he begged God to provide for them, and he encouraged them to cast all their cares on him (1Pe 5:7): "Whatever you need, go to God. Let this be your comfort, that you have a God to go to, a God who is all-sufficient." Although we may be separated from our family and friends, God is still near us (1Pe 4:19).

5.1.2. He commended them *to the word of his grace,* which some understand to mean Christ: he is *the word* (Jn 1:1). He is called here *the word of God's grace* because *from his fulness we receive grace for grace* (Jn 1:16). Paul commended them not only to God and his providence but also to Christ and his grace. It comes to much the same thing if we understand *the word of his grace* to refer to the Gospel of Christ. "You will find much relief by acting with faith on the providence of God, but much more by acting with faith on the promises of the Gospel." He commended them to the word of God's grace not only as the foundation of their hope and the fountain of their joy but also as the rule of their walking: "*I commend you to God* as your Master, *and to the word of his grace.* Observe the commands of the word, and then live on its promises."

5.2. Notice here what he commended them to the word of God's grace for. They had received the Gospel of the grace of God and were entrusted to preach it. Now he commended them to that Gospel:

5.2.1. For their edification: *"It is able to build you up."* Although you have already been supplied with good gifts, there is something in the Gospel that you need to be better acquainted with and more affected by." Ministers must aim at building up themselves as well as others. The most advanced Christians, as long as they are in this world, still need to grow.

5.2.2. For their glorification: *It is able to give you an inheritance among all those who are sanctified.* The word of God's grace gives this inheritance not only by giving the knowledge of it but also by giving the promise of it, the promise of a God *that cannot lie* (Tit 1:2). And by the word the Spirit of grace is given (10:44) as the seal of the promise.

5.2.2.1. Heaven is an inheritance that gives all the heirs a right that cannot be annulled.

5.2.2.2. This inheritance is secured to all those, and only those, who are sanctified, because just as those who are unsanctified cannot be welcome guests to the holy God, so heaven would really not be heaven to them; but *to all that are sanctified*, all who are born again, it is as guaranteed as almighty power and eternal truth can make it. We cannot expect to be among the glorified in the future unless we are among the sanctified here.

6. He commended himself to them as an example of being indifferent to the things of this world. He had commended them to God for spiritual blessings, which are the best blessings, but what would they do for food for their families? "As to these," Paul said, "do as I did."

6.1. He never aimed at worldly wealth (v. 33): *I have coveted no man's silver, or gold, or apparel* (clothing). Many in Ephesus were rich and looked fine.

6.1.1. Paul was not ambitious to live like them. We may take it in this sense: "I never longed to have as much silver and gold at my disposal as I see others have. I neither condemn them nor envy them. I can live comfortably and usefully without living such a fine life." He knew how to be in need, *how to be abased* (Php 4:2).

6.1.2. He was not greedy to receive silver, gold, or fine clothing from them; far from always craving such things, he did not even long for them. "Whose kindness have I coveted or asked for? Or whom have I been a burden to?"

6.2. He had worked hard for his living, so as to earn it (v. 34): *"Yea, you yourselves know that these hands of mine have ministered to my necessities, and to those that were with me."*

6.2.1. Paul was sometimes in need, lacking even the ordinary supports of life. What an unthinking, unkind, and ungrateful world this is, when it could let such a man as Paul be poor!

6.2.2. He wanted nothing more than to have his basic needs supplied.

6.2.3. When he was to earn his living, he did it by undertaking manual work. Paul had a mind and a tongue that he could have earned money from, but "it was these hands," he said, "that ministered to my necessities." Paul reminded these elders — and others through them — of this so that they would not think it strange if they were neglected. The less encouragement they had from other people, the more they would receive from God.

6.2.4. He worked not only for himself but also for the support of those who were with him. This was really hard. It would have been better for them to have worked for him. But it was so; those who are willing to take the working oar will find those around them willing for them to take it up.

6.3. Even when he worked to supply his own necessities, he still spared something from what he earned to help and relieve others, as he here obliged them to do (v. 35): *"I have shown you all things, that so labouring you ought to support the weak."* Some understand this as referring to supporting the faith of weak believers by removing their prejudices against Christianity; however, I understand it as referring to the elders' helping to support the sick, the poor, and those who could not work, because this agrees with Paul's appeal elsewhere: *Let him labour, working with his hands, that he may have to give to him that needeth* (Eph 4:28). We must work at an honest job not only to live but also to give. This might seem a hard saying, and so Paul backed it up with a saying of our Master's. It is an excellent saying, containing

something of a paradox: *It is more blessed to give than to receive.* It is more blessed to give to others than to receive from others, not only more blessed to be rich, and so be on the giving end, than to be poor, and so on the receiving end — everyone acknowledges this — but also more blessed to do good with what we have, whether it is much or little, than to increase it and make it more. The attitude of the children of this world is contrary to this; they are afraid of giving. They live in hope of getting. With them, making a clear gain is the most blessed thing possible, but Christ says, *It is more blessed to give than to receive.* It makes us more like God, who gives to everyone and receives from no one, and more like the Lord Jesus, *who went about doing good* (10:38). It is more blessed to make an effort than to receive pay for it. It is more pleasant to do good to the grateful, but it is more honorable to do good to the ungrateful, because then we have God as our paymaster.

Verses 36–38

After the parting sermon that Paul preached to the elders of Ephesus, we have here the parting prayer and tears.

1. They parted with prayer (v. 36): *And, when he had thus spoken, he kneeled down, and prayed with them all.*

1.1. It was a joint prayer. He prayed not only for them but also with them, *prayed with them all.* Public prayers are in no way intended to replace our own private prayers, but to inspire and encourage them.

1.2. It was a humble, reverent prayer. This was expressed by the position they assumed: *He kneeled down, and prayed with them,* signifying both adoration and petition, and especially asking for the forgiveness of sin.

1.3. It was a prayer after a sermon. He had committed the care of the church at Ephesus to those elders, and now he prayed that God would enable them faithfully to discharge this great trust that had been given them. He prayed for the flock *that the great Shepherd of the sheep* (Heb 13:20) would take care of them all and keep them from being attacked by savage wolves. In this way he taught these ministers to pray for those they preached to.

1.4. It was a parting prayer. When friends part, it is good for them to part with prayer, so that by praying together when they part, they may be enabled to pray more feelingly for one another when they are separated. Paul followed the example of Christ here, who, when he took leave of his disciples after preaching to them, prayed with them all (Jn 17:1).

2. They parted with tears and most affectionate embraces (vv. 37–38).

2.1. *They all wept sorely.* The one who was so often tearful while he was with them (vv. 19, 31) no doubt shed many tears where they parted. However, notice is also taken of their tears: *They all wept sorely;* there was not a dry eye among them. These were tears of love and mutual fondness.

2.2. *They fell upon Paul's neck* (they embraced him), *and kissed him.* Those who are most loving are usually also most loved. Paul, who was a most affectionate friend himself, had friends who were very affectionate to him.

2.3. What cut them to the heart so much was *that word which Paul spoke, that* he was certain *they would see his face no more* (v. 38). When they were told that they would never see him again in this world, that it was a final farewell they were now giving and taking, this made it a great mourning. When our friends are separated from us by death, this is the consideration that we raise up in our mourning, that we will never see their faces again; yet we do not complain about this as those who have no hope (1Th 4:13). Although we will not see their faces again in this world, we trust we will see them again in a better world, and to be there forever with them and the Lord.

3. The elders *accompanied him unto the ship,* so that they could enjoy a little more of his company and conversation, delaying their parting as long as possible, as those who are reluctant to part say their farewells often. It was a comfort to both sides, however, that the presence of Christ both went with him and remained with them.

CHAPTER 21

Now we go with Paul to Jerusalem, and there into lasting chains. It is a great pity that such a worker would be set aside; yet this is how it is, and we must not only accept, but also believe, that Paul in prison was as truly glorifying God as Paul in the pulpit. We have here: 1. A journal of Paul's voyage from Ephesus to Caesarea (vv. 1–7). 2. The struggles he had with his friends at Caesarea, who strongly opposed his going to Jerusalem (vv. 8–14). 3. Paul's journey from Caesarea to Jerusalem (vv. 15–17). 4. His compliance with the urging of the believers there to go and purify himself with an offering in the temple, so that it would be clear that he was not an enemy of the Mosaic rituals and ceremonies, as he was reported to have been (vv. 18–26). 5. The turning of this very thing against him by the Jews (vv. 27–30). 6. His narrow escape from being torn to pieces by the rabble, and the taking of him into custody by the commander, who allowed him to speak up for himself to the people (vv. 31–40).

Verses 1–7

We may notice here:

1. How difficult it was for Paul to get clear of Ephesus, as suggested by the first words of the chapter, *after we had gotten* (torn ourselves away) *from them.* Paul was reluctant to leave them, and they were reluctant to part with him; it had to be so.

2. What a successful voyage they then had. *They came with a straight course to Cos, the next day to Rhodes,* and *thence to Patara,* a famous port, the chief city of Lycia (v. 1); here they very fortunately *found a ship sailing over into Phenicia,* the very course they were steering (v. 2). Providence must be acknowledged when things happen so opportunely. This ship that they took was bound for Phoenicia, that is, Tyre, and they *went on board, and set sail.* On this voyage *they discovered Cyprus,* the island that Barnabas came from and that he took care of, which Paul therefore did not visit; rather, *we left it on the left hand* (v. 3), *sailed* on the coast of *Syria, and* eventually landed at *Tyre, for there the ship was to unlade her burden* (unload its cargo).

3. The stop that Paul made at Tyre.

3.1. *At Tyre he found disciples.* Wherever Paul went, he asked what disciples were there and associated with them, because birds of a feather know how to conduct themselves with one another. When Christ was on earth, although he sometimes went into the region of Tyre, he never went there to preach the Gospel. However, after the enlarging of the Gospel commission, Christ was preached at Tyre and had disciples there.

3.2. Paul, *finding* those *disciples at Tyre, tarried there seven days.* He stayed seven days at Troas (20:6), and that many days at Tyre, in order to be sure to spend one Lord's Day with them.

3.3. The disciples at Tyre were endowed with such gifts that by the Spirit they could foretell the troubles Paul would face at Jerusalem, for *the Holy Spirit witnessed it in every city* (20:23). God saw fit to have these troubles prophesied of often in advance, so that people's faith, instead of being offended, would be strengthened. Foreseeing his troubles, out of love for him, these disciples begged him *that he would not go up to Jerusalem,* because they hoped the decree was conditional. *If* he went up, they thought, he would face trouble there. They therefore said to him, *by the Spirit, that he should not go up.* It was no fault in them at all to think so, but it was their mistake, because his trial would be for the glory of God and the furtherance of the Gospel, and he knew it.

3.4. Although the disciples of Tyre were not Paul's converts, they still showed great respect for him. Although they had known him for only seven days, they all came together, *with their wives and children,* to solemnly take their leave of him. We should pay respect not only to our own ministers but also, as there is need, to all the faithful ministers of Christ. It is good to train children to respect good people and good ministers. Gracious notice was no doubt taken of the children of the disciples at Tyre, who honored an apostle, just as Christ accepted the hosannas of the little children (Mt 21:15). We should use well the opportunities that present themselves to us, making the most we can of them for the good of our souls. *They brought Paul on his way* in order to have as much of his company and prayers as possible.

3.5. They parted with prayer, as Paul and the Ephesian elders had done (20:36). *We kneeled down on the shore and prayed.* Just as he was often in prayer, so he was also mighty in prayer. Those who are going to sea should commit themselves to God in prayer, putting themselves under his protection, as those who, even when they leave firm ground, hope to find firm footing for their faith in the providence of God. They knelt down on the shore, even though it was probably stony or dirty, and there they prayed. Where he lifted up his prayer, he bowed his knees. Mr. George Herbert says, "Kneeling never spoiled silk stockings."

3.6. They parted at last (v. 6): *When we had taken our leave one of another, we took* (went aboard the) *ship,* and *they returned home again.* Paul left his blessing behind him with those who went to their homes, and those who stayed sent their prayers after those who went to sea.

4. Their arrival at Ptolemais (v. 7): *We came to Ptolemais.* Paul asked to be allowed to go ashore there *to salute the brethren.* He would not pass by them without paying his respects to them, and he *abode with them one day;* better a short visit than none at all.

Verses 8–14

We have here Paul and his company arriving eventually at Caesarea, because it was the place where the Gospel was first preached to the Gentiles and where *the Holy Spirit fell upon them* (10:1, 44). Notice:

1. Who received Paul and his company at Caesarea. He rarely needed to go to an inn; wherever he went, some friend or other took him in and made him welcome. "We who belonged to Paul's group went where he went, and we came to Caesarea." Those who travel together through this world will separate at death, and then it will be clear who belongs to Paul's group and who does not.

1.1. They were received by Philip the evangelist. We left Philip at Caesarea many years before, after he had baptized the eunuch (8:40), and now we find him there again. He was originally a deacon (6:5). He was now, and had long been, an evangelist. He had a house in Caesarea, and he made Paul and his company very welcome to it: *We entered into the house of Philip the evangelist, and we abode with him.*

1.2. This Philip *had four virgin daughters, who did prophesy* (v. 9). They prophesied about Paul's troubles at Jerusalem, or perhaps they prophesied for his comfort and encouragement.

2. A clear and full prediction of the sufferings of Paul by a noted prophet (vv. 10–11).

2.1. Paul and his friends stayed many days in Caesarea. We do not know why Paul wanted to stay there so long, but we are sure he did not stay either there or anywhere else to be lazy.

2.2. *Agabus the prophet came to Caesarea from Judea*; this was the one about whom we read before, who came *from Jerusalem to Antioch* to foretell a general famine (11:27–28). Notice how God distributes his gifts widely. The word of wisdom and knowledge, as well as the gifts of healing, was given to Paul by the Spirit. The gift of prophecy—the foretelling of things to come—was given to Agabus and to Philip's daughters by the same Spirit. The foretelling of things to come, the most renowned gift of the Spirit under the Old Testament, was completely surpassed by other gifts in the New Testament. It seems as if Agabus deliberately came to Caesarea to meet Paul with this prophetic news.

2.3. He foretold Paul's bonds at Jerusalem:

2.3.1. By a sign, as the prophets in former times did. *Agabus took Paul's girdle,* and with it he *bound* first *his own hands, and then his own feet.* What we see usually makes a greater impression on us than what we only hear about.

2.3.2. By an explanation of the sign: *Thus saith the Holy Spirit, so shall the Jews at Jerusalem bind the man that owneth this girdle* and *shall deliver him into the hands of the Gentiles.* Paul was given this explicit warning of his troubles to enable him to prepare for them.

3. The great boldness of his friends in trying to dissuade him from going to Jerusalem (v. 12). "Not only those of that place but also we who were of Paul's company pleaded with him tearfully not to go to Jerusalem."

3.1. Here can be seen a commendable affection for Paul. Good people who are very active sometimes need to be dissuaded from overworking, and good people who are very bold need to be dissuaded from exposing themselves to unnecessary risks.

3.2. Frailty, however, was mixed in with this affection, especially in those of Paul's friends who knew he undertook this journey by divine direction. We see in them, however, the weakness that is part of us all; when we see trouble in the distance, we can make light of it, but when it comes near, we begin to shrink back.

4. The holy bravery with which Paul persisted in his determination (v. 13).

4.1. He rebuked them for trying to dissuade him. Here was a quarrel of love on both sides. They love him dearly and therefore opposed his resolution; he loved them dearly and therefore scolded them for opposing it: *What mean you to weep and to break my heart?* Their weeping about him broke his heart.

4.1.1. It was a temptation to him; it began to weaken his resolution. "I know I have been appointed to suffer; you should encourage me. You, with your tears, are really breaking my heart and discouraging me. Has not our Master told us to take up our cross (Mt 16:24)? Would you have me avoid mine?"

4.1.2. It was a trouble to him that they would urge him so passionately to do something that would wrong his conscience. Just as he was very tearful himself, so he also had compassionate regard for the tears of his friends. But it was now really breaking his heart, when he had to deny the request of his weeping friends. It was unkind to torment him in this way with their attempts to dissuade him. When our friends are called to suffer, we will show our love by comforting them rather than by grieving for them. Notice, however, that if these Christians at Caesarea could have foreseen the details of what would happen, they would have come to terms with it better for their own sakes, because when Paul was made a prisoner at Jerusalem, he was immediately sent to Caesarea (23:33), and he remained there for at least *two years* (24:27). He was a prisoner with great freedom, as is clear from 24:23. The church at Caesarea enjoyed more of Paul's company and help when he was imprisoned than they could have if he had been at liberty. What we oppose, thinking it will work very much against us, may be overruled by the providence of God to work for us.

4.2. He repeated his resolution to go forward: "*What mean you to weep thus? I am ready* to suffer whatever has been appointed for me. I am willing to suffer, and so why are you unwilling to have me suffer? For my part, *I am ready.* I was told originally *what great things I must suffer* (9:16). I am prepared for it; I can welcome it. I can, through the Lord's grace, not only bear it but even rejoice in it."

4.2.1. Notice how far his resolution extended: "I tell you, I am ready not only to be bound, but to die at Jerusalem." We would be wise to think of the worst that may happen to us, and to prepare for it accordingly.

4.2.2. Notice what made him willing to suffer and die: it is *for the name of the Lord Jesus.* All that a person has they will give for their life (Job 2:4), but Paul would give even life itself for the service and honor of the name of Christ.

5. His friends' patient acceptance of his decision (v. 14).

5.1. They submitted to the wisdom of a good man. "*When he would not be persuaded, we ceased* trying to dissuade him. Paul knows his own mind best, and what he has to do. It befits us to leave it to him. No doubt Paul has a good reason for his decision, and God has in his gracious purpose to serve in strengthening him in it." When a person refuses to be persuaded in a matter of their own affairs, it is good manners not to press them too much.

5.2. They submitted to the will of a good God: *We ceased,* saying, *The will of the Lord be done.* They did not say, "Ah, Paul is being his usual stubborn self," but attributed his decision to his willingness to suffer and to submit to God's will. *The will of the Lord be done* may refer here:

5.2.1. To Paul's present firmness; he was inflexible, and in this they saw the will of the Lord done.

5.2.2. To his approaching suffering: "If there is no other way, may the will of the Lord Jesus be done. We leave matters to God, leave them with Christ, and so we will do not as we want but as he wills." God is wise, and he knows how to make all work together for good (Ro 8:28), and that is why we should welcome his holy will. Not only, "The will of the Lord must be done, and there is no other way, but also, "Let the will of the Lord be done, for his will is his wisdom." When a trouble has come, knowing that the will of the Lord is done must lessen our griefs; when we see it coming, knowing that the will of the Lord will be done must silence our fears; let the will of the Lord all be done.

Verses 15–26

In these verses we have:

1. Paul's journey to Jerusalem from Caesarea, and the company who went with him.

1.1. They *took up their carriages*, their bag and baggage; it seems they had so little baggage with them that, like poor travelers or soldiers, they were their own porters. If they could have persuaded Paul to go some other way, they would gladly have gone along with him, but if he was determined go to Jerusalem, they would not say, "Let him go there by himself then," but, "*Let us go and die with him* (Jn 11:16)." Paul's boldness made them bolder.

1.2. Some of the disciples of Caesarea went along with them. The less time Paul was likely to enjoy his liberty, the more diligent they would be to use every opportunity to be with him.

1.3. They brought with them an honest old man who had a house of his own at Jerusalem, in which he would gladly receive Paul and his company, *one Mnason of Cyprus, with whom we should lodge* (v. 16). There were so many people who came to the feast that it was hard to find somewhere to stay; the inns would be taken by those of the better sort, and it was looked on as scandalous for those who had private houses to rent their rooms out at those times. Everyone then would choose their friends to be their guests, and Mnason took Paul and his company in as his lodgers. Knowing what trouble Paul was likely to fall into, he still welcomed him, whatever came of it. This Mnason is called an *old disciple*—a disciple from the beginning. He had been a Christian for a long time and was now advanced in years. It is honorable to be an old disciple of Jesus Christ, to have been enabled by the grace of God to continue for a long time in the course of duty, firm in the faith. One would choose to lodge with these old disciples, for *the multitude of their years will teach wisdom* (Job 32:7).

2. Paul's welcome at Jerusalem.

2.1. The believers there *received him gladly* (v. 17). The words used here for the welcome they gave to the apostles are used for the welcome of the apostles' teaching (2:41). They *gladly received his word*. We think if we had Paul among us we would gladly receive him, but that may be doubted if, having his teaching, we do not gladly receive that.

2.2. Paul and his company paid a visit to James and the elders of the church (v. 18): "*The day following, Paul went in unto James*, and took us with him." It seems that James was now the only apostle who lived in Jerusalem, the others having dispersed to preach the Gospel in other places. They decided to keep one apostle in Jerusalem, because a great many people went there from all parts. James now filled that role, and all the elders were present. Paul *saluted them*. The proper meaning of *salutation* is "a wish for the salvation of another." It is very befitting for Christians to give such mutual greetings as a sign of their love for one another and their joint regard for God.

3. The account they received from him of his ministry among the Gentiles, and the satisfaction they took in this.

3.1. He gave them a detailed report of the success of the Gospel in those countries where he had been working: *He declared particularly what things God had wrought among the Gentiles by his ministry* (v. 19), not what things he had done but what God had done through his ministry. It was *not I, but the grace of God which was with me* (1Co 15:10). He gave a detailed report so that the grace of God

would be seen to be more important in the circumstances of his success.

3.2. They used the occasion to give praise to God (v. 20): *When they heard it, they glorified the Lord.* Paul attributed all that he had done to God, and they gave God the praise for it. They gave glory to the grace of God, which was extended to the Gentiles. They were not jealous of him or of his growing reputation; on the contrary, they *glorified the Lord*. If God was praised, Paul was pleased.

4. The request of James and the elders to Paul, or rather their advice to him, that he satisfy the believing Jews by submitting in some way to the ceremonial law and appearing in public in the temple to offer sacrifice. Although the ceremonial law was in no way to be imposed on the Gentile converts, it had not yet become unlawful to those who had been brought up to observe it. It was dead, but not buried; dead, but not yet deadly.

4.1. They wanted him to take notice of the great numbers of Jewish converts: *Thou seest, brother, how many thousands of the Jews there are who believe.* They called him brother. Although they were conformists and he a nonconformist, they were still brothers and acknowledged that relationship. The number of the names at first was only 120 (1:15), but now how many thousands. Let no one, therefore, despise the day of small things (Zec 4:10), for although the beginning may be small, God can make the end great. The account of the success of the Gospel among the Jews was no doubt as pleasing to Paul as the account he gave them of the conversion of the Gentiles was to them, because his heart's desire and prayer to God for the Jews was *that they might be saved* (Ro 10:1).

4.2. They informed him of a prevailing weakness these believing Jews labored under: *they are all zealous of the law.* They believed in Christ as the true Messiah, but they knew that the Law of Moses came from God. They had found spiritual benefit in its institutions, and so they could not think of parting with it. It was a great weakness to be so fond of the shadows when the reality had come (Col 2:17; Heb 8:5; 10:1). But see:

4.2.1. The power of education and of having long observed a custom or tradition, and especially of having obeyed a ceremonial law.

4.2.2. The loving allowance that must be made in consideration of this. Their zeal for the law could be interpreted favorably, and love would so interpret it, and it could be well excused.

4.3. They gave him to understand that these Jews were ill disposed toward him (v. 21). Paul himself could not receive a good word from some who belonged to Christ's family. "*They are informed of thee*, that you not only do not teach the Gentiles to observe the law, but *dost teach all the Jews who are among the Gentiles to forsake Moses, not to circumcise their children nor to walk after the customs* of our nation." It was true that Paul preached the annulment of the Law of Moses; he had taught them that it was impossible to be justified by it. However, it was false that he taught them to turn away from Moses, for the religion he preached did not tend to destroy the law, but to fulfill it. Even the believing Jews, having acquired this idea that Paul was an enemy of Moses, were very much angered against him. The elders present here loved and honored Paul and called him brother, but the people could hardly be induced to have such favorable thoughts of him, for it is certain that the least judicious are the most critical, and that the weak-headed are the hotheaded.

4.4. They wanted Paul to demonstrate by some public act, therefore, that the charge against him was false, that he did not teach people to break the customs of the Jewish church, since he himself observed them.

4.4.1. They concluded that something of this kind must be done: "*What is it therefore?* What must be done? The *multitude will hear that thou art come* to town. When they hear that you have come, *they must needs come together,* expecting to hear you.*"* Now something must be done to satisfy them that Paul did not teach the people to turn away from Moses, and the elders thought it necessary:

4.4.1.1. For Paul's sake, so that his reputation would be cleared.

4.4.1.2. For the people's sake, so that they would not continue to be prejudiced against such a good man.

4.4.1.3. For their own sake, so that, since they knew it was their duty to recognize Paul, their doing so would not be turned to their discredit.

4.4.2. They came up with a good opportunity that Paul could use to clear himself: "*Do this that we say unto thee. We have four men,* Jews who believe, and *they have a vow on them,* a vow of Nazariteship for a certain time; their time has now expired (v. 23), and they are to offer their offering according to the law when they *shave the head of separation* (Nu 6:18); they are to offer a male lamb as a burnt offering, a ewe lamb as a sin offering, and a ram as a fellowship offering.*"* Now because Paul had just complied with the law so far as to take on himself the vow of a Nazarite, and to show the expiration of that by having his hair cut off at Cenchrea (18:18), they wanted him to go a little further and join these four in offering the sacrifices of a Nazarite: *Purify thyself with them* according to the law, and share the expense of buying sacrifices for this solemn occasion, and join with them in the sacrifice.*"* This, they thought, would effectively silence the accusations of slander, and everyone would be convinced that Paul had not taught the Jews to turn away from Moses, but that he himself kept the law.

4.5. They pleaded that this would in no way infringe the decree just issued in favor of the Gentile converts (v. 25): "*As touching the Gentiles* who *believe, we have written and concluded that they observe no such things,* but only that they must keep themselves from *things offered to idols, and from blood, and from things strangled, and from fornication.*" The elders knew how concerned Paul was to preserve the liberty of the converted Gentiles, and so they expressly covenanted to remain faithful to that. This was their proposal.

5. Paul's submission to this request or advice. Although he would not be persuaded not to go to Jerusalem, nevertheless, when he was there, he was persuaded to do as they did there (v. 26). *Then Paul took the men,* and the very next day, *purifying himself with them,* and not *with multitude nor tumult,* as he himself pleads (24:18), he *entered into the temple,* to show the fulfillment of the days of purification to the priests. It has been questioned whether James and the elders did well to give Paul this advice and whether he did well to take it.

5.1. Some have blamed this occasional conformity of Paul's as indulging the Jews too much in their loyalty to the ceremonial law and discouraging those who stood firm in the liberty with which Christ had set them free (Gal 5:1). Would it not have been better to take pains with their people to convince them of their error and show them that they had been set free from the law? To urge him to encourage them in it by his example seems to contain more of fleshly wisdom than of the grace of God.

5.2. Others think the advice was wise and good. It was Paul's avowed principle, *To the Jews became I as a Jew, that I might gain the Jews* (1Co 9:20). He had circumcised

Timothy to please the Jews. Those who are weak in the faith are to be borne patiently, while those who subvert the faith must be opposed. It is true that this compliance of Paul's turned out badly for him, but this is not a sufficient basis for continuing to condemn it: it was possible for Paul to do well but still suffer for it. Integrity and uprightness are more likely to preserve us than petty compliance. Moreover, when we consider what a great trouble it must have been to James and the elders that by their advice they had brought Paul into trouble, it should be a warning to us not to urge people to please us by doing anything contrary to their own way of thinking.

Verses 27–40

Here Paul is brought into a custody that we are not likely to see the end of. When we see the beginning of trouble, we do not know either how long it will last or what its result will be.

1. We have Paul seized here.

1.1. He was seized in the temple when he was there for the solemn services of the days of his purifying (v. 27). It was not until *the seven days were almost ended* that he was noticed at all. In the temple, where he should have been protected, as in a sanctuary, he was violently attacked by those who did what they could to have his blood mixed with his sacrifices (Lk 13:1). They themselves corrupted the temple.

1.2. The informers against him were the Jews of Asia, not those of Jerusalem—the Jews of the dispersion, who were most angry with him. Those who seldom came to worship at the temple in Jerusalem themselves still wanted to appear most zealous for the temple, as if in so doing they would make up for their habitual neglect of it.

1.3. The strategy they used was to raise a mob: *They stirred up all the people.* The people who are governed least by reason and most by passion are the best ones to act against Christ and Christianity.

1.4. The arguments with which they incited the people against him were popular, but false and unjust. They cried out, *Men of Israel, help.* Since the enemies of Christianity could never prove it to be evil, they have always worked very hard to give it a bad reputation by provoking outrage and uproar against it. What is lacking in right is made up for in noise.

1.5. They accused him of both bad teaching and bad practice.

1.5.1. They accused him of bad teaching, not here in Jerusalem, indeed, but in other places, in fact in all places: *he teaches all men everywhere*—as if, because he was an itinerant preacher, he was ubiquitous. "He is spreading certain damnable and heretical positions with all his power:

1.5.1.1. "Against the Jewish people." He had taught that Jews and Gentiles stand on the same level before God, *and* that *neither circumcision avails any thing nor uncircumcision* (Gal 5:6); in fact, he had taught against the unbelieving Jews that they were rejected—and therefore he had separated from them and their synagogues. Those who are Christians in name only often seem to be most jealous for the church's name.

1.5.1.2. "Against the law." His teaching people to believe the Gospel as the end of the law, and its completion, was interpreted as his preaching against the law.

1.5.1.3. "Against *this place*, the temple." Because he taught people to pray everywhere, he was criticized as an enemy of the temple. Paul himself had been active in persecuting Stephen and putting him to death for words spoken *against this holy place* (6:13), and now he was accused of the same thing. The one who had earlier been used as the tool of Jewish rage and hatred was now set up as its target.

1.5.2. They accused him of bad practice. He was accused of defiling the temple himself. He *has brought Gentiles also into the temple*, into the inner court of the temple, into which no one who was uncircumcised was allowed to come. Paul himself was a Jew and had the right to enter the court of the Jews, and they, seeing some with him there who joined him in his devotions, concluded that Trophimus, who was an Ephesian and a Gentile, was one of them. Did they see him there? Certainly not. They had seen him with Paul in the city, and so they supposed that Paul had brought him with him into the temple, which was completely false. See here:

1.5.2.1. Innocence is no protection against slander and false accusation.

1.5.2.2. Scoundrels plot evil, and they will go far in search of ways to back up their false accusations, as they did here. By such unjust and baseless suggestions evildoers have thought they were justified in committing the cruelest outrages.

1.5.2.3. Evildoers often use against the wise and good the very things with which the latter had hoped to please them and win their favor. Paul thought he could commend himself to their good opinion by going into the temple, and they took advantage of that to accuse him. If he had kept farther away from them, he would not have been so maligned by them.

2. We have Paul in danger of being torn to pieces by the mob. The execution would be consistent with the prosecution—as quick as possible, and entirely unjust and irregular. As those who neither feared God nor had any respect for human beings (Lk 18:2), they were determined to deal with him immediately.

2.1. The whole city was in complete uproar (v. 30). When the people heard the hue and cry from the temple, they were up in arms. *All the city was moved* (aroused) when they were called for from the temple with, *Men of Israel, help.* The Jews showed just such a zeal for God's temple here as the Ephesians did for Diana's temple when Paul was informed against as its enemy: *The whole city was full of confusion* (19:29).

2.2. They dragged Paul out of the temple and shut the doors. In dragging him furiously out of the temple:

2.2.1. They showed their real detestation of him as unfit to be considered a member of the Jewish nation.

2.2.2. They claimed respect for the temple. They condemned Paul for drawing people away from the temple, and yet when he himself was devoutly worshiping in the temple, they dragged him out of it. The officers of the temple shut the doors in case the crowd, growing as more and more ran in to join them, were thrown back into the temple, with the result that some outrage was committed that desecrated that holy place.

2.3. They set about killing him by beating (vv. 31–32), having decided to beat him to death by "blows without number." Now Paul was like a lamb thrown into the den of lions. No doubt he was still of the same mind as when he said, *I am ready not only to be bound, but to die at Jerusalem* (v. 13).

3. We have here Paul rescued from the hands of his Jewish enemies by a Roman enemy.

3.1. News of the disturbance was brought *to the chief captain of the band.* Somebody who was concerned not for Paul but for the public peace and safety gave this information to the commander, who always kept a jealous and watchful eye on these turbulent Jews, and he was the

one who was instrumental in saving Paul's life when no friend could help him.

3.2. The commander got his forces together as quickly as possible and went out to suppress the mob: *He took soldiers* and *centurions* and *ran down to them.* He had them close at hand, and *he ran down unto the multitude*, for delays are dangerous at such times.

3.3. The very sight of the Roman general frightened Paul's persecutors from beating him. The power of the Romans deterred them from doing what they should have been restrained from doing by the justice of God. God often gives protection to his people by means of those who have no affection for his people. The shepherd uses even his dogs to defend his sheep. The commander took Paul into custody. He rescued him not out of concern for him but out of a concern for justice, because Paul should not be put to death without trial. He therefore took Paul out of the hands of the mob and into the hands of the law (v. 33): *He took him, and commanded him to be bound with two chains, for he demanded who he was, and what he had done.* This forceful taking of Paul out of their hands by the commander was, said the mob, a crime: *The chief captain Lysias came with great violence, and took him out of our hands* (24:7).

4. We have the provision the commander made to allow Paul to speak for himself. It would almost have been easier to enter into a struggle with the winds and the waves than with such a mob, but Paul made provision to gain liberty of speech among them.

4.1. There was no getting any sense from the people, because when the commander asked about Paul, *some cried one thing, and some another*, so that it was impossible for the commander to know what they thought, since they knew neither their own minds nor one another's. Those who listen to the shouts of the crowd will know nothing certain.

4.2. The rage and fury of the people could not be quelled. When *the chief captain commanded that Paul should be carried into the castle* (barracks)—the tower of Antonia, where the Roman soldiers kept the garrison, near the temple—the soldiers themselves had great difficulty getting him there safely, because the people were so violent (v. 35). *When he came upon the stairs* leading up to the barracks, the soldiers were forced to carry him to keep him from the people, who would have torn him limb from limb if possible. When they could not reach him with their cruel hands, *They followed, crying, Away with him* (v. 36). "Take him out of the land of the living," is how the old commentators explain it; "chase him out of the world."

4.3. Paul finally asked the commander if he could say something to him (v. 37): *As he was to be led into the castle, he said unto the chief captain, May I speak unto thee?* What a humble, modest question this was! Paul knew how to speak to the greatest people, yet he humbly begged to be allowed to speak to this commander.

4.4. The commander revealed what idea he had of him: *Canst thou speak Greek? Art not thou that Egyptian who made an uproar?* It seems that somewhere in that country there had just been an insurrection led by an Egyptian. The commander said here *that* this Egyptian *led out into the wilderness four thousand men that were murderers.* It happened in the thirteenth year of Claudius, about three years before the events narrated in this passage. The ringleader of this rebellion had made his escape, and the commander concluded that Paul could not be a criminal of less significance than this Egyptian. Notice how good people are exposed to ill will by mistake.

4.5. Paul put right the commander's mistake about him by telling him specifically what he was: *I am a man who is a Jew; I am of Tarsus, a city of Cilicia, a citizen of no mean city*. Whether by *no mean city* he meant Tarsus or Rome is not certain; neither of them was insignificant, and he was a freeman of both. Although the commander had suspected him so offensively and unjustly, Paul did not repay insult with insult, but mildly denied the charge and acknowledged who he really was.

4.6. He humbly sought permission to speak to the people. He sought it as a favor, which he would be thankful for: *I beseech thee, suffer* (allow) *me to speak to the people*. The commander rescued him with no other intention than to give him a fair hearing. Now, therefore, he asked to be allowed to defend himself immediately, since his case needed nothing more than to be set in a true light.

4.7. He obtained permission to plead his own cause. He needed no attorney to be assigned him, because the Spirit of the Father was ready to dictate to him (Mt 10:20). *The chief captain gave him license* (permission) (v. 40). That justice that he could not obtain from his compatriots, the Jews, was given him by this commander. With this permission obtained:

4.7.1. The people listened attentively: *Paul stood on the stairs*. It was a sad pulpit, but it was better than none. There he *beckoned with the hand unto the people*, motioned to them to be quiet, and persuaded them so effectively that a deep silence came on them all. When the cause of Christ and his Gospel is to be pleaded, there should be a great silence, so that we may *give the more earnest heed* (Heb 2:1), and all will be little enough.

4.7.2. Paul prepared himself to speak: he *spoke unto them in the Hebrew tongue*, that is, in their own ordinary language, the language of their country, which he here showed he had not only an enduring relationship with but also enduring respect for.

CHAPTER 22

At the end of the previous chapter we had Paul bound, but with his tongue set free. As a result, he was so intent on using his liberty of speech to the honor of Christ that he forgot the chains he was in and spoke of the great things Christ had done for him with as much ease as if nothing had been done to disturb him. We have here: 1. His address to the people, and their attention to it (vv. 1–2). 2. The account he gave of himself. 2.1. What a bigoted Jew he had been (vv. 3–5). 2.2. How he was miraculously converted (vv. 6–11). 2.3. How he was strengthened and baptized by the ministry of Ananias (vv. 12–16). 2.4. How he was later called to be the apostle of the Gentiles (vv. 17–21). 3. The interruption of his speech by the mob, and the violent passion they flew into on hearing it (vv. 22–23). 4. Paul's second rescue from the hands of the mob, and the further course the commander took to find the true reason for this great outcry against Paul (vv. 24–25). 5. Paul's pleading his privilege as a Roman citizen (vv. 26–29). 6. The commander's moving the case to the high priest's court (v. 30).

Verses 1–2

In 21:40, Paul had gained a good point by commanding such a profound silence after such a loud noise. Now notice here:

1. What wonderful composure he had as he began to speak. There appeared no hint of panic; his mind was calm and composed. Nor did there appear any anger. He still did not break out into angry expressions.

2. What respectful titles he gave even to those who had mistreated him: "*Men, brethren, and fathers*" (v. 1). *To you, O men, I call* (Pr 8:4): men, who should listen to reason and be ruled by it; men, from whom one may expect humanity. You, *brethren* of the common people; you, *fathers* of the priests." He let them know that he was one of them. Although we must not give flattering titles to anyone, we should give titles of due respect to all (Ro 13:7), and we should not seek to provoke those to whom we want to do good. Although he was rescued out of the hands of these Jews and was taken under the protection of the commander, he did not fall foul of them, but asked simply, *Hear you my defense*. This is a just and reasonable request, because everyone who is accused has a right to defend themselves.

3. The language he spoke in, which commended what he said to the audience: *He spoke in the Hebrew tongue*, that is, the common language of the Jews, which at this time was not the pure Old Testament Hebrew, but Aramaic, a dialect of Hebrew. Paul's use of this dialect showed his continued respect for his compatriots, the Jews, because it showed that he himself was a Jew. Moreover, by using it he would be more generally understood. To speak in that language was truly to appeal to the people. *When they heard that he spoke in the Hebrew tongue, they kept the more silence*. The commander was surprised to hear him speak Greek (21:37), and the Jews were surprised to hear him speak Aramaic, and so both thought better of him. Many wise and good people are shown disrespect only because they are unknown.

Verses 3–21

Paul here gave an account of himself not only to satisfy the commander that he was not that Egyptian he took him to be, but also to satisfy the Jews that he was not the enemy of their law and temple that they took him to be. Notice:

1. What his background and education were.

1.1. He was one of their own nation. "*I am verily a man who is a Jew*. I am a sincere friend of your nation, because I belong to it."

1.2. He was born in a creditable and reputable place, *in Tarsus, a city of Cilicia*, and was by his birth a freeman of that city. This was only a small matter to make any boast about, but it was necessary to mention now to those who arrogantly trampled all over him.

1.3. He had a learned and liberal education. He *was brought up* in Jerusalem, the chief seat of Jewish learning, and *at the feet of Gamaliel*. He could not be ignorant of their law, therefore, nor be thought to insult it because he did not know it.

1.4. In his early days he was a very eager and eminent professor of the Jews' religion.

1.4.1. He was an intelligent professor of their religion. He was very attentive at Gamaliel's feet and was there *taught according to the perfect manner of the law of the fathers*. Such departures as he had made from the law were not owing to any confused or mistaken ideas of it, for he understood its finer points. Paul had as great a value for antiquity and tradition as any of these Jews, and there was never a Jew who understood his religion better than Paul did, or could give a better account of it.

1.4.2. He was an active professor of their religion: *I was zealous toward God, as you all are this day*. Many who are very skilled in the theory of religion are willing to leave the practice of it to others, but Paul was as much a zealot as he was a rabbi. Here he complimented his hearers by saying *that they all were this day zealous toward*

God; he bore them record (Ro 10:2) *that they had a zeal for God, but not according to knowledge.* Although this in no way justified their rage, it enabled those who prayed, *Father, forgive them,* to plead, as Christ did, *for they know not what they do* (Lk 23:34).

2. What a fiery, furious persecutor he had been at the beginning of his life (vv. 4–5). He mentioned this to make it clearer that the change that came on him when he was converted to the Christian faith was purely the effect of a divine power. Immediately before that sudden change was brought about in him, he had had the most intense hatred possible toward Christianity. He may further have intended to invite and encourage those persecuting him to repent, because he himself had been *a blasphemer, and a persecutor,* but had obtained mercy. Let us view Paul's picture of himself when he was a persecutor.

2.1. He hated Christianity with mortal enmity: *I persecuted this way unto the death.* He *breathed out slaughter against the disciples* (9:1). When *they were put to death, he gave his voice against them* (26:10). He *persecuted it to the death;* that is, he would have been willing to die himself in his fight against Christianity, as some understand it. He would have been content to lose his life in defense of the laws and traditions of the ancestors.

2.2. He did all he could to frighten people from this way and make them leave it, by *binding and delivering into prison both men and women.* Now that he himself was bound, he emphasized particularly this part of his charge against himself, that he had bound the Christians and taken them prisoner; and he reflected with special regret that he had imprisoned not only the men but also the women.

2.3. He was employed by the great Sanhedrin, the high priest and all the Council of the elders, in suppressing this new sect (v. 5). When they heard that many of the Jews at Damascus had accepted the Christian faith, they resolved to proceed against them, and could not think of a better person to do that work than Paul. That was why they sent him, and letters through him, to the Jews at Damascus, here called *the brethren,* ordering them to help Paul arrest those among them who had become Christians and bring them as prisoners to Jerusalem to be punished, thereby either compelling them to recant their faith or putting them to death to terrorize others. "I was like this at first," said Paul, "just as you are now. I know the heart of a persecutor, and that is why I pity you, and pray that you may know the heart of a convert, which God soon gave to me."

3. How he was converted. It was not from any natural or external causes. It was all the Lord's doing (Ps 118:23; Mt 21:42), and the circumstances in which it was done were enough to justify him in the change. No one could condemn him for it without reflecting on that divine energy. He told the story of his conversion here in detail, as we had it before (9:1–19), aiming to show that it was purely the act of God.

3.1. Just before Christ stopped him, he was as fully intent on persecuting the Christians as ever. He *made his journey, and was come nigh to Damascus* (v. 6), and had no other thought than to carry out the cruel plans he was sent to fulfill.

3.2. It was *a light from heaven* that startled him at first, *a great light,* which *shone suddenly round about him;* the Jews knew that God is light, and that such a light as this, shining at noon, must come from God. It shone on him on the open road, at noon, and so strongly *that it struck him*—and all *that were with him* (26:14)—*to the ground* (v. 7).

3.3. It was a *voice from heaven* that first produced in him fearful thoughts of Jesus Christ. The voice called to

him by name, saying, *Saul, Saul, why persecutest thou me?* When he asked, *Who art thou, Lord?* the answer came, *I am Jesus of Nazareth, whom thou persecutest* (v. 8).

3.4. In case the objection should be raised, "How come this light and voice worked such a change on him, and not on those who journeyed with him?"—he commented *that his fellow travellers saw indeed the light, and were afraid,* but although the light made them afraid, they did not hear the voice of the One who spoke to Paul. Now faith comes by hearing (Ro 10:17), and so the change was performed on the one who heard the words, and heard them directed to himself, but it was not performed on those who only saw the light.

3.5. He assured them that when he was so stunned, he referred himself completely to divine guidance, asking, "*What shall I do, Lord?* May the same voice from heaven that has stopped me from pursuing the wrong way now guide me on the right way (v. 10)." Immediately he received directions to go to Damascus, and there *it shall be told thee all things which are appointed for thee to do.* The extraordinary ways of divine revelation, by visions, voices, and the appearance of angels, were intended only to introduce and establish the ordinary method of the Scriptures and a constant ministry. The voice here did not tell Paul what he must do, except to go to Damascus, where he would be told further.

3.6. As a demonstration of the greatness of the light that fastened on him, he told them of the immediate effect it had on his eyesight (v. 11): *I could not see for the glory of that light.* It struck him blind for the present. Condemned sinners are struck blind by the power of darkness, and it is a lasting blindness. Convinced sinners are struck blind, as Paul was here, not by darkness, but by light, so that they may be enlightened. Those who were with Paul were not blinded, and so they, with their sight, led *Paul by the hand into the city.* Paul, being a Pharisee, had been proud of his spiritual sight. The Pharisees said, *Are we blind also?* (Jn 9:40). Paul was struck with physical blindness to make him aware of his spiritual blindness.

4. How he was strengthened in the change he had made, and further instructed in what he should do, by Ananias. Notice:

4.1. The description of Ananias. He was not in any way prejudiced against the Jewish nation or religion, but was himself *a devout man according to the law,* and from the devoutness he had he was advanced further to the faith of Christ. He had *a good report of* (was highly respected by) *all the Jews that dwelt at Damascus.* This was the first Christian whom Paul had any friendly communication with.

4.2. The healing immediately performed by him on Paul's eyes. Ananias *came to him* (v. 13), and to assure him that he came to him from Christ, he *stood by him, and said, Brother Saul, receive thy sight.* Power went along with this word, and *the same hour* Saul recovered his sight and *looked up upon* Ananias, ready to receive from him the instructions sent through him.

4.3. The declaration that Ananias made to him of the favor that the Lord Jesus intended for him, which was greater than that intended for any other person. The Lord would show him favor:

4.3.1. In the present revelation of himself to him (v. 14): *The God of our fathers has chosen thee.* This powerful call was the result of a particular choice; Ananias's calling God *the God of our fathers* shows that Ananias was himself a Jew by birth. *This God of our fathers has chosen thee that thou shouldst know his will.* Those whom God has chosen he has chosen to know his will and to do it. *That thou shouldst see that Just One, and shouldst hear the voice of his mouth*, and so know his will directly from him. It was a distinctive favor that he would see Christ here on earth after his ascension to heaven. Stephen saw him *standing at the right hand of God* (7:56), but Paul saw him standing at his own right hand. Stephen saw him, but we do not find that he heard words from his mouth, as Paul did. Christ was called here *that Just One* because he is Jesus Christ the Righteous One (1Jn 2:1), and the One who suffered wrongfully. Those whom God has chosen to know his will must look to Christ, and they must see him and hear words from his mouth.

4.3.2. In the later revelation of himself by Paul to others (v. 15): *"Thou shalt be his witness unto all men*, Gentiles as well as Jews, *of what thou hast seen and heard."* Finding Paul relating his conversion in such detail both here and in his defense of himself in ch. 26, we have reason to think that he frequently related the same narrative in his preaching for the conversion of others. He told them what God had done for his soul (Ps 66:16) to encourage them to hope that God would do something for their souls.

4.4. The advice Ananias gave him to join the Lord Jesus by baptism (v. 16): *Arise, and be baptized.* In his circumcision Paul been given up to God, but he must now by baptism be given up to God in Christ.

4.4.1. The great Gospel privilege that is sealed for us by baptism is the remission of sins: *Be baptized and wash away thy sins* (v. 16); that is, "Receive the assurance of the forgiveness of your sins in and through Jesus Christ, and receive power against sin," for our being washed includes our being both justified and sanctified (1Co 6:11).

4.4.2. The great Gospel duty that we are committed to by our baptism is *to call on the name of the Lord, the Lord Jesus*, to acknowledge him to be our Lord and our God and to turn to him accordingly. We must *wash away our sins, calling on the name of the Lord;* that is, we must seek the forgiveness of our sins in Christ's name.

4.4.3. We must do this quickly. *Why tarriest thou?* Our making a covenant with God in Christ is a necessary work that must not be put off. If a thing must done sometime or else we are ruined, why should it not be done now?

5. How he was commissioned to go and preach the Gospel to the Gentiles. This was the great reason why they were so angry with him, and so it was necessary for him to produce his divine authority. He did not receive this commission immediately on his conversion, for he received it at Jerusalem.

5.1. He received his orders to do it when he was praying, begging God to appoint his work for him and show him the course he should steer. He was *at prayer in the temple*, which was to be called *a house of prayer for all people* (Isa 56:7), not only a house in which all people should pray but also a house in which all people should be prayed for. Paul's praying in the temple was evidence that he had respect for the temple. It would be a great satisfaction to Paul later, in fulfilling this commission, to recall that he received it when he was praying.

5.2. He received it in a vision. He fell *into a trance* (v. 17). In this trance he saw Jesus Christ (v. 18): *I saw him saying unto me.*

5.3. Before Christ gave him a commission to go to the Gentiles, he told him it was unproductive for him to think of doing any good at Jerusalem, and so the Jews of Jerusalem must not blame him, but themselves, if he was sent to the Gentiles. *"Make haste,"* Christ had said, *"and get thee quickly out of Jerusalem.* You will find that they *will not receive thy testimony concerning me."* As God knows

beforehand who will receive the Gospel, so he also knows those who will reject it.

5.4. Paul renewed his request that he be employed at Jerusalem, because the people there knew what he had been like before his conversion, and so would have to attribute such a great change in him to the power of almighty grace. He reasoned both with himself and with the Lord, and he thought he reasoned reasonably (vv. 19–20): *"Lord,"* he said, *"they know* that I was as bitter an enemy as any of them to those who believed in you, that I *imprisoned them* and *beat them in every synagogue.* Especially in Stephen's case, they know that when he was being stoned, I was standing by, *consenting to his death,* and I *kept the clothes of those that stoned him.* If I appear among them preaching the message Stephen preached and suffered for, they will no doubt receive my testimony." "No," Christ said to him, "they will not; rather, they will become even angrier against you as a deserter."

5.5. Paul's request for authority to preach the Gospel at Jerusalem was overruled (v. 21): *Depart, for I will send thee far hence, unto the Gentiles.* God often gives gracious answers to the prayers of his people not in the thing itself that they pray for, but in something better. It is God who appoints his laborers both their day and their place, and it befits them to accept his appointment, even though it may go against their own inclinations. Paul longed for Jerusalem; to be a preacher there was the summit of his ambitions. But Christ had plans for his greater advancement. So often Providence works things better for us than we do for ourselves. Paul would not go to preach among the Gentiles without a commission: *I will send thee.* If Christ sent him, his Spirit would accompany him and allow him to see the fruit of his labors. Paul was sent to places far away. Surely these Jews would see that they had no reason to be angry with Paul for preaching among the Gentiles, because he was compelled to it by an overruling command from heaven.

Verses 22–30

Paul was continuing to give this account of himself. However, whatever he intended to say, they were determined that he would say nothing more to them: *They gave him audience to this word.* Up to this time they had listened to him patiently, giving him some attention, but when he spoke of being sent to the Gentiles, they could not bear it. On the mere mention of this, they lost all patience and forgot all rules of decency and justice. Now here we are told how furious the people were against Paul for mentioning the Gentiles as embraced within the scope of divine grace.

1. They interrupted him so that nobody could hear a word he said. Angry consciences strike out at the slightest touch, and those who are determined not to be ruled by reason are often determined not to listen to it if they can help it.

2. They shouted out against him as one who was unworthy of life. They cried out with a confused noise, *"Away with such a fellow* as this *from the earth; it is not fit that he should live."* Here, as at other times, the people who have been the greatest blessings of their age have been represented not only as the burdens of the earth but even as the plague of their generation. The ungodly Jews said here about Paul that he was not fit to live, and so he must be gotten rid of, so that the world could be relieved of the burden of having him living.

3. They went raving mad against Paul and against the commander (v. 23). They cried out, howling like those whose reason was completely lost in their anger; they *cast*

off their clothes. This was how they showed how ready they were to stone him; those who stoned Stephen threw off their clothes (v. 20). Or they tore their clothes apart to indicate their judgment that he had spoken blasphemy, and they *threw dust into the air* in detestation. All they intended was to make the commander aware how angry they were with Paul.

4. The commander took care of Paul's safety by ordering that he be brought into the barracks (v. 24). A prison has sometimes protected good people from popular rage. Paul's hour had not yet come (Jn 7:30; 8:20), and so God raised up a person who took care of him.

5. He ordered him to be flogged. *He ordered that he should be examined by scourging,* so that *he might know wherefore they cried so against him.* Here the commander did not act fairly; he should have singled out some of the people who were making the complaint, should have tried them to see what they had to lay to the charge of one who could give such a good account of himself. It was proper to ask them, but not at all proper to ask Paul, *wherefore they cried so against him.* No one is bound to accuse themselves, even if they are guilty, and much less should Paul be compelled to accuse himself when he was innocent. Was this a fair or just reason to flog Paul, that a rude, violent mob cried out against him but could not tell why?

6. Paul pleaded his privilege as a Roman citizen, by which he was exempted from all trials and punishments of this kind (v. 25). *As they bound him with thongs,* he did not cry out against the injustice of their proceedings against an innocent man, but explained to them the illegality of their proceedings against him as a citizen of Rome. He *said to the centurion that stood by, Is it lawful for you to scourge a man that is a Roman, and uncondemned?* The expression he used clearly showed what a holy security and peace of mind this good man enjoyed, not disturbed either by anger or by fear of all the humiliation he had suffered and the danger he was in.

7. The commander was surprised and put into a panic at this. He had taken Paul to be a wandering Egyptian. How many people of great worth and merit are despised because they are not known! The commander had centurions, under-officers, with him (21:32). One of these reported this matter to the commander (v. 26): *Take heed what thou doest, for this man is a Roman.* They all knew what value was put on the privilege of being a Roman citizen.

7.1. The commander wanted to be satisfied of the truth of this from Paul's own mouth (v. 27): "*Tell me, art thou a Roman?* Are you entitled to the privileges of a Roman citizen?" "Yes," Paul replied, "*I am.*"

7.2. The commander compared notes with him on this matter, and it appeared that the privilege Paul had as a Roman citizen was more honorable than the commander's, because the commander acknowledged that his had been bought: "I am a freeman of Rome, but *with a great sum obtained I this freedom.*" Paul said, *I was freeborn.* He pleaded it for his own preservation, and from Paul's action here we may conclude that we not only may but ought to use all lawful means.

7.3. This put an immediate end to Paul's troubles. Those who were appointed to examine him by flogging *departed from him* (v. 29). The commander himself was afraid when he heard that Paul was a Roman citizen, because although he had not beaten Paul, he had bound him in order to beat him. Many who would not be restrained from evil practices by the fear of God are restrained from them by the fear of human beings. Notice here the benefit of human

laws and judiciary, and what reason we have to be thankful to God for them. By the general support of justice and fair dealing between people, these institutions have served to restrain the rage of evildoers. We need to pray for everyone in authority, therefore, because we have reason to expect this benefit from them.

7.4. The next day the commander brought Paul before the Sanhedrin (v. 30). He first *loosed him from his bands* and then summoned the chief priests and all their council to come together to consider Paul's case, for he found it to be a religious matter. He kept Paul in custody and appealed the judgment of the mob, bringing the matter before the general assembly. We may hope that in so doing he intended Paul's safety, thinking the chief priests and elders would grant him justice and clear him, because their court governed by rules of justice; but what he is said here to have aimed at is satisfying his own curiosity: he *would have known* (wanted to know) *the certainty wherefore he was accused of the Jews.*

CHAPTER 23

The end of the previous chapter left Paul in the high priest's court, and if his enemies acted against him there with less noise, it was with greater subtlety. We have here: 1. Paul's pleading his own integrity and a civil respect to the high priest, however heatedly, though justly, he had just spoken to that official (vv. 1–5). 2. Paul's wisdom in getting himself clear of them by setting the Pharisees and Sadducees in conflict with one another (vv. 6–9). 3. The commander's timely intervention (v. 10). 4. Christ's comforting and strengthening appearance to him (v. 11). 5. A bloodthirsty conspiracy of some desperate Jews to kill Paul (vv. 12–15). 6. The revealing of this conspiracy to Paul, and through him to the commander (vv. 16–22). 7. The commander's concern for Paul's safety; he sent Paul away from Jerusalem to Caesarea, and there Paul safely arrived (vv. 23–35).

Verses 1–5

Perhaps Paul thought that, though pagan magistrates and councils had shown him great disrespect, if he were brought before the Sanhedrin in Jerusalem, he would be able to deal with them effectively, but we do not find that he had any positive effect on them. Here we have:

1. Paul's pleading his own integrity, and appearing:

1.1. With good courage. He was not at all discouraged by being brought before such an impressive assembly: *he earnestly beheld the council.* When Stephen was brought before them, they thought they could intimidate him, but they could not, because of his holy confidence. Now that Paul was brought before them, he thought he could intimidate them, but he could not, because of their evil arrogance.

1.2. With a good conscience. He said, *Men and brethren, I have lived in all good conscience before God unto this day.*

1.2.1. He had always been well disposed toward religion, and he had always distinguished between moral good and evil. He had been neither reckless nor scheming.

1.2.2. Even when he persecuted the church of God, it was because that was what he thought he ought to do. Although his conscience was misinformed, he ought to be given credit for acting according to its dictates.

1.2.3. Yet it seems more likely that he was speaking of the time since his conversion, since he fell under their displeasure. "Even *to this day, I have lived in all good conscience before God.*" He had aimed at nothing but to please God and do his duty. We see here the character of an honest man. He set God before him; he lived in his sight. He was careful about what he said and did, though he might make some mistakes. He had been universally conscientious and continued to be so, persevering in it: "I have lived *so until this day.*" Whatever changes had come to him, he had remained the same, strictly conscientious.

2. The outrage of which Ananias the high priest was guilty: he *commanded those that stood by to smite him on the mouth* (v. 2).

2.1. The high priest was highly offended at Paul. Some think Paul provoked Ananias by the way he looked at the Council or by not addressing the high priest directly, but the pleading of his integrity was enough of a provocation to one who was determined to defeat him. When the high priest could not accuse Paul of any crime, he thought it was criminal enough that he asserted his own innocence.

2.2. In his rage he ordered Paul to be struck, and to be struck on the mouth as one who had given offense with his lips, and as a sign of his commanding Paul to be silent. If we, therefore, see such indignities done to good people, or if they are done to us for doing good and saying good words, we must not think it strange: Christ will give the *kisses of his mouth* (SS 1:2) to those who for his sake receive blows on the mouth.

3. The declaration of the wrath of God (Ro 1:18) against the high priest: *God shall smite thee, thou whited* (whitewashed) *wall* (v. 3). Paul did not speak this out of any sinful anger; he spoke in a holy zeal against the high priest's abuse of his power, and not at all with a spirit of revenge.

3.1. He described the high priest's true character: *Thou whited wall*; that is, "you hypocrite—you mud wall, with trash, dirt, and rubbish underneath, but plastered over, or whitewashed, on the surface." Those who daubed with mortar not properly mixed (Eze 13:10–11, 14, etc.) did not fail to daub themselves over with something that made them look not only clean but also bright.

3.2. He read out the high priest's just condemnation to him: "*God shall smite thee,* will bring on you his severe judgment, especially spiritual judgment."

3.3. He assigned a good reason for that condemnation: "For *sittest thou* pretending *to judge me after the law,* but *commandest me to be smitten* before any crime has been proved against me, which is *contrary to the law?*" It is against all law, human and divine, natural and positive, to prevent someone from making their defense and thus condemn them without their case being heard. It was inexcusable in a high priest, who had been appointed to judge according to the law.

4. The offense that was taken at this bold word of Paul's (v. 4): *Those that stood by said, Revilest thou God's high priest?* It is a good guess that those who blamed Paul for what he said were believing Jews, who were nevertheless zealous for the law and were therefore zealous for the honor of the high priest. See here then:

4.1. What a hard game Paul had to play: when his enemies were so abusive to him, his friends were so far from standing by him that they were ready to find fault with his conduct.

4.2. How even the disciples of Christ themselves tend to overvalue external pomp and power. Because the high priest had been God's high priest and was a significant figure, these people were disgusted at Paul for giving him what he deserved, even though he was an inveterate enemy of Christianity.

5. The excuse that Paul made for what he had said, because he found it was a stumbling block. Although he

had taken the liberty to tell the high priest his fault, nevertheless, when he found it gave offense, he cried out, "I have done wrong." He wished he had not done it.

5.1. He excused his remark by saying that when he spoke, he had not considered to whom he was speaking (v. 5): "*I wist not* (did not know), *brethren, that he was the high priest.* When I was speaking, I was not thinking of the dignity of his place; otherwise I would have spoken more respectfully to him." I do not see how we can think that Paul did not know him to be the high priest, and yet he said he had not realized it. On the other hand, the Jews acknowledged that prophets were entitled to speak freely of rulers in a way that others were not entitled to do (Isa 1:10, 23).

5.2. He took care that what he had said would not be considered a precedent, to weaken the obligation of that law in the least: *For it is written, Thou shalt not speak evil of the ruler of thy people* (Ex 22:28). It is for the public good that the honor of magistracy should be supported, so that it will not suffer because of the failures of those who are entrusted with it. It is not as if great people must not hear of their faults, or as if public grievances should not be complained of to the proper persons, but a particular sensitivity for the honor of those in authority must be exercised, because the law of God requires that particular reverence be paid to them, as God's vice-regents.

Verses 6–11

Now Paul found that the One who had rescued did and would rescue still. The One who rescued him from the tumult of the people here rescued him from that of the elders.

1. His own wisdom and ingenuity stood him in good stead and contributed much to his escape. Paul's greatest honor, which he esteemed himself most for, was that he was a Christian and an apostle of Christ, and yet he sometimes had occasion to make use of his other honors. His being a citizen of Rome saved him from being flogged by the commander, and here his being a Pharisee saved him from being condemned by the Sanhedrin. It fits very well with our willingness to suffer for Christ to use all lawful methods both to prevent suffering and to extricate ourselves from it. The honest way Paul followed here to preserve his own life was to divide his judges; by provoking one section of them to oppose him more strongly, he engaged the other part for him.

1.1. The great council was made up of Sadducees and Pharisees, and Paul knew this (v. 6): *One part were Sadducees, and the other Pharisees.* Now these groups were very different from one another, but they usually agreed enough to do the business of the council together.

1.1.1. The Pharisees were bigots, zealous for ceremony, but at the same time very orthodox in their adherence to the beliefs the Jewish church held concerning the spiritual world, the resurrection of the dead, and the future life.

1.1.2. The Sadducees were deists—no friends of Scripture or divine revelation. They accepted the books of Moses as containing good history and good law, but had little regard for the other books of the Old Testament.

1.1.2.1. They *denied the resurrection,* not only the return of the body to life but also a future state of rewards and punishments.

1.1.2.2. They denied the existence of angels and spirits and accepted no being except matter. They thought that God himself was physical. When they read about angels in the Old Testament, they supposed that they were impressions on the imaginations of those they were sent to, but that they did not really exist—that they were this, or that, or anything rather than what they really were. As for human souls, they denied their existence in a separate state from the body and denied any difference between the soul of a human being and that of an animal. These no doubt claimed to be freethinkers, but really they thought as poorly as possible. It is strange how people with such evil principles could have a place in the great Sanhedrin, but many of them had prestige and good estates, and they complied with the rules of the establishment, and so they got in and stayed in. How degenerate was the character of the Jewish church, when such profane men were among their rulers!

1.2. In the matter of differences between the Pharisees and Sadducees, Paul openly declared himself to be on the Pharisees' side against the Sadducees (v. 6): "He *cried out, I am a Pharisee, the son of a Pharisee. I hope for the resurrection of the dead*, and this is why I am now *called in question.*"

1.2.1. Paul acknowledged himself to be a Pharisee insofar as the Pharisees were in the right. Although to the extent that Pharisaism was opposed to Christianity, he set himself against it, nevertheless, to the extent that it was opposed to Sadducism, he remained faithful to it. We must never think the worse of any truth of God because it is held by people who are otherwise corrupt.

1.2.2. He could truthfully say that in being persecuted as a Christian, he was on trial for being a Pharisee, for holding to the hope of the resurrection of the dead, as he later pleaded (24:15; 26:6–7).

1.3. This led to a division in the council. There arose *a dissension between the Pharisees and the Sadducees* (v. 7), because this word of Paul's made the Sadducees hotter in their prosecution of him, and the Pharisees cooler. The result was that *the multitude was divided.* All the cry had been against Paul, but now there arose a great cry against one another (v. 9). Everything was done with clamor and noise, and the great principles of their religion were argued about chaotically. Those who contradict the truth may be convinced by fair reasoning, but never by a great hue and cry.

1.4. The Pharisees then—who would have thought it?—took Paul's side (v. 9): *They strove, saying, We find no evil in this man.* He had given a good account of himself and had now declared himself orthodox in the great principles of religion, and so they could not see he had *done any thing worthy of death or of bonds.* In fact, they went even further: *"If a spirit or an angel hath spoken to him, we should not oppose him, lest we be found fighting against God,"* as Gamaliel, himself a Pharisee, had argued (5:39).

1.4.1. We may notice, to the honor of the Gospel, that it was witnessed to even by its adversaries, and confessions not only of its innocence but also of its excellence were drawn out sometimes by the power of truth even from those who persecuted it. Pilate found no fault in Christ, though he put him to death. The Pharisees here supposed it possible that Paul might have received a commission from heaven through an angel to do what he did, but it seems they later joined the high priest in prosecuting him (24:1). They sinned against the knowledge that they not only had but sometimes acknowledged. Yet:

1.4.2. We hope that some of them at least then developed a higher opinion of Paul than they had had, and were favorable toward him. It must then be noticed, to their honor, that their zeal for the traditions of the elders was so far swallowed up in a zeal for the fundamental doctrines of religion that if Paul would sincerely join them against the Sadducees and stand by the hope of the resurrection

of the dead, they would charitably hope that he was walking according to the light God had given him, and, far from persecuting him, they would be ready to support and protect him.

2. The commander's care and conduct stood Paul in even better stead, because when he had thrown this bone of contention between the Pharisees and Sadducees, he was no closer to safety, but was in danger of being torn to pieces by them. The commander was forced to come with his soldiers and rescue him, as he had done before (21:32; 22:24). We see here:

2.1. Paul's danger. Between his friends and his enemies, he was nearly torn to pieces, the one hugging him to death, the other crushing him to death.

2.2. Paul's rescue. *The chief captain ordered his soldiers to go down, to take him by force from among them* and *bring him into the castle* (v. 10).

3. Divine encouragement stood him in the best stead of all. The commander had rescued him from the hands of cruel men, but he was still in custody. The barracks was a good protection to him, but it also meant confinement, and just as it was now his preservation from such a great death, it might also be his reservation for a greater one. On the following night, Paul was perhaps full of thoughts and concerns about what would become of him, and how his present troubles might be turned to some good purpose. It was then that the Lord Jesus paid him a kindly visit (v. 11): *The Lord stood by him*, came to his bedside. No matter who is against us, we need not fear if the Lord stands by us (Ro 8:31).

3.1. Christ told him to take courage: *"Be of good cheer, Paul"*; do not be discouraged." It is the will of Christ that his servants who are faithful be always cheerful. Christ, by his word, satisfied Paul that God approved of his conduct.

3.2. It is a strange argument that he used to encourage Paul: *As thou hast testified of me in Jerusalem, so must thou bear witness also at Rome.* One would have thought this was cold comfort, but it was intended to encourage him, for by it he was given to understand:

3.2.1. That he had been serving Christ as a witness for him in what he had endured up to that time. It was not a punishment for anything; rather, Paul was still continuing with his work.

3.2.2. That he had not yet finished his testimony (Rev 11:7), and so he was reserved for further service. Nothing discouraged Paul so much as the thought of being taken away from serving Christ and from doing good to souls: "Fear not," Christ said; "I have not finished with you." Paul seems to have had a particular inclination to go to Rome to preach the Gospel there. Because he was a Roman citizen, he longed to go there, and had intended it (19:21): *After I have been at Jerusalem, I must also see Rome.* Now he was ready to conclude that these recent experiences had upset his plans and that he would never see Rome, but even in that, Christ told him he would be satisfied.

Verses 12–35

We have here the account of a conspiracy against Paul's life. We see:

1. How this plot was hatched. The Jews found they could gain nothing either by popular uprising or by due process of law, and so they turned to the barbaric method of assassination. Notice:

1.1. Who formed this conspiracy. They were *certain Jews* (v. 12), *more than forty* (v. 13).

1.2. When the conspiracy was formed: *when it was day.* At night Christ appeared to Paul to protect him, and when it was day forty men appeared against him to destroy him; they were not up soon enough, however, to have risen before Christ.

1.3. What the conspiracy was. These men *banded together*; they committed themselves to stand by one another, and each one, according to his ability, would play his part in helping to murder Paul. How terrible an idea these men must have formed of Paul before they could have been capable of forming such a monstrous plot against him! Are there any laws of truth and justice, however sacred, however strong, that hatred and bigotry will not break through?

1.4. How firmly they were set on their course of action. *They bound themselves under a curse* (with an oath), calling down the heaviest curses on themselves if they did not kill Paul, and so quickly *that they would not eat nor drink till they had done it.* What a complex web of evil this was! To conspire to kill an innocent man who had done them no harm was *going in the way of Cain* (Jude 11); yet, as if this by itself were a small thing:

1.4.1. They bound themselves to it. To incline to do evil, and intend to do it, is bad enough, but to commit yourself on oath to do it is far worse. This is entering into covenant with the Devil; it is leaving no room for repentance.

1.4.2. They committed one another to do it, and did all they could to secure the condemnation not only of their own souls but also of the souls of those whom they drew into the conspiracy.

1.4.3. They showed great contempt for the providence of God to do such a thing within such a short time. When we say, *Tomorrow we will do this or that*, we must add, *If the Lord will* (Jas 4:13–15). But how could they have the nerve to insert a condition relating to the permission of God's providence when what they were doing was directly against the prohibitions of God's work?

1.4.4. They showed great contempt for their own souls and bodies. They showed contempt for their own souls by calling down a curse on themselves if they did not succeed in this desperate plot. What a terrible dilemma they fell into! God would certainly meet them with his curse if they succeeded in it, and they wished he would if they did not! They showed great contempt for their own bodies by binding themselves to abstain from the necessary supports of life until they had accomplished what they might never be able to do.

1.4.5. They showed a most eager desire to achieve this purpose.

1.5. How they undertook to bring it about. Paul could not be approached in the barracks. Therefore the chief priests and elders would ask the governor of the barracks to let Paul come to them to be further examined, and then, on his way from the barracks to the council, they would put an end to the whole matter by killing him (vv. 14–15). They came to the principal members of the great Sanhedrin. They were so confident of the council's approval of this villainous act that they were not ashamed to acknowledge to them *that they had bound themselves under a great curse, that they would eat nothing till they had killed Paul.* They intended to eat breakfast the next morning having shed his blood. They did not doubt that the chief priests would help them, that they would be the plotters' tools, pretending to *the chief captain that they would inquire something more perfectly concerning him.* What a low opinion they had of their priests, that they could turn to them on such a mission as this! Yet the priests and elders consented to it without any scruples. Instead of rebuking them, they supported them in it, because it was Paul whom they hated.

2. How the plot was discovered. Providence so arranged matters that it was brought to light and thereby brought to nothing. Notice:

2.1. How it was revealed to Paul (v. 16). A young man who was related to Paul, *his sister's son*, somehow *heard* of the Jews' *lying in wait*, and *he went into the castle* and *told Paul* what he had heard. God has many ways of bringing to light the hidden works of darkness (1Co 4:5; Eph 5:11).

2.2. How it was revealed to the commander.

2.2.1. By his peaceful behavior, Paul had gained good influence with the officers who attended him. He could call one of the centurions to him, and he was ready to come at his call (v. 17). Paul wanted him to introduce this young man to the commander so that the young man could give information.

2.2.2. The centurion agreed to his wish very readily (v. 18). He went himself to commend the young man's mission to the commander: *"Paul the prisoner—*this was his title now*—called me to him, and prayed me to bring this young man to thee; he has something to say to thee."* It is a true kindness to poor prisoners to act for them as well as to give to them. *"I was sick and in prison,* and you went on an errand for me," will be as valid in giving an account of our lives as, *"I was sick and in prison, and you came unto me* (Mt 25:36)." Those who know people and have influence should be ready to use their influence to help those in distress. This centurion helped save Paul's life by this act of civility. Those who cannot give a good gift to God's prisoners may still speak a good word for them.

2.2.3. The commander received the information with a great deal of sensitivity (v. 19). He *took the young man by the hand* to encourage him, so that he would not be disheartened, but assured of receiving a favorable hearing. The notice that is taken of this detail should encourage leaders to make themselves available. The familiarity with which this Roman commander received Paul's nephew is recorded here to his honor. Let no one think they are disparaging themselves by their humility or kindness. He *went with (took)* him *aside privately and asked him, What is it that thou hast to tell me?*

2.2.4. The young man delivered his message to the commander very readily (vv. 20–21): *"The Jews have agreed to desire* (ask) *thee that thou wouldst bring down Paul tomorrow into the council, but do not thou yield unto them, for there lie in wait for him of them more than forty men,* who have sworn to put him to death, *and now are they ready looking for a promise from thee."*

2.2.5. The commander dismissed the young man, telling him to keep the secret: *See that thou tell no man that thou hast shown these things unto me* (v. 22). Those who cannot keep a secret are not fit to be employed in business.

3. How the plot was defeated: when the commander realized how relentless the Jews were in their intentions to cause trouble for Paul, and how close he himself had come to being accessory to it, he decided to send Paul away, out of their reach, as fast as possible. He seemed afraid that if he detained Paul in his barracks there, they would find some way or other to carry out their plan. Whatever happened, he wanted to protect Paul, because he did not deserve such treatment. What a sad observation it is that when the Jewish chief priests knew of this assassination plot, they supported it, while a Roman chief captain, purely out of a natural sense of justice and humanity, set himself to thwart it.

3.1. He ordered a considerable detachment of the Roman forces under his command *to go to Caesarea* as quickly as possible and take Paul there *to Felix the governor.* It seems clear to me that the commander could legitimately have set Paul free, allowing him to fend for himself. He himself acknowledged *that nothing was laid to his charge worthy of bonds* (v. 29), and he should have had the same compassion for Paul's liberty that he had for his life, but he feared that this would have enraged the Jews too much against Paul. *Two centurions* were employed in this business (vv. 23–24). They must *get ready two hundred soldiers to go to Caesarea,* and besides these, *seventy horse and two hundred spearmen.*

3.1.1. The commander intended to expose the Jews as headstrong and turbulent, people who needed to be awed by such a retinue. Also, he thought nothing less would be enough to defeat their attempt.

3.1.2. God intended to encourage Paul. Paul, however, did not desire such a guard, because he trusted in God's all-sufficiency; it was because of the governor's own concern, however. But Paul was also made significant here, for in this way his *bonds in Christ* were revealed throughout the country (Php 1:13). When his enemies hated him—and I suppose his friends neglected him—then a Roman commander carefully provided:

3.1.2.1. For his comfort: *Let them provide beasts, that they set Paul on.* If his Jewish persecutors had ordered that he be transferred to Caesarea, they would have made him walk on foot or have dragged him there in a cart. But the commander treated him as a gentleman and ordered him a good horse to ride on.

3.1.2.2. For his security. Strict orders were given *to bring him safely to Felix the governor,* who was supreme in all civil affairs among the Jews, as this commander was in military affairs. The Roman historians speak much about this Felix, as a man of humble extraction, but one who raised himself by his own efforts to become governor of Judea. Poor Paul was turned over to the judgment of such a man, but better to him than into the hands of Ananias the high priest!

3.2. The commander ordered that he be taken away at *the third hour of the night,* three hours after sunset, so that they would have the cool of the night to march in.

3.3. *He wrote a letter to Felix the governor* of this province, by which he left the whole matter with Felix. This letter is inserted verbatim here (v. 25). Notice:

3.3.1. The compliments the commander gave to *the governor* (v. 26). He was *the most excellent governor Felix,* this title being proper to the office of governor. The commander sent him *greeting.*

3.3.2. The just and fair account that he gave Felix of Paul's case:

3.3.2.1. Paul was one whom the Jews were angry with: *They had taken him* and would *have killed him,* and perhaps Felix did not think any the worse of Paul for that (v. 27).

3.3.2.2. He had protected Paul because he was a Roman: "When they were about to kill him, *I came with an army and rescued him*"—an action on behalf of a citizen of Rome that would commend the commander to the Roman governor.

3.3.2.3. He could not understand the merits of Paul's case. He followed the proper method to find out: he *brought him forth into their council* (v. 28) to be examined there, but he found *that he was accused of questions of their law* (v. 29), about *the hope of the resurrection of the dead* (v. 6). The Romans allowed the nations they conquered to exercise their own religion, and never tried to impose theirs on them, but as those who wanted to keep the public peace, they would not allow them, in the name of their religion, to mistreat their neighbors.

3.3.2.4. He had understood enough to know that there was *nothing laid to his charge worthy of death or of bonds.*

3.3.3. His referring Paul's case to Felix (v. 30): "*When it was told me that the Jews laid wait for the man* to kill him, *I sent straightaway to thee.* Let *his accusers* pursue him and *say before thee what they have against him,* for, having been brought up as a soldier, I will never claim to be a judge, and so *farewell.*"

3.4. Accordingly, Paul was led to Caesarea; the soldiers got him safely out of Jerusalem by night and left the conspirators to consider whether they should eat and drink or not. If they would not repent of the wickedness of their oath, they were now at leisure to repent of its rashness. If any of them did starve themselves to death, they fell unpitied. Paul was led to Antipatris, which was about midway to Caesarea (v. 31). From there *the two hundred foot-soldiers* and *the two hundred spearmen returned* to their quarters in the barracks. There was no need for such a strong guard; *the horsemen* would be enough to take him to Caesarea and would do it more quickly.

3.5. He was handed over to Felix (v. 33). The officers *presented the letter,* and *Paul with it, to Felix.* Paul had never desired the familiarity or the company of great people, but Providence oversaw his sufferings so as to make them give him an opportunity to witness to Christ before leaders. *The governor* inquired as to *what province* the prisoner originally came from, and he was told *that* Paul *was a native of Cilicia* (v. 34). He promised him a speedy trial (v. 35): *I will hear thee when thine accusers have come.* He ordered him to be taken into custody, that he *be kept* a prisoner *in Herod's judgment hall.*

CHAPTER 24

We left Paul a prisoner at Caesarea, and now we have his accusation and trial before Felix the governor. Here is:
1. The appearing of the prosecutors against him (vv. 1–2).
2. The opening of the charges against him by Tertullus (vv. 2–8). 3. The corroborating of the charge by the testimony of the witnesses (v. 9). 4. The prisoner's defense, in which, with all due deference to the governor (v. 10), he denied the charge (vv. 11–13), acknowledged the truth and made an unexceptionable profession of his faith (vv. 14–16), and gave a more detailed account of what had taken place from their first seizing him (vv. 17–21). 5. The adjourning of the case (vv. 22–23). 6. The private conversation that took place between the prisoner and the judge (vv. 24–26). 7. The extension of Paul's imprisonment for two years, until another governor came (v. 27).

Verses 1–9

We must suppose *that Lysias, the chief captain,* gave notice to the chief priests that they must follow him to Caesarea and that there they would find a judge ready to hear them.

1. We have here the case brought against Paul. No time was lost, for they were ready for a hearing *after five days.* He said here (v. 11) *that it was but twelve days since he came up to Jerusalem,* and he had *spent seven in his purifying in the temple.* Those who had been his judges themselves appeared here as his prosecutors. *Ananias the high priest* himself now stood to inform against him. It is surprising:

1.1. That he would so disparage himself, forgetting the dignity of his position.

1.2. That he would so reveal himself and his enmity against Paul! Ananias was not ashamed to acknowledge he was a sworn enemy of Paul. The elders accompanied him to show their agreement with him. The pains evildoers take in pursuing evil—their tireless diligence—should shame us out of our coldness and indifference toward doing what is good.

2. We have here the case pleaded against Paul. The prosecutors brought *with them a certain orator named Tertullus*, who was a Roman and therefore the most suitable person to employ in a case before *the Roman governor*, and most likely to gain favor. Although the hearts of the high priest and elders were spiteful enough, they did not think their own tongues were sharp enough. Paul was brought to the bar before Felix the governor: *He was called forth* (v. 2). Tertullus's business was to open up the information against Paul on behalf of the prosecutors. His speech was made up of flattery and falsehood; it calls evil good, and good evil (Isa 5:20).

2.1. One of the worst people was applauded here as one of the best and most generous, only because he was the judge. Felix is represented by the historians of his own nation, as well as by Josephus the Jew, as a very bad man, who allowed himself to indulge all kinds of evil. He was noted as a great oppressor, very cruel and very greedy. But Tertullus here, in the name of the high priest and elders, complimented him, praising him to the skies as if there had never been such a good magistrate. To engage Felix to satisfy their malice against Paul, they exalted him as the greatest blessing to their church and nation who had ever come among them.

2.1.1. They were very ready to acknowledge it (v. 2): *By thee we enjoy great quietness, and very worthy deeds are done to the whole nation of the Jews by thy providence.* To give him his due, he had been instrumental in suppressing the insurrection of that Egyptian about whom the commander had spoken (21:38). See here:

2.1.1.1. What a great misfortune it is to great men to have their services exalted immeasurably, and never to be faithfully told of their faults. Here, they are hardened and encouraged in committing evil.

2.1.1.2. The shrewdness of evildoers, who, by flattering rulers in what they do wrong, draw them on to do even worse.

2.1.2. They promised to continue being grateful for it (v. 3): *We accept it always, and in all places, most noble Felix, with all thankfulness.* If it had been true that he was such a governor, it would have been just for them to accept his help with great thankfulness. The benefits that we enjoy through the government, especially through the administration of wise and good governors, are what we should be thankful for both to God and humanity.

2.1.3. They therefore expected his favor in this case (v. 4). They pretended to be very concerned not to intrude on his time—we will *not be further tedious to thee* (not weary you further)—but to be sure of his patience: *I pray thee that thou wouldest hear us of thy clemency a few words* (I would request that you be kind enough to hear us briefly). They were so aware that their cause would soon be shown to contain more hatred than substance that they found it necessary to insinuate themselves in this way into his favor. Everybody knew that the high priest and the elders hated Felix, but to pursue their ends against Paul, they showed him all this respect. Rulers cannot always judge the affections of their people by their applause; flattery is one thing, and true loyalty is another.

2.2. One of the best people was accused here as one of the worst evildoers. After a flourish of flattery, the Jews' attorney got down to business. This part of his speech is as nauseous for its insults as the former part is for its flat-

tery. As we cannot help being sorry that a man of wit and sense would have such a mercenary tongue, so we cannot help being angry at those men of high position who put such words into his mouth. Tertullus here complained of two things to Felix:

2.2.1. The peace of the nation had been disturbed by Paul. They could not have baited Christ's disciples if they had not first dressed them up in the skins of wild beasts. Innocence—indeed, excellence and usefulness—are no protection against slander, not even against the impressions of slander on the minds of both magistrates and multitudes. Even if the representation is very unjust, when it is enforced, as here, with a note of seriousness and assurance, something will stick. The Jews did not say, "We suspect him of being a dangerous man," but, as if the thing were beyond dispute, "*We have found him to be so,*" as if he were a traitor and rebel who had already been convicted.

2.2.1.1. Paul was a useful man and a great blessing to his country, but he was called here *a pestilent fellow* (v. 5): "*We have found him the plague* of the nation, a walking disease." They wanted it thought that he had done more trouble in his time than a plague could do, that the trouble he caused was spreading and infectious, that it had exactly the sort of fatal consequences that a plague has, that it was as much to be dreaded and guarded against as plague.

2.2.1.2. Paul was a peacemaker; he himself lived peacefully and quietly, and he taught others to do so too, but here he was represented as *a mover of sedition among all the Jews throughout all the world*. The Jews were discontent with the Roman government, and Felix knew this. Now they wanted to make him believe that this Paul was the man who made them so. They tried to cause a rebellion wherever he went, and then put the blame unjustly on him.

2.2.1.3. Paul was a man of wide love and kindness, who made himself the servant of everyone for their good, but he was accused here of being *a ringleader of the sect of the Nazarenes*. Now it was true that Paul was an active, leading man in spreading Christianity, but:

2.2.1.3.1. It was completely false that this was a sect. True Christianity establishes what is of common concern to the whole human race; it declares goodwill to all people and therefore cannot be thought to arise from such narrow opinions as sects owe their origin to. True Christianity leads directly to uniting all people, and as far as it obtains its just influence on people's minds, it will make them peaceful and loving, and is therefore far from being a narrow sect. True Christianity aims at no worldly benefit or advantage and must therefore by no means be called a sect. Those who accept the teaching of a sect aim at wealth and honor, but the professors of Christianity risk the loss of all that is dear to them in this world.

2.2.1.3.2. It was invidiously called *the sect of the Nazarenes*, by which Christ was represented as coming from Nazareth, from where nothing good was expected to come (Jn 1:46), whereas he came from Bethlehem, where the Messiah was to be born (Mic 5:2; Mt 2:6).

2.2.1.3.3. It was false that Paul was the author or standard-bearer of this so-called sect, because he did not draw people to himself, but to Christ.

2.2.1.4. Paul had respect for the temple and had just reverently attended the temple service, and yet he was accused here of having *profaned the temple* (v. 6).

2.2.2. The course of justice against Paul had been obstructed by the commander.

2.2.2.1. The Jews pleaded that they *took him, and would have judged him according to their law*. This was false; they did not go about judging him according to their law, but went about to beat him to death or tear him to pieces, to throw him into the hands of ruffians who lay in wait to destroy him. When people know what they should have done, it is easy for them to say that in other circumstances they would have done something else, when in reality they fully intended to do nothing less than what they in fact did.

2.2.2.2. They reflected on the commander. *The chief captain Lysias came upon us and with great violence took him out of our hands* (v. 7). Notice how persecutors are enraged at their disappointments, which they should really be thankful for. These cruel men justified themselves and regarded as their enemy the one who kept them from shedding blood with their own hands.

2.2.2.3. They referred the matter to Felix and his judgment, though uneasy about having to do so, the commander having made them do it (v. 8). "He *commanded his accusers to come to thee*, so that you could hear the charges. He has left it to you to examine him and see what you can get out of him."

3. We have the assent of the Jews to this charge (v. 9): *They confirmed it, saying that those things were so.* Some think this expresses testimony by which witnesses, examined under oath, attested to the Jews' charges. Yet it seems rather to show the approval the high priest and the elders gave to what Tertullus said. Those who do not have the wit and gifts that some others have for causing trouble still make themselves guilty of the troubles others cause by assenting to what others do. Many who do not have enough learning to plead for Baal still have enough wickedness to vote for Baal.

Verses 10–21

We have here Paul's defense of himself, and it contains a fulfillment of Christ's promise to his followers that when they stood before governors and kings for his sake, it would be *given them in that same hour what they should speak* (Mt 10:19). Although Tertullus had said a great many offensive things, Paul did not interrupt him, but let him continue to the end of his speech. Moreover, when the lawyer had finished, Paul waited for permission from the judge to speak in his turn, and gained it. The *governor beckoned to him to speak* (v. 10). Paul made no references at all to Tertullus, but directed his defense against those who employed him.

1. He addressed himself very respectfully to the governor. Here were no such flattering compliments as Tertullus soothed him with, but Paul's profession that he *cheerfully answered for himself* before him, looking on him as one who would be fair and impartial. It was also the language of one who was aware of his own integrity. He did not stand trembling at the bar; he was very cheerful because he had a judge who was not biased but impartial. In fact, when he considered who his judge was, *I the more cheerfully answer for myself*, because *I know thou hast been many years a judge to this nation*; this was very true.

1.1. The governor could say of his own knowledge that there had never been any complaints against Paul before. He never had Paul brought before him until now, and so Paul was not so dangerous a criminal as he was made out to be.

1.2. He was familiar with the Jewish nation. He knew what furious zealots they were against all who did not comply with them, and so he would make allowances for that. Although he did not know Paul, he knew his prosecutors, and by this he could guess what kind of person Paul was.

2. He denied the charges against him, on which their characterization of him was based. Stirring up riots and desecrating the temple were the crimes for which he stood accused (v. 5), crimes that they knew the Roman governors were not accustomed to look into, and so the Jews had hoped that the governor would return him to them. Paul, however, hoped that although he would not inquire into the crimes, he would protect one who had been unjustly accused of them. Now he wanted Felix to understand:

2.1. That he had come to Jerusalem deliberately to worship God in peace and holiness. He came to maintain his fellowship with the Jews, not to show them any disrespect.

2.2. That it was only twelve days since he had come to Jerusalem; he had been a prisoner six days, and it could not be supposed that in such a short time he could cause the trouble the Jews accused him of.

2.3. That if he had behaved very quietly and peaceably at Jerusalem. If it had been true that he was *a mover of sedition among all the Jews*, surely he would have worked hard to assemble a group and worked subversively to incite a rebellion in Jerusalem, but he had not. He was in the temple, attending the public service there. He was in the synagogues, where the law was read and explained. He went about in the city among his relatives and friends. The Jews could not accuse him of bringing anything either against the faith or against the peace of the Jewish church.

2.3.1. His spirit was not at all perverse, like that of those who incite rebellion. They never found him *disputing with any man* (v. 12). He was ready, if asked, to give a reason for his own hope (1Pe 3:15), and to teach others, but he never picked a quarrel with anyone about their religion.

2.3.2. His spirit was not at all turbulent: "They never found me *raising up the people*." He behaved as was fitting for a Christian, with love and quietness and appropriate submission to lawful authority. Nor did he ever mention or think of such a thing as taking up arms to spread the Gospel.

2.4. That as to what they had accused him of, of inciting rebellion in other countries, he was completely innocent, and they could not prove the charge (v. 13): *Neither can they prove the things whereof the now accuse me.*

2.4.1. He maintained his own innocence. He was not an enemy of the public peace.

2.4.2. He was sad about his own personal difficulty, that he was accused of things that could not be proved against him. It has often been the lot of very worthy and good people to be wronged in this way, to be accused of things that they hate the mere thought of.

2.4.3. He showed the sin of his prosecutors, who said what they knew they could not prove and thereby wronged him, and did the judge wrong too, by trying to deceive him.

2.4.4. He appealed to the fairness of his judge. A judge must give sentence according to what is not only alleged but proved.

3. He gave a fair and just account of himself, which indicated the true reason they were prosecuting him.

3.1. He acknowledged that they looked on him as a heretic. The commander had noticed, and the governor now must surely notice, an unusual violence and fury in Paul's prosecutors. Guessing at the crime from the uproar, they concluded he must have been a very bad man. Now Paul here cleared up the confusion: *In the way which they call heresy*—or a *sect* (v. 5)—*so worship I the God of my fathers*. It is nothing new for the right way of worshiping

God to be called heresy. Let us, therefore, never be driven away from pursuing any good way by its being given a bad name.

3.2. He vindicated himself against this accusation. They called Paul a heretic, but he was not so.

3.2.1. He *worshiped the God of his fathers* and was therefore right in the object of his worship. He worshiped the God of Abraham, Isaac, and Jacob (Ex 3:6; Mt 22:32), the God who took them into covenant with himself. Paul was faithful to that covenant and set up no other god in opposition to it. "*I worship* the same God whom all my ancestors worshiped." Paul's religion gloried in its antiquity and in an uninterrupted succession of those who professed it. It is very comforting in our worship of God to look to him as the God of our ancestors. He showed himself to be their God, and so if we serve him as they did, he will be our God.

3.2.2. He *believed all things which were written in the law and the prophets* and was therefore right in the rule of his worship. He accepted the Scriptures as whole and pure. He did not set up any rule of faith or practice but the Scriptures. Divine revelation, as it is in the Scriptures, was what he was determined to live and die by, and for this reason, too, he was not a heretic.

3.2.3. He had his eye on the future state and was therefore right in the purpose of his worship. Those who turn aside to heresy have regard to this world, but Paul aimed to make heaven his religion, nothing more nor less (v. 15): "*I have hope toward God*; my hope is toward God and not toward the world. I depend on God and his power, that *there shall be a resurrection of the dead*, of all, both *the just and unjust.*" Notice here:

3.2.3.1. There will be a resurrection of the dead, of all people from the beginning to the end of time. Not only do we have another life to live when our present life comes to an end; there is also to be another world.

3.2.3.2. It will be a resurrection *both of the just and of the unjust*; it will be a resurrection of those who did well, and our Savior has told us that to them it will be *a resurrection of life*; it will be a resurrection of those who did evil, and he has told us that it will be a resurrection of condemnation (Jn 5:29; Da 12:2). This implies that it will be a resurrection to a final judgment. The just will rise because of their union with Christ as their head; the unjust will rise because of Christ's dominion over them as their Judge.

3.2.3.3. God is to be depended on for the resurrection of the dead: "I have *hope toward God* that there will be a resurrection"; it will be brought about by the almighty power of God.

3.2.3.4. The resurrection of the dead is a fundamental article of our creed, as it was also of that of the Jewish church. It was what *they themselves also allowed* (accept), but it was more clearly revealed by the Gospel.

3.2.3.5. In every aspect of our religion we should serve God with confidence that in him *there will be a resurrection of the dead*, and we should expect our reward in that.

3.2.4. His conduct was consistent with his devotion (v. 16): *And herein do I exercise myself, to have always a conscience void of offense toward God and toward men.* This pleading of Paul's was to the same effect as what he presented before the high priest (23:1): *I have lived in all good conscience.* Notice:

3.2.4.1. What was Paul's aim and desire: to *have a conscience void of offense.* Either:

3.2.4.1.1. "A conscience not offending, not informing me wrongly or misleading me in anything." Or:

3.2.4.1.2. A conscience that is not offended. "This is what I am ambitious to have, to keep on good terms with my own conscience. I am as careful not to offend my conscience as I am not to offend a friend whom I am with daily."

3.2.4.2. How he was concerned to conduct himself in pursuing this: "*I exercise myself,* I make it my constant business." Those who did so were called ascetics, from the word used here; *asko,* "I strive; I strive to keep my own conscience clear."

3.2.4.3. The extent of this objective:

3.2.4.3.1. At all times: *To have always a conscience void of offense.* Paul was conscious in himself that he had not yet attained perfection (Php 3:12), and the evil that he would not do he still did (Ro 7:19). Sins of weakness make the conscience uneasy, but they do not wound it as presumptuous sins do; although offense may be given to the conscience, care must be taken that it is not a lasting offense. This requires, however, that we always *exercise ourselves* in faith and repentance.

3.2.4.3.2. In all things: *both toward God, and toward man.* The care he took of his conscience extended to the whole of his duty, and he was afraid of breaking the law of love either toward God or toward his neighbor. We must be very careful not to think, speak, or do anything wrong either against God or against other people (2Co 8:21).

3.2.4.4. The motivation to do it: *Herein do I exercise myself. Herein: en touto,* "for this cause," as it may read. "Because I look for the resurrection of the dead and the future life of the world, I exercise myself."

4. Having made confession of his faith, he gave a clear account of his situation and of the wrong done him by his persecutors. He challenged them to prove him guilty:

4.1. In the temple. Here they had seized him violently as an enemy of their nation and the temple (21:28).

4.1.1. It was very hard to accuse him as an *enemy to their nation*, since he came to *bring alms to his nation*, to help the poor in Jerusalem. He had no malice toward that people and was ready to do them all the good he could.

4.1.2. It was very hard to accuse him of having defiled the temple, since he brought offerings, and at his own expense (21:24), and was found *purifying himself in the temple* according to the law (v. 18), *neither with multitude nor with tumult* (no crowd being with him, and he not being involved any disturbance). It was Jews from Asia, his enemies, who caused him to be noticed; they did not even have a pretense for raising a mob and a tumult against him, since he had neither a mob nor a tumult supporting him. As for the charge that Paul had brought Greeks into the temple, he challenged these Jews from Asia to prove it (v. 19): "Those Jews of Asia should have been *here before thee,* so that they could have been examined, whether *they had aught against me.*"

4.2. In the council: "Let *these same* who are *here* say whether they have *found any evil doing in me when I stood before the council* (v. 20). When I was there, all I said was, *Touching the resurrection of the dead I am called in question by you this day* (v. 21), which caused no offense to anyone except the Sadducees. I stood by what is the faith of the whole Jewish church, except those whom they themselves call heretics."

Verses 22–27

We have here the result and consequences of Paul's trial before Felix.

1. Felix adjourned the case (v. 22): he *had a more perfect knowledge of* (was better acquainted with) *that way* than the high priest and the elders thought he had. He

had gained an idea of Christianity, that it was not such an evil thing as it was here said to be, and so he put the prosecutors off with an excuse: "*When the chief captain shall come down, I will know the uttermost of your matter*; I will know the truth. Either Paul deserves to be punished for inciting the people to riot, or you do for doing it yourselves. I will hear what he says and will determine the matter between you accordingly."

1.1. It was a disappointment to the high priest and the elders that Paul was not condemned or subjected to their judgment. But this is how God sometimes restrains the wrath of his people's enemies (Ps 76:10) by means not of their friends but of those who are strangers to them.

1.2. It was a wrong to Paul that he was not released. But Felix was a judge who neither feared God nor respected other people (Lk 18:2), and what good could be expected from him?

2. He detained the prisoner in custody. Felix thought a man of such a public character as Paul had many friends, and he might have an opportunity of pleasing them or making use of them. He continued to detain him as prisoner and commanded a centurion to guard him (v. 23). He took care that Paul would be a prisoner with some freedom; his keeper must allow him some liberty, and make his confinement as comfortable for him as possible. The high priest and the elders begrudged him his life, but Felix generously allowed him some degree of liberty. He also gave orders that none of his friends should be hindered from coming to him, and a man's prison is like his own house if only he has his friends around him.

3. He had frequent conversations with him later in private (v. 24–25). Notice:

3.1. Why *Felix sent for Paul*. He had in mind that he wanted to talk with him *concerning the faith in Christ*. Felix wanted to talk with Paul more freely than he could in open court *concerning the faith of Christ*. He did this to satisfy his curiosity, or rather the curiosity of *his wife Drusilla, who was a Jewess*, daughter of Herod Agrippa. Being educated in the Jewish religion, she was more inquisitive about the Christian religion. However, it was not significant what religion she belonged to, for, whatever it was, she was a reproach and scandal to it—a Jew, but also an adulterer; she was noted for being arrogant. Many are fond of new ideas and speculations in religious matters but hate to come under the power or influence of true religion.

3.2. What account Paul gave him of the Christian faith. Felix expected to be amused with a mystical divinity, but he was alarmed with a practical divinity. When Paul was asked *concerning the Christ, he reasoned* concerning *righteousness, temperance, and judgment to come*. He spoke with clarity and warmth *of righteousness, temperance, and judgment to come*. Faith in Christ is intended to reinforce in people the great laws of justice and self-control. Justice and self-control were celebrated virtues among the pagan moralists; if the doctrine Paul preached would only free him from an obligation to cultivate these, Felix would readily accept it. "It is so far from doing that that it actually strengthens the obligations of those sacred laws." *Paul reasoned of righteousness and temperance* to convince Felix of his unrighteousness and lack of self-control, so that, seeing how repugnant they were, he would seek the faith of Christ and accept it fully. Through the message of Christ the judgment to come is revealed to us. People have their day now, Felix has his, but God's day is coming (Ps 37:13). From this account of the main subjects of Paul's discussion we may gather that in his preaching Paul showed no favoritism to people, because the word of

God does not. Rather, he aimed at the human conscience and led people to see their sins. Paul put serving Christ and saving souls before thoughts of his own safety. Paul was willing to run risks in his work even where there was little probability of doing good. Felix and Drusilla were such hardened sinners that it was not at all likely they would be brought to repentance by Paul's preaching, but Paul still dealt with them as one who did not despair of them. Let the watchman give fair warning, and then he has saved his own soul, even if he does not succeed in saving the souls he watches for (Eze 33:1–10).

3.3. What impressions Paul's words made on this great but evil man: *Felix trembled*, "being made afraid." Paul never trembled in his presence, but he was made to tremble in Paul's. We do not find that Drusilla trembled, even though she was equally guilty. See here the power of the word of God. It is searching and startling; it can strike terror on the heart of the proudest and most daring sinner. See too the workings of natural conscience; when that is startled and awakened, it fills the soul with stunned horror. A prospect of the future judgment is enough to make the strongest heart tremble.

3.4. How Felix struggled to get clear of these impressions. He acted toward them as he did to Paul's prosecutors (v. 25), *he deferred them*; he said, Go thy way for this time; when I have a convenient season, I will call for thee. He trembled and that was all. Many are startled by the word of God but not effectively changed by it. Many people fear the consequences of sin but continue to be in love and alliance with sin. Felix did not fight against his convictions. He skillfully shifted his convictions by delaying pursuing them to another time. Like a sad debtor, he begged for another day; Paul was spent, and he had tired out the governor and his lady, too, and so, "*Go thy way for this time; when I have a convenient season, I will call for thee*." Many people lose all the benefit of their convictions because they do not strike while the iron is hot. By dropping his convictions now, he lost them forever, and himself with them. In spiritual matters, delays are dangerous. The matter is delayed to a more convenient time, and then convictions cool off and die down. Felix put off this matter to a more convenient time, but we do not find that this more convenient time ever came. The present time—now—is without doubt the most convenient time.

4. After all this, he still detained Paul as a prisoner, and he left him so when, two years later, he was removed from the government (vv. 26–27). He was convinced in his conscience that Paul had done *nothing worthy of death or of bonds*, but he did not have the honesty to release him. Here we are told what principles he was governed by in this.

4.1. The love of money. He would not release Paul because he hoped that eventually Paul's friends would buy his liberty. Felix could not find it in his heart to do his duty as a judge unless he gained money from it: *He hoped that money would have been given him of Paul*. In the hope of this, he detained him as a prisoner *and sent for him the oftener, and communed with him*. He sent for him to take his pulse, to give him the opportunity to ask what the governor would accept to release him.

4.1.1. Now we see what became of his promise both to Paul and to himself that he would hear more about Christ at some other convenient time. His only concern now was to get money from Paul.

4.1.2. Paul was a poor man, but Felix knew there were those who wished him well who were able to help him. Although Paul is to be commended for not offering money to Felix, I am not sure whether his friends are to be commended for not doing it for him. We should not bribe someone to do something unjust, but if they will not do me justice without a fee, it is only doing myself justice to give it to them, and if Paul's friends could have done it, it was a shame they did not. The Christians here at Caesarea had parted with their tears to prevent his going into prison (21:13), and could they not find it in their hearts to part with their money to help him out of prison?

4.1.3. The providence of God in using Paul to further the Gospel even in his chains will not excuse Felix. The judge who will not do right without a bribe will no doubt do wrong with a bribe.

4.2. The desire to please other people. Felix was recalled from his government about *two years after this*, and Porcius Festus was put in his place. Felix *left Paul bound*, and the reason given here is that he was *willing to do the Jews a pleasure*. He did it in the hope that it would make up for the many offenses he had committed against them. Those who do some evil things are tempted to do more to protect themselves. But when Felix had done this, it seems it did not have the intended effect. The Jews, despite this, accused him to the emperor. Those who aim to please God by doing good will have what they aim at, but those who seek to please people by doing evil will not.

CHAPTER 25

We have here much the same management of Paul's case as we had in the previous chapter. It was here considered: 1. By Festus, the governor who succeeded Felix (vv. 1–3). The hearing of it was appointed to be not at Jerusalem, as the Jews wanted, but at Caesarea (vv. 4–6). The Jews appeared against Paul (v. 7), but Paul insisted on his innocence (v. 8), and to avoid the moving of the case to Jerusalem, he eventually appealed to Caesar (vv. 9–12). 2. By King Agrippa (vv. 13–21), and Agrippa asked to hear the case himself (v. 22). Accordingly, Paul was brought to the bar (v. 23), and Festus explained the case (vv. 24–27).

Verses 1–12

We sometimes say, "New lords mean new laws and new customs." Here, however, with a new governor, Paul still received the same treatment. Festus, like Felix, did not release him. Here is:

1. The urgent attempt of the high priest and other Jews to persuade the governor to abandon Paul.

1.1. Notice how quick they were in applying to Festus. As soon as he *had come into the province*, within *three days he went up to Jerusalem*, and immediately the priests urged him to proceed against Paul. Having probably been installed in office at Caesarea, he stayed *three days at Caesarea*, where Paul was a prisoner, and we are not told that during that time Paul asked to be released, but as soon as Festus came to Jerusalem, the priests were quick to use their influence with him against Paul.

1.2. Notice how spiteful they were in their request. They *informed the governor against Paul* (v. 2) before he was brought to fair trial, in order to get Festus on their side, since he was to be the judge. But they could not trust in this trick, even though it was very corrupt. They formed another project, therefore, which was even more corrupt, and that was to assassinate Paul before he came to trial.

1.3. Notice how false their pretense was. Now that *the governor was himself at Jerusalem, they desired* (requested) *he would send for Paul thither* and try him there. Paul was charged with having desecrated the temple

at Jerusalem, and it is usual for criminals to be tried in the court that has jurisdiction over the place. However, what they intended was to ambush him and murder him on the road. *They desired favour against Paul.* The business of prosecutors is to demand justice against one whom they think to be a criminal. To ask a favor against a prisoner, and to ask it of the judge, who should be trustworthy and impartial, is very arrogant. If any favor is to be shown, it should be shown to the prisoner, but here they sought it against him.

2. The governor's decision that Paul would stand trial at Caesarea (vv. 4–5). He gave orders *that Paul should be kept at Caesarea.*

2.1. He would not do the Jews the kindness of having Paul sent to Jerusalem. Whatever his reason for refusing the Jews' request, God used it as a means of preserving Paul from the hands of his enemies. God did not bring it to light, but he found another way to bring it to nothing, by inclining the heart of the governor not to move Paul to Jerusalem. God is not limited to one method in working out salvation for his people.

2.2. He would do them the justice, however, of hearing what they had to say against Paul if they would go down to Caesarea: "*Let those among you who are able go down with me, and accuse this man*; let them go and give evidence." Festus would not assume that there was evil in him until it was proved against him. If he was guilty, the responsibility lay on them to prove him so.

3. Paul's trial before Festus. Festus stayed *at Jerusalem about ten days* and then *went down to Caesarea*. Since the Jews were so eager in the prosecution, Festus was willing to call this case first; he would deal with it *the next day*. We have here:

3.1. The court set and the prisoner called to the bar. Festus *sat in the judgment seat* and *commanded Paul to be brought.*

3.2. The prosecutors bringing their charges against the prisoner (v. 7): *The Jews stood round about*, which shows they were many. They *stood round about* so that if possible they might frighten the judge into agreeing to their evil intent, or at least frighten the prisoner, but it was in vain. He had too just and strong an assurance to be frightened by them. When they stood around Paul, they brought many serious accusations against him. They drew for the court as dreadful and vile a picture of him as their intelligence and hatred could contrive, but when they came to the evidence, there they failed: *they could not prove* their allegations against him, for they were all false. It is nothing new for the most excellent people on earth to have all kinds of evil said against them falsely, even *before the judgment-seat.*

3.3. The prisoner's insistence on justifying himself (v. 8). He insisted on his general plea of not guilty: *Neither against the law of the Jews, nor against the temple, nor yet against Caesar, have I offended anything at all.*

3.3.1. He had not broken the law of the Jews; he established the law (Ro 3:31). Preaching Christ, *the end of the law* (Ro 10:4), was not an offense against the law.

3.3.2. He had not defiled the temple; his helping set up the Gospel temple was in no way an offense against the temple that was its type.

3.3.3. He had not committed any offense against Caesar or his government. This shows that his prosecutors had charged Paul with actions that reflected discontent with the present higher powers, which made it necessary for him to deny having done any such things.

4. Paul's appeal to the emperor. This brought a new turn to the case. God put it into his heart to do it in order

to bring about what he had said to him, *that he must bear witness to Christ at Rome* (23:11). We have here:

4.1. The proposal Festus made to Paul to go and stand trial at Jerusalem (v. 9). *Festus* was *willing to do the Jews a pleasure*, disposed to satisfy the prosecutors rather than the prisoner, and he asked Paul whether he would be willing to go to Jerusalem and clear himself there. He would not offer to turn Paul over to the high priest and the Sanhedrin, but, *Wilt thou go thither, and be judged of these things before me?* Festus, as the one who presided over the court, could have ordered Paul to go, but he would not send him without his own consent.

4.2. Paul's refusal to agree to this, and his reasons for refusing.

4.2.1. Since he was a citizen of Rome, it was most proper for him to be tried in the Roman court, which sat at Caesarea: *I stand at Caesar's judgment-seat, where I ought to be judged.* Because the court was held in Caesar's name and by his authority and commission, before one who was delegated by him, it could well be said to be Caesar's judgment seat. Paul's acknowledging that he should be judged at Caesar's court clearly proves that Christ's ministers are not exempt from the jurisdiction of the civil powers, and if they are guilty of a real crime, they should submit to the judgment of those powers; if innocent, then they should submit to their investigation.

4.2.2. As a member of the Jewish nation, he had done nothing to make himself abhorrent to them: *To the Jews have I done no wrong, as thou very well knowest.* It is good for those who are innocent to plead their innocence, and to insist on it.

4.2.3. He was willing to stand by the rules of the law and to let that take its course (v. 11). If he was guilty of any capital crime that deserved death, he would neither flee from justice nor fight against it: "I do not refuse to die." If he was innocent, as he pleaded he was — "*If there be none of these things whereof these accuse me, no man may deliver me unto them,* not even the governor himself, because it is his business as much to protect the innocent as to punish the guilty"; and so he claimed the governor's protection.

4.3. His appeal to the court. Since he was continually in danger from the Jews, and one attempt after another had been made to get him into their hands, since he could not have justice done him in any other way, "*I appeal unto Caesar.* Rather than be handed over to the Jews, let me be handed over to Nero." It was a sad case when a son of Abraham was forced to appeal the judgment of those who called themselves the descendants of Abraham and appeal to a Nero — when he would be safer in Rome than in Jerusalem.

5. The judgment declared on the whole matter. His enemies hoped the case would end in his death, and his friends hoped it would end in his release, but they were both disappointed, and matters were left as they were. It shows the slow steps Providence sometimes takes, by which we are often made ashamed of both our hopes and our fears and are kept waiting on God.

5.1. The president of the court took advice on the matter: *He conferred with the council,* not with the council of the Jews but with his own counselors.

5.2. He decided to send Paul to Rome. A Roman citizen could appeal at any time to a superior court, even to the supreme court. *Hast thou appealed unto Caesar? Unto Caesar thou shalt go.* In our judgment before God, those who by justifying themselves appeal to the law will be sent to the law, and it will condemn them, but those

who by repentance and faith appeal to the Gospel will be sent to the Gospel, and it will save them.

Verses 13 – 27

We have here the preparations that were made for another hearing of Paul before King Agrippa, merely to satisfy his curiosity. Here is:

1. The friendly visit King Agrippa made to Festus upon his installation as governor of that province (v. 13): *After certain days, king Agrippa came to Caesarea.* Notice:

1.1. Who the visitors were:

1.1.1. King Agrippa II, the son of Herod Agrippa I, who killed James the apostle and was himself eaten by worms (12:23), and the great grandson of Herod the Great, under whom Christ was born.

1.1.2. Bernice, this king's own sister and the widow of his uncle Herod, after whose death she lived with this brother of hers. After she was married a second time, to Polemon, king of Cilicia, she got divorced from him and returned to her brother King Agrippa. The Roman historians Tacitus (c. 56–c. 117) and Suetonius (69–122) speak of a criminal intimacy afterward between her and the Roman Emperor Titus Vespasian (A.D. 9–79). Drusilla, the wife of Felix, was another sister of Agrippa's. Great people were often so immoral in those times!

1.2. The purpose of this visit: they *came to salute Festus,* to compliment him on his accession to the government. However, they probably came as much to divert themselves and share in the hospitality of his court as to show respect to him.

2. The account Festus gave King Agrippa of Paul and his case, which he gave:

2.1. To amuse him. It would be particularly acceptable to Agrippa, not only because he was a judge, and it contained some points of law and practice that were well worth his notice, but much more because he was a Jew, and it contained some points of religion that deserved his attention much more.

2.2. To obtain his advice. Festus had only recently become a judge, and so he was willing to receive the advice of those who were older and more experienced. Let us consider the particular account he gave King Agrippa about Paul (vv. 14–21):

2.2.1. Festus found Paul to be a prisoner when he came into the government of this province: *There is a certain man left in bonds by Felix,* and so if there had been anything wrong in the first taking of him into custody, Festus could not answer that.

2.2.2. The Jewish Sanhedrin was very much against him: "The *chief priests and the elders informed me* against him as a dangerous man, and they wanted him condemned to die."

2.2.3. He had insisted on the Roman law in favor of the prisoner, and would not condemn him without his case having been heard (v. 16): *It is not the manner of the Romans to deliver any man to die before the accused has the accusers face to face.* "Hear the other side" had become a proverb among them. We must not describe people in bad terms, nor condemn their words and actions, until we have heard what is to be said to vindicate them.

2.2.4. He had brought him to trial, according to the duty of his position (v. 17). He had acted quickly and efficiently: *as soon as ever they had come, without any delay, on the morrow,* he had heard the case. He had also tried Paul in the most solemn manner: he *sat on the judgment seat.* He convened a great court deliberately for Paul's trial, so that the sentence would be definitive, and the case brought to an end.

2.2.5. He was extremely disappointed at the charges the Jews brought against Paul (vv. 18–19): *When the accusers stood up against him, they brought no accusations of such things as I supposed.* He imagined from the eagerness of their prosecution, and their urging it upon one Roman governor after another:

2.2.5.1. That they had something to accuse Paul of that was dangerous either to private property or to the public peace. Such were the outcries against the first Christians; they were so loud and fierce that the bystanders must have concluded that Christians were the worst evildoers, and to describe them in these terms was the intention of that clamor, as it was of the clamor against our Savior.

2.2.5.2. That they had something to accuse him of that was recognized in the Roman courts and that the governor was properly the judge of, as Gallio expected (18:14). He found, however, that the matter was not so; they had *certain questions against him,* instead of proof and evidence against him. Moreover, these were questions *of their own superstition,* as he called their religion. By their law, the Romans protected the Jews' religion but not their superstition. It seems the great question here, however, was *concerning one Jesus that was dead, whom Paul affirmed to be alive.* Notice how disrespectfully this Roman spoke about Christ and his death and resurrection, about the great controversy between the Jews and the Christians as to whether Jesus was the promised Messiah or not, and about the great proof that he was the Messiah, his resurrection from the dead. What Paul affirmed about Jesus, that he was now alive, is a matter of such immense importance that if it is not true, we are all ruined.

2.2.6. He had proposed to Paul that the case be adjourned to the Jewish courts, that they were best able to consider such a matter (v. 20): *Because I doubted of such manner of questions, I asked him whether he would go to Jerusalem and there be judged of these matters.*

2.2.7. Paul had chosen to transfer his case to Rome rather than to Jerusalem: "He *appealed to be reserved to the hearing of Augustus* (v. 21), and so I *commanded him to be kept till I might send him to Caesar.*"

3. The bringing of Paul before Agrippa.

3.1. The king requested it (v. 22): *I would also hear the man myself.* Agrippa knew more of this matter than Festus did; he had heard of Paul. Nothing would please him more than to hear Paul. Agrippa would not for all the world have gone to a meeting to hear Paul preach, any more than Herod would have gone to listen to Jesus, but they were both glad to have them brought before them to satisfy their curiosity (Lk 9:9; 23:7–8).

3.2. Festus granted it: *Tomorrow thou shalt hear him.* There was a good providence in this; it would encourage Paul, who seemed buried alive in his imprisonment, and deprived of all opportunities to do good. This gave him an opportunity to preach Christ to a great congregation, and—what is more—to a congregation of leading people. Felix had heard him speak in private about the faith of Christ, but Agrippa and Festus agreed he would be heard in public.

3.3. Great preparation was made for it (v. 23): *The next day* there was a great number of people *in the place of hearing* (audience room).

3.3.1. Agrippa and Bernice took this opportunity to show themselves in pomp; *they came with great pomp,* or "with great fancy." Great pomp is only great fancy. It neither adds any real excellence nor gains any real respect, but feeds a vain attitude. It is mere show, a dream, something fantastic. The pomp that Agrippa and Bernice appeared in was:

3.3.1.1. Stained by their immoral characters, and all its beauty sullied, and all the good people who knew them must have condemned them as evildoers in the middle of all this pomp (Ps 15:4).

3.3.1.2. Surpassed by the real glory of the poor prisoner at the bar. His chains for such a good cause were more glorious than their chains of gold. Who would be fond of worldly pomp after seeing here such a bad woman loaded down with it and such a good man loaded down with its opposite?

3.3.2. The commanders and leaders of the city took this opportunity to pay their respects to Festus and his guests. I tend to think that those who were to appear in pomp perplexed themselves more with concern about their clothes than Paul, who was to appear as a prisoner, perplexed himself with concern about his case.

4. The speech with which Festus introduced the case.

4.1. He addressed himself respectfully to the company: *King Agrippa, and all men who are here present with us.* He spoke *to all the men,* as if he intended a tacit reflection on Bernice. The word used is not the one for "men" in the sense "human beings," but for "men" in contrast to "women"; what was Bernice doing here?

4.2. He represented the prisoner as one whom the Jews had great spite against. *The multitude of them, both at Jerusalem and here at Caesarea, cry out that he ought not to live any longer.*

4.3. He confessed the prisoner's innocence (v. 25): *I found that he had committed nothing worthy of death.* On a full hearing of the case, his own conscience declared Paul not guilty. Why did he not release him then, since he had stood up for his deliverance? Why, just because he was clamored against so much, and he feared the clamor would turn on him if he were to release him. It is a pity that everyone who has a conscience does not have the courage to act on it.

4.4. He told them about the present state of the case, that the prisoner had appealed to the emperor himself and that he, Festus, had allowed the appeal: *I have determined to send him.* This was how the case now stood.

4.5. He requested their help in examining the matter calmly and impartially, so that he could have at least such insight into the case as was necessary for him to state it to the emperor (vv. 26–27).

4.5.1. He thought it *unreasonable to send a prisoner and not withal* (also) *to signify the crimes laid against him;* the matter should be gotten ready for the emperor's decision.

4.5.2. He could not as yet write anything certain about Paul; the information given against him was so confused that Festus could make nothing of it at all. He wanted Paul to be publicly examined, therefore, so that he could be advised by them what to write about him.

CHAPTER 26

We have here: 1. The account Paul gave of himself, in which we have: 1.1. His humble address to king Agrippa (vv. 1–3). 1.2. His account of his origins and education, his profession as a Pharisee, and his continued loyalty to what had then been the main article of his creed, the "resurrection of the dead" (vv. 3–8). 1.3. His description of his zeal, in his early years, against Christianity (vv. 9–11). 1.4. His account of his miraculous conversion (vv. 12–16). 1.5. His commission to preach the Gospel to the Gentiles (vv. 17–18). 1.6. His actions according to that commission (vv. 19–21). 1.7. The doctrine he had made it his business to preach to the

Gentiles (vv. 22–23). 2. The remarks that were made on his defense. 2.1. Festus considered him insane (v. 24). In answer to Festus, Paul appealed to King Agrippa (vv. 25–27). 2.2. King Agrippa acknowledged himself to be almost converted (v. 28), and Paul sincerely wished he would be (v. 29). 2.3. They all agreed that Paul was innocent, that he should be set free, and that it was a pity he was appealing to Caesar (vv. 30–32).

Verses 1–11

Agrippa was the most honored person in the whole gathering, having the title of king—though otherwise having only the power of other governors under the emperor—and being senior to Festus, though not superior to him, and so, Festus having opened the case, Agrippa intimated to Paul that he had permission to *speak for himself* (v. 1). This was a favor the Jews would not allow Paul, but Agrippa freely gave it to him. Notice is taken of Paul's gesture: he *stretched forth his hand*, as one who had complete freedom and command of himself.

1. Paul addressed himself with great respect to Agrippa (vv. 2–3). He answered cheerfully before Felix, because he knew he had been *many years a judge to that nation* (24:10), but his opinion of Agrippa was higher.

1.1. Being accused by the Jews, and having been charged with many corrupt things, he was glad to have an opportunity to clear his name.

1.2. Since he was forced to answer for himself, he was glad it was before king Agrippa, who, being himself a convert to the Jewish religion, understood all matters that concerned it better than the other Roman governors did: *I know thee to be expert in all customs and questions which are among the Jews.* It seems Agrippa was an expert both in the customs of the Jewish religion and in the questions that arose from those customs. He was also well versed in the Old Testament Scriptures and could therefore reach a better judgment on the dispute about Jesus' being the Messiah than another could. It is encouraging for a preacher to be able to speak to those who are intelligent and can discern matters.

1.3. He begged him, therefore, to *hear him patiently.* Paul knew he would speak for a long time, and so he begged Agrippa to hear him out and not become weary. Paul intended to speak plainly, and so he begged Agrippa to listen to him with mildness and not become angry. Surely the least we can expect when we preach Christianity is to be listened to patiently.

2. He professed that although he was branded an apostate, he still remained faithful to all the good that he was first trained up in.

2.1. Notice here what his religion had been in his youth: his *manner of life was well known* (vv. 4–5). He was not born among his own nation, but he was brought up among them at Jerusalem. His education was neither foreign nor obscure. Those who *knew him from the beginning* could testify for him that he was a Pharisee and that he was of the *most strict sect of that religion.* He was not only called a Pharisee; he also *lived a Pharisee.* He was of the better kind of Pharisee, for he was brought up at the feet of Gamaliel (22:3), an eminent rabbi of the school or house of Hillel. Now if Paul was a Pharisee and lived as a Pharisee:

2.1.1. Then he was a scholar, a man of learning; the Pharisees knew the law and were well versed in it. It was a criticism of the other apostles that they had not had an academic education, but had been brought up as unschooled fishermen (4:13). Here an apostle was raised up who had sat at the feet of their most eminent teacher.

2.1.2. Then he was a moral, good man, not immoral or corrupt. He was, *as touching the righteousness which is in the law, blameless* (Php 3:6). As he could not be thought of as having deserted his religion because he did not know it—because he was learned—so he could not be thought of as having deserted it because he did not love it.

2.1.3. Then he was orthodox, sound in the faith. He was a Pharisee, as opposed to a Sadducee. The Jews could not say that he had abandoned his religion for lack of due regard to divine revelation. No, he had always respected the ancient *promise made of God unto the fathers.* Now although Paul knew very well that all this would not justify him before God, he also knew his reputation among the Jews and knew that a personal argument, *such as Agrippa would feel*, would show that he was not the kind of man they described him as. Although he counted this reputation as loss so that he could gain Christ (Php 3:7–8), he still mentioned it when it might serve to honor Christ. He reflected with some satisfaction on the knowledge that before his conversion he had *lived in all good conscience before God* (23:1).

2.2. Notice here what his religion was. He did not have such a zeal for the ceremonial law as he had had in his youth. However, he was as zealous for the main principles of his religion as ever.

2.2.1. His religion was built on the *promise made of God unto the fathers*, that is, on divine revelation and divine grace, on grace revealed and conveyed by promise. The promise of God was the guide and basis of his religion, the promise *made to the fathers*, which was older than the ceremonial law. Christ and heaven are the two great doctrines of the Gospel—that *God has given to us eternal life, and this life is in his Son* (1Jn 5:11); and these two are the substance of the promise made to the fathers.

2.2.2. His religion consisted in the hopes of this promise. He did not define his religion, as the Jews did, in terms of food and drink (Ro 14:17), but as a faithful dependence on God's grace promised in the covenant.

2.2.2.1. He had a firm hope in Christ as the promised offspring; he hoped to be blessed in Christ.

2.2.2.2. He had a firm hope of heaven. Paul had no confidence in the flesh (Php 3:3–4); all his confidence was in Christ.

2.2.3. In this matter, he agreed with all the devout Jews. *"Our twelve tribes, instantly* (earnestly) *serving God day and night*, hope to *come to this promise*, and all Israelites profess to believe in this promise, which is a promise of both Christ and heaven. They all hope for a Messiah to come, and we who are Christians hope in a Messiah who has already come; we all agree, therefore, to build on the same promise. They look for the *resurrection of the dead*, and this is what I look for too. Why should I be looked on as one who has turned away from the faith and worship of the Jewish church, when I agree with them on this fundamental article? I hope eventually to come to the same heaven that they hope to come to, and if we expect to meet so happily in the end, why then should we fall out so unhappily on the way?" Paul earnestly served God day and night in the Gospel of his Son, and the twelve tribes by their representatives did so in the Law of Moses, but he and they did it in the hope of the same promise. Much more should Christians, who hope in the same Jesus, for the same heaven, though having different modes and ceremonies of worship, live together in holy love. It is only those who are diligent and constant in serving God who have good grounds to hope for eternal life, and the prospect of that eternal life should make us diligent and faithful in all religious exercises. We should exercise charitable judgment toward those who earnestly serve God day and night, though not in our way.

2.2.4. This was what he was now suffering for: *I am judged for the hope of the promise made unto the fathers.* He stood by the promise, against the ceremonial law, while his persecutors stood by the ceremonial law, against the promise. It is common for people to hate and persecute in others the power of the religious faith that they pride themselves in the form of (2Ti 3:5). Paul's hope was what *they themselves also allowed* (24:15), and yet they were so enraged against him for practicing according to that hope.

2.2.5. This was what he would try to persuade all who heard him to warmly embrace (v. 8): *Why should it be thought a thing incredible with you that God should raise the dead?* He probably explained the *promise made to the fathers* to be the promise of the resurrection and eternal life and proved that he was pursuing that happiness in the right way because he believed in Christ, who had *risen from the dead* and whose resurrection was a pledge of the resurrection that the ancestors had hoped for. Now many of his hearers were Gentiles, especially Festus, and when they heard him speak so much about Christ's resurrection and the resurrection from the dead, they probably mocked. Yet if it is beyond the power of nature, it is not above the power of the God of nature. Do we not see a kind of resurrection in nature at the return of every spring? Since the sun has such power to raise dead plants, should it seem incredible to us that God would raise dead bodies?

3. He acknowledged that as long as he continued to be a Pharisee, he was a bitter enemy of Christians and Christianity, and thought he should be so. He mentioned this:

3.1. To show that his becoming a Christian and a preacher was not the result of any previous inclination in that direction. He did not reason himself into Christianity, but was brought into the highest assurance of it directly from the highest prejudice against it. His conversion in such a miraculous way was a convincing proof of the truth of Christianity not only to himself but also to others.

3.2. Perhaps intending it as an excuse for his persecutors. Paul himself once thought he was doing what he should do when he persecuted Christ's disciples, and he charitably thought his own persecutors were laboring under the same mistake. Notice:

3.2.1. How foolish he had been in his opinion (v. 9): he *thought with himself that he ought to do many things contrary to the name of Jesus of Nazareth.* Because Christianity did not fit in with the idea he had of the kingdom of the Messiah, he wanted to do all he could against it. He thought he was doing God a good service by persecuting those who called on the name of Jesus Christ. It is possible for people to be confident that they are doing right when they are clearly doing wrong,

3.2.2. How ruthless he had been in his practice (vv. 10–11). There is no more violent principle in the world than a misinformed conscience. He gave an account of what he did, emphasizing it as one who was truly penitent for it.

3.2.2.1. He filled the jails with Christians. *Many of the saints did I shut up in prison* (v. 10), *both men and women* (8:3).

3.2.2.2. He made himself the tool of the chief priests. He *received authority* from them, and he was proud enough to have authority for such a purpose.

3.2.2.3. He was very careful to vote in favor of putting Christians to death, particularly Stephen, to whose death Saul agreed (8:1).

3.2.2.4. He brought them under punishments of a lesser nature *in the synagogues*, where they were lashed for disobeying the rules of the synagogue.

3.2.2.5. He not only punished them for their religion but also tried to force them to deny it by torturing them: "*I compelled them to blaspheme* Christ." Nothing will lie more heavily on persecutors than violating human consciences.

3.2.2.6. His rage swelled so much against Christians and Christianity that Jerusalem itself was too small a stage for it to be acted out on; rather, being *exceedingly mad against them, he persecuted them even to strange* (foreign) *cities.* He was obsessed by them, furious when he saw them multiply even more when they were afflicted. He was *exceedingly mad* (v. 11); the tide of his fury could not be stopped or limited. Persecutors are furious and obsessive; some of them are *exceedingly mad.* There is no more restless principle than malice, especially malice that claims to have right on its side. This was what Paul was like at the beginning of his life. All imaginable external objections lay against his being a Christian.

Verses 12–23

All who have faith in God must acknowledge that those who speak and act by his direction are not to be opposed, because that *is fighting against God* (23:9). Here Paul explained how he received a direct call from heaven to preach the Gospel of Christ to the Gentile world.

1. He became a Christian by divine power. He was brought into it by a sudden act from heaven, by a divine and spiritual power, by a revelation of Christ from heaven. This happened while he was careering toward Damascus in his sin. He was not tempted to give it all up by the failing of his friends, because he had at this time as full an *authority and commission from the chief priests* to persecute Christianity as ever. Two things brought about this surprising change, a vision and a voice from heaven.

1.1. He saw a heavenly vision: it was undoubtedly a divine appearance. He *saw a great light, a light from heaven,* such as could not be produced by any human skill, *at midday*; it was not in a house, where tricks could have been played on him, but was *in the way*, in the open air. It was a light *above the brightness of the sun,* and this could not have been the result of Paul's own imagination, since it *shone round about those that journeyed with him*; it made the sun itself, in their eyes, shine less brightly. It shocked them so powerfully that they all fell to the ground when they saw it. In the creation of grace, as in the creation of the world, the first thing created was light (2Co 4:6). Christ himself appeared to Paul (v. 16): *I have appeared to thee for this purpose.* Christ was in this light, even though those who traveled with Paul saw only the light, not Christ in it.

1.2. He heard a heavenly voice *speaking to him*; it is said here to have been *in the Hebrew tongue,* his native language. Notice:

1.2.1. Christ called him by his name, and repeated it: *Saul, Saul* (v. 14).

1.2.2. He convicted him of sin, the sin of persecuting Christians.

1.2.3. He interested himself in the sufferings of his followers: *Thou persecutest me* (v. 14), and again, *I am Jesus whom thou persecutest* (v. 15). Little did Paul think, when he was trampling on those whom he looked on as the blemishes of this earth, that he was insulting the One who was so much the glory of heaven.

1.2.4. He restrained him for his willful resistance to those convictions: *It is hard for thee to kick against the pricks.*

1.2.5. In response to Paul's question, Christ made himself known to him. Paul asked (v. 15), *"Who art thou, Lord?"* And he said, *"I am Jesus,* the One whom you have despised, hated." Paul thought Jesus was buried in the earth and, though stolen from his own grave, nevertheless placed in some other. All the Jews were taught to say so, and that was why he was amazed to hear Christ speak from heaven, to see him surrounded by all this glory. This convinced him that the teaching of Jesus was divine and heavenly, not to be opposed, but, on the contrary, to be warmly accepted. This was enough to make him a Christian immediately.

2. He was made a minister by divine authority: *the same Jesus that appeared to him in that glorious light* ordered him *to go and preach the Gospel to the Gentiles.* What was said of his being an apostle is here joined directly to what was said to him on the road. Compare 9:15; 22:15. He put the two together for the sake of brevity: *Rise, and stand upon thy feet.* He must stand up, for Christ had work for him to do: *I have appeared to thee to make thee a minister* (v. 16). Christ is responsible for making his own ministers, and he will reveal himself to all those whom he makes his ministers, for how can those who do not know him preach him? How can people know him if he does not, by his Spirit, make himself known to them? Notice:

2.1. The position to which Paul was appointed: he was made a minister, to be with Christ and to act for him as a witness. Christ appeared to him so that he would appear for Christ before people.

2.2. The subject of Paul's testimony: he must give an account to the world *of the things which he had seen.* He saw these things so that he could make them known, and he used every occasion to speak about them, as here, and before (ch. 22). He must speak *of those things in which* Christ *would appear to him.* Paul at first had confused ideas of the Gospel, until Christ appeared to him and gave him fuller instructions. *The Gospel he preached he received from Christ* directly (Gal 1:12), but he received it gradually. Christ often appeared to Paul, continuing to teach him.

2.3. The spiritual protection he was taken under (v. 17): *delivering thee from the people of the Jews and from the Gentiles.* Christ had shown Paul at this time *what great things he must suffer* (9:16), but here Paul told Agrippa that Jesus had promised to *deliver him from the people.* Great sufferings are reconcilable to God's promise to rescue his people. Sometimes God delivers them into the hands of their persecutors so that he may have the honor of rescuing them out of their hands.

2.4. The special commission given him to go among the Gentiles, though, as far as we can tell, years passed before he was sent to the Gentiles.

2.4.1. There was great work to be done among the Gentiles, and Paul must be instrumental in doing it.

2.4.1.1. A world that sat in darkness must be enlightened. Paul would be *sent to open their eyes, and to turn them from darkness to light* (v. 18). He would open their eyes, which before were shut to the light, and they would be willing to understand. Christ opens the heart by opening the eyes; he does not lead people blindfolded, but allows them to see their own way. He would be sent not only to open their eyes for the present but also to keep them open, *to turn them from darkness to light,* that is, from following false and blind guides to following a divine revelation of unquestionable certainty and truth. This was turning them from darkness to light, from the ways of darkness to those on which the light shines. The great purpose of the Gospel

is to put right the mistakes of those who are in error so that things may be set and seen in their true light.

2.4.1.2. A world that lay in evil must be reformed; it would not be enough for them to have their eyes opened; they must also have their hearts renewed. Satan rules by the power of darkness, and God by the convincing evidence of light. Sinners are under the power of Satan; converting grace gets them out from under the power of Satan and brings them into submission to God. When gracious dispositions are strong in the soul, as corrupt and sinful dispositions had been, it is then *turned* from the power of Satan to God.

2.4.2. A great happiness was intended for the Gentiles through this work — *that they may receive forgiveness of sins, and inheritance among those who are sanctified;* they would be turned away from the slavery of Satan to the service of God:

2.4.2.1. So that they would be able to be restored to his favor, which they had forfeited by their sin: *that they may receive forgiveness of sins.* They are persuaded to lay down their weapons and return to their allegiance, so that they may enjoy the benefits of the act of indemnity.

2.4.2.2. So that they might enjoy the fruit of that favor, so *that they may have an inheritance among those who are sanctified by faith that is in me.* This shows us:

2.4.2.2.1. Heaven is an inheritance; it is given to all the children of God, because *if children, then heirs* (Ro 8:17); "that they may have a right," as some read it; not by merit, but purely by grace.

2.4.2.2.2. All who are powerfully turned away from sin to God are not only pardoned but also advanced.

2.4.2.2.3. All who will be saved in the future are sanctified now. No one can be happy who is not holy; nor will anyone be a saint in heaven who is not first a saint on earth.

2.4.2.2.4. We need nothing more to make us happy than to be among those who are sanctified, to fare as they do. Those who are sanctified will be glorified. Let us, therefore, now cast in our lot among them.

2.4.2.2.5. We are sanctified and saved by faith in Christ. Some read *by faith* as modifying *sanctified,* the word immediately before: we are *sanctified by faith,* for faith purifies the heart. Others read *by faith* as modifying *receive forgiveness of sins and inheritance:* we must receive these gifts by faith. It all comes to the same thing, because it is by faith that we are justified, sanctified, and glorified. It is expressed emphatically and may be translated, "by faith, that faith which is in me." This faith focuses specifically on Jesus Christ and his mediation, by which we depend on Christ and submit ourselves to him.

3. He had discharged his ministry with God's help and under his direction and protection.

3.1. God gave him a heart to comply with the call (v. 19): *I was not disobedient to the heavenly vision.* If Paul had *conferred with flesh and blood* (Gal 1:16) and been influenced by worldly interests, he would have done as Jonah did, gone anywhere rather than pursue this God-given errand. But he accepted the commission and applied himself to his task accordingly.

3.2. God enabled him to get through a great deal of work, though in it he grappled with a great deal of difficulty (v. 20). He applied himself to preaching the Gospel with great vigor. He began at Damascus, where he was converted. When he reached Jerusalem, where he had been educated, he witnessed for Christ where he had earlier most ruthlessly set himself against him (9:29). He preached *throughout all the coasts of Judea;* he made the first offer of the Gospel to the Jews, as Christ had appointed, and did not leave them until they had willfully rejected the Gospel. Finally, he turned to the Gentiles.

3.3. His preaching was practical. He showed people that they ought:

3.3.1. To *repent of their sins,* to be sorry for them and enter into covenant against them. They should change their minds and their ways.

3.3.2. To *turn to God.* They must not only conceive hatred for sin but also want to be like God. They must turn to God in love and affection and return to God in duty and obedience, turning and returning from the world and the flesh.

3.3.3. To *do works meet for repentance.* This was what John preached, who was the first Gospel preacher (Mt 3:8). Those who profess repentance must practice it; they must lead a life of repentance. It is not enough to say penitent words; we must also do works that are consistent with those words. Now what fault could be found with such preaching as this?

3.4. The Jews had no quarrel with him except that he did all he could to persuade people to be religious and to bring them to God by bringing them to Christ (v. 21): it was for these reasons, and no other, *that the Jews caught* (seized) *me in the temple, and went about to kill me,* and let anyone judge whether these were crimes worthy of death or chains. They caught him in the temple worshiping God, and they attacked him there, as if the better the place, the better the deed.

3.5. He had no help except from heaven (v. 22): "*Having therefore obtained help of God, I continue unto this day.* I have stood by what I said and have not been afraid or ashamed to persist in it." What was it that supported him? Not any strength of his own resolutions, but *having obtained help of God*; without that help, he could not have gone on with the work. Those who are employed in work for God will obtain help from God. Our continuation to this day must be attributed to help that we have obtained from God. The preachers of the Gospel could never have done as they did unless they had received direct help from heaven.

3.6. He preached no message except what was consistent with the Old Testament Scriptures: he *witnessed both to small and great.* The condescending grace of the Gospel was evidenced by its being witnessed to the most insignificant people; the poor were welcome to come to know it for themselves. The incontestable truth and power of the Gospel were shown in its being neither afraid nor ashamed to reveal itself to the greatest. The enemies of Paul objected against him that he preached something more than *that men should repent, and turn to God, and do works meet for repentance.* Besides this, which the Old Testament prophets had preached, he had also preached Christ, his death, and his resurrection, and this was what they quarreled with him for. "I did so," said Paul, "and I do so, but here, too, I say *no other than that which Moses and the prophets said should come* (v. 22), and what greater honor can be done to them than to reveal that what they foretold has been fulfilled?" There were three things that were both prophesied by them and preached by Paul:

3.6.1. *That Christ would suffer* (v. 23), that the Messiah would be "a sufferer." His ignominious death would be not only consistent with but also in accordance with his undertaking. The cross of Christ was a stumbling block to the Jews (1Co 1:23), but Paul stood by it, so that in preaching it, he preached the fulfilling of the Old Testament predictions.

3.6.2. *That he would be the first that would rise from the dead,* that he would be the chief of the resurrection, the head, or principal one. He was the first person who rose from the dead to die no more.

3.6.3. *That he would show light unto the people, and to the Gentiles,* to the Jewish people in the first place. To them he showed light by himself, and then to the Gentiles by the ministry of his apostles. Here Paul was alluding to his own commission (v. 18) *to turn them from darkness to light.* Christ rose from the dead so that he could show light to the people. This also was foretold by the Old Testament prophets, that the Gentiles would be brought to the knowledge of God by the Messiah (Isa 9:2), and what was there in all this that the Jews could justly be displeased at?

Verses 24–32

We have reason to think that Paul had a great deal more to say. He had just come to the crux of the matter—the death and resurrection of Jesus Christ. Once led to this subject, he would not know when to finish, because the power of Christ's death and the fellowship of his sufferings (Php 3:10) were inexhaustible subjects to him. It was a great pity that he would be interrupted while speaking on this subject, and that, being allowed to speak for himself (v. 1), he would not be permitted to say all he intended.

1. Festus, the Roman governor, thought the poor man was insane. He took him to be a lunatic, one who should be pitied but at the same time should not be heeded. He thought he had found a way to excuse himself both from condemning Paul as a prisoner and from believing him as a preacher, for if he was not sane, he was to be neither condemned nor credited. Notice:

1.1. What Festus said about him (v. 24): *He said with a loud voice,* to make Paul stop speaking and to distract the audience from listening to it, "*Paul, thou art beside thyself. Much learning hath made thee mad*; you have broken your mind with too much studying." He said this not so much in anger as in scorn and contempt. He did not understand what Paul said; it was all puzzling to him, and so he attributed it to a fevered imagination.

1.1.1. He acknowledged Paul to be a scholar, one who had studied greatly. The apostles, who were fishermen, were despised because they had no learning; Paul, who had been to college, was despised as having too much learning. The enemies of Christ's ministers will always have something or other to criticize them for.

1.1.2. He insulted him as being mad. John the Baptist (Mt 11:18) and Christ (Jn 7:20; 8:48; 10:20; Mk 3:21) were represented as having a demon and being insane. Paul probably now spoke more earnestly than at the beginning of his speech, with gestures to express his zeal, and probably that was why Festus described him so invidiously, which perhaps no one else in the court would have thought of doing.

1.2. How Paul cleared himself from this invidious imputation.

1.2.1. He denied the charge, declaring there was neither ground nor reason for it (v. 25): "*I am not mad, most noble Festus.* I do not ramble, *but speak the words of truth and soberness* (reasonableness)." He showed Festus every possible respect, complimenting him with his title of honor, *most noble Festus,* to teach us not to repay insult for insult, but to speak politely to those who speak insultingly about us.

1.2.2. He appealed to Agrippa about what he spoke (v. 26): *For the king knows of these things.* He *spoke freely before* Agrippa because Agrippa knew that these were no mere products of Paul's imagination, but matters of fact, and would therefore be willing to know more. *For I am persuaded that none of these things are hidden from him; for this thing was not done in a corner*; the whole country rang with its news, and so it was unreasonable to censure him for talking about it as if it showed he was insane; and it was much more unreasonable to censure him in this way for speaking about the death and resurrection of Christ, which was so universally spoken of. Agrippa could not be ignorant of it, and it was to Festus's shame that he was so.

2. Agrippa was so far from thinking Paul mad that he thought that he never heard a man talk more to the point.

2.1. Paul applied himself closely to Agrippa's conscience. He would speak to those who understood him, those whom he was likely to fasten something on, and that was why he continued to address *Agrippa*: *King Agrippa, believest thou the prophets?* He did not wait for an answer, but, as a compliment to Agrippa, assumed it: *I know that thou believest*, because everyone knew that Agrippa professed the Jews' religion and that he therefore both knew the writings of the prophets and believed them. It is good to deal with those who know the Scriptures and believe them, for one has some influence on such people.

2.2. Agrippa acknowledged there was a great deal of reason in what Paul said (v. 28): *Almost thou persuadest me to be a Christian.* Some understand this as spoken ironically: "Would you persuade me in such a short time to be a Christian?" But if it is taken this way, it is an acknowledgment that Paul spoke very much to the point. Others think it was spoken seriously. Agrippa was as close to being persuaded to believe in Christ as Felix, when he trembled, was to leaving his sins (24:25). Many are almost persuaded to be religious but not quite persuaded; they are under strong convictions but are still overruled by some external inducements and therefore do not fully pursue their convictions.

2.3. Paul concluded with a devout wish that all his hearers were Christians, and this wish was turned into a prayer: *I pray to God for it* (v. 29), *that not only thou but all that hear me this day were both almost, and altogether, such as I am, except these bonds.* Here:

2.3.1. He professed his determination to remain faithful to his religious faith. In wishing that they were all as he was, he in effect declared his determination never to be as they were, however much it might be to his worldly advantage.

2.3.2. He intimated his satisfaction not only in the truth of Christianity but also in its benefits and advantages. He could not wish better to the best friend he had in the world than to wish them a faithful, zealous disciple of Jesus Christ.

2.3.3. He intimated how troubled and concerned he was that Agrippa went no further than being almost a Christian—what good would that do?

2.3.4. He intimated that it would be the inexpressible happiness of each one of them to become a true Christian—that there is enough grace in Christ for all, even if they are very many.

2.3.5. He intimated the hearty goodwill he had for them all; he wished them as well as he wished his own soul, and better than he now was as to his outward condition. He wished they would all be encouraged Christians as he was, but not persecuted Christians as he was. When he wished them in chains *to* Christ, he hoped they would never be in chains *for* Christ; nothing could be said more tenderly or with better grace.

3. They all agreed that Paul was innocent.

3.1. The court broke up precipitously (v. 30): when *he had spoken*, the king was afraid that he would say some-

thing even more moving. The king himself found that his own heart began to yield, and he dared not trust himself to hear more, but, as Felix had done before (24:25), dismissed Paul for this time. *The king rose up, and the governor, and Bernice and those that sat with them.*

3.2. They all agreed in the opinion that Paul was innocent (v. 31). The court withdrew to consider, and *they talked among themselves*, and all had the same thought, *that this man does nothing worthy of death*; in fact, he had done *nothing worthy of bonds.* And so, though his listeners would not receive his message, his character was nevertheless revealed in their consciences (2Co 5:11), and thus the shouts of the hotheaded Jews, who cried out, *Away with him, it is not fit he should live* (22:22), were shamed by the moderate counsels of this court.

3.3. *Agrippa* gave his judgment *that* Paul *might have been set at liberty, if he had not himself appealed to Caesar* (v. 32), but that by that appeal he had put a bar on his own door. Some think that Agrippa and Festus, being unwilling to displease the Jews, made this an excuse for continuing to hold him even though they knew they could have justified discharging him. And so Agrippa, who was almost persuaded to become a Christian, proved no better than if he had not been persuaded at all. Now we cannot tell:

3.3.1. Whether Paul repented of having appealed to Caesar now that he saw that it was the only thing preventing him from being discharged. What we think is for our welfare often proves to be a trap; we are so shortsighted. Or:

3.3.2. Whether, despite this, he remained satisfied in what he had done, believing that there was a providence in it and that things would finally turn out well. Besides, he was told in a vision that he must *bear witness at Rome* (23:11). It was all the same to him whether he went there as a prisoner or free.

CHAPTER 27

We have here an account of Paul's voyage toward Rome. 1. The beginning of the voyage was calm and successful (vv. 1–8). 2. Paul gave the centurion and the captain notice of an approaching storm (vv. 9–11). 3. They met with a great deal of stormy weather, and they expected nothing but to be driven along by the wind (vv. 12–20). 4. Paul assured them that by the good providence of God they would be brought safely through it (vv. 21–26). 5. Finally, at midnight, they were driven onto an island, which proved to be Malta (vv. 27–36). 6. They narrowly escaped with their lives, the ship being wrecked but all the people wonderfully preserved (vv. 37–44).

Verses 1–11

We are not told how long after his meeting with Agrippa Paul was sent away to Rome to pursue his appeal to Caesar, but those who had custody of him probably took the first opportunity to take him; in the meantime Paul was among his friends at Caesarea; they were an encouragement to him, and he was a blessing to them. Here we are told:

1. How Paul was shipped off to Italy. This was a long voyage, but there was no other way. He had appealed to Caesar, and to Caesar he must go (25:12): *It was determined that we should sail into Italy.* It was determined in the purposes of God before Festus determined it; Paul must go to Rome because God had work for him to do there. Notice:

1.1. Whose custody he was committed to—to *one named Julius, a centurion of Augustus's band.* He had soldiers under him, who guarded Paul.

1.2. What ship he embarked on. They went on board a ship of Adramyttium (v. 2), a port of Africa.

1.3. What company he had on this voyage, some prisoners who were committed to the custody of the same centurion. As Christ was linked with the thieves who were crucified with him, Paul was linked with these, and had to share with them on this voyage. We find (v. 42) that for their sakes he was nearly killed, but they were preserved for his sake. But he had also some of his friends with him, including Luke, whose presence we can infer from his use of *we* throughout this passage: "We sailed into Italy," and, "We launched" (v. 2). Aristarchus, a Thessalonian, is named specifically as one of Paul's company now. It was an encouragement to Paul to have the company of some of his friends on this long and tedious voyage. Those who go on long voyages at sea need wisdom, so that they may do good to the bad company they are in—may make them better, or at least not be made any worse by them.

2. What course they steered and what places they passed by.

2.1. They landed at Sidon *the next day.* Significantly, Julius, the centurion, was extraordinarily polite to Paul. Julius probably was one of the *chief captains, or principal men,* who heard Paul plead his own cause before Agrippa (25:23), and was convinced of his innocence. Although Paul was committed to him as a prisoner, he treated him as a friend and as a gentleman: he *gave him liberty to go among his friends to refresh himself.* Julius here gave an example to those in power to be respectful to those whom they find worthy of their respect. God here encourages those who suffer for him to trust in him, since he can move the hearts of those from whom they least expect goodwill, causing them to befriend his people. The passage also shows Paul's faithfulness. He did not set about trying to escape. If the centurion was so polite as to take his word, he would be so just and honest as to keep his word.

2.2. They then *sailed under* (to the lee of) *Cyprus* (v. 4). If the wind had been fair, they would have left Cyprus on the right hand, but because the wind did not favor them, they were driven to sailing with a side wind, and left it on the left hand. Sailors must do as they can when they cannot do as they want, making the best of their wind, whatever direction it is in; we must live in the same way in all our journeys over the ocean of this world.

2.3. At a port called Myra they changed ships. They went aboard an Alexandrian ship bound for Italy (vv. 5–6). There was great trading between that city and Italy. From Alexandria ships took grain to Rome, and the East Indian and Persian goods they imported at the Red Sea were exported by them especially to Italy. The ports of Italy showed the Alexandrian ships the particular favor of not obliging them to lower the sail when they came into port.

2.4. With much trouble they made Fair Havens, a port of the island of Crete (vv. 7–8). They *sailed slowly many days.* It was a long time before they arrived at Cnidus, and from there they were forced to sail to the lee of Crete, as they had earlier been forced to the lee of Cyprus. They had great difficulty passing by Salmone, a promontory on the eastern shore of the island of Crete. Although the voyage up to that time was not stormy, it was still very tedious. Many who are not driven backward in their affairs by adverse providences still sail on slowly and do not move forward by favorable providences. The place they came to was called Fair Havens. It is known to this day by the same name, and its name corresponds to the pleasantness of its situation and prospect. Yet:

2.4.1. It was not the harbor they were bound for; it was a fair haven, but not their haven.

2.4.2. It was not a *commodious* (suitable) *haven to winter in* (v. 12). Not every fair haven is safe; in fact, there may be most danger where there is most pleasure.

3. What advice Paul gave the centurion and the captain: they should be content to winter where they were.

3.1. It was now a bad time for sailing; they had lost much time while struggling with contrary winds. Sailing was now dangerous, because *the fast was already past* (v. 9), that is, the famous yearly fast of the Jews, the Day of Atonement, which was on the tenth day of the seventh month; it was about September 20 in our calendar. Strangely, we never have any mention of its observance in all the Scripture history, unless it is meant here, where it serves only to describe the season of the year. Today, Michaelmas is reckoned by mariners to be as a bad time of the year to be at sea as any other.

3.2. Paul reminded them of it and warned them of their danger (v. 10): *I perceive that this voyage will be with hurt and damage.* There were some good men aboard the ship, and many more bad men, but in matters of this nature, *all things come alike to all* (Ecc 9:2). If both were in the same ship, they were both in the same danger.

3.3. They refused to be advised by Paul in this matter (v. 11). They thought it impertinent of him to interfere in such a matter, and the centurion to whom it was referred to decide the matter took it on himself to overrule. The centurion paid more attention to the opinion of the master and owner of the ship than to Paul's, for normally a person's judgment in matters of their own profession is to be trusted. The centurion was very polite to Paul (v. 3), but he would not be guided by his advice.

Verses 12–20

In these verses we have:

1. The ship putting to sea again, at first with a promising wind. Notice:

1.1. What persuaded them to leave the Fair Havens: they thought the harbor not suitable to winter in. They ran toward harm to avoid inconvenience, as we often do. Some of the ship's crew wanted to stay there. It is better to be safe in an unsuitable harbor than to be lost in a stormy sea. But the dissenters were outvoted, and the *greater part advised to depart thence also.* They aimed not to go far, but only to another port of the same island, here called *Phenice* (Phoenix). It is described here as lying toward the southwest and northwest. Probably the haven was between two promontories, one of which pointed to the northwest and the other to the southwest, by which it was guarded against the east winds. Nature would have provided us with waters to sail on in vain if it had not also provided us with natural harbors to shelter in.

1.2. What encouragement they had at first on their voyage. They set out with a fair wind (v. 13); the *south wind blew softly,* and seeing this, they flattered themselves with the hope that they would reach their destination, and so they sailed close by the coast of Crete. Those who put to sea with a breeze do not know what storms they may still encounter, and so they must not be self-confident.

2. The ship suddenly coming into a terrible storm. They imagined that because the south wind now blew softly, it would always blow so; putting their confidence in this, they put out to sea. But they were soon made aware of their foolishness in trusting more in a smiling wind than in the word of God in Paul's mouth. Notice:

2.1. What their danger and distress was.

2.1.1. There *arose against them a tempestuous wind.* This wind the sailors called *Euroclydon,* a northeast wind, which on those seas was especially troublesome and dangerous.

2.1.2. The ship was *exceedingly tossed* (v. 18); it was kicked from wave to wave like a football. The ship could not possibly *bear up into the wind* (v. 15), and so the crew folded up their sails, which would put them in danger in such a storm rather than do them any good, and so *let the ship drive* (be driven along). When this storm arose, they probably were very near the haven of Phoenix and thought they would soon be at a quiet harbor, but suddenly they were in this distress.

2.1.3. They saw neither sun nor stars for many days. Their situation was all the more dangerous because the magnetic compass to direct sailors was not then in use, which meant that they had no guide at all when they could not see either sun or stars. This is how sad the condition of the people of God sometimes is for a spiritual reason; but light is sown for them (Ps 97:11).

2.1.4. They had more than their fair share of winter weather: *no small tempest*, so that they were about to die for cold, and all this went on for many days. Notice what hardships those who sail often have to go through, besides the dangers they face. Yet to gain profit, some will make nothing of all this, and it is an example of divine Providence that some people are disposed to this kind of job despite its difficulties. Perhaps Christ chose ministers from among sailors because they had learned to endure hardship (2Ti 2:3).

2.2. What methods they followed to help themselves.

2.2.1. When they could make no headway against the wind, they let the ship run adrift. When it is fruitless to struggle, it is wise to yield.

2.2.2. They nevertheless did what they could to avoid the present danger. There was a small island called *Clauda*, and when they neared it, they took care to prevent the ship from being wrecked, arranging matters so that they did not run against the island, but quietly passed its calmer side (v. 16).

2.2.3. When they were afraid they would scarcely save the ship, they busied themselves to save the lifeboat. They had *much work to come by the boat* (v. 16), but eventually they hoisted it aboard (v. 17).

2.2.4. They used methods that were proper in those times; they *undergirded the ship* (v. 17). They passed strong ropes under the ship to hold it together in the storm.

2.2.5. For fear of falling *into the quicksands* (sandbars), they *struck sail* (lowered the gear) and then let the ship be driven along. It is strange how a ship will survive at sea, even in stormy weather, if it has space.

2.2.6. The next day they lightened the ship of its cargo, throwing the goods and merchandise overboard. Notice what the wealth of this world consists of; the time may come when it will be a burden not only too heavy to carry safely but also heavy enough to sink those who have it. Notice the foolishness of the children of this world; they can give away their goods when it is to save their lives. But notice how ungenerous they are in spending them on works of godliness and charity, and in suffering for Christ. Anyone will prefer losing their goods to losing their life, but many would rather make *shipwreck of faith and a good conscience* than of their goods (1Ti 1:19).

2.2.7. The third day they *cast out the tacklings of the ship.*

2.3. The despair that they were eventually brought to (v. 20): *All hope that we should be saved was then taken away.* The storm continued, and they saw no signs that it would abate. The means they had used were ineffective,

so that they were at their wits' end. They had the heart neither to eat nor to drink. They had enough provisions on board (v. 38), but they were so enthralled by the fear of death that they could not even accept the supports of life.

Verses 21–44

We have here the outcome of the distress of Paul and his fellow travelers; they escaped with their lives, and that was all. We are told (v. 37) how many there were on board: 276; such a large number, and Paul among them worth more than all the rest. We left them in despair, giving themselves up for lost. Among these sailors, Paul was not, like Jonah, the cause of the storm, but the comforter in the storm. Notice:

1. The encouragement Paul gave them by assuring them that their lives would all be saved. Paul rescued them from their despair first, so that they would not die of that, and then they were in a good position to be rescued from their distress. *After long abstinence, Paul stood forth in the midst of them.* During the distress up to that time Paul was one of the crowd, helping with the rest to *throw out the tackling* (v. 19), but now, though a prisoner, he undertook to be their counselor and comforter.

1.1. He rebuked them for not taking his advice (v. 8): *"You should have hearkened to me and not have loosed from Crete,* and then we would not have *gained this harm and loss.* They did not listen to Paul when he warned them of their danger, but he would speak words of comfort and relief to them now that they were in danger. God is so compassionate to those who are in misery, even when they bring themselves into it by their own willfulness. Before administering comfort, Paul would make them aware of their sin in not following his advice. What they were blamed for was sailing from Crete, where they were safe. Most people cause some trouble for themselves because they do not know when they are well off, but they incur real damage and loss by acting against advice to better themselves.

1.2. He assured them that although they would lose the ship, none of them would lose their lives. "Your situation is sad, but it is not desperate. Now, I *exhort you to be of good cheer."* This is how we can speak to sinners who are convicted of their sin and foolishness. "You should have listened to us and have had nothing to do with sin. Yet we now urge you to be of good cheer. Although you would not follow our advice when we said, 'Do not presume,' take it now when we say, 'Do not despair.'" The travelers would use no further means, because *all hope that they should be saved was taken away* (v. 20). Now Paul encouraged them to get busy. If they would resume their vigor, they would keep their lives. They must count on the loss of the ship; it would be wrecked. Yet *not a life would be lost.* This would be good news to those who were about to die for fear of dying.

1.3. He told them what basis he had for this assurance; it was backed up by divine revelation. An angel of God had appeared to him at night and told him that for his sake they would all be preserved (vv. 23–25). They would have it not only by providence but also by promise, and as a special favor to Paul. Notice:

1.3.1. The solemn profession Paul made of his relationship with God. It is he *whose I am, and whom I serve.* He looked on God:

1.3.1.1. As his rightful owner, who had a sovereign, incontestable title to him and power over him: *Whose I am.* We are more his than our own.

1.3.1.2. As his sovereign ruler and master, who had the right to give him law: *Whom I serve.* Because we are his, we are bound to serve him. Paul did not say, "Whose *we* are, and whom *we* serve," since most who were present were strangers to him. He said this to the company so that they might be drawn to accept him as their God and serve him too.

1.3.2. The account he gave of the vision he had: *There stood by me this night an angel of God*. Though Paul was *afar off upon the sea* (Ps 65:5), even this could not break his fellowship with God. He could direct a prayer to God wherever he was, and God could direct an angel to him there. The ship was tossed with winds and waves, but the angel found a way into it. No storms can prevent the giving of God's favor to his people, because he is an ever-present help (Ps 46:1). We may suppose that Paul, being a prisoner, did not have a cabin of his own in the ship, but was put down into the hold—any dark or dirty place in common with the rest of the prisoners was thought good enough for him—but even there the angel of God stood by him. Lowliness and poverty set no one far away from God and his favor. Paul had this vision only *this last night*. He had this fresh vision to assure him of the safety of those with him.

1.3.3. The encouragements given him in the vision (v. 14).

1.3.3.1. He was forbidden to fear. Although everyone around him was at their wits' end and lost in despair, *Fear not, Paul*. Let not the saints be afraid, not even at sea, in a storm, for *the Lord of hosts is with them* (Ps 46:7, 11).

1.3.3.2. He was assured that he would come safely to Rome: *Thou must be brought before Caesar*. God's witnesses cannot be defeated until they have finished their testimony (Rev 11:7); so it is with the rage of the stormiest sea. This is an assurance to faithful servants of God in difficulties, that as long as God has any work for them to do, their lives will be extended.

1.3.3.3. For his sake all who were in the ship with him would be saved too: *God hath given thee all those that sail with thee*. By preserving them all for his sake, God chose to show what great blessings good people are to the world. Paul rescued a whole ship's crew here, almost 300 souls. God often spares evildoers for the sake of the godly. The good people are hated and persecuted in the world as if they were unworthy to live in it, but really it is for their sakes that the world stands. It was a great favor to Paul—and he looked on it as such—that others were saved for his sake: *They are given thee*. There is no greater satisfaction to a good person than to know that they are a public blessing.

1.4. He comforted them (v. 25): *Wherefore, Sirs, be of good cheer, for I believe God, that it shall be even as it was told me*. He would not require them to believe what he himself did not believe, and so he solemnly professed that he believed it himself. Will it be as God has said? Then take heart; be very courageous (Nu 13:20; Dt 31:6–7; Jos 1:6, 9, 18; etc.). If with God saying and doing are not two things, then believing and enjoying should not be so with us.

1.5. He gave them a sign, telling them specifically what this stormy voyage would result in (v. 26): "*We must be cast upon* (run aground on) *a certain island*, and that will both break the ship and save the passengers." Providence still undertook to bring them to an island that would be a refuge for them.

2. Their eventual coming to drop anchor on an unknown shore (vv. 27–29). They had been in the storm a full two weeks, continually expecting death: *The fourteenth night they came near land*; they were *that night driven up and down in Adria*, on the Adriatic Sea, a part of the Mediterranean extending to the African shore, but they did not know where they were. *About midnight the mariners apprehended that they drew near to some shore*. To find out whether they really were or not, they took soundings. The water would be shallower as they neared the shore. When they first took soundings, *they found they drew twenty fathoms* (about 120 feet, about thirty-seven meters) *deep of water*, and by *the next, fifteen fathoms* (about ninety feet, about twenty-seven meters), which showed they were near the shore. They took the hint and, fearing rocks near the shore, *cast anchor and wished for the day*. When they had light, no land could be seen; now that land was near, they had no light to see by; it is hardly surprising that they wished for daylight to come. When those who fear God walk in darkness, let them do as these sailors did: drop anchor, wish for the day, and be assured that the day will dawn.

3. The defeating of the sailors' attempt to escape from the ship. Notice:

3.1. The treacherous plan of the sailors to leave the sinking ship (v. 30): *They were about to flee out of the ship*, to save themselves and leave all the rest to perish. They pretended that they were going to *cast anchors out of the fore-ship* (lower some anchors from the bow), and that for that reason they needed to *let down the boat*. Paul had assured them in God's name that they would safely reach land, but they would rather trust in their own refuge of lies (Isa 28:17) than in God's word and truth.

3.2. Paul's revelation of the plan (v. 31). Paul saw through it and told the centurion and the soldiers about it, speaking to them plainly, *Except these abide in the ship, you cannot be saved*. Now the greatest difficulty of all was before them, and so the sailors were now more necessary than ever. Now that the ship was near land, the sailors must use their skill to bring the ship to it. When God has done for us what we could not do, we must then help ourselves in his strength. God, who appointed the ending, that they would be saved, also appointed the means, that they would be saved by the help of these sailors. Duty is ours; outcomes are God's. We are not trusting God, but tempting him, when we do not use the proper means that are within our power to preserve our own lives.

3.3. The effective defeat of the plan by the soldiers (v. 32). It was no time to stand arguing the case with the sailors, and so they made no further trouble, *but cut the ropes of the boat* (lifeboat) *to let it fall off*. Now because the sailors were forced to stay in the ship, they were also forced to work toward the safety of the ship, because if the others perished, they would perish with them.

4. The new life that Paul put into the company. Those who have one like Paul in their company are fortunate. The day was coming on. The dawning of the day revived them a little, and then Paul got them together.

4.1. He rebuked them for their neglect of themselves: *This is the fourteenth day that you have tarried, and continued fasting, having taken nothing* (v. 33). They had eaten very little, next to nothing. "*You have continued fasting*; that is, you have lost your stomach; you have had neither appetite nor appreciation for your food because of your overwhelming fear and despair." How foolish it is to die for fear of dying!

4.2. He urged them to eat food (v. 34): "*Wherefore I pray you to take some meat*. We have a hard struggle in front of us: if our bodies are weak from not eating, we will be unable to help ourselves." Paul wanted these people to eat, for otherwise the waves would be too strong for them: "*I pray you* take some nourishment, *for this is for your health*"—or rather "for your preservation" or "for your safety." "It is for your salvation." "Without nourishment you will not have strength to preserve your lives." *He that will not labour, let him not eat* (2Th 3:10); similarly, those who want to work must eat. Weak and trembling Christians, who give way to doubts and fears, continue to fast from the Lord's Supper and from divine encouragements, and then they complain that they cannot continue in their spiritual work, and it is all their own fault. If they would eat and feast as they should, they would be strengthened, and it would be for their souls' health and salvation.

4.3. He assured them that their lives would be preserved: *There shall not a hair fall from the head of any of you.* "You cannot eat for fear of dying; I tell you, you are sure to live, and so you must eat."

4.4. He himself spread their table for them: *When he had thus spoken, he took bread.* They were not reduced to short rations; they had plenty. But what good did that do them if they had no stomach to eat? We have reason to be thankful to God that we have not only food for our appetite but also appetite for our food.

4.5. He was chaplain to the ship, and they had reason to be proud of their chaplain. *He gave thanks to God in presence of them all.* Whether he had prayed with the whole company together before this is uncertain. Now *he gave thanks to God, in presence of them all,* thanking him that they were alive and that they had a promise that their lives would be preserved. He gave thanks for the provision they had, and he sought a blessing on it. We must *in everything give thanks* (1Th 5:18), and must especially look to God in receiving our food. *He gave thanks in presence of them all,* not only to show that he served a Master he was unashamed of but also to invite them into his service. If we seek a blessing on our food and give thanks for it rightly, we will also be a credit to our profession and commend it to the good opinion of others.

4.6. He set them a good example: *When he had given thanks, he broke the bread* (it was sea-biscuit) and *he began to eat.* Whether they would be encouraged or not, he would still eat his food and be thankful. The most effective way of preaching is by example.

4.7. It had a beneficial effect on them all (v. 36): *Then were they all of good cheer.* They dared to believe the message God sent them through Paul when they realized Paul believed it himself. People feel encouraged to commit themselves to Christ as their Savior when those who invite them to do so make it clear that they have done so themselves. It is here that the number of the people is recorded: *they were in all two hundred threescore and sixteen souls.* Notice how many people may be influenced by the good example of one. *They did all eat;* in fact, *they did all eat enough* (v. 38).

4.8. They once more lightened the ship. Before, they had thrown *the wares and the tackle overboard*, and now they threw out *the wheat*; it was better to sink the food than be sunk by it. We ourselves, in order to save our lives, may need to throw away something that we have gathered and stored to support our lives.

5. Their putting ashore, and the breaking up of the ship in the process. When it was fully day, they began to look around them, and:

5.1. *They knew not where they were*; they could not tell what country they were now on the coast of. These sailors had probably often sailed this way before, and but here they were at a loss.

5.2. *They discovered a creek with a level shore* (a bay with a sandy beach), *into which they hoped to thrust the ship* (run the ship aground) (v. 39). Even though they did not know which country it was or whether the inhabitants

were civil or cruel, they decided to throw themselves on their mercy. It was at least dry land, which would be very welcome to those who had been so long at sea. It was a pity that they lacked some help from the shore. Those who live on the coast often have the opportunity to help those who are in distress at sea, saving precious lives, and they should do their utmost to that end. The crew of this ship made straight for the shore (v. 40):

5.3. *They took up the anchors. They then committed themselves to the sea* and *loosed the rudder-bands* (untied the ropes that held the rudders); these ropes had been fastened during the storm to give the ship greater steadiness, but now that the travelers were *putting into the port*, the ropes *were loosed* so that the pilot could steer with more freedom. *They then hoisted up the main-sail to the wind, and made toward shore.* When they saw the shore, they rushed toward it as fast as they could, perhaps "making more haste and less speed," as the proverb says. Should not poor souls who have long been struggling with winds and storms in this world long to put into the safe and quiet harbor of eternal rest? Should the soul not also lift up the foresail of faith to the wind of the Spirit, and so make for the shore with longing desires?

5.4. They used all means *to run the ship aground* on a sandbank, or on a peninsula, a neck of land washed by the sea on both sides—about which it is therefore said *two seas met* on it (v. 41)—and *there the foreport stuck fast. The hinder part* would soon be broken *by the violence of the waves.* The ship, which had strangely weathered the storm in the vast ocean, where it had room to roll, was dashed to pieces when it stood fast. If the heart is established in the world, it is lost; Satan's temptations beat against it, and it is gone. But as long as it keeps above the world, even if it is tossed about with worries and disturbances, there is hope for it. The travelers had the shore in view but suffered shipwreck in the harbor, to teach us never to be secure.

6. A particular danger that Paul and the rest of the prisoners were in.

6.1. In this critical moment *the soldiers advised the killing of the prisoners*—whom they were to give an account of—*lest any of them should swim out and escape* (v. 42). There was no great danger of that, since the prisoners could not go far, being weak and weary; and since they were in the full view of so many soldiers who had responsibility for them, it was unlikely they would attempt it. But in any case, this suggestion by the soldiers was cruel and barbaric, and so much the worse because it showed that they were so ready to throw away other people's lives when without a miracle of mercy they would have lost their own.

6.2. The centurion, for Paul's sake, quashed this idea. Paul, who was his prisoner, had found favor with him. Although this Julius had earlier despised Paul's advice (v. 11), now, being *willing to save Paul*, he prevented the execution of that gory plan. Just as God had saved all in the ship for Paul's sake, so here the centurion saved all the prisoners for Paul's sake; such a widely generous man is a good man.

7. The saving of the lives of all the people in the ship.

7.1. Some were saved by swimming: *The centurion commanded his soldiers, as many of them as could swim, to get to land* first, and to be ready to receive the prisoners and prevent their escape.

7.2. The rest scrambled to the shore with much trouble, some on planks and others on the *broken pieces of the ship*, and exerting themselves all the more because they were assured that their labor would not be in vain (1Co

15:58), and *so it came to pass* that through the good providence of God they *escaped all safely to land.* They were rescued from the dreadful sea and *brought to the desired haven.* Although there are great difficulties on the way of promised salvation, that salvation will be brought about without fail, and even a shipwreck may provide a means of saving lives, so that when all seems to be lost, everything proves to be safe, even though it is *on boards, and broken pieces of the ship.*

CHAPTER 28

After the account of this chapter we hear no more about Paul in the sacred history, though we hear a great deal from him in his letters, which are still to come. It would have been good if we could have taken our final leave of him with more pleasure, if we had left him at liberty, but in this chapter we are to grieve with him, yet also congratulate him. 1. We grieve with him as a poor, shipwrecked passenger, yet we also congratulate him: 1.1. As especially honored by his God in his distress. First he was preserved from being harmed by a viper that fastened on his hand (vv. 1–6), and then he was made an instrument of much good on the island on which they were shipwrecked (vv. 7–9). 1.2. As highly respected by the people there (v. 10). 2. We grieve with him as a poor, confined prisoner (vv. 11–16), but we also congratulate him: 2.1. On the respect shown him by the Christians at Rome (v. 15). 2.2. On the favor he found with the captain of the guard (v. 16). 2.3. On the free meetings he had with the Jews at Rome, both about his own affairs (vv. 17–22) and about the Christian faith in general (v. 23). The outcome of these meetings was that God was glorified and the apostles were justified in preaching the Gospel to the Gentiles (vv. 24–29). 2.4. On the undisturbed liberty he had to preach the Gospel in his own house for two years (vv. 30–31).

Verses 1–10

What a wide range of places and circumstances we have found Paul in! He was a moving planet (literally, a "wanderer"), not a fixed star. It is truly an ill wind that blows nobody any good, as the proverb says. This ill wind blew good to the island of *Melita* (Malta), giving it for three months the company of Paul, who was a blessing to every place he went to. We have here:

1. The kind reception the inhabitants of this island gave the strangers (v. 2): *The barbarous people showed us no little kindness.* Providence continued its care of them. Whatever benefits we receive by human hands must be acknowledged as having come from the hand of God. Just as he can bring about peace between enemies, so he can make strangers friends, true friends in need, and those are friends indeed. See here:

1.1. The general notice taken of the kind welcome the islanders of Malta gave to Paul and his company. The islanders are called *barbarous people* because they did not, in language and customs, conform either to the Greeks or to the Romans, who looked on everyone except themselves as *barbarians*, though otherwise civilized enough, and perhaps in some cases more civil than they were. These people were full of humanity: they *showed us no little kindness.* So far were they from taking advantage of this shipwreck that they grasped it as an opportunity to show mercy. Such a comment is written for our imitation, so that we may learn from it to be compassionate to those who are in distress and misery, helping and relieving them to the best of our ability. If Providence has so

appointed the bounds of our habitation (17:26) as to give us frequent opportunities to help people who are at a loss, we should not consider it an inconvenience to our life, but an advantage.

1.2. A particular example of their kindness: *"They kindled a fire,* and *they received us every one*—made room for us around the fire and welcomed us all warmly." Waters from above met those from below, and it rained so hard that they must have been wet to the skin immediately. *It was a cold rain too,* so that they needed nothing so much as a good fire—*to warm them, and dry their clothes. Be you warmed* is as necessary as *Be you filled* (Jas 2:16).

2. The further danger that Paul was put in when a viper attached itself to his hand.

2.1. When the fire was to be made, and to be made bigger, Paul was as busy as any of them in gathering sticks (v. 3). Paul was industrious and active and loved to be busy doing things that needed to be done. He would stoop to anything in which he could make himself useful, even including gathering sticks to make a fire. We should be willing to condescend to the most humble work for the good of our brothers and sisters. Those who receive benefit from the fire should help carry fuel to it.

2.2. A viper happened to be among the sticks, and it played dead until it came to the heat, and then it revived and flew at the one who had thrown it unawares into the fire, and *fastened upon his hand* (v. 3). Just as there is sometimes a snake in the green grass, so there is often one under dry leaves. Notice how many dangers human life is exposed to, and what danger we are in from the lesser creatures. We often meet with what is troublesome where we expect what is good, and many incur harm when they are honestly employed and fulfilling their duty.

2.3. The islanders concluded that this viper was sent by divine justice to be the avenger of blood. *When they saw the venomous animal hang on his hand,* they concluded, *"No doubt this man is a murderer,* and so, *though he has escaped the sea, yet* divine *vengeance* pursues him and will *not suffer* (allow) *him to live."* Here we may see:

2.3.1. Some of the revelations of natural light. The islanders were a primitive people, but they naturally knew:

2.3.1.1. That there is a God who governs the world, that not even such a thing as this happens except by divine command.

2.3.1.2. That evil pursues sinners, that there are good works that God will reward and evil works he will punish.

2.3.1.3. That murder is a detestable crime that will not go unpunished for long. Those who think they will go unpunished in any evil action will be judged out of the mouth of these islanders. Learn from these illiterate people that although evildoers have escaped the vengeance of the sea, it is impossible to outrun divine justice.

2.3.2. Some of the mistakes of natural light. Their knowledge was defective in two things:

2.3.2.1. They thought all evildoers were punished in this life. The day of vengeance is to come in the other world; although some are made examples of in this world, to prove that there is a God, many are left unpunished, to prove that there is a judgment to come.

2.3.2.2. They thought that all who were remarkably afflicted in this life were evil. Divine revelation sets this matter in its true light, telling us that, ordinarily, all things come alike to all (Ecc 9:2), that good people often suffer greatly in this life, so that they will exercise their faith and patience.

2.4. When he shook the viper from his hand, they expected *that he would swell* or *that he would fall down dead suddenly.* Notice how people tend, once they have gained a poor opinion of a person, to stand by it, and to think that God must necessarily confirm their perverse judgment.

3. Paul's rescue from the danger, and the improper interpretation the people put on this.

3.1. It does not appear that it frightened or unsettled him at all. He did not shriek or start. He had a wonderful presence of mind, such as no one could have had in response to such a sudden misfortune except by the special help of divine grace.

3.2. He *shook off the viper into the fire.* Believers, similarly, in the power of the grace of Christ, shake off the temptations of Satan. When we despise human criticism and insult, having the testimony of conscience for us, then, like Paul here, we *shake off the viper into the fire,* and it does us no harm.

3.3. He was none the worse. Those who thought it would be the death of him *looked a great while, but saw no harm at all come to him.* God here intended to make way for the reception of the Gospel among them.

3.4. They then praised him as much as they had insulted him before: *They changed their minds, and said that he was a god,* for they thought it impossible that a mere mortal would have a viper hang on their hand so long and not be any the worse for it. Notice the uncertainty of popular opinion, how it turns with the wind and tends to run to extremes.

4. Paul's miraculous healing of an old man who was sick with a fever, and of others. Notice:

4.1. The kind reception which *Publius, the chief man of the island,* gave to these distressed strangers; he *received them and lodged them three days very courteously.* It is fortunate when God gives a generous heart to those to whom he has given great possessions. It was commendable of the chief official of the island, the richest man, to be rich in good works.

4.2. The illness of *the father of Publius*: he *lay sick of a fever and a bloody flux* (dysentery). Providence so arranged matters that he would be ill just at that time, so that his healing would be a reward to Publius for his generosity, and a reward especially for his kindness toward Paul.

4.3. The healing of him. Paul heard about his case, and he came, not as a doctor to heal him with medicines, but as an apostle to heal him by a miracle. He prayed for his healing and then laid his hands on him, and the elderly man was completely well in a moment. Although he must have been getting on in years, he still recovered his health.

4.4. The healing of many others. If Paul could heal diseases so effectively, he would soon have enough patients, and he *bade them all welcome.* He did not plead that he was a stranger there, thrown by accident among them and waiting to be gone at the first opportunity, who therefore should therefore be excused. No, a good person will try to do good wherever the providence of God places them. Paul thanked God for the opportunity to be useful among them. In this way, he in effect paid for his quarters, which should encourage us to receive strangers, since in so doing some have entertained angels, and some apostles, unawares (Heb 13:2). God will not be in arrears in repaying anyone for the kindness they show to his people in distress. Never were any people so enriched by a shipwreck on their coasts as these islanders of Malta were.

5. The islanders' grateful acknowledgement of the kindness Paul had done them (v. 10). They *honoured us with many honours.* They showed them all possible respect; indeed, they justly thought no expression of respect for them to be too much. *"When we departed, they loaded us with such things as were necessary;* they put on board such things as we needed." Paul accepted the kindness of the good people of Malta not as a fee for his cures—he had received freely, so he gave freely (Mt 10:8)—but as the relief of his needs, and of the needs of those who were with him.

Verses 11–16

Here is the account of the progress of Paul's voyage toward Rome and his eventual arrival there. After a storm came a calm: the latter part of his voyage was easy and quiet. We have here:

1. The travelers' departure from Malta. When they were refreshed, they must put to sea again. The difficulties and discouragements we have met with in our Christian life must not hinder us from pressing onward. Notice:

1.1. The time of their departure. It was *after three months,* the three winter months. It was better to wait than to go forward while the season was dangerous. Paul had warned the centurion and his soldiers against risking going to sea in winter, and they had refused to pay any attention to the warning, but now he had no need to warn them again. Experience is called the mistress of fools because those who will not learn until experience has taught them are fools.

1.2. The ship in which they departed. It was in an Alexandrian ship. This ship had *wintered in that isle* and was safe. Here were two ships, both from Alexandria, but one was wrecked there and the other was saved. Events are varied in this way so that we may learn both how to be in need and how to have plenty (Php 4:12). The writer takes notice of the ship's sign, which probably gave it its name: its figurehead was of the twin sea gods Castor and Pollux. The travelers superstitiously hoped they would have better sailing conditions under this badge than they had had before.

2. Their landing in or near Italy and pursuing their journey toward Rome.

2.1. They landed first at Syracuse, the chief city of the island of Sicily. There they *tarried three days.*

2.2. From Syracuse they went to Rhegium, a city in Italy. There, it seems, they stayed one day. It does not appear that they even went ashore, but only came to cast anchor briefly.

2.3. From Rhegium they went to Puteoli, a seaport not far from Naples. The Alexandrian ship was bound for that port, and so Paul and the rest who were bound for Rome were put ashore there and took the remainder of their journey by land. At Puteoli they *found brethren.* We are not told who brought the knowledge of Christ there, but it was in that port: the yeast of the Gospel spreads its influence so wonderfully (Mt 13:33). God has many people to serve and worship him in places where we little think he has.

2.3.1. Although there were probably only a few believers in Puteoli, Paul still found them. By instinct, as it were, they got together. Brothers and sisters in Christ should seek one another, as those of the same country do in a foreign land.

2.3.2. They wanted Paul and his companions to *tarry with them seven days,* that is, to plan on staying at least one Lord's Day with them. Paul was willing to allow them that much of his time, and the centurion agreed to stay one week there to please Paul.

2.4. From Puteoli they went on toward Rome. This was the final stage of their journey.

3. The meeting the Christians at Rome arranged for Paul. Notice:

3.1. The great honor they paid Paul. They had heard much of his fame and what distinguished service he had done for the kingdom of Christ, and they had heard about his sufferings and how God had acknowledged him in them; they thought themselves obliged, therefore, to show him all possible respect. He had some time before written a long letter to them, in return for which they showed him this respect. They *went to meet him* so that they could bring him in state, even though he was a prisoner. Some of them went as far as the Forum of Appius, which was fifty-one miles (about eighty-two kilometers) from Rome; others to a place called the Three Taverns. Far from being ashamed of him because he was a prisoner, they counted him worthy of double honor for that very reason.

3.2. The great encouragement Paul had in this. Now that he was drawing near to Rome, he began to have some misgivings about his appeal to Caesar and its consequences. What things might happen to him here he could not tell, but he began to lose his sense of excitement about it, until he met these good people who came from Rome, and *when he saw them*:

3.2.1. He *thanked God*. If our friends are kind to us, it is God who makes them so, and we must give him the glory for it. When he saw so many Christians who were from Rome, he thanked God that the Gospel of Christ had had such wonderful success there in the center of the empire. When we go out into the world and meet, even in strange places, those who bear Christ's name and fear God, we should lift our hearts to heaven in thanksgiving; let us thank God that there are so many excellent ones on this earth (Ps 16:3), bad though it is.

3.2.2. He *took courage*. It put new life into him, and now he could enter Rome in custody as cheerfully as he had ever entered Jerusalem at liberty. He found that there were those there who loved and valued him here. It is an encouragement to those who are traveling toward heaven to meet with their fellow travelers. When we see the numerous and earnest assemblies of good Christians, we should not only give thanks to God but also take encouragement to ourselves.

4. The delivering of Paul into custody at Rome (v. 16). He had now come to his journey's end. However:

4.1. He was still a prisoner. He had longed to see Rome, but when he arrived there, he was delivered to the *captain of the guard* and could see no more of Rome than the captain would allow him to. How many great people had made their entry into Rome crowned and in triumph, though they were really the plagues of their generation! Here a good man, however, made his entry into Rome chained and gloated over as a poor prisoner. This thought is enough to make a person dissatisfied forever with this world.

4.2. He had some favor shown him. He was a prisoner, but not a confined prisoner: *Paul was suffered* (allowed) *to dwell by himself*, and a soldier was appointed to be his guard, who, we hope, let him take all the freedom that could be allowed to a prisoner. God's prisoners can take encouragement from knowing that he can give them favor in the eyes of those who take them captive. If he either makes their captivity comfortable for them or makes them comfortable in it, they have reason to be thankful.

Verses 17–22

Paul had to convene his own case; here he explained it to the leaders of the Jews at Rome: these *chief of the Jews* were the most distinguished men of that religion.

Paul called them together so that he could come to a good understanding with them. Notice:

1. What explanation he gave them of his case.

1.1. He professed his own innocence: "I have *committed nothing against the people* of the Jews, nor have I committed anything *against the customs of our fathers*." Paul did not impose the customs of the ancestors on the Gentiles; those customs were never intended for them. Nor did he ever oppose the Jews' following of those customs; indeed, he himself conformed to them.

1.2. He complained of the harsh treatment he had met with. *He was delivered prisoner from Jerusalem into the hands of the Romans*. If he had spoken the whole truth in this matter, the Jews would have looked worse than they did in this account, for the whole truth was that they would have murdered him if the Romans had not protected him. However, since they accused him as a criminal before Felix the governor, they were in effect delivering him as prisoner into the hands of the Romans.

1.3. He declared the judgment of the Roman governors about him (v. 18). They had examined him, inquiring into his case. The *chief captain* had examined him, as did Felix, Festus, and Agrippa, and they could not find him guilty of any crime deserving death; on the contrary, they wanted to release him. Those who most carefully examined his case acquitted him, and no one condemned him except those who were prejudiced against him, those who refused to hear his case.

1.4. He pleaded that he had had to move his case to Rome, and that it was only in his own defense, and not with any intention of raising recriminations. *When the Jews spoke against it* (v. 19), he was *constrained to appeal unto Caesar.* His aim in this appeal was not to accuse his nation, but only to vindicate himself. It is invidious to accuse, especially to accuse a nation. Paul interceded for them, but never against them. The Roman government had at this time a poor opinion of the Jewish nation, and it would have been easy to anger the emperor. Paul, however, would not do this for anything; he wanted to make the best of what everyone was, not make bad things even worse.

1.5. He put his sufferings on their true footing (v. 20): "*For this cause I have called for you*, not to quarrel with you but to *see you and speak with you* as my compatriots, because *for the hope of Israel I am bound with this chain.*" He carried the mark of his imprisonment with him, and was probably chained to the soldier who kept him, and it was:

1.5.1. Because he preached that the Messiah had come, the One whom Israel hoped for. "Do not all the Jews agree that the Messiah will be the glory of his people Israel? I preach and prove that this Messiah has come. I preach a hope in a Messiah who has already come, a hope that must lead to joy in him."

1.5.2. Because he preached that the resurrection of the dead would come. This also was the hope of Israel. "The Jews who accuse me want you to continue to expect a Messiah who will free you from the Roman burden and make you great and prosperous on earth. This is what they hate me for, that I want to take you away from the idea of a worldly Messiah and lead you to what is the true and real hope of Israel, a spiritual kingdom of holiness and love set up in human hearts, to be the pledge of and preparation for the joyful resurrection of the dead and the life of the world to come."

2. What their reply was. They acknowledged:

2.1. That they had nothing to say in particular against him; nor did they have any instructions either by letter or word of mouth (v. 21): "*We have neither received letters out of Judea concerning thee—nor have any of the brethren shown or spoken any harm of thee.*" This was very strange, that that restless rage of the Jews that had followed Paul wherever he went did not follow him to Rome. Some think they told a lie here, that they had orders to prosecute him but dared not admit it. But I am inclined to think that what they said was true, and that Paul now found he had gained the point he aimed at in appealing to Caesar, which was to transfer his case to a court to which they dared not follow it.

2.2. That they wanted to know in more detail about the religion he spent so much effort spreading in the face of so much opposition (v. 22): "*We desire to hear of thee what thou thinkest.* Although we know little else of Christianity, we know *it is a sect every where spoken against.*" This was all they knew about the Christian religion, that it was *a sect every where spoken against.* Its enemies gave it a bad name and then criticized it.

2.2.1. They looked on it as a sect, and this was false. True Christianity establishes what is of common concern to the whole human race; it is not built on such narrow opinions as sects commonly owe their origin to. All its gains are spiritual and eternal. It leads directly to uniting people, not dividing them.

2.2.2. They said it was everywhere spoken against, and this was too true. It is and always has been the lot of Christ's holy faith to be spoken against everywhere.

Verses 23–29

Here is a short account of a long meeting Paul had with the Jews at Rome about the Christian faith. They were still willing to give it a hearing, which was more than the Jews at Jerusalem would. We are told here:

1. How Paul managed this conference. The Jews appointed the time and date (v. 23). They seemed well disposed to receive conviction, but it turned out that not all of them were.

1.1. There were *many got together to Paul.* Although he was a prisoner, they were still willing to come to him at his house. The confinement he was now under, instead of making them prejudiced against his message, should have confirmed it to them, since it was a sign that he thought this message worth suffering for. One would visit such a man as Paul in his prison rather than miss the opportunity to receive instruction from him.

1.2. He was very full in his talk with them, seeking their conviction more than his own vindication.

1.2.1. He explained the kingdom of God to them, showing them the nature of that kingdom, that it is heavenly and spiritual and that it does not shine in worldly show but in purity of heart and life. If that was explained to them and set in its true light, they would be brought to obey it.

1.2.2. He not only explained the kingdom of God but also testified to it; he declared it plainly to them and confirmed it by undeniable proofs. He declared to them the extraordinary powers in the kingdom of grace by which the kingdom of God had been set up, and the miracles in the kingdom of nature by which it was confirmed. He bore testimony to it from his own experience of its power.

1.2.3. He not only explained and declared the kingdom of God; he pleaded with them earnestly to accept the kingdom of God for themselves. His message was given with a warm and lively application to his hearers.

1.2.4. He tried to persuade them about Jesus. The whole purpose of his talk was to bring them to Christ, to convince them that he was the Messiah. He urged on

them *the things concerning Jesus, out of the law of Moses and out of the prophets,* showing how they all had their fulfillment in this Jesus. He spoke to them out of the Old Testament Scriptures.

1.3. He spoke long, from *morning till evening.* The subject was exciting—it was of vast importance—and he was serious about it. He did not know if and when he would have another such opportunity, and so he spoke to them all day.

2. What the effect of this talk was. One would have thought that such a good cause, promoted by such a skillful hand as Paul's, would surely be effective, but it did not prove so: the child Jesus was set to make some fall and others rise again (Lk 2:34), to be a foundation stone to some (1Co 3:11) and a stumbling block to others (1Pe 2:8).

2.1. *They did not agree among themselves* (v. 25). His hearers could not agree on the meaning of what he preached or on the adequacy of the evidence in support of it.

2.2. *Some believed the things that were spoken, and some believed not* (v. 24). Some are persuaded by the word, and others are hardened; some receive the light, and others close their eyes to it. This is how it was among Christ's hearers; some believed and some blasphemed.

3. The arousing word that Paul said to them when they parted. He perceived from what they were muttering that many of them were stubborn and refused to yield. "Hold on a moment," Paul said; "take one word with you before you go. What do you think will be the effect of your stubborn unfaithfulness? Where will it all lead?

3.1. "By the righteous judgment of God you will be sealed in your unbelief. Turn to the Scripture (Isa 6:9–10) and tremble, for fear that the situation described there may prove to be yours." Just as the Old Testament contains Gospel promises, which will be fulfilled in all who believe, so also the Gospel threatens spiritual judgments, which will be fulfilled in those who do not believe. Isaiah the prophet was sent to make worse those who would not be made better. *Well spoke the Holy Spirit by* Isaiah *the prophet unto our fathers.* Although what was said there contained terror for the people and grief for the prophet, it was said here to have been spoken well. *He that believes not shall be damned* is Gospel as well as *He that believes shall be saved* (Mk 16:16). "*Well did Esaias prophesy of you.* The Holy Spirit said to your ancestors what would be fulfilled in you: *Hearing you shall hear, and shall not understand.*

3.1.1. "Their great sin against God is also yours, namely, that *your eyes you have closed* (v. 27). Just as your ancestors would not see God's hand lifted against them in his judgments, so you will not see God's hand stretched out to you in the grace of the Gospel." They did not see because they were determined not to, and there are none so blind as those who will not see. They had deliberately *closed their eyes, lest they should see with their eyes* the great things that concerned their eternal peace (Lk 19:42). They would not receive the evidence *lest they should hear with their ears.* What they were afraid of, that made them shut their eyes and ears, was that *they would understand with their heart, and would be converted, and I would heal them.* They kept their minds in the dark, or at least in constant confusion and disturbance. God's method is, first, to bring people to see and hear and so understand with their hearts; then to convert them, so that they submit their wills; and so to heal them; this is the normal way of dealing with a reasonable soul, and that is why Satan prevents the conversion of souls to God by blinding the mind and darkening the understanding (2Co 4:4). The situation is very sad when the sinner joins with Satan in this matter, blinding his own eyes. They were in love with their disease and afraid that God might heal them. This was the sin.

3.1.2. "The great judgment of God on them for this sin is also his judgment on you, namely, that you will be blind. *Hearing you shall hear — but you shall not understand* it, because you will not allow your minds to understand it; God will not give you strength and grace to understand it. *Seeing you shall see, but you shall not perceive.*" What with their resisting the grace of God and rebelling against the light, and God's withdrawing and withholding his grace and light from them, what with their not receiving the love of the truth (2Th 2:10), and God's giving them up for that to strong delusions, to believe a lie (2Th 2:11), *the heart of this people was waxed gross, and their ears were dull of hearing.* No living doctor could operate on them, and so their disease must be considered incurable. How can people be healed if they will not be converted to use the methods of healing? How can people be converted if they will not be convinced either of their disease or of their remedy? How can people be convinced if they *shut their eyes and stop their ears?* Once they are given over to hardness of heart, they are already near hell.

3.2. "Your unbelief will justify God in sending the Gospel to the Gentile world (v. 28). Since you push the grace of God away from you and refuse to submit to the power of divine truth and love, *be it known unto you that the salvation of God is sent unto the Gentiles.* They will hear it, receive it, and be happy in it." Now here Paul intended:

3.2.1. To lessen their displeasure at the preaching of the Gospel to the Gentiles by showing them the absurdity of that displeasure. They were angry that the salvation of God was sent to the Gentiles, but if they thought that salvation was so insignificant as not to be worthy of their own acceptance, then surely they could not begrudge the Gentiles the benefit of it. The salvation of God was sent into the world; the Jews had the first offer of it. They would not accept the invitation to the wedding banquet that was given to them first, and so they would have only themselves to blame if other guests were invited (Mt 22:1 – 14).

3.2.2. To make the most of the Jews' displeasure at the favor shown to the Gentiles, for the Jews' advantage — to bring good out of that evil. The Jews had rejected the Gospel of Christ, but it was still not too late to repent of their refusal; they could say "No" but then accept it, like the elder brother in the parable (Mt 21:29). "Is the Gospel sent to the Gentiles? Let us go after it rather than fall short of it. Will those who are thought to be beyond hearing hear it? Shall we then not hear it, whose privilege it is to have God so near us whenever we pray to him (Dt 4:7)?" In this way he wanted to shame them into believing the Gospel by the welcome it received among the Gentiles. If it did not have that effect on them, however, it would worsen their condemnation.

4. The breaking up of the gathering — in some disorder, it seems.

4.1. They turned their backs on Paul. *When Paul had said these words*, he had said enough for them, and *they departed*, no more affected, either by those terrible words at the close of his talk or all the encouraging words he had spoken before, than the seats they sat on.

4.2. They set their faces one against another, disputing with one another. Those who agreed to leave Paul did not agree on the reasons why they left, but had *great reasoning among themselves.* Many argue vigorously but do not

reason rightly. Nor will arguments among them convince them unless the grace of God opens their understandings (Lk 24:45).

Verses 30 – 31

We take our leave of the record of the apostle Paul's life here. We should carefully take note of every detail of the circumstances in which we leave him.

1. It must trouble us that we leave him in chains for Christ. *Two whole years* of his good life were spent here in confinement. He appealed to Caesar in the hope of gaining a speedy release from imprisonment, but he was still detained as a prisoner. Then his chains in Christ were revealed in Caesar's court, as he says in Php 1:13. During these two years' imprisonment he wrote his letters to the Ephesians, Philippians, Colossians, and to Philemon. We are not told how he obtained his freedom, only that he was a prisoner for two years. Tradition has it that after his release he went from Italy to Spain, from there to Crete, and from there, with Timothy, into Judea; from there he went to visit the churches in Asia, eventually coming to Rome a second time, where he was beheaded in the last year of Nero.

1.1. It grieves us to think that such a useful person as Paul was detained for so long. He was a prisoner under Felix for two years (24:27), and he was a prisoner under Nero for two more. How many churches might Paul have planted if he had been at liberty! However, God will show that he is not indebted even to the most useful instruments he employs, but will carry on his own interest both without their services and by their sufferings. Even Paul's chains meant *the furtherance of the Gospel* (Php 1:12 – 14).

1.2. Paul's imprisonment was in some respects even a kindness to him; for these *two years he dwelt in his own hired house,* doing more, for all we know, than he had ever done before. Such a retirement would be a refreshment to one who had been traveling throughout his life. Now he lived for two years in the same house; his being brought into this prison was like Christ's call to his disciples *to come into a desert place, and rest awhile* (Mk 6:31). When he was at liberty, he was in continual fear because of *the lying in wait of the Jews* (20:19), but now his prison was his castle.

2. Yet it is a pleasure to us that although we leave him in chains for Christ, we also leave him at work for Christ. His prison became a temple, a church, and then it was a palace to him. Thanks be to God, Paul's mouth was not silenced; a faithful, zealous minister can bear any hardship better than being silenced. Paul was bound, but the word of the Lord is not bound (2Ti 2:9). He was glad to *see some of them* (v. 15), but it would only be half his joy unless he could pass on to them some spiritual gift, which here he had an opportunity to do. Notice:

2.1. To whom he preached. Whoever wanted to come to his house to hear was welcome. Ministers' doors should be open to those who want to receive instruction from them. When we cannot do what we want to do in serving God, we must still do all that we can. *He received all that came to him*; he was neither afraid of the greatest nor ashamed of the humblest. He might hope to be more effective because *they came in unto him*, which presumed a desire to be instructed and a willingness to learn, and where these are, it is probable that some good may be done.

2.2. What he preached.

2.2.1. He was God's ambassador, and so he *preached the kingdom of God.* He did not interfere with the affairs of human kingdoms; let those whose work it was deal with them. He preached the kingdom of God; he centered on this in his public preaching, just as he did in his public debates, *testifying the kingdom of God* (v. 23), which will make us all wise and good, wiser and better, which is the purpose of preaching.

2.2.2. He was an ambassador for Christ, and so he *taught those things which concern the Lord Jesus Christ*—the whole account of the life of Christ, all that concerns the mystery of godliness (1Ti 3:16). Paul stood by his aim—to know and preach *nothing but Christ, and him crucified* (1Co 2:2).

2.3. With what liberty he preached. Divine grace gave him a free spirit. He preached *with all confidence.* He spoke boldly, *not ashamed of the Gospel of Christ* (Ro 1:16). Divine Providence gave him freedom of speech: *No man forbidding him.* The Jews who used to forbid him to speak to the Gentiles had no authority here, and the Roman government as yet did not consider the profession of Christianity a crime. It set limits on the rage of persecutors; there were many in Rome, both Jews and Gentiles, who hated Christianity, and yet, though Paul was a prisoner, he was ignored when he preached the Gospel. Though there were very many who had it in their power to forbid Paul's preaching, God so controlled it *that no man did forbid him.* See God providing comfort for the relief of the persecuted here. Although it was not a wide door that was opened up for him, still, it was kept open, and to many it was an effective door, one they benefited from by walking through it, so that there were saints even in Caesar's household (Php 4:22). Therefore, when the place where we have our meetings is at any time made a quiet home, we must give thanks to God for it, still longing for the holy mountain on which there will never be any pricking brier or painful thorn (Eze 28:24).

A PRACTICAL AND DEVOTIONAL EXPOSITION OF

Romans

D avid's Psalms are the stars of the first magnitude in the Old Testament, and Paul's Letters in the New, the stars in each of these clusters differing from the other stars in glory (1Co 15:41). Scripture is a letter from heaven to earth, but within it we have several specific letters, more of Paul's than of any other person's. His understanding was quick and insightful; his expressions were fluent and copious; his affections were very warm and zealous, and his resolutions no less bold and daring. Before his conversion, these made him a very keen and bitter persecutor, but after it, he became the most skillful, zealous preacher; no one was better fitted to win souls, nor more effective.

This letter to the Romans is placed first not because of the priority of its date but because of its superlative excellence, it being one of the longest and fullest of all. We gather from some passages in the letter that it was written in AD 56, from Corinth. Paul was now going to Jerusalem with the money that was given for the poor saints there, and he speaks about that (15:26). The great mysteries written about in this letter necessarily produced many things that are difficult to understand (2Pe 3:16). The first eleven chapters are doctrinal; the last five are practical. 1. The doctrinal part of the letter instructs us: 1.1. About the way of salvation. 1.2. About the people who have been saved, those who belong to the *election of grace* (11:5), Gentiles and Jews. The Jews then stumbled at two things—justification by faith apart from the works of the law, and the admission of the Gentiles into the church, and that is why he seeks to clarify and uphold both of these truths. 2. The practical part follows. 3. As he draws toward a conclusion, he defends his decision to write to them, sends particular greetings to many friends there, adds the greetings of his friends who are with him, and ends with a blessing to his readers and a doxology to God.

CHAPTER 1

In this chapter we may notice: 1. The introduction to the whole letter (vv. 1–16). 2. A description of the wretched condition of the Gentile world, which begins the proof of the teaching of justification by faith (vv. 17–32).

Verses 1–7

In this paragraph:

1. The person who is writing the letter is described (v. 1): *Paul, a servant of Jesus Christ;* this is his title of honor, which he glories in, a servant. *Called to be an apostle.* Christ sought him to make an apostle out of him (Ac 9:15). He builds his authority on his call here; he did not go off without being sent. *Called an apostle,* as if this were the name he wanted to be called by, even though he acknowledged himself not fit to be called by this title (1Co 15:9). *Separated to the Gospel of God.* The Pharisees also had their name from their separation, because they *separated themselves to the study of the law.* Paul had formerly been such a person, but he had now changed his studies, was a Gospel Pharisee, separated by the purpose of God (Gal 1:15), *separated from his mother's womb.* He was wholeheartedly devoted to the Gospel of God.

2. Having mentioned the Gospel of God, he digresses to commend it. We have here:

2.1. Its antiquity. It was *promised before* (v. 2); it had an ancient origin in the promises and prophecies of the Old Testament.

2.2. Its subject matter: it is about Christ (vv. 3–4). The prophets and apostles all bear witness to him (Ac 10:43). Notice how, when Paul mentions Christ, he heaps up his names and titles: *his Son Jesus Christ our Lord.* And then he cannot continue without including some expression of love and honor, showing us that in one person Christ has two distinct natures.

2.2.1. His human nature: *made of the seed of David* (v. 3), that is, born of the Virgin Mary, who was a descendant of David (Lk 1:27).

2.2.2. His divine nature: *declared to be the Son of God* (v. 4), *according to the Spirit of holiness. According to the flesh,* that is, his human nature, *he was of the seed of David,* but *according to the Spirit of holiness,* that is, the divine nature, he is the Son of God. The great proof or demonstration of this is *his resurrection from the dead.* Those who would not be convinced by that would be convinced by nothing. So here we have a summary of the Gospel teaching about Christ's two natures in one person.

2.3. Its fruit (v. 5); *by whom we have received grace and apostleship.* Paul counts the apostleship as a favor. We may justly count it a great favor to be employed in any work or service for God. This apostleship was received *for obedience to the faith*, that is, to bring people to that obedience. Paul's obedience was for the sake of bringing about this obedience *among all nations*, because he was the *apostle of the Gentiles* (11:13). Notice the description given here of the Christian profession: it is *obedience to the faith*. It does not consist in an intellectual knowledge, and much less does it consist in contrary disputes, but in obedience. The act of faith is the obedience of the understanding to God's revelation, and the result of that is the obedience of the will to God's commands. Paul speaks of Christianity as obedience here. Christ has a yoke (Mt 11:29–30). "*Among whom are you* (v. 6). You Romans here stand on the same level as other Gentile nations who are less famous and less wealthy; you are all one in Christ." God shows no favoritism (Lev 19:15; Dt 1:17; 16:19; 1Pe 1:17). *The called of Jesus Christ*; all those, and only those, who are effectively called by Jesus Christ are brought to an obedience of the faith.

3. The people to whom it is written are identified (v. 7): *To all that are in Rome, beloved of God, called to be saints*, that is, to all the professing Christians who were in Rome, slave or free, clever or ignorant. Rich and poor meet together in Christ Jesus (Pr 22:2). Here is:

3.1. The privilege of Christians: they are *beloved of God*. He has a common love for the whole human race and a special love for true believers.

3.2. The duty of Christians, which is to be holy, because they are called to that, *called to be saints*. Saints, and only saints, are loved by God with a special and distinctive love. They are *called saints* by profession, and it would be good if all who are called saints were true saints. To have been called saints will be of little use on the great day if we have not really been saints.

4. The apostolic blessing is given (v. 7): *Grace to you and peace*. It has not only the affection of good wishes but also the authority of a blessing. The favors desired are *grace and peace*. The Old Testament greeting was, *Peace be to you*, but now grace is added. Paul prays for *grace*, that is, the favor of God toward us. All Gospel blessings are included in these two: *grace and peace*. He also prays for *peace*, that is, all good. The source of those favors is *God our Father, and the Lord Jesus Christ*. All good comes:

4.1. From God as a Father. We are taught that when we come for grace and peace, we should call him our Father.

4.2. *From the Lord Jesus Christ* as Mediator. We have grace and peace from his fullness (Jn 1:16), peace from the fullness of his merit, grace from the fullness of his Spirit.

Verses 8–15

Notice here:

1. His thanksgiving for them (v. 8): *First, I thank my God*. It is good to begin everything with blessing God. He says this with delight and triumph. *Through Jesus Christ*. All our duties and actions—and all our praises as well as prayers—are pleasing to God only through Jesus Christ. *For you all*. We must express our love for our friends not only by praying for them but also by praising God for them. When some of the Roman Christians met him (Ac 28:15), he thanked God for them and was encouraged, but here his true, wide love extends itself further, and he *thanks God for them all. That your faith is spoken of.* Wherever he went, he heard great commendations of the Christians at Rome, which he mentions not to make them proud but to stir them to fulfill the general characterization people give of them. The greater a person's reputation

for their religious faith, the more careful they should be to preserve it. *Throughout the whole world*, that is, the Roman Empire. This was indeed a good name, a reputation for good things with God and good people. It is desirable to be well known for faith. Rome was a city on a hill (Mt 5:14): everyone took notice of what was done there. Those who are looked at by many need to walk carefully, since what they do, good or bad, will be spoken about.

2. His prayer for them (v. 9). Although they were famous and flourishing, they still needed to be prayed for. One of the greatest kindnesses we can do for our friends, and sometimes the only kindness that is in our power to do, is to commend them to the loving-kindness of God through prayer. We may learn from Paul's example here:

2.1. Faithfulness in prayer: *Always, without ceasing*.

2.2. Love in prayer: *I make mention of you*. He not only prayed for all saints in general but also expressly mentioned these Roman Christians. It is not inappropriate sometimes to be explicit in our prayers for specific churches and places, not to inform God, but to move ourselves. We are likely to have the most encouragement in those friends we pray for most. Paul makes a solemn appeal to the One who searches hearts (8:27): *For God is my witness*. It is encouraging to be able to call God to witness our faithfulness in fulfilling our duty. God is especially a witness to our private prayers. *God, whom I serve with my spirit*. Those who serve God with their spirits may appeal to him with humble confidence; hypocrites, who trust merely in physical exercise (1Ti 4:8), cannot. His particular prayer was that he would have an opportunity to pay them a visit (v. 10): *Making request, if by any means*. The expressions used here show (1) that Paul wanted such an opportunity very much: *if by any means*; (2) that he had long and often been disappointed: *now at length*; but (3) that he submitted the matter to divine Providence: *a prosperous journey by the will of God*. Our journeys are successful or not according to the will of God, comfortable or not as he pleases.

3. His great desire to see them, and the reasons for this desire (vv. 11–15). Fruitful Christians are as much the joy of faithful ministers as barren professors are their grief. Paul wants to get to know the Roman Christians more, and so he has *often purposed to come, but was let* (prevented) *hitherto* (v. 13), for we have our plans, but it is God's will that is done. Paul had been prevented from making this visit by other business. He wanted to do that first; he would not do what was most pleasant—in that case he would have gone to Rome—but what was most necessary. Paul wants to visit these Romans:

3.1. So that they will be edified (v. 11): *that I may impart unto you*. He has received so that he can pass on to others (Ps 68:18). *To the end you may be established*—so that as they grow upward in the branches they will also grow downward in their roots (2Ki 19:30). The best saints need to become stronger and stronger.

3.2. So that he will be *comforted* (v. 12). What he has heard of their flourishing in grace has been so much a joy to him that he wants very much to see it for himself. *By the mutual faith both of you and me*. When there is a mutual confidence between minister and people, they confiding in him as a faithful minister, and he in them as a faithful people, then both are greatly encouraged. It is very refreshing for Christians to compare notes about their spiritual concerns. *That I might have some fruit* (v. 13). The more good he did, the greater his reward would be.

3.3. So that he may fulfill his trust as the apostle of the Gentiles (v. 14): *I am a debtor*. His receipts have made him a debtor. When we seek great things, we should remember that all that we have received puts us in debt; we are simply managers of our Lord's goods. Paul's position made him a debtor. He had made the most of his talent, labored hard in his work, and done as much good as anyone had ever done, but he still describes himself as a *debtor. Debtor to the Greeks, and to the barbarians, to the wise and to the unwise.* The Greeks thought they had a monopoly on wisdom, and they looked on the rest of the world as *barbarians.* Paul was a debtor to both, looking on himself as obliged to do all the good he could possibly do to both the one and the other. We find him, therefore, repaying his debt, doing good *both to Greeks and barbarians.* For these reasons, when he had the opportunity, he would be ready *to preach the Gospel at Rome* (v. 15). Although it was a dangerous place, Paul was still ready to run the risk if called to it: *I am ready*—ready in his mind. What he did was not for dishonest gain, but from a ready mind.

Verses 16–18

Paul begins a detailed discussion on justification here, describing the deplorable condition of the Gentile world. He is ready to preach the Gospel at Rome, *for I am not ashamed of it* (v. 16). There is a great deal about the Gospel that such a person as Paul might be tempted to be ashamed of, especially that the One whose Gospel it is was hanged on a tree (Dt 21:23; Gal 3:13). Nonetheless, Paul was not ashamed to confess it. I count someone a true Christian if they are neither ashamed of the Gospel nor a shame to it. Here is:

1. The proposition (vv. 16–17). The Gospel reveals to us:

1.1. The salvation of believers as the aim: *It is the power of God unto salvation.* Paul is not ashamed of the Gospel; it shows us *the way of salvation* (Ac 16:17). *It is through the power of God;* without that power the Gospel is only a dead letter. It is to those, and only those, who believe. The medicine prepared will not heal the patient if it is not taken. *To the Jew first. The lost sheep of the house of Israel* had the first offer made to them, both by Christ (Mt 10:6) and by his apostles. On the Jews' refusal, the apostles turned to the Gentiles (Ac 13:46). Jews and Gentiles now stand on the same level; both are equally welcome to the Savior (Col 3:11). The long-expected Messiah proves to be *a light to enlighten the Gentiles* as well as *the glory of his people Israel* (Lk 2:32).

1.2. The justification of believers as the way (v. 17): *For therein is the righteousness of God revealed.* What will show us the way of salvation must show us the way of justification, and so the Gospel makes known a righteousness. This righteousness under the Gospel:

1.2.1. Is called the *righteousness of God;* it is appointed by God. It is so called to cut off all claims to a righteousness resulting from what we think our own works might deserve. It is the righteousness of Christ.

1.2.2. Is said to be *from faith to faith.* From the first faith, by which we are put into a justified state, to the faith by which we live, from faith engrafting us into Christ (Ro 11:17) to faith deriving resources from him as our root. Both are implied in the next words, *The just shall live by faith. Just by faith:* there is faith justifying us; *live by faith:* there is faith maintaining us. Faith is all in all, in both the beginning and the progress of a Christian life. It is increasing, continuing, persevering faith. To show that this is no new, upstart teaching, Paul quotes in support of it that famous Scripture in the Old Testament: *The just shall live by faith* (Hab 2:4). Being justified by faith, the just person will live by it both the life of grace and the life of glory.

This is how righteousness under the Gospel is from faith to faith—from Old Testament faith in a Christ to come to New Testament faith in a Christ already come.

2. The proof of this proposition. Justification must be either by faith or by works. Paul proves that it cannot be by works, and so he concludes that it must be by faith (3:20, 28). The apostle, like a skillful surgeon, examines the wound before applying the salve—he tries first to convict of guilt and wrath, and then to show the way of salvation. This makes the Gospel more welcome. In general (v. 18), *the wrath of God is revealed.* The light of nature and the light of the law reveal the wrath of God from sin to sin. It is good for us that the Gospel reveals the justifying righteousness of God from faith to faith.

2.1. Human sinfulness is described; he reduces it to two headings, *ungodliness and unrighteousness.*

2.2. The cause of that sinfulness is identified, namely, *holding the truth in unrighteousness.* Human beings had some common ideas of the difference between good and evil, but they held them in unrighteousness. They held the truth as a captive or prisoner, so that it would not influence them. An unrighteous, evil heart is the dungeon in which many good truths are detained and buried.

2.3. The displeasure of God against it is expressed: *The wrath of God is revealed from heaven;* it is revealed not only in the written word but also in the providences of God, in his judgments executed on sinners, which are a revelation from heaven. Or, *wrath from heaven is revealed;* it is not human wrath like ours, but *wrath from heaven,* and therefore the more terrible.

Verses 19–32

In this last part of the chapter the apostle applies his foregoing words to the Gentile world in particular, and here we may notice:

1. The means and helps they had to come to the knowledge of God. *He left not himself without witness* among them (Ac 14:17). Notice:

1.1. What revelations they did have: *That which may be known of God is manifest among them;* that is, there were some even among them who had the knowledge of God. *That which may be known* implies that there is a great deal that cannot be known. God's being may be apprehended, but it cannot be fully comprehended. Finite understanding cannot know an infinite being perfectly, but there is something that can be known.

1.2. From where they received these revelations: *God hath shown it to them.* Those common, natural ideas they had of God were imprinted on their hearts by the God of nature himself.

1.3. By what means these revelations were confirmed, namely, by the work of creation (v. 20): *For the invisible things of God.* Notice:

1.3.1. What they knew: *The invisible things of him, even his eternal power and Godhead.* The power and divine nature of God are invisible, but they are clearly seen in their results. He works in secret but reveals what he has created, so making known his power and divine nature. They did come to the knowledge of God's nature, at least enough knowledge to have kept them from idolatry. This was the truth that they held in their unrighteousness.

1.3.2. How they knew it: *by the things that are made,* which could not make themselves and so must have been produced by some first cause or intelligent agent, which could be nothing other than an eternal, powerful God. Workers are known by their work. The harmony of all parts for the good and beauty of the whole abundantly proves a Creator and his eternal power and nature. This is how the light shone in the darkness. And *this from the creation of the world.* We may understand this either:

1.3.2.1. As the subject from which the knowledge of the invisible things of God is drawn: "To demonstrate this truth, we turn to the great work of creation." Or:

1.3.2.2. As the date of the revelation. It is as old as the creation of the world. These revelations of God are ancient truths. The way of acknowledging God is a good and old way (Jer 6:16); it was from the beginning. Truth got a head start on error.

2. Their gross idolatry (vv. 21–23, 25). We will wonder less at the ineffectiveness of these natural revelations for preventing the idolatry of the Gentiles if we remember how much even the Jews tended to follow idols; corrupt human beings had so miserably plunged into the mire of sin. Notice:

2.1. The inward cause of their idolatry (vv. 21–22). They are without excuse, because they did know God. Although some have greater light and means of knowledge than others, all have enough to leave them without excuse. They *glorified him not as God.* To glorify him as God is to glorify only him. They did not glorify him in this way, however, because they set up many other gods. To glorify him as God is to worship him with spiritual worship, but they made images of him. Not to glorify God as God is in effect not to glorify him at all. *Neither were they thankful.* Being unmoved by God's blessings lies at the root of our sinful departures from him. *But they became vain in their imaginations,* "in their reasonings," in their practical inferences. They had a great deal of knowledge of general truths (v. 19) but did not have the wisdom to apply them to particular cases. They soon disputed among themselves in a thousand futile and foolish thoughts. When truth is forsaken, errors multiply. *And their foolish heart was darkened.* The foolishness and practical evil of the heart cloud and darken the intellectual powers and faculties. *Professing themselves to be wise, they became fools* (v. 22). Those who had the widest imaginations, framing for themselves the idea of a God, fell into the most gross and absurd errors. This is how the *world by wisdom knew not God* (1Co 1:21). A proud belief in one's own wisdom is the cause of much foolishness. Paul's preaching was nowhere so laughed at and ridiculed as among the learned Athenians (Ac 17:18–32). *Professing themselves to be wise,* or "conceiting themselves to be wise": the plain truth of the existence of God was not enough for them; they thought themselves above that, and so fell into the greatest error.

2.2. Their outward acts of idolatry (vv. 23–25).

2.2.1. Making images of God (v. 23), by which they *changed the glory of the incorruptible God.* It was the greatest honor God did to human beings that he made them in the image of God, but it is the greatest dishonor human beings have done to God that they have made God in a human image. This is called (v. 25) *changing the truth of God into a lie.* Idols are called lies (Jnh 2:8), because they tell lies about God, as if he had a physical body, whereas he is a Spirit (Jer 23:14; Hos 7:1; Jn 4:24). See also Hab 2:18.

2.2.2. Giving divine honor to created things: *worshiped and served the creature more than the Creator,* or "besides the Creator." They disowned him in effect by the worship they gave to created things, because God wants all or nothing. Or they worshiped creatures *above* the Creator, thinking the supreme God was inaccessible. The sin itself was their worshiping created things in any way, but to emphasize the sin it is mentioned that they worshiped created things more than they did the Creator. This was the general corruption of the Gentile world. Even the wisest among them, who knew and acknowledged a supreme God and were convinced of the nonsense and absurdity of their polytheism and idolatry, did as their neighbors did. I mention this because I think it fully explains the thought of the apostle in v. 18: *who hold the truth in unrighteousness.* After mentioning the dishonor shown to God by the idolatry of the Gentiles, the apostle expresses himself in awesome adoration of God: *who is blessed for ever. Amen.* When we see or hear of any contempt shown to God or his name, we should think and speak highly and honorably of him. In this, as in other things, the worse others are, the better we should be.

3. The judgments of God on them for this idolatry, not many temporal judgments, but spiritual judgments, giving them over to the most shameful and unnatural lusts. *He gave them up*; it is mentioned three times here (vv. 24, 26, 28). Spiritual judgments are the most painful of all judgments. Notice:

3.1. By whom they were given over. God gave them over, by way of righteous judgment, leaving them to themselves—letting them alone, for his grace is his own, and he may give or withhold his grace as he wishes. We are sure that it is nothing new for God to give people over to their own hearts' sinful desires. However, God is not the author of sin, because although the greatest evil follows this giving over, the blame for it is to be laid fairly and squarely on the sinner's evil heart. If the patient will not submit to the methods prescribed, but willfully does what is harmful, the doctors are not to be blamed. The fatal symptoms that follow may not be attributed to the doctors, but must be attributed to the disease itself and to the foolishness of the patient.

3.2. To what they were given over.

3.2.1. *To uncleanness and vile affections* (sexual impurity and shameful lusts) (vv. 24, 26, 27). It is, as is said here, *through the lusts of their own hearts*—all the blame is to be laid on them. Those who dishonored God were given over to dishonoring themselves. Human beings cannot be delivered over to a greater slavery than slavery to their own lusts. The particular instances of their immorality and shameful lusts are their unnatural relations, for which many pagans, even those among them who passed for wise, were infamous. Perhaps the apostle is referring especially to the detestable practices committed in the worship of their idol gods. Rubbish service for rubbish gods. Notice what evil there is in human nature. How much we are indebted to the restraining grace of God! Were it not for this, human beings, who have been made only a little lower than the angels (Ps 8:5), would make themselves a great deal lower than the demons. This is said to be that *recompence of their error which was meet.*

3.2.2. To a *reprobate* (depraved) *mind* in these detestable practices (v. 28).

3.2.2.1. They *did not like to retain God in their knowledge.* The blindness of their understandings was caused by the stubborn hostility of their wills and affections. They would neither know nor do anything but what pleased themselves. There are many who have some knowledge of God but do not keep it, because it thwarts their sinful desires; they do not like it. There is a difference between the "knowledge" and the "acknowledgment" of God; the pagans knew God but would not acknowledge him.

3.2.2.2. In accordance with their willfulness, God gave them over to a willfulness in the most corrupt sins, here called *a reprobate mind.* See where the way of sin leads, into what a chasm it plunges the sinner eventually. This depraved mind was a blind, seared conscience, having lost all sensitivity (Eph 4:19). Willful hardness is justly punished with judicial hardness. *To do those things which are not convenient.* Here Paul adds a black list of those terrible things the Gentiles were guilty of. There is no evil so contrary to the light of nature that a depraved mind will not comply with it. From the accounts of those times it appears that the sins mentioned here were dominant national sins. No fewer than twenty-three different sorts of sins and sinners are specified here (vv. 29–31). It was time to have the Gospel preached among them, because the world needed reformation. They committed:

3.2.2.2.*1.* Sins against the first table of the Ten Commandments: *Haters of God.* Here the Devil is seen in his true colors, sin appearing as sin. Every sin contains a hatred of God. *Proud men and boasters* put on their own heads those crowns that must be placed before his throne (Rev 4:10).

3.2.2.2.*2.* Sins against the second table of the Ten Commandments. In general, here is a charge of unrighteousness. This is put first, since every sin is unrighteousness. The word stands especially for sins of the second table, not doing to others as we would have them do to us. They sinned against the fifth commandment, being *disobedient to parents* and *without natural affection.* Disobedient children are justly punished with unnatural parents, and unnatural parents are justly punished with disobedient children. They sinned against the sixth commandment, being guilty of *wickedness* (causing trouble its own sake), *maliciousness, envy, murder, debate,* and *malignity*; being *despiteful, implacable,* and *unmerciful*; and expressing all kinds of hatred toward brothers and sisters, which is murder in the heart. They sinned against the seventh commandment, committing *fornication.* They sinned against the eighth commandment by *unrighteousness* and *covetousness.* They sinned against the ninth commandment by *deceit* and by being *back-biters, covenant-breakers, inventors of evil things, and without understanding*; they were wise for doing evil but without knowledge of how to do good. They were so quick to devise sinful acts, being foolish and without understanding in their thoughts of God. Every heart by nature has in it the seed and offspring of all these sins. At the close Paul mentions worse expressions of the sins (v. 32).

3.2.2.2.2.*1.* They *knew the judgment of God.* They knew the law. They knew the penalty; they knew *that those who commit such things were worthy of death*; their own consciences must have suggested this to them. It greatly emphasizes sin when it is committed against knowledge. It is daring and presumptuous to run toward the point of the sword.

3.2.2.2.2.*2.* They *not only did the same, but had pleasure in those that did them.* To be pleased with other people's sins is to love sin for sin's sake: it is joining in an alliance for the Devil's kingdom. Our own sins are made even worse by our agreement with the sins of others. If we put all this together, we can then say whether the Gentile world could be justified before God by any works of their own.

CHAPTER 2

The theme of the first two chapters of this letter may be seen from 3:9: We have before proved both Jews and Gentiles, that they are all under sin. *We have proved this for the Gentiles (ch. 1); in this chapter he proves it for the Jews. 1. Jews and Gentiles stand on the same level before the justice of God (vv. 1–11). 2. God is just in his proceedings*

with both Jews and Gentiles (vv. 12–16). 3. Paul shows especially what sins the Jews were guilty of (vv. 17–29).

Verses 1–16

In the previous chapter the apostle showed the state of the Gentile world to be as bad and corrupt as the Jews were ready enough to declare it. Intending to show that the state of the Jews is very bad too, he now sets himself to show that God will proceed on equal terms of justice with Jews and Gentiles.

1. He calls the Jews to account for their judgmental spirit and conceit (v. 1): *Thou art inexcusable, O man, whosoever thou art that judgest.* He has in mind especially the Jews, and he applies this general charge to them particularly: *Thou who teachest another, teachest thou not thyself?* The Jews looked down with great contempt on the poor Gentiles, while in the meantime they themselves were as bad and immoral—though not idolaters. *Therefore thou art inexcusable.* If the Gentiles, who had only the light of nature, were without excuse, then much more so the Jews, who had the light of the law.

2. He asserts the fixed justice of divine government (vv. 2–3). He shows here how righteous the God with whom we have to do is (Heb 4:13). The *judgment of God is according to truth*, according to the heart, and not according to the outward appearance; it is according to the works and without partiality, because he would not be God if he were not just. However, it is especially good for people to remember this when they condemn others for those things they themselves are guilty of, supposing they can bribe divine justice by pleading against sin in others, while they themselves practice sin and persist in that practice—as if preaching against sin would atone for its guilt. But notice how Paul puts it to the sinner's conscience (v. 3): *Thinkest thou this, O man?* The situation is so clear that we may dare appeal to the sinner's own thoughts: "Canst thou think that *thou shalt escape the judgment of God*? Can the heart-searching God be deceived by formal pretense, the righteous Judge of all be bribed in such a way?"

3. He draws up a charge against them (vv. 4–5), consisting of two parts:

3.1. Insulting the goodness of God (v. 4), *the riches of his goodness.* The more light we sin against, the more love we sin against. Every willful sin contains implicit contempt of the goodness of God, especially the goodness of his patience, taking advantage of that to be bold in committing sin (Ecc 8:11). *Not knowing* that the *goodness of God leadeth thee to repentance.* Notice how God brings sinners to repentance. He leads them; he does not drive them like animals, but draws them. It is goodness that leads, with cords of love (Hos 11:4). The consideration of the goodness of God, of his common goodness to all, should be effective in bringing us all to repentance.

3.2. Provoking the wrath of God (v. 5). The cause of this provocation is *a hard and impenitent heart.* To sin is to walk in the way of the heart (Ecc 11:9; Jer 23:17; Eze 11:21), and when that is a hard and unrepentant heart, how desperate the course must be! The provocation is expressed as *treasuring up wrath. Treasure* denotes abundance. It is a treasure that will be spent to eternity, but sinners are still adding to it as to a treasure, *Treasure* also denotes secrecy, and reservation for some further occasion. These treasures will be broken open. They are stored up *against the day of wrath.* Although the present day is a day of patience toward sinners, a day of wrath is coming. That day of wrath will be *the day of the revelation of the righteous judgment of God.* The wrath of God is not like our wrath, wild and passionate. It is a righteous judgment, his will to punish sin. God's righteous judgment is now concealed many times in the prosperity of sinners, but soon it will be revealed before the whole world.

4. Having mentioned the righteous judgment of God in v. 5, he illustrates that judgment and its righteousness here.

4.1. He will *render to every man according to his deeds* (v. 6), for the Judge of all the earth does right (Ge 18:25):

4.1.1. In showing his favor, and this is mentioned here twice, in vv. 7 and 10: God delights to show mercy. Notice:

4.1.1.1. The objects of his favor: *those who by patient continuance.* Those whom the righteous God will reward are:

4.1.1.1.*1.* Those who set out toward the right goal, who *seek for glory, and honor, and immortality.* A holy ambition lies at the root of all practical religious faith. This is looking at our desires and aiming as high as heaven, being determined, with God's help, not to fall short of it. This seeking implies a loss, a desire to retrieve it, and pursuits and endeavors consistent with that desire.

4.1.1.1.*2.* Those who, having set out toward the right goal, remain faithful to the right way: *A patient continuance in well-doing* (doing good). There must be well-doing (v. 10). It is not enough to know well, to promise well; we must also do well. There must be a persistence in well-doing. We are not to do good in fits and starts, like the morning cloud and the early dew (Hos 6:4); it is perseverance that wins the crown. This persistence must be a patient persistence, and this patience is concerned not only with the length of the work but also with its difficulties. Those who want to do good and persist in it must do so with a great deal of patience.

4.1.1.2. The result of his favor. He will repay such people with eternal life. Heaven is life, eternal life, and it is called *glory, honor, and peace* (v. 10). Those who seek the worldly glory and honor often miss them, but those who seek immortal glory and honor will have them, and not only *glory and honor,* but also *peace.* Heavenly glory and honor have peace with them, undisturbed eternal peace.

4.1.2. In showing his disapproval (vv. 8–9). Notice:

4.1.2.1. The objects of his disapproval: *such as are contentious and do not obey the truth, contentious* toward God. Every willful sin is a quarrel with God. *Contentious, and do not obey the truth.* The truths of religious faith are not only to be known but also to be obeyed. Disobedience to the truth is interpreted as striving against it. *But obey unrighteousness.* Those who refuse to be the servants of truth will soon become the slaves of unrighteousness.

4.1.2.2. The results of this disapproval: *indignation and wrath, tribulation and anguish.* These are the wages of sin (6:23). This is *upon the soul;* souls are the objects of that wrath. Sin qualifies the soul for this wrath. Hell is eternal trouble and distress, the result of wrath and righteous anger. This is what comes of contending against God. Those who refuse to submit to his golden scepter will certainly be broken by his iron rod (Ps 2:9).

4.2. *There is no respect of persons with God* (v. 11). As to the spiritual state, there is a distinguishing between persons, but not as to outward relation or condition. God does not save people because of their external privileges, but according to their true state and disposition. He shows both his disapproval and his favors to both Jews and Gentiles. If to *the Jews first,* who had greater privileges, it is also *to the Gentiles,* whose lack of such privileges will neither excuse them from the punishment of their ill-doing nor exclude them from the reward of their doing good.

5. He proves that God is just in his proceedings with everyone (vv. 12–16). Three degrees of light are revealed to human beings:

5.1. The light of nature. The Gentiles have this, and they will be judged by this: *As many as have sinned without law shall perish without law;* that is, the unbelieving Gentiles, who had no guide but natural conscience, will not be judged for disobedience of the law they never had. They will be judged by the law of nature. For the Gentiles, the light of nature took the place of a written law. Paul has said (v. 12) they *sinned without law* (apart from law), which looks like a contradiction, since where there is no law there is no disobedience (4:15), but, he says, although they did not have the written law, they had its equivalent. They *had the work of the law,* that is, both the work that the law tells us to do—its requirements—and the work that the law does, examining in us what we have done.

5.1.1. They had what guided their actions by the light of nature. They grasped a clear and vast difference between good and evil. They *did by nature the things contained in the law.* They had a sense of justice, honor, purity, and love. In this way, they were *a law unto themselves.*

5.1.2. They had what examined their actions: *Their conscience also bearing witness.* They had within them something that approved what was done well and that blamed them for what was done wrong. Conscience is a witness, and sooner or later it will bear witness, testifying about what is most secret, and so the Gentiles' *thoughts accused or excused,* passing judgment on the basis of the testimony of conscience. Conscience is the candle of the Lord (Pr 20:27) that was not completely put out, not even in the Gentile world. Their *thoughts the meanwhile.* Their consciences either acquitted or condemned them according to how they observed or broke these natural laws and dictates. All this showed they had what functioned for them in place of a law. So the guilty Gentiles are left without excuse. God is justified in condemning them. They cannot plead ignorance.

5.2. The light of the law. The Jews had this, and they will be judged by this (v. 12): *As many as have sinned in the law shall be judged by the law.* They sinned in the face and light of such a pure and clear law. These will be judged *by the law;* their punishment will be, as their sin is, so much greater because they have the law. *The Jew first* (v. 9). The apostle shows (v. 13) that their having, hearing, and knowing the law will not justify them if they did not obey it. It is a great privilege that they have the law, but not a saving privilege unless they live up to the law they have. We may apply it to the Gospel: it is not hearing that will save us, but doing (Jn 13:17; Jas 1:22).

5.3. The light of the Gospel, and it is according to this that those who enjoyed the Gospel will be judged (v. 16): *According to my Gospel.* They will be judged by the Gospel in general, but here Paul calls it his because he preaches it. Some refer the words *according to my Gospel* to what he says about the Day of Judgment. It is good for us to come to know what is revealed about that day. A day is set for a general judgment. The judgment of that day will be put into the hands of Jesus Christ. Nothing speaks more terror to sinners or more comfort to saints than that Christ will be the Judge. People's secrets will then be judged. That will be the great day of revelation.

Verses 17–29

Paul has said (v. 13) that not the hearers but the doers of the law are justified, and here he applies that great truth to the Jews. Notice:

1. He accepts their profession (vv. 17–20), so that they will see that he does not condemn them out of ignorance. He knows the best of their case.

1.1. They are a distinctive people, having had the written law and the special presence of God among them. *Thou art called a Jew.* It was a very honorable title. Salvation was from the Jews (Jn 4:22), and they were very proud of this, but many who were called that were great evildoers. It is nothing new for the worst practices to be covered up under the best names. *And restest in* (rely on) *the law.* They were greatly puffed up by this privilege and thought it was enough to take them to heaven, even though they did not live up to the law. It is dangerous to rely on external privileges and not make the most of them. *And makest thy boast of God.* A faithful, humble, and thankful glorying in God is the summary of all religious faith (Ps 34:2; Isa 45:15; 1Co 1:31). A proud boasting in God, on the other hand, a boasting in the outward profession of his name, is the summary of all hypocrisy. Spiritual pride is the most dangerous form of pride.

1.2. They are a knowledgeable people (v. 18): *and knowest his will.* In the Greek it is literally "the will." God's will is *the* will. The world will be set to rights when God's will is the only will and all other wills are melted into it. The Jews knew not only the truth of God but also the will of God, what he wanted them to do. *And approvest the things that are more excellent.* We may understand this approval as referring to:

1.2.1. A good understanding of *the things of God*, reading it as "you can discern things that differ," that is, "you know how to distinguish between good and evil." Good and bad are sometimes so close together that it is difficult to distinguish them, but the Jews were—or at least thought they were—able to distinguish, to split hairs in doubtful cases. Or the phrase that our translation renders *the things that are more excellent* may be translated as "controversies." A person may be skilled in the arguments of religious faith but still be a stranger to the power of godliness (2Ti 3:5).

1.2.2. A warm affection for the things of God, as our translation reads it: *approvest the things that are excellent.* A person's practical judgment may give consent *to the law*, affirming *that it is good*, but that consent may be overpowered by the sinful desires of the flesh and of the heart: "I see the better but pursue the worse." The Jews became acquainted with what is good by being *instructed out of the law.* It was the custom of the Jews to take a great deal of effort in teaching their children, and all their lessons were *out of the law*; it would be good if Christians were as diligent in teaching their children out of the Gospel. Now this is called (v. 20) *the form of knowledge, and of the truth in the law.* A form of knowledge produces a mere form of godliness (2Ti 3:5). A form of knowledge may deceive people, but it cannot deceive the heart-searching God.

1.3. They are a teaching people, or at least think they are (vv. 19–20): *And art confident that thou thyself art a guide of the blind.* We may apply this:

1.3.1. To the Jews in general. They thought they were guides to the poor blind Gentiles who sat in darkness. All other nations must come to their school to learn what is good.

1.3.2. To their rabbis, teachers. The apostle expresses this in several different ways—*a guide of the blind, a light of those who are in darkness, an instructor of the foolish, a teacher of babes*—the better to set out these leaders' proud conceit. This was a string they loved to harp on. Even the best work becomes unacceptable to God when it is bragged about. It is good to instruct the foolish, but

considering our own inability to make our teaching effective without God, there is nothing to be proud of.

2. He underlines their offenses (vv. 21–24) by referring to two things:

2.1. That sin against their knowledge, that they themselves do the things they teach others to avoid: *Thou that teachest another, teachest thou not thyself?* Teaching is an act of love that begins at home, though it must not end there. The Pharisees pulled down with their lives what they built up with their preaching. The greatest obstructions to the success of the word are those whose bad lives contradict their good teaching, who preach so well in the pulpit that it is a great pity they ever leave it, because once they leave it they lead such a corrupt life that it is a pity they ever entered it. Paul specifies three particular sins that are prevalent among the Jews:

2.1.1. Stealing.

2.1.2. Adultery (v. 22). Many of the Jewish rabbis are said to have been notorious for this sin.

2.1.3. Sacrilege. This was the accusation against those who professed to loathe idols. It was in the later days of the Old Testament church that the Jews were accused of *robbing God in tithes and offerings* (Mal 3:8–9), converting to their own use what was set apart for God. This is almost equivalent to idolatry.

2.2. They dishonor God by their sin (vv. 23–24). While God and his law are outwardly held in honor by them, and they boast of the honor they give it, they dishonor God and his law by giving outsiders occasion to think that their religion supports and allows such things. *As it is written* (v. 24). He does not mention the place, because he is writing this to those who have been instructed in the law. The great evil of the sins of professors is the dishonor shown to God and religious faith by their profession. *"Blasphemed through you.* The shame you bring on yourselves reflects badly on your God, and religious faith is wounded because of you." This is a good warning to professors of faith to walk carefully.

3. He asserts the complete insufficiency of their profession to clear them from the guilt of these offenses (vv. 25–29): *Circumcision verily profiteth, if thou keep the law*; that is, obedient Jews will not lose the reward of their obedience. He is speaking to the Jews here, whose Judaism would benefit them if they would only live up to its laws, but if not, "*thy circumcision is made uncircumcision.* You will be no more justified than the uncircumcised Gentiles, but more condemned for sinning against greater light."

3.1. He shows that if the uncircumcised Gentiles live up to the light they have—if *they keep the righteousness of the law* (v. 26), if they *fulfil the law* (v. 27), that is, if by submitting sincerely to the direction of natural light they fulfill the matter of the law—then they stand on the same level as the Jews. This seems to refer to a kind of obedience that some of the Gentiles actually reached. Doubtless there were many such examples, and *they were the uncircumcision, that kept the righteousness of the law.* They were accepted with God. *Their uncircumcision was counted for circumcision.* Their obedience greatly emphasized the disobedience of the Jews (v. 27). *And shall not uncircumcision judge thee*, who *by the letter and circumcision dost transgress?* To worldly professors, the law is simply the letter; they read it as bare words but are not ruled by it as a law. If external privileges do not do us good, they do us harm. The obedience of those who enjoy fewer means and make less profession will help condemn those who enjoy greater means and make a greater profession but do not live up to it.

3.2. He describes the true circumcision (vv. 28–29).

3.2.1. It is *not that which is outward in the flesh and in the letter.* This is not to drive us away from the observances of external institutions—which are good in their place—but from trusting in them and being satisfied to be thought alive while not truly alive. *He is not a Jew.* To be Abraham's children is to do the works of Abraham (Jn 8:39–40).

3.2.2. It is *that which is inward, of the heart, and in the spirit.* It is the heart that God looks at.

3.2.3. The *praise* for this, though *not of men,* who judge according to outward appearance, is still *of God,* because *he seeth not as man seeth* (1Sa 16:7). Fair claims and a plausible profession may deceive people, but God sees through our pretense, to the reality. This is as true of a person's Christianity as it was of a person's circumcision. A merely outward Christian is not a Christian, nor is a baptism that is only in the flesh a baptism.

CHAPTER 3

In this chapter: 1. The apostle answers some objections that might be made against what he has said about the Jews (vv. 1–8). 2. He asserts the guilt and corruption of the human race in general (vv. 9–18). 3. He then argues that justification must be by faith, not by the law (vv. 19–31).

Verses 1–18

1. Here the apostle answers several objections. Divine truths must be cleared from faults.

1.1. Objection: If Jew and Gentile stand on the same level before God, *what advantage then hath the Jew?* Does not this leveling doctrine deny them all privileges and reflect dishonor on the ordinance of circumcision?

1.2. Answer: The Jews are, despite this, a people who remain greatly privileged and honored (v. 2): *Much every way.* The door is open to the Gentiles as well as to the Jews, but the Jews have a clearer path to this door. Paul counts up many of the Jews' privileges in 9:4–5; here he mentions just one—*that unto them were committed the oracles of God,* that is, the Scriptures of the Old Testament. The Scriptures are the *lively oracles,* or living words, of God: they are a divine revelation. We must turn to the law and to the testimony (Isa 8:20) as to an oracle. Now these words were committed to the Jews. The Old Testament was deposited in their hands, to be carefully preserved pure and uncorrupt. The Jews were entrusted with that sacred treasure for their own use and benefit in the first place, and then for the advantage of the world. The Jews had the means of salvation, but they did not have a monopoly on salvation. Now Paul mentions this with a *chiefly:* this was their prime and principal privilege. The enjoyment of God's word and ordinances is the chief benefit of a people.

1.3. Objection: Why were the oracles of God committed to them, when so many of them continued to be strangers to Christ and enemies to his Gospel? *Some did not believe* (v. 3).

1.4. Answer: *But shall their unbelief make the faith of God without effect?* The apostle was startled at such a thought: *God forbid!* The obstinacy of the Jews could not nullify those prophecies of the Messiah that were contained in the words entrusted to them. Christ will be glorious, *though Israel be not gathered* (Isa 49:5); God's words will be fulfilled even though there is a generation who by their unbelief try to make God a liar. *Let God be true, but every man a liar;* let us stand by this principle, that God is true to every word he has spoken. Better to question the reputation of all the people in the world than

to doubt the faithfulness of God. Everyone is a liar, compared with God. When we find that everyone is a liar and we are to trust no one, it is very encouraging that God is faithful. Paul quotes Ps 51:4, *that thou mightest be justified,* to show:

1.4.1. That God will preserve his own honor in the world, despite human sins.

1.4.2. That it is our duty to justify God and to assert and maintain his justice, truth, and goodness, however difficult things become. This is how God is justified in his words and vindicated when *he is judged.*

1.5. Objection: Worldly hearts might use the foregoing truth to encourage themselves in sin. If all our sin is so far from overthrowing God's honor that it commends it, and his ends are secured, is it not unjust for God to punish our sin and unbelief so severely? If *our unrighteousness commend the righteousness of God, what shall we say?* (v. 5). What conclusion may be drawn from this? *Is God unrighteous*—"Is not God unrighteous"—*who taketh vengeance* (in bringing his wrath on us)? *I speak as a man;* that is, "I raise this objection as that of a worldly heart."

1.6. Answer: *God forbid.* Suggestions that reflect dishonor on God, his justice, and his holiness are to be responded to with shock rather than discussed. *For then how shall God judge the world?* (v. 6). A sin never has any less evil in it because God brings glory to himself out of it. It is only accidentally that sin commends God's righteousness. No thanks to sinners for that. It is not for us to argue against the ways of such an absolute Sovereign. The sentence of the supreme court, after which there is no appeal, is not to be called into question.

1.7. Objection: The previous objection is repeated (vv. 7–8). However, Paul's setting off the objection in its own colors is sufficient to answer it: "*If the truth of God has more abounded through my lie,* why *should I be judged as a sinner, and not rather* take encouragement from it to continue in my sin, so that grace may abound?" *Let us do evil that good may come* is more often in the heart than in the mouth of sinners; it is how they justify themselves to themselves in their evil ways. There were those who accused Paul and his fellow ministers of such teaching: "Some affirm that we are saying this." It is nothing new for the best of God's people and ministers to be accused of holding and teaching things that they most detest, and it is not to be thought strange, since our Master himself was said to be in league with Beelzebub (Mt 12:24). It is an old trick of Satan to sling mud at Christ's ministers. "Spread the slander thick, for some are sure to stick."

1.8. Answer: Paul says no more by way of repudiation except that the condemnation of such people is just. Those who deliberately commit evil so that good may come from it will be so far from escaping under the shelter of that excuse that it will rather justify their condemnation. Sinning on the basis of such a surmise, and with such confidence, shows a great deal of both knowledge and the will in the sin. The condemnation of those who sin with this attitude is just, and whatever excuses of this kind they may now comfort themselves with, none of those excuses will be valid on the great day, but God will be justified in his proceedings.

2. Paul returns to his assertion of the general guilt of the human race, both Jews and Gentiles (vv. 9–18). "*Are we better than they,* we Jews, or will this justify us? No, by no means." Or, "Were we Christians—Jews and Gentiles—so much better than those who are unfaithful that we deserved God's grace? Alas! No." They *are all under sin,* under the guilt of sin. We are guilty before God (v. 19). He has proved this. It is a legal expression: "We have accused them of it and have proved our charge." He

illustrates here this charge and conviction by citing several Scriptures from the Old Testament. Vv. 10–12 are taken from Ps 14:1–3 (which is repeated in Ps 53:1–3). The rest that follows here is found in the Septuagint (the Greek version of the Old Testament) translation of Ps 14:1–7. What is said in Ps 14:1–7 is expressly spoken of *all the children of men*. The *Lord looked down*, as he did on the old world (Ge 6:5). The One who, when he himself had made everything, looked on all he had made, and saw that it was very good (Ge 1:31), now looked and saw that all was very bad, since human beings had spoiled it all. Notice:

2.1. What is inherent, which is described in two ways:

2.1.1. An inherent failure in everything good.

2.1.1.1. *There is none righteous*; no one has an honest motivating principle of goodness, *no, not one*; here Paul implies that if there had been only one, God would have found them. When the whole world was corrupt, God had his eye on one righteous Noah (Ge 6:8–9). No righteousness is born with us.

2.1.1.2. *There is none that understandeth* (v. 11). The fault lies in the corruption of the understanding. Religion and righteousness have so much reason on their side that if people had only had a little understanding they would be better and do better. Sinners are fools.

2.1.1.3. *None that seeketh after God*, that is, no one who has any desire for him.

2.1.1.4. *They are together become unprofitable* (v. 12). Those who have forsaken God soon become good for nothing.

2.1.1.5. *There is none that doeth good*; not one just person on earth, who does good and does not sin (Ecc 7:23).

2.1.2. An inherent bias toward everything that is evil: *They are all gone out of the way*. God made human beings to follow his ways, setting them to do right, but they have forsaken that way.

2.2. What is actual. Paul gives examples:

2.2.1. From their words (vv. 13–14), especially in three things:

2.2.1.1. Cruelty: *Their throat is an open sepulchre*, waiting for an opportunity to cause trouble. When they do not express it publicly, they still plot trouble secretly: the *poison of asps is under their lips*, the most venomous and incurable poison, with which they damage the good name of their neighbor.

2.2.1.2. Cheating: *With their tongues they have used deceit*. Here they show themselves to be the Devil's children. They *have used* (practiced) it: it suggests they make a business of lying.

2.2.1.3. Cursing, reflecting badly on God and blaspheming his holy name, wishing evil to their brothers and sisters: *Their mouth is full of cursing and bitterness*. How many who are called Christians show by these sins that they are still under the reign and controlling power of sin.

2.2.2. From their ways (vv. 15–17): *Their feet are swift to shed blood*. Wherever they go, *destruction and misery* accompany them; these are their companions — destruction and misery for others, and finally for themselves. Destruction and misery are in their ways; their sin is its own punishment: people need nothing more to make themselves miserable than to be a slave to their sins. *And the way of peace have they not known*. They are strangers to all true peace; they do not know the things that will bring about their peace (Lk 19:42).

3. Here is the root of all this: *There is no fear of God before their eyes* (v. 18). The fear of God here stands for all practical religion. Evildoers do not have this in their sights; they are guided by other rules and aim at fulfilling other purposes. Where there is no fear of God, no good can be expected. When the fear of God is undermined, devotion is hindered, and then all goes quickly to wrack and ruin. Here we have a short account of the general depraved condition and corruption of the whole human race.

Verses 19–31

From all this Paul concludes that it is futile to look for justification by the works of the law, and that it is to be obtained only by faith, which is the point he establishes (v. 28) as the summary of his discourse. *We conclude that a man is justified by faith, without the deeds of the law.* Humans, under the power of such corruption, could never gain acceptance with God by any works of their own; rather, justification must be seen purely in the light of the free grace of God, given through Jesus Christ. There are two things from which the apostle argues here: he argues from the guiltiness of human beings to prove that we cannot be justified by the works of the law, and he argues from the glory of God to prove that we must be justified by faith.

1. He argues from human guiltiness. The argument is clear: we can never be justified and saved by the law that we have broken. Now concerning the guiltiness of human beings:

1.1. He fastens it specifically on the Jews (v. 19). *This that the law says, it says to those who are under the law*; this conviction belongs to the Jews as well as others, because it is written in their law. "The law convicts and condemns you — you see it does." That *every mouth may be stopped*. Those who are justified have their mouths silenced by humble conviction; those who are condemned have their mouths silenced too, since they will eventually be convinced (Jude 15).

1.2. He extends it in general to the whole world: *That all the world may become guilty before God. May become guilty*; that is, may be proved guilty. They must all plead guilty. "Guilty before God" is a fearful sentence. All are guilty, and so all need a righteousness in which to appear before God. *For all have sinned* (v. 23) and *have come short of the glory of* God — have failed in what is the chief aim of their humanity. They have *come short*, as an archer shoots an arrow that falls short of the target, and as a runner comes short of winning the prize; they have come short in such a way that they not only do not win but also are great losers. All have:

1.2.1. Come short of glorifying God. *They glorified him not as God*. Through sin, humanity comes short of this and, instead of glorifying God, dishonors him.

1.2.2. Come short of glorying *before God*. There is no boasting of innocence: if we go about glorifying ourselves before God, we all have sinned, and that will silence us. We may glorify ourselves in front of other people, who cannot search our hearts, but there is no glorying before God.

1.2.3. Come short of being glorified by God, come short of justification, which is glory begun, come short of sanctification, which is the glorious image of God on humanity. It is impossible now to reach heaven by way of spotless innocence. That passage is blocked.

1.3. To drive us further away from expecting justification by the law, he attributes this conviction to the law (v. 20): *For by the law is the knowledge of sin*. That law which convicts and condemns us can never justify us. It is the proper use and intention of the law to open up our wound, and so it is unlikely to be the remedy. What is probing does not heal. Paul makes this use of the law (7:9): *Therefore by the deeds of the law shall no flesh be justified in his sight.*

1.3.1. *No flesh shall be justified.* The corruption that remained in our nature will forever obstruct any justification by our own works.

1.3.2. No one will be justified *in his sight.* As the conscience stands in relationship to God, *in his sight*, we cannot be justified by observing the law.

2. He argues from God's glory to prove that justification must be expected only by faith in Christ's righteousness. Is there no hope? Has the wound become incurable because of disobedience? No, thank God, it has not (vv. 21–22); another way has been opened for us; *the righteousness of God without* (apart from) *the law is manifested* now under the Gospel. This is called *the righteousness of God,* righteousness that he has ordained, provided, and accepted, righteousness that he confers on us.

2.1. Notice about this righteousness of God:

2.1.1. It is revealed. The Gospel way of justification is a highway; it is opened for us.

2.1.2. It is *without* (apart from) *the law.* The righteousness that Christ has brought in is a complete righteousness.

2.1.3. Yet *it is witnessed by the law and the prophets.* The law, far from justifying us, directs us to another way of justification; it points to Christ as our righteousness, to whom all the prophets bear witness (Ac 10:43).

2.1.4. It is by the *faith of Jesus Christ,* the faith that has Jesus Christ as its object. It is by this that we share in the privilege of enjoying the righteousness that God has ordained and that Christ has brought in.

2.1.5. It is *to all, and upon all, those that believe.* Jews and Gentiles are equally welcome to God through Christ, *for there is no difference.* It is *to all*; the Gospel excludes none who do not exclude themselves, but is *upon all that believe,* not only offered to them, but also put on them as a robe or a crown.

2.2. Yet how is this for God's glory?

2.2.1. It is for the glory of his grace (v. 24): *Justified freely by his grace.* We are justified *by his grace.* Moreover, to make it even more emphatic, he says we are justified *freely by his grace.* The grace of God comes *freely, freely*; nothing in us deserves such favors. No, we are saved purely *through the redemption that is in Jesus Christ.* This redemption comes freely to us, but Christ bought it and paid dearly for it. And yet Christ's purchase is no bar to the freeness of God's grace, for it was grace that both provided and accepted this vicarious atonement.

2.2.2. It is for the glory of his justice and righteousness (vv. 25–26): *Whom God hath set forth to be a propitiation.*

2.2.2.1. Jesus Christ is the great atoning sacrifice. He is our throne of grace, in and through whom atonement is made for sin. He is in every way our reconciliation, not only its maker but also the reconciliation itself. God was in Christ reconciling the world to himself (2Co 5:19).

2.2.2.2. *God hath set him forth.* God, the offended party, takes the initiative toward reconciliation. God *fore-ordained* Christ to be this, in the purposes of his love from eternity, and has presented him to a guilty world as their atoning sacrifice.

2.2.2.3. *By faith in his blood* we share in the benefits of this atoning sacrifice. There the healing salve is provided. Faith is the applying of this salve to the wounded soul. This faith looks specifically to *the blood of Christ.* Without the shedding of blood there would be no forgiveness of sins (Heb 9:22), and no blood but this could do this effectively.

2.2.2.4. All who through faith share in the benefits of his atoning sacrifice have *the remission of their sins that are past.* Christ was presented as an atoning sacrifice in order to bring about remission. *Through the forbearance of God.* Divine patience has kept us out of hell, so that we could have the opportunity to repent and reach heaven. *Past through the forbearance of God.* It is owing to God's patience that we were not seized in the very act of sin. It is because of the master's goodness and the gardener's mediation that barren trees are left alone in the vineyard (Lk 13:6–9). It is because of Christ that there is even one sinner on this side of hell.

2.2.2.5. In all this, God *declares his righteousness.* Paul insists on this with great emphasis: *To declare, I say, at this time his righteousness.* God declares his righteousness:

2.2.2.5.1. In the atoning sacrifice itself. It shows that he hates sin, since nothing less than the blood of Christ would make atonement for it. Finding sin, even though only imputed, on his own Son, he did not spare him, because the Son had made himself sin for us (2Co 5:21).

2.2.2.5.2. In the pardon issued upon the offering of that atoning sacrifice, for it follows, *that he might be just, and the justifier of him that believeth.* It has now become not only an act of grace and mercy but also an act of righteousness for God to pardon the sins of penitent believers, having accepted the atonement Christ's death made for them in fulfillment of the demands of God's justice. God is just, that is, faithful to his word.

2.2.3. It is for the glory of God himself, since boasting is excluded (v. 27). Now, if justification were by the works of the law, boasting would not be excluded. If we were saved by our own works, we could put the crown on our own heads. However, the *law of faith* forever excludes boasting, because faith is a dependent, self-emptying, and self-denying grace, and casts every crown before the throne (Rev 4:10). Paul speaks of *the law of faith.* Believers are not left without law: faith is a law; it is a working grace. He concludes from all this *that a man is justified by faith without the deeds of the law* (v. 28).

3. He shows the extent of this privilege of justification by faith, and that it is not the special privilege of only the Jews, but applies also to the Gentiles; for he has said (v. 22) that there is no difference.

3.1. He asserts and proves it (vv. 29–30): *Is he the God of the Jews only?* It is one God of grace who *justifies the circumcision by faith, and the uncircumcision through faith.* The Jews, in favor of themselves, want to imagine a difference, but really there is no more difference than between *by* and *through.*

3.2. He deals with an objection (v. 31), namely, that this teaching nullifies the law. "No," he says, "although we do say that the law will not justify us, we do not therefore say that it was given in vain. *We establish the right use of the law* and secure its standing by establishing it on the right basis. Although we cannot be saved by it as a covenant, we still recognize it and submit to it as a rule in the hand of the Mediator, subordinate to the law of grace, and are therefore so far from overthrowing the law that we establish it."

CHAPTER 4

The great Gospel teaching of justification by faith apart from the works of the law was so contrary to the ideas the Jews had learned that it would hardly go down well with them. Now in this chapter Paul proves it by example. The example he chooses is that of Abraham, and the whole chapter is taken up with his discussion of this. 1. He proves that Abraham was justified not by works but by faith (vv. 1–8). 2. He comments on when and why Abraham was so justified (vv. 9–17). 3. He describes and commends Abraham's faith (vv. 17–22). 4. He applies all this to us (vv. 23–25).

Verses 1–8

Here the apostle proves that Abraham was justified not by works but by faith. He appeals to the case of Abraham, the Jews' father, including his own name in that relation, since he is a Hebrew of the Hebrews (Php 3:5): *Abraham our father.* Now *what has he found?* The whole world is seeking, but no one can be truly reckoned to have discovered something except those who are justified before God, and this is how Abraham discovered this one pearl of great price (Mt 13:46). What has he found *as pertaining to the flesh,* that is, by circumcision and his external privileges? Was he justified by them? Was it the merit of his works that commended him to God's acceptance? No, not at all.

1. If he had been justified by works, there would have been room left for boasting. If so, *he hath whereof to glory* (v. 2). "But was not his name made great (Ge 12:2), and is he not then permitted to boast?" Yes, but not before God; he might deserve favor from other people, but he could never merit anything from God. Paul himself had *whereof to glory* (something to boast about) before men (Php 3:4), and we have him sometimes boasting about it, but he had nothing to glory in before God. People must not claim to glory in anything before God; not even Abraham may do so.

2. It is explicitly said that Abraham's faith was credited to him as righteousness. *What saith the scripture?* (v. 3). In all religious controversies we must ask this question. It is not what this great person or that good person says, but *What saith the scripture?* Now the Scripture says that *Abraham believed, and this was counted to him for righteousness* (Ge 15:6); that is why he had nothing to glory in before God, because it was purely by free grace that his righteousness was imputed in this way. It is mentioned in Genesis on the occasion of a significant act of faith about the promised offspring, and it followed a serious conflict Abraham had with unbelief. What is required for justification is not perfect faith, but an effective faith, faith that has the upper hand over unbelief.

3. If he had been justified by works, the reward would have been *of debt, and not of grace.* This is Paul's argument (vv. 4–5): Abraham's reward was God himself; God had told him this just before (Ge 15:1): *I am thy exceeding great reward.* Now if Abraham had deserved this through his perfect obedience, it would not have been an act of grace by God. God wants free grace to have all the glory. Therefore, *to him that worketh not* — who cannot claim to have such merit, but throws himself wholly on the free grace of God in Christ by a living, active, and obedient faith — to such a person *faith is counted for righteousness. Him that justifieth the ungodly,* that is, the one who was ungodly before, Abraham: his former ungodliness was no barrier to his being justified when he believed. No room is left, therefore, for despair; even though God does not clear the unrepentant guilty (Ex 34:7), through Christ he justifies the ungodly.

4. Paul further illustrates this by a passage from the Psalms where David speaks of the forgiveness of sins as constituting the blessedness of a person, declaring that the blessed person is not the one who has no sin, but *the man to whom the Lord imputeth not sin.* In this passage, from Ps 32:1–2, notice:

4.1. The nature of forgiveness. It is the remission of a debt; it is the covering of sin. God is said *to cast sin behind his back* (Isa 38:17), *to hide his face from it* (Ps

51:9), which implies that the basis of our blessedness is not our innocence, but God's not blaming us. Our justification consists in God's *not imputing sin* (v. 8), which makes it completely a gracious act of God. The reward (Ge 15:1) of being accepted by God cannot be expected as a debt, and so Paul concludes (v. 6) that this reward is the crediting of righteousness apart from works.

4.2. Its blessedness: *Blessed are they.* When it is said, *Blessed are the undefiled in the way* (Ps 119:1), the intention is to describe character, but when it is said, *Blessed are those whose iniquities are forgiven,* the intention is to show what that blessedness is and what is its basis. Forgiven people are the only blessed people. Oh how much it is in our interests, therefore, to make sure that our sins are pardoned, since this is the foundation of all other benefits.

Verses 9–17

In this paragraph, the apostle Paul comments on when and why Abraham was justified.

1. It was before he was circumcised (v. 10). His faith was credited to him as righteousness while he was uncircumcised. It was reckoned in Ge 15:6, and he was not circumcised until Ge 17. The apostle takes notice of this in answer to the question (v. 9), *Cometh this blessedness then on the circumcision only, or on the uncircumcision also?* Abraham was forgiven and accepted when he was still uncircumcised. Here are two reasons why Abraham was justified by faith while uncircumcised:

1.1. So that circumcision could be *a seal of the righteousness of faith* (v. 11). To confirm Abraham's faith, God appointed a sealing ceremony, and Abraham received *the sign of circumcision* as a special favor. We may notice from this:

1.1.1. The nature of sacraments in general; they are signs and seals. They are signs of absolute grace and favor; they are seals of conditional promises. In the sacraments God seals himself to us to be our God, and we seal ourselves to him to be his people.

1.1.2. The nature of circumcision in particular: it was the initiating sacrament of the Old Testament, and it is said to be here:

1.1.2.1. *A sign* of that original corruption that we are all born with and that is cut off by spiritual circumcision. In the words of the *Westminster Larger Catechism,* Answer 163, concerning sacraments, circumcision was "an outward and sensible sign of an inward and spiritual grace signified thereby."

1.1.2.2. *A seal of the righteousness of the faith.* In general, it was a seal of the covenant of grace, especially of justification by faith. Now if infants were then capable of receiving a seal of the covenant of grace, which proves that they were then within that covenant, how they now come to be rejected by the covenant is a question that must be answered by those who reject the baptism of the offspring of believers.

1.2. *That he might be the father of all those that believe.* In Abraham a much clearer and fuller dispensation of the covenant of grace began than any that had existed before that. And that is why he is called *the father of all that believe. The father of all those that believe,* that is, a constant example of faith, as parents are examples to their children, and a constant precedent of justification by faith, as the liberties of ancestors pass to their children. He was:

1.2.1. The father of believing Gentiles, *though they be not circumcised.* Because Abraham himself was uncircumcised when he was justified by faith, uncircumcision can never be a reason for exclusion. In this way, the doubts and fears of the poor Gentiles were anticipated.

1.2.2. The father of believing Jews, because they *are not of the circumcision only but* also *walk in the steps of that faith*; they not only are of Abraham's family but also follow the example of Abraham's faith. Notice here who are the genuine children of those who were the church's fathers: those who follow in their footsteps; this is the line of succession. Those who have most reason to call Christ Father (Isa 9:6; 53:10) are those who show by their lives that they follow in his steps, not those who bear his name by being Christians only in their profession.

2. It was before the giving of the Law (vv. 13–16). Notice:

2.1. What the promise was—*that he would be the heir of the world*. The meek are said to *inherit the earth* (Mt 5:5), and the world is theirs. Although Abraham possessed so little of the world (Ge 23), he was still heir of it all. Or, rather, it points to Christ, the descendant mentioned here. *To thy seed, which is Christ* (Gal 3:16). Now Christ is the heir of the world (Ps 2:8), and it is in him that Abraham was so.

2.2. How it was made to him: *Not through the law, but through the righteousness of faith. Not through the law*; rather, the promise was made to him upon that believing of his that was credited to him as righteousness; it was upon his trusting God by leaving his own country when God commanded him (Heb 11:8). Now, because it was by faith, it could not have been done by the law (vv. 14–15): *If those who are of the law be heirs*, then *faith is made void*, because if perfect fulfillment of the whole law were necessary for participation in the promise, then the promise could never take effect, since the way to life by perfect obedience to the Law and spotless, sinless innocence is wholly blocked, and the Law in itself opens up no other way. Paul proves this in v. 15: *The law worketh* (brings) *wrath*. It brings about wrath in us toward God; it stirs up the worldly heart that is set against God, as the damming of a river makes it swell. It also brings about wrath in God against us. Now it is certain that we can never expect the inheritance through a law that brings wrath. Paul shows how the Law brings wrath in the second part of the verse: *Where no law is, there is no transgression*—an acknowledged maxim that implies that where there is a law, there is transgression.

2.3. Why the promise was made to him by faith; for three reasons (v. 16):

2.3.1. *That it might be by grace and not by the law; by grace, and not of debt, nor of merit*. Faith has particular reference to grace being granted, as grace has reference to faith receiving. God wants to have every crown thrown at the feet of grace (Rev 4:10), free grace.

2.3.2. *That the promise might be sure* (guaranteed). The first covenant was not guaranteed, and through human failure its benefits were cut off, and so another way was found, to more effectively guarantee the conveyance of the new covenant. This way is *not by works but by faith*, which receives all from Christ, in whose keeping it is safe.

2.3.3. *That it might be sure to all the seed*. If it had been through the law, it would have been limited to the Jews. It was through faith that Gentiles as well as Jews, the spiritual as well as the natural descendants of faithful Abraham, would share in the privileges provided under the promise. God would arrange the promise in such a way as to include all true believers, and this is why (v. 17) Paul refers us to Ge 17:5, where the reason is given for the change of name from *Abram*, "exalted father," to *Abra-*

ham, "father of many": *for a father of many nations have I made thee*; that is, all believers should take Abraham as their pattern and call him *father*.

Verses 17–22

Having commented on when Abraham was justified by faith, and why, for the honor of Abraham and as an example to us who call him father, the apostle here describes and commends the faith of Abraham. Notice:

1. Whom he believed: *God, who quickeneth*. It is God himself that faith focuses on. Now notice what Abraham's faith looked to in God.

1.1. *God, who quickeneth the dead*. It was promised that Abraham would be *the father of many nations* (v. 17; Ge 17:5) when he and his wife were *as good as dead* (Heb 11:11–12), and so he looked on God as a God who could breathe life into dry bones (Eze 37:1–10). The One who gives life to the dead can do anything; he can give a child to Abraham when he is old; he can bring in the Gentiles, who are *dead in trespasses and sins*, to give them a divine and spiritual life (Eph 2:1).

1.2. *God, who calleth things which are not as though they were*. The justification and salvation of sinners, the embracing of the Gentiles who had not been a people (Hos 1:9; 2:23; 1Pe 2:10), were a gracious calling of things which are not as though they were. This expresses the sovereignty of God and his absolute power and dominion, which is a mighty support to faith when all other props fail and sink. It is true faith that depends on the all-sufficiency of God to accomplish what is impossible, on nothing apart from that all-sufficiency. This is how Abraham became *the father of many nations before him whom he believed*. It is through faith in God that we are accepted by him.

2. How he believed.

2.1. *Against hope, he believed in hope* (v. 18). There was a hope against him, a natural hope. All the arguments of sense, reason, and experience, which usually produce and support hope in such cases, were against him. But despite all those motivations to the contrary, he still believed, because he had a hope on his side: *He believed in hope*, which arose, as his faith did, from considering God's all-sufficiency. *That he might become the father of many nations*. That is why God, by his almighty grace, enabled him to believe against all hope. It was fitting that the one who was to be the father of the faithful would have something extraordinary in his faith. Or, rather than *why* he believed, this was *what* he believed when his believing was credited to him as righteousness (v. 6).

2.2. *Being not weak in faith, he considered not his own body* (v. 19). His own body was now dead—it was highly improbable that he could have children. When God intends to give some special blessing to his people, he often puts a sentence of death on the blessing itself. However, Abraham did not consider this; "he did not dwell in his thoughts upon it." His faith thought of nothing except the faithfulness of the promise, and this kept up his faith. Although it may seem to be the wisdom of worldly reason to delve deeply into all the difficulties that arise against the promise, it is really the weakness of faith.

2.3. *He staggered not* (did not waver) *at the promise of God through unbelief* (v. 20). "He did not decide"; he did not hold any self-consultation about it; he did not take time to consider whether he should accept it or not, but by a resolute act of his soul, with a holy boldness, risked everything on the promise. He did not consider it a point worthy of argument or debate. He *staggered not through unbelief*. Unbelief lies at the root of all our waverings at

God's promises. When we waver, it is not the promise that fails, but our faith.

2.4. He *was strong in faith, giving glory to God*; "he was strengthened" in faith: his faith gained ground by being exercised. Although weak faith will not be rejected, strong faith will be commended and honored. The strength of his faith appeared in the victory it won over his fears. Abraham's faith gave God the glory, especially for his faithfulness. Abraham gave glory to God by trusting him. We never hear our Lord Jesus commending anything as much as great faith (Mt 8:10; 15:28): God gives honor to great faith because great faith gives honor to God.

2.5. He was *fully persuaded that what God had promised he was able to perform*; "he was carried on with the greatest confidence" and assurance; it is a metaphor taken from ships that come into the harbor with full sail. Abraham saw the storms of doubts, fears, and temptations that were likely to rise up against the promise. However, because he had taken God as his pilot, and the promise as his guide and compass, like a bold adventurer he set up all his sails and paid no attention to winds or clouds; he simply trusted in the wisdom and faithfulness of his pilot, bravely made his way to the harbor, and came home with unspeakable gain. This was his full persuasion, built on the almighty power of God: *He was able.* Our waverings arise mainly from our distrust of God's power. We must believe not only that he is faithful but also that he is able (Heb 10:23; 11:11). *And therefore it was imputed to him for righteousness* (v. 22). Because he risked everything on the divine promise, God graciously accepted him, and not only fulfilled but surpassed his expectation. He justified him even though there was nothing in his believing that deserved such acceptance. This shows why faith is chosen to be the primary condition of our justification: it is a grace that gives glory to God more than all others.

Verses 23–25

At the close of the chapter, Paul applies his whole argument to us. He concludes here that Abraham's justification was to be the pattern of ours: *It was not written for his sake alone.* It was not intended only as a historical commendation of Abraham, or as a description of something peculiar to him. The accounts we have of the Old Testament saints were not intended as mere historical accounts, but as precedents to guide us, as examples (1Co 10:11) for *our learning* (15:4). This account of Abraham was particularly written *for us also*, to assure us of the righteousness that God requires. It is written for us on whom the fulfillment of the ages has come (1Co 10:11), as well as for the patriarchs, for the grace of God is the same yesterday, today, and forever (Heb 13:8). Notice:

1. Our common privilege; righteousness will be credited to us. *It shall be imputed*; he uses a future verb to show the continuation of this mercy in the church, that just as it is the same now, so it will be as long as God has a church in the world. There is a fountain opened up (Zec 13:1) that is inexhaustible.

2. Our common duty, the condition of this privilege, and that is believing. The proper object of this believing is divine revelation. The revelation to Abraham was about a Christ to come; the revelation to us is about a Christ who has already come; but this difference between the two revelations does not change the case. Now we are to believe in the One who raised up Christ, and we must not only believe in his power but also depend on his grace. This is how Paul explains it in v. 25.

2.1. He was *delivered for our offenses.* He died as an evildoer, because he died for sin, but it was not his own sin. He died to make atonement for our sins.

2.2. He was *raised again for our justification.* He paid our debt by the merit of his death; he secured our acquittal in his resurrection. The apostle especially emphasizes Christ's resurrection; it is Christ who died, *yea, rather, that has risen again* (8:34). On the whole matter it is clear, therefore, that we are not justified by the merit of our own works, but by dependence on Jesus Christ and his righteousness, which is the truth that Paul in this and the previous chapter has been establishing as the great foundation of all our comfort.

CHAPTER 5

In this chapter: 1. The apostle shows the fruits of justification (vv. 1–5). 2. He shows the fountain and foundation of justification in the death of Jesus Christ (vv. 6–21).

Verses 1–5

The precious benefits and privileges that flow from justification should inspire us all to make sure that we ourselves are justified. The fruits of this tree of life are exceedingly precious:

1. *We have peace with God* (v. 1). It is sin that is the origin of the quarrel between us and God. Justification takes away that guilt; as soon as that obstacle is removed, peace is made. By faith we take hold of God's strength, and so we are at peace (Isa 27:4–5). There is more in this peace than a bare cessation of enmity; there is friendship and unfailing love, because God is either the worst enemy or the best friend. Christ has called his disciples *friends* (Jn 15:13–15). Surely we need nothing more to make us happy than to have God as our friend! However, this is *through our Lord Jesus Christ—through him* as the great peacemaker, *the Mediator between God and man* (1Ti 2:5). *He is our peace*, not only the maker of our peace but also its content and maintainer (Col 1:20).

2. *We have access by faith into this grace wherein we stand* (v. 2). This is a further privilege, not only peace but grace. Notice:

2.1. The saints' fortunate state. It is a state of grace, God's loving-kindness to us and our conformity to God; we have access into this grace. We were not born in this state, but brought into it. We could not have gotten into it by ourselves; we are led into it as blind, lame, or weak people are led. *We have had access.* Paul, in his conversion, gained this access; he was then brought near (Eph 2:13). It was Christ who introduced and led him by the hand into this grace. *By whom we have access by faith*, by Christ as the author, by faith as the means of this access.

2.2. Their fortunate standing in this state: *Wherein we stand.* Not only in which we are, but in which we stand. The expression shows our progress; as long as we are standing, we are moving on. We must not lie down, as if we had *already attained* (Php 3:12), but stand as those who are pressing forward, stand as servants waiting on Christ our master. The expression also shows our perseverance: we stand firmly and safely; we stand as soldiers do, who keep their ground. Things are different in the court of heaven than in worldly courts, where high places are slippery.

3. *We rejoice in hope of the glory of God.* Besides the happiness in hand, there is also a happiness in hope, *the glory of God.* Those who have access through faith into

the grace of God may now hope for the glory of God in the future. Grace is glory begun, the pledge and assurance of glory. Those who hope for the glory of God in the future have enough to rejoice about now.

4. *We glory in tribulations* (sufferings) *also*; we glory not only despite our sufferings, but even in our sufferings. Notice what growing and increasing happiness the happiness of the saints is: *Not only so. We glory in tribulations also*, especially in sufferings for righteousness' sake. Because this is the hardest point, Paul sets himself to show its basis and reasons. Sufferings, by a series of causes, greatly befriend hope, which he shows in the way tribulation influences us.

4.1. *Tribulation worketh patience* (suffering produces perseverance), by the powerful grace of God working in and with the suffering. It tests patience and, by testing it, increases it, as steel is hardened by fire. What produces perseverance is a matter of joy; for perseverance does us more good than suffering can do us harm. Suffering in itself produces impatience, but as it is sanctified to the saints, it produces perseverance.

4.2. *Patience, experience* (perseverance produces character) (v. 4). Perseverance produces character through an experience of God; patient sufferers have the greatest experience of divine comfort. Perseverance also produces an experience of ourselves. It is through suffering that we test our own sincerity. Perseverance produces "an approval," as those who have passed the test are approved.

4.3. *Experience* (character), *hope*. These who, being tested in this way, come out as gold (Job 23:10) will be encouraged to hope. Experience of God supports our hope. Experience of ourselves helps to bring evidence of our sincerity.

4.4. This *hope maketh not ashamed*; it will not disappoint or deceive us. Nothing defeats us more than disappointment. This hope does not make us ashamed of or disappointed in our suffering. It is in a good cause, for a good Master, and in a good hope, and that is why we are not ashamed. *Because the love of God is shed abroad.* This hope will not disappoint us because it is sealed with the Holy Spirit as a Spirit of love. *The love of God* refers to the assurance of God's love to us, drawing out our love toward him in return. The basis of all our comfort and holiness, and of our perseverance in both, is laid in the *shedding abroad of the love of God in our hearts.* An assurance of God's love toward us will not make us ashamed, either of our hope in him or of our sufferings for him.

Verses 6–21

The apostle describes here the fountain and foundation of justification that is laid in the death of the Lord Jesus. He enlarges on this expression of the love of God that is poured out. We have here:

- The people Christ died for (vv. 6–8).
- The precious fruits of his death (vv. 9–11).
- The parallel Paul draws between the communication of sin and death by the First Adam and the communication of righteousness and life by the Second Adam (vv. 12–21). Notice:

1. What we were like when Christ died for us.

1.1. *We were without strength* (v. 6), in a sad condition, totally unable to help ourselves out of that condition. Therefore, our salvation is said here to come *in due time* (at the right time). God's time to help and save is when those who are to be saved are powerless. God's way is to help in a crisis.

1.2. *He died for the ungodly*, for creatures who were not only helpless and therefore likely to perish but also guilty and sinful and therefore deserving to perish. Because they were ungodly, they needed someone to die for them. Paul illustrates this (vv. 7–8) as an unparalleled expression of love; here God's thoughts and ways were far above ours (Isa 55:8–9).

1.2.1. One would scarcely *die for a righteous man*, that is, one who is unjustly condemned; everybody will pity such a person, but few will risk their own life for them.

1.2.2. One might perhaps be persuaded *to die for a good man*, one who is more than merely righteous. Many who are good themselves do only a little good to others, but those who are useful often become well loved. But notice how Paul qualifies this: it is only some who would do so, and ultimately it is only *a peradventure* (possibly).

1.2.3. *But Christ died for sinners* (v. 8), those who were neither righteous nor good, who were not only useless but also guilty. Now here *God commended his love*, not only proved but also exalted it and made it shine brightly, not only put it beyond dispute but also rendered it the object of the greatest wonder. He *commendeth his love* in order to bring about the pouring out of his love in our hearts by the Holy Spirit. *While we were yet sinners.* He died to save us not in our sins but from our sins, but we were still sinners when he died for us.

1.2.4. In fact, what is more, *we were enemies* (v. 10), not only evildoers but even traitors and rebels. That Christ died for such people is such a mystery, such an unprecedented expression of love, that it may well be our business to eternity to admire and wonder at it. The One who had loved us in this way could justly make it one of the laws of his kingdom that we should love our enemies.

2. The precious fruits of his death.

2.1. Justification and reconciliation are the fruit of the death of Christ: *We are justified by his blood* (v. 9), *reconciled by his death* (v. 10). Sin is forgiven, hostility brought to an end, sin dealt with, and eternal righteousness brought in. As soon as we believe, we are actually put into a state of justification and reconciliation. *Justified by his blood.* Our justification is attributed to the blood of Christ because *without blood there is no remission* (Heb 9:22). In all sacrifices of atonement, the giving up of the lifeblood was the essential part of the sacrifice (Lev 17:11).

2.2. The result of this is salvation from wrath: *Saved from wrath* (v. 9), *saved by his life* (v. 10). If God justified and reconciled us when we were enemies, much more will he then save us when we are justified and reconciled. The One who has done the greater, which is to change us from enemies to friends, will certainly do the less, which is to treat us in a kind and friendly way when we are friends. Twice, therefore, the apostle speaks of it with *a much more. We shall be saved from wrath.* It is the wrath of God that is the fire of hell. *Reconciled by his death, saved by his life.* His life spoken of here is not to be understood as his life in the flesh, but his life in heaven. We are reconciled by Christ humbled; we are saved by Christ exalted. The dying Jesus laid the foundation by making atonement for sin and bringing the enmity to an end. It is the living Jesus who completes the work. Christ dying was the testator (the One who made the will [Heb 9:16–17]), who bequeathed us the legacy, but Christ living is the executor, who pays it.

2.3. All this produces, as a further privilege, our *joy in God* (v. 11). God is now so far from being a terror to us that he is our *joy. We are reconciled and saved from wrath. And not only so*; this joy contains even more, a constant flow of God's favors; we not only reach the harbor but come in with full sails: *We joy in God*, basking in his love. All this—which Paul repeats as a string he loves to pluck—is because of the atonement, for through Christ we *received the atonement*. To *receive the atonement* is:

2.3.1. To give our consent to the atonement, being willing and glad to be saved by the Gospel and on Gospel terms.

2.3.2. To take encouragement from the atonement. Now *we joy in God*; now we do indeed *receive the atonement*, boasting in it.

3. The parallel that the apostle draws between the communication of sin and death by the First Adam and the communication of righteousness and life by the Second Adam (vv. 12–21), showing a correspondence between our fall and our recovery. Here is:

3.1. A general truth laid down as the foundation of his discussion—that Adam was a type of Christ (v. 14): *who is the figure of him that was to come.* God dealt with Adam as a representative, and Adam acted as such, as a common father of and for all his descendants. Similarly, Jesus Christ, the Mediator, acted as a representative, as the head of all the elect: he dealt with God for them as their father (Isa 9:6; 53:10), died for them, rose for them, entered within the veil for them, did all for them.

3.2. A more specific explanation of the parallel. Notice:

3.2.1. How Adam passed on sin and death to all his descendants (v. 12): *By one man sin entered.* We see the world inundated with sin and death, full of sins and full of disasters. The spring that feeds this flood is our corrupt nature, and the gap through which it entered was Adam's first sin. It was *by one man*, and he was the first man.

3.2.1.1. Through him *sin entered.* When God declared all to be very good (Ge 1:31), there was no sin in the world. Sin had entered earlier into the world of angels, but it never entered into humanity until Adam sinned. That was when the guilt of Adam's sin entered, the guilt that was reckoned to his descendants, along with a general depravedness of nature. *Eph' ho* is rendered *for that* by our translation, that is, "because"; a better translation would be "in whom": "in whom *all have sinned.*" Sin entered the world through Adam, because in him we all sinned. God, as the author of nature, had made it a law of nature that a man would father others in his own likeness. In Adam, therefore, as in a common container, the whole human nature was deposited. When Adam sinned and fell, therefore, the nature became guilty and corrupt. In this way, all have sinned in him.

3.2.1.2. *Death* entered *by sin*, because death is the wages of sin (6:23). When sin came, death came naturally with it.

3.2.1.3. *So death passed, passed through* all people, as an infectious disease passes through a city, so that no one escapes it. It is the universal fate, without exception. *Death reigned* (v. 14). No one is exempt from its scepter. It is the last enemy (1Co 15:26).

3.2.1.4. Paul shows that sin did not begin with the Law of Moses, but was *in the world until*, or before, that law. Sin was in the world before the Law, as can be seen from Cain's murder (Ge 4:8), the apostasy of the old world (Ge 6:5–6, 11–12), the evil of Sodom (Ge 19:1–29). His conclusion from this is that, therefore, there was a law, for *sin is not imputed where there is no law.* Original sin is a lack of conformity to the law of God, and actual sin is disobedience to it: therefore all were under some law. Paul's proof is, *Death reigned from Adam to Moses* (v. 14). This proves that sin was in the world before the

Law, and that it was original sin, because death reigned over those who had not sinned any actual sin, those who *had not sinned after the similitude of Adam's transgression* (in the likeness of Adam's offense).

3.2.2. How, corresponding to this, Christ communicates righteousness and life to all true believers. Paul shows not only how the resemblance holds, but also how the communication of grace and love through Christ *goes beyond* the communication of guilt and wrath through Adam. Notice:

3.2.2.1. How the resemblance holds (vv. 18–19).

3.2.2.1.*1.* *By the offense and disobedience of one many were made sinners, and judgment came upon all men to condemnation.*

3.2.2.1.*1.1.* Adam's sin was disobedience. The thing he did was evil only because it was forbidden, but although it seemed very small, it opened the door to other sins.

3.2.2.1.*1.2.* The evil and poison of sin are strong and spreading; otherwise the guilt of Adam's sin would not have reached so far. Who would have thought there would be so much evil in sin?

3.2.2.1.*1.3.* By Adam's sin many are made sinners: *many*, that is, all his descendants. They are said to have been *made sinners*, which refers to making us such by a judicial act.

3.2.2.1.*1.4.* Judgment has come on all those who by Adam's disobedience were made sinners. The whole human race lies under a sentence, as when, under our law, a whole family lose their estate because of the crime of the father.

3.2.2.1.*2.* Similarly, *by the righteousness and obedience of one are many made righteous*, and so the *free gift comes upon all.* Notice:

3.2.2.1.*2.1.* The nature of Christ's righteousness, how it is brought in; it is by his obedience. The disobedience of the First Adam ruined us; the obedience of the Second Adam saves us. By his obedience he brought about a righteousness for us, satisfying God's justice.

3.2.2.1.*2.2.* Its fruit. There is *a free gift that has come upon all men.* The salvation brought is a *common salvation* (Jude 3); whoever wants to may come and drink of these waters of life (Isa 55:1). This free gift is given *unto justification of life.* It is a justification that not only frees from death but also entitles those who receive it to life. *Many shall be made righteous.* It could also be translated, "They shall be constituted righteous," as those who are officially declared so in writing.

3.2.2.2. How the communication of grace and love through Christ goes beyond the communication of guilt and wrath through Adam (vv. 15–17). It is intended to exalt Christ's love and to strengthen believers.

3.2.2.2.*1.* If guilt and wrath are communicated, then much more will grace and love be: *Much more the grace of God, and the gift by grace.* Of all his qualities, God's goodness is especially his glory (Ex 33:18–19). We know that God is inclined to show mercy; punishing is *his strange work* (Isa 28:21).

3.2.2.2.*2.* If the sin of one human being had so much power and effectiveness for condemning us, then much more did the righteousness and grace of Christ have power and effectiveness to justify and save us. Surely Adam could not spread such a strong poison unless Jesus Christ could spread as strong an antidote, and even stronger.

3.2.2.2.*3.* It is only the guilt of a single offense of Adam's that we are accused of: *The judgment was by one*, that is, "by one offense" (vv. 16–17, margin). But from Jesus Christ we receive and derive an *abundance of grace, and of the gift of righteousness.* The flow of grace and righteousness is deeper and broader than the flow of guilt. God in Christ forgives all our sins (Col 2:13).

3.2.2.2.*4.* Through Adam's sin *death reigned*, but through Christ's righteousness believers are advanced to *reign in life* (v. 17). Through Christ and his righteousness we are entitled to and given more and greater privileges than we ever lost through the offense of Adam. The salve is wider than the wound, and more healing than the wound is killing.

4. An anticipation, it seems, in vv. 20–21 of an objection that is expressed in Gal 3:19: *Wherefore then serveth* (what then was the purpose of) *the law?* Answer:

4.1. *The law entered that the offense might abound.* Not to make sin increase more in itself, but to reveal its abundant sinfulness. The mirror reveals the spots, but it does not cause them. The letting in of a clearer light into a room reveals the dust and filth that were already there but not seen.

4.2. *That grace might much more abound*—that the terrors of the law would make Gospel comforts so much sweeter. The greater the strength of the enemy, the greater the honor of the conqueror. Paul illustrates this increase of grace in v. 21. *Sin reigned unto death*; it was a cruel and bloody reign. But *grace reigns* to life, *eternal life*, and this *through righteousness* by *Jesus Christ our Lord*, through the power and efficacy of Christ.

CHAPTER 6

Having proved in detail the great doctrine of justification by faith, the apostle now urges, with similar powerful arguments, the absolute necessity of sanctification and a holy life as the inseparable fruit of justification. Wherever Jesus Christ is made by God to be righteousness to any soul, he is also made by God to be sanctification to that soul (1Co 1:30).

Verses 1–23

The apostle's transition, which joins this discussion with the former, is significant: *What shall we say then?* (v. 1). *Shall we continue in sin that grace may abound?* Shall we take encouragement from this to sin, because the more sin we commit, the more the grace of God will be exalted in our forgiveness? The apostle is shocked at the mere thought of it (v. 2): *God forbid.* Opinions that give any support to sin are to be rejected with the greatest detestation. The apostle is detailed in urging the necessity of holiness in this chapter, which may be reduced to two headings: his exhortations to holiness and his arguments to support those exhortations, which show its necessity.

1. As to the first, we may notice here the nature of sanctification. It contains two aspects, mortification and renewal—dying to sin and living to righteousness.

1.1. Mortification, putting off the old self, is expressed as follows:

1.1.1. We must *live no longer in sin* (v. 2). Although no one lives without sin (1Ki 8:46; Ecc 7:20), nevertheless, there are those who do not live in sin, who do not make it their business.

1.1.2. *The body of sin must be destroyed* (v. 6). The corruption that dwells in us is the body of sin. This is the root to which the ax must be laid (Mt 3:10). We must not only stop committing acts of sin; we must also have the corrupt habits and inclinations weakened and destroyed. *That henceforth we should not serve sin.* It is the body of sin that is powerful; destroy this, and the yoke will be broken (Isa 9:4; 10:27; 58:6).

1.1.3. *We must be dead indeed unto sin* (v. 11). As the death of the oppressor is a release, so much more is the death of the oppressed (Job 3:17–18). This is how we must be dead to sin, fulfilling its will no more. Those who are dead to sin are separated from their former company. Death makes a powerful change; sanctification makes such a change in the soul; it cuts off all dealings with sin.

1.1.4. *Sin must not reign in our mortal bodies, that we should obey it* (v. 12). Although sin may remain as an outlaw, we are not to let it reign as a king. Do not let it make laws, so that we obey it. Although we may sometimes be overtaken and overcome by it, let us never be obedient to it. *In the lusts thereof.* Sin lies very much in satisfying the desires of the body. There is a reason implied in the phrase *your mortal body.* It was sin that made our bodies mortal, and so do not yield obedience to such an enemy.

1.1.5. We must not *yield our members as instruments of unrighteousness* (v. 13). The members of the body are used by the corrupt nature as tools; we must not submit to such abuse. One sin leads to another. Beginning to sin is like breaching a dam; therefore leave it right away (Pr 17:14). Perhaps the members of the body will be forced to be instruments of sin, but do not surrender them to be so; do not submit to it. This is one branch of sanctification, putting sin to death.

1.2. Renewal, or living for righteousness—what is that?

1.2.1. It is to *walk in newness of life* (v. 4). Newness of life presupposes a new heart; there is no way to make the stream sweet except by making the spring so. Walk according to new rules. Choose a new way, new paths to walk on, new leaders to follow, new companions to walk with.

1.2.2. It is to be *alive unto God through Jesus Christ our Lord* (v. 11). To talk with God, to have regard for him, to delight in him—to have this is to be alive to God. It is to have the affections and desires alive toward God. Or the phrase may be understood as "*living* our life in the flesh *unto God*," to his honor and glory as our aim, by his word and will as our rule; this is to live to God. *Through Jesus Christ our Lord.* Christ is our spiritual life; there is no living for God except through him. He is the Mediator; there is no fellowship between sinful souls and a holy God except through the mediation of the Lord Jesus. In living to God, Christ is all in all (Eph 1:23; Col 3:11).

1.2.3. It is to *yield ourselves to God, as those that are alive from the dead* (v. 13). The very life and being of holiness lie in the dedication of ourselves to the Lord, giving ourselves to the Lord (2Co 8:5). "Do not give your possessions to him, but give yourselves, nothing less than your whole selves. Not only submit to him but also comply with him; be always ready to serve him. Yield yourselves to him as wax to the seal, to take any impression, to be, have, and do what he pleases." *As those that are alive from the dead.* To offer a dead carcass to a living God is not to please him, but to mock him: "Offer yourselves as those who are alive and good for something, *a living sacrifice*" (12:1). The surest evidence of our spiritual life is the dedication of ourselves to God.

1.2.4. It is to offer *our members as instruments of righteousness to God.* When the members of our bodies are withdrawn from serving sin, they are not to lie idle, but are to be used to serve God. The body must always be ready to serve the soul in the service of God. Therefore (v. 19), "*Yield your members servants to righteousness unto holiness.* Let them be under the command and guidance of the righteous law of God." *Righteousness unto holiness* indicates growth, progress, and ground that is won. As every sinful act confirms the sinful habit and makes the old nature more and more inclined to sin, so every gracious act confirms the gracious habit. One duty prepares us for another, and the more we do for God, the more we can do for him.

2. Then we have the motives or arguments to show the necessity of sanctification. There is such opposition in our hearts by nature to holiness that it is not easy to bring them into submission to it; it is the Spirit's work.

2.1. He argues from our sacramental conformity to Jesus Christ. Our baptism carried in it a great reason why we should die to sin and live to righteousness. Notice his reasoning:

2.1.1. In general, we are *dead to sin.* Our baptism represents our being cut off from the kingdom of sin. We are dead to sin by our union with Christ, in and by whom it is killed. All this is futile if we persist in sin, if we return to what we were dead to, like walking ghosts. For *he that is dead is freed from sin* (v. 7); those who are dead to sin are freed from its rule and controlling power. Now shall we be such fools as to return to the slavery from which we have been discharged?

2.1.2. In particular, being *baptized into Jesus Christ, we were baptized into his death* (v. 3). Baptism binds us to Christ. In particular, we were baptized into his death. As Christ died for sin, so we should die to sin. This was the profession and promise of our baptism, and we do not do well if we do not live up to this profession and fulfill this promise.

2.1.2.1. Our conformity to the death of Christ obliges us to die to sin. We are here, therefore, said to be *planted together in the likeness of is death* (v. 5), as the engrafted stock is planted into the likeness of the shoot, whose nature it participates in (11:17–24). We are planted in the vineyard in likeness to Christ, and we should show this likeness in our sanctification. Our creed concerning Jesus Christ is, among other things, that he was "crucified, dead, and buried"; now baptism is a sacramental conformity to him in each of these.

2.1.2.1.1. *Our old man is crucified with him* (v. 6). The death of the cross was a slow death, but a sure one. Such is the putting to death of sin in believers. It was a cursed death (Gal 3:13). Sin dies as an evildoer, devoted to destruction, *accursed. Crucified with him.* The crucifying of Christ for us has an influence on the crucifying of sin in us.

2.1.2.1.2. We are dead with Christ (v. 8). Christ was obedient to death (Php 2:8), and when he died, we can be said to have died with him. Baptism signifies and seals our union with Christ, so that we are dead with him and have committed ourselves to have nothing more to do with sin than he had.

2.1.2.1.3. *We are buried with him by baptism* (v. 4). Our conformity is complete. We are by profession completely cut off from all dealings and fellowship with sin. This is how we must live, as Christ did, separate from sin and sinners. We are sealed to be the Lord's, and therefore to be cut off from sin. Just as Christ was buried so that he could rise again to a new and more heavenly life, so we too in baptism are buried so that we may rise again to a new life of faith and love.

2.1.2.2. Our conformity to the resurrection of Christ obligates us to rise again to *newness of life* (v. 4). Christ was raised *up from the dead by the glory of the Father,* that is, by the Father's power. Now in baptism we com-

mit ourselves to conform to that pattern, to be planted in the *likeness of his resurrection* (v. 5), to *live with him* (v. 8). Conversion is the first resurrection from the death of sin to the life of righteousness, and this resurrection is like Christ's resurrection. We have all risen with Christ. We must conform to the resurrection of Christ in two respects:

2.1.2.2.1. He rose never to die again (v. 9). Over Christ *death has no more dominion;* he was truly dead, but he is alive, and so alive that he lives for ever and ever (Rev 1:18). We, similarly, must rise from the grave of sin never to return to it.

2.1.2.2.2. He rose to live to God (v. 10), to lead a heavenly life. He rose again to leave the world. *Now I am no more in the world* (Jn 13:1; 17:11). He rose to *live to God.* We, similarly, must rise to live to God: this is what Paul calls *newness of life* (v. 4), to live by other rules, with other aims, than we have done. A life devoted to God is a new life; before, self was the chief and highest aim, but now God is.

2.2. He argues from the precious promises of the new covenant (v. 14). It might be objected that we cannot subdue sin, that it is unavoidably too hard for us. "No," he says, "you wrestle with an enemy who can be dealt with and subdued; it is an enemy who is already thwarted and defeated. *Sin shall not have dominion.*" Sin may struggle in a believer, and may create a great deal of trouble in their life; it may trouble them, but it will not rule them. *For we are not under the law, but under grace,* not under the law of sin and death, but under the law of the spirit of life, which is in Christ Jesus. New lords, new laws. Or, *we are not under* the covenant of works, which requires bricks and gives no straw, but under the covenant of grace, which accepts sincerity as our Gospel perfection, which requires nothing except what it promises power to perform. It does not leave our salvation in our own keeping, but puts it in the hands of the Mediator, who undertakes for us that sin will not have mastery over us, who has himself condemned it and will destroy it. Christ rules by the golden scepter of grace. We are under grace, which accepts the willing mind, leaves room for repentance, and promises forgiveness upon repentance. Shall we sin against so much goodness, abuse such love? See how the apostle is shocked at such a thought (v. 15): *Shall we sin because we are not under the law, but under grace? God forbid.*

2.3. He argues from the fact that our obedience or disobedience will be evidence of our state, evidence either for us or against us (v. 16): *To whom you yield yourselves servants to obey, his servants you are.* All people are either the servants of God or the servants of sin. We must ask which of these masters we yield obedience to. Our obeying the laws of sin will be evidence against us, evidence that we belong to the family that will inherit death. Our obeying the laws of Christ will be evidence of our relationship with Christ's family.

2.4. He argues from their former sinfulness (vv. 17–21), from:

2.4.1. What they have been and done formerly. *You were the servants of sin.* Those who are now the servants of God would do well to remember the time when they were the servants of sin, to keep them humble and stir them in their service of God. It brings shame to the service of sin that so many thousands have abandoned that service and that no one who has sincerely deserted it and given themselves up to the service of God has returned to their former drudgery. "*God be thanked that you were so*—that we can speak about it as something past." *You* have yielded your members servants to uncleanness (impurity), *and to iniquity unto iniquity* (v. 19). It is the misery of a sinful state that the body is made a drudge to sin. *You have yielded.* Sinners willingly serve sin. The Devil could not force them into that service unless they surrendered themselves to it. *To iniquity unto iniquity.* To iniquity as the work, to iniquity as the wages. If you sow the wind, you will reap the whirlwind (Hos 8:7), growing worse and worse (2Ti 3:13), more and more hardened. Paul speaks *after the manner of men*, using a comparison common among human beings. *You were free from righteousness* (v. 20); not free by any liberty given, but by a liberty taken, which is licentiousness. But a freedom from righteousness is the worst form of slavery.

2.4.2. How the godly change was made and what it consisted of.

2.4.2.1. *You have obeyed from the heart that form of doctrine which was delivered to you* (v. 17). This, according to the margin, describes conversion; it is our conformity to and compliance with the Gospel. The end of the verse could also be translated, "*the doctrine* into which you were delivered." Notice:

2.4.2.1.1. The rule of grace, that form of doctrine. The Gospel is the great rule of both truth and holiness. The Gospel is the stamp, and grace is the impression of that stamp.

2.4.2.1.2. Our conformity to that rule.

2.4.2.1.2.1. It is to obey from the heart. The Gospel is a doctrine to be obeyed from the heart, not only in profession but also in power—from the heart, the commanding part of us.

2.4.2.1.2.2. It is—again using our alternative translation of v. 17—to be "delivered into it," as into a mold, or as the wax receives the impression of the seal, corresponding to it line for line.

2.4.2.2. *Being made free from sin, you became servants of righteousness* (v. 18), *servants to God* (v. 22). Conversion is:

2.4.2.2.1. Freedom from the service of sin.

2.4.2.2.2. Submission of ourselves to the service of God. When we are made free from sin, it is not so that we may live as we wish and be our own masters. We cannot be made the servants of God until we have been freed from the controlling power of sin; we cannot serve two masters (Mt 6:24).

2.4.3. What understanding they now have of their former way. He appeals to them as to whether they did not find the service of sin (v. 21):

2.4.3.1. An unfruitful service: "*What fruit had you then?* Did you ever gain anything by it?" Besides the future losses, which are infinitely great, even the present gains of sin are not worth mentioning. *What fruit?* Nothing that deserves to be called fruit.

2.4.3.2. An unbecoming service; it is what we *are now ashamed* of. Shame came into the world with sin and is still the inevitable product of it. Who would willfully do what sooner or later they are sure to be ashamed of?

2.5. He argues from the results of all these things. To persuade us to move from sin to holiness, Paul sets before us good and evil, life and death, and we are given a choice (Dt 30:15, 19).

2.5.1. The result of sin is death (v. 21): *The end of those things is death.* Although the way may seem pleasant and inviting, it will be bitterness in the end (2Sa 2:26). *The wages of sin is death* (v. 23). Death is due to sinners as wages are to servants. All who are sin's servants and do sin's work must expect to be paid in this way.

2.5.2. If the fruit is holiness, the result will be eternal life—the happiest result possible! Even if the way is uphill, eternal life is guaranteed at its destination. So (v. 23), *the gift of God is eternal life.* Heaven is life, and it is eternal life, with no illness or weakness, no death to put an end to it. This is the gift of God. Death is the wages of sin, but life is a gift. Sinners deserve hell, but saints do not deserve heaven. We must thank God, and not ourselves, if ever we get to heaven. This gift is *through Jesus Christ our Lord.* It is Christ who purchased it, prepares us for it, and keeps us safe for it.

CHAPTER 7

We have here: 1. Our freedom from the law urged as an argument to impress sanctification on us (vv. 1–6). 2. The excellence and usefulness of the law asserted, nevertheless (vv. 7–14). 3. The conflict between grace and corruption in the heart (vv. 14–25).

Verses 1–6

Among other arguments to persuade us against sin and to holiness was the argument (6:14) that *we are not under the law*, and this argument is here further insisted on (v. 6): *We are delivered from the law.*

1. What is meant by this?

1.1. We are delivered from the power of the law that condemns us for the sin committed by us. The law says, *The soul that sins shall die* (Eze 18:4, 20), but we are delivered from the law.

1.2. We are released from the power of the law that provokes the sin that lives in us. The apostle seems especially to refer to this (v. 5): *the motions of sins* (sinful passions) *which were by* (aroused by) *the law.* The law, by threatening corrupt and fallen humanity but offering no grace to heal, only stirred up the corruption. Because we are lamed by the Fall, the law comes and directs us, but it provides nothing to heal and help our lameness. We are under grace, which promises power to do what it commands and promises forgiveness upon repentance when we do wrong. Paul illustrated earlier the difference between a law state and a Gospel state by the analogy of serving a new master; now here he speaks using the analogy of being married to a new husband.

2. Our first marriage was to the law. The law of marriage is binding until the death of one of the parties, no matter which, and no longer. For this Paul appeals to his readers themselves, as people who know the law (v. 1): *I speak to those that know the law.* Many of the Christians at Rome had been Jews and were therefore familiar with the law. One has some hold on knowing people. *The law hath power over a man as long as he liveth*; in particular, the law of marriage has power. The obligation of laws extends no further, and the condemnation of laws extends no further; death is the finishing of the law. The severest laws can only kill the body, and after that there is nothing more that they can do. So while we were alive to the law, we were under its power. Such is the law of marriage (v. 2): the woman is bound to her husband during life; she cannot marry another man. If she does, she will be considered an adulteress (v. 3). This is how we were married to the law (v. 5): *When we were in the flesh*, then *the motions of sins which were by the law did work in our members*; we followed the stream of sin, and the law was as an imperfect dam, which made the stream swell higher. Our desire was toward sin, and sin ruled over us (Ge 3:16; 4:7). We were under a law of sin and death, as the wife is under the law

of marriage, and the result of that marriage was fruit that resulted in death. Sinful desire, having been conceived by the law, *bringeth forth sin, and sin, when it is finished, bringeth forth death* (Jas 1:15). This is the offspring that springs from this marriage to sin and the law. This comes of the sinful passions working in our bodies.

3. Our second marriage is to Christ.

3.1. We are freed by death from our obligation to the law as a covenant (v. 3). *You are become dead to the law* (v. 4). He does not say, "The law is dead"—but, *You are dead to the law*; it all comes to the same thing. We are *delivered from the law* (v. 6); our obligation to it is made void, like the obligation to a deceased husband. Paul then speaks of the law as being dead as far as it was a law of mastery to us: *that being dead wherein we were held.* It is dead; it has lost its controlling power, and it has done so (v. 4) *by the body of Christ*, that is, by the sufferings of Christ in his body, by his crucified body. We are dead to the law by our union with the mystical body of Christ, having nothing more to do with it than dead servants have to do with their master's burden.

3.2. We are married to Christ. On the day we believe, we enter a life of dependence on him and duty to him: *Married to another, even to him who is raised from the dead.* Just as our dying to sin and the law is in conformity to the death of Christ and the crucifying of his body, so our devotion to Christ in *newness of life* (6:4) is in conformity to the resurrection of Christ. We are married to the raised, exalted Jesus. We are married to Christ:

3.2.1. So *that we may bring forth fruit unto God* (v. 4). One purpose of marriage is fruitfulness. The great purpose of our marriage to Christ is our fruitfulness in love, grace, and every good work. Just as our old marriage to sin bears fruit toward death, so our second marriage, to Christ, bears fruit for God. Good works are the children of the new nature. Whatever we may profess or claim, no fruit is produced for God until we are married to Christ. This distinguishes the good works of believers from the good works of hypocrites and self-justifiers: those done by believers are done in union with Christ.

3.2.2. So *that we may serve in newness of spirit, and not in the oldness of the letter* (v. 6). We must continue to serve, but it is a service that is perfect freedom, whereas the service of sin was perfect drudgery. A renewal in our spirits must be brought about by the Spirit of God, and we must serve in that. *Not in the oldness of the letter*; that is, we must not rest in mere external services. The letter is said to kill with its slavery and terror (2Co 3:6), but we have been rescued from that burden so that we may serve God without fear, in holiness and righteousness (Lk 1:74–75). We can now worship in the inner sanctuary behind the curtain, no longer in the outward court.

Verses 7–14

What shall we say then? Is the law sin? He has said so much about the contribution of the law to the controlling power of sin that what he said might easily be misinterpreted as a reflection on the law, and to prevent this he shows the excellence of the law as a guide. Notice:

1. The excellence of the law in itself. Far be it from Paul to reflect badly on the law.

1.1. It is *holy, just, and good* (v. 12). Laws are like those who made them. God, the great Lawgiver, is holy, just, and good, and so his law must also be so. The law commands holiness, encourages holiness, and is itself holy, because it conforms to the holy will of God, the origin of holiness. The law is just, because it is consistent with the rules of equity and right reason: the ways of the

Lord are right (Hos 14:9). The law is good in its intention; it was given for the good of the human race. It makes its observers good. Wherever there is true grace, there is an agreement that the law is holy, just, and good.

1.2. *The law is spiritual* (v. 14), not only in regard to its effect but also in regard to its extent; it reaches our spirits. It is given to us, whose main part is spiritual; the soul is the best part, and so the law must be a law to our soul. The law of God is above all other laws in that it is a spiritual law. The law of God takes notice of the sin considered in the heart. *We know this*: wherever there is true grace, there is an experience of the knowledge of the spirituality of the law of God.

2. The great advantage he has found through the law.

2.1. It was revealing: *I had not known sin but by the law* (I would not have known what sin really was except through the law) (v. 7). Just as what is straight reveals what is crooked, so there is no way of coming to that knowledge of sin which is necessary for our repentance except by comparing our hearts and lives with the law. Paul especially came to the knowledge of the sinfulness of coveting. By coveting and sinful desire he means sin living in us. He came to recognize this sin when the law said, *Thou shalt not covet.* The law spoke in the spiritual sense and meaning. He knew that coveting was sin and was very sinful. Paul had a very quick and piercing judgment, but he never reached the right knowledge of indwelling sin until the Spirit made it known to him through the law. There is nothing about which natural humanity is blinder than about original corruption. This is how *the law is a schoolmaster to bring us to Christ.* This is how, through the commandment, sin is recognized as sin (v. 13); it appears in its true colors. This is how, by the commandment, sin *becomes exceedingly sinful*: it is seen to be so.

2.2. It was humbling (v. 9): *I was alive.* He thought himself to be in a very good condition, self-confident of the goodness of his state. This is how he was *once*, in former times, when he was a Pharisee, and the reason was that he was then *without* (apart from) *the law.* Though brought up at the feet of Gamaliel (Ac 22:3), a teacher of the law, though himself a strict observer of it, nevertheless, he was *without the law.* He had the letter of the law, but he did not have its spiritual meaning—he had the shell but not the kernel. He had the law in his hand and in his head, but he did not have it in his heart. *But when the commandment came*—not only to his eyes but to his heart—*sin revived* (sprang to life), as the dust in a room rises, or appears, when sunshine is let into the room. Paul then saw in sin what he had never seen before: sin in its terrible consequences, sin with death at its heels, sin and its inherited curse. "The Spirit, by the commandment, convinced me that I was in a state of sin, and in a state of death because of sin." The law has this excellent use: it is a lamp and a light (Ps 119:105); it opens the eyes (Ps 19:8) and prepares the way of the Lord (Isa 40:3; Mal 3:1; Mt 3:3).

3. The bad use his corrupt nature made of the law.

3.1. *Sin, taking occasion by the commandment, wrought in me all manner of concupiscence* (sin, seizing the opportunity given by the commandment, produced in me all kinds of covetous desire) (v. 8). Paul had in him all kinds of covetous desires; concerning the righteousness of the law, he was blameless (Php 3:6), but he was still aware of all kinds of covetous desires. It was sin that performed it, indwelling sin, and it seized the opportunity given by the commandment. The corrupt nature would not have swelled and raged so much if it had not been for the restraints of the law. Ever since Adam ate the forbidden fruit, we have all been fond of forbidden paths. *Without* (apart from) *the law sin was dead*, like a snake in winter, which the sunbeams of the law stimulate and irritate.

3.2. It *deceived men*. Sin deceives sinners, and it is a fatal deception (v. 11). It deceived Paul and put him to death.

3.3. It *worked* (produced) *death in me by that which is good* (v. 13). There is nothing so good that a corrupt and evil nature cannot pervert it and make an opportunity for sin. Now in this, sin is recognized as sin. The worst thing that sin does is to pervert the law. This is how the commandment, which was ordained to life, proved to lead to death (v. 10). The same word that leads to life in some leads to death in others (2Co 2:16). The same sun that makes the garden of flowers more fragrant makes the rubbish heap more offensive. The way to prevent this trouble is to submit to the commanding authority of the law of God.

Verses 14–25

Here is a description of the conflict between grace and corruption in the heart. It may be applied in two ways: (1) To the struggles that are in a convicted but still unregenerate soul, in whose voice some think Paul is speaking when he uses the first person singular in this passage. (2) To the struggles that are in a renewed, sanctified soul, which is still in a state of imperfection, as others think. There is a great debate about which the apostle is writing about here.

1. We may apply it to the struggles that are felt in a convicted soul, one that is still in a state of sin, *knowing the Lord's will* but not doing it (2:18), continuing to be a slave to controlling sinful desires. The apostle said earlier (6:14), *Sin shall not have dominion, because you are not under the law, but under grace*, and to prove this he shows here that someone under the law but not under grace may be under the controlling power of sin. The law may reveal sin and convict of sin, but it cannot conquer and subdue sin. It reveals the defilement but will not wash it away. It makes a person weary and burdened (Mt 11:28), burdened with sin, but it provides no help toward shaking off that burden; this help is to be found only in Christ. The law may make a person cry out, *O wretched man that I am! Who shall deliver me?* but leave them chained. Now a soul advanced so far by the law is in a good position to enter a state of freedom through Christ, but many rest here and go no further. It is possible for a person to go to hell with their eyes open, carrying with them a self-accusing conscience—even while remaining in the service of the Devil. That person may *consent to the law that it is good*, may have within them that bears witness against sin and seeks holiness, but all this is overpowered by the dominant love of sin. Drunkards and immoral people have some faint desires to leave their sins and yet persist in them. It is very hard to imagine why, if this was what the apostle meant, he would speak all along about himself, and not only so, but also in the present tense.

2. It seems rather to be understood as referring to the struggles that are maintained between grace and corruption in sanctified souls. That there are remnants of indwelling corruption even where there is a living motivation of grace is beyond dispute. If we say that we have no sin, we deceive ourselves (1Jn 1:8, 10). That true grace strives against these sins and corruptions is also certain (Gal 5:17): *The flesh lusteth against the spirit, and the spirit against the flesh, and these are contrary the one to the other, so that you cannot do the things that you would.*

His intention is to further open up the nature of sanctification, to show that it does not achieve sinless perfection in this life. We will not be accused of what we sincerely strive against, and through grace ultimate victory is certain. Notice:

2.1. What he complains about—the remnant of indwelling sinfulness. The law is insufficient to justify even a regenerate person, which is not the fault of the law, but of our own corrupt nature, which cannot fulfill the law. Notice the details of this complaint.

2.1.1. *I am carnal* (unspiritual), *sold under sin* (v. 14). Even where there is spiritual life, worldly, unspiritual affections still linger; so far may a person be *sold under sin*.

2.1.2. *What I would, that I do not*, but *what I hate, that do I* (v. 15); and to the same effect (vv. 19, 21): *When I would do good, evil is present with me*. He presses forward toward perfection, but he acknowledges he has not already *attained*, nor is he *already perfect* (Php 3:12). He wants to do the will of God perfectly, but his corrupt nature draws him another way: it is like the bias of a ball in lawn bowling, which draws the ball aside even when it is thrown straight.

2.1.3. *In me, that is, in my flesh, dwelleth no good* (v. 18). As far as the flesh goes, no good is to be expected, any more than one would expect to have grain grow well on a rock (Mt 13:5–6). As the new nature cannot commit sin (1Jn 3:9), so the flesh, the old nature, cannot perform a good duty. How could it? For *the flesh serveth the law of sin* (v. 25).

2.1.4. *I see another law in my members warring against the law of my mind* (v. 23). Now that Christ has set up his throne in Paul's heart, it is only the rebellious members of the body that are the instruments of sin—all the corrupt nature that is the seat not only of sensory but also of more refined sinful desires. This corrupt disposition and inclination wars against the law of the mind, the new nature, and is as great a burden and grief to the soul as the worst drudgery and captivity could be. *It brings me into captivity.* And to the same effect (v. 25): *With the flesh I serve the law of sin*; that is, the unregenerate part of him is continually working toward sin.

2.1.5. We have his general complaint (v. 24): *O wretched man that I am! Who shall deliver me from the body of this death?* The thing he complains about is a body of death, which is either the body of flesh, which is mortal and dying, or the body of sin, the corrupt nature, which leads to death. This corrupt nature is as troublesome to Paul as if he had a dead body tied to him. This made him cry out, *O wretched man that I am!* If we had been required to speak about Paul, we would have said, "How blessed you are." But in his own account he was wretched because of the corruption of nature. *Who shall deliver me?* He speaks as one who is sick of it. The remnants of indwelling sin are a very heavy burden to a gracious soul.

2.2. What he comforts himself with. Three things comfort him:

2.2.1. His conscience witnesses for him that he has a good motive ruling and prevailing in him, nevertheless. The rule of this good motive that he has is the law of God, which he speaks about here from three different points of view

2.2.1.1. *I consent unto the law that it is good* (v. 16). Here is the approval of the judgment. Wherever there is grace, there is not only a dread of the severity of the law but also an agreement that the law is good. This is a sign that the law is written on the heart (Jer 31:33). The sanctified judgment agrees not only that the law is equitable but also that it is excellent.

2.2.1.2. *I delight in the law of God after the inward man* (v. 22). He delighted not only in the promises of the word but also in the precepts and prohibitions of the word. All who are born again truly delight in the law of God; they are never better pleased than when heart and life are in the strictest conformity to the law and will of God. *After the inward man;* that is:

2.2.1.2.1. The mind or rational faculties. The soul is the inner being, and that is the seat of gracious delights, which are sincere and serious, but secret.

2.2.1.2.2. The new nature. The new man is called the *inner man* (Eph 3:16).

2.2.1.3. *With the mind I myself serve the law of God* (v. 25). It is not enough to agree with the law and delight in the law; we also must serve the law. This is the situation of Paul's mind; this is how it is with every sanctified, renewed mind.

2.2.2. The fault lies in that corruption of his nature which he really does mourn and strive against: *It is no more I that do it, but sin that dwelleth in me.* He mentions this twice (vv. 17, 20), not to excuse himself from the guilt of sin, but so that he will not sink into despair, because he takes comfort from the covenant of grace, which accepts the willingness of the spirit and has provided pardon for the weakness of the flesh. He professes here his dissent from the law of sin. "It is not I; it is against my mind that it is done."

2.2.3. His great comfort lies in Jesus Christ (v. 25): *I thank God, through Jesus Christ our Lord.* In the middle of his complaints, he breaks out into praise. It is a special remedy against fears and sorrows to praise God often: many poor, drooping souls have found it to be so. *Who shall deliver me?* he says (v. 24), as one who is at a loss for help. He finally finds an all-sufficient friend: Jesus Christ. If it were not for Christ, the sin that lives in us would certainly be our ruin. It is Christ who purchased our rescue at just the right time (5:6). *Blessed be God that giveth us this victory through our Lord Jesus Christ!* (1Co 15:57).

CHAPTER 8

The apostle turns in this chapter to the comfort of the Lord's people. It is the will of God that his people be comforted. Many of the people of God have therefore found this chapter to be a spring of inexpressible comfort to their souls, living and dying. This chapter contains three things: 1. The particular expressions of Christians' privileges (vv. 1–28). 2. The basis of these in predestination (vv. 29–30). 3. The apostle's triumph in these in the name of all the saints (vv. 31–39).

Verses 1–9

1. The apostle begins here with one significant privilege of true Christians and describes the character of those to whom it belongs: *There is therefore now no condemnation to those that are in Christ Jesus* (v. 1). This is his triumph after that depressing complaint and conflict. He makes the complaint his, but humbly transfers the comfort to all true believers.

1.1. It is the inexpressible privilege of all those who are in Christ Jesus that there is, therefore, now no condemnation for them. He does not say, "There is no accusation against them," for there is, but the accusation is thrown out. He does not say, "There is nothing in them that deserves condemnation," for there is, and they see it and acknowledge it, but it will not be their ruin. He does not say, "There is no cross, no suffering for them," for there may be. Rather, he says that there is *no condemnation.* Now this arises from their being *in Christ Jesus;* because of their union with him through faith they are kept in this way.

1.2. The undoubted character of all those who are in Christ Jesus is that *they walk not after the flesh, but after the Spirit.* Notice that they are characterized in terms of their walk, not any one particular act.

2. Paul now illustrates this truth in vv. 2–9, showing how we may fulfill this character. Notice:

2.1. How these privileges become ours—the privilege of justification, the privilege of sanctification.

2.1.1. The law could not do it (v. 3). It could neither justify nor sanctify. The law made nothing perfect (Heb 7:19): *it was weak.* Yet that weakness was not through any defect in the law, but *through the flesh,* through the corruption of human nature. In a case of failure, the law, as a covenant of works, made no provision, and so left us as it found us.

2.1.2. *The law of the Spirit of life in Christ Jesus* does it (v. 2). The covenant of grace in Christ is a treasure of merit and grace, and it is from that that we receive pardon and a new nature, *are freed from the law of sin and death,* from both the guilt and the power of sin. We are under another covenant, under the *law of the Spirit,* the law that gives the Spirit, spiritual life to qualify us for eternal life. The foundation of this freedom is laid in Christ's undertaking for us (1Co 3:11), about which Paul speaks in v. 3: *God sending his own Son.* When the law failed, God provided another way. Christ comes to do what the law could not do. The best explanation of this verse is Heb 10:1–10. Notice:

2.1.2.1. How Christ appeared: *in the likeness of sinful flesh.* It does not say he appeared sinful, but that he appeared in the likeness of that flesh. He took on himself the nature that was corrupt, though he remained completely separate from its corruptions. It was a great condescension that the One who was God would be made in the likeness of flesh, but much greater that the One who was holy would be made in the likeness of sinful flesh. *And for sin.* God sent him *in the likeness of sinful flesh, and* as a sacrifice *for sin.* The Greek has only *for sin,* but "as a sacrifice" is to be supplied.

2.1.2.2. What was done through this appearance of his: sin *was condemned.* For all who are Christ's, both the condemning and the controlling power of sin is broken. Although it lives and remains, its life in the saints is no greater than that of a condemned evildoer. The condemning of sin saved sinners from condemnation. Christ was made sin for us (2Co 5:21). When Christ was condemned, sin was condemned in his flesh. In this way, he made satisfaction to divine justice and made way for the salvation of sinners.

2.1.2.3. The good effects of this on us (v. 4): *That the righteousness of the law might be fulfilled in us.* A righteousness of satisfaction for disobedience to the law is fulfilled by the crediting of Christ's perfect righteousness. A righteousness of obedience to the law is fulfilled in us when by the Spirit the law of love is written on the heart, because that love is the fulfilling of the law (13:10). *Us, who walk not after the flesh, but after the Spirit.* This is the description of all those who enjoy this privilege.

2.2. How we may fulfill this character (v. 5).

2.2.1. By looking to our minds, by examining what we have our minds set on, the things of the flesh or the things of the Spirit. The favor of God, the welfare of the soul, and the concerns of eternity are the things of the Spirit. People are according to what their minds are set on. The mind is the forge of thoughts. Which way do the thoughts move with greatest pleasure? The mind is the seat of wisdom. Are we more informed about the world or about our souls? *They mind the things of the flesh.* The same Greek verb, *phroneo,* is translated *savour* in Mt 16:23: *they savor the things of the flesh.* It is important to note what we savor, which truths, news, comforts, we truly relish. Now, to warn us against this worldly-mindedness, Paul shows its great misery and compares it with the indescribable comfort of spiritual-mindedness.

2.2.1.1. Worldly-mindedness is death (v. 6). It is the death of the soul, for it is the soul's separation from God, and the life of the soul consists in union and fellowship with God. An unspiritual, worldly soul is dead—dead as a soul can be. Death includes complete misery; worldly, unspiritual souls are miserable. But to be *spiritually minded* is *life and peace.* A sanctified soul is a living soul, and that life is peace; it is a contented life. It is life and peace in the other world as well as in this. Spiritual-mindedness is eternal life and peace begun.

2.2.1.2. It is enmity toward God (v. 7), and this is worse than the first evil. To be dead is bad, but to be his enemy is to be a devil of a person. The condition referred to here is not only the separation of the soul from God, but the opposition of the soul to God. To prove this, Paul urges that worldly-mindedness *is not subject to the law of God, neither indeed can be.* The holiness of the law of God and the unholiness of the worldly, unspiritual mind are as irreconcilable as light and darkness. The *carnal* (worldly, unspiritual) person may, by the power of divine grace, be made subject to the law of God, but the *carnal mind* never can be; this must be broken and expelled. Paul concludes, therefore (v. 8), *Those that are in the flesh cannot please God.* Pleasing God is our highest purpose, and those who are in the flesh must fall short of it; they cannot please him—in fact, they cannot do anything but displease him.

2.2.2. By asking whether we have the Spirit of God and Christ or not (v. 9): *You are not in the flesh, but in the Spirit.* It refers to our being overcome and subdued by one of these principles. Now the great question is whether we are in the flesh or in the Spirit, and how can we come to know? Why, by asking whether the Spirit of God dwells in us. The Spirit visits many people who are unregenerate, but he dwells in all who are sanctified. Will we ask our own hearts this question, "Who lives, rules, and keeps house here?" Paul adds to this a general rule of testing: *If any man has not the Spirit of Christ, he is none of his.* To be Christ's is a privilege and honor claimed by many who have no share in the matter (Ac 8:21). No one is his except those who have his Spirit. The attitude of our souls must conform to Christ's example. Those who belong to him are moved and guided by the Holy Spirit of God. Having the Spirit of Christ is the same as having the Spirit of God live in us. All who are guided by the Spirit of God as their rule conform to the spirit of Christ as their example.

Verses 10–16

Here are two more excellent benefits that belong to true believers.

1. Life. The happiness we have is not merely a negative happiness, that of not being condemned; it is also positive (vv. 10–11): *if Christ be in you.* Now we are told here what happens to the bodies and souls of those in whom Christ is.

1.1. We have to say that *the body is dead;* it is a frail, mortal, and dying body. In the middle of life, we are in death: even if our bodies are very strong, they are as good as dead, and this is *because of sin.* It is sin that kills the body. It seems to me that if there were no other argument, love for our bodies would make us hate sin, because it is such an enemy to our bodies.

1.2. The spirit, however, is life. The life of the saint lies in the soul, while the life of the sinner goes no further than the body. When the body dies, *the spirit is life.* To the saints, death is simply the freeing of the heaven-born spirit from the burden and load of this body, so that it may be fit to share in eternal life. This was *because of righteousness.* The righteousness of Christ that is credited to the saints protects the soul from death; the righteousness of Christ that is inherent in them preserves it, and at death raises it, making it fit to share in the inheritance of the saints in light (Col 1:12).

1.3. There is a life reserved for the poor body eventually as well: *he shall also quicken your mortal bodies* (v. 11). The body will be reunited to the soul and clothed with a glory that is fit for it. Two great assurances of the resurrection of the body are mentioned:

1.3.1. The resurrection of Christ: *he that raised up Christ from the dead shall also quicken.* Christ rose as the forerunner of all the saints (1Co 15:20). It is because of the power of Christ's resurrection that we will rise.

1.3.2. The indwelling of the Spirit. The same Spirit who raises the soul now will raise the body soon: *by his Spirit that dwelleth in you.* The Spirit, breathing on dead and dry bones, will make them live (Eze 37:1–10), and even in their flesh the saints will see God (Job 19:26). From this the apostle infers how much it is in our duty to live according to the Spirit, not the flesh (vv. 12–13). He mentions two motives here:

1.3.2.1. We are not indebted to the flesh. We are certainly bound to clothe, feed, and take care of the body as a servant to the soul in the service of God, but no further. We do not have an obligation to it. We have an obligation to Christ and the Spirit: we owe them our all. See 1Co 6:19–20.

1.3.2.2. Consider what will come at the end of the course of our life. *If you live after the flesh, you shall die;* that is, die eternally. True dying is in fact the soul's dying; the death of the saints is merely a sleep. But on the other hand, *You shall live*—that is the true life—*if you through the Spirit mortify the deeds of the body.* We cannot do it without the Spirit working it in us, and the Spirit will not do it without our doing our part. We are confronted by this dilemma: we must either displease the body or destroy the soul.

2. The *Spirit of adoption* (vv. 14–16).

2.1. All who are Christ's are brought into the relation of children of God (v. 14). Notice:

2.1.1. The One who owns them: they are *led by the Spirit of God,* not driven as wild animals, but led as reasonable creatures. It is the undoubted character of all true believers that they are led by the Spirit of God. In their obedience they follow that guidance and are sweetly led into all truth and all duty.

2.1.2. Their privilege: *they are the sons of God,* recognized and loved by him as his children.

2.2. Those who are the *sons of God* have the Spirit:

2.2.1. To produce in them the nature of children.

2.2.1.1. *You have not received the spirit of bondage again to fear* (v. 15). We may understand this to refer to:

2.2.1.1.1. The spirit of slavery that the Old Testament church was under because of the darkness of that age. "You are no longer living in that age; you have not received that spirit."

2.2.1.1.2. The spirit of slavery that many of the saints themselves were under at their conversion. At that time the Spirit himself was a spirit of slavery to the saints: "But," the apostle says, "this is over with you."

2.2.1.2. Rather, you *have received the Spirit of adoption.* It is God's right, when he adopts, to give a spirit of adoption — the nature of children. A sanctified soul bears the image of God as the child bears the image of the father. *Whereby we cry, Abba, Father.* Praying is here called *crying.* Children who cannot speak express their desires by crying. Now, the Spirit teaches us to come to God as a Father in prayer. Why both *Abba* and *Father* (Greek *pater*), since *Abba* means "father"? Because Christ said this in prayer (Mk 14:36). It denotes an affectionate, endearing boldness. Little children, begging their parents, can say little except "Father, Father," and that is a suitable enough expression. It also shows that the adoption is common to both Jews and Gentiles, since both an Aramaic and a Greek word are used.

2.2.2. To testify that they stand in the relation of children (v. 16). *Beareth witness with our spirit.* There are many who speak peace to themselves to whom the God of heaven does not speak peace. Those who are sanctified, however, have God's Spirit testifying with their spirits. This testimony always agrees with the written word and is therefore always based on sanctification. The Spirit testifies of the privileges of children to no one who does not have the nature and disposition of a child.

Verses 17–25

Having described the freedom from condemnation, the life, and the Spirit of adoption that belong to believers, here the apostle describes a fourth branch of their happiness, namely, an entitlement to future glory. *If children, then heirs* (v. 17). In earthly inheritances this rule does not hold; only the firstborn are heirs. But heaven is an inheritance that all the saints inherit. They do not come into it by any merit of their own, but as heirs, purely by the act of God. Their present state is a state of education and preparation for the inheritance.

1. But what is the nature of their inheritance? They are:

1.1. *Heirs of God.* The Lord himself is the saints' inheritance (Ps 16:5). Seeing and enjoying God make up the inheritance the saints are heirs to.

1.2. *Joint-heirs with Christ.* True believers *shall inherit all things* (Rev 21:7). Those who now share in the Spirit of Christ as his brothers and sisters will, as his brothers and sisters, share in his glory. Lord, *what is man,* that you exalt us in this way (Ps 8:4–5)! Now this future glory is the reward of present sufferings, the fulfillment of present hopes. It is:

2. The reward of the saints' present sufferings, *If so be that we suffer with him* (v. 17), or *forasmuch as we suffer with him.* The state of the church in this world is always an afflicted state. Paul tells them that they are suffering with Christ and will be glorified with him. Although we may lose some things for him, in the end we will not, we cannot, lose by him. The Gospel is filled with assurances of this. Paul holds up the balance (v. 18), significantly comparing the two.

2.1. In one scale he puts the *sufferings of this present time.* The sufferings of the saints last no longer than the present; they are light troubles, lasting only for a moment (2Co 4:17). On the sufferings, therefore, he writes *tekel,* "weighed in the balance and found light" (Da 5:25, 27).

2.2. In the other scale he puts the glory, and finds that to be an exceeding and eternal weight (2Co 4:17): *glory that shall be revealed.* In our present state we fall short not only in the enjoyment of that glory but also in the

knowledge of it (1Co 2:9; 1Jn 3:2), but it will be revealed. It surpasses all that we have ever seen and known. There is something to come, something behind the curtain (Heb 6:19–20), that will surpass them all. This glory *shall be revealed in us,* not only revealed to us, to be seen, but also revealed in us, to be enjoyed.

2.3. He concludes that the sufferings are *not worthy to be compared with the glory.* They cannot deserve that glory, and if suffering for Christ will not deserve it, much less will doing anything for him. The sufferings are relatively slight and short, and concern only the body, but the glory is rich and great, concerns the soul, and is eternal. Paul *reckons* this, like an accountant balancing an account. He first sums up what has been spent for Christ in the sufferings of this present time, and he finds it comes to very little; he then adds up what has been made secure for us by Christ in the glory that will be revealed, and he finds this to be an infinite sum. Who, then, will be afraid to suffer for Christ, who, as he is in advance of us in suffering, will not be in arrears in rewarding us? Paul could reckon not only by skill but also by experience, because he knew both, and when he considered both, he gave this judgment. The disgrace of Christ is of greater value to those who are looking ahead to the reward (Heb 11:26).

3. The fulfillment of the saints' present hopes and expectations (v. 19). Just as the saints are suffering for this reward, so they are also waiting for it. He will fulfill to his servants that word by which he has given them hope (Ps 119:49). If hope deferred makes the heart sick, surely when the longing is fulfilled, it will be a tree of life (Pr 13:12). Now Paul notices an expectation of this glory:

3.1. In the creation (vv. 19–22). A glory that the whole creation is so earnestly expecting and longing for must indeed be a great, transcendent glory. We understand the *creature* here to mean the whole frame of nature, the whole creation. We may understand the apostle's sense in these four verses to be:

3.1.1. There is a present futility to which the creation, because of human sin, is made subject (v. 20). When Adam and Eve sinned, the ground was cursed for their sake (Ge 3:17–19), and with it the whole creation: *under the bondage of corruption* (v. 21). The creation is sullied and stained; much of the beauty of the world has gone. It is not the least part of the creatures' futility and bondage that they are used, or abused rather, by people as instruments of sin. Moreover, this is *not willingly,* not of their own choice. All the creatures desire their own perfection. When they become instruments of sin, it is not by their own choice. They are held captive in this way not because of any sin of their own, but for human sin: *by reason of him who hath subjected the same.* These poor creatures bear this burden in the hope that it will not remain forever. We have reason to pity the poor creatures who for our sin have become subject to futility.

3.1.2. *The creation,* that is, all the creatures, *groan and travail in pain together* under this futility and decay (v. 22). Sin is a burden on the whole creation. There is a general outcry of the whole creation against human sin.

3.1.3. The creation will be *delivered from this bondage into the glorious liberty of the children of God* (v. 21). The creatures will no longer be subject to futility and decay. This lower world will be renewed. When there is a new heaven, there will be a new earth.

3.1.4. The creation, therefore, earnestly expects the *manifestation* (revelation) *of the children of God* (v. 19). Now the saints are God's hidden ones (Ps 83:3), and the wheat seems lost in a heap of worthless chaff, but then they will be revealed. The children of God will then appear in their true colors. This redemption of the creation is reserved until then. The whole creation longs for this, and it may serve as a reason why now good people should be merciful to their animals (Pr 12:10).

3.2. In the saints, who are new creations (2Co 5:17; Gal 6:15) (vv. 23–25). Notice:

3.2.1. The basis of this expectation in the saints. It is our having received *the firstfruits of the Spirit*. Grace is the firstfruits of glory; it is glory begun. Because we have received such clusters of grapes in this desert, we must long for the full grape harvest in the heavenly Canaan. *Not only they*—not only the parts of the creation that are incapable of receiving the firstfruits of the Spirit—but even we must long for something more and greater. In having the firstfruits of the Spirit, we have what is very precious, but we do not have all we want to have. *We groan within ourselves* with silent groans, the kind that pierce heaven soonest of all. Or, "We groan among ourselves." It is the unanimous vote of the whole church. Present receipts and comforts are consistent with very many groans, groans like those of a woman in the throes of labor—groans that are signs of life, not death.

3.2.2. The object of this expectation: *the adoption, to wit, the redemption of our body*. The resurrection is called here *the redemption of the body*. At the resurrection the body will be rescued from the power of death and the grave and made like the glorious body of Christ (Php 3:21; 1Co 15:42). This is called *the adoption*.

3.2.2.1. It is the adoption revealed before all the world, before angels and human beings. By the resurrection from the dead, the saints will be, as Christ was, declared to be the *sons of God with power* (1:4).

3.2.2.2. It is the adoption perfected and completed. The children of God have bodies as well as souls, and until those bodies are brought into the glorious freedom of the children of God, the adoption is not perfect.

3.2.3. How this corresponds with our present state (vv. 24–25). We do not now possess our happiness: *We are saved by hope*. Our reward is out of sight. Those who want to have dealings with God must do so on trust. Faith concerns the promise; hope concerns what is promised. Faith is the evidence of things unseen, hope the expectation of them. Faith is the mother of hope. *We do with patience wait*. In hoping for his glory we need patience. Our way is rough and long, but the One who is coming will certainly come (Heb 10:37), and so, although he seems to delay, it is good for us to wait for him.

Verses 26–28

Here are two more privileges to which true Christians are entitled:

1. The help of the Spirit in prayer. Notice:

1.1. Our weakness in prayer: *We know not what we should pray for as we ought*. We do not know what to ask for in our requests. We are shortsighted. We are like foolish children, who are ready to cry out for fruit before it is ripe and fit for them. Nor do we know how to pray as we should. The apostle speaks of this in the first person, including himself among the rest: *We know not*. If such a great saint as Paul did not know what to pray for, what little reason have we to go about that duty in our own strength!

1.2. The help the Spirit gives us. He *helps our infirmities*; the word refers especially to our infirmities in praying. The Spirit in the Word helps. The Spirit in the heart helps; this is why the Holy Spirit was poured out. The Spirit "takes hold with us," helps as one helps a person who wants to lift a heavy object, by lifting up with them at

the other end. We must not sit back and expect the Spirit to do everything; when the Spirit goes before us, we must also stir ourselves. We cannot do without God, and he will not work without us. The *Spirit itself makes intercession for us*. Christ intercedes for us in heaven, and the Spirit intercedes for us in our hearts; so graciously has God provided encouragement for the praying remnant. Now this intercession that the Spirit makes is:

1.2.1. *With groanings that cannot be uttered*. There may be praying in the Spirit where a word is not spoken. It is not the rhetoric or eloquence of our prayers, but their faith and fervency, that the Spirit, as an intercessor, produces in us. *Cannot be uttered*; we do not know what to say or how to express ourselves. When we can only cry, *Abba, Father*, with a holy, humble boldness, this is the work of the Spirit.

1.2.2. *According to the will of God* (v. 27). The Spirit interceding in us always melts our wills into the will of God.

1.3. The guaranteed success of these intercessions: *He that searcheth the heart knoweth what is the mind of the Spirit* (v. 27). To hypocrites, whose religion lies entirely in their tongue, nothing is more terrible than that God searches the heart. To a sincere Christian, who makes heart work of their duty, nothing is more encouraging. God will hear and answer those desires that we lack words to express. He knows what we need before we ask. Christ said, "Whatever you ask the Father according to his will he will give you." But how will we learn to ask according to his will? Why, the Spirit will teach us that.

2. The working of all providences for the good of those who are Christ's (v. 28). Despite all these privileges, we see believers surrounded by many adversities; yet the Spirit's intercession is always effective in that everything is working together for their good. Notice:

2.1. The characterization of the saints, who enjoy this privilege: *They love God*. Those who love God make the best of all he does and accept everything with a good attitude. *They are the called according to his purpose*, not according to anything we have deserved, but according to God's own gracious purposes.

2.2. The privilege of the saints, that *all things work together for good to them*. All the providences of God are theirs—merciful providences, suffering providences. They are all for good; perhaps for temporal good, but at least for spiritual and eternal good. Either directly or indirectly, every providence leads to the spiritual good of those who love God. Things *work together*, as different ingredients in a medicine work in harmony to fulfill the intention. "He works all things together for good," as some read it. All this *we know*—know it as certain, from the word of God, from our own experience, and from the experience of all the saints.

Verses 29–30

Having considered the many ingredients of the happiness of true believers, the apostle comes here to represent the basis of them all, which he locates in predestination. He sets before us here the order of the causes of our salvation, a golden chain that cannot be broken. It contains four links:

1. *Whom he did foreknow, he also did predestinate to be conformed to the image of his Son*. All whom God intended to bring to glory and happiness as their end were ordained by his decree to follow grace and holiness as their way. God's foreknowledge of the saints is the same as that eternal love with which he is said to have loved them (Jer 31:3). *Whom he did foreknow*, that is, whom he

intended to be his friends and favorites. Now those whom God foreknew in this way he predestined to be conformed to the likeness of Christ.

1.1. Holiness consists in our conformity to the likeness of Christ. This conforming takes in the whole of sanctification. Christ is the exact representation of his Father (Heb 1:3), and the saints are conformed to the likeness of Christ. In this way, God's love is restored to us and God's likeness is renewed on us (Col 3:10).

1.2. All whom God has foreknown from eternity with favor he has predestined to conform to this likeness. It is not we who can make ourselves conform to Christ. No one can know their election except by their conformity to the likeness of Christ, because all who are chosen are chosen for sanctification.

1.3. What is chiefly intended here is the honor of Jesus Christ, that he would be the *first-born among many brethren*, that is, that Christ would have the honor of being the great model, that he would have the supremacy (Col 1:18). We thank God that there are many brothers and sisters; although they seem only a few in one place at one time, nevertheless, when they all come together, there will be very many of them. In spite of all the opposition of the powers of darkness, Christ will be the firstborn among very many brothers and sisters.

2. *Whom he did predestinate, those he also called*, not only with the external call but also with the internal and effective call. The external call comes only to the ear, but the effective call comes to the heart. The call is effective when we respond to it, and we respond by coming when the Spirit draws us, persuading and enabling us to accept Christ in the promises. It is an effective call away from self and earth to God and Christ, away from sin and futility to grace and holiness. This is the Gospel call. *Them he called*, so that the purpose of God according to election would stand.

3. *Whom he called, those he also justified.* All who are effectively called are accepted as righteous through Jesus Christ. They are no longer dealt with as criminals, but acknowledged and loved as friends and favorites.

4. *Whom he justified, those he also glorified.* Because the power of corruption has been broken in the effective calling, and the guilt of sin removed in justification, nothing can come between that soul and glory. It is spoken of as something already done, because of its certainty: *He glorified*; he *hath* saved us (2Ti 1:9). In the eternal glorification of all the elect, God's intention of love has its complete fulfillment. This was what he aimed at all along—to bring them to heaven. Have they been chosen? It is for salvation. Have they been called? It is to his kingdom and glory. Have they been born again (Jn 3:3, 7)? It is to an incorruptible inheritance (1Pe 1:4). Are they suffering? It is to produce for them this exceeding and eternal weight of glory (2Co 4:17). The author of all these is the same One. God himself has undertaken to do it from first to last. This is a mighty encouragement to our faith and hope.

Verses 31–39

The apostle closes with a note of holy triumph in the name of all the saints. *What shall we then say to these things?* What use shall we make of all that has been said? He speaks as one wondering at the height and depth, the length and breadth, of the love of Christ, which passes knowledge (Eph 3:18–19). The more we know of other things, the less we wonder at them, but the further we are led to know the mysteries of the Gospel, the more we are moved with wonder at them. If ever Paul rode in a trium-phant chariot on this side of heaven, it was here. He issues a challenge here. He dares all the enemies of the saints to do their worst: *If God be for us, who can be against us?* That *God is for us* includes everything. All that he is, has, and does is for his people. If that is so, *who can be against us*, so as to succeed against us? Even if they are very strong, very many, what can they do? As long as God is for us, and we remain in his love (Jn 15:10), we can defy all the powers of darkness. Let Satan do his worst; he is chained. Who then dares to fight against us, as long as God himself is fighting for us? And this is what *we*, too, *say to these things.*

1. We have supplies that are ready for all our needs (v. 32): *He that spared.* Who can cut off our streams as long as we have a fountain to go to? Notice:

1.1. What God has done for us, on which our hopes are built: *He spared not his own Son.* Now we can know that he loves us, because he has not withheld his Son. If nothing less will save human beings, then, rather than let them perish, the Father says, "Let him go"—though he had been at the Father's very side (Jn 1:18). God the Father *delivered him up for us all*, not only for our good but also in our place, as a sacrifice of atonement for sin. He did not *spare his own Son that served him*, so that he could spare us.

1.2. What we can expect, therefore, that he will do: he will *with him freely give us all things*. It is implied that he will give us Christ, for other things are given *with him*. He will graciously give us all things with him, all good things, and we should not desire more (Ps 34:10). Freely, without reluctance; freely, without recompense. *How shall he not?* Can it be imagined that he would give such a great gift for us when we were enemies (5:10), and then deny us any good thing, now that we are friends and children? The One who has prepared a crown and kingdom for us will be sure to give us enough to pay the expenses on our way to it.

2. We have an answer ready for all accusations and a security against all condemnations (vv. 33–34): *Who shall lay any thing* (bring any charge)? This is enough: *It is God that justifieth.* If God justifies, this answers all. We may challenge all our accusers, therefore, to come and bring their charges. This overthrows them all; it is God, the righteous, faithful God, who justifies. *Who is he that condemneth?* Even if they cannot substantiate the charges, they will still be ready to condemn, but we have a plea ready, one that cannot be overruled. *It is Christ that died.* It is by virtue of our share in Christ and our union with him that we are kept safe, that is:

2.1. By his death: *It is Christ that died.* He paid our debt by the merit of his death.

2.2. By his resurrection: *yea, rather, that has risen again.* This is a much greater encouragement. Therefore the apostle mentions it with a *yea, rather.* If Christ had died and not risen again, we would have remained where we were.

2.3. By his sitting at the right hand of God: he is *even at the right hand of God*, and this is a powerful encouragement to us in reference to all accusations, that we have such a friend in the court of heaven. Our friend is himself the judge.

2.4. By the intercession he makes there. While there, he is not unconcerned about us, not forgetful of us, but *making intercession.* Is this not plentiful matter to encourage us? What room is left for doubting and disquiet? Some understand the accusation and condemnation here spoken of as what the suffering saints met with from other people. The early Christians were accused of many black crimes. The ruling powers condemned them. "It does not matter," says the apostle; "as long as we are in the right as we stand at God's bar, it is not important how we stand in a human court."

3. We have good assurance that we will be preserved and will continue in this blessed state (vv. 35–39). The fears of the saints that they might lose their hold of Christ are often very discouraging and unsettling; here is what can silence their fears: nothing can separate them. We have here:

3.1. A daring challenge to all the enemies of the saints to separate them, if they can, from the love of Christ. *Who shall?* None (vv. 35–37). Because God has revealed his love by giving his own Son for us, can we imagine that anything else could divert or hinder that love? Notice here:

3.1.1. The present adversities of Christ's beloved ones mentioned—that they meet with *tribulation*, are in *distress*, are followed by *persecution* from an angry, evil world that always hated those whom Christ loved (Jn 15:19), suffer *famine*, are starved with *nakedness*, and are exposed to the greatest *perils*, with the *sword* of the magistrate drawn against them. Can a blacker, more dismal case be imagined? It is illustrated (v. 36) by a passage quoted from Ps 44:22, *For thy sake we are killed all the day long*, that is, continually exposed to and expecting the fatal blow. *Accounted as sheep for the slaughter*; persecutors think no more of killing a Christian than they do of butchering a sheep.

3.1.2. The inability of all these things to separate us from the love of Christ. All this will not cut the bond of love and friendship between Christ and true believers.

3.1.2.1. Christ does not, will not, love us the less for all this. All these troubles are neither a cause nor evidence of the lessening of his love. These things separate us from the love of other friends. When Paul was brought before Nero, everyone abandoned him. But then the Lord stood by him (2Ti 4:16–17). Whatever persecuting enemies may rob us of, they cannot rob us of the love of Christ, and so, even if they do their worst, they cannot make true believers miserable.

3.1.2.2. We do not, will not, love him the less for this, because we do not think that he loves us any less. True Christians love Christ no less even if they suffer for him; they never think the worse of Christ even if they lose everything for him.

3.1.3. The triumph of believers in this (v. 37): *Nay, in all these things we are more than conquerors.*

3.1.3.1. We are *conquerors*. It is a strange way of conquering, but it was Christ's way. Faith and patience are a surer and a nobler way of conquest than fire and the sword. The enemies have sometimes confessed themselves to be confounded and overcome by the invincible courage and faithfulness of martyrs.

3.1.3.2. We are *more than conquerors*. People are more than conquerors when they conquer:

3.1.3.2.1. With little loss. Many conquests are dearly bought, but what do suffering saints lose? Why, they lose what gold loses in the furnace, nothing but dross.

3.1.3.2.2. With great gain. The plunder is exceedingly rich; glory, honor, and peace, a crown of righteousness that does not fade away (1Pe 5:4). In this, the suffering saints have triumphed. As adversities increase, comforts overflow (2Co 1:5). Those who have gone smiling to the stake and stood singing in the flames—these were more than conquerors.

3.1.3.3. It is only *through Christ that loved us*. We are conquerors not in our own strength but in the grace that is in Christ Jesus. We are conquerors because of Christ's victory. We have nothing to do but to pursue the victory and divide the spoils, and so are more than conquerors.

3.2. A direct and positive conclusion of the whole matter (Ecc 12:13): *For I am persuaded* (vv. 38–39). He lists here all those things that might come between Christ and believers, and concludes that it cannot be done.

3.2.1. *Neither death nor life*, neither the fear of death nor the hope of life. We will not be separated from that love in either death or life.

3.2.2. *Nor angels, nor principalities, nor powers.* The good angels do not wish to do it, the bad will not be permitted to do it, and neither can. The good angels are committed friends; the bad are restrained enemies.

3.2.3. *Nor things present, nor things to* come—neither the awareness of present troubles nor the fear of future troubles. Time will not separate us, and neither will eternity, from the love of Christ, whose favor is an integral part of both present and future things.

3.2.4. *Nor height, nor depth*—neither the height of prosperity nor the depth of disgrace, nothing from heaven above, nothing on earth below.

3.2.5. *Nor any other creature*—anything that can be named or thought of. It will not, it cannot, separate us from the love of God that is in Christ Jesus our Lord. Nothing does it, can do it, except sin. This is the basis of the firmness of the love, because Jesus Christ, in whom he loves us, is the same yesterday, today, and forever (Heb 13:8).

CHAPTER 9

What happens to the Jews, especially those of them who do not accept Christ or believe the Gospel? What becomes of the promise made to the fathers, which passed the inheritance of salvation on to the Jews? Paul grants that the consequence of the rejection of the unbelieving Jews follows from his teaching, but he tries to soften it (vv. 1–5). He denies, however, that it follows from this that the word of God is ineffective (v. 6), and he proves the denial in the rest of the chapter, which also serves to illustrate the great doctrine of predestination.

Verses 1–5

Here the apostle solemnly professes a great concern for the Jewish people and nation—that he is greatly troubled in his heart that so many of them are enemies of the Gospel. He has *great heaviness and continual sorrow* for this. It is wise to soften as far as possible those truths that sound harsh: dip the nail in oil, and it will drive home better. He introduces his words with this affectionate profession so that they will not think he gloats over the rejected Jews. He is so far from desiring the woeful day (Jer 17:16) that he prays against it most passionately.

1. He asserts it with a solemn pleading (v. 1): *I say the truth in Christ*, "I speak it as one of God's people, children who will not lie (Isa 63:8). I appeal to Christ about it." He also appeals to his own conscience. What he is going to assert is a secret; it is about a sorrow within his own heart to which no one is a competent witness except God and his own conscience; *I have great heaviness* (great sorrow) (v. 2). Even the mention of it was unpleasant.

2. He backs it up with a very serious oath that he is ready to take out of love for the Jews. *I could wish*; he does not say, "I do wish," for it was not a proper means appointed for such an end, but if it were, *I could wish that myself were accursed from Christ for my brethren*—a very high expression of zeal and affection for his com-

patriots. Love tends to be so bold, adventurous, and self-denying. Because the glory of God's grace in the salvation of many is to be preferred to the welfare and happiness of a single person, Paul would be content to forgo all his own happiness to purchase theirs.

2.1. He would be content to be cut off from the land of the living as a curse. The Jews thirsted for his blood, persecuting him as the most terrible person in the whole world. And yet he says, "I am willing to bear all this, and a great deal more, for your good. Your unbelief and rejection create in my heart an anguish that is so much greater than all troubles that I could look on them not only as tolerable, but even as desirable, compared to seeing this rejection."

2.2. He would be content to be excommunicated from the society of the faithful if that would do them any good. He could wish that he were forgotten among the saints. He would be content to have his name buried in oblivion or reproach for the good of the Jews.

2.3. He could be content to be cut off from all his share of happiness in Christ if that would be a means of their salvation.

3. He gives us the reason for this affection and concern.

3.1. Because of their relationship to the church: *My brethren, my kinsmen, according to the flesh.* Although they have been bitter against him on all occasions, he still speaks about them respectfully. It shows him to be a man of forgiving spirit. *My kinsmen.* Paul was a Hebrew of the Hebrews (Php 3:5). We should be especially concerned for the spiritual good of our relatives. We must give a particular account concerning our usefulness to them.

3.2. Especially because of their relationship with God (vv. 4–5): *Who are Israelites,* set apart by visible church privileges, many of which are mentioned here:

3.2.1. *The adoption,* not the saving kind of adoption, which gives an entitlement to eternal happiness, but the external kind.

3.2.2. *And the glory,* the many signs of the divine presence and guidance: the cloud, the *Shechinah,* the distinctive favors shown them—these were the glory.

3.2.3. *And the covenants*—the covenant made with Abraham and renewed with his descendants on several occasions. These still concerned Israel.

3.2.4. *And the giving of the law.* It is a great privilege to have the law of God among us, and it is to be counted so (Ps 147:19–20).

3.2.5. *And the services of God.* They had the ordinances of God's worship among them—the temple, the altars, the priests, the sacrifices, the festivals. While other nations were worshiping and serving sticks, stones, demons, and all kinds of other idols of their own invention, the Israelites were serving the true God in his appointed way.

3.2.6. *And the promises* relating to the Messiah and the Gospel age. Notice that the promises accompanied the giving of the Law and the service of God, for the encouragement of the promises is to be found in obedience to that Law and in seeing to that service.

3.2.7. *Whose are the fathers* (v. 5), Abraham, Isaac, and Jacob, who stood so high in the favor of God. It was for the fathers' sake that they were taken into the covenant (11:28).

3.2.8. But the greatest honor of all was that *of them as concerning the flesh Christ came.* This was the great privilege of the Jews, that Christ came from their family. Mentioning Christ, Paul writes a great word about him, that he is *over all, God blessed for ever.* It is a very full proof of the godhead of Christ; he is not only over all, as Mediator, but *God blessed forever* (God over all, forever praised). It was similarly to the honor of the Jews that if *God blessed forever* would be a man, he would be a Jew.

Verses 6–13

The rejection of the Jews by the establishment of the Gospel age in no way invalidated the word of God's promise to the patriarchs: *Not as though the word of God hath taken no effect* (v. 6). We are not to think of any word of God as ineffective: nothing that he has spoken does or can fall to the ground; see Isa 55:10–11. This is to be understood especially as referring to the promise of God, which to a wavering faith may come to seem very doubtful, but is not, cannot be, made null and void. Now the difficulty is to reconcile the rejection of the unbelieving Jews with the word of God's promise. Paul does this in four ways:

- By explaining the true meaning and intention of the promise (vv. 6–13).
- By asserting the absolute sovereignty of God (vv. 14–24).
- By showing how this rejection of the Jews and inclusion of the Gentiles were foretold in the Old Testament (vv. 25–29).
- By establishing the true reason for the Jews' rejection (v. 30–33).

In this paragraph the apostle explains the true meaning and intention of the promise. When we misunderstand the promise, it is hardly surprising if we are ready to quarrel with God about the fulfillment. When God said he would be *a God to Abraham, and to his seed,* he was not referring to all Abraham's natural descendants. He intended it with a limitation. Just as it was assigned from the beginning to Isaac and not to Ishmael, to Jacob and not to Esau—but for all this the word of God was not made of no effect—so now the same promise is assigned to believing Jews who embrace Christ, and although this removes many who refuse Christ, the promise is not therefore invalidated.

1. He lays down the proposition that *they are not all Israel who are of Israel* (v. 6), *neither because they are the seed of Abraham are they all children* (v. 7). Not all who are Israel in name and profession are really Israel. Grace does not run in the blood.

2. He proves this by examples. Some of Abraham's descendants were chosen, and others not. God there acted according to the purpose of his own will. Paul specifies:

2.1. The case of Isaac and Ishmael. Both of them were offspring of Abraham, but only Isaac was taken into covenant with God, and Ishmael rejected. For this, Paul quotes Ge 21:12, *In Isaac shall thy seed be called,* because the covenant was to be established with Isaac (Ge 17:19). Since God was the benefactor who had blessings to bestow according to that great word, he was free to determine on whose head they would rest, and accordingly he settled them on Isaac. Paul explains this further (vv. 8–9):

2.1.1. The natural children are not, as such, because of their natural relation to Abraham, the children of God, because then Ishmael would have had a good claim. This remark would have hit home with the unbelieving Jews. They had confidence in the flesh (Php 3:3). Ishmael was a physical descendant, representing those who expect justification and salvation by their own strength and righteousness.

2.1.2. The *children of the promise are counted for the seed* (are regarded as Abraham's offspring). Those who have the privilege of being regarded as Abraham's offspring do not have it because of any merit of their own, but purely because of the promise. Isaac was a child of promise; Paul proves this in v. 9. He was also conceived and born by virtue of the promise, and so was a type of those who are now regarded as that offspring, namely, true believers, who are born not of the natural descent, nor of human decision or a husband's will, but of God (Jn 1:13).

2.2. The case of Jacob and Esau (vv. 10–13), which is much stronger. In the case of Ishmael and Isaac, there was a difference before Ishmael was driven out: Ishmael was of a fierce disposition and had mocked or persecuted Isaac (Ge 21:9). But the case of Jacob and Esau was not so; they were both the sons of Isaac by one mother. The distinction was made between them by the divine purpose before they were born or had committed any good or evil. Both lay struggling alike in their mother's womb, and then it was said, *The elder shall serve the younger, that the purpose of God according to election might stand*—so that this great truth would be established, that God chooses some and refuses others by his own absolute and sovereign will. Paul further illustrates the distinction made between Jacob and Esau by a quotation from Mal 1:2–3, where it is said, not about Jacob and Esau but about the Edomites and Israelites, their descendants, *Jacob have I loved, and Esau have I hated*. The people of Israel were taken into the covenant, while the Edomites were rejected. God put a distinction between those two nations, which both descended from the bodies of Abraham and Isaac, just as in the beginning a distinction was made between Jacob and Esau.

2.2.1. Some understand it as referring to the election and rejection of conditions or qualifications. Just as God chose Isaac and Jacob and rejected Ishmael and Esau, so he could and did choose faith to be the condition of salvation and reject the works of the law.

2.2.2. Others understand it as referring to the election and rejection of particular individuals—some loved, and others hated, from eternity. But the apostle speaks about Jacob and Esau not in their own persons, but as ancestors. Nor does God condemn any merely because he wants to, without any reason taken from what they themselves have deserved.

2.2.3. Others understand it, therefore, as referring to the election and rejection of people considered as a whole. Paul's intention is to justify God—his mercy and his truth—in calling the Gentiles while he allowed the obstinate part of the Jews to persist in their unbelief. The choosing of Jacob the younger and the preferring of him to Esau the elder, so crossing hands (Ge 48:14), was to show that the Jews, though the natural descendants of Abraham, would be set aside, and the Gentiles, who were like the younger brother, would be included in their place. The Jews had for many ages been the favorites of heaven. Now that the Gospel was preached, Christian churches—and in the course of time Christian nations—became their successors in God's favor.

Verses 14–24

The apostle here undertakes to maintain the absolute sovereignty of God in dealing with people. Here God is to be considered as an owner and benefactor, giving people such grace and favor as he has decided in and by his secret and eternal will. Now this part of Paul's discourse is in answer to two objections.

1. It might be objected, *Is there unrighteousness with God?* The apostle is shocked at the mere thought of this: *God forbid!* Far be it from us to think such a thing. Paul denies this conclusion and proves the denial:

1.1. With respect to those to whom God shows mercy (vv. 15–16). The reason he quotes the Scripture he does (Ex 33:19) is to show God's sovereignty in dispensing his favors (Ex 33:19): *I will be gracious to whom I will be gracious*. All God's reasons of mercy come from within himself. He dispenses his gifts to those to whom he wants to, without giving us any reason. The expression is emphatic, and the repetition makes it more so: *I will have mercy on whom I will have mercy*. God will do what he wishes. God's mercy endures forever (1Ch 16:34, 41; 2Ch 5:13; etc.) because its reason is drawn from within himself; his gifts and callings are therefore irrevocable. Paul concludes from this (v. 16), *It is not of him that willeth*. The glory for God's goodness is not to be ascribed to even the most generous desire of human beings, or to their most diligent work, but purely to the free grace and mercy of God. In Jacob's case it was *not of him that willeth, nor of him that runneth*, but only the mercy and grace of God. The reason why the unworthy, undeserving Gentiles are called, while most of the Jews are left to perish in unbelief, is not that those Gentiles were more deserving or better disposed to receive such a favor, but because God's free grace made that difference. Such is the way of God's grace toward all who share in it, because he is found by those who did not seek him (Isa 65:1).

1.2. With respect to those who perish (v. 17). God's sovereignty is shown here in the example of Pharaoh. Notice:

1.2.1. What God did with Pharaoh. He raised him up, as in general he raises up sinners, makes them for himself, even for a day of disaster (Pr 16:4); he raises them up in outward prosperity, external privileges.

1.2.2. What he intended in it: *that I might show my power in thee*. By all this, God would serve the honor of his name by revealing his power.

1.2.3. Paul's conclusion about both of these (v. 18). *He hath mercy on whom he will have mercy, and whom he will he hardeneth*. The various dealings of God must be seen in the light of his absolute sovereignty. He is indebted to no one; his grace is his own. None of us has deserved it; in fact, we have all justly forfeited it a thousand times. Those who are saved have only God to thank, and those who perish have only themselves to blame. We are committed to do all we can for the salvation of all we come into contact with, but God is committed no further than he has been pleased to commit himself, namely, that he will receive, and not drive out, those who come to Christ. Did he have mercy on the Gentiles? It was because he wanted to have mercy on them.

2. It might be objected, *Why doth he yet find fault? For who hath resisted his will?* (v. 19). He might well find fault if people refused to fulfill the terms on which such a salvation is offered; because the salvation is so great, the terms could not be hard. But when God withholds distinguishing and prevenient grace from some, gives effective grace to some and denies it to others before they do anything, why does he find fault with those to whom he denies it? Paul answers this objection in some detail:

2.1. By reproving the objector (v. 20): *Nay but, O man*. This objection is not fitting for a created being to bring against the Creator, for human beings to bring against God. Notice how contemptibly Paul speaks of human beings when they come to argue with God their Maker: "*Who art thou*, you who are so foolish, so incompetent a judge of God's purposes? Are you able to fathom such depths?" *That repliest against God*. We should submit to him, not talk back to him, fly in his face, or accuse him of foolishness.

2.2. By seeing everything in the light of God's sovereignty. We are the thing formed, and he is the One who forms, and we are not to accuse his wisdom in ordering and arranging us into a certain form or figure. God's sovereignty over us is fitly illustrated by the power that the potter has over the clay; compare Jer 18:6.

2.2.1. Paul gives us the comparison (v. 21). Out of any given lump, the potter may make either a fashionable object or a contemptible one, and here he acts arbitrarily.

2.2.2. He applies the comparison (vv. 22–24). God forms two kinds of objects out of the great lump of the fallen human race:

2.2.2.1. *Vessels of wrath.* In these God has willed to show his wrath. God will make it clear that he hates sin. He will also make his power known. In order to do this, God *endured them with much long-suffering*—exercised a great deal of patience toward them—and so they became *fitted for destruction*, fitted by their own sin and self-hardening. The reigning corruption and evil of the soul are its preparation for hell.

2.2.2.2. *Vessels of mercy.* The happiness shown to the saved remnant is the fruit not of their goodness—they have none—but of God's mercy. Objects of honor must acknowledge themselves to be objects of mercy for all eternity. Notice:

2.2.2.2.1. What he intends for them: to *make known the riches of his glory,* that is, of his goodness, for God's goodness is his greatest glory (Ex 33:18–19). God reveals his glory, his goodness, in the preservation and supply of all the creation; the earth is full of his goodness (Ps 119:64; 104:24). When he wants to demonstrate the riches of his goodness, he does so in the salvation of the saints.

2.2.2.2.2. What he does for them: he *prepares them to glory.* This is God's work. We can destroy ourselves quickly enough, but we cannot save ourselves. Sinners prepare themselves for hell, but it is God who prepares saints for heaven. Do you want to know who these *vessels of mercy* are? Those whom he has called (v. 24), because those whom he predestined, he also called with an effective call (8:30), and these not only from the Jews but also from the Gentiles. The question now is not whether one is from the descendants of Abraham, but whether one is called according to his purpose (8:28).

Verses 25–29

The apostle here shows how the rejection of the Jews and the inclusion of the Gentiles were foretold in the Old Testament. The Jews would no doubt willingly refer to the Old Testament. Now he shows how this was spoken of there:

1. By the prophet Hosea. The Gentiles had not been the people of God. "But," God says, "*I will call them my people,* make them such and acknowledge them as such, despite all their unworthiness." Former badness is no barrier to God's present grace and mercy. *And* call *her beloved which was not beloved.* Those whom God calls his people he calls "my loved one": he loves those who are his own. *In the place where it was said . . . , there shall they be called.* Wherever they are scattered over the face of the earth, God will acknowledge them. *Behold, what manner of love!* (1Jn 3:1). All his saints have this honor (Ps 149:9).

2. By the prophet Isaiah, who speaks of the rejecting of many of the Jews, in two places:

2.1. One is Isa 10:22–23, which speaks about the saving of a remnant, that is, only a remnant. It is in no way strange for god to abandon to ruin a great many of the

descendants of Abraham but also maintain his word of promise to Abraham in full force and effect. This is suggested in the supposition that the number of children of Israel was as the sand of the sea. Only a remnant, however, will be saved, for many are called, but few are chosen (Mt 20:16). We are told, from the prophet (v. 28), that in this salvation of the remnant:

2.1.1. God will complete the work: *He will finish the work.* When God begins a work, he will complete it (1Sa 3:12), whether in ways of judgment or ways of mercy. As for God, his work is perfect (Dt 32:4; 2Sa 22:31). "He will finish the account" (v. 28, margin). God has taken an account of people, and he will finish the account, calling in as many as belong to the election of grace (11:5), and then the account will be finished.

2.1.2. He will finish it quickly. Now he will *cut it short;* he will *make short work on the earth* (v. 28). But he will cut it short *in righteousness.* When people cut short, they commit wrong; when God cuts short, it is always in righteousness. *The work*—"the word," the law—was very long under the Old Testament. Our duty now, under the Gospel, is summed up in much less space than it was under the law; religion can now be summed up more briefly. With us, contractions tend to confuse things, but it is not so in this case. Although the work will be cut short, it is clear and plain, and because it is short, it is easier.

2.2. The other quotation is from Isa 1:9, where the prophet showed how God would preserve a remnant. It was not strange for God to leave most of the Jewish people to ruin and to reserve for himself only a small remnant, and they must not be amazed if he did so now. Notice:

2.2.1. What God is. He is *the Lord of sabaoth,* that is, the Lord of Hosts. When God keeps a remnant for himself, he acts as Lord of Hosts. When God keeps a remnant for himself, it is an act of almighty power and infinite sovereignty.

2.2.2. What his people are; they are *a seed,* a small number. But they are a useful number. It is a wonder of divine power and mercy that any are saved, because even those who are left to be a seed would have perished with the rest if God had dealt with them according to their sins.

Verses 30–33

Here the apostle establishes the true reason for the reception of the Gentiles and the rejection of the Jews. There was a difference in how they sought, and that was why they had different success. He concludes like an orator: *What shall we say then?*

1. Notice about the Gentiles:

1.1. How they had been separated from righteousness: they had not pursued it. God was *found of those that sought him not* (Isa 65:1). Here we see how God delights to give grace in his sovereignty and absolute rule.

1.2. How they obtained that righteousness, nevertheless: by *faith,* by accepting Christ, believing in Christ. They obtained it by the shortcut of believing sincerely in Christ, for which the Jews had been beating about the bush in vain for a long time.

2. Notice about the Jews:

2.1. How they missed their objective: they *followed after the law of righteousness* (v. 31). As many as stood by their old Jewish principles and ceremonies, accepting the shadows now that the reality had come—these fell short of acceptance with God.

2.2. How they mistook their way, which was the cause of their missing the objective (vv. 32–33). They sought, but not in the right way. *Not by faith*, not by depending on Christ, submitting to the terms of the Gospel, which were the very life and goal of the law. Rather, they sought by the *works of the law*. This was the *stumbling-stone at which they stumbled*. They could in no way be reconciled to the message of Christ, which directed them to expect justification through the goodness of another. Christ himself is a stumbling block to some, and to show this, Paul quotes Isa 8:14; 28:16. It is sad that Christ should be set for the fall of any, but it is so (Lk 2:34). He was set for the fall of the unbelieving Jews. However, there is still a remnant who do believe in him, and they *shall not be ashamed*. Their hopes and expectations of justification through him will not be disappointed, as are the hopes of those who expect justification through the law. The unbelieving Jews have no reason to quarrel with God for rejecting them; they had a fair offer made to them on Gospel terms, which they did not accept. If they perish, they have only themselves to blame.

CHAPTER 10

We may reduce this chapter to two great truths: 1. That there is a great difference between the righteousness of the law, which the unbelieving Jews were devoted to, and the righteousness of faith offered in the Gospel (vv. 1–11). 2. That there is no difference between Jews and Gentiles; the Gospel sets them both on the same level (vv. 12–21).

Verses 1–11

The scope of the apostle in this part of the chapter is to show the great preeminence of the righteousness of faith above that of the law in order to persuade the Jews to believe in Christ.

1. Paul professes here his deep affection for the Jews (vv. 1–2), offering them good wishes and a good witness. He offers:

1.1. Good wishes (v. 1), that they will be saved. Although Paul preaches against them, he still prays for them. This, he says, is *his heart's desire and prayer*, which shows:

1.1.1. The strength and sincerity of his desire. It is *his heart's desire*; it is not a formal compliment, as good wishes are with many, only from the mouth, but his real, heartfelt desire. The soul of prayer is the heart's desire. Cold desires will lead to denials.

1.1.2. The offering of this desire to God. It is not only his desire but also his prayer. There may be desires in the heart but no prayer. To wish and will, if that is all our desires are, is not praying.

1.2. A good witness, as a reason for his good wish (v. 2): *I bear them record that they have a zeal of God.* The unbelieving Jews were the bitterest enemies Paul had in the world, but he describes them in the best terms the truth will bear. Love teaches us to give the words and actions of others the best interpretation that they will bear. We should take notice of what is commendable even in bad people. *They have a zeal of God.* Their opposition to the Gospel is from a motive of respect for the law. There is such a thing as a blind and misguided zeal: such was that of the Jews.

2. He shows here the fatal mistake that the unbelieving Jews are guilty of. Their zeal is *not according to knowledge*. It is true that God gave them the law for which they are so zealous, but they should have known by the appearance of the promised Messiah that an end had been put to it. He gave the most convincing evidence possible that he was the Messiah, yet they would not acknowledge him,

but shut their eyes to the clear light, so that their zeal for the law was blind. Paul shows this further in v. 3, where we may notice:

2.1. The nature of their unbelief. They *have not submitted themselves to the righteousness of God*. Unbelief is nonsubmission to the righteousness of God. They *have not submitted*. In true faith, there is need for a great deal of submission.

2.2. The causes of their unbelief, and these are two:

2.2.1. Ignorance of God's righteousness. They did not consider how much we need a righteousness in which to appear before him. If they had, they would never have expected justification through their own works, as if they could satisfy God's justice.

2.2.2. Proud thoughts of their own righteousness: *going about to establish their own*—a righteousness of their own working out, by the "goodness"—or so they thought—of their works. They thought they did not need to be indebted to the goodness of Christ.

3. He shows here the foolishness of that mistake, how unreasonable it is, considering:

3.1. The subservience of the law to the Gospel (v. 4): *Christ is the end of the law for righteousness*. The purpose of the law was to lead people to Christ. The use of the law was to direct people so that they would find righteousness in Christ.

3.1.1. Christ is the end of the ceremonial law, because he is its perfection.

3.1.2. Christ is the end of the moral law in that he did what the law could not do (8:3). The aim of the law was to bring people to perfect obedience, and so to obtain for them justification. The law is not destroyed, but because full atonement has been made by the death of Christ for our disobedience to the law, the end has been reached, and now he justifies in another way. Christ is thus the end of the law, but only to *every one that believeth*.

3.2. The excellence of the Gospel above the law.

3.2.1. What is the righteousness that is through the law? He shows this (v. 5). Its thrust is, *Do, and live*. It acknowledges nothing as a righteousness that is sufficient to justify a person except the righteousness of perfect obedience. Here Paul quotes the Scripture (Lev 18:5), *You shall therefore keep my statutes and my judgments, which if a man do, he shall live in them*. The supposed action must be perfect and sinless, without the least disobedience or violation. Now, was it not extremely foolish of the Jews to remain so strictly faithful to this way of justification and salvation when a new and living way had been opened (Heb 10:20)?

3.2.2. What is that righteousness that is through faith (v. 6)? He describes it in the words of Moses in Dt 30:11–14, showing:

3.2.2.1. It is not at all hard or difficult. The way of justification and salvation contains no such depths or knots as may discourage us, and no insuperable difficulties accompany it.

3.2.2.1.*1*. We need not go up to heaven to inquire into the secrets of God's purposes. It is true that Christ is in heaven, but we can be justified and saved without going there.

3.2.2.1.2. We need not go down to the deep to take Christ out of the grave: *into the deep, to bring up Christ from the dead*. It is true that Christ was in the grave, and it is just as true that he is now in heaven, but we need not perplex ourselves with imagined difficulties. No, salvation is not put such a long way from us.

3.2.2.2. It is very clear and easy: *The word is nigh thee.* Christ is near you because the word is near you. It is in *thy mouth, and in thy heart.* The work you have to do lies within you. All that has to be done for us is already in our hands. Those who were under the law were to do everything themselves—*Do this, and live*—but the Gospel reveals that the greatest part of the work has already been done, and that what remains to be achieved in righteousness and salvation has been brought to our door, as it were. It is in our mouth—we are reading it daily; it is in our heart—we are, or should be, thinking about it daily. Yes, *the word of faith.* Now what is this word of faith? We have the gist of it in vv. 9–10. Notice:

3.2.2.2.*1.* What is promised to us: *thou shalt be saved.* It is salvation that the Gospel reveals and offers, a salvation of which the author is Christ, a Savior *to the uttermost* (Heb 7:25).

3.2.2.2.*2.* On what terms.

3.2.2.2.2.*1.* Two things are required as the conditions of salvation:

3.2.2.2.2.1.*1.* *Confessing the Lord Jesus*—openly professing a relationship with him and a dependence on him, standing by him forever. Our Lord Jesus emphasizes this confessing of him before human beings; see Mt 10:32–33. It was a very great deed, especially when the profession of Christ endangered life and all that is dear in this world, which was the case in the early times.

3.2.2.2.2.1.*2.* *Believing in the heart that God raised him from the dead.* The profession of faith with the mouth is a mockery if its power is not in the heart—if it is not rooted in a sincere assent to the Gospel revelation, especially concerning his resurrection, which is the fundamental article of the Christian faith.

3.2.2.2.2.*2.* This is further illustrated (v. 10), and the order inverted, because faith in the heart must come before there can be an acceptable confession with the mouth.

3.2.2.2.2.2.*1.* Concerning faith: it is *with the heart that man believeth,* which implies more than a mere assent of the understanding; it includes the submission of the will. This is *unto righteousness.* There is the righteousness of justification and the righteousness of sanctification. Faith leads to both.

3.2.2.2.2.2.*2.* Concerning profession: it is with *the mouth that confession* is made—confession to God in prayer and praise, confession to people by acknowledging the ways of God before others. This is said to be *unto salvation* because it is the fulfillment of the condition of that promise Jesus made in Mt 10:32. Justification by faith lays the foundation of our entitlement to salvation, but by confession we build on that foundation. We have here then a brief summary of the terms of salvation: we must give up to God our souls and our bodies—our souls in believing with the heart, and our bodies in confessing with the mouth. For this (v. 11) he quotes Isa 28:16: *Whosoever believeth on him shall not be ashamed.*

3.2.2.2.2.2.2.*1.* They will not be ashamed to acknowledge the Christ in whom they trust; those who believe in the heart will not be ashamed to confess with their mouth.

3.2.2.2.2.2.2.*2.* They will not be ashamed of their hope in Christ (1:16). They will never have cause to repent of the confidence they showed by putting such trust in the Lord Jesus.

Verses 12–21

There is no difference between Jews and Gentiles; they stand on the same level as regards acceptance with God. In Jesus Christ there is neither Greek nor Jew (Col 3:11). *There is no difference.*

1. God is the same to all: *The same Lord over all is rich unto all.* There is not one God to the Jews who is more kind, and another to the Gentiles who is less kind; rather, he is the same God to all. When he made known his name, *The Lord, the Lord God, gracious and merciful* (Ex 34:6), he showed not only what he was to the Jews but also what he is and will be to all his creatures who seek him: generous in dispensing his favors *to all that call upon him* (v. 12). Something must be done by us, and it is as little as can be: we must call on him. We have nothing to do but to receive through prayer.

2. The promise is the same to all (v. 13): *Whoever shall call.* Calling on the name of the Lord here stands for all practical religion. What is the life of a Christian but a life of prayer? Those who call on God with their whole hearts will be saved. It is simply "ask and have"; what more could we want? To illustrate this further, Paul shows:

2.1. How necessary it is for the Gospel to be preached to the Gentiles (vv. 14–15). This was what the Jews were so angry with Paul about. He shows how necessary it is to bring the Gentiles within the reach of the promise.

2.1.1. *They cannot call on him in whom they have not believed.* Unless they believe God is God, they will not call on him through prayer. The grace of faith is absolutely necessary for the duty of prayer; we cannot pray rightly without it. Those who come to God in prayer must believe (Heb 11:6).

2.1.2. *They cannot believe in him of whom they have not heard.* One way or another, the divine revelation must be made known to us before we can receive it and give our agreement to it; it is not born with us.

2.1.3. *They cannot hear without a preacher.* Somebody must tell them what they are to believe.

2.1.4. *They cannot preach except* (unless) *they be sent.* How can people act as ambassadors unless they have received both credentials and instructions from a sending ruler? It is God's prerogative to send out ministers. Only he can qualify people for and incline them toward the work of the ministry. But the competency for that qualification and the sincerity of that inclination must not be left for each person to judge concerning themselves. Rather, this matter must be submitted to the judgment of those who are presumed to be the most able judges and are empowered to set apart those they consider qualified and inclined. Moreover, those who are set apart in this way not only may but also must preach as those who are sent.

2.2. How welcome the Gospel should be to those to whom it is preached, because it shows the way to salvation (v. 15). For this Paul quotes Isa 52:7. Notice:

2.2.1. What the Gospel is: it is *the Gospel of peace.* Peace stands in general for all that is good, as it is explained here; it is *glad tidings of good things.* The things of the Gospel are truly good things, the best things, the best news that ever came from heaven to earth.

2.2.2. What the work of ministers is: to *bring these glad tidings,* to bring good news of peace. Every preacher is an evangelist in this sense.

2.2.3. How acceptable they should be, therefore, for their work's sake: *How beautiful are the feet,* that is, how welcome they are! Those who preach the Gospel of peace should see to it that their feet—their way of life—are beautiful; the holiness of ministers' lives is the beauty of their feet. *How beautiful,* namely, in the eyes of those who hear them. Those who welcome the message must love the messengers.

2.3. How a certain objection to all this is to be answered (v. 16): *But they have not all obeyed the Gospel.* All the Jews have not, all the Gentiles have not; by far the greater part of both remain in unbelief and disobedience. The Gospel is given to us not only to be known and believed but also to be obeyed. It is in no way strange, but it is very sad and uncomfortable, for the ministers of Christ to bring the report of the Gospel and not be believed.

2.3.1. Paul shows that the word preached is the ordinary means of producing faith (v. 17): *So then, though many who hear do not believe, those who believe have first heard. Faith cometh by hearing.* The beginning, progress, and power of faith are brought about by hearing. The word of God is therefore called *the word of faith.* God gives faith, but he uses the word as the instrument. *Hearing is by the word of God.* It is not hearing the enticing words of human wisdom that will befriend faith, but hearing the word of God.

2.3.2. He shows that those who will not believe the report of the Gospel when they hear it are left without excuse, *to the end* (v. 18).

2.3.2.1. The Gentiles have heard it (v. 18): *Have they not heard?* They have either heard the Gospel or at least heard of it. *Their sound went into all the earth*—the sound of the heavens declaring the glory of God (the apostle is quoting Ps 19:4), the sound of the Gospel; and not merely a confused sound, but their *words* have gone *unto the ends of the world.* The commission the apostles received is *Go you into all the world and preach to every creature* (Mk 16:15), *disciple all nations* (Mt 28:19), and they pursued that commission with indefatigable diligence and great success. It was to this end that the gift of tongues was poured out so plentifully on the apostles.

2.3.2.2. The Jews have also heard it (vv. 19–21). For this Paul appeals to two passages of the Old Testament. *Did not Israel know* that the Gentiles were to be called in? They should have known it from Moses and Isaiah.

2.3.2.2.1. One quotation is taken from Dt 32:21: *I will provoke you to jealousy.* The Jews not only had the offer; they had the right to refuse it. In all places where the apostles went, the Jews had the first offer, and the Gentiles had what was left over. If one would not accept it, then another would. Now this *provoked them to jealousy.* The Gentiles are called *no people* and *a foolish nation* here. However much there is of the knowledge and wisdom of the world, those who are not the people of God are a foolish people, a people without true understanding. Such was the state of the Gentile world, and yet they were made the people of God, and Christ to them was the wisdom of God (1Co 1:24). We can see what a provocation it was to the Jews to see the Gentiles taken into God's favor (Ac 22:22). It showed the great wickedness of the Jews that they were so enraged; God often makes people's sin their punishment. A person needs no greater plague than to be left to the impetuous rage of their own sinful desires.

2.3.2.2.2. Another quotation is taken from Isa 65:1–2, and in it Isaiah is very bold. Those who want to be found faithful need to be very bold. Those who are determined to please God must not be afraid of displeasing any human being. Isaiah speaks boldly and plainly:

2.3.2.2.2.1. About the prevenient grace and favor of God in the reception of the Gentiles (v. 20): *I was found of those that sought me not.* The prescribed method is, "Seek and find"; but this is a rule for us, not a rule for God, who is often found by those who do not seek. This is how he revealed himself to the Gentiles, by sending the light of the Gospel among them. Was not this our own particular situation? Did not God begin to move toward us in love, and reveal himself to us when we did not ask after him? Was not that a time of true love, often to be remembered with much thankfulness?

2.3.2.2.*2.2.* About the stubbornness and perversity of Israel (v. 21). Notice:

2.3.2.2.2.2.1. God's great goodness to them: *All day long I have stretched forth my hands.* Notice his offers: *I have stretched forth my hands,* offering them life and salvation. Holding out the hands is the gesture of those who seek an audience or acceptance. Christ was crucified with his hands stretched out. *Stretched forth my hands* offering reconciliation—"Come, let us shake hands and be friends"—and our duty is to give our hand to him. Notice his patience in making these offers: *All day long.* He waits to be gracious (Isa 30:18). He is patient for a long time, but he will not always be patient.

2.3.2.2.2.2.2. Their great badness to him. They were *a disobedient, gainsaying* (obstinate) *people,* not only *disobedient* to the call but also *gainsaying,* perversely quarreling with it. The Jews contradicted and blasphemed. It is a wonder of mercy in God that his goodness is not overcome by human badness, and it is a wonder of human evil that our badness is not overcome by God's goodness.

CHAPTER 11

It might be said, "Has God then rejected his people?" The apostle sets himself, therefore, to reply to this objection, and he does so in two ways: 1. He shows in detail what the mercy is that is mixed with this wrath (vv. 1–32). 2. He infers from this the infinite wisdom and sovereignty of God, with the adoration of which he concludes this chapter and subject (vv. 33–36).

Verses 1–32

The apostle proposes here a plausible objection that might be raised against God's way (v. 1): *Hath God cast away his people?* Is the rejection total and final? Will he no longer have a distinctive people for himself? Paul shows that a great deal of goodness and mercy is expressed along with this apparent harshness:

- Although some of the Jews are rejected, they are not all so.
- Although most of the Jews are rejected, the Gentiles are still taken in. And:
- Although the Jews are rejected at present, in God's appropriate time they will be taken into his church again.

1. Many of the Jews, it is true, have been rejected, but not all. Paul introduces such a supposition with a *God forbid.*

1.1. There is a chosen remnant of believing Jews who have obtained righteousness and life through faith in Jesus Christ (vv. 1–7). These are said to be those whom God *foreknew* (v. 2), and those whom he foreknew, he predestined (8:29). Here lies the basis of the difference. They are called the *election* (v. 7). Believers are the *election,* all those and only those whom God has chosen.

1.1.1. Paul shows that he himself is one of them: *For I also am an Israelite.* Paul was a chosen instrument (Ac 9:15), but he was of the *seed of Abraham.*

1.1.2. He suggests that as in Elijah's time, so now, this chosen remnant was really more and greater than one would think it was. Notice:

1.1.2.1. Elijah's mistake concerning Israel; he spoke as if he himself were the only faithful servant God had in the world. Paul refers to 1Ki 19:14, where—it is said here—*he maketh intercession to God against Israel.* A strange kind of intercession. "He deals with God against Israel," as it may read. In prayer, we make requests to God, have dealings with him. It is said of Elijah (Jas 5:17) that "he prayed in praying." We are likely to pray in praying when we pray as those who are dealing with God. In this prayer, Elijah spoke as if no one faithful were left in Israel except himself. Notice to what a low ebb the profession of religion may sometimes be brought. The powers of Israel were then persecuting powers: they had *killed thy prophets, and digged* (torn) *down thine altars*, and they *seek my life*. Most people in Israel were idolatrous: *I am left alone*. Those few who were faithful to God were not only lost in the crowd of idolaters but also crushed and driven into corners. "They have *digged down thine altars*." When altars were set up for Baal, it is hardly surprising if God's altars were torn down; the Israelites could not endure that constant testimony against their idolatry. This was Elijah's intercession *against Israel*. It is very sad for any person or people to have the prayers of God's people against them, for God embraces, and sooner or later will visibly acknowledge, the cause of his praying people.

1.1.2.2. The rectifying of this mistake (v. 4): *I have reserved*. Things are often much better with the church of God than wise and good people think. In times of general apostasy, there is usually a remnant who keep their integrity: all do not go the same way. When there is a remnant who keep their integrity, it is God who reserves that remnant for himself. It is his free and almighty grace that makes the difference between them and others. The remnant were *seven thousand*, an adequate number, but, when compared with the many thousands of Israel, a very small number. Now the description of this remnant is that *they had not bowed the knee to the image of Baal*. In court, city, and country, Baal was dominant, and most of the people, more or less, paid their respect to Baal. The best evidence of integrity is to swim against the tide when it is strong. It is commendable not to bow the knee to Baal when everyone else is (1Pe 2:19). Sober nonconformity is often the badge of true sincerity.

1.1.2.3. The application of this example to the situation in hand: *Even so at this present time* (vv. 5–7). As it has been, so it is now. In Elijah's time, there was a remnant, and so is there now. There was *a remnant*, a few out of many, a remnant of believing Jews. This is called *a remnant according to the election of grace* (v. 5). If the difference between them and others is made purely by the grace of God, as certainly it is—*I have reserved them*, he says, *to myself*—then it must be according to the election. We may notice about this remnant:

1.1.2.3.*1*. Where it comes from: from the free grace of God (v. 6), that grace which excludes works. Election is purely in accordance with his pleasure and his will (Eph 1:5). Paul's heart is so full of the freeness of God's grace that he turns aside to comment, *If of grace, then not of works*.

1.1.2.3.*2*. What it obtains, namely, what Israel sought in vain (v. 7): *Israel hath not obtained that which he seeketh for*—that is, justification and acceptance with God—but *the election have obtained it*. It is in the elect that the promise of God is fulfilled and God's ancient kindness for the people of Israel is remembered. The elect were the people whom God had in his eye in the purposes of his love.

1.2. *The rest were blinded* (v. 7). Some are chosen and called (Mt 20:16; 22:14), but others are left to perish in their unbelief. The Gospel, which to those who believed was the fragrance of life, was to the unbelieving the smell of death (2Co 2:16). The same sun softens wax and hardens clay. The rest *were blinded*; "they were hardened," according to some. They could neither see the light nor

feel the touch of Gospel grace. Blindness and hardness express the same spiritual insensitivity and foolishness. This seems a harsh teaching. To qualify it, therefore, Paul appeals to two witnesses from the Old Testament:

1.2.1. To Isaiah, who spoke about such a judgment in his day (Isa 6:9; 29:10). God gave Israel the *spirit of slumber*. They were under the power of a prevailing lack of concern, like people who are asleep. They had *eyes, that they should not see, and ears, that they should not hear*. They had the senses, but in regard to the things that would bring about their peace (Lk 19:42) they did not have the use of those faculties. They saw Christ, but they did not believe in him; they heard his word, but they did not accept it. They were no different than if they had neither seen nor heard anything or anyone. *Unto this day.* "Ever since Isaiah prophesied, this hardening work has been going on; some among them have been blind and senseless." It is still true of many of them, even to the day in which we live.

1.2.2. To David (vv. 9–10), quoted from Ps 69:22–23, where, having foretold the sufferings of Christ at the hands of his own people, the Jews, especially their giving him *vinegar to drink*, he foretold the fearful judgments of God on them for it: *Let their table become a snare*. The apostle applies this here to the present blindness of the Jews and the offense they took at the Gospel. David spoke here:

1.2.2.1. Of the ruin of their comforts: *Let their table be made a snare*, that is, as the psalmist explains it, "May what should be for their welfare be a trap to them." The curse of God will turn food to poison. Their food, which should nourish them, will choke them.

1.2.2.2. Of the ruin of their powers and faculties (v. 10), of their eyes going blind and their backs being bent over, so that they could not find the right way, and would not be able to walk along it even if they could find it. *They mind earthly things*. We have our eyes blinded if we are bent down in worldliness.

2. Another thing that qualifies this teaching of the rejection of the Jews is that although they have been rejected, the Gentiles are still taken in (vv. 11–14), which Paul applies by way of warning to the Gentiles (vv. 17–22).

2.1. The Jews' leftovers are a feast for the poor Gentiles (v. 11): "*Have they stumbled that they should fall?* Had God no other goal in rejecting them than their destruction?" Paul is shocked at this, as he usually is when anything is suggested that seems to reflect badly on the wisdom, righteousness, or goodness of God: *God forbid!* Not at all; *through their fall salvation is come to the Gentiles*. By the divine appointment it was so ordered that the Gospel was to be preached to the Gentiles when the Jews refused it. So it was in the history (Ac 13:46): *It was necessary that the word of God should first have been spoken to you, but, seeing you put it from you, lo, we turn to the Gentiles*. The Jews refused it, and so the offer was made to the Gentiles. See how Infinite Wisdom brings light out of darkness, good out of evil. To the same effect, Paul also says (v. 12), *The fall of them was the riches of the world*. The riches of the Gentiles were the great number of converts among them. True believers are God's jewels. V. 15 is also to the same effect: *The casting away of them is the reconciling of the world*. God's displeasure toward the Jews made way for his favor toward the Gentiles. God was in Christ *reconciling the world* (2Co 5:19). In every nation those who feared God and did what was right would be accepted by him (Ac 10:34–35).

2.2. He applies this teaching.

2.2.1. As a relative of the Jews, he offers a word of exhortation to stir them to receive the Gospel offer. God intended this in his favor to the Gentiles, to *provoke the Jews to jealousy* (v. 11), and, accordingly, Paul tries to reinforce it (v. 14): *If by any means I might provoke to emulation those who are my flesh.* "Will the despised Gentiles run away with all the comforts and privileges of the Gospel, and shall not we repent of our refusal, and now finally seek a share?" There is a commendable imitation in spiritual matters; why should we not be as holy and happy as any of our neighbors? The blessings are not lessened by the great number of those who share in them. *And might save some of them.* Notice that Paul's business was to save souls, but the most he promised himself was to save some. Of the many he dealt with, he could save only some. Ministers must think their effort well spent if they can be instrumental in saving even some.

2.2.2. As an apostle to the Gentiles, he offers a word of warning for them: "*I speak to you Gentiles.* You believing Romans, you hear what riches of salvation have come to you through the fall of the Jews, but make sure you do nothing to forfeit it." Paul uses this occasion, as he does others, to apply his discussion to the Gentiles, because he was the apostle to the Gentiles. This was the purpose of his extraordinary mission (Ac 22:21): *I will send thee far hence unto the Gentiles.* It should be our great and special care to do good to those who are our responsibility: we must especially be concerned for our own work. The Gentile world was a wider province, and the work to be done in it required a very able, courageous worker. God calls to special work those whom he either sees to be fit for it or makes fit for it. *I magnify my office.* There were those who hated it and jeered at Paul's office, and who hated and insulted him because of it. It is a sign of true love toward Jesus Christ to count as truly honorable that service for him which the world looks down on with scorn. The office of minister is an office to be *magnified.* Ministers are stewards of the mysteries of God (1Co 4:1), and for their work's sake they are to be highly regarded in love. He calls it *my office,* that is, "my ministry," "my service." It was not the prestige and power of an apostle, but the duty and work, that Paul was so much in love with. Next he encourages the Gentiles to do two things:

2.2.2.1. To have respect for the Jews and desire their conversion. A great advantage would come to the church by their conversion (vv. 12, 15). It would be like life from the dead, and so the Gentiles must long for them to be received again.

2.2.2.2. To watch themselves so that they do not stumble and fall, as the Jews did (vv. 17–22). Notice:

2.2.2.2.1. The privilege the Gentiles had by being included in the church. They were grafted in (v. 17), like a branch of a wild olive shoot into a good olive tree, which is contrary to the custom of the farmer, who grafts the good olive shoot into the bad tree. But those whom God grafts into the church are those whom he has found to be wild and barren, good for nothing. People graft to mend the tree, but God grafts to mend the branch. The church of God is an olive tree, flourishing and fruitful, and the fruit is useful. Those who are outsiders to the church are like wild olive trees; not only are they themselves useless, but what they do produce is sour and unsavory; they are *wild by nature* (v. 24). It is the natural state of each one of us to be wild by nature. Conversion is the grafting of wild branches into the good olive tree. Those who are grafted into the good olive tree share in the root and *fatness* (nourishing sap) of the olive. All who through a living faith are grafted into Christ partake of him as the branches of a tree partake of the root. Because the Gentiles are grafted into the church, they share in the same privileges that the

Jews did, *the root and fatness.* Christ is that root. Now the believing Gentiles share in this root.

2.2.2.2.2. A warning not to abuse these privileges.

2.2.2.2.2.1. "Do not be proud (v. 18): *Boast not against the branches.*" Grace is given not to make us proud but to make us thankful. The law of faith excludes all boasting either about ourselves or against others. "Do not say (v. 19), *They were broken off that I might be grafted in*; that is, do not think that you deserved more at the hand of God than they did. Remember, *thou bearest not* (you do not support) *the root, but the root* (the root supports) *thee.* Although you are grafted in, you are still only a branch supported by the root; in fact, you are an engrafted branch, brought into the good olive *contrary to nature* (v. 24), not freeborn, but by an act of grace. Therefore, *if thou boast,* know"—"know" must be supplied to clarify the sense—"*thou bearest not the root, but the root thee.*"

2.2.2.2.2.2. "Do not be self-confident (v. 20): *Be not high-minded, but fear.* Don't be confident of your own strength and standing." A holy fear is an excellent protection against arrogance: fortunate are those who always fear in this way. *Fear* what? "Fear that you may lose the privileges you now enjoy, as the Jews have lost theirs." The evils that come to others should be warnings to us. The right that churches have to their privileges does not last for a certain term; it runs as long as they behave themselves well, and no longer. Consider:

2.2.2.2.2.2.1. "How they were broken off. It was not undeservedly, but *because of unbelief.*" Not only did their unbelief provoke God to cut them off, but by it they cut themselves off. They were *natural branches* (v. 21), yet when they sank into unbelief, God did not spare them. Tradition, time-honored customs, and the faithfulness of their ancestors would not protect them. It was futile to plead—though they insisted very much on it—that they were Abraham's descendants. This is called here *severity* (v. 22). *Severity* is a harsh-sounding word, and I do not remember that it is attributed to God anywhere else in Scripture. If those who have been closest to God in their profession rebel against him, they will be the ones toward whom he is the severest. Of all judgments, spiritual judgments are the severest, and these are what Paul is speaking of here (v. 8).

2.2.2.2.2.2.2. "How you stand: you are grafted in. Consider, then, by what means you stand: *by faith,* which is a trusting grace. You do not stand in any strength of your own: you are nothing more than the free grace of God makes you. What ruined the Jews was their unbelief, and you stand by faith. Consider also on what terms you stand (v. 22): *toward thee, goodness, if thou continue in his goodness,* that is, continue in dependence on the free grace of God." The condition of our happiness is to keep ourselves in the love of God.

3. Another thing that qualifies this doctrine of the Jews' rejection is that the rejection is not final. Notice:

3.1. How this conversion of the Jews is described here.

3.1.1. It is said to be their fullness (v. 12), that is, their addition to the church. This would be the enriching of the world—with much light, strength, and beauty.

3.1.2. It is called receiving them. They will be received into the love of Christ. This will be like *life from the dead*—so strange and surprising, and yet also so welcome and acceptable.

3.1.3. It is called the *grafting of them in again* (v. 23). What is grafted in receives nourishing sap from the root; so does a soul that is truly grafted into the church receive life, strength, and grace from Christ, the life-giving root of the church. They will be *grafted into their own olive tree* (v. 24), to recover the privileges they so long enjoyed but have now sinned away and lost by their unbelief.

3.1.4. It is called the *saving of all Israel* (v. 26). The adding of them to the church is the saving of them (Ac 2:47).

3.2. What it is based on, why we should look for it.

3.2.1. Because of the holiness of the firstfruits and the root (v. 16). A good beginning promises a good ending. The firstfruits may be the same as the root, namely, the patriarchs, Abraham, Isaac, and Jacob. Now, if they were holy — if they were in the covenant — then we have reason to conclude that God has a kind intention for the whole batch, that is, the whole of that people, and for the *branches*, that is, its particular members. *If the root be holy, so are the branches.* Although a wise man does not beget a wise man, a free man begets a free man. Although grace does not run in the blood, external privileges do, until they are forfeited. The Jewish branches are reckoned holy because the root was so. This is expressed more clearly in v. 28: *They are beloved for the fathers' sakes.* This same love would also revive their privileges, because the ancient, unfailing love continues to be remembered. Although, as for the Gospel, the Jews are enemies to it *for your sakes*, that is, for the sake of the Gentiles, against whom they have such hostility, nevertheless, when God's time comes, this will wear off, and God's love for their fathers will be remembered. Many fare better for the sake of their godly ancestors. This is why the church is called the Jews' own *olive tree*, which is some encouragement to us to hope that there may be room for them in it again, for the sake of old acquaintance. What has been may be again.

3.2.2. Because of the power of God (v. 23): *God is able to graft them in again.* Our comfort is that God is able to produce a change. He is able to graft into the tree those who have long been rejected and withered. *If they abide not still in unbelief.* Nothing has to be done except remove the unbelief, and God is able to take that away, though nothing less than almighty power will do it.

3.2.3. Because of the grace of God revealed to the Gentiles. This is Paul's argument in v. 24: "If you, who were wild by nature, were grafted into a good olive, much more will these who were the natural branches." This suggestion was very proper for restraining the arrogance of those Gentile Christians who looked down with disdain on the rejected Jews. This is his argument in vv. 30–31: *as you in times past have not.* It is good for those who have found mercy with God to think often about what they were in previous times and how they obtained that mercy. Paul argues further from the occasion of the Gentiles' call: "*You have obtained mercy through their unbelief*; much more will they obtain mercy through your mercy. *That through your mercy they might obtain mercy*, that is, so that they may be indebted to you, as you have been to them." True grace hates a monopoly. Those who have found mercy themselves should seek through their mercy to see that others also obtain mercy.

3.2.4. Because of the promises and prophecies of the Old Testament. He quotes a remarkable one (v. 26, from Isa 59:20–21), in which we may notice:

3.2.4.1. The coming of Christ promised: *There shall come out of Zion the deliverer.* Jesus Christ is the great deliverer. In Isaiah it is, *the Redeemer shall come to Zion.* There he is called the Redeemer; here, the Deliverer; he delivers by way of redemption, by paying a price. There he is said to come to Zion, because when the prophet prophesied, Christ was still to come into the world. When the apostle wrote this, Christ had come, and Paul is speak-

ing of the fruits of his appearing, which will come *out of Zion.*

3.2.4.2. The purpose of this coming: *He shall turn away ungodliness from Jacob.* Christ's mission into the world was to turn away ungodliness, so that evil would not be either our ruin or our ruler. Especially, he came to turn it away from Jacob. What greater kindness could he do them than to turn away ungodliness from them, and then make way for complete goodness? In Isaiah it is, *The Redeemer shall come to Zion, and unto those that turn from transgression in Jacob,* only those who leave their sins and turn to God; to them Christ would come as a Redeemer. *For this is my covenant with them — this*, that the Deliverer will come to them, and *this*, that *my Spirit shall not depart* from them (Isa 59:21). The apostle adds, *When I shall take away their sins.* Forgiveness of sin is laid as the foundation. *For I will be merciful.* Paul concludes from all this that without doubt God has great mercy in store for that people, and he proves his conclusion (v. 29) by this truth: *For the gifts and callings of God are without repentance* (irrevocable). These gifts and callings are unchangeable; those whom God loves in this way are loved by him to the end (Jn 13:1). We never find God repenting that he had given people grace or effectively called them.

3.3. The time and extent of this conversion, when and where it is to be expected. It is called a mystery (v. 25), something that was not obvious and that you would not expect if you looked at the present state of that people. The case of the rejected Jews seemed as bad now as that of the Gentiles had been. Now Paul wanted the Gentiles to know enough about this mystery to keep them humble: *lest you be wise in your own conceit.* Ignorance is the cause of our pride and conceit. Notice:

3.3.1. The present state of Israel: *Blindness, in part, is happened to Israel* (v. 25). There is a remnant who see the things that would bring about their peace (Lk 19:42), though the far greater part remain in blindness (vv. 7–8). V. 32 is to the same effect (v. 32): *God has concluded them all in unbelief*, shut them up as in a prison. They all stand before God convicted of unbelief. They refused to believe. "Why then," God says, "you shall not."

3.3.2. When this wonderful change would be: when the *fulness of the Gentiles shall come in*, when the Gospel has had its intended success, having made its progress in the Gentile world. The Jews will continue in blindness until God has fulfilled his whole work among the Gentiles. God will take them again not because he needs them but because of his own free grace.

3.3.3. Its extent: *All Israel shall be saved* (v. 26). He *will have mercy upon all* (v. 32). They would be brought to believe in Christ the true Messiah, whom they crucified. They would become one fold with the Gentiles under Christ the great Shepherd (Heb 13:20). Some think it has been done already, when before, in, and after the destruction of Jerusalem by the Romans, many of the Jews were convinced of their unfaithfulness and became Christians. Others think that it is still to have its fulfillment toward the end of the world.

Verses 33–36

Having insisted at such great length on reconciling the rejection of the Jews with God's goodness, the apostle concludes here with an acknowledgment of the divine wisdom in it all. He adores:

1. The mystery of the divine purposes: *O the depth!* — in general, the whole mystery of the Gospel, which we cannot fully grasp. Notice:

1.1. The *riches of the wisdom and knowledge of God*, a depth that the angels look into (1Pe 1:12). Much more may it puzzle any human understanding. Paul confesses himself at a loss as he contemplates it, and, despairing of seeing the bottom, he humbly sits down at the edge and adores its depth. Those who know most in this state of imperfection must also be most aware of their own weakness and shortsightedness.

1.2. The *depth of the riches*. Human riches are shallow — you can soon see the extent — but God's riches are deep. There is not only depth in his purposes, but also riches, and they are beyond knowledge (v. 19). They are the riches *of the wisdom and knowledge of God*, his seeing all things — the *knowledge and wisdom* before which all lie exposed and open to him: his knowledge is there. His ruling, arranging all things, and bringing about his own purposes in everything: this is his *wisdom*.

1.3. *How unsearchable are his judgments!* that is, his deliberations and purposes; and his *ways*, that is, the execution of these plans and purposes. We do not know what he has in view; it *is past finding out*. Secret things are not for us to know (Dt 29:29). What he does we do not know now (Jn 13:7). We cannot give a reason for God's proceedings.

1.4. The judgments of God's mouth (1Ch 16:12) and the way of our duty are, thank God, clear and easy. The judgments of his hands, however, and the ways of his providence are dark and mysterious, and these, therefore, we must not pry into, but silently adore. The apostle says this especially with reference to that strange turn, the rejection of the Jews and the reception of the Gentiles in order to include the Jews again in due time.

1.5. These are methods that cannot be explained, about which we must say, *O the depth! Past finding out*; or "cannot be traced." God leaves no footprints behind him; the paths of his providence are new every morning (La 3:23). He does not follow the same path often enough to leave tracks. It follows (v. 34), *For who hath known the mind of the Lord?* Is any creature appointed to his cabinet? Is there anyone to whom he has communicated his purposes, or who is able to recognize now the way that he takes?

1.6. The apostle issues the same challenge in 1Co 2:16: *For who hath known the mind of the Lord?* Although there he adds, *But we have the mind of Christ*. The One who knew the mind of the Lord has declared him (Jn 1:18). Therefore, though we do not know the mind of the Lord, if we have the mind of Christ, we have enough. Or *who has been his counsellor?* It is nonsense for anyone to give orders to God or presume to teach him how to govern the world.

2. The sovereignty of God's purposes. In all these things, God does what he wants, because he wants to, and yet there is no unrighteousness in him (Ps 92:15).

2.1. Paul challenges anyone to prove that God is indebted to them (v. 35): *Who hath first given to him?* Who of all the creatures can prove God is indebted to them? *Of thine own we have given thee* (1Ch 29:14). All the duties we can perform are not repayments, but rather restitutions. If anyone can prove that God is indebted to them, the apostle here declares in God's name that payment is ready: *It shall be recompensed to him again.* It is certain that God will let no one lose through him, but never has anyone yet dared make such a demand. This is suggested here:

2.1.1. To silence the shouts of the Jews. When God took their visible church privileges away from them, he was only taking his own.

2.1.2. To silence the insults of the Gentiles. When God sent the Gospel among them, it was not because he owed them so much favor, but out of his own good pleasure.

2.2. He sees everything in the light of the sovereignty of God (v. 36): *For of him, and through him, and to him, are all things*; that is, God is all in all (1Co 15:28). All things are from God as the source and fountain of all; they are through Christ, as the guide; and they are to God as the ultimate goal. If everything is from him and through him, there is all the reason in the world that everything should be to him and for him. To do everything to the glory of God is to make a virtue of necessity, because all will in the end be to him, whether we wish it so or not. Paul concludes, therefore, with a short doxology: *To whom be glory for ever. Amen.* Paul has been discussing in detail the purposes of God concerning humanity; in the end, he concludes with the acknowledgment that all these things must ultimately be determined by divine sovereignty. It is best for us to turn our arguments into fearful and serious adoration, especially when we come to talk about his purposes and actions.

CHAPTER 12

The apostle next undertakes to urge the main duties of Christianity. We are mistaken in our religious faith if we consider it only as a system of ideas and a guide to thought. No, it is also a practical religion. These duties are drawn from the privileges by way of deduction. The foundation of Christian practice must be laid in Christian knowledge and faith. This chapter is joined to the previous discussion by the word therefore. *It is the practical application of doctrinal truths that is the life of preaching. The faith that justifies is a faith that "works through love" (Gal 5:6). There is no way to heaven except through holiness and obedience. The particular exhortations of this chapter may be reduced to the three main headings of Christian duty: our duty to God, to ourselves, and to our brothers and sisters. The grace of God teaches us, in general, to live godly, soberly (with self-control), and righteously (Tit 2:12). Now this chapter explains to us what godliness, sobriety, and righteousness are.*

Verses 1–21

We may notice here, according to the outline mentioned above, the apostle's exhortations:

1. About our duty to God. We see what godliness is like.

1.1. To be godly means to surrender ourselves to God and so lay a good foundation. This is urged here as the spring of all duty and obedience (vv. 1–2).

1.1.1. The body must be presented to him (v. 1). The exhortation is introduced here with great emotion: *I beseech you, brethren.* Although he was a great apostle, he still calls the humblest Christians *brethren*, a term of affection and concern. He begs; this is the way of the Gospel. He does this to sweeten the exhortation, so that it may come with more pleasant power. Many are sooner persuaded if they are spoken to kindly; they are more easily led than driven. Notice here:

1.1.1.1. The duty urged — to present our *bodies a living sacrifice. Your bodies* refers to our whole selves. What is meant is "your bodies and spirits." Sacrifice here stands for whatever is dedicated to God by his own appointment. Christ, who was once offered to bear the sins of many, is the only sacrifice of atonement, but our persons and actions, offered to God through Christ, are like sacrifices of acknowledgment to the honor of God. *Present* shows that it is a voluntary act. It must be a freewill offering. The presenting of the body to God implies not only the avoiding of the sins that are committed with or against the body, but also the use of the body as a servant of the soul in the service of God. It is to yield the members of our bodies as instruments of righteousness (6:13). Although physical training is of little value (1Ti 4:8), in its place it is a proof of the dedication of our souls to God.

1.1.1.1.1. Present them as a living sacrifice. Christians make their bodies sacrifices to God. A body sincerely devoted to God is a living sacrifice. It is Christ living in the soul by faith that makes the body a living sacrifice (Gal 2:20). Holy love kindles the sacrifices, puts life into duties. We must be sacrificed *alive*, that is, *alive to God* (6:11; v. 11).

1.1.1.1.2. They must be holy; that is, they must have that real holiness that consists of a complete integrity of heart and life; our bodies must not be made the instruments of sin and immorality, but set apart for God and put to holy uses. It is the soul that is the proper subject of holiness, but a sanctified soul gives a holiness to the body. What is holy is according to the will of God; when the bodily actions are holy, the body is holy.

1.1.1.2. The three arguments to support this:

1.1.1.2.1. Consider the mercies of God: *I beseech you by the mercies of God.* This is a sweet and powerful argument. There is the mercy that is in God and the mercy that comes from God—mercy in the spring and mercy in the streams: both are included here. God is a merciful God, and so may we present our bodies to him; he will be sure to use them kindly. We receive from him the fruits of his mercy every day, especially mercy for our bodies: he made them, he maintains them, he bought them. The greatest mercy of all is that Christ has made not only his body, but also his soul, an offering for sin (Isa 53:10). Let us give ourselves as an acknowledgment of all these favors—all we are, all we have, and all we can do, and after all, that is a poor response; and yet, because it is what we have:

1.1.1.2.2. It is *acceptable to God.* These living sacrifices are acceptable to God. If the presenting of ourselves will please him, we may easily conclude that there is nothing and no one we would do better to give ourselves to.

1.1.1.2.3. It is our *reasonable service.* There is an act of reason in it, because it is the soul that presents the body. Our God must be served in the spirit (Jn 4:24) and with the understanding (Ps 47:7). God does not impose on us anything hard or unreasonable, but what is completely agreeable to the principles of right reason. A reasonable service is one that we are able and ready to give a reason for.

1.1.2. The mind must be renewed for him. This is urged in v. 2: *Be you transformed by the renewing of your mind.* Conversion and sanctification are the renewing of the mind, a change not in substance, but in spiritual qualities. We are not what we once were—old things have passed away; all things become new (2Co 5:17; Rev 21:4–5). The renewing of the mind, therefore, is the renewing of the whole person, for out of the heart are the *issues of life* (Pr 4:23). The progress of sanctification, dying to sin more and more and living to righteousness more and more, is the continuation of this renewing work. This is called our transformation. The same word is used in 2Co 3:18, where we are said to be *changed into the same image from glory to glory.* Not that we can produce such a change ourselves: we could as soon make a new world as make a new heart by our own power; it is God's work. Rather, "Use the means God has appointed and ordained

for it." It is God who turns us, and then we are turned (Jer 31:18). "Put your souls under the changing, transforming influences of the Holy Spirit." Although the new being is created by God, we must still put it on (Eph 4:24) and be pressing forward toward perfection. Notice:

1.1.2.1. What the great enemy to this renewing is, namely, conformity to this world: *Be not conformed to this world.* All the disciples and followers of the Lord Jesus must be nonconformists with respect to this world. "Do not fashion yourselves" according to the world. We must not conform to the things of the world. We must not conform to other people in the world; we must not follow the crowd to commit evil (Ex 23:2). If sinners entice us (Pr 1:10), we must not follow them, but witness against them where we are. True Christianity consists of a sober nonconformity. We must, however, beware the extremes of affected rudeness and moroseness, which some fall into. The rule of the Gospel calls for us to let ourselves be directed, not to be contrary.

1.1.2.2. What the great effect of this renewing is: *That you may prove what is that good, and acceptable, and perfect will of God.* By *will of God*, we are here to understand his revealed will about our duty, which we pray may be done by us as it is done by the angels.

1.1.2.2.1. The will of God is *good, and acceptable, and perfect*—three excellent properties for a law to have. It is good in itself. It is good for us. It is acceptable; it is pleasing to God. The only way to obtain his favor, which is the goal of our life, is to conform to his will, which is the rule of our life. It is perfect, and nothing can be added to it.

1.1.2.2.2. Christians should test and approve what is the will of God that is good, acceptable, and perfect, that is, know it from experience, know the excellence of the will of God by the experience of conforming to it. This means to approve *things that are excellent* (Php 1:10), to *be of quick understanding in the fear of the Lord* (Isa 11:3).

1.1.2.2.3. Those who are being transformed by the renewing of their mind are best able to prove what is the good, acceptable, and perfect will of God. A living motive of grace in the soul inclines the soul to receive the revelations of God's will. The promise is (Jn 7:17), *If any man will do his will, he shall know of the doctrine.* An expert may dispute the will of God; an honest, humble heart, however, loves it.

1.2. To be godly means that when this is done, we serve God (vv. 11–12), that we are continually *serving the Lord.* To be religious is to serve God.

1.2.1. We must make it our business, and *not be slothful in that business.* We must not make slow progress in religious matters. Slothful servants will be reckoned as wicked servants (Mt 25:26).

1.2.2. We must be *fervent in spirit, serving the Lord.* God must be *served with the spirit* (1:9; Jn 4:24), under the influences of the Holy Spirit. We must have a fervency in spirit—a holy zeal and warmth, as those who love God not only with the heart and soul, but with all our hearts and with all our souls. This is the holy fire that kindles the sacrifice and carries it up to heaven, an offering of a sweet smelling savor (Ex 29:18; Lev 1:9, 13; etc.).

1.2.3. We must be *rejoicing in hope.* God is honored by our hope and trust in him, especially when we rejoice in that hope.

1.2.4. We must be *patient in tribulation.* In this way, too, we serve God, not only by working for him when he calls us to work but also by sitting quietly when he calls us to suffer. Those who rejoice in hope are likely to be patient in suffering.

1.2.5. We must be *continuing instant* (faithful) *in prayer.* Prayer is a friend of hope and patience, and in it we serve the Lord.

2. About our duty with respect to ourselves; this is *sobriety* (self-control).

2.1. We must hold a sober opinion of ourselves (v. 3). *I say, through the grace given unto me.* It is said to each one of us, to one as well as another. Pride is a sin that is bred in the bone of each one of us. *Not to think of himself more highly than he ought to think.* We must beware having too high an opinion of ourselves. We must not be self-conceited or pay too much attention to our own wisdom. There is a high thought of ourselves that we may and must have, which is to think ourselves too good to be the slaves of sin and drudges to this world. We should think soberly, that is, have a modest opinion of ourselves and our own abilities, valuing them as what we have received from God, and not otherwise. The words will bear yet another sense. *Of himself* is not in the original; it may therefore read, "That no man be wise above what he should be wise, but be wise unto sobriety." There is a knowledge that puffs up (1Co 8:1). We must be aware of this, and seek that knowledge that tends to sobriety. Under this heading comes that exhortation (v. 16), *Be not wise in your own conceits.* It is good to be wise, but it is bad to think ourselves so, for there is more hope for a fool than for a person who is wise in their own eyes (Pr 26:12). It was excellent for Moses to have his face shine and not know it (Ex 34:29). Now the reasons are these:

2.1.1. Because whatever we have that is good, *God hath dealt* it to us. The best and most useful person in the world is no more, no better, than what the free grace of God makes them every day. When we think about ourselves, we must remember to think not about how much we have achieved, but about how kind God has been to us.

2.1.2. Because God gives his gifts in a certain measure: according to *the measure of faith.* Paul calls the measure of spiritual gifts the measure of faith, because this is the radical grace. What we have and do that is good is right and acceptable insofar as it is based on faith. Christ had the Spirit given him without measure (Jn 3:34), but the saints have the Spirit in a limited way. Christ, who had gifts without measure, was humble and lowly, and shall we, who are limited, become proud and conceited?

2.1.3. Because God has given gifts to others as well as to us: *Dealt to every man.* If we had a monopoly on the Spirit, there might be some excuse for this self-conceit, but others have their share as well as we. It is wrong, therefore, for us to lift up ourselves and despise others as if we were the only people in favor with heaven. He illustrates this reasoning by a comparison taken from the members of the natural body: *as we have many members in one body* (vv. 4–5).

2.1.3.1. All the saints make up one body in Christ, who is the head of the body. Believers do not lie in the world as a confused and disorderly heap, but are organized and knit together (Col 2:2).

2.1.3.2. Individual believers are members of this body, deriving life and spirits from the head. Some members in the body are bigger and more useful than others, and each receives according to its proportion. If the little finger were to receive as much nourishment as the leg, it would be ugly and harmful! We must remember that we are not the whole body; we are merely parts.

2.1.3.3. All *the members have not the same office* (v. 4), but each has its respective place and work assigned to it. This is what happens in the mystical body: some are called to one sort of work; others are called to another.

2.1.3.4. Each member has its own place and role for the good of the whole and of every other member. We are not only members of Christ; we are also *members one of another* (v. 5). We are committed to do all the good we can to one another. Whatever we have received not for ourselves but for the good of others.

2.2. We must make sober use of the gifts God has given us. Just as we must not, on the one hand, become proud of our talents, so, on the other hand, we must not bury them. We must not say, "I am nothing, and so I will sit back and do nothing," but, "I am nothing in myself, and so I will give all I can in the power of the grace of Christ." *Having gifts,* let us use them. *Gifts differing.* The immediate intention of each gift is different from that of all the others, though the ultimate aim of all is the same. *According to the grace.* It is grace that appoints the position and qualifies and inclines the person. Paul specifies seven gifts (vv. 6–8), which seem to refer to so many distinct roles that were used in the early churches. Two general gifts are expressed here by *prophesying* and *ministering,* the former the work of the bishops (overseers and elders), the latter the work of the deacons. The last five gifts are to be understood in terms of the first two.

2.2.1. *Prophecy. Whether prophecy, let us prophesy according to the proportion of faith.* This does not refer to the extraordinary gifts of foretelling future things, but to the ordinary role of preaching the word. The work of the Old Testament prophets was not only to foretell future things but also to warn the people about their sin and duty. This is how Gospel preachers are prophets. Those who preach the word must do it *according to the proportion of faith.*

2.2.1.1. As to the method of prophesying, it must be according to the proportion of the grace of faith. Let the one who preaches set all the faith they have to work, so as to impress the truths they preach on their own heart firstly. Just as people cannot listen well without faith, so ministers cannot preach well without faith. We must remember the proportion of faith—that although not all people have faith, very many do have it besides us. "*Hast thou faith? Have it to thyself,* and do not make it a controlling rule to others, remembering that you have only your proportion."

2.2.1.2. As to the content of our prophesying, it must be according to the proportion of the doctrine of faith. There are some basic truths, as we may call them, clearly and uniformly taught in Scripture, which are the touchstone of preaching, by which we must *prove all things,* and then we must *hold fast that which is good* (1Th 5:20–21). Truths that are less clear must be examined in the light of those that are clearer, because it is certain that one truth can never contradict another. See here what the great concern of preachers should be—to preach sound doctrine. It is necessary for it to be according to the proportion of faith, because it is the word of faith that we preach. Now there are two particular tasks that the one who prophesies has to consider—teaching and encouraging.

2.2.1.2.1. Let the one who teaches get on with their teaching. Teaching is the simple explaining and proving of Gospel truths, without practical application. Now to one who has been given a skill in teaching and has undertaken that responsibility: let them stick to it. It is a good gift; let them use it and give their mind to it.

2.2.1.2.2. Let the one who exhorts get on with their exhorting. Let them give themselves to that. This is the work of the pastor; it is to apply Gospel truths and rules more closely to the people, to urge on them what is more practical. Many who are very accurate in their teaching may be cold and unskillful in encouraging, and the opposite too. The one requires a clearer mind, the other a warmer heart. To give ourselves to our work is to give it the best of our time and thoughts, and to seek not only to do it but to do it well.

2.2.2. *Ministry.* If someone has *the office of a deacon*, let them fulfill that office well. It includes all those positions that form part of the external work of the house of God. *Serving tables* (Ac 6:2). Now let those who undertake this care of ministering pursue it with faithfulness and diligence.

2.2.2.1. *He that giveth, let him do it with simplicity.* Those church officers who managed the church's gifts were to do it *generously* and faithfully and with all sincerity and integrity, having no other intention than to glorify God and do good. Let those who have the resources give generously and plentifully. God loves a cheerful, generous giver (2Co 9:7).

2.2.2.2. *He that ruleth, with diligence.* It seems he is referring to those who assisted the pastors in exercising church discipline. They must govern with diligence. The word shows both care and hard work to discover what is wrong and keep the church pure.

2.2.2.3. *He that showeth mercy, with cheerfulness.* Some think this refers in general to all who show mercy in anything. Let them be willing to do it and take pleasure in it. However, it seems to refer to some particular church officers whose work it was to take care of the sick and strangers. Now this must be done cheerfully. A pleasant face when undertaking acts of mercy is a great relief and comfort to the miserable — when they see that it is not done grudgingly and unwillingly, but with pleasant looks and gentle words. Those who have to do with the sick and ill, who may be bad tempered, need to put on not only patience but also cheerfulness.

3. About that part of our duty that concerns our brothers and sisters. All our duty toward one another is summed up in one sweet word: *love.* That is why the apostle mentions it first. *Let love be without dissimulation*; let it not be shown in mere compliment and pretense, but in reality and sincerity. There is a love due to our friends and a love due to our enemies. Paul mentions both.

3.1. We must show love to our friends. There is a mutual love that Christians owe and must pay. It is:

3.1.1. An affectionate love (v. 10): *Be kindly affectioned one to another, with brotherly love.* It refers not only to love but also to a readiness and inclination to love, kindness flowing as from a spring. It properly refers to the love of parents toward their children. This is how we are to love one another, and there will be such love where there is a new nature and the law of love is written on the heart. *One to another.* It may commend the grace of love to us to know that it is just as much the duty of others to love us as it is our duty to love others. What can be sweeter on this side of heaven than to love and be loved?

3.1.2. A respectful love: *In honour preferring one another.* Let us be forward to give others the preeminence. We should be eager to take notice of the gifts, graces, and actions of our brothers and sisters, and value them accordingly, being more pleased to hear another praised than to be praised ourselves. Some read it, "going before, or leading, one another in honor" — not in taking honor, but in giving it. Though we must prefer others (as our translation reads) as being more capable and deserving than we are, we must still not make that an excuse for doing nothing nor are we permitted to claim to honor others in order to indulge ourselves in ease and slothfulness. Paul adds immediately, therefore (v. 11), *Not slothful in business.*

3.1.3. A liberal love (v. 13): *Distributing to the necessities of saints.* It is a false love that limits itself to mere verbal expressions of kindness and respect, while the needs of our brothers and sisters demand real supplies and it is in our power to provide them.

3.1.3.1. It is in no way strange for saints in this world to lack the necessities to support their natural lives. Surely the things of this world are not the best things; if they were, the saints would not have so few of them.

3.1.3.2. Those who have resources have the duty to *distribute*, or — as the verb form *koinonountes* may better be read — to share those necessities.

3.1.3.2.1. It is not enough to draw out the soul to give to the hungry (Isa 58:10); we must bring out our wallets and purses for them too. *Communicating,* sharing. Our poor brothers and sisters have a kind of interest in what God has given us, and our relieving them should come from a fellow feeling for their needs. The charitable benevolence of the Philippians toward Paul is called their sharing in his troubles (Php 4:14). We are especially bound to share with the saints. There is a common love owing to our fellow creatures, but a special love owing to our fellow Christians.

3.1.3.2.2. Paul mentions another branch of this generous love: *given to hospitality.* As there is opportunity, we must welcome strangers. *I was a stranger, and you took me in* (Mt 25:35), is mentioned as one instance of the mercifulness of those who will obtain mercy (Mt 5:7). It shows that we must not only take opportunities to show mercy but also actively seek such opportunities.

3.1.4. A sympathizing love (v. 15): *Rejoice with those that do rejoice, and weep with those that weep.* True love will be interested in the sorrows and joys of one another and will teach us to make them our own. In this world, some are always rejoicing, and others weeping; God allows this so that our mutual love and Christian sympathy, as well as other graces, may be tested. It is not that we are to participate in the sinful merriment or mourning of any, yet we must not envy those who prosper, but rejoice with them; we must not despise those who are in trouble, but be concerned for them and ready to help them.

3.1.5. A united love: "*Be of the same mind one toward another* (v. 16). Agree in friendliness; seek to be united." Some understand it, "*wishing the same good* for others that you wish for yourselves." This is to love our brothers and sisters as ourselves.

3.1.6. A gracious love: *Mind not high things, but condescend to men of low estate* (v. 16). True love cannot be without humility. To love one another rightly is to be willing to stoop to the most humble roles of kindness for one another's good. Love is gracious.

3.1.6.1. *Mind not high things.* We must not seek honor and advancement. The Romans were perhaps ready to think better of themselves because they lived in the imperial city. The apostle often warns the Roman Christians, therefore, against high-mindedness; compare 11:20.

3.1.6.2. *Condescend to men of low estate.*

3.1.6.2.1. The phrase translated *men of low estate* means literally "the low ones" and may refer not to low persons but to low things — menial work that we must condescend to undertake. If our condition in the world is poor and lowly, we must still put our mind to it and accept it. The margin reads: "Be contented with mean things." Be reconciled to the position God in his providence has put us in. We must consider nothing beneath us except sin.

3.1.6.2.2. The phrase may refer to people of a low position, as our translation reads it: *Condescend to men of low estate.* We need not be ashamed to talk with the poor, as long as the great God looks from heaven to earth to consider such (Ps 53:2; 102;19–20). True love values grace in rags as well as in scarlet. A jewel is a jewel, even if it lies in the dirt. *Condescend*; that is, adjust yourselves to them, stoop down to them for their good. He adds, *Be not wise in your own conceits*, to the same effect as v. 3. We will never find it in our own hearts to *condescend* to others as long as we find self-conceit there, and so this pride must be put to death. "Do not be wise by yourselves; do not be confident that your own wisdom is enough; do not be reluctant to share what you have with others. It is the business of wisdom that we profess, and business consists of commerce, giving and receiving."

3.1.7. A love that commits us, as much as it depends on us, *to live peaceably with all men* (v. 18). We must live peaceably even with those with whom we cannot live closely and familiarly. We must seek to preserve the peace, that is, to see that it is not broken and to put it back together when it is broken. This is not expressed so as to oblige us to undertake something impossible: *If it be possible, as much as lies in you*. Seek the things that make for peace (14:19). *If it be possible*. It is not possible to preserve the peace when we cannot do it without offending God and wounding conscience. The wisdom from above is first pure and then peace-loving (Jas 3:17). Peace without purity is the peace of Satan's palace. *As much as lieth in you*. There must be two sides to the negotiation of peace. We may be unavoidably fought against. Our concern must be to see that nothing is lacking on our part to preserve the peace (Ps 120:7).

3.2. We must show love to our enemies. Those who embrace religion have reason to expect to encounter enemies in a world whose smiles rarely harmonize with Christ's. Now Christianity teaches us how to behave toward our enemies, and it is completely different from all other rules of conduct; they generally aim at victory and dominion, but this rule aims at inner peace. Whoever our enemies are, our rule is to do them all the good we can.

3.2.1. We must do them no harm (v. 17): *Recompense to no man evil for evil*. We have *not so learned God*, who does so much for his enemies (Mt 5:45), and much less have we *so learned Christ* (Eph 4:20), who died for us when we were enemies (5:8, 10). "Respond this way *to no man*: not to one who has been your friend, for by repaying evil for evil you will certainly lose them, and not to one who has been your enemy, for by not repaying evil for evil you may win their friendship." V. 19 is to the same effect (v. 19): *Dearly beloved, avenge not yourselves*. Paul addresses himself to such people in this endearing language to soften and mollify them. Anything that breathes love sweetens the blood. Do you want to pacify a *brother offended* (Pr 18:19)? Then call him *dearly beloved*. Such a soft word may be effective in turning away wrath (Pr 15:1). *Avenge not yourselves*. This forbids private revenge, which flows from anger and hatred. Notice how strict the law of Christ is in this matter (Mt 5:38–40). It is forbidden not only to take it into our own hands to avenge ourselves, but even to thirst after that judgment that the law affords in our case, to satisfy a vengeful attitude. This is a hard lesson for our corrupt nature to learn, and so Paul adds:

3.2.1.1. A remedy against revenge: *Rather give place unto wrath*; make room for it. Not for our own wrath; to make room for that is to make room for the devil. We must resist and suppress this; but we must make room for:

3.2.1.1.*1*. The wrath of our enemy. "Make room for that; do not answer wrath with wrath, but rather with love." When people's passions run high, and the stream is

strong, let it take its course, so that it is not made to rage and swell even more strongly. When others are angry, let us be calm.

3.2.1.1.1.*2*. The wrath of God, according to many: "Leave room for the wrath of God, and let him alone deal with your adversary."

3.2.1.2. A reason against it: *For it is written, Vengeance is mine*. God is the sovereign King, the righteous Judge, and it is his right to administer justice. Some of this power he has entrusted to the civil magistrates; their legal punishments, therefore, are to be looked on as a branch of God's revenge. If vengeance is God's, we may not exercise it; if we do, we step into God's throne. Nor do we need to exercise it. God will do so, if we humbly leave the matter with him.

3.2.2. We must not only not do harm to our enemies; we are to do them all the good we can. This is a command that is distinctive to Christianity: *Love your enemies* (Mt 5:44). We are taught here to show them that love in both word and action. We must show it:

3.2.2.1. In word: *Bless those who persecute you* (v. 14). It has been the common fate of God's people to be persecuted. Now we are taught here to bless those who so persecute us. *Bless* them: "Speak well of them and speak respectfully to them, not repaying insult for insult (1Pe 3:9)." We must wish them well, and then, if we cannot do anything else for them, we can still show our goodwill by offering up that desire to God in prayer for them, just as our master commanded, supporting his command by his example (Lk 23:34). *Bless, and curse not*. It shows a thorough goodwill; not, "Bless them when you are praying, and curse them at other times," but, "Bless them always, and do not curse at all." Cursing is wrong for those whose work is to bless God.

3.2.2.2. In action (v. 20): "*If thine enemy hunger*, be ready to show them any kindness, and never be any less eager because they are your enemy, so that you may show by your kindness that you sincerely forgive them." Notice here:

3.2.2.2.*1*. What we must do. We must do good to our enemies. "*If he hunger*, do not say, 'Now God is avenging me against him.' Instead, *feed him*." Even then, when he needs your help and you have an opportunity to starve him, *feed him*. "Feed him abundantly; feed him as we feed children and sick people, with much tenderness. Seek to do it so as to express your love. *If he thirst, give him drink* as a sign of reconciliation and friendship. Confirm your love to him."

3.2.2.2.*2*. Why we must do this. *Thou shalt heap coals of fire on his head*; that is, "You will either:

3.2.2.2.2.*1*. "Melt him into repentance and friendship"—alluding to those who melt metals; they not only put fire under them but also heap fire on them. "You will win a friend by it, and if your kindness does not have that effect, then:

3.2.2.2.2.*2*. "It will make his hatred toward you even more inexcusable." Not that this must be our intention in showing him kindness, but such will be the effect. Those who avenge are the conquered, and those who forgive are the conquerors.

3.2.2.2.2.2.*1*. "*Be not overcome of evil*. Let the evil of any provocation that is given you not have such power over you as to disturb your peace, destroy your love, or cause you to seek or attempt to take any revenge." Those who cannot quietly bear an injury are completely conquered by it.

3.2.2.2.2.2.*2*. "*But overcome evil with good*, with the good of patience—indeed, with the good of kindness and generosity to those who wrong you." Those who have this rule over their spirit are better than the powerful (Pr 16:32).

3.2.2.2.2.3. There remain two exhortations that commend all the others as good in themselves and praiseworthy.

3.2.2.2.2.3.1. One commends them as good in themselves (v. 9): *Abhor that which is evil; cleave to that which is good.* We must not only not commit evil; we must *abhor that which is evil.* We must hate sin with a complete and irreconcilable hatred. We must not only do what is good; we must cling to it. This refers to a deliberate choice of, a sincere devotion for, and a constant perseverance in what is good.

3.2.2.2.2.3.2. The other commends them as praiseworthy (v. 17): "*Provide things honest in the sight of all men;* seek and be careful to do what commends religious faith to all with whom you have dealings."

CHAPTER 13

We are taught three good lessons in this chapter. 1. A lesson of submission to lawful authority (vv. 1–6). 2. A lesson of justice and love to our brothers and sisters (vv. 7–10). 3. A lesson of self-control and godliness in ourselves (vv. 11–14).

Verses 1–6

We are taught here how to behave toward magistrates and all those who are in authority over us, called here the *higher powers,* showing their authority (*powers*) and their position (*higher powers*). The just power they have must be submitted to and obeyed. Notice:

1. The duty commanded: *Let every soul be subject.* Every soul—every person, one as well as another, not excluding the clergy. *Every soul.* Not that our consciences are to submit to the will of any human being. It is God's right to make laws that directly bind our conscience. But this expression shows that our submission must be free and voluntary, sincere and genuine. The submission of the soul required here includes inner honor and outer reverence and respect to these powers, honor and respect both in speaking to them and in speaking about them. "They are *higher powers;* be content to have them be so, and submit to them accordingly." Now there was good reason to urge this duty:

1.1. Because of the reproach the Christian religion lay under in the world, as an enemy of public peace, order, and government. Our Lord Jesus was reproached in this way (Lk 23:2; Jn 19:12), even though he declared that his kingdom was not of this world (Jn 18:36). It is hardly surprising, then, if his followers have been burdened through the ages with similar misrepresentations, called *factious, seditious,* and *turbulent.* The apostle, therefore, showed that obedience to civil magistrates is one of the laws of Christ, whose religion helps make people good subjects.

1.2. Because of the temptation the Christians lay under to be otherwise disposed toward civil magistrates. The apostle commanded obedience to the civil authorities, which it was more necessary to urge now because the magistrates were pagans and unbelievers, though that did not destroy their civil power and authority.

2. Paul himself offers reasons to support this duty.

2.1. For *wrath's sake.* Magistrates wield the sword; it is useless to oppose those who hold the sword. The least show of resistance in a Christian would be very damaging to the whole society of Christians. They had greater need than others, therefore, to be exact in their submis-

sion. We must add here that argument (v. 2), *Those that resist shall receive to themselves damnation:* they will be called to account for it. God will judge them for it, because the resistance reflects on him. The magistrates will judge them for it. Therefore it follows (v. 3), *Rulers are a terror.* This is a good argument, but a Christian has a higher one.

2.2. *Not only for wrath, but for conscience's sake,* not so much from the fear of punishment as from the love of virtue (v. 5). Now to oblige his readers' consciences to give this submission, Paul argues (vv. 1–4, 6):

2.2.1. From the instituting of magistracy: *There is no power but of God.* God, as the ruler of the world, has appointed the institution of magistracy, so that all civil authority is derived from him. The usurpation of power and the abuse of power do not come from God, but the power itself does. The most unjust and oppressive rulers in the world have no power except what is given them from above (Jn 19:11). It is an instance of God's wisdom, power, and goodness in the management of humanity that he has put the Roman Christians into a state that distinguishes governors and governed, and has not left them like fish of the sea, where the greater devour the less. The *powers that be:* whatever the particular form and method of government is, it is an institution of God and is to be received and submitted to accordingly. *Ordained of God.* It follows, therefore (v. 2), that whoever *resisteth* (rebels against) *the power resisteth* (is rebelling against) *the ordinance of God.* Magistracy is from God as an ordinance; that is, it is a great law, and it is a great blessing. Those who defy the power of magistrates reflect on God himself. Magistrates are again and again called God's ministers here. *He is the minister of God* (vv. 4, 6). Magistrates are God's servants in a particular way; the position they have calls for duty. Although they are lords to us, they are servants of God.

2.2.2. From the intention of magistracy: *Rulers are not a terror to good works, but to the evil.* Magistracy was intended to be:

2.2.2.1. A terror to evil works and evildoers. Magistrates wield the sword, not only the sword of war but also the sword of justice. Such is the power of sin and corruption that many will not be restrained from the greatest crimes by any regard for the law of God and nature, but only by the fear of temporal punishments. Laws with penalties for the lawless and disobedient (1Ti 1:9) must be constituted in Christian nations, and are in harmony with, and not contradictory to, the Gospel. In this work the magistrate is the *minister of God* (v. 4). They act as God's agent, and so they must beware infusing into their judgments any private, personal resentments. To *execute wrath upon him that doeth evil.* The judicial processes of the most vigilant, faithful magistrates still come far short of the judgment of God: they reach only to the evil act, but God's judgment extends to the evil thought. *He beareth not the sword in vain.* It is not for nothing that God has put such power into the magistrate's hand. Therefore, "*If thou do that which is evil, be afraid,*" for civil powers have quick eyes and long arms." It is a good thing when the punishment of evildoers is managed as a law of God, because he is a holy God, who hates sin, he is King of nations and the God of peace and order, he is the protector of the good, and he is One who determines to terrify some by the punishment of others, and so prevent similar wickedness.

2.2.2.2. A source of praise to those who do well. "Do what is good (v. 3), and you need not be *afraid of the power;* in fact, you will be commended by it." This is the intention of magistracy, and so we must, for conscience's sake, submit to it, as a constitution intended for the public good. However, it is a pity that this gracious intention should ever be perverted, so that those who wield the sword become a terror to those who do well. Even then, the blessing and benefit of common protection and an appearance of government and order are such that it is our duty to submit to persecution for well-doing, rather than attempt redress by pursuing any irregular and disorderly practice. Better a bad government than none at all.

2.2.3. From our interests in it: "He is *the minister of God to thee for good.*" Protection draws allegiance. By upholding the government, we maintain our own protection. This submission is also consented to by the tax we pay (v. 6): "*For this cause pay you tribute*, as a sign of your submission and an acknowledgment that in conscience you think it is due. By paying tax you acknowledge not only the magistrate's authority but also the blessing of that authority to yourselves and the pains the magistrate takes in the work of government, because honor is a burden. If the magistrate does as he should, *he is attending continually upon this very thing*, and in consideration of this hard work, we pay tax." Paul does not say, "You give it as a gift," but, "You pay it as a just debt." This is the lesson the apostle teaches, and it is good for all Christians to learn and practice it: that the godly in the land—whatever others are like—may be found to be the quiet and the peace-loving people of the land (1Ti 2:2).

Verses 7 – 10

We are taught here a lesson of justice and love.

1. Justice (v. 7): *Render therefore to all their dues.* What we have we have as stewards; others have an interest in it, and so they must have their dues. Give to everyone what you owe them, and do so readily and cheerfully, not waiting until you are compelled by law to do it. Paul specifies:

1.1. Due taxes: *Tribute to whom tribute is due, custom to whom custom.* He wrote this to the Romans, who, being rich, were drained by taxes and duties, which the apostle here urges them to pay honestly, as is just. Our Lord was born when his mother went to be taxed, and he commanded the payment of tax to Caesar (Mt 22:21). Many who in other things seem to be just are unconcerned to do this, but pass it off with the false, ill-favored maxim that it is not a sin to cheat the king.

1.2. Due respect: *Fear to whom fear, honour to whom honour.* This sums up the duty we owe not only to magistrates but to all who are over us in the Lord, according to the fifth commandment: *Honour thy father and mother.* Where there is not this respect in the heart toward our superiors, no other duty will be paid rightly.

1.3. Due payment of debts (v. 8): "*Owe no man any thing*; do not continue in anyone's debt as long as you are able to pay it." Many who are very aware of the trouble of being in debt think little of the sin of it.

2. Love: *Owe no man any thing.* "Whatever you owe, it is eminently summed up in this debt of love. However, *loving one another* is a debt that must be always being paid and is always still owing." Love is a debt. Love is *the fulfilling of the law*; not perfectly, but it is a good step toward it. It includes all the duties of the second table of the Ten Commandments, which Paul specifies in v. 9, and these presuppose the love of God. If love is sincere, it is accepted as the *fulfilling of the law*. Surely we serve a good master, who has summed up all our duty in one word, and that short, sweet word is *love*, the beauty and

harmony of the universe. Loving and being loved is all the delight, joy, and happiness of an intelligent being. *God is love* (1Jn 4:16), and love is his image on the soul. Now, to prove that love is the fulfilling of the law, Paul gives us:

2.1. A list of particular commands (v. 9). He specifies the last five of the Ten Commandments, which he declares to be all summed up in this royal law: *Thou shalt love thy neighbour as thyself.* On this is built the golden rule of doing to others as we would have them do to us (Mt 7:12). If there were no restraints of human laws in these things, the law of love would by itself be effective to keep peace and good order among us. The apostle puts the seventh commandment—*Thou shalt not commit adultery*—before the sixth, mentioning it first, because although adultery commonly goes under the name of love—it is a great pity that such a good word should be so abused—it is really as great a violation of the law as killing and stealing. Those who tempt others to sin, though they may claim the most passionate love, really hate them.

2.2. A general rule about the nature of mutual love: *Love worketh no ill* (v. 10); one who walks in love *works no ill* (does no harm) *to his neighbour*, to anyone he has anything to do with. Love intends no harm to anybody. More is implied than is expressed: love not only does no wrong; it does all the good possible. Love is a living, active principle of obedience to the whole law. The whole law is written on the heart if the law of love is there.

Verses 11 – 14

We are taught here a lesson of self-control and godliness, a guide to a Christian's daily life including four things: when to wake up, how to get dressed, how to behave, and what provision to make.

1. When to wake up: *Now it is high time to awake* (v. 11). We need to be stirred often to keep awake. The word of command to all Christ's disciples is, *Watch.* "*Awake*—be concerned about your souls and your eternal interests, considering:

1.1. "The time we are now in: *Knowing the time.* Consider what time of day it is with us, and you will see that the hour has come to wake up. It is Gospel time, a time when more is expected than was expected in the times of ignorance that God overlooked (Ac 17:30), when people sat in darkness (Lk 1:79; Ro 2:19). Now is the time to wake up, because the sun has been up a long time and is shining in our faces. It is time to wake up, because others around us are awake and up and about. Know that the time is to be a busy one; we have a great deal of work to do. Know that the time is a dangerous time. We are among enemies and snares. It is time to wake up, for we have slept enough.

1.2. "The salvation we are on the verge of: *Now is our salvation nearer than when we believed.* The eternal happiness we chose as our portion is now nearer to us than it was when we first became Christians. Let us be concerned for the path we take, and let us exert ourselves. The nearer we are to our center, the quicker our movement should be. Is there only one step between us and heaven, and shall we be so very slow and dull in our Christian course?"

2. How to get dressed. This is our next concern, once we are awake and up: "The *night is far spent, the day is at hand*; therefore it is time to get dressed. Clearer revelations of Gospel grace than have been made up to this time will soon be made, as the day becomes lighter and lighter. Notice, then:

2.1. "What we must put off: our night clothes, which it is a shame to walk around in: *Cast off the works of darkness.*" Sinful works are works of darkness. Let us, therefore, who belong to the day (1Th 5:8), set them aside and have nothing more to do with them.

2.2. "What we must put on." We are to be eager to wear the appropriate clothes: how shall we dress our souls?

2.2.1. *Put on the armour of light.* Christians are soldiers among enemies; they must therefore wear their armor. Christians may consider themselves undressed if they are unarmed. The graces of the Spirit are this armor, to protect the soul from Satan's temptations. This is called the armor of light; the graces of the Spirit are suitable, splendid ornaments.

2.2.2. *Put on the Lord Jesus Christ* (v. 14). This stands in opposition to very many corrupt, sinful desires mentioned in v. 13. *Rioting and drunkenness* must be set aside. "*Put on Christ*; this includes everything. Put on the righteousness of Christ for justification; be found in him (Php 3:9) as a person is found wearing clothes. Put on the spirit and grace of Christ for sanctification; put on the *new man* (Eph 4:24)." Jesus Christ is the best clothing for Christians to adorn themselves with, to arm themselves with. All other things are filthy rages (Isa 64:6). In our profession and through baptism we have put on Christ (Gal 3:27). Let us do so in truth and sincerity. *The Lord Jesus Christ.* "Put him on as Lord to rule you, as Jesus to save you, and in both as Christ, appointed by the Father to this ruling, saving work."

3. How to walk. When we are up and dressed, we are not to sit still. What have we good clothes for, but to go out in them? *Let us walk.* Christianity teaches us how to walk, how to live, so as to please God. Our lives must be consistent with the Gospel. *Walk honestly,* decently. Christians should be careful to conduct themselves well in those things in which people are watching them, and to seek what is lovely and praiseworthy (Php 4:8). We must not walk:

3.1. *In rioting* (orgies) *and drunkenness*; we must abstain from all excess in eating and drinking. We must not give the least support to reveling or carousing.

3.2. *In chambering and wantonness* (sexual immorality and debauchery), not in any of those sinful desires of the flesh, those works of darkness, whatever is against the sacred law of purity and modesty.

3.3. *In strife and envying* (dissension and jealousy). These are works of darkness too, because although the acts and instances of dissension and jealousy are common, no one is willing to acknowledge themselves to be jealous or quarrelsome. Dissension and jealousy in Christ's disciples and followers are inconsistent with the humble and peace-loving Jesus. Where there are orgies and drunkenness, there is usually sexual immorality and debauchery, dissension and jealousy.

4. What provision to make (v. 14): "*Make not provision for the flesh* (do not think about how to gratify the desires of the sinful nature). Don't be concerned for the body." Our great desire must be to provide for our souls, but must we be completely unconcerned for our bodies? Two things are forbidden here:

4.1. Perplexing ourselves by excessive concern: "In making this provision, do not stretch your mind or indulge in anxious thoughts." It forbids an anxious, burdensome concern.

4.2. Indulging in an irregular desire. The needs of the body must be considered, but its desires must not be gratified. Natural desires must be satisfied, but immoral appetites must be restrained and denied.

CHAPTER 14

Having directed our conduct toward one another in civil things, the apostle undertakes in this chapter to direct our behavior toward one another in sacred things. It seems there was something wrong among the Roman Christians that he sought here to redress. The rules are general, however, and perpetually to be followed in the church. Nothing is more threatening, nor more often fatal, to Christian communities than the disagreements and divisions of their members.

Verses 1–23

We have in this chapter:

1. An account of the sad disagreement that had broken out in the Christian church.

1.1. There was a disagreement among them about distinctions between foods and between days; some of the members of the Christian church at Rome were originally Gentiles, and others were originally Jews. Now those who had been Jews were brought up to observe the ceremonial appointments concerning food and days, and so they clung to them, while other Christians made no such distinction:

1.1.1. About food (v. 2): *One believeth that he may eat all things*—he is well satisfied that everything created by God is good, and nothing is to be refused; nothing is *unclean of itself* (v. 14). The strong Christian is clear about this and practices it accordingly, eating what is set before him. On the other hand, *another, who is weak,* is dissatisfied on this point; he will eat no meat at all, but *eateth herbs* (eats only vegetables), being content with only the fruits of the earth.

1.1.2. About days (v. 5). Those who thought themselves still under some kind of obligation to the ceremonial law considered *one day above another*—continued to pay respect to the times of the Passover, Pentecost, New Moon festivals, and the Feasts of Tabernacles. Those who knew that all these things were abolished by Christ's coming considered every day alike. We must understand this abolition with the exception of the Lord's Day, which all Christians unanimously observed. The apostle seems willing to allow the ceremonial law to wither gradually and to let it have an honorable burial.

1.2. It was not so much the difference itself that caused the trouble as the mismanagement of the difference, making it a bone of contention. Those who were strong, who knew their Christian liberty, despised the weak, who did not. The strong should have pitied the weak and helped them. Those who have knowledge tend to be easily puffed up by it (1Co 8:1) and to look down on their brothers and sisters disdainfully and scornfully. Those who were weak, on the other hand, and dared not use their Christian liberty judged and censured the strong, who did dare, as if the strong were lax Christians. They judged them as law breakers. Well, this was the illness, and we see it remaining in the church to this day.

2. Proper suggestions laid down to quell this disagreement. He does not excommunicate, suspend, or silence either side, but seeks to persuade them to exercise patience with one another, arguing with the strong that they should not be so scornful, and with the weak that they should not be so censorious. Let us notice the rules he gives, some to the strong and some to the weak and some to both.

2.1. Those who are weak must be *received* (accepted), *but not to doubtful disputations* (without passing judgment on disputable matters) (v. 1). "Use your zeal in those things on which you and all the people of God are agreed."

Receive him, or "accept him," or "lend him your hand" to help him. Receive him into your company. Receive him not to quarrel with him, not to argue about uncertain, controversial points. Let your Christian friendship not be disturbed by such meaningless talk and quarrels about words (1Ti 6:4). "Not to judge his doubtful thoughts" (margin). Receive him not to expose him but to instruct and strengthen him.

2.2. Those who are strong must in no way despise the weak, nor are those who are weak to judge the strong (v. 3). This is directed against the fault of each side. It is rare that any such contention exists without there being a fault on both sides. We must not despise or judge our brothers and sisters. Why should we not?

2.2.1. Because God has received them. Strong believers and weak believers, if they are true believers, are accepted by God. "In fact, God not only receives him but *holds him up* (v. 4). Both, if they have true faith, will be supported—the one in his integrity, and the other in his comfort. This hope is built on the power of God, for *God is able to make him stand.*"

2.2.2. Because they are servants of their own master (v. 4): *Who art thou that judgest another man's servant?* We would consider it bad manners to interfere with other people's servants. Weak and strong Christians are indeed our brothers and sisters, but they are not our servants (Mt 23:8). We make ourselves the masters of our brothers and sisters, and in effect usurp the throne of God, when we take it upon ourselves to judge them in this way. God does not see as people see (1Sa 16:7), and he is their Master, not we. If we must judge something, let us exercise that faculty on our own hearts and ways. To *his own master he stands or falls.* How good it is for us that we will not stand or fall by the judgment of one another, but by the judgment of God.

2.2.3. Because both the strong and the weak, if they are true believers, look to God and submit themselves to God's judgment in what they do (v. 6).

2.2.3.1. He who *regards the day*—it is good. We have reason to think, because in other things he behaves as a good Christian, that *he regards it* (regards it as special) *unto the Lord,* and God will accept his honest intention. The sincerity and uprightness of the heart were never rejected because of the weakness of the mind: we serve such a good master.

2.2.3.2. On the other hand, he who *regards not the day,* but considers every day alike—he does not do it out of a spirit of contradiction or contempt of his brothers and sisters. If he is a true Christian, we charitably conclude that to the *Lord he does not regard it.* He makes no such distinction between days only because he knows God has made none, and that is why he seeks God's honor by endeavoring to dedicate every day to him. It is the same in the other example: *He that eats* whatever is set before him *eats to the Lord.* He understands the liberty that God has given him and uses it to the glory of God. He *gives God thanks* for the variety of food available and the liberty he has to eat it. On the other hand, he who does not eat, *to the Lord he eats not.* It is for God's sake, because he is afraid of offending God by eating what he is sure was once prohibited, and he *gives God thanks,* too, that there is enough besides the food from which he abstains. Consequently, as long as both approve themselves to God in their integrity, why should either be judged or despised?

2.2.3.3. Whether we eat meat or only vegetables, it is with a thankful response to God, the author and giver of all our mercies, who sanctifies and sweetens our food. It is clear from this that saying grace, as we commonly call it,

before and after eating was the commonly known practice of the early church. Before we eat, we bless in God's name what God has created, and afterward we bless the name of God for it; both are included. Notice Paul's description of true Christians, taken from their goal (vv. 7–8) and its basis (v. 9).

2.2.3.3.*1.* Our goal: not ourselves, but the Lord. If we want to know what path we are walking on, we must ask what goal we are walking toward.

2.2.3.3.*1.1.* Not to ourselves. We have learned to deny ourselves (Mt 16:24): *None of us liveth to himself.* This is something about which all the people of God agree, however much they may differ in other things. No one who has given themselves to Christ is allowed to be a self-seeker; it is contrary to the foundation of true Christianity. We neither *live to ourselves nor die to ourselves.* The business of our lives is not to please ourselves, but to please God. When it is time for us to die, we die to the Lord, so that we may depart and be with Christ.

2.2.3.3.*1.2.* But *to the Lord* (v. 8), to the Lord Jesus Christ. Christ is the gain we seek, whether we live or die (Php 1:21). We live to glorify him; we die to glorify him, and to go to be glorified with him. Christ is the center, in which all the lines of life and death meet. *Whether we live or die,* then, *we are the Lord's.* Although some Christians are weak and others strong, they are all the Lord's, and acknowledged and accepted by him. Is it for us, then, to judge or despise them, as if we were their masters?

2.2.3.3.*2.* The basis of this (v. 9). It is based on Christ's absolute sovereignty, the fruit and purpose of his death and resurrection. *To this end he both died, and rose, and revived, that he might be Lord both of the dead and living.* He is head over all things for the church (Eph 1:22). He is Lord of those who are living, to rule them, and of those who have died, to receive them and raise them up. We must consider that Christ is Lord of the dead as well as of the living. If they have died, they have already given their account, and let that be enough. This leads to another reason against judging and despising.

2.2.4. Because both the one and the other must soon give an account of themselves (vv. 10–12). *Why dost thou* who are weak *judge thy brother* who is strong? *Why dost thou* who are strong *set at nought* (look down on) *thy brother* who is weak? Why is there all this conflict, argument, and criticism among Christians? *We shall all stand before the judgment seat of Christ* (2Co 5:10). Christ will be the Judge, and before him we will stand as people on trial. To illustrate this (v. 11), Paul quotes a passage from the Old Testament, which speaks of Christ's universal sovereignty, establishing it with an oath: *As I live* (says the Lord), *every knee shall bow to me.* It is a prophecy, in general, of Christ's authority (Php 2:10). Here is a proof of Christ's godhead. Divine honor is due to him, and it must be given. The bowing of the knee to him and the confession made with the tongue are outward expressions of inner adoration and praise. *Every knee* and *every tongue,* either freely or by force.

2.2.4.1. All his friends do it freely. Bowing to him means the understanding is submitted to his truths, the will to his laws, and the whole being to his authority, and this is expressed by bowing the knee, the position of adoration and prayer. Confessing to him means acknowledging his glory, grace, and greatness, acknowledging our own inferiority and corruption, and, according to some, confessing our sins to him.

2.2.4.2. All his enemies will be constrained to do it. Paul concludes, therefore (v. 12), *Every one of us shall give account of himself to God.* We must not give an account for others, nor they for us, but each one for himself. We have little to do to judge others, since they are not accountable to us and we are not accountable to them. They must give account to their own master, not to us; if we can be helpers of their joy in any way (2Co 1:24), it is good, but we do not have authority over their faith. We have more to do to judge ourselves. We have our own account to give. Let this occupy our thoughts, and then those who are strict in judging themselves will tend not to judge and despise their brothers and sisters.

2.2.5. Because the emphasis in Christianity is not to be put on these things, nor are they at all essential to religious faith. Why should you spend your zeal either for or against things that are so insignificant in religion? *The kingdom of God is not meat* (not a matter of eating). Notice here:

2.2.5.1. The nature of true Christianity. It is called here *the kingdom of God*; it is a religion intended to rule us.

2.2.5.1.*1*. It is *not meat* (food) *and drink*: it does not consist either in using or in abstaining from certain foods or drinks. Christianity gives no rule in that case. Matters are left open. Every *creature of God is good* (1Ti 4:4). It is not belonging to this or that party and persuasion, or holding this or that opinion in minor things, that will commend us to God. Rather, it will be asked, "Who feared God and acted righteously, and who did not?"

2.2.5.1.*2*. It is *righteousness, and peace, and joy in the Holy Spirit.* These are some of the essentials of Christianity, in the pursuit of which we must spend our zeal. Righteousness, peace, and joy are comprehensive words. As to God, our great concern is *righteousness*, for the righteous Lord loves righteousness (Ps 11:7). As to our brothers and sisters, it is *peace*—to live in peace and love with them. Christ came into the world to be the great peacemaker. As to ourselves, it is *joy in the Holy Spirit.* Next to our submission to God, religious life consists in our delighting ourselves always in the Lord (Ps 37:4). Surely we serve a good Master, who makes peace and joy so essential to our religion.

2.2.5.1.*3*. It is to *serve Christ* in all these things (v. 18), to do all this out of respect to Christ himself as our Master, to do his will as our rule and look to his glory as our goal. What is Christianity but serving Christ?

2.2.5.2. The advantages of true Christianity. Those who properly observe these things:

2.2.5.2.*1*. Are acceptable to God. They enjoy the love and favor of God, and we need nothing more to make us happy. Those who are most pleased with God are most pleasing to him.

2.2.5.2.*2*. Are approved by other people—by all wise and good people, and the opinion of others is not to be taken notice of. Human approval is not to be ignored, because we must take pains to do what is right in the sight of all (2Co 8:21), but the acceptance of God is to be aimed at in the first place.

2.3. In these controversial matters on which people differ, everyone not only may but also must walk according to the light that God has given them. This is laid down in v. 5: *Let every man be fully persuaded in his own mind*; that is, "Practice according to your own judgment in these things, and leave others to do so too. If your thoughts are sincerely different, do not make their practice a rule to you, any more than you must prescribe yours as a rule to them. First be persuaded that what you do is lawful, before you embark on it." In controversial matters, it is good to keep to the safe side of the hedge. Paul argues to this effect in vv. 14 and 23, which explain this verse and give us a rule not to act against the dictates:

2.3.1. Of a mistaken conscience (v. 14). If we really think it is a sin to do a certain thing, then it is a sin to us, because we are acting against our consciences, even though they are mistaken and misinformed. Notice:

2.3.1.1. Paul's own clear stand on this matter. "*I know and am persuaded*—I am fully persuaded—that there *is nothing unclean of itself*; that is, no kind of food is ceremonially unclean in itself, nor is it forbidden." Sin brought a curse on the whole creation. Now that Christ has removed the curse, the matter is set free again. Paul says, therefore, that he is convinced by the Lord Jesus, not only as the author of that conviction, but also as its basis. Now, therefore, nothing is unclean in itself; every creature of God is good; nothing is "common"; or "nothing profane"; this is the sense in which the Jews used the word *common*. This was Paul's own clear stand, and he practiced it accordingly.

2.3.1.2. A warning, however: *To him that esteemeth any thing to be unclean, to him it is unclean.* To those who do something that they truly believe to be unlawful, whatever the true character of the thing in itself, it is a sin to them. Our wills, in all their choices, should follow the dictates of our minds. This order is broken if the mind (though misguided) tells us that such and such a thing is a sin and yet we still do it. This is a *will* to do evil; there is the same corruption of the will in doing it as if it really were a sin. It must be understood with this condition as well: although human judgments and opinions may make what is good in itself become evil to them, they cannot make what is evil in itself become good.

2.3.2. Of a doubting conscience.

2.3.2.1. He *that doubteth is damned if he eat* (v. 23); that is, it becomes a sin to him; *he is* condemned by his own conscience, because his eating is not from faith, because he does what he is not fully convinced he may lawfully do. Here his own heart must condemn him for having disobeyed. *For whatsoever is not of faith is sin.* Whatever is done while we are not clearly convinced of its lawfulness is a sin against our conscience. Those who dare to do what their own conscience suggests to them is unlawful, when it is not so in itself, will by a similar temptation be brought to do what their conscience tells them is unlawful when it really is. It is dangerous to act against the conscience, even though it is mistaken.

2.3.2.2. *Happy is he that condemns not himself in that thing which he allows* (v. 22). Many people allow themselves to do what in their judgment and conscience they condemn themselves for. While they do it, and argue in favor of it, their own heart tells them they are lying, and their conscience condemns them for it. Now, blessed are those who live their lives in such a way that they do not expose themselves to the reproaches of their own conscience. Blessed is the person who has peace and quietness within (Isa 32:17).

2.4. Those who know their Christian liberty should beware using it so as to give offense to a weak brother or sister. This is laid down in v. 13: *Let us not judge one another any more.* "*Judge* (determine) *this rather*: instead of criticizing the practice of others, let us look to our own, so that no *man* may *put a stumbling-block, or an occasion to fall, in his brother's way*." We must beware saying or doing anything that may cause our brother or sister to stumble or fall, anything that may be an occasion:

2.4.1. Of grief to our brother or sister. "One who is weak and thinks it unlawful to eat certain foods will be greatly troubled to see you eat them." Christians should make sure they do not grieve one another, that they do not sadden the hearts of Christ's little ones.

2.4.2. Of guilt to our brother or sister. An occasion of grief is a *stumbling block*, which disturbs our brother or sister greatly, but this is an *occasion to fall*. "If your weak brother or sister, purely following your example and influence, is drawn to act against their conscience and to walk against the light they have, and so becomes guilty in their soul, you are to be blamed for putting that obstacle in their way." In v. 21 Paul recommends, to the same effect, that we take care not to give offense by the use of lawful things: *It is good neither to eat flesh nor to drink wine*; these are not necessary to support human life, and so we must deny ourselves the use of them rather than give offense. To deny ourselves in this way *is good*—pleasing to God, profitable to our brother or sister, and no harm to us. This is to be extended to all things by which your brother or sister stumbles or is caused to fall—by which they may be involved in either sin or trouble or be *made weak*, weakened as to their resolutions. Notice the motives to support this warning.

2.4.2.1. Consider the royal law of Christian love, which is broken by giving such an offense (v. 15). *If thy brother be grieved with thy meat*. You may be ready to say, "Now he is talking foolishly and weakly." We tend in such cases to put all the blame on that side. But the rebuke is given here to the stronger: now *walkest thou not charitably*. The apostle takes the part of the weakest, and condemns the defect in love on the one side more than the defect in knowledge on the other. Love toward the souls of our brothers and sisters is the best kind of love. True love would make us sensitive toward their peace and purity and would engender a regard for their consciences as well as for our own. Christ deals gently with those who have true grace, even though they are weak in it.

2.4.2.2. Consider the purpose of Christ's death: *Destroy not him with thy meat for whom Christ died* (v. 15).

2.4.2.2.1. Drawing a soul to sin threatens the destruction of that soul. It refers to a complete destruction.

2.4.2.2.2. The consideration of the love of Christ in dying for souls should make us very sensitive toward the happiness and salvation of souls. Did Christ give up a life for souls—such a life—and will not we give up a small piece of food for them? Did he think it worthwhile to deny himself so much for them as to die for them, and will not we think it worthwhile to deny ourselves so little for them? *With thy meat*. "You plead that it is your own food, but remember that although the food is yours, the brother or sister who is offended by it is Christ's. While you are destroying your brother or sister, you are actually helping to advance the Devil's purpose and, as much as it depends on you (12:18), going against the purpose of Christ, and it offends not only your brother or sister but also Christ. But are any destroyed for whom Christ died? It is no thanks to you if they are not; by doing what has a tendency to it, you reveal a great opposition to Christ."

2.4.2.3. Consider the work of God (v. 20): *For meat* (food) *destroy not the work of God*. Do not undo what God has done. You should work together with God (2Co 6:1), not undermine his work. The work of grace and peace is the work of God. The people for whom Christ died (v. 15) are called here the work of God; besides the work that is done for us there is also a work to be done in us. Every saint is God's workmanship (Eph 2:10). We must be very careful to do nothing that leads to the destruction of this work, either in ourselves or in others. We must deny ourselves rather than obstruct and harm our own or others' grace and peace. Many destroy the work of God in themselves for the sake of food and drink—and many destroy it in others by willful offense. Think of what

you are destroying—the *work of God*; think of what you are destroying it for—*for meat* (food), which was only for the stomach, and the stomach for it (1Co 6:13).

2.4.2.4. Consider the evil of giving offense. Paul grants that *all things indeed are pure*. But if we abuse this liberty, it turns into sin to us: *It is evil to him that eats with offense*. Lawful things may be done unlawfully. It is significant that the apostle directs his rebuke most against those who gave the offense. He directs his speech to the strong, because they are more able to bear the rebuke and begin the reformation. To urge this rule further, we may notice here two instructions:

2.4.2.4.1. *Let not then your good be evil spoken of* (v. 16)—be careful not to do anything that may give an opportunity to others to speak ill of either the Christian religion in general or your Christian liberty in particular. It is true that we cannot hinder loose and uncontrolled tongues from speaking ill of us, and of the best things we have, but we must not, if we can help it, give them any cause to do so. In many cases, we must deny ourselves to preserve our reputation; when our doing something that we rightly know we may lawfully do may harm our good name, we will refrain from doing it. In such cases we must cross ourselves rather than shame ourselves. We should manage all our good duties in such a way that they may not be spoken ill of. As we offer the reputation of the good we profess and practice, let us live our lives in such a way that they may not be spoken ill of.

2.4.2.4.2. *Hast thou faith? Have it to thyself before God* (v. 22). "Are you satisfied that you may eat all foods and observe all days (except the Lord's Day) alike? *Have it to thyself*, and do not trouble others by unwise expression of your clarity." In these neutral matters, though we must never go against our conviction, we may still sometimes conceal it, when confessing it will do more harm than good. Keep it as rule to yourself, not to be imposed on others or made a rule to them; or keep it "as a rejoicing to yourself." Paul had faith in these things: *I am persuaded that there is nothing unclean of itself*; but he kept it to himself, so as not to use his liberty to offend others. In things necessary let there be unity, in things unnecessary let there be liberty, and in both let there be *charity. Have it to thyself before God*. The purpose of such knowledge is that we may have a conscience clear of any offense toward God. Those who are right in God's sight are truly right.

2.5. Generally, *Let us therefore follow after the things which make for peace, and things wherewith one may edify another* (v. 19).

2.5.1. We must seek mutual peace. Many who wish for peace and talk loudly about it do not actually follow the things that make for peace. Humility, self-denial, and love are the springs of peace, the things that make for our peace. We are not always so happy as to obtain peace; there are so many who delight in war (Ps 68:30). But the God of peace (15:33; 16:20) will accept us if we pursue the things that make for peace.

2.5.2. We must seek mutual edification. We cannot edify one another while we are quarreling and competing with one another. We are God's building (1Co 3:9), God's temple (1Co 3:16), and need to be edified. No one is so strong that they do not need to be further built up; no one is so weak that they cannot build others up.

CHAPTER 15

In this chapter, the apostle continues the discussion he began in the previous chapter about mutual forbearance in neutral but controversial matters, and so he is com-

ing to the conclusion of his letter. We have here: 1. His commands to them (vv. 1–4). 2. His prayers for them (vv. 5–6). 3. His reasons for writing to them (vv. 7–16). 4. His account of himself and his own life (vv. 17–21). 5. The declaration of his purpose to come and see them (vv. 22–29). 6. His request for a share in their prayers (vv. 30–33).

Verses 1–4

The apostle lays down here two commands, showing the duty of the strong Christian to consider the weakest.

1. We must *bear the infirmities of the weak* (v. 1). We all have our infirmities, but the weak are more subject to them than others. We must bear with their weaknesses and not let our affection for them cool. Christ, similarly, bore with his weak disciples. We must also bear with their weaknesses by sympathizing with them and strengthening them. This is bearing one another's burdens (Gal 6:2).

2. We must please not ourselves but our neighbor (vv. 1–2).

2.1. Christians must not please themselves. It is good for us to go against our own wishes sometimes, and then we will be better able to bear others going against us. We will be spoiled if we are always indulged. The first lesson we have to learn is to deny ourselves (Mt 16:24).

2.2. Christians must please their brothers and sisters. Christians should seek to please others. How pleasant and beneficial a community the church of Christ would be if Christians would seek to please one another! *Please his neighbour*, not in everything, but *for his good*, especially for the good of his soul. *To edification*, that is, not only for his benefit but also for the benefit of others, to build up the body of Christ (Eph 4:12). The closer the stones lie, and the more square they are cut to fit with one another, the stronger the building. *For even Christ pleased not himself.* The self-denial of our Lord Jesus is the best argument against the selfishness of Christians.

2.2.1. Christ did not please himself. He did not consider his own worldly reputation, ease, safety, or pleasure; he emptied himself, making himself nothing (Php 2:7). He did all this for our sakes and to set us an example. His whole life was a self-denying, self-displeasing life.

2.2.2. Here the Scripture was fulfilled: *as it is written, The reproaches of those that reproached thee fell on me* (the insults of those who insulted you have fallen on me). The verse is quoted to show that Christ was so far from pleasing himself that he displeased himself to the highest degree possible. In his humiliation the contentment and satisfaction of his natural inclination were thwarted and denied. He put our benefit before his own comfort and pleasure. The apostle chooses to express this in the words of Scripture. These reproaches were:

2.2.2.1. The shame of those insults that Christ experienced. Whatever dishonor was shown to God troubled the Lord Jesus. Christ himself also endured the greatest indignities; he faced much abuse in his suffering.

2.2.2.2. The sin of those insults. Every sin is a kind of insult to God; the guilt of these sins fell on Christ when he was made a sin offering for us (2Co 5:21). Nothing could be more against him than to be made sin and a curse for us (2Co 5:21; Gal 3:13), and to have the insults against God fall on him. We must not please ourselves, because Christ did not please himself; we must bear the failings of the weak, because Christ bore the insults of those who insulted God. He bore the guilt of sin and the curse for it; we are called to bear only a little of its trouble. He bore the presumptuous sins of evildoers; we are called only to bear the failings of the weak. *Even Christ*, who had enough

reasons to please himself, and no reason to be concerned for us—*even he* did not please himself; *even he* bore our sins. Should not we then be humble, self-denying, and ready to consider one another?

2.2.3. Therefore we must go and do likewise (Lk 10:37): *For whatsoever things were written aforetime were written for our learning.*

2.2.3.1. What is written about Christ *is written for our learning*; he has left us an example. The example of Christ is recorded for our imitation.

2.2.3.2. What is written in the Scriptures of the Old Testament is written *for our learning* (to teach us). What happened to the Old Testament saints happened to them as examples (1Co 10:11). The Scriptures are *written*, so that they will remain for our use and benefit. They are written:

2.2.3.2.1. For our learning. We must seek, therefore, not only to understand the literal meaning of Scripture but also to apply it to ourselves so that it will do us good. Practical observations are more necessary than critical explanations.

2.2.3.2.2. So *that we through patience and comfort of the scriptures might have hope.* Scripture was written in order that we might know what to hope for from God. Now the way to attain this hope is *through patience and comfort* (endurance and encouragement) *of the scripture.* Endurance and encouragement presuppose trouble and sorrow; such is the lot of the saints in this world. But both of these are friends of the hope that is the life of our souls. Perseverance produces character, and character produces hope, which does not disappoint us (5:3–5). The more perseverance we exercise in suffering, the more hopefully we may look through our troubles; nothing is more destructive to hope than impatience. The *comfort of the scriptures*, the encouragement that springs from the word of God, is also a great support to our hope, for it is a pledge of the good that is hoped for.

Verses 5–6

Having delivered two exhortations, the apostle writes a prayer here for the success of what he has said. Notice:

1. The title he gives to God: *The God of patience and consolation* (endurance and encouragement). God gives the grace of endurance; he confirms and maintains it as the God of encouragement. When Paul comes to seek the outpouring of the spirit of love and unity, he addresses himself to God as the God of endurance and encouragement, that is:

1.1. As a God who bears with us and comforts us, who does not keep a record of what we do wrong (Ps 130:3)—to teach us to show our love to our brothers and sisters in the same way God does. Or:

1.2. As a God who gives us endurance and encouragement. Paul spoke in v. 4 of the endurance and encouragement of the Scriptures; these gifts come through Scripture as the channel, but from God as the fountain. Nothing breaks peace more than an impatient, perverse, downheartedness.

2. The mercy he seeks from God: *grant you to be like-minded* (have a spirit of unity) *one toward another, according to Christ have Jesus.*

2.1. The foundation of Christian love and peace is laid in a spirit of unity.

2.2. This unity must be *according to Christ Jesus*, according to the command of Christ, the royal law of love, according to the model and example of Christ, which Paul gave them for their imitation in v. 3. The method of our prayer must be first for truth, and then for peace, because this is the way of the wisdom that comes from above: *it is first pure, then peaceable* (Jas 3:17). This is to have a spirit of unity according to Christ Jesus.

2.3. Unity among Christians according to Christ Jesus is the gift of God. We are taught to pray that the will of God may be done on earth as it is done in heaven (Mt 6:10); there it is done unanimously, among the angels, and our desire must be that the saints on earth may do so too.

3. The goal of his desire: that God may be glorified (v. 6). We should have the glory of God in view whenever we pray. The purpose of unity among Christians is to glorify God:

3.1. *With one mind and one mouth.* It is not enough that there be one mouth; there must also be one mind. In fact, there will hardly be one mouth where there is not one mind.

3.2. As *the Father of our Lord Jesus Christ.* God must be glorified as he has now revealed himself in the person of Jesus Christ, in whom God is our Father. The unity of Christians glorifies *God as the Father of our Lord Jesus Christ.*

Verses 7–12

Paul has encouraged the strong to *receive* the weak (14:1), and here again he urges, *Receive* (accept) *one another*, because sometimes the prejudices of the weak Christian make them suspicious of the strong, as much as the pride of the strong Christian makes them suspicious of the weak, neither of which should happen. Let there be a mutual acceptance among Christians. Now the reason why Christians must accept one another is taken, as before, from the gracious love of Christ toward us: *as Christ also received us, to the glory of God.* If Christ has been so kind to us, shall we be unkind to those who are his? Christ has received us into the closest and dearest relationship with himself. He has received us—even though we were strangers (Eph 2:12, 19) and enemies (5:10) and had gone astray like the prodigal son (Lk 15:11–32)—into fellowship with himself. The words *to the glory of God* may refer both to Christ's acceptance of us, which is our model, and to our accepting of one another, which is our practice according to that model.

1. Christ has accepted us for the glory of God. The goal of our acceptance in Christ is for us to be able to glorify God in this world and be glorified with Christ in the future world. We are called to an eternal glory through Christ Jesus (Jn 17:24).

2. We must accept one another for the glory of God. This must be our great goal in all our actions, that God may be glorified, and nothing leads more to this than the mutual love and kindness of those who profess religious faith; compare v. 6: *That you may with one mind and one mouth glorify God.* Paul shows how Jesus Christ has accepted both Jews and Gentiles; they are both one in him, *one new man* (Eph 2:14–16). Those who agree in Christ may well afford to agree among themselves.

2.1. Christ accepted the Jews (v. 8). Let not anyone think harshly or scornfully, therefore, of those who were originally Jews.

2.1.1. Jesus Christ was *a minister of the circumcision.* He was *a minister, a servant.* Christ blessed the Jews, looked on himself as primarily sent to the *lost sheep of the house of Israel* (Mt 15:24), "took hold of the seed of Abraham" (Heb 2:16, margin), and through them, as it were, took hold of the whole human race. Christ's personal ministry was reserved for them.

2.1.2. He was such a minister *for the truth of God,* to fulfill the promises given to the patriarchs about the special mercy God had in store for their descendants. *To confirm the promises made unto the fathers.* The best confirmation of promises is their fulfillment. When Messiah the Prince (Da 9:25) appeared in the fullness of time (Gal 4:4; Eph 1:10), as a *minister of the circumcision,* all these promises were confirmed. In Christ all the promises of God are *Yea,* and in him *Amen* (2Co 1:20).

2.2. He accepted the Gentiles as well. Paul shows this in vv. 9–12. Notice:

2.2.1. Christ's favor to the Gentiles. One of Christ's purposes was that the Gentiles, too, would be converted. Here is a good reason why the Roman Christians should not think the worse of any Christian for their having been formerly a Gentile: Christ has accepted them. Notice how their conversion is expressed here: *that the Gentiles might glorify God for his mercy.*

2.2.1.1. They will have cause to praise: the mercy of God. Considering the wretched and miserable condition that the Gentile world was in, their acceptance appears more as an act of mercy than the acceptance of the Jews does. The greatest mercy of God to any people is their acceptance into covenant with him.

2.2.1.2. They will have a heart to praise God. They will glorify God for his mercy. God intended to reap a harvest of glory from the Gentiles, because they had for so long turned his glory into shame (Ps 4:2).

2.2.2. The fulfilling of the Scriptures in this. The favor of God to the Gentiles was not only mercy but also truth. Though promises were not directly given to them, many prophesies were made about their being called, and Paul mentions some of these. By referring the Jews to the Old Testament, he seeks to qualify their dislike of the Gentiles. It was foretold that:

2.2.2.1. The Gentiles would have the Gospel preached to them: "*I will confess to thee among the Gentiles* (v. 9); your name will be known and acknowledged in the Gentile world." Christ, in and through his apostles and ministers, whom he sent to disciple all nations (Mt 28:19–20), confessed allegiance to God among the Gentiles. Christ's declaring God's name to his brothers and sisters is called *his praising God in the midst of the congregation* (Ps 22:22). When David's psalms are read and sung among the Gentiles, to the praise and glory of God, it may be said that David is *confessing to God among the Gentiles, and singing to his name.* The one who was the sweet psalmist of Israel (2Sa 23:1) is now the sweet psalmist of the Gentiles. Converting grace makes people greatly in love with David's psalms. If anyone confesses allegiance to God among the Gentiles and sings to his name, it is not they who do so, but Christ and his grace in them who does so.

2.2.2.2. The Gentiles would *rejoice with his people* (v. 10). Those Jews who remain prejudiced against the Gentiles will in no way accept them into any of their joyful festivities. However, because the wall of hostility has been taken down (Eph 2:14), the Gentiles are welcome to rejoice with God's people.

2.2.2.3. They would praise God (v. 11): *Praise the Lord, all ye Gentiles.* Converting grace sets people praising God. The Gentiles long praised their idols of wood and stone, but now they have been brought to praise the Lord.

2.2.2.4. They would believe in Christ (v. 12). This is quoted from Isa 11:10, where we may notice:

2.2.2.4.1. The revelation of Christ as the Gentiles' king. He is called here *the root of Jesse.* Christ, as God, was David's root; Christ, as man, was David's *offspring. And he that shall rise to reign over the Gentiles.* When Christ rose from the dead, *when he ascended on high* (Eph 4:8; Ps 68:18), it was to reign over the Gentiles.

2.2.2.4.2. The turning of the Gentiles to him: *In him shall the Gentiles trust.* Paul quotes from the Septuagint (the Greek translation of the Old Testament); Isa 11:10 itself, translated from the Hebrew, says, *to him shall the Gentiles seek.* The way of faith is first to seek Christ, as One who is offered to us as a Savior, and then, finding him able and willing to save, to trust him. Those who know him will trust in him. Or, this seeking him is the effect of trusting him. We will never find Christ until we trust him. Trust is the parent; diligence in the use of means is the child. Because Jews and Gentiles are so united in Christ's love, why should they not be united in one another's love?

Verse 13

Here is another prayer directed to God, as the God of hope. Notice:

1. How Paul addresses God, as the *God of hope.* He is the foundation on which our hope is built, and he is the builder who himself raises our hope: he is both the object of our hope and its author. Hope that it is not focused on God and brought about by his working in us is mere fancy.

2. What he asks of God, not for himself, but for his readers.

2.1. *That they may be filled with all joy and peace in believing.* Joy and peace are two of the things that the kingdom of God consists of (14:17). Notice:

2.1.1. How desirable this joy and peace are; they fill the soul. Worldly joy puffs up the soul but cannot fill it. True, heavenly, and spiritual joy fills the soul; it has a delight and satisfaction in it, responding to the soul's vast and just desires. Nothing more than this joy, only more of it, as well as its perfection in glory, is the desire of the soul that has it.

2.1.2. How they may be obtained.

2.1.2.1. By prayer. Prayer draws in resources of spiritual joy and peace.

2.1.2.2. By believing. True, substantial, and lasting joy is the fruit of faith. It is because of the weakness of our faith that we lack so much joy and peace. Only believe (Mk 5:36); believe the goodness of Christ, the love of Christ, and the result must be joy and peace. It is *all* joy and peace — all kinds of true joy and peace. When we come to God in prayer, we must enlarge our desires. We are to ask for complete joy.

2.2. That they will *abound* (overflow) *in hope through the power of the Holy Spirit.* What is laid out on them is only a little, compared with what is stored up for them; therefore, the more hope they have, the more joy and peace they have. Christians should seek an overflow of hope, such hope as will not disappoint us (5:5). This comes about through the power of the Holy Spirit. Our own power will never achieve it, and so where this hope is, and overflows, the Holy Spirit must receive all the glory.

Verses 14–16

Here:

1. Paul commends these Christians. He began his letter by praising them (1:8): *Your faith is spoken of throughout the world.* Now, because he has sometimes rebuked them sharply, he concludes with a similar commendation, so that they may part as friends. It was not merely to flatter and compliment them, but to acknowledge their worth and the grace of God in them. We must be eager to observe

and commend in others what is excellent and praiseworthy. Paul had no personal acquaintance of these Christians, and yet he says he is convinced of their excellent qualities, though he knows them only by hearsay. As we must not, on the one hand, be so simple as to believe every word, so, on the other hand, we must not be so skeptical as to believe nothing, but we must be especially eager to believe good about others. It is safer to err on this side. Paul commended them because they were:

1.1. *Full of goodness,* and therefore more likely to accept with a good attitude what he had written, to count it a kindness; and not only so, but also to put it into practice, especially what related to the healing of their differences. A good understanding of one another and a goodwill toward one another would soon put an end to conflict.

1.2. *Filled with all knowledge.* Goodness and knowledge together! What a rare and excellent combination, the head and the heart of the new self.

1.3. *Able to admonish one another.* Those who have goodness and knowledge should share what they have. "You who excel so much in good gifts may think you have no need of any of my teaching." How gladly ministers would leave their admonishing work if people were able and willing to *admonish* (advise, teach) one another! If only all the Lord's people were prophets (Nu 11:29).

2. He clears himself from the suspicion of interfering with what did not concern him (v. 15). Notice how warmly he speaks to them: *My brethren* (v. 14), and again, *brethren* (v. 15). He himself had, and he taught others, the art of pleasing one another. He acknowledges he has written *boldly in some sort.*

2.1. He has done it only to remind them: *as putting you in mind.* People commonly excuse themselves from hearing the word by saying that the minister can tell them nothing but what they already know. Do they not need to be reminded of it so that they may know it better?

2.2. He has done it as the apostle of the Gentiles. It was according to his position: *because of the grace given to me of God* to be the minister *of Jesus Christ to the Gentiles* (v. 16). Now, he gave himself to the Gentiles so that he would not receive the grace of God in vain (2Co 6:1). Christ received so that he could give (Ps 68:18; Eph 4:8), as did Paul; we have talents that must not be buried (Mt 25:24–30). Paul was a minister, and it is good for ministers to remember often the grace that has been given them by God. Notice here:

2.2.1. Whose minister he was: the *minister of Jesus Christ* (1Co 4:1); we are his, and we serve him.

2.2.2. Whom he served: the Gentiles. These Romans were Gentiles: "Now," he says, "I don't thrust myself on you; I am appointed to this task. My commission is my authority."

2.2.3. What he ministered: the *Gospel of God;* "ministering holy things about the Gospel."

2.2.4. For what purpose: *that the offering up of the Gentiles might be acceptable.* Paul gave his life seeking to bring about something that would be acceptable to God. It is the *offering up of the Gentiles;* "the sacrifice of the Gentiles," an expression in which the Gentiles are looked on either:

2.2.4.1. As the priests, offering the sacrifice of prayer and praise. The Jews had long been the holy nation, the kingdom of priests (Ex 19:6), but now the Gentiles are made priests to God. Or:

2.2.4.2. As the sacrifice itself, offered to God by Paul. Paul gathered in souls by his preaching not to keep them to himself but to offer them to God. Moreover, it is an acceptable offering, *being sanctified by the Holy Spirit.*

What made the Gentiles sacrifices to God was their sanctification, and this was not Paul's work, but the work of the Holy Spirit. No one is acceptably offered to God except those who are sanctified.

Verses 17–21

Here the apostle exalts his position for its effectiveness, mentioning to the glory of God the wonderful things God has done through him. He does this to show that although, compared with the multitude of their idolatrous neighbors, the Christian church at Rome are only a little flock (Lk 12:32), nevertheless, they have many companions in the patient endurance that is theirs in the kingdom of Jesus Christ (Rev 1:9). And it was a great confirmation of the truth of the Christian message that it had such strange success. That is why Paul gives them this account, which he makes the subject of his glorying—not boasting, but holy, gracious glorying, for it is *through Jesus Christ.* And so he centers all his glorying on Christ. *I have therefore whereof I may glory*; I would rather read it, "Therefore I have a rejoicing." *In those things which pertain to God*; I would rather read it, "concerning the things of God." The whole of v. 17 would then read: "Therefore I have a rejoicing in Christ Jesus concerning the things of God." Paul wants the Roman Christians to rejoice with him in the effectiveness of his ministry, about which he speaks not only with the greatest possible deference to the power of Christ, but also with a pleading of the truth of what he is saying (v. 18): *I will not dare to speak of any of those things which Christ hath not wrought by me.* He will not take the praise for another person's work, "for"—he says—"I dare not do so." Notice here:

1. Paul's untiring diligence in his work.

1.1. He preached in many places: *from Jerusalem and round about unto Illyricum.* We have an account of Paul's travels in the book of the Acts. We find him there, after he was sent out to preach to the Gentiles (Ac 13:1–52), laboring in Seleucia, Cyprus, Pamphylia, Pisidia, and Lycaonia (Ac 13:1–14:28), afterward traveling through Syria and Cilicia, Phrygia, Galatia, Mysia, Troas, and from there called over to Macedonia, and so into Europe (Ac 15–16). Then we find him very busy at Thessalonica, Berea, Athens, Corinth, Ephesus, and adjacent regions. Now it might be suspected that if Paul undertook so much work, surely he could not have finished it. "No," he says, *"I have fully preached the Gospel of Christ*—have given them a full account of the truth and terms of the Gospel, have not hesitated to declare the whole will of God (Ac 20:27)."

1.2. He preached in places that had not heard the Gospel before (vv. 20–21). He broke up the fallow ground, introducing Christianity where nothing had reigned for years except idolatry and witchcraft. Paul broke the ice, and so must have met with many difficulties and discouragements in his work. He was called to fulfill the hardest work. He was a bold man who launched the first attack on the palace of the fully armed strong man in the Gentile world (Lk 11:21); it was he who ventured the first assault in many places, and he suffered greatly for it. He mentions this as a proof of his apostleship, for the task of the apostles was especially to bring in outsiders. He principally extended himself for the good of those who sat in darkness (Mt 4:16; Lk 1:79). He was concerned not to *build upon another man's foundation.* He quotes a Scripture for this from Isa 52:15: *To whom he was not spoken of, they shall see.* The transition from darkness to light is more perceptible than the later growth and increase of that light. Commonly the Gospel has its greatest success when it first comes to a place; afterward most people become sermon-proof.

2. The great success that he had in his work: it was effective to *make the Gentiles obedient.* The purpose of the Gospel is to bring people to obedience. This was Paul's aim in all his travels. Now how was this great work undertaken?

2.1. Christ was the main agent. He does not say, "which I did," but "which Christ did through me" (v. 18). Whatever good we do, it is not we who do it, but Christ who does it through us. Paul takes every opportunity to acknowledge this.

2.2. Paul was a very active instrument: *by word and deed*, that is, by his preaching and by the miracles he performed, or by his preaching and his living. Those ministers who preach both by word and by action are likely to win souls. This is according to the example of Christ, who *began both to do and teach* (Ac 1:1). *Through mighty signs and wonders.* These were what made the preaching of the word so effective.

2.3. The *power of the Spirit of God* made this effective (v. 19).

2.3.1. It was the power of the Spirit in Paul, as in the other apostles, to perform those miracles. Miracles were performed by the power of the Holy Spirit. Or:

2.3.2. It was the power of the Spirit in the hearts of those who saw the miracles. Paul himself could not make one soul obedient further than the power of the Spirit of God made it by accompanying his labors. This is an encouragement to faithful ministers, who labor under a sense of great weakness. The same almighty Spirit who worked with Paul often makes strength perfect in weakness (2Co 12:9). The converted nations were his joy and crown of rejoicing (Php 4:1). He tells them about it so that they will rejoice with him.

Verses 22–29

The apostle Paul here declares his plan to come and see the Christians at Rome. The way he expresses himself is gracious, and for our imitation. Even our ordinary talk should show an air of grace; this will show what country we belong to (Heb 11:14–16). It seems that Paul's company was very much desired at Rome. Should the apostle of the Gentiles be a stranger to Rome, the center of the Gentile world? He promises to come shortly and gives a good reason why he cannot come now.

1. He excuses himself for not having come yet.

1.1. He assures them that he very much wants to see them; not to see Rome, but *to come unto you* (v. 3), a company of poor, despised saints in Rome. These are the ones whose acquaintance Paul is ambitious to make at Rome. He has a special desire to see them because in all the churches he has heard of their great reputation for faith and holiness. He has had this desire for many years but has never been able to fulfill it. Even God's dearest servants are not always given everything they want.

1.2. He tells them that the reason why he cannot come to them is that he has so much work cut out for him elsewhere. *For which cause*, that is, because of his work in other regions, into which God has opened a wide door for him, so turning him aside. Notice:

1.2.1. The gracious providence of God to his ministers, which puts them in a certain place not according to their own will but according to his own purpose. "Man proposes, but God disposes" (Thomas à Kempis, *The Imitation of Christ*, 1.19; see Pr 16:9; 19:21; Jer 10:23). The Gospel does not come by chance to any place, but by the will and purpose of God.

1.2.2. The gracious wisdom of Paul in spending his time and effort where there was most need. Had Paul considered his own honor, the greatness of the work would never have prevented him from seeing Rome, but Paul sought the things of Christ more than his own things (Php 2:21). There was now a wind of opportunity; the fields were ripe for harvest (Jn 4:35); the season that was slipping by was such as might never come again. We should all do first what is most necessary. Paul mentions this as a sufficient and satisfying reason. We must not take it wrong if our friends prefer necessary work, which is pleasing to God, over unnecessary visits and compliments.

2. He promises to come and see them soon (vv. 23–24, 29), *having no more place in these parts*, namely, in Greece, where he then lived. He had driven the chariot of the Gospel to the coast, and having conquered Greece, he was ready to seek another Greece to conquer. Notice:

2.1. How he forecast his intended visit. His plan was to see them on his way to Spain. This shows that Paul intended to make a journey to Spain. It is not certain, however, whether he ever fulfilled his purpose and went to Spain. He did, it is true, come to Rome, but he was taken there as a prisoner and was detained there two years. Where he went afterward is uncertain. The grace of God often accepts the sincere intention with favor even when the providence of God in wisdom prohibits the intention from being actually fulfilled. Now, he proposed that on his way to Spain he would come to see the Christians at Rome. *I trust to see you*: not, "I am determined I will," but, "I hope I will." We must plan all our goals with submission to divine Providence.

2.2. What he expected in his intended visit.

2.2.1. What he expected from them. He expected that they would help him on his way toward Spain. He did not expect a grand entrance, but a loving attendance, such as friends give. They might be helpful to Paul in his voyage there. It was not merely their accompanying him part of the way, but their furthering him on his expedition, that he counted on.

2.2.2. What he expected in them: to *be somewhat filled with* (to enjoy) *their company*. What Paul wanted was their company and friendship. Paul was himself a man of great achievements in knowledge and grace, but see how he pleased himself with the thoughts of good company. He intended to stay some time with them, because he wanted to enjoy their company, not just to look at them and go on his way. It is only *somewhat filled*; he thought he would leave them with a desire of more of their company. The satisfaction we have in fellowship with the saints in this world is not complete. It is incomplete compared with our fellowship with Christ; only that will fill the soul. It is incomplete compared with the fellowship we hope to have with the saints in the other world.

2.2.3. What he expected from God with them (v. 29). He expected to come *in the fulness of the blessing of the Gospel of Christ*. He speaks doubtfully about what he expects from *them*: *I trust to be brought on my way, and to be filled with your company*. Paul had learned not to place too much confidence in even the best people. These very people later slipped from him (2Ti 4:16): *At my first answer, no man stood by me*—none of the Christians at Rome. However, he speaks confidently about what he expects from God: *I am sure that, when I do come, I shall come in the fulness*. We cannot expect too little from people or too much from God. Now Paul expects that God will bring him to them loaded with blessings. Compare 1:11: *that I may impart unto you some spiritual gift*. The blessing of the Gospel of Christ is the best and most desir-

able blessing. There is a happy meeting between people and ministers when they are both under the fullness of the blessing. When ministers are fully prepared to give this blessing, and people are fully prepared to receive it, both are happy.

3. He gives them a good reason why he cannot come and see them now. He must first make a journey to Jerusalem (vv. 25–28) as the messenger of the church's love. Notice what he says:

3.1. About this love itself. His reason for speaking of this mission now was probably to stir the Roman Christians to contribute similarly. Examples are moving, and Paul was skilled at begging, not for himself, but for others. Notice:

3.1.1. For whom the *contribution* was intended: *For the poor saints which are at Jerusalem* (v. 26). It is in no way strange for saints to be poor. Riches are not the best things, nor is poverty a curse. It seems the saints at Jerusalem were poorer than other saints, perhaps because the famine that prevailed throughout the world in the times of Claudius Caesar was especially prevalent in Judea. This was the occasion of that contribution mentioned in Ac 11:28–30. Although the saints at Jerusalem lived far away from the Christians at Macedonia and Achaia, the latter were still so good and generous toward their needy brothers and sisters, to teach us to extend the hand of our love to all who belong to the household of faith (Gal 6:10), even though they live far away from us. We must extend our goodness, as the sun extends its rays.

3.1.2. By whom it was collected: by *those of Macedonia*, the chief of whom were the Philippians, *and by those of Achaia*, the chief of whom were the Corinthians. It seems the Christians of Macedonia and Achaia were wealthy, while those at Jerusalem were poor and needy; Infinite Wisdom had ordered things in this way so that some would supply the lack of others, and so that a mutual dependence of Christians on one another would thereby be maintained. It *pleased them*. This shows how ready the Christians of Macedonia and Achaia were to contribute and how cheerful they were in it. It pleased them *to make a certain* (some) *contribution*, as a sign of the communion of the saints, as in the natural body one member relieves another, as need be. There was a time when the saints at Jerusalem were on the giving end, when they sold their land and brought the money to the apostles for charitable uses, taking special care that the Grecian widows were not neglected in the daily distribution (Ac 6:1). Now that the providence of God had tipped the scales and made them needy, they found the Grecians kind to them, because the merciful will obtain mercy (Mt 5:7).

3.1.3. What reason there was for it (v. 27): *and their debtors they are*. The Gentiles were greatly indebted to the Jews and were bound in gratitude to be very kind to them. Christ himself came from the people of Israel; the prophets, apostles, and first preachers of the Gospel came from the same people. The Jews, having had the *lively oracles committed* to them (Ac 7:38), were the Christians' librarians. They were cut off so that the Gentiles could be admitted. The Gentiles, then, shared the Jews' spiritual things, receiving the Gospel of salvation secondhand from them, as it were, and therefore *their duty was to minister unto them in carnal things* (material blessings). It was the least they could do.

3.2. About his agency in this business. He *ministered unto the saints* (v. 25) by encouraging others, receiving what was gathered, and passing it on to Jerusalem. Many such good works stand still for lack of someone active to take the lead in them, to set the wheels in motion. Besides this, Paul had other work on his journey, to visit and strengthen the churches. Paul was one who, like his Master (Ac 10:38), gave himself in doing good in every possible way, to the bodies of people as well as to their souls. Paul has undertaken this, and so he has resolved that he will complete it before he embarks on other work (v. 28): *When I have sealed to them this fruit.* He calls the gifts *fruit* because giving is one of the fruits of righteousness; it springs from a root of grace in the givers. His *sealing it to them* shows his great care for it. Paul was very concerned to show himself faithful in managing this matter.

Verses 30–33

Here we have:

1. The apostle Paul's request for a share in the prayers of the Romans, fervently expressed (vv. 30–32). He has prayed much for them, and he desires that in response to this kindness they also pray for him. Praying for one another is an excellent way of expressing love for one another. How careful we should be to make sure we do nothing to forfeit our interests in the love and prayers of God's praying people! Notice:

1.1. Why they must pray for him. "*I beseech you, for the Lord Jesus Christ's sake. You* love Christ and acknowledge Christ; for his sake, then, do me this kindness. *For the love of the Spirit*: as a proof of the love that the Spirit works in the hearts of believers to one another, pray for me. If you have ever experienced the Spirit's love to you, and you want to respond to this love in the Spirit, do not neglect to pursue this work of kindness."

1.2. How they must pray for him: *that you strive together.*

1.2.1. *That you strive in prayer.* We must exert all that is within us (Ps 103:1) to undertake that duty; pray with firmness, faith, and fervency. We are to do this not only when we pray for ourselves but also when we pray for our friends. True love for our brothers and sisters should make us as fervent for them as a sense of our own need makes us for ourselves.

1.2.2. "*That you strive together with me,* who am wrestling with God daily, for myself and my friends." He wants them to share in the same task. Those who are far away according to God's providence may still meet together at the throne of his grace (Heb 4:16).

1.3. What they must ask of God for him. In praying both for ourselves and for our friends, it is good to be specific. He commends himself to their prayers with reference to three things:

1.3.1. The dangers he is exposed to: *That I may be delivered from those that do not believe in Judea.* He had some prospect of trouble from unbelieving Jews on his journey; the Roman Christians must pray, therefore, that God will rescue him. We may and must pray against persecution.

1.3.2. His services: *Pray that my service which I have for Jerusalem may be accepted of the saints.* Why? Was there any danger that it would not be accepted? Paul was the apostle to the Gentiles, and just as the unbelieving Jews looked spitefully at him, which was their evil, so those who believed were suspicious of him, which was their weakness. "Pray that it may be accepted." As God must be sought for the restraining of the ill will of our enemies, so he must also be sought for the preserving and increasing of the goodwill of our friends.

1.3.3. His journey to them. To oblige their prayers for him, he invokes their own interest in his concerns (v. 32): *That I may come unto you with joy.* If he does not do well and prosper in one visit, he thinks he will find little joy in

the next. *May come with joy, by the will of God.* All our joy depends on the will of God.

2. Another prayer of the apostle for them (v. 33): *Now the God of peace be with you all. Amen.* Paul describes God using this title here because of the divisions among the Roman Christians; if God is the God of peace, let us be people of peace. Those who have the fountain cannot lack any of the streams. *With you all,* both weak and strong. Those who are united in the blessing of God should be united in affection for one another.

CHAPTER 16

Paul is now coming to the end of his long and excellent letter, and he does so with a great deal of affection. It is clear that he was very loving. It is significant how often Paul speaks as if he were concluding, but then starts again. These repeated blessings, which stand for farewells, show that Paul is reluctant to part. We have here: 1. His commendation of one friend to the Roman Christians, and his particular greeting of several among them (vv. 1–16). 2. A warning to beware of those who cause divisions (vv. 17–20). 3. Greetings added from some people who are with Paul (vv. 21–24). 4. A final conclusion with a solemn celebration of the glory of God (vv. 25–27).

Verses 1–16

Such best wishes as are contained in these verses are common in letters between friends, but Paul, by the use of such warm expressions, sanctifies these common compliments.

1. Here is the commendation of a friend, by whom (some think) this letter was delivered—one *Phebe* (Phoebe) (vv. 1–2). It seems she was a person of good social position and wealth who had business that called her to Rome, where she was a stranger; that is why Paul commends her to the acquaintance of the Christians there. Courtesy and Christianity are in harmony with one another.

1.1. He describes her as having a very good character.

1.1.1. As a sister to him: she is Phoebe *our sister,* not in nature but in grace. Both Christ and his apostles had some of their best friends among the devout, and therefore honorable, women.

1.1.2. As *a servant to the church at Cenchrea*: a servant by office, not one who was to preach the word—that was forbidden to women—but one who was to serve by acts of love and hospitality. Phoebe seems to have been a person of some significance, and it was no disparagement to her to be a servant to the church. Everyone should seek to serve the church in their place, for in doing so they are serving Christ. Cenchrea was a small seaport town next to Corinth.

1.1.3. As one who helped many, especially Paul (v. 2). She helped many people in need and distress. Her goodness was extensive. Notice the gratitude of Paul in mentioning her particular kindness to him: *and of myself also.* Acknowledging favors is the least response we can make.

1.2. He commends her to their care: "*Receive her in the Lord.* Entertain her; make her welcome, as a servant and friend of Christ. Do it *as it becometh saints* to receive, because they love Christ and therefore love all who are his for his sake." Or, "Do it as *becometh saints* to be received, with love and honor." *Assist her in whatsoever business she has need of you.* Being a woman, a stranger, a Christian, she needed help, and Paul called on them to help her. It is good for Christians to be helpful to one another in their dealings, especially to be helpful to strangers, because we are members of one body (12:4–5; 1Co 12:12–27; Eph 4:25). Paul arranged for help to one who had been so helpful to many.

2. Here are commendations to some particular friends among those to whom he wrote. Although Paul felt daily the burden of caring for all the churches—which was enough to distract an ordinary person—he could still retain the memory of so many people. His heart was so full of love and affection that he sent greetings to each of them. *Greet* them, *salute* them; they are translations of the same word. "Let them know that I remember them."

2.1. Aquila and Priscilla were a famous couple whom Paul felt a special kindness for. They originally came from Rome but were banished from there by order of Claudius (Ac 18:2). Paul came to know them at Corinth and undertook the trade of tent making with them. After some time, they returned to Rome. He calls them his *helpers in Christ Jesus.* In fact, they not only did much for Paul but also risked much for him: "they have *for my life laid down their own necks.*" They risked their lives to protect Paul, putting their own lives in danger to preserve his. Paul was in a great deal of danger at Corinth, but they sheltered him. It has been a good while since they showed Paul this kindness, but he speaks as feelingly of it as if it had been only yesterday. *To whom not only I give thanks, but also all the churches of the Gentiles*, who were all indebted to these good people for helping save the life of the one who was the apostle to the Gentiles. He also sends a greeting to the *church in their house* (v. 5). Religion reigning in a family will turn a house into a church. No doubt their house gained a good reputation because Priscilla, the good wife of the family, was so very well known and enthusiastic in her religious faith, so well known that she is often named first. When Priscilla and Aquila were at Ephesus, even though they were only *sojourners*, there, too, they hosted a church in their house (1Co 16:19). Truly godly people will be careful to take religious faith along with them wherever they go.

2.2. Epenetus (v. 5) is called Paul's *well-beloved* (my dear friend). Endearing language should be used among Christians both to express love and to engage love. This is why Paul calls Ampliatus *beloved in the Lord* (v. 8) and why he calls Stachys his *beloved* (v. 9). About Epenetus it is also said that he is the *firstfruits* (the first convert) *of Achaia unto Christ*, one who was offered to God by Paul as the firstfruits of his ministry there. Epenetus was the pledge of a great harvest, because God had many people in Corinth, the chief city of Achaia (Ac 18:10). Special respect is to be paid to those who set out early, who come to work in the vineyard at the first hour (Mt 20:1–2).

2.3. He commends Mary and some others: *Mary*, who *bestowed much labor on us.* True love does not mind hard work, but rather takes pleasure in it; where there is great love, there will be a great deal of hard work. He says of Tryphena and Tryphosa that they *labour in the Lord* (v. 12), and about the beloved Persis, that *she laboured much in the Lord*; she gave herself fully to the work of the Lord (1Co 15:58).

2.4. About Andronicus and Junia (v. 7). Some consider them husband and wife.

2.4.1. They were Paul's *cousins*, related to him, as was Herodion (v. 11). Religion does not take away our respect for our relatives, but sanctifies and increases it, engaging us to rejoice in them even more, since we find them related to Christ through faith.

2.4.2. They were his fellow prisoners. Partnership in suffering sometimes does much toward uniting souls and knitting affections.

2.4.3. They were *of note among the apostles.* They were distinguished for knowledge, gifts, and graces, which made them famous among the apostles.

2.4.4. *Who also were in Christ before me.* As regards actual time, they were converted to Christ before Paul. How ready was Paul to acknowledge in others any kind of precedence!

2.5. Apelles is said here to be *approved in Christ* (v. 10), a high characterization! He was one who had been tested; his friends and enemies had tested him, and he was as gold (Job 23:10), trustworthy.

2.6. About Aristobulus and Narcissus, notice is taken of their household (vv. 10–11), those of their household who *are in the Lord*, those who were Christians, for it is limited (v. 11). Note how careful Paul was to leave no one out of his greetings whom he knew at all!

2.7. About Rufus (v. 13), Paul says that he is *chosen in the Lord.* He was a fine Christian, whose gifts and graces showed that he had been eternally chosen in Christ Jesus. Paul also commends "*his mother and mine*, his mother by nature and mine by Christian love." This good woman, on some occasion or other, has been like a mother to Paul, and Paul gratefully acknowledges it here.

2.8. As for the rest, he greets the *brethren who are with them* (v. 14) and the *saints who are with them* (v. 15). It is good when saints delight in being together, and Paul joins them together in his greetings to endear them to one another. In Christian congregations there should be smaller groups linked together in love and fellowship.

2.9. He concludes by commending them to the love and embraces of one another: *Salute one another with a holy kiss.* Mutual greetings both express love and increase and strengthen love. Paul encourages the use of them here, therefore, requiring only that they be holy. He adds, in closing, a general greeting to them all, in the name of the churches of Christ (v. 16): "*The churches of Christ salute you*; that is, the churches whom I am with want me to show their affection for you and send their good wishes to you." This is one way of maintaining the fellowship of the saints.

Verses 17–20

Here is a warning to his readers that they should beware of those whose principles and practices are destructive to Christian love. Notice:

1. The warning itself: *I beseech you, brethren.* He does not will and command, but urges for the sake of love. He teaches them:

1.1. To see their danger: *Mark those who cause divisions and offenses.* Our Master himself foretold that divisions and offenses would come, and here we are warned against the people who cause them. Those who burden the church with dividing and offending impositions cause divisions and offenses, teachings contrary to or different from "the teaching we have learned." Once truth is deserted, unity and peace will not last long. Now, *mark* those who cause such divisions. We need a piercing, watchful eye to discern the danger we are in from such people, for often their pretenses are plausible, but their plans very harmful. A danger discovered is half prevented.

1.2. To shun it: "*Avoid them.* Avoid all unnecessary fellowship and communication with them, so that you may not become leavened and defiled *by them. Their word will eat as doth a canker.*" Some think Paul is especially warning his readers to beware of the Judaizing teachers.

2. The reasons to support this warning.

2.1. The harmful ways of these deceivers (v. 18). Notice two things in Paul's description of them:

2.1.1. The master they serve: not *our Lord Jesus Christ.* Although they call themselves Christians, they do not serve Christ, whatever they may claim; rather, they *serve their own belly.* It is some sinful desire that they please. Their *God is their belly* (Php 3:19). What an evil master they serve, and how unworthy they are to rival Christ.

2.1.2. The way they follow to fulfill their purposes: *By good words and fair speeches they deceive the hearts of the simple.* Their words and speeches have an appearance of holiness and zeal for God—it is easy to appear godly on the outside—and an appearance of kindness and love toward those into whom they instill their corrupt teachings. We have a great need, therefore, to keep our hearts with unqualified diligence (Pr 4:23).

2.2. The danger we are in: *"For your obedience has come abroad unto all men*—you are noted in all the churches as willing, teachable, complying people."

2.2.1. Therefore, because it is so, these deceiving teachers will be more likely to attack them. "The false teachers hear that you are an obedient people, and so they will be likely to come among you, to see if you will obey them."

2.2.2. Even though things are so, they are in danger from these deceivers. Paul suggests this not as one who is suspicious of them, but as one who is concerned for them: *your obedience has come abroad unto* (is known to) *all men*; *I am glad therefore on your behalf.* This is how he introduces their commendation, to make way for the warning. "You must not become self-confident: *I would have you wise unto that which is good, and simple concerning evil.*" An impressionable temperament is good when well controlled, but otherwise it may be very ensnaring, and so he gives two general rules:

2.2.2.1. To be *wise unto that which is good.* We need a great deal of wisdom to be faithful to good truths, good duties, and good people, so that we may not be deceived or deluded with regard to any of these.

2.2.2.2. To be *simple* (innocent) *concerning evil*—so wise as not to be *deceived*, but so innocent as not to be deceivers. It is good for Christians to have the wisdom of the serpent (Mt 10:16), but not the subtlety of the old Serpent (Rev 12:9; 20:2). It is a wisely innocent person who does not know how to do anything against the truth. Now Paul was even more concerned for the Roman church because it was so famous; it was a city set on a hill (Mt 5:14), and many eyes were looking at the Christians there.

2.3. The promise of God that we will gain the final victory (v. 20): *The God of peace shall bruise Satan under your feet.* Notice:

2.3.1. The title he gives to God: *the God of peace.* When we come to God for spiritual victories, we must look on him not only as the Lord of Hosts but also as the God of peace, a God who is at peace with us, who creates peace for us. Victory comes from God more as the God of peace than as the God of war.

2.3.2. The blessing he expects from God—victory over Satan. Satan tempting and troubling, acting as a deceiver and as a destroyer: him the *God of peace will bruise under our feet.* "Although you cannot overcome in your own strength and wisdom, nevertheless, the God of peace will do it for you."

2.3.2.1. The victory will be complete: *He shall bruise Satan under your feet*; here Paul clearly alludes to the first promise the Messiah made in Paradise (Ge 3:15). Christ

has overcome for us, and we have nothing to do but to pursue the victory. Let this encourage us in our spiritual conflict; let it encourage us to fight the good fight of faith (1Ti 6:12).

2.3.2.2. The victory will be quick: God will bring it about *shortly.* Soldiers are encouraged when they know that the war will end quickly in such a victory. It is the victory that all the saints will have over Satan when they reach heaven, together with the present victories that they obtain through grace as a pledge of that final victory. Hold out, therefore, with faith and patience for a little while. *The grace of our Lord Jesus Christ be with you.* If the grace of Christ is with us, who can be against us so as to defeat us? Paul, not only as a friend but also as an apostle, blesses them with his authority, and he repeats the blessing (v. 24).

Verses 21–24

The apostle adds here that some individuals who are now with him remember the believers in Rome with affection. He mentions:

1. Some who are his particular friends: *Timotheus my workfellow.* Paul sometimes calls Timothy his son, but here he describes him as his fellow worker, equal to him. He also mentions *Lucius,* probably Lucius of Cyrene, a noted man in the church of Antioch (Ac 13:1), and *Sosipater,* probably the same as Sopater from Berea, mentioned in Ac 20:4. Paul calls these friends his relatives. It is very encouraging to see the holiness and usefulness of our relatives.

2. One who is Paul's secretary (v. 22): *I Tertius, who wrote this epistle.* Paul made use of a scribe because his handwriting was bad and not very legible, which he excuses when he writes to the Galatians with his own hand (Gal 6:11). The least bit of service done to the church will not pass unremembered or unrewarded.

3. Some others who are noted among the Christians (v. 23). There is *Gaius my host.* Paul commends him for his great hospitality, not only as his host but also as the host for the *whole church. Erastus, the chamberlain of the city* (the city's director of public works), is also mentioned; the city Paul refers to is Corinth. It seems Erastus was a person of some honor and significance, one who held a public position. Not many who are influential, not many who are noble, are called (1Co 1:26), but some are. *Quartus,* too, is mentioned, and called a brother.

Verses 25–27

Here the apostle solemnly closes his letter with a magnificent ascription of glory to the blessed God. He, as it were, breathes out his heart to the Romans in praising God. Notice here:

1. A description of the Gospel of God, which is included in parenthesis, as it were, as the means by which God strengthens souls: *To establish you according to my Gospel.* Paul calls it his Gospel because he is its preacher. Paul has his mind and heart so full of the Gospel that he can scarcely mention it without digressing to express its nature and excellence.

1.1. It is the *preaching of Jesus Christ.* The sum and substance of the whole Gospel is Jesus Christ and him crucified (1Co 2:2). We do not preach ourselves, Paul says, but Christ Jesus the Lord (2Co 4:5). What strengthens souls is the clear, direct preaching of Jesus Christ.

1.2. *It is the revelation of the mystery which was kept secret since the world began, and by the scriptures of the prophets made known.* The subject matter of the Gospel is a mystery. Praise God, enough of this mystery is made clear to us to bring us to heaven, if we do not willfully neglect such a great salvation (Heb 2:3).

1.2.1. This mystery was kept secret since the world began: it "was wrapped up in silence from eternity." Before the foundation of the world was laid, the mystery was kept hidden in God (Eph 3:9). Or, *since the world began* may mean "throughout Old Testament times": this mystery was kept comparatively secret in the ceremonial law and the prophets. This is how it was kept hidden from ages and generations (Col 1:26), even among the Jews, and much more among the Gentiles. Even the disciples of Christ themselves, before his resurrection and ascension, were very much in the dark about the mystery of redemption.

1.2.2. It is now revealed. The shadows of the evening are over, and the Sun of righteousness has risen on the world (Mal 4:2; Lk 1:78). But how is it revealed by the *scriptures of the prophets* (prophetic writings)? Surely, because now the fulfillment has given the best explanation of the prophecies of the Old Testament. Being fulfilled, they are explained. The Old Testament not only borrows light from the revelation of the New Testament; it also returns light to it. Now Christ is seen to have been the treasure hidden in the field of the Old Testament (Mt 13:44). To him bear *all the prophets witness* (Ac 10:43). See Lk 24:27.

1.2.3. It is revealed *according to the commandment of the everlasting God*. In case anyone should object, "Why was this mystery kept hidden for so long, and why is revealed now?" Paul responds that he sees it in the light of the will of God. *The everlasting God*. He is from everlasting and is to everlasting. We must never look for any new revelation, but must stand by this one, because it is according to the commandment of the eternal God. Christ, in the Gospel, is the same yesterday, today, and forever (Heb 13:8).

1.2.4. It is *made known to all nations for the obedience of faith*. Paul often takes note of the extent of this revelation. Christ is salvation to the ends of the earth (Ac 13:47), to all nations. The purpose of this revelation, too, is significant; it is *for the obedience of faith*. The Gospel is revealed not to be talked about and discussed but to be submitted to. Notice here what the right kind of faith is—what leads to obedience; notice what the right kind of obedience is—what comes from faith; and notice what is the purpose of the Gospel—to lead us to both.

2. A doxology to the God whose Gospel it is, giving glory to him forever (v. 27). Notice:

2.1. The subject of this praise. In thanking God, we focus on his favors to us; in praising and adoring God, we focus on his perfections in himself. Two of his principal qualities are taken notice of here:

2.1.1. His power (v. 25): *to him that is of power to establish you*. It is no less than a divine power that strengthens the saints. In giving God the glory of this power, we may and must take to ourselves the comfort of it—that whatever our doubts, difficulties, and fears, our God, whom we serve, is powerful to strengthen us.

2.1.2. His wisdom (v. 27): *To God only wise*. Power to carry something out without the wisdom to plan it, and wisdom to plan something without the power to carry it out, are both worthless and useless, but both together, and both infinite, make a perfect being. God alone is perfectly and infallibly wise. He is the spring and fountain of all the wisdom of the creatures. With him are strength and wisdom (Job 26:5).

2.2. The Mediator of this praise: *through Jesus Christ*. "To God only wise through Jesus Christ," as some read it. It is in and through Christ that God is revealed to the world as the only wise God. Or rather, as our translation reads it, *glory through Jesus Christ*. All the glory that comes from fallen humanity to God must pass through the hands of the Lord Jesus. Just as he is the Mediator of all our prayers, so he is and, we believe, will be to eternity the Mediator of all our praises.

A PRACTICAL AND DEVOTIONAL
EXPOSITION OF
1 Corinthians

1. Corinth was a main city of Greece, situated on the isthmus that joined the Peloponnese to the rest of Greece, with two adjoining ports, one called Lechaeum, not far from the city, from where they traded to Italy and the west, and the other called Cenchrea, farther away, from where they traded to Asia. From this situation, it is hardly surprising that Corinth would be a place of great trade and wealth, or that a place so famous for its wealth and arts would also be infamous for its vice. Yet in this immoral city Paul planted and raised a Christian church, chiefly among the Gentiles. *You know that you were Gentiles, carried away to those dumb idols even as you were led* (12:2). On the other hand, it is not improbable that many Jewish converts were among them, for we are told that *Crispus, the chief ruler of the synagogue, believed on the Lord, with all his house* (Ac 18:8). Paul remained in this city for nearly two years, being encouraged by a divine vision assuring him God *had much people in that city* (Ac 18:9–10).

2. Some time after he left, he wrote this letter to them to nurture what he had planted and put right some gross disorders that had been introduced during his absence. Pride, greed, self-indulgence, and lust are all fueled and prompted by outward affluence, and here the apostle charges either most of these people or some individuals among them with these vices.

2.1. Their pride revealed itself in their different factions. This vice was not wholly fueled by their wealth; it was also supported by the insight they had into Greek learning and philosophy.

2.2. Their greed was revealed in their lawsuits before pagan judges.

2.3. Their self-indulgence appeared in more instances than one; it appeared in the clothes they wore and in their defiling themselves even at the Lord's Table.

2.4. Their lust broke out in a most flagrant and notorious example—a man had his father's wife.

2.5. It is clear from other passages of the letter that they were not so entirely free from their former immoral inclinations that they did not need very strict cautions against sexual immorality. The pride of their learning had also taken many of them so far that they disbelieved or argued against the teaching of the resurrection.

3. It is clear that there was much that deserved blame and needed correction in this church. The apostle sets himself to do both with great wisdom and faithfulness, and with a mixture of tenderness and authority. After a short introduction:

3.1. He blames them, in the first four chapters, for their discord and factions, and prescribes humility as a remedy for the evils that are so evident among them.

3.2. In chapter 5 he discusses the case of the incestuous man.

3.3. In chapter 6 he blames them for the lawsuits they have brought before worldly judges, and in 6:9–20 he accuses them of the sin of sexual immorality.

3.4. In chapter 7 he gives advice on a case of conscience about marriage and gives some guidance about virgins.

3.5. In chapter 8 he gives them instructions about food offered to idols. From this he also takes the opportunity, in chapter 9, to expand a little on his own conduct in regard to Christian liberty.

3.6. In chapter 10 he undertakes to dissuade them from having fellowship with idolaters by eating their sacrifices, because they could not have a place at the Lord's Table and a place at the table of demons at the same time.

3.7. In chapter 11 he gives instructions about their clothing in public worship, blaming them for their gross irregularities and scandalous disorders in receiving the Lord's Supper.

3.8. In chapter 12 he begins his consideration of spiritual gifts, which were poured out in great abundance on this church. Toward the close he informs them that he can commend to them something far more excellent, upon which he breaks out, in chapter 13, into a commendation and characterization of love.

3.9. Then, in chapter 14, he instructs them on how to maintain decency and order in the churches in the use of their spiritual gifts.

3.10. Chapter 15 is taken up in confirming and explaining the great teaching of the resurrection.

3.11. The last chapter consists of some individual pieces of advice and greetings.

CHAPTER 1

Here we have: 1. The introduction to the whole letter (vv. 1–9). 2. One main reason for writing it, namely, their divisions and the origin of those divisions (vv. 10–13). 3. An account of Paul's ministry among them (vv. 14–17). 4. The way in which he preached the Gospel (vv. 17–31).

Verses 1–9

We have here the apostle's introduction to his whole letter, in which we may notice:

1. The opening greeting. It is a letter from Paul to the church of Corinth, which he himself had planted, though some among them now questioned his apostleship (9:1–2). The most faithful and useful ministers are not safe from such contempt. *Paul, called to be an apostle of Jesus Christ, through the will of God.* He had not taken this honor for himself, but had received a divine commission for it. It was now necessary to assert his character and *magnify his office* (Ro 11:13), when false teachers made a virtue of defaming him. At such a time, for Paul to maintain his legitimacy and authority as an apostle showed not pride but faithfulness to his trust. To make it clearer that faithfulness is his aim, he represented Sosthenes as writing the letter with him, because Sosthenes, once a ruler of the Jewish synagogue, later a convert to Christianity, was probably a Corinthian by birth and dear to this people. Throughout the rest of the letter, however, Paul speaks in the first person singular. The people to whom this letter was directed were *the church of God that was at Corinth, sanctified in Christ Jesus, and called to be saints.* All Christians are sanctified in Christ Jesus insofar as they are dedicated and devoted to him by their baptism. If they are not holy in fact, it is their own fault and shame. It is the purpose of Christianity to sanctify us in Christ. Paul directs the letter also *to all that in every place call on the name of Christ Jesus our Lord, both theirs and ours.* God has his remnant in every place, and we should have a common concern for and hold fellowship with all who call on Christ's name.

2. The apostolic blessing. *Grace be to you, and peace, from God our Father, and from the Lord Jesus Christ. Grace and peace*—the favor of God and reconciliation to him. It is the summary of all blessings. We have this advantage under the Gospel:

2.1. We are instructed how to obtain that peace from God: it is in and through Christ.

2.2. We are told what must qualify us for this peace, namely, grace: first grace, and then peace.

3. The apostle's thanksgiving to God on their behalf. Paul begins most of his letters by giving thanks to God for his friends and praying for them. He gives thanks:

3.1. For their conversion to the faith of Christ: *for the grace which was given you through Jesus Christ* (v. 4). Those who are united to Christ through faith are the objects of divine favor. God loves them.

3.2. For the abundance of their spiritual gifts. They did not fall short of any other church in any gift (v. 7). He specifies *utterance* (speaking) *and knowledge* (v. 5). Many are able to speak well but do not have a sound basis in knowledge, and their words are barren. Many have the

treasure of knowledge but lack the ability to employ it for the good of others, and then it is hidden. But the person to whom God gives both is qualified for great usefulness. These gifts were a confirmation of the testimony of Christ among them (v. 6). The more plentifully the gifts were poured out on any church, the more confirming evidence that church had of their divine mission. It is hardly surprising that when the Corinthian Christians had such a foundation for their faith, they would live in expectation of the coming of their Lord Jesus Christ (v. 7). It is the character of Christians that they wait for Christ's second coming. The stronger we are in the Christian faith, the more eager is our expectation of Christ's return.

4. The encouraging hopes the apostle has for their future, based on the power and love of Christ and the faithfulness of God (vv. 8–9). The One who has begun a good work in them will not leave it unfinished (Php 1:6). Those who wait for the coming of our Lord Jesus Christ will be kept by him, and those who are so *will be blameless in the day of Christ.* How glorious are the hopes of such a privilege, whether for ourselves or for others! O glorious expectation, especially when the faithfulness of God supports our hopes! Those who come at his call will never be disappointed in their hopes in him. If we show ourselves to be faithful to God, we will never find him unfaithful to us.

Verses 10–13

Here the apostle gets to the heart of his subject.

1. He encourages them to have unity and mutual love and rebukes them for their divisions. From some who wish the Corinthian church well, he has received an account about some sad divisions among them. He writes to them in a very engaging way: *"I beseech you, brethren, by the name of our Lord Jesus Christ,* be united. Speak all the same thing; avoid divisions or schisms. *Be perfectly joined together in the same mind.* In the great things of religion be united in mind, but when there is not a unity of attitude, let there be a unity of affection."

2. He hints at the origin of these quarrels. Pride lay at their root, and this caused them to split into factions. They quarreled about their ministers. Those who were inclined to be quarrelsome broke into different groups, setting their ministers at the head of their different factions: some praised Paul, others praised Apollos, some Cephas, or Peter, and some wanted none of them, but only Christ. The best things in the world—including the Gospel and its institutions—are liable to be corrupted in this way—though they are in perfect harmony with themselves and one another—and to become the means of dissension, discord, and conflict. How far will pride carry Christians in their opposition to one another! It will go even so far as to set Christ and his own apostles in conflict, making them rivals and competitors.

3. He pleads with them about their discord and quarrels: *"Is Christ divided? No*; there is only one Christ, and so Christians should be united. *Was Paul crucified for you?* Was he your sacrifice and atonement? Or, *were you baptized in the name of Paul?* By that sacred ritual were you devoted to my service, or committed to be my disciples?"

Ministers, however much they may be instrumental in doing us good, are not to be put in place of Christ. It would be good for the churches if their members did not distinguish themselves from each other by the names of parties they belonged to, for Christ is not divided.

Verses 14–16

Here the apostle gives an account of his ministry among them. He thanks God he has baptized only a few among them; *Crispus*, who was once a ruler of a synagogue at Corinth (Ac 19:8), *Gaius, and the household of Stephanas*, besides whom, he says, he does not remember that he has baptized any. He is not to be understood to mean that he was thankful for not having baptized at all, but for not having done it in the present circumstances. He left it to other ministers to baptize, while he occupied his time with preaching the Gospel. This, he thought, was more his business. In this sense he said, *Christ sent him not to baptize, but to preach the Gospel* (v. 17) — not so much to baptize as to preach. Ministers should consider themselves set apart more especially to that service in which Christ will be most honored and the salvation of souls furthered, and for which they are best fitted. The chief business Paul did among them was to preach *the Gospel* (v. 17), *the cross* (v. 18), *Christ crucified* (v. 23). He did not preach his own thoughts, but the Gospel. Christ crucified is the foundation of all our hopes and the fountain of all our joys. We live through his death. This is what Paul preached, what all ministers should preach, and what all the saints live on.

Verses 17–31

We have here:

1. The way in which Paul preached the Gospel and the cross of Christ: *Not with the wisdom of words* (v. 17), *the enticing words of man's wisdom* (2:4), so that *the cross of Christ would* not *be of no effect*, so that its success would not be attributed to the power of human skill rather than to truth, to the powerful oratory of those who declared it rather than to the simple doctrine of a crucified Jesus. He preached a crucified Jesus in clear, direct, plain language, telling the people that the Jesus who was crucified at Jerusalem was the Son of God and Savior of humanity, and that all who want to be saved must repent of their sins and believe in this Jesus. This truth did not need to be dressed up; it shone out with the greatest splendor in its own light and was effective in the world by its divine authority, without any human help. The clear and direct preaching of a crucified Jesus was more powerful than all the oratory and philosophy of the pagan world.

2. The different effects of this preaching: to those who perish it is foolishness, *but to those who are saved it is the power of God* (v. 18). *It is to the Jews a stumblingblock, and to the Greeks foolishness*, but *unto those who are called, both Jews and Greeks, Christ the power of God and the wisdom of God* (vv. 23–24).

2.1. Christ crucified was a stumbling block to the Jews. They despised him, looking on him as detestable because he did not satisfy them with a sign to their liking — though his divine power shone out in innumerable miracles. The Jews demanded a sign (v. 22).

2.2. He was foolishness to the Greeks. They laughed at the story of a crucified Savior. They sought human wisdom, and there was nothing in the plain message of the cross to suit their taste; they received it, therefore, with scorn and contempt. What, hope to be saved by a man who could not save himself (Mk 15:31)! Trust in one who was condemned and crucified as an evildoer, a man of humble birth and lowly condition in life! This was what

the pride of human reason and learning could not accept. It is just of God to leave to themselves those who pour such proud contempt on divine wisdom and grace.

2.3. To those who are saved, *he is the wisdom of God, and the power of God*. Those who are enlightened by the Spirit of God discern more glorious revelations of God's wisdom and power in the message of Christ crucified than in all God's other works.

3. The triumphs of the cross over human wisdom, according to the ancient prophecy (Isa 29:14): *I will destroy the wisdom of the wise, and bring to nothing the understanding of the prudent. Where is the wise? Where is the scribe? Where is the disputer of this world? Hath not God made foolish the wisdom of this world?* (vv. 19–20). All the valuable learning of this world was frustrated by the Christian revelation and the glorious triumphs of the cross. When God wanted to save the world, he used his own way, and with good reason, too, because *the world by wisdom knew not God* (v. 21). All the boasted worldly knowledge did not — indeed, could not — effectively bring the world back to God. People were puffed up by their imaginary knowledge (8:1), and so *it pleased him, by the foolishness of preaching, to save those that believe*.

3.1. The message preached was foolishness in the eyes of the worldly-wise. To those who were blinded by self-conceit, our living through One who died, our being blessed by One who was made a curse, our being justified by One who was himself condemned, was all foolishness.

3.2. The way of preaching the Gospel was foolishness to them too. None of the people who were famous for wisdom or eloquence were employed. A few fishermen were called and sent on this mission. They were commissioned to disciple the nations. Those who proudly claimed to have learning and wisdom despised the message of the Gospel for the sake of those who spoke it. But *the foolishness of God is wiser than men* (v. 25). *You see your calling, brethren, how that not many wise men after the flesh, not many mighty, not many noble, are called* (v. 26). There is a great deal of lowliness and weakness in the outward appearance of our religion.

3.2.1. Few people of distinguished character in any of these respects were chosen for the work of the ministry: not those who were wise by human standards, not the powerful and influential. God looks on things differently than human beings look on them (1Sa 16:7). God has chosen the foolish things of the world, the weak things of the world, the lowly and contemptible things of the world — people of humble birth, low rank, or no great education — to be the preachers of the Gospel. He is a better judge than we as to what instruments and ways will best serve the purposes of his glory.

3.2.2. Few people of distinguished rank and character were called to be Christians. As the preachers were poor and lowly, so, generally, were the converts. Few wise, powerful, and influential people accepted the message of the cross. What glorious revelations there are of divine wisdom in the whole plan of the Gospel!

4. An account of how wonderfully everything works:

4.1. To humble human pride and boasting. God has chosen *the foolish things of the world to confound the wise, the weak things of the world to confound the mighty, and base things, and things which are despised, things which are not, to bring to nought* (to nullify) *things that are*. The conversion of the Gentiles was to open up a way to abolish the constitution that the Jews prided themselves so much on. It is common for the Jews to speak of the Gentiles as "things that are not." The Gospel is ready to humble the pride of both Jews and Greeks, so *that no flesh may glory in his presence* (v. 29), so that there may be no room for boasting. Only divine wisdom planned the way of redemption; only divine grace revealed it and made it known. It lay, in both respects, out of human reach. The Gospel era is a way of humbling humanity.

4.2. To glorify God. The hand of the Lord accompanied the preachers and worked powerfully in the hearts of the hearers, and Jesus Christ was made what was truly great and honorable to both ministers and Christians. All that we have we have received from God as the source, and in and through Christ as the channel. Christ is *made by God to us wisdom, righteousness, sanctification, and redemption* (v. 30). We are foolishness, and he is made wisdom to us. We are guilty, and he is made righteousness. We are depraved and corrupt, and he is made our sanctification. We are in chains, and he is made our redemption. What is intended in everything is *that all flesh may glory in the Lord* (v. 31). And by the whole plan, people are humbled and God is glorified.

CHAPTER 2

The apostle: 1. Reminds the Corinthians of the clear and direct way in which he communicated the Gospel to them (vv. 1–5). 2. Shows them that he has communicated to them a treasure of the highest wisdom, such as could never have entered the human heart unless it had been revealed, nor can be received except by the light and influence of that Spirit who revealed it (vv. 6–16).

Verses 1–5

The apostle pursues his intention, reminding the Corinthians how he acted when he first preached the Gospel among them. He writes about:

1. Its subject (v. 2): *I determined to know nothing among you but Jesus Christ, and him crucified.* Christ, in his person and work, is the essence of the Gospel and should be the great subject of a Gospel minister's preaching. Anyone who heard Paul preach found him to speak so constantly about this that they would say he knew nothing except Christ, and him crucified.

2. The way in which he preached Christ.

2.1. Negatively. *I came not among you with excellency of speech or wisdom* (v. 1). *My speech and preaching were not with enticing words of man's wisdom* (v. 4). He did not set himself to charm them into listening to him by eloquent expressions or to entertain their imagination with grand ideas. Divine wisdom did not need to be displayed with such human ornaments.

2.2. Positively. He came among them *declaring the testimony of God* (v. 1). He made known a divine revelation. Fine speech and philosophical skill and argument could add no value to what came commended by such authority. He was also *among them in weakness and fear, and in much trembling*; however, his *speech and preaching were in demonstration of the Spirit and of power* (vv. 3–4). His enemies in the church of Corinth spoke contemptuously about him: *His bodily presence, say they, is weak, and his speech contemptible* (2Co 10:10). Possibly he was short in stature and had a quiet voice, but it is clear that he was no mean speaker. Nor did he lack courage or determination: he was *in nothing terrified by his adversaries*. But he was not one who boasted. He did not go around bragging, as his opponents did. No one knows the fear and trembling experienced by faithful ministers; a deep sense of their own weakness brings about this fear and trembling. They know how inadequate they are for the great task before them. Paul also spoke with authority: *in the demonstra-*

tion of the Spirit and of power. He preached the truths of Christ in the native language of his hearers, with clear, direct speech. He taught as the Spirit enabled him to, and he left the Spirit to demonstrate the truth of his message.

3. The goal for which he preached Christ crucified: *That your faith should not stand in the wisdom of man, but the power of God* (v. 5), so that they would not be drawn by human motives or overcome by mere human arguments. But when nothing but Christ crucified was clearly preached, the success must be entirely attributed to God's power.

Verses 6–16

The apostle shows the Corinthians that he has communicated to them a treasure of the truest and the highest wisdom: *We speak wisdom among those who are perfect* (v. 6). Those who receive the message as divine and have looked well into it discover true wisdom in it. Although what we preach is foolishness to the world, it is wisdom to them. Those who are wise themselves are the only proper judges of what is wisdom—*not*, indeed, *the wisdom of this world, nor of the princes of this world*, but the *wisdom of God in a mystery* (vv. 6–7); not worldly wisdom, but divine; not such as worldly people, destitute of the Spirit of God, could have discovered or can receive. How different the judgment of God is from that of the world! The wisdom he teaches is of a completely different kind from what passes by that name in the world. It is *the wisdom of God in a mystery, the hidden wisdom of God*, the depths of which, now that it is revealed, no one but God himself can fathom. Notice about this wisdom:

1. Its origin: *It was ordained of God, before the world, to our glory* (v. 7). It was ordained by God; he had determined long ago to make it known, and he determined to do so *to our glory*, or "the glory of us," either us apostles or us Christians. It was a great honor to the apostles to be entrusted with the revelation of this wisdom. It was a great privilege for Christians to have this glorious wisdom revealed to them; the wisdom of God taught by the Gospel prepares for our eternal glory and happiness in the future world. What honor he puts on his saints!

2. The ignorance of the great people of the world about it: *Which none of the princes of this world knew* (v. 8). The Roman governor and the rulers of the Jewish nation seem to be the people chiefly referred to here. Jesus Christ is the Lord of Glory, and the reason he was hated was that he was not known. If his crucifiers had known him, known who and what he was, they would have withheld their ungodly hands. This is how he pleaded with his Father for their pardon: *Father, forgive them, for they know not what they do* (Lk 23:34).

3. It is such wisdom as could not have been made known without revelation, according to what the prophet Isaiah says (Isa 64:4): *Eye hath not seen, nor ear heard, nor have entered into the heart of man the things which God hath prepared for those that love him.* So it is in Paul's quotation; Isa 64:4 itself ends with, *for him that waiteth for him*, and the Septuagint (the Greek version of the Old Testament) reads, "for him who waits for his mercy." Waiting for God is evidence of love for him. There are things that God has prepared for those who love him and wait for him. However, the apostle speaks here about divine revelation under the Gospel. The great truths of the Gospel are things that lie outside the sphere of human discovery: *Eye hath not seen, nor ear heard them, nor have they entered into the heart of man.* If they were objects we could sense, there would have been no need for revelation. But because they lie outside the sphere of nature, we cannot discover them except by the light of revelation.

4. By whom this wisdom is revealed to us: *God hath revealed them to us by his Spirit* (v. 10). The Scripture is given by inspiration of God. The apostles spoke by inspiration of the same Spirit. What Paul taught was revealed by God through his Spirit, *that Spirit that searches all things, yea, the deep things of God, and knows the things of God, as the spirit of a man that is in him knows the things of a man* (v. 11). A double argument is drawn from these words as proof of the divinity of the Holy Sprit:

4.1. Omniscience is attributed to him: *He searches all things, even the deep things of God.* He enters into the very depths of God, penetrating into his most hidden purposes. Now who can have such a thorough knowledge of God except God?

4.2. This allusion seems to imply that the Holy Spirit is as much in God as *a man's* mind is in himself. The Spirit is as much and as intimately one with God as the human mind is with a human being. The Spirit of God knows the things of God because he is one with God. Nor can we know the secret purposes of God until they are made known to us by his Holy Spirit. It was through this Spirit that the apostles had received the *wisdom of God in a mystery*. "*Now we have received not the spirit of the world, but the Spirit which is of God, that we might know the things freely given to us of God* (v. 12). We have what we communicate in the name of God by inspiration from him, and it is through his gracious illumination that *we know the things freely given to us of God* for salvation" — that is, "the great privileges of the Gospel." Although these things are given to us, we cannot know them to any saving purpose until we have the Spirit.

5. How this wisdom was taught: *Which things we speak, not in the words which man's wisdom teaches, but which the Holy Spirit teaches* (v. 13). The wisdom the apostles taught was what they had received from the Spirit of God. Nor did they dress it up in human adornments, but openly declared the message of Christ in terms taught them by the Holy Spirit. The truths of God need no garnishing by human skill or eloquence, but look best in the words the Holy Spirit teaches. *Comparing spiritual things with spiritual* — one part of revelation with another. When spiritual things are brought together, they will help illustrate one another, but if the principles of human art and inquiry are made a test of revelation, we will certainly judge revelation wrongly. The language of the Spirit of God is the most proper way to convey his meaning.

6. How this wisdom is received.

6.1. *The natural man receiveth not the things of God, for they are foolishness to him, neither can he know them, because they are spiritually discerned* (v. 14). The *natural man* refers either:

6.1.1. To the person under the power of corruption, not yet enlightened by the Spirit of God. Unsanctified people do not receive the things of God. The truths of God are foolishness to such a heart. Evil inclinations and principles make the person unwilling to enter the mind of God. It is the quickening rays of the Spirit of truth and holiness that must help the heart to discern the excellence of spiritual things. The natural person, then, cannot know them, because they are spiritually discerned. Or:

6.1.2. To the natural person, that is, the wise person in the world (1:19–20), one who has the wisdom of the world, human wisdom (vv. 4–6), someone who wants to receive nothing by faith, nor acknowledge any need for supernatural help. This was very much the character of those who claimed great knowledge and the Greek learning and wisdom of that day. Such people do not receive the things of the Spirit of God. With them, revelation is

not a matter of knowledge; they look on it as the wild thoughts of deluded dreamers. For that reason they can have no knowledge of things revealed, because those things are only spiritually discerned.

6.2. *But he that is spiritual judgeth all things, yet he himself is judged of no man* (v. 15). Either:

6.2.1. Those who are sanctified are capable of judging matters of human wisdom and also have an appreciation and relish for divine truths. It is the sanctified heart that discerns the real beauty of holiness (1Ch 16:29; 2Ch 20:21; etc.), and yet it does not lose its power to discern common and natural things. Spiritual people may judge all things, natural and supernatural, human and divine. They themselves, however, are not judged or discerned by anyone; they are not subject to merely human judgments. Worldly people know no more about spiritual people than they do about other spiritual matters. Spiritual people do not lie open to their observation. Or:

6.2.2. *He that is spiritual* — who has had divine revelations made to him — can judge both common things and divine things. He does not lose the power of reasoning by basing his religion on revelation. But *he himself is judged of no man* — he cannot be judged, so as to be overcome, by anyone. Those who base all their knowledge on principles of human inquiry and the mere light of human reason can never judge the truth or falsehood of what is received only by revelation. *For who hath known the mind of the Lord, that he may instruct him* (v. 16; Isa 40:13), that is, the *spiritual man?* Who can enter so far into the mind of God as to instruct those who have the Spirit of God and are under his inspiration? Very few have known anything of the mind of God by means of natural power. *But,* adds the apostle, *we have the mind of Christ,* and the mind of Christ is the mind of God. It is the great privilege of Christians that they have the mind of Christ.

CHAPTER 3

The apostle: 1. Rebukes the Corinthians for their worldliness and divisions (vv. 1–4). 2. Instructs them how to put right what is wrong among them, by remembering: 2.1. That their ministers are no more than ministers (v. 5). 2.2. That their ministers pursue the same intention (vv. 6–10). 2.3. That they build on one and the same foundation (vv. 11–15). 3. Encourages them to give appropriate honor to their bodies (vv. 16–17) and to be humble (vv. 18–20). 4. Tries to dissuade them from boasting in particular ministers (vv. 21–23).

Verses 1–4

Here:

1. Paul blames the Corinthians for their weakness. Those who are renewed to a spiritual life may still be defective in many things. The apostle tells them, *I could not speak to you as unto spiritual* people, *but as unto carnal* (worldly) people, *as to babes in Christ* (v. 1). It was only too evident they were still very much under the command of worldly and corrupt feelings. They were still mere infants in Christ. They had received some of the basic principles of Christianity but had not grown up to maturity, and this was why he had communicated no more of its deep things to them than he had. They could not stomach such food; they needed to be fed milk, not *meat* (solid food) (v. 2). It is the duty of faithful ministers of Christ to consider the abilities of their hearers and teach them only what they can bear (Jn 16:12). It is natural for infants to grow up to become adults; infants in Christ should seek to grow in stature and become mature in Christ (Eph 4:13).

Christians are completely to blame when they do not try to grow in grace and knowledge (2Pe 3:18).

2. He blames them for their worldliness, and he mentions their strife and discord about their ministers as evidence: *For you are yet carnal; for whereas there are among you envyings, and strifes, and divisions, are you not carnal, and walk as men?* (v. 3). *One said, I am of Paul,* and *another, I am of Apollos* (v. 4). Conflicts and quarrels about religion are sad evidence of remaining worldliness. True religion makes people peace-loving, not quarrelsome. *Do you not walk as men?* It is a sad fact that many who should walk as Christians, above merely ordinary human ways, still walk as worldly people, as those who do not belong to the Lord.

Verses 5–10

Here the apostle instructs them how to heal this disease:

1. By reminding them that the ministers about whom they quarrel are simply ministers: *Who then is Paul, and who is Apollos, but ministers by whom you believed? Even as the Lord gave to every man* (v. 5). Ministers are mere instruments used by the God of all grace (1Pe 5:10). We should take care not to look on our ministers as gods or put them in place of God. All the gifts and powers that even apostles applied and exerted in the work of the ministry came from God. Those gifts were intended to reveal the apostles' mission and message to be divine. *Paul had planted and Apollos had watered* (v. 6). Both were useful, one for one purpose, the other for another. Paul was equipped for the work of planting, and Apollos for watering, but God makes things grow. The success of the ministry must be derived from God's blessing: *Neither he that planteth is any thing, nor he that watereth, but God who giveth the increase* (v. 7). Even apostolic ministers can do nothing effectively and successfully unless God gives growth. Paul and Apollos are nothing at all in themselves; rather, God is all in all (12:6; 15:28).

2. By representing to them the unanimity of Christ's ministers:

2.1. *He that planteth and he that watereth are one* (v. 8), employed by one Master, busy in the same one work, in harmony with one another, however much they may be set in opposition to each other by those who lead the petty factions. All the faithful ministers of Christ are one in the great business and intention of their ministry.

2.2. All such people may expect a glorious reward for their faithfulness, and in proportion to it: *Every man shall receive his own reward, according to his own labor.* Those who work hardest will fare best. Those who are most faithful will have the greatest reward.

2.3. *They are laborers with God, fellow laborers* (v. 9); that is, they are working for him. They are working together with God, and the One who knows their work will take care that they do not labor in vain. The judgment of God is based on truth (Ro 2:2). He always rewards in proportion to the diligence and faithfulness of his servants.

2.4. They are always under his eye and employed in his field and building, and so he will definitely look after them: *You are God's husbandry, you are God's building,* and therefore you are neither *of Paul* nor *of Apollos.* What we have been doing among you is all for God." *According to the grace of God which is given unto me, as a wise master-builder, I have laid the foundation, and another buildeth thereon.* It was honorable to be an expert builder in the edifice of God, but it added to his character to be wise.

2.5. And yet Paul does not characterize himself in this way to satisfy his own pride, but to exalt divine grace. He

was an expert builder, but it was the grace of God that made him such. Spiritual pride is detestable, but to take notice of the favors of God in order to advance our gratitude to him and speak of them to his honor is simply a proper expression of the duty and regard we owe him. Ministers should not be proud of their gifts or graces, but the more qualified they are for their work, and the more success they have in it, the more thankful they should be to God.

2.6. *I have laid the foundation, and another buildeth thereon.* It was Paul who laid the foundation of a church among them. He would detract from no one who had given service among them, but neither would he be robbed of his own honor and respect. Faithful ministers may and should have a concern for their own reputation. Their usefulness depends much on it. *But let every man take heed how he buildeth thereon.* A very poor building may be built on a good foundation. Nothing must be laid on it except what the foundation will bear and what belongs on it. Gold and dirt must not be mixed together. Ministers of Christ should take great care that they do not build according to their own fancies or false reasoning on the foundation of divine revelation.

Verses 11–15

Here the apostle informs us what foundation he has laid. *Other foundation can no man lay besides what is laid—even Jesus Christ.* The teaching of our Savior and his mediation are the main teaching of Christianity. It lies under and is the foundation of all the others. Of those who hold on to the foundation there are two kinds:

1. Some build on this foundation with *gold, silver, and precious stones* (v. 12), namely, those who hold nothing but the *truth as it is in Jesus* (Eph 4:21) and preach nothing else. This is building well on a good foundation.

2. Others *build wood, hay, and stubble* on this foundation; that is, although they remain faithful to the foundation, they depart from the mind of Christ in many details. They build on the good foundation what will not stand the test when the day of testing comes. A time is coming when what people have built on this foundation will be revealed: *Every man's work shall be made manifest.* Everyone's work will be revealed both to them and to others, both to those who have been misled by them and to those who have escaped their errors. A day is coming that will show us our true selves and show us our actions in their true light, without covering or disguise: *For the day shall declare it* (that is, every person's work), *because it shall be revealed by fire,* and the *fire shall try every man's work, of what sort it is* (v. 13). The day, the last day, the appointed great day of testing, will declare and reveal it; see 4:5. A day is coming that will distinguish one person from another, and one person's work from another's, as fire separates gold from dross or separates metal that will withstand fire from other materials that will be consumed by it.

2.1. Some people's works will *abide the trial.* It will be clear that they not only held on to the foundation but also built regularly and well on it. The foundation and the superstructure were all in harmony. Those who build in that way will not, cannot, fail to receive a reward. They will have praise and honor on that day and have an eternal reward after it. Faithfulness in the ministers of Christ will meet with a full and ample reward in a future life. And, Lord, how great that reward will be!

2.2. Others' *works shall be burnt* (v. 15). The great day will peel away all disguises and make things appear as they really are: *He whose work shall be burnt will suffer loss.* If he has built on the right foundation with wood, hay, and straw, he will suffer loss, even though he may generally have been an honest and upright Christian. This part of his work will be lost even though he himself may be saved. Those who hold to the foundation of Christianity can be saved even if they build with hay, wood, and straw on it. This may help release our love: nothing will condemn people but their wickedness. The one who builds with inferior materials will be saved, *yet so as by fire*, escaping through the flames. God will have no mercy on their works, though he may snatch them as burning sticks out of the fire (Am 4:11).

Verses 16–17

Here the apostle resumes his argument, basing it on his earlier metaphor, *You are God's building* (v. 9), and adding here, *Know you not that you are the temple of God, and the Spirit of God dwelleth in you? If any man defile* (corrupts and destroys) *the temple of God, him shall God destroy*—the same word is translated *defile* in the first clause and *destroy* in the second—*for the temple of God is holy, which temple you are.* From other parts of the letter (see 6:13–20), it looks as if the false teachers among the Corinthians not only led loose lives but also taught licentious doctrines. Such teaching was not to be counted among hay and straw, which would be consumed while the person who laid them on the foundation escaped burning. Those who spread principles of this sort would provoke God to destroy them. *Know you not that you are the temple of God, and that the Spirit of God dwelleth in you?* Christian churches are temples of God. He lives among them through his Holy Spirit. Every Christian is also a living temple of the living God. Christ through his Spirit lives in all true believers. The temple was set apart from every common use for a holy use, for the immediate service of God. In the same way, all Christians are separated from common uses and set apart for God and his service. They are sacred to him: Christians are holy by profession and should be pure and clean in both heart and life.

Verses 18–20

Here Paul prescribes humility as the remedy for the irregularities in the church at Corinth:

1. *"Let no man deceive himself* (v. 18). Do not be led away from the truth and simplicity of the Gospel." We are in a great danger of deceiving ourselves when we have too high an opinion of human wisdom and knowledge.

2. But *he who seems to be wise must become a fool, that he may be wise.* He must be aware of his own ignorance and mourn it; he must distrust his own understanding and not depend on it. He who submits his own understanding to the instruction of God is in line to receive true and eternal wisdom. Those who have a low opinion of their own knowledge and powers will submit to better information.

3. But the proud, those who are conceited in their own wisdom and understanding, will undertake to correct even divine wisdom itself. We must humble ourselves before God if we want to be either truly wise or good: *For the wisdom of this world is foolishness with God* (v. 19).

4. *His understanding is infinite* (Ps 147:5). There can be no greater comparison between his wisdom and ours than between his power and being and ours. There is no common measure by which we may compare our finite selves and his infinite nature. Much more is human wisdom foolishness with God when set in competition with his. How justly does he despise it, how easily can he frustrate and overcome it!

5. *He knows the thoughts of the wise, that they are vain* (v. 20). God has perfect knowledge of human thoughts,

their most secret purposes. He knows them to be futile. Should not all of this teach us modesty and a deference to the wisdom of God? Those who want to be truly wise must learn from God, and not set their own wisdom up to compete with God's.

Verses 21–23

Here Paul exhorts the Corinthians not to overrate their teachers, considering that the church has an equal interest in all their ministers. *Therefore let no man glory in men* (v. 21): they should not forget that their ministers are human, pay them that respect that is due only to God, or set them at the heads of their competing parties.

1. Faithful ministers are a great blessing to any people, but the foolishness and weakness of human beings may cause much trouble by what is in itself a blessing. The only way to avoid this trouble is to have a due sense of the common weakness of human understanding and a wholehearted submission to the wisdom of God. Ministers are not to set themselves up in competition with one another. They were appointed by Christ for the common benefit of the church: "*Paul, and Apollos, and Cephas, are all yours.* All are to be valued and used for your own spiritual benefit."

2. Paul also takes this occasion to give an inventory of the church's possessions, the spiritual riches of a true believer: "*All is yours.* In fact, the world itself is yours. *Life is yours*, so that you may prepare for the life of heaven, and *death is yours*, so that you may go to possess it. Death is the kind messenger who will take you to your Father's house. *Things present* are yours, for your support on the road; *things to come* are yours, to enrich you forever at your destination." All is ours, time and eternity, earth and heaven, life and death.

3. However, it must be remembered at the same time *that we are Christ's.* All things are ours simply because we are Christ's. Those who want to be safe for time and happy to eternity must be Christ's. *And Christ is God's.* He is the Christ of God (Lk 9:20), anointed by God and commissioned by him. God in Christ reconciling a sinful world to himself (2Co 5:19), and pouring out the riches of his grace on a reconciled world, is the essence of the Gospel.

CHAPTER 4

Here: 1. The apostle tells them how to consider him and his fellow ministers (vv. 1–6). 2. He warns them against pride and self-exaltation (vv. 7–13). 3. He claims their respect for him as their father in Christ (vv. 14–16). 4. He tells them he has sent Timothy to them and that he himself plans to come to them soon (vv. 17–21).

Verses 1–6

Here:

1. The apostle claims the respect due to him because of his position and office: *Let a man so account of us as of the ministers of Christ, and stewards of the mysteries of God* (v. 1). In our opinion of ministers, we should be careful to avoid extremes. Apostles themselves were:

1.1. Not to be overvalued, because they were ministers, not masters. They were servants of Christ, nothing more. They had no authority to spread their own ideas, but were to spread the Christian faith.

1.2. Not to be undervalued, because they were ministers of Christ. They were not stewards of the ordinary things of the world, but of divine mysteries. They did not set themselves up as masters, but they deserved respect in this honorable service.

2. He asserts that apostles especially deserve this respect when they do their duty in this service: *It is required in stewards that a man be found faithful* (v. 2), trustworthy. The stewards in Christ's family must appoint what he has appointed. They must teach what he has commanded. When they have the testimony of a good conscience and the approval of their Master, they must take no notice of the opinions and censures of their fellow servants: *But with me*, the apostle writes, *it is a small thing that I should be judged of you, or of man's judgment* (v. 3). Indeed, reputation and respect among people are a good step toward usefulness in the ministry. However, those who want to make it their chief endeavor to please people would hardly show themselves to be faithful servants of Christ (Gal 1:10). Those who want to be faithful to Christ must despise human censures for his sake. Even the best people tend to judge rashly, harshly. It is encouraging that people are not our final judges. In fact, we are not to judge ourselves in this way: *"Yea, I judge not myself. For though I know nothing by myself*, cannot charge myself with unfaithfulness, *yet am I not thereby justified*, but *he that judgeth me is the Lord*. It is his judgment that must determine me. He will find and judge me to be as I am."

3. The apostle uses this opportunity to warn the Corinthians against a censorious spirit: *Therefore judge nothing before the time, until the Lord come* (v. 5).

3.1. What he is warning against is judging at the wrong time, judging people's future state or the secret motives of their actions. To judge in these cases is to assume the seat of God. How bold a sinner is the eager and severe criticizer! How ill-timed and arrogant is their criticism!

3.2. But there is one who will judge both the censurer and those he censures. This should make the Corinthians hesitant now to judge others, and careful in judging themselves. A time is coming when the *Lord will bring to light the hidden things of darkness, and make manifest the counsels of the hearts.* A day is coming that will make known people's secret sins, the secrets of their hearts, bringing them into broad daylight.

3.3. The Lord Jesus Christ will reveal the intentions of the heart, of all hearts. The Lord Jesus Christ must have the knowledge of the intentions of the heart, for otherwise he could not reveal them. We should be very careful about how we criticize others, since we have to deal with a Judge from whom we cannot conceal ourselves.

3.4. When he comes to judge, *every man shall have praise of God. Every man*, that is, everyone qualified for it. Christians may well be patient under unjust censures when they know such a day is coming. But how fearful they should be of loading censures now onto anyone whom their common Judge will commend later.

4. The apostle shows us the reason why he has used his own name and that of Apollos in his discussion. He has done *it in a figure* (figuratively), and *he has done it for their sakes*. He chose to mention his own name and the name of a faithful fellow laborer rather than the names of any heads of factions among them in order to avoid what would offend. The apostle's advice is *that they learn not to think of men above what is written, nor be puffed up for one against another* (v. 6). Apostles were not to be regarded as anything other than servants of Christ. We must be very careful not to transfer the honor and authority of the Master to his servant. We must not think of our ministers beyond what is written. Pride commonly lies at the root of these quarrels. We will not become *puffed up for one against another* if we remember they are all instruments employed by God in his field and building (3:6–15) and endowed by him with their various talents and qualifications.

Verses 7–13

Here the apostle applies the foregoing hint to a warning against pride and arrogance.

1. He warns them against pride; all the distinctions made among them were owing to God: *Who maketh thee to differ? And what hast thou that thou didst not receive?* (v. 7). Here the apostle turns his discussion to the ministers who set themselves as leaders of these little groups. What had they to glory in, when all their special gifts came from God? It may be taken as a general rule: we have no reason to be proud of our achievements or actions; all that we have, are, or do that is good is because of the free and rich grace of God. Boasting is forever excluded. Those who receive everything should be proud of nothing (Ps 115:1). Proper attention to our obligations to divine grace would heal us of pride and arrogance.

2. He urges the duty of humility on them by a very clever irony: *"You are full, you are rich, you have reigned as kings without us.* You not only have enough spiritual gifts; you are affluent in them; in fact, you can make them the matter of your glory *without us.*" There is a very well-expressed gradual development from sufficiency to wealth to royalty, to show how much the Corinthians were proud of the abundance of their wisdom and spiritual gifts: *"You have reigned as kings,"* the apostle says, "that is, in your own conceit, and *I would to God you did reign, that we also might reign with you.* I wish you had as much of the true glory of a Christian church on you as you take to yourselves." Those who think best of themselves do not commonly know themselves best. The Corinthians might have reigned, and the apostle with them, if they had not been blown up by their imaginary royalty. Pride is the great prejudice to our improvement. Those who think they have arrived are stopped from growing wiser or better; they are not only full but rich. In fact, they think they are royalty.

3. He undertakes to set out his own circumstances and those of the other apostles and compares them with the circumstances of the Corinthians.

3.1. He sets out the case of the apostles: *For I think it hath pleased God to set forth us the apostles last, as it were appointed to death. For we are made a spectacle to the world, and to angels, and to men.* Never were any men in this world so hunted and harassed.

3.1.1. An allusion is made to some of the bloody spectacles in the Roman amphitheaters, where the victor did not escape with his life, but was only reserved for another combat, so that such wretched criminals could very properly be called "persons devoted or appointed to death." The apostles are said to be put on display last because those who fought against one another in the afternoon were most exposed, being obliged to fight naked.

3.1.2. The general meaning is that the apostles were exposed to continual danger of death: God had put them on display. The apostles were shown in order to reveal the power of God's grace, to confirm the truth of their mission and message. These were ends worthy of God—noble views, fit to encourage them to fight.

3.1.3. The role of an apostle was harsh and dangerous as well as honorable: *"For we are made a spectacle"*—or "a show"—*"to the world, and to angels, and to men* (v. 9). Angels and human beings are witnesses to our persecution, patience, and generosity. They all see that we suffer for our faithfulness to Christ, how intense our suffering is, and how patiently we endure it by the power of divine grace. We work hard, but honorably; the work is hazardous, but also glorious. The world must see and wonder at our undaunted resolution, our invincible patience."

3.2. He compares his own situation with that of the Corinthians: "*We are fools for Christ's sake, but you are wise in Christ; we are weak, but you are strong; you are honorable, but we are despised* (v. 10). We don't mind being thought fools in the world, and despised as such, so that the honor of the Gospel may by this means be secured and displayed. *But you are wise in Christ.* You have the reputation of being wise and learned Christians, and you take no little pride in that. *We are weak, but you are strong.* We are suffering for Christ's sake when you are in easy and flourishing circumstances." All Christians are not exposed to the same difficulties. The standard bearers in an army are the ones most attacked. In times of persecution, ministers are usually the ones who suffer first and most. "You look on yourselves as adults, as much more advanced." Those who think of themselves in this way or consider others to be such are not always the ones who are most proficient in Christianity. The Corinthians may think themselves, and be regarded by others, as wiser and stronger in Christ than the apostles themselves. But, oh, how great is their mistake!

4. He describes some details of their sufferings:

4.1. *Even to this present hour we hunger and thirst, and are naked, and are buffeted, and have no certain dwelling place, and labor, working with our own hands* (vv. 11–12). In fact, they were *made as the filth of the world, and the offscouring of all things* (v. 13). Poor circumstances these were—for the prime ministers of our Savior's kingdom to have neither house nor home, and to be without food and clothing! But they were no poorer than the One who had nowhere to lay his head (Lk 9:58). But what glorious love and devotion they had to carry them through all these hardships! How ardent was their love for God. They thought they had a rich compensation for all the outward good things they lacked, if only they could serve Christ and save souls.

4.2. In fact, they *were made the filth of the world, and the offscouring of all things.* They were treated as people not fit to live. Apostles could not expect any better treatment. They suffered in their bodies and reputations as the very worst evildoers—in fact, as the *offscouring of all things.* To be the scum of anything is bad, but what is it to be the scum of all things! How much were the apostles like their Master! They suffered for him, and they suffered according to his example. Those whom people may think unworthy to live, and whom they abuse and scorn as the very dirt and refuse of the world, may be very dear to God, and honorable in his estimation.

5. We have here the apostles' behavior in all these circumstances: *Being reviled, we bless; being persecuted, we suffer it; being defamed, we entreat* (answer kindly) (vv. 12–13). They responded to curses with blessings and were patient in the most intense persecution. The disciples of Christ, especially his ministers, should hold fast to their integrity and maintain a good conscience. They must be content to be despised and mistreated with him (Ro 6:8) and for him.

Verses 14–16

Here Paul claims the right to be regarded as the father of the Corinthian church.

1. He tells them that what he has written, he has written not to reproach them, but to admonish them (v. 14): *I write not to shame you, but as my beloved children I warn you.* Rebukes that expose often exasperate, whereas those that warn kindly and affectionately are likely to reform. To lash like an enemy or executioner will provoke and make obstinate. To expose to open shame is the way to make people shameless.

2. He shows them on what foundation he calls them his sons. He is their father, *for in Christ Jesus he has begotten them by the Gospel* (v. 15). They were made Christians by his ministry. He was the instrument of their new birth, and that is why he claims the relation of a father to them. There commonly is, and always should be, a binding affection between faithful ministers and the children they beget in Christ Jesus through the Gospel. They should love like parents and children.

3. He urges special advice on them: *Wherefore I beseech you, be you followers of me* (v. 16). He explains and limits this elsewhere (11:1): "*Be you followers of me, as I also am of Christ.* Follow me as far as I follow Christ. I don't want you to be my disciples, but his." Ministers should live in such a way that their people may see them as models and justly follow their example. They should guide their people by their lives as well as by their words, going before them on the way to heaven, not content merely to point it out.

Verses 17–21

Here:

1. Paul tells his readers that he has sent Timothy to them, *to bring you into remembrance of my ways in Christ, as I teach every where in every church* (v. 17). Those who have received very good teaching tend to forget and need to have their memories refreshed. His teaching *is the same every where, and in every church.* Paul did not have one teaching for one place and people, and another for another. What he taught was the Gospel revelation, which was the equal concern of all and did not vary from place to place. He taught the same things in every church, therefore, and lived in the same way at all times and in all places. The truth of Christ is one and invariable. What one apostle taught at one time and in one place, he taught at all times and in all places. To make their regard for Timothy even greater, he describes his character to them. Timothy is *his beloved son,* his spiritual child, just as they are his spiritual children. The children of one father should have one heart. But he adds, "*He is faithful in the Lord*—trustworthy, as one who fears the Lord." It is a great commendation of any minister that they are faithful in the Lord; this must go a long way in obtaining respect for their message.

2. He rebukes those who imagine he will not come to them, by telling them this is his plan: "*I will come to you shortly.*" He adds, however, *if the Lord will.* All our plans must be formed with a dependence on Providence.

3. He lets them know what will follow his coming to them: *I will know, not the speech of those that are puffed up, but the power* (v. 19). He will test the great boasters among them, will know what they are really like by the authority and effectiveness of what they teach and by whether it is accompanied by divine power and saving effects on the hearts of listeners, because, he adds, *the kingdom of God is not in word, but in power,* the powerful influence of divine truth on people's minds and ways. A good way in general of judging a preacher's message is to see whether the effects of it on people's hearts are truly divine. What is most likely to have come from God is what in its own nature is most fit and what in its outcome is found to produce most likeness to God.

4. He lets them choose how he will come among them, *whether with a rod or in love and the spirit of meekness* (v. 21); that is, he will conduct himself in accordance with how they have conducted themselves. Stubborn offenders must be treated severely. In families, in Christian communities, parental compassion and tenderness, Christian love and compassion, will sometimes force the use of the rod.

But this is far from being desirable if it can be prevented. *Or in love and the spirit of meekness.* It is as much as if he had said, "Take warning, stop your unchristian fighting, and you will find me as gentle and kind as you can wish. I would rather come and show the tenderness of a father among you than assert my authority." In a well-tempered minister, the spirit of love and humility is dominant, but just authority is maintained.

CHAPTER 5

Here the apostle: 1. Rebukes his readers for their leniency toward the person who has committed incest (vv. 1–6). 2. Exhorts them to cultivate Christian purity (vv. 7–8). 3. Instructs them to avoid Christians who are guilty of any notorious and detestable wickedness (vv. 9–13).

Verses 1–6

Here the apostle states the case:

1. He tells them he has heard that one of their community is guilty of sexual immorality (v. 1). It is told everywhere to their dishonor. The detestable sins of professing Christians are noted quickly and reported widely. We should walk circumspectly, because many people are watching us. This was not a common example of sexual immorality, but *such as was not so much as named among the Gentiles, that a man should have his father's wife.* Not that there were no such instances of incestuous marriages among the ungodly, but whenever they happened, they shocked every good and upright person among them; they could not mention them without detestation. But such a horrible wickedness was committed by a member of the church at Corinth. The best churches, in this imperfect earthly state, are liable to very great corruptions.

2. He severely rebukes them for their own behavior in response to this: they are *puffed up* (v. 2); they *glory* (v. 6) in it (boasted about it).

2.1. Perhaps they were proud of this scandalous person, because he was greatly respected. Instead of mourning his fall and their own shame on his account, they continued to praise him and pride themselves in him. Pride or self-confidence often lies at the root of our excessive respect for others, and this makes us as blind to their faults as to our own. Or else:

2.2. Some who belonged to a party that opposed his had become proud. It is wicked to glory over the failures and sins of others. Probably this was one effect of the divisions among them. The opposite party took advantage of this scandalous lapse, seized it as an opportunity. The sins of others should be our sorrow.

3. He instructs them as to how they should now proceed with this scandalous sinner.

3.1. He wants the man excommunicated and handed over to Satan (vv. 3–5): *For I verily, as absent in body, but present in spirit, have judged already, as though I were present.* He says this to let them know that although he is far away, he does not pass an unrighteous sentence, nor judge without having as full an understanding of the case as if he had been on the spot.

3.2. The apostle adds, *him who hath so done this deed.* He has *so* committed the evil as to increase the guilt by the way he committed it. In dealing with scandalous sinners, we must charge them not only with the facts but also with the aggravating circumstances of the sin.

3.3. Paul has judged that *he should be delivered* (handed over) *to Satan* (v. 5), and this is to be done *in the name of Christ,* and in a full assembly, where the apostle will also be present in spirit.

3.3.1. Some think that this is to be understood as merely ordinary excommunication, and that handing him over to Satan meant only disowning him so that he might be brought to repentance and so that his flesh might be mortified. Those who live in sin while professing to know Christ actually belong to another master, to whom they should be handed over by excommunication—and this in the name of Christ. It was to be done also *when they were gathered together.* The more public, the more solemn, and the more solemn, the more likely it will be to have a good effect on the offender.

3.3.2. Others think the apostle is not to be understood as referring to mere excommunication, but to a miraculous power or authority the church had, by which it handed over a scandalous sinner to the power of Satan to be subjected to physical disease or pain, which is the meaning of the *destruction of the flesh.* The destruction of the flesh in this sense has been a beneficial occasion of the salvation of the spirit. The great goal of church discipline is the good of those who fall under it. It is so that their spirit may be saved on the day of the Lord Jesus (v. 5).

4. Paul hints at the danger of contagion from this example: *Your glorying is not good. Know you not that a little leaven leaveneth the whole lump?* The bad example of a man in a high position and reputation is very troublesome, spreading the contagion far and wide. A little yeast will quickly ferment a great batch.

Verses 7–8

Here the apostle exhorts them to lead pure lives. We have here:

1. The advice itself, addressed either:

1.1. To the church in general. In this case, getting rid of the old yeast so that they could be a new batch refers to *putting away from themselves that wicked person* (v. 13). Or:

1.2. To each particular member of the church. In this case, it implies that they should cleanse themselves of all impurity of heart and life. Christians should be careful to keep themselves clean as well as to remove corrupt members from their community. They must also cleanse themselves from malice and wickedness. This is yeast that greatly sours the mind and heart. Christians should be careful to keep free from hatred and trouble. Love is the actual essence and life of the Christian religion. It is the fairest image of God, *for God is love* (1Jn 4:8, 16), and it is therefore hardly surprising if it is the greatest beauty and ornament of a Christian.

2. The reason with which this advice is enforced: *For Christ our passover is sacrificed for us* (v. 7). After the Jews killed the Passover lamb, they kept the Feast of Unleavened Bread. So must we, not only for seven days but for all our days. The whole Christian life must be a feast of unleavened bread. We must *purge out the old leaven, and keep the feast of unleavened bread of sincerity and truth.* Christians must be without guilt in their behavior toward God and other people. In a gracious heart, the sacrifice of our Redeemer is, on the whole, the strongest argument for purity and sincerity. Detestable evil, which could be atoned for only by the blood of the Son of God! Will a Christian love the murderer of his Lord? God forbid.

Verses 9–13

Here the apostle advises them not to associate with those who profess Christian faith but conduct themselves scandalously. Notice:

1. The advice itself: *I wrote to you in a letter not to company with fornicators* (v. 9). Some think this was a

letter written to them before, which has been lost. Some think it is to be understood as referring to this particular letter—that he had written this advice earlier in the letter, but thought it necessary now to be more detailed. Therefore, he told them that if any believer, anyone who was a member of a Christian church, were *a fornicator, or covetous* (sexually immoral or greedy), *or an idolater, or a railer* (swindler), they should not *keep company with him, not so much as eat with such a one.* They were to avoid all familiarity with such people, but, in order to shame them and bring them to repentance, must disown and avoid them. Such people may call themselves *brethren in Christ,* but they are not true Christian brothers. To Christian brothers, they are only fit to be companions in sin.

2. How he limits this advice. He does not forbid their eating or associating with the *fornicators of this world.* They know no better. They profess no better. *"You must needs go out of the world* if you wish to have no contact at all with such people. As long as you are in the world, it is impossible to avoid falling into their company."

3. The reason for this limitation is given here. Christians would need to leave the world entirely to avoid the company of loose ungodly people. Besides, Christians carry an antidote against the infection of the bad example of worldly people and are naturally on their guard in their presence. The dread of sin wears off, however, by frequent association with corrupt Christians. And the ungodly are those whom it is not the place of Christians to judge and censure, or to avoid on the basis of a censure imposed, for *they are without* (v. 12) and must be left to *God's judgment* (v. 13). As to members of the church, they are within and have professed to be bound by the laws and rules of Christianity, and when they break those rules, they are liable not only to the judgment of God but also to the censures of their fellow members of the same body. They are to be punished by having this mark of disgrace put on them so that they may be shamed and, if possible, reclaimed. Although the church has nothing to do with outsiders, it must try to keep clear of the guilt and shame of those within.

4. How he applies the argument to the case before him: *"Therefore put away from among yourselves that wicked person* (v. 13). Expel him from your fellowship."

CHAPTER 6

In this chapter: 1. The apostle rebukes the Corinthians for going to court with one another, bringing their causes before ungodly judges (vv. 1–8). 2. He uses the occasion to warn them against many gross sins (vv. 9–11). 3. He passionately advises them against sexual immorality (vv. 12–20).

Verses 1–8

Here the apostle rebukes them for taking legal action against one another before ungodly judges for trivial matters, and in this way he condemns all unwarranted lawsuits. Notice:

1. The fault he blames them for:

1.1. *Brother goes to law with brother* (v. 6). The bonds of family love were broken through. Christians should not fight with one another, because they are brothers and sisters.

1.2. They brought the matter before the ungodly magistrates: *they went to law before the unjust, not before the saints* (v. 1); they brought the controversy before unbelievers (v. 6). This brought great shame to Christianity. Therefore, the apostle says, *"Dare any of you,* having a dispute with another believer, go to law before the ungodly?"

1.3. Here is at least a hint that they went to court for trivial matters, because the apostle rebukes them for not being willing to be cheated rather than go to court (v. 7). Christians should have a forgiving temperament. It is more for their honor to suffer small wrongs than to appear quarrelsome.

2. The aggravations of their fault: *Do you not know that the saints shall judge the world* (v. 2), *shall judge angels?* (v. 3). Are they unworthy, then, *to judge the smallest matters, the things of this life?* It was a dishonor to their Christian character as saints for them to pursue before ungodly magistrates such trivial matters, matters about the things of this life. Some think that *judging the world and angels* refers to their being assistants to Christ on the great Day of Judgment. Not that they will be partners in their Lord's commission, but they will see his proceeding against the evil world and approve it. Given that they were to judge the world—indeed, to judge angels—it was inexplicable that the Corinthian believers could not settle little controversies among one another. Others understand the phrase as referring to believers' condemning the world by their faith and practice, but the first sense seems most natural. "Will Christians have the honor of sitting with the sovereign Judge, and if so, are they not worthy to judge the trifles about which you contend before ungodly magistrates? Cannot Christians make up among themselves such mutual differences as you have? Must you, concerning *the affairs of this life, set those to judge who are* of no esteem *in the church?"* that is, *ungodly* magistrates—some believe "of no esteem" is a better translation here than *least esteemed,* and perhaps it is (v. 4). "Must those whom you should have such a low opinion of be called on to give judgment in your disputes? Is not this shameful?" (v. 5). Some who read it as our translators do consider it ironic: "If you have such disputes pending, set those to judge who are of least account among yourselves. Your disputes are trifles not worth fighting over. *Bear and forbear,* and the people of least skill among you will be able to end your quarrels. *I speak it to your shame"* (v. 5).

3. The way he shows them for putting right this fault. They can choose one of two ways:

3.1. They can refer the matter to a person among them to help them make up: *"Is it so, that there is no wise man among you, no one able to judge between his brethren?* (v. 5). You who pride yourselves so much on your wisdom and knowledge, is there no one among you who has enough wisdom to judge these differences? Must brothers and sisters quarrel, and the ungodly magistrate judge, in a church as famous as yours for knowledge and wisdom?"

3.2. They can suffer wrong rather than use this method to right themselves: *It is utterly a fault among you to go to law in this matter:* it is always a fault of one side to go to court unless the entitlement is really doubtful and there is a friendly agreement between the parties to refer the matter to the judgment of experts in the law to settle it. *Should you not rather take wrong, rather suffer yourselves to be defrauded?* Christians should put up with a little injury rather than disturb themselves and provoke others by a legal battle. Peace in their own mind and the calm of their neighborhood are more valuable than winning a victory in such a contest. The apostle tells them, however, that they are so far from bearing injuries *that they actually do wrong, and defraud, and that their brethren.* It is certainly not right to wrong and defraud anyone, but we aggravate this fault if we defraud our Christian brothers and sisters.

Verses 9–11

Here the apostle takes the opportunity to warn them against many detestable evils to which they were once addicted.

1. He puts it to them as a clear and direct truth that such sinners will not inherit the kingdom of God. The simplest among them must know this much, that *the unrighteous shall not inherit the kingdom of God* (v. 9). He specifies several kinds of sinners: violators of the first and second commandments, as *idolaters*; violators of the seventh, as *adulterers, fornicators* (NIV: the sexually immoral), *effeminate* (NIV: male prostitutes), and *Sodomites* (NIV: homosexual offenders)—for this is what is meant by *abusers of themselves with mankind*; violators of the eighth, as *thieves* and *extortioners* (NIV: swindlers), who use force or fraud to wrong their neighbors; violators of the ninth, as *revilers* (NIV: slanderers); and violators of the tenth, as *covetous* (NIV: the greedy) and *drunkards*. Heaven could never be intended for these. The scum of the earth are in no way fit to fill the heavenly mansions.

2. He also warns them against deceiving themselves: *Be not deceived.* Those who must surely know the truth just mentioned are all too inclined to neglect it, to flatter themselves that they can live in sin but die in Christ, lead the life of the Devil's children but still go to heaven with the children of God. However, this is all gross deception. We cannot hope to sow in the flesh but still reap eternal life (Gal 6:7–8).

3. He reminds them what a change the Gospel and grace of God has made in them: *Such were some of you* (v. 11). Some who are eminently good after their conversion have been as remarkably evil before. Grace makes glorious changes! It changes the most corrupt evildoers into saints and children of God. "You are not what you once were. *You are washed, you are sanctified, you are justified in the name of Christ, and by the Spirit of our God.*" The washing of regeneration can cleanse all guilt and defilement. *You are sanctified, you are justified*; for rhetorical effect, Paul puts them in the opposite of the natural order of events, in which justification comes first. Yet none are cleansed from the guilt of sin and reconciled to God through Christ except those who are also sanctified by his Spirit. All who are made righteous in the sight of God are made holy by the grace of God.

Verses 12–20

1. V. 12 and first part of v. 13 seem to relate to that early dispute among Christians about distinguishing between different kinds of food, and yet they also seem to introduce the warning that follows against sexual immorality. The connection seems clear enough if we read the famous decision of the apostles in Ac 15:19–29, where the prohibition of certain foods was joined with that of sexual immorality.

1.1. Now some among the Corinthians seem ready to say, even in the case of fornication, *All things are lawful for me*, because fornication was not a sin condemned by the laws of their country. Paul here sets himself to oppose this dangerous thought: he tells them that many things that are *lawful* (permissible) in themselves are not *expedient* (beneficial). Christians should consider not only what is in itself permitted to be done but also what is beneficial for them to do.

1.2. They should be very careful that they do not, by taking this maxim too far, let themselves be mastered by anything, whether by a crafty deceiver or by a worldly inclination. *All things are lawful for me*, he says, *but I will not be brought under the power of any* (v. 12). There is a liberty

with which Christ has set us free (Gal 5:1), in which we must stand firm, but surely Paul would never take this liberty so far as to put himself into the power of any physical appetite. He would not become a glutton or a drunkard.

1.3. Much less would he abuse the maxim concerning permissible liberty to support the sin of sexual immorality. And he would not abuse this maxim about eating and drinking to encourage any excessive practice or the indulging of any worldly appetite: "*Though meats are for the belly, and the belly for meats* (v. 13), nevertheless, if I am in danger of being subjected to my stomach and appetite, I will abstain. *But God shall destroy both it and them.*"

1.4. A time is coming when the need and use of food will be abolished. The transition to his arguments against sexual immorality seems natural: *But the body is not for fornication, but for the Lord, and the Lord for the body* (v. 13). Food and the stomach are meant for one another, but not so with sexual immorality and the body.

2. The body is not meant for sexual immorality, but for the Lord. This is the first argument he uses against this sin, for which the ungodly inhabitants of Corinth were infamous. The *body is not for fornication*; it was never formed for any such purpose, *but for the Lord.* It is to be a member of Christ, and so must not be united with a prostitute (v. 15). *The Lord is for the body*; that is, as some think, Christ is to be Lord of the body, to own it and control it. We must take care that we do not use what belongs to Christ as if it were our own, much less use it to his dishonor.

3. Some understand this last passage, *The Lord is for the body*, as meaning he is on the side of its resurrection and glorification, according to what follows (v. 14), which is a second argument against this sin, the honor intended to be put on our bodies: *God hath raised up our Lord, and will raise us up by his power* (v. 14). It will be an honor to our bodies that they will be raised. Therefore, let us not, by sin, abuse the bodies that, if kept pure, will be made like *Christ's glorious body*.

4. A third argument is the honor already shown to our bodies: *Know you not that your bodies are the members of Christ?* (v. 15). If the soul is united to Christ by faith, the whole person has become a member of his mystical body. The body, as well as the soul, is united with Christ.

4.1. *But now*, says the apostle, *shall I take the members of Christ, and make them the members of a harlot? God forbid.* Would it not be extremely dishonoring to Christ as well as to ourselves? What, unite Christ's members to a prostitute? *God forbid.* Never.

4.2. *Know you not that he who is joined to a harlot is one body* with hers? *For two*, he says, *shall be one flesh* (Ge 2:24; Mt 19:5–6). *But he who is joined to the Lord is one spirit* (vv. 16–17). Christians are joined to the Lord in union with Christ and are made to share by faith in his Spirit. Now shall one in such close union with Christ as to be one spirit with him be so united to a prostitute as to become one flesh with her? Can anything be more inconsistent with our profession or relation with Christ?

4.3. It is hardly surprising, therefore, that the apostle would say, *Flee fornication* (v. 18). "Other vices may be conquered by fighting, but this one only by fleeing"; these are the words of many of the church fathers.

5. A fourth argument is that it is a sin against our own bodies. *Every sin that a man does is without* (outside) *the body; he that committeth fornication sinneth against his own body* (v. 18); every sin, that is, every external act of sin besides this one, is outside the body. This sin is especially called immorality and defilement because no

sin contains such external depravity, especially in a Christian. In committing this sin, they sin against their own body; they defile it, degrade it. They pour great shame on what their Redeemer has highly dignified by taking it into union with himself. We should not make our present corrupt bodies more corrupt by sinning against them.

6. The fifth argument against this sin is that the bodies of Christians are *the temples of the Holy Ghost which is in them, and which they have of God* (v. 19). The believer who is joined to Christ is one spirit. They are yielded to him and are then possessed, inhabited by his Holy Spirit. This is the proper idea of a temple—a place where God lives, which is set apart for his use. Real Christians are such temples of the Holy Spirit. We are not our own. We are possessed by and for God; indeed, and this is because we have been purchased: *You are bought with a price.* In short, our bodies were made for God and bought for him. Shall we desecrate his temple and offer it for the use and service of a prostitute? The temple of the Holy Spirit must be kept holy. Our bodies must be kept for the One to whom they belong, kept fit for his use and residence.

7. The apostle argues from the obligation we are under *to glorify God with both our body and our spirit, which are his* (v. 20). He made both; he bought both. They must be kept as vessels fit for our Master's use. We must look on our whole selves as *holy to the Lord* (Ex 28:36; 39:30; etc.). We are to honor *him with our bodies and spirits, which are his.* Body and spirit are to be kept pure, so that God may be honored by both. God is dishonored when either is defiled by such a terrible sin. Therefore *flee fornication*; indeed, flee every sin. Use your bodies for the glory and service of your Lord and Maker.

CHAPTER 7

In this chapter the apostle answers some cases proposed to him by the Corinthians about marriage. 1. He shows them that marriage was appointed as a remedy against sexual immorality (vv. 1–9). 2. He instructs those who are married to remain together even if they have an unbelieving partner, unless the unbeliever wants to part (vv. 10–16). 3. He shows them that becoming a Christian does not change their external state (vv. 17–24). 4. He advises them to remain unmarried because of the present distress, and he shows them how worldly cares distract them in the service of God (vv. 25–35). 5. He gives guidance on the course they should take with their virgins (vv. 36–38). 6. He closes the chapter with advice to widows on how to conduct themselves in their widowhood (vv. 39–40).

Verses 1–9

The apostle now undertakes to answer some questions of practical application that the Corinthians have asked him. They are *things whereof they wrote to him* (v. 1). The apostle was as ready to give guidance as they were to ask questions about their doubts. In the previous chapter he warns them to avoid sexual immorality; here he gives some instructions on marriage.

1. He tells them that it is good to abstain from marriage completely: *It is good for a man not to touch a woman* (not to take her as his wife). *Good* here does not mean that it is not in harmony with the mind of God to do otherwise, that to do otherwise is a sin—an extreme to which many people in former times have run in favor of celibacy and virginity. For now, rather, it would be beneficial for Christians to keep themselves single, provided they can keep themselves chaste.

2. He informs them that marriage, with the comforts and satisfactions of that state, is prescribed by divine wisdom for preventing sexual immorality (v. 2). When a man and a woman marry, then, let each give the other *due benevolence* (v. 3). They should not deprive one another of the use of their bodies unless it be *with mutual consent* (v. 5) and *for a time* only, while they employ themselves in some extraordinary duties of religion *or give themselves to fasting and prayer.* Seasons of profound self-denial require abstinence from lawful pleasures.

3. The apostle limits what he said in v. 2. Paul did not oblige everyone to get married. No, he *could wish all men were as himself* (v. 7). Natural constitutions vary.

4. He sums up (vv. 9–10). Marriage, with all its disadvantages, is much better than burning with impure and lustful passions.

Verses 10–16

In this paragraph the apostle answers a question that must have arisen frequently at that time: whether they were to remain married to an ungodly spouse. Moses' law permitted divorce, and on one occasion the Jewish people had been obliged to send away their idolatrous wives (Ezr 10:3). This might raise a scruple in many minds.

1. Marriage, by Christ's command, is for life. The wife *must not depart from the husband* (v. 10), nor the *husband put away his wife* (v. 11). The Lord himself forbade such separation (Mt 5:32; 19:9; Mk 10:11; Lk 16:18). They must not separate for any other cause than what Christ allows. Husbands and wives should not quarrel at all, or they should be quickly reconciled. They are committed to each other for life. They cannot throw off the commitment and so should set their shoulder to the task, seeking to make the commitment as light for each other as possible.

2. He applies this principle to the situation of those who have an unbelieving partner (v. 12): *But to the rest speak I, not the Lord.* It does not mean that the apostle decided this case by his own wisdom. He closes this subject with a declaration to the contrary (v. 40). Notice:

2.1. The advice itself, that if an unbelieving husband or wife is happy to live with a Christian partner, the latter should not separate (vv. 12–13). The Christian calling did not dissolve the marriage covenant, but rather bound it more firmly. If the unbelieving partner deserts the believer, *in such a case a brother or sister is not in bondage* (is not bound in such circumstances) (v. 15). In such cases the deserted person must be free to marry again. However, the apostle says (v. 11), *If the woman depart from her husband, let her remain unmarried.*

2.2. The reasons for this advice.

2.2.1. The relationship is sanctified by the holiness of either party (v. 14). The apostle told them that even if they were yoked with unbelievers, if they themselves were holy, to them marriage was a holy state. He was sanctified for the wife's sake. She was sanctified for the husband's sake. *Else were your children unclean, but now are they holy* (v. 14). A pair of parents of whom one is a Christian and the other a non-Christian are not to be counted as part of the world because of the non-Christian parent, but as part of the church.

2.2.2. Another reason is that *God hath called Christians to peace* (v. 15).

2.2.3. It is possible for the believing partner to be an instrument of the other's salvation (v. 16). Should a Christian desert a partner when an opportunity offers itself to give the most glorious proof of love? Seek to save a soul. It is not impossible. " 'Who knows? I may save his soul,' should move me to attempt it."

Verses 17–24

Here the apostle uses the occasion to advise them to remain in the state and condition in which Christianity found them, the state in which they were converted. Here:

1. He lays down this rule in general: *as God hath distributed to every one*. Again, *As the Lord hath called every one, so let him walk*. A person can live in any state so as to be a credit to that state. The apostle adds that this is a general rule to be observed in all places: *So ordain I in all churches*.

2. He specifies particular cases, namely:

2.1. That of circumcision. It does not matter whether a man is a Jew or a Gentile (v. 19). External observances without internal godliness are nothing. Therefore let everyone abide *in the calling* (the state) *wherein he was called* (v. 20).

2.2. That of slavery and freedom. "Now," the apostle says, "*art thou called being a servant? Care not for it.* It is not inconsistent with your duty, profession, or hopes as a Christian. *Yet if thou mayest be made free, use it rather*" (v. 21). The state of freedom has many advantages over that of slavery. However, people's outward condition neither hinders nor furthers their acceptance with God. Those who are slaves can still be free in Christ; those who are free in human society can still be Christ's servants. But believers must not become servants of human beings so much that they fail in anything to obey Christ's will. Christ's will must be regarded more than their master's. The servants of Christ should be at the absolute command of no other master than him.

3. He sums up his advice (v. 24). They should quietly remain in the condition they are in, and they may well do this, given that remaining in that condition does not in itself prevent them from living before God. The presence and favor of God are not limited to any outward condition. Slaves can enjoy it as much as those who are free. The favor of God is not limited.

Verses 25–35

The apostle here gives directions to virgins as to how to act. Notice:

1. How he introduces these directions (v. 25). Although Christ had previously given no universal law on that matter, he now gave direction by an inspired apostle.

2. His judgment. He judges that at present, a state of celibacy is preferable. His judgment is worded with modesty but given with apostolic authority. Ministers do not lose their authority by prudent condescension. In those days, the married state would bring greater concern and distraction with it (vv. 33–34) and would therefore make persecution more terrible.

3. That he is very careful to assure them that he does not condemn marriage, declaring it unlawful. Although he says, "If you *are loosed from a wife, do not seek a wife*," he adds, "*If thou art bound to a wife, do not seek to be loosed*." Duty must be done, and God is to be trusted with outcomes. Marrying is not a sin in itself, but marrying at that time was likely to add to the adversities of the times.

4. That he instructs all Christians that, in general, they ought to have a holy indifference toward the world. Those *that have wives must be as though they had none*. They do not know how soon they will have none. Those with children should act as though they had none. Those who are their comfort now may prove their greatest cross. Those *that weep must be as though they wept not*. Even in sorrow the heart may be joyful, and the end of our grief may be gladness. Those *that rejoice should be as though they rejoiced not*. Their rest is not here (Heb 4:1–11), nor are

these things their inheritance. Those *that buy must be as though they possessed not*. Buying and possessing should not take up too much of our minds. They stop many people from being concerned with something better. Those *that use this world, as not abusing* (not engrossed in) *it* (v. 31). The world may be used, but it must not totally preoccupy us. It engrosses us when, instead of being oil to the wheels of our obedience, it fuels our sinful desires. We must keep the world out of our hearts, so that we may not be too engrossed in it when it is in our hands.

5. Two reasons to back up this advice.

5.1. *The time is short* (v. 29). We have only a short time to remain in this world. That is why we are not to set our hearts on worldly enjoyments. We are not to be overwhelmed by worldly cares and troubles.

5.2. *The fashion*—or form or appearance—*of this world passeth away* (v. 31). It is not so much a world as the appearance of one. All is show, with nothing solid in it, a transient show, which will soon be gone.

6. That he warns them against the burden of worldly concerns (v. 32). A wise concern for worldly interests is a duty, but to be anxious and overconcerned about them is a sin. God must *be attended upon without distraction* (with undivided devotion) (v. 35). But how is this possible when the heart is overtaken by the worries of this life? This is the general principle by which the apostle wants Christians to govern themselves. Christian prudence must direct us. The unmarried man and woman are concerned about the things of the Lord, about how they can please the Lord, remaining holy in both body and spirit (vv. 32, 34). Those who are married can also be holy in both body and spirit, of course. But the unmarried would have been able to spend more time on their religion in those days, whereas it is the constant concern of the married to please each other. At that season, therefore, the apostle advised that those who were single refrain from marriage. The same rule may lead people to decide in favor of marriage if in the unmarried state they are likely to be more distracted in the service of God than if they are married. The Christian should choose that condition of life in which they are most likely to have the best helps and the fewest hindrances in the service of God.

Verses 36–38

1. In this passage the apostle is commonly thought to give advice about the disposal of children in marriage. In that age, it was reckoned a disgrace for a woman to remain unmarried beyond a certain age. "Now," the apostle says, "if any man thinks he is behaving wrongly toward his daughter, he may do what he wants. It is no sin for him to direct her toward a suitable partner. But if a man has decided to keep her as a virgin with her consent, he does well."

2. But I think the apostle is continuing here his former teaching, advising unmarried people who are at liberty to govern their own lives, the man's *virgin* referring to his virginity. It was a common matter of shame among Jews and the civilized ungodly for a man to remain single beyond a certain age. The general meaning of the apostle is the same as in the foregoing interpretation, namely, that it was no sin for a man to marry if he thought he must in order to avoid popular censure, and much less if he thought he must in order to avoid the passions of lust.

Verses 39–40

The whole matter is closed here with advice to widows. Only death can annul the bond of marriage, but upon the death of one partner, a second marriage is not unlawful. A widow is at liberty in this matter, the only limitation being that *she marry in the Lord* (v. 40). Yet it will be much more for the peace and quiet of such women, and give them less hindrance in serving God, to remain unmarried.

CHAPTER 8

Here the apostle considers eating those things that have been sacrificed to idols. 1. He warns them against too high an opinion of their knowledge (vv. 1–3). 2. He asserts the futility of idols (vv. 4–6). 3. He tells them that consideration must be given to the weakness of Christian brothers and sisters (vv. 7–13).

Verses 1–3

Regarding things that had been offered to idols, we must note that it was a custom among the pagans to make feasts of their sacrifices. These were usually held in the temple where the sacrifice was offered (v. 10). What remained at the end belonged to the priests, who sometimes sold it in the markets. See 10:25. It was considered very worldly among the pagans to eat at their private tables any meat that they had not first sacrificed. Now, what should the Corinthian Christians do if anything that had been sacrificed was put in front of them? What should they do if they were invited to eat with pagans in their temples? The Corinthians had the idea that even this could be done because they knew an idol was *nothing in the world* (v. 4). But, *"We know*, the apostle says, *that we all have knowledge. We* who abstain know as much of the futility of idols as you do; we too know that they are nothing. But we also know that the liberty you take is reprehensible, and that even permissible liberty must be used with love and not to the prejudice of weaker brothers and sisters" *Knowledge puffeth up, but charity edifieth"* (v. 1). Notice:

1. Love is to be preferred over proud knowledge. A high opinion of our own knowledge leads to no good in ourselves and leads to the harm of others. True love, however, will make us act so as to build them up.

2. There is no proof of ignorance that is more common than proud knowledge. Those who understand their own ignorance are the ones who know best. One who imagines that he is knowledgeable, on the other hand, has reason to suspect that he knows nothing truly. Much may be known when nothing is known to any good effect. *But*, the apostle adds, *if any man love God, the same is known* by God. Some read it, "He will be approved by God; God will accept him and delight in him." The loving person is most likely to receive God's favor. How much better it is to be approved by God than to have a proud opinion of ourselves!

Verses 4–6

In this passage Paul shows the futility of idols. Pagan idols have no divinity in them; they are merely imaginary gods. The gods of the nations have nothing of real godhead belonging to them, for there is no God but one. All their divinity and mediation were imaginary, because:

1. *To us there is but one God*, says the apostle, *the Father, of whom are all things, and we in him.* We Christians well know there is only one God. All things come from him, and we and everything else are for him. He is called the *Father* here not in contrast with the other persons of the Holy Trinity, to exclude them from the Godhead, but in contrast with all the creatures made by God, whose formation is attributed to each of these three in other places of Scripture, not only to the Father.

2. To us there is only one Lord, one Mediator between God and humanity, the Lord Jesus Christ. It is the great privilege we have as Christians that we know the true God and the true Mediator between God and humanity.

Verses 7–13

Having granted that idols are nothing, the apostle now proceeds to show the Corinthians that they are not just in the conclusion they draw from this premise, namely, that they can therefore go into the idol temple and feast there with their ungodly neighbors. He does not insist so much on the unlawfulness of the thing in itself as on the trouble such freedom might cause to weaker Christians.

1. He informs them that every Christian is not yet fully convinced that an idol is nothing. Weak Christians may be ignorant of, or have confused knowledge of, the greatest and clearest truths.

1.1. Some Corinthian converts to Christianity seem to have maintained their worship of their idols and continued to eat things offered to idols. *So their conscience, being weak, was defiled*; that is, they ate out of respect to the idol and so committed idolatry. They were weak in their understanding, and whenever they ate what was sacrificed, they contracted the guilt of idolatry, so polluting themselves.

1.2. Some interpreters, on the other hand, understand this verse as referring to Christians who were weak in a different way. Believing that the sacrificing of food to an idol made it unclean, these Christians ate it anyway, thus violating their consciences. We should be careful to do nothing that may cause weak Christians to defile their consciences.

2. He tells them that merely eating and drinking contains nothing either virtuous or offensive (v. 8). Some of the Corinthians thought it commendable to eat what had been offered to idols, even in their temples (v. 10), because it clearly showed that they thought the idols were nothing. But eating this food and refusing that one do not in themselves commend a person to God.

3. He warns them against abusing their supposed liberty. That they misunderstood this matter, and did not really have this liberty, seems clear from 10:20, but the apostle argues that even supposing they did have it, they must be careful how they use it; it might be a *stumblingblock to the weak* (v. 9). The apostle backs up this warning with two considerations:

3.1. The danger that might come to weak brothers and sisters. We must deny ourselves rather than do things that might lead to their stumbling and endanger their souls (v. 11): *Through thy knowledge shall thy weak brother perish, for whom Christ died?* If he had such compassion as to die for them, we should have so much compassion for them as to deny ourselves for their sakes. A person who would prefer to let their brother or sister perish rather than be restricted in their own liberty has very little of the spirit of the Redeemer.

3.2. That Christ takes the harm done to them as done to him (v. 12). Injuries done to Christians are injuries to Christ. Shall we be so devoid of compassion for those for whom Christ has shown so much? Shall we sin against Christ, who suffered so much for us?

4. He backs all this up with his own example (v. 13). We must not rigorously claim our own rights, to the harm and ruin of the soul of a brother or sister, so wronging our Redeemer, who died for them. If we must be so careful not to cause other people to sin, how much more careful should we be to avoid sin in ourselves also!

CHAPTER 9

In this chapter: 1. The apostle asserts his apostolic mission and authority (vv. 1–2). 2. He claims a right to be supported in his ministry (vv. 3–14). 3. He shows that he has willingly waived this privilege (vv. 15–18). *4. He specifies several other instances in which he has denied himself (vv. 19–23). 5. He concludes his argument by showing what motivates him on this course (vv. 24–27).*

Verses 1–2

Paul faced not only opposition from outsiders but also discouragement from those inside the churches. Some members of the church at Corinth questioned, if they did not openly disown, his apostolic character. Here he responded.

1. He asserted his apostolic mission and character: *Am I not an apostle? Have I not seen Jesus Christ our Lord?* To be a witness of his resurrection was one great criterion for being commissioned as an apostle. *Am I not free?* It was not because he had no right to live by the Gospel that he supported himself with his own hands.

2. He offered the success of his ministry among the Corinthians as proof of his apostleship.

3. He justly rebuked them for their lack of respect (v. 2). "You, above all others, should recognize my character and not question it." It emphasized their ingratitude that some of them questioned his authority.

Verses 3–14

He proceeds to claim the rights belonging to his position.

1. He states these rights (vv. 3–6).

2. He proceeds to prove his claim.

2.1. He argues from common human practices. Those who give themselves to any form of business in the world expect to earn their living from it (vv. 7–9). It is very reasonable for ministers to expect to earn a livelihood from their labors (v. 8).

2.2. He argues it from the Jewish law: *Saith not the law the same also?* (v. 8). Indeed, it is also consistent with the old law. God had ordered there that oxen should not be muzzled while treading out the grain (Dt 25:4). However, this law was not chiefly given out of God's regard for oxen, but to teach people that all appropriate encouragement should be given to those who are laboring for our good — that the laborers should enjoy the fruit of their labors (v. 10). Those who give themselves to do good to our souls should not have their mouths muzzled.

2.3. He argues from common justice (v. 11). What the apostles had sown was much better than what they expected to reap. They had been instruments of conveying to the Corinthians the greater, spiritual blessings, and had they no claim to a share in their material things? What, had the converts obtained so much good from them, and would they begrudge doing so little good for them!

2.4. He argues from the support they give others. "Who has as just a claim as I have on the church at Corinth? Who has worked so hard for your good?" He preferred to renounce his right rather than claim it and so hinder his success, and yet he asserted his right so that his self-denial would not damage the ministry.

2.5. He argues from the old Jewish establishment: *"Do you not know that those who minister about holy things live of the things of the temple, and those who wait at the altar are partakers with the altar?"* (v. 13). He asserts that Christ instituted this right: *"Even so hath the Lord ordained that those who preach the Gospel should live of the Gospel"* (v. 14). Those who deny or withhold this right, therefore, break an appointed principle of Christ.

Verses 15–18

Here Paul tells the Corinthian Christians that he has, nevertheless, waived his privilege, and lays down his reason for having done so.

1. He tells them that he has neglected to claim his right in the past. Nor is he writing this to make his claim now.

2. He tells them why he has exercised this self-denial. He does not want to be deprived of his boast (v. 15). *Better to die* than to have it justly said that he preferred his wages to his work. It is the glory of ministers to deny themselves so that they may serve Christ and save souls.

3. This self-denial gives him much more contentment than his preaching does (v. 16). *"Though I preach the Gospel, I have nothing whereof to glory; for necessity is laid upon me* (v. 16). My preaching is a duty expressly committed to me." Those who are set apart for the ministry are commissioned to preach the Gospel. How terrible it would be if they did not! Not all, however — and not any preacher of the Gospel — are commissioned to do their work for nothing. It may be their duty to preach under some circumstances without receiving support for it, but they have a right to support. It may sometimes be their duty to insist on their support, and whenever they refrain, they part with their right.

4. *If I do this thing willingly, I have a reward.* Indeed, it is only willing service that is capable of receiving a reward from God. If we leave the heart out of our duties, God abhors them: they are merely carcasses, without any life and spirit of religion. Ministers have the stewardship of the Gospel committed to them. Christ's willing servants will not fail to receive a reward, and his slothful and unwilling servants will all be called to account (Mt 25:26).

5. *What is my reward then?* (v. 18). *That when I preach the Gospel, I may make it without charge, that I abuse not my power in the Gospel.* It is an abuse of power to apply it against the very reasons for which it is given. The apostle would never use his so as to frustrate the purposes of his ministry, but would willingly and cheerfully deny himself.

Verses 19–23

The apostle takes occasion from the subject of the foregoing passage to mention some other instances of his self-denial and his giving up liberty for the benefit of others.

1. He asserts his liberty (v. 19). He was born a free citizen of Rome. He was the slave of no one. *Yet he made himself a servant to all, that he might gain the more.* He made himself a servant so that they could be made free.

2. He specifies some ways in which he has made himself a servant. He has accommodated himself to all sorts of people.

2.1. *To the Jews, and those under the law, I became a Jew.* He submitted to the law in order to be effective with them and win them to Christ.

2.2. *To those that are without the law, as without law,* that is, to the Gentiles. In innocent things he could comply with people's customs for their advantage. He behaved among them as one who was not enslaved to the Jewish laws. He did not insist on privileges and fine points.

2.3. *To the weak I became as weak, that I might gain the weak* (v. 22). He did not despise or judge them, but became like one of them. He denied himself for their sakes so that he might gain their souls. He could not give up the rights of God, but he would resign his own rights, and he did this very often for the good of others.

3. He presents his reason for acting in this way (v. 23): *This I do for the Gospel's sake, and that I may be partaker thereof with you.* A heart warmed with zeal for God and longing for the salvation of others will not plead and insist on rights and privileges.

Verses 24–27

The apostle has a glorious prize, an incorruptible crown, in view. *"Know you not that those who run in a race run all, but one obtaineth the prize? (v. 24)."*

1. He stirs them to their duty: *"So run that you may obtain.* It is completely different in the Christian race from in your races. In the latter, only one wins the prize, but you, as Christians, may all run so as to win. You cannot fail if you run well. It is a glorious contest to see who will get to heaven first."

2. He instructs them on their course by setting out more fully his own example.

2.1. Those who ran in their games kept to a strict diet (v. 25). "The fighters and wrestlers in your athletic events have self-control. They adhere to a strict diet and deny themselves much; so do I; so should you."

2.2. They not only exercised self-control but also got used to hardship. Those who fought with one another prepared themselves by *beating the air,* as the apostle calls it. There is no room for any such exercise in Christian warfare; Christians are always in close combat. The apostle mentions one enemy here, namely, the body; this must be disciplined, beaten into submission.

3. The apostle urges this advice by proper arguments drawn from the same contenders.

3.1. They endured hardships *to obtain a corruptible crown* (v. 25), *but we an incorruptible.* Those who were winners in these games were crowned only with the withering leaves or boughs of olive, bay, or laurel trees, but Christians have the prospect of an incorruptible crown. Could those who had no more in view than the trifling cheers of a fickle crowd or a crown of leaves expose their bodies to so much hardship? If they could do that, could not Christians, who hoped for a crown of glory, apply themselves to subdue and discipline their physical inclinations?

3.2. The racers in these games ran with uncertainty. All the competitors ran, but only one received the prize (v. 24). But the Christian racer is under no such uncertainty; everyone may run here so as to win. But then they must keep to the path of prescribed duty, which is the meaning of *running not as uncertainly* (aimlessly) (v. 26). Would the Greek racers exert themselves to the end when only one could win? Will not Christians, therefore, be much more vigorous in their running, since everyone is sure they will win a crown?

3.3. He sets out for himself and them the danger of surrendering to physical inclinations: *I keep under my body, lest by any means, when I have preached to others, I myself should be a castaway* (v. 27), disqualified, rejected, one to whom the *judge* or *umpire* will not decree the crown. A preacher of salvation may still miss the crown. Preachers may show others the way to heaven but never get there themselves. If a holy fear of himself was necessary to preserve the faithfulness of an apostle, how much more necessary is it to preserve us?

CHAPTER 10

In this chapter: 1. The apostle uses the example of the Jews to warn the Corinthians against self-confidence (vv. 1–14). 2. He resumes his earlier argument (ch. 8)

about eating food offered to idols (vv. 15–22). 3. He lets them know that they can buy such meat in the market or eat it at the table of ungodly acquaintances without asking any questions. Yet liberty of this kind must be used with due regard to weak consciences (vv. 23–33).

Verses 1–5

He sets out for them the example of the Jews. They enjoyed great privileges, but they were severely punished.

1. He begins with a note of affection: *Moreover, brethren, I would not that you should be ignorant.* God's providence toward the people of Israel and what happened to them despite their privileges should be a warning to us.

2. He specifies some of their privileges.

2.1. He begins with their rescue from Egypt. They were miraculously led through the Red Sea, where the pursuing Egyptians were drowned: it was an avenue to them, but a grave to the Egyptians. That God performed such miracles to rescue the Israelites shows that they were very precious to him.

2.2. They had sacraments like ours. *They were all baptized unto Moses in the cloud, and in the sea* (v. 2). *They did all eat of the same spiritual meat, and drink of the same spiritual drink.* These were great privileges. One would have thought that this would have saved them, but it did not (v. 5). People may enjoy many and great spiritual privileges in this world and yet fall short of eternal life. Let no one presume on their great privileges.

Verses 6–14

1. Several of Israel's sins are specified as warnings to us.

1.1. We should not set our hearts on material things (v. 6). God fed the Israelites with manna, but they had to have meat (Nu 11:4). Physical desires gain control if they are indulged. Once they triumph and gain control in us, we do not know where they will take us.

1.2. He warns against idolatry (v. 7). The apostle is speaking to the situation of the Corinthians, who are tempted to eat the pagan sacrifices.

1.3. He warns against sexual immorality, a sin to which the inhabitants of Corinth were especially addicted. How necessary it was to bring a warning against sexual immorality to those who lived in such a corrupt city. Spiritual prostitution led in many cases to physical prostitution. Many think that such worship was given to Baal-Peor (Nu 25), bringing on the Israelites a plague that killed 23,000 in one day. Let us fear the sins of Israel if we want to avoid their plagues.

1.4. He warns us against *tempting* (testing) *Christ—as some of them tempted, and were destroyed of serpents* (v. 9)—or arousing the Lord's jealousy (v. 22). God sent venomous snakes among them for this sin (Nu 21:5–6). It is only just to fear that those who test Christ in the present age will be left by him in the power of the old Serpent (Rev 12:9; 20:2).

1.5. He warns against grumbling (v. 10). When the Israelites met discouragements on their way to Canaan, they tended to attack their leaders. Something like this seems to have been the situation of the Corinthians; they grumbled against Paul, and in him against Christ.

2. The apostle adds to these particular warnings a more general one (v. 11). The Israelites' sins against God were types of the unfaithfulness of many under the Gospel. God's judgments on the Israelites were types of present spiritual judgments. The history of Israel was written

down as a constant reminder to the church. Nothing in Scripture is written in vain, and we would be wise and responsible to accept instruction from it. On this the apostle bases a warning (v. 12). Others have fallen, and so may we. God has not promised to keep us from falling if we do not look to ourselves; his protection presupposes our own care.

3. He adds a word of comfort (v. 13). Although God is displeased when we presume, he is not pleased when we despair. Although we must take heed, we should not be dismayed, for either our testings will be in proportion to our strength, or strength will be supplied in proportion to our temptations.

3.1. "*No temptation*," says the apostle, "*hath yet taken you, but such as is common to man,* what is human." Others have similar temptations; what they endure and break through, we may too.

3.2. *God is faithful.* People may be false, and the world may be false, but God remains faithful, and our strength and security are in him.

3.3. He is wise as well as faithful. He knows what we can bear. He will take care that we are not overcome if we depend on him. *He will make a way to escape.* There is no valley so dark that he cannot find a way through it.

4. And on this argument he bases another warning against idolatry: "*Wherefore, flee idolatry*; run away from it." Idolatry is the most detestable affront to the true God. "Since you have such encouragement to trust God, do not be shaken by any discouragements. God will both help you in your trials and help you out of them." We cannot fall by a temptation if we remain close to him.

Verses 15–22

In this passage the apostle urges the general warning against idolatry.

1. He begins with an appeal to their own reason and judgment: *I speak to wise men; judge you what I say* (v. 15).

2. He lays down his argument from the Lord's Supper. Is not this sacred ceremony a sign by which we professedly have fellowship with Christ? To eat the feast is to share in the sacrifice, and so to be the guests of the One to whom the sacrifice was offered, and all this as a sign of friendship with him. So to share in the Lord's Table is to profess ourselves to be his guests and covenant people; we do this together with all true Christians, with whom we have fellowship also in this ceremony (v. 17).

3. He confirms this from the Jewish worship and customs. Those who were admitted to eat the offerings were reckoned as participating in the sacrifice itself, and therefore as worshiping God.

4. He applies this to the argument against eating with idolaters, that is, eating their sacrifices. An idol was nothing. What was sacrificed to idols was nothing. But eating it as a part of a pagan sacrifice was:

4.1. Sharing with the idolaters in their idolatry, just as those who eat the Lord's Supper are thought to share in the Christian sacrifice. "Therefore do not eat their sacrifices. I would not have you be in fellowship with demons."

4.2. Virtually renouncing Christianity (v. 21). Fellowship with Christ and fellowship with demons could never be had at the same time. One must be renounced if the other is to be maintained. How much reason we have to make sure that every sin and idol is renounced by us when we eat and drink at the Lord's Table.

5. He warns them that God is a jealous God (v. 22). Those who have fellowship with other gods arouse him to jealousy. And before they do that, they should con-

sider whether they are stronger than he. It is dangerous to arouse God's anger—unless we suppose we can withstand his power. Will we arouse almighty wrath? Are we a match for God?

Verses 23–33

In this passage the apostle shows in what examples Christians can lawfully eat what has been sacrificed to idols.

1. Something *lawful* (permissible) may not be *expedient* (not be beneficial), may not *edify* (not be constructive). An individual Christian *must not seek his own only, but his neighbour's wealth* (good). He must be concerned not to harm his neighbor; in fact, he must be concerned to promote his neighbor's welfare. Those who allow themselves everything not clearly sinful in itself will often commit sin by accident. The welfare of others, as well as our own convenience, must be considered in many things we do.

2. He tells them that what is *sold in the shambles* (meat market) *they may eat without asking questions.* They need not be so scrupulous as to ask the butcher whether the meat sold in the market has been offered to an idol. It is sold there as common food, and as such can be bought and used, *for the earth is the Lord's, and the fulness thereof* (v. 26; Ps 24:1).

3. If they are invited by any ungodly friends to a meal, *they may go, and eat what is set before them, without asking questions* (v. 27). Politeness is due even to unbelievers and the ungodly. The Corinthian Christians could lawfully eat anything fit to be eaten that was put in front of them. It is to be understood as referring to civil meals, not religious ones. At an ordinary feast they could expect ordinary food.

4. Yet if anyone were to say that the food had been offered to idols, they should refrain from eating it. They should refrain both for the sake of the person who suggested this to them and *for conscience' sake,* out of regard for conscience. Christians should be very careful about doing something that may harm the consciences of others.

5. He urges them to refrain where they will cause offense. Christians should take care not to use their liberty either to the harm of others or to their own disgrace.

6. The apostle takes this discussion as an opportunity to establish a general rule for Christian behavior (vv. 31–32): In all we do, we should aim at the glory of God. Nothing should be done by us to offend anyone, *whether Jew, or Gentile, or the church* (v. 32). Not our own attitudes and desires, but the honor of God and the good and edification of the church, must determine our practice.

7. He urges everything on them by his own example (v. 33). This shows us that preachers may urge their advice with boldness and authority when they can enforce it with their own example. It is highly commendable in ministers to neglect their own personal advantage so that they may promote the salvation of their hearers.

CHAPTER 11

In this chapter the apostle blames and tries to put right some clear irregularities in the church at Corinth: 1. He blames them for misconduct in the public assembly by their women, who have been taking off their veils. He rebukes this behavior and asserts the authority of the husband, but does this in such a way as to remind the husband that men and women were made for each other's help and comfort (vv. 1–16). 2. He blames them for their conflict and contempt of the poor at the Lord's Supper (vv. 17–22). 3. He sets before them the intentions of this holy institution (vv. 23–34).

Verses 1–16

V. 1 seems more properly put at the end of the previous chapter to enforce Paul's warnings against the abuse of liberty by his own example: *Be ye followers of me, as I also am of Christ* (v. 1). But whichever chapter this verse belongs to, it is clear that Paul not only preached a doctrine that the Corinthian Christians should believe but also led a life that they should imitate. Ministers are likely to preach most effectively when they can urge their hearers to follow their example. But Paul does not want to be followed blindly; he wants to be followed no further than he follows Christ. Christ's example is perfect; no one else's is. Now, having urged his readers to follow his example, Paul passes on to find fault with what is improper among them, of which the women are especially guilty. Notice:

1. He commends what is good among them (v. 2): when we rebuke what is wrong in anyone, it is very wise and fit to commend what is good in them.

2. He asserts the authority of the man over the woman. Christ is the head of the whole human race. In this high office he has one over him in authority, God being his head. Just as God is the head of Christ, and Christ the head of the whole human race, so the man is the head of the two sexes, and the woman should be in submission and not usurp the man's place. The women of the church at Corinth prayed and prophesied even in their meetings (v. 5), whereas it is actually an apostolic principle that the women *should keep silence in the churches* (14:34; 1Ti 2:12). Here, however, the apostle does not prohibit the thing itself, but how it is done. The morality of a thing depends partly on how it is done. We must be concerned not only to do good but also to do well the good that we do.

3. The thing he rebukes is the woman's praying or prophesying uncovered, or the man's doing either covered (vv. 4–5).

4. The reasons on which he bases his rebuke.

4.1. *The man that prays or prophesies with his head covered dishonoureth his head*, namely, Christ, the head of every man (v. 3). *The woman who prays or prophesies with her head uncovered dishonoureth her head*, namely, the man (v. 3). She appears clothed like the one who has authority over her, thereby throwing off the sign of her submission. The sexes should not seek to change places. The woman should keep to the position God has chosen for her.

4.2. *The man is the image and glory of God.* It is the man who is set at the head of this lower creation, and in that role he bears a resemblance to God. The woman, on the other hand, is *the glory of the man* (v. 7). She is the image of God inasmuch as she is the image of the man.

4.3. *The woman was made for the man, and not the man for the woman.* She should do nothing that seems to assert equality. *She ought to have power on her head, because of the angels. Power*, that is, a veil, the sign that she is under the power, or authority, of her husband. And she is to have this sign *because of the angels*. Both Jews and Christians have had an opinion that these ministering spirits (Heb 1:14) are present in their meetings. Their presence should restrain Christians from all indecency in worshiping God.

5. A warning so that his readers will not infer too much (vv. 11–12). Man and woman were made to be a mutual comfort and blessing to one another, not one a slave and the other a tyrant. Just as it is the will of God that the woman know her place, so it is also his will that the man should not abuse his power.

6. He enforces his argument by reference to the fact that the woman's hair is a natural covering; to wear it long is her glory. But for a man to have long hair is a sign of weakness and effeminacy.

7. He sums up everything by referring to the customs of the churches (v. 16). The common practice of the churches is what he would have them govern themselves by.

Verses 17–22

In this passage the apostle sharply rebukes the Corinthian Christians for much greater improprieties than in the previous passage, improprieties in partaking in the Lord's Supper. Notice:

1. How he introduces his charge: *I praise you not* (v. 17). Such scandalous practices as they were guilty of called for sharp rebuke. This shows us that if the ordinances of Christ do not make us better, they will very likely make us worse; if they do not melt and mend, they will harden.

2. His charge against them.

2.1. He tells them that when they come together, they fall into *divisions*. They started to quarrel with one another. The apostle had heard a report of the Corinthians' divisions, and he told them he had too much reason to believe it. There must also be heresies. No wonder there are breaches of Christian love in the churches when such offenses come. Such offenses must come (Mt 18:7). God allows them so that those who are approved—such honest hearts as will endure the test—may be put on view and seen to be faithful. The wisdom of God can make the evil of others a contrast to the integrity of the saints.

2.2. He accuses them of scandalous disorder. They would not wait for one another, and so some lacked what they needed while others had more than enough. The poor were deprived of the food prepared for them, and the rich defiled a feast of love.

3. The apostle lays the blame for this conduct strictly on them:

3.1. Their conduct has completely destroyed the purpose and use of such an institution. They might as well have stayed away.

3.2. Their behavior carries with it a contempt for the church (v. 22). If they wanted to have a feast, they could have done it in their own houses. Religious feasts should be attended religiously.

Verses 23–34

To put right these gross corruptions and irregularities, the apostle explains how the sacrament was instituted.

1. He tells us how he came to know it. He *received from the Lord what he delivered to them* (v. 23).

2. He gives us a more detailed account of the institution than we meet with elsewhere.

2.1. The author is our Lord Jesus Christ.

2.2. The time of the instituting *was the very night wherein he was betrayed*, just as he was beginning his sufferings that are commemorated in it.

2.3. In the institution itself, our Savior took bread, and when he had given thanks, *he broke, and said, Take, eat; this is my body, broken for you; this do in remembrance of me. And in like manner he took the cup, when he had supped, saying, This cup is the New Testament in my blood; this do, as oft as you drink it, in remembrance of me* (vv. 24–25). Notice here:

2.3.1. The materials of this sacrament. We have an account of:

2.3.1.1. The visible signs; these are bread and the cup. What is eaten is called *bread* even though it is at the same time said to be *the body of the Lord*. Bread and the cup are both used because it is a holy feast. It is in no way unlawful to have a sacred ceremony when wine cannot be obtained; the cup stands for what was in it, without any specification of what the liquid was.

2.3.1.2. The things represented by these outward signs: they are Christ's body and his blood, his body broken, his blood shed.

2.3.2. The sacramental actions. At the institution, our Savior gave his disciples his body and blood, with all the benefits gained by his death, and he continues to do the same every time the sacraments are administered to true believers. They are to take him as their Lord and life, to give themselves to him and live on him.

2.3.3. The purposes of this institution. It was appointed to be done *in remembrance of Christ*, to keep fresh in our minds his dying for us as well as to remember an absent friend, Christ, interceding for us. The motto connected with this ceremony, with its very meaning, is, *When this you see, remember me.* It was *to show forth Christ's death.* It is not merely in remembrance of Christ but also to commemorate his glorious condescension and grace in our redemption. We acknowledge before the world by this very service that we are the disciples of Christ, who trust only in him for salvation and acceptance with God.

2.3.4. It should be frequent. Our physical meals come around often. It is right, therefore, that this spiritual meal should be taken often too. It must be perpetual. It is to be celebrated *till the Lord shall come.* The Lord's Supper is not a temporary decree, but a constant and perpetual one.

3. He lays before the Corinthians the danger of receiving the supper unworthily and using it for the purposes of feasting and faction.

3.1. Those who do so will *be guilty of the body and blood of the Lord* (v. 27). Instead of being cleansed by his blood, they will be guilty of his blood.

3.2. *They eat and drink judgment to themselves* (v. 29). They offend God and are likely to bring punishment on themselves.

3.2.1. Fearful believers should not, however, be discouraged by the sound of these words from attending this holy ceremony. The Holy Spirit never inspired this to deter serious Christians from their duty, though the Devil has often taken advantage of it to rob good Christians of their finest strengths and encouragements.

3.2.2. The Corinthians came to the Lord's Table *not discerning the Lord's body*—not making a distinction between this and ordinary food. *For this cause many are weak and sickly among you, and many sleep.*

3.2.3. Yet even those who were so punished were in a state of favor with God: *They were chastened of the Lord, that they should not be condemned with the world* (v. 32). God frequently punishes those whom he tenderly loves (Heb 12:6). It is kindness to discipline children to prevent their ruin. They were punished by him out of fatherly goodwill, punished now so that they would not perish forever.

4. He points out the duty of those who wish to come to the Lord's Table: *Let a man examine himself* (v. 28). Such self-examination is necessary for a right attendance at this holy service. Those who want to be welcomed at this marriage banquet should have the wedding garments on (Mt 22:11–12)—both grace in habits and grace in

exercise. To be exact and severe on ourselves is the most proper way to avoid falling under the just severity of our heavenly Father. We must not judge others, so that we will not be judged (Mt 7:1), but we must judge ourselves to prevent our being judged and condemned by God.

5. He closes the chapter with a warning against the irregularities they are guilty of (vv. 33–34). They are to eat for hunger and pleasure only at home. Through our own abuse, our holy duties may prove a cause for condemnation. Holy things are to be used in holy ways, for otherwise they are desecrated.

CHAPTER 12

In this chapter the apostle: 1. Considers the case of spiritual gifts: their origin—that they come from God—and their variety and use (vv. 1–11). 2. Illustrates this by an analogy to the human body (vv. 12–26). 3. Tells us that the church is the body of Christ (vv. 27–30). 4. Closes with an exhortation to seek something more beneficial than these gifts (v. 31).

Verses 1–11

The apostle comes now to discuss spiritual gifts. Where grace is given, it is for the salvation of those who have it. Gifts are granted for the advantage and salvation of others. There may be great gifts where there is not a gram of grace. This church was rich in gifts, but many things were scandalously out of order in it.

1. The apostle tells the Corinthian believers that gifts come from God and are to be used for him.

2. He reminds them of the sad state from which they were recovered (v. 2). Notice:

2.1. Their former standing: they *were Gentiles*. Not God's distinctive people, but belonging to the nations whom he had in a way abandoned. What a change there was! Christian Corinthians were once Gentiles. It is very useful to Christians, and a consideration proper for stirring them up both to do their duty and to be thankful, to think about what they once were.

2.2. Their former behavior: *carried away to these dumb idols, even as you were led.* How miserable, worthless, and contemptible! And even the pagans who despised these corrupt conceptions still supported them in practice. Could the Spirit of God live among such stupefied idolaters?

3. He shows them how they can discern the gifts that are from the Spirit of God: *No man, speaking by the Spirit, calls Jesus accursed.* This is what both Jews and Gentiles did: they blasphemed Christ as an imposter and cursed his name. No one could act under the influence or by the power of the Spirit of God if they disowned and blasphemed Christ, because the Spirit of God could never so greatly contradict himself as to declare Christ cursed. No one can call Christ *Lord*, with a believing dependence on him, unless that faith is brought about by the Holy Spirit.

4. The same giver may grant various gifts (v. 4). There are different kinds of service or positions, and different officers to discharge them (see vv. 28–30), but the same Lord, who appointed all (v. 6). *There are diversities of operations* (v. 10), *but it is the same God that worketh all in all.* However different the gifts may be in themselves, they harmonize in that all come from God. The apostle specifies several different kinds here (vv. 8–10). To one was given the *word of wisdom*, a knowledge of the secrets of the Gospel and an ability to explain them. *To another the word of knowledge by the same Spirit,* that is,

according to some, the knowledge of mysteries (2:13), according to others, a skill and readiness to give advice and counsel in confusing situations. *To another faith by the same Spirit*, by which they were enabled to trust God in any emergency. *To another the gift of healing*, that is, healing the sick, *by the same Spirit. To another the working of miracles. To another prophecy*, to explain Scripture by a special gift of the Spirit. *To another the discerning of spirits*, power to distinguish between true and false prophets. *To another divers kinds of tongues*, or the ability to speak languages by inspiration. *To another the interpretation of tongues*, or the ability to render foreign languages into their own.

5. He states the purpose for which these gifts were given (v. 7). They were not distributed for the advantage of those who had them, but for the benefit of the church. Whatever gifts God gives to anyone, he gives them so that those who have them may do good with them. Gifts are a trust put into their hands, given not for show but for service.

6. *All these worketh one and the same Spirit, dividing to every man as he will.* Shall not the Spirit of God do what he wishes with what belongs to him? He does not give as people wish, nor as they may think fit, but as he, the Spirit, pleases.

Verses 12–26

The apostle reminds the gifted among the Corinthians of their duty by comparing the church of Christ to a human body.

1. One body may have many members; the many members make up a unit (v. 12). All the members are *baptized into the same body, and made to drink of the same Spirit* (v. 13). Christians become members of this body by baptism; they are baptized into one body. We are sustained by participating in the Lord's Supper, by drinking one Spirit. It is baptism by the Spirit and internal renewal and drinking of the same Spirit that makes us true members of Christ's body. All who have the spirit of Christ are the members of Christ, whether Jew or Gentile, slave or free.

2. Each member has its particular form, place, and use.

2.1. The most insignificant member is a part of the body. The foot and ear are less useful, perhaps, than the hand and eye, but will they therefore say that they do not belong to the body (vv. 15–16)? Every member of the mystical body cannot have the same place and office. The lowliest member of Christ's body is as much a member as the noblest is. All his members are dear to him.

2.2. There must be a distinction of members in the body: *They are many members, and yet are but one body* (v. 20). So it is in the body of Christ. Variety in the members of the body contributes to its beauty. Similarly, it is for the beauty and good appearance of the church that there be a diversity of gifts.

2.3. The disposal and situation of members of a natural body are as God pleases (v. 18). So it is in the members of Christ's body. Each of us should be actively fulfilling the duties of our own station and not quarreling with others because we are not in their shoes.

2.4. All the members of the body are useful and necessary to each other. Those members of the body *which seem to be more feeble are necessary* (vv. 21–22). Every member serves some good purpose or other. Nor is there a member of the body of Christ who is never useful to their fellow members, and in some cases, indispensable to them. Those who excel in any gift cannot say that they do not need those who are inferior to them in that gift,

for those inferior to them in one gift may excel them in other gifts. The eye needs the hand, and the head needs the feet.

2.5. Such is a person's concern for their whole body that *on the less honourable members more abundant honour is bestowed* (the less honorable members are treated with special modesty), *and our uncomely* (unpresentable) *parts have more abundant comeliness* (are treated with special modesty) (v. 24). The members of Christ's body should behave toward their fellow members in the same way.

2.6. Divine wisdom has ordered things in this way so that the members of the body will not be divided, so that *there might be no schism in the body* (v. 25). The members of the natural body are made to have a care and concern for one another. So should it be in Christ's body. Christian sympathy is a great branch of Christian duty.

Verses 27–31

1. Here the apostle applies this comparison to the church of Christ. Notice:

1.1. The relation in which Christians stand to Christ and one another. *Now you are the body of Christ, and members in particular.* All have a common relationship with one another.

1.2. The variety of ministries instituted by Christ and the gifts or favors given by him (v. 28), in which notice:

1.2.1. The wide variety of these gifts and ministries. God was not stingy in giving his benefits and favors. The early church had no lack, but a generous store at their disposal—all that was necessary, and even more.

1.2.2. The order of these ministries and gifts. Those of most value have the first place. God values things, and so should we, according to their real worth. What holds the last and lowest rank in this list is those speaking different kinds of tongues. The gift of speaking in tongues is by itself the least significant of all these gifts. The Corinthians prided themselves exceedingly on this gift. This shows us how proper it is to beat down pride in order to inform people of the true value of what they pride themselves in! It is only too common for people to pride themselves most in what is least valuable.

1.2.3. The various distribution of these gifts. All members and officers did not have the same endowments (vv. 29–30). The Spirit distributes to everyone as he wishes. We must be content with our own rank and share. All are to minister to one another and advance the good of the body in general.

2. He closes this chapter with a piece of advice and a hint.

2.1. He advises them to seek the best gifts: we should desire most what is best and most valuable. Grace is therefore to be preferred before gifts. But some read this passage not as advice but as accusation: "You are envious of each other's gifts. You quarrel and fight about them." The Corinthian Christians certainly did this. They quarreled about who had precedence, and it is no wonder that a quarrel about precedence would snuff out love. When everyone wanted to be first, no wonder they jostled.

2.2. He hints at a more excellent way, namely, the way of *charity*, of mutual love and goodwill. To have the heart aglow with love is vastly better than to glare with the most pompous titles, positions, or powers.

CHAPTER 13

In this chapter the apostle goes on to discuss the more excellent way of charity *(love): 1. By showing its necessity (vv. 1–3). 2. By describing its qualities (vv. 4–7).*

3. By showing how much it excels the best gifts and other graces in its power to continue when those others no longer exist (vv. 8–13).

Verses 1–3

Here the apostle shows what more excellent way he meant, *charity*, or *love* in its fullest meaning, true love to God and people. Without this, the most glorious gifts are nothing. He specifies:

1. The gift of tongues (v. 1). It is the loving heart, not the fluent tongue, that is acceptable with God.

2. Prophecy, and the understanding of mysteries, and complete knowledge. This gift, without love, is as nothing (v. 2). A clear and deep mind is of no significance without a generous and loving heart. It is not great knowledge that God values, but true and sincere devotion and love.

3. Miraculous faith. Moving mountains is a great achievement in human reckoning, but in God's estimation one gram of charity is much more valuable than all the faith of this kind in the world. Saving faith always goes together with love, but the faith of miracles may be without it.

4. Performing outward acts of love (v. 3). There may be an open and lavish hand where there is no generous and loving heart. If we give away all we have while we withhold the heart from God, it will gain us nothing.

5. Even suffering (v. 3). If we sacrifice our lives for the faith of the Gospel, this will have no true value without love. True love is the very heart and spirit of Christian faith. If we feel none of its sacred heat in our hearts, we will gain nothing, even if we have been burned to ashes for the truth.

Verses 4–7

Notice some of the qualities and effects of love:

1. *It is long-suffering.* It can bear evil and provocation without being filled with resentment or a desire for revenge. It will put up with many insults from the person it loves and will wait long to see the good effect of such patience on them.

2. *It is kind. The law of kindness is in her lips* (Pr 31:26). It seeks to be useful, not only grasping hold of opportunities to do good but actively looking out for them.

3. *It envieth not*; it is not grieved at the good of others. Envy is the effect of ill will. The heart that is set on doing good to everyone can never seek to harm anyone.

4. *It vaunteth not itself* (does not boast), *is not puffed up* (is not proud), is not bloated with self-conceit. True love will give us respect for our brothers and sisters, and this will limit our esteem for ourselves. The word translated *vaunteth itself* has other meanings, but in every sense true love stands in opposition to it. The Aramaic renders it "does not raise tumults" and disturbances. Love calms down angry passions, instead of raising them. Others translate it, "It does not act insidiously with anyone," does not seek to trap them. It is not perverse, nor is it inclined to be irritable or rebellious. Some understand this word as referring to pretense and flattery. Love detests these.

5. *It behaveth not unseemly.* It does nothing out of place or time, but behaves with courtesy and goodwill toward all.

6. Love is the complete enemy of selfishness: *It seeketh not its own.* Self-love is indeed, to some extent, natural to all. A reasonable love of self is considered by our Savior to be the measure of our love to others: *Thou shalt love thy neighbour as thyself* (Mt 22:39; Lev 19:18). But love never seeks its own advantage to the harm of others. It often neglects its own interest for the sake of others.

7. It is *not easily provoked*, "is not exasperated." Where the fire of love is sustained, the flames of wrath will not easily ignite, nor keep burning for long. Anger cannot rest within a person where love reigns. It is hard to be angry with those we love.

8. Love *thinks no evil.* It cherishes no hatred, nor does it give way to revenge. It does not become angry quickly or for long. It does not suspect evil of others. It will hide faults that become apparent instead of hunting down and raking out those that lie covered and concealed.

9. The subject of its joy and pleasure is suggested here: *It rejoiceth not in iniquity.* It wishes no one any wrong, much less will it make this a substance of its delight, and least of all will it rejoice in doing harm and causing trouble. The sins of others stir all its compassion, but can give it no entertainment. *It rejoiceth in the truth.* It gives love much satisfaction to see truth and justice triumph among people, to see mutual faith and trust established.

10. *It beareth all things, it endureth all things.* Some read the first clause, "It covers all things." It does not wish to display or make known the faults of a brother or sister. Although a loving person is free to tell their brother or sister their own faults in private, they are very unwilling to expose those faults by making them public. This is how we would like our own faults dealt with, and this is how love would teach us to respond to the faults of others. Or, it *beareth all things*: it will be patient under provocation and for a long time. What bravery and determination passionate love will give the heart! What cannot a lover endure for the beloved and for their sake!

11. *It believeth all things, hopeth all things.* Indeed, love will by no means destroy wisdom. Wisdom may dwell with love, and love will always be cautious. Yet love is inclined to believe well of everyone and make the best of everything. It will judge well and trust well. When, despite inclination, it cannot trust others, it will still hope. How lovely is a heart that is tinged throughout with such kindness! Happy are those who have this heavenly fire glowing in their heart!

Verses 8–13

Here the apostle shows how preferable love is to the gifts the Corinthians tended to boast about:

1. *Charity never faileth.* It is a permanent and perpetual grace, lasting to eternity. *Prophecy must fail. Tongues will cease.* There will be only one language in heaven; there is no confusion of tongues in the region of perfect tranquility. Also, *knowledge will vanish away.* Not that holy and happy souls will be ignorant; it is a very poor form of happiness that can exist alongside complete ignorance. Rather, the apostle is here contrasting the grace of love with supernatural gifts. Love is more valuable because it is more durable; *it* will enter into heaven, where *they* will have no place.

2. *We know in part, and we prophesy in part* (v. 9). How little a portion of God was heard even by apostles and other inspired people! These gifts were fitted to the present imperfect state of the church, whereas love was to last forever.

3. How much better it will be with the church in the future (v. 10). Once the end is reached, the means will of course be abolished. Then the church will be in a state of perfection, complete in both knowledge and holiness. God will then be known clearly. What confused and unclear ideas of things children have in comparison to adults! How naturally adults despise and abandon their infant thoughts! In the future state, the things to be known will be open to our eyes, and our knowledge will be free

from all obscurity and error. God is to be seen *face to face*, and we *are to know him* as *we are known by him*. What a glorious change, to pass from darkness to light, from clouds to the clear sunshine of our Savior's face, and to see light in God's own light (Ps 36:9)! It is at best dusk while we remain in this world; there it will be perfect and eternal day.

4. Faith, hope, and love are the three main graces, of which love is the chief. Faith fixes on the divine revelation and gives its approval to that; hope fastens on future happiness and waits for that. But love focuses on the divine perfections themselves, which will all shine brightly in the most glorious splendors in another world, where love will be made perfect. There we will love God perfectly. There we will love one another perfectly. When faith and hope come to an end, true love will burn forever with the brightest flame. Where God is to be seen as he is, and face to face, love is there at its greatest height—there, and only there, will it be perfected.

CHAPTER 14

In this chapter the apostle instructs his readers on spiritual gifts: 1. He begins by advising them to prefer prophesying over all other spiritual gifts (vv. 1–5). 2. He goes on to show them how unbeneficial speaking in tongues is (vv. 6–14). 3. He advises that worship should be celebrated in such a way that the most ignorant can understand (vv. 15–20). 4. He advises that tongues are a sign for unbelievers (vv. 21–25). 5. He blames them for the disorder they have brought into the meeting (vv. 26–33). 6. He forbids women to speak in the church (vv. 34–40).

Verses 1–5

He teaches them which spiritual gifts they should prefer.

1. He begins the chapter with a command to love. "See that you do not lack this main grace."

2. He guides them as to which spiritual gift to prefer: *Desire spiritual gifts, but rather that you may prophesy.* Gifts are the fitting objects for our desire and pursuit, in subordination to grace and love.

3. He designates the reasons for this preference. He compares prophesying only with speaking in tongues. The latter was more ostentatious than the plain interpretation of Scripture, but less fitting for pursuing the purposes of Christian love.

3.1. Those who speak in tongues must only speak with God (v. 2). What cannot be understood can never edify. Those who prophesy, however, speak to the advantage of their hearers, who may be exhorted and comforted by it (v. 3).

3.2. *He that speaks in a tongue may edify himself* (v. 4). Others can reap no benefit from his speech, whereas the purpose of speaking in church is to edify the church (v. 4), which is the very purpose of prophesying.

3.3. The best gifts are to be preferred. The best gift is one that does most good. Every gift of God is a favor from God, but those that are most useful are to be most valued. Greater are those who interpret Scripture to edify the church than those who speak in tongues to commend themselves. What is most for the church's edification—not what shows a person's gifts to the greatest advantage—is most for the honor of a minister.

Verses 6–14

Here the apostle shows how vain it is to show off one's ability to speak in an unknown and unintelligible lan-

guage (v. 6): *If I come to you speaking with tongues, what will it profit you, unless I speak to you by revelation, or by knowledge, or by prophesying, or by doctrine?* It would mean nothing to speak these in an unknown tongue:

1. He illustrates this by several metaphors:

1.1. A flute or harp always playing the same note: Unintelligible language gives no more direction than a flute with only one stop or a harp with only one string can give directions to dancers as to how they should regulate their steps (v. 7).

1.2. A trumpet giving an *uncertain sound*. If instead of sounding an attack it sounded a retreat, or sounded something unknown, who would prepare for battle? Words without meaning can convey no ideas or instruction to the mind, and words that are not understood have no meaning.

1.3. A foreign language. There are (v. 10) many kinds of *voices* (languages) in the world, none of which is without its proper meaning. But whatever the proper meaning of the words in any language to those who understand them, they are complete gibberish to people who speak another language. In such a case, the speaker and hearers are barbarians to each other (v. 11); they talk and hear sounds but no sense. To speak in the church in an unknown tongue is to talk gibberish.

2. Having established his point:

2.1. He applies it, by advising them to desire chiefly those gifts that are most for the church's edification (v. 12). "Seek most those gifts that will best serve people's souls."

2.2. He applies it to the matter in hand: if they did speak a foreign language, they should seek God for the gift of interpreting it (v. 13). The church must understand in order to be built up. The essence was that they should perform all religious activities in their meetings in such a way that everyone could join in them and benefit from them.

2.3. He reinforces this advice: *If I pray in an unknown tongue, my spirit might pray*—that is, a spiritual gift might be exercised in prayer, or his own mind might be devoutly engaged—*but my understanding would be unfruitful* (v. 14); he would not be understood, and so others could not join in the devotions. Language that is clearest and most easily understood is the most proper for public devotion.

Verses 15–20

1. The apostle tells them how they should sing and pray in public (v. 15). He wants them to perform both so as to be understood by others, so that others can join them. Public worship should be performed so as to be understood.

2. He reinforces the argument with several reasons.

2.1. Otherwise the *unlearned* (ignorant) cannot say "Amen" to their fellow believers' prayers or thanksgiving; they cannot join in the worship, for they will not understand it (v. 16). Everyone should say *Amen* inwardly, and it is not improper to show this inner agreement in public prayers and devotions by an audible *Amen*. Now, how could the people say *Amen* to something they did not understand? The intention of public devotions is completely undermined if they are performed in an unknown language. Others are not, and cannot be, edified (v. 17) by something they do not understand.

2.2. He cites his own example to make a greater impression.

2.2.1. He did not lag behind any of them in this spiritual gift. It was not jealousy that made Paul depreciate what they valued so highly and boasted about so much; he surpassed them all in this gift of tongues. There was more reason for them to envy him for this than for him to envy them. When we overthrow people's unreasonable esteem for themselves, we should let them see that this does not come from an envious and grudging spirit.

2.2.2. He would rather *speak five words with understanding than ten thousand words in an unknown tongue* (v. 19). Genuine Christian ministers will esteem themselves much more for doing good to people's souls than for obtaining the greatest praise.

2.2.3. The fondness then being shown for this gift clearly indicated the immaturity of their judgment (v. 20). Children love novelties and things that look curious. "Do not act like them, preferring noise and show to worth and substance; be like children in nothing but an innocent and inoffensive disposition. Christians should have wisdom and knowledge that are ripe and mature.

Verses 21–25

The apostle pursues his argument.

1. Tongues, as the Corinthians used them, were a sign of judgment from God rather than of mercy to any people (v. 21). When God gives a people over to the discipline of those who speak in another language, it is evidence that that people has been abandoned by God. They can never benefit from such teaching, and when they are left to it, it is a sad sign that God has given them over as beyond healing. This, however, was what the Corinthian preachers did when they always wanted to deliver their inspirations in an unknown tongue.

2. Tongues were a sign to unbelievers rather than to believers (v. 22). The gift of tongues was necessary to spread Christianity. It was proper and was intended for convincing unbelievers. Interpreting Scripture in their own language was best for the edification of those who already believed; for gifts to be rightly used, it is necessary to know the purpose they are intended to serve. To seek the conversion of unbelievers would have been in vain without the gift of tongues, but in a meeting of Christians, using that gift would be totally inappropriate.

3. The reputation of their meetings required them to prefer prophesying to speaking in tongues.

3.1. If their ministers, or all employed in public worship, talked in an unintelligible language, and unbelievers dropped in, the latter would conclude that the believers were insane. What kind of religion is it that leaves out sense and understanding? Would not this make Christianity ridiculous to the ungodly?

3.2. If, instead of speaking in tongues, those who ministered clearly interpreted Scripture, then if an unbeliever or *unlearned* (ignorant) person came in, they would probably be convinced and become converted to Christianity (vv. 24–25), and so would be led to confess their guilt, pay homage to God, and acknowledge that he was truly among them. Prophesying would certainly edify the church and probably convert unbelievers. The ministry was not instituted to show off gifts and talents, but to save souls.

Verses 26–33

In these verses the apostle rebukes them for their disorder and seeks to correct and regulate their future behavior.

1. He blames them for the confusion they have introduced into the assembly (v. 26). "You tend to confuse the different parts of worship"; or, "You tend to be confused in a single aspect of worship, many of you having words to give at the same time, and not waiting for one another.

Can this be edifying? *Let all things be done unto edifying* (v. 26)."

2. He corrects their faults.

2.1. As to speaking in an unknown tongue, he orders that no more than two or three people should do it at one meeting, one after another. Moreover, even this was not to be done unless there was someone to interpret (vv. 27–28). But if there was no one to interpret, the one who wished to speak in tongues was to be silent in church, exercising the gift only between God and themselves (v. 28).

2.2. As to prophesying, he orders:

2.2.1. That only two or three should speak at one meeting (v. 29). There might be false prophets, and the true prophets were to judge these and discover who was divinely inspired and who was not.

2.2.2. That if any assistant prophet has a revelation while another is prophesying, the first speaker should stop and be silent (v. 30). The one who has the new revelation can claim freedom of speech in their turn (v. 31): *For you may all prophesy one by one*, one after another. Divine inspirations are not, like the satanic possessions of ungodly priests, violent and uncontrollable, but are sober and calm and capable of being expressed in an orderly manner. The person who is inspired by the Spirit of God may still observe the rules of natural order and decency in delivering revelations.

3. The apostle gives the reasons for these regulations.

3.1. They will be for the church's benefit, for their instruction and encouragement.

3.2. *God is not the God of confusion, but of peace and good order* (v. 33). Divine inspiration, therefore, should in no way throw Christian meetings into confusion. If they are managed in a disorderly and confused way, what an idea must this give of the God who is worshiped! Does it look as if God were the author of peace and order, and an enemy of confusion?

3.3. Things are managed in an orderly way in all the other churches. And it would be completely scandalous for them, who surpassed most churches in spiritual gifts, to be more disorderly than any of them in exercising the gifts.

Verses 34–35

Here the apostle:

1. Commands women to remain silent in public meetings; they must not ask questions for their own information at church, but ask their husbands at home. There is in fact an indication (11:5) that the women sometimes prayed and prophesied in their meetings. But here the apostle seems to forbid all public spoken participation in worship by women. They are not permitted to speak (v. 34) in the church. The connection seems clearly to include prophesying, which would be a kind of teaching and therefore be an exercise of authority, which is not allowed for the woman to have over the man. She must not, therefore, be allowed to teach in a congregation, nor even ask questions in the church, but must learn in silence there and, if difficulties arose, *ask her own husband at home*. Just as it is the woman's duty to learn in submission, so it is the man's duty to maintain his authority by being able to instruct her. If it is disgraceful for her to speak in the church, where she should be silent, it is disgraceful for him to be silent when he should speak, and not be able to give an answer when she asks him at home.

2. Gives the reason for this command: it is God's law. The apostle concludes, therefore, that it would be *a shame* (disgraceful) for women to speak in the church. Shame is the mind's uneasy reflection on having done something

indecent, and what could be more indecent than for a woman to leave her position? The woman was made subject to the man, and she should keep her position and be content with it.

Verses 36–40

Here:

1. Paul begins with a just rebuke of the Corinthians for their extravagant pride and arrogance. "Are you the only church favored with divine revelations?" How intolerably arrogant is such behavior!

2. He lets them know that what he is saying to them is the command of God, and no true prophet would dare deny it (v. 37): "If their revelations contradict mine, they do not come from the same Spirit; either I or they must be false prophets. But if anyone remains uncertain or ignorant as to whether they or I am speaking by the Spirit of God, they must be left under the power of this ignorance." God is just to leave to the blindness of their own hearts those who deliberately shut out the light.

3. He sums up everything.

3.1. Although they should not despise the gift of tongues, they should still prefer prophesying. It was the more useful gift.

3.2. All things should be done decently and in order (v. 40). They must do nothing that was clearly immature (v. 20) or that would give others occasion to say they were out of their minds (v. 23), nor must they act so as to breed confusion (v. 33). All parts of divine worship should be carried on in a composed and orderly way.

CHAPTER 15

In this chapter: 1. The apostle establishes the certainty of our Savior's resurrection (vv. 1–11). 2. He sets himself to refute those who say there is no resurrection of the dead (vv. 12–19). 3. On the basis of our Savior's resurrection he establishes the resurrection of the dead (vv. 20–34). 4. He answers an objection and uses the occasion to show what a vast change will occur in the bodies of believers at the resurrection (vv. 35–50). 5. He informs us what a change will occur in those who will be living when the last trumpet sounds (vv. 51–57). 6. He sums up the argument with a very serious exhortation to Christians (v. 58).

Verses 1–11

It is the apostle's task in this chapter to establish the teaching of the resurrection of the dead, which some of the Corinthians flatly denied (v. 12). And by denying the resurrection of the dead, they also rejected a future state of rewards. Paul begins with a summary of the Gospel. Notice about the Gospel:

1. What emphasis he puts on it (vv. 1–2).

1.1. It was what he constantly preached. Paul continued to teach the doctrine he had taught up to that time.

1.2. It was what they had received. It was no strange message; it was the true Gospel on which they had taken their stand up to that time, and they must continue to stand by it. The teaching of Christ's death and resurrection is at the heart of Christianity. If we take away this foundation, the whole structure falls.

1.3. It was only through this Gospel that they were saved (v. 2). There is *no salvation in any other name* (Ac 4:12), and there is no salvation in his name except on the basis of his death and resurrection. These are the saving truths of our holy religious faith. They must be kept in mind; they must be held firmly. We believe in vain unless we continue

and persevere in the faith of the Gospel. We will never be any better for a short-lived, temporary faith. It is futile to profess faith in Christ if we deny the resurrection. Take this away, and we make nothing of Christianity.

2. What this Gospel is. It was the message he had received and delivered to them *among the first*, a teaching of the first rank, a most necessary truth. Christ's death and resurrection are the essence and substance of evangelical truth.

3. How this truth is confirmed:

3.1. By Old Testament predictions. Christ died for our sins; he was buried and rose from the dead, according to the Scripture prophecies. It is a great confirmation of our faith in the Gospel to see how it corresponds with ancient prophecies.

3.2. By the testimony of many eyewitnesses, who saw Christ after he had risen from the dead. How powerfully clear Christ's resurrection from the dead was, since so many eyes saw him at so many different times. Even Paul himself, last of all, was favored with seeing him. The Lord Jesus appeared to him on the road to Damascus (Ac 9:17). He was highly favored by God, but he always sought to maintain a humble opinion of himself. He does this here:

3.2.1. By commenting that he was *one born out of due time* (v. 8). He was not matured for the apostolic function, as the others were, who had personal dealings with our Lord. He was too late for that.

3.2.2. By acknowledging that he is inferior to the other apostles. He calls himself *the least*, and even unworthy to be called an apostle, having once been *a persecutor of the church of God* (v. 9). In a person who has achieved great things, a humble spirit is a great jewel. What kept Paul humble was the memory of his former evil ways, his raging zeal against Christ and his followers. How easily God can bring good out of the greatest evil! When sinners become saints by divine grace, he makes the memory of their former sins very useful, to keep them humble, diligent, and faithful.

3.2.3. By attributing all that is valuable in him to divine grace. We are nothing except what God has made us. Although Paul was conscious of his own zeal and service, he still thought himself very much indebted to divine grace. *Yet not I, but the grace of God which was with me.* The harder he worked, and the more good he did, the humbler he was, and the more disposed to acknowledge the favor of God toward him. The apostle tells them (v. 11) that not only does he preach the same Gospel himself at all times and in all places; all the apostles preach the same message. All agree that Jesus Christ, and him crucified and put to death (2:2), and then rising from the dead, was the essence of Christianity. They live by this belief; they die in this belief.

Verses 12–19

If Christ be preached that he rose from the dead, how say some among you that there is no resurrection of the dead? (v. 12). Against this the apostle produces an incontestable fact, namely, the resurrection of Christ.

1. It was foretold in the ancient prophecies that he would rise, and it has been proved by many eyewitnesses that he arose.

2. If this supposition that there is no resurrection were accepted, it would destroy the main evidence of Christianity, and so it would:

2.1. Make preaching useless. "*We* apostles would *be found false witnesses of God.* Would not all our hard work be completely in vain? If Christ is not raised, the Gospel is a joke; it is empty and worthless."

2.2. Make the faith of Christians useless, because it is only through his death and sacrifice for sin that forgiveness is to be obtained. If he had remained under the power of death, how could he have saved us from its power? Furthermore, how useless faith in him would be. There would have been no justification or salvation if Christ had not risen.

3. It would also follow that *those who have fallen asleep in Christ have perished.* Those who denied the resurrection took death to mean the destruction and extinction of the person, not merely of the physical life. "Supposing there is no resurrection, no after-state and afterlife, then dead Christians are completely lost. How useless our faith and religion would be on this supposition!" Moreover:

4. From this it would follow that Christ's ministers and servants were *of all men most miserable, having hope in him in this life only* (v. 19). If there is no resurrection or state of future reward, and if all their hopes in Christ lie within the bounds of this life only, they are in a much worse condition than the rest of humanity. On these terms, it would be better to be anything else than a Christian. They fare with much greater difficulty than others in this life if they have no further hopes, nor any better ones. By their religion, Christians are crucified to this world and taught to live on basis of the hope of another.

Verses 20–34

In these verses, the apostle establishes the truth of the resurrection of the dead, the dead in Christ:

1. He establishes it on the basis of the resurrection of Christ.

1.1. Christ has actually risen himself, as the firstfruits of those who sleep in him. As he has risen, they will rise. Christ's resurrection is a pledge of ours. This is the first argument used by the apostle in confirmation of the truth.

1.2. He illustrates this argument by a parallel between the First Adam and the Second. All who die, die through the sin of Adam; all who are raised rise through the merit and power of Christ. But the meaning is not that just as all people died in Adam, so all people, without exception, will be made alive in Christ. Christ rose as the firstfruits; therefore *those that are Christ's* (v. 23) will rise too. All who rise in this way rise because of Christ's resurrection, and so just as death came through a human being, so deliverance came through a human being too.

1.3. He states that an order will be observed in their resurrection. What that precisely will be we are not told anywhere. It is said here only that when Christ comes again, the firstfruits are expected to rise first, and afterward all others who are his.

2. He argues for the resurrection from the truth that Christ's rule as Mediator-King will continue until all his enemies are destroyed, the last of which is death (vv. 24–26).

2.1. This argument implies:

2.1.1. That our Savior rose from the dead to have all authority given into his hands.

2.1.2. That this mediatorial kingdom is to have an end (v. 24).

2.1.3. That it is not to come to an end until all opposing powers are destroyed (vv. 24–25).

2.1.4. That, among other enemies, death must be destroyed (v. 26). The apostle is explicit up to this point, but he leaves it to us to draw the conclusion that the saints must rise, for otherwise death and the grave would have power over them. When saints live again, and never die, then—and not until then—death will be abolished.

2.2. The apostle drops several noteworthy hints.

2.2.1. Our Savior, as man and mediator between God and humanity, has a delegated royalty. Since he is a human being, all his authority must be delegated. As Mediator he has the character of a middle person, between God and humanity, sharing both natures, since he was to reconcile the two parties, God and humanity. On his ascension, he was made head over all things to the church (Eph 1:22), that is, given power to govern and protect it against all its enemies and, in the end, destroy them and complete the salvation of all who believe in him.

2.2.2. This delegated royalty must finally *be delivered up to the Father,* from whom it was received (v. 24), for it is a power received for particular purposes (vv. 25–26). The Redeemer must reign until his enemies are destroyed, and when this goal has been reached, he will then hand over the power.

2.2.3. The Redeemer will certainly reign until the last enemy of his people is destroyed, until death itself is abolished. Until then he will have all power in heaven and on earth. What a support this should be to his saints in every time of distress and temptation! When this is done, *and all things are put under his feet* (v. 28), then the man Christ Jesus (2Ti 2:5) will, on giving it up, be seen to be a subject of the Father. And this will be seen to the glory of God, *so that God may be all in all,* so that the accomplishment of our salvation may be seen to be altogether divine. Although the human nature must be employed in the work of our redemption, nevertheless, God was all in all in it.

3. He argues for the resurrection from the case of those who are baptized for the dead (v. 29). But what is this baptism for the dead? Some understand the passage as referring to the martyrs: why do they suffer martyrdom for their religion, *if the dead rise not at all?* Early believers sometimes called martyrdom the baptism of blood. See Mt 20:22; Lk 12:50. Some understand this baptism as referring to a custom that was observed among many who professed the Christian name in the first ages, a custom of baptizing some in the name and place of new converts who died without having been baptized. But whether this is the meaning, or whatever else it may be, no doubt the apostle's argument was good and intelligible to the Corinthians. His next argument is as clear to us as that one must have been to them.

4. He argues that his own behavior and that of other Christians is absurd if the dead are not raised.

4.1. It would be foolish for them to put themselves in so much danger (v. 30).

4.1.1. Christianity would be a foolish profession if it offered no hopes beyond this life, if it required people to risk all the blessings and comforts of this life, and to face and endure all its evils, without any future prospects. And yet must they not characterize it in this way if they are to give up their future hopes by denying the resurrection of the dead?

4.1.2. The apostle brings home this argument to himself: *I die daily* (v. 31). He was in continual danger of death, taking his life, as we say, in his own hands. He had met very great difficulties and fierce enemies; he had *fought with beasts at Ephesus* (v. 32)—been in danger of being torn to pieces by an enraged crowd (Ac 19:24). I take it that *fought with beasts* is a figurative expression, that the animals referred to were people of a fierce and wild disposition. "Now," he says, "what advantage have I gained from such contests if the dead do not rise? *If I am to perish by death* and expect nothing after it, could anything be weaker?" Was Paul so foolish? Could anything but the confident hopes of a better life after death have extinguished the love of life in him to this degree? *What advantageth it me* (what have I gained), *if the dead rise not?* It is lawful and fitting for Christians to expect to gain a personal advantage by their faithfulness to God. Paul did.

4.2. It would be much wiser to take the comforts of this life (v. 32). Let us also live like the animals, if we must die like them. If there were no resurrection, this would indeed be wiser. If there were no hopes after death, would not every wise person prefer an easy, comfortable life, and seek to enjoy the comforts of life as much as possible, because it was so short-lived? Nothing but the hopes of better things in the future can enable a person to renounce all the comforts and pleasures in this one.

5. The apostle ends his argument with a warning, an exhortation, and a rebuke.

5.1. He gives a warning against people of loose lives and principles (v. 33). Perhaps some of those who said that there was no resurrection of the dead were those who led loose lives; perhaps it was from their mouths that the saying was heard, *Let us eat and drink, for tomorrow we die.* Having disproved their principle, the apostle now warns the Corinthians how dangerous associating with such people must turn out to be. The believers would probably be corrupted by them and fall in with their way of life if they gave in to their evil principles. Those who want to keep their innocence must keep good company. Error and vice are infectious.

5.2. Here is an exhortation to break away from their sins and lead a more holy and righteous life (v. 34): "Come to your senses; stir yourselves, break away from your sins. Do not, by your laziness or foolishness, be led away into a way of life that will sap your Christian hope." Disbelief in a future state destroys all goodness and godliness. If there is a resurrection and a future life, we should live and act as those who believe it.

5.3. Here is a rebuke to at least some among them. It is a shame in Christians not to have the knowledge of, to be ignorant of, God. Those who profess this religion disgrace themselves by remaining ignorant of God, because it must be due to their own laziness. It must be ignorance of God that leads people to disbelieve in the resurrection and future life. Those who know God know that he is not so unfaithful nor so unkind as to forget their hard work and patience, their faithful service and cheerful suffering, or to allow their *labour to be in vain.* Those who acknowledge God and notice how unequal the distributions of the present life are, and how frequently the best people fare the worst, can hardly doubt an afterlife, where everything will be set right.

Verses 35–50

Here is a reasonable objection to the teaching of the resurrection of the dead (v. 35). The objection is plainly twofold:

- *How are they raised up?* That is, "By what means? What power is able to effect this?" This objection is that of those who opposed the doctrine.
- The other part concerns the quality of their bodies: *With what body will they come?* This objection is the question of curious doubters.

1. The apostle replies to the first objection by telling his readers this is to be brought about by divine power, that very power which they have all observed doing something very similar to it, year after year, in the death and revival of the grain (v. 36). It not only sprouts after it is dead; it must die so that it may live. It is foolish to question the divine power to raise the dead when we see it every day giving life to and reviving dead things.

2. He takes longer, however, to reply to the second question.

2.1. He comments that a change occurs in the grain that is sown. God gives it the body he determines. Every seed sown has its *own body.* It is certain that the grain undergoes a great change, and so will the dead when they rise again.

2.2. He proceeds to comment that there is a great deal of variety among other bodies:

2.2.1. There is variety in bodies of flesh (v. 39).

2.2.2. There is variety in heavenly and earthly bodies. The true glory of every being consists in its fitness for its rank and state.

2.2.3. There is a variety of glory among heavenly bodies themselves (v. 41). This is to suggest to us that when the bodies of the dead rise, they will be changed so much that there will be a variety of glories. It must be as easy for divine power to raise the dead as to form from the same materials so many different kinds of flesh and plants, and heavenly bodies as well as earthly ones. Can he form such a variety of beings out of the same materials, but not raise the dead?

2.3. *So also,* Paul says, *is the resurrection of the dead.*

2.3.1. *It is sown in corruption; it is raised in incorruption.* Burying the dead is like sowing them; it is like committing the seed to the earth so that it may spring up from it again. When we rise, they will be out of the power of the grave, and never again be liable to corruption.

2.3.2. *It is sown in dishonour; it is raised in glory.* Ours is at present a *vile* (lowly) body (Php 3:21). But at the resurrection it will be made like the glorious body of our Savior (Php 3:21) and shine with a splendor resembling his.

2.3.3. *It is sown in weakness; it is raised in power.* It is laid in the earth, poor and helpless, wholly in the power of death. But when we rise, our bodies will have a heavenly life and vigor given to them.

2.3.4. *It is sown a natural,* or animal, body, but when we rise, our body will rise spiritual. At the resurrection we will have bodies made fit to be perpetual associates of spirits made perfect. Why should it not be as much in the power of God to raise imperishable spiritual bodies as it was in his power to make matter out of nothing in the beginning, and then produce such an immense variety of creatures, both on earth and in heaven? *To God all things are possible* (Mt 19:26).

2.4. He illustrates this by a comparison of the First Adam and the Second.

2.4.1. As we have our natural body from the First Adam, we expect our spiritual body from the Second.

2.4.2. *The first Adam was made a living soul,* a being like us. The *second Adam is a quickening Spirit*; he is the resurrection and the life (Jn 11:25). If the First Adam could communicate to us natural and physical bodies, cannot the Second Adam make our bodies spiritual ones?

2.4.3. We must have natural bodies from the First Adam before we can have spiritual bodies from the Second (v. 49).

2.4.4. Yet it is as certain that we will have spiritual bodies as it is that we now have natural or physical ones. It is as certain that we are intended to bear the one as that we have borne the other.

2.5. He assigns the reason for this change (v. 50). *Corruption* (the perishable) cannot inherit *incorruption* (imperishable). When the bodies of the saints rise again, they will be greatly changed from what they are now, and much for the better. They are now perishable; they will then be imperishable, glorious, spiritual bodies, fitted to the heavenly world, where from then on they will always live and enjoy their eternal inheritance.

Verses 51–57

To confirm what he has said of this change:

1. He tells them here that not all the saints will die, but all will be changed. Those who are alive at our Lord's coming will be caught up into the clouds without dying (1Th 4:17), but it will not be without changing from perishable to imperishable (v. 52). They must be changed as well as the dead, because flesh and blood cannot inherit the kingdom of God. The apostle reveals here a truth that was unknown before, which is that the saints living at our Lord's second coming will not die, but be changed, that this change will be made in a moment, in the twinkling of an eye, and *at the sound of the last trump*. At this summons, the graves will open, the dead saints will rise imperishable, and the living saints be changed to the same imperishable state (v. 52).

2. He assigns the reason for this change (v. 52). This perishable body must be made imperishable; this mortal body must be changed into an immortal one. What is sown must receive new life.

3. He lets us know what will follow this change of the living and dead in Christ: *Then shall be brought to pass that saying, Death is swallowed up in victory*. Christ prevents death from swallowing up his saints when they die, but when they rise again, death will be swallowed up forever.

3.1. They will glory over death as a vanquished enemy: "*O death! Where is thy sting?* We fear no further trouble from you, but defy your power: *O grave! Where is thy victory?* Once we were your prisoners, but the prison doors have been flung open, and we are released forever. Captivity has been taken captive (Ps 68:18; Eph 4:8). Your triumphs, grave, have come to an end."

3.2. The foundation for this triumph is intimated here.

3.2.1. In the account of the source of death's power to harm: *The sting of death is sin*. This gives venom to its dart. Sin is the parent of death and gives it all its harmful power. Death is sin's cursed offspring.

3.2.2. In the account of the victory saints gain over it through Jesus Christ (v. 56). *The sting of death is sin*, but Christ, by dying, has taken out this sting. Death may hiss, therefore, but it cannot harm. *The strength of sin is the law*, but the curse of the law is removed by our Redeemer's *becoming a curse for us* (Gal 3:13), so that sin is robbed of its power and sting through Christ. A day is coming when the grave will open and the dead saints will revive, become immortal, and be put out of the reach of death forever. They often rejoice in advance in the hope of this victory, and when they rise glorious from the grave, they will boldly triumph over death. It is entirely because of the grace of God in Christ that sin is pardoned and death disarmed.

3.2.3. This triumph of the saints over death should lead to thanksgiving to God: *Thanks be to God, who giveth us the victory through Christ Jesus, our Lord* (v. 57). Only when God receives the glory he is due from our joy do we enjoy our blessings and honors. And this truly exalts our satisfaction and makes it profitable to us. We are conscious both of having done our duty and of having enjoyed our pleasure. Those who remain under the power of death can have no heart to praise, but such conquests and triumphs will certainly make the tongues of the saints sing with thankfulness and praise. With what acclamations will saints rising from the dead praise him! "Thanks be to God" will be the theme of their song, and angels will join

the chorus and declare their joyful consent with a loud "Amen, Hallelujah."

Verse 58

In this verse we have the application of the whole argument in an exhortation, backed up by a motive resulting clearly from it.

1. We have an exhortation, and this has three aspects:

1.1. They should stand firm, established in the faith of the Gospel. "Do not let your belief of these truths be shaken. They are most certain and of the greatest importance." Christians should be firm believers in this great article of their faith, the resurrection of the dead. Disbelief in a future life will open a way to all kinds of licentiousness. It will be easy and natural to infer from such a disbelief that we may live like animals, eating and drinking because tomorrow we die (v. 32; Isa 22:13).

1.2. They must be *immovable* in their expectation of being raised imperishable and immortal. Christians should not be moved from this hope of the Gospel (Col 1:23). This hope should be an anchor to their souls, firm and secure (Heb 6:19).

1.3. They must *abound in the work of the Lord*, and do so *always*. What vigor and resolution, what faithfulness and patience, should those hopes inspire!

2. They have the best reasons in the world to build on. As certainly as Christ is risen, they will rise. The hard work of Christians will not be lost; they may lose for God, but they will lose nothing by him. He will never be found to be so unjust as to forget their labor of love (Heb 6:10). In fact, he will do immeasurably more than all they ask or imagine (Eph 3:20). Those who serve God have good wages; they cannot do too much nor suffer too much for such a good Master. If they serve him now, they will see him in the future; they will rise again from the dead, be crowned with glory, honor, and immortality, and inherit eternal life.

CHAPTER 16

In this chapter: 1. The apostle gives directions about some charitable collection to be taken for the churches in Judea (vv. 1–4). 2. He talks about paying the Corinthian church a visit (vv. 5–9). 3. He commends Timothy to them and tells them Apollos intends to come to them (vv. 10–12). 4. He urges them to be watchful, faithful, and loving, and to pay proper regard to all his fellow laborers (vv. 13–18). 5. After greetings from others and himself, he closes the letter (vv. 19–24).

Verses 1–4

In this chapter Paul closes this long letter. He begins by giving the church instructions for taking a charitable collection for a particular need, the distress and poverty of Christians in Judea. Notice:

1. How he introduces his instructions. He has given similar *orders to the churches of Galatia* (v. 1). He asks them only to conform to the same guidelines he has given to other churches on a similar occasion. And it was wise of him to mention his orders to the churches of Galatia, because this would stir them up to imitation, to generosity. Those who surpassed most churches in spiritual gifts surely would not allow themselves to fall behind anyone else in their goodness toward their suffering brothers and sisters. It is becoming to a Christian to be unable to bear being outdone by fellow Christians in anything good and commendable, provided this consideration only makes them exert themselves, not envy others. The church at

Corinth should not be outdone in this service of love by the churches of Galatia.

2. The instructions themselves. Notice:

2.1. The way in which the collection is to be made: *let everyone lay by him in store* (v. 2). Each should set aside such a sum of money as they could spare from time to time. Those who are rich in this world should be rich in good works (1Ti 6:17–18), and the best way to be so is to regularly set aside from their income, in a fund that they keep for this purpose, a supply of money for the poor as well as for themselves. Many who work with their own hands for a living should work in such a way that they may have something to share with those in need (Eph 4:28), and the best way in the world for them to gain a fund for this purpose is to set aside a sum of money from time to time, as they can afford. As the proverb says, "Many a little makes a mickle (much)." We can give cheerfully when we know that we can spare because we have been setting aside.

2.2. The measure according to which they are to set aside their gifts: *as God hath prospered them*. All our business and work are what God makes them to us. It is not the diligent hand that will make someone rich by itself, but the diligent hand blessed by God (Pr 10:4, 22). It is his goodness and blessing to which we owe all we have. And what argument could be more proper to stir us to give to the people of God than to consider all we have as his gift? When his goodness flows out on us, we should not confine it to ourselves, but let it flow out to others. The more good we receive from God, the more good we should do to others. The Corinthian believers were to set aside an amount of money *as* God had blessed them, in proportion to that. God expects our generosity to others to bear some proportion to his goodness to us. The greater ability he gives, the more generous our hearts should be, and the more open our hands, but where the ability is less, the hands cannot be as open, however willing the mind and however large the heart; nor does God expect it.

2.3. The time when this is to be done: *The first day of the week*, the Lord's Day. It is a day of holy rest, and the more rest the mind has from worldly cares and toils, the more inclination it has to show mercy. The other duties of the day should stir us up to perform this; works of love to others should always accompany works of love toward God. Works of mercy are the genuine fruits of true love for God and are therefore a proper service on his own day.

2.4. That the apostle wanted everything to be ready for his coming. He would leave it to them to decide how the collection would be delivered. Paul no more tried to lord it over the purses of his hearers than over their faith; he would not involve himself in their contributions without their agreement.

2.4.1. He told them that they should give letters of introduction and send messengers of their own with their gift (v. 3). This would be a proper testimony of their respect and mutual love for their distressed brothers and sisters. It would argue that they were very sincere in this service if they sent some of their own group on such a long and dangerous journey to convey their gift. We can learn from this that we should not only charitably relieve our poor fellow Christians but also do it in such a way as will best show our compassion to them.

2.4.2. He offers to go with their messengers if they think it advisable (v. 4). Ministers are doing their proper business when they are furthering or helping works of charity.

Verses 5–9

The apostle announces his intention to visit them. Notice:

1. His intention: he intended to leave Asia and go through Macedonia to Achaia, where Corinth lay, and to stay with them some time, perhaps even spend the winter with them (vv. 5–6). He had worked long in this church and done much good among them. The heart of truly Christian ministers must be very much set on the people among whom they have worked long and with remarkable success. Although some among this people set up a faction against him, no doubt many also loved him dearly. Is it any wonder, then, that he would be willing to visit them and stay with them? It is clear that he hoped his visit would be useful, because he said he intended to stay so *that they might bring him on his journey whithersoever he went* (v. 6); not so that they would accompany him a little way on the road, but so that they would help him on his way, encouraging and providing for him on it. His stay among them, he hoped, would heal their factious attitudes.

2. His excuse for not seeing them now (v. 7), namely, that if he visited them now, he could not stay with them long. Such a visit would give neither him nor them any satisfaction. He loved them so much that he longed for an opportunity to stay with them for some time. This would be more pleasant to him and more useful to them than a brief, passing visit.

3. The limitation of this purpose: I *trust to tarry awhile with you, if the Lord permit* (v. 7). We should always say, "We will carry our plans out if the Lord permits." It is not *in us* to fulfill our own intentions without divine permission (Jer 10:23). It is by God's power and permission.

4. His plan to stay at Ephesus for the present. He says he will stay there until Pentecost (v. 8). Probably when he wrote this letter he was in Ephesus, as we can see from this verse and as is hinted in v. 19, where he says, *The churches of Asia salute you*.

5. The reason given for his staying at Ephesus for the present (v. 9). God gave him great success among them. Success, and a fair prospect of more, was a just reason to make an apostle decide to stay and work in a particular place. On the other hand, many there opposed him, too. Great success in the work of the Gospel commonly creates many enemies. The Devil opposes most those who most sincerely set themselves to destroy his kingdom. Many opposed the apostle; therefore, he was determined to stay. True courage is increased by opposition, and the opposition of Paul's enemies only increased his zeal. We can learn from this that adversaries and opposition do not break the spirits of faithful ministers; they only kindle their zeal. To work in vain is discouraging and disheartening; it dampens the spirits and breaks the heart. But success gives life and vigor to a minister. It is not the opposition of enemies, but the hardness of their hearers, and the backslidings of those who make a profession of their faith, that dampen faithful ministers and break their heart.

Verses 10–12

In this passage:

1. Paul commends Timothy to them (v. 10).

1.1. Timothy is to be *among them without fear* (v. 10). The young minister was to be sent by the apostle to correct the abuses that had crept in among them, and not only to direct but also to rebuke those who were responsible. No doubt the mutual strife and hatred ran very high among them. Proud spirits cannot easily bear rebuke. It was reasonable, therefore, to think young Timothy might be mistreated. It was their duty to behave well toward him and not discourage him in his Lord's work. They should not leap to resentment at his rebukes.

1.2. The church must not despise him (v. 11). He was only a young man, and his own youthful face and years commanded little reverence. Pride was a dominant sin among the Corinthians, and such a warning was only too necessary. Christians should be very careful not to pour contempt on anyone, but especially on ministers.

1.3. They should treat him well while he was with them, and they should send him away in friendship, well prepared for his journey back to Paul. This is the meaning of helping him on his way in peace (v. 11).

2. He gives the reasons why they should behave in this way toward Timothy.

2.1. Because he is employed in the same work as Paul and acts in it by the same authority (v. 10). He is not coming on Paul's mission among them, nor to do Paul's work, but the work of the Lord. While pastors and teachers, as well as apostles and evangelists, are doing their duty, which is the Lord's work, they are to be treated with honor and respect.

2.2. Another reason is implied: they are to respect Timothy not only for his work's sake but also for the sake of Paul, who is sending him to Corinth (v. 11): "I am expecting his return, and I will judge by your conduct toward him what your respect for me will be." They would hardly dare send back Timothy with a report that would grieve or provoke the apostle.

3. He informs them of Apollos's plan to see them.

3.1. He himself had wanted very much for Apollos to come to them (v. 12). Although one party among them had declared themselves for Apollos and against Paul, Paul did not prevent Apollos from going to Corinth in his absence. Faithful ministers tend not to entertain jealousies of each other. True mutual love thinks no evil.

3.2. Apollos could not be persuaded to go at present. He would not go to be put at the head of a party. When the church's divisiveness had subsided, he might conclude that a visit would be more proper. Apostles did not compete with each other, but considered one another's comfort and usefulness. Apollos showed his respect to Paul by declining the journey until the Corinthians were in a better frame of mind.

Verses 13–18

In this passage the apostle gives:

1. Some general pieces of advice:

1.1. To be watchful (v. 13). The Corinthians were clearly in danger for many reasons: their feuds ran high, the irregularities among them were very great, and deceivers had gotten in among them. In such dangerous circumstances it was their responsibility to be watchful. If Christians want to be secure, they must be on their guard.

1.2. To *stand fast in the faith*. Christians should be firm in the faith of the Gospel. It is only by this faith that they will be able to stand their ground in times of temptation; it is by this that we must overcome the world (1Jn 5:4), both in its disapproval and in its delights.

1.3. To be men of courage (*quit you like men*) and be strong: "Show yourselves strong in Christ by your steadiness, sound judgment, and firm resolution." Christians should be strong and firm in defending their faith.

1.4. To do everything in love (v. 14). When the apostle wants us to be strong in our faith or religion, he warns us against causing trouble in it. Christians should be careful that love not only reigns in their hearts but also shines

out in their lives. Christianity never appears to so much advantage as when the love of Christians is clearest, when they can bear with their mistaken brothers and sisters and show love in opposing the open enemies of their holy faith.

2. Particular instructions on how they should behave toward some who had been particularly useful among them.

2.1. He describes them.

2.1.1. The household of Stephanas is mentioned by him, and he describes them as *the firstfruits of Achaia* (v. 15). It is an honorable description to anyone to be among the first to become Christians in an area. But it was also to the honor of this household that they devoted themselves *to the ministry of the saints*, to serving the saints. It is not meant to refer to the ministry of the word as such, but to serving them in other respects and assisting them on all occasions.

2.1.2. He mentions Stephanas, Fortunatus, and Achaicus as coming to him from the church of Corinth. They supplied the deficiencies of the church toward him and, by so doing, *refreshed his spirit and theirs* (vv. 17–18). These men gave him a more complete account of the state of the church by word of mouth than he could have acquired by the church's letter. Reports had represented the church's case as much worse than it actually was, but he had been put at greater ease by his dealings with these men. They came to him as peacemakers. It is a great refreshment to the spirit of a faithful minister to hear better of a people they wise and good members of their own body than by rumor. It is a grief to him to hear ill of those he loves; it brings joy to his heart to hear that the report is false.

2.2. He instructs them on how they should behave toward these messengers. He wants them to be acknowledged (v. 11), that is, recognized and respected. They deserve it for their good works. Those who reveal such a good spirit cannot easily be overvalued (v. 16). These men were owed particular respect and should be held in high regard.

Verses 19–24

The apostle closes his letter:

1. With greetings to the church at Corinth, first from those of Asia, from *Priscilla* and *Aquila*—who seem to have lived in Ephesus at this time (Ac 18:26)—*with the church in their house* (v. 19), and from *all the brethren* (v. 20) at Ephesus. Even in a letter discussing very important matters, Paul could find room to send the greetings of friends. Religion should promote a polite and pleasing attitude toward everyone. Those who want to take any encouragement from it to be unpleasant and morose misrepresent and disgrace it. Some of these who send greetings *salute them much in the Lord*. Christian greetings are accompanied by sincere commendations to God's grace and blessing. We read also of a church in a private home (v. 19). Every Christian family should in some respects be a Christian church. Wherever two or three are gathered together, and Christ is among them (Mt 18:20), there is a church. He adds:

1.1. A piece of advice, that *they should greet one another with a holy kiss* (v. 20), or with sincere goodwill—an unspoken rebuke of their feuds and factions. The love of brothers and sisters should be a powerful incentive to mutual love.

1.2. His own greeting: *The salutation of me Paul with my own hand* (v. 21). At the end, it was fitting that he himself sign the letter, so that they would know it was genuine. He wrote this in every letter he did not wholly write, such as the letter to the Galatians (Gal 6:11).

2. With a very solemn warning to them (v. 22). We sometimes need threatening words so that we may fear. Holy fear is a very good friend of both holy faith and holy living. Notice:

2.1. The person described, the one who is liable to this condemnation: *He that loveth not the Lord Jesus Christ.* It stands here as a warning to the Corinthians and a rebuke of their offensive behavior. By contempt of Christ and rebellion from him, professed Christians may bring on themselves the most dreadful destruction. Many who often have his name in their mouths have no true love for him in their hearts. No one loves him in truth who does not love his laws and keep his commandments. What, not love the most glorious lover in the world! What have we got a power of loving for if we are unmoved by such love, if we are without affection for such a Savior?

2.2. The condemnation of the person described: "*Let him be Anathema, Maran-atha,* lie under the heaviest and most fearful curse." *Maran-atha* is Aramaic and means

"The Lord is coming." That very Lord whom they do not love is coming to execute judgment, and those who fall under his condemning sentence must perish. True faith in Christ will always produce sincere love for him. Those who do not love him cannot be believers in him.

3. With his good wishes for them and expressions of goodwill toward them.

3.1. With his good wishes (v. 23). The grace of our Lord Jesus Christ includes everything that is good, for time and eternity. We can wish our friends nothing more, and we should wish them nothing less. The most solemn warnings are the result of the tenderest affection and the greatest goodwill. No wonder, then, that the apostle would close the whole letter:

3.2. With the declaration of his love for them in Christ Jesus (v. 24). He parts with them in love. His heart would be with them and he would show them warm affection as long as their hearts were with Christ. We should be warmly friendly to all who are in Christ. We should love all, of course, but those who are dear to Christ and love him must have our warmest affection. Let our love be with all those who are in Christ Jesus! Amen.

A Practical and Devotional
Exposition of
2 Corinthians

◀━━━━━━◆

The apostle has expressed his intentions of *coming to Corinth, as he passed through Macedonia* (1Co 16:5), but, being providentially hindered, he writes this second letter to them. There seem to have been two urgent occasions for this letter. One was the case of the incestuous person. Paul therefore gave directions about this (2:1–11), and later (7:1–16) he declared the satisfaction he felt on receiving news of the Corinthians' good behavior in that matter. The other occasion was the contribution now being made for the poor saints at Jerusalem; Paul exhorted the Corinthians to participate (chs. 8–9). Other things are significant in this letter: 1. The account the apostle gives of his labors and success in preaching the Gospel in several places (1:3–24; 2:12–17). 2. The comparison he makes between the Old and New Testament eras (ch. 3). 3. The many sufferings that he and his fellow workers met with (chs. 4–5). 4. The warning he gives the Corinthians against mixing with unbelievers (ch. 6). 5. The way in which he justifies himself and his apostleship in chs. 10–12, and indeed throughout the whole letter.

CHAPTER 1

After the introduction (vv. 1–2), the apostle begins with an account of his troubles and God's goodness as an occasion for giving thanks to God (vv. 3–6) and edifying the Corinthians (vv. 7–11). He then affirms his and his fellow workers' integrity (vv. 12–14) and vindicates himself (vv. 15–24).

Verses 1–2

This is the introduction to this letter, in which we have:

1. The opening greeting, in which are named:

1.1. The sender, Paul, *an apostle of Jesus Christ by the will of God.* The apostleship itself was ordained by Jesus Christ according to the will of God, and Paul was called to it by Jesus Christ according to the will of God. He includes Timothy with himself in writing this letter. His dignifying Timothy with the title of *brother* shows the great apostle's humility and his desire to commend Timothy to the respect of the Corinthians.

1.2. Those to whom this letter was sent, *the church of God at Corinth* and *all the saints in all Achaia,* that is, all the Christians who lived in the surrounding region.

2. The blessing. The apostle desires for the Corinthians the two great and comprehensive blessings, grace and peace. He puts these two great benefits together because there is no good and lasting peace without true grace, and both of them come *from God our Father, and from the Lord Jesus Christ.*

Verses 3–6

The apostle begins by telling of God's goodness to him and his fellow workers in their many distresses, which he speaks of by way of thanksgiving to God (vv. 3–6).

1. The object of the apostle's thanksgiving is the holy God.

1.1. He is *the God and Father of our Lord Jesus Christ.* He is so called in the New Testament to show his covenant relationship with the Mediator and his spiritual offspring (Gal 3:16).

1.2. He is *the Father of mercies.* All mercies come from God originally: mercy is his genuine offspring and his delight.

1.3. He is *the God of all comfort;* the *Comforter* (Counselor) comes from him (Jn 15:26). All our comforts come from God.

2. The reasons for the apostle's thanksgivings:

2.1. The benefits he himself and his friends have received from God (v. 4). In the world they had trouble, but in Christ they had peace. Their sufferings, called *the sufferings of Christ* (v. 5), were great, but the comfort they received from Christ was also great. We speak best of God and his goodness when we speak from our own experience, when, in telling others, we also tell God what he has done for our souls (Ps 66:16).

2.2. The benefit others can receive (v. 4). The favors God gives us are intended not only to make us cheerful ourselves but also to enable us to be useful to others.

Verses 7–11

In these verses the apostle speaks for the encouragement of the Corinthians. He tells them (v. 7) of his firm hope that they will benefit by the troubles he and his friends have met with. To this end, he tells them:

1. What he and his fellow workers have suffered (v. 8). It is uncertain what particular troubles in Asia are being referred to here, because the apostle was *in deaths often* (11:23). It is clear, however, that the troubles were great. They *despaired even of life* (v. 8).

2. What they did in their distress: *They trusted in God.* This was why they were brought to this extremity (v. 9).

God often brings his people into great difficulties so that they may be led to put their trust and hope in his all-sufficiency. Our extremity is God's opportunity. We may safely trust in *God, who raiseth the dead* (v. 9). The One who can do this can do anything, and he deserves to be trusted at all times.

3. What deliverance they gained. Their hope and trust were not in vain. God rescued them, and he continues to rescue them (v. 10).

4. What use they are making of this deliverance: *We trust that he will yet deliver us* (v. 10). Past experiences are great encouragements to faith and hope. We show contempt for our experiences if we distrust God in future difficulties when he has rescued us in previous troubles.

5. What is needed from the Corinthians on this account (v. 11). Paul desires the help of others' prayers. If we help one another by our prayers in this way, we may hope for an opportunity to *give thanks by many* in answer to prayer.

Verses 12–14

In these verses the apostle affirms his and his fellow workers' integrity on the basis of the godly sincerity of their conduct.

1. He appeals to the testimony of conscience with joy (v. 12). Notice:

1.1. The witness appealed to is conscience. This is God's deputy in the soul, and the voice of conscience is the voice of God. Paul and his fellow workers rejoiced at the testimony of conscience. The testimony of conscience for us will be a matter of joy at all times and in all conditions.

1.2. The testimony this witness gave. Conscience witnessed:

1.2.1. To their conduct, to the constant course of their life, for that is a basis on which we may judge ourselves; we ought not judge ourselves by one or another single act.

1.2.2. To the nature or way of their conduct, that it was in integrity and godly sincerity. This dear apostle was one who dealt plainly; you knew where you were with him. He was not a man who seemed to be one thing but in reality was another; he was a man of sincerity.

1.2.3. To the motivation of all their conduct, and that was not worldly wisdom, but the grace of God.

2. He appeals to the knowledge of the Corinthians with hope and confidence (vv. 13–14). They have never found anything in Paul and his fellow workers that was unbecoming to an honorable person. They have acknowledged this in part already, and he does not doubt that they will do so to the end. And so they and Paul will have joy in one another.

Verses 15–24

The apostle vindicates himself here against the accusation that he is fickle and unfaithful because he did not hold to his plan of coming to them at Corinth.

1. He asserts the sincerity of his intention (vv. 15–17), and he does this in the confidence that they have a good opinion of him and will therefore believe him when he assures them he *was minded to come* to them, and not so that he might receive, but so that they might receive *a second benefit*. He tells them that he has not here *used lightness* (done so lightly) (v. 17), because his purpose was not *according to the flesh*. It was for some significant reasons that he changed his plans; with him there was not *yea yea, and nay nay* (v. 17).

2. He does not want the Corinthians to conclude that his Gospel is false or uncertain (vv. 18–19). For *God is true*, and *the Son of God, Jesus Christ*, is true. Jesus Christ is not *yea* and *nay*, but in him was *yea* (v. 19), nothing but infal-

lible truth. Moreover, the promises of God in Christ are not "Yes" and "No," but "Yes" and "Amen" (v. 20). There is an unbreakable firmness and certainty in all the parts of the Gospel of Christ. The promises of the Gospel covenant still stand firm and inviolable. Evildoers are false; good people are fickle; but *God is true*, neither false nor fickle. The promises of God are "Yes" and "Amen," because:

2.1. They are the promises of the God of truth (v. 20).

2.2. They are made in Christ Jesus (v. 20), the Amen, the true and faithful witness (Rev 3:14).

2.3. They are confirmed by the Holy Spirit. He is given *as an earnest in their hearts* (vv. 21–22). An *earnest*, or deposit, secures and guarantees the promise and is part of the payment. The fulfillment of the promises will be to the *glory of God* (v. 20).

3. The apostle gives a good reason why he did not come to Corinth (v. 23). It was in order to spare them. He knew some things were wrong among them, things that deserved censure, but he wanted to show them compassion. He assures them that this was the true reason. He adds that he does not pretend to lord it over their faith (v. 24). Only Christ is the Lord of our faith. He reveals to us what we must believe. Paul and Apollos were *but ministers by whom they believed* (1Co 3:5) and were thus the *helpers of their joy*, the joy of faith. Our strength and ability are because of faith, and our comfort and joy must flow from faith.

CHAPTER 2

In this chapter: 1. The apostle continues to explain the reasons why he did not come to Corinth (vv. 1–4). 2. He then writes about the incestuous person (vv. 5–11) 3. He informs them of his hard work and success in preaching the Gospel (vv. 12–17).

Verses 1–4

In these verses the apostle proceeds to explain why he did not come to Corinth. He was unwilling to either grieve them or be grieved by them (vv. 1–2). If he had caused them sorrow, that would have been a sorrow to him, for then there would have been no one to make him glad. He tells them that he refrained from visiting them for the same reason that he wrote his previous letter, *that I might not have sorrow from those of whom I ought to rejoice* (vv. 3–4). The particular thing referred to is the case of the incestuous person. He assures them that he did not intend to grieve them. He wrote to them with much *anguish and affliction* in his own heart and with great affection for them.

Verses 5–11

In these verses the apostle discusses the case of the incestuous person.

1. He tells the Corinthians that the punishment that has been inflicted on this offender is sufficient (v. 6). The desired effect has been obtained.

2. He tells them that they should therefore receive the man back into their fellowship as quickly as possible (vv. 7–8). He urges them to forgive him, *confirm* (reaffirm) their love to him, and show that their rebukes proceeded from love for his person as well as from hatred of his sin.

3. He uses several significant arguments.

3.1. The penitent is in danger of being *swallowed up with overmuch sorrow* (overwhelmed by excessive sorrow) (v. 7) and falling into despair. When sorrow is excessive, it hurts deeply, and even sorrow for sin is too great when it drives people to despair.

3.2. The Corinthians have obeyed Paul by censuring the offender; now he wants them to comply with his desire to restore him (v. 9).

3.3. He mentions his readiness to concur with them in their forgiveness of him (v. 10). He will do this for their sakes and for Christ's sake, in conformity to Christ's message and example, which are so full of kindness and tender mercy toward all those who truly repent.

3.4. He is concerned *lest Satan get an advantage against us* (v. 11). Not only was there danger that Satan might take advantage of the penitent by driving him to despair; Satan might also take advantage of the apostles or ministers of Christ by representing them as too strict and severe. Satan is a subtle enemy, and we should *not be ignorant of his devices* (not be unaware of his schemes); he is also a watchful adversary, ready to take every advantage of us.

Verses 12–17

The apostle here digresses at length to give the Corinthians an account of his travels and labors, informing them at the same time how he *had no rest in his spirit* when he did not find Titus at Troas (v. 13). We find later (7:5–7) that when the apostle had come to Macedonia, he was comforted by the coming of Titus. Notice here:

1. Paul's unwearied exertion and diligence in his work (vv. 12–13). He went to Troas from Philippi by sea (Ac 20:6), and from there he went to Macedonia. Although he was prevented from working where he had intended, he was still tireless in his work.

2. His success in his work (v. 12). God *made manifest the savour of his knowledge* through him everywhere he went. The apostle speaks of this as a cause of gratitude to God. In ourselves we are weak and have neither joy nor victory, but in Christ we may rejoice and triumph.

3. The comfort, strength, and encouragement that the apostle found even when the Gospel did not bring about the salvation of some who heard it (vv. 15–17). Notice here:

3.1. The success of the Gospel is varying, for some are saved by it while others perish under it.

3.1.1. To some it is *a savour of death unto death*, as people find a smell unpleasant and are therefore blinded and hardened by it. They reject the Gospel and are therefore ruined, even sentenced to spiritual death.

3.1.2. To others the Gospel is a *savour of life unto life*. To humble and gracious souls the preaching of the word is most delightful and profitable. Just as it gave them life at first, *when they were dead in trespasses and sins* (Eph 2:1), so it will lead to eternal life.

3.2. The fearful impressions this matter made on the apostle (v. 16). Who is *worthy* to be employed in such a significant work? Who is able to perform such a difficult work? The work is great and our strength is small; *all our sufficiency is of God* (3:5).

3.3. The comfort that the apostle had:

3.3.1. Because faithful ministers will be accepted by God, whatever their success is: *We are*, if faithful, *unto God a sweet savour of Christ* (v. 15), in both those who are saved and those who perish. Ministers will be accepted and rewarded not according to their success but according to their faithfulness.

3.3.2. Because his conscience witnessed to his faithfulness (v. 17), although many *corrupted the word of God*. His aim was to show himself approved to God; he always spoke and acted sincerely, therefore, as one who knew he was *in the sight of God*.

CHAPTER 3

The apostle makes an apology for apparently commending himself (vv. 1–5). He then draws a comparison between the Old Testament and the New (vv. 6–11), from which he concludes what is the duty of Gospel ministers and what advantage those who live under the Gospel have over those who lived under the Law (vv. 12–18).

Verses 1–5

In these verses:

1. The apostle makes an apology for apparently commending himself. He neither needs nor desires any verbal commendation to them, nor letters of recommendation from them, as some others do; here he refers to the false apostles or teachers (v. 1). The Corinthians themselves are his real commendation (v. 2). They are written *in his heart, known and read of all men.*

2. The apostle is careful to ascribe all the praise to God. He says the Corinthians are the *epistle of Christ* (v. 3). The apostle and others are simply instruments. This letter was not written with *ink, but with the Spirit of the living God*; nor was it written in *tables of stone*, but on the *heart*, on the *fleshy* (not *fleshly*, as fleshliness denotes sensuality) *tables of the heart*, that is, on hearts that are softened by divine grace. He completely denies that he and his fellow workers have taken any praise for themselves, and he ascribes all the glory to God (v. 5). *All our sufficiency is of God*; to him, therefore, is due all the praise and glory for the good that is done. The best are no more than what the grace of God makes them.

Verses 6–11

Here the apostle draws a comparison between the Old Testament and the New and esteems himself and his fellow workers on the basis of their being *able* (competent) *ministers of the New Testament*, made such by God (v. 6).

1. He distinguishes between the letter and the spirit even of the New Testament (v. 6). They are ministers not merely of the letter but also of the Spirit. The *letter killeth*, but the Spirit of the Gospel gives spiritual and eternal life.

2. He shows how much more excellent the Gospel is than the Law. The Old Testament age was the *ministration* (ministry) *of death* (v. 7), whereas that of the New Testament is the ministry of life. The Law was the *ministration of* (ministry that brought) *condemnation*; the Gospel is the *ministration of* (ministry that brings) *righteousness*. The Gospel reveals the grace and mercy of God through Jesus Christ for obtaining forgiveness of sins and eternal life, and therefore so excels in glory that it eclipses, in a way, the glory of the legal dispensation (v. 10). The Law is done away with, but the Gospel does and will *remain* (v. 11). The age of the Law was to continue only for a time, whereas the Gospel will remain to the end of the world.

Verses 12–18

In these verses the apostle draws two conclusions from what he has said about the Old and New Testament:

1. It is the duty of the ministers of the Gospel to use great clearness of speech. The Gospel is a clearer dispensation than the Law. Although the Israelites could not look *steadfastly to the end* of what was commanded, we can.

2. The privilege of those who enjoy the Gospel is far above that of those who lived under the Law. Those who lived under the legal dispensation had their minds blinded (v. 14), and there was a *veil upon their hearts* (v. 15).

A time is coming when this *veil also shall be taken away*, and *when it* (most of that people) *shall turn to the Lord* (v. 16). The condition of those who believe the Gospel is much happier. They have freedom (v. 17) and *light*, because with *open face we behold the glory of the Lord* (v. 18). It was the special privilege of Moses for God to converse with him face to face (Ex 33:11), but now all true Christians see him with open face. This light and freedom *are transforming* (v. 18); we are changed *from glory to glory* until the grace we enjoy here is consummated in glory forever.

CHAPTER 4

In this chapter we have an account: 1. Of the faithfulness of the apostle and his fellow laborers in their work (vv. 1–7). 2. Of their courage and patience in suffering (vv. 8–18).

Verses 1–7

In this chapter the apostle's intention is to vindicate his and his fellow workers' ministry against the accusation of false teachers. He tells the Corinthians how he and his colleagues believed and how they show the value of their office as ministers of the Gospel.

1. We have an account of two virtues reflected in their work:

1.1. Their faithfulness and perseverance in their work (v. 1). Their endurance is owing to the *mercy of God*. The best people in the world would lose heart in their work and under their burdens if they did not receive mercy from God.

1.2. Their sincerity in their work (v. 2). They have no corrupt and evil intentions covered with a veneer of fair and fine-sounding claims of something good. Nor do they, in their preaching, *handle the word of God deceitfully* (distort the word of God); rather, they use *great plainness of speech*. They *manifest the truth to every man's conscience*, declaring nothing but what in their own conscience they believe to be true. They do all this *in the sight of God*, wanting to commend themselves to God and to people's consciences.

2. The apostle anticipates the objection, "How then does it happen that the Gospel is hidden from some who hear it?" The true reasons for this are:

2.1. *Those souls* to whom the Gospel is hidden *are lost souls* (v. 3).

2.2. *The god of this world hath blinded their minds* (v. 4). They are under the influence of the Devil, who is called here *the god of this world* because of the great influence he has on this world. Just as he is the prince of darkness and ruler of the darkness of this world (Eph 6:12), so he darkens people's minds. Christ's intention is to make a glorious revelation of God to the minds of human beings through his Gospel. The intention of the Devil is to keep people in ignorance.

3. He gives proof of their integrity (v. 5). The apostles have made it their business to preach Christ, not themselves. They have *preached Christ Jesus the Lord*, because they are Christ's servants. All the lines of Christian doctrine center on Christ, and in preaching Christ we preach all we should preach. Ministers should not have proud spirits; they are servants of people's souls. Yet at the same time they must avoid becoming servants of human inclinations or desires. There is good reason:

3.1. Why they should preach Christ. It is through Gospel light that we have the *knowledge of the glory of God*, which shines in the *face of Jesus Christ* (v. 6). It is pleasant for the eye to look at the sun in the sky, but it is more pleasant and profitable to see the Gospel shine in the heart.

3.2. Why they should not preach themselves: because they are merely *earthen vessels*. The ministers of the Gospel are weak and frail creatures; they are mortal and soon break into pieces. God has so arranged things that the weaker the vessels are, the stronger his power will appear to be, so that the treasure itself will be valued even more.

Verses 8–18

In these verses Paul gives an account of the apostles' courage and patience in all their suffering, and we may notice:

1. How their sufferings and their patience in them are noted (vv. 8–12). *"We are troubled* (hard pressed) *on every side, yet not distressed* (v. 8), because we can see help in God and help from God. We are *perplexed, yet not in despair* (v. 8), knowing that God is able to support us, to rescue us. We are *persecuted, but not forsaken* by God (v. 9). We are *cast* (struck) *down, but not destroyed"* (v. 9). They are still preserved and keep their heads above water. Whatever condition the children of God may be in on earth, they still have a *but not* to comfort themselves with. The apostle speaks of their sufferings as a counterpart of the sufferings of Christ (v. 10). This is how they *bear about* (carried around) *the dying of the Lord Jesus* in their body, so *that the life of Jesus might also be made manifest*, though they are always *delivered to death* (v. 11) and though *death works in them* (v. 12). *Death worketh in us*, but *life in you* (v. 12).

2. What keeps them from sinking and losing heart in their suffering (vv. 13–18).

2.1. Faith keeps them from losing heart (v. 13): the grace of faith is a sovereign medicine against losing heart in times of trouble. As the apostle had the example of David to imitate, who said (Ps 116:10), *I have believed, and therefore have I spoken*, so he also leaves us his own example to imitate: *We also believe*, he says, *and therefore speak*.

2.2. Hope of the resurrection keeps them from sinking (v. 14). Their hope that the One who raised up Christ the head will also raise up all his members is firm, being well founded. What reason have good Christians to fear death, since they die in hope of a joyful resurrection?

2.3. Consideration of the benefits of the church keeps them from losing heart (v. 15). We may well afford to bear sufferings patiently when we see that others are better off because of them.

2.4. The thoughts of the benefits their souls will keep them from losing heart (v. 16). It is our happiness if when the body is sick, the soul is vigorous. Even the best people need constant renewal of their inner being day by day. As things become worse and worse every day in evildoers, so in godly people they become better and better.

2.5. The prospect of eternal life and happiness keeps them from losing heart. The apostle and his fellow sufferers saw their adversities working toward heaven, as eventually coming to an end (v. 17), and on the basis of this hope they weighed things up rightly in the balance of the sanctuary (Ex 30:13, 24; 38:24–26; etc.). They found adversities to be light, and the glory of heaven to be *a far more exceeding weight*. What the mind guided by the senses was ready to declare heavy and long, faith perceived to be light, short, and momentary. Their faith enabled them to make this right judgment of things (v. 18). Unseen things are eternal; seen things only temporary. By faith we not only discern these things, and the great difference between them, but also take our aim at unseen things.

CHAPTER 5

The apostle proceeds to show the reason why he and his fellow workers do not lose heart in their suffering, namely, their assurance of happiness after death (vv. 1–5), and he draws a conclusion to encourage believers (vv. 6–8), and another to stir them to fulfill their duty (vv. 9–11). He then makes an apology for seeming to commend himself (vv. 12–15). He also mentions two things that are necessary in order for us to live for Christ (vv. 16–21).

Verses 1–11

The apostle in these verses pursues the argument of the previous chapter concerning the basis of the apostles' courage and patience in suffering.

1. He mentions their expectation, desire, and assurance of eternal happiness (vv. 1–5). Notice particularly:

1.1. Believers' expectation of eternal happiness after death (v. 1). "We know that *we have a building of God*; we have a firm expectation of future happiness." Let us take note:

1.1.1. What heaven is in the eyes and hope of believers. They look on it as a house or home, our Father's house and our eternal home. It is a house in the heavens. It is a building made by God (Heb 11:10). It is *eternal in the heavens*, not like the earthly tents, the poor cottages of clay in which our souls now live.

1.1.2. When it is expected that this happiness will be enjoyed—as soon as *our house of this earthly tabernacle is dissolved* (destroyed). Then the *house not made with human hands* comes. Those who have walked with God here will live with God forever.

1.2. The believers' passionate desire for this future blessedness: *we groan*, which shows:

1.2.1. A groaning of sorrow under a heavy burden (v. 2). *We that are in this tabernacle groan, being burdened* (v. 4). Believers groan because they know they are burdened by a body of sin.

1.2.2. A groaning of desire for the happiness of another life. The believer is *willing rather to be absent from the body, that he may be present with the Lord* (v. 1), to take off these rags of mortality so that he may put on the robes of glory. Gracious souls are not found naked in the other world. No, they are clothed with garments of praise (Isa 61:3).

1.3. Believers' assurance of this future blessedness, for two reasons:

1.3.1. The experience of the grace of God making them fit for it (v. 5). All who are intended for heaven in the future are made or prepared for heaven while they are here; the stones of that spiritual building above are formed and fashioned here below (1Pe 2:5). No hand less than the hand of God himself can work this thing for and in us.

1.3.2. The *earnest* (pledge) *of the Spirit*. An *earnest* is the deposit, a partial payment that guarantees full payment.

2. The apostle draws a conclusion to encourage believers in their present state in this world (vv. 6–8). Notice here:

2.1. What their present state is: they *are absent from the Lord* (v. 6). God is with us here, but we are not at home with him as we hope to be, *for we walk by faith, not by sight* (v. 7). Faith is for this world, and sight is reserved for the other world.

2.2. How encouraged and courageous we should be in the hour of death (vv. 6, 8). We should be willing to die rather than live when it is the will of God that we put off *this tabernacle*, that we close our eyes to all things in this world and open them in a world of glory. Faith will be turned into sight.

3. He draws a conclusion to encourage himself and others to fulfill their duty (vv. 9–11). Here we see how well-founded hopes of heaven will be far from giving the least encouragement to laziness; on the contrary, they should be a great incentive to apply our care and diligence to our religious faith (v. 9). *Wherefore we labour*—or "make it our ambition"—*that we may be accepted of the Lord.* Notice here:

3.1. What the apostle was so ambitious for—*acceptance with God*. It was the goal of the apostles' ambition.

3.2. What further incentives they had to stir their diligence from a consideration of the judgment to come (vv. 10–11): the certainty of this judgment, at which we must appear; its universality, because we must all appear; the great Judge before whose judgment seat we must appear, the Lord Jesus Christ; the reward to be received then *for things done while in the body*. The apostle calls this fearful judgment *the terror of the Lord* (v. 11) and is stirred to persuade people to repent and live a holy life so that when Christ appears fearfully, they may appear before him with assurance.

Verses 12–15

Notice here:

1. The apostle makes an apology for seeming to commend himself and his fellow workers (v. 13). The true reason he spoke of their faithfulness and diligence in vv. 1–11 was to put an argument in the mouths of the Corinthians with which to answer his accusers.

2. He gives good reasons for their great zeal and diligence:

2.1. It is for the glory of God and the good of the church that he is so zealous and industrious (v. 13).

2.2. *The love of Christ constrains them* (v. 14). Love has a compelling power to stir ministers and individual Christians to fulfill their duty. Our love for Christ will have this power, and Christ's love for us will have this effect on us. Notice how the apostle argues, declaring:

2.2.1. What we would have continued to be if Christ had not died for us (v. 14). *If one died for all, then were all dead*, dead in sins and trespasses (Eph 2:1), spiritually dead.

2.2.2. What people for whom Christ died should do, namely, live for him. They should not live *to themselves* (v. 15). We will live as we should live when we live for Christ, who died for us.

Verses 16–21

In these verses the apostle mentions two things that are necessary in order for us to live for Christ: regeneration and reconciliation.

1. We must be regenerated, which means:

1.1. Being cut off from our dependence on the world (v. 16). The love of Christ must be in our hearts, and the world under our feet. *Yea, though we have known Christ after the flesh* (although we once regarded Christ in this way), *yet*, the apostle says, *we know him no more* (we do so no longer). We must live on his spiritual presence and the strength and encouragement it brings.

1.2. A thorough change of heart: *He is a new creature* (v. 17). Some read it, *Let him be a new creature*, not only wear a new uniform but also have a new heart and nature. *Old things are passed away*, and *all* these *things must become new*.

2. We must be reconciled, which is here spoken of:

2.1. As an unquestionable privilege (vv. 18–19). Reconciliation presupposes a quarrel or break in friendship. But see, there may be a reconciliation. He has reconciled us to himself through Jesus Christ (v. 18). All things concerning our reconciliation through Jesus Christ come from God, who by the mediation of Jesus Christ has reconciled the world to himself. He has appointed the *ministry of reconciliation* (v. 18). He has appointed the work of the ministry, which is *a ministry of reconciliation*.

2.2. As our indispensable duty (v. 20). Just as God is willing to be reconciled to us, we should be reconciled to God. Although God can be no loser by the quarrel, nor gainer by the peace, yet by his ministers he urges sinners to be reconciled to him. Furthermore, to encourage us to do this, the apostle adds what should be well known by us (v. 21):

2.2.1. The purity of the Mediator: *He knew no sin*.

2.2.2. The sacrifice he offered: *He was made sin*, that is, a sin offering, a sacrifice for sin (the Hebrew word most commonly translated *sin* is sometimes translated *sin offering* [Ex 29:14, 36; 30:10]).

2.2.3. The purpose of all this: that *we might be made the righteousness of God in him*. Just as Christ, who knew no sin of his own, was made sin for us, so we, who have no righteousness of our own, are made the righteousness of God in him.

CHAPTER 6

We have here the apostle's account of his general mission to all to whom he preaches (vv. 1–10). He then addresses himself particularly to the Corinthians with great affection (vv. 11–18).

Verses 1–10

Here we have an account of the apostle's general mission and exhortation to all to whom he preached. Notice:

1. The mission or exhortation itself (v. 1). As it is the duty of the ministers of the Gospel to urge their hearers to accept grace and mercy, so they are honored with this high title of *coworkers with God*. They are workers with God, but under him. If they are faithful, they may hope to find God working with them, and their labor will be effective. Notice the way of the Gospel: it is not with harshness and severity, but with great mildness and gentleness; it begs and urges.

2. The arguments and method that the apostle uses. He tells them:

2.1. The present time is the only proper season to accept the grace that is offered: now *is the accepted time*; now *is the day of salvation* (v. 2). Tomorrow does not belong to us: we do not know what will happen tomorrow.

2.2. How careful he and his fellow workers are to avoid putting in anyone's path a stumbling block that might hinder the success of their preaching (v. 3). When others tend to take offense easily, we should be careful not to give offense. Ministers especially should be careful.

2.3. Their constant aim in everything is to show themselves faithful, as befits ministers of God (v. 4). Paul's great desire was to be the servant of God and to commend himself as such, and he did so:

2.3.1. With much patience in suffering. He suffered greatly, meeting with many *afflictions*, but he exercised

great patience in them all (vv. 4–5). Those who want to commend themselves to God must show that they are faithful in times of trouble as well as in times of peace, not only in doing God's work diligently but also in bearing the will of God patiently.

2.3.2. By acting from good principles. Here he tells the Corinthians what his principles are (vv. 6–7). First, purity, and there is no godliness without purity. *Knowledge* (understanding) is another of his principles, and zeal without this is sheer madness (Ro 10:2). He also acts with *long-suffering* (patience) *and kindness*, bearing with people's hardness of heart and with harsh treatment from their hands. He acts under the influence of the Holy Spirit, from the noble principle of sincere love, according to the rule of the word of truth, under the power of God, having put on the *armor of righteousness*, which is the best defense against the temptations of prosperity *on the right hand* and the temptations of adversity *on the left*.

2.3.3. By a proper attitude and behavior in all kinds of conditions (vv. 8–10). The apostles met with *honor and dishonor, good reports and bad reports*. We stand in need of the grace of God to arm us against the temptations of honor on the one hand, so as to bear a good report about us without pride, and of dishonor on the other hand, so as to bear reproach without recrimination. Some represented the apostles as the best people, and others as the worst: some considered them *deceivers*; others said they were *true* and genuine. They were insulted by worldly people as *unknown*, beneath notice. In all the churches of Christ, however, they were *well known* and considered significant; they were looked on as dying, "but *behold, we live*." They were rebuked and often fell under the punishment of the law, but *not killed*, and though it was thought that they were *sorrowful*, a company of foolish and sad people, they were *always rejoicing* in God. They were despised as *poor*, but they *made many* people *rich* by preaching the unsearchable riches of Christ (Eph 3:8). They were thought to *have nothing*, and in themselves they had nothing, but they *possessed all things* in Christ. A Christian's life is such a paradox.

Verses 11–18

The apostle warns them against being united to unbelievers. Notice:

1. The warning is introduced with a profession of very tender affection for them (vv. 11–13). He seems unable to find just the right words to express the warm affections he has for these Corinthians. We want to advance the spiritual welfare of all to whom we preach, but *our mouth is open unto you, and our heart is enlarged unto you*, in a special way. "*You are not*," he says, "*straitened in us* (we are not withholding our affection from you); we would gladly do you all the service we can, and if we cannot, the fault is in you, because you are restricted in yourselves. All we desire as a reward is that you respond with proportionate affection, as children to their father."

2. The warning itself, not to make close alliances with unbelievers, not to be *unequally yoked* with them (v. 14), either:

2.1. In constant relationships. It is wrong for good people to join in marriage with those who are worldly or irreligious. There is more danger that the bad will damage the good than there is hope that the good will benefit the bad.

2.2. In our ordinary interactions with others. We should not mix closely in friendship with evildoers and unbelievers.

2.3. Much less in religious fellowship.

2.3.1. It is very absurd (vv. 14–15). Believers are righteous, but unbelievers are unrighteous. Believers are made light in the Lord (Eph 5:8), but unbelievers remain in the darkness, and what encouraging fellowship can they have together? *Christ and Belial* oppose one other.

2.3.2. It is a dishonor to the Christian's profession (v. 16), because Christians are the *temples of the living God*. Now there can be no agreement between *the temple of God and idols*.

2.3.3. There is a great deal of danger in associating closely with unbelievers, danger of being made unclean and of being rejected; therefore the exhortation is (v. 17) *to come out from among them, to be separate,* as one would avoid the company of those who have the leprosy or the plague, and not *to touch the unclean thing*. Who can touch tar without being stained by it? We must take care not to make ourselves unclean by closely associating with those who pollute themselves with sin.

2.3.4. It shows corrupt ingratitude to God for all the favors he has given and promised to believers (v. 18). God has promised to *be a Father to them* and that they will be *his sons and his daughters*, and is there a greater honor or happiness than this?

CHAPTER 7

This chapter begins with an exhortation to progressive holiness (vv. 1–4). The apostle then returns to speak further of the incestuous person, telling the Corinthians what comfort he received on meeting Titus (vv. 5–7) and how he rejoiced in their repentance (vv. 8–11). He concludes by seeking to comfort them (vv. 12–16).

Verses 1–4

These verses contain a double exhortation:

1. To make progress in holiness (v. 1). *Having these promises* of God is a strong inducement to sanctification, both to:

1.1. Dying to sin. We must *cleanse ourselves from all filthiness of flesh and spirit* (purify ourselves from everything that contaminates body and spirit). There are sins of the flesh, which are committed with the body, and sins of the spirit; and we must cleanse ourselves from the filthiness of both.

1.2. Living for righteousness and holiness. We must continue to *perfect our holiness* and not be contented with sincerity—which is our Gospel perfection—without aiming at sinless perfection. We must do this *in the fear of God* (out of reverence for God); there is no holiness without this fear.

2. To show proper respect for the ministers of the Gospel: *Receive us* (make room for us in your hearts) (v. 2). If the ministers of the Gospel are thought contemptible because of their position, there is danger that the Gospel itself will be regarded with contempt. Paul tells them:

2.1. He has done nothing to forfeit their esteem (v. 2). But:

2.2. He does not here reflect on their lack of affection toward him (vv. 3–4). He assures them again of his great affection for them, which is such that he would give his last breath for them and *live and die with them*. It was his great affection for them that both made him use such *boldness* of *speech toward them* and, on the other hand, caused him to *glory* in them, or make his boast of them.

Verses 5–11

There seems to be a connection between 2:13, where the apostle said he had no rest in his spirit when he did not find Titus at Troas, and v. 5 of this chapter, and so great was his affection for the Corinthians, and his concern for their behavior relative to the incestuous person, that in his further travels he still had no rest until he heard from them. He now tells them:

1. How distressed he was (v. 5). He was troubled when he did not meet with Titus at Troas, and also later when for some time he did not meet with him in Macedonia. There were *fightings without*, and there were *fears within*.

2. How he was comforted (vv. 6–7). The coming of Titus was some comfort to him, and the good news Titus brought about the Corinthians was a matter of even greater encouragement. He found Titus to be comforted in them, and this filled the apostle with comfort. He ascribes all his comfort to God, who is the God of all comfort (1:3). It was God who comforted him by the coming of Titus (v. 6).

3. How greatly he rejoiced at their repentance. The apostle was sorry that it was necessary for him to make sorry those whom he would rather have made glad (v. 8). Now, however, he rejoices, having found that they have *sorrowed to repentance* (v. 9). It was the nature and effect of their sorrow—*repentance unto salvation* (v. 10)—that made him rejoice.

3.1. Godly sorrow comes before true repentance. The sorrow of the Corinthians was a godly sorrow because it was a sorrow for sin. Godly sorrow will end in salvation, but worldly sorrow produces death. The sorrows of worldly people for worldly things will bring gray hairs sooner to the grave. Humiliation and godly sorrow are necessary in order to bring about repentance, and both of them come from God, the giver of all grace.

3.2. The beneficial fruits and effects of true repentance are mentioned (v. 11). Where the heart is changed, the life and actions will also be changed. The Corinthians' sorrow produced *indignation* at sin. It also produced *fear*: the fear that consists of reverence for God, the watchful fear of sin, and a jealous fear of themselves. It brought about a *vehement desire* for a thorough reformation of what had been wrong in their lives. It brought about *zeal*, a mixture of love and anger, a zeal for duty and against sin. This is how *in all things they had approved themselves to be clear in that matter*. They were penitent, and so were clear of guilt before God, who would pardon and not punish them.

Verses 12–16

In these verses the apostle seeks to encourage the Corinthians. He had a good intention in his previous letter, which might have been thought severe (v. 12). He did not write in this way chiefly *for his cause that did the wrong* (on account of the one who did wrong), nor was it merely *for his cause that suffered wrong* (on account of the one who suffered wrong); no, it was also to show his sincere concern and *care for them*. Titus was glad, and his spirit refreshed, with their comfort, and this comforted the apostle, making him glad too (v. 13). Just as Titus was comforted while he was with them, so when he remembered his reception among them, the thoughts of these things increased his affection for them (v. 15). Great comfort and joy follow godly sorrow. Paul and Titus were glad, and the Corinthians were comforted. Well may all this joy be on earth, considering that there is joy in heaven over one sinner who repents (Lk 15:7). Paul is *not ashamed* (not embarrassed) of his boasting about the Corinthians to Titus (v. 14), because he was not disappointed in his expectation concerning them, and he can now declare with great joy what confidence he still has in them concerning everything.

CHAPTER 8

In this chapter and the next Paul urges and instructs the Corinthians about a particular work of charity—to relieve the needs of the poor saints at Jerusalem and in Judea. The apostle stirs them up to contribute generously for their relief. He begins, in this chapter, by commending to the Corinthians the good example of the Macedonians and telling them that Titus is being sent to Corinth to collect their offering (vv. 1–6). He then proceeds to urge this duty (vv. 7–15) and recommends the people who are to be employed in this matter (vv. 16–24).

Verses 1–6

Notice here:

1. The apostle applies the good example of the churches in Macedonia to encourage the Corinthians toward the good work of charity.

1.1. He tells the Corinthians about the Macedonians' great generosity (v. 1). It is a great grace and favor from God to be made useful to others.

1.2. He commends the charity of the Macedonians.

1.2.1. The Macedonians themselves were in distress, and yet they contributed to the relief of others (v. 2). As they had great joy in the midst of troubles, they were generous in their gifts; they gave out of a little, trusting God to provide for them.

1.2.2. They gave very fully, with *the riches of liberality* (v. 2); it was *according to*, even *beyond, their power* (v. 3), as much as could have properly been expected from them, if not more.

1.2.3. *They were willing of themselves* (v. 3); they were so far from needing Paul to urge and press them that they *prayed us with much entreaty* (urgently pleaded with us) *to receive the gift* (v. 4).

1.2.4. Their charity was founded on true godliness. They solemnly made a fresh commitment of themselves and all they had to the Lord Jesus Christ, sanctifying their contributions to God's honor by first giving themselves to the Lord. We should give ourselves to God; we cannot give ourselves to anyone better. What we give for charitable uses will not be accepted by God unless we first give ourselves to the Lord.

2. The apostle tells them that Titus was urged to go and make a collection among them (v. 6). Titus had already begun this work among them, and so he wanted to finish it. When such a good work had already prospered in such good hands, it would be a pity if it was not continued and finished. The work of charity will often succeed best when the most proper people are employed to seek contributions and distribute them.

Verses 7–15

In these verses the apostle uses several powerful arguments to stir the Corinthians to perform this good work of charity.

1. He urges on them the consideration of their eminence in other gifts and graces, wanting them to excel in this work of charity too (v. 7). When he wants to persuade the Corinthians to do this good thing, he commends them for other good things. Most people love to be complimented, especially when we ask a gift from them, and it is a justice we owe to those in whom God's grace shines so appropriately commend them.

1.1. Notice what it was that the Corinthians overflowed in. *Faith* is mentioned first, for that is the root. Those who have much faith will have much of the other graces and good works too. To their faith was added *utterance*

(speech). Many who have faith lack speech. With their speech appeared *knowledge*. They excelled also in all *diligence* (complete earnestness or commitment). Those who have great knowledge and ready speech are not always the most committed Christians, and great talkers are not always the best doers, but these Corinthians were committed to doing good as well as knowing and talking well. Further, they had much love for their ministers. Now to all these good things the apostle wants them to add this grace also: to excel in love for the poor.

1.2. The apostle takes care to prevent any misapprehension: he does not speak by commandment (v. 8), but gives his *advice* (v. 10). Many things that are good for us to do cannot be said, by express and indispensable commandment, to be our duty at a particular time.

2. Another argument is taken from the consideration of the grace of our Lord Jesus Christ. *You know*, the apostle says, *the grace of our Lord Jesus Christ* (v. 9), *that though he was rich, yet for your sakes he became poor*, in order to make us rich: rich in the love of God, rich in the blessings of the new covenant, rich in the hopes of eternal life. We should be kind, loving, and generous to the poor with what we have, because we ourselves live on the lovingkindness of the Lord Jesus Christ.

3. Another argument is taken from their eagerness to begin this good work.

3.1. It is fitting for them to finish what they have begun (vv. 10–11). Good plans and intentions, indeed, are good; they are like buds and blossoms, pleasant to look at, giving hope of good fruit; but they are lost and mean nothing without fulfillment.

3.2. It would be acceptable to God (v. 12). When people intend what is good and also seek to perform it, God will accept what they can do, and not reject them for what is not in their power to do. Yet this Scripture will in no way justify those who think good intentions are enough.

4. Another argument is taken from the distribution of the things of this world and the changeability of human affairs (vv. 13–15). Providence gives to some more of the good things of this world, and to some less, so that those who have a greater *abundance may supply those who are in want*, so that there may be opportunity for acts of charity. It is the will of God that, by our mutually supplying one another, there *be some sort of equality*. All should consider whether they should be concerned to supply those in need. This is illustrated by the instance of gathering and distributing manna in the desert (Ex 16): *he that had gathered much* had nothing left over when a share was given to the one *that had gathered little*.

Verses 16–24

In these verses the apostle commends the brothers who are being sent to Corinth to collect their kind gift and, as it were, gives them letters of recommendation, so that if they *are inquired after* (v. 23), if anyone is inquisitive or suspicious about them, it will be known who they are and how safely they can be trusted.

1. He commends Titus for his *earnest care* for them. This is mentioned with thankfulness to God (v. 16), and it is a cause of thankfulness if God has put it into the hearts of anyone to do us or others any good. Paul commends Titus for his readiness to carry out this present service (v. 17). Asking charity for the relief of others is looked on as a thankless task, but it is a good task.

2. He commends another brother who is being sent with Titus. It is generally thought that this was Luke. He is commended as a man whose *praise is in the Gospel*

through all the churches (v. 18) and as one chosen by the churches (v. 19) and included with the apostle in his ministry. He was probably chosen at the request of Paul himself, so *that no man might blame him in that abundance which was administered by him* (v. 20). Paul would not give anyone cause to accuse him of favoritism, and thought it his duty *to provide for things honest, not only in the sight of the Lord, but also in the sight of men.* We live in a censorious world and should avoid anything that might give opportunity to those who seek to reproach us.

3. He also commends another brother, who is thought to have been Apollos. Whoever he was, he had *approved himself diligent* (zealous) *in many things* and was therefore suitable to be employed in this way.

4. He concludes with a generally good characterization of them all (v. 23). This characterization is the reason he urges the Corinthians to show their generosity—so that these messengers of the churches, and the churches themselves, will see a full *proof of* the Corinthians' *love*, and that it is with good reason the apostle has even *boasted on their behalf* (v. 24).

CHAPTER 9

In this chapter the apostle seems to excuse his earnestness in urging the Corinthians to fulfill the duty of giving (vv. 1–5), and he proceeds to give directions about the acceptable way in which it should be performed (vv. 6–15).

Verses 1–5

1. The apostle tells the Corinthians it is unnecessary to urge them with further arguments to give relief to their poor brothers and sisters (v. 1). He knows their *forwardness* (eagerness) to do every good work, and how they began this good work *a year ago.* He has boasted of their zeal to the Macedonians, and this has stirred many of them to do as the Corinthians have done. And he is persuaded that just as they began well, so they will continue well.

2. He seems to apologize for sending Titus and the other brothers to them, and he gives his true reasons for doing so, namely:

2.1. So that, having received this timely notice, the Corinthians will be fully prepared (v. 3) when he comes to them. When we want others to do what is good, we must address them tenderly and give them time.

2.2. So that he will not be ashamed of his boasting about them because they are found unready (vv. 3–4). Some from Macedonia might *haply come with him*, and if the collection could not then be made, this would make him—and no doubt them as well—ashamed.

Verses 6–15

Here we have:

1. Proper instructions to be observed about the right manner of giving money. It should be given generously. People who expect a good return at harvest do not sow their seed sparingly. It should be given thoughtfully: *Every man, according as he purposes in his heart* (v. 7). Acts of giving, like other good works, should be done with thought and intention. It should be given freely: *Not grudgingly, nor of necessity*, but cheerfully (v. 7). People sometimes will give merely to satisfy the persistence of those who ask for their charity, and what they give is in a way squeezed or forced out of them, and this unwillingness spoils all they do.

2. Good encouragement to perform this loving act.

2.1. They themselves will not lose by what they give in charity. What is given to the poor is far from being lost, just as the precious seed that is planted in the ground is not lost; it will spring up and bear fruit; the sower will receive it back, with much more, in the crop it produces (v. 6).

2.1.1. God loves a cheerful giver (v. 7). Can a person be a loser by doing something God is pleased with?

2.1.2. God is able to make our charity return to our advantage (v. 8). We have no reason to distrust the goodness of God; he is *able to make all grace abound.* Its honor is lasting; its reward eternal.

2.1.3. The apostle offers a prayer to God that the Corinthians' will be gainers, not losers (vv. 10–11). The prayer is made to God, *who ministereth seed to the sower,* who gives such a harvest of the crops of the earth that we have not only enough bread to eat for one year but also enough to sow again for a future supply. What he asks in his prayer is that the Corinthians may have *bread for their food*, always enough for themselves; that God *will multiply their seed sown*, so that they may be able to do even more good; and that there may be *an increase of the fruits of righteousness*, so that they may reap plentifully and be *enriched in everything to all bountifulness* (v. 11). Works of charity are so far from impoverishing us that they are the proper means to truly enrich us or make us truly rich.

2.2. While they will not be losers, the poor will be gainers (v. 12).

2.3. This will lead to the praise and glory of God. All who wish the Gospel well will *glorify God for this* proof *of subjection* (their obedience) *to the Gospel of Christ* and true love to all (v. 13).

2.4. Those whose needs are supplied will make the best response they can by offering many prayers to God for those who have helped them (v. 14). This is the only response the poor can make, and it is often greatly for the advantage of the rich.

3. A conclusion of this whole matter in this doxology: *Thanks be to God for his unspeakable* (indescribable) *gift* (v. 15). This seems to refer to Jesus Christ, who really is the indescribable gift of God to this world.

CHAPTER 10

In this chapter the apostle asserts the power of his preaching, his power to punish offenders (vv. 1–6), his relation to Christ, and his authority as an apostle of Christ (vv. 7–11), and he refuses to justify himself or to act by such rules as the false teachers do (vv. 12–18).

Verses 1–6

Here we may notice:

1. That the apostle addresses the Corinthians in a very mild and humble manner (v. 1).

1.1. In the middle of the greatest provocations he shows mildness. How humbly this great apostle speaks of himself, as *one in presence base* (timid) *among them!* This is what his enemies say of him, with contempt (v. 10), and he seems to acknowledge it.

1.2. He wants to be given no reason to deal harshly (v. 2). *He beseeches* (begs) *them* to give him no reason to be bold or to exercise his authority against them in general.

2. That he asserts the power of his preaching and his power to punish offenders.

2.1. He asserts the power of his preaching (vv. 3, 5).

2.1.1. The work of the ministry is warfare, but it is certainly not *after the flesh* (worldly), because it is a spiritual warfare with spiritual enemies and is engaged for spiritual purposes.

2.1.2. The doctrines of the Gospel are weapons, and the way of the Gospel is not outward force but strong persuasion. People must be persuaded to pursue God and their duty, not driven to do so by force of arms. Great opposition is raised against the Gospel by the powers of sin and Satan in human hearts. Ignorance, prejudice, and sinful desires are his strongholds in soul. But these strongholds are demolished by the Gospel through the grace and power of God.

2.2. He asserts his power to punish offenders (v. 6). Although the apostle showed meekness and gentleness, he would not betray his authority.

Verses 7–11

The apostle proceeds to reason the case with the Corinthians: "*Do you,*" he says, "*look on things after the outward appearance* (look only on the surface of things)? (v. 7). Is this a fitting rule to value either people or things by?" In outward appearance, Paul seemed to some to be lowly and contemptible (v. 10). But appearances are often false. The apostle asserts two things about himself:

1. His relation to Christ (v. 7). It seems from this that Paul's opponents boasted that they were Christ's ministers and servants. "Now," the apostle reasons, "suppose they are: they should also allow us to say confidently that *we are Christ's.*" There is room in Christ for many, and those who differ much from one another may still be one in him. It would help heal the differences among us if we remembered that those who differ from us may also belong to Christ. We must not think that only *we are the people* (Job 12:2) and that no one else belongs to him except us. On the other hand, against those who judge us and despise us we may plead that, however weak we are, we are Christ's just as they are.

2. His authority from Christ as an apostle. The *Lord has given it to him,* and this is more than his opponents can justly claim. It is certainly what he will not be ashamed of (v. 8). Notice:

2.1. The nature of his authority: it is for *edification* (to build you up), *and not for destruction* (not to pull you down).

2.2. The caution with which he speaks about his authority, professing that his intention is not to terrify them with big words or angry letters (v. 9). He does not intend to frighten those who are obedient. Yet he wants his adversaries to *know this* (v. 11): by the exercise of his apostolic power, he will make it clear that that power is truly effective.

Verses 12–18

Notice in these verses:

1. The apostle refuses to justify himself as the false apostles do (v. 12). He clearly shows they are following a wrong method to commend themselves. They are pleased with and pride themselves on their own achievements. We should be pleased and thankful for the gifts or graces we have, but never pride ourselves on them, as if no one else could be compared with us. The apostle refused to belong to such vain people.

2. He establishes a better rule for his behavior (v. 13). He will not go beyond the sphere prescribed to him, which the false apostles do when they *boast of other men's labors.*

3. He acts according to this rule: *We stretch not ourselves beyond our measure* (we are not going too far)

(v. 14). He acted according to this rule especially in preaching at Corinth, because he went there by divine direction. Therefore, in boasting of them as those who have been given into his responsibility, he does not boast of *other men's labours* (the work done by others) (v. 15).

4. He declares his success in observing this rule. His hope is that their faith is increased and that others will also accept the Gospel.

5. He seems to restrain himself as if he had spoken too much in his own praise. He is afraid of boasting or taking any praise to himself (v. 17). Ministers especially must be careful not to boast of what they have done, but must give God the glory for their work and its success. Self-flattery is the worst form of flattery. Instead of praising or commending ourselves, we should seek to approve ourselves to God, and his approval will be our best commendation.

CHAPTER 11

In this chapter the apostle continues his discourse in opposition to the false apostles. 1. He apologizes for commending himself (vv. 1–4). 2. He mentions his equality with the other apostles, and with the false apostles in the particular matter of preaching the Gospel to the Corinthians without wages (vv. 5–15). 3. He makes another introduction to what he is about to say further in his own justification (vv. 16–21). 4. He gives an extensive account of his labors and sufferings, in which he has surpassed the false apostles (vv. 22–33).

Verses 1–4

Notice here:

1. The apology the apostle makes for commending himself (v. 1). Just as it goes against the grain for a proud man to acknowledge his weaknesses, so it goes very much against the grain for a humble man to speak his own praise.

2. The reasons for what he did:

2.1. To preserve the Corinthians from being corrupted by the insinuations of the false apostles (vv. 2–3). He is *jealous over them with godly jealousy.* He has *espoused* (promised) *them to one husband,* and he wishes to *present them as a chaste virgin,* pure, spotless, and faithful, not having *their minds corrupted* by false teachers.

2.2. To vindicate himself against the false apostles. They cannot claim they have another Jesus, another Spirit, or another Gospel to preach to the Corinthians (v. 4). And since there is only one Jesus, one Spirit, and one Gospel preached to them and received by them, what reason could there be for the Corinthians to be prejudiced against Paul, who first converted them to the faith?

Verses 5–15

Having given the foregoing introduction to what he is about to say, the apostle here:

1. Mentions his equality with the other apostles (v. 5). Although he could have spoken very positively, he expresses this very modestly—*I suppose so*—and humbly acknowledges his personal weakness, that he is *rude* (unskilled) *in speech.* He was not, however, unskilled in *knowledge,* and much less was he ignorant of the mysteries of the kingdom of heaven.

2. Mentions his equality with the false apostles in one particular matter. The Corinthians must not only recognize him as a minister of Christ but also acknowledge he has been a good friend to them. He has preached the Gospel freely to them (vv. 7–10). He says he has *taken wages of other churches* (v. 8), so that he had a right to ask

for and receive wages from them. He waived this right, however, and chose rather to deny himself. He chose to be supplied from Macedonia rather than be a burden to the Corinthians. He informs them of the reason. It is not because *he does not love them* (v. 11), but to avoid giving offense. He will not give anyone opportunity to accuse him of worldly intentions in preaching the Gospel, or to say that he intends to enrich himself (v. 12).

3. Charges the false apostles with being *deceitful workers* (v. 13), because although they are the ministers of Satan, they want to appear to be the *ministers of righteousness*. Hypocrisy is something not to be wondered at in this world, especially when we consider the great influence Satan has. Just as Satan can turn himself into any shape, and look sometimes *like an angel of light* (v. 14) in order to advance his kingdom of darkness, so he will teach his instruments to do the same. However, it follows, *Their end is according to their works* (their end will be what their actions deserve) (v. 15).

Verses 16–21

Here Paul further excuses what he is about to say.

1. He does not want the Corinthians to think he is guilty of foolishness. *Let no man think me a fool* (v. 16). Boasting about ourselves is usually not only a sign of pride but also a mark of foolishness (v. 17). "*Yet*," the apostle says, "*as a fool receive me*; still heed what I say."

2. He warns them that *he does not speak after the Lord* (v. 17). He does not want them to think that boasting about ourselves is something the Lord commands Christians to do in general. It is the duty and practice of Christians to humble and deny themselves. When, on the other hand, we consider in what circumstances it may be necessary to speak of what God has done for us, in us, and by us, wisdom must guide us (v. 18; Ecc 10:10).

3. He gives a good reason why they should allow him to boast a little: because they allow others to do so who have less reason. *Seeing many glory after the flesh* (glory in worldly privileges, or outward advantages and achievements), *I will glory also* (v. 18). He, however, will boast in his weaknesses, as he later tells them (12:9–10). These words, *You suffer fools gladly, seeing you yourselves are wise* (v. 19), may be ironic: "Despite all your wisdom, you willingly allow yourselves to be *brought into bondage*, or allow others to lord it over you" (v. 20). The circumstances of the case made it necessary that *whereinsoever any were bold*, he should be *bold also* (v. 21).

Verses 22–33

Here the apostle gives a detailed account of his own qualifications, labors, and sufferings—not out of pride, but to the honor of God, who has enabled him to do and suffer so much for the cause of Christ—and of the things in which he surpasses the false apostles, who want to lessen his character and usefulness among the Corinthians. Notice:

1. He mentions the privileges of his birth (v. 22). He is a Hebrew of the Hebrews, of a family among the Jews that has never intermarried with Gentiles. He is also an Israelite and a descendant of Abraham.

2. He also mentions his apostleship (v. 23). The Corinthians have found full proofs of his ministry: *Are they*, the false apostles, *ministers of Christ? I am more so.*

3. He mainly insists that he has suffered extraordinarily for Christ (v. 23). When the apostle wanted to prove himself an extraordinary minister, he proved that he had suffered extraordinarily. Chains and imprisonment were familiar to him. He says that *thrice he suffered*

shipwreck. A night and a day he had been in the deep (v. 25). Wherever he went, he was in danger. If he made a journey by land or a voyage by sea, he was in danger of bandits. His own compatriots tried to kill him. The Gentiles were no kinder to him, for he was in danger among them too. Whether he was in the city or in the desert, he was in constant danger. He was in danger not only among his open enemies but even among false believers who called themselves brothers and sisters (v. 26). He was in *watchings often* (had many sleepless nights) and exposed to *hunger and thirst*; he was *in fastings* (without food) *often* and endured *cold and nakedness* (v. 27). Thus he was treated like a burden to the earth and the plague of his generation. As an apostle, he bore the *care of* (pressure of his concern for) *all the churches* (v. 28). He mentions this last, as if it lay the heaviest on him (v. 29). There was not a weak Christian with whom he did not sympathize, nor anyone led into sin without him being moved by it. Nor was he ashamed of all this; it was what he counted his honor (v. 30).

4. He mentions one particular aspect of his sufferings out of place, as if he had forgotten it before, namely, the danger he was in at Damascus soon after he was converted. This was his first great danger and difficulty, and the rest of his life was like this. The apostle confirms this account with a solemn oath (v. 31). It is a great encouragement to good people that *the God and Father of our Lord Jesus Christ* knows the truth of all they say and knows all they do and all they suffer for his sake.

CHAPTER 12

In this chapter the apostle continues to defend the honor of his apostleship. He mentions the favor God has shown him, the methods God has taken to keep him humble, and the use he has made of this means (vv. 1–10). He then addresses himself to the Corinthians, giving a detailed account of his behavior and kind intentions toward them (vv. 11–21).

Verses 1–10

Notice here:

1. The account the apostle gives of the favors God has shown him, for no doubt he himself is the *man in Christ* about whom he is writing. Notice:

1.1. The honor itself: he was *caught up into the third heaven* (v. 2). We cannot say when this took place, and much less can we claim to say *how* it happened. In some sense he was caught up into the *third heaven*. This third heaven is called *paradise* (v. 4). The apostle does not mention what he saw in the third heaven or paradise, but he tells us that *he heard unspeakable words* (inexpressible things), words that it was not permissible to speak.

1.2. The modest way in which the apostle mentions this matter: *It is not expedient for me doubtless to glory* (v. 1). That is why he has not mentioned this until *above fourteen years* later (v. 2). His humility appears by the restraint he seems to put on himself (v. 6). It is excellent to have a humble spirit in the midst of high advancements, and those who humble themselves will be exalted (Mt 23:12).

2. The methods God has taken to prevent his *being lifted up above measure* (becoming conceited). When God's people share their experiences, let them always remember to take notice of what God has done to keep them humble.

2.1. The apostle was distressed by *a thorn in the flesh* and *buffeted* with (tormented by) a messenger of Satan

(v. 7). We are very much in the dark about what this was. Some think it was an acute physical pain or sickness. It is certain, though, that what the apostle calls *a thorn in his flesh* was very painful to him for a time. The thorns Christ wore for us, however, sanctify to us and make bearable to us all the thorns in the flesh we may be afflicted with at any time.

2.2. The purpose of this was to keep the apostle humble (v. 7). If God loves us, he will keep pride from us and keep us from being *exalted above measure* (conceited). This thorn in the flesh is said to be a messenger of Satan, which he did not send with a good purpose, but with bad intentions. But God overruled it for good.

2.3. The apostle prayed fervently to God for the removal of this severe distress. If an answer is not given to our first prayer or to our second, we must hold on and hold out until we receive an answer. Just as troubles are sent to teach us to pray, so they are continued to teach us to continue faithfully in prayer (Ro 12:12).

2.4. *My grace is sufficient for thee.* Although God accepts the prayer of faith, he does not always answer it to the letter; just as he sometimes grants in wrath, so he also sometimes denies in love. It is a great encouragement to us to know that, whatever thorns in the flesh we suffer, God's grace is sufficient for us. Grace means two things:

2.4.1. The goodwill of God toward us, and this is sufficient to strengthen and encourage us.

2.4.2. The good work of God in us. Christ Jesus will give the remedy in proportion to our illness.

3. The use the apostle has made of this means: "*I glory* (boast) *in my infirmities* (v. 9) and *take pleasure* (I delight) in them for Christ's sake" (v. 10). They were good opportunities for Christ to reveal the power and sufficiency of his grace in Paul. When we are weak in ourselves, we are strong in the grace of our Lord Jesus Christ.

Verses 11 – 21

Here the apostle addresses the Corinthians in two ways:

1. He blames them for not standing up to defend him. They compelled him to commend himself (v. 11), even though they in particular had good reason to speak well of him. We owe it to good people to stand up in defense of their reputation. On the other hand, however highly we are regarded by others, we should always think humbly of ourselves. We see here an example of this in this great apostle, who thought himself to be nothing, though in truth he did not fall short of the greatest apostles.

2. He gives a detailed account of his behavior and kind intentions toward them.

2.1. He says (v. 13) he has not been a burden to them in the past, and he tells them (v. 14) he will not be a burden to them when he comes to them. He will spare their purses to save their souls. Those who aim at clothing themselves with the fleece of the flock but who have no care for the sheep are hired workers (Jn 10:12 – 13), not good shepherds (Jn 10:11, 14).

2.2. He will gladly spend and be spent for them (v. 15); in fact, he will spend himself in such a way that in the end he is spent, like a candle, which consumes itself to give light to others.

2.3. He has not lessened his love for them (v. 15).

2.4. He is careful not only that he himself will not be a burden but also that no one he employs will.

2.5. He is a man who does everything to build others up (v. 19).

2.6. He will not shrink from his duty. He has decided, therefore, to be faithful in rebuking sin (v. 20). Faithful ministers must not fear offending the guilty by administering sharp rebukes as necessary, in public and in private.

2.7. He is grieved at the thought that he will find scandalous sins among them not properly repented of. This will be the cause of great humiliation and mourning. We have reason to *bewail* (mourn) *many that have sinned, and have not repented* (v. 21). Those who love God and love those sinners should mourn for them.

CHAPTER 13

In this chapter the apostle threatens to be severe with stubborn sinners (vv. 1 – 6). He then offers a suitable prayer to God on behalf of the Corinthians (vv. 7 – 10). He concludes his letter with greetings and a blessing (vv. 11 – 14).

Verses 1 – 6

Notice in these verses:

1. The apostle threatens to deal severely with stubborn sinners when he comes. Notice:

1.1. His warning. He has not been hasty to deal severely, but has given a first and second warning (v. 1). This is how some understand *the third time I am coming to you*, as referring to his first and second letters, by which he warned them as if he were present with them even though he was absent in person (v. 2). We should go or send to our brother or sister twice to tell them their fault (Mt 18:16). Now Paul tells them to exercise severity.

1.2. The threat itself: "*I will not spare* the unrepentant." Although it is God's gracious method to be patient with sinners for a long time, he will not be patient forever.

2. Why he will be so severe (v. 3). It was the intention of the false teachers to make the Corinthians call the authority of Paul's preaching into question, though they had not weak, but strong and mighty, proofs of it (v. 3). Even as Christ himself *was crucified through weakness but liveth by the power of God* (v. 4), so the apostles still revealed the power of God, especially the power of his grace, in converting the world to Christianity. Paul encourages the Corinthians to prove their Christianity (v. 5). If Jesus Christ is in them, this is proof that Christ speaks in him. If, therefore, they can prove themselves *not to be reprobates, he trusts they will know that he is not a reprobate* (v. 6). We should examine ourselves to see whether we are in the faith, *prove our own selves*, ask ourselves whether Christ is in us or not.

Verses 7 – 10

We have here:

1. The apostle's prayer to God for the Corinthians (v. 7). We should be more concerned to pray that we may not commit evil than that we may not suffer evil.

2. The reasons why the apostle offers this prayer to God (v. 7).

2.1. It is not so much for his own personal reputation as for the honor of religious faith: "*that you should do that which is honest*, right or decent, and for the good reputation of religious faith" (v. 7). The best way to grace our holy religious faith is *to do that which is honest* and right and good.

2.2. It is so that they will be free from all blame when he comes to them. This is suggested in v. 8. If they do not commit evil, the apostle has no power to punish them. See how glad the apostle is at this blessed powerlessness:

We are glad when we are weak and you are strong (v. 9); that is, "Although we are weak through persecutions and contempt, we bear them joyfully, as long as we see that you are strong and persevering in well-doing."

2.3. He desires their perfection (v. 9). He wants them not only to be kept from sin but also to grow in grace. This is his great goal in writing this letter.

Verses 11–14

The apostle concludes this letter with:

1. A farewell greeting.

1.1. He appeals to them with several good requests. He calls on them to be perfect, or to be knit together in love (Col 2:2); to be encouraged; to be united, because the more comfortable we are with our brothers and sisters, the more encouragement we have in our own souls; and to live in peace, that they do not let differences in opinion cause a lack of love between them.

1.2. He encourages them with the promise of God's presence among them (v. 11). God is the God of love and peace. He will be with those who live in love and peace, and he will love those who love peace.

1.3. He gives instructions to them to greet each other, sending kind greetings to them from those who are with him (vv. 12–13).

2. The apostolic blessing (v. 14). This is how the apostle concludes his letter. This is a very solemn blessing, and we should be very diligent to make sure we inherit it.

A Practical and Devotional Exposition of

Galatians

While he was with the Galatians, they had expressed the greatest respect and affection for both his person and his ministry, but some Judaizing teachers got in among them. The main aim of these false teachers was to draw the Galatians away from the truth as it is in Jesus (Eph 4:21), especially in the great teaching of justification, asserting the necessity of adding the observance of the Law of Moses to faith in Christ. They did all they could to diminish the character and reputation of the apostle, representing him as one who, if indeed he was to be recognized as an apostle, was much inferior to others, especially to Peter, James, and John. In both these attempts the false teachers had too much success. This was the occasion of Paul's writing this letter, in which he expresses his great concern that they have allowed themselves to be turned aside so quickly. Paul defends his own character and authority as an apostle and shows he is not *behind the very chief of the apostles* (2Co 11:5). He then undertakes to assert and declare the great Gospel teaching of justification by faith apart from the works of the Law, and he appeals to them to stand firm in the freedom with which Christ has set them free (5:1), gives them several very necessary pieces of advice and directions, and then concludes the letter.

CHAPTER 1

In this chapter, after the introduction (vv. 1–5), the apostle severely rebukes these churches (vv. 6–9), and then proves his own apostleship. He defends it on the basis of: 1. His purpose in preaching the Gospel (v. 10). 2. His having received it by direct revelation (vv. 11–12). For the proof of the latter, he informs them: 2.1. How he formerly conducted himself (vv. 13–14). 2.2. How he was converted (vv. 15–16). 2.3. How he behaved afterward (vv. 16–24).

Verses 1–5

In these verses we have the introduction to the letter, in which notice:

1. The person or persons from whom this letter is sent—Paul, *an apostle, and all the brethren which are with me.*

1.1. At the very outset he gives a general account of both his ministry and the way in which he was called to it. As to his position, he is an apostle. He tells them how he was called to this office and assures them that his commission to undertake it was wholly divine. He is an apostle *by Jesus Christ.* He received his commission directly from him, and so from *God the Father.* Furthermore, his call to the apostleship was received after Christ's resurrection from the dead. He received his call from Christ when Christ was in heaven.

1.2. He includes in the opening greeting of the letter *all the brethren* (all the brothers and sisters) who are with him. He wants it to be seen that he has their agreement in the message he has preached and is now to confirm.

2. To whom this letter is sent—*to the churches of Galatia,* all of whom, it seems, were more or less cor-

rupted through the cunning of those deceivers who had crept in among them.

3. The apostolic blessing (v. 3). Grace includes God's goodwill toward us and his good work on us; peace implies in it all the inner comfort or outward prosperity that is really necessary for us. The apostle wishes both of these for these Christians. Grace comes first, then peace, because there can be no true peace without grace. Having mentioned the Lord Jesus Christ, he cannot go on without enlarging on his love (v. 4): *Who gave himself for our sins, that he might deliver us from this present evil world.* This present world is an evil world; it has become so through human sin. But Jesus Christ has died to rescue us from this present evil age, not to remove his people from it but to rescue them from its power. This, the apostle informs us, he has done *according to the will of God and our Father.* We may draw encouragement from this to look on God as our Father. Just as he is the Father of our Lord Jesus, so in and through him he is also the Father of all true believers.

4. The conclusion of this introduction, in which the apostle solemnly ascribes the praise and glory to him—either to Christ or both to him and to the Father (v. 5).

Verses 6–9

Here the apostle comes to the body of the letter, and he begins it with a more general rebuke of these churches for their unsteadiness in the faith, which he further enlarges on several times later in the letter. Here we may notice:

1. How much he is concerned at their defection. Their defection is greatly aggravated by several things:

1.1. That *they have been removed from* (have deserted) *him that called them,* not only from the apostle but from

God himself. They have become guilty of a great abuse of God's kindness and mercy toward them.

1.2. That they had been called by the Gospel to share in the greatest blessings and benefits. Their sin and foolishness in abandoning the privilege they enjoyed were in proportion to the greatness of that privilege.

1.3. That they have so quickly turned away. In a very short time they lost that respect for the grace of Christ that they had seemed to have. This both showed their weakness and emphasized their guilt.

1.4. That they have turned to *"another Gospel, which yet is not another*. You will find it to be no Gospel at all, but the perverting of the Gospel of Christ." Those who seek to establish any other way to heaven than the one the Gospel of Christ has revealed will find themselves wretchedly mistaken.

2. The Gospel he has preached to them is the only true Gospel. He declares a curse on those who claim to preach any other gospel (v. 8). "If you have any other Gospel preached to you under our name, or even under pretext of having it from an angel himself, you must conclude that you are being deceived, and whoever preaches another gospel puts himself under a curse."

Verses 10–24

What Paul said in the introduction of this letter, he now proceeds to enlarge on. There he declared himself to be an apostle of Christ; here he comes to more directly support his claim to that position and mission:

1. From the scope and intention of his ministry. Just as he professes to act by a commission from God, so his chief aim is to advance his glory, by reclaiming sinners to a state of submission to him. He does not seek to win human approval; his great concern is to gain the approval of God. No one could serve two such masters (Mt 6:24); therefore he dare not allow himself to satisfy people at the expense of his faithfulness to Christ. This is how he proves that he is a true apostle of Christ. The great end that ministers of the Gospel should aim at is to bring people to God. They must not be concerned to please people if they wish to show they are faithful servants of Christ.

2. From the way in which he received the Gospel he preaches to them (vv. 11–12). One thing that was special in the character of an apostle was that he had been called to and instructed for this ministry directly by Christ himself. Accordingly, Paul tells the Galatians that he received both his knowledge of the Gospel and his authority to preach it directly from the Lord Jesus himself.

2.1. He tells them what his conduct once had been (vv. 13–14). It had to be something extraordinary to make such a great change in him, to bring him not only to profess, but even to preach, the doctrine that he had opposed so vehemently before.

2.2. He tells them in what a wonderful way he was brought to the knowledge and faith of Christ and appointed to the office of an apostle (vv. 15–16). There was something distinctive in the case of Paul, both in the suddenness and in the greatness of the change brought about in him, and also in the way in which it was carried out. Christ was revealed not only to him but also *in him*. It will do us little good if we have Christ revealed to us unless he is also revealed in us. It pleased God *to reveal his Son in him* so that he would preach him among the Gentiles. It was by revelation, therefore, that he was both a Christian and an apostle.

2.3. He tells them how he behaved himself then (vv. 16–24): *He conferred not with flesh and blood*. It cannot, therefore, be well claimed that he is indebted to any

other person either for his knowledge of the Gospel or for his authority to preach it. Because this account is important to establish his claim to this position, he confirms it by a solemn oath (v. 20). Although this will not justify us in making solemn appeals to God on every occasion, it shows that in significant matters doing so may sometimes be not only lawful but also our duty. He had no communication at that time with the *churches of Christ in Judea*; they had not even *seen his face*—he was not known to them personally. But the mere report of this radical change in him both filled them with joy and excited them to praise God.

CHAPTER 2

Here the apostle makes it clear that he is not indebted to the other apostles either for his knowledge of the Gospel or for his authority as an apostle; he is recognized and approved even by them as having a commission equal to theirs. 1. He tells the Galatians in detail about another journey he took to Jerusalem (vv. 1–10). 2. He gives them an account of another meeting he had with the apostle Peter at Antioch, and how he was obliged to behave toward him there. He proceeds to discuss the great teaching of justification through faith in Christ, apart from the works of the law, which it is the main intention of this letter to establish (vv. 11–21).

Verses 1–10

From the very first preaching of Christianity there was a difference of understanding between those Christians who had previously been Jews and those who had previously been Gentiles. Peter was *the apostle of the circumcision* (the Jews), but Paul was the apostle of the Gentiles. He tells us about another journey that he took to Jerusalem (vv. 1–10).

1. He gives us an account of some circumstances concerning his journey:

1.1. Its time: it was not until *fourteen years* after the earlier journey (mentioned in 1:18). That he had been absent from the other apostles for so long and was all that time employed in preaching pure Christianity, without being called into question by them for it, was some evidence that he did not depend on the other apostles at all.

1.2. His companions: *I went up with Barnabas, and took with me Titus also.* If the journey spoken of here was the one recorded in Ac 15:36–41, then we have a clear reason why Barnabas went along with him, namely, that he was chosen by the Christians at Antioch as Paul's companion and associate. As for Titus, although he had now become not only a convert to the Christian faith but also a preacher of it, he was still by birth a Gentile and uncircumcised, and so by making Titus his companion, Paul made it clear that their message and practice were in harmony.

1.3. The reason for it: *I went up by revelation*. This apostle was often favored with the privilege of receiving a special divine direction. It should teach us that in everything significant that we undertake, we should endeavor to see our way made clear before us and commit ourselves to the guidance of Providence.

2. He gives us an account of his behavior while he was at Jerusalem.

2.1. *He there communicated the Gospel to them, which he preached among the Gentiles, but privately.* Notice both the faithfulness and the prudence of our great apostle.

2.1.1. He showed faithfulness by giving the believers at Jerusalem a reasonable account of the message he had preached all along among the Gentiles, and was still determined to preach.

2.1.2. He showed prudence and caution in this. He chose to do it in a more private rather than in a public way, so that he would not stir up opposition against himself, with the result that either the success of his past labors would be lessened or his future usefulness would be obstructed. It fulfilled his purpose enough to have his message recognized by those who were in positions of the greatest authority, whether it was approved by others or not.

2.2. In his practice he remained faithful to the message he had preached. Although he had Titus with him, who was a Gentile, he would not let him be circumcised. Nor does it seem that the apostles exerted any pressure on Titus to be circumcised; they did not want to impose this on the Gentiles. Others did want to, however—*false brethren, unawares* (secretly) *brought in, to spy out their liberty which they had in Christ Jesus*. The intention of these false brothers was *to bring* Paul and his companions *into bondage*. If they had persuaded Paul to have Titus circumcised, they could easily have imposed circumcision on other Gentiles, and so have made them slaves to the Law of Moses. Paul, however, would not *give place by subjection, no, not for an hour* (did not give in to them even for a moment), *that the truth of the Gospel might continue with them*. He refused to yield to those who wanted to keep Mosaic rituals and ceremonies, and he was determined to stand firm in the liberty with which Christ has set us free (5:1).

2.3. Although he had dealings with the other apostles, he did not receive from them any addition to his knowledge or authority (v. 6). That they were apostles first did not prejudice his equality as an apostle with them. They told him nothing except what he already knew before by revelation, nor could they take exception to the message he set out before them.

2.4. The other apostles were fully convinced of his divine mission and authority and therefore acknowledged him as their fellow apostle (vv. 7–10). They justly concluded *that the Gospel of the uncircumcision was committed to Paul, as the Gospel of the circumcision was to Peter. They gave unto him and Barnabas the right hand of fellowship* and agreed that *these should go to the heathen* (Gentiles), *while they continued to preach to the circumcision* (Jews). This meeting therefore ended in complete harmony and agreement; they approved both Paul's teaching and his behavior and had nothing further to add, except *that* Paul and Barnabas *should remember the poor*, which Paul *was very forward to do* of his own accord. Here he has given us an excellent model of Christian love, and we should in no way confine our love to those who share our sentiments precisely, but be ready to extend it to all whom we have reason to consider Christ's disciples.

Verses 11–21

1. He tells the Galatians what took place in another meeting he had with the apostle Peter, at Antioch (vv. 11–14). In their earlier meeting, there had been good harmony and agreement. But here Paul found himself obliged to oppose Peter. Notice:

1.1. Peter's error. When he came among the Gentile churches, he complied with them and ate with them. But when some Jewish Christians came from Jerusalem, he *withdrew, and separated himself; and the other Jews also dissembled with him* (joined him in his hypocrisy). His fault here had a bad influence on others. Barnabas himself—one of the apostles to the Gentiles—*was carried away with their dissimulation* (led astray by their hypocrisy). This shows us:

1.1.1. The weakness and inconsistency of even the best people, and how they tend to falter in fulfilling their duty to God out of an undue desire to please people.

1.1.2. The great strength of bad examples, especially the examples of good leaders.

1.2. The rebuke Paul gave him. When he saw Peter behaving in this way, he was not afraid to rebuke him for it. Paul stuck faithfully to his principles when others faltered in theirs. He was as good a Jew as any, but as the apostle to the Gentiles, he refused to see them discouraged and trampled on. Peter's behavior in effect signified that Gentiles must comply with Jews, or else they would not be admitted into Christian fellowship.

2. He takes the opportunity to speak about that great basic teaching of the Gospel—that justification is only through faith in Christ, not by the works of the law. This was the doctrine Paul had preached among the Galatians, to which he remained faithful and which it was the great task of this letter to confirm. Now concerning this, Paul tells us:

2.1. What is the practice of the Jewish Christians themselves: "What did we believe in Christ for? Was it not so that we would be justified through faith in Christ? If so, is it not foolish to return to the Law?" To give greater significance to this, he adds (v. 17), "*But if, while we seek to be justified by Christ, we ourselves also are found sinners, is Christ the minister of sin?* Will it not follow that he is, if he requires us to receive a teaching by which we are so far from being justified that we remain impure sinners?" But he rejects this with loathing: "*God forbid*," he says, "that by it he would direct us to a way of justification that is defective and ineffective. *For*," he says (v. 18), "*if I build again the things which I destroyed, I make myself a transgressor*; I acknowledge that I remain under the guilt of sin despite my faith in Christ."

2.2. What his own judgment and practice are.

2.2.1. He is dead to the Law, *through the law itself*. He sees that justification is not to be expected by the works it produces and that there is now no further need for its sacrifices, since they were abolished in Christ by his offering himself as a sacrifice for us. But although he is *dead to the law* in this way, he does not look on himself as *without law*. He is dead to the law so *that he may live unto God*. The teaching of the Gospel, rather than weakening the bond that ties him to obedience, serves to strengthen and confirm it even more. Therefore, although he is dead to the law, it is only so that he may live a new and better life for God.

2.2.2. As he is dead to the law, so he is alive to God through Jesus Christ (v. 20). He is crucified, but he lives; the old self has been crucified, and the new self is alive. Sin is put to death, and grace is given life. *I live, and yet not I*. He has the strengths, encouragements, and triumphs of grace, but that grace does not come from himself, but from another. *He is crucified with Christ*, but *Christ lives in him*. He shares in the death of Christ, so as to die to sin, but also shares in the life of Christ and therefore lives to God. *He lives in the flesh*, and *yet lives by faith*; to all outward appearances he lives as other people do, but a higher and nobler principle supports him, that of faith in Christ. Those who have true faith live by that faith.

3. The apostle concludes by informing us that with the doctrine of justification through faith in Christ, apart from the works of the law, he avoids two great difficulties:

3.1. *He does not frustrate* (set aside) *the grace of God*, which the teaching of justification through the works of the Law does.

3.2. He does not set aside the death of Christ; for if we look for salvation through the Law of Moses, then we make the death of Christ unnecessary.

CHAPTER 3

In this chapter: 1. The apostle rebukes the Galatians for their foolishness in allowing themselves to be drawn away from the faith of the Gospel (vv. 1–5). 2. He proves the doctrine of justification through faith apart from observing the law: 2.1. From the example of Abraham's justification. 2.2. From the nature of the Law. 2.3. From the clear testimony of the Old Testament. 2.4. From the covenant of God with Abraham (vv. 6–18). In case anyone should then say, "What purpose does the Law then have?" he answers that it was added because of sin, it was given to convict the world of the necessity of a Savior, and it was intended as a schoolteacher to bring us to Christ. He concludes the chapter by reminding us of the privileges of being Christians (vv. 19–29).

Verses 1–5

The apostle is dealing here with those who, having accepted the faith of Christ, still continue to seek justification through observing the Law. He rebukes them, calling them *foolish Galatians* (v. 1). He asks, *Who hath bewitched you* (who has put you under an evil spell)? They are not being faithful to the Gospel way of justification that they were taught. It is not enough to know the truth and to say we believe it; we must also obey it. Several things prove the foolishness of these Christians:

1. *Jesus Christ was evidently set forth* (clearly portrayed) *as crucified among them*; they have had the message of the cross preached to them and the sacrament of the Lord's Supper administered to them, in both of which Christ crucified has been set out for them.

2. They have experienced the activity of the Spirit on their souls (v. 2). He wants to know how they came by these gifts and graces: was it *by the works of the law*, or was it by the *hearing of faith*? If they want to say the truth, they will be obliged to confess the latter.

3. He calls on them to consider their past and present behavior (vv. 3–4). They began well, but now they are turning to the Law and expecting to be advanced to higher degrees of perfection by adding the observance of it to faith in Christ in order to justify themselves. This, rather than improving on the Gospel, really perverts it. Far from being more perfect Christians, they are more in danger of becoming no Christians at all. And they have not only accepted the Christian message but also suffered for it; their foolishness will be even more extreme, therefore, if they desert it now.

4. They have had ministers among them who have *ministered the Spirit to them, and wrought miracles among them*. He appeals to them as to whether these people have ministered to them *by the works of the law or by the hearing of faith*. The Galatians know very well that it was not the former but the latter, and that it is therefore inexcusable of them to abandon a teaching that has been so significantly recognized and confirmed.

Verses 6–18

He fully proves the teaching that he has rebuked them for rejecting.

1. He does this by appealing to the example of Abraham's justification (v. 6). His faith had as its object the promise of God, and because he trusted God, he was acknowledged and accepted by God as righteous. *Those who are of faith are the children of Abraham* (v. 7). Abraham was justified through faith, and so are they (v. 8). God would justify the Gentile world through faith, and so justify them in Abraham; that is, in the offspring of Abraham, namely, Christ, not only the Jews but also the Gentiles would be blessed as Abraham was, being justified as he was. It was through faith in the promise of God that Abraham was blessed, and it is only in the same way that others obtain this privilege.

2. He shows that we cannot be justified except by faith in the Gospel, because the Law condemns us. If we put ourselves on trial in the court of the Law, we are certainly lost and ruined. The condition on which we may have life under the Law is perfect, personal, and perpetual obedience; unless our obedience is total and perpetual, we fall under the curse of the Law. If, as transgressors of the law, we are under its curse, it must be futile to look for justification through it. The apostle later tells us that a way is open for us to escape this curse, namely, through faith in Christ (v. 13). Christ followed a strange method to redeem us from the curse of the Law; it was *by being himself made a curse for us*. The purpose of this was *that the blessing of Abraham might come on the Gentiles through Jesus Christ*—so that all who believed in Christ could become heirs of Abraham's blessing, especially of the great promise of the Spirit. It became clear from this that it was not by putting themselves under the Law, but through faith in Christ, that the Galatians became the people of God and heirs of the promise.

3. The apostle brings as evidence the clear testimony of the Old Testament (v. 11): the *just shall live by faith* (Hab 2:4). It is only through faith that people become righteous and, as such, obtain life and happiness. *The law is not of faith*; rather, its language is, *The man that doeth them shall live in them* (Lev 18:5). The Law requires perfect obedience as the condition of life and therefore cannot now, by any means, be the rule of our justification.

4. The apostle urges the stability of the covenant that God made with Abraham, which was not annulled by the giving of the Law to Moses (v. 15). Faith preceded the Law, because Abraham was justified by faith. God entered into a covenant with Abraham (v. 8). The Greek word *diatheke*, translated "covenant" in vv. 15, 17, can also mean "a testament or will" (see also Heb 10:15–18). If it should be said that a testament may be defeated for lack of people to claim its benefit (v. 16), Paul shows that there is no danger of that here. Abraham is dead, and the prophets are dead, but the covenant is made with Abraham and his *seed*. "And this is in the singular," the apostle says; "it points at a single *person*—*that seed is Christ*." The covenant is therefore still in force, because Christ lives forever. The subsequent law could not annul the covenant or promise already made (v. 18). If the inheritance was given to Abraham by promise, we may be sure that God would not withdraw that promise, because he *is not a man that he should lie* (Nu 23:19).

Verses 19–29

It might be asked, "If that promise is sufficient for salvation, what is the purpose of the Law? Or, Why did God give the Law through Moses?"

1. The *law was added because of transgressions* (human sin) (v. 19). The Israelites were sinners as much as others, and so the Law was given both to convict them of their sin and to restrain them from committing sin, *till the seed should come to whom the promise was made*, till this fullness of time came (4:4). But when a fuller revelation was made of the divine grace contained in the promise, then the Law, as given by Moses, was to come to an end. Moreover, although the Law, considered as the law of nature, is always in force, we are now no longer enslaved to it and under the terror of that legal covenant.

The Law, then, was only to lead people to see their need of the promise by showing them the sinfulness of sin, and then to point them to Christ. As a further proof that the Law was not intended to abolish the promise, the apostle adds, *It was ordained by angels in the hand of a mediator*, whereas the promise was given directly by God himself. It was clear from this that the Law could not be intended to set aside the promise, for (v. 20) *God is one*; only one party, God, made the promise to Abraham, and so it is not to be supposed that by a transaction that took place only between him and the nation of the Jews, through a mediator, he would annul a promise that he had made long before to Abraham and all his spiritual offspring, whether Jews or Gentiles, without a mediator. This would not have been consistent with his truth and faithfulness. Moses was only a mediator; the Law that was given by him could not, therefore, affect the promise.

2. The Law was given to convince people of their absolute need of a Savior (v. 21). The Law is in no way inconsistent with the promise. Its purpose is to reveal human sin and show people how much they need a better righteousness than that of the Law. *The scripture hath concluded all under sin* (v. 22). The Law revealed their wounds but could not give them a remedy. The great purpose of the Law, therefore, was *that the promise by faith of Jesus Christ might be given to those that believe*, so that, being convicted of the insufficiency of the Law to bring about a righteousness for them, they might be persuaded to believe in Christ and so obtain the benefit of the promise.

3. The Law was intended to be *a schoolmaster to bring men to Christ* (v. 24). They were confined, held under its terror and discipline, as prisoners are in a state of confinement, so that they would be more readily inclined to accept Christ when he came into the world. It was also a proper means to convince them of their lost and ruined condition in themselves and to let them see the weakness and insufficiency of their own righteousness. In this way, it was their schoolteacher, to instruct and govern them as children, or a "servant" charged with leading them to Christ—as children were led to school by those servants who were charged with caring for them—so that they would be more fully instructed by him as their Teacher in the true way of justification and salvation, which is only through faith in him. The apostle adds (v. 25) that *after faith has come, we are no longer under a schoolmaster*—we no longer have the need there was then for the Law to direct us to him. From this we may notice:

3.1. The goodness God showed to his people in former times by giving them the Law. It provided them with sufficient helps both to direct them in fulfilling their duty to God and to encourage their hope in him.

3.2. The great fault and foolishness of the Jews in mistaking the intention of the Law. They expected to be justified by performing its works, whereas it was never intended to be the rule of their justification, but only a means of convicting them of their guilt and of their need of a Savior.

3.3. The great advantage the Gospel age has over the legal age. We are no longer treated as children, but as sons grown up into adults.

3.3.1. *We are the children of God by faith in Christ Jesus* (v. 26). Notice:

3.3.1.1. The great privilege that real Christians enjoy under the Gospel: they are no longer considered servants, but *sons*. They are admitted to the number of his children and have a right to all the privileges of children.

3.3.1.2. How they come to obtain this privilege: *by faith in Christ Jesus*. This faith in Christ, by which the Galatians became children of God (v. 27), was what they professed in baptism. Having become members of Christ, they were recognized as the children of God. Notice here:

3.3.1.2.1. Baptism is now the solemn ceremony of our admission to the Christian church. *Those who are baptized into Christ have put on Christ*; under the Gospel, baptism comes in place of circumcision.

3.3.1.2.2. In our baptism we put on Christ; we oblige ourselves to behave as his faithful servants. Being baptized into Christ, we are baptized into his death, so that as he died and rose again, so we might die to sin and live a new life. It would be of great advantage to us if we remembered this more often.

3.3.2. This privilege of being the children of God is now enjoyed in common by all true Christians. The Law distinguished between Jews and Gentiles, between *bond and free*, and between *male and female*. But it is not so now; now *all* stand on the same level *and are one in Christ Jesus*. All who sincerely believe in Christ, from whatever nation, sex, or condition, are accepted by him and become the children of God through faith in him.

3.3.3. *Being Christ's, we are Abraham's seed, and heirs according to the promise.* "If you sincerely believe in Christ, you become the true *seed of Abraham* and, as such, *are heirs according to the promise*, and so are entitled to the promise's great blessings and privileges." The Galatians were very unreasonable and unwise in listening to those who tried to deprive them of the truth and liberty of the Gospel.

CHAPTER 4

The apostle continues to pursue the same general purpose as in the previous chapter. He now draws in various considerations: 1. The superiority of the Gospel age to the legal (vv. 1–7). 2. The favorable change that was brought about in the Galatians at their conversion (vv. 8–11). 3. The affection they once had for him (vv. 12–16). 4. The character of the false teachers (vv. 17–18). 5. The warm affection he has for the Galatians (vv. 19–20). 6. The account of Isaac and Ishmael (vv. 21–31).

Verses 1–7

In this chapter the apostle deals plainly with those who listen to the Judaizing teachers.

1. He tells us about the state of the Old Testament church: it was like a young child. That was indeed an age of grace, but it was comparatively an age of darkness, because as an heir, being a minor, is *under tutors and governors till the time appointed of his father*, so it was with the Old Testament church. Moreover, it was an age of slavery as well as of darkness. The church then bore more of the character of *a servant*. When the time appointed by the Father had come, that darkness and slavery were removed, and now we are in an age of greater light and freedom.

2. He tells us about the much happier state in the Gospel age (vv. 4–7). *When the fulness of time had come, he sent forth his Son*, and in accordance with the great purpose the Son had undertaken, he submitted both to being *made of a woman* and to being *made under the Law*; there is his incarnation, and there is his submission.

2.1. One great purpose of this was *to redeem those that were under the law*.

2.2. He was sent to redeem us so *that we might receive the adoption of sons*—so that we would no longer be counted as servants, but as sons who have grown into mature adults. Under the Gospel, individual believers *receive the adoption*, the full rights of sons. And along with that, they have received the Spirit of adoption, enabling them to look on God in prayer as a Father (v. 6): *Because you are sons, God hath sent forth the Spirit of his Son into your hearts, crying Abba, Father.* Here (v. 7) the apostle concludes this argument: *Wherefore thou art no more a servant, but a son, and, if a son, then an heir of God through Christ*; now, we are no longer enslaved to the Law; now, when we believe in Christ, we become sons of God and, being sons of God, are also heirs of God. From vv. 1–7 we may notice:

2.2.1. The wonders of divine love and mercy toward us, especially that of God the Father in sending his Son into the world to redeem and save us; that of the Son of God in suffering so much for us; and that of the Holy Spirit in condescending to live in the hearts of believers for such gracious purposes.

2.2.2. The great and invaluable benefits Christians enjoy under the Gospel. We receive *the adoption of sons.* We who by nature are children of wrath and disobedience (Eph 2:2–3) have by grace become children of love. And we receive not only the adoption but also *the Spirit of adoption.* All who are received into God's family share in the nature of his children, because he wants all his children to resemble him. And those who have the nature of sons will receive the inheritance of sons.

Verses 8–11

1. He reminds them what they were before the Gospel was preached to them. Then *they knew not God.* They were under the worst form of slavery, because *they did service to those which by nature were no gods* and which were therefore completely unable to hear and help them. Those who are ignorant of the true God cannot help being inclined toward false gods.

2. He calls on them to consider the beneficial change brought about in them by the preaching of the Gospel. *They have known God, or rather, have been known of God.* This fortunate change in their state was not owing to them but to him. All our friendship with God begins with him; we know him because we are first known by him.

3. He infers from this the unreasonableness of their allowing themselves to be brought again into a state of slavery. *How turn you again,* he says (v. 9). "How is it that you, who have been taught to worship God in the Gospel way, could now be persuaded to submit to the ceremonial way of worship?" It is more inexcusable in them than in the Jews, who might have been expected to have some fondness for what lasted so long among them. Besides, what they have allowed themselves to be enslaved to are only *weak and beggarly elements* (weak and miserable principles), things that have no power in them to purify the soul. Both a comparison with the Jews and the consideration of the weakness of these principles, then, aggravate the Galatians' weakness and foolishness in submitting to the ceremonial law and in observing the Jews' various festivals—*days, and months, and times, and years.* Note here:

3.1. It is possible for those who have made great professions of faith to be later led terribly astray from its purity and simplicity.

3.2. The greater the mercy God has shown to anyone in leading them to a knowledge of the Gospel, the greater their sin and foolishness in allowing themselves to be deprived of the Gospel. This is what the apostle especially emphasizes with the Galatians.

4. He expresses his fears for them, that *he has bestowed on them labour in vain.* He has gone to a great deal of effort with them; now they are making all his efforts among them worthless, and he cannot help being deeply moved by this.

Verses 12–16

1. He addresses them warmly, calling them *brethren*, even though he knows their hearts are largely alienated from him. He wants them *to be as he is, for he is as they are*; and he assures them that *they have not injured* (wronged) *him at all.* He has no quarrel with them on his own account. This is how he seeks to soften their spirits toward him, so that they will receive the warnings he is giving them. In rebuking others we should take care to convince them that our rebukes do not come from any private animosity, but from a sincere desire for the honor of God and their truest welfare.

2. He praises their former affection. He reminds them of the difficulty he labored under when he first came among them: *You know how through infirmity of the flesh* (NIV: that it was because of an illness that) *I preached the Gospel unto you at the first.* We do not know for certain what this *infirmity of the flesh* was, but it seems to have made no disadvantageous impression on them. They did not despise him or treat him with contempt or scorn because of it, but, on the contrary, *received him as an angel of God, even as Christ Jesus*; they welcomed him as a messenger among them. In fact, their respect for him was so great that *they could have plucked out their own eyes, and have given them to him.* How uncertain the respect of human beings is, how easily they change their minds: they are ready to tear out the eyes of those for whom they would earlier have torn out their own!

3. He pleads with them about this: *Where is then the blessedness you spoke of?* "You once thought yourselves fortunate in receiving the Gospel; have you now any reason to think otherwise?" Those who have left their first love (Rev 2:4) would do well to ask themselves where all the joy that they once spoke of has gone. He again asks (v. 16), "*Am I become your enemy, because I tell you the truth?* How is it that I, who till now was your favorite, am now considered your enemy?" It is not uncommon for people to count as their enemies those who are really their best friends—for that is undoubtedly the proper name for those who tell them the truth. Ministers sometimes create enemies for themselves by faithfully discharging their duty, but they must not stop speaking the truth for fear of offending others. Indeed, they may rest easy when they know that if they have made any enemies, it was only by telling them the truth.

Verses 17–18

Here the apostle describes for the Galatians the character of those false teachers. He tells them those teachers are scheming men who aim to set themselves up. "*They zealously affect you* (they are zealous to win you over)," he says, "and claim to have a great deal of affection for you, *but not well*; they are not sincere, because *they would exclude you* (want to take you away from us), *that you might affect them* (so that you may be zealous for them). Their chief aim is to engage your affection for them." A great deal of zeal may be apparent where there is little truth and sincerity. Here the apostle gives us the excellent rule (v. 18), *It is good to be zealously affected always in a good thing* (it is fine to be zealous, provided the purpose is good). Some render the expression translated *in a good thing* as "to a good man," inferring that the apostle is referring to himself; they think this sense is favored by what immediately follows: *and not only when I am present with you*. It is a very good rule that zeal should be exercised only on what is good, for zeal is good only when it is for a good purpose. It is good to be zealous for a good purpose always; not only for a while, or now and then, sometimes blowing hot and sometimes blowing cold, but remaining as constant as the natural heat of the body is. It would be good for the church of Christ if this rule were observed more often among Christians!

Verses 19–20

1. The apostle here expresses his great affection for the Galatians. He is not like them—one thing when among them and completely different when absent from them. Nor is he like their false teachers, who claim to have a great deal of affection for them even though they are considering only their own interests. He calls them *his children*, as he justly may. In fact, he calls them his *little children*, which possibly alludes to their present behavior, by which they have shown themselves too much like little children. He expresses his concern for them. *He travails in birth for them, that Christ might be formed in them*, so that they may become true Christians. From this we may notice:

1.1. The warm affection that faithful ministers have toward those among whom they are employed; it is like that of the most affectionate parents toward their little children.

1.2. The chief thing ministers desire for their flocks: that Christ may be formed in them. How unreasonable must those people be who allow themselves to be prevailed on to abandon or dislike such ministers!

2. The apostle adds (v. 20) that *he desires to be present with them now*, so that he may find an opportunity to *change his voice* (change his tone) toward them, because at present *he stands in doubt of* (is perplexed about) *them*. He does not know what to think of them, but he would be glad to find that matters are better with them than he fears and to have an opportunity to commend them instead of rebuking them.

Verses 21–31

In these verses the apostle illustrates the difference between believers who rest only in Christ and those Judaizers who trust in the Law, using a comparison taken from the story of Isaac and Ishmael. *Tell me*, he says, *you that desire to be under the law, do you not hear* (are you not aware of) *the law?*

1. He sets before them the account itself (vv. 22–23): *For it is written, Abraham had two sons*. The one, Ishmael, *was by a bondmaid* (slave woman), and the other, Isaac, *by a free woman*. The first *was born after the flesh*, or by the ordinary course of nature; the second *was by promise*, when in the course of nature there was no reason to expect Sarah to have a son.

2. He tells them the meaning of this account (vv. 24–27): *These things*, he says, *are an allegory*. These two, Hagar and Sarah, *are the two covenants*. Hagar represents what was given from Mount Sinai and *gendereth to bondage* (bears children who are to be slaves). *For this Agar is mount Sinai in Arabia, and it answereth to Jerusalem which now is* (corresponds to the present city of Jerusalem), *and which is in bondage with her children*; that is, it justly represents the present state of the Jews, who, standing by that covenant, are still in slavery with their children. But Sarah was intended to prefigure the

Jerusalem that is above, which is free from both the curse of the moral law and the slavery of the ceremonial law, and *is the mother of us all*—a state into which all, both Jews and Gentiles, are admitted when they believe in Christ. To explain this greater freedom, the apostle refers to the prophet (Isa 54:1), where it is written, *Rejoice, thou barren that bearest not; break forth and cry, thou that travailest not* (you who have no labor pains); *for the desolate hath many more children than she who hath a husband*.

3. He applies the history to the present case (v. 28): *Now we, brethren, as Isaac was, are the children of the promise*. We Christians, who have accepted Christ and look for justification and salvation only through him, are also entitled to the promised inheritance. Paul tells them that *as then he that was born after the flesh persecuted him that was born after the Spirit*, they must expect that it will be *so now*. But he wants them to consider what the Scripture says (Ge 21:10): *Cast out* (get rid of) *the bondwoman and her son, for the son of the bondwoman shall not be heir with the son of the freewoman*. He concludes (v. 31), *So then, brethren, we are not children of the bondwoman, but of the free*.

CHAPTER 5

In applying his foregoing message, the apostle begins by issuing a general exhortation (v. 1), which he later supports by several considerations (vv. 2–12). He then urges them to exercise serious practical godliness. 1. He recommends that they not fight with one another (vv. 13–15). 2. He recommends that they fight against sin. Here he shows: 2.1. There is in everyone a struggle between the flesh and spirit (v. 17). 2.2. It is our duty to side with the better part (vv. 16, 18). 3. He specifies the works of the flesh and the fruit of the Spirit (vv. 19–24). He then concludes the chapter with a warning against pride and envy (vv. 25–26).

Verses 1–12

Since it is clear from what he has said that we can be justified only through faith in Jesus Christ, and that the Law of Moses is no longer in force, he wants them to *stand fast in the liberty wherewith Christ hath made us free, and not to be again entangled with* (not be burdened again by) *the yoke of bondage*. Under the Gospel we are set free, brought into a state of freedom. We owe this freedom to Jesus Christ. It is he who *has made us free*. It is our duty, therefore, to *stand fast in this liberty* and not to allow ourselves *to be again entangled* (not be burdened again).

1. The Galatians' submitting to circumcision and depending on the works of the Law for righteousness are a forfeiture of all the advantages they have gained by Jesus Christ (vv. 2–4). Notice the solemnity with which the apostle declares this: *Behold, I Paul say unto you* (v. 2); and he repeats it (v. 3): *I testify unto you that if you be circumcised, Christ shall profit you nothing* (if you let yourselves be circumcised, Christ will be of no value to you). He looks on it as a matter of the greatest importance that they not submit to it. That this is his meaning is clear from v. 4, where *if ye be circumcised* is replaced with *whosoever of you are justified by the law*. If they submit to circumcision in this sense, *Christ will profit them nothing* (Christ will be of no value to them); *they are debtors to do* (under an obligation to keep) *the whole law*. *Christ has become of no effect to them* (they have become separated from Christ), and *they are fallen*

from grace. They have renounced the way of justification that God has established. They are under an obligation to keep the whole law, which requires an obedience they are incapable of. Having rebelled from Christ and built their hopes on the law, they will neither gain anything nor be helped in any way by Christ. He will not be the Savior of anyone who will not confess and depend on him as their only Savior.

2. To persuade them to stand firm, he sets before them his own example and tells them what their hopes are: *through the Spirit they are waiting for the hope of righteousness by faith*. Notice:

2.1. What it is that Christians are waiting for: it is *the hope of righteousness*; the phrase is chiefly to be understood as referring to the happiness of the other world. This is the great object of their hope, which they desire and pursue above everything else, and it is only the righteousness of Christ that has obtained this world for us and assures us that we will be brought into possession of it.

2.2. How they hope to obtain this happiness, namely, through faith in our Lord Jesus Christ, not by observing the law.

2.3. Where they are waiting for the hope of righteousness to come from: *through the Spirit*. It is under his guidance and by his assistance they are enabled to believe in Christ and look for the hope of righteousness through him.

3. He tells them (v. 6) that *in Christ Jesus neither circumcision availeth any thing nor uncircumcision*. Now that Christ, who is *the end of the law*, has come, it is not significant whether a man is circumcised or not. He is neither better off for being circumcised nor worse off for not being so, nor will either the one or the other commend him to God. Paul informs the Galatians what will, and that is *faith, which worketh by love*. Without faith, nothing else will mean anything, and faith, where it is true, is a working grace, expressed in love for God and love for our brothers and sisters. Faith expressing itself by love is what is most important in our Christianity.

4. To reclaim them from their backsliding, he reminds them of their good beginnings.

4.1. He tells them that *they did run well*. The life of a Christian is a race, in which we must run and keep on running if we wish to obtain the prize. And it is not enough to run; we must run well. These Christians had done this for a while, but they were caused either to turn aside from that way or at least to falter in it.

4.2. He asks them, and calls on them to ask themselves, *Who did hinder you?* He knows very well who and what have hindered them, but he wants them to ask themselves the question. Many who set out promisingly in religious faith and run well for a while are still by some means or other hindered in their progress or turned aside from the path. Those who have run well but have now begun either to turn aside from the path or to tire in it should ask themselves what hinders them. Young converts must expect Satan to do all he can to divert them from the course they are following. The apostle tells the Galatians that by listening to the false teachers, they are kept from *obeying the truth*. The Gospel that he has preached to them is the truth. They must obey it and continue to govern their lives and hopes according to its directions. The truth is to be not only believed but also obeyed, to be received not only in its light but also in its love and power. Those who do not remain faithful to the truth do not rightly obey it.

5. To support his argument, he refers to the bad source of that *persuasion* (distraction) that has drawn them away

(v. 8): *This persuasion*, he says, *cometh not of him that calleth you*, that is, either God or the apostle himself. It could not have come from God, because it is against the way of justification and salvation he established; nor could it have come from Paul himself, because he has all along opposed, not preached, circumcision; he has never urged it on Christians, much less imposed it on them as necessary for salvation. He leaves them to judge from where it must have arisen; it could be owing to no one but Satan and his instruments. The Galatians have every reason to reject it and to remain firm in the truth they have embraced.

6. The danger that this infection might spread is a further argument that the apostle urges against the Galatians' complying with the false teachers. To convince them that they are endangering themselves more than they know, he tells them (v. 9) that *a little leaven leaveneth the whole lump*. The whole batch of the Christian community may be infected by one member, and so they should be greatly concerned to purify the infection from among them. The doctrine that the false teachers are assiduously spreading, and that some people in these churches have been drawn into, is subversive to Christianity itself, and therefore, considering its fatal tendency, he does not want them to rest easy and unconcerned.

7. He expresses the hopes he has for them (v. 10): *I have confidence in you, through the Lord, that you will be none otherwise minded* (that you will take no other view). He hopes that they will be brought to share his view, to acknowledge and remain faithful to the truth and freedom of the Gospel that he has preached to them. We should hope the best even of those about whom we have cause to fear the worst.

7.1. He lays the blame for it more on others than on the Galatians themselves, adding, *But he that troubleth you shall bear his judgment* (the one who is throwing you into confusion will pay the penalty), *whosoever he be*. In rebuking sin and error, we should always distinguish between the leaders and those who are led. In this way the apostle softens the fault of these Christians, even while he is rebuking them.

7.2. However, as for the one or ones who troubled them, he declares they *should bear their judgment*. He does not doubt that God will deal with these according to their deserts. He wishes that *they were even cut off*—not cut off from Christ and all hopes of salvation by him, but cut off by the discipline of the church, which should testify against those teachers who have corrupted the purity of the Gospel.

8. To dissuade these Christians from listening to their Judaizing teachers, he represents the teachers as people who have used corrupt methods to fulfill their purposes. They have misrepresented him. They have started the rumor among the Galatians that Paul himself is a preacher of circumcision, for when he says (v. 11), *And I, brethren, if I yet preach circumcision*, it is clear that they had reported him to have done so; but he utterly denies it. If he had preached circumcision, he might have avoided persecution. "If I still preach circumcision," he says, *why do I yet suffer persecution?* If he had fallen in with the Jews in this matter, then instead of being exposed to their rage, he might have been received into their favor. But he is so far from preaching the doctrine he is accused of that, rather than do so, he is willing to expose himself to the greatest dangers. If he had yielded to the Jews in this matter, *then would the offense of the cross have ceased*. But he chose instead to risk his comfort and reputation—indeed, even

his life—rather than corrupt Gospel truth and give up Gospel freedom.

Verses 13–26

In the second part of this chapter the apostle exhorts these Christians to exercise serious practical godliness.

1. They should not fight against one another, but love one another. He tells them (v. 13) that *they have been called unto liberty*, but he wants them to be very careful that they do not *use this liberty as an occasion to* (an opportunity to indulge) *the flesh*. On the contrary, he wants them *to serve one another by love*. The freedom we enjoy as Christians is not one that allows us to act presumptuously: although Christ has redeemed us from the curse of the Law, he has not freed us from obligation to it. Although we should stand firm in our Christian freedom, we should not insist on it in such a way that it leads to a breach in Christian love, but should always maintain an attitude toward one another that will incline us to serve one another in love. To persuade these Christians to follow this way, he sets out two considerations:

1.1. *That all the law is fulfilled in one word, even in this, Thou shalt love thy neighbour as thyself* (v. 14; Mt 19:19; Lev 19:18). Love is the essence of the whole law. It will be seen that we are the true disciples of Christ when we love one another (Jn 13:35), and if this attitude does not wholly extinguish those unfortunate conflicts among Christians, at least it will prevent their fatal consequences.

1.2. The dangerous tendency of a contrary disposition (v. 15): But, he says, *if you bite and devour one another, take heed that you be not consumed one of another.* If mutual conflicts among brothers and sisters are persisted in, they are likely to be the ruin of them all. Christian churches can be ruined only by their own hands, but if Christians act like wild animals, biting and devouring each other, what can be expected but that the God of love will deny his grace to them, that the Spirit of love will depart from them, and that the evil spirit will triumph?

2. They should all fight against sin, and it would be good for the church if Christians would let all their quarrels be swallowed up by a quarrel against sin. This is what we are chiefly concerned to fight against.

2.1. There is in everyone a struggle between the flesh and the spirit (v. 17): *The flesh lusts against the spirit.* On the other hand, *the spirit*—the renewed part of us—strives *against the flesh*, and so it happens *that we cannot do the things that we would.* Even as in a natural person there is something of this struggle—with the convictions of conscience and the corruption of the heart fighting against one another—so also in a renewed person there is a struggle between the old nature and the new nature, between the remnants of sin and the beginnings of grace. Christians must expect this as long as they remain in this world.

2.2. It is our responsibility and in our interests in this struggle to side with the better part, to side with our graces against our sinful desires. The apostle gives us this one general rule, to walk in the Spirit (v. 16): *This I say, then, Walk in the Spirit, and you shall not fulfil the lust of the flesh.* The duty commended to us here is that we set ourselves to act under the guidance and influence of the Holy Spirit. We may be assured that although we may not be freed from the stirrings of our corrupt nature, we will be kept from gratifying its sinful desires. Although it remains in us, it will not gain control of us. The best antidote to the poison of sin is to live by the Spirit. In the Galatians, it would also be good evidence that they were true Christians, because, as the apostle says (v. 18), *If you*

be led by the Spirit, you are not under the law. "If, in the prevailing course and tenor of your lives, you are *led by the Spirit*, it will be clear that you are not under the law, not under its condemning power, although you are still under its commanding power."

2.3. The apostle specifies the works of the flesh, which must be put to death, and the fruit of the Spirit, which must be lovingly tended and produced (v. 19).

2.3.1. He begins with *the works of the flesh*, which are both many and clear. Some are sins against the seventh commandment, such as *adultery, fornication, uncleanness, and lasciviousness* (sexual immorality, impurity, and debauchery). Some are sins against the first and second commandments, such as *idolatry* and *witchcraft*. Others are sins against our neighbor, such as *hatred, variance* (discord), *emulations* (jealousy), *wrath* (fits of rage), *strife, seditions* (dissension), *heresies*, and *envyings*, which sometimes break out into *murders*, not only of the names and reputations of our fellow creatures, but even of their lives. Others are sins against ourselves, such as *drunkenness and revellings* (orgies). Of these and *such like*, he says, *I tell you before, as I have also told you in times past*, that *those who do such things shall not inherit the kingdom of God.* These are sins that will undoubtedly shut people out of heaven.

2.3.2. He specifies the fruit of the Spirit, which it is our concern as Christians to produce (vv. 22–23). Just as sin is called *the work of the flesh*, because the flesh is the principle that moves people to it, so grace is said to be *the fruit of the Spirit*, because it wholly proceeds from the Spirit, as the fruit proceeds from the root.

2.3.2.1. Specifically, he commends to us *love; joy*, which may refer to constant delight in God; *peace* with God or a peaceful attitude toward others; *longsuffering*, or patience; *gentleness*, a kind attitude, which inclines us to be easy to deal with when anyone has wronged us; *goodness*, readiness to do good to everyone as we have opportunity; *faith*, faithfulness in what we profess and promise to others; *meekness*, or gentleness, by which we humbly control our passions so as not to be easily provoked and, when provoked, are quickly pacified; and *temperance*, or self-control.

2.3.2.2. Concerning those in whom this fruit of the Spirit is found, the apostle says, *There is no law against them.* They are not under the law, but under grace, because this fruit of the Spirit, in whomever it is found, plainly shows that such persons are *led by the Spirit*. Having told us by these lists both what to avoid and what to produce, the apostle informs us (v. 24) that this is the sincere concern and endeavor of all real Christians: *And those that are Christ's have crucified the flesh with the affections and lusts.* They are now sincerely seeking to die to sin (Ro 6:1), as Christ died for it. They have not yet obtained complete victory over it; they still have flesh as well as Spirit in them, and the flesh has its passions and desires, which continue to give them no little disturbance. But they are seeking the complete ruin and destruction of the flesh.

2.3.2.3. If we want to show ourselves to be approved as Christ's, we must make it our constant concern to put to death the flesh. Christ will never acknowledge as his those who yield themselves to be servants of sin (Ro 6:19): it is not enough that we stop doing evil; we must also learn to do good (Isa 1:16–17). Our Christianity obliges us not only to oppose the works of the flesh but also to produce the fruit of the Spirit. It must be our sincere desire and endeavor to do both.

2.3.2.4. That it was the apostle's intention to represent both as our duty may be gathered from what follows

(v. 25): *If we live in the Spirit, let us also walk in the Spirit.* He told us earlier that the Spirit of Christ is a privilege given to all the children of God (4:6). Let us show it by behavior that is consistent with that privilege; let us give evidence of our good principles by good practices. It must be by our *walking not after the flesh, but after the spirit.* We must set ourselves seriously both to put to death the sins the body commits and to live a new life.

2.4. The apostle concludes this chapter with a warning against pride and envy (v. 26). He warns them against becoming conceited, because this would certainly lead them to provoke and envy one another, laying a foundation for those quarrels and conflicts that are inconsistent with the love that Christians should have for each other. The apostle therefore wants us to watch against this in everything. This shows us:

2.4.1. The glory that comes from other people is worthless conceit, which, rather than seek, we should be dead to.

2.4.2. An undue desire for the applause of other people is one great basis of the unhappy strife and conflicts that arise among Christians.

CHAPTER 6

This chapter consists of two parts. 1. In the first part, the apostle gives us several practical instructions intended to teach Christians about their duties toward one another (vv. 1–10). 2. In the second part, he goes back to the main purpose of the letter, which is to strengthen the Galatians against the undermining work of their Judaizing teachers, to which end: 2.1. He gives the true description of these teachers (vv. 11–14). 2.2. He tells the Galatians about his own attitude and behavior. He then concludes the letter with a solemn blessing (vv. 15–18).

Verses 1–10

1. We are taught here to deal sympathetically with those who are *overtaken in a fault* (caught in a sin) (v. 1), that is, in sin because of an unexpected temptation. It is one thing to fall into sin by a deliberate act, another thing to be caught in a sin. Great sensitivity should be exercised. *Those who are spiritual* must *restore such a one with the spirit of meekness.* Notice:

1.1. The duty we are directed to—to restore such people. The original word means "to set (for example, a dislocated bone) in joint." We should seek to set the dislocated bone back in its proper condition, comforting such persons with a sense of forgiving mercy, confirming our love to them.

1.2. The way in which this is to be done: *with the spirit of meekness* (gentleness), not in wrath and passion, as those who gloat over the fall of a brother or sister. Many necessary rebukes lose their effectiveness by being given in anger, but when they are handled with sensitivity and from a sincere concern for the welfare of those to whom they are given, they are likely to make a proper impression.

1.3. A very good reason why this should be done with gentleness: *Considering thyself, lest thou also be tempted.* We should deal very sensitively with those who are caught in sin, knowing that we too may be caught up in a sin some time. This will make us do to others as we would wish to have them do to us in such a situation (Mt 7:12).

2. We are told here *to bear one another's burdens* (v. 2). This may be considered either as referring to what has gone before, thus teaching us to exercise patience and compassion toward one another, or as a more general command, instructing us to sympathize with one another in the various trials and troubles that we face. In doing so, we will *fulfil the law of Christ*, the law of his command, which is the law of love. We will also then conform with his pattern and example, which have the force of a law to us. Although as Christians we are freed from the Law of Moses, we are still under the law of Christ, and so, instead of putting unnecessary burdens on others, it is much better for us to fulfill the law of Christ by carrying one another's burdens. Knowing how great a hindrance pride is to the mutual grace he has been commending (v. 3), the apostle takes care to warn us against this. He thinks it very possible for a person to think of themselves as *something* when in truth they are nothing. Such a person is only deceiving themselves, even as they deceive others by pretending to be what they are not. They will not be either freer from mistakes or more secure against temptations because of the good opinion they have of their own sufficiency, but rather will be more liable to fall into the one and be overcome by the other, because *he that thinks he stands has need to take heed lest he fall* (1Co 10:12). Self-conceit is simply self-deceit. There is not a more dangerous deceit in the world than self-deceit.

3. Everyone is advised to *prove his own work* (test his own actions) (v. 4). By our *own work* is meant our own actions or behavior. The apostle tells us to test these, that is, seriously examine them by the rule of God's word. Instead of being eager to judge and criticize others, it would be much better if we examined ourselves and tested our own actions; our business lies more at home than away, more with ourselves than with other people. The best way to keep from being proud is to test ourselves: the more familiar we are with our own hearts and ways, the less liable we will be to despise others and the more inclined we will be to be compassionate toward them and help them. To persuade us to test ourselves, the apostle urges two considerations:

3.1. This is the way to *have rejoicing* (take pride) *in ourselves alone.* If we set ourselves seriously to test our own actions, this, he indicates, would be a much better basis for joy and satisfaction than to be able to rejoice *in another*, either in the good opinion others may have of us or in a comparison of ourselves with others. The joy that results from such things is nothing compared to what arises from testing ourselves by the rule of God's word and then being able to show ourselves approved by him. Although we have nothing to boast about in ourselves, we may still have things to rejoice about. If our consciences testify in our favor, we may find them to be a good basis for rejoicing. The true way to have *rejoicing in ourselves* is to be much involved in *proving our own works.* If we have the testimony of our consciences that we are accepted by God, we need not be very much concerned about what others think or say of us.

3.2. A day is coming when we must all give an account of ourselves to God (v. 5), and Paul declares that then the judgment will proceed, and the sentence pass, according to what our state and behavior have really been in the sight of God. If we are definitely to be called to account in the future, surely we should often be calling ourselves to account here, to see whether or not we are such as God will acknowledge and approve then. If this were more our practice, then instead of being harsh toward one another, we would be more ready to fulfill that law of Christ by which we must be judged on whether we have carried one another's burdens.

4. Christians are encouraged here to be free and generous in supporting their ministers (v. 6): *Let him that is taught in the word communicate to him that teacheth in all good things* (share all good things with his instructor). Notice:

4.1. As some are to be taught, so others are appointed to teach them. Reason itself directs us to distinguish between the teachers and the taught, and the Scriptures sufficiently declare that it is the will of God that we do so.

4.2. It is the word of God that ministers are to teach and instruct others in. It is the word of God that is the only rule of faith and life. Ministers are to be valued, then, only insofar as they speak according to this rule.

4.3. It is the duty of those who are taught the word to support those who are appointed to teach them, for they are to share *all good things*. It is only right and just that, while ministers are *sowing to others spiritual things, they should reap their carnal* (material) *things* (1Co 9:11).

5. Here is a warning to beware of mocking God or deceiving ourselves by imagining that he can be deceived by mere professions (v. 7): *Be not deceived; God is not mocked.* Many people tend to excuse themselves from undertaking the work of religious faith, though at the same time they may make an outward show of it, and in so doing they may deceive others, but they are only deceiving themselves if they think they can deceive God. Just as he cannot be deceived, so he will not be mocked. *Whatsoever a man soweth, that shall he also reap.* The present time is a time of sowing: in the other world there will be a great harvest. We will reap then as we now sow. Paul also informs us (v. 8) that just as there are two kinds of sowing, so there will be two kinds of reaping in the future: *If we sow to the flesh, we shall of the flesh reap corruption*; we will receive a paltry and short-lived satisfaction at present and ruin and misery in the end. On the other hand, *those who sow to the Spirit* may be assured that *of the Spirit they shall reap life everlasting*—they will have the truest comfort in their present way of life and have eternal life and happiness in the end. The God with whom we have to do (Heb 4:13) will certainly deal with us in the future not according to what we have professed but according to what we have actually practiced.

6. Here is a further warning, *not to be weary in well doing* (v. 9). There is in all of us too great a tendency to do this; we tend to flag and tire in fulfilling duty, but *in due season we shall reap, if we faint not* (if we do not give up). There is a reward in reserve for all who sincerely employ themselves in doing good, and even though our reward may be delayed, it will definitely come.

7. Here is an exhortation to all Christians to do good where they are (v. 10): *As we have therefore an opportunity.* It is not enough for us to be good ourselves; we must also do good to others.

7.1. The objects of this duty are all people. We are not to confine our love, kindness, and generosity within too narrow limits, but should be ready to extend it to all as far as we are capable. And yet we are to take special notice of *the household of faith.* Although others are not to be excluded, these are to be favored.

7.2. The rule we are to observe in doing good is *as we have opportunity.*

7.2.1. We should be sure to do it while we have opportunity, that is, while our life lasts. We must not, as too many do, neglect it in our lifetime and delay it until we come to die, under the pretense that we will do something good then by leaving something behind us for the good of others when we can no longer keep it ourselves. We should take care to do good in our lifetime, therefore; in fact, we should make this the work of our lives.

7.2.2. We should be ready to make the most of every opportunity. Whenever God gives us an opportunity to be useful to others, he expects us to make the most of it, according to our abilities. No one who stands in need of us is to be completely overlooked, yet a distinction is to be made between some and others.

Verses 11–18

The apostle seems to intend to end the letter here in v. 11, because he notes that as a particular mark of his respect for them, he has written this long letter with his own hand, not using another person as his secretary. But such is his affection for them that he cannot finish until he has once again given them a true description of their false teachers and an account of his own different attitude and behavior.

1. False teachers were those who *desired to make a fair show in the flesh* (make a good impression outwardly) (v. 12). They were very zealous for the externals of religion, though they had little or no regard for real godliness, because *neither do they themselves keep the law.* Frequently those who are most concerned to make a good outward show have least of the substance of religious faith. These teachers compelled the Gentile Christians to be circumcised *only lest they should suffer persecution* (to avoid being persecuted) *for the cross of Christ.* They wished to save their skins and all their worldly cargo, and did not care in the slightest if they shipwrecked their faith and a good conscience (1Ti 1:19). They had no more zeal for the Law than served their worldly intentions, because they wanted to have these Christians circumcised so *that they might glory in their flesh* (v. 13), so that they could say they had won them over to their side.

2. He tells us, on the other hand, about his own attitude and behavior.

2.1. His chief glory is the cross of Christ: *God forbid that I should glory* (boast), *save in the cross of our Lord Jesus Christ* (v. 14). This was what the Jews stumbled at and the Greeks considered foolishness (1Co 1:23), and the Judaizing teachers themselves wanted to mix the observance of the Law of Moses with faith in Christ as necessary to salvation. But Paul was so far from being offended by the cross of Christ that he boasted in it and rejected with the greatest abhorrence the thought of setting up anything to compete with it: *God forbid.* This was the basis for all his hope as a Christian, and whatever trials his faithfulness to it might bring on him, he was ready not only to submit to them but even to rejoice in them. There is the greatest reason why we should glory in the cross, for we owe all our joys and hopes to it.

2.2. He is dead to the world. Through Christ *the world has been crucified to him, and he to the world.* He has risen above both its smiles and its frowns and become as indifferent to it as one who is dying from it. The more we contemplate the sufferings that our dear Redeemer met with from the world, the less likely will we be to be in love with it.

2.3. He does not emphasize one or another aspect of his religious faith that is favored by one or another side among conflicting interests; instead his emphasis is on sound Christianity (v. 15).

2.3.1. What the false teachers emphasized so much Paul saw as insignificant. He knew very well that *in Jesus Christ neither circumcision avails any thing nor uncircumcision* (neither circumcision nor uncircumcision means anything) as to people's acceptance with God, *but a new creature* (what counts is a new creation).

2.3.2. Here he instructs us both as to what true religious faith consists in and as to what it does not consist in. It does not consist in our belonging to a certain denomination of Christians; it consists in our being new creations, in our being renewed in the spirit of our minds (Eph 4:23) and having Christ formed in us (Gal 4:19). It is a change of mind and heart, by which we are enabled to believe in the Lord Jesus and live a life of devotion to God. No external professions or particular names will ever be sufficient to commend us to him. If Christians were properly concerned to experience this in themselves and advance it in others, then even if it did not make them set aside their distinctive names, it would at least stop them from emphasizing them as much as they too often do.

2.3.3. The apostle declares a blessing on all who follow this rule: *And as many as walk according to this rule, peace be upon them, and mercy, and upon the Israel of God.* The blessings that he seeks or that he gives them the hope and prospect of—the words may be taken either as a prayer or a promise—are *peace and mercy.* A foundation is laid for these in the gracious change that is performed in believers. He declares that these will be the reward of *all the Israel of God,* all sincere Christians, whether Jews or Gentiles, all who are true Israelites. The Jews and Judaizing teachers wanted to confine these blessings to those who were circumcised. We can learn from this:

2.3.3.1. Real Christians are those who follow a rule, not a rule that they themselves have devised, but what God himself has prescribed for them.

2.3.3.2. Even those who walk according to this rule stand in need of the mercy of God.

2.3.3.3. All who sincerely seek to follow this rule may be assured that peace and mercy will be on them. This is the best way to have peace with God, and, having that

peace, we may be assured both of the favor of God now and of his mercy in the future.

2.4. He has cheerfully suffered persecution for the sake of Christ and Christianity (v. 17). He has already suffered much in the cause of Christ, because *he bears in his body the marks of the Lord Jesus,* the scars of the wounds he has sustained from enemies who have persecuted him because of his faithfulness to him. With a fitting warmth and passion, appropriate to his authority as an apostle and his deep concern, he insists that no one trouble him from now on by opposing his message or authority, or by any such insults as have been hurled at him. It may justly be presumed that people are fully convinced of those truths in the defense of which they are willing to suffer, and it is very unjust to accuse others of things that are contrary not only to their profession but also to their sufferings.

3. The apostle concludes the letter with his apostolic blessing (v. 18). He calls them his *brethren* and takes his leave of them with a very affectionate prayer that *the grace of our Lord Jesus Christ may be with their spirit.* This was a usual farewell wish of the apostle's (see Ro 16:20; 1Co 16:23). Here he prays that they would enjoy the favor of Christ, all the grace that is necessary to establish them in their Christian journey and to encourage and comfort them in all the trials of life and the prospect of death itself. Although these churches have done enough to forfeit their grace, nevertheless, out of his great concern for them, he sincerely desires it for them, that it will *be with their spirit,* that they will continually experience its influence on their souls. We need desire nothing more to make us happy than the grace of our Lord Jesus Christ. He then adds his *Amen,* to encourage both them and us to hope for this grace.

A PRACTICAL AND DEVOTIONAL
EXPOSITION OF

Ephesians

Some think that this letter to the Ephesians was a circular letter sent to several churches. It is the only one of all Paul's letters that has nothing in it especially adapted to the case of that particular church, but it has much of common concern to all Christians. It is a letter written from prison, and some have noticed that what this apostle wrote when he was a prisoner contained matters concerning the things of God that he most delighted in. When his troubles were many, his comforts were even greater. The apostle's intention is to settle and establish the Ephesians in the truth, and he therefore informs them further about the mystery of the Gospel. In the first part he represents the great privilege of the Ephesians, who are now converted to Christianity and received into covenant with God (chs. 1–3). In the second part he instructs them about the main duties of religion (chs. 4–6).

CHAPTER 1

We have here: 1. *The introduction to the whole letter (vv. 1–2). 2. The apostle's thanksgivings and praises to God for his inestimable blessings given to the believing Ephesians (vv. 3–14). 3. His fervent prayers to God for them (vv. 15–23).*

Verses 1–2

Here is:

1. The title Paul takes for himself—Paul, *an apostle of Jesus Christ*. He was such *by the will of God*. Every faithful minister of Christ may, with our apostle, reflect on it as an honor that they are what they are *by the will of God* (1Co 15:10).

2. The people to whom this letter is sent: *to the saints who are at Ephesus.* He called them saints because that was what they professed, and many of them were such. All Christians must be saints. He called them *the faithful in Christ Jesus.* Those who are not faithful are not saints. They were saints *in Christ Jesus*, from whom they derived all their grace and spiritual strength.

3. The apostolic blessing: *Grace be to you.* By *grace* we are to understand the free and undeserved love and favor of God and the graces of the Spirit that come from that love and favor; by *peace*, all other blessings, the fruits and product of grace. There can be no peace without grace. No peace or grace comes except *from God the Father, and from the Lord Jesus Christ.* These distinctive blessings come from God not as a Creator but as a Father, and they come from our Lord Jesus Christ, who has a right to give them. The saints and the faithful in Christ Jesus have already received grace and peace, but even the best saints stand in constant need of fresh supplies of the graces of the Spirit. They should pray, therefore, each for themselves and all for one another, that such blessings may continue to overflow to them. The Spirit of God saw fit that Paul's discussion of divine things in this chapter would be put in the form of prayers and praises. Prayer may preach, and so may praise.

Verses 3–14

He begins with thanksgiving and praise, discoursing at length on the extremely great and precious benefits we enjoy through Jesus Christ.

1. He blesses God for *spiritual* blessings (v. 3), calling him *the God and Father of our Lord Jesus Christ*. All blessings come from God as the Father of our Lord Jesus Christ. *He hath blessed us with all spiritual blessings.* Spiritual blessings are the best blessings. He blesses us by giving us things that make us truly blessed. We cannot bless God in the same way in response, but we can bless him by praising. Those whom God blesses with some spiritual blessings he blesses with all spiritual blessings, though it is not so with temporal blessings. These blessings are *spiritual blessings in heavenly places*. Or it may read "in heavenly things," referring to things that come from heaven and are intended to prepare people for it. We should learn from this to be concerned for spiritual and heavenly blessings as the best blessings, with which we cannot be miserable and without which we must be.

2. Particular spiritual blessings are enlarged on.

2.1. Election and predestination (vv. 4–5, 11). *Election*, or choice, concerns that whole batch or mass of the human race from which believers are set apart. Predestination concerns the blessings they are intended for, especially *the adoption of children*, that at the appropriate time we would become his adopted children and so enjoy the right to all the privileges of children. The Ephesians were chosen *before the foundation of the world*; they were chosen in the purpose of God from all eternity. The gifts one gives beggars at the door come from a sudden decision, but the provision parents make for their children is the result of much thought. God acts in accordance with his eternal purposes in giving spiritual blessings to his people. *He hath blessed us according as he hath chosen us in him*, in Christ, the great head of election. One great purpose and intention in this choice was *so that we would be holy*. All who are chosen for eternal life as their goal are chosen for holiness as the means. They were chosen to be *without blame before him* — so that their holiness would not be merely external and in outward appearance but also internal and real, the holiness that comes from love for God and our fellow creatures, this charity being the source of all true holiness. Here is also the rule and the primary cause of God's election: it is *according to the good pleasure of his will* (v. 5); he chose them because it was his sovereign will. It is *according to the purpose of him who worketh all things after the counsel of his own will* (v. 11). The last and great purpose is his own glory: *To the praise of the glory of his grace* (v. 6), *that we should be to the praise of his glory* (v. 12). The glory of God is his own ultimate aim, and it should also be ours in everything we do.

2.2. Acceptance with God through Jesus Christ: *Wherein he hath made us accepted in the beloved* (v. 6). We cannot be accepted by God except in and through Jesus Christ. God loves his people for the sake of *the beloved*.

2.3. Forgiveness of sins and redemption through the blood of Jesus (v. 7). There can be no forgiveness without redemption. The guilt and the stain of sin could be removed only by the blood of Jesus. All our spiritual blessings flow to us in that stream. And they flow to us according to the riches of God's grace. It was rich grace that provided such a security as his own Son, when nothing of that nature could have entered into our thoughts or have been found for us in any other way. He has not only revealed the riches of grace but *has abounded toward us in all wisdom and prudence* (understanding) (v. 8).

2.4. Divine revelation — that God has *made known to us the mystery of his will* (v. 9). We owe this revelation to Christ, who came to declare God's will to human beings. God made it known *according to his good pleasure which he had purposed*. It is described (v. 13) *as the word of truth* and *the Gospel of our salvation*. Oh, how we should value this glorious Gospel and bless God for it!

2.5. Union in and with Christ, which is a great privilege. *He gathers* (brings) *together in one all things in Christ* (v. 10). All the lines of divine revelation meet in Christ; all religion centers on him. Jews and Gentiles were united with each other by both being united with Christ. *Things in heaven and things on earth* are brought together in him; through him peace is made between heaven and earth. The innumerable company of angels become one with the church through Christ: God *purposed* this *in himself*.

2.6. The eternal inheritance, which is the great blessing with which we are blessed in Christ: *In whom also we have obtained an inheritance* (v. 11). Heaven is the inheritance, the gift of a Father to his children. *If children, then heirs* (Ro 8:17). All the blessings we have in our hands are only small in comparison with the inheritance. What is spent on heirs when they are children is nothing compared to what is reserved for them when they come of age.

2.7. The seal and pledge of the Spirit (2Co 1:22; 5:5). We are said to be *sealed with that Holy Spirit of promise*, that is, the promised Spirit (v. 13). He makes us holy. By him believers are sealed and set apart for God. The Spirit is *the earnest* (pledge) *of our inheritance* (v. 14). An earnest is a partial payment, a deposit that guarantees the full sum. All the Spirit's influences are heaven begun, glory in the seed and bud. His comforts are a deposit guaranteeing eternal joys. He is said to be the deposit *until the redemption of the purchased possession*. This deposit makes it as certain to the heirs as though they already possessed it, and it has been purchased for them by the blood of Christ. The great purpose and intention of God in giving all these spiritual privileges *was that we who first trusted in Christ would be to the praise of his glory*. Seniority in grace is an advancement: those who have experienced the grace of Christ for a longer time are under more special obligations to glorify God. This is the great intention of God in everything he has done for us: it is *unto the praise of his glory* (v. 14).

Verses 15–23

We have here Paul's heartfelt prayer to God on behalf of the Ephesians. He gives thanks for spiritual blessings and prays for more of them. God has stored up these spiritual blessings for us in the hands of his Son, and he has appointed us to draw them out in prayer. We have no share in the matter (Ac 8:21) unless we claim it by faith and prayer. One incentive Paul had to pray for the Ephesians was the good account he had received *of their faith in the Lord Jesus and love to all the saints* (v. 15). Those who love the saints as saints love all of them, however much some of them may be weak in grace, however insignificant in the world, or even however perverse some of them may be. Another incentive the apostle had to pray for them was that they had received the deposit of their inheritance. *Wherefore I cease not to give thanks for you, making mention of you in my prayers* (v. 16). While he blessed God for giving them the Spirit, he did not stop praying (v. 17) that God would give greater measures of the Spirit. The great thing he prayed for was the enlightenment of their understandings and the increase of their knowledge; he is referring to a practical, experiential knowledge. The graces, strengths, and encouragements of the Spirit are communicated to the soul by the enlightening of the understanding. Satan takes an opposite way: he gains possession through the senses and passions; Christ does so through the understanding. Notice:

1. From where this knowledge must come: from *the God of our Lord Jesus Christ* (v. 17). *The Lord is a God of knowledge* (1Sa 2:3), and there is no sound, saving knowledge except what comes from him. He gives knowledge by giving the Spirit of knowledge, because the Spirit of God is the teacher of the saints, *the Spirit of wisdom and revelation*. We have the revelation of the Spirit in the word, but what good will that do us if we do not have the wisdom of the Spirit in the heart? Paul prays that God will give the Ephesians this Spirit *in the knowledge of him*. This knowledge is first in the *understanding* (heart). He prays that *the eyes of their understanding* (heart) *may be enlightened* (v. 18). Christians should not think it enough to have warm affections; they should also seek to have clear understandings; they should seek to be knowledgeable, discerning Christians.

2. What it is that he more especially desires they grow in the knowledge of.

2.1. *The hope of his calling* (v. 18). There is a hope in this calling, for those who deal with God deal on trust. We should seek and pray fervently for a clearer insight into and a fuller knowledge of the great objects of a Christian's hopes.

2.2. *The riches of the glory of his inheritance in the saints.* Besides the heavenly inheritance prepared for the saints, there is also a present inheritance in the saints, because grace is glory begun, and holiness is budding happiness. There is a glory in this inheritance, and it is good to know this in our own experience. The phrase may be understood as referring to the glorious inheritance in heaven, where God, as it were, displays all his riches. Let us seek, therefore, by reading, contemplation, and prayer, to know as much of heaven as we possibly can, so that we may desire and long to be there.

2.3. *The exceeding greatness of God's power toward those who believe* (v. 19). It is difficult to bring a soul to believe in Christ. It is something that nothing less than God's almighty power will work in us. The apostle speaks as if he lacked words to express the *exceeding greatness of God's almighty power*, the power that God exerts toward his people and by which *he raised Christ from the dead* (v. 20). That indeed was the great proof of the truth of the Gospel to the world, but the copy of that in ourselves, our sanctification and our rising from the death of sin, is the great proof to us. Many people understand the apostle here as speaking about the *exceeding greatness of power* that God will exert to raise believers to eternal life, even the same *mighty power which he wrought in Christ when he raised him*. How good it must be to finally come to know that power by being raised by it to receive eternal life!

3. The apostle digresses a little to make mention of the Lord Jesus and his exaltation. He sits at the Father's *right hand in the heavenly places* (vv. 20–21). The Father *hath put all things under his feet* (v. 22). God *gave him to be head over all things*. It was a gift to Christ. It was also a gift to the church to be provided with a head endowed with so much power and authority. The Father gave him all power both in heaven and on earth (Mt 28:18). *The Father loves the Son, and hath given all things into his hands* (Jn 3:35). But what completes the comfort of this is that Christ is the head over all things *for the church*. The same power that supports the world supports the church, and we are sure he loves his church, because it *is his body* (v. 23), and he will care for it. It is *the fulness of him that filleth all in all*. Jesus Christ fills everything in every way. Christ as Mediator would not be complete if he did not have a church. How could he be a king if he did not have a kingdom?

CHAPTER 2

This chapter contains an account: 1. Of the miserable condition of these Ephesians in their natural state (vv. 1–3 and again vv. 11–12). 2. Of the glorious change that was brought about in them (vv. 4–10 and again v. 13). 3. Of the great privileges that both converted Jews and Gentiles receive from Christ (vv. 14–22). We have here, therefore, a vivid description of both the misery of unregenerate people and the happy condition of converted souls.

Verses 1–3

The miserable condition of the Ephesians by nature is described in part here.

1. Unregenerate souls are *dead in trespasses and sins*. All those who are in their sins are dead in sins. Sin is the death of the soul. Wherever that reigns, there is a deprivation of all spiritual life.

2. A state of sin is a state of conformity to this world (v. 2). "*Wherein in time past you walked*; you lived and behaved as the people of the world do."

3. We are by nature slaves to sin and Satan. Those who follow the course of this world live *according to the prince of the power of the air*. Evildoers are slaves to Satan. The course and tendency of their lives are according to his suggestions; they are subject to him and are led captive by him at his will, which is why he is called the god of this world and *the spirit that now worketh in the children of disobedience*. As the good Spirit produces what is good in obedient souls, so this evil spirit produces what is evil in evildoers. He *now works*; he has been working as long as

the world has been blessed with the light of the glorious Gospel. *Among whom also we all had our conversation in times past.*

4. We are by nature slaves to the flesh and to our corrupt feelings (v. 3). By *fulfilling the desires* (gratifying the cravings) *of the flesh and of the mind*, people succumb to everything that defiles flesh and spirit. We lived in the actual committing of all the sins to which corrupt nature inclined us. The sinful mind makes a person a complete slave to their evil appetite. The words may also be rendered, "the fulfilling of the wills of the flesh."

5. We are *by nature the children of wrath, even as others*. One person is so as much as another by nature, not only by custom and imitation but also because of our natural inclinations and appetites. Our state and way of life are such as deserve wrath, and they would end in eternal wrath if divine grace did not intervene. What reason have sinners, then, to look for that grace that will turn them from children of wrath to children of God and heirs of glory!

Verses 4–10

We have here the glorious change that was brought about in the Ephesians by converting grace. Notice:

1. By whom and how it was brought about: *Not of yourselves* (v. 8). *Not of works, lest any man should boast* (v. 9). These things do not come about by anything we have done. There is no room for anyone to boast of their own abilities and power, or as though they themselves had done anything that might deserve such immense favors from God. *But God, who is rich in mercy* (v. 4). God himself is the author of this great and happy change. Love is his inclination to do us good simply because we are creatures; mercy deals with us as apostate and miserable creatures. That love of God is great, and his mercy is *rich*. *By grace you are saved* (v. 5), and *by grace are you saved through faith—it is the gift of God* (v. 8). All converted sinners are saved sinners. The grace that saves them is the free undeserved goodness and favor of God. He saves them not *by the works of the law* but through faith in Christ Jesus. Both that faith and that salvation are the gift of God. God has arranged everything so that the whole will be seen to be of grace.

2. In what this change consists.

2.1. We who were dead are *quickened* (made alive) (v. 5). Grace in the soul is new life there. Just as death seals up all the powers and faculties, so does a state of sin as to anything that is good. Grace unlocks and opens everything; it releases the soul. A regenerate sinner becomes a living soul (Ge 2:7), being born of God (Jn 1:13). *He hath quickened us together with Christ*. It is in Christ that we live: *Because I live, you shall live also.*

2.2. We who were buried are raised up (v. 6). When he raised Christ from the dead, he in effect raised up all believers together with him, and when he put him at his right hand in the heavenly realms, he advanced and glorified them in and with *him. And made us sit together in heavenly places in Christ Jesus*. Sinners roll in the dust; sanctified souls are seated in the heavenly realms; the world is as nothing to them, compared with what it has been and compared with what the other world is. They are also exalted to reign with him; they sit on the throne with Christ.

3. The great purpose of God in bringing about this change.

3.1. With respect to others: *That in the ages to come he might show* (v. 7), so that he could give proof of his great goodness and mercy to encourage sinners in the future. The goodness of God in saving sinners up to that time is a proper encouragement to others in later times to hope in his grace and mercy. Because this is God's purpose, poor sinners should take great encouragement from it.

3.2. With respect to the regenerated sinners themselves: *For we are his workmanship, created in Christ Jesus unto good works* (v. 10). *We are his workmanship* not only as people but also as saints. The new being is a new creature; God is its Creator. We are created *in Christ Jesus,* that is, on account of what he has done and suffered. We are created *unto good works.* So as not to seem to discourage good works, the apostle comments here that God, in his new creation, has intended us for good works: we were *created unto good works.* They are good works *which God hath before ordained that we should walk in them,* or glorify God by an exemplary life and by our perseverance in holiness.

Verses 11 – 13

1. The apostle proceeds to describe the miserable natural condition of these Ephesians. *Wherefore remember* (v. 11). Converted sinners should frequently reflect on the sinfulness and misery of the state they were in by nature. The Ephesians were *Gentiles in the flesh,* that is, living in the sinfulness of their natures. They were *called uncircumcision by that*; that is, "You were criticized and rebuked for it by the formal Jews." Here is the misery of their case (v. 12). "*At that time* you were:

1.1. "In a Christless condition, without any saving relationship with the Messiah." It is sad and deplorable for a soul to be without Christ. Being without Christ, they were:

1.2. *Aliens from the commonwealth of* (excluded from citizenship in) *Israel*; they did not belong to Christ's church. It is a marvelous privilege to be placed in the church of Christ and to share in its special advantages.

1.3. *Strangers from* (foreigners to) *the covenants of promise,* so called because it is made up of promises. The Ephesians, being Gentiles, were foreigners to this covenant. All unregenerate sinners are strangers to it.

1.4. Without hope. Those who are without Christ and are foreigners to the covenant can have no good hope. The Ephesians were in a state of separation from God: *without God in the world.* The words mean literally "atheists in the world," because although they worshiped many gods, they were still without the true God.

2. The favorable change that was made in their state: *But now, in Christ Jesus, you who sometimes were far off.* They had been far off from Christ and from God himself, and therefore from all good. "*But now in Christ Jesus,* you have been brought near." They were brought back home to God. God is an ever-present help (Ps 46:1) to his people. His people are brought near *by the blood of Christ.* Every believing sinner owes their closeness to God to the death and sacrifice of Christ.

Verses 14 – 22

We now come to the great privileges that converted Jews and Gentiles both receive from Christ. Those who were in a state of enmity have been reconciled. Jesus Christ is our peace (v. 14).

1. He made peace, and he came to reconcile Jews and Gentiles to each other. He *made both one.* He *broke down the middle wall of partition* (the dividing wall of hostility), the ceremonial law, which is called *the partition wall* by way of allusion to the partition in the temple that separated the court of the Gentiles from the one into which

only the Jews were free to enter. By this sacrifice *he abolished in his flesh the enmity* (v. 15). Through his sufferings in the flesh, he took away the binding power of the ceremonial law, *the law of commandments contained in ordinances.* By removing these, he formed one church of believers, whether they had been Jews or Gentiles before. This is how he made *in himself of twain* (two) *one new man.* He joined both these parties into one new community, *so making peace.*

2. There is a hostility between God and sinners, whether Jews or Gentiles. Christ came to put to death that enmity and to reconcile them both to God (v. 16). Sin breeds a quarrel between God and humanity. Christ came to take up the quarrel, and to bring it to an end, and this by *the cross, having slain the enmity thereby.*

2.1. The apostle illustrates the great advantages that both parties gain (v. 17). Christ came partly in his own person, as to the Jews, who are said here to have been near, and partly in his apostles to the Gentiles, who are said to have been far off. *And preached peace,* reconciliation with God.

2.2. Now the effect of this peace is the free access that both Jews and Gentiles have to God (v. 18): *For through him we both have access.* The throne of grace has been set up for us to come to, and we are free to approach that throne. Christ purchased for us permission to come to God, and the Spirit gives us a heart to come.

2.3. Since the Ephesians have now gained such access, the apostle tells them, *Now therefore you are no more strangers and foreigners* (v. 19). They were now no longer *aliens from the commonwealth of Israel, but fellowcitizens with the saints, and of the household of God.* The church is compared to a city, and every converted sinner has been given the privileges of freedom of that city. The church is also compared to a house, and every converted sinner is one of the family, a servant and a child in God's house.

2.4. In v. 20 the church is compared to a building. The apostles and prophets are *the foundation* of that building, *Jesus Christ himself being the chief corner stone.* Christ supports the building by his strength: *In whom all the building, fitly framed* (joined) *together* (v. 21). Because all believers are united to Christ through faith and have among themselves Christian love, they *grow unto a holy temple,* in which there is much fellowship between God and his people. The church is the place where God has chosen to put his name (1Ki 8:29), and it becomes such a temple by grace and power derived from him. It becomes a temple *in the Lord, in whom you also are built together* (v. 22). Every true believer is a living temple, a *habitation* (dwelling place) *of God through the Spirit.* God lives in all believers now, which is a pledge of their living with him to eternity.

CHAPTER 3

This chapter consists of two parts. 1. The account Paul gives the Ephesians about himself (vv. 1 – 13). 2. His devout and affectionate prayer to God for the Ephesians (vv. 14 – 21). We may notice that it was very much the practice of this apostle to mix his instructions and advice with intercessions and prayers to God. All his instructions and teachings would be worthless and futile unless God cooperated with them, making them effective.

Verses 1 – 13

We have here the account Paul gives the Ephesians of himself as one who was appointed by God to be the apostle to the Gentiles.

1. He tells them about the troubles and sufferings he has endured (v. 1). The first clause may be understood in either of two ways:

1.1. "*For this cause*—for asserting that the great privileges of the Gospel belong not only to the Jews but also to believing Gentiles, for this reason I am now a prisoner, but *a prisoner of Jesus Christ*." If Christ's servants come to be prisoners, they are his prisoners (Ps 69:33). Even when Paul was in prison, he remained faithful to Christ and Christ recognized him. *For you, Gentiles*: the Jews persecuted and imprisoned him because he was the apostle to the Gentiles and preached the Gospel to them. The faithful ministers of Christ are to communicate his sacred truths, whatever they themselves may suffer for doing so.

1.2. "*For this cause*, since *you are no more strangers and foreigners* (2:19) but are united with Christ, I pray that you may be enabled to act as befits people who have been favored in this way." He speaks again about his sufferings: *Wherefore I desire that you faint not* (not be discouraged) *at my tribulation for you, which is your glory* (v. 13). While he was in prison, he suffered much; he did not want them to be discouraged or dismayed at this. The apostle seems to have been more concerned that they might become discouraged because of his sufferings than about what he himself was going through. His sufferings were their glory. God sent his apostles not only to preach the Gospel to them but even to suffer for them.

2. He informs them about God's appointing him to this ministry by a special revelation.

2.1. God appointed him to the ministry: *If you have heard of the dispensation* (administration) *of the grace of God, which is given me to you-ward* (v. 2). He calls the Gospel *the grace of God* because it is the gift of divine grace to sinners. It is also the great instrument in the hands of the Spirit by which God works grace in human souls. *Whereof I was made a minister* (v. 7). He was *made a minister*—he did not give himself such an honor—*according to the gift of the grace of God unto* him. God equipped him for his work *by the effectual working of his power*, in Paul himself especially, and also in great numbers of those to whom he preached. What God calls people to, he equips them for, and he does so with his almighty power.

2.2. God qualified him eminently for it by a special revelation

2.2.1. The mystery revealed is *that the Gentiles would be fellow heirs, and of the same body, and partakers of his promise in Christ, by the Gospel* (v. 6). And they would be so joined to one another *in Christ*—being united to Christ, *in whom all the promises are yea and amen* (2Co 1:20)—and *by the Gospel*. This was the great truth revealed to the apostles.

2.2.2. He received this truth by revelation (vv. 3–5). The coalition of Jews and Gentiles in the Gospel church was a mystery. It is called a mystery because its many different circumstances were concealed and kept secret within God's own heart. It is called *the mystery of Christ* because it was revealed by him and concerns him so much. The apostle has given some hints about this *afore*, in the preceding chapters. *Whereby, when you read*, or, as those words may read, "giving attention to which"—it is not enough for us merely to read the Scriptures; we must also give our attention to them—*whereby* you *may understand my knowledge in the mystery of Christ. This mystery in other ages was not made known unto the sons of men, as it is now revealed unto his holy apostles and prophets by the Spirit* (v. 5). Who would have imagined that those who had been so long in the dark and so far

away would be enlightened with the marvelous light and be brought near? Let us learn from this not to despair of the worst, of the worst people and the worst nations. No one is so unworthy that God may not be pleased to lavish his great grace on them.

3. He informs them how he was employed in this ministry for the Gentiles and all people.

3.1. Concerning the Gentiles, he has *preached* to them *the unsearchable riches of Christ* (v. 8). Notice:

3.1.1. How humbly he speaks of himself: *I am less than the least of all saints.* The apostle Paul, who was the chief of the apostles, calls himself *less than the least of all saints*. What can be less than the least? To make himself appear as insignificant as possible, he speaks of himself as less significant than possible. Where God gives grace to be humble, he also gives all other graces. While Paul magnifies his office (Ro 11:13), he humbles himself.

3.1.2. How highly he speaks of Jesus Christ: *The unsearchable riches of Christ.* There is a vast treasure of mercy, grace, and love stored in Christ Jesus for both Jews and Gentiles. They are *unsearchable* riches, which we cannot fathom the bottom of. It was the apostle's business and employment to *preach* these *unsearchable riches of Christ among the Gentiles.* "*Unto me is this grace given*; this special favor God has given to such an unworthy creature as I." It is also an indescribable favor to the Gentile world that *the unsearchable riches of Christ* are preached to them. Although many remain poor, not made rich with these riches, if we are not made rich by them, we have only ourselves to blame.

3.2. Concerning all people (v. 9), he was employed *to make all men see what is the fellowship of the mystery which from the beginning of the world hath been hid in God, who created all things by Jesus Christ.* It is hardly surprising that he saves the Gentiles as well as the Jews, because he is the common Creator of them both. *To the intent that now unto the principalities and powers in heavenly places might be known, by the church, the manifold wisdom of God* (v. 10). God wanted the good angels to be informed *of the manifold wisdom of God*, that is, of the wide range of ways in which God wisely dispenses things, or of many different ways he uses in organizing his church, especially in receiving the Gentiles into it. All this is *according to the eternal purpose which he purposed in Christ Jesus our Lord* (v. 11). Having mentioned our Lord Jesus Christ, the apostle adds about him, *In whom we have boldness and access with confidence by the faith of him* (v. 12). We are permitted to open our hearts freely to God, as to a Father. We may come with humble boldness to hear from God, and we may expect to hear *good words and comfortable words* (Zec 1:13) from him.

Verses 14–21

Here is Paul's affectionate prayer to God for his dear Ephesians. *For this cause.* This may refer to the immediately previous verse (v. 13), *that you faint not* (not be discouraged), or, rather, the apostle is here resuming what he began at v. 1. Notice:

1. To whom he prays—to God, as *the Father of our Lord Jesus Christ.*

2. His posture: *I bow my knees.* When we draw near to God, we should have reverence for him in our hearts and express our reverence in the best behavior. The universal church depends on the Lord Jesus Christ: *Of whom the whole family in heaven and earth is named.* This refers to the saints in heaven, who wear the crown of glory, and the saints on earth, who are continuing the work of grace

here. The one and the other make up only one family, and from him they are *named* Christians.

3. What the apostle asks God to give these friends—spiritual blessings. He prays:

3.1. For spiritual power for the work to which they are called. *That he would grant you, according to the riches of his grace, to be strengthened.* The apostle prays that this may be *according to the riches of his glory,* or according to his glorious riches, and through his Spirit. Power from the Spirit of God in the inner being is the best and most desirable form of power.

3.2. For the indwelling of Christ in their hearts (v. 17). Christ dwells in the soul of every true Christian. Where his Spirit dwells, there he dwells, and he dwells in the heart through faith. Faith opens up the door of the soul to receive Christ; faith admits him and submits to him. Through faith we are united with Christ.

3.3. For the establishing of devotions in the soul: *That you, being rooted and grounded in love.* Many have some love for God and his people, but it is like a flash, like the burning of thorns under a pot (Ecc 7:6): it makes a great noise but is quickly gone. We should wholeheartedly wish for good affections to be established in us. Some understand this as referring to the Ephesians' being settled and established in the sense of God's love for them. It is very good to have an established assurance of the love of God and Christ toward our souls, so that we can say with the apostle at all times, *He has loved me!* (Gal 2:20). The best way to obtain this is to be careful that we maintain a constant love for God in our souls.

3.4. That they may know the love of Jesus Christ in their own experience. *That you may be able to comprehend with all saints* (vv. 18–19). Christians should not aim to grasp more than all the saints, but we should try to grasp *with all saints,* to have as much knowledge as the saints are allowed in this world. How magnificently the apostle speaks of the love of Christ. The dimensions of redeeming love are wonderful: *the breadth, and length, and depth, and height.* By listing these dimensions, the apostle wants to show the surpassing greatness of the love of Christ, the unsearchable riches of his love (v. 8). We should seek to grasp this love: it is a characteristic of all saints to do so. He prays that they may *know the love of Christ which passeth knowledge* (v. 19). If it surpasses knowledge, how can we know it? We must pray and want to know something of it and should continually seek to know more and more of it, even though no one can fully grasp it, because in its full extent it surpasses knowledge.

3.5. That they may *be filled with all the fulness of God.* It is an exalted expression: we would not dare use it if we did not find it in the Scriptures. It refers to God's fullness as a God in covenant relationship with us. God is ready to give such a fullness; he is willing to fill the Ephesians all to maximum capacity with all the gifts and graces he sees they need. Those who receive grace upon grace from Christ's fullness (Jn 1:16) may be said to be *filled with the fulness of God,* according to their capacity.

4. The apostle closes the chapter with a doxology (vv. 20–21). Notice how he describes God and how he ascribes glory to him. He describes him as a God who *is able to do exceedingly abundantly above all that we ask or think.* There is an inexhaustible fullness of grace and mercy in God, which the prayers of all the saints can never exhaust. We should encourage our faith by considering his all-sufficiency and almighty power: *according to the power which worketh in us.* We already have proof of this power of God in what he has done in and for us. The power that continues to work for the saints is according to the power that has been at work in them. Paul ascribes glory to him: *Unto him be glory in the church by Christ Jesus.* The seat of God's praises is the church. That little payment of praise that God receives from this world is from the church, every individual member of which, both Jew and Gentile, is in agreement in this work of praising God. The Mediator of these praises is Jesus Christ. All God's gifts come from him to us through the hand of Christ, and all our praises pass from us to him through the same hand. God should and will be praised in this way *throughout all ages, world without end. Amen.* So be it, and it will certainly be so.

CHAPTER 4

In what has gone before, we have read about Christian privileges. In what follows we will read about Christian duties. Christian faith and Christian practice go together. In this chapter we have various exhortations to fulfill important duties. 1. One that is more general (v. 1). 2. An exhortation to mutual love (vv. 2–16). 3. An exhortation to Christian purity and holiness of life, both in a general way (vv. 17–24) and then in several distinct expressions (vv. 25–32).

Verse 1

This is a general exhortation to lead lives that are consistent with our Christian profession. Paul was now a prisoner at Rome, and he was the *prisoner of the Lord.* He mentions this more than once, to show that he is not ashamed of his chains. Here is the petition of a poor prisoner: "*I, therefore, the prisoner of the Lord, beseech* (urge) *you.* Considering what God has done for you, I now come, not urging you to send me relief or use your influence to obtain my liberty, but with a heartfelt request that you show yourselves to be good Christians, that you *walk worthily.*" We are called Christians; we must fulfill that name and live as Christians. We are called to God's kingdom and glory; we must live a life that befits heirs of them.

Verses 2–16

Here is an exhortation to mutual love and unity. Love is the law of Christ's kingdom, the lesson of his school, the uniform of his family. We have here:

1. The means of unity: *Lowliness and meekness* (humility and gentleness), *longsuffering, and forbearing* (patience and bearing with) *one another in love* (v. 2). By *lowliness* we are to understand humility, the opposite of pride. *Meekness* is the humble and gentle attitude that makes people unwilling to provoke others and not easily provoked themselves. *Longsuffering* implies patient bearing with wrongs, not seeking revenge for them. *Forbearing one another in love.* Even the best Christians need to make the best of one another, to provoke one another's graces, not their passions. We find very much in ourselves that is hard to forgive ourselves for, and so we must not think it too much if we find in others something we think hard to forgive them for; we must forgive them. Now without these things unity cannot be preserved. The first step toward unity is humility. Pride and passion break the peace and cause all kinds of trouble. Humility and gentleness restore the peace. The more humble our attitude is, the greater our unity will be.

2. The nature of the unity: it is *the unity of the Spirit* (v. 3). The seat of Christian unity is in the heart or spirit:

it does not lie in one set of thoughts, nor in one form of worship, but in one heart and one soul. We should seek to keep this. *Endeavouring* is a Gospel word. We must do all we can to keep the unity of the Spirit. If others want to quarrel with us, we must take all possible care that we do not quarrel with them. *In the bond of peace.* Peace is a bond. Many slender twigs bound together become strong. The bond of peace is the strength of a community. Not that it can be imagined that all good people would share all the same attitudes and minds, but the bond of peace unites them. Like a bundle of sticks, they may have different lengths and different strengths, but when they are tied together by one bond, they are stronger than any one stick by itself, even the thickest and strongest.

3. The motives that are proper to advance this Christian unity and harmony.

3.1. Consider how many unities there are. There should be one heart, as *there is one body, and one spirit* (v. 4). Two hearts in one body would be grotesque. If there is only one body, all who belong to that body should have one heart. If we belong to Christ, we are all motivated by one and the same Spirit and should therefore be one. *Even as you are called in one hope of your calling.* There is one Christ that they all hope in and one heaven they all hope for, and so they should be of one heart. *One Lord* (v. 5), that is, Christ. *One faith*, that is, the Gospel, or, it is the same grace of faith through which all Christians are saved. *One baptism*, by which we profess our faith. *One God and Father of all* (v. 6). One God, who acknowledges all the true members of the church as his children, and he *is above all and through all* by his providence upholding them, *and in you all*, in all believers, by his Spirit. If, then, there are so many *ones*, it would be a pity if there were not one more: one heart, or one soul.

3.2. Consider the variety of gifts that Christ has given Christians: *But unto everyone of us is given grace according to the measure of the gift of Christ.* Although the members of Christ's church agree in many things, there are some things about which they differ. This should not, however, breed any difference of affection among them, since all gifts are derived from the same bountiful author.

3.2.1. Some gift of grace is given to every Christian, to some a greater gift, to some a lesser. The Ephesians have no reason to quarrel about their ministers, because all that their ministers have has been given *according to the measure of the gift of Christ.* All the ministers and all the members of Christ owe to him all the gifts and graces they have been given, and this is a good reason why we should love one another, *because to every one of us is given grace.* All to whom Christ has given grace, and all on whom he has bestowed any gifts, *ought to love one another.* The apostle uses this occasion to specify some of the gifts.

3.2.2. The apostle makes it clear that these gifts were given by Christ by quoting the words of David (Ps 68:18): *Wherefore he saith* (v. 8), *When he ascended up on high, he led captivity captive, and gave gifts unto men.* Let us set ourselves to think of the ascension of Jesus Christ: that our blessed Redeemer, having risen from the dead, has gone to heaven, where he sits at the right hand of the Majesty on high (Heb 1:3).

3.2.3. Christ, when he ascended into heaven as a triumphant conqueror, *led captivity captive.* It is a phrase used in the Old Testament to refer to a conquest over enemies, especially over those who formerly held others captive. Christ conquered those who had conquered us; he defeated sin, the Devil, and death. Indeed, he triumphed over these *on the cross*, but the triumph was completed at his ascension, when he became Lord over all.

3.2.4. *And he gave gifts unto men*: in the psalm it is, *He received gifts for men.* He received for them so that he could give to them.

3.2.5. The apostle takes notice that Christ *descended first into the lower parts of the earth* (v. 9). He descended to the earth in his incarnation. He descended into the earth in his burial. *He that descended is the same also that ascended up far above all heavens* (v. 10), into the heaven of heavens, *that he might fill all things*, all the members of his church, with gifts and graces.

3.3. The apostle next tells us what Christ's gifts were at his ascension: *He gave some apostles* (v. 11). The great gift Christ gave to the church at his ascension was that of the ministry of peace and reconciliation (2Co 5:18–19). The gift of the ministry is the fruit of Christ's ascension. The officers that Christ gave to his church were of two sorts:

3.3.1. There are *extraordinary* ones: such were *apostles*, *prophets*, and *evangelists*. The apostles were the chief ones. Having witnessed his miracles and message, they were sent out by him to spread the Gospel. The *prophets* seem to have been persons who explained the writings of the Old Testament. The evangelists were ordained persons whom the apostles took as their companions on their travels.

3.3.2. Then there are *ordinary* ministers, *pastors* and *teachers*. Some take these two names to stand for one position. Others think they refer to two distinct posts, and in that case pastors are the established leaders of particular churches, who are frequently called *bishops*, or overseers, and elders. The teachers are those whose work it is to instruct the people by way of exhortation. How rich is the church that still has such a variety of gifts! How kind Christ is to his church!

3.4. Consider Christ's great goal and intention in giving gifts to human beings. The gifts of Christ were intended for the good of his church. All are *for the perfecting of the saints* (v. 12), to bring into an orderly spiritual state those who were once dislocated and put out of joint by sin (see commentary on Gal 6:1), and then to advance them in that so that each can contribute to the good of the whole. For *the work of the ministry, for the edifying of the body of Christ*, that is, to build up the church, which is Christ's mystical body, by an increase in their graces and the addition of new members. All the offices are intended to prepare us for heaven: *Till we all come in the unity of the faith, and of the knowledge of the Son of God*, not a merely speculative knowledge, but a knowledge that is taken hold of and received with love. To *a perfect man*, to a maturity of growth in gifts and graces and a freedom from those childish weaknesses we are subject to in the present world. *Unto the measure of the stature of the fulness of Christ*: so as to be Christians who are fully mature in all the graces that come from Christ's fullness. Yet we will never come to *the perfect man* until we come to the perfect world. As long as God's children are in this world, they are growing.

3.5. Now see God's intention in his sacred institutions, and what effect they should have on us.

3.5.1. *We should henceforth be no more children* (v. 14), no longer children in knowledge, weak in the faith and fickle in our judgments, easily giving in to every temptation and being at everyone's beck and call. Children are easily deceived. We must beware of this, that we are not *tossed to and fro*, like ships without ballast, *and carried about*, like clouds, with doctrines that have no truth or solidity in them and are therefore compared to the wind. *By the sleight* (trickery) *of men and cunning craftiness, whereby they lie in wait to deceive,* as in an ambush, in order to lead astray the weak. The best method we can use to strengthen ourselves against such people is to study the sacred writings and pray for the enlightenment and grace of the Spirit of Christ.

3.5.2. We should *speak the truth in love* (v. 15). Love is excellent, but we must be careful to preserve truth together with it. Truth is excellent, but we must speak it in love, and not in strife. These two should go together: truth and peace.

3.5.3. We should *grow up into Christ in all things*. Into Christ, so as to be more deeply rooted in him. In all things: in knowledge, love, faith. We should grow up to maturity, which is the opposite of being infants. The more we come to know Christ and to increase our faith in him, our love for him, and our dependence on him, the more we will flourish in every grace.

3.5.4. We should help one another, as members of the same body (v. 16). Here the apostle draws a comparison between the natural body and Christ's mystical body. Just as there must be fellowship of the members of the body among themselves, so there also must be mutual love and unity among Christians so that they may make spiritual progress and grow in grace. Individual Christians receive their gifts and graces from Christ for the sake and benefit of the whole body. *Unto the edifying of itself in love.* Mutual love among Christians is a great friend to spiritual growth: the body edifies itself in love.

Verses 17–32

There follows an exhortation to Christian purity and holiness in heart and life, both generally (vv. 17–24) and in specific instances (vv. 25–32). This is solemnly introduced: *This I say therefore, and testify in the Lord.* Consider:

1. The more general exhortation to purity and holiness in heart and life.

1.1. It begins: "*That you henceforth walk not as other Gentiles walk.*" Converted Gentiles must not live like unconverted Gentiles. Although they live among them, they must not live like them. Here:

1.1.1. We see the evil of the Gentile world.

1.1.1.1. Their *understandings were darkened* (v. 18). They were devoid of all saving knowledge. They sat in darkness, preferring it to the light (Jn 3:19), and by their ignorance they were *alienated from the life of God*. They were separated from a life of holiness. Their deliberate ignorance was the cause of their separation from this life of God. What was the cause of their being ignorant in this way? It was *because of the blindness* or the hardness *of their heart*. It was not because God had not revealed himself to them through his works (Ro 1:20). They were ignorant because they wanted to be so. Their ignorance derived from their stubbornness.

1.1.1.2. Their consciences were defiled and seared: *Who being past feeling* (having lost all sensitivity) (v. 19). They had no sense of their sin or of the danger of their situation. They *gave themselves over unto lasciviousness* (sensuality). They indulged in evil pleasures of their bodies. They became the slaves of sin and the Devil, *working all uncleanness with greediness* (so as to indulge in every kind of impurity, with a continual lust for more). Once people's consciences are seared, there are no limits to their sins.

1.1.2. The apostle instructs these Christians that they must set themselves apart from such Gentiles: *You have not so learned Christ* (v. 20). It may be read, "But you are not so; you have learned Christ." Those who have come to know Christ are saved from the darkness others lie under, and just as they know more than others, so they are also obliged to lead better lives than others. *Learn Christ.* Is Christ a book, a lesson, a way, a business? The meaning is, "You have not learned or come to know Christianity in this way—the teachings of Christ and the rules of life he gives. In learning Christianity, you have not learned to do as others do, *if so be that you have heard him* (v. 21)—that is, "since you have heard him"—*and have been taught by him.* Christ is the lesson; we must come to know Christ more. Christ is the teacher; we are taught by him. *As the truth is in Jesus.* "You have been taught the real truth, as offered by Christ himself, both in his teaching and in his life." The truth of Christ appears in its beauty and power when it appears as in Jesus.

1.2. Another aspect of the general exhortation follows: *That you put off, concerning the former conversation* (way of life), *the old man* (vv. 22–24). Here the apostle expresses himself in metaphors taken from clothing. There must be sanctification, which consists of these two things:

1.2.1. The *old man* (old self) must be taken off. The corrupt nature is called *a man*. It is the *old man*, as old Adam, from whom we derive it. It is innate in us, and we brought it into the world with us. It is said to be corrupt because sin in the soul is the corruption of its faculties, and where it is not put to death, it grows daily worse and worse. *According to the deceitful lusts.* They promise people happiness but instead make them more miserable. These must be taken off, therefore, like an old piece of clothing that we are ashamed to be seen in. These sinful desires triumphed in the Ephesians' former way of life.

1.2.2. The *new man* (new self) must be put on. It is not enough to shake off corrupt principles; we must be motivated by gracious ones. "*Be renewed in the spirit of your mind* (v. 23), more and more." *And that you put on the new man* (v. 24). By the *new man* is meant the new nature, the new creation. This new self *is created*, or produced out of confusion and emptiness, by God's almighty power. *After God.* The loss of God's image on the soul was both the sinfulness and the misery of humanity's fallen state, and the likeness that it bears to God is the glory and happiness of the new creation. The *new man* is created *in righteousness* toward people *and in holiness* toward God. *True holiness* is in contrast to the ceremonial holiness of the Jews. We are said to put on this new self when we are seeking to lead lives according to this divine nature.

2. Those particular limbs of the old self that must be put to death, those filthy rags of the old nature that must be put off, and what are the distinctive ornaments of the new self.

2.1. Beware of lying and be very careful to speak the truth (v. 25): *Wherefore, putting away lying.* The ungodly were very guilty of this sin, saying that a profitable lie was better than a hurtful truth. That branch of the new self that must be put on in opposition to this part of the old self is *speaking the truth* in all our conversation with others. All who have grace are conscientious about speaking the truth. The reason given is, *We are members one of another.* Truth is a debt we owe one another, and if we love one another, we will not deceive one another. We belong to the same community or body, which falsehood or lying tends to dissolve, and so we should avoid it and speak truth. Lying is a very great sin.

2.2. "Beware of anger and uncontrolled passions. *Be you angry, and sin not*" (v. 26). Here is an easy allowance, for that is how we should consider it, rather than as a command. *Be you angry.* We tend to be angry all too easily, God knows, but we find it difficult enough to observe the restriction, *and sin not*. If we want to be angry and not sin — according to one commentator — we must be angry at nothing but sin. One great and common sin in anger is to allow it to turn into wrath, and then to let it rest. Before night, calm and quiet your spirits, be reconciled to the offender: *Let not the sun go down upon your wrath*. Although anger in itself is not sinful, there is the greatest danger of its becoming so unless it is carefully watched. *Neither give place to the devil* (do not give the devil a foothold) (v. 27). Those who persevere in sinful anger and in wrath let the Devil into their hearts. "*Neither give place to the* one who speaks slander, or the false accuser" — as some understand the words — "let your ears be deaf to whisperers, gossips, and slanderers."

2.3. We are warned here against the sin of stealing and advised to work hard, honestly, and with kindness: *Let him that stole steal no more* (v. 28). We must not only beware of the sin, however, but also conscientiously overflow in the opposite duty; each must not only not steal, *but rather let him labour, working with his hands the thing that is good*. Idleness makes thieves. People should therefore be conscientious and industrious, not in any unlawful way, but in pursuing an honest calling, *working the thing which is good*. Industriousness in honest work will keep people out of the temptation of wrongdoing. But there is another reason why people should work hard, namely, that they may be capable of doing some good: *that he may have to give to him that needeth*. They must labor not only so that they themselves may live, but also so that they may share with others. Even those who have only a little for themselves must put their few copper coins into the treasury (Mk 12:42). God must receive his dues, and the poor are authorized to receive them on his behalf.

2.4. We are warned here against *corrupt communication* (unwholesome talk) and told to say what is useful and edifying (v. 29). Impure words and speech are poisonous and infectious, like putrid, rotten meat. Christians should beware of all such speech. We must not only put off unwholesome talk but also *put on that which is good to the use of edifying*. Christians should seek to promote a useful conversation: *that it may minister grace unto the hearers*. It is the great duty of Christians to take care that they do not offend with their lips and that they use speech for the good of others.

2.5. Here is another warning against wrath and anger, with further advice to show mutual love (vv. 31–32). By *bitterness*, *wrath*, and *anger* are meant violent inner rage, resentment, against others; and by *clamour* are meant immoderate speech and actions, which are expressed in bitterness, rage, and anger. Christians should not harbor these corrupt passions in their hearts, nor clamor with their tongues. *Evil speaking* signifies all insulting speech against those we are angry with. *Malice* is that deep-rooted hatred that prompts people to plan trouble to others. The opposite of all this follows: *Be you kind one to another*. This implies that the motivating principle in the heart is love and that it is expressed outwardly in kind, humble, and polite behavior. *Tender-hearted*, that is, compassionate and merciful, so as to be quickly moved to compassion and pity. *Forgiving one another*. Occasions of difference will come among Christ's disciples,

and so they must be forgiving, like God himself, who *for Christ's sake hath forgiven them*. Those who are forgiven by God should have a forgiving spirit and should forgive as God forgives.

2.6. All these detailed exhortations that the apostle has insisted on belong to the second table of the Ten Commandments. Those who do not conscientiously fulfill them do not fear or love God in truth and in sincerity, whatever they may claim.

2.7. In the middle of these exhortations the apostle includes a general one: *And grieve not the Holy Spirit of God* (v. 30). We must not do what is contrary to his holy nature and his will; we must not refuse to listen to his advice or rebel against his rule. Do not provoke the Holy Spirit of God to withdraw his presence and his gracious influences from you. A good reason not to grieve him is that *by him we are sealed unto the day of redemption*, that is, the day of resurrection, when the body is to be redeemed from the power of the grave; then our full and complete happiness begins. All true believers are sealed for that day. God has set them apart from others, and the Spirit of God is the seal. We would be ruined if God were to take away his Holy Spirit from us (Ps 51:11).

CHAPTER 5

We have here: 1. An exhortation to mutual love (vv. 1–2). 2. An exhortation against all kinds of immorality, with some further warnings added and other duties commended (vv. 3–20). 3. A direction to conscientiously fulfill our duties in our relationships (vv. 21–6:9).

Verses 1–2

Here we have the exhortation to mutual love. "Because God, for Christ's sake, has forgiven you, you should be followers of God, or 'imitators' of him." To say that practical religion is imitating God puts great honor on it. We must be holy as God is holy (Lev 11:44–45; 1Pe 1:16), merciful as he is merciful (Lk 6:36), perfect as he is perfect (Mt 5:48). However, no single attribute of God is more commended to our imitation than his goodness. We are to imitate God especially in his love. *As dear children*: as children — who are usually greatly loved by their parents — are usually like them in the facial features and in the character of their hearts. Children are obliged to imitate their parents in what is good, especially when they are dearly loved by them. Our position as God's children makes us want to be like him. Only those who imitate God are his dear children. *And walk in love* (v. 2). Love should be the driving principle that motivates our actions; it should direct the goals we aim at. *As Christ also hath loved us*. We all share jointly in that love, and we should love one another because Christ has loved us all. *He hath given himself for us an offering and a sacrifice to God*, or, as it may also be read, "an offering, even a sacrifice," a sacrifice that atoned; and this offering was to be *for a sweet-smelling* (fragrant) *savour*. As he offered himself with the intention of being accepted by God, so God accepted and was pleased with that sacrifice. His example should persuade us, and we should carefully imitate it.

Verses 3–20

Impure desires must be suppressed in order to support holy love. *Walk in love* and *shun fornication and all uncleanness*. These sins must be dreaded and detested most intensely: *Let it not be once named among you, as becometh saints.* The apostle warns not only against the gross acts of sin but also against what some people may make light of and think excusable: *neither filthiness* (v. 4) *nor foolish talking*—empty conversation that shows much foolishness and indiscretion—*nor jesting.* No doubt there is an innocent, harmless, and inoffensive kind of joking, which we cannot suppose the apostle forbids here. But the context seems to restrict the meaning to filthy and obscene kinds of speech. *They are not convenient* (they are out of place). Indeed, they are more than out of place: they contain a great deal of trouble. These things do not befit a Christian. Christians are allowed to be cheerful and pleasant, but they must be happy and wise. *But rather giving of thanks.* Christians may give joy to their heart and make themselves cheerful by remembering with thanksgiving God's goodness and mercy to them, and by blessing and praising him for these. Reflections on the grace and goodness of God toward us, stirring up our thankfulness to him, are proper to delight the Christian's heart and make us cheerful. If people were fuller of good and devout expressions, they would not tend so much to use bad and improper language.

1. To strengthen us against the sins of *uncleanness* and the like, the apostle urges several arguments and prescribes several remedies.

1.1. He urges several arguments against these sins:

1.1.1. Consider that these are sins that exclude people from heaven: *For this you know* (v. 5). There is spiritual idolatry in the love of this world. Just as epicures make a god of their stomach (Php 3:19), so those who are greedy make a god of their money. They serve Mammon instead of God (Mt 6:24). It is said of these people that they *have no inheritance in the kingdom of Christ and of God.* In this kingdom, the saints and servants of God have an inheritance. But those who indulge themselves either in the lustful desires of the flesh or the love of the world do not belong to the kingdom of grace, nor will they ever reach the kingdom of glory. Let us be on our guard, then, against sins that would shut us out of heaven.

1.1.2. Consider that these sins bring the wrath of God on those who are guilty of them: *"Let no man deceive you with vain words* (v. 6). Those who flatter themselves with hopes of impunity in sin are only deceiving themselves. They are truly *vain words, for because of these things cometh the wrath of God upon the children of disobedience.* Disobedience is the very evil heart of sin. *The wrath of God comes upon* such, sometimes in this world, but especially in the next. Dare we make light of what will put us under the wrath of God? *Be not you therefore partakers with them* (v. 7). "Do not share with them in their sins, so that you may not share with them in their punishment."

1.1.3. Consider what obligations Christians are under to live differently. *For you were sometimes darkness, but now* (v. 8). A state of sin is a state of darkness. Sinners, like people in the dark, do not know where they are going or what they are doing. *Now are you light in the Lord. Walk as children of light.* "Now, because you are such, live out the obligation to which you are subjected by the knowledge and advantages you enjoy." *Proving what is acceptable unto the Lord* (v. 10): searching diligently what God has revealed to be his will. We must not only dread and avoid what is displeasing to God but also seek to find out what will be acceptable to him.

1.2. He prescribes some remedies against them.

1.2.1. We must produce *the fruit of the Spirit* (v. 9). It is expected of the children of light that they will be sancti-fied by the Spirit and then produce his fruit, which *is in all goodness and righteousness.* All religion is goodness and righteousness, and with these must be *truth.*

1.2.2. We must have no fellowship with sin or sinners (v. 11). Sinful works are works of darkness. These works of darkness are *unfruitful works*; there is nothing to be gained by them in the long run. Whatever profit is claimed by sin, it will in no way balance out the loss. We must, therefore, *have no fellowship* with these unfruitful works. If we share with others in their sin, we must also expect to share with them in their punishment. Rather than have fellowship with them, we must *reprove them.* We must witness against the sins of others and seek to convince them of their sinfulness in our words, but especially by the holiness of our lives. Rebuke their sins by being full of the opposite duties. *For it is a shame even to speak of those things* (v. 12), and much more must it be a shame to have any fellowship with them. *The things which are done of them in secret.* A good person is ashamed to speak what many evildoers are not ashamed to do. *"But all things that are reproved are made manifest by the light* (v. 13), by the instructive light that is diffused by the holiness of your lives and by your exemplary walk." *For whatsoever doth make manifest is light*; it befits those who are *children of light,* therefore, who are *light in the Lord,* to expose to others their sins, thus shining as lights in the world. The apostle further urges this duty from the example of God or Christ: *Wherefore he saith* (v. 14), *Awake, thou that sleepest, and arise from the dead.* Sinners should break away from their sins by repentance, and God encourages them to do all they can to that end according to that gracious promise, *And Christ shall give thee light.* When we are seeking to convict sinners and reform them from their sins, we are imitating God and Christ in what is their great intention throughout the Gospel.

1.2.3. Another remedy against sin is carefulness (v. 15): *See then that ye walk circumspectly, not as fools, but as wise.* "If you are to expose others for their sins, you must look well to yourselves and your own behavior." We have here another preservative from the sins mentioned before. It is impossible to maintain purity and holiness of heart and life without great carefulness. *Walk circumspectly,* "exactly, in the right way," and to this end we must be frequently consulting our Christian rule of conduct. *Not as fools,* who walk recklessly, and who through neglect and carelessness fall into sin and destroy themselves, but *as wise,* as people taught by God. Careful living is the effect of true wisdom, but the opposite is the effect of foolishness. *Redeeming the time* (v. 16), literally, "buying up the opportunity." It is a metaphor taken from business, referring to traders who carefully note and make the most of opportunities for selling and trade. Good Christians must be good managers of their time. They should make the best use they can of the present seasons of grace. Our time is a talent given us by God for some good purpose, and it is misspent and lost when it is not used according to his purposes. If we have wasted our time till now, we must seek to redeem it by redoubling our diligence in future. *Because the days are evil.* The time when the apostle wrote this was a time of persecution: the Christians were in jeopardy every hour. When the days are evil, we should consider that we do not know how soon they may become worse. People tend to complain about bad times; it would be good if that would stir them to make the most of the opportunities that are presented to them. *Wherefore* (v. 17), *be you not unwise, but understanding what the will of the Lord is.* Knowledge of the will of God, together with a concern to follow it, are signs of the best and truest wisdom.

2. The apostle warns against some other particular sins, urging some other duties.

2.1. He warns against the sin of drunkenness: *And be not drunk with wine* (v. 18). The apostle adds, therefore, *wherein is excess.* Drunkenness is a sin that rarely goes alone; it often involves people in other expressions of guilt. It is a great hindrance to the spiritual life.

2.2. He exhorts the Ephesians, instead of being filled with wine, to be *filled with the Spirit.* Those who are full of drink are unlikely to be full of the Spirit. People should seek a plentiful measure of the graces of the Spirit, which would fill their souls with great joy and courage, things that worldly people expect their wine to inspire them with. We should not be satisfied with a little of the Spirit, but be filled with the Spirit. Now by this means we will come to *understand what the will of the Lord is.*

2.3. The apostle, therefore, urges them to sing to the Lord (v. 19). Drunkards often sing their obscene and sacrilegious songs. The joy of Christians should express itself in songs of praise to their God. In these they should *speak to themselves* in their meetings. Although Christianity is an enemy of worldly merriment, it still encourages joy and gladness. God's people have reason to rejoice and to sing for joy. They are to *sing and to make melody in their hearts,* not only with their voices but also with inward joy, and then it will be done *to the Lord.*

2.4. Finally, he exhorts them to be *always giving thanks,* for thanksgiving is another duty (v. 20). We should give thanks *for all things.* It is our duty in *every thing to give thanks unto God and the Father.*

Verses 21–33

Here the apostle begins his exhortation to the fulfillment of duties in relationships. As a general foundation for these duties, he lays down a basic rule (v. 21). There is a mutual submission that Christians owe one another. *In the fear of God* means "for his sake, so that we may show in our lives that we sincerely fear him." Where there is this mutual submission, the duties of all relationships will be better performed.

1. The duty prescribed to wives is submission to their husbands in the Lord (v. 22). The reason for wives' submission is, *For the husband is the head of the wife* (v. 23). By creation God has given the man the preeminence and a right to direct and lead. Generally, too, the man has—what he should have—greater wisdom and knowledge. He is the head, therefore, *even as Christ is the head of the church, and he is the Saviour of the body.* Christ's authority is exercised over the church to save her from evil and supply her with everything good for her. Similarly, the husband should seek the protection and comfort of his spouse. *Therefore as the church is subject unto Christ* (v. 24), with cheerfulness, faithfulness, and humility, *so let the wives be to their own husbands in every thing.*

2. The duty of husbands is to love their wives (v. 25), for without this they would abuse their authority, and wherever this prevails, it will lead to the performance of the other duties of the relationship, because it is a special affection that is required on her behalf.

2.1. The love of Christ to the church is offered as an example for this love; Christ's love is a constant affection, despite the imperfections and failures the church is guilty of. The greatness of his love for it was shown in his giving himself up to die for it. The love that God requires from the husband for his wife will make up for the sub-

mission to her husband that he demands of her, and the prescribed submission of the wife will be an abundant response for the love of the husband that God has declared is due to her.

2.2. The reason why he gave himself for it was so *that he might sanctify and cleanse it with the washing of water by the word, that he might present it to himself a glorious church, not having spot, nor wrinkle, nor any such thing, holy and without blemish* (vv. 26–27), free from the slightest remnant of sin. Both the church in general and individual believers will not be without stain or wrinkle until they reach glory. Those, and only those, who are sanctified now will be glorified in the future.

2.3. So *ought men to love their wives* as *their own bodies* (v. 28). The wife's being made one with her husband is an argument why he should love her with as warm and as ardent an affection as the love with which he loves himself. *For no man ever yet hated his own flesh*; on the contrary, *he nourishes and cherishes it, even as the Lord the church. For we are members of his body, of his flesh and of his bones* (vv. 29–30).

2.4. *For this cause*—because they are one, as Christ and his church are one—*shall a man leave his father and mother* (v. 31). This relationship is to be preferred to all others, there being a closer union between these two than between any others. And *they two shall be one flesh* (v. 31; Ge 2:24). *This is a great mystery* (v. 32). Those words of Adam are spoken literally about marriage, but they also have a hidden, mystical sense in them, relating to the union between Christ and his church. *I speak concerning Christ and the church.*

3. The apostle concludes this chapter with a brief summary of the duty of husbands and wives (v. 33). *Nevertheless let every one of you in particular so love his wife even as himself; and the wife see that she reverence her husband.* Reverence consists of love, esteem, and fear, which awakens a carefulness to avoid giving offense. That the wife should respect her husband in this way is the will of God and the law of that relationship.

CHAPTER 6

1. The apostle continues his exhortation concerning duties in relationships, especially insisting on the duties of children and parents and of servants and masters (vv. 1–9). 2. He tells Christians how to behave in the spiritual warfare with the enemies of their souls, and he tells them to exercise various Christian graces, which he sets before them as various pieces of spiritual armor (vv. 10–18). 3. We have here the conclusion of the letter (vv. 19–24).

Verses 1–9

Here are further instructions concerning duties in relationships, in which the apostle is very detailed.

1. The first duty of children is to obey their parents (v. 1). The obedience that God demands from children includes an inner reverence as well as outward expressions and acts. *Obey in the Lord.* "Obey your parents, especially in matters that relate to the Lord. Your parents teach you good manners, and you must obey them. They teach you what is for your good, and you must obey them in this. But the chief things in which you are to do it are the things concerning the Lord." In these things, especially, they must see to it that they are obedient. *For this is right*; there is a natural justice about it, and God has commanded it. It is the order of nature that parents command and children obey. The apostle quotes the law of

the fifth commandment: *Honour thy father and mother* (v. 2), *which is the first commandment with promise*. The promise is *That it may be well with thee* (v. 3). Outward prosperity and long life are blessings promised to those who keep this commandment. Obedient children are often rewarded with outward prosperity. Not that it is always so, but *ordinarily* obedience is rewarded in this way.

1.1. The Gospel has its temporal promises as well as its spiritual ones.

1.2. Although the authority of God is sufficient to obligate us to do our duty, we are still allowed to look forward to the promised reward, and:

1.3. Although doing our duty contains some temporal advantage, even this may be considered as a motive and encouragement to our obedience.

2. The duty of parents: *And you fathers* (v. 4).

2.1. "*Do not provoke your children to wrath.* Your children are parts of yourselves and should therefore be governed with great tenderness and love. When you warn them, give them advice, or rebuke them, do it in such a way as not to *provoke them to wrath*, but to seek to convince their judgments and have an effect on their reason.

2.2. "*Bring them up* well, *in the nurture and admonition* (training and instruction) *of the Lord.* Train them well; give them a good education." It is the great duty of parents to be careful how they bring up their children. Bring them up not merely as the animals do, but as human beings, who have rational natures, and not only as human beings but as Christians, in the fear of the Lord. Let them have a religious education.

3. The duty of servants. This is also summed up in one word: *obedience.* These servants were generally slaves. Civil submission is not inconsistent with Christian freedom. Those who are slaves may be the Lord's free people (1Co 7:22). "Obey *your masters according to the flesh* (v. 5), who have command of your bodies, but not of your souls and consciences." The apostle exhorts servants:

3.1. To obey *with fear and trembling.* They are to revere those who are over them.

3.2. To be sincere in their obedience, serving *in singleness of heart*, with sincerity and faithfulness.

3.3. To look to Jesus Christ in all the service they give their masters (vv. 5–7), *doing service as to the Lord, and not to men*. Service they do for their earthly masters while looking to God becomes acceptable service to him also.

3.4. Not to serve their masters *with eyeservice* (v. 6)—that is, not only when their master is looking at them. Their Master in heaven sees them; they must not act, therefore, as *menpleasers*. A steady regard for the Lord Jesus Christ will make people faithful and sincere in every position in life.

3.5. To do their duty cheerfully: *doing the will of God from the heart*, serving their masters as God wants them to. This is *doing it with goodwill* (v. 7). Service performed with a good conscience and from a regard for God, even though it is done to unrighteous masters, will be counted by Christ as service done to himself.

3.6. If they are faithful, to trust God for their wages while doing their duty in fear of him: *Knowing that whatsoever good thing any man does* (v. 8), *the same shall he receive of the Lord*. Even if his master on earth neglects or abuses him instead of rewarding him, he will certainly be rewarded by the Lord Christ, *whether he be bond or free*. Christ pays no attention to these differences among people at present, nor will he in the great and final judgment.

4. The duty of masters: *And you masters, do the same things unto them* (v. 9). Masters are under just as strict obligations to fulfill their duty to their servants as servants are to be obedient and dutiful to them. "*Forbearing threatening*: do not be tyrannical and imperious toward them, *knowing that your Master also is in heaven*; you and they are merely fellow servants with respect to Christ. You are to show favor to others, therefore, if you expect ever to find favor with him. You will never be a match for him, even though you may be too harsh on your servants." *Neither is there respect of persons with him* (God does not show partiality). He will call masters and servants to give an impartial account for their behavior toward one another. If both masters and servants consider their relationship to God and the account they must soon give him, they will be more careful about their duty toward each other.

Verses 10–18

Is our life not a warfare? It is, because we struggle against the common adversities of human life. Is our religion not much more a warfare? It is, because we struggle with the opposition of the powers of darkness. "*Finally, my brethren* (v. 10), you still need to apply yourselves to your work and duty as Christian soldiers."

1. They must see to it that they are bold. *Be strong in the Lord.* Those who have many battles to fight, and who, on their way to heaven, must struggle over every pass wielding a sword, need a great deal of courage. *Be strong therefore.* If soldiers do not have within them a strong heart, their armor will do them little good, no matter how well armed they are on the outside. Spiritual strength and courage are necessary for our spiritual warfare. We have no adequate strength in ourselves. All our sufficiency is from God (2Co 3:5). We must go out and on in his strength. We must draw in supplies of grace and help from heaven to enable us to do what we by ourselves cannot do in our Christian work and warfare.

2. They must be well armed: "*Put on the whole armour of God* (v. 11). Obtain and exercise all the Christian graces, the whole armor, so that no part of you lies exposed to the enemy." Those who want to have true grace must aim at all grace, putting on the whole armor. We have no armor of our own that will be strong enough to protect us in times of trial and testing. Nothing will stand us in good stead except the armor of God. This armor is prepared for us, but we must put it on. Christians should be completely armed so *that they may be able to stand against the wiles of the devil*—so that they may be able to hold out and overcome. The apostle shows here:

2.1. What our danger is, and what need we have to put on this whole armor. *For we wrestle not against flesh and blood* (v. 12). The combat is not against ordinary human enemies, not merely against people made up of *flesh and blood*.

2.1.1. We have to deal with an enemy who uses wiles and stratagems (v. 11). He has a thousand different ways of deceiving unstable souls.

2.1.2. He is a powerful enemy: *principalities, powers,* and *rulers*. They are numerous and vigorous; they rule in the ungodly nations that are still in darkness. Satan's is a kingdom of darkness, whereas Christ's is a kingdom of light.

2.1.3. They are spiritual enemies: *spiritual wickedness in high places*, or "evil spirits," or "spiritual forces of evil," as some translate it. Our danger is the greater from our enemies because they are unseen and attack us before we are aware of them. These enemies are said to be *in high places*, or "in the heavenly realms." Our enemies fight to prevent our ascent to heaven. They attack us in the things that belong to our souls. We need faith in our Christian warfare, because we grapple with spiritual enemies; we also need faith in our Christian work, because we need to draw in supplies of spiritual strength.

2.2. What our duty is: to put on the whole armor of God, and then to stand our ground and withstand our enemies.

2.2.1. We must *withstand* (v. 13). We must not yield to the Devil's temptations and attacks, but oppose them. If he stands up against us, we must stand our ground against him. To stand our ground against Satan is to fight against sin. *That you may be able to withstand in the evil day*, in the day of temptation, or the day of any severe affliction.

2.2.2. We must stand our ground: *And, having done all, to stand.* Resist the Devil, and he will flee (Jas 4:7). If we give way, he will gain ground. Our present task is to withstand his attacks and outlast them; then our warfare will be fulfilled (Isa 40:2) and we will finally be victorious.

2.2.3. We must stand armed. Here is a Christian in complete armor; the armor is divine: *armour of God.* The apostle specifies the parts of this armor, both offensive and defensive: the military girdle or belt, the breastplate, the shoes (or greaves), the shield, the helmet, and the sword. It is significant that among them all there is none for the back; if we turn our back on the enemy, we are exposed.

2.2.3.1. Truth is our *girdle* (belt) (v. 14). This is the strength of our waist; it secures all other pieces of our armor and therefore is mentioned first. I know of no religion without sincerity.

2.2.3.2. Righteousness must be our breastplate. The breastplate protects the vital organs; it protects the heart. The righteousness of Christ implanted in us is our breastplate to strengthen the heart against the attacks Satan launches against us.

2.2.3.3. Resolution must be like the shoes to our feet: *And their feet shod with the preparation of the Gospel of peace* (v. 15). Shoes, or bronze greaves, were once part of the military armor, to defend the feet against the traps and sharp sticks that were often laid to obstruct the marching of the enemy, those who fell on them being made unfit to march. *The preparation of the Gospel of peace* refers to a determined attitude of heart that will enable us to walk steadily on the path of religious faith. It is called *the Gospel of peace* because it brings all kinds of peace. "Seek that peaceful and quiet heart that the Gospel calls for, and this will certainly preserve you from many great temptations and persecutions, as those bronze shoes protected the soldiers from those traps" (Dr. Whitby).

2.2.3.4. Faith must be our shield: *Above all, taking the shield of faith* (v. 16). This is more necessary than any of them. Faith is everything in the hour of temptation. The breastplate protects the vital organs, but we can turn the shield in every direction. Faith is like a shield, a kind of universal defense. Our enemy the Devil is called here *the wicked one.* He is wicked himself, and he seeks to make us wicked. His temptations are called *fiery darts*, by way of allusion to the poisonous arrows that often inflamed the parts that were wounded. Violent temptations, by which the soul is set on fire by hell (Jas 3:6), are the arrows that Satan shoots at us. Faith is the shield with which we must extinguish these flaming arrows so that they may not hit us, or at least not harm us.

2.2.3.5. Salvation must be our helmet (v. 17); that is, *hope*, which has salvation as its object. The Devil wants

to tempt us to despair, but good hope keeps us trusting and rejoicing in God.

2.2.3.6. The word of God is the sword of the Spirit. It is called *the sword of the Spirit* because the Spirit makes it effective and powerful. When Scripture is hidden in the heart, it will protect us from sin (Ps 119:11).

2.2.3.7. Prayer must buckle on all the other parts of our Christian armor (v. 18). We must add prayer to all these graces, and we must pray always. It is not as though we were to do nothing else but pray, because there are other duties that are to be undertaken in the right place and at the right time, but we should keep up constant times of prayer. We must pray on all occasions. We must mix exclamatory prayers with other duties and with ordinary business. Although set and solemn prayer may sometimes be inopportune, godly exclamatory prayers can never be so. We must pray *with all prayer and supplication*, with all kinds of prayer. We must pray *in the Spirit*, by the grace of God's good Spirit. We must *watch thereunto*, seeking to keep our hearts in a prayerful attitude, taking every opportunity for this duty. We must pray *with all perseverance*, continuing with it as long as we live in the world. We must pray *with supplication*, not only for ourselves but also *for all saints*. No one is such a saint, and in such a good condition in this world, that they do not need our prayers; and they should have them.

Verses 19–24

Here:

1. He wants the Ephesians to pray for him (v. 19). Having mentioned *supplication for all saints*, he includes himself in that number. We must pray for all saints, especially for God's faithful ministers. *That utterance may be given unto me* and *that I may open my mouth boldly to make known the mystery of the Gospel.* The whole Gospel was a mystery until it was made known by divine revelation. Paul had a great command of language; they called him *Mercury*, because he was the chief speaker (Ac 14:12); but he still wanted his friends to ask God for the gift of utterance, that words would be given him. He was a man of great courage, but he wanted them to pray that God would give him boldness. He knew as well as anyone what to say, but he wanted them to pray for him, that he might *speak as he ought to speak.* He reinforces his request by noting that for the sake of the Gospel he is *an ambassador in bonds* (v. 20). He was persecuted and imprisoned for preaching the Gospel, and yet he continued in the mission committed to him by Christ. The best ministers may benefit from the prayers of good Christians and should therefore earnestly desire those prayers.

2. He commends Tychicus to them (vv. 21–22). He is sending Tychicus with this letter so that Tychicus may inform the Ephesians how Paul is doing and what he is doing. It is desirable for good ministers that their Christian friends know their state, and also that ministers themselves know better the condition of their friends, for this is how they can help each other better in their prayers. "*And that he might comfort your hearts* by giving such an account of my sufferings as will prevent your becoming discouraged at my troubles and even minister reasons for joy and thanksgiving to you." Tychicus was *a beloved brother and faithful minister in the Lord.* He was very dear to Paul, which made Paul's love for these Christian Ephesians more remarkable, in that he was willing now to part with such a good and dear friend for their sakes. But faithful servants of Jesus Christ tend to prefer the public good to their own personal interests.

3. He concludes with his good wishes and prayers for the Ephesians, and not only for them but also for all the brothers and sisters (vv. 23–24). *Peace be to the brethren, and love with faith*; faith and love including all the streams of God's grace. It is the continuation and increase of these that he wants for them, in whom these blessings have already begun. *From God the Father*. The closing blessing is more extensive than the previous one, because in this one he prays for all true believers at Ephesus and everywhere else. All believers *love our Lord Jesus Christ in sincerity*. Our love for Christ is not acceptable unless it is sincere; in fact, there is no such thing as love for Christ where there is not sincerity, whatever people may claim. Grace, that is, the favor of God, and all the good things that are the product of that favor, are and will be with all those who love our Lord Jesus Christ in this way. It is, or should be, the prayer of every lover of Christ that it may be so with all fellow Christians. *Amen*, so be it.

A Practical and Devotional Exposition of

Philippians

Philippi was a chief city of the western part of Macedonia. It is most remarkable among Christians for this letter, which was written when Paul was a prisoner at Rome. Paul seems to have had a particular fondness, a fatherly, tender care, for the church at Philippi, which he himself had been instrumental in planting. He looked on them as his children, and, having *begotten them through the Gospel* (1Co 4:15), he wanted to nurture and build them up through the same Gospel. 1. He was called in an extraordinary way to preach the Gospel at Philippi. A vision appeared to him at night: *There stood a man of Macedonia, and prayed him, saying, Come over into Macedonia, and help us.* He saw God going before him. 2. At Philippi he suffered hardships; yet he did not for that reason have any less affection for the place. We must never love our friends any less for the ill treatment that we receive from our enemies. 3. The beginnings of that church were very small, yet that did not discourage him. If good is not done at the beginning, it may be done later, and the last works may be more than the first (Rev 2:19). 4. It seems that this church eventually flourished, and especially that the brothers and sisters were very kind to Paul. He acknowledges receipt of a gift they have sent him (4:18), a gift given when no other church shared with him in giving and receiving (4:15).

CHAPTER 1

We have here: 1. The apostle Paul's opening greeting and blessing (vv. 1−2). 2. His thanksgiving for the saints at Philippi (vv. 3−6). 3. A description of his great affection (vv. 7−8). 4. His prayers for them (vv. 9−11). 5. His concern to prevent their taking offense at his sufferings (vv. 12−20). 6. His readiness to glorify Christ in life or death (vv. 21−26). 7. His concluding exhortation to live a consistently faithful life (vv. 27−30).

Verses 1−2

We have here the greeting and blessing. We see:

1. The people writing the letter—*Paul and Timotheus, the servants of Jesus Christ.* The highest honor of the greatest apostle was, and that of the most eminent ministers is, to be the servants of Jesus Christ; not the masters of the churches, but the servants of Christ.

2. The people to whom the letter is sent.

2.1. *To all the saints in Christ who are at Philippi.* He mentions the church before the ministers, because the ministers exist for the church, not the other way around. Ministers are not only the servants of Christ but also servants of the church for his sake. The letter is sent to *all the saints,* one as well as another, even the weakest, the poorest, and those with the smallest gifts. Christ makes no distinction; rich and poor meet together in him (Pr 22:2), *saints in Christ Jesus.* Outside of Christ the best saints will remain sinners, unable to stand before God.

2.2. *With the bishops and deacons.* First the *bishops* (overseers), or elders, are mentioned, whose role was to teach and lead; and second, the deacons, or those with oversight of the poor, who took care of the outward busi-

ness of the house of God (Ne 11:16). These were all the leadership roles that were then known in the church and that were divinely appointed.

3. The apostolic blessing: *Grace be unto you, and peace, from God our Father, and from the Lord Jesus Christ* (v. 2). This is the same, almost word for word, in all the letters; we must not shun prescribed orders of words, though we are not to be tied to them. *Grace and peace*—the free favor and goodwill of God and all its blessed fruits and effects; and it is wished *from God our Father, and from the Lord Jesus Christ.* There is no peace without grace; inner peace springs from a sense of divine favor. Nor is there grace and peace except those that come from God our Father, the fountain and origin of all blessings. And there is no grace and peace from God our Father except in and through our Lord Jesus Christ.

Verses 3−6

The apostle proceeds to give thanks for the saints at Philippi.

1. Paul remembered them; they were frequently in his thoughts: *upon every remembrance of you.* Just as he thought about them often, so he also often spoke about them and was delighted to hear them spoken about. It is a pleasure to hear how an absent friend is doing.

2. He remembered them with joy. He had been maltreated in Philippi, and yet, far from being ashamed of them or reluctant to hear about the scene of his sufferings, he remembered the city with joy.

3. He remembered them in prayer: *Always in every prayer of mine for you all* (v. 4). The best way we can remember our friends is to remember them in prayer at the

throne of grace. Paul had times of prayer specifically for the church at Philippi. God allows us to be free with him in this way, and it is comforting that he knows whom we are thinking of even when we do not name them.

4. He thanked God for every joyful memory of them. Thanksgiving must have a part in every prayer. God must receive the glory for what we have an assurance of. Paul thanked God, as well as asking with joy.

5. *I thank my God.* It encourages us in prayer and releases the heart in prayer to see every blessing coming from the hand of God as our God. *I thank my God upon every remembrance of you.* He gave thanks to God:

5.1. For the comfort he had from them: for *your fellowship in the Gospel, from the first day until now* (v. 5). Gospel fellowship is good fellowship. Those who sincerely receive the Gospel have fellowship with it *from the very first day.* Newly born Christians, if they are really born again, share in all the promises of the Gospel from the first day they become Christians. *Until now.* It is a great assurance to ministers when those who begin well continue and persevere.

5.2. For the confidence he had for them (v. 6): *Being confident of this very thing.* The confidence of Christians is a great encouragement to Christians, and we may draw matter for praise from our hopes as well as from our joys. Paul speaks with great confidence. *That he who has begun a good work in you will perform it unto the day of Jesus Christ.* It may also be read "a good work among you." The One who has planted Christianity in the world will preserve it as long as the world stands. But it should rather be applied to particular individuals, and in that case Paul is speaking of the certain fulfillment of the work of grace wherever it has begun.

5.2.1. The work of grace is a good work. It makes us like God and fits us to enjoy God.

5.2.2. Wherever this good work has begun, it is God who began it: *He has begun a good work in you.* We could not begin it by ourselves, for we are by nature *dead in trespasses and sins:* and what can dead people do toward raising themselves to life? It is God who gives life to those who are spiritually dead.

5.2.3. The work of grace is only begun in this life. It is not finished here.

5.2.4. If the same God who begins the good work did not undertake to continue and finish it, it would lie unfinished forever.

5.2.5. We may be confident that God will finish the work of his own hands (Ps 138:8).

5.2.6. The work of grace will never be completed *till the day of Jesus Christ.* When he comes to judge the world, this work will be complete.

Verses 7–8

The apostle expresses his warm feelings for the Philippians: *I have you in my heart* (v. 7). Notice:

1. Why he had them in his heart: *Inasmuch as both in my bonds and in the defense and confirmation of the Gospel, you are all partakers of my grace*; they had shared in the grace of God because it had been given to them by means of him. This makes people dear to their ministers—their receiving good from their ministry. Or, "*You are partakers of my grace*; you have joined with me in my actions and my suffering." The Philippians had shared in his suffering by showing sympathy and concern and a readiness to help him. Those who bear their part of a burden will share in the reward. He loved them because they remained faithful to him in his chains and in the *defense and confirmation of the Gospel*: they were

as ready to appear in their places to defend the Gospel as the apostle was to play his part. Fellow sufferers should be dear one to another.

2. The evidence of his affection: *It is meet for me to think this of you all, because I have you in my heart.* It was clear that he had them in his heart by the good opinion he had of them. It is very proper to think the best of other people—as highly as we can.

3. An appeal to God concerning the truth of this (v. 8): *For God is my record how greatly I long after you all in the bowels* (affection) *of Jesus Christ.* Having them in his heart, he longed for them. He had *joy in them* (v. 4), because of the good he saw and heard among them. He *longed after them all*, not only those among them who were clever and excellent, but even the most insignificant and the poorest; he *longed greatly* after them. This was *in the bowels* (affection) *of Jesus Christ*, with the tender concern that Christ himself has and has shown to precious souls. Paul was a follower of Christ in this matter, and all good ministers should aim to be so too. Shall we not pity and love those souls whom Christ had such a love and pity for? He appeals to God for this: *God is my record.* "Whether you know it or not, God, who knows the heart, knows it."

Verses 9–11

Here we have the prayers Paul offered for the Philippians. Paul often let his friends know what he begged of God for them, so that they would know what to ask for themselves and be encouraged to hope they would receive from God the encouraging grace that Paul asked of God for them. He prayed that they would be:

1. A loving people. *That your love might abound yet more and more.* Those who overflow in any grace still need more and more of it, because we are imperfect in our best achievements.

2. A knowing and wisely judging people, that love would overflow *in knowledge and in all judgment.* It is not a blind love that will commend us to God. Strong passions without knowledge and a settled judgment will not make us complete in the will of God (Col 4:12), and will sometimes do more harm than good.

3. A discerning people. *That you may approve the things which are excellent* (v. 10); or, as it is in the margin, "test the things that differ"; we should be able to discern the things that are excellent by testing them, distinguishing differences. The truths and laws of Christ are excellent. We need only test them to approve them.

4. A pure, honest, and upright people: *That you may be sincere.* Purity is our Gospel perfection. If our *eye is single* (Mt 6:22), if we really are what we appear to be and our intentions are honest, then we are sincere.

5. A blameless people: "that you may be *without offense until the day of Christ,* not inclined to take offense and very careful not to give offense either to God or to your brothers and sisters." We must continue to be blameless to the end so that we may be presented so at the day of Christ.

6. A fruitful, useful people (v. 11): *Being filled with the fruits of righteousness.* Our fruit comes from God and therefore must be asked for from him. *Being filled with* them. Do not fear being emptied by producing the fruits of righteousness, because you will be filled with them. These fruits come *by Jesus Christ*, and they are *unto the glory and praise of God.* We must not seek our own glory in our fruitfulness. It is much for the honor of God when Christians not only are good but also do good, *abounding in good works* (1Ti 6:18).

Verses 12–20

Paul was now a prisoner at Rome; this might be a stumbling block to those who had received the Gospel by his ministry. They might be reluctant to acknowledge this message, fearing they might become involved in the same trouble themselves. Now to remove the offense of the cross (Gal 5:11), he explained this mysterious and hard account of his sufferings.

1. He suffered at the hands of the sworn enemies of the Gospel, but the Philippians should not be shaken by this, because good was brought out of it, and it led to the advance of the Gospel (v. 12): *The things which happened unto me have fallen out rather unto the furtherance of the Gospel.* A strange outworking of Providence is seen here, that such a great good as the advancement of the Gospel could be drawn out of such a great evil as the confinement of the apostle.

1.1. His imprisonment alarmed outsiders (v. 13): *My bonds in Christ are manifest in all the palace and in all other places.* Paul's sufferings made him known at court, and this might lead some people to ask about the Gospel for which he suffered, which they might otherwise have never heard of. When it became known in the palace that his chains were for Christ, it became known everywhere else too.

1.2. It gave boldness to those within the church. Just as his enemies were stunned by his sufferings, so his friends were encouraged by them. *Many of the brethren in the Lord waxing confident by my bonds* (v. 14). When they saw Paul imprisoned for Christ, then, far from being deterred from preaching Christ and praising his name, they were emboldened. If they were hurriedly rushed away from the pulpit to the prison, they could come to terms with it because they knew that there they would be in good company. Besides, the comfort that Paul had in his sufferings greatly encouraged them. They saw that those who served Christ served a good Master, who could both support them and strengthen them. What was intended by the enemy to discourage the preachers of the Gospel was overruled for their encouragement. Moreover, Christians *were much more bold to speak the word without fear*; they saw the worst of what might happen and were therefore not afraid to take a risk.

2. He suffered from false friends as well as from enemies (vv. 15–16): *Some preach Christ even of envy and strife. The one preach Christ of contention* (out of selfish ambition), *not sincerely.* There were those who envied Paul's reputation in the churches and who therefore tried to supplant and undermine him. *Supposing to add affliction to my bonds* (supposing they would stir up trouble for me while I am in chains). But there were also others who were encouraged by Paul's sufferings to preach Christ even more strongly: *Some also of good will, and love.* And they did so *knowing that I am set for the defense of the Gospel.* They were afraid the Gospel might suffer through his confinement, and this made them bolder to preach the word.

3. See how calm he was in the midst of all: *Notwithstanding every way* (what does it matter), *whether in pretense or in truth* (from false motives or true), *Christ is preached, and I therein do rejoice, yea, and I will rejoice* (v. 18). It is God's prerogative to judge the motives by which people act; this is beyond us. Far from envying those who were free to preach the Gospel, Paul rejoiced in its preaching even by those who did so out of selfish ambition, and not in truth.

3.1. It led to the salvation of people's souls: *I know that this shall turn to my salvation* (v. 19). God can bring good out of evil. What reward can be expected by those who preach Christ out *of strife, and envy, and contention*, and to add suffering to a faithful minister's chains, those who preach Christ out of selfish ambition, not in truth? But even this may lead to the salvation of others, and Paul's joy at it turned to his salvation too. *Through your prayers, and the supply of the Spirit of Christ* (v. 19). The prayers of the people may bring the Holy Spirit's help to their ministers, to support them in their suffering as well as in preaching the Gospel.

3.2. It would lead to the glory of Christ (v. 20): *According to my earnest expectation and hope, that in nothing I shall be ashamed.* The great desire of every true Christian is that Christ may be exalted and glorified. Those who really want Christ to be exalted want him to be *magnified in their body.* They are willing to serve his purposes with every part of their body as well as with their soul. *That in nothing I shall be ashamed, but that with all boldness Christ may be magnified.* The boldness of Christians is the honor of Christ. Those who make Christ's glory their desire may make it their expectation and hope. If it is really aimed at, it will certainly be reached. Those who want Christ to be exalted in their bodies have a holy indifference concerning *whether it be by life or by death.* They leave it to him to decide whether they will be useful for his glory by labor or by suffering, by diligence or by patience, by living for his honor in working for him or by dying for his honor in suffering for him.

Verses 21–26

We have here an account of the life and death of the apostle Paul: his life was Christ, and his death was gain (v. 21). It is the undoubted character of all true Christians that for them to live is Christ. The glory of Christ should be the goal of our life. On the other hand, death *will be gain* to all those for whom *to live is Christ.* Death is a great loss to worldly people, but it is gain to true Christians. It delivers them from all the evils of life and brings them into possession of the chief good. Some read the whole expression in this way: "To me, living and dying, Christ is gain"; that is, "I wish for no more, either while I am living or when I die, than to win Christ and be found in him (3:8–9)."

1. *If I live in the flesh, this is the fruit of my labour* (v. 22); that is, Christ is. He considered his work well done if he could only be instrumental in advancing the kingdom of Christ in the world. It is worthwhile for true Christians and good ministers to live in the world as long as they can glorify God and do good for his church. *Yet what I shall choose I wot not* (I do not know); *for I am in a strait betwixt* (torn between the) *two.* It was a wonderful difficulty Paul was in, not between two evil things, but between two good things. Paul was in a difficulty between two blessings—living for Christ and being with him.

1.1. His inclination was for death. We naturally have an aversion to death, but he had an inclination to it (v. 23): *having a desire to depart, and to be with Christ.* It is being with Christ that makes a departure desirable to good people. If I cannot be with Christ without departing, I will count it desirable on that account to depart. *Which is far better.* Those who know the value of Christ and heaven will readily acknowledge that it is far better to be in heaven than to be in this world, far better to be with Christ. If we go to be with Christ, we say farewell to sin and temptation, sorrow and death, forever.

1.2. His preference was rather to live awhile longer in this world to serve the church (v. 24): *Nevertheless to abide in the flesh is more needful for you.* Paul's difficulty was not between living in this world and living in heaven—there is no comparison between these two—but between serving Christ in this world and enjoying him in another. To advance the influence of Christ and his church, he chose rather to stay here, where he met with opposition and difficulties, and to deny himself the satisfaction of his reward for a while.

2. *And, having this confidence, I know that I shall abide and continue with you all for your furtherance and joy of faith* (v. 25). Notice:

2.1. What great confidence Paul had in divine Providence, that it would arrange all for the best to him.

2.2. We may be sure God will do whatever is best for the church.

2.3. What ministers remain here for: *For our furtherance and joy of faith*, our further progress in holiness and comfort.

2.4. What promotes our *faith and joy of faith* is very much for our progress on the way to heaven. The more faith, the more joy; the more faith and joy, the more progress we make on our Christian path.

3. *That your rejoicing may be more abundant in Jesus Christ for me, by my coming to you again* (v. 26). They rejoiced in the hope of seeing him and enjoying his further work among them. All our joys should lead to Christ. Our joy in good ministers should be our joy *in Christ Jesus for them.*

Verses 27–30

The apostle concludes the chapter with two exhortations:

1. He exhorts them to strict conduct (v. 27): *Only let your conversation* (behavior) *be as becometh* (in a manner worthy of) *the Gospel of Christ.* Let their conduct be in all respects becoming to those who belong to the kingdom of God. It adds grace to our profession of faith when our conduct corresponds to it. *That whether I come and see you, or else be absent, I may hear of your affairs.* Our religious faith must not be based on our ministers. Whether ministers come or not, Christ is always near (4:5). Let me hear about you *that you stand fast in one spirit, with one mind striving together for the faith of the Gospel.* He wanted to hear three things of them, all worthy of the Gospel:

1.1. It befits those who profess the Gospel to strive for it. There is much opposition, and there is a need for a great deal of striving. A man may fall asleep and go to hell, but those who are on the way to heaven must diligently look around them.

1.2. The unity and unanimity of Christians is consistent with the Gospel: *Strive together*, not against one another. To have one spirit and one mind is consistent with the Gospel.

1.3. Standing firm is consistent with the Gospel: *Stand fast in one spirit, with one mind.* Shame is brought to religion when its professors are bold one moment and cool the next, unfixed in their hearts (Ps 57:7) and unstable as water (Ge 49:4). Those who want to fight for the faith of the Gospel must stand by it firmly.

2. He exhorts them to be courageous and faithful in suffering: *And in nothing terrified by your adversaries* (v. 28). Whatever opposition we meet with, we must not be frightened by it. Persecuting, on the other hand, is a sure sign of destruction. Those who oppose the Gospel of Christ are destined for destruction, but being persecuted is a sign of salvation. It is not a certain mark; many hypocrites have suffered for their religion. But it is a good sign that we are serious about our religious faith when we are enabled to rightly suffer for the cause of Christ. For *to you it is given on the behalf of Christ not only to believe, but also to suffer for his name* (v. 29). Here are two precious gifts:

2.1. To believe in him; faith is God's gift on behalf of Christ.

2.2. To suffer for the sake of Christ. If we suffer shame and loss for Christ, we are to consider it a great gift, provided, always, that we behave in our suffering with the genuine attitude of martyrs (v. 30): "*Having the same conflict which you saw in me, and now hear to be in me*; suffering in the same way as you saw and now hear that I am suffering." It is not simply the suffering, but the cause, and not only the cause, but the spirit, that makes a martyr.

CHAPTER 2

1. The apostle proceeds to exhort the Philippians to several other duties: 1.1. To be in agreement with one another and humble, which he urges from the example of Christ (vv. 1–11). 1.2. To be diligent and sincere (vv. 12–13). 1.3. To adorn their Christian profession with suitable graces (vv. 14–18). 2. He then concludes with particular notice and commendation of Timothy and Epaphroditus, whom he intends to send to them (vv. 19–30).

Verses 1–11

Here are further exhortations to fulfill Christian duties. Notice:

1. The great Gospel command urged on us to love one another. Paul represents love (v. 2) as being *like-minded, having the same love, being of one accord, of one mind.* Christians should be one in love, whether they can be one in thought or not. *Having the same love.* Christian love should be mutual. Love, and you will be loved. *Being of one accord, and of one mind*, unanimously agreeing on the great things of God and keeping the *unity of the Spirit* (Eph 4:3) in other differences. Notice here:

1.1. The passionate urging of this duty. The incentives to mutual love are:

1.1.1. "*If there is any consolation in* (encouragement from being united to) *Christ.* Have you experienced encouragement in Christ? Prove that experience by loving one another." Do we expect encouragement from being united to Christ? If we do not want to be disappointed, we must love one another.

1.1.2. "*If there is any comfort of* (comfort from his) *love.* If there is any comfort in God's love for you, in your love for God, or in the love of your brothers and sisters to us, be like-minded."

1.1.3. "*If there is any fellowship of* (fellowship with) *the Spirit.* If there is such a thing as fellowship with God and Christ through the Spirit, such a thing as the communion of saints, be of the same mind."

1.1.4. "*If there is any any bowels and mercies* (tenderness and compassion) in God and Christ toward you. If you expect to enjoy God's compassion toward yourselves, be compassionate to one another."

1.1.5. The encouragement it would be to him: *Fulfil you my joy.* It is the joy of ministers to see people living in harmony and love. Paul has been instrumental in bringing the Philippians to the grace of Christ and the love of God. "Now," he says, "*fulfil the joy* of your poor minister, who preached the Gospel to you."

1.2. Some means to advance it.

1.2.1. *Do nothing through strife and vain glory* (selfish ambition or vain conceit) (v. 3). Christ came to put to death all hostilities (Eph 2:16); among Christians, therefore, let there not be a spirit of opposition. Christ came to humble us, and so let there not be a spirit of pride among us.

1.2.2. We must, *in lowliness of mind, esteem others better than ourselves*, be strict toward ourselves as regards our own faults and charitable in our judgments of others. We must consider the good that is in others as greater than what is in ourselves, for we are the best ones to know our own unworthiness and imperfections.

1.2.3. We must be concerned for others in Christian love and sympathy: *Look not every man on his own things, but every man also on the things of others* (v. 4). A selfish spirit destroys Christian love. We must love our neighbor as ourselves (Lev 19:18; Mk 12:31) and make their case our own.

2. A Gospel pattern proposed, and that is the example of our Lord Jesus Christ: *Let this mind be in you which was also in Christ Jesus* (v. 5). Christians must have Christ's attitude. We must display a resemblance to his life if we want to benefit from his death. He had a very humble attitude, and it is this that we are especially to learn from him. If we were humble, we would all be of one mind, and if we were like Christ, we would be humble. Walk in the same spirit as the Lord Jesus, who humbled himself to suffer and die for us.

2.1. Here are the two natures of Christ. His divine nature: *Who being in the form of God* (v. 6), sharing in the divine nature as the eternal Son of God. *He thought it no robbery to be equal with God*; he did not think himself guilty of invading what did not belong to him. It is the highest degree of robbery for any mere mortal or mere creature to claim to be equal with God. His human nature: he was *made in the likeness of men* and *found in fashion as a man*. He was really and truly human. He voluntarily assumed human nature; it was his own act. We cannot say that of our own participation in human nature. Here, he *made himself of no reputation*—literally, "emptied himself"—to clothe himself with the rags of human nature.

2.2. Here are his two states, his humiliation and his exaltation.

2.2.1. His humiliation. The *form of a servant*. He was not only God's servant but also a minister to people, among them as one who serves. One would have thought that the Lord Jesus, if he was going to be a human being, would have been a ruler. But quite the contrary: *He took upon him the form of a servant*. He was brought up in humble, lowly circumstances, probably working with his supposed father at his trade. His whole life was a life of humiliation. But the lowest step of his humiliation was when he died on the cross: *He became obedient to death, even the death of the cross*. He not only suffered but was voluntarily obedient. An emphasis is put here on the way in which he died, which was humbling in every circumstance: *Even the death of the cross*, a cursed, shameful death (Dt 21:23; Gal 3:13)—full of pain, the death of an evildoer and a slave, not of a freeman, exposing him as a public spectacle.

2.2.2. His exaltation: *Wherefore God also hath highly exalted him*. Because he humbled himself, God exalted him (Lk 14:11); he *highly exalted him*. He exalted his whole person, the human nature as well as the divine. His exaltation here is said to consist in honor and power. *He had a name above every name. Every knee must bow to him*. The whole creation must be put in submission to him: *things in heaven, and things in earth, and things under the earth*, the inhabitants of heaven and earth, the living and the dead. *At the name of Jesus* all would give solemn homage. *Every tongue would confess that Jesus Christ is Lord*. The kingdom of Christ reaches to

heaven and earth, and to all the creatures in each, and to the dead as well as the living. *To the glory of God the Father*. Whatever respect is given to Christ leads to the honor of the Father.

Verses 12–13

1. He exhorts the Philippians to live the Christian life conscientiously and seriously: *Work out your own salvation*. We should be concerned above everything else to protect the welfare of our souls; whatever becomes of other things, let us take care of our best interests. It is our own salvation. It is not for us to judge other people; we have enough to do in looking to ourselves. We are required to *work out our salvation*. The word means "working thoroughly" and "taking true pains over it." We must not only work *at* our salvation, doing something occasionally about it; we must work *out* our salvation, doing all that is to be done and persevering in it to the end. We cannot attain salvation without the greatest care and diligence. *With fear and trembling*, that is, with great care and carefulness. Fear is a great guard and preservation from evil.

2. He urges this from the consideration of their readiness always to obey the Gospel: "*As you have always obeyed, not as in my presence only, but now much more in my absence*" (v. 12). They were not merely in awe at the apostle's presence, but obeyed even *much more in his absence*. "And because *it is God who worketh in you*, you are to work out your salvation. Work because he is working in you." God is ready to agree with his grace and to help our faithful endeavors. The actions of God's grace in us, far from excusing us, are intended to spur us on in our endeavors. "And work out your salvation *with fear and trembling*, for *he worketh in you*. Work with *fear*, because he works from his *good pleasure*." *To will and to do*. It is the grace of God that inclines the will to do what is good; it is the grace of God that then enables us to perform it. *Of his good pleasure*. Just as we cannot act without God's grace, so we cannot pretend to deserve that grace.

Verses 14–18

The apostle exhorts the Philippians to grace their Christian profession with a suitable attitude and behavior.

1. By a cheerful obedience to the commands of God (v. 14): "*Do all things without murmurings*. Be taken up with your work, and do not quarrel with it." God's commands were given to be obeyed, not argued with.

2. By being peaceful and loving to one another. "*Do all things without disputing*. The light of truth and the life of religious faith are often lost in the anger and mists of an argument."

3. By leading a blameless life toward all (v. 15): *That you may be blameless and harmless, the sons of God, without rebuke*. We should seek not only not to do harm, but also not to come under any just suspicion of it. The *sons of God*. The children of God should be different from the children of the world.

3.1. *Without rebuke*. We should endeavor not only to get to heaven but also to get there faultless.

3.2. *In the midst of a crooked and perverse generation*. Where there is no true religious faith, little is to be expected but sinfulness and perverseness, and the more sinful and perverse others are among whom we live, the more careful we should be to keep ourselves blameless and pure. *Among whom you shine as lights in the world*. True Christians are lights in the world (Mt 5:14). When God raises up a good person in any place, he sets up a light in that place. Christians must shine as well as be sincere.

3.3. *Holding forth the word of life* (v. 16). It is our duty not only to hold firmly to the word of life but also to hold it out for the benefit of others, to hold it out as a lampstand holds out the light. "*That I may rejoice in the day of Christ*, rejoice not only in your firmness but also in your usefulness." He wanted them to believe that *he had not run in vain, nor laboured in vain.* Notice:

3.3.1. The work of the ministry requires the exertion of the whole person. *Running* shows intensity and vigor; *labor* shows faithfulness and close application.

3.3.2. It is a great joy to ministers to realize that they have not *run in vain, nor laboured in vain*, and it will be their rejoicing on the day of Christ, when their converts will be their crown. The apostle not only ran and labored for them with satisfaction; he was also ready to suffer for their good (v. 17): *Yea, and if I be offered upon the sacrifice and service of your faith, I joy and rejoice with you all.* He could willingly be a sacrifice at their altars to serve the faith of God's chosen ones. If Paul thought it worthwhile to die for the service of the church, shall we think it too much to take a few pains? He could rejoice to seal his doctrine with his blood (v. 18): *For the same cause also do you joy and rejoice with me.* It is the will of God that true Christians be joyful, and those who are fortunate to have good ministers have great reason to *joy and rejoice with him.*

Verses 19–30

Paul takes particular notice of two good ministers, for although he himself was a great apostle, who *laboured more abundantly than they all* (1Co 15:10), he still took the opportunity to speak with great respect of those less able than he. He speaks of:

1. Timothy, whom he intends to send to the Philippians. *For I have no man like minded, who will naturally care for your state.* Timothy was unique; none was comparable to him. He was a man with an excellent spirit and a tender heart. *Who will naturally care for your state.* Things go best with us when our duty becomes, in a way, natural to us. *Naturally*, that is, sincerely, not in pretense, taking a genuine interest in the Philippians' welfare. This shows us:

1.1. It is the duty of ministers to be genuinely concerned for the state and welfare of their people.

1.2. It is rare to find a minister who does so naturally.

1.2.1. *All seek their own, not the things which are Jesus Christ's* (v. 21). Did Paul say this in haste, as David said, *All men are liars* (Ps 116:11)? No, he is referring to the general situation; *all* here means either most or all in comparison with Timothy. Many put their own reputation, comfort, and security first, before truth, holiness, and duty.

1.2.2. But Timothy was not like that. *You know the proof of him* (he has proved himself) (v. 22). Timothy was a man who had been tried and tested and was faithful in all that happened to him. He had proved himself in all the churches he knew. He was as good as he seemed to be. *As a son with a father, he hath served with me in the Gospel.* He was Paul's helper in many places. They ministered together with great respect and with great warmth and kindness—a wonderful example to elder and younger ministers united in the same service.

1.2.3. Paul wanted to send Timothy soon: *Him therefore I hope to send presently, as soon as I shall see how it will go with me* (v. 23). Paul was now a prisoner, and he did not know how events would turn out. He hoped to come himself too (v. 24): *But I trust in the Lord that I also myself shall come shortly.* Paul wanted to be set free not

so that he could sit back and do nothing for the rest of his life, but so that he could do good. *I trust in the Lord.* He expressed his hope of seeing them with a humble submission to God's will.

2. Epaphroditus, whom he calls *his brother, and companion in labour, and fellow soldier, who ministered to my wants* (took care of my needs). Epaphroditus passionately wanted to come to them, and Paul was willing that he do so.

2.1. Epaphroditus had been ill: *They had heard that he had been sick* (v. 26); *indeed he was sick, nigh unto death* (v. 27).

2.2. The Philippians were very sad to hear about his illness. He was one for whom they had a particular respect and affection, one whom they thought fit to send to the apostle.

2.3. It pleased God to restore and spare him: *But God had mercy on him* (v. 27). The apostle acknowledges it as a great mercy to himself as well as to Epaphroditus and others. He was greatly touched by the thoughts of such a great loss: *Lest I should have sorrow upon sorrow*, that is, "fearing that, besides the sorrow of my own imprisonment, I would also have the sorrow of his death."

2.4. Epaphroditus was willing to visit the Philippians so that he could be comforted with those who had been sorrowful for him when he was ill: "*That when you see him again, you may rejoice*" (v. 28). He gave himself the pleasure of comforting them by the sight of such a dear friend.

2.5. Paul commends him to their respect and affection: "*Receive him therefore in the Lord with all gladness, and hold such in reputation*: consider such zealous and faithful people valuable; let them be loved and held in high regard." It seems Epaphroditus had caught his illness in the work of God: *It was for the work of Christ that he was nigh to death, and to supply your lack of service to me* (make up for the help you could not give me). The apostle believes they should love him all the more for risking his life to serve the Gospel. What is given us in answer to prayer should be received with great thankfulness and joy.

CHAPTER 3

Here: 1. The apostle warns the Philippians against Judaizing deceivers (vv. 1–3). 2. He proposes himself as an example to them, and in so doing: 2.1. He lists the privileges he rejected (vv. 4–8). 2.2. He describes the content of his own choice (vv. 9–16). 3. He closes with an exhortation to watch out for evildoers and follow his example (vv. 17–21).

Verses 1–3

It seems the Philippian church, though a faithful and flourishing church, was disturbed by the Judaizing teachers.

1. He exhorts to them to *rejoice in the Lord* (v. 1). The more we enjoy our religious faith, the more closely we will remain faithful to it; the more we rejoice in Christ, the more willing we will be to suffer for him, and the less danger we will be in of being drawn away from him.

2. He warns them to watch out for those false teachers: *To write the same thing to you to me indeed is not grievous* (is no trouble), *but for you it is safe* (it is a safeguard for you). Ministers must not think anything a trouble to them that they have reason to believe is safe and edifying to the people. It is good for us to hear the same truths often. To always want to hear something new shows unrestrained

curiosity (Ac 17:21). *Beware of dogs* (v. 2). The Judaizing teachers are *dogs* in their malice toward the faithful professors of the Gospel of Christ, barking at them and biting them. They praise good works in opposition to the faith of Christ, but Paul calls them evildoers: they boast that they themselves belong to the circumcision, but he calls them the *concision* (mutilators of the flesh).

3. He describes true Christians. *We are the circumcision, who worship God in the spirit, and rejoice in Christ Jesus, and have no confidence in the flesh.* Here are three characteristics:

3.1. They worshiped in the spirit, in opposition to the external regulations of the Old Testament. Christianity teaches us to be internal, to have a heart relationship with God in all the duties of religious worship. The work of religion is futile if the heart is not employed in it.

3.2. They *rejoiced in Christ Jesus*. Now that the substance has come, the shadows are done away with (Col 2:17; Heb 8:5; 10:1), and we are to rejoice only in Jesus Christ.

3.3. They had no *confidence in the flesh*, in those external regulations and actions. Our confidence, as well as our joy, is all in him.

Verses 4–8

The apostle here suggests himself as an example of trusting only in Christ.

1. He shows what he has to boast of as a Jew and a Pharisee. *If any other man thinketh that he hath whereof to trust in the flesh, I more* (v. 4). He had as much to boast of as any Jew had.

1.1. He could boast of his birthright privileges. He was not a convert, but a native Israelite: *of the stock of Israel.* He came from the *tribe of Benjamin.* He was *a Hebrew of the Hebrews*, an Israelite on both sides, and from one generation to another; none of his ancestors had married Gentiles.

1.2. He could boast of his relationship with the covenant, because he was *circumcised the eighth day.*

1.3. In his learning, he had been a Pharisee, brought up at the feet of Gamaliel (Ac 22:3). He was *a Pharisee, the son of a Pharisee* (Ac 23:6).

1.4. His conduct had been blameless: *Touching the righteousness which is of the law* (as for legalistic righteousness), *blameless*. As to the mere letter of the law and its outward observance, he could acquit himself from disobedience to it and could not be accused by anyone of breaking it.

1.5. He had been active for his religion. *Concerning zeal, persecuting the church.*

1.6. He showed that he was serious, though he had a zeal without knowledge (Ro 10:2). With all this, he was fully provisioned to undertake his own justification.

2. He tells us here how insignificant he considers these: *But what things were gain to me, those have I counted loss for Christ* (v. 7). "I would have considered myself an overwhelming loser if, to remain faithful to those things, I had not known Jesus Christ." The apostle did not try to persuade them to abandon anything except what he himself had abandoned. *Yea doubtless, and I count all things but loss for the excellency of the knowledge of* (the surpassing greatness of knowing) *Christ Jesus my Lord.*

2.1. He tells us what he reaches for: to know Christ Jesus his Lord, to believingly know Christ as Lord in his own experience, to have not a speculative but a practical knowledge of him. And what he values is not merely the knowing of Christ, but the surpassing greatness of knowing him. There is an abundant, transcendent, surpassing greatness in the teaching of Christ, above all the knowledge of nature and all the improvements of human wisdom.

2.2. He shows how he abandoned his privileges as a Jew and a Pharisee: *Yea doubtless* (what is more); his expression rises in holy triumph and elevation: "But indeed even also do *I count all things but loss.*" He has just spoken of *those things*, his Jewish privileges (v. 7): here he speaks of *all things*. He said there that he counted them loss, but it might be asked, "Did he still continue to think the same?" Now he speaks in the present tense: *Yea doubtless, I do count them but loss.* He tells us that he himself has lived according to this view: *For whom I have suffered the loss of all things.* When he embarked on the path of the Christian faith, he risked all for it, and he suffered the loss of all to enjoy instead the privileges of being a Christian. He counted his earthly honors not only loss but even *dung*, offal thrown to dogs. Worldly things are not only less valuable than Christ; they are utterly contemptible when they compete with him.

Verses 9–14

What the apostle took hold of were Christ and heaven.

1. The apostle had his heart set on Christ as his righteousness.

1.1. He wanted to gain Christ. "That I may gain him," as a runner wins a prize, as sailors reach the port they are bound for.

1.2. He wanted to *be found in him* (v. 9). We are ruined without a righteousness in which to appear before God, and a righteousness is provided for us in Jesus Christ. *Not having my own righteousness, which is of the law.* "Not thinking that my outward observances and good deeds can atone for my bad ones. No; the righteousness that I depend on is that *which is through the faith of Christ*, not a legal righteousness, based on keeping the Law, but an evangelical righteousness, based on accepting the Gospel: *The righteousness which is of God by faith*, ordained and appointed by God." Faith is the ordained means of sharing in the saving benefits of what has been purchased by Christ's blood.

1.3. He wanted to know Christ (v. 10): *That I may know him, and the power of his resurrection, and the fellowship of his sufferings.* Knowing him here on earth means believing in him: it is an experiential knowledge. The apostle was as ambitious to be sanctified as he was to be justified.

1.4. He wanted to become like him. We are made like Christ in his death when we die to sin as he did, when we are crucified with Christ and the *world is crucified to us.*

2. The apostle had his heart set on heaven as his happiness: *If by any means I might attain to the resurrection of the dead* (v. 11).

2.1. The happiness of heaven is here called the resurrection of the dead. The apostle had his eyes set on this; he wanted to attain it. There will be a resurrection of the unjust (Da 12:2), and we must be concerned to escape that, but the joyful and glorious resurrection of saints is a resurrection by virtue of Christ, as their head and firstfruits, whereas that of evildoers is a resurrection only by the power of Christ, as their judge. There will be a true resurrection for the saints, while the resurrection of evildoers is a rising only to return to a second death (Rev 20:14).

2.2. Toward this joyful resurrection the apostle pressed on. He speaks as if the Philippians were in danger of missing it and falling short of it. A holy fear of falling short is an excellent means of perseverance. Even Paul himself did not hope to attain it through his own merit, but through the merit of Jesus Christ. Notice:

2.2.1. He looks on himself as in a state of imperfection and testing: *Not as though I had already attained, or were already perfect* (v. 12). The best people in the world will readily acknowledge their imperfection in the present state. If Paul had not attained perfection, then much less have we. *Brethren, I count not myself to have apprehended* (do not consider myself to have taken hold) (v. 13). Thinking that one has enough grace proves only that one does not, or rather that one has none at all, because wherever there is true grace, there is a desire for more grace.

2.2.2. What were the apostle's actions under this conviction. "*I follow after* (v. 12), I pursue with vigor, *if that I may apprehend that for which also I am apprehended of Christ Jesus* (to take hold of that for which Christ Jesus took hold of me)." It is not our taking hold of Christ first, but his taking hold of us, that is our happiness and salvation. Our security is not in our keeping hold of Christ, but in his keeping hold of us. *To apprehend that for which we are apprehended of Christ.* To take hold of that for which Christ Jesus took hold of us is to attain the perfection of our bliss. Paul adds further (v. 13): *This one thing I do, forgetting those things which are behind, and reaching forth to those things which are before.* Paul forgot the things that were behind; he always wanted more and more. So he *reached forth.*

2.2.3. The apostle's aim: *I press towards the mark, for the prize of the high calling of God in Christ Jesus* (v. 14). The fitter we become for heaven, the faster we must press on toward it. Heaven is the *prize of the high calling,* what we aim at in all we do and what will be the reward of all our effort. It is from God; we are to expect it from him. But it is in Christ Jesus; it must come to us through his hand. We cannot go to heaven as our home except through Christ as the way.

Verses 15–16

Having offered himself as an example, the apostle urges the Philippians to follow it. Let us be of the same mind. He shows that:

1. The thing on which all true Christians agree is that they must make Christ all in all and set their hearts on another world. This is the point we have all attained. Let us follow the same rule, therefore, and be concerned with the same thing. Having made Christ our all, *to us to live must be Christ* (1:21).

2. This is a good reason why Christians who differ in less significant matters should still bear with one another, because they agree on the main point: "*If in any thing you be otherwise minded,* you still must not judge one another, as long as you all now meet in Christ as your center and hope to meet soon in heaven as your home. *God shall reveal even this unto you.* Whatever it is that you differ about, you must wait until God gives you a better understanding. *As far as you have attained,* you must travel together in the things of God, waiting for further light in the insignificant points on which you differ."

Verses 17–21

He closes the chapter with warnings and appeals.

1. He warns them against following the examples of evil teachers (vv. 18–19): *Many walk, of whom I have told you often, and now tell you weeping, that they are the enemies of the cross of Christ.*

1.1. Many who are called by Christ's name are in fact enemies of Christ's cross. Their life is more reliable evidence than their profession of faith. *I have told you often.* We take so little notice of the warnings given us that we need them repeated to us often. *I now tell you weeping.* What we say often we may say again, if we say it with feeling.

1.2. He describes those who are the enemies of the cross of Christ.

1.2.1. Their god is their stomach. Their only concern is their physical appetite. The same service that good people render to God is rendered by Epicures to their appetites.

1.2.2. They glory in their shame. "They pride themselves on what is their blemish and disgrace."

1.2.3. They are taken up with worldly things. Those whose hearts and affections are set on worldly things (Col 3:2) act directly contrary to the cross of Christ. How absurd it would be for Christians to follow the example of such people. To deter us all from doing so, Paul reads out their destiny.

1.2.4. Their destiny is destruction. Their way of life seems pleasant, but death and hell lie at its end (Pr 14:12). If we choose their way of life, we have reason to fear their end.

2. He suggests himself and his brothers as an example: *Brethren, be followers together of me, and mark those who walk as you have us for an example* (take note of those who live according to the pattern we gave you) (v. 17). In v. 20 he explains himself as referring to their regard for Christ and heaven: *For our conversation* (citizenship) *is in heaven.* Even while true Christians are here on earth, their citizenship is in heaven. This world is not our home, but that one is. The life of Christians is in heaven, where their home is and where they hope to be soon. It is good to have fellowship with those who have fellowship with Christ, to share with those whose citizenship is in heaven.

2.1. We look for the Savior from heaven (v. 20): *Whence also we look for the Saviour, the Lord Jesus Christ.* We expect his second coming from there.

2.2. At the second coming of Christ we expect to be happy and glorified there. *Who shall change our vile bodies, that they may be fashioned like unto his glorious body* (v. 21). There is a glory reserved for the saints, a glory in which they will be instated at the resurrection. The body is now at best a *vile body,* "the body of our humiliation." But it will be made a glorious body. *According to the working whereby he is able even to subdue all things unto himself.* It is a matter of encouragement to us that he can subdue all things under himself. The resurrection will be brought about by this power. Let our faith in the resurrection be strengthened by the assurance that we not only have the Scriptures, which assure us it will happen, but also *know the power of God,* which can carry it out (Mt 22:29). Just as Christ's resurrection was a glorious example of divine power, so will our resurrection be. Then all the enemies of the Redeemer's kingdom will be completely conquered.

CHAPTER 4

We have here: 1. Exhortations to various Christian duties (vv. 1–9). 2. The apostle's grateful acknowledgments of the Philippians' kindness to him (vv. 10–19). 3. The apostle's concluding with praise, greetings, and blessing (vv. 20–23).

Verses 1–9

The apostle begins the chapter with exhortations to do various Christian duties.

1. To stand firm in our Christian profession (v. 1). Since our citizenship is in heaven (3:20), and we look for

the Savior to come from there and take us there, *therefore let us stand fast*. A faithful expectation of eternal life should make us consistent in our Christian way of life. Notice:

1.1. The apostle's endearing expressions: *my brethren, dearly beloved and longed for, my joy and crown*; and again, *my dearly beloved*. This is how he expresses the delight he takes in them in order to convey his exhortations to them with so much greater advantage. Because they are brothers and sisters:

1.1.1. He loves them dearly: *dearly beloved*; and again, *my dearly beloved*. Mutual love must always go along with family relationships.

1.1.2. He loves them and longs for them.

1.1.3. He loves them and rejoices in them. They are his joy.

1.1.4. He loves them and glories in them. They are his crown as well as his *joy*.

1.2. The exhortation itself: *So stand fast in the Lord*. Because they are in Christ, they must stand firm in him, faithful to the end. Or to *stand fast in the Lord* is to stand firm in his strength and through his grace. We must not trust in ourselves, but in his sufficiency.

2. To agree with and help one another (vv. 2–3): *I beseech Euodias and Syntyche that they be of the same mind in the Lord*. This is directed to some particular individuals. Sometimes the general commands of the Gospel need to be applied to particular individuals and cases. Euodia and Syntyche, it seems, disagreed, either with one another or with the church. "I beg you," Paul writes, "to agree in the Lord, to keep the peace and live in love, to agree with the rest of the church." He then exhorts certain particular individuals to help each other (v. 3):

2.1. *I entreat thee also, true yoke fellow*. Who this *true yoke fellow* was is uncertain. He exhorts his yokefellow to *help the women who laboured with him*. Whoever the yokefellow of the apostle was, they must also have been a yokefellow of his friends. It seems there were women who worked hard with Paul in the cause of the Gospel. Women may help ministers in the work of the Gospel. *Do thou help them*. Those who help others should themselves be helped when necessary.

2.2. With *Clement also, and other my fellow labourers*. Paul cared for all his fellow workers, *whose names are in the book of life*. There is a Book of Life; there are names, not only characters and conditions, written in that book. We cannot look into that book or know whose names are written there, but we can conclude that those who work hard for the Gospel have their names written in the Book of Life.

3. To *rejoice in the Lord always, and again I say, Rejoice* (v. 4). All our joy must lead to God, and our thoughts of God must be delightful. It is our duty and privilege to rejoice in God, and to rejoice in him always, at all times, in all conditions. There is enough in God to provide us with matter for joy in the worst circumstance on earth. Paul said it before (3:1): *Finally, my brethren, rejoice in the Lord*. He says it here again. If good people do not have a continual feast (Pr 15:15), they only have themselves to blame.

4. To be kind and gentle, showing a good attitude toward our brothers and sisters: "*Let your moderation be known to all men* (v. 5). In neutral things do not go to extremes; have loving thoughts about one another." Some understand it as referring to the patient bearing of suffering or the sober enjoyment of worldly good; *the Lord is at hand*. "He will take vengeance on your enemies and reward your patience."

5. Not to yield to disturbing, perplexing worries (v. 6): "*Be careful for nothing*, do not have anxious and distracting thoughts about the needs and difficulties of life." It is the duty and concern of Christians to live without worries. There is a care to be diligent that consists of foresight, which is our duty, but there is also a care that consists of distrust, which is our sin and foolishness.

6. To pray constantly: *In everything by prayer and supplication, with thanksgiving, let your requests be made known to God*. Notice:

6.1. We must pray not only regularly but also in response to every pressing need: *In everything by prayer*. When anything burdens our spirits, we must relieve our hearts by prayer; when our affairs are bewildering or distressing, we must seek direction and support from God in prayer.

6.2. We must add thanksgiving to our prayers and supplications. We must not only seek supplies of good but also acknowledge receipts of mercy.

6.3. Prayer is the offering of our desires to God: *Let your requests be made known to God*. It is not that God needs to be told either our needs or our desires, but he wants to know them from us.

6.4. The effect of this will be the *peace of God keeping our hearts* (v. 7). The *peace of God which passeth all understanding* is a greater good than can be sufficiently valued or properly expressed. This peace *will keep our hearts and minds through Christ Jesus*; it will keep us from sinning in our troubles and from sinking under them.

7. To obtain and keep a good name. We must seek *whatsoever things are true and honest* (noble) (v. 8), having regard for truth and for consistency in behavior; whatever things are *just and pure*, without the impurity of sin; whatever things are *lovely and of good report*, which will make us loved and well spoken of. *If there is any virtue, if there is any praise*, we must think about such things. Notice:

7.1. The apostle wanted the Christians to learn anything that was good from their ungodly neighbors: "*If there be any virtue, think of these things*—imitate them in what is really excellent among them." We should not be ashamed to learn good things from bad people.

7.2. Goodness is commendable. *Those things which you have learned, and received, and heard and seen in me, do*. Paul's message and life were in harmony. He could suggest himself as well as his message for them to imitate. We give great force to what we say to others when we can appeal to what they have seen in us.

Verses 10–19

Here is a grateful acknowledgment of the kindness of the Philippians.

1. Paul uses the occasion to acknowledge their past kindnesses to him (vv. 15–16). See what a grateful spirit Paul had. Wherever this letter is read, their act of kindness toward Paul will be told in memory of them (Mt 26:13). Surely never was a present so well repaid. *In the beginning of the Gospel no church communicated* (shared) *with me as to giving and receiving, but ye only* (v. 15). They supported him not only while he was with them but even when *he departed from Macedonia*; they did this when no other church did. They were the only church that was so fair and generous. *Even in Thessalonica you sent once and again to my necessity* (v. 16). Notice:

1.1. They sent only such things as he needed; he did not desire an excessive amount or delicacies.

1.2. It is excellent to see those to whom God has given many gifts of his grace overflowing with gratitude to their ministers, according to their own ability and their needs. *You sent once and again.* Many people excuse themselves from charity by saying that they have given once; why should they have to give again? But the Philippians sent again and again.

2. He excuses their recent neglect. *Now at the last your care of me hath flourished again* (v. 10), like a tree in the spring, which seemed quite dead all winter. He makes an excuse for them: *wherein you were also careful, but you lacked opportunity.* They would have done it if a fair opportunity had offered itself.

3. He commends their present generosity: *Notwithstanding, you have well done that you did communicate* (share) *with my affliction* (v. 14). See here the nature of true Christian sympathy: not only to be concerned for our friends in their troubles but also to do what we can to help them. The apostle rejoiced greatly in it (v. 10), because it was evidence of their affection toward him and the success of his ministry among them.

4. He takes care to prevent the bad use some might make of his taking so much notice of what was sent him. His recognition of the gift did not proceed either from discontent and distrust (v. 11) or from greed and love of the world (v. 12).

4.1. Not from discontent or distrust: *Not that I speak in respect of want* (v. 11); he was not referring to any need he felt or any lack he feared. As to the former, he was content with the little he had; it satisfied him. As to the latter, he depended on the providence of God to provide for him from day to day, and that satisfied him: *For I have learned, in whatsoever state I am, therewith to be content.* That was the lesson he needed to learn as much as most people, considering the hardships and sufferings with which he was exercised. *I know both how to be abased and I know how to abound* (v. 12). This is a special act of grace, to come to terms with every condition of life:

4.1.1. To come to terms with our miserable condition—to know how to be in need so as not to be overcome by the temptations associated with it.

4.1.2. To accept prosperity—to know how to have plenty so as not to become proud or self-confident. This is as hard a lesson as the other, because the temptations of fullness and prosperity are no less than those of suffering and need. But how must we learn it? *I can do all things through Christ who strengthens me* (v. 13). We need his strength to teach us to be content in every condition. Just now the apostle seemed to boast about himself and his own strength: *I know how to be abased* (v. 12); but here he transfers all the praise to Christ. "It is through his constant and renewed strength I am enabled to act in everything."

4.2. Not from greed: *"Not because I desired a gift* (v. 17). I welcome your kindness because it is credited to your account. *I desire fruit that may abound to your account. I have all, and abound* (v. 18). What can anyone want more than enough?" *I am full, having received from Epaphroditus the things which were sent by you.* Covetous worldly people always want more, no matter how much they have, but heavenly Christians have enough even if they have only a little.

5. The apostle assures them that God has accepted and will reward their kindness to him.

5.1. He has accepted it: *It is an odour of a sweet smell, a sacrifice acceptable, well-pleasing to God.* It was a sacrifice of acknowledgment, *well pleasing to God.* It was more acceptable to God as the fruit of their grace than it was to Paul as the supply of his needs.

5.2. He will reward it: *But my God shall supply all your wants according to his riches in glory by Christ Jesus* (v. 19). Paul writes a check, as it were, drawn on the treasury in heaven, and leaves it to God to pay the Philippians back. "You have supplied my needs according to your poverty; he will supply yours according to his riches." But it is still through Christ Jesus; through him we have grace to do what is good. What God gives, he gives not as a debt but as grace.

Verses 20–23

The apostle concludes the letter in these verses with:

1. Praise to God: *Now unto God and our Father be glory for ever and ever. Amen* (v. 20). God is to be considered by us as our Father. This is a favor distinctive to the Gospel age. In all our weaknesses and fears, we should look on God not as a tyrant, but as a Father, who pities us and helps us (Ps 103:13; Mk 9:22). Accordingly, we must thankfully acknowledge the receipt of all we are and have from him, and we must give the praise for everything to him. And our praise must be constant and perpetual; it must be *glory for ever and ever.*

2. Greetings to his friends at Philippi: *Salute every saint in Christ Jesus* (v. 21). Paul had a love for all Christians.

3. Greetings from those who are at Rome: *"The brethren who are with me,* all the saints here, *salute you. Chiefly those who are of Caesar's household,* the Christian converts who belong to the emperor's court." There were saints in Caesar's household. The Gospel was successful at an early age among some rich and great people.

4. The usual apostolic blessing: "The grace of our Lord Jesus Christ be with you all. Amen."

A Practical and Devotional Exposition of

Colossians

Colosse was a significant city in Phrygia, probably not far from Laodicea and Hierapolis; we find these mentioned together (4:13). It is now in ruins, its memory chiefly preserved in this letter. The purpose of the letter is to warn the readers of the danger of the Jewish zealots. Paul takes great satisfaction in the Colossians' firmness and faithfulness. The letter was written while he was a prisoner at Rome. He was not idle in his confinement, and the word of God was not bound (2Ti 2:9). The letter, like that to the Romans, was written to people he had never seen. The church was planted at Colosse not by Paul's ministry, but by the ministry of Epaphras, whom he delegated to preach the Gospel among the Gentiles (1:7), and yet: 1. There was a flourishing church at Colosse, and one that was famous among the other churches. God sometimes uses the ministry of those who are less notable and have lower gifts to do great service for his church. God uses whatever hands he pleases and is not limited to those who are notable. 2. Although Paul did not plant this church, he did not for that reason neglect it. The Colossians were as dear to him as the Philippians or any others who were converted through his ministry.

CHAPTER 1

We have here: 1. The apostle's opening greeting (vv. 1–2). 2. His thanksgiving to God for the Colossians' faith, love, and hope (vv. 3–8). 3. His prayer for their knowledge, fruitfulness, and strength (vv. 9–11). 4. An admirable summary of Christian doctrine concerning the activity of the Spirit, the person of the Redeemer, the work of redemption, and the preaching of it in the Gospel (vv. 12–29).

Verses 1–2

1. Paul calls himself an *apostle of Jesus Christ by the will of God.* He thought himself obligated to do all he could as an apostle because he was designated such by the will of God. He links Timothy with himself in the commission and, though elsewhere he calls him *his son,* here he calls him his brother. He calls the Christians at Colosse *saints, and faithful brethren in Christ.* All true Christians are brothers and sisters of one another, and they must be saints toward God. In both these aspects, as saints toward God and as brothers and sisters toward one another, they must be faithful. Faithfulness runs through every characteristic and relationship of the Christian life and is the crown and glory of them all.

2. The apostolic blessing is the same as usual: *Grace be unto you, and peace, from God our Father, and the Lord Jesus Christ.* He wishes them *grace and peace,* the free favor of God and all its blessed fruits.

Verses 3–8

1. In his prayers for the Colossians, Paul gives thanks for them. Thanksgiving should be a part of every prayer. Notice:

1.1. Whom he gives thanks to: *to God, even the Father of our Lord Jesus Christ.* In our thanksgiving we must look to God as God and as the Father of our Lord Jesus Christ, in and through whom all good comes to us.

1.2. What he gives thanks to God for—for the graces of God in them. *Since we heard of your faith in Christ Jesus, and of the love you have to all the saints, for the hope which is laid up for you in heaven* (vv. 4–5). Faith, hope, and love are the three principal graces in the Christian life. He gives thanks:

1.2.1. For their faith in Christ Jesus, that they were brought to believe in him.

1.2.2. For their love. Besides the general love that is due to all, there is a particular love owing to the saints. We must love all the saints, despite any minor differences and many real weaknesses.

1.2.3. For their hope: *The hope which is laid up for you in heaven* (v. 5). What is given to believers in this world is much, but what is stored up for them in heaven is very much more. The more we fix our hopes on the reward in the next world, the freer we will be with our earthly treasure in taking every opportunity to do good.

2. He blesses God for the means of grace they enjoy: *Wherein you heard before in the word of the truth of the Gospel.*

2.1. The Gospel is the word of truth, and we may safely trust our immortal souls to it. He calls it *the grace of God in truth* (v. 6).

2.2. It is a great blessing to hear this word of truth, *which has come unto you, as it hath to all the world, and bringeth forth fruit, as it doth also in you* (v. 6). All who hear the word of the Gospel should bear the fruit of the Gospel. Wherever the Gospel comes, it will bear fruit to the honor and glory of God. We are mistaken if we think we can keep the comforts and benefits of the Gospel to ourselves.

3. He mentions the minister through whom they believed (vv. 7–8): *As you also learned of Epaphras, our*

dear fellowservant, who is for you a faithful minister of Christ. He calls Epaphras his *fellowservant.* They were fellow workers in the work of the Lord. He calls him his *dear fellowservant:* it is an appealing consideration that they are engaged in the same service. He describes him as a faithful minister of Christ to them. He does not say "who is your minister," but *who is the minister of Christ for you.* It is by Christ's authority and appointment that Epaphras is a minister. Paul describes him as one who gave them a good word: *Who also declared unto us your love in the Spirit* (v. 8). He commends Epaphras to their affection from the good report he made of their sincere love, which was produced in them by the Spirit. Faithful ministers are glad to be able to speak well of their people.

Verses 9–11

He heard that they were good, and he prayed that they would be even better. *We do not cease to pray for you.* It may be that he heard about them only rarely, but he constantly prayed for them. He asks of God:

1. That they will be knowing Christians, *filled with the knowledge of his will, in all wisdom and spiritual understanding.* Mere empty ideas of the greatest truths are insignificant. Our knowledge of the will of God must always be practical: we must know the truth in order to do it. Our knowledge is a true blessing when it is in wisdom, when we know how to apply our general knowledge to particular occasions. Christians should seek to be *filled with* knowledge, not only to know the will of God but also to know more of it, to *increase in the knowledge of God* (v. 10).

2. That their way of life will be good. Good knowledge without a good life is useless. *That you may walk worthy of the Lord unto all pleasing* (v. 10). A harmony between how we live and what we believe is pleasing to God as well as to good people. *Being fruitful in every good work.* Good words are not enough without good works. We must be full of good works (Ac 9:36), doing *every good work.* We must pay a consistent, unvarying attention to all the will of God. The more fruitful we are in doing good works, the more we will *increase in the knowledge of God.*

3. That they will be strengthened, *strengthened with all might, according to his glorious power* (v. 11). Where there is spiritual life, there is still a need for spiritual strength. To be strengthened is to be supplied with the grace of God with his resources for every good work, and strengthened by that grace against every evil work. In praying for spiritual strength, we are not restricted in the promises, and so we should not be restricted in our own hopes and desires. Notice:

3.1. Paul prays that the Colossians will be *strengthened with might* (power), that they will be mightily strengthened.

3.2. It is with *all might*, "with all the power that we need to enable us to fulfill our duty or preserve our innocence," "with the grace that is sufficient for us in all the trials of life."

3.3. It is *according to his glorious power.* The grace of God in the hearts of believers is the power of God, and there is a glory in this power. The conveyance of strength is not according to our weakness, but according to his power. *That you may be strengthened unto all patience and long-suffering with joyfulness.* He prays not only that they may be supported in their troubles but also that they may be *strengthened* in them, strengthened:

3.3.1. To *all patience.* We are strengthened to all patience when we not only bear our troubles patiently but also receive them as gifts from God and are thankful for them.

3.3.2. To *long-suffering,* not only to bear trouble for a while but also to bear it as long as God pleases to continue it.

3.3.3. To receive *all patience and long-suffering with joyfulness,* to rejoice in troubles, to rejoice that we are counted worthy to suffer for his name (Ac 5:41), to have joy as well as patience in the troubles of life. We could never do all this with any strength of our own, but only as we are strengthened by the grace of God.

Verses 12–29

Here is a summary of the doctrine of the Gospel concerning the great work of our redemption by Christ. It is included here as the subject of thanksgiving: *Giving thanks unto the Father* (v. 12). The apostle speaks of:

1. The activities of the Spirit of grace on us (vv. 12–13). Those in whom the work of grace is performed must give thanks to the Father. It is described as the work of the Father because the Spirit of grace is the Spirit of the Father (Mt 10:20). Now how has the Spirit redeemed us?

1.1. "He has *delivered us from the power of darkness* (v. 13). He has saved us from the power of sin, which is darkness.

1.2. "He has *translated* (brought) *us into the kingdom of his dear Son,* made us members of the church of Christ, which is a state of light and purity." The conversion of a sinner is the transfer of a soul from the kingdom of the Devil to the kingdom of Christ, the kingdom of his dear Son.

1.3. "He has *made us meet to partake of* (qualified us to share in) *the inheritance of the saints in light* (v. 12)." God gives both grace and glory.

1.3.1. That glory is the *inheritance of the saints in light.* It is an inheritance and therefore belongs to them as children. It is also an inheritance of the saints. Those who are not saints on earth will never be saints in heaven. It is an inheritance in light, by fellowship with God, who is light.

1.3.2. This grace is qualification for the inheritance: *He hath made us meet to be partakers.* All who are destined for heaven later are prepared for heaven now. Those who are sanctified and renewed leave the world with their heaven around them. Those who have the inheritance of sons have the education of sons. This qualification for heaven is the pledge of the Spirit in our hearts (2Co 1:22; 5:5), which is a down payment, an assurance of full payment.

2. The Redeemer. Glorious things are here said about him, for the apostle Paul was full of Christ. He speaks of him distinctly as God and as Mediator.

2.1. He speaks of him as God (vv. 15–17).

2.1.1. He is the *image of the invisible God.* He is the image of God just as a son is the image of his father, having a natural likeness to him.

2.1.2. He is the *firstborn of every creature,* that is, "born, or begotten, before all the creation," which is the Scripture's way of representing eternity. It shows Christ's authority over all things; just as the firstborn in a family is heir and lord of everything, so Christ is the *heir of all things* (Heb 1:2).

2.1.3. He is so far from being himself a creature that he is the Creator: *For by him were all things created, which are in heaven and earth, visible and invisible* (v. 16). Paul speaks here as if there were several orders of angels: *whether thrones, or dominions, or principalities, or powers. All things are created by him and for him.* He is the goal as well as the cause of all things.

2.1.4. He *was before all things.* He existed before the world was made, and, therefore, from all eternity. He not only had existence before he was born from the Virgin; he had existence before all time.

2.1.5. *By him all things consist.* By the power of the Son of God, the whole creation is kept together and caused to consist in its proper order and arrangement.

2.2. He speaks of him as Mediator (vv. 18–19).

2.2.1. He is the *head of the body, the church.* He is not only a head for the sake of government and direction, but also a head of vital influence, as the head is in the natural body, because all grace and strength come from him.

2.2.2. He is the *beginning, the firstborn from the dead*, the original principle of our resurrection. He was the first and only one who rose by his own power, and he has given us evidence that we too will rise from the dead.

2.2.3. He has in *all things the pre-eminence*, being advanced above angels and all the powers in heaven, so that in all the matters of the kingdom of God on earth he has the supremacy.

2.2.4. All fullness dwells in him, and it pleased the Father to have it do so (v. 19), not only a fullness of abundance for himself but also a fullness overflowing to us.

3. The work of redemption.

3.1. What it consists of.

3.1.1. The remission of sin: *In whom we have redemption, even the forgiveness of sins* (v. 14). If we are redeemed, we are redeemed from sin. This is brought about by forgiveness.

3.1.2. Reconciliation to God. God *reconciled all things to himself* through Christ (v. 20). He is the Mediator of reconciliation, who obtains peace as well as pardon for sinners and will bring all holy creatures, *things in earth, or things in heaven*, into one blessed community in the end. The Gentiles, who were separated and were *enemies in their minds by wicked works, yet now hath he reconciled* (v. 21). This *enmity is slain* (Eph 2:16), and we are now reconciled. The greatest enemies of God may be reconciled, and if they are not, it is their own fault.

3.2. How the redemption is obtained: *it is through his blood* (v. 14); he has *made peace through the blood of his cross* (v. 20), and it is in *the body of his flesh through death* (v. 22). There was such a value in the blood of Christ that, on account of Christ's shedding it, God was willing to deal with humanity on new terms and to pardon and accept into favor all who submit to those terms.

4. The preaching of this redemption.

4.1. To whom it was preached: *To every creature under heaven* (v. 23). The Gospel excludes no one who does not exclude themselves.

4.2. By whom it was preached: *Whereof I Paul am made a minister.* He looks on it as the highest title of honor to be a minister of the Gospel of Jesus Christ. Notice:

4.2.1. From where Paul received his ministry: it was *according to the dispensation of God which was given to him* (v. 25). He received it from God as a gift and accepted it as a favor.

4.2.2. For whose sake he had his ministry: *It is for you.* We are Christ's ministers for the good of his people, to *fulfill the word of God* (that is, fully to preach it).

4.2.3. What kind of preacher Paul was.

4.2.3.1. He was a suffering preacher: *Who now rejoice in my sufferings for you* (v. 24). He suffered for preaching the Gospel to them, and while he suffered in such a good cause, he could rejoice in his sufferings. *And fill up that which is behind of the afflictions of Christ in my flesh.* The sufferings of Paul and other good ministers made them *conformable* with Christ (Php 3:10), like him. They are therefore said to fill up what was still lacking in the sufferings of Christ, as the wax fills up the empty spaces of

the seal when it receives its impression. Or it may refer to his suffering for Christ. He *filled that which was behind.* He was still filling up further what was lacking or what remained of them as his share.

4.2.3.2. He was a personal preacher. *Whom we preach, warning every man, and teaching every man in all wisdom* (v. 28). When we warn people about what they are dong wrong, we must teach them to do better: warning and teaching must go together. People must be warned and taught *in all wisdom.* We must choose the best times and adjust to the different abilities of those we have to do with. What he aimed at was to *present every man perfect in Christ Jesus.* Ministers should aim at the perfection, maturity, and salvation of every individual person who hears them.

4.2.3.3. He was a hardworking preacher (v. 29): *Whereunto I also labour, striving according to his working, which worketh in me mightily.* As Paul exerted himself to do much good, he enjoyed the favor of the power of God working in him even more and more effectively.

4.3. The Gospel that was preached. *Even the mystery which hath been hid from ages, and from generations, but is now made manifest to his saints* (vv. 26–27). The mystery of the Gospel was kept hidden for a long time. This mystery is now revealed to the saints. What is this mystery? It is the riches of God's glory among the Gentiles. This mystery, made known in this way, *is Christ in you, the hope of glory.* Christ is the hope of glory. The basis of our hope is Christ in the world. The evidence of our hope is Christ in the heart.

4.4. The responsibility of those who share in this redemption: *If you continue in the faith, grounded and settled* (established and firm), *and be not moved away from the hope of the Gospel which you have heard* (v. 23). We can expect the favorable end of our faith only when we continue in the faith, and are so firmly established that we are not moved from it.

CHAPTER 2

1. The apostle expresses his concern for the Colossians (vv. 1–3). 2. He repeats that concern (v. 5). 3. He warns them against false teachers among the Jews (vv. 4, 6–7) and against the Gentile philosophy (vv. 8–12). 4. He describes the privileges of Christians (vv. 13–15). 5. He concludes with a warning against those who want to introduce the worship of angels (vv. 16–23).

Verses 1–3

1. The apostle had never been to Colosse, but he had as tender a concern for it as if it had been the only church entrusted to him (v. 1): *For I would that you knew what great conflict I have for you, and for those at Laodicea, and for as many as have not seen my face in the flesh.* Notice:

1.1. Paul's care for the church amounted to a conflict. He was in a kind of anguish.

1.2. We may maintain fellowship by faith, hope, and holy love even with those whom we do not know personally. Those we never saw in the flesh we may hope to meet in heaven.

2. What the apostle wanted for them: *That their hearts might be comforted, being knit together in love* (v. 2). *Their hearts*: it was their spiritual welfare that he was concerned for. The prosperity of the soul is the best prosperity. Here is a description of soul prosperity.

2.1. When our knowledge grows to an understanding of the mystery of God and of the Father and of Christ, then the soul prospers—when we *understand the mystery*, not merely speaking about it by rote, but entering into its meaning and intention.

2.2. Our soul prospers when our faith grows to a full assurance and bold acknowledgment of this mystery. To a *full assurance*, or a well-established judgment. To a bold *acknowledgment*, a believing with the heart and also a ready confessing with our mouth (Ro 10:9). This is called the *riches of the full assurance of understanding*. Great knowledge and strong faith make a soul rich.

2.3. The soul prospers when it is filled with joy and peace (Ro 15:13): *That their hearts might be comforted.*

2.4. The more intimate the fellowship we have with our fellow Christians, the more the soul prospers: *being knit together* (united) *in love*. The stronger our faith, and the warmer our love, the greater our encouragement. Mentioning Christ (v. 2), Paul comments to his honor (v. 3): *In whom are hidden all the treasures of wisdom and knowledge.* The treasures of wisdom are hidden not from us, but for us, in Christ. We must spend the resources that are stored for us in him, and we must draw from the treasures that are hidden in him.

3. His concern for them is repeated (v. 5): *Though I am absent in the flesh, yet am I with you in the spirit, joying and beholding your order* (delighting to see how orderly you are), *and the steadfastness of your faith in Christ.* We may be present in spirit with those from whom we are absent in body. Although Paul had never seen the Colossians, he told them he could easily think of himself as being among them and could look on their good behavior with pleasure. The firmer our faith in Christ, the better order there will be in our whole way of life.

Verses 4–12

The apostle warns the Colossians against deceivers: *And this I say lest any man beguile you with enticing words* (v. 4); and, *lest any man spoil you* (so that no one may take you captive) (v. 8). Satan takes souls captive by deceiving them, and by the same means he puts them to death. He could not ruin us if he did not deceive us, and he could not deceive us except through our own foolishness. Satan's agents deceive people with *enticing words* (fine-sounding arguments). Many are ruined by the flattery of those who lie in wait to deceive them (Eph 4:14). "What they aim at is to take you captive." Notice:

1. A sovereign remedy against deceivers (vv. 6–7): *As you have therefore received Christ Jesus the Lord, so walk you in him, rooted and built up.* All Christians have, in profession at least, *received Jesus Christ the Lord*, submitted to him, taken him as theirs in every relationship and every capacity in which they act. The great concern of those who have received Christ is *to walk in him*. We must walk with him in our daily lives and maintain our fellowship with him. The more closely we walk with Christ, the more we are *rooted and established in the faith*. If we walk in him, we will be rooted in him; the more firmly we are rooted in him, the more closely we will walk with him. *Rooted and built up, as you have been taught.* A good education contributes much to our being established. We must be *established in the faith, as we have been taught, abounding therein*. And this with thanksgiving.

2. The fair warning given us of our danger: *Beware lest any man spoil you* (Beware, so that no one will take you captive) *through philosophy and vain deceit* (hollow and deceptive philosophy), *after the tradition of men after the rudiments* (which depends on human tradition and the basic principles) *of the world, and not after Christ* (v. 8). There is a philosophy that is a noble exercise of the faculty of our reason. But there is also a philosophy that is hollow and deceptive. *After the tradition of men, after the rudiments of the world.* The Jews governed themselves by the traditions of their elders. The Gentiles mixed their maxims of philosophy with their Christian principles. Both separated their minds from Christ. Those who pin their faith on human beings have turned away from following Christ.

2.1. In Christ we have the substance of all the shadows of the ceremonial law.

2.1.1. Did those who were under the ceremonial law have the *Shechinah,* or the special, visible presence of God? So do we now, in Jesus Christ (v. 9): *For in him dwelleth all the fulness of the Godhead bodily.* It *dwells in him bodily*; not the body as opposed to the spirit, but the body as opposed to the shadow (v. 17). The fullness of the Godhead dwells in Christ really, not figuratively.

2.1.2. Did they have circumcision, which was the seal of the covenant? In Christ we are *circumcised with the circumcision made without hands* (v. 11). *It is made without hands*; not through the power of any creature, but through the power of the Holy Spirit of God. Again, the Jews thought they were complete in the ceremonial law, but we are *complete in Christ* (v. 10). The ceremonial law was imperfect and defective, but all its defects are made up for in the Gospel of Christ. *Which is the head of all principality and power* (who is the head over every power and authority). Just as the Old Testament priesthood had its perfection in Christ, so did the kingdom of David. He is the Lord and head of all the powers in heaven and earth.

2.2. We have fellowship with Christ in his whole work (v. 12): *Buried with him in baptism, wherein also you have risen with him.* We both are buried and rise with him, and both of these are represented by our baptism. Paul is speaking of the *circumcision made without hands*, and he says this is done *through the faith of the operation* (through your faith in the power) *of God*. In our baptism, God commits himself to be our God and we are obligated to be his people and, by his grace, to die to sin and live to righteousness.

Verses 13–15

See how much greater are the privileges we Christians have than those of the Jews:

1. Christ's death is our life: *And you, being dead in your sins and the uncircumcision of your flesh, hath he quickened together with him* (v. 13). A state of sin is a state of spiritual death. Those who are in sin are dead in sin. Just as the death of the body is its corruption, so sin is the corruption of the soul. Just as dead people are unable to help themselves by any power of their own, so habitual sinners are morally powerless. This is our state. Now through Christ we who were dead in sins are *quickened*. *Quickened together with him.* Christ's death was the death of our sins; Christ's resurrection gives life to our souls.

2. Through him we have forgiveness of sins: *Having forgiven you all trespasses.* The pardon of the crime is the life of the criminal.

3. Whatever was in force against us is taken out of the way. He has obtained for us a legal release from the *handwriting of ordinances* (the written code), *which was against us* (v. 14), which may be understood as referring to:

3.1. An obligation to be punished: *Cursed is every one who continues not in everything* (Dt 27:26; Gal 3:10). This was a written code that was *against us, and contrary to us*. When Christ was nailed to the cross, the curse was, as it were, nailed to the cross as well.

3.2. The ceremonial law, the *handwriting of ordinances*. The Lord Jesus *took it out of the way, nailed it to his cross*; he annulled its obligation. When the substance came, the shadows rushed away.

4. He has obtained a glorious victory for us over the powers of darkness: *And, having spoiled principalities and powers, he made a show of them openly, triumphing over them in it* (v. 15). Just as the curse of the law was against us, so the power of Satan was also against us. Christ redeemed us powerfully and boldly out of the hands of Satan the executioner. The Devil and all the powers of hell were conquered and disarmed by the dying Redeemer. The Redeemer conquered by dying. See his crown of thorns turned into a crown of laurels. He *spoiled them* and *made a show of them openly*. Never did the Devil's kingdom received such a mortal blow as was given by the Lord Jesus. *Triumphing over them in it*: in his cross and by his death.

Verses 16–23

The apostle concludes the chapter with exhortations to the Colossians to fulfill their duty, which he bases on the foregoing discussion. We have here:

1. A warning to watch out for Judaizing teachers: *Let no man therefore judge you in meat nor in drink* (v. 16). "Let no one impose these things on you, because God has not imposed them." These things *were shadows of things to come* (v. 17). They are now done away with. *But the body* (reality) *is of Christ*: the reality has now come, of which they were merely shadows. They had shadows; we have the substance.

2. A warning to watch out for those who wanted to introduce the worship of angels, as the Gentile philosophers did: *Let no man beguile you of your reward, in a voluntary humility and worshiping of angels* (do not let anyone who delights in false humility and the worship of angels disqualify you for the prize) (v. 18). It looked like an act of humility to make use of the mediation of angels, but it was a false and self-imposed, not a commanded humility. It was therefore not acceptable; in fact, it is not warrantable. Besides, the ideas on which this practice was based were merely human inventions, the proud thoughts of human reason: *intruding into those things which he hath not seen, vainly puffed up by his fleshly mind*. Although there was a show of humility in practice, there was a real pride in the motive. Pride lies at the root of very many errors and corruptions—and even many evil practices—that give the appearance of humility. Those who engage in such practices do *not hold* (have lost connection with) *the head* (v. 19). When people let go of their connection with Christ, they catch hold of whatever lies closest to them, which will do them no good. *From which all the body, by joints and bands, having nourishment ministered, and knit together, increaseth with the increase of God*. Jesus Christ is not only a head of government over the church, but also a head of living influence to it. The body of Christ is a growing body: *it increaseth with the increase of God*, with a large and plentiful increase.

3. A further warning: "*Wherefore, if you be dead with Christ from the rudiments of the world, why, as though living in the world, are you subject to ordinances* (v. 20)—such observances as *Touch not, taste not, handle not* (vv. 21–22), *which all are to perish with the using*, having no other authority than the human traditions and commands?" *Which things have indeed a show of wisdom in will worship and humility.* Those who promoted such observances thought themselves wiser than their neighbors. But there is no true devotion in these things, because the Gospel teaches us to worship God in spirit and truth (Jn 4:24), not by ritual observances, and only through the mediation of Christ, not of any angels. Such things appear to be wise, but in reality they are foolish. It is true wisdom to keep close to the worship and commands of the Gospel and remain in complete submission to Christ, the only head of the church.

CHAPTER 3

1. The apostle exhorts us 1. To set our hearts on heaven (vv. 1–4). 2. To put to death sin (vv. 5–11). 3. To mutual love and compassion (vv. 12–17). He concludes with exhortations to duties in relationships (vv. 18–25).

Verses 1–4

Although we have been set free from the ceremonial law, it does not follow that we may therefore live as we wish. Rather, we must walk more closely with God: *If you then have risen with Christ, seek those things which are above.* We must be more concerned with the other world than with the concerns of this one. *Christ sits at the right hand of God.* The One who is our best friend has gone before us to protect heavenly happiness for us; we should therefore seek what he has purchased at such an immense expense.

1. Paul explains this duty (v. 2): *Set your affections on things above, not on things on the earth.* The heart soars upward on the wings of affection. *Things on earth* are here set in opposition to *things above*. Heaven and earth are set in contrast with one another, and the predominance of our affection for one will proportionally weaken our affection for the other.

2. He gives three reasons for this (vv. 3–4).

2.1. We are dead toward present things. If we are dead to the earth and have renounced it as our goal and source of happiness, it is absurd for us to *set our affections* on it and *seek* it.

2.2. Our true life lies in the other world: *You are dead, and your life is hid with Christ in God* (v. 3). The new self has its livelihood from there. It is *hid with Christ*, not only hidden from us, in secrecy, but also hidden for us, kept secure. This is our assurance, that our *life is hid with him*, stored up safely with him.

2.3. At the second coming of Christ we hope for the perfection of our happiness. *When Christ, who is our life, shall appear, we shall also appear with him in glory* (v. 4). Christ is a believer's life. He is the motivating principle and goal of the Christian's life. Christ will appear again. He is now *hid*, but he will appear in *his own glory and his Father's glory* (Mk 8:38; Lk 9:26). We will then appear with him in glory. It will be his glory to have his redeemed ones with him. It will also be their glory to come with him. Do we look for such a happiness, and if so, should we not set our affections on that world and live above this one? Our head is there, our home is there, our treasure is there, and we hope to be there forever.

Verses 5–7

It is our duty to put to death our *members which are upon the earth*, which naturally incline us to the things of the world. He specifies:

1. The sinful desires of the flesh: *Fornication, uncleanness, inordinate affection, evil concupiscence* (sexual immorality, impurity, lust, evil desires)—which are so against the Christian state and the heavenly hope.

2. The love of the world: *and covetousness* (greed), *which is idolatry*, that is, excessive love of present

good and outward enjoyments. Greed is spiritual idolatry: it is giving to worldly wealth the love and respect that are due only to God. Among all the expressions of sin that good people are recorded in Scripture as having fallen into, there is no instance of any good person accused of greed. How necessary it is to put sins to death (vv. 6–7):

2.1. Because if we do not kill them, they will kill us: *For which things' sake the wrath of God cometh on the children of disobedience* (v. 6). Notice what we all more or less are by nature: *children of disobedience*. The wrath of God comes on all such. Those who do not obey the commands of the law incur its penalties.

2.2. Because they have lived in us: *In which you also walked some time, when you lived in them* (v. 7). The consideration that we formerly lived in sin is a good argument why we should now abandon it. We have been led astray into bypaths; therefore, let us no longer walk along them. Some understand the last part of v. 7 as saying, "when you lived among them," that is, among those who did such things: "You followed those evil practices when you lived among those who did such things." Let us keep out of the way of evildoers.

Verses 8–11

1. We are to put to death immoderate passions as well as immoderate appetites.

1.1. *But now you also put off all these, anger, wrath, malice* (v. 8). Anger and wrath are bad, but malice is even worse; it is anger settled and heightened. Just as the corrupt principles in the heart must be cut off, so must their result in the tongue, such as *blasphemy*, which seems here to mean not so much speaking wrong about God as speaking slanderously about people. *Filthy communication* refers to lying and to dirty or abusive speech, which spreads the same defilements in the hearers. *Lie not one to another* (v. 9). Lying makes us like the Devil, the *father of lies* (Jn 8:44).

1.2. *Seeing you have put off the old man with his deeds, and have put on the new man* (v. 10). Those who have put off the old self have put it off with its actions, and those who have put on the new self must put on all its deeds. We must also be *renewed in knowledge*, because an ignorant soul cannot be good. Light is the first thing in the new creation, just as it was in the first (Ge 1:3): *after the image of him who created him*. It was the honor of human beings in their innocence that they were made in the image of God.

2. In the privilege of sanctification, *there is neither Greek nor Jew, circumcision nor uncircumcision, Barbarian, Scythian, bond nor free* (v. 11). It is as much the duty of the one as of the other to be holy, and as much the privilege of the one as of the other to receive from God the grace to be so. *Christ is all in all.* Christ is the "all" of Christians, all their hope and happiness.

Verses 12–17

Put on therefore bowels of mercy (compassion) (v. 12). We must not only put off anger and wrath (as v. 8) but also put on compassion and kindness.

1. The argument used here is moving: *Put on, as the elect of God, holy and beloved.* Those who are the chosen ones of God are dearly loved and should conduct themselves in everything as befits them. Notice what we must put on:

1.1. Compassion toward those in misery: *bowels of mercy* (compassion). Those who owe so much to mercy should be merciful.

1.2. *Kindness.* The purpose of the Gospel is not only to soften human hearts but also to sweeten them, to promote friendship among people as well as reconciliation with God.

1.3. *Humbleness of mind.* There must not only be a humble outward behavior but also a humble heart.

1.4. *Meekness* (gentleness). We must wisely restrain our anger and patiently bear the anger of others.

1.5. *Longsuffering* (patience). Many people can bear a provocation for a short time but become weary of being patient when it continues long. If God is patient toward us, we should exercise patience toward others.

1.6. Bearing with one another: *Forbearing one another.* All of us have something that needs to be put up with. We need the same good turn from others that we are bound to show them.

1.7. *Forgiving one another, if any man have a quarrel against any.* Quarrels will sometimes happen, even among God's chosen ones, who are holy and dearly loved (v. 12). But it is our duty to forgive one another in such cases. *Even as Christ forgave you, so also do you.* It is a branch of his example that we are obliged to follow if we ourselves want to be forgiven.

2. So that we may do all these things, we are urged:

2.1. To clothe ourselves with love (v. 14): *Above all things put on charity.* He lays the foundation in faith and the capstone in love, *which is the bond of perfectness* (which binds them all together in perfect unity). Christian unity consists of being of one mind and mutual love.

2.2. To submit ourselves to the government of the *peace of God* (v. 15): "*Let the peace of God rule in your hearts,* reign and govern there, or, like an umpire, decide all differences among you." To *which you are called in one body.* Being united in one body, we are called to be at peace one with another. To preserve in us this peaceful attitude, we must be thankful. The work of thanksgiving to God is such a sweet and pleasant work that it will help make us sweet and pleasant toward all people.

2.3. To let the *word of Christ dwell in us richly* (v. 16). It must *keep house* in us, not as a servant but as a master. And it must be always available to us in everything. It must live in us as a rich treasure: not only live in our hearts, but live well there. In many who have the word of Christ in them, it lives in them poorly. The soul prospers when the word of God *dwells in us richly*. And this *in all wisdom*. The word of Christ must live in us richly not in ideas, to make us walking encyclopedias, but *in all wisdom*, to make us true Christians.

2.4. To teach and correct one another. We sharpen ourselves by spurring others on. We must *admonish one another in psalms and hymns.* Religious poetry seems supported by these expressions and is very useful to build up others. But when we sing psalms, we make no melody (Eph 5:19) unless we sing with grace in our hearts, and we must not only spur on and encourage ourselves but also *teach and admonish one another.*

2.5. To do all this in the name of Christ (v. 17): *And whatsoever you do in word or deed, do all in the name of the Lord Jesus, giving thanks to God and the Father by him.* Those who do everything in Christ's name will never lack topics of thanksgiving to God the Father.

Verses 18–25

We have here exhortations to duties in relationships. We must never separate the privileges and responsibilities of the Gospel faith.

1. The apostle begins with the duties of wives and husbands (v. 18): *Wives, submit yourselves unto your own*

husbands, as it is fit in the Lord. Submission is the duty of wives. It is in accordance with the order of nature and the reason of things, as well as the appointment and will of God. It is submission to a husband, and to her *own* husband, who stands in the closest relationship to her and is under strict obligation to fulfill his proper duty too. In addition, *this is fit in the Lord. Husbands must love their wives, and not be bitter against them* (v. 19). They must love them with a warm, tender, and faithful love, as Christ loved the church. They must not be bitter against them, but be kind and considerate to them in everything.

2. He proceeds to the duties of children and parents: *Children, obey your parents in all things, for this is well-pleasing unto the Lord* (v. 20). Children must be willing to do all their parents' lawful commands, because their parents have a natural right and are fitter to direct them than they are to direct themselves. This is *well pleasing to God.* Parents must be caring and encouraging, just as children must be obedient (v. 21): "*Fathers, provoke not your children to anger, lest they be discouraged.* Let your authority over them not be exercised with harshness, rigor, or severity, but with kindness and gentleness, so that you may not, by holding the reins too tight, make them fly out with greater fierceness."

3. Finally, he addresses servants and masters: *Servants, obey your masters in all things according to the flesh* (v. 22). Servants must fulfill the duty of the relationship in which they stand in *all things,* not only when their master is watching them, but *in singleness of heart, fearing God.* Reverence for God ruling in the heart will make people good in every relationship. "*And whatsoever you do, do it heartily* (v. 23), with diligence, not laziness," *as to the Lord, and not as to men.* It sanctifies a servant's work when it is done as for God, and not merely for people. We are really doing our duty to God when we are faithful in our duty to others. Good and faithful servants are never further from heaven simply because they are servants: "*Knowing that of the Lord you shall receive the reward of the inheritance, for you serve the Lord Christ*" (v. 24). Serving your masters according to the command of Christ, you serve Christ, and he will be the One who repays you. Although you are servants now, you will receive the inheritance of sons. *He who does wrong,* on the other hand, *will receive for the wrong which he has done*" (v. 25). God will be sure to punish the unjust as well as reward faithful servants, and masters will be treated in the same way if they wrong their servants. *And there is no respect of persons with him.* The righteous Judge of the earth will be impartial, treating master and servant without favoritism. How happy would the Gospel faith make the world if it were successful everywhere; how much it would influence every situation and every relationship in life!

CHAPTER 4

1. The apostle Paul continues his account of the responsibility of masters (v. 1). 2. He exhorts us to fulfill the duty of prayer (vv. 2–4) and to conduct ourselves wisely toward those with whom we are involved (vv. 5–6). 3. He ends the letter by mentioning several of his friends (vv. 7–18).

Verse 1

The apostle continues to describe the duty of masters toward their servants. Justice is required of them: *Give unto your servants that which is just and equal* (v. 1), not only strict justice, but fairness and kindness. "*Knowing*

that you also have a Master in heaven. You who are masters of others have a Master yourself; you are accountable to One above you. Deal with your servants as you expect God to deal with you. You are both servants of the same Lord and are equally accountable to him in the end."

Verses 2–4

It is the duty of everyone to *continue in prayer. Watching the same.* Christians should grasp every opportunity for prayer, choosing the best times and keep their minds active in the duty. *With thanksgiving.* Thanksgiving must have a part in every prayer. *Withal* (also) *praying for us* (v. 3). The people must pray especially for their ministers, keeping them on their hearts at all times when they come to the throne of grace. It is as if Paul said, "Do not forget us whenever you pray for yourselves." *That God would open to us a door of utterance,* that is, either give opportunities to preach the Gospel or give ability and courage. *And for me, that utterance may be given to me, that I may open my mouth boldly, to speak the mystery of Christ, for which I am also in bonds.* He wanted them to pray for him so that he would neither be discouraged in his work nor be driven from it by his sufferings: *That I may make it manifest, as I ought to speak* (v. 4). He has been detailed in telling them what he prays for on their behalf (1:9–11); here he tells them specifically what he wants them to pray for on his behalf. Paul knew as well as anyone how to speak, and yet he asked them to pray that he would be taught to speak.

Verses 5–6

The apostle exhorts the Colossians to behave wisely toward the pagan world, those outside the Christian church but among whom they lived (v. 5): "*Walk in wisdom toward those who are without.* Be careful not to be harmed by them; also avoid doing any harm to them or doing anything that might increase their prejudice against religion. Do them all the good you possibly can, and by all the best means commend religious faith to them." *Redeeming the time:* either "making the best of every opportunity to do them good" or "walking with carefulness, to give them no advantage over you." "*Let your speech be always with grace* (v. 6). Let all your speech be fitting for Christians—wholesome, tactful, appropriate." Although we may not always be talking about grace, we must always talk *with grace, seasoned with salt*—Christianly. Grace is the salt that seasons our speech, makes it wholesome, and keeps it from decay. *That you may know how to answer every man.* We need a great deal of wisdom and grace to give proper answers to everyone, especially to answer the questions and objections of enemies of our Christian faith, giving the reasons for our faith.

Verses 7–18

At the end of this letter the apostle honors several of his friends by recording their names with some testimony of his respect, which will be spoken of wherever the Gospel comes, and eventually to the end of the world. We read here:

1. About Tychicus (v. 7). This letter was delivered by him. Paul knew the Colossians would be glad to hear how he was doing. The churches must be concerned for good ministers and want to know their news. *A beloved brother and faithful minister.* Faithfulness in anyone is a really lovely characteristic, making them worthy of our affection and respect. *And a fellowservant in the Lord.* Much is added to the beauty and strength of the Gospel ministry when ministers are loving toward one another. *Whom*

I have sent unto you for the same purpose, that he might know your estate, and comfort your hearts (v. 8). Paul was as willing to hear from the Colossians as they could be to hear from him. It is a great encouragement to have the mutual concern of fellow Christians.

2. About Onesimus (v. 9): *With Onesimus, a faithful and beloved brother, who is one of you*. This was the one who had become Paul's son in his chains (Phm 10). He was converted at Rome, to which he had fled from his master's service. Although he was a poor servant and had been bad, nevertheless, now that he had been converted, Paul called him *a faithful and beloved brother*. The lowliest circumstance of life, and greatest evil of a former life, make no difference in the spiritual relationship among sincere Christians.

3. About *Aristarchus, a fellow prisoner*. Those who join one another in services and sufferings should be committed to one another in holy love.

4. About *Marcus, sister's son to* (the cousin of) *Barnabas*, who wrote the Gospel that bears his name. *If he come unto you, receive him*. Paul had a quarrel with Barnabas on account of this Mark (Ac 15:38–39), but Paul now not only was reconciled to him himself but also commended him to the respect of the churches. If people have been found guilty of a fault, it must not be always remembered against them. We must forget as well as forgive.

5. About one who is called *Jesus*, which is the Greek name for the Hebrew *Joshua. Who is called Justus. These are my fellow labourers unto the kingdom of God, who have been a comfort unto me*. One is Paul's fellow servant, another his fellow prisoner, and all are his fellow workers.

6. About *Epaphras* (v. 12). He is *one of you; he salutes you. Always labouring fervently for you in prayers*. Epaphras has learned from Paul to pray very much for his friends. We must be fervent in prayer not only for ourselves but also for others. *That you may stand perfect* (mature) *and complete* (fully assured) *in all the will of God*. To stand *perfect and complete* in the will of God is what we should earnestly seek both for ourselves and for others. Paul bore witness that Epaphras had a great zeal for the Colossians: *I bear him record*. His zeal also extended to all around them, to *those who are in Laodicea and Hierapolis*.

7. About *Luke*, whom he calls the *beloved physician*. This is the Luke who wrote the Gospel and Acts and was Paul's companion.

8. About *Demas*. We read in 2Ti 4:10, *Demas hath forsaken me, having loved this present world*. Many who have made a significant profession of faith and gained a great name among Christians have later shamefully committed apostasy.

9. About the *brethren in Laodicea*, who lived in the neighborhood of Colosse. Paul sends greetings to them and gives orders that this letter be read in their church (v. 16). Some think Paul sent another letter at this time to Laodicea and that he here told the Colossians to send to Laodicea for that letter: *and that you likewise read the epistle from Laodicea*. If so, that letter is now lost.

10. About *Nymphas* (v. 15), one who lived in Colosse and had a church *in his house*.

11. About *Archippus*. The Colossians are told to admonish him to complete his work as a minister, to *take heed to it, and to fulfil it*. The ministry we have received is a great honor, because it is *received in the Lord* and is by his appointment. The people may remind their ministers of their duty and stir them to fulfill it: *Say to Archippus, Take heed to the ministry*.

12. About himself (v. 18): *The salutation of me Paul. Remember my bonds*. He wrote these words with his own hand: "*Grace be with you*. The favor of God, and all goodness, be with you and be your inheritance."

A PRACTICAL AND DEVOTIONAL
EXPOSITION OF

1 Thessalonians

Thessalonica was formerly the chief city in Macedonia. The apostle Paul, being directed in an extraordinary way to preach the Gospel in Macedonia (Ac 16:9–10), went from Troas to Samothrace, from there to Neapolis, and then to Philippi, where his ministry was successful but where he was treated harshly, being thrown into prison with Silas. They were wonderfully rescued from there, encouraged the brothers and sisters, and departed. Passing through Amphipolis and Apollonia, they came to Thessalonica, where the apostle planted a church. But when a riot was instigated in the city, Paul and Silas were sent away by night to Berea for their safety, and later Paul was taken to Athens, leaving Silas and Timothy behind. When they later joined him, Timothy was sent to Thessalonica to ask how the church there was doing and to strengthen them in the faith (3:2), and when he returned to Paul in Athens, he was sent again, with Silas, to visit the churches in Macedonia. Paul, being *left alone* at Athens (3:1), departed from there to Corinth, where he stayed for a year and a half, and then he wrote this letter to the church of Christ at Thessalonica, which, though placed after the other letters of this apostle, is thought to be first he wrote.

CHAPTER 1

After the opening greeting (v. 1), the apostle begins by giving thanks to God (vv. 2–5). He then mentions the effectiveness of the Gospel among them (vv. 6–10).

Verse 1

Here we have:

1. The title, naming the people from whom this letter came and those to whom it was written. Paul was the writer of this letter, but to his own name he adds those of *Silvanus* (Silas) and Timothy. Those to whom this letter was written were the church of the Thessalonians, the converted Jews and Gentiles in Thessalonica. This church is said to *be in God the Father and in the Lord Jesus Christ.* The Gentiles among them had turned to God from idols, and the Jews among them believed Jesus to be the promised Messiah. All of them were devoted and dedicated to God the Father and the Lord Jesus Christ.

2. The greeting: *Grace be with you, and peace from God our Father and the Lord Jesus Christ.* The free grace or favor of God is the spring of all the peace and prosperity we can enjoy. Just as all good comes from God, so no good can be hoped for by sinners except from God in Christ. The best good may be expected from God as our Father for the sake of Christ.

Verses 2–5

1. The apostle begins by giving thanks to God. Being about to mention the things that are a matter of joy to him and highly commendable in them, he chooses to do this by way of thanksgiving to God. Even when we do not actually give thanks to God by our words, we should have a grateful sense of God's goodness in our hearts.

2. He attaches prayer to his praise or thanksgiving. When we give thanks for any benefit we receive, we should add prayer to our thanksgiving. Just as there is much that we should be thankful for, so we are continually supplied with new occasions to seek further supplies of good in prayer.

3. He mentions the particulars for which he is so thankful to God.

3.1. He mentions the saving benefits given them:

3.1.1. Their faith and their work of faith. Their faith was a true and living faith, because it was a working faith. Wherever there is a true faith, it will work effectively.

3.1.2. Their love and labor of love. Love shows itself through work.

3.1.3. Their hope and the patience of hope. Wherever there is a well-founded hope of eternal life, it will be seen by the exercise of patience.

3.2. The apostle not only mentions these three cardinal graces, faith, hope, and love, but also takes notice of the sincerity of them: being in the *sight of God even our Father.* The work of faith or labor of love is sincere when it is done as under the eye of God, and the patience of hope is sincere when it is exercised as under the eye of God. Note the fountain from which these graces flow, God's electing love: *Knowing, brethren beloved, your election of God* (v. 4). This is how he traces these streams back to the fountain, to God's eternal election. He calls them *brethren beloved* (brothers who are loved). That we are all loved by God is a good reason why we should *love one another* (1Jn 4:11). The election of God is of his own good pleasure and sheer grace, not for the sake of any merit in those who are chosen. Note that the election of God may be known by its fruits, by our sincere faith, hope, and love.

3.3. Another ground for the apostle's thanksgiving is the success of his ministry among them. He is thankful on his own account as well as theirs that his hard work has not been in vain. Their ready reception of the Gospel he preached to them was evidence of their being elected and loved by God. He notes with thankfulness:

3.3.1. That the Gospel came to them not only in word but also in power. It did not merely tickle their ears and please their fancy, but deeply affected their hearts. God's power accompanied it. We can know that we are elect if we do not speak of the things of God by rote, like parrots, but sense the influence of these things in our hearts.

3.3.2. That it came in the Holy Spirit. Unless the Spirit of God accompanies the word of God, it will be a dead letter to us; the letter kills, but it is the Spirit who gives life (2Co 3:6).

3.3.3. That the Gospel came to them in much assurance. They were fully convinced of its truth; they were willing to leave everything for Christ and to trust their souls on the truthfulness of the Gospel revelation. By the evidence of their own faith, the Thessalonians knew what kind of people the apostle and his fellow laborers were and what those ministers had done for their sake.

Verses 6–10

Here we have the evidence of the apostle's effectiveness among the Thessalonians.

1. They were careful to imitate the good examples of the apostles and ministers of Christ (v. 6), showing a conscientious concern to follow them. In so doing, they also became followers of the Lord, who is the perfect example we must strive to imitate. The Thessalonians acted in this way despite their *much affliction*. They were willing to share in the sufferings that attended their accepting and professing Christianity. Perhaps it made the word more precious that they paid dearly for accepting it. They accepted it *with joy in the Holy Spirit*, who, when our adversities are many, makes our comforts even greater.

2. They themselves were examples to everyone around them (vv. 7–8).

2.1. Their example was effective in making good impressions on many others. They were *ensamples* (NIV: a model)—or literally, "stamps," instruments to make an impression with. They themselves had received good impressions, and they made good impressions. Christians should be so good that they influence others by their example.

2.2. Their example was extensive, reaching beyond the confines of Thessalonica to the believers of all Macedonia, and even further, into Achaia.

2.3. Their example was eminent. The word of the Lord was famous and well known in the regions around that city and *in every place*, so that by the effectiveness of the Gospel among them many others were encouraged to receive it and to be willing, when called, to suffer for it.

2.3.1. The readiness of their faith was famous over a wide area. These Thessalonians accepted the Gospel as soon as it was preached to them.

2.3.2. The effects of their faith were famous. They abandoned their idolatry. They gave themselves to God, to the living and true God. And they set themselves to wait for the Son of God from heaven (v. 10). It is one of the distinctive aspects of our holy faith to wait for Christ's second coming, as those who believe he will come and hope his coming will bring us joy.

CHAPTER 2

In this chapter the apostle reminds the Thessalonians of the way he preached among them (vv. 1–6), how he lived among them (vv. 7–12), and the success of his ministry

(vv. 13–16), and then he expresses regret for his absence (vv. 17–20).

Verses 1–6

Paul can appeal to the Thessalonians as to how faithfully he, Silas, and Timothy have fulfilled their ministry: *You yourselves, brethren, know our entrance in* (our visit) *unto you. His preaching was not in vain*, or, as some read it, "was not vain." It was not fruitless or *in vain*—as our translation reads it—or, as others think, it was not vain in the sense of "empty." The subject matter of the apostle's preaching was sound and solid truth. Much less was his preaching itself futile or deceitful. He had no worldly intentions in his preaching, which, he reminds them, was undertaken:

1. With courage and resolution: *We were bold in our God to speak unto you the Gospel of God* (v. 2). The apostle was inspired with a holy boldness. He was not discouraged by the suffering he met with. He was treated harshly at Philippi, as these Thessalonians well know. It was there that he and Silas were insulted and put in the stocks, but no sooner were they set free than they went to Thessalonica and preached the Gospel as boldly as ever. Suffering in a good cause should sharpen rather than blunt the edge of holy determination. Those who first preached the Gospel preached it *with contention*, an expression that shows either the apostles' striving in their preaching or their striving against the opposition they faced. Paul was neither daunted in his work nor driven away from it.

2. With great simplicity and godly sincerity: *Our exhortation was not of deceit, nor of uncleanness, nor in guile* (error, impure motives, or trickery) (v. 3). No doubt the apostle's awareness of his own sincerity was a source of great encouragement to him and was one reason for his success. The Gospel he preached was without deceit; it was true and faithful. Nor was it of *uncleanness*. His Gospel was pure and holy, and, just as the subject of his exhortation was true and pure, the way in which he spoke was free from deceit and trickery. The apostle not only asserts his sincerity but also adds the reasons for it and the evidence of it.

2.1. The reasons for it:

2.1.1. The apostles were stewards, entrusted with the Gospel. The Gospel Paul preached was not his own, but the Gospel of God. Ministers have a great favor given them, honor shown them, and trust committed to them.

2.1.2. Their intention was to please God, not people. If sincerity is lacking, all we do cannot please God. The Gospel of Christ will not be accommodated to the futile imaginations or sinful desires of human beings; on the contrary, it was intended to put to death their corruption, so that they would be brought under the power of faith.

2.1.3. They acted as those who knew they acted in the sight of the One who *tries* (tests) *our hearts*. He knows full well all our aims and purposes, as well as our actions and desires. It is from this God who tests our hearts that we must receive our reward.

2.2. The evidence of it:

2.2.1. He avoided flattery: *Neither at any time used we flattering words, as you know* (v. 5). He and his fellow workers preached Christ, and him crucified (1Co 2:2), and did not aim to influence the affections of human beings; nor did he flatter people in their sins. He did not flatter them with vain hopes.

2.2.2. He avoided greed. He did not make the ministry *a cloak*, a mask or a coverup, for *covetousness* (greed), *as God was witness* (v. 5). His intention was not to make himself rich by preaching the Gospel; he was so far from this that he did not demand compensation from them.

2.2.3. He avoided boasting and ambition: *Nor of men sought we glory, neither of you nor yet of others* (v. 6). They did not expect people either to open their wallets or to tip their hats.

Verses 7–12

Here the apostle reminds the Thessalonians of how he lived among them:

1. He mentions the gentleness of his and his fellow apostles' behavior: *We were gentle among you* (v. 7). He showed the kindness and care of nurses cherishing their children. This is the way to win people, rather than by ruling them harshly. Just as a nursing mother bears with contrariness in a child, condescending to do the lowliest tasks for his or her good and nourishing the child at her breast, so in the same way ministers of Christ should care for their people. The apostle showed this gentleness in several ways:

1.1. By the fondest affection for their welfare: *Being affectionately desirous of you* (v. 8). It was their spiritual and eternal welfare that he passionately sought.

1.2. By great readiness to do them good, willingly imparting to them *not the Gospel of God only, but also our own souls* (v. 8). He was willing to give himself in the service of people.

1.3. By laboring with his hands to avoid being a burden to them: *You remember our labour and travail; for, labouring night and day* (v. 9). To the hard work of the ministry he added the work of his calling as a tentmaker, so that he could earn his own living. He spent part of the night as well as the day in this work, forgoing some rest at night so that he would have opportunity to do good to people during the day.

1.4. By the holiness of his and the other apostles' way of life, about which he appeals not only to the Thessalonians' but also to God (v. 10): *You are witnesses, and God also.* The Thessalonians have observed the apostles' outward way of life in public, and God is witness not only to their behavior in private but also to the motives from which they acted.

2. He mentions their faithful fulfillment of the work of the ministry (vv. 11–12). Paul and his fellow workers were not only good Christians but also faithful ministers. Paul both exhorted the Thessalonians and comforted them, *charging every one* of them by addressing each one personally: this is what is intended by the comparison of a father's relationship with his children. He was their spiritual father, and just as he nurtured them like a nursing mother, so he charged them as a father to do their duty, with a father's affection rather than a father's authority. Ministers should note both the manner and the content of the apostle's exhortation here, urging their people to *walk worthy of God, who hath called them to his kingdom and glory* (v. 12). Notice:

2.1. What our great Gospel privilege is—that God has called us to his kingdom and glory.

2.2. What our great Gospel duty is—to live lives worthy of God.

Verses 13–16

Notice here:

1. The success of Paul's ministry among these Thessalonians (v. 13).

1.1. The way in which they received the word of God: *When you received the word of God, which you heard of us, you received it, not as the word of men, but—as it is in truth—the word of God.* The word of the Gospel is preached by people like us, people *of like passions* (Jas

5:17) and weaknesses. And yet it is truly the word of God. Such was the word the apostles preached by divine inspiration, and such is what is left on record. Such is the word that is preached in our days. Those who dispense their own commandments or the products of the own imaginations as if those things were the word of God are greatly to blame. Those who, on hearing the word, look no further than to the ministry or the words of human beings are also to blame. We should receive the word of God as the word of God. The words of human beings are frail and perishing, like human beings themselves, and are sometimes false, foolish, and fickle, but God's word is holy, wise, just, and faithful, and lasts forever.

1.2. The wonderful activity of the word they received: *It effectually worketh* (is at work) *in those that believe* (v. 13). And people who have this inner testimony of the truth of the Scriptures have within their own hearts the best evidence of the Scriptures' divine origin, though this testimony is not sufficient to convince others who are strangers to it.

2. The good effects his successful preaching had:

2.1. On him and fellow workers. This was a constant cause of thankfulness: *For this cause thank we God without ceasing* (v. 13). Paul could never be thankful enough that God had considered him faithful (1Ti 1:12) and made his service effective.

2.2. On the Thessalonians. The word was at work powerfully in them, enabling them to be faithful and patient in suffering: *You became followers of the churches of God, and have suffered like things as they have done* (v. 14). The cross is the mark of a Christian. It is a good effect of the Gospel when we are enabled to suffer for its sake. The apostle mentions the sufferings of the churches of God that *in Judea are in Christ Jesus*. Those in Judea heard the Gospel first and suffered for it first, because the Jews were the bitterest enemies of Christianity. Bitter zeal and fiery persecution will set compatriots at each other's throats. The Jews were the ringleaders of persecution everywhere, and especially at Thessalonica. On this occasion, the apostle gives enough of a description of the unbelieving Jews to justify their final rejection (v. 15).

2.2.1. They *killed the Lord Jesus*.

2.2.2. They killed *their own prophets*.

2.2.3. They hated the apostles and caused them all the trouble they could. And if they killed the Lord Jesus, no wonder they persecuted his followers.

2.2.4. They *pleased not God*. They had completely lost all sense of religion.

2.2.5. They were *contrary* (hostile) *to all men*. Their persecuting spirit was perverse.

2.2.6. They had a hardened hostility toward the Gentiles, envying them the offers of the Gospel: *Forbidding the apostles to speak to the Gentiles, that they might be saved.* They were envious of the Gentiles, angry that they would be admitted to share in salvation. This is how the Jews *filled up* (reached the limit of) their sins (Mt 23:32). For the sake of these things *wrath has come upon them to the uttermost*; wrath was determined against them and would soon overcome them. It was not many years after this that Jerusalem was destroyed and the Jewish nation cut off by the Romans.

Verses 17–20

The apostle expresses regret for his absence:

1. He tells the Thessalonians that he and his fellow apostles were unwillingly forced away from them: *We, brethren, were taken from you* (v. 17). He was unwillingly sent away by night to Berea.

2. Although he was absent in body, he was still present *in heart* (in thought).

3. Even his physical absence was brief. This world is not a place where we are always together, nor are we together for long. It is in heaven that holy souls will meet, never to part again.

4. He passionately desired and sought to see them again: *We endeavoured more abundantly to see your face with great desire* (v. 17). But businesspeople are not masters of their own time. Paul did his best, but he could do no more (v. 18).

5. Satan stopped him from returning (v. 18). Satan is a constant enemy to the work of God and does all he can to obstruct it.

6. Paul assures them of his affection and high regard for them. They are his *hope, and joy, and crown of rejoicing, his glory and joy*. It will be good when those who sow and those who reap rejoice together (Jn 4:36) *in the presence of our Lord Jesus Christ at his coming*. Even if Paul is never able to come to the Thessalonians, our Lord Jesus Christ will come.

CHAPTER 3

In this chapter the apostle gives further evidence of his love for the Thessalonians (vv. 1–5) and tells them of his great satisfaction at hearing good news about them (vv. 6–10). He concludes with heartfelt prayer for them (vv. 11–13).

Verses 1–5

Here is an account of his sending Timothy to the Thessalonians. Paul was content, for their good, *to be left alone at Athens*. Notice:

1. His description of Timothy (v. 2): *We sent Timotheus, our brother*. Elsewhere he calls him his son; here, *brother*, and also *minister of God* and *fellow labourer* in the Gospel of Christ. Ministers should strengthen each other, not fight with one another—which will hinder their work. They should strive together to continue the great work they are engaged in.

2. Paul's purpose in sending Timothy: *To establish you and to comfort you concerning your faith* (v. 2). He wanted to strengthen and encourage the Thessalonians concerning their faith, specifically, concerning the object of their faith and the reward of faith. The more we are encouraged, the more we will be strengthened.

3. Paul's motive, a godly fear that they might be moved from faith in Christ (v. 3).

3.1. He knew there was danger, and he feared the consequences.

3.1.1. There was danger because of *affliction* (trials) and persecution for the sake of the Gospel (v. 3). Those who professed the Gospel were persecuted, and without doubt these Thessalonians themselves had suffered. The apostle was afraid that the tempter had tempted them in some way (v. 5). The Devil is a subtle and tireless tempter. He has often been successful in his attacks on people who are suffering.

3.1.2. The consequence the apostle feared was *lest his labour should be in vain* (that all his efforts might be useless). It is the Devil's purpose to hinder the good fruit and effects of the preaching of the Gospel. If he cannot hinder ministers from laboring, he will, if he is able, hinder them in the effectiveness of their labor.

3.2. The apostle tells them what he had in mind in sending Timothy:

3.2.1. To remind them of what he told them earlier about suffering in trials (v. 4), he says (v. 3), *We are appointed thereunto*. Their troubles and persecutions did not come merely from the hatred of the enemies of religion, but by the *appointment of God*. Being forewarned, they should be forearmed. Besides, their faith might be confirmed when they realized that what happened to them was only what had been predicted in advance.

3.2.2. To know their faith, whether they remained firm. If their faith did not fail, they would be able to stand their ground against the tempter and all his temptations.

Verses 6–10

Paul's great satisfaction on the return of Timothy with good news. Notice:

1. The good report Timothy made about them (v. 6) and their faith, that they were not unsettled and had not turned aside. *Their love* also continued, their love for the Gospel and the ministers of the Gospel. They *desired greatly to see the apostles again*, and there was a mutual love between them, because the apostle wanted to see them too.

2. The great comfort the apostle had in this good news (vv. 7–8): *Therefore, brethren, we were comforted in all our affliction and distress*. The apostle considered this good news of them sufficient to make up for all the troubles he met with. This put new life and spirit into him; it not only encouraged him but also greatly inspired him to rejoice: *Now we live, if you stand fast in the Lord* (v. 8). It would have been a crushing blow to the apostles to see the professors of religious faith become unsteady, whereas nothing was more encouraging than their faithfulness.

3. The effects of this were thankfulness and prayer to God on their behalf. Notice:

3.1. How thankful the apostle was (v. 9). When we are most cheerful, we should also be most thankful. Paul speaks as if he did not know how to express either his thankfulness to God or his joy and rejoicing for their sakes. His heart was released in love to them and in thanksgiving to God.

3.2. He prayed for them night and day (v. 10), lifting up his heart to God in prayer in the middle of the business of the day or the sleep of the night. He prayed much. When we are most thankful, we should always give ourselves to prayer. There was something still lacking in their faith; Paul wanted this to be perfected, and to that end he wanted to see them again. The best people have something lacking in their faith. Perhaps it is lacking in content, there being some things they know or believe insufficiently; perhaps it is lacking in its clearness and certainty.

Verses 11–13

The apostle wanted to be instrumental in the further benefiting of the Thessalonians, and the only way to do so while he was far away from them was by praying for them and sending a letter to them. Notice:

1. Whom he prays to, namely, God and Christ. Prayer is to be offered not only in the name of Christ but to Christ himself, as our Lord and our Savior.

2. What he prays for.

2.1. He prays that he and his fellow workers will be directed to them (v. 11). One would have thought that the taking of a journey to this or that place would depend on a person's own will and lie in their own power, but the apostle knew that God our Father directs and orders where his children go to and what they do. Let us acknowledge God in all our ways, and he will direct our paths (Pr 3:6).

2.2. He prays for the prosperity of the Thessalonians.

2.2.1. That they will *increase and abound* (overflow) in love (v. 12), in love for one another and in love for everyone. Love comes from God and is the fulfilling of the Gospel as well as of the Law (Ro 13:10). Timothy brought good news of their faith, but something was lacking in it. He also brought good news of their love, but the apostle prays that this will increase and overflow. We are indebted to God not only for the supply put into our hands at the beginning but also for how we use it. To our prayer we must add endeavor. The apostle again mentions his overflowing love toward them. The more we are dearly loved, the more affectionate we should be.

2.2.2. That they will be established so that they may be blameless in holiness (v. 13). *To the end that he* (the Lord) *may establish your hearts.* Holiness is required of all those who want to go to heaven, and there we must be blameless. Our desire should be to have our hearts strengthened in holiness before God — to be, already now, blameless *before God, even our Father*, and then be presented blameless when the Lord Jesus comes with all his saints.

CHAPTER 4

In this chapter: 1. The apostle issues passionate exhortations to holiness (vv. 1–8). 2. He then mentions the great duties of mutual love and quietness with diligence in our callings (vv. 9–12). 3. He concludes by comforting those who mourn their relatives and friends who have died in the Lord (vv. 13–18).

Verses 1–8

Here we have:

1. An exhortation to *abound more and more in* what is good (vv. 1–2). Notice:

1.1. The way in which the exhortation is given: very warmly. The apostle deals with them as brothers; he exhorts them passionately: *We beseech and exhort you.*

1.2. The content of his exhortation — that they excel in leading holy lives. The apostle wants them to excel others even more. Those who most surpass others still fall short of perfection. We must not only persevere to the end, but become even better.

1.3. The arguments the apostle uses to back up his exhortation.

1.3.1. The Thessalonians have been informed of their duty. They have *received*, or been taught, *how they ought to walk.* The intention of the Gospel is to teach people not only what they should believe, but also how they should live. The apostle taught them how to walk, not simply how to talk. To talk well without living a good life will never take us to heaven.

1.3.2. The apostle has taught and exhorted them in the name of the Lord Jesus Christ.

1.3.3. They will please God in it. We should not live as *menpleasers* (Eph 6:6; Col 3:22), but should walk so as to please God.

1.3.4. The rule according to which they should walk and act is *the commandments the apostles have given them by the Lord Jesus Christ.* Although the apostles received great authority from Christ, they received it to teach people what Christ had commanded, not to issue their own commandments. The Thessalonians knew what commandments Paul gave them, that they were nothing other than what he had received from the Lord Jesus himself.

2. A warning against sexual immorality, which the apostle states and then supports with arguments.

2.1. He states it: *That you should abstain from fornication* (v. 3), by which we are to understand all sexual immorality whatsoever. All that is contrary to purity in heart, speech, and behavior is contrary to the command of God and contrary to the holiness that the Gospel requires.

2.2. He supports it.

2.2.1. This aspect of sanctification in particular is the will of God (v. 3). God requires not only holiness in the heart but also purity in our bodies.

2.2.2. This will be greatly for our honor (v. 4). The body is called here the *vessel* of the soul; the soul lives in the body (1Sa 21:5), and so the body must be kept pure from defiling sinful desires. What can be more dishonorable than for a rational soul to be enslaved by bodily affections and sensual appetites?

2.2.3. To indulge passionate lusts is to live and act like the pagans: *even as the Gentiles who know not God* (v. 5). Christians should not walk like unconverted Gentiles.

2.2.4. The sin of sexual immorality, especially adultery, is a great act of injustice that God will punish; this is how we may understand those words, *That no man go beyond* (wrong) *or defraud* (take advantage of) *his brother* (v. 6) *in any matter.* Some understand these words as a further warning against injustice and oppression, which are certainly against the Gospel. But the intention may rather be to show the injustice and wrong that are done by the sin of sexual immorality. Since this sin is so detestable, God will certainly punish it.

2.2.5. The sin of sexual immorality is contrary to the intention of our Christian calling: *For God hath called us not unto uncleanness, but unto holiness* (v. 7).

2.2.6. The contempt shown by this sin to God's law and his Gospel, therefore, is contempt of God himself: *He that despises, despises God, not man* only. *God hath given us his Spirit.* The Holy Spirit is given to us to protect us against these sins.

Verses 9–12

In these words the apostle mentions the great duties:

1. Of love for one another. He urges the Thessalonians to grow in their love for one another more and more. They are already remarkable in the exercise of it, which makes it less necessary for him to write to them about it (v. 9). Here we see how, by his high opinion of them, he appeals to their affections and so opens the way for his exhortation. Notice:

1.1. What the apostle commends in them. It is not so much their own goodness as God's grace; God has taught them this good lesson: *You yourselves are taught of God to love one another* (v. 9). Whoever does what is good is taught by God to do it. All who are savingly taught by God are taught the lesson of loving one another. This is the uniform of Christ's family. By *their love to the brethren in all Macedonia* (v. 10), the Thessalonians give good evidence of having been taught by God. They do not love only their own; no, their love is wider than that. A true Christian's love is toward all the saints.

1.2. The exhortation itself: that they increase more and more in love for one another (v. 10). They must still be exhorted to pray for more and seek more. No one on this side of heaven loves perfectly.

2. Of quietness and diligence in their callings.

2.1. The apostle exhorts them to these duties: *Study to be quiet* (v. 11). It is most desirable to have a calm and quiet temper and to display peaceable and quiet behavior. Satan is very busy trying to disturb us, and we have in our own hearts things that incline us to be unsettled; therefore, let us seek to be quiet. *Do your own business.* Those who are busybodies, interfering in other people's affairs, generally have little quiet within them and greatly unsettle their neighbors. At least they seldom take any notice of the other exhortation, to be diligent in their own calling, *to work with their own hands.* Christianity does not discharge us from the responsibility of the work of our particular callings, but teaches us to pursue them diligently.

2.2. He argues that by following this exhortation:

2.2.1. We will walk honestly, that is, decently and creditably toward outsiders (v. 12). This will be behaving as befits those who profess to believe the Gospel, and it will gain a good reputation from those who are strangers or even enemies to it.

2.2.2. We will live comfortably and lack nothing (v. 12). Those who diligently mind their own business live comfortably and lack nothing. They earn their own living and have great pleasure in doing so.

Verses 13–18

In these words the apostle comforts the Thessalonians who mourn the death of their relatives and friends who have died in the Lord. His intention is to dissuade them from grieving excessively. It is far from true that *all* grief for the death of friends is unlawful; we may weep for our own loss, even though it may be their gain. But we must not be excessive in our sorrow, because:

1. This seems to show that we have no hope (v. 13). It is to act too much like the Gentiles, who have no hope of a better life after this. We have the hope of eternal life after this one, which is more than enough to counterbalance all our griefs.

2. This reflects ignorance about the dead (v. 13). Of some things about those who are asleep we must remain ignorant, and yet there are some things, especially about those who die in the Lord, that we need not be ignorant of. They will be sufficient to soften our sorrow for those who die in the Lord.

2.1. They sleep in Jesus (v. 13). They have withdrawn from this troublesome world to rest from all their toil and sorrow, and they are asleep in Jesus (v. 14). They are not lost by death, therefore, nor are they losers, but in fact great gainers, and their transfer from this world is to a better one.

2.2. They will be raised up from the dead and woken up from their sleep, for *God will bring them with him* (v. 14). They are now with God, and are therefore better off where they are than when they were here, and when God comes he will take them with him. The doctrine of the resurrection and the second coming of Christ is a great remedy for the fear of death and excessive sorrow for the death of our Christian friends. We have full assurance of this teaching because we *believe that Jesus died and rose again* (v. 14).

2.3. Their state and condition will be glorious and happy at the second coming of Christ. The apostle informs the Thessalonians of this *by the word of the Lord* (v. 15). The Lord Jesus will come down from heaven in all the glory and power of the higher world (v. 16): *The Lord himself shall descend from heaven with a shout.* He will descend from heaven into our own atmosphere (v. 17). The appearance will be with glory and power, *with a shout, with the voice of the archangel.* The glorious appearance of this great Redeemer and Judge will be declared and ushered in by the *trump of God.* The dead will be raised: *The dead in Christ shall rise first*

(v. 16). Those who are then *found alive shall not prevent* (precede) *those that are asleep* (v. 15). Those who are found alive will then be changed. They will *be caught up together with the* others *in the clouds, to meet the Lord in the air* (v. 17). Those who are raised and those who are changed in this way will meet together in the clouds, and there they will meet with their Lord. Here is the happiness of the saints on that day: they will *be ever with the Lord* (v. 17). The main happiness of heaven is *to be with the Lord,* to see him, live with him, and enjoy him forever. This should comfort the saints on the death of their friends. We and our loved ones who have died in the Lord, with all the saints, will meet our Lord and be with him forever, never again to be separated either from him or from one another. The apostle wants us to *comfort one another with these words* (v. 18).

CHAPTER 5

The apostle, having spoken at the end of the previous chapter about the resurrection and second coming of Christ, now comes to speak about the futility of asking questions about the particular time of Christ's coming, which will be sudden and terrible to evildoers but an encouragement to the saints (vv. 1–5). He then urges the Thessalonians to fulfill the duties of watchfulness, sobriety, and the exercise of faith, love, and hope, as befits their converted state (vv. 6–10). Next, he exhorts them to fulfill several duties to others, or to one another (vv. 11–15), then to fulfill several other important Christian duties (vv. 16–22), and then he concludes this letter (vv. 23–28).

Verses 1–5

In these words notice:

1. The apostle tells the Thessalonians it is unnecessary or useless to ask questions about the particular time of Christ's coming: *Of the times and seasons you need not that I write unto you* (v. 1). A certain time has been appointed for his coming, but no revelation of that time had been given to Paul; nor should they inquire into this secret, and nor should we. There are times and seasons for us to do our work in: it is our duty and in our interests to know and observe these. But we do not know the time and season when we must give an account. Our vain curiosity would like to know many things that there is no need at all for us to know and that it would do us no good to know.

2. He tells them that the coming of Christ will be a great surprise to most people (v. 2). His coming will be *as a thief in the night.* Just as thieves usually come at the dead of night, when least expected, the day of the Lord will be such a surprise.

3. He tells them how terrible Christ's coming will be to the ungodly (v. 3). It will be for their destruction on that day of the Lord. It will overtake them suddenly in the middle of their worldly self-confidence and mirth, when they say in their hearts, *Peace and safety,* and do not expect it, *as travail cometh upon a woman with child*—actually at the set time, but not perhaps at the expected time. Their destruction will be unavoidable: *They shall not escape.*

4. He tells them how comfortable this day will be for the righteous (vv. 4–5). Notice:

4.1. Their character and privilege. They are the *children of the light.* This was the fortunate condition of the Thessalonians, as it is of all true Christians. They were not in a state of sin and ignorance as the ungodly were. They were the *children of the day,* because the Morning Star had risen on them (2Pe 1:19). They were no longer in pagan darkness, but under the Gospel, which brings life and immortality to light (2Ti 1:10).

4.2. Their great advantage on this account: that *that day would not overtake them as a thief* (v. 4). They had received fair warning and sufficient help to prepare, and could hope to stand with comfort and confidence before the Son of Man, as a friend in the day, not as a thief in the night.

Verses 6–10

On what has been said the apostle bases several timely exhortations.

1. To be watchful and sober (v. 6). These duties are distinct, but they are linked with one another. We will not remain sober unless we are watchful, and, unless we remain sober, we will not long be watchful.

1.1. Then *let us not sleep as do others, but let us watch*; we must not be self-confident and careless, nor indulge in spiritual laziness. Most people are too negligent of their duty and heedless of their spiritual enemies. Either they do not consider the things of another world at all, because they are asleep, or they do not consider them rightly, because they are dreaming. But let us keep watch, like those who are awake and stand on guard.

1.2. Let us also *be sober*. Let us keep our natural desires and appetites for worldly things within appropriate limits. Watchfulness and sobriety are most suitable to the character and privilege of Christians, as *children of the day*; for *those that sleep, sleep in the night, and those that are drunken are drunken in the night* (v. 7). Such people were not aware of their danger, and that is why they *slept*; they were not aware of their duty, and that is why they were drunk: but it is inconsistent for Christians to do such things.

2. To be well armed as well as watchful. Our spiritual enemies are many, mighty, and malicious. We must therefore arm ourselves against their attempts. Our spiritual armor consists of the three great graces of Christians: faith, love, and hope (v. 8).

2.1. We must live by faith, and this will keep us watchful and sober. Faith will be our best defense against the attacks of our enemies.

2.2. We must have a heart inflamed with love. True and fervent love for God and the things of God will keep us watchful and sober.

2.3. We must make salvation our hope. This good hope of eternal life will be like a helmet to protect the head and prevent us from being intoxicated with the pleasures of sin, which last merely a short time (Heb 11:25). The apostle shows what basis Christians have to hope for this salvation. Note that he says nothing of their having deserved it. No, the doctrine of human merit is altogether unscriptural and antiscriptural. Our hopes are based on:

2.3.1. God's appointment: because *God hath not appointed us to wrath, but to obtain salvation* (v. 9). If we were to trace our salvation back to its first cause, we would see that that cause is God's appointment. We build unshaken hope on it, therefore, especially when we consider:

2.3.2. Christ's merit and grace, and consider that salvation is through our Lord Jesus Christ, who died for us. Our salvation is therefore owing to, and our hopes of it are based on, Christ's atonement as well as God's appointment. We should think often about Christ's death and sufferings, with this goal in mind, *that whether we wake or sleep, we shall live together with Christ*, live in union and in glory with him forever. Christ died for us so that, living and dying, we could belong to him, so that we could

live for him while we are here and live with him when we leave here.

Verses 11–15

In these words the apostle urges the Thessalonians to fulfill their duties:

1. Toward those who are closely related to them. Those who are closely related should comfort themselves, encourage one another, and edify one another (v. 11). They must encourage or *comfort* themselves and one another. We should be concerned not only about our own comfort and welfare but about that of others. The Thessalonians must build one another up. We should share our knowledge and experiences with one another. We should join in prayer and praise with one another. We should set a good example before one another. The Thessalonians did this: *which also you do*. Those who do what is good need further exhortations to stir them to do more good as well as to continue in doing what they already do.

2. Toward their ministers (vv. 12–13). Let them notice:

2.1. How the ministers of the Gospel are described by the work of their ministry. Ministers must work conscientiously among their people, to the point of weariness, as the original implies. They are called to *labour*, not to be lazy. Ministers are to "rule" (direct) their people too; the word that is here translated *are over* may also be translated "rule." They must direct their people lovingly, not harshly. They must direct as spiritual guides, by setting a good example to the flock (1Pe 5:3). They *are over* the people *in the Lord* and must direct the people according to Christ's laws. They must also *admonish* (correct) the people. They must instruct them to do right and should rebuke when they do wrong.

2.2. What the duty of the people is toward their ministers. The people must *know* (appreciate) them. Just as the shepherd should know his flock, so the sheep must know their shepherd. They must respect their ministers highly in love for their work's sake, because their business is to advance the honor of Christ and the welfare of people's souls. Far from being lightly respected because of their work, faithful ministers should be highly respected on account of it.

3. Toward one another in general.

3.1. They must *be at peace among themselves* (v. 13). The people should be at peace among themselves, doing all they can to prevent any differences from arising or continuing among them, and using all proper means to preserve peace and harmony.

3.2. They must *warn the unruly* (v. 14). There will be in every community some who *walk disorderly* (2Th 3:6, 11). Such should be rebuked and told clearly of the wrong they are doing their own souls and of the hurt they may cause others.

3.3. They must *comfort the feebleminded* (v. 14), the timid and shy, or those who are discouraged or downcast. Such people should be encouraged. We should not despise them, but encourage them, and who knows what good a kind and comforting word may do them?

3.4. They must *support the weak* (v. 15). Some are unable to fulfill their work or cope with burdens; we should therefore help them in their weaknesses; we should lift one end of the burden and so help them to bear it.

3.5. They must *be patient toward all men* (v. 14). We must bear people and bear with them. We must exercise this duty toward all people, good and bad, noble and ordinary. We must seek to make the best we can of everything and to think the best we can of everyone.

3.6. They must not *render evil for evil to any man* (v. 15). We must in no way take revenge ourselves. As those who are and hope to be forgiven by God, we ought to forgive.

3.7. They must *ever follow that which is good* (v. 15). We must try to do what is pleasing to God. Whatever people do to us, we must do good to others, both among ourselves and then, *as we have opportunity, unto all men* (Gal 6:10).

Verses 16–22

Here we have various short exhortations. The duties are very important, and we may notice how they are all connected:

1. *Rejoice evermore* (v. 16). If we rejoice in God, we may do that forever. A religious life is a pleasant one; it is a life of constant joy.

2. *Pray without ceasing* (v. 17). The way to be always joyful is to pray continually. We would be more joyful if we prayed more. The meaning is not that people should do nothing but pray, but that nothing else we do should prevent prayer at its proper time. Prayer will help advance and not hinder all other lawful business and every good work.

3. *In every thing give thanks* (v. 18). If we pray continually, we will not lack reasons for giving thanks *in every thing*. We should be thankful in every circumstance, in adversity as well as prosperity. Things are never so bad with us that they might not be worse. Even if we have reasons to humbly complain to God, we can never have any reason to complain about God, and we always have many reasons to praise and give thanks. This is the *will of God in Christ Jesus concerning us, that we give thanks*. He allows us to always be joyful and commands us to give thanks in all circumstances.

4. *Quench not the Spirit* (v. 19). Christians are said to *be baptized with the Holy Spirit and with fire* (Mt 3:11). We must be careful not to put out this holy fire. Just as fire is put out by withdrawing fuel, so we *quench the Spirit* if we do not stir up our spirits. Just as fire is quenched when water is poured on it or a great quantity of dirt is piled on it, so we must be careful not to quench the Holy Spirit by gratifying sinful desires or by being taken up with worldly things.

5. *Despise not prophesyings* (v. 20). By *prophesyings* here we are to understand the preaching of the word. We must not treat preaching with contempt, even though it is direct and though we are told no more than what we knew before. It is useful, and many times necessary, to have our love and resolutions aroused to those things that we already knew before to be our duty and in our interests.

6. *Prove all things, but hold fast that which is good* (v. 21). We must not take things on trust from the preacher. We must search the Scriptures to see whether what they say is true or not (Ac 17:11). But we must not be always testing, always unsettled; no, in the end we must become settled and hold firmly to what is good. Our reason for testing everything must be in order to hold on to what is good.

7. *Abstain from all appearance of evil* (v. 22). Corrupt attitudes enjoyed in the heart and evil practices allowed in the life will greatly tend to promote fatal errors in the mind, whereas purity of heart and integrity of life will incline people to receive the truth in love. We should therefore avoid evil and every appearance of evil. Those who are not shy of appearances of sin will not long abstain from actually committing sin.

Verses 23–28

Notice in these words, which conclude this letter:

1. Paul's prayer for the Thessalonians (v. 23). Notice:

1.1. To whom the apostle prays, *the very God of peace*. The things he prays for will best be obtained by the Thessalonians' peacefulness and unity.

1.2. The things he prays for: he prays for their sanctification, that *God would sanctify them wholly*; and he prays for their preservation, that they would be *preserved blameless*. All those *who are sanctified in Christ Jesus* (1Co 1:2) will be *preserved until the coming of our Lord Jesus Christ* (v. 23). We should pray to God to complete and perfect his work and *preserve us blameless*, until we are finally *presented faultless before the throne of his glory with exceeding joy* (Jude 24).

2. His comforting assurance that God will hear his prayer: *Faithful is he who calleth you, who will also do it* (v. 24). The faithfulness of God is their security, assuring them that they will persevere to the end, that God will do what the apostle desires. God will fulfill all the good purposes of his goodness toward them. Our faithfulness toward God depends on his faithfulness toward us.

3. His request for their prayers: *Brethren, pray for us* (v. 25). In this way, brothers and sisters should express their mutual love. The more people pray for their ministers, the more good things ministers may receive from God, and the more benefit people may receive from their ministry.

4. His greeting: *Greet all the brethren with a holy kiss* (v. 26). This is how the apostle sends a friendly greeting from himself, Silas, and Timothy, and he wants the Thessalonians to pass that greeting on to each other. This is how he wants them to show their mutual love and affection for one another.

5. His solemn command for the reading of this letter (v. 27). This is not only an exhortation but a solemn command or charge under oath by the Lord. This letter was to be read to *all the holy brethren*. To read the Scriptures is the indispensable duty of ordinary people, and to that end, these holy, living words should not be kept concealed in an unknown tongue, but translated into the common languages. As the Law was read among the Jews in public in their synagogues, the Scriptures should also be read in the public meetings of Christians.

6. The apostolic greeting that is usual in other letters: *The grace of our Lord Jesus Christ be with you. Amen* (v. 28). We need nothing more to make us happy than to know the grace that our Lord Jesus Christ has revealed. This is an ever-flowing and overflowing fountain of grace to supply all our needs.

A Practical and Devotional
Exposition of
2 Thessalonians

This Second Letter to the Thessalonians was written soon after the first and seems to have been intended to prevent a mistake about the second coming of Christ. Some, it seems, thought that that event was close at hand. The apostle informs them that many intermediate purposes are still to be fulfilled before that day of the Lord will come, although, because it is definite, he earlier spoke of it as close.

CHAPTER 1

After the introduction (vv. 1–2): 1. The apostle begins this letter with an account of his great respect for these Thessalonians (vv. 3–4). 2. He then encourages them in their suffering and persecutions (vv. 5–10). 3. He tells them what his prayers to God for them are (vv. 11–12).

Verses 1–4

Here we have:

1. The introduction (vv. 1–2), in the same words as in the previous letter. This Thessalonian church was built, as all true churches are, *in God our Father and the Lord Jesus Christ.*

2. The apostle's expression of the great respect he had for them. Notice:

2.1. How his respect for them was expressed.

2.1.1. He praised God for them (v. 3). We should be thankful to God for all the good that is found in us or others. To thank God on behalf of our fellow Christians is not only an act of kindness toward them but also our duty.

2.1.2. He also *gloried* (boasts) *in them before the churches of God* (v. 4). The apostle never flattered his friends, but he took pleasure in speaking well about them, to the glory of God.

2.2. What he respected and thanked God for in them. In his previous letter (1Th 1:3) he gave thanks for their faith, love, and endurance; here he gives thanks for the increase of all those graces. Where there is the truth of grace, there will be an increase in it. Where there is an increase of grace, God must receive all the glory for it. We may be tempted to think that although when we were bad we could not make ourselves good, nevertheless, when we are good we can easily make ourselves better, but we depend as much on the grace of God for increasing the grace we have as for planting grace when we did not have it.

2.2.1. Their faith grew very much (v. 3). The growth of their faith could be seen in the works of their faith, and where faith grows, all other graces grow in proportion.

2.2.2. Their love increased (v. 3). Where faith grows, love will increase.

2.2.3. Their *patience* (perseverance) as well as their faith increased in all their persecution and troubles. Perseverance matures when it extends to all trials. The Thessalonians endured all their suffering by faith. They endured it with patience, that is, not with indifference, but with perseverance arising from Christ's resources within them.

Verses 5–10

Having mentioned the persecutions and trials that the Thessalonians endured for the cause of Christ, the apostle proceeded to offer several things to encourage them:

1. The present blessedness and advantage of their sufferings (v. 5). They became better people through their suffering; they were *counted worthy of the kingdom of God.* If religious faith is worth anything, it is worth everything, and those who cannot find it in their hearts to suffer for it either have no faith at all or do not know how to value it.

2. The future reward that will be given to persecutors and persecuted.

2.1. In this future reward there will be:

2.1.1. A punishment inflicted on persecutors (v. 6). Nothing more infallibly marks a person out for eternal ruin than a spirit of persecution. God will pay people back, and he will trouble those who trouble his people (Jos 7:25).

2.1.2. A reward for those who are persecuted (v. 7). There remains a rest for the people of God (Heb 4:9), a rest from sin and sorrow. The future rest will greatly make up for all their present troubles. There is more than enough in heaven to make up for all that we may lose or suffer for the name of Christ in this world.

2.2. About this future reward we may further notice:

2.2.1. Its certainty: *It is a righteous thing with God* (v. 6). God's suffering people will lose nothing by their sufferings, and their enemies will gain nothing.

2.2.2. Its timing (v. 7). The Lord Jesus will appear from heaven on that day. He will be revealed with his *mighty angels* (v. 7). He will come in *flaming fire* (v. 8), to the saints a refining fire to purify them, to evildoers a consuming fire (Dt 4:24; Heb 12:29). The effects of this appearance will be fearful to some and joyful to others.

2.2.2.1. They will be fearful to some: those who sinned against the principles of natural religion and rebelled against the light of nature (v. 8), and those who rebelled against the light of revelation. To such people, the revelation of our Lord Jesus Christ will be fearful, because of their fate (v. 9): they will then be punished. They did the work of sin and must therefore receive the wages of sin (Ro 6:23). Their punishment will be no less than destruction. This destruction will come from the *presence of the Lord*, from the *glory of his power*.

2.2.2.2. It will be a joyful day to some, to saints. Christ Jesus will be glorified and marveled at both by his saints and in them. His grace and power will be exalted in their salvation. How they will be wondered at on this great and glorious day, or rather, how Christ will be marveled at!

Verses 11–12

Here the apostle told his readers of his wholehearted and faithful prayer for them: *Wherefore also we pray*. Notice:

1. What the apostle prayed for (v. 11).

1.1. That God would begin his good work of grace in the Thessalonians; this is how we may understand this expression: *that our God would count you* (or, as it might read, "make you") *worthy of this calling*. We are called to God's kingdom and glory. Now if this is our calling, our great concern should be to lead lives that are worthy of it. We should pray that he would make us worthy.

1.2. That God would continue the good work that had been begun. *The good pleasure* of God refers to his gracious purposes toward his people. God has various purposes of grace and goodwill toward his people, and the apostle prayed that all of them might be *fulfilled* toward these Thessalonians. In particular, the apostle prayed that God would fulfill in them the *work of faith with power*.

2. Why the apostle prayed for these things (v. 12). Our good works should so shine out in the sight of others that they may glorify God (Mt 5:16), that Christ may be glorified in and by us, and then we will be glorified in and with him.

CHAPTER 2

1. The apostle takes great care to prevent the spreading of an error into which some of the Thessalonians have fallen, a belief that the coming of Christ is very near (vv. 1–3). 2. He then proceeds to refute the error he has warned them against (vv. 4–12). 3. He then encourages them and exhorts them to stand firm (vv. 13–15). 4. He concludes with a prayer for them (vv. 16–17).

Verses 1–3

Some of the Thessalonians had mistaken the apostle's meaning about the coming of Christ and thought that that coming was close at hand. The apostle is careful to put right this mistake. If errors and mistakes arise among Christians, we should take the first opportunity to deal with them and put them right. Good people will be especially careful to suppress errors that may arise from a mistake in their words and actions. We have a subtle adversary, who will sometimes promote errors even by using words of Scripture. Notice:

1. How eager this apostle is to prevent mistakes (v. 1). He who could have commanded them as a father commands his children speaks to them as brothers. This is the best way to deal with people when we want to preserve or restore them from errors—gently and affectionately. We may notice from this form of request—*by the coming of Christ*:

1.1. It is most certain that the Lord Jesus Christ will come to judge the world. Whatever mistakes may arise about the time of his coming, his coming itself is certain.

1.2. At the second coming of Christ all the saints will be gathered together to him. It will be the completing of the happiness of his saints. There will then be a general meeting of all the saints, and no one except saints. All the Old Testament saints and all the New Testament saints will be gathered *together to Christ*. He will be the great center of their unity, and they will gather to be with him forever, completely happy in his presence to all eternity.

2. What the apostle warns the Thessalonians against: they should not be deceived about the time of Christ's coming and so *be shaken in mind, or be troubled*. Errors in the mind tend to greatly weaken our faith, and those who are weak in faith and have troubled minds often tend to be deceived.

2.1. He does not want them to be deceived (v. 3). Many lie in wait to deceive others (Eph 4:14), and they have many ways of deceiving. We must therefore stand on our guard. He warns them not to be deceived about the time of Christ's coming, which they think will be in the apostle's days.

2.2. He does not want them *be soon shaken or troubled* (become easily unsettled or alarmed) (v. 2).

2.2.1. He does not want their faith to be weakened. They ought not to waver in their thinking about the great matter of Christ's second coming, which is the faith and hope of all the saints. False doctrines are like winds (Eph 4:14), which toss the water to and fro, and they tend to unsettle people, who are sometimes as unstable as water (Ge 49:4).

2.2.2. He does not want to see their assurances diminished by false alarms. The coming of Christ was probably represented with terror among these Christians, but in itself it should be a matter of the believer's hope and joy. We should always watch and pray (Mt 26:41), but we must not be discouraged or uncomfortable at the thought of Christ's coming.

Verses 3–12

The apostle denies the error against which he has warned them. Several events will precede the second coming of Christ, under these two headings:

1. A general apostasy (v. 3). The apostle speaks of some very great apostasy that will give occasion for the revelation or rise of that *man of sin* (man of lawlessness). This, he says (v. 5), he told them about when he was with them. No sooner was Christianity planted and rooted in the world than some began to defect from the Christian church. It was so in the Old Testament church; it was in no way strange, therefore, that after Christianity had been planted there would come a general falling away.

2. A revelation of *that man of sin* (v. 3). The apostle later speaks of *the revelation of that Wicked* one (v. 8). Here he seems to speak about his rise: Notice:

2.1. The names of this person. He is called the *man of sin*, to refer to his flagrant evil. He is the *son of perdition*, because he himself is devoted to certain destruction (Dt 7:2; 20:16–17; Jos 6:17–18) and is the instrument of destroying many others.

2.2. The descriptions given here (v. 4). The Antichrist is some usurper of God's authority who claims divine honors.

2.3. His rise (vv. 6–7).

2.3.1. There was something that hindered, or *let, until it was taken away*. This is thought to be the power of the Roman Empire, which for a time prevented the advances of the bishops of Rome to the tyranny that they later reached.

2.3.2. This mystery of lawlessness reached its height gradually. The apostle calls it a *mystery of iniquity*. This secret power of lawlessness *doth already work*. While the apostles were still living, *the enemy came, and sowed tares* (Mt 13:25).

2.4. How the fall or ruin of the state of the Antichrist is declared (v. 8). The head of this kingdom is called *that wicked one*, and the revelation of his character to the world will be the sure sign of his forthcoming ruin. The apostle assures the Thessalonians that the Lord will destroy him. In due time the power of the Antichrist will be totally and finally destroyed, and this will be by the *brightness of Christ's coming*.

2.5. How the apostle further describes the rule of this man of lawlessness. Notice:

2.5.1. A description of *his coming*, that is, of his rule. A divine power will be claimed for the support of this kingdom, but it will only be in accordance with the working of Satan—false signs and wonders, visions and miracles. By these the papal kingdom was first set up and is kept up. The apostle calls it *all deceivableness of unrighteousness* (every kind of evil that deceives) (v. 10). The man of lawlessness has used many subtle tricks.

2.5.2. A description of those who will be his willing subjects (v. 10). If they had loved the truth, they would have persevered in it and been preserved by it, but it is hardly surprising if they easily parted with what they never had any love for.

2.6. How the sin and ruin of the subjects of the Antichrist's kingdom are declared (vv. 11–12). An erroneous mind and corrupt life often go together and spur each other on. God will punish people for their unbelief, for their dislike of the truth and their love for sin and evil. He sometimes withdraws his grace from such sinners as are mentioned here; he gives them over to their own hearts' sinful desires and leaves them to themselves, and then sin will follow its natural course.

Verses 13–15

Notice here:

1. The encouragement the Thessalonians could take because they were chosen for salvation (vv. 13–14). The apostle considered himself bound to be thankful to God on this account, and there was good reason for this, because they were loved by the Lord. This preservation of the saints is owing to:

1.1. The stability of the election of grace (v. 13). God had chosen them from the beginning. He had loved them with an eternal love. Notice about God's election:

1.1.1. Its eternal date—it is *from the beginning*.

1.1.2. The purpose for which the Thessalonians were chosen—complete and eternal salvation.

1.1.3. How this purpose would be achieved—*sanctification of the spirit and belief of the truth*. We have not been chosen by God because we were holy, but in order that we may become holy. Being chosen by God, we must not live as we wish. Faith and holiness, as well as holiness and happiness, must be joined together.

1.2. The effectiveness of the Gospel call (v. 14). They were called to salvation by the Gospel. It is a call to honor and happiness, even the *glory of our Lord Jesus Christ*. Those who believe in Christ and obey his Gospel will be with him to see his glory, and they will be glorified with him and share in his glory.

2. He does not say, "You are chosen for salvation, and so you can sit back in your self-confidence and do whatever you want," but *therefore stand fast*. The Thessalonians are urged to stand firm in their Christian profession.

Verses 16–17

Here we have the apostle's passionate prayer for the Thessalonians, in which we may notice:

1. To whom he prays: *Our Lord Jesus Christ himself, and God, even our Father.* We may and should direct our prayers not only to God the Father but also *to our Lord Jesus Christ himself.*

2. From what he takes encouragement—from the consideration of what God has already done for him and them (v. 16). The love of God is the spring and fountain of all the good we have or hope for. From this fountain flows all our encouragement. The encouragement of the saints is eternal; the comforts of the saints do not die. Their encouragement is based on the hope of eternal life. The free grace and mercy of God are what they hope for and what their hopes are founded on.

3. What he asks of God for them (v. 17). He prays that they will have even greater encouragement and that they will be strengthened. True comfort is a means of strengthening, because the more pleasure we take in the ways of God, the more likely we will be to persevere in them. Our strengthening in the ways of God, on the other hand, is a likely means of comfort. If we are halting and faltering in fulfilling our responsibility, it is hardly surprising if we are strangers to the pleasures and joys of our religious faith. We must be strengthened in every good word and work. Christ must be honored by both our good works and our good words.

CHAPTER 3

1. The apostle has prayed passionately for the Thessalonians, and now he seeks their prayers (vv. 1–5). 2. He gives commands and directions to correct some things that are wrong among them (vv. 6–15). 3. He concludes with blessings and prayers (vv. 16–18).

Verses 1–5

In these words notice:

1. The apostle seeks the prayers of his friends (v. 1). He always remembers them in his prayers, and he also does not want them to forget him and his fellow workers. The communion of saints is maintained not only by their praying together but also by their praying for one another when they are apart. They are told to pray for:

1.1. The success of the Gospel ministry (v. 1). He wants the word of the Lord to "run," as it is in the original, to spread and gain ground, not only to go forward but to go forward rapidly. We should pray that the Gospel may have free access to the hearts and the consciences of people and that it may be glorified in the conversion of sinners. God will glorify the Gospel and so glorify his own name.

1.2. The safety of Gospel ministers. He requests their prayers not for promotion but for preservation (v. 2). Those who are enemies to the preaching of the Gospel are *unreasonable and wicked*. There is the greatest absurdity in the world in such enmity. Godly and faithful ministers, on the other hand, are like the standard-bearers, who are most attacked. *For all men have not faith.* Many do not believe the Gospel, and then no wonder if they are restless in their endeavors to oppose the Gospel and disgrace the ministers of the word. Too many have no common faith or honesty; we cannot safely put any confidence in them at all, and we should pray to be saved from those who have no conscience or honor.

2. He encourages them to trust in God. Notice:

2.1. What the good is that we may expect from the grace of God—*establishment* (strengthening) and preservation from evil. We stand no longer than God holds us up. We have as much need of the grace of God for our perseverance to the end as for the beginning of the good work.

2.2. What encouragement we have to depend on the grace of God. He is faithful to his promises. Once he has made a promise, its fulfillment is sure and certain. He is a faithful God and a faithful friend. Let us be concerned to remain true and faithful in our promises and to the relationship we stand in with this faithful God.

2.3. A further basis for the hope that God will do this for the Thessalonians, namely, that they both do and will do the things they have been commanded (v. 4). The apostle has this confidence in them, and it is founded on his confidence in God, for otherwise no confidence is to be put in human beings (Ps 118:8).

3. He prays a short prayer for them (v. 5):

3.1. That their hearts may be brought into the love of God. This is not only a most reasonable and necessary requirement for us to be happy; it is our happiness itself. We can never reach this unless God by his grace directs our hearts rightly, for our love tends to go astray after other things all too easily.

3.2. That a *patient waiting for Christ* may be added to this love for God. We must wait for Christ, which implies our faith in him, that we believe he came once in flesh and will come again in glory. We *have need of patience*, patience for Christ's sake and patience in following Christ's example.

Verses 6–15

Here are commands and directions to some who are at fault, correcting some things that are wrong among them. The best community of Christians may have some faulty people among them. Perfection is not to be found on this side of heaven. And yet, as the saying goes, "From evil conduct spring good laws." Notice:

1. What was wrong among the Thessalonians.

1.1. There were some who *walked disorderly, not after the tradition they received* from the apostle (v. 6).

1.2. There were among them some *idle persons and busybodies* (v. 11).

1.2.1. It does not appear that the *idle persons* were gluttons or drunkards, but simply lazy, and therefore *disorderly*. It is not enough for a person to say they are doing no harm; all are required to do good. These people probably had the idea that Christ's return was imminent and used that as an excuse to leave their jobs and lead idle lives. Diligence in our particular callings as ordinary people is a duty required of us by our general calling as Christians.

1.2.2. There were also busybodies among them, and it seems from the context that they were the same people who were lazy. Often those people who have no business of their own to do, or who neglect it, busy themselves in other people's lives. If we are idle, the Devil will soon find us something to do. The human mind needs to be kept busy; if it is not employed in doing good, it will be doing evil.

2. The good laws that were brought about by this evil conduct. Notice:

2.1. Whose laws they are: they are commands of the apostles of our Lord, that is, the commands of our Lord himself (vv. 6, 12). The authority of Christ should awe

our minds into obedience, and his grace and goodness should attract us.

2.2. What the good laws and rules are.

2.2.1. His commands and directions to the whole church concern:

2.2.1.1. Their behavior toward the disorderly people (v. 6). We must ascertain whether a person charged with not obeying the word of God is doing so. We must have sufficient proof of their fault before we proceed further. Warn them in a friendly manner; remind them of their sin and of their duty. If they will not listen, do not keep company with them, for two reasons: first, to avoid learning their evil ways, for those who follow worthless people are in danger of becoming like them; and second, to shame and thereby reform them. Even when we withdraw from our offending brothers and sisters because we hate their vices, therefore, we must be motivated by love for their persons. Even those who are under the discipline of the church must not be counted as enemies (v. 15).

2.2.1.2. Their general conduct, which should be according to the good example the apostle has given them (v. 7). The particular good example the apostle mentions is his and his fellow apostles' diligence: "*We behaved not ourselves disorderly among you* (v. 7); we did not spend our time idly." The apostles took pains in their ministry and in earning their own living (v. 8). Those who preach the Gospel may rightly expect to live by the Gospel (1Co 9:14). This is a just debt that people owe their ministers, and the apostle had authority to demand it (v. 9), but he waived his right out of love for the Thessalonians, and so that he would be an example for them to follow (v. 9).

2.2.2. He commands those who lead idle lives to reform their ways (v. 10). Workers are worthy of their food, but what are those who are lazy worthy of? No one should live like a useless sluggard in the world. That *with quietness we work, and eat our own bread* (v. 12) was not the mere whim of the apostle; it was the command of our Lord Jesus Christ. People should earn their own living some way or other; otherwise they do not eat their own bread. We must seek to be quiet and keep to our own business. This is an excellent but rare combination, to be active yet quiet, active in our own business but quiet as to other people's.

2.2.3. He urges *those that do well not* to be *weary in well doing* (v. 13). "You must never give up or become tired in your work. There will be time enough for rest when you come to heaven."

Verses 16–18

Here we have the apostle's blessing and prayers for these Thessalonians. He prays:

1. That God will give them peace. Peace is the blessing declared or desired. This peace is desired for them always and by all means, for peace is often difficult, just as it is always desirable. If we are to have any peace that is desirable, God must give it.

2. That the presence of God will be with them. We need nothing more to make us safe and happy, nor can we wish anything better for ourselves and our friends. It is the presence of God that makes heaven heaven, and the same presence will make this earth like heaven.

3. That the *grace of our Lord Jesus Christ may be with them*. It is through the grace of our Lord Jesus Christ that we may comfortably hope to have peace with God and enjoy the presence of God. It is this grace that is everything we need to make us happy.

A PRACTICAL AND DEVOTIONAL EXPOSITION OF

1 Timothy

Up to this time Paul's letters have been directed to churches; now come some to particular individuals: two to Timothy, one to Titus, and one to Philemon. Timothy and Titus were evangelists. Their commission and work was much the same as that of the apostles, namely, to plant churches and to water the churches that were planted; they were itinerant ministers, therefore, as we find Timothy was. Timothy was first converted through Paul, which is why Paul calls him his *own son in the faith* (1:2). The scope of these two letters was to instruct Timothy on how to fulfill his duty as an evangelist at Ephesus, where he now was.

CHAPTER 1

After the opening greeting (vv. 1–2) we have: 1. The command given to Timothy (vv. 3–4). 2. The true goal of the law (vv. 5–11). 3. A mention of his own call to be an apostle (vv. 12–16). 4. His doxology (v. 17). 5. A renewal of the command to Timothy (v. 18). 6. A remark about Hymenaeus and Alexander (vv. 19–20).

Verses 1–4

Here is:

1. The opening greeting of the letter. Paul's credentials were unquestionable. He had a command not only from God our Savior but also from *Jesus Christ, who is our hope.* Jesus Christ is a Christian's hope; all our hope of eternal life rests on him. Paul calls Timothy his own son because he was instrumental in Timothy's conversion and because Timothy has been a son by serving him. Timothy has not failed to fulfill the duty of a son to Paul, and Paul is not lacking in the care and tenderness of a father to him.

2. The blessing: in all the letters to the churches the apostolic blessing is *grace and peace*; in these two letters to Timothy and the one to Titus it is *grace, mercy, and peace*, as if ministers had greater need of mercy than others. If Timothy needed the increase and continuation of God's mercy, then how much more do we ministers.

3. The purpose for which Paul appointed Timothy to this position. Timothy's business was to take care to establish both the ministers and the people of the church at Ephesus, to charge them not to add to the Christian doctrine or change it, but remain faithful to it as it was delivered to them. In the times of the apostles, attempts were made to corrupt Christianity; otherwise this command to Timothy could have been spared. Timothy must not only see to it that he does not preach false doctrine; he must also command others to preach it pure and uncorrupted. "Beware of these people," Paul says; "or they will corrupt and ruin religious faith among you, because *they minister questions* (promote controversies) *rather than edifying.*" What gives rise to differences of opinion pulls down the church rather than builds it up. *Godly edifying* is the goal ministers should aim at in all their sermons and discussions, and it must be done in faith. It is by faith that we come to God in the beginning, and we must be built up in the same way and by the same principle of faith. Ministers should avoid what will cause disputes. Even disputes about great and necessary truths eat up the vital parts of religious faith, which consist in practice and obedience as well as in faith.

Verses 5–11

Here the apostle shows the use of the law and the glory of the Gospel.

1. He shows the purpose and uses of the law: it is intended to promote love.

1.1. The main scope and thrust of the divine law is to urge us to love God and one another. Surely the Gospel, which obliges us to love our enemies and do good to those who hate us (Mt 5:44), does not intend to supersede a commandment of which the purpose is love. Those, therefore, who boasted of their knowledge of the law but used it only as a disguise for the disturbance they caused in the preaching of the Gospel defeated what was the very purpose of the commandment. and that is love, love *out of a pure heart.* Our hearts must be cleansed from all sinful love; our love must arise *out of a good conscience*, a real belief in the truth of the word of God, here called *a faith unfeigned* (sincere). The three qualities that accompany the grace of love are:

1.1.1. A pure heart.

1.1.2. A good conscience, in which we must exercise ourselves daily.

1.1.3. A faith that is *unfeigned*, or sincere, for the love that is required is elsewhere called *love without dissimulation*, or pretense (Ro 12:9): the faith that works by it (Gal 5:6) must be of the same nature, genuine and sincere. When people wander away from the great law of love, they will turn aside to meaningless talk; and when people mistake their goal and aim, no wonder if every step they take is off the path. Mere talk, especially in religion, is vain, but many people's religion consists of little else but meaningless talk.

1.2. The use of the law (v. 8). The Jews set it up for justification, and so used it unlawfully. We are to return to its right use and remove the abuses, for the law is still very useful as a rule of life. It is good to teach us what is sin and what is duty. It is the grace of God that changes people's hearts, but the terrors of the law may be useful to tie their hands and restrain their tongues. The law is not made primarily for the righteous, but for sinners of all kinds, to a greater or less extent (vv. 9–10).

2. He shows the glory and grace of the Gospel. He calls it *the glorious gospel*, for that is what it is: much of the glory of God appears in the works of creation and providence, but much more in the Gospel, where it shines in the face of Jesus Christ (2Co 4:6). Paul considered it a great honor and a great favor to be entrusted with this glorious Gospel.

Verses 12–17

Here the apostle:

1. Thanks Jesus Christ for putting him in the ministry. It is Christ's work to put people into the ministry (Ac 26:16–17). Ministers cannot make themselves ministers, because it is Christ's work. He also equips those whom he puts into the ministry; he qualifies those he calls. Christ gives not only ability but also faithfulness to those whom he puts in the ministry. Christ's ministers are trustworthy servants. A call to the ministry is a great favor.

2. Gives an account of his conversion. Notice:

2.1. What he was before his conversion. Frequently those who are intended for great and distinguished services are left to themselves before their conversion. The greatness of sin is no bar to our acceptance with God or to our being employed for him, if it is truly repented of. True penitents will not be reluctant to acknowledge their former condition. This good apostle often confessed what his former life had been.

2.2. The great favor of God to him.

2.2.1. Because Paul sinned ignorantly and in unbelief, he obtained mercy. What we do ignorantly is less a crime than what we do knowingly, and yet a sin of ignorance is a sin. In some cases ignorance will extenuate a crime, even though it does not take it away. Unbelief lies at the root of what sinners do in ignorance. For these reasons Paul obtained mercy: he sinned *ignorantly, in unbelief.*

2.2.2. He takes notice of the abundant grace of Jesus Christ (v. 14), the grace of Christ that appears in his glorious Gospel (v. 15). Here we have a summary of the whole Gospel: *that Jesus Christ came into the world.* It is good news, which deserves full acceptance, but it is not too good to be true, because it is a dependable saying. Paul was the worst sinner; he acknowledges it. Persecutors are some of the worst sinners, Paul had been one. He who elsewhere calls himself the *least of all saints* (Eph 3:8) calls himself here the *chief of sinners.* Yet the chief of sinners may become the chief of saints. This is a trustworthy saying, one that can be relied on.

2.2.3. He speaks of the mercy he found with God. He speaks of it:

2.2.3.1. To encourage others to repent and believe (v. 16). It demonstrated the patience of Christ that he would bear so much with one who had been so greatly offensive, and it was intended as an example to all others, to show that the greatest sinners should not despair of mercy with God.

2.2.3.2. To give glory to God. He cannot continue with his letter without inserting a thankful acknowledgment

of God's goodness to him. Those who are aware of their obligations to the mercy and grace of God will have their hearts released in his praise. When we have found God to be good, we must not forget to declare that he is also great; his kind thoughts of us must not lessen our high thoughts of him at all, but rather increase them. God's gracious dealings with us should fill us with wonder at his glorious attributes. *To him be glory for ever and ever.*

Verses 18–20

Here is the *charge* Paul gives Timothy to proceed in his work with perseverance (v. 18). It seems, there had been prophecies before about Timothy. This encouraged Paul to give him this charge. Notice:

1. The ministry is a good fight (6:12; 2Ti 4:7) against sin and Satan.

2. Ministers must wage this good war conscientiously and courageously.

3. The prophecies in the past about Timothy are mentioned here as a motive to stir him to a vigorous fulfillment of his duty. In the same way, the good hopes that others have received about us should stir us to fulfill our duty.

4. We must *hold* both *faith and a good conscience* (v. 19). Those who abandon a good conscience will soon shipwreck their faith; we must aim for the one as well as the other. As for those who have shipwrecked their faith, he mentions two, *Hymenaeus and Alexander*, who have professed the Christian faith but abandoned their profession, and Paul has handed them over to Satan, has declared them to belong to the Devil's kingdom, so *that they may learn not to blaspheme.* God can, if he pleases, work by opposites: *Hymenaeus and Alexander* are handed over to Satan to learn not to blaspheme, when one would rather have thought they would learn from Satan to blaspheme even more. Let us hold on to our faith and a good conscience, because once we let go our hold of these, we do not know where we will stop.

CHAPTER 2

In this chapter Paul: 1. Speaks of prayer (vv. 1–8). 2. Speaks of women's clothing (vv. 9–10). 3. Speaks of women's submission (vv. 11–14). 4. Conveys a promise given for their encouragement in childbirth (v. 15).

Verses 1–8

Here is:

1. A command given to Christians to pray for everyone in general, and especially for people in authority. Paul does not give Timothy any prescribed form of prayer; he thought it enough to give general headings of prayer. If ministers have the Scriptures to direct them in prayer and the Spirit of prayer poured out on them, they needed no further directions.

1.1. Notice that the disciples of Christ must be praying people. There must be prayers for ourselves in the first place; this is implied here. We must also pray *for all men.* Notice how far the Christian religion was from being a sect, since it taught people this generous act of love, to pray for everyone.

1.2. Pray *for kings* (v. 2). Even though the kings at that time were ungodly, Christians must still pray for them. *For kings, and all that are in authority.* We must give thanks for them, praying for their welfare and for the welfare of their kingdoms, so that we may enjoy peace in our community.

1.3. Notice that he does not say, "so that we may be advanced under them, so that we may grow rich and be given honor and power under them. No, the highest ambition of a true Christian is to lead a peaceful and quiet life. We cannot expect to be kept peaceful and quiet unless we keep up *all godliness and honesty* (respect). Here our duty as Christians is summed up in two words: *godliness*, that is, the right worship of God, and *honesty*, that is, good conduct toward all people. These two must go together. Christians are to be people who are much given to prayer. In our prayers we are to have a generous concern for others as well as for ourselves; we are to pray for everyone and give thanks for everyone. Even kings themselves, and all others in authority, are to be prayed for. They need our prayers, for they face many difficulties and snares which their high positions expose them to.

2. A reason why, namely, God's love to humanity in general (v. 4).

2.1. God bears goodwill to the whole human race. There is one God (v. 5), and only one. This one *God will have all men to be saved and to come to the knowledge of the truth* (v. 4). We should seek to obtain the knowledge of the truth, because that is the way to be saved.

2.2. There is one Mediator, and that Mediator gave himself as a *ransom for all.* Just as the mercy of God extends to all his works (Ps 145:9), so the mediation of Christ extends to all people, so that now they are not under the law as a covenant of works, but as a rule of life. They are under grace. We deserved to die. Christ died for us. He put himself into the office of Mediator between God and humanity. A mediator implies a dispute. Sin had made a quarrel between us and God; Jesus Christ is a Mediator who undertakes to make peace, to bring God and humanity together. He is a ransom that *was to be testified in due time.* Paul was entrusted to preach this message of Christ's mediation to the whole creation (Mk 16:15). He was commissioned especially to preach *in faith and truth*, or faithfully and truly, to the Gentiles. We can learn from this:

2.2.1. God has goodwill for the salvation of all, so that if any are not saved, it is not so much for lack of a will in God to save them as it is for lack of a will in people to be saved in God's way.

2.2.2. Those who are saved must come to the knowledge of the truth. Without knowledge, the heart cannot be good; if we do not know the truth, we cannot be ruled by it.

2.2.3. Paul was appointed to be a minister to declare this to the Gentiles, that Christ is the one Mediator between God and humanity, who gave himself as a ransom for all.

2.2.4. Ministers must preach the truth; they are, like our apostle, to preach in faith and truthfulness, and they must also be faithful and trustworthy.

3. A direction as to how to pray (v. 8). People must pray everywhere: no place is unsuitable for prayer; no place is more acceptable to God than another (Jn 4:21). *Lifting up holy hands*, or pure hands, pure from the defilement of sin. We must pray in love: *without wrath*, or anger or malice toward anyone. We must pray in faith, *without doubting*, or as some read it, "without disputing."

Verses 9–15

1. Women who profess the Christian religion should be modest, sober, silent, and submissive.

1.1. They must be very modest in their clothing—you can read the futility of a person's heart in the showiness of their clothes—because they have better graces with which they should *adorn themselves.* Good works are the best adornment. Those who profess godliness should, in the clothes they wear as well as in other things, act as befits their profession.

1.2. Women must learn the principles of their religion, learn Christ (Eph 4:20), learn the Scriptures.

1.3. They must be silent and submissive, not usurping authority. *Adam was first formed, then Eve* from him. Just as she was the last to be created, so she was first to disobey. Here is a word of encouragement (v. 15) that those who continue in sobriety will be *saved in child-bearing*, or "through childbearing" or "with childbearing." The sentence they are under for sin will be no bar to their acceptance with Christ.

2. Notice here:

2.1. The extensiveness of the rules of Christianity; they reach not only men but also women.

2.2. Women are to profess godliness as much as men, and to their honor let it be said that many of them were eminent professors of Christianity in the days of the apostles, as the book of Acts tells us.

2.3. The best ornaments for those who profess godliness are good works.

2.4. Women must be learners and are not allowed to be public teachers in the church. The woman must not exercise authority over the man but is to remain silent. However, despite this prohibition, good women should teach their children at home the principles of religion. Timothy had known the Holy Scriptures from his childhood, and who taught him but his mother and grandmother?

2.5. Two very good reasons are given for the man's authority over the woman and her submission to the man (vv. 13–14).

2.6. Here is much for the woman's support and encouragement. Although in sorrow, she will still give birth, and be a living mother of living children (Ge 3:20).

CHAPTER 3

We have here: 1. The qualifications required of a person who is to be admitted to the office of a bishop (overseer) (vv. 1–7). 2. The qualifications for deacons (vv. 8–10), their wives (v. 11), and again for deacons (vv. 12–13). 3. The reasons for writing to Timothy (vv. 14–16).

Verses 1–7

Timothy was probably an evangelist who was left at Ephesus. The Ephesian overseers were very reluctant to part with Paul, especially because he told them they would *see his face no more* (Ac 20:38), and that is why Paul left Timothy with them. Here we have the character of a Gospel minister, whose office it is, as an overseer, to lead a particular congregation of Christians. Notice:

1. The ministry is a work. The office of overseer in Scripture is an office that has been divinely appointed, not one of human invention. That the office is a work implies that it requires diligence and application. Ministers should always look more to their work than to the honor and advantage of their office. It is *a good work*, a work of the greatest importance. The ministry is concerned with nothing less than the life and happiness of immortal souls. Those who wish to be put into that office should desire it earnestly.

2. The worker must be duly qualified. A minister must be *blameless*, not connected to any scandal; *the husband of one wife*; *vigilant*, that is, watchful against Satan; *sober*, that is, self-controlled, moderate in all his actions and in the use of all creature comforts; *of good behaviour*, not shallow, proud, or frivolous; *given to hospitality*; *apt to teach*, both able and willing to share with others the

knowledge God has given him; no drunkard; *no striker*, not quarrelsome, but doing everything with love and gentleness; *not greedy of filthy lucre*, but dead to the wealth of this world and living above it; *patient, not a brawler*, but having a gentle disposition, not violent with his hands and not destructive with his tongue; and *not covetous*, for greed is bad in anyone, but worst in a minister. He must also be one who keeps his family in good order. The families of ministers should be examples of good to all others families. *With all gravity.* The best way for parents to induce their children to submit to them is to be grave, or serious and dignified, with them. The overseer must *have his children in subjection* not with all harshness, but with due dignity. He must not be *a novice*, who has only a superficial knowledge of religion, for such a person is likely to become conceited: the more ignorant people are, the prouder they are. We should beware of pride, because it is a sin that turned angels into devils. Finally, he must be of good reputation among his neighbors.

3. What great reason we have to cry out, as Paul does, *Who is sufficient for these things?* (2Co 2:16). What holy watchfulness is necessary in this work! Have not the most faithful and conscientious ministers just reason to complain against themselves? How far short the best of them come as regards what they should be and what they should do! But let God be blessed and thanked by those whom he has enabled and counted faithful (1:12). He will equip us for our work and reward our faithfulness with a crown of glory (1Pe 5:4).

Verses 8–13

1. We have here:

1.1. The character of deacons. They must be *grave* (dignified or worthy of respect). Dignity is fitting for all Christians, but especially those who are to hold office in the church. *Not doubled-tongued.* A double tongue comes from an insincere heart; flatterers and slanderers are insincere. *Not given to much wine*, for this opens the door to many temptations. *Not greedy of filthy lucre.* This would especially be bad in deacons, who were entrusted with the church's money (v. 9). If we keep a clear conscience, our souls will be preserved in the deep truths of the faith. The soundness of the candidates' judgments, their zeal for Christ, and the blamelessness of their way of life must be tested. Their wives must also have a good character (v. 11). All who are related to ministers must redouble their concern to live as is appropriate to the Gospel of Christ, so that the ministry may not come into disrepute. Just as Paul said before of overseers or ministers, so he says here of deacons, that they must be *the husband of one wife*; they must *rule their children and their own houses well*: the families of deacons should be examples to other families.

1.2. The reason why the deacons must be so qualified (v. 13): it is a step toward the higher office. Or this verse may refer to the good reputation that a person would gain by faithfulness in this office.

2. Notice that in the early church there were only two orders of ministers or officers, *bishops* (overseers) and *deacons* (Php 1:1). The intention of the deacon's office was to take care of the temporal concerns of the church, such as the salaries of ministers and providing for the poor. Integrity and uprightness in a subordinate office are the way to be advanced to a higher office in the church: *They purchase to themselves a good degree.* And these same virtues will give a person great boldness in the faith, whereas a lack of integrity and uprightness will make a person timid.

Verses 14–16

Paul hoped to come to Timothy soon to give him further directions and help in his work, and so he wrote more briefly than he otherwise might have. But he wrote *lest he should tarry long, that* Timothy *might know how to behave himself in the house of God.*

1. Ministers should behave well. Their office obligates them to behave well, for not just any behavior will do in this case. The church is the house of God; he dwells there.

2. The great support of the church is that it is the church of the living *God*, the true God.

2.1. It is *the pillar and ground* (foundation) *of truth.*

2.1.1. The church itself is the pillar and foundation of truth. The church holds out Scripture and the doctrine of Christ as a pillar to which a proclamation is affixed holds out the proclamation.

2.1.2. Others understand it as referring to Timothy and other faithful ministers. As evangelists, they are the pillars and foundation of the truth; it is their work to maintain the truths of Christ in the church. Let us be diligent and impartial in our own search for truth; let us buy the truth at any cost (Pr 23:23) and not think much of any work required to discover it. Let us be careful to keep and preserve it and to proclaim it.

2.2. But what is the truth that churches and ministers are the pillars and foundation of? The apostle tells us (v. 16):

2.2.1. Christianity is a mystery that could not have been discovered by reason or the light of nature, because it is beyond reason, though not contrary to it. It is a mystery of godliness, and here it surpasses all the mysteries of the Gentiles.

2.2.2. It is Christ.

2.2.2.1. He is God revealed in the flesh.

2.2.2.2. He is *justified in the Spirit.* Whereas he was reproached as a sinner and put to death as an evildoer, when he was raised again, he was justified in the Spirit.

2.2.2.3. He was *seen of angels.* Angels ministered to him (Mk 1:13), for he is the Lord of angels.

2.2.2.4. He is *preached unto the Gentiles.* This is a great part of the mystery of godliness, that Christ was offered to the Gentiles as Redeemer and Savior.

2.2.2.5. He was *believed on in the world.* Who would have thought that the world, which lay in evil, would believe in the Son of God, would take as their Savior the One who was himself crucified at Jerusalem?

2.2.2.6. He was *received up into glory.* It is not only his ascension that is referred to but also his being seated at the right hand of God, where he always lives to make intercession (Heb 7:25). The One who was revealed in flesh was God, really and truly God. This makes it a mystery. Godliness is a mystery in all its aspects. Because it is a great mystery, we should humbly adore it, rather than curiously pry into it.

CHAPTER 4

1. Paul foretells a dreadful apostasy (vv. 1–3). 2. He discusses Christian liberty (vv. 4–5). 3. He gives Timothy various directions (vv. 6–16).

Verses 1–5

We have here a prophecy of the apostasy of later times.

1. The prophecies concerning the Antichrist, as well as those about Christ, came from the Spirit: *the Spirit speaketh expressly. Some shall depart from the faith*; there

will be an apostasy from the faith. *Some*, not all, for in the worst times God will still have a remnant (Ro 11:5). Notice:

1.1. One of the great expressions of the apostasy: following *doctrines of devils*, or about devils.

1.2. The instruments of promoting and spreading this apostasy and delusion. It will be done by the hypocrisy of those who speak lies (v. 2), who have *their consciences seared with a hot iron*, who are completely lost to the basic principles of virtue and moral honesty. Another part of their character is that they will forbid people to marry and will order them *to abstain from meats* (certain foods), defining religion as abstinence at certain times and seasons.

1.3. The apostasy of the later times should not surprise us, because it was clearly foretold by the Spirit. The Spirit speaks clearly, but the words of the ungodly were always doubtful and uncertain. In such general apostasies, all do not abandon the faith, but only some. People must be hardened, and their consciences seared, before they can depart from the faith and draw others to follow them.

2. The apostle uses the occasion to establish the doctrine of Christian liberty, that whereas under the Law there was a distinction between clean and unclean foods, all this is now taken away. Notice:

2.1. We are to look on our food as what God has created; we have received it from him and must therefore use it for him.

2.2. We must not refuse the gifts of God's goodness, not have scruples that lead us to make distinctions where God has made none, but receive those gifts and be thankful.

2.3. Everything created by God is good, and it is doubly sweet to us when it is received with thanksgiving (v. 5). It is desirable to have consecrated use of our creature comforts. They are sanctified to us:

2.3.1. *By the word of God.*

2.3.2. *By prayer*, which blesses our food to us. Everything is God's, because he created everything; and everything created by God is good. The blessing of God makes every part of the creation nourishing to us, and so nothing should be refused. We should therefore consecrate by prayer the created things we receive by prayer.

Verses 6–16

The apostles considered it a main part of their work to *put the brethren in remembrance of those things* (v. 6) *which they had received and heard* (Php 4:9; Rev 3:3), for we tend to forget, and are slow to learn and remember, the things of God. The best way for ministers to grow in knowledge and faith is to remind the brothers and sisters; when we teach others, we also teach ourselves. Notice:

1. Godliness is here urged on Timothy and others (vv. 7–8). Those who want to be godly must train themselves in godliness; it requires constant exercise. What good will it do us to mortify the body if we do not mortify sin? There is a great deal to be gained by godliness. *The promises* made to godly people concern the present life, but especially the life to come. If godly people have only a little of the good things of the present life, it will be made up to them in the good things of the life to come. It is not enough to have nothing to do with godless myths and old wives' tales; we must also train ourselves in godliness.

2. The encouragement that we have to proceed in ways of godliness (v. 8). Will the profit balance out the loss? Yes, here is another of Paul's trustworthy sayings, deserving full acceptance (1:15; 4:9)—that all our work and losses in the service of God will be abundantly rewarded,

so that even though we lose things for Christ, we will not lose by him (v. 10).

2.1. We are to expect toil and trouble in this world not only as people but as saints.

2.2. Those who work hard and suffer reproach in the service of God may depend on the living God to ensure that they will not lose by it. Let this encourage them. He is *the Saviour of all men*. Now, if he is the Savior of all people in this way, we may reason from this that much more will he be the rewarder of those who seek and serve him. The salvation he has in store for those who believe is sufficient to reward them for all their services and sufferings. The life of a Christian is a life of hard work and suffering: *We labour and suffer.* The best we can expect to suffer in the present life is reproach for our well-doing, for our work of faith and labor of love (1Th 1:3).

3. The apostle concludes with an exhortation to Timothy.

3.1. *To command and teach these things* that he, Paul, has now been teaching him.

3.2. To behave with that dignity and wisdom which may gain him respect despite his youth. A person will not be despised for their youth if they do not, by youthful follies, make themselves despicable. Nor do only young people act foolishly; old people may do so as well, and then they have only themselves to thank if they are despised.

3.3. To confirm his message by setting a good example. Those who teach with words must also make sure that their teaching is supported by their life, for otherwise they pull down with one hand what they are building up with the other.

3.4. To study hard (vv. 13, 15). Although Timothy has extraordinary gifts, he must still use ordinary means. Or it may refer to the public reading of Scriptures; he must *read and exhort.* He must teach the people both what to do and also what to believe. The best way for ministers to avoid being despised is to teach and practice the things that are entrusted to them. Those ministers who are the best qualified for their work must still be concerned with their studies; they must devote themselves to their work.

3.5. To beware of negligence (v. 14). The gifts of God will wither if they are neglected. We see here the Scripture way of ordination: it was by the laying on of hands, and it was the laying on of the hands of the elders. The office of ministry is a gift; it is the gift of Christ, and this was a very kind gift to his church. Ministers should not neglect the gift given to them, whether by *gift* we understand the office of the ministry or the qualifications for the office.

3.6. Having this work committed to him, to *give himself wholly* to it, making it clear that he is increasing in knowledge. Ministers must meditate often. They are to meditate on the great trust committed to them. They must be wholly given to these things, and then their progress will be apparent in everything.

3.7. To be very cautious. This will be the way to *save thyself, and those that hear thee.* "Save yourself first of all, and then you will be instrumental in saving those who listen to you." The best way to fulfill both these goals is to watch ourselves, our own life and doctrine, closely.

CHAPTER 5

Here the apostle: 1. Directs Timothy how to rebuke people (vv. 1–2). 2. Gives advice to widows (vv. 3–16). 3. Gives advice to elders (vv. 17–19). 4. Discusses pub-

lic rebukes (v. 20). 5. Gives a solemn command about ordination (vv. 21–22). 6. Refers to his health (v. 23) and states that people's sins are different in their effects (vv. 24–25).

Verses 1–2

Ministers are those who rebuke by office; it is a part, though the least pleasant part, of their office. They are to be very tender in rebuking elders, showing respect for the dignity of their years and position. The younger men must be rebuked as brothers, with love and tenderness. Great humility is needed in rebuking those who deserve it. The elder women must be rebuked as mothers; the younger women as *sisters, with all purity.*

Verses 3–16

Directions are here given about taking widows into the number of those who are employed and supported by the church: *Honour widows that are widows indeed,* to maintain and relieve them with respect and tenderness.

1. Only those widows who are devout should be relieved. She who, being *desolate* (left all alone), *trusteth in God* (v. 5) is to be considered a *widow indeed* and therefore eligible to be maintained at the church's expense. Those who trust in God must *continue in prayer.* But she whose sensual desires overcome her dedication to Christ is not a true widow (v. 6). Nor is a merry widow a true widow; *she that lives in pleasure is dead while she lives,* is no living member of the church, but is a carcass in it, or a mortified member. More generally, all who live in pleasure are dead while they live; their lives in the world serve no substantial purpose. They are, as it were, buried alive as to the great purpose of living.

2. The church should not be burdened with the maintenance of those widows whose own relatives are able to maintain them (vv. 4, 16). The respect children show their parents by looking after them is rightly called *piety.* Children can never sufficiently repay their parents for the care they have taken of them, but they must try. The apostle speaks of this again (v. 8). If people spend on their sinful desires what should be used to maintain their families, they have denied the faith (v. 16). And if the rich maintain their poor relatives and do not burden the church with them, the church *may relieve those who are widows indeed.* Wisdom should be exercised in choosing the objects of charity, so that it may not be thrown away on those who are not its proper objects, but may be reserved for those who are truly in need.

3. Here are directions about the characters of the widows who are to receive the church's charity. Particular care should be taken to relieve those who, when they had the means, actually did good with it. Those who want to find mercy when they are in distress must show mercy when they are in prosperity.

4. He warns the church to be wary of admitting among the widows those who are likely to be untrustworthy (v. 11): *The younger widows refuse;* they will be weary of the rules they must follow in exercising the office of widow; they *will marry, and cast off their first faith* (break their first pledge). The apostle here advises the younger widows to marry (v. 14). It is rare that those who are idle are only idle; they learn to cause trouble among their neighbors and sow seeds of discord among brothers and sisters (Pr 6:14, 19). If housekeepers do not mind their business, but are gossips, they give cause to the enemies of Christianity to reproach the Christian name. We can learn from this:

4.1. In the early church, care was taken of poor widows. The churches of Christ in these days should follow such a good example.

4.2. Great care should be taken that those who need and deserve the church's charity share in the funds.

4.3. The reputation of religion and Christian churches is greatly affected by the character and behavior of those who receive gifts from the church.

4.4. Christianity obliges its professors to help their needy friends. Rich people should be ashamed to burden the church with their poor relatives.

Verses 17–25

Here are directions:

1. About supporting ministers. Care must be taken that they are honorably maintained (v. 17). The early church did not have one office holder to preach to them and another to direct their affairs; rather, directing the affairs of the church and teaching were performed by the same people. Notice:

1.1. The work of ministers consists mainly in two things: directing the affairs of the church well, and preaching and teaching.

1.2. Those who were not idle, but labored at this work, were worthy of double honor. *Thou shalt not muzzle the ox that treads out the corn* (Dt 25:4). Does God take care of oxen? Will he not, then, take care of his own servants? The ox only treads out the grain from which people make the bread that perishes, but ministers break the bread of life, which lasts forever (Jn 6:27). Those who want to see ministers starved, or not comfortably provided for, will be judged by God one day.

2. About the accusation of ministers (v. 19).

2.1. There must be a proper accusation. The church is not to accept an uncertain report that is flying around.

2.2. This accusation is not to be *received,* or entertained, unless supported by two or three credible witnesses. The accusation must be *received* before them; that is, the accused must see the accusers face to face. Great care should be taken that the thing alleged against him is well proved, "but (v. 20) *those that sin, rebuke before all;* that is, those who sin before all should be rebuked before all, so that the bandage may be as wide as the wound—so that those who are in danger of sinning by following the example of the fallen may take warning by the rebuke the latter receive for it, so *that others also may fear.*" Public rebuke is intended for the good of others as well as for the good of the party rebuked.

3. About the ordination of ministers (v. 22). This seems to refer to the ordaining of men to the office of the ministry. Some understand it as referring to absolution. "Do not be too hasty in laying hands on anyone; do not refrain from inflicting church discipline on anyone. Those who are hasty will share in other people's sins."

4. About absolution, to which vv. 24–25 seems to refer. Some people's sins are so plain and obvious that there is no dispute about bringing them under the discipline of the church. *Others they follow after* (the sins of others trail behind them); their evil does not appear immediately, but only after due search has been made. The same is true of the evidence of repentance. Notice:

4.1. There are secret sins as well as open ones.

4.2. Some are humbled and brought to repentance by church discipline, while with others it is the opposite.

4.3. Persistent sins cannot be hidden.

5. About Timothy himself. He is commanded to be a good steward of his office (v. 21), and especially to stay on his guard against favoritism. Ministers must give an

account to God and the Lord Jesus Christ. Woe to those who have shown favoritism in their ministry. For Timothy's health, Paul advises him to use wine to help his stomach and recover his strength. It is the will of God that people take all due care of their bodies, that they use them so that they may be fittest and most helpful to us in the service of God. Wine should be used as a help, not a hindrance, to our work and usefulness.

CHAPTER 6

Here the apostle: 1. Discusses the duty of slaves (vv. 1–2). 2. Discusses false teachers (vv. 3–5). 3. Discusses godliness and greed (vv. 6–10). 4. Tells Timothy what to flee and what to follow (vv. 11–12). 5. Gives a solemn command (vv. 13–16). 6. Gives a command about the rich (vv. 17–19). 7. Gives a command to Timothy (vv. 20–21).

Verses 1–5

1. Here is the duty of *servants* (slaves). They are yoked to their work; they are not to be idle. They must respect their masters, counting them worthy of all the honor due them as masters. If slaves who accepted the Christian religion became disobedient to their masters, they would reflect badly on the message of Christ. If the professors of religion misbehave, *the name of God and his doctrine* are in danger of being slandered. This is a good reason why we should all behave well. Or suppose the master was a Christian, a believer, and the slave was also a believer: the slave must think themselves even more obliged to serve them, because the faith and love that make people Christians oblige them to do good. Believing masters and slaves are brothers and share in the same benefits.

2. Paul here warns Timothy to withdraw from those who pervert the teaching of Christ. *If any man teach otherwise* (vv. 3–5). We are not required to accept any words as sound except the words of our Lord Jesus Christ, but those who do not agree with the words of Christ are *proud* (v. 4), *knowing nothing*. Often those who know least are the proudest. Those who fall away from the direct, practical doctrines of Christianity have an unhealthy interest in controversies. When people are not content with the words of the Lord Jesus Christ, but are determined to make up their own ideas and impose them on others, they sow the seeds of all trouble in the church (Pr 6:14, 19) (v. 5). From these come disputes that are all aimed at deception, not at building people up. People with corrupt minds are *destitute of the truth*. The words of our Lord Jesus Christ are sound words, those most suitable to prevent or heal the church's wounds as well as to heal a wounded conscience. When people leave the sound words of our Lord Jesus Christ, they will never agree on other words, either their own or other people's, but will constantly wrangle and quarrel about them. People who are given to perverse disputes are shown to have corrupt minds, to be devoid of the truth, especially those who act in this way for the sake of gain, which is their kind of godliness. Christians will withdraw themselves from such people.

Verses 6–12

From the mention of the abuse to which religion is subjected by some, who make it serve their own worldly advantages, the apostle:

1. Shows the excellence of contentment and the evil of greed.

1.1. The excellence of contentment (vv. 6–8). Although Christianity is the worst trade, it is the best calling in the world. Those who make a trade out of it, merely to serve their own personal advantage in this world, will find it a sorry trade, but those who consider it their calling and make it their business will find it a gainful calling.

1.1.1. The truth he lays down is that *godliness with contentment is great gain*. Godliness is itself great gain; wherever there is true godliness, there will also be contentment. Christian contentment is great gain. Those who are godly are sure to be happy in another world, and if they also by contentment come to terms with their condition in this world, they have enough. It is not like the little gains of worldly people, who are so fond of small worldly advantages. Godliness is always accompanied by contentment. All truly godly people have learned with Paul to be content whatever the circumstances (Php 4:11).

1.1.2. The reason he gives for it is in v. 7. We can consider nothing as a debt that is due to us, for we came into the world naked (Job 1:21). Whatever we have gained since, we are obliged to the providence of God for it. We cannot be any poorer than when we came into this world—and yet even then we were provided for. Let us trust in God, therefore, for the remaining part of our pilgrimage on earth. We will take nothing with us out of this world. Why should we not be content with a little, since, however much we have, we must leave it behind us (Ecc 5:15–16)?

1.1.3. He infers from this, *having food and raiment, let us be therewith content* (v. 8). If God gives us the necessary supports of life, we should be content with them. What will worldly people do when death strips them of their happiness and wealth and they must say an eternal farewell to all these things that they have been so much devoted to? The necessities of life are the limits of a true Christian's desire. A few comforts of this life will be enough for them, and so they may justly hope to enjoy these.

1.2. The evil of greed (v. 9). It is not said that those who are rich fall into temptation, but those who want to be rich, those who put their happiness in worldly wealth. When the Devil sees which way their sinful desires take them, he will soon put bait on this hook accordingly.

1.2.1. Some want to get rich; they are determined to do so. Such people will be neither safe nor innocent. Worldly, sinful desires are foolish and harmful, because they plunge people into ruin and destruction.

1.2.2. The apostle affirms that the *love of money is the root of all evil* (v. 10). People may have money but not love it, but if they love it excessively, it will urge them on to pursue all evil. Greedy people will abandon the faith if that is the way to obtain money. Those who abandon God are storing up sorrows for themselves.

2. Uses this occasion to warn Timothy. He addresses himself to him as *a man of God*. Ministers are God's special people, and they should conduct themselves accordingly. He charges Timothy to beware of the love of money. It is unfitting for God's ministers to set their hearts on the things of this world; they should be taken up with the things of God. To protect Timothy against the love of the world, Paul directs him to follow what is good. It is not enough that God's ministers flee these things; they must also pursue what is directly contrary to them. How excellent are God's ministers who pursue righteousness! They are *the excellent ones of the earth* (Ps 16:3), and they should be approved by human beings. He exhorts Timothy to fulfill the role of a soldier. Those who want to get to heaven must fight their way there. It is a good fight, a good cause, and it will have a good outcome. It is the fight of faith. Eternal life is the crown offered us. We must

take hold of this, as those who are afraid of falling short of it and losing it. "Take hold, and make sure you do not lose your hold."

Verses 13–21

The apostle here charges Timothy *to keep this commandment*—that is, the whole work of his ministry, all the trust rested in him, all the service expected from him—*without spot, unrebukable*. He must conduct himself in his ministry in such a way that he will not lay himself open to any blame nor incur any blemish. What are the motives to move him to this?

1. Paul gives him a solemn command. He commands him in accordance with the way he will answer for his stewardship on the great day to the God who sees us all, who sees what we are and what we do. We should be quickened, or enlivened, to serve God by the knowledge that the God we serve quickens, or gives life to, everything. Paul commands Timothy before Christ Jesus. Christ died not only as a sacrifice but also as a martyr, for the word *martyr* literally means "witness"; he witnessed a good confession when he was brought before Pilate. His good confession before Pilate, *My kingdom is not of this world*, should be effective in drawing all his followers away from the love of this world.

2. He reminds Timothy of the confession that Timothy himself made (v. 12). That obligation is still on him, and he must live up to it.

3. He reminds him of Christ's second coming. The Lord Jesus Christ will appear, and it will be a glorious appearing (Tit 2:13). Ministers should look to this appearing of the Lord Jesus Christ, and until he appears, they are to keep this commandment without spot or blame. The appearing of Christ is certain, but it is not for us to know its time and season (Ac 1:7); let us simply know that he will *show it* in due time.

3.1. The apostle here speaks great things of Christ and God the Father. God is the *only Potentate* (only Ruler); the powers of worldly rulers are all derived from him. He is the blessed and the only Ruler, infinitely happy. Only he is immortal. He dwells in inaccessible light; no one can reach heaven except those whom he is pleased to bring there and accept into his kingdom. He is invisible. It is impossible for mortal eyes to bear the brightness of divine glory. No one can see God and live (Ex 33:20).

3.2. He concludes with a doxology. What an evil sin is, since it is committed against such a God. What are we then, that the blessed God, the King of kings and Lord of lords, should seek us? Blessed are those who are accepted to dwell with this great and blessed Ruler.

4. The apostle adds a lesson for rich people (vv. 17–19).

4.1. Timothy must command those who are rich to beware of the temptations, and make the best use of the opportunities, of their prosperous state. He must warn them to beware of pride. He must warn them against futile confidence in their wealth. Nothing is more uncertain than the wealth of this world; many have had much of it one day but then been stripped of everything the next. Those who are rich must see God giving them their riches, and giving them everything to enjoy richly, for many people have riches but enjoy them poorly, not having the heart to use them. Timothy must command them to do good with what they have. Those who are rich in good works are truly rich. Timothy must command them to think of another world and prepare for what is to come by works of charity.

4.2. We may notice from this:

4.2.1. Ministers must not be afraid of the rich. They must warn them against pride and futile confidence in their riches.

4.2.2. A lesson for ministers in the command given to Timothy: *Keep that which is committed to thy trust.* Every minister is a trustee. Guard the truths of God, the ordinances of God. Keep close to the written word, for that is committed to our trust. Some who have been very proud of their learning, their *science* (knowledge), *which is falsely so called*, have by that been drawn away from faith in Christ, which is a good reason why we should keep to the plain word of the Gospel. *O Timothy, keep that which is committed to thy trust!* It is as if Paul had said, "I cannot conclude without commanding you again: whatever you do, be sure to guard what has been entrusted to you, for it is too great a trust to be betrayed." The "knowledge" that opposes the truth of the Gospel is falsely so called. Those who want to advance reason above faith are in danger of leaving the faith.

5. Our apostle concludes with a solemn prayer and blessing. Grace is a pledge—indeed, a beginning—of glory, for wherever God gives grace, he will give glory. *Grace be with you* all. Amen.

A PRACTICAL AND DEVOTIONAL
EXPOSITION OF

2 Timothy

Paul wrote this second letter to Timothy from Rome, when he was a prisoner there and his life was in danger; *I am now ready to be offered, and the time of my departure is at hand* (4:6). He had been brought before the emperor Nero, which he calls *his first answer, when no man stood with him, but all men forsook him* (4:16). And interpreters agree that this was the last letter he wrote. Where Timothy now was is uncertain.

CHAPTER 1

After the introduction (vv. 1–2) we have: 1. Paul's sincere love for Timothy (vv. 3–5). 2. Various exhortations given to him (vv. 6–14). 3. His words about Phygelus and Hermogenes, as well as others, closing with Onesiphorus (vv. 15–18).

Verses 1–5

Here is:

1. The opening greeting of the letter. The Gospel is the promise of life in Christ Jesus; life is the goal, and Christ the way (Jn 14:6). Paul was an apostle of Jesus Christ by the will of God. His commission to be an apostle did not come from human will; God called him to be an apostle. We have the promise of life. This, as well as all other promises, is in and through Jesus Christ. The grace, mercy, and peace that Timothy needed, come from God the Father and Christ Jesus our Lord. Even the best people need these blessings, and they are the best we can ask for our dear friends.

2. Paul's thanksgiving to God for Timothy's faith and holiness. Paul was very prayerful; he prayed night and day. Prayer was his constant activity, and he never forgot his friends in his prayers, as we often do. It was a comfort to him that he was among the descendants of those who served God, just as it was a comfort to him that he had served God with a clear conscience. Timothy was sorry to part with Paul; he wept when they parted company, and so Paul wanted to see him again, because he had perceived the true affection Timothy had for him. He thanks God that Timothy is keeping up the religion of his ancestors (v. 5). It is encouraging when children imitate the faith and holiness of their godly parents and follow in their steps (3Jn 4). The faith that lives in real believers is sincere. It is a faith that will stand the trials of life, and it lives in them as a motivating principle. Paul gave thanks that Timothy inherited the faith of his mother Eunice and his grandmother Lois.

Verses 6–14

Here is an exhortation to Timothy to fulfill his duty (v. 6). Even the best people need to be reminded.

1. He exhorts him to stir up the gift that is in him as a fire is fanned into flame. Use gifts and have gifts. Timothy must take every opportunity to use these gifts, for that is the best way to increase them. The great hindrance to our being useful in the increase of our gifts is slavish fear. Paul therefore warns Timothy against this (v. 7). God has saved us from the spirit of fear, and has given us the spirit *of power, and of love, and of a sound mind* (self-discipline): the spirit of power, or of courage and resolution, the spirit of love for God, which will set us above fearing people, and the spirit of a sound mind, or self-discipline, for we are often discouraged in our work by the figments of our own imagination, which a self-controlled, thoughtful mind would deal with easily.

2. He exhorts him to remember that afflictions will surely come and that he should get ready for them. Don't be ashamed of the Gospel.

2.1. We must not be ashamed of those who are suffering for the Gospel of Christ. Timothy must not be ashamed of blessed Paul even though he was now in chains. The Gospel is the testimony of our Lord; he testifies about himself to us and by this, and by professing our faithfulness to it we testify about him and for him. Paul was the Lord's prisoner. He was in chains for his sake. If we are ashamed of either now, Christ will be ashamed of us in the future (Mk 8:38). "Expect afflictions for the Gospel's sake; be willing to share with the suffering saints in this world. *Be partaker of the afflictions of the Gospel.*"

2.2. He takes notice of what great things God has done for us by the Gospel (vv. 9–10), urging two considerations:

2.2.1. The nature of the Gospel and its glorious intentions. Notice:

2.2.1.1. The Gospel aims at our salvation, and we must not hesitate to suffer for what we hope to be saved by.

2.2.1.2. It is intended for our sanctification. All who will be saved in the future are sanctified now. Wherever the call of the Gospel is effective, it is found to be a holy call.

2.2.1.3. Its origin is the free grace and eternal purpose of God in Christ Jesus. If we had deserved it, it would have been hard to suffer for it, but our salvation by it comes about by free grace, so we must not hesitate to suffer for it. *In Christ Jesus*, for all the gifts that come from God to sinful humanity come in and through Christ Jesus.

2.2.1.4. The Gospel is the revelation of this purpose and grace. Did Jesus Christ suffer for it? Will we, then, hesitate to suffer for it?

2.2.1.5. By the Gospel of Christ death is abolished. Death, once an enemy, has now become a friend; it is the gate by which we pass out of this troublesome, sinful world into a world of perfect peace and purity. Death does not triumph over those who believe the Gospel; they triumph over it.

2.2.1.6. He has *brought life and immortality to light by the Gospel*. By the Gospel, he has brought it to light, not only set it before us but also offered it to us.

2.2.2. His own example (vv. 11–12). He was appointed to preach the Gospel, specifically to teach the Gentiles. He thought it a cause worth suffering for, and why should not Timothy think so too? No one need be afraid or ashamed to suffer for the cause of the Gospel.

2.2.2.1. Good people often suffer many things for the best cause in the world.

2.2.2.2. They need not be ashamed; the cause will support them.

2.2.2.3. Those who trust in Christ know the One whom they have trusted. What must we commit to Christ? The salvation of our souls and their preservation for the heavenly kingdom; he will keep what we commit to him in this way. A day is coming when we must give account of our souls. Now, if by an active obedient faith we commit it to Jesus Christ, we may be sure he is able to keep it.

3. He exhorts him to *hold fast* (keep) *the form of sound words* (v. 13). "Remain faithful to it in opposition to all the heretical and false doctrines." But how must it be kept? Faith and love must go together; it is not enough to believe the sound words; we must also love them, believe their truth and love their goodness. It must be faith and love focusing on Jesus Christ. "Of healing words," as it may read; there is a healing power in the word of God. V. 14 is to the same effect: *That good thing* (the good deposit) *which was committed unto thee keep by the Holy Spirit*. The good deposit was the pattern of sound teaching, Christian doctrine, which was committed to Timothy in his baptism and in his ordination. Christian teaching is a trust that is committed to us. It is a good thing, unspeakably valuable in itself and of unspeakable advantage to us. It is committed to us to be preserved and guarded pure and whole and transmitted to those who will follow us. Even those who are very well taught cannot keep and guard what they have learned—any more than they could learn it originally—without the help of the Holy Spirit. We must not think we can keep it in our own strength, but must keep it by the Holy Spirit. The help and indwelling of the Holy Spirit do not exclude human endeavors; rather, they exist alongside each other very well.

Verses 15–18

Having (vv. 13–14) urged Timothy to stand firm:

1. He mentions the apostasy of many from the teaching of Christ (v. 15), though he does not say that they have turned away from the teaching of Christ, but that they have turned away from him, Paul.

2. He mentions the faithfulness of Onesiphorus. He often refreshed Paul, and he was not ashamed of his chains. When Onesiphorus was at Rome, he took care to search hard for Paul (v. 17). Good people will search out opportunities to do good. At Ephesus he had ministered to him and been very kind to him. Paul returns his kindness (vv. 16–18): he repays him with his prayers.

3. He prays for Onesiphorus himself as well as for his household: *That he may find mercy in that day*, on the day of death and of judgment. We need desire nothing more to make us happy than to find mercy of the Lord on that day. If you want to have mercy then, you must seek it from the Lord now. The best thing we can seek, either for ourselves or for our friends, is that the Lord will grant to them that they may find the mercy of the Lord on that day.

CHAPTER 2

1. *The apostle encourages Timothy in his work, showing him from where he must draw help (v. 1). 2. Timothy must make sure of succession in the ministry (v. 2). 3. Paul urges him to remain faithful and persevere in this work, considering what will be the end of all his suffering (vv. 3–15). 4. Timothy must avoid godless, futile chatter (vv. 16–18). 5. Paul speaks of the foundation of God, which stands firm (vv. 19–21). 6. He tells Timothy what he is to avoid and what he is to do (vv. 22–26).*

Verses 1–7

Paul encourages Timothy to remain faithful and persevere in his work (v. 1). Those who have work to do for God must strengthen themselves for it. Where there is the truth of grace, there must be a seeking of the power of grace. We need to become stronger and stronger in what is good. Or it may be understood in opposition to our being strong in our own strength: "Be strong, not trusting in your own resources, but in the grace that is in Jesus Christ." There is enough grace in him for all of us. We must be strong in this grace; not in ourselves, or in the grace we have already received, but in the grace that is in him.

1. Timothy must count on sufferings, even to the point of shedding his blood (Heb 12:4), and he must therefore train up others to succeed him in the ministry of the Gospel (v. 2). He must entrust them with the Gospel, so committing to them the things he has heard. He must consider two things in ordaining ministers: their faithfulness or integrity and their ministerial ability. They must not only be knowledgeable themselves but also be able to teach.

2. He must *endure hardness* (v. 3). All Christians, but especially ministers, *are soldiers of Jesus Christ*. Soldiers of Jesus Christ must prove themselves to be good soldiers, faithful to their captain, resolute in his cause. Those who want to prove themselves to be good soldiers of Jesus Christ must endure hardship; we must count on it in this world and bear it patiently when it comes.

3. He must not *entangle himself in the affairs of this world* (get involved in civilian affairs) (v. 4). If we have given ourselves to be Christ's soldiers, we must sit loose to the things of this world, and though we have to take some part in the affairs of this life while we are here—we have something to do here—we must not become involved in, our hearts must not be set on, those matters. The great concern of soldiers should be to please their general; in the same way, the great concern of Christians should be to please Christ.

4. He must see to it that in pursuing spiritual warfare he followed the rules, that he observed the laws of war (v. 5). In doing what is good we must take care that we do it rightly, so that our good may not be spoken of as evil. Those who do so will be crowned at last.

5. He must be willing to wait for a reward (v. 6). If we want to share in the crops, we must work hard. We must do the will of God before we receive the promises. The apostle further commends what he has said to the

attention of Timothy. Timothy must be reminded to use his faculties to reflect on the things of God. Reflection is as necessary to a good life as to a sound conversion. He prays for Timothy: *The Lord give thee understanding in all things*. Even the most intelligent person needs more and more of this gift. If the One who gave the revelation in the word does not also give the understanding in the heart, we are nothing.

Verses 8–13

1. To encourage Timothy in suffering, the apostle reminds him of the resurrection of Christ (v. 8). Considering that should make us faithful to our Christian profession. The incarnation and resurrection of Jesus Christ, sincerely believed and rightly considered, will support a Christian in all sufferings in the present life.

2. Another thing to encourage Timothy in suffering was that he had Paul as an example. Notice:

2.1. How the apostle suffered (v. 9). We must not think it strange if those who do well fare badly in this world, and if the best people face the worst treatment, but Paul was assured *that the word of God was not bound*. Persecuting powers cannot prevent the operation of the word of God on human hearts and consciences; that cannot be bound by any human force. This could encourage Timothy not to be afraid of chains for the testimony of Jesus.

2.2. Why he suffered cheerfully (v. 10). Next to the salvation of our own souls, we should be willing to do and suffer anything to advance the salvation of the souls of others.

3. Another thing with which he encourages Timothy is the prospect of a future state.

3.1. Those who remain faithful to Christ, whatever it may cost them, will certainly receive the reward for it in another world (v. 11). If we are dead to this world, we will go to live with him in a better world, to be with him forever. *Those who suffer for Christ* on earth will reign with Christ in heaven (v. 12).

3.2. Our lives are in danger if we prove unfaithful to him. Those whom Christ disowns must in the end be miserable forever. This will certainly be the outcome, whether we believe it or not (v. 13). If we are faithful to Christ, he will certainly be faithful to us. If we are false to him, he will be faithful to his threats. This is a faithful saying and may be depended on and should be trusted in.

Verses 14–18

He comes next to direct Timothy in his work.

1. Timothy must make it his business to edify those under his charge. This is the work of ministers, not to tell people what they never knew before, but to remind them of what they already know, *charging them that they strive not about words*. If people only stopped to consider how unimportant most religious disputes are, they would not be so zealous in their quarrels about words. People are very prone to quarrel about words, and such conflicts only disturb some and ruin others. *Show thyself approved unto God, a workman that need not be ashamed* (v. 15). Workers who are unskillful, unfaithful, or lazy need to be ashamed, but those who are concerned with their business and keep to their work need not be ashamed. And what is their work? Not to invent a new Gospel, but to correctly handle the Gospel they have been entrusted with.

2. He must beware of what might hinder him in his work (v. 16). He must beware of error: *Shun profane and vain babblings* (avoid godless chatter). Once people become fond of those, *they will increase unto more ungodliness*. The way of error is downhill. The infecting of one

often leads to the infecting of many, or the infecting of the same person with one error often leads to the infecting of that same person with many errors. The apostle mentions some people who have recently advanced erroneous doctrines: *Hymeneus and Philetus*. They did not deny the resurrection, but they put a corrupt interpretation on that true doctrine, saying that the resurrection had already taken place. By this they *overthrew the faith of some*. Whatever takes away the doctrine of a future state destroys the faith of Christians. Notice:

2.1. Error is prolific, and therefore more dangerous.

2.2. When people go astray concerning the truth, they always try to have some plausible pretense for it.

Verses 19–21

Here we see what we may comfort ourselves with in reference both to this and to the small errors and heresies that infect and infest the church and cause trouble.

1. Human unbelief cannot cancel out the promises of God (Ro 4:14; Gal 3:17). The prophets and apostles, that is, the doctrines of the Old and New Testament, continue to stand firm. They have a seal with two mottoes on it, one on the one side, and the other on the other, as is usual in an authenticating seal. One expresses our comfort—that *the Lord knows those that are his*. He will never lose them. Another declares our duty—that *everyone who names the name of Christ must depart from iniquity*. We must depart from evil, for otherwise he will not acknowledge us.

2. Although the faith of some is destroyed, others keep their integrity and hold it firmly (v. 20). Some professors of religion are like the articles of wood and earth; they are instruments of dishonor. Yet not all are instruments of dishonor. When we are discouraged by the badness of some, we must encourage ourselves by the goodness of others. Now we should make sure that we are instruments of honor, *sanctified for our Master's use*. Everyone in the church whom God approves must be devoted to their Master's service and fit for his use.

Verses 22–26

1. Paul here exhorts Timothy to beware *of youthful lusts* (v. 22). The *lusts of the flesh* (1Pe 2:18) are the evil desires of youth, which young people must carefully watch against. Paul prescribes an excellent remedy against these desires, which are very dangerous, waging war against the soul (1Pe 2:11): *Follow righteousness, faith, charity, peace*. The stirring of our graces will extinguish our corruptions; the more we follow what is good, the faster and further we will flee what is evil. Christians do this by *calling on the Lord Jesus Christ out of a pure heart*. Our prayers to God and Christ are not acceptable unless they come from a pure heart.

2. He warns him against conflict and (v. 23) against *foolish and unlearned questions*, which produce quarrels about words. Those who advanced such questions thought they were wise and learned, but Paul calls them *foolish and unlearned*. They produce disputes and quarrels among Christians. Religion consists more in believing and practicing what God requires than in subtle disputes. *The servant of the Lord must not strive* (v. 24). The servant of the Lord must be *gentle to all men, apt* (able) *to teach*. Those who are quarrelsome are unable to teach. *In meekness instructing* (v. 25) not only those who submit themselves but also those who *oppose themselves*. This is the way to convey truth in its light and power and to overcome evil with good (Ro 12:21). What ministers must have in view in instructing those who oppose themselves is their recovery. Notice:

2.1. Repentance is God's gift.

2.2. In the case of those who *oppose themselves*, it is a gift with a *peradventure*. We must make sure we do not presume on the grace of God.

2.3. The same God who gives us the revelation of the truth brings us by his grace *to the acknowledging of the truth*; otherwise our hearts would continue in rebellion against it. This is how sinners come to their senses and escape from the trap of Satan. See the misery of sinners (v. 26): they are slaves to the worst of taskmasters, caught in a trap, and in the worst trap, because it is the Devil's. See the happiness of those who repent: they escape from this trap; those who before were held captive by the Devil at his will come to be led into the glorious freedom of the children of God (Ro 8:21).

CHAPTER 3

1. The apostle warns Timothy what the last days will be like (vv. 1–9). 2. He gives various remedies against those days (vv. 10–17), especially his own example and the knowledge of the Holy Scriptures. Paul tells Timothy how bad others will be and how good he should therefore be.

Verses 1–9

Timothy must not think it strange if there were bad people in the church, for the net of the Gospel was to catch both good and bad fish (Mt 13:47–48). Even gold ore contains dross, and there is a great deal of chaff among the wheat when it lies on the floor.

1. In the *last days* (v. 1), in Gospel times, there *would come perilous times*, not so much because of persecution from outside as because of internal corruptions. Two traitors within the garrison may do it more harm than two thousand besiegers outside. Terrible times will come, for people are evil. Sin makes the times terrible.

2. Paul tells Timothy what will be the marks and signs by which these times may be known (vv. 1–2). The times will be terrible when people:

2.1. Are *lovers of themselves*. Instead of Christian love, which is concerned for the good of others, they will look after themselves only.

2.2. Are *covetous* (NIV: loving money). When people love themselves excessively, no good can be expected from them, as good may be expected from those who love God. When everyone is out to get what they can and keep what they have, people become dangerous to one another.

2.3. Are *boasters* and *proud* and *blasphemers*. When people do not fear God, they will have no regard for people.

2.4. Are, as children, *disobedient to their parents*. What evil will those stop at who will abusive and rebel against their own parents?

2.5. Are full of *unthankfulness* and *unholiness*. Why are people unholy and without the fear of God, except that they are ungrateful for the mercies of God?

2.6. Are *without natural affection* (without love) and are *truce-breakers* (unforgiving) (v. 3). The times are terrible when children are disobedient toward their parents (v. 2) and when parents have no natural love for their children (v. 3). With those who will not be bound by natural affection, it is hardly surprising that they will not be bound by the most solemn alliances and covenants. *They are truce-breakers*.

2.7. Are *false accusers* one of another, demons to one another.

2.8. Lack control over themselves and their own appetites and their own passions, when they are *incontinent* and *fierce* (brutal).

2.9. Generally despise and regard with contempt what is good and should be honored.

2.10. Are generally treacherous, stubborn, and proud (v. 4). When people are proud, behaving scornfully to everyone around them, then the times are terrible.

2.11. Are generally *lovers of pleasure more than lovers of God*. People have a worldly heart, one full of enmity toward him, when they prefer anything to him, especially something so corrupt as worldly pleasure.

2.12. *Have the form of godliness* (v. 5). A form of godliness is very different from its power; people may have the one but be wholly destitute of the other.

3. Paul warns Timothy to beware of certain deceivers. He shows how diligent they are to make converts (v. 6). They creep into houses to worm their way into the good opinion of people and so to draw them over to their side. See what kind of people they gained: those who were weak and evil. A gullible mind and a corrupt heart make people easy prey to deceivers. He shows how far they are from coming to the knowledge of the truth, even though they pretend to be *ever learning* (v. 7). He foretells the certain end that will be put to their progress (vv. 8–9). Those heretics *resist the truth* and are people *of corrupt minds, reprobate concerning the faith*, and *they shall proceed no further*. Although the spirit of error may be let loose for a time, God has it on a chain. *Their folly shall be manifest*; it will become clear that they are impostors, and everyone will abandon them.

Verses 10–17

Here, to confirm Timothy in that way in which he lived:

1. The apostle set before him his own example (v. 10). Christ's apostles had no enemies except those who did not know them, or did not know them fully; those who knew them best loved and honored them the most. Timothy had fully known:

1.1. The message Paul preached. Paul kept back nothing from his hearers, but declared to them the whole will of God (Ac 20:27), so that unless they themselves were at fault, they could fully know it.

1.2. His way of life. His way of life was consistent with his teaching and did not contradict it. Those who preach well but lead a bad life cannot expect to benefit the people.

1.3. The great thing Paul had in view: "You have known *my purpose*, what I am driving at."

1.4. Paul's good character.

1.5. That Paul had suffered wrong for doing well (v. 11). Paul mentions only those afflictions that happened to him while Timothy was with him, *at Antioch, at Iconium, at Lystra*.

1.6. What care God had taken of him. Just as Paul never failed his cause, so his God never failed him. "You have known full well my *afflictions*." When *we fully* know the afflictions of good people, not only how they suffer but also how they are supported and comforted in their suffering, then, instead of being discouraged, we will be encouraged by them, especially considering that we have been told before that we must count on such things (v. 12). Those who want to lead godly lives must expect it; especially those who want to live godly lives *in Christ Jesus*, especially when they are determined in their way of life. Notice:

1.6.1. The apostle's life was exemplary for three things: his *doctrine*, his *life*, and his *persecutions and sufferings*.

1.6.2. His life was a life of great usefulness, yet also of great suffering.

1.6.3. For Timothy's and our encouragement under sufferings, the apostle mentions the Lord's rescuing him from them all.

2. He warned Timothy of the fatal end of deceivers (v. 13). Just as good people, by the grace of God, grow better and better, so also bad people, through the subtlety of Satan and the power of their own corruptions, grow worse and worse.

3. He directed him especially to what he had learned from the Holy Scriptures (vv. 14–15). It is not enough to learn what is good; we must also continue in it and persevere in it to the end. If Timothy remained faithful to the truth as he had been taught it, this would protect him against the traps and insinuations of deceivers.

3.1. It is a great happiness to know the certainty of the things in which we have been instructed (Lk 1:4). "Consider from *whom thou hast learned them*; not from evildoers and deceivers, but good people, who themselves had experienced the power of the truths they taught you. *Knowing* especially the firm foundation on which you have built (v. 15): *That from a child thou hast known the holy scriptures.*"

3.2. Those who want to acquaint themselves with the things of God must know the holy Scriptures.

3.3. It is a great happiness to know the Holy Scriptures from childhood. The age of children is the age for learning, and those who want to gain true learning must gain it from of the Scriptures.

3.4. They must not be neglected by us, seldom or never looked into. Notice:

3.4.1. What is the excellence of Scripture (v. 16). The prophets and apostles did not speak from themselves, but passed on to us what they received from the Lord (1Co 11:23).

3.4.2. How useful it will be to us. *It is able to make us wise to salvation.* Those who are wise to salvation are truly wise. *Through faith.* The Scriptures will make us wise to salvation if we add faith to them (Heb 4:12). For if we do not believe their truth and goodness, they will do us no good. It is *profitable* to us for all the purposes of the Christian life. It instructs us in what is true, rebukes us for what is wrong, and directs us in what is good. *That the man of God may be perfect* (v. 17). What equips believers in this world is Scripture. By it we are *thoroughly furnished for every good work.* Scripture has various uses and fulfills various goals and purposes. Scripture is a perfect rule of faith and practice. If we consider Scripture, which was given by inspiration of God, and if we follow its directions, we will be made *perfect and thoroughly furnished to every good work.* Oh that we would love our Bibles more and keep closer to them than ever!

CHAPTER 4

In this chapter: 1. Paul fervently and seriously urges Timothy to conscientiously do his work and fulfill his office as an evangelist (vv. 1–5). 2. He gives the reason for his concern in this case: his departure is close (vv. 6–8). 3. He discusses various matters (vv. 9–15). 4. He informs Timothy of what happened to him at his first defense; although people left him, the Lord stood by him (vv. 16–18). He then concludes with greetings and a blessing (vv. 19–22).

Verses 1–8

Notice:

1. How fearfully this command is introduced (v. 1). Even the best people need to be awed into doing their duty. The eyes of God and Jesus Christ were on Timothy: *I charge thee before God and the Lord Jesus Christ.* Paul commands him as one who will answer for it at the great day, reminding him of the future judgment. Christ will appear; he will come again, a second time, and it will be a glorious appearance. Then his kingdom will appear in its glory, and he will appear in it: *At his appearing and kingdom.*

2. The content of the command (vv. 2–5). Timothy is commanded:

2.1. To *preach the word.* This is the work of ministers. What they must preach are not their own ideas and things they have imagined, but the pure, plain word of God.

2.2. To urge what he preaches on his hearers with all seriousness: "*Be instant in season and out of season, reprove, rebuke, exhort*; do this work with all fervency of spirit: *in season*, when some special opportunity to speak to them with advantage offers itself, and even *out of season*, because you do not know what the Spirit of God has in mind to make them respond to."

2.3. To tell people of their faults: "*Reprove them, rebuke them.* Try, by dealing plainly with them, to bring them to repentance."

2.4. To direct, encourage, and motivate those who began well. "*Exhort them* (urge them to keep going, to persevere to the end), and do this *with all long-suffering and doctrine.*" He must do it very patiently. While God shows all patience to them, let ministers also urge with all patience. Timothy must do it reasonably, not with passion, but *with doctrine.* "Teach them the truth as it is in Jesus (Eph 4:21), and this will be a means both to restore them from evil and to bring them to good."

2.5. To *watch in all things*, and so must all ministers. "Guard your work; watch against the temptations of Satan. Watch over the souls of those who are committed to your trust."

2.6. To count on afflictions, to endure them and make the best of them, and so must all ministers. "Get used to hardships."

2.7. To remember his work and discharge its duties, and so must all ministers. The office of the evangelist, as the apostles' deputy, was to water the churches the apostles planted. This was Timothy's work.

2.8. To fulfill his ministry, and so must all ministers: he must *make full proof of it*, performing all the parts of his office with diligence and care. The best way to discharge our ministry is to fulfill it, to fill up all its parts with proper work.

3. The reasons to reinforce the charge.

3.1. Errors and heresies are likely to creep into the church, which will corrupt the minds of many professing Christians (vv. 3–4). "Make the most of the present time, when they will endure it. They will become weary of the old paths of the plain, direct Gospel of Christ, and then they will be greedy to hear myths." These false teachers were not sent by God, but chosen by the people themselves to please their *itching ears.* People do this when they will not put up with sound doctrine, the preaching that is searching, plain, and to the point. There is a wide difference between the word of God and the word of such teachers. The one is sound doctrine, the word of truth; the other is only myths.

3.2. Paul, for his part, has almost completed his work. *I am now ready to be offered* (vv. 5–6). And:

3.2.1. "Therefore you will be needed more." The fewer the hands available to work, the more diligent those hands that work must be.

3.2.2. "I have completed the work of my day and generation; you, likewise, must complete the work of your day and generation."

3.2.3. The comfort and cheerfulness of Paul as he faced the prospect of his approaching departure might encourage Timothy. "I can look back on my service with a great deal of pleasure and satisfaction; therefore do not be afraid of the difficulties you must face. The crown of life is as sure to you as if it were already on your head." Here the apostle looks forward to his approaching death; he looks on it now as close at hand: I am *already poured out.*

3.2.3.1. With what pleasure he speaks of dying. He calls it *his departure* or his release. Death to a good person is a release from the imprisonment of this world and a departure to the enjoyments of another world; they do not stop existing, but are only taken from one world to another.

3.2.3.2. With what pleasure he looks back on the life he has lived (v. 7). He does not fear death, because he has the testimony of his conscience that by the grace of God he has in some measure fulfilled the purpose of living. He has fought a good fight. His life has been a course, and he has now finished it; just as his warfare has been accomplished (Isa 40:2), so his race is run. *I have kept the faith.* We too must fight this good fight; we must fight it to the end and finish our course. To be able to speak in this way toward the end of our days—what unspeakable comfort it will bring!

3.2.3.3. With what pleasure he looks forward to the life he is to live in the future (v. 8). Let this encourage Timothy to endure hardship as a good soldier of Jesus Christ, that there is a crown of life before us. It is called *a crown of righteousness* because in the heavenly kingdom our holiness and righteousness will be perfected and will be our crown. And yet this crown of righteousness did not belong only to Paul—as if it were proper only for apostles and well-known ministers and martyrs—but *to all those also that love his appearing.* It is the character of all the saints that they long for the appearing of Jesus Christ. They love his second appearing at the great day; they love it and long for it. This crown that believers will wear is in store for them; they do not have it at present, for here they are simply heirs; they do not have it in their possession. And yet it is sure.

Verses 9–15

1. Paul tells Timothy to come quickly to him, if possible (v. 9). He wants Timothy's company and help, because, he says, several people have left him (v. 10): *Demas hath forsaken me, having loved this present world.* Love for this present world is often the reason why people turn away from the truths and ways of Jesus Christ. *Crescens* has gone one way, and *Titus* another. *Luke,* however, remains with Paul (vv. 11–12).

2. He speaks respectfully of *Mark*: *He is profitable to me for the ministry.* It is supposed that this Mark was the one about whom Paul and Barnabas had had a dispute (Ac 15:39). Paul refused to take him with him *to the work,* because he had once drawn back: but now, he says,

Take Mark, and bring him with thee. This shows that Paul was now reconciled with Mark. We must not, therefore, forever disown those who are profitable and useful, even though they may have done wrong in the past.

3. Paul orders Timothy to come to him, and he tells him that as he comes through Troas he should bring with him from there the things Paul left behind (v. 13), including a cloak, which Paul perhaps needed more now that he was in a cold prison. Paul also wanted to have his books with him. Having exhorted Timothy to devote himself to reading, he also does so himself.

4. He mentions *Alexander* and the trouble he has caused him (vv. 14–15). This is the one who is spoken about in Ac 19:33. Paul foretells that God will judge him. It is a prophetic pronouncement of the just judgment of God that will come on him: The Lord *will reward him according to his works.* Some who were once Paul's hearers and admirers did not give him reason to remember them with much pleasure, for one abandoned him and another did him a great deal of harm. Yet he mentions some with pleasure; the evil of some did not make him forget the goodness of others.

Verses 16–22

Here:

1. Paul gives Timothy an account of his own present circumstances.

1.1. He has just been called to appear before the emperor (v. 16). The Christians at Rome were eager to go and meet him (Ac 28), but in a pinch, facing the prospect of suffering with him, they all abandoned him. Paul's trials included being forsaken by friends in a time of danger as well as being opposed by enemies: everyone abandoned him. And yet, knowing that God might hold it against them, Paul tries to prevent that by his fervent prayers.

1.2. When he had no one to help him keep his chin up, God made his face shine (Ex 34:29). Paul knew how to preach at the bar as well as in the pulpit. *And that all the Gentiles might hear.* The emperor himself and some other leaders would never have heard Paul preach if he had not been brought before them. *And I was delivered out of the mouth of the lion. And the Lord shall deliver me from every evil work.* Notice how Paul made the most of every experience. *And shall preserve me to his heavenly kingdom.* If the Lord stands by us, he will strengthen us, and his presence will more than make up for the absence of everyone. We should give God the glory for all past, present, and future deliverances: *to whom be glory for ever and ever. Amen.*

2. He sends greetings (v. 19). He mentions his leaving *Trophimus sick at Miletum* (v. 20).

3. He wants Timothy to *come to him before winter* (v. 21).

4. He sends salutations to Timothy from *Eubulus, Pudens, Linus, Claudia,* and all the *brethren.*

5. He concludes with a prayer that the *Lord Jesus would be with* Timothy's *spirit.* We need nothing more to make us happy than to have the Lord Jesus Christ with our spirits. It is the best prayer we can offer for our friends. *Grace be with you. Amen.* If grace is with us here to convert and change us, to make us holy, to keep us humble, and to enable us to persevere to the end, glory will crown us in the future.

A Practical and Devotional Exposition of

Titus

᪗———᪗

T his Letter of Paul to Titus is of much the same nature as those to Timothy. We read much about this Titus. He was a Greek (Gal 2:3). Paul called him *his son* (1:4), *his brother* (2Co 2:13), *his partner and fellow-helper* (2Co 8:23). He went up with the apostles to the church at Jerusalem (Gal 2:1) and was familiar with Corinth, for which church he had *a deep concern* (2Co 8:16). Paul's second letter to them was sent by Titus's hand (2Co 8:16–18, 23; 9:2–4; 12:18). He was with the apostle at Rome and went from there to Dalmatia (2Ti 4:10), after which we read nothing more about him in Scripture. The Gospel had gained some footing in Crete, and Paul and Titus went here on one of their travels, but the apostle could not himself stay long there. He left Titus there for some time, therefore, to continue the work that had been begun, in which Titus probably met with greater difficulty than usual, prompting Paul to write this letter to him. Perhaps, however, Paul did not write this letter so much for Titus's own sake as for the people's, so that the endeavors of Titus would be more significant and effective among them.

CHAPTER 1

In this chapter we have: 1. The introduction to the letter with the apostle's greetings and prayer for Titus (vv. 1–4). 2. The purpose of Titus's being left at Crete (v. 5). 3. How that purpose should be pursued in reference to both good and bad ministers (vv. 6–16).

Verses 1–4

1. Here is the writer. His name is *Paul*, a Gentile name taken by the apostle of the Gentiles (Ac 13:9, 46–47). Ministers will be accommodating even in small matters if they see a possibility of furthering the acceptance of their work.

1.1. *A servant of God, and an apostle of Jesus Christ.* The highest officers in the church are simply servants. As we can see, much divinity and devotion are included in the opening greetings of the letters.

1.2. *According to the faith of God's elect.* The apostles' message agreed with the faith of all the chosen ones. There are ones chosen by God, *chosen to salvation through sanctification of the Spirit and belief of the truth* (2Th 2:13–14). Faith is the first principle of sanctification.

1.3. *And the acknowledging of the truth which is after godliness.* The Gospel is truth, the great, faithful, and saving truth. Divine faith does not rest on fallible reasonings and probable opinions, but on the truth itself, *which is after godliness.* All Gospel truth leads to godliness. It is truth not only to be known but also to be acknowledged; it must be held out in word and practice. The great goal of the Gospel ministry is to lead people to this knowledge and faith and to the acknowledging and professing of the truth that leads to godliness (v. 2).

1.4. *In* (or "for") *hope of eternal life* (v. 2). This is the further purpose of the Gospel, to produce hope as well as faith. The faith and godliness of Christians lead to eternal life and give hope of it, because *God, that cannot lie, hath promised it.*

1.5. But how is God said to promise *before the world began* (v. 2)? Some understand *promise* to refer to his eternal decree, his promise in embryo. Here is the stability and antiquity of the promise of eternal life to the saints. God, who cannot lie, has promised before the world began.

1.6. No wonder if contempt of this promise is punished severely, since God has not only given it of old, *but* (v. 3) *has in due times manifested his word through preaching.* So highly has God honored what some called *foolishness of preaching* (1Co 1:21).

1.7. *Which is committed unto me.* The ministry is a trust. No one takes this honor on themselves (Heb 5:4); it is given them by divine appointment; and whoever is appointed and called must preach the word.

1.8. *According to the commandment of God our Saviour.* Let no one rest on mere human calling, therefore, without God's.

2. Here is the person written to, *Titus*, a Gentile, a Greek, but called to both the faith and the ministry. The grace of God is free and powerful. What worthiness or preparation was ever bestowed on someone with a Gentile background and education? And yet Paul calls him *my own* (or my true) *son*, not by natural generation, but by supernatural regeneration. "*After the common faith*, that faith which is common to all those who have been born again and which you have in truth and express in life."

3. Here is the opening greeting and prayer, wishing all blessings to Titus. The blessings wished are *grace, mercy, and peace.* Grace is the fountain of all blessings. Mercy, peace, and all good spring from this. If we gain God's favor, then all must be well, for the persons of the Trinity from whom the blessings are wished are *God the Father and the Lord Jesus Christ our Saviour.* God the Father is the fountain of all good. Every blessing, every comfort,

comes to us from God as a Father. And all comes from the Father by the Son.

Verse 5

Up to this point we have had the introduction to the letter; then the body of the letter begins with the statement of the purpose of Titus's being left in Crete.

1. The purpose is expressed more generally. Titus was to continue to straighten out what the apostle himself did not have time for in his short stay there. Notice:

1.1. The apostle's great diligence in the Gospel; when he had set things in motion in one place, he went quickly to another.

1.2. His faithfulness and wisdom. He did not neglect the places that he went away from, but left others to water the young, growing church.

1.3. His humility; he did not look down on being helped in his work by those who did not have such great gifts as himself.

1.4. Titus, though subordinate to an apostle, was still above the ordinary, regular pastors or bishops, whose distinctive responsibility was to look after particular churches. Titus was in a higher sphere, to ordain such ordinary pastors where lacking, and to settle things in their first state and form, and then to move to other places. Titus was only occasionally here in Crete, and for a short time; Paul wanted him to deal with the business he had left him there for, and then come to him at Nicopolis, where he intended to spend the winter. After this Titus was sent to Corinth, was with the apostle at Rome, and was sent from there to Dalmatia, which is the last time we read of him in Scripture. But did not the apostle and evangelist encroach on the rights of civil rulers? No, their work was spiritual. The *things wanting* (unfinished) were divine and spiritual ordinances, and appointments for spiritual purposes, derived from Christ. Titus was left to settle these. It was not easy to raise churches and bring them to maturity. Paul himself had worked hard here, but there were things that were unfinished. Even the best churches tend to deteriorate and go out of order. This in general was Titus's work in Crete.

2. It is expressed more specifically: *to ordain elders in every city.* These presbyters or elders were to have the ordinary and regular care and responsibility of the churches. Elders here, therefore, are Gospel ministers, to direct Christ's ordinances and to *feed the church of God.* A church without a fixed and constant ministry is imperfect and lacking. Where there is a suitable number of believers, presbyters or elders must be appointed; for the *perfecting of the saints and the edifying of the body of Christ,* their continuation in the churches is as necessary as their first appointment. *Faith comes by hearing,* and is preserved through it as well. Ignorance and corruption, decrease of good and increase of every evil, come about by a lack of a teaching and stimulating ministry. That is why *Titus was left in Crete, to set in order the things that were wanting.*

3. The rule by which Titus is to proceed is given. As under the Law all things were to be made according to the pattern shown to Moses on the mountain (Ex 25:40; Heb 8:5), so also under the Gospel all things must be ordered and managed according to the direction of Christ and his chief ministers. Human traditions and ideas may not be brought into the church of God. If an evangelist could not do anything except by appointment, then much less may others.

Verses 6–16

The apostle here gives Titus directions about ordination, showing whom he should ordain and whom not.

1. Those he should ordain.

1.1. Their qualifications concerning their life.

1.1.1. More generally: *If any be blameless*; not absolutely without fault, because no one is, nor altogether unblamed, because this is rare and difficult. Even Christ himself and his apostles were blamed. Rather, elders must not be people who have a bad reputation.

1.1.2. More specifically.

1.1.2.1. There is the elder's character in relationships. In his own person, he must be pure with respect to marriage. As to his children, he must *have faithful children,* obedient and good, brought up in the true Christian faith and living according to it, at least as far as the endeavors of the parents are effective. His children must *not be accused of riot, nor unruly,* nor even give ground and occasion for such an accusation, because in this way even the most innocent may be falsely charged. Children who are faithful and obedient will be a good sign of faithfulness and diligence in the parents. And the parent's faithfulness in small matters may encourage those who are over him to commit to him greater ones—the direction of the church of God. The basis for this qualification is shown from the nature of the position (v. 7). Because such bishops and overseers of the flock were to be examples to the flock (1Pe 5:3), God's stewards to take care of the affairs of his house, there was great reason for them to be blameless.

1.1.2.2. There is his character in more absolute terms, expressed:

1.1.2.2.1. Negatively. *Not self-willed.* The prohibition is wide-ranging and excludes all of the following: a high opinion of oneself; self-love, making self the center of everything; excessive self-confidence and self-pleasing; and being set on one's own personal will and way. It is a great honor to a minister to be ready to request and take advice, to be ready to defer to the mind and will of others, becoming all things to all people so that he may gain some (1Co 9:22). *Not soon angry.* How unfit to lead a church are those who cannot discipline themselves. *Not given to wine.* Moderate use of alcohol, as of the other good things God has created, is not unlawful, but excessive drinking is shameful in all, especially in a minister. *Not given to filthy lucre,* not entering into the ministry with corrupt, worldly views. Nothing is more inconsistent in a minister, who is to direct his own and others' eyes to another world, than to be too intent on this one.

1.1.2.2.2. Positively: he must be (v. 8) *a lover of hospitality.* Such a spirit and practice, according to ability and occasion, are consistent with those who should be examples of good works. *A lover of good men,* or of *good things*; ministers should be exemplary in loving what is good. *Sober,* or self-controlled or wise, a necessary grace in a minister for both his ministerial and his personal behavior and management. *Just,* upright in things that concern civil life. *Holy* in what concerns religion. *Temperate,* disciplined; the term comes from a word that means "strength," and describes one who has power over his appetite and affections.

1.2. As to his teaching:

1.2.1. Here is his duty: *Holding fast the faithful word, as he has been* taught, holding it firmly in his own belief and profession and in teaching others. Ministers must hold firmly to, and hold out, the faithful word in their teaching and life.

1.2.2. Here is its goal: *that he may be able by sound doctrine both to exhort and to convince the gainsayers* (those who oppose it). How could he do this if he was uncertain or unstable, not holding firmly to the *faithful word and sound doctrine*?

2. Whom he should reject or avoid. He takes reasons from both bad teachers and hearers among them (vv. 10–16).

2.1. From bad teachers.

2.1.1. Those false teachers are described. They are *unruly*, that is, headstrong and ambitious for power; and they are rebellious. *And vain* (mere) *talkers and deceivers*, falling into errors and mistakes, which they are fond of, and seeking to draw others into the same false ways. There were many such people, *especially those of the circumcision*, who still wanted to mix Judaism and Christianity together, so making a corrupt combination.

2.1.2. Here are the apostle's instructions on how to deal with them (v. 11): *Their mouths must be stopped* by confutation and conviction.

2.1.3. Reasons are given for this from the harmful effects of their errors and from their corrupt purpose in what they do, serving worldly interests while pretending to be religious.

2.2. In reference to their people or hearers, who are described from the ancient testimony given of them:

2.2.1. Here is the witness (v. 12). He is *one of themselves, even a prophet of their own*, that is, Epimenides, a Greek poet, who was likely to know the Cretans and unlikely to slander them. Their poets were considered prophets.

2.2.2. Here is the matter of Epimenides' testimony: *The Cretans are always liars, evil beasts, slow bellies*. They were proverbially notorious for falsehood and lying; "to play the Cretan" and "to lie" meant the same. They were compared to evil brutes for their sly harmfulness and savage nature, and called *slow bellies* (lazy gluttons) because of their laziness and sensuality; they were more inclined to eat than work.

2.2.3. Here is the verification of this by the apostle himself (v. 13). The apostle saw too much basis for the poet's description.

2.2.4. He tells Titus how to deal with them. When Paul wrote to Timothy he told him to instruct with humility, but now when he writes to Titus he tells him to rebuke them sharply. Timothy perhaps had more refined people to deal with, and so he must rebuke them with humility, whereas Titus may have had to deal with people who were more rough and uncultivated. Their sins were many and gross and should therefore be dealt with accordingly. In rebuking, there must be a distinguishing between some sins and others; some are more gross and detestable. A distinction should also be made between some sinners and others. Some have a more tender and obedient attitude, more likely to be persuaded by gentleness; others are harder and more stubborn and need more incisive language.

2.2.5. Here is noted the purpose Titus must pursue by such rebukes: that these Cretans may show themselves truly and effectively changed. The sharpest rebukes must aim at the good of those who are rebuked, to restore and reform the erroneous and the guilty. Soundness in the faith is most desirable and necessary. This is the soul's health and vigor. A special means to soundness in the faith is to turn away from listening to myths and merely human commands. Merely human commands and thoughts about the worship of God are against truth and godliness.

2.2.6. He gives the reasons for this: to good Christians who are sound in the faith and so are purified, *all things are pure, but to those that are defiled and unbelieving, nothing is pure*. They suck poison out of what others draw sweetness from. When their minds and consciences are defiled, a taint is passed on to all they do. Many profess to know God but reject and deny him in their lives;

their practice contradicts their profession of faith. When the apostle instructs Titus to rebuke sharply, he himself rebukes sharply; he describes the Cretans in harsh words, but no doubt no harder than their case warranted and their need required. *Being abominable*, detestable, deserving to have God and good people turn away their eyes from them as nauseous and offensive. *And disobedient*. They could do various things, but it was not the obedience of faith. *To every good work reprobate* (unfit for anything good), without the skill or judgment needed to do anything right. Notice the miserable condition of hypocrites. And yet let us not be as ready to direct this charge at others as to be careful that it does not describe us.

CHAPTER 2

Here the apostle gives Titus directions about faithfully discharging his own ministry generally (v. 1), and especially as regards different kinds of people (vv. 2–10), giving the reasons for these and other directions (vv. 11–14), with a general direction at the end (v. 15).

Verses 1–10

Here Paul urges Titus:

1. Generally, to faithfully discharge his own ministry. His appointing others to preach will not excuse him from preaching, nor must he look after only ministers and elders, but also instruct private Christians in their duty. The true doctrines of the Gospel are *sound doctrines*; in themselves they are good and holy, and they make believers so.

2. Specifically and in detail, to apply this sound doctrine to different kinds of people (vv. 2–10). Ministers must be particular as well as practical in their preaching. They must teach people their duty, all people and each person. Here is an excellent Christian guide:

2.1. For the older men. Older disciples of Christ must conduct themselves in everything in a way consistent with the Christian message. *That the aged men be sober* (moderate). They must remain moderate in their behavior, for the sake of both their health and their fitness for service, to advise and set an example to younger men. *Grave*: serious, worthy of respect, for irreverence is unfitting in anyone, but especially in older people. *Temperate, sound in faith*, sincere and steadfast. Those who are mature in years should also be mature in grace and goodness, the inner self being renewed more and more (Eph 3:16; 4:23–24; Col 3:10) as the outer self deteriorates. *In charity*, or love; this is appropriately attached to *faith*, which works by and must be seen in love (Gal 5:6). And love must be sincere, without pretense (Ro 12:9), loving God for himself and loving people for God's sake. *In patience*: older people tend to get bad tempered easily; they must therefore be on their guard against such weaknesses. Faith, love, and endurance are three main Christian graces, and soundness in these goes far toward soundness in the Gospel.

2.2. For the older women: they too must be instructed and warned. Those qualities mentioned before—*sobriety, gravity, temperance, soundness in the faith, charity, and patience*—which are commended to older men, are not proper for them only, but applicable to both sexes. There is not one way of salvation for one sex or kind of person, and another for another; rather, both must learn and practice the same things; the qualities and duties are common. *That the aged women likewise be in behaviour as becometh holiness*, or as is right for holy people, such as they profess to be. Whatever things are fitting or unfitting form a standard and rule of conduct to be embraced. *Not false accusers*, slandering and backbiting their neighbors, which is too common a fault; they must not be those who not only love to speak but love to speak bad things about people, and to come between close friends. *Not given to much wine.* This is unfitting and evil in anyone, but especially in this sex and age, and was found too often among the Greeks at that time and place. *Teachers of good things.* Not that they must preach in public, which is forbidden to them, but otherwise they may and should teach, by example and their good life. Those whose actions and behavior are consistent with holiness are in that way teachers of good things. Besides this, the older women may and should teach by doctrinal instruction at home and privately. Their business is — and they may be called on to fulfill it — to be teachers of what is good.

2.3. For the young women. There are lessons for them too, that the older women must teach. Older women often have better access for teaching such things than men, even than ministers.

2.3.1. Younger women must have a good personal character. *To be sober and discreet*, self-controlled, in contrast to the vanity and rashness that younger people are usually subject to. *Discreet* and *chaste* (pure) go well together; many expose themselves to fatal temptations by what at first might be "merely indiscretion." *Chaste* and *keepers at home* are well joined too. Of course there are occasions to go out, but to gad about carelessly here, there, and everywhere for the sake of merriment and company is the opposite evil that is intended. *Good*: both generally, in opposition to all evil, and specifically, in kindness, helpfulness, and love. It may also have a more particular sense, referring to a humble but cheerful spirit and attitude, not angry or bitter.

2.3.2. They have duties with regard to their husband and children. *To love their husbands, and to be obedient to them*; where there is true love, this command will not be difficult. God wants to have a resemblance of Christ's authority over the church displayed in the husband's authority over the wife. Christ is the head of the church, to protect and save it, to provide it with all that is good and protect it from evil (Eph 5:22 – 33). In the same way, the husband is over the wife, to keep her from harm and provide comfortably for her. What is required, then, is not a slavish submission, but a loving subordination. *And to love their children*, not only with a natural affection but also with a spiritual love. It must not be a fond and foolish love, neglecting appropriate rebuke and correction where necessary, but a consistent Christian love, forming their children's life and conduct rightly, taking care of their souls as well as their bodies. *That the word of God may not be blasphemed* (maligned). "In what ways are these people better because of their new religion?" the ungodly are ready to ask. "Judge what kind of God he is by his servants. See what his word, message, and religion are like by looking at his followers."

2.4. For the young men. They tend to be eager and rash; they must be seriously urged, therefore, to be self-controlled; considerate, not rash; humble, not haughty or proud, because more young people are ruined by pride than by any other sin.

2.5. For Titus. Along with these instructions, the apostle inserts some directions for Titus himself. Here is:

2.5.1. Guidance for his conduct. He must be *a pattern of good works* (v. 7). Without this, he will tear down with one hand what he builds with the other. Good doctrine and good life must go together. *In all things*; some read,

"above all things." Above all things, example, especially that of the teacher himself, is necessary; in this way light and influence are more likely to go together. Ministers must be good examples to the flock (1Pe 5:3), and the people must be followers of them, as they are of Christ (1Co 11:1).

2.5.2. Guidance for his teaching and doctrine as well as for his life (vv. 7 – 8). Ministers must make it clear that the purpose of their preaching is purely to advance the honor of God, the interests of Christ and his kingdom, and the welfare and happiness of souls. In their preaching, therefore, they must not display their wit or intellect, their fine human learning or rhetorical ability; rather, they must use sound speech, and they must use Scripture, as far as possible, to express Scripture truths. "In this way, be an example *in word* and *in conversation*, your life corresponding to your teaching."

2.5.3. The reason for both the strictness of the minister's life and the seriousness and soundness of his preaching. These who seek to oppose the truth will seek opportunities to misrepresent Titus, trying to find something wrong in his teaching or life. Faithful ministers will have enemies watching, those who will try to find or pick holes in their teaching or behavior. There is greater need, therefore, for them to examine themselves.

2.6. For *servants* (slaves). Slaves must know and do their duty to their worldly masters, but do it while looking to their heavenly One.

2.6.1. The duties themselves are:

2.6.1.1. Obedience (v. 9). This is the primary duty, the one by which they are to be characterized. Their will must be subject to their master's will, and their time and labor at their master's disposal and command. If a person is a master, the duties of a slave are to be given to him as such.

2.6.1.2. *To please them well in all things.* We are not to understand it as referring to either obeying or pleasing them without any restrictions, but always with a reservation of God's right. If God's command and the earthly master's compete with each other, we are instructed to obey God rather than a human being (Ac 5:29). Not only must the will of God be the measure of the slave's obedience; it must also be its reason. All must be done with respect to him, because of his authority, and to please him primarily and mainly (Col 3:22 – 24). Notice, Christian liberty is certainly harmonious with civil slavery and submission. People may serve their masters and yet be the servants of Christ. Slaves should not, therefore, be troubled at their condition, but be faithful and cheerful in the position in which God has put them, striving to please their masters in everything. It may be hard, but it must be aimed at as far as possible.

2.6.1.3. *Not answering again.* When one is aware of a fault in oneself, to try to extenuate it or justify it actually doubles it. Yet the not answering back that is referred to here does not exclude turning away wrath with a soft answer (Pr 15:1), when time and circumstances allow. Good and wise masters will be ready to listen and do the right thing.

2.6.1.4. *Not purloining* (not stealing from them), *but showing all good fidelity.* This is another essential quality in slaves, honesty. They must be just and true, doing for their masters as they would or should for themselves. Even if the master is strict and difficult, hardly making sufficient provision for slaves, their slaves must not take matters into their own hands, nor go about stealing what does not belong to them. They must not only not steal or waste; they must look after their master's goods and advance their prosperity to the best of their ability. The servant who did not increase his master's talent is accused of unfaithfulness (Mt 25:26), even though he did not embezzle or lose it.

2.6.2. The consideration with which Titus is to back up these duties: *that they may adorn the doctrine of God our Saviour in all things.* If they are careful to do their duty, it will lead to the glory of God and the good name of religion. The unbelieving masters will think better of that despised way (Ac 28:22) when they find that those of their slaves who are Christians are better than their other servants. True religion is an honor to those who profess it; they should see that they do not dishonor it in any way.

Verses 11–14

The grounds on which all the previous instructions are urged.

1. From the nature and purpose of the Gospel. Let all kinds of people fulfill their respective duties, for this is the aim and work of Christianity, to instruct people to live right lives and behave well.

1.1. They are put under the dispensation of *the grace of God.* Now grace obliges and compels to goodness those who receive it. Without this effect, grace is received in vain (1Co 15:2, 10; 2Co 6:1).

1.2. This Gospel grace *brings salvation.* That is why it is called *the word of life*; it brings people to faith, and so to life.

1.3. *It hath appeared.* The old age was comparatively dark and shadowy; the Gospel is a clear and shining light.

1.4. It has appeared *to all men.* Gospel grace is open to all, and all are invited to come and share in its benefits. The teaching of grace and salvation through the Gospel is for all ranks and conditions of people—slaves and servants as well as masters.

1.5. This Gospel revelation is to *teach.* It gives directions about what to shun and what to follow, what to avoid and what to do. The Gospel is not for speculation only or chiefly, but for practice and right managing of life, for it teaches:

1.5.1. *Denying ungodliness and worldly lusts.* "Put away ungodliness, irreligion, all unbelief, worldly passions toward God; put away not loving him, fearing him, trusting in him, or obeying him as we should. *And worldly lusts*, all corrupt and evil desires and affections that exist in worldly people." A worldly, immoral way of life is not consistent with a heavenly calling.

1.5.2. *To live soberly, righteously* (in a self-controlled, upright way), *and godly.* Religion is not made up only of negatives; there must be doing good as well as avoiding evil.

1.5.2.1. We should live soberly with respect to ourselves, keeping the limits of moderation and restraint.

1.5.2.2. We should live uprightly toward all others, rendering to everyone their due and harming no one, doing good to others. Selfishness is a kind of unrighteousness; it robs others of the share in us that is their due. Live righteously, therefore, as well as soberly.

1.5.2.3. And we should be godly toward God. Respect for him should actually run through everything, but there is also a clear and direct duty that we owe to God: belief and acknowledgment of his being and qualities, loving, fearing, and trusting in him, depending on him and devoting ourselves to him, praying to him, praising him, and meditating on his word and works. This is godliness, looking to and coming to God as he has revealed himself in

Christ. This is how we must train ourselves in godliness, without which there can be no *adorning* of the Gospel (v. 10). The Gospel teaches us not only how to believe and hope in the right way but also how to live well, as is consistent with faith and hope in this present world, and as those who expect another and better one.

1.5.3. *Looking for that blessed hope, and the glorious appearing of the great God and our Saviour Jesus Christ.* Hope stands for the thing hoped for, heaven and its happiness, which is here called *that hope* because it is the great thing we look for, and is called a *blessed hope* because when we reach it we will be completely happy forever. This shows both the time of the fulfilling of our hope and the certainty and greatness of that hope. *The great God and our Saviour* (or "even our Savior") *Jesus Christ.* Christ, then, is the *great God*, not figuratively, but properly and absolutely; he is *the true God.* At his second coming he will reward his servants and bring them to glory with him. This shows us:

1.5.3.1. There is a common and blessed hope for all true Christians in the other world. By *hope* is meant the thing hoped for—namely, Christ himself, who is called *our hope* (1Ti 1:1)—and blessedness in and through him, here appropriately called *that blessed hope.*

1.5.3.2. The intention of the Gospel is to stir up everyone to lead a good life through this blessed hope. *Denying ungodliness and worldly lusts, live soberly, righteously, and godly, in this present world, looking for the blessed hope*, not as mercenaries, but as dutiful and thankful Christians.

1.5.3.3. At the glorious appearing of Christ, the blessed hope of Christians will be reached. The glory of the great God and our Savior will then break out like the sun. The work and intention of the Gospel are to raise the heart to wait for this second coming of Christ. Let us then pay attention to this hope.

1.5.3.4. The strength, encouragement, and joy of Christians is that their Savior is the great God, and he will gloriously reveal himself.

2. From the purpose of Christ's death (v. 14). To bring us to holiness and happiness was the purpose of Christ's death as well as the scope of his teaching. We have here:

2.1. The purchaser of salvation—Jesus Christ, *that great God and our Saviour*, who does not save simply as God, much less only as man, but as God-man. Man, so that he could obey, suffer, and die, for humanity; God, so that he could support the humanity.

2.2. The price of our redemption: *He gave himself.* The Father gave him, but he gave himself too, and in the freeness and voluntariness of the offering, as well as in its greatness, lay in its acceptableness and merit. The human nature was the offering, and the divine the altar, sanctifying the gift.

2.3. The people for whom he died. He gave himself *for us*, not only for our good but also in our place. *He loved us, and gave himself for us.* What can we do but love him and give ourselves back to him?

2.4. The purpose of his giving himself for us:

2.4.1. *That he might redeem us from all iniquity.* This corresponds to the first lesson, *denying ungodliness and worldly lusts.* Christ gave himself to redeem us from these; therefore put them away. To love and live in sin is to trample underfoot redeeming blood (Heb 10:29). But how could the short sufferings of Christ redeem us from all iniquity? Through the infinite dignity of his person. The One who was God suffered, though not as God. The *great God and our Saviour gave himself for us*; this accounts for the great effectiveness of his redemption. The glorious goal and fruit of Christ's death is redemption from all iniquity! Christ died for this.

2.4.2. *To purify to himself a peculiar people* (a people that are his very own). This backs up the second lesson: *to live soberly, righteously, and godly, in this present world.* Christ died to purify as well as to pardon, to heal our nature as well as to free us from guilt and condemnation. This is how his people are set apart from the world that lies in wickedness. Redemption from sin and sanctification of the nature go together, and both make a people distinctive to God. And:

2.4.3. *Zealous of good works* (eager to do what is good). This distinctive people must be distinguished by doing good and being eager to do it.

Verse 15

Here is a general instruction to Titus in which we have the matter and manner of ministers' teaching.

1. The subject matter of ministers' teaching. *These things,* namely, those mentioned before: the truths and duties of the Gospel, the duties of avoiding sin and living lives that are self-controlled, upright, and godly in this present world.

2. The manner: by doctrine, encouragement, and rebuke with all authority. The great and necessary truths and duties of the Gospel—especially *speak and exhort* these; *parakalei,* urge them with great earnestness. Ministers must not be cold or lifeless in communicating heavenly teaching and commands, as if they were ordinary things, but must urge them with great fervency. *And rebuke;* convict and correct those who oppose, contradict, or neglect, who do not receive the truth as they should. *Rebuke with all authority,* as one who comes in the name of God. Ministers are to rebuke in their churches.

3. "*Let no man despise thee. Speak and exhort these things,* urge them on everyone, rebuke sin boldly and faithfully, but be careful to examine yourself and your own behavior, and then no one will despise you." The most effective way for ministers to protect themselves from contempt is to keep close to the teaching of Christ and do their duty with wisdom and courage. Perhaps a warning is intended to the people here, too—that Titus, though young, should not be shown contempt by them.

CHAPTER 3

This chapter deals with: 1. Duties that concern Christians more generally (vv. 1–8). 2. What Titus should avoid in teaching, along with some other instructions (vv. 9–14), and greetings at the end (v. 15).

Verses 1–8

The apostle has instructed Titus with reference to the particular duties of several different kinds of people; now he tells him to exhort the Christian he is among to duties that concern them more generally. Forgetfulness of duty is a common weakness; the people need to be reminded and encouraged, therefore, to undertake these things, and their minister is the proper person to do so.

1. The duties themselves. Titus must *put them in mind:*

1.1. *To be subject to principalities and powers, to obey magistrates.* They must be subject to all civil rulers and obey them when what the latter require is lawful and honorable. The Christian faith was misrepresented by its opponents as harmful to the rights of rulers and civil powers and as leading to factions and rebellion against lawful authority. Christians must be reminded to show themselves to be examples of proper submission and obedience to the government they are under.

1.2. *To be ready to every good work.* This command concerns doing good of every kind and on every occasion that may present itself, whether it concerns God, ourselves, or our neighbor. Mere harmlessness, or only good words and good meanings, are not enough without good works. "Not only take, but also seek, opportunity to do good. Remind them of this."

1.3. *To speak evil of no man.* If no good can be spoken, say nothing rather than speak evil unnecessarily. We must never take pleasure in speaking ill of others, nor make the worst of anything, but think the best that we can. We must not go about gossiping, saying, "Have you heard the latest about so-and-so?" Just as this evil is all too common, so it is very harmful. This is among the sins to be gotten rid of (Eph 4:31) because if it is indulged in, it unfits a person for Christian fellowship here and for the community of the blessed in heaven. "Remind them, therefore, to avoid this."

1.4. *To be no brawlers,* to be no fighters, either with the hand or with the tongue. Contention and strife arise from sinful desires, which must be restrained, not indulged. Christians need to be reminded of these things.

1.5. *But gentle,* fair, not taking words or actions in their worst sense, and sometimes yielding what we are strictly entitled to for the sake of peace.

1.6. *Showing all meekness to all men.* We must have humility not only in our hearts but also in our speech and conduct. *All meekness*—humility on all occasions, not only toward friends but *to all men.* Humility in spirit and behavior makes religion pleasant; it is a commanded imitation of Christ and brings its own reward.

2. He adds the reasons:

2.1. From their own past condition. *We ourselves also were sometimes:*

2.1.1. *Foolish,* lacking true spiritual understanding, ignorant of heavenly things. Those who can remember many of their own foolish ways should be most disposed to bear with those of others.

2.1.2. *Disobedient,* headstrong and hardhearted, resisting the word. These often go together, *foolish* and *disobedient,* for what foolishness is there like disobeying God and his laws, natural or revealed?

2.1.3. *Deceived,* or wandering, wandering from the ways of truth and holiness. Human beings in their natural, degenerate state tend to go astray. People are weak and ready to be deceived by the schemes of Satan and of people who lie in wait ready to deceive and mislead (Eph 4:14).

2.1.4. *Serving divers lusts* (enslaved by all kinds of passions) *and pleasures.* Worldly people think they simply enjoy their pleasures; the Word calls it slavery. It is the misery of the servants of sin that they have many masters, one sinful desire rushing them one way, and another, another way. The sinful desires that tempt them promise them freedom, but in yielding to them they become the servants of corruption.

2.1.5. *Living in malice.* Malice desires another's harm and rejoices in it.

2.1.6. *And envy,* which begrudges and complains at another's good. Both are roots of bitterness, from which many evils spring (Dt 29:18; Heb 12:15). These were some of the sins in which we lived in our natural state.

2.1.7. *Hateful, and hating one another.* It is the misery of sinners that they hate one another, as it is the duty and happiness of saints to love one another. The consideration of this past of ours should incline us to be more humble and tenderhearted toward those who are still like this.

2.2. From their present state. "We have been rescued from such a miserable condition by no merit or strength of our own." The apostle again lays out the circumstances of our salvation (vv. 4–7).

2.2.1. The prime author of our salvation: God the Father, who is therefore called here *God our Saviour*. All things belonging to the new creation and to the restoration of fallen humanity to life and happiness come from God the Father. The Father begins, the Son directs, and the Holy Spirit works and perfects all.

2.2.2. Its origin: the divine *kindness and love of God to man*. By grace we are saved from first to last. This is the ground and motive. The occasion for this grace is in humanity, namely, our misery and wretchedness. Because sin brought that misery, wrath might have been the outcome rather than compassion, but God wanted to pity and save rather than destroy. He delights in mercy (Mic 7:18).

2.2.3. The means: the shining out of this love and grace of God in the Gospel, *after it appeared*. Through the Spirit, the appearing of love and grace has great power to change and turn people to God.

2.2.4. False grounds removed: *Not by works of righteousness which we have done, but according to his mercy, he saved us*. Works must be in those who are saved, but they are not among the motives for salvation; they are the way of the kingdom, not its meriting price. Faith and all saving graces are God's free gift and his work; the beginning, growth, and perfection of them in glory all come from him.

2.2.5. The formal cause of salvation, or what it consists in: regeneration or spiritual renewal, as it is called here. A new controlling principle of grace and holiness is brought in, which makes the person a new creation (Gal 6:15), with new thoughts, desires, and affections. *He saved us* (v. 5): what is begun in this way is sure to be perfected in time and is expressed as if it already were so. We must be initially saved now, by regeneration, if we want good reason to expect complete salvation in heaven. The change then will be one of degree, not in kind. Grace is glory begun, as glory is simply grace in its perfection.

2.2.6. Its outward sign and seal in baptism, which because of its outwardness is called *the washing of regeneration*. The work itself is inside and spiritual, but it is externally signified and sealed in this ritual. Baptism saves figuratively and sacramentally where it is rightly used. Do not show disrespect to this outward sign and seal, but do not trust in the outward washing. The covenant sealed in baptism commits the person to duties as well as conveying benefits and privileges; if the duties are not done, the benefits are expected in vain.

2.2.7. The principal cause, *the renewing of the Holy Spirit*. In the plan of our salvation, the applying and effecting part is attributed especially to the Holy Spirit. We are said to be born of the Spirit (Jn 3:8), to be given life (2Co 3:6) and sanctified by the Spirit (2Th 2:13), to be led (Gal 5:18) and guided (Jn 16:13), strengthened (Eph 3:16) and helped (Ro 8:26) by the Spirit. He is to be passionately sought, therefore, and carefully heeded, so that we do not quench his holy movements (1Th 5:19). We can expect that he will act toward us as we act toward him; if we disrespect, resist, or oppose his activities, he will lessen them; if we continue to trouble him, he will withdraw.

2.2.8. How God communicates this Spirit in his gifts and graces: not with a stingy hand, but very freely and plentifully: *Which he shed on us abundantly*. More of the Spirit in his gifts and graces is poured out under the Gospel than was under the Law. The church has had a measure of the Spirit in all ages, but more since the coming of Christ than before. In the early church there was a great abundance of common gifts of illumination, outward calling and profession, and general faith, and also of more special gifts of sanctification, such as faith, hope, and love. Let us share in these! What will it mean if much is poured out but we remain dry? This is how God shares his grace and all the spiritual blessings under the Gospel—*plentifully*; he is not limited toward us.

2.2.9. The prevailing channel of everything, namely, Christ: *Through Jesus Christ our Saviour.* Everything comes through him, and through him as Savior. Let us therefore praise God for him above all; let us go to the Father through him. Have we grace? Then let us thank him with the Father and Spirit for it, and grow and increase in it more and more (2Pe 3:18).

2.2.10. The reasons why we are brought into this new spiritual condition, namely, justification, inheritance, and the hope of eternal life: *That being justified by his grace, we should be made heirs according to the hope of eternal life.*

2.2.10.1. Justification is the free acquittal of sinners and the accepting of them as righteous through the righteousness of Christ received by faith. God does all this freely for us, but through the intervention of Christ's sacrifice and righteousness, taken hold of by faith. Justification is by grace, as the spring and origin, *through the redemption that is in Christ*; and then faith applies that redemption. We must have an indwelling righteousness and its fruits in obedient works; works are the fruits of our justification and evidence of our union with Christ and our qualification for life and happiness; they are part of that happiness and its beginning.

2.2.10.2. But all this is obtained by Christ so that, *being justified by his grace, we should be made heirs*. Our justification is *by the grace of God*, and our justification by that grace is necessary for us to be made *heirs of eternal life*. Eternal life is set before us in the promise. The Spirit produces in us faith and the hope of that life, and in this way we are made heirs of it. Faith and hope bring it near, and its well-established expectation fills us with joy. The humblest believer is a great heir.

2.2.10.3. Although we do not have our inheritance in our hands, we have good hope through grace. All this is a good reason why we should *show all meekness to all men*, because we have experienced so much good from the kindness and love of God to us, and so we may hope that they, in God's time, may also share in the same grace as we do.

3. Having laid out the grace of God toward us, Paul immediately urges the necessity of good works, because we must not expect the benefit of God's mercy unless we carefully fulfill our duty (v. 8). Faith must be an active, working faith. The Cretan Christians must be eager *to maintain good works*, not to do them only occasionally. *These things are good and profitable unto men*; "these good works," according to some, or "the teaching of these things," rather than idle questions (v. 9).

Verses 9–15

Here we have what Titus should avoid in teaching, how he should deal with a *heretic* (divisive person), and some other instructions.

1. He tells Titus what he should avoid in teaching (v. 9). Idle and *foolish* controversies must be avoided. *And genealogies*. Some lawful and useful inquiries can be made into

these things, to see the fulfilling of the Scriptures in some cases, and especially in the family of Christ the Messiah, but all that serve pride and feed vanity, enabling people to boast of a long, fine background—these Titus must withstand as foolish and useless. *And contentions* (arguments), *and strivings* (quarrels) *about the law.* There were those who wanted the Mosaic rituals and ceremonies, and wanted to see them continue in the church. Titus must give no support to these, but avoid and oppose them, *for they are unprofitable and vain*: this refers to all those *foolish questions and genealogies*, as well as those *strivings about the law.* Far from instructing and building up people in godliness, they are hindrances. Ministers must not only teach things that are good and useful, but they are also to avoid and oppose the contrary. Nor should people have itching ears (2Ti 4:3), but love and embrace sound doctrine.

2. The apostle next instructs Titus on how to deal with heresies and *heretics* (NIV: divisive persons) when they do arise (v. 10). "Warn that person more than once, so that if possible they may be brought back, and you may gain your brother or sister, but if this will not subdue them, reject them from the fellowship." Those who will not be reclaimed by warnings, but remain stubborn in their sins and errors, *are subverted and self-condemned.* How great an evil real heresy is. Such a person is *subverted*, or perverted—it is a metaphor from a building ruined in such a way as to render it difficult, if not impossible, to repair and rebuild. Real heretics have rarely been restored to the true faith, not so much because of a defect of judgment as because of an obstinacy of the will. Great care and patience must be exercised toward those who err most. They must be warned and instructed. On finding that the corrupt member stubbornly refuses to be reclaimed, the church is obliged to preserve its own purity by severing them. By God's blessing, such discipline may become effective in reforming the offender.

3. The apostle adds some further commands (vv. 12–13). Here are two personal instructions:

3.1. Titus should keep himself ready to come to Paul at *Nicopolis* as soon as *Artemas* or *Tychicus* has been sent to Crete to take his place. We read little about Artemas, but Tychicus is mentioned on many occasions with respect. Paul calls him *a beloved brother, and faithful minister, and fellow-servant in the Lord* (Col 4:7); he was therefore fit for the service suggested.

3.2. Titus should do his best to help two of his friends on their journey, to see that they were well taken care of and had everything they needed. *Zenas* is described as *the lawyer. Apollos* was an eminent and faithful minister. Accompanying such people part of the way and supplying their needs for their work and journeys was a godly and necessary service. Let Christians learn to devote themselves to doing good works, *that they be not unfruitful* (v. 14). Christianity is not a fruitless profession. It is not enough that they be harmless; they must be profitable, doing good as well as avoiding evil. "Let them set up and maintain some honest work and employment to provide for themselves and their families, so that they do not become unprofitable burdens on the earth," as some understand it (compare Lk 13:7). Let them not think Christianity gives them the right to sit back and take it easy. *To maintain good works for necessary uses*, not, like drones, living off the labors of others, but themselves being fruitful, to everyone's benefit.

4. The apostle concludes with greetings and blessings (v. 15). It is a great comfort and encouragement to have the hearts and prayers of other Christians with and for us. *Grace be with you all. Amen.* This is the apostle's wish and prayer. Grace is the chief thing to be wished and asked for, whether for ourselves or for others; it is, in summary, all that is good. *Amen* closes the prayer, expressing desire and hope that it may be so, and it will be so.

A Practical and Devotional Exposition of

Philemon

Philemon, a man of note and probably a minister in the church of Colosse, a city of Phrygia, had a servant named *Onesimus*, who, having stolen some of his goods, ran away from him and came to Rome, where Paul was then a prisoner for the Gospel. By the blessing of God, he was converted through Paul, after which he ministered to the apostle for a while as the latter remained in chains. Understanding him to be another man's servant, Paul would not detain him without his master's consent, but sent him back with this letter of recommendation, in which he passionately seeks a pardon and kind reception for Onesimus. There is no reason to doubt that Paul persuaded Philemon to forgive and receive Onesimus.

CHAPTER 1

In this letter we have: 1. Its introduction (vv. 1–7). 2. Its substance (vv. 8–21). Its conclusion (vv. 22–25).

Verses 1–7

1. In the first two verses of the introduction we have the people from and to whom it is written.

1.1. The people writing. Paul is the main person writing, and he calls himself *a prisoner of Jesus Christ*. To be such a prisoner was true glory, and it would be proper for Philemon to be persuaded by this glory to grant the request made to him by the one who had it, especially when the request was also strengthened with the agreement of Timothy. What could be denied two such petitioners?

1.2. The people written to. These are *Philemon and Apphia*, and with them Archippus and the church in Philemon's house. Philemon, the master of Onesimus, was the person principally addressed; he was a good man, and probably a minister too, and on both accounts dearly loved by Paul. To Philemon is added Apphia, probably his wife. She was a party who had been offended and wronged by Onesimus, and so it was right that proper notice be taken of her in a letter for reconciliation and forgiveness. These are the main parties written to. The secondary ones are *Archippus, and the church in Philemon's house*. Archippus was a minister in the church of Colosse (Col 4:17) and Philemon's friend. Paul may have thought Archippus was one whom Philemon would discuss matters with and who might be capable of furthering the good work of peacemaking and forgiveness. *And to the church in thy house*, Philemon's whole family, in which the worship of God was maintained. Families that are generally most godly and orderly may still have one or another member who is ungodly and evil. Onesimus's sin was made worse by the fact that he had lived where he could have learned better. Yet this one evil servant did not hinder Philemon's house from being called a church. All families should be like this—a place where religious faith is nurtured. Wicked families are a place where hell is nurtured, just as good ones are nurtured for heaven. Paul, because of a

concern that all in that household may have in this matter of Onesimus, addresses his instruction to them all, so that their affection as well as Philemon's may be restored to Onesimus, and so that they will advance, not hinder, the reconciliation wished for and sought.

2. Then we have the apostle's greeting of those named by him (v. 3). He wishes the best things for them; not gold, silver, or any earthly benefit, but *grace and peace from God in Christ. Grace*, the spring and fountain of all blessings, *and peace*, all that is good, as the fruit and result of that grace. *From God our Father and the Lord Jesus Christ.* We have grace from the Father, who is our Father in Christ, and from Christ comes his own favor and goodwill as God, and its fruits come through him as Mediator. Just as the favor of God and peace with him in itself are the best and most desirable good, so they are also the cause of all other goods, and what gives sweetness to every mercy and can make happy even those who lack all worldly things.

3. Paul expresses the special affection he has for Philemon by giving thanks and prayer to God on his behalf and expressing great joy for the many good things he knows and has heard to be in him (vv. 4–7). Here is:

3.1. The object of Paul's praises and prayers for Philemon (v. 4). It is the privilege of good people that in their praises and prayers they come to God as their God: *I thank my God*, said Paul. We should offer God prayers and praises not only for ourselves but also for others. This is no small part of the communion of saints. In his private thanksgivings and prayers, Paul was often specific in remembering his friends. This is a means of exercising love and obtaining good for others.

3.2. The circumstance: *Always making mention of thee.* This is how we must remember Christian friends: much and often, as their situation may require.

3.3. The matter both of his praises and prayers in reference to Philemon.

3.3.1. His praises. He thanks God for the love that he has heard Philemon has toward the Lord Jesus. He also gives thanks for his faith in Christ. Love for Christ and faith in him are primary Christian graces for which there is great reason for praise to God. He also praises God for Philemon's love for all the saints. These two must go together. Different attitudes and ways in nonessentials will not make any difference in our affection for those in whom we see the truth. Mere external differences are nothing here. Paul calls a poor converted slave *his bowels* (his very heart) (v. 8). We must love all the saints, as God does. *Hearing of thy love and faith, which thou hast toward the Lord Jesus, and toward all saints.* If love for the saints is sincere, it will be a general and universal love toward all saints; although faith and love are hidden things in the heart, they are known by their effects.

3.3.2. His prayer, that the fruits of Philemon's faith and love will be more and more evident, so that his sharing of them might constrain others to acknowledge all the good things that are in him and in his house *toward* Christ Jesus.

3.4. He adds a reason for both his prayer and his praises (v. 7). "The good you have done and still do is an abundant matter of joy and comfort to me and others, who therefore want you to continue and be fuller and fuller of such good fruits."

Verses 8–25

We have here:

1. The main business of this letter, which is to plead with Philemon on behalf of Onesimus. Paul urges many arguments for this purpose (vv. 8–21).

1.1. The first argument is taken from what was noted before: "Since so much good is reported of you and found in you, especially your love for all the saints, now let me see it on a fresh and further occasion." A disposition to do good, together with its past expressions, is a good handle to take hold of for urging even more.

1.2. The second argument is taken from the authority of the one who is making this request (v. 8). This was a matter within the range of the apostle's authority to require, even though in this instance he would not exercise that authority.

1.3. He chooses rather to appeal to Philemon (v. 9). He argues on the basis of love rather than authority, which no doubt must carry a persuasive influence with it.

1.4. *Being such a one as Paul the aged* (an old man), *and now also a prisoner of Jesus Christ.* Years call for respect. The request of an old apostle, one now suffering for Christ and his Gospel, should be sympathetically considered.

1.5. He argues from the spiritual relationship he now has with Onesimus (v. 10). *My son, whom I have begotten in my bonds*; Onesimus is dear to him, and he hopes that this consideration will make him so to Philemon. Onesimus became his son while he was in his chains; prison blessings are sweet.

1.6. He argues from Philemon's own interests (v. 11). Unsanctified people are unprofitable, but grace makes a person good for something: *"In time past unprofitable, but now profitable,* as he has been to me here since his conversion, ministering to me in my confinement." Here is an allusion to the name *Onesimus*, which means "useful." Now he will fulfill the meaning of his name. Notice how tenderly Paul speaks here when he is pleading with Philemon not to harshly reflect on his servant's misconduct, but to forgive him. What happy changes conversion makes—making what is evil good! Making what is useless useful!

1.7. He urges Philemon from the strong affection he has for Onesimus (v. 12). Even good people may sometimes need to be begged earnestly to forgive those who have wronged and offended them.

1.8. The apostle argues from his denying himself in sending back Onesimus (vv. 13–14). Paul was now in prison and wanted a friend or servant to assist him, for which he found Onesimus fit and ready, and so he could have detained him to minister to him. But he would not take this liberty, even though his circumstances needed it: *"I have sent him back* to you, so that any good service of yours to me will not be *of necessity, but willingly* (spontaneous, not forced)." He might indeed have presumed on Philemon's willingness, but, despite his need, he would rather deny himself than follow that way.

1.9. He argues that such a change has now been brought about in Onesimus that Philemon need not fear his ever running away from him or harming him again (v. 15). Love would hope for this and judge that, yes, it would be so. How tenderly the sins of penitents are spoken of: Paul calls Onesimus's running away *a departure for a season*, instead of giving it the term it deserves. True penitents will not return to their folly (Pr 26:11). Notice the goodness and power of God in that the one who had fled from the way of salvation was led to it, and the one who had been so hardened under means used at Colosse found them effective at Rome.

1.10. He argues from the capacity in which Onesimus will now return, and in which he must therefore be received by Philemon (v. 16). There is a spiritual fellowship between all true believers, however different they may be from one another in civil and outward respects; they are all children of the same heavenly Father. Christianity does not nullify or confuse respective civil duties, but strengthens our obligations to them. Religious servants are more than mere ordinary servants; they have grace in their hearts and have found grace in God's sight, and will therefore also find it in the sight of religious masters. *"A brother beloved, specially to me, but how much more to thee, both in the flesh and in the Lord.* He is God's servant and yours too; here are more ties than he is under to me."

1.11. He argues from the communion of saints (v. 17). "Recognize and treat him as you would me, with as ready and true, though perhaps not equal, affection."

1.12. Yet, it might be objected, Onesimus had not only offended his master but also wronged him materially. Paul anticipates this objection with a promise of restitution to Philemon (vv. 18–19). Here are three things:

1.12.1. A confession of Onesimus's debt to Philemon. True penitents will be open in acknowledging their faults; this is to be done especially in cases of wrong to others.

1.12.2. Paul here promises restitution. Notice:

1.12.2.1. The fellowship of saints does not destroy distinct ownership of property: Onesimus is still Philemon's servant and indebted to him for the wrongs that he has done.

1.12.2.2. Putting up security is not in all cases unlawful; in some cases it is a good and merciful undertaking.

1.12.2.3. Here he expresses his real and great affection for Onesimus and his full belief in the sincerity of his conversion.

1.12.3. The position of things between him and Philemon: *Albeit I do not say to thee how thou owest unto me even thy own self besides.* The apostle glances at the benefits he has given Philemon. "I have been the instrument of all spiritual good to you, and I leave you to consider what your obligation to me on this account is."

1.13. He argues from the joy and comfort he will have on Philemon's own account, as well as on Onesimus's (v. 20). Philemon is Paul's son in the faith, but he treats him as a brother; Onesimus is a poor slave, but Paul asks on his behalf as if he were seeking some great thing for himself. Christians should do the things that may give joy to the hearts of one another. From the world they expect trouble (Jn 16:33); where can they look for comfort and joy except in one another? "It is not a desire for any selfish respect that motivates me, but what is pleasing to Christ."

1.14. A final argument lies in the good hope he has for Philemon and the good opinion he has of him (v. 21). Good thoughts and expectations of us strongly move and engage us to do the things expected from us. Good people will be ready for good works; they will not be tightfisted and miserly, but abundant, in them.

2. The conclusion.

2.1. Paul signifies his good hope that, through their prayers, he will be delivered, and that soon he might see them, and so he wants Philemon to make provision for him (v. 22).

2.1.1. *Prepare me also a lodging.* He wants Philemon to do it, intending to be his guest. Who would not show the greatest affectionate regards to such a person?

2.1.2. *For I trust that through your prayers I shall be given unto you.* He did not know how God might deal with him, but with the benefit of prayer he had often found, and hoped he would again find, deliverance and freedom to come to them. Trust must be exercised along with the proper use of means, especially prayer; this has unlocked heaven and opened prison doors. The least may in this way be helpful to the greatest. But note that although prayer is effective, it still does not deserve the things obtained: they are God's gift and Christ's purchase. *I trust that through your prayers* "I shall be freely bestowed on you." In praying for faithful ministers, people are in effect praying for themselves: "*I trust I shall be given unto you,* for your service and comfort."

2.2. He sends salutations from one who is his fellow prisoner, and from four more who are his fellow workers (vv. 23–24). *Epaphras, my fellowprisoner in Christ Jesus.* He came from Colosse and was therefore a compatriot and fellow citizen of Philemon, and, being at Rome, perhaps accompanying Paul, he was confined in the same prison, and for the same cause. The expression *my fellowprisoner in Christ Jesus* is mentioned as Epaphras's glory and the apostle's comfort. This is how God sometimes lightens the sufferings of his servants through the fellowship of saints, the sweet fellowship they have with one another in their chains. No greater enjoyment of God have people found than when suffering together for God. *Marcus, Aristarchus, Demas, Lucas, my fellowlabourers.* The mention of these people seems in a way to make them involved in the work of this letter. How bad it would look to insult, by denying this letter's request, so many worthy names as most of these, at least, were! *Marcus* was the cousin of Barnabas and son of Mary who was so hospitable to the saints at Jerusalem. Although there seems to have been some failing in him when Paul and he went their separate ways (Ac 13:13; 15:37–38), nevertheless, together with Barnabas, Mark continued his work, and here Paul and he, we may infer, were reconciled. *Aristarchus* is mentioned with Mark in Col 4:10, and there Paul calls him his *fellowprisoner.* Next is *Demas*: no mark of disgrace is laid on him here — though in 2Ti 4:10 he is censured — and he is joined with others who were faithful. *Lucas* is the last, that *beloved physician* and evangelist who came to Rome as a companion to Paul.

2.3. The apostle gives a closing prayer and blessing (v. 25). What is wished and prayed for is *grace,* the free favor and love of God; the apostle begins and ends with this. It is grace from *our Lord Jesus Christ.* All grace to us is from Christ; he purchased it, and he gives it. It is grace to *your spirit,* not only to the spirit of Philemon but also to those of all who were named in the opening greeting. All the members of the house who are greeted are joined here in the closing blessing, to stimulate all to fulfill the purpose of the letter. *Amen* is added, not only as a strong and affectionate summing up of the prayer and wish — *so let it be* — but also as an expression of faith that it will be heard: *so shall it be.* The grace of Christ with their spirits, especially Philemon's, would sweeten and soften them, and encourage Philemon to forgive others as God for Christ's sake has forgiven us (Eph 4:32).

A Practical and Devotional
Exposition of
Hebrews

Concerning this letter, we must ask: 1. About its divine authority, for this has been questioned by some. But its divine origin shines out with such strong and unclouded rays that it may be well read as an eminent part of the canon of Scripture. Its general reception by the church of God in all ages is the evidence of its divine authority. 2. About the writer of this letter. About this we are not so certain; it does not bear the name of any person at the beginning, as the rest of the letters do, and some dispute has therefore raged among the learned as to the identity of its writer. Some have assigned it to Clement of Rome; others to Luke; many to Barnabas. But it has generally been attributed to the apostle Paul. In the early church it was generally ascribed to him. (Since the Reformation it has been widely recognized that Paul could not have been the writer [Ed. note]). 3. About the theme of this letter. It is clear that it was written to inform the minds of the Hebrews, and to strongly confirm their judgment, that the Gospel was transcendentally superior to the Law. The purpose of this letter was to urge the believing Hebrews to remain loyal to the Christian faith and persevere in it despite all the sufferings they might face in so doing. It must be acknowledged that many things in this letter are hard to understand, but the sweetness we will find in it will more than make up for all the hard work that is necessary to understand it.

CHAPTER 1

In this chapter a twofold comparison is stated: 1. A comparison between the dispensation of the Gospel and that of the Law (vv. 1–3). 2. A comparison between the glory of Christ and that of the highest creatures, the angels (vv. 4–14).

Verses 1–3

The writer begins with a general declaration of the superiority of the Gospel dispensation above that of the Law. Notice:

1. How God communicated himself and his will to humanity in the Old Testament.

1.1. The people by whom God made known his mind in the Old Testament were *the prophets*, that is, people chosen and qualified by God for the work of revealing his will to humanity.

1.2. The people to whom God spoke by the prophets were *the fathers*, all the Old Testament saints.

1.3. The order in which God spoke to people in those past times was *at sundry times and in divers manners*. The phrase translated *at sundry times* could also be translated "by several parts," referring either to the different ages of the Old Testament era or to the several gradual openings of God's mind concerning the Redeemer. *In divers manners*, according to the different ways in which God thought right to communicate his mind to his prophets.

2. How God communicated his mind and will in the New Testament, in *these last days*, as they are called. Now that we have the Gospel revelation, we must expect no new revelation, but only more of the Spirit of Christ to help us to understand better what has already been revealed. Now the superiority of this revelation consists in two things:

2.1. It is the final, finishing revelation; the canon of Scripture was now to be settled and sealed.

2.2. It is a revelation that God has made by his Son, the most excellent messenger who was ever sent into the world. Consider the glory of our Lord Jesus Christ.

2.2.1. Here is the glory of his office. God has appointed him to be heir of all things. By him God made the worlds, both visible and invisible, the heavens and the earth. By him he made the old creation, and by him he makes the new creation, and by him he rules and governs both. He upholds all things by the word of his power. The weight of the whole creation is laid on Christ: he supports the whole and all its parts.

2.2.2. The writer passes from this to the glory of the person of Christ (v. 3). He is the only begotten Son of God (Jn 1:14, 18), and as such he must have the same nature as God. The person of the Son is the glory of the Father, shining out with a truly divine splendor. Jesus Christ in his person is God revealed in the flesh. The person of the Son is the true image and character of the person of the Father. In seeing the power, wisdom, and goodness of the Lord Jesus Christ, we see the power, wisdom, and goodness of the Father. This is the glory of the person of Christ; the fullness of the Godhead dwells in him (Col 2:9).

2.2.3. From the glory of the person of Christ he proceeds to mention the glory of his grace. The sufferings of Christ had the great honor of making full atonement for the sins of his people: *By himself he purged away our sins*; he has made atonement for sin. He himself, the glory of his person and nature, gave to his sufferings such merit as was a sufficient reparation of honor to God, who had suffered injury and dishonor by the sins of humanity.

2.2.4. From the glory of his sufferings we are finally led to consider the glory of his exaltation. Having assumed our nature and suffered in it on earth, he has taken it up with him to heaven. Now it was by no less a person than this that God spoke to us in these last days. The dispensation of the Gospel must therefore exceed, by far, the dispensation of the Law.

Verses 4–14

The writer now proceeds to show that the Lord Jesus Christ is much superior not only to the prophets, but even to angels. Both in nature and office, Christ is vastly superior to the angels themselves.

1. The superior nature of Christ is proved from his superior name. He is *made better*; that is, he "is more excellent."

2. The superiority of the name and nature of Christ above the angels is declared in the Holy Scriptures, and is to be concluded from them. Now here several passages of Scripture are quoted in which those things that were never said about the angels are said about Christ.

2.1. It was said about Christ, *Thou art my Son; this day have I begotten thee* (Ps 2:7). Now this was never said about the angels, and so by inheritance he has a more excellent nature and name than they have.

2.2. It is said about Christ, but never about the angels, *I will be to him a Father, and he shall be to me a Son* (2Sa 7:14).

2.3. It is said about Christ, *When God bringeth his First-begotten into the world, let all the angels of God worship* him. The proof of this is taken from Ps 97:7, *Worship him, all you gods*; that is, "All you who are superior to people, acknowledge yourselves to be inferior to Christ in nature and power."

2.4. God has said about Christ, *Thy throne, O God, is for ever and ever* (vv. 8–12). But about the angels he has only said that *he hath made them spirits, and his ministers a flame of fire* (v. 7).

2.4.1. What does God say here about the angels? *He maketh his angels spirits, and his ministers a flame of fire.* Notice the office of the angels: they are God's ministers, or *servants, to do his pleasure.* He gives them light and zeal, readiness and resolution to do his pleasure; they are no more than what God has made them to be.

2.4.2. How much greater things the Father says about Christ. Here two passages of Scripture are quoted.

2.4.2.1. One of these is Ps 45:6–7, where:

2.4.2.1.*1.* God declares Christ's true and real divinity: *Thy throne, O God.* And if God the Father declares him to be so, he must be really and truly so.

2.4.2.1.*2.* God declares his dignity and authority, as One who has a throne, a kingdom, and a scepter of that kingdom.

2.4.2.1.*3.* God declares the eternal duration of the authority and dignity of Christ: *Thy throne, O God, is for ever and ever.* This distinguishes Christ's throne from all earthly thrones, which waver and will eventually fall; it will endure as the days of heaven.

2.4.2.1.*4.* God declares about Christ the perfect justice of his administration (v. 8). He came to the scepter righteously, and he uses it in perfect righteousness (v. 9). Christ came to fulfill all righteousness (Mt 3:15). He came to deal with transgression and to make an end of sin (Da 9:24) as something hateful as well as harmful.

2.4.2.1.*5.* God declares about Christ how he was qualified for the office of Mediator and how he was installed and confirmed in it (v. 9). Christ has the name *Messiah* because he is anointed. This anointing was *with the oil of gladness*, the joy that was set before him as the reward of his service and sufferings (12:2), the crown of glory and gladness he would wear forever after the sufferings of his death. This anointing of Christ was above the anointing of his companions. All God's other anointed ones had the Spirit only in a limited measure; Christ had the Spirit without limit (Jn 3:34).

2.4.2.2. The other is Ps 102:25–27 and is given in vv. 10–12, where the almightiness of the Lord Jesus Christ is declared as it appears both in creating the world and in changing it.

2.4.2.2.*1.* In creating the world (v. 10). His right, as God with the Father, was absolute, resulting from his creating power. He had this power before the beginning of the world, and he exerted it in giving a beginning and existence to the world. He founded not only the earth but also the heavens, including the inhabitants of the heavens, the angels themselves; he therefore must be infinitely superior to them.

2.4.2.2.*2.* In changing the world that he has made. This world is changeable; all created nature is. This world has passed through many changes and will pass through more (vv. 11–12). Not only human beings and animals and trees grow old, but also this world itself grows old, and is moving on quickly to its dissolution; it changes like a garment that has lost much of its beauty and strength. It bears the symptoms of a dying world. But then its dissolution will not be its complete destruction, but its change. Christ will roll up this world as a robe, not to be abused any longer. Sin has made a great change in the world for the worse, and Christ will make a great change in it for the better. But Christ himself is unchangeable. The Father testifies this of him: *Thou remainest; thy years shall not fail.* Christ is the same in himself and the same to his people in all the changes of time. Christ is unchangeable and immortal: his years will never end. Christ lives to take care of us while we live, and of our families when we are gone.

3. The superiority of Christ to the angels appears in the fact that God never said to the angels what he has said to Christ (vv. 13–14).

3.1. What has God said to Christ? He has said, *Sit thou at my right hand, till I make thy enemies thy footstool* (Ps 110:1). Christ Jesus has his enemies even among human beings. Let us not think it strange, then, if we have enemies. Christ never did anything to make people his enemies, but has done a great deal to make them all his friends and his Father's friends, and yet he still has his enemies. All the enemies of Christ will be made his footstool. God the Father has undertaken this, and though it is not done immediately, it will certainly be done. Christ will continue to rule and reign until this is done; he will not leave any of his great purposes unfinished. It is therefore good for his people to continue in their duty until he makes them more than conquerors over all their spiritual enemies (Ro 8:37).

3.2. What has God said to the angels? *They are ministering spirits, sent forth to minister for those who shall be the heirs of salvation.* Notice:

3.2.1. What the angels are as to their nature: they are spirits.

3.2.2. What the angels are as to their work: they are ministering spirits. They are ministers of divine Providence. The angels are sent out to minister to those who will be the heirs of salvation. Notice:

3.2.2.1. The description of the saints: they are *heirs of salvation*; at present they are underage, heirs, not inheritors. They are heirs because they are children of God.

3.2.2.2. The dignity and privilege of the saints: the angels are sent out to minister for them. Thank God for the ministry of angels.

CHAPTER 2

The writer: 1. Applies the teaching laid down about the superiority of the person of Christ (vv. 1–4). 2. Enlarges further on the superiority of Christ above the angels (vv. 5–9). 3. Proceeds to deal with the scandal of the cross (vv. 10–13). 4. Asserts the incarnation of Christ, that he took on himself the seed of Abraham. The writer gives the reason why Christ did this (vv. 14–18).

Verses 1–4

Here we have the application of the truths asserted and proved in the previous chapter.

1. By way of exhortation (v. 1). Everyone who lives in the age of the Gospel should give most careful attention to all Gospel revelations and directions. We must accept them in our hearts and affections, retain them in our memories, and finally regulate our words and actions by them.

2. By way of argument. He adds strong motives to back up this exhortation:

2.1. From the great loss we will sustain if we do not give such careful attention to the things we have heard: *We shall let them slip.* Our minds and memories are like a leaky vessel; only if we take care will they retain what is poured into them. Those who drift away from the Gospel truths meet with an inconceivable loss. All is lost if the Gospel is lost. If we do not listen well, we will not retain the word of God for long; inattentive hearers soon forget what they have heard.

2.2. From the fearful punishment we will incur if we do not fulfill this duty (vv. 2–3). Notice:

2.2.1. How the law is described: it was the *word spoken by angels, and declared to be steadfast.* It is like the promise, *yea and amen* (2Co 1:20); it is true and trustworthy. It will remain in force whether people obey it or not, *for every transgression and disobedience will receive a just recompense of reward.* If people play around with the law of God, the law will not play around with them. Punishments are as just, and are as fitting payments for sin, as rewards are for obedience.

2.2.2. How the Gospel is described. It is salvation, a great salvation, so great that no one can fully express, or even conceive, how great it is. It shows how we may be saved from such great sin and such great misery and how we may be restored to such great holiness and such great happiness.

2.2.3. How sinning against the Gospel is described: it is declared to be *a neglect of this great salvation;* it is a contempt shown to the saving grace of God in Christ, making light of it, not being concerned with it. Let us all make sure that we are not found among those evil, wretched sinners who neglect the grace of the Gospel.

2.2.4. How the misery of such sinners is described: it is declared to be unavoidable (v. 3): *How shall we escape?* Those who reject this salvation are already condemned; they are already under arrest and in the hands of justice. There is no escape from this condemned state except by accepting the great salvation revealed in the Gospel. As for those who neglect it, the wrath of God is on them, and

it remains on them (Jn 3:36). No door of mercy is left open for them; no further sacrifice for sin will be made.

2.3. From the person by whom the Gospel began to be spoken (v. 3), that is, the Lord Jesus Christ. Now surely it may be expected that all will fear this Lord, that they will give their attention to a Gospel that began to be spoken by One who spoke in a way no one had ever spoken before (Jn 7:46).

2.4. From the character of those who were witnesses to Christ and the Gospel (vv. 3–4).

2.4.1. The declaration of the Gospel was continued and confirmed by the evangelists and apostles, who were eyewitnesses and ear-witnesses of what Jesus Christ began both to do and to teach (Ac 1:1). These witnesses could have no worldly purpose to serve. They exposed themselves by their testimony to the loss of all that was dear to them in this life, and many of them sealed it with their blood.

2.4.2. *God himself bore witness* to those who were witnesses for Christ. He bore witness to them by giving them great inner peace and *by signs, and wonders, and divers miracles, and gifts of the Holy Spirit, according to his will.* It was the will of God that we have a firm footing for our faith and a strong foundation for our hope in receiving the Gospel. Just as at the giving of the Law there were signs and wonders, so God witnessed to the Gospel by more and greater miracles, as to a superior and more abiding age.

Verses 5–9

Having applied the teaching of Christ's superiority to the angels, the writer now returns to that pleasant subject.

1. Here the writer lays down a negative proposition that entails a positive one: that the state of the Gospel church, which is called here *the world to come, is not subjected to the angels.* This new world is committed to Christ and put in absolute submission only to him. His angels were too weak for such a responsibility.

2. We have a Scripture account of the blessed Jesus taken from Ps 8:4–6. These words are to be considered both as applicable to the human race in general and as applied here to the Lord Jesus Christ.

2.1. As applicable to the human race in general. Considered in this sense, they express affectionate gratitude to God for his kindness to humanity:

2.1.1. In remembering them, or being mindful of them. God always remembers us, so let us never forget him.

2.1.2. In coming to them. He comes to see us, to see how things are going with us, and by his coming our spirit is preserved.

2.1.3. In making human beings the head of all the creatures in this lower world.

2.1.4. In crowning humanity with glory and honor, the honor of having noble powers and senses.

2.1.5. In giving humanity the authority over the lower creatures.

2.2. As applied to the Lord Jesus Christ (vv. 8–9).

2.2.1. The original cause of all the kindness God shows to humanity is his grace.

2.2.2. The fruits of this free grace of God are:

2.2.2.1. That God was *mindful* of Christ for us.

2.2.2.2. That God came to Christ on our account.

2.2.2.3. That God made him a little lower than the angels in his being made human.

2.2.2.4. That God crowned the human nature of Christ with glory and honor in his being perfectly holy, so that by his sufferings he might make atonement, tasting death for everyone.

2.2.2.5. That as a reward for his humiliation in suffering death, Christ was advanced to the highest honor in heaven.

Verses 10–13

The writer here proceeds to deal with the scandal of the cross.

1. He shows how it was fitting to God that Christ suffer (v. 10).

1.1. God is described as the final end and primary cause of all things, and because he is such, it was fitting that he safeguard his own glory in all he did.

1.2. He is declared to have acted according to the glorious characterization of him here in the work of redemption. He acted according to his character:

1.2.1. In the choice of the purpose, which was to bring many sons and daughters to glory. We must be the children of God by both adoption and regeneration before we can be brought to the glory of heaven. Although the children of God are only a few in one place and at one time, nevertheless, when they all are brought together, it will be clear that they are many.

1.2.2. In the choice of the means, specifically, in finding such a person to be the *captain* (author) of our salvation and in making this author of our salvation perfect through sufferings. Christ perfected the work of our redemption by shedding his blood. He found his way to the crown by the cross, and so must his people.

2. He shows how much humanity would benefit from the cross and sufferings of Christ. By those sufferings they are brought into close union with Christ and into a precious relationship with him.

2.1. Into a close union (v. 11). Christ, who is the agent in this work of sanctification, and Christians, who are the subjects who receive this, are *all of one* (of the same family). They all come from one heavenly Father, and they all come from one earthly father, Adam. Christ and believers have the same human nature. They are of one spirit; the same mind is in believers that was in Christ (Php 2:5).

2.2. Into a precious relationship.

2.2.1. He declares what this relationship is: Christ is not ashamed to call them *brethren*. Christ and believers are brothers and sisters in what is heavenly as well as in what is earthly, since they share the same heavenly Father and all have earthly mothers. He will never be ashamed of anyone who is not ashamed of him (Ro 8:38) and who takes care not to be a shame and disgrace to him and to themselves.

2.2.2. He illustrates this from three texts of Scripture.

2.2.2.1. The first is Ps 22:22. Christ would have a church or *congregation* in the world, a community of willing believers who would freely follow him. These would be brothers and sisters not only of one another but also of Christ himself. He would declare his Father's name to them.

2.2.2.2. The second Scripture quoted is Ps 18:2. Like David, Christ passed through many troubles. But as Dr. Owen puts it [probably the Puritan theologian John Owen, 1616–83], Christ suffered and trusted as our head and president. Now, his brothers and sisters must suffer and trust too.

2.2.2.3. The third Scripture is Isa 8:18. Christ's children are given him by the Father. They are given to Christ at their conversion. Christ receives them, rejoices in them, takes them up to heaven, and there presents them to his Father.

Verses 14–18

Here the writer proceeds to assert the incarnation of Christ as Christ's taking on himself the nature not of angels, but of the descendants of Abraham, and he shows the reason and intention of his doing so.

1. The incarnation of Christ is asserted (v. 16): *Verily he took not upon him the nature of angels, but he took upon him the seed of Abraham.* He took our nature into union with his divine nature and became really and truly human. The word here translated *took upon* may be translated "took hold of": he did not take hold of angels, but he took hold of the seed of Abraham. The angels fell, and he let them go, and let them lie under their deserved punishment. The nature of angels could not be an atoning sacrifice for the sin of humanity. To restore the descendants of Abraham, therefore, he took on himself the human nature from one descended from Abraham's body, so that the same nature that had sinned might suffer. Now there is hope and help for the worst sinners in and through Christ.

2. The reasons and intentions of the incarnation of Christ are declared.

2.1. No higher or lower nature than the human nature that had sinned could suffer for human sin so as to satisfy God's justice and raise humanity up to a state of hope.

2.2. He became human so that he might die. God could not accept the legal sacrifices and offerings as an atoning sacrifice. Therefore, a body was prepared for Christ (10:5).

2.3. So that *through death he might destroy him that had the power of death* (v. 14). The Devil was the first sinner and the first tempter to sin, and sin was the prevailing cause of death. He draws people to sin, the ways of which are death. In these respects he may be said to have had the power of death. But now Christ has to such an extent destroyed the one who had the power of death that the latter can keep no one under the power of spiritual death; nor can he draw any into sin.

2.4. So that he might save his own people from the slavish fear of death to which they are often subject. Christ became human and died to save them from fears of the soul by telling them that death is not only a conquered enemy but even a reconciled friend. Death is not now in the hands of Satan, but in the hands of Christ.

2.5. Christ had to be made like his brothers and sisters so that he might be faithful to God and merciful to people.

2.5.1. He must be faithful in things concerning God, his justice, and his honor. He must make atonement for the sins of the people in order to fully reconcile them to God.

2.5.2. He must be merciful in things concerning his people, to their support and comfort (v. 18). Notice Christ's passion: *He suffered being tempted*; his temptations were not the least part of his sufferings. Notice also his compassion: *He is able to succour* (help) *those that are tempted.* He knows how to deal with sad, tempted souls, because he himself has been sick with the same disease—not the disease of sin, but that of temptation and trouble in his spirit. Even the best Christians are subject to many temptations. Temptations bring our souls into such distress and danger that they need help and support.

CHAPTER 3

The writer applies what he said about the priesthood of Christ (vv. 1–6). He then adds many significant words of advice and warnings (vv. 7–19).

Verses 1–6

Here we have the application of the teaching about the priesthood of our Lord Jesus Christ. Notice:

1. How fervently the writer urges Christians to have this high priest much in their thoughts. Consider:

1.1. The writer's honorable description of those to whom he writes: *Holy brethren, partakers of the heavenly calling.* He means not only "my brothers and sisters" but also the brothers and sisters of Christ, and in him brothers and sisters of all the saints. They are holy brothers and sisters, holy not only in profession and title but also in principle and practice, in heart and life. *Partakers of the heavenly calling*—sharing in the means of grace and the Spirit of grace, who came from heaven and by whom Christians are effectively called, by that calling which brings heaven down into human souls.

1.2. The titles he gives Christ, whom he wants them to consider:

1.2.1. As the apostle of our profession, the One who revealed the faith we profess to hold and the hope we profess to have.

1.2.2. As not only the apostle but also the high priest of our profession, on whose atonement and intercession we profess to depend for pardon of sin and acceptance with God.

1.2.3. As Christ, the Messiah, anointed and therefore qualified in every way.

1.2.4. As Jesus, our Savior, our healer.

2. The duty we owe the One who bears all these high and honorable titles. Look to Jesus, the author and finisher of your faith (12:2). Even those who are holy brothers and sisters, who share in the heavenly calling, need to encourage one another to think more of Christ than they do; the best people think too rarely and too disrespectfully about him.

3. Several arguments to support this duty of considering Christ, the apostle and high priest of our profession.

3.1. The first is taken from his faithfulness (v. 2). He was faithful to the One who appointed him, as Moses was in all his house. Moses was faithful in discharging his office to the Jewish church in the Old Testament, and so is Christ in the New; this was a proper argument to urge on the Jews.

3.2. Another is taken from the superiority of Christ's glory and excellence to that of Moses (vv. 3–6).

3.2.1. Christ is a builder of the house, Moses only a member in it. Christ, who is God, drew the ground plan of the church, provided the materials, and arranged them to receive the form; he has put together and united this house of his and has crowned it all with his own presence, which is the true glory of this house of God.

3.2.2. Christ was the master of this house as well as the maker (vv. 5–6), whereas Moses was only a faithful servant. As the eternal Son of God, Christ is the rightful owner and sovereign ruler of the church. Christ is therefore worthy of more glory than Moses, and of greater regard and consideration. The writer concludes this argument with an encouraging application of it to himself and all true believers: *Whose house we are.* He also characterizes those who constitute this house: "We are his house *if we hold fast the confidence, and the rejoicing of the hope, firmly to the end.*" There must not only be a setting out well in the ways of Christ but also a steady perseverance in them to the end.

Verses 7–19

Here the writer continues to exhort the Hebrews with serious words of advice and warnings; he recalls Ps 95:7–11. Notice:

1. What he advises them to do—to give prompt and present attention to the call of Christ. "Listen to his voice; apply it to yourselves and set about doing what he tells you to this very day, for tomorrow may be too late."

2. What he warns them against—hardening their hearts, turning a deaf ear to the calls and advice of Christ. The hardening of our hearts is the spring of all our other sins.

3. Whose example he warns them by—that of the Israelites, their ancestors, in the desert: *As in the provocation and day of temptation*; this refers to Ex 17:2–7. Notice:

3.1. Days of testing are often days of rebellion.

3.2. The sins of others should be a warning to us. We should remember our ancestors' sins and punishments to deter ourselves from following their bad examples. Notice concerning the sin of the Hebrews' ancestors:

3.2.1. The sin they were guilty of: they distrusted God, complained against Moses, and would not listen to the voice of God.

3.2.2. The aggravations of their sin: they sinned when they saw his works—works of wonder performed for their deliverance from Egypt and for their support and provision in the desert. They continued to sin in this way against God for forty years.

3.2.3. The source and spring of such terrible sins. They went astray in their hearts; these heart errors produced many other errors in their lips and lives. They did not know God's ways, even though he had walked before them. They did not notice either his providences or his ordinances rightly.

3.2.4. The just anger God expressed toward their sins, and yet also the great patience he exercised toward them (v. 10). All sin not only angers and affronts God; it also grieves him. If they by their sins continue to grieve the Spirit of God, their sins will oppress their own spirits, either by way of judgment or by way of mercy.

3.2.5. The irreversible condemnation passed on them eventually. God declared on oath in his anger that they would not enter into his rest. Sin long continued in will kindle God's anger. His wrath will make the condition of the impenitent restless; there is no resting under the wrath of God.

4. What use the writer makes of the fearful example of these ancestors (vv. 12–13).

4.1. He gives the Hebrews a proper warning; the word is, *Take heed*, or "See to it." "Look around you; be on your guard against enemies both within and without." The ruin of others should be a warning to us to watch out for the rock they stumbled over.

4.2. He enlarges on the matter of the warning: *Take heed, brethren, lest there be in any of you an evil heart of unbelief in departing from the living God.* A heart of unbelief is an evil heart, and an evil heart of unbelief is at the root of all our sinful departures from God; once we allow ourselves to distrust God, we may soon desert him.

4.3. He advises them as to what will be a remedy against this evil heart of unbelief (v. 13). Notice:

4.3.1. Since tomorrow does not belong to us, we must make the most of today.

4.3.2. If Christians do not encourage one another daily, they will be in danger of being hardened through the deceitfulness of sin. This shows us:

4.3.2.1. There is a great deal of deceitfulness in sin; it promises much but performs nothing.

4.3.2.2. The deceitfulness of sin leads to a hardening of the nature of the soul. Every act of sin confirms the habit.

4.4. He comforts those who not only set out well but also hold on well, and hold out to the end (v. 14). Notice here the saints' privilege: they share in Christ, in all that he is and in all that he has done or can do. But notice also the condition on which they hold that privilege: their perseverance. This is not to deny that they will persevere, being kept by the almighty power of God through faith to salvation; but to be urged to do so is one means by which Christ helps his people to persevere. Christians should maintain to the end the same spirit with which they set out on the ways of God. Very many who at the beginning show a great deal of courage and confidence do not hold to them firmly to the end.

4.5. The writer resumes what he quoted before (vv. 15–16), telling the Hebrews that although some who had heard the voice of God offended him, not all did. God will have a remnant who will be obedient to his voice.

4.6. The writer raises and gives proper answers to some questions concerning what he has mentioned before (vv. 17–19). God is angry only with those of his people who sin against him and continue in sin. Unbelief—with rebellion as its consequence—is the great condemning sin of the world. This sin shuts up the heart of God and the gate of heaven against them.

CHAPTER 4

Here the writer: 1. Proceeds to declare that our privileges through Christ under the Gospel surpass the privileges of the Jewish church under Moses (vv. 1–4). 2. Assigns the cause of the ancient Hebrews' failure to benefit from their religious privileges (v. 2). 3. Confirms the privileges of those who believe and the misery of those who continue in disobedience and unbelief (vv. 3–10). 4. Concludes with arguments and motives to faith and obedience (vv. 11–16).

Verses 1–10

Here:

1. The writer declares that our privileges through Christ under the Gospel are not only as great as, but even greater than, those enjoyed under the Mosaic Law. We have a *promise left to us of entering into his rest.* This promise of spiritual rest is a promise left to us by the Lord Jesus Christ in his last will and testament as a precious legacy (9:15–17). Our task is to make sure that we inherit it, and so have the prospect and pledge of perfect and eternal rest in heaven.

2. He demonstrates this truth that we have as great advantages as they (v. 2). The same Gospel substantially was preached in both Testaments. We have the Gospel as well as they, and in greater purity and clarity than they had.

3. He again assigns the reason why so few of the ancient Jews benefited from that era of the Gospel: it was their lack of faith. The word is preached to us so that we may benefit from it; it is *a price put into our hands to get wisdom* (Pr 17:16). In all ages there have been very many unprofitable hearers, and those who do not gain by hearing lose out greatly. What is at the root of all our unprofitableness is our unbelief. If the hearers do not have faith in their souls to combine with the word, they will be never any better for it. This faith must combine with every word and be exercised while we are actually listening.

4. On these considerations the writer bases his repeated and fervent warning and advice that those who enjoy the Gospel should maintain a holy fear and jealousy over themselves (v. 1), remembering that those who may obtain salvation by faith may instead fall short by unbelief. It is fearful even to *seem* to fall short of the Gospel salvation; it is much more fearful really to fall short. Let us maintain

a holy and religious fear of falling short. Presumption is the highway to ruin.

5. The writer confirms the happiness of all those who truly believe the Gospel.

5.1. He does this by positively asserting its truth, from his own experience and that of others: *We who have believed, do enter into rest* (v. 3).

5.2. He illustrates and confirms it:

5.2.1. From God's finishing his work of creation, and so entering his rest (vv. 3–4). He will also cause those who believe to finish their work and then enjoy their rest.

5.2.2. From God's continuing the observance of the Sabbath. There is a more spiritual Sabbath remaining for the people of God than the one into which Joshua led the Jews (vv. 6–9). Believers will enter their rest (v. 10).

6. The writer confirms the misery of those who refuse to believe; they will never enter this spiritual rest, either of grace here or of glory in the future. It remains only for the people of God; others, by their sin, abandon themselves to eternal restlessness.

Verses 11–16

In this second part of the chapter the writer concludes, first, with a serious repeated exhortation, and then with proper and powerful motives.

1. A serious exhortation (v. 11). The end offered is rest in Christ on earth and with Christ in heaven. The way to this end is *labour*, making every effort, diligently exerting ourselves; this is the only way to enter that rest; those who will not work now will not rest in the future. Let us therefore exert ourselves, and let us all call on one another to exert ourselves. Now is the time to make an effort; our rest remains for us.

2. Powerful motives to make the advice effective:

2.1. *Lest any man fall after the same unbelief.* To have seen so many fall before us will greatly emphasize our sin if we will take no notice of the warning.

2.2. The great help we may have from the word of God to strengthen our faith and stir our diligence, so that we may obtain this rest (v. 12). That word is *quick*; it is lively and active, in seizing hold of the conscience of sinners, in cutting them to the heart, and in encouraging them and binding up the wounds of the soul (Hos 6:1). It is *powerful*. It convinces powerfully, converts powerfully, and comforts powerfully. It is powerful enough to defeat Satan's kingdom and to set up the kingdom of Christ on its ruins. It is *sharper than any two-edged sword.* It will enter where no other sword can, and make a more critical dissection: it *pierces to the dividing asunder of* (penetrates even to dividing) *the soul and the spirit*, the soul and its habitual, prevalent character. It makes humble a soul that has long been proud. It turns a perverse spirit into one that is gentle, humble, and obedient. This sword divides between *the joints and the marrow*; it can make people willing to undergo the sharpest operation to put sin to death. It is *a discerner of the thoughts and intents of the heart*, turning sinners inside out and letting them see all that is in their heart.

2.3. The perfections of the Lord Jesus Christ.

2.3.1. His person, particularly his omniscience (v. 13). Nothing in all creation can be hidden from Christ. All of the actions and thoughts of our hearts and minds are open, uncovered, and laid bare to him. This omniscience of Christ should encourage us to persevere in faith and obedience.

2.3.2. His office, particularly the office of our high priest. Notice:

2.3.2.1. What kind of high priest Christ is (v. 14).

2.3.2.1.*1*. A great high priest. The greatness of our high priest is shown by his having *passed into the heavens*. Christ fulfilled one part of his priesthood on earth, by dying for us; the other he fulfills in heaven, by pleading the cause of his people. His greatness is shown also by his name, *Jesus*—a physician and a Savior, able to save completely all who come to God by him (7:25).

2.3.2.1.*2*. He is not only a great but also a gracious high priest, one who is merciful, compassionate, and sympathizing with his people (v. 15). He is able to sympathize with our weaknesses. He was tested by all the suffering and troubles that happen to us in our fallen state, and he did this not only to make atonement for us but also so that he would be able to sympathize with us.

2.3.2.1.*3*. He is a sinless high priest: *He was in all things tempted as we are, yet without sin.* We rarely meet with temptations without being disturbed by them in some way. They tend to set us back even if we do not yield. But our great high priest came away clear, not guilty, in his encounter with the Devil (Mt 4:1–11).

2.3.2.2. How we should behave toward him.

2.3.2.2.*1*. Let us hold firmly to the faith we profess (v. 14). Let us never deny him; let us never be ashamed of him before others. Christians must not only set out well; they must also persevere.

2.3.2.2.*2*. We should encourage ourselves to come boldly to the throne of grace (v. 16). Notice:

2.3.2.2.2.*1*. A throne of grace has been set up. God might have set up a tribunal of strict justice, but he has chosen to set up a throne of grace. Grace reigns there, and acts with sovereign freedom, power, and goodness.

2.3.2.2.2.*2*. It is our duty to come often to this throne of grace. It is good for us to be there (Mt 17:4).

2.3.2.2.2.*3*. Our business at the throne of grace should be to *obtain mercy and find grace to help in time of need*. Mercy and grace are the things we need: mercy to pardon all our sins, and grace to cleanse our souls.

2.3.2.2.2.*4*. Whenever we approach this throne of grace for mercy, we should come with a humble freedom and boldness; we should ask in faith, with no doubts. We are, it is true, to come to him with reverence and godly fear, but not with terror and dismay.

2.3.2.2.2.*5*. The office of Christ, since he is our high priest—and such a high priest—should be the basis of all our confidence whenever we come to the throne of grace.

CHAPTER 5

The writer continues his discussion of the priesthood of Christ. 1. He explains: 1.1. The nature of the priestly office in general (vv. 1–3). 1.2. The proper call there must be to this office (vv. 4–6). 1.3. The necessary qualifications for this work (vv. 7–9). 1.4. The distinctive order of the priesthood of Christ (vv. 6–7, 10). 2. He rebukes the Hebrews for not making the most of their knowledge, which might have made them capable of looking into the deeper parts of Scripture (vv. 11–14).

Verses 1–9

We have here an account of the nature of the priestly office in general. We are told:

1. What kind of person the high priest must be. He must be taken from among the people; he must be a man, one of us. This implies that God would not allow sinful people to come to him directly and alone, and that God was pleased to take from among human beings themselves one by whom the rest could approach God in hope.

2. For whom every high priest is selected: *for men in things pertaining to God* (to represent them in matters relating to God), for the glory of God and the good of people.

3. For what purpose every high priest was selected: *that he might offer both gifts and sacrifices for sin*, that is:

3.1. So that he might offer gifts or freewill offerings, which were brought to him to be offered as an acknowledgment that everything we have comes from God. All we bring to God must be free, not forced; it must be a gift.

3.2. So that he might offer sacrifices for sin, that is, the offerings that were appointed for atonement so that sin might be pardoned and sinners accepted. Christ is constituted a high priest for both these purposes. Our good deeds must be presented by Christ, and our evil deeds must be atoned for by his sacrifice of himself.

4. How this high priest must be qualified (v. 2).

4.1. He must be one who can have compassion on two sorts of persons:

4.1.1. On *the ignorant*. He must be one who can find it in his heart to pity them, one who is willing to instruct those who are slow in understanding.

4.1.2. *On those that are out of the way.* He must be one who has enough tenderness to lead them back from the byways of error, sin, and misery onto the right path. This requires great patience and compassion, even the compassion of a God.

4.2. He must also be *compassed with infirmity* (subject to weakness), and so be able to sympathize with us from within himself. This is how Christ was qualified.

5. How the high priest was to be called by God (v. 4). The office of the priesthood was a very great honor. It is only those who have been called by God who can expect his presence and blessing on them and their service; others may expect to receive blame instead of blessing.

6. How this is brought home and applied to Christ (v. 5). Although Christ reckoned it his glory to be made a high priest, he would not take that glory to himself. He did not take up this office without being called to it, and if he did not, surely others should be afraid to do so.

7. The writer prefers Christ to Aaron:

7.1. In the way in which he was called: God said to him, *Thou art my Son; this day have I begotten thee*. Now God never said this to Aaron. We have another expression God used in calling Christ in Ps 110:4 (v. 6). God the Father appointed Christ as priest of a higher order than that of Aaron. The priesthood of Aaron was to be only temporary; the priesthood of Christ was to be eternal.

7.2. In the holiness of his person. Other priests were to offer up sacrifices, as for the *sins of others, so for themselves* (v. 3). But Christ did not need to make an offering for his own sins.

8. Christ's fulfillment of this office and the consequences of that fulfillment (vv. 7–9).

8.1. The fulfillment of his office of the priesthood (v. 7). Notice:

8.1.1. He took to himself flesh; he became a mortal human being.

8.1.2. In the days of his flesh, Christ submitted to death; he was a tempted, bleeding, dying Jesus!

8.1.3. God the Father was able to save him from death, but what would have become of us if God had saved Christ from dying? It was in kindness to us that the Father would not allow that bitter cup to pass from him, for if he had, we would have had to drink its dregs.

8.1.4. Christ, in the days of his life on earth, offered up prayers and petitions to his Father. We have very many examples of Christ's praying. This verse refers to his prayer in his anguish (Mt 26:39; 27:46) and to that before his anguish (Jn 17).

8.1.5. The prayers and petitions that Christ offered were joined with loud cries and tears, so setting us an example. How many dry prayers, and how few wet ones, do we offer to God!

8.1.6. Christ *was heard in that he feared* (was heard because of his reverent submission). He was answered by immediate support in his anguish, by being taken well through death, and by being rescued from it by a glorious resurrection. He was carried through death, and there is no real rescue from death except to be carried well through it. We may be restored from sickness often, but we are never saved from death until we are carried well through it.

8.2. The consequences of this fulfillment of his office (vv. 8–9).

8.2.1. By these his sufferings *he learned obedience, though he was a Son* (v. 8). Let none, then, who are the children of God by adoption expect absolute freedom from suffering. Though he was never disobedient, he never performed such an act of obedience as when he became obedient to the point of death, even the death of the cross. We should learn by all our afflictions to humbly obey the will of God.

8.2.2. In doing so, he has become the author of eternal salvation to humanity. This salvation is actually given to none except those who obey Christ. We must listen to his word and obey him. He is exalted to be a ruler to rule us as well as to be a Savior to save us, and he will be a Savior to none except to those to whom he is a ruler. But to those who obey him, he will be the author—*aitios*, cause or source—of their salvation.

Verses 10–14

Here the writer returns to what he cited from Ps 110:4 in v. 6 concerning the distinctive order of the priesthood of Christ, that is, the order of Melchizedek. Here the writer tells the Hebrews:

1. He has many things that he could say to them about this mysterious person called Melchizedek, whose priesthood was eternal. There are great mysteries in the person and offices of the Redeemer; Christianity is the great mystery of godliness (1Ti 3:16).

2. The reason why he is not saying all those things about Christ, our Melchizedek, that he wants to say is, *You are dull of hearing.* Slow learners make the preaching of the Gospel difficult, and even many who have some faith are slow to learn.

3. This is not a mere natural weakness in them, but a sinful weakness (v. 12). Notice here:

3.1. What might have been expected of these Hebrews: they might have been so well instructed in the doctrine of the Gospel that they could teach others.

3.2. The sad disappointment of those expectations: *you have need that one should teach you again.* In God's word there are some elementary truths that are clear and necessary to learn. There are also deep and sublime mysteries.

4. The church has infants and adults (vv. 12–14), and the Gospel has milk and *strong meat* (solid food).

4.1. Those who are infants, *unskillful in the word of righteousness,* must be fed with milk. Christ does not despise his infants; he has provided suitable food for them.

4.2. There is strong food for those who are mature (v. 14). Notice:

4.2.1. The deeper mysteries of religion belong to those who are in a higher class in the school of Christ.

4.2.2. Every true Christian stands in need of nourishment.

4.2.3. The word of God is food and nourishment to the life of grace.

4.2.4. There are spiritual senses as well as natural ones. The soul has its senses, as well as the body; these are much depraved and lost by sin, but they are restored by grace.

4.2.5. It is by use and exercise that these senses are improved, made stronger and more alert to taste the sweetness of what is good and true and the bitterness of what is false and evil.

CHAPTER 6

1. The writer seeks to persuade the Hebrews to make better progress in religion (vv. 1–8). 2. He then expresses his good hopes for them and sets before them the great encouragement they have from God (vv. 9–20).

Verses 1–8

In order to grow, Christians must *leave the principles of the doctrine of Christ* (the elementary teachings of Christ) (v. 1). They must not lose them; they must not despise them; they must not forget them. But they must not rest in them. They must not be constantly laying the same foundation, doing the beginners' course every year—they must move on and build on it. Although some of the Hebrews were weak, others had gained more strength, and they must be provided for suitably. He hoped they would be growing and making progress and so be able to digest solid food.

1. The writer mentions several elementary teachings that must first be well laid and then be built on.

1.1. *Repentance from dead works.* "Make sure you do not return to your former way of sin, for then you would have to lay a foundation again. Repentance for and from dead works is an elementary teaching, which must not be laid again, even though we must renew our repentance daily.

1.2. *Faith towards* (in) *God.* Repentance from dead works and faith toward God are connected and always go together. They are inseparable twins: the one cannot live without the other.

1.3. *The doctrine of baptisms.* The ordinance of baptism is a foundation that is to be laid rightly and remembered daily, but not repeated.

1.4. *Laying on of hands,* on people passing out of the state they were initiated into by baptism, and into the confirmed state. Or this may refer to ordaining people to the ministerial office. This is to be done only once.

1.5. *The resurrection of the dead.*

1.6. *Eternal judgment.* These are the great elementary teachings, and the Hebrews must never depart from these.

2. The writer declares his readiness to help the Hebrews build themselves up on these foundations (v. 3). A resolution is right when it is made with sincerity in our hearts but also with humble dependence on God. Ministers should not only teach people what to do, but also go before them and along with them in fulfilling their own duty.

3. He shows that spiritual growth is the surest way to prevent apostasy from the faith.

3.1. He shows how far people may go in religion and still, after all, fall away and perish forever (vv. 4–5).

3.1.1. They may be *enlightened.* This refers to knowledge of ideas and common illumination, which people may have a great deal of and yet fall short of heaven.

3.1.2. They may *taste of the heavenly gift*, like people at a market, who taste what they will not buy, who only take a taste and leave it.

3.1.3. They may be *made partakers of the Holy Spirit*, of his extraordinary and miraculous gifts. In the apostolic age such gifts were sometimes given to those who had no true saving grace.

3.1.4. They may *taste of the good word of God*; they may hear the word with pleasure and talk well about it but never have it dwelling richly in them (Col 3:16).

3.1.5. They may have *tasted of the powers of the world to come*. Hypocrites may go to these lengths and in the end still commit apostasy.

3.2. The writer describes the fearful situation of those who fall away after having gone so far in the profession of religion. Notice:

3.2.1. The greatness of the sin of apostasy. It is *crucifying the Son of God afresh, and putting him to open shame* (subjecting him to public disgrace). By their apostasy such sinners declare that they approve of what the Jews did in crucifying Christ and that they would be glad to do the same thing all over again; they want him to be a public disgrace.

3.2.2. The great misery of apostates.

3.2.2.1. It is impossible to renew them to repentance. God can bring them back to repentance, but he seldom does, and with people themselves it is impossible (Mk 10:27).

3.2.2.2. Their misery is exemplified by a proper comparison (v. 8). To give the comparison greater impact, the difference is observed here between good land and bad land. A good land *drinketh in the rain that cometh often upon it* (v. 7). Believers not only taste of the word of God but also drink it in; this good land produces fruit and receives the blessing. Bad land, on the other hand, *bears briers and thorns* (thorns and thistles); it is not only barren of good fruit but also fruitful in what is bad, producing thorns and thistles. Such ground is then rejected; indeed, it is so far from receiving the blessing that it is in danger of being cursed.

3.2.2.3. In the end, it will be burned. This is the sad end to which apostasy leads, and so Christians should persevere and grow in grace (2Pe 3:18), for fear that if they do not go forward, they will go backward.

Verses 9–20

The writer proceeds to apply himself to their hopes.

1. He declares the good hope he has for them (v. 9). There are things that accompany salvation, things that are never separated from it. Ministers must sometimes speak by way of warning to those about whose salvation they have good hopes. Those who have good hopes for themselves should still seriously consider how fatal a disappointment it would be if they were to fall short. This is how they are to work out their salvation with fear and trembling (Php 2:12).

2. He offers them arguments and encouragements to induce them to persevere.

2.1. God has brought about a motive of holy love in them (v. 10). Good works and labor that come from love for God are commendable, and what is done to anyone in the name of God will not go unrewarded.

2.2. Those who expect a gracious reward for their labor of love must continue in it as long as they have ability and opportunity.

2.3. Those who persevere in diligently fulfilling their duty will reach full assurance of hope in the end. Full assurance is a higher degree *of* hope; assurance and hope

do not differ in nature, but only in degree. Full assurance may be obtained by great diligence and perseverance to the end.

3. He sets before them a warning and advice on how to obtain this full assurance of hope to the end. They should not be lazy. They must neither love their ease nor lose their opportunities. They should follow the good examples of those who have gone before (v. 12). We can learn from this that there are some who on the basis of assurance have gone on to inherit the promises. The way by which they came into the inheritance was that of faith and patience. We must follow them on the path of faith and patience.

4. The writer ends the chapter with an account of the assured truth of the promises of God (vv. 13–18).

4.1. They are all confirmed by the oath of God. The writer specifies the oath of God to Abraham (Ge 22:16–17), which remains in full force to all true believers. Those whom he has blessed truly he will continue to bless. *He swore by himself.* No greater security can be given or desired. Notice that this promise was made good to Abraham after he had patiently endured. There is always an interval, sometimes a long one, between the promise and the fulfillment. That interval is a testing time for believers. Those who patiently endure will certainly obtain the promised blessedness as surely as Abraham did (v. 16). The purpose and intention of an oath is to make the promise sure and to encourage those to whom it is made to wait patiently until the time of fulfillment comes (v. 16). To this end, people swear by someone greater, by the Lord himself. Now, if God would condescend to take an oath to his people, he will surely remember its nature and intention.

4.2. The promises of God are all based in his eternal purpose, and his purpose is unchangeable. God never needs to change his purposes.

4.3. The promises of God may safely be depended on. This shows us:

4.3.1. The people to whom God has given such full security of happiness. They are the heirs of the promise, and they are those who have fled for refuge to the hope set before them (12:2). Here is a refuge for all sinners who will have the heart to flee to it.

4.3.2. What God's intention toward them is: *that they might have strong consolation* (encouragement) (v. 18). God is concerned for the encouragement of believers, and his encouragements are strong enough to support his people in their strongest tests. The encouragements of this world are too weak, but the encouragements of the Lord are neither few nor small.

4.3.3. What use the people of God should make of their hope and comfort (v. 19). In this world, we are like a ship at sea that is in danger of being shipwrecked. Heaven is the harbor to which we sail. We need an anchor to keep us firm and secure. The Gospel hope is our firm and secure anchor. It is secure in its own nature—not a flattering hope made out of a spider's web, but a true work of God. And it is firm as to its object; it is an anchor that has taken good hold. It does not seek to be fixed to sand, but enters *within the veil*, to the inner sanctuary, and fixes there on Christ. He is the anchor-hold of the believer's hope.

CHAPTER 7

The writer here assures his readers that by receiving the Lord Jesus they will have a much better high priest, a priesthood of a higher order. We have: 1. A fuller account of Melchizedek (vv. 1–3). 2. The superiority of his priesthood to that of Aaron (vv. 4–10). 3. Application of all this to Christ, to show the superior excellence of his person, office, and covenant (vv. 11–28).

Verses 1–10

Here the writer sets before the Hebrews some of the solid food he spoke of before.

1. The first question to consider is, Who was this Melchizedek? All the account we have of him in the Old Testament is in Ge 14:18–20 and Ps 110:4. We are very much in the dark about him.

1.1. The opinions about him that are most worthy our consideration are these:

1.1.1. The rabbis, and most of the Jewish writers, think he was Shem the son of Noah.

1.1.2. Many Christian writers have thought him to be Jesus Christ himself.

1.1.3. The most widely held opinion is that he was a Canaanite king who reigned in Salem.

1.2. But let us seek to understand how Christ is represented here (vv. 1–3).

1.2.1. Melchizedek was a king, as is the Lord Jesus.

1.2.2. He was *king of righteousness*: his name means "the righteous king." Jesus Christ is a rightful and a righteous king.

1.2.3. He was king of Salem, that is, king of peace; first king of righteousness, and after that king of peace. So is our Lord Jesus.

1.2.4. He was *priest of the most high God*. So is the Lord Jesus.

1.2.5. The Scripture has chosen to set him before us as an extraordinary person, without giving us his genealogy, so that he might be a more suitable type of Christ, whose priesthood did not descend either to him from another human being or from him to another human being, but is personal and perpetual.

1.2.6. He *met Abraham returning from the slaughter of the kings, and blessed him*. He gave as a king and blessed as a priest. In the same way, our Lord Jesus meets his people, refreshes them, renews their strength, and blesses them.

1.2.7. *Abraham gave him a tenth part of all* (v. 2). In the same way, we are obliged to make every possible response of love and gratitude to the Lord Jesus for all the favors we receive from him.

1.2.8. This Melchizedek was *made like unto the Son of God, and abideth a priest continually*. He bore the image of God in his godliness and authority, and stands on record as an immortal high priest, as the ancient type of him who remains a priest forever.

2. Let us now consider how great this Melchizedek was, and how far his priesthood was superior to that of the order of Aaron (vv. 4–5). The greatness of this man and his priesthood appears from Abraham's giving the tenth of the plunder from him; it is well observed that *in Abraham*, Levi paid tithes to Melchizedek (v. 9), as to a greater and higher priest than himself. Melchizedek's greatness is also clear from his blessing of Abraham, *who had the promises* (vv. 6–7). Notice:

2.1. Abraham's great dignity and happiness was that he had the promises. Those who have deeds and certificates signed with God's own hand and seal are truly rich and happy.

2.2. Melchizedek's greater honor was his privilege of blessing Abraham; and it is an uncontested maxim *that the less is blessed of the greater* (v. 7).

Verses 11–28

Notice the necessity there was of raising up another priest, in the order of Melchizedek and not in the order of Aaron (vv. 11–12).

1. It is asserted that perfection could not come through the Levitical priesthood and the law.

2. Therefore, another priest must be raised up, in the order of Melchizedek, by whom perfection might come.

3. It is asserted that because the priesthood is changed, there must be a change in the law.

4. It is not only asserted but also proved that the priesthood and law are changed (vv. 13–14). A new dispensation has been established, by which true believers may be made perfect.

4.1. There is a change in the tribe from which the priesthood comes (v. 14). This change of the family shows a real change of the law of priesthood.

4.2. There is a change in the form and order for making the priests. The law by which Christ was constituted a priest, in the order of Melchizedek, was the power of an indestructible life. This gives preference infinitely to Christ and the Gospel. The high priest of our profession (3:1) holds his office by the innate power of endless life that he has in himself, a power to communicate eternal life to all those who trust in his sacrifice and intercession.

4.3. There is a change in the effectiveness of the priesthood (vv. 18–19). The Levitical priesthood brought nothing to perfection, but the priesthood of Christ brings along with it a better hope. It shows us the true foundation of all the hope we have toward God for pardon and salvation. By this hope we are encouraged to draw near to God, to live a life of fellowship with him.

4.4. There is a change in God's way of acting in this priesthood. Christ was made a priest with the oath of God (v. 21).

4.5. There is a change in the dispensation of that covenant. The Gospel dispensation is fuller, freer, and more effective than that of the law. As surety, Christ has united the divine and human natures together in his own person, thereby giving assurance of reconciliation; as surety, he has united God and humanity together in the commitment of the eternal covenant.

4.6. There is a remarkable change in the number of priests. In the order of Aaron, there were many priests, but in the order of Christ there is only one and the same. *They were not suffered* (allowed) *to continue by reason of death*, but our high priest continues forever, and his priesthood is *unchangeable*. There can be no vacancy in this priesthood, no hour or moment in which the people are without a priest to negotiate their spiritual concerns in heaven. This ever-living high priest is able to save completely all who come to God by him (v. 25).

4.7. There is a remarkable difference in the moral qualifications of the priests. He is *such a high priest as became us, holy, harmless, and undefiled* (vv. 26–28). Our situation, as sinners, needed a high priest to make atonement and intercession for us. No priest could be suitable or sufficient for our reconciliation to God except One who was perfectly righteous. The Lord Jesus was exactly such a high priest as we needed, for he has a personal holiness and is absolutely perfect.

4.7.1. He is holy. No sin dwells in him, even though it does in the best Christians.

4.7.2. He is harmless. He never did the least wrong to God or people.

4.7.3. He is undefiled. Although he took on himself the guilt of our sins, he never involved himself in their act or blame.

4.7.4. He is separate from sinners. Although he took on himself a true human nature, the miraculous way in which he was conceived set him apart from the rest of humanity.

4.7.5. He is *made higher than the heavens* (v. 26), for he is exalted at the right hand of God, to perfect the intention of his priesthood. The phrase may also be read as referring to the personal holiness of Christ, especially considering that in v. 27 the validity and prevailing of Christ's priesthood are placed in its impartiality and selflessness. He had no need to make an offering for himself: it was a selfless mediation; he mediated for the mercy for others that he did not need for himself.

CHAPTER 8

The writer continues to discuss the priesthood of Christ. 1. He sums up what he already said (vv. 1–2). 2. He sets before his readers the necessary aspects of the priestly office (vv. 3–5). 3. He fully illustrates the excellence of the priesthood of Christ (vv. 6–13).

Verses 1–5

Here:

1. We have a summary of what was said before about the excellence of Christ's priesthood (vv. 1–2). Notice:

1.1. What we have in Christ. We have such a high priest as no other people ever had; all others were simply types and shadows of this high priest.

1.2. Where he now resides: *He sits on the right hand of the throne of the Majesty on high.* This is the reward of his humiliation.

1.3. In what sanctuary he is a minister (v. 2). In the tabernacle set up by human beings, there was an outer part where stood the altar where they were to offer their sacrifices, which was a type of Christ dying, and there was an interior part within the curtain, the inner sanctuary, which was a type of Christ interceding for the people in heaven. Having finished the work of atonement in the true tabernacle of his own body, he is now a minister in the inner sanctuary, the Most Holy Place, the true tabernacle in heaven. He is in heaven not only enjoying great authority and dignity but also serving as the high priest of his church.

2. The writer sets before his readers what belongs to Christ's office as high priest (vv. 3–4): *Every high priest is ordained to offer gifts and sacrifices.* It then necessarily belongs to the priesthood of Christ to have something to offer, and he did: he had himself to offer as the great atoning sacrifice. Christ must now fulfill his priesthood in heaven; having finished the work of sacrificing here, he must go into heaven to present his righteousness and to make intercession there. *If Christ were on earth, he would not be a priest* (v. 4), that is, not according to the Levitical law. If he had still remained on earth, he could not have been a either a perfect priest or an imperfect one.

Verses 6–13

The writer illustrates and confirms the superior excellence of the priesthood of Christ. His ministry is more excellent to the extent that he is the Mediator of a better covenant. Notice:

1. What is here said about the old covenant.

1.1. That it was made with the ancestors of the Jewish nation at Mount Sinai (v. 9).

1.2. That this covenant was not found to be without defect (vv. 7–8). It was perfect in its kind, and suitable to fulfill its purpose, but very imperfect in comparison with the Gospel.

1.3. That it was not firm or steadfast, for the Jews dealt unfaithfully (v. 9). God will regard those who remain in his covenant, but will reject those who *cast away his yoke from them* (Ps 2:3).

1.4. That it is decayed, aging, and vanishing away (v. 13). It is antiquated, of no more use in Gospel times than candles are when the sun has risen.

2. What is here said about the New Testament dispensation.

2.1. That it is a better covenant (v. 6). It is without fault, well ordered in all things (2Sa 23:5). It requires nothing except what it promises grace to fulfill. All is put into good and safe hands.

2.2. That it is established on better promises. This covenant contains promises of help and acceptance in duty, promises of progress and perseverance in grace and holiness, of happiness and glory in heaven.

2.3. That it is a new covenant. It will always be a new covenant, in which all who truly take hold of it will always be found preserved by the power of God.

2.4. That the articles of this covenant are sealed between God and his people by baptism and the Lord's Supper.

2.4.1. God makes the terms known to his people (v. 10). He once wrote his laws to them; now he will write his laws in them. Their souls will be a charter and copy of the Law of God.

2.4.2. He declares that he will take them into a close and very honorable relationship with himself. He will be a God to them. Nothing more can be said in a thousand volumes than is included in these few words: *I will be a God to them.* They will be his people, to love, honor, observe, and obey him in all things. Those who have God as their God must do and will do these things: they are obligated to do them as their part of the contract, and they will do them because God will enable them to. It is God himself who first establishes the relationship, and then it is he who fills it with grace that is suitable and sufficient, helping them to fill it with love and duty.

2.4.3. He declares to them that they will know God more and more (v. 11). Under the New Testament, there will not be so much need of one neighbor teaching another the knowledge of God as there was under the Old. There will be such an abundance of public, qualified preachers of the Gospel, and so many will flock to them, with such a plentiful outpouring of the Spirit, that there will be a great growth and spreading of Christian knowledge in people of all kinds, of each sex, and of all ages. Oh that this promise would be fulfilled in our days!

2.4.4. God declares his terms concerning the pardon of their sins (v. 12). Notice the freeness of this pardon. It does not result from anything people deserve, but only from God's mercy. Notice the fullness of this pardon; it extends to all kinds of sin. And see the firmness of this pardon. It is so final and firm that God will no longer remember his people's sins; he will not revoke his pardon. It is the effect of mercy from eternity, and it is the pledge of mercy that will last to eternity. We have great reasons, therefore, to rejoice that the former age has now become old and has vanished.

CHAPTER 9

The Old Testament was never intended to be rested in, but to prepare for the institutions of the Gospel. Here the writer discusses: 1. The tabernacle, the place of worship (vv. 1–5). 2. The worship and services performed in the tabernacle (vv. 6–7). 3. The spiritual sense and main intention of all this (vv. 8–28).

Verses 1–7

Here:

1. The writer gives an account of the tabernacle, which was divided into two parts, called a first and a second tabernacle, an inner and an outer part. We are also told what was placed in each part of the tabernacle.

1.1. In the outer part were several things:

1.1.1. The *candlestick* (lampstand), no doubt not empty and unlit, but one whose lamps were always burning. There was a need for it, for there were no windows in the sanctuary. The light the Jews had was only candlelight in comparison to the fullness of light that Christ, the Sun of righteousness (Mal 4:2; Lk 1:78), would bring with him.

1.1.2. The table and the consecrated bread set on it. This table was set directly opposite the lampstand. We must not come in the dark to Christ's table, but by light from him must *discern the Lord's body* (1Co 11:29). He is the bread of life (Jn 6:35, 48); in our Father's house there is enough bread and to spare (Lk 15:17); we may have fresh supplies from Christ, especially every Lord's Day.

1.2. We have an account of what was in the inner part of the sanctuary, which was within the second curtain, and is called *the holiest of all*, the Most Holy Place. Now in this part were:

1.2.1. The *golden censer*, which was to hold the incense, or perhaps the word refers to the golden altar set up to burn the incense on.

1.2.2. The ark of the covenant, covered with pure gold (v. 4). Now here we are told both what was in this ark and what was over it.

1.2.2.1. What was in it:

1.2.2.1.*1. The golden pot that had* (the gold jar of) *manna.* This was a reminder of God's miraculously feeding his people in the desert, so that they might never forget such a special favor in the future.

1.2.2.1.*2. Aaron's rod* (staff) *that budded.* This was the rod of God with which Moses and Aaron performed such wonders, and this was a type of Christ, by whom God has performed wonders for his people.

1.2.2.1.*3. The tables of the covenant*, on which the moral law was written, showing the regard God has for the preservation of his holy law and the care we all should take that we keep the law of God.

1.2.2.2. What was over the ark (v. 5): the mercy seat, which was the covering of the ark. It was made of pure gold, as long and as broad as the ark in which the tablets of the law were laid. It was an eminent type of Christ and of his perfect righteousness, sufficient for the dimensions of the law of God and covering all our transgressions. There were also *the cherubim of glory* overshadowing the atonement cover, representing the holy angels of God.

2. The writer proceeds to speak about the duties and services performed in those places (v. 6).

2.1. The ordinary priests *went always into the first tabernacle* to fulfill the service of God. None except priests were to enter into the first part of the tabernacle. But the ordinary priests were to enter only into the first part of the tabernacle; it would have been fatally presumptuous of them to go into the Most Holy Place.

2.2. Into the second, the inner part, the high priest went alone (v. 7). Notice:

2.2.1. No one except the high priest must go into the Most Holy Place; in the same way, no one except Christ could enter into heaven by his own right and by his own merits.

2.2.2. The high priest must not enter without blood. None of us can enter either God's gracious presence here or his glorious presence in the future except by the blood of Jesus.

2.2.3. The high priest offered up blood *for himself* and his own errors first, and then *for the errors of the people* (v. 7). Christ is a more excellent person and high priest than any high priest under the law, for he has no errors of his own to offer for. When ministers intercede for others in the name of Christ, they must first apply the blood of Christ to themselves for their pardon.

2.2.4. When the high priest under the law had offered a sacrifice for himself, he must not stop there, but must also offer one for the errors of the people. Although our high priest need not make an offering for himself, he does not forget to make an offering for his people; he pleads the merit of his sufferings for the benefit of his people on earth.

Verses 8–14

In these verses the writer undertakes to pass on to us the mind and meaning of the Holy Spirit in all the ordinances of the tabernacle.

1. The way into the Most Holy Place was not yet revealed (v. 8). There was not that free access to God then that there is now; God has now opened a wider door.

2. The first tabernacle was a temporary figure, or type, only for that time (v. 9).

3. None of the gifts and sacrifices offered there could make those bringing the offerings perfect in regard to their conscience (v. 9). Those offerings could not save a conscience from a fear of the wrath of God. A person could be saved by them from physical punishments, but not from sin.

4. The Old Testament institutions were *imposed on* the Old Testament people of God *until the time of reformation* (v. 10). These were never intended to last forever, but only until the better things that were provided for the people were actually given them. We have far greater advantages under the Gospel than they had under the law, and we must be better because of these advantages, or we will be worse.

5. Since the writer is addressing those who believe that Jesus is the Christ, he very justly concludes that Christ is infinitely above all those who were high priests under the law (vv. 11–12).

5.1. *Christ is a high priest of good things to come*, by which may be understood:

5.1.1. All the good things that during the Old Testament were *things to come* and that now under the New have come.

5.1.2. All the good things still to come in a Gospel state, when the promises will be fulfilled; all these depend on Christ and his priesthood.

5.1.3. All the good things to come in the heavenly state, which will perfect both of the Testaments. The state of glory will perfect the state of grace.

5.2. Christ is a high priest *by a greater and more perfect tabernacle* (v. 11), his own body, or rather human nature, conceived by the Holy Spirit overshadowing the Blessed Virgin. This was a new structure, a new order of building, a new creation.

5.3. Christ, our high priest, has entered heaven, not as the high priest under the law entered the Most Holy

Place, with the blood of bulls and of goats, but by his own blood.

5.4. He did this not for one year only; no, our high priest entered heaven *once for all*, and has obtained eternal redemption.

5.5. The Holy Spirit showed what effect the blood of the Old Testament sacrifices had. The effectiveness of that blood extended to purifying the flesh (v. 13): it freed the outward person from ceremonial uncleanness. The writer justly infers from this the far greater effectiveness of the blood of Christ (v. 14).

5.5.1. What gave such effectiveness to the blood of Christ was his offering himself to God through the eternal Spirit without blemish, without any sinful stain.

5.5.2. The effectiveness of Christ's blood is very great. It is sufficient to cleanse the conscience from dead works; it reaches the very soul and conscience. It is also sufficient to enable us to serve the living God, because it sanctifies and renews the soul through the gracious influences of the Holy Spirit.

Verses 15 – 22

In these verses the writer considers the Gospel using the concept of a will or testament, the new or last will and testament of Christ, and shows the necessity and effectiveness of the blood of Christ for making this testament valid and effective.

1. The Gospel is here considered as a testament. A covenant is an agreement between two or more parties about things that are in their own power; this agreement takes effect at such time and in such a way as is declared in the covenant. A testament or will is a voluntary act and deed of a single person, granting legacies to such other persons as are described by the one who made the will, and which can take effect only on that person's death. Christ is the Mediator of a New Testament (v. 15), to redeem people from their transgressions committed against the law or first testament, and to qualify all those who are effectively called so that they can receive the promise of an eternal inheritance.

2. To make this New Testament effective, it was necessary for Christ to die. The writer proves this by two arguments:

2.1. One argument is from the general nature of every will or testament (v. 16). No estate, no right, is conveyed by will until the death of the one who has made the will has made it effective.

2.2. Another is from the particular way used by Moses to confirm the first testament, which was not done without blood (vv. 18 – 19). God accepted the shed blood of bulls and goats; by these means the covenant of grace was confirmed under the former dispensation. Moses spoke every command to all the people, according to the law (v. 19). Then he took the blood of calves and of goats, together with water, scarlet wool, and hyssop, and applied this blood by sprinkling it. With these Moses sprinkled:

2.2.1. The book of the law and covenant.

2.2.2. The people. The blood of Christ will be no advantage to us unless it is applied to us. Moses at the same time used these words: *This is the blood of the testament which God hath enjoined unto you.*

2.2.3. The tabernacle and all its vessels. All the sacrifices offered and all the services performed there were accepted only through the blood of Christ.

Verses 23 – 28

In this last part of the chapter, the writer goes on to tell us what the Holy Spirit has shown us by the legal purifications of the copies of the heavenly things, inferring from this the necessity of better sacrifices to consecrate the heavenly things themselves.

1. The copies of the heavenly things had to be purified (v. 23). The sanctuary of God on earth is a copy of heaven, and fellowship with God in his sanctuary is to his people a heaven on earth.

2. The heavenly things themselves had to be purified, and since the things themselves are better than the copies, they must be consecrated with better sacrifices. These heavenly things are the privileges of the Gospel state, begun in grace and perfected in glory. Now it is clear that the sacrifice of Christ is infinitely better than those of the law. This is clear:

2.1. From the places in which the sacrifices were offered. Those offered under the law were offered in the holy places made with human hands (v. 24). Christ's sacrifice, though offered on earth, was taken by him up to heaven, for he appears in the presence of God for us.

2.2. From the sacrifices themselves (v. 26). The sacrifices under the law were the lives and blood of other creatures, but the sacrifice of Christ was the offering of himself. He offered his own blood; it was therefore of infinite value.

2.3. From the frequent repetition of the legal sacrifices. This showed the imperfection of that law, but it is the perfection of Christ's sacrifice that, having been offered once, it was sufficient for all its purposes. *But now once in the end of the world hath he appeared, to put away sin by the sacrifice of himself.*

2.4. From the ineffectiveness of the legal sacrifices and the effectiveness of Christ's sacrifice. The legal sacrifices could not by themselves do away with sin, but Jesus Christ by one sacrifice has made an end of sin.

3. The writer illustrates the argument from the appointment of God concerning humanity (vv. 27 – 28). Notice:

3.1. The appointment of God concerning humanity. Human beings must *once die*. It is a matter of comfort to the godly that they will die well and die only once, but it is a matter of terror to evildoers, who die in their sins, that they cannot return to do that great work better. After death all will come to judgment. This is the unalterable decree of God concerning humanity.

3.2. The appointment of God concerning Christ. He must be *once offered* to take away the sins of many. He was not offered for any sin of his own; he was wounded for our transgressions (Isa 53:5). Christ will *appear a second time without sin*, for the salvation of those who look for him. At his first appearance, though he had no sin of his own, he still stood charged with sin, and he appeared in the form of sinful flesh, but his second appearance will be without any such charge on him. This will be for the salvation of all who look for him; he will then perfect their holiness, their happiness.

CHAPTER 10

The writer: 1. Plays down the Levitical priesthood and sacrifice (vv. 1 – 6). 2. Exalts the priesthood of Christ very highly (vv. 7 – 18). 3. Shows believers the honors of their state, urging them to fulfill their duties (vv. 19 – 39).

Verses 1 – 6

Here the writer sets himself to play down the Levitical dispensation:

1. The law was only a shadow of good things to come. Under the Old Testament, these good things were things to come, not clearly revealed. The Jews then had only the

shadow of the good things of Christ; under the Gospel we have the reality.

2. The law was *not the very image* of the good things to come, but was merely a shadow. The law was a very rough draft of the great design of divine grace, and people should therefore not be so fond of it.

3. Because the legal sacrifices were offered year by year, they could never make those who drew near to worship perfect (vv. 1–2). Now, on the other hand, under the Gospel, the atonement is complete; sinners, once pardoned, are always in a pardoned state, and only need to renew their repentance and faith to receive continued pardon.

4. Just as the legal sacrifices did not by themselves take away sin, so it was impossible for them to do so (v. 4). The atoning sacrifice must be made by one capable of consenting, and he must voluntarily substitute himself for the sinner. Christ did.

5. A time was fixed and foretold by the great God—and that time had now come—when these legal sacrifices would no longer be accepted by him or useful to people. This time of the repeal of the Levitical laws was foretold by David (Ps 40:6–7).

Verses 7–18

The writer commends Christ to them as the true high priest, the true atoning sacrifice. He illustrates this:

1. From the purpose and promise of God about Christ, which are frequently recorded in the scroll of the book of God (v. 7).

2. From what God had done in *preparing a body* for Christ—that is, a human nature—so that he might be qualified to be our Redeemer and Advocate (1Jn 2:1).

3. From the readiness and willingness that Christ showed in this work, when no other sacrifice would be accepted (vv. 7–9). Christ voluntarily came into it: *Lo, I come! I delight to do thy will, O God!* This should endear Christ and our Bibles to us, that in Christ we have the fulfilling of the Scriptures.

4. From Christ's mission and the intention with which he came, which was to do the will of God in two ways:

4.1. By taking away the first priesthood, which God had no pleasure in.

4.2. By establishing the second, his own priesthood, and the eternal Gospel. This is the great intention on which the heart of God was set from all eternity. And it is not more agreeable to the divine will than it is advantageous to human souls.

5. From the perfect effectiveness of the priesthood of Christ (v. 14): *By one offering he hath for ever perfected those that are sanctified.* This is what the Levitical priesthood could never do, and if we are in fact aiming at a perfect state, we must receive the Lord Jesus as the only high priest who can ever bring us to that state.

6. From the position to which our Lord Jesus is now exalted (vv. 12–13). Notice:

6.1. To what honor Christ is exalted—to the right hand of God, the position of authority, the giving hand, the receiving hand, the working hand—this is the highest position of honor.

6.2. How Christ came to this honor—as a reward due him for his sufferings. He will never abandon this honor or cease to employ it for his people's good.

6.3. How he enjoys this honor—with the greatest satisfaction and rest. This is his rest forever (Ps 132:14).

6.4. He has further expectations, which will not be disappointed. One would think that such a person as Christ could have no enemies except in hell, but it is certain that he has enemies on earth. Let not Christians, then, wonder that they have enemies. But Christ's enemies will be made his footstool (Ps 110:1); he is expecting this. When his enemies are subdued, his people's enemies will also be subdued.

7. From the witness the Holy Spirit has given in the Scriptures about him (v. 15): *Whereof the Holy Spirit is a witness.* The passage cited comes from Jer 31:33–34. God promises that he will pour out his Spirit on his people; he will put his laws in their hearts and write them on their minds (v. 16). Their sins and lawless acts he will remember no more (v. 17), which will alone show the sufficiency of Christ's atonement—that it need not be repeated (v. 18). This was much more than the Levitical priesthood and sacrifices could ever bring about.

Verses 19–39

We have now completed the doctrinal part of the letter, in which we have met with many things that have been dark and difficult to understand (2Pe 3:16), which we must attribute to the weakness and slowness of our own minds. The writer now proceeds to apply this great teaching so as to influence his readers' affections and direct their practice, setting before them the dignities and duties of the Gospel state.

1. Here the writer sets out the dignities of the Gospel state. The privileges are:

1.1. *Boldness to enter the holiest* (confidence to enter the Most Holy Place). Believers have access into God's very presence until they are prepared to enter his glorious presence in heaven.

1.2. A high priest over the house of God, namely, this blessed Jesus. God is willing to live with people on earth (1Ki 8:27; Rev 21:3) and to have them live with him in heaven, but fallen humanity cannot live with God without a high priest.

2. The writer tells us the way and means by which Christians enjoy such privileges: *by the blood of Jesus.* The writer describes this in detail (v. 20):

2.1. It is the only way.

2.2. It is a new way, and it is a way that will always be effective.

2.3. It is a living way. This way we may come to God and live. It is made by a living Savior who, though he was dead, is alive; it is a way that gives life and a living hope to those who enter it.

2.4. It is a way that Christ has consecrated for us through the curtain, that is, his body. Our way to heaven is by a crucified Savior; his death is the way of life to us.

3. Here are the duties binding on them on account of these privileges (vv. 22–23).

3.1. They must draw near to God, and do so rightly. They must draw near in conformity to God and in communion with him, continually seeking to draw nearer and nearer until they come to live in his presence, but they must make their approach to God rightly:

3.1.1. With a true heart. God searches hearts (Jer 17:10), and he requires truth in the inner being (Ps 51:6).

3.1.2. In full assurance of faith. We should set aside all sinful distrust. Without faith it is impossible to please God (11:6).

3.1.3. *Having our hearts sprinkled from an evil conscience.* Our hearts can be cleansed from guilt and whatever evils human consciences are subject to because of sin.

3.1.4. Having *our bodies washed with pure water*, that is, with the water of baptism or with the sanctifying power of the Holy Spirit, cleansing us from the defilement of the flesh as well as of the spirit.

3.2. The writer urges believers to hold firmly to the profession of their faith (v. 23). Here we have:

3.2.1. The duty itself to hold firmly to the profession of our faith. Our spiritual enemies will do what they can to wrest our faith and hope out of our hands, but we must hold firm.

3.2.2. The way in which we must do this—*without wavering*. Those who begin to waver are in danger of falling away.

3.2.3. The motive or reason enforcing this duty: *He is faithful that hath promised*. There is no fickleness with God, and there should be none with us. We must depend more on his promises to us than on our promises to him.

4. We have the means prescribed for advancing our faithfulness and perseverance (vv. 24–25).

4.1. We should *consider one another, to provoke to love and to good works*. Christians should have a tender consideration and concern for one another. A good example given to others is the best and most effective incentive to love and good works.

4.2. We should *not forsake the assembling of ourselves together* (v. 25). Even in those times there were some who did not bother to come to meetings for discussion and prayer and for worship and participation in the Gospel ordinances. The communion of saints is a great help and privilege, and a good means of advancing firmness and perseverance.

4.3. We should encourage one another, watch over one another, and care for ourselves and one another with a godly jealousy. This would be the best friendship.

4.4. We should notice the approaching of times of testing. Christians should observe the signs of the times, such as God has foretold. A day of testing is coming on us all, the day of our death, and we should observe all the signs of its approaching and make the most of them to be more watchful and diligent in pursuing our duty.

5. The writer proceeds to back up his exhortations (vv. 26–27):

5.1. From the description he gives of the sin of apostasy. It is *sinning wilfully after we have received the knowledge of the truth*. The sin mentioned here is a total and final apostasy, when people reject Christ, the only Savior, and renounce the Gospel, the only way of salvation, and the words of eternal life, after they have professed the Christian religion.

5.2. From the fearful condemnation of such apostates.

5.2.1. There *remains no more sacrifice for such sins* (v. 26), no other Christ to come to save such sinners. Those under the Gospel who will not accept Christ, so that they may be saved by him, have no other refuge left to them.

5.2.2. There remains for them only *a certain fearful looking-for of judgment* (v. 27). God gives some notorious sinners, while on earth, a fearful foreboding in their own consciences, with despair of ever being able to either endure or escape it.

5.3. From the methods of divine justice with those who despised Moses' Law. These, when convicted by two or three witnesses, were put to death (Dt 17:6–7); they died without mercy. From that, the writer infers the fearful condemnation that will fall on those who turn in defiance away from Christ. They have *trodden under foot the Son of God*. What punishment can be too great for such people? They have *counted the blood of the covenant, wherewith he was sanctified, an unholy thing*; that is, they have so accounted the blood of Christ, with which he

was consecrated, or with which the apostate was sanctified, that is, baptized. People who seemed before to have a high opinion of the blood of Christ may come to count it unholy. *Those have done despite unto the Spirit of grace.* They have grieved (Eph 4:30), resisted (Ac 7:51), indeed insulted him, which is the highest act of evil, and makes the case of sinners desperate—that they refuse to have the Gospel salvation applied to them.

5.4. From the description we have of the nature of God's vindictive justice (v. 30). This is taken from Ps 94:1: *Vengeance belongs unto me* (also Dt 32:35). The terrors of the Lord are known both by revelation and by reason. The other quotation is from Dt 32:36: *The Lord will judge his people*; he will search and test his visible church and will punish the sinners in Zion with the greatest severity. Now those who know the One who has said, *Vengeance belongeth to me, I will recompense*, must conclude, as the writer does (v. 31), *It is a fearful thing to fall into the hands of the living God.* Those who know the joy that comes from the favor of God can judge the power and dread of his vindictive wrath.

5.5. From a consideration of their past sufferings for Christ (v. 32). The writer wanted them to remember:

5.5.1. When they had suffered: *In former days, after* they were *illuminated*. A natural state is dark, and those who continue in that state are not disturbed by Satan and the world, but a state of grace is a state of light, and so the powers of darkness will oppose it violently.

5.5.2. What they suffered: they *endured a great fight of afflictions*. They were afflicted in themselves, in their own persons and in their names and reputations (v. 33), by many insults and persecution. Christians should value their own reputation because the reputation of religion is connected with it: this makes insults a great affliction. They were afflicted in the suffering of their brothers and sisters. The Christian spirit is a sympathizing spirit; not a selfish spirit, but a compassionate spirit. Christians are one body, the children of the God who is distressed in all the distress of his people (Isa 63:9). If one member of the body suffers, all the rest suffer with it (1Co 12:26). The writer takes particular notice of how the Hebrews have sympathized with him (v. 34).

5.5.3. How they had suffered. They endured their sufferings patiently, and not only so, but also joyfully received them from God, honored to be thought worthy to suffer reproach for the name of Christ (Ac 5:41).

5.5.4. What enabled them to endure such suffering. They *knew in themselves* that they had *in heaven a better and a more enduring substance* (better and lasting possessions) (v. 34). The happiness of the saints in heaven is substantial, whereas all things here are merely shadows. That happiness is a better substance than anything they can have or lose here. It will survive time and run parallel with eternity. In heaven, everything will be better. Christians should know this *in themselves*: they should obtain assurance of it in themselves, for the assured knowledge of this will help them endure any *fight of suffering* they may encounter in this world.

5.6. From the rich reward that awaits all true Christians (v. 35). He exhorts them not to throw away their confidence, but to hold firmly to the profession for which they have suffered so much. The reward of their holy confidence will be rich. It carries a present reward in it, in holy peace and joy, and it will bring a rich reward in the future. He shows them how necessary a grace the grace of patience is in our present state (v. 36). They must first do the will of God before they receive the promise, and after they have done the will of God, they need patience to wait for the time when the promise will be fulfilled. We must be God's waiting servants when we can no longer be his working servants. To help the Hebrews' patience, the writer assures them of the nearness of Christ's coming (v. 37). A time has been appointed, and beyond that time he will not delay (Hab 2:3).

5.7. From the knowledge that this will be their happiness, whereas apostasy is the reproach, and will be the ruin, of all who are guilty of it (vv. 38–39): *Now the just shall live by faith*. It is the honorable character of the just that in times of the greatest affliction they can live by faith. Faith puts life and energy into them. They can trust God, living on him. As their faith maintains their spiritual life now, it will be crowned with eternal life in future. Apostasy, on the other hand, is the mark of those in whom God takes no pleasure, and it is a cause of God's severe displeasure and anger. The writer concludes by declaring his good hope about himself and these Hebrews (v. 39). Notice that professors may go a long way and still in the end shrink back; this shrinking back from God is moving toward destruction: the further we depart from God, the nearer we go to ruin. Those who have been kept faithful in past times of great testing have reason to hope that the same grace will be sufficient to help them continue to live by faith. If we live by faith and die in faith, our souls will be safe forever.

CHAPTER 11

The writer now enlarges on the nature and fruits of faith. We have here: 1. The nature of faith (vv. 1–3). 2. The great examples we have in the Old Testament of those who lived by faith (vv. 4–38). 3. The advantages that we have in the Gospel for exercising this grace, which are greater than the advantages of those who lived in Old Testament times (vv. 39–40).

Verses 1–3

Here we have:

1. A definition of the grace of faith in two parts. It *is the substance of things hoped* (being sure of what we hope) *for*. Faith and hope go together, and the same things that are the object of our hope are the object of our faith. Faith is a firm conviction and expectation that God will fulfill all he has promised to us in Christ. When believers exercise faith, they *are filled with joy unspeakable and full of glory* (1Pe 1:8). It is also *the evidence of things not seen* (being certain of what we do not see). Faith demonstrates to the mind the reality of those things that cannot be discerned by the physical sight. It is intended to serve the believer in the place of sight, and to be to the soul all that the senses are to the body.

2. An account of the honor faith reflects on all those who have lived by exercising it (v. 2). *By it the elders* (ancients) *obtained a good report*. True faith is an old grace, and of all graces it has the best claim of being ancient: it is not a new invention, a modern idea. The most ancient and best people who ever were in the world were believers. They were an honor to their faith, and their faith was an honor to them. Their faith was an incentive for them to do *the things that were of good report*.

3. One of the first articles of faith, the assertion that the *worlds* (universe) were created *by the word of God*, not out of preexistent matter, but out of nothing (v. 3). The grace of faith looks back as well as forward; it looks not only forward to the end of the world but also back to the beginning of the world. Now what does faith lead us to understand concerning *the worlds*?

3.1. *That these worlds were* not eternal, nor did they produce themselves; rather, they were made by another being.

3.2. That the Maker of the worlds exists.

3.3. That God made the world by his word, that is, by his essential wisdom and eternal Son, and by his active will.

3.4. That the world, therefore, was formed out of nothing. We understand these things by faith.

Verses 4–31

The writer now proceeds to set before us some notable examples of faith in the Old Testament times, and these may be divided into two groups:

- Those whose names are mentioned, and the particular activities of whose faith are specified.
- Those whose names are barely mentioned, and the exploits of whose faith an account is given of in general.

1. The faith of Abel. God would not enroll our first parents in this blessed roll of honor, though the church of God has generally assumed that God gave them repentance and faith. The list begins, rather, with Abel, one who lived by faith and died for it, and is therefore a fit model for the Hebrews to imitate. Notice:

1.1. What Abel did by faith: *He offered up a more acceptable sacrifice than Cain*. After the Fall, God opened up a new way for people to return to him in religious worship, and this new way required sacrifices. Ever since, there has been a remarkable difference between worshipers. Cain was the elder brother, but Abel was preferred. It is not seniority of birth, but grace, that makes people truly honorable. Abel brought a sacrifice of atonement, *brought of the firstlings of the flock*. Cain brought only a sacrifice of acknowledgment, a mere thank offering, *the fruit of the ground*.

1.2. What Abel gained by his faith. Here we are told that he obtained some special advantages by his faith.

1.2.1. *He obtained witness that he was righteous* (was commended as righteous).

1.2.2. It was God who gave this testimony to the righteousness of his person, by showing his acceptance of his gifts.

1.2.3. *By it he, being dead, yet speaketh*. He had the honor to leave behind him an instructive speaking case, and what does it say to us? That fallen humanity may worship God with hope of acceptance, and that God will not allow the wrongs done to his people to remain unpunished, nor their sufferings unrewarded.

2. The faith of Enoch (v. 5).

2.1. What is here reported of him: *that he walked with God*; that *he was translated* (taken from this life), so *that he should not see death*, nor any part of him be found on earth; and that *before his translation* (he was taken), *he had this testimony, that he pleased God*. He bore the evidence of it in his own conscience, and the Spirit of God witnessed with his spirit (Ro 8:16).

2.2. What is here said about his faith (v. 6): that *without this faith it is impossible to please God*—without such a faith as helps us walk with God, an active faith—*and that he is a rewarder of those that diligently seek him*. Although by the Fall we have lost God, he is again to be found by us through Christ, and God has ordered means and ways in which he may be found. Those who want to find God must *seek him diligently*, and once they have found him, they will never repent of the effort they spent in seeking him.

3. The faith of Noah (v. 7).

3.1. The basis of Noah's faith: a warning he received from God of things not yet seen. God usually warns sinners before he strikes, and where his warnings are disrespected, the blow will fall more heavily.

3.2. The activities of Noah's faith, and the influence it had both on his mind and on his practice. He was *moved with fear*. Faith first influences our affections, then our actions, and faith works on those affections that are suitable to the matter that is revealed. If it is something good, faith stirs up love and desire; if something evil, faith stirs up fear. Noah's faith influenced his practice. His fear moved him to prepare an ark. His faith set him to work in earnest.

3.3. The rewards of Noah's faith.

3.3.1. He himself and his house were saved, when a whole world of sinners were perishing around them.

3.3.2. He judged and condemned the world: his holy fear condemned their self-confidence; his faith condemned their unbelief; his obedience condemned their contempt. Good examples will either convert sinners or condemn them. This is the best way the people of God can use to condemn evildoers — not by harsh and critical language, but by holy, exemplary conduct.

3.3.3. He *became an heir of the righteousness which is by faith*. He was given a true, justifying righteousness; he was *heir to it*.

4. The faith of Abraham, the friend of God (2Ch 20:7; Isa 41:8; Jas 2:23) and father of the faithful, in whom the Hebrews boasted. The writer enlarges more on the heroic achievements of Abraham's faith than on those of any of the other patriarchs; and in the middle of his account of the faith of Abraham he inserts the story of Sarah's faith.

4.1. The basis of Abraham's faith, the call and promise of God (v. 8).

4.1.1. This call was the call of God. This was an effective call, by which he was converted from the idolatry of his father's house (Ge 12:1). The grace of God is absolutely free, taking in some of the worst people. God must come to us before we come to him. The glorious work he does in the soul calls us to leave not only sin but also sinful company.

4.1.2. The promise of God was that the place Abraham was called to would later be given him as an inheritance. God calls his people to an inheritance. This inheritance is not immediately possessed by them, but the promise is sure.

4.2. The exercise of Abraham's faith. *He went out, not knowing whither he went.* He put himself into the hands of God, to send him wherever he pleased. All who are effectively called submit their own will and wisdom to the will and wisdom of God. Although they do not always know their way, they know their guide. *He sojourned in the land of promise as in a strange country.* This was an exercise of his faith. Abraham lived in Canaan only as a stranger. He lived in tents with Isaac and Jacob, heirs with him of the same promise. The promise is made to believers and their children (Ac 2:39), and it is pleasant to see parents and children staying together in this world as heirs of the heavenly inheritance.

4.3. The supports of Abraham's faith (v. 10): *He looked for a city*, a city with firm *foundations*, namely, the unchangeable purposes and almighty power of God. Notice the due regard that Abraham had for this heavenly city. He looked for it and waited for it, and in the meantime he lived by his faith, which was a support to him in all the tests of his wandering state.

5. The faith of Sarah.

5.1. The difficulties of her faith. Her unbelief prevailed for a time: she laughed at the promise as something impossible to fulfill. The thing promised, that she would be the mother of a child, was very improbable.

5.2. The activity of her faith. Her unbelief is forgiven and forgotten, but her faith was victorious and is recorded (v. 11).

5.3. The rewards of her faith. *She received strength to conceive seed* (v. 11). God can make the barren soul fruitful, as well as the barren womb. *She was delivered of a child*, a child of the promise. From Abraham and Sarah, by this son, sprang eminent descendants, numerous *as the stars of the sky* (v. 12).

6. The faith of the other patriarchs (v. 13).

6.1. The testing of their faith. When they died, they *had not received the promises*. One imperfection of the present state of the saints on earth is that their happiness lies more in promise than in actual enjoyment and possession.

6.2. The activities of their faith. Although they had not received the promises, nevertheless:

6.2.1. They saw them from a distance. Faith has a clear and strong eye and can see promised mercies a long way off.

6.2.2. They were convinced by them, that they were true and would be fulfilled.

6.2.3. They welcomed them. Faith has a long arm, and can take hold of blessings that are far away.

6.2.4. They *confessed that they were strangers and pilgrims on earth*. They were strangers as saints, whose home was heaven; they were pilgrims, traveling home.

6.2.5. Here they declared clearly that they were looking for another country (v. 14), heaven.

6.2.6. They gave full proof of their sincerity. They did not think about the country from which they came (v. 15). Those who are once savingly called out of a sinful life do not think about returning to it; they now know better things. These saints did not take the opportunity to return that offered itself. They remained faithful to God. We must show the truth of our faith and profession by remaining faithful to him. Their sincerity appeared not only in their not returning to their former country, but also in desiring a better country, that is, a heavenly one. All true believers desire this better country. The stronger the faith, the more fervent those desires will be.

6.2.7. They died believing in those promises (v. 13). That faith remained firm to the end.

6.3. The gracious reward of their faith (v. 16). God is called their God. He calls himself so; he allows them to call him so. God is not ashamed to be called *their God*: such is his love for them. Let them take care that they do not shame and disgrace their God, and so provoke him to be ashamed of them. As proof of his willingness to be called their God, God has prepared a city for them, a happiness suitable to the relationship he has taken them into. If God neither could nor would give his people anything better than this world offers, he would be ashamed to be called their God.

7. Now having given this account of the faith that others shared with Abraham, the writer returns to him, giving us an instance of the greatest test and act of faith that is recorded: his offering Isaac (v. 17). Notice:

7.1. The test of Abraham's faith. God had tested the faith of Abraham before, but this test was the greatest; he was commanded to offer his son Isaac. "*Take now thy son*, your only son by Sarah, Isaac, 'your laughter' (Ge 21:3–6), the child of your joy and delight; take him away to the land of Moriah; not only leave him there, but offer him as a burnt offering." Here are some things that very much added to the greatness of this test:

7.1.1. He was commanded to do it after he had received the promises (v. 18). In being called to offer his Isaac, he seemed to be called to cut off his own family, to cancel the promises of God.

7.1.2. This Isaac was his only-born son by his wife Sarah, the only one he was to have by her, and the only one who was to be the child and heir of the promise. Besides his most tender affection for his son, all his expectations were caught up in him, and if he perished, all those expectations must perish with him. To have this son offered as a sacrifice—and by his own hand, too—was a trial that would have overcome the firmest and the strongest mind.

7.2. The activity of Abraham's faith in such a great test. He obeyed. He went as far as to the critical moment, and would have gone through with it if God had not prevented him.

7.3. The supports of his faith (v. 19). He knew that God was able to raise Isaac from the dead, and he believed that God would do so. God is able to raise the dead, both dead bodies and dead souls.

7.4. The reward of his faith in this great test (v. 19). He received his son. He had left him to God, and God gave him back again. He received him from the dead, for he had given him up as dead.

8. The faith of Isaac (v. 20).

8.1. The activities of his faith: he *blessed Jacob and Esau concerning things to come*. Both Jacob and Esau were blessed as Isaac's children, though Jacob had precedence and the principal blessing. If one member of a family has their inheritance in this world, and another in the better world, it is God who makes the difference, for even the comforts of this life are more and better than any deserve.

8.2. The difficulties Isaac's faith struggled with. He seemed to have forgotten how God had determined the matter at the birth of his sons (Ge 25:23). When he came to declare the blessing on Esau, *he trembled very exceedingly* (Ge 27:33), and he accused Jacob of deceitfully taking away Esau's blessing. But despite this, Isaac's faith recovered, and he confirmed the blessing: *I have blessed him, yea, and he shall be blessed*. Now because the faith of Isaac prevailed over his unbelief, it has pleased the God of Isaac to overlook the weakness of his faith and to commend its sincerity.

9. The faith of Jacob (v. 21). There were a great many examples of the faith of Jacob; his life was a life of faith. But here notice:

9.1. The activities of his faith.

9.1.1. *He blessed both the sons of Joseph*, Ephraim and Manasseh. He made them both leaders of tribes, as if they had been his own direct sons. As Isaac did before, so now Jacob prefers the younger, Ephraim, although Joseph had placed them in such a way that it would be natural for his father to lay his right hand on Manasseh, the elder.

9.1.2. *He worshiped, leaning on his staff*; he praised God for what he had done for him and for the prospect he had of approaching blessedness. He was not able to support himself so far as to sit up without a staff, but he would not make this an excuse for neglecting to worship God; he would do it as well as he could with his body, as well as with his spirit.

9.2. When Jacob showed his faith: when he was dying. He lived by faith, and he died by faith and in faith.

10. The faith of Joseph (v. 22).

10.1. What he did by his faith. By faith he mentioned the departure of the children of Israel, that the time would come when they would be rescued from Egypt. Though he would not live to see their rescue, he could still die believing in it. By faith he gave instructions about his bones, that his people should preserve them unburied in Egypt. Although he had lived and died in Egypt, he did not live and die an Egyptian, but an Israelite. He preferred a significant burial in Canaan to a magnificent one in Egypt.

10.2. When the faith of Joseph acted in this way: when he was dying. God often gives his people living comforts in their dying moments.

11. The faith of the parents of Moses.

11.1. The activity of their faith: they hid their son for three months. Moses was persecuted from an early age and had to be concealed; here he was a type of Christ, who was persecuted almost as soon as he was born, and his parents had to flee with him to Egypt to preserve his life.

11.2. Their reasons for acting in this way. No doubt natural affection must have moved them, but there was something more. They *saw he was a goodly* (fine) *child*. There appeared to be something unusual in him; the beauty of the Lord rested on him (Ps 27:4). Sometimes, not always, the face is a sign of the mind.

11.3. The victory of their faith over their fear. They were not afraid of the king's commandment. They believed that God would preserve his people, and that the time was coming when it would be worthwhile for an Israelite to live. Some must risk their own lives to preserve their children, and these parents were determined to do so. Faith is a great preservation against the sinful, slavish fear of human beings.

12. The faith of Moses himself (vv. 24–25).

12.1. The faith he showed in conquering the world.

12.1.1. He *refused to be called the son of Pharaoh's daughter*, whose dear foundling he was. Notice how glorious the triumph of his faith was. He *refused to be called the son of Pharaoh's daughter* in case he should undervalue the truer honor of being a son of Abraham, the father of the faithful, and in case it would look like renouncing his religion as well as his relationship with Israel. No doubt he would have had to do both of these if he had accepted this honor.

12.1.2. He was willing to take his lot with the people of God here, even though it meant mistreatment and suffering, so that he might share his portion with them in the future. Here he acted reasonably as well as religiously. The pleasures of sin last for only a short time; they must end in speedy repentance or in speedy ruin. The pleasures of this world, especially those of a court, are too often the pleasures of sin, and a true believer will despise them. Suffering is to be chosen rather than sin, because there is more evil in the smallest sin than there can be in the greatest suffering.

12.1.3. Notice how Moses weighed matters up: in one scale he put the worst of religion, the *reproaches of Christ*; in the other scale the best of the world, *the treasures of Egypt*. The worst of religion weighed heavier than the best of the world. The disgrace faced by the church of God is disgrace suffered for the sake of Christ. God's people are and always have been a disgraced people. Christ considers himself disgraced in their disgrace, and while he shares in their disgrace, they become rich. Faith discerns this, and acts accordingly.

12.2. The time when Moses by his faith gained this victory: *when he had come to years* (v. 24), not only to years of discretion but to years of experience, to the age of forty years. He made this choice when he had grown mature in judgment and wisdom, able to know what he did and why he did it. It was not the act of a child, but proceeded from mature deliberation. It is excellent for people to despise the world when they are most capable of relishing and enjoying it.

12.3. What supported and strengthened the faith of Moses: *He had respect unto the recompense of* (he was looking ahead to his) *reward.* Believers can and should look ahead to this reward. It will prove a landmark to direct their course, a magnet to draw their hearts, and a drink to refresh them.

12.4. The faith Moses showed by leaving Egypt (v. 27).

12.4.1. The result of his faith: *he forsook Egypt.* Moses left Egypt twice: once as a supposed criminal, when the king's wrath was enraged against him for killing the Egyptian, and then as a commander, after God had employed him to humble Pharaoh and make him willing to let Israel go.

12.4.2. The victory of his faith. It lifted him above the fear of the king's wrath. Those who have left Egypt must expect human wrath, but they need not fear it.

12.4.3. The principle on which his faith acted in these his movements: *he endured, as seeing him that was invisible.* By faith we can see this invisible God. We may be fully assured of his existence and of his gracious and powerful presence with us. Such a sight of God will enable believers to persevere to the end.

12.5. The faith Moses showed by keeping *the passover and sprinkling of blood* (v. 28). The Passover was one of the most sacred institutions of the Old Testament, and a very significant type of Christ. To entitle the Israelites to this distinguishing favor, a lamb had to be killed, and its blood must be sprinkled with a bunch of hyssop on the top of the doorframe and on both its sides. Christ is that Lamb: he is our Passover (1Co 5:7), who was sacrificed for us. His blood must be sprinkled; it must be applied to those who have the saving benefit of it. It is not because of our inherent righteousness that we are saved from the wrath of God, but because of the blood of Christ and his imputed righteousness. Wherever this blood is applied, the soul receives Christ by faith and lives on him. All our spiritual privileges on earth should stir us to set out early and go forward on our way to heaven.

13. The faith of the Israelites passing through the Red Sea under the leadership of Moses (v. 29).

13.1. Their safe passage through the Red Sea when there was no other way to escape from Pharaoh and his forces. Israel's danger was very great, and their deliverance was very glorious. The grace of faith will help us through all the dangers we meet with on our way to heaven.

13.2. The destruction of the Egyptians. Their rashness was great, and their ruin was massive. When God judges, he will overcome (Ro 3:4; Ps 51:4), and it is clear that the destruction of sinners is brought on by themselves.

14. The faith of the Israelites under Joshua before the walls of Jericho. We have the account in Jos 6:5–21. The means prescribed by God to bring down the walls of Jericho was a great test of their faith, a means that seemed unlikely to fulfill such a purpose. But this was the way God commanded, and he loves to do great things by small and lowly means so that his own power may be made known. See the powerful success of the prescribed means: the walls of Jericho fell before them. God can in his own time cause all the powerful opposition that is raised against his interests to fall down, and the grace of faith is *mighty through God to the pulling down of strongholds*

(2Co 10:4). When he has some great thing to do for his people, he raises up great and strong faith in them.

15. The faith of Rahab (v. 31). Notice:

15.1. Who this Rahab was. She was a Canaanite, a *stranger to the commonwealth of Israel* (Eph 2:12), who had only a little help for her faith, but she was a believer. She was a prostitute, living in sin. Christ has saved the worst sinners. *Where sin has abounded, grace has superabounded* (Ro 5:20).

15.2. What she did by her faith: *She received the spies in peace.* She not only made them welcome but also concealed them from their enemies, and she made a noble confession of her faith.

15.2.1. True faith will show itself in good works, especially toward the people of God.

15.2.2. Faith will risk everything in the cause of God and his people.

15.2.3. True believers want not only to be in covenant with God but also to be in fellowship with the people of God.

15.3. What she gained by her faith. She escaped perishing with those who did not believe. The city was completely destroyed, men and women, young and old. Her preservation was significant. One who distinguishes herself by having faith when most people are unbelievers will be rewarded with distinctive favors in times of general disaster. Joshua gave a strict order that she be spared, and none except her and her relatives.

Verses 32–40

The writer now concludes his narrative with a summary account of another group of believers. He introduces this part of the narrative with elegant pleading: *What shall I say more? Time would fail me.* We should be pleased to think how great the number of believers was under the Old Testament, and how strong their faith was. We should mourn the fact that now, when the rule of faith is clearer and more perfect, the number of believers is so small and their faith so weak.

1. The writer mentions:

1.1. Gideon. He was an eminent instrument raised up by God to deliver his people from the oppression of the Midianites. God confused the whole army of the Midianites.

1.2. Barak, who obtained a great victory by his faith over all the forces of Sisera.

1.3. Samson. If Samson had not had strong faith as well as a strong arm, he would never have performed such exploits. True faith is acknowledged and accepted even when combined with many failings. The faith of believers endures to the end, and when they die, it gives them victory over death and all their mortal enemies; they gain their greatest conquest by dying.

1.4. Jephthah. As various and new enemies rise up against the people of God, various and new deliverers are raised up for them. The grace of God often finds out and focuses on the most undeserving and ill-deserving people, to do great things for them and by them. Jephthah was the son of a prostitute. Faith will not only call on people to make their vows to God; it will also make them pay their vows after the mercy has been received, even if they have vowed to their own great grief (Ps 15:4), as in the case of Jephthah and his daughter.

1.5. David, that great man after God's own heart (1Sa 13:14). Few ever met with greater tests, and few ever revealed a more living faith. The same faith made him a very successful and victorious ruler, and after a long life of good and honor—though not without some foul stains of sin—he died in faith. He left behind him, in the book of Psalms, such excellent memoirs of the tests and acts of faith as will always be held in great respect and used often.

1.6. Samuel, raised up to be a most eminent prophet of the Lord to Israel, as well as a ruler over them. God revealed himself to Samuel when he was only a child, and continued to do so until his death.

1.7. To Samuel the writer adds, *and of the prophets*, who were employed by God sometimes to declare judgment, sometimes to promise mercy, always to rebuke sin; sometimes to foretell remarkable events, and chiefly to announce the coming of the Messiah. A true faith was necessary to rightly fulfill such an office.

2. The writer proceeds to tell what things were done by their faith.

2.1. *By faith they subdued kingdoms* (v. 33). The influence and power of kings and kingdoms are often set up in opposition to God and his people, but God can easily subdue all such powers.

2.2. They *wrought righteousness* (administered justice). They believed God, and it was credited to them as righteousness (Ge 15:6). It is a greater happiness to administer justice than to perform miracles.

2.3. They *obtained promises* (gained what was promised). It is by faith that we are prepared to wait for the promises and to receive them in due time.

2.4. They *stopped the mouths of lions*. Whenever it will be for God's glory, faith engages God's power for his people to overcome wild animals and cruel human beings.

2.5. They *quenched the violence of the fire* (quenched the fury of the flames) (v. 34). The three children, or rather mighty champions, in the fiery furnace did this (Da 3:17–27). Never was the grace of faith more severely tested, never more nobly exerted, nor ever more gloriously rewarded, than theirs was.

2.6. They *escaped the edge of the sword*. The swords of human beings are held in the hand of God. Faith takes hold of the hand of God that has hold of human swords, and God has often allowed himself to be prevailed on by the faith of his people.

2.7. *Out of weakness they were made strong* (their weakness was turned to strength). It is the same grace of faith that helps people to recover from spiritual weakness and renew their strength.

2.8. They *grew valiant in fight* (became powerful in battle). True faith gives truest courage and patience, for it discerns the power of God and therefore also the weakness of all his enemies. These believers were not only powerful but also effective. As a reward and encouragement of their faith, God *put to flight the armies of the aliens* (routed foreign armies); God made them flee and fall before his faithful servants.

2.9. *Women received their dead raised to life again* (v. 35). Many women have been strong in faith. God has sometimes yielded so far to the tender affections of sorrowful women as to restore their dead children to life.

3. The writer tells us what these believers endured by faith. They *were tortured, not accepting deliverance* (v. 35). What inspired them in their suffering was their hope of *obtaining a better resurrection*. They endured *trials of cruel mockings* (jeers) *and scourgings, and bonds and imprisonment* (v. 36). They were persecuted in their reputation by jeers, which are cruel to innocent minds; persecuted in their bodies by flogging, the punishment of slaves; persecuted in their liberty by *bonds and imprisonment*. They were put to death in the cruelest manner. Their

enemies clothed death in all the array of cruelty and terror, but they boldly met it and endured it. Those who escaped death were so mistreated that death may have seemed better than such a life. Their enemies spared them only to prolong their misery (vv. 37–38). They endured such suffering for their faith, and they endured these through the power of the grace of faith; and which will we be most astonished at, the evil of human nature, or the excellence of divine grace, which is able to support the faithful in such cruelties and to carry them safely through all?

4. He tells us what they obtained by their faith.

4.1. They obtained a most honorable commendation from God, namely, that *the world was not worthy* of such people; the world did not deserve such blessings. The wicked say that the righteous are not worthy to live in the world, and God declares that the world is unworthy of them.

4.2. They *obtained a good report* (were all commended) (v. 39) from all good people, and indeed from the truth itself.

4.3. They obtained a share in the promises, even though they did not receive the great things that were promised. They had shadows, but had not seen the reality; and yet, under this imperfect dispensation, they revealed this precious faith. The writer insists on this to render their faith more illustrious. He tells the Hebrews that God has *provided some better things for* them (v. 40), and that they can therefore be assured that God expects at least as good things from them. Their faith will be much more perfect than the faith of the Old Testament saints, because their state and dispensation are more perfect than the earlier state and dispensation.

CHAPTER 12

Here the writer presses his argument home: 1. From a greater example than he had mentioned till now, Christ himself (vv. 1–3). 2. From the gentle nature of the suffering the Hebrews have endured in their Christian lives (vv. 4–17). 3. From the conformity between the state of the Gospel church in the world and the triumphant church in heaven (vv. 18–29).

Verses 1–3

Notice here the great duty the writer urges on the Hebrews. The duty consists of two parts.

1. One that prepares: *Lay aside every weight, and the sin.* Every weight (everything that hinders) refers to all excessive affection and concern for the body and the present life and world. *The sin that doth so easily beset us* is the sin that has the greatest advantage over us because of the circumstances we are in, our constitution, and our company.

2. One that perfects: *Run with patience the race that is set before us.*

2.1. Christians have a race to run.

2.2. This race is set before them; it is marked out for them by both the word of God and the examples of faithful servants of God, the *cloud of witnesses* by whom they are surrounded.

2.3. This race must be run with patience and perseverance. Faith and patience are the graces that overcome, and they must therefore always be cultivated.

2.4. Christians have a greater example to encourage them than any who have been mentioned before, the Lord Jesus Christ (v. 2). Notice:

2.4.1. What our Lord Jesus is to his people: he is *the author and finisher of* their *faith*. He is not only the object but also the author, the great leader and example of our faith. And he is *the finisher of our faith*, completing the work of grace and the work of faith with power in the souls of his people. He is the judge and rewarder of their faith.

2.4.2. What trials Christ met with in his race and course. He *endured the contradiction* (opposition) *of sinners against himself* (v. 3). He endured all their evil ways with great patience. He *endured the* cross—all the sufferings he met with in the world, for he took up his cross early in life and was finally nailed to it. He endured all this with invincible patience and resolution. And he *despised the shame*. All the insults that were hurled at him, both in his life and at his death, he despised.

2.4.3. What supported the human soul of Christ: *the joy that was set before him*. He rejoiced to see that by his suffering he would satisfy the wronged justice of God, that he would make peace between God and humanity, that he would open a way of salvation.

2.4.4. The reward of his suffering: he *has sat down at the right hand of the throne of God. He ever lives to make intercession for* his people (7:25).

2.4.5. What is our duty with respect to this Jesus: we must look to him; we must set him continually before us as our example. We must consider him, meditating much on him. We will find that just as his sufferings far exceeded ours, so his patience far excels ours.

2.4.6. The advantage we will reap if we do this: it will be a way of preventing us from becoming weary and losing heart (v. 3). There is a tendency even in the best people to become weary and lose heart under their trials and afflictions. The best way to prevent this is to look to Jesus. Faith and meditation will draw in fresh resources of his strength, comfort, and courage.

Verses 4–17

Here the writer presses on to his readers a word of exhortation to be patient and persevering. He argues from the gentle measure and gracious nature of the suffering that the faithful Hebrews have endured in their Christian lives.

1. He argues from the gentle and moderate measure of their suffering (v. 4). He recognizes that they have suffered much; they have been *striving* against sin to the point of agony. Yet he reminds them that they might have suffered more, for they have not yet resisted to the point of shedding their blood. Our Lord Jesus does not call his people to the hardest trials at first, but wisely trains them up (Pr 22:6) by lesser sufferings to be prepared for greater ones. Notice the gentleness of Christ in adjusting the trials of Christians to their strength. They should not exalt their afflictions, but take notice of the mercy that is with them.

2. He argues from the nature of those sufferings. They are still forms of divine correction; their heavenly Father has his hand in all of them. He has given them due notice of this, and they should not forget it (v. 5).

2.1. Those afflictions that may truly be persecution as far as other people are concerned are fatherly rebukes and chastisements as far as God is concerned in them. People persecute the believers because they are religious; God rebukes them because they are not more so.

2.2. God has directed his people as to how they should behave themselves in all their suffering and adversities. They must not despise the Lord's discipline. Those who make light of suffering make light of God and sin. Yet neither must they lose heart when they are rebuked.

2.3. Though afflictions may be the fruits of God's displeasure, they are still proofs of his fatherly love and care for his people (vv. 6–7). The best of God's children have

their faults and follies that need to be corrected, and he will correct them, because the children belong to his family. In this he acts as befits a father. No wise and good father will turn a blind eye to faults in his own children, as he would to faults he sees in others. To be allowed to continue in sin without rebuke is a sad sign of alienation from God; children who are allowed to do so are illegitimate, not true, children. They are the false offspring, belonging to another father, not God (vv. 7–8).

2.4. Those who are impatient under the discipline of their heavenly Father behave worse toward him than they would toward their earthly parents (vv. 9–10). It is the duty of children to give their parents the reverence of submission to their correction when they have been disobedient. The writer recommends that we humble ourselves and submit to our heavenly Father when we are disciplined by him.

2.4.1. Our earthly fathers are simply *the fathers of our flesh*, but God is *the Father of our spirits*. Our fathers on earth were instrumental in producing our bodies, which are merely flesh. We must owe much more to the One who is the Father of our spirits.

2.4.2. Our earthly parents *chastened us after*, or "for," *their own pleasure*. Sometimes they did it to satisfy their passion rather than to reform our conduct. This is a weakness our natural fathers are subject to. Our heavenly Father's correction, however, is always for our benefit. God loves his children so much that he wants them to be as like him as possible, and this is why he disciplines them when they need it.

2.4.3. Our natural fathers corrected us for *a few days*, when we were children. When we reached maturity, we loved and honored them all the more for it. Our whole life here is a state of childhood. When we come to a state of perfection, we will be fully reconciled to all the ways in which God has disciplined us now.

2.4.4. God's correction is not condemnation. He disciplines his children now in order to prevent the death and destruction of their souls, so that they may live to God, be like God, and be with him forever.

2.5. The children of God should not judge his dealings with them by how it seems at the present time, but by reason, faith, and experience (v. 11). Notice:

2.5.1. The judgment of the senses. To them, afflictions are not pleasant, but painful.

2.5.2. The judgment of faith. Affliction produces peace by producing further righteousness, for the harvest of righteousness is peace. The great concern of believers is to endure discipline with patience and make the most of it to grow in holiness. They must:

2.5.2.1. Endure their affliction with patience (v. 12). A burden of affliction tends to make a Christian's hands hang down, and their knees feeble, to bring discouragement, but they must strive against sin so that they may better run their spiritual race. Faith, patience, holy courage, and determination will make them walk more steadily. They must encourage and not discourage others. Many who are on their way to heaven walk weakly and lamely on that path. Such believers tend to discourage one another, but it is their duty to help one another move forward on their way to heaven.

2.5.2.2. Make the most of it to grow in holiness (v. 14). Faith and patience will enable them to follow peace and holiness. Sufferings tend to sour the spirit and sharpen the passions, but the children of God must follow peace with everyone. Notice that peace and holiness are connected; true Christian peaceableness is never found separate from holiness. *Without holiness no man shall see the Lord.*

2.6. Where afflictions and sufferings for the sake of Christ are not considered the discipline of our heavenly Father, they will become a dangerous temptation to apostasy (vv. 15–16).

2.6.1. Here the writer gives a serious warning against apostasy, backing it up with a terrible example. Notice:

2.6.1.1. The warning, in which is set forth:

2.6.1.1.*1*. The nature of apostasy (v. 15). It is *failing of* (missing) *the grace of God*, coming short of a principle of true grace in the soul, and so coming short of the love and favor of God here and in the future.

2.6.1.1.*2*. The consequences of apostasy: where people miss the true grace of God, a root of bitterness will spring up in them (v. 15; Dt 28:18), and corruption will prevail and break out from them, producing corrupt motives in them and bitter fruits in others. *Many are defiled*, that is, tainted with those bad principles and drawn into defiling practices.

2.6.1.2. The fearful example, that of Esau. Notice:

2.6.1.2.*1*. Esau's sin. He godlessly despised and sold his birthright and all its accompanying advantages. This is what apostates do.

2.6.1.2.*2*. Esau's punishment: his conscience was convicted of his sin and foolishness when it was too late. He now saw that the blessing he had made so light of was worth having, but he was rejected by God: *he found no place of repentance* (could bring about no change of mind). In his great godlessness Esau had made the bargain, and God in his righteous judgment confirmed it.

2.6.2. We can learn from this:

2.6.2.1. Apostasy from Christ is the fruit of preferring indulgence of the flesh to the blessing of God.

2.6.2.2. Sinners will not always have such corrupt thoughts of God's blessing and inheritance as they now have.

2.6.2.3. When the day of grace is over, they will find no place for repentance: they will not be able to repent rightly of their sin, and God will not change his mind about their sentence. Christians should never give up their hope of their Father's blessing by deserting their holy religion to avoid suffering.

Verses 18–29

Here the writer goes on to urge the professing Hebrews to persevere in their Christian lives and conflict and not fall back into Judaism. He does this by showing them how different the state of the Gospel church is from that of the Jewish church, how much it resembles the state of the church in heaven, and how much, therefore, on both accounts, it demands and deserves our diligence, patience, and perseverance in the Christian way.

1. He shows how different the Gospel church is from the Jewish church and how much it surpasses it (vv. 18–21).

1.1. The church in the Mosaic age was a physical, visible state. Mount Sinai was *a mount that might be touched* (v. 18), a physical, perceptible place, in accordance with the nature of that age. The state of the Gospel church on Mount Zion is more spiritual.

1.2. It was a dark age. On that mountain there was darkness and gloom; the Gospel state is clearer and brighter.

1.3. It was a dreadful and terrible age; the Jews could not bear its terror (v. 19). In fact, even Moses said, I *exceedingly fear and quake* (v. 21; Dt 9:19). The Gospel state is mild, kind, suited to our weak frame.

1.4. It was a limited age; not everyone was permitted to approach that mountain. Under the Gospel, on the other hand, we all have access to come boldly and with

confidence to God (Eph 3:12). This was the state of the Jewish church, fitted to set out the strict and awesome justice of God.

2. He shows how much the Gospel church represents the triumphant church in heaven. The Gospel church is called *Mount Zion, the heavenly Jerusalem*. In coming to Mount Zion, believers come into heavenly places (Eph 1:3) and into a heavenly community.

2.1. Into heavenly places.

2.1.1. *Unto the city of the living God.* God has taken up his gracious home in the Gospel church, which is therefore an emblem of heaven.

2.1.2. To *the heavenly Jerusalem*, as its free citizens.

2.2. To a heavenly community.

2.2.1. *To an innumerable company of angels.* Those who by faith are joined to the Gospel church are joined to the angels, and they will ultimately be like them.

2.2.2. *To the general assembly and church of the firstborn, that are written in heaven*, to the universal church, however much dispersed. By faith we come to them, have fellowship with them in the same blessed hope, and walk in the same way of holiness. Here will be the general assembly of the firstborn, the saints of earlier times. Their names are written in heaven: they have a name in God's house and are enrolled in the Lamb's book of life (Rev 21:27), as citizens are enrolled in government record books.

2.2.3. *To God the Judge of all*, the great God who will judge both Jews and Gentiles according to the law they are under.

2.2.4. *To the spirits of just men made perfect*, to the best people, the righteous; to the best part of just people, their spirits; and to these in their best state, made perfect.

2.2.5. *To Jesus the Mediator of the new covenant, and to the blood of sprinkling, that speaketh better things than that of Abel.* This is not the least of the many encouragements there are to persevere.

2.2.5.1. The Gospel covenant is the new covenant, distinct from the covenant of works.

2.2.5.2. Christ is the Mediator of this new covenant.

2.2.5.3. This covenant is confirmed by the blood of Christ sprinkled on our consciences. This blood of Christ pacifies God and purifies human consciences.

2.2.5.4. This is the blood that speaks a better word than that of Abel. It speaks to God on behalf of sinners, pleading not for vengeance but for mercy. It speaks to sinners in the name of God. It speaks forgiveness of their sins and peace to their souls.

3. The writer closes the chapter by applying the argument in a way that befits its significance (v. 25). In those earlier days, God spoke on earth; now he speaks from heaven.

3.1. When God speaks to people most excellently, he justly expects from them the strictest attention. He now speaks from a higher and more glorious throne in heaven. He now speaks more powerfully and effectively. At that time, his voice shook the earth, but now he has shaken not only the earth but also the heavens. It is by the Gospel from heaven that God shook to pieces the Jewish nation. He shook them in their church state, which in Old Testament times was a heaven on earth, and he introduced a new state of the church.

3.2. When God speaks to people in the most excellent way, the guilt of those who refuse him is greater. By the sound of the Gospel trumpet a new kingdom was set up for God in the world, a kingdom that can never be shaken so as to be removed. This was a change made once for all. The writer therefore justly concludes:

3.2.1. How necessary it is for us to obtain *grace from God, to serve him acceptably*. We lose all our effort in religion if we are not accepted by God.

3.2.2. We cannot worship God acceptably unless we worship him with *godly reverence and fear*. Holy fear, as well as faith, is necessary for acceptable worship.

3.2.3. It is only the grace of God that enables us to worship God rightly.

3.2.4. God is the same just and righteous God under the Gospel that he showed himself to be under the Law. He remains in himself a consuming fire, that is, a God of strict justice.

CHAPTER 13

The writer commends several excellent duties to the Hebrews as the appropriate results of faith (vv. 1–17). He then asks for their prayers for him and offers his prayers to God for them, giving them some hope of seeing both him and Timothy, and ending with the general greeting and blessing (vv. 18–25).

Verses 1–17

The writer calls the faithful Hebrews to carry out many excellent duties.

1. To brotherly love (v. 1). The spirit of Christianity is a spirit of love. Faith works by love (Gal 5:6), and true religion is the strongest bond of friendship. Yet this love for one another was in danger of being lost in a time of persecution, when it would be most necessary. Christians should always love and live as brothers and sisters, and the more they grow in devout love for God their heavenly Father, the more they will grow in love for one another for his sake.

2. To hospitality (v. 2). To brotherly kindness we must add charity (2Pe 1:7). The duty required is *to entertain strangers*. Since strangers do not have a certain home, we should allow them room in our hearts and in our houses as we have opportunity and ability to do so. The motive is that *thereby some have entertained angels unawares*. God has often given his hospitable servants honors and favors beyond all their thoughts, *unawares*.

3. To Christian sympathy (v. 3).

3.1. The duty. Those who are themselves at liberty must sympathize with those who are in prison and adversity, as if they were bound with them in the same prison.

3.2. The reason for the duty: *as being yourselves in the body*, not only in the natural body but also in the same mystical body, the church. It would be unnatural if Christians did not bear one another's burdens.

4. To purity and chastity (v. 4). Here is a commendation of God's ordinance of marriage, that it *is honourable in all*. It is *honourable* and happy when people who are pure come together and keep the marriage bed pure. Here also is a dreadful but just censure of impurity and sexual immorality: *Whoremongers and adulterers* (adulterers and sexually immoral) *God will judge*. He will call such sins by their proper names, not "love" and "romance," but sexual immorality and adultery. He will judge them, convict them, and condemn them.

5. To Christian contentment (vv. 5–6). The sin that goes against this grace and duty is *covetousness*. We must take care not only to keep this sin down but to uproot it from our souls. The duty that is against greed and love of money is being satisfied and pleased *with such things as we have*. We must be content with what God gives us from day to day. We must come to terms with our present condition; those who cannot do this would not be content even

if God raised their condition to what is in their minds, for the mind would rise with the condition. Paul, though in need and empty, had *learned in* every *state, in* any *state, therewith to be content* (Php 4:11). Notice what reason Christians have to be contented with their lot: *God hath said, I will never leave thee, nor forsake thee* (vv. 5–6). This promise contains the essence of all the promises. From this comprehensive promise believers may assure themselves of help from God (v. 6). People can do nothing against God, and God can make all that people do against his own ones turn to their good.

6. To the duty Christians owe their ministers, both those who are dead and those still alive.

6.1. They owe a duty to those who have died (v. 7). Notice:

6.1.1. The description given of them. They were those who had led the Hebrews, who had spoken the word of God to them.

6.1.2. The duties owing to them.

6.1.2.1. "*Remember them*—their preaching, praying, advice, example.

6.1.2.2. "*Follow* (imitate) their *faith*; seek the grace of faith by which they lived and died so well. *Consider the end of their conversation* (the outcome of their way of life)." The writer now enlarges on the Hebrews' duty of following the same true faith in which they have been instructed by referring to:

6.1.2.2.1. The unchangeableness and eternity of the Lord Jesus Christ. The great head of the church lives forever, remaining the same. They should remain firm and immovable, imitating Christ.

6.1.2.2.2. The nature and tendency of the erroneous doctrines they must avoid.

6.1.2.2.2.1. They are many and various (v. 9), different from those the Hebrews have received and inconsistent with themselves.

6.1.2.2.2.2. They are strange doctrines.

6.1.2.2.2.3. They have an unsettling and distracting nature. They are completely against the grace of God that establishes the heart (1Th 3:13).

6.1.2.2.2.4. They concern external, small, perishing things, such as ceremonial *meats and drinks*.

6.1.2.2.2.5. They are unprofitable. They do not make people more holy, more humble, more thankful, or more heavenly.

6.1.2.2.2.6. They will exclude those who accept them from the privileges of the Christian altar (v. 10). *We have an altar*—the Christian church has its altar, not a physical altar but a personal one, and that is Christ; he is both our altar and our sacrifice. This altar provides a feast for true believers. The Lord's Supper is the feast of the Gospel Passover. Those who remain faithful to the tabernacle or the Levitical age, or return to it, exclude themselves from the privileges of this altar. The writer first proves this part of the argument and then applies it. He proves that this servile loyalty to the Jewish state is a bar to the privileges of the Gospel altar. The Gospel feast is the fruit of the sacrifice, which those who do not acknowledge the sacrifice itself have no right to. He proceeds to apply the argument (vv. 13–15): *Let us go forth* (go out) *therefore unto him without* (outside) *the camp*; let us be willing to *bear his reproach* (disgrace). We must submit to it, and we have greater reason to do so because we must necessarily soon go out by death, for *here we have no continuing city*. We should go out now by faith and seek in Christ the rest and settlement that this world cannot give us (v. 14). And let us make right use of this altar. Let us bring our sacrifices to it (vv. 15–16), sacrifices not of atonement but of acknowledgment, of which there are two. One is the sacrifice of praise to God, which we should offer to him continually. This includes all adoration and prayer as well as thanksgiving; this is *the fruit of our lips*. The other is the sacrifice of gifts to the needy, the sacrifice of Christian charity (v. 16). We must not be content to offer only the sacrifice of our lips, mere words; we must also offer the sacrifice of good deeds.

6.2. They owe a duty also to their living ministers (v. 17). Here we have:

6.2.1. Their duty: to obey and submit to their ministers. Christians must submit to being instructed by their ministers, not thinking themselves too wise, good, or great to learn from them, and they must obey them.

6.2.2. The motives to fulfill this duty.

6.2.2.1. Ministers *have the rule over* the people; their office is truly authoritative.

6.2.2.2. They *watch* over *the souls* of the people. They are to guard against everything that may harm the people and to seek every opportunity to move them on their way to heaven.

6.2.2.3. They must give an account of how they have fulfilled their duty, and they would be glad to give a good account. If they can give an account of their own faithfulness and success, it will be a joyful day to them. If they give their account with grief, it will be to the people's loss as well as theirs.

Verses 18–25

Here:

1. The writer commends himself and his fellow sufferers to the prayers of the Hebrew believers (v. 18).

1.1. This is one part of the duty that people owe their ministers. Ministers need the prayers of the people, and the more fervently the people pray for their ministers, the more benefit they may expect to reap from their ministry.

1.2. There are good reasons why people should pray for their ministers.

1.2.1. *We trust we have a good conscience* (v. 18). Many of the Jews had a low opinion of Paul. Here he modestly asserts his own integrity. *We trust*: he might have said, "We know," but he chose to speak in a humble style. "We trust, we are sure, we have a clear conscience *in all things*. We wish to act with sincerity and integrity in all things." A clear conscience has respect for all God's commands and all our duty, but those who have this clear conscience still need the prayers of others.

1.2.2. He hopes to be restored to them sooner (v. 19). Here he intimates that he is now absent from them, that he has a great desire and real intention to return to them, and that the best way to facilitate his return to them is for them to make it a matter of prayer.

2. He offers his prayers to God for them: now *the God of peace* (v. 20). Notice:

2.1. The title given to God—*the God of peace*, who has found a way to make peace and reconciliation between himself and sinners.

2.2. The great work attributed to him: *He hath brought again from the dead our Lord Jesus.* That divine power by which Christ was raised is able to do everything for us that we need.

2.3. The titles given to Christ—our Lord Jesus, our sovereign, our Savior, and the Great Shepherd of the sheep. Believers are the flock of his pasture (Ps 74:1), and his care and concern are for them.

2.4. The way in which God was reconciled and Christ raised from the dead: *through the blood of the everlasting covenant.* This blood is the sanction and seal of an eternal covenant between God and his people.

2.5. The mercy prayed for (v. 21). The perfecting and equipping of the saints with everything good is the great thing desired by them and for them. The way in which God equips his people is by working in them always what is pleasing in his sight. Eternal glory is due to Christ, who is the cause of all the good in us and all the good done by us. Everyone should say *Amen* to this.

3. He is pleased with the hope of not only seeing Timothy but also seeing the Hebrews with him.

4. He closes with a greeting and a solemn, though short, blessing.

4.1. He sends a greeting from himself to them all, to both ministers and people, and he sends them a greeting from the Christians in Italy.

4.2. He gives a blessing (v. 25). It is good to part with prayer.

A PRACTICAL AND DEVOTIONAL
EXPOSITION OF

James

The writer of this letter was not James the son of Zebedee, because he was put to death by Herod (Ac 12:1–2). Rather, he was James the son of Alphaeus, one of Jesus' cousins and another of the twelve apostles (Mt 10:3). (It is generally thought now that James the brother of Jesus wrote this letter [Ed. note].) It is called a general letter because in the opinion of some it was not directed to any particular person or church, but was what we call a circular letter. The time when this letter was written is uncertain. Its intention was to rebuke Christians for their great degeneracy in both their faith and their way of life, and especially to awaken the Jewish nation to a sense of the greatness and nearness of the judgments that were coming on them, and to support all true Christians in fulfilling their duty in all the adversities and persecution they might face.

CHAPTER 1

After the opening greeting (v. 1), Christians are taught how to behave when they face different kinds of trials. Those who come through times of testing and adversity are declared blessed (vv. 2–12). But the sins that bring suffering are by no means to be attributed to God, who cannot be the author of sin, but is the author of all good (vv. 13–18). The word of God should be what we chiefly study, and we must take care that we practice what we hear and know of it. To this is added an account of what pure religion is (vv. 19–27).

Verse 1

We have here the opening greeting of this letter, showing:

1. The characteristics by which the writer wishes to be known: *James, a servant of God, and of the Lord Jesus Christ.* Although James is called by the evangelist *the brother of our Lord* (Gal 1:19; see also Mt 15:53), it was his glory to serve Christ in the spirit rather than to boast of being one of his relatives. Let us learn from this to prize the title *servant* above all others in the world—*the servants of God and of Christ.* We cannot acceptably serve the Father unless we are also servants of the Son.

2. The condition of those to whom he writes: they are *the twelve tribes which are scattered abroad* (among the nations). They were dispersed in mercy, scattered in several countries to spread the light of divine revelation. They began now to be scattered in wrath, when the Jewish nation crumbled into factions and many were forced to leave their country. Even good people among them shared in the general disaster. These Jews of the dispersion, however, were those who had accepted the Christian faith. It is often the lot even of God's own tribes to be scattered among the nations, but when they are, he will send help for them. Here is a writer writing to the scattered ones, writing a letter from God to them. When we suffer outward calamities, we should not become despondent and think we have been rejected; God remembers and sends his encouragement to his scattered people.

3. The respect God has even for the dispersed ones, reflected in his *greeting* them. It was the desire of this writer's heart that those who were scattered among the nations be encouraged.

Verses 2–12

Here:

1. The suffering state of Christians in this world is represented. It is implied that troubles and adversities may come even to the best Christians. Believers who are entitled to the greatest joy may also endure severe suffering. The trials of good people are ones that they do not create for themselves or sinfully pull on themselves, but ones that they *fall into*.

2. The graces and duties of a state of trial and suffering are described.

2.1. One Christian grace to be exercised is joy (v. 2). We must not become sad and miserable, which would make us lose heart in the trials we face. Philosophy may instruct people to remain calm in troubles, but Christianity teaches us to be joyful in them. Our trials will brighten our graces now, and it will brighten our crown in the end. There is greater reason for joy in adversities if we consider the other graces that are developed by them.

2.2. There must be a wholesome trust in the great truths of Christianity and a firm clinging to them in times of testing (vv. 3, 6).

2.3. There must be patience and perseverance: *The trial of faith worketh patience* (perseverance). The testing of one grace produces another. To exercise Christian perseverance rightly:

2.3.1. We must let it work. Stoical apathy and Christian perseverance are very different: by the one, people become to some extent unaware of their sufferings, but by the other they become triumphant in and over them. Let us allow it to work, and it will do wonders in a time of trouble.

2.3.2. We must let it finish its work. When we endure all that God appoints, and as long as he appoints, when we not only endure troubles but even rejoice in them, then perseverance has finished its work.

2.3.3. When the work of perseverance is complete, then the Christian is mature, and nothing will be lacking.

2.4. There must be prayer, and the writer shows:

2.4.1. What we should especially pray for—wisdom. We should not pray so much for the removal of an adversity as for wisdom to make right use of it. To be wise in times of testing is a special gift of God.

2.4.2. How this is to be obtained—we are to ask for it. Let the foolish become beggars at the throne of grace, and then they are set to be wise.

2.4.3. That we have the greatest encouragement to do this: *he giveth to all men liberally, and upbraideth not.* The One to whom we go has it to give; he has a generous disposition, nor need we fear at all that his favors will be limited to some, because *he gives to all men.* If you say you need a great deal of wisdom, that a small portion will not be enough for you, know that he *gives liberally.* Moreover, if you are afraid of being put to shame for your foolishness, he *upbraideth not.* Ask when you wish, and as often as you want; he does not reproach or find fault. The promise is: *It shall be given him.*

2.4.4. One thing is necessary to observe when we ask. There must be *no wavering,* no wavering at the promise of God through unbelief (Ro 4:20).

2.5. Sincerity of intention and single-mindedness constitute another duty required under adversity: *He that wavereth is like a wave of the sea, driven with the wind, and tossed.* To be sometimes lifted up by faith and then thrown down again by distrust is very appropriately compared to the waves of the sea, which rise and fall, swell and sink, just as the wind tosses them higher or lower, that way or this. By such a wavering spirit the effectiveness of prayer is spoiled (v. 7). Such a distrustful, unstable, unsettled person is unlikely to value a favor from God as they should, and therefore cannot expect to receive. A wavering faith and spirit also has a bad influence on our conduct, making it very unsteady. Those who are as unstable as water will not excel (Ge 49:4).

3. Both poor and rich are told on what basis to build their joy and comfort (vv. 9–11).

3.1. Those in humble circumstances are to be looked on as brothers and sisters.

3.2. Good Christians may be rich in the world (v. 10). Grace and wealth are not wholly inconsistent.

3.3. Both of these kinds of Christians—those in humble circumstances and those who are rich—are allowed to rejoice. No condition of life puts us beyond the position to rejoice in God. All who are brought low, made lowly by grace, may rejoice in the ultimate prospect of their exaltation in heaven.

3.4. Notice what reason a rich person has to be lowly in his own eyes: *As the flower of the grass he shall pass away;* he, and his wealth with him (v. 11). *For the sun has no sooner risen with a burning heat than it withereth the grass.* Just as a flower fades in the face of the heat of the scorching sun, *so shall the rich man fade away in his ways.* Therefore let those who are rich rejoice not so much in the providence of God, which makes them rich, as in the grace of God that makes and keeps them humble.

4. A blessing is declared on those who persevere in trials and temptations (v. 12).

4.1. It is not those who simply suffer who are blessed, but those who persevere.

4.2. Adversities cannot make us miserable unless it is our own fault. A blessing may rise up from them.

4.3. Sufferings and temptations are the way to eternal blessedness: *When he is tried, he shall receive the crown of life;* or he shall receive this crown "when he is approved," when his graces are found to be true and most valuable, as metals are tried for excellence by fire. Tested Christians will be crowned, and the crown they will wear will be a crown of life. We carry the cross only for a while (Mt 10:38; 16:24), but we will wear the crown for eternity.

4.4. This blessedness that is implied in a crown of life is promised to righteous sufferers. It is therefore what we may depend on most surely.

4.5. Our enduring of temptations must come from a motive of love for God and our Lord Jesus Christ: *the Lord hath promised to those that love him.*

4.6. The crown of life is promised to all who have the love of God reigning in their hearts.

Verses 13–18

1. We are taught that God is not the author of anyone's sin. Some who profess faith might fall in the hour of temptation. If they do, the blame for their misbehavior must lie entirely with them. There is nothing either in the nature of God or in his providential ways that they can lay the blame on (v. 13). Just as God cannot be tempted by evil himself, so neither can he be One who tempts others. It is very bad to sin, but it is much worse, when we have done wrong, to accuse God of it, to say it was because of him. Afflictions are intended to draw out our graces, not our corruptions.

2. We are taught where the true cause of evil lies and where the blame should therefore be put (v. 14). The true origin of evil and temptation is in our own hearts. The combustible matter is in us, even though the flames may be blown up by some outward causes. Notice:

2.1. The method by which sin proceeds. First it draws away, then it entices. The heart is drawn away from what is good and enticed to cling to what is evil; it is separated from the life of God, and then gradually fixed on a course of sin.

2.2. The power and scheming of sin. The word rendered here *drawn away* signifies being forcibly dragged or compelled. The word translated *enticed* signifies being wheedled and beguiled. The force and power of sin could never be effective if it were not for its craftiness and guile.

2.3. The effectiveness of corruption in the heart (v. 15). When sin is allowed to excite desires in us, it will soon develop those desires into agreement, and then it is said to have *conceived.* The *sin, when it is finished* (full-grown), *bringeth forth* (gives birth to) *death.* Death lies on the soul, and death comes on the body.

3. We are taught further that *God is the Father and fountain of all good* (vv. 16–17). We should take particular care not to go astray in our conceptions of God: "*Do not err, my beloved brethren,* God is not and cannot be the author of evil, but must be acknowledged as the cause and spring of everything good.

3.1. God is the *Father of lights* (v. 17). "Just as the sun is constant in its nature and influences, though it sometimes seems to change, so God is unchangeable, and our changes and shadows are not from any variability or shadowy changes in him, but from us ourselves." *With him there is no variableness, neither shadow of turning.*

3.2. Every good gift comes from him. He gives both the light of reason and the light of learning. The light of divine revelation also comes directly from above. We have nothing good, therefore, except what we receive from God.

3.3. Our regeneration and all its holy, happy consequences must be attributed to him (v. 18). True Christians are those who have been born again (Jn 3:3, 7). Their new birth comes about by God's own will; it comes about not by our own skill or power, but purely from the goodwill and grace of God. The means by which this is effected is *the word of truth*, that is, the Gospel. This Gospel is indeed a word of truth; otherwise it could never produce such real, lasting, great, and noble effects. The purpose of God's giving renewing grace is *that we should be a kind of firstfruits* of creation.

Verses 19–27

1. We are required to restrain the activity of passion: *Wherefore, let every man be swift to hear, slow to speak, slow to wrath* (v. 19). We will learn this lesson if we have been truly born again by the word of truth (v. 18).

1.1. The *Wherefore* here may refer to the adversities and temptations spoken of at the beginning of the chapter. We are to be ready to listen and consider what God's word teaches. Instead of censuring God in our times of testing and temptation, let us open our ears and hearts to listen to what he wants to say to us.

1.2. It may also refer to the disputes and differences that Christians were running into among themselves. We should be quick to listen to reason and truth on all sides and be slow to speak. When we do speak, there should be no trace of anger. We may also notice that if people are to control their tongues, they must also control their passions. If we want to be slow to speak, we must be slow to become angry.

2. A very good reason is given for suppressing anger (v. 20). The worst thing we can bring to a religious dispute is anger. *Wrath* is human, and our anger stands in opposition to the righteousness of God. Those who claim to serve the cause of God by becoming angry show that they know neither God nor his cause.

3. We are called on to suppress other corrupt desires, as well as rash anger. We are taught here, as Christians, to watch against and get rid of all the disorders of a corrupt heart that would influence it against the word and ways of God. There is a prevalence of what is evil in us, which is to be guarded against; there is a *superfluity of naughtiness*. It is not enough to restrain evil desires; they must be *laid apart*, or "cast away," from us. This must extend not only to outward sins but to all sin in our minds and hearts as well as in our speech and practice.

4. Here we are instructed about hearing the word of God.

4.1. We are required to prepare ourselves for it (v. 21).

4.2. We are told how to listen to it: *Receive with meekness* (humbly accept) *the engrafted word, which is able to save your souls.* In hearing the word of God, we are to *receive* it, as a branch receives a grafted-in shoot, so that the fruit produced may not be according to the nature of the sour branch, but according to the nature of the Gospel that is planted in our souls. We must therefore yield ourselves to the word of God with a most submissive temper; this is to *receive it with meekness.* We must be willing to listen to our faults, and to do so not only patiently but also thankfully. And in all our listening we should aim at the salvation of our souls, for it is the purpose of the word of God to make us wise for salvation (2Ti 3:15).

4.3. We are taught what is to be done after we have listened to it (v. 22). We listen in order to do what the word says; the most attentive and the most frequent hearing of the word of God will do us no good unless we also do what it says. It is not enough to remember what we hear.

Those who merely hear the word deceive themselves, and self-deceit will ultimately be found to be the worst form of deceit.

4.4. The writer shows what the proper use of the word of God is, who they are who do not use it as they should, and who they are who make right use of it (vv. 23–25).

4.4.1. The use we are to make of God's word may be learned from its being compared to a mirror in which someone looks at their face. Just as a mirror shows us the spots and blemishes on our faces, so the word of God shows us our sins. It shows us what is wrong so that it may be put right. When we give our attention to the word of God, so as to see our true state and condition and dress ourselves afresh by the mirror of God's word, we make proper use of it.

4.4.2. We have here an account of those who do not use the mirror of the word as they should. We hear God's word and look into the Gospel mirror in vain if we go away and forget our blemishes and forget the remedy. This is the case of those who do not listen to the word as they should.

4.4.3. Those who hear rightly, who use the mirror of God's word as they should, are also described (v. 25).

4.4.3.1. The Gospel is a law of freedom, the law "of liberation," whereas the ceremonial law was a burden of slavery.

4.4.3.2. It is a perfect law, and in hearing the word, we look into this perfect law.

4.4.3.3. We look into the law of freedom as we should only when we *continue therein.*

4.4.3.4. Those who do this, who *continue in the law and word of God*, are and *shall be blessed in their deed*. This blessedness does not lie in knowing the will of God, but in doing it. It is not talking, but walking, that will bring us to heaven.

5. The writer informs us how we may distinguish between a worthless religion and one that is pure and approved by God. James plainly and definitively declares:

5.1. What religion is worthless: *If any man among you seemeth to be religious, and bridleth not his tongue, but deceives his own heart, this man's religion is vain.*

5.1.1. In a worthless religion there is much that is show. When people are more concerned to *seem* religious than really to be so, it is a sign that their religion is worthless.

5.1.2. In a worthless religion there is much criticizing. When we hear people all too ready to speak about the faults of others, so that they themselves may seem wiser and better, this is a sign that they have a worthless religion. Those who have a tongue that devalues others cannot have a truly humble, gracious heart. In the religion that does not enable a person to restrain their tongue, there is no power.

5.1.3. In a worthless religion a person deceives their own heart. Once religion becomes worthless, how great is that worthlessness (Mt 6:23)!

5.2. What true religion consists of (v. 27).

5.2.1. It is the glory of religion to be pure and undefiled. A holy life and a loving heart show a true religion.

5.2.2. The religion that is pure and undefiled is so *in the presence of God and the Father*. True religion teaches us to do everything as in the presence of God.

5.2.3. Compassion and love for the poor and distressed form a great and necessary part of true religion: *visiting the fatherless and widow in their affliction.* By James's reference to such persons we are to understand all who are appropriate objects of charity, all who suffer. If the essence of religion is drawn up in two articles, this is one—to be charitable and relieve those who suffer.

5.2.4. An undefiled life must accompany sincere love: *to keep himself unspotted from the world.* The world tends to blemish the soul; it is hard to live in it and have to do with it and yet not be defiled, but we must constantly try. Pure and undefiled religion consists of this.

CHAPTER 2

The writer condemns showing favoritism toward the rich and despising the poor (vv. 1–7). Mercy as well as justice should be pursued (vv. 8–13). He exposes the error and foolishness of those who boast of their faith without works (vv. 14–26).

Verses 1–7

The writer shows how much trouble is in the sin of favoritism. We have here:

1. A warning against this sin in general. First, the characteristics of Christians are broadly implied: they are those who *have the faith of our Lord Jesus Christ.* They have received it as a trust; they have it as a treasure. Notice how honorably James speaks of Jesus Christ: he calls him *the Lord of glory.* Knowing that Christ is the Lord of glory should teach us not to respect Christians for anything so much as for conformity to Jesus Christ. We should not show favoritism to certain people and thereby obscure or lessen the glory of our glorious Lord. This is certainly a detestable sin.

2. A description of it and a warning against it by way of an example (vv. 2–3). "You act with favoritism and determine wrongly simply because one person looks better than another." Notice from this:

2.1. God has his remnant among all kinds of people, among those who wear rich and fine clothing and among those who wear coarse and shabby clothes. In matters of religion, rich and poor stand on the same level; no one's riches set them closer to God in the least, nor does anyone's poverty set them further away from God.

2.2. All undue honoring of worldly greatness and riches should be especially guarded against in Christian communities. If a poor person is good, we must not value that person any less because they are poor, and if a rich person is bad, we must not value them any more because of their riches. There are many humble, heavenly, good Christians who wear inferior clothes, but neither they nor their Christianity should be thought of any the worse because of this.

3. The greatness of this sin (vv. 4–5).

3.1. This sin contains shameful favoritism: *Are you not then partial in* (Have you not discriminated among) *yourselves?* According to the strict rendering of the original, the question is, "Have you not made a distinction? Moreover, in making that distinction, are you not judging according to a false rule, going by false standards?"

3.2. This favoritism is owing to the evil and injustice of thoughts. "*You have become judges of evil thoughts*; you are judges according to the unjust and corrupt opinions that you have formed in yourselves. You secretly prefer outward show to inner grace and prefer the things that are seen to those that are unseen." The defilement of sin is never truly and fully discerned until the evil of our thoughts is disclosed.

3.3. This favoritism is a detestable sin, because in committing it we show ourselves most directly to be going against God (vv. 5–6). "Those whom you have such a low opinion of are those whom God has made the heirs of a kingdom." Many of the poor of this world are the ones who have been chosen by God. Their being God's chosen does not prevent their being poor; their being poor

does not at all prejudice the evidence that they have been chosen. God intended to commend his holy faith not by the external advantages of a fine outward show, but by its inner worth; that is why he chose the poor of this world. Many who are poor in this world are rich in faith; the poorest may become rich in this way. It is expected of those who have wealth that they be rich in good works, but it is expected of the poor in the world that they be rich in faith. Believing Christians are heirs of a kingdom, even though they may be poor according to their present possessions. Where anyone is rich in faith, there will be also divine love. We read in the previous chapter about the crown promised to those who love God (1:12); here we find there is a kingdom too. Just as the crown is a crown of life, so the kingdom will be an eternal kingdom. After such considerations, the charge is truly cutting (v. 6).

3.4. Favoritism based on people's riches or outward appearance is shown to be a great sin because of the troubles that come about through worldly wealth and greatness. "Your sin will be shown to be extremely sinful (Ro 7:13) and foolish when it is seen to be setting up what tends to pull you down, what dishonors the worthy name by which you are called."

Verses 8–13

The writer now shows how this matter may be put right.

1. We have the law that is to guide us. Scripture teaches us to love all our neighbors, whether rich or poor, as ourselves (Lev 19:18; Mt 19:19); in having a firm respect for this rule, therefore, *we shall do well.* The rule for Christians to walk by is established in Scripture, Scripture gives us this rule as a law, and that law is to love our neighbor as ourselves. This law is a royal law; it comes from the King of Kings. By its own value and position it deserves to be honored. When this royal law is interpreted with favoritism, a pretense of observing it will not excuse people for any unjust proceedings.

2. This general law is to be considered together with a particular law (v. 9). The royal law itself, rightly explained, will serve to convict James's readers, because it teaches them to put themselves as much in the position of the poor as in that of the rich.

3. We are shown the extent of the law and how far obedience must be given to it. The readers must fulfill the royal law with regard to one part as well as another. "Do you plead that you show different respect for the rich because you are to love your neighbor as yourselves? If so, then show also a just and proper regard for the poor because you are to love your neighbor as yourself, or else your offending in one point will spoil your claim of observing the whole law." This is further illustrated by putting forward a different situation from the one mentioned before (v. 11). "You may be very severe in cases of adultery but less ready to condemn murder. Another person has an unnatural dread of murder but a more lenient attitude toward adultery. But when you consider the authority of the Lawgiver, you will see that the same reason is given for condemning one as for condemning the other. If we offend in one point, we show contempt for the authority of the One who gave the whole law and are therefore guilty of breaking it all.

4. James directs Christians to be governed by and behave themselves by the law of Christ. Notice:

4.1. The Gospel is called a law. It sets out duties as well as administering comfort. Christ is a king to rule us as well as a prophet to teach us and a priest to sacrifice and intercede for us.

4.2. It is *a law of liberty*; the service of God according to the Gospel is perfect freedom.

4.3. We must all be judged by this law of freedom.

4.4. We should therefore speak and act now as befits those who must soon be judged by this law of freedom; we are to keep a Gospel attitude and see that our lives are molded according to the Gospel.

4.5. The consideration that we will be judged by the Gospel should make us more merciful in our behavior toward the poor (v. 13). Those who show no mercy now will find no mercy on the great day, but there will be those who will become expressions of the triumph of mercy, in whom *mercy rejoices over judgment*.

Verses 14–26

The writer shows the error of those who rest in a bare profession of the Christian faith, as if that would save them. It is proved in detail here that people are justified not only by faith but also by works.

1. Here a great question arises, namely, how to reconcile Paul and James. Paul, in his letters to the Romans and Galatians, seems to assert the direct opposite of James, *that we are justified by faith only, and not by the works of the law* (Ro 3–4; Gal 3). To reconcile the two, it may be sufficient only to notice that:

1.1. When Paul says that *a man is justified by faith, without the deeds of* (apart from observing) *the law* (Ro 3:28), he is clearly speaking of a kind of work that is different from the one James is speaking about, but not of a different kind of faith. Paul is speaking of works performed in obedience to the Law of Moses, and before people's acceptance of the faith of the Gospel. James is speaking of works done in obedience to the Gospel. Both apostles are concerned to exalt the faith of the Gospel as that which alone can save us and justify us.

1.2. Paul speaks of a quite different use that is made of good works from what is urged and intended here. He was dealing with those who depended on the merit of their works in the sight of God. James was dealing with those who praised faith but would not allow works to be used even as evidence. Those who praise the Gospel so much as to set aside the Law and those who praise the Law so much as to set aside the Gospel are both wrong.

1.3. The justification of which Paul speaks is different from the one spoken of by James. The one speaks of our persons being justified before God; the other, of our faith being justified before human beings. *Show me thy faith by thy works*, says James. But Paul speaks of justification in the sight of God.

2. Let us see what is more particularly to be learned from this great passage of James. We are taught:

2.1. That faith without works will do no good and cannot save us. *What doth it profit, my brethren, if a man say he hath faith, and have not works? Can faith save him?* Faith that does not save will not really do us any good. All things should be considered profitable or unprofitable to us as they tend to advance or hinder the salvation of our souls. To say that one has faith and actually to have faith are two different things. People may boast to others about having faith, being proud of what they do not really have.

2.2. That as love is a practical motive, so is faith. By seeing how it looks for people to pretend they are very loving but never actually do any loving, you may judge what sense there is in claiming to have faith without its fruits (vv. 15–17). What good will such "love," which consists in mere words, do for either you or the poor? You might as well claim that your love will stand the test

without acts of mercy as think that a profession of faith will support you before God without works of godliness and obedience (v. 17). We tend to rest too much in a mere profession of faith, and think that will save us. Mock-faith is as detestable as mock-love, and both show a heart that is dead to all real godliness.

2.3. To compare a faith that boasts about itself without works and a faith that is evidenced by works, and, by looking at them together, to see how this comparison will work on our minds. "You make a profession and say you have faith; I make no such boast, but leave my works to speak for me." This is the evidence by which the Scriptures throughout teach people to judge both themselves and others. This is also the evidence according to which Christ will proceed on the Day of Judgment.

2.4. To look on a faith that is mere speculation and knowledge as the faith of demons (v. 19). The instance of faith that the writer chooses to mention here is the basic principle of all religion—to *believe that there is a God*. "But if you rest there, and form a good opinion of your situation toward God merely on account of your believing in him, it will put you in a bad state: *The devils also believe, and tremble*. If you content yourself with a mere assent to articles of faith, and some speculations on them, note that demons go that far. They tremble not out of reverence for the one God in whom they believe but out of hatred and opposition to him.

2.5. That those who boast about faith without works are to be looked on at present as foolish and condemned people. Faith without works is said to be *dead*, not only devoid of all the activities that are the proofs of spiritual life but also unable to bring eternal life.

2.6. That a justifying faith cannot be without works. Here are two examples.

2.6.1. The first is that of Abraham. By what Abraham did it was made clear that he truly believed; his faith was an active faith (v. 22). By this means you come to the true sense of the Scripture that says Abraham believed God, *and it was imputed unto him for* (credited it him as) *righteousness* (v. 23); this is how he became the *friend of God*. You see then (v. 24) how *by works a man is justified, and not by faith only*; not by believing without obeying, but by having a faith that produces good works. Those who want to have Abraham's blessings must be careful to copy his faith: merely to boast of being Abraham's descendants will do no good. And those works that are evidence of true faith must be such as God himself commands, not the mere fruits of our own imagination and devising. Such works complete faith, just as the truth of faith causes it to act. Such an active faith will make others, as well as Abraham, friends of God.

2.6.2. The second is that of Rahab (v. 25). The previous example was of a person renowned for his faith all his life. This example is of one noted for her sin. The strongest faith will not suffice by itself, nor the lowest be allowed to go without works. What proved Rahab's faith to be sincere was that, risking her life, she *received the messengers, and sent them out another way*. Where great sins are pardoned, there must be great acts of self-denial. Her former acquaintances must be set aside, and her former way of life must be completely abandoned, and she must give significant proof and evidence of this.

2.7. The writer draws this conclusion: *As the body without out the spirit is dead, so faith without works is dead also* (v. 26). The best works, without faith, are dead; they lack their root and principle. It is through faith that anything we do is really good. But the most plausible profession of faith, without works, is dead, as the root is dead when it produces nothing green, nothing fruitful. Faith is the root, good works are the fruits, and we must make sure that we have both. We must not think that either without the other will justify and save us.

CHAPTER 3

Those who profess a religious faith should especially control their tongues (vv. 1–12). True wisdom makes people humble, and it may easily be distinguished from a wisdom that is earthly (vv. 13–18).

Verses 1–12

The previous chapter shows how unprofitable and dead faith is without works. Such faith tends, however, to make people conceited in their attitude and their words. Even the best people need to be warned against a dictatorial, critical use of their tongues. We are taught, therefore:

1. Not to use our tongues so as to lord it over others. We must not desire to speak and act as those who are continually assuming the chair; we must not prescribe to one another so as to make our own thoughts a standard by which we try everyone else. "Therefore be not many *masters*" — or "teachers," as some read it — "but rather speak with the humility and spirit of learners." Those who set themselves up as judges and critics *shall receive the greater condemnation*. Our judging others will only make our own judgment stricter and more severe (Mt 7:1–2). We are all sinners; if we were to think more about our own mistakes and offenses, we would be less inclined to judge others. Self-justifiers are commonly self-deceivers. Their arrogance and critical tongues may prove worse than any faults they condemn in others.

2. To control our tongues so as to prove ourselves *perfect*, upright, and in complete control of ourselves. However, on the other hand, *if a man seemeth to be religious and bridleth not his tongue, that man's religion is vain.* Further, those who are never at fault in what they say will prove themselves to be not only sincere Christians but also very advanced and good Christians, for the wisdom and grace that enable them to control their tongue will enable them also to rule all their actions. We have this illustrated by two comparisons:

2.1. The controlling and guiding of all the movements of a horse by the bit that is put into its mouth (v. 3). There is a great deal of wild rebellion and fierceness in us. This shows itself very much in the tongue, and so it must be bridled. Otherwise, just as an unruly and wild horse runs away with its rider, or throws them, so an uncontrolled tongue will treat those who have no command over it.

2.2. The directing of a ship by the right control of the rudder (vv. 4–5). Just as the rudder is a very small part of the ship, so the tongue is a very small part of the body, but the right control of the rudder will steer and turn the ship, and a right control of the tongue is to a large extent the control of the whole person. Things that are small may be immensely useful. We should learn from this that it must be our aim to take proper control of our tongues, because although they are small parts of the body, they are capable of doing a great deal of good or harm.

3. To dread an uncontrollable tongue as one of the greatest and most harmful evils (vv. 5–6). There is such great sin in the tongue that it may be called a *world of iniquity. So is the tongue among the members that it defileth the whole body.* The whole body is often drawn into sin and guilt by the tongue. *It setteth on fire the course of nature.* The affairs of the human race and of communities are often thrown into confusion and all set on fire by

human tongues. *And it is set on fire of hell.* Hell has more to do in furthering the fire of the tongue than people are generally aware of. When it is set on fire by hell, as it is in all undue passion, it is troublesome, producing rage and hatred and those things that serve Satan's purposes.

4. How difficult it is to control the tongue: *For every kind of beasts is tamed of mankind. But the tongue can no man tame* (vv. 7–8). And these creatures have not been subdued or tamed only by miracles. What is spoken of here is something commonly done: every beast not merely 'has been tamed,' but *is tamed* by humanity. But the tongue is worse than all these and cannot be tamed by the human power and skill that can tame the animals, birds, reptiles, and so on. The writer does not intend to represent the taming of the tongue as something impossible, but as something extremely difficult, which therefore requires great watchfulness, effort, and prayer. Sometimes all is too little, *for it is an unruly evil, full of deadly poison.* The tongue tends to break through all limits and rules and to spit out its poison on one occasion or another despite the greatest care we may exercise.

5. To think of the use we make of our tongues in religion and in the service of God (vv. 9–10). How absurd it is that those who use their tongues in prayer and praise should also use them in cursing, slandering, and the like! The tongue that addresses the divine Being with reverence cannot, without the greatest inconsistency, turn on fellow creatures with abusive and brawling words. *These things ought not so to be,* and if such considerations were always in our thoughts, surely they would not be. Furthermore, to drive home this thought, the writer shows that contrary effects from the same causes are grotesque, not to be found in nature, and therefore inconsistent with grace (vv. 11–12). True religion will not allow contradictions, and one who is truly religious can never allow them in either their words or their actions.

Verses 13–18

In these verses James shows the difference between pretending to be wise and really being so, and between the wisdom that comes from below and the kind that comes from above.

1. We have an account of true wisdom. Truly wise people will not esteem themselves for simply knowing things, but only for having the wisdom to rightly apply their knowledge. These two things must be put together to make up true wisdom: *Who is wise, and endued with knowledge among you?* In anyone who is so, there will be the following:

1.1. *Good conversation*, or conduct. If we are wiser than others, this should be shown by the goodness of our conduct, not by its coarseness or pride.

1.2. Good works. The conduct referred to here is not only words but the whole of a person's practice; it is therefore said, *Let him show out of a good conversation his works.* Those who think well or talk well are not considered wise unless they also live and act well.

1.3. Humility. It is a great expression of wisdom to wisely restrain our own anger and patiently to bear the anger of others. When we are gentle and calm, we are best able to listen to reason and best able to speak it. Wisdom produces humility, and humility increases wisdom.

2. The glorying of those who have a different character is taken away. Notice:

2.1. Envying and strife are opposed to the humility that comes from wisdom. The heart is the seat of both envy and wisdom, but the two cannot dwell together in the same heart.

2.2. The order of things is laid down here. Envying comes first and stirs up strife; strife boasts and lies, and then (v. 16) come confusion, disorder, and every evil practice. One sin leads to another, and it cannot be imagined how much trouble is produced: evil practices are all around us.

2.3. From where such wisdom comes (v. 15). It springs from earthly principles and comes from the Devil. Therefore those who are *lifted up* (Eze 28:2–5; 1Ti 3:6) with such "wisdom" must fall under the same judgment as the Devil.

3. The lovely picture of the wisdom that comes from above, from heaven, is more fully drawn. True wisdom is God's gift and comes from above.

3.1. It is *pure*, without elements of corruption that would debase it, seeking holiness in both heart and life.

3.2. It is *peaceable*. Those who are truly wise do what they can to keep the peace so that it may not be broken, and to make peace so that where it has been lost it may be restored. Heavenly wisdom makes people peace-loving.

3.3. It is *gentle*: not rude and arrogant in speaking or harsh and cruel in attitude.

3.4. It is *easy to be entreated*—the word could be translated "submissive"—easy to be entreated either *to* what is good or *from* what is evil. There is an easygoing nature that is weak and mistaken, but it is not a blameworthy easygoing nature to submit ourselves to the convictions of God's word and to all just requests made by others.

3.5. It is *full of mercy and good fruits*, inwardly disposed both to relieve those in need and to forgive those who offend.

3.6. It is *without partiality*. The margin reads "without wrangling." The wisest people are least likely to be those who criticize.

3.7. It is *without hypocrisy*. It is sincere; it has no disguises nor deceits. It is sincere and open, steady and uniform, and consistent with itself.

3.8. It will go on to sow the fruits of righteousness in peace and will thereby make peace in the world (v. 18). What is sown in peace will produce a harvest of joy.

CHAPTER 4

Here we are directed: 1. To consider some causes of fights and quarrels (vv. 1–5). 2. To abandon friendship with this world (vv. 4–10). 3. To carefully avoid all detraction and rash judgment of others (vv. 11–12). 4. To maintain a constant regard to the commands of divine Providence (vv. 13–17).

Verses 1–10

This chapter speaks of a sinful desire for worldly things as what has taken the divisions of James's readers to a shameful excess.

1. James here reproves the Jewish Christians both for their fights and for their sinful desires as the cause of them. The origin of their fights and quarrels was not—as they claimed—a true zeal for their country and for the honor of God; rather, their widespread sinful desires were the cause of them all. What is shrouded under a false pretense of zeal for God and religion often comes from human pride.

1.1. Worldly lusts make war within a person as well as battle outside them. All the fighting, wars, and battles of the world arise from the sinful desires for power and dominion, pleasure, or riches. The right way to heal the contention, therefore, is to lay the ax to the root (Mt 3:10) and put to death those sinful desires that are at war within us.

1.2. Thinking of the defeat of these sinful desires should put them to death. Immoderate desires are either completely disappointed or not to be satisfied by obtaining the things desired. Worldly, sinful desires are the disease that will not allow contentment or satisfaction in the heart.

1.3. Sinful desires and feelings generally exclude prayer: "*You fight and war, yet you have not, because you ask not.* You do not consider God in your undertakings. You do not commit your way to him (Ps 37:5), but follow your own corrupt views and inclinations: that is why you meet with continual disappointments.

1.4. "Your sinful desires spoil your prayers. Pride, self-indulgence, and worldliness are what you aim to serve by your successes and your prayers. You disgrace devotion and dishonor God because you pursue such corrupt goals; that is why your prayers are rejected." When people ask God for prosperity in their callings or undertakings and do not receive what they ask for, it is because they ask not so that they may glorify their heavenly Father and do good with what they have, but so that they may *consume it upon their lusts*. When we are not effective in our prayers, it is *because we ask amiss*; either we do not ask for the right reasons or we are not asking in the right way. When our prayers are full of the language of our sinful desires rather than our graces, they will not be answered.

2. We have fair warning to avoid all destructive friendships with this world.

2.1. Worldly-mindedness is branded as hostility toward God. A person can have enough of the good things of this life and also keep themselves in the love of God, but it is destructive treason and rebellion against God to set the world on his throne in our hearts. *Whosoever therefore is the friend of the world is the enemy of God.* From this adulterous, idolatrous love of the world, and from the serving of it, arise fights and quarrels. What peace can there be among people as long as there is hostility toward God?

2.2. "Think seriously what the spirit of the world is. *Do you think that the scripture saith in vain, The spirit that dwelleth in us lusteth to envy?*" (v. 5). Natural corruption shows itself mainly by envying, and there is a continual tendency in us toward this. Now this way of the world, with all its ostentatious pomp and pleasure and its tendency to make us fall into fights and quarrels for the sake of these things, is the certain consequence of being friends with the world. To avoid fights and quarrels, therefore, Christians must avoid friendship with the world. If we belong to God, he gives us enough grace to live and act better than most of the world does. The grace of God will correct and heal the spirit that naturally lives in us; where he gives grace, he gives a spirit that is different from that of the world.

3. We are taught to notice the distinction God makes between pride and humility (v. 6). This is represented as the language of Scripture in the Old Testament. Notice here:

3.1. The disgrace shown to the proud: God *resists* them. Let proud spirits hear this and tremble—God *resists them*. He will certainly fill with shame the faces of those who have filled their hearts with pride.

3.2. The honor and help God gives the humble. Grace, as opposed to disgrace, is honor; God gives this grace to the humble. Wherever God gives true grace, he will give more. God will especially give more grace to the humble, because they see their need of it; they will pray for it and be thankful for it.

4. We are taught to submit ourselves completely to God (v. 7). Christians should forsake the friendship of the

world and learn by grace to glory in their submission to God. We are to be submissive in both reverence and love. Now just as this submission to God is what Satan works extremely hard to hinder, so we should exercise great care and control to resist his suggestions. *Resist him and he will flee from you.* If we sinfully give in to temptations, the Devil will continually pursue us, but if we withstand him, he will go away from us. Resolution shuts and bolts the door against temptation.

5. We are told how to act toward God in becoming submissive to him (vv. 8–10).

5.1. *Draw nigh to God.* The heart that has rebelled must be brought to the feet of God; the spirit that was separated from a life of fellowship with God must come to know him.

5.2. *Cleanse your hands.* Those who come to God must have clean hands. Hands must be cleansed, or it will be useless for us to draw near to God.

5.3. The hearts of the double-minded must be purified. To *purify the heart* is to be sincere.

5.4. *Be afflicted* (grieve), *and mourn, and weep* (wail). "Take any afflictions God sends as he would have you take them. Times of contention and division are times in which to mourn, and the sins that bring fights and quarrels should be mourned. *Let your laughter be turned to mourning, and your joy to heaviness* (gloom)." This may be taken either as a prediction of sorrow or as a prescription of seriousness. The unconcerned Christians James writes to are told to set aside their worthless merriment and their worldly pleasures before the worst happens, so that they may indulge in godly sorrow and repentant tears.

5.5. "*Humble yourselves in the sight of the Lord.* Let there be a thorough humiliation expressed in mourning everything evil; let there be great humility shown in doing what is good."

6. We have great encouragement to act in this way toward God (vv. 8–10). Those who draw near to God in duty will find God drawing near to them in mercy. If there is not close fellowship between God and us, we are at fault, not he. *He shall lift up the humble.* If we are truly penitent and humble under God's displeasure, we will soon know the benefits of his favor; he will lift us up out of trouble, or he will lift us up in our spirits. The highest honor in heaven will be the reward of the greatest humility on earth.

Verses 11–17

1. We are warned here against the sin of slander. We must not speak evil of other people, even if it is true, unless there is some necessary occasion for it. Much less must we report evil things when they are false. Our lips must be guided by the law of kindness as well as by truth and justice. *Speak not evil one of another:*

1.1. Because you are brothers and sisters. We are to be sensitive to the good name of our brothers and sisters; when we cannot speak good things, it is better to say nothing than to speak evil.

1.2. Because this is to judge the law. Those who quarrel with their brothers and sisters and condemn them concerning any matter not determined in the word of God are bringing dishonor on that word, as if it were not a perfect rule. Let us be on our guard against judging the law, for the law of the Lord is perfect (Ps 19:7). If people break the law, we may leave the law to judge them; if they do not break it, let us not judge them. Those who are most ready to set themselves up as judges of the law generally fail most in their obedience to it.

1.3. Because God, the Lawgiver, has reserved wholly to himself the power of passing the final sentence on people. God is to be acknowledged as the only supreme Lawgiver; he is the only One who can administer law to the conscience. He is the only One who is to be obeyed absolutely. No one can question his right to enact laws, because he has such authority to enforce them. He *is able to save and to destroy.* He has full authority to reward the observance of his laws and to punish all disobedience. James here warns against many becoming judges. Let us not boss our brothers and sisters around; it is enough that we have the law of God, which is a rule for us all. We should not, therefore, set up other rules.

2. We are warned against a presumptuous confidence of the continuation of our lives (vv. 13–14). "Reflect a little on this way of thinking and talking; call yourselves to account for it." There were some who used to say, as many say still do, *We will go to such a city and do this or that,* ignoring all serious regard to the ways of Providence. Notice:

2.1. How in much worldly business, people tend to leave God out of their schemes.

2.2. How much worldly happiness lies in the promises people make to themselves in advance. Their heads are full of fine visions as to what they will do in the future.

2.3. How pointless it is to look for anything good in the future without the agreement of Providence. *We will go to such a city,* they say. But something that happens on the way might prevent them from getting to their destination or call them to go somewhere else. Many people who have set out on their journey have gone to their distant home without reaching their earthly destination. But suppose they reached the city they intended, how did they know they would remain there? Something might happen to shorten their stay. Nor could they be certain they would buy and sell there. Suppose they went to that city and remained there a year: they might not make a profit; making money in this world is at best uncertain. The frailty, shortness, and uncertainty of life should restrain the arrogant confidence of those who plan for the future in such a way. God has wisely left us in the dark about future events. We *know not what shall be on the morrow;* we may know what we intend to do and to be, but a thousand things may happen to prevent us. We are not sure of life itself, since it is simply like a mist. *It appears but for a little time, and then vanishes away.*

3. We are taught to maintain a constant sense of our dependence on the will of God (v. 15). James now tells his readers how to be and do better: "You should say in your hearts at all times that if it is the Lord's will, you have such and such intentions to fulfill." "With the will and blessing of God" was used by the Greeks at the beginning of every undertaking. *If the Lord will, we shall live.* We must remember that our times are not in our own hands, but are at God's disposal (Ps 31:15); that is why we must submit to him. *If the Lord will, we shall do this or that.* All our actions and designs are under the direction of heaven. Both all of our plans and all of what we actually do, therefore, should be referred to God.

4. We are told to avoid worthless boasting (v. 16). James's readers promised themselves life and prosperity and great things in the world, without any just regard for God, and then they boasted about these things. *Such rejoicing is evil;* it is foolish and harmful. If we rejoice in God that our times are in his hand, that all events are at his disposal, and that he is our God, this rejoicing is good. If, however, we rejoice in our own worthless confidence and arrogant boasting, this is evil.

5. We are taught that we should act according to our own convictions, that we should never act against our own knowledge (v. 17). To do so is to commit an aggravated sin; it is sinning while being witnessed—and with the worst possible witness, one's own conscience. Notice that omissions, as well as commissions, are sins that will be judged. Those who do not do the good they know should be done, as well as those who commit the evil they know should not be done, will be condemned.

CHAPTER 5

James declares the judgments of God on rich people who oppress the poor (vv. 1–6). Then all the faithful are urged to be patient in their trials and sufferings (vv. 7–11). The sin of swearing is warned against (v. 12). We are instructed how to act in both adversity and prosperity (v. 13). Commands are given about praying for the sick and anointing with oil (vv. 14–15). Christians are instructed to acknowledge their faults to one another and pray for one another (vv. 16–18). Finally, we are commended to do what we can to bring back those who wander from the truth (vv. 19–20).

Verses 1–11

James addresses first sinners here, and then saints.

1. Let us consider what he writes to sinners. Here James supports what his great Teacher said: *Woe unto you that are rich; for you have received your consolation* (Lk 6:24). The poor among the Jews received the Gospel, and many of them believed, but most of the rich rejected Christianity, persecuting those who believed in Christ.

1.1. He foretells the judgments of God that will come on them (vv. 1–3). Misery will come on them, misery that will arise from the very things in which they put their happiness. *Go to now* (now listen), *you rich men*. Rich people tend to say to themselves—and others are ready to say to them—*Eat, drink, and be merry*, but God says, *Weep and howl*. Those who live like animals are called to wail as such. "Corruption, decay, rust, and ruin will come on all your fine things (v. 2). The things that you now have inordinate affection for will be useless" (v. 3). They think they can heap up treasure for their final days, but alas! They are only heaping up treasures that will eventually turn out to be treasures of wrath (Ro 2:5).

1.2. He shows what those sins are that will bring such miseries.

1.2.1. These rich people are accused of greed. God gives us our worldly possessions so that we may honor him and do good with them, but if instead we sinfully hoard them up, this is a detestable offense and will be witnessed against by the rust and corruption of the treasure that are heaped together.

1.2.2. He accuses them of oppression (v. 4). Those who have wealth gain power, and then they are tempted to abuse that power to oppress those under them. These rich people probably made as hard bargains with the poor as possible, and even afterward would not fulfill their agreements as they should have.

1.2.3. He mentions the sin of luxurious self-indulgence (v. 5). God does not forbid us the right use of pleasures, but to live in them as if we lived for nothing else is offensive. Luxury makes people self-indulgent. Self-indulgence and luxury are commonly the effects of great plenty and abundance. "*You have nourished your hearts as in a day of slaughter*; you live as if every day were a day of sacrifices, a festival." Some may say, "What harm is there in people enjoying themselves, provided they do not spend

more than they have?" What! Is it not harmful for people to make gods of their stomachs (Php 3:19), and to spend everything on their stomachs instead of being full of acts of love and godliness? Pride, idleness, and an abundant supply of food and drink mean the same thing as living in luxury and self-indulgence, nourishing the heart as in a day of slaughter.

1.2.4. He accuses them of persecution (v. 6). This reaches the limit of their sins (Mt 23:32). When the just suffer, and when they yield without resistance to the unjust sentence of oppressors, this is noticed by God, to the honor of the sufferers and the infamy of their persecutors.

2. Next we have his words to saints. James's words concerning evil and oppressive rich people give him occasion to administer comfort to God's suffering people. "Be patient; see what your duty is and where your greatest encouragement lies.

2.1. "Attend to your duty.

2.1.1. *"Be patient.* Although God may not appear for you immediately, wait for him." When we have completed our work, we need patience to wait for our reward. This Christian patience is not, like the moral patience taught by some philosophers, a mere yielding to necessity, but a humble coming to terms with the wisdom and will of God. *Be patient to* (until) *the coming of the Lord.* Because this is a lesson that, though difficult, must be learned, it is repeated in v. 8.

2.1.2. *"Establish your hearts*—let your faith be firm, let your practice of what is good be constant and continued, and let your resolutions for God and heaven be firmly established in spite of all the sufferings or temptations.

2.1.3. *"Grudge not one against another* (v. 9); don't 'groan' against one another. Don't make yourselves or one another anxious by groaning to and grieving one another." Those who are among common enemies and in similar circumstances of suffering should be especially careful not to groan against one another, for otherwise judgments will come on them as well as others.

2.2. Consider what encouragement is here for Christians to be patient.

2.2.1. "Look to the example of the farmer: *He waits for the precious fruit of the earth, and has long patience.* When you sow your grain in the ground, you wait many months for the harvest; will you not wait for a crown of glory? If you should be called to wait a little longer than the farmer, is it not for something that is proportionately greater and infinitely more worth waiting for?

2.2.2. "Think how short your waiting time may be (vv. 8–9). Don't be impatient, don't quarrel with one another; the great Judge is at hand, as near as someone who is knocking on the door."

2.2.3. The danger of our being condemned should stir us to fulfill our duty: *Grudge not, lest you be condemned* (don't grumble against one another, or you will be judged).Worry and discontent expose us to the righteous judgment of God, and we bring more suffering on ourselves by our groans and complaints against one another than we are aware of.

2.2.4. We are also encouraged to be patient by the example of the prophets (v. 10). When we think that the best people have met with the harshest treatment in this world, we should come to terms with suffering. Those who were the greatest examples of experiencing suffering were also the best and greatest examples of patience (v. 11): *We count those happy who endure.*

2.2.5. Job also is offered as an example (v. 11). In everything he could bless God, and what happened to him in the end? God accomplished for him the things that clearly prove that *the Lord is very pitiful, and of tender mercy*. The tender mercy of God is such that he will abundantly make up for all his people's sufferings. Let us, then, serve our God and endure our trials as those who believe the end will crown it all.

Verses 12–20

This letter is now drawing to a close, and so the writer moves quickly from one thing to another: that is why a range of matters is insisted on in these few verses.

1. The sin of swearing is warned against (v. 12). Some have translated the words *pro panton* as "before all things" rather than *above all things*, and as therefore instructing that the readers should not, in ordinary conversation, put an oath "before every thing they say." All customary, needless swearing is condemned throughout Scripture as a detestable sin. Worldly swearing was customary among the Jews, and some of the looser sort of those who called themselves Christians might also be guilty of this. James says here:

1.1. *Above all things, swear not*. But how many there are who heed this command less than any other, who make light of nothing so much as common, profane swearing! But why is this forbidden *above all things*? First, because it strikes most directly at the honor of God and throws contempt most expressly on his name and authority. Second, there is less to tempt us to this sin than to any other. Third, it is stopped with great difficulty once people get used to it. Finally, how can we expect the name of God to be a strong tower to us (Pr 18:10) in our distress if we abuse it and play with it at other times? And yet all this is so far from forbidding necessary oaths that it simply confirms them by preserving the appropriate reverence for them. The Jews thought that if they simply omitted the greatest oaths they were safe. But they grew so worldly as to swear by the creation, as if it were God. On the other hand, those who swear commonly by the name of God are putting him on the same level as every common thing.

1.2. *"But let your yea be yea, and your nay nay, lest you fall into condemnation.* Be sure to stand by your word and be true to it, so as to give no cause for suspicion of falsehood." It is being suspected of falsehood that leads people to swear.

2. As Christians we are taught to reconcile ourselves to the ways of Providence (v. 13). Our condition in this world varies, and we are wise if we submit to its doing so, behaving as is fitting in both prosperity and adversity. Adversities should make us pray, and prosperity should make us full of praise.

2.1. In times of suffering nothing is more timely than prayer. Times of adversity should be prayerful times. The reason God sends suffering is so that we may become committed to seeking him early (Ps 63:1; Pr 8:17; Isa 26:9); then those who at other times have neglected him may be brought to seek him. Adversities naturally draw out complaints, and to whom should we complain except to God in prayer? In suffering, it is necessary to exercise faith and hope, and prayer is the appointed means to both obtain and increase these graces in us.

2.2. In times of happiness and success, singing psalms is very proper and appropriate. We are sure that the singing of Psalms is a Gospel ordinance, and that our joy should be holy joy, consecrated to God. Holy celebration befits family worship and solitary devotions as well as public meetings.

3. We have particular instructions given concerning sick people (vv. 14–15). It is the responsibility of sick people to send for ministers and seek their help and

prayers. When ministers are sought and called for in this way, it is their duty to pray over the sick. The sick were to be *anointed with oil in the name of the Lord*. Expositors generally believe that when miracles ceased, this institution also ceased. Some, however, have thought that it should not be wholly set aside in any age, but that where there are extraordinary measures of faith in both the person who is anointing and those who are anointed, an extraordinary blessing may attend the observance of this instruction for the sick. One thing is to be carefully noted here, and that is that the saving of the sick is not ascribed to the *anointing with oil*, but to prayer (v. 15). Prayer for the sick must proceed from and be accompanied by a living faith. There must be faith both in the person praying and in the person prayed for. *And if he have committed sins, they shall be forgiven him.* The great thing we should seek from God in times of sickness, both for ourselves and for others, is forgiveness of sin. Sin is both the root of sickness and its sting. If sin is forgiven, either the affliction will be removed in mercy or we will see that there is mercy in its continuance.

4. Christians are told to *confess their faults one to another* (v. 16). The confession required here is that of Christians to one another. Where people have wronged one another, or tempted one another to sin, or consented in the same evil actions (Ac 8:1), they should confess these sins and encourage one another to do so. Yet we need not confess everything that we are aware is wrong in ourselves. Rather, so far as confession is necessary for our reconciliation with those we disagree with, or for reparation of wrongs, or to make our own spirits quiet and at ease—so far should we be ready to confess our faults. Sometimes it may also be useful to Christians to disclose their individual weaknesses to one another where there is a deep, trusting friendship, and where friends may by their prayers help each other obtain forgiveness of their sins and power against them.

5. The great advantage and effectiveness of prayer is declared and proved (vv. 17–18). The one who prays must be righteous, and the prayer itself must be fervent, genuine, and heartfelt; such prayer is powerful and effective. It is very useful to us ourselves, it may be very beneficial to our friends, and we are assured that it is acceptable to God. To prove the power of prayer and encourage us, James points us to the example of Elijah, who, though zealous and great, was *a man of like passions with us*; he had weaknesses. In prayer we must not look to what we deserve—which is nothing—but to the grace of God. Elijah prayed fervently, or, as it is in the original, "in prayer he prayed." It is not enough simply "to say a prayer"; we must pray hard, earnestly, fervently. Elijah *prayed that it might not rain*, and God heard him, so that *it rained not on the earth for the space of three years and six months. Again he prayed, and the heaven gave rain.* This is recorded to encourage even ordinary Christians to be constant and fervent in prayer. Where there may not be so much of a miracle in God's answering our prayers, there still may be as much grace.

6. The letter concludes with an exhortation to do all we can to advance the conversion and salvation of others (vv. 19–20). "If anyone wanders from the truth, and someone brings them back, let it be acknowledged that whoever did this good deed for another is an instrument in saving a soul from death." Even if the wanderer is very famous, you must not be afraid to point out to them their error, and if they are very weak and insignificant, you must not disdain to seek to make them wiser and better. If they wander from the truth, whether in opinion or prac-

tice, you must seek to bring them back to that standard. Errors in judgment and in life generally go together. If we are instrumental in bringing any back, *we* are said to bring them back, though this is the work of God. If we can do nothing more toward bringing sinners to Christ, we can still pray for the grace and Spirit of God to turn and change them. Those who in v. 19 are said to *err from the truth* are described in v. 20 as *erring in their way*, and we cannot be said to restore anyone simply by changing their opinions, but only if we can also bring them to correct and amend their ways. This is conversion. Those who turn sinners from the error of their ways *shall save a soul from death*. By such conversion of heart and life, a *multitude of sins shall be hidden* (covered). Although our sins are many, even *a multitude*, they can still be covered, or pardoned. If people seek to cover up their own sin, there is no effective way to do so except by giving it up. Some read this text as stating that conversion will "prevent" a multitude of sins, and there is a certain truth in that: many sins are prevented in the person who has been converted, and many also may be prevented in others whom that person may influence.

A Practical and Devotional Exposition of

1 Peter

We have two letters registered in the sacred canon of Scripture written by Peter. When our Savior called and commissioned his apostles, he named Peter first in the list, and his behavior toward Peter seems to suggest that he set him apart as a special favorite among the Twelve. Many examples of our Lord's affection for him, both during his life and after his resurrection, are recorded. He modestly calls himself an *apostle of Jesus Christ*, and when he writes to the elders of the church, he humbly places himself in the same rank as them: *The elders who are among you I exhort, who am also an elder* (5:1). The intention of this first letter is: 1. To explain the doctrines of Christianity more fully to these newly converted Jews. 2. To instruct and persuade them to lead holy lives. 3. To prepare them for suffering. This last seems to be his main intention, for he has something to this effect in every chapter.

CHAPTER 1

The apostle describes the people to whom he is writing, greets them (vv. 1–2), and blesses God for their new birth to a living hope of eternal salvation (vv. 3–5). He shows that in the hope of this salvation they have great cause for joy (vv. 6–9). This is the salvation that the ancient prophets foretold and that the angels long to look into (vv. 10–12). He urges them to lead lives of self-control, holiness (vv. 13–21), and mutual love (vv. 22–25).

Verses 1–2

1. Here the writer of the letter is described:
1.1. By his name. As a commendation of his faith, Jesus Christ gave him the surname *Peter*, which means "a rock."
1.2. By his position—an *apostle of Jesus Christ. Apostle* refers to the highest position in the Christian church. To claim something we do not have is hypocrisy, but to deny what we do have is ingratitude. Besides asserting his position as an apostle, Peter hereby mentions his apostolic function as the authority and call he has for writing this letter to these people.
2. The people to whom this letter was addressed are described:
2.1. By their external condition—*strangers dispersed throughout Pontus, Galatia*, and so on. Their circumstances were poor and adverse. The best of God's servants may, through the hardships of times, be dispersed and forced to leave their native countries. The value of good people should not be gauged by their present external condition.
2.2. By their spiritual condition. They are:
2.2.1. *Elect according to the foreknowledge of God the Father.* Now, people may be *elect*, or chosen and appointed, to any of three things. A person may be chosen to an office. A people may be chosen to be a church-state and thereby to enjoy special privileges, and a person may be chosen to eternal salvation. This last is the election spoken of here.

2.2.1.1. This election is said to be *according to the foreknowledge of God. Foreknowledge* may be taken in two ways. On the one hand, it may mean mere prescience, foresight, or understanding that such and such a thing will happen. This is how a mathematician can know with certainty that at such and such a time there will be an eclipse. Such a foreknowledge is not, however, the cause of any event. On the other hand, *foreknowledge* sometimes signifies purpose, appointment, and approval. The death of Christ was not only foreseen but also foreordained (v. 20). This is the sense here, so the meaning is, "elect according to the counsel, ordination, and free grace of God."
2.2.1.2. To *the foreknowledge of God* is added *the Father*. In the matter of human redemption, election is attributed to the Father, as reconciliation is attributed to the Son and sanctification to the Holy Spirit.
2.2.2. Chosen *through sanctification of the Spirit, unto obedience, and sprinkling of the blood of Jesus Christ.* Every elect person must be sanctified by the Spirit and justified by the blood of Jesus. By *sanctification* we understand here living for God in all the duties of a Christian life, which are summed up here in one word, *obedience. The Spirit* refers to the Holy Spirit, the author of sanctification. *Unto obedience* refers to what has gone before it, showing the goal of sanctification, which is to bring rebellious sinners back to obedience: *You have purified your souls in obeying the truth through the Spirit* (v. 22).
2.2.3. Chosen also to the *sprinkling of the blood of Jesus.* Here is a clear allusion to the typical sprinklings of blood under the Law. It is not enough that the blood of Christ, the great all-sufficient sacrifice, be shed; it must also be sprinkled and passed on to every one of these chosen Christians. All who are chosen for eternal life as the goal are chosen for obedience as the way. Unless a person is sanctified by the Spirit and sprinkled with the blood of Jesus, there will be no true obedience in the life.
3. The greeting follows. The blessings wished for them are *grace and peace. Grace* is the free favor of God, with

all its appropriate effects. *Peace.* All kinds of peace may be intended here, but especially peace with God, with the assurance of it on our own consciences. The request or prayer in relation to these blessings is that they may be multiplied. Peter wishes them to continue, increase, and become abundant. The best blessings we can desire for ourselves or one another are grace and peace in abundance. Peace cannot be enjoyed where there is no true grace; first grace, then peace. Peace without grace is foolishness, but grace may be true where there is for a time no real peace; Christ was once in anguish. The increase of grace and peace, as well as the initial giving of them, comes from God.

Verses 3–5

1. The apostle begins the main part of the letter with thanksgiving to God. We have here:

1.1. The duty performed, which is blessing God.

1.2. The object of this blessing described by his relationship with Jesus Christ: *The God and Father of our Lord Jesus Christ.* Here are three names of one person, showing his life and work in three different ways. He is *Lord*, a universal king; *Jesus*, a priest or Savior; and *Christ*, a prophet.

1.3. The reasons that lead us to fulfill this duty of blessing God, which center on *his abundant mercy*. God *hath begotten us again* (he has given us new birth), and the best response to this is thanksgiving, especially if we consider the fruit it produces in us, which is the excellent grace of hope, a living, durable hope, which has such a solid foundation as *the resurrection of Jesus Christ from the dead.*

1.3.1. A true Christian's condition is never so bad that they do not have good reason to bless God.

1.3.2. In our prayers and praises we should address God as *the Father of our Lord Jesus Christ*; it is only through him that we and our services are accepted.

1.3.3. Even the best people owe their best blessings to the great mercy of God. All the evil in the world comes from human sin, but all the good in the world comes from *God's mercy*. We owe all we have to divine mercy.

1.3.4. The new birth produces a living hope of eternal life. Those who have been born again to a new and spiritual life have been born to a new and spiritual hope.

1.3.5. The hope of a Christian has this excellence: it is a living hope. The hope of eternal life in a true Christian is a hope that keeps that person alive, gives them life, supports them, and leads them to heaven. The delusive hopes of those who have not been born again are worthless and perishing; hypocrites and their hope expire and die together.

1.3.6. *The resurrection of Jesus Christ from the dead* is the basis of a Christian's hope. Because there is an inseparable union between Christ and his flock, they rise because of his resurrection as a head, rather than because of his power as judge.

2. The apostle goes on to describe that life under the idea of *an inheritance.* He tells them they have been born again to receive a new inheritance, one that is infinitely better than the one they lost. They are reminded of the noble inheritance kept in heaven for them. Notice:

2.1. Heaven is the undoubted inheritance of all the children of God. God gives his gifts to everyone, but he gives the inheritance to none except his children. This inheritance is not something we can buy; we can receive it only as our Father's gift. It is not a wage that we deserve, but the gift of grace.

2.2. The incomparable excellence of this inheritance. It is incorruptible, like its Maker. All corruption is a change from better to worse, but heaven has no changes and no

end; the sanctuary is eternal in heaven. This inheritance is undefiled; it does not fade, but always keeps its vigor and beauty: *reserved in heaven for you.* It is certain, a possession in another world, safely kept and preserved until we come to possess it. The people for whom it is reserved are described by their character: everyone who has been *begotten again to a lively hope.*

3. He imagines some doubt or uneasiness that may remain in his readers as to whether they might fall by the way and thus fall short of this inheritance. He answers this question by stating that they will be kept and preserved from all such destructive temptations as would prevent their safe arrival at eternal life. The heirs of heaven will certainly be securely led to possess it. The blessing promised here is preservation: you *are kept*; the author of the blessing is *God*; the means used to preserve this blessing is our own *faith* and care; the goal for which we are preserved is *salvation*; and the time when we will see the safe outcome of everything is *the last time.*

3.1. The fact that they are kept implies both danger and deliverance; they may be attacked, but they will not be overcome.

3.2. The preservation of those who have been born again to receive eternal life is the effect of God's power.

3.3. Preservation by God's power does not replace the endeavor and care of human beings for their own salvation; here we see both God's power and human faith. Faith is God's sovereign means of preserving the soul through grace to glory.

3.4. This salvation is *ready to be revealed in the last time.* It is now prepared and reserved in heaven for them. Although it is ready now, it is still largely hidden and unrevealed, even to the heirs of salvation (Heb 1:14) themselves. It will be fully and completely *revealed in the last time. Life and immortality are now brought to light by the Gospel* (2Ti 1:10), but this life will be revealed more gloriously at death, when the soul will be received into the presence of Christ and see his glory.

Verses 6–9

The opening expression *wherein* (in which) refers to the apostle's foregoing discussion of the excellence of his readers' present state and their great expectations for the future (v. 6). "In this condition *you greatly rejoice.*"

1. Here are several things to mitigate their sorrows.

1.1. All true Christians always have something in which they may greatly rejoice.

1.2. The chief joy of true Christians arises from their relationship with God and heaven, which is their treasure, and their entitlement to it is certain.

1.3. Even the best Christians may still be troubled and feel grief in many trials. All kinds of adversities are temptations or tests. These seldom come singly, but are many, coming from different quarters, and their effects are trouble and grief.

1.4. The adversities and sorrows of good people last only a short while. The shortness of any adversity does much to lessen its sorrow.

1.5. Great sorrow is often necessary for a Christian's good: *If need be, you are in heaviness.* God does not trouble his people willingly, but he acts with judgment, in proportion to our needs. These troubles, which cause sorrow, never come to us except when we need them, and they never remain any longer than necessary.

2. He expresses the goal of their adversities and the basis of their joy in them (v. 7).

2.1. The adversities of serious Christians are designed to test their faith to see if it is genuine. God's intention in afflicting his people is to examine and refine them, not to destroy them. This test is administered to their faith principally, because the testing of this is, in effect, the testing of all that is good in us. Christ prays for this apostle *that his faith might not fail* (Lk 22:32); if that is supported, everything else will stand firm.

2.2. A tested faith is much more precious than refined gold. Here is a double comparison of faith and gold, a comparison between faith and gold and between the testing of the one and the testing of the other. Gold is the most valuable and durable of all metals; so is faith among the Christian virtues. It lasts until it brings the soul to heaven. The testing of faith is much more precious than the testing of gold. Gold does not increase and multiply by being tested in fire; rather, it becomes less. But *faith* is established and multiplied by the adversity that it meets with. *Gold* must perish in the end — *gold that perisheth* — but *faith* never will. The testing of faith will be found *to praise, and honour, and glory.* If a tested faith is found to result in praise, honor, and glory, let this commend faith to you as much more precious than gold, even though it is attacked and tested by adversities.

2.3. Jesus Christ will appear again in glory. The time of testing will soon be over, but the glory, honor, and praise will last to eternity.

3. He particularly commends the faith of these early Christians for two reasons:

3.1. The excellence of its object, the unseen Jesus (v. 8). It is one thing to believe God, or Christ — even demons believe (Jas 2:19) — and another thing to trust in him.

3.2. The two notable results or effects of their faith, *love* and *joy*, and this joy is so great that it defies description.

3.2.1. The senses deal with things that are visible and present; reason is a higher guide; faith rises further still. It is *the evidence of things not seen* (Heb 11:1).

3.2.2. True faith is never alone; it produces a strong love for Jesus Christ. True Christians have a sincere love for Jesus, because they believe in him.

3.2.3. Where there are true faith and love for Christ, there is *joy unspeakable and full of glory.* It cannot be described in words. The best way to discover it is by tasting it for ourselves in our own experience; it is *full of glory*, full of heaven. There is much of heaven and the future glory in the present joys of growing Christians; their faith removes the causes of sorrow and offers the best reasons for joy. Well might these early Christians rejoice with joy inexpressible, since they were every *day receiving the end of their faith, the salvation of their souls* (v. 9). Notice:

3.2.3.1. The blessing they received: *The salvation of their souls*, salvation here being called *The end of their faith*, the goal of their faith.

3.2.3.2. The word used alludes to the games at which the conqueror received a crown or reward. The salvation of the soul was the prize these Christians sought, the goal they aimed at, which came nearer and more within their reach every day. Every faithful Christian is daily receiving the salvation of their soul. These believers had the beginnings of heaven in their possession of holiness and a heavenly mind. They were on the losing side in the world, but the apostle reminds them of what they are receiving; if they lose things that are less good, they are all the time receiving the salvation of their souls. The glory of God and our own happiness are connected in such a way that if we regularly seek one, we must obtain the other.

Verses 10–12

Peter goes on to show his readers what authority he has for what he has written. He produces the authority of the prophets to convince them that the doctrine of salvation through faith in Jesus Christ is not a new doctrine. The old prophets searched into it intently. Notice:

1. Who made this diligent search — the *prophets*, who were inspired by God.

2. The object of their search, which was *salvation* and *the grace of God which would come unto you.* They foresaw glorious times of light, grace, and comfort, which made them and other righteous people want to see and hear the things that came to pass in the days of the Gospel.

3. How they inquired: they *inquired and searched diligently.* The words are strong and emphatic, alluding to miners, who dig to the bottom of a pit, breaking through not only earth but also rock to reach the ore. In the same way, these holy prophets had a passionate desire to know and were proportionately diligent in their seeking. Their being inspired did not make their diligent search unnecessary. The doctrine of human salvation through Jesus Christ has been the study and wonder of the greatest and wisest people, and those who want to come to know this great salvation and the grace that shines in it must inquire and search diligently into it.

4. The particular matters into which the ancient prophets chiefly searched (v. 11). Jesus Christ was the main subject of their studies. They inquired most intently into:

4.1. His humiliation and death and its glorious consequences. This inquiry would lead them to consider the whole Gospel.

4.2. The time in which the Messiah was to appear. Undoubtedly these holy prophets earnestly desired to see the days of the Son of Man (Mt 13:17; Lk 17:22); their minds, therefore, were set on the time of its accomplishment, so far as the Spirit of Christ, which was in them, had shown anything on that subject. The nature of the times was also under their strict consideration. Note, from the example of Christ Jesus we may learn to expect a time of service and suffering before we are received in glory. It was so with him, and *the disciple is not above his Lord* (Mt 10:24).

5. The success with which their inquiries were crowned. God gave them a satisfactory revelation to quiet and comfort their minds. They were informed that these things would not come to pass in their time: "*not unto themselves, but to us,* and we must report them, under the infallible direction of the Holy Spirit, to the whole world." *Which things the angels desire to look into* (v. 12).

6. We have here three kinds of inquirer: *the prophets*, who *searched diligently* into it; the apostles, who consulted all the prophecies, were witnesses of their fulfillment, and reported what they knew to others by preaching the Gospel; and the angels, who most attentively look into these matters. We can learn from this:

6.1. A diligent endeavor for the knowledge of Christ will certainly be answered with success.

6.2. Even the holiest and best people sometimes have their lawful and godly requests denied. God is pleased to answer our needs rather than all our requests.

6.3. In many cases it is the honor and practice of Christians to be useful to others rather than to themselves. The prophets ministered to others, not to themselves.

6.4. The revelations of God to his church are all perfectly consistent; the doctrine of the prophets and that of the apostles agree exactly, since they come from the same Spirit of God.

6.5. The Gospel is the ministry of the Spirit; its success depends on his activity and blessing.

6.6. The mysteries of the Gospel are so glorious that the holy angels long to look into them.

Verses 13–23

1. Peter exhorts his readers to lead lives of self-control and holiness.

1.1. *"Wherefore gird up the loins of your mind* (prepare your minds for action) (v. 13). Let the strength and vigor of your minds be exerted in your duty; disentangle yourselves from everything that would hinder you, and continue resolutely in obedience. *Be sober*, self-controlled, watchful against all spiritual dangers and enemies, and be modest in the whole of your lives. Further, be self-controlled in the formation of your opinions as well as in your practices." The main work of Christians lies in the right management of their heart and mind. Even the best Christians need to be exhorted to self-control. A Christian's work is not finished as soon as they are in a state of grace; they must still hope for and seek more grace. We must settle our hopes fully, but also prepare our minds for action, vigorously setting about the work we have to do, encouraging ourselves from the grace of Jesus Christ.

1.2. *As obedient children* (v. 14). It may be taken as an argument to urge Peter's readers to holiness from the consideration of what they now are, children of obedience, and what they were when they lived in their sinful desires and ignorance. The children of God should prove they are such by their obedience to God. The best of God's children have had their times of evil desires and ignorance, but on the whole, when people are converted, they are very different from what they were before.

1.3. *But as he who hath called you* (vv. 15–16). Here is a noble rule enforced by three strong arguments, taken from the grace of God in calling us, from his command *it is written*, and from his example: *Be you holy, for I am holy*. This shows us:

1.3.1. It is a great favor to be called effectively by divine grace into the possession of all the blessings of the new covenant, and great favors are strong incentives; they enable as well as motivate us to be holy.

1.3.2. Complete holiness is the duty of every Christian. Its extent must be universal: we must *be holy* and be so *in all manner of conversation* (in all we do), toward all people, friends and enemies; in all our dealings and business we must be holy.

1.3.3. Its example is God himself: we must *be holy, as God is holy*: we must imitate him, even though we can never equal him. The consideration of the holiness of God should be an incentive to us to attain the highest degree of holiness possible.

1.4. If *you call on the Father* (v. 17). The whole time of our living here is to be spent in reverent fear of God. Holy confidence in God as Father and a reverential fear of him as Judge are consistent with each other. The judgment of God will be undertaken impartially, *according to every man's work*. God will not show partiality; he will not favor the cause of the Jews out of personal considerations, but judge them according to their work.

1.5. Peter adds (v. 18) a second argument. Here, he reminds his readers:

1.5.1. That they were redeemed by a ransom paid to the Father.

1.5.2. What the price paid for their redemption was.

1.5.3. What they were redeemed from: the empty way of life handed down from their ancestors (v. 18).

1.5.4. They know this, and cannot pretend ignorance. This shows us:

1.5.4.1. The consideration of our redemption should be a constant and powerful incentive to holiness and the fear of God.

1.5.4.2. God expects Christians to live responsibly according to what they know.

1.5.4.3. Neither silver nor gold nor anything perishable in this world can redeem even one soul. They are perishable and therefore cannot redeem an imperishable and immortal soul.

1.5.4.4. The blood of Jesus Christ is the only price of human redemption.

1.5.4.5. The intention of Christ in shedding his most precious blood was to redeem us not only from eternal misery in the future but also from an empty way of life in this world. Not only the open evils but also the emptiness and unprofitableness of our way of life are highly dangerous.

1.5.4.6. A person's way of life may plead long custom and tradition in its defense and yet in the end be empty. Antiquity is no certain rule of truth.

1.6. The apostle goes on to speak about some things relating to both the Redeemer and the redeemed (vv. 20–21).

1.6.1. The Redeemer is further described as one:

1.6.1.1. Who was *fore-ordained before the foundation of the world. Fore-ordained* refers to an act of the will, a resolution that the thing will happen (Ac 2:23).

1.6.1.2. Who was *manifested in these last days for them*. He was revealed to be the Redeemer whom God had foreordained. "This was done in these last times of the New Testament and of the Gospel. You have the encouragement of the revelation and appearance of Christ if you believe in him."

1.6.1.3. Who was raised from the dead by the Father, who *gave him glory*, declaring to the whole world by his resurrection from the dead that he is his Son (Ro 1:4), and who glorified him with the glory that he had with God before the world existed (Jn 17:5).

1.6.2. The redeemed are also described here, by their faith and hope, the basis of which is Jesus Christ: *You do by him believe in God.*

1.6.3. We can learn from all this:

1.6.3.1. The decree of God to send Christ to be a Mediator was from eternity. God had purposes of special favor toward his people long before he made any revelations of such grace to them.

1.6.3.2. Great is the happiness of the last times in comparison with what the former ages of the world enjoyed. Our gratitude and service should correspond to the favors with which we have been blessed in this latter age.

2. He exhorts them to show mutual love.

2.1. He presumes that the Gospel has already produced at least an *unfeigned love of the brethren* (v. 22). It is not to be doubted that all sincere Christians purify their soul. The apostle assumes this: *Seeing you have*. Many people hear the truth but are never purified by it, because they will not submit to it or obey it. The Spirit of God is the great agent in the purification of the human soul. He provides those virtues and graces that both adorn and purify, and he stirs up our endeavors, making them effective. Yet the help of the Spirit does not replace our own diligence; these people purified their own souls, but it was through the Spirit. The souls of Christians must be purified before they can love one another sincerely. There is no love except what comes out of a pure heart.

2.2. He further urges this duty of love on the basis of a consideration of their spiritual relationship (v. 23). All Christians are born again. They have been brought into a new and a close relationship with one another, that of brothers and sisters. This new and second birth is much more desirable and excellent than the first. By the one we become human beings; by the other, the sons and daughters of the Most High God. Natural brothers and sisters are bound to love one another, but the obligation is double where there is a spiritual relationship.

Verses 24–25

He now sets before us the futility of human beings in their natural state. Nothing can make them solid and substantial except being born again of the imperishable seed, the word of God, and this word is daily set before us in the preaching of the Gospel. People, in their greatest flourishing and glory, are still withering, fading, and dying creatures. Their knowledge, beauty, strength, vigor, wealth, and honor—these are merely like the flower of grass, which soon withers and falls. The only way for this perishing creature to become solid and imperishable is to receive the word of God, for this will preserve them to eternal life and remain with them forever.

CHAPTER 2

The general exhortation to holiness is continued. The means of obtaining it, the word of God, is commended (vv. 1–12). Particular instructions are given (vv. 13–25).

Verses 1–3

The apostle continues his recommendation of mutual love from the previous chapter.

1. His advice is to get rid of or put off what is evil.

1.1. The sins to be put off, or thrown aside, are *malice*, which is settled, excessive anger, retained until it inflames a person to intend trouble; *guile*, or deceit in words; *hypocrisies*, which, because the word is plural, includes all kinds of hypocrisy; *envies*, all instances of grieving at the good and welfare of another; and *evil speaking*, speaking against another or defaming them.

1.2. We can learn from this:

1.2.1. Even the best Christians need to be warned against the worst sins. They are only partly sanctified, and are still liable to succumb to temptations.

1.2.2. Even our best services toward God will neither please him nor profit us if we are not conscientious in fulfilling our duties to others.

1.2.3. Even one sin, if not set aside, will hinder our spiritual profit and eternal welfare.

2. The apostle, like a wise physician, goes on to instruct his readers to digest wholesome food so that they may grow. The duty urged is a strong and constant desire for the *word of God*. This milk of the word must be *sincere*, not adulterated by mixtures from people. The readers must desire it *as new-born babes*. A new life requires the right food. Infants desire ordinary milk, and their desires for it are passionate and frequent. This must be how Christians desire the word of God, so that they may grow by it. Strong desires and love for the word of God are a sure sign of a person's being born again. And once born again, every Christian desires growth and improvement in wisdom and grace. Nor will the word of God leave a person as it finds them; it will fulfill this desire.

3. He adds an argument from their own experience (v. 3): *If so be you have tasted*. The *if* is more like "since"; the apostle is not expressing a doubt, but affirming that these good Christians have tasted the goodness of God. Our Lord Jesus Christ is very gracious to his people; he has in him a fullness of grace (Jn 1:16). This graciousness is best revealed by tasting it for ourselves, but we cannot taste from a distance, as we may see, hear, and smell; to truly taste the graciousness of Christ, then, implies our being united to him by faith. And yet even the best of God's servants have in this life only a taste of the grace of Christ.

Verses 4–12

1. The apostle gives us here a description of Jesus Christ as a *living stone*.

1.1. The apostle calls him a stone to refer to his invincible strength and eternity, and to teach his servants that he is the foundation on which they are built. He is the living stone, having eternal life in himself. The reputation and respect he has with God and humanity are different. He has been rejected by people, but he was chosen by God. We are to come to this person: *To whom coming*. And we come to him by faith, by which we first are united to him and afterward draw near to him. This shows us:

1.1.1. Jesus Christ is the actual foundation stone of all our hopes and happiness.

1.1.2. In general, people reject Jesus Christ (Isa 53:3).

1.1.3. However much Christ may be rejected by an ungrateful world, he is still the One chosen by God and precious in his account.

1.1.4. Those who expect to receive mercy from this gracious Redeemer must come to him, which is our act, though done by God's grace; it is a real endeavor, not a fruitless wish.

1.2. The apostle goes on to speak about the superstructure, the materials built on Christ (v. 6). The apostle is commending the Christian church and constitution to these dispersed Jews. The Christian church is a much nobler fabric than the Jewish temple; it is a living temple. Christ, the foundation, is a living stone. Christians are *lively* (living) *stones*, and they are a holy priesthood. They offer spiritual sacrifices, acceptable to God through Jesus Christ. This shows us:

1.2.1. All sincere Christians have in them a motivation of spiritual life communicated to them from Christ; they are not dead in trespasses and sins (Eph 2:1), but alive to God.

1.2.2. The church of God is a *spiritual house*. This house is being built up, every part of it growing daily, and the whole is supplied in every age by the addition of new members.

1.2.3. All good Christians are a holy priesthood.

1.2.4. This holy priesthood must and will offer spiritual sacrifices to God.

1.2.5. Even the most spiritual sacrifices of the best people are unacceptable to God except through Jesus Christ; that is why we are to bring all our sacrifices to Christ, and by him present them to God.

2. He confirms what he has asserted about Christ being a *living stone* from Isa 28:16. Notice how the apostles, in their quotations, kept to the sense rather than always to the precise words of Scripture. The true sense of Scripture may be justly and fully expressed in words other than Scripture, but in the weighty matters of religion we must depend entirely on Scriptural proof, because the word of God is the only rule God has given us. Accordingly,

the accounts that God has given us in Scripture about his Son Jesus Christ are what require our strictest attention: *Behold, I lay.* The constituting of Christ Jesus as head of the church is an eminent work of God: *I lay in Zion.* Jesus Christ is the chief cornerstone that God has laid in his spiritual building. The cornerstone remains an inseparable part of the building; it supports, unites, and adorns it. So does Christ stay by his holy church, his spiritual house.

3. He draws an important conclusion (v. 7). "You who believe will be so far from being ashamed of Christ that you will boast of him and glory in him forever." The disobedient will go on to reject Jesus Christ, but God is determined that he will remain, despite all opposition, the head of the corner. The apostle draws a conclusion from the prophet's testimony. The prophet did not explicitly say to whom this stone was precious, but he said something from which this consequence drawn by the apostle was unavoidable. The business of a faithful minister is to apply general truths to the particular condition and state of his hearers. The apostle quotes a passage (v. 6) from the prophet Isaiah, applying it differently to good and bad people. This requires wisdom, courage, and faithfulness, but it is profitable to the hearers. Disobedient people have no true faith. They may have some right ideas, but no solid faith. Those who should build the church of Christ are often the worst enemies that Christ has in the world. Yet God will continue his own work despite the falseness of unfaithful friends and the opposition of his worst enemies.

4. The apostle adds a further description, still preserving the metaphor of a stone (v. 8). The words are taken from Isa 8:13–14. Notice:

4.1. The builders, the chief priests, rejected Christ, and the people followed their leaders. Therefore, Christ became to them *a stone of stumbling, and a rock of offense.* All those who are disobedient take offense at the word of God. They are offended by Christ himself, by his teaching and by the purity of his commands, but especially by the lowliness of his appearance. The same blessed Jesus who is the author of salvation to some is the occasion of others' sin and destruction. Those who reject him as a Savior will be split on him as a Rock (Mt 21:44).

4.2. Those who accepted him were greatly privileged (v. 9). The Jews were very fond of their ancient privileges. "Now," they say, "if we submit to the Gospel constitution, we will lose all this." The apostle responds that if they do not submit, they are ruined (vv. 7–8), but if they do submit, they will lose no real advantage, but remain still *a chosen generation, a royal priesthood.* All true Christians *are a chosen generation*; they all form one family, a kind of people distinct from the common world. All the true servants of Christ are a royal priesthood, separated from sin and sinners, dedicated to God, and offering God spiritual services and sacrifices, acceptable to God through Jesus Christ. All Christians, wherever they are, form one *holy nation.* It is the honor of the servants of Christ that they are God's *peculiar people*, the people he has acquired, chosen, cared for, and delighted in. These four excellencies of Christians are not natural to them, because their first state is a state of terrible darkness, but they have been effectively called out of darkness into a state of *marvelous light*, so that they may declare the greatness and praise of the One who has called them. The apostle advises his readers to compare their former state and their present one. There was a time when they were not a people and had not obtained mercy, but now they have been taken in again to be the people of God and have obtained mercy.

5. He warns them to beware of sinful desires (v. 11). Knowing both the difficulty and the importance of the duty, he pleads his strongest relationship with them: *Dearly beloved, I beseech you.* The duty is to keep away from these desires. These Christians should avoid these, considering:

5.1. The respect they have from God: They are *dearly beloved.*

5.2. Their condition in the world: they are *strangers and pilgrims* and should not impede their passage by giving in to the sinful desires of the country through which they pass.

5.3. The great trouble these sins cause: they *war against the soul.* Of all kinds of sin, none are more harmful to the soul than *fleshly lusts.*

6. He urges them, further, to conduct themselves honorably. They live among the Gentiles, who are their hardened enemies and constantly speak evil of them *as of evildoers.* "A good life may not only silence their mouths but also be a means of bringing them to glorify God and turn to you when they see that you surpass others in good works. Vindicate yourselves by good works: this is the way to convince them. When the Gospel comes among them and takes effect, good conduct on your part will encourage them in their conversion, but evil conduct will obstruct it."

Verses 13–25

A Christian life must be honorable. We must discharge all our duties to other people. Here the apostle deals with each of these duties.

1. The duty of citizens to their government. Christians were not only reputed to be innovators in religion but also considered to be disturbers of the state. It was highly necessary, therefore, that the apostle settle the rules of obedience to civil magistrates.

1.1. The duty required is submission.

1.2. The people or objects to whom this appropriate submission is due are described. Generally, *every ordinance of man* must be obeyed. Authority is certainly divinely instituted. This is a general rule, binding on all nations, whatever the established form of government. Particularly, submission is due *to the king, as supreme, or unto governors*, who *are sent by him*, commissioned by him to govern.

1.3. The reasons in support of this duty:

1.3.1. *For the Lord's sake*, for the Lord has ordained magistracy for the good of the human race.

1.3.2. For the goals and use of the magistrate's office, which are to punish evildoers and to praise and encourage all who do well. True religion is the best support of civil government. The best way magistrates can discharge their duty and change the world is to punish well and reward well.

1.3.3. Because it *is the will of God*, and God's will is by definition the duty of Christians. To good people, *the will of God* is the strongest reason to carry out any duty. Christians must try in all their relationships to behave so as to silence the unreasonable reproaches of the most ignorant and foolish people.

1.3.4. Because of the spiritual nature of Christian freedom. The apostle tells the Christians that they are free, but free from what? Not from duty or obedience to God's law, which requires submission to civil magistrates. They are free spiritually; they must still remember they are *the servants of God.* All the servants of Christ are free, but the servants of Jesus Christ should be very careful not to abuse their Christian freedom.

1.4. The apostle concludes with four wonderful commands:

1.4.1. *Honour all men.* Proper respect is to be given to everyone; the poor are not to be despised, and even evildoers must be honored, not for their evil, but for qualities such as knowledge, courage, high rank, or great age.

1.4.2. *Love the brotherhood* (your fellow believers). All Christians are a community. They should therefore love one another with special affection.

1.4.3. *Fear God* with the greatest reverence. If this is lacking, none of the other three duties can be performed as they should be.

1.4.4. *Honour the king.*

2. The duty of servants. Servants thought their Christian freedom set them free from their unbelieving and cruel masters, but:

2.1. The apostle orders them to *be subject*—and *not only to the good and gentle,* but even to the crooked and perverse. Sinful behavior by one party in a relationship does not justify sinful behavior in another; servants are bound to do their duty even if their master is sinfully unreasonable. But good people are humble and gentle toward their servants and subordinates.

2.2. He condescends to reason with them about it.

2.2.1. If they are patient under their hardships while they suffer unjustly (vv. 19–20), this will be acceptable to God. There is no condition so low that a person cannot glorify God in it; the most insignificant person can do so. The most conscientious people are often the ones who suffer most. *For conscience toward God, they suffer wrongfully*; *they do well, and suffer for it*; but sufferers of this kind are to be commended; they honor God and they are accepted by him. Deserved sufferings, on the other hand, must be endured with patience.

2.2.2. More reasons are given to encourage Christian servants to endure unjust sufferings patiently (v. 21). They must do so because of their Christian calling and because of the example of Christ. Good Christians are a kind of people who are called to suffer and must therefore expect it; they are bound to deny themselves and take up the cross (Mt 16:24). Jesus Christ *suffered for you,* or *for us,* in our place and for our good (v. 24). The sufferings of Christ should quiet us under the most unjust and cruel sufferings we encounter in the world. He suffered for us willingly and with the greatest readiness. Shall not we sinners submit to the light adversities of this life, which work for us inexpressible advantages afterward (2Co 4:17)?

2.3. The example of Christ's submission and patience is explained here. *Christ suffered*:

2.3.1. Wrongfully; he *did no sin* (v. 22), *neither was guile found in his mouth* (Isa 53:9). His words as well as his actions were all sincere, just, and right.

2.3.2. Patiently. Provocations to sin can never justify commission of sin. The reasons to sin can never be so great that we do not always have stronger reasons to avoid it.

2.4. In case anyone should think that Christ's death was intended to be merely an example of patience in suffering, the apostle here adds a more glorious intention and effect of it: *Who his own self bore our sins.* Notice in this:

2.4.1. The person suffering—Jesus Christ: *His own self—in his own body.* The expression *his own self* is emphatic, to distinguish him from the Levitical priests, who offered the blood of other creatures.

2.4.2. The sufferings he experienced were *stripes and the death of the* cross—servile and ignominious punishment.

2.4.3. The reason for his suffering was that he *bore our sins.* He bore them when he stood charged with them, and he bore them by being punished for them on our behalf. Just as the scapegoat symbolically bore the sins of the people on his head, and then took them completely away, so the Lamb of God first bears our sins in his own body, taking away the sins of the world.

2.4.4. The results of Christ's sufferings are our sanctification and our justification: *By his stripes we are healed.*

2.5. The apostle concludes by reminding Christian servants of the difference between their former and present condition (v. 25). Formerly, they *were as sheep going astray,* which represents:

2.5.1. The sin of human beings: people go astray; it is their own act.

2.5.2. Their misery: people go astray from the shepherd and the flock.

2.5.3. The recovery of these by conversion: *but are now returned.* This return is to Christ, who is the true caring Shepherd, who loves his sheep, who is the most watchful pastor—*pastor* literally means "shepherd"—and *bishop,* or Overseer, of souls.

CHAPTER 3

The apostle describes the duties of husbands and wives to one another (vv. 1–7). He exhorts Christians to unity and patience in suffering, and he exhorts them to oppose the slander of their enemies (vv. 8–17). To encourage them to do this, he offers the example of Christ (vv. 18–22).

Verses 1–7

1. In case Christian women should imagine that their conversion to Christ exempts them from submission to their pagan or Jewish husbands, the apostle here:

1.1. Tells them what the duty of wives consists in, namely:

1.1.1. *Subjection,* or an affectionate submission. This obliging behavior will be the likeliest way to win those unbelieving husbands who have rejected the word or who will pay attention to no other evidence of its truth than what they see in the exemplary *conversation* (behavior) *of their wives.* A cheerful submission and a loving, reverential respect are duties that Christian women owe their husbands, whether the latter are good or bad. For winning people to the Gospel, there is nothing more powerful, next to the word of God, than a good life.

1.1.2. *Fear,* or reverence to their husbands.

1.1.3. *A chaste way of life.* Evildoers are strict observers of the conduct of those who profess a religious faith. Purity of life is an excellent means of winning them to the faith of the Gospel.

1.1.4. Preferring the adornments of the inner life to those of outward appearance (v. 3).

1.1.4.1. Peter establishes a rule forbidding three kinds of decorative features: *plaiting of hair,* which was common in those times among immoral women; *wearing of gold*; and *putting on of apparel* (fine clothes) when it is too expensive and too elaborate. Religious people should take care that all their external behavior corresponds to their profession of faith. The outward adorning of the body is often worldly and excessive. Pure Christian women should not wear the clothes that prostitutes wear.

1.1.4.2. He tells Christian wives to put on much more excellent and beautiful adornments (v. 4). Notice:

1.1.4.2.*1*. The part to be adorned: *the hidden man of the heart*. "Take care to grace and beautify your souls rather than your bodies."

1.1.4.2.*2*. The adornment prescribed. It must be something *not corruptible*. The adornments of the body perish when they are used, but the longer we wear the grace of God, the brighter and better it is. The finest adornment of Christian women is *a meek and quiet spirit*. If the husband is harsh and averse to religion, there is no way that is so likely to win him as wise, gentle behavior.

1.1.4.2.*3*. Its excellence. In the sight of God, a gentle, quiet spirit is *of great price* (v. 4). A true Christian's main concern lies in the right controlling and commanding of their own spirit (Pr 16:32). Where the hypocrite's work ends, the true Christian's work begins. The endowments of the inner being are the chief adornments of a Christian, but especially a gentle, composed, and calm spirit makes the man or woman beautiful and lovely.

1.2. Backs up his argument by giving examples:

1.2.1. Of the greatest and best women in the world who trusted in God.

1.2.2. Of Sarah in particular, who obeyed her husband Abraham, following him. "*Whose daughters you are* if you imitate her in faith and good works." The submission of wives to their husbands is a duty that has been practiced universally by holy women in all ages. Christians should fulfill their duty to one another not out of fear or because they are forced, but from a willing mind and in obedience to the command of God.

2. He next considers the husband's duty to the wife.

2.1. The details are, first, *dwelling with the wife according to knowledge*, as wise and self-controlled men, who know the word of God and their own duty, and, second, *giving honour to the wife*, giving her proper respect and placing an appropriate trust and confidence in her (Pr 31:11).

2.2. The reason is that she is *the weaker vessel* by nature and constitution. But apart from that, in other and higher respects, the wife is equal to her husband; they are *heirs together of the grace of life* and should therefore live peacefully and quietly with one another, and if they do not, their praying with one another and for one another will be hindered.

Verses 8 – 15

The apostle moves on to more general exhortations.

1. He teaches us how Christians and friends should treat one another. Christians should seek to be in agreement on the great points of faith, in genuine affection, and in Christian practice. If they cannot be exactly in agreement, they should still have compassion on one another and love one another as brothers and sisters. Christianity requires pity for the distressed and civility to all.

2. He instructs us how to behave toward enemies.

2.1. He warns his readers not to repay *evil for evil*. "When they hurl insults at you, bless them; when they speak to you with evil words, respond to them with good ones, because Christ has called you to bless those who curse you (Mt 5:44) and has established a blessing on you as your eternal inheritance." The laws of Christ make us respond to insults with blessing. We must pity, pray for, and love those who insult us. As the calling of Christians invests them with glorious privileges, so it obliges them to fulfill difficult duties.

2.2. He gives an excellent prescription for a worthwhile, happy life in this quarrelsome, ill-natured world (vv. 10 – 12). The verses quoted come from Ps 34:12 – 16.

2.2.1. It is lawful to consider physical advantages as motives and encouragements to religious faith.

2.2.2. The practice of religious faith, especially the right control of the tongue, is the best way to make this life encouraging and prosperous; a sincere, inoffensive, discreet tongue is a uniquely effective means of getting us through life in this world peaceably and comfortably.

2.2.3. It is the duty of Christians not only to accept peace when it is offered but also to seek and pursue it when it is denied.

2.3. He shows that Christians need not fear that such patient, inoffensive behavior will invite their enemies to be cruel. God's *ears are open to their prayers. But the face of the Lord is against those that do evil.* He is more an enemy to evil persecutors than people are. God takes special care and offers fatherly love toward all his righteous people. God always hears the prayers of the faithful

2.4. This patient, humble behavior of Christians is further urged from two considerations.

2.4.1. It will be the best and surest way to prevent suffering, "Usually, there will only be a few people who are so diabolical and godless as to harm those who live so innocently and usefully as you."

2.4.2. It is the way to learn from suffering. "*If you be followers of that which is good*, and yet *suffer* (v. 14), it will be for your glory and your happiness. Therefore, you need not be afraid of anything your enemies can do to strike you with terror; don't be very much troubled or concerned about their rage or force." Notice, always to follow what is good is the best way we can take to keep out of harm's way, and yet to suffer for righteousness' sake is the honor and happiness of a Christian, for Christians have no reason to fear the threats or rage of any of their enemies. Instead of terrifying yourselves with human fear, be sure to *sanctify the Lord God* (set apart Christ as Lord) *in your hearts* (v. 15). And, "when this principle is set deeply in your hearts, the next thing is to be always ready, with regard to others, *to give an answer to every man that asketh a reason of your hope.* The hope and faith of a Christian are defensible against the whole world, and every Christian is bound to answer for the hope that is in them, and to have reasons readily available to offer for their Christian faith, so that it may be seen that they are not motivated by either foolishness or fancy. These confessions of our faith should be made *with meekness and fear.*

Verses 16 – 17

The confession of a Christian's faith cannot be supported credibly except by *a good conscience* and a *good conversation* (conduct). Conscience is good when it is kept clear from guilt. *A good conversation in Christ* is a holy life. "Look well to your conscience and your behavior, and then, even if people falsely accuse you as evildoers, you will put them to shame. Don't be discouraged, for it is better for you, though worse for your enemies, that you suffer for doing good than for doing evil." The most conscientious people cannot escape the censures and slander of evildoers; Christ and his apostles were treated in this way. Yet false accusation generally turns to the accuser's shame. Just as doing good sometimes exposes good people to suffering, so doing evil will not exempt evildoers from it. If the sufferings of good people for doing good are so severe, what will the sufferings of evildoers be for doing evil?

Verses 18–20

1. The example of Christ is given as an argument for patience. Jesus Christ himself was not exempt from suffering in this life. Note the particular words of this argument.

1.1. The reason for Christ's suffering was human sins: *Christ suffered for sins.*

1.2. In the case of our Lord's suffering, it was the *just* One who suffered for the *unjust* (the righteous for the unrighteous). The One who had no sin suffered instead of those who had no righteousness.

1.3. The merit and perfection of Christ's sacrifice were such that for him to suffer *once* was enough. The legal sacrifices were repeated; the sacrifice of Christ, once suffered, cleanses from sin.

1.4. The blessed purpose of our Lord's sufferings was to *bring us to God.*

1.5. The outcome of Christ's suffering as to himself was that he was *put to death* in his human nature but was *quickened* and raised again *by the Spirit.* If Christ was not exempt from suffering, why should Christians expect to be? If he suffered, though perfectly just, why should we not, who are all criminals? If he suffered once and then entered glory, shall we not be patient in trouble?

2. The apostle passes from this example of Christ to the example of his preaching to the people in the old world. Like them, the Jews to whom Peter writes now have an offer of mercy; those who accept it will be saved, but those who reject Christ will just as certainly be destroyed as the disobedient people in the times of Noah were.

2.1. For the explanation of this we may notice:

2.1.1. The preacher: Christ Jesus. *He went and preached,* striving with them by his Spirit (Ge 6:3).

2.1.2. The hearers. Being dead and disembodied when the apostle speaks about them, they are properly called spirits now *in prison,* though they were not yet in prison when Christ preached to them.

2.1.3. The sin of these people: they were *disobedient.* Their sin is emphasized by the patience and *longsuffering of God.*

2.1.4. The outcome of it all: their bodies were drowned, while Noah and his family, who believed and were obedient, *were saved in the ark.*

2.2. From all this we may learn that although the patience of God waits a long time for sinners, it will eventually expire; it is beneath the majesty of the great God always to wait for people in vain. We may also learn that the way of most people is neither the best, the wisest, nor the safest way to follow: it is better to follow the eight people in the ark.

Verses 21–22

Noah's salvation in the ark on the water was a symbol of the salvation of all good Christians through baptism. To prevent mistakes:

1. The apostle declares what he means by saving baptism. It is not the external ceremony of washing with water, but the baptism in which there is a faithful answer of a resolved good conscience.

2. The effectiveness of baptism for salvation depends not on the work done by human hands, but on the resurrection of Christ. The sacrament of baptism, rightly received, is a means and a promise of salvation, and so the apostle can say that *baptism now saveth us,* and yet the external participation in baptism will save no one without a corresponding clear conscience and good conduct. There must be the response of a good conscience toward God.

3. The apostle proceeds to speak of Christ's ascension and his sitting at the right hand of the Father (v. 22). If the advancement of Christ was so glorious after his deep humiliation, let his followers not despair; let them expect to be advanced to transcendent joy and glory after these short times of distress. Upon his ascension into heaven, Christ was enthroned at the right hand of the Father. Angels, authorities, and powers are all made subject to Christ Jesus.

CHAPTER 4

The work of a Christian is twofold: doing the will of God and suffering according to his will. This chapter instructs us in both. The duties we are here exhorted to apply ourselves to are putting to death sin, living for God, self-control, prayer, love, hospitality, and the best use of our gifts (vv. 1–11). The instructions for suffering are that we should not be surprised at it, but rejoice in it. The apostle tells his readers that the best way to preserve their souls is to commit them to God while doing good (vv. 12–19).

Verses 1–3

The apostle uses a consideration of Christ's sufferings to persuade his readers to put to death sin. Notice:

1. How the exhortation is expressed. *Christ suffered* for us in the flesh, or in his human nature. "Therefore, *arm* and strengthen *yourselves likewise with the same mind.* As Christ suffered in his human nature, you are to make your corrupt nature suffer, by putting to death the body of sin (Ro 6:6) by self-denial. Some of the strongest and best arguments against all kinds of sin are taken from the suffering of Christ. All sympathy and tenderness for Christ as a sufferer are lost if you do not put away sin. The beginning of all true putting to death of sin lies in the mind, not in doing penance and treating the body harshly.

2. How it is further explained (v. 2). Negatively, Christians should *no longer live the rest of their time in the flesh.* Positively, they should conform themselves to the revealed will of the holy God. Sinful desires of human beings are the springs of all their evil. No matter how strong the temptations we are subject to from time to time, they could not conquer if it were not for our own corruptions. True conversion makes a marvelous change in the heart and life of a person who has experienced it.

3. How it is supported (v. 3). "It is only just that as up to this time, in the entire first part of your life, you have served sin and Satan, so you should now serve the living God." When a person is really converted, it is very painful to them to think how their past life has been spent. While the will of a person is unsanctified and corrupt, they walk continually in evil ways, making a bad condition daily worse and worse. One sin that is allowed leads to another. Here six sins are named: *lasciviousness,* expressed in looks, gestures, or behavior (Ro 13:13); *lusts,* acts of sexual immorality; *excess of wine; revellings,* feasts that are too frequent, excessive, or expensive; *banquetings,* by which is meant gluttony; and *abominable idolatry,* the detestable idol worship of the Gentiles. It is a Christian's duty to abstain not only from what is grossly evil but also from those things that generally cause sin.

Verses 4–6

1. Here we have the visible change brought about in those who were represented as having been evil in the first part of their lives. Notice the behavior of their evil acquaintances toward them.

1.1. *They think it strange* that their old friends do not rush with as much force as they used to *into the same excess of riot* (flood of dissipation).

1.2. *They speak evil of them.* Their surprise leads them to blasphemy. But those who are truly converted will not return to their former course of life; neither persuasion nor insults will be effective with them. The attitude and behavior of true Christians seem very strange to the ungodly; the ungodly cannot understand. Even the best actions of religious people, therefore, cannot escape the criticism and slander of those who are irreligious. The world will speak evil of good people even though they themselves reap the fruits of their love, devotion, and goodness.

2. For the comfort of the servants of God, it is added here:

2.1. That all evildoers will *give an account* to the One who is ready to judge. The evil world will soon have to give to the great God an account of all the harsh words they have spoken against his people.

2.2. That *for this cause was the Gospel preached also to those that are dead.* Some understand *to those that are dead* as meaning "to all the faithful of old, who are now dead in Christ." The Gospel was preached to them so that, having put to death their sins, they would live a new and spiritual life, according to God. Putting sins to death and living for God are the expected effects of the Gospel that is preached to us. God will certainly judge all those who have had the Gospel preached to them but have not been affected in this way. It does not matter how we are judged according to human standards as regards the body, if only we will live according to God in the Spirit.

Verses 7–11

We have here a fearful position and a conclusion drawn from it. The position is that the *end of all things is at hand.* The destruction of the Jewish church and nation is now very close; the time of persecution for Peter's readers is therefore short. "Your own life and the lives of your enemies will soon come to an end." In fact, the world itself will not continue very long. The conclusion from this consists of exhortations:

1. To sobriety and watchfulness. Do not allow yourselves to be caught up with your former sins and temptations (v. 3). *And watch unto prayer.* Take care that you frequently pray, so that the end may not come on you unawares. Those who want to pray relevantly must *watch unto prayer.*

2. To love. Christians should love one another. This mutual affection must not be cold, but wholehearted, that is, sincere, strong, and lasting. This sort of wholeheartedness is commended *above all things*, which shows its importance. One excellent effect of it is that it will *cover a multitude of sins. Have charity among yourselves.* There is a special relationship between all sincere Christians, and a particular loveliness and good in them that require special affection. It is not enough for Christians not to bear hatred, nor to have ordinary respect for one another; they must love one another deeply and wholeheartedly. It is the quality of true love *to cover a multitude of sins.* It makes people forgive and forget offenses against them, covering the sins of others rather than emphasizing them and making them known. It prepares for mercy from God, who has promised to forgive those who forgive others.

3. To hospitality (v. 9). The proper objects of Christian hospitality are one another. The way in which this duty is to be performed is that it must be done in an easy, kind,

generous manner, *without grudging* or grumbling at the expense or trouble. Christians should show each other not only love but also hospitality.

4. To the stewardship of talents (Mt 25:14–30) (v. 11).

4.1. Whatever power of doing good has been given to us, we should use it to minister *to one another.* In receiving and using the various gifts of God, we must consider ourselves simply stewards.

4.2. The apostle enlarges on his instructions about gifts by giving two examples, speaking and ministering, about which he gives his readers these rules:

4.2.1. *If any man speaks*, he must do it *as the oracles of God.* Whatever Christians teach and speak in private, or ministers in public, must be the pure word of God.

4.2.2. "*If any man minister, let him do it as of the ability which God giveth*; let him give according to his ability, so that God may be glorified *through Jesus Christ*, to whom *be praise and dominion for ever and ever. Amen.*" This teaches us:

4.2.2.1. It is the duty of Christians in private, as well as ministers in public, to speak to one another about the things of God.

4.2.2.2. All preachers of the Gospel should keep close to the word of God and treat that word as befits *the oracles of God.*

4.2.2.3. Whatever we are called to do for the honor of God and the good of others, we should do it with all our strength.

4.2.2.4. In all the duties and services of life we should aim at the glory of God; all other aims must be subservient to this.

4.2.2.5. *God in all things must be glorified through Jesus Christ, who* is the only way to the Father.

Verses 12–19

The frequent repetition, in every chapter of this letter, of advice and encouragement to Christians as those who suffer shows that the greatest danger these new converts were in arose from the persecutions that their acceptance of Christianity exposed them to. The apostle comes here to instruct them in the necessary duty of patience in suffering. Notice:

1. The apostle's kind way of addressing his readers: they are his *beloved* (v. 12).

2. His advice to them about their suffering.

2.1. They should not think it strange or be surprised at it.

2.1.1. Although their trial is sharp and *fiery*, it is intended to test them, not ruin them. They should rejoice in their suffering, then, because theirs may properly be called suffering for Christ. He suffers in our sufferings and feels our weaknesses, and if we share in his suffering, we will also be made *partakers of his glory.*

2.1.1.1. True Christians love and recognize the children of God in their lowliest circumstances. The apostle acknowledges these poor afflicted Christians and calls them his *beloved* (dear friends). True Christians never look more kindly on one another than in their adversities.

2.1.1.2. There is no reason for Christians to wonder at the unkindness and persecution of the world, because they have been forewarned of them. Christ himself endured them.

2.1.1.3. Even in their most painful trials for Christ, Christians should not merely be patient, but rejoice. Those who rejoice in their sufferings for Christ will triumph eternally and rejoice with him in glory.

2.1.2. The apostle descends to speak of a lower form of persecution. They will be verbally abused, insulted, misrepresented, and slandered for the name or sake of Christ. "In such cases," he asserts, "*Happy are you. You have the Spirit of God with you, and the Spirit of God is also the Spirit of glory.* This glorious Spirit *resteth upon you.* By your patience and courage in suffering, *he is on your part glorified,* but by the contempt and insults shown to you, the Spirit himself is slandered and blasphemed." The happiness of good people is not only consistent with, but even flows from, their adversities: *Happy are you.* Those who have the Spirit of God resting on them cannot be miserable, even if their adversities are very great. When good people are insulted *for the name of Christ,* his Holy Spirit is glorified in them.

2.2. They should take care that they do not suffer justly, as murderers, thieves, or evildoers (v. 15). Their enemies accused them of these and other foul crimes; therefore, the apostle thought these warnings necessary. *If any man suffer* for the cause of Christianity, and with a patient Christian spirit, he should not consider it a shame, and he should glorify God who has dignified him in this way (v. 16). But there is very little comfort in sufferings when we bring them on ourselves by our own sin and foolishness. It is not the suffering, but the cause, that makes the martyr.

2.3. Their trials are now at hand, and they should get ready accordingly (vv. 17–18).

2.3.1. Peter tells them the time has come when *judgment must begin at the house of God.* "This makes all the foregoing exhortations to patience necessary for you. Consider:

2.3.1.1. "These judgments will only *begin* with you who are God's house, and will soon be over.

2.3.1.2. "Your troubles will be only light and short in comparison with what will happen to the wicked world. *What shall the end be of those who obey not the Gospel of God?*" Even the best of God's servants have so much wrong in them that it is sometimes necessary for God to correct and punish them, and so *judgment begins at the house of God.* Yet those who belong to the family of God have their worst things in this life; their worst condition is tolerable and will soon be over. The apostle distinguishes the disobedient from the house of God.

2.3.2. He intimates the irremediable destiny of evildoers.

2.3.2.1. The painful suffering of good people in this world is a sad sign of much harsher judgments coming on unrepentant sinners.

2.3.2.2. It is as much as the righteous can do to be saved, but let the absolute necessity of salvation balance out its difficulties. "Your difficulties are greatest at first, and God offers his grace and help."

2.4. When called to suffer *according to the will of God,* they should look chiefly to the security of their *souls, committing them to God.* He will take custody of our souls, because he is their Creator (v. 19). All the suffering that comes to good people comes on them *according to the will of God.* It is the duty of Christians to look more to the keeping of their souls than to the preserving of their bodies. They have great encouragement to commit their souls to God, because he is their Creator, and he remains faithful to all his promises.

CHAPTER 5

In this chapter the apostle gives specific instructions, first to the elders (vv. 1–4), then to those who are younger (vv. 5–7). He then exhorts them all to self-

control, watchfulness against temptations, and firmness in the faith, praying wholeheartedly for them, and concludes his letter (vv. 8–14).

Verses 1–4

We may notice here:

1. The people to whom this exhortation is given: to the elders, elders by position rather than by age, the ministers of the churches to whom he is writing this letter.

2. The person who gives this exhortation. He tells them he is their fellow elder, so laying on them no burden except what he himself is ready to fulfill. He is also *a witness of the sufferings of Christ* and *a partaker of the glory* that will be completely enjoyed at his second coming. It was the distinctive honor of Peter and a few others to have been the witnesses of Christ's sufferings, but it is the privilege of all true Christians to share in the glory that will be revealed.

3. The pastor's duty, which is threefold: *to feed the flock* by preaching to them the sincere word of God (2:2), to *take the oversight thereof,* and to be *examples to the flock,* practicing the holiness that they preach and commend to their people. These duties must be performed *not by constraint* but from a willing mind that takes pleasure in the work. They must be performed *not for filthy lucre* (not greedy for money), *but of a ready mind,* regarding the flock more than the fleece. Nor must they be performed *as being lords over God's heritage,* lording it over them. These poor, dispersed, suffering Christians were the flock of God. The rest of the world is a wild herd. These are an orderly flock, redeemed to God by the Great Shepherd. They are also honored with the title of God's *heritage,* chosen from the general population to be his own people. They are God's people and should be treated with love, humility, and tenderness for the sake of the One to whom they belong.

4. The crown of glory that the apostle tells them is intended by the Great Shepherd for all his faithful ministers, in opposition to the greed for money. Jesus Christ is *the chief shepherd* of the whole flock and *heritage of God.* He is also the chief shepherd over all lesser shepherds. This Chief Shepherd will appear to judge all ministers and undershepherds. Those who are found to have done their duty will receive from the Chief Shepherd *a crown of glory that fadeth not away.*

Verses 5–7

1. The apostle comes now to instruct the flock how to behave themselves toward their ministers and one another. He exhorts those who are younger and subordinate to *submit themselves to the elder.* As to one another, the instruction is that they should all *be subject* (be submissive) *one to another,* so far as to receive the rebukes and advice of one another. He advises them to *be clothed with humility.* "If you are disobedient and proud, God will set himself to oppose you, because *he resisteth the proud* when he *giveth grace to the humble.*" Humility is the great preserver of peace and order in all Christian communities, and so pride disturbs them greatly. There is a mutual opposition between God and the proud. Where God gives grace to be humble, he will give more and more grace and humility. That is why the apostle adds, "Since God opposes the proud but gives grace to the humble, humble yourselves not only to one another but also to the great God. His hand is almighty, and can easily humble you if you become proud or exalt you if you are humble." Humbling ourselves to God under his hand is the best way to deliverance and exaltation.

2. The apostle rightly supposes that what he has foretold of greater hardships still coming might arouse great anxiety in his readers. Foreseeing that these troubles will be a great burden and a severe temptation, he gives them the best advice. His advice is to *cast all their care*, or "all anxiety for themselves," *upon God*. They must trust in him with a firm, composed mind, *for he careth for you*. He is willing to release you from your anxiety and take it from you onto himself. Even the best Christians tend to labor under the burden of anxious and excessive worry. The worries even of good people are burdensome, and are too often sinful. The best solution for anxiety is to *cast our care upon God*. A firm belief in the uprightness of God's will calms the human spirit.

Verses 8–9

Here the apostle does three things:

1. He shows his readers their danger from an enemy whom he describes:

1.1. By his characteristics and names. He is an adversary: *That adversary of yours, the devil*, the accuser of all the brothers (Rev 12:10). He is *a roaring lion*, the fierce and greedy pursuer of souls.

1.2. By his work: *He walks about, seeking whom he may devour*; his whole purpose is to devour and destroy souls.

2. He reasons from this that it is their duty to *be sober* (self-controlled) and *vigilant*, diligent to prevent the Devil from carrying out his designs on them and to save their soul. They must resist him by being *steadfast in the faith*. It is the faith of these people that Satan aims at. They must resist this strong trial and temptation by being firm in the faith.

3. He tells them that their case is not special, because they know that similar adversities have come to their brothers and sisters throughout the world; all the people of God are their fellow soldiers in this warfare. The Devil is the great persecutor *of the brethren* as well as their great *deceiver and accuser*. Self-control and watchfulness are necessary virtues at all times, but especially in times of suffering and persecution. If your faith gives way, you are gone. The consideration of what others suffer rightly encourages us to bear our own share in any suffering: *The*

same afflictions are accomplished (experienced) *in your brethren.*

Verses 10–14

We come now to the conclusion of this letter.

1. The apostle begins with a significant prayer, which he addresses to God as *the God of all grace*. Notice:

1.1. What Peter prays for on his readers' account: that *after they have suffered awhile*, God would perfect his work in them. Those who are called to be heirs of eternal life through Jesus Christ must nevertheless suffer in this world, but their sufferings will last only a little while. God must be wholeheartedly sought, therefore, in constant prayer and dependence on his promises.

1.2. His doxology (v. 11).

2. He sums up his purpose for writing this letter (v. 12). The doctrine of salvation that he has explained and they have embraced is the true account of the grace of God, foretold by the prophets and declared by Jesus Christ. As they embraced the Gospel, they are to continue firm in it. A firm persuasion that we are on the true way to heaven will be the best motivation to stand firm and persevere on that path.

3. He commends *Silvanus* (Silas), the person through whom he is sending them this brief letter. The prejudices that some of these Jews might have had against Silas, as one who, being partner of Paul's, was a minister to the Gentiles (Ac 15:23, 27, 40), would soon wear off once they were convinced that he was a faithful brother.

4. He closes with greetings and a solemn blessing. Peter, being in Babylon, in Assyria, sends the greeting of that church to the other churches to whom he is writing (v. 13). In his greeting he particularly includes Mark the evangelist, who is with him and is *his son* in a spiritual sense. All the churches of Jesus Christ should have a most affectionate concern for one another; they should love and pray for one another. Peter urges his readers to have wholehearted love toward one another and to express this by giving *the kiss of peace* (v. 14), and with this he comes to his concluding blessing, which he confines to those *that are in Christ Jesus*. The blessing he declares on them is *peace*, by which he means all necessary good.

A PRACTICAL AND DEVOTIONAL
EXPOSITION OF
2 Peter

The purpose of this second letter is the same as that of the previous one, as is clear from 3:1, and in this we notice that in the things of God we need *precept upon precept, and line upon line* (Isa 28:10), and all is scarcely enough for us to remember them, but these are the things that should be most faithfully recorded and frequently remembered by us.

CHAPTER 1

In this chapter: 1. We have an introduction leading to what is the main intention of the apostle (vv. 1–4). 2. We have an exhortation to make progress in all Christian graces (vv. 5–7). 3. To support this exhortation, the apostle adds a representation of the great advantage that will come to his readers (vv. 8–11), a promise of the best help the apostle can give (vv. 12–15), and a declaration of the certain truth of the Gospel of Christ (vv. 16–21).

Verses 1–4

1. We have here a description of the person who wrote the letter, by the name of *Simon* as well as *Peter*, and by the title of *servant* as well as that of *apostle*. How great an honor it is to be the servants of this Master! This is what we cannot, without sin, be ashamed of.

2. We have an account of the people to whom the letter is written. They are described as *having obtained precious faith in our Lord Jesus Christ*. True saving faith is a precious grace, on the one hand very scarce, and on the other hand excellent and very useful and advantageous to those who have it. *The just live by faith* (Hab 2:4; Ro 1:17). Faith is equally precious in the private Christian and in the apostle; it produces the same precious effects in the one as in the other. Faith, wherever it is found, takes hold of the same *precious* Savior and applies the same precious promises. This precious faith is obtained from God, as his gift. The preciousness of faith, as well as our obtaining it, is through the righteousness of Christ.

3. We have the apostolic blessing.

3.1. An account of the way by which *grace and peace are multiplied*—it is *through the knowledge of God and Jesus Christ*.

3.2. The basis of his own faith in asking for the increase of grace and the basis of every Christian's hope in expecting it. What we have already received should encourage us to ask for more. All things that have any relation to and influence on the true spiritual life, the life and power of godliness, come from Jesus Christ. Knowledge of God and faith in him are the channels through which all spiritual resources and encouragements are communicated to us, but then we must acknowledge God as the author of our effective calling, for he is described in that way here: *him that hath called us to glory and virtue*. The inten-

tion of God in calling or converting people is to bring them to *glory and virtue*. It is the glory of God's power to convert sinners. The apostle goes on to encourage his readers' faith and hope in looking for an increase in grace and peace.

3.2.1. The good things that the promises declare are great. Pardon of sin is one of the blessings meant here. To forgive sins that are numerous and detestable is wonderful.

3.2.2. The promised blessings of the Gospel are very precious. The great promise of the New Testament is the *Holy Spirit*.

3.2.3. Those who receive the promises of the Gospel *partake of* (share in) *the divine nature*. Their hearts are set on God and his service.

3.2.4. Those in whom the Spirit produces the divine nature are freed from the slavery of corruption. The power that sin has in the people of the world is *through lust*, sinful desires; the desires of human beings are for sin, and that is why it rules over them (Ge 4:7). The controlling power that sin has over us is according to the delight we have in it.

Verses 5–11

Having already obtained precious faith and been enabled to share in the divine nature is a good beginning, but it is not to be rested in, as if we were already perfect. Peter therefore urges his readers to move on to obtain more grace. Those who want to make any progress in religious faith must be very industrious in their endeavors. Without *giving all diligence*, there is no gaining any ground in holiness.

1. The believer's way is marked out step by step.

1.1. They must gain *virtue*, by which some understand justice or goodness. With the *knowledge, temperance, and patience* that follow, the apostle may then be thought to be urging them to seek the four cardinal virtues. On the other hand, in light of Tit 3:8, we may understand *virtue* here to refer to strength and courage, without which believers cannot stand up for good works. Cowardly Christians must expect Christ to be ashamed of them on the great day. We need *virtue* while we live, and it will be very useful when we come to die.

1.2. Believers must add *knowledge* to their *virtue*, wisdom to their courage. Christian wisdom takes note of the people we have to do with and the place and company we are in.

1.3. We must add *temperance*, or self-control, *to our knowledge*. We must be moderate in desiring and using the good things of natural life; an inordinate desire for these is inconsistent with a wholehearted desire for God and Christ.

1.4. Believers are to add to self-control *patience*, which must *have its perfect work*. We are born to trouble (Job 5:7) and must enter into the kingdom of heaven through many sufferings (Ac 14:22). Our sufferings are less than our sins deserve.

1.5. To patience we must add *godliness*. When Christians bear adversities patiently, they experience the *knowledge of the loving-kindness of their heavenly Father*, by which they are brought to the childlike fear and reverential love that true godliness consists of.

1.6. We must add *brotherly-kindness*, a mutual tender affection for all our fellow Christians, who are children of the same Father. They are to be loved as those who are especially near and dear to us.

1.7. *Charity*, or a love consisting of goodwill to all people, must be added to the joyful love we have for the children of God. God has made all nations from one man, and all human beings share in the same human nature, are capable of the same mercies, and are liable to the same adversities. All believers in Christ, then, must show they are the children of God, who is good to all.

2. All the graces just mentioned must be gained, or we will not be *thoroughly furnished for all good works* (2Ti 3:17). To lead us to pursue them, therefore, the apostle sets out the advantages that come to all who successfully labor to get them—who get the graces to *be in them and abound in them* (vv. 8–11).

2.1. These are suggested more generally (v. 8).

2.1.1. When it is said here that the possession and overflowing of all Christian graces in us will make us neither ineffective nor unfruitful, we are to infer that it will make us very zealous and active and very effective and productive in righteous works. These will bring much glory to God by producing much fruit among human beings, making them *fruitful in knowledge*, or the acknowledging, *of our Lord Jesus Christ*. This is the necessary effect of adding one grace to another, because where all Christian graces are in the heart, they improve and strengthen one another. Wherever grace overflows, there will be many good works.

2.1.2. The apostle shows in v. 9 how desirable it is to be in such a situation.

2.1.2.1. He who does not have these active, faithful graces is *blind. He cannot see far off.* He can see and is devoted to this present evil world, but he has no discernment at all about the world to come. How wretched is the condition of those who are so blind to the fearfully great things of the other world!

2.1.2.2. Yet this is not all the misery of those who do not *add to their faith virtue, knowledge*, and so on They are as unable to look backward as to look forward; their memories are slippery and unable to retain what has past. We should often remember and seriously meditate on our solemn engagement to be the Lord's, to lay aside *all filthiness of flesh and spirit*.

2.2. The apostle proposes two particular advantages: stability in grace and a triumphant entrance into glory. We must *give diligence to make our calling and election sure*. It requires a great deal of diligence and labor to make sure of our calling and election; there must be a very close examination of ourselves. "But, however great the work,

do not think it too much, for the advantage you gain by it is great.

2.2.1. "By this you will be kept from falling." When many fall into error, those who are diligent will be kept sound in the faith and stand mature and complete in all the will of God (Col 4:12).

2.2.2. Those who are diligent in their religious faith, who are *growing in grace* and *abounding in the work of the Lord*, will have an *abundant entrance into the joy of their Lord*, and they will *reign with him for ever and ever*.

Verses 12–15

1. Peter *will not be negligent* but will be an example of diligence, especially in reminding others. We need to be reminded of what we already know so that we do not forget it, and so that we improve our knowledge and put everything into practice. We must be firmly established in the belief of the truth so that we may not be shaken by every wind of doctrine (Eph 4:14). We are to be firmly established in the *present truth*, the truth we now have, the truth that is more especially necessary for us to know in our day (Lk 19:42). If the people need teaching and encouragement while they are in the body, it is right and just that ministers, as long as they are *in this tabernacle*, instruct and exhort them, reminding them of those truths that they have heard before.

2. The apostle tells us (v. 14) what makes him serious in pursuing this matter. The body is simply the tent of the soul, and this tent must be put aside. We are not to remain long in this earthly house. The nearness of death makes the apostle diligent in the work of life. He will soon be removed from those to whom he is writing, and because he wants them to remember the teaching he has delivered to them after he himself has been taken away from them, he commits his exhortation to writing.

Verses 16–18

These things are not idle tales or worthless things, but have guaranteed truth and immense significance. The Gospel is not *a cunningly devised fable* (cleverly invented story). Salvation through Jesus Christ is eminently the purpose of God, and the apostle's preaching made this known.

1. The preaching of the Gospel is a declaration of the power of Christ.

2. The coming of Christ is also made known through the preaching of the Gospel. The Gospel sets out very clearly and in detail the first coming of Christ, but there is a second coming, which it also mentions, namely, his coming to judge the world in righteousness by the eternal Gospel.

3. Although this Gospel of Christ has been blasphemously called a *fable* by one of those who call themselves the successors of Peter, our apostle proves that it is the most certain and real thing in the world, inasmuch as during our Savior's time here on earth he sometimes revealed himself to be God, especially to our apostle and the two sons of Zebedee. They *were eyewitnesses of his divine majesty, when he was transfigured before them*. Besides this, there was an audible voice from heaven. Notice here:

3.1. What a gracious declaration was made: *This is my beloved Son, in whom I am well pleased*—the best voice that ever came from heaven to earth; God is pleased with Christ.

3.2. The intention of this voice was to give our Savior a special honor while he was here on earth: *he received honour and glory from God the Father.* This is the person God delights to honor.

3.3. This voice is from heaven, called here *the excellent* (Majestic) *glory*.

3.4. This voice was heard so as to be understood by Peter, James, and John. They not only heard a sound but understood the sense. God opens the ears and understandings of his people to receive what it concerns them to know. Blessed are those who not only hear but also understand, who believe the truth and feel the power of the voice from heaven.

Verses 19–21

In these words the apostle lays down another argument to prove the truth and reality of the Gospel. The doctrine of *the power and coming of our Lord Jesus Christ* is not a mere fable, but the wise and wonderful plan of the holy and gracious God. This doctrine was foretold by the prophets of the Old Testament, who spoke and wrote according to the direction of the Spirit of God. Notice:

1. The description given of the Old Testament Scriptures: they are called *a more sure word of prophecy*. The Old Testament is a prophetic declaration of the power and coming of our Savior. But the New Testament is a historical record of what the Old Testament is a prophecy of. We should read the Old Testament as a prophecy of Christ and use the New Testament with diligence and thankfulness as the best exposition of the Old. How firm and sure should our faith be then, since we have such a firm and sure word to trust in! All the prophecies of the Old Testament are more sure and certain to us who have the history of their fulfillment.

2. The encouragement the apostle gives us to search the Scriptures. *We do well if we take heed to them*, if we apply our minds to understand the sense, and our hearts to believe the truth, of this faithful word. If we apply ourselves to the word of God in this way, we certainly do well in all respects: we do what is pleasing to God and useful to ourselves. The apostle suggests some things that are especially useful to those who want to attend to the Scriptures to any good purpose.

2.1. They must regard and use Scripture as a light that God has sent into the world to dispel the darkness that covers the face of the whole earth.

2.2. They must acknowledge their own darkness. Every person in the world is naturally without the knowledge that is necessary for eternal life.

2.3. If people are ever to become wise for salvation (2Ti 3:15), it is by the shining of the word of God into their hearts. Natural ideas of God are not sufficient for fallen humanity.

2.4. When the light of Scripture shoots into the dark understanding through the Holy Spirit of God, then the spiritual *day dawns and the daystar arises in* that soul. This enlightening of a dark mind is like a dawn that spreads itself through the whole soul until it comes to the full light of day (Pr 4:18). It is an increasing knowledge. All who act honestly come to this light, while evildoers keep far away from it.

3. The one thing the apostle lays down as necessary beforehand if we are to heed and benefit from the Scriptures: knowing that all prophecy has a divine origin.

3.1. No Scripture prophecy comes about by private interpretation; rather, it is the revelation of the mind of God. This was the difference between the prophets of the Lord and the false prophets. The prophets of the Lord did not speak or do anything that came from their own mind. They, and all the writers of Scripture, spoke and wrote what was in the mind of God. Every person should search

the Scripture and come to understand and apply its sense and meaning.

3.2. This important truth of the divine origin of the Scriptures is to be known and acknowledged by everyone who wants to give their attention to the faithful word of prophecy. Just as a person does not merely believe, but also definitely knows, that a particular person in whom they see all the proper, distinctive marks and characteristics of their friend is indeed their friend, so the Christian knows that that book in and on which they see all the proper marks and characteristics of a divinely inspired book is indeed the word of God.

3.3. The divinity of the Scriptures must be known and acknowledged in the first place, before people can profitably use them.

4. The apostle (v. 21) tells us how the Old Testament came to be compiled.

4.1. Those who were employed in making the book that we receive as the word of God—all the writers of the Scriptures—were the holy people of God.

4.2. *These holy men were moved by the Holy Spirit.* The Holy Spirit is the supreme agent; his holy people are merely the instruments. The Holy Spirit inspired and dictated to them what they were to deliver of the mind of God. He effectively inspired them to speak—and write—what he had put into their mouths. We, then, must combine faith with what we find in the Scriptures (Heb 4:2); we are to respect and reverence our Bible as a book written by holy people, inspired, influenced, and helped by the Holy Spirit.

CHAPTER 2

The apostle now moves on to consider what might prevent his readers from complying with his exhortation. He therefore gives them a fair warning against false teachers. 1. He describes these deceivers as ungodly in themselves and very harmful to others (vv. 1–3). 2. He assures his readers of the punishment that will be inflicted on the deceivers (vv. 3–6). 3. He tells us how opposite is the method that God takes with those who fear him (vv. 7–9). 4. He gives further description of those deceivers (vv 10–22).

Verses 1–3

1. In all ages of the church the Devil sends some of his servants to deceive: false prophets in the Old Testament and deceiving teachers in the New. Their work is to introduce destructive errors, *even damnable* (destructive) *heresies*. Those who introduce destructive heresies *deny the Lord that bought them*. Those who introduce errors that are destructive to others bring swift—and therefore definite—*destruction upon themselves*. Self-destroyers are soon destroyed.

2. The apostle proceeds to tell us the consequences that these *damnable heresies* have on others.

2.1. Corrupt leaders seldom fail to have many follow them. People drink in sin like water; they are happy to live in error.

2.2. The spreading of error will bring into disrepute the way of truth, the way of salvation through Jesus Christ.

3. Notice the method deceivers follow to draw disciples after them: they use *feigned words* (stories they have made up); they flatter, speaking good words and giving plausible speeches that deceive the hearts of the simple (Ro 16:18). All this is through greed, with the intention of increasing in wealth, reputation, or commendation by increasing the number of their followers.

Verses 3–6

However successful and prosperous false teachers may be, their *judgment lingereth not* (is not idle). Such unbelievers are condemned already. To prove this assertion, several examples of the righteous judgment of God are given:

1. Notice how God dealt with the angels who sinned. No superiority will exempt sinners from punishment: God did not spare the angels. If the offenders are more important, the punishment will be more severe. Sin corrupts and degrades the people who commit it. The angels of heaven are robbed of all their glory. Sin is the work of darkness, and darkness is the wages of sin. Those who refuse to walk according to the light and direction of God's Law will be deprived of the light of God's face.

2. Notice how God dealt with the old world; he did not spare it. If sin is universal, punishment will also extend to everyone. But if there are only a few righteous, they will be preserved. God does not destroy the good with the bad. In wrath he remembers mercy (Hab 3:2). The prevalent cause of destruction was that *it was a world of ungodly men.* Ungodliness puts people outside God's protection, exposing them to complete destruction.

3. Notice how God dealt with Sodom and Gomorrah.

3.1. He can use opposite kinds of creatures to punish hardened sinners. He destroyed the *old world by water*, and Sodom by fire. The One who keeps fire and water from harming his people can make either destroy his enemies; they are therefore never safe.

3.2. Those who are gross sinners before the Lord must expect the most dreadful vengeance.

3.3. The punishment of sinners in earlier ages is intended as an example to those who come later. People who lead ungodly lives must see what they are to expect if they continue in a course of ungodliness.

Verses 7–9

When God sends destruction on the ungodly, he commands that the righteous be rescued. We have an example of this in his preservation of Lot. Notice:

1. The description of Lot; he is called *a just man.* He does not follow the many who commit evil, but walks uprightly in a city of injustice.

2. The impression the sins of others made on this righteous man. In bad company, we cannot escape becoming either guilty or grieved.

3. The duration and continuation of this good man's trouble and torment: it was *from day to day* (day after day). Being used to hearing and seeing their evil did not reconcile him to it. Notice here:

3.1. *The Lord knows those that are his* (2Ti 2:19). He has set apart for himself those who are godly, and if there is only one person in five cities, he knows that person.

3.2. The wisdom of God is never at a loss about his ways and means to rescue his people. They are often completely at a loss, but he can rescue very many.

3.3. The rescue of the godly is the work of God: by his wisdom he devises the way, and by his power he works out the rescue *out of temptation.*

3.4. The unrighteous have no share in the salvation God works for the righteous. Evildoers are *reserved to the day of judgment.*

Verses 10–22

Since his intention is to warn us of deceivers, the apostle now returns to discuss them in more detail.

1. *These walk after the flesh.* In their lives, they act directly against God's righteous commands and comply with the demands of their corrupt nature. Evil opinions are often accompanied by evil practices, and those who want to spread error also want to become even worse in their evil. They continue in their sinful ways, increasing in ungodliness. They also pour contempt on those whom God has set in authority over them and requires them to honor.

2. He emphasizes this by setting out the very different behavior of superior creatures, namely, *angels.* They *are greater in power and might* than even those who have authority and power among human beings. *Angels bring* their *accusations* against sinful creatures *before the Lord*, who is the Judge of, and will be the avenger of, all ungodliness and injustice. Good angels mix no bitter insults or corrupt reproaches with any of the accusations they bring. Let us imitate the angels. If we complain about evildoers, let it be to God, and not with rage and insults, but with compassion, which will show that we belong to the One who is humble and merciful.

3. The apostle proceeds (v. 12) to show how deceiving teachers are like the most inferior creatures. Human beings under the power of sin are so far from heeding divine revelation that they do not even exercise reason. Unreasoning animals follow the instinct of their physical appetite, and sinners follow the inclination of their sinful mind. They are ignorant of what they could and should know. Notice, therefore:

3.1. Ignorance is the cause of speaking evil.

3.2. Destruction will be its effect. These people will be completely destroyed in their own corruption. Whatever they meet with is the just *reward of their unrighteousness.*

3.2.1. Sinners who revel in causing trouble deceive themselves and disgrace all they belong to, because by one kind of sin they prepare themselves for another, so that their *eyes are full of adultery*; their immoral looks show their own impure desires and are directed to kindle the same in others. This is what they *cannot cease* from. Those who are themselves incessant in sin work very hard, often successfully, to draw others into the same riotous living (1Pe 4:4). Those who are in the greatest danger of being led away into error and impiety are the *unstable.* Those whose hearts are not established with grace are easily turned aside to the way of sin.

3.2.2. These deceiving teachers are not only riotous and immoral but also *covetous*; they yearn for riches, and the desire of their souls is the wealth of this world. If people abandon themselves to all kinds of sinful desires, it is hardly surprising that the apostle calls them *cursed children* (accursed brood).

4. The apostle (vv. 15–16) proves that they are *cursed children.* They *have forsaken the right way*; they have gone astray; they have erred from the way of life. He demonstrates this by showing it to be *the way of Balaam, the son of Bosor.* The love of riches and honor turned Balaam astray from his duty, even though he knew that the path he took displeased the Lord. Hardened sinners sometimes meet with rebukes for their sin. God stops them on their path. If rebuking sinners for their sin could have made a person return to their duty, surely the rebuking of Balaam would have produced this effect: a *dumb ass* was enabled to speak and thereby expose *the madness* of Balaam's conduct and oppose his continuing on his evil way. But all in vain.

5. The apostle proceeds to a further description of deceiving teachers (v. 17), whom he describes:

5.1. *As wells*, or fountains, *without water*. The word of truth is the water of life; these deceivers are set on spreading and promoting error, and that is why they are described as empty, because they contain no truth.

5.2. *As clouds* (mists) *carried with a tempest.* These are clouds that produce no rain, for they are driven by the wind, the stormy wind of their own ambition, not by the Spirit. Clouds obstruct the light of the sun and darken the air, and since these people want to promote darkness in this world, it is very just for the mist of darkness to be their portion in the next. God is just to deal with them in this way, because:

5.2.1. They *allure* those they deal with.

5.2.2. They do this *with great swelling words of vanity*, which make a great sound but little sense.

5.2.3. They work on *the corrupt affections* and *carnal fleshly lusts of men.*

5.2.4. They deceive people who have kept at a distance from those who spread destructive errors. Notice:

5.2.4.1. By application and diligence, people become skilled at promoting error. They are as skillful and as successful as fishermen, who make fishing their daily practice.

5.2.4.2. People who for a while have remained faithful to the truth and kept clear of errors may be deceived so much as to fall into those errors they had for a while *clean escaped.*

5.2.4.2.1. To prevent these people from gaining converts, the apostle tells us that they are the servants of corruption; their own sinful desires have gained complete victory over them, and they are actually enslaved to them.

5.2.4.2.2. How shameful it is to be overcome and commanded by those who are themselves *the servants of corruption!* This consideration should prevent our being led away by these deceivers; and the apostle adds another thought to this (v. 20): to be so led away is a real disadvantage to those who have just escaped from those who live in error, because their end is made worse than their beginning. Notice:

5.2.4.2.2.1. Some people are for a time *kept from the pollutions of the world by the knowledge of Christ.* Many who have been restrained by a religious upbringing have not been renewed by the grace of God. We must receive the love of the truth (2Th 2:10) and hide God's word in our heart (Ps 119:11); otherwise it will not sanctify and save us.

5.2.4.2.2.2. Once people get caught up, they are easily overcome. If people who once *escaped are again entangled, the latter end is worse with them than the beginning.*

6. In vv. 21–22, the apostle sets himself to prove that a state of apostasy is worse than a state of ignorance, because it is *a condemning of the way of righteousness* after one has had some knowledge of it. The misery of such deserters of Christ and his Gospel is more intolerable than that of other offenders. God is more greatly offended by those who, by their conduct, despise the Gospel as well as disobey the Law, hurling contempt on it. And no wonder, when they have licked up *their own vomit* (v. 22; Pr 26:11), returning to the same ungodliness they had once rejected, and *wallowing* in the filthiness from which they appeared once to have been really cleansed.

CHAPTER 3

1. The apostle begins this last chapter by repeating the account of his intention in writing a second time to them (vv. 1–2). 2. He mentions one thing that motivated him to write this second letter, namely, the coming of scoffers *(vv. 3–7). 3. He instructs them in the coming of our Lord Jesus Christ for judgment (vv. 8–10). 4. He explains how Christians should apply to their lives the doctrine of Christ's second coming (vv. 11–18).*

Verses 1–2

Here, to better fulfill his purpose, which is to make his readers firm in their trust and to give a practical reminder of the doctrine of the Gospel, the apostle first expresses his special affection for them, calling them *beloved.* Second, he shows his sincere love and genuine concern for them by *writing the same thing to them* (Php 3:1). Finally, to better commend the matter, he tells them what he wants them to remember, namely, *the words spoken by the holy prophets*, who were divinely inspired, and *the commandments of the apostles of the Lord and Saviour.* What God has spoken through the prophets of the Old Testament and what Christ has commanded through the apostles of the New deserves and calls to be frequently remembered. It is by these things that the pure minds of Christians are to be stirred up.

Verses 3–7

There will be *scoffers*, those who make fun of sin and salvation. God's way of saving sinners through Jesus Christ is something people will laugh at—and *in the last days*, too, under the Gospel. The spirituality and simplicity of New Testament worship are set directly against the sinful human mind. This is mentioned as something well known to all Christians. Notice:

1. What kind of people these scoffers are: they *walk after their own lusts*, they follow the evil devices and desires of their own hearts. They live as they wish and speak as they wish. Just as they follow their own way and talk their own language, so they also think their own thoughts and form principles that are completely their own.

2. They will scoffingly say, *Where is the promise of his coming?* (v. 4). Without this, all the other articles of the Christian faith will mean very little; this is what fills up and gives the finishing stroke to all the others. Since this apostle and the others have given us the most sure and satisfying evidence of the doctrines concerning Christ's first coming, it is probable that these enemies will eventually grow weary of their opposition. However, as long as one of the main articles of our faith refers to what is still to come and is a promise to trust in, they continue to attack us here, even to the end of time. Until our Lord comes, they refuse to believe that he will come; in fact, they laugh at the very mention of his second coming. Believers not only desire that Christ come, but, having a promise that he will come, they are also firmly and fully persuaded that he will come. These deceivers, on the other hand, because they wish him never to come, do all they can to deceive themselves and others into being convinced he will never come. They will laugh at the promise itself: *Where is the promise*, they say, *of his coming?*

3. While they laugh, they will pretend also to argue (v. 4). This is a subtle, though not a solid, way of reasoning; it tends to make an impression on weak minds, and especially on wicked hearts. "Those to whom *the promise was made* are all dead," the scoffers say, "and it was never fulfilled in their time, and it is unlikely that it will ever be in any time; so why should we trouble ourselves about it? To this very day *all things continue as they were*, without any change, even *from the beginning of the creation*."

They conclude that what he never has done is something he never can do or never will.

4. The apostle reminds us of a change that has already happened—the flood of the world in Noah's time: *this* the scoffers are *willingly ignorant of* (v. 5); they choose to ignore it in silence. It is hard to persuade people to believe what they are unwilling to find true. They do not know because they do not care to know. But let sinners not think that such ignorance will be accepted as an excuse for whatever sin it may lead them into.

4.1. We begin with the apostle's account of the destruction that has already come on the world once (vv. 5–6). At creation, the waters were divided most wisely; at the time of the universal flood, however, the case was strangely altered; the waters that God had divided before, he now, in anger, threw together again in a heap. All this was done by the word of God. It was by his powerful word that the world was originally made: by *the word of the Lord the heavens were of old and the earth standing out of the water and in the water*. The later confusion and ruin of the world in the Flood, as well as the complete destruction of its inhabitants in that calamity, were by the same word. This was the change that God had brought on the world before and that these scoffers overlooked.

4.2. We proceed to what the apostle says about the destructive change that is still to come (v. 7). Here we have a fearful account of the final dissolution of the world. The judgment spoken of here is still to come, and will definitely come, though we do not know when. That the world has been destroyed once by a universal deluge makes it more believable that it may again be ruined by a universal conflagration. Therefore, let the scoffers who laugh at the coming of our Lord to judgment at least consider that it may be possible. *The heavens and the earth, which now are, are kept in store.* They are *reserved unto fire*. The Day of Judgment is the day of the destruction of the ungodly. Those who now scoff at a future judgment will find it a day of vengeance. "Make sure you are found in Christ, so that that may be a time of refreshment (Ac 3:19) and a day of redemption for you."

Verse 8

Here we may clearly discern the tenderness and affection with which the apostle speaks to his readers, calling them *beloved*. He has a compassionate concern, love, and goodwill for the ungodly who refuse to believe divine revelation, but he has a special respect for true believers. Notice:

1. The truth the apostle asserts—that *with the Lord one day is as a thousand years, and a thousand years are as one day*. All things past, present, and future are always before him.

2. The importance of this truth: this is the *one thing* the apostle wants us not to be ignorant of. This is a truth that concerns our peace, and so he seeks to make sure it is not hidden from our eyes (Lk 19:42); as it is in the original, "Let not this one thing be hidden from you." How hard it is to conceive of eternity!

Verses 9–10

We are told here that *the Lord is not slack*—he does not delay beyond the appointed time in coming to judge the world. Good people tend to think God is delaying beyond the appointed time, that is, the time they have set, but they set one time and God sets another.

1. What people consider slowness is actually God's *longsuffering* (patience) toward us; it is giving more time to his own people so that they may bring him glory and become fitter for heaven, because God does not want any of these to perish; he wants them all to repent. God does not delight in the death of sinners. His goodness and patience by nature call to repentance all those toward whom they are exercised. If people remain impenitent when God gives them opportunity to repent, he will deal more severely with them.

2. *The day of the Lord will come as a thief in the night* (v. 10). Notice:

2.1. The certainty of the day of the Lord. The day still has not come, but there is no doubt that it will come. God has *appointed a day*, and he will keep his appointment.

2.2. The suddenness of this day: it *will come as a thief in the night*, at a time when people are sleeping and feeling secure. The time people think of as the most inappropriate and unexpected, and when they therefore feel most secure, will be the time when the Lord comes again.

2.3. The solemnity of this coming. *The heavens shall pass away with a great noise. The elements shall melt with fervent heat. The earth also, and all the works that are therein, shall be burnt up.* All must pass through the fire, which will be a consuming fire to all that sin has brought into the world, though it may be only a refining fire to the works of God's hand. What a difference there will be between the first coming of Christ and the second! Let us be so wise as to prepare for it, so that it may not be a day of vengeance and destruction for us.

Verses 11–18

Having instructed his readers in the teaching of Christ's second coming:

1. The apostle uses the opportunity to exhort them to lead lives of purity and godliness. *Seeing all these things must be dissolved, how holy should we be.* Inasmuch as this dissolution is undertaken to enable them to be restored to their original beauty and excellence, how pure and holy we should be, so that we may be prepared for the *new heaven and new earth, wherein dwelleth righteousness!* Those things that we now see must soon pass away, no longer to exist as they do now. Let us, therefore, look at what will remain. This *looking for the day of God* is one of the instructions the apostle gives us, so that we may be eminently *holy and godly in all manner of conversation. The coming of the day of God* is what every Christian must hope for and passionately expect. Although it must terrify the ungodly to see the visible heavens and the elements melting, believers can rejoice in the hope of more glorious heavens after these have been refined by the dreadful fire that will burn up all the dross of this visible creation. Notice:

1.1. What true Christians look for: *new heavens and a new earth*. In these new heavens and earth only righteousness will dwell.

1.2. What the ground and basis of this expectation and hope is—the promise of God. To look for anything that God has not promised is presumption, but if our expectations are according to the promise, we cannot meet with a disappointment.

2. In v. 14 he resumes his exhortation from the consideration that the heavens and the earth will be renewed. "Make sure you consider the condition you will be in when the Judge of all the world comes to pass sentence on all people, and get ready to *appear before the judgment-seat of Christ* (Ro 14:10; 2Co 5:10).

2.1. "See that you are *found of him in peace*, in a state of peace and reconciliation with God through Christ. Those whose sins are pardoned and who have had their peace made with God are the only safe and happy people; therefore *follow peace*, and do so *with all* (Heb 12:14)." Let us pursue peace with God through our Lord Jesus Christ, peace in our own consciences, and peace with other people.

2.2. "See that you are *found of Christ without spot, and blameless*. Pursue holiness as well as peace." We must not only watch out for all spots that are not the spots of God's children (Dt 32:5); we must also press on toward spotless purity, absolute perfection. Christians must be *perfecting holiness* (2Co 7:1). It is only diligent Christians who will be happy on the day of the Lord. He will certainly reward us if we are diligent in the work he has assigned us; now, so that you may be diligent, consider that the patience of our Lord means salvation. "Does your Lord delay his coming? He does so to give more opportunity to repent, so that people may have time to prepare for eternity." Our apostle quotes the apostle Paul as telling people to make the same good use of divine patience. What an honorable mention this apostle to the Jews gives of the very man who openly, *before all, reproved him* (Gal 2:11). He calls him *brother*, signifying not only that he is a fellow Christian but also that he is a fellow apostle. Although many deceiving teachers have denied Paul's apostleship, Peter still recognizes him to be an apostle. He also calls him *beloved*, indicating a fitting affection. Finally, he mentions Paul as one who has been given an uncommon measure of wisdom. How desirable it would be for those who preach the same Gospel to treat one another according to the pattern Peter here sets for them! Notice also:

2.2.1. The great wisdom that was in Paul is said to have been *given* him. The understanding and knowledge that qualify people to preach the Gospel are the gift of God.

2.2.2. Paul communicates to people according to what he has received from God. He seeks to lead others as far as he himself was led into the knowledge of the mysteries of the Gospel. But the apostle Peter proceeds to tell us that Paul's letters contain some things that are hard to under-

stand. Some are not easy to understand because of their obscurity; others because of their excellent sublimity; others because of the weakness of the human mind. Here the *unlearned* (ignorant) *and unstable* do their wretched work in distorting the Scriptures. Those who are not well instructed and well established in the truth are in great danger of perverting the word of God. Where there is a divine power to establish as well as to instruct people in divine truth, people are effectively protected from falling into error. We see how great a blessing this is by observing what is the harmful consequence of the errors that the ignorant and unstable fall into, namely, their own destruction.

3. The apostle gives them a word of caution (vv. 17–18).

3.1. The knowledge we have of these things should make us very watchful, inasmuch as there is a twofold danger (v. 17).

3.1.1. We are in great danger *of* being deceived and turned away from the truth. Many who have the Scriptures and read them do not understand what they read; too many of those who have a right understanding are not established in the belief of the truth, and all these are liable to fall into error.

3.1.2. We are in great danger *by* being deceived. If people corrupt the word of God, it leads to their own complete ruin. When people distort the word of God, *they fall into the error of the wicked*. If we take in their opinions, we too will soon imitate their practices. Those who are led away by error *fall from their own steadfastness*. They are wholly confused and unsettled and do not know where to rest.

3.2. The apostle tells us what to do (v. 18). We must *grow in grace*. We will be as firm in the truth as the strength of grace that is in us. We must grow *in the knowledge of our Lord Jesus Christ*. Such a knowledge of Christ as makes us more like him and endears him more to us must preserve us from falling away in times of general apostasy, and those who experience this effect of knowing the Lord will join with our apostle in saying, *To him be glory both now and for ever. Amen.*

1 John

The continued tradition of the church affirms that this letter was written by John the apostle. There is scarcely a critic or competent judge of writing or of style of argument and spirit who will not attribute this letter to the writer of the Gospel that bears the name of the apostle John. The letter is called *general* because it was not written to any particular church; it is like a circular letter sent to various churches in order to strengthen them in their faithfulness to the Lord Christ, to strengthen them against deceivers, and to encourage them to adorn the sacred doctrines concerning him by their love for God and people, and especially for each other.

CHAPTER 1

Here: 1. We are given evidence about Christ's person and excellence (vv. 1–2). 2. We are told that the knowledge of that gives us fellowship with God and Christ (v. 3), and joy (v. 4). 3. We have a description of God (v. 5). 4. We are told how we ought therefore to live (v. 6). 5. We are told the benefit of such a life (v. 7). 6. We are told the way to forgiveness (v. 9). 7. We are told the evil of denying our sin (vv. 8–10).

Verses 1–4

The apostle begins:

1. With an account of the Mediator's person. He is not a mere vocal word, but a living one. He should be well known:

1.1. As *the Word of life*, the living Word.

1.2. As *eternal life* (v. 2), the Word of the eternal, living Father.

1.3. As *life manifested* (v. 2), revealed in the flesh. What kindness—that eternal life should come to visit us mortals, and obtain eternal life for us, and then give that to us!

2. With the evidence that the apostle and his fellow apostles have of the Mediator's presence. *The life, the word of life, the eternal life*, as such, could not be seen and felt, but the life revealed could be and was (vv. 1, 3). The life assumed a mouth and tongue in order to speak words of life. The divine word would use the ear, and the ear would be devoted to the word of life (vv. 1–3). The Word became visible, so as to be not only heard but also seen *with our eyes*—with all the use and exercise that we could make of our eyes. His apostles must be eyewitnesses as well as ear-witnesses of him. His life was also revealed:

2.1. To their inner, spiritual sense, to the eyes of their heart, for the next clause may be interpreted in this way: *which we have looked upon.* The Greek word here was not applied to the immediate object of the eye, but to what was rationally gathered from what they saw. The senses are to inform the mind.

2.2. To their hands and sense of feeling: *and our hands have handled of the Word of life.* The invisible life and Word did not despise the testimony of sense. Sense is a means that God has appointed for us to inform ourselves with. Our Lord took care to satisfy all the senses of his apostles, so that they would be more authentic witnesses of him to the world. The apostles could not be deceived in such a long and various exercise of their senses. Sense must minister to reason and judgment, and reason and judgment must serve to welcome the Lord Jesus Christ and his Gospel.

3. With a solemn affirmation of these reasons for the Christian truth. The apostles declare these assurances for our satisfaction (vv. 2–3). It was right that they open up to the disciples the evidence by which they were led. The disciples needed to be well assured of the truth of the institution they had accepted. They should see the evidence of their holy religious faith.

4. With the reason for the apostle's asserting this summary of sacred faith.

4.1. So that believers in it may be advanced to the same happiness as they, as the apostles themselves. The apostle is referring to such fellowship as is compatible with being physically distant from one another: communion with heaven, and in blessings that come from there and lead there. There is a fellowship, a common participation of privilege and position, that belongs to all the saints, from the highest apostle to the lowest believer. The apostles want the disciples to know what it is and where it is: *and truly our fellowship is with the Father and his Son Jesus Christ.* See what the Gospel revelation leads to—to the advancing of us far above sin and earth, into blessed fellowship with the Father and the Son. See what the goal of eternal life made flesh is—that the Son might advance us to eternal life in fellowship with the Father and him.

4.2. So that believers may be released and advanced in holy joy. The mystery of the Christian faith is directly calculated for the joy of mortals. Those who are not filled with spiritual joy are living below the true purpose and goal of the Christian revelation. If they were truly strong in their holy faith, how much they would rejoice.

Verses 5–7

1. Here is the message from the Lord Jesus Christ. The apostles are the messengers of the Lord Jesus; it is their honor to bring his messages to the world. The One who assumed human nature will honor jars of clay such as we are (2Co 4:7). It was the aim of the apostles to faithfully communicate the messages they had received. The present message is *that God is light, and in him is no darkness at all* (v. 5). He is all the beauty and perfection that can be represented to us by light. There is no defect or imperfection in him. It is fitting that the great God would be represented as the pure and perfect light to this dark world. How much more could be included in a single statement than is included in the statement *God is light, and in him is no darkness at all?*

2. A just conclusion is to be drawn from this message.

2.1. To convict those professors who have no true fellowship with God, it is said, *If we say we have fellowship with him, and walk in darkness, we lie, and do not the truth.* To *walk in darkness* is to live and act according to such ignorance and wrong ways as go against our holy faith. There may be those who profess to have fellowship with God but whose lives are irreligious, immoral, and impure. The apostle is not afraid to contradict such people: *They lie, and do not the truth.* Their practice shows that their profession and pretenses are false, demonstrating their foolishness.

2.2. To convict and thereby assure those who are near to God, it is said, *But, if we walk in the light, we have fellowship one with another, and the blood of Jesus Christ his Son cleanseth us from all sin.* Those who walk in this way show that they know God. *Then we have fellowship one with another,* others with us and we with them, and both with God. *The blood of Jesus Christ his Son cleanseth us from all sin. His* blood obtains for us those sacred influences by which sin is to be subdued more and more, until it is completely abolished.

Verses 8–10

1. Having supposed that even those of this heavenly fellowship still have their sin, the apostle proceeds here to justify that supposition (v. 8). We must beware of deceiving ourselves by denying or excusing our sins. The Christian faith is the religion of sinners. The Christian life is a life of continual repentance, of constant faith in and thankfulness and love for the Redeemer (v. 10). The denial of our sin not only deceives us ourselves but also challenges God's truthfulness. God has given his testimony to the continued sinfulness of the world by providing a sacrifice for sin that will be needed in every age, and he has given his testimony to the continued sinfulness of believers themselves by requiring them constantly to confess their sins.

2. The apostle then instructs believers in the way to the continued pardon of their sin. We have here:

2.1. The duty we must do in order to enjoy this: *confess our sins* (v. 9). Penitent confession and acknowledgment of sin are the work of believers and the means of their deliverance from guilt.

2.2. Our encouragement in this: the righteousness and mercy of God, to whom we make such confession (v. 9). God is faithful to his word, in which he has promised forgiveness to penitent, believing confessors. He is also merciful and gracious and will therefore forgive contrite confessors all their sins and cleanse them from the guilt of all unrighteousness.

CHAPTER 2

Here the apostle exhorts against sins of weakness (vv. 1–2), shows the true knowledge and love of God (vv. 3–6), renews the command of mutual love (vv. 7–11), addresses Christians of various ages (vv. 12–14), warns against worldly love (vv. 15–17) and against deceivers (vv. 18–19), shows the security of true Christians (vv. 20–27), and exhorts Christians to continue in Christ (vv. 28–29).

Verses 1–2

Here the apostle seeks to dissuade the disciples from one thing and support them in another.

1. He seeks to dissuade them from sin. He wants to leave no room for sin (v. 1), and the intention of this letter is to dissuade and drive them from sin. Notice the familiar, affectionate description of the disciples with which he introduces his warning: *My little children.* Certainly the Gospel was most effective where such ministerial love abounded most.

2. He reminds them of the believer's support and relief in cases of sin (v. 1). Even believers have their sins, though in comparison with others they are said *not to sin* (3:9). And when they do sin, this must be their support and refuge: *we have an Advocate.* Besides having the Holy Spirit within us, here we have an advocate outside of us, in heaven with the Father. Notice, the Judge with whom our advocate pleads is the Father. He who was our Judge in the legal court — the court of the Law that we disobeyed — is our Father in the Gospel court, the court of heaven and of grace. His throne or tribunal is the mercy seat (Ex 25:17, 20). Our advocate is commended to us on these considerations:

2.1. By his person and personal names. *It is Jesus Christ the Son of the Father,* anointed by the Father for the whole work of salvation, and therefore for that of the intercessor.

2.2. By his qualification for the work. *It is Jesus Christ the righteous.* The clients are guilty; their innocence and legal righteousness cannot be pleaded. It is the advocate's own righteousness that he must plead for the offenders. He has been righteous to death, righteous for them. And it is on this basis that the Advocate pleads that the clients' sins be not imputed to them.

2.3. By the plea he has to make, the ground and basis of his advocacy. Contrary to the distinction made by some Roman Catholics, the Mediator of intercession, the Advocate for us, is also the Mediator of redemption, the atoning sacrifice for our sins. It is his atoning sacrifice that he pleads. *He ever lives to make intercession for those that come to God through him* (Heb 7:25).

2.4. By the extent of his plea. It is not confined to one nation, nor is it only for the past, or for us present believers, but also for the sins of all who in the future come to God through him. The extent and intent of the Mediator's death reach all tribes, nations, and countries.

Verses 3–6

It may seem that these verses relate to 1:7, and that the verses between that one and these are to be taken parenthetically. Here now comes the test of our light and our love that were referred to in 1:7.

1. The test of our light (v. 3). Divine light and knowledge are the beauty and improvement of the mind. Young Christians tend to exalt their new light and commend their own knowledge, and older ones tend to doubt the sufficiency and fullness of their knowledge. Here, however, is the evidence that we have sound knowledge: that it compels us to *keep God's commandments.* A careful, conscientious obedience to his commands shows that the

understanding and knowledge of these things are graciously impressed on the soul; the converse must, therefore, follow, namely, that *he that saith* (claims), *I know him, and keepeth not his commandments, is a liar, and the truth is not in him* (v. 4). A disobedient life is the denial and shame of claimed religious knowledge.

2. The test of our love (v. 5). To keep the word of God, or of Christ, is to sacredly give it attention in every aspect of our lives; in the person who does so, the love of God is perfected. The phrase *the love of the Father* shows here our love for God, as in v. 15, rather than, as some suppose, God's love for us. We know that we belong to him and that we are united to him by that Spirit who raises us and helps us in this obedience. If we acknowledge our relationship with him and our union with him, that acknowledgment must motivate us in this way: *He that saith* (claims) he *abideth in him ought himself to walk even as he walked* (v. 6). Those who claim to be on his side and to live with him must walk with him, following his example.

Verses 7–11

The command of mutual love is commended:

1. As an old one: *I write no new commandment unto you, but an old commandment, which you had from the beginning* (v. 7). The command of love must be as old as human nature, and so it is the *old commandment.*

2. As a new one: *"Again, a new commandment I write unto you, which thing is true in him.* It is also true *in you;* this law is written on your hearts to some extent (Jer 31:33; Heb 10:16); you have been taught by God to love one another, and you have been so taught *because the darkness is past,* that is, because your deplorable ignorance of God and of Christ is now in the past, *and the true light now shineth* (v. 8). We should make sure that that grace that was true in Christ is true also in us. The more our darkness is passing and the Gospel light is shining on us, the deeper our submission should be to the commandments of our Lord, whether considered old or new. Here, then, is another test of our Christian light: before, it was to be approved by obedience to God; here, it is by Christian love.

2.1. Those who lack such love show the falseness of their claim to have light. They cannot be swayed by the sense of the love of Christ toward their brothers and sisters, and so they remain in darkness.

2.2. He whose life is directed by such love shows his light to be good and genuine. He sees how fitting it is that we love those whom Christ has loved. *There is no occasion of stumbling in him* (there is nothing in him to make him stumble) (v. 10). Christian love teaches us to value our brothers and sisters highly and to dread everything that will harm their purity and peace.

2.3. Hatred is a sign of spiritual darkness (v. 11). He, then, who has hatred toward a Christian brother or sister must be devoid of spiritual light; therefore *he walks in darkness, and he knows not whither he goes.* It is the Lord Jesus Christ who is the great Master of love; it is his school that is the school of love, his disciples are the disciples of love, and his family must be the family of love.

Verses 12–17

1. We have the address itself. All Christians do not have the same standing and stature; there are infants in Christ, adults in Christ, and old disciples. And yet there are commands and a corresponding obedience that are common to all, especially mutual love and a disregard for the world. The apostle addresses:

1.1. The class of beginners in the Christian school (v. 12). There are new converts to religious faith, infants in Christ. He addresses these as *children* in Christianity, and he addresses them for two reasons:

1.1.1. *Because their sins were forgiven them for his name's sake* (v. 12). The youngest sincere disciple is forgiven. Sins are forgiven *for his name's sake,* that is, either for God's or for Christ's name's sake, and those who have been forgiven by God are strongly obliged to relinquish this world.

1.1.2. Because of their knowledge of God. We have a proverb, "It is a wise child that knows his own father." These children must know theirs. Those who know the Father may well withdraw from the love of this world.

1.2. Those of the highest position, seniors in Christianity (vv. 13–14). The apostle moves immediately from the bottom class to the top class at school. Those who are of longest standing in Christ's school need further advice and instruction. No one is too old to learn. He writes to them because of their knowledge. Those who know the One who was from the beginning may well be motivated to relinquish this world.

1.3. The middle age of Christians, those who are in bloom and flower (vv. 13–14). There are the adults in Christ Jesus. The apostle turns to them:

1.3.1. On account of their military exploits. They are skillful soldiers in the camp of Christ. Those who have been well taught in Christ's school can handle their arms and overcome the evil one, and those who can overcome him can justly be called to overcome the world too.

1.3.2. On account of their strength, revealed in their achievement (v. 14). Young men usually boast about their strength. It will be their glory, and it will test their strength, to overcome the Devil. Let them show the same strength in overcoming the world as in overcoming the Devil.

1.3.3. Because of their acquaintance with the word of God (v. 14). Those in whom the word of God abides are well equipped to conquer the world.

2. We have the dissuasion that is thereby introduced, a warning that is basic to vital, practical religious faith (v. 15): "Be crucified to the world" (Gal 5:24; 6:14). If all Christians were united in this, their love would be reserved for God; it would not be thrown away on the world. The reasons for this dissuasion and caution:

2.1. The inconsistency of this love with the love of God (v. 15). The human heart is limited and cannot contain both loves.

2.2. The prohibition of worldly love or sinful desires; such love is not appointed by God (v. 16), but intrudes itself from the world. The things of this world are distinguished in three different groups, according to the three main inclinations of depraved nature:

2.2.1. There is *the lust of the flesh.* This sort of *lust* is usually called *luxury.*

2.2.2. There is *the lust of the eyes.* This is the *lust* of covetousness.

2.2.3. There is *the pride of life.* This is ambition. The objects of all these appetites must be abandoned and renounced (v. 16). The Father rejects them. The craving or appetite for these things must be conquered and subdued.

2.3. The worthless and vanishing state of earthly things (v. 17). The things of the world are fading and dying quickly.

2.4. The immortality of those who love God (v. 17). *He that doeth the will of God abideth for ever.* The object of his love, in contrast to *the world* that *passeth away,* lives forever. Love will never fail (1Co 13:8); and he himself is an heir of immortality and eternal life.

Verses 18–19

Here is:

1. A moral forecast of the time. The end is coming. It was fitting that the disciples be warned about the coming end of time and be taught as much as possible about the prophetic periods of time.

2. The sign of this last time, that *even now* there were many who opposed the kingdom of Christ. It should be no great offense or harm to the disciples that there are such antichrists, for:

2.1. One great one has been foretold: *as you have heard that antichrist shall come*; and there are many forerunners of that great one: *even now there are many antichrists*; the *mystery of iniquity* is already at work (2Th 2:7).

2.2. They were foretold also as the sign of this last time (v. 18).

3. Some account of these deceivers or antichrists. *"They went out from us* (v. 19), from our community and fellowship." The purest churches may have their apostates. *"For if they had been of us, they would have continued with us* (v. 19). If the sacred truth had been rooted in their hearts, it would have kept them with us." Those who commit apostasy from religion show sufficiently that before they did, they were hypocrites in religion. *But* this was done (or *they went out) that they* (it) *might be made manifest that they were not all of us* (their going showed that none of them belonged to us) (v. 19). Some of the hypocritical must be revealed here on earth in their belittling of the truth; this must be done both for their own shame and for their benefit.

Verses 20–27

1. The apostle encourages the disciples in this hour of deceivers. *But you have an unction from the Holy One, and you know all things.* We see:

1.1. The blessing with which they were enriched: *You have an unction.* True Christians are anointed ones; their name intimates as much.

1.2. From whom this blessing comes: *from the Holy One,* either from the Holy Spirit or from the Lord Jesus Christ. Christ gives the graces of his Holy Spirit, and he anoints the disciples to make them like him.

1.3. The effect of this anointing: *And by it you know all things* (v. 20), all these things about Christ and his religious faith.

2. The apostle explains to them the mind and meaning with which he is writing to them:

2.1. Negatively. He does not doubt their knowledge. It is good to have good thoughts about our Christian brothers and sisters. A just confidence in religious people may both encourage and contribute to their faithfulness.

2.2. Positively: *but because you know it*—you know *the truth in Jesus—and that no lie is of the truth.* Those who know the truth in any respect are prepared by it to discern what is contrary to it. No lie belongs to or comes from natural or revealed religion. *No lie is of the truth;* frauds and counterfeits are most inappropriate means to support and spread the truth.

3. He further accuses these deceivers.

3.1. They are *liars: Who is a liar, but he that denieth that Jesus is the Christ?* There is no truth so sacred and fully affirmed that someone or other will not contradict or deny it.

3.2. They are enemies of God as well as the Lord Jesus Christ (v. 22). The person who opposes Christ denies the witness and testimony of the Father. The apostle may well conclude, therefore, that *whosoever denies the Son, the same has not the Father.* However, as some copies add, *he that acknowledgeth the Son has the Father also* (v. 23).

4. The apostle advises the disciples to remain in the old doctrines first communicated to them (v. 24). Truth is older than error. The truth about Christ that was originally delivered to the saints is not to be exchanged for novelties. The Christian truth can plead antiquity, and it is commended by that. This exhortation is enforced by these considerations:

4.1. The sacred benefit the disciples will receive by remaining faithful to the original truth and faith.

4.1.1. They will thereby remain in holy union with God and Christ (v. 24). It is the truth of Christ remaining in us that is the means of separating us from sin and uniting us to the Son of God (Jn 15:3–4).

4.1.2. They will by this means secure the promise of eternal life (v. 25). The promise that God makes to those who remain faithful to him is great. It is *eternal life,* which no one but God can give.

4.2. The purpose of the apostle's writing to them. This letter is to strengthen them against the deceivers of the age (v. 26), "and so if you do not remain in what *you have heard from the beginning,* my writing and service will be in vain."

4.3. The instructive blessing they have received from heaven (v. 27). True Christians have an inner confirmation of the divine truth they have taken in: the Holy Spirit has imprinted it on their minds and hearts. This sacred anointing, or divine *unction* (v. 20), is commended because:

4.3.1. It is durable and lasting (v. 27). Divine enlightenment must be something continual. Temptations, snares, and deceptions arise. The anointing must remain.

4.3.2. It is better than human instruction (v. 27): *"and you need not that any man teach you* (v. 27). You were instructed by us before you were anointed, but now our teaching is nothing in comparison to the teaching you receive through this anointing."

4.3.3. It is a sure sign of truth (v. 27). The Holy Spirit must be *the Spirit of truth.* The Spirit of truth will not lie, and he *teaches all things.*

4.3.4. It has an influence that preserves: those in whom the anointing remains will be preserved by it against deceivers and their deception (v. 27). "It teaches you to remain in Christ, and as it teaches you, it also protects you."

Verses 28–29

And now, little children—or, better, "dear children"—*abide* (continue) *in him* (v. 28). The apostle wishes to persuade by love; he seeks to be effective by endearment as well as by reason. Those who have been anointed by the Lord Jesus Christ are greatly obliged to continue with him. This duty of perseverance and faithfulness is strongly urged:

1. From the consideration of Christ's return on the great Day of Judgment (v. 28). It is assumed here that the Lord Jesus will come again. This was part of the truth the disciples had. Those who have remained faithful to him throughout all their temptations will have confidence and joy when they see him. Those who have deserted him, on the other hand, *shall be ashamed before him.* The apostle includes himself in the number: "Let us not be ashamed of you," as well as, "You will not be ashamed of yourselves."

2. From the consideration of the honor of those who remain faithful to Christ. The phrase *every one that doeth righteousness* may here be justly assumed to be another description of those who continue in Christ. Such people

must necessarily *be born of him*. They are renewed by the Spirit of Christ, in the image of Christ. Those who are faithful in their practice of Christianity in times of testing give good evidence that they have been born from above (Jn 3:3), from the Lord Jesus Christ.

CHAPTER 3

The apostle here exalts the love of God in adopting us as his children (vv. 1–2). On that basis, he argues for holiness (v. 3) and against sin (vv. 4–10). He urges mutual love (vv. 11–18) and shows us how to assure our hearts before God (vv. 19–22). We are given the precept of faith (v. 23) and shown the benefits of obedience (v. 24).

Verses 1–3

The apostle:

1. Breaks out in an expression of wonder at the grace that is the spring of such a marvelously condescending gift: *Behold what manner of love the Father hath bestowed upon us, that we should be called the sons of God!* It is because of the wonderful condescending love of the eternal Father that people like us are made and called his children. How wonderful that God in his holiness is not ashamed to call himself our Father and to call us his children!

2. Concludes that the honor of believers is above the notice of the world (v. 1). Little does the world perceive the happiness of the genuine followers of Christ. Little does the world think that these poor, humble, condemned ones are the favorites of heaven and will live there before long. Moreover, believers can bear their situation better because their Lord was unknown here as much as they are. Let the followers of Christ be content with being treated harshly here, since they are in a land of strangers, among those who know them little, and since their Lord was treated the same way before them.

3. Exalts these persevering disciples in the prospect of the certain revelation of their honor and position.

3.1. Their present honorable relationship is affirmed. "*Beloved*—dearly loved friends because loved by God—*now are we the sons of God* (v. 2)."

3.2. The glory of their sonship and adoption is reserved for another world. Children of God must walk by faith (2Co 5:7) and live by hope.

3.3. The time of the revelation of the children of God is determined: *but we know that when he shall appear, we shall be like him*. The children of God will be known and be revealed by their likeness to their head.

3.4. Their likeness to him is argued from their seeing him: *We shall be like him, for we shall see him as he is*. All will see him, but not as his disciples will, not as *he is*, namely, to those in heaven. Evildoers will see him with his frowns, but his people will see him in the smiles and beauty of his face. Their likeness to him will enable them to see him as the blessed people of God do in heaven.

4. Urges them to commit themselves to pursuing holiness (v. 3). The children of God know that their Lord is holy and pure. Those, then, who hope to live with him must seek the greatest purity; their hope of heaven will urge and compel them to do so. It is a contradiction to such hope, therefore, to indulge in sin and impurity. As we are sanctified by faith, we must also be sanctified by hope. And we must be purified by hope so that we may be saved by hope.

Verses 4–10

The apostle now proceeds to fill his own mouth and the believer's mind with many arguments (Job 23:4) against sin and all fellowship with the works of darkness (Eph 5:11). He argues:

1. From the nature of sin. It is contrary to God's law. Commission of sin is the rejecting of God's law, which is the rejecting of his authority and therefore of God himself.

2. From the mission of the Lord Jesus Christ in this world, which was to take away sin. He takes sin away so that he may make us like himself, *and in him is no sin*. Those who expect to enjoy fellowship with Christ above should seek fellowship with him here in the greatest purity.

3. From the opposition between sin and a real union with the Lord Christ. Those who remain in Christ do not keep on sinning. Those who remain in Christ remain in their covenant relationship with him. They remain in his powerful light and knowledge; it may therefore be concluded *that he that sinneth hath not seen him neither known him*. Practical renunciation of sin is the great evidence of saving knowledge of the Lord Christ.

4. From the connection between the practice of righteousness and a state of righteousness. The practice of sin and a justified state are inconsistent. *Little children, he that doeth righteousness is righteous*. It seems that in several parts of Scripture, righteousness may justly be rendered "religion." For instance, *Blessed are those that are persecuted for righteousness' sake* (Mt 5:10), that is, for religion's sake. To do what is right, then, is to practice religion. The practice of religion cannot exist without a principle of integrity and conscience.

5. From the relationship between the sinner and the Devil, and then from the purpose of the Lord Christ against the Devil.

5.1. From the relationship between the sinner and the Devil. *To commit sin* is here to live under its power and dominion, and those who do so are *of the devil*.

5.2. From the purpose and work of the Lord Christ against the Devil. He came to our world so that he could conquer the Devil. He will loosen and dissolve sin more and more until he has completely destroyed it. Let us, then, not indulge in or serve what the Son of God came to destroy.

6. From the connection between regeneration and the relinquishment of sin: *Whosoever is born of God doth not commit sin*. To be born of God is to be inwardly renewed and restored to a holy rightness of nature by the power of the Spirit of God. *Such a one committeth not sin*, because *his seed remaineth in him*; the spiritually significant principle of holiness *remaineth in him*. Compare 1Pe 1:23. Renewing grace is a prevalent principle. Religion is not an art, not an acquired skill, but a new nature. Consequently, the regenerate person *cannot sin*. This must refer to not continuing in the course and practice of sin. The reason is that *he is born of God*. There is a light in his mind that shows him the evil of sin. There is that bias in his heart that inclines him to hate sin. There is the spiritual disposition that breaks the force and extensiveness of sinful acts. It is not reckoned the person's sin, in the Gospel account, when the whole attitude of the mind and spirit are against it. The unregenerate person is morally unable to do what is religiously good. The regenerate person is happily disabled from sin.

7. From the discrimination between the children of God and the children of the Devil. They have their distinct characteristics. Now the offspring of the serpent are known:

7.1. By neglect of religion: *whosoever doeth not righteously is not of God*, but of the Devil.

7.2. By hatred of fellow Christians.

Verses 11–13

The apostle:

1. Commends mutual Christian love (v. 11). We should love the Lord Jesus and value his love, and so we should love all those who receive his love.

2. Tries to dissuade from what is contrary to this by using the example of Cain. Cain's envy and hatred should deter us from harboring a similar passion, for these reasons:

2.1. He was of the Serpent's offspring, of *the wicked one*. He imitated and resembled the first wicked one, the Devil.

2.2. His hatred had no restraint; it led all the way to murder (v. 12). When sin is indulged in, it knows no bounds.

2.3. It contained so much of the Devil that he murdered his brother for religion's sake. He was angry at the superiority of Abel's service, envying him the favor and acceptance he enjoyed with God. This is why he martyred his brother (v. 12). Hatred will teach us to take revenge on what we should wonder at and imitate.

3. Concludes that it is no wonder good people are treated in this way now (v. 13). The nature of the Devil still remains in the world. Do not be surprised, then, that the Serpent's world hates and hisses at you.

Verses 14–19

The dear apostle can scarcely mention sacred love without speaking at length in favor of it.

1. It is a mark of our transition to life. We can know *that we have passed from death to life* by the signs of our faith in Christ, of which this love for our brothers and sisters is one. This love:

1.1. Presupposes a general love for the whole human race. People are to be loved:

1.1.1. Because they are the excellent work of God, made by him and made in wonderful likeness to him.

1.1.2. Because they are, in some measure, loved in Christ. A world loved in this way by God should, for that reason, be loved by us. This love will even include all proper love for enemies.

1.2. Includes a distinctive love for members of the Christian community. They are not to be loved so much for their own sakes as for the sake of God and Christ, who have loved them. This is the result of faith in Christ, of our passage from death to life.

2. Hatred of our brothers and sisters, on the other hand, is a sign that we are in a deadly state. The apostle argues this. Hatred of the person is a hatred of their life and welfare and naturally tends to desire its extinction. Now the one who by the frame and disposition of his heart is a murderer *cannot have eternal life abiding in him*.

3. The example of God and Christ should kindle holy love in our hearts (v. 16). The great God has given his Son to die for us. Surely, then, we should love those whom God has loved, and loved so much.

4. The apostle then proceeds to show us what should be the attitude and effect of such Christian love.

4.1. It must be so wholehearted as to make us willing to suffer even death for the safety and salvation of the dear brothers and sisters. How dead should Christians be to this life! How well assured we should also be of a better one!

4.2. It must be compassionate and generous, eager to fulfill the needs of our brothers and sisters. Those who have this world's goods must love a good God even more, and their good brothers and sisters more, and be ready to distribute those goods for their sakes. This love for brothers and sisters is love for God in them, and where there is none of this love for them, there is no true love for

God at all. There may be other fruits of this love (v. 18). Compliments and flatteries do not befit Christians, but the sincere expressions of holy affection and the services or labors of love do.

5. This love will be evidence of our sincerity in our faith and will give us hope toward God (v. 19). It is a great happiness to be assured of our integrity in our Christian faith. The way to secure our inner peace is to be full of love and the works of love.

Verses 20–22

Here the apostle proceeds:

1. To establish the court of conscience (v. 20). *Our heart* here refers to our self-reflecting judicial power, by which we can become aware of ourselves and so pass judgment on our state toward God; it is the same as our conscience, which is God's vice-regent, calling the court to order in his name and acting for him.

1.1. If our conscience condemns us, God does so too. God, in fact, is a greater witness than our conscience and knows more against us than it does: *he knoweth all things*.

1.2. If our conscience acquits us, God does so too. Then we have assurance that he accepts us now and will acquit us on the great Day of Judgment. Let conscience, therefore, be well informed, listened to, and diligently acted on.

2. To show the privilege of those who have a good conscience toward God. They have influence in heaven; their cases are heard there (v. 22). Obedient souls are prepared for blessings, and they have the promise that they will be listened to.

Verses 23–24

The apostle proceeds to describe to us:

1. What God's commandments are:

1.1. To recognize what Jesus Christ is, according to his name, that he is the Son of God and the anointed Savior of the world.

1.2. To approve him in judgment and conscience.

1.3. To submit to him as our Redeemer.

1.4. To trust in him for the full discharge of his saving work. This faith is necessary for those who want to have their requests answered by God, because it is through the Son that we must come to the Father. We are to *love one another, as he gave us commandment* (v. 23). As goodwill to human beings was declared from heaven (Lk 2:14), so goodwill to human beings must be carried in the hearts of those who go to God and heaven.

2. The blessing of obedience to these commands. Those who are obedient enjoy fellowship with God (v. 24). We dwell in God by a happy relationship with him, and God dwells in us through his word. *And hereby we know that he abideth in us, by the Spirit which he hath given us* (v. 24), by the sacred disposition and frame of soul that he has given us.

CHAPTER 4

The apostle urges us to test the spirits (v. 1), gives us a standard to use in such tests (vv. 2–3), shows who belongs to the world and who belongs to God (vv. 4–6), urges Christian love (vv. 7–16), and describes our love for God and its effects (vv. 17–21).

Verses 1–3

1. The apostle urges the disciples to be careful and examine the spirits that have now arisen.

1.1. He urges caution: "*Beloved, believe not every spirit; do not follow* everyone who claims to have the

Spirit of God." There had been real communications from God's Spirit to some, and therefore others pretended to have had such communications.

1.2. He urges the disciples to examine the claims that are attributed to the Spirit. Disciples are allowed to use their discretion to judge spirits. The reason for this testing is that *many false prophets have gone out into the world* (v. 1). It should not seem strange to us that false teachers set themselves up in the church; it was so already in the apostles' times.

2. He gives a test the disciples may apply to these professing spirits. The spirits are to be tested by their teaching. Those who recognize, acknowledge, and preach Christ do so through the Spirit of God. The summary of revealed religion is included in the teaching about Christ, his person and work. We see, then, how terrible is a systematic opposition toward him and it. But we have been forewarned that such opposition will arise, and the more we see the word of Christ fulfilled, the more confirmed we should be in its truth.

Verses 4–6

The apostle encourages the disciples against this deceiving spirit of antichrist.

1. He assures them that there is a more divine principle in them (vv. 4, 6). *We are born of God.*

2. He gives them hope of victory (v. 4), a hope founded on two reasons. First: "There is a strong preserver within you (v. 4). The Spirit of God lives in you, and that Spirit is more powerful than human beings." Second: "The Spirit of God has formed your mind for God and heaven, but *they are of the world, and therefore speak they of the world.* Their worldly intentions win them converts (v. 5). They are followed by people like themselves: the world loves its own, and its own love it."

3. He tells them that they have greater divine and holy knowledge: *He that knoweth God heareth us.* Those who know the purity and holiness of God, the love and grace of God, must know that he is with us, and those who know this will listen to us and remain with us. There is a distinction, therefore, between us and others."

Verses 7–13

The Spirit of truth is known by doctrine (v. 1) and also by love (v. 7). The apostle wants to unite the disciples in his love in order to unite them in love for one another. They should love one another because:

1. Love has a high and heavenly origin: *for love is of God* (v. 7). The Spirit of God is the Spirit of love. Love comes from heaven.

2. Love evidences a true understanding of the divine nature (v. 8). What attribute of the divine Majesty is communicated so clearly to the whole world as that of love? *He that loveth not*, therefore, *knoweth not God*; knowledge of God does not live in such a soul. Love is natural and essential to God's majesty: *God is love.* He has loved us as we are. How amazing and wonderful that God would love impure dust and ashes—and that he has loved us at such a price, has placed such an incomparable value on us. What a mystery and miracle of divine love—that such a Son would be sent to our world for us (v. 10)! He loved us even when we had no love for him, when we were in our guilt and blood (Eze 16:6). He gave us his Son for such a service, such a purpose, *to be the propitiation for our sins*, so that we might live with God, live in eternal glory and blessedness with him. O what love is this!

3. God's love for our brothers and sisters should compel our love for them (v. 11). This should be an invincible argument. Will we refuse to love those whom the eternal God has loved? We should wonder at his love, and love his love, and therefore love those whom he loves.

4. Christian love is an assurance that God lives in us. The sacred lovers of brothers and sisters are the temples of God; God's majesty has a special residence there.

5. In such love, God's love accomplishes a significant purpose in us. God's love is not made complete in him, but in us and with us. Faith is made complete by its works (Jas 2:18–26), and love is made complete by its actions. When God's love has produced in us the love for God, and then love for brothers and sisters for his sake, it is complete. How ambitious we should be to gain this love, since God reckons his own love to us as made complete by it. One would have thought that to speak of God living in us and we in him would be to use words too high for mortals, if God had not gone before us in such a matter. What this indwelling fully is must be left to the revelation of the blessed future world. And yet we *know* it, says the apostle, *because he hath given us of his spirit.*

Verses 14–16

The apostle confirms that the primary article of the Christian faith is the foundation of our love for God and fellow human beings.

1. He declares the fundamental article of the Christian religion: *the Father sent the Son to be the Saviour of the world* (v. 14). We see here:

1.1. The Lord Jesus' relationship with God; he is the Son of the Father.

1.2. His relationship with and work for us—*the Saviour of the world.*

1.3. The basis on which he became so: *The Father sent the Son.*

1.4. The apostle's assurance of this—he and his brothers have seen it; they have seen the Son of God in his human nature.

1.5. The apostle's affirmation of this: *We have seen and do testify.*

2. The apostle states the excellent privilege that accompanies the due acknowledgment of this truth: those who acknowledge Christ, and God in him, are possessed by the Spirit of God.

3. The apostle applies this same truth, *that the Father sent the Son to be the Saviour of the world*, in order to stir up the disciples to holy love. God's love is seen and exerted in Christ Jesus (v. 16). The Christian revelation is the revelation of God's love; the articles of our revealed faith are simply the many articles relating to his love. The record of the Lord Jesus Christ is the record of God's love for us. We can learn from this:

3.1. *God is love* (v. 16); he is essential, boundless love; he has incomprehensible love for us who live in this world, and he has demonstrated this in the mission of his dear Son. What will he not do when he intends to demonstrate his love, that he himself is love? In such a dispensation as that of giving an eternal Son for us and to us, he will demonstrate his love to us indeed. Then may it well be inscribed on the whole creation of God, *God is love.*

3.2. *He that dwelleth in love dwelleth in God, and God in him.* Those who live in sacred love have *the love of God shed abroad upon their heart* (Ro 5:5) and will before long go to live with God forever.

Verses 17–21

Here the apostle recommends both branches of holy love, love for God and love for our brothers and sisters.

1. He recommends love for God.

1.1. It will give us peace and spiritual assurance on the day when that will be most needed (v. 17). A day of universal judgment is coming. Those who have a boldness and confidence before the Judge on that day will be happy; they will be able to lift up their heads and look him in the face, knowing he is their friend. We have this boldness toward Christ because we are like him (v. 17). Love has made us like him.

1.2. It prevents servile fear (v. 18); insofar as love triumphs, fear comes to an end. We must here distinguish between the fear of God and being afraid of him. The fear of God is often mentioned and commanded as the substance of religion (1Pe 2:17; Rev 14:7). Such fear is consistent with love—indeed, with perfect love. But then there is also a being-afraid of God that arises from a sense of guilt, and so *fear* may here be rendered "dread": "There is no dread in love." Love sets aside dread and puts on joy in him, and just as love grows, so joy grows too; the result is that *perfect love casteth out fear* or dread. Those who love God perfectly know well that God loves them, and they then triumph in his love. The apostle then points out that what casts out torment must also cast out fear or dread, *because fear hath torment* (v. 18); it is known to be a disturbing passion. But perfect love casts out torment, because it teaches the mind a perfect acceptance of the loved One, and that is why *perfect love casteth out fear. He that feareth is not made perfect in love* (v. 18); it is a sign that our love is far from being perfect.

1.3. The only fitting response to the love of such a good God is to love him; he loved us when we were both unloving and unlovely. God's love stamped love on our souls.

2. He recommends love for our brothers and sisters in Christ, for these reasons:

2.1. It is consistent with our Christian profession. In the profession of Christianity we profess to love God as the root of religious faith. *If then a man say, I love God, but hate his brother*, whom he should love for God's sake, *he is a liar* (v. 20). The apostle proves that such a person does not love God (v. 20). The eye naturally affects the heart; things unseen are less likely to catch the mind and therefore less likely to catch the heart. A fellow Christian has something of God visible in them. How then will the person who hates a visible image of God claim to love the invisible God himself?

2.2. It is consistent with the explicit law of God. We must love God originally and supremely, and we must love others in him. It must surely be a natural, suitable obligation *that he who loves God should love his brother also* (v. 21).

CHAPTER 5

The apostle asserts: 1. The honor of believers (v. 1). 2. Their obligation to love (vv. 1–3). 3. Their victory (vv. 4–5). 4. The confirmation of their faith (vv. 6–10). 5. That eternal life is a benefit of their faith (vv. 11–13). 6. That their prayers are heard (vv. 14–17). 7. Their preservation from sin and Satan (v. 18). 8. Their beneficial separation from the world (v. 19). 9. Their true knowledge of God (v. 20), which requires them to keep themselves from idols (v. 21).

Verses 1–5

1. The apostle urges Christian love because our Christian brothers and sisters are closely related to God; they are his children (v. 1). Here the Christian brother is:

1.1. Described by his faith; he *believes that Jesus is the Christ*. Accordingly he gives himself to Christ's care and direction.

1.2. Dignified by the new birth (v. 1). All believers, though by nature sinners, are spiritually born of God and are therefore to be loved (v. 1). It seems only natural that those who love the Father would love the children too.

2. The apostle shows:

2.1. How we can discern the truth of our love for those who have been born again. The basis of that love must be our love for God (v. 2). Our love for God's children is seen to be sound and genuine when we love them simply because they are God's children, and because therefore God himself is loved in them.

2.2. How we can learn the truth of our love for God (v. 2). We truly, and for the Gospel's sake, love God when we carry out his commandments: *For this is the love of God, that we keep his commandments*, and the keeping of his commandments requires a spirit that delights to do so (v. 3). Or, his love for us makes his commandments easy and pleasant to us.

2.3. What is the result of regeneration (v. 4). Those who are born of God are born for God and therefore for another world. They can repel and conquer this world (v. 4). Faith is the cause, or means, of victory. In and by faith we cling to Christ in opposition to the world. Faith receives and derives strength for conquering the world from its object, the Son of God.

3. Real Christians are the true conquerors of the world (v. 5). The world is a great hindrance to our entering heaven, but *he that believeth that Jesus is the Son of God* believes that Jesus came from God to be the Savior of the world. And he who believes this must overcome the world by this faith, because:

3.1. He must be assured that this world is a vehement enemy of his soul.

3.2. He sees that the redeeming and rescuing of him from this evil world must be a great part of the Savior's work and of his own salvation.

3.3. He realizes that the Lord Jesus conquered the world not only for himself but also for his followers.

3.4. He has been given a spirit and disposition that cannot be satisfied with this world, that look beyond it. It is the Christian revelation that is the great means of conquering the world and of gaining another that is blessed and eternal. The Savior does not intend this world to be the inheritance of his saved community. It is the real Christian who is the real hero, who overcomes the world. Who in all the world but the believer in Jesus Christ can overcome the world in this way?

Verses 6–9

The faith of Christian believers needs to be well founded, and it is. Christ brings his credentials with him. He brought them in the way by which he came, and he still brings them in the witness that accompanies him.

1. He brought them in the way by which he came: *This is he that came by water and blood* (v. 6).

1.1. We are inwardly and outwardly defiled. We are defiled inwardly by the pollution of sin in our nature. To be cleansed from this, we need spiritual water. We are defiled outwardly by the guilt of sin in our lives. We must be purged from this by his atoning blood.

1.2. Both of these ways of cleansing were represented in the old ceremonial institutions of God. Both people and things must be purified by water and blood.

1.3. On the death of Jesus Christ, because his side was pierced by a soldier's spear, water and blood flowed immediately out of the wound. The beloved apostle saw this. Now this water and blood include all that is necessary for our salvation. By the water our souls are washed and purified. By the blood God is glorified and his law is honored. By the blood we are justified, reconciled, and presented righteous to God. The water and the blood, then, include all things that are needed for our salvation.

2. He still brings them in the witness that accompanies him, and that is the divine Spirit (v. 6). The apostle adds the commendation of this witness. He is the Spirit of God and cannot lie (Tit 1:2). He is truly the Spirit of truth. That the Spirit is truth and is a witness that deserves to be fully accepted can be seen in that he is a heavenly witness. But here:

2.1. We are stopped in our tracks by the dispute about the genuineness of v. 7. It is alleged that many old Greek manuscripts do not have this verse. We will not here enter the controversy. We will only note that it can scarcely be supposed that when the apostle was representing the Christian's faith as it is shown in their overcoming the world, and representing the foundation that that faith relies on in remaining faithful to Jesus Christ, he would omit the supreme testimony, mentioned in v. 7, that accompanied Christ, namely, the *three that bear record in heaven*. But in our own version, we have here a noble listing of the different witnesses and testimonies supporting the truth of the Lord Jesus.

2.2. Having told us that the Spirit who bears witness to Christ is truth, the apostle shows us that he is so by assuring us that he is in heaven (v. 7).

2.2.1. Here is a trinity of heavenly witnesses who have testified and vouched to the world the authority of the Lord Jesus in his claims. The first named is *the Father*; he set his seal to the commission of the Lord Christ all the while he was here. The second witness is *the Word*, a mysterious name. He must bear witness to the human nature, or to the man Christ Jesus (1Ti 2:5). The third witness is the Holy Spirit. He must be true and faithful to the One on whom the Spirit of holiness (Ro 1:4) sets his seal (Jn 3:33). These are witnesses in heaven; they testify from heaven, and they are one.

2.2.2. Set opposite these, though joined with them, are a trinity of witnesses on earth (v. 8).

2.2.2.1. Of these witnesses, the first is the *spirit*, not the Holy Spirit, but the spirit of which Jesus speaks when, in this apostle's Gospel, he says, *that which is born of the Spirit is spirit* (Jn 3:6). The regeneration or renewal of souls—their being *born of the Spirit*—is a testimony to the Savior. It is a testimony *on earth*, because it continues with the church here. To this Spirit belong not only the regeneration and conversion of the church but also its progressive sanctification, its victory over the world.

2.2.2.2. The second is the *water*. This was considered before as a means of salvation, now as a testimony to the Savior himself, and it shows his purity and purifying power. It seems to include, therefore:

2.2.2.2.1. The testimony of the baptism of John, who testified about him.

2.2.2.2.2. The purity of his own message, by which souls are purified and washed.

2.2.2.2.3. The baptism that he has appointed for the initiation of his disciples.

2.2.2.3. The third witness is the blood; he shed this, and this was our ransom. This testifies for Jesus Christ:

2.2.2.3.1. In that it demonstrated his indescribable love for us, and no one will deceive those whom they love completely (Jn 14:13–15).

2.2.2.3.2. In that it also places an obligation on his disciples to suffer and die for him. This shows that neither he nor his kingdom is like this world (Jn 18:36).

2.2.2.3.3. In that the benefits obtained and coming through his blood are signified and sealed in the institution of his own supper. These are the witnesses on earth. These three witnesses *agree in one*; they say one and the same thing among themselves.

3. The apostle concludes (v. 9): *Here is the witness* by which *God has testified about his Son*. Here we have:

3.1. A supposition that is well based on the premises. *This is the witness of God*, which must surely indicate some direct, indisputable testimony. God has by himself declared him to the world.

3.2. The authority and acceptableness of his testimony. It is truth itself, of the highest authority and most unquestionable infallibility.

3.3. The application of the rule to the present case. *God, that cannot lie* (Tit 1:2), has given sufficient assurance to the world that Jesus Christ is his Son, the Son of his love, to reconcile the world to himself (2Co 5:19). He testified, therefore, the truth and divine origin of the Christian faith, and that it is the sure and appointed way of bringing us to God.

Verses 10–13

Here, we may notice:

1. The privilege and stability of true Christians (v. 10). *He that believeth on the Son of God* not only has the outward evidence that others have; he also has in his own heart a testimony for Jesus Christ. He can affirm what Christ and the truth of Christ have done for his soul and what he has seen and found in him. Christ is formed in him (Gal 4:19), and he is growing up to the fullness and maturity, or perfect likeness, of Christ (Eph 4:13), in heaven.

2. The charging of the unbeliever with the sin of unbelief (v. 10). *He that believeth not God* in effect believes that God did not send his Son to the world, or that Jesus Christ was not the Son of God.

3. The content of all this divine testimony about Jesus Christ (v. 11). This is the summary of the Gospel.

3.1. *God hath given to us eternal life*. He has intended it for us, and he has given it to us.

3.2. *This life is in the Son*. He is eternal life to us. It must follow, therefore:

3.2.1. Those who are united to the Son are united to life (v. 12).

3.2.2. Those (v. 12) who refuse the Son, who is life itself and the way to it, refuse life.

4. The goal of the apostle's preaching this to believers. He has preached it:

4.1. For their assurance and encouragement. These believers have eternal life. Furthermore, they can come to know that they do, and they should be encouraged and strengthened as they gaze on it.

4.2. For their confirmation and progress in their holy faith (v. 13). Believers must persevere, or they do nothing.

Verses 14–17

We have here:

1. A privilege belonging to faith in Christ, namely, the hearing of believers' prayers (v. 14). The Lord Christ makes us bold when we come to God in all circumstances. Through him, our petitions are accepted by God. The content of our prayer must of course be in harmony with the declared will of God, but if it is, we may have confidence that the prayer of faith will be heard in heaven.

2. The benefit coming to us from such privilege (v. 15). For those who bring holy petitions to know that their requests are heard or accepted is as good as to know that they are answered.

3. Guidance in prayer concerning the sins of others (v. 16).

3.1. We should pray for others as well as for ourselves.

3.2. There is a great distinction between the evil and guilt of one sin and that of another (vv. 16–17).

3.2.1. *There is a sin unto death.* All sin, as to its merit and legal sentence, leads to death, but there is also a sin that leads to death in contrast to other sin that is said here *not to be unto death.* There is, therefore:

3.2.2. *A sin not unto death.* The Gospel does not positively and conclusively threaten death to the more visible sins of the members of Christ; it threatens only some Gospel discipline. There is room left for divine wisdom or goodness, or even Gospel severity, to determine how far the discipline or the scourge will proceed. There are sins that lead to spiritual and Gospel death, that is, sins that are inconsistent with spiritual life in the soul and with a Gospel right to life above. Such are total impenitence and unbelief.

4. The application of this guidance on prayer according to the different kinds of sin. It is supposed that the prayer is for life: *He shall ask, and he shall give them life.* Life is to be asked for from God. He is the God of life; he gives it when and to whom he pleases. In the case of the sin of a brother or sister that does not lead to death, we may in faith and hope pray for them. But in cases of sin that lead to death we have no permission to pray. Perhaps the apostle's expression *I do not say, He shall pray for it* means no more than, "In that case, I have no promise for you." The removal of Gospel penalties or the prevention of death can be prayed for only conditionally or provisionally. As long as the impenitent and unbelieving remain such, we cannot pray that their sins be forgiven them. Yet we may pray for their repentance, for them to be enriched with faith in Christ and then to receive all other saving mercies. The apostle seems to argue that there is sin that does not lead to death (v. 17). Indeed, if all unrighteousness led to death, we would all certainly be bound over to death. Since it is not so, there must be sin that does not lead to death.

Although there is no venial sin—in the sense in which the term is commonly used—there is pardoned sin.

Verses 18–21

We have here:

1. A repetition of the privileges of true Christian believers.

1.1. They are protected against sin (v. 18), against the sin that leads to death. The new nature, and the indwelling of the Holy Spirit that attends that nature, prevent the committing of such unpardonable sin.

1.2. They are strengthened against the Devil's attempts to destroy them (v. 18). It seems not to be simply an account of the duty of the regenerate, but an indication of their power.

1.3. They are on God's side and against the world (v. 19). The human race is divided into two great sides, one that belongs to God and another that belongs to evil. Christian believers belong to God. They come from God and live for him. In contrast, *the whole world*, the rest, by far the major part, *lieth in wickedness.* May the God of the Christian world continually destroy the Devil's dominion and transfer souls to *the kingdom of his dear Son* (Col 1:13)!

1.4. They are enlightened in the knowledge of the true, eternal God (v. 20). The Son of God has come to our world, and we have seen him and know him. He has revealed to us the true God, and he has also opened our minds to understand that revelation, and we are assured that it is the true God whom he has revealed to us. It is a great joy to know the true God, to know him in Christ; it is eternal life (Jn 17:3).

1.5. They have a joyful union with God and his Son (v. 20). The Son leads us to the Father, and we are *in* both, in the love and favor of both. In union with either—and much more with both—we are united to *the true God and eternal life.*

2. The apostle's concluding warning (v. 21): "Since you know the true God and are in him, let your light and love guard you. Flee from the false gods of the pagan world. The God whom you have known is the One who redeemed you through his Son. He is the one who has pardoned your sins and given you eternal life. Hold on to him in faith, love, and constant obedience. To this living and true God be glory and power for ever and ever. Amen."

A Practical and Devotional Exposition of

2 John

Here we find a canonical letter written, chiefly, not to a church but to an individual—and to a woman. And why not? In the Gospel redemption, the Gospel privilege, and the Gospel dignity, *there is neither male nor female*; they are both one *in Christ Jesus* (Gal 3:28). No wonder, then, that a heroine in the Christian faith would be dignified by an apostolic letter.

CHAPTER 1

The apostle here greets an honorable lady and her children (vv. 1–3), recommends faith and love to them (vv. 5–6), warns them of deceivers (v. 7), warns them to keep watch over themselves (v. 8), teaches them how to deal with those who do not bring the teaching of Christ (vv. 10–11), and concludes the letter (vv. 12–13).

Verses 1–4

Letters in the past began, like this one, with greetings and good wishes: religious faith consecrates, as far as possible, old forms, turning compliments into real expressions of life and love. We have here, as usual:

1. The writer, referred to not by name but by a chosen description: *The elder.* The expression, style, and love show that the writer was the same as that of the previous letter, possibly the oldest apostle then living. He was now old in holy service and experience, had seen and tasted much of heaven, and was much nearer to heaven than when he believed in the beginning.

2. The ones addressed in the letter: *to the elect* (chosen) *lady and her children,* a lady, a person of eminent quality. It is good that the Gospel has gained ground among such people. It is a pity if lords and ladies are not acquainted with the Lord Jesus Christ and his religious faith. *The elect lady:* not only a chosen one, but one chosen by God. *And her children:* probably the lady was a widow. We see that children may well be taken notice of in Christian letters, and they should know it too; it may encourage them. Notice the respect paid them:

2.1. By the apostle himself: *whom I love in the truth,* "whom I sincerely love." The one who was the beloved disciple had learned to exercise love.

2.2. By all her Christian acquaintances: *And not I only, but also all those that have known the truth* (v. 1). Truth demands recognition, and those who see the evidences of pure religion should acknowledge and affirm them. The basis of this love and respect was their respect for the truth: *For the truth's sake which dwelleth in us, and shall be with us for ever.* Those who love truth and godliness in themselves should love it in others too. Religious faith should continue to live in us, in our minds and hearts, in our constant faith and love.

3. The greeting, which is a true apostolic blessing (v. 3). Sacred love pours out blessings on this honorable Christian family; to those who have, more will be given (Mk 4:25). Notice:

3.1. From whom these blessings are sought:

3.1.1. *From God the Father.* He is the fountain of blessedness.

3.1.2. *From the Lord Jesus Christ.* He is also author and communicator of these heavenly blessings, since he is *the Son of the Father.*

3.2. What the apostle seeks.

3.2.1. *Grace*—divine favor and goodwill.

3.2.2. *Mercy*—free pardon and forgiveness; even those who are already rich in grace need constant forgiveness.

3.2.3. *Peace*—tranquility of spirit and serenity of conscience. These are desired *in truth and love.* These blessings will continually preserve true faith and love *in the elect lady and her children.*

4. The apostle's rejoicing upon learning of the exemplary behavior of other children of this excellent lady (v. 4). Possibly the lady's sons traveled abroad, and in their travels they may have come to Ephesus, where the apostle is thought then to have been living, and perhaps they were blessed to have contact with him there. Let young travelers learn to take their religious faith along with them, and not leave it at home or learn the bad customs of the countries they visit. It is pleasing to see children following in their good parents' footsteps. How great a joy it must have been to her ladyship to hear such a good account of them from such a good judge! We see here also the rule for true walking in the faith: *the commandment of the Father.* Our walk is true, our life right, when it is directed by the word of God.

Verses 5–6

We come now more into the purpose and substance of the letter, and we have:

1. The apostle's request: whether out of respect for her ladyship or out of apostolic humility or both, he condescends to ask: *And now I beseech thee, lady.* Love will succeed where authority will not, and we often see that the more authority is urged, the more it is disrespected.

2. The thing requested: Christian sacred love. Those who are distinguished in any Christian virtue still have room to grow in it.

A Practical and Devotional

2.1. This love is encouraged on the basis of the obligation to fulfill it—the *commandment*—and on the basis of the great age of the obligation (v. 5). The commandment that disciples love one another must be part of Christianity everywhere.

2.2. This love is illustrated (v. 6). That we follow all God's commands is the evidence of our sincere mutual Christian love. Universal obedience is the proof of the sincerity of Christian virtues, and to walk in this love is a fundamental duty in the Gospel charter.

Verses 7–9

In this main part of the letter we find:

1. The bad news communicated to the lady: "*For many deceivers have entered into the world*, and your stability is likely to be tested." Notice:

1.1. The description of the deceivers and their deceit (v. 7); they bring in some error about the person of the Lord Jesus. It is strange that after such evidence as was provided, anyone would deny that the Lord Jesus Christ is the Son of God and Savior of the world!

1.2. The charge brought against such people (v. 7); they delude souls and undermine the kingdom of the Lord Christ.

2. The advice then given (v. 8). They must beware of two things:

2.1. *That they lose not what they have wrought* (worked for) (v. 8), what they have done or what they have gained. Some people begin well but in the end are still lost. Those who profess religious faith should take care not to lose the ground that they have already gained. It is sad that reasonable and splendid achievements in the school of Christ should all ultimately be lost.

2.2. That they do not lose their reward, none of it. *That we receive a full reward.* The way to receive the full reward is to remain true to Christ and constant in religious faith to the end.

3. The reason for the apostle's advice.

3.1. The danger and evil of departing from Gospel light. It is in reality a departure from God himself: *Whosoever transgresseth and abideth not in the doctrine of Christ, hath not God.* Those who abandon that doctrine are in fact abandoning God.

3.2. The advantage and happiness of constant faithfulness to Christian truth. *He that abideth in the doctrine of Christ, he hath both the Father and the Son.* We must keep that holy teaching in faith and love if we hope or desire to reach that blessed fellowship with the Father and the Son.

Verses 10–11

1. The apostle gives guidance about the treatment of such deceivers: *If there come any unto you, and bring not this doctrine, receive him not into your house. Neither bid him God speed.* Bad work should not be consecrated or commended to God's blessing. God will not support falsehood and sin. We must not dare support the spreading of fatal error.

2. The reason for such an instruction: *For he that biddeth him God speed is partaker of his evil deeds.* To give favor and affection is to share in the sin. It is possible to share in the sins of others.

Verses 12–13

The apostle concludes this letter. Some things are better spoken face to face than written in a letter. The use of pen and ink may be a mercy and a pleasure, but a personal meeting even more so. *The children of thy elect sister greet thee.* Grace was plentiful toward this family; here are two chosen sisters, and probably their chosen children. Let there be many such gracious ladies who express their joy in their gracious descendants and other relatives! Amen.

A Practical and Devotional
Exposition of
3 John

The apostle sends this encouraging letter to his public-spirited friend Gaius, in which he also complains about the completely opposite spirit of a certain minister. He confirms the good report about another.

CHAPTER 1

In this letter: 1. The apostle congratulates Gaius on the prosperity of his soul (vv. 1–2), on the good reputation he has among true Christians (vv. 3–4), and on his hospitality toward Christ's servants (vv. 5–8). 2. He complains about Diotrephes (vv. 9–11), commends Demetrius (v. 12), and expresses his hope of visiting Gaius soon (vv. 13–14).

Verses 1–2

Here we see:

1. The sacred writer who composes and sends the letter, who is identified here by the title *The elder*. Some have questioned whether the writer is John the apostle, but his style and spirit seem to shine out in this letter. Gaius could not question from whom the letter came.

2. The person greeted and honored by the letter. He is described:

2.1. By his name, *Gaius*. We read of several people with that name, especially one the apostle Paul baptized at Corinth.

2.2. By the kind expressions by which the apostle refers to him: *The well-beloved* and *whom I love in the truth.* Love that is expressed usually kindles further love. To love our friends for the truth's sake is true love, Gospel love.

3. The greeting, containing:

3.1. The apostle's good opinion of his friend, that his *soul prospers*, the greatest blessing this side of heaven.

3.2. His good wish for his friend, that his body may *prosper and be in health* as well as his soul. Grace will improve health, and health will apply grace.

Verses 3–8

In these verses we have:

1. The good report that the apostle had received about his friend (vv. 3, 6).

1.1. The testimony about Gaius—the truth that was in him, which was shown by his love. Faith should show itself in acts of love (Gal 5:6).

1.2. The witnesses—brothers and sisters who came from Gaius testifying. A good report is due from those who have received good.

1.3. The audience before which this report and testimony were given—*before the church.* This seems to refer to the church that the apostle was now part of. They could only testify what they found and felt.

2. The report the apostle himself gives of him (v. 5). He was hospitable, good to the brothers and sisters, even to strangers. All who belonged to the household of faith were welcome to him. He was conscientious in what he did: *"Thou doest faithfully whatsoever thou doest*; you do it as a faithful servant, and you can expect the reward from the Lord Jesus Christ."

3. The apostle's joy in this matter (v. 3). The best evidence of our having the truth is our *walking in the truth.*

4. Guidance about further treatment of the brothers and sisters who are with him. It seems to have been usual in those days of love to accompany traveling ministers and Christians on at least part of their way (1Co 16:6). It is a kind act to guide strangers on their way, and it is a pleasure for travelers to have good company. This is a work that may be done *after a godly sort.*

5. The reasons for following this way: *Because that for his name's sake these brethren went forth, taking nothing of the Gentiles* (receiving no help from the pagans). They went out to preach the Gospel; perhaps they were sent out by this apostle himself. They went out to convert the Gentiles for God and his name's sake. They went out also to take a free Gospel with them: *taking nothing of the Gentiles.* Some who are not called to preach the Gospel themselves can still contribute to its progress. The Gospel should be made available without charge to those to whom it is preached for the first time. *We ought therefore to receive such, that we may be fellow-helpers to the truth.* Those who cannot themselves make it known can still help and support those who do.

Verses 9–11

1. Here is a very different example and character. Notice:

1.1. His name: *Diotrephes*, a Gentile name belonging to an unchristian spirit.

1.2. His attitude and spirit—full of pride and ambition: *He loves to have the pre-eminence.*

1.3. His contempt for the apostle's authority, letter, and friends.

1.3.1. His contempt for his authority: *the deeds which he doeth, prating against us with malicious words* (gossiping maliciously about us). Hatred and malice in the heart tend to express themselves in words.

1.3.2. His contempt for his letter (v. 9). To an ambitious, aspiring spirit, apostolic authority or an apostolic letter means very little.

1.3.3. His contempt for his friends, the brothers and sisters the apostle has commended (v. 10). There may have been some differences or different customs between the Jewish and Gentile Christians. Many who should be received there with joy and welcome in the church are put out of it.

1.4. The apostle's threat against this proud, domineering man (v. 10). This seems to show his apostolic authority.

2. Here is a word of advice concerning that different character (v. 11). Caution and advice are not unnecessary to those who are already good. Reasons are added to both the warning and the word of advice. To the word of advice: *Follow that which is good*, for *he that doeth good is of God*. To the warning: *Follow not that which is evil*, for *he that doeth evil hath not seen God*. Evildoers falsely claim or boast that they know God.

Verses 12–14

We have here:

1. The description of another person, one *Demetrius*. Not much else is known about him, but his name lives on here. His commendation was:

1.1. General: *Demetrius has a good report of all men*. Few are well spoken of by everyone, but universal integrity and goodness are the way to—and sometimes gain—universal commendation.

1.2. Deserved and well founded (v. 12).

1.3. Confirmed by the apostle's and his friends' testimony: *Yea, and we also bear record; and you know that our record is true*. It is good to be *well* known, or known for good.

2. The conclusion of this letter. Notice:

2.1. The deferring of some things to a personal meeting (vv. 13–14). Many things can be communicated more suitably face to face than by letter. True Christians may well be glad to see one another.

2.2. The blessing: *Peace be to you*.

2.3. The public greeting sent to Gaius: *Our friends salute thee*.

2.4. The apostle's particular greeting to the Christians in Gaius's church or nearby: *Greet thy friends by name*. Those who hope to live together in heaven may well greet one another on earth.

A Practical and Devotional Exposition of

Jude

This letter is called—as are a few others—*general* or *catholic*, because it is not directed in the first place to any particular person, family, or church, but to the whole community of Christians. Its general theme is much the same as that of 2Pe 2. It is intended to warn us against deceivers and to inspire us to have a warm love and a sincere concern for truth—keeping truth closely joined with holiness, of which love is a most essential characteristic.

CHAPTER 1

We have here: 1. An account of the writer of this letter (vv. 1–2). 2. The occasion for writing it (v. 3). 3. A characterization of certain evil and perverse people (v. 4). 4. A warning against listening to and following such people (vv. 5–7). 5. A comparison likening the deceivers he is warning his readers against to certain ancient sinners (vv. 8–13). 6. A citation of an ancient prophecy of Enoch (vv. 14–15). 7. Further characterization of the deceivers (vv. 16–19). 8. An exhortation that his readers persevere in the faith (vv. 20–21). 9. Direction as to how to act toward what is erroneous and scandalous (vv. 22–23). 10. A wonderful doxology to conclude the letter (vv. 24–25).

Verses 1–2

Here we have the introduction, in which:

1. We have an account of the writer of this letter, *Jude*, or *Judas*. He was a namesake of one of his ancestors, the patriarch son of Jacob. This name was highly valued, eminent, and honorable, but:

1.1. He also had an evil namesake. There was one Judas who was the betrayer of his and our Lord. The same names may be held by the best and worst people. It may be instructive to be called after the names of eminently good people, but no conclusion can be drawn from that as to how we will turn out, though we can conclude from it what our good parents hoped we would be. However:

1.2. Our Judas was quite another person. He was a faithful servant of Jesus Christ; the other one was his betrayer and murderer. Our apostle here calls himself a servant of Jesus Christ, considering that to be a most honorable title. He could have claimed to be related to Christ as to his human nature, but he waives this claim and prefers to glory in being his servant. It is a great honor to the most insignificant sincere ministers—and, in proportion, to every upright Christian—to be a *servant of Christ Jesus*. The apostles were servants before they were apostles, but they remained servants after they became apostles. Jude was also a *brother of James*, namely, the James whom the ancient writers call the first bishop of Jerusalem. Our Jude was a *brother* of this James, though we cannot determine whether in the narrowest or the wider sense.

2. We are informed here to whom this letter is directed: to all those *who are sanctified by God the Father, and preserved in Jesus Christ, and called.*

2.1. By *called*, the apostle may mean *called to be Christians*. Christians are the called ones, the ones called out of the world, called to turn away from sin to Christ.

2.2. They are sanctified: *sanctified by God the Father.* All who are effectively called are sanctified. Our sanctification is not our own work. Our corruption and defilement come about from ourselves, but our sanctification and renewal come from God and his grace.

2.3. The called and sanctified ones are *preserved in Christ Jesus.* Where he begins, he will complete; even though we are fickle, he remains constant.

3. We have the apostolic blessing: *Mercy to you.* The *mercy* of God is the fountain of all the good we have or hope for. Next to mercy is *peace*, which we have from the assurance of having obtained mercy. Just as from mercy springs peace, so from peace springs *love*, his love for us, our love for him, and our mutual love for one another. The apostle prays that these goods may be multiplied, that Christians may not be content with scraps and small bits of them.

Verses 3–7

Here we have:

1. The purpose of the apostle in writing this letter: to strengthen his readers in the Christian faith as well as in a way of life truly conforming to it and in an open and bold profession of it. Notice:

1.1. The Gospel salvation is a *common salvation*, in that a most sincere offer of it is made to all human beings to whom news of it reaches. None are excluded from benefiting from these gracious offers and invitations except those who exclude themselves.

1.2. This *common salvation* is the subject of the faith of all the saints. It applies to all believers; the invitation is made to the weak as well as the strong. Let us remain in this faith; we are safe here; if we move a step away from it, we are in danger of being either entangled or deceived.

1.3. The apostles and evangelists all wrote to us of this salvation in which we share. They have fully declared to us all that is necessary for everyone to believe and do in order to obtain a personal share in the *common salvation.*

1.4. Though inspired, the apostle was still *diligent* in writing about the common salvation. Those who speak of sacred things should always speak of them with the greatest reverence, care, and diligence.

1.5. Those who have received the message of this salvation in which we share must fight earnestly for it. *Earnestly*, not furiously. But how? As the apostles did, by suffering patiently and courageously for it.

2. The occasion the apostle had for writing to this effect. Just as evil conduct gives rise to good laws, so dangerous errors often give just opportunity for the proper defense of important truths.

2.1. Ungodly people are the great enemies of the faith of Christ and the peace of the church. Those who deny or corrupt that faith or disturb that peace are here explicitly called *ungodly*. Ungodly people raise scruples and questions, cause divisions, and widen breaches. Nothing cuts us off from the church except what cuts us off from Christ, namely, prevalent unfaithfulness and ungodliness. Those who live *without God in the world* (Eph 2:12), who have no regard for God and conscience, are ungodly.

2.2. The *worst of ungodly men* are those *who turn the grace of God into lasciviousness* (v. 4), who take encouragement to sin more boldly because the grace of God has abounded (Ro 6:1).

2.3. Those who change the grace of God into a license for immorality in effect *deny the Lord God, and our Lord Jesus Christ*; they deny both natural and revealed religion. They strike at the very roots of natural religion because they *deny the only Lord God*, and they overturn all the framework of revealed religion because they deny *the Lord Jesus Christ*. Natural and revealed religion stand or fall together, and they give light and support to each other. Never did two accounts correspond more exactly to each other than these do.

2.4. Those who change the grace of God into a license for immorality are marked out for condemnation. Those who sin in this way must necessarily die of their wounds, of their disease.

2.5. We should *contend earnestly for the faith* (v. 3), in opposition to those who want to corrupt or distort it, those who have *crept in unawares*. The busier and more scheming the instruments and agents of Satan are to rob us of the truth, the more careful we should be to hold it firmly.

3. The fair warning that the apostle, in Christ's name, gives to those who, having professed his holy faith, later prove false to it (vv. 5 – 7). *I will put you in remembrance.* What we already know, we still need to be reminded of. Preaching is not intended to teach us something new in every sermon, but *to put us in remembrance*, to call to mind things that we have forgotten. *"Though you know these things,"* you still need to know them better." We Christians need to be reminded of:

3.1. The destruction of the unfaithful Israelites in the desert (v. 5). They had many miracles: miracles were their daily bread (Ex 16:14 – 35). But they still perished in unbelief. We have much greater advantages than they had; let their fatal error be a fearful warning to us.

3.2. The fall of the angels (v. 6). There were very many angels who *left their own habitation*. They abandoned their positions and rebelled against God, their Creator and sovereign Lord. But God did not spare them. Those who refused to be servants to their Maker and his will in their original state were made captives to his justice and are *reserved in everlasting chains under darkness*. Hear and fear (Dt 17:13), O sinful mortals!

3.3. The destruction of Sodom and Gomorrah (v. 7). Their ruin is a particular warning to all people to be on their guard against and flee *from fleshly lusts that war against the soul* (1Pe 2:11). God is the same holy, just, and pure Being now as he was then, and can the wild pleasures of a moment make up for your suffering the vengeance of eternal fire?

Verses 8 – 15

The apostle brings a charge against deceivers who are now deceiving the disciples of Christ. He calls them *filthy dreamers*, inasmuch as delusion is a dream and is the beginning of and inlet to all kinds of defilement. *These filthy dreamers* dream themselves into a fool's paradise on earth and into a real hell in the end.

1. The character of these deceivers is described.

1.1. They *defile the flesh*. The flesh or body is the immediate origin, and often the provoking occasion, for many horrid defilements, but these, though done in and against the body, greatly defile and grievously harm and wound the soul.

1.2. They *despise dominion, and speak evil of dignities* (reject authority and slander celestial beings). Such evil-speakers despise the authority of conscience and make fun of it, wanting to banish it from the world, and as for the word of God, the rule of conscience, they despise that too. Religious faith and those who seriously profess it have always and everywhere been slandered. The apostle mentions *Michael the archangel* (v. 9). Interpreters are at a loss as to what is here meant by *the body of Moses*. It is said that Michael *durst* (dared) *not bring a railing* (slanderous) *accusation*. It was not that he was afraid of the Devil, but that he believed God would be offended if, in such a dispute, he pursued that way. This should serve as a word of advice to all those involved in disputes, never to bring slanderous accusations into their disputes. Truth does not need any support from falsehood or slander. Instead, therefore, Michael said, *The Lord rebuke thee.* He would not stand disputing with the Devil. Divine rebukes are harder to endure than careless sinners now think.

1.3. *They speak evil of the things which they know not* (v. 10). If they had known them, they would have spoken well about them, for nothing but what is good and excellent can be truthfully said about the Christian faith. People tend to speak evil of those people and things that they know least about. On the other hand, by staying out of the public eye some people avoid even just criticism. *But what they know naturally.* The apostle likens such people to *brute beasts* (unreasoning animals), even though they often think and boast about themselves as if they were, if not the wisest, then at least as the wittiest, part of the human race. *In those things they corrupt themselves.* The fault, whatever it is, lies in their depraved wills.

1.4. In v. 11 the apostle represents them as followers *of Cain*, and in vv. 12 – 13 as unbelieving and worldly people, and as greedy people who, so long as they can gain present worldly advantages, do not care what comes next, and who, like Korah, rush into actions in which they will certainly perish, as he did.

1.4.1. *These* deceivers *are spots in your feasts of charity*, or *love-feasts*. Yet how common such blemishes are in all Christian communities here on earth, including the very best ones!

1.4.2. *When they feast with you, they feed themselves without fear.* They were undoubtedly outright gluttons, concerned only to satisfy their appetites. Even in ordinary eating and drinking, holy fear is necessary, and much more so in feasting.

1.4.3. They are *clouds without water*, which promise rain in a time of drought but fulfill nothing of what they promise. Such is the case with those who profess Christian faith merely out of tradition. *Carried about of winds*, easily driven whichever way the wind happens to be blowing; such people are empty, unfounded professors, easy targets to every deceiver. How fortunate would our world be if people either knew more or practically knew how little they know.

1.4.4. They are *trees whose fruit withereth*. They are trees, for they have been planted in the Lord's vineyard, but they do not bear fruit. *Twice dead*. One would have thought that to be dead once would be enough. They were once dead in their natural state, but when they took on themselves the profession of the Christian faith, they seemed to recover and be brought back to life. But now, by the clear proofs they give of their hypocrisy, they are seen to be dead again: whatever they appear to be, they have nothing truly living in them: they are *plucked up by the roots*, as we commonly deal with dead trees, from which we expect no more fruit.

1.4.5. They are *raging waves of the sea*, full of talk and turbulence, *foaming out their own shame*, creating much uneasiness to people with calmer tempers, which will in the end turn to the greater shame and just discredit of the deceivers. Raging waves are a terror to passengers in ships, but when they have reached the harbor, the waves are forgotten and their noise and terror are ended forever.

1.4.6. They are *wandering stars*. Here is a vivid picture of false teachers, who are now here, now there, so that one does not know what they really think or even how to figure that out.

2. The destiny of these evildoers is declared. False teachers are to expect the worst form of punishment in this and a future world. If this will not make both ministers and people cautious, I do not know what will. No other Scripture mentions the prophecy of Enoch (vv. 14–15), but notice:

2.1. Christ's coming to judgment was prophesied as early as the middle of the patriarchal age. *The Lord cometh with* his holy myriads, including both angels and the spirits of the righteous made perfect (Heb 12:23). What a glorious time that will be, when Christ *cometh with ten thousand of these*!

2.2. It was spoken of even then as something close at hand: he *cometh*. He comes:

2.2.1. *To execute judgment upon* evildoers.

2.2.2. *To convince* them. They will have no excuse or apology that they either can or will then dare to stand on. We cannot pass v. 15 without taking notice how often and how emphatically the word *ungodly* is repeated in it, no fewer than four times: *ungodly* people, *ungodly sinners*, *ungodly deeds*, *ungodly committed*. *Godly* and *ungodly* mean little nowadays except as objects of ridicule, but it is not so with the language of the Holy Spirit. Harsh words about one another, especially if ill founded, will most certainly be judged at *the judgment of the great day*.

Verses 16–25

Here:

1. The apostle enlarges further on his description of these evildoers and deceivers (v. 16). A grumbling, fault-finding attitude earns people a very bad reputation; such people are very weak at least, and they are often evil too.

They get angry at everything that happens and are never pleased with their own condition in the world, not thinking it good enough for them. Their will, appetite, and imagination are their only rule.

2. He then comes to warn and exhort his readers (vv. 17–23).

2.1. He urges them to remember how they have been forewarned (v. 17). "The fulfillment of what the apostles foretold should confirm your faith rather than shake or unsettle you in it at all." Those who seek to persuade must make it evident that they sincerely love those whom they are seeking to persuade. Bitter words and harsh treatment never did and never will convince, much less persuade, anybody. We must not think it strange, but assure ourselves with the thought that in the middle of all this confusion Christ will keep his church and fulfill his promise. The more religion is ridiculed and persecuted, the more firmly we should take and keep hold of it. Being forewarned, we should show that we are forearmed; under such tests we should stand firm.

2.2. He guards them against deceivers by a further description of their repugnant character (v. 19). These worldly deceivers do not have the Spirit, that is, the Spirit of God and Christ, the Spirit of holiness. The worse others are, the better we should seek to be; the busier Satan is, the more firmly we should hold on to sound doctrine and good conduct.

2.3. He exhorts them to a persevering constancy in truth and holiness.

2.3.1. *Building up yourselves in your most holy faith* (v. 20). Having laid a good foundation in a sound faith, we must build on it. We should also be careful what materials we continue to build with. Right principles will stand even the test of fire.

2.3.2. *Praying in the Holy Ghost*. Prayer nurtures faith. Our prayers are most likely to prevail when we *pray in the Holy Ghost*, under his direction, guidance, and influence.

2.3.3. *Keep yourselves in the love of God* (v. 21). "Keep yourselves in God's way if you want to continue in his love."

2.3.4. *Looking for the mercy*. Eternal life is to be looked for only through *mercy*; mercy, not our merit, is our only plea. And we must look for this life through the mercy of *our Lord Jesus Christ* as Redeemer; all who come to heaven must come there through our Lord Jesus Christ. A living faith in the blessed hope will help us to put to death our cursed sinful desires.

2.4. He tells them how to behave toward brothers and sisters who are going astray (vv. 22–23). We should do all we can to rescue others from the snares of the Devil. We are not only our own keepers; everyone should be, as far as they are able, their *brother's keeper*. This must be done with *compassion, making a difference*. We must distinguish between the weak and the willful. *Of some we must have compassion*, treating them with great sensitivity, not being unnecessarily harsh and severe in our criticism of them. If God has forgiven them, why should not we? We need his forgiveness infinitely more than they need ours. *Others save with fear*, urging on them *the terrors of the Lord*; "Seek to frighten them out of their sins. Yet also *fear*, so that you may not frustrate your own good intentions by hardening instead of reclaiming." We often tend to overdo things when we are sure we mean honestly and think we are generally right. "*Hating even the garment spotted with the flesh*, keeping yourselves farthest away from what is or appears evil."

3. The apostle concludes this letter with a solemn attribution of glory to the great God (vv. 24–25). God is able, and he is as willing as able, *to keep us from falling and to present us faultless before the presence of his glory,* not as those who never have been faulty, but as those whose faults will not be imputed to us. *Before the presence of his glory.* The glory of the Lord will soon be present. This is now the object of our faith, but soon it will be the object of our senses; the One whom we now believe in will soon be seen by us. When believers are presented faultless, it will be with exceeding joy. Where there is no sin, there will be no sorrow; where there is the perfection of holiness, there will be the perfection of joy. Surely, the God who can and will do all this is worthy to have *glory, majesty, dominion, and power* attributed to him, *both now and for ever! Amen.*

A Practical and Devotional
Exposition of
Revelation

It should not prejudice the credit or authority of this book to note that it has been rejected by people with corrupt minds. The church of God has generally accepted it and found great wisdom and comfort in it. Christ himself prophesied about the destruction of Jerusalem, and about the time when that prophecy was fulfilled, he entrusted the apostle John with this book of Revelation to support the faith of his people and direct their hope.

CHAPTER 1

This chapter is a general introduction to the whole book and contains: 1. Its title (vv. 1–2). 2. The apostolic blessing (vv. 3–8). 3. A glorious appearance of the Lord Jesus Christ that the apostle John saw when Christ delivered this revelation to him (vv. 9–20).

Verses 1–2

1. It is *the revelation of Jesus Christ.* As the prophet of the church, he has revealed to us the things that will come in the future. It is a revelation *which God gave unto Christ.* Our Lord Jesus is the great trustee of divine revelation; it is to him that we owe our knowledge of what we are to expect from God and what he expects from us. Christ *sent and signified* this revelation to the churches *by his angel.* The angels are God's messengers. The angels *signified it to the apostle John,* the apostle chosen for this service. Some think he was the only surviving apostle, the rest having sealed their testimony with their blood. John was to deliver this revelation to the church, to all Christ's servants. They all have a right to the word of God.

2. The subject matter of this revelation is the *things that must shortly come to pass.* It gives us a general idea of the ways of divine Providence. These events would come to pass not only *surely* but *shortly.*

3. Here is a testimony to the truth of the prophecy (v. 2). John testified to the word of God in general and to the testimony of Jesus in particular, and to everything that he saw; he was an eyewitness, and he concealed nothing that he saw. As he added nothing to it, so he also kept back no part of the purposes of God.

Verses 3–8

We have here an apostolic blessing on those who give proper attention to this divine revelation.

1. The blessing is given more generally, to all who either read or hear the words of the prophecy. It is a blessed privilege to enjoy the word of God. It is a blessed thing to study the Scriptures. It is a privilege not only to read the Scriptures ourselves but also to hear them read by others. It is not enough for our blessedness that we read and hear the Scriptures; we must also *keep the things that are written.*

2. It is declared more particularly to the seven churches in the province of Asia (v. 4). These seven churches are named in v. 11, and a distinct message is sent to each. Notice:

2.1. What the blessing is: *Grace,* that is, the goodwill of God toward us and his good work in us, and *peace,* that is, the sweet evidence and assurance of this grace.

2.2. Where this blessing is to come from: it is spoken in the name of God, of the whole Trinity.

2.2.1. The Father is named first: God the Father, *who is, and who was, and who is to come,* eternal, unchangeable.

2.2.2. Then the Holy Spirit is invoked. He is called *the seven spirits,* the infinite, perfect Spirit of God, in whom there is a diversity of gifts and activities. He is before the throne, because, just as God made, so he also governs, all things by his Spirit.

2.2.3. The blessing is spoken, finally, in the name of the Lord Jesus Christ. Notice the particular account we have here of Christ (v. 5).

2.2.3.1. He is *the faithful witness.* We may safely depend on his testimony, because he is a faithful witness: he cannot be deceived and he cannot deceive us.

2.2.3.2. He is *the first begotten,* or firstborn, from the dead.

2.2.3.3. He is the ruler of the kings of the earth; their power is limited by him; their purposes are overruled by him, and they are accountable to him.

2.2.3.4. He is the great friend of his church and people. He has loved them. *He has washed them from their sins in his own blood.* Sins leave a stain on the soul, a stain that nothing except the blood of Christ can take away, and rather than let it not be washed out, Christ was willing to shed his own blood. Having justified and sanctified them, he has *made them kings and priests to God and his Father.* As kings, they overcome the world. He has made them priests, giving them access to God. Because of these high honors and favors, they must give him praise, power, and glory forever.

2.2.3.5. He will be the Judge of the world (v. 7). This book, Revelation, begins and ends with a prediction of the second coming of the Lord Jesus Christ. John speaks as if he saw that day: "*Behold, he cometh,* as surely as if you looked at him with your eyes. *He cometh with clouds,* which are his chariot and canopy. *Every eye shall see him,* the eye of his people, the eye of his enemies, every eye, yours and mine." His coming will arouse terror in those who have pierced him and have not repented and in all who have wounded and crucified him afresh by their apostasy from him, and it will arouse the horror of the pagan world.

2.2.3.6. This account of Christ is confirmed by Christ himself (v. 8). He is the beginning and the end; all things come from him and are for him; he is the Almighty One; he is the same eternal and unchangeable One.

Verses 9–20

We now come to the glorious vision that the apostle had of the Lord Jesus Christ when the Lord came to deliver this revelation to him, in which notice:

1. The person who was favored with this vision. He describes himself:

1.1. By his present state and condition. He was persecuted, banished, and perhaps imprisoned for his faithfulness to Christ. To these churches for whom Christ had messages he was a *brother*, even though he was an apostle. He was their companion in suffering; the persecuted servants of God did not suffer alone. He was their companion in *patience*, sharing with them not only in suffering circumstances but also in suffering graces. By this account he acknowledges his commitment to sympathize with them and to seek to give them advice and encouragement.

1.2. By the place where he was when he was favored with this vision: he was in *the isle Patmos*. In this confinement it was the apostle's encouragement that he did not suffer as an evildoer, but for the testimony of Jesus. This was a cause worth suffering for, and the Spirit of glory and of God rested on this persecuted apostle.

1.3. By the day and time when he had this vision: it was on *the Lord's day*.

1.4. By the attitude of his soul at that time: *He was in the Spirit*. He was in a rapture not only when he received the vision but even before he received it. God usually prepares the souls of his people for uncommon revelations of himself by the life-giving influence of his good Spirit.

2. What he heard. An alarm was sounded as with the blast of a trumpet, and then *he heard a voice*, the voice of Christ, *the first and the last*, commanding the apostle to commit to writing the things that were now to be revealed to him and to send it immediately *to the seven Asian churches*.

3. What he saw. *He turned to see the voice* (v. 12), and then in a vision he saw a wonderful scene open before him.

3.1. He saw a representation of the church in the form of an emblem of *seven golden candlesticks*. The churches are compared to *candlesticks* (lampstands) because they hold out the light of the Gospel to great advantage.

3.2. He saw a representation of the Lord Jesus Christ among the golden lampstands. Notice:

3.2.1. The glorious form in which Christ appeared.

3.2.2. The impression this appearance of Christ made on the apostle John (v. 17). He was overpowered with the greatness of the brightness and glory in which Christ appeared, even though he had been very familiar with him before.

3.2.3. The condescending goodness of the Lord Jesus to his disciple (v. 17). He raised him up; he put strength into him, speaking kind words to him, words of comfort and encouragement—*Fear not*—and words of instruction, telling him specifically who it was who appeared to him in this way. Christ revealed to him:

3.2.3.1. His divine nature: *The first and the last*.

3.2.3.2. His former sufferings: *I was dead*.

3.2.3.3. His resurrection and life: "*I live, and am alive for evermore*; I have conquered death, and now I partake of an eternal life."

3.2.3.4. His office and authority: *I have the keys of hell and of death*, sovereign power in and over the invisible world.

3.2.3.5. His will and pleasure: *Write the things which thou hast seen, and the things which are, and which shall be hereafter.*

3.2.3.6. The meaning of the seven stars: they are *the angels*, or ministers, *of the churches*; and he revealed the meaning of the seven lampstands: *they are the seven churches.*

CHAPTER 2

In this chapter we have the messages sent to: 1. Ephesus (vv. 1–7). 2. Smyrna (vv. 8–11). 3. Pergamum (vv. 12–17). 4. Thyatira (vv. 18–29).

Verses 1–7

We have here:

1. The title.

1.1. It is to *the church of Ephesus*.

1.2. It is from him *that holds the stars in his right hand*. The ministers of Christ are under his special care and protection, in his hand. He supports them, for otherwise they would soon be falling stars; and all the good they do is done by his hand with them. His *walking in the midst of the golden candlesticks* shows his relationship with his churches. Although Christ is in heaven, he walks among his churches on earth.

2. The contents of the letter.

2.1. Christ's commendation of this church, which, as usual, he introduces by declaring that he knows their works. Therefore both his commendation and his censures are to be strictly regarded, because he does not speak either at random: he knows what he says. The church of Ephesus is commended:

2.1.1. For their diligence in fulfilling their duty (vv. 2–3).

2.1.2. For their patience in suffering (v. 2). It is not enough to be diligent; we must also have patience. No Christian can be without it. They must have both enduring patience and waiting patience, so that they may receive the promise (v. 3).

2.1.3. For their zeal against evil (v. 2). We must show great humility toward people, but we must also show just zeal against their sins. True zeal proceeds with discretion; no one should be rejected until they are tried.

2.2. The rebuke he gives it (v. 4). Those who have much good in them may also have something wrong in them. *Thou hast left thy first love*; they have not left and forsaken its object, but lost the passion they had shown at first. The first affections people have toward Christ are usually vibrant and warm, but these vibrant affections will decline and cool unless great care is taken.

2.3. His advice to it. Those who have lost their first love *must remember whence they have fallen*; they must compare their present state with their former and consider how much better it was with them then than now. They must repent. They must return and do their *first works*. They must, as it were, begin again. They must endeavor to revive and recover their first zeal.

2.4. The reinforcing and urging of this good advice:

2.4.1. By a severe threat that if it is neglected, Christ will come and *remove their candlestick out of its place.*

If the presence of Christ's grace and Spirit is shown disrespect, we may expect the presence of his displeasure.

2.4.2. By an encouraging mention of what is still good among them (v. 6). "Although you have declined in your love for what is good, you still keep your hatred for what is evil." An indifference of spirit between truth and error, good and evil, may be called *charity* and *meekness*, but it does not please Christ.

3. The conclusion of this letter, in which we have:

3.1. A call to attention. What is said to one church concerns all the churches in every place and age.

3.2. A promise of great mercy to those who overcome. We must never yield to our spiritual enemies, but continue to fight the good fight (1Ti 6:12; 2Ti 4:7) until we gain the victory, and the warfare and victory will have a glorious triumph and reward. They will *eat of the tree of life which is in the midst of the paradise of God*, not in the earthly Paradise, but the heavenly one (22:1–2).

Verses 8–11

We now proceed to the second letter, sent to another of the churches in Asia, where, as before, notice:

1. The introduction or inscription, again in two parts.

1.1. The title: *To the angel of the church in Smyrna.*

1.2. The subtitle: Jesus Christ is the *first and the last.* Only a short time is allowed us in this world, but our Redeemer is the first and the last. He *was dead and is alive.* He was dead, and he died for our sins. He is alive, and he always lives to make intercession for us (Heb 7:25).

2. The body of this letter, in which the apostle takes notice:

2.1. Of the improvement these Christians have made in their spiritual state. *But thou art rich.* Some who are outwardly poor are inwardly rich, rich in faith and good works. Where there is spiritual plenty, outward poverty may be better coped with.

2.2. Of their sufferings: *I know thy tribulation and thy poverty.* Jesus Christ takes particular notice of all their troubles.

2.3. Of the evil and falsehood of their enemies: *I know the blasphemy* (slander) *of those that say they are Jews, but are not,* that is, of those who claim to be the only special covenant people of God when in fact *they are the synagogue of Satan.* For the synagogues of Satan to declare themselves to be the church or Israel of God is no less than blasphemy.

2.4. Of the future trials of his people that he foresees.

2.4.1. He forewarns them of future trials (v. 10). They have been impoverished by their troubles before; now they will have to be imprisoned.

2.4.2. Christ forearms them against these approaching troubles:

2.4.2.1. By his advice: *Fear none of these things.* This is a word not only of command but also of efficacy.

2.4.2.2. By showing them how their sufferings will be reduced and limited. Some, not all, of them will be thrown into prison. Their sufferings will not last forever, but for a short time: *ten days.* It will be to test them, not destroy them.

2.4.2.3. By proposing a glorious reward for their faithfulness: *Be thou faithful to death, and I will give thee a crown of life.* The One who has said it is able to do it, and he has undertaken to do it. Notice the suitableness of this reward: it is *a crown,* to reward their poverty, faithfulness, and conflict, and it is *a crown of life,* to reward those who are faithful even to death

3. The conclusion of this message with:

3.1. A call to universal attention. All the people of the world should take notice of God's dealings with his own people.

3.2. A gracious promise to conquering Christians (v. 11). There is not only a first death but also a second. This second death is unspeakably worse than the first; it is *eternal death.* Christ will save all his faithful servants from this death. The first death will not harm them, and the second death will have no power over them.

Verses 12–17

1. Here we are to consider the title of this message.

1.1. It is sent *to the angel of the church of Pergamos.*

1.2. It is sent by the one who *hath the sharp sword with two edges* (v. 12). The church at Pergamum was infested with people with corrupt minds, and because Christ was determined to fight against them with the sword of his word, he took this title. The word of God is a *sword*; it is a weapon that is both offensive and defensive. It is a *sharp* sword; no heart is so hard that it is unable to wound it. And it is *a sword with two edges*; there is the edge of the law against those who are disobedient under that age, and the edge of the Gospel against those who despise that age.

2. We proceed to the body of the letter.

2.1. Christ takes notice of the trials and difficulties this church has experienced (v. 13). Now what added very much brightness to the good works of this church was the circumstance of the place where it was planted, a place where *Satan's seat* was. Satan's *circuit* is throughout the world; his *seat* is in some places that are infamous for evil, error, and cruelty.

2.2. He commends their faithfulness: "*Thou holdest fast my name*; you are not ashamed of your relationship with me, but count it your honor that you are named with my name. What has made you so faithful is the grace of faith: *thou hast not denied* or departed from the Christian faith." They have been faithful *even in those days wherein Antipas his faithful martyr was slain among them.* This Antipas sealed his faith and faithfulness with his blood in the place where Satan lived, and yet the rest of the believers were not discouraged or drawn away from their faithfulness.

2.3. He rebukes them for their sinful failures (v. 14). The defilement of the spirit and the defilement of the flesh often go together. To continue in fellowship with people who have corrupt principles and practices draws guilt and blemish on the whole community.

2.4. He calls them to repentance (v. 16). Repentance is the duty of churches and communities as well as individual people; those who sin together should repent together. When God comes to punish the corrupt members of a church, he rebukes that church itself for allowing such people to continue in its fellowship, and some drops of the storm fall on the whole community. The word of God will take hold of sinners sooner or later, either to convict them or to confuse them.

3. There is the promise of great favor to those who overcome (v. 17).

3.1. They will eat the hidden manna, the influences and encouragements of the Spirit of Christ coming down from heaven into the soul from time to time. This is hidden from the rest of the world and stored in Christ.

3.2. They will have the white stone with a new name engraved on it. This white stone is absolution from the guilt of sin, alluding to the ancient custom of giving a white stone to those acquitted on trial and a black stone to those condemned. The new name is the name of adoption. No one can read the evidence of a person's spiritual adoption but that person himself or herself.

Verses 18–29

The form of each letter is very much the same, and here, as in the others, we have to consider the title, contents, and conclusion.

1. The title: *To the angel of the church of Thyatira*, by *the Son of God*, who is described here as having *eyes like a flame of fire, and feet like as fine brass* (burnished bronze). He has piercing insight into all people and all things, and just as he judges with perfect wisdom, so he also acts with perfect strength and steadiness.

2. We have the body of this letter, which includes:

2.1. The honorable characterization and commendation Christ gives of this church. Christ mentions honorably:

2.1.1. Their *charity*. There is no religion where there is no love.

2.1.2. Their *service*, their ministry, the officers' hard work in the word and doctrine.

2.1.3. Their *faith*, which is the grace that motivates all the rest.

2.1.4. Their *patience*, for even those who are most loving must expect to have their patience tested.

2.1.5. Their growing fruitfulness: their last works were better than the first. It should be the ambition and passionate desire of all Christians that their last works may be their best works.

2.2. A faithful rebuke for what is wrong. These wicked deceivers are compared to Jezebel and called by her name. Their sin is that they have attempted to draw the servants of God into sexual immorality and the offering of sacrifices to idols. They have abused the patience of God to harden themselves in their evil. God has given them opportunity to repent, but they have refused to.

2.3. The punishment of these deceivers, who, being one in their spirit and intention, are spoken of as one person, Jezebel (vv. 22–23). *I will cast her into a bed*, into a bed of pain, not of pleasure: *I will kill her children with death*, that is, the second death.

2.4. The intention of Christ in the destruction of these evil deceivers, which is that others, especially his churches, will be instructed by it. God is known *by the judgments that he executes* (Ps 9:16).

2.5. The encouragement given to those who keep themselves pure and undefiled (v. 24). Notice:

2.5.1. What these deceivers call their teachings: *depths*, deep secrets, profound mysteries.

2.5.2. What Christ calls them: *depths of Satan*, satanic delusions and devices.

2.5.3. How tender Christ is toward his faithful servants (vv. 24–25). "I only require your attention to what you have received." If they hold firmly to their faith and a good conscience until he comes, all difficulties and dangers will cease.

3. The conclusion of this message (vv. 26–29).

3.1. The promise of a full reward to persevering victorious believers. They will be given very great power and authority over the rest of the world: *power over the nations*. They will also be given knowledge and wisdom suitable to such power and authority: *I will give him the morning star*. Christ is the Morning Star. He brings day with him into the soul, the light of grace and of glory.

3.2. The end of the letter with the usual call for attention.

CHAPTER 3

Here we have three more letters of Christ to the churches:
1. To Sardis (vv. 1–6). 2. To Philadelphia (vv. 7–13).
3. To Laodicea (vv. 14–22).

Verses 1–6

Here is:

1. The introduction. The letter is sent *to the angel of the church of Sardis*, said to have been the first city in that part of the world that was converted by the preaching of John. Some say it was also the first that rebelled from Christianity. This message was sent by the Lord Jesus, *he that hath the seven spirits of God, and the seven stars.*

1.1. He has seven spirits, that is, the Holy Spirit with his various powers. Because this letter is sent to a languishing ministry and church, they are appropriately reminded that Christ has the seven spirits, the Spirit without limit (Jn 3:34) and in perfection, and they may turn to that Spirit and ask him to revive his work among them.

1.2. He has seven stars, the *angels*, or ministers, of the churches. The Holy Spirit usually works through the ministry, and the ministry will be ineffective without the Spirit; the same divine hand holds them both.

2. The main part of this letter.

2.1. In this—and in the letter to Laodicea—he begins with a rebuke, and a very severe one. Hypocrisy and a lamentable decline in religious faith are the sins that this church is accused of. It had gained a great reputation; it had a name of being a flourishing church. We do not read about any unhappy divisions among them. Everything appeared to be going fine on the surface, as far as could be seen by ordinary human observation. Yet this church was not really what it was reputed to be. There was a form of godliness, but not the power (2Ti 3:5), *a name to live* (a reputation for being alive), but not a vital principle of life. What little life was still left among them was expiring, on the point of dying.

2.2. Our Lord proceeds to give this degenerate church the best advice (v. 2). He advises them:

2.2.1. To wake up. Whenever we sleep, we lose ground and must therefore return to our wakefulness against sin and Satan.

2.2.2. To strengthen what remains and is ready to die. Some understand this as referring to people. It is difficult to maintain the life and *power of godliness* (2Ti 3:5) ourselves when we see a general deadness and decline all round us. Or it may be understood as referring to practices: *I have not found thy works perfect before God*; there is something lacking in them; there is a shell but no kernel. The inward thing is lacking: "Your works are hollow and empty." When the spirit is lacking, the form cannot exist for long.

2.2.3. To collect their thoughts (v. 3), to remember what they have received and heard, how welcome the Gospel and the grace of God were to them when they first received them.

2.2.4. To hold firmly to what they have received so that they will not lose everything, and to *repent*.

2.3. Christ reinforces his counsel with a fearful threat (v. 3).

2.3.1. When Christ leaves a people as to his gracious presence, he comes to them in judgment.

2.3.2. His judicial approach to a dead, declining people will be surprising; their deadness will keep them trusting themselves and prevent their discerning and preparing for this coming.

2.4. Our dear Lord does not leave this sinful people without some comfort and encouragement (v. 4). He makes honorable mention of the faithful remnant in Sardis, even though it is only small. God takes notice of the smallest number of those who remain faithful to him; the fewer they are, the more precious they are in his sight. Christ makes a very gracious promise to the faithful remnant. They will walk with Christ, and what delightful conversation there will be between Christ and them when they walk together in this way! Those who walk with Christ will walk with him in the white robes of honor and glory in the other world.

3. The end of this letter.

3.1. A great reward is promised to conquering Christians (v. 5). The purity of grace will be rewarded with the perfect purity of glory. When holiness is perfected, it will be its own reward; glory is the perfection of grace. To this is added another promise: Christ has his Book of life. He will never blot the names of his chosen and faithful ones, those who overcome, out of this Book of Life. Christ will produce this Book of Life before God and all the angels, and he will acknowledge the names of the faithful who stand there. How great this honor and reward will be!

3.2. The call for universal attention concludes the message. Every word from God deserves attention.

Verses 7–13

We now come to the sixth letter sent to one of the churches in Asia, in which notice:

1. The title.

1.1. For whom it was intended: *the angel of the church of Philadelphia*. This was its ancient name, given to it because of the love and kindness that the citizens had and showed one another. This was an excellent spirit and would render them an excellent church, as in fact they were, for here not a single fault is found with them.

1.2. By whom this letter was signed: by the same Jesus. We have his personal character: *he that is holy* and *he that is true*, holy in his nature and therefore necessarily true to his word. Notice:

1.2.1. The acts of his government.

1.2.1.1. He opens. He opens a door of opportunity to his churches; he opens a door for the message; he opens the heart; he opens the door of admission into the church triumphant.

1.2.1.2. He shuts the door. When he pleases, he shuts the door of opportunity. He shuts the door of heaven against the evildoers.

1.2.2. The way in which he performs these acts is by his absolute sovereignty. When he works, no one can stop him.

2. The body of this letter.

2.1. Christ reminds the church of what he has done for them (v. 8). "I have opened a door *before thee* and kept it open, even though there are many adversaries." Evildoers envy God's people their door of freedom and would be glad to shut it against them, but if we do not provoke Christ to shut this door against us, people cannot do it.

2.2. This church is commended (v. 8). In this there seems to be couched a gentle rebuke: "*Thou hast a little strength*, a little grace." True grace, even though it is weak, still has divine approval, but believers should not remain satisfied with a little, but should seek to grow in grace (2Pe 3:18). True grace, even if weak, will enable Christians to keep faithful to the word of Christ and not deny his name.

2.3. God will do this church a great favor (vv. 9–10).

2.3.1. Christ will make this church's enemies subject to her.

2.3.1.1. Those enemies are described as those who *say they are Jews* but are really *the synagogue of Satan*.

2.3.1.2. Their submission to the church is described: *They shall worship at thy feet*; they will be convinced that they have been wrong. How will this great change be brought about? By the power of God on the hearts of

his enemies and by significant revelation of his special favor to his church: *They shall know that I have loved thee*. Christ can reveal his favor to his people in such a way that even their enemies will see it and be forced to acknowledge it. This, by the grace of Christ, will soften the hearts of their enemies.

2.3.2. As the reward for their past faithfulness, he will give them persevering grace in the most trying times (v. 10). Notice:

2.3.2.1. The Gospel of Christ is *the word of his patience*. It is the fruit of the patience of God to a sinful world.

2.3.2.2. After a time of patience we must expect an hour of temptation.

2.3.2.3. Those who remain faithful to the Gospel in a time of peace will be kept by Christ in an hour of temptation.

2.4. Christ calls the church to persevere: "*Hold fast that which thou hast*. You have been given this excellent treasure; hold it firmly. *Behold, I come quickly*. I am coming to relieve those who are faithful under the trial, to reward their faithfulness and punish those who fall away. Persevering Christians will win the prize from backsliding professors of faith."

3. The conclusion of this letter (vv. 12–13).

3.1. Our Savior promises victorious believers a glorious reward, in two parts:

3.1.1. They will be monumental *pillars in the temple of God*; not pillars to support the temple, but monuments to the grace of God, monuments that will never be defaced or removed, as many stately pillars erected in honor of Roman emperors and generals have been.

3.1.2. On these there will be honorable titles, as is usual in such cases:

3.1.2.1. *The name of God, and the name of the city of God, the new Jerusalem, which came down from heaven.*

3.1.2.2. The *new name* of Christ; from this it will be seen under whose banner conquering believers enlisted and under whose influence they fought the good fight (1Ti 6:12; 2Ti 4:7) and were victorious.

3.2. The letter closes with a call for attention.

Verses 14–22

We now come to the last and worst of all the seven churches in Asia. Here nothing is commended.

1. The title: *To the angel of the church of Laodicea*. The apostle Paul was instrumental in planting the Gospel in this city, from which he wrote a letter, as he mentions in his letter to the Colossians (Col 2:1; 4:13, 15–16). Here our Lord Jesus describes himself as *the Amen, the faithful and true witness, the beginning of the creation of God*. As *the Amen*, he is the One who is steady and unchangeable in all his purposes and promises. As *the faithful and true witness*, he is the One whose testimony of God to people should be received. And he is *the beginning of the creation of God*, either of the first creation or of the second, the church, as it is in 1:5.

2. The body, in which notice:

2.1. The severe accusation brought against this church (v. 15). Lukewarmness or indifference in religious faith is the worst attitude in the world. If religious faith is worth anything, it is worth everything. Here is no room for being neutral. Christ expects people to declare themselves seriously either for him or against him.

2.2. A severe punishment threatened: *I will spew thee out of my mouth*. Just as lukewarm water turns the stomach and provokes vomiting, so lukewarm professors turn the heart of Christ against them. He is sick of them and cannot bear them any longer. They will be rejected.

2.3. One cause of this indifference named, and that is pride or self-delusion (v. 17). What a difference there was between the thoughts they had of themselves and the thoughts that Christ had of them. They had high thoughts of themselves. Perhaps they were well provided for physically, and this made them overlook the needs of their souls. Or they thought themselves well provided for in their souls. How careful we should be not to deceive our own souls! No doubt many in hell once thought they were on their way to heaven. But Christ had low thoughts of them. They were actually very *poor*, though they said and thought they were rich. Their souls were starving in the middle of their plenty. They were *blind*, though they thought they could see; they could not see their state or their way; they could not look into themselves; they could not see Christ; they could not see God. They were *naked*, having neither the garment of justification nor that of sanctification.

2.4. Good advice given by Christ to this sinful people (v. 18). Notice:

2.4.1. Our Lord Jesus Christ continues to give good advice even to those who have rejected his purposes.

2.4.2. Our dear Lord, the Counselor, always gives the best advice.

2.4.2.1. These people are poor; Christ advises them to buy from him gold refined in the fire, so that they will become rich. He lets them know both where they can get true riches and how: they can get them from him, and they must buy them. "Abandon your self-sufficiency and come to Christ with your poverty and emptiness, so that you may be filled with his hidden treasure."

2.4.2.2. These people are naked; Christ tells them where they can get clothing: again, from Christ. They must take off their filthy rags in order to put on the white garment he has provided for them.

2.4.2.3. They are blind, and he *counsels them to buy of him eye-salve, that they might see.* They must give up their own wisdom and reason and submit to his word and Spirit, and then their eyes will be opened.

2.5. Great and gracious encouragement given to this sinful people to accept the warning that Christ has given them (vv. 19–20). He tells them:

2.5.1. It is being given in true and tender affection: "You may think I have spoken hard words and severe reproofs to you, but it is all out of love for your souls." Sinners should accept the rebukes of God's word as signs of his goodwill to their souls. Better are the frowns and wounds of a friend than the flattering smiles of an enemy (Pr 27:6).

2.5.2. If they comply with his warnings, he is ready to apply them to their souls (v. 20). Christ is graciously pleased to come, by his word and Spirit, to the door of the heart of sinners. He finds this door shut against him; the human heart is by nature shut up against Christ. When he finds the heart shut, he does not immediately withdraw, but waits to be gracious (Isa 30:18). Those who open up their hearts to him will enjoy his presence. He will *sup* (eat) with them; he will accept what is good in them, and he will bring the best part of the reception with him.

3. The conclusion of this letter, including:

3.1. The promise made to conquering believers. It is possible that by the rebukes and advice of Christ they may be inspired with fresh zeal and vigor and come off conquerors in their spiritual warfare. If they do, they will have a great reward (v. 21). Christ himself met with his temptations and conflicts, and he overcame them all and was more than a conqueror (Ro 8:37). Those who are conformed to Christ in his trials and victories will be conformed to him in his glory.

3.2. The closing of the whole issue with the general call for attention (v. 22). We have now come to the end of the messages of Christ to the churches in Asia.

CHAPTER 4

In this chapter the prophetic scene opens, and John records: 1. The heavenly sight he saw (vv. 1–7), and then: 2. The heavenly songs he heard (vv. 8–11).

Verses 1–8

We have here an account of a second vision with which the apostle John was favored, including:

1. The preparation made for the apostle's having this vision.

1.1. *A door was opened in heaven.* We can know nothing of future events except what God wishes to reveal to us; they are within the veil until God opens the door.

1.2. To prepare John for the vision, a trumpet was sounded, and he was called up into heaven to see there the things that were to be in the future.

1.3. To prepare for this vision, the apostle was *in the Spirit*, in a rapture. His spirit was possessed with the spirit of prophecy, wholly under divine influence.

2. The vision itself.

2.1. He saw *a throne set in heaven*, the seat of honor, authority, and judgment. All earthly thrones are under the jurisdiction of this throne in heaven.

2.2. He saw a glorious One on the throne, One who filled it, and that was God. *His countenance was like a jasper and a sardine stone* (carnelian). He is not described by any human features, so as to be represented by an image, but only by his transcendent brightness.

2.3. He saw *a rainbow about the throne, like unto an emerald* (v. 3). The rainbow was the seal and token of the covenant of providence that God made with Noah (Ge 9:12–16). This rainbow looked like *the emerald*; the most prevalent color was a pleasant green, to show the reviving and refreshing nature of the new covenant.

2.4. He saw *four-and-twenty seats* around the throne, with *four-and-twenty elders. They were clothed in white raiment*, the righteousness of the saints (19:8); they *had on their heads crowns of gold*, signifying the honor and authority given them by God and the glory they have with him.

2.5. He saw flashes of lightning and voices coming from the throne. This was how God declared the Law on Mount Sinai (Ex 19:16–19), and the Gospel has no less glory and authority than the law.

2.6. He saw *seven lamps of fire burning before the throne* (v. 5), the various gifts, graces, and activities of the Spirit of God.

2.7. He saw *before the throne a sea of glass, like unto crystal.* All who are admitted into the gracious presence of God must be washed in this, which represents the blood of the Lord Jesus Christ.

2.8. He saw *four animals*, living creatures, probably between the throne and the circle of the elders, standing between God and the people. These seem to signify the ministers of the Gospel. The elders sit and are ministered to; these creatures stand and minister: they do not rest night or day.

Verses 8–11

We have considered the sights the apostle saw in heaven: now let us consider the songs he heard.

1. He heard the song of the four living creatures, which alludes to the prophet Isaiah's vision of God (Isa 6:1–4).

They adored one God, and only one God, *the Lord God Almighty*. They adored three holies in this one God.

2. He heard the adoration of the *four-and-twenty elders* (vv. 10–11). Notice:

2.1. The object of their worship: *Him that sat on the throne*, the eternal, ever-living God. There is only one God, and he alone is worshiped as God by the church on earth and in heaven.

2.2. The acts of adoration. They *fell down before him that sat on the throne* and *cast their crowns before the throne*; they gave God the glory of the holiness with which he had crowned their souls on earth and the honor and happiness with which he crowned them in heaven. It is their glory to be glorifying God.

2.3. The words of adoration (v. 11). In this they tacitly acknowledged that God is exalted far above all blessing and praise (Ne 9:5). He was worthy to receive glory, but they were not worthy to praise.

2.4. The basis of their adoration.

2.4.1. He is the Creator of all things. No one except the Creator of all things should be adored; something that has been made cannot be the object of religious worship.

2.4.2. He is the preserver of all things. All beings except God are dependent on the will and power of God, and no dependent being must be set up as an object of religious worship.

2.4.3. He is the final cause of all things: *For thy pleasure they are and were created*. It was his will and pleasure to create all things.

CHAPTER 5

Now the purposes and decrees of God were set before the apostle as in a book, and this book was represented: 1. As sealed in the hand of God (vv. 1–9). 2. As taken into the hand of Christ the Redeemer to be unsealed and opened (vv. 6–14).

Verses 1–5

Up to this time the apostle had seen only the great God, the Ruler of all things. Now:

1. He was favored with a sight of the ways of his rule, represented as all written down in a book that God held in his hand; we are now to consider this as closed and sealed. But there is a transcript of as much as was necessary to be known, and this is found in the book of Scripture in general, especially in the prophetic part of Scripture. God held this book in his right hand, to declare the authority of the book. It is known to no one except himself until he allows it to be opened. It is *sealed with seven seals*. Each part seems to have its own particular seal. These seven parts are not unsealed and opened all at once, but successively, one scene of Providence introducing another and explaining it.

2. He heard a declaration about this sealed book. The crier was *a strong angel*, who seems to have come out also as a champion, with a challenge to any or all the creatures to test the power of their wisdom in opening the purposes of God. The challenge was, *Who is worthy?* (v. 2). No one in heaven or on earth could accept the challenge and undertake the task. Nor any *under the earth*, none of the fallen angels. Satan himself, with all his subtlety, could not do it; the creatures can neither open it nor look on it; they cannot read it. Only God can.

3. The apostle *wept much*; it was a grave disappointment to him. From what he had seen in him who sat on the throne, he wanted very much to see and know more

of his mind and will. Those who have seen his glory wish to know his will.

4. The apostle was comforted and encouraged to hope this sealed book would still be opened. Notice who gave John the hint: *one of the elders*. God had revealed it to his church. Notice who would do it—the Lord Jesus Christ, called *the lion of the tribe of Judah* (Ge 49:10), according to his human nature, and *the root of David* according to his divine nature. The One who bears the office of Mediator between God and humanity is fit and worthy to open and fulfill all the purposes of God toward people.

Verses 6–14

Here:

1. The apostle saw this book taken into the hands of the Lord Jesus Christ. Christ is described:

1.1. By his position. He was on the same throne with the Father. Christ, as a human being and as our mediator, is subordinate to God the Father, but is closer to him than all the creatures.

1.2. By the form in which he appeared. Earlier he was called *a lion*; here he appeared *as a lamb slain*. He is a lion to conquer Satan, a lamb to satisfy the justice of God. He appeared as *a lamb, having seven horns and seven eyes*, perfect power to fulfill all the will of God and perfect wisdom to understand it all, *for he hath the seven Spirits of God*, he has received the Holy Spirit without limit (Jn 3:34).

1.3. By his act (v. 7). He did not do this by violence, nor by deception; rather, he *prevailed* to do it (v. 5); he triumphed by his merit and worthiness.

2. No sooner had Christ received this book from the Father's hand than he received the praise and adoration of angels and people—in fact, of *every creature*.

2.1. The church began the doxology, being most directly concerned in it (v. 8). Notice:

2.1.1. The object of their *worship: the Lamb*, the Lord Jesus Christ.

2.1.2. Their posture: they *fell down before him*, giving him the deepest adoration.

2.1.3. The instruments used in their adoration: *harps and vials* (bowls). The harps were the instruments of praise, and the bowls were full of incense, signifying *the prayers of the saints*.

2.1.4. The subject of their song: *Thou art worthy to take the book, and to open the seals thereof*. In stating the basis of this worthiness, though they did not exclude the standing of his person as God, they chiefly insisted on the merit of his sufferings; these struck their souls more with thankfulness and joy: *Thou wast slain*. The fruits of his sufferings were their redemption to God and their high exaltation (v. 10).

2.2. The doxology was continued by the angels (v. 11). They are said to have been *innumerable* and to have been the attendants on the throne of God. Although they did not need a Savior themselves, they still rejoiced in the redemption and salvation of sinners, and they agreed with the church that the Lord Jesus is *worthy to receive power, and riches, and wisdom, and strength, and honour, and glory, and blessing* (v.12).

2.3. This doxology was resounded by the whole creation (v. 13). Heaven and earth ring with the high praises of the Redeemer. The whole creation fares the better for Christ, and here it is personified as singing a song of *blessing, and honour, and glory, and power*. It is sung *to him that sits on the throne*, that is, God the Father, and *to the Lamb*, the Mediator of the new covenant. We worship and glorify one and the same God for our creation and for our redemption. Here, then, we have seen this sealed book passing with great solemnity from the hand of the Creator into the hand of the Redeemer.

CHAPTER 6

Now we are to launch out into the deep, and our task is not so much to fathom the depths as to let down our net for a catch (Lk 5:4). We will only hint at what seems most obvious. In this chapter, six of the seven seals are opened and the visions accompanying them are related: the first seal (vv. 1–2), the second seal (vv. 3–4), the third seal (vv. 5–6), the fourth seal (vv. 7–8), the fifth seal (vv. 9–11), the sixth seal (vv. 12–17).

Verses 1–2

Here:

1. Christ, the Lamb, opened the first seal.

2. One of the ministers called on the apostle to notice what then appeared.

3. We have the vision itself (v. 2).

3.1. The Lord Jesus appeared riding on *a white horse.*

3.2. *He had a bow* in his hand. The convictions impressed by the word of God are sharp arrows, and they reach far.

3.3. *A crown was given him.* When Christ was going to war, one would have thought a helmet would be more appropriate than a crown, but a crown was given him as the pledge of victory.

3.4. *He went forth conquering, and to conquer.* As long as the church continues to be militant, Christ will be conquering. He conquers his enemies in his people; their sins are their enemies and his enemies. When Christ comes with power into their soul, he begins to conquer these enemies, and he continues to conquer in the progressive work of sanctification until he has gained us a complete victory. He also conquers his enemies in the world, evildoers. The successful progress of the Gospel of Christ in the world is a glorious sight, worth looking at. Christ's work is not all done at once. We are ready to think that when the Gospel is declared it should defeat all in its path, but it often meets with opposition and makes slow progress. Christ will do his own work effectively, in his own time and way.

Verses 3–8

The next three seals give us a sad prospect of judgments with which God punishes those who abuse the eternal Gospel.

1. Upon the opening of the second seal *another horse* appeared, *a red horse* (v. 4). This represents the devastating judgment of war. The sword of war is a fearful judgment; it takes away peace from the earth. In a state of war, human beings, who should love one another and help one another, are bent on killing one another.

2. Upon the opening of the third seal, another horse appeared, *a black horse,* signifying famine (v. 5). One judgment seldom comes alone; the judgment of war naturally brings after it the judgment of famine. The famine of bread is a terrible judgment, but the famine of the word is even worse (Am 8:11).

3. Upon the opening of the fourth seal there appeared another horse, of a pale color. Notice:

3.1. The name of the *rider: Death,* the king of terrors (Job 18:14).

3.2. The attendants of this king of *terrors: hell.* There is a natural connection between one judgment and another: war is a devastating calamity and brings scarcity and famine with it; famine draws the plague after it. God has declared threats against evildoers as well as promises to the righteous, and it is our duty to believe the threats as well as the promises.

4. After the opening of these seals, we have the general observation in v. 8. To the three great judgments of war, famine, and the plague is here added *the beasts of the earth,* another of God's harsh judgments. When a nation is depopulated by the sword, famine, and the plague, the small remnant who continue become an easy prey. Others understand *the beasts of the field* to mean cruel, savage evildoers.

Verses 9–17

In the remaining part of this chapter we have the opening of the fifth and the sixth seals.

1. Here we have the fifth seal opened. No mention is made of anyone who called the apostle to take notice, perhaps because the part of the scroll that was revealed here did not contain a new prophecy, but rather opened a spring of consolation to those who still were under great tribulation. Notice:

1.1. The sight this apostle saw at the opening of the fifth seal (v. 9). He saw the souls of the martyrs in the Most Holy Place—in heaven, at the foot of Christ. God has provided a good place in the better world for those who are faithful to death and are not allowed a place any longer on earth. The cause for which they suffered was *the word of God and the testimony which they held,* a noble cause, the best that anyone can lay down their life for.

1.2. The call can be heard (v. 10). Even *the spirits of just men made perfect* (Heb 12:23) retain a proper indignation at the wrong they have sustained from their cruel enemies. They commit their cause to the One to whom vengeance belongs (Dt 32:35; Heb 10:30); they do not seek to take vengeance themselves, but leave everything to God.

1.3. The kind response that was made to this call (v. 11). What was given to *them* was *white robes,* the robes of victory and of honor. What was said to them was that they must be satisfied and at ease, because it would not be long before the number of their fellow sufferers *would be fulfilled.* God will repay tribulation on those who trouble his people, and he will reward those who are troubled with full and uninterrupted *rest.*

2. We have here the sixth seal opened (v. 12). Notice:

2.1. The terrible events that were coming quickly, and here are several incidents that contribute to making that day and time dreadful (v. 13). It would be a judgment that would dismay the whole world.

2.2. The dread and terror that would seize all kinds of people on that great and fearful day (v. 15). This terror would be so widespread as to make them call *to the mountains to fall upon them, and to the hills to cover them,* and its cause would be *the wrath of the Lamb.* Though God is invisible, he can make the inhabitants of this world aware of his terrible displeasure. Though Christ is a lamb, he can still be angry, and *the wrath of the Lamb* is extremely terrible. Just as people have their day of opportunity and their seasons of grace, so God has his day of righteous wrath.

CHAPTER 7

This encouraging chapter secures the graces and comforts of the people of God in times of general disaster. We have here: 1. An account of the restraint laid on the winds (vv. 1–3). 2. The sealing of the servants of God (vv. 4–8). 3. The songs of angels and saints on this occasion (vv. 9–12). 4. A description of the honor and happiness of those who had faithfully served Christ and suffered for him (vv. 13–17).

Verses 1–12

We have here:

1. An account of the restraint put on the winds. I think these winds refer to errors that would cause a great deal of trouble to the church of God. The spirits of error are compared to *the four winds*, contrary to one another but doing much harm to the garden and vineyard of God (Isa 5:1–7; Mt 21:33–44). Errors are like wind, by which those who are unstable are shaken (Eph 4:14). These winds are restrained by the ministry of angels *standing on the four corners of the earth*; the spirit of error cannot go out until God permits it. Angels minister to the good of the church by restraining its enemies. Their restraint was only for a season, *till the servants of God were sealed in their foreheads.*

2. An account of the sealing of the servants of God. Notice:

2.1. To whom this work was committed: an angel. An angel was employed to mark out and distinguish the faithful servants of God.

2.2. How they were set apart: the seal of God was set on their foreheads. By this mark they were set apart for mercy and safety in the worst times.

2.3. The number of those who were sealed. We have a particular account of those who were sealed from the twelve tribes of Israel: 12,000 from every tribe. We have a general account of those who were saved out of other nations (v. 9). Although the church of God is only a little flock (Lk 12:32) in comparison to the wicked world, it is no contemptible community; rather, it is large and is to be enlarged still more.

3. An account of the songs of saints and angels (vv. 9–12). Here are:

3.1. The praises offered by the saints. Notice:

3.1.1. The posture of these praising saints: they *stood before the throne, and before the Lamb*, before the Creator and the Mediator. The throne of God would be inaccessible to sinners if it were not for a Mediator.

3.1.2. Their clothes: they were *clothed with white robes, and had palms in their hands*, as conquerors used to appear in their triumphs.

3.1.3. Their work: they *cried with a loud voice, saying, Salvation to our God who sitteth upon the throne, and to the Lamb*. This may be understood either as a hosanna or as a hallelujah. The Father and the Son are joined together in these praises; the Father planned this salvation, the Son purchased it, and those who enjoy it must and will bless the Lord and the Lamb.

3.2. The song of the angels (vv. 11–12): *They fell before the throne on their faces, and worshiped God.* What humility, then, and what profound reverence should we as weak and corrupt creatures have when we come into the presence of God! The angels agreed with the praises of the saints, saying their *Amen* to them and then adding more of their own. Here we see what the work of heaven is, and we should get our hearts tuned for it and should long for that world where our praises, as well as our happiness, will be perfected.

Verses 13–17

Here is a description of the happiness of those who have faithfully served the Lord Jesus Christ. Notice:

1. A question asked by one of the elders, not for his own information, but for John's instruction. The lowest saint in heaven knows more than the greatest apostle in the world.

2. The answer given by the apostle, in which he tacitly acknowledged his own ignorance: *Thou knowest*.

3. The account the apostle was given of the noble army of martyrs. We see:

3.1. The low and desolate state they had formerly been in. They had been in the great tribulation. The way to heaven lies through many tribulations (Ac 14:22), but tribulation will not *separate us from the love of God* (Ro 8:39).

3.2. The means by which they had been prepared for the great happiness they now enjoyed (v. 14). The blood of the Lamb is the only blood that makes the robes of the saints white and clean.

3.3. The blessedness to which they were now advanced.

3.3.1. They were happy in their position, for *they were before the throne of God night and day*, and he *dwelt among them.*

3.3.2. They were happy in their work, because they served God continually.

3.3.3. They were happy in their freedom from all the inconveniences of this present life. They were free from all need and sense of need: *They hungered and thirsted no more*; all their needs were supplied. They were free from all sickness and pain: they would never be scorched *by the heat of the sun any more.*

3.3.4. They were happy in the love and guidance of the Lord Jesus: *He shall feed them; he shall lead them to living fountains of waters.*

3.3.5. They were happy in being saved from all sorrow. *God shall wipe away all tears from their eyes.* God himself, with his own gentle and gracious hand, would wipe those tears away, and they would not have wanted to be without those tears, since it was God who came to wipe them away. Here he dealt with them as a tender father who finds his dear child in tears: he comforted them. He wiped their eyes and turned their sorrow into joy.

CHAPTER 8

In this chapter we have: 1 The introduction to the sounding of the trumpets (vv. 1–6). 2. The sounding of four of the trumpets (vv. 7–13).

Verses 1–6

In these verses we have, in several parts, the introduction to the sounding of the trumpets.

1. The opening of the last seal. This was to introduce a new set of events.

2. A profound *silence in heaven for the space of half an hour.* It was a silence of expectation; great things were in motion on the wheels of providence, and the church of God, both in heaven and on earth, stood silent to see what God was doing.

3. The trumpets being passed to the angels who were to sound them.

4. Another angel offering incense before the trumpet was blown (v. 3). He was to offer this incense, *with the prayers of all the saints, upon the golden altar*. Notice:

4.1. All the saints are a praying people; none of the children of God are born mute.

4.2. Times of danger should be times of prayer, as should times of great expectation; both our fears and our hopes should lead us to pray.

4.3. The prayers of the saints themselves stand in need of the incense and intercession of Christ to make them acceptable and effective, nor has any prayer commended in this way ever been denied a hearing or acceptance. Note that these prayers that were accepted in this way in heaven led to great changes on earth. The same angel *took of the fire of* (from) *the altar* in the same censer *and cast it into the earth*, and this immediately caused a strange commotion, *voices, and thunderings, and lightnings, and an earthquake*. Now, all things being prepared in this way, the angels fulfilled their duty.

Verses 7–13

Notice:

1. *The first angel sounded* the first trumpet (v. 7). It was a terrible storm—fire, and hail, and blood: a strange mixture! Yet it was limited: it fell on *the third part of the trees* and a third *of the grass* and withered and burned it up. The most severe adversities have their bounds and limits set on them by the great God.

2. *The second angel sounded* (v. 8). Again the destruction was limited to one third, for *in the midst of judgment* God remembers mercy (Hab 3:2).

3. *The third angel sounded* (v. 10), and a star from heaven fell *upon a third part of the rivers, and upon the fountains of waters*. It turned those springs and streams into *wormwood*, making them very bitter so that people were poisoned by them. The people found ruin where they sought refreshment.

4. *The fourth angel sounded*. Notice the nature of this calamity. It was darkness; it therefore fell on the great lights of the sky that illuminate the world: *the sun, and the moon, and the stars*. But notice the limit: it was confined to a third of these lights; there was some light of both the sun by day, and of the moon and stars by night. Where the Gospel comes to a people and is only coldly received, it is usually followed by dreadful judgments. God warns people of his judgments before he sends them, so that if a people are surprised, it is their own fault. Yet God does not in this world stir up all his wrath, but sets limits to the most terrible judgments.

5. Before the other three trumpets were sounded, a solemn warning was given about how terrible the disasters that would follow them would be (v. 13). The messenger was *an angel flying in the midst of heaven*, as in haste. Here are three woes, to show how much the coming disasters would exceed those that had come already. If lesser judgments do not take effect, and the church and the world become worse under them, they must expect greater ones.

CHAPTER 9

Here we have an account of the sounding of the fifth (vv. 1–12) and sixth (vv. 13–21) trumpets, the appearances that accompanied them, and the events that were to follow.

Verses 1–12

1. *A star fell from heaven to the earth*. Some think this star represents some eminent overseer or elder in the Christian church, some *angel of the church* (1:20), but expositors do not agree on whom this refers to precisely.

2. To this fallen star *was given the key of the bottomless pit*. Having ceased to be a minister of Christ, he became the Antichrist, the Devil's jailer, to let loose the powers of hell against the churches of Christ.

3. On the opening of the bottomless pit, *there arose a great smoke*, which darkened the sun and the air. The Devil pursues his intentions by extinguishing light and knowledge. Wretched souls follow him in the dark, or they dare not follow him.

4. Out of this dark smoke came a swarm of locusts. These, by the just permission of God, had power to harm those who did not have the mark of God on their foreheads.

5. The harm they were to do was not physical, but spiritual. They must not in a military way destroy everything by fire and sword; the trees and the grass must be untouched, and those the locusts harmed must not be killed.

6. They had no power even to hurt those who had the seal of God on their foreheads.

7. The power given to these agents of hell was limited in time: *five months*, a definite season, and only a short season.

8. Although it would be short, it would be very sharp (v. 6).

9. These locusts were monstrous in size and shape (vv. 7–8). They were equipped for their work like horses prepared for battle. *They had crowns like gold on their heads*; it was not, however, a true authority, but a counterfeit one. They had the appearance of wisdom, *the faces of men*, but they had the spirit of demons. They had all the allurement of apparent *beauty—hair like women*. Although they looked as if they had the tenderness of women, in reality they were cruel creatures. They had the defense and protection of earthly powers: *breastplates of iron*. They made a great noise in the world, and the noise of their movement was like that of an army with chariots and horses. Although at first they soothed and flattered people with a fair appearance, there was a sting in their tails. The king and commander of this hellish squadron is described here as an angel, *the angel of the bottomless pit*; he was still an angel, but a fallen one, fallen into the bottomless pit. His true name is *Abaddon, Apollyon*, "a destroyer," as that is his work, to which he gives his diligent attention.

Verses 13–21

Here let us consider the introduction to this vision, and then the vision itself.

1. The introduction to this vision (vv. 13–14). When nations are ready for punishment, those instruments of God's anger that were restrained before are let loose on them (v. 14).

2. The vision itself (vv. 15–16). Notice:

2.1. The time of their military operations was limited to *an hour, and a day, and a month, and a year*. Prophetic characterizations of time are difficult for us to understand, but we know that God has fixed a certain hour when this work will begin and a certain hour when it will end. Notice how far the execution will be effective: to a third of the inhabitants of the earth.

2.2. The army that was to execute this great commission was mustered, and the number was found to be *two hundred thousand thousand* horsemen, but we are left to guess what the infantry must be. In general, the text tells us that the armies would be immensely great.

2.3. Their equipment and appearance were formidable (v. 17). Just as the horses were fierce like lions, so those who sat on them were clothed in bright and fine armor.

2.4. They made colossal havoc and desolation.

2.5. Their artillery, with which they made such slaughter, is described by *fire, smoke, and brimstone* coming out of the mouths of their horses and the stings in their tails.

2.6. The Antichristian generation was generally impenitent under these fearful judgments (v. 20). They still persisted in those sins for which God was punishing them so severely. Although God had revealed his wrath from heaven against them (Ro 1:18), they remained obstinate and impenitent.

3. From this sixth trumpet we learn that impenitence under divine judgments is a sin that will be the ruin of sinners, because where God judges, he will overcome (Ro 3:4; Ps 51:4).

CHAPTER 10

This chapter is an introduction to the latter part of the prophecies of this book. Here is: 1. A remarkable description of a glorious angel with an open book in his hand (vv. 1–3). 2. An account of seven thunders that the apostle heard echoing the voice of this angel (v. 4). 3. The solemn oath taken by the one who had the book in his hand (vv. 5–7). 4. The command given to the apostle and observed by him (vv. 8–11).

Verses 1–7

Here is another vision the apostle was favored with. Notice:

1. The person communicating this revelation to John: an angel from heaven, *another mighty angel.*

2. The angel's position: *He set his right foot upon the sea and his left foot upon the earth, and he held in his hand a little book opened,* probably the same one that earlier was sealed; now it was opened and was gradually fulfilled by him.

3. His awesome voice (v. 3), which was echoed by *seven thunders,* seven solemn and terrible ways of revealing the mind of God.

4. The prohibition given to the apostle (v. 4). The apostle wanted to preserve and declare everything he saw and heard in these visions, but the time had not yet come.

5. The solemn oath taken by this mighty angel. *He lifted up his hand to heaven, and swore by him that liveth for ever* that *there shall be time no longer,* that is, either:

5.1. That there would now no longer be any delay in fulfilling the predictions of this book than until the last angel sounded his trumpet (v. 7). Or:

5.2. That when this mystery of God is accomplished, time itself will be no more.

Verses 8–11

Here we have:

1. A command given to the apostle that he must *go and take the little book* out of the hands of the mighty angel and eat it. Before he could declare what he had discovered, he must more thoroughly digest the predictions.

2. An account of the taste this little book would have. At first, while *in his mouth,* it would be *sweet,* but when it was more thoroughly digested, the contents would be bitter; these were things so terrible that the foresight of them would not be pleasant.

3. The apostle's carrying out the duty he was called to (v. 10): he found it as enjoyable as he had been told.

4. The apostle's learning that this book of prophecy was not given him simply to satisfy his own curiosity, but to be communicated by him to the world. He was ordered to prepare for another mission, to convey those declarations of the mind and will of God to the whole world to be read and recorded in many languages.

CHAPTER 11

In this chapter we have an account: 1. Of the measuring rod given to the apostle to take the dimensions of the temple (vv. 1–2). 2. Of the two witnesses of God (vv. 3–13).

3. Of the sounding of the seventh trumpet and what followed (vv. 14–19).

Verses 1–2

This prophetic passage about measuring the temple is a clear reference to what we find in Ezekiel's vision in Eze 40:3–47. The purpose of this measurement seems to be the preservation of the temple in those times of public danger and disaster that are foretold here. Notice:

1. How much was to be measured.

1.1. *The temple,* the Gospel church in general.

1.2. *The altar.* It must be determined whether the church had the true altars.

1.3. The worshipers, too, must be measured, to determine whether they made God's glory their goal and his word their rule.

2. What was not to be measured (v. 2): *The court which is without the temple, measure it not.* Herod, in making additions to the temple, built an outer court and called it the Court of the Gentiles. That was not part of the temple, and so God did not give it his attention. Both that and the city were trampled on for *forty and two months.* Those who worship in the outer court are those who worship either falsely or with hypocritical hearts. Those who worship in the outer court will be rejected, and only those who worship in God's inner sanctuary will be accepted.

Verses 3–13

God has reserved for himself his faithful witnesses. Notice:

1. The number of these witnesses.

1.1. It is only small. One person who is willing to be a witness when the cause is being tested is worth many who are willing at other times.

1.2. It is a sufficient number, because by the testimony of two witnesses every cause will be established (Dt 17:6; 19:15; Mt 18:16). Christ sent out his disciples two by two to preach the Gospel (Lk 10:1).

2. The time of their prophesying: *a thousand two hundred and threescore days,* that is, as many think, the period of the reign of the Antichrist.

3. Their garments: they prophesy in sackcloth, as those who have been deeply moved by the low and distressed state of the churches.

4. How they are supported: they stand before the God of the whole earth. He makes them be like Zerubbabel and Joshua, the two olive trees and lampstand in the vision of Zechariah (Zec 4:2–14).

5. Their security and defense during the time of their prophesying (v. 5). Some think this alludes to Elijah's calling for fire from heaven to consume the captains and their associates who came to seize him (2Ki 1:12). God will restrain the dew of heaven, shutting heaven so that no rain will fall for many days, as he did in response to the prayers of Elijah (1Ki 17:1).

6. The killing of the witnesses. To make their testimony stronger, they must seal it with their blood. Notice:

6.1. The time when they will be killed: *when they have finished their testimony* (v. 7). They are immortal until their work is complete.

6.2. The enemy that will overcome and kill them: the *beast that ascendeth out of the bottomless pit.* The Antichrist will wage war on them with open force and violence, and God will allow his enemies to succeed against his witnesses for a time.

6.3. The cruel treatment of these slain witnesses. The hatred of their enemies will pursue even their dead bodies. They will not allow them a quiet grave; their bodies will be hurled out onto the open streets. Their death will be a matter of joy and celebration to the Antichristian world (v. 10).

7. The resurrection of these witnesses. They will rise after they have been dead *three days and a half* (v. 11). God's witnesses may be put to death, but they will rise again. God will revive his work when it seems to be dead in the world. *The spirit of life from God entered into them, and they stood upon their feet.* God put not only life but also courage into them. The effect of their resurrection on their enemies will be that *great fear will fall upon them.* A persecuting spirit, though cruel, is not a courageous, but a cowardly, spirit.

8. The ascension of the witnesses into heaven (vv. 12–13).

8.1. Their ascension. To this honor they did not attempt to ascend until God called them, saying, *Come up hither.* The Lord's witnesses must wait for their advancement until God calls them.

8.2. The consequences of their ascension: a mighty shock and tremor and the fall of *a tenth part of the city. The fear of God fell upon many. They gave glory to the God of heaven.* This is how, when God's work and witnesses are revived, the Devil's work and witnesses fall before him.

Verses 14–19

What he expected before he now heard: the seventh angel sounding.

1. Here were loud and joyful acclamations of the saints and angels in heaven. They rose from their seats *and fell upon their faces, and worshiped God.* They recognized with thankfulness the right of our God and Savior to rule and reign over the whole world (v. 15). They gave him thanks because he had taken to himself his great power. They rejoiced that this his reign would never end. No one will ever force the scepter out of his hand.

2. Here was angry resentment in the world at these actions of the power of God (v. 18): *The nations were angry*; their hearts rose up against God. They were angry with God and thereby increased their guilt and speeded their destruction.

3. Another consequence was the opening of the temple of God in heaven. Notice what was seen there: the *ark of God's testament.* This was in the Most Holy Place; the tablets of the Law were kept in this ark. Just as before Josiah's time the Law of God had been lost but was then found (2Ki 22), so in the reign of the Antichrist God's law was set aside. But now the Scriptures are opened up, brought to the view of all. Notice also what was heard and felt there: *lightnings, voices, thunderings, an earthquake, and great hail. By terrible things in righteousness* (Ps 65:5) God would answer those prayers that were presented in his holy temple, which had now opened up.

CHAPTER 12

In this chapter we have an account of the contest between the church and the Antichrist, the offspring of the woman and the offspring of the Serpent: 1. As it began in heaven (vv. 1–11). 2. As it was pursued in the desert (vv. 12–17).

Verses 1–11

Here we see eminently fulfilled that early prophecy in which God said he would *put enmity between the seed* (offspring) *of the woman and the seed of the serpent* (Ge 3:15). We may notice:

1. The attempts of Satan to prevent the increase of the church.

1.1. The church is represented:

1.1.1. As a *woman*, the bride of Christ and the mother of the saints.

1.1.2. As *clothed with the sun.* Having put on Christ (Ro 13:14), who is *the Sun of righteousness* (Mal 4:2), she shone in his rays.

1.1.3. As having *the moon under her feet.* Her heart and hope were not set on sublunary things—literally, "things under the moon"—but on the things that are in heaven (Col 3:2), where her head was.

1.1.4. As having on her head *a crown of twelve stars*, that is, the doctrine of the Gospel preached by the twelve apostles.

1.1.5. As in labor, in pain to give birth to a holy descendant of Christ (Isa 53:10).

1.2. The great enemy of the church is represented:

1.2.1. As a dragon, having the strength and terror, the fierceness and cruelty, of a dragon.

1.2.2. As *having seven heads.* It is probable, therefore, that pagan Rome is meant here.

1.2.3. As having *ten horns*, being divided into ten provinces, as the Roman Empire was by the emperor Augustus Caesar (reigned 27 BC–AD 14).

1.2.4. As having *seven crowns upon his head*, which are later explained as seven kings (17:10).

1.2.5. As drawing with his tail a *third part of the stars in heaven* and *casting them down to the earth.*

1.2.6. As standing *before the woman, to devour her child as soon as it should be born*, watching to crush the Christian faith at birth.

2. The failure of these attempts. She safely gave birth to a *man child* (male child) (v. 5), and care was taken of this child. The Christian faith has been from its infancy the special care of *the great God and our Saviour Jesus Christ* (Tit 2:13). Care was taken of the mother as well as of the child (v. 6). Yet her obscure and private state lasted only a limited time.

3. The attempts of the dragon turning out to be not only unsuccessful against the church but also fatal to his own interests (v. 7). Heaven will embrace the quarrel of the church.

3.1. The place of this war: in *heaven*, in the church, which is *the kingdom of heaven* on earth, being under the care of heaven.

3.2. The parties: on the one side, Christ, the great Angel of the covenant, and his faithful followers, and on the other, Satan and all his instruments. The strength of the church lies in having the Lord Jesus Christ as the *captain of their salvation* (Heb 2:10).

3.3. The outcome of the battle: *The dragon and his angels fought and prevailed not.* The victory fell to Christ and his church, and the dragon and his angels were not only conquered but hurled down.

3.4. The triumphant song that was composed and used on this occasion (vv. 10–11). The conqueror was adored. The salvation and strength of the church are all to be attributed to the king and head of the church. The conquered enemy is described by his hatred and his disappointment. His hatred was shown in his appearing before God as an adversary to the church. Although he hates the presence of God, he is willing to appear there to accuse the people of God. His disappointment was shown in the victory gained over him. The servants of God overcame Satan:

3.4.1. *By the blood of the Lamb.*

3.4.2. *By the word of their testimony*, by a resolute, powerful preaching of the eternal Gospel and by their courage and patience in suffering for that preaching. *They loved not their lives unto the death*: their love for their own lives was overcome by stronger feelings of another nature.

Verses 12–17

Now that this war had been so happily finished in heaven, or in the church, it was renewed and pursued in the desert, where the church had fled and been for some time protected by the special care of her God and Savior. Notice:

1. The warning given of the distress that would fall on the inhabitants of the world in general. Defeated in his purposes against the church, the Devil is determined to disturb the world in general as much as possible (v. 12).

2. His second attempt on the church, now in the desert (v. 13). Notice:

2.1. The care that God had taken of his church. He had conveyed her as on eagles' wings (Isa 40:31) into a place of safety provided for her.

2.2. The continual hatred of the dragon against the church. Her obscurity could not protect her completely.

2.3. The timely help provided at this dangerous point (v. 16).

2.4. The dragon's malice against the woman pushed him on to *make war with the remnant of her seed.* Faithfulness will continue to expose people to the rage of Satan until the end of the world, when *the last enemy shall be destroyed.*

CHAPTER 13

Here we have a further description of the church's enemies in another way. They are represented as two beasts. We have an account of the first in vv. 1–10 and of the second in vv. 11–18.

Verses 1–10

We have here an account of the first beast. Notice:

1. From what position the apostle saw him. It seemed to the apostle that he was standing on *the sea shore.*

2. From where this beast came: *out of the sea.*

3. The form and shape of this beast. In some part of this description there seems to be an allusion to Daniel's vision of the four beasts, which represented the four monarchies (Da 7:1–3). The seven heads and the ten horns seem to suggest its different powers; the ten crowns, its subject rulers; the word *blasphemy* on its forehead proclaims its direct hostility to the glory of God.

4. The source and spring of its authority: *the dragon.* This beast was set up by the Devil, and the Devil gave him all possible help.

5. A dangerous wound given him, but unexpectedly healed (v. 3). Some think that this wound represents the abolition of pagan idolatry and that the healing of the wound represents the introduction of Roman Catholic idolatry.

6. The honor and worship paid to this diabolical monster: *All the world wondered after the beast.* They gave honor and submission to the Devil and his agents and thought no power was able to withstand them.

7. How he exercised his diabolical power and knowledge: he had a *mouth, speaking great things, and blasphemies* (v. 5); *and he made war with the saints, and overcame them* (v. 7). The beast's hatred was directed *against those that dwell in heaven.* The hatred of the Devil shows itself against heaven and the blessed inhabitants of heaven, but these are above the reach of his power; all he can do is to slander and blaspheme them. The saints on earth are more exposed to his cruelty, and he sometimes is permitted to triumph over them.

8. The limitation of the Devil's power and success. He is limited in time (v. 5). He is also limited as to the people that he will entirely subject to his will; it will be only those *whose names are not written in the Lamb's book of life.*

9. A call for attention to what is revealed here and an assurance that God will ultimately turn his hand against the enemies of his people. Those who have killed with the sword will themselves fall by the sword (v. 10), and those who led the people of God into captivity will themselves be taken captive.

Verses 11–18

Notice here:

1. The form and shape of this second beast: *He had two horns like a lamb,* but a mouth that *spoke like the dragon.* All agree that this must be some great impostor who, under the pretense of religion, will deceive human souls.

2. The power that he exercises (v. 12) to draw people away from worshiping the true God to worship those who by nature are not gods (Gal 4:8).

3. The ways by which this second beast pursued his intentions. He used counterfeit wonders, pretended miracles, by which people would be deceived. The beasts would claim to call down fire from heaven. God sometimes permits his enemies to do things that seem wonderful, by which unwary people may be deluded. Under the papacy, people would have to have *the mark of the beast in their forehead* and *in their right hand,* and to have *the name of the beast* and *the number of his name.* They would make an open profession of their submission and obedience to the papacy.

4. We have here *the number of the beast,* given in such a way as will sufficiently exercise all human wisdom and accuracy: *The number is the number of a man,* and it is 666. To me the time referred to here seems to be one of those times that God has reserved to himself (Ac 1:7). We know only that God has written *Mene Tekel* on all his enemies (Da 5:25–27); he has numbered their days, and they will be finished, but his own kingdom will endure forever.

CHAPTER 14

The day begins to dawn, and here is represented: 1. The Lord Jesus Christ at the head of his faithful followers (vv. 1–5). 2. Three angels sent successively to proclaim the fall of Babylon (vv. 6–12). 3. The vision of the harvest (vv. 13–20).

Verses 1–5

Here is the Lord Jesus Christ at the head of his faithful. Notice:

1. How Christ appeared: as a Lamb standing on *Mount Zion.* In the previous chapter a false lamb was mentioned as rising out of the earth, but it was really a dragon; here Christ appeared as the true paschal Lamb.

2. How his people appeared: very honorably.

2.1. They were many, all who were sealed; not one of them was lost in all the tribulations through which they went.

2.2. They had *the name of God written in their foreheads.*

2.3. Their songs of praise (v. 3) are characterized:

2.3.1. By their purity: *They are virgins.* They had not defiled themselves either with physical or spiritual adultery.

2.3.2. By their loyalty and faithfulness to Christ: *They follow the Lamb withersoever he goes.*

2.3.3. By their earlier designation to this honor: *These were the firstfruits to God and to the Lamb* (v. 4) and were the pledge of many more who would *be followers of them, as they were of Christ* (1Co 11:1).

2.3.4. By their integrity: *There was no guile found in them,* and *they were without fault* (blameless) *before the throne of God.* Their hearts were right with God, and they were freely pardoned in Christ.

Verses 6–12

Here we have three angels or messengers sent from heaven to announce the fall of Babylon.

1. The first angel was sent on an errand before that great event (vv. 6–7). The Gospel is an eternal Gospel, and the preaching of it is therefore a work fit for an angel. The eternal Gospel is of great concern to the whole world, for it is the great means by which people are brought to fear God and give him glory. It is by the preaching of the Gospel that people are *turned from idols to serve the living God* (v. 7).

2. The second angel followed the first and declared the actual fall of Babylon. Babylon is generally understood as referring to Rome. The evil of Babylon will make her fall just (v. 8).

3. A third angel followed the other two (vv. 9–10). If after this anyone persisted in idolatry, they must expect *to drink* deep *of the wine of the wrath of God.* Those who refuse to come out of Babylon must receive her plagues. When the treachery and rebellion of others is punished, it will then be said, to the honor of the faithful (v. 12): *"Here is the patience of the saints;* before, you have seen their patience exercised, and now you see it rewarded."

Verses 13–20

Here we have the vision of the harvest of grain and of grapes. Notice:

1. The introduction (v. 13). This prophecy came from heaven, not from people, and it is therefore certainly true. It was to be preserved and made known by writing; it was to be a matter of record, so that the people of God could turn to it for their encouragement on all occasions. It was principally intended to show the blessedness of all the faithful servants of God, both in death and after death: *Blessed are the dead that die in the Lord from henceforth.* Here we see the description of those who are and who will be blessed: they are those who die in the Lord. They are blessed in their rest, and they are blessed in their reward. *Their works follow them* as evidence of their having lived and died in the Lord.

2. The vision itself. It is:

2.1. A harvest of grain (vv. 14–15), a sign that sometimes represents the cutting down of evildoers, and sometimes the gathering of the righteous. In this case it seems to represent God's judgments against evildoers. Notice:

2.1.1. The Lord of the harvest, who was one so *like unto the Son of man* that that was who he was, the Lord Jesus Christ. The chariot in which he sat was a *white cloud,* a cloud that had a bright side turned to the church, however dark it might be to evildoers (Ex 14:20). The symbol of his power was a *golden crown on his head,* authority to do whatever he wanted to do. The instrument of his providences was *a sharp sickle in his hand.*

2.1.2. The harvest work, to put the sickle into the grain and reap the field.

2.1.3. The harvest time, when the grain was ripe, when the limit of people's sins had been reached (Ge 15:16; Mt 23:32). Then he will no longer spare them; he will put in his sickle, and the earth will be reaped.

2.2. A harvest of grapes (v. 17). This harvesting of the vintage was *committed* to *another angel that came out from the altar.* The work of the vintage consists of two parts:

2.2.1. *Gathering the clusters of the vine, fully ripe* (v. 18).

2.2.2. Throwing grapes *into the winepress* (v. 19). The winepress was *the wrath of God,* which was located *without* (outside) *the city,* where the army that came against Babylon lay. Notice the great quantity of wine, that is, of the blood that was drawn by this judgment (v. 20). Here we are left to make doubtful speculations, but *the vision is for an appointed time* (Hab 2:3), and so we are still to wait for it.

CHAPTER 15

Here we have the vision of the seven bowls: 1. A sight of the angels in heaven who were to execute this great work (vv. 1–4). 2. A sight of these angels coming out of heaven to receive the bowls they were to pour out (vv. 5–8).

Verses 1–4

Here is the pouring out of the seven bowls that were committed to seven angels. The work they had to do was to finish the destruction of the Antichrist. The spectators and witnesses of their commission, all *that had gotten the victory over the beast,* stood on *a sea of glass singing the song of Moses,* extolling the greatness of God's works, calling on all nations to render to God the fear due to such a revelation of his truth and justice: *Who shall not fear thee?* (v. 4).

Verses 5–8

Notice:

1. How these angels appeared (v. 5). Here is an allusion to the Most Holy Place in the tabernacle and temple, where *the mercy seat, covering the ark of the testimony* (Ex 30:6), was. In the judgments God was now about to execute, he was fulfilling the prophecies and promises of his word and covenant, which were always before him (Pr 8:30).

2. How they were equipped. Their garments (v. 6) were like those of the high priests when they went in to inquire of God and came out with an answer from him. Angels do everything in a pure and holy manner. Their artillery was *seven vials* (bowls) *filled with the wrath of God;* they were armed with the wrath of God against his enemies.

3. They were all wrapped up in clouds of smoke that filled the temple because of the glorious and powerful presence of God, so that *no man was able to enter into the temple* until the work was completed (v. 8; Ex 40:34–35). God himself was now preaching to the church and the whole world *by terrible things in righteousness* (Ps 65:5), but when this work was completed, the temple would be opened.

CHAPTER 16

Here we have the pouring out of these bowls that were filled with the wrath of God (v. 1). 1. The first bowl was poured out on the land (v. 2). 2. The second on the sea (v. 3). 3. The third on the rivers and springs of water (v. 4). Here the heavenly hosts applauded the righteousness of the judgments of God (vv. 5–7). 4. The fourth was poured out on the sun (vv. 8–9). 5. The fifth on the throne of the beast (vv. 10–11). 6. The sixth on the Euphrates River (vv. 12–16). 7. The seventh in the air, and then the cities of the nations fell (vv. 17–21).

Verses 1–7

1. Although everything was made ready before, nothing was to be executed without an order from God, and he gave this from the temple.

2. No sooner was the word of command given than it was immediately obeyed. God says, *Go your ways, and pour out the vials* (v. 1), and immediately the work begins. We have here a reference and allusion to several of the plagues of Egypt. The sins of the two peoples were similar, and so were their punishments. These bowls clearly correspond to the seven trumpets that represented the rise of the Antichrist. The fall of the Antichrist will be gradual; just as Rome was not built in one day, so neither will it fall in one day. The fall of the Antichristian influence will be universal. Everything that in any way belonged to it is consigned to ruin; it is all cursed because of the evil of that people.

2.1. The first angel poured out his bowl (v. 2). The bowl fell *upon the earth*, on the ordinary people, and it produced *noisome and grievous* (ugly and painful) *sores on all who had the mark of the beast*. They had marked themselves by their sin; now God marked them out by his judgments.

2.2. *The second angel poured out his vial*, and it turned the sea into blood, *as the blood of a dead man, and every living soul died in the sea*. God revealed not only the worthlessness and falsehood of their religion but also its deadly and harmful nature.

2.3. The next angel poured out his bowl, and it fell *upon the rivers, and upon the fountains of waters*, turning them into *blood*. Some think this stirred up Christian rulers to take just revenge on those who had caused the shedding of the blood of armies and martyrs. The following doxology (vv. 5–6) favors this sense. The instrument God employed in this work is called here *the angel of the waters*, who extolled the righteousness of God in this act of retaliation and was answered in full agreement by another angel (v. 7).

Verses 8–11

The fourth angel poured out his bowl, and that fell on the sun, perhaps some eminent ruler of the Roman Catholic communion. This sun, which previously favored them with warm and kind influences, would now grow hot against these idolaters and sear them, which would be so far from bringing them to repentance that it would cause them to curse God. They would be hardened to their ruin. Then the fifth angel poured out his bowl (v. 10), and this bowl fell *upon the seat* (throne) *of the beast*, on Rome itself. The whole kingdom of the beast *was full of darkness*. Darkness is opposed to wisdom and insight, and so here it points to the coming confusion and foolishness that idolaters would discover at that time. It is also opposed to pleasure and joy.

Verses 12–16

The sixth angel poured out his vial, and it fell *upon the great river Euphrates*. Some take it literally; others think it refers to the Tiber River. And what did this bowl produce? The drying up of the river. And so a way was prepared *for the kings of the east*. This would lead to the last effort of

the great dragon; he was determined to make another push for it. He would employ *three unclean spirits like frogs* to engage the powers of the earth in his cause. These would gather the Devil's forces for a decisive battle and would pursue their aim by performing pretended miracles. The place of battle would be *Armageddon*, that is, according to some, the Mount of Megiddo. The further account of this battle is suspended until we reach 19:19–20. Note the warning God gave of this great and decisive trial (v. 15). When God's cause comes to be tested, and his battles to be fought, all his people will be ready and faithful and courageous in his service.

Verses 17–21

Here is an account of the seventh and last angel pouring out his bowl, which was the finishing stroke. Notice where this plague fell: on *the air*, on the prince of the power of the air (Eph 2:2), that is, the Devil. A bowl was poured out on his kingdom, and he could not support his tottering cause and interests any longer. The plague produced a thankful voice from heaven, declaring that now the work was done. "*It is done* (v. 17). It is finished (Jn 19:30)." It also produced an earthquake greater than any there had ever been, and this was introduced by thunder and lightning. Finally, the plague produced the fall of Babylon (v. 19). God now remembered this great and evil city and gave her *the cup of the wine of the fierceness of his wrath*, and every island and every mountain, which seemed naturally to be most secure because of its situation, was carried away in the deluge of this ruin. Notice how the Antichristian group were affected by it: although it fell on them as a dreadful storm, as if the stones of the city, tossed up into the air, were coming down on their heads, like hailstones weighing *a talent* (a hundred pounds or around 40 kilograms) each, they were so far from repenting that they cursed the God who punished them.

CHAPTER 17

This Antichrist is now described as a great prostitute. 1. The apostle was invited to see this evil woman (vv. 1–2). 2. He tells us what her appearance was (vv. 3–6). 3. Its mystery was explained to him (vv. 7–12). 4. Her ruin is foretold (vv. 13–18).

Verses 1–6

Here we have a new vision. Notice:

1. The invitation given to the apostle to see the *judgment of the great whore* (v. 1). This is an infamous name. She had been a prostitute to the kings of the earth, whom she had intoxicated with the wine of her adulteries (v. 2)

2. Her appearance (v. 4), which was bright and showy.

3. Her principal seat and residence: on *the beast that had seven heads and ten horns*, that is, Rome, the city on seven hills.

4. Her name, which *was written on her forehead*. She was named from her place of residence and from her infamous way and practices, as not only a prostitute but a mother of prostitutes.

5. Her diet: she satiated herself with *the blood of the saints and martyrs of Jesus*. She drank their blood with such greediness that she intoxicated herself with it.

Verses 7–13

Here the mystery of this vision is explained. However, it is explained in such a way as still requires further explanation.

1. This beast *was, and is not, and yet is.* That is, it *was* a seat of idolatry and persecution, *and is not,* not idolatry in the ancient form, *and yet it is* truly the seat of idolatry and tyranny. *It ascends out of the bottomless pit,* and it will return there and go into destruction.

2. *This beast had seven heads,* which have a double meaning. They are *seven mountains,* the seven hills on which Rome stands. They are also *seven kings,* seven kinds of government. Five of these were extinct: kings, consuls, tribunes, judges, and dictators; one was then in existence: the pagan emperor; and the other was still to come: the Christian emperor (v. 10). This beast, the papacy, was the eighth.

3. This beast had ten horns, which are said to be *ten kings which have as yet received no kingdoms.*

Verses 14–18

1. War was begun between the beast and his followers on one side and the Lamb and his followers on the other. One would have thought an army with a lamb at their head could not stand before *the great red dragon.* Yet:

2. Victory was gained by the Lamb: *The Lamb shall overcome.* He will be sure to face many enemies, but he will also be sure to gain the victory.

3. The basis or reason for the victory is taken:

3.1. From the character of the Lamb: *He is King of kings and Lord of lords.* All the powers of earth and hell are subject to his restraint and control.

3.2. From the description of his followers: *They are called, and chosen, and faithful.* Such an army, under such a commander, will ultimately carry the whole world before them.

4. The victory is justly emphasized:

4.1. By the vast multitude who paid obedience and submission to the beast and to the prostitute (vv. 15, 18).

4.2. By the powerful influence that God thus showed he had over the minds of great people. These kings' *agreeing to give their kingdom unto the beast* came from God, and to fulfill his will. It also came from God that later their hearts were turned against the prostitute.

CHAPTER 18

We have here: 1. An angel proclaiming the fall of Babylon (vv. 1–2). 2. An angel specifying the reasons for her fall (v. 3). 3. An angel warning all who belonged to God to come out of her (vv. 4–5) and assist in her destruction (vv. 6–8). 4. Great mourning for her by those who had largely shared in her sinful pleasures and profits (vv. 9–19). 5. Great joy among others at the sight of her irrevocable ruin (vv. 20–24).

Verses 1–8

1. Here another angel was sent from heaven. The light he had was given him not only for himself, to enable him to discern the truth of his own prediction, but also for the world, to inform and enlighten it about the destruction of Babylon.

2. This angel declared the fall of Babylon as something that had already taken place. This seems to be an allusion to the prediction of the fall of pagan Babylon in Isa 21:9, where the word is repeated as it is here: *has fallen, has fallen.* The following words—*has become the habitation of devils* (a home for demons), *and the hold* (haunt) *of every foul spirit, and the cage of every unclean and hateful bird*—are also borrowed from Isa 21:9, and seem to describe not so much her sin as her punishment, it being a common idea that unclean spirits,

as well as ominous and hateful birds, haunted a ruined city or house.

3. The reason for this ruin was declared (v. 3). She had not only abandoned the true God and set up idols herself; she had also drawn all kinds of people into spiritual adultery and had kept them pursuing her interests by her wealth and her indulgence of them.

4. Fair warning was given to all who expected mercy from God, that they should not only *come out of her* but also help in her destruction (vv. 4–5). Notice:

4.1. God may have a people even in Babylon, but those who are determined to share with evildoers in their sins must receive their plagues.

4.2. Though private revenge is forbidden, God will still have his people act under him when he calls them to it, to pull down his and their implacable enemies (v. 6).

4.3. God will proportion the punishment of sinners to the measure of their pride and self-confidence (v. 7).

4.4. When destruction comes on a people unexpectedly, the surprise greatly emphasizes their misery (v. 8).

Verses 9–24

1. Here is a grievous lamentation made by Babylon's friends at her fall.

1.1. The mourners were those who had been bewitched by her immorality and those who had profited from her wealth and trade, the kings and the merchants of the earth.

1.2. When they mourned, they stood at a distance, even though they were Babylon's friends. Even though they had shared with her in her sinful pleasures and profits, they were unwilling to endure a share in her plagues. They cried out in terror, for those who have most indulged themselves in pride and pleasure are the least able to bear calamities.

1.3. The cause of their mourning was not their sin but their punishment. The spirit of the Antichrist is a worldly spirit, and the sorrow of his followers is a mere worldly sorrow (2Co 7:10). The wealth and merchandise of this city was all lost suddenly (vv. 12–13) and irrevocably (v. 14). The church of God may fall for a time, but she will rise again, but the fall of Babylon will be a complete overthrow. Godly sorrow is some support in suffering, but mere worldly sorrow adds to the adversity.

2. Here is the joy and triumph there was both in heaven and on earth at the irrevocable fall of Babylon (v. 20). Notice:

2.1. How universal this joy would be: heaven and earth, angels and saints, would join in it.

2.2. How just and reasonable it was:

2.2.1. Because the fall of Babylon was an act of God. Though God's people did not take pleasure in the miseries of anyone, they still had reason to rejoice in the revelation of the glorious justice of God.

2.2.2. Because it was an irrevocable ruin. The place would be no longer fit for human habitation; no work would be done there, no comfort enjoyed, no light seen there, but rather total darkness and desolation, as the reward of her great evil. Such detestable sins deserved such a great destruction.

CHAPTER 19

In this chapter we have: 1. A further account of the triumphant song of angels and saints at the fall of Babylon (vv. 1–4). 2. The marriage between Christ and the church declared (vv. 5–10). 3. Another warlike expedition of the glorious head of the church (vv. 11–21).

Verses 1–4

The fall of Babylon being finished and declared irrevocable, this chapter begins with a holy triumph over her by all the residents of heaven. The form of their thanksgiving is *Alleluia,* "Praise the Lord." They began with this, they continued with this, and they ended with this (v. 4); their prayers now became praise; their hosannas ("Save!") ended in hallelujahs. They praised him for the truth of his word and the righteousness of his providence, especially in the great event of the downfall of Babylon (v. 2). When the angels and saints cried *Alleluia,* Babylon's fire burned more fiercely (v. 3). Praising God for what we already have is praying most effectively for what is still to be done for us; the praises of the saints fan the fire of God's wrath against the common enemy. Notice the blessed harmony between the angels and the saints in this triumphant song (v. 4).

Verses 5–10

A marriage song began (v. 6). Notice:

1. The concert of heavenly music. The chorus was large and loud, *as the voice of many waters and of mighty thunderings.*

2. The occasion of this song (v. 7), which was the reign of the almighty God. We have here a description of:

2.1. The bride, how she appeared, not in the bright, showy dress of the mother of prostitutes, but *in fine linen, clean and white,* which *is the righteousness of saints,* in the robes of Christ's righteousness. She did not buy these marriage ornaments with any money of her own, but received them as the gift of her dear Lord.

2.2. The wedding supper, which is declared to be such as would make all those happy who were called to it—a banquet made up of the promises of the Gospel, *the true sayings of God* (v. 9).

2.3. The spellbound joy the apostle felt. *He fell down at the feet of the angel, to worship him.* The angel refused it, and with a note of offense, too: "*See thou do it not: I am thy fellow-servant, and of thy brethren which have the testimony of Jesus.* You, as an apostle, having *the Spirit of prophecy,* have the same testimony to give; we are therefore brothers and fellow servants in this. *Worship God,* and only him."

Verses 11–21

The glorious head of the church was called out on a new expedition, which seems to be the great battle that was to be fought at Armageddon, foretold in 16:16. Notice:

1. The description of the great Commander. The seat of his empire is *heaven.* He is again described as sitting *on a white horse,* and he *is faithful and true,* righteous in all his acts. He has a penetrating insight into all the strength of his enemies. He has a large and extensive dominion, *many crowns.* His armor is *a vesture* (robe) *dipped in blood.* His name is *The Word of God,* a name that no one fully knows except him. His perfections cannot be comprehended by any creature.

2. The army he commands (v. 14).

3. The weapons of his warfare (2Co 10:4): a *sharp sword* proceeding from *his mouth* (v. 15).

4. The symbols of his authority, his coat of arms (v. 16).

5. An invitation given *to the fowls of heaven* to come and share in the plunder and pillage of the field (vv. 17–18).

6. The battle joined. The enemy attacked with great fury; the powers of earth and hell gathered to exert themselves to the utmost (v. 19).

7. The victory gained by the great head of the church: *The beast and the false prophet* were taken prisoners and *cast into the burning lake.* Their followers were given up to military execution and made a feast for *the fowls of heaven.*

CHAPTER 20

Here we have an account of: 1. The binding of Satan for a thousand years (vv. 1–3). 2. The reign of the saints with Christ for the same time (vv. 4–6). 3. The release of Satan and the conflict between the church on one side and Gog and Magog on the other (vv. 7–10). 4. The Day of Judgment (vv. 11–15).

Verses 1–10

We have here:

1. A prophecy of *the binding of Satan.* Notice to whom this work of binding Satan was committed: *an angel from heaven.* Christ never lacks appropriate powers and instruments to break Satan's power. Neither the strength of the dragon nor the subtlety of the serpent was enough to rescue him from the hands of Christ; Christ *cast him into the bottomless pit.* He had been permitted to break out, disturb the churches, and deceive the nations, but now he was brought back to that prison and there laid in chains. He was *shut up, and a seal was set upon him.* The term of this confinement was to be a *thousand years,* after which he was to *be loosed* again for *a little season.*

2. An account of the reign of the saints for the same length of time that Satan remained bound (vv. 4–6). Those who received such honor were those who had suffered for Christ and all who had remained faithful to him. The honor given them was that they were raised from the dead and restored to life, and *they reigned with Christ a thousand years.* Those who suffer with Christ will reign with Christ (2Ti 2:12). This is called *the first resurrection,* which none except those who have served Christ and suffered for him will be favored with. These servants of God will be *blessed and holy* (v. 6). None can be blessed except those who are holy, and all who are holy will be blessed. They are kept safe from the power of the second death. Those who have experienced a spiritual resurrection are saved from the power of the second death.

3. An account of another mighty conflict, which is very sharp, but short and decisive. The restraints laid on Satan were eventually taken away. While this world lasts, Satan's power in it will not be wholly destroyed. No sooner was Satan let loose than he fell to his old work of *deceiving the nations,* so stirring them up to make a war against the saints and servants of God. His final efforts seemed to be the greatest (v. 8). The principal commanders in this army under the dragon were *Gog and Magog.* We read about *Gog and Magog* together in Eze 38:2, a prophecy from which this one in Revelation borrows many of its images. Notice the march and military disposition of this formidable army (v. 9). The condemnation and punishment of the grand enemy, *the devil,* was that he was now thrown into hell with his two great officers, *the beast and the false prophet,* to be *tormented night and day, for ever and ever.*

Verses 11–15

The complete destruction of the devil's kingdom leads to an account of the Day of Judgment. This will be a great day, *the great day, when all shall appear before the judgment seat of Christ* (2Co 5:10). We see:

1. *The throne, great* and *white,* very glorious and perfectly just and righteous.

2. The Judge, the Lord Jesus Christ. *The earth and the heaven fled from his face, and there was no place found for them.*

3. The people to be judged (v. 12). No one is so lowly that they do not have some talents to account for (Mt 25:14–30), and no one is so great as to avoid the jurisdiction of this court; not only those who are alive at the coming of Christ will be judged, but all who have died before.

4. The rule of judgment settled: *The books were opened.* One is the book of God's omniscience; another is the book of the sinner's conscience. *And another book* will be *opened*: the book of the Scriptures, the statute book of heaven, the rule of life.

5. The case to be tried, *the works of men*, what they have done and whether it is good or evil.

6. The outcome of the trial and judgment. All those who have *made a covenant with death* and an *agreement with hell* (Isa 28:15, 18) will then be condemned with their diabolic associates and thrown with them into the lake of fire. But those whose names are written in that book will then be justified and acquitted by the Judge.

CHAPTER 21

The day breaks, and the shadows flee away; a new world now appears, the former having passed away. Here we have: 1. An introduction to the vision of the New Jerusalem (vv. 1–8). 2. The vision itself (vv. 9–27).

Verses 1–8

1. A new world now opens to our view (v. 1). To make way for the beginning of this new world, the old world *passed away.*

2. In this new world, the apostle *saw the holy city, the new Jerusalem, coming down from heaven.* This New Jerusalem is the church of God in its new and perfect state, *prepared as a bride adorned for her husband.*

3. The blessed presence of God with his people is declared here (v. 3). The presence of God with his church is the glory of the church. The presence of God with his people in heaven will not be interrupted as it is on earth; he will live with them continually. *They shall be his people. God himself will be their God.*

4. This new and blessed state will be free from all trouble and sorrow. *All tears shall be wiped away.* God himself, as their tender Father, with his own kind hand, *shall wipe away the tears* of his children, and they would not have wanted to be without those tears when God himself comes and wipes them away. All causes of future sorrow will be removed forever: *There shall be neither death nor pain*, and therefore *no sorrow nor crying; former things have passed away.*

5. The truth and certainty of this blessed state are confirmed by the word and promise of God (vv. 5–6). God wanted this word and promise committed to writing so that his people would remember it always and use it continually. *These words are faithful and true*; it follows, *It is done*, as sure as if it were done already. We can and should take God's promise as present payment; if he has said that he *makes all things new, it is done.* His titles of honor are a pledge of the complete fulfillment; he is *Alpha and Omega, the beginning and the end.* As his power and will were the first cause of all things, so his pleasure and glory are the final goal, and he will not fail to fulfill his intentions. People may begin projects that they never complete, but *the counsel of God shall stand*

(Isa 44:28; 46:10). The desires of his people toward this blessed state provide further evidence of its truth: it would be inconsistent with the goodness of God and his love for his people to create in them holy desires and then deny them their proper satisfaction; they may be assured, therefore, that *he will give them of the fountain of the water of life freely* (v. 6).

6. The greatness of this future happiness is declared by:

6.1. Its freeness: *He gives of the water of life freely.*

6.2. Its fullness. The people of God then *inherit all things* (v. 7). In that blessed state, God is all in all (1Co 15:28).

6.3. The terms and entitlement by which they enjoy this blessedness as *the sons of God* (v. 7; Jn 1:12; Ro 8:14, 19; Php 2:15; 1Jn 3:1–2), a title most sure and certain.

6.4. The vastly different state of evildoers (v. 8). Notice the sins of those who perish. *The fearful* lead the vanguard in this list. But those who were so cowardly as not to dare to take up the cross of Christ were still so desperate as to pursue all kinds of detestable wickedness. Notice their punishment: they could not burn at a stake for Christ, but they must burn in hell for sin. They must die another death after their natural death; the agonies and terrors of the first death will consign them to far greater terrors and agonies of eternal death.

Verses 9–27

We now come to the vision itself. Notice:

1. The person who opened the vision to the apostle (v. 9). God has a variety of work and employment for his holy angels. They readily fulfill every commission they receive from God.

2. The place from which the apostle had this glorious view. He was taken to *a high mountain.* Those who want to have clear views of heaven must get as close to heaven as they can, onto the mount of vision.

3. The subject of the vision (v. 10); the church of God in her glorious, perfect, triumphant state.

3.1. Notice the exterior of the *city, the wall* and *the gates.*

3.1.1. It has a wall for security; heaven is a safe state. Notice:

3.1.1.1. The wall is high enough for both decoration and security (v. 17), and its material *was as jasper* (v. 11); it is both impregnable and precious.

3.1.1.2. Its form: in the New Jerusalem all will be equal in purity and perfection.

3.1.1.3. The length and breadth of the wall (vv. 15–16). Here is enough room for all the people of God—*many mansions in their Father's house* (Jn 14:2).

3.1.1.4. The foundation of the wall (v. 19). The foundations are described by their number: twelve, referring to the twelve apostles (v. 14). The material of these foundations is varied and precious, as shown by twelve kinds of precious stones.

3.1.2. It has gates for entrance. Heaven is not inaccessible; there is a free admission to all those who are sanctified. There are *twelve gates*, corresponding to the twelve tribes of Israel. All the true Israel of God will have access into the New Jerusalem. The gates are guarded by *twelve angels*, to admit and receive the different tribes of the spiritual Israel. Inscribed on the *gates* are *the names of the twelve tribes*, to show that they have a right to the tree of life (22:14) and to enter through the gates into the city. Notice the locations of the gates: just as the city had four equal sides, corresponding to the four directions of the world, so on each side there were three gates, showing that there is as free entrance from one part of the world as from another. These gates were all made of pearl: *every gate one pearl.* Christ is the pearl of great price (Mt 13:46), and he is our way to God. There is nothing magnificent enough in this world to declare fully the glory of heaven.

3.2. See the interior of the New Jerusalem (vv. 22–27). The first thing we notice there is the street of the city (v. 21). The saints in heaven walk on gold. The saints are then at rest, and yet it is not a merely passive rest, but a state of delightful movement: *The nations that are saved walk in the light of it.* They walk with Christ in white. They have fellowship not only with God but also with one another. Notice:

3.2.1. The temple of the New Jerusalem, which was no physical temple, *for the Lord God Almighty, and the Lamb, are the temple thereof.*

3.2.2. The light of this city (v. 23). No sun or moon shines there (v. 23), yet the sun's light is not missed, *for the glory of God lightens that city, and the Lamb is the light thereof.* There is no need for the sun or moon, any more than we here need to light a candle at noon.

3.2.3. The inhabitants of this city. They are whole nations of saved souls. All those many who were sealed on earth are saved in heaven. Some of the kings, queens, and rulers of the earth will enter, for God will have some of all ranks and kinds of people to fill the heavenly homes. Notice their continual accession and entrance into this city: *The gates shall never be shut.* Those who are sanctified always find the gates open.

3.2.4. The resources in this city: all the *glory and honour of the nations shall be brought into it.* Whatever is excellent and valuable in this world will be enjoyed there in a more refined way and to a far greater extent.

3.2.5. The unmixed purity of all who belong to the New Jerusalem (v. 27). There the saints will have nothing impure remaining in them. Now they feel a sad mixture of corruption with their graces, but at their entrance into the Most Holy Place they are washed in the basin of Christ's blood and presented to the Father blameless. There the saints will have no one impure admitted among them. In the New Jerusalem the community is perfectly pure. It is free from those who are openly worldly, for no one is admitted into heaven who practices detestable acts. And it is free from hypocrites, those who utter lies; they cannot intrude on the New Jerusalem.

CHAPTER 22

Here is: 1. A further description of the heavenly state of the church (vv. 1–5). 2. A confirmation of this and all the other visions of this book (vv. 6–19). 3. The conclusion (vv. 20–21).

Verses 1–5

The heavenly state is here described as a paradise. A paradise in a city, or a whole city in a paradise! In the first paradise, there were only two people to see its beauty, but in this second paradise whole cities and nations will find abundant delight and satisfaction. Notice:

1. The river of paradise. Its origin is the *throne of God and the Lamb.* All our springs of grace, comfort, and glory come from God, and all our streams from him are through the Lamb. This river is *pure and clear as crystal.* All the streams of earthly comfort are muddy, but these are clear, giving life to those who drink them.

2. The tree of life in this paradise. There was such a tree in the earthly paradise (Ge 2:9), but this paradise far excels it. This tree is *in the midst of the street, and on* *either side* the river. It is fed by the pure waters of the river that flows from the throne of God. It is very fruitful, producing *twelve sorts* of fruit and producing fruit at all times: it *yields its fruit every month.* The fruit is not only pleasant but also wholesome. The presence of God in heaven is the health and happiness of the saints.

3. The perfect freedom of this paradise from everything evil (v. 3). There is no serpent there, as there was in the earthly paradise. The Devil has nothing to do there.

4. The supreme happiness of this state of paradise. There the saints will see the face of God. God will recognize them because they have his seal and name on their foreheads. *They shall reign with him for ever.* All this will be with perfect knowledge and joy. They will continually walk in the light of the Lord, and not just for a time, *but for ever and ever.*

Verses 6–19

Here is a solemn confirmation of the contents of this book.

1. It is confirmed by the name and nature of that God who gave these revelations: he is *the Lord God, faithful and true.*

2. It is confirmed by the messengers he chose. The holy angels showed these things to God's holy people.

3. It will soon be confirmed by their fulfillment. Christ will come quickly.

4. It is confirmed by the integrity of the angel who had been the apostle's guide and interpreter in these visions.

5. It is confirmed by the order given to leave the book of the prophecy open to be read by all. God does not speak in secret (Jn 18:20).

6. It will be confirmed by the effect this book will have on people; those who are vile and who do wrong will take the opportunity from this to be more so, but it will further sanctify those who are upright with God.

7. It will be confirmed when it is Christ's rule of judgment on the great day; he will dispense rewards and punishments to people according to how their works agree or disagree with the word of God.

8. It is confirmed by the fact that it is the word of the One who is the author, finisher (Heb 12:2), and rewarder (Heb 11:6) of the faith and holiness of his people (vv. 13–14). He is *the first and the last.* He will by this word give to his people *a right to the tree of life* and entrance into heaven.

9. It is confirmed by the fact that it is a book that condemns and excludes from heaven all evildoers, especially *those that love and make lies* (v. 15).

10. It is confirmed by *the testimony of Jesus, which is the Spirit of prophecy* (19:10). He is the fountain of all light, the *bright and the morning star* (v. 22), and has given to his churches this morning light of prophecy to assure them of the light of the coming perfect day (Pr 4:18).

11. It is confirmed by an open invitation to all to come and share in the streams of the water of life; these are offered to all who feel in their souls a thirst that nothing in this world can quench.

12. It is confirmed by the joint testimony of the Spirit of God and the gracious Spirit that is in all the true members of the church of God; *the Spirit and the bride* join in testifying.

13. It is confirmed by a most solemn warning (vv. 18–19). This warning is like a flaming sword to guard the canon of Scripture from sinners (Ge 3:24).

Verses 20–21

We have now come to the conclusion of the whole:

1. Christ's farewell to his church. *Behold, I come quickly.* Just as he left with a promise of his gracious presence when he ascended into heaven after his resurrection, so here he leaves with a promise of a speedy return. The vision is for an appointed time and will not be delayed. *He will come quickly.*

2. The church's hearty echo to Christ's promise. She declares her firm belief in it: *Amen, so it is,* so it will be. She expresses her passionate desire for it: *Even so, come, Lord Jesus.* We should never be satisfied until we find such a spirit breathing in us. This is the language of the church of the firstborn (Heb 12:23), and we should join

with them. What comes from heaven in a promise should return to heaven in a prayer: "*Come, Lord Jesus.* Finish your great purpose and fulfill all of the word in which you have caused your people to hope (Ps 119:49)."

3. The apostolic blessing, which closes the whole: *The grace of our Lord Jesus Christ be with you all. Amen.* Nothing should be more desired by us than that the grace of Christ may be with us in this world to prepare us for the glory of Christ in the other world. We should all add our hearty *Amen* to this comprehensive prayer, most earnestly thirsting for greater measures of the gracious influences of the blessed Lord Jesus Christ in our souls and for his gracious presence with us, until glory has completed all his grace toward us.

We want to hear from you. Please send your comments about this book to us in care of zreview@zondervan.com. Thank you.

ZONDERVAN.com/
AUTHORTRACKER
follow your favorite authors